D1177393

# Webster's
# Universal
# Encyclopedic
# Dictionary

# Webster's
# Universal
# Encyclopedic
# Dictionary

Created in Cooperation with the Editors of
**MERRIAM-WEBSTER**

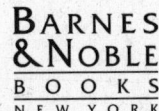

BARNES
&NOBLE
BOOKS
NEW YORK

This 2002 edition published by Barnes & Noble, Inc., by arrangement with
Federal Street Press, a division of Merriam-Webster, Incorporated

2002 Barnes & Noble Books

ISBN 0-7607-2911-5

Printed in the United States of America

02 03 04 05 06     5 4 3 2 1

# Contents

Preface     4a

Explanatory Notes     5a

New Words     21a

Guide to Pronunciation     28a

**A Dictionary of the English Language**     1

Abbreviations and Symbols for Chemical Elements     2157

Biographical Names     2169

Geographical Names     2182

Handbook of Style     2211

# Preface

This dictionary has been specially created to serve the needs of a broad audience: everyone who uses English to communicate. It is produced in cooperation with the editors of Merriam-Webster, and it draws on the scholarship and reputation of a company that is the oldest and most respected publisher of dictionaries in America.

The book you are holding incorporates all of the essential features of a general purpose dictionary and a good deal more. The heart and soul of any dictionary is its main vocabulary and its ever-expanding stock of new words and uses. New words and senses come into use far more rapidly than older uses die out, and in the front of the book is a section of recently established words and senses, set aside to highlight these new additions to the language.

Entries known to be trademarks or service marks are so labeled and are treated in accordance with a formula approved by the United States Trademark Association. No entry in this dictionary, however, should be regarded as affecting the validity of any trademark or service mark.

Of particular note in this dictionary is the easy-to-read type, the abundance of pictorial illustrations, and the many set-off paragraphs with discussions of the shades of difference among synonyms, pointed discussions of some matters of confused or disputed usage, and brief stories of the interesting histories of certain words, giving more information than can be presented in the etymologies. Another feature that has proved popular with people interested in the histories of words is the date of first recorded use of a word, given before the first definition. Similarly, each letter section of the main vocabulary is introduced by a short history of the letter itself.

Other features meant to make this dictionary more inviting to the eye than dictionaries commonly are include the placing of numbered definitions on a new line, to make them easier to locate, and the spelling out of words typically abbreviated in other dictionaries.

The explantions in the front of this book establish a context for understanding what this dictionary is and how it may be used most effectively. The Explanatory Notes answer the user's questions about the conventions, devices, and techniques by which the editors have been able to present large amounts of information in a single volume. All users of the dictionary are urged to read this section through and then consult it for special information as the need arises.

In order to fit as much information as possible into a convenient size, the dictionary contains less-often referenced material in smaller sections in the back of the book including Abbreviations and Symbols, Biographical Names, Geographical Names, and a Handbook of Style, in which various stylistic conventions are explained.

The publisher is happy to offer this work in the belief that this single-volume reference will serve the user as a reliable resource for many years.

# Explanatory Notes

## Entries

### MAIN ENTRIES

A boldface letter or a combination of such letters, including punctuation marks and diacritics where needed, that is set flush with the left-hand margin of each column of type is a main entry or entry word. The main entry may consist of letters set solid, of letters joined by a hyphen or a diagonal, or of letters separated by one or more spaces:

**¹alone** . . . *adjective*

**au·to-da-fé** . . . *noun*

**and/or** . . . *conjunction*

**automatic pilot** *noun*

The material in lightface type that follows each main entry on the same line and on succeeding indented lines explains and justifies its inclusion in the dictionary.

Variation in the styling of compound words in English is frequent and widespread. It is often completely acceptable to choose freely among open, hyphenated, and closed alternatives (as *lifestyle, life-style,* or *life style*). However, to show all the stylings that are found for English compounds would require space that can be better used for other information. So this dictionary limits itself to a single styling for a compound:

**peace·mak·er**

**pell–mell**

**boom box**

When a compound is widely used and one styling predominates, that styling is shown. When a compound is uncommon or when the evidence indicates that two or three stylings are approximately equal in frequency, the styling shown is based on the analogy of parallel compounds.

### ORDER OF MAIN ENTRIES

The main entries follow one another in alphabetical order letter by letter without regard to intervening spaces or hyphens: *battle royal* follows *battlement* and *earth-shattering* follows *earthshaking.* Those containing an Arabic numeral are alphabetized as if the numeral were spelled out: *3-D* comes between *three-color* and *three-decker.* Those that often begin with the abbreviation *St.* in common usage have the abbreviation spelled out: *Saint Anthony's fire.*

Full words come before parts of words made up of the same letters. Solid compounds come first and are followed by hyphenated compounds and then open compounds. Lowercase entries come before entries that begin with a capital letter:

**semi** . . . *noun*

**semi-** . . . *prefix*

**take·out** . . . *noun*

**take–out** . . . *adjective*

**take out** . . . *transitive verb*

**tim·o·thy** . . . *noun*

**Tim·o·thy** . . . *noun*

### HOMOGRAPHS

When one main entry has exactly the same written form as another, the two are distinguished by superscript numerals preceding each word:

**¹melt** . . . *verb*          **¹pine** . . . *noun*

**²melt** *noun*          **²pine** *intransitive verb*

Sometimes such homographs are related: the two entries *melt* are derived from the same root. Sometimes there is no relationship: the two entries *pine* are unrelated beyond the accident of spelling. The order of homographs is usually historical: the one first used in English is entered first. A homograph derived from an earlier homograph by functional shift, however, follows its parent immediately, with the result that occasionally one homograph appears ahead of another that is older in usage. For example, of the three entries *kennel* the second (a verb) is derived from the first (a noun). Even though the unrelated third entry *kennel* was used in English many years before the second, it follows the two related entries.

### GUIDE WORDS

A pair of guide words is printed at the top of each page. The entries that fall alphabetically between the guide words are found on that page.

It is important to remember that alphabetical order rather than position of an entry on the page determines the selection of guide words. The first guide word is the alphabetically first entry on the page. The second guide word is usually the alphabetically last entry on the page:

**game**          **gamut**

The entry need not be a main entry. Another boldface word—a variant, an inflected form, or a defined or undefined run-on—may be selected as a guide word. For this reason the last printed main entry on a page is not always the last entry alphabetically:

**Gentoo**          **geomagnetism**

On the page where these guide words are used, *geomagnetic storm* is the last printed entry, but *geomagnetism,* an undefined run-on at *geomagnetic,* is the last entry alphabetically and so has been chosen as the second guide word.

All guide words must themselves be in alphabetical order from page to page throughout the dictionary; thus, the alphabetically last entry on a page is not used if it follows alphabetically the first guide word on the next page:

**Giemsa stain**          **gillied**

On the page where these guide words are found, *gillying,* an inflected form at the entry ²*gillie,* is the last entry alphabetically, but it is not used as the second guide word because it follows alphabetically the entry *gillnet,* which is the first guide word on the next page. To use *gillying* would violate the alphabetical order of guide words from page to page, and so the inflected form *gillied* is the second guide word instead.

# END-OF-LINE DIVISION

The centered dots within entry words indicate division points at which a hyphen may be put at the end of a line of print or writing. Thus the noun *pos·si·bil·i·ty* may be ended on one line with:

*pos-*
*possi-*
*possibil-*
*possibili-*

and continued on the next with:

*sibility*
*bility*
*ity*
*ty*

Centered dots are not shown after a single initial letter or before a single terminal letter because printers seldom cut off a single letter:

**aswirl** . . . *adjective*

**mouthy** . . . *adjective*

**idea** . . . *noun*

Nor are they shown at second and succeeding homographs unless these differ among themselves:

**¹re·form** . . . *verb*      **¹min·ute** . . . *noun*

**²reform** *noun*      **²minute** *transitive verb*

**³reform** *adjective*      **³mi·nute** . . . *adjective*

There are acceptable alternative end-of-line divisions just as there are acceptable variant spellings and pronunciations. It is, for example, all but impossible to produce a convincing argument that either of the divisions *aus·ter·i·ty, au·ster·i·ty* is better than the other. But space cannot be taken for entries like *aus·ter·i·ty or au·ster·i·ty,* and *au·ster·i·ty* would likely be confusing to many. No more than one division is, therefore, shown for an entry in this dictionary.

Many words have two or more common pronunciation variants, and the same end-of-line division is not always appropriate for each of them. The division *pi·an·ist,* for example, best fits the variant \pē-'a-nist\ whereas the division *pi·a·nist* best fits the variant \'pē-ə-nist\. In instances like this, the division falling farther to the left is used, regardless of the order of the pronunciations:

**pi·a·nist** \pē-'a-nist, 'pē-ə-\

A double hyphen ⸗ at the end of a line in this dictionary (as in the etymology at *dally*) stands for a hyphen that belongs at that point in a hyphenated word and that is retained when the word is written as a unit on one line.

# VARIANTS

When a main entry is followed by the word *or* and another spelling, the two spellings are equal variants. Both are standard, and either one may be used according to personal inclination:

**ocher** *or* **ochre**

If two variants joined by *or* are out of alphabetical order, they remain equal variants. The one printed first is, however, slightly more common than the second:

**plow** *or* **plough**

When another spelling is joined to the main entry by the word *also,* the spelling after *also* is a secondary variant and occurs less frequently than the first:

**can·cel·la·tion** *also* **can·cel·ation**

Secondary variants belong to standard usage and may be used according to personal inclination. If there are two secondary variants, the second is joined to the first by *or.* Once the word *also* is used to signal a secondary variant, all following variants are joined by *or:*

**¹Shake·spear·ean** *or* **Shake·spear·ian**
*also* **Shak·sper·ean** *or* **Shak·sper·ian**

Variants whose spelling places them alphabetically more than a column away from the main entry are entered at their own alphabetical places and usually not at the main entry:

**¹jibe** . . . *variant of* GIBE

**³rime, rimester** *variant of* RHYME, RHYMESTER

Variants having a usage label appear only at their own alphabetical places:

**metre** . . . *chiefly British variant of* METER

**agin** . . . *dialect variant of* AGAINST

# RUN-ON ENTRIES

A main entry may be followed by one or more derivatives or by a homograph with a different functional label. These are run-on entries. Each is introduced on a new line by a boldface dash and each has a functional label. They are not defined, however, since their meanings are readily derivable from the meaning of the root word:

**slay** . . . *verb* . . .
— **slay·er** *noun*

**spir·it·ed** . . . *adjective* . . .
— **spir·it·ed·ly** *adverb*
— **spir·it·ed·ness** *noun*

**stac·ca·to** . . . *adjective* . . .
— **staccato** *adverb*
— **staccato** *noun*

A main entry may be followed by one or more phrases containing the entry word or an inflected form of it. These are also run-on entries. Each is introduced on a new line by a boldface dash but there is no functional label. They are, however, defined since their meanings are more than the sum of the meanings of their elements:

**¹hole** . . . *noun* . . .
— **in the hole :** . . .

**¹live** . . . *verb* . . .
— **live it up :** . . .

Defined phrases of this sort are run on at the entry constituting the first major element in the phrase. The first major element is ordinarily a verb or a noun, but when these are absent another part of speech may serve instead:

**¹but** . . . *conjunction* . . .
— **but what :** . . .

When there are variants, however, the run-on appears at the entry constituting the first major invariable element in the phrase:

**¹clock** . . . *noun* . . .
— **kill the clock** *or* **run out the clock**
**:** . . .

**¹hand** . . . *noun* . . .
  **— on all hands** *or* **on every hand**
  **:** . . .

A run-on entry is an independent entry with respect to function and status. Labels at the main entry do not apply unless they are repeated.

Attention is called to the definition of *vocabulary entry* in this book. The term *dictionary entry* includes all vocabulary entries as well as all boldface entries in the separate sections of the back matter headed "Abbreviations and Symbols for Chemical Elements," "Foreign Words and Phrases," "Biographical Names," and "Geographical Names."

# Pronunciation

Pronunciation is indicated between a pair of reversed virgules \ \ following the entry word. The symbols used are listed in the chart printed on the page facing the first page of the dictionary proper. An abbreviated list appears at the bottom of the third column of each right-hand page of the vocabulary. Explanations of the symbols are given in the Guide to Pronunciation.

## SYLLABLES

A hyphen is used in the pronunciation to show syllabic division. These hyphens sometimes coincide with the centered dots in the entry word that indicate end-of-line division; sometimes they do not:

**ab·sen·tee** \ˌab-sən-'tē\

**¹met·ric** \'me-trik\

## STRESS

A high-set mark \'\ indicates primary (strongest) stress or accent; a low-set mark \ˌ\ indicates secondary (medium) stress or accent:

**heart·beat** \'härt-ˌbēt\

The stress mark stands at the beginning of the syllable that receives the stress.

Stress marks are an indication of the relative prominence of the syllables in a word. In running speech the primary stress can vary in English words for several contextual and semantic reasons. Because the variation is so great, this book shows the primary stress of a word in its pronunciation as a single word out of context.

## VARIANT PRONUNCIATIONS

The presence of variant pronunciations indicates that not all educated speakers pronounce words the same way. A second-place variant is not to be regarded as less acceptable than the pronunciation that is given first. It may, in fact, be used by as many educated speakers as the first variant, but the requirements of the printed page make one precede the other:

**apri·cot** \'a-prə-ˌkät, 'ā-\

**for·eign** \'fȯr-ən, 'fär-\

A variant that is appreciably less common than the preceding variant is preceded by the word *also* :

**¹al·loy** \'a-ˌlȯi *also* ə-'lȯi\

A variant preceded by *sometimes* is even less common, though it does occur in educated speech:

**in·vei·gle** \in-'vā-gəl *sometimes* -'vē-\

Sometimes a regional label precedes a variant:

**¹great** \'grāt, *Southern also* 'gre(ə)t\

The label *dial* precedes a variant that is noteworthy or common in a dialect or dialects of American English, but that is not considered to be a standard pronunciation:

**ask** \'ask, 'ȧsk; *dialect* 'aks\

The symbol \÷\ is placed before a pronunciation variant that occurs in educated speech but that is considered by some to be unacceptable:

**cu·po·la** \'kyü-pə-lə, ÷-ˌlō\

This symbol refers only to the immediately following variant and not to subsequent variants separated from it by a comma or a semicolon.

## PARENTHESES IN PRONUNCIATIONS

Symbols enclosed by parentheses represent elements that are present in the pronunciation of some speakers but are absent from the pronunciation of other speakers, or elements that are present in some but absent from other utterances of the same speaker:

**¹twin·kle** \'twiŋ-kəl\ *verb* . . . **twin·kling** \-k(ə-)liŋ\

**sat·is·fac·to·ry** \ˌsa-təs-'fak-t(ə-)rē\

**re·sponse** \ri-'spän(t)s\

Thus, the parentheses at *twinkling* mean that there are some who pronounce the \ə\ between \k\ and \l\ and others who do not pronounce it.

## PARTIAL AND ABSENT PRONUNCIATIONS

When a main entry has less than a full pronunciation, the missing part is to be supplied from a pronunciation in a preceding entry or within the same pair of reversed virgules:

**cham·pi·on·ship** \-ˌship\

**Ma·dei·ra** \mə-'dir-ə, -'der-\

The pronunciation of the first three syllables of *championship* is found at the main entry *champion* :

**¹cham·pi·on** \'cham-pē-ən\

The hyphens before and after \'der\ in the pronunciation of *Madeira* indicate that both the first and the last parts of the pronunciation are to be taken from the immediately preceding pronunciation.

Partial pronunciations are usually shown when two or more variants have a part in common. When a variation of stress is involved, a partial pronunciation may be terminated at the stress mark which stands at the beginning of a syllable not shown:

**di·verse** \dī-'vərs, də-', 'dī-ˌ\

**an·cho·vy** \'an-ˌchō-vē, an-'\

In general, no pronunciation is indicated for open compounds consisting of two or more English words that have own-place entry:

**witch doctor** *noun*

A pronunciation is shown, however, for any element of an open compound that does not have entry at its own alphabetical place:

**Oc·cam's razor** \'ä-kəmz-\

**sieve of Er·a·tos·the·nes** \-,er-ə-'täs-thə-,nēz\

Only the first entry in a sequence of numbered homographs is given a pronunciation if their pronunciations are the same:

¹**re·ward** \ri-'wȯrd\

²**reward**

Pronunciations are shown for obsolete words only if they occur in Shakespeare:

**clois·tress** \'klȯi-strəs\ *noun . . . obsolete*

The pronunciation of unpronounced derivatives and compounds run on at a main entry is a combination of the pronunciation at the main entry and the pronunciation of the suffix or final element as given at its alphabetical place in the vocabulary:

— **oval·ness** *noun*

— **shot in the dark**

Thus, the pronunciation of *ovalness* is the sum of the pronunciations given at *oval* and *-ness* ; that of *shot in the dark,* the sum of the pronunciation of the four elements that make up the phrase.

# Functional Labels

An italic label indicating a part of speech or some other functional classification follows the pronunciation or, if no pronunciation is given, the main entry. The eight traditional parts of speech are indicated as follows:

¹**bold** . . . *adjective*           **bo·le·ro** . . . *noun*

**hand·some·ly** . . . *adverb*    ²**under** . . . *preposition*

¹**but** . . . *conjunction*         **some·one** . . . *pronoun*

**oops** . . . *interjection*        ¹**shrink** . . . *verb*

If a verb is both transitive and intransitive, the labels *transitive verb* and *intransitive verb* introduce the subdivisions:

**flat·ten** . . . *verb . . .*
*transitive verb . . .*
*intransitive verb . . .*

If there is no subdivision, *transitive verb* or *intransitive verb* takes the place of *verb*:

²**fleece** *transitive verb*

**ap·per·tain** . . . *intransitive verb*

Labeling a verb as transitive, however, does not preclude occasional intransitive use (as in absolute constructions).

Other italicized labels used to indicate functional classifications that are not traditional parts of speech are:

**poly-** *combining form*        **-iferous** *adjective combining form*

**-logy** *noun combining form*   **super-** *prefix*

**Gram·my** . . . *service mark*      **Ly·cra** . . . *trademark*

¹**-ic** *adjective suffix*           **-nd** *symbol*

²**-ward** *or* **-wards** *adverb suffix*     ¹**may** . . . *verbal auxiliary*

**-itis** *noun suffix*               **gid·dap** . . . *verb imperative*

**-ize** *verb suffix*                **me·thinks** . . . *impersonal verb*

**NC–17** . . . *certification mark*

Two functional labels are sometimes combined:

**zilch** . . . *adjective or noun*

**afloat** . . . *adjective or adverb*

# Inflected Forms

In comparison with some other languages English does not have many inflected forms. Of those which it has, several are inflected forms of words belonging to small, closed groups (as the personal pronouns or the demonstratives). These forms can readily be found at their own alphabetical places with a full entry (as *whom,* the objective case form of *who*) or with a cross-reference in small capital letters to another entry (as *those,* the plural form of *that*).

Most other inflected forms, however, are covered explicitly or by implication at the main entry for the base form. These are the plurals of nouns, the principal parts of verbs (the past tense, the past participle when it differs from the past tense, and the present participle), and the comparative and superlative forms of adjectives and adverbs. In general, it may be said that when these inflected forms are created in a manner considered regular in English (as by adding *-s* or *-es* to nouns, *-ed* and *-ing* to verbs, and *-er* and *-est* to adjectives and adverbs) and when it seems that there is nothing about the formation likely to give the dictionary user doubts, the inflected form is not shown in order to save space for information more likely to be sought. Inflected forms are also not shown at undefined run-ons or at some entries bearing a limiting label:

**gour·mand** . . . *noun . . .*
— **gour·man·dize** . . . *intransitive verb*

¹**fem·i·nine** . . . *adjective . . .*
— **fem·i·nine·ness** . . . *noun*

²**lake** *noun . . .*
— **laky** . . . *adjective*

²**cote** . . . *transitive verb . . . obsolete* **:** to pass by

**crouse** . . . *adjective . . .*
*chiefly Scottish* **:** BRISK, LIVELY

On the other hand, if the inflected form is created in an irregular way or if the dictionary user is likely to have doubts about it (even though it is formed regularly), the inflected form is shown in boldface, either in full or cut back to a convenient and easily recognizable point. Full details about the kinds of entries at which inflected forms are shown and the kinds at which they are not shown are given in the three following sections.

## NOUNS

The plurals of nouns are shown in this dictionary when suffixation brings about a change of final *-y* to *-i-,* when the noun ends in a consonant plus *-o* or in *-ey,* when the noun ends in *-oo,* when the noun has an irregular plural or a zero plural or a foreign plural, when the noun is a compound that pluralizes any element but the last, when a final consonant is doubled, when the noun has variant plurals, and when it is believed that the dictionary user might have reasonable doubts about the spelling of the plural or when the plural is spelled in a way contrary to expectations:

²**spy** *noun, plural* **spies**

**si·lo** . . . *noun, plural* **silos**

¹**ro·deo** . . . *noun, plural* **ro·de·os**

²**shampoo** *noun, plural* **shampoos**

¹**mouse** . . . *noun, plural* **mice**

**moose** . . . *noun, plural* **moose**

**cri·te·ri·on** . . . *noun, plural* **-ria**

**son–in–law** . . . *noun, plural* **sons–in–law**

¹**quiz** . . . *noun, plural* **quiz·zes**

¹**fish** . . . *noun, plural* **fish** *or* **fish·es**

**cor·gi** . . . *noun, plural* **corgis**

³**dry** *noun, plural* **drys**

Cutback inflected forms are used when the noun has three or more syllables:

**ame·ni·ty** . . . *noun, plural* **-ties**

The plurals of nouns are usually not shown when the base word is unchanged by suffixation, when the noun is a compound whose second element is readily recognizable as a regular free form entered at its own place, or when the noun is unlikely to occur in the plural:

¹**night** . . . *noun*

²**crunch** *noun*

**fore·foot** . . . *noun*

**mo·nog·a·my** . . . *noun*

Nouns that are plural in form and that regularly occur in plural construction are labeled *noun plural*:

**munch·ies** . . . *noun plural*

Nouns that are plural in form but that are not always construed as plurals are appropriately labeled:

**ro·bot·ics** . . . *noun plural but singular in construction*

**two bits** *noun plural but singular or plural in construction*

A noun that is singular in construction takes a singular verb when it is used as a subject; a noun that is plural in construction takes a plural verb when it is used as a subject.

# VERBS

The principal parts of verbs are shown in this dictionary when suffixation brings about a doubling of a final consonant or an elision of a final -*e* or a change of final -*y* to -*i*-, when final -*c* changes to -*ck* in suffixation, when the verb ends in -*ey*, when the inflection is irregular, when there are variant inflected forms, and when it is believed that the dictionary user might have reasonable doubts about the spelling of an inflected form or when the inflected form is spelled in a way contrary to expectations:

²**snag** *transitive verb* **snagged; snag·ging**

¹**move** . . . *verb* **moved; mov·ing**

¹**cry** . . . *verb* **cried; cry·ing**

²**frolic** *intransitive verb* **frol·icked; frol·ick·ing**

¹**sur·vey** . . . *verb* **sur·veyed; sur·vey·ing**

¹**drive** . . . *verb* **drove** . . . ; **driv·en** . . . ; **driv·ing**

²**bus** *verb* **bused** *or* **bussed; bus·ing** *or* **bus·sing**

²**visa** *transitive verb* **vi·saed** . . . ; **vi·sa·ing**

²**chagrin** *transitive verb* **cha·grined** . . . ; **cha·grin·ing**

The principal parts of a regularly inflected verb are shown when it is desirable to indicate the pronunciation of one of the inflected forms:

**learn** . . . *verb* **learned** \'lərnd, 'lərnt\; **learn·ing**

**rip·en** . . . *verb* **rip·ened; rip·en·ing** \'rī-pə-niŋ, 'rīp-niŋ\

Cutback inflected forms are often used when the verb has three or more syllables, when it is a disyllable that ends in -*l* and has variant spellings, and when it is a compound whose second element is readily recognized as an irregular verb:

**elim·i·nate** . . . *transitive verb* **-nat·ed; -nat·ing**

³**quarrel** *intransitive verb* **-reled** *or* **-relled; -rel·ing** *or* **-rel·ling**

¹**re·take** . . . *transitive verb* **-took** . . . ; **-tak·en** . . . ; **-tak·ing**

The principal parts of verbs are usually not shown when the base word is unchanged by suffixation or when the verb is a compound whose second element is readily recognizable as a regular free form entered at its own place:

¹**jump** . . . *verb*

**pre·judge** . . . *transitive verb*

Another inflected form of English verbs is the third person singular of the present tense, which is regularly formed by the addition of -*s* or -*es* to the base form of the verb. This inflected form is not shown except at a handful of entries (as *have* and *do*) for which it is in some way anomalous.

# ADJECTIVES & ADVERBS

The comparative and superlative forms of adjectives and adverbs are shown in this dictionary when suffixation brings about a doubling of a final consonant or an elision of a final -*e* or a change of final -*y* to -*i*-, when the word ends in -*ey*, when the inflection is irregular, and when there are variant inflected forms:

¹**red** . . . *adjective* **red·der; red·dest**

¹**tame** . . . *adjective* **tam·er; tam·est**

¹**kind·ly** . . . *adjective* **kind·li·er; -est**

¹**ear·ly** . . . *adverb* **ear·li·er; -est**

**dic·ey** . . . *adjective* **dic·i·er; -est**

¹**good** . . . *adjective* **bet·ter** . . . ; **best**

¹**bad** . . . *adjective* **worse** . . . ; **worst**

¹**far** . . . *adverb* **far·ther** . . . *or* **fur·ther** . . . ; **far·thest** *or* **fur·thest**

The superlative forms of adjectives and adverbs of two or more syllables are usually cut back:

³**fancy** *adjective* **fan·ci·er; -est**

The comparative and superlative forms of regularly inflected adjectives and adverbs are shown when it is desirable to indicate the pronunciation of the inflected forms:

¹**young** . . . *adjective* **youn·ger** \'yəŋ-gər\; **youn·gest** \'yəŋ-gəst\

The inclusion of inflected forms in -*er* and -*est* at adjective and adverb entries means nothing more about the use of *more* and *most* with these adjectives and adverbs than that their comparative and superlative degrees may be expressed in either way; *lazier* or *more lazy; laziest* or *most lazy.*

At a few adjective entries only the superlative form is shown:

³**mere** . . . *adjective, superlative* **mer·est**

The absence of the comparative form indicates that there is no evidence of its use.

The comparative and superlative forms of adjectives and adverbs are not shown when the base word is unchanged by suffixation or when the word is a compound whose second element is readily recognizable as a regular free form entered at its own place:

¹**near** . . . *adverb*

**un·wary** . . . *adjective*

The comparative and superlative forms of adverbs are not shown when they are identical with the inflected forms of a preceding adjective homograph:

¹**hot** . . . *adjective* **hot·ter; hot·test**

²**hot** *adverb*

# Capitalization

Most entries in this dictionary begin with a lowercase letter. A few of these have an italicized label *often capitalized,* which indicates that the word is as likely to be capitalized as not, that it is as acceptable with an uppercase initial as it is with one in lowercase. Some entries begin with an uppercase letter, which indicates that the word is usually capitalized. The absence of an initial capital or of an *often capitalized* label indicates that the word is not ordinarily capitalized:

**lunk·head** . . . *noun*

**gar·gan·tuan** . . . *adjective, often capitalized*

**Mo·hawk** . . . *noun*

The capitalization of entries that are open or hyphenated compounds is similarly indicated by the form of the entry or by an italicized label:

**obstacle course** *noun*

**neo-Dar·win·ian** . . . *adjective, often N capitalized*

**off–off–Broadway** *noun, often both Os capitalized*

**un–Amer·i·can** . . . *adjective*

**Dutch oven** *noun*

**Old Glory** *noun*

A word that is capitalized in some senses and lowercase in others shows variations from the form of the main entry by the use of italicized labels at the appropriate senses:

**re·nais·sance** . . . *noun* . . . **1** *capitalized* . . . **2** *often capitalized*

**Shet·land** . . . *noun* . . . **2** *often not capitalized*

**Trin·i·ty** . . . *noun* . . . **2** *not capitalized*

# Attributive Nouns

The italicized label *often attributive* placed after the functional label *noun* indicates that the noun is often used as an adjective equivalent in attributive position before another noun:

**gold** . . . *noun, often attributive*

**busi·ness** . . . *noun, often attributive*

Examples of the attributive use of these nouns are *gold chain* and *business ethics.*

While any noun may occasionally be used attributively, the label *often attributive* is limited to those having broad attributive use. This label is not used when an adjective homograph (as *iron* or *paper*) is entered. And it is not used at open compounds (as *X ray*) that may be used attributively with an inserted hyphen (as in *X-ray therapy*).

# Etymology

The matter in square brackets preceding the definition is the etymology. Meanings given in roman type within these brackets are not definitions of the entry, but are meanings of the Middle English, Old English, or non-English words within the brackets.

The etymology traces a vocabulary entry as far back as possible in English (as to Old English), tells from what language and in what form it came into English, and (except in the case of such words outside the general vocabulary of English as *bascule* and *zloty*) traces the pre-English source as far back as possible if the source is an Indo-European language. These etyma are printed in italics.

## OLD, MIDDLE, AND MODERN ENGLISH

The etymology usually gives the Middle English and the Old English forms of words in the following style:

¹**nap** . . . *intransitive verb* . . . [Middle English *nappen,* from Old English *hnappian* . . . ]

¹**old** . . . *adjective* [Middle English, from Old English *eald* . . . ]

An etymology in which a word is traced back to Middle English but not to Old English indicates that the word is found in Middle English but not in those texts that have survived from the Old English period:

¹**slab** . . . *noun* [Middle English *slabbe* ]

¹**stale** . . . *adjective* . . . [Middle English, aged (of ale), not fresh; akin to Middle Dutch *stel* stale]

An etymology in which a word is traced back directly to Old English with no intervening mention of Middle English indicates that the word has not survived continuously from Old English times to the present. Rather, it died out after the Old English period and has been revived in modern times:

**ge·mot** . . . *noun* [Old English *gemōt* . . . ]

**thegn** . . . *noun* [Old English . . . ]

An etymology is not usually given for a word created in English by the combination of existing constituents or by functional shift. This indicates that the identity of the constituents is expected to be self-evident to the user.

**book·shelf** . . . *noun* . . . : an open shelf for holding books

¹**fire·proof** . . . *adjective* . . . : proof against or resistant to fire

**off–put·ting** . . . *adjective* . . . : that puts off : REPELLENT, DISCONCERTING

**penal code** *noun* . . . : a code of laws concerning crimes and offenses and their punishment

³**stalk** *noun* . . . 1 : the act of stalking

In the case of a family of words obviously related to a common English word but differing from it by containing various easily recognizable suffixes, an etymology is usually given only at the base word, even though some of the derivatives may have been formed in a language other than English:

¹**equal** . . . *adjective* [Middle English, from Latin *aequalis,* from *aequus* level, equal] . . . 1 **a** (1) : of the same measure, quantity, amount, or number as another

**equal·i·ty** . . . *noun* . . . 1 : the quality or state of being equal

**equal·ize** . . . *transitive verb* 1 : to make equal

While *equalize* was formed in Modern English, *equality* was actually borrowed into Middle English (via Middle French) from Latin *aequalitas.*

## LANGUAGES OTHER THAN ENGLISH

The etymology gives the language from which words borrowed into English have come. It also gives the form or a transliteration of the word in that language if the form differs from that in English:

¹**mar·ble** . . . *noun* [Middle English, from Old French *marbre,* from Latin *marmor,* from Greek *marmaros* ]

**pome·gran·ate** . . . *noun* [Middle English *poumgrenet,* from Middle French *pomme grenate,* literally, seedy apple]

**souk** . . . *noun* [Arabic *sūq* market]

In a few cases the expression "ultimately from" replaces the more usual "from." This expression indicates that one or more intermediate steps have been omitted in tracing the derivation of the form preceding the expression from the form following it:

**tri·lo·bite** . . . *noun* [ultimately from Greek *trilobos* three-lobed, from *tri-* + *lobos* lobe]

Words cited from certain American Indian languages and from some other languages that are infrequently printed have been rendered with the phonetic symbols used by scholars of those languages. These symbols include the following: a raised dot to the right of a vowel letter to mark vowel length; a hook below a vowel letter to mark nasality; an apostrophe over a consonant letter to mark glottal release; a superscript *w* to the right of a consonant letter to mark labialization; the symbol ɔ to render \ò\; the symbol ɨ to render a high central vowel; the Greek letters β, δ, and γ to render voiced labial, dental, and velar fricatives; the symbol *x* to render \k\; the symbol ʔ to render a glottal stop; and the symbol ƛ ("crossed lambda") for a voiceless lateral affricate. Examples of these symbols can be found at etymologies for the words *Athabascan, babassu, coho, geoduck, muskellunge, obeah, potlatch,* and *sego lily.*

## WORDS OF UNKNOWN ORIGIN

When the source of a word appearing as a main entry is unknown, the expression "origin unknown" is usually used. Only in exceptional circumstances (as with some ethnic names) does the absence of an etymology mean that it has not been possible to furnish an informative etymology. More often, it means that no etymology is believed to be necessary. This is the case, for instance, with most of the entries identified as variants and with many derivatives.

## ETYMOLOGIES OF TECHNICAL WORDS

Much of the technical vocabulary of the sciences and other specialized studies consists of words or word elements that are current in two or more languages, with only such slight modifications as are necessary to adapt them to the structure of the individual language in each case. Many words and word elements of this kind have become sufficiently a part of the general vocabulary of English as to require entry in an abridged dictionary. Because of the vast extent of the relevant published material in many languages and in many scientific and other specialized fields, it is impracticable to ascertain the language of origin of every such term. Yet it would not be accurate to formulate a statement about the origin of any such term in a way that could be interpreted as implying that it was coined in English. Accordingly, whenever a term that is entered in this dictionary belongs recognizably to this class of internationally current terms and whenever no positive evidence is at hand to show that it was coined in English, the etymology recognizes its international status and the possibility that it originated elsewhere than in English by use of the label International Scientific Vocabulary:

**mega·watt** . . . *noun* [International Scientific Vocabulary]

**phy·lo·ge·net·ic** . . . *adjective* [International Scientific Vocabulary, from New Latin *phylogenesis* . . .]

¹**-ol** *noun suffix* [International Scientific Vocabulary, from *alcohol* ]

## COMPRESSION OF INFORMATION

An etymology giving the name of a language (including Middle English or Old English) and not giving the foreign (or Middle English or Old English) form indicates that this form is the same as that of the entry word:

**ka·pok** . . . *noun* [Malay]

¹**po·grom** . . . *noun* [Yiddish, from Russian . . .]

**¹dumb** . . . *adjective* [Middle English, from Old English . . .]

An etymology giving the name of a language (including Middle English or Old English) and the form in that language but not giving the foreign (or Middle English or Old English) meaning indicates that this meaning is the same as that expressed in the first definition in the entry:

**¹wea·ry** . . . *adjective* . . . [Middle English *wery,* from Old English *wērig* . . .] . . .
**1 :** exhausted in strength . . .

When a word from a foreign language (or Middle English or Old English) is a key element in the etymologies of several related entries that are found close together, the meaning of the word is usually given at only one of the entries:

**ve·lo·ce** . . . *adverb or adjective* [Italian, from Latin *veloc-, velox* ]

**ve·loc·i·pede** . . . *noun* [French *vélocipède,* from Latin *veloc-, velox* + *ped-, pes* foot — more at FOOT]

**ve·loc·i·ty** . . . *noun* . . . [Middle French *velocité,* from Latin *velocitat-, velocitas,* from *veloc-, velox* quick; probably akin to Latin *vegēre* to enliven — more at WAKE]

When an etymology includes the expression "by alteration" and the altered form is not cited, the form is the term given in small capital letters as the definition:

**crit·ter** . . . *noun* [by alteration] . . .
**:** CREATURE

When the origin of a word is traced to the name of a person or place not further identified, additional information may be found in the Biographical Names or Geographical Names section in the back matter:

**far·ad** . . . *noun* [Michael *Faraday* ]

**jodh·pur** . . . *noun* [*Jodhpur,* India]

## RELATED WORDS

When a word of Indo-European origin has been traced back to the earliest language in which it is attested, words descended from the same Indo-European base in other languages (especially Old High German, Latin, Greek, and Sanskrit) are usually given:

**na·vel** . . . *noun* [Middle English, from Old English *nafela;* akin to Old High German *nabalo* navel, Latin *umbilicus,* Greek *omphalos* ]

**¹wind** . . . *noun* . . . [Middle English, from Old English; akin to Old High German *wint* wind, Latin *ventus,* Greek *aēnai* to blow, Sanskrit *vāti* it blows ]

Sometimes, however, to avoid space-consuming repetition, the expression "more at" directs the user to another entry where the cognates are given:

**ho·ly** . . . *adjective* . . . [Middle English, from Old English *hālig;* akin to Old English *hāl* whole — more at WHOLE]

Besides the use of "akin to" to denote relatedness, some etymologies make special use of "akin to" as part of a longer formula "of — origin; akin to —." This formula indicates that a word was borrowed from some language belonging to a group of languages whose name is inserted in the blank before the word *origin,* that it is impossible to say that the word in question is a borrowing of a particular attested word in a particular language of the source group, and that the form cited in the blank after the expression *akin to* is related to the word in question as attested within the source group:

**ba·nana** . . . *noun* . . . [Spanish or Portuguese; Spanish, from Portuguese, of African origin; akin to Wolof *banäna* banana]

**²brier** *noun* [French *bruyère* heath, from Middle French *bruiere,* from (assumed) Vulgar Latin *brucaria,* from Late Latin *brucus* heather, of Celtic origin; akin to Old Irish *froech* heather; akin to Greek *ereikē* heather]

This last example shows the two contrasting uses of "akin to." The word cited immediately after "of Celtic origin; akin to" is an attested Celtic word descended from the same etymon as the unattested Celtic source of the Latin word. The word cited after the second "akin to" is evidence that the Celtic etymon has deeper relations within Indo-European.

# Word History Paragraphs

Word history paragraphs are provided for a number of words with especially interesting origins. Such paragraphs explain word origins in greater detail than is possible in etymologies. A brown-shaded diamond after the last definition of a word signals that a word history paragraph discussing that word can be found in the right-hand column on that page or on the facing page to the right:

**den·im** . . . *noun* [French (*serge*) *de Nîmes* serge of Nîmes, France] (1965)
**1 a :** a firm durable twilled usually cotton fabric woven with colored warp and white filling threads **b :** a similar fabric woven in colored stripes
**2** *plural* **:** overalls or trousers usually of blue denim ◆

The paragraph itself is set on a light-brown background:

◇ WORD HISTORY
**denim** It is not unusual for fabrics to be named after the places where they were originally made. Nîmes is a city in France known traditionally for its textiles. A heavy serge produced there became known as *serge de Nîmes,* meaning literally, "serge from Nîmes." The "s" in *Nîmes* is not pronounced in French, so when the name of the fabric came into English in the late 17th century, it was often written *serge de Nim* and later *serge denim.* In time the latter was shortened to *denim.*

When a word is included in the word history paragraph of a different entry, the main entry for that word is followed by a run-on "**word history** see _____" which refers to the entry where the word history paragraph appears.

# Dates

At most main entries a date will be found enclosed in parentheses before the boldface colon or number that introduces the first sense:

**som·bre·ro** . . . *noun* . . . [Spanish, from *sombra* shade] (1599)

**:** a high-crowned hat of felt or straw with a very wide brim worn especially in the Southwest and Mexico

This is the date of the earliest recorded use in English, as far as it could be determined, of the sense which the date precedes. Several caveats are appropriate at this point. First, a few classes of main entries that are not complete words (as prefixes, suffixes, and combining forms) or are not generic words (as trademarks and names of figures from mythology) are not given dates. Second, the date given applies only to the first sense of the word entered in this dictionary and not necessarily to the word's very earliest meaning in English. Many words, especially those with long histories, have obsolete, archaic, or uncommon senses that are not entered in this dictionary, and such senses have been excluded from consideration in determining the date:

**¹slur** . . . *noun* [obsolete English dialect *slur* thin mud, from Middle English *sloor;* akin to Middle High German *slier* mud] (1609)
**1 a :** an insulting or disparaging remark or innuendo **:** ASPERSION

The 1609 date is for a sense of *slur* synonymous with *aspersion. Slur* also has an obsolete sense, "thin mud," that was recorded as early as the fifteenth century; but since this sense is not entered, it is ignored for purposes of dating. Third, the printed date should not be taken to mark the very first time that the word—or even the sense—was used in English. Many words were certainly in spoken use for decades or even longer before they passed into the written language. The date is for the earliest written or printed use that the editors have been able to discover. This fact means further that any date is subject to change as evidence of still earlier use may emerge, and many dates given now can confidently be expected to yield to others in future printings and editions.

A date will appear in one of three different styles:

**put·tee** . . . *noun* [Hindi *paṭṭī* strip of cloth, from Sanskrit *paṭṭikā* ] (1886)
**1 :** a cloth strip wrapped around the leg from ankle to knee

**¹moon·light** . . . *noun* (14th century) **:** the light of the moon

**¹thrall** . . . *noun* [Middle English *thral,* from Old English *thræl,* from Old Norse *thræll* ] (before 12th century)
**1 a :** a servant slave **:** BONDMAN; *also* **:** SERF

The style that names a year (as 1886) is the one used for the period from the sixteenth century to the present. The style that names only a century (as 14th century) is the one used for the period from the twelfth century through the fifteenth century, a span that roughly approximates the period of Middle English. The style (before 12th century) is used for the period before the twelfth century back to the earliest records of English, a span that approximates the period of Old English. Words first attested after 1500 can usually be dated to a single year because the precise dates of publication of modern printed texts are known. If a word must be dated from a modern text of uncertain chronology, it will be assigned the latest possible date of the text's publication prefixed by the word *circa.* For words from the Old and Middle English periods the examples of use on which the dates depend very often occur in manuscripts which are themselves of uncertain date and which may record a text whose date of composition is highly conjectural. To date words from these periods by year would frequently give a quite misleading impression of the state of our knowledge, and so the broader formulas involving centuries are used instead.

Each date reflects a particular instance of the use of a word, most often within a continuous text. In cases where the earliest appearance of a word dated by year is not from continuous text but from a source (as a dictionary or glossary) that defines or explains the word instead of simply using it, the year is preceded by *circa:*

**magnesium sulfate** *noun* (circa 1890)
**:** a sulfate of magnesium . . .

In such instances, *circa* indicates that while the source providing the date attests that the word was in use in the relevant sense at that time, it does not offer an example of the normal use of the word and thus gives no better than an approximate date for such use. For the example above no use has so far been found that is earlier than its appearance (spelled *magnesium sulphate*) as an entry in Webster's International Dictionary, published in 1890, so the date is given with the qualifying abbreviation.

# Usage

## USAGE LABELS

Three types of status labels are used in this dictionary—temporal, regional, and stylistic—to signal that a word or a sense of a word is not part of the standard vocabulary of English.

The temporal label *obsolete* means that there is no evidence of use since 1755:

**¹per·du** . . . *noun* . . .
*obsolete*

**gov·ern·ment** . . . *noun* . . .
**2** *obsolete*

The label *obsolete* is a comment on the word being defined. When a thing, as distinguished from the word used to designate it, is obsolete, appropriate orientation is usually given in the definition:

**¹cat·a·pult** . . . *noun* . . .
**1 :** an ancient military device for hurling missiles

**far·thin·gale** . . . *noun* . . .
**:** a support (as of hoops) worn especially in the 16th century beneath a skirt to expand it at the hipline

The temporal label *archaic* means that a word or sense once in common use is found today only sporadically or in special contexts:

**¹goody** . . . *noun* . . .
*archaic*

**lon·gi·tude** . . . *noun* . . .
**2** *archaic*

A word or sense limited in use to a specific region of the U.S. has a regional label. Some regional labels correspond loosely to areas defined in Hans Kurath's *Word Geography of the Eastern United States.* The adverb *chiefly* precedes a label when the word has some currency outside the specified region, and a double label is used to indicate considerable currency in each of two specific regions:

**pung** . . . *noun* . . .
*New England*

**ban·quette** . . . *noun* . . .
**1** . . . **b** *Southern*

**³pas·tor** . . . *noun* . . .
*chiefly Southwest*

**do·gie** . . . *noun* . . .
*chiefly West*

**gal·lery** . . . *noun* . . .
**2** . . . **b** *Southern & Midland*

**¹pot·latch** . . . *noun* . . .
  **2** *Northwest*

**smear·case** . . . *noun* . . .
  *chiefly Midland*

**crul·ler** . . . *noun* . . .
  **2** *Northern & Midland*

Words current in all regions of the U.S. have no label.

A word or sense limited in use to one of the other countries of the English-speaking world has an appropriate regional label:

**cutty sark** . . . *noun* . . .
  *chiefly Scottish*

**lar·ri·kin** . . . *noun* . . .
  *chiefly Australian*

**in·da·ba** . . . *noun* . . .
  *chiefly South African*

**spal·peen** . . . *noun* . . .
  *chiefly Irish*

**¹bon·net** . . . *noun* . . .
  **2 a** *British*

**book off** *intransitive verb* . . .
  *Canadian*

**¹din·kum** . . . *adjective* . . .
  *Australian & New Zealand*

**gar·ron** . . . *noun* . . .
  *Scottish & Irish*

The label *dialect* indicates that the pattern of use of a word or sense is too complex for summary labeling: it usually includes several regional varieties of American English or of American and British English:

**least·ways** . . . *adverb* . . .
  *dialect*

The label *dialect British* indicates currency in several dialects of the Commonwealth; *dialect English* indicates currency in one or more provincial dialects of England:

**bo·gle** . . . *noun* . . .
  *dialect British*

**¹hob** . . . *noun* . . .
  **1** *dialect English*

The stylistic label *slang* is used with words or senses that are especially appropriate in contexts of extreme informality, that usually have a currency not limited to a particular region or area of interest, and that are composed typically of shortened or altered forms or extravagant or facetious figures of speech:

**⁴barb** *noun* . . .
  *slang* **:** BARBITURATE

**²skin·ny** *noun* . . .
  *slang* **:** inside information **:** DOPE

**main squeeze** *noun* . . .
  *slang* **:** one's principal romantic partner

There is no satisfactory objective test for slang, especially with reference to a word out of context. No word, in fact, is invariably slang, and many standard words can be given slang applications.

The stylistic label *nonstandard* is used for a few words or senses that are disapproved by many but that have some currency in reputable contexts:

**learn** . . . *verb* . . .
  **2 a** *nonstandard*

**ir·re·gard·less** . . . *adverb* . . .
  *nonstandard*

The stylistic label *substandard* is used for those words or senses that conform to a widespread pattern of usage that differs in choice of word or form from that of the prestige group of the community:

**is** . . . *present 3d singular of* BE, *dialect present 1st & 2d singular of* BE, *substandard present plural of* BE

A subject label or guide phrase is sometimes used to indicate the specific application of a word or sense:

**knock·about** . . . *adjective* . . .
  **3** *of a sailing vessel*

**²break** *noun* . . .
  **5** . . . **d** *mining*

**²up** *adjective* . . .
  **5** *of a quark*

In general, however, subject orientation is given in the definition:

**Di·do** . . . *noun* . . .
  **:** a legendary queen of Carthage in Virgil's *Aeneid* who kills herself when Aeneas leaves her

**je·té** . . . *noun* . . .
  **:** a springing jump in ballet made from one foot to the other in any direction

# ILLUSTRATIONS OF USAGE

Definitions are sometimes followed by verbal illustrations that show a typical use of the word in context. These illustrations are enclosed in angle brackets:

**¹key** . . . *noun* . . .
  **3 a** . . . <the *key* to a riddle>

**nary** . . . *adjective*
  . . . <*nary* a person wanted to go>

**²plummet** *intransitive verb* . . .
  **2** . . . <prices *plummeted*>

**¹true** . . . *adjective* . . .
  **8** . . . <in the *truest* sense>

**turn off** *transitive verb* . . .
  **4** . . . <*turn* the water *off*>

Illustrative quotations are also used to show words in typical contexts:

**con·flict·ed** . . . *adjective*
  . . . <this unhappy and *conflicted* modern woman —John Updike>

Omissions in quotations are indicated by suspension points:

**alien·ation** . . . *noun*
  . . . <*alienation* . . . from the values of one's society and family —S.L. Halleck>

# USAGE NOTES

Definitions are sometimes followed by usage notes that give supplementary information about such matters as idiom, syntax, semantic relationship, and status. A usage note is introduced by a lightface dash:

**²cry** *noun* . . .
  **11 :** . . . — usually used in the phrase *a far cry*

**²drum** . . . *transitive verb* . . .
  **2 :** . . . — usually used with *out*

**¹so** . . . *adverb* . . .
  **1 a** : . . . — often used as a substitute for a preceding clause

**¹sfor·zan·do** . . . *adjective or adverb* . . . **:** . . . — used as a direction in music

**grin·go** . . . *noun* . . .
  **:** . . . — often used disparagingly

**pissed** . . . *adjective* . . .
  **1** . . . **:** . . . — sometimes considered vul gar

**hajji** . . . *noun* . . .
  **:** . . . — often used as a title

Two or more usage notes are separated by a semicolon:

**²thine** *pronoun* . . .
  **:** that which belongs to thee — used without a following noun as a pronoun equivalent in meaning to the adjective *thy*; used especially in ecclesiastical or literary language and still surviving in the speech of Friends especially among themselves

Sometimes a usage note calls attention to one or more terms with the same denotation as the main entry:

**water moccasin** *noun* . . .
  **1 :** a venomous semiaquatic pit viper (*Agkistrodon piscivorus*) chiefly of the southeastern U.S. that is closely related to the copperhead — called also *cottonmouth, cottonmouth moccasin*

The called-also terms are shown in italic type. If such a term falls alphabetically more than a column away from the main entry, it is entered at its own place with the sole definition being a synonymous cross-reference to the entry where it appears in the usage note:

**cot·ton·mouth** . . . *noun* . . .
  **:** WATER MOCCASIN

**cottonmouth moccasin** *noun* . . .
  **:** WATER MOCCASIN

Sometimes a usage note is used in place of a definition. Some function words (as conjunctions and prepositions) have little or no semantic content; most interjections express feelings but are otherwise untranslatable into meaning; and some other words (as oaths and honorific titles) are more amenable to comment than to definition:

**¹of** . . . *preposition* . . .
  **1** — used as a function word to indicate a point of reckoning

**¹oyez** . . . *verb imperative* . . .
  — used by a court or public crier to gain attention before a proclamation

**¹or** . . . *conjunction* . . .
  **1** — used as a function word to indicate an alternative

**gol·ly** . . . *interjection* . . .
  — used as a mild oath or to express surprise

**sir** . . . *noun* . . .
  **2 a** — used as a usually respectful form of address

## USAGE PARAGRAPHS

Brief usage paragraphs are provided for a number of entries that are considered to present problems of confused or disputed usage. A usage paragraph typically summarizes the historical background of the item and its associated body of opinion, compares these with available evidence of current usage, and often adds a few words of suitable advice for the dictionary user.

A small green-shaded square after the last definition of a word signals that a usage paragraph discussing that word can be found in the right-hand column on that page or on the facing page to the right:

**ag·gra·vate** . . . *transitive verb* . . .
  **1** *obsolete* **a :** to make heavy **:** BURDEN **b** **:** INCREASE
  **2 :** to make worse, more serious, or more severe **:** intensify unpleasantly <problems have been *aggravated* by neglect>
  **3 a :** to rouse to displeasure or anger by usually persistent and often petty goading **b** **:** to produce inflammation in ■

The paragraph itself is set on a green background. Where appropriate, discussion in the paragraph is keyed by sense number to the definition of the meaning in question. Most paragraphs incorporate appropriate verbal illustrations and illustrative quotations to clarify and exemplify the points being made:

□ USAGE
**Aggravate** Although *aggravate* has been used in sense 3a since the 17th century, it has been the object of disapproval only since about 1870. It is used in expository prose <when his silly conceit . . . about his not-very-good early work has begun to *aggravate* us —William Styron> but seems to be more common in speech and casual writing <a good profession for him, because bus drivers get *aggravated* —Jackie Gleason (interview, 1986)> <& now this letter comes to *aggravate* me a thousand times worse —Mark Twain (letter, 1864)>. Sense 2 is far more common than sense 3a in published prose. Such is not the case, however, with *aggravation* and *aggravating. Aggravation* is used in sense 3 somewhat more than in its earlier senses; *aggravating* has practically no use other than to express annoyance.

When a second word is also discussed in a paragraph, the main entry for that word is followed by a run-on "*usage* see_____" which refers to the entry where the paragraph may be found:

**²af·fect** . . . *verb* . . .
  . . . *usage* see EFFECT

When a word that has its own usage paragraph is also discussed in a usage paragraph at another entry, the word's usage paragraph is followed by a cross-reference to the other entry.

# Definitions

## DIVISION OF SENSES

A boldface colon is used in this dictionary to introduce a definition:

**¹coo·per** . . . *noun* . . .
  **:** one that makes or repairs wooden casks or tubs

It is also used to separate two or more definitions of a single sense:

**un·cage** . . . *transitive verb* . . .
  **:** to release from or as if from a cage **:** free from restraint

Boldface Arabic numerals separate the senses of a word that has more than one sense:

> ²**savage** *noun* . . .
> **1 :** a person belonging to a primitive society
> **2 :** a brutal person
> **3 :** a rude or unmannerly person

Boldface lowercase letters separate the subsenses of a word:

> ¹**grand** . . . *adjective* . . .
> **5 a :** LAVISH, SUMPTUOUS . . . **b :** marked by a regal form and dignity **c :** fine or imposing in appearance or impression **d :** LOFTY, SUBLIME

Lightface numerals in parentheses indicate a further division of subsenses:

> **take out** . . . *transitive verb* . . .
> **1 a** (1) **:** DEDUCT, SEPARATE (2) **:** EXCLUDE, OMIT (3) **:** WITHDRAW, WITHHOLD

A lightface colon following a definition and immediately preceding two or more subsenses indicates that the subsenses are subsumed by the preceding definition:

> ²**crunch** *noun* . . .
> **3 :** a tight or critical situation: as **a :** a critical point in the buildup of pressure between opposing elements . . . **b :** a severe economic squeeze . . . **c :** SHORTAGE

> **se·quoia** . . . *noun* . . .
> **:** either of two huge coniferous California trees of the bald cypress family that may reach a height of over 300 feet (90 meters): **a :** BIG TREE **b :** REDWOOD 3a

The word *as* may or may not follow the lightface colon. Its presence (as at ²*crunch*) indicates that the following subsenses are typical or significant examples. Its absence (as at *sequoia*) indicates that the subsenses which follow are exhaustive.

The system of separating the various senses of a word by numerals and letters is a lexical convenience. It reflects something of their semantic relationship, but it does not evaluate senses or set up a hierarchy of importance among them.

Sometimes a particular semantic relationship between senses is suggested by the use of one of four italic sense dividers: *especially, specifically, also,* or *broadly.*

The sense divider *especially* is used to introduce the most common meaning subsumed in the more general preceding definition:

> ²**slick** *adjective* . . .
> **3 a :** characterized by subtlety or nimble wit **:** CLEVER; *especially* **:** WILY

The sense divider *specifically* is used to introduce a common but highly restricted meaning subsumed in the more general preceding definition:

> **pon·tiff** . . . *noun* . . .
> **2 :** BISHOP; *specifically* **:** POPE

The sense divider *also* is used to introduce a meaning that is closely related to but may be considered less important than the preceding sense:

> **chi·na** . . . *noun* . . .
> **1 :** PORCELAIN; *also* **:** vitreous porcelain wares (as dishes, vases, or ornaments) for domestic use

The sense divider *broadly* is used to introduce an extended or wider meaning of the preceding definition:

> **flot·sam** . . . *noun* . . .
> **1 :** floating wreckage of a ship or its cargo; *broadly* **:** floating debris

# ORDER OF SENSES

The order of senses within an entry is historical: the sense known to have been first used in English is entered first. This is not to be taken to mean, however, that each sense of a multisense word developed from the immediately preceding sense. It is altogether possible that sense 1 of a word has given rise to sense 2 and sense 2 to sense 3, but frequently sense 2 and sense 3 may have arisen independently of one another from sense 1.

When a numbered sense is further subdivided into lettered subsenses, the inclusion of particular subsenses within a sense is based upon their semantic relationship to one another, but their order is likewise historical: subsense 1a is earlier than 1b, 1b is earlier than 1c, and so forth. Divisions of subsenses indicated by lightface numerals in parentheses are also in historical order with respect to one another. Subsenses may be out of historical order, however, with respect to the broader numbered senses:

> ¹**job** . . . *noun* . . . (circa 1627)
> **1 a :** a piece of work; *especially* **:** a small miscellaneous piece of work undertaken on order at a stated rate **b :** the object or material on which work is being done **c :** something produced by or as if by work <do a better *job* next time> **d :** an example of a usually specified type **:** ITEM <this *job* is round-necked and sleeveless —Lois Long>
> **2 a :** something done for private advantage <suspected the whole incident was a put-up *job*> **b :** a criminal enterprise; *specifically* **:** ROBBERY **c :** a damaging or destructive bit of work <did a *job* on him>
> **3 a** (1) **:** something that has to be done **:** TASK (2) **:** an undertaking requiring unusual exertion <it was a real *job* to talk over that noise> **b :** a specific duty, role, or function **c :** a regular remunerative position **d** *chiefly British* **:** state of affairs — used with *bad* or *good* <it was a good *job* you didn't hit the old man —E. L. Thomas>

At *job* the date indicates that the earliest unit of meaning, sense 1a, was born in the seventeenth century, and it is readily apparent how the following subsenses are linked to it and to each other by the idea of work. Even subsense 1d is so linked, because while it does not apply exclusively to manufactured items, it often does so, as the illustrative quotation suggests. Yet 1d did not exist before the 1920s, while 2a and 3a(1) both belong to the seventeenth century, although they are later than 1a. Even the very last subsense, 3d, is earlier than 1d, as it is found in the works of Dickens.

Historical order also determines whether transitive or intransitive senses are given first at verbs which have both kinds. If the earliest sense is transitive, all the transitive senses precede all the intransitive senses.

# OMISSION OF A SENSE

Occasionally the dictionary user, having turned to an entry, may not find a particular sense that was expected or hoped for. This usually means no more than that the editors judged the sense insufficiently common or otherwise important to include in a dictionary of this scope. Such a sense will frequently be found at the appropriate entry in a dictionary (as Webster's Third New International Dictionary) that has room for less common words and meanings. One special case is worth noting, however.

At times it would be possible to include the definition of a meaning at more than one entry (as at a simple verb and a verb-adverb collocation or at a verb and an adjective derived from a participle of that verb). To save space for other information such double coverage is avoided, and the meaning is generally defined only at the base form. For the derivative term the meaning is then considered to be essentially self-explanatory and is not defined. For example *cast off* has a sense "to get rid of" in such typical contexts as "cast off all restraint," and so has the simple verb *cast* in contexts like "cast all restraint to the winds." This meaning is defined as sense 1e(2) of *cast* and is omitted from the entry *cast off*, where the dictionary user will find a number of senses that cannot be considered self-explanatory in relation to the entries for *cast* and *off*. Likewise, the entry for the adjective *picked* gives only one sense—"CHOICE, PRIME"—which is not the meaning of *picked* in such a context as "the picked fruit lay stacked in boxes awaiting shipment." A definition suitable for this use is not given at *picked* because one is given at the first homograph *pick*, the verb from which the adjective *picked* is derived, as sense 3a—"to gather by plucking."

## INFORMATION AT INDIVIDUAL SENSES

Information coming between the entry word and the first definition of a multisense word applies to all senses and subsenses. Information applicable only to some senses or subsenses is given between the appropriate boldface numeral or letter and the symbolic colon. A variety of kinds of information is offered in this way:

> **²palm** *noun* . . .
> **3** [Latin *palmus,* from *palma*]

> **²rally** *noun* . . .
> **4** *also* **ral·lye**

> **¹disk** *or* **disc** . . . *noun* . . .
> **4** . . . **b** *usually disc*

> **cru·ci·fix·ion** . . . *noun* . . .
> **1 a** *capitalized*

> **¹tile** . . . *noun* . . .
> **1** *plural* **tiles** *or* **tile a** . . .

> **del·i·ca·tes·sen** . . . *noun plural* . . .
> **1** . . .
> **2** *singular, plural* **delicatessens**

> **fix·ing** . . . *noun* . . .
> **2** *plural*

> **²die** . . . *noun, plural* **dice** . . . *or* **dies**
> . . .
> **1** *plural* **dice** . . .
> **2** *plural* **dies** . . .
> **3** *plural* **dies**

> **¹folk** . . . *noun, plural* **folk** *or* **folks** . . .
> **4** *folks plural*

At *palm* the subetymology indicates that the third sense, while ultimately derived from the same source (Latin *palma*) as the other senses of the word, has a different immediate etymon (Latin *palmus*), from which it receives its meaning. At *rally* one is told that in the fourth sense the word has a variant spelling not used for other senses and that this variant is a secondary or less common one. At *disk* the italic label of sense 4b indicates that, while the spelling *disk* is overall somewhat the more common (since it precedes *disc* out of alphabetical order at the beginning of the entry), *disc* is the usual spelling for this particular sense. At *crucifixion* the label *capitalized* points out the one meaning of the word in which it is capitalized. At the first homograph *tile* no plural is shown at the beginning of the entry because the usual plural, *tiles,* is regular. The subsenses of sense 1, however, have a zero plural as well as the usual one, and so both plurals appear in boldface at sense 1. At *delicatessen* the situation is different: the entry as a whole is labeled a plural noun, but sense 2 is used as a singular. In this sense *delicatessen* can take the plural ending *-s* when needed, a fact that is indicated by the appearance of the plural in boldface at the sense. At *fixing* the italic abbreviation simply means that when used in this sense the word is always written in its plural form, *fixings.* At the second homograph *die* the actual distribution of the variant plurals can be given sense by sense in italic type because both variants are shown in boldface earlier in the entry. At the first homograph *folk* a singular noun is

shown with variant plurals of nearly equal frequency, when all senses are taken into account. The fourth sense, however, is unique in being always plural in form and construction. The form of the plural for this sense is *folks,* as shown, and the placement of the form before the label instead of after it (as at the senses of *die*) means that this sense is always plural.

When an italicized label or guide phrase follows a boldface numeral, the label or phrase applies only to that specific numbered sense and its subsenses. It does not apply to any other boldface numbered senses:

> **¹boot** . . . *noun* . . .
> **1** *archaic* . . .
> **2** *chiefly dialect* . . .
> **3** *obsolete* . . . .

> **¹fa·vor** . . . *noun* . . .
> **2** *archaic* **a** . . . **b** (1) . . . (2) . . .
> **3**

At *boot* the *archaic* label applies only to sense 1, the *chiefly dialect* label only to sense 2, and the *obsolete* label only to sense 3. At *favor* the *archaic* label applies to all the subsenses of sense 2 but not to sense 3.

When an italicized label or guide phrase follows a boldface letter, the label or phrase applies only to that specific lettered sense and its subsenses. It does not apply to any other boldface lettered senses:

> **²stour** *noun* . . .
> **1 a** *archaic* . . . **b** *dialect British*

The *archaic* label applies to sense 1a but not to sense 1b. The *dialect British* label applies to sense 1b but not to sense 1a.

When an italicized label or guide phrase follows a parenthesized numeral, the label or phrase applies only to that specific numbered sense:

> **in·car·na·tion** . . . *noun* . . .
> **1a** (1) . . . (2) *capitalized*

The label *capitalized* applies to sense 1a(2) and to no other subsenses of the word.

# Names of Plants & Animals

The entries that define the common or vernacular names (as *peach* and *lion*) of plants and animals or sometimes a related term (as *streptomycin*), if a common name is rare or does not exist, employ in part the formal, codified, New Latin vocabulary of biological systematics. This vocabulary has been developed and used by biologists in accordance with international codes of botanical and zoological nomenclature for the purpose of identifying and indicating the relationships of plants and animals. This system of names classifies organisms into a hierarchy of groups—taxa—with each kind of organism having one—and only one—correct name and belonging to one—and only one—taxon at each level of classification in the hierarchy.

This contrasts with the system of common or vernacular names which is determined by popular usage and in which one organism may have several names (as *mountain lion, cougar,* and *painter*), different organisms may have the same name (as *dolphin*), and there may be variation in meaning or overlapping of the categories denoted by the names (as *whale, dolphin,* and *porpoise*).

The fundamental taxon is the genus. It includes a group of closely related kinds of plants (as *Prunus,* which includes the wild and cultivated cherries, apricots, peaches, and almonds) or animals (as *Canis,* which includes domestic dogs, coyotes, jackals, and wolves). The genus name is a capitalized singular noun.

The unique name of each kind of organism or species—the binomial or species name—consists of a singular capitalized genus name combined with an uncapitalized specific epithet. The name for a variety or subspecies—the trinomial, variety name, or subspecies name—adds a similar varietal or subspecific epithet. The cultivated cabbage (*Brassica oleracea capitata*), the cauliflower (*Brassica oleracea botrytis*), and brussels sprouts (*Brassica oleracea gemmifera*) belong to the same species (*Brassica oleracea*) of cole.

Names of taxa higher than the genus (as family, order, and class) are capitalized plural nouns that are often used with singular verbs and that are not abbreviated in normal use. No two genera of animals in good standing are permitted to have the same name, nor are any two genera of plants in good standing. Since the botanical and zoological codes are independent, however, a plant genus and an animal genus may have the same name. Thus, a number of cabbage butterflies (as *Pieris rapae*) are placed in a genus of animals with the same name as the plant genus to which the Japanese andromeda (*Pieris japonica*) belongs. Although no two higher taxa of plants are permitted to have the same name, the rules of zoological nomenclature do not apply to taxa above the family so that rarely some widely separated groups may receive the same taxonomic name (as the ordinal name Decapoda in the entry *decapod*) from different specialists.

The taxonomic names of biological nomenclature used in this dictionary are enclosed in parentheses and usually come immediately after the primary orienting noun. Genus names as well as binomials and trinomials are italicized, but names of taxa above the genus are not italicized:

> **¹bee·tle** . . . *noun* . . .
> **1 :** any of an order (Coleoptera) of insects having four wings of which the outer pair are modified into stiff elytra that protect the inner pair when at rest
>
> **rob·in** . . . *noun* . . .
> **1 a :** a small chiefly European thrush (*Erithacus rubecula*) resembling a warbler and having a brownish olive back and orangish face and breast **b :** any of various Old World songbirds that are related to or resemble the European robin
> **2 :** a large North American thrush (*Turdus migratorius*) with olivaceous to slate gray upperparts, blackish head and tail, black and whitish streaked throat, and dull reddish breast and underparts
>
> **strep·to·my·cin** . . . *noun* . . .
> **:** an antibiotic organic base $C_{21}H_{39}N_7O_{12}$ produced by a soil actinomycete (*Streptomyces griseus*), active against many bacteria, and used especially in the treatment of infections (as tuberculosis) by gram-negative bacteria

Sometimes two or more different New Latin names can be found used in current literature for the same organism or group. This happens when older monographs and field guides are kept in print after name changes occur, when there are legitimate differences of opinion about the validity of names, and when the rules of priority do not apply or are not applied. To help the reader in recognizing an organism or group, some entries in this dictionary give two taxonomic names connected by the word *synonym*:

> **li·on** . . . *noun* . . .
> **1 a** . . . **:** a large heavily-built social cat (*Panthera leo* synonym *Leo leo*) of open or rocky areas chiefly of sub-Saharan Africa . . .

Taxonomic names are used in this dictionary to provide precise technical identifications through which defined terms may be pursued in technical writings. Because of their specialized nature taxonomic names do not have separate entry. However, many common names are derived directly from the names of taxa and especially genera with little or no modification. It is particularly important to distinguish between a common name and the genus name from which it is derived without a change in spelling, as these names appear in print. The common name (as clostridium

or drosophila) is not usually capitalized or italicized but does have a plural (as clostridia or drosophilas) which often has an ending different from that of the singular. In contrast the genus name (as *Clostridium* or *Drosophila*) is capitalized and italicized but never takes a plural. A common name in plural form (as coleoptera) may sometimes be spelled like the name of a taxon, but it is not usually capitalized.

The entries defining the names of plants and animals are usually oriented to higher taxa by other vernaculars (as by *alga* at *seaweed* or *thrush* at *robin*) or by technical adjectives (as by *composite* at *daisy*, *leguminous* at *pea*, or *oscine* at *warbler*) so that the name of a higher taxon may often be found by consulting an entry defining a more inclusive common name or a term related to it. Among the higher plants, except for the composites and legumes and a few tropical groups, such orientation is by a vernacular family name linked at the corresponding taxonomic entry to its technical equivalent:

> **²rose** . . . *noun* . . .
> **1 a :** any of a genus (*Rosa* of the family Rosaceae, the rose family) of usually prickly shrubs with pinnate leaves and showy flowers . . .
>
> **ap·ple** . . . *noun, often attributive* . . .
> **1 :** the fleshy usually rounded and red, yellow, or green edible pome fruit of a tree (genus *Malus*) of the rose family; *also* **:** an apple tree

A genus name may be abbreviated to its initial letter when it is used more than once in senses not separated by a boldface number:

> **nas·tur·tium** . . . *noun* . . .
> **:** any of a genus (*Tropaeolum* of the family Tropaeolaceae, the nasturtium family) of herbs of Central and South America with showy spurred flowers and pungent seeds; *especially* **:** either of two widely cultivated ornamentals (*T. majus* and *T. minus*)

# Cross-Reference

Four different kinds of cross-references are used in this dictionary: directional, synonymous, cognate, and inflectional. In each instance the cross-reference is readily recognized by the lightface small capitals in which it is printed.

A cross-reference following a lightface dash and beginning with *see* or *compare* is a directional cross-reference. It directs the dictionary user to look elsewhere for further information. A *compare* cross-reference is regularly appended to a definition; a *see* cross-reference may stand alone:

> **wel·ter·weight** . . . *noun*
> . . . — compare LIGHTWEIGHT, MIDDLEWEIGHT
>
> **¹ri·al** . . . *noun*
> . . . — see MONEY table

A cross-reference immediately following a boldface colon is a synonymous cross-reference. It may stand alone as the only definitional matter for an entry or for a sense or subsense of an entry; it may follow an analytical definition; it may be one of two synonymous cross-references separated by a comma:

> **gar·ban·zo** . . . *noun* . . .
> **:** CHICKPEA
>
> **¹ne·glect** . . . *transitive verb* . . .
> **1 :** to give little attention or respect to
> **:** DISREGARD

**²main** *adjective* . . .
  **1 :** CHIEF, PRINCIPAL

A synonymous cross-reference indicates that a definition at the entry cross-referred to can be substituted as a definition for the entry or the sense or subsense in which the cross-reference appears.

A cross-reference following an italic *variant of* is a cognate cross-reference:

**kaf·tan** *variant of* CAFTAN

Sometimes a cognate cross-reference has a limiting label preceding *variant of* as a specific indication that the variant is not standard English:

**haul·ier** . . . *British variant of* HAULER

**²hist** . . . *dialect variant of* HOIST

**sher·ris** . . . *archaic variant of* SHERRY

A cross-reference following an italic label that identifies an entry as an inflected form of a noun, of an adjective or adverb, or of a verb is an inflectional cross-reference. Inflectional cross-references appear only when the inflected form falls at least a column away from the entry cross-referred to:

**calves** *plural of* CALF

**³wound** . . . *past and past participle of* WIND

When guidance seems needed as to which one of several homographs or which sense of a multisense word is being referred to, a superscript numeral may precede the cross-reference or a sense number may follow it or both:

**¹toss** . . . *transitive verb* . . .
  **3** . . . **c :** MATCH 5a

# Synonyms

Brief paragraphs discriminating words of closely associated meaning from one another have been placed at a number of entries. A small blue-shaded star after the last definition of a word signals that a synonym paragraph discussing that word can be found in the right-hand column on that page or on the facing page to the right:

**²answer** . . . *intransitive verb* . . .
  **6 :** to offer a solution for; *especially* **:** SOLVE ☆

The paragraph itself is set on a blue background and begins with a list of the words to be discussed in it, followed by a concise statement of the element of meaning that the words have in common. The discriminations are amplified with verbal illustrations:

> ☆ SYNONYMS
> **Answer, respond, reply, rejoin, re-tort** mean to say, write, or do something in return. ANSWER implies the satisfying of a question, demand, call, or need <*an-swered* all the questions>. RESPOND may suggest an immediate or quick reaction <*responded* eagerly to a call for volunteers>. REPLY implies making a return commensurate with the original question or demand <an invitation that requires you to *reply*>. REJOIN often implies sharpness or quickness in answering <"who asked you?" she *rejoined*>. RETORT suggests responding to an explicit charge or criticism by way of retaliation <he *retorted* to the attack with biting sarcasm>.

When a word is included in a synonym paragraph, the main entry for that word is followed by a run-on "**synonym** see _____" which refers to the entry where the synonym paragraph appears:

**²respond** *verb* . . . **synonym** see ANSWER

When a word is a main entry at which there is a synonym paragraph and is also included in another paragraph elsewhere, the paragraph at the main entry is followed by a run-on "See in addition _____" which refers to the entry where the other paragraph may be found:

**¹nat·u·ral** . . . *adjective* . . .
  **15 :** of an off-white or beige color ☆

> ☆ SYNONYMS
> **Natural, ingenuous, naive, unsophisticated, artless** mean free from pretension or calculation . . . See in addition REGULAR.

**¹reg·u·lar** . . . *adjective* . . .
  **5 :** of, relating to, or constituting the permanent standing military force of a state <*regular* army> <*regular* soldiers> ☆

> ☆ SYNONYMS
> **Regular, normal, typical, natural** mean being of the sort or kind that is expected as usual, ordinary, or average . . .

# Combining Forms, Prefixes & Suffixes

An entry that begins or ends with a hyphen is a word element that forms part of an English compound:

**mega-** *or* **meg-** *combining form* . . .
  **1** . . . **b** . . . <*mega*hit>

**-logy** *noun combining form* . . .
  **1** . . . <phrase*ology*>

**-lyze** *verb combining form*
  . . . <electro*lyze*>

**-like** *adjective combining form*
  . . . <bell-*like*> <lady*like*>

**pre-** *prefix* . . .
  **1 a** (1) . . . <*pre*historic>

**¹-ory** . . . *noun suffix* . . .
  **1** . . . <observat*ory*>

**¹-ic** *adjective suffix* . . .
  **2 a** . . . <alderman*ic*>

**²-ly** *adverb suffix* . . .
  **1 a** . . . <slow*ly*>

**-ize** *verb suffix* . . .
  **2 a** . . . <crystall*ize*>

Combining forms, prefixes, and suffixes are entered in this dictionary for three reasons: to make easier the writing of etymologies of words in which these word elements occur over and over again; to make understandable the meaning of many undefined run-ons which for reasons of space would be omitted if they had to be given etymologies and definitions; and to make recognizable the meaningful elements of new words that are not well enough established in the language to warrant dictionary entry.

# Lists of Undefined Words

Lists of undefined words occur after the entries of these prefixes and combining forms:

| | | |
|---|---|---|
| **anti-** | **multi-** | **re-** |
| **co-** | **non-** | **self-** |

| | | |
|---|---|---|
| **counter-** | **out-** | **sub-** |
| **hyper-** | **over-** | **super-** |
| **inter-** | **post-** | **ultra-** |
| **mis-** | **pre-** | **un-** |

These words are not defined because they are self-explanatory; their meanings are simply the sum of a meaning of the prefix or combining form and a meaning of the root word. Centered dots are shown to save the dictionary user the trouble of consulting another entry. The lists are not exhaustive of all the words that might be, or actually have been, formed with these prefixes and combining forms. The dictionary has room for only the most common or important examples.

# New Words and Senses

Cross-references to other entries or tables refer you to the main body of the book unless otherwise specified. Entries here, except for abbreviations, which contain the date of first recorded use are new words; those without dates shown are new meanings of words already entered in the main vocabulary section.

**acid snow** *noun* (1981)
: acid precipitation in the form of snow
**ac·tion·er** \'ak-sh(ə-)nər\ *noun* (1973)
: a film dominated by a high degree of exciting action
**action figure** *noun* (1987)
: a small-scale figure usu. of a superhero used especially as a toy
**ADHD** *abbreviation* attention deficit/hyperactivity disorder
**adren·al·ized** \ə-'dre-n°l-īzd\ *adjective* (1973)
: filled with a sudden rush of energy : EXCITED
**advance directive** *noun* (1984)
: a legal document (as a living will) signed by a competent person in order to provide guidance for medical and health-care decisions (as the termination of life support or organ donation) in the event the person becomes incompetent to make such decisions
**aer·o·bi·cize** \ā(-ə)r-'ō-bə-,sīz, ,e(-ə)r-\ *verb*
**aer·o·bi·cized; aer·o·bi·ciz·ing**
*transitive verb* (1981)
: to bring to good physical condition through aerobics
*intransitive verb*
: to engage in aerobics
**agree** *transitive verb*
: to consent to as a course of action ⟨agreed to sell him the house⟩
**AHA** \ā-(,)āch-'ā\ *noun* (1991)
: ALPHA HYDROXY ACID (in this list)
**all–ter·rain vehicle** *noun* (1969)
: a small motor vehicle with three or four wheels that is designed for use on various types of terrain — called also *ATV*
**alpha hydroxy acid** *noun* (1986)
: any of various carboxylic acids with a hydroxyl group attached at the alpha position; *specifically* : one (as malic acid or lactic acid) that occurs in natural products (as fruits, sugar cane, or yogurt) and is used in cosmetics for its exfoliating effect on the surface layer of skin — called also *AHA*
**al·ter·na·tive** *adjective*
: of, relating to, or being rock music that is regarded as an alternative to conventional rock and is typically influenced by punk rock, hard rock, hip-hop, or folk music
**alternative medicine** *noun* (1977)
: any of various systems of healing or treating disease (as chiropractic, homeopathy, or faith healing) not included in the traditional medical curricula taught in the U.S. and Britain
**aluminum oxide** *noun* (1907)
: ALUMINA
**an·i·ma·tron·ic** \,a-nə-mə-'trä-nik\ *adjective* [short for *audio-animatronic*] (1978)
: of, relating to, or being a puppet or similar figure that is animated by means of electromechanical devices
— **an·i·ma·tron·i·cal·ly** \-ni-k(ə-)lē\ *adverb*
**an·ti·choice** \,an-ti-'chȯis, ,an-,tī-\ *adjective* (1978)

: ANTIABORTION
— **an·ti·choic·er** \-'chȯi-sər\ *noun*
**ap·o·pto·sis** \,a-pəp-'tō-səs, -pə-'tō-\ *noun, plural* **ap·o·pto·ses** \-,sēz\ [New Latin, from Greek *apoptōsis* a falling off, from *apopiptein* to fall off, from *apo-* + *piptein* to fall — more at FEATHER] (1972)
: a genetically determined destruction of cells from within due to activation of a stimulus or removal of a suppressing agent or stimulus that is postulated to exist to explain the orderly elimination of superfluous cells — called also *programmed cell death*
— **ap·o·pto·tic** \-'tä-tik\ *adjective*
**app** \'ap\ *noun* (1987)
: APPLICATION 1a(3)
**ap·plet** \'a-plət, -(,)plet\ *noun* [*application* + *-et*] (1990)
: a short application program especially for performing a simple specific task
**ar·chaea** \är-'kē-ə\ *plural noun* [New Latin, from Greek *archaios*] (1990)
: microorganisms of a domain (Archaea) comprising the archaebacteria when considered as equal in taxonomic rank to the other prokaryotes and the eukaryotes
— **ar·chae·al** \-əl\ *adjective*
— **ar·chae·an** \-ən\ *adjective or noun*
**ar·mored** \'är-mərd\ *adjective* (1862)
**1 a :** equipped or protected with armor **b** : equipped with armored fighting vehicles ⟨an *armored* division⟩
**2 :** marked by the use of armor ⟨*armored* combat⟩
**assault weapon** *noun* (1973)
: any of various automatic or semiautomatic firearms; *especially* : ASSAULT RIFLE
**attention deficit/hyperactivity disorder** *noun* (1987)
: ATTENTION DEFICIT DISORDER — abbreviation *ADHD*
**ATV** \ā-(,)tē-'vē\ *noun* (1969)
: ALL-TERRAIN VEHICLE (in this list)
**au·dio·book** \'ȯ-dē-ō-,bùk\ *noun* (1988)
: TALKING BOOK
**Azer·bai·ja·ni** \,a-zər-,bī-'jä-nē, ,ä-\ *noun, plural* **Azerbaijanis** *also* **Azerbaijani** [Persian *āzarbāyjānī*, from *Āzarbāyjān* Azerbaijan] (circa 1909)
**1 :** a member of a Turkic-speaking people of Azerbaijan and northwest Iran
**2 :** the Turkic language of the Azerbaijanis
— **Azerbaijani** *adjective*
**baf·fle·gab** \'ba-fəl-,gab\ *noun* (1952)
: GOBBLEDYGOOK
**bench·mark·ing** \-,mär-kiŋ\ *noun* (1976)
: the study of a competitor's product or business practices in order to improve the performance of one's own company
**beta test** *noun* (1978)
: a field test of a prototype version of a product (as software) especially by testers outside the

company developing it that is conducted prior to commercial release
— **beta test** *transitive verb*
— **beta tester** *noun*
**Bh** *symbol* **bohrium**
**big crunch** *noun, often capitalized B&C* (1979)
: a hypothetical cosmological event in which all matter in the universe collapses to a singularity and which is posited to be a possible fate of the universe if the density of matter in it is sufficiently high — compare BIG BANG
**big–time** \'big-,tīm\ *adjective* (1930)
: relating to or involved in the big time ⟨*big-time* sports⟩; *also* : MAJOR 4 ⟨*big-time* operators⟩
**big–time** *adverb* (1980)
: in a major or large-scale manner : to a great extent or degree ⟨owes me *big-time*⟩
**bio·mark·er** \'bī-ō-,mär-kər\ *noun* (1982)
: a distinctive usually biochemical indicator (as a metabolite) of a biological or geochemical process or event (as aging, poisoning, fossilization, or oil formation)
**bio·mi·met·ics** \,bī-ō-mə-'me-tiks, -mī-\ *noun plural but singular in construction* (1974)
: the study of the formation, structure, or function of biologically produced substances and materials (as enzymes or silk) and biological mechanisms and processes (as protein synthesis or photosynthesis) especially for the purpose of synthesizing similar products by artificial mechanisms which mimic natural ones
— **bio·mi·met·ic** \-tik\ *adjective*
**bio·re·gion** \'bī-ō-,rē-jən\ *noun* (1978)
: a region whose limits are naturally defined by topographic and biological features (as mountains and ecosystems)
— **bio·re·gion·al** \,bī-ō-'rēj-nəl, -'rē-jə-n°l\ *adjective*
**bio·re·gion·al·ism** \,bī-ō-'rēj-nə-,li-zəm, -'rē-jə-n°l-i-\ *noun* (1981)
: an environmentalist movement to make political boundaries coincide with bioregions
— **bio·re·gion·al·ist** \-list, -ist\ *noun or adjective*
**bio·re·me·di·a·tion** \-ri-,mē-dē-'ā-shən\ *noun* (1986)
: the treatment of pollutants or waste (as in an oil spill, contaminated groundwater, or industrial process) by the use of microorganisms (as bacteria) that break down the undesirable substances
**bio·sol·id** \'bī-ō-,sä-ləd\ *noun* (1990)
: solid organic matter recovered from a sewage treatment process and used especially as fertilizer — usually used in plural
**bis·cot·to** \bi-'skät-ō\ *noun, plural* **bis·cot·ti** \-ē\ [Italian, biscuit, cookie, from (*pane*) *biscotto*, literally, bread baked twice] (1973)
: a crisp cookie or biscuit of Italian origin that is flavored usu. with anise and filberts or almonds
**bit–map** \'bit-,map\ *noun* (1982)
: an array of binary data representing a bit-mapped image or display; *also* : the image or display itself

**bit–mapped** \'bit-,mapt\ *adjective* (1978)
**:** of, relating to, or being a digital image or display for which an array of binary data specifies the value of each pixel ⟨*bit-mapped* graphics⟩
**blo·vi·ate** \'blō-vē-,āt\ *intransitive verb*
**blo·vi·at·ed; blo·vi·at·ing** [perhaps irregularly from *blow*] (circa 1897)
**:** to speak or write verbosely and windily
— **blo·vi·a·tion** \,blō-vē-'ā-shən\ *noun*
**blow off** *transitive verb*
**1 :** to outperform in a contest
**2 :** to end a relationship with
**blue screen** *noun* (1977)
**:** a photographic technique in which a subject is filmed in front of a blue background so as to allow compositing with other footage; *also*
**:** the blue background
**bohr·i·um** \'bōr-ē-əm, 'bȯr-\ *noun* [New Latin, from Niels *Bohr*] (1994)
**:** a short-lived radioactive element that is artificially produced — see ELEMENT table
**bo·lus** *noun*
**:** a dose of a substance (as a drug) that is administered intravenously; *specifically* **:** a large dose given intravenously so that the desired therapeutic concentration in the blood is reached rapidly
**bo·no·bo** \bə-'nō-bō; 'bä-nə-bō, -nō-\ *noun* [origin unknown] (1954)
**:** PYGMY CHIMPANZEE
**book·mark** *noun*
**:** a menu entry or icon on a computer that is most often created by the user and that serves as a shortcut to a previously viewed location (as an Internet address)
**boot** *intransitive verb*
**:** to become ready for use especially by booting a program ⟨the computer *boots* quickly⟩ — often used with *up*
**bot·tom–feed·er** \'bä-təm-,fē-dər\ *noun* (1920)
**1 :** a fish that feeds at the bottom
**2 :** one that is of the lowest status or rank
**3 :** an opportunist who seeks quick profit usually at the expense of others or from their misfortune
**bovine spon·gi·form encephalopathy**
\-'spən-ji-,fȯrm-\ *noun* (1987)
**:** a fatal disease of cattle affecting the nervous system, resembling or identical with scrapie of sheep and goats, and probably caused by a prion transmitted by infected tissue in food — abbreviation *BSE*; called also *mad cow disease*
**brain·i·ac** \'brā-nē-,ak\ *noun* [probably from *Brainiac*, superintelligent villain in the *Superman* comic-book series] (1982)
**:** a person characterized by unusual brainpower
**breakout** *adjective* (1977)
**:** being or relating to a sudden or smashing success especially in comparison to previous efforts ⟨a *breakout* book⟩
**brown·field** \'braȯn-,fē(ə)ld\ *noun, often attributive* (1977)
**:** a tract of land that has been developed for industrial purposes, polluted, and then abandoned
**brows·er** \'braȯ-zər\ *noun* (1845)
**1 :** one that browses
**2 :** a computer program used for accessing sites or information on a network (as the World Wide Web)
**BSE** *abbreviation* bovine spongiform encephalopathy
**buff** *or* **buffed** *adjective*
**:** having a physique enhanced by bodybuilding exercises
**buffalo wing** *noun* [*Buffalo*, New York] (1984)
**:** a deep-fried chicken wing coated with a spicy sauce and usually served with a blue cheese dressing
**bust·er** *noun, chiefly Midland* **:** someone or something extraordinary ⟨a *buster* of a breakfast —Harriet B. Stowe⟩
**caf·fein·at·ed** \'ka-fə-,nā-təd, -fē-ə\ *adjective* (1970)
**1 :** stimulated by or as if by caffeine ⟨*caffeinated* workers⟩
**2 :** containing caffeine
**camp·out** \'kam-,paȯt\ *noun* (1879)
**:** an occasion on which a group camps out
**ca·noo·dle** \kə-'nü-dᵊl\ *intransitive verb*
**ca·noo·dled; ca·noo·dling** \-'nü-dliŋ, -'nü-dᵊl-iŋ\ [perhaps from English dialect *canoodle*, noun, donkey, fool, foolish lover] (1859)

**:** PET, FONDLE ⟨lovers *canoodling* in the park⟩
**car seat** *noun* (1968)
**:** a portable seat for a small child that attaches to an automobile seat and holds the child safely
**cellophane noodle** *noun* (1977)
**:** a translucent noodle made from mung beans
**cell phone** *noun* (1984)
**:** a cellular telephone
**cen·tas** \'sen-,täs\ *noun, plural* **cen·tai** \-,tī\ *or* **cen·tu** \-,tü\ [Lithuanian (nominative plural *centai*, genitive plural *centų*), probably from French *centime* or English *cent*] (circa 1934)
— see *litas* at MONEY table
**CFS** *abbreviation* chronic fatigue syndrome
**challenged** *adjective* (1983)
**:** having a disability or deficiency
**charter school** *noun* (1992)
**:** a tax-supported school established by a charter between a granting body (as a school board) and an outside group (as of teachers and parents) which operates the school without most local and state educational regulations so as to achieve set goals
**chat room** *noun* (1986)
**:** a real-time on-line interactive discussion group
**chat·ter** *intransitive verb*
**:** to vibrate especially audibly as a consequence of repeated sticking and slipping ⟨the brakes were *chattering*⟩
**cher·ry–pick** \'cher-ē-,pik\
*intransitive verb* (1965)
**:** to select the best or most desirable
*transitive verb*
**:** to select as being the best or most desirable
**chip** *noun*
**:** a small piece of food ⟨chocolate *chips*⟩
**chronic fatigue syndrome** *noun* (1986)
**:** a group of symptoms of unknown cause that include fatigue, cognitive dysfunction, and sometimes fever and affect especially people between the ages of 20 and 40 — abbreviation *CFS*
**cine·plex** \'si-nə-,pleks\ *noun* [*cinema* + *-plex*] (1983)
**:** a complex that houses several movie theaters
**click**
*transitive verb*
**:** to select especially on a computer by pressing a button on a control device (as a mouse)
*intransitive verb*
**:** to select something by clicking — often used with *on* ⟨*click* on the icon⟩
**click** *noun*
**:** an instance of clicking ⟨a mouse *click*⟩
**click·er** \'kli-kər\ *noun* (1985)
**:** REMOTE CONTROL 2
**cli·ent** *noun*
**:** a computer in a network that uses the services (as access to files or shared peripherals) provided by a server
**clip art** *noun* (1968)
**:** ready-made usually copyright-free illustrations sold in books or as part of a software package from which they may be cut and pasted or inserted as artwork
**clip·board** *noun*
**:** a section of computer memory that temporarily stores data (as text) especially to facilitate its movement or duplication
**co·in·ci·den·tal·ly** \-'dent-lē, -'den-tᵊl-ē\ *adverb* (1837)
**1 :** in a coincidental manner **:** by coincidence ⟨lonely singles who meet *coincidentally* and click —People⟩
**2 :** it is or seems coincidental that ⟨*coincidentally*, the dog died exactly one year after his owner did⟩
**comfort food** *noun* (1977)
**:** food prepared in a traditional style having a usually nostalgic or sentimental appeal
**com·mod·i·ty** *noun*
**:** one that is subject to ready exchange or exploitation within a market ⟨the sensitive female singer-songwriter as a viable pop *commodity* —Elysa Gardner⟩
**cook·ie** *noun*
**:** a small file or part of a file stored on a World Wide Web user's computer, created and subsequently read by a Web site server, and containing personal information (as a user identification code, customized preferences, or a record of pages visited)
**creative** *noun* (1962)

**1 :** one (as an artist or writer) that is creative; *especially* **:** one directly involved in the creation of advertisements
**2 :** creative activity or the material produced by it especially in advertising
**cred** \'kred\ *noun* (1981)
**:** CREDIBILITY; *specifically* **:** the quality of being deserving of acceptance as a member of a particular group or class ⟨used . . . his new street *cred* to develop contacts —Dale Keiger⟩
**cre·mi·ni** \kri-'mē-nē\ *noun* [Italian, plural of *cremino*, from *crema* cream, from Middle French *cresme*; probably from their color — more at CREAM] (1984)
**:** a meaty cultivated brown or tan mushroom belonging to the same variety of button mushroom as the larger and more mature portobello
**cri·mi·ni** \kri-'mē-nē\ *noun* (1986)
**:** CREMINI (in this list)
**cryp·to·spo·rid·i·o·sis** \,krip-tō-spȯr-,id-ē-'ō-səs\ *noun, plural* **cryp·to·spo·rid·i·o·ses** \-,sēz\ [New Latin] (1982)
**:** a disease caused by cryptosporidia
**cryp·to·spo·rid·i·um** \,krip-tō-spȯr-'id-ē-əm\ *noun, plural* **cryp·to·spo·rid·ia** \-ē-ə\ [New Latin, from *crypto-* + *spora* spore + *-idium*] (1982)
**:** a protozoan (genus *Cryptosporidium* of the order Coccidia) that is parasitic in the gut of vertebrates including humans and sometimes causes diarrhea
**cut** *noun*
**:** an edited version of a film ⟨a director's *cut*⟩
**cu·vée** *also* **cu·vee** \kü-'vā, kyü-; kū̄e-vä\ *noun* [French, from *cuve*] (1833)
**1 :** bulk wine; *especially* **:** wine in casks or vats so blended as to ensure uniformity and marketability
**2 :** a blend of still wines used in the production of champagne
**cyber–** *combining form* [*cybernetic*]
**:** computer **:** computer network ⟨*cyber*space⟩
**cy·ber·sex** \-,seks\ *noun* (1991)
**1 :** on-line sex-oriented conversations and exchanges
**2 :** sex-oriented material available on the Internet and on CD-ROMs
**date** *intransitive verb*
**:** to go out on usually romantic dates
**day job** *noun* (1977)
**:** one's regular employment as contrasted with an occasional, secondary, or coveted job
**day trader** *noun* (1953)
**:** a speculator who seeks profit from the intraday fluctuation in the price of a security or commodity by completing double trades of buying and selling or selling and covering during a single session of the market
— **day–trade** \'dā-,trād\ *noun or verb*
**Db** *symbol* dubnium
**dear** *adverb* (before 12th century)
**1 :** DEARLY 3 ⟨the effort cost them *dear*⟩
**2 :** DEARLY 1 ⟨so *dear* I loved the man —Shak.⟩
**dear·ly** *adverb* (13th century)
**1 :** with affection **:** FONDLY
**2 :** HEARTILY, EARNESTLY ⟨prayed so *dearly* for peace⟩
**3 :** at a high rate or price ⟨paid *dearly* for the error⟩
**delt** \'delt\ *noun* (1980)
**:** DELTOID — usually used in plural
**de·nar** \'de-,när, 'dā-\ *noun, plural* **de·nars** \-,närz\ *also* **denar** *or* **de·na·ri** \'de-nä-,rē, 'dā-\ [Macedonian, alteration of *dinar* dinar, ultimately from Arabic *dīnār* — more at DINAR] (15th century)
— see MONEY table
**de·ni** \'de-nē, 'dā-\ *noun plural* [Macedonian, probably alteration of *denari*, plural of *denar* denar] (1992)
— see *denar* at MONEY table
**di·ge·ra·ti** \di-jə-'rä-(,)tē\ *noun plural* [*digital* + *-erati* (as in *literati*)] (1992)
**:** persons well versed in computer use and technology
**digital versatile disc** *or* **digital video disc** *noun* (1982)
**:** DVD (in this list)
**diminishing returns** *noun*
**:** benefits that beyond a certain point fail to increase in proportion to extended efforts

**disconnect** *noun* (1976)
**:** a lack of or break in connection, consistency, or agreement

**distance learning** *noun* (1972)
**:** learning that takes place via electronic media linking instructors and students who are not together in a classroom

**DNA virus** *noun* (1963)
**:** a virus whose genome consists of DNA

**do·main** *noun*
**:** the highest taxonomic category in biological classification ranking above the kingdom

**domestic partner** *noun* (1975)
**1 :** a company especially in a developing country that joins in a commercial venture with an international company
**2 :** either one of an unmarried heterosexual or homosexual cohabiting couple especially when considered as to eligibility for spousal benefits

**dot–com** \'dät-ˌkäm\ *noun, often attributive* [from the use of *.com* in the URLs of such companies] (1994)
**:** a company that markets its products or services on-line via a Web site

**download** *noun* (1980)
**:** the act or an instance of downloading something; *also* **:** the item downloaded

**dram** \'dräm\ *noun* [Armenian, literally, coin, money, ultimately from Greek *drachmē* drachma] (1993)
**—** see MONEY table

**dub·ni·um** \'düb-nē-əm, 'dəb-\ *noun* [New Latin, from *Dubna*, city in Russia where a center for investigation of heavy elements is located] (1994)
**:** a short-lived radioactive element that is artificially produced **—** see ELEMENT table

**duh** \'də, *usually with prolonged* ə\ *interjection* (1974)
**1 —** used to express actual or feigned ignorance or stupidity
**2 —** used derisively to indicate that something just stated is all too obvious or self-evident

**DVD** \ˌdē-(ˌ)vē-'dē\ *noun* [*d*igital *v*ideo *d*isc] (1993)
**:** a high-capacity optical disk format; *also* **:** an optical disk using such a format and containing especially a video recording (as a movie) or computer data

**e-** *combining form* [*E-mail*]
**:** electronic ⟨*e*-commerce⟩

**eating disorder** *noun* (1984)
**:** any of several psychological disorders (as anorexia nervosa or bulimia) characterized by serious disturbances of eating behavior

**eau de toi·lette** \ˌō-də-twä-'let\ *noun, plural* **eaux de toilette** \ˌō(z)-\ *or* **eaux de toi·lettes** \ˌō(z)-də-twä-'let(s)\ *or* **eau de toi·lettes** \ˌō-də-twä-'let(s)\ [French, literally, water for washing and dressing] (1907)
**:** a perfumed liquid containing a lower percentage of fragrant oils than does ordinary perfume
**—** called also *toilet water*

**Ebon·ics** \ē-'bä-niks, i-, e-\ *noun plural but singular in construction* [blend of *ebony* and *phonics*] (1973)
**:** BLACK ENGLISH

**ech·i·na·cea** \ˌe-ki-'nā-sē-ə, -shə\ *noun* [New Latin, genus name, from *echin-* + *-acea* (feminine of *-aceus* -aceous)] (1921)
**:** the dried rhizome, roots, or other parts of any of three composite herbs (*Echinacea angustifolia, E. pallida,* and *E. purpurea*) used in folk medicine and some patent medicines especially for a supposed beneficial effect on the immune system

**eco·fem·i·nism** \ˌē-kō-'fe-mə-ˌni-zəm, ˌe-kō-\ *noun* (1987)
**:** a movement or theory that applies feminist principles and ideas to ecological issues
**— eco·fem·i·nist** \-nist\ *noun or adjective*

**E. coli** \ˌē-'kō-ˌlī\ *noun, plural* **E. coli** (1926)
**:** a straight rod-shaped gram-negative bacterium (*Escherichia coli* of the family Enterobacteriaceae) occurring in various strains that are used in medical and genetic research, live as harmless inhabitants of the human lower intestine, are used in public health as indicators of fecal pollution (as of water or food), or produce a toxin causing intestinal illness

**eco·ter·ror·ism** \ˌē-kō-'ter-ər-i-zəm, ˌe-kō-\ *noun* (1987)
**1 :** sabotage intended to hinder activities that are considered damaging to the environment
**2 :** political terrorism intended to damage an enemy's natural environment
**— eco·ter·ror·ist** \-ər-ist\ *noun or adjective*

**eco·tour** \-ˌtůr\ *noun* (1987)
**:** a trip conducted by the principles of ecotourism

**edge city** *noun* (1988)
**:** a suburb that has developed its own political, economic, and commercial base independent of the central city

**edu** *abbreviation* educational organization

**elec·tron·i·ca** \i-ˌlek-'trä-ni-kə\ *noun* [probably from *New Electronica,* recording label of the British firm Beechwood Music Ltd.] (1994)
**:** dance music featuring extensive use of synthesizers, electronic percussion, and samples of recorded music or sound

**E-mail** \'ē-ˌmāl\ *noun* (1982)
**:** a means or system for transmitting messages electronically (as between terminals linked by telephone lines or microwave relays)
**— e-mail** *verb*
**— e-mail·er** \-ˌmā-lər\ *noun*

**emo·ti·con** \i-'mō-ti-ˌkän\ *noun* [*emotion* + *icon*] (1990)
**:** a group of keyboard characters (as :-)) typically representing a facial expression or an emotion or otherwise conveying tone or attitude that is used especially in computerized communications (as E-mail)

**en·abler** \i-'nā-blər, -bᵊl-ər\ *noun* (1615)
**:** one that enables another to achieve an end; *especially* **:** one who enables another to persist in self-destructive behavior (as substance abuse) by providing excuses or by helping that individual avoid the consequences of such behavior

**en·cul·tur·a·tion** \in-ˌkəl-chə-'rā-shən, (ˌ)en-\ *noun* (1948)
**:** the process by which an individual learns the traditional content of a culture and assimilates its practices and values
**— en·cul·tur·ate** \-'kəl-chə-ˌrāt\ *verb*

**era** *noun*
**:** a stage in development (as of a person or thing)

**euro** *noun, plural* **euros** *also* **euro** [short for the equivalent of *Europe* or *European* in the languages of the European Union] (1981)
**:** the basic monetary unit shared by countries of the European Union since 1999

**Eu·ro** \'yůr-(ˌ)ō\ *adjective* (1963)
**:** EUROPEAN
**— Euro** *noun*

**ex·treme** *adjective*
**1 :** of, relating to, or being an outdoor activity or a form of a sport (as skiing) that involves an unusually high degree of physical risk ⟨*extreme* mountain biking down steep slopes⟩
**2 :** involved in an extreme sport ⟨an *extreme* snowboarder⟩

**eye candy** *noun* (1981)
**:** something superficially attractive to look at

**face time** *noun* (1978)
**1 :** the amount of time one spends appearing on television
**2 :** time spent in a face-to-face meeting with someone
**3 :** time spent at one's place of employment especially beyond normal work hours

**family leave** *noun* (1981)
**:** a usually unpaid leave of absence for an employee to attend to family concerns (as care of an infant or a serious illness)

**far·fal·le** \fär-'fä-(ˌ)lā, -lē\ *noun* [Italian, plural of *farfalla,* literally, butterfly] (1941)
**:** butterfly-shaped pasta

**fash·ion·is·ta** \ˌfa-shə-'nēs-tə\ *noun* [*fashion* + *-ista* (as in *Sandinista*)] (1993)
**:** a designer, promoter, or follower of the latest fashions

**feng shui** \'fəŋ-ˌshwē, -'shwä\ *noun* [Chinese (Beijing) *fēngshui* geomantic omen, literally, wind-water] (1797)
**:** a Chinese geomantic practice in which a structure or site is chosen or configured so as to harmonize with the spiritual forces that inhabit it; *also* **:** auspicious orientation, placement, or arrangement as determined by feng shui

**fi·bro·my·al·gia** \ˌfī-brō-ˌmī-'al-j(ē)ə\ *noun* [New Latin] (1983)
**:** a painful rheumatic condition of uncertain cause that is characterized by diffuse or localized pain, tenderness, and stiffness of skeletal muscles and associated connective tissue and that is usually accompanied by fatigue

**fire·wall** \'fīr-ˌwól\ *noun*
**:** a computer or computer software that prevents unauthorized access to private data (as on a company's local area network or intranet) by outside computer users (as of the Internet)

**fitting** *noun*
**:** something used in fitting up **:** ACCESSORY

**flat·line** \'flat-ˌlīn\ *intransitive verb* (1980)
**1 a :** to register on an electronic monitor as having no brain waves or heartbeat **b :** DIE
**2 a :** to be in a state of no progress or advancement **b :** to come to an end
**— flat·lin·er** *noun*

**flu·ox·e·tine** \flü-'äk-sə-ˌtēn\ *noun* [International Scientific Vocabulary, probably from *fluor-* + *oxy* + *methyl* + *amine*] (1976)
**:** an antidepressant drug $C_{17}H_{18}F_3NO$ that enhances serotonin activity

**focus group** *noun* (1985)
**:** a small group of people whose response to something (as a new product or a politician's image) is studied to determine the response that can be expected from a larger population

**foos·ball** \'füz-ˌból\ *noun, often capitalized* [probably modification of German *Tischfussball,* from *Tisch* table + *Fussball* soccer, from *Fuss* foot + *Ball* ball] (1977)
**:** a table game resembling soccer in which the ball is moved by manipulating rods to which small figures of players are attached

**401(k)** \ˌfór-(ˌ)ō-(ˌ)wən-'kā, ˌfór-\ *noun* [from the section of the Internal Revenue Code that established it] (1989)
**:** a retirement account to which employee and employer contribute, on which taxes are deferred until withdrawal, and for which the employee selects the types of investments

**free·ware** \'frē-ˌwar, -ˌwer\ *noun* (1983)
**:** software that is available for use at no cost or for a nominal usually voluntary fee

**fric·tion** *noun*
**:** sound produced by the movement of air through a narrow constriction in the mouth or glottis

**fri·sée** *also* **fri·sé** \frē-'zā\ *noun* [French, short for *chicorée frisée* curly chicory] (1982)
**:** curly endive leaves that have finely dissected edges and are used in salads **—** called also *frisée lettuce*

**FTP** *abbreviation* file transfer protocol

**ful·fill** *transitive verb*
**:** to meet the requirements of (a business order)

**full bore** *adverb* (1927)
**:** with maximum effort or speed

**full–bore** \'fůl-ˌbór, -'bór\ *adjective* (1974)
**1 :** FULL-BLOWN 2
**2 :** made with maximum effort

**function key** *noun* (1964)
**:** any of a set of keys on a computer keyboard that have or can be programmed to have special functions

**fusion cuisine** *noun* (1986)
**:** food prepared using techniques and ingredients of various ethnic or regional cuisines

**F/X** *or* **FX** \ˌef-'eks\ *noun plural* [letter names *ef* and *ex* representing *effects*] (1985)
**:** SPECIAL EFFECTS

**gang·sta rap** \'gaŋ(k)-stə-\ *noun* [*gangsta* gang member, alter. of *gangster*] (1991)
**:** rap music with lyrics explicitly relating to urban gangs, violence, drug use, and the degradation of women

**gated community** *noun* (1981)
**:** a residential area protected by a private security force, enclosed by physical barriers, and entered through a controlled gate

**ga·zil·lion** \gə-'zil-yən\ *noun* [alteration of *zillion*] (1978)
**:** an indeterminately large number
**— gazillion** *adjective*

**ga·zoo** \gə-'zü\ *noun, plural* **gazoos** [origin unknown] (1965)
*slang* **:** WAZOO (in this list)

**GDP** *abbreviation* gross domestic product

**giga·flop** \-ˌfläp\ *noun* [*floating-point operation*] (1976)

**:** a unit of measure for the speed of calculation of a computer equal to one billion floating-point operations per second

**giv·en** *adjective*
**:** assumed as actual or hypothetical **:** GRANTED ⟨*given* that all are equal before the law⟩

**Global Positioning System** *noun* (1975)
**:** GPS

**go·pik** \gō-'pēk, -'pik\ *noun, plural* **gopik** [Azerbaijani *gəpik* kopeck, from Russian *kopeĭka*] (1992)
— see *manat* at MONEY table

**got·cha** \'gä-chə\ *noun* [alteration of *got you*] (1974)
**:** an unexpected usually disconcerting challenge, revelation, or catch

**GPS** \jē-(,)pē-'es\ *noun* [*Global Positioning System*] (1975)
**:** a navigational system using satellite signals to fix the location of a radio receiver on or above the earth's surface; *also* **:** the radio receiver so used

**graphical user interface** *noun* (1988)
**:** a computer program designed to allow a computer user to interact easily with the computer typically by using a mouse to make choices from menus or groups of icons

**green** *adjective*
**:** tending to preserve environmental quality (as by being recyclable, biodegradable, or nonpolluting)

**green·field** \'grēn-,fēld\ *noun, often attributive* (1972)
**:** undeveloped land especially when unpolluted ⟨a *greenfield* site⟩

**gross domestic product** *noun* (1970)
**:** the gross national product excluding the value of net income earned abroad

**ha·ba·ne·ro** *also* **ha·ba·ñe·ro** \,(h)ä-bə-'n(y)er-ō\ *noun* [American Spanish (*chile*) *habanero*, literally, Havanan chili] (1988)
**:** a very hot roundish chili pepper (*Capsicum chinense*) that is usually orange when mature

**Hail Mary** *noun*
**:** a long forward pass in football thrown into or near the end zone in a last-ditch attempt to score as time runs out

**half–pipe** \'haf-,pīp, 'háf-\ *noun* (1984)
**:** a V-shaped high-sided ramp or runway used in snowboarding, skateboarding, or in-line skating

**half·tone** *noun*
**:** an image (as one printed on an offset press or laser printer) that renders smooth variations of color in an original by means of dots assigned to areas of the image electronically

**han·ta·vi·rus** \'hän-tə-,vī-rəs, 'hən-, 'han-\ *noun* [New Latin, from *hanta-* (from *Hantaan*, river in South Korea near where rodents carrying the virus were collected 1974–78) + *virus*] (1984)
**:** any of a genus (*Hantavirus* of the family Bunyaviridae) of RNA viruses that are transmitted by rodent feces and urine and cause acute respiratory illness and hemorrhagic fever marked by renal necrosis

**has·si·um** \'ha-sē-əm\ *noun* [New Latin, from *Hassia* Hesse (German state), location of the laboratory that first produced the element] (1992)
**:** a short-lived radioactive element that is artificially produced — see ELEMENT table

**he·li·o·sphere** \'hē-lē-ə-,sfir, -ō-\ *noun* [International Scientific Vocabulary] (1976)
**:** the region in space influenced by the sun or solar wind

**hepatitis C** *noun* (1980)
**:** a hepatitis caused by a single-stranded RNA virus (family Flaviviridae) that is usually transmitted by parenteral means (as injection of an illicit drug, blood transfusion, or exposure to blood or blood products)

**Hib** \'hib\ *noun, often attributive* [*Hi-* (from the species name *Haemophilus influenzae* + type *B*] (1984)
**:** a bacterial serotype (*Haemophilus influenzae* type B) that causes bacterial meningitis and pneumonia especially in children ⟨*Hib* disease⟩ ⟨*Hib* vaccine⟩

**high–definition** *adjective* (1981)
**:** being or relating to a television system that has twice as many scan lines per frame as a conventional system, a proportionally sharper image, and a wide-screen format

**hit** *noun*
**:** an instance of connecting to a particular Web site ⟨a million *hits* per day⟩

**Hmong** \'məŋ\ *noun, plural* **Hmong** [Hmong *hmoŋ* (with high level tone), a self-designation] (1977)
**1 :** a member of a mountain-dwelling people inhabiting southeastern China and the northern parts of Vietnam, Laos, and Thailand
**2 :** the language of the Hmong people

**home·girl** \'hōm-,gərl\ *noun* (1934)
**1 :** a girl or woman from one's neighborhood, hometown, or region
**2 :** a girl or woman who is a member of one's peer group

**home page** *noun* (1992)
**:** the page typically encountered first at a World Wide Web site that usually contains links to the other pages of the site or to other sites

**home·school·er** \-,skü-lər\ *noun* (1981)
**1 :** one that homeschools
**2 :** a child who is homeschooled

**ho·mo·so·cial** \-'sō-shəl\ *adjective* (1968)
**:** of, relating to, or involving social relationships between persons of the same sex and especially between men
— **ho·mo·so·ci·al·i·ty** \-,sō-shē-'a-lə-tē\ *noun*

**hryv·nia** \'(h)riv-nē-ə\ *also* **hryv·na** \'(h)riv-na\ *noun, plural* **hryvnia** *or* **hryvnias** *also* **hryvna** *or* **hryvnas** [Ukrainian *gryvnya* 3-kopeck coin of pre-independent Ukraine, from Old Russian *grivĭna* necklace, ring, weight, coin, from *griva* mane] (1991)
— see MONEY table

**Hs** *symbol* hassium

**HTML** \,āch-(,)tē-(,)em-'el\ *noun* [*hypertext markup language*] (1992)
**:** a markup language that is a subset of SGML and is used to create hypertext and hypermedia documents on the World Wide Web incorporating text, graphics, sound, video, and hyperlinks

**hy·per·link** \'hī-pər-,liŋk\ *noun* (1989)
**:** an electronic link providing direct access from one distinctively marked place in a hypertext or hypermedia document to another in the same or a different document
— **hyperlink** *transitive verb*

**hy·per·me·dia** \-,mē-dē-ə\ *noun* (1965)
**:** a database format similar to hypertext in which text, sound, or video images related to that on a display can be accessed directly from the display

**IBS** *abbreviation* irritable bowel syndrome

**IDDM** *abbreviation* insulin-dependent diabetes mellitus

**im·pel·ler** *noun*
**:** a rotor located in a conduit to impart motion to a fluid

**in·ar·gu·ably** \-blē\ *adverb* (1925)
**:** it cannot be argued ⟨*inarguably*, December is the best month for retailers⟩

**in·cen·tiv·ize** \in-'sen-tə-,vīz\ *transitive verb* **in·cen·tiv·ized; in·cen·tiv·iz·ing** (1970)
**:** to provide with an incentive

**insulin–dependent diabetes** *noun* (1980)
**:** TYPE I DIABETES

**insulin–dependent diabetes mellitus** *noun* (1980)
**:** TYPE I DIABETES — abbreviation *IDDM*

**in·ter·est** *noun*
**:** the profit in goods or money that is made on invested capital

**In·ter·net** \'in-tər-,net\ *noun* (1986)
**:** an electronic communications network that connects computer networks and organizational computer facilities around the world

**in·ter·tex·tu·al·i·ty** \-,teks-chə-'wa-lə-tē\ *noun, plural* **in·ter·tex·tu·al·i·ties** [French *intertextualité*, from *inter-* + *textuel* textual + *-ité* -ity] (1975)
**:** the complex interrelationship between a text and other texts taken as basic to the creation or interpretation of the text
— **in·ter·tex·tu·al** \-'teks-chə-wəl\ *adjective*
— **in·ter·tex·tu·al·ly** *adverb*

**in·tra·net** \'in-trə-,net\ *noun* (1983)
**:** a network operating like the World Wide Web but having access restricted to a limited group of authorized users (as employees of a company)

**irritable bowel syndrome** *noun* (1943)
**:** a chronic functional disorder of the colon that is characterized especially by constipation or diarrhea, cramping abdominal pain, and the passage of mucus in the stool — abbreviation *IBS*

**ISP** *abbreviation* Internet service provider

**jar·gon·ish** \'jär-gə-nish\ *adjective* (1816)
**:** JARGONISTIC

**jar·gon·is·tic** \,jär-gə-'nis-tik\ *adjective* (1929)
**:** characterized by the use of jargon **:** phrased in jargon

**joke·ster** \'jōk-stər\ *noun* (1877)
**:** JOKER 1

**jones** \'jōnz\ *noun* [origin unknown] (1965)
**1** *slang* **:** HABIT, ADDICTION; *especially* **:** addiction to heroin
**2** *slang* **:** HEROIN
**3** *slang* **:** an avid desire or appetite for something **:** CRAVING

**kazoo** *noun, plural* **kazoos** [origin unknown] (1968)
*slang* **:** WAZOO (in this list)

**ki·net·o·chore** *noun*
**:** a specialized structure on the centromere to which the microtubular spindle fibers attach during mitosis and meiosis

**ko·piy·ka** \,kō-'pē-kä\ *noun* [Ukrainian, literally, kopeck] (1996)
— see *hryvnia* at MONEY table

**kroon** \'krōn\ *noun, plural* **kroo·ni** \'krō-nē\ *or* **kroons** [Estonian (partitive singular *krooni*), literally, crown, from Swedish *krona* or German *Krone*] (1928)
— see MONEY table

**ku·na** \'kü-,nä, -nə\ *noun, plural* **kuna** *or* **ku·ne** \-nä\ [Serbo-Croatian (nominative plural *kune*, genitive plural *kunā*), literally, marten (the skin of which was used as currency in medieval Slavic cultures)] (1951)
— see MONEY table

**La Ni·ña** \lä-'nē-nyə, -nyä\ *noun, plural* **La Ni·ñas** [Spanish, the (female) child] (1988)
**:** an irregularly recurring upwelling of unusually cold water to the surface along the western coast of South America that often occurs following an El Niño and that disrupts typical regional and global weather patterns especially in a manner opposite to that of El Niño

**laptop** *noun* (1984)
**:** a portable microcomputer having its main components (as processor, keyboard, and display screen) integrated into a single unit capable of battery-powered operation

**lari** \'lä-rē\ *noun, plural* **lari** [Georgian, literally, treasury, valuables] (1995)
— see MONEY table

**La·ti·na** \lə-'tē-nə\ *noun* [American Spanish, feminine of *latino* Latino] (1983)
**1 :** a woman who is a native or inhabitant of Latin America
**2 :** a woman of Latin-American origin living in the U.S.
— **Latina** *adjective*

**lats** \'läts\ *noun, plural* **la·ti** \'lä-tē\ *or* **la·tu** \'lä-tü\ [Latvian (nominative plural *lati*, genitive plural *latu*), from *Latvija* Latvia] (1923)
— see MONEY table

**lead·er·board** \-,bōrd, -,bòrd\ *noun* (1963)
**:** a large board for displaying the ranking of the leaders in a competitive event (as a golf tournament)

**learning curve** *noun*
**:** the course of progress while learning something

**line dance** *noun* (1948)
**1 :** CONTREDANSE 1
**2 :** a dance performed by a group usually in single file
**3 :** a dance in which the dancers stand in ranks while performing a particular set of steps in unison
— **line dancer** *noun*
— **line dancing** *noun*

**li·pa** \'lē-,pä, -pə\ *noun, plural* **lipa** *also* **lipe** \-,pä\ [Serbo-Croatian (nominative plural *lipe*, genitive plural *lipā*), literally, linden tree] (1993)
— see *kuna* at MONEY table

**li·tas** \'lē-,täs\ *noun, plural* **li·tai** \-,tī\ *or* **li·tu** \-,tü\ [Lithuanian (nominative plural *litai*, genitive plural *litų*), from initial letters of New Latin *Lituania*, French *Lituanie*, etc.] (1923)
— see MONEY table

**LLC** *abbreviation* limited liability company

**lu·ma** \,lü-'mä\ *noun, plural* **luma** [Armenian *luma, lumay*, literally, small coin, mite, from Syriac *lūmā*] (1999)
— see *dram* at MONEY table

**mad cow disease** *noun* (1988)
**:** BOVINE SPONGIFORM ENCEPHALOPATHY
**managed care** *noun* (1982)
**:** a system of health care (as by an HMO) that controls costs by placing limits on physicians' fees and by restricting the patient's choice of physicians
**ma·nat** \mä-'nät\ *noun, plural* **manat** *or* **manats** [Azerbaijani, ruble, from Persian *munāt*, from Russian *moneta, monet* coin, silver ruble coin, from Polish *moneta* coin, from Latin — more at MINT] (1990) — see MONEY table
**markup language** *noun* (1980)
**:** a system (as HTML or SGML) for marking or tagging a document that indicates its logical structure (as paragraphs) and gives instructions for its layout on the page for electronic transmission and display
**mas·cu·lin·ist** \'mas-kyə-lə-(,)nist\ *noun* (1918)
**:** an advocate of male superiority or dominance
— **masculinist** *adjective*
**max out**
*intransitive verb* (1967)
**:** to be at the upper limit ⟨the car *maxed out* at 85 mph⟩
*transitive verb*
**:** to use up all the available credit on ⟨*maxed out* the credit cards⟩
**med** *noun* (1982)
**:** MEDICATION 2 — usually used in plural
**med·i·gap** \'me-də-,gap\ *noun, often capitalized, often attributive* [*Medicare* + *gap*] (1975)
**:** supplemental health insurance that covers costs (as of medical care or a hospital stay) not covered by Medicare
**mei·ster** \'mīs-tər\ *noun* [Yiddish *mayster* & German *Meister* master, from Middle High German *meister,* from Old High German *meistar,* from Latin *magister* — more at MASTER] (1979)
**:** one who is knowledgeable about something specified — often used in combination ⟨puzzle-*meister*⟩
**meit·ner·i·um** \mīt-'nir-ē-əm, -'ner-\ *noun* [New Latin, from Lise *Meitner*] (1992)
**:** a short-lived radioactive element that is artificially produced — see ELEMENT table
**meme** \'mēm\ *noun* [alteration of *mimeme,* from *mim-* (as in *mimesis*) + *-eme*] (1976)
**:** an idea, behavior, style, or usage that spreads from person to person within a culture
**mes·clun** \'mes-klən\ *noun* [French, from Provençal, literally, mixture, from *mescla* to mix, from Old Provençal *mesclar,* from (assumed) Vulgar Latin *misculare* — more at MEDDLE] (1980)
**:** a salad consisting of a mixture of young tender greens (as lettuces, arugula, and chicory)
**mif·e·pris·tone** \,mi-fə-'pris-,tōn\ *noun* [*mife-* (perhaps alteration of *dimethyl* and *phenyl* + *-pristone* (alteration of *progesterone*)] (1985)
**:** RU 486
**mini·bar** \'mi-nē-,bär\ *noun* (1984)
**:** a small refrigerator in a hotel room that is stocked with especially alcoholic beverages and snacks for guests
**mini·dress** \'mi-nē-,dres\ *noun* (1965)
**:** a short close-fitting dress
**monstrous** *adverb, chiefly dialect* (1663)
**:** VERY, EXTREMELY ⟨a *monstrous* long raft— Mark Twain⟩
**morph** *verb* [short for *metamorphose*]
*transitive verb* (1975)
**:** to change the form or character of **:** TRANSFORM
*intransitive verb*
**:** to undergo transformation
**mosh** \'mäsh\ *intransitive verb* [perhaps alteration of *mash* or *mush*] (1987)
**:** to engage in uninhibited often frenzied activities (as intentional collision) with others near the stage at a rock concert
— **mosh·er** *noun*
**NAFTA** *abbreviation* North American Free Trade Agreement
**nano·tube** \-,tüb\ *noun* (1992)
**:** a microscopic tube whose diameter is measured in nanometers ⟨carbon *nanotubes*⟩
**net** *noun, often capitalized*
**:** INTERNET (in this list)

**net·i·quette** \'ne-ti-kət, -,ket\ *noun* [blend of *net* and *etiquette*] (1988)
**:** etiquette governing communication on the Internet
**net·i·zen** \'ne-tə-zən *also* -sən\ *noun* [blend of *net* and *citizen*] (1994)
**:** an active participant in the on-line community of the Internet
**new·bie** \'nü-bē, 'nyü-\ *noun* [irregular from *new*] (1985)
**:** BEGINNER, NOVICE; *especially* **:** a newcomer to cyberspace
**New Historicism** *noun* (1986)
**:** a method of literary criticism that emphasizes the historicity of a text by relating it to the configurations of power, society, or ideology in a given time
— **New Historicist** *adjective or noun*
**news·group** \-,grüp\ *noun* (1993)
**:** an electronic bulletin board on the Internet that is devoted to a particular topic
**NIDDM** *abbreviation* non-insulin-dependent diabetes mellitus
**non–insulin–dependent diabetes** *noun* (1984)
**:** TYPE II DIABETES (in this list)
**non–insulin–dependent diabetes mellitus** *noun* (1979)
**:** TYPE II DIABETES (in this list) — abbreviation *NIDDM*
**nu·tra·ceu·ti·cal** \,nü-trə-'sü-ti-kəl\ *noun* [*nutritive* + *pharmaceutical*] (1990)
**:** a foodstuff (as a fortified food or dietary supplement) that provides health benefits
**out** *transitive verb*
**:** to identify publicly as being such secretly ⟨wanted to *out* pot smokers⟩; *especially* **:** to identify as being a closet homosexual
**out** *adjective*
**:** publicly known or identified as a homosexual
**pac·li·tax·el** \,pa-kli-'tak-sᵊl\ *noun* [*Pacific yew* + *-litax-* (perhaps from *Taxus brevifolia*) + *-el* (alteration of *-ol* or *-ol*)] (1992)
**:** an antineoplastic drug $C_{47}H_{51}NO_{14}$ derived especially from a yew tree of the western U.S. (*Taxus brevifolia*) and used to treat ovarian cancer
**page** *noun*
**:** the block of information found at a single World Wide Web address
**Para·lym·pics** \,par-ə-'lim-piks\ *noun plural* [*paraplegic* + *Olympics*] (1953)
**:** a series of international contests for athletes with disabilities that are associated with and held following the summer and winter Olympic Games — called also *Paralympic Games*
— **Para·lym·pi·an** \-pē-ən\ *noun*
— **Para·lym·pic** \-pik\ *adjective*
**passive–aggressive** *adjective* (1946)
**:** being, marked by, or displaying behavior characterized by expression of negative feelings, resentment, and aggression in an unassertive passive way (as through procrastination and stubbornness)
— **passive–aggressive** *noun*
**peck** *noun*
**:** a quick light kiss ⟨a *peck* on the cheek⟩
**peel** *noun*
**:** a cosmetic operation for the removal of skin blemishes by the application of a caustic chemical and especially an acid to the skin
**perp** \'pərp\ *noun* (1981)
**:** a perpetrator especially of a crime
**phone sex** *noun* (1982)
**1 :** prerecorded sex-oriented telephone messages available by calling a commercial service
**2 :** sex-oriented conversations with an operator employed by a commercial service
**plat·form** *noun*
**:** a computer architecture that uses a particular operating system
**plyo·met·rics** \,plī-ə-'me-triks\ *plural noun but singular or plural in construction* [perhaps irregular from *plio-* + *-metrics* (as in *isometrics*)] (1981)
**:** exercise involving repeated rapid stretching and contracting of muscles (as by jumping and rebounding) to increase muscle power
— **plyo·met·ric** \-trik\ *adjective*
**por·to·bel·lo** \,pȯr-tə-'be-(,)lō\ *also* **por·ta·bel·la** \-lə\ *or* **por·ta·bel·lo** \,pȯr-tə-'be-(,)lō\ *noun, plural* **por·to·bel·los** *also* **por·ta-**

**bel·las** *or* **por·ta·bel·los** [perhaps alteration of Italian *prataiolo, prataiuolo* or dialect Italian *pratarolo* meadow mushroom, from *prato* meadow, from Latin *pratum*] (1986)
**:** a large dark mature cultivated mushroom noted for its meaty texture and belonging to a variety of the button mushroom — compare CREMINI (in this list)
**poster boy** *noun* (1978)
**:** a male poster child
**poster child** *noun* (1969)
**1 :** a child afflicted with a disease who is pictured in posters to solicit funds for combating the disease
**2 :** a person having a public image that is identified with something (as a cause or group)
**poster girl** *noun* (1969)
**:** a female poster child
**post–struc·tur·al·ism** \,pōs(t)-'strək-chə-rə-,li-zəm, -'strək-shrə-\ *noun* (1980)
**:** a movement or theory (as in literary theory or psychoanalysis) that sees inquiry not as the objective exploration of stable structures and categories (as the self) but rather as a relative undertaking shaped by discursive and interpretive practices
— **post–struc·tur·al·ist** \-list\ *adjective or noun*
**pre·press** \'prē-,pres\ *adjective* (1965)
**:** of or relating to the processing of copy preparatory to printing ⟨*prepress* costs⟩ ⟨*prepress* equipment⟩
**pri·ma·vera** \,prē-mə-'ver-ə\ *adjective* [Italian *(alla) primavera* in the style of springtime] (1976)
**:** served with a mixture of fresh vegetables (as zucchini, snow peas, and broccoli) ⟨pasta *primavera*⟩
**programmed cell death** *noun* (1982)
**:** APOPTOSIS (in this list)
**prostate–specific antigen** *noun* (1981)
**:** a protease secreted by epithelial cells of the prostate that is used in the diagnosis of prostate cancer since its concentration in blood serum tends to be proportional to the clinical stage of the disease — abbreviation *PSA*
**protease inhibitor** *noun* (1981)
**:** a substance that inhibits the action of a protease; *specifically* **:** any of a group of drugs that inhibit the protease of HIV so that the cleavage of viral proteins into mature infectious particles is prevented and that are used especially in combination with other antiviral agents in the treatment of HIV infection
**qua·si·crys·tal** \'kwä-,zī-,kris-tᵊl, -,sī-, 'kwä-zē-, -sē-\ *noun* (1984)
**:** a body of solid material that resembles a crystal in being composed of repeating structural units but that incorporates two or more unit cells into a quasiperiodic structure
— **qua·si·crys·tal·line** \-'kris-tə-lən *also* -,līn, -,lēn\ *adjective*
**ra·men** \'rä-mən\ *noun* [Japanese *rāmen*] (1974)
**:** quick-cooking egg noodles usually served in a broth with bits of meat and vegetables
**Rf** *symbol* rutherfordium
**right–size** \'rīt-,sīz\
*transitive verb* (1989)
**:** to reduce (as a workforce) to an optimal size
*intransitive verb*
**:** to undergo a reduction to an optimal size
**rig·or** *noun*
**:** RIGOR MORTIS
**RNA virus** *noun* (1963)
**:** a virus (as a paramyxovirus or a retrovirus) whose genome consists of RNA
**rosy periwinkle** *noun* (1982)
**:** PERIWINKLE 1b
**royal antler** *noun* (circa 1727)
**:** the third tine above the base of a stag's antler
**ruth·er·ford·ium** \,rə-thə(r)-'fȯr-dē-əm\ *noun* [New Latin, from Ernest *Rutherford* †1937 British physicist] (1969)
**:** a short-lived radioactive element that is artificially produced — see ELEMENT table
**san·tims** \'sän-,tims\ *noun, plural* **san·ti·mi** \-ti-mē\ *or* **san·ti·mu** \-ti-mü\ [Latvian (nominative plural *santimi,* genitive plural *santimu,* from French *centime* centime] (1924) — see *lats* at MONEY table
**screen saver** *noun* (1982)
**:** a computer program that usually displays various images on the screen of a computer that is on

but not in use so as to prevent damage to the screen's phosphors

**sea·borg·i·um** \sē-'bȯr-gē-əm\ *noun* [New Latin, from Glenn T. *Seaborg* †1999 American chemist] (1994)
**:** a short-lived radioactive element that is artificially produced — see ELEMENT table

**search engine** *noun* (1984)
**:** computer software used to search data (as text or a database) for specified information

**sent** \'sent\ *noun, plural* **sen·ti** \'sen-tē\ [Estonian (partitive singular *senti*), probably from French *centime* or English *cent*] (1930)
— see kroon at MONEY table

**sen·sei** \'sen-ˌsā\ *noun, plural* **sensei** *or* **senseis** [Japanese, teacher, master] (1968)
**:** a teacher of martial arts (as karate or judo)

**Sg** *symbol* seaborgium

**SGML** \ˌes-(ˌ)jē-(ˌ)em-'el\ *noun* [*standard generalized markup language*] (1983)
**:** a markup language used to define the structure of and manage documents in electronic form — compare HTML (in this list)

**sick building syndrome** *noun* (1983)
**:** a set of symptoms (as headache, fatigue, and eye irritation) typically affecting workers in modern airtight office buildings that is believed to be caused by indoor pollutants (as formaldehyde fumes or microorganisms)

**site** *noun*
**:** one or more Internet addresses at which an individual or organization provides information to others often including links to other locations where related information may be found

**skanky** \'skan-kē\ *adjective* [origin unknown] (1982)
**1** *slang* **:** repugnantly filthy or squalid
**2** *slang* **:** of low or sleazy character

**SKU** *abbreviation* stock-keeping unit

**smooth·ie** \'smü-thē\ *noun*
**:** a creamy beverage made of fruit blended with juice, milk, or yogurt

**snail mail** *noun* (1983)
**1 :** mail delivered by a postal system
**2 :** MAIL 3

**soccer mom** *noun* (1987)
**:** a typically suburban mother who accompanies her children to their soccer games and is considered as part of a significant voting bloc or demographic group

**som** \'sōm\ *noun, plural* **som** [Kirghiz, crude iron casting, ruble] (1993)
— see MONEY table

**sophomore** *adjective* (1953)
**:** being the second in a series 〈their *sophomore* album〉

**spam** \'spam\ *noun* [from a skit on the British television series *Monty Python's Flying Circus* in which chanting of the word *Spam* (trademark for a canned meat product) overrides the other dialogue] (1994)
**:** unsolicited usually commercial E-mail sent to a large number of addresses

**spam** *verb* **spammed; spam·ming** *transitive verb* (1994)
**:** to send spam to
*intransitive verb*
**:** to send spam
— **spam·mer** *noun*

**spelling checker** *noun* (1981)
**:** a computer program that identifies possible misspellings in a text file by comparing the contents of the file with a database of accepted spellings — called also *spell check, spell checker*

**sport–util·i·ty vehicle** \'spȯrt-yü-'ti-lə-tē-, 'spȯrt-\ *noun* (1987)
**:** a rugged automotive vehicle similar to a station wagon but built on a light-truck chassis

**stay** *noun*
**:** a thin firm strip (as of plastic) used for stiffening a garment or part (as a shirt collar)

**stent** \'stent\ *noun* [Charles Thomas *Stent* †1885 English dentist] (1961)
**:** a short narrow metal or plastic tube that is inserted into the lumen of an anatomical vessel (as an artery or a bile duct) especially to keep a formerly blocked passageway open

**sto·tin** \stō-'tēn\ *noun, plural* **sto·ti·nov** \stō-'tēn-ˌnȯv\ [Slovenian (nominative plural *stotini*, genitive plural *stotinov*), from *sto* hundred] (1991)

— see *tolar* at MONEY table

**stretch** *adjective*
**:** longer than the standard size 〈*stretch* limousine〉

**surf** *intransitive verb*
**:** to scan a wide range of offerings for something of interest
*transitive verb*
**:** to scan the offerings of (as television or the Internet) for something that is interesting or fills a need

**SUV** *abbreviation* sport-utility vehicle

**switch–hit·ter** *noun*
**:** one that is flexible or adaptable; *especially* **:** a person who can work equally well in either of two jobs or capacities

**syn·er·gy** *noun*
**:** a mutually advantageous conjunction or compatibility of distinct business participants or elements (as resources or efforts)

**syn·the·size** *transitive verb*
**:** to produce (as music) by an electronic synthesizer

**tac·rine** \'ta-ˌkrēn\ *noun* [*tetra*- + *acridine*] (1965)
**:** an anticholinesterase $C_{13}H_{14}N_2$ used especially in the palliative treatment of cognitive deficits occurring early in Alzheimer's disease

**tan·ga** \'tän-'gä\ *noun, plural* **tanga** [Tajik, from Tajik & Persian, a silver coin, cash] (1998)
— see *ruble* at MONEY table

**ta·pe·nade** \ˌtä-pə-'näd\ *noun* [French *tapénade*, from Provençal *tapenado*, from *tapeno* caper, ultimately from Latin *capparis* — more at CAPER] (1952)
**:** a seasoned spread made chiefly with mashed black olives, capers, and anchovies

**Tax·ol** \'tax-ˌsȯl\ *trademark* — used for a preparation of paclitaxel

**tech·no** \'tek-nō\ *noun* [*techno*- (as in *techno-pop* or *techno-rock*, styles of popular music utilizing electronically created sounds)] (1987)
**:** electronic dance music that features a fast beat and synthesized sounds usually without vocals or a conventional popular song structure

**tel·e·com** \'tel-i-ˌkäm\ *noun* (1948)
**1 :** TELECOMMUNICATION
**2 :** the telecommunications industry

**tel·net** \'tel-ˌnet\ *noun* [*tel*etype *net*work] (1971)
**:** a telecommunications protocol providing specifications for emulating a remote computer terminal so that one can access a distant computer and function on-line using an interface that appears to be part of the user's local system
— **telnet** *intransitive verb*

**tenge** \'teŋ-ˌgä\ *noun, plural* **tenge** [Kazakh *teŋge* coin, ruble] (1992)
— see MONEY table

**tera·byte** \'ter-ə-ˌbīt\ *noun* (1982)
**:** a unit of computer information storage capacity equal to about one trillion bytes; *specifically* **:** 1,099,511,627,776 bytes

**tes·tos·ter·one** *noun*
**:** qualities (as brawn and aggressiveness) usually associated with males **:** MANLINESS

**tet·ri** \'te-trē\ *noun, plural* **tetri** [Georgian, literally, white, silver, a silver coin] (1994)
— see *lari* at MONEY table

**thong** *noun*
**:** a garment consisting of a narrow strip of fabric fitting between the legs and a waistband that is worn as underwear or the bottom piece of a bikini

**three–peat** \'thrē-ˌpēt\ *noun* [blend of *three* and *repeat*] (1988)
**:** a third consecutive championship

**toast** *noun*
*slang* **:** one that is finished or done for 〈soon their relationship was *toast* —Rick Reilly〉

**tobacco mosaic virus** *noun* (1938)
**:** a single-stranded RNA virus (genus *Tobamovirus*) that occurs worldwide and causes mosaic disease in tobacco and numerous other plants

**toggle**
*intransitive verb*
**:** to switch between two options especially of an electronic device usually by pressing a single button or a simple key combination

**to·lar** \'tȯ-lär\ *noun, plural* **to·lar·jev** \'tȯ-lär-ˌyev\ *or* **tolars** [Slovenian (nominative plural *tolarji*, genitive plural *tolarjev*), from German *Taler* taler] (1991)
— see MONEY table

**trans·gen·der** \-'jen-dər\ *or* **trans·gen·dered** \-dərd\ *adjective* (1979)
**:** exhibiting the appearance and behavioral characteristics of the opposite sex

**trash talk** *noun* (1981)
**:** disparaging, taunting, or boastful comments especially between opponents trying to intimidate each other
— **trash–talk** \'trash-ˌtȯk\ *verb*

**tro·phy** *noun*
**:** one that is prized for qualities that enhance prestige or social status — usually used attributively 〈a *trophy* wife〉 〈a *trophy* house〉

**tsu·ris** *also* **tsou·ris** \'tsü-ris, 'tsu̇r-is\ *noun* [Yiddish *tsures, tsores*, plural of *tsure, tsore* trouble, distress, from Hebrew *ṣārāh*] (1941)
**:** TROUBLE, DISTRESS

**24–7** *or* **24/7** \ˌtwen-tē-'fȯr-'se-vən, 'twən-, -'fȯr-\ *adverb or adjective* (1986)
**:** for twenty-four hours seven days a week 〈can now shop *24-7*〉

**tyin** \'tēn\ *noun, plural* **tyin** [Kazakh *tiin, tiyin* kopeck, literally, squirrel, squirrel skin (formerly used as currency)] (1994)
— see *tenge* at MONEY table

**ty·iyn** \tē-'yen\ *noun, plural* **tyiyn** [Kirghiz *tiyin* kopeck, literally, squirrel, squirrel skin (formerly used as currency)] (1993)
— see *som* at MONEY table

**type I diabetes** \'tīp-'wən-\ *noun* (1982)
**:** a form of diabetes mellitus that usually develops during childhood or adolescence and is characterized by a severe deficiency in insulin resulting from atrophy of the islets of Langerhans and causing hyperglycemia and a marked tendency toward ketoacidosis — called also *insulin-dependent diabetes, insulin-dependent diabetes mellitus*

**type II diabetes** \-'tü-\ *noun* (1982)
**:** a common form of diabetes mellitus that develops especially in adults and most often in obese individuals and that is characterized by hyperglycemia resulting from impaired insulin utilization coupled with the body's inability to compensate with increased insulin production — called also *non-insulin-dependent diabetes, non-insulin-dependent diabetes mellitus*

**un·ar·gu·able** \ˌən-'är-gyə-wə-bəl\ *adjective* (1881)
**:** not arguable

**un·ar·gu·ably** \-blē\ *adverb* (1929)
**:** it cannot be argued **:** UNQUESTIONABLY

**uniform resource locator** *noun* (1993)
**:** URL

**universal resource locator** *noun* (1993)
**:** URL

**urban legend** *noun* (1979)
**:** an often lurid story or anecdote that is based on hearsay and widely circulated as true 〈the *urban legend* of alligators living in the sewers〉 — called also *urban myth*

**URL** \ˌyü-(ˌ)är-'el, 'ər(-ə)l\ *noun* (1992)
**:** the address of a computer or a document on the Internet that consists of a communications protocol followed by a colon and two slashes (as http://), the identifier of a computer (as www.m-w.com), and usually a path through a directory to a file — called also *uniform resource locator, universal resource locator*

**ve·loc·i·rap·tor** \və-'lä-sə-ˌrap-tər\ *noun* [New Latin, from Latin *veloc-, velox* + *raptor* plunderer, predator — more at RAPTOR] (1990)
**:** any of a genus (*Velociraptor*) of theropod dinosaurs of the late Cretaceous having a long head with a flat snout and a large sickle-shaped claw on the second toe of each foot

**vision quest** *noun* (1922)
**:** a solitary vigil by an adolescent American Indian boy to seek spiritual power and learn through a vision the identity of his usually animal or bird guardian spirit

**wait·staff** \'wāt-ˌstaf\ *noun* (1983)
**:** the staff of servers at a restaurant

**wake·board** \'wāk-ˌbȯrd\ *noun* (1991)
**:** a short board with foot bindings on which a rider is towed by a motorboat across its wake and especially up off the crest for aerial maneuvers
— **wake·board·er** *noun*
— **wake·board·ing** *noun*

**walk** *intransitive verb*

: to avoid criminal prosecution or conviction

**warp speed** *noun* [from the use in science fiction of space-time warps to allow faster-than-light travel] (1980)
: the highest possible speed

**wa·zoo** \(ˌ)wä-ˈzü\ *noun* [origin unknown] (1983)
*slang* : the posterior opening of the alimentary canal : ANUS
   **— up the wazoo** *also* **out the wazoo**
: in excess ⟨we've got lawyers *up the wazoo* —Steven Bochco⟩

**web** *noun, capitalized*
: WORLD WIDE WEB

**Web·mas·ter** \ˈweb-ˌmas-tər\ *noun* (1994)
: a person responsible for the creation or maintenance of a World Wide Web site especially for a company or organization

**wet·ware** \ˈwet-ˌwar, -ˌwer\ *noun* [*wet* + *software*] (1977)
: the human brain or a human being considered especially with respect to human logical and computational capabilities

**Wic·ca** \ˈwi-kə\ *noun* [probably from Old English *wicca* wizard — more at WITCH] (1959)

: a religion influenced by pre-Christian beliefs and practices of western Europe that affirms the existence of supernatural power (as magic) and of both male and female deities who inhere in nature, and that emphasizes ritual observance of seasonal and life cycles
   **— Wic·can** \ˈwi-kən\ *adjective or noun*

**witch** *noun*
: a practitioner of Wicca

**witch·craft** *noun*
: WICCA

**World Wide Web** *noun* (1992)
: a part of the Internet designed to allow easier navigation of the network through the use of graphical user interfaces and hypertext links between different addresses — called also *Web*

**yeast infection** *noun* (1979)
: infection of the female genital tract that is caused by a yeast fungus (*Candida albicans*) and is characterized by a discharge and inflammation; *broadly* : an infection (as thrush) caused by a yeast fungus

**yoc·to-** *combining form* [International Scientific Vocabulary, blend of *yotta-* and *octo-*]

: one septillionth ($10^{-24}$) part of ⟨*yocto*second⟩

**yoc·to·sec·ond** \ˈyäk-tə-ˌse-kənd, -ˌkänt\ *noun* (1996)
: one septillionth of a second

**yot·ta-** *combining form* [International Scientific Vocabulary, alteration of Greek *iōta* (representing *y*, next-to-last letter of Latin alphabet)]
: septillion ⟨*yotta*byte⟩

**yot·ta·byte** \ˈyä-tə-ˌbīt\ *noun* (1993)
: one septillion bytes

**yuppie flu** *noun* (1987)
: CHRONIC FATIGUE SYNDROME (in this list)

**zep·to-** *combining form* [International Scientific Vocabulary, blend of *zetta-* and *hepta-*]
: one sextillionth ($10^{-21}$) part of ⟨*zepto*second⟩

**zep·to·sec·ond** \ˈzep-tə-ˌse-kənd, -ˌkänt\ *noun* (1994)
: one sextillionth of a second

**zet·ta-** *combining form* [International Scientific Vocabulary, alteration of Greek *zēta* (representing *z*, last letter of Latin alphabet)]
: sextillion ⟨*zetta*byte⟩

**zet·ta·byte** \ˈze-tə-ˌbīt\ *noun* (1993)
: one sextillion bytes

# Guide to Pronunciation

ə ... b**a**n**a**n**a**, c**o**llide, **a**but

ˈə, ˌə ... h**u**mdr**u**m, ab**u**t
ə̣

... immediately preceding \l\, \n\, \m\, \ŋ\, as in batt**le**, mitt**en**, eat**en**, and sometimes op**en** \'ō-p°m\, lock **and** key \-°ŋ-\; immediately following \l\, \m\, \r\, as often in French tab**le**, pris**me**, tit**re**

ər ... furth**er**, merg**er**, b**ir**d

ˈər-⎫ ... as in two different pronunciations of h**urr**y \'hər-ē,
ˈə-r⎭ 'hə-rē\

a ... m**a**t, m**a**p, m**a**d, g**a**g, sn**a**p, p**a**tch

ā ... d**ay**, f**a**de, d**a**te, **a**orta, dr**a**pe, c**a**pe

ä ... b**o**ther, c**o**t, and, with most American speakers, f**a**ther, c**a**rt

ȧ ... f**a**ther as pronounced by speakers who do not rhyme it with *bother*; French p**a**tte

aú ... n**ow**, l**ou**d, **ou**t

b ... **b**a**b**y, ri**b**

ch ... **ch**in, natu**r**e \'nā-chər\

d ... **d**i**d**, a**dd**er

e ... b**e**t, b**e**d, p**e**ck

ˈē, ˌē ... b**ea**t, nosebl**ee**d, **e**venly, **ea**sy

ē ... eas**y**, meal**y**

f ... **f**i**f**ty, cu**ff**

g ... **g**o, bi**g**, **g**ift

h ... **h**at, a**h**ead

hw ... **wh**ale as pronounced by those who do not have the same pronunciation for both *whale* and *wail*

i ... t**i**p, ban**i**sh, act**i**ve

ī ... s**i**te, s**i**de, b**uy**, tr**i**pe

j ... **j**ob, **g**em, ed**ge**, **j**oin, **j**u**dg**e

k ... **k**in, **c**ook, a**ch**e

k̲ ... German i**ch**, Bu**ch**; one pronunciation of lo**ch**

l ... **l**i**l**y, poo**l**

m ... **m**ur**m**ur, di**m**, ny**m**ph

n ... **n**o, ow**n**
n

... indicates that a preceding vowel or diphthong is pronounced with the nasal passages open, as in French un bon vin blanc \œⁿ-bōⁿ-vaⁿ-blä<sup>n</sup>\

ŋ ... si**ng** \'siŋ\, si**ng**er \'siŋ-ər\, fi**ng**er \'fiŋ-gər\, i**n**k \'iŋk\

ō ... b**o**ne, kn**ow**, b**eau**

ȯ ... s**aw**, **a**ll, gn**aw**, c**au**ght

œ ... French b**oeu**f, German H**ö**lle

œ̄ ... French f**eu**, German H**öh**le

ȯi ... c**oi**n, destr**oy**

p ... **p**e**pp**er, li**p**

r ... **r**ed, ca**r**, **r**a**r**ity

s ... **s**ource, le**ss**

sh ... as in **sh**y, mi**ss**ion, ma**ch**ine, spe**ci**al (actually, this is a single sound, not two); with a hyphen between, two sounds as in *grasshopper* \'gras-ˌhä-pər\

t ... **t**ie, a**tt**ack, la**t**e, la**t**er, la**tt**er

th ... as in **th**in, e**th**er (actually, this is a single sound, not two); with a hyphen between, two sounds as in *knighthood* \'nīt-ˌhu̇d\

t̲h̲ ... **th**en, ei**th**er, **th**is (actually, this is a single sound, not two)

ü ... r**u**le, y**ou**th, uni**o**n \'yün-yən\, f**ew** \'fyü\

u̇ ... p**u**ll, w**oo**d, b**oo**k, curable \'kyu̇r-ə-bəl\, fury \'fyu̇r-ē\

ᴜe ... German f**ü**llen, h**ü**bsch

ᴜ̄e ... French r**u**e, German f**üh**len

v ... **v**i**v**id, gi**v**e

w ... **w**e, a**w**ay

y ... **y**ard, **y**oung, cue \'kyü\, mute \'myüt\, union \'yün-yən\

y ... indicates that during the articulation of the sound represented by the preceding character the front of the tongue has substantially the position it has for the articulation of the first sound of *yard*, as in French digne \dēnʸ\

z ... **z**one, rai**s**e

zh ... as in vi**si**on, azure \'a-zhər\ (actually, this is a single sound, not two); with a hyphen between, two sounds as in *hogshead* \'hȯgz-ˌhed, 'hägz-\

\ ... slant line used in pairs to mark the beginning and end of a transcription: \'pen\

ˈ ... mark preceding a syllable with primary (strongest) stress: \'pen-mən-ˌship\

ˌ ... mark preceding a syllable with secondary (medium) stress: \'pen-mən-ˌship\

- ... mark of syllable division

, ... mark separating variant pronunciations

; ... mark separating groups of variant pronunciations

( ) ... indicate that what is symbolized between is present in some utterances but not in others: *factory* \'fak-t(ə-)rē\

÷ ... indicates that many regard as unacceptable the pronunciation variant immediately following: *cupola* \'kyü-pə-lə, ÷-ˌlō\

# A

**A** *is the first letter of the English Alphabet and of most alphabets that are closely related. It comes from Latin A, which was itself descended, via Etruscan, from Greek A (alpha). The Greek letter, in turn, was borrowed from the first letter of the Phoenician alphabet, ' aleph. That letter represented a consonant sound called the glottal stop, pronounced something like a cough. Since the Greeks did not use the glottal stop, they assigned the letter to their own equivalent of the vowel sound (pronounced "ah") following the glottal stop in Phoenician ' aleph. In modern English, A represents various sounds, including the short a in bad and the long a in fate. The two small forms of a developed through gradual transformation of the capital form. First, the horizontal bar of A dropped out; next, it was replaced by a line slanting upward from the bottom of the left leg to the center of the right leg; then, the triangle thus formed was rounded to the left to form a loop; and, eventually, the right upward stroke was curved leftward or shortened and straightened to a vertical position.*

---

**¹a** \'ā\ *noun, plural* **a's** *or* **as** \'āz\ *often capitalized, often attributive* (before 12th century)
**1 a :** the 1st letter of the English alphabet **b :** a graphic representation of this letter **c :** a speech counterpart of orthographic *a*
**2 :** the 6th tone of a C-major scale
**3 :** a graphic device for reproducing the letter *a*
**4 :** one designated *a* especially as the 1st in order or class
**5 a :** a grade rating a student's work as superior in quality **b :** one graded or rated with an A
**6 :** something shaped like the letter A

**²a** \ə, (')ā, *Canadian* 'a\ *indefinite article* [Middle English, from Old English *ān* one — more at ONE] (before 12th century)
**1** — used as a function word before singular nouns when the referent is unspecified ⟨*a* man overboard⟩ and before number collectives and some numbers ⟨*a* dozen⟩
**2 :** the same ⟨birds of *a* feather⟩ ⟨swords all of *a* length⟩
**3 a** — used as a function word before a singular noun followed by a restrictive modifier ⟨*a* man who was here yesterday⟩ **b :** ANY ⟨*a* man who is sick can't work⟩ **c** — used as a function word before a mass noun to denote a particular type or instance ⟨*a* bronze made in ancient times⟩ ⟨glucose is *a* simple sugar⟩ **d** — used as a function word before a proper noun representing an example or type ⟨the attractions of *a* Boston or *a* Cleveland⟩
**4** — used as a function word with nouns to form adverbial phrases of quantity, amount, or degree ⟨felt *a* little tired⟩ ∎

**³a** \ə *also* (')ā\ *preposition* [Middle English, from Old English *a-, an, on*] (before 12th century)
**1** *chiefly dialect :* ON, IN, AT
**2 :** in, to, or for each ⟨twice *a* week⟩ ⟨five dollars *a* dozen⟩
**usage** see ²A

**⁴a** \ə, (,)ā\ *verb* [Middle English, contraction of *have*] (14th century)
*archaic :* HAVE ⟨I might *a* had husbands afore now —John Bunyan⟩

**⁵a** \ə\ *preposition* [Middle English, by contraction] (15th century)
**:** OF — often attached to the preceding word ⟨kind*a*⟩ ⟨lott*a*⟩

**¹a-** \ə\ *prefix* [Middle English, from Old English]
**1 :** on : in : at ⟨*a*bed⟩
**2 :** in (such) a state or condition ⟨*a*fire⟩
**3 :** in (such) a manner ⟨*a*loud⟩
**4 :** in the act or process of ⟨gone *a*-hunting⟩ ⟨*a*tingle⟩

**²a-** \(')ā *also* (')a *or* (')ä\ *or* **an-** \(')an\ *prefix* [Latin & Greek; Latin, from Greek — more at UN-]
**:** not : without ⟨*a*sexual⟩ — *a-* before consonants other than *h* and sometimes even before *h*, *an-* before vowels and usually before *h* ⟨*a*chromatic⟩ ⟨*a*historical⟩ ⟨*an*astigmatic⟩ ⟨*an*hydrous⟩

**-a-** *combining form* [International Scientific Vocabulary]
**:** replacing carbon especially in a ring ⟨*aza*-⟩

**-a** \ə\ *noun suffix* [New Latin, from *-a* (as in *magnesia*)]
**:** OXIDE ⟨silic*a*⟩

**aah** \'ä, *often prolonged and/or followed by* ə\ *intransitive verb* (1953)
**:** to exclaim in amazement, joy, or surprise ⟨one finds oneself oohing and *aah*ing over the exciting new TV commercials —Walter Goodman⟩
**— aah** *noun*

**aard·vark** \'ärd-,värk\ *noun* [obsolete Afrikaans, from Afrikaans *aard* earth + *vark* pig] (1827)
**:** a large burrowing nocturnal ungulate mammal (*Orycteropus afer*) of sub-Saharan Africa that has a long snout, extensible tongue, powerful claws, large ears, and heavy tail and feeds especially on termites and ants

**aardvark**

**aard·wolf** \-,wůlf\ *noun* [Afrikaans, from *aard* + *wolf*] (1833)
**:** a maned striped nocturnal mammal (*Proteles cristatus*) of southern and eastern Africa that resembles the related hyenas and feeds chiefly on insects and especially termites

**aardwolf**

**Aar·on** \'ar-ən, 'er-\ *noun* [Late Latin, from Greek *Aarōn*, from Hebrew *Ahărōn*]
**:** a brother of Moses and high priest of the Hebrews

**Aa·ron·ic** \a-'rä-nik, e-\ *adjective* (circa 1828)
**1 :** of or stemming from Aaron
**2 :** of or relating to the lower order of the Mormon priesthood

---

**ab** \'ab\ *noun* (1983)
**:** an abdominal muscle — usually used in plural

**Ab** \'äb, 'äv, 'ȯv\ *noun* [Hebrew *Ābh*] (circa 1771)
**:** the 11th month of the civil year or the 5th month of the ecclesiastical year in the Jewish calendar — see MONTH table

**ab-** \(,)ab, əb\ *prefix* [Middle English, from Old French & Latin; Old French, from Latin *ab-, abs-, a-,* from *ab, a* — more at OF]
**:** from : away : off ⟨*ab*axial⟩

**aba** \ə-'bä, ä-'ba\ *noun* [Arabic *'abā*] (1811)
**1 :** a loose sleeveless outer garment worn as traditional dress by men in the Middle East
**2 :** a fabric woven from the hair of camels or goats

**ab·a·ca** \,a-bə-'kä, 'a-bə-,\ *noun* [Spanish *abacá,* from Tagalog *abaká*] (circa 1818)
**1 :** a strong fiber obtained from the leafstalk of a banana (*Musa textilis*) native to the Philippines — called also *Manila hemp*
**2 :** the plant that yields abaca

**aback** \ə-'bak\ *adverb* (before 12th century)
**1** *archaic :* BACKWARD, BACK
**2 :** in a position to catch the wind upon the forward surface of a square sail
**3 :** by surprise : UNAWARES ⟨was taken *aback* by her sharp retort⟩

**abac·te·ri·al** \,ā-(,)bak-'tir-ē-əl\ *adjective* (circa 1935)
**:** not caused by or characterized by the presence of bacteria ⟨*abacterial* prostatitis⟩

**ab·a·cus** \'a-bə-kəs, ə-'ba-\ *noun, plural* **aba·ci** \'a-bə-,sī, -,kē; ə-'ba-,kī\ *or* **aba·cus·es** [Latin, from Greek *abak-, abax,* literally, slab] (14th century)
**1 :** an instrument for performing calculations by sliding counters along rods or in grooves
**2 :** a slab that forms the uppermost member or division of the capital of a column

**abacus 1**

**¹abaft** \ə-'baft\ *preposition* [¹*a-* + *baft* (aft)] (1594)
**:** to the rear of; *specifically :* toward the stern from

**²abaft** *adverb* (1628)
**:** toward or at the stern : AFT

**ab·a·lone** \,a-bə-'lō-nē, 'a-bə-,\ *noun* [American Spanish *abulón,* from Rumsen (American

---

---

\ə\ **abut** \ə\ **kitten** \ər\ **further** \a\ **ash** \ā\ **ace**
\ä\ **mop, mar** \au̇\ **out** \ch\ **chin** \e\ **bet** \ē\ **easy**
\g\ **go** \i\ **hit** \ī\ **ice** \j\ **job** \ŋ\ **sing** \ō\ **go**
\ȯ\ **law** \ȯi\ **boy** \th\ **thin** \t̶h\ **the** \ü\ **loot** \u̇\ **foot**
\y\ **yet** \zh\ **vision** *see also* Guide to Pronunciation

Indian language of Monterey Bay, Calif.) *au-lon*] (1850)
**:** any of a genus (*Haliotis*) of edible rock-clinging gastropod mollusks that have a flattened shell slightly spiral in form, lined with mother-of-pearl, and with a row of apertures along its outer edge

¹**aban·don** \ə-'ban-dən\ *transitive verb* [Middle English *abandounen*, from Middle French *abandoner*, from *abandon*, noun, surrender, from *a bandon* in one's power] (14th century)
**1 a :** to give up to the control or influence of another person or agent **b :** to give up with the intent of never again claiming a right or interest in
**2 :** to withdraw from often in the face of danger or encroachment ⟨*abandon* ship⟩
**3 :** to withdraw protection, support, or help from
**4 :** to give (oneself) over unrestrainedly
**5 a :** to cease from maintaining, practicing, or using ⟨*abandoned* their native language⟩ **b :** to cease intending or attempting to perform ⟨*abandoned* the escape⟩ ☆
— **aban·don·er** *noun*
— **aban·don·ment** \-dən-mənt\ *noun*

²**abandon** *noun* (1822)
**:** a thorough yielding to natural impulses; *especially* **:** ENTHUSIASM, EXUBERANCE ⟨with reckless *abandon*⟩

**aban·doned** \ə-'ban-dənd\ *adjective* (14th century)
**1 :** wholly free from restraint
**2 :** given up **:** FORSAKEN

**à bas** \ä-'bä\ [French] (circa 1897)
**:** down with ⟨*à bas* the profiteers⟩

**abase** \ə-'bās\ *transitive verb* **abased; abas·ing** [Middle English *abassen*, from Middle French *abaisser*, from *a-* (from Latin *ad-*) + (assumed) Vulgar Latin *bassiare* to lower] (15th century)
**1** *archaic* **:** to lower physically
**2 :** to lower in rank, office, prestige, or esteem
— **abase·ment** \-'bā-smənt\ *noun*

**abash** \ə-'bash\ *transitive verb* [Middle English *abaishen*, from (assumed) Middle French *abaiss-, abair* to astonish, alteration of Middle French *esbair*, from *ex-* + *baer* to yawn — more at ABEYANCE] (14th century)
**:** to destroy the self-possession or self-confidence of **:** DISCONCERT
*synonym* see EMBARRASS
— **abash·ment** \-mənt\ *noun*

**abate** \ə-'bāt\ *verb* **abat·ed; abat·ing** [Middle English, from Old French *abattre* to beat down — more at REBATE] (13th century)
*transitive verb*
**1 a :** to put an end to ⟨*abate* a nuisance⟩ **b :** NULLIFY ⟨*abate* a writ⟩
**2 a :** to reduce in degree or intensity **:** MODERATE **b :** to reduce in value or amount **:** make less especially by way of relief ⟨*abate* a tax⟩
**3 :** DEDUCT, OMIT ⟨*abate* part of the price⟩
**4 a :** to beat down or cut away so as to leave a figure in relief **b** *obsolete* **:** BLUNT
**5 :** DEPRIVE
*intransitive verb*
**1 :** to decrease in force or intensity
**2 a :** to become defeated or become null or void **b :** to decrease in amount or value ☆
— **abat·er** *noun*

**abate·ment** \ə-'bāt-mənt\ *noun* (14th century)
**1 :** the act or process of abating **:** the state of being abated
**2 :** an amount abated; *especially* **:** a deduction from the full amount of a tax

**ab·a·tis** \'a-bə-ˌtē, 'a-bə-təs\ *noun, plural* **ab·a·tis** \'a-bə-ˌtēz\ *or* **ab·a·tis·es** \'a-bə-tə-səz\ [French, from *abattre*] (1766)
**:** a defensive obstacle formed by felled trees with sharpened branches facing the enemy

**ab·at·toir** \'a-bə-ˌtwär, -ˌtwȯr, -ˌtȯr\ *noun* [French, from *abattre*] (1820)
**:** SLAUGHTERHOUSE

**ab·ax·i·al** \(ˌ)a-'bak-sē-əl\ *adjective* (1857)

**:** situated out of or directed away from the axis ⟨the *abaxial* or lower surface of a leaf⟩

**ab·ba·cy** \'a-bə-sē\ *noun, plural* **-cies** [Middle English *abbatie*, from Late Latin *abbatia*] (15th century)
**:** the office, dignity, jurisdiction, or tenure of an abbot

**Ab·bas·id** \ə-'ba-səd, 'a-bə-səd\ *noun* (1788)
**:** a member of a dynasty of caliphs (750–1258) ruling the Islamic empire especially from their capital Baghdad and claiming descent from Abbas the uncle of Muhammad

**ab·ba·tial** \ə-'bā-shəl, a-\ *adjective* (circa 1642)
**:** of or relating to an abbot, abbess, or abbey

**ab·bé** \a-'bā, 'a-ˌbā\ *noun* [French, from Late Latin *abbat-, abbas*] (1530)
**:** a member of the French secular clergy in major or minor orders — used as a title

**ab·bess** \'a-bəs\ *noun* [Middle English *abbesse*, from Old French, from Late Latin *abbatissa*, feminine of *abbat-, abbas*] (13th century)
**:** a woman who is the superior of a convent of nuns

**Abbe·vil·li·an** \ˌab-'vi-lē-ən, ˌa-bə-\ *adjective* [*Abbeville*, France] (circa 1934)
**:** of or relating to an early Lower Paleolithic culture of Europe characterized by bifacial stone hand axes

**ab·bey** \'a-bē\ *noun, plural* **abbeys** [Middle English, from Old French *abaïe*, from Late Latin *abbatia* abbey, from *abbat-, abbas*] (13th century)
**1 a :** a monastery ruled by an abbot **b :** a convent ruled by an abbess
**2 :** an abbey church

**ab·bot** \'a-bət\ *noun* [Middle English *abbod*, from Old English, from Late Latin *abbat-, abbas*, from Late Greek *abbas*, from Aramaic *abbā* father] (before 12th century)
**:** the superior of a monastery for men

**ab·bre·vi·ate** \ə-'brē-vē-ˌāt\ *transitive verb* **-at·ed; -at·ing** [Middle English, from Late Latin *abbreviatus*, past participle of *abbreviare* — more at ABRIDGE] (15th century)
**:** to make briefer; *especially* **:** to reduce to a shorter form intended to stand for the whole
*synonym* see SHORTEN
— **ab·bre·vi·a·tor** \-ˌā-tər\ *noun*

**ab·bre·vi·a·tion** \ə-ˌbrē-vē-'ā-shən\ *noun* (15th century)
**1 :** the act or result of abbreviating **:** ABRIDGMENT
**2 :** a shortened form of a written word or phrase used in place of the whole ⟨*amt* is an *abbreviation* for *amount*⟩

**ABC** \ˌā-(ˌ)bē-'sē\ *noun, plural* **ABC's** *or* **ABCs** \-'sēz\ (13th century)
**1 :** ALPHABET — usually used in plural
**2 a :** the rudiments of reading, writing, and spelling — usually used in plural **b :** the rudiments of a subject

**ABD** \ˌā-(ˌ)bē-'dē\ *noun, plural* **ABDs** *also* **ABD's** [*all but d*issertation] (1965)
**:** a doctoral candidate who has completed required courses and examinations but not a dissertation

**Ab·di·as** \ab-'dī-əs\ *noun* [Late Latin, from Greek]
**:** OBADIAH

**ab·di·cate** \'ab-di-ˌkāt\ *verb* **-cat·ed; -cat·ing** [Latin *abdicatus*, past participle of *abdicare*, from *ab-* + *dicare* to proclaim — more at DICTION] (1541)
*transitive verb*
**1 :** to cast off **:** DISCARD
**2 :** to relinquish (as sovereign power) formally
*intransitive verb*
**:** to renounce a throne, high office, dignity, or function ☆
— **ab·di·ca·ble** \-kə-bəl\ *adjective*
— **ab·di·ca·tion** \ˌab-di-'kā-shən\ *noun*
— **ab·di·ca·tor** \'ab-di-ˌkā-tər\ *noun*

**ab·do·men** \'ab-də-mən, -ˌdō-; ab-'dō-mən, ab-\ *noun* [Middle French & Latin; Middle French, from Latin] (1615)
**1 :** the part of the body between the thorax and the pelvis; *also* **:** the cavity of this part of the trunk containing the chief viscera
**2 :** the posterior section of the body behind the thorax in an arthropod — see INSECT illustration
— **ab·dom·i·nal** \ab-'dä-mə-nᵊl, əb-, -'däm-nᵊl\ *adjective*
— **ab·dom·i·nal·ly** \-ē\ *adverb*

**ab·du·cens nerve** \ab-'dü-ˌsenz-, -'dyü-\ *noun* [New Latin *abducent-, abducens*, from Latin, present participle of *abducere*] (1947)
**:** either of the 6th pair of cranial nerves that are motor nerves supplying the rectus on the outer and lateral side of each eye — called also *abducens*

**ab·du·cent nerve** \ab-'dü-sᵊnt-, -'dyü-\ *noun* (1875)
**:** ABDUCENS NERVE

**ab·duct** \ab-'dəkt, əb-; 2 *also* 'ab-\ *transitive verb* [Latin *abductus*, past participle of *abducere*, literally, to lead away, from *ab-* + *ducere* to lead — more at TOW] (1834)
**1 :** to carry off (as a person) by force
**2 :** to draw or spread away (as a limb or the fingers) from a position near or parallel to the median axis of the body or from the axis of a limb
— **ab·duc·tor** \-'dək-tər\ *noun*

**ab·duc·tion** \ab-'dək-shən, əb-\ *noun* (1666)
**1 :** the action of abducting **:** the condition of being abducted
**2 :** the unlawful carrying away of a woman for marriage or intercourse

**abeam** \ə-'bēm\ *adverb or adjective* (circa 1836)
**:** off to the side of a ship or plane especially at a right angle to the middle of the ship or plane's length

¹**abe·ce·dar·i·an** \ˌā-bē-(ˌ)sē-'der-ē-ən\ *noun* [Middle English *abecedary*, from Medieval Latin *abecedarium* alphabet, from Late Latin,

---

☆ SYNONYMS
**Abandon, desert, forsake** mean to leave without intending to return. ABANDON suggests that the thing or person left may be helpless without protection ⟨*abandoned* children⟩. DESERT implies that the object left may be weakened but not destroyed by one's absence ⟨a *deserted* town⟩. FORSAKE suggests an action more likely to bring impoverishment or bereavement to that which is forsaken than its exposure to physical dangers ⟨a *forsaken* lover⟩. See in addition RELINQUISH.

**Abate, subside, wane, ebb** mean to die down in force or intensity. ABATE stresses the idea of progressive diminishing ⟨the storm *abated*⟩. SUBSIDE implies the ceasing of turbulence or agitation ⟨the protests *subsided* after a few days⟩. WANE suggests the fading or weakening of something good or impressive ⟨*waning* enthusiasm⟩. EBB suggests the receding of something (as the tide) that commonly comes and goes ⟨the *ebbing* of daylight⟩. See in addition DECREASE.

**Abdicate, renounce, resign** mean to give up a position with no possibility of resuming it. ABDICATE implies a giving up of sovereign power or sometimes an evading of responsibility such as that of a parent ⟨*abdicated* the throne⟩. RENOUNCE may replace it but often implies additionally a sacrifice for a greater end ⟨*renounced* her inheritance by marrying a commoner⟩. RESIGN applies to the giving up of an unexpired office or trust ⟨*resigned* from the board⟩.

neuter of *abecedarius* of the alphabet, from the letters *a + b + c + d*] (1603)
**:** one learning the rudiments of something (as the alphabet)
**²abecedarian** *adjective* (1665)
**1 a :** of or relating to the alphabet **b :** alphabetically arranged
**2 :** RUDIMENTARY
**abed** \ə-'bed\ *adverb or adjective* (13th century)
**:** in bed
**Abel** \'ā-bəl\ *noun* [Late Latin, from Greek, from Hebrew *Hebhel*]
**:** a son of Adam and Eve killed by his brother Cain
**abe·lia** \ə-'bēl-yə\ *noun* [New Latin, from Clarke *Abel* (died 1826) English botanist] (circa 1899)
**:** any of a genus (*Abelia*) of shrubs of Asian or Mexican origin having opposite leaves and white, red, or pink flowers
**abe·li·an** \ə-'bē-lē-ən\ *adjective, often capitalized* [Niels *Abel* (died 1829) Norwegian mathematician] (circa 1909)
**:** COMMUTATIVE 2 〈*abelian* group〉 〈*abelian* ring〉
**Abe·na·ki** \ˌa-bə-'nä-kē\ *noun, plural* **Abe·naki** *or* **Abenakis** (1721)
**1 :** a member of a group of American Indian peoples of northern New England and adjoining parts of Quebec
**2 :** either of the two Algonquian languages spoken by the Abenaki peoples
**Ab·er·deen An·gus** \'a-bər-ˌdēn-'aŋ-gəs\ *noun* [*Aberdeen & Angus*, counties in Scotland] (1862)
**:** ANGUS
**¹ab·er·rant** \a-'ber-ənt, ə-; 'a-bə-rənt, -ˌber-ənt\ *adjective* [Latin *aberrant-, aberrans*, present participle of *aberrare* to go astray, from *ab-* + *errare* to wander, err] (circa 1780)
**1 :** straying from the right or normal way
**2 :** deviating from the usual or natural type **:** ATYPICAL
— **ab·er·rance** \-ən(t)s\ *noun*
— **ab·er·ran·cy** \-ən(t)-sē\ *noun*
— **ab·er·rant·ly** *adverb*
**²aberrant** *noun* (1938)
**1 :** an aberrant group, individual, or structure
**2 :** a person whose behavior departs substantially from the standard
**ab·er·rat·ed** \'a-bə-ˌrā-təd\ *adjective* [Latin *aberratus,* past participle of *aberrare*] (1893)
**:** ABERRANT
**ab·er·ra·tion** \ˌa-bə-'rā-shən\ *noun* [Latin *aberrare*] (1594)
**1 :** the fact or an instance of being aberrant especially from a moral standard or normal state
**2 :** failure of a mirror, refracting surface, or lens to produce exact point-to-point correspondence between an object and its image
**3 :** unsoundness or disorder of the mind
**4 :** a small periodic change of apparent position in celestial bodies due to the combined effect of the motion of light and the motion of the observer
**5 :** an aberrant individual
— **ab·er·ra·tion·al** \-shnəl, -shə-nᵊl\ *adjective*
**abet** \ə-'bet\ *transitive verb* **abet·ted; abet·ting** [Middle English *abetten,* from Middle French *abeter,* from Old French, from *a-* (from Latin *ad-*) + *beter* to bait, of Germanic origin; akin to Old English *bǣtan* to bait] (14th century)
**1 :** to actively second and encourage (as an activity or plan) **:** FORWARD
**2 :** to assist or support in the achievement of a purpose 〈*abetted* the thief in his getaway〉
**synonym** *see* INCITE
— **abet·ment** \-mənt\ *noun*
— **abet·tor** *or* **abet·ter** \ə-'be-tər\ *noun*
**abey·ance** \ə-'bā-ən(t)s\ *noun* [Middle French *abeance* expectation, from *abaer* to desire, from *a-* + *baer* to yawn, from Medieval Latin *batare*] (1660)

**1 :** temporary inactivity **:** SUSPENSION
**2 :** a lapse in succession during which there is no person in whom a title is vested
**abey·ant** \-ənt\ *adjective* [back-formation from *abeyance*] (circa 1859)
**:** being in abeyance
**ab·hor** \əb-'hȯr, ab-\ *transitive verb* **abhorred; ab·hor·ring** [Middle English *abhorren,* from Latin *abhorrēre,* from *ab-* + *horrēre* to shudder — more at HORROR] (15th century)
**:** to regard with extreme repugnance **:** LOATHE
**synonym** *see* HATE
— **ab·hor·rer** \-'hȯr-ər\ *noun*
**ab·hor·rence** \əb-'hȯr-ən(t)s, -'här-\ *noun* (1660)
**1 a :** the act or state of abhorring **b :** the feeling of one who abhors
**2 :** one that is abhorred
**ab·hor·rent** \-ənt\ *adjective* [Latin *abhorrent-, abhorrens,* present participle of *abhorrēre*] (1599)
**1 a** *archaic* **:** strongly opposed **b :** feeling or showing abhorrence
**2 :** not agreeable **:** CONTRARY 〈a notion *abhorrent* to their philosophy〉
**3 :** being so repugnant as to stir up positive antagonism 〈acts *abhorrent* to every right-minded person〉
— **ab·hor·rent·ly** *adverb*
**Abib** \ä-'vēv\ *noun* [Hebrew *Ābhībh,* literally, ear of grain] (1535)
**:** the 1st month of the ancient Hebrew calendar corresponding to Nisan — see MONTH table
**abid·ance** \ə-'bī-dᵊn(t)s\ *noun* (1647)
**1 :** an act or state of abiding **:** CONTINUANCE
**2 :** COMPLIANCE 〈*abidance* by the rules〉
**abide** \ə-'bīd\ *verb* **abode** \-'bōd\ *or* **abid·ed; abid·ing** [Middle English, from Old English *ābīdan,* from *ā-,* perfective prefix + *bīdan* to bide; akin to Old High German *ir-,* perfective prefix] (before 12th century)
*transitive verb*
**1 :** to wait for **:** AWAIT
**2 a :** to endure without yielding **:** WITHSTAND **b :** to bear patiently **:** TOLERATE 〈cannot *abide* such bigots〉
**3 :** to accept without objection 〈will *abide* your decision〉
*intransitive verb*
**1 :** to remain stable or fixed in a state
**2 :** to continue in a place **:** SOJOURN
**synonym** *see* BEAR, CONTINUE
— **abid·er** *noun*
— **abide by 1 :** to conform to **2 :** to acquiesce in
**abid·ing** \ə-'bī-diŋ\ *adjective* (14th century)
**:** ENDURING, CONTINUING 〈an *abiding* interest in nature〉
— **abid·ing·ly** *adverb*
**ab·i·gail** \'a-bə-ˌgāl\ *noun* [*Abigail,* servant in *The Scornful Lady,* a play by Francis Beaumont & John Fletcher] (1671)
**:** a lady's personal maid
**abil·i·ty** \ə-'bi-lə-tē\ *noun, plural* **-ties** [Middle English *abilite,* from Middle French *habilité,* from Latin *habilitat-, habilitas,* from *habilis* apt, skillful — more at ABLE] (14th century)
**1 a :** the quality or state of being able 〈*ability* of the soil to hold water〉; *especially* **:** physical, mental, or legal power to perform **b :** competence in doing **:** SKILL
**2 :** natural aptitude or acquired proficiency 〈children whose *abilities* warrant higher education〉
**-ability** *also* **-ibility** *noun suffix* [Middle English *-abilite, -ibilite,* from Middle French *-abilité, -ibilité,* from Latin *-abilitas, -ibilitas,* from *-abilis, -ibilis -able + -tas -ty*]
**:** capacity, fitness, or tendency to act or be acted on in a (specified) way 〈agglutin*ability*〉
**ab in·i·tio** \ˌab-ə-'ni-shē-ˌō\ *adverb* [Latin] (1599)
**:** from the beginning

**abio·gen·e·sis** \ˌā-bī-ō-'je-nə-səs\ *noun* [New Latin, from ²*a-* + *bio-* + Latin *genesis*] (1870)
**:** the supposed spontaneous origination of living organisms directly from lifeless matter
— **abi·og·e·nist** \ˌā-(ˌ)bī-'ä-jə-nist\ *noun*
**abio·gen·ic** \ˌā-bī-ō-'je-nik\ *adjective* (1891)
**:** not produced by the action of living organisms
— **abio·gen·i·cal·ly** \-ni-k(ə-)lē\ *adverb*
**abi·o·log·i·cal** \ˌā-bī-ə-'lä-ji-kəl\ *adjective* (1868)
**:** not biological; *especially* **:** not involving or produced by organisms 〈*abiological* synthesis of amino acids〉
**abi·ot·ic** \ˌā-(ˌ)bī-'ä-tik\ *adjective* (circa 1893)
**:** not biotic **:** ABIOLOGICAL 〈the *abiotic* environment〉
— **abi·ot·i·cal·ly** \-ti-k(ə-)lē\ *adverb*
**ab·ject** \'ab-ˌjekt\ *adjective* [Middle English, from Latin *abjectus,* from past participle of *abicere* to cast off, from *ab-* + *jacere* to throw — more at JET] (15th century)
**1 :** sunk to or existing in a low state or condition 〈to lowest pitch of *abject* fortune thou art fallen —John Milton〉
**2 a :** cast down in spirit **:** SERVILE, SPIRITLESS 〈a man made *abject* by suffering〉 **b :** showing utter hopelessness or resignation 〈*abject* surrender〉
**3 :** expressing or offered in a humble and often ingratiating spirit 〈*abject* flattery〉 〈an *abject* apology〉
**synonym** *see* MEAN
— **ab·ject·ly** \'ab-ˌjekt-lē, ab-'\ *adverb*
— **ab·ject·ness** \-ˌjekt-nəs, -'jekt-\ *noun*
**ab·jec·tion** \ab-'jek-shən\ *noun* (14th century)
**1 :** a low or downcast state **:** DEGRADATION
**2 :** the act of making abject **:** HUMBLING, REJECTION 〈I protest . . . this vile *abjection* of youth to age —G. B. Shaw〉
**ab·ju·ra·tion** \ˌab-jə-'rā-shən\ *noun* (15th century)
**1 :** the act or process of abjuring
**2 :** an oath of abjuring
**ab·jure** \ab-'jur\ *transitive verb* **ab·jured; ab·jur·ing** [Middle English, from Middle French or Latin; Middle French *abjurer,* from Latin *abjurare,* from *ab-* + *jurare* to swear — more at JURY] (15th century)
**1 a :** to renounce upon oath **b :** to reject solemnly
**2 :** to abstain from **:** AVOID 〈*abjure* extravagance〉 ☆
— **ab·jur·er** *noun*
**ab·late** \a-'blāt\ *verb* **ab·lat·ed; ab·lat·ing** [Latin *ablatus* (past participle of *auferre* to remove), from *ab-* + *latus,* past participle of

---

☆ **SYNONYMS**
**Abjure, renounce, forswear, recant, retract** mean to withdraw one's word or professed belief. ABJURE implies a firm and final rejecting or abandoning often made under oath 〈*abjured* the errors of his former faith〉. RENOUNCE often equals ABJURE but may carry the meaning of disclaim or disown 〈*renounced* abstract art and turned to portrait painting〉. FORSWEAR may add to ABJURE an implication of perjury or betrayal 〈I cannot *forswear* my principles〉. RECANT stresses the withdrawing or denying of something professed or taught 〈if they *recant* they will be spared〉. RETRACT applies to the withdrawing of a promise, an offer, or an accusation 〈the newspaper had to *retract* its allegations against the mayor〉.

---

\ə\ **abut** \ᵊ\ **kitten** \ər\ **further** \a\ **ash** \ā\ **ace**
\ä\ **mop, mar** \aù\ **out** \ch\ **chin** \e\ **bet** \ē\ **easy**
\g\ **go** \i\ **hit** \ī\ **ice** \j\ **job** \ŋ\ **sing** \ō\ **go**
\ò\ **law** \òi\ **boy** \th\ **thin** \t̲h̲\ **the** \ü\ **loot** \ù\ **foot**
\y\ **yet** \zh\ **vision** *see also* Guide to Pronunciation

*ferre* — more at UKASE, BEAR, TOLERATE]
(1542)
*transitive verb*
**:** to remove especially by cutting, abrading, or evaporating
*intransitive verb*
**:** to become ablated; *especially* **:** VAPORIZE 1
**ab·la·tion** \a-'blā-shən\ *noun* (15th century)
**:** the process of ablating: as **a :** surgical removal **b :** loss of a part (as ice from a glacier or the outside of a nose cone) by melting or vaporization
**¹ab·la·tive** \'a-blə-tiv\ *adjective* (15th century)
**:** of, relating to, or constituting a grammatical case expressing typically the relations of separation and source and also frequently such relations as cause or instrument
— **ablative** *noun*
**²ab·la·tive** \a-'blā-tiv\ *adjective* (circa 1569)
**1 :** of or relating to ablation
**2 :** tending to ablate ⟨*ablative* material on a nose cone⟩
— **ab·la·tive·ly** *adverb*
**ablative absolute** \'a-blə-tiv-\ *noun* (circa 1828)
**:** a construction in Latin in which a noun or pronoun and its adjunct both in the ablative case form together an adverbial phrase expressing generally the time, cause, or an attendant circumstance of an action
**ab·laut** \'ä-blaut, 'a-; 'äp-,laut\ *noun* [German, from *ab* away from + *Laut* sound] (1849)
**:** a systematic variation of vowels in the same root or affix or in related roots or affixes especially in the Indo-European languages that is usually paralleled by differences in use or meaning (as in *sing, sang, sung, song*)
**ablaze** \ə-'blāz\ *adjective or adverb* (1801)
**1 :** being on fire
**2 :** radiant with light or emotion ⟨his face all *ablaze* with excitement —Bram Stoker⟩
**able** \'ā-bəl\ *adjective* **abler** \-b(ə-)lər\;
**ablest** \-b(ə-)ləst\ [Middle English, from Middle French, from Latin *habilis* apt, from *habēre* to have — more at HABIT] (14th century)
**1 a :** having sufficient power, skill, or resources to accomplish an object **b :** susceptible to action or treatment
**2 :** marked by intelligence, knowledge, skill, or competence
— **ably** \'ā-b(ə-)lē\ *adverb*
**-able** *also* **-ible** *adjective suffix* [Middle English, from Old French, from Latin *-abilis*, *-ibilis*, from *-a-*, *-i-*, verb stem vowels + *-bilis* capable or worthy of]
**1 :** capable of, fit for, or worthy of (being so acted upon or toward) — chiefly in adjectives derived from verbs ⟨break*able*⟩ ⟨collect*ible*⟩
**2 :** tending, given, or liable to ⟨agree*able*⟩ ⟨perish*able*⟩
— **-ably** *also* **-ibly** *adverb suffix*
**able–bod·ied** \,ā-bəl-'bä-dēd\ *adjective* (circa 1622)
**:** having a sound strong body
**able–bodied seaman** *noun* (circa 1909)
**:** ABLE SEAMAN
**able seaman** *noun* (1702)
**:** an experienced deck-department seaman qualified to perform routine duties at sea
**abloom** \ə-'blüm\ *adjective* (1855)
**:** abounding with blooms **:** BLOOMING ⟨parks *abloom* with roses⟩
**ab·lut·ed** \ə-'blü-təd, a-\ *adjective* [back-formation from *ablution*] (1650)
**:** washed clean
**ab·lu·tion** \ə-'blü-shən, a-\ *noun* [Middle English, from Middle French or Latin; Middle French, from Latin *ablution-, ablutio*, from *abluere* to wash away, from *ab- + luere* to wash; akin to Latin *lavere* to wash — more at LYE] (1533)
**1 a :** the washing of one's body or part of it (as in a religious rite) **b** *plural* **:** the act or action of bathing

**2** *plural, British* **:** a building housing bathing and toilet facilities on a military base
— **ab·lu·tion·ary** \-shə,ner-ē\ *adjective*
**ABM** \,ā-(,)bē-'em\ *noun, plural* **ABM's** *or* **ABMs** \-'emz\ (1963)
**:** ANTIBALLISTIC MISSILE
**Ab·na·ki** \ab-'nä-kē\ *variant of* ABENAKI
**ab·ne·gate** \'ab-ni-,gāt\ *transitive verb* **-gat·ed; -gat·ing** [back-formation from *abnegation*] (1623)
**1 :** DENY, RENOUNCE ⟨*abnegated* their God⟩
**2 :** SURRENDER, RELINQUISH ⟨*abnegated* her powers⟩
— **ab·ne·ga·tor** \-,gā-tər\ *noun*
**ab·ne·ga·tion** \,ab-ni-'gā-shən\ *noun* [Late Latin *abnegation-, abnegatio*, from Latin *abnegare* to refuse, from *ab- + negare* to deny — more at NEGATE] (14th century)
**:** DENIAL; *especially* **:** SELF-DENIAL
**¹ab·nor·mal** \(,)ab-'nȯr-məl, əb-\ *adjective* [alteration of French *anormal*, from Medieval Latin *anormalis*, from Latin *a- +* Late Latin *normalis* normal] (circa 1836)
**:** deviating from the normal or average **:** UNUSUAL, EXCEPTIONAL ⟨*abnormal* behavior⟩
— **ab·nor·mal·ly** \-mə-lē\ *adverb*
**²abnormal** *noun* (1912)
**:** an abnormal person
**ab·nor·mal·i·ty** \,ab-nər-'ma-lə-tē, -(,)nȯr-\ *noun, plural* **-ties** (1854)
**1 :** the quality or state of being abnormal
**2 :** something abnormal
**abnormal psychology** *noun* (circa 1903)
**:** a branch of psychology concerned with mental and emotional disorders (as neuroses, psychoses, and mental deficiency) and with certain incompletely understood normal phenomena (as dreams and hypnosis)
**abo** \'a-(,)bō\ *noun, plural* **ab·os** (1908)
*Australian* **:** ABORIGINE — often used disparagingly
**¹aboard** \ə-'bōrd, -'bȯrd\ *adverb or adjective* (14th century)
**1 :** ALONGSIDE
**2 a :** on, onto, or within a vehicle (as a car or ship) **b :** in or into a group, association, or organization ⟨her second promotion since coming *aboard*⟩
**3** *baseball* **:** on base
**²aboard** *preposition* (15th century)
**:** ON, ONTO, WITHIN ⟨go *aboard* ship⟩ ⟨*aboard* a plane⟩
**ABO blood group** \,ā-(,)bē-'ō-\ *noun* (1949)
**:** any of the four blood groups A, B, AB, and O comprising the ABO system
**abode** \ə-'bōd\ *noun* [Middle English *abod*, from *abiden* to abide] (13th century)
**1** *obsolete* **:** WAIT, DELAY
**2 :** a temporary stay **:** SOJOURN
**3 :** the place where one abides **:** HOME
**aboil** \ə-'bȯi(ə)l\ *adjective or adverb* (1810)
**1 :** being at the boiling point **:** BOILING
**2 :** intensely excited or stirred up ⟨the meeting was *aboil* with controversy⟩
**abol·ish** \ə-'bä-lish\ *transitive verb* [Middle English *abolisshen*, from Middle French *aboliss-*, stem of *abolir*, from Latin *abolēre*; probably akin to *adolescere* to grow up — more at ADULT] (15th century)
**1 :** to end the observance or effect of **:** ANNUL
**2 :** DESTROY
— **abol·ish·able** \-li-shə-bəl\ *adjective*
— **abol·ish·er** *noun*
— **abol·ish·ment** \-mənt\ *noun*
**ab·o·li·tion** \,a-bə-'li-shən\ *noun* [Middle French, from Latin *abolition-, abolitio*, from *abolēre*] (1529)
**1 :** the act of abolishing **:** the state of being abolished
**2 :** the abolishing of slavery
— **ab·o·li·tion·ary** \-'li-shən-,er-ē\ *adjective*
**ab·o·li·tion·ism** \-'li-shən-,i-zəm\ *noun* (1808)
**:** principles or measures fostering abolition especially of slavery

— **ab·o·li·tion·ist** \-ist\ *noun or adjective*
**ab·oma·sum** \,a-bō-'mā-səm\ *noun, plural* **-sa** \-sə\ [New Latin, from Latin *ab- + omasum* ox's tripe] (circa 1706)
**:** the fourth compartment of the ruminant stomach that follows the omasum and has a true digestive function — compare RUMEN, RETICULUM
— **ab·oma·sal** \-səl\ *adjective*
**A–bomb** \'ā-,bäm\ *noun* (1945)
**:** ATOMIC BOMB 1
**abom·i·na·ble** \ə-'bäm-nə-bəl, -'bä-mə-\ *adjective* (14th century)
**1 :** worthy of or causing disgust or hatred **:** DETESTABLE ⟨the *abominable* treatment of the poor⟩
**2 :** quite disagreeable or unpleasant ⟨*abominable* weather⟩
— **abom·i·na·bly** \-blē\ *adverb*
**abominable snow·man** \-'snō-mən, -,man\ *noun, often A&S capitalized* (1921)
**:** a mysterious creature with human or apelike characteristics reported to exist in the high Himalayas — called also *yeti*
**abom·i·nate** \ə-'bä-mə-,nāt\ *transitive verb* **-nat·ed; -nat·ing** [Latin *abominatus*, past participle of *abominari*, literally, to deprecate as an ill omen, from *ab- + omin-, omen* omen] (1644)
**:** to hate or loathe intensely **:** ABHOR
*synonym* see HATE
— **abom·i·na·tor** \-,nā-tər\ *noun*
**abom·i·na·tion** \ə-,bä-mə-'nā-shən\ *noun* (14th century)
**1 :** something abominable
**2 :** extreme disgust and hatred **:** LOATHING
**ab·oral** \(,)a-'bōr-əl, -'bȯr-\ *adjective* (1857)
**:** situated opposite to or away from the mouth ⟨a sea urchin's *aboral* surface⟩
— **ab·oral·ly** \-ə-lē\ *adverb*
**¹ab·orig·i·nal** \,a-bə-'rij-nəl, -'ri-jə-n°l\ *adjective* (1667)
**1 :** being the first or earliest known of its kind present in a region ⟨*aboriginal* forests⟩ ⟨*aboriginal* rocks⟩
**2 a :** of or relating to aborigines **b** *often capitalized* **:** of or relating to the indigenous peoples of Australia
*synonym* see NATIVE
— **ab·orig·i·nal·ly** *adverb*
**²aboriginal** *noun* (1767)
**1 :** ABORIGINE 1
**2** *often capitalized* **:** ABORIGINE 2
**ab·orig·i·ne** \,a-bə-'rij-(,)nē, -'ri-jə-\ *noun* [Latin *aborigines*, plural, from *ab origine* from the beginning] (1533)
**1 :** an aboriginal inhabitant especially as contrasted with an invading or colonizing people
**2** *often capitalized* **:** a member of any of the indigenous peoples of Australia
**¹aborn·ing** \ə-'bȯr-niŋ\ *adverb* [¹a- + English dialect *borning* (birth)] (1916)
**:** while being born or produced ⟨a resolution that died *aborning*⟩
**²aborning** *adjective* (1943)
**:** being born or produced ⟨the *aborning* fiasco⟩
**¹abort** \ə-'bȯrt\ *verb* [Latin *abortus*, past participle of *aboriri* to miscarry, from *ab- + oriri* to rise, be born — more at ORIENT] (1580)
*intransitive verb*
**1 :** to bring forth premature or stillborn offspring
**2 :** to become checked in development so as to degenerate or remain rudimentary
*transitive verb*
**1 a :** to induce the abortion of or give birth to prematurely **b :** to terminate the pregnancy of before term
**2 a :** to terminate prematurely **:** CANCEL ⟨*abort* a project⟩ ⟨*abort* a spaceflight⟩ **b :** to stop in the early stages ⟨*abort* a disease⟩
— **abort·er** *noun*
**²abort** *noun* (1944)
**:** the premature termination of a flight (as of

an aircraft or spacecraft), a mission, or an action or procedure relating to a flight ⟨a launch *abort*⟩

**abor·ti·fa·cient** \ə-ˌbȯr-tə-ˈfā-shənt\ *noun* (1873)
: an agent (as a drug) that induces abortion
— **abortifacient** *adjective*

**abor·tion** \ə-ˈbȯr-shən\ *noun* (1547)
**1 :** the termination of a pregnancy after, accompanied by, resulting in, or closely followed by the death of the embryo or fetus: as **a :** spontaneous expulsion of a human fetus during the first 12 weeks of gestation — compare MISCARRIAGE **b :** induced expulsion of a human fetus **c :** expulsion of a fetus by a domestic animal often due to infection at any time before completion of pregnancy — compare CONTAGIOUS ABORTION
**2 :** MONSTROSITY
**3 :** arrest of development (as of a part or process) resulting in imperfection; *also* : a result of such arrest

**abor·tion·ist** \-sh(ə-)nist\ *noun* (1871)
: one who induces abortions

**abor·tive** \ə-ˈbȯr-tiv\ *adjective* (14th century)
**1** *obsolete* **:** prematurely born
**2 :** FRUITLESS, UNSUCCESSFUL
**3 :** imperfectly formed or developed
**4 :** tending to cut short ■
— **abor·tive·ly** *adverb*
— **abor·tive·ness** *noun*

**ABO system** \ˌā-(ˌ)bē-ˈō-\ *noun* (1944)
: the basic system of antigens of human blood behaving in heredity as an allelic unit to produce any of the ABO blood groups

**abound** \ə-ˈbau̇nd\ *intransitive verb* [Middle English, from Middle French *abonder*, from Latin *abundare*, from *ab-* + *unda* wave — more at WATER] (14th century)
**1 :** to be present in large numbers or in great quantity **:** be prevalent
**2 :** to be copiously supplied ⟨life *abounded* in mysteries —Norman Mailer⟩ ⟨institutions *abound* with evidence of his success —*Johns Hopkins Magazine*⟩

**¹about** \ə-ˈbau̇t\ *adverb* [Middle English, from Old English *abūtan*, from ¹*a-* + *būtan* outside — more at BUT] (before 12th century)
**1 a :** reasonably close to ⟨*about* a year ago⟩ **b : ALMOST** ⟨*about* starved⟩ **c :** on the verge of — usually used with *be* and a following infinitive ⟨is *about* to join the army⟩; used with a negative to express intention or determination ⟨not *about* to quit⟩
**2 :** on all sides **:** AROUND
**3 a :** in rotation **b :** around the outside
**4 :** HERE AND THERE
**5 :** in the vicinity **:** NEAR
**6 :** in succession **:** ALTERNATELY ⟨turn *about* is fair play⟩
**7 :** in the opposite direction ⟨face *about*⟩ ⟨the other way *about*⟩

**²about** *preposition* (before 12th century)
**1 :** in a circle around **:** on every side of **:** AROUND
**2 a :** in the immediate neighborhood of **:** NEAR **b :** on or near the person of **c :** in the makeup of ⟨a mature wisdom *about* him⟩ **d :** at the command of ⟨has his wits *about* him⟩
**3 :** engaged in ⟨act as if they know what they're *about* —T. S. Matthews⟩
**4 a :** with regard to **:** CONCERNING **b :** concerned with **c :** fundamentally concerned with or directed toward ⟨poker is *about* money —David Mamet⟩
**5 :** over or in different parts of

**³about** *adjective* (1815)
**1 :** moving from place to place; *specifically* **:** being out of bed
**2 :** AROUND 2

**about–face** \ə-ˈbau̇t-ˈfās\ *noun* [from the imperative phrase *about face*] (1861)
**1 :** a 180° turn to the right from the position of attention

**2 :** a reversal of direction
**3 :** a reversal of attitude, behavior, or point of view
— **about–face** *intransitive verb*

**about–turn** \-ˈtərn\ *noun* (1893)
*British* **:** ABOUT-FACE

**¹above** \ə-ˈbəv\ *adverb* [Middle English, from Old English *abufan*, from *a-* + *bufan* above, from *be-* + *ufan* above; akin to Old English *ofer* over] (before 12th century)
**1 a :** in the sky **:** OVERHEAD **b :** in or to heaven
**2 a :** in or to a higher place **b :** higher on the same page or on a preceding page **c :** UPSTAIRS **d :** above zero ⟨10 degrees *above*⟩
**3 :** in or to a higher rank or number ⟨30 and *above*⟩
**4** *archaic* **:** in addition **:** BESIDES
**5 :** UPSTAGE

**²above** *preposition* (before 12th century)
**1 :** in or to a higher place than **:** OVER
**2 a :** superior to (as in rank, quality, or degree) **b :** out of reach of **c :** in preference to **d :** too proud or honorable to stoop to
**3 :** exceeding in number, quantity, or size **:** more than
**4 :** as distinct from and in addition to ⟨heard the whistle *above* the roar of the crowd⟩

**³above** *noun, plural* **above** (13th century)
**1 a :** something that is above **b :** a person whose name is written above
**2 a :** a higher authority **b :** HEAVEN ■

**⁴above** *adjective* (1604)
: written or discussed higher on the same page or on a preceding page
*usage* see ³ABOVE

**above all** *adverb* (14th century)
: before every other consideration **:** ESPECIALLY

**¹above·board** \ə-ˈbəv-ˌbōrd, -ˌbȯrd\ *adverb* [from the difficulty of cheating at cards when the hands are above the table] (1594)
: in a straightforward manner **:** OPENLY

**²aboveboard** *adjective* (1648)
: free from all traces of deceit or duplicity

**above·ground** \ə-ˈbəv-ˌgrau̇nd\ *adjective* (1878)
**1 :** located or occurring on or above the surface of the ground
**2 :** existing, produced, or published by or within the establishment ⟨*aboveground* movies⟩

**ab ovo** \ab-ˈō-(ˌ)vō\ *adverb* [Latin, literally, from the egg] (circa 1586)
: from the beginning

**ab·ra·ca·dab·ra** \ˌa-brə-kə-ˈda-brə\ *noun* [Late Latin] (1565)
**1 :** a magical charm or incantation
**2 :** unintelligible language

**abrade** \ə-ˈbrād\ *verb* **abrad·ed; abrad·ing** [Latin *abradere* to scrape off, from *ab-* + *radere* to scrape — more at RODENT] (1677)
*transitive verb*
**1 a :** to rub or wear away especially by friction **:** ERODE **b :** to irritate or roughen by rubbing
**2 :** to wear down in spirit **:** IRRITATE, WEARY
*intransitive verb*
: to undergo abrasion
— **abrad·able** \-ˈbrā-də-bəl\ *adjective*
— **abrad·er** *noun*

**Abra·ham** \ˈā-brə-ˌham\ *noun* [Late Latin, from Greek *Abraam*, from Hebrew *ʾAbhrāhām*] 
: an Old Testament patriarch regarded by Jews as the founder of the Hebrew people through his son Isaac and by Muslims as the founder of the Arab peoples through his son Ishmael

**abra·sion** \ə-ˈbrā-zhən\ *noun* [Medieval Latin *abrasion-, abrasio,* from Latin *abradere*] (circa 1656)
**1 a :** a wearing, grinding, or rubbing away by friction **b :** IRRITATION
**2 :** an abraded area of the skin or mucous membrane

**¹abra·sive** \ə-ˈbrā-siv, -ziv\ *noun* (1853)
: a substance (as emery or pumice) used for abrading, smoothing, or polishing

**²abrasive** *adjective* (1875)
**1 :** tending to abrade
**2 :** causing irritation ⟨*abrasive* manners⟩
— **abra·sive·ly** *adverb*
— **abra·sive·ness** *noun*

**ab·re·ac·tion** \ˌa-brē-ˈak-shən\ *noun* [part translation of German *Abreagierung* catharsis, from *ab* off, away (from Old High German *aba*) + *Reagierung* reaction, from Latin *reagere* to react — more at OF, REACT] (1912)
: the expression and emotional discharge of unconscious material (as a repressed idea or emotion) by verbalization especially in the presence of a therapist
— **ab·re·act** \-ˈakt\ *verb*

**abreast** \ə-ˈbrest\ *adverb or adjective* (15th century)
**1 :** beside one another with bodies in line ⟨columns of men five *abreast*⟩
**2 :** up to a particular standard or level especially of knowledge of recent developments ⟨keeps *abreast* of the latest trends⟩

**abridge** \ə-ˈbrij\ *transitive verb* **abridged; abridg·ing** [Middle English, from Middle French *abregier,* from Late Latin *abbreviare,* from Latin *ad-* + *brevis* short — more at BRIEF] (14th century)
**1 a** *archaic* **:** DEPRIVE **b :** to reduce in scope **:** DIMINISH ⟨attempts to *abridge* the right of free speech⟩
**2 :** to shorten in duration or extent ⟨modern transportation that *abridges* distance⟩
**3 :** to shorten by omission of words without sacrifice of sense **:** CONDENSE
*synonym* see SHORTEN
— **abridg·er** *noun*

**abridg·ment** *or* **abridge·ment** \ə-ˈbrij-mənt\ *noun* (15th century)
**1 :** the action of abridging **:** the state of being abridged
**2 :** a shortened form of a work retaining the general sense and unity of the original

**abroach** \ə-ˈbrōch\ *adverb or adjective* (14th century)
**1 :** in a condition for letting out a liquid (as wine) ⟨a cask set *abroach*⟩
**2 :** in action or agitation **:** ASTIR ⟨mischiefs that I set *abroach* —Shakespeare⟩

**abroad** \ə-ˈbrȯd\ *adverb or adjective* (13th century)
**1 :** over a wide area **:** WIDELY

□ USAGE
**abortive** Sense 2 has been objected to occasionally since the 1880s. These objections depend upon an etymological argument that the suffix *-ive* implies continuation, repetition, or tendency, rather than completion; therefore, something unsuccessful must be *aborted,* rather than *abortive.* This argument ignores the whole history of the word in English; from Shakespeare's time and earlier *abortive* has meant, literally and figuratively, "aborted." One may safely ignore this objection, as other writers have ⟨our first design, my friend, has prov'd *abortive* —Joseph Addison⟩ ⟨the *abortive* coup against him in October —Elizabeth Drew⟩.

**above** Although still objected to by some, the use of *above* as a noun in sense 1a ⟨none of the *above*⟩ ⟨the *above* is Theseus's opinion —William Blake⟩ and as an adjective ⟨without the *above* reserve —O. W. Holmes (died 1935)⟩ ⟨I was brought up on the *above* words —Viscount Montgomery⟩ has been long established as standard.

\ə\ abut \ᵊ\ kitten \ər\ further \a\ ash \ā\ ace \ä\ mop, mar \au̇\ out \ch\ chin \e\ bet \ē\ easy \g\ go \i\ hit \ī\ ice \j\ job \ŋ\ sing \ō\ go \ȯ\ law \ȯi\ boy \th\ thin \tẖ\ the \ü\ loot \u̇\ foot \y\ yet \zh\ vision    *see also* Guide to Pronunciation

**2 :** away from one's home
**3 :** beyond the boundaries of one's country
**4 :** in wide circulation **:** ABOUT
**5 :** wide of the mark **:** ASTRAY

**ab·ro·gate** \'a-brə-ˌgāt\ *transitive verb* **-gat·ed; -gat·ing** [Latin *abrogatus,* past participle of *abrogare,* from *ab-* + *rogare* to ask, propose a law — more at RIGHT] (1526)
**1 :** to abolish by authoritative action **:** ANNUL
**2 :** to treat as nonexistent ⟨*abrogating* their responsibilities⟩
**synonym** see NULLIFY
— **ab·ro·ga·tion** \ˌa-brə-'gā-shən\ *noun*

**abrupt** \ə-'brəpt\ *adjective* [Latin *abruptus,* from past participle of *abrumpere* to break off, from *ab-* + *rumpere* to break — more at REAVE] (1591)
**1 a :** characterized by or involving action or change without preparation or warning **:** UNEXPECTED ⟨came to an *abrupt* stop⟩ ⟨an *abrupt* turn to the left⟩ ⟨an *abrupt* decision to retire⟩ **b :** unceremoniously curt ⟨an *abrupt* manner⟩ **c :** lacking smoothness or continuity ⟨an *abrupt* transition⟩
**2 :** giving the impression of being cut or broken off; *especially* **:** involving a sudden steep rise or drop ⟨*abrupt* hills⟩ ⟨a high *abrupt* bank bounded the stream⟩
**synonym** see PRECIPITATE, STEEP
— **abrupt·ly** \ə-'brəp(t)-lē\ *adverb*
— **abrupt·ness** \ə-'brəp(t)-nəs\ *noun*

**abrup·tion** \ə-'brəp-shən\ *noun* (1606)
**:** a sudden breaking off or away

**ABS** \ˌā-(ˌ)bē-'es\ *noun* [*acrylonitrile·butadiene-styrene*] (1966)
**:** a tough rigid plastic used especially for automobile parts and building materials

**ab·scess** \'ab-ˌses\ *noun, plural* **ab·scess·es** \'ab-ˌse-səz, -ˌsēz; -sə-səz\ [Latin *abscessus,* literally, act of going away, from *abscedere* to go away, from *abs-, ab-* + *cedere* to go] (1615)
**:** a localized collection of pus surrounded by inflamed tissue
— **ab·scessed** \-ˌsest\ *adjective*

**ab·scise** \ab-'sīz\ *verb* **ab·scised; ab·scis·ing** [Latin *abscisus,* past participle of *abscidere,* from *abs-* + *caedere* to cut] (1612)
*transitive verb*
**:** to cut off by abscission
*intransitive verb*
**:** to separate by abscission

**ab·scis·ic acid** \ab-ˌsi-zik-, -sik-\ *noun* [*abscision* (variant of *abscission*) + *-ic*] (1968)
**:** a plant hormone $C_{15}H_{20}O_4$ that is a sesquiterpene widespread in nature and that typically promotes leaf abscission and dormancy and has an inhibitory effect on cell elongation

**ab·sci·sin** \'ab-sə-sən, ab-'si-s°n\ *noun* [*abscision* + *-in*] (1961)
**:** ABSCISIC ACID

**ab·scis·sa** \ab-'si-sə\ *noun, plural* **abscis·sas** *also* **ab·scis·sae** \-'si-(ˌ)sē\ [New Latin, from Latin, feminine of *abscissus,* past participle of *abscindere* to cut off, from *ab-* + *scindere* to cut — more at SHED] (1694)
**:** the horizontal coordinate of a point in a plane Cartesian coordinate system obtained by measuring parallel to the x-axis — compare ORDINATE

**AP** abscissa of point *P*

**ab·scis·sion** \ab-'si-zhən\ *noun* [Latin *abscission-, abscissio,* from *abscindere*] (15th century)
**1 :** the act or process of cutting off **:** REMOVAL
**2 :** the natural separation of flowers, fruit, or leaves from plants at a special separation layer

**ab·scond** \ab-'skänd, əb-\ *intransitive verb* [Latin *abscondere* to hide away, from *abs-* + *condere* to store up, conceal — more at CONDIMENT] (circa 1578)
**:** to depart secretly and hide oneself
— **ab·scond·er** *noun*

**ab·seil** \'ab-ˌsāl, -ˌsīl\ *intransitive verb* [German *abseilen,* from *ab* down, off + *Seil* rope] (1941)
*chiefly British* **:** RAPPEL

**ab·sence** \'ab-sən(t)s\ *noun* (14th century)
**1 :** the state of being absent
**2 :** the period of time that one is absent
**3 :** WANT, LACK ⟨an *absence* of detail⟩
**4 :** inattention to present surroundings or occurrences ⟨*absence* of mind⟩

**¹ab·sent** \'ab-sənt\ *adjective* [Middle English, from Middle French, from Latin *absent-, absens,* present participle of *abesse* to be absent, from *ab-* + *esse* to be — more at IS] (14th century)
**1 :** not present or attending **:** MISSING
**2 :** not existing **:** LACKING ⟨danger in a situation where power is *absent* —M. H. Trytten⟩
**3 :** INATTENTIVE, PREOCCUPIED
— **ab·sent·ly** *adverb*

**²ab·sent** \ab-'sent, 'ab-ˌ\ *transitive verb* (15th century)
**:** to keep (oneself) away

**³ab·sent** \'ab-sənt\ *preposition* (1945)
**:** in the absence of **:** WITHOUT

**ab·sen·tee** \ˌab-sən-'tē\ *noun* (1605)
**:** one that is absent: as **a :** a proprietor that lives away from his or her estate or business **b :** one missing from work or school
— **absentee** *adjective*

**absentee ballot** *noun* (1932)
**:** a ballot submitted (as by mail) in advance of an election by a voter who is unable to be present at the polls

**ab·sen·tee·ism** \ˌab-sən-'tē-ˌi-zəm\ *noun* (1829)
**1 :** prolonged absence of an owner from his or her property
**2 :** chronic absence (as from work or school); *also* **:** the rate of such absence

**ab·sent-mind·ed** \ˌab-sənt-'mīn-dəd\ *adjective* (1854)
**1 :** lost in thought and unaware of one's surroundings or actions **:** PREOCCUPIED; *also* **:** given to absence of mind
**2 :** indicative of or resulting from preoccupation or absence of mind
— **ab·sent-mind·ed·ly** *adverb*
— **ab·sent-mind·ed·ness** *noun*

**absent without leave** *adjective* (circa 1919)
**:** absent without authority from one's place of duty in the armed forces

**ab·sinthe** *also* **ab·sinth** \'ab-(ˌ)sin(t)th\ *noun* [French *absinthe,* from Latin *absinthium,* from Greek *apsinthion*] (1612)
**1 :** WORMWOOD 1; *especially* **:** a common European wormwood (*Artemisia absinthium*)
**2 :** a green liqueur flavored with wormwood or a substitute, anise, and other aromatics

**ab·so·lute** \'ab-sə-ˌlüt, ˌab-sə-'\ *adjective* [Middle English *absolut,* from Latin *absolutus,* from past participle of *absolvere* to set free, absolve] (14th century)
**1 a :** free from imperfection **:** PERFECT **b :** free or relatively free from mixture **:** PURE ⟨*absolute* alcohol⟩ **c :** OUTRIGHT, UNMITIGATED ⟨an *absolute* lie⟩
**2 :** being, governed by, or characteristic of a ruler or authority completely free from constitutional or other restraint
**3 a :** standing apart from a normal or usual syntactical relation with other words or sentence elements ⟨the *absolute* construction *this being the case* in the sentence "this being the case, let us go"⟩ **b** *of an adjective or possessive pronoun* **:** standing alone without a modified substantive ⟨*blind* in "help the blind" and *ours* in "your work and ours" are *absolute*⟩ **c** *of a verb* **:** having no object in the particular construction under consideration though normally transitive ⟨*kill* in "if looks could kill" is an *absolute* verb⟩
**4 :** having no restriction, exception, or qualification ⟨an *absolute* requirement⟩ ⟨*absolute* freedom⟩

**5 :** POSITIVE, UNQUESTIONABLE ⟨*absolute* proof⟩
**6 a :** independent of arbitrary standards of measurement **b :** relating to or derived in the simplest manner from the fundamental units of length, mass, and time ⟨*absolute* electric units⟩ **c :** relating to, measured on, or being a temperature scale based on absolute zero ⟨*absolute* temperature⟩; *specifically* **:** KELVIN ⟨10° *absolute*⟩
**7 :** FUNDAMENTAL, ULTIMATE ⟨*absolute* knowledge⟩
**8 :** perfectly embodying the nature of a thing ⟨*absolute* justice⟩
**9 :** being self-sufficient and free of external references or relationships ⟨an *absolute* term in logic⟩ ⟨*absolute* music⟩
**10 :** being the true distance from an aircraft to the earth's surface ⟨*absolute* altitude⟩
— **absolute** *noun*
— **ab·so·lute·ness** *noun*

**absolute ceiling** *noun* (circa 1920)
**:** the maximum height above sea level at which a particular airplane can maintain horizontal flight under standard air conditions — called also *ceiling*

**absolute convergence** *noun* (circa 1909)
**:** convergence of a mathematical series when the absolute values of the terms are taken

**absolute humidity** *noun* (1867)
**:** the amount of water vapor present in a unit volume of air — compare RELATIVE HUMIDITY

**ab·so·lute·ly** \'ab-sə-ˌlüt-lē, ˌab-sə-'\ *adverb* (14th century)
**1 :** in an absolute manner or condition — often used as an intensive ⟨*absolutely* brilliant⟩
**2 :** with respect to absolute values ⟨an *absolutely* convergent series⟩

**absolute magnitude** *noun* (1902)
**:** the intrinsic luminosity of a celestial body (as a star) if viewed from a distance of 10 parsecs — compare APPARENT MAGNITUDE

**absolute pitch** *noun* (1864)
**1 :** the position of a tone in a standard scale independently determined by its rate of vibration
**2 :** the ability to recognize or sing a given isolated note

**absolute space** *noun* (circa 1889)
**:** SPACE 4b

**absolute value** *noun* (1907)
**1 :** a nonnegative number equal in numerical value to a given real number
**2 :** the positive square root of the sum of the squares of the real and imaginary parts of a complex number

**absolute zero** *noun* (1848)
**:** a theoretical temperature characterized by complete absence of heat and equivalent to exactly −273.15°C or −459.67°F

**ab·so·lu·tion** \ˌab-sə-'lü-shən\ *noun* (13th century)
**:** the act of absolving; *specifically* **:** a remission of sins pronounced by a priest (as in the sacrament of reconciliation)

**ab·so·lut·ism** \'ab-sə-ˌlü-ˌti-zəm\ *noun* (1830)
**1 a :** a political theory that absolute power should be vested in one or more rulers **b :** government by an absolute ruler or authority **:** DESPOTISM
**2 :** advocacy of a rule by absolute standards or principles
**3 :** an absolute standard or principle
— **ab·so·lut·ist** \-ˌlü-tist\ *noun or adjective*
— **ab·so·lu·tis·tic** \ˌab-sə-(ˌ)lü-'tis-tik\ *adjective*

**ab·so·lu·tive** \ˌab-sə-'lü-tiv\ *adjective* (1952)
**:** of, being, or relating to an inflectional morpheme that typically marks the subject of an intransitive verb or the direct object of a transitive verb in an ergative language

**ab·so·lut·ize** \'ab-sə-ˌlü-ˌtīz\ *transitive verb* **-ized; -iz·ing** (1919)
**:** to make absolute **:** convert into an absolute

**ab·solve** \əb-'zälv, -'sälv, -'zölv, -'sölv *also* without l\ *transitive verb* **ab·solved; ab-**

**solv·ing** [Middle English, from Latin *absolvere*, from *ab-* + *solvere* to loosen — more at SOLVE] (15th century)
**1** : to set free from an obligation or the consequences of guilt
**2** : to remit (a sin) by absolution
***synonym*** see EXCULPATE
— **ab·solv·er** *noun*
**ab·sorb** \əb-'sȯrb, -'zȯrb\ *transitive verb* [Middle French *absorber*, from Latin *absorbēre*, from *ab-* + *sorbēre* to suck up; akin to Lithuanian *surbti* to sip, Greek *rophein* to gulp down] (15th century)
**1** : to take in and make part of an existent whole ⟨the capacity of China to *absorb* invaders⟩
**2 a** : to suck up or take up ⟨a sponge *absorbs* water⟩ ⟨charcoal *absorbs* gas⟩ ⟨plant roots *absorb* water⟩ **b** : to take in : ACQUIRE, LEARN ⟨convictions *absorbed* in youth —M. R. Cohen⟩ **c** : USE UP, CONSUME ⟨the fever *absorbed* her strength⟩
**3** : to engage or engross wholly ⟨*absorbed* in thought⟩
**4 a** (1) : to receive without recoil or echo ⟨provided with a sound-*absorbing* surface⟩ (2) : ENDURE, SUSTAIN ⟨*absorbing* hardships⟩ (3) : ASSUME, BEAR ⟨the expenses were *absorbed* by the company⟩ **b** : to transform (radiant energy) into a different form usually with a resulting rise in temperature ⟨the earth *absorbs* the sun's rays⟩
— **ab·sorb·abil·i·ty** \əb-ˌsȯr-bə-'bi-lə-tē, -ˌzȯr-\ *noun*
— **ab·sorb·able** \əb-'sȯr-bə-bəl, -'zȯr-\ *adjective*
— **ab·sorb·er** *noun*
**ab·sor·bance** \əb-'sȯr-bən(t)s, -'zȯr-\ *noun* (1947)
: the ability of a layer of a substance to absorb radiation expressed mathematically as the negative common logarithm of transmittance
**ab·sor·ben·cy** \əb-'sȯr-bən(t)-sē, -'zȯr-\ *noun, plural* **-cies** (1859)
**1** : the quality or state of being absorbent
**2** *or* **ab·sor·ban·cy** : ABSORBANCE
**ab·sor·bent** *also* **ab·sor·bant** \-bənt\ *adjective* [Latin *absorbent-, absorbens*, present participle of *absorbēre*] (1718)
: able to absorb ⟨as *absorbent* as a sponge⟩
— **absorbent** *also* **absorbant** *noun*
**ab·sorb·ing** *adjective* (1876)
: fully taking one's attention : ENGROSSING ⟨an *absorbing* novel⟩
— **ab·sorb·ing·ly** \-biŋ-lē\ *adverb*
**ab·sorp·tance** \əb-'sȯrp-tən(t)s, -'zȯrp-\ *noun* [*absorption* + *-ance*] (circa 1931)
: the ratio of the radiant energy absorbed by a body to that incident upon it
**ab·sorp·tion** \əb-'sȯrp-shən, -'zȯrp-\ *noun* [French & Latin; French, from Latin *absorption-, absorptio*, from *absorbēre*] (1741)
**1 a** : the process of absorbing or of being absorbed — compare ADSORPTION **b** : interception of radiant energy or sound waves
**2** : entire occupation of the mind ⟨*absorption* in his work⟩
— **ab·sorp·tive** \-tiv\ *adjective*
**absorption band** *noun* (1867)
: a dark band in an absorption spectrum
**absorption line** *noun* (circa 1889)
: a dark line in an absorption spectrum
**absorption spectrum** *noun* (1879)
: an electromagnetic spectrum in which a decrease in intensity of radiation at specific wavelengths or ranges of wavelengths characteristic of an absorbing substance is manifested especially as a pattern of dark lines or bands
**ab·sorp·tiv·i·ty** \əb-ˌsȯrp-'ti-və-tē, -ˌzȯrp-\ *noun, plural* **-ties** (circa 1859)
: the property of a body that determines the fraction of incident radiation absorbed by the body

**ab·stain** \əb-'stān, ab-\ *intransitive verb* [Middle English *absteinen*, from Middle French *abstenir*, from Latin *abstinēre*, from *abs-, ab-* + *tenēre* to hold — more at THIN] (14th century)
: to refrain deliberately and often with an effort of self-denial from an action or practice
— **ab·stain·er** *noun*
**ab·ste·mi·ous** \ab-'stē-mē-əs\ *adjective* [Latin *abstemius*, from *abs-* + *-temius*; akin to Latin *temetum* intoxicating drink] (1609)
: marked by restraint especially in the consumption of food or alcohol; *also* : reflecting such restraint ⟨an *abstemious* diet⟩
— **ab·ste·mi·ous·ly** *adverb*
— **ab·ste·mi·ous·ness** *noun*
**ab·sten·tion** \əb-'sten(t)-shən, ab-\ *noun* [Late Latin *abstention-, abstentio*, from Latin *abstinēre*] (1521)
: the act or practice of abstaining
— **ab·sten·tious** \-shəs\ *adjective*
**ab·sti·nence** \'ab-stə-nən(t)s\ *noun* [Middle English, from Middle French, from Latin *abstinentia*, from *abstinent-, abstinens*, present participle of *abstinēre*] (14th century)
**1** : voluntary forbearance especially from indulgence of an appetite or craving or from eating some foods : ABSTENTION
**2** : habitual abstaining from intoxicating beverages
— **ab·sti·nent** \-nənt\ *adjective*
— **ab·sti·nent·ly** *adverb*
**¹ab·stract** \ab-'strakt, 'ab-ˌ\ *adjective* [Medieval Latin *abstractus*, from Latin, past participle of *abstrahere* to drag away, from *abs-, ab-* + *trahere* to pull, draw] (14th century)
**1 a** : disassociated from any specific instance ⟨*abstract* entity⟩ **b** : difficult to understand : ABSTRUSE ⟨*abstract* problems⟩ **c** : insufficiently factual : FORMAL ⟨possessed only an *abstract* right⟩
**2** : expressing a quality apart from an object ⟨the word *poem* is concrete, *poetry* is *abstract*⟩
**3 a** : dealing with a subject in its abstract aspects : THEORETICAL ⟨*abstract* science⟩ **b** : IMPERSONAL, DETACHED ⟨the *abstract* compassion of a surgeon —*Time*⟩
**4** : having only intrinsic form with little or no attempt at pictorial representation or narrative content ⟨*abstract* painting⟩
— **ab·stract·ly** \ab-'strak(t)-lē, 'ab-ˌ\ *adverb*
— **ab·stract·ness** \ab-'strak(t)-nəs, 'ab-ˌ\ *noun*
**²ab·stract** \'ab-ˌstrakt, *in sense 2 also* ab-'\ *noun* [Middle English, from Latin *abstractus*] (15th century)
**1** : a summary of points (as of a writing) usually presented in skeletal form; *also* : something that summarizes or concentrates the essentials of a larger thing or several things
**2** : an abstract thing or state
**3** : ABSTRACTION 4a
**³ab·stract** \ab-'strakt, 'ab-ˌ, *in sense 3 usually* 'ab-ˌ\ (1542)
*transitive verb*
**1** : REMOVE, SEPARATE
**2** : to consider apart from application to or association with a particular instance
**3** : to make an abstract of : SUMMARIZE
**4** : to draw away the attention of
**5** : STEAL, PURLOIN
*intransitive verb*
: to make an abstraction
— **ab·stract·able** \-'strak-tə-bəl, -ˌstrak-\ *adjective*
— **ab·strac·tor** *or* **ab·stract·er** \-tər\ *noun*
**ab·stract·ed** \ab-'strak-təd, 'ab-ˌ\ *adjective* (1643)
**1** : PREOCCUPIED, ABSENTMINDED ⟨the *abstracted* look of a professor⟩
**2** : ABSTRACT 4 ⟨*abstracted* geometric shapes⟩
— **ab·stract·ed·ly** *adverb*
— **ab·stract·ed·ness** *noun*
**abstract expressionism** *noun* (1951)

: an artistic movement of the mid-20th century comprising diverse styles and techniques and emphasizing especially an artist's liberty to convey attitudes and emotions through nontraditional and usually nonrepresentational means
— **abstract expressionist** *noun or adjective*
**ab·strac·tion** \ab-'strak-shən, əb-\ *noun* (1549)
**1 a** : the act or process of abstracting : the state of being abstracted **b** : an abstract idea or term
**2** : absence of mind or preoccupation
**3** : abstract quality or character
**4 a** : an abstract composition or creation in art **b** : ABSTRACTIONISM
— **ab·strac·tion·al** \-shnəl, -shə-n°l\ *adjective*
— **ab·strac·tive** \ab-'strak-tiv, 'ab-ˌ\ *adjective*
**ab·strac·tion·ism** \ab-'strak-shə-ˌni-zəm, əb-\ *noun* (1926)
: the principles or practice of creating abstract art
— **ab·strac·tion·ist** \-sh(ə-)nist\ *adjective or noun*
**abstract of title** (1858)
: a summary statement of the successive conveyances and other facts on which a title to a piece of land rests
**ab·struse** \əb-'strüs, ab-\ *adjective* [Latin *abstrusus*, from past participle of *abstrudere* to conceal, from *abs-, ab-* + *trudere* to push — more at THREAT] (1599)
: difficult to comprehend : RECONDITE ⟨the *abstruse* calculations of mathematicians⟩
— **ab·struse·ly** *adverb*
— **ab·struse·ness** *noun*
**ab·stru·si·ty** \-'strü-sə-tē\ *noun, plural* **-ties** (1646)
**1** : the quality or state of being abstruse : ABSTRUSENESS
**2** : something that is abstruse
**¹ab·surd** \əb-'sərd, -'zərd\ *adjective* [Middle French *absurde*, from Latin *absurdus*, from *ab-* + *surdus* deaf, stupid] (1557)
**1** : ridiculously unreasonable, unsound, or incongruous
**2** : having no rational or orderly relationship to human life : MEANINGLESS; *also* : lacking order or value
**3** : dealing with the absurd or with absurdism
— **ab·surd·ly** *adverb*
— **ab·surd·ness** *noun*
**²absurd** *noun* (1946)
: the state or condition in which human beings exist in an irrational and meaningless universe and in which human life has no ultimate meaning — usually used with *the*
**ab·surd·ism** \əb-'sər-ˌdi-zəm, -'zər-\ *noun* (1946)
: a philosophy based on the belief that the universe is irrational and meaningless and that the search for order brings the individual into conflict with the universe — compare EXISTENTIALISM
— **ab·surd·ist** \-dist\ *noun or adjective*
**ab·sur·di·ty** \əb-'sər-də-tē, -'zər-\ *noun, plural* **-ties** (1528)
**1** : the quality or state of being absurd : ABSURDNESS
**2** : something that is absurd
**abub·ble** \ə-'bə-bəl\ *adjective* (circa 1869)
**1** : being in the process of bubbling
**2** : being in a state of agitated activity or motion : ASTIR
**abuild·ing** \ə-'bil-diŋ\ *adjective* (1535)
: being in the process of building or of being built

| | | |
|---|---|---|
| \ə\ abut | \ə\ kitten | \ər\ further | \a\ ash | \ā\ ace |
| \ä\ mop, mar | \au̇\ out | \ch\ chin | \e\ bet | \ē\ easy |
| \g\ go | \i\ hit | \ī\ ice | \j\ job | \ŋ\ sing | \ō\ go |
| \ȯ\ law | \ȯi\ boy | \th\ thin | \t͟h\ the | \ü\ loot | \u̇\ foot |
| \y\ yet | \zh\ vision | *see also* Guide to Pronunciation |

**abu·lia** \ə-'bü-lē-ə, -'byü-, -ə-\ *noun* [New Latin, from ²*a-* + Greek *boulē* will] (circa 1864)
**:** abnormal lack of ability to act or to make decisions
— **abu·lic** \-lik\ *adjective*

**abun·dance** \ə-'bən-dən(t)s\ *noun* (14th century)
**1 :** an ample quantity **:** PROFUSION
**2 :** AFFLUENCE, WEALTH
**3 :** relative degree of plentifulness ⟨low *abundances* of uranium and thorium —H. C. Urey⟩

**abun·dant** \-dənt\ *adjective* [Middle English, from Middle French, from Latin *abundant-, abundans,* present participle of *abundare* to abound] (14th century)
**1 a :** marked by great plenty (as of resources) ⟨a fair and *abundant* land⟩ **b :** amply supplied **:** ABOUNDING ⟨an area *abundant* with bird life⟩
**2 :** occurring in abundance **:** AMPLE ⟨*abundant* rainfall⟩
**synonym** see PLENTIFUL
— **abun·dant·ly** *adverb*

**¹abuse** \ə-'byüs\ *noun* [Middle English, from Middle French *abus,* from Latin *abusus,* from *abuti* to consume, from *ab-* + *uti* to use] (15th century)
**1 :** a corrupt practice or custom
**2 :** improper or excessive use or treatment **:** MISUSE ⟨drug *abuse*⟩
**3** *obsolete* **:** a deceitful act **:** DECEPTION
**4 :** language that condemns or vilifies usually unjustly, intemperately, and angrily
**5 :** physical maltreatment ☆

**²abuse** \ə-'byüz\ *transitive verb* **abused; abus·ing** (15th century)
**1 :** to put to a wrong or improper use ⟨*abuse* a privilege⟩
**2** *obsolete* **:** DECEIVE
**3 :** to use so as to injure or damage **:** MALTREAT
**4 :** to attack in words **:** REVILE
— **abus·able** \-'byü-zə-bəl\ *adjective*
— **abus·er** *noun*

**abu·sive** \ə-'byü-siv, -ziv\ *adjective* (1583)
**1 :** characterized by wrong or improper use or action; *especially* **:** CORRUPT ⟨*abusive* financial practices⟩
**2 a :** using harsh insulting language **:** characterized by or serving for abuse **b :** physically injurious ⟨*abusive* behavior⟩
— **abu·sive·ly** *adverb*
— **abu·sive·ness** *noun*

**abut** \ə-'bət\ *verb* **abut·ted; abut·ting** [Middle English *abutten,* partly from Old French *aboter* to border on, from *a-* (from Latin *ad-*) + *bout* blow, end, from *boter* to strike; partly from Old French *abuter* to come to an end, from *a-* + *but* end, aim — more at ¹BUTT, ⁴BUTT] (15th century)
*intransitive verb*
**1 :** to touch along a border or with a projecting part ⟨land *abuts* on the road⟩
**2 a :** to terminate at a point of contact **b :** to lean for support
*transitive verb*
**1 :** to border on
**2 :** to cause to abut

**abu·ti·lon** \ə-'byü-t⁰l-ˌän, -t⁰l-ən\ *noun* [New Latin, genus name, from Arabic *awbūtīlūn* abutilon] (circa 1578)
**:** any of a genus (*Abutilon*) of plants of the mallow family often having lobed leaves and solitary bell-shaped flowers

**abut·ment** \ə-'bət-mənt\ *noun* (1644)
**1 :** the place at which abutting occurs
**2 :** the part of a structure (as an arch or a bridge) that directly receives thrust or pressure

**abut·tals** \ə-'bə-t⁰lz\ *noun plural* (1630)
**:** the boundaries of lands with respect to adjacent lands

**abut·ter** \ə-'bə-tər\ *noun* (1673)
**:** one that abuts; *specifically* **:** the owner of a contiguous property

**abut·ting** *adjective* (1599)
**:** that abuts or serves as an abutment **:** ADJOINING, BORDERING

**abuzz** \ə-'bəz\ *adjective* (1859)
**:** filled or resounding with or as if with a buzzing sound ⟨a lake *abuzz* with outboards⟩ ⟨a town *abuzz* with excitement⟩

**aby** *or* **abye** \ə-'bī\ *transitive verb* [Middle English *abien,* from Old English *ābycgan,* from *ā-* + *bycgan* to buy — more at ABIDE, BUY] (before 12th century)
*archaic* **:** to suffer a penalty for

**abysm** \ə-'bi-zəm\ *noun* [Middle English *abime,* from Middle French *abisme,* modification of Late Latin *abyssus*] (14th century)
**:** ABYSS ⟨the dark backward and *abysm* of time —Shakespeare⟩

**abys·mal** \ə-'biz-məl, -a-\ *adjective* (circa 1656)
**1 a :** having immense or fathomless extension downward, backward, or inward ⟨an *abysmal* cliff⟩ **b :** immeasurably great **:** PROFOUND ⟨*abysmal* ignorance⟩ **c :** immeasurably low or wretched ⟨*abysmal* living conditions of the poor⟩
**2 :** ABYSSAL
— **abys·mal·ly** \-mə-lē\ *adverb*

**abyss** \ə-'bis, a- *also* 'a-(ˌ)bis\ *noun* [Middle English *abissus,* from Late Latin *abyssus,* from Greek *abyssos,* from *abyssos,* adjective, bottomless, from *a-* + *byssos* depth; perhaps akin to Greek *bathys* deep] (14th century)
**1 :** the bottomless gulf, pit, or chaos of the old cosmogonies
**2 a :** an immeasurably deep gulf or great space **b :** intellectual or moral depths

**abys·sal** \ə-'bi-səl\ *adjective* (1691)
**1 :** UNFATHOMABLE a
**2 :** of or relating to the bottom waters of the ocean depths

**abyssal plain** *noun* (1954)
**:** any of the great flat areas of ocean floor

**Ab·ys·sin·i·an cat** \ˌa-bə-'si-nē-ən-, -'sin-yən-\ *noun* [Abyssinia, kingdom in Africa] (1876)
**:** any of a breed of small slender cats of African origin with short brownish hair ticked with bands of darker color

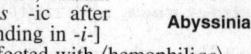

**Abyssinian cat**

**ac-** — see AD-

**-ac** *noun suffix* [New Latin *-acus,* from Greek *-akos,* variant of *-ikos* *-ic* after stems ending in *-i-*]
**:** one affected with ⟨hemophili*ac*⟩

**aca·cia** \ə-'kā-shə\ *noun* [New Latin, genus name, from Latin, acacia tree, from Greek *akakia*] (14th century)
**1 :** GUM ARABIC
**2 :** any of a large genus (*Acacia*) of leguminous shrubs and trees of warm regions with leaves pinnate or reduced to phyllodes and white or yellow flower clusters

**ac·a·deme** \'a-kə-ˌdēm, ˌa-kə-'\ *noun* [Latin *Academus* (in the phrase *inter silvas Academi* among the groves of Academus), from Greek *Akadēmos* — more at ACADEMY] (1588)
**1 a :** a place of instruction **:** SCHOOL **b :** the academic life, community, or world ⟨in the halls of *academe*⟩
**2 :** ACADEMIC; *especially* **:** PEDANT

**ac·a·de·mia** \ˌa-kə-'dē-mē-ə\ *noun* [New Latin, from Latin, academy] (1946)
**:** ACADEME 1b

**¹ac·a·dem·ic** \ˌa-kə-'de-mik\ *noun* (1587)
**1 :** a member of an institution of learning
**2 :** one who is academic in background, outlook, or methods
**3** *plural* **:** academic subjects

**²academic** *also* **ac·a·dem·i·cal** \-mi-kəl\ *adjective* (1588)
**1 a :** of, relating to, or associated with an academy or school especially of higher learning **b :** of or relating to performance in academic courses ⟨*academic* excellence⟩ **c :** very learned but inexperienced in practical matters

⟨*academic* thinkers⟩ **d :** based on formal study especially at an institution of higher learning
**2 :** of or relating to literary or artistic rather than technical or professional studies
**3 a :** THEORETICAL, SPECULATIVE ⟨an *academic* question⟩ **b :** having no practical or useful significance
**4 :** conforming to the traditions or rules of a school (as of literature or art) or an official academy **:** CONVENTIONAL
— **ac·a·dem·i·cal·ly** \-mi-k(ə-)lē\ *adverb*

**academic freedom** *noun* (1901)
**:** freedom to teach or to learn without interference (as by government officials)

**ac·a·de·mi·cian** \ˌa-kə-də-'mi-shən, ə-ˌka-də-\ *noun* (1748)
**1 a :** a member of an academy for promoting science, art, or literature **b :** a follower of an artistic or philosophical tradition or a promoter of its ideas
**2 :** ACADEMIC

**ac·a·dem·i·cism** \ˌa-kə-'de-mə-ˌsi-zəm\ *also* **acad·e·mism** \ə-'ka-də-ˌmi-zəm\ *noun* (1610)
**1 :** the doctrines of Plato's Academy; *specifically* **:** the skeptical doctrines of the later Academy holding that nothing can be known — compare PYRRHONISM
**2 :** a formal academic quality (as in art or music)
**3 :** purely speculative thoughts and attitudes

**academic year** *noun* (circa 1934)
**:** the annual period of sessions of an educational institution usually beginning in September and ending in June

**acad·e·my** \ə-'ka-də-mē\ *noun, plural* **-mies** [Latin *academia,* from Greek *Akadēmeia,* from *Akadēmeia,* gymnasium where Plato taught, from *Akadēmos* Attic mythological hero] (1549)
**1 a :** a school usually above the elementary level; *especially* **:** a private high school **b :** a high school or college in which special subjects or skills are taught **c :** higher education — used with *the* ⟨the functions of the *academy* in modern society⟩
**2** *capitalized* **a :** the school for advanced education founded by Plato **b :** the philosophical doctrines associated with Plato's Academy
**3 :** a society of learned persons organized to advance art, science, or literature
**4 :** a body of established opinion widely accepted as authoritative in a particular field ◆

**Aca·di·an** \ə-'kā-dē-ən, a-\ *noun* (1705)
**1 :** a native or inhabitant of Acadia
**2 :** a descendant of the French-speaking inhabitants of Acadia expelled after the French loss of the colony in 1755; *especially* **:** CAJUN
— **Acadian** *adjective*

**acan·tho·ceph·a·lan** \ə-ˌkan(t)-thə-'se-fə-lən\ *noun* [ultimately from Greek *akantha* thorn, spine + *kephalē* head — more at CEPHALIC] (circa 1909)
**:** SPINY-HEADED WORM

---

☆ **SYNONYMS**
**Abuse, vituperation, invective, obloquy, billingsgate** mean vehemently expressed condemnation or disapproval. ABUSE, the most general term, usually implies the anger of the speaker and stresses the harshness of the language ⟨scathing verbal *abuse*⟩. VITUPERATION implies fluent and sustained abuse ⟨a torrent of *vituperation*⟩. INVECTIVE implies a comparable vehemence but suggests greater verbal and rhetorical skill and may apply to a public denunciation ⟨blistering political *invective*⟩. OBLOQUY suggests defamation and consequent shame and disgrace ⟨subjected to *obloquy* and derision⟩. BILLINGSGATE implies practiced fluency and variety of profane or obscene abuse ⟨directed a stream of *billingsgate* at the cabdriver⟩.

— **acanthocephalan** *adjective*

**acan·thus** \ə-'kan(t)-thəs\ *noun, plural* **acanthus** [New Latin, genus name, from Greek *akanthos,* an acanthus, from *akantha* thorn] (1616)
**1** : any of a genus (*Acanthus* of the family Acanthaceae, the acanthus family) of prickly herbs of the Mediterranean region
**2** : an ornamentation (as in a Corinthian capital) representing or suggesting the leaves of the acanthus

**acanthus 2**

**a cap·pel·la** *also* **a ca·pel·la** \ˌä-kə-'pe-lə\ *adverb or adjective* [Italian *a cappella* in chapel style] (circa 1864)
: without instrumental accompaniment

**ac·a·ri·a·sis** \ˌa-kə-'rī-ə-səs\ *noun* (1828)
: infestation with or disease caused by mites

**acar·i·cide** \ə-'kar-ə-ˌsīd\ *noun* [*acar*us + -*i*- + -*cide*] (circa 1879)
: a pesticide that kills mites and ticks
— **acar·i·cid·al** \ə-ˌkar-ə-'sī-d°l\ *adjective*

**ac·a·rid** \'a-kə-rəd\ *noun* (1881)
: any of an order (Acarina) of arachnids including the mites and ticks; *especially* : a typical mite (family Acaridae)
— **acarid** *adjective*

**ac·a·rus** \'a-kə-rəs\ *noun, plural* **-ri** \-ˌrī\ [New Latin, genus name, from Greek *akari,* a mite] (1658)
: MITE; *especially* : one of a formerly extensive genus (*Acarus*)

**acat·a·lec·tic** \(ˌ)ā-ˌka-tə-'lek-tik\ *adjective* [Late Latin *acatalecticus,* from *acatalectus,* from Greek *akatalēktos,* from *a-* + *katalēgein* to leave off — more at CATALECTIC] (1589)
: not catalectic ⟨*acatalectic* verse⟩
— **acatalectic** *noun*

**acau·les·cent** \ˌā-kȯ-'le-s°nt\ *adjective* [*a-* + Latin *caulis* stem — more at HOLE] (1854)
: having no stem or appearing to have none

**ac·cede** \ak-'sēd, ik-\ *intransitive verb* **ac·ced·ed; ac·ced·ing** [Middle English, from Latin *accedere* to go to, be added, from *ad-* + *cedere* to go] (15th century)
**1 a** : to become a party (as to an agreement) **b** : to express approval or give consent : give in to a request or demand
**2** *archaic* : APPROACH
**3** : to enter upon an office or position
**synonym** see ASSENT

¹**ac·ce·le·ran·do** \(ˌ)ä-ˌche-lə-'rän-(ˌ)dō; ik-ˌse-, (ˌ)ak-\ *adverb or adjective* [Italian, literally, accelerating, from Latin *accelerandum,* gerund of *accelerare*] (circa 1842)
: gradually faster — used as a direction in music

²**accelerando** *noun, plural* **-dos** (1889)
: a gradual increase in tempo

**ac·cel·er·ant** \ik-'se-lə-rənt, ak-\ *noun* (1916)
: a substance used to accelerate a process (as the spreading of a fire)

**ac·cel·er·ate** \-lə-ˌrāt\ *verb* **-at·ed; -at·ing** [Latin *acceleratus,* past participle of *accelerare,* from *ad-* + *celer* swift — more at HOLD] (circa 1530)
*transitive verb*
**1** : to bring about at an earlier time
**2** : to cause to move faster; *also* : to cause to undergo acceleration
**3 a** : to hasten the progress or development of **b** : INCREASE ⟨*accelerate* food production⟩
**4 a** : to enable (a student) to complete a course in less than usual time **b** : to speed up (as a course of study)
*intransitive verb*
**1 a** : to move faster : gain speed **b** : GROW, INCREASE ⟨inflation was *accelerating*⟩
**2** : to follow an accelerated educational program

— **ac·cel·er·at·ing·ly** \-ˌrā-tiŋ-lē\ *adverb*

**ac·cel·er·a·tion** \ik-ˌse-lə-'rā-shən, (ˌ)ak-\ *noun* (1531)
**1** : the act or process of accelerating : the state of being accelerated
**2** : the rate of change of velocity with respect to time; *broadly* : change of velocity

**acceleration of gravity** (circa 1889)
: the acceleration of a body in free fall under the influence of earth's gravity expressed as the rate of increase of velocity per unit of time and assigned the standard value of 980.665 centimeters per second per second

**acceleration principle** *noun* (circa 1941)
: a theory in economics: an increase or decrease in income induces a corresponding but magnified change in investment

**ac·cel·er·a·tive** \ik-'se-lə-ˌrā-tiv, ak-\ *adjective* (1751)
: of, relating to, or tending to cause acceleration : ACCELERATING

**ac·cel·er·a·tor** \ik-'se-lə-ˌrā-tər, ak-\ *noun* (1611)
: one that accelerates: as **a** : a muscle or nerve that speeds the performance of an action **b** : a device (as a pedal) for controlling the speed of a motor vehicle engine **c** : a substance that speeds a chemical reaction **d** : an apparatus for imparting high velocities to charged particles (as electrons)

**ac·cel·er·om·e·ter** \ik-ˌse-lə-'rä-mə-tər, ak-\ *noun* [International Scientific Vocabulary *accel*eration + -*o*- + -*meter*] (circa 1890)
: an instrument for measuring acceleration or for detecting and measuring vibrations

¹**ac·cent** \'ak-ˌsent, ak-\ *transitive verb* [Middle French *accenter,* from *accent* intonation, from Latin *accentus,* from *ad-* + *cantus* song — more at CHANT] (1530)
**1 a** : to pronounce with accent : STRESS **b** : to mark with a written or printed accent
**2** : to give prominence to : make more prominent

²**ac·cent** \'ak-ˌsent, *chiefly British* -sənt\ *noun* (1538)
**1** : a distinctive manner of expression: as **a** : an individual's distinctive or characteristic inflection, tone, or choice of words — usually used in plural **b** : a way of speaking typical of a particular group of people and especially of the natives or residents of a region
**2** : an articulative effort giving prominence to one syllable over adjacent syllables; *also* : the prominence thus given a syllable
**3** : rhythmically significant stress on the syllables of a verse usually at regular intervals
**4** *archaic* : UTTERANCE
**5 a** : a mark (as ´, `, ^) used in writing or printing to indicate a specific sound value, stress, or pitch, to distinguish words otherwise identically spelled, or to indicate that an ordinarily mute vowel should be pronounced **b** : an accented letter
**6 a** : greater stress given to one musical tone than to its neighbors **b** : ACCENT MARK 2
**7 a** : emphasis laid on a part of an artistic design or composition **b** : an emphasized detail or area; *especially* : a small detail in sharp contrast with its surroundings **c** : a substance or object used for emphasis
**8** : a mark placed to the right of a letter or number and usually slightly above it: as **a** : a double prime **b** : PRIME
**9** : special concern or attention : EMPHASIS ⟨an *accent* on youth⟩
— **ac·cent·less** \-ləs\ *adjective*

**accent mark** *noun* (circa 1889)
**1** : ACCENT 5a, 8
**2 a** : a symbol used to indicate musical stress **b** : a mark placed after a letter designating a note of music to indicate in which octave the note occurs

**ac·cen·tu·al** \ak-'sen(t)-sh(ə-)wəl, ik-\ *adjective* [Latin *accentus*] (1610)
: of, relating to, or characterized by accent; *specifically* : based on accent rather than on quantity or syllabic recurrence ⟨*accentual* poetry⟩
— **ac·cen·tu·al·ly** *adverb*

**ac·cen·tu·ate** \ik-'sen(t)-shə-ˌwāt, ak-\ *transitive verb* **-at·ed; -at·ing** [Medieval Latin *accentuatus,* past participle of *accentuare,* from Latin *accentus*] (circa 1731)
: ACCENT, EMPHASIZE; *also* : INTENSIFY ⟨*accentuates* the feeling of despair⟩
— **ac·cen·tu·a·tion** \ik-ˌsen(t)-shə-'wā-shən, (ˌ)ak-\ *noun*

**ac·cept** \ik-'sept, ak-\ *also* ek-\ *verb* [Middle English, from Middle French *accepter,* from Latin *acceptare,* frequentative of *accipere* to receive, from *ad-* + *capere* to take — more at HEAVE] (14th century)
*transitive verb*
**1 a** : to receive willingly ⟨*accept* a gift⟩ **b** : to be able or designed to take or hold (something applied or added) ⟨a surface that will not *accept* ink⟩
**2** : to give admittance or approval to ⟨*accept* her as one of the group⟩
**3 a** : to endure without protest or reaction ⟨*accept* poor living conditions⟩ **b** : to regard as proper, normal, or inevitable ⟨the idea is widely *accepted*⟩ **c** : to recognize as true : BELIEVE ⟨refused to *accept* the explanation⟩
**4 a** : to make a favorable response to ⟨*accept* an offer⟩ **b** : to agree to undertake (a responsibility) ⟨*accept* a job⟩
**5** : to assume an obligation to pay; *also* : to take in payment ⟨we don't *accept* personal checks⟩
**6** : to receive (a legislative report) officially
*intransitive verb*
: to receive favorably something offered — usually used with *of*
— **ac·cept·ing·ly** \-'sep-tiŋ-lē\ *adverb*
— **ac·cept·ing·ness** \-tiŋ-nəs\ *noun*

**ac·cept·able** \ik-'sep-tə-bəl, ak- *also* ek-\ *adjective* (14th century)
**1** : capable or worthy of being accepted ⟨no compromise would be *acceptable*⟩
**2 a** : WELCOME, PLEASING ⟨compliments are always *acceptable*⟩ **b** : barely satisfactory or adequate ⟨performances varied from excellent to *acceptable*⟩
— **ac·cept·abil·i·ty** \ik-ˌsep-tə-'bi-lə-tē, (ˌ)ak-, ek-\ *noun*
— **ac·cept·able·ness** \ik-'sep-tə-bəl-nəs, ak-\ *noun*
— **ac·cept·ably** \-blē\ *adverb*

**ac·cep·tance** \ik-'sep-tən(t)s, ak-\ *noun* (1574)
**1** : an agreeing either expressly or by conduct to the act or offer of another so that a contract is concluded and the parties become legally bound

\ə\ abut  \ᵊ\ kitten  \ər\ further  \a\ ash  \ā\ ace
\ä\ mop, mar  \aů\ out  \ch\ chin  \e\ bet  \ē\ easy
\g\ go  \i\ hit  \ī\ ice  \j\ job  \ŋ\ sing  \ō\ go
\ȯ\ law  \ȯi\ boy  \th\ thin  \ṯh\ the  \ü\ loot  \ů\ foot
\y\ yet  \zh\ vision  *see also* Guide to Pronunciation

**2** : the quality or state of being accepted or acceptable
**3** : the act of accepting : the fact of being accepted : APPROVAL
**4 a** : the act of accepting a time draft or bill of exchange for payment when due according to the specified terms **b** : an accepted draft or bill of exchange
**5** : ACCEPTATION 2

**ac·cep·tant** \-tənt\ *adjective* (1851)
: willing to accept : RECEPTIVE
**ac·cep·ta·tion** \ˌak-ˌsep-ˈtā-shən\ *noun* (15th century)
**1** : ACCEPTANCE; *especially* : favorable reception or approval
**2** : a generally accepted meaning of a word or understanding of a concept
**ac·cept·ed** *adjective* (15th century)
: generally approved or used
— **ac·cept·ed·ly** *adverb*
**ac·cept·er** \ik-ˈsep-tər, ak-\ *noun* (1585)
**1** : one that accepts
**2** : ACCEPTOR 2
**ac·cep·tive** \ak-ˈsep-tiv\ *adjective* (1596)
**1** : ACCEPTABLE
**2** : RECEPTIVE
**ac·cep·tor** \ik-ˈsep-tər, ak-\ *noun* (14th century)
**1** : ACCEPTER 1
**2** : one that accepts an order or a bill of exchange
**3** : an atom, molecule, or subatomic particle capable of receiving another entity (as an electron) especially to form a compound — compare DONOR 3a
**¹ac·cess** \ˈak-ˌses *also* ik-ˈses\ *noun* [Middle English, from Middle French & Latin; Middle French *acces* arrival, from Latin *accessus* approach, from *accedere* to approach — more at ACCEDE] (14th century)
**1 a** : ONSET 2 **b** : a fit of intense feeling : OUTBURST
**2 a** : permission, liberty, or ability to enter, approach, communicate with, or pass to and from **b** : freedom or ability to obtain or make use of **c** : a way or means of access **d** : the act or an instance of accessing
**3** : an increase by addition ⟨a sudden *access* of wealth⟩
**²access** *transitive verb* (1962)
: to get at : gain access to ⟨*accessed* the computer by phone⟩
**ac·ces·si·ble** \ik-ˈse-sə-bəl, ak-, ek-\ *adjective* (15th century)
**1** : providing access
**2 a** : capable of being reached ⟨*accessible* by rail⟩; *also* : being within reach ⟨fashions at *accessible* prices⟩ **b** : easy to speak or deal with ⟨*accessible* people⟩
**3** : capable of being influenced : OPEN
**4** : capable of being used or seen : AVAILABLE
**5** : capable of being understood or appreciated ⟨the author's most *accessible* stories⟩ ⟨an *accessible* film⟩
— **ac·ces·si·bil·i·ty** \-ˌse-sə-ˈbi-lə-tē\ *noun*
— **ac·ces·si·ble·ness** \-ˈse-sə-bəl-nəs\ *noun*
— **ac·ces·si·bly** \-blē\ *adverb*
**¹ac·ces·sion** \ik-ˈse-shən, ak-\ *noun* (1588)
**1 a** : increase by something added **b** : acquisition of additional property (as by growth or increase of existing property)
**2** : something added : ACQUISITION
**3** : the act of assenting or agreeing
**4 a** : the act of becoming joined : ADHERENCE **b** : the act by which one nation becomes party to an agreement already in force between other powers
**5 a** : an act of coming near or to : APPROACH, ADMITTANCE **b** : the act of coming to high office or a position of honor or power
**6** : a sudden fit or outburst : ACCESS
— **ac·ces·sion·al** \-ˈsesh-nəl, -ˈse-shə-nᵉl\ *adjective*
**²accession** *transitive verb* (1892)
: to record in order of acquisition

**ac·ces·so·ri·al** \ˌak-sə-ˈsōr-ē-əl, -ˈsȯr-\ *adjective* (1726)
**1** : of or relating to an accessory ⟨*accessorial* liability⟩
**2** : of, relating to, or constituting an accession : SUPPLEMENTARY ⟨*accessorial* services⟩
**ac·ces·so·rise** *British variant of* ACCESSORIZE
**ac·ces·so·rize** \ik-ˈse-sə-ˌrīz, ak-\ *verb* **-rized; -riz·ing** (1939)
*transitive verb*
: to furnish with accessories
*intransitive verb*
: to wear clothing accessories
**¹ac·ces·so·ry** *also* **ac·ces·sa·ry** \ik-ˈse-sə-rē, ak-, ek-, -ˈses-rē, *also* ə-ˈse-\ *noun, plural* **-ries** (15th century)
**1 a** : a person not actually or constructively present but contributing as an assistant or instigator to the commission of an offense — called also *accessory before the fact* **b** : a person who knowing that a crime has been committed aids or shelters the offender with intent to defeat justice — called also *accessory after the fact*
**2 a** : a thing of secondary or subordinate importance : ADJUNCT **b** : an object or device not essential in itself but adding to the beauty, convenience, or effectiveness of something else ⟨auto *accessories*⟩ ⟨clothing *accessories*⟩
**²accessory** *adjective* (1607)
**1** : assisting as a subordinate; *especially* : contributing to a crime but not as the chief agent
**2** : aiding or contributing in a secondary way : SUPPLEMENTARY
**3** : present in a minor amount and not essential as a constituent ⟨an *accessory* mineral in a rock⟩
**accessory fruit** *noun* (circa 1900)
: a fruit (as the apple) of which a conspicuous part consists of tissue other than that of the ripened ovary
**accessory nerve** *noun* (circa 1842)
: either of a pair of motor nerves that are the 11th cranial nerves of higher vertebrates, arise from the medulla and the upper part of the spinal cord, and supply chiefly the pharynx and muscles of the upper chest, back, and shoulders
**access time** *noun* (1950)
: the time lag between the time stored information (as in a computer) is requested and the time it is delivered
**ac·ciac·ca·tu·ra** \(ˌ)ä-ˌchä-kə-ˈtu̇r-ə\ *noun* [Italian, literally, crushing] (circa 1819)
: a discordant note sounded with a principal note or chord and immediately released
**ac·ci·dence** \ˈak-sə-dən(t)s, -ˌden(t)s\ *noun* [Middle English, from Middle French, from Latin *accidentia* inflections of words, nonessential qualities, plural of *accident-, accidens*, noun] (15th century)
: a part of grammar that deals with inflections
**ac·ci·dent** \ˈak-sə-dənt, -ˌdent; ˈaks-dənt\ *noun* [Middle English, from Middle French, from Latin *accident-, accidens* nonessential quality, chance, from present participle of *accidere* to happen, from *ad-* + *cadere* to fall — more at CHANCE] (14th century)
**1 a** : an unforeseen and unplanned event or circumstance **b** : lack of intention or necessity : CHANCE ⟨met by *accident* rather than by design⟩
**2 a** : an unfortunate event resulting especially from carelessness or ignorance **b** : an unexpected and medically important bodily event especially when injurious ⟨a cerebrovascular *accident*⟩ **c** : an unexpected happening causing loss or injury which is not due to any fault or misconduct on the part of the person injured but for which legal relief may be sought
**3** : a nonessential property or quality of an entity or circumstance ⟨the *accident* of nationality⟩
**¹ac·ci·den·tal** \ˌak-sə-ˈden-tᵉl\ *adjective* (14th century)

**1** : arising from extrinsic causes : INCIDENTAL, NONESSENTIAL
**2 a** : occurring unexpectedly or by chance **b** : happening without intent or through carelessness and often with unfortunate results ☆
— **ac·ci·den·tal·ly** \-ˈdent-lē, -ˈden-tᵉl-ē\ *also* **ac·ci·dent·ly** \-ˈdent-lē\ *adverb*
— **ac·ci·den·tal·ness** \-ˈden-tᵉl-nəs\ *noun*
**²accidental** *noun* (1651)
**1** : a nonessential property
**2 a** : a note foreign to a key indicated by a signature **b** : a prefixed sign indicating an accidental
**accident insurance** *noun* (1866)
: insurance against loss through accidental bodily injury to the insured
**accident–prone** *adjective* (1926)
**1** : having a greater than average number of accidents
**2** : having personality traits that predispose to accidents
**ac·cid·ie** \ˈak-sə-dē\ *noun* (13th century)
: ACEDIA
**ac·cip·i·ter** \ak-ˈsi-pə-tər, ik-\ *noun* [New Latin, genus name, from Latin, hawk] (circa 1828)
: any of a genus (*Accipiter*) of medium-sized forest-inhabiting hawks that have short broad wings and a long tail and a characteristic flight pattern of several quick flaps and a glide
— **ac·cip·i·trine** \-ˈsi-pə-ˌtrīn\ *adjective or noun*
**¹ac·claim** \ə-ˈklām\ *verb* [Latin *acclamare*, literally, to shout at, from *ad-* + *clamare* to shout — more at CLAIM] (1633)
*transitive verb*
**1** : APPLAUD, PRAISE
**2** : to declare by acclamation
*intransitive verb*
: to shout praise or applause
— **ac·claim·er** *noun*
**²acclaim** *noun* (1667)
**1** : the act of acclaiming
**2** : PRAISE, APPLAUSE
**ac·cla·ma·tion** \ˌa-klə-ˈmā-shən\ *noun* [Latin *acclamation-, acclamatio*, from *acclamare*] (1585)
**1** : a loud eager expression of approval, praise, or assent
**2** : an overwhelming affirmative vote by cheers, shouts, or applause rather than by ballot
**ac·cli·mate** \ˈa-klə-ˌmāt; ə-ˈklī-mət, -ˌmāt\ *verb* **-mat·ed; -mat·ing** [French *acclimater*, from *a-* (from Latin *ad-*) + *climat* climate] (1792)
: ACCLIMATIZE
**ac·cli·ma·tion** \ˌa-klə-ˈmā-shən, -ˌklī-\ *noun* (1826)
: ACCLIMATIZATION; *especially* : physiological adjustment by an organism to environmental change
**ac·cli·ma·tise** *British variant of* ACCLIMATIZE
**ac·cli·ma·ti·za·tion** \ə-ˌklī-mə-tə-ˈzā-shən\ *noun* (1830)
: the process or result of acclimatizing
**ac·cli·ma·tize** \ə-ˈklī-mə-ˌtīz\ *verb* **-tized; -tiz·ing** (1836)
*transitive verb*

: to adapt to a new temperature, altitude, climate, environment, or situation
*intransitive verb*
: to become acclimatized
— **ac·cli·ma·tiz·er** *noun*
**ac·cliv·i·ty** \ə-'kli-və-tē, a-\ *noun*, *plural*
**-ties** [Latin *acclivitas*, from *acclivis* ascending, from *ad-* + *clivus* slope — more at DECLIVITY] (1614)
: an ascending slope (as of a hill)
**ac·co·lade** \'a-kə-,lād, -,läd\ *noun* [French, from *accoler* to embrace, from (assumed) Vulgar Latin *accollare*, from Latin *ad-* + *collum* neck — more at COLLAR] (1623)
**1 a :** a ceremonial embrace **b :** a ceremony or salute conferring knighthood
**2 a :** a mark of acknowledgment : AWARD **b :** an expression of praise
**3 :** a brace or a line used in music to join two or more staffs carrying simultaneous parts
**ac·com·mo·date** \ə-'kä-mə-,dāt\ *verb* **-dated; -dat·ing** [Latin *accommodatus*, past participle of *accommodare*, from *ad-* + *commodare* to make fit, from *commodus* suitable — more at COMMODE] (1550)
*transitive verb*
**1 :** to make fit, suitable, or congruous
**2 :** to bring into agreement or concord : RECONCILE
**3 :** to provide with something desired, needed, or suited (as a helpful service, a loan, or lodgings)
**4 a :** to make room for **b :** to hold without crowding or inconvenience
**5 :** to give consideration to : allow for ⟨*accommodate* the special interests of various groups⟩
*intransitive verb*
: to adapt oneself; *also* : to undergo visual accommodation
**synonym** see ADAPT, CONTAIN
— **ac·com·mo·da·tive** \-,dā-tiv\ *adjective*
— **ac·com·mo·da·tive·ness** *noun*
**ac·com·mo·dat·ing** *adjective* (1775)
: HELPFUL, OBLIGING
— **ac·com·mo·dat·ing·ly** \-,dā-tiŋ-lē\ *adverb*
**ac·com·mo·da·tion** \ə-,kä-mə-'dā-shən\ *noun* (1603)
**1 :** something supplied for convenience or to satisfy a need: as **a :** lodging, food, and services or traveling space and related services — usually used in plural ⟨tourist *accommodations* on the boat⟩ ⟨overnight *accommodations*⟩ **b :** a public conveyance (as a train) that stops at all or nearly all points **c :** LOAN
**2 :** the act of accommodating : the state of being accommodated: as **a :** the providing of what is needed or desired for convenience **b :** ADAPTATION, ADJUSTMENT **c :** a reconciliation of differences : SETTLEMENT **d :** the automatic adjustment of the eye for seeing at different distances effected chiefly by changes in the convexity of the crystalline lens; *also* : the range over which such adjustment is possible
— **ac·com·mo·da·tion·al** \-shnəl, -shə-n°l\ *adjective*
**¹ac·com·mo·da·tion·ist** \-'dā-sh(ə-)nist\ *noun* (1964)
: a black who adapts to the ideals or attitudes of whites ⟨making Uncle Toms, compromisers, and *accommodationists* . . . thoroughly ashamed —Ossie Davis⟩
**²accommodationist** *adjective* (1964)
: favoring or practicing accommodation or compromise
**accommodation ladder** *noun* (1769)
: a light ladder or stairway hung over the side of a ship for ascending from or descending to small boats
**ac·com·mo·da·tor** \ə-'kä-mə-,dā-tər\ *noun* (circa 1630)
: one that accommodates; *especially* : a part-time or special-occasion domestic worker
**ac·com·pa·ni·ment** \ə-'kəm-pə-nē-mənt, -'kəmp-nē-\ *noun* (circa 1744)

**1 :** an instrumental or vocal part designed to support or complement a melody
**2 a :** an addition (as an ornament) intended to give completeness or symmetry : COMPLEMENT **b :** an accompanying situation or occurrence : CONCOMITANT
**ac·com·pa·nist** \ə-'kəmp-nist, -'kəm-pə-\ *noun* (circa 1828)
: one (as a pianist) who plays an accompaniment
**ac·com·pa·ny** \ə-'kəmp-nē, -'kämp-; -'kəm-pə-, -'käm-\ *verb* **-nied; -ny·ing** [Middle English *acompanien*, from Middle French *acompaignier*, from *a-* (from Latin *ad-*) + *compaing* companion — more at COMPANION] (15th century)
*transitive verb*
**1 :** to go with as an associate or companion
**2 :** to perform an accompaniment to or for
**3 a :** to cause to be in association ⟨*accompanied* their advice with a warning⟩ **b :** to be in association with ⟨the pictures that *accompany* the text⟩
*intransitive verb*
: to perform an accompaniment
**ac·com·plice** \ə-'käm-pləs, -'kəm-\ *noun* [alteration (from incorrect division of *a complice*) of *complice*] (1589)
: one associated with another especially in wrongdoing
**ac·com·plish** \ə-'käm-plish, -'kəm-\ *transitive verb* [Middle English *accomplisshen*, from Middle French *accompliss-*, stem of *acomplir*, from (assumed) Vulgar Latin *accomplēre*, from Latin *ad-* + *complēre* to fill up — more at COMPLETE] (14th century)
**1 :** to bring about (a result) by effort ⟨have much to *accomplish* today⟩ ⟨regretted that he had never *accomplished* a marriage for her —Francis Hackett⟩
**2 :** to bring to completion : FULFILL ⟨we can *accomplish* the job in an hour⟩
**3 :** to succeed in reaching (a stage in a progression) ⟨would starve before *accomplishing* half the distance —W. H. Hudson (died 1922)⟩
**4** *archaic* **a :** to equip thoroughly **b :** PERFECT
**synonym** see PERFORM
— **ac·com·plish·able** \-pli-shə-bəl\ *adjective*
— **ac·com·plish·er** *noun*
**ac·com·plished** *adjective* (15th century)
**1 :** proficient as the result of practice or training ⟨an *accomplished* dancer⟩ **b :** having many social accomplishments
**2 :** established beyond doubt or dispute ⟨an *accomplished* fact⟩
**ac·com·plish·ment** \ə-'käm-plish-mənt, -'kəm-\ *noun* (15th century)
**1 :** the act of accomplishing : COMPLETION
**2 :** something that has been accomplished : ACHIEVEMENT
**3 a :** a quality or ability equipping one for society **b :** a special skill or ability acquired by training or practice
**¹ac·cord** \ə-'kȯrd\ *verb* [Middle English, from Old French *acorder*, from (assumed) Vulgar Latin *accordare*, from Latin *ad-* + *cord-, cor* heart — more at HEART] (12th century)
*transitive verb*
**1 :** to bring into agreement : RECONCILE
**2 :** to grant or give especially as appropriate, due, or earned
*intransitive verb*
**1** *archaic* : to arrive at an agreement
**2** *obsolete* : to give consent
**3 :** to be consistent or in harmony : AGREE
**synonym** see GRANT
**²accord** *noun* [Middle English, from Old French *acort*, from *acorder*] (14th century)
**1 a :** AGREEMENT, CONFORMITY ⟨acted in *accord* with the company's policy⟩ **b :** a formal reaching of agreement : COMPACT, TREATY
**2 :** balanced interrelationship : HARMONY
**3** *obsolete* : ASSENT
**4 :** voluntary or spontaneous impulse to act ⟨gave voluntarily of their own *accord*⟩

**ac·cor·dance** \ə-'kȯr-d°n(t)s\ *noun* (14th century)
**1 :** AGREEMENT, CONFORMITY ⟨in *accordance* with a rule⟩
**2 :** the act of granting
**ac·cor·dant** \-d°nt\ *adjective* (14th century)
**1 :** CONSONANT, AGREEING
**2 :** HARMONIOUS, CORRESPONDENT
— **ac·cor·dant·ly** *adverb*
**according as** *conjunction* (1500)
**1 :** in accord with the way in which
**2 a :** depending on how **b :** depending on whether : IF
**ac·cord·ing·ly** \ə-'kȯr-diŋ-lē\ *adverb* (14th century)
**1 :** in accordance : CORRESPONDINGLY
**2 :** CONSEQUENTLY, SO
**according to** *preposition* (14th century)
**1 :** in conformity with
**2 :** as stated or attested by
**3 :** depending on
**¹ac·cor·di·on** \ə-'kȯr-dē-ən\ *noun* [German *Akkordion*, from *Akkord* chord, from French *accord*, from Old French *acort*] (1831)
: a portable keyboard wind instrument in which the wind is forced past free reeds by means of a hand-operated bellows
— **ac·cor·di·on·ist** \-dē-ə-nist\ *noun*
**²accordion** *adjective* (1885)
: folding or creased or hinged to fold like an accordion ⟨an *accordion* pleat⟩ ⟨an *accordion* door⟩

accordion

**ac·cost** \ə-'kȯst, -'käst\ *transitive verb* [Middle French *accoster*, ultimately from Latin *ad-* + *costa* rib, side — more at COAST] (1612)
: to approach and speak to often in a challenging or aggressive way
**ac·couche·ment** \,a-,küsh-'mäⁿ, ə-'küsh-,\ *noun* [French] (1803)
: the time or act of giving birth
**ac·cou·cheur** \,a-,kü-'shər\ *noun* [French] (1759)
: one that assists at a birth; *especially* : OBSTETRICIAN
**¹ac·count** \ə-'kaùnt\ *noun* (14th century)
**1** *archaic* : RECKONING, COMPUTATION
**2 a :** a record of debit and credit entries to cover transactions involving a particular item or a particular person or concern **b :** a statement of transactions during a fiscal period and the resulting balance
**3 a :** a statement explaining one's conduct **b :** a statement or exposition of reasons, causes, or motives ⟨no satisfactory *account* of these phenomena⟩ **c :** a reason for an action : BASIS ⟨on that *account* I must refuse⟩
**4 a :** a formal business arrangement providing for regular dealings or services (as banking, advertising, or store credit) and involving the establishment and maintenance of an account; *also* : CLIENT, CUSTOMER **b :** money deposited in a bank account and subject to withdrawal by the depositor
**5 a :** VALUE, IMPORTANCE ⟨it's of no *account* to me⟩ **b :** ESTEEM ⟨stood high in their *account*⟩
**6 :** ADVANTAGE ⟨turned her wit to good *account*⟩
**7 a :** careful thought : CONSIDERATION ⟨have to take many things into *account*⟩ **b :** a usually mental record : TRACK ⟨keep *account* of all you do⟩

\ə\ abut \ᵊ\ kitten \ər\ further \a\ ash \ā\ ace \ä\ mop, mar \aù\ out \ch\ chin \e\ bet \ē\ easy \g\ go \i\ hit \ī\ ice \j\ job \ŋ\ sing \ō\ go \ò\ law \òi\ boy \th\ thin \t̲h̲\ the \ü\ loot \ù\ foot \y\ yet \zh\ vision *see also* Guide to Pronunciation

**8 :** a description of facts, conditions, or events **:** REPORT, NARRATIVE ⟨the newspaper *account* of the fire⟩ ⟨by all *accounts* they're well-off⟩; *also* **:** PERFORMANCE ⟨a straightforward *account* of the sonata⟩
**— on account :** with the price charged to one's account
**— on account of :** for the sake of **:** by reason of
**— on no account :** under no circumstances
**— on one's own account 1 :** on one's own behalf **2 :** at one's own risk **3 :** by oneself **:** on one's own

²**account** *verb* [Middle English, from Middle French *acompter*, from *a-* (from Latin *ad-*) + *compter* to count] (14th century)
*transitive verb*
**1 :** to think of as **:** CONSIDER ⟨*accounts* himself lucky⟩
**2 :** to probe into **:** ANALYZE
*intransitive verb*
**1 :** to furnish a justifying analysis or explanation — used with *for* ⟨couldn't *account* for the loss⟩
**2 a :** to be the sole or primary factor — used with *for* ⟨the pitcher *accounted* for all three putouts⟩ **b :** to bring about the capture, death, or destruction of something ⟨*accounted* for two rabbits⟩

**ac·count·abil·i·ty** \ə-ˌkaün-tə-ˈbi-lə-tē\ *noun* (1794)
**:** the quality or state of being accountable; *especially* **:** an obligation or willingness to accept responsibility or to account for one's actions ⟨public officials lacking *accountability*⟩

**ac·count·able** \ə-ˈkaün-tə-bəl\ *adjective* (14th century)
**1 :** subject to giving an account **:** ANSWERABLE
**2 :** capable of being accounted for **:** EXPLAINABLE
*synonym* SEE RESPONSIBLE
— **ac·count·able·ness** \-ˈkaün-tə-bəl-nəs\ *noun*
— **ac·count·ably** \-blē\ *adverb*

**ac·coun·tan·cy** \ə-ˈkaün-tᵊn(t)-sē\ *noun* (1854)
**:** the profession or practice of accounting

¹**ac·coun·tant** \ə-ˈkaün-tᵊnt\ *noun* (15th century)
**1 :** one that gives an account or is accountable
**2 :** one who is skilled in the practice of accounting or who is in charge of public or private accounts
— **ac·coun·tant·ship** \-tᵊn(t)-ˌship\ *noun*
²**accountant** *adjective* (15th century)
*obsolete* **:** ACCOUNTABLE, ANSWERABLE ⟨I stand *accountant* for as great a sin —Shakespeare⟩

**account executive** *noun* (1931)
**:** a business executive (as in an advertising agency) responsible for dealing with a client's account

**ac·count·ing** \ə-ˈkaün-tiŋ\ *noun* (circa 1716)
**1 :** the system of recording and summarizing business and financial transactions and analyzing, verifying, and reporting the results; *also* **:** the principles and procedures of accounting
**2 a :** work done in accounting or by accountants **b :** an instance of applied accounting or of the settling or presenting of accounts

**account payable** *noun, plural* **accounts payable** (circa 1936)
**:** the balance due to a creditor on a current account

**account receivable** *noun, plural* **accounts receivable** (1936)
**:** a balance due from a debtor on a current account

**ac·cou·tre** *or* **ac·cou·ter** \ə-ˈkü-tər\ *transitive verb* **-cou·tred** *or* **-cou·tered; -cou·tring** *or* **-cou·ter·ing** \-ˈkü-tə-riŋ, -ˈkü-triŋ\ [French *accoutrer*, from Middle French *acoustrer*, from *a-* + *costure* seam, from (assumed) Vulgar Latin *consutura* — more at COUTURE] (1596)
**:** to provide with equipment or furnishings **:** OUTFIT
*synonym* SEE FURNISH

**ac·cou·tre·ment** *or* **ac·cou·ter·ment** \ə-ˈkü-trə-mənt, -ˈkü-tər-mənt\ *noun* (1549)
**1 a :** EQUIPMENT, TRAPPINGS; *specifically* **:** a soldier's outfit usually not including clothes and weapons — usually used in plural **b :** an accessory item of clothing or equipment — usually used in plural
**2** *archaic* **:** the act of accoutring
**3 :** an identifying and often superficial characteristic or device — usually used in plural ⟨*accoutrements* of power that define our diplomacy —Elizabeth Drew⟩

**ac·cred·it** \ə-ˈkre-dət\ *transitive verb* [Latin *accreditus*, past participle of *accredere* to give credence to, from *ad-* + *credere* to believe — more at CREED] (1535)
**1 :** to give official authorization to or approval of: **a :** to provide with credentials; *especially* **:** to send (an envoy) with letters of authorization **b :** to recognize or vouch for as conforming with a standard **c :** to recognize (an educational institution) as maintaining standards that qualify the graduates for admission to higher or more specialized institutions or for professional practice
**2 :** to consider or recognize as outstanding
**3 :** ATTRIBUTE, CREDIT
*synonym* SEE APPROVE
— **ac·cred·i·table** \-də-tə-bəl\ *adjective*
— **ac·cred·i·ta·tion** \ə-ˌkre-də-ˈtā-shən, -ˈdā-\ *noun*

**ac·crete** \a-ˈkrēt\ *verb* **ac·cret·ed; ac·cret·ing** [back-formation from *accretion*] (1784)
*intransitive verb*
**:** to grow or become attached by accretion
*transitive verb*
**:** to cause to adhere or become attached; *also* **:** ACCUMULATE

**ac·cre·tion** \ə-ˈkrē-shən\ *noun* [Latin *accretion-, accretio*, from *accrescere* — more at ACCRUE] (1615)
**1 :** the process of growth or enlargement by a gradual buildup: as **a :** increase by external addition or accumulation (as by adhesion of external parts or particles) **b :** the increase of land by the action of natural forces
**2 :** a product of accretion; *especially* **:** an extraneous addition ⟨*accretions* of grime⟩
— **ac·cre·tion·ary** \-shə-ˌner-ē\ *adjective*
— **ac·cre·tive** \ə-ˈkrē-tiv\ *adjective*

¹**ac·cru·al** \ə-ˈkrü-əl\ *noun* (1880)
**1 :** the action or process of accruing
**2 :** something that accrues or has accrued
²**accrual** *adjective* (1917)
**:** being a method of accounting that recognizes income when earned and expenses when incurred regardless of when cash is received or disbursed

**ac·crue** \ə-ˈkrü\ *verb* **ac·crued; ac·cru·ing** [Middle English *acreuen*, probably from Middle French *acreue* increase, from *acreistre* to increase, from Latin *accrescere*, from *ad-* + *crescere* to grow — more at CRESCENT] (15th century)
*intransitive verb*
**1 :** to come into existence as a legally enforceable claim
**2 a :** to come about as a natural growth, increase, or advantage ⟨the wisdom that *accrues* with age⟩ **b :** to come as a direct result of some state or action ⟨rewards due to the feminine will *accrue* to me —Germaine Greer⟩
**3 :** to accumulate or be added periodically ⟨interest *accrues* on a daily basis⟩
*transitive verb*
**:** to accumulate or have due after a period of time ⟨*accrue* vacation time⟩
— **ac·cru·able** \-ˈkrü-ə-bəl\ *adjective*
— **ac·crue·ment** \-ˈkrü-mənt\ *noun*

**ac·cul·tur·ate** \ə-ˈkəl-chə-ˌrāt, a-\ *transitive verb* **-at·ed; -at·ing** [back-formation from *acculturation*] (1930)
**:** to change through acculturation

**ac·cul·tur·a·tion** \ə-ˌkəl-chə-ˈrā-shən, a-\ *noun* (1880)
**1 :** cultural modification of an individual, group, or people by adapting to or borrowing traits from another culture; *also* **:** a merging of cultures as a result of prolonged contact
**2 :** the process by which a human being acquires the culture of a particular society from infancy
— **ac·cul·tur·a·tion·al** \-shnəl, -shə-nᵊl\ *adjective*
— **ac·cul·tur·a·tive** \ə-ˈkəl-chə-ˌrā-tiv, a-\ *adjective*

**ac·cu·mu·late** \ə-ˈkyü-m(y)ə-ˌlāt\ *verb* **-lat·ed; -lat·ing** [Latin *accumulatus*, past participle of *accumulare*, from *ad-* + *cumulare* to heap up — more at CUMULATE] (15th century)
*transitive verb*
**:** to gather or pile up especially little by little **:** AMASS ⟨*accumulate* a fortune⟩
*intransitive verb*
**:** to increase gradually in quantity or number

**ac·cu·mu·la·tion** \ə-ˌkyü-m(y)ə-ˈlā-shən\ *noun* (15th century)
**1 :** something that has accumulated or has been accumulated
**2 :** the action or process of accumulating **:** the state of being or having accumulated
**3 :** increase or growth by addition especially when continuous or repeated ⟨*accumulation* of interest⟩

**ac·cu·mu·la·tive** \ə-ˈkyü-m(y)ə-ˌlā-tiv, -lə-\ *adjective* (circa 1651)
**1 :** CUMULATIVE ⟨an age of rapid and *accumulative* change⟩
**2 :** tending or given to accumulation
— **ac·cu·mu·la·tive·ly** *adverb*
— **ac·cu·mu·la·tive·ness** *noun*

**ac·cu·mu·la·tor** \ə-ˈkyü-m(y)ə-ˌlā-tər\ *noun* (1748)
**:** one that accumulates: as **a :** a device (as in a hydraulic system) in which a fluid is collected and especially in which it is kept under pressure as a means of storing energy **b** *British* **:** STORAGE BATTERY **c :** a part (as in a computer) where numbers are totaled or stored

**ac·cu·ra·cy** \ˈa-kyə-rə-sē, ˈa-k(ə-)rə-\ *noun, plural* **-cies** (1662)
**1 :** freedom from mistake or error **:** CORRECTNESS
**2 a :** conformity to truth or to a standard or model **:** EXACTNESS **b :** degree of conformity of a measure to a standard or a true value — compare PRECISION 2a

**ac·cu·rate** \ˈa-kyə-rət, ˈa-k(ə-)rət\ *adjective* [Latin *accuratus*, from past participle of *accurare* to take care of, from *ad-* + *cura* care] (1596)
**1 :** free from error especially as the result of care ⟨an *accurate* diagnosis⟩
**2 :** conforming exactly to truth or to a standard **:** EXACT ⟨providing *accurate* color⟩
**3 :** able to give an accurate result ⟨an *accurate* gauge⟩
*synonym* SEE CORRECT
— **ac·cu·rate·ly** \ˈa-kyə-rət-lē, ˈa-k(ə-)rət-, ˈa-k(y)ərt-\ *adverb*
— **ac·cu·rate·ness** \-kyə-rət-nəs, -k(ə-)rət-nəs\ *noun*

**ac·cursed** \ə-ˈkərst, -ˈkər-səd\ *or* **ac·curst** \ə-ˈkərst\ *adjective* [Middle English *acursed*, from past participle of *acursen* to consign to destruction with a curse, from *a-* (from Old English *ā*, perfective prefix) + *cursen* to curse — more at ABIDE] (13th century)
**1 :** being under or as if under a curse
**2 :** DAMNABLE
— **ac·curs·ed·ly** \-ˈkər-səd-lē\ *adverb*
— **ac·curs·ed·ness** \-ˈkər-səd-nəs\ *noun*

**ac·cus·al** \ə-ˈkyü-zəl\ *noun* (1594)
**:** ACCUSATION

**ac·cu·sa·tion** \,a-kyə-'zā-shən, -(,)kyü-\ *noun* (14th century)
**1** : the act of accusing : the state or fact of being accused
**2** : a charge of wrongdoing

**¹ac·cu·sa·tive** \ə-'kyü-zə-tiv\ *adjective* [Middle English, from Middle French or Latin; Middle French *accusatif*, from Latin *accusativus*, from *accusatus*, past participle of *accusare*] (15th century)
**1** : of, relating to, or being the grammatical case that marks the direct object of a verb or the object of any of several prepositions
**2** : ACCUSATORY

**²accusative** *noun* (circa 1620)
: the accusative case of a language : a form in the accusative case

**ac·cu·sa·to·ry** \ə-'kyü-zə-,tōr-ē, -,tȯr-\ *adjective* (14th century)
: containing or expressing accusation : ACCUSING

**ac·cuse** \ə-'kyüz\ *verb* **ac·cused; ac·cus·ing** [Middle English, from Old French *acuser*, from Latin *accusare* to call to account, from *ad-* + *causa* lawsuit] (14th century)
*transitive verb*
**1** : to charge with a fault or offense : BLAME
**2** : to charge with an offense judicially or by a public process
*intransitive verb*
: to bring an accusation
— **ac·cus·er** \ə-'kyü-zər\ *noun*
— **ac·cus·ing·ly** \-'kyü-ziŋ-lē\ *adverb*

**ac·cused** *noun, plural* **accused** (1593)
: one charged with an offense; *especially* : the defendant in a criminal case

**ac·cus·tom** \ə-'kəs-təm\ *transitive verb* [Middle English, from Middle French *acostumer*, from *a-* (from Latin *ad-*) + *costume* custom] (15th century)
: to make familiar with something through use or experience
— **ac·cus·tom·ation** \-,kəs-tə-'mā-shən\ *noun*

**ac·cus·tomed** \ə-'kəs-təmd\ *adjective* (15th century)
**1** : often used or practiced : CUSTOMARY ⟨her *accustomed* cheerfulness⟩
**2** : adapted to existing conditions ⟨eyes *accustomed* to the dark⟩
**3** : being in the habit or custom ⟨*accustomed* to making decisions⟩
*synonym* see USUAL
— **ac·cus·tomed·ness** \-təm(d)-nəs\ *noun*

**AC/DC** \'ā-(,)sē-'dē-(,)sē\ *adjective* [from the likening of a bisexual person to an electrical appliance which can operate on either alternating or direct current] (circa 1960)
: BISEXUAL 1b

**¹ace** \'ās\ *noun* [Middle English *as*, from Middle French, from Latin, unit, a copper coin] (14th century)
**1 a** : a die face marked with one spot **b** : a playing card marked in its center with one pip **c** : a domino end marked with one spot
**2** : a very small amount or degree : PARTICLE
**3** : a point scored especially on a service (as in tennis or handball) that an opponent fails to touch
**4** : a golf score of one stroke on a hole; *also* : a hole made in one stroke
**5** : a combat pilot who has brought down at least five enemy airplanes
**6** : one that excels at something
— **ace in the hole 1** : an ace dealt face down to a player (as in stud poker) and not exposed until the showdown **2** : an effective and decisive argument or resource held in reserve
— **within an ace of** : on the point of : very near to ⟨came *within an ace of* winning⟩

**²ace** *transitive verb* **aced; ac·ing** (1923)
**1** : to score an ace against (an opponent)
**2** : to make (a hole in golf) in one stroke
**3** : to gain a decisive advantage over : DEFEAT — usually used with *out*

**4** : to earn a high grade on (as an examination); *especially* : to get an A on

**³ace** *adjective* (1926)
: of first or high rank or quality

**-aceae** *noun plural suffix* [New Latin, from Latin, feminine plural of *-aceus* -aceous]
: plants of the nature of ⟨Rosac*eae*⟩ — in names of families of plants

**ace·dia** \ə-'sē-dē-ə\ *noun* [Late Latin, from Greek *akēdeia*, from *a-* + *kēdos* care, grief — more at HATE] (1607)
: APATHY, BOREDOM

**ACE inhibitor** \,ā-(,)sē-'ē-; 'ās-\ *noun* [*a*ngiotensin *c*onverting *e*nzyme] (1985)
: any of a group of antihypertensive drugs (as captopril) that relax arteries and promote renal excretion of salt and water by inhibiting the activity of angiotensin converting enzyme

**Acel·da·ma** \ə-'sel-də-mə\ *noun* [Greek *Akeldama*, from Aramaic *ḥăqēl dĕmā*, literally, field of blood]
: the potter's field bought with the money Judas had been paid for betraying Christ

**acel·lu·lar** \(,)ā-'sel-yə-lər\ *adjective* (1940)
**1** : containing no cells ⟨*acellular* vaccines⟩
**2** : not divided into cells : consisting of a single complex cell — used especially of protozoa and ciliates

**acen·tric** \(,)ā-'sen-trik\ *adjective* (1937)
: lacking a centromere ⟨*acentric* chromosomes⟩

**-aceous** *adjective suffix* [Latin *-aceus*]
**1 a** : characterized by : full of ⟨set*aceous*⟩ **b** : consisting of ⟨diatom*aceous*⟩ : having the nature or form of ⟨tuff*aceous*⟩
**2 a** : of or relating to a group of animals typified by (such) a form ⟨cet*aceous*⟩ or characterized by (such) a feature ⟨crust*aceous*⟩ **b** : of or relating to a plant family ⟨solan*aceous*⟩

**aceph·a·lous** \(,)ā-'se-fə-ləs, ə-'se-\ *adjective* [Greek *akephalos*, from *a-* + *kephalē* head — more at CEPHALIC] (circa 1731)
**1** : lacking a head or having the head reduced
**2** : lacking a governing head or chief

**ace·quia** \ə-'sā-kē-ə, ä-\ *noun* [Spanish, from Arabic *as-sāqiyah* the irrigation stream] (1844)
*Southwest* : an irrigation ditch or canal

**acerb** \ə-'sərb, a-\ *adjective* [French or Latin; French *acerbe*, from Latin *acerbus*; akin to Latin *acer* sharp — more at EDGE] (1622)
: ACERBIC

**ac·er·bate** \'a-sər-,bāt\ *transitive verb* **-bat·ed; -bat·ing** (circa 1731)
: IRRITATE, EXASPERATE

**acer·bic** \ə-'sər-bik, a-\ *adjective* (1865)
: acid in temper, mood, or tone
— **acer·bi·cal·ly** \-bi-k(ə-)lē\ *adverb*

**acer·bi·ty** \-bə-tē\ *noun, plural* **-ties** (1572)
: the quality of being acerbic

**ac·er·o·la** \,a-sə-'rō-lə\ *noun* [American Spanish, from Spanish, fruit of a shrub (*Crataegus azarolus*), from Arabic *az-zu'rūr*] (1945)
: any of various West Indian shrubs (genus *Malpighia*) with mildly acid cherrylike fruits very rich in vitamin C

**acet-** *or* **aceto-** *combining form* [French & Latin; French *acét-*, from Latin *acet-*, from *acetum* vinegar; akin to *acēre* to be sour, *acer* sharp — more at EDGE]
: acetic acid : acetic ⟨*acetyl*⟩

**ac·e·tab·u·lum** \-'ta-byə-ləm\ *noun, plural* **-lums** *or* **-la** \-lə\ [Latin, literally, vinegar cup, from *acetum* vinegar] (1661)
**1** : a ventral sucker of a trematode
**2** : the cup-shaped socket in the hipbone
— **ac·e·tab·u·lar** \-lər\ *adjective*

**ac·e·tal** \'a-sə-,tal\ *noun* [German *Azetal*, from *azet-* acet- + *A*lkohol alcohol] (1853)
: any of various compounds characterized by the grouping C(OR)$_2$ and obtained especially by heating aldehydes or ketones with alcohols

**ac·et·al·de·hyde** \,a-sə-'tal-də-,hīd\ *noun* [International Scientific Vocabulary] (1877)
: a colorless volatile water-soluble liquid aldehyde C$_2$H$_4$O used chiefly in organic synthesis

**acet·amide** \ə-'se-tə-,mīd, ,a-sə-'ta-,mīd\ *noun* [International Scientific Vocabulary] (1873)
: a white crystalline amide C$_2$H$_5$NO of acetic acid used especially as a solvent and in organic synthesis

**acet·amin·o·phen** \ə-,sē-tə-'mi-nə-fən, ,a-sə-tə-\ *noun* [*acet-* + *amino* + *phen*ol] (1958)
: a crystalline compound C$_8$H$_9$NO$_2$ that is a hydroxy derivative of acetanilide and is used in chemical synthesis and in medicine to relieve pain and fever

**ac·et·an·i·lide** *or* **ac·et·an·i·lid** \,a-sə-'ta-nə-,līd, -ləd\ *noun* [International Scientific Vocabulary] (circa 1864)
: a white crystalline compound C$_8$H$_9$NO that is derived from aniline and acetic acid and is used especially to relieve pain or fever

**ac·e·tate** \'a-sə-,tāt\ *noun* (1827)
**1** : a salt or ester of acetic acid
**2** : CELLULOSE ACETATE; *also* : something (as a textile fiber) made from cellulose acetate
**3** : a phonograph recording disk made of an acetate or coated with cellulose acetate

**ac·et·azol·amide** \,a-sə-tə-'zō-lə-,mīd, -'zä-,məd\ *noun* [*acet-* + *azole* + *amide*] (1954)
: a diuretic drug C$_4$H$_6$N$_4$O$_3$S$_2$ used especially in the treatment of edema associated with congestive heart failure and of glaucoma

**ace·tic acid** \ə-'sē-tik-\ *noun* [probably from French *acétique*, from Latin *acetum* vinegar] (1808)
: a colorless pungent liquid acid C$_2$H$_4$O$_2$ that is the chief acid of vinegar and that is used especially in synthesis (as of plastics)

**acetic anhydride** *noun* (1876)
: a colorless liquid C$_4$H$_6$O$_3$ with a pungent odor used in organic synthesis (as of cellulose acetate and aspirin)

**ace·ti·fy** \ə-'sē-tə-,fī, -'se-\ *transitive verb* **-fied; -fy·ing** (circa 1828)
: to turn into acetic acid or vinegar
— **ace·ti·fi·ca·tion** \-,sē-tə-fə-'kā-shən, -,se-\ *noun*

**ace·to·ace·tic acid** \,a-sə-(,)tō-ə-,sē-tik-, ə-,sē-tō-\ *noun* [part translation of German *Azetessigsäure*, from *azet-* acet- + *Essigsäure* acetic acid] (circa 1900)
: an unstable acid C$_4$H$_6$O$_3$ that is a ketone body found in abnormal quantities in the blood and urine in some conditions (as diabetes)

**ac·e·tone** \'a-sə-,tōn\ *noun* [German *Azeton*, from Latin *acetum*] (circa 1839)
: a volatile fragrant flammable liquid ketone C$_3$H$_6$O used chiefly as a solvent and in organic synthesis and found in abnormal quantities in diabetic urine
— **ac·e·ton·ic** \,a-sə-'tä-nik\ *adjective*

**ace·to·ni·trile** \ə-,sē-tō-'nī-trəl, ,a-sə-tō-, -,trīl\ *noun* (circa 1869)
: the colorless liquid nitrile CH$_3$CN of acetic acid used chiefly in organic synthesis and as a solvent

**ace·to·phe·net·i·din** \,a-sə-(,)tō-fə-'ne-tə-dən, ə-,sē-tō-\ *noun* [International Scientific Vocabulary] (1910)
: PHENACETIN

**ace·tous** \ə-'sē-təs, 'a-sə-təs\ *adjective* (1778)
: relating to or producing vinegar ⟨*acetous* fermentation⟩; *also* : SOUR, VINEGARY

**ace·tyl** \ə-'sē-t°l, 'a-sə-; 'a-sə-,tēl\ *noun* (circa 1864)
: the radical CH$_3$CO— of acetic acid — often used in combination

**acet·y·late** \ə-'se-t°l-,āt\ *transitive verb* **-lat·ed; -lat·ing** (circa 1900)
: to introduce the acetyl radical into (a compound)
— **acet·y·la·tion** \-,se-t°l-'ā-shən\ *noun*

— **acet·y·la·tive** \-'set-ᵊl-ˌā-tiv\ adjective
**ace·tyl·cho·line** \ə-ˌse-tᵊl-'kō-ˌlēn, -ˌsē-; 'a-sə-ˌtēl-\ noun [International Scientific Vocabulary] (1906)
: a neurotransmitter $C_7H_{17}NO_3$ released at autonomic synapses and neuromuscular junctions and formed enzymatically in the tissues from choline
**ace·tyl·cho·lin·es·ter·ase** \-ˌkō-lə-'nes-tə-ˌrās, -ˌrāz\ noun (1947)
: an enzyme that occurs especially in some nerve endings and in the blood and promotes the hydrolysis of acetylcholine
**acetyl CoA** \-ˌkō-'ā\ noun (circa 1959)
: ACETYL COENZYME A
**acetyl coenzyme A** noun (1952)
: a compound $C_{25}H_{38}N_7O_{17}P_3S$ formed as an intermediate in metabolism and active as a coenzyme in biological acetylations
**acet·y·lene** \ə-'se-tᵊl-ən, -tᵊl-ˌēn\ noun (1864)
: a colorless gaseous hydrocarbon HC≡CH used chiefly in organic synthesis and as a fuel (as in welding and soldering)
— **acet·y·le·nic** \ə-ˌse-tᵊl-'ē-nik, -'e-nik\ adjective
**ace·tyl·sa·lic·y·late** \ə-ˌsē-tᵊl-sə-'li-sə-ˌlāt\ noun (circa 1960)
: a salt or ester of acetylsalicylic acid
**ace·tyl·sal·i·cyl·ic acid** \ə-ˌsē-tᵊl-ˌsa-lə-ˌsi-lik-\ noun [International Scientific Vocabulary] (1897)
: ASPIRIN 1
**ac·ey–deuc·ey** also **ac·ey–deu·cy** \ˌā-sē-'dü-sē, -'dyü-\ noun (1925)
: a variation of backgammon in which a throw of a 1-2 wins extra turns
¹**Achae·an** \ə-'kē-ən\ or **Achai·an** \-'kī-ən, -'kā-ən\ adjective (1567)
: of, relating to, or characteristic of Achaea; broadly : of or relating to Greece
²**Achaean** or **Achaian** noun (1607)
: a native or inhabitant of Achaea; broadly : GREEK
**Ach·ae·me·ni·an** \ˌa-kə-'mē-nē-ən\ adjective (1717)
: of or relating to the Achaemenids
**Achae·me·nid** \ə-'kē-mə-nəd\ noun, plural **-menids** also **-men·i·dae** \ˌa-kə-'me-nə-ˌdē\ [Greek Achaimenides, from Achaimenes, 7th century B.C. Persian king, founder of the dynasty + -ides (patronymic suffix)] (1889)
: a member of the ruling house of ancient Persia generally considered historically important from the assumption of power by Cyrus the Great (559 B.C.) to the overthrow of Darius III (330 B.C.)
**acha·la·sia** \ˌā-kə-'lā-zh(ē-)ə\ noun [New Latin, from a- + Greek chalasis slackening + New Latin -ia] (1914)
: failure of a ring of muscle (as the anal sphincter or one of the esophagus) to relax
**Acha·tes** \ə-'kā-tēz\ noun [Latin]
: a faithful companion of Aeneas in Virgil's Aeneid
¹**ache** \'āk\ intransitive verb **ached; ach·ing** [Middle English aken, from Old English acan] (before 12th century)
**1 a** : to suffer a usually dull persistent pain **b** : to become distressed or disturbed (as with anxiety or regret) **c** : to feel compassion
**2** : to experience a painful eagerness or yearning
²**ache** noun (before 12th century)
**1** : a usually dull persistent pain
**2** : a condition marked by aching
**achene** \ə-'kēn\ noun [New Latin achaenium, from a- + Greek chainein to yawn — more at YAWN] (1855)
: a small dry indehiscent one-seeded fruit (as of a sunflower) developing from a simple ovary and usually having a thin pericarp attached to the seed at only one point
**Ach·er·on** \'a-kə-ˌrän, -rən\ noun [Greek Acherōn]
: a river in Hades

**Acheu·le·an** or **Acheu·li·an** \ə-'shü-lē-ən\ adjective [French acheuléen, from Saint Acheul, near Amiens, France] (circa 1909)
: of or relating to a Lower Paleolithic culture typified by bifacial tools with round cutting edges
**à che·val** \ˌä-shə-'väl\ adverb [French, literally, on horseback] (1832)
**1** : with a leg on each side : ASTRIDE
**2** : in such a way as to be played or chanced simultaneously on two numbers or events (as in roulette)
**achieve** \ə-'chēv\ verb **achieved; achiev·ing** [Middle English acheven, from Middle French achever to finish, from a- (from Latin ad-) + chief end, head — more at CHIEF] (14th century)
transitive verb
**1** : to carry out successfully : ACCOMPLISH ⟨achieve a gradual increase in production⟩
**2** : to get or attain as the result of exertion : REACH ⟨achieved a high degree of skill⟩ ⟨achieved greatness⟩
intransitive verb
: to attain a desired end or aim : become successful
synonym see PERFORM
— **achiev·able** \-'chē-və-bəl\ adjective
— **achiev·er** noun
**achieved** adjective (1918)
: brought to or marked by a high degree of development or refinement : FINISHED ⟨fully achieved poems⟩
**achieve·ment** \ə-'chēv-mənt\ noun (15th century)
**1** : the act of achieving : ACCOMPLISHMENT
**2 a** : a result gained by effort **b** : a great or heroic deed
**3** : the quality and quantity of a student's work
synonym see FEAT
**Achil·les** \ə-'ki-lēz\ noun [Latin, from Greek Achilleus]
: the greatest warrior among the Greeks at Troy and slayer of Hector
**Achilles' heel** noun [from the story that Achilles was vulnerable only in the heel] (1864)
: a vulnerable point
**Achilles tendon** noun (circa 1879)
: the strong tendon joining the muscles in the calf of the leg to the bone of the heel
**ach·ing** \'ā-kiŋ\ adjective (13th century)
**1** : that aches ⟨an aching back⟩
**2** : causing or reflecting distress, deep emotion, or longing ⟨aching country ballads⟩
— **ach·ing·ly** adverb
**achlor·hy·dria** \ˌā-ˌklōr-'hi-drē-ə, -ˌklȯr-\ noun [New Latin, from a- + International Scientific Vocabulary chlor- + hydr- + New Latin -ia] (1898)
: absence of hydrochloric acid from the gastric juice
— **achlor·hy·dric** \-'hi-drik, -'hī-\ adjective
**achon·drite** \(ˌ)ā-'kän-ˌdrīt\ noun (circa 1904)
: a stony meteorite without rounded grains
— **achon·drit·ic** \ˌā-ˌkän-'dri-tik\ adjective
**achon·dro·pla·sia** \ˌā-ˌkän-drə-'plā-zh(ē-)ə\ noun [New Latin, from a- + chondr- + -plasia] (circa 1893)
: a genetic disorder disturbing normal growth of cartilage, resulting in a form of dwarfism characterized by a usually normal torso and shortened limbs, and usually inherited as an autosomal dominant
— **achon·dro·plas·tic** \-'plas-tik\ adjective
**ach·ro·mat** \'a-krə-ˌmat\ noun (1900)
: ACHROMATIC LENS
**ach·ro·mat·ic** \ˌa-krə-'ma-tik, (ˌ)ā-\ adjective (1766)
**1** : refracting light without dispersing it into its constituent colors : giving images practically free from extraneous colors ⟨an achromatic telescope⟩

**2** : not readily colored by the usual staining agents
**3** : possessing no hue : being or involving black, gray, or white : NEUTRAL ⟨achromatic visual sensations⟩
**4** : being without accidentals or modulation : DIATONIC
— **ach·ro·mat·i·cal·ly** \-ti-k(ə-)lē\ adverb
— **achro·ma·tism** \(ˌ)ā-'krō-mə-ˌti-zəm, a-\ noun
— **achro·ma·tize** \(ˌ)ā-'krō-mə-ˌtīz, a-\ transitive verb
**achromatic lens** noun (circa 1864)
: a lens made by combining lenses of different glasses having different focal powers so that the light emerging from the lens forms an image practically free from unwanted colors
**achy** \'ā-kē\ adjective **ach·i·er; ach·i·est** (1875)
: afflicted with aches
— **ach·i·ness** noun
**acic·u·lar** \ə-'si-kyə-lər\ adjective [Late Latin acicula (diminutive of Latin acus needle) + English -ar — more at ACUTE] (1794)
: shaped like a needle ⟨acicular leaves⟩ ⟨acicular crystals⟩
¹**ac·id** \'a-səd\ adjective [French or Latin; French acide, from Latin acidus, from acēre to be sour — more at ACET-] (1626)
**1 a** : sour, sharp, or biting to the taste **b** : sharp, biting, or sour in manner, disposition, or nature ⟨an acid individual⟩ **c** : sharply clear, discerning, or pointed ⟨an acid wit⟩ **d** : piercingly intense and often jarring ⟨acid yellow⟩
**2 a** : of, relating to, or being an acid; also : having the reactions or characteristics of an acid ⟨acid soil⟩ ⟨an acid solution⟩ **b** of salts and esters : derived by partial exchange of replaceable hydrogen ⟨acid sodium carbonate $NaHCO_3$⟩ **c** : containing or involving the use of an acid (as in manufacture) **d** : marked by or resulting from an abnormally high concentration of acid ⟨acid indigestion⟩
**3** : relating to or made by a process (as in making steel) in which the furnace is lined with acidic material and an acidic slag is used
**4** : rich in silica ⟨acid rocks⟩
— **ac·id·ly** adverb
— **ac·id·ness** noun
²**acid** noun (1696)
**1** : a sour substance; specifically : any of various typically water-soluble and sour compounds that in solution are capable of reacting with a base to form a salt, redden litmus, and have a pH less than 7, that are hydrogen-containing molecules or ions able to give up a proton to a base, or that are substances able to accept an unshared pair of electrons from a base
**2** : something incisive, biting, or sarcastic ⟨a social satire dripping with acid⟩
**3** : LSD
— **ac·idy** \'a-sə-dē\ adjective
**ac·id–fast** \'a-səd-ˌfast\ adjective (1903)
: not easily decolorized by acids
**ac·id·head** \-ˌhed\ noun (1966)
: an individual who uses LSD
**acid·ic** \ə-'si-dik, a-\ adjective (1880)
**1** : acid-forming
**2** : ACID
**acid·i·fi·er** \ə-'si-də-ˌfī(-ə)r, a-\ noun (circa 1828)
: one that acidifies; especially : a substance used to increase soil acidity
**acid·i·fy** \-ˌfī\ transitive verb **-fied; -fy·ing** (1797)
**1** : to make acid
**2** : to convert into an acid
— **acid·i·fi·ca·tion** \-ˌsi-də-fə-'kā-shən\ noun
**acid·i·met·ric** \ə-ˌsi-də-'me-trik\ adjective (1900)
: of or relating to the precise determination of the amount of acid present in a solution
— **ac·i·dim·e·ter** \ˌa-sə-'di-mə-tər\ noun
— **ac·i·dim·e·try** \-'di-mə-trē\ noun

**ac·id·i·ty** \ə-'si-də-tē, a-\ *noun, plural* **-ties** (1620)
**1** : the quality, state, or degree of being acid
**2** : the state of being excessively acid

**ac·id·o·phil** \ə-'si-də-ˌfil, a-\ *also* **ac·id·o·phile** \-ˌfīl\ *noun* (circa 1900)
` : a substance, tissue, or organism that stains readily with acid stains
— **acidophil** *also* **acidophile** *adjective*

**ac·i·do·phil·ic** \ˌa-sə-dō-'fi-lik\ *adjective* (circa 1900)
**1** : staining readily with acid stains : ACIDOPHIL
**2** : preferring or thriving in a relatively acid environment

**ac·i·doph·i·lus milk** \ˌa-sə-'dä-f(ə-)ləs-\ *noun* [New Latin *Lactobacillus acidophilus,* literally, acidophilic lactobacillus] (1921)
: milk fermented by any of several bacteria and used therapeutically to change the intestinal flora

**ac·i·do·sis** \ˌa-sə-'dō-səs\ *noun* [New Latin] (1900)
: an abnormal condition characterized by reduced alkalinity of the blood and of the body tissues
— **ac·i·dot·ic** \-'dä-tik\ *adjective*

**acid phosphatase** *noun* (1949)
: a phosphatase (as the phosphomonoesterase from the prostate gland) optimally active in acid medium

**acid precipitation** *noun* (1979)
: precipitation (as rain or snow) having increased acidity caused by environmental factors (as atmospheric pollutants)

**acid rain** *noun* (1858)
: acid precipitation in the form of rain

**acid rock** *noun* (1966)
: rock music with lyrics and sound relating to or suggestive of drug-induced experiences

**acid test** *noun* (1912)
: a severe or crucial test

**acid·u·late** \ə-'si-jə-ˌlāt\ *transitive verb* **-lat·ed; -lat·ing** [Latin *acidulus*] (1732)
: to make acid or slightly acid
— **ac·id·u·la·tion** \-ˌsi-jə-'lā-shən\ *noun*

**acid·u·lent** \ə-'si-jə-lənt\ *adjective* [French *acidulant,* from present participle of *aciduler* to acidulate, from Latin *acidulus*] (1834)
: ACIDULOUS

**acid·u·lous** \ə-'si-jə-ləs\ *adjective* [Latin *acidulus,* from *acidus*] (1769)
: somewhat acid or harsh in taste or manner

**ac·i·nar** \'a-sə-nər, -ˌnär\ *adjective* (1936)
: of, relating to, or comprising an acinus ⟨pancreatic *acinar* cells⟩

**ac·i·nus** \'a-sə-nəs\ *noun, plural* **-ni** \-ˌnī\ [New Latin, from Latin, berry, berry seed] (circa 1751)
: any of the small sacs terminating the ducts of some exocrine glands and lined with secretory cells
— **ac·i·nous** \-nəs\ *adjective*

**ack–ack** \'ak-ˌak\ *noun* [British signalmen's former telephone pronunciation of *AA,* abbreviation of *antiaircraft*] (1926)
: an antiaircraft gun; *also* : antiaircraft fire

**ackee** *variant of* AKEE

**ac·knowl·edge** \ik-'nä-lij, ak-\ *transitive verb* **-edged; -edg·ing** [*ac-* (as in *accord*) + *knowledge*] (15th century)
**1** : to recognize the rights, authority, or status of
**2** : to disclose knowledge of or agreement with
**3 a** : to express gratitude or obligation for **b** : to take notice of **c** : to make known the receipt of
**4** : to recognize as genuine or valid ⟨*acknowledge* a debt⟩ ☆

**ac·knowl·edged** \-lijd\ *adjective* (1598)
: generally recognized, accepted, or admitted
— **ac·knowl·edged·ly** \-lijd-lē, -li-jəd-\ *adverb*

**ac·knowl·edg·ment** *or* **ac·knowl·edge·ment** \ik-'nä-lij-mənt, ak-\ *noun* (1594)
**1 a** : the act of acknowledging **b** : recognition or favorable notice of an act or achievement
**2** : a thing done or given in recognition of something received
**3** : a declaration or avowal of one's act or of a fact to give it legal validity

**ac·me** \'ak-mē\ *noun* [Greek *akmē* point, highest point — more at EDGE] (1620)
: the highest point or stage; *also* : one that represents perfection of the thing expressed
**synonym** *see* SUMMIT

**ac·ne** \'ak-nē\ *noun* [Greek *aknē* eruption of the face, manuscript variant of *akmē,* literally, point] (circa 1828)
: a disorder of the skin caused by inflammation of the skin glands and hair follicles; *specifically* : a form found chiefly in adolescents and marked by pimples especially on the face
— **ac·ned** \-nēd\ *adjective*

**acock** \ə-'käk\ *adjective or adverb* (1846)
: being in a cocked position

**acoe·lo·mate** \(ˌ)ā-'sē-lə-ˌmāt\ *noun* (circa 1889)
: an invertebrate lacking a coelom; *especially* : one belonging to the group comprising the flatworms and nemerteans and characterized by bilateral symmetry and a digestive cavity that is the only internal cavity
— **acoelomate** *adjective*

**acold** \ə-'kōld\ *adjective* (14th century)
*archaic* : COLD, CHILLED ⟨the owl, for all his feathers, was *acold* —John Keats⟩

**ac·o·lyte** \'a-kə-ˌlīt\ *noun* [Middle English, from Middle French & Medieval Latin; Middle French, from Medieval Latin *acoluthus,* from Middle Greek *akolouthos,* from Greek, adjective, following, from *a-, ha-* together (akin to Greek *homos* same) + *keleuthos* path] (14th century)
**1** : one who assists the clergyman in a liturgical service by performing minor duties
**2** : one who attends or assists : FOLLOWER

**ac·o·nite** \'a-kə-ˌnīt\ *noun* [Middle French or Latin; from Latin *aconitum,* from Greek *akoniton*] (1578)
**1** : MONKSHOOD
**2** : the dried tuberous root of a common monkshood (*Aconitum napellus*) formerly used as a sedative and anodyne

**acorn** \'ā-ˌkórn, -kərn\ *noun* [Middle English *akern,* from Old English *æcern;* akin to Old English *æcer* field, Middle High German *ackeran* acorns collectively, Old Irish *áirne* sloe, Lithuanian *uoga* berry] (before 12th century)
: the nut of the oak usually seated in or surrounded by a hard woody cupule of indurated bracts

acorn

**acorn squash** *noun* (1937)
: an acorn-shaped dark green winter squash with a ridged surface and sweet yellow to orange flesh

**acorn worm** *noun* (circa 1889)
: any of a class (Enteropneusta) of burrowing wormlike marine animals having an acorn-shaped proboscis and classified with the hemichordates

acorn squash

**acous·tic** \ə-'kü-stik\ *or* **acous·ti·cal** \-sti-kəl\ *adjective* [Greek *akoustikos* of hearing, from *akouein* to hear — more at HEAR] (1605)
**1** : of or relating to the sense or organs of hearing, to sound, or to the science of sounds ⟨*acoustic* apparatus of the ear⟩ ⟨*acoustic* energy⟩: as **a** : deadening or absorbing sound ⟨*acoustic* tile⟩ **b** : operated or utilizing sound waves

**2** : of, relating to, or being a musical instrument whose sound is not electronically modified
— **acous·ti·cal·ly** \-k(ə-)lē\ *adverb*

**ac·ous·ti·cian** \ˌa-ˌkü-'sti-shən, ə-ˌkü-\ *noun* (1859)
: a specialist in acoustics

**acous·tics** \ə-'kü-stiks\ *noun plural* (1683)
**1** *singular in construction* : a science that deals with the production, control, transmission, reception, and effects of sound
**2** *also* **acoustic** : the qualities that determine the ability of an enclosure (as an auditorium) to reflect sound waves in such a way as to produce distinct hearing

**ac·quaint** \ə-'kwānt\ *transitive verb* [Middle English, from Old French *acointier,* from *acointe* familiar, from Latin *accognitus,* past participle of *accognoscere* to recognize, from *ad-* + *cognoscere* to know — more at COGNITION] (14th century)
**1** : to cause to know personally ⟨was *acquainted* with the mayor⟩
**2** : to make familiar : cause to know firsthand
**synonym** *see* INFORM

**ac·quain·tance** \ə-'kwān-t°n(t)s\ *noun* (14th century)
**1 a** : the state of being acquainted **b** : personal knowledge : FAMILIARITY
**2 a** : the persons with whom one is acquainted ⟨should auld *acquaintance* be forgot —Robert Burns⟩ **b** : a person whom one knows but who is not a particularly close friend
— **ac·quain·tance·ship** \-ˌship\ *noun*

**ac·qui·esce** \ˌa-kwē-'es\ *intransitive verb* **-esced; -esc·ing** [French *acquiescer,* from Latin *acquiescere,* from *ad-* + *quiescere* to be quiet — more at QUIESCENT] (circa 1620)
: to accept, comply, or submit tacitly or passively — often used with *in* and sometimes with *to*
**synonym** *see* ASSENT

**ac·qui·es·cence** \-'e-s°n(t)s\ *noun* (1612)
**1** : the act of acquiescing : the state of being acquiescent
**2** : an instance of acquiescing

**ac·qui·es·cent** \-'e-s°nt\ *adjective* [Latin *acquiescent-, acquiescens,* present participle of *acquiescere*] (1753)
: inclined to acquiesce
— **ac·qui·es·cent·ly** *adverb*

**ac·quir·able** \ə-'kwī-rə-bəl\ *adjective* (1646)
: capable of being acquired

**ac·quire** \ə-'kwīr\ *transitive verb* **ac·quired; ac·quir·ing** [Middle English *aqueren,* from Middle French *aquerre,* from Latin *acquirere,* from *ad-* + *quaerere* to seek, obtain] (15th century)

☆ SYNONYMS
**Acknowledge, admit, own, avow, confess** mean to disclose against one's will or inclination. ACKNOWLEDGE implies the disclosing of something that has been or might be concealed ⟨*acknowledged* an earlier peccadillo⟩. ADMIT implies reluctance to disclose, grant, or concede and refers usually to facts rather than their implications ⟨*admitted* the project was over budget⟩. OWN implies acknowledging something in close relation to oneself ⟨must *own* I know little about computers⟩. AVOW implies boldly declaring, often in the face of hostility, what one might be expected to be silent about ⟨*avowed* that he was a revolutionary⟩. CONFESS may apply to an admission of a weakness, failure, omission, or guilt ⟨*confessed* a weakness for sweets⟩.

**1** : to get as one's own: **a** : to come into possession or control of often by unspecified means **b** : to come to have as a new or added characteristic, trait, or ability (as by sustained effort or natural selection) ⟨*acquire* fluency in French⟩ ⟨bacteria that *acquire* tolerance to antibiotics⟩
**2** : to locate and hold (a desired object) in a detector ⟨*acquire* a target by radar⟩

**acquired immune deficiency syndrome** *noun* (1982)
: AIDS

**acquired immunodeficiency syndrome** *noun* (1982)
: AIDS

**acquired taste** *noun* (1858)
: one that is not easily or immediately liked or appreciated

**ac·quire·ment** \ə-'kwīr-mənt\ *noun* (1630)
**1** : a skill of mind or body usually resulting from continued endeavor
**2** : the act of acquiring

**ac·qui·si·tion** \ˌa-kwə-'zi-shən\ *noun* [Middle English *acquisicioun*, from Middle French or Latin; Middle French *acquisition*, from Latin *acquisition-*, *acquisitio*, from *acquirere*] (14th century)
**1** : the act of acquiring
**2** : something acquired or gained
— **ac·qui·si·tion·al** \-shnəl, -shə-nᵊl\ *adjective*
— **ac·quis·i·tor** \ə-'kwi-zə-tər\ *noun*

**ac·quis·i·tive** \ə-'kwi-zə-tiv\ *adjective* (1846)
: strongly desirous of acquiring and possessing
**synonym** see COVETOUS
— **ac·quis·i·tive·ly** *adverb*
— **ac·quis·i·tive·ness** *noun*

**ac·quit** \ə-'kwit\ *transitive verb* **ac·quit·ted; ac·quit·ting** [Middle English *aquiten*, from Old French *aquiter*, from *a-* (from Latin *ad-*) + *quite* free of — more at QUIT] (13th century)
**1 a** *archaic* : to pay off (as a claim or debt) **b** *obsolete* : REPAY, REQUITE
**2** : to discharge completely (as from an obligation or accusation) ⟨the court *acquitted* the prisoner⟩
**3** : to conduct (oneself) usually satisfactorily especially under stress ⟨the recruits *acquitted* themselves like veterans⟩
**synonym** see BEHAVE, EXCULPATE
— **ac·quit·ter** *noun*

**ac·quit·tal** \ə-'kwi-tᵊl\ *noun* (15th century)
: a setting free from the charge of an offense by verdict, sentence, or other legal process

**ac·quit·tance** \ə-'kwi-tᵊn(t)s\ *noun* (14th century)
: a document evidencing a discharge from an obligation; *especially* : a receipt in full

**acr-** or **acro-** *combining form* [Middle French or Greek; Middle French *acro-*, from Greek *akr-*, *akro-*, from *akros* topmost, extreme; akin to Greek *akmē* point — more at EDGE]
**1** : beginning : end : tip ⟨*acro*nym⟩
**2 a** : top : peak : summit ⟨*acro*petal⟩ **b** : height ⟨*acro*phobia⟩

**acre** \'ā-kər\ *noun* [Middle English, from Old English *æcer*; akin to Old High German *ackar* field, Latin *ager*, Greek *agros*, and perhaps to Latin *agere* to drive — more at AGENT] (before 12th century)
**1 a** *archaic* : a field especially of arable land or pastureland **b** *plural* : LANDS, ESTATE
**2** : any of various units of area; *specifically* : a unit in the U.S. and England equal to 43,560 square feet (4047 square meters) — see WEIGHT table
**3** : a broad expanse or great quantity ⟨*acres* of free publicity⟩

**acre·age** \'ā-k(ə-)rij\ *noun* (1859)
: area in acres : ACRES

**acre–foot** \'ā-kər-'fut\ *noun* (1900)
: the volume (as of irrigation water) that would cover one acre to a depth of one foot

**acre–inch** \'ā-kər-'inch\ *noun* (circa 1909)
: one twelfth of an acre-foot

**ac·rid** \'a-krəd\ *adjective* [modification of Latin *acr-*, *acer* sharp — more at EDGE] (1712)
**1** : sharp and harsh or unpleasantly pungent in taste or odor : IRRITATING
**2** : deeply or violently bitter : ACRIMONIOUS ⟨an *acrid* denunciation⟩
**synonym** see CAUSTIC
— **acrid·i·ty** \a-'kri-də-tē, ə-\ *noun*
— **ac·rid·ly** \'a-krəd-lē\ *adverb*
— **ac·rid·ness** *noun*

**ac·ri·dine** \'a-krə-ˌdēn\ *noun* (circa 1877)
: a colorless crystalline compound $C_{13}H_9N$ occurring in coal tar and important as the parent compound of dyes and pharmaceuticals

**acridine orange** *noun* (circa 1909)
: a basic orange dye structurally related to acridine and used especially to stain nucleic acids

**ac·ri·fla·vine** \ˌa-krə-'flā-ˌvēn, -vən\ *noun* [*acridine* + *flavine*] (1917)
: a yellow dye $C_{14}H_{14}N_3Cl$ used as an antiseptic especially for wounds

**Ac·ri·lan** \'a-krə-ˌlan, -lən\ *trademark*
— used for an acrylic fiber

**ac·ri·mo·ni·ous** \ˌa-krə-'mō-nē-əs\ *adjective* (1775)
: caustic, biting, or rancorous especially in feeling, language, or manner ⟨an *acrimonious* dispute⟩
— **ac·ri·mo·ni·ous·ly** *adverb*
— **ac·ri·mo·ni·ous·ness** *noun*

**ac·ri·mo·ny** \'a-krə-ˌmō-nē\ *noun*, *plural* **-nies** [Middle French or Latin; Middle French *acrimonie*, from Latin *acrimonia*, from *acr-*, *acer*] (1542)
: harsh or biting sharpness especially of words, manner, or disposition

**ac·ri·tarch** \'a-kri-ˌtärk\ *noun* [Greek *akritos* uncertain (from *a-* + *kritos*, verbal of *krinein* to decide) + *archē* beginning — more at CERTAIN, ARCH-] (1963)
: any of a group of fossil one-celled marine planktonic organisms of uncertain and possibly various taxonomic affinities held to represent the earliest known eukaryotes

**ac·ro·bat** \'a-krə-ˌbat\ *noun* [French & Greek; French *acrobate*, from Greek *akrobatēs*, from *akros* + *bainein* to go — more at COME] (1825)
**1** : one that performs gymnastic feats requiring skillful control of the body
**2 a** : one skillful at exercises of intellectual or artistic dexterity **b** : one adept at swiftly changing or adapting a position or viewpoint ⟨a political *acrobat*⟩
— **ac·ro·bat·ic** \ˌa-krə-'ba-tik\ *adjective*
— **ac·ro·bat·i·cal·ly** \-ti-k(ə-)lē\ *adverb*

**ac·ro·bat·ics** \ˌa-krə-'ba-tiks\ *noun plural but singular or plural in construction* (1882)
**1** : the art, performance, or activity of an acrobat
**2** : a spectacular, showy, or startling performance or demonstration involving great agility or complexity

**ac·ro·cen·tric** \ˌa-krō-'sen-trik\ *adjective* (1945)
: having the centromere situated so that one chromosomal arm is much shorter than the other
— **acrocentric** *noun*

**ac·ro·lect** \'a-krə-ˌlekt\ *noun* [*acr-* + *-lect* (as in *dialect*)] (1964)
: the language variety of a speech community closest to the standard or prestige form of a language

**acro·le·in** \ə-'krō-lē-ən\ *noun* [International Scientific Vocabulary *acr-* (from Latin *acr-*, *acer*) + Latin *olēre* to smell — more at ODOR] (circa 1857)
: a colorless irritant pungent liquid aldehyde $C_3H_4O$ used chiefly in organic synthesis

**ac·ro·meg·a·ly** \ˌa-krō-'me-gə-lē\ *noun* [International Scientific Vocabulary] (1889)
: chronic hyperpituitarism marked by progressive enlargement of hands, feet, and face

— **ac·ro·me·gal·ic** \-mə-'ga-lik\ *adjective or noun*

**ac·ro·nym** \'a-krə-ˌnim\ *noun* [*acr-* + *-onym*] (1943)
: a word (as *radar* or *snafu*) formed from the initial letter or letters of each of the successive parts or major parts of a compound term
— **ac·ro·nym·ic** \ˌa-krə-'ni-mik\ *adjective*
— **ac·ro·nym·i·cal·ly** \-mi-k(ə-)lē\ *adverb*

**acrop·e·tal** \ə-'krä-pə-tᵊl, a-\ *adjective* [*acr-* + *-petal* (as in *centripetal*)] (1875)
: proceeding from the base toward the apex or from below upward ⟨*acropetal* development of floral buds⟩
— **acrop·e·tal·ly** \-tᵊl-ē\ *adverb*

**ac·ro·pho·bia** \ˌa-krə-'fō-bē-ə\ *noun* [New Latin] (circa 1892)
: abnormal dread of being at a great height
— **ac·ro·phobe** \'a-krə-ˌfōb\ *noun*

**acrop·o·lis** \ə-'krä-pə-ləs\ *noun* [Greek *akropolis*, from *akr-* acr- + *polis* city — more at POLICE] (1662)
: the upper fortified part of an ancient Greek city (as Athens); *also* : a usually fortified height of a city or district elsewhere (as in Central America)

**ac·ro·some** \'a-krə-ˌsōm\ *noun* [International Scientific Vocabulary] (1899)
: an anterior prolongation of a spermatozoon that releases egg-penetrating enzymes
— **ac·ro·so·mal** \ˌa-krə-'sō-məl\ *adjective*

**¹across** \ə-'krós, *chiefly dialect* -'króst\ *adverb* [Middle English *acros*, from Anglo-French *an crois*, from *an* in (from Latin *in*) + *crois* cross, from Latin *crux*] (14th century)
**1** : in a position reaching from one side to the other : CROSSWISE
**2** : to or on the opposite side
**3** : so as to be understandable, acceptable, or successful ⟨get an argument *across*⟩

**²across** *preposition* (1591)
**1 a** : from one side to the opposite side of : OVER, THROUGH ⟨swam *across* the river⟩ **b** : on the opposite side of ⟨lives *across* the street from us⟩
**2** : so as to intersect or pass through at an angle ⟨sawed *across* the grain of the wood⟩
**3** : so as to find or meet ⟨came *across* your football in the hall closet⟩
**4 a** : THROUGHOUT ⟨obvious interest *across* the nation —Robert Goralski⟩ **b** : so as to include or take into consideration all classes or categories ⟨*across* differences, they insist, there can be no rational dialogue —Huston Smith⟩

**³across** *adjective* (1646)
: being in a crossed position

**across–the–board** *adjective* (1945)
**1** : placed to win if a competitor wins, places, or shows ⟨an *across-the-board* racing bet⟩
**2** : embracing or affecting all classes or categories : BLANKET ⟨an *across-the-board* price increase⟩

**acros·tic** \ə-'krós-tik, -'kräs-\ *noun* [Middle French & Greek; Middle French *acrostiche*, from Greek *akrostichis*, from *akr-* acr- + *stichos* line; akin to *steichein* to go — more at STAIR] (1530)
**1** : a composition usually in verse in which sets of letters (as the initial or final letters of the lines) taken in order form a word or phrase or a regular sequence of letters of the alphabet
**2** : ACRONYM
— **acrostic** *also* **acros·ti·cal** \-ti-kəl\ *adjective*
— **acros·ti·cal·ly** \-ti-k(ə-)lē\ *adverb*

**ac·ryl·am·ide** \ˌa-krᵊl-'a-ˌmīd, ə-'kri-lə-\ *noun* [*acrylic* + *amide*] (1946)
: an amide $C_3H_5NO$ that is derived from acrylic acid, that polymerizes readily, and that is used in the manufacture of synthetic textile fibers

**ac·ry·late** \'a-krə-ˌlāt\ *noun* (1873)
**1** : a salt or ester of acrylic acid
**2** : ACRYLIC RESIN

**¹acryl·ic** \ə-'kri-lik\ *adjective* [International Scientific Vocabulary *acrolein* + -*yl* + ¹-*ic*] (1855)
**1 :** of or relating to acrylic acid or its derivatives ⟨*acrylic* polymers⟩
**2 :** made or consisting of an acrylic ⟨an *acrylic* window⟩

**²acrylic** *noun* (1942)
**1 a :** ACRYLIC RESIN **b :** a paint in which the vehicle is an acrylic resin **c :** a painting done in an acrylic resin
**2 :** ACRYLIC FIBER

**acrylic acid** *noun* (circa 1855)
**:** an unsaturated liquid acid $C_3H_4O_2$ that polymerizes readily to form useful products (as constituents for varnishes and lacquers)

**acrylic fiber** *noun* (1951)
**:** a quick-drying synthetic textile fiber made by polymerization of acrylonitrile usually with other monomers

**acrylic resin** *noun* (1936)
**:** a glassy thermoplastic made by polymerizing acrylic or methacrylic acid or a derivative of either and used for cast and molded parts or as coatings and adhesives

**ac·ry·lo·ni·trile** \ˌa-krə-lō-'nī-trəl, -ˌtrēl\ *noun* (1893)
**:** a colorless volatile flammable liquid nitrile $C_3H_3N$ used chiefly in organic synthesis and for polymerization

**¹act** \'akt\ *noun* [Middle English, partly from Latin *actus* doing, act, from *agere* to drive, do; partly from Latin *actum* thing done, record, from neuter of *actus,* past participle of *agere* — more at AGENT] (14th century)
**1 a :** the doing of a thing **:** DEED **b :** something done voluntarily
**2 :** a state of real existence rather than possibility
**3 :** the formal product of a legislative body **:** STATUTE; *also* **:** a decision or determination of a sovereign, a legislative council, or a court of justice
**4 :** the process of doing **:** ACTION ⟨caught in the *act*⟩
**5** *often capitalized* **:** a formal record of something done or transacted
**6 :** one of the principal divisions of a theatrical work (as a play or opera)
**7 a :** one of successive parts or performances (as in a variety show or circus) **b :** the performer or performers in such an act **c :** a performance or presentation identified with a particular individual or group **d :** the sum of a person's actions or effects that serve to create an impression or set an example ⟨a hard *act* to follow⟩
**8 :** a display of affected behavior **:** PRETENSE

**²act** (1594)
*transitive verb*
**1 a :** to represent or perform by action especially on the stage **b :** FEIGN, SIMULATE **c :** IMPERSONATE
**2** *obsolete* **:** ACTUATE, ANIMATE
**3 :** to play the part of as if in a play ⟨*act* the man of the world⟩
**4 :** to behave in a manner suitable to ⟨*act* your age⟩
*intransitive verb*
**1 a :** to perform on the stage **b :** to behave as if performing on the stage **:** PRETEND
**2 :** to take action **:** MOVE ⟨think before *acting*⟩ ⟨*acted* favorably on the recommendation⟩
**3 :** to conduct oneself **:** BEHAVE ⟨*act* like a fool⟩
**4 :** to perform a specified function **:** SERVE ⟨trees *acting* as a windbreak⟩
**5 :** to produce an effect **:** WORK ⟨wait for a medicine to *act*⟩
**6** *of a play* **:** to be capable of being performed ⟨the play *acts* well⟩
**7 :** to give a decision or award ⟨adjourned without *acting* on the bill⟩
**— act·abil·i·ty** \ˌak-tə-'bi-lə-tē\ *noun*
**— act·able** \'ak-tə-bəl\ *adjective*

**Ac·tae·on** \ak-'tē-ən\ *noun* [Latin, from Greek *Aktaiōn*]
**:** a hunter turned into a stag and killed by his own hounds for having seen Artemis bathing

**ACTH** \ˌā-(ˌ)sē-(ˌ)tē-'āch\ *noun* [*a*dreno*c*ortico*t*ropic *h*ormone] (1944)
**:** a protein hormone of the anterior lobe of the pituitary gland that stimulates the adrenal cortex — called also *adrenocorticotropic hormone*

**ac·tin** \'ak-tən\ *noun* [International Scientific Vocabulary, from Latin *actus*] (1942)
**:** a cellular protein found especially in microfilaments (as those comprising myofibrils) and active in muscular contraction, cellular movement, and maintenance of cell shape

**actin-** *or* **actini-** *or* **actino-** *combining form* [New Latin, ray, from Greek *aktin-, aktino-,* from *aktin-, aktis;* perhaps akin to Old English *ūhte* morning twilight, Latin *noct-, nox* night — more at NIGHT]
**1 :** having a radiate form ⟨*actino*lite⟩
**2 :** actinic radiation (as X rays) ⟨*actino*meter⟩

**¹act·ing** \'ak-tiŋ\ *noun* (1664)
**:** the art or practice of representing a character on a stage or before cameras

**²acting** *adjective* (1797)
**1 :** holding a temporary rank or position **:** performing services temporarily ⟨*acting* president⟩
**2 a :** suitable for stage performance ⟨an *acting* play⟩ **b :** prepared with directions for actors ⟨an *acting* text of a play⟩

**ac·tin·i·an** \ak-'ti-nē-ən\ *noun* [New Latin *actinia,* from Greek *aktin-, aktis*] (1888)
**:** SEA ANEMONE

**ac·tin·ic** \ak-'ti-nik\ *adjective* (1844)
**:** of, relating to, resulting from, or exhibiting actinism
**— ac·tin·i·cal·ly** \-ni-k(ə-)lē\ *adverb*

**ac·ti·nide** \'ak-tə-ˌnīd\ *noun* [International Scientific Vocabulary] (1945)
**:** any of the series of elements that begins with actinium or thorium and ends with lawrencium — see PERIODIC TABLE table

**ac·ti·nism** \'ak-tə-ˌni-zəm\ *noun* (1844)
**:** the property of radiant energy especially in the visible and ultraviolet spectral regions by which chemical changes are produced

**ac·tin·i·um** \ak-'ti-nē-əm\ *noun* [New Latin] (1900)
**:** a radioactive trivalent metallic element that resembles lanthanum in chemical properties and that is found especially in pitchblende — see ELEMENT table

**ac·tin·o·lite** \ak-'ti-nºl-ˌīt\ *noun* (circa 1828)
**:** a bright or grayish green amphibole occurring in fibrous, radiate, or columnar forms

**ac·ti·nom·e·ter** \ˌak-tə-'nä-mə-tər\ *noun* (1833)
**:** any of various instruments for measuring the intensity of incident radiation; *especially* **:** one in which the intensity of radiation is measured by the speed of a photochemical reaction
**— ac·ti·no·me·tric** \-nō-'me-trik\ *adjective*
**— ac·ti·nom·e·try** \-'nä-mə-trē\ *noun*

**ac·ti·no·mor·phic** \ˌak-(ˌ)ti-nō-'mór-fik, -tə-nō-; ak-ˌti-nō-\ *adjective* [International Scientific Vocabulary] (1900)
**:** being radially symmetrical and capable of division by any longitudinal plane into essentially symmetrical halves ⟨an *actinomorphic* tulip flower⟩
**— ac·ti·no·mor·phy** \'ak-tə-nō-ˌmór-fē, ak-'ti-nō-\ *noun*

**ac·ti·no·my·ces** \ˌak-(ˌ)ti-nō-'mī-ˌsēz, -tə-nō-; ak-ˌti-nō-\ *noun, plural* **actinomyces** [New Latin, genus name, from *actin-* + Greek *mykēt-, mykēs* fungus; akin to Greek *myxa* mucus — more at MUCUS] (1882)
**:** any of a genus (*Actinomyces*) of filamentous or rod-shaped bacteria that includes usually commensal and sometimes pathogenic forms inhabiting mucosal surfaces especially of the oral cavity of warm-blooded vertebrates

**ac·ti·no·my·cete** \-'mī-ˌsēt, -ˌmī-'sēt\ *noun* [ultimately from Greek *aktin-, aktis* + *mykēt-, mykēs*] (1911)
**:** any of an order (Actinomycetales) of filamentous or rod-shaped bacteria (as the actinomyces and streptomyces)
**— ac·ti·no·my·ce·tous** \-ˌmī-'sē-təs\ *adjective*

**ac·ti·no·my·cin** \-'mī-sºn\ *noun* (1940)
**:** any of various red or yellow-red mostly toxic polypeptide antibiotics isolated from soil bacteria (especially *Streptomyces antibioticus*); *specifically* **:** one used to inhibit DNA or RNA synthesis

**ac·ti·no·my·co·sis** \-ˌmī-'kō-səs\ *noun* [New Latin] (1882)
**:** infection with or disease caused by actinomycetes; *especially* **:** a chronic disease of cattle, swine, and humans characterized by hard granulomatous masses usually in the mouth and jaw
**— ac·ti·no·my·cot·ic** \-'kä-tik\ *adjective*

**ac·ti·non** \'ak-tə-ˌnän\ *noun* [New Latin, from *actinium*] (1926)
**:** a gaseous radioactive isotope of radon that has a half-life of about 4 seconds

**ac·tion** \'ak-shən\ *noun* (14th century)
**1 :** the initiating of a proceeding in a court of justice by which one demands or enforces one's right; *also* **:** the proceeding itself
**2 :** the bringing about of an alteration by force or through a natural agency
**3 :** the manner or method of performing: **a** **:** the deportment of an actor or speaker or his expression by means of attitude, voice, and gesture **b :** the style of movement of the feet and legs (as of a horse) **c :** a function of the body or one of its parts
**4 :** an act of will
**5 a :** a thing done **:** DEED **b :** the accomplishment of a thing usually over a period of time, in stages, or with the possibility of repetition **c** *plural* **:** BEHAVIOR, CONDUCT ⟨unscrupulous *actions*⟩ **d :** INITIATIVE, ENTERPRISE ⟨a man of *action*⟩
**6 a** (1) **:** an engagement between troops or ships (2) **:** combat in war ⟨gallantry in *action*⟩ **b** (1) **:** an event or series of events forming a literary composition (2) **:** the unfolding of the events of a drama or work of fiction **:** PLOT (3) **:** the movement of incidents in a plot **c :** the combination of circumstances that constitute the subject matter of a painting or sculpture
**7 a :** an operating mechanism **b :** the manner in which a mechanism or instrument operates
**8 a :** the price movement and trading volume of a commodity, security, or market **b :** the process of betting including the offering and acceptance of a bet and determination of a winner **c :** an opportunity for financial gain ⟨a piece of the *action*⟩
**9 :** the most vigorous, productive, or exciting activity in a particular field, area, or group ⟨they itch to go where the *action* is —D. J. Henahan⟩

**ac·tion·able** \'ak-sh(ə-)nə-bəl\ *adjective* (1591)
**:** subject to or affording ground for an action or suit at law
**— ac·tion·ably** \-blē\ *adverb*

**ac·tion·less** \'ak-shən-ləs\ *adjective* (circa 1817)
**:** marked by inaction **:** IMMOBILE

**action painting** *noun* (1952)
**:** abstract expressionism marked especially by the use of spontaneous techniques (as dribbling, splattering, or smearing)
**— action painter** *noun*

**action potential** *noun* (1926)
**:** a momentary change in electrical potential

\ə\ **abut** \ºº\ **kitten** \ər\ **further** \a\ **ash** \ā\ **ace**
\ä\ **mop, mar** \au̇\ **out** \ch\ **chin** \e\ **bet** \ē\ **easy**
\g\ **go** \i\ **hit** \ī\ **ice** \j\ **job** \ŋ\ **sing** \ō\ **go**
\ȯ\ **law** \ȯi\ **boy** \th\ **thin** \th\ **the** \ü\ **loot** \u̇\ **foot**
\y\ **yet** \zh\ **vision** *see also* Guide to Pronunciation

(as between the inside of a nerve cell and the extracellular medium) that occurs when a cell or tissue has been activated by a stimulus

**ac·ti·vate** \'ak-tə-ˌvāt\ verb **-vat·ed; -vat·ing** (1626)
*transitive verb*
**:** to make active or more active: as **a** (1) **:** to make (as molecules) reactive or more reactive (2) **:** to convert (as a provitamin) into a biologically active derivative **b :** to make (a substance) radioactive **c :** to treat (as carbon or alumina) so as to improve adsorptive properties **d** (1) **:** to set up or formally institute (as a military unit) with the necessary personnel and equipment (2) **:** to put (an individual or unit) on active duty
*intransitive verb*
**:** to become active
— **ac·ti·va·tion** \ˌak-tə-'vā-shən\ *noun*
— **ac·ti·va·tor** \'ak-tə-ˌvā-tər\ *noun*

**activated carbon** *noun* (1921)
**:** a highly adsorbent powdered or granular carbon made usually by carbonization and chemical activation and used chiefly for purifying by adsorption — called also *activated charcoal*

**activation analysis** *noun* (1949)
**:** NEUTRON ACTIVATION ANALYSIS

**activation energy** *noun* (1940)
**:** the minimum amount of energy required to convert a normal stable molecule into a reactive molecule

**ac·tive** \'ak-tiv\ *adjective* [Middle English, from Middle French or Latin; Middle French *actif*, from Latin *activus*, from *actus*, past participle of *agere* to drive, do — more at AGENT] (14th century)
**1 :** characterized by action rather than by contemplation or speculation
**2 :** producing or involving action or movement
**3 a** *of a verb form or voice* **:** asserting that the person or thing represented by the grammatical subject performs the action represented by the verb ⟨*hits* in "he hits the ball" is *active*⟩ **b :** expressing action as distinct from mere existence or state
**4 :** quick in physical movement **:** LIVELY
**5 :** marked by vigorous activity **:** BUSY ⟨the stock market was *active*⟩
**6 :** requiring vigorous action or exertion ⟨*active* sports⟩
**7 :** having practical operation or results **:** EFFECTIVE ⟨an *active* law⟩
**8 a :** disposed to action **:** ENERGETIC ⟨took an *active* interest⟩ **b :** engaged in an action or activity ⟨an *active* club member⟩ **c** *of a volcano* **:** currently erupting or likely to erupt — compare DORMANT 2a, EXTINCT 1b **d :** characterized by emission of large amounts of electromagnetic energy ⟨an *active* galactic nucleus⟩
**9 :** engaged in full-time service especially in the armed forces ⟨*active* duty⟩
**10 :** marked by present operation, transaction, movement, or use ⟨*active* account⟩
**11 a :** capable of acting or reacting **:** reacting readily ⟨*active* nitrogen⟩ **b :** tending to progress or to cause degeneration ⟨*active* tuberculosis⟩ **c** *of an electronic circuit element* **:** capable of controlling voltages or currents **d** (1) **:** requiring the expenditure of energy ⟨*active* calcium ion uptake⟩ (2) **:** functioning by the emission of radiant energy ⟨radar is an *active* sensor⟩
**12 :** still eligible to win the pot in poker
**13 :** moving down the line **:** visiting in the set — used of couples in contredanses or square dances
— **active** *noun*
— **ac·tive·ly** *adverb*
— **ac·tive·ness** *noun*

**active immunity** *noun* (circa 1903)
**:** usually long-lasting immunity that is acquired through production of antibodies within the organism in response to the presence of antigens — compare PASSIVE IMMUNITY

**active transport** *noun* (1963)
**:** movement of a chemical substance by the expenditure of energy through a gradient (as across a cell membrane) in concentration or electrical potential and opposite to the direction of normal diffusion

**ac·tiv·ism** \'ak-ti-ˌvi-zəm\ *noun* (1915)
**:** a doctrine or practice that emphasizes direct vigorous action especially in support of or opposition to one side of a controversial issue
— **ac·tiv·ist** \-vist\ *noun or adjective*
— **ac·tiv·is·tic** \ˌak-ti-'vis-tik\ *adjective*

**ac·tiv·i·ty** \ak-'ti-və-tē\ *noun, plural* **-ties** (1530)
**1 :** the quality or state of being active
**2 :** vigorous or energetic action **:** LIVELINESS
**3 :** natural or normal function: as **a :** a process (as digestion) that an organism carries on or participates in by virtue of being alive **b :** a similar process actually or potentially involving mental function; *specifically* **:** an educational procedure designed to stimulate learning by firsthand experience
**4 :** an active force
**5 a :** a pursuit in which a person is active **b :** a form of organized, supervised, often extracurricular recreation
**6 :** an organizational unit for performing a specific function; *also* **:** its function or duties

**act of God** (circa 1859)
**:** an extraordinary interruption by a natural cause (as a flood or earthquake) of the usual course of events that experience, prescience, or care cannot reasonably foresee or prevent

**ac·to·my·o·sin** \ˌak-tə-'mī-ə-sən\ *noun* [International Scientific Vocabulary *actin* + *-o-* + *myosin*] (1942)
**:** a viscous contractile complex of actin and myosin concerned together with ATP in muscular contraction

**ac·tor** \'ak-tər *also* -ˌtȯr\ *noun* (15th century)
**1 :** one that acts **:** DOER
**2 a :** one who represents a character in a dramatic production **b :** a theatrical performer **c :** one that behaves as if acting a part
**3 :** one that takes part in any affair
— **ac·tor·ish** \-tə-rish\ *adjective*

**act out** *transitive verb* (1611)
**1 a :** to represent in action ⟨children *act out* what they read⟩ **b :** to translate into action ⟨unwilling to *act out* their beliefs⟩
**2 :** to express (as an impulse or a fantasy) directly in overt behavior without modification to comply with social norms

**ac·tress** \'ak-trəs\ *noun* (1676)
**:** a woman who is an actor
— **ac·tressy** \-trə-sē\ *adjective*
**usage** see -ESS

**Acts** \'akts\ *noun plural but singular in construction*
**:** a book in the New Testament narrating the beginnings of the Christian Church — called also *Acts of the Apostles;* see BIBLE table

**ac·tu·al** \'ak-ch(ə-w)əl, -sh(ə-w)əl\ *adjective* [Middle English *actuel*, from Middle French, from Late Latin *actualis*, from Latin *actus* act] (14th century)
**1** *obsolete* **:** ACTIVE
**2 a :** existing in act and not merely potentially **b :** existing in fact or reality ⟨*actual* and imagined conditions⟩ **c :** not false or apparent ⟨*actual* costs⟩
**3 :** existing or occurring at the time **:** CURRENT ⟨caught in the *actual* commission of a crime⟩

**actual cash value** *noun* (circa 1946)
**:** money equal to the cost of replacing lost, stolen, or damaged property after depreciation

**ac·tu·al·i·ty** \ˌak-chə-'wa-lə-tē, ˌak-shə-\ *noun, plural* **-ties** (1652)
**1 :** the quality or state of being actual
**2 :** something that is actual **:** FACT, REALITY ⟨possible risks which have been seized upon as *actualities* —T. S. Eliot⟩

**ac·tu·al·ize** \'ak-ch(ə-w)ə-ˌlīz, -sh(ə-w)ə-ˌlīz\ *verb* **-ized; -iz·ing** (1701)
*transitive verb*
**:** to make actual **:** REALIZE
*intransitive verb*
**:** to become actual
— **ac·tu·al·iza·tion** \ˌak-ch(ə-w)ə-lə-'zā-shən, -sh(ə-w)ə-lə-\ *noun*

**ac·tu·al·ly** \'ak-ch(ə-w)ə-lē, -sh(ə-w)ə-lē; 'aksh-lē, 'aks-\ *adverb* (15th century)
**1 :** in act or in fact **:** REALLY ⟨nominally but not *actually* independent —Karl Loewenstein⟩ ⟨don't know how old they *actually* are⟩ ⟨*actually*, they just arrived⟩
**2 :** in point of fact **:** in truth — used to suggest something unexpected ⟨I have *actually* been invited⟩ ⟨he could *actually* read the Greek⟩

**ac·tu·ar·i·al** \ˌak-chə-'wer-ē-əl, -shə-\ *adjective* (1869)
**1 :** of or relating to actuaries
**2 :** relating to statistical calculation especially of life expectancy
— **ac·tu·ar·i·al·ly** \-ē-ə-lē\ *adverb*

**ac·tu·ary** \'ak-chə-ˌwer-ē, -shə-\ *noun, plural* **-ar·ies** [Latin *actuarius* shorthand writer, alteration of *actarius,* from *actum* record — more at ACTIVE] (1553)
**1** *obsolete* **:** CLERK, REGISTRAR
**2 :** one who calculates insurance and annuity premiums, reserves, and dividends

**ac·tu·ate** \'ak-chə-ˌwāt, -shə-\ *transitive verb* **-at·ed; -at·ing** [Medieval Latin *actuatus,* past participle of *actuare* to execute, from Latin *actus* act] (1645)
**1 :** to put into mechanical action or motion
**2 :** to move to action
*synonym* see MOVE
— **ac·tu·a·tion** \ˌak-chə-'wā-shən, -shə-\ *noun*

**ac·tu·a·tor** \'ak-chə-ˌwā-tər, -shə-\ *noun* (circa 1864)
**:** one that actuates; *specifically* **:** a mechanical device for moving or controlling something

**act up** *intransitive verb* (1903)
**1 :** to act in a way different from that which is normal or expected: as **a :** to behave in an unruly, recalcitrant, or capricious manner **b :** SHOW OFF **c :** to function improperly ⟨this typewriter is *acting up* again⟩
**2 :** to become active or acute after being quiescent ⟨her rheumatism started to *act up*⟩

**acu·ity** \ə-'kyü-ə-tē, a-\ *noun, plural* **-ities** [Middle French *acuité,* from Late Latin *acuitat-, acuitas,* from Latin *acuere*] (1543)
**:** keenness of perception **:** SHARPNESS

**acu·le·ate** \ə-'kyü-lē-ət\ *adjective* [Latin *aculeatus* having stings, from *aculeus* sting, from *acus*] (1875)
**:** relating to or being hymenopterans (as bees, ants, and many wasps) of a division (Aculeata) typically having the ovipositor modified into a sting

**acu·men** \ə-'kyü-mən, 'a-kyə-mən\ *noun* [Latin *acumin-, acumen,* literally, point, from *acuere*] (circa 1580)
**:** keenness and depth of perception, discernment, or discrimination especially in practical matters **:** SHREWDNESS
*synonym* see DISCERNMENT

**acu·mi·nate** \ə-'kyü-mə-nət\ *adjective* (1646)
**:** tapering to a slender point

**acu·pres·sure** \'a-kyə-ˌpre-shər, 'a-kə-\ *noun* (1958)
**:** SHIATSU

**acu·punc·ture** \-ˌpəŋ(k)-chər\ *noun* [Latin *acus* + English *puncture*] (1684)
**:** an originally Chinese practice of puncturing the body (as with needles) at specific points to cure disease or relieve pain (as in surgery)
— **acu·punc·tur·ist** \-ˌpəŋ(k)-chə-rist\ *noun*

**acute** \ə-'kyüt\ *adjective* **acut·er; acut·est** [Latin *acutus,* past participle of *acuere* to sharpen, from *acus* needle; akin to Latin *acer* sharp — more at EDGE] (14th century)

**1 a** (1) **:** characterized by sharpness or severity ⟨*acute* pain⟩ (2) **:** having a sudden onset, sharp rise, and short course ⟨*acute* disease⟩ **b :** lasting a short time ⟨*acute* experiments⟩
**2 :** ending in a sharp point: as **a :** being or forming an angle measuring less than 90 degrees ⟨*acute* angle⟩ **b :** composed of acute angles ⟨*acute* triangle⟩
**3 a** *of an accent mark* **:** having the form ´ **b :** marked with an acute accent **c :** of the variety indicated by an acute accent
**4 a :** marked by keen discernment or intellectual perception especially of subtle distinctions **:** PENETRATING ⟨an *acute* thinker⟩ **b :** responsive to slight impressions or stimuli ⟨*acute* hearing⟩
**5 :** felt, perceived, or experienced intensely ⟨*acute* distress⟩
**6 :** seriously demanding urgent attention ☆
— **acute·ly** *adverb*
— **acute·ness** *noun*
**acy·clic** \(ˌ)ā-ʹsī-klik, -ʹsi-\ *adjective* (1878)
**:** not cyclic: as **a :** not disposed in whorls or cycles **b :** having an open-chain structure **:** ALIPHATIC ⟨an *acyclic* compound⟩
**acy·clo·vir** \(ˌ)ā-ʹsī-klō-ˌvir\ *noun* [²*a*- + *cycl*- + *virus*] (1979)
**:** a cyclic nucleoside $C_8H_{11}N_5O_3$ used especially to treat the symptoms of the genital form of herpes simplex
**ac·yl** \ʹa-səl\ *noun, often attributive* [International Scientific Vocabulary, from *acid*] (1899)
**:** a radical RCO− derived usually from an organic acid by removal of the hydroxyl from all acid groups — often used in combination
**ac·yl·ate** \ʹa-sə-ˌlāt\ *transitive verb* **-at·ed; -at·ing** (1907)
**:** to introduce an acyl group into
— **ac·yl·a·tion** \ˌa-sə-ʹlā-shən\ *noun*
**¹ad** \ʹad\ *noun, often attributive* (1841)
**1 :** ADVERTISEMENT 2
**2 :** ADVERTISING
**²ad** *noun* (1947)
**:** ADVANTAGE 4
**ad-** *or* **ac-** *or* **af-** *or* **ag-** *or* **al-** *or* **ap-** *or* **as-** *or* **at-** *prefix* [Middle English, from Middle French, Old French & Latin; Middle French, from Old French, from Latin, from *ad* — more at AT]
**1 :** to **:** toward — usually *ac-* before *c, k,* or *q* ⟨*ac*culturation⟩ and *af-* before *f* ⟨*af*fluent⟩ and *ag-* before *g* ⟨*ag*gradation⟩ and *al-* before *l* ⟨*al*literation⟩ and *ap-* before *p* ⟨*ap*portion⟩ and *as-* before *s* ⟨*as*suasive⟩ and *at-* before *t* ⟨*at*tune⟩ and *ad-* before other sounds but sometimes *ad-* even before one of the listed consonants ⟨*ad*sorb⟩
**2 :** near **:** adjacent to — in this sense always in the form *ad-* ⟨*ad*renal⟩
**¹-ad** \ˌad, əd\ *adverb suffix* [Latin *ad*]
**:** in the direction of **:** toward ⟨cephal*ad*⟩
**²-ad** *noun suffix* [probably from New Latin *-ad-, -as,* from Greek, suffix denoting descent from or connection with]
**:** member of a botanical group ⟨bromeli*ad*⟩
**Ada** \ʹā-də\ *trademark*
— used for a structured computer programming language
**ad·age** \ʹa-dij\ *noun* [Middle French, from Latin *adagium,* from *ad-* + *-agium* (akin to *aio* I say); akin to Greek *ē* he said] (1548)
**:** a saying often in metaphorical form that embodies a common observation ■
**¹ada·gio** \ə-ʹdä-j(ē-ˌ)ō, ä-, -zh(ē-ˌ)ō\ *adverb or adjective* [Italian, from *ad* to + *agio* ease] (1724)
**:** at a slow tempo — used chiefly as a direction in music
**²adagio** *noun, plural* **-gios** (1754)
**1 :** a musical composition or movement in adagio tempo
**2 :** a ballet duet by a man and woman or a mixed trio displaying difficult feats of balance, lifting, or spinning
**¹Ad·am** \ʹa-dəm\ *noun* [Middle English, from Late Latin, from Greek, from Hebrew *Ādhām*]

**1 :** the first man and father by Eve of Cain and Abel
**2 :** the unregenerate nature of man — used especially in the phrase *the old Adam*
— **Adam·ic** \ə-ʹda-mik\ *or* **Adam·i·cal** \-mi-kəl\ *adjective*
**²Adam** *adjective* [Robert *Adam* & James *Adam*] (1872)
**:** of, relating to, or being an 18th century decorative style (as of furniture) characterized by straight lines, surface decoration, and conventional designs (as festooned garlands and medallions)
**ad·a·mance** \ʹa-də-mən(t)s\ *noun* (1954)
**:** ADAMANCY
**ad·a·man·cy** \-mən(t)-sē\ *noun* [²*adamant* + *-cy*] (1937)
**:** OBSTINACY
**adam–and–eve** \ˌa-də-mən-ʹ(d)ēv\ *noun* (1807)
**:** PUTTYROOT
**¹ad·a·mant** \ʹa-də-mənt, -ˌmant\ *noun* [Middle English, from Middle French, from Latin *adamant-, adamas* hardest metal, diamond, from Greek] (14th century)
**1 :** a stone (as a diamond) formerly believed to be of impenetrable hardness
**2 :** an unbreakable or extremely hard substance
**²adamant** *adjective* (1923)
**:** unshakable or immovable especially in opposition **:** UNYIELDING
**synonym** see INFLEXIBLE
— **ad·a·mant·ly** *adverb*
**ad·a·man·tine** \ˌa-də-ʹman-ˌtēn, -ˌtīn, -ʹman-t°n\ *adjective* [Middle English, from Latin *adamantinus,* from Greek *adamantinos,* from *adamant-, adamas*] (13th century)
**1 :** made of or having the quality of adamant
**2 :** rigidly firm **:** UNYIELDING
**3 :** resembling the diamond in hardness or luster
**Adam's apple** *noun* (circa 1775)
**:** the projection in the front of the neck formed by the largest cartilage of the larynx
**Adam's needle** *noun* (circa 1760)
**:** an often cultivated yucca (*Yucca filamentosa*) of coastal pine barrens of the eastern U.S. with a basal rosette of sharp-tipped leaves having loose threads along the margins
**adapt** \ə-ʹdapt, a-\ *verb* [French or Latin; French *adapter,* from Latin *adaptare,* from *ad-* + *aptare* to fit, from *aptus* apt, fit] (15th century)
*transitive verb*
**:** to make fit (as for a specific or new use or situation) often by modification
*intransitive verb*
**:** to become adapted ☆
— **adapt·ed·ness** *noun*
**adapt·able** \ə-ʹdap-tə-bəl, a-\ *adjective* (1800)
**:** capable of being adapted **:** SUITABLE
**synonym** see PLASTIC
— **adapt·abil·i·ty** \-ˌdap-tə-ʹbi-lə-tē\ *noun*
**ad·ap·ta·tion** \ˌa-ˌdap-ʹtā-shən, -dəp-\ *noun* (1610)
**1 :** the act or process of adapting **:** the state of being adapted
**2 :** adjustment to environmental conditions: as **a :** adjustment of a sense organ to the intensity or quality of stimulation **b :** modification of an organism or its parts that makes it more fit for existence under the conditions of its environment
**3 :** something that is adapted; *specifically* **:** a composition rewritten into a new form
— **ad·ap·ta·tion·al** \-shnəl, -shə-n°l\ *adjective*
— **ad·ap·ta·tion·al·ly** *adverb*
**adapt·er** *also* **adap·tor** \ə-ʹdap-tər, a-\ *noun* (1801)
**1 :** one that adapts
**2 a :** a device for connecting two parts (as of different diameters) of an apparatus **b :** an attachment for adapting apparatus for uses not originally intended

**adap·tion** \ə-ʹdap-shən, a-\ *noun* (1704)
**:** ADAPTATION
**adap·tive** \ə-ʹdap-tiv, a-\ *adjective* (1824)
**:** showing or having a capacity for or tendency toward adaptation
— **adap·tive·ly** *adverb*
— **adap·tive·ness** *noun*
— **ad·ap·tiv·i·ty** \ˌa-ˌdap-ʹti-və-tē\ *noun*
**adaptive radiation** *noun* (1902)
**:** evolutionary diversification of a generalized ancestral form with production of a number of adaptively specialized forms
**Adar** \ä-ʹdär, ʹä-\ *noun* [Middle English, from Hebrew *Ădhār*] (14th century)
**:** the 6th month of the civil year or the 12th month of the ecclesiastical year in the Jewish calendar — see MONTH table
**Adar She·ni** \ä-ˌdär-shä-ʹnē\ *noun* [Hebrew *Ădhār Shēnī* second Adar] (circa 1901)
**:** VEADAR
**ad·ax·i·al** \(ˌ)a-ʹdak-sē-əl\ *adjective* (circa 1900)

---

☆ **SYNONYMS**
**Acute, critical, crucial** mean of uncertain outcome. ACUTE stresses intensification of conditions leading to a culmination or breaking point ⟨an *acute* housing shortage⟩. CRITICAL adds to ACUTE implications of imminent change, of attendant suspense, and of decisiveness in the outcome ⟨the war has entered a *critical* phase⟩. CRUCIAL suggests a dividing of the ways and often a test or trial involving the determination of a future course or direction ⟨a *crucial* vote⟩. See in addition SHARP.

**Adapt, adjust, accommodate, conform, reconcile** mean to bring one thing into correspondence with another. ADAPT implies a modification according to changing circumstances ⟨*adapted* themselves to the warmer climate⟩. ADJUST suggests bringing into a close and exact correspondence or harmony such as exists between parts of a mechanism ⟨*adjusted* the budget to allow for inflation⟩. ACCOMMODATE may suggest yielding or compromising to effect a correspondence ⟨*accommodated* his political beliefs in order to win⟩. CONFORM applies to bringing into accordance with a pattern, example, or principle ⟨refused to *conform* to society's idea of morality⟩. RECONCILE implies the demonstration of the underlying compatibility of things that seem to be incompatible ⟨tried to *reconcile* what they said with what I knew⟩.

---

□ **USAGE**
**adage** Quite a few commentators call *old adage* redundant because they say *adage* means "an old saying," a phrase Noah Webster did use in his definition of 1828. But *old* has been absent from Merriam-Webster definitions for more than 50 years—adages simply are not always old ⟨the popular *adage* is that 12 years is the ideal median age —Michael Jackson⟩. Even so, *old* has gone with *adage* from the beginning ⟨that old *adage* 'Much courtesy, much subtlety' —Thomas Nashe (1594)⟩. It is sometimes used actually to impute age ⟨racegoers remembered the old *adage,* "Second in the Trial, first in the Derby" —Audax Minor⟩ and is sometimes merely casual ⟨the old *adage* "misery loves company" —Natalie Babbitt⟩. It may be used where it seems apt.

---

\ə\ abut  \ᵊ\ kitten  \ər\ further  \a\ ash  \ā\ ace
\ä\ mop, mar  \au̇\ out  \ch\ chin  \e\ bet  \ē\ easy
\g\ go  \i\ hit  \ī\ ice  \j\ job  \ŋ\ sing  \ō\ go
\ȯ\ law  \ȯi\ boy  \th\ thin  \th\ the  \ü\ loot  \u̇\ foot
\y\ yet  \zh\ vision  *see also* Guide to Pronunciation

: situated on the same side as or facing the axis (as of an organ) ⟨the *adaxial* or upper surface of a leaf⟩

**add** \'ad\ *verb* [Middle English, from Latin *addere*, from *ad-* + *-dere* to put — more at DO] (14th century)
*transitive verb*
**1 :** to join or unite so as to bring about an increase or improvement ⟨*adds* 60 acres to his land⟩ ⟨wine *adds* a creative touch to cooking⟩
**2 :** to say further **:** APPEND
**3 :** to combine (numbers) into an equivalent simple quantity or number
**4 :** to include as a member of a group ⟨don't forget to *add* me in⟩
*intransitive verb*
**1 a :** to perform addition **b :** to come together or unite by addition
**2 a :** to serve as an addition ⟨the movie will *add* to his fame⟩ **b :** to make an addition ⟨*added* to her savings⟩
— **add·able** *or* **add·ible** \'a-də-bəl\ *adjective*

**ad·dax** \'a-ˌdaks\ *noun, plural* **ad·dax·es** [Latin] (1693)
**:** a large light-colored Saharan antelope (*Addax nasomaculatus*) that has long spiralling horns

**ad·dend** \'a-ˌdend, ə-'dend\ *noun* [short for *addendum*] (1674)
**:** a number to be added to another

**ad·den·dum** \ə-'den-dəm\ *noun, plural* **-den·da** \-'den-də\ [Latin, neuter of *addendus*, gerundive of *addere*] (1684)
**1 :** a thing added **:** ADDITION
**2 :** a supplement to a book — often used in plural but singular in construction

**¹ad·der** \'a-dər\ *noun* [Middle English, alteration (by false division of *a naddre*) of *naddre*, from Old English *nædre*; akin to Old High German *nātara* adder, Latin *natrix* water snake] (14th century)
**1 :** the common venomous viper (*Vipera berus*) of Europe; *broadly* **:** a terrestrial viper (family Viperidae)
**2 :** any of several North American snakes (as the hognose snakes) that are harmless but are popularly believed to be venomous

**²add·er** \'a-dər\ *noun* (1580)
**:** one that adds; *especially* **:** a device (as in a computer) that performs addition

**ad·der's–tongue** \'a-dərz-ˌtəŋ\ *noun* (1578)
**1 :** any of a genus (*Ophioglossum*, family Ophioglossaceae) of small ferns having a spore-bearing stalk resembling a serpent's tongue
**2 :** DOGTOOTH VIOLET

**¹ad·dict** \ə-'dikt\ *transitive verb* [Latin *addictus*, past participle of *addicere* to favor, from *ad-* + *dicere* to say — more at DICTION] (1534)
**1 :** to devote or surrender (oneself) to something habitually or obsessively ⟨*addicted* to gambling⟩
**2 :** to cause addiction to a substance in

**²ad·dict** \'a-(ˌ)dikt\ *noun* (1909)
**1 :** one who is addicted to a substance
**2 :** DEVOTEE ⟨a detective novel *addict*⟩

**ad·dic·tion** \ə-'dik-shən, a-\ *noun* (1599)
**1 :** the quality or state of being addicted ⟨*addiction* to reading⟩
**2 :** compulsive need for and use of a habit-forming substance (as heroin, nicotine, or alcohol) characterized by tolerance and by well-defined physiological symptoms upon withdrawal; *broadly* **:** persistent compulsive use of a substance known by the user to be harmful

**ad·dic·tive** \-'dik-tiv\ *adjective* (1939)
**:** causing or characterized by addiction

**Ad·di·son's disease** \'a-də-sənz-\ *noun* [Thomas *Addison* (died 1860) English physician] (circa 1856)
**:** a destructive disease marked by deficient adrenocortical secretion and characterized by extreme weakness, loss of weight, low blood pressure, gastrointestinal disturbances, and brownish pigmentation of the skin and mucous membranes

**ad·di·tion** \ə-'di-shən, a-\ *noun* [Middle English, from Middle French, from Latin *addition-, additio*, from *addere*] (14th century)
**1 :** a part added (as to a building or residential section)
**2 :** the result of adding **:** INCREASE
**3 :** the act or process of adding; *especially* **:** the operation of combining numbers so as to obtain an equivalent simple quantity
**4 :** direct chemical combination of substances into a single product
— **in addition :** ²BESIDES, ALSO
— **in addition to :** combined or associated with **:** ¹BESIDES 2

**ad·di·tion·al** \-'dish-nəl, -'di-shə-nəl\ *adjective* (1646)
**:** existing by way of addition **:** ADDED

**ad·di·tion·al·ly** \-'dish-nə-lē, -'di-shən-lē, 'di-shə-nəl-ē\ *adverb* (circa 1665)
**:** in or by way of addition **:** FURTHERMORE

**¹ad·di·tive** \'a-də-tiv\ *adjective* (1699)
**1 :** of, relating to, or characterized by addition
**2 :** produced by addition
**3 :** characterized by, being, or producing effects (as drug responses or gene products) that when the causative factors act together are the sum of their individual effects
— **ad·di·tive·ly** *adverb*
— **ad·di·tiv·i·ty** \ˌa-də-'ti-və-tē\ *noun*

**²additive** *noun* (1945)
**:** a substance added to another in relatively small amounts to effect a desired change in properties ⟨food *additives*⟩

**additive identity** *noun* (1960)
**:** an identity element (as 0 in the group of whole numbers under the operation of addition) that in a given mathematical system leaves unchanged any element to which it is added

**additive inverse** *noun* (1958)
**:** a number that when added to a given number gives zero ⟨the *additive inverse* of 4 is −4⟩ — compare OPPOSITE 3

**¹ad·dle** \'a-dᵊl\ *adjective* [Middle English *adel* filth, from Old English *adela*; akin to Middle Low German *adele* liquid manure] (1592)
**1** *of an egg* **:** ROTTEN
**2 :** CONFUSED

**²addle** *verb* **ad·dled; ad·dling** \'ad-liŋ, 'a-dᵊl-iŋ\ (circa 1712)
*transitive verb*
**:** to throw into confusion **:** CONFOUND
*intransitive verb*
**1 :** to become rotten **:** SPOIL
**2 :** to become confused

**ad·dle·pat·ed** \'a-dᵊl-ˌpā-təd\ *adjective* (1630)
**1 :** being mixed up **:** CONFUSED
**2 :** ECCENTRIC

**¹add–on** *noun* (1946)
**:** something added on: as **a :** a sum or amount added on **b :** something (as an accessory or added feature) that enhances the thing it is added to

**²add–on** \'a-ˌdän, -ˌdȯn\ *adjective* (1955)
**1 :** being or able to be added on
**2 :** able to be added to ⟨*add-on* certificates of deposit⟩

**¹ad·dress** \ə-'dres, a- *also* 'a-ˌdres\ *verb* [Middle English *adressen*, from Middle French *adresser*, from *a-* (from Latin *ad-*) + *dresser* to arrange — more at DRESS] (14th century)
*transitive verb*
**1** *archaic* **a :** DIRECT, AIM **b :** to direct to go **:** SEND
**2 a :** to direct the efforts or attention of (oneself) ⟨will *address* himself to the problem⟩ **b**

: to deal with **:** TREAT ⟨intrigued by the chance to *address* important issues —I. L. Horowitz⟩
**3** *archaic* **:** to make ready; *especially* **:** DRESS
**4 a :** to communicate directly ⟨*addresses* his thanks to his host⟩ **b :** to speak or write directly to; *especially* **:** to deliver a formal speech to
**5 a :** to mark directions for delivery on ⟨*address* a letter⟩ **b :** to consign to the care of another (as an agent or factor)
**6 :** to greet by a prescribed form
**7 :** to adjust the club preparatory to hitting (a golf ball)
**8 :** to identify (as a peripheral or memory location) by an address or a name for information transfer
*intransitive verb*
*obsolete* **:** to direct one's speech or attentions
— **ad·dress·er** *noun*

**²ad·dress** \ə-'dres, *for* 5 & 7 & 4 *also* 'a-ˌdres\ *noun* (1539)
**1 :** dutiful and courteous attention especially in courtship — usually used in plural
**2 a :** readiness and capability for dealing (as with a person or problem) skillfully and smoothly **:** ADROITNESS **b** *obsolete* **:** a making ready; *also* **:** a state of preparedness
**3 a :** manner of bearing oneself ⟨a man of rude *address*⟩ **b :** manner of speaking or singing **:** DELIVERY
**4 :** a formal communication; *especially* **:** a prepared speech delivered to a special audience or on a special occasion
**5 a :** a place where a person or organization may be communicated with **b :** directions for delivery on the outside of an object (as a letter or package) **c :** the designation of place of delivery placed between the heading and salutation on a business letter
**6 :** a preparatory position of the player and club in golf
**7 :** a location (as in the memory of a computer) where particular information is stored; *also* **:** the digits that identify such a location
*synonym* see TACT

**ad·dress·able** \ə-'dre-sə-bəl\ *adjective* (1953)
**1 :** able to be addressed **:** directly accessible ⟨*addressable* registers in a computer⟩
**2 :** of or relating to a subscription television system that uses decoders addressable by the system operator
— **ad·dress·abil·i·ty** \ə-ˌdre-sə-'bi-lə-tē\ *noun*

**ad·dress·ee** \ˌa-ˌdre-'sē, ə-ˌdre-'sē\ *noun* (1810)
**:** one to whom something is addressed

**ad·duce** \ə-'düs *also* -'dyüs\ *transitive verb* **ad·duced; ad·duc·ing** [Latin *adducere*, literally, to lead to, from *ad-* + *ducere* to lead — more at TOW] (15th century)
**:** to offer as example, reason, or proof in discussion or analysis
— **ad·duc·er** *noun*

**¹ad·duct** \ə-'dəkt, a-\ *transitive verb* [Latin *adductus*, past participle of *adducere*] (circa 1839)
**:** to draw (as a limb) toward or past the median axis of the body; *also* **:** to bring together (similar parts) ⟨*adduct* the fingers⟩
— **ad·duc·tive** \-'dək-tiv\ *adjective*

**²ad·duct** \'a-ˌdəkt\ *noun* [German *Addukt*, from Latin *adductus*] (1941)
**:** a chemical addition product

**ad·duc·tion** \ə-'dək-shən, a-\ *noun* (14th century)
**1 :** the action of adducting **:** the state of being adducted
**2 :** the act or action of adducing

**ad·duc·tor** \-'dək-tər\ *noun* [New Latin, from Latin, one that draws to, from *adductus*] (1615)
**1 :** a muscle that draws a part toward the median line of the body or toward the axis of an extremity
**2 :** a muscle that closes the valves of a bivalve mollusk

**add up** (1850)
*intransitive verb*
**1 a :** to come to the expected total ⟨the bill doesn't *add up*⟩ **b :** to form an intelligible pattern **:** make sense ⟨her story just doesn't *add up*⟩
**2 a :** AMOUNT 1b — used with *to* ⟨the play *adds up* to a lot of laughs⟩ **b :** to amount to a lot ⟨just a little each time, but it all *adds up*⟩
*transitive verb*
**:** to form an opinion of ⟨*added* him *up* at a glance⟩

**-ade** *noun suffix* [Middle English, from Middle French, from Old Provençal *-ada,* from Late Latin *-ata,* from Latin, feminine of *-atus* -ate]
**1 :** act **:** action ⟨block*ade*⟩
**2 :** product; *especially* **:** sweet drink ⟨lime*ade*⟩

**Adé·lie penguin** \ə-'dā-lē-\ *noun* [*Adélie* Coast, Antarctica] (1907)
**:** a small antarctic penguin (*Pygoscelis adeliae*) — called also *Adélie*

**Adélie penguin**

**-adelphous** *adjective combining form* [probably from New Latin *-adelphus,* from Greek *adelphos* brother, from *ha-, a-* together (akin to *homos* same) + *delphys* womb — more at SAME, DOLPHIN]
**:** having (such or so many) stamen fascicles ⟨mon*adelphous*⟩

**aden-** *or* **adeno-** *combining form* [New Latin, from Greek, from *aden-, adēn;* akin to Latin *inguen* groin]
**:** gland ⟨*aden*ine⟩ **:** adenoid ⟨*adeno*virus⟩

**ad·e·nine** \'a-d°n-,ēn\ *noun* [International Scientific Vocabulary, from its presence in glandular tissue] (1885)
**:** a purine base $C_5H_5N_5$ that codes hereditary information in the genetic code in DNA and RNA — compare CYTOSINE, GUANINE, THYMINE, URACIL

**ad·e·ni·tis** \,a-d°n-'ī-təs\ *noun* [New Latin] (circa 1848)
**:** inflammation of a gland; *especially* **:** LYMPH-ADENITIS

**ad·e·no·car·ci·no·ma** \,a-d°n-(,)ō-,kär-s°n-'ō-mə\ *noun* [New Latin] (circa 1889)
**:** a malignant tumor originating in glandular epithelium
— **ad·e·no·car·ci·no·ma·tous** \-mə-təs\ *adjective*

**ad·e·no·hy·poph·y·sis** \-hī-'pä-fə-səs\ *noun, plural* **-y·ses** \-fə-,sēz\ [New Latin] (1935)
**:** the anterior glandular lobe of the pituitary gland
— **ad·e·no·hy·poph·y·se·al** \-(,)hī-,pä-fə-'sē-əl\ *or* **ad·e·no·hy·po·phys·i·al** \-,hī-pə-'fi-zē-əl\ *adjective*

**¹ad·e·noid** \'a-d°n-,óid, 'ad-,nóid\ *noun* [Greek *adenoeidēs* glandular, from *adēn*] (circa 1890)
**:** an enlarged mass of lymphoid tissue at the back of the pharynx characteristically obstructing breathing — usually used in plural

**²adenoid** *adjective* (circa 1947)
**1 :** of or relating to the adenoids
**2 :** relating to, affected with, or associated with abnormally enlarged adenoids ⟨a severe *adenoid* condition⟩ ⟨*adenoid* facies⟩

**ad·e·noi·dal** \,a-d°n-'ói-d°l\ *adjective* (1919)
**:** exhibiting the characteristics (as snoring, mouth breathing, and voice nasality) of one affected with abnormally enlarged adenoids **:** ADENOID ⟨an *adenoidal* tenor⟩ — not usually used technically

**ad·e·no·ma** \,a-d°n-'ō-mə\ *noun, plural* **-mas** *also* **-ma·ta** \-mə-tə\ [New Latin *adenomat-, adenoma*] (1870)
**:** a benign tumor of a glandular structure or of glandular origin
— **ad·e·no·ma·tous** \-mə-təs\ *adjective*

**aden·o·sine** \ə-'de-nə-,sēn, -sən\ *noun* [International Scientific Vocabulary, blend of *adenine* and *ribose*] (circa 1909)
**:** a nucleoside $C_{10}H_{13}N_5O_4$ that is a constituent of RNA yielding adenine and ribose on hydrolysis

**adenosine diphosphate** *noun* (1938)
**:** ADP

**adenosine mo·no·phos·phate** \-,mä-nə-'fäs-,fāt, -,mō-\ *noun* (1950)
**:** AMP

**adenosine 3',5'–monophosphate** \-,thrē-,fīv-\ *noun* (1970)
**:** CYCLIC AMP

**adenosine tri·phos·pha·tase** \-trī-'fäs-fə-,tās, -,tāz\ *noun* (1943)
**:** ATPASE

**adenosine tri·phos·phate** \-trī-'fäs-,fāt\ *noun* (1938)
**:** ATP

**ad·e·no·vi·rus** \,a-d°n-ō-'vī-rəs\ *noun* (1956)
**:** any of a group of DNA-containing viruses originally identified in human adenoid tissue, causing respiratory diseases (as catarrh), and including some capable of inducing malignant tumors in experimental animals
— **ad·e·no·vi·ral** \-rəl\ *adjective*

**ad·e·nyl·ate cy·clase** \ə-,de-n°l-ət-'sī-,klās, -,āt-, -,klāz; ,a-d°n-,i-lət-, -ə-,lāt-\ *noun* (1968)
**:** an enzyme that catalyzes the formation of cyclic AMP from ATP

**ad·e·nyl cyclase** \'a-d°n-,il\ *noun* [*adenine* + *-yl*] (1968)
**:** ADENYLATE CYCLASE

**ad·e·nyl·ic acid** \'a-d°n-,i-lik-\ *noun* (1894)
**:** AMP

**¹ad·ept** \'a-,dept, ə-'dept, a-'\ *noun* [New Latin *adeptus* alchemist who has attained the knowledge of how to change base metals into gold, from Latin, past participle of *adipisci* to attain, from *ad-* + *apisci* to reach — more at APT] (1709)
**:** a highly skilled or well-trained individual **:** EXPERT ⟨an *adept* at chess⟩

**²adept** \ə-'dept *also* 'a-,dept\ *adjective* (circa 1691)
**:** thoroughly proficient **:** EXPERT
*synonym* see PROFICIENT
— **adept·ly** \ə-'dep-(t)lē, a-\ *adverb*
— **adept·ness** \-'dep(t)-nəs\ *noun*

**ad·e·qua·cy** \'a-di-kwə-sē\ *noun, plural* **-cies** (1808)
**:** the quality or state of being adequate

**ad·e·quate** \-kwət\ *adjective* [Latin *adaequatus,* past participle of *adaequare* to make equal, from *ad-* + *aequare* to equal — more at EQUABLE] (circa 1617)
**1 :** sufficient for a specific requirement ⟨*adequate* taxation of goods⟩; *also* **:** barely sufficient or satisfactory ⟨her first performance was merely *adequate*⟩
**2 :** lawfully and reasonably sufficient
*synonym* see SUFFICIENT
— **ad·e·quate·ly** *adverb*
— **ad·e·quate·ness** *noun*

**ad eun·dem** \,a-dē-'ən-dəm\ *or* **ad eundem gra·dum** \-'grā-dəm\ *adverb or adjective* [New Latin *ad eundem gradum*] (1711)
**:** to, in, or of the same rank — used especially of the honorary granting of academic standing or a degree by a university to one whose actual work was done elsewhere

**¹à deux** \(,)ä-'də(r), (,)ä-dœ̄\ *adjective* [French] (1886)
**:** involving two people especially in private ⟨a cozy evening *à deux*⟩

**²à deux** *adverb* (1927)
**:** privately or intimately with only two present ⟨dined *à deux*⟩

**ad·here** \ad-'hir, əd-\ *verb* **ad·hered; ad·her·ing** [Middle French or Latin; Middle French *adhérer,* from Latin *adhaerēre,* from *ad-* + *haerēre* to stick] (1536)
*intransitive verb*
**1 :** to give support or maintain loyalty
**2** *obsolete* **:** ACCORD 3

**3 :** to hold fast or stick by or as if by gluing, suction, grasping, or fusing
**4 :** to bind oneself to observance
*transitive verb*
**:** to cause to stick fast
*synonym* see STICK

**ad·her·ence** \-'hir-ən(t)s\ *noun* (1531)
**1 :** the act, action, or quality of adhering
**2 :** steady or faithful attachment **:** FIDELITY

**¹ad·her·ent** \ad-'hir-ənt, əd-\ *adjective* [Middle English, from Middle French or Latin; Middle French *adhérent,* from Latin *adhaerent-, adhaerens,* present participle of *adhaerēre*] (15th century)
**1 :** able or tending to adhere
**2 :** connected or associated with especially by contract
**3 :** ADNATE
— **ad·her·ent·ly** *adverb*

**²adherent** *noun* (15th century)
**:** one that adheres: as **a :** a follower of a leader, party, or profession **b :** a believer in or advocate especially of a particular idea or church
*synonym* see FOLLOWER

**ad·he·sion** \ad-'hē-zhən, əd-\ *noun* [French or Latin; French *adhésion,* from Latin *adhaesion-, adhaesio,* from *adhaerēre*] (1624)
**1 :** steady or firm attachment **:** ADHERENCE
**2 :** the action or state of adhering
**3 :** the abnormal union of separate tissue surfaces by new fibrous tissue resulting from an inflammatory process; *also* **:** the newly formed uniting tissue
**4 :** agreement to join ⟨*adhesion* of all nations to a copyright convention⟩
**5 :** the molecular attraction exerted between the surfaces of bodies in contact
— **ad·he·sion·al** \-'hēzh-nəl, -'hē-zhə-n°l\ *adjective*

**¹ad·he·sive** \-'hē-siv, -ziv\ *adjective* (1670)
**1 :** tending to remain in association or memory
**2 :** tending to adhere or cause adherence
**3 :** prepared for adhering
— **ad·he·sive·ly** *adverb*
— **ad·he·sive·ness** *noun*

**²adhesive** *noun* (1912)
**1 :** an adhesive substance (as glue or cement)
**2 :** a postage stamp with a gummed back

**adhesive binding** *noun* (1955)
**:** PERFECT BINDING
— **ad·he·sive–bound** \-,baùnd\ *adjective*

**adhesive tape** *noun* (1928)
**:** tape coated on one side with an adhesive mixture; *especially* **:** one used for covering wounds

**¹ad hoc** \'ad-'häk, -'hōk; 'äd-'hōk\ *adverb* [Latin, for this] (1659)
**:** for the particular end or case at hand without consideration of wider application

**²ad hoc** *adjective* (1879)
**1 a :** concerned with a particular end or purpose ⟨an *ad hoc* investigating committee⟩ **b :** formed or used for specific or immediate problems or needs ⟨*ad hoc* solutions⟩
**2 :** fashioned from whatever is immediately available **:** IMPROVISED ⟨large *ad hoc* parades and demonstrations —Nat Hentoff⟩

**¹ad ho·mi·nem** \(')ad-'hä-mə-,nem, -nəm\ *adjective* [New Latin, literally, to the person] (1598)
**1 :** appealing to feelings or prejudices rather than intellect
**2 :** marked by an attack on an opponent's character rather than by an answer to the contentions made

**²ad hominem** *adverb* (1962)
**:** in an ad hominem manner ⟨was arguing *ad hominem*⟩

**adi·a·bat·ic** \ˌa-dē-ə-'ba-tik, ˌā-ˌdī-ə-\ *adjective* [Greek *adiabatos* impassable, from *a-* + *diabatos* passable, from *diabainein* to go across, from *dia-* + *bainein* to go — more at COME] (1870)
: occurring without loss or gain of heat ⟨*adiabatic* expansion of a body of air⟩
— **adi·a·bat·i·cal·ly** \-ti-k(ə-)lē\ *adverb*

**adieu** \ə-'dü, -'dyü\ *noun, plural* **adieus** *or* **adieux** \-'düz, -'dyüz\ [Middle English, from Middle French, from *a* (from Latin *ad*) + *Dieu* God, from Latin *Deus* — more at DEITY] (14th century)
: FAREWELL — often used interjectionally

**ad in·fi·ni·tum** \ˌad-ˌin-fə-'nī-təm *also* ˌäd-\ *adverb or adjective* [Latin] (1610)
: without end or limit

**¹ad in·ter·im** \'ad-'in-tə-rəm, -ˌrim *also* 'äd-\ *adverb* [Latin] (1787)
: for the intervening time : TEMPORARILY

**²ad interim** *adjective* (1818)
: made or serving ad interim

**adi·os** \ˌä-dē-'ōs, ˌa-\ *interjection* [Spanish *adiós*, from *a* (from Latin *ad*) + *Dios* God, from Latin *Deus*] (1837)
— used to express farewell

**adip-** *or* **adipo-** *combining form* [Latin *adip-, adeps*, probably from Greek *aleipha* fat, oil, from *aleiphein* to rub with oil — more at ALIPHATIC]
: fat ⟨*adip*ocyte⟩

**adip·ic acid** \ə-'di-pik-\ *noun* [International Scientific Vocabulary] (1877)
: a white crystalline dicarboxylic acid $C_6H_{10}O_4$ formed by oxidation of various fats and also made synthetically for use especially in the manufacture of nylon

**ad·i·po·cyte** \'a-di-pō-ˌsīt\ *noun* (1959)
: FAT CELL

**ad·i·pose** \'a-də-ˌpōs\ *adjective* [New Latin *adiposus*, from Latin *adip-, adeps*] (1743)
: of or relating to animal fat; *broadly* : FAT
— **ad·i·pos·i·ty** \ˌa-də-'pä-sə-tē\ *noun*

**adipose tissue** *noun* (1854)
: connective tissue in which fat is stored and which has the cells distended by droplets of fat

**ad·it** \'a-dət\ *noun* [Latin *aditus* approach, from *adire* to go to, from *ad-* + *ire* to go — more at ISSUE] (1602)
: a nearly horizontal passage from the surface in a mine

**ad·ja·cen·cy** \ə-'jā-s°n(t)-sē\ *noun, plural* **-cies** (1646)
**1** : something that is adjacent
**2** : the quality or state of being adjacent : CONTIGUITY

**ad·ja·cent** \ə-'jā-s°nt\ *adjective* [Middle English, from Middle French or Latin; Middle French, from Latin *adjacent-, adjacens,* present participle of *adjacēre* to lie near, from *ad-* + *jacēre* to lie; akin to Latin *jacere* to throw — more at JET] (15th century)
**1 a** : not distant : NEARBY ⟨the city and *adjacent* suburbs⟩ **b** : having a common endpoint or border ⟨*adjacent* lots⟩ ⟨*adjacent* sides of a triangle⟩ **c** : immediately preceding or following
**2** *of two angles* : having the vertex and one side in common ☆
— **ad·ja·cent·ly** *adverb*

**ad·jec·ti·val** \ˌa-jik-'tī-vəl\ *adjective* (1797)
**1** : ADJECTIVE
**2** : characterized by the use of adjectives
— **ad·jec·ti·val·ly** \-və-lē\ *adverb*

**¹ad·jec·tive** \'a-jik-tiv *also* ˌa-jik-'tiv\ *adjective* [Middle English, from Middle French or Late Latin; Middle French *adjectif,* from Late Latin *adjectivus,* from Latin *adjectus,* past participle of *adjicere* to throw to, from *ad-* + *jacere* to throw — more at JET] (14th century)
**1** : of, relating to, or functioning as an adjective ⟨an *adjective* clause⟩
**2** : not standing by itself : DEPENDENT
**3** : requiring or employing a mordant ⟨*adjective* dyes⟩

**4** : PROCEDURAL ⟨*adjective* law⟩
— **ad·jec·tive·ly** *adverb*

**²adjective** *noun* (14th century)
: a word belonging to one of the major form classes in any of numerous languages and typically serving as a modifier of a noun to denote a quality of the thing named, to indicate its quantity or extent, or to specify a thing as distinct from something else

**ad·join** \ə-'jóin, a-\ *verb* [Middle English, from Middle French *adjoindre,* from Latin *adjungere,* from *ad-* + *jungere* to join — more at YOKE] (14th century)
*transitive verb*
**1** : to add or attach by joining
**2** : to lie next to or in contact with
*intransitive verb*
: to be close to or in contact with one another

**ad·join·ing** *adjective* (15th century)
: touching or bounding at a point or line
**synonym** see ADJACENT

**ad·joint** \'a-ˌjóint\ *noun* [French, from past participle of *adjoindre* to adjoin] (1907)
: the transpose of a matrix in which each element is replaced by its cofactor

**ad·journ** \ə-'jərn\ *verb* [Middle English *ajournen,* from Middle French *ajourner,* from *a-* (from Latin *ad-*) + *jour* day — more at JOURNEY] (15th century)
*transitive verb*
: to suspend indefinitely or until a later stated time
*intransitive verb*
**1** : to suspend a session indefinitely or to another time or place
**2** : to move to another place

**ad·journ·ment** \-mənt\ *noun* (1607)
**1** : the act of adjourning
**2** : the state or interval of being adjourned

**ad·judge** \ə-'jəj\ *transitive verb* **ad·judged; ad·judg·ing** [Middle English *ajugen,* from Middle French *ajugier,* from Latin *adjudicare,* from *ad-* + *judicare* to judge — more at JUDGE] (14th century)
**1 a** : to decide or rule upon as a judge : ADJUDICATE **b** : to pronounce judicially : RULE
**2** *archaic* : SENTENCE, CONDEMN
**3** : to hold or pronounce to be : DEEM ⟨*adjudge* the book a success⟩
**4** : to award or grant judicially in a case of controversy

**ad·ju·di·cate** \ə-'jü-di-ˌkāt\ *verb* **-cat·ed; -cat·ing** (1775)
*transitive verb*
: to settle judicially
*intransitive verb*
: to act as judge
— **ad·ju·di·ca·tive** \-ˌkā-tiv, -kə-\ *adjective*
— **ad·ju·di·ca·tor** \-ˌkā-tər\ *noun*

**ad·ju·di·ca·tion** \ə-ˌjü-di-'kā-shən\ *noun* [French or Late Latin; French, from Late Latin *adjudicatio,* from Latin *adjudicare*] (1691)
**1** : the act or process of adjudicating
**2 a** : a judicial decision or sentence **b** : a decree in bankruptcy
— **ad·ju·di·ca·to·ry** \-'jü-di-kə-ˌtōr-ē, -ˌtór-\ *adjective*

**¹ad·junct** \'a-ˌjəŋ(k)t\ *noun* [Latin *adjunctum,* from neuter of *adjunctus,* past participle of *adjungere*] (1588)
**1** : something joined or added to another thing but not essentially a part of it
**2 a** : a word or word group that qualifies or completes the meaning of another word or other words and is not itself a main structural element in its sentence **b** : an adverb or adverbial (as *heartily* in "Most children eat heartily" or *at noon* in "We will leave at noon") attached to the verb of a clause especially to express a relation of time, place, frequency, degree, or manner — compare DISJUNCT 2
**3** : an associate or assistant of another
— **ad·junc·tive** \a-'jəŋ(k)-tiv, ə-\ *adjective*

**²adjunct** *adjective* (1595)
**1** : added or joined as an accompanying object or circumstance

**2** : attached in a subordinate or temporary capacity to a staff ⟨an *adjunct* psychiatrist⟩
— **ad·junct·ly** \'a-ˌjəŋ(k)-tlē, -ˌjəŋ-klē\ *adverb*

**ad·junc·tion** \a-'jəŋ(k)-shən\ *noun* (1618)
: the act or process of adjoining

**ad·ju·ra·tion** \ˌa-jə-'rā-shən\ *noun* (1611)
**1** : a solemn oath
**2** : an earnest urging or advising
— **ad·jur·a·to·ry** \ə-'jur-ə-ˌtōr-ē, -ˌtór-\ *adjective*

**ad·jure** \ə-'jur\ *transitive verb* **ad·jured; ad·jur·ing** [Middle English, from Middle French & Latin; Middle French *ajurer,* from Latin *adjurare,* from *ad-* + *jurare* to swear — more at JURY] (14th century)
**1** : to command solemnly under or as if under oath or penalty of a curse
**2** : to urge or advise earnestly
**synonym** see BEG

**ad·just** \ə-'jəst\ *verb* [Middle English *ajusten,* from Middle French *ajuster* to gauge, adjust, from *a-* (from Latin *ad-*) + *juste* right, exact — more at JUST] (14th century)
*transitive verb*
**1 a** : to bring to a more satisfactory state: (1) : SETTLE, RESOLVE (2) : RECTIFY **b** : to make correspondent or conformable : ADAPT **c** : to bring the parts of to a true or more effective relative position ⟨*adjust* a carburetor⟩
**2** : to reduce to a system : REGULATE
**3** : to determine the amount to be paid under an insurance policy in settlement of (a loss)
*intransitive verb*
**1** : to adapt or conform oneself (as to new conditions)
**2** : to achieve mental and behavioral balance between one's own needs and the demands of others
**synonym** see ADAPT
— **ad·just·abil·i·ty** \-ˌjəs-tə-'bi-lə-tē\ *noun*
— **ad·just·able** \-'jəs-tə-bəl\ *adjective*
— **ad·jus·tive** \-'jəs-tiv\ *adjective*

**adjustable rate mortgage** *noun* (1981)
: a mortgage having an interest rate which is usually initially lower than that of a mortgage with a fixed rate but is adjusted periodically according to the cost of funds to the lender

**ad·just·ed** *adjective* (circa 1674)
**1** : accommodated to suit a particular set of circumstances or requirements
**2** : having achieved an often specified and usually harmonious relationship with the environment or with other individuals ⟨a well-*adjusted* schoolchild⟩

**ad·just·er** *also* **ad·jus·tor** \ə-'jəs-tər\ *noun* (1673)
: one that adjusts; *especially* : an insurance agent who investigates personal or property damage and makes estimates for effecting settlements

**ad·just·ment** \ə-'jəs(t)-mənt\ *noun* (1644)
**1** : the act or process of adjusting
**2** : a settlement of a claim or debt in a case in which the amount involved is uncertain or full payment is not made
**3** : the state of being adjusted
**4** : a means (as a mechanism) by which things are adjusted one to another

---

☆ **SYNONYMS**
**Adjacent, adjoining, contiguous, juxtaposed** mean being in close proximity. AD-JACENT may or may not imply contact but always implies absence of anything of the same kind in between ⟨a house with an *adjacent* garage⟩. ADJOINING definitely implies meeting and touching at some point or line ⟨had *adjoining* rooms at the hotel⟩. CONTIGUOUS implies having contact on all or most of one side ⟨offices in all 48 *contiguous* states⟩. JUXTAPOSED means placed side by side especially so as to permit comparison and contrast ⟨a skyscraper *juxtaposed* to a church⟩.

**5 :** a correction or modification to reflect actual conditions
— **ad·just·men·tal** \ə-,jəs(t)-'men-t<sup>ə</sup>l, ,a-,jəs(t)-\ *adjective*

**ad·ju·tan·cy** \'a-jə-tən(t)-sē\ *noun* (1775)
**:** the office or rank of an adjutant

**ad·ju·tant** \'a-jə-tənt\ *noun* [Latin *adjutant-, adjutans,* present participle of *adjutare* to help — more at AID] (1539)
**1 :** a staff officer in the army, air force, or marine corps who assists the commanding officer and is responsible especially for correspondence
**2 :** one who helps **:** ASSISTANT

**adjutant general** *noun, plural* **adjutants general** (1645)
**1 :** the chief administrative officer of an army who is responsible especially for the administration and preservation of personnel records
**2 :** the chief administrative officer of a major military unit (as a division or corps)

**¹ad·ju·vant** \'a-jə-vənt\ *adjective* [French or Latin; French, from Latin *adjuvant-, adjuvans,* present participle of *adjuvare* to aid — more at AID] (1574)
**1 :** serving to aid or contribute **:** AUXILIARY
**2 :** assisting in the prevention, amelioration, or cure of disease ⟨*adjuvant* chemotherapy following surgery⟩

**²adjuvant** *noun* (1609)
**:** one that helps or facilitates: as **a :** an ingredient (as in a prescription or a solution) that modifies the action of the principal ingredient **b :** something (as a drug or method) that enhances the effectiveness of medical treatment **c :** a substance enhancing the immune response to an antigen

**Ad·le·ri·an** \äd-'lir-ē-ən, ad-\ *adjective* [Alfred *Adler*] (1924)
**:** of, relating to, or being a theory and technique of psychotherapy emphasizing the importance of feelings of inferiority, a will to power, and overcompensation in neurotic processes

**¹ad·lib** \'ad-'lib\ *verb* **ad–libbed; ad–lib·bing** [*ad lib*] (1919)
*transitive verb*
**:** to deliver spontaneously
*intransitive verb*
**:** to improvise especially lines or a speech
— **ad–lib** *noun*

**²ad–lib** *adjective* (1935)
**:** spoken, composed, or performed without preparation

**ad lib** *adverb* [New Latin *ad libitum*] (circa 1811)
**1 :** in accordance with one's wishes
**2 :** without restraint or limit

**¹ad li·bi·tum** \(,)ad-'li-bə-təm\ *adverb* [New Latin, in accordance with desire] (1610)
**:** AD LIB ⟨rats fed *ad libitum*⟩

**²ad libitum** *adjective* (circa 1801)
**:** omissible according to a performer's wishes — used as a direction in music; compare OBBLIGATO

**ad·man** \'ad-,man\ *noun* (1909)
**:** a person who writes, solicits, or places advertisements

**ad·mass** \'ad-,mas\ *noun, often attributive* [*advertising* + *mass*] (1955)
*chiefly British* **:** mass-media advertising; *also* **:** the society influenced by it

**ad·mea·sure** \ad-'me-zhər, -'mā-\ *transitive verb* **-sured; -sur·ing** [Middle English *amesuren,* from Middle French *amesurer,* from *a-* (from Latin *ad-*) + *mesurer* to measure] (1641)
**:** to determine the proper share of **:** APPORTION

**ad·mea·sure·ment** \-'me-zhər-mənt, -'mā-\ *noun* (1523)
**1 :** determination and apportionment of shares
**2 :** determination or comparison of dimensions
**3 :** DIMENSIONS, SIZE

**Ad·me·tus** \ad-'mē-təs\ *noun* [Latin, from Greek *Admētos*]
**:** a king of Pherae who is saved by Apollo from his fated death when his wife Alcestis offers to die in his place

**ad·min·is·ter** \əd-'mi-nə-stər\ *verb* **-is·tered; -is·ter·ing** \-st(ə-)riŋ\ [Middle English *administren,* from Middle French *administrer,* from Latin *administrare,* from *ad-* + *ministrare* to serve, from *minister* servant — more at MINISTER] (14th century)
*transitive verb*
**1 :** to manage or supervise the execution, use, or conduct of ⟨*administer* a trust fund⟩
**2 a :** to mete out **:** DISPENSE ⟨*administer* punishment⟩ **b :** to give ritually ⟨*administer* the last rites⟩ **c :** to give remedially ⟨*administer* a dose of medicine⟩
*intransitive verb*
**1 :** to perform the office of administrator
**2 :** to furnish a benefit **:** MINISTER ⟨*administer* to an ailing friend⟩
**3 :** to manage affairs
— **ad·min·is·tra·ble** \-strə-bəl\ *adjective*
— **ad·min·is·trant** \-strənt\ *noun*

**ad·min·is·trate** \-,strāt\ *verb* **-trat·ed; -trat·ing** [Latin *administratus,* past participle of *administrare*] (circa 1617)
**:** ADMINISTER

**ad·min·is·tra·tion** \əd-,mi-nə-'strā-shən, (,)ad-\ *noun* (14th century)
**1 :** performance of executive duties **:** MANAGEMENT
**2 :** the act or process of administering
**3 :** the execution of public affairs as distinguished from policy-making
**4 a :** a body of persons who administer **b** *often capitalized* **:** a group constituting the political executive in a presidential government **c :** a governmental agency or board
**5 :** the term of office of an administrative officer or body

**ad·min·is·tra·tive** \əd-'mi-nə-,strā-tiv, -strə-\ *adjective* (circa 1731)
**:** of or relating to administration or an administration **:** EXECUTIVE
— **ad·min·is·tra·tive·ly** *adverb*

**administrative county** *noun* (1949)
**:** a British local administrative unit often not coincident with an older county

**administrative law** *noun* (1896)
**:** law dealing with the establishment, duties, and powers of and available remedies against authorized agencies in the executive branch of the government

**ad·min·is·tra·tor** \əd-'mi-nə-,strā-tər, -,strā-,tȯr\ *noun* (15th century)
**1 :** a person legally vested with the right of administration of an estate
**2 a :** one that administers especially business, school, or governmental affairs **b :** a priest appointed to administer a diocese or parish temporarily

**ad·min·is·tra·trix** \-,mi-nə-'strā-triks\ *noun, plural* **-tra·tri·ces** \-'strā-trə-,sēz\ [New Latin] (circa 1623)
**:** a woman administrator especially of an estate

**ad·mi·ra·ble** \'ad-m(ə-)rə-bəl\ *adjective* (15th century)
**1 :** deserving the highest esteem **:** EXCELLENT
**2** *obsolete* **:** exciting wonder **:** SURPRISING
— **ad·mi·ra·bil·i·ty** \,ad-m(ə-)rə-'bi-lə-tē\ *noun*
— **ad·mi·ra·ble·ness** \'ad-m(ə-)rə-bəl-nəs\ *noun*
— **ad·mi·ra·bly** \-blē\ *adverb*

**ad·mi·ral** \'ad-m(ə-)rəl\ *noun* [Middle English, from Middle French *amiral* admiral & Medieval Latin *admiralis* emir, *admirallus* admiral, from Arabic *amīr-al-* commander of the (as in *amīr-al-baḥr* commander of the sea)] (15th century)
**1** *archaic* **:** the commander in chief of a navy
**2 a :** FLAG OFFICER **b :** a commissioned officer in the navy or coast guard who ranks above a vice admiral and whose insignia is four stars — compare GENERAL

**3** *archaic* **:** FLAGSHIP
**4 :** any of several brightly colored butterflies (family Nymphalidae) ◆

**admiral of the fleet** (1660)
**:** the highest-ranking officer of the British navy

**ad·mi·ral·ty** \'ad-m(ə-)rəl-tē\ *noun* (15th century)
**1** *capitalized* **:** the executive department or officers formerly having general authority over British naval affairs
**2 :** the court having jurisdiction over questions of maritime law; *also* **:** the system of law administered by admiralty courts

**ad·mi·ra·tion** \,ad-mə-'rā-shən\ *noun* (15th century)
**1** *archaic* **:** WONDER
**2 :** an object of esteem
**3 :** delighted or astonished approbation

**ad·mire** \əd-'mīr\ *verb* **ad·mired; ad·mir·ing** [Middle French *admirer,* from Latin *admirari,* from *ad-* + *mirari* to wonder, from *mirus* astonishing] (1579)
*transitive verb*
**1** *archaic* **:** to marvel at
**2 :** to regard with admiration
*intransitive verb*
*dialect* **:** to like very much ⟨I would *admire* to know why not —A. H. Lewis⟩
*synonym* see REGARD
— **ad·mir·er** *noun*
— **ad·mir·ing·ly** \-'mī-riŋ-lē\ *adverb*

**ad·mis·si·ble** \əd-'mi-sə-bəl, ad-\ *adjective* [French, from Medieval Latin *admissibilis,* from Latin *admissus,* past participle of *admittere*] (circa 1611)
**1 :** capable of being allowed or conceded **:** PERMISSIBLE ⟨evidence legally *admissible* in court⟩
**2 :** capable or worthy of being admitted ⟨*admissible* to the university⟩
— **ad·mis·si·bil·i·ty** \-,mi-sə-'bi-lə-tē\ *noun*

**ad·mis·sion** \əd-'mi-shən, ad-\ *noun* (15th century)
**1 a :** the act or process of admitting **b :** the state or privilege of being admitted **c :** a fee paid at or for admission
**2 a :** the granting of an argument or position not fully proved **b :** acknowledgment that a fact or statement is true
*synonym* see ADMITTANCE

◇ WORD HISTORY
**admiral** It is a curiosity of history that *admiral,* a word meaning "naval commander," ultimately has its source in Arabic, the language of a desert people who acquired their seafaring skills largely from the Mediterranean peoples they dominated after the great Islamic expansion of the 7th century. As a name for a Muslim chieftain, the Arabic word *amīr* "commander" appears as early as the 9th century in Medieval Latin documents, in forms such as *amiratus, amirandus,* and *admirallus.* These display a variety of suffixes and an extraneous *d* through confusion with the Latin verb *admirari* "to admire." The ending *-allus* is probably from the Arabic definite article *al,* which actually belongs to the following word in phrases such as *amīr al-ʿalī* "supreme commander." The specific application of *admirallus* to a commander of a fleet originated in 12th century Sicily, when it was ruled by the Normans. This usage was acquired by the Genoese and then spread to the rest of western Europe, including France and England.

\ə\ **abut** \<sup>ə</sup>\ **kitten** \ər\ **further** \a\ **ash** \ā\ **ace**
\ä\ **mop, mar** \au̇\ **out** \ch\ **chin** \e\ **bet** \ē\ **easy**
\g\ **go** \i\ **hit** \ī\ **ice** \j\ **job** \ŋ\ **sing** \ō\ **go**
\ȯ\ **law** \ȯi\ **boy** \th\ **thin** \t͟h\ **the** \ü\ **loot** \u̇\ **foot**
\y\ **yet** \zh\ **vision** *see also* Guide to Pronunciation

— **ad·mis·sive** \-'mi-siv\ *adjective*

**ad·mit** \əd-'mit, ad-\ *verb* **ad·mit·ted; ad·mit·ting** [Middle English *admitten*, from Latin *admittere*, from *ad-* + *mittere* to send] (15th century)
*transitive verb*
**1 a :** to allow scope for **:** PERMIT ⟨*admits* no possibility of misunderstanding⟩ **b :** to concede as true or valid ⟨*admitted* making a mistake⟩
**2 :** to allow entry (as to a place, fellowship, or privilege) ⟨an open window had *admitted* rain⟩ ⟨*admitted* to the club⟩
*intransitive verb*
**1 :** to give entrance or access
**2 a :** ALLOW, PERMIT ⟨*admits* of two interpretations⟩ **b :** to make acknowledgment — used with *to*
**synonym** *see* ACKNOWLEDGE

**ad·mit·tance** \əd-'mi-t°n(t)s, ad-\ *noun* (1536)
**1 :** permission to enter (as a place or office) **:** ENTRANCE
**2 :** the reciprocal of the impedance of a circuit ☆

**ad·mit·ted·ly** \əd-'mi-təd-lē, ad-\ *adverb* (1804)
**1 :** as has been or must be admitted ⟨an *admittedly* inadequate treatment⟩
**2 :** it must be admitted ⟨*admittedly*, we took a chance⟩

**ad·mix** \ad-'miks\ *transitive verb* [back-formation from obsolete *admixt* mingled (with), from Middle English, from Latin *admixtus*] (1533)
**:** to mix in

**ad·mix·ture** \ad-'miks-chər\ *noun* [Latin *admixtus*, past participle of *admiscēre* to mix with, from *ad-* + *miscēre* to mix — more at MIX] (1605)
**1 a :** the action of mixing **b :** the fact of being mixed
**2 a :** something added by mixing **b :** a product of mixing **:** MIXTURE

**ad·mon·ish** \ad-'mä-nish\ *transitive verb* [Middle English *admonesten*, from Middle French *admonester*, from (assumed) Vulgar Latin *admonestare*, alteration of Latin *admonēre* to warn, from *ad-* + *monēre* to warn — more at MIND] (14th century)
**1 a :** to indicate duties or obligations to **b :** to express warning or disapproval to especially in a gentle, earnest, or solicitous manner
**2 :** to give friendly earnest advice or encouragement to
**synonym** *see* REPROVE
— **ad·mon·ish·er** *noun*
— **ad·mon·ish·ing·ly** \-ni-shiŋ-lē\ *adverb*
— **ad·mon·ish·ment** \-mənt\ *noun*

**ad·mo·ni·tion** \ˌad-mə-'ni-shən\ *noun* [Middle English *amonicioun*, from Middle French *amonition*, from Latin *admonition-, admonitio*, from *admonēre*] (14th century)
**1 :** gentle or friendly reproof
**2 :** counsel or warning against fault or oversight

**ad·mon·i·to·ry** \əd-'mä-nə-ˌtōr-ē, -ˌtȯr-\ *adjective* (1594)
**:** expressing admonition **:** WARNING
— **ad·mon·i·to·ri·ly** \-ˌmä-nə-'tōr-ə-lē, -'tȯr-\ *adverb*

**ad·nate** \'ad-ˌnāt\ *adjective* [Latin *adnatus, adgnatus*, past participle of *adgnasci* to be born in addition, grow later — more at AGNATE] (1661)
**:** grown to a usually unlike part especially along a margin ⟨a calyx *adnate* to the ovary⟩
— **ad·na·tion** \ad-'nā-shən\ *noun*

**ad nau·se·am** \ad-'nȯ-zē-əm *also* -ˌam\ *adverb* [Latin] (1647)
**:** to a sickening or excessive degree

**ad·nexa** \ad-'nek-sə\ *noun plural* [New Latin, from Latin *annexa*, neuter plural of *annexus*, past participle of *annectere* to bind to — more at ANNEX] (1899)

**:** conjoined, subordinate, or associated anatomic parts
— **ad·nex·al** \-səl\ *adjective*

**ado** \ə-'dü\ *noun* [Middle English, from *at do*, from *at* + *don, do* to do] (14th century)
**1 :** fussy bustling excitement **:** TO-DO
**2 :** time-wasting bother over trivial details ⟨wrote the paper without further *ado*⟩
**3 :** TROUBLE, DIFFICULTY

**adobe** \ə-'dō-bē\ *noun* [Spanish, from Arabic *aṭ-ṭūb* the brick, from Coptic *tōbe* brick] (1748)
**1 :** a brick or building material of sun-dried earth and straw
**2 :** a structure made of adobe bricks
**3 :** a heavy clay used in making adobe bricks; *broadly* **:** alluvial or playa clay in desert or arid regions
— **ado·be·like** \-ˌlīk\ *adjective*

adobe 2

**ado·bo** \ə-'dō-bo, ä-'thō-bō\ *noun, plural* **-bos** [Spanish] (circa 1951)
**:** a Philippine dish of fish or meat marinated in a sauce usually containing vinegar and garlic, browned in fat, and simmered in the marinade

**ad·o·les·cence** \ˌa-d°l-'e-s°n(t)s\ *noun* (15th century)
**1 :** the state or process of growing up
**2 :** the period of life from puberty to maturity terminating legally at the age of majority
**3 :** a stage of development (as of a language or culture) prior to maturity

**¹ad·o·les·cent** \-s°nt\ *noun* [French, from Latin *adolescent-, adolescens*, present participle of *adolescere* to grow up — more at ADULT] (15th century)
**:** one that is in the state of adolescence

**²adolescent** *adjective* (1785)
**1 :** of, relating to, or being in adolescence
**2 :** emotionally or intellectually immature
— **ad·o·les·cent·ly** *adverb*

**Ado·nai** \ˌä-də-'nói, -'nī\ *noun* [Hebrew *ădhōnāy*] (14th century)
— used as a name of the God of the Hebrews

**Ado·nis** \ə-'dä-nəs, -'dō-\ *noun* [Latin, from Greek *Adōnis*]
**1 :** a youth loved by Aphrodite who is killed at hunting by a wild boar and restored to Aphrodite from Hades for a part of each year
**2 :** a very handsome young man

**adopt** \ə-'däpt\ *transitive verb* [Middle English, from Middle French or Latin; Middle French *adopter*, from Latin *adoptare*, from *ad-* + *optare* to choose] (1500)
**1 :** to take by choice into a relationship; *especially* **:** to take voluntarily (a child of other parents) as one's own child
**2 :** to take up and practice or use ⟨*adopted* a moderate tone⟩
**3 :** to accept formally and put into effect ⟨*adopt* a constitutional amendment⟩
**4 :** to choose (a textbook) for required study in a course ☆
— **adopt·abil·i·ty** \-ˌdäp-tə-'bi-lə-tē\ *noun*
— **adopt·able** \-'däp-tə-bəl\ *adjective*
— **adopt·er** *noun*

**adopt·ee** \ə-ˌdäp-'tē\ *noun* (1892)
**:** one that is adopted

**adop·tion** \ə-'däp-shən\ *noun* (14th century)
**:** the act of adopting **:** the state of being adopted

**adop·tion·ism** *or* **adop·tian·ism** \-shə-ˌni-zəm\ *noun, often capitalized* (1874)
**:** the doctrine that Jesus of Nazareth became the Son of God by adoption
— **adop·tion·ist** \-sh(ə-)nist\ *noun, often capitalized*

**adop·tive** \ə-'däp-tiv\ *adjective* (15th century)
**1 :** made or acquired by adoption ⟨the *adoptive* father⟩
**2 :** tending to adopt

**3 :** of or relating to adoption
— **adop·tive·ly** *adverb*

**ador·able** \ə-'dȯr-ə-bəl, -'dȯr-\ *adjective* (1611)
**1 :** worthy of being adored
**2 :** extremely charming ⟨an *adorable* child⟩
— **ador·abil·i·ty** \-ˌdȯr-ə-'bi-lə-tē, -ˌdȯr-\ *noun*
— **ador·able·ness** \-'dȯr-ə-bəl-nəs, -'dȯr-\ *noun*
— **ador·ably** \-blē\ *adverb*

**ad·o·ra·tion** \ˌa-də-'rā-shən\ *noun* (1528)
**:** the act of adoring **:** state of being adored

**adore** \ə-'dȯr, -'dȯr\ *transitive verb* **adored; ador·ing** [Middle English *adouren*, from Middle French *adorer*, from Latin *adorare*, from *ad-* + *orare* to speak, pray — more at ORATION] (14th century)
**1 :** to worship or honor as a deity or as divine
**2 :** to regard with loving admiration and devotion ⟨*adored* his daughter⟩
**3 :** to be extremely fond of ⟨*adores* pecan pie⟩
**synonym** *see* REVERE
— **ador·er** *noun*
— **ador·ing·ly** *adverb*

**adorn** \ə-'dȯrn\ *transitive verb* [Middle English, from Middle French *adorner*, from Latin *adornare*, from *ad-* + *ornare* to furnish — more at ORNATE] (14th century)
**1 :** to enhance the appearance of especially with beautiful objects
**2 :** to enliven or decorate as if with ornaments ⟨people of fashion who *adorned* the Court⟩ ☆

---

☆ **SYNONYMS**
**Admittance, admission** mean permitted entrance. ADMITTANCE is usually applied to mere physical entrance to a locality or a building ⟨members must show their cards upon *admittance* to the club⟩. ADMISSION applies to entrance or formal acceptance (as into a club) that carries with it rights, privileges, standing, or membership ⟨two recommendations are required for *admission* to the club⟩.

**Adopt, embrace, espouse** mean to take an opinion, policy, or practice as one's own. ADOPT implies accepting something created by another or foreign to one's nature ⟨forced to *adopt* new policies⟩. EMBRACE implies a ready or happy acceptance ⟨*embraced* the customs of their new homeland⟩. ESPOUSE adds an implication of close attachment to a cause and a sharing of its fortunes ⟨*espoused* the cause of women's rights⟩.

**Adorn, decorate, ornament, embellish, beautify, deck, garnish** mean to enhance the appearance of something by adding something unessential. ADORN implies an enhancing by something beautiful in itself ⟨a diamond necklace *adorned* her neck⟩. DECORATE suggests relieving plainness or monotony by adding beauty of color or design ⟨*decorate* a birthday cake⟩. ORNAMENT and EMBELLISH imply the adding of something extraneous, ORNAMENT stressing the heightening or setting off of the original ⟨a white house *ornamented* with green shutters⟩, EMBELLISH often stressing the adding of superfluous or adventitious ornament ⟨*embellish* a page with floral borders⟩. BEAUTIFY adds to EMBELLISH a suggestion of counterbalancing plainness or ugliness ⟨will *beautify* the grounds with flower beds⟩. DECK implies the addition of something that contributes to gaiety, splendor, or showiness ⟨a house all *decked* out for Christmas⟩. GARNISH suggests decorating with a small final touch and is used especially in referring to the serving of food ⟨an entrée *garnished* with parsley⟩.

**adorn·ment** \-mənt\ *noun* (14th century)
**1 :** the action of adorning **:** the state of being adorned
**2 :** something that adorns
**ADP** \ˌā-(ˌ)dē-ˈpē\ *noun* [adenosine *d*iphosphate] (1944)
**:** an ester of adenosine that is reversibly converted to ATP for the storing of energy by the addition of a high-energy phosphate group — called also *adenosine diphosphate*
**ad rem** \(ˌ)ad-ˈrem\ *adverb or adjective* [Latin, to the thing] (1599)
**:** to the point or purpose **:** RELEVANTLY
**adren-** *or* **adreno-** *combining form* [*adrenal*]
**1 :** adrenal glands ⟨*adreno*cortical⟩
**2 :** adrenaline ⟨*adren*ergic⟩
¹**ad·re·nal** \ə-ˈdrē-n°l\ *adjective* [*ad-* + *renal*] (1875)
**:** of, relating to, or derived from the adrenal glands or their secretions ⟨*adrenal* steroids⟩
²**adrenal** *noun* (1882)
**:** ADRENAL GLAND
**ad·re·nal·ec·to·my** \ə-ˌdrē-n°l-ˈek-tə-mē\ *noun* (circa 1910)
**:** surgical removal of one or both adrenal glands
— **ad·re·nal·ec·to·mized** \-ˌmīzd\ *adjective*
**adrenal gland** *noun* (1875)
**:** either of a pair of complex endocrine organs near the anterior medial border of the kidney consisting of a mesodermal cortex that produces glucocorticoid, mineralocorticoid, and androgenic hormones and an ectodermal medulla that produces epinephrine and norepinephrine — called also *adrenal, suprarenal gland*
**Adren·a·lin** \ə-ˈdre-n°l-ən\ *trademark*
— used for a preparation of levorotatory epinephrine
**adren·a·line** \ə-ˈdre-n°l-ən\ *noun* (1901)
**:** EPINEPHRINE — often used in nontechnical contexts ⟨the fans were jubilant, raucous, their *adrenaline* running high —W. P. Kinsella⟩
**ad·ren·er·gic** \ˌa-drə-ˈnər-jik\ *adjective* [*adren-* + *ergic*] (1934)
**1 :** liberating or activated by adrenaline or a substance like adrenaline ⟨an *adrenergic* nerve⟩
**2 :** resembling adrenaline especially in physiological action ⟨*adrenergic* drugs⟩
— **ad·ren·er·gi·cal·ly** \-ji-k(ə-)lē\ *adverb*
**ad·re·no·chrome** \ə-ˈdrē-nō-ˌkrōm\ *noun* (circa 1913)
**:** a red-colored mixture of quinones derived from epinephrine by oxidation
**ad·re·no·cor·ti·cal** \ə-ˌdrē-nō-ˈkȯr-ti-kəl\ *adjective* (1936)
**:** of, relating to, or derived from the cortex of the adrenal glands
**ad·re·no·cor·ti·co·ste·roid** \-ˌkȯr-ti-kō-ˈstir-ˌȯid *also* -ˈster-\ *noun* (1960)
**:** a steroid obtained from, resembling, or having physiological effects like those of the adrenal cortex
**ad·re·no·cor·ti·co·tro·pic** \ə-ˌdrē-nō-ˌkȯr-ti-kō-ˈtrō-pik\ *also* **ad·re·no·cor·ti·co·tro·phic** \-ˈtrō-fik\ *adjective* (1936)
**:** acting on or stimulating the adrenal cortex ⟨*adrenocorticotropic* activity⟩
**adrenocorticotropic hormone** *noun* (1937)
**:** ACTH
**ad·re·no·cor·ti·co·tro·pin** \-ˈtrō-pən\ *also* **ad·re·no·cor·ti·co·tro·phin** \-ˈtrō-fən\ *noun* (1952)
**:** ACTH
**Adria·my·cin** \ˌā-drē-ə-ˈmī-s°n, ˌa-drē-\ *trademark*
— used for a preparation of the hydrochloride of doxorubicin
**adrift** \ə-ˈdrift\ *adverb or adjective* (1624)
**1 :** without motive power and without anchor or mooring
**2 :** without ties, guidance, or security
**3 :** free from restraint or support

**adroit** \ə-ˈdrȯit\ *adjective* [French, from Old French, from *a-* (from Latin *ad-*) + *droit* right, droit] (1652)
**:** having or showing skill, cleverness, or resourcefulness in handling situations ⟨an *adroit* leader⟩
**synonym** see CLEVER, DEXTEROUS
— **adroit·ly** *adverb*
— **adroit·ness** *noun*
**ad·sci·ti·tious** \ˌad-sə-ˈti-shəs\ *adjective* [Latin *adscitus*, from past participle of *adsciscere* to admit, adopt, from *ad-* + *sciscere* to get to know, from *scire* to know — more at SCIENCE] (1620)
**:** derived or acquired from something extrinsic **:** ADVENTITIOUS
**ad·sorb** \ad-ˈsȯrb, -ˈzȯrb\ *verb* [*ad-* + ab*sorb*] (1882)
*transitive verb*
**:** to take up and hold by adsorption
*intransitive verb*
**:** to become adsorbed
— **ad·sorb·able** \-ˈsȯr-bə-bəl, -ˈzȯr-\ *adjective*
— **ad·sorb·er** \-ˈsȯr-bər, -ˈzȯr-\ *noun*
**ad·sor·bate** \ad-ˈsȯr-bət, -ˈzȯr-, -ˌbāt\ *noun* (1928)
**:** an adsorbed substance
**ad·sor·bent** \-bənt\ *noun* (1917)
**:** a usually solid substance that adsorbs another substance
— **adsorbent** *adjective*
**ad·sorp·tion** \ad-ˈsȯrp-shən, -ˈzȯrp-\ *noun* [*ad-* + ab*sorption*] (1882)
**:** the adhesion in an extremely thin layer of molecules (as of gases, solutes, or liquids) to the surfaces of solid bodies or liquids with which they are in contact — compare ABSORPTION
— **ad·sorp·tive** \-ˈsȯrp-tiv, -ˈzȯrp-\ *adjective*
**ad·u·lar·ia** \ˌa-jə-ˈlar-ē-ə, ˌa-dyə-, -ˈler-\ *noun* [Italian, from French *adulaire*, from *Adula*, Swiss mountain group] (1798)
**:** a transparent or translucent orthoclase
**ad·u·late** \ˈa-jə-ˌlāt, ˈa-dyə-; ˈa-d°l-ˌāt\ *transitive verb* **-lat·ed; -lat·ing** [back-formation from *adulation*, from Middle English, from Middle French, from Latin *adulation-, adulatio*, from *adulari* to fawn on (of dogs), flatter] (1777)
**:** to flatter or admire excessively or slavishly
— **ad·u·la·tion** \ˌa-jə-ˈlā-shən, ˌa-dyə-; ˌa-d°l-ˈā-\ *noun*
— **ad·u·la·tor** \ˈa-jə-ˌlā-tər, ˈa-dyə-; ˈa-d°l-ˌā-\ *noun*
— **ad·u·la·to·ry** \-lə-ˌtȯr-ē, -ˌtȯr-\ *adjective*
¹**adult** \ə-ˈdəlt, ˈa-ˌdəlt\ *adjective* [Latin *adultus*, past participle of *adolescere* to grow up, from *ad-* + *-olescere* (from *alescere* to grow) — more at OLD] (1531)
**1 :** fully developed and mature **:** GROWN-UP
**2 :** of, relating to, intended for, or befitting adults ⟨an *adult* approach to a problem⟩
**3 :** dealing in or with explicitly sexual material ⟨*adult* bookstores⟩ ⟨*adult* movies⟩
— **adult·hood** \ə-ˈdəlt-ˌhu̇d\ *noun*
— **adult·ly** \ə-ˈdəlt-lē\ *adverb*
— **adult·ness** \ə-ˈdəlt-nəs, ˈa-ˌdəlt-\ *noun*
²**adult** *noun* (1658)
**:** one that is adult; *especially* **:** a human being after an age (as 21) specified by law
— **adult·like** \ə-ˈdəlt-ˌlīk\ *adjective*
**adult education** *noun* (1851)
**:** CONTINUING EDUCATION
**adul·ter·ant** \ə-ˈdəl-t(ə-)rənt\ *noun* (circa 1755)
**:** an adulterating substance or agent
— **adulterant** *adjective*
¹**adul·ter·ate** \ə-ˈdəl-tə-ˌrāt\ *transitive verb* **-at·ed; -at·ing** [Latin *adulteratus*, past participle of *adulterare*, from *ad-* + *alter* other — more at ELSE] (1531)
**:** to corrupt, debase, or make impure by the addition of a foreign or inferior substance or

element; *especially* **:** to prepare for sale by replacing more valuable with less valuable or inert ingredients
— **adul·ter·a·tor** \-ˌrā-tər\ *noun*
²**adul·ter·ate** \ə-ˈdəl-t(ə-)rət\ *adjective* (1590)
**1 :** tainted with adultery **:** ADULTEROUS
**2 :** being adulterated **:** SPURIOUS
**adul·ter·a·tion** \ə-ˌdəl-tə-ˈrā-shən\ *noun* (1506)
**1 :** the process of adulterating **:** the condition of being adulterated
**2 :** an adulterated product
**adul·ter·er** \ə-ˈdəl-tər-ər\ *noun* (1513)
**:** a person who commits adultery; *especially* **:** a man who commits adultery
**adul·ter·ess** \ə-ˈdəl-t(ə-)rəs\ *noun* (1611)
**:** a woman who commits adultery
**adul·ter·ine** \ə-ˈdəl-tə-ˌrīn, -ˌrēn\ *adjective* (1542)
**1 a :** marked by adulteration **:** SPURIOUS **b :** ILLEGAL
**2 :** born of adultery
**adul·ter·ous** \ə-ˈdəl-t(ə-)rəs\ *adjective* (1606)
**:** relating to, characterized by, or given to adultery
— **adul·ter·ous·ly** *adverb*
**adul·tery** \ə-ˈdəl-t(ə-)rē\ *noun, plural* **-ter·ies** [Middle English, alteration of *avoutrie*, from Middle French, from Latin *adulterium*, from *adulter* adulterer, back-formation from *adulterare*] (15th century)
**:** voluntary sexual intercourse between a married man and someone other than his wife or between a married woman and someone other than her husband; *also* **:** an act of adultery
**ad·um·brate** \ˈa-dəm-ˌbrāt, a-ˈdəm-\ *transitive verb* **-brat·ed; -brat·ing** [Latin *adumbratus*, past participle of *adumbrare*, from *ad-* + *umbra* shadow — more at UMBRAGE] (1581)
**1 :** to foreshadow vaguely **:** INTIMATE
**2 a :** to give a sketchy representation or outline of **b :** to suggest or disclose partially
**3 :** OVERSHADOW, OBSCURE
— **ad·um·bra·tion** \ˌa-(ˌ)dəm-ˈbrā-shən\ *noun*
— **ad·um·bra·tive** \a-ˈdəm-brə-tiv\ *adjective*
— **ad·um·bra·tive·ly** *adverb*
**adust** \ə-ˈdəst\ *adjective* [Middle English, from Latin *adustus*, past participle of *adurere* to set fire to, from *ad-* + *urere* to burn — more at EMBER] (15th century)
**1 :** SCORCHED, BURNED
**2** *archaic* **:** of a sunburned appearance
**3** *archaic* **:** of a gloomy appearance or disposition
**ad va·lo·rem** \ˌad-və-ˈlȯr-əm, -ˈlȯr-\ *adjective* [Latin, according to the value] (1698)
**:** imposed at a rate percent of value ⟨*ad valorem* tax on goods⟩
¹**ad·vance** \əd-ˈvan(t)s\ *verb* **ad·vanced; ad·vanc·ing** [Middle English *advauncen*, from Old French *avancier*, from (assumed) Vulgar Latin *abantiare*, from Late Latin *abante* in front, from Latin *ab-* + *ante* before — more at ANTE-] (15th century)
*transitive verb*
**1 :** to accelerate the growth or progress of
**2 :** to bring or move forward
**3 :** to raise to a higher rank
**4** *archaic* **:** to lift up **:** RAISE
**5 a :** to bring forward in time; *especially* **:** to make earlier ⟨*advance* the date of the meeting⟩ **b :** to place later in time
**6 :** to bring forward for notice, consideration, or acceptance **:** PROPOSE
**7 :** to supply or furnish in expectation of repayment
**8 :** to raise in rate **:** INCREASE ⟨*advance* the rent⟩

*intransitive verb*
**1 :** to move forward **:** PROCEED
**2 :** to make progress **:** INCREASE ⟨*advance* in age⟩
**3 :** to rise in rank, position, or importance
**4 :** to rise in rate or price ☆
— **ad·vanc·er** *noun*
²**advance** *noun* (1668)
**1 :** a moving forward
**2 a :** progress in development ⟨mistaking material *advance* for spiritual enrichment —H. J. Laski⟩ **b :** a progressive step **:** IMPROVEMENT ⟨an *advance* in medical technique⟩
**3 :** a rise in price, value, or amount
**4 :** a first step or approach made ⟨her attitude discouraged all *advances*⟩
**5 :** a provision of something (as money or goods) before a return is received; *also* **:** the money or goods supplied
— **in advance :** before a deadline or an anticipated event
— **in advance of :** AHEAD OF
³**advance** *adjective* (1701)
**1 :** made, sent, or furnished ahead of time ⟨*advance* sales⟩
**2 :** going or situated before ⟨an *advance* party of soldiers⟩
**ad·vanced** *adjective* (1534)
**1 :** far on in time or course ⟨a man *advanced* in years⟩
**2 a :** being beyond others in progress or ideas ⟨tastes a bit too *advanced* for the times⟩ **b :** being beyond the elementary or introductory ⟨*advanced* chemistry⟩ **c :** greatly developed beyond an initial stage ⟨the most *advanced* scientific methods⟩ ⟨*advanced* weapons systems⟩
**advanced degree** *noun* (1928)
**:** a university degree (as a master's or doctor's degree) higher than a bachelor's
**Advanced level** *noun* (1947)
**:** A LEVEL
**advance man** *noun* (1906)
**:** an employee who makes arrangements and handles publicity in advance of an appearance or engagement by the employer (as a political candidate or a circus)
**ad·vance·ment** \əd-'van(t)-smənt\ *noun* (1599)
**1 :** the action of advancing **:** the state of being advanced: **a :** promotion or elevation to a higher rank or position **b :** progression to a higher stage of development
**2 :** an improved feature **:** IMPROVEMENT
¹**ad·van·tage** \əd-'van-tij\ *noun* [Middle English *avantage*, from Middle French, from *avant* before, from Late Latin *abante*] (1523)
**1 :** superiority of position or condition ⟨higher ground gave the enemy the *advantage*⟩
**2 :** a factor or circumstance of benefit to its possessor ⟨lacked the *advantages* of an education⟩
**3 a :** BENEFIT, GAIN; *especially* **:** benefit resulting from some course of action ⟨a mistake which turned out to our *advantage*⟩ **b** *obsolete* **:** INTEREST 2a
**4 :** the first point won in tennis after deuce
— **to advantage :** so as to produce a favorable impression or effect
²**advantage** *transitive verb* **-taged; -tag·ing** (1549)
**:** to give an advantage to **:** BENEFIT
**ad·van·ta·geous** \ˌad-ˌvan-'tā-jəs, -vən-\ *adjective* (1598)
**:** giving an advantage **:** FAVORABLE
— **ad·van·ta·geous·ly** *adverb*
— **ad·van·ta·geous·ness** *noun*
**ad·vec·tion** \ad-'vek-shən\ *noun* [Latin *advection-, advectio* act of bringing, from *advehere* to carry to, from *ad-* + *vehere* to carry — more at WAY] (1910)
**:** the usually horizontal movement of a mass of fluid (as air or an ocean current); *also* **:** transport (as of pollutants or plankton) by such movement
— **ad·vect** \-'vekt\ *transitive verb*

— **ad·vec·tive** \-'vek-tiv\ *adjective*
**Ad·vent** \'ad-ˌvent, *chiefly British* -vənt\ *noun* [Middle English, from Medieval Latin *adventus*, from Latin, arrival, from *advenire*] (12th century)
**1 :** the period beginning four Sundays before Christmas and observed by some Christians as a season of prayer and fasting
**2 a :** the coming of Christ at the Incarnation **b :** SECOND COMING
**3** *not capitalized* **:** a coming into being or use ⟨the *advent* of spring⟩ ⟨the *advent* of pasteurization⟩ ⟨the *advent* of personal computers⟩
**Ad·vent·ism** \'ad-ˌven-ˌti-zəm\ *noun* (1874)
**1 :** the doctrine that the second coming of Christ and the end of the world are near at hand
**2 :** the principles and practices of Seventh-Day Adventists
— **Ad·vent·ist** \əd-'ven-tist, ad-', 'ad-ˌ\ *adjective or noun*
**ad·ven·ti·tia** \ˌad-vən-'ti-shə, -(ˌ)ven-\ *noun* [New Latin, alteration of Latin *adventicia*, neuter plural of *adventicius* coming from outside, from *adventus*, past participle] (1876)
**:** an external chiefly connective tissue covering of an organ; *especially* **:** the external coat of a blood vessel
— **ad·ven·ti·tial** \-shəl\ *adjective*
**ad·ven·ti·tious** \ˌad-(ˌ)vən-'ti-shəs, -vən-\ *adjective* [Latin *adventicius*] (1603)
**1 :** coming from another source and not inherent or innate
**2 :** arising or occurring sporadically or in other than the usual location ⟨*adventitious* roots⟩
— **ad·ven·ti·tious·ly** *adverb*
**ad·ven·tive** \ad-'ven-tiv\ *adjective* (circa 1859)
**1 :** introduced but not fully naturalized
**2 :** ADVENTITIOUS 2
— **adventive** *noun*
**Advent Sunday** *noun* (15th century)
**:** the first Sunday in Advent
¹**ad·ven·ture** \əd-'ven-chər\ *noun* [Middle English *aventure*, from Old French, from (assumed) Vulgar Latin *adventura*, from Latin *adventus*, past participle of *advenire* to arrive, from *ad-* + *venire* to come — more at COME] (14th century)
**1 a :** an undertaking usually involving danger and unknown risks **b :** the encountering of risks ⟨the spirit of *adventure*⟩
**2 :** an exciting or remarkable experience ⟨an *adventure* in exotic dining⟩
**3 :** an enterprise involving financial risk
²**adventure** *verb* **ad·ven·tured; ad·ven·tur·ing** \-'ven-ch(ə-)riŋ\ (14th century)
*transitive verb*
**1 :** to expose to danger or loss **:** VENTURE
**2 :** to venture upon **:** TRY
*intransitive verb*
**1 :** to proceed despite risk
**2 :** to take the risk
**ad·ven·tur·er** \əd-'ven-ch(ə-)rər\ *noun* (1539)
**1 :** one that adventures: as **a :** SOLDIER OF FORTUNE **b :** one that engages in risky commercial enterprises for profit
**2 :** one who seeks unmerited wealth or position especially by playing on the credulity or prejudice of others
**ad·ven·ture·some** \əd-'ven-chər-səm\ *adjective* (circa 1731)
**:** inclined to take risks **:** VENTURESOME
— **ad·ven·ture·some·ness** *noun*
**ad·ven·tur·ess** \əd-'ven-ch(ə-)rəs\ *noun* (1754)
**:** a female adventurer; *especially* **:** one who seeks position or livelihood by questionable means
**ad·ven·tur·ism** \əd-'ven-chə-ˌri-zəm\ *noun* (1932)
**:** improvisation or experimentation (as in politics or military or foreign affairs) in the absence or in defiance of accepted plans or principles
— **ad·ven·tur·ist** \-'ven-ch(ə-)rist\ *noun*

— **ad·ven·tur·is·tic** \-ˌven-chə-'ris-tik\ *adjective*
**ad·ven·tur·ous** \əd-'ven-ch(ə-)rəs\ *adjective* (14th century)
**1 a :** disposed to seek adventure or to cope with the new and unknown ⟨an *adventurous* explorer⟩ **b :** INNOVATIVE ⟨an *adventurous* artistic style⟩
**2 :** characterized by unknown dangers and risks ⟨an *adventurous* journey⟩ ☆
— **ad·ven·tur·ous·ly** *adverb*
— **ad·ven·tur·ous·ness** *noun*
¹**ad·verb** \'ad-ˌvərb\ *noun* [Middle English *adverbe*, from Middle French, from Latin *adverbium*, from *ad-* + *verbum* word — more at WORD] (14th century)
**:** a word belonging to one of the major form classes in any of numerous languages, typically serving as a modifier of a verb, an adjective, another adverb, a preposition, a phrase, a clause, or a sentence, expressing some relation of manner or quality, place, time, degree, number, cause, opposition, affirmation, or denial, and in English also serving to connect and to express comment on clause content — compare ADJUNCT, CONJUNCT, DISJUNCT
²**adverb** *adjective* (1879)
**:** ADVERBIAL
**ad·ver·bi·al** \ad-'vər-bē-əl\ *adjective* (1611)
**:** of, relating to, or having the function of an adverb
— **adverbial** *noun*
— **ad·ver·bi·al·ly** \-ə-lē\ *adverb*
**ad ver·bum** \(ˌ)ad-'vər-bəm\ *adverb* [Latin] (circa 1580)
**:** to a word **:** VERBATIM
**ad·ver·sar·i·al** \ˌad-və(r)-'ser-ē-əl\ *adjective* (1926)
**:** of, relating to, or characteristic of an adversary or adversary procedures **:** ADVERSARY
¹**ad·ver·sary** \'ad-və(r)-ˌser-ē\ *noun, plural* **-sar·ies** (14th century)
**:** one that contends with, opposes, or resists **:** ENEMY
— **ad·ver·sari·ness** *noun*

---

☆ **SYNONYMS**
**Advance, promote, forward, further** mean to help (someone or something) to move ahead. ADVANCE stresses effective assisting in hastening a process or bringing about a desired end ⟨*advance* the cause of peace⟩. PROMOTE suggests an encouraging or fostering and may denote an increase in status or rank ⟨a campaign to *promote* better health⟩. FORWARD implies an impetus forcing something ahead ⟨a wage increase would *forward* productivity⟩. FURTHER suggests a removing of obstacles in the way of a desired advance ⟨used the marriage to *further* his career⟩.

**Adventurous, venturesome, daring, daredevil, rash, reckless, foolhardy** mean exposing oneself to danger more than required by good sense. ADVENTUROUS implies a willingness to accept risks but not necessarily imprudence ⟨*adventurous* pioneers⟩. VENTURESOME implies a jaunty eagerness for perilous undertakings ⟨*venturesome* stunt pilots⟩. DARING heightens the implication of fearlessness in courting danger ⟨*daring* mountain climbers⟩. DAREDEVIL stresses ostentation in daring ⟨*daredevil* motorcyclists⟩. RASH suggests imprudence and lack of forethought ⟨a *rash* decision⟩. RECKLESS implies heedlessness of probable consequences ⟨a *reckless* driver⟩. FOOLHARDY suggests a recklessness that is inconsistent with good sense ⟨only a *foolhardy* sailor would venture into this storm⟩.

**²adversary** *adjective* (14th century)
**1** : of, relating to, or involving an adversary
**2** : having or involving antagonistic parties or opposing interests ⟨divorce can be an *adversary* proceeding⟩
**ad·ver·sa·tive** \əd-'vər-sə-tiv, ad-\ *adjective* (15th century)
: expressing antithesis, opposition, or adverse circumstance ⟨the *adversative* conjunction *but*⟩
— **adversative** *noun*
— **ad·ver·sa·tive·ly** *adverb*
**ad·verse** \ad-'vərs, 'ad-\ *adjective* [Middle English, from Middle French *advers*, from Latin *adversus*, past participle of *advertere*] (14th century)
**1** : acting against or in a contrary direction : HOSTILE ⟨hindered by *adverse* winds⟩
**2 a** : opposed to one's interests ⟨an *adverse* verdict⟩ ⟨heard testimony *adverse* to their position⟩; *especially* : UNFAVORABLE ⟨*adverse* criticism⟩ **b** : causing harm : HARMFUL ⟨*adverse* drug effects⟩
**3** *archaic* : opposite in position ■
— **ad·verse·ly** *adverb*
— **ad·verse·ness** *noun*
**ad·ver·si·ty** \ad-'vər-sə-tē\ *noun, plural* **-ties** (13th century)
**1** : a state or condition contrary to one of well-being
**2** : an instance of adversity
**synonym** *see* MISFORTUNE
**¹ad·vert** \ad-'vərt\ *intransitive verb* [Middle English *adverten*, from Middle French & Latin; Middle French *advertir*, from Latin *advertere*, from *ad-* + *vertere* to turn — more at WORTH] (15th century)
**1** : to turn the mind or attention — used with *to* ⟨*adverted* to the speaker⟩
**2** : to call attention in the course of speaking or writing : make reference — used with *to* ⟨*adverted* to foreign-language sources⟩
**²ad·vert** \'ad-,vərt\ *noun* (1860)
*chiefly British* : ADVERTISEMENT
**ad·ver·tence** \ad-'vər-t°n(t)s\ *noun* (14th century)
**1** : the action or process of adverting : ATTENTION
**2** : ADVERTENCY 1
**ad·ver·ten·cy** \-t°n(t)-sē\ *noun, plural* **-cies** (1646)
**1** : the quality or state of being advertent : HEEDFULNESS
**2** : ADVERTENCE 1
**ad·ver·tent** \-t°nt\ *adjective* [Latin *advertent-, advertens*, present participle of *advertere*] (1671)
: giving attention : HEEDFUL
— **ad·ver·tent·ly** *adverb*
**ad·ver·tise** \'ad-vər-,tīz\ *verb* **-tised; -tis·ing** [Middle English, from Middle French *advertiss-*, stem of *advertir*] (15th century)
*transitive verb*
**1** : to make something known to : NOTIFY
**2 a** : to make publicly and generally known ⟨*advertising* their readiness to make concessions⟩ **b** : to announce publicly especially by a printed notice or a broadcast **c** : to call public attention to especially by emphasizing desirable qualities so as to arouse a desire to buy or patronize : PROMOTE
*intransitive verb*
: to issue or sponsor advertising ⟨*advertise* for a secretary⟩
— **ad·ver·tis·er** *noun*
**ad·ver·tise·ment** \,ad-vər-'tīz-mənt; əd-'vər-təz-mənt, -tə-smənt\ *noun* (15th century)
**1** : the act or process of advertising
**2** : a public notice; *especially* : one published in the press or broadcast over the air
**ad·ver·tis·ing** *noun* (1762)
**1** : the action of calling something to the attention of the public especially by paid announcements
**2** : ADVERTISEMENTS ⟨the magazine contains much *advertising*⟩

**3** : the business of preparing advertisements for publication or broadcast
**ad·ver·tize, ad·ver·tize·ment** *British variant of* ADVERTISE, ADVERTISEMENT
**ad·ver·to·ri·al** \,ad-vər-'tōr-ē-əl, -'tòr-\ *noun* [blend of *advertisement* and *editorial*] (1946)
: an advertisement that imitates editorial format
**ad·vice** \əd-'vīs\ *noun* [Middle English, from Middle French *avis* opinion, probably from the phrase *ce m'est a vis* that appears to me, part translation of Latin *mihi visum est* it seemed so to me, I decided] (14th century)
**1** : recommendation regarding a decision or course of conduct : COUNSEL ⟨he shall have power, by and with the *advice* and consent of the Senate, to make treaties —*U.S. Constitution*⟩
**2** : information or notice given — usually used in plural
**3** : an official notice concerning a business transaction
**ad·vis·able** \əd-'vī-zə-bəl\ *adjective* (1582)
: fit to be advised or done : PRUDENT
**synonym** *see* EXPEDIENT
— **ad·vis·abil·i·ty** \-,vī-zə-'bi-lə-tē\ *noun*
— **ad·vis·able·ness** \-'vī-zə-bəl-nəs\ *noun*
— **ad·vis·ably** \-blē\ *adverb*
**ad·vise** \əd-'vīz\ *verb* **ad·vised; ad·vis·ing** [Middle English, from Middle French *aviser*, from *avis*] (14th century)
*transitive verb*
**1 a** : to give advice to : COUNSEL ⟨*advise* her to try a drier climate⟩ **b** : CAUTION, WARN ⟨*advise* them of the consequences⟩ **c** : RECOMMEND ⟨*advise* prudence⟩
**2** : to give information or notice to : INFORM ⟨*advise* them of their rights⟩
*intransitive verb*
**1** : to give advice ⟨*advise* on legal matters⟩
**2** : to take counsel : CONSULT ⟨*advise* with your parents⟩
— **ad·vis·er** *also* **ad·vi·sor** \-'vī-zər\ *noun*
**ad·vised** \əd-'vīzd\ *adjective* (14th century)
: thought out : CONSIDERED — often used in combination ⟨ill-*advised* plans⟩
— **ad·vis·ed·ly** \-'vī-zəd-lē\ *adverb*
**ad·vis·ee** \əd-,vī-'zē\ *noun* (1824)
: one that is advised
**ad·vise·ment** \əd-'vīz-mənt\ *noun* (14th century)
**1** : careful consideration : DELIBERATION
**2** : the act or process of advising (as a college student)
**¹ad·vi·so·ry** \əd-'vīz-rē, -'vī-zə-\ *adjective* (1778)
**1** : having or exercising power to advise
**2** : containing or giving advice
**²advisory** *noun, plural* **-ries** (1936)
: a report giving information (as on the weather) and often recommending action to be taken
**ad·vo·ca·cy** \'ad-və-kə-sē\ *noun* (15th century)
: the act or process of advocating or supporting a cause or proposal
**advocacy journalism** *noun* (1970)
: journalism that advocates a cause or expresses a viewpoint
— **advocacy journalist** *noun*
**¹ad·vo·cate** \'ad-və-kət, -,kāt\ *noun* [Middle English *advocat*, from Middle French, from Latin *advocatus*, from past participle of *advocare* to summon, from *ad-* + *vocare* to call, from *voc-, vox* voice — more at VOICE] (14th century)
**1** : one that pleads the cause of another; *specifically* : one that pleads the cause of another before a tribunal or judicial court
**2** : one that defends or maintains a cause or proposal
**²ad·vo·cate** \-,kāt\ *transitive verb* **-cat·ed; -cat·ing** (1599)
: to plead in favor of
**synonym** *see* SUPPORT
— **ad·vo·ca·tion** \,ad-və-'kā-shən\ *noun*

— **ad·vo·ca·tive** \'ad-və-,kā-tiv\ *adjective*
— **ad·vo·ca·tor** \-,kā-tər\ *noun*
**ad·vow·son** \əd-'vaù-z°n\ *noun* [Middle English, from Old French *avoueson*, from Medieval Latin *advocation-, advocatio*, from Latin, act of calling, from *advocare*] (14th century)
: the right in English law of presenting a nominee to an ecclesiastical benefice
**ady·nam·ic** \,ā-(,)dī-'na-mik, ,a-də-'na-\ *adjective* [Greek *adynamia* lack of strength, from *a-* + *dynamis* power, from *dynasthai* to be able] (1829)
: characterized by or causing a loss of strength or function ⟨*adynamic* ileus⟩
**ad·y·tum** \'a-də-təm\ *noun, plural* **-ta** \-tə\ [Latin, from Greek *adyton*, neuter of *adytos* not to be entered, from *a-* + *dyein* to enter] (1611)
: the innermost sanctuary in an ancient temple open only to priests : SANCTUM
**adze** *also* **adz** \'adz\ *noun* [Middle English *adse*, from Old English *adesa*] (before 12th century)
: a cutting tool that has a thin arched blade set at right angles to the handle and is used chiefly for shaping wood
**ad·zu·ki bean** \ad-'zü-kē-\ *noun* [Japanese *azuki*] (1795)
: an annual bushy leguminous plant (*Vignis angularis* synonym *Phaseolus angularis*) widely grown in Japan and China for its seeds which are used as food and to produce a flour; *also* : its seed — called also *adzuki*

adze

**ae** \'ā\ *adjective* [Middle English (northern dialect) *a*, alteration of *an*] (1737)
*chiefly Scottish* : ONE
**Ae·a·cus** \'ē-ə-kəs\ *noun* [Latin, from Greek *Aiakos*]
: a son of Zeus who is given the Myrmidons as followers and becomes on his death a judge of the underworld
**ae·cio·spore** \'ē-shə-,spōr, 'ē-sə-, -,spòr\ *noun* (1905)
: one of the spores arranged within an aecium in a series like a chain
**ae·ci·um** \'ē-shē-əm, 'ē-sē-\ *noun, plural* **-cia** \-shē-ə, -sē-\ [New Latin, from Greek *aikia* outrage, assault, from *aikēs, aeikēs* unseemly, from *a-* + *-eikēs*, from *eikenai* to seem] (1905)

---

☐ USAGE
**adverse**   Here are a few observations to help with the use of *adverse* and *averse*. *Adverse* is often used attributively ⟨under *adverse* circumstances⟩ ⟨an *adverse* reaction⟩ while *averse* is rarely so used. It is more often a thing than a person that is adverse ⟨the whole Parliamentary tradition . . . is adverse to it —Sir Winston Churchill⟩. When used with *to* and of people, *adverse* and *averse* are pretty much synonymous, but *adverse* generally refers to opinion or intention ⟨was *adverse* to his union with this young lady —George Meredith⟩ and *averse* to feeling or inclination ⟨I am not *averse* to pillorying the innocent —John Barth⟩. But this is a subtle distinction and is not observed universally, even by respected writers ⟨liked to settle herself and was *adverse* to complications —Carson McCullers⟩ ⟨Her Majesty . . . was by no means *averse* to reforms —Edith Sitwell⟩.

---

: the fruiting body of a rust fungus in which the first binucleate spores are usually produced
— **ae·cial** \-sh(ē-)əl\ *adjective*

**ae·des** \ā-'ē-(,)dēz\ *noun, plural* **aedes** [New Latin, genus name, from Greek *aēdēs* unpleasant, from *a-* + *ēdos* pleasure; akin to Greek *hēdys* sweet — more at SWEET] (circa 1909)
: any of a genus (*Aedes*) of mosquitoes including the vector of yellow fever, dengue, and other diseases
— **ae·dine** \-'ē-,dīn\ *adjective*

**ae·dile** \'ē-,dīl, 'ē-dᵊl\ *noun* [Latin *aedilis*, from *aedes* temple — more at EDIFY] (1540)
: an official in ancient Rome in charge of public works and games, police, and the grain supply

**Ae·ge·an** \i-'jē-ən\ *adjective* [Latin *Aegaeus*, from Greek *Aigaios*] (1550)
**1** : of or relating to the arm of the Mediterranean Sea east of Greece
**2** : of or relating to the chiefly Bronze Age civilization of the islands of the Aegean Sea and the countries adjacent to it

**ae·gis** \'ē-jəs *also* 'ā-\ *noun* [Latin, from Greek *aigis*, literally, goatskin, from *aig-, aix* goat; akin to Armenian *ayc* goat] (1611)
**1** : a shield or breastplate emblematic of majesty that was associated with Zeus and Athena
**2 a** : PROTECTION ⟨under the *aegis* of the constitution⟩ **b** : controlling or conditioning influence ⟨many American mothers, under the *aegis* of benevolent permissiveness . . . actually neglect their children —*Time*⟩
**3 a** : AUSPICES, SPONSORSHIP ⟨under the *aegis* of the museum⟩ **b** : control or guidance especially by an individual, group, or system ⟨acted under the court's *aegis*⟩ ◆

**Ae·gis·thus** \i-'jis-thəs\ *noun* [Latin, from Greek *Aigisthos*]
: a lover of Clytemnestra slain with her by her son Orestes

**-aemia** *chiefly British variant of* -EMIA

**Ae·ne·as** \i-'nē-əs\ *noun* [Latin, from Greek *Aineias*]
: a son of Anchises and Aphrodite, defender of Troy, and hero of Virgil's *Aeneid*

**Ae·ne·o·lith·ic** \ā-,nē-ō-'li-thik\ *adjective* [Latin *aeneus* of copper or bronze, from *aes* copper, bronze — more at ORE] (1901)
: of or relating to a transitional period between the Neolithic and Bronze ages in which some copper was used

**¹ae·o·lian** \ē-'ō-lē-ən, ē-'ōl-yən\ *adjective* (1605)
**1** *often capitalized* : of or relating to Aeolus
**2** : giving forth or marked by a moaning or sighing sound or musical tone produced by or as if by the wind

**²aeolian** *variant of* EOLIAN

**¹Ae·o·lian** \ē-'ō-lē-ən, ā-, -'ōl-yən\ *adjective* (1589)
: of or relating to Aeolis or its inhabitants

**²Aeolian** *noun* (circa 1889)
**1** : a member of a group of Greek peoples of Thessaly and Boeotia that colonized Lesbos and the adjacent coast of Asia Minor
**2** : AEOLIC

**aeolian harp** *noun* (1791)
: a box-shaped musical instrument having stretched strings usually tuned in unison on which the wind produces varying harmonics over the same fundamental tone

**¹Ae·ol·ic** \ē-'ä-lik\ *adjective* (1674)
: AEOLIAN

**²Aeolic** *noun* (1902)
: a group of ancient Greek dialects used by the Aeolians

**Ae·o·lus** \'ē-ə-ləs\ *noun* [Latin, from Greek *Aiolos*]
: the Greek god of the winds

**ae·on** *or* eon \'ē-,än, 'ē-ən\ *noun* [Latin, from Greek *aiōn* — more at AYE] (1647)
**1** : an immeasurably or indefinitely long period of time : AGE
**2 a** *usually* eon : a very large division of geo-

logic time usually longer than an era **b** : a unit of geologic time equal to one billion years

**ae·o·ni·an** \ē-'ō-nē-ən\ *or* **ae·on·ic** \-'ä-nik\ *adjective* (1765)
: lasting for an immeasurably or indefinitely long period of time

**ae·py·or·nis** \ē-pē-'ȯr-nəs\ *noun* [New Latin, genus name, from Greek *aipys* high + *ornis* bird — more at ERNE] (1851)
: any of a group (genus *Aepyornis* or order Aepyornithiformes) of gigantic ratite birds known only from remains found in Madagascar — called also *elephant bird*

**aer-** *or* **aero-** *combining form* [Middle English *aero-*, from Middle French, from Latin, from Greek *aer-, aero-*, from *aēr*]
**1 a** : air : atmosphere ⟨aerate⟩ ⟨aerobiology⟩ **b** : air and ⟨aerospace⟩
**2** : gas ⟨aerosol⟩
**3** : aviation ⟨aerodrome⟩

**aer·ate** \'a(-ə)r-,āt, 'e(-ə)r-\ *transitive verb* **aer·at·ed; aer·at·ing** (1794)
**1** : to supply (the blood) with oxygen by respiration
**2** : to supply or impregnate (as the soil or a liquid) with air
**3 a** *British* : CARBONATE 2 **b** : to make light or sparkling
— **aer·a·tion** \,a(-ə)r-'ā-shən, ,e(-ə)r-\ *noun*

**aer·a·tor** \'a(-ə)r-,ā-tər, 'e(-ə)r-\ *noun* (1861)
: one that aerates; *especially* : an apparatus for aerating something (as sewage)

**aer·en·chy·ma** \,ar-'eŋ-kə-mə, ,er-\ *noun* [New Latin] (circa 1893)
: the spongy modified cork tissue of many aquatic plants that facilitates gaseous exchange and maintains buoyancy

**¹aer·i·al** \'ar-ē-əl, 'er-; ā-'ir-ē-əl\ *adjective* [Latin *aerius*, from Greek *aerios*, from *aēr*] (1604)
**1 a** : of, relating to, or occurring in the air or atmosphere **b** : existing or growing in the air rather than in the ground or in water **c** : high in the air ⟨aerial spires⟩ **d** : operating or operated overhead on elevated cables or rails ⟨an aerial tram⟩
**2** : suggestive of air: as **a** : lacking substance **b** : FANCIFUL, ETHEREAL ⟨visions of aerial joy —P. B. Shelley⟩
**3 a** : of or relating to aircraft ⟨aerial navigation⟩ **b** : designed for use in, taken from, or operating from or against aircraft ⟨aerial transportation⟩
**4** : of, relating to, or gained by the forward pass in football
— **aer·i·al·ly** \-ə-lē\ *adverb*

**²aer·i·al** \'ar-ē-əl, 'er-\ *noun* (1902)
**1** : ANTENNA 2
**2** : FORWARD PASS

**aer·i·al·ist** \'ar-ē-ə-list, 'er-, ā-'ir-\ *noun* (1905)
: one that performs feats in the air or above the ground especially on the trapeze

**aerial ladder** *noun* (1904)
: a mechanically operated extensible ladder usually mounted on a fire truck

**aerial perspective** *noun* (1720)
: the expression of space in painting by gradation of color and distinctness

**ae·rie** \'ar-ē, 'er-, 'ir-, 'ā-(ə-)rē\ *noun* [Medieval Latin *aerea*, from Old French *aire*, probably from (assumed) Vulgar Latin *agrum* origin, nest, lair, from Latin *ager* field — more at ACRE] (1581)
**1** : the nest of a bird on a cliff or a mountaintop
**2** *obsolete* : a brood of birds of prey
**3** : an elevated often secluded dwelling, structure, or position

**aero** \'a(-ə)r-(,)ō, 'e(-ə)r-\ *adjective* [aero-] (1874)
: of or relating to aircraft or aeronautics ⟨an aero engine⟩

**aer·o·bat·ics** \,ar-ō-'ba-tiks, ,er-\ *noun plural but singular or plural in construction* [aer- + acrobatics] (circa 1911)

: spectacular flying feats and maneuvers (as rolls and dives)
— **aer·o·bat·ic** \-tik\ *adjective*

**aer·obe** \'a(-ə)r-,ōb, 'e(-ə)r-\ *noun* [French *aérobie*, from *aéro-* aer- + *-bie* (from Greek *-bion*, from *bios* life) — more at QUICK] (1886)
: an organism (as a bacterium) that lives only in the presence of oxygen

**aer·o·bic** \,a(-ə)r-'ō-bik, ,e(-ə)r-\ *adjective* (1884)
**1** : living, active, or occurring only in the presence of oxygen ⟨aerobic respiration⟩
**2** : of, relating to, or induced by aerobes ⟨aerobic fermentation⟩
**3** : involving, utilizing, or used in aerobics ⟨an aerobic workout⟩ ⟨aerobic fitness⟩
— **aer·o·bi·cal·ly** \-bi-k(ə-)lē\ *adverb*

**aer·o·bics** \-biks\ *noun plural* (1967)
**1** *singular or plural in construction* : a system of physical conditioning involving exercises (as running, walking, swimming, or calisthenics) strenuously performed so as to cause marked temporary increase in respiration and heart rate
**2** : aerobic exercises

**aero·bi·ol·o·gy** \,ar-ō-bī-'ä-lə-jē\ *noun* [aer- + biology] (circa 1937)
: the science dealing with the occurrence, transportation, and effects of airborne materials (as viruses, pollen, or pollutants)
— **aero·bi·o·log·i·cal** \-,bī-ə-'lä-ji-kəl\ *adjective*

**aero·bi·o·sis** \,ar-ō-bī-'ō-səs, ,er-, -bē-\ *noun, plural* **-o·ses** \-,sēz\ [New Latin] (circa 1900)
: life in the presence of air or oxygen

**aero·brake** \'ar-ō-,brāk, 'er-\ *transitive verb* (1965)
: to decelerate (as a spacecraft) by passage through a planetary atmosphere

**aero·drome** \'ar-ə-,drōm, 'er-\ *noun* (1908)
*chiefly British* : AIRFIELD

**aero·dy·nam·i·cist** \,ar-ō-dī-'na-mə-sist, ,er-\ *noun* (1926)
: one who specializes in aerodynamics

**aero·dy·nam·ics** \-'na-miks\ *noun plural but singular or plural in construction* (circa 1837)
: a branch of dynamics that deals with the motion of air and other gaseous fluids and with the forces acting on bodies in motion relative to such fluids
— **aero·dy·nam·ic** \-mik\ *also* **aero·dy·nam·i·cal** \-mi-kəl\ *adjective*
— **aero·dy·nam·i·cal·ly** \-mi-k(ə-)lē\ *adverb*

**aero·dyne** \'ar-ə-,dīn, 'er-\ *noun* [aerodynamic] (circa 1906)
: a heavier-than-air aircraft (as an airplane, helicopter, or glider) — compare AEROSTAT

**aero·elas·tic·i·ty** \,ar-ō-ē-,las-'ti-sə-tē, ,er-, -i-,las-\ *noun* (1935)

◊ WORD HISTORY
**aegis** When we speak of something as being "under the aegis of" another, we mean that it is under the authority, sponsorship, or control of another. The basic idea is that whatever is in the subordinate position is being protected. In ancient Greece the word *aigis* meant literally "goatskin," but literal usage was uncommon. More frequently, *aigis* referred to a protective mantle, presumably of goat hide, or perhaps a shield, brandished by the god Zeus. Sometimes he entrusted the aegis to other deities, especially his daughter Athena. In its center the aegis bore an image of the Gorgon Medusa's head, and its border was decorated with golden fringe according to Homer. The aegis became a familiar classical reference in English literature, and by the 18th century the word *aegis* was being used figuratively for other kinds of seemingly impregnable protection.

: distortion (as from bending or flexing) in a structure (as an airplane wing or a building) caused by aerodynamic forces
— **aero·elas·tic** \-'las-tik\ *adjective*
**aero·em·bo·lism** \ar-ō-'em-bə-,li-zəm, ,er-\ *noun* (circa 1939)
: a condition equivalent to bends caused by rapid ascent to high altitudes and resulting exposure to rapidly lowered air pressure
**aero·foil** \'ar-ə-,fóil, 'er-\ *noun* (1907)
*chiefly British* : AIRFOIL
**aero·gram** *or* **aero·gramme** \'ar-ə-,gram, 'er-\ *noun* (1899)
: AIR LETTER 2
**aer·og·ra·pher's mate** \a-'rä-grə-fərz-, ,e-\ *noun* (circa 1952)
: a navy petty officer specializing in meteorology
**aer·o·lite** \'ar-ə-,līt, 'er-\ *noun* (circa 1815)
: a stony meteorite
**aero·mag·net·ic** \ar-ō-mag-'ne-tik, ,er-\ *adjective* (1948)
: of, relating to, or derived from a study of the earth's magnetic field especially from the air ⟨an *aeromagnetic* survey⟩
**aero·me·chan·ics** \-mə-'ka-niks\ *noun plural but singular or plural in construction* (circa 1909)
: mechanics that deals with the equilibrium and motion of gases and of solid bodies immersed in them
**aero·med·i·cine** \-'me-də-sən\ *noun* (1942)
: a branch of medicine that deals with the diseases and disturbances arising from flying and the associated physiological and psychological problems
— **aero·med·i·cal** \-'me-di-kəl\ *adjective*
**aer·om·e·ter** \,a(-ə)r-'ä-mə-tər, ,e(-ə)r-\ *noun* [probably from French *aéromètre*, from *aér-* + *-mètre* -meter] (1794)
: an instrument for ascertaining the weight or density of air or other gases
**aero·naut** \'ar-ə-,nòt, 'er-, -,nät\ *noun* [French *aéronaute*, from *aér-* aer- + Greek *nautēs* sailor — more at NAUTICAL] (1784)
: one that operates or travels in an airship or balloon
**aero·nau·tics** \,ar-ə-'nò-tiks, ,er-, -'nä-\ *noun plural but singular in construction* (circa 1824)
**1** : a science dealing with the operation of aircraft
**2** : the art or science of flight
— **aero·nau·ti·cal** \-ti-kəl\ *also* **aero·nau·tic** \-tik\ *adjective*
— **aero·nau·ti·cal·ly** \-ti-k(ə-)lē\ *adverb*
**aer·on·o·my** \,a(-ə)r-'ä-nə-mē, ,e(-ə)r-\ *noun* (1957)
: a science that deals with the physics and chemistry of the upper atmosphere of planets
— **aer·on·o·mer** \-mər\ *noun*
— **aer·o·nom·ic** \,ar-ə-'nä-mik, ,er-\ *or* **aer·o·nom·i·cal** \-mi-kəl\ *adjective*
— **aer·on·o·mist** \,a(-ə)r-'ä-nə-mist, ,e(-ə)r-\ *noun*
**aero·plane** \'ar-ə-,plān, 'er-\ *noun* [French *aéroplane*, from *aéro-* aer- + *-plane*, probably from feminine of *plan* flat, level, from Latin *planus* — more at FLOOR] (1873)
*chiefly British* : AIRPLANE
**aero·sol** \'ar-ə-,säl, 'er-, -,sòl\ *noun* (1923)
**1** : a suspension of fine solid or liquid particles in gas ⟨smoke, fog, and mist are *aerosols*⟩
**2** : a substance (as an insecticide or cosmetic) dispensed from a pressurized container especially as an aerosol; *also* : the container for this
**aero·sol·ize** \-,sä-,līz, -,sò-, -sə-\ *transitive verb* **-ized; -iz·ing** (1944)
: to disperse as an aerosol
— **aero·sol·iza·tion** \,ar-ə-,sä-lə-'zā-shən, -,sò-, -sə-\ *noun*
¹**aero·space** \'ar-ō-,spās, 'er-\ *noun* (circa 1958)
**1** : space comprising the earth's atmosphere and the space beyond

---

**2** : a physical science that deals with aerospace
**3** : the aerospace industry
²**aerospace** *adjective* (1958)
: of or relating to aerospace, to vehicles used in aerospace or the manufacture of such vehicles, or to travel in aerospace ⟨*aerospace* research⟩ ⟨*aerospace* profits⟩ ⟨*aerospace* medicine⟩
**aerospace plane** *noun* (1960)
: an airplane designed to be able to reach low earth orbit
**aero·stat** \-,stat\ *noun* [French *aérostat*, from *aér-* + *-stat*] (1784)
: a lighter-than-air aircraft (as a balloon or blimp) — compare AERODYNE
**aero·stat·ics** \ar-ō-'sta-tiks, ,er-\ *noun plural but singular or plural in construction* [modification of New Latin *aerostatica*, from *aer-* + *statica* statics] (1784)
: a branch of statics that deals with the equilibrium of gaseous fluids and of solid bodies immersed in them
**aero·ther·mo·dy·nam·ics** \-,thər-mə-(,)dī-'na-miks\ *noun plural but singular or plural in construction* (1949)
: the thermodynamics of gases and especially of air
— **aero·ther·mo·dy·nam·ic** \-mik\ *adjective*
¹**aery** \'ar-ē, 'er-ē, 'ā-ə-rē\ *adjective* **aer·i·er; -est** [Latin *aerius* — more at AERIAL] (14th century)
: having an aerial quality : ETHEREAL ⟨*aery* visions⟩
— **aer·i·ly** \'ar-ə-lē, 'er-\ *adverb*
²**aery** *like* AERIE *variant of* AERIE
**Aes·cu·la·pi·an** \,es-k(y)ə-'lā-pē-ən\ *adjective* [*Aesculapius*, Greco-Roman god of medicine, from Latin, from Greek *Asklēpios*] (1605)
: of or relating to Aesculapius or the healing art ◆
**Ae·sir** \'ā-,zir, -,sir\ *noun plural* [Old Norse *Æsir*, plural of *āss* god]
: the principal race of Norse gods
**Ae·so·pi·an** \ē-'sō-pē-ən, -'sä-\ *also* **Ae·sop·ic** \-'sä-pik\ *adjective* (1728)
**1** : of, relating to, or characteristic of Aesop or his fables
**2** : conveying an innocent meaning to an outsider but a hidden meaning to a member of a conspiracy or underground movement ⟨*Aesopian* language⟩
**aes·thete** \'es-,thēt, *British usually* 'ēs-\ *noun* [back-formation from *aesthetic*] (1881)
: one having or affecting sensitivity to the beautiful especially in art
¹**aes·thet·ic** \es-'the-tik, is-, *British usually* ēs-\ *or* **aes·thet·i·cal** \-ti-kəl\ *adjective* [German *ästhetisch*, from New Latin *aestheticus*, from Greek *aisthētikos* of sense perception, from *aisthanesthai* to perceive — more at AUDIBLE] (1798)
**1 a** : of, relating to, or dealing with aesthetics or the beautiful ⟨*aesthetic* theories⟩ **b** : ARTISTIC ⟨a work of *aesthetic* value⟩ **c** : pleasing in appearance : ATTRACTIVE ⟨easy-to-use keyboards, clear graphics, and other ergonomic and *aesthetic* features —Mark Mehler⟩
**2** : appreciative of, responsive to, or zealous about the beautiful; *also* : responsive to or appreciative of what is pleasurable to the senses
— **aes·thet·i·cal·ly** \-ti-k(ə-)lē\ *adverb*
²**aesthetic** *noun* (1822)
**1** *plural but singular or plural in construction* : a branch of philosophy dealing with the nature of beauty, art, and taste and with the creation and appreciation of beauty
**2** : a particular theory or conception of beauty or art : a particular taste for or approach to what is pleasing to the senses and especially sight ⟨modernist *aesthetics*⟩ ⟨staging new ballets which reflected the *aesthetic* of the new nation —Mary Clarke & Clement Crisp⟩

---

**3** *plural* : a pleasing appearance or effect : BEAUTY ⟨appreciated the *aesthetics* of the gemstones⟩
**aesthetic distance** *noun* (1938)
: the frame of reference that an artist creates by the use of technical devices in and around the work of art to differentiate it psychologically from reality
**aes·the·ti·cian** \,es-thə-'ti-shən\ *noun* (1829)
: a specialist in aesthetics
**aes·thet·i·cism** \es-'the-tə-,si-zəm, is-\ *noun* (1855)
**1** : a doctrine that the principles of beauty are basic to other and especially moral principles
**2** : devotion to or emphasis on beauty or the cultivation of the arts
**aes·thet·i·cize** \-,sīz\ *transitive verb* **-cized; -ciz·ing** (1864)
: to make aesthetic
**aes·ti·val** \'es-tə-vəl\ *variant of* ESTIVAL
**aes·ti·vate, aes·ti·va·tion** *variant of* ESTIVATE, ESTIVATION
**aether** *variant of* ETHER 2a
**ae·ti·ol·o·gy** *chiefly British variant of* ETIOLOGY
**af-** — see AD-
¹**afar** \ə-'fär\ *adverb* [Middle English *afer*, from *on fer* at a distance and *of fer* from a distance] (14th century)
: from, to, or at a great distance ⟨roamed *afar*⟩
: far away
²**afar** *noun* (14th century)
: a great distance ⟨saw him from *afar*⟩
**afeard** *or* **afeared** \ə-'fird\ *adjective* [Middle English *afered*, from Old English *āfǣred*, past participle of *āfǣran* to frighten, from *ā-*, perfective prefix + *fǣran* to frighten — more at ABIDE, FEAR] (before 12th century)
*dialect* : AFRAID
**afe·brile** \(,)ā-'fe-,brīl *also* -'fē-\ *adjective* (1875)
: not marked by fever
**af·fa·ble** \'a-fə-bəl\ *adjective* [Middle French, from Latin *affabilis*, from *affari* to speak to, from *ad-* + *fari* to speak — more at BAN] (15th century)
**1** : being pleasant and at ease in talking to others
**2** : characterized by ease and friendliness
*synonym* see GRACIOUS
— **af·fa·bil·i·ty** \,a-fə-'bi-lə-tē\ *noun*
— **af·fa·bly** \-blē\ *adverb*
**af·fair** \ə-'far, -'fer\ *noun* [Middle English & Middle French; Middle English *affaire*, from Middle French, from *a faire* to do] (14th century)
**1 a** *plural* : commercial, professional, public, or personal business **b** : MATTER, CONCERN
**2** : a procedure, action, or occasion only

---

\ə\ **abut** \ə\ **kitten** \ər\ **further** \a\ **ash** \ā\ **ace**
\ä\ **mop, mar** \aů\ **out** \ch\ **chin** \e\ **bet** \ē\ **easy**
\g\ **go** \i\ **hit** \ī\ **ice** \j\ **job** \ŋ\ **sing** \ō\ **go**
\ò\ **law** \òi\ **boy** \th\ **thin** \t̲h̲\ **the** \ü\ **loot** \ů\ **foot**
\y\ **yet** \zh\ **vision**   *see also* Guide to Pronunciation

vaguely specified; *also* **:** an object or collection of objects only vaguely specified ⟨their house was a 2-story *affair*⟩
**3** *also* **af·faire a :** a romantic or passionate attachment typically of limited duration **:** LIAISON 2b **b :** a matter occasioning public anxiety, controversy, or scandal **:** CASE
¹**af·fect** \'a-ˌfekt\ *noun* [Middle English, from Latin *affectus*, from *afficere*] (14th century)
**1** *obsolete* **:** FEELING, AFFECTION
**2 :** the conscious subjective aspect of an emotion considered apart from bodily changes
**usage** see EFFECT
²**af·fect** \ə-'fekt, a-\ *verb* [Middle English, from Middle French & Latin; Middle French *affecter*, from Latin *affectare*, frequentative of *afficere* to influence, from *ad-* + *facere* to do — more at DO] (15th century)
*transitive verb*
**1** *archaic* **:** to aim at
**2 a** *archaic* **:** to have affection for **b :** to be given to **:** FANCY ⟨*affect* flashy clothes⟩
**3 :** to make a display of liking or using **:** CULTIVATE ⟨*affect* a worldly manner⟩
**4 :** to put on a pretense of **:** FEIGN ⟨*affect* indifference, though deeply hurt⟩
**5 :** to tend toward ⟨drops of water *affect* roundness⟩
**6 :** FREQUENT
*intransitive verb*
*obsolete* **:** INCLINE 2
**synonym** see ASSUME
**usage** see EFFECT
³**affect** *transitive verb* [Middle English, from *affectus*, past participle of *afficere*] (15th century)
**:** to produce an effect upon: as **a :** to produce a material influence upon or alteration in ⟨paralysis *affected* his limbs⟩ **b :** to act upon (as a person or a person's mind or feelings) so as to effect a response **:** INFLUENCE ☆
**usage** see EFFECT
— **af·fect·abil·i·ty** \-ˌfek-tə-'bi-lə-tē\ *noun*
— **af·fect·able** \-'fek-tə-bəl\ *adjective*
**af·fec·ta·tion** \ˌa-ˌfek-'tā-shən\ *noun* (1548)
**1 a :** the act of taking on or displaying an attitude or mode of behavior not natural to oneself or not genuinely felt **b :** speech or conduct not natural to oneself **:** ARTIFICIALITY
**2** *obsolete* **:** a striving after
**synonym** see POSE
**af·fect·ed** \ə-'fek-təd, a-\ *adjective* (1587)
**1 :** INCLINED, DISPOSED ⟨was well *affected* toward her⟩
**2 a :** given to affectation **b :** assumed artificially or falsely **:** PRETENDED ⟨an *affected* interest in art⟩
— **af·fect·ed·ly** *adverb*
— **af·fect·ed·ness** *noun*
**af·fect·ing** \ə-'fek-tiŋ, a-\ *adjective* (1720)
**:** evoking a strong emotional response
**synonym** see MOVING
— **af·fect·ing·ly** \-tiŋ-lē\ *adverb*
**af·fec·tion** \ə-'fek-shən\ *noun* [Middle English, from Old French *affection*, from Latin *affection-*, *affectio*, from *afficere*] (13th century)
**1 :** a moderate feeling or emotion
**2 :** tender attachment **:** FONDNESS ⟨she had a deep *affection* for her parents⟩
**3 a** (1) **:** a bodily condition (2) **:** DISEASE, MALADY **b :** ATTRIBUTE ⟨shape and weight are *affections* of bodies⟩
**4** *obsolete* **:** PARTIALITY, PREJUDICE
**5 :** the feeling aspect (as in pleasure) of consciousness
**6 a :** PROPENSITY, DISPOSITION **b** *archaic* **:** AFFECTATION 1
**7 :** the action of affecting **:** the state of being affected
**synonym** see FEELING
— **af·fec·tion·less** \-ləs\ *adjective*
**af·fec·tion·al** \ə-'fek-shnəl, -shə-nᵊl\ *adjective* (1859)
**:** of or relating to the affections
— **af·fec·tion·al·ly** *adverb*

**af·fec·tion·ate** \ə-'fek-sh(ə-)nət\ *adjective* (15th century)
**1** *obsolete* **:** INCLINED, DISPOSED
**2 :** having affection or warm regard **:** LOVING
**3 :** proceeding from affection **:** TENDER ⟨*affectionate* care⟩
— **af·fec·tion·ate·ly** *adverb*
**af·fec·tioned** \-shənd\ *adjective* (1555)
*archaic* **:** having a tendency, disposition, or inclination **:** DISPOSED
**af·fec·tive** \a-'fek-tiv\ *adjective* (1623)
**1 :** relating to, arising from, or influencing feelings or emotions **:** EMOTIONAL ⟨*affective* disorders⟩
**2 :** expressing emotion ⟨*affective* language⟩
— **af·fec·tive·ly** *adverb*
— **af·fec·tiv·i·ty** \ˌa-ˌfek-'ti-və-tē\ *noun*
**af·fect·less** \'a-ˌfekt-ləs, a-'fekt-\ *adjective* (1967)
**:** showing or expressing no emotion; *also* **:** UNFEELING ⟨a ruthless *affectless* society⟩
— **af·fect·less·ness** *noun*
**af·fen·pin·scher** \'a-fən-ˌpin-chər\ *noun* [German, from *Affe* ape + *Pinscher*, a breed of hunting dog] (1903)
**:** any of a breed of toy dogs with a wiry black, red, tan, or gray coat, erect ears, large round eyes, and bushy eyebrows, chin tuft, and mustache
¹**af·fer·ent** \'a-fə-rənt, -ˌfer-ənt\ *adjective* [Latin *afferent-*, *afferens*, present participle of *afferre* to bring to, from *ad-* + *ferre* to bear — more at BEAR] (circa 1847)
**:** bearing or conducting inward; *specifically* **:** conveying impulses toward a nerve center (as the brain or spinal cord) — compare EFFERENT
— **af·fer·ent·ly** *adverb*
²**afferent** *noun* (1949)
**:** an afferent anatomical part (as a nerve)
¹**af·fi·ance** \ə-'fī-ən(t)s\ *noun* [Middle English, from Middle French, from *affier* to pledge, trust, from Medieval Latin *affidare* to pledge, from Latin *ad-* + (assumed) Vulgar Latin *fidare* to trust — more at FIANCÉ] (14th century)
*archaic* **:** TRUST, CONFIDENCE
²**affiance** *transitive verb* **-anced; -anc·ing** (1555)
**:** to solemnly promise (oneself or another) in marriage **:** BETROTH
**af·fi·ant** \ə-'fī-ənt\ *noun* [Middle French, from present participle of *affier*] (1807)
**:** one that swears to an affidavit; *broadly* **:** DEPONENT
**af·fi·cio·na·do** *variant of* AFICIONADO
**af·fi·da·vit** \ˌa-fə-'dā-vət\ *noun* [Medieval Latin, he has made an oath, from *affidare*] (1593)
**:** a sworn statement in writing made especially under oath or on affirmation before an authorized magistrate or officer
¹**af·fil·i·ate** \ə-'fi-lē-ˌāt\ *verb* **-at·ed; -at·ing** [Medieval Latin *affiliatus*, past participle of *affiliare* to adopt as a son, from Latin *ad-* + *filius* son — more at FEMININE] (1761)
*transitive verb*
**1 a :** to bring or receive into close connection as a member or branch **b :** to associate as a member ⟨*affiliates* herself with the local club⟩
**2 :** to trace the origin of
*intransitive verb*
**:** to connect or associate oneself **:** COMBINE
— **af·fil·i·a·tion** \-ˌfī-lē-'ā-shən\ *noun*
²**af·fil·i·ate** \ə-'fi-lē-ət, -ˌāt\ *noun* (1879)
**:** an affiliated person or organization
**af·fil·i·at·ed** \-lē-ˌā-təd\ *adjective* (1795)
**:** closely associated with another typically in a dependent or subordinate position ⟨the university and its *affiliated* medical school⟩
¹**af·fine** \a-'fīn, ə-\ *noun* [Middle French *affin*, from Latin *affinis*, from *affinis* related] (circa 1509)
**:** a relative by marriage **:** IN-LAW
²**affine** *adjective* [Latin *affinis*, adjective] (1918)

**:** of, relating to, or being a transformation (as a translation, a rotation, or a uniform stretching) that carries straight lines into straight lines and parallel lines into parallel lines but may alter distance between points and angles between lines ⟨*affine* geometry⟩
— **af·fine·ly** *adverb*
**af·fined** \a-'fīnd, ə-\ *adjective* (1597)
**1 :** joined in a close relationship **:** CONNECTED
**2 :** bound by obligation
**af·fin·i·ty** \ə-'fi-nə-tē\ *noun, plural* **-ties** [Middle English *affinite*, from Middle French or Latin; Middle French *afinité*, from Latin *affinitas*, from *affinis* bordering on, related by marriage, from *ad-* + *finis* end, border] (14th century)
**1 :** relationship by marriage
**2 a :** sympathy marked by community of interest **:** KINSHIP **b** (1) **:** an attraction to or liking for something ⟨people with an *affinity* to darkness —Mark Twain⟩ ⟨pork and fennel have a natural *affinity* for each other —Abby Mandel⟩ (2) **:** an attractive force between substances or particles that causes them to enter into and remain in chemical combination **c :** a person especially of the opposite sex having a particular attraction for one
**3 a :** likeness based on relationship or causal connection ⟨found an *affinity* between the teller of a tale and the craftsman —Mary McCarthy⟩ ⟨this investigation, with *affinities* to a case history, a psychoanalysis, a detective story and a novel — Oliver Sacks⟩ **b :** a relation between biological groups involving resemblance in structural plan and indicating a common origin
**synonym** see ATTRACTION
**affinity chromatography** *noun* (1970)
**:** chromatography in which a macromolecule (as a protein) is isolated and purified by passing it in solution through a column treated with a substance having a ligand for which the macromolecule has an affinity that causes it to be retained on the column
**affinity group** *noun* (1970)
**:** a group of people having a common interest or goal or acting together for a specific purpose (as for a chartered tour)
**af·firm** \ə-'fərm\ *verb* [Middle English *affermen*, from Middle French *afermer*, from Latin *affirmare*, from *ad-* + *firmare* to make firm, from *firmus* firm — more at FIRM] (14th century)
*transitive verb*
**1 a :** VALIDATE, CONFIRM **b :** to state positively
**2 :** to assert (as a judgment or decree) as valid or confirmed
**3 :** to express dedication to

---

☆ **SYNONYMS**
**Affect, influence, touch, impress, strike, sway** mean to produce or have an effect upon. AFFECT implies the action of a stimulus that can produce a response or reaction ⟨the sight *affected* her to tears⟩. INFLUENCE implies a force that brings about a change (as in nature or behavior) ⟨our beliefs are *influenced* by our upbringing⟩ ⟨a drug that *influences* growth rates⟩. TOUCH may carry a vivid suggestion of close contact and may connote stirring, arousing, or harming ⟨plants *touched* by frost⟩ ⟨his emotions were *touched* by her distress⟩. IMPRESS stresses the depth and persistence of the effect ⟨only one of the plans *impressed* him⟩. STRIKE, similar to but weaker than *impress*, may convey the notion of sudden sharp perception or appreciation ⟨*struck* by the solemnity of the occasion⟩. SWAY implies the acting of influences that are not resisted or are irresistible, with resulting change in character or course of action ⟨politicians who are *swayed* by popular opinion⟩.

*intransitive verb*
**1 :** to testify or declare by affirmation as distinguished from swearing an oath
**2 :** to uphold a judgment or decree of a lower court
**synonym** see ASSERT
— **af·firm·able** \ə-'fər-mə-bəl\ *adjective*
— **af·fir·mance** \ə-'fər-mən(t)s\ *noun*
**af·fir·ma·tion** \ˌa-fər-'mā-shən\ *noun* (15th century)
**1 a :** the act of affirming **b :** something affirmed **:** a positive assertion
**2 :** a solemn declaration made under the penalties of perjury by a person who conscientiously declines taking an oath
**¹af·fir·ma·tive** \ə-'fər-mə-tiv\ *adjective* (15th century)
**1 :** asserting a predicate of a subject
**2 :** asserting that the fact is so
**3 :** POSITIVE ⟨*affirmative* approach⟩
**4 :** favoring or supporting a proposition or motion
— **af·fir·ma·tive·ly** *adverb*
**²affirmative** *noun* (15th century)
**1 :** an expression (as the word *yes*) of affirmation or assent
**2 :** an affirmative proposition
**3 :** the side that upholds the proposition stated in a debate
**affirmative action** *noun* (1965)
**:** an active effort to improve the employment or educational opportunities of members of minority groups and women
**¹af·fix** \ə-'fiks, a-\ *transitive verb* [Latin *affixus*, past participle of *affigere* to fasten to, from *ad-* + *figere* to fasten — more at FIX] (1533)
**1 :** to attach physically ⟨*affix* a stamp to a letter⟩
**2 :** to attach in any way **:** ADD, APPEND ⟨*affix* a signature to a document⟩
**3 :** IMPRESS ⟨*affixed* my seal⟩
**synonym** see FASTEN
— **af·fix·able** \-'fik-sə-bəl\ *adjective*
— **af·fix·a·tion** \ˌa-ˌfik-'sā-shən\ *noun*
— **af·fix·ment** \ə-'fik-smənt, a-\ *noun*
**²af·fix** \'a-ˌfiks\ *noun* (1612)
**1 :** one or more sounds or letters occurring as a bound form attached to the beginning or end of a word, base, or phrase or inserted within a word or base and serving to produce a derivative word or an inflectional form
**2 :** APPENDAGE
— **af·fix·al** \-ˌfik-səl\ *or* **af·fix·i·al** \a-'fik-sē-əl\ *adjective*
**af·fla·tus** \ə-'flā-təs, a-\ *noun* [Latin, act of blowing or breathing on, from *afflare* to blow on, from *ad-* + *flare* to blow — more at BLOW] (1660)
**:** a divine imparting of knowledge or power **:** INSPIRATION
**af·flict** \ə-'flikt\ *transitive verb* [Middle English, from Latin *afflictus*, past participle of *affligere* to cast down, from *ad-* + *fligere* to strike — more at PROFLIGATE] (14th century)
**1** *obsolete* **a :** HUMBLE **b :** OVERTHROW
**2 a :** to distress so severely as to cause persistent suffering or anguish **b :** TROUBLE, INJURE
☆
**af·flic·tion** \ə-'flik-shən\ *noun* (14th century)
**1 :** the state of being afflicted
**2 :** the cause of persistent pain or distress
**3 :** great suffering
**af·flic·tive** \ə-'flik-tiv\ *adjective* (circa 1611)
**:** causing affliction **:** DISTRESSING, TROUBLESOME
— **af·flic·tive·ly** *adverb*
**af·flu·ence** \'a-(ˌ)flü-ən(t)s *also* a-'flü- *or* ə-\ *noun* (14th century)
**1 a :** an abundant flow or supply **:** PROFUSION
**b :** abundance of property **:** WEALTH
**2 :** a flowing to or toward a point **:** INFLUX
**af·flu·en·cy** \-ən(t)-sē\ *noun, plural* **-cies** (1664)
**:** AFFLUENCE

**¹af·flu·ent** \-ənt\ *adjective* [Middle English, from Middle French, from Latin *affluent-*, *affluens*, present participle of *affluere* to flow to, flow abundantly, from *ad-* + *fluere* to flow — more at FLUID] (15th century)
**1 :** flowing in abundance ⟨*affluent* streams⟩ ⟨*affluent* creativity⟩
**2 :** having a generously sufficient and typically increasing supply of material possessions ⟨our *affluent* society⟩
**synonym** see RICH
— **af·flu·ent·ly** *adverb*
**²affluent** *noun* (1828)
**1 :** a tributary stream
**2 :** an affluent person
**af·ford** \ə-'fōrd, -'förd\ *transitive verb* [Middle English *aforthen*, from Old English *geforthian* to carry out, from *ge-*, perfective prefix + *forthian* to carry out, from *forth* — more at CO-, FORTH] (14th century)
**1 a :** to manage to bear without serious detriment ⟨you can't *afford* to neglect your health⟩
**b :** to be able to bear the cost of ⟨can't *afford* to be out of work long⟩ ⟨able to *afford* a new car⟩
**2 :** to make available, give forth, or provide naturally or inevitably ⟨the sun *affords* warmth to the earth⟩ ⟨the roof *afforded* a fine view⟩
**synonym** see GIVE
— **af·ford·abil·i·ty** \-ˌfōr-də-'bi-lə-tē, -ˌför-\ *noun*
— **af·ford·able** \-'fōr-də-bəl, -'för-\ *adjective*
— **af·ford·ably** \ə-'fōr-də-blē, -'för-\ *adverb*
**af·for·es·ta·tion** \ə-ˌfōr-ə-'stā-shən, ə-, -ˌfär-\ *noun* [Medieval Latin *afforestation-*, *afforestatio*, from *afforestare* to put under forest laws, from Latin *ad-* + Medieval Latin *foresta*, *forestis* forest] (1615)
**:** the act or process of establishing a forest especially on land not previously forested
— **af·for·est** \a-'fōr-əst, -'fär-\ *transitive verb*
**¹af·fray** \ə-'frā\ *noun* [Middle English, from Middle French, from *affreer* to startle] (14th century)
**:** FRAY, BRAWL
**²affray** *transitive verb* [Middle English *affraien*, from Middle French *affreer*] (14th century)
*archaic* **:** STARTLE, FRIGHTEN
**af·fri·cate** \'a-fri-kət\ *noun* [probably from German *Affrikata*, from Latin *affricata*, feminine of *affricatus*, past participle of *affricare* to rub against, from *ad-* + *fricare* to rub — more at FRICTION] (1880)
**:** a stop and its immediately following release into a fricative that are considered to constitute a single phoneme (as the \t\ and \sh\ of \ch\ in *choose*)
— **af·fric·a·tive** \a-'fri-kə-tiv, ə-\ *noun or adjective*
**¹af·fright** \ə-'frīt\ *transitive verb* [Middle English *afyrht*, *afright* frightened, from Old English *āfyrht*, past participle of *āfyrhtan* to frighten, from *ā-*, perfective prefix + *fyrhtan* to fear; akin to Old English *fyrhto* fright — more at ABIDE, FRIGHT] (before 12th century)
**:** FRIGHTEN, ALARM
**²affright** *noun* (1596)
**:** sudden and great fear **:** TERROR
**¹af·front** \ə-'frənt\ *transitive verb* [Middle English *afronten*, from Middle French *afronter* to defy, from (assumed) Vulgar Latin *affrontare*, from Latin *ad-* + *front-*, *frons* forehead] (14th century)
**1 a :** to insult especially to the face by behavior or language **b :** to cause offense to ⟨a system of law about both family and marriage that *affronted* lay society —J. H. Mundy⟩
**2 a :** to face in defiance **:** CONFRONT ⟨*affront* death⟩ **b** *obsolete* **:** to encounter face-to-face
**3 :** to appear directly before
**synonym** see OFFEND

**²affront** *noun* (1533)
**1** *obsolete* **:** a hostile encounter
**2 :** a deliberate offense **:** INSULT ⟨an *affront* to his dignity⟩
**af·fu·sion** \a-'fyü-zhən\ *noun* [Late Latin *affusion-*, *affusio*, from Latin *affundere* to pour on, from *ad-* + *fundere* to pour — more at FOUND] (1615)
**:** an act of pouring a liquid on (as in baptism)
**Af·ghan** \'af-ˌgan *also* -gən\ *noun* [Persian *afghān* Pashtun] (1767)
**1 a** (1) **:** PASHTUN (2) **:** PASHTO **b :** a native or inhabitant of Afghanistan
**2** *not capitalized* **:** a blanket or shawl of colored wool knitted or crocheted in strips or squares
**3** *not capitalized* **:** a Turkoman carpet of large size and long pile woven in geometric designs
**4 :** AFGHAN HOUND
— **Afghan** *adjective*
**Afghan hound** *noun* (1925)
**:** any of a breed of tall slim swift hunting dogs of Near Eastern origin with a coat of silky thick hair and a long silky topknot

**af·ghani** \af-'ga-nē, -'gä-\ *noun* [Persian *afghānī*, literally, of the Pashtuns] (1927)

**Afghan hound**

— see MONEY table
**afi·cio·na·da** \ə-ˌfi-sh(ē-)ə-'nä-də, -fē-, -sē-ə-, -ˌdä\ *noun* [Spanish, feminine of *aficionado*] (1952)
**:** a female aficionado
**afi·cio·na·do** \-'nä-(ˌ)dō\ *noun, plural* **-dos** [Spanish, from past participle of *aficionar* to inspire affection, from *afición* affection, from Latin *affection-*, *affectio* — more at AFFECTION] (1845)
**:** a person who likes, knows about, and appreciates a usually fervently pursued interest or activity **:** DEVOTEE ⟨*aficionados* of the bullfight⟩ ⟨movie *aficionados*⟩
**afield** \ə-'fē(ə)ld\ *adverb or adjective* (before 12th century)
**1 :** to, in, or on the field ⟨was weak at bat but strong *afield*⟩
**2 :** away from home **:** ABROAD
**3 :** out of the way **:** ASTRAY ⟨irrelevant remarks that carried us far *afield*⟩
**afire** \ə-'fīr\ *adjective or adverb* (13th century)
**:** being on fire **:** BLAZING
**aflame** \ə-'flām\ *adjective or adverb* (1555)
**:** AFIRE

\ə\ abut \ᵊ\ kitten \ər\ further \a\ ash \ā\ ace
\ä\ mop, mar \aů\ out \ch\ chin \e\ bet \ē\ easy
\g\ go \i\ hit \ī\ ice \j\ job \ŋ\ sing \ō\ go
\ô\ law \ói\ boy \th\ thin \th̲\ the \ü\ loot \ů\ foot
\y\ yet \zh\ vision *see also* Guide to Pronunciation

**af·la·tox·in** \ˌa-flə-'täk-sən\ *noun* [New Latin *Aspergillus flavus,* species of mold + English *toxin*] (1962)
: any of several carcinogenic mycotoxins that are produced especially in stored agricultural crops (as peanuts) by molds (as *Aspergillus flavus*)

**afloat** \ə-'flōt\ *adjective or adverb* [Middle English *aflot,* from Old English *on flot,* from *on* + *flot,* from *flot* deep water, sea; akin to Old English *flēotan* to float — more at FLEET] (before 12th century)
**1 a :** borne on or as if on the water **b :** being at sea
**2 :** free of difficulties **:** SELF-SUFFICIENT ⟨the inheritance kept them *afloat* for years⟩
**3 a :** circulating about ⟨nasty stories were *afloat*⟩ **b :** ADRIFT

**aflut·ter** \ə-'flə-tər\ *adjective* (1830)
**1 :** being in a flutter **:** FLUTTERING
**2 :** nervously excited
**3 :** filled with or marked by the presence of fluttering things ⟨roofs *aflutter* with flags⟩

**afoot** \ə-'fut\ *adverb or adjective* (13th century)
**1 :** on foot
**2 :** in the process of development **:** UNDER WAY ⟨something out of the ordinary was *afoot* —Hamilton Basso⟩

**afore** \ə-'fōr, -'for\ *adverb or conjunction or preposition* [Middle English, from Old English *onforan,* from *on* + *foran* before — more at BEFORE] (before 12th century)
*chiefly dialect* **:** BEFORE

**afore·men·tioned** \-'men(t)-shənd\ *adjective* (1587)
: mentioned previously

**afore·said** \-ˌsed\ *adjective* (14th century)
: said or named before or above

**afore·thought** \-ˌthȯt\ *adjective* (1581)
: previously in mind **:** PREMEDITATED, DELIBERATE ⟨with malice *aforethought*⟩

**a for·ti·o·ri** \ˌä-ˌfȯr-shē-'ȯr-ˌī, -ä-ˌfȯr-shē-'ȯr-ē, -ˌfȯr-tē-, -'ȯr-\ *adverb* [New Latin, literally, from the stronger (argument)] (1588)
: with greater reason or more convincing force — used in drawing a conclusion that is inferred to be even more certain than another ⟨the man of prejudice is, *a fortiori,* a man of limited mental vision⟩

**afoul of** \ə-'faủ-ləv\ *preposition* (1824)
**1 :** in or into conflict with
**2 :** in or into collision or entanglement with

**Afr-** *or* **Afro-** *combining form*
: African ⟨*Afro*-American⟩ **:** African and ⟨*Afro*-Asiatic⟩

**afraid** \ə-'frād, *Southern also* ə-'fred\ *adjective* [Middle English *affraied,* from past participle of *affraien* to frighten — more at AFFRAY] (14th century)
**1 :** filled with fear or apprehension ⟨*afraid* of machines⟩ ⟨*afraid* for his job⟩
**2 :** filled with concern or regret over an unwanted situation ⟨I'm *afraid* I won't be able to go⟩
**3 :** having a dislike for something ⟨*afraid* of hard work⟩
**synonym** see FEARFUL

**A–frame** \'ā-ˌfrām\ *noun* (circa 1909)
**1 :** a support structure shaped like the letter A
**2 :** a building typically having triangular front and rear walls and a roof reaching to the ground

**afreet** *or* **afrit** \'a-ˌfrēt, ə-'frēt\ *noun* [Arabic *'ifrīt*] (1786)
: a powerful evil jinni, demon, or monstrous giant in Arabic mythology

**afresh** \ə-'fresh\ *adverb* (15th century)
: from a fresh beginning **:** ANEW, AGAIN

**¹Af·ri·can** \'a-fri-kən *also* 'ä-\ *noun* (before 12th century)
**1 :** a native or inhabitant of Africa
**2 :** a person and especially a black person of African ancestry

**²African** *adjective* (1564)

: of, relating to, or characteristic of the continent of Africa or its people
**— Af·ri·can·ness** \-kə(n)-nəs\ *noun*

**Af·ri·ca·na** \ˌa-fri-'ka-nə, -'kä-, -'kā- *also* ˌä-\ *noun plural* (1908)
: materials (as books, documents, or artifacts) relating to African history and culture

**Af·ri·can–Amer·i·can** \ˌa-fri-kə-nə-'mer-ə-kən *also* ˌä-\ *noun* (1984)
: AFRO-AMERICAN
**— African–American** *adjective*

**African buffalo** *noun* (1902)
: CAPE BUFFALO

**African daisy** *noun* (circa 1889)
: any of a genus (*Arctotis*) of widely cultivated composite herbs

**Af·ri·kan·der** *or* **Af·ri·kan·der** \ˌa-fri-'kan-dər\ *noun* [Afrikaans *Afrikaner, Afrikaander,* literally, Afrikaner] (1852)
: any of a breed of tall red large-horned humped southern African cattle used chiefly for meat or draft

**African elephant** *noun* (1607)
: ELEPHANT 1a

**Af·ri·can·ise** *British variant of* AFRICANIZE

**Af·ri·can·ism** \'a-fri-kə-ˌni-zəm *also* 'ä-\ *noun* (1641)
**1 :** a characteristic feature (as a custom or belief) of African culture
**2 :** a characteristic feature of an African language occurring in a non-African language
**3 :** allegiance to the traditions, interests, or ideals of Africa

**Af·ri·can·ist** \-nist\ *noun* (1895)
: a specialist in African languages or cultures

**Af·ri·can·ize** \-ˌnīz\ *transitive verb* **-ized; -izing** (1853)
**1 :** to cause to acquire a distinctively African trait
**2 :** to bring under the influence, control, or cultural or civil supremacy of Africans and especially black Africans
**— Af·ri·can·iza·tion** \ˌa-fri-kə-nə-'zā-shən *also* ˌä-\ *noun*

**Africanized bee** *noun* (1974)
: a honeybee that originated in Brazil as an accidental hybrid between an aggressive African subspecies (*Apis mellifera scutellata*) and previously established European honeybees and has spread to Mexico and the southernmost U.S. by breeding with local bees producing populations retaining most of the African bee's traits — called also *Africanized honeybee, killer bee*

**African mahogany** *noun* (1842)
: MAHOGANY 1b

**African violet** *noun* (1902)
: any of several tropical African gesneriads (especially *Saintpaulia ionantha*) widely grown as houseplants for their velvety fleshy leaves and showy purple, pink, or white flowers

**¹Af·ri·kaans** \ˌa-fri-'kän(t)s, ˌä-, -'känz, 'a-fri-ˌ, 'ä-\ *noun* [Afrikaans, from *afrikaans,* adjective, African, from obsolete Afrikaans *afrikanisch,* from Latin *africanus*] (1908)
: a language developed from 17th century Dutch that is one of the official languages of the Republic of South Africa

**²Afrikaans** *adjective* (1923)
: of or relating to Afrikaners or Afrikaans

**Af·ri·ka·ner** \ˌa-fri-'kä-nər\ *noun, often attributive* [Afrikaans, literally, African, from Latin *africanus*] (1824)
: a South African of European descent whose native language is Afrikaans
**— Af·ri·ka·ner·dom** \-dəm\ *noun*

**¹Af·ro** \'a-(ˌ)frō\ *adjective* [probably from *Afro-American*] (1938)
: characterized by or being a hairstyle of tight curls in a full evenly rounded shape

**²Afro** *noun, plural* **Afros** (1968)
: an Afro hairstyle

**Af·ro–Amer·i·can** \ˌa-frō-ə-'mer-ə-kən\ *noun* (1853)

*Afro*

: an American of African and especially of black African descent
**— Afro–American** *adjective*

**Af·ro–Asi·at·ic** \ˌa-frō-ˌā-zhē-'a-tik, -zē- *also* -shē-\ *adjective* (1953)
: of, relating to, or being a family of languages widely distributed over southwestern Asia and Africa comprising the Semitic, Egyptian, Berber, Cushitic, and Chadic subfamilies

**Af·ro·cen·tric** \ˌa-frō-'sen-trik\ *adjective* (1966)
: centered on or derived from Africa or the Africans
**— Af·ro·cen·trism** \-ˌtri-zəm\ *noun*

**¹aft** \'aft\ *adverb* [Middle English *afte* back, from Old English *æftan* from behind, behind; akin to Old English *æfter*] (1628)
: near, toward, or in the stern of a ship or the tail of an aircraft **:** ABAFT ⟨called all hands *aft*⟩

**²aft** *adjective* (1816)
: REARWARD, AFTER 2 ⟨the *aft* decks⟩

**³aft** *Scottish variant of* OFT

**¹af·ter** \'af-tər\ *adverb* [Middle English, from Old English *æfter;* akin to Old High German *aftar* after, and probably to Old English *of* of] (before 12th century)
: following in time or place **:** AFTERWARD, BEHIND, LATER ⟨we arrived shortly *after*⟩ ⟨returned 20 years *after*⟩

**²after** *preposition* (before 12th century)
**1 a :** behind in place **b** (1) **:** subsequent to in time or order (2) **:** subsequent to and in view of ⟨*after* all our advice⟩
**2 —** used as a function word to indicate the object of a stated or implied action ⟨go *after* gold⟩ ⟨was asking *after* you⟩
**3 :** so as to resemble: as **a :** in accordance with **b :** with the name of or a name derived from that of **c :** in the characteristic manner of **d :** in imitation of

**³after** *conjunction* (before 12th century)
: subsequently to the time when

**⁴after** *adjective* (before 12th century)
**1 :** later in time ⟨in *after* years⟩
**2 :** located toward the rear and especially toward the stern of a ship or tail of an aircraft

**⁵af·ter** \'äf-tər\ *verbal auxiliary* (1800)
*chiefly Irish —* used with a present participle to indicate action completed and especially just completed ⟨the poor old man is *after* dying on me —J. M. Synge⟩

**⁶after** *noun* (circa 1902)
: AFTERNOON

**after all** *adverb* (1846)
**1 :** in spite of considerations or expectations to the contrary **:** NEVERTHELESS ⟨decided to take the train *after all*⟩ ⟨didn't rain *after all*⟩
**2 —** used as a sentence modifier to emphasize something to be taken into consideration ⟨literature which is *after all* only a special department of reading —W. W. Watt⟩

**af·ter·birth** \'af-tər-ˌbərth\ *noun* (1587)
: the placenta and fetal membranes that are expelled after delivery

**af·ter·burn·er** \-ˌbər-nər\ *noun* (1947)
**1 :** a device incorporated into the tail pipe of a turbojet engine for injecting fuel into the hot exhaust gases and burning it to provide extra thrust
**2 :** a device for burning or catalytically destroying unburned or partially burned carbon compounds in exhaust (as from an automobile)

**af·ter·care** \-ˌker, -ˌkar\ *noun* (1894)
: the care, treatment, help, or supervision given to persons discharged from an institution (as a hospital)

**af·ter·clap** \-ˌklap\ *noun* (14th century)

: an unexpected damaging or unsettling event following a supposedly closed affair

**af·ter·deck** \-,dek\ *noun* (1897)
: the part of a deck abaft amidships

**af·ter·ef·fect** \'af-tə-rə-,fekt\ *noun* (1817)
: an effect that follows its cause after an interval

**af·ter·glow** \'af-tər-,glō\ *noun* (1871)
**1** : a reflection of past splendor, success, or emotion
**2** : a glow remaining where a light has disappeared

**af·ter–hours** \,af-tər-'au̇(-ə)rz\ *adjective* (1929)
: engaged in or operating after a legal or conventional closing time ⟨*after-hours* drinking⟩ ⟨an *after-hours* club⟩

**af·ter·im·age** \'af-tər-,i-mij\ *noun* (1874)
: a usually visual sensation occurring after stimulation by its external cause has ceased

**af·ter·life** \'af-tər-,līf\ *noun* (circa 1593)
**1** : an existence after death
**2** : a later period in one's life

**af·ter·mar·ket** \-,mär-kət\ *noun* (1940)
**1** : the market for parts and accessories used in the repair or enhancement of a product (as an automobile)
**2** : a secondary market available after sales in the original market are finished ⟨a movie in the videocassette *aftermarket*⟩

**af·ter·math** \-,math\ *noun* [⁴*after* + *math* (mowing, crop)] (1523)
**1** : a second-growth crop — called also *rowen*
**2** : CONSEQUENCE, RESULT ⟨stricken with guilt as an *aftermath* of the accident⟩
**3** : the period immediately following a usually ruinous event ⟨in the *aftermath* of the war⟩

**af·ter·most** \-,mōst\ *adjective* (1773)
: farthest aft

**af·ter·noon** \,af-tər-'nün\ *noun* (13th century)
**1** : the part of day between noon and sunset
**2** : a relatively late period (as of time or life) ⟨in the *afternoon* of the 19th century⟩
**— afternoon** *adjective*

**af·ter·noons** \-'nünz\ *adverb* (1896)
: in the afternoon repeatedly : on any afternoon

**af·ter·piece** \'af-tər-,pēs\ *noun* (1779)
: a short usually comic entertainment performed after a play

**af·ters** \'af-tərz\ *noun plural* (circa 1909)
*British* : DESSERT

**af·ter·shave** \'af-tər-,shāv\ *noun* (1946)
: a usually scented lotion for use on the face after shaving

**af·ter·shock** \-,shäk\ *noun* (1894)
**1** : a minor shock following the main shock of an earthquake
**2** : an aftereffect of a distressing or traumatic event

**af·ter·taste** \-,tāst\ *noun* (circa 1798)
: persistence of a sensation (as of flavor or an emotion) after the stimulating agent or experience has gone

**af·ter–tax** \-'taks\ *adjective* (1954)
: remaining after payment of taxes and especially of income tax ⟨an *after-tax* profit⟩

**af·ter·thought** \-,thȯt\ *noun* (circa 1661)
**1** : an idea occurring later
**2** : a part, feature, or device not thought of originally

**af·ter·time** \-,tīm\ *noun* (1597)
: FUTURE

**af·ter·ward** \'af-tə(r)-wərd\ *or* **af·ter·wards** \-wərdz\ *adverb* (13th century)
: at a later or succeeding time : SUBSEQUENTLY, THEREAFTER

**af·ter·word** \-,wərd\ *noun* (1890)
: EPILOGUE 1

**af·ter·world** \-,wərld\ *noun* (1596)
: a future world : a world after death

**ag** \'ag\ *adjective* (circa 1918)
: of or relating to agriculture ⟨*ag* schools⟩

**ag-** — see AD-

**Aga·da** \ə-'gä-də, -'gȯ-\ *variant of* HAGGADAH

**again** \ə-'gen, -'gin, -'gān\ *adverb* [Middle English, opposite, again, from Old English *ongēan* opposite, back, from *on* + *gēn, gēan* still, again; akin to Old English *gēan-* against, Old High German *gegin* against, toward] (13th century)
**1** : in return : BACK ⟨swore he would pay him *again* when he was able —Shakespeare⟩
**2** : another time : once more : ANEW ⟨I shall not look upon his like *again* —Shakespeare⟩
**3** : on the other hand ⟨he might go, and *again* he might not⟩
**4** : in addition : BESIDES ⟨*again*, there is another matter to consider⟩

**again and again** *adverb* (1604)
: OFTEN, REPEATEDLY

**¹against** \ə-'gen(t)st, -'gin(t)st, -'gān(t)st\ *preposition* [Middle English, alteration of *againes*, from *again*] (13th century)
**1 a** : in opposition or hostility to **b** : contrary to ⟨*against* the law⟩ **c** : in competition with **d** : as a basis for disapproval of ⟨had nothing *against* him⟩
**2 a** : directly opposite : FACING **b** *obsolete* : exposed to
**3** : compared or contrasted with
**4 a** : in preparation or provision for **b** : as a defense or protection from
**5 a** : in the direction of and into contact with **b** : in contact with
**6** : in a direction opposite to the motion or course of : counter to
**7 a** : as a counterbalance to **b** : in exchange for **c** : as a charge on
**8** : before the background of

**²against** *conjunction* (14th century)
*archaic* : in preparation for the time when ⟨throw on another log of wood *against* father comes home —Charles Dickens⟩

**Ag·a·mem·non** \,a-gə-'mem-,nän, -nən\ *noun* [Latin, from Greek *Agamemnōn*]
: a king of Mycenae and leader of the Greeks in the Trojan War

**aga·mete** \(,)ā-'ga-,mēt *also* -gə-'mēt\ *noun* [International Scientific Vocabulary, from Greek *agametos* unmarried, from *a-* + *gamein* to marry, from *gamos* marriage] (circa 1920)
: an asexual reproductive cell (as a spore)

**agam·ic** \(,)ā-'ga-mik\ *adjective* [Greek *agamos* unmarried, from *a-* + *gamos*] (1850)
: ASEXUAL, PARTHENOGENETIC

**agam·ma·glob·u·lin·emia** \,ā-,ga-mə-,glä-byə-lə-'nē-mē-ə\ *noun* [New Latin, from *a-* + International Scientific Vocabulary *gamma globulin* + New Latin *-emia*] (circa 1952)
: a condition in which the body forms few or no gamma globulins or antibodies
**— agam·ma·glob·u·lin·emic** \-'nē-mik\ *adjective*

**aga·mo·sper·my** \(,)ā-'ga-mə-,spər-mē, 'a-gə-mō-,spər-\ *noun* [Greek *agamos* + English *-spermy*] (1944)
: APOGAMY; *specifically* : apogamy in which sexual union is not completed and the embryo is produced from the innermost layer of the integument of the female gametophyte

**ag·a·pan·thus** \,a-gə-'pan(t)-thəs\ *noun, plural* **-thus** *also* **-thuses** [New Latin, genus name, from Greek *agapē* + *anthos* flower — more at ANTHOLOGY] (circa 1789)
: any of several African plants (genus *Agapanthus*) of the lily family cultivated for their umbels of showy blue or purple flowers

**¹aga·pe** \ä-'gä-(,)pā, 'ä-gə-,pā\ *noun* [Late Latin, from Greek *agapē*, literally, love] (1607)
**1** : LOVE FEAST
**2** : LOVE 4a

**²agape** \ə-'gāp *also* -'gap\ *adjective or adverb* (1667)
**1** : wide open : GAPING
**2** : being in a state of wonder

**agar** \'ä-gər\ *noun* [Malay *agar-agar*] (1889)
**1** : a gelatinous colloidal extractive of a red alga (as of the genera *Gelidium, Gracilaria,* and *Eucheuma*) used especially in culture media or as a gelling and stabilizing agent in foods

**2** : a culture medium containing agar

**agar–agar** \,ä-gər-'ä-gər\ *noun* [Malay] (1820)
: AGAR

**aga·ric** \'a-gər-ik, ə-'gar-ik\ *noun* [Latin *agaricum*, a fungus, from Greek *agarikon*] (15th century)
**1** : the dried fruiting body of a fungus (*Fomes officinalis* synonym *Polyporus officinalis*) formerly used in medicine
**2** : any of a family (Agaricaceae) of fungi with the sporophore usually resembling an umbrella and with numerous gills on the underside of the cap

**aga·rose** \'a-gə-,rōs, 'ä-, -,rōz\ *noun* (1964)
: a polysaccharide obtained from agar and used especially as a supporting medium in gel electrophoresis

**ag·ate** \'a-gət\ *noun, often attributive* [Middle French, from Latin *achates*, from Greek *achatēs*] (1570)
**1** : a fine-grained variegated chalcedony having its colors arranged in stripes, blended in clouds, or showing mosslike forms
**2** : something made of or fitted with agate: as **a** : a drawplate used by gold-wire drawers **b** : a playing marble of agate
**3** : a size of type approximately 5½ point

**agate line** *noun* (circa 1935)
: a space one column wide and ¹⁄₁₄ inch deep used as a unit of measurement in classified advertising

**agate ware** *noun* (1857)
**1** : pottery veined and mottled to resemble agate
**2** : an enameled iron or steel ware for household utensils

**aga·ve** \ə-'gä-vē\ *noun* [New Latin *Agave*, genus name, from Latin, a daughter of Cadmus, from Greek *Agauē*] (circa 1797)
: any of a genus (*Agave* of the family Agavaceae, the agave family) of plants having spiny-margined leaves and flowers in tall spreading panicles and including some cultivated for their fiber or sap or for ornament

**agaze** \ə-'gāz\ *adjective* (circa 1902)
: engaged in the act of gazing

agave

**¹age** \'āj\ *noun* [Middle English, from Old French *aage*, from (assumed) Vulgar Latin *aetaticum*, from Latin *aetat-, aetas*, from *aevum* lifetime — more at AYE] (13th century)
**1 a** : the time of life at which some particular qualification, power, or capacity arises or rests ⟨the voting *age* is 18⟩; *specifically* : MAJORITY **b** : one of the stages of life **c** : the length of an existence extending from the beginning to any given time ⟨a boy 10 years of *age*⟩ **d** : LIFETIME **e** : an advanced stage of life
**2** : a period of time dominated by a central figure or prominent feature ⟨the *age* of Pericles⟩: as **a** : a period in history or human progress ⟨the *age* of reptiles⟩ ⟨the *age* of exploration⟩ **b** : a cultural period marked by the prominence of a particular item ⟨entering the atomic *age*⟩ **c** : a division of geologic time that is usually shorter than an epoch
**3 a** : the period contemporary with a person's lifetime or with his or her active life **b** : a long time — usually used in plural ⟨haven't seen him in *ages*⟩ **c** : GENERATION
**4** : an individual's development measured in terms of the years requisite for like development of an average individual
**synonym** see PERIOD

**²age** *verb* **aged; ag·ing** *or* **age·ing** (14th century)
*intransitive verb*
**1** : to become old **:** show the effects or the characteristics of increasing age
**2** : to acquire a desirable quality (as mellowness or ripeness) by standing undisturbed for some time ⟨letting cheese *age*⟩
*transitive verb*
**1** : to cause to become old
**2** : to bring to a state fit for use or to maturity
— **ag·er** \'ā-jər\ *noun*
**-age** *noun suffix* [Middle English, from Old French, from Latin *-aticum*]
**1** : aggregate : collection ⟨track*age*⟩
**2 a** : action : process ⟨haul*age*⟩ **b** : cumulative result of ⟨break*age*⟩ **c** : rate of ⟨dos*age*⟩
**3** : house or place of ⟨orphan*age*⟩
**4** : state : rank ⟨peon*age*⟩
**5** : charge ⟨post*age*⟩
**aged** \'ā-jəd, 'ājd; 'ājd *for 1b*\ *adjective* (15th century)
**1** : grown old: as **a** : of an advanced age **b** : having attained a specified age ⟨a man *aged* 40 years⟩
**2** : typical of old age
— **ag·ed·ness** \'ā-jəd-nəs\ *noun*
**age–group** \'āj-,grüp\ *noun* (1904)
: a segment of a population that is of approximately the same age or is within a specified range of ages
**age·ism** *also* **ag·ism** \'ā-,ji-zəm\ *noun* (1969)
: prejudice or discrimination against a particular age-group and especially the elderly
— **age·ist** *also* **ag·ist** \-jist\ *adjective*
**age·less** \'āj-ləs\ *adjective* (1651)
**1** : not growing old or showing the effects of age
**2** : TIMELESS, ETERNAL ⟨*ageless* truths⟩
— **age·less·ly** *adverb*
— **age·less·ness** *noun*
**age·long** \'āj-,lȯn\ *adjective* (1810)
: lasting for an age : EVERLASTING
**age·mate** \-,māt\ *noun* (1583)
: one who is of about the same age as another
**agen·cy** \'ā-jən(t)-sē\ *noun, plural* **-cies** (1658)
**1** : the capacity, condition, or state of acting or of exerting power : OPERATION
**2** : a person or thing through which power is exerted or an end is achieved : INSTRUMENTALITY ⟨communicated through the *agency* of the ambassador⟩
**3 a** : the office or function of an agent **b** : the relationship between a principal and his agent
**4** : an establishment engaged in doing business for another ⟨an advertising *agency*⟩
**5** : an administrative division (as of a government) ⟨the *agency* for consumer protection⟩
**agency shop** *noun* (circa 1946)
: a shop in which the union serves as the agent for and receives dues and assessments from all employees in the bargaining unit regardless of union membership
**agen·da** \ə-'jen-də\ *noun* [Latin, neuter plural of *agendum*, gerundive of *agere*] (1871)
**1** : a list or outline of things to be considered or done ⟨*agendas* of faculty meetings⟩
**2** : an underlying often ideological plan or program ⟨a political *agenda*⟩
— **agen·da·less** \-də-ləs\ *adjective*
**agen·dum** \-dəm\ *noun, plural* **-da** \-də\ *or* **-dums** [Latin] (circa 1847)
**1** : AGENDA
**2** : an item on an agenda
**agen·e·sis** \(,)ā-'je-nə-səs\ *noun* [New Latin] (circa 1879)
: lack or failure of development (as of a body part)
**agent** \'ā-jənt\ *noun* [Middle English, from Medieval Latin *agent-, agens*, from Latin, present participle of *agere* to drive, lead, act, do; akin to Old Norse *aka* to travel in a vehicle, Greek *agein* to drive, lead] (15th century)

**1** : one that acts or exerts power
**2 a** : something that produces or is capable of producing an effect : an active or efficient cause **b** : a chemically, physically, or biologically active principle
**3** : a means or instrument by which a guiding intelligence achieves a result
**4** : one who is authorized to act for or in the place of another: as **a** : a representative, emissary, or official of a government ⟨crown *agent*⟩ ⟨federal *agent*⟩ **b** : one engaged in undercover activities (as espionage) : SPY ⟨secret *agent*⟩ **c** : a business representative (as of an athlete or entertainer) ⟨a theatrical *agent*⟩
**agent–general** *noun, plural* **agents–general** (1833)
: a chief agent; *specifically* : the representative in England of a British dominion
**agent·ing** \'ā-jən-tiŋ\ *noun* (1681)
: the business or activities of an agent
**Agent Orange** *noun* [so called from the identifying color stripe on its container] (1970)
: an herbicide widely used as a defoliant in the Vietnam War that is composed of 2,4-D and 2,4,5-T and contains dioxin as a contaminant
**agent pro·vo·ca·teur** \'ä-,zhä⁼-prō-,vä-kə-'tər, 'ä-jənt-\ *noun, plural* **agents provocateurs** \'ä-,zhä⁼-prō-,vä-kə-'tər, 'ä-jən(t)s-prō-\ [French, literally, provoking agent] (1877)
: one employed to associate with suspected persons and by pretending sympathy with their aims to incite them to some incriminating action
**agent·ry** \'ā-jən-trē\ *noun, plural* **-ries** (1925)
: the office, duties, or activities of an agent
**age of consent** (1504)
: the age at which one is legally competent to give consent especially to marriage or to sexual intercourse
**age of reason** (circa 1794)
**1** : a period characterized by a prevailing belief in the use of reason; *especially* : the 18th century in England and France
**2** : the time of life when one begins to be able to distinguish right from wrong
**age–old** \'ā-'jōld\ *adjective* (1904)
: having existed for ages : ANCIENT
**ag·er·a·tum** \,a-jə-'rā-təm\ *noun, plural* **-tum** *also* **-tums** [New Latin, genus name, from Greek *agēratos* ageless, from *a-* + *gēras* old age — more at GERONT-] (1866)
: any of a genus (*Ageratum*) of tropical American composite herbs often cultivated for their small showy heads of blue or white flowers; *also* : a related blue-flowered plant (*Eupatorium coelestinum*)
**Ag·ga·dah** \ə-'gä-də, -'gȯ-\ *variant of* HAG-GADAH
**Ag·ge·us** \a-'gē-əs\ *noun* [Late Latin *Aggaeus*, from Greek *Aggaios*, from Hebrew *Ḥaggai*] : HAGGAI
**¹ag·gie** \'a-gē\ *noun, often capitalized* [*agricultural* + *-ie*] (1902)
: an agricultural school or college; *also* : a student at such an institution
**²aggie** *noun* [*agate* + *-ie*] (1915)
: a playing marble; *specifically* : AGATE 2b
**ag·gior·na·men·to** \ə-,jȯr-nə-'men-(,)tō\ *noun, plural* **-tos** [Italian, from *aggiornare* to bring up to date, from *a-* (from Latin *ad-*) + *giorno* day, from Late Latin *diurnum* day — more at JOURNEY] (1963)
: a bringing up to date : MODERNIZATION ⟨dedicated to the *aggiornamento* of the church⟩
**¹ag·glom·er·ate** \ə-'glä-mə-,rāt\ *transitive verb* **-at·ed; -at·ing** [Latin *agglomeratus*, past participle of *agglomerare* to heap up, join, from *ad-* + *glomer-, glomus* ball — more at CLAM] (1684)
: to gather into a ball, mass, or cluster
**²ag·glom·er·ate** \-rət\ *adjective* (1828)
: gathered into a ball, mass, or cluster; *specifically* : clustered or growing together but not coherent ⟨an *agglomerate* flower head⟩

**³ag·glom·er·ate** \-rət\ *noun* (1830)
**1** : a rock composed of volcanic fragments of various sizes and degrees of angularity
**2** : a jumbled mass or collection : AGGLOMERATION
**ag·glom·er·a·tion** \ə-,glä-mə-'rā-shən\ *noun* (1774)
**1** : the action or process of collecting in a mass
**2** : a heap or cluster of usually disparate elements ⟨urban *agglomerations* knit together by the new railways —*Times Literary Supplement*⟩
— **ag·glom·er·a·tive** \-'glä-mə-,rā-tiv\ *adjective*
**ag·glu·ti·na·bil·i·ty** \ə-,glü-t⁼n-ə-'bi-lə-tē\ *noun* (1901)
: capacity (as of red blood cells) to be agglutinated
— **ag·glu·ti·na·ble** \ə-'glü-t⁼n-ə-bəl\ *adjective*
**¹ag·glu·ti·nate** \ə-'glü-t⁼n-,āt\ *verb* **-nat·ed; -nat·ing** [Latin *agglutinatus*, past participle of *agglutinare* to glue to, from *ad-* + *glutinare* to glue, from *glutin-, gluten* glue — more at CLAY] (1586)
*transitive verb*
**1** : to cause to adhere : FASTEN
**2** : to combine into a compound : attach to a base as an affix
**3** : to cause to undergo agglutination
*intransitive verb*
**1** : to unite or combine into a group or mass
**2** : to form words by agglutination
**²ag·glu·ti·nate** \-t⁼n-ət, -t⁼n-,āt\ *noun* (1952)
: a clump of agglutinated material (as blood cells or mineral particles in soil)
**ag·glu·ti·na·tion** \ə-,glü-t⁼n-'ā-shən\ *noun* (1541)
**1** : the action or process of agglutinating
**2** : a mass or group formed by the union of separate elements
**3** : the formation of derivational or inflectional words by putting together constituents of which each expresses a single definite meaning
**4** : a reaction in which particles (as red blood cells or bacteria) suspended in a liquid collect into clumps and which occurs especially as a serologic response to a specific antibody
**ag·glu·ti·na·tive** \ə-'glü-t⁼n-,ā-tiv, -ə-tiv\ *adjective* (1634)
**1** : ADHESIVE
**2** : characterized by linguistic agglutination
**ag·glu·ti·nin** \ə-'glü-t⁼n-ən\ *noun* [International Scientific Vocabulary *agglutin*ation + *-in*] (1902)
: a substance (as an antibody) producing agglutination
**ag·glu·ti·no·gen** \ə-'glü-t⁼n-ə-jən\ *noun* [*agglutin*in + *-o-* + *-gen*] (1904)
: an antigen whose presence results in the formation of an agglutinin
— **ag·glu·ti·no·gen·ic** \-,glü-t⁼n-ə-'je-nik\ *adjective*
**ag·gra·da·tion** \,a-grə-'dā-shən\ *noun* [*ad-* + *gradation*] (1898)
: a modification of the earth's surface in the direction of uniformity of grade by deposition
**ag·gran·dise** *British variant of* AGGRANDIZE
**ag·gran·dize** \ə-'gran-,dīz *also* 'a-grən-\ *transitive verb* **-dized; -diz·ing** [French *agrandiss-*, stem of *agrandir*, from *a-* (from Latin *ad-*) + *grandir* to increase, from Latin *grandire*, from *grandis* great] (1634)
**1** : to make great or greater : INCREASE, ENLARGE
**2** : to make appear great or greater : praise highly
**3** : to enhance the power, wealth, position, or reputation of ⟨exploited the situation to *aggrandize* himself⟩
— **ag·gran·dize·ment** \ə-'gran-dəz-mənt, -,dīz- *also* ,a-grən-'dīz-\ *noun*
— **ag·gran·diz·er** \ə-'gran-,dī-zər *also* 'a-grən-\ *noun*

**ag·gra·vate** \'a-grə-ˌvāt\ *transitive verb* **-vat·ed; -vat·ing** [Latin *aggravatus,* past participle of *aggravare* to make heavier, from *ad-* + *gravare* to burden, from *gravis* heavy — more at GRIEVE] (1530)
**1** *obsolete* **a :** to make heavy **:** BURDEN **b :** INCREASE
**2 :** to make worse, more serious, or more severe **:** intensify unpleasantly 〈problems have been *aggravated* by neglect〉
**3 a :** to rouse to displeasure or anger by usually persistent and often petty goading **b :** to produce inflammation in ■
**aggravated assault** *noun* (1925)
**:** an assault that is more serious than a common assault: as **a :** an assault combined with an intent to commit a crime **b :** any of various assaults so defined by statute
**aggravating** *adjective* (1775)
**:** arousing displeasure, impatience, or anger
*usage* see AGGRAVATE
**ag·gra·va·tion** \ˌa-grə-'vā-shən\ *noun* (circa 1555)
**1 :** an act or circumstance that intensifies or makes worse
**2 :** the act, action, or result of aggravating; *especially* **:** an increasing in seriousness or severity
**3 :** IRRITATION, PROVOCATION
*usage* see AGGRAVATE
**¹ag·gre·gate** \'a-gri-gət\ *adjective* [Middle English *aggregat,* from Latin *aggregatus,* past participle of *aggregare* to add to, from *ad-* + *greg-, grex* flock] (15th century)
**:** formed by the collection of units or particles into a body, mass, or amount **:** COLLECTIVE: as **a** (1) **:** clustered in a dense mass or head 〈an *aggregate* flower〉 (2) **:** formed from several separate ovaries of a single flower 〈*aggregate* fruit〉 **b :** composed of mineral crystals of one or more kinds or of mineral rock fragments **c :** taking all units as a whole 〈*aggregate* sales〉
— **ag·gre·gate·ly** *adverb*
— **ag·gre·gate·ness** *noun*
**²ag·gre·gate** \-ˌgāt\ *transitive verb* **-gat·ed; -gat·ing** (15th century)
**1 :** to collect or gather into a mass or whole
**2 :** to amount in the aggregate to **:** TOTAL
**³ag·gre·gate** \-gət\ *noun* (15th century)
**1 :** a mass or body of units or parts somewhat loosely associated with one another
**2 :** the whole sum or amount **:** SUM TOTAL
**3 a :** an aggregate rock **b :** any of several hard inert materials (as sand, gravel, or slag) used for mixing with a cementing material to form concrete, mortar, or plaster **c :** a clustered mass of individual soil particles varied in shape, ranging in size from a microscopic granule to a small crumb, and considered the basic structural unit of soil
**4 :** SET 21
**5 :** MONETARY AGGREGATE
— **in the aggregate :** considered as a whole **:** COLLECTIVELY 〈dividends for the year amounted *in the aggregate* to 25 million dollars〉
**ag·gre·ga·tion** \ˌa-gri-'gā-shən\ *noun* (1547)
**1 :** a group, body, or mass composed of many distinct parts or individuals
**2 a :** the collecting of units or parts into a mass or whole **b :** the condition of being so collected
— **ag·gre·ga·tion·al** \-shnəl, -shə-nᵊl\ *adjective*
**ag·gre·ga·tive** \'a-gri-ˌgā-tiv\ *adjective* (1644)
**1 :** of or relating to an aggregate
**2 :** tending to aggregate
— **ag·gre·ga·tive·ly** *adverb*
**ag·gress** \ə-'gres\ *intransitive verb* (circa 1714)
**:** to commit aggression **:** act aggressively
**ag·gres·sion** \ə-'gre-shən\ *noun* [Latin *aggression-, aggressio* attack, from *aggredi* to attack, from *ad-* + *gradi* to step, go — more at GRADE] (1611)

**1 :** a forceful action or procedure (as an unprovoked attack) especially when intended to dominate or master
**2 :** the practice of making attacks or encroachments; *especially* **:** unprovoked violation by one country of the territorial integrity of another
**3 :** hostile, injurious, or destructive behavior or outlook especially when caused by frustration
**ag·gres·sive** \ə-'gre-siv\ *adjective* (1824)
**1 a :** tending toward or exhibiting aggression 〈*aggressive* behavior〉 **b :** marked by combative readiness 〈an *aggressive* fighter〉
**2 a :** marked by obtrusive energy **b :** marked by driving forceful energy or initiative **:** ENTERPRISING 〈an *aggressive* salesman〉
**3 :** strong or emphatic in effect or intent 〈*aggressive* colors〉 〈*aggressive* flavors〉
**4 :** more severe, intensive, or comprehensive than usual especially in dosage or extent 〈*aggressive* chemotherapy〉 ☆
— **ag·gres·sive·ly** *adverb*
— **ag·gres·sive·ness** *noun*
— **ag·gres·siv·i·ty** \ˌa-ˌgre-'si-və-tē\ *noun*
**ag·gres·sor** \ə-'gre-sər\ *noun* (1646)
**:** one that commits or practices aggression
**ag·grieve** \ə-'grēv\ *transitive verb* **ag·grieved; ag·griev·ing** [Middle English *agreven,* from Middle French *agrever,* from Latin *aggravare* to make heavier] (14th century)
**1 :** to give pain or trouble to **:** DISTRESS
**2 :** to inflict injury on
*synonym* see WRONG
**ag·grieved** \ə-'grēvd\ *adjective* (14th century)
**1 :** troubled or distressed in spirit
**2 :** suffering from an infringement or denial of legal rights 〈*aggrieved* minority groups〉 **b :** showing or expressing grief, injury, or offense 〈an *aggrieved* plea〉
— **ag·griev·ed·ly** \-'grē-vəd-lē\ *adverb*
**ag·grieve·ment** \ə-'grēv-mənt\ *noun* (1847)
**:** the quality or state of being aggrieved
**ag·gro** \'a-(ˌ)grō\ *noun, plural* **aggros** [probably *aggra*vation + ¹-*o*] (1969)
**1** *British* **:** deliberately aggressive, provoking, or violent behavior
**2** *British* **:** EXASPERATION, IRRITATION
**aghast** \ə-'gast\ *adjective* [Middle English *agast,* from past participle of *agasten* to frighten, from *a-* (perfective prefix) + *gasten* to frighten — more at ABIDE, GAST] (13th century)
**:** struck with terror, amazement, or horror **:** SHOCKED
**ag·ile** \'a-jəl, -ˌjīl\ *adjective* [Middle French, from Latin *agilis,* from *agere* to drive, act — more at AGENT] (1581)
**1 :** marked by ready ability to move with quick easy grace
**2 :** having a quick resourceful and adaptable character 〈an *agile* mind〉
— **ag·ile·ly** \-jə(l)-lē, -ˌjī(l)-lē\ *adverb*
**agil·i·ty** \ə-'ji-lə-tē\ *noun, plural* **-ties** (15th century)
**:** the quality or state of being agile **:** NIMBLENESS, DEXTERITY 〈played with increasing *agility*〉
**agin** \ə-'gin\ *dialect variant of* AGAINST
**aging** *present participle of* AGE
**ag·ism** *variant of* AGEISM
**ag·i·tate** \'a-jə-ˌtāt\ *verb* **-tat·ed; -tat·ing** [Latin *agitatus,* past participle of *agitare,* frequentative of *agere* to drive — more at AGENT] (15th century)
*transitive verb*
**1 a** *obsolete* **:** to give motion to **b :** to move with an irregular, rapid, or violent action 〈the storm *agitated* the sea〉
**2 :** to excite and often trouble the mind or feelings of **:** DISTURB
**3 a :** to discuss excitedly and earnestly **b :** to stir up public discussion of

*intransitive verb*
**:** to attempt to arouse public feeling 〈*agitated* for better schools〉
*synonym* see SHAKE, DISCOMPOSE
— **ag·i·tat·ed·ly** *adverb*
— **ag·i·ta·tion** \ˌa-jə-'tā-shən\ *noun*
— **ag·i·ta·tion·al** \-shnəl, -shə-nᵊl\ *adjective*
**ag·i·ta·tive** \'a-jə-ˌtā-tiv\ *adjective* (1687)
**:** causing or tending to cause agitation
**ag·i·ta·to** \ˌa-jə-'tä-(ˌ)tō\ *adverb or adjective* [Italian, literally, agitated, from Latin *agitatus*] (circa 1801)
**:** in a restless and agitated manner — used as a direction in music
**ag·i·ta·tor** \'a-jə-ˌtā-tər\ *noun* (circa 1734)
**:** one that agitates: as **a :** one who stirs up public feeling on controversial issues 〈political *agitators*〉 **b :** a device or an apparatus for stirring or shaking
**ag·it·prop** \'a-jət-ˌpräp\ *noun* [Russian, from *agit*atsiya agitation + *prop*aganda] (1935)
**:** PROPAGANDA; *especially* **:** political propaganda promulgated chiefly in literature, drama, music, or art
— **agitprop** *adjective*
**Aglaia** \ə-'glī-ə, -'glā-ə\ *noun* [Latin, from Greek]
**:** one of the three Graces
**aglare** \ə-'glar, -'gler\ *adjective* (1872)
**:** GLARING 〈his eyes *aglare* with fury〉
**agleam** \ə-'glēm\ *adjective* (1870)
**:** gleaming especially with reflected light

---

☆ **SYNONYMS**

**Aggressive, militant, assertive, self-assertive** mean obtrusively energetic especially in pursuing particular goals. AGGRESSIVE implies a disposition to dominate often in disregard of others' rights or in determined and energetic pursuit of one's ends 〈was taught to be *aggressive* in his business dealings〉. MILITANT also implies a fighting disposition but suggests not self-seeking but devotion to a cause, movement, or principle 〈*militant* protesters held a rally against racism〉. ASSERTIVE suggests bold self-confidence in expression of opinion 〈the more *assertive* speakers dominated the forum〉. SELF-ASSERTIVE connotes forwardness or brash self-confidence 〈a *self-assertive* young executive climbing the corporate ladder〉.

---

□ **USAGE**

**aggravate** Although *aggravate* has been used in sense 3a since the 17th century, it has been the object of disapproval only since about 1870. It is used in expository prose 〈when his silly conceit . . . about his not-very-good early work has begun to *aggravate* us —William Styron〉 but seems to be more common in speech and casual writing 〈a good profession for him, because bus drivers get *aggravated* —Jackie Gleason (interview, 1986)〉 〈& now this letter comes to *aggravate* me a thousand times worse —Mark Twain (letter, 1864)〉. Sense 2 is far more common than sense 3a in published prose. Such is not the case, however, with *aggravation* and *aggravating. Aggravation* is used in sense 3 somewhat more than in its earlier senses; *aggravating* has practically no use other than to express annoyance.

---

\ə\ **abut** \ᵊ\ **kitten** \ər\ **further** \a\ **ash** \ā\ **ace**
\ä\ **mop, mar** \au̇\ **out** \ch\ **chin** \e\ **bet** \ē\ **easy**
\g\ **go** \i\ **hit** \ī\ **ice** \j\ **job** \ŋ\ **sing** \ō\ **go**
\ȯ\ **law** \ȯi\ **boy** \th\ **thin** \t̶h̶\ **the** \ü\ **loot** \u̇\ **foot**
\y\ **yet** \zh\ **vision** *see also* Guide to Pronunciation

**ag·let** \'a-glət\ *noun* [Middle English, from Middle French *aguillette, aiguillette,* diminutive of *aguille, aiguille* needle, from Late Latin *acicula, acucula* ornamental pin, diminutive of Latin *acus* needle, pin — more at ACUTE] (15th century)
**1 :** the plain or ornamental tag covering the ends of a lace or point
**2 :** any of various ornamental studs, cords, or pins worn on clothing

**agley** \ə-'glā, -'glē, -'glī\ *adverb* [Scots, from [1]*a*- + *gley* to squint] (1785)
*chiefly Scottish* **:** AWRY, WRONG ⟨the best-laid schemes o' mice an' men gang aft *agley* —Robert Burns⟩

**aglit·ter** \ə-'gli-tər\ *adjective* (1865)
**:** glittering especially with reflected light

**aglow** \ə-'glō\ *adjective* (1817)
**:** glowing especially with warmth or excitement

**agly·cone** \a-'glī-ˌkōn\ *also* **agly·con** \-ˌkän\ *noun* [International Scientific Vocabulary *a*- (from Greek *ha-, a-* together) + *glyc-* + *-one, -on*] (1925)
**:** an organic compound (as a phenol or alcohol) combined with the sugar portion of a glycoside

**¹ag·nate** \'ag-ˌnāt\ *noun* [Latin *agnatus,* from past participle of *agnasci* to be born in addition to, from *ad-* + *nasci* to be born — more at NATION] (1534)
**1 :** a relative whose kinship is traceable exclusively through males
**2 :** a paternal kinsman

**²agnate** *adjective* (1782)
**1 :** ALLIED, AKIN
**2 :** related through male descent or on the father's side
— **ag·nat·ic** \ag-'na-tik\ *adjective*

**Ag·ne·an** \'äg-nē-ən\ *noun* [*Agni,* ancient kingdom in Turkestan] (1939)
**:** TOCHARIAN A

**ag·nize** \ag-'nīz\ *transitive verb* **ag·nized; ag·niz·ing** [Latin *agnoscere* to acknowledge (from *ad-* + *noscere* to know) + English *-ize* (as in *recognize*) — more at KNOW] (1535)
*archaic* **:** RECOGNIZE, ACKNOWLEDGE

**ag·no·men** \ag-'nō-mən\ *noun, plural* **-nom·i·na** \-'nä-mə-nə\ *or* **-no·mens** [Latin, irregular from *ad-* + *nomen* name — more at NAME] (1665)
**:** an additional cognomen given to a person by the ancient Romans (as in honor of some achievement)

**ag·no·sia** \ag-'nō-zhə, -shə\ *noun* [New Latin, from Greek *agnōsia* ignorance, from *a-* + *gnōsis* knowledge, from *gignōskein*] (circa 1900)
**:** loss or diminution of the ability to recognize familiar objects or stimuli usually as a result of brain damage

**¹ag·nos·tic** \ag-'näs-tik, əg-\ *noun* [Greek *agnōstos* unknown, unknowable, from *a-* + *gnōstos* known, from *gignōskein* to know — more at KNOW] (1869)
**:** a person who holds the view that any ultimate reality (as God) is unknown and probably unknowable; *broadly* **:** one who is not committed to believing in either the existence or the nonexistence of God or a god ◆
— **ag·nos·ti·cism** \-tə-ˌsi-zəm\ *noun*

**²agnostic** *adjective* (1873)
**1 :** of, relating to, or being an agnostic or the beliefs of agnostics
**2 :** NONCOMMITTAL, UNDOGMATIC

**Ag·nus Dei** \ˌäg-nùs-'dā(-ˌē), -ˌnüs-; ˌän-yùs-; ˌag-nəs-\ *noun* [Middle English, from Late Latin, lamb of God; from its opening words] (14th century)
**1 :** a liturgical prayer addressed to Christ as Savior
**2 :** an image of a lamb often with a halo and a banner and cross that is used as a symbol of Christ

**ago** \ə-'gō\ *adjective or adverb* [Middle English *agon, ago,* from past participle of *agon*

to pass away, from Old English *āgān,* from *ā-* (perfective prefix) + *gān* to go — more at ABIDE, GO] (14th century)
**:** earlier than the present time ⟨10 years *ago*⟩

**agog** \ə-'gäg\ *adjective* [Middle French *en gogues* in mirth] (1559)
**:** full of intense interest or excitement **:** EAGER ⟨kids all *agog* over new toys⟩

**¹a-go-go** \ä-'gō-(ˌ)gō, ə-\ *noun* [*Whisky à Gogo,* café and discotheque in Paris, France, from French *à gogo* galore, from Middle French] (1965)
**:** a nightclub for dancing to pop music **:** DISCO

**²a-go-go** *adjective* (1965)
**1 :** GO-GO 1
**2 :** being in a whirl of motion
**3 :** being up-to-date — often used postpositively

**-agogue** *noun combining form* [French & New Latin; French, from Late Latin *-agogus* promoting the expulsion of, from Greek *-agōgos,* from *agein* to lead; New Latin *-agogon,* from Greek, neuter of *-agōgos* — more at AGENT]
**:** substance that promotes the secretion or expulsion of ⟨emmen*agogue*⟩

**agon** \'ä-ˌgän, ä-'gōn\ *noun* [Greek *agōn*] (1600)
**:** CONTEST, CONFLICT; *especially* **:** the dramatic conflict between the chief characters in a literary work

**ag·o·nal** \'a-gə-nᵊl\ *adjective* (1901)
**:** of, relating to, or associated with agony and especially the death agony

**agone** \ə-'gòn *also* -'gän\ *adjective or adverb* (14th century)
*archaic* **:** AGO

**ag·o·nise, agonised, agonising** *British variant of* AGONIZE, AGONIZED, AGONIZING

**ag·o·nist** \'a-gə-nist\ *noun* [Late Latin *agonista* competitor, from Greek *agōnistēs,* from *agōnizesthai* to contend, from *agōn*] (circa 1623)
**1 :** one that is engaged in a struggle
**2** [from *antagonist*] **a :** a muscle that is controlled by the action of an antagonist with which it is paired **b :** a chemical substance capable of combining with a receptor on a cell and initiating a reaction or activity — compare ANTAGONIST 2b

**ag·o·nis·tic** \ˌa-gə-'nis-tik\ *adjective* (1648)
**1 :** of or relating to the athletic contests of ancient Greece
**2 :** ARGUMENTATIVE
**3 :** striving for effect **:** STRAINED
**4 :** of, relating to, or being aggressive or defensive social interaction (as fighting, fleeing, or submitting) between individuals usually of the same species
— **ag·o·nis·ti·cal·ly** \-ti-k(ə-)lē\ *adverb*

**ag·o·nize** \'a-gə-ˌnīz\ *verb* **-nized; -niz·ing** (1583)
*transitive verb*
**:** to cause to suffer agony **:** TORTURE
*intransitive verb*
**1 :** to suffer agony, torture, or anguish ⟨*agonizes* over every decision⟩
**2 :** STRUGGLE

**agonized** *adjective* (1583)
**:** characterized by, suffering, or expressing agony

**agonizing** *adjective* (1593)
**:** causing agony **:** PAINFUL
— **ag·o·niz·ing·ly** *adverb*

**ag·o·ny** \'a-gə-nē\ *noun, plural* **-nies** [Middle English *agonie,* from Late Latin *agonia,* from Greek *agōnia* struggle, anguish, from *agōn* gathering, contest for a prize, from *agein* to lead, celebrate — more at AGENT] (14th century)

**Agnus Dei**

**1 a :** intense pain of mind or body **:** ANGUISH, TORTURE **b :** the struggle that precedes death
**2 :** a violent struggle or contest
**3 :** a strong sudden display (as of joy or delight) **:** OUTBURST ◆
*synonym* see DISTRESS

**agony column** *noun* (1863)
**:** a newspaper column of personal advertisements relating especially to missing relatives or friends

**¹ag·o·ra** \'a-gə-rə\ *noun, plural* **-ras** *or* **-rae** \-ˌrē, -ˌrī\ [Greek, from *ageirein* to gather] (1589)
**:** a gathering place; *especially* **:** the marketplace in ancient Greece

**²ago·ra** \ˌä-gə-'rä\ *noun, plural* **ago·rot** \-'rōt\ [New Hebrew *ăgōrāh,* from Hebrew, a small coin] (1963)
**:** see *shekel* at MONEY table

**ag·o·ra·pho·bia** \ˌa-g(ə-)rə-'fō-bē-ə\ *noun* [New Latin, from Greek *agora* + New Latin *-phobia*] (1873)
**:** abnormal fear of being helpless in an embarrassing or unescapable situation that is characterized especially by the avoidance of open or public places
— **ag·o·ra·phobe** \'a-g(ə-)rə-ˌfōb\ *noun*
— **ag·o·ra·pho·bic** \-'fō-bik\ *adjective or noun*

**agou·ti** \ə-'gü-tē\ *noun* [French, from Spanish *agutí,* from Tupi] (1625)
**1 :** any of a genus (*Dasyprocta*) of tropical American rodents about the size of a rabbit
**2 :** a grizzled color of fur resulting from the barring of each hair in several alternate dark and light bands

agouti 1

**agrafe** *or* **agraffe** \ə-'graf\ *noun* [French *agrafe*] (1643)
**:** a hook-and-loop fastening; *especially* **:** an ornamental clasp used on armor or costumes

---

◇ WORD HISTORY

**agnostic** The word *agnostic* owes its origin to a particular occasion on the evening of April 21, 1869, when it was coined by the English biologist Thomas Henry Huxley at an organizational meeting of the Metaphysical Society. The precise etymological route by which Huxley arrived at his coinage has been a matter of debate. Two decades after the fact, the coiner himself recalled that the word seemed "suggestively antithetic to the 'gnostic' of church history" and so he chose it on that basis. In any event, *agnostic* is undoubtedly rooted in *agnōstos,* a Greek word meaning "unknown" or "unknowable." The ending *-ic* was probably suggested by the previously established English word *gnostic.*

**agony** In ancient Greece the word *agōn* denoted any large public assembly. As the Greeks placed a high value on athletic skills, assemblies on festival days featured athletic contests, the prototype of our modern Olympic Games. The word *agōn* by association with public games came to denote any competitive event. The struggle to win, as well as the pain accompanying the struggle, was called *agōnia,* which began also to be applied to any intense pain, physical or mental. The irony is that English *agony,* a word synonymous with intense pain of mind or body, ultimately comes from a word for a festive game.

**agran·u·lo·cyte** \(ˌ)ā-'gran-yə-lō-ˌsīt\ *noun* (circa 1923)
: a white blood cell without cytoplasmic granules

**agran·u·lo·cy·to·sis** \ˌā-ˌgran-yə-lō-ˌsī-'tō-səs\ *noun, plural* **-to·ses** \-'tō-ˌsēz\ [New Latin] (1927)
: an acute febrile condition marked by severe decrease in blood granulocytes and often associated with the use of certain drugs

**ag·ra·pha** \'a-grə-fə\ *noun plural* [Greek, neuter plural of *agraphos* unwritten, from *a-* + *graphein* to write — more at CARVE] (1890)
: sayings of Jesus not in the canonical gospels but found in other New Testament or early Christian writings

**agraph·ia** \(ˌ)ā-'gra-fē-ə\ *noun* [New Latin, from ²*a-* + Greek *graphein* to write] (1871)
: the pathologic loss of the ability to write

¹**agrar·i·an** \ə-'grer-ē-ən, -'grar-\ *adjective* [Latin *agrarius,* from *agr-, ager* field — more at ACRE] (1618)
**1 :** of or relating to fields or lands or their tenure
**2 a :** of, relating to, or characteristic of farmers or their way of life **b :** organized or designed to promote agricultural interests ⟨an *agrarian* political party⟩ ⟨*agrarian* reforms⟩

²**agrarian** *noun* (1818)
: a member of an agrarian party or movement

**agrar·i·an·ism** \-ē-ə-ˌni-zəm\ *noun* (1830)
: a social or political movement designed to bring about land reforms or to improve the economic status of the farmer

**agree** \ə-'grē\ *verb* **agreed; agree·ing** [Middle English, from Middle French *agreer,* from *a gre* at will, from *a* (from Latin *ad*) + *gre* will, pleasure, from Latin *gratum,* neuter of *gratus* pleasing, agreeable — more at GRACE] (15th century)
*transitive verb*
**1 :** ADMIT, CONCEDE ⟨*agrees* that he is right⟩
**2** *chiefly British* **:** to settle on by common consent **:** ARRANGE ⟨I *agreed* rental terms with him —Eric Bennett⟩
*intransitive verb*
**1 :** to accept or concede something (as the views or wishes of another) ⟨*agree* to a plan⟩
**2 a :** to achieve or be in harmony (as of opinion, feeling, or purpose) ⟨we *agree* in our taste in music⟩ **b :** to get along together **c :** to come to terms
**3 a :** to be similar **:** CORRESPOND ⟨both copies *agree*⟩ **b :** to be consistent ⟨the story *agrees* with the facts⟩
**4 :** to be fitting, pleasing, or healthful **:** SUIT ⟨this climate *agrees* with him⟩
**5 :** to have an inflectional form denoting identity or other regular correspondence in a grammatical category (as gender, number, case, or person) ☆

**agree·able** \ə-'grē-ə-bəl\ *adjective* (14th century)
**1 :** pleasing to the mind or senses especially as according well with one's tastes or needs ⟨an *agreeable* companion⟩ ⟨an *agreeable* change⟩
**2 :** ready or willing to agree or consent
**3 :** being in harmony **:** CONSONANT
— **agree·abil·i·ty** \-ˌgrē-ə-'bi-lə-tē\ *noun*
— **agree·able·ness** \-'grē-ə-bəl-nəs\ *noun*
— **agree·ably** \-blē\ *adverb*

**agree·ment** \ə-'grē-mənt\ *noun* (15th century)
**1 a :** the act or fact of agreeing **b :** harmony of opinion, action, or character **:** CONCORD
**2 a :** an arrangement as to a course of action **b :** COMPACT, TREATY
**3 a :** a contract duly executed and legally binding **b :** the language or instrument embodying such a contract

**ag·ri·busi·ness** \'a-grə-ˌbiz-nəs, -ˌnəz\ *noun* [*agriculture* + *business*] (circa 1955)
: an industry engaged in the producing operations of a farm, the manufacture and distribu-

tion of farm equipment and supplies, and the processing, storage, and distribution of farm commodities

**ag·ri·busi·ness·man** \ˌa-grə-'biz-nəs-ˌman, -mən, -ˌnəz-\ *noun* (1961)
: a person who works in or manages an agribusiness

**ag·ri·cul·tur·al** \ˌa-gri-'kəl-ch(ə-)rəl\ *adjective* (1776)
: of, relating to, used in, or concerned with agriculture
— **ag·ri·cul·tur·al·ly** *adverb*

**ag·ri·cul·ture** \'a-gri-ˌkəl-chər\ *noun* [Middle English, from Middle French, from Latin *agricultura,* from *ager* field + *cultura* cultivation — more at ACRE, CULTURE] (15th century)
: the science, art, or practice of cultivating the soil, producing crops, and raising livestock and in varying degrees the preparation and marketing of the resulting products **:** FARMING
— **ag·ri·cul·tur·ist** \ˌa-gri-'kəl-ch(ə-)rist\ *or* **ag·ri·cul·tur·al·ist** \-ch(ə-)rə-list\ *noun*

**ag·ri·mo·ny** \'a-grə-ˌmō-nē\ *noun, plural* **-nies** [Middle English, from Middle French & Latin; Middle French *aigremoine,* from Latin *agrimonia,* manuscript variant of *argemonia,* from Greek *argemōnē*] (14th century)
: any of a genus (*Agrimonia* and especially *A. eupatoria*) of herbs of the rose family having compound leaves, slender spikes of small yellow flowers, and fruits like burs

**agro-** *combining form* [French, from Greek, from *agros* field — more at ACRE]
**1 :** of or belonging to fields or soil **:** agricultural ⟨*agro*chemical⟩
**2 :** agricultural and ⟨*agro*-industrial⟩

**ag·ro·chem·i·cal** \ˌa-grō-'ke-mi-kəl\ *also* **ag·ri·chem·i·cal** \ˌa-gri-\ *noun* (1956)
: an agricultural chemical (as an herbicide or an insecticide)

**ag·ro·for·est·ry** \ˌa-grō-'fȯr-ə-strē, -'fär-\ *noun* (1977)
: land management for the simultaneous production of food, crops, and trees; *also* **:** the science of agroforestry
— **ag·ro·for·est·er** \-stər\ *noun*

**ag·ro·in·dus·tri·al** \ˌa-grō-in-'dəs-trē-əl\ *adjective* (1940)
: of or relating to production (as of power for industry and water for irrigation) for both industrial and agricultural purposes

**agron·o·my** \ə-'grä-nə-mē\ *noun* [probably from French *agronomie,* from *agro-* + *-nomie* -nomy] (1814)
: a branch of agriculture dealing with field-crop production and soil management
— **ag·ro·nom·ic** \ˌa-grə-'nä-mik\ *adjective*
— **ag·ro·nom·i·cal·ly** \-mi-k(ə-)lē\ *adverb*
— **agron·o·mist** \ə-'grä-nə-mist\ *noun*

**aground** \ə-'graund\ *adverb or adjective* (14th century)
**1 :** on the ground ⟨planes aloft and *aground*⟩
**2 :** on or onto the shore or the bottom of a body of water ⟨a ship run *aground*⟩

**ague** \'ā-(ˌ)gyü\ *noun* [Middle English, from Middle French *aguë,* from Medieval Latin (*febris*) *acuta,* literally, sharp fever, from Latin, feminine of *acutus* sharp — more at ACUTE] (14th century)
**1 :** a fever (as malaria) marked by paroxysms of chills, fever, and sweating that recur at regular intervals
**2 :** a fit of shivering **:** CHILL
— **agu·ish** \'ā-ˌgyü-ish\ *adjective*

**ah** \'ä\ *interjection* [Middle English] (13th century)
— used to express delight, relief, regret, or contempt

**aha** \ä-'hä\ *interjection* [Middle English] (14th century)
— used to express surprise, triumph, or derision

**ahead** \ə-'hed\ *adverb or adjective* (1596)
**1 a :** in a forward direction or position **:** FORWARD **b :** in front
**2 :** in, into, or for the future ⟨plan *ahead*⟩

**3 :** in or toward a more advantageous position ⟨helped others to get *ahead*⟩
**4 :** at or to an earlier time **:** in advance ⟨make payments *ahead*⟩

**ahead of** *preposition* (1748)
**1 :** in front or advance of
**2 :** in excess of

**ahem** \a throat-clearing sound; often read as ə-'hem\ *interjection* [imitative] (1763)
— used especially to attract attention

**ahim·sa** \ə-'him-ˌsä\ *noun* [Sanskrit *ahiṁsā* noninjury] (1875)
: the Hindu and Buddhist doctrine of refraining from harming any living being

**ahis·tor·i·cal** \ˌā-his-'tȯr-i-kəl, -'tär-\ *or* **ahis·tor·ic** \-ik\ *adjective* (1945)
: not concerned with or related to history, historical development, or tradition ⟨the *ahistorical* attitudes of the radicals⟩

**ahold** \ə-'hōld\ *noun* [probably from the phrase *a hold*] (1872)
: HOLD ⟨if you could get *ahold* of a representative —Norman Mailer⟩

**A horizon** \'ā-\ *noun* (1936)
: the uppermost dark-colored layer of a soil consisting largely of partly disintegrated organic debris

**ahoy** \ə-'hȯi\ *interjection* [*a-* (as in *aha*) + *hoy*] (1751)
— used in hailing ⟨ship *ahoy*⟩

**Ah·ri·man** \'är-i-mən, -ˌmän\ *noun* [Persian, modification of Avestan *aṅrō mainyuš* hostile spirit]
: Ahura Mazda's antagonist who is a spirit of darkness and evil in Zoroastrianism

**Ahu·ra Maz·da** \ə-ˌhu̇r-ə-'maz-də, ä-ˌhu̇r-\ *noun* [Avestan *Ahuramazda,* literally, wise god]
: the Supreme Being represented as a deity of goodness and light in Zoroastrianism

**Ai·as** \'ī-əs\ *noun* [Greek]
: AJAX

**ai·blins** \'ā-blənz\ *adverb* [*able* + *-lings, -lins* -lings] (circa 1605)
*chiefly Scottish* **:** PERHAPS

¹**aid** \'ād\ *verb* [Middle English *eyden,* from Middle French *aider,* from Latin *adjutare,* frequentative of *adjuvare,* from *ad-* + *juvare* to help] (15th century)
*transitive verb*
: to provide with what is useful or necessary in achieving an end
*intransitive verb*
: to give assistance
— **aid·er** *noun*

²**aid** *noun* (15th century)
**1 :** a subsidy granted to the king by the English parliament until the 18th century for an extraordinary purpose
**2 a :** the act of helping **b :** help given **:** ASSISTANCE; *specifically* **:** tangible means of assistance (as money or supplies)

---

☆ **SYNONYMS**
**Agree, concur, coincide** mean to come into or be in harmony regarding a matter of opinion. AGREE implies complete accord usually attained by discussion and adjustment of differences ⟨on some points we all can *agree*⟩. CONCUR tends to suggest cooperative thinking or acting toward an end but sometimes implies no more than approval (as of a decision reached by others) ⟨if my wife *concurs,* it's a deal⟩. COINCIDE, used more often of opinions, judgments, wishes, or interests than of people, implies an agreement amounting to identity ⟨their wishes *coincide* exactly with my desire⟩. See in addition ASSENT.

---

\ə\ abut \ᵊ\ kitten \ər\ further \a\ ash \ā\ ace
\ä\ mop, mar \au̇\ out \ch\ chin \e\ bet \ē\ easy
\g\ go \i\ hit \ī\ ice \j\ job \ŋ\ sing \ō\ go
\ȯ\ law \ȯi\ boy \th\ thin \t͟h\ the \ü\ loot \u̇\ foot
\y\ yet \zh\ vision *see also* Guide to Pronunciation

**3 a :** an assisting person or group — compare AIDE **b :** something by which assistance is given **:** an assisting device ⟨an *aid* to understanding⟩ ⟨a visual *aid*⟩; *especially* **:** HEARING AID
**4 :** a tribute paid by a vassal to his lord

**aide** \'ād\ *noun* [short for *aide-de-camp*] (1777)
**:** a person who acts as an assistant; *specifically* **:** a military officer acting as assistant to a superior

**aide–de–camp** \,ād-di-'kamp, -'käⁿ\ *noun*, *plural* **aides–de–camp** \,ād(z)-di-\ [French *aide de camp*, literally, camp assistant] (1670)
**:** a military aid; *also* **:** a civilian aide usually to an executive

**aide–mé·moire** \,ād-mām-'wär\ *noun*, *plural* **aide–mémoire** [French, from *aider* to aid + *mémoire* memory] (1846)
**1 :** an aid to the memory; *especially* **:** a mnemonic device
**2 :** a written summary or outline of important items of a proposed agreement or diplomatic communication

**aid·man** \'ād-,man\ *noun* (1944)
**:** an army medical corpsman attached to a field unit

**AIDS** \'ādz\ *noun* [acquired *i*mmuno*d*eficiency *s*yndrome] (1982)
**:** a disease of the human immune system that is caused by infection with HIV, that is characterized cytologically especially by severe reduction in the numbers of helper T cells, that in modern industrialized nations occurs especially in homosexual and bisexual men and in intravenous users of illicit drugs, that is commonly transmitted in blood and bodily secretions (as semen), and that renders the subject highly vulnerable to life-threatening conditions (as Pneumocystis carinii pneumonia) and to some that become life-threatening (as Kaposi's sarcoma)

**AIDS–related complex** *noun* (1984)
**:** a group of symptoms (as fever, weight loss, and lymphadenopathy) that is associated with the presence of antibodies to HIV and is followed by the development of AIDS in a certain proportion of cases

**AIDS virus** *noun* (1985)
**:** HIV

**ai·grette** \ā-'gret, 'ā-,\ *noun* [French, plume, egret, from Middle French — more at EGRET] (1630)
**1 :** a spray of feathers (as of the egret) for the head
**2 :** a spray of gems worn on a hat or in the hair

**ai·guille** \ā-'gwē(ə)l, -'gwē\ *noun* [French, literally, needle — more at AGLET] (1816)
**:** a sharp-pointed pinnacle of rock

**ai·guil·lette** \,ā-gwi-'let\ *noun* [French — more at AGLET] (1816)
**:** AGLET; *specifically* **:** a shoulder cord worn by designated military aides — compare FOUR-RAGÈRE

**ai·ki·do** \,ī-ki-'dō, ī-'kē-(,)dō\ *noun* [Japanese *aikidō*, from *ai-* match, coordinate + *ki* breath, spirit + *dō* art, way] (1956)
**:** a Japanese art of self-defense employing locks and holds and utilizing the principle of nonresistance to cause an opponent's own momentum to work against him

**¹ail** \'ā(ə)l\ *verb* [Middle English *eilen*, from Old English *eglan*; akin to Gothic *agljan* to harm] (before 12th century)
*transitive verb*
**:** to give physical or emotional pain, discomfort, or trouble to
*intransitive verb*
**:** to have something the matter; *especially* **:** to suffer ill health

**²ail** *noun* (13th century)
**:** AILMENT

**ai·lan·thus** \ā-'lan(t)-thəs\ *noun* [New Latin, from Ambonese *ai lanito*, literally, tree (of) heaven] (1807)

**:** any of a small Asian genus (*Ailanthus* of the family Simaroubaceae, the ailanthus family) of chiefly tropical trees and shrubs with bitter bark, pinnate leaves, and terminal panicles of ill-scented greenish flowers

**ai·le·ron** \'ā-lə-,rän\ *noun* [French, from diminutive of *aile* wing — more at AISLE] (1909)
**:** a movable airfoil at the trailing edge of an airplane wing that is used for imparting a rolling motion especially in banking for turns — see AIRPLANE illustration

**ail·ment** \'ā(ə)l-mənt\ *noun* (circa 1706)
**1 :** a bodily disorder or chronic disease
**2 :** UNREST, UNEASINESS

**ai·lu·ro·phile** \ī-'lur-ə-,fīl, ā-\ *noun* [Greek *ailouros* cat] (1927)
**:** a cat fancier **:** a lover of cats

**ai·lu·ro·phobe** \-,fōb\ *noun* (1905)
**:** a person who hates or fears cats

**¹aim** \'ām\ *verb* [Middle English, from Middle French *aesmer* & *esmer*; Middle French *aesmer*, from Old French, from *a-* (from Latin *ad-*) + *esmer* to estimate, from Latin *aestimare*] (14th century)
*intransitive verb*
**1 :** to direct a course; *specifically* **:** to point a weapon at an object
**2 :** ASPIRE, INTEND ⟨*aims* to reform the government⟩
*transitive verb*
**1** *obsolete* **:** GUESS, CONJECTURE
**2 a :** POINT **b :** to direct to or toward a specified object or goal ⟨a program *aimed* at reducing pollution⟩

**²aim** *noun* (14th century)
**1** *obsolete* **:** MARK, TARGET
**2 a :** the pointing of a weapon at a mark **b :** the ability to hit a target **c :** a weapon's accuracy or effectiveness
**3** *obsolete* **:** CONJECTURE, GUESS **b :** the directing of effort toward a goal
**4 :** a clearly directed intent or purpose
*synonym* see INTENTION
— **aim·less** \-ləs\ *adjective*
— **aim·less·ly** *adverb*
— **aim·less·ness** *noun*

**ain** \'ān\ *adjective* [probably from Old Norse *eiginn*] (1721)
*Scottish* **:** OWN

**ain't** \'ānt\ [contraction of *are not*] (1778)
**1 :** am not **:** are not **:** is not
**2 :** have not **:** has not
**3 :** do not **:** does not **:** did not — used in some varieties of Black English ▪

**Ai·nu** \'ī-(,)nü\ *noun*, *plural* **Ainu** *or* **Ainus** [Ainu *aynu* person] (1819)
**1 :** a member of an indigenous people of the Japanese archipelago, the Kuril Islands, and part of Sakhalin Island
**2 :** the language of the Ainu people

**ai·o·li** \(,)ī-'ō-lē, (,)ä-\ *noun* [Provençal, from *ai* garlic + *oli* oil] (circa 1900)
**:** a sauce made of crushed garlic, egg yolks, olive oil, and lemon juice and sometimes potato **:** garlic mayonnaise

**¹air** \'ar, 'er\ *noun*, *often attributive* [Middle English, from Middle French, from Latin *aer*, from Greek *aēr*] (14th century)
**1 a** *archaic* **:** BREATH **b :** the mixture of invisible odorless tasteless gases (as nitrogen and oxygen) that surrounds the earth **c :** a light breeze
**2 a :** empty space **b :** NOTHINGNESS ⟨vanished into thin *air*⟩ **c :** a sudden severance of relations ⟨she gave me the *air*⟩
**3** [probably translation of Italian *aria*] **a :** TUNE, MELODY **b** *Elizabethan & Jacobean music* **:** an accompanied song or melody in usually strophic form **c :** the chief voice part or melody in choral music
**4 a :** outward appearance of a thing ⟨an *air* of luxury⟩ **b :** a surrounding or pervading influence **:** ATMOSPHERE ⟨an *air* of mystery⟩ **c :** the look, appearance, or bearing of a person especially as expressive of some personal quality

or emotion **:** DEMEANOR ⟨an *air* of dignity⟩ **d :** an artificial or affected manner ⟨put on *airs*⟩
**5 :** public utterance ⟨he gave *air* to his opinion⟩
**6 :** COMPRESSED AIR
**7 a (1) :** AIRCRAFT ⟨go by *air*⟩ **(2) :** AVIATION ⟨*air* safety⟩ ⟨*air* rights⟩ **(3) :** AIR FORCE ⟨*air* headquarters⟩ **b :** the medium of transmission of radio waves; *also* **:** RADIO, TELEVISION ⟨went on the *air*⟩
**8 :** a football offense utilizing primarily the forward pass ⟨trailing by 20 points, the team took to the *air*⟩
**9 :** an air-conditioning system
*synonym* see POSE
— **air·less** \-ləs\ *adjective*
— **air·less·ness** *noun*
— **in the air :** in wide circulation **:** ABOUT
— **up in the air :** not yet settled

**²air** (1530)
*transitive verb*
**1 :** to expose to the air for drying, purifying, or refreshing **:** VENTILATE — often used with *out*
**2 :** to expose to public view or bring to public notice
**3 :** to transmit by radio or television ⟨*air* a program⟩
*intransitive verb*
**1 :** to become exposed to the open air
**2 :** to become broadcast ⟨the program *airs* daily⟩
*synonym* see EXPRESS

**air bag** *noun* (1969)
**:** an automobile safety device consisting of a bag designed to inflate automatically in front of an occupant in case of collision

**air ball** *noun* (1981)
**:** a missed shot in basketball that fails to touch the rim and backboard

**air base** *noun* (1915)
**:** a military base intended chiefly for the operation of aircraft

**air bladder** *noun* (1731)
**:** a sac containing gas and especially air; *especially* **:** a hydrostatic organ present in most fishes that serves as an accessory respiratory organ

**air·boat** \'ar-,bōt, 'er-\ *noun* (1946)
**:** a shallow-draft boat driven by an airplane propeller and steered by an airplane rudder

**air·borne** \-,bōrn, -,bȯrn\ *adjective* (1641)
**1 :** done or being in the air **:** being off the ground: as **a :** carried through the air (as by an

aircraft) **b :** supported especially by aerodynamic forces or propelled through the air by force

**2 :** trained for deployment by air and especially by parachute

**air brake** *noun* (1871)

**1 :** a brake operated by a piston driven by compressed air

**2 :** a surface that may be projected into the airstream for increasing drag and lowering the speed of an airplane

**¹air·brush** \-ˌbrəsh\ *noun* (circa 1889)
**:** an atomizer for applying by compressed air a fine spray (as of paint or liquid color)

**²airbrush** *transitive verb* (1938)
**:** to paint, treat, or alter with an airbrush

**air·burst** \-ˌbərst\ *noun* (1917)
**:** the burst of a shell or bomb in the air

**air·bus** \-ˌbəs\ *noun* (1945)
**:** a short-range or medium-range subsonic jet passenger airplane

**air chief marshal** *noun* (1919)
**:** a commissioned officer in the British air force who ranks with a general in the army

**air commodore** *noun* (1919)
**:** a commissioned officer in the British air force who ranks with a brigadier in the army

**air–con·di·tion** \ˌar-kən-'di-shən, ˌer-\ *transitive verb* [back-formation from *air conditioning*] (1933)
**:** to equip (as a building) with an apparatus for washing air and controlling its humidity and temperature; *also* **:** to subject (air) to these processes
— **air con·di·tion·er** \-'di-sh(ə-)nər\ *noun*
— **air–con·di·tion·ing** \-'di-sh(ə-)niŋ\ *noun*

**air·craft** \'ar-ˌkraft, 'er-\ *noun, plural* **aircraft** *often attributive* (1850)
**:** a vehicle (as an airplane or balloon) for traveling through the air

**aircraft carrier** *noun* (1919)
**:** a warship with a flight deck on which airplanes can be launched and landed

**air·crew** \'ar-ˌkrü, 'er-\ *noun* (1921)
**:** the crew manning an airplane

**air–cush·ion vehicle** *noun* (circa 1962)
**:** HOVERCRAFT

**air dam** *noun* (1965)
**:** a device attached to the underside of the front of an automobile to improve stability, aerodynamic performance, and engine cooling by redirecting the flow of air

**air·date** \-ˌdāt\ *noun* (1971)
**:** the scheduled date of a broadcast

**air·drome** \'ar-ˌdrōm, 'er-\ *noun* [alteration of *aerodrome*] (1917)
**:** AIRPORT

**air·drop** \-ˌdräp\ *noun* (circa 1945)
**:** delivery of cargo or personnel by parachute from an airplane in flight
— **air–drop** *transitive verb*
— **air–drop·pa·ble** \-ˌdrä-pə-bəl\ *adjective*

**air–dry** \-'drī\ *adjective* (1856)
**:** dry to such a degree that no further moisture is given up on exposure to air

**Aire·dale terrier** \'ar-ˌdāl-, 'er-\ *noun* [*Airedale*, valley of the Aire river, England] (1880)
**:** any of a breed of large terriers with a hard, wiry, black-and-tan coat — called also *Airedale*

**air·er** \'ar-ər, 'er-\ *noun* (circa 1847)
*British* **:** a frame on which clothes are aired or dried

**air·fare** \'ar-ˌfar, 'er-ˌfer\ *noun* (1918)
**:** fare for travel by airplane

**air·field** \-ˌfēld\ *noun* (1927)
**:** an area of land from which aircraft operate: as **a :** AIRPORT **b :** AIR BASE

**air·flow** \-ˌflō\ *noun* (circa 1911)
**:** a flow of air; *specifically* **:** the motion of air (as around parts of an airplane in flight) relative to the surface of a body immersed in it

**air·foil** \-ˌfȯil\ *noun* (circa 1922)
**:** a body (as an airplane wing or propeller

blade) designed to provide a desired reaction force when in motion relative to the surrounding air

**air force** *noun* (1917)
**1 :** the military organization of a nation for air warfare

**2 :** a unit of the U.S. Air Force higher than a division and lower than a command

**air·frame** \-ˌfrām\ *noun* (1931)
**:** the structure of an aircraft, rocket vehicle, or missile without the power plant

**air·freight** \-'frāt\ *noun* (1929)
**:** freight transport by air in volume; *also* **:** the charge for this service
— **airfreight** *transitive verb*

**air·glow** \-ˌglō\ *noun* (circa 1950)
**:** light that is observed especially during the night, that originates in the high atmosphere of a planet (as the earth), and that is associated with photochemical reactions of gases caused by solar radiation

**air gun** *noun* (circa 1753)
**1 :** a gun from which a projectile is propelled by compressed air

**2 :** any of various hand tools that work by compressed air; *especially* **:** AIRBRUSH

**¹air·head** \-ˌhed\ *noun* [*¹air* + *-head* (as in *beachhead*)] (circa 1944)
**:** an area in hostile territory secured usually by airborne troops for further use in bringing in troops and materiel by air

**²airhead** *noun* (1972)
**:** a mindless or stupid person
— **air·head·ed** \-ˌhe-dəd\ *adjective*

**air·hole** \-ˌhōl\ *noun* (1766)
**:** a hole to admit or discharge air

**air·ing** \'ar-iŋ, 'er-\ *noun* (circa 1606)
**1 :** exposure to air or heat for drying or freshening

**2 :** exposure to or exercise in the open air especially to promote health or fitness

**3 :** exposure to public view or notice

**4 :** a radio or television broadcast

**air lane** *noun* (circa 1910)
**:** a path customarily followed by airplanes

**air letter** *noun* (1920)
**1 :** an airmail letter

**2 :** a sheet of airmail stationery that can be folded and sealed with the message inside and the address outside

**air·lift** \'ar-ˌlift, 'er-\ *noun* (1945)
**:** a system of transporting cargo or passengers by aircraft usually to or from an otherwise inaccessible area
— **airlift** *transitive verb*

**air·line** \-ˌlīn\ *noun* (1910)
**:** an air transportation system including its equipment, routes, operating personnel, and management

**air line** *noun* (1813)
**:** a straight line through the air between two points

**air·lin·er** \-ˌlī-nər\ *noun* (1908)
**:** an airplane operated by an airline

**air lock** *noun* (1857)
**1 :** an intermediate chamber with two airtight doors or openings to permit passage between two dissimilar spaces (as two places of unequal atmospheric pressure)

**2 :** a stoppage of flow caused by air being in a part where liquid ought to circulate

**air·mail** \'ar-ˌmā(ə)l, 'er-\ *noun* (1913)
**:** the system of transporting mail by aircraft; *also* **:** the mail thus transported
— **airmail** *transitive verb*

**air·man** \-mən\ *noun* (1873)
**1 :** a civilian or military pilot, aviator, or aviation technician

**2 :** an enlisted man in the air force: as **a :** an enlisted man of the three ranks below sergeant **b :** an enlisted man ranking above an airman basic and below an airman first class

**airman basic** *noun* (circa 1961)
**:** an enlisted man of the lowest rank in the air force

**airman first class** *noun* (1952)

**:** an enlisted man in the air force ranking above an airman and below a sergeant

**air·man·ship** \'ar-mən-ˌship, 'er-\ *noun* (1908)
**:** skill in piloting or navigating airplanes

**air marshal** *noun* (1919)
**:** a commissioned officer in the British air force who ranks with a lieutenant general in the army

**air mass** *noun* (1893)
**:** a body of air extending hundreds or thousands of miles horizontally and sometimes as high as the stratosphere and maintaining as it travels nearly uniform conditions of temperature and humidity at any given level

**air mattress** *noun* (1926)
**:** MATTRESS 1b

**Air Medal** *noun* (1942)
**:** a U.S. military decoration awarded for meritorious achievement while participating in an aerial flight

**air mile** *noun* (1919)
**:** a mile in air travel

**air–mind·ed** \'ar-'mīn-dəd, 'er-\ *adjective* (1924)
**:** interested in aviation or in air travel
— **air–mind·ed·ness** *noun*

**air·mo·bile** \-ˌmō-bəl, -ˌbēl, -ˌbīl\ *adjective* (1965)
**:** of, relating to, or being a military unit whose members are transported to combat areas usually by helicopter

**air·park** \-ˌpärk\ *noun* (1929)
**:** a small airport usually near an industrial area

**air piracy** *noun* (1948)
**:** the hijacking of a flying airplane **:** SKYJACKING

**air·plane** \'ar-ˌplān, 'er-\ *noun* [alteration of *aeroplane*] (1907)
**:** a powered heavier-than-air aircraft that has fixed wings from which it derives most of its lift

airplane: *1* weather radar, *2* cockpit, *3* jet engine, *4* engine pod, *5* pylon, *6* wing, *7* vertical stabilizer, *8* rudder, *9, 10* tabs, *11* elevator, *12* horizontal stabilizer, *13* inboard flap, *14* inboard spoiler, *15, 16* tabs, *17* aileron, *18* outboard flap, *19* outboard spoiler, *20* sound suppressor, *21* thrust reverser, *22* cabin air intake, *23* fuselage, *24* nose landing gear

**air plant** *noun* (1841)
**1 :** EPIPHYTE
**2 :** BRYOPHYLLUM

**air·play** \-ˌplā\ *noun* (1966)
**:** the playing of a musical recording on the air by a radio station

**air pocket** *noun* (1912)
**:** a condition of the atmosphere (as a local down current) that causes an airplane to drop suddenly

**air police** *noun* (1944)
**:** the military police of an air force

**air·port** \'ar-ˌpōrt, 'er-, -ˌpȯrt\ *noun* (1919)
**:** a place from which aircraft operate that usually has paved runways and maintenance facilities and often serves as a terminal

\ə\ abut \ᵊ\ kitten \ər\ further \a\ ash \ā\ ace
\ä\ mop, mar \au̇\ out \ch\ chin \e\ bet \ē\ easy
\g\ go \i\ hit \ī\ ice \j\ job \ŋ\ sing \ō\ go
\ȯ\ law \ȯi\ boy \th\ thin \t͟h\ the \ü\ loot \u̇\ foot
\y\ yet \zh\ vision *see also* Guide to Pronunciation

**air·post** \-'pōst\ *noun* (circa 1927)
: AIRMAIL

**air·pow·er** \-,paù(-ə)r\ *noun* (1908)
: the military strength of a nation's air force

**air pump** *noun* (1660)
: a pump for exhausting air from a closed space or for compressing air or forcing it through other apparatus

**air raid** *noun* (1914)
: an attack by armed airplanes on a surface target — usually hyphened when used attributively ⟨*air-raid* shelter⟩

**air rifle** *noun* (1886)
: a rifle whose projectile (as a BB or pellet) is propelled by compressed air or carbon dioxide

**air right** *noun* (1922)
: a property right to the space above a surface area or object

**air sac** *noun* (circa 1828)
**1 :** one of the air-filled spaces in the body of a bird connected with the air passages of the lungs
**2 :** ALVEOLUS 1b
**3 :** a thin-walled dilation of a trachea occurring in many insects

**air·screw** \'ar-,skrü\ *noun* (1894)
*chiefly British* **:** an airplane propeller

**air·ship** \-,ship\ *noun* (1819)
: a lighter-than-air aircraft having propulsion and steering systems

**air show** *noun* (1950)
: an exhibition of aircraft and aviation skills

**air·sick** \-,sik\ *adjective* (1785)
: affected with motion sickness associated with flying
— **air·sick·ness** *noun*

**air·space** \-,spās\ *noun* (1911)
: the space lying above the earth or above a certain area of land or water; *especially* **:** the space lying above a nation and coming under its jurisdiction

**air·speed** \-,spēd\ *noun* (circa 1909)
: the speed (as of an airplane) with relation to the air — compare GROUND SPEED

**air·stream** \-,strēm\ *noun* (1869)
: a current of air; *specifically* **:** AIRFLOW

**air·strip** \-,strip\ *noun* (1942)
: a runway without normal air base or airport facilities

**¹airt** \'ärt, 'ert\ *noun* [Middle English *art*, from Scottish Gaelic *àirt*] (15th century)
*chiefly Scottish* **:** compass point **:** DIRECTION

**²airt** *transitive verb* (circa 1782)
*chiefly Scottish* **:** DIRECT, GUIDE

**air taxi** *noun* (1920)
: a small commercial airplane used for short flights between localities not served by scheduled airlines

**air·tight** \'ar-,tīt, 'er-\ *adjective* (1760)
**1 :** impermeable to air or nearly so
**2 a :** having no noticeable weakness, flaw, or loophole ⟨an *airtight* argument⟩ **b :** permitting no opportunity for an opponent to score ⟨an *airtight* defense⟩
— **air·tight·ness** *noun*

**air·time** \-,tīm\ *noun* (1942)
**1 :** the time at which a radio or television broadcast is scheduled to begin
**2 :** the time or any part thereof that a radio or television station is on the air

**air-to-air** \,ar-tə-'(w)ar, ,er-tə-'(w)er\ *adjective* (1941)
: launched from one airplane in flight at another ⟨*air-to-air* missiles⟩; *also* **:** involving aircraft in flight ⟨*air-to-air* combat⟩

**air vice–marshal** *noun* (1919)
: a commissioned officer in the British air force who ranks with a major general in the army

**air·wave** \'ar-,wāv, 'er-\ *adjective* (1944)
: of, created for, or heard on the airwaves

**air·waves** \-,wāvz\ *noun plural* (1928)
: the medium of radio and television transmission — not used technically

**air·way** \-,wā\ *noun* (1849)
**1 :** a passage for a current of air (as in a mine or to the lungs)
**2 :** a designated route along which airplanes fly from airport to airport; *especially* **:** such a route equipped with navigational aids
**3 :** AIRLINE
**4 :** a channel of a designated radio frequency for broadcasting or other radio communication

**air·wor·thy** \-,wər-thē\ *adjective* (1829)
: fit for operation in the air ⟨an *airworthy* airplane⟩
— **air·wor·thi·ness** *noun*

**airy** \'ar-ē, 'er-\ *adjective* **air·i·er; -est** (14th century)
**1 a :** of or relating to air **:** ATMOSPHERIC **b :** high in the air **:** LOFTY ⟨*airy* perches⟩ **c :** performed in air **:** AERIAL ⟨*airy* leaps⟩
**2 :** UNREAL, ILLUSORY ⟨*airy* romances⟩
**3 a :** being light and graceful in movement or manner **:** SPRIGHTLY, VIVACIOUS ⟨an *airy* laugh⟩ **b :** ETHEREAL ⟨*airy* fantasy⟩
**4 a :** open to the free circulation of air ⟨an *airy* front porch⟩ **b :** having openings or spaces ⟨*airy* lacework⟩
**5 :** AFFECTED, PROUD ⟨*airy* condescension⟩
— **air·i·ly** \'ar-ə-lē, 'er-\ *adverb*
— **air·i·ness** \-ē-nəs\ *noun*

**airy–fairy** \-'far-ē, -'fer-ē\ *adjective* (1869)
**1** *chiefly British* **:** DELICATE, FAIRYLIKE
**2** *chiefly British* **:** lacking substance or purpose ⟨in . . . an *airy-fairy*, unserious, insufficiently careful fashion —*Times Literary Supplement*⟩

**aisle** \'ī(ə)l\ *noun* [Middle English *ile*, alteration of *ele*, from Middle French, wing, from Latin *ala*; akin to Old English *eaxl* shoulder, Latin *axis* axletree — more at AXIS] (15th century)
**1 :** the side of a church nave separated by piers from the nave proper
**2 a :** a passage (as in a theater or railroad passenger car) separating sections of seats **b :** a passage (as in a store or warehouse) for inside traffic

**aisle·way** \-,wā\ *noun* (1926)
: AISLE 2b

**ait** \'āt\ *noun* [Middle English *eyt*, alteration of Old English *īggoth*, from *īg* island — more at ISLAND] (before 12th century)
*British* **:** a little island

**aitch** \'āch\ *noun* [French *hache*, from (assumed) Vulgar Latin *hacca*] (circa 1580)
: the letter *h*

**aitch·bone** \'āch-,bōn\ *noun* [Middle English *hachbon*, alteration (resulting from incorrect division of *a nachebon*) of (assumed) Middle English *nachebon*, from Middle English *nache* buttock (from Middle French, from Late Latin *natica*, from Latin *natis*) + *bon* bone] (15th century)
**1 :** the hipbone especially of cattle
**2 :** the cut of beef containing the aitchbone

**ajar** \ə-'jär\ *adjective or adverb* [earlier *on char*, from *on* + *char* turn — more at CHARE] (15th century)
: slightly open ⟨a door *ajar*⟩

**Ajax** \'ā-,jaks\ *noun* [Latin, from Greek *Aias*]
**1 :** a Greek hero in the Trojan War who kills himself because the armor of Achilles is awarded to Odysseus
**2 :** a fleet-footed Greek hero in the Trojan War

**aju·ga** \'a-jə-gə\ *noun, plural* **-ga** *or* **-gas** [New Latin, from ²*a*- + Latin *jugum* yoke — more at YOKE] (circa 1899)
: ¹BUGLE

**Akan** \'ä-,kän\ *noun, plural* **Akan** *or* **Akans** (1694)
**1 :** a member of any of the Akan-speaking peoples (as the Ashanti)
**2 :** a Kwa language of southern Ghana and the southeast Ivory Coast

**akee** \'a-,kē, a-'kē\ *noun* [origin unknown] (1794)
: the fleshy fruit of an African tree (*Blighia sapida*) of the soapberry family grown in the

Caribbean area, Florida, and Hawaii that is edible when ripe but has a toxic pink raphe attaching the aril to the seed and toxic arils when immature or overripe; *also* **:** the tree

**AK–47** \'ā-,kā-,fȯr-tē-'se-vˀn, -,fȯr-\ *noun* [Russian *avtomat Kalashnikova* 1947 Kalashnikov automatic rifle of 1947] (1968)
: a Soviet-designed 7.62 mm (.30 cal.) gas-operated magazine-fed rifle for automatic or semiautomatic fire

**akim·bo** \ə-'kim-(,)bō\ *adjective or adverb* [Middle English *in kenebowe*] (15th century)
**1 :** having the hand on the hip and the elbow turned outward
**2 :** set in a bent position ⟨a tailor sitting with legs *akimbo*⟩

**akin** \ə-'kin\ *adjective* (1586)
**1 :** related by blood **:** descended from a common ancestor or prototype
**2 :** essentially similar, related, or compatible

**Aki·ta** \ə-'kē-tə, ä-\ *noun* [from *Akita*, Japan] (1928)
: any of a breed of large muscular dogs of Japanese origin

**Ak·ka·di·an** \ə-'kā-dē-ən\ *noun* (circa 1855)
**1 :** an extinct Semitic language of ancient Mesopotamia
**2 :** a Semitic inhabitant of central Mesopotamia before 2000 B.C.
— **Akkadian** *adjective*

**ak·va·vit** \'ä-kwə-,vēt, 'äk-və-\ *variant of* AQUAVIT

**al-** — see AD-

**¹-al** *adjective suffix* [Middle English, from Old French & Latin; Old French, from Latin *-alis*] **:** of, relating to, or characterized by ⟨directional⟩ ⟨fictional⟩

**²-al** *noun suffix* [Middle English *-aille*, from Old French, from Latin *-alia*, neuter plural of *-alis*] **:** action **:** process ⟨rehearsal⟩

**³-al** *noun suffix* [French, from *alcool* alcohol, from Medieval Latin *alcohol*] **:** aldehyde ⟨furfural⟩

**ala** \'ā-lə\ *noun, plural* **alae** \-,lē\ [Latin — more at AISLE] (1738)
: a wing or a winglike anatomic process or part
— **alar** \'ā-lər\ *adjective*
— **ala·ry** \-lə-rē\ *adjective*

**à la** *also* **a la** \ä-(,)lä, ,ä-lə, ,a-lə\ *preposition* [French *à la*] (1589)
: in the manner of

**al·a·bas·ter** \'a-lə-,bas-tər\ *noun* [Middle English *alabastre*, from Middle French, from Latin *alabaster* vase of alabaster, from Greek *alabastros*] (14th century)
**1 :** a compact fine-textured usually white and translucent gypsum often carved into vases and ornaments
**2 :** a hard compact calcite or aragonite that is translucent and sometimes banded
— **alabaster** *or* **al·a·bas·trine** \,a-lə-'bas-trən\ *adjective*

**à la carte** *also* **a la carte** \,ä-lə-'kärt, ,a-lə-\ *adverb or adjective* [French, by the bill of fare] (1826)
: according to a menu that prices each item separately

**alack** \ə-'lak\ *interjection* [Middle English] (15th century)
— used to express sorrow or regret

**alac·ri·ty** \ə-'la-krə-tē\ *noun* [Latin *alacritas*, from *alacr-, alacer* lively, eager] (15th century)
: promptness in response **:** cheerful readiness ⟨accepted the invitation of the president with *alacrity*⟩
— **alac·ri·tous** \-krə-təs\ *adjective*

**Alad·din** \ə-'la-dˀn\ *noun*
: a youth in the *Arabian Nights' Entertainments* who comes into possession of a magic lamp

**à la grecque** \,ä-lə-'grek, ,a-lə-\ *adjective, often G capitalized* [French, in the Greek manner] (circa 1925)

**:** served in a sauce made of olive oil, lemon juice, and several seasonings (as fennel, coriander, sage, and thyme)

**à la king** \ˌä-lə-'kiŋ, ˌa-lə-\ *adjective* (1919)
**:** served in a cream sauce with mushrooms and pimiento or green peppers ⟨chicken *à la king*⟩

**al·a·me·da** \ˌa-lə-'mē-də, -'mā-\ *noun* [Spanish, from *álamo* poplar] (1797)
**:** a public promenade bordered with trees

**à la mode** *also* **a la mode** \ˌä-lə-'mōd, ˌa-lə-\ *adjective* [French, according to the fashion] (1650)
**1 :** FASHIONABLE, STYLISH
**2 :** topped with ice cream

**al·a·nine** \'a-lə-ˌnēn\ *noun* [German *Alanin,* irregular from *Aldehyd* aldehyde] (circa 1879)
**:** a simple nonessential crystalline amino acid $C_3H_7NO_2$

**al·a·nyl** \'a-lə-ˌnil\ *noun* [International Scientific Vocabulary *alanine* + *-yl*] (circa 1928)
**:** an acyl radical of alanine

**¹alarm** \ə-'lärm\ *also* **ala·rum** \ə-'lär-əm, -'lar-, *British also* -'ler-\ *noun* [Middle English *alarme, alarom,* from Middle French *alarme,* from Old Italian *all'arme,* literally, to the arms] (14th century)
**1** *usually* **alarum,** *archaic* **:** a call to arms ⟨the angry trumpet sounds *alarum* —Shakespeare⟩
**2 :** a signal (as a loud noise or flashing light) that warns or alerts; *also* **:** a device that signals ⟨set the *alarm* to wake me at seven⟩
**3 :** sudden sharp apprehension and fear resulting from the perception of imminent danger
**4 :** a warning notice
**synonym** see FEAR

**²alarm** *also* **alarum** *transitive verb* (1605)
**1 :** DISTURB, EXCITE
**2 :** to give warning to
**3 :** to strike with fear
— **alarm·ing·ly** \-'lär-miŋ-lē\ *adverb*

**alarm clock** *noun* (1697)
**:** a clock that can be set to sound an alarm at a desired time

**alarm·ism** \ə-'lär-ˌmi-zəm\ *noun* (1867)
**:** the often unwarranted exciting of fears or warning of danger
— **alarm·ist** \-mist\ *noun or adjective*

**alarm reaction** *noun* (1936)
**:** the initial reaction of an organism (as increased hormonal activity) to stress

**alarums and excursions** *noun plural* (1592)
**1 :** martial sounds and the movement of soldiers across the stage — used as a stage direction in Elizabethan drama
**2 :** clamor, excitement, and feverish or disordered activity

**alas** \ə-'las\ *interjection* [Middle English, from Old French, from *a* ah + *las* weary, from Latin *lassus* — more at LASSITUDE] (13th century)
— used to express unhappiness, pity, or concern

**Alas·kan malamute** \ə-'las-kən-\ *noun* (1938)
**:** any of a breed of powerful heavy-coated deep-chested dogs of Alaskan origin that have erect ears, heavily cushioned feet, and a plumy tail

**Alas·ka time** \ə-'las-kə-\ *noun* (1945)
**:** the time of the 9th time zone west of Greenwich that includes most of Alaska

**¹alate** \'ā-ˌlāt\ *adjective* [Latin *alatus,* from *ala*] (1668)
**:** having wings or a winglike part

**²alate** *noun* (1941)
**:** a winged insect (as an aphid) of a kind having winged and wingless forms

**alb** \'alb\ *noun* [Middle English *albe,* from Old English, from Medieval Latin *alba,* from Latin, feminine of *albus* white; akin to Greek *alphos* white leprous spot] (before 12th century)
**:** a full-length white linen ecclesiastical vestment with long sleeves that is gathered at the waist with a cincture

**al·ba·core** \'al-bə-ˌkȯr, -ˌkȯr\ *noun, plural* **-core** *or* **-cores** [Portuguese *albacor,* from Arabic *al-bakūrah* the albacore] (1579)
**:** a large pelagic tuna (*Thunnus alalunga*) with long pectoral fins that is a source of canned tuna; *broadly* **:** any of various tunas (as a bonito)

albacore

**Al·ba·nian** \al-'bā-nē-ən, -nyən *also* ȯl-\ *noun* (1579)
**1 :** a native or inhabitant of Albania
**2 :** the Indo-European language of the Albanian people — see INDO-EUROPEAN LANGUAGES table
— **Albanian** *adjective*

**al·ba·tross** \'al-bə-ˌtrȯs, -ˌträs\ *noun, plural* **-tross** *or* **-tross·es** [probably alteration of obsolete *alcatrace* frigate bird, from Spanish or Portuguese *alcatraz* pelican, from Arabic *al-ghaṭṭās,* a kind of sea eagle] (1672)
**1 :** any of a family (Diomedeidae) of large web-footed seabirds that have long slender wings, are excellent gliders, and include the largest seabirds
**2 a :** something that causes persistent deep concern or anxiety **b :** something that greatly hinders accomplishment **:** ENCUMBRANCE

albatross 1

**al·be·do** \al-'bē-(ˌ)dō\ *noun, plural* **-dos** [Late Latin, whiteness, from Latin *albus*] (circa 1859)
**:** reflective power; *specifically* **:** the fraction of incident radiation (as light) that is reflected by a surface or body (as the moon or a cloud)

**al·be·it** \ȯl-'bē-ət, al-\ *conjunction* [Middle English, literally, all though it be] (14th century)
**:** conceding the fact that **:** even though

**Al·bi·gen·ses** \ˌal-bə-'jen-ˌsēz\ *noun plural* [Medieval Latin, plural of *Albigensis,* literally, inhabitant of Albi, from *Albiga* (Albi), France] (1625)
**:** members of a Catharistic sect of southern France flourishing primarily in the 12th and 13th centuries
— **Al·bi·gen·sian** \-'jen(t)-shən, -'jen(t)-sē-ən\ *adjective or noun*
— **Al·bi·gen·sian·ism** \-shə-ˌni-zəm, -sē-ə-ˌ\ *noun*

**al·bi·nism** \'al-bə-ˌni-zəm, al-'bī-\ *noun* (1836)
**:** the condition of an albino
— **al·bi·nis·tic** \ˌal-bə-'nis-tik\ *adjective*

**al·bi·no** \al-'bī-(ˌ)nō\ *noun, plural* **-nos** [Portuguese, from Spanish, from *albo* white, from Latin *albus*] (1777)
**:** an organism exhibiting deficient pigmentation; *especially* **:** a human being or nonhuman mammal that is congenitally deficient in pigment and usually has a milky or translucent skin, white or colorless hair, and eyes with pink or blue iris and deep-red pupil

**al·bi·not·ic** \ˌal-bə-'nä-tik\ *adjective* [*albino* + *-tic* (as in *melanotic*)] (1872)
**1 :** of, relating to, or affected with albinism
**2 :** tending toward albinism

**Al·bi·on** \'al-bē-ən\ *noun* [Latin] (before 12th century)
**1 :** Great Britain
**2 :** England

**al·bite** \'al-ˌbīt\ *noun* [Swedish *albit,* from Latin *albus*] (circa 1843)
**:** a triclinic usually white feldspar consisting of a sodium aluminum silicate

**— al·bit·ic** \al-'bit-ik\ *adjective*

**al·bum** \'al-bəm\ *noun* [Latin, a white tablet, from neuter of *albus*] (1612)
**1 a :** a book with blank pages used for making a collection (as of autographs, stamps, or photographs) **b :** a paperboard container for a phonograph record **:** JACKET **c :** one or more recordings (as on tape or disc) produced as a single unit ⟨a 2-record *album*⟩
**2 :** a collection usually in book form of literary selections, musical compositions, or pictures **:** ANTHOLOGY

**al·bu·men** \al-'byü-mən; 'al-ˌbyü-, -byə-\ *noun* [Late Latin, from *albus*] (1599)
**1 :** the white of an egg — see EGG illustration
**2 :** ALBUMIN

**al·bu·min** \al-'byü-mən; 'al-ˌbyü-, -byə-\ *noun* [International Scientific Vocabulary *albumen* + *-in*] (1869)
**:** any of numerous simple heat-coagulable water-soluble proteins that occur in blood plasma or serum, muscle, the whites of eggs, milk, and other animal substances and in many plant tissues and fluids

**al·bu·min·ous** \al-'byü-mə-nəs\ *adjective* (1791)
**:** relating to, containing, or having the properties of albumen or albumin

**al·bu·min·uria** \ˌ(ˌ)al-ˌbyü-mə-'nu̇r-ē-ə, -'nyu̇r-\ *noun* [New Latin] (circa 1842)
**:** the presence of albumin in the urine often symptomatic of kidney disease
— **al·bu·min·uric** \-'nu̇r-ik, -'nyu̇r-\ *adjective*

**al·ca·ic** \al-'kā-ik\ *adjective, often capitalized* [Late Latin *Alcaicus* of Alcaeus, from Greek *Alkaïkos,* from *Alkaios* Alcaeus, (flourished about 600 B.C.) Greek poet] (circa 1637)
**:** relating to or written in a verse or strophe marked by complicated variation of a dominant iambic pattern
— **alcaic** *noun, often capitalized*

**al·cai·de** *or* **al·cay·de** \al-'kī-dē\ *noun* [Spanish *alcaide,* from Arabic *al-qā'id* the captain] (1502)
**:** a commander of a castle or fortress (as among Spaniards, Portuguese, or Moors)

**al·cal·de** \al-'käl-dē\ *noun* [Spanish, from Arabic *al-qāḍī* the judge] (1565)
**:** the chief administrative and judicial officer of a Spanish town

**al·ca·zar** \al-'kä-zər, -'ka-\ *noun* [Spanish *alcázar,* from Arabic *al-qaṣr* the castle] (circa 1615)
**:** a Spanish fortress or palace

**Al·ces·tis** \al-'ses-təs\ *noun* [Latin, from Greek *Alkēstis*]
**:** the wife of Admetus who dies for her husband and is restored to him by Hercules

**al·che·mist** \'al-kə-mist\ *noun* (15th century)
**:** a person who studies or practices alchemy
— **al·che·mis·tic** \ˌal-kə-'mis-tik\ *also* **al·che·mis·ti·cal** \-ti-kəl\ *adjective*

**al·che·mize** \'al-kə-ˌmīz\ *transitive verb* **-mized; -miz·ing** (1597)
**:** to change by alchemy **:** TRANSMUTE

**al·che·my** \'al-kə-mē\ *noun* [Middle English *alkamie, alquemie,* from Middle French or Medieval Latin; Middle French *alquemie,* from Medieval Latin *alchymia,* from Arabic *al-kīmiyā',* from *al* the + *kīmiyā'* alchemy, from Late Greek *chēmeia*] (14th century)
**1 :** a medieval chemical science and speculative philosophy aiming to achieve the transmutation of the base metals into gold, the discovery of a universal cure for disease, and the discovery of a means of indefinitely prolonging life
**2 :** a power or process of transforming something common into something special

\ə\ **abut** \ᵊ\ **kitten** \ər\ **further** \a\ **ash** \ā\ **ace**
\ä\ **mop, mar** \au̇\ **out** \ch\ **chin** \e\ **bet** \ē\ **easy**
\g\ **go** \i\ **hit** \ī\ **ice** \j\ **job** \ŋ\ **sing** \ō\ **go**
\ȯ\ **law** \ȯi\ **boy** \th\ **thin** \t͟h\ **the** \ü\ **loot** \u̇\ **foot**
\y\ **yet** \zh\ **vision** *see also* Guide to Pronunciation

**3 :** an inexplicable or mysterious transmuting
— **al·chem·i·cal** \-mi-kəl\ *also* **al·chem·ic** \al-'ke-mik\ *adjective*
— **al·chem·i·cal·ly** \-mi-k(ə-)lē\ *adverb*
**Alc·me·ne** \alk-'mē-nē\ *noun* [Greek *Alkmēnē*]
**:** the mother of Hercules by Zeus in the form of her husband Amphitryon
**al·co·hol** \'al-kə-ˌhȯl\ *noun* [New Latin, from Medieval Latin, powdered antimony, from Old Spanish, from Arabic *al-kuḥul* the powdered antimony, from *koḥl* kohl] (1672)
**1 a :** ethanol especially when considered as the intoxicating agent in fermented and distilled liquors **b :** drink (as whiskey or beer) containing ethanol **c :** a mixture of ethanol and water that is usually 95 percent ethanol
**2 :** any of various compounds that are analogous to ethanol in constitution and that are hydroxyl derivatives of hydrocarbons
**¹al·co·hol·ic** \ˌal-kə-'hȯ-lik, -'hä-\ *adjective* (1790)
**1 a :** of, relating to, or caused by alcohol **b :** containing alcohol
**2 :** affected with alcoholism
— **al·co·hol·i·cal·ly** \-li-k(ə-)lē\ *adverb*
**²alcoholic** *noun* (circa 1890)
**:** a person affected with alcoholism
**al·co·hol·ism** \'al-kə-ˌhȯ-ˌli-zəm, -kə-hə-\ *noun* (1860)
**1 :** continued excessive or compulsive use of alcoholic drinks
**2 :** poisoning by alcohol; *especially* **:** a complex chronic psychological and nutritional disorder associated with excessive and usually compulsive drinking
**Al·co·ran** \ˌal-kə-'ran\ *noun* [Middle English, from Middle French or Medieval Latin; Middle French & Medieval Latin, from Arabic *al-qur'ān*, literally, the reading] (14th century) *archaic* **:** KORAN
**al·cove** \'al-ˌkōv\ *noun* [French *alcôve*, from Spanish *alcoba*, from Arabic *al-qubbah* the arch] (1676)
**1 a :** a small recessed section of a room **:** NOOK **b :** an arched opening (as in a wall) **:** NICHE
**2 :** SUMMERHOUSE 2
— **al·coved** \-ˌkōvd\ *adjective*
**al·cy·o·nar·i·an** \ˌal-sē-ə-'nar-ē-ən\ *noun* [ultimately from Greek *alkyoneion*, a zoophyte, from neuter of *alkyoneios* of a kingfisher, from *alkyon* kingfisher; from its resemblance to a kingfisher's nest] (1878)
**:** any of a subclass (Alcyonaria) of colonial anthozoans (as the sea pen) having polyps with eight branched tentacles and eight septa
**Al·cy·o·ne** \al-'sī-ə-(ˌ)nē\ *noun* [Latin, from Greek *Alkyonē*]
**:** the brightest star in the Pleiades
**Al·deb·a·ran** \al-'de-bə-rən\ *noun* [Arabic *al-dabarān*, literally, the follower]
**:** a red star of the first magnitude that is seen in the eye of Taurus and is the brightest star in the Hyades
**al·de·hyde** \'al-də-ˌhīd\ *noun* [German *Aldehyd*, from New Latin *al. dehyd.*, abbreviation of *alcohol dehydrogenatum* dehydrogenated alcohol] (circa 1846)
**:** ACETALDEHYDE; *broadly* **:** any of various highly reactive compounds typified by acetaldehyde and characterized by the group CHO
— **al·de·hy·dic** \ˌal-də-'hī-dik\ *adjective*
**al den·te** \äl-'den-(ˌ)tā, al-\ *adjective* [Italian; literally, to the tooth] (1935)
**:** cooked just enough to retain a somewhat firm texture
**al·der** \'ȯl-dər\ *noun* [Middle English, from Old English *alor*; akin to Old High German *elira* alder, Latin *alnus*] (before 12th century)
**:** any of a genus (*Alnus*) of toothed-leaved trees or shrubs of the birch family that have catkins which become woody, that grow in moist ground, and that have wood used in turnery

**al·der·man** \'ȯl-dər-mən\ *noun* [Middle English, from Old English *ealdorman*, from *ealdor* parent (from *eald* old) + *man* — more at OLD] (before 12th century)
**1 :** a person governing a kingdom, district, or shire as viceroy for an Anglo-Saxon king
**2 a :** a magistrate formerly ranking next below the mayor in an English or Irish city or borough **b :** a high-ranking member of a borough or county council in Ireland or formerly in England chosen by elected members
**3 :** a member of a city legislative body
— **al·der·man·ic** \ˌȯl-dər-'ma-nik\ *adjective*
**al·der·wom·an** \'ȯl-dər-ˌwu̇-mən\ *noun* [*alder-* (as in *alderman*) + *woman*] (1768)
**:** a female member of a city legislative body
**al·dol** \'al-ˌdȯl, -ˌdōl\ *noun* [International Scientific Vocabulary *ald*ehyde + *¹-ol*] (1874)
**:** a colorless beta-hydroxy aldehyde $C_4H_8O_2$ used especially in organic synthesis; *broadly* **:** any of various similar aldehydes
— **al·dol·iza·tion** \ˌal-ˌdȯ-lə-'zā-shən, -ˌdō-\ *noun*
**al·dol·ase** \'al-də-ˌlās, -ˌlāz\ *noun* [*aldol* + *-ase*] (1940)
**:** a crystalline enzyme that occurs widely in living systems and catalyzes reversibly the cleavage of a phosphorylated fructose into triose sugars
**al·dose** \'al-ˌdōs, -ˌdōz\ *noun* [International Scientific Vocabulary *ald*ehyde + *-ose*] (1894)
**:** a sugar containing one aldehyde group per molecule
**al·do·ste·rone** \al-'däs-tə-ˌrōn; ˌal-dō-'ster-ˌōn, -'stir-; 'al-dō-stə-ˌrōn\ *noun* [*ald*ehyde + *-o-* + *-sterone*] (1954)
**:** a steroid hormone $C_{21}H_{28}O_5$ of the adrenal cortex that functions in the regulation of the salt and water balance of the body
**al·do·ste·ron·ism** \al-'däs-tə-rə-ˌni-zəm; ˌal-dō-'ster-(ˌ)ō-, -'stir-; ˌal-dō-stə-'rō-\ *noun* (1955)
**:** a condition that is characterized by excessive secretion of aldosterone and typically by loss of body potassium, muscular weakness, and elevated blood pressure
**al·drin** \'ȯl-drən, 'al-\ *noun* [Kurt *Alder* (died 1958) German chemist + English *¹-in*] (1949)
**:** an exceedingly poisonous cyclodiene insecticide $C_{12}H_8Cl_6$
**ale** \'āl\ *noun* [Middle English, from Old English *ealu*; akin to Old Norse *ǫl* ale, Lithuanian *alus*] (before 12th century)
**1 :** an alcoholic beverage brewed especially by rapid fermentation from an infusion of malt with the addition of hops
**2 :** an English country festival at which ale is the principal beverage
**ale·a·tor·ic** \ˌā-lē-ə-'tȯr-ik, -'tär-\ *adjective* [Latin *aleatorius*] (1961)
**:** characterized by chance or indeterminate elements ⟨*aleatoric* music⟩
**ale·a·to·ry** \'ā-lē-ə-ˌtȯr-ē, -ˌtȯr-\ *adjective* [Latin *aleatorius* of a gambler, from *aleator* gambler, from *alea* a dice game] (1693)
**1 :** depending on an uncertain event or contingency as to both profit and loss ⟨an *aleatory* contract⟩
**2 :** relating to luck and especially to bad luck
**3 :** ALEATORIC
**alee** \ə-'lē\ *adverb* (14th century)
**:** on or toward the lee — compare AWEATHER
**ale·house** \'ā(ə)l-ˌhau̇s\ *noun* (before 12th century)
**:** a place where ale is sold to be drunk on the premises
**Al·e·man·nic** \ˌa-lə-'ma-nik\ *noun* [Late Latin *alemanni*, of Germanic origin; akin to Gothic *alamans* totality of people] (circa 1797)
**:** the group of dialects of German spoken in Alsace, Switzerland, and southwestern Germany
**alem·bic** \ə-'lem-bik\ *noun* [Middle English, from Middle French & Medieval Latin; Middle French *alambic* & Medieval Latin *alem-*

*bicum*, from Arabic *al-anbīq*, from *al* the + *anbīq* still, from Late Greek *ambik-, ambix* alembic, from Greek, cap of a still] (14th century)
**1 :** an apparatus used in distillation
**2 :** something that refines or transmutes as if by distillation ⟨philosophy . . . filtered through the *alembic* of Plato's mind —B. T. Shropshire⟩

alembic 1

**alen·çon** \ə-'len-ˌsän, -'len(t)-sən\ *noun, often capitalized* [*Alençon*, France] (1865)
**:** a delicate needlepoint lace
**aleph** \'ä-ˌlef, -ˌläf\ *noun* [Hebrew *āleph*, probably from *eleph* ox] (14th century)
**:** the 1st letter of the Hebrew alphabet — see ALPHABET table
**aleph–null** \-'nəl\ *noun* (circa 1909)
**:** the number of elements in the set of all integers which is the smallest transfinite cardinal number
**¹alert** \ə-'lərt\ *adjective* [Italian *all'erta*, literally, on the ascent] (1618)
**1 a :** watchful and prompt to meet danger or emergency **b :** quick to perceive and act
**2 :** ACTIVE, BRISK
**synonym** see WATCHFUL, INTELLIGENT
— **alert·ly** *adverb*
— **alert·ness** *noun*
**²alert** *noun* (1796)
**1 :** the state of readiness of those warned by an alert
**2 :** an alarm or other signal of danger
**3 :** the period during which an alert is in effect
— **on the alert :** on the lookout especially for danger or opportunity
**³alert** *transitive verb* (circa 1868)
**1 :** to call to a state of readiness **:** WARN
**2 :** to make aware of ⟨*alerted* the public to the dangers of pesticides⟩
**-ales** *noun plural suffix* [New Latin, from Latin, plural of *-alis -al*]
**:** plants consisting of or related to — in the names of orders of plants ⟨Conifer*ales*⟩
**al·eu·rone** \'al-yə-ˌrōn\ *noun* [German *Aleuron*, from Greek, flour; akin to Armenian *ałam* I grind] (1869)
**:** protein matter in the form of minute granules or grains occurring in seeds in endosperm or in a special peripheral layer
**Aleut** \ˌa-lē-'üt, 'a-lē-ˌ; ə-'lüt\ *noun* [Russian] (1780)
**1 :** a member of a people of the Aleutian and Shumagin islands and the western part of Alaska Peninsula
**2 :** the language of the Aleuts
**A level** *noun* (1951)
**1 :** the second of three standardized British examinations in a secondary school subject used as a qualification for university entrance; *also* **:** successful completion of an A-level examination in a particular subject — called also *Advanced level*; compare O LEVEL, S LEVEL
**2 a :** the level of education required to pass an A-level examination **b :** a course leading to an A-level examination
**ale·vin** \'a-lə-vən\ *noun* [French, from Old French, from *alever* to lift up, rear (offspring), from Latin *allevare*, from *ad-* + *levare* to raise — more at LEVER] (1868)
**:** a young fish; *especially* **:** a newly hatched salmon when still attached to the yolk sac
**¹ale·wife** \'ā(ə)l-ˌwīf\ *noun* (15th century)
**:** a woman who keeps an alehouse
**²alewife** *noun* [perhaps alteration of obsolete *allowes*, a kind of shad, from French *alose* shad, from Old French, from Late Latin *alausa*] (1633)
**:** a clupeid food fish (*Alosa pseudoharengus*) very abundant along the Atlantic coast; *also* **:** any of several related fishes (as the menhaden)

**al·ex·an·der** \ˌa-lig-ˈzan-dər, ˌe-\ *noun, often capitalized* (1928)
**:** an iced cocktail made from crème de cacao, sweet cream, and gin or brandy

**Al·ex·an·dri·an** \ˌa-lig-ˈzan-drē-ən, ˌe-\ *adjective* (circa 1860)
**1 :** of or relating to Alexander the Great
**2 :** HELLENISTIC

**al·ex·an·drine** \-ˈzan-ˌdrēn, -drən, -ˌdrīn\ *noun, often capitalized* [Middle French *alexandrin*, adjective, from *Alexandre* Alexander the Great; from its use in a poem on Alexander] (1667)
**:** a line of verse of 12 syllables consisting regularly of 6 iambs with a caesura after the 3d iamb
**— alexandrine** *adjective*

**al·ex·an·drite** \-ˈzan-ˌdrīt\ *noun* [German *Alexandrit*, from *Alexander I* Russian emperor] (circa 1880)
**:** a grass-green chrysoberyl that shows a red color by transmitted or artificial light

**alex·ia** \ə-ˈlek-sē-ə\ *noun* [New Latin, from *a*- + Greek *lexis* speech, from *legein* to speak — more at LEGEND] (1878)
**:** aphasia marked by loss of ability to read

**Al·fa** \ˈal-fə\ (1952)
**—** a communications code word for the letter *a*

**al·fal·fa** \al-ˈfal-fə\ *noun* [Spanish, modification of Arabic dialect *al-faṣfaṣah* the alfalfa] (1845)
**:** a deep-rooted European leguminous plant (*Medicago sativa*) widely grown for hay and forage

**alfalfa weevil** *noun* (1912)
**:** a small dark brown European weevil (*Hypera postica*) that is now a widespread pest of alfalfa in North America

**al·fi·la·ria** \ˌ(ˌ)al-ˌfi-lə-ˈrē-ə\ *noun* [American Spanish *alfilerillo*, from Spanish, diminutive of *alfiler* pin, modification of Arabic *al-khilāl* the thorn] (1868)
**:** a European weed (*Erodium cicutarium*) of the geranium family grown for forage in the western U.S.

**al·for·ja** \al-ˈfȯr-(ˌ)hä\ *noun* [Spanish, from Arabic *al-khurj*] (1611)
*West* **:** SADDLEBAG

**al·fres·co** \al-ˈfres-(ˌ)kō\ *adjective or adverb* [Italian] (1753)
**:** taking place or located in the open air **:** OUTDOOR, OUTDOORS ⟨an *alfresco* lunch⟩ ⟨an *alfresco* restaurant⟩
**word history** see FRESCO

**al·ga** \ˈal-gə\ *noun, plural* **al·gae** \ˈal-(ˌ)jē\ *also* **algas** [Latin, seaweed] (1551)
**:** a plant or plantlike organism of any of several phyla, divisions, or classes of chiefly aquatic usually chlorophyll-containing nonvascular organisms of polyphyletic origin that usually include the green, yellow-green, brown, and red algae in the eukaryotes and the blue-green algae in the prokaryotes
**— al·gal** \-gəl\ *adjective*

**al·ga·ro·ba** *also* **al·gar·ro·ba** \ˌal-gə-ˈrō-bə\ *noun* [Spanish *algarroba*, from Arabic *al-kharrūbah* the carob] (1577)
**1 :** CAROB 1
**2** [Mexican Spanish, from Spanish] **:** MESQUITE; *also* **:** its pods

**al·ge·bra** \ˈal-jə-brə\ *noun* [Medieval Latin, from Arabic *al-jabr*, literally, the reduction] (1551)
**1 :** a generalization of arithmetic in which letters representing numbers are combined according to the rules of arithmetic
**2 :** any of various systems or branches of mathematics or logic concerned with the properties and relationships of abstract entities (as complex numbers, matrices, sets, vectors, groups, rings, or fields) manipulated in symbolic form under operations often analogous to those of arithmetic — compare BOOLEAN ALGEBRA
**— al·ge·bra·ist** \-ˌbrā-ist\ *noun*

**al·ge·bra·ic** \ˌal-jə-ˈbrā-ik\ *adjective* (1662)
**1 :** relating to, involving, or according to the laws of algebra
**2 :** involving only a finite number of repetitions of addition, subtraction, multiplication, division, extraction of roots, and raising to powers ⟨*algebraic* equation⟩ — compare TRANSCENDENTAL
**— al·ge·bra·i·cal·ly** \-ˈbrā-ə-k(ə-)lē\ *adverb*

**algebraic number** *noun* (1904)
**:** a root of an algebraic equation with rational coefficients

**-algia** *noun combining form* [Greek, from *algos* pain]
**:** pain ⟨neur*algia*⟩

**al·gi·cide** *or* **al·gae·cide** \ˈal-jə-ˌsīd\ *noun* (1904)
**:** an agent used to kill algae
**— al·gi·cid·al** \ˌal-jə-ˈsī-dᵊl\ *adjective*

**al·gid** \ˈal-jəd\ *adjective* [Latin *algidus*, from *algēre* to feel cold] (circa 1623)
**:** COLD

**al·gin** \ˈal-jən\ *noun* (1883)
**:** any of various colloidal substances (as an alginate or alginic acid) derived from marine brown algae and used especially as emulsifiers or thickeners

**al·gi·nate** \ˈal-jə-ˌnāt\ *noun* (circa 1909)
**:** a salt or ester of alginic acid

**al·gin·ic acid** \(ˌ)al-ˈji-nik-\ *noun* [International Scientific Vocabulary *algin* + ¹-*ic*] (1885)
**:** an insoluble colloidal acid $(C_6H_8O_6)n$ that in the form of its salts is a constituent of the cell walls of brown algae

**Al·gol** \ˈal-ˌgäl, -ˌgȯl\ *noun* [Arabic *al-ghūl*, literally, the ghoul]
**:** a binary star in the constellation Perseus whose larger member orbits and eclipses the smaller brighter star causing periodic variation in brightness

**AL·GOL** *or* **Al·gol** \ˈal-ˌgäl, -ˌgȯl\ *noun* [*algo*rithmic *l*anguage] (1959)
**:** an algebraic computer programming language used especially in mathematical and scientific applications

**al·go·lag·nia** \ˌal-gō-ˈlag-nē-ə\ *noun* [New Latin, from Greek *algos* pain + Greek *lagneia* lust, from *lagnos* lustful — more at SLACK] (circa 1900)
**:** a perversion (as sadism or masochism) characterized by pleasure and especially sexual gratification in inflicting or suffering pain
**— al·go·lag·ni·ac** \-ˈlag-nē-ˌak\ *noun*

**al·gol·o·gy** \al-ˈgä-lə-jē\ *noun* (1849)
**:** the study or science of algae — called also *phycology*
**— al·go·log·i·cal** \ˌal-gə-ˈlä-ji-kəl\ *adjective*
**— al·gol·o·gist** \al-ˈgä-lə-jist\ *noun*

**Al·gon·qui·an** \al-ˈgän-kwē-ən, -ˈgän-\ *or* **Al·gon·quin** \-kwən\ *or* **Al·gon·ki·an** \-ˈgän-kē-ən\ *also* **Al·gon·kin** \-ˈgän-kən\ *noun* [Canadian French *Algonquin*] (1625)
**1** *usually* Algonquin **a :** an American Indian people of the Ottawa river valley **b :** the dialect of Ojibwa spoken by these people
**2** *usually* Algonquian **a :** a family of American Indian languages spoken by peoples from Labrador to Carolina and westward into the Great Plains **b :** a member of the peoples speaking Algonquian languages

**al·go·rithm** \ˈal-gə-ˌri-t͟həm\ *noun* [alteration of Middle English *algorisme*, from Old French & Medieval Latin; Old French, from Medieval Latin *algorismus*, from Arabic *al-khuwārizmi*, from *al-Khuwārizmi* (flourished A.D. 825) Arab mathematician] (circa 1894)
**:** a procedure for solving a mathematical problem (as of finding the greatest common divisor) in a finite number of steps that frequently involves repetition of an operation; *broadly* **:** a step-by-step procedure for solving a problem or accomplishing some end especially by a computer

**— al·go·rith·mic** \ˌal-gə-ˈrit͟h-mik\ *adjective*
**— al·go·rith·mi·cal·ly** \-mi-k(ə-)lē\ *adverb*

**Al·ham·bra** \al-ˈham-brə\ *noun* [Spanish, from Arabic *al-ḥamrā'* the red house] (1612)
**:** the palace of the Moorish kings at Granada, Spain

**¹alias** \ˈā-lē-əs, ˈāl-yəs\ *adverb* [Latin, otherwise, from *alius* other — more at ELSE] (15th century)
**:** otherwise called **:** otherwise known as

**²alias** *noun* (1605)
**:** an assumed or additional name

**Ali Ba·ba** \ˌa-lē-ˈbä-bə, ˌä-lē-\ *noun*
**:** a woodcutter in the *Arabian Nights' Entertainments* who enters the cave of the Forty Thieves by using the password *Sesame*

**¹al·i·bi** \ˈa-lə-ˌbī\ *noun* [Latin, elsewhere, from *alius*] (1743)
**1 :** the plea of having been at the time of the commission of an act elsewhere than at the place of commission; *also* **:** the fact or state of having been elsewhere at the time
**2 :** an excuse usually intended to avert blame or punishment (as for failure or negligence) ◆
**synonym** see APOLOGY

**²alibi** *verb* **-bied; -bi·ing** (1909)
*transitive verb*
**:** to exonerate by an alibi **:** furnish an excuse for
*intransitive verb*
**:** to offer an excuse

**Al·ice-in-Won·der·land** \ˈa-lə-sən-ˈwən-dər-ˌland\ *adjective* [from *Alice's Adventures in Wonderland* (1865) by Lewis Carroll] (1925)
**:** suitable to a world of fantasy or illusion **:** UNREAL

**ali·cy·clic** \ˌa-lə-ˈsī-klik, -ˈsi-klik\ *adjective* [International Scientific Vocabulary *ali*phatic + *cyclic*] (1891)
**:** of, relating to, or being an organic compound that contains a ring but is not aromatic — compare ALIPHATIC

**al·i·dade** \ˈa-lə-ˌdād\ *noun* [Middle English *alidatha*, from Medieval Latin *alhidada*, from Arabic *al-'iḍādah* the revolving radius of a circle] (15th century)
**:** a rule equipped with simple or telescopic sights and used for determination of direction: as **a :** a part of an astrolabe **b :** a part of a surveying instrument consisting of the telescope and its attachments

**¹alien** \ˈā-lē-ən, ˈāl-yən\ *adjective* [Middle English, from Middle French, from Latin *alienus*, from *alius*] (14th century)

\ə\ abut \ᵊ\ kitten \ər\ further \a\ ash \ā\ ace
\ä\ mop, mar \aù\ out \ch\ chin \e\ bet \ē\ easy
\g\ go \i\ hit \ī\ ice \j\ job \ŋ\ sing \ō\ go
\ȯ\ law \ȯi\ boy \th\ thin \t͟h\ the \ü\ loot \ù\ foot
\y\ yet \zh\ vision *see also* Guide to Pronunciation

**1 a :** belonging or relating to another person, place, or thing **:** STRANGE **b :** relating, belonging, or owing allegiance to another country or government **:** FOREIGN
**2 :** differing in nature or character typically to the point of incompatibility
*synonym* see EXTRINSIC
— **alien·ly** *adverb*
— **alien·ness** \-lē-ən-nəs, -yən-nəs\ *noun*
**²alien** *noun* (14th century)
**1 :** a person of another family, race, or nation
**2 :** a foreign-born resident who has not been naturalized and is still a subject or citizen of a foreign country; *broadly* **:** a foreign-born citizen
**3 :** EXTRATERRESTRIAL
**³alien** *transitive verb* (14th century)
**1 :** ALIENATE, ESTRANGE
**2 :** to make over (as property)
**alien·able** \'āl-yə-nə-bəl, 'ā-lē-ə-nə-\ *adjective* (1611)
**:** transferable to another's ownership
— **alien·abil·i·ty** \'āl-yə-nə-'bi-lə-tē, ,ā-lē-ə-nə-\ *noun*
**alien·age** \'āl-yə-nij, 'ā-lē-ə-nij\ *noun* (1809)
**:** the status of an alien
**alien·ate** \'ā-lē-ə-,nāt, 'āl-yə-\ *transitive verb* **-at·ed; -at·ing** (circa 1509)
**1 :** to make unfriendly, hostile, or indifferent where attachment formerly existed
**2 :** to convey or transfer (as property or a right) usually by a specific act rather than the due course of law
**3 :** to cause to be withdrawn or diverted
*synonym* see ESTRANGE
— **alien·ator** \-,nā-tər\ *noun*
**alien·ation** \,ā-lē-ə-'nā-shən, ,āl-yə-\ *noun* (14th century)
**1 :** a withdrawing or separation of a person or a person's affections from an object or position of former attachment **:** ESTRANGEMENT ⟨*alienation* . . . from the values of one's society and family —S. L. Halleck⟩
**2 :** a conveyance of property to another
**alien·ee** \-'nē\ *noun* (1531)
**:** one to whom property is transferred
**alien·ism** \'ā-lē-ə-,ni-zəm, 'āl-yə-\ *noun* (1808)
**:** ALIENAGE
**alien·ist** \-nist\ *noun* [French *aliéniste*, from *aliéné* insane, from Latin *alienatus*, past participle of *alienare* to estrange, from *alienus*] (1864)
**:** PSYCHIATRIST
**alien·or** \,ā-lē-ə-'nor, ,āl-yə-\ *noun* (circa 1552)
**:** one who transfers property to another
**¹alight** \ə-'līt\ *intransitive verb* **alight·ed** *also* **alit** \ə-'lit\; **alight·ing** [Middle English, from Old English *ālīhtan*, from *ā-* (perfective prefix) + *līhtan* to alight — more at ABIDE, LIGHT] (before 12th century)
**1 :** to come down from something (as a vehicle): as **a :** DISMOUNT **b :** DEPLANE
**2 :** to descend from or as if from the air and come to rest **:** LAND, SETTLE
**3** *archaic* **:** to come by chance
— **alight·ment** *noun*
**²alight** *adjective* (15th century)
**1** *chiefly British* **:** being on fire
**2 :** lighted up
**align** *also* **aline** \ə-'līn\ *verb* [French *aligner*, from Old French, from *a-* (from Latin *ad-*) + *ligne* line, from Latin *linea*] (circa 1693)
*transitive verb*
**1 :** to bring into line or alignment
**2 :** to array on the side of or against a party or cause
*intransitive verb*
**1 :** to get or fall into line
**2 :** to be in or come into precise adjustment or correct relative position
— **align·er** *noun*
**align·ment** *also* **aline·ment** \ə-'līn-mənt\ *noun* (1790)
**1 :** the act of aligning or state of being

aligned; *especially* **:** the proper positioning or state of adjustment of parts (as of a mechanical or electronic device) in relation to each other
**2 a :** a forming in line **b :** the line thus formed
**3 :** the ground plan (as of a railroad or highway) in distinction from the profile
**4 :** an arrangement of groups or forces in relation to one another ⟨new *alignments* within the political party⟩
**¹alike** \ə-'līk\ *adverb* (14th century)
**:** in the same manner, form, or degree **:** EQUALLY ⟨was denounced by teachers and students *alike*⟩
**²alike** *adjective* [Middle English *ilik, ilich* (from Old English *gelīc*) & *alik*, alteration of Old English *onlīc*, from *on* + *līc* body — more at LIKE] (15th century)
**:** exhibiting close resemblance without being identical ⟨*alike* in their beliefs⟩
— **alike·ness** *noun*
**¹al·i·ment** \'a-lə-mənt\ *noun* [Middle English, from Latin *alimentum*, from *alere* to nourish — more at OLD] (15th century)
**:** FOOD, NUTRIMENT; *also* **:** SUSTENANCE ⟨there was nothing there of conversational *aliment* —Kingsley Amis⟩
**²al·i·ment** \-,ment\ *transitive verb* (15th century)
**:** to give aliment to **:** NOURISH, SUSTAIN
**al·i·men·ta·ry** \,a-lə-'men-t(ə-)rē\ *adjective* (1615)
**1 :** of or relating to nourishment or nutrition
**2 :** furnishing sustenance or maintenance
**alimentary canal** *noun* (1764)
**:** the tubular passage that extends from mouth to anus and functions in digestion and absorption of food and elimination of residual waste
**al·i·men·ta·tion** \,a-lə-mən-'tā-shən, -,men-\ *noun* (circa 1656)
**:** the act or process of affording nutriment or nourishment ⟨intravenous *alimentation*⟩
**al·i·mo·ny** \'a-lə-,mō-nē\ *noun, plural* **-nies** [Latin *alimonia* sustenance, from *alere*] (1656)
**1 :** an allowance made to one spouse by the other for support pending or after legal separation or divorce
**2 :** the means of living **:** MAINTENANCE
**A-line** \'ā-,līn\ *adjective* (1964)
**:** having a flared bottom and a close-fitting top — used of a garment ⟨an *A-line* skirt⟩
**al·i·phat·ic** \,a-lə-'fa-tik\ *adjective* [International Scientific Vocabulary, from Greek *aleiphat-, aleiphar* oil, from *aleiphein* to smear; perhaps akin to Greek *lipos* fat — more at LEAVE] (1889)
**:** of, relating to, or being an organic compound having an open-chain structure (as an alkane) — compare ALICYCLIC, AROMATIC 2
**al·i·quot** \'a-lə-,kwät, -kwət\ *adjective* [Medieval Latin *aliquotus*, from Latin *aliquot* some, several, from *alius* other + *quot* how many — more at ELSE, QUOTE] (1570)
**1 :** contained an exact number of times in something else — used of a divisor or part ⟨5 is an *aliquot* part of 15⟩ ⟨an *aliquot* portion of a solution⟩
**2 :** FRACTIONAL ⟨an *aliquot* part of invested capital⟩
— **aliquot** *noun*
**A-list** \'ā-,list\ *noun* (1980)
**:** a list or group of individuals of the highest level of society, excellence, or eminence
**alit·er·a·cy** \,ā-'li-tər-ə-,sē, ə-'\ *noun* (1984)
**:** the quality or state of being able to read but uninterested in doing so
— **alit·er·ate** \-'li-tər-ət\ *adjective or noun*
**alive** \ə-'līv\ *adjective* [Middle English, from Old English *on life,* from *on* + *līf* life] (before 12th century)
**1 :** having life **:** not dead or inanimate
**2 :** still in existence, force, or operation **:** ACTIVE ⟨kept hope *alive*⟩
**3 :** knowing or realizing the existence of **:** SENSITIVE ⟨*alive* to the danger⟩
**4 :** marked by alertness, energy, or briskness

**5 :** marked by much life, animation, or activity **:** SWARMING ⟨streets *alive* with traffic⟩
**6 :** — used as an intensive following the noun ⟨the proudest boy *alive*⟩
*synonym* see AWARE
— **alive·ness** *noun*
**ali·yah** *or* **ali·ya** \ä-'lē-(,)yä, ,ä-lē-'yä\ *noun* [New Hebrew *'alīyāh,* from Hebrew, ascent] (circa 1934)
**:** the immigration of Jews to Israel
**aliz·a·rin** \ə-'li-zə-rən\ *noun* [probably from French *alizarine*] (circa 1835)
**1 :** an orange or red crystalline compound $C_{14}H_8O_4$ formerly prepared from madder and now made synthetically and used especially to dye Turkey reds and in making red pigments
**2 :** any of various acid, mordant, and solvent dyes derived like alizarin proper from anthraquinone
**al·ka·hest** \'al-kə-,hest\ *noun* [New Latin *alchahest*] (1641)
**:** the universal solvent believed by alchemists to exist
— **al·ka·hes·tic** \,al-kə-'hes-tik\ *adjective*
**al·ka·li** \'al-kə-,lī\ *noun, plural* **-lies** *or* **-lis** [Middle English, from Medieval Latin, from Arabic *al-qili* the ashes of the plant saltwort] (14th century)
**1 :** a soluble salt obtained from the ashes of plants and consisting largely of potassium or sodium carbonate; *broadly* **:** a substance (as a hydroxide or carbonate of an alkali metal) having marked basic properties — compare BASE 7a
**2 :** ALKALI METAL
**3 :** a soluble salt or a mixture of soluble salts present in some soils of arid regions in quantity detrimental to agriculture
**alkali metal** *noun* (circa 1885)
**:** any of the univalent mostly basic metals of group I of the periodic table comprising lithium, sodium, potassium, rubidium, cesium, and francium — see PERIODIC TABLE table
**al·ka·lim·e·ter** \,al-kə-'li-mə-tər\ *noun* [French *alcalimètre,* from *alcali* alkali + *-mètre* -meter] (circa 1828)
**:** an apparatus for measuring the strength or the amount of alkali in a mixture or solution
— **al·ka·lim·e·try** \-'lim-ə-trē\ *noun*
**al·ka·line** \'al-kə-lən, -,līn\ *adjective* (1677)
**:** of, relating to, containing, or having the properties of an alkali or alkali metal **:** BASIC; *especially, of a solution* **:** having a pH of more than 7
— **al·ka·lin·i·ty** \,al-kə-'li-nə-tē\ *noun*
**alkaline battery** *noun* (1941)
**:** a long-lived dry cell that has an alkaline electrolyte which decreases corrosion of the cell — called also *alkaline cell*
**alkaline earth metal** *noun* (circa 1903)
**:** any of the bivalent strongly basic metals of group II of the periodic table comprising beryllium, magnesium, calcium, strontium, barium, and radium — called also *alkaline earth;* see PERIODIC TABLE table
**alkaline phosphatase** *noun* (1949)
**:** any of the phosphatases that are optimally active in alkaline medium and occur in especially high concentrations in bone, the liver, the kidneys, and the placenta
**al·ka·lin·ize** \'al-kə-lə-,nīz\ *transitive verb* **-ized; -iz·ing** (1800)
**:** to make alkaline
— **al·ka·lin·iza·tion** \,al-kə-,li-nə-'zā-shən, -lə-nə-\ *noun*
**al·ka·loid** \'al-kə-,loid\ *noun* (circa 1831)
**:** any of numerous usually colorless, complex, and bitter organic bases (as morphine or codeine) containing nitrogen and usually oxygen that occur especially in seed plants
— **al·ka·loi·dal** \,al-kə-'loi-d°l\ *adjective*
**al·ka·lo·sis** \,al-kə-'lō-səs\ *noun* (1911)
**:** an abnormal condition of increased alkalinity of the blood and tissues
— **al·ka·lot·ic** \-'lä-tik\ *adjective*
**al·kane** \'al-,kān\ *noun* [*alk*yl + *-ane*] (1899)

: any of numerous saturated hydrocarbons; *specifically* : any of a series of open-chain hydrocarbons $C_nH_{2n+2}$ (as methane and butane) — called also *paraffin*

**al·ka·net** \'al-kə-ˌnet\ *noun* [Middle English, from Old Spanish *alcaneta*, diminutive of *alcana* henna shrub, from Medieval Latin *alchanna*, from Arabic *al-ḥinnā'* the henna] (14th century)
**1 a** : a European plant (*Alkanna tinctoria*) of the borage family; *also* : its root **b** : a red dyestuff prepared from the root
**2** : a plant (*Anchusa officinalis*) of the borage family with delicate usually blue flowers

**al·kene** \'al-ˌkēn\ *noun* [International Scientific Vocabulary *alkyl* + *-ene*] (1899)
: any of numerous unsaturated hydrocarbons having one double bond; *specifically* : any of a series of open-chain hydrocarbons $C_nH_{2n}$ (as ethylene)

**alk·ox·ide** \al-'käk-ˌsīd, -səd\ *noun* [*alkyl* + *oxide*] (circa 1889)
: a basic salt derived from an alcohol by the replacement of the hydroxyl hydrogen with a metal

**alk·oxy** \'al-ˌkäk-sē\ *adjective* [International Scientific Vocabulary *alkyl* + *oxygen*] (circa 1925)
: of, relating to, or containing a univalent radical composed of an alkyl group united with oxygen — often used in combination

**al·kyd** \'al-kəd\ *noun* [blend of *alkyl* and *acid*] (1929)
**1** : any of numerous synthetic resins that are used especially for protective coatings and in paint
**2** : a paint in which the vehicle is an alkyd resin

**¹al·kyl** \'al-kəl\ *adjective* (1882)
: having a monovalent organic group and especially one $C_nH_{2n+1}$ (as methyl) derived from an alkane (as methane)

**²alkyl** *noun* [probably from German, from *Alkohol* alcohol] (1952)
: a compound of one or more alkyl groups with a metal (mercury *alkyls*)

**alkylating agent** *noun* (1900)
: a substance that causes replacement of hydrogen by an alkyl group especially in a biologically important molecule; *specifically* : one with mutagenic activity that inhibits cell division and growth and is used to treat some cancers

**al·kyl·a·tion** \ˌal-kə-'lā-shən\ *noun* (1900)
: the act or process of introducing one or more alkyl groups into a compound (as to increase octane number in a motor fuel)
— **al·kyl·ate** \'al-kə-ˌlāt\ *transitive verb*

**al·kyne** \'al-ˌkīn\ *noun* [*alkyl* + *-yne*, alteration of *-ine*] (circa 1909)
: any of a series of open-chain hydrocarbons $C_nH_{2n-2}$ (as acetylene) having one triple bond

**¹all** \'òl\ *adjective* [Middle English *all, al*, from Old English *eall*; akin to Old High German *all* all] (before 12th century)
**1 a** : the whole amount or quantity of (needed *all* the courage they had) (sat up *all* night) **b** : as much as possible (spoke in *all* seriousness)
**2** : every member or individual component of (*all* men will go) (*all* five children were present)
**3** : the whole number or sum of (*all* the angles of a triangle are equal to two right angles)
**4** : EVERY (*all* manner of hardship)
**5** : any whatever (beyond *all* doubt)
**6** : nothing but : ONLY : **a** : completely taken up with, given to, or absorbed by (became *all* attention) **b** : having or seeming to have (some physical feature) in conspicuous excess or prominence (*all* legs) **c** : paying full attention with (*all* ears)
**7** *dialect* : used up : entirely consumed — used especially of food and drink

**8** : being more than one person or thing (who *all* is coming)
**synonym** see WHOLE
— **all the** : as much of . . . as : as much of a . . . as (*all the* home I ever had)

**²all** *adverb* (before 12th century)
**1 a** : WHOLLY, QUITE (sat *all* alone) — often used as an intensive (*all* out of proportion) (*all* over the yard) **b** : selected as the best (as at a sport) within an area or organization — used in combination (*all*-league halfback)
**2** *obsolete* : ONLY, EXCLUSIVELY
**3** *archaic* : JUST
**4** : so much (*all* the better for it)
**5** : for each side : APIECE (the score is two *all*)

**³all** *pronoun* (before 12th century)
**1** : the whole number, quantity, or amount : TOTALITY (*all* that I have) (*all* of us) (*all* of the books)
**2** : EVERYBODY, EVERYTHING (gave equal attention to *all*) (that is *all*)
— **all in all** : on the whole : GENERALLY (*all* in all, things might have been worse)
— **and all** : and everything else especially of a kind suggested by a previous context (cards to fill out with . . . numbers and all —Sally Quinn)

**⁴all** *noun* (1593)
: the whole of one's possessions, resources, or energy (gave his *all* for the cause)

**all-** *or* **allo-** *combining form* [Greek, from *allos* other — more at ELSE]
**1** : other : different : atypical (*allogamous*) (*allotropy*)
**2** *allo-* : isomeric form or variety of (a specified chemical compound) (*allopurinol*)
**3** *allo-* : being one of a group whose members together constitute a structural unit especially of a language (*allophone*)

**¹al·la breve** \ˌä-lə-'brev, ˌä-lə-'bre-(ˌ)vā\ *noun* [Italian, literally, according to the breve] (circa 1740)
: the sign marking a piece or passage to be played alla breve; *also* : a passage so marked

**²alla breve** *adverb or adjective* (circa 1823)
: in duple or quadruple time with the beat represented by the half note    **alla breve**

**Al·lah** \'ä-lə, 'a-lə, 'ä-ˌlä, ä-'lä\ *noun* [Arabic *allāh*] (1584)
: GOD 1a — used in Islam

**all along** *adverb* (1670)
: all the time (knew the truth *all along*)

**¹all–Amer·i·can** \ˌò-lə-'mer-ə-kən\ *adjective* (1888)
**1 a** *also* **all–Amer·i·ca** : selected (as by a poll of journalists) as one of the best in the U.S. in a particular category at a particular time (an *all-American* quarterback) **b** : having only all-American participants (an *all-American* basketball team)
**2** : composed wholly of American elements
**3** : representative or typical of the U.S. or its ideals (an *all-American* boy) (her *all-American* optimism)
**4** : of or relating to the American nations as a group

**²all–American** *noun* (1920)
: one (as an athlete) that is voted all-American

**al·lan·to·in** \ə-'lan-tə-wən\ *noun* [probably from German, from New Latin *allantois* + German *-in*] (circa 1845)
: a crystalline oxidation product $C_4H_6N_4O_3$ of uric acid used to promote healing of local wounds and infections

**al·lan·to·is** \ə-'lan-tə-wəs\ *noun, plural* **al·lan·to·ides** \ˌa-lən-'tō-ə-ˌdēz, ˌa-ˌlan-\ [New Latin, ultimately from Greek *allant-, allas* sausage] (1646)
: a vascular fetal membrane of reptiles, birds, and mammals that is formed as a pouch from the hindgut and that in placental mammals is intimately associated with the chorion in formation of the placenta

— **al·lan·to·ic** \ˌa-lən-'tō-ik, ˌa-ˌlan-\ *adjective*

**al·lar·gan·do** \ˌä-lär-'gän-(ˌ)dō\ *adjective or adverb* [Italian, widening, verbal of *allargare* to widen, from *al-* (from Latin *ad-*) + *largare* to widen] (circa 1893)
: becoming gradually slower and more stately — used as a direction in music

**all–around** \ˌò-lə-'raùnd\ *adjective* (1867)
**1** : considered in or encompassing all aspects : COMPREHENSIVE (the best *all-around* performance so far)
**2** : competent in many fields (an *all-around* performer)
**3** : having general utility or merit

**al·lay** \ə-'lā, ə-\ *verb* [Middle English *alayen*, from Old English *ālecgan*, from *ā-* (perfective prefix) + *lecgan* to lay — more at ABIDE, LAY] (14th century)
*transitive verb*
**1** : to subdue or reduce in intensity or severity : ALLEVIATE (expect a breeze to *allay* the heat)
**2** : to make quiet : CALM
*intransitive verb*
*obsolete* : to diminish in strength : SUBSIDE
**synonym** see RELIEVE

**all but** *adverb* (1593)
: very nearly : ALMOST (would be *all but* impossible)

**all clear** *noun* (1902)
: a signal that a danger has passed

**all–day** \'òl-'dā\ *adjective* (circa 1870)
: lasting for, occupying, or appearing throughout an entire day (an *all-day* trip)

**al·lée** \ä-'lā, a-\ *noun* [French, from Middle French *alee* — more at ALLEY] (1759)
: a walkway lined with trees or tall shrubs

**al·le·ga·tion** \ˌa-li-'gā-shən\ *noun* (15th century)
**1** : the act of alleging
**2** : a positive assertion; *specifically* : a statement by a party to a legal action of what the party undertakes to prove
**3** : an assertion unsupported and by implication regarded as unsupportable (vague *allegations* of misconduct)

**al·lege** \ə-'lej\ *transitive verb* **al·leged; al·leg·ing** [Middle English *alleggen*, from Middle French *alleguer*, from Latin *allegare* to dispatch, cite, from *ad-* + *legare* to depute — more at LEGATE] (14th century)
**1** *archaic* : to adduce or bring forward as a source or authority
**2** : to assert without proof or before proving (the newspaper *alleges* the mayor's guilt)
**3** : to bring forward as a reason or excuse

**al·leged** \ə-'lejd, -'le-jəd\ *adjective* (1509)
**1** : asserted to be true or to exist (an *alleged* miracle)
**2** : questionably true or of a specified kind : SUPPOSED, SO-CALLED (bought an *alleged* antique vase)
**3** : accused but not proven or convicted (an *alleged* gangster)
— **al·leg·ed·ly** \-'le-jəd-lē\ *adverb*

**Al·le·ghe·ny spurge** \'a-lə-ˌgā-nē- *also* -ˌge-nē-\ *noun* [*Allegheny* Mountains, U.S.A.] (circa 1936)
: a low herb or subshrub (*Pachysandra procumbens*) of the box family widely grown as a ground cover

**al·le·giance** \ə-'lē-jən(t)s\ *noun* [Middle English *allegeaunce*, modification of Middle French *ligeance*, from Old French, from *lige* liege] (14th century)
**1 a** : the obligation of a feudal vassal to his liege lord **b** (1) : the fidelity owed by a subject or citizen to a sovereign or government (2) : the obligation of an alien to the government under which the alien resides

\ə\ abut \ᵊ\ kitten \ər\ further \a\ ash \ā\ ace \ä\ mop, mar \aù\ out \ch\ chin \e\ bet \ē\ easy \g\ go \i\ hit \ī\ ice \j\ job \ŋ\ sing \ō\ go \ò\ law \òi\ boy \th\ thin \t̷h\ the \ü\ loot \ù\ foot \y\ yet \zh\ vision    *see also* Guide to Pronunciation

**2 :** devotion or loyalty to a person, group, or cause
**synonym** see FIDELITY
— **al·le·giant** \-jənt\ *adjective*
**al·le·gor·i·cal** \ˌa-lə-'gȯr-i-kəl, -'gär-\ *adjective* (1528)
**1 :** of, relating to, or having the characteristics of allegory
**2 :** having hidden spiritual meaning that transcends the literal sense of a sacred text
— **al·le·gor·i·cal·ly** \-k(ə-)lē\ *adverb*
— **al·le·gor·i·cal·ness** \-kəl-nəs\ *noun*
**al·le·go·rise** *British variant of* ALLEGORIZE
**al·le·go·rist** \'a-lə-ˌgȯr-əst, -ˌgȯr-\ *noun* (1684)
**:** a creator of allegory
**al·le·go·ri·za·tion** \ˌa-lə-ˌgȯr-ə-'zā-shən, -ˌgȯr-, -gər-\ *noun* (1847)
**:** allegorical representation or interpretation
**al·le·go·rize** \'a-lə-ˌgȯr-ˌīz, -ˌgȯr-, -gər-\ *verb* **-rized; -riz·ing** (1581)
*intransitive verb*
**1 :** to give allegorical explanations
**2 :** to compose or use allegory
*transitive verb*
**1 :** to treat or explain as an allegory
**2 :** to make into allegory
— **al·le·go·riz·er** *noun*
**al·le·go·ry** \'a-lə-ˌgȯr-ē, -ˌgȯr-\ *noun, plural* **-ries** [Middle English *allegorie*, from Latin *allegoria*, from Greek *allēgoria*, from *allēgorein* to speak figuratively, from *allos* other + *-ēgorein* to speak publicly, from *agora* assembly — more at ELSE, AGORA] (14th century)
**1 :** the expression by means of symbolic fictional figures and actions of truths or generalizations about human existence; *also* **:** an instance (as in a story or painting) of such expression
**2 :** a symbolic representation **:** EMBLEM 2
**¹al·le·gret·to** \ˌa-lə-'gre-(ˌ)tō, ˌä-lə-'\ *adverb or adjective* [Italian, diminutive of *allegro*] (circa 1740)
**:** faster than andante but not so fast as allegro — used as a direction in music
**²allegretto** *noun, plural* **-tos** (circa 1846)
**:** a musical composition or movement in allegretto tempo
**¹al·le·gro** \ə-'le-(ˌ)grō, -'lā-\ *noun, plural* **-gros** (1683)
**:** a musical composition or movement in allegro tempo
**²allegro** *adverb or adjective* [Italian, merry, from (assumed) Vulgar Latin *alecrus* lively, alteration of Latin *alacr-, alacer*] (circa 1721)
**:** at a brisk lively tempo — used as a direction in music
**al·lele** \ə-'lē(ə)l\ *noun* [German *Allel*, short for *Allelomorph*] (1928)
**1 :** any of the alternative forms of a gene that may occur at a given locus
**2 :** either of a pair of alternative Mendelian characters (as smooth and wrinkled seed in the pea)
— **al·le·lic** \-'lē-lik, -'le-\ *adjective*
— **al·lel·ism** \-'lē(ə)-ˌli-zəm, -'le-\ *noun*
**allelo-** *combining form* [Greek *allēlōn* of each other, from *allos* . . . *allos* one . . . the other, from *allos* other — more at ELSE]
**1 :** alternative ⟨*allelo*morph⟩
**2 :** reciprocal ⟨*allelo*pathy⟩
**al·le·lo·morph** \ə-'lē-lə-ˌmȯrf, -'le-lə-\ *noun* (1902)
**:** ALLELE
— **al·le·lo·mor·phic** \ə-ˌlē-lə-'mȯr-fik, -ˌle-lə-\ *adjective*
— **al·le·lo·mor·phism** \ə-'lē-lə-ˌmȯr-ˌfi-zəm, -'le-lə-\ *noun*
**al·le·lop·a·thy** \ə-'lē-lə-ˌpa-thē, -'le-lə-; *also* ˌa-lə-'lä-pə-thē\ *noun* [International Scientific Vocabulary] (1948)
**:** the suppression of growth of one plant species by another due to the release of toxic substances

— **al·le·lo·path·ic** \ə-ˌlē-lə-'pa-thik, -ˌlə-\ *adjective*
**al·le·lu·ia** \ˌa-lə-'lü-yə\ *interjection* [Middle English, from Late Latin, from Greek *allēlouia*, from Hebrew *halălūyāh* praise ye Jehovah] (14th century)
**:** HALLELUJAH
**al·le·mande** \'a-lə-ˌman(d), -mən, -ˌmänd, *1a & 2 also* ˌa-lə-'\ *noun, often capitalized* [French, from feminine of *allemand* German] (1685)
**1 :** a musical composition or movement (as in a baroque suite) in moderate tempo and duple or quadruple time
**2 a :** a 17th and 18th century court dance developed in France from a German folk dance
**b :** a dance step with arms interlaced
**all–em·brac·ing** \ˌȯ-lim-'brā-siŋ\ *adjective* (circa 1649)
**:** COMPLETE, SWEEPING
**Al·len wrench** \'a-lən-\ *noun* [Allen Manufacturing Co., Hartford, Conn.] (1943)
**:** an L-shaped hexagonal metal bar either end of which fits the socket of a screw or bolt
**al·ler·gen** \'a-lər-jən\ *noun* [International Scientific Vocabulary *allergy* + *-gen*] (1910)
**:** a substance that induces allergy
— **al·ler·gen·ic** \ˌa-lər-'je-nik\ *adjective*
— **al·ler·ge·nic·i·ty** \ˌa-lər-jə-'ni-sə-tē\ *noun*
**al·ler·gic** \ə-'lər-jik\ *adjective* (1911)
**1 :** of, relating to, inducing, or affected by allergy
**2 :** having an aversion ⟨*allergic* to work⟩
**al·ler·gist** \'a-lər-jist\ *noun* (1928)
**:** a specialist in allergy
**al·ler·gy** \'a-lər-jē\ *noun, plural* **-gies** [German *Allergie*, from *all-* + Greek *ergon* work — more at WORK] (1910)
**1 :** altered bodily reactivity (as hypersensitivity) to an antigen in response to a first exposure ⟨a bee venom *allergy* so severe that a second sting may be fatal⟩
**2 :** exaggerated or pathological reaction (as by sneezing, respiratory embarrassment, itching, or skin rashes) to substances, situations, or physical states that are without comparable effect on the average individual
**3 :** medical practice concerned with allergies
**4 :** a feeling of antipathy or repugnance
**al·le·thrin** \'a-lə-thrən\ *noun* [*allyl* + *pyrethrin*] (1950)
**:** a light yellow viscous oily synthetic insecticide $C_{19}H_{26}O_3$ used especially in household aerosols
**al·le·vi·ate** \ə-'lē-vē-ˌāt\ *transitive verb* **-at·ed; -at·ing** [Late Latin *alleviatus*, past participle of *alleviare*, from Latin *ad-* + *levis* light — more at LIGHT] (15th century)
**:** RELIEVE, LESSEN: as **a :** to make (as suffering) more bearable ⟨her sympathy *alleviated* his distress⟩ **b :** to partially remove or correct
**synonym** see RELIEVE
— **al·le·vi·a·tion** \-ˌlē-vē-'ā-shən\ *noun*
— **al·le·vi·a·tor** \-'lē-vē-ˌā-tər\ *noun*
**¹al·ley** \'a-lē\ *noun, plural* **alleys** [Middle English, from Middle French *alee*, from Old French, from *aler* to go] (14th century)
**1 :** a garden or park walk bordered by trees or bushes
**2 a** (1) **:** a grassed enclosure for bowling or skittles (2) **:** a hardwood lane for bowling; *also* **:** a room or building housing a group of such lanes **b :** the space on each side of a tennis doubles court between the sideline and the service sideline **c :** an area in a baseball outfield between two outfielders when they are in normal positions
**3 :** a narrow street; *especially* **:** a thoroughfare through the middle of a block giving access to the rear of lots or buildings
— **up one's alley** *also* **down one's alley :** suited to one's own tastes or abilities
**²alley** *noun, plural* **alleys** [by shortening and alteration from *alabaster*] (1720)

**:** a playing marble; *especially* **:** one of superior quality
**al·ley–oop** \ˌa-lē-'yüp\ *noun* [alteration of *allez-oop*, cry of a circus acrobat about to leap, probably from French *allez*, 2d person plural imperative of *aller* to go + English *-oop*, perhaps alteration of *up*] (1967)
**:** a basketball play in which a leaping player catches a pass above the basket and immediately dunks the ball; *also* **:** the usually looping pass thrown on such a play
**al·ley·way** \'a-lē-ˌwā\ *noun* (1788)
**1 :** a narrow passageway
**2 :** ALLEY 3
**All Fools' Day** *noun* (1712)
**:** APRIL FOOLS' DAY
**all fours** *noun plural* (1563)
**1 a :** all four legs of a quadruped **b :** the two legs and two arms of a person when used to support the body
**2** *singular in construction* **:** any of various card games in which points are scored for the high trump, low trump, jack of trumps, and game
**all get–out** \ˌȯl-'get-ˌaut, -'git-\ *noun* (1884)
**:** the utmost conceivable degree — used in comparisons to suggest something superlative ⟨is handsome as *all get-out* and has a deft way with the ladies —John McCarten⟩
**all hail** *interjection* (14th century)
— used to express greeting, welcome, or acclamation
**All·hal·lows** \ȯl-'ha-(ˌ)lōz, -ləz\ *noun, plural* **Allhallows** [short for *All Hallows' Day*] (1503)
**:** ALL SAINTS' DAY
**al·li·a·ceous** \ˌa-lē-'ā-shəs\ *adjective* [Latin *allium* garlic] (1792)
**:** resembling garlic or onion especially in smell or taste
**al·li·ance** \ə-'lī-ən(t)s\ *noun* (13th century)
**1 a :** the state of being allied **:** the action of allying **b :** a bond or connection between families, states, parties, or individuals ⟨a closer *alliance* between government and industry⟩
**2 :** an association to further the common interests of the members; *specifically* **:** a confederation of nations by treaty
**3 :** union by relationship in qualities **:** AFFINITY
**4 :** a treaty of alliance
**al·lied** \ə-'līd, 'a-ˌlīd\ *adjective* (14th century)
**1 :** having or being in close association **:** CONNECTED ⟨a strong personal pride *allied* with the utmost probity⟩ ⟨two families *allied* by marriage⟩
**2 :** joined in alliance by compact or treaty; *specifically, capitalized* **:** of or relating to the nations united against Germany and its allies in World War I or those united against the Axis powers in World War II
**3 a :** related especially by common properties or qualities ⟨heraldry and *allied* subjects⟩ **b :** related genetically
**allies** *plural of* ALLY
**al·li·ga·tor** \'a-lə-ˌgā-tər\ *noun* [Spanish *el lagarto* the lizard, from *el* the (from Latin *ille* that) + *lagarto* lizard, from (assumed) Vulgar Latin *lacartus*, from Latin *lacertus, lacerta* — more at LIZARD] (1579)
**1 a :** either of two crocodilians (genus *Alligator*) having broad heads not tapering to the snout and a special pocket in the upper jaw for reception of

alligator 1a

the enlarged lower fourth tooth **b :** CROCODILIAN
**2 :** leather made from alligator hide
**alligator clip** *noun* (circa 1941)

**:** a spring-loaded clip that has jaws resembling an alligator's and is used for making temporary electrical connections

alligator clip

**alligator pear** *noun* [by folk etymology from Spanish *aguacate* — more at AVOCADO] (1763)
**:** AVOCADO

**alligator snapper** *noun* (1884)
**:** a snapping turtle (*Macrochelys temminckii*) of the rivers of the Gulf states that may reach nearly 150 pounds (68 kilograms) in weight and 5 feet (1.5 meters) in length

**all–im·por·tant** \ˌȯ-lim-'pȯr-t°nt, -tənt\ *adjective* (1839)
**:** of very great or greatest importance ⟨an *all-important* question⟩

**all–in** \'ȯ-'lin\ *adjective* (1890)
**1** *chiefly British* **:** ALL-INCLUSIVE
**2** *chiefly British* **:** being almost without restrictions ⟨*all-in* wrestling⟩

**all in** *adjective* (1903)
**:** TIRED, EXHAUSTED ⟨after a day of wood-splitting he was *all in*⟩

**all–in·clu·sive** \ˌȯ-lin-'klü-siv, -ziv\ *adjective* (circa 1855)
**:** including everything ⟨a broader and more nearly *all-inclusive* view⟩
— **all–in·clu·sive·ness** *noun*

**al·lit·er·ate** \ə-'li-tə-ˌrāt\ *verb* **-at·ed; -at·ing** [back-formation from *alliteration*] (1816)
*intransitive verb*
**1 :** to form an alliteration
**2 :** to write or speak alliteratively
*transitive verb*
**:** to arrange or place so as to make alliteration ⟨*alliterate* syllables in a sentence⟩

**al·lit·er·a·tion** \ə-ˌli-tə-'rā-shən\ *noun* [*ad-* + Latin *littera* letter] (circa 1656)
**:** the repetition of usually initial consonant sounds in two or more neighboring words or syllables (as *w*ild and *w*oolly, *thr*eatening *thr*ongs) — called also *head rhyme, initial rhyme*

**al·lit·er·a·tive** \ə-'li-tər-ə-tiv, -tə-ˌrā-tiv\ *adjective* (1764)
**:** of, relating to, or marked by alliteration
— **al·lit·er·a·tive·ly** *adverb*

**al·li·um** \'a-lē-əm\ *noun* [New Latin, genus name, from Latin, garlic] (1807)
**:** any of a large genus (*Allium*) of bulbous herbs of the lily family including the onion, garlic, chive, leek, and shallot

**all–night** \'ȯl-'nīt\ *adjective* (1888)
**1 :** lasting throughout the night ⟨an *all-night* poker game⟩
**2 :** open throughout the night ⟨an *all-night* diner⟩

**all–night·er** \'ȯl-'nī-tər\ *noun* (1967)
**:** something that lasts all night; *specifically* **:** an all-night study session

**allo-** — see ALL-

**al·lo·an·ti·body** \ˌa-lō-'an-ti-ˌbä-dē\ *noun* (1964)
**:** an antibody produced following introduction of an alloantigen into the system of an individual of a species lacking that particular antigen — called also *isoantibody*

**al·lo·an·ti·gen** \ˌa-lō-'an-ti-jən\ *noun* (1964)
**:** an antigen present only in some individuals (as of a particular blood group) of a species and capable of inducing the production of an isoantibody by individuals which lack it — called also *isoantigen*

**al·lo·ca·ble** \'a-lə-kə-bəl\ *adjective* (1916)
**:** capable of being allocated

**al·lo·cate** \'a-lə-ˌkāt\ *transitive verb* **-cat·ed; -cat·ing** [Medieval Latin *allocatus*, past participle of *allocare*, from Latin *ad-* + *locare* to place, from *locus* place — more at STALL] (circa 1641)
**1 :** to apportion for a specific purpose or to particular persons or things **:** DISTRIBUTE ⟨*allo-*

cate tasks among human and automated components⟩
**2 :** to set apart or earmark **:** DESIGNATE ⟨*allocate* a section of the building for special research purposes⟩
— **al·lo·cat·able** \-ˌkā-tə-bəl\ *adjective*
— **al·lo·ca·tion** \ˌa-lə-'kā-shən\ *noun*
— **al·lo·ca·tor** \'a-lə-ˌkā-tər\ *noun*

**al·lo·cu·tion** \ˌa-lə-'kyü-shən\ *noun* [Latin *allocution-, allocutio*, from *alloqui* to speak to, from *ad-* + *loqui* to speak] (1615)
**:** a formal speech; *especially* **:** an authoritative or hortatory address

**all of** *adverb* (1829)
**:** FULLY ⟨she's *all of* 20 years old⟩

**al·log·a·mous** \ə-'lä-gə-məs\ *adjective* (circa 1890)
**:** reproducing by cross-fertilization
— **al·log·a·my** \-mē\ *noun*

**al·lo·ge·ne·ic** \ˌa-lō-jə-'nē-ik\ *also* **al·lo·gen·ic** \-'je-nik\ *adjective* [*all-* + *-geneic* (as in *syngeneic*)] (1961)
**:** involving, derived from, or being individuals of the same species that are sufficiently unlike genetically to interact antigenically

**al·lo·graft** \'a-lə-ˌgraft\ *noun* (1961)
**:** a homograft between allogeneic individuals
— **allograft** *transitive verb*

**al·lo·graph** \'a-lə-ˌgraf\ *noun* (1951)
**1 :** a letter of an alphabet in a particular shape (as A or a)
**2 :** a letter or combination of letters that is one of several ways of representing one phoneme (as *pp* in *hopping* representing the phoneme \p\)
— **al·lo·graph·ic** \ˌa-lə-'gra-fik\ *adjective*

**al·lom·e·try** \ə-'lä-mə-trē\ *noun* (1936)
**:** relative growth of a part in relation to an entire organism or to a standard; *also* **:** the measure and study of such growth
— **al·lo·me·tric** \ˌa-lə-'me-trik\ *adjective*

**allomorph** *noun* [*allo-* + *morph*eme] (1945)
**:** one of a set of forms that a morpheme may take in different contexts (the *-s* of *cats*, the *-en* of *oxen*, and the zero suffix of *sheep* are *allomorphs* of the English plural morpheme)
— **al·lo·mor·phic** \ˌa-lə-'mȯr-fik\ *adjective*
— **al·lo·mor·phism** \'a-lə-ˌmȯr-ˌfi-zəm\ *noun*

**al·longe** \a-'lōⁿzh\ *noun* [French, literally, lengthening] (circa 1859)
**:** RIDER 2a

**al·lo·pat·ric** \ˌa-lə-'pa-trik\ *adjective* [*all-* + Greek *patra* fatherland, from *patēr* father — more at FATHER] (1942)
**:** occurring in different geographical areas or in isolation ⟨*allopatric* speciation⟩ — compare SYMPATRIC
— **al·lo·pat·ri·cal·ly** \-tri-k(ə-)lē\ *adverb*
— **al·lop·a·try** \ə-'lä-pə-trē\ *noun*

**al·lo·phane** \'a-lə-ˌfān\ *noun* [Greek *allophanēs* appearing otherwise, from *all-* + *phainesthai* to appear, middle voice of *phainein* to show — more at FANCY] (circa 1821)
**:** an amorphous translucent mineral of various colors often occurring in incrustations or stalactite forms and consisting of a hydrous aluminum silicate

**al·lo·phone** \'a-lə-ˌfōn\ *noun* [*allo-* + *phone*] (1938)
**:** one of two or more variants of the same phoneme ⟨the aspirated \p\ of *pin* and the unaspirated \p\ of *spin* are *allophones* of the phoneme \p\⟩
— **al·lo·phon·ic** \ˌa-lə-'fä-nik\ *adjective*

**al·lo·poly·ploid** \ˌa-lō-'pä-li-ˌplȯid\ *noun* (1928)
**:** a polyploid individual or strain having a chromosome set composed of two or more chromosome sets derived more or less complete from different species
— **allopolyploid** *adjective*
— **al·lo·poly·ploi·dy** \-ˌplȯi-dē\ *noun*

**al·lo·pu·ri·nol** \ˌa-lō-'pyùr-ə-ˌnȯl, -ˌnōl\ *noun* [*all-* + *purine* + [1]-*ol*] (1964)

**:** a drug $C_5H_4N_4O$ used to promote excretion of uric acid

**all–or–none** \ˌȯ-lər-'nən\ *adjective* (1900)
**:** marked either by entire or complete operation or effect or by none at all ⟨*all-or-none* response of a nerve cell⟩

**all–or–noth·ing** \-'nə-thin\ *adjective* (1765)
**1 :** ALL-OR-NONE
**2 a :** accepting no less than everything ⟨he's an *all-or-nothing* perfectionist⟩ **b :** risking everything ⟨an *all-or-nothing* combat strategy⟩

**al·lo·sau·rus** \ˌa-lə-'sȯr-əs\ *noun* [New Latin, from Greek *all-* + *sauros* lizard] (1899)
**:** any of a genus (*Allosaurus*) of huge carnivorous North American theropod dinosaurs of the Upper Jurassic period

**al·lo·ste·ric** \ˌa-lō-'ster-ik, -'stir-\ *adjective* [*all-* + *steric*] (1962)
**:** of, relating to, or being a change in the shape and activity of a protein (as an enzyme) that results from combination with another substance at a point other than the chemically active site
— **al·lo·ste·ri·cal·ly** \-i-k(ə-)lē\ *adverb*
— **al·lo·ste·ry** \'a-lō-ˌster-ē, ə-'lä-stə-rē\ *noun*

**al·lot** \ə-'lät\ *transitive verb* **al·lot·ted; al·lot·ting** [Middle English *alotten*, from Middle French *aloter*, from *a-* (from Latin *ad-*) + *lot*, of Germanic origin; akin to Old English *hlot* lot] (15th century)
**1 :** to assign as a share or portion ⟨*allot* 10 minutes for the speech⟩
**2 :** to distribute by or as if by lot ⟨*allot* seats to the press⟩
— **al·lot·ter** *noun*

**al·lo·te·tra·ploid** \ˌa-lō-'te-trə-ˌplȯid\ *noun* (1930)
**:** AMPHIDIPLOID
— **al·lo·te·tra·ploi·dy** \-ˌplȯi-dē\ *noun*

**al·lot·ment** \ə-'lät-mənt\ *noun* (1574)
**1 :** the act of allotting **:** APPORTIONMENT
**2 :** something that is allotted; *especially, chiefly British* **:** a plot of land let to an individual for cultivation

**al·lo·trope** \'a-lə-ˌtrōp\ *noun* [International Scientific Vocabulary, back-formation from *allotropy*] (circa 1889)
**:** a form showing allotropy

**al·lot·ro·py** \ə-'lä-trə-pē\ *noun, plural* **-pies** (1850)
**:** the existence of a substance and especially an element in two or more different forms (as of crystals) usually in the same phase
— **al·lo·trop·ic** \ˌa-lə-'trä-pik\ *adjective*

**all' ot·ta·va** \ˌa-lə-'tä-və, ä-lō-\ *adverb or adjective* [Italian, at the octave] (circa 1823)
**:** OTTAVA

**al·lot·tee** \ə-ˌlä-'tē\ *noun* (1846)
**:** one to whom an allotment is made

**al·lo·type** \'a-lə-ˌtīp\ *noun* (1960)
**:** an alloantigen that is part of a plasma protein (as an antibody)
— **al·lo·typ·ic** \ˌa-lə-'ti-pik\ *adjective*
— **al·lo·typ·i·cal·ly** \-pi-k(ə-)lē\ *adverb*
— **al·lo·typy** \'a-lə-ˌtī-pē\ *noun*

**all–out** \'ȯ-'laùt\ *adjective* (1908)
**1 :** made with maximum effort **:** THOROUGHGOING ⟨an *all-out* effort to win the contest⟩
**2 :** FULL-BLOWN 2

**all out** *adverb* (1895)
**:** with full determination or enthusiasm **:** with maximum effort — used chiefly in the phrase *go all out*

**[1]all–over** \'ȯ-ˌlō-vər\ *adjective* (1859)
**:** covering the whole extent or surface ⟨a sweater with an *allover* pattern⟩

**[2]allover** *noun* (1838)
**1 :** an embroidered, printed, or lace fabric with a design covering most of the surface

\ə\ abut \°\ kitten \ər\ further \a\ ash \ā\ ace \ä\ mop, mar \aù\ out \ch\ chin \e\ bet \ē\ easy \g\ go \i\ hit \ī\ ice \j\ job \ŋ\ sing \ō\ go \ȯ\ law \ȯi\ boy \th\ thin \th\ the \ü\ loot \ù\ foot \y\ yet \zh\ vision   *see also* Guide to Pronunciation

**2 :** a pattern or design in which a single unit is repeated so as to cover an entire surface
**all over** *adverb* (1577)
**1 :** over the whole extent ⟨decorated *all over* with a flower pattern⟩
**2 :** EVERYWHERE ⟨looked *all over* for the book⟩
**3 :** in every respect **:** THOROUGHLY ⟨she is her mother *all over*⟩
**al·low** \ə-'lau̇\ *verb* [Middle English, from Middle French *alouer* to place, (from Medieval Latin *allocare*) & *allouer* to approve, from Latin *allaudare* to extol, from *ad-* + *laudare* to praise — more at ALLOCATE] (14th century)
*transitive verb*
**1 a :** to assign as a share or suitable amount (as of time or money) ⟨*allow* an hour for lunch⟩ **b :** to reckon as a deduction or an addition ⟨*allow* a gallon for leakage⟩
**2 a** *chiefly Southern & Midland* **:** to be of the opinion **:** THINK **b** *dialect* **:** SAY, STATE **c :** to express an opinion — usually used with *as how* or *that*
**3** *chiefly Southern & Midland* **:** INTEND, PLAN
**4 :** ADMIT, CONCEDE ⟨must *allow* that money causes problems in marriage⟩
**5 a :** PERMIT ⟨doesn't *allow* people to smoke in his home⟩ **b :** to forbear or neglect to restrain or prevent ⟨*allow* the dog to roam⟩
*intransitive verb*
**1 :** to make a possibility **:** ADMIT — used with *of* ⟨evidence that *allows* of only one conclusion⟩
**2 :** to give consideration to circumstances or contingencies — used with *for* ⟨*allow* for expansion⟩
**al·low·able** \ə-'lau̇-ə-bəl\ *adjective* (15th century)
**:** PERMISSIBLE
— **al·low·ably** \-blē\ *adverb*
**¹al·low·ance** \ə-'lau̇-ən(t)s\ *noun* (14th century)
**1 a :** a share or portion allotted or granted **b :** a sum granted as a reimbursement or bounty or for expenses ⟨salary includes cost-of-living *allowance*⟩; *especially* **:** a sum regularly provided for personal or household expenses ⟨each child has an *allowance*⟩ **c :** a fixed or available amount ⟨provide an *allowance* of time for recreation⟩ **d :** a reduction from a list price or stated price ⟨a trade-in *allowance*⟩
**2 :** an imposed handicap (as in a horse race)
**3 :** an allowed dimensional difference between mating parts of a machine
**4 :** the act of allowing **:** PERMISSION
**5 :** a taking into account of mitigating circumstances or contingencies
**²allowance** *transitive verb* **-anced; -anc·ing** (circa 1828)
**1** *archaic* **:** to put on a fixed allowance (as of food and drink)
**2** *archaic* **:** to supply in a fixed or regular quantity
**al·low·ed·ly** \ə-'lau̇-əd-lē\ *adverb* (1602)
**:** by allowance **:** ADMITTEDLY
**al·lox·an** \ə-'läk-sən\ *noun* [German, from *Allantoin* + *Oxalsäure* oxalic acid + *-an*] (1853)
**:** a crystalline compound $C_4H_2N_2O_4$ causing diabetes mellitus when injected into experimental animals
**¹al·loy** \'a-,lȯi *also* ə-'lȯi\ *noun* [French *aloi*, from Old French *alei*, from *aleir* to combine, from Latin *alligare* to bind — more at ALLY] (1604)
**1 :** the degree of mixture with base metals **:** FINENESS
**2 :** a substance composed of two or more metals or of a metal and a nonmetal intimately united usually by being fused together and dissolving in each other when molten; *also* **:** the state of union of the components
**3 a :** an admixture that lessens value **b :** an impairing alien element
**4 :** a compound, mixture, or union of different things ⟨an ethnic *alloy* of many peoples⟩

**5** *archaic* **:** a metal mixed with a more valuable metal to give durability or some other desired quality
**²al·loy** \ə-'lȯi *also* 'a-,lȯi\ (1661)
*transitive verb*
**1 a :** TEMPER, MODERATE **b :** to impair or debase by admixture
**2 :** to reduce the purity of by mixing with a less valuable metal
**3 :** to mix so as to form an alloy
*intransitive verb*
**:** to lend itself to being alloyed ⟨iron *alloys* well⟩
**all-pow·er·ful** \'ȯl-'pau̇(-ə)r-fəl\ *adjective* (1667)
**:** having complete or sole power
**all-pur·pose** \-'pər-pəs\ *adjective* (1928)
**:** suited for many purposes or uses
**¹all right** *adjective* (1701)
**1 :** SATISFACTORY, AGREEABLE ⟨whatever you decide is *all right* with me⟩
**2 :** SAFE, WELL ⟨he was ill but he's *all right* now⟩
**3 :** GOOD, PLEASING — often used as a generalized term of approval ⟨an *all right* guy⟩
*usage* see ALRIGHT
**²all right** *adverb* (1837)
**1 :** very well ⟨*all right*, let's go⟩
**2 :** beyond doubt **:** CERTAINLY ⟨she has pneumonia *all right*⟩
**3 :** well enough **:** SATISFACTORILY ⟨does *all right* in school⟩
*usage* see ALRIGHT
**all-round** \'ȯl-'rau̇nd\ *variant of* ALL-AROUND
**all-round·er** \'ȯl-'rau̇n-dər\ *noun* (1875)
*British* **:** one that is all-around
**All Saints' Day** *noun* (circa 1798)
**:** November 1 observed in Western liturgical churches as a Christian feast in honor of all the saints
**All Souls' Day** *noun* (14th century)
**:** November 2 observed in some Christian churches as a day of prayer for the souls of the faithful departed
**all·spice** \'ȯl-,spīs\ *noun* (1621)
**1 :** the berry of a West Indian tree (*Pimenta dioica*) of the myrtle family; *also* **:** the allspice tree
**2 :** a mildly pungent and aromatic spice prepared from allspice berries
**¹all-star** \'ȯl-'stär\ *adjective* (1889)
**:** composed wholly or chiefly of stars or of outstanding performers or participants ⟨an *all-star* cast⟩
**²all-star** \'ȯl-,stär\ *noun* (circa 1934)
**:** a member of an all-star team
**all that** *adverb* (1945)
**:** to an indicated or suggested extent or degree **:** SO ⟨didn't take his threats *all that* seriously⟩
**all-time** \'ȯl-,tīm\ *adjective* (1914)
**1 :** FULL-TIME 1
**2 :** being for or of all time up to and including the present; *especially* **:** exceeding all others of all time ⟨an *all-time* best-seller⟩
**all told** *adverb* (1850)
**:** with everything taken into account **:** in all
**al·lude** \ə-'lüd\ *intransitive verb* **al·lud·ed; al·lud·ing** [Latin *alludere*, literally, to play with, from *ad-* + *ludere* to play — more at LUDICROUS] (1533)
**:** to make indirect reference ⟨*alluded* vaguely to personal problems⟩; *broadly* **:** REFER
**¹al·lure** \ə-'lu̇r\ *transitive verb* **al·lured; al·lur·ing** [Middle English *aluren*, from Middle French *alurer*, from Old French, from *a-* (from Latin *ad-*) + *loire* lure — more at LURE] (15th century)
**:** to entice by charm or attraction
*synonym* see ATTRACT
— **al·lure·ment** \-'lu̇r-mənt\ *noun*
— **al·lur·ing·ly** *adverb*
**²allure** *noun* (1548)
**:** power of attraction or fascination **:** CHARM
**al·lu·sion** \ə-'lü-zhən\ *noun* [Late Latin *allusion-, allusio*, from Latin *alludere*] (1548)

**1 :** an implied or indirect reference especially in literature; *also* **:** the use of such references
**2 :** the act of alluding or hinting at
— **al·lu·sive** \-'lü-siv, -ziv\ *adjective*
— **al·lu·sive·ly** *adverb*
— **al·lu·sive·ness** *noun*
**¹al·lu·vi·al** \ə-'lü-vē-əl\ *adjective* (1802)
**:** relating to, composed of, or found in alluvium ⟨*alluvial* soil⟩ ⟨*alluvial* diamonds⟩
**²alluvial** *noun* (1866)
**:** an alluvial deposit
**alluvial fan** *noun* (1873)

**alluvial fan**

**:** the alluvial deposit of a stream where it issues from a gorge upon a plain or of a tributary stream at its junction with the main stream
**al·lu·vi·on** \ə-'lü-vē-ən\ *noun* [Latin *alluvion-, alluvio*, from *alluere* to flow past, from *ad-* + *lavere* to wash — more at LYE] (1536)
**1 :** the wash or flow of water against a shore
**2 :** FLOOD, INUNDATION
**3 :** ALLUVIUM
**4 :** an accession to land by the gradual addition of matter (as by deposit of alluvium) that then belongs to the owner of the land to which it is added; *also* **:** the land so added
**al·lu·vi·um** \-vē-əm\ *noun, plural* **-vi·ums** *or* **-via** \-vē-ə\ [Medieval Latin, alteration of Latin *alluvio*] (circa 1656)
**:** clay, silt, sand, gravel, or similar detrital material deposited by running water
**¹al·ly** \ə-'lī, 'a-,lī\ *verb* **al·lied; al·ly·ing** [Middle English *allien*, from Old French *alier*, from Latin *alligare* to bind to, from *ad-* + *ligare* to bind — more at LIGATURE] (14th century)
*transitive verb*
**1 :** to unite or form a connection between **:** ASSOCIATE ⟨*allied* himself with a wealthy family by marriage⟩
**2 :** to connect or form a relation between (as by likeness or compatibility) **:** RELATE
*intransitive verb*
**:** to form or enter into an alliance
**²al·ly** \'a-,lī, ə-'lī\ *noun, plural* **allies** (1598)
**1 :** a sovereign or state associated with another by treaty or league
**2 :** a plant or animal linked to another by genetic or taxonomic proximity
**3 :** one that is associated with another as a helper **:** AUXILIARY
**-ally** *adverb suffix* [¹-*al* + -*ly*]
**:** ²-LY ⟨terrific*ally*⟩ — in adverbs formed from adjectives in -*ic* with no alternative form in -*ical*
**al·lyl** \'a-ləl\ *adjective* [International Scientific Vocabulary, from Latin *allium* garlic] (1854)
**:** being or containing the unsaturated univalent group $C_3H_5$—
**al·lyl·ic** \ə-'li-lik, a-\ *adjective* (1857)
**:** involving or characteristic of an allyl group
**al·ma·gest** \'al-mə-,jest\ *noun* [Middle English *almageste*, from Middle French & Medieval Latin, from Arabic *al-majusti*, the Arabic version of Ptolemy's astronomy treatise, from *al* the + Greek *megistē* (*syntaxis*), literally, greatest (composition)] (14th century)
**:** any of several early medieval treatises on a branch of knowledge
**al·ma ma·ter** \,al-mə-'mä-tər\ *noun* [Latin, fostering mother] (1696)
**1 :** a school, college, or university which one has attended or from which one has graduated
**2 :** the song or hymn of a school, college, or university
**al·ma·nac** \'ȯl-mə-,nak, 'al-\ *noun* [Middle

English *almenak*, from Medieval Latin *almanach*, probably from Arabic *al-manākh* the almanac] (14th century)
**1 :** a publication containing astronomical and meteorological data for a given year and often including a miscellany of other information
**2 :** a usually annual publication containing statistical, tabular, and general information

**al·man·dine** \'al-mən-ˌdēn, -ˌdīn\ *noun* [Middle English *alemaundine*, from Middle French *alemandine*, alteration of *alabandine*, from Medieval Latin *alabandina*, from *Alabanda*, ancient city in Asia Minor] (15th century)
**:** ALMANDITE

**al·man·dite** \'al-mən-ˌdīt\ *noun* [alteration of *almandine*] (circa 1868)
**:** a deep red garnet consisting of an iron aluminum silicate

**¹al·mighty** \ȯl-'mī-tē\ *adjective* [Middle English, from Old English *ealmihtig*, from *eall* all + *mihtig* mighty] (before 12th century)
**1** *often capitalized* **:** having absolute power over all ⟨*Almighty* God⟩
**2 :** relatively unlimited in power
**3 :** great in magnitude or seriousness
**— al·mighti·ness** *noun*

**²almighty** *adverb* (1833)
**:** to a great degree **:** EXTREMELY ⟨although he did not precisely starve, he was *almighty* hungry —W. A. Swanberg⟩

**Almighty** *noun* (before 12th century)
**:** GOD 1 — used with *the*

**al·mond** \'ä-mənd, 'a-, 'äl-, 'al-\ *noun* [Middle English *almande*, from Middle French, from Late Latin *amandula*, alteration of Latin *amygdala*, from Greek *amygdalē*] (14th century)
**1 a :** the drupaceous fruit of a small tree (*Prunus dulcis* synonym *P. amygdalus*) of the rose family with flowers and young fruit resembling those of the peach; *especially* **:** its ellipsoidal edible kernel used as a nut **b :** any of several similar fruits
**2 :** a tree that produces almonds

almond 1a

**al·mond–eyed** \-ˌīd\ *adjective* (1870)
**:** having narrow slant almond-shaped eyes

**al·mo·ner** \'al-mə-nər, 'ä-mə-\ *noun* [Middle English *almoiner*, from Middle French *almosnier*, from *almosne* alms, from Late Latin *eleemosyna*] (15th century)
**1 :** one who distributes alms
**2** *British* **:** a social-service worker in a hospital

**¹al·most** \'ȯl-ˌmōst, ȯl-'\ *adverb* [Middle English, from Old English *ealmǣst*, from *eall* + *mǣst* most] (before 12th century)
**:** very nearly but not exactly or entirely

**²almost** *adjective* (1709)
**:** very near but not quite ⟨an *almost* failure⟩

**alms** \'ä(l)mz, *New England also* 'àmz\ *noun*, *plural* **alms** [Middle English *almesse*, *almes*, from Old English *ælmesse*, *ælmes*, from Late Latin *eleemosyna* alms, from Greek *eleēmosynē* pity, alms, from *eleēmōn* merciful, from *eleos* pity] (before 12th century)
**1** *archaic* **:** CHARITY
**2 :** something (as money or food) given freely to relieve the poor
**— alms·giv·er** \-ˌgi-vər\ *noun*
**— alms·giv·ing** \-ˌgi-viŋ\ *noun*

**alms·house** \-ˌhaus\ *noun* (14th century)
**1** *British* **:** a privately financed home for the poor
**2 :** POORHOUSE

**alms·man** \-mən\ *noun* (before 12th century)
**:** a recipient of alms

**al·ni·co** \'al-ni-ˌkō\ *noun* [*al*uminum + *ni*ckel + *co*balt] (1935)
**:** a powerful permanent-magnet alloy containing iron, nickel, aluminum, and one or more of the elements cobalt, copper, and titanium

**al·oe** \'a-(ˌ)lō\ *noun* [Middle English, from Late Latin, from Latin, dried juice of aloe leaves, from Greek *aloē*] (before 12th century)
**1** *plural* **:** the fragrant wood of an East Indian tree (*Aquilaria agallocha*) of the mezereon family
**2 a :** any of a large genus (*Aloe*) of succulent chiefly southern African plants of the lily family with basal leaves and spicate flowers **b :** the dried juice of the leaves of various aloes used especially formerly as a purgative — usually used in plural but singular in construction

**aloe vera** \-'ver-ə, -'vir-\ *noun* [New Latin, species name, from *Aloe* + Latin *vera*, feminine of *verus* true — more at VERY] (circa 1936)
**:** an aloe (*Aloe barbadensis* synonym *A. vera*) whose leaves furnish an emollient extract used especially in cosmetics and skin creams; *also* **:** such a preparation

**¹aloft** \ə-'lȯft\ *adverb* [Middle English, from Old Norse *ā lopt*, from *ā* on, in + *lopt* air — more at ON, LOFT] (13th century)
**1 :** at or to a great height
**2 :** in the air; *especially* **:** in flight (as in an airplane) ⟨meals served *aloft*⟩
**3 :** at, on, or to the masthead or the higher rigging

**²aloft** *preposition* (14th century)
**:** on top of **:** ABOVE ⟨bright signs *aloft* hotels⟩

**alog·i·cal** \(ˌ)ā-'lä-ji-kəl\ *adjective* (1694)
**:** being outside the bounds of that to which logic can apply
**— alog·i·cal·ly** \-k(ə-)lē\ *adverb*

**alo·ha** \ə-'lō-ˌ(h)ä, ä-, -(h)ə\ *interjection* [Hawaiian, from *aloha* love] (1820)
**—** used as a greeting or farewell

**aloha shirt** *noun* (1940)
**:** HAWAIIAN SHIRT

**¹alone** \ə-'lōn\ *adjective* [Middle English, from *al* all + *one* one] (13th century)
**1 :** separated from others **:** ISOLATED
**2 :** exclusive of anyone or anything else **:** ONLY
**3 a :** considered without reference to any other ⟨the children *alone* would eat that much⟩ **b :** INCOMPARABLE, UNIQUE ⟨*alone* among their contemporaries in this respect⟩ ☆
**— alone·ness** \-'lōn-nəs\ *noun*

**²alone** *adverb* (13th century)
**1 :** SOLELY, EXCLUSIVELY
**2 :** without aid or support

**¹along** \ə-'lȯŋ\ *preposition* [Middle English, from Old English *andlang*, from *and-* against + *lang* long — more at ANTE-] (before 12th century)
**1 :** in a line parallel with the length or direction of
**2 :** in the course of
**3 :** in accordance with **:** IN

**²along** *adverb* (14th century)
**1 :** FORWARD, ON ⟨move *along*⟩
**2 :** from one to another ⟨word was passed *along*⟩
**3 a :** in company **:** as a companion ⟨brought his wife *along*⟩ — often used with *with* ⟨walked to school *along* with her friends⟩ **b :** in association — used with *with* ⟨work *along* with colleagues⟩
**4 a :** sometime within a specified or implied extent of time — usually used with *about* ⟨*along* about July 17⟩ **b :** at or to an advanced point ⟨plans are far *along*⟩
**5 :** in addition **:** ALSO — often used with *with* ⟨a bill came *along* with the package⟩
**6 :** at hand **:** as a necessary or useful item ⟨brought an extra one *along*⟩ ⟨had his gun *along*⟩
**7 :** on hand **:** THERE ⟨tell him I'll be *along* to see him⟩

**along of** *preposition* [Middle English *ilong on*, from Old English *gelang on*, from *ge-*, associative prefix + *lang* — more at CO-] (before 12th century)
*dialect* **:** BECAUSE OF

**along·shore** \ə-'lȯŋ-ˌshōr, -ˌshȯr\ *adverb or adjective* (1779)
**:** along the shore or coast ⟨walked *alongshore*⟩ ⟨*alongshore* currents⟩

**¹along·side** \-ˈsīd\ *adverb* (1707)
**1 :** along the side **:** in parallel position
**2 :** at the side **:** close by ⟨a guard with a prisoner *alongside*⟩

**²alongside** *preposition* (1793)
**1 a :** along the side of **b :** BESIDE 1
**2 a :** in company with ⟨men she has been working *alongside* —Richard Halloran⟩ **b :** in addition to ⟨a special category *alongside* the awards it annually presents —*Horizon*⟩

**alongside of** *preposition* (1781)
**:** ALONGSIDE

**¹aloof** \ə-'lüf\ *adverb* [obsolete *aloof* to windward, from ¹*a-* + *loof, luf* luff] (circa 1540)
**:** at a distance

**²aloof** *adjective* (1608)
**:** removed or distant either physically or emotionally ⟨the *aloof* composer neither worried nor cared about public opinion —Mary Jane Matz⟩ ⟨he stood *aloof* from worldly success —John Buchan⟩
*synonym* see INDIFFERENT
**— aloof·ly** *adverb*
**— aloof·ness** *noun*

**al·o·pe·cia** \ˌa-lə-'pē-sh(ē-)ə\ *noun* [Middle English *allopicia*, from Latin *alopecia*, from Greek *alōpekia*, from *alōpek-, alōpēx* fox; akin to Armenian *ałuēs* fox, Sanskrit *lopāśa*] (14th century)
**:** loss of hair, wool, or feathers **:** BALDNESS
**— al·o·pe·cic** \-'pē-sik\ *adjective*

**aloud** \ə-'laud\ *adverb* [Middle English, from ¹*a-* + *loud*] (13th century)
**1** *archaic* **:** in a loud manner **:** LOUDLY
**2 :** with the speaking voice

**alow** \ə-'lō\ *adverb* [Middle English, from ¹*a-* + *low*] (13th century)
**:** BELOW ⟨*alow* in the ship's hold⟩

**alp** \'alp\ *noun* [back-formation from *Alps*, mountain system of Europe] (15th century)
**1 :** a high rugged mountain
**2 :** something suggesting an alp in height, size, or ruggedness

**al·pa·ca** \al-'pa-kə\ *noun* [Spanish, from Aymara *allpaqa*] (1811)
**1 :** a domesticated mammal (*Lama pacos*) especially of Peru that is probably descended from the guanaco
**2 a :** wool of the alpaca **b** (1) **:** a thin cloth

☆ **SYNONYMS**
**Alone, solitary, lonely, lonesome, lone, forlorn, desolate** mean isolated from others. ALONE stresses the objective fact of being by oneself with slighter notion of emotional involvement than most of the remaining terms ⟨everyone needs to be *alone* sometimes⟩. SOLITARY may indicate isolation as a chosen course ⟨glorying in the calm of her *solitary* life⟩ but more often it suggests sadness and a sense of loss ⟨left *solitary* by the death of his wife⟩. LONELY adds to SOLITARY a suggestion of longing for companionship ⟨felt *lonely* and forsaken⟩. LONESOME heightens the suggestion of sadness and poignancy ⟨an only child often leads a *lonesome* life⟩. LONE may replace LONELY or LONESOME but typically is as objective as ALONE ⟨a *lone* robin pecking at the lawn⟩. FORLORN stresses dejection, woe, and listlessness at separation from one held dear ⟨a *forlorn* lost child⟩. DESOLATE implies inconsolable grief at loss or bereavement ⟨*desolate* after her brother's death⟩.

\ə\ abut \ᵊ\ kitten \ər\ further \a\ ash \ā\ ace \ä\ mop, mar \au̇\ out \ch\ chin \e\ bet \ē\ easy \g\ go \i\ hit \ī\ ice \j\ job \ŋ\ sing \ō\ go \ȯ\ law \ȯi\ boy \th\ thin \t͟h\ the \ü\ loot \u̇\ foot \y\ yet \zh\ vision *see also* Guide to Pronunciation

made of or containing this wool (2) **:** a rayon or cotton imitation of this cloth

**al·pen·glow** \'al-pən-ˌglō\ *noun* [part translation of German *Alpenglühen,* from *Alpen* Alps + *Glühen* glow] (1871)
**:** a reddish glow seen near sunset or sunrise on the summits of mountains

alpaca 1

**al·pen·horn** \'al-pən-ˌhòrn\ *or* **alp·horn** \'alp-ˌhòrn\ *noun* [German, from *Alpen* + *Horn* horn] (1864)
**:** a straight wooden horn 5 to 14 feet (about 1.5 to 4.3 meters) in length used chiefly by Swiss herdsmen

**al·pen·stock** \'al-pən-ˌstäk\ *noun* [German, from *Alpen* + *Stock* staff] (1829)
**:** a long iron-pointed staff used in mountain climbing

¹**al·pha** \'al-fə\ *noun* [Middle English, from Latin, from Greek, of Semitic origin; akin to Hebrew *āleph* aleph] (13th century)
**1 :** the 1st letter of the Greek alphabet — see ALPHABET table
**2 :** something that is first **:** BEGINNING
**3 :** ALPHA WAVE
**4 :** ALPHA PARTICLE

²**alpha** *adjective* (1863)
**1 :** closest in the structure of an organic molecule to a particular group or atom — symbol α 〈α-substitution〉
**2 :** socially dominant especially in a group of animals
**3 :** ALPHABETIC

**al·pha–ad·ren·er·gic** \'al-fə-ˌa-drə-'nər-jik\ *adjective* (1966)
**:** of, relating to, or being an alpha-receptor 〈*alpha-adrenergic* blocking action〉

**alpha and omega** *noun* [from the fact that alpha and omega are respectively the first and last letters of the Greek alphabet] (1526)
**1 :** the beginning and ending
**2 :** the principal element

**al·pha·bet** \'al-fə-ˌbet, -bət\ *noun* [Middle English *alphabete,* from Late Latin *alphabetum,* from Greek *alphabētos,* from *alpha* + *bēta* beta] (1513)
**1 a :** a set of letters or other characters with which one or more languages are written especially if arranged in a customary order **b :** a system of signs or signals that serve as equivalents for letters
**2 :** RUDIMENTS, ELEMENTS

**al·pha·bet·ic** \ˌal-fə-'be-tik\ *or* **al·pha·bet·i·cal** \-ti-kəl\ *adjective* (1567)
**1 :** arranged in the order of the letters of the alphabet
**2 :** of, relating to, or employing an alphabet
— **al·pha·bet·i·cal·ly** \-ti-k(ə-)lē\ *adverb*

**al·pha·bet·iza·tion** \ˌal-fə-ˌbe-tə-'zā-shən\ *noun* (1889)
**1 :** the act or process of alphabetizing
**2 :** an alphabetically arranged series, list, or file

**al·pha·bet·ize** \'al-fə-bə-ˌtīz\ *transitive verb* **-ized; -iz·ing** (1796)
**1 :** to arrange alphabetically
**2 :** to furnish with an alphabet
— **al·pha·bet·iz·er** *noun*

**alphabet soup** *noun* (1934)
**:** a hodgepodge especially of initials (as of the names of organizations)

**al·pha–fe·to·pro·tein** \ˌal-fə-ˌfē-tō-'prō-ˌtēn, -'prō-tē-ən\ *noun* (1968)
**:** a fetal blood protein present abnormally in adults with some cancers (as of the liver) and normally in the amniotic fluid of pregnant women with high or low levels tending to be associated with certain birth defects (as spina bifida or Down's syndrome)

**alpha globulin** *noun* [International Scientific Vocabulary] (1923)
**:** any of several globulins of plasma or serum that have at alkaline pH the greatest electrophoretic mobility next to albumin — compare BETA GLOBULIN, GAMMA GLOBULIN

**al·pha–he·lix** \ˌal-fə-'hē-liks\ *noun* (1955)
**:** the coiled structural arrangement of many proteins consisting of a single chain of amino acids stabilized by hydrogen bonds
— **al·pha–he·li·cal** \-'he-li-kəl, -'hē-li-\ *adjective*

**alpha iron** *noun* (1902)
**:** the form of iron stable below 910°C

**al·pha–mer·ic** \ˌal-fə-'mer-ik\ *adjective* [*alphabetic* + *numeric*] (circa 1952)
**:** ALPHANUMERIC

**al·pha·nu·mer·ic** \-nü-'mer-ik, -nyü-\ *also* **al·pha·nu·mer·i·cal** \-i-kəl\ *adjective* [*alphabetic* + *numeric, numerical*] (1950)
**1 :** consisting of both letters and numbers and often other symbols (as punctuation marks and mathematical symbols) 〈an *alphanumeric* code〉; *also* **:** being a character in an alphanumeric system
**2 :** capable of using or displaying alphanumeric characters
— **al·pha·nu·mer·i·cal·ly** \-i-k(ə-)lē\ *adverb*
— **al·pha·nu·mer·ics** \-iks\ *noun plural*

**alpha particle** *noun* (1903)
**:** a positively charged nuclear particle identical with the nucleus of a helium atom that consists of two protons and two neutrons and is ejected at high speed in certain radioactive transformations — called also *alpha, alpha ray*

**alpha privative** *noun* (1590)
**:** the prefix *a-* or *an-* expressing negation in Greek and in English

**al·pha–re·cep·tor** \'al-fə-ri-ˌsep-tər\ *noun* (1961)
**:** any of a group of receptors postulated to exist on nerve cell membranes of the sympathetic nervous system to explain the specificity of certain adrenergic agents in affecting only some sympathetic activities (as vasoconstriction, relaxation of intestinal muscle, and contraction of most smooth muscle)

**alpha wave** *noun* (1936)
**:** an electrical rhythm of the brain with a frequency of 8 to 13 cycles per second that is often associated with a state of wakeful relaxation — called also *alpha, alpha rhythm*

**Al·phe·us** \al-'fē-əs\ *noun* [Latin, from Greek *Alpheios*]
**:** a Greek river-god who pursues the nymph Arethusa and is finally united with her

**al·pine** \'al-ˌpīn\ *noun* (circa 1828)
**1 :** a plant native to alpine or boreal regions that is often grown for ornament
**2** *capitalized* **:** a person possessing Alpine physical characteristics

**Alpine** *adjective* (15th century)
**1** *often not capitalized* **:** of, relating to, or resembling the Alps or any mountains
**2** *often not capitalized* **:** of, relating to, or growing in the biogeographic zone including the elevated slopes above timberline
**3 :** of or relating to a physical type characterized by a broad head, stockiness, medium height, and brown hair or eyes often regarded as constituting a branch of the Caucasian race
**4 :** of or relating to competitive ski events consisting of slalom and downhill racing — compare NORDIC

**al·pin·ism** \'al-pə-ˌni-zəm\ *noun, often capitalized* (1884)
**:** mountain climbing in the Alps or other high mountains
— **al·pin·ist** \-nist\ *noun*

**al·ready** \òl-'re-dē, 'òl-\ *adverb* [Middle English *al redy,* from *al redy,* adjective, wholly ready, from *al* all + *redy* ready] (14th century)
**1 :** prior to a specified or implied past,

present, or future time **:** by this time **:** PREVIOUSLY 〈he had *already* left when I called〉
**2** — used as an intensive 〈all right *already*〉 〈enough *already*〉

**al·right** \(ˌ)òl-'rīt, 'òl-\ *adverb or adjective* (1887)
**:** ALL RIGHT ■

**Al·sa·tian** \al-'sā-shən\ *noun* [Medieval Latin *Alsatia* Alsace] (1917)
**:** GERMAN SHEPHERD

**al·sike clover** \'al-ˌsak-, -ˌsīk-\ *noun* [*Alsike,* Sweden] (1852)
**:** a European perennial clover (*Trifolium hybridum*) much used as a forage plant

**al·so** \'òl(t)-(ˌ)sō, 'ò-\ *adverb* [Middle English, from Old English *eallswā,* from *eall* all + *swā* so — more at so] (before 12th century)
**1 :** LIKEWISE 1
**2 :** in addition **:** BESIDES, TOO

**al·so–ran** \-ˌran\ *noun* (1896)
**1 :** a horse or dog that finishes out of the money in a race
**2 :** a contestant that does not win
**3 :** one that is of little importance especially competitively 〈was just an *also-ran* in the scramble for . . . privileges —C. A. Buss〉

**Al·ta·ic** \al-'tā-ik\ *adjective* (circa 1828)
**1 :** of or relating to the Altai Mountains
**2 :** of, relating to, or constituting the Turkic, Tungusic, and Mongolian language families collectively

**Al·tair** \al-'tīr, -'tar, -'ter, 'al-,\ *noun* [Arabic *al-ṭā'ir,* literally, the flier]
**:** the brightest star in the constellation Aquila

**al·tar** \'òl-tər\ *noun, often attributive* [Middle English *alter,* from Old English *altar,* from Latin *altare;* probably akin to Latin *adolēre* to burn up] (before 12th century)
**1 :** a usually raised structure or place on which sacrifices are offered or incense is burned in worship
**2 :** a table on which the eucharistic elements are consecrated or which serves as a center of worship or ritual

**altar boy** *noun* (1772)
**:** a boy who assists the celebrant in a liturgical service

**altar call** *noun* (1946)
**:** an appeal by an evangelist to worshipers to come forward to signify their decision to commit their lives to Christ

**altar of repose** *often A&R capitalized* (circa 1872)
**:** REPOSITORY 2

**al·tar·piece** \'òl-tər-ˌpēs\ *noun* (1644)
**:** a work of art that decorates the space above and behind an altar

**altar rail** *noun* (1860)
**:** a railing in front of an altar separating the chancel from the body of the church

**altar stone** *noun* (14th century)
**:** a stone slab with a compartment containing the relics of martyrs that forms an essential part of a Roman Catholic altar

**alt·az·i·muth** \(ˌ)al-'taz-məth, -'ta-zə-\ *noun, often attributive* [International Scientific Vocabulary *altitude* + *azimuth*] (1860)
**:** a telescope mounted so that it can swing horizontally and vertically; *also* **:** any of several other similarly mounted instruments

□ USAGE
**alright** The one-word spelling *alright* appeared some 75 years after *all right* itself had reappeared from a 400-year-long absence. Since the early 20th century some critics have insisted *alright* is wrong, but it has its defenders and its users. It is less frequent than *all right* but remains in common use especially in journalistic and business publications. It is quite common in fictional dialogue, and is used occasionally in other writing (the first two years of medical school were *alright* —Gertrude Stein).

# ALPHABET TABLE

Showing the letters of five non-Roman alphabets and the transliterations used in the etymologies

## HEBREW[1,4]

| Letter | Name | Translit. |
|---|---|---|
| א | aleph | ' [2] |
| ב | beth | b, bh |
| ג | gimel | g, gh |
| ד | daleth | d, dh |
| ה | he | h |
| ו | waw | w |
| ז | zayin | z |
| ח | heth | ḥ |
| ט | teth | ṭ |
| י | yod | y |
| כ ך | kaph | k, kh |
| ל | lamed | l |
| מ ם | mem | m |
| נ ן | nun | n |
| ס | samekh | s |
| ע | ayin | ' |
| פ ף | pe | p, ph |
| צ ץ | sadhe | ṣ |
| ק | qoph | q |
| ר | resh | r |
| שׂ | sin | ś |
| שׁ | shin | sh |
| ת | taw | t, th |

## ARABIC[3,4]

| (alone) | (joined prec.) | (joined both) | (joined foll.) | Name | Translit. |
|---|---|---|---|---|---|
| ا | ل | | | alif | [5] |
| ب | ب | ـبـ | بـ | bā | b |
| ت | ت | ـتـ | تـ | tā | t |
| ث | ث | ـثـ | ثـ | thā | th |
| ج | ج | ـجـ | جـ | jīm | j |
| ح | ح | ـحـ | حـ | ḥā | ḥ |
| خ | خ | ـخـ | خـ | khā | kh |
| د | د | | | dāl | d |
| ذ | ذ | | | dhāl | dh |
| ر | ر | | | rā | r |
| ز | ز | | | zāy | z |
| س | س | ـسـ | سـ | sīn | s |
| ش | ش | ـشـ | شـ | shīn | sh |
| ص | ص | ـصـ | صـ | ṣād | ṣ |
| ض | ض | ـضـ | ضـ | ḍād | ḍ |
| ط | ط | ـطـ | طـ | ṭā | ṭ |
| ظ | ظ | ـظـ | ظـ | ẓā | ẓ |
| ع | ع | ـعـ | عـ | 'ayn | ' |
| غ | غ | ـغـ | غـ | ghayn | gh |
| ف | ف | ـفـ | فـ | fā | f |
| ق | ق | ـقـ | قـ | qāf | q |
| ك | ك | ـكـ | كـ | kāf | k |
| ل | ل | ـلـ | لـ | lām | l |
| م | م | ـمـ | مـ | mīm | m |
| ن | ن | ـنـ | نـ | nūn | n |
| ه | ه | ـهـ | هـ | hā | h[6] |
| و | و | | | wāw | w |
| ي | ي | ـيـ | يـ | yā | y |

## GREEK[7]

| Letter | Name | Translit. |
|---|---|---|
| A α | alpha | a |
| B β | beta | b |
| Γ γ | gamma | g, n |
| Δ δ | delta | d |
| E ε | epsilon | e |
| Z ζ | zeta | z |
| H η | eta | ē |
| Θ θ | theta | th |
| I ι | iota | i |
| K κ | kappa | k |
| Λ λ | lambda | l |
| M μ | mu | m |
| N ν | nu | n |
| Ξ ξ | xi | x |
| O o | omicron | o |
| Π π | pi | p |
| P ρ | rho | r, rh |
| Σ σ s | sigma | s |
| T τ | tau | t |
| Υ υ | upsilon | y, u |
| Φ φ | phi | ph |
| X χ | chi | ch |
| Ψ ψ | psi | ps |
| Ω ω | omega | ō |

## RUSSIAN[8]

| Letter | Translit. |
|---|---|
| А а | a |
| Б б | b |
| В в | v |
| Г г | g |
| Д д | d |
| Е е | e |
| Ж ж | zh |
| З з | z |
| И и Й й | i, ĭ |
| К к | k |
| Л л | l |
| М м | m |
| Н н | n |
| О о | o |
| П п | p |
| Р р | r |
| С с | s |
| Т т | t |
| У у | u |
| Ф ф | f |
| Х х | kh |
| Ц ц | ts |
| Ч ч | ch |
| Ш ш | sh |
| Щ щ | shch |
| Ъ ъ[9] | " |
| Ы ы | y |
| Ь ь[10] | ' |
| Э э | e |
| Ю ю | yu |
| Я я | ya |

## SANSKRIT[11]

| Letter | Translit. | Letter | Translit. |
|---|---|---|---|
| अ | a | ञ | ñ |
| आ | ā | ट | ṭ |
| इ | i | ठ | th |
| ई | ī | ड | ḍ |
| उ | u | ढ | dh |
| ऊ | ū | ण | ṇ |
| ऋ | r | त | t |
| ॠ | ṝ | थ | th |
| ऌ | ḷ | द | d |
| ॡ | ḹ | ध | dh |
| ए | e | न | n |
| ऐ | ai | प | p |
| ओ | o | फ | ph |
| औ | au | ब | b |
| ं | ṁ | भ | bh |
| ः | ḥ | म | m |
| क | k | य | y |
| ख | kh | र | r |
| ग | g | ल | l |
| घ | gh | व | v |
| ङ | ṅ | श | ś |
| च | c | ष | ṣ |
| छ | ch | स | s |
| ज | j | ह | h |
| झ | jh | | |

1 See ALEPH, BETH, etc., in the vocabulary. Where two forms of a letter are given, the one at the right is the form used at the end of a word. 2 Not represented in transliteration when initial. 3 The left column shows the form of each Arabic letter that is used when it stands alone, the second column its form when it is joined to the preceding letter, the third column its form when it is joined to both the preceding and the following letter, and the right column its form when it is joined to the following letter only. In the names of the Arabic letters, ā, ī, and ū respectively are pronounced like a in *father*, i in *machine*, u in *rude*. 4 Hebrew and Arabic are written from right to left. The Hebrew and Arabic letters are all primarily consonants; a few of them are also used secondarily to represent certain vowels, but full indication of vowels, when provided at all, is by means of a system of dots or strokes adjacent to the consonantal characters. 5 Alif represents no sound in itself, but is used principally as an indicator of the presence of a glottal stop (transliterated ' medially and finally; not represented in transliteration when initial) and as the sign of a long a. 6 When ة has two dots above it ( ة ), it is called tā marbūta and, if it immediately precedes a vowel, is transliterated t instead of h. 7 See ALPHA, BETA, GAMMA, etc., in the vocabulary. The letter gamma is transliterated n only before velars; the letter upsilon is transliterated u only as the final element in diphthongs. 8 See CYRILLIC in the vocabulary. 9 This sign indicates that the immediately preceding consonant is not palatalized even though immediately followed by a palatal vowel. 10 This sign indicates that the immediately preceding consonant is palatalized even though not immediately followed by a palatal vowel. 11 The alphabet shown here is the Devanagari. When vowels are combined with preceding consonants they are indicated by various strokes or hooks instead of by the signs here given, or, in the case of short a, not written at all. Thus the character क represents ka; the character का, kā; the character कि, ki; the character की, kī; the character कु, ku; the character कू, kū; the character कृ, kr; the character कॄ, kṝ; the character के, ke; the character कै, kai; the character को, ko; the character कौ, kau; and the character क्, k without any following vowel. There are also many compound characters representing combinations of two or more consonants.

**al·ter** \'ȯl-tər\ *verb* **al·tered; al·ter·ing** \-t(ə-)riŋ\ [Middle English, from Middle French *alterer*, from Medieval Latin *alterare*, from Latin *alter* other (of two); akin to Latin *alius* other — more at ELSE] (14th century)
*transitive verb*
**1 :** to make different without changing into something else
**2 :** CASTRATE, SPAY
*intransitive verb*
**:** to become different
*synonym* see CHANGE
— **al·ter·abil·i·ty** \ˌȯl-t(ə-)rə-'bi-lə-tē\ *noun*
— **al·ter·able** \'ȯl-t(ə-)rə-bəl\ *adjective*
— **al·ter·ably** \-blē\ *adverb*
— **al·ter·er** \-tər-ər\ *noun*

**al·ter·ation** \ˌȯl-tə-'rā-shən\ *noun* (14th century)
**1 :** the act or process of altering **:** the state of being altered
**2 :** the result of altering **:** MODIFICATION

**al·ter·cate** \'ȯl-tər-ˌkāt\ *intransitive verb* **-cat·ed; -cat·ing** [Latin *altercatus*, past participle of *altercari*, from *alter*] (1530)
**:** to dispute angrily or noisily **:** WRANGLE

**al·ter·ca·tion** \ˌȯl-tər-'kā-shən\ *noun* (14th century)
**:** a noisy heated angry dispute; *also* **:** noisy controversy

**al·ter ego** \ˌȯl-tər-'ē-(ˌ)gō *also* -'e-(ˌ)gō\ *noun* [Latin, literally, second I] (1537)
**:** a second self: as **a :** a trusted friend **b :** the opposite side of a personality **c :** COUNTERPART 3

**¹al·ter·nate** \*US & Canadian* 'ȯl-tər-nət *also* 'al-; *chiefly British* ȯl-'tər-\ *adjective* [Latin *alternatus*, past participle of *alternare*, from *alternus* alternate, from *alter*] (1513)
**1 :** occurring or succeeding by turns ⟨a day of *alternate* sunshine and rain⟩
**2 a :** arranged first on one side and then on the other at different levels or points along an axial line ⟨*alternate* leaves⟩ — compare OPPOSITE **b :** arranged one above or alongside the other
**3 :** every other **:** every second ⟨he works on *alternate* days⟩
**4 :** constituting an alternative ⟨took the *alternate* route home⟩
**5 :** ALTERNATIVE 3
— **al·ter·nate·ly** *adverb*

**²al·ter·nate** \'ȯl-tər-ˌnāt *also* 'al-\ *verb* **-nat·ed; -nat·ing** (1599)
*transitive verb*
**1 :** to perform by turns or in succession
**2 :** to cause to alternate
*intransitive verb*
**:** to change from one to another repeatedly ⟨rain *alternated* with sun⟩

**³al·ter·nate** \*same as* ¹\ *noun* (1717)
**1 :** ALTERNATIVE
**2 :** one that substitutes for or alternates with another

**alternate angle** *noun* (1660)
**:** one of a pair of angles with different vertices and on opposite sides of a transversal at its intersection with two other lines: **a :** one of a pair of angles inside the two intersected lines — called also *alternate interior angle* **b :** one of a pair of angles outside the two intersected lines — called also *alternate exterior angle*

alternate interior angles *a, a', b, b'*; alternate exterior angles *c, c', d, d'*

**alternating current** *noun* (1839)
**:** an electric current that reverses its direction at regularly recurring intervals — abbreviation *AC*

**alternating group** *noun* (1904)
**:** a permutation group whose elements comprise those permutations of *n* objects which can be formed from the original order by making consecutively an even number of interchanges of pairs of objects

**alternating series** *noun* (circa 1909)
**:** a mathematical series in which consecutive terms are alternatively positive and negative

**al·ter·na·tion** \ˌȯl-tər-'nā-shən *also* ˌal-\ *noun* (15th century)
**1 a :** the act or process of alternating or causing to alternate **b :** alternating occurrence **:** SUCCESSION
**2 :** INCLUSIVE DISJUNCTION
**3 :** the occurrence of different allomorphs or allophones

**alternation of generations** (1858)
**:** the occurrence of two or more forms differently produced in the life cycle of a plant or animal usually involving the regular alternation of a sexual with an asexual generation

**¹al·ter·na·tive** \ȯl-'tər-nə-tiv, al-\ *adjective* (1540)
**1 :** ALTERNATE 1
**2 :** offering or expressing a choice ⟨several *alternative* plans⟩
**3 :** existing or functioning outside the established cultural, social, or economic system ⟨*alternative* newspaper⟩ ⟨*alternative* lifestyles⟩; *also* **:** different from the usual or conventional ⟨*alternative* fuels⟩
— **al·ter·na·tive·ly** *adverb*
— **al·ter·na·tive·ness** *noun*

**²alternative** *noun* (1624)
**1 a :** a proposition or situation offering a choice between two or more things only one of which may be chosen **b :** an opportunity for deciding between two or more courses or propositions
**2 a :** one of two or more things, courses, or propositions to be chosen **b :** something which can be chosen instead ⟨the only *alternative* to intervention⟩ ■
*synonym* see CHOICE

**alternative school** *noun* (1972)
**:** an elementary or secondary school with a nontraditional curriculum

**al·ter·na·tor** \'ȯl-tər-ˌnā-tər *also* 'al-\ *noun* (1892)
**:** an electric generator for producing alternating current

**alt·horn** \'alt-ˌhȯrn\ *noun* [German, from *alt* alto + *Horn* horn] (1859)
**:** an alto saxhorn

**al·though** *also* **al·tho** \ȯl-'thō\ *conjunction* [Middle English *although*, from *al* all + *though*] (14th century)
**:** in spite of the fact that **:** even though

**al·tim·e·ter** \al-'ti-mə-tər, 'al-tə-ˌmē-tər\ *noun* [Latin *altus* + English *-meter*] (circa 1828)
**:** an instrument for measuring altitude; *especially* **:** an aneroid barometer designed to register changes in atmospheric pressure accompanying changes in altitude
— **al·tim·e·try** \al-'ti-mə-trē\ *noun*

**al·ti·pla·no** \ˌal-ti-'plä-(ˌ)nō\ *noun, plural* **-nos** [American Spanish, from Latin *altus* + *planum* plain] (1919)
**:** a high plateau or plain **:** TABLELAND

**al·ti·tude** \'al-tə-ˌtüd *also* -ˌtyüd\ *noun* [Middle English, from Latin *altitudo* height, depth, from *altus* high, deep — more at OLD] (14th century)
**1 a :** the angular elevation of a celestial object above the horizon **b :** the vertical elevation of an object above a surface (as sea level or land) of a planet or natural satellite **c** (1) **:** a perpendicular line segment from a vertex of a geometric figure (as a triangle or a pyramid) to the opposite side or the opposite side extended or from a side or face to a parallel side or face or the side or face extended (2) **:** the length of an altitude
**2 :** a high level (as of quality or feeling) ⟨the *altitudes* of his anger⟩

**3 a :** vertical distance or extent **b :** position at a height **c :** an elevated region **:** EMINENCE — usually used in plural
*synonym* see HEIGHT
— **al·ti·tu·di·nal** \ˌal-tə-'tü-dᵊn-əl, -'tyü-\ *adjective*
— **al·ti·tu·di·nous** \-dᵊn-əs\ *adjective*

**altitude sickness** *noun* (1920)
**:** the effects (as nosebleed or nausea) of oxygen deficiency in the blood and tissues developed in rarefied air at high altitudes

**¹al·to** \'al-(ˌ)tō\ *noun, plural* **altos** [Italian, literally, high, from Latin *altus*] (circa 1724)
**1 a :** COUNTERTENOR **b :** CONTRALTO
**2 :** the second highest voice part in a 4-part chorus
**3 :** a member of a family of instruments having a range lower than that of the treble or soprano; *especially* **:** an alto saxophone

**²alto** *adjective* (circa 1724)
**:** relating to or having the range or part of an alto

**al·to·cu·mu·lus** \ˌal-tō-'kyü-myə-ləs\ *noun, plural* **-li** \-ˌlī, -ˌlē\ [New Latin, from Latin *altus* + New Latin *-o- + cumulus*] (1894)
**:** a fleecy cloud formation consisting of large whitish globular cloudlets with shaded portions — see CLOUD illustration

**¹al·to·geth·er** \ˌȯl-tə-'ge-thər\ *adverb* [Middle English *altogedere*, from *al* all + *togedere* together] (13th century)
**1 :** WHOLLY, COMPLETELY ⟨an *altogether* different problem⟩ ⟨stopped crying *altogether*⟩
**2 :** in all **:** ALL TOLD ⟨spent a hundred dollars *altogether*⟩
**3 :** on the whole **:** in the main ⟨*altogether* their efforts were successful⟩

**²altogether** *noun* (1894)
**:** NUDE — used with *the* ⟨posed in the *altogether*⟩

**al·to–re·lie·vo** *or* **al·to–ri·lie·vo** \ˌal-(ˌ)tō-ri-'lē-(ˌ)vō, ˌäl-(ˌ)tō-rēl-'yä-(ˌ)vō\ *noun, plural* **alto–relievos** *or* **al·to–ri·lie·vi** \ˌäl-(ˌ)tō-rēl-'yä-(ˌ)vē\ [Italian *altorilievo*] (1664)
**1 :** HIGH RELIEF
**2 :** a sculpture in high relief

**al·to·stra·tus** \ˌal-tō-'strā-təs, -'stra-\ *noun, plural* **-ti** \-ˌtī\ [New Latin, from Latin *altus* + New Latin *-o- + stratus*] (1894)
**:** a cloud formation similar to cirrostratus but darker and at a lower level — see CLOUD illustration

**al·tri·cial** \al-'tri-shəl\ *adjective* [Latin *altric-, altrix*, feminine of *altor* one who nourishes, from *alere* to nourish — more at OLD] (1872)
**:** being hatched or born or having young that are hatched or born in a very immature and helpless condition so as to require care for some time ⟨*altricial* birds⟩ — compare PRECOCIAL

**al·tru·ism** \'al-trù-ˌi-zəm\ [French *altruisme*, from *autrui* other people, from Old French, oblique case form of *autre* other, from Latin *alter*] (1853)
**1 :** unselfish regard for or devotion to the welfare of others
**2 :** behavior by an animal that is not beneficial to or may be harmful to itself but that benefits others of its species

☐ USAGE
**alternative** Sometime during the 19th century the notion arose that *alternative* could not properly be applied to a choice of more than two. This notion, based on the word's derivation from Latin *alter* "other of two," has come down to modern times ⟨*alternatives*, like the horns of a dilemma, come only in pairs —Heywood Hale Broun⟩. But modern usage largely ignores the stricture ⟨anyone who doesn't like the other *alternatives —Reader's Digest Success with Words*⟩ and many modern authorities dismiss the etymological objection as pedantry.

— **al·tru·ist** \-trü-ist\ *noun*
— **al·tru·is·tic** \,al-trü-'is-tik\ *adjective*
— **al·tru·is·ti·cal·ly** \-ti-k(ə-)lē\ *adverb*
**al·u·la** \'al-yə-lə\ *noun, plural* **-lae** \-,lē, -,lī\ [New Latin, from Latin, diminutive of *ala* wing — more at AISLE] (1772)
: the process of a bird's wing corresponding to the thumb and bearing a few short quills — called also *bastard wing*
¹**al·um** \'a-ləm\ *noun* [Middle English, from Middle French *alum, alun*, from Latin *alumen*] (14th century)
**1** : a potassium aluminum sulfate KAl(SO₄)₂·12H₂O or an ammonium aluminum sulfate NH₄Al(SO₄)₂·12H₂O used especially as an emetic and as an astringent and styptic
**2** : any of various double salts isomorphous with potassium aluminum sulfate
**3** : ALUMINUM SULFATE
²**alum** \ə-'ləm\ *noun* [by shortening] (1930)
: ALUMNUS, ALUMNA
**alu·mi·na** \ə-'lü-mə-nə\ *noun* [New Latin, from Latin *alumin-, alumen* alum] (1801)
: aluminum oxide Al₂O₃ occuring native as corundum and in hydrated forms (as in bauxite)
**alu·mi·nate** \-nət\ *noun* (1841)
: a compound of alumina with a metallic oxide
**al·u·min·i·um** \,al-yə-'mi-nē-əm\ *noun* [New Latin, from *alumina*] (1812)
*chiefly British* : ALUMINUM
**alu·mi·nize** \ə-'lü-mə-,nīz\ *transitive verb* **-nized; -niz·ing** (1934)
: to treat or coat with aluminum
**alu·mi·no·sil·i·cate** \ə-,lü-mə-nō-'si-lə-,kāt, -'si-li-kət\ *noun* [International Scientific Vocabulary *alumin-, alumen* + *-o-* + International Scientific Vocabulary *silicate*] (1907)
: a combined silicate and aluminate
**alu·mi·nous** \ə-'lü-mə-nəs\ *adjective* (15th century)
: of, relating to, or containing alum or aluminum
**alu·mi·num** \ə-'lü-mə-nəm\ *noun, often attributive* [New Latin, from *alumina*] (1812)
: a bluish silver-white malleable ductile light trivalent metallic element that has good electrical and thermal conductivity, high reflectivity, and resistance to oxidation and is the most abundant metal in the earth's crust where it always occurs in combination — see ELEMENT table
**aluminum sulfate** *noun* (1873)
: a white salt Al₂(SO₄)₃ usually made by treating bauxite with sulfuric acid and used in making paper, in water purification, and in tanning
**alum·na** \ə-'ləm-nə\ *noun, plural* **-nae** \-(,)nē *also* -,nī\ [Latin, feminine of *alumnus*] (1879)
**1** : a girl or woman who has attended or has graduated from a particular school, college, or university
**2** : a girl or woman who is a former member, employee, contributor, or inmate
**alum·nus** \ə-'ləm-nəs\ *noun, plural* **-ni** \-,nī\ [Latin, foster son, pupil, from *alere* to nourish — more at OLD] (1645)
**1** : one who has attended or has graduated from a particular school, college, or university
**2** : one who is a former member, employee, contributor, or inmate
**al·um·root** \'a-ləm-,rüt, -,rùt\ *noun* (1813)
: any of a genus (*Heuchera*) of North American herbs of the saxifrage family having basal rounded or lobed toothed leaves; *especially* : one (*H. americana*) of eastern North America
**al·u·nite** \'al-yə-,nīt, 'a-lə-\ *noun* [French, from *alun* alum] (1868)
: a mineral that consists of a hydrous potassium aluminum sulfate and occurs in massive form or in rhombohedral crystals
**al·ve·o·lar** \al-'vē-(ə-)lər\ *adjective* (1799)
**1** : of, relating to, resembling, or having alveoli; *especially* : of, relating to, or consti-

tuting the part of the jaws where the teeth arise, the air-containing cells of the lungs, or glands with secretory cells about a central space
**2** : articulated with the tip of the tongue touching or near the teethridge
— **al·ve·o·lar·ly** *adverb*
**al·ve·o·late** \-lət\ *adjective* (circa 1823)
: pitted like a honeycomb ⟨*alveolate* pollen⟩
**al·ve·o·lus** \al-'vē-ə-ləs\ *noun, plural* **-li** \-,lī, -(,)lē\ [New Latin, from Latin, diminutive of *alveus* cavity, hollow, from *alvus* belly, beehive; akin to Lithuanian *aulys* beehive, Greek *aulos* tube, flute] (circa 1706)
**1** : a small cavity or pit: as **a** : a socket for a tooth **b** : an air-containing cell of the lungs **c** : an acinus of a compound gland **d** : a cell or compartment of a honeycomb
**2** : TEETHRIDGE
**al·way** \'ol-(,)wā\ *adverb* [Middle English *alwey, alneway*, from Old English *ealne weg*, literally, all the way, from *ealne* (accusative of *eall* all) + *weg* (accusative) way — more at WAY] (14th century)
*archaic* : ALWAYS
**al·ways** \'ol-wēz, -wəz, -(,)wāz *also* 'o-\ *adverb* [Middle English *alwayes*, from *alwey*] (14th century)
**1** : at all times : INVARIABLY
**2** : FOREVER, PERPETUALLY
**3** : at any rate : in any event ⟨as a last resort one can *always* work⟩
**Al·yce clover** \'a-ləs-\ *noun* [probably by folk etymology from New Latin *Alysicarpus*, genus name, from Greek *halysis* chain + *karpos* fruit] (1941)
: a low spreading annual Old World legume (*Alysicarpus vaginalis*) used in the southern U.S. as a cover crop and for hay and forage
**alys·sum** \ə-'li-səm\ *noun* [New Latin, from Greek *alysson*, plant believed to cure rabies, from neuter of *alyssos* curing rabies, from *a-* + *lyssa* rabies] (1548)
**1** : any of a genus (*Alyssum*) of Old World herbs of the mustard family with small usually yellow racemose flowers
**2** : SWEET ALYSSUM
**Alz·hei·mer's disease** \'älts-,hī-mərz-, 'alts-\ *noun* [Alois *Alzheimer* (died 1915) German physician] (1912)
: a degenerative disease of the central nervous system characterized especially by premature senile mental deterioration — called also *Alzheimer's* ◆
**am** [Middle English, from Old English *eom*; akin to Old Norse *em* am, Latin *sum*, Greek *eimi* present 1st singular of BE
**AM** \'ā-,em\ *noun, often attributive* [amplitude modulation] (1940)
: a broadcasting system using amplitude modulation; *also* : a radio receiver of such a system
**ama** \'ä-(,)mä\ *noun, plural* **amas** *or* **ama** [Japanese] (1946)
: a Japanese diver especially for pearls
**amah** \'ä-(,)mä\ *noun* [Portuguese *ama* wet nurse, from Medieval Latin *amma*] (1839)
: an Oriental female servant; *especially* : a Chinese nurse
**amain** \ə-'mān\ *adverb* (1540)
**1** : with all one's might ⟨attacking a huge rack of beef with a cleaver, she flailed away *amain* —Jay Jacobs⟩
**2** *archaic* **a** : at full speed **b** : in great haste
**3** *archaic* : to a high degree : EXCEEDINGLY ⟨they whom I favour thrive in wealth *amain* —John Milton⟩
**Ama·le·kite** \'a-mə-,le-,kīt, ə-'ma-lə-,kīt\ *noun* [Hebrew *'Ămālēqī*, plural from *'Ămālēq* Amalek, grandson of Esau] (1560)
: a member of an ancient nomadic people living south of Canaan
**amal·gam** \ə-'mal-gəm\ *noun* [Middle English *amalgame*, from Middle French, from Medieval Latin *amalgama*] (15th century)
**1** : an alloy of mercury with another metal that

is solid or liquid at room temperature according to the proportion of mercury present and is used especially in making tooth cements
**2** : a mixture of different elements : COMBINATION
**amal·gam·ate** \-gə-,māt\ *transitive verb* **-at·ed; -at·ing** (1617)
**1** : to unite in or as if in an amalgam; *especially*
: to merge into a single body
*synonym* see MIX
— **amal·gam·ator** \-,mā-tər\ *noun*
**amal·gam·ation** \ə-,mal-gə-'mā-shən\ *noun* (1612)
**1 a** : the action or process of amalgamating : UNITING **b** : the state of being amalgamated
**2** : the result of amalgamating : AMALGAM
**3** : CONSOLIDATION, MERGER ⟨*amalgamation* of two corporations⟩
**aman·dine** \,ä-,män-'dēn\ *adjective* [French] (1945)
: prepared or served with almonds
**am·a·ni·ta** \,a-mə-'nī-tə, -'nē-\ *noun* [New Latin, genus name, from Greek *amanitai*, plural, a kind of fungus] (1899)
: any of a genus (*Amanita*) of white-spored fungi that typically have a volva and an annulus about the stipe and that includes some deadly poisonous forms

amanita

**am·a·ni·tin** \-'nī-t°n, -'nē-\ *noun* [*amanita* + *-in*] (circa 1847)
: a highly toxic peptide that is produced by the death cap and that selectively inhibits mammalian RNA polymerase
**aman·ta·dine** \ə-'man-tə-,dēn\ *noun* [International Scientific Vocabulary *amantad-* (alteration of *adamantane*, C₁₀H₁₆) + *amine*] (1964)
: a drug used especially as the hydrochloride C₁₀H₁₇N·HCl to prevent infection (as by an influenza virus) by interfering with virus penetration into host cells
**aman·u·en·sis** \ə-,man-yə-'wen(t)-səs\ *noun, plural* **-en·ses** \-(,)sēz\ [Latin, from (*servus*) *a manu* slave with secretarial duties] (1619)
: one employed to write from dictation or to copy manuscript
**am·a·ranth** \'a-mə-,ran(t)th\ *noun* [Latin *amarantus*, a flower, from Greek *amaranton*, from neuter of *amarantos* unfading, from *a-* + *marainein* to waste away] (1548)

**1 :** any of a large genus (*Amaranthus* of the family Amaranthaceae, the amaranth family) of coarse herbs including forms cultivated as food crops and various pigweeds
**2 :** a flower that never fades
**3 :** a red azo dye
**am·a·ran·thine** \ˌa-mə-ˈran(t)-thən, -ˈranˌthīn\ *adjective* (1667)
**1 a :** of or relating to an amaranth **b :** UNDYING
**2 :** of the color amaranth
**am·a·ret·to** \ˌa-mə-ˈre-(ˌ)tō, -ˈä-\ *noun* [Italian, diminutive of *amaro* bitter, from Latin *amarus*] (1945)
**1 am·a·ret·ti** \-(ˌ)tē\ *plural* **:** macaroons made with bitter almonds
**2** *often capitalized* **:** an almond-flavored liqueur
**am·a·ryl·lis** \ˌa-mə-ˈri-ləs\ *noun* [New Latin, genus name, probably from Latin, name of a shepherdess in Virgil's *Eclogues*] (circa 1794)
**:** an autumn-flowering South African bulbous herb (*Amaryllis belladonna* of the family Amaryllidaceae, the amaryllis family) widely grown for its deep red to whitish umbellate flowers; *also* **:** a plant of any of several related genera (as *Hippeastrum* or *Sprekelia*)
**amass** \ə-ˈmas\ *verb* [Middle French *amasser*, from Old French, from *a-* (from Latin *ad-*) + *masser* to gather into a mass, from *masse* mass] (15th century)
*transitive verb*
**1 :** to collect for oneself **:** ACCUMULATE ⟨*amass* a great fortune⟩
**2 :** to collect into a mass **:** GATHER ⟨must select rather than simply *amass* details⟩
*intransitive verb*
**:** to come together **:** ASSEMBLE
— **amass·er** *noun*
— **amass·ment** \-mənt\ *noun*
**am·a·teur** \ˈa-mə-(ˌ)tər, -ˌtùr, -ˌtyùr, -ˌchùr, -chər\ *noun, often attributive* [French, from Latin *amator* lover, from *amare* to love] (1784)
**1 :** DEVOTEE, ADMIRER
**2 :** one who engages in a pursuit, study, science, or sport as a pastime rather than as a profession
**3 :** one lacking in experience and competence in an art or science ☆
— **am·a·teur·ish** \ˌa-mə-ˈtər-ish, -ˈt(y)ùr-, -ˈchùr-, -ˈchər-\ *adjective*
— **am·a·teur·ish·ly** *adverb*
— **am·a·teur·ish·ness** *noun*
— **am·a·teur·ism** \ˈa-mə-ˌtər-ˌi-zəm, -ˌt(y)ùr-, -ˌchùr-; -ˌtə-ˌri-, -ˌchə-ˌri-\ *noun*
**Ama·ti** \ä-ˈmä-tē, ə-\ *noun, plural* **Amatis** (1833)
**:** a violin made by a member of the Amati family of Cremona
**am·a·tive** \ˈa-mə-tiv\ *adjective* [Medieval Latin *amativus*, from Latin *amatus*, past participle of *amare*] (1636)
**:** AMOROUS 1, 3
— **am·a·tive·ly** *adverb*
— **am·a·tive·ness** *noun*
**am·a·to·ry** \ˈa-mə-ˌtōr-ē, -ˌtòr-\ *adjective* (1599)
**:** of, relating to, or expressing sexual love
**am·au·ro·sis** \ˌa-mò-ˈrō-səs\ *noun, plural* **-ro·ses** \-ˌsēz\ [New Latin, from Greek *amaurōsis*, literally, dimming, from *amauroun* to dim, from *amauros* dim] (circa 1657)
**:** partial or complete loss of sight occurring especially without an externally perceptible change in the eye
— **am·au·rot·ic** \-ˈrä-tik\ *adjective*
**amaurotic idiocy** *noun* (1896)
**:** any of several recessive genetic conditions characterized by the accumulation of lipid-containing cells in the viscera and nervous system, mental retardation, and impaired vision or blindness; *especially* **:** TAY-SACHS DISEASE
**¹amaze** \ə-ˈmāz\ *verb* **amazed; amaz·ing** [Middle English *amasen*, from Old English

*āmasian*, from *ā-* (perfective prefix) + (assumed) *masian* to confuse — more at ABIDE] (before 12th century)
*transitive verb*
**1** *obsolete* **:** BEWILDER, PERPLEX
**2 :** to fill with wonder **:** ASTOUND
*intransitive verb*
**:** to show or cause astonishment
**synonym** *see* SURPRISE
— **amaz·ed·ly** \-ˈmā-zəd-lē\ *adverb*
**²amaze** *noun* (15th century)
**:** AMAZEMENT
**amaze·ment** \ə-ˈmāz-mənt\ *noun* (1595)
**1** *obsolete* **:** CONSTERNATION, BEWILDERMENT
**2 :** the quality or state of being amazed
**3 :** something that amazes
**amaz·ing·ly** \ə-ˈmā-ziŋ-lē\ *adverb* (1673)
**1 :** to an amazing degree ⟨*amazingly* low prices⟩
**2 :** what is amazing ⟨*amazingly*, the runnerup was only two seconds behind —Jim Doherty⟩
**am·a·zon** \ˈa-mə-ˌzän, -zən\ *noun* [Middle English, from Latin, from Greek *Amazōn*] (14th century)
**1** *capitalized* **:** a member of a race of female warriors of Greek mythology
**2 :** a tall strong often masculine woman
**Am·a·zo·nian** \ˌa-mə-ˈzō-nē-ən, -nyən\ *adjective* (1594)
**1 :** relating to, resembling, or befitting an Amazon or an amazon
**2 :** of or relating to the Amazon River or its valley
**am·a·zon·ite** \ˈa-mə-zə-ˌnīt\ *noun* [*Amazon* River] (circa 1879)
**:** an apple-green or bluish-green microcline
**am·a·zon·stone** \-zən-ˌstōn\ *noun* (1836)
**:** AMAZONITE
**am·bage** \ˈam-bij\ *noun, plural* **am·ba·ges** \am-ˈbā-(ˌ)jēz, ˈam-bi-jəz\ [back-formation from Middle English *ambages*, from Middle French or Latin; Middle French, from Latin, from *ambi-* + *agere* to drive — more at AGENT] (14th century)
**1** *archaic* **:** AMBIGUITY, CIRCUMLOCUTION — usually used in plural
**2** *plural, archaic* **:** indirect ways or proceedings
**am·bas·sa·dor** \am-ˈba-sə-dər, əm-, im-, -ˌdòr, -ˈbas-dər\ *noun* [Middle English *ambassadour*, from Middle French *ambassadeur*, ultimately of Germanic origin; akin to Old High German *ambaht* service] (14th century)
**1 :** an official envoy; *especially* **:** a diplomatic agent of the highest rank accredited to a foreign government or sovereign as the resident representative of his own government or sovereign or appointed for a special and often temporary diplomatic assignment
**2 a :** an authorized representative or messenger **b :** an unofficial representative ⟨traveling abroad as *ambassadors* of goodwill⟩
— **am·bas·sa·do·ri·al** \-ˌba-sə-ˈdòr-ē-əl, -ˈdòr-\ *adjective*
— **am·bas·sa·dor·ship** \-ˈba-sə-dər-ˌship\ *noun*
**ambassador–at–large** *noun, plural* **ambassadors–at–large** (1908)
**:** a minister of the highest rank not accredited to a particular foreign government or sovereign
**am·bas·sa·dress** \am-ˈba-sə-drəs, əm-, im-\ *noun* (1594)
**1 :** a woman who is an ambassador
**2 :** the wife of an ambassador
**am·beer** \ˈam-ˌbir\ *noun* [probably alteration of *amber;* from its color] (1848)
*chiefly Southern & southern Midland* **:** TOBACCO JUICE
**¹am·ber** \ˈam-bər\ *noun* [Middle English *ambre*, from Middle French, from Medieval Latin *ambra*, from Arabic *'anbar* ambergris] (14th century)
**1 :** a hard yellowish to brownish translucent fossil resin that takes a fine polish and is used chiefly in making ornamental objects (as beads)

**2 :** a variable color averaging a dark orange yellow
**²amber** *adjective* (15th century)
**1 :** consisting of amber
**2 :** resembling amber; *especially* **:** having the color amber
**am·ber·gris** \ˈam-bər-ˌgris, -ˌgrē(s)\ *noun* [Middle English *ambregris*, from Middle French *ambre gris*, from *ambre* + *gris* gray — more at GRIZZLE] (15th century)
**:** a waxy substance found floating in or on the shores of tropical waters, believed to originate in the intestines of the sperm whale, and used in perfumery as a fixative
**am·ber·i·na** \ˌam-bə-ˈrē-nə\ *noun* [from *Amberina*, a trademark] (1885)
**:** a late 19th century American clear glassware of a graduated color that shades from ruby to amber
**am·ber·jack** \-ˌjak\ *noun* [from its color] (circa 1893)
**:** any of several carangid fishes (genus *Seriola*); *especially* **:** a large vigorous sport fish (*S. dumerili*) of the western Atlantic
**ambi-** *prefix* [Latin *ambi-, amb-* both, around; akin to Latin *ambo* both, Greek *amphō* both, *amphi* around — more at BY]
**:** both ⟨*ambivalence*⟩
**am·bi·dex·ter·i·ty** \ˌam-bi-(ˌ)dek-ˈster-ə-tē\ *noun* (1593)
**:** the quality or state of being ambidextrous
**am·bi·dex·trous** \ˌam-bi-ˈdek-strəs\ *adjective* [Late Latin *ambidexter*, from Latin *ambi-* + *dexter* right-hand — more at DEXTER] (1646)
**1 :** using both hands with equal ease
**2 :** unusually skillful **:** VERSATILE
**3 :** characterized by duplicity **:** DOUBLE-DEALING
— **am·bi·dex·trous·ly** *adverb*
**am·bi·ence** *or* **am·bi·ance** \ˈam-bē-ən(t)s, ˈäm-bē-än(t)s; äⁿ-byäⁿs\ *noun* [French *ambiance*, from *ambiant* ambient] (1889)
**:** a feeling or mood associated with a particular place, person, or thing **:** ATMOSPHERE
**¹am·bi·ent** \ˈam-bē-ənt\ *adjective* [Latin *ambient-, ambiens*, present participle of *ambire* to go around, from *ambi-* + *ire* to go — more at ISSUE] (1596)
**:** existing or present on all sides **:** ENCOMPASSING
**²ambient** *noun* (1624)
**:** an encompassing atmosphere **:** ENVIRONMENT
**am·bi·gu·i·ty** \ˌam-bə-ˈgyü-ə-tē\ *noun, plural* **-ties** (15th century)
**1 a :** the quality or state of being ambiguous especially in meaning **b :** an ambiguous word or expression
**2 :** UNCERTAINTY
**am·big·u·ous** \am-ˈbi-gyə-wəs\ *adjective* [Latin *ambiguus*, from *ambigere* to be undecided, from *ambi-* + *agere* to drive — more at AGENT] (1528)

**1 a :** doubtful or uncertain especially from obscurity or indistinctness ⟨eyes of an *ambiguous* color⟩ **b :** INEXPLICABLE
**2 :** capable of being understood in two or more possible senses or ways
**synonym** see OBSCURE
— **am·big·u·ous·ly** *adverb*
— **am·big·u·ous·ness** *noun*
**am·bi·sex·u·al** \,am-bi-'sek-sh(ə-)wəl, -'sek-shəl\ *adjective* (1939)
**:** BISEXUAL
— **ambisexual** *noun*
— **am·bi·sex·u·al·i·ty** \-,sek-shə-'wa-lə-tē\ *noun*
**am·bit** \'am-bət\ *noun* [Middle English, from Latin *ambitus*, from *ambire*] (1597)
**1 :** CIRCUIT, COMPASS
**2 :** the bounds or limits of a place or district
**3 :** a sphere of action, expression, or influence **:** SCOPE
¹**am·bi·tion** \am-'bi-shən\ *noun* [Middle English, from Middle French or Latin; Middle French, from Latin *ambition-, ambitio*, literally, act of soliciting for votes, from *ambire*] (14th century)
**1 a :** an ardent desire for rank, fame, or power **b :** desire to achieve a particular end
**2 :** the object of ambition
**3 :** a desire for activity or exertion ⟨felt sick and had no *ambition*⟩ ☆ ◆
— **am·bi·tion·less** \-ləs\ *adjective*
²**ambition** *transitive verb* (1664)
**:** to have as one's ambition **:** DESIRE
**am·bi·tious** \am-'bi-shəs\ *adjective* (14th century)
**1 a :** having or controlled by ambition **b :** having a desire to achieve a particular goal **:** ASPIRING
**2 :** resulting from, characterized by, or showing ambition
— **am·bi·tious·ly** *adverb*
— **am·bi·tious·ness** *noun*
**am·biv·a·lence** \am-'bi-və-lən(t)s\ *noun* [International Scientific Vocabulary] (1918)
**1 :** simultaneous and contradictory attitudes or feelings (as attraction and repulsion) toward an object, person, or action
**2 a :** continual fluctuation (as between one thing and its opposite) **b :** uncertainty as to which approach to follow
— **am·biv·a·lent** \-lənt\ *adjective*
— **am·biv·a·lent·ly** *adverb*
**am·bi·ver·sion** \,am-bi-'vər-zhən, -shən\ *noun* [*ambi-* + *-version* (as in *introversion*)] (1927)
**:** the personality configuration of an ambivert
**am·bi·vert** \'am-bi-,vərt\ *noun* [*ambi-* + *-vert* (as in *introvert*)] (1927)
**:** a person having characteristics of both extrovert and introvert
¹**am·ble** \'am-bəl\ *intransitive verb* **am·bled; am·bling** \-b(ə-)liŋ\ [Middle English, from Middle French *ambler*, from Latin *ambulare* to walk, from *ambi-* + *-ulare* (verb base akin to Middle Welsh *el* he may go, Greek *ēlythe* he went) — more at ELASTIC] (14th century)
**:** to go at or as if at an amble **:** SAUNTER
— **am·bler** \-b(ə-)lər\ *noun*
²**amble** *noun* (14th century)
**1 a :** an easy gait of a horse in which the legs on the same side of the body move together **b :** ⁷RACK b
**2 :** an easy gait
**3 :** a leisurely walk
**am·blyg·o·nite** \am-'bli-gə-,nīt\ *noun* [German *Amblygonit*, from Greek *amblygōnios* obtuse-angled, from *amblys* blunt, dull + *gōnia* angle — more at MOLLIFY, -GON] (circa 1828)
**:** a mineral that consists of basic lithium aluminum phosphate commonly containing sodium and fluorine and occurs in white cleavable masses
**am·bly·opia** \,am-blē-'ō-pē-ə\ *noun* [New Latin, from Greek *amblyōpia*, from *amblys* + *-ōpia* -opia] (circa 1706)

**:** dimness of sight especially in one eye without apparent change in the eye structures — called also *lazy eye*
— **am·bly·opic** \-'ō-pik, -'ä-pik\ *adjective*
**Am·boi·nese** \,am-,bòi-'nēz, -'nēs, am-'bòi-,\ *or* **Am·bo·nese** \,am-bə-'nēz, -'nēs\ *noun, plural* **Amboinese** *or* **Ambonese** (circa 1864)
**1 :** a native or inhabitant of Ambon
**2 :** the group of closely related Austronesian languages spoken on Ambon
— **Amboinese** *or* **Ambonese** *adjective*
**am·boy·na** *or* **am·boi·na** \am-'bòi-nə\ *noun* [*Amboina*, Moluccas, Indonesia] (circa 1859)
**:** a mottled curly-grained wood of a leguminous tree (*Pterocarpus indicus*) of southeastern Asia
**am·bro·sia** \am-'brō-zh(ē-)ə\ *noun* [Latin, from Greek, literally, immortality, from *ambrotos* immortal, from *a-* + *-mbrotos* (akin to *brotos* mortal) — more at MURDER] (15th century)
**1 a :** the food of the Greek and Roman gods **b :** the ointment or perfume of the gods
**2 :** something extremely pleasing to taste or smell
**3 :** a dessert made of oranges and shredded coconut ◆
— **am·bro·sial** \-zh(ē-)əl\ *adjective*
— **am·bro·sial·ly** \-zh(ē-)ə-lē\ *adverb*
**ambrosia beetle** *noun* (circa 1900)
**:** any of various small wood-boring beetles (family Scolytidae) that cultivate a fungus on which they feed and raise their larvae
**am·bro·type** \'am-brə-,tīp\ *noun* [Greek *ambrotos* + English *type*] (1858)
**:** a positive picture made of a photographic negative on glass backed by a dark surface
**am·bry** \'am-brē; 'äm-rē, 'óm-\ *noun, plural* **ambries** [Middle English *almery*, from Middle French *almarie, armarie*, from Latin *armarium*, from *arma* weapons — more at ARM] (14th century)
**1** *dialect chiefly British* **:** PANTRY
**2 :** a recess in a church wall (as for holding sacramental vessels)
**ambs·ace** \'ām-,zās\ *noun* [Middle English *ambes as*, from Old French, from *ambes* both + *as* aces] (13th century)
*archaic* **:** the lowest throw at dice; *also* **:** something worthless or unlucky
**am·bu·la·cral** \,am-byə-'la-krəl, -'lā-\ *adjective* (1836)
**:** of, relating to, or being any of the radial areas of echinoderms along which run the principal nerves, blood vessels, and elements of the water-vascular system ⟨*ambulacral* grooves⟩
**am·bu·la·crum** \-krəm\ *noun, plural* **-cra** \-krə\ [New Latin, from Latin, alley, from *ambulare* to walk — more at AMBLE] (1837)
**:** an ambulacral area or part
**am·bu·lance** \'am-byə-lən(t)s, -bə- *also* -,lan(t)s\ *noun* [French, from (*hôpital*) *ambulant*, literally, ambulant field hospital, from *ambulant* itinerant, from Latin *ambulant-, ambulans*, present participle of *ambulare*] (1809)
**:** a vehicle equipped for transporting the injured or sick
**ambulance chaser** *noun* (1897)
**:** a lawyer or lawyer's agent who incites accident victims to sue for damages
— **ambulance chasing** *noun*
**am·bu·lant** \'am-byə-lənt\ *adjective* (1619)
**:** moving about **:** AMBULATORY
**am·bu·late** \-,lāt\ *intransitive verb* **-lat·ed; -lat·ing** [Latin *ambulatus*, past participle of *ambulare*] (circa 1623)
**:** to move from place to place **:** WALK
— **am·bu·la·tion** \,am-byə-'lā-shən\ *noun*
¹**am·bu·la·to·ry** \'am-byə-lə-,tōr-ē, -,tòr-\ *adjective* (1622)
**1 :** of, relating to, or adapted to walking; *also* **:** occurring during a walk
**2 :** moving from place to place **:** ITINERANT

**3 :** capable of being altered ⟨a will is *ambulatory* until the testator's death⟩
**4 a :** able to walk about and not bedridden **b :** performed on or involving an ambulatory patient or an outpatient ⟨*ambulatory* medical care⟩ ⟨an *ambulatory* electrocardiogram⟩
— **am·bu·la·to·ri·ly** \,am-byə-lə-'tōr-ə-lē, -'tòr-\ *adverb*
²**ambulatory** *noun, plural* **-ries** (circa 1616)
**:** a sheltered place (as in a cloister or church) for walking
**am·bus·cade** \'am-bə-,skād, ,am-bə-'\ *noun* [Middle French *embuscade*, modification of Old Italian *imboscata*, from *imboscare* to place in ambush, from *in* (from Latin) + *bosco* forest, of Germanic origin; akin to Old High German *busc* forest — more at IN, BUSH] (circa 1588)
**:** AMBUSH
— **ambuscade** *verb*
— **am·bus·cad·er** *noun*

---

---

◇ **WORD HISTORY**
**ambition** When candidates for public office in ancient Rome wanted to be elected, they had to make the rounds of their districts urging citizens to vote for them, just as modern political candidates must do. The Latin word for this effort was *ambitio*, which came from *ambire*, a verb meaning literally "to go around." Because the act of canvassing votes was motivated by a desire for honor or power, the word came to denote this desire itself. *Ambitio* entered French and English as *ambition* in the late Middle Ages. Later its meaning broadened to include any desire for advancement or improvement and still later the object of this desire.

**ambrosia** The Greek and Roman gods all too often behaved like mere mortals, but what set them apart was the gift of immortality. This they enjoyed as a result of their peculiar diet. Their food, ambrosia, and their drink, nectar, had the power to prevent death. In Greek *ambrosia* literally means "immortality" and is a derivative of *ambrotos* "immortal." The notion of ambrosia as something fit for the gods has resulted in the name being given to various things whose taste or smell is especially pleasing. The ancient Greeks and Romans called several aromatic-leaved plants *ambrosia*, but in modern botany *ambrosia* is the scientific name for the genus of plants commonly known as the ragweeds—which have neither flavor nor fragrance to recommend them. Indeed, to allergy sufferers they are among the most unappealing of plants.

---

\ə\ **abut** \ᵊ\ **kitten** \ər\ **further** \a\ **ash** \ā\ **ace**
\ä\ **mop, mar** \aú\ **out** \ch\ **chin** \e\ **bet** \ē\ **easy**
\g\ **go** \i\ **hit** \ī\ **ice** \j\ **job** \ŋ\ **sing** \ō\ **go**
\ó\ **law** \ói\ **boy** \th\ **thin** \t͟h\ **the** \ü\ **loot** \ú\ **foot**
\y\ **yet** \zh\ **vision** *see also* Guide to Pronunciation

**¹am·bush** \'am-ˌbush\ *verb* [Middle English *embushen,* from Middle French *embuschier,* from *en* in (from Latin *in*) + *busche* stick of firewood] (14th century)
*transitive verb*
**1 :** to station in ambush
**2 :** to attack from an ambush **:** WAYLAY
*intransitive verb*
**:** to lie in wait **:** LURK
— **am·bush·er** *noun*
— **am·bush·ment** \-mənt\ *noun*
**²ambush** *noun* (15th century)
**1 :** a trap in which concealed persons lie in wait to attack by surprise
**2 :** the persons stationed in ambush; *also*
**:** their concealed position
**3 :** an attack especially from an ambush
**ame·ba, ame·boid** *variant of* AMOEBA, AMOEBOID
**am·e·bi·a·sis** \ˌa-mi-'bī-ə-səs\ *noun, plural* **-a·ses** \-ˌsēz\ (1905)
**:** infection with or disease caused by amoebas (especially *Entamoeba histolytica*)
**ame·bic dysentery** \ə-'mē-bik-\ *noun* (1891)
**:** acute human intestinal amebiasis caused by an amoeba (*Entamoeba histolytica*) and marked by dysentery, gripes, and erosion of the intestinal wall
**ame·bo·cyte** *variant of* AMOEBOCYTE
**ameer** *variant of* EMIR
**ame·lio·rate** \ə-'mēl-yə-ˌrāt, -'mē-lē-ə-\ *verb* **-rat·ed; -rat·ing** [alteration of *meliorate*] (1767)
*transitive verb*
**:** to make better or more tolerable
*intransitive verb*
**:** to grow better
*synonym* SEE IMPROVE
— **ame·lio·ra·tion** \-ˌmēl-yə-'rā-shən, -ˌmē-lē-ə-\ *noun*
— **ame·lio·ra·tive** \-'mēl-yə-ˌrā-tiv, -'mē-lē-ə-\ *adjective*
— **ame·lio·ra·tor** \-ˌrā-tər\ *noun*
— **ame·lio·ra·to·ry** \-rə-ˌtōr-ē, -ˌtȯr-\ *adjective*
**am·e·lo·blast** \'a-mə-lō-ˌblast\ *noun* [obsolete *amel* enamel (Middle English, ultimately from Old French *esmail*) + *-o-* + *-blast* — more at ENAMEL] (1882)
**:** one of a group of columnar cells that produce and deposit enamel on the surface of a developing vertebrate tooth
**amen** \(')ä-'men, (')ā-; 'ä- *when sung*\ *interjection* [Middle English, from Old English, from Late Latin, from Greek *amēn,* from Hebrew *āmēn*] (before 12th century)
— used to express solemn ratification (as of an expression of faith) or hearty approval (as of an assertion)
**ame·na·ble** \ə-'mē-nə-bəl, -'me-\ *adjective* [probably from (assumed) Anglo-French, from Middle French *amener* to lead up, from Old French, from *a-* (from Latin *ad-*) + *mener* to lead, from Late Latin *minare* to drive, from Latin *minari* to threaten — more at MOUNT] (1596)
**1 :** liable to be brought to account **:** ANSWERABLE ⟨citizens *amenable* to the law⟩
**2 a :** capable of submission (as to judgment or test) **:** SUITED ⟨the data is *amenable* to analysis⟩ **b :** readily brought to yield, submit, or cooperate **c :** WILLING 1 ⟨was *amenable* to spending more time at home⟩
*synonym* SEE RESPONSIBLE, OBEDIENT
— **ame·na·bil·i·ty** \-ˌmē-nə-'bil-ət-ē, -ˌme-\ *noun*
— **ame·na·bly** \-'mē-nə-blē, -'me-\ *adverb*
**amen corner** \'ā-ˌmen-\ *noun* (1860)
**:** a conspicuous corner in a church occupied by fervent worshipers
**amend** \ə-'mend\ *verb* [Middle English, from Old French *amender,* modification of Latin *emendare,* from *e, ex* out + *menda* fault; akin

to Latin *mendax* lying, *mendicus* beggar, and perhaps to Sanskrit *mindā* physical defect] (13th century)
*transitive verb*
**1 :** to put right; *especially* **:** to make emendations in (as a text)
**2 a :** to change or modify for the better **:** IMPROVE ⟨*amend* the situation⟩ **b :** to alter especially in phraseology; *especially* **:** to alter formally by modification, deletion, or addition ⟨*amend* the constitution⟩
*intransitive verb*
**:** to reform oneself
*synonym* see CORRECT
— **amend·able** \-'men-də-bəl\ *adjective*
— **amend·er** *noun*
**amen·da·to·ry** \ə-'men-də-ˌtōr-ē, -ˌtȯr-\ *adjective* [*amend* + *-atory* (as in *emendatory*)] (circa 1828)
**:** CORRECTIVE
**amend·ment** \ə-'men(d)-mənt\ *noun* (13th century)
**1 :** the act of amending **:** CORRECTION
**2 :** a material (as compost or sand) that aids plant growth indirectly by improving the condition of the soil
**3 a :** the process of amending by parliamentary or constitutional procedure **b :** an alteration proposed or effected by this process ⟨the 18th *amendment*⟩
**amends** \ə-'men(d)z\ *noun plural but singular or plural in construction* [Middle English *amendes,* from Middle French, plural of *amende* reparation, from *amender*] (14th century)
**:** compensation for a loss or injury **:** RECOMPENSE ⟨make *amends*⟩
**ame·ni·ty** \ə-'me-nə-tē, -'mē-\ *noun, plural* **-ties** [Middle English *amenite,* from Latin *amoenitat-, amoenitas,* from *amoenus* pleasant] (14th century)
**1 a :** the quality of being pleasant or agreeable **b (1) :** the attractiveness and value of real estate or of a residential structure **(2) :** a feature conducive to such attractiveness and value
**2 :** something (as a conventional social gesture) that conduces to smoothness or pleasantness of social relationships
**3 :** something that conduces to comfort, convenience, or enjoyment
**amen·or·rhea** \ˌā-ˌme-nə-'rē-ə, ˌä-\ *noun* [New Latin, from *a-* + Greek *mēn* month + New Latin *-o-* + *-rrhea* — more at MOON] (1804)
**:** abnormal absence or suppression of menses
— **amen·or·rhe·ic** \-'rē-ik\ *adjective*
**ament** \'a-mənt, 'ā-\ *noun* [New Latin *amentum,* from Latin, thong, strap] (1791)
**:** CATKIN
— **amen·tif·er·ous** \-mən-'ti-f(ə-)rəs\ *adjective*
**amen·tia** \ā-'men(t)-sh(ē-)ə, (ˌ)ä-\ *noun* [New Latin, from Latin, madness, from *ament-, amens* mad, from *a-* (from *ab-*) + *ment-, mens* mind — more at MIND] (14th century)
**:** MENTAL RETARDATION; *specifically* **:** a condition of lack of development of intellectual capacity
**Am·er·asian** \ˌa-mə-'rā-zhən, -shən\ *noun* [*American* + *Asian*] (1953)
**:** a person of mixed American and Asian descent; *especially* **:** one fathered by an American and especially an American serviceman in Asia
**amerce** \ə-'mərs\ *transitive verb* **amerced; amerc·ing** [Middle English *amercien,* from Anglo-French *amercier,* from Old French *a merci* at (one's) mercy] (15th century)
**:** to punish by a fine whose amount is fixed by the court; *broadly* **:** PUNISH
— **amerce·ment** \-'mər-smənt\ *noun*
— **amer·cia·ble** \-'mər-sē-ə-bəl, -'mər-shə-bəl\ *adjective*
**¹Amer·i·can** \ə-'mer-ə-kən, -'mər-, -'mar-, -i-kən\ *noun* (1578)

**1 :** an American Indian of North America or South America
**2 :** a native or inhabitant of North America or South America
**3 :** a citizen of the U.S.
**4 :** AMERICAN ENGLISH
**²American** *adjective* (1598)
**1 :** of or relating to America
**2 :** of or relating to the U.S. or its possessions or original territory
— **Amer·i·can·ness** \-kə(n)-nəs\ *noun*
**Amer·i·ca·na** \ə-ˌmer-ə-'kä-nə, -ˌmər-, -ˌmar-, -'ka-nə\ *noun plural* (1841)
**1 :** materials concerning or characteristic of America, its civilization, or its culture; *broadly* **:** things typical of America
**2 :** American culture
**American chameleon** *noun* (1881)
**:** a lizard (*Anolis carolinensis*) of the southeastern U.S. that can vary its skin color from green to brown and is often kept as a pet
**American cheese** *noun* (1804)
**:** a process cheese made from American cheddar
**American dog tick** *noun* (1927)
**:** a common North American ixodid tick (*Dermacentor variabilis*) especially of dogs and humans that is an important vector of Rocky Mountain spotted fever and tularemia — called also *dog tick*
**American dream** *noun, often D capitalized* (1931)
**:** an American social ideal that stresses egalitarianism and especially material prosperity
**American eel** *noun* (circa 1949)
**:** a yellow to greenish-brown eel (*Anguilla rostrata*) that is lighter below, has 103 to 111 vertebrae, is found in fresh and coastal waters along the Atlantic coasts of North America, and is held to spawn in or near the Sargasso Sea
**American elm** *noun* (1813)
**:** a large elm (*Ulmus americana*) with gradually spreading branches and pendulous branchlets that is common in eastern North America
**American English** *noun* (1806)
**:** the English language as spoken in the U.S. — used especially with the implication that it is clearly distinguishable from British English yet not so divergent as to be a separate language
**Amer·i·ca·nese** \ə-ˌmer-ə-kə-'nēz, -ˌmər-, -ˌmar-, -i-kə-, -'nēs\ *noun* (1882)
**:** AMERICAN ENGLISH
**American foxhound** *noun* (circa 1891)
**:** any of an American breed of foxhounds smaller than the English foxhound but with longer ears and a short glossy coat usually of black, tan, and white
**American Indian** *noun* (1732)
**:** a member of any of the aboriginal peoples of the western hemisphere except usually the Eskimos; *especially* **:** an American Indian of North America and especially the U.S.
**Amer·i·can·isa·tion, Amer·i·can·ise** *British variant of* AMERICANIZATION, AMERICANIZE
**Amer·i·can·ism** \ə-'mer-ə-kə-ˌni-zəm, -'mər-, -'mar-\ *noun* (1781)
**1 :** a characteristic feature of American English especially as contrasted with British English
**2 :** attachment or allegiance to the traditions, interests, or ideals of the U.S.
**3 a :** a custom or trait peculiar to America **b :** the political principles and practices essential to American culture
**Amer·i·can·ist** \-kə-nist\ *noun* (1881)
**1 :** a specialist in American culture or history
**2 :** a specialist in the languages or cultures of the aboriginal inhabitants of America
**Amer·i·can·iza·tion** \ə-ˌmer-ə-kə-nə-'zā-shən, -ˌmər-, -ˌmar-\ *noun* (1858)
**1 :** the act or process of Americanizing

**2 :** instruction of foreigners (as immigrants) in English and in U.S. history, government, and culture

**Amer·i·can·ize** \ə-'mer-ə-kə-,nīz, -'mər-, -'mar-\ *verb* **-ized; -iz·ing** (1797) *transitive verb*
**1 :** to cause to acquire or conform to American characteristics
**2 :** to bring (as an area) under the political, cultural, or commercial influence of the U.S. *intransitive verb*
**:** to acquire or conform to American traits **:** assimilate to American life or culture

**American pit bull terrier** *noun* (1950)
**:** any of a breed of dogs developed to combine the traits of terriers and bulldogs that have extremely powerful jaws and great strength and tenacity — called also *pit bull terrier*

**American plan** *noun* (1856)
**:** a hotel plan whereby the daily rates cover the costs of the room and three meals — compare EUROPEAN PLAN

**American saddlebred** *noun* (1948)
**:** any of a breed of 3-gaited or 5-gaited saddle horses developed chiefly in Kentucky from Thoroughbreds and smoothgaited stock — called also *American saddle horse*

American saddlebred

**American short·hair** *noun* (1974)
**:** any of a breed of cats with a usually solidcolored or tabby coat; *broadly* **:** SHORTHAIR

**American Sign Language** *noun* (1960)
**:** a sign language for the deaf in which meaning is conveyed by a system of articulated hand gestures and their placement relative to the upper body

**American Staffordshire terrier** *noun* (1971)
**:** a strong stocky terrier of a breed originally developed for dogfighting

**American Standard Version** *noun* (1901)
**:** an American version of the Bible that is based on the Revised Version and was published in 1901 — called also *American Revised Version*

**American trotter** *noun* (1894)
**:** STANDARDBRED

**American water spaniel** *noun* (1947)
**:** any of a breed of medium-sized spaniels of American origin that have a thick curly chocolate or liver-colored coat

**am·er·i·ci·um** \,a-mə-'ri-shē-əm, -sē-\ *noun* [New Latin, from *America* + New Latin *-ium*] (1946)
**:** a radioactive metallic element produced by bombardment of plutonium with high-energy neutrons — see ELEMENT table

**Am·er·in·di·an** \,a-mə-'rin-dē-ən\ *noun* [*American* + *Indian*] (circa 1898)
**:** AMERICAN INDIAN
— **Am·er·ind** \'a-mə-,rind\ *noun or adjective*
— **Amerindian** *adjective*

**Ame·slan** \'a-məs-,lan, 'am-,slan\ *noun* (1972)
**:** AMERICAN SIGN LANGUAGE

**Ames test** \'āmz-\ *noun* [Bruce N. *Ames* (born 1928) American biochemist] (1977)
**:** a test for identifying potential carcinogens by studying their mutagenic effect on bacteria

**am·e·thyst** \'a-mə-thəst, -(,)thist\ *noun* [Middle English *amatiste*, from Old French & Latin; Old French, from Latin *amethystus*, from Greek *amethystos*, literally, remedy against drunkenness, from *a-* + *methyein* to be drunk, from *methy* wine — more at MEAD] (13th century)

**1 a :** a clear purple or bluish violet variety of crystallized quartz that is much used as a jeweler's stone **b :** a deep purple variety of corundum
**2 :** a moderate purple ◆
— **am·e·thys·tine** \,a-mə-'this-tən\ *adjective*

**am·e·tro·pia** \,a-mə-'trō-pē-ə\ *noun* [New Latin, from Greek *ametros* without measure (from *a-* + *metron* measure) + New Latin *-opia* — more at MEASURE] (1875)
**:** an abnormal refractive condition (as myopia, hyperopia, or astigmatism) of the eye in which images fail to focus upon the retina
— **am·e·tro·pic** \-'trō-pik, -'trä-\ *adjective*

**Am·har·ic** \am-'har-ik; am-'här-, äm-\ *noun* (1813)
**:** a Semitic language that is the official language of Ethiopia
— **Amharic** *adjective*

**ami·a·ble** \'ā-mē-ə-bəl\ *adjective* [Middle English, from Middle French, from Late Latin *amicabilis* friendly, from Latin *amicus* friend; akin to Latin *amare* to love] (14th century)
**1** *archaic* **:** PLEASING, ADMIRABLE
**2 a :** generally agreeable ⟨an *amiable* comedy⟩ **b :** being friendly, sociable, and congenial ☆
— **ami·a·bil·i·ty** \,ā-mē-ə-'bi-lə-tē\ *noun*
— **ami·a·ble·ness** \'ā-mē-ə-bəl-nəs\ *noun*
— **ami·a·bly** \-blē\ *adverb*

**am·i·ca·ble** \'a-mi-kə-bəl\ *adjective* [Middle English, from Late Latin *amicabilis*] (15th century)
**:** characterized by friendly goodwill **:** PEACEABLE ☆
— **am·i·ca·bil·i·ty** \,a-mi-kə-'bi-lə-tē\ *noun*
— **am·i·ca·ble·ness** \'a-mi-kə-bəl-nəs\ *noun*
— **am·i·ca·bly** \-blē\ *adverb*

**am·ice** \'a-məs\ *noun* [Middle English *amis*, probably from Middle French, plural of *amit*, from Medieval Latin *amictus*, from Latin, cloak, from *amicire* to wrap around, from *am-, amb-* around + *jacere* to throw — more at AMBI-, JET] (13th century)
**:** a liturgical vestment made of an oblong piece of cloth usually of white linen and worn about the neck and shoulders and partly under the alb

**ami·cus** \ə-'mē-kəs, -'mī-\ *noun, plural* **ami·ci** \-'mē-,kē, -'mī-,sī\ (1951)
**:** AMICUS CURIAE

**amicus cu·ri·ae** \-'kyùr-ē-,ī, -'kùr-, -i-,ē\ *noun, plural* **amici curiae** [New Latin, literally, friend of the court] (1612)
**:** one (as a professional person or organization) that is not a party to a particular litigation but that is permitted by the court to advise it in respect to some matter of law that directly affects the case in question

**amid** \ə-'mid\ *or* **amidst** \-'midst, -'mitst\ *preposition* [*amid* from Middle English *amidde*, from Old English *onmiddan*, from *on* + *middan*, dative of *midde* mid; *amidst* from Middle English *amiddes*, from *amidde* + *-es* -s] (before 12th century)
**1 :** in or into the middle of **:** surrounded by **:** AMONG
**2 a :** DURING **b :** with the accompaniment of ⟨resigned *amid* rumors of misconduct⟩

**am·i·dase** \'a-mə-,dās, -,dāz\ *noun* [International Scientific Vocabulary] (1921)
**:** an enzyme that hydrolyzes acid amides usually with the liberation of ammonia

**am·ide** \'a-,mīd, -məd\ *noun* [International Scientific Vocabulary, from New Latin *ammonia*] (circa 1847)
**1 :** an inorganic compound derived from ammonia by replacement of an atom of hydrogen with another element (as a metal)
**2 :** an organic compound derived from ammonia or an amine by replacement of ammoniacal hydrogen with an acyl group — compare AMINE, IMIDE

**ami·do** \ə-'mē-(,)dō, 'a-mə-,dō\ *adjective* [International Scientific Vocabulary *amide* + *-o-*] (1877)
**:** relating to or containing an organic amide group — often used in combination

**am·i·dol** \'a-mə-,dòl, -,dōl\ *noun* [German, from *Amidol*, a trademark] (1892)
**:** a colorless crystalline salt $C_6H_8N_2O \cdot 2HCl$ used chiefly as a photographic developer

**amid·ships** \ə-'mid-,ships\ *adverb* (1692)
**1 :** in or toward the part of a ship midway between bow and stern
**2 :** in or toward the middle

**ami·go** \ə-'mē-(,)gō, ä-\ *noun, plural* **-gos** [Spanish, from Latin *amicus* — more at AMIABLE] (1837)
**:** FRIEND

**amine** \ə-'mēn, 'a-,mēn\ *noun* [International Scientific Vocabulary, from New Latin *ammonia*] (1863)
**:** any of a class of organic compounds derived from ammonia by replacement of hydrogen with one or more alkyl groups — compare AMIDE 2

**ami·no** \ə-'mē-(,)nō\ *adjective* [International Scientific Vocabulary *amine* + *-o-*] (1904)
**:** relating to, being, or containing an amine group — often used in combination

---

☆ SYNONYMS
**Amiable, good-natured, obliging, complaisant** mean having the desire or disposition to please. AMIABLE implies having qualities that make one liked and easy to deal with ⟨an *amiable* teacher not easily annoyed⟩. GOOD-NATURED implies cheerfulness or helpfulness and sometimes a willingness to be imposed upon ⟨a *good-natured* girl who was always willing to pitch in⟩. OBLIGING stresses a friendly readiness to be helpful ⟨our *obliging* innkeeper found us a bigger room⟩. COMPLAISANT often implies passivity or a yielding to others because of weakness ⟨was too *complaisant* to protest a decision he thought unfair⟩.

**Amicable, neighborly, friendly** mean exhibiting goodwill and an absence of antagonism. AMICABLE implies a state of peace and a desire on the part of the parties not to quarrel ⟨maintained *amicable* relations⟩. NEIGHBORLY implies a disposition to live on good terms with others and to be helpful on principle ⟨*neighborly* concern⟩. FRIENDLY stresses cordiality and often warmth or intimacy of personal relations ⟨sought *friendly* advice⟩.

---

◇ WORD HISTORY
**amethyst** For the ancient Greeks and Romans, gemstones had medical as well as ornamental value. The violet-colored variety of quartz known as amethyst, for example, was believed to protect against the effects of overdrinking, and this quality is reflected in its name. The Greek word *amethystos* means literally "not inducing drunkenness" and is a derivative of the verb *methyein* "to be drunk," itself from the noun *methy* "wine" (which is related to the English word *mead*). The Roman author Pliny associated the stone's supposed magical property with its color, for to him it resembled wine that had been heavily diluted with water and was hence not very intoxicating.

---

\ə\ **abut**  \ᵊ\ **kitten**  \ər\ **further**  \a\ **ash**  \ā\ **ace**
\ä\ **mop, mar**  \aù\ **out**  \ch\ **chin**  \e\ **bet**  \ē\ **easy**
\g\ **go**  \i\ **hit**  \ī\ **ice**  \j\ **job**  \ŋ\ **sing**  \ō\ **go**
\ò\ **law**  \òi\ **boy**  \th\ **thin**  \t̲h̲\ **the**  \ü\ **loot**  \ù\ **foot**
\y\ **yet**  \zh\ **vision**      *see also* Guide to Pronunciation

**amino acid** *noun* (1898)
**:** an amphoteric organic acid containing the amino group NH₂; *especially* **:** any of the alpha-amino acids that are the chief components of proteins and are synthesized by living cells or are obtained as essential components of the diet

**ami·no·ac·id·uria** \ə-ˌmē-nō-ˌa-sə-ˈdu̇r-ē-ə, -ˈdyu̇r-\ *noun* [New Latin] (circa 1923)
**:** a condition in which one or more amino acids are excreted in excessive amounts

**ami·no·ben·zo·ic acid** \ə-ˌmē-nō-ben-ˈzō-ik-\ *noun* [International Scientific Vocabulary] (1904)
**:** any of three crystalline derivatives C₇H₇NO₂ of benzoic acid; *especially* **:** PARA-AMINO-BENZOIC ACID

**ami·no·pep·ti·dase** \ə-ˌmē-nō-ˈpep-tə-ˌdās, -ˌdāz\ *noun* (1943)
**:** an enzyme that hydrolyzes peptides by acting on the peptide bond next to a terminal amino acid containing a free amino group

**am·i·noph·yl·line** \ˌa-mə-ˈnä-fə-lən\ *noun* [*amino* + *theophylline*] (1934)
**:** a theophylline derivative C₁₆H₂₄N₁₀O₄ used especially to stimulate the heart in congestive heart failure and to dilate the air passages in respiratory disorders

**am·i·nop·ter·in** \ˌa-mə-ˈnäp-tə-rən\ *noun* [*amino* + *pteroylglutamic acid* + *-in*] (1948)
**:** a derivative of glutamic acid C₁₉H₂₀N₈O₅ used especially as a rodenticide

**ami·no·py·rine** \ə-ˌmē-nō-ˈpīr-ˌēn\ *noun* [International Scientific Vocabulary, from *amino* + *antipyrine*] (circa 1936)
**:** a crystalline compound C₁₃H₁₇N₃O formerly used to relieve pain and fever but now largely abandoned for this purpose because of the occurrence of fatal agranulocytosis as a side effect in some users

**ami·no·sal·i·cyl·ic acid** \ə-ˌmē-nō-ˌsa-lə-ˈsi-lik-\ *noun* (1925)
**:** any of four isomeric derivatives C₇H₇NO₃ of salicylic acid that have a single amino group; *especially* **:** PARA-AMINOSALICYLIC ACID

**ami·no·trans·fer·ase** \-ˈtran(t)s-fə-ˌrās, -ˌrāz\ *noun* (circa 1965)
**:** TRANSAMINASE

**amir** *variant of* EMIR

**Amish** \ˈä-mish, ˈa-, ˈā-\ *adjective* [probably from German *amisch*, from Jacob *Amman* or *Amen* (flourished 1693) Swiss Mennonite bishop] (1844)
**:** of or relating to a strict sect of Mennonite followers of Amman that settled in America chiefly in the 18th century
— **Amish** *noun*

¹**amiss** \ə-ˈmis\ *adverb* (13th century)
**1 a :** in a mistaken way **:** WRONGLY ⟨if you think he is guilty, you judge *amiss*⟩ **b :** ASTRAY ⟨something had gone *amiss*⟩
**2 :** in a faulty way **:** IMPERFECTLY

²**amiss** *adjective* (14th century)
**1 :** not being in accordance with right order
**2 :** FAULTY, IMPERFECT
**3 :** out of place in given circumstances — usually used with a negative ⟨a few remarks may not be *amiss* here⟩

**ami·to·sis** \ˌā-mī-ˈtō-səs\ *noun* [New Latin, from ²*a-* + *mitosis*] (1894)
**:** cell division by simple cleavage of the nucleus and division of the cytoplasm without spindle formation or appearance of chromosomes
— **ami·tot·ic** \-ˈtä-tik\ *adjective*
— **ami·tot·i·cal·ly** \-ti-k(ə-)lē\ *adverb*

**am·i·trip·ty·line** \ˌa-mə-ˈtrip-tə-ˌlēn\ *noun* [*amino* + *tryptophan* + *-yl* + ²*-ine*] (1961)
**:** a tricyclic antidepressant drug C₂₀H₂₃N

**am·i·trole** \ˈa-mə-ˌtrōl\ *noun* [*amino* + *triazole*] (circa 1960)
**:** a systemic herbicide C₂H₄N₄ used in areas other than food croplands

**am·i·ty** \ˈa-mə-tē\ *noun, plural* **-ties** [Middle English *amite*, from Middle French *amité*,

from Medieval Latin *amicitas*, from Latin *amicus* friend — more at AMIABLE] (15th century)
**:** FRIENDSHIP; *especially* **:** friendly relations between nations

**am·me·ter** \ˈa-ˌmē-tər\ *noun* [*ampere* + *-meter*] (1882)
**:** an instrument for measuring electric current in amperes

**am·mine** \ˈa-ˌmēn, a-ˈmēn\ *noun* [International Scientific Vocabulary *ammonia* + ²*-ine*] (1897)
**1 :** a molecule of ammonia as it exists in a coordination complex ⟨hex-*ammine*-cobalt chloride Co(NH₃)₆Cl₃⟩
**2 :** a compound that contains an ammine

**am·mo** \ˈa-(ˌ)mō\ *noun* [by shortening & alteration] (1911)
**:** AMMUNITION

**am·mo·nia** \ə-ˈmō-nyə\ *noun* [New Latin, from Latin *sal ammoniacus* sal ammoniac, literally, salt of Ammon, from Greek *ammōniakos* of Ammon, from *Ammōn* Ammon, Amen, an Egyptian god near one of whose temples it was prepared] (circa 1799)
**1 :** a pungent colorless gaseous alkaline compound of nitrogen and hydrogen NH₃ that is very soluble in water and can easily be condensed to a liquid by cold and pressure
**2 :** AMMONIA WATER

**am·mo·ni·ac** \ə-ˈmō-nē-ˌak\ *noun* [Middle English & Latin; Middle English, from Latin *ammoniacum*, from Greek *ammōniakon*, from neuter of *ammōniakos* of Ammon] (15th century)
**:** the aromatic gum resin of a Persian herb (*Dorema ammoniacum*) of the carrot family used as an expectorant and stimulant and in plasters

**am·mo·ni·a·cal** \ˌa-mə-ˈnī-ə-kəl\ *also* **am·mo·ni·ac** \ə-ˈmō-nē-ˌak\ *adjective* (1798)
**:** of, relating to, containing, or having the properties of ammonia

**am·mo·ni·ate** \ə-ˈmō-nē-ˌāt\ *transitive verb* **-at·ed; -at·ing** (circa 1928)
**1 :** to combine or impregnate with ammonia or an ammonium compound
**2 :** to subject to ammonification
— **am·mo·ni·a·tion** \-ˌmō-nē-ˈā-shən\ *noun*

**ammonia water** *noun* (circa 1928)
**:** a water solution of ammonia

**am·mo·ni·fi·ca·tion** \ə-ˌmä-nə-fə-ˈkā-shən, -ˌmō-nə-\ *noun* (1886)
**1 :** the act or process of ammoniating
**2 :** decomposition with production of ammonia or ammonium compounds especially by the action of bacteria on nitrogenous organic matter
— **am·mo·ni·fy** \-ˌfī\ *verb*

**am·mo·nite** \ˈa-mə-ˌnīt\ *noun* [New Latin *ammonites*, from Latin *cornu Ammonis*, literally, horn of Ammon] (1758)
**:** any of a subclass (Ammonoidea) of extinct cephalopods with flat spiral shells that were especially abundant in the Mesozoic age
— **am·mo·nit·ic** \ˌa-mə-ˈni-tik\ *adjective*

ammonite

**Am·mon·ite** \ˈa-mə-ˌnīt\ *noun* [Late Latin *Ammonites*, from Hebrew '*Ammōn* Ammon (son of Lot), descendant of Ammon] (1537)
**:** a member of a Semitic people who in Old Testament times lived east of the Jordan between the Jabbok and the Arnon
— **Ammonite** *adjective*

**am·mo·ni·um** \ə-ˈmō-nē-əm\ *noun* [New Latin, from *ammonia*] (1808)
**:** an ion NH₄⁺ derived from ammonia by combination with a hydrogen ion and known in compounds (as salts) that resemble in properties the compounds of the alkali metals

**ammonium carbonate** *noun* (circa 1881)

**:** a carbonate of ammonium; *specifically* **:** the commercial mixture of the bicarbonate and carbamate used especially in smelling salts

**ammonium chloride** *noun* (1869)
**:** a white crystalline volatile salt NH₄Cl that is used in dry cells and as an expectorant — called also *sal ammoniac*

**ammonium cyanate** *noun* (circa 1881)
**:** an inorganic white crystalline salt NH₄CNO that can be converted into organic urea

**ammonium hydroxide** *noun* (1904)
**:** a weakly basic compound NH₄OH that is formed when ammonia dissolves in water and that exists only in solution

**ammonium nitrate** *noun* (circa 1881)
**:** a colorless crystalline salt NH₄NO₃ used in explosives and fertilizers and in veterinary medicine

**ammonium phosphate** *noun* (circa 1881)
**:** a phosphate of ammonium; *especially* **:** DI-AMMONIUM PHOSPHATE

**ammonium sulfate** *noun* (circa 1881)
**:** a colorless crystalline salt (NH₄)₂SO₄ used chiefly as a fertilizer

**am·mo·noid** \ˈa-mə-ˌnȯid\ *noun* (1884)
**:** AMMONITE

**am·mu·ni·tion** \ˌam-yə-ˈni-shən\ *noun* [obsolete French *amunition*, from Middle French, alteration of *munition*] (circa 1626)
**1 a :** the projectiles with their fuses, propelling charges, or primers fired from guns **b :** CARTRIDGES **c :** explosive military items (as grenades or bombs)
**2 :** material for use in attacking or defending a position ⟨*ammunition* for the defense lawyers⟩

**am·ne·sia** \am-ˈnē-zhə\ *noun* [New Latin, from Greek *amnēsia* forgetfulness, alteration of *amnēstia*] (1786)
**1 :** loss of memory due usually to brain injury, shock, fatigue, repression, or illness
**2 :** a gap in one's memory
**3 :** the selective overlooking or ignoring of those events or acts that are not favorable or useful to one's purpose or position
— **am·ne·si·ac** \-zhē-ˌak, -zē-\ *or* **am·ne·sic** \-zik, -sik\ *adjective or noun*

**am·nes·ty** \ˈam-nə-stē\ *noun, plural* **-ties** [Greek *amnēstia* forgetfulness, from *amnēstos* forgotten, from *a-* + *mnasthai* to remember — more at MIND] (1580)
**:** the act of an authority (as a government) by which pardon is granted to a large group of individuals
— **amnesty** *transitive verb*

**am·nio·cen·te·sis** \ˌam-nē-ō-(ˌ)sen-ˈtē-səs\ *noun, plural* **-te·ses** \-ˌsēz\ [New Latin, from *amnion* + *centesis* puncture, from Greek *kentesis*, from *kentein* to prick — more at CENTER] (1957)
**:** the surgical insertion of a hollow needle through the abdominal wall and into the uterus to obtain amniotic fluid especially for the determination of fetal sex or chromosomal abnormality

**am·ni·on** \ˈam-nē-ˌän, -ən\ *noun, plural* **am·nions** *or* **am·nia** \-nē-ə\ [New Latin, from Greek, caul, from *amnos* lamb — more at YEAN] (1667)
**1 :** a thin membrane forming a closed sac about the embryos of reptiles, birds, and mammals and containing a serous fluid in which the embryo is immersed
**2 :** a membrane analogous to the amnion and occurring in various invertebrates
— **am·ni·ot·ic** \ˌam-nē-ˈä-tik\ *adjective*

**am·ni·ote** \ˈam-nē-ˌōt\ *noun* [New Latin *Amniota*, from *amnion*] (1909)
**:** any of a group (Amniota) of vertebrates that undergo embryonic development within an amnion and include the birds, reptiles, and mammals
— **amniote** *adjective*

**amniotic fluid** *noun* (1855)
**:** the serous fluid in which the embryo is suspended within the amnion

**amniotic sac** *noun* (circa 1881)

: AMNION
**amo·bar·bi·tal** \ə-mō-'bär-bə-,tȯl\ *noun*
[*amyl* + *-o-* + *barbital*] (1949)
: a barbiturate $C_{11}H_{18}N_2O_3$ used as a hypnotic
and sedative; *also* : its sodium salt
**amoe·ba** \ə-'mē-bə\ *noun, plural* **-bas** *or*
**-bae** \-(,)bē\ [New Latin, genus name, from
Greek *amoibē* change, from *ameibein* to
change — more at MIGRATE] (1855)
: any of a large genus
(*Amoeba*) of naked
rhizopod protozoans
with lobed and never
anastomosing pseu-
dopodia, without per-
manent organelles or
supporting structures,
and of wide distribu-
tion in fresh and salt
water and moist ter-
restrial environments;
*broadly* : a naked rhi-
zopod or other amoe-
boid protozoan
— **amoe·bic** \-bik\
*adjective*

amoeba:
*1* pseudopodium,
*2* nucleus, *3* contractile
vacuole, *4* food
vacuole

**am·oe·bi·a·sis** *variant of* AMEBIASIS
**amoe·bo·cyte** \ə-'mē-bə-,sīt\ *noun* (1892)
: a cell (as a phagocyte) having amoeboid
form or movements
**amoe·boid** \ə-'mē-,bȯid\ *adjective* (1856)
: resembling an amoeba specifically in moving
or changing in shape by means of protoplasmic flow
**¹amok** \ə-'mək, -'mäk\ *noun* [Malay *amok*]
(1665)
: a murderous frenzy that occurs chiefly
among Malays ◆
**²amok** *adverb* (1672)
**1** : in a murderously frenzied state
**2 a** : in a violently raging manner ⟨a virus that
had run *amok*⟩ **b** : in an undisciplined, uncontrolled, or faulty manner ⟨films . . . about
computers run *amok* —*People*⟩
**³amok** *adjective* (1944)
: possessed with or motivated by a murderous
or violently uncontrollable frenzy
**amo·le** \ə-'mō-lē\ *noun* [American Spanish,
from Nahuatl *ahmōlli* soap] (1831)
: a plant part (as a root) possessing detergent
properties and serving as a substitute for soap;
*also* : a plant (as a yucca or agave) so used
**among** \ə-'məŋ\ *also* **amongst** \-'məŋ(k)st\
*preposition* [*among* from Middle English,
from Old English *on gemonge*, from *on* + *ge-*
*monge*, dative of *gemong* crowd, from *ge-* (associative prefix) + *-mong* (akin to Old English
*mengan* to mix); *amongst* from Middle English *amonges*, from *among* + *-es* -s — more
at CO-, MINGLE] (before 12th century)
**1** : in or through the midst of : surrounded by
**2** : in company or association with ⟨living
*among* artists⟩
**3** : by or through the aggregate of ⟨discontent
*among* the poor⟩
**4** : in the number or class of ⟨wittiest *among*
poets⟩ ⟨*among* other things she was president
of her college class⟩
**5** : in shares to each of ⟨divided *among* the
heirs⟩
**6 a** : through the reciprocal acts of ⟨quarrel
*among* themselves⟩ **b** : through the joint action
of ⟨made a fortune *among* themselves⟩
**usage** *see* BETWEEN
**amon·til·la·do** \ə-,män-tə-'lä-(,)dō, -ti(l)-'yä-
(,)thō\ *noun, plural* **-dos** [Spanish, literally,
done in the manner of *Montilla*, town in An-
dalusia] (1825)
: a medium dry sherry
**amor·al** \(,)ā-'mȯr-əl, (,)a-, -'mär-\ *adjective*
(1882)
**1 a** : being neither moral nor immoral; *specifically* : lying outside the sphere to which moral judgments apply ⟨science as such is completely *amoral* —W. S. Thompson⟩ **b** : lacking
moral sensibility ⟨infants are *amoral*⟩

**2** : being outside or beyond the moral order or
a particular code of morals ⟨*amoral* customs⟩
— **amor·al·ism** \-ə-,li-zəm\ *noun*
— **amo·ral·i·ty** \,ā-mə-'ra-lə-tē, ,a-, -(,)mȯ-\
*noun*
— **amor·al·ly** \,ā-'mȯr-ə-lē, (,)a-, -'mär-\
*adverb*
**amo·ret·to** \,a-mə-'re-(,)tō, ,ä-\ *noun, plural*
**-ti** \-(,)tē\ *or* **-tos** [Italian, diminutive of
*amore* love, cupid, from Latin *amor*] (1622)
: CUPID, CHERUB 2
**am·or·ist** \'a-mə-rist\ *noun* (1581)
**1** : a devotee of love and especially sexual
love : GALLANT
**2** : one that writes about romantic love
— **am·or·is·tic** \,a-mə-'ris-tik\ *adjective*
**Am·o·rite** \'a-mə-,rīt\ *noun* [Hebrew *Ĕmōrī*]
(1535)
: a member of one of various Semitic peoples
living in Mesopotamia, Syria, and Palestine
during the 3d and 2d millennia B.C.
— **Amorite** *adjective*
**am·o·rous** \'a-mə-rəs, 'am-rəs\ *adjective*
[Middle English, from Middle French, from
Medieval Latin *amorosus*, from Latin *amor*
love, from *amare* to love] (14th century)
**1** : strongly moved by love and especially sexual love ⟨*amorous* women⟩
**2** : being in love : ENAMORED — usually used
with *of* ⟨*amorous* of the girl⟩
**3 a** : indicative of love ⟨received *amorous*
glances from her partner⟩ **b** : of or relating to
love ⟨an *amorous* novel⟩
— **am·o·rous·ly** *adverb*
— **am·o·rous·ness** *noun*
**amor·phous** \ə-'mȯr-fəs\ *adjective* [Greek
*amorphos*, from *a-* + *morphē* form] (circa
1731)
**1 a** : having no definite form : SHAPELESS ⟨an
*amorphous* cloud mass⟩ **b** : being without definite character or nature : UNCLASSIFIABLE ⟨an
*amorphous* segment of society⟩ **c** : lacking organization or unity ⟨an *amorphous* style⟩
**2** : having no real or apparent crystalline form
: UNCRYSTALLIZED ⟨an *amorphous* mineral⟩
— **amor·phous·ly** *adverb*
— **amor·phous·ness** *noun*
**amort** \ə-'mȯrt\ *adjective* [short for *all-a-mort*,
by folk etymology from Middle French *a la
mort* to the death] (1590)
*archaic* : being at the point of death
**am·or·ti·za·tion** \,a-mər-tə-'zā-shən *also*
ə-,mȯr-\ *noun* (circa 1859)
**1** : the act or process of amortizing
**2** : the result of amortizing
**am·or·tize** \'a-mər-,tīz *also* ə-'mȯr-\ *transitive
verb* **-tized; -tiz·ing** [Middle English *amor-
tisen* to deaden, alienate in mortmain, modification of Middle French *amortiss-*, stem of
*amortir*, from (assumed) Vulgar Latin *ad-
mortire* to deaden, from Latin *ad-* + *mort-*,
*mors* death — more at MURDER] (1882)
**1** : to provide for the gradual extinguishment
of (as a mortgage) usually by contribution to a
sinking fund at the time of each periodic interest payment
**2** : to amortize an expenditure for ⟨*amortize*
intangibles⟩ ⟨*amortize* the new factory⟩
— **am·or·tiz·able** \-,tī-zə-bəl\ *adjective*
**Amos** \'ā-məs\ *noun* [Hebrew *Āmōs*]
**1** : a Hebrew prophet of the 8th century B.C.
**2** : a prophetic book of canonical Jewish and
Christian Scripture — see BIBLE table
**am·o·site** \'a-mə-,sīt, -,zīt\ *noun* [*Amosa*
(from *Asbestos Mines of South Africa*) + *¹-ite*]
(circa 1918)
: an iron-rich amphibole that is a variety of asbestos
**¹amount** \ə-'maùnt\ *intransitive verb* [Middle
English, from Middle French *amonter*, from
*amont* upward, from *a-* (from Latin *ad-*) +
*mont* mountain — more at MOUNT] (14th century)
**1 a** : to be equivalent ⟨acts that *amount* to
treason⟩ **b** : to reach in kind or quality ⟨wants

her son to *amount* to something⟩ ⟨doesn't
*amount* to much⟩
**2** : to reach a total : add up ⟨the bill *amounts*
to $10⟩
**²amount** *noun* (1710)
**1 a** : the total number or quantity : AGGREGATE
**b** : the quantity at hand or under consideration
⟨has an enormous *amount* of energy⟩
**2** : the whole effect, significance, or import
**3** : a principal sum and the interest on it ■
**amour** \ə-'mùr, ä-, a-\ *noun* [Middle English,
love, affection, from Middle French, from Old
Provençal *amor*, from Latin, from *amare* to
love] (14th century)
: a usually illicit love affair; *also* : LOVER
**amour pro·pre** \,a-,mùr-'prȯprᵊ, ,ä-, -'prȯprᵊ\
*noun* [French *amour-propre*, literally, love of
oneself] (1775)
: SELF-ESTEEM
**amox·i·cil·lin** \ə-,mäk-sē-'si-lən\ *noun* [*amino*
+ *ox-* + *penicillin*] (1973)
: a semisynthetic penicillin $C_{16}H_{19}N_3O_5S$ derived from ampicillin
**amox·y·cil·lin** *British variant of* AMOXICILLIN
**Amoy** \ä-'mȯi, a-, ə-\ *noun* (1904)
: the dialect of Chinese spoken in and near
Amoy in southeastern China
**amp** \'amp\ *noun* [by shortening] (1886)
**1** : AMPERE
**2** : AMPLIFIER; *also* : a unit consisting of an
electronic amplifier and a loudspeaker
**AMP** \,ā-,em-'pē\ *noun* [adenosine *mono*phos-
phate] (1951)
: a mononucleotide of adenine $C_{10}H_{12}$-
$N_5O_3H_2PO_4$ that was originally isolated from
mammalian muscle and is reversibly convert-

□ **USAGE**
**amount**   *Number* is regularly used with
count nouns ⟨a large *number* of mistakes⟩
⟨any *number* of times⟩ while *amount* is mainly used with mass nouns ⟨annual *amount* of
rainfall⟩ ⟨a substantial *amount* of money⟩.
The use of *amount* with count nouns has
been frequently criticized; it usually occurs
when the number of things is thought of as a
mass or collection ⟨glad to furnish any
*amount* of black pebbles —*New Yorker*⟩ ⟨a
substantial *amount* of film offers —Lily Tom-
lin⟩ or when money is involved ⟨a substantial
*amount* of loans —E. R. Black⟩.

◇ **WORD HISTORY**
**amok**   From the earliest Portuguese contacts with Southeast Asia in the sixteenth
century, travelers have reported on a psychiatric disorder peculiar to the region that afflicts only men and is known in Malay as
*amok*. In its typical modern manifestation, a
man affected by amok first goes through a
period of brooding and then explodes into
homicidal frenzy, seizing a parang (a short
sword) and cutting down everyone in his
path, whether relative, friend, or stranger. If
the man is not first killed by efforts to stop
him, he eventually collapses in exhaustion,
with no recollection of the episode. The
phrase *run amuck* (translating the Malay verb
*mengamok*) was being used in English to
describe any undisciplined behavior by the
late 17th century, and it occurs in the poetry
of Alexander Pope ("Satire's my weapon, but
I'm too discreet/To run a muck, and tilt at all I
meet"). Most English speakers are probably
no longer aware of the literal violence that
the Malay word describes.

ible to ADP and ATP in metabolic reactions — called also *adenosine monophosphate, adenylic acid;* compare CYCLIC AMP

**am·per·age** \'am-p(ə-)rij, -ˌpir-ij\ *noun* (1893) : the strength of a current of electricity expressed in amperes

**am·pere** \'am-ˌpir *also* -ˌper\ *noun* [André-Marie *Ampère*] (1881)
**1** : the practical meter-kilogram-second unit of electric current that is equivalent to a flow of one coulomb per second or to the steady current produced by one volt applied across a resistance of one ohm
**2** : the base unit of electric current in the International System of Units that is equal to a constant current which when maintained in two straight parallel conductors of infinite length and negligible circular sections one meter apart in a vacuum produces between the conductors a force equal to $2 \times 10^{-7}$ newton per meter of length ◆

**ampere–hour** *noun* (1885) : a unit quantity of electricity equal to the quantity carried past any point of a circuit in one hour by a steady current of one ampere

**ampere–turn** *noun* (1884) : the meter-kilogram-second unit of magnetomotive force equal to the magnetomotive force around a path that links with one turn of wire carrying an electric current of one ampere

**am·per·o·met·ric** \ˌam-pir-ə-'me-trik\ *adjective* [*ampere* + *-o-* + *-metric*] (1940) : relating to or being a chemical titration in which the measurement of the electric current flowing under an applied potential difference between two electrodes in a solution is used for detecting the end point

**am·per·sand** \'am-pər-ˌsand\ *noun* [alteration of *and* (&) *per se and*, literally, (the character) & by itself (is the word) *and*] (1835) : a character typically & standing for the word *and* ◆

**am·phet·amine** \am-'fe-tə-ˌmēn, -mən\ *noun* [International Scientific Vocabulary *alpha* + *methyl* + *phen-* + *ethyl* + *amine*] (1938) : a racemic compound $C_9H_{13}N$ or one of its derivatives (as dextroamphetamine or methamphetamine) frequently abused as a stimulant of the central nervous system but used clinically especially as the sulfate or hydrochloride salt to treat hyperactive children and the symptoms of narcolepsy and as a short-term appetite suppressant in dieting

**amphi-** *or* **amph-** *prefix* [Latin *amphi-* around, on both sides, from Greek *amphi-, amph-*, from *amphi* — more at AMBI-] : on both sides *or* of both kinds : both ⟨*amphi*-brach⟩ ⟨*amphi*diploid⟩

**am·phib·ia** \am-'fi-bē-ə\ *noun plural* (1607) : AMPHIBIANS

**am·phib·i·an** \-bē-ən\ *noun* [ultimately from Greek *amphibion* amphibious being, from neuter of *amphibios*] (1835)
**1** : an amphibious organism; *especially* : any of a class (Amphibia) of cold-blooded vertebrates (as frogs, toads, or salamanders) intermediate in many characters between fishes and reptiles and having gilled aquatic larvae and air-breathing adults
**2** : an airplane designed to take off from and land on either land or water
— **amphibian** *adjective*

**am·phib·i·ous** \am-'fi-bē-əs\ *adjective* [Greek *amphibios*, literally, living a double life, from *amphi-* + *bios* mode of life — more at QUICK] (1643)
**1** : combining two characteristics
**2 a** : relating to or adapted for both land and water ⟨*amphibious* vehicles⟩ **b** : executed by coordinated action of land, sea, and air forces organized for invasion; *also* : trained or organized for such action ⟨*amphibious* forces⟩
**3** : able to live both on land and in water ⟨*amphibious* plants⟩
— **am·phib·i·ous·ly** *adverb*
— **am·phib·i·ous·ness** *noun*

**am·phi·bole** \'am(p)-fə-ˌbōl\ *noun* [French, from Late Latin *amphibolus*, from Greek *amphibolos* ambiguous, from *amphiballein* to throw round, doubt, from *amphi-* + *ballein* to throw — more at DEVIL] (circa 1823)
**1** : HORNBLENDE
**2** : any of a group of complex silicate minerals with like crystal structures that contain calcium, sodium, magnesium, aluminum, and iron ions or a combination of them

**am·phib·o·lite** \am-'fi-bə-ˌlīt\ *noun* (1833) : a usually metamorphic rock consisting essentially of amphibole

**am·phi·bol·o·gy** \ˌam(p)-fə-'bä-lə-jē\ *noun, plural* **-gies** [Middle English *amphibologie*, from Late Latin *amphibologia*, alteration of Latin *amphibolia*, from Greek, from *amphibolos*] (14th century) : a sentence or phrase (as "nothing is good enough for you") susceptible of more than one interpretation

**am·phib·o·ly** \am-'fi-bə-lē\ *noun, plural* **-lies** [Late Latin *amphibolia*] (circa 1588) : AMPHIBOLOGY

**am·phi·brach** \'am(p)-fə-ˌbrak\ *noun* [Latin *amphibrachys*, from Greek, literally, short at both ends, from *amphi-* + *brachys* short — more at BRIEF] (1589) : a metrical foot consisting of a long syllable between two short syllables in quantitative verse or of a stressed syllable between two unstressed syllables in accentual verse ⟨*romantic* is an accentual *amphibrach*⟩
— **am·phi·brach·ic** \ˌam(p)-fə-'bra-kik\ *adjective*

**am·phic·ty·o·ny** \am-'fik-tē-ə-nē\ *noun, plural* **-nies** [Greek *amphiktyonia*] (1835) : an association of neighboring states in ancient Greece to defend a common religious center; *broadly* : an association of neighboring states for their common interest
— **am·phic·ty·on·ic** \(ˌ)am-ˌfik-tē-'ä-nik\ *adjective*

**am·phi·dip·loid** \ˌam(p)-fi-'di-ˌplȯid\ *noun* (1930) : an interspecific hybrid having a complete diploid chromosome set from each parent form — called also *allotetraploid*
— **amphidiploid** *adjective*
— **am·phi·dip·loi·dy** \-ˌplȯi-dē\ *noun*

**am·phim·a·cer** \am-'fi-mə-sər\ *noun* [Latin *amphimacrus*, from Greek *amphimakros*, literally, long at both ends, from *amphi-* + *makros* long — more at MEAGER] (1589) : a metrical foot consisting of a short syllable between two long syllables in quantitative verse or of an unstressed syllable between two stressed syllables in accentual verse ⟨*twenty-two* is an accentual *amphimacer*⟩

**am·phi·mix·is** \ˌam(p)-fi-'mik-səs\ *noun, plural* **-mix·es** \-ˌsēz\ [New Latin, from *amphi-* + Greek *mixis* mingling, from *mignynai* to mix — more at MIX] (1893) : the union of gametes in sexual reproduction

**Am·phi·on** \am-'fi-ən\ *noun* [Latin, from Greek *Amphiōn*] : a musician of Greek mythology who builds the walls of Thebes by charming the stones into place with his lyre

**am·phi·ox·us** \ˌam(p)-fē-'äk-səs\ *noun, plural* **-oxi** \-ˌsī\ *or* **-ox·us·es** [New Latin, from *amphi-* + Greek *oxys* sharp] (1847) : any of a genus (Branchiostoma) of lancelets; *broadly* : LANCELET

**am·phi·path·ic** \ˌam(p)-fə-'pa-thik\ *adjective* [*amphi-* + *-pathic* (as in *empathic*)] (1945) : AMPHIPHILIC

**am·phi·phil·ic** \-'fi-lik\ *adjective* (1950) : of, relating to, or being a compound (as a surfactant) consisting of molecules having a polar water-soluble group attached to a water-insoluble hydrocarbon chain; *also* : being a molecule of such a compound
— **am·phi·phile** \'am(p)-fə-ˌfīl\ *noun*

**am·phi·ploid** \'am(p)-fi-ˌplȯid\ *adjective* (1945)

*of an interspecific hybrid* : having at least one complete diploid set of chromosomes derived from each parent species
— **amphiploid** *noun*
— **am·phi·ploi·dy** \-ˌplȯi-dē\ *noun*

**am·phi·pod** \-ˌpäd\ *noun* [ultimately from Greek *amphi-* + *pod-, pous* foot — more at FOOT] (1835) : any of a large order (Amphipoda) of small crustaceans (as the beach flea) with a laterally compressed body
— **amphipod** *adjective*

**am·phi·pro·style** \ˌam(p)-fi-'prō-ˌstīl\ *adjective* [Latin *amphiprostylos*, from Greek, from *amphi-* + *prostylos* having pillars in front, from *pro-* + *stylos* pillar — more at STEER] (1850) : having columns at each end only ⟨an *amphiprostyle* building⟩
— **amphiprostyle** *noun*

**am·phis·bae·na** \ˌam(p)-fəs-'bē-nə\ *noun* [Latin, from Greek *amphisbaina*, from *amphis* on both sides (from *amphi* around) + *bainein* to walk, go — more at BY, COME] (14th century) : a serpent in classical mythology having a head at each end and capable of moving in either direction
— **am·phis·bae·nic** \-nik\ *adjective*

**am·phi·the·ater** \'am(p)-fə-ˌthē-ə-tər *also* 'am-pə-ˌthē-\ *noun* [Latin *amphitheatrum*, from Greek *amphitheatron*, from *amphi-* + *theatron* theater] (14th century)
**1** : an oval or circular building with rising tiers of seats ranged about an open space and used in ancient Rome especially for contests and spectacles
**2 a** : a very large auditorium **b** : a room with a gallery from which doctors and students may observe surgical operations **c** : a rising gallery in a modern theater **d** : a flat or gently sloping area surrounded by abrupt slopes
**3** : a place of public games or contests
— **am·phi·the·at·ric** \ˌam(p)-fə-thē-'a-trik *also* ˌam-pə-thē-\ *or* **am·phi·the·at·ri·cal** \-tri-kəl\ *adjective*
— **am·phi·the·at·ri·cal·ly** \-tri-k(ə-)lē\ *adverb*

◇ WORD HISTORY

**ampere** The *ampere* was named in honor of the French physicist André-Marie Ampère (1775–1836). Ampère is credited with founding, naming, and developing the science of electrodynamics. He was the formulator of two laws in electromagnetism relating magnetic fields to electric currents. The first person to develop techniques for measuring electricity, he invented an instrument that was a forerunner of the galvanometer. In 1881 an international congress on electricity adopted *ampere* as a term for the standard unit of electric current.

**ampersand** For pupils studying Latin in the grammar schools of late medieval and Tudor England, the traditional practice was to spell words by syllables. When a single letter formed a whole word (like *I*) or a complete syllable (like the first *i-* in *iris*), it was followed by the words *per se*, which in Latin means "by itself." Thus in the schoolroom *I* became *I per se, I.* Because the character &, a symbol for *and*, was placed after *z* in primers and treated like any other letter of the alphabet, it too was spelled out orally as "and per se, and." Frequent use of the phrase and diminishing recognition of its literal meaning shrank it to *ampersand* by the 19th century. The character & is a development of &, a ligature of *et*, the Latin word for "and."

**Am·phit·ry·on** \am-'fi-trē-ən\ *noun* [Greek *Amphitryōn*]
: the husband of Alcmene

**am·pho·ra** \'am(p)-fə-rə\ *noun, plural* **-rae** \-,rē, -,rī\ *or* **-ras** [Latin, modification of Greek *amphoreus, amphiphoreus,* from *amphi-* + *phoreus* bearer, from *pherein* to bear — more at BEAR] (14th century)
**1** : an ancient Greek jar or vase with a large oval body, narrow cylindrical neck, and two handles that rise almost to the level of the mouth
**2** : a 2-handled vessel shaped like an amphora

**amphora 1**

**am·pho·ter·ic** \,am(p)-fə-'ter-ik\ *adjective* [International Scientific Vocabulary, from Greek *amphoteros* each of two, from *amphō* both — more at AMBI-] (circa 1849)
: partly one and partly the other; *specifically* : capable of reacting chemically either as an acid or as a base

**am·pho·ter·i·cin B** \,am(p)-fə-'ter-ə-sən-'bē\ *noun* [*amphoteric* + -¹*in*] (1955)
: an antifungal antibiotic obtained from a soil actinomycete (*Streptomyces nodosus*) and used especially to treat systemic fungal infections

**am·pi·cil·lin** \,am-pə-'si-lən\ *noun* [*amino* + *penicillin*] (1961)
: a penicillin $C_{16}H_{19}N_3O_4S$ that is effective against gram-negative and gram-positive bacteria and is used to treat various infections of the urinary, respiratory, and intestinal tracts

**am·ple** \'am-pəl\ *adjective* **am·pler** \-p(ə-)lər\; **am·plest** \-p(ə-)ləst\ [Middle French, from Latin *amplus*] (15th century)
**1** : generous or more than adequate in size, scope, or capacity ⟨there was room for an *ample* garden⟩
**2** : generously sufficient to satisfy a requirement or need ⟨they had *ample* money for the trip⟩
**3** : BUXOM, PORTLY ⟨an *ample* figure⟩
**synonym** *see* SPACIOUS, PLENTIFUL
— **am·ple·ness** \-pəl-nəs\ *noun*
— **am·ply** \-plē\ *adverb*

**am·plex·us** \am-'plek-səs\ *noun* [New Latin, from Latin, embrace, from *amplecti* to embrace, from *am-, amb-* around + *plectere* to braid — more at AMBI-, PLY] (circa 1927)
: the mating embrace of a frog or toad during which eggs are shed into the water and there fertilized

**am·pli·dyne** \'am-plə-,dīn\ *noun* [*amplifier* + Greek *dynamis* power — more at DYNAMIC] (1940)
: a direct-current generator that precisely controls a large power output whenever a small power input is varied in the field winding of the generator

**am·pli·fi·ca·tion** \,am-plə-fə-'kā-shən\ *noun* (1546)
**1 a** : an act, example, or product of amplifying **b** : a usually massive replication especially of a gene or DNA sequence (as in a polymerase chain reaction)
**2 a** : the particulars by which a statement is expanded **b** : an expanded statement

**am·pli·fi·er** \'am-plə-,fī(-ə)r\ *noun* (1542)
: one that amplifies; *specifically* : an electronic device (as in a stereo system) for amplifying voltage, current, or power

**am·pli·fy** \-,fī\ *verb* **-fied; -fy·ing** [Middle English *amplifien,* from Middle French *amplifier,* from Latin *amplificare,* from *amplus*] (15th century)
*transitive verb*
**1** : to expand (as a statement) by the use of detail or illustration or by closer analysis
**2 a** : to make larger or greater (as in amount,

importance, or intensity) : INCREASE **b** : to increase the strength or amount of; *especially* : to make louder **c** : to cause (a gene or DNA sequence) to undergo amplification
*intransitive verb*
: to expand one's remarks or ideas
**synonym** *see* EXPAND

**am·pli·tude** \-,tüd, -,tyüd\ *noun* (1542)
**1** : the quality or state of being ample : FULLNESS
**2** : the extent or range of a quality, property, process, or phenomenon: as **a** : the extent of a vibratory movement (as of a pendulum) measured from the mean position to an extreme **b** : the maximum departure of the value of an alternating current or wave from the average value
**3** : ARGUMENT 6b

**amplitude modulation** *noun* (1921)
: modulation of the amplitude of a radio carrier wave in accordance with the strength of the audio or other signal; *also* : a broadcasting system using such modulation — compare FREQUENCY MODULATION

**am·poule** *or* **am·pule** *also* **am·pul** \'am-,pyü(ə)l, -pül\ *noun* [Middle English *ampulle* flask, from Old English & Old French; Old English *ampulle* & Old French *ampoule,* from Latin *ampulla*] (1886)
**1** : a hermetically sealed small bulbous glass vessel that is used to hold a solution for hypodermic injection
**2** : a vial resembling an ampoule

**am·pul·la** \am-'pù-lə, 'am-,pyü-lə\ *noun, plural* **-lae** \-(,)lē, -,lī\ [Middle English, from Latin, from Latin, diminutive of *amphora*] (before 12th century)
**1** : a glass or earthenware flask with a globular body and two handles used especially by the ancient Romans to hold ointment, perfume, or wine
**2** : a saccular anatomic swelling or pouch
— **am·pul·la·ry** \am-'pù-lər-ē, 'am-pyə-,ler-ē\ *adjective*

**am·pu·tate** \'am-pyə-,tāt\ *transitive verb* **-tat·ed; -tat·ing** [Latin *amputatus,* past participle of *amputare,* from *am-, amb-* around + *putare* to cut, prune — more at AMBI-] (1638)
: to remove by or as if by cutting; *especially* : to cut (as a limb) from the body
— **am·pu·ta·tion** \,am-pyə-'tā-shən\ *noun*

**am·pu·tee** \,am-pyə-'tē\ *noun* (1910)
: one that has had a limb amputated

**am·trac** *or* **am·track** \'am-,trak\ *noun* [*amphibious* + *tractor*] (1944)
: a flat-bottomed military vehicle that moves on tracks on land or water

**amuck** \ə-'mək\ *variant of* AMOK

**am·u·let** \'am-yə-lət\ *noun* [Latin *amuletum*] (1584)
: a charm (as an ornament) often inscribed with a magic incantation or symbol to protect the wearer against evil (as disease or witchcraft) or to aid him

**amuse** \ə-'myüz\ *verb* **amused; amus·ing** [Middle French *amuser,* from Old French, from *a-* (from Latin *ad-*) + *muser* to muse] (15th century)
*transitive verb*
**1 a** *archaic* : to divert the attention of so as to deceive **b** *obsolete* : to occupy the attention of : ABSORB **c** *obsolete* : DISTRACT, BEWILDER
**2 a** : to entertain or occupy in a light, playful, or pleasant manner ⟨*amuse* the child with a story⟩ **b** : to appeal to the sense of humor of ⟨the joke doesn't *amuse* me⟩
*intransitive verb*
*obsolete* : MUSE ☆
— **amus·ed·ly** \-'myü-zəd-lē\ *adverb*
— **amus·er** *noun*
— **amus·ive** \ə-'myü-zəv, -səv\ *adjective*

**amuse·ment** \ə-'myüz-mənt\ *noun* (1603)
**1** : a means of amusing or entertaining ⟨what are her favorite *amusements*⟩
**2** : the condition of being amused ⟨his *amusement* knew no bounds⟩

**3** : pleasurable diversion : ENTERTAINMENT ⟨plays the piano for *amusement*⟩

**amusement park** *noun* (1909)
: a commercially operated park having various devices for entertainment (as a merry-go-round and roller coaster) and usually booths for the sale of food and drink

**amus·ing** \ə-'myü-zin\ *adjective* (1712)
: giving amusement : DIVERTING
— **amus·ing·ly** \-zin-lē\ *adverb*
— **amus·ing·ness** *noun*

**amyg·da·la** \ə-'mig-də-lə\ *noun, plural* **-lae** \-,lē, -,lī\ [New Latin, from Latin, almond, from Greek *amygdalē*] (circa 1860)
: the one of the four basal ganglia in each cerebral hemisphere that is part of the limbic system and consists of an almond-shaped mass of gray matter in the anterior extremity of the temporal lobe — called also *amygdaloid nucleus*

**amyg·da·lin** \-lən\ *noun* [Latin *amygdala*] (1651)
: a white crystalline cyanogenetic glucoside $C_{20}H_{27}NO_{11}$ found especially in the seeds of the apricot, peach, and bitter almond

**amyg·da·loid** \-,lòid\ *adjective* [Greek *amygdaloeidēs,* from *amygdalē*] (1836)
**1** : almond-shaped
**2** : of, relating to, or affecting an amygdala

**amyg·da·loi·dal** \ə-,mig-də-'lòi-d°l\ *adjective* (1813)
: of, being, or containing small cavities in igneous rock that are filled with deposits of different minerals (as chalcedony or calcite)
— **amyg·da·loid** \ə-'mig-də-,lòid\ *noun*

**am·yl** \'a-məl\ *noun* [Latin *amylum* + English -*yl*] (1850)
: a univalent hydrocarbon radical $C_5H_{11}$ — that occurs in various isomeric forms and is derived from pentane

**amyl-** *or* **amylo-** *combining form* [Latin *amylum,* from Greek *amylon,* from neuter of *amylos* unmilled (of grain), from *a-* + *mylē* mill — more at MEAL]
: starch ⟨*amyl*oplast⟩

**amyl acetate** *noun* (circa 1881)
: BANANA OIL

**amyl alcohol** *noun* (1863)
: any of eight isomeric alcohols $C_5H_{12}O$ used especially as solvents and in making esters; *also* : a commercially produced mixture of amyl alcohols used especially as a solvent

**am·y·lase** \'a-mə-,lās, -,lāz\ *noun* (1893)
: any of a group of enzymes (as amylopsin) that catalyze the hydrolysis of starch and glycogen or their intermediate hydrolysis products

**amyl nitrite** *noun* (circa 1881)
: a pale yellow pungent flammable liquid ester $C_5H_{11}NO_2$ of commercial amyl alcohol and nitrous acid — compare POPPER 2

**am·y·loid** \-,lòid\ *noun* (1872)
: a waxy translucent substance consisting of protein in combination with polysaccharides

---

☆ **SYNONYMS**
**Amuse, divert, entertain** mean to pass or cause to pass the time pleasantly. AMUSE suggests that one's attention is engaged lightly or frivolously ⟨*amuse* yourselves while I prepare dinner⟩. DIVERT implies the distracting of the attention from worry or routine occupation especially by something funny ⟨a light comedy to *divert* the tired businessman⟩. ENTERTAIN suggests supplying amusement or diversion by specially prepared or contrived methods ⟨a magician *entertaining* children at a party⟩.

---

\ə\ **abut** \°\ **kitten** \ər\ **further** \a\ **ash** \ā\ **ace**
\ä\ **mop, mar** \aù\ **out** \ch\ **chin** \e\ **bet** \ē\ **easy**
\g\ **go** \i\ **hit** \ī\ **ice** \j\ **job** \ŋ\ **sing** \ō\ **go**
\ò\ **law** \òi\ **boy** \th\ **thin** \th\ **the** \ü\ **loot** \ù\ **foot**
\y\ **yet** \zh\ **vision**    *see also* Guide to Pronunciation

that is deposited in some animal organs and tissues under abnormal conditions (as Alzheimer's disease)
— **amyloid** *adjective*

**am·y·loid·osis** \,a-mə-,lȯi-'dō-səs\ *noun* [New Latin] (circa 1900)
: a disorder characterized by the deposition of amyloid in bodily organs and tissues

**am·y·lo·lyt·ic** \,a-mə-lō-'li-tik\ *adjective* [New Latin *amylolysis,* from *amyl-* + *-lysis*] (1876)
: characterized by or capable of the enzymatic splitting of starch into soluble products ⟨*amylolytic* enzymes⟩ ⟨*amylolytic* activity⟩

**am·y·lo·pec·tin** \,a-mə-lō-'pek-tən\ *noun* (1905)
: a component of starch that has a high molecular weight and branched structure and does not tend to gel in aqueous solutions

**am·y·lo·plast** \'a-mə-(,)lō-,plast\ *noun* (1886)
: a colorless plastid that forms and stores starch

**am·y·lop·sin** \,a-mə-'läp-sən\ *noun* [*amyl-* + *-psin* (as in *trypsin*)] (circa 1881)
: the amylase of the pancreatic juice

**am·y·lose** \'a-mə-,lōs, -,lōz\ *noun* (1877)
: a component of starch characterized by its straight chains of glucose units

**amyo·to·nia** \,ā-,mī-ə-'tō-nē-ə\ *noun* [New Latin] (circa 1919)
: deficiency of muscle tone

**amyo·tro·phic lateral sclerosis** \,ā-,mī-ə-'trō-fik-, -'trä-\ *noun* [²*a-* + *my-* + *-trophic*] (circa 1889)
: a rare progressive degenerative fatal disease affecting the spinal cord, usually beginning in middle age, and characterized especially by increasing and spreading muscular weakness — called also *Lou Gehrig's disease*

**Am·y·tal** \'a-mə-,tȯl\ *trademark*
— used for amobarbital

¹**an** \ən, (')an\ *indefinite article* [Middle English, from Old English *ān* one — more at ONE] (before 12th century)
: ²A
*usage* see ²A

²**an** \ən, an\ *preposition* (before 12th century)
: ³A 2
*usage* see ²A

³**an** *or* **an'** *conjunction* (12th century)
**1** \*see* AND\ : AND
**2** \'an\ *archaic* : IF

**an-** — see ²A-

¹**-an** *or* **-ian** *also* **-ean** *noun suffix* [*-an* & *-ian* from Middle English *-an,* from Old French & Latin; Old French *-ien,* from Latin *-ianus,* from *-i-* + *-anus,* from *-anus,* adjective suffix; *-ean* from such words as *Mediterranean, European*]
**1** : one that is of or relating to ⟨American⟩ ⟨Boston*ian*⟩
**2** : one skilled in or specializing in ⟨phoneti*cian*⟩

²**-an** *or* **-ian** *also* **-ean** *adjective suffix*
**1** : of or belonging to ⟨American⟩ ⟨Florid*ian*⟩
**2** : characteristic of : resembling ⟨Mozart*ean*⟩

³**-an** *noun suffix* [International Scientific Vocabulary *-an, -ane,* alteration of *-ene, -ine,* & *-one*]
**1** : unsaturated organic compound ⟨fur*an*⟩
**2** : anhydride of a carbohydrate ⟨dextr*an*⟩

¹**ana** \'a-nə\ *adverb* [Middle English, from Medieval Latin, from Greek, at the rate of, literally, up] (14th century)
: of each an equal quantity — used in prescriptions

²**ana** \'a-nə, 'ä-, 'ā-\ *noun, plural* **ana** *or* **anas** [*-ana*] (circa 1751)
**1** : a collection of the memorable sayings of a person
**2** : a collection of anecdotes or interesting information about a person or a place

**ana-** *or* **an-** *prefix* [Latin, from Greek, up, back, again, from *ana* up — more at ON]
**1** : up : upward ⟨*ana*bolism⟩
**2** : back : backward ⟨*ana*tropous⟩

**-ana** *or* **-iana** *noun plural suffix* [New Latin, from Latin, neuter plural of *-anus -an* & *-ianus -ian*]
: collected items of information especially anecdotal or bibliographical concerning ⟨Ameri*cana*⟩

**ana·bap·tism** \,a-nə-'bap-,ti-zəm\ *noun* [New Latin *anabaptismus,* from Late Greek *anabaptismos* rebaptism, from *anabaptizein* to rebaptize, from Greek *ana-* again + *baptizein* to baptize] (1577)
**1** *capitalized* **a** : the doctrine or practices of the Anabaptists **b** : the Anabaptist movement
**2** : the baptism of one previously baptized

**Ana·bap·tist** \-'bap-tist\ *noun* (1532)
: a Protestant sectarian of a radical movement arising in the 16th century and advocating the baptism and church membership of adult believers only, nonresistance, and the separation of church and state
— **Anabaptist** *adjective*

**anab·a·sis** \ə-'na-bə-səs\ *noun, plural* **-a·ses** \-,sēz\ [Greek, inland march, from *anabainein* to go up or inland, from *ana-* + *bainein* to go — more at COME] (circa 1706)
**1** : a going or marching up : ADVANCE; *especially* : a military advance
**2** [from the retreat of Greek mercenaries in Asia Minor described in the *Anabasis* of Xenophon] : a difficult and dangerous military retreat

**an·a·bat·ic** \,a-nə-'ba-tik\ *adjective* [Greek *anabatos,* verbal of *anabainein*] (1853)
: moving upward : RISING ⟨an *anabatic* wind⟩

**anabolic steroid** *noun* (1961)
: any of a group of usually synthetic hormones that increase constructive metabolism and are sometimes abused by athletes in training to increase temporarily the size of their muscles

**anab·o·lism** \ə-'na-bə-,li-zəm\ *noun* [International Scientific Vocabulary *ana-* + metab*olism*] (1886)
: the constructive part of metabolism concerned especially with macromolecular synthesis — compare CATABOLISM
— **an·a·bol·ic** \,a-nə-'bä-lik\ *adjective*

**anach·ro·nism** \ə-'na-krə-,ni-zəm\ *noun* [probably from Middle Greek *anachronismos,* from *anachronizesthai* to be an anachronism, from Late Greek *anachronizein* to be late, from Greek *ana-* + *chronos* time] (circa 1646)
**1** : an error in chronology; *especially* : a chronological misplacing of persons, events, objects, or customs in regard to each other
**2** : a person or a thing that is chronologically out of place; *especially* : one from a former age that is incongruous in the present
— **anach·ro·nis·tic** \ə-,na-krə-'nis-tik\ *also* **ana·chron·ic** \,a-nə-'krä-nik\ *adjective*
— **anach·ro·nis·ti·cal·ly** \ə-,na-krə-'nis-ti-k(ə-)lē\ *adverb*
— **anach·ro·nous** \ə-'na-krə-nəs\ *adjective*
— **anach·ro·nous·ly** *adverb*

**an·a·clit·ic** \,a-nə-'kli-tik\ *adjective* [Greek *anaklitos,* verbal of *anaklinein* to lean upon, from *ana-* + *klinein* to lean — more at LEAN] (1922)
: of, relating to, or characterized by the direction of love toward an object (as the mother) that satisfies nonsexual needs (as hunger)

**an·a·co·lu·thon** \,a-nə-kə-'lü-,thän\ *noun, plural* **-tha** \-thə\ *also* **-thons** [Late Latin, from Late Greek *anakolouthon* inconsistency in logic, from Greek, neuter of *anakolouthos* inconsistent, from *an-* + *akolouthos* following, from *ha-, a-* together + *keleuthos* path] (circa 1706)
: syntactical inconsistency or incoherence within a sentence; *especially* : a shift in an unfinished sentence from one syntactic construction to another (as in "you really ought—well, do it your own way")
— **an·a·co·lu·thic** \-'thik\ *adjective*
— **an·a·co·lu·thi·cal·ly** \-thi-k(ə-)lē\ *adverb*

**an·a·con·da** \,a-nə-'kän-də\ *noun* [probably modification of Sinhalese *henakandayā,* a slender green snake] (1768)
: a large semiaquatic constricting snake (*Eunectes murinus*) of the boa family of tropical South America that may reach a length of 30 feet (9.1 meters); *broadly* : any of the large constricting snakes

**anac·re·on·tic** \ə-,na-krē-'än-tik\ *noun* (1656)
: a poem in the manner of Anacreon; *especially* : a drinking song or light lyric
◆

anaconda

**Anacreontic** *adjective* [Latin *anacreonticus,* from *Anacreont-, Anacreon* Anacreon, from Greek *Anakreont-, Anakreōn*] (1611)
**1** : of, relating to, or resembling the poetry of Anacreon
**2** : convivial or amatory in tone or theme

**an·a·cru·sis** \,a-nə-'krü-səs\ *noun, plural* **-cru·ses** \-,sēz\ [New Latin, from Greek *anakrousis* beginning of a song, from *anakrouein* to begin a song, from *ana-* + *krouein* to strike, beat; akin to Lithuanian *kraušyti* to strike] (1830)
**1** : one or more syllables at the beginning of a line of poetry that are regarded as preliminary to and not a part of the metrical pattern
**2** : UPBEAT; *specifically* : one or more notes or tones preceding the first downbeat of a musical phrase

**an·a·dama bread** \,a-nə-'da-mə-\ *noun* [origin unknown] (1954)
: a leavened bread made with flour, cornmeal, and molasses

**an·a·dem** \'a-nə-,dem\ *noun* [Latin *anadema,* from Greek *anadēma,* from *anadein* to wreathe, from *ana-* + *dein* to bind — more at DIADEM] (1604)
*archaic* : a wreath for the head : GARLAND

**ana·di·plo·sis** \,a-nə-də-'plō-səs, ,a-nə-(,)dī-'plō-\ *noun, plural* **-plo·ses** \-,sēz\ [Late Latin, from Greek *anadiplōsis,* literally, repetition, from *anadiploun* to double, from *ana-* + *diploun* to double — more at DIPLOMA] (circa 1550)
: repetition of a prominent and usually the last word in one phrase or clause at the beginning of the next (as in "rely on his honor—honor such as his?")

**anad·ro·mous** \ə-'na-drə-məs\ *adjective* [Greek *anadromos* running upward, from

*anadramein* to run upward, from *ana-* + *dramein* to run — more at DROMEDARY] (circa 1753)
**:** ascending rivers from the sea for breeding (shad are *anadromous*) — compare CATADROMOUS

**anae·mia, anae·mic** *chiefly British variant of* ANEMIA, ANEMIC

**an·aer·obe** \'a-nə-ˌrōb; (ˌ)an-'a(-ə)r-ˌōb, -'e(-ə)r-\ *noun* [International Scientific Vocabulary] (1884)
**:** an anaerobic organism

**an·aer·o·bic** \ˌa-nə-'rō-bik; ˌan-ˌa(-ə)-, -ˌe(-ə)-\ *adjective* (circa 1881)
**1 a :** living, active, occurring, or existing in the absence of free oxygen 〈*anaerobic* respiration〉 **b :** of, relating to, or being activity in which the body incurs an oxygen debt 〈*anaerobic* exercise〉
**2 :** relating to or induced by anaerobes
— **an·aer·o·bi·cal·ly** \-bi-k(ə-)lē\ *adverb*

**an·aer·o·bi·o·sis** \ˌa-nə-rō-(ˌ)bī-'ō-səs, -bē-; ˌan-ˌa(-ə)-, -ˌe(-ə)-\ *noun, plural* **-o·ses** \-'ō-ˌsēz\ [New Latin] (circa 1889)
**:** life in the absence of air or free oxygen

**an·aes·the·sia, an·aes·thet·ic** *chiefly British variant of* ANESTHESIA, ANESTHETIC

**ana·gen·e·sis** \ˌa-nə-'je-nə-səs\ *noun* [New Latin] (1889)
**:** evolutionary change producing a single lineage in which one taxon replaces another without branching — compare CLADOGENESIS

**ana·glyph** \'a-nə-ˌglif\ *noun* [Late Latin *anaglyphus* embossed, from Greek *anaglyphos*, from *anaglyphein* to emboss, from *ana-* + *glyphein* to carve — more at CLEAVE] (1651)
**1 :** a sculptured, chased, or embossed ornament worked in low relief
**2 :** a stereoscopic motion or still picture in which the right component of a composite image usually red in color is superposed on the left component in a contrasting color to produce a three-dimensional effect when viewed through correspondingly colored filters in the form of spectacles
— **ana·glyph·ic** \ˌa-nə-'gli-fik\ *adjective*

**an·ag·no·ri·sis** \ˌa-ˌnag-'nòr-ə-səs\ *noun, plural* **-ri·ses** \-ˌsēz\ [Greek *anagnōrisis*, from *anagnōrizein* to recognize, from *ana-* + *gnōrizein* to make known; akin to Greek *gnōrimos* well-known, *gignōskein* to come to know — more at KNOW] (circa 1800)
**:** the point in the plot especially of a tragedy at which the protagonist recognizes his or her or some other character's true identity or discovers the true nature of his or her own situation

**an·a·go·ge** *or* **an·a·go·gy** \'a-nə-ˌgō-jē\ *noun, plural* **-ges** *or* **-gies** [Late Latin *anagoge*, from Late Greek *anagōgē*, from Greek, reference, from *anagein* to refer, from *ana-* + *agein* to lead — more at AGENT] (15th century)
**:** interpretation of a word, passage, or text (as of Scripture or poetry) that finds beyond the literal, allegorical, and moral senses a fourth and ultimate spiritual or mystical sense
— **an·a·gog·ic** \ˌa-nə-'gä-jik\ *or* **an·a·gog·i·cal** \-ji-kəl\ *adjective*
— **an·a·gog·i·cal·ly** \-ji-k(ə-)lē\ *adverb*

**¹an·a·gram** \'a-nə-ˌgram\ *noun* [probably from Middle French *anagramme*, from New Latin *anagrammat-, anagramma*, modification of Greek *anagrammatismos*, from *anagrammatizein* to transpose letters, from *ana-* + *grammat-, gramma* letter — more at GRAM] (1589)
**1 :** a word or phrase made by transposing the letters of another word or phrase
**2** *plural but singular in construction* **:** a game in which words are formed by rearranging the letters of other words or by arranging letters taken (as from a stock of cards or blocks) at random
— **an·a·gram·mat·ic** \ˌa-nə-grə-'ma-tik\ *also* **an·a·gram·mat·i·cal** \-ti-kəl\ *adjective*

— **an·a·gram·mat·i·cal·ly** \-ti-k(ə-)lē\ *adverb*

**²anagram** *transitive verb* **-grammed; -gram·ming** (1630)
**1 :** ANAGRAMMATIZE
**2 :** to rearrange (the letters of a text) in order to discover a hidden message

**an·a·gram·ma·tize** \ˌa-nə-'gra-mə-ˌtīz\ *transitive verb* **-tized; -tiz·ing** (1588)
**:** to transpose (as letters in a word) so as to form an anagram
— **an·a·gram·ma·ti·za·tion** \-ˌgra-mə-tə-'zā-shən\ *noun*

**anal** \'ā-nᵊl\ *adjective* (1769)
**1 :** of, relating to, or situated near the anus 〈*anal* fin〉
**2 a :** of, relating to, characterized by, or being the stage of psychosexual development in psychoanalytic theory during which the child is concerned especially with its feces **b :** of, relating to, characterized by, or being personality traits (as parsimony, meticulousness, and ill humor) considered typical of fixation at the anal stage of development 〈*anal* disposition〉 〈*anal* neatness〉
— **anal·ly** \-nᵊl-ē\ *adverb*

**anal·cime** \ə-'nal-ˌsēm\ *noun* [French, from Greek *analkimos* weak, from *an-* + *alkimos* strong, from *alkē* strength] (1803)
**:** a white or slightly colored mineral that consists of hydrated silicate of sodium and aluminum and occurs in various igneous rocks in massive form or in crystals

**anal·cite** \ə-'nal-ˌsīt\ *noun* (1868)
**:** ANALCIME

**an·a·lects** \'a-nᵊl-ˌek(t)s\ *also* **an·a·lec·ta** \ˌa-nᵊl-'ek-tə\ *noun plural* [New Latin *analecta*, from Greek *analekta*, neuter plural of *analektos*, verbal of *analegein* to collect, from *ana-* + *legein* to gather — more at LEGEND] (1652)
**:** selected miscellaneous written passages

**an·a·lem·ma** \ˌa-nə-'le-mə\ *noun* [Latin, sundial on a pedestal, from Greek *analēmma*, lofty structure, sundial, from *analambanein* to take up, restore, from *ana-* + *lambanein* to take — more at LATCH] (1832)
**:** a plot or graph of the position of the sun in the sky at a certain time of day (as noon) at one locale measured at regular intervals throughout the year that has the shape of a figure 8; *also* **:** a scale (as on a globe or sundial) based on such a plot that shows the sun's position for each day of the year or that allows local mean time to be determined
— **an·a·lem·mat·ic** \ˌa-nə-le-'ma-tik, -lə-\ *adjective*

**an·a·lep·tic** \ˌa-nə-'lep-tik\ *noun* [Greek *analēptikos*, from *analambanein*] (1671)
**:** a drug that stimulates the central nervous system
— **analeptic** *adjective*

**an·al·ge·sia** \ˌa-nᵊl-'jē-zh(ē-)ə, -zē-ə\ *noun* [New Latin, from Greek *analgēsia*, from *an-* + *algēsis* sense of pain, from *algein* to suffer pain, from *algos* pain] (circa 1706)
**:** insensibility to pain without loss of consciousness
— **an·al·ge·sic** \-'jē-zik, -sik\ *adjective or noun*
— **an·al·get·ic** \-'je-tik\ *adjective or noun*

**anal·i·ty** \ā-'na-lə-tē\ *noun, plural* **-ties** (1939)
**:** the psychological state or quality of being anal

**an·a·log** \'a-nᵊl-ˌòg, -ˌäg\ *adjective* (1948)
**1 :** of, relating to, or being an analogue
**2 a :** of, relating to, or being a mechanism in which data is represented by continuously variable physical quantities **b :** of or relating to an analog computer **c :** being a timepiece having hour and minute hands

**analog computer** *noun* (1948)
**:** a computer that operates with numbers represented by directly measurable quantities (as voltages or rotations) — compare DIGITAL COMPUTER, HYBRID COMPUTER

**an·a·log·i·cal** \ˌa-nᵊl-'ä-ji-kəl\ *also* **an·a·log·ic** \-jik\ *adjective* (1609)
**1 :** of, relating to, or based on analogy
**2 :** expressing or implying analogy
— **an·a·log·i·cal·ly** \-ji-k(ə-)lē\ *adverb*

**anal·o·gist** \ə-'na-lə-jist\ *noun* (circa 1828)
**:** one who searches for or reasons from analogies

**anal·o·gize** \-ˌjīz\ *verb* **-gized; -giz·ing** (1655)
*intransitive verb*
**:** to use or exhibit analogy
*transitive verb*
**:** to compare by analogy

**anal·o·gous** \ə-'na-lə-gəs\ *adjective* [Latin *analogus*, from Greek *analogos*, literally, proportionate, from *ana-* + *logos* reason, ratio, from *legein* to gather, speak — more at LEGEND] (1646)
**1 :** showing an analogy or a likeness that permits one to draw an analogy
**2 :** being or related to as an analogue
*synonym* see SIMILAR
— **anal·o·gous·ly** *adverb*
— **anal·o·gous·ness** *noun*

**¹an·a·logue** *or* **an·a·log** \'a-nᵊl-ˌòg, -ˌäg\ *noun* [French *analogue*, from *analogue* analogous, from Greek *analogos*] (1826)
**1 :** something that is analogous or similar to something else
**2 :** an organ similar in function to an organ of another animal or plant but different in structure and origin
**3** *usually* **analog :** a chemical compound that is structurally similar to another but differs slightly in composition (as in the replacement of one atom by an atom of a different element or in the presence of a particular functional group)
**4 :** a food product made by combining a less expensive food (as soybeans or whitefish) with additives to give the appearance and taste of a more expensive food (as beef or crab)

**²an·a·logue** *chiefly British variant of* ANALOG

**anal·o·gy** \ə-'na-lə-jē\ *noun, plural* **-gies** (15th century)
**1 :** inference that if two or more things agree with one another in some respects they will probably agree in others
**2 a :** resemblance in some particulars between things otherwise unlike **:** SIMILARITY **b :** comparison based on such resemblance
**3 :** correspondence between the members of pairs or sets of linguistic forms that serves as a basis for the creation of another form
**4 :** correspondence in function between anatomical parts of different structure and origin — compare HOMOLOGY
*synonym* see LIKENESS

**an·al·pha·bet** \(ˌ)an-'al-fə-ˌbet, -bət\ *noun* [Greek *analphabētos* not knowing the alphabet, from *an-* + *alphabētos* alphabet] (circa 1889)
**:** one who cannot read **:** ILLITERATE
— **an·al·pha·bet·ic** \ˌan-ˌal-fə-'be-tik\ *adjective or noun*
— **an·al·pha·bet·ism** \(ˌ)an-'al-fə-bə-ˌti-zəm\ *noun*

**anal·y·sand** \ə-'na-lə-ˌsand\ *noun* [*analyse* + *-and* (as in *multiplicand*)] (1917)
**:** one who is undergoing psychoanalysis

**an·a·lyse** *chiefly British variant of* ANALYZE

**anal·y·sis** \ə-'na-lə-səs\ *noun, plural* **-y·ses** \-ˌsēz\ [New Latin, from Greek, from *analyein* to break up, from *ana-* + *lyein* to loosen — more at LOSE] (1581)

**1 :** separation of a whole into its component parts
**2 a :** the identification or separation of ingredients of a substance **b :** a statement of the constituents of a mixture
**3 a :** proof of a mathematical proposition by assuming the result and deducing a valid statement by a series of reversible steps **b** (1) **:** a branch of mathematics concerned mainly with functions and limits (2) **:** CALCULUS 1b
**4 a :** an examination of a complex, its elements, and their relations **b :** a statement of such an analysis
**5 a :** a method in philosophy of resolving complex expressions into simpler or more basic ones **b :** clarification of an expression by an elucidation of its use in discourse
**6 :** the use of function words instead of inflectional forms as a characteristic device of a language
**7 :** PSYCHOANALYSIS
**analysis of variance** (circa 1939)
**:** analysis of variation in an experimental outcome and especially of a statistical variance in order to determine the contributions of given factors or variables to the variance
**anal·y·sis si·tus** \-'sī-təs, -'sē-, -ˌtüs\ *noun* [New Latin, literally, analysis of situation] (circa 1909)
**:** TOPOLOGY 2a(1)
**an·a·lyst** \'a-n°l-əst\ *noun* [French *analyste,* from *analyse* analysis] (1656)
**1 :** a person who analyzes or who is skilled in analysis
**2 :** PSYCHOANALYST
**an·a·lyt·ic** \ˌa-n°l-'i-tik\ *or* **an·a·lyt·i·cal** \-ti-kəl\ *adjective* [Late Latin *analyticus,* from Greek *analytikos,* from *analyein*] (1601)
**1 :** of or relating to analysis or analytics; *especially* **:** separating something into component parts or constituent elements
**2 :** being a proposition (as "no bachelor is married") whose truth is evident from the meaning of the words it contains — compare SYNTHETIC
**3 :** skilled in or using analysis especially in thinking or reasoning ⟨a keenly *analytic* person⟩
**4 :** characterized by analysis rather than inflection ⟨*analytic* languages⟩
**5 :** PSYCHOANALYTIC
**6 :** treated or treatable by or using the methods of algebra and calculus
**7 a** *of a function of a real variable* **:** capable of being expanded in a Taylor's series in powers of *x − h* in some neighborhood of the point *h* **b** *of a function of a complex variable* **:** differentiable at every point in some neighborhood of a given point or points
— **an·a·lyt·i·cal·ly** \-ti-k(ə-)lē\ *adverb*
— **an·a·ly·tic·i·ty** \ˌa-n°l-ə-'ti-sə-tē\ *noun*
**analytic geometry** *noun* (circa 1886)
**:** the study of geometric properties by means of algebraic operations upon symbols defined in terms of a coordinate system — called also *coordinate geometry*
**analytic philosophy** *noun* (1936)
**:** a philosophical movement that seeks the solution of philosophical problems in the analysis of propositions or sentences — called also *philosophical analysis; compare* ORDINARY-LANGUAGE PHILOSOPHY
**an·a·lyt·ics** \ˌa-n°l-'i-tiks\ *noun plural but singular or plural in construction* (circa 1590)
**:** the method of logical analysis
**an·a·ly·za·tion** \ˌa-n°l-ə-'zā-shən\ *noun* (1742)
**:** ANALYSIS
**an·a·lyze** \'a-n°l-ˌīz\ *transitive verb* **-lyzed; -lyz·ing** [probably irregular from *analysis*] (1587)
**1 :** to study or determine the nature and relationship of the parts of by analysis ⟨*analyze* a traffic pattern⟩
**2 :** to subject to scientific or grammatical analysis

**3 :** PSYCHOANALYZE ☆
— **an·a·lyz·abil·i·ty** \ˌa-n°l-ˌī-zə-'bi-lə-tē\ *noun*
— **an·a·lyz·able** \'a-n°l-ˌī-zə-bəl\ *adjective*
— **an·a·lyz·er** \-ˌī-zər\ *noun*
**an·am·ne·sis** \ˌa-ˌnam-'nē-səs\ *noun, plural* **-ne·ses** \-ˌsēz\ [New Latin, from Greek *anamnēsis,* from *anamimnēskesthai* to remember, from *ana-* + *mimnēskesthai* to remember — more at MIND] (circa 1593)
**1 :** a recalling to mind **:** REMINISCENCE
**2 :** a preliminary case history of a medical or psychiatric patient
**an·am·nes·tic** \-'nes-tik\ *adjective* [Greek *anamnēstikos* easily recalled, from *anamimnēskesthai*] (circa 1753)
**1 :** of or relating to an anamnesis
**2 :** of or relating to a secondary response to an immunogenic substance after serum antibodies can no longer be detected in the blood
**ana·mor·phic** \ˌa-nə-'mȯr-fik\ *adjective* [New Latin *anamorphosis* distorted optical image] (circa 1925)
**:** producing, relating to, or marked by intentional distortion (as by unequal magnification along perpendicular axes) of an image ⟨an *anamorphic* lens⟩
**An·a·ni·as** \ˌa-nə-'nī-əs\ *noun* [Greek, probably from Hebrew *Ḥānanyāh*]
**1 :** an early Christian struck dead for lying
**2 :** LIAR
**an·a·pest** \'a-nə-ˌpest\ *noun* [Latin *anapaestus,* from Greek *anapaistos,* literally, struck back (a dactyl reversed), from *ana-* + *-paistos,* verbal of *paiein* to strike] (circa 1678)
**:** a metrical foot consisting of two short syllables followed by one long syllable or of two unstressed syllables followed by one stressed syllable (as *unabridged*)
— **an·a·pes·tic** \ˌa-nə-'pes-tik\ *adjective or noun*
**ana·phase** \'a-nə-ˌfāz\ *noun* [International Scientific Vocabulary] (1887)
**:** the stage of mitosis and meiosis in which the chromosomes move toward the poles of the spindle
— **ana·pha·sic** \ˌa-nə-'fā-zik\ *adjective*
**ana·phor** \'a-nə-ˌfȯr\ *noun, plural* **anaphors** *also* **anaph·o·ra** \ə-'na-f(ə-)rə\ [back-formation from *anaphoric*] (1975)
**:** a word or phrase with an anaphoric function
**anaph·o·ra** \ə-'na-f(ə-)rə\ *noun* [Late Latin, from Late Greek, from Greek, act of carrying back, reference, from *anapherein* to carry back, refer, from *ana-* + *pherein* to carry — more at BEAR] (circa 1589)
**1 :** repetition of a word or expression at the beginning of successive phrases, clauses, sentences, or verses especially for rhetorical or poetic effect ⟨Lincoln's "we cannot dedicate—we cannot consecrate—we cannot hallow—this ground" is an example of *anaphora*⟩ — compare EPISTROPHE
**2 :** use of a grammatical substitute (as a pronoun or a pro-verb) to refer to the denotation of a preceding word or group of words; *also* **:** the relation between a grammatical substitute and its antecedent
**an·a·phor·ic** \ˌa-nə-'fȯr-ik, -'fär-\ *adjective* (1904)
**:** of or relating to anaphora ⟨an *anaphoric* usage⟩; *especially* **:** being a word or phrase that takes its reference from another word or phrase and especially from a preceding word or phrase — compare CATAPHORIC
— **an·a·phor·i·cal·ly** \-i-k(ə-)lē\ *adverb*
**an·aph·ro·di·si·ac** \ˌa-ˌna-frə-'dē-zē-ˌak, -zhē-, -'di-zē-\ *adjective* (1823)
**:** inhibiting or discouraging sexual desire
— **anaphrodisiac** *noun*
**ana·phy·lac·tic** \ˌa-nə-fə-'lak-tik\ *adjective* (1907)
**:** of, relating to, affected by, or causing anaphylaxis or anaphylactic shock
— **ana·phy·lac·ti·cal·ly** \-ti-k(ə-)lē\ *adverb*

— **ana·phy·lac·toid** \-'lak-ˌtȯid\ *adjective*
**anaphylactic shock** *noun* (1910)
**:** an often severe and sometimes fatal systemic reaction in a susceptible individual upon exposure to a specific antigen (as wasp venom or penicillin) after previous sensitization that is characterized especially by respiratory symptoms, fainting, itching, and urticaria
**ana·phy·lax·is** \-'lak-səs\ *noun, plural* **-lax·es** \-ˌsēz\ [New Latin, from *ana-* + pro*phylax*is] (1907)
**1 :** hypersensitivity (as to foreign proteins or drugs) resulting from sensitization following prior contact with the causative agent
**2 :** ANAPHYLACTIC SHOCK
**ana·pla·sia** \ˌa-nə-'plā-zh(ē-)ə\ *noun* [New Latin] (circa 1909)
**:** reversion of cells to a more primitive or undifferentiated form
— **ana·plas·tic** \-'plas-tik\ *adjective*
**ana·plas·mo·sis** \ˌa-nə-ˌplaz-'mō-səs\ *noun, plural* **-mo·ses** \-ˌsēz\ [New Latin, from *Anaplasma,* genus name, from *ana-* + *plasma* (protoplasm)] (1920)
**:** a tick-borne disease of cattle and sheep caused by a bacterium (*Anaplasma marginale*) and characterized especially by anemia without blood-tinged urine and by jaundice
**an·arch** \'a-ˌnärk\ *noun* [back-formation from *anarchy*] (1667)
**:** a leader or advocate of revolt or anarchy
**an·ar·chic** \a-'när-kik, ə-\ *also* **an·ar·chi·cal** \-ki-kəl\ *adjective* (1649)
**1 a :** of, relating to, or advocating anarchy **b :** likely to bring about anarchy ⟨*anarchic* violence⟩
**2 :** lacking order, regularity, or definiteness ⟨*anarchic* art forms⟩
— **an·ar·chi·cal·ly** \-k(ə-)lē\ *adverb*
**an·ar·chism** \'a-nər-ˌki-zəm, -ˌnär-\ *noun* (1642)
**1 :** a political theory holding all forms of governmental authority to be unnecessary and undesirable and advocating a society based on voluntary cooperation and free association of individuals and groups
**2 :** the advocacy or practice of anarchistic principles
**an·ar·chist** \'a-nər-kist, -ˌnär-\ *noun* (1678)
**1 :** one who rebels against any authority, established order, or ruling power
**2 :** one who believes in, advocates, or promotes anarchism or anarchy; *especially* **:** one who uses violent means to overthrow the established order
— **anarchist** *or* **an·ar·chis·tic** \ˌa-nər-'kis-tik, -ˌ)när-\ *adjective*
**an·ar·cho–syn·di·cal·ism** \a-ˌnär-kō-'sin-di-kə-ˌli-zəm, ˌa-nər-kō-\ *noun* (circa 1928)
**:** SYNDICALISM
— **an·ar·cho–syn·di·cal·ist** \-kə-list\ *noun or adjective*
**an·ar·chy** \'a-nər-kē, -ˌnär-\ *noun* [Medieval Latin *anarchia,* from Greek, from *anarchos* having no ruler, from *an-* + *archos* ruler — more at ARCH-] (1539)

☆ SYNONYMS
**Analyze, dissect, break down** mean to divide a complex whole into its parts or elements. ANALYZE suggests separating or distinguishing the component parts of something (as a substance, a process, a situation) so as to discover its true nature or inner relationships ⟨*analyzed* the problem of the trade deficit⟩. DISSECT suggests a searching analysis by laying bare parts or pieces for individual scrutiny ⟨commentators *dissected* every word of the President's statement⟩. BREAK DOWN implies a reducing to simpler parts or divisions ⟨*break down* the budget⟩.

**1 a :** absence of government **b :** a state of law-lessness or political disorder due to the absence of governmental authority **c :** a utopian society of individuals who enjoy complete freedom without government
**2 a :** absence or denial of any authority or established order **b :** absence of order **:** DISORDER ⟨not manicured plots but a wild *anarchy* of nature —Israel Shenker⟩
**3 :** ANARCHISM

**ana·sar·ca** \,a-nə-'sär-kə\ *noun* [New Latin, from *ana-* + Greek *sark-, sarx* flesh — more at SARCASM] (14th century)
**:** generalized edema with accumulation of serum in the connective tissue
— **ana·sar·cous** \-kəs\ *adjective*

**An·a·sa·zi** \,ä-nə-'sä-zē\ *noun, plural* **Ana·sazi** [Navajo *anaasází*, literally, enemy ancestors] (1938)
**:** a prehistoric American Indian inhabitant of the canyons of northern Arizona and New Mexico and southwestern Colorado

**an·as·tig·mat** \a-'nas-tig-,mat, ,a-nə-'stig-\ *noun* [German, back-formation from *anastigmatisch* anastigmatic] (1890)
**:** an anastigmatic lens

**an·a·stig·mat·ic** \,a-nə-(,)stig-'ma-tik, ,a-,nas-tig-\ *adjective* [International Scientific Vocabulary] (1890)
**:** not astigmatic — used especially of lenses that are able to form approximately point images of object points

**anas·to·mose** \ə-'nas-tə-,mōz, -,mōs\ *verb* **-mosed; -mos·ing** [probably back-formation from *anastomosis*] (1697)
*transitive verb*
**:** to connect or join by anastomosis
*intransitive verb*
**:** to communicate by anastomosis

**anas·to·mo·sis** \ə-,nas-tə-'mō-səs\ *noun, plural* **-mo·ses** \-,sēz\ [Late Latin, from Greek *anastomōsis*, from *anastomoun* to provide with an outlet, from *ana-* + *stoma* mouth, opening — more at STOMACH] (1541)
**1 :** the union of parts or branches (as of streams, blood vessels, or leaf veins) so as to intercommunicate **:** INOSCULATION
**2 :** a product of anastomosis **:** NETWORK
— **anas·to·mot·ic** \-'mä-tik\ *adjective*

**anas·tro·phe** \ə-'nas-trə-(,)fē\ *noun* [Medieval Latin, from Greek *anastrophē*, literally, turning back, from *anastrephein* to turn back, from *ana-* + *strephein* to turn] (circa 1550)
**:** inversion of the usual syntactical order of words for rhetorical effect — compare HYSTERON PROTERON

**an·a·tase** \'a-nə-,tās, -,tāz\ *noun* [French, from Greek *anatasis* extension, from *anateinein* to extend, from *ana-* + *teinein* to stretch — more at THIN] (circa 1828)
**:** a tetragonal form of titanium dioxide used especially as a white pigment

**anath·e·ma** \ə-'na-thə-mə\ *noun* [Late Latin *anathemat-, anathema*, from Greek, thing devoted to evil, curse, from *anatithenai* to set up, dedicate, from *ana-* + *tithenai* to place, set — more at DO] (1526)
**1 a :** one that is cursed by ecclesiastical authority **b :** someone or something intensely disliked or loathed — usually used as a predicate nominative ⟨this notion was *anathema* to most of his countrymen —S. J. Gould⟩
**2 a :** a ban or curse solemnly pronounced by ecclesiastical authority and accompanied by excommunication **b :** the denunciation of something as accursed **c :** a vigorous denunciation **:** CURSE ◆

**anath·e·ma·tize** \-,tīz\ *transitive verb* **-tized; -tiz·ing** (1566)
**:** to pronounce an anathema upon
**synonym** see EXECRATE

**An·a·to·lian** \,a-nə-'tō-lē-ən, -'tōl-yən\ *noun* (1590)
**1 :** a native or inhabitant of Anatolia and specifically of the western plateau lands of Turkey in Asia

**2 :** a branch of the Indo-European language family that includes a group of extinct languages of ancient Anatolia — see INDO-EUROPEAN LANGUAGES table
— **Anatolian** *adjective*

**anat·o·mise** *British variant of* ANATOMIZE

**anat·o·mist** \ə-'na-tə-mist\ *noun* (1543)
**1 :** a student of anatomy; *especially* **:** one skilled in dissection
**2 :** one who analyzes minutely and critically ⟨an *anatomist* of urban society⟩

**anat·o·mize** \-,mīz\ *transitive verb* **-mized; -miz·ing** (15th century)
**1 :** to cut in pieces in order to display or examine the structure and use of the parts **:** DISSECT
**2 :** ANALYZE

**anat·o·my** \ə-'na-tə-mē\ *noun, plural* **-mies** [Late Latin *anatomia* dissection, from Greek *anatomē*, from *anatemnein* to dissect, from *ana-* + *temnein* to cut] (14th century)
**1 :** a branch of morphology that deals with the structure of organisms
**2 :** a treatise on anatomic science or art
**3 :** the art of separating the parts of an organism in order to ascertain their position, relations, structure, and function **:** DISSECTION
**4** *obsolete* **:** a body dissected or to be dissected
**5 :** structural makeup especially of an organism or any of its parts
**6 :** a separating or dividing into parts for detailed examination **:** ANALYSIS
**7 a** (1) **:** SKELETON (2) **:** MUMMY **b :** the human body
— **an·a·tom·ic** \,a-nə-'tä-mik\ *or* **an·a·tom·i·cal** \-mi-kəl\ *adjective*
— **an·a·tom·i·cal·ly** \-mi-k(ə-)lē\ *adverb*

**anat·ro·pous** \ə-'na-trə-pəs\ *adjective* (circa 1846)
**:** having or being an ovule inverted so that the micropyle is bent down to the funiculus to which the body of the ovule is united

**-ance** *noun suffix* [Middle English, from Old French, from Latin *-antia*, from *-ant-, -ans* *-ant* + *-ia* -y]
**1 :** action or process ⟨further*ance*⟩ **:** instance of an action or process ⟨perform*ance*⟩
**2 :** quality or state **:** instance of a quality or state ⟨protuber*ance*⟩
**3 :** amount or degree ⟨conduct*ance*⟩

**an·ces·tor** \'an-,ses-tər *also* -səs-\ *noun* [Middle English *ancestre*, from Old French, from Latin *antecessor* predecessor, from *antecedere* to go before, from *ante-* + *cedere* to go — more at CEDE] (13th century)
**1 a :** one from whom a person is descended and who is usually more remote in the line of descent than a grandparent **b :** FOREFATHER 2
**2 :** FORERUNNER, PROTOTYPE
**3 :** a progenitor of a more recent or existing species or group

**ancestor worship** *noun* (1854)
**:** the custom of venerating deceased ancestors who are considered still a part of the family and whose spirits are believed to have the power to intervene in the affairs of the living

**an·ces·tral** \an-'ses-trəl\ *adjective* (15th century)
**:** of, relating to, or inherited from an ancestor ⟨*ancestral* estates⟩
— **an·ces·tral·ly** \-trə-lē\ *adverb*

**an·ces·tress** \'an-,ses-trəs\ *noun* (1580)
**:** a female ancestor

**an·ces·try** \'an-,ses-trē\ *noun* (14th century)
**1 :** line of descent; *especially* **:** honorable, noble, or aristocratic descent
**2 :** persons initiating or comprising a line of descent **:** ANCESTORS

**An·chi·ses** \an-'kī-(,)sēz, aŋ-\ *noun* [Latin, from Greek *Anchisēs*]
**:** the father of Aeneas rescued by his son from the burning city of Troy

**¹an·chor** \'aŋ-kər\ *noun, often attributive* [Middle English *ancre*, from Old English *ancor*, from Latin *anchora*, from Greek *ankyra*;

akin to Old English *anga* hook — more at ANGLE] (before 12th century)
**1 :** a device usually of metal attached to a ship or boat by a cable and cast overboard to hold it in a particular place by means of a fluke that digs into the bottom
**2 :** a reliable or principal support **:** MAINSTAY
**3 :** something that serves to hold an object firmly
**4 :** an object shaped like a ship's anchor
**5 :** an anchorman or anchorwoman
**6 :** the member of a team (as a relay team) that competes last
**7 :** a large business (as a department store) that attracts customers and other businesses to a shopping center or mall
— **an·chor·less** \-ləs\ *adjective*
— **at anchor :** being anchored

anchor 1: *A* yachtsman's: *1* ring, *2* stock, *3* shank, *4* bill, *5* fluke, *6* arm, *7* throat, *8* crown; *B* grapnel; *C* mushroom

**²anchor** *verb* **an·chored; an·chor·ing** \-k(ə-)riŋ\ (13th century)
*transitive verb*
**1 :** to hold in place in the water by an anchor
**2 :** to secure firmly **:** FIX
**3 :** to act or serve as an anchor for ⟨it is she who is *anchoring* the rebuilding campaign —G. D. Boone⟩ ⟨*anchoring* the evening news⟩
*intransitive verb*
**1 :** to cast anchor
**2 :** to become fixed

**an·chor·age** \'aŋ-k(ə-)rij\ *noun* (15th century)

---

◇ WORD HISTORY

**anathema** The word *anathema* is of Greek origin, a derivative of the verb *anatithenai*, which means "to set up, dedicate." In the Septuagint, an influential Greek translation of the Hebrew scriptures, *anathema* was used to mean "something offered to God," and could refer either to a revered object or an object representing destruction brought about in the name of the Lord. Since the objects symbolic of consecrated destruction were often the spoils of war stripped from the bodies of despised enemies, *anathema* came to signify something odious or accursed. In the New Testament, Paul uses the term in the sense of a curse and the forced exclusion of a person from the Christian community. In Medieval Latin *anathema* was used interchangeably with *excommunicatio* and was pronounced chiefly against unrepentant heretics. In English the word *anathema* has been and continues to be used in its ecclesiastical sense. By the 18th century, however, its use in a broadened sense for "the denunciation of anything as accursed" is attested. That secular use continues to be common, as does the transferred sense, "someone or something intensely disliked."

---

\ə\ abut \ᵊ\ kitten \ər\ further \a\ ash \ā\ ace
\ä\ mop, mar \aù\ out \ch\ chin \e\ bet \ē\ easy
\g\ go \i\ hit \ī\ ice \j\ job \ŋ\ sing \ō\ go
\ò\ law \òi\ boy \th\ thin \th\ the \ü\ loot \ù\ foot
\y\ yet \zh\ vision *see also* Guide to Pronunciation

**1 a :** a place where vessels anchor **:** a place suitable for anchoring **b :** the act of anchoring **:** the condition of being anchored
**2 :** a means of securing **:** a source of reassurance ⟨this *anchorage* of Christian hope —T. O. Wedel⟩
**3 :** something that provides a secure hold
**an·cho·ress** \'aŋ-k(ə-)rəs\ *or* **an·cress** \-krəs\ *noun* [Middle English *ankeresse*, from *anker* hermit, from Old English *ancor*, from Old Irish *anchara*, from Late Latin *anachoreta*] (14th century)
**:** a woman who is an anchorite
**an·cho·rite** \'aŋ-kə-,rīt\ *also* **an·cho·ret** \-,ret\ *noun* [Middle English, from Medieval Latin *anchorita*, alteration of Late Latin *anachoreta*, from Late Greek *anachōrētēs*, from Greek *anachōrein* to withdraw, from *ana-* + *chōrein* to make room, from *chōros* place] (15th century)
**:** one who lives in seclusion usually for religious reasons
— **an·cho·rit·ic** \,aŋ-kə-'ri-tik\ *adjective*
— **an·cho·rit·i·cal·ly** \-ti-k(ə-)lē\ *adverb*
**an·chor·man** \'aŋ-kər-,man\ *noun* (1911)
**1 :** one who is last: as **a :** the member of a team who competes last ⟨the *anchorman* on a relay team⟩ **b :** one who has the lowest scholastic standing in a graduating class
**2 :** a broadcaster (as on a news program) who introduces reports by other broadcasters and usually reads the news
**3 :** MODERATOR 2c
**an·chor·peo·ple** \-,pē-pəl\ *noun plural* (1974)
**:** ANCHORPERSONS
**an·chor·per·son** \-,pər-s°n\ *noun* (1973)
**:** an anchorman or anchorwoman
**an·chor·wom·an** \-,wu̇-mən\ *noun* (1973)
**:** a woman who anchors a broadcast
**an·cho·veta** *also* **an·cho·vet·ta** \,an-chō-'ve-tə\ *noun* [Spanish *anchoveta*, diminutive of *anchova*] (1940)
**:** a small anchovy (*Cetengraulis mysticetus*) of the Pacific coast of North America
**an·cho·vy** \'an-,chō-vē, an-'\ *noun, plural* **-vies** *or* **-vy** [Spanish *anchova*] (1596)
**:** any of a family (Engraulidae) of small fishes resembling herrings; *especially* **:** a common Mediterranean fish (*Engraulis encrasicholus*) used especially in appetizers, as a garnish, and for making sauces and relishes
**an·cien ré·gime** \ä<sup>n</sup>s-ya<sup>n</sup>-rā-'zhēm\ *noun* [French, literally, old regime] (1794)
**1 :** the political and social system of France before the Revolution of 1789
**2 :** a system or mode no longer prevailing
**¹an·cient** \'ān(t)-shənt, 'āŋ(k)-shənt\ *adjective* [Middle English *ancien*, from Middle French, from (assumed) Vulgar Latin *anteanus*, from Latin *ante* before — more at ANTE-] (14th century)
**1 :** having had an existence of many years
**2 :** of or relating to a remote period, to a time early in history, or to those living in such a period or time; *especially* **:** of or relating to the historical period beginning with the earliest known civilizations and extending to the fall of the western Roman Empire in A.D. 476
**3 :** having the qualities of age or long existence: **a :** VENERABLE **b :** OLD-FASHIONED, ANTIQUE
**synonym** see OLD
— **an·cient·ness** *noun*
**²ancient** *noun* (1502)
**1 :** an aged living being ⟨a penniless *ancient*⟩
**2 :** one who lived in ancient times: **a** *plural* **:** the civilized people of antiquity; *especially* **:** those of the classical nations **b :** one of the classical authors ⟨Plutarch and other *ancients*⟩
**3 :** an ancient coin
**³ancient** *noun* [alteration of *ensign*] (1554)
**1** *archaic* **:** ENSIGN, STANDARD, FLAG
**2** *obsolete* **:** the bearer of an ensign
**ancient history** *noun* (1595)
**1 :** the history of ancient times

**2 :** knowledge or information that is widespread and has lost its initial freshness or importance **:** common knowledge
**an·cient·ly** *adverb* (1502)
**:** in ancient times **:** long ago
**an·cient·ry** \-shən-trē\ *noun* (1580)
**:** ANTIQUITY, ANCIENTNESS
**an·cil·la** \an-'si-lə\ *noun, plural* **-lae** \-(,)lē\ [Latin, female servant] (1902)
**:** an aid to achieving or mastering something difficult
**an·cil·lary** \'an(t)-sə-,ler-ē, *especially British* an-'si-lə-rē\ *adjective* (1667)
**1 :** SUBORDINATE, SUBSIDIARY ⟨the main factory and its *ancillary* plants⟩
**2 :** AUXILIARY, SUPPLEMENTARY ⟨the need for *ancillary* evidence⟩
— **ancillary** *noun*
**an·con** \'aŋ-,kän\ *noun, plural* **an·co·nes** \aŋ-'kō-nēz\ [Latin, from Greek *ankōn* elbow; akin to Old English *anga* hook — more at ANGLE] (circa 1706)
**:** a bracket, elbow, or console used as an architectural support
**-ancy** *noun suffix* [Latin *-antia* — more at -ANCE]
**:** quality or state ⟨piqu*ancy*⟩
**an·cy·lo·sto·mi·a·sis** \,aŋ-ki-,lō-stə-'mī-ə-səs, ,an(t)-sə-\ *noun, plural* **-a·ses** \-,sēz\ [New Latin, from *Ancylostoma*, genus of hookworms, from Greek *ankylos* hooked (akin to Old English *anga* hook) + *stoma* mouth — more at ANGLE, STOMACH] (1887)
**:** infestation with or disease caused by hookworms; *especially* **:** a lethargic anemic state in humans due to blood loss from hookworms feeding in the small intestine
**and** \ən(d), (')an(d), *usually* °n(d) *after* t, d, s *or* z, *often* °m *after* p *or* b, *sometimes* °ŋ *after* k *or* g\ *conjunction* [Middle English, from Old English; akin to Old High German *unti* and] (before 12th century)
**1** — used as a function word to indicate connection or addition especially of items within the same class or type; used to join sentence elements of the same grammatical rank or function
**2 a** — used as a function word to express logical modification, consequence, antithesis, or supplementary explanation **b** — used as a function word to join one finite verb (as *go, come, try*) to another so that together they are logically equivalent to an infinitive of purpose ⟨come *and* see me⟩
**3** *obsolete* **:** IF
**4** — used in logic to form a conjunction
— **and so forth** \ən-'sō-,fȯrth, -,fȯrth\ **1 :** and others or more of the same or similar kind **2 :** further in the same or similar manner **3 :** and the rest **4 :** and other things
— **and so on** \ən-'sō-,ȯn, -,än\ **:** and so forth
**AND** \'and\ *noun* (1949)
**:** a logical operator that requires both of two inputs to be present or two conditions to be met for an output to be made or a statement to be executed
**An·da·lu·sian** \,an-də-'lü-zhən\ *noun* [*Andalusia*, Spain] (1966)
**:** any of a breed of horses of Spanish origin that have a high-stepping gait
**an·da·lu·site** \,an-də-'lü-,sīt\ *noun* [French *andalousite*, from *Andalousie* Andalusia, region in Spain] (circa 1828)
**:** a mineral consisting of a silicate of aluminum usually in thick orthorhombic prisms of various colors
**¹an·dan·te** \än-'dän-(,)tā, -'dän-tē; an-'dan-tē\ *adverb or adjective* [Italian, literally, going, present participle of *andare* to go] (1724)
**:** moderately slow — usually used as a direction in music
**²andante** *noun* (1784)
**:** a musical composition or movement in andante tempo

**¹an·dan·ti·no** \än-,dän-'tē-(,)nō\ *adverb or adjective* [Italian, diminutive of *andante*] (1819)
**:** slightly faster than andante — used as a direction in music
**²andantino** *noun, plural* **-nos** (1845)
**:** a musical composition or movement in andantino tempo
**an·des·ite** \'an-di-,zīt\ *noun* [German *Andesit*, from *Andes*] (1850)
**:** an extrusive usually dark grayish rock consisting essentially of oligoclase or feldspar
— **an·des·it·ic** \,an-di-'zi-tik\ *adjective*
**and how** *adverb* (1865)
— used to emphasize the preceding idea ⟨having a great time—*and how!*⟩
**and·iron** \'an-,dī(-ə)rn\ *noun* [Middle English *aundiren*, modification of Middle French *andier*] (14th century)
**:** either of a pair of metal supports for firewood used on a hearth and made of a horizontal bar mounted on short legs with usually a vertical shaft surmounting the front end
**and/or** \'an-'dȯr\ *conjunction* (1853)
— used as a function word to indicate that two words or expressions are to be taken together or individually ⟨language comprehension *and/or* production —David Crystal⟩
**an·douille** \än-'dü-ē, än-dü-ē\ *noun* [French, from Old French *andoille*, from (assumed) Vulgar Latin *inductilia*, neuter plural of *inductilis* made by insertion, from Latin *inductus*, past participle of *inducere* to insert, bring in — more at INDUCE] (1605)
**:** a highly spiced smoked pork sausage
**an·douill·ette** \,än-dü-'yet\ *noun* [French, diminutive of *andouille*] (1611)
**:** a fresh pork sausage made with tripe or chitterlings
**andr-** *or* **andro-** *combining form* [Latin, from Greek, from *andr-, anēr;* akin to Oscan *ner-* man, Sanskrit *nar-*, Old Irish *nert* strength]
**1 :** male human being ⟨*andro*centric⟩
**2 :** male ⟨*andro*ecium⟩
**an·dra·dite** \an-'drä-,dīt, 'an-drə-,dīt\ *noun* [José B. de *Andrada* e Silva (died 1838) Brazilian geologist] (1868)
**:** a garnet of any of various colors ranging from yellow and green to brown and black
**an·dro·cen·tric** \,an-drə-'sen-trik\ *adjective* (1903)
**:** dominated by or emphasizing masculine interests or a masculine point of view
**An·dro·cles** \'an-drə-,klēz\ *noun* [Latin, from Greek *Androklēs*]
**:** a fabled Roman slave spared in the arena by a lion from whose foot he had years before extracted a thorn
**an·droe·ci·um** \an-'drē-shē-əm, -sē-əm\ *noun, plural* **-cia** \-shē-ə, -sē-ə\ [New Latin, from *andr-* + Greek *oikion*, diminutive of *oikos* house — more at VICINITY] (circa 1839)
**:** the aggregate of stamens in the flower of a seed plant
**an·dro·gen** \'an-drə-jən\ *noun* [International Scientific Vocabulary] (1936)
**:** a male sex hormone (as testosterone)
— **an·dro·gen·ic** \,an-drə-'je-nik\ *adjective*
**an·dro·gen·e·sis** \,an-drō-'je-nə-səs\ *noun* [New Latin] (circa 1900)
**:** development of an embryo containing only paternal chromosomes due to failure of the egg to participate in fertilization
— **an·dro·ge·net·ic** \-jə-'ne-tik\ *adjective*
**an·dro·gyne** \'an-drə-,jīn\ *noun* [Middle French, from Latin *androgynus*] (1552)
**:** one that is androgynous
**an·drog·y·nous** \an-'drä-jə-nəs\ *adjective* [Latin *androgynus* hermaphrodite, from Greek *androgynos*, from *andr-* + *gynē* woman — more at QUEEN] (1651)
**1 :** having the characteristics or nature of both male and female
**2 a :** neither specifically feminine nor masculine ⟨the *androgynous* pronoun *them*⟩ **b :** suitable to or for either sex ⟨*androgynous* clothing⟩

**3** : having traditional male and female roles obscured or reversed ⟨an *androgynous* marriage⟩
— **an·drog·y·ny** \-nē\ *noun*
**an·droid** \'an-ˌdrȯid\ *noun* [Late Greek *androeidēs* manlike, from Greek *andr-* + *-oeidēs* -oid] (circa 1751)
: a mobile robot usually with a human form
**An·drom·a·che** \an-'drä-mə-(ˌ)kē\ *noun* [Latin, from Greek *Andromachē*]
: the wife of Hector
**an·drom·e·da** \an-'drä-mə-də\ *noun* [New Latin *Andromeda*, genus name, from Latin] (circa 1760)
: any of several evergreen shrubs (genera *Pieris* and *Andromeda*) of the heath family; *especially* : JAPANESE ANDROMEDA
**An·drom·e·da** \an-'drä-mə-də\ *noun* [Latin, from Greek *Andromedē*]
**1** : an Ethiopian princess of Greek mythology rescued from a monster by her future husband Perseus
**2** [Latin (genitive *Andromedae*)] : a northern constellation directly south of Cassiopeia between Pegasus and Perseus
**an·dros·ter·one** \an-'drä-stə-ˌrōn\ *noun* [International Scientific Vocabulary] (1934)
: an androgenic hormone that is a hydroxy ketone $C_{19}H_{30}O_2$ found in human male and female urine
**ane** \'ān\ *adjective or noun or pronoun* (before 12th century)
*chiefly Scottish* : ONE
**-ane** *noun suffix* [International Scientific Vocabulary *-an, -ane,* alteration of *-ene, -ine,* & *-one*]
**1** : ³-AN 1 ⟨fur*ane*⟩
**2** : saturated hydrocarbon ⟨alk*ane*⟩ ⟨meth*ane*⟩
**an·ec·dot·age** \'a-nik-ˌdō-tij\ *noun* (1823)
**1** : the telling of anecdotes; *also* : ANECDOTES
**2** : garrulous old age
**an·ec·dot·al** \ˌa-nik-'dō-t°l\ *adjective* (1836)
**1 a** : of, relating to, or consisting of anecdotes ⟨an *anecdotal* biography⟩ **b** : ANECDOTIC 2 ⟨my *anecdotal* uncle⟩
**2** : based on or consisting of reports or observations of usually unscientific observers ⟨*anecdotal* evidence⟩
**3** : of, relating to, or being the depiction of a scene suggesting a story ⟨*anecdotal* painting⟩ ⟨*anecdotal* detail⟩
— **an·ec·dot·al·ly** \-t°l-ē\ *adverb*
**an·ec·dot·al·ist** \ˌa-nik-'dō-t°l-ist\ *or* **an·ec·dot·ist** \'a-nik-ˌdō-tist\ *noun* (1837)
: one who is given to or is skilled in telling anecdotes
— **an·ec·dot·al·ism** \-t°l-ˌi-zəm\ *noun*
**an·ec·dote** \'a-nik-ˌdōt\ *noun, plural* **anec·dotes** *also* **an·ec·dota** \ˌa-nik-'dō-tə\ [French, from Greek *anekdota* unpublished items, from neuter plural of *anekdotos* unpublished, from *a-* + *ekdidonai* to publish, from *ex* out + *didonai* to give — more at EX-, DATE] (circa 1721)
: a usually short narrative of an interesting, amusing, or biographical incident ◆
**an·ec·dot·ic** \ˌa-nik-'dä-tik\ *or* **an·ec·dot·i·cal** \-'dä-ti-kəl\ *adjective* (circa 1744)
**1** : ANECDOTAL 1a
**2** : given to or skilled in telling anecdotes
— **an·ec·dot·i·cal·ly** \-'dä-ti-k(ə-)lē\ *adverb*
**an·echo·ic** \ˌa-ni-'kō-ik\ *adjective* (1946)
: free from echoes and reverberations ⟨an *anechoic* chamber⟩
**an·elas·tic** \ˌa-n°l-'as-tik\ *adjective* (1947)
: relating to the property of a substance in which there is no definite relation between stress and strain
— **an·elas·tic·i·ty** \-n°l-ˌas-'ti-sə-tē, -'tis-tē\ *noun*
**anem-** *or* **anemo-** *combining form* [Greek, from *anemos* — more at ANIMATE]
: wind ⟨*anem*ometer⟩

**ane·mia** \ə-'nē-mē-ə\ *noun* [New Latin, from Greek *anaimia* bloodlessness, from *a-* + *-aimia* -emia] (1824)
**1 a** : a condition in which the blood is deficient in red blood cells, in hemoglobin, or in total volume **b** : ISCHEMIA
**2** : lack of vitality
**ane·mic** \ə-'nē-mik\ *adjective* (1858)
**1** : relating to or affected with anemia
**2 a** : lacking force, vitality, or spirit ⟨an *anemic* rendition of the song⟩ ⟨*anemic* efforts at enforcement⟩ **b** : lacking interest or savor : INSIPID ⟨*anemic* wines⟩ **c** : lacking in substance or quantity ⟨*anemic* returns on an investment⟩ ⟨*anemic* attendance⟩
— **ane·mi·cal·ly** \-mi-k(ə-)lē\ *adverb*
**anemo·graph** \ə-'ne-mə-ˌgraf\ *noun* (1865)
: a recording anemometer
**an·e·mom·e·ter** \ˌa-nə-'mä-mə-tər\ *noun* (circa 1751)
: an instrument for measuring and indicating the force or speed of the wind
**an·e·mom·e·try** \ˌa-nə-'mä-mə-trē\ *noun* (1847)
: the process of ascertaining the force, speed, and direction of wind or an airflow
**anem·o·ne** \ə-'ne-mə-nē\ *noun* [Latin, from Greek *anemōnē*] (1548)
**1** : any of a large genus (*Anemone*) of the buttercup family having lobed or divided leaves and showy flowers without petals but with conspicuous often colored sepals — called also *windflower*
**2** : SEA ANEMONE
**an·e·moph·i·lous** \ˌa-nə-'mä-fə-ləs\ *adjective* (1874)
: pollinated by wind
**an·en·ceph·a·ly** \ˌan-(ˌ)en-'se-fə-lē\ *noun, plural* **-lies** [²*a-* + *encephal-* + ²*-y*] (circa 1889)
: congenital absence of all or a major part of the brain
— **an·en·ce·phal·ic** \-ˌen(t)-sə-'fa-lik\ *adjective*
**anent** \ə-'nent\ *preposition* [Middle English *onevent, anent,* from Old English *on efen* alongside, from *on* + *efen* even] (13th century)
: ABOUT, CONCERNING
**an·er·oid** \'a-nə-ˌrȯid\ *adjective* [French *anéroïde,* from Greek *a-* + Late Greek *nēron* water, from Greek, neuter of *nearos, nēros* fresh; akin to Greek *neos* new — more at NEW] (circa 1848)
: using no liquid; *specifically* : operating by the effect of outside air pressure on a diaphragm forming one wall of an evacuated container ⟨*aneroid* barometer⟩
**an·es·the·sia** \ˌa-nəs-'thē-zhə\ *noun* [New Latin, from Greek *anaisthēsia* insensibility, from *a-* + *aisthēsis* perception, from *aisthanesthai* to perceive — more at AUDIBLE] (circa 1721)
: loss of sensation with or without loss of consciousness
**an·es·the·si·ol·o·gist** \-ˌthē-zē-'ä-lə-jist\ *noun* (1942)
: ANESTHETIST; *specifically* : a physician specializing in anesthesiology
**an·es·the·si·ol·o·gy** \-jē\ *noun* (circa 1914)
: a branch of medical science dealing with anesthesia and anesthetics
¹**an·es·thet·ic** \ˌa-nəs-'the-tik\ *adjective* (1846)
**1** : of, relating to, or capable of producing anesthesia
**2** : lacking awareness or sensitivity ⟨unmoved and quite *anesthetic* to his presence —S. J. Perelman⟩
— **an·es·thet·i·cal·ly** \-ti-k(ə-)lē\ *adverb*
²**anesthetic** *noun* (1848)
**1** : a substance that produces anesthesia
**2** : something that brings relief : PALLIATIVE
**anes·the·tist** \ə-'nes-thə-tist, *British* -'nēs-\ *noun* (1882)
: one who administers anesthetics

**anes·the·tize** \-thə-ˌtīz\ *transitive verb* **-tized; -tiz·ing** (1848)
: to subject to anesthesia
**an·es·trous** \(ˌ)an-'es-trəs\ *adjective* (circa 1909)
**1** : not exhibiting estrus
**2** : of or relating to anestrus
**an·es·trus** \-trəs\ *noun* [New Latin] (1927)
: the period of sexual quiescence between two periods of sexual activity in cyclically breeding mammals
**an·eu·ploid** \'an-yủ-ˌploid\ *adjective* (1926)
: having or being a chromosome number that is not an exact multiple of the usually haploid number — compare EUPLOID
— **aneuploid** *noun*
— **an·eu·ploi·dy** \-ˌploi-dē\ *noun*
**an·eu·rysm** *also* **an·eu·rism** \'an-yə-ˌri-zəm\ *noun* [Greek *aneurysma,* from *aneurynein* to dilate, from *ana-* + *eurynein* to stretch, from *eurys* wide — more at EURY-] (15th century)
: an abnormal blood-filled dilatation of a blood vessel and especially an artery resulting from disease of the vessel wall
— **an·eu·rys·mal** \ˌan-yə-'riz-məl\ *adjective*
**anew** \ə-'nü, -'nyü\ *adverb* [Middle English *of newe,* from Old English *of nīwe,* from *of* + *nīwe* new] (before 12th century)
**1** : for an additional time : AFRESH
**2** : in a new or different form
**an·frac·tu·os·i·ty** \(ˌ)an-ˌfrak-chə-'wä-sə-tē, -shə-\ *noun, plural* **-ties** (1596)
**1** : the quality or state of being anfractuous
**2** : a winding channel or course; *especially* : an intricate path or process (as of the mind)
**an·frac·tu·ous** \an-'frak-chə-wəs, -shə-\ *adjective* [French *anfractueux,* from Late Latin *anfractuosus,* from Latin *anfractus* coil, bend, from *an-* (from *ambi-* around) + *-fractus,* from *frangere* to break — more at AMBI-, BREAK] (1621)
: full of windings and intricate turnings : TORTUOUS
**an·gel** \'ān-jəl\ *noun* [Middle English, from Old English *engel* & Old French *angele;* both from Late Latin *angelus,* from Greek *angelos,* literally, messenger] (before 12th century)
**1 a** : a spiritual being superior to man in power and intelligence; *especially* : one in the lowest rank in the celestial hierarchy **b** *plural* : an order of angels — see CELESTIAL HIERARCHY

◇ **WORD HISTORY**
**anecdote** Procopius, a 6th century historian and official at the court of the eastern Roman emperor Justinian, published two important historical works in his lifetime. A third work, however, did not begin to circulate until after his death. Entitled *Anekdota,* "unpublished things," it contained bitter attacks on the emperor Justinian and his wife, Theodora, as well as on many other noted officials in Constantinople. Some of these attacks are in the form of juicy bits of scandalous gossip. Procopius's work is often referred to as *Historia Arcana* or *Secret History.* It was the original title that became a byword, however. Procopius's title first appeared in English in its Medieval Latin form, *anecdota,* and then as *anecdotes,* borrowed from French. When first used in the latter half of the 17th century, these plurals meant "unpublished secret history." By the 18th century, the word was being used in the singular, *anecdote,* and in the sense familiar to us today.

\ə\ **abut** \°\ **kitten** \ər\ **further** \a\ **ash** \ā\ **ace**
\ä\ **mop, mar** \aủ\ **out** \ch\ **chin** \e\ **bet** \ē\ **easy**
\g\ **go** \i\ **hit** \ī\ **ice** \j\ **job** \ŋ\ **sing** \ō\ **go**
\ȯ\ **law** \ȯi\ **boy** \th\ **thin** \th̲\ **the** \ü\ **loot** \ủ\ **foot**
\y\ **yet** \zh\ **vision** *see also* Guide to Pronunciation

**2 :** an attendant spirit or guardian
**3 :** a white-robed winged figure of human form in fine art
**4 :** MESSENGER, HARBINGER ⟨*angel* of death⟩
**5 :** a person like an angel (as in looks or behavior)
**6** *Christian Science* **:** inspiration from God
**7 :** one (as a backer of a theatrical venture) who aids or supports with money or influence
**8 :** ANGELFISH
— **an·gel·ic** \an-'je-lik\ *or* **an·gel·i·cal** \-li-kəl\ *adjective*
— **an·gel·i·cal·ly** \-li-k(ə-)lē\ *adverb*
**angel dust** *noun* (1973)
**:** PHENCYCLIDINE
**An·ge·le·no** \ˌan-jə-'lē-(ˌ)nō\ *noun, plural* **-nos** [American Spanish *angeleño*, from Los Angeles, Calif.] (1888)
**:** a native or resident of Los Angeles, Calif.
**an·gel·fish** \'ān-jəl-ˌfish\ *noun* (1668)
**1 :** any of several compressed bright-colored bony fishes (family Pomacanthidae) of warm seas
**2 :** SCALARE
**angel food cake** *noun* (1920)
**:** a usually white sponge cake made of flour, sugar, and whites of eggs
**angel–hair pasta** \'an-jəl-ˌher-, -ˌhar-\ *noun* (1981)
**:** pasta smaller in diameter than vermicelli
**an·gel·i·ca** \an-'je-li-kə\ *noun* [New Latin, genus name, from Medieval Latin, from Late Latin, feminine of *angelicus* angelic, from Late Greek *angelikos*, from Greek, of a messenger, from *angelos*] (1527)
**1 a :** any of a genus (*Angelica*) of herbs of the carrot family; *especially* **:** a Eurasian biennial or perennial (*A. archangelica*) whose roots and fruit yield a flavoring oil **b :** a confection prepared from angelica
**2** *capitalized* **:** a sweet fortified wine produced in California
**angelica tree** *noun* (1785)
**:** HERCULES'-CLUB 1
**an·gel·ol·o·gy** \ˌān-jə-'lä-lə-jē\ *noun, often capitalized* (circa 1828)
**:** the theological doctrine of angels or its study
— **an·gel·ol·o·gist** \-jist\ *noun*
**An·ge·lus** \'an-jə-ləs\ *noun* [Medieval Latin, from Late Latin, angel; from the first word of the opening versicle] (1658)
**1 :** a devotion of the Western church that commemorates the Incarnation and is said in the morning, at noon, and in the evening
**2 :** a bell announcing the time for the Angelus
**¹anger** *verb* **an·gered; an·ger·ing** \-g(ə-)riŋ\ (13th century)
*transitive verb*
**:** to make angry
*intransitive verb*
**:** to become angry
**²an·ger** \'aŋ-gər\ *noun* [Middle English, affliction, anger, from Old Norse *angr* grief; akin to Old English *enge* narrow, Latin *angere* to strangle, Greek *anchein*] (14th century)
**1 :** a strong feeling of displeasure and usually of antagonism
**2 :** RAGE 2 ☆
— **an·ger·less** \-ləs\ *adjective*
**An·ge·vin** \'an-jə-vən\ *adjective* [French, from Old French, from Medieval Latin *andegavi-nus*, from *Andegavia* Anjou] (1769)
**:** of, relating to, or characteristic of Anjou or the Plantagenets
— **Angevin** *noun*
**angi-** *or* **angio-** *combining form* [New Latin, from Greek *angei-*, *angeio-*, from *angeion* vessel, blood vessel, diminutive of *angos* vessel]
**1 :** blood or lymph vessel **:** blood vessels and ⟨*angioma*⟩ ⟨*angiocardiography*⟩
**2 :** pericarp ⟨*angiosperm*⟩
**an·gi·na** \an-'jī-nə, 'an-jə-\ *noun* [Latin, throat inflammation, from Greek *anchonē* strangling, from *anchein* to strangle] (1578)
**:** a disease marked by spasmodic attacks of in-

tense suffocative pain: as **a :** a severe inflammatory or ulcerated condition of the mouth or throat **b :** ANGINA PECTORIS
— **an·gi·nal** \an-'jī-nᵊl, 'an-jə-\ *adjective*
**angina pec·to·ris** \-'pek-t(ə-)rəs\ *noun* [New Latin, literally, angina of the chest] (1744)
**:** a disease marked by brief paroxysmal attacks of chest pain precipitated by deficient oxygenation of the heart muscles
**an·gio·car·di·og·ra·phy** \'an-jē-ō-ˌkär-dē-'ä-grə-fē\ *noun* (1938)
**:** the roentgenographic visualization of the heart and its blood vessels after injection of a radiopaque substance
— **an·gio·car·dio·graph·ic** \-dē-ə-'graf-ik\ *adjective*
**an·gio·gen·e·sis** \ˌan-jē-ō-'je-nə-səs\ *noun* [New Latin] (1899)
**:** the formation and differentiation of blood vessels
— **an·gio·gen·ic** \-'je-nik\ *adjective*
**an·gio·gram** \'an-jē-ə-ˌgram\ *noun* (1933)
**:** a roentgenogram made by angiography
**an·gi·og·ra·phy** \ˌan-jē-'ä-grə-fē\ *noun* (1933)
**:** the roentgenographic visualization of the blood vessels after injection of a radiopaque substance
— **an·gio·graph·ic** \ˌan-jē-ə-'gra-fik\ *adjective*
**an·gi·o·ma** \ˌan-jē-'ō-mə\ *noun* [New Latin] (1871)
**:** a tumor composed chiefly of blood vessels or lymph vessels
— **an·gi·o·ma·tous** \-mə-təs\ *adjective*
**an·gio·plas·ty** \'an-jē-ə-ˌplas-tē\ *noun, plural* **-ties** (circa 1919)
**:** surgical repair of a blood vessel; *especially* **:** BALLOON ANGIOPLASTY
**an·gio·sperm** \'an-jē-ə-ˌspərm\ *noun* [ultimately from New Latin *angi-* + Greek *sperma* seed — more at SPERM] (circa 1828)
**:** any of a class (Angiospermae) or division (Magnoliophyta) of vascular plants (as magnolias, grasses, oaks, roses, and daisies) that have the ovules and seeds enclosed in an ovary, form the embryo and endosperm by double fertilization, and typically have each flower surrounded by a perianth composed of two sets of floral envelopes comprising the calyx and corolla — called also *flowering plant*
— **an·gio·sper·mous** \ˌan-jē-ə-'spər-məs\ *adjective*
**an·gio·ten·sin** \ˌan-jē-ō-'ten(t)-sən\ *noun* [*angi-* + hyper*tension* + *-in*] (circa 1961)
**:** either of two forms of a kinin of which one has marked vasoconstrictive action; *also* **:** a synthetic amide derivative of the physiologically active form used to treat some forms of hypotension
**angiotensin converting enzyme** *noun* (1970)
**:** a proteolytic enzyme that converts the physiologically inactive form of angiotensin to the active vasoconstrictive form
**¹an·gle** \'aŋ-gəl\ *noun* [Middle English, from Middle French, from Latin *angulus*] (14th century)
**1 :** a corner whether constituting a projecting part or a partially enclosed space ⟨they sheltered in an *angle* of the building⟩
**2 a :** the figure formed by two lines extending from the same point; *also* **:** DIHEDRAL ANGLE **b :** a measure of an angle or of the amount of turning necessary to bring one line or plane into coincidence with or parallel to another
**3 a :** the precise viewpoint from which something is observed or considered; *also* **:** the aspect seen from such an angle **b** (1) **:** a special approach, point of attack, or technique for accomplishing an objective (2) **:** an often improper or illicit method of obtaining advantage ⟨he always had an *angle* to beat the other fellow⟩
**4 :** a sharply divergent course ⟨the road went off at an *angle*⟩

**5 :** a position to the side of an opponent in football from which a player may block his opponent more effectively or without penalty — usually used in the phrases *get an angle* or *have an angle*
— **an·gled** \-gəld\ *adjective*
**²angle** *verb* **an·gled; an·gling** \-g(ə-)liŋ\ (1741)
*intransitive verb*
**:** to turn or proceed at an angle
*transitive verb*
**1 :** to turn, move, or direct at an angle
**2 :** to present (as a news story) from a particular or prejudiced point of view **:** SLANT
**³angle** *intransitive verb* **an·gled; an·gling** \-g(ə-)liŋ\ [Middle English *angelen*, from *angel* fishhook, from Old English, from *anga* hook; akin to Old High German *ango* hook, Latin *uncus*, Greek *onkos* barbed hook, *ankos* glen] (15th century)
**1 :** to fish with a hook
**2 :** to use artful means to attain an objective ⟨*angled* for an invitation⟩
**An·gle** \'aŋ-gəl\ *noun* [Latin *Angli*, plural, of Germanic origin; akin to Old English *Engle* Angles] (before 12th century)
**:** a member of a Germanic people that invaded England along with the Saxons and Jutes in the 5th century A.D. and merged with them to form the Anglo-Saxon peoples
**angle bracket** *noun* (circa 1956)
**:** BRACKET 3b
**angle iron** *noun* (circa 1853)
**1 :** an iron cleat for joining parts of a structure at an angle
**2 :** a piece of structural steel rolled with an L-shaped section
**angle of attack** (1908)
**:** the acute angle between the direction of the relative wind and the chord of an airfoil
**angle of depression** (1790)
**:** the angle formed by the line of sight and the horizontal plane for an object below the horizontal
**angle of elevation** (circa 1737)
**:** the angle formed by the line of sight and the horizontal plane for an object above the horizontal
**angle of incidence** (1628)
**:** the angle that a line (as a ray of light) falling on a surface or interface makes with the normal drawn at the point of incidence — see CRITICAL ANGLE illustration
**angle of reflection** (1638)
**:** the angle between a reflected ray and the normal drawn at the point of incidence to a reflecting surface
**angle of refraction** (circa 1737)
**:** the angle between a refracted ray and the normal drawn at the point of incidence to the interface at which refraction occurs

---

☆ SYNONYMS
**Anger, ire, rage, fury, indignation, wrath** mean an intense emotional state induced by displeasure. ANGER, the most general term, names the reaction but in itself conveys nothing about intensity or justification or manifestation of the emotional state ⟨tried to hide his *anger*⟩. IRE, more frequent in literary contexts, may suggest greater intensity than *anger*, often with an evident display of feeling ⟨cheeks flushed dark with *ire*⟩. RAGE suggests loss of self-control from violence of emotion ⟨screaming with *rage*⟩. FURY is overmastering destructive rage that can verge on madness ⟨in her *fury* she accused everyone around her of betrayal⟩. INDIGNATION stresses righteous anger at what one considers unfair, mean, or shameful ⟨a refusal to listen that caused general *indignation*⟩. WRATH is likely to suggest a desire or intent to revenge or punish ⟨rose in his *wrath* and struck his tormentor to the floor⟩.

**an·gler** \'aŋ-glər\ *noun* (15th century)
**1 :** one that angles
**2 :** ANGLERFISH
**ang·ler·fish** \-ˌfish\ *noun* (circa 1889)
**:** any of several pediculate fishes (as the goosefishes); *especially* **:** MONKFISH
**angle shot** *noun* (circa 1922)
**:** a picture taken with the camera pointed at an angle from the horizontal
**an·gle·site** \'aŋ-gəl-ˌsīt, -glə-\ *noun* [French *anglésite*, from *Anglesey* Island, Wales] (circa 1841)
**:** a mineral consisting of lead sulfate formed by the oxidation of galena
**an·gle·worm** \'aŋ-gəl-ˌwərm\ *noun* (1832)
**:** EARTHWORM
**An·gli·an** \'aŋ-glē-ən\ *noun* (1726)
**1 :** a member of the Angles
**2 :** the Old English dialects of Mercia and Northumbria
— **Anglian** *adjective*
**An·gli·can** \'aŋ-gli-kən\ *adjective* [Medieval Latin *anglicanus*, from *anglicus* English, from Latin *Angli* Angles] (1635)
**1 :** of or relating to the established episcopal Church of England and churches of similar faith and order in communion with it
**2 :** of or relating to England or the English nation
— **Anglican** *noun*
— **An·gli·can·ism** \-kə-ˌni-zəm\ *noun*
**an·gli·ce** \'aŋ-glə-(ˌ)sē\ *adverb, often capitalized* [Medieval Latin, adverb of *anglicus*] (1602)
**:** in English; *especially* **:** in readily understood English ⟨the city of Napoli, *anglice* Naples⟩
**an·gli·cise** *often capitalized, variant of* ANGLICIZE
**an·gli·cism** \'aŋ-glə-ˌsi-zəm\ *noun, often capitalized* [Medieval Latin *anglicus* English] (1642)
**1 :** a characteristic feature of English occurring in another language
**2 :** adherence or attachment to English customs or ideas
**An·gli·cist** \'aŋ-glə-sist\ *noun* (1930)
**:** a specialist in English linguistics
**an·gli·cize** \'aŋ-glə-ˌsīz\ *transitive verb* **-cized; -ciz·ing** *often capitalized* (1710)
**1 :** to make English in quality or characteristics
**2 :** to adapt (a foreign word or phrase) to English usage; *especially* **:** to borrow into English without alteration of form or spelling and with or without change in pronunciation
— **an·gli·ci·za·tion** \ˌaŋ-glə-sə-ˈzā-shən\ *noun, often capitalized*
**an·gling** \'aŋ-gliŋ\ *noun* (15th century)
**:** the action of one who angles; *especially* **:** the action or sport of fishing with hook and line
**An·glist** \'aŋ-glist\ *noun* (1888)
**:** ANGLICIST
**An·glo** \'aŋ-(ˌ)glō\ *noun, plural* **Anglos** [in sense 2, from American Spanish, short for Spanish *angloamericano* Anglo-American] (1800)
**1 :** ANGLO-AMERICAN
**2 :** a white inhabitant of the U.S. of non-Hispanic descent
— **Anglo** *adjective*
**An·glo-** *combining form* [New Latin, from Late Latin *Angli*]
**1** \'aŋ-(ˌ)glō, -glə\ **:** English ⟨*Anglo*-Norman⟩
**2** \-(ˌ)glō\ **:** English and ⟨*Anglo*-Japanese⟩
**An·glo-Amer·i·can** \ˌaŋ-glō-ə-ˈmer-ə-kən\ *noun* (circa 1782)
**:** a North American whose native language is English; *especially* **:** an inhabitant of the U.S. of English origin or descent
— **Anglo-American** *adjective*
**An·glo-Cath·o·lic** \-ˈkath-lik, -ˈka-thə-\ *adjective* (1838)
**:** of or relating to a High Church movement in Anglicanism emphasizing its continuity with historic Catholicism and fostering Catholic dogmatic and liturgical traditions

— **Anglo-Catholic** *noun*
— **An·glo-Ca·thol·i·cism** \-kə-ˈthä-lə-ˌsi-zəm\ *noun*
**An·glo-French** \-ˈfrench\ *noun* (circa 1884)
**:** the French language used in medieval England
**An·glo·ma·nia** \-ˈmā-nē-ə, -nyə\ *noun* (1787)
**:** an absorbing or pervasive interest in England or things English
**An·glo-Nor·man** \-ˈnȯr-mən\ *noun* (1735)
**1 :** any of the Normans living in England after the Norman conquest of 1066
**2 :** the form of Anglo-French used by Anglo-Normans
— **Anglo-Norman** *adjective*
**An·glo·phile** \'aŋ-glə-ˌfīl\ *also* **An·glo·phil** \-ˌfil\ *noun* [French, from *anglo-* + *-phile*] (1883)
**:** one who greatly admires or favors England and things English
— **Anglophile** *or* **An·glo·phil·ic** \ˌaŋ-glə-ˈfi-lik\ *adjective*
**An·glo·phil·ia** \ˌaŋ-glə-ˈfi-lē-ə\ *noun* (1896)
**:** unusual admiration or partiality for England, English ways, or things English
— **An·glo·phil·i·ac** \-lē-ˌak\ *adjective*
**An·glo·phobe** \'aŋ-glə-ˌfōb\ *noun* [probably from French, from *anglo-* + *-phobe*] (1866)
**:** one who is averse to or dislikes England and things English
— **An·glo·pho·bia** \ˌaŋ-glə-ˈfō-bē-ə\ *noun*
— **An·glo·pho·bic** \-bik\ *adjective*
**an·glo·phone** \'aŋ-glə-ˌfōn\ *adjective, often capitalized* (1965)
**:** consisting of or belonging to an English-speaking population especially in a country where two or more languages are spoken
— **Anglophone** *noun*
**An·glo-Sax·on** \ˌaŋ-glō-ˈsak-sən\ *noun* [New Latin *Anglo-Saxones*, plural, alteration of Medieval Latin *Angli Saxones*, from Latin *Angli* Angles + Late Latin *Saxones* Saxons] (before 12th century)
**1 :** a member of the Germanic peoples conquering England in the 5th century A.D. and forming the ruling class until the Norman conquest — compare ANGLE, JUTE, SAXON
**2 a :** ENGLISHMAN; *specifically* **:** a person descended from the Anglo-Saxons **b :** a white gentile of an English-speaking nation
**3 :** OLD ENGLISH 1
**4 :** direct plain English; *especially* **:** English using words considered crude or vulgar
— **Anglo-Saxon** *adjective*
**an·go·ra** \aŋ-ˈgȯr-ə, an-, -ˈgȯr-\ *noun* (1852)
**1 :** the hair of the Angora rabbit or Angora goat — called also *angora wool*
**2 :** a yarn of Angora rabbit hair used especially for knitting
**3** *capitalized* **a :** ANGORA CAT **b :** ANGORA GOAT **c :** ANGORA RABBIT
**Angora cat** *noun* [*Angora* (Ankara), Turkey] (1819)
**:** a long-haired domestic cat; *specifically* **:** any of a breed that differs from the Persian in having a narrower head and slighter body
**Angora goat** *noun* (1833)
**:** any of a breed or variety of the domestic goat raised for its long silky hair which is the true mohair
**Angora rabbit** *noun* (1849)
**:** any of a breed of long-haired usually white rabbits with red eyes that is raised for fine wool

*Angora goat*

**an·gry** \'aŋ-grē\ *adjective* **an·gri·er; -est** (14th century)
**1 :** feeling or showing anger **:** WRATHFUL
**2 a :** indicative of or proceeding from anger ⟨*angry* words⟩ **b :** seeming to show anger or to threaten in an angry manner ⟨an *angry* sky⟩
**3 :** painfully inflamed ⟨an *angry* rash⟩

— **an·gri·ly** \-grə-lē\ *adverb*
— **an·gri·ness** \-grē-nəs\ *noun*
**angry young man** *noun* (1941)
**1 :** an outspoken critic of or protester against an economic condition or social injustice
**2 :** one of a group of mid-20th century British authors whose works express the bitterness of the lower classes toward the established sociopolitical system and toward the mediocrity and hypocrisy of the middle and upper classes

*Angora rabbit*

**angst** \'äŋ(k)st, 'aŋ(k)st\ *noun* [Danish & German; Danish, from German] (circa 1942)
**:** a feeling of anxiety, apprehension, or insecurity
**ang·strom** \'aŋ-strəm *also* 'ȯŋ-\ *noun* [Anders J. *Ångström*] (1892)
**:** a unit of length equal to one ten-billionth of a meter
**¹an·guish** \'aŋ-gwish\ *noun* [Middle English *angwisshe*, from Old French *angoisse*, from Latin *angustiae*, plural, straits, distress, from *angustus* narrow; akin to Old English *enge* narrow — more at ANGER] (13th century)
**:** extreme pain, distress, or anxiety
**synonym** see SORROW
**²anguish** (14th century)
*intransitive verb*
**:** to suffer anguish
*transitive verb*
**:** to cause to suffer anguish
**an·guished** *adjective* (14th century)
**1 :** suffering anguish **:** TORMENTED ⟨the *anguished* martyrs⟩
**2 :** expressing anguish **:** AGONIZED ⟨*anguished* cries⟩
**an·gu·lar** \'aŋ-gyə-lər\ *adjective* [Middle French or Latin; Middle French *angulaire*, from Latin *angularis*, from *angulus* angle] (15th century)
**1 a :** forming an angle **:** sharp-cornered **b :** having one or more angles
**2 :** measured by an angle ⟨*angular* distance⟩
**3 a :** stiff in character or manner **:** lacking smoothness or grace **b :** lean and having prominent bone structure
— **an·gu·lar·ly** *adverb*
**angular acceleration** *noun* (1883)
**:** the rate of change per unit time of angular velocity
**an·gu·lar·i·ty** \ˌaŋ-gyə-ˈlar-ə-tē\ *noun, plural* **-ties** (1642)
**1 :** the quality of being angular
**2** *plural* **:** angular outlines or characteristics
**angular momentum** *noun* (1870)
**:** a vector quantity that is a measure of the rotational momentum of a rotating body or system, that is equal in classical physics to the product of the angular velocity of the body or system and its moment of inertia with respect to the rotation axis, and that is directed along the rotation axis
**angular velocity** *noun* (1819)
**:** the rate of rotation around an axis usually expressed in radians or revolutions per second or per minute
**an·gu·la·tion** \ˌaŋ-gyə-ˈlā-shən\ *noun* (1869)
**1 :** the action of making angular
**2 :** an angular position, formation, or shape
**An·gus** \'aŋ-gəs\ *noun* [*Angus*, county in Scotland] (1842)
**:** any of a breed of usually black hornless beef cattle originating in Scotland

\ə\ abut \ᵊ\ kitten \ər\ further \a\ ash \ā\ ace
\ä\ mop, mar \au̇\ out \ch\ chin \e\ bet \ē\ easy
\g\ go \i\ hit \ī\ ice \j\ job \ŋ\ sing \ō\ go
\ȯ\ law \ȯi\ boy \th\ thin \t̲h̲\ the \ü\ loot \u̇\ foot
\y\ yet \zh\ vision *see also* Guide to Pronunciation

**an·he·do·nia** \,an-(,)hē-'dō-nē-ə, -nyə\ *noun* [New Latin, from ²*a-* + Greek *hēdonē* pleasure — more at HEDONISM] (1897)
: a psychological condition characterized by inability to experience pleasure in normally pleasurable acts
— **an·he·don·ic** \-'dä-nik\ *adjective*

**an·hin·ga** \an-'hiŋ-gə\ *noun* [Portuguese, from Tupi] (1769)
: any of a genus (*Anhinga*) of fish-eating birds related to the cormorants but distinguished by a longer neck and sharply pointed rather than hooked bill; *especially* : one (*A. anhinga*) occurring from the southern U.S. to Argentina

**an·hy·dride** \(,)an-'hī-,drīd\ *noun* (1863)
: a compound derived from another (as an acid) by removal of the elements of water

**an·hy·drite** \-,drīt\ *noun* [German *Anhydrit*, from Greek *anydros*] (circa 1823)
: a mineral consisting of an anhydrous calcium sulfate that is usually massive and white or slightly colored

**an·hy·drous** \-drəs\ *adjective* [Greek *anydros*, from *a-* + *hydōr* water — more at WATER] (1819)
: free from water and especially water of crystallization

**ani** \ä-'nē\ *noun* [Spanish *aní*, or Portuguese *ani*, from Tupi *ani*] (circa 1823)
: any of a genus (*Crotophaga*) of black cuckoos of the warmer parts of America

**anile** \'a-,nīl, 'ā-\ *adjective* [Latin *anilis*, from *anus* old woman] (1652)
: of or resembling a doddering old woman; *especially* : SENILE
— **anil·i·ty** \a-'ni-lə-tē, ā-, ə-\ *noun*

**an·i·line** \'a-n°l-ən\ *noun* [German *Anilin*, from *Anil* indigo, from French, from Portuguese, from Arabic *an-nīl* the indigo plant, from Sanskrit *nīlī* indigo, from feminine of *nīla* dark blue] (1850)
: an oily liquid poisonous amine $C_6H_5NH_2$ obtained especially by the reduction of nitrobenzene and used chiefly in organic synthesis (as of dyes)

**aniline dye** *noun* (1864)
: a dye made by the use of aniline or one chemically related to such a dye; *broadly* : a synthetic organic dye

**ani·lin·gus** \,ā-ni-'liŋ-gəs\ *or* **ani·linc·tus** \-'liŋ(k)-təs\ *noun* [New Latin, from *anus* + -*i-* + *-lingus, -linctus* (as in *cunnilingus, cunnilinctus*)] (1949)
: erotic stimulation achieved by contact between mouth and anus

**an·i·ma** \'a-nə-mə\ *noun* [New Latin, from Latin, soul] (1923)
: an individual's true inner self that in the analytic psychology of C. G. Jung reflects archetypal ideals of conduct; *also* : an inner feminine part of the male personality — compare ANIMUS, PERSONA

**an·i·mad·ver·sion** \,a-nə-,mad-'vər-zhən, -məd-, -'vər-shən\ *noun* [Latin *animadversion-, animadversio*, from *animadvertere*] (1599)
**1** : a critical and usually censorious remark — often used with *on*
**2** : adverse criticism

**an·i·mad·vert** \-'vərt\ *verb* [Latin *animadvertere* to pay attention to, censure, from *animum adverte*, literally, to turn the mind to] (15th century)
*transitive verb*
*archaic* : NOTICE, OBSERVE
*intransitive verb*
: to make an animadversion

**¹an·i·mal** \'a-nə-məl\ *noun* [Latin, from *animale*, neuter of *animalis* animate, from *anima* soul — more at ANIMATE] (14th century)
**1** : any of a kingdom (Animalia) of living things including many-celled organisms and often many of the single-celled ones (as protozoans) that typically differ from plants in having cells without cellulose walls, in lacking chlorophyll and the capacity for photosynthe-

sis, in requiring more complex food materials (as proteins), in being organized to a greater degree of complexity, and in having the capacity for spontaneous movement and rapid motor responses to stimulation
**2 a** : one of the lower animals as distinguished from human beings **b** : MAMMAL; *broadly* : VERTEBRATE
**3** : a human being considered chiefly as physical or nonrational; *also* : this nature
**4** : an individual with a particular interest or aptitude ⟨a political *animal*⟩
**5** : MATTER, THING ⟨the theater . . . is an entirely different *animal* —Arthur Miller⟩; *also* : CREATURE 1c ◆
— **an·i·mal·like** \-mə(l)-,līk\ *adjective*

**²animal** *adjective* (1615)
**1** : of, relating to, resembling, or derived from animals
**2 a** : of or relating to the physical or sentient as contrasted with the intellectual or rational **b** : SENSUAL, FLESHLY
**3** : of or relating to the animal pole of an egg or to the part from which ectoderm normally develops
*synonym* see CARNAL
— **an·i·mal·ly** \-mə-lē\ *adverb*

**animal control** *noun* (1957)
: an office or department responsible for enforcing ordinances relating to the control, impoundment, and disposition of animals

**animal cracker** *noun* (1898)
: a small cookie in the shape of an animal

**an·i·mal·cule** \,a-nə-'mal-(,)kyü(ə)l\ *also* **an·i·mal·cu·lum** \-'mal-kyə-ləm\ *noun, plural* **-cules** *also* **-cu·la** \-kyə-lə\ [New Latin *animalculum*, diminutive of Latin *animal*] (1662)
: a minute usually microscopic organism

**animal heat** *noun* (1779)
: heat produced in the body of a living animal by functional chemical and physical activities

**animal husbandry** *noun* (1919)
: a branch of agriculture concerned with the production and care of domestic animals

**an·i·mal·ier** \,a-nə-mə-'lir\ *noun* [French, from *animal* animal, from Latin] (1912)
: a sculptor or painter of animal subjects

**an·i·mal·ism** \'a-nə-mə-,li-zəm\ *noun* (1831)
: ANIMALITY
— **an·i·mal·is·tic** \,a-nə-mə-'lis-tik\ *adjective*

**an·i·mal·i·ty** \,a-nə-'ma-lə-tē\ *noun* (1615)
**1** : qualities associated with animals: **a** : VITALITY **b** : a natural unrestrained unreasoned response to physical drives or stimuli
**2** : the animal nature of human beings

**an·i·mal·ize** \'a-nə-mə-,līz\ *transitive verb* **-ized; -iz·ing** (1741)
**1** : to represent in animal form
**2** : to cause to be or act like an animal
— **an·i·mal·iza·tion** \,a-nə-mə-lə-'zā-shən\ *noun*

**animal kingdom** *noun* (1776)
: a basic group of natural objects that includes all living and extinct animals — compare MINERAL KINGDOM, PLANT KINGDOM

**animal magnetism** *noun* (1784)
**1** : a mysterious force claimed by Mesmer to enable him to hypnotize patients
**2** : a magnetic charm or appeal; *especially* : SEX APPEAL

**animal model** *noun* (1976)
: an animal sufficiently like humans in its anatomy, physiology, or response to a pathogen to be used in medical research in order to obtain results that can be extrapolated to human medicine

**animal pole** *noun* (1887)
: the point on the surface of an egg that is diametrically opposite to the vegetal pole and usually marks the most active part of the protoplasm or the part containing least yolk

**animal rights** *noun plural but singular in construction* (1879)
: fair and humane treatment of animals — often used attributively

**animal spirits** *noun plural* (1543)
**1** *sometimes* **animal spirit** *obsolete* : the nervous energy that is the source of physical sensation and movement
**2** : vivacity arising from physical health and energy

**animal starch** *noun* (circa 1860)
: GLYCOGEN

**¹an·i·mate** \'a-nə-mət\ *adjective* [Middle English, from Latin *animatus*, past participle of *animare* to give life to, from *anima* breath, soul; akin to Old English *ōthian* to breathe, Latin *animus* spirit, Greek *anemos* wind, Sanskrit *aniti* he breathes] (15th century)
**1** : possessing or characterized by life : ALIVE
**2** : full of life : ANIMATED
**3** : of or relating to animal life as opposed to plant life
**4** : referring to a living thing ⟨an *animate* noun⟩
— **an·i·mate·ly** *adverb*
— **an·i·mate·ness** *noun*

**²an·i·mate** \-,māt\ *transitive verb* **-mat·ed; -mat·ing** (15th century)
**1** : to give spirit and support to : ENCOURAGE
**2 a** : to give life to **b** : to give vigor and zest to
**3** : to move to action
**4 a** : to make or design in such a way as to create apparently spontaneous lifelike movement **b** : to produce in the form of an animated cartoon
*synonym* see QUICKEN

**an·i·mat·ed** \-,mā-təd\ *adjective* (1534)
**1 a** : endowed with life or the qualities of life : ALIVE ⟨viruses that can behave as *animated* bodies or inert crystals⟩ **b** : full of movement and activity **c** : full of vigor and spirit : LIVELY ⟨an *animated* discussion⟩
**2** : having the appearance of something alive
**3** : made in the form of an animated cartoon
*synonym* see LIVELY
— **an·i·mat·ed·ly** *adverb*

**animated cartoon** *noun* (1915)
**1** : a motion picture made from a series of drawings simulating motion by means of slight progressive changes in the drawings
**2** : ANIMATION 2a

**an·i·ma·tion** \,a-nə-'mā-shən\ *noun* (1597)
**1** : the act of animating : the state of being animate or animated
**2 a** : a motion picture made by photographing successive positions of inanimate objects (as puppets or mechanical parts) **b** : ANIMATED CARTOON 1
**3** : the preparation of animated cartoons

**an·i·ma·to** \,ä-nə-'mä-(,)tō, ,a-\ *adverb or adjective* [Italian, from Latin *animatus*] (circa 1724)
: with animation — used as a direction in music

**an·i·ma·tor** \'a-nə-,mā-tər\ *noun* (1611)
**1** : one that animates ⟨the prime *animator* of the movement⟩
**2** : an artist who creates drawings for an animated cartoon

**an·i·mism** \'a-nə-,mi-zəm\ *noun* [German *Animismus*, from Latin *anima* soul] (1832)
**1** : a doctrine that the vital principle of organic development is immaterial spirit

◇ WORD HISTORY
**animal** Latin *anima* means "breath," the vital principle that distinguishes living things from dead ones, and the adjective derivative *animalis* means "having breath, living." Though plants may be said to breathe insofar as they take in certain gases from the atmosphere and release others, this is not a process seen by the naked eye. Thus the Latin noun *animal*, derived from *animalis*, is used to designate those living beings that breathe perceptibly, and so is our word, borrowed from Latin.

**2 :** attribution of conscious life to objects in and phenomena of nature or to inanimate objects
**3 :** belief in the existence of spirits separable from bodies
— **an·i·mist** \-mist\ *noun*
— **an·i·mis·tic** \ˌa-nə-'mis-tik\ *adjective*
**an·i·mos·i·ty** \ˌa-nə-'mä-sə-tē\ *noun, plural* **-ties** [Middle English *animosite*, from Middle French or Late Latin; Middle French *animosité*, from Late Latin *animositat-, animositas*, from Latin *animosus* spirited, from *animus*] (1605)
**:** ill will or resentment tending toward active hostility **:** an antagonistic attitude
*synonym* see ENMITY
**an·i·mus** \'a-nə-məs\ *noun* [Latin, spirit, mind, courage, anger] (1816)
**1 :** basic attitude or governing spirit **:** DISPOSITION, INTENTION
**2 :** a usually prejudiced and often spiteful or malevolent ill will
**3 :** an inner masculine part of the female personality in the analytic psychology of C. G. Jung — compare ANIMA
*synonym* see ENMITY
**an·ion** \'a-ˌnī-ən\ *noun* [Greek, neuter of *aniōn*, present participle of *anienai* to go up, from *ana-* + *ienai* to go — more at ISSUE] (1834)
**:** the ion in an electrolyzed solution that migrates to the anode; *broadly* **:** a negatively charged ion
**an·ion·ic** \ˌa-(ˌ)nī-'ä-nik\ *adjective* (circa 1920)
**1 :** of or relating to anions
**2 :** characterized by an active and especially surface-active anion
**anis-** *or* **aniso-** *combining form* [New Latin, from Greek, from *anisos*, from *a-* + *isos* equal]
**:** unequal ⟨*aniso*tropic⟩
**an·ise** \'a-nəs\ *noun* [Middle English *anis*, from Middle French, from Latin *anisum*, from Greek *annēson, anison*] (14th century)
**:** an herb (*Pimpinella anisum*) of the carrot family having carminative and aromatic seeds; *also* **:** ANISEED
**ani·seed** \'a-nə(s)-ˌsēd\ *noun* [Middle English *anis seed*, from *anis* + *seed*] (14th century)
**:** the seed of anise often used as a flavoring in liqueurs and in cooking
**an·is·ei·ko·nia** \ˌa-ˌnī-ˌsī-'kō-nē-ə\ *noun* [New Latin, from *anis-* + Greek *eikōn* image — more at ICON] (1934)
**:** a defect of binocular vision in which the two retinal images of an object differ in size
— **an·is·ei·kon·ic** \-'kä-nik\ *adjective*
**an·is·ette** \ˌa-nə-'set, -'zet\ *noun* [French, from *anis*] (1837)
**:** a usually colorless sweet liqueur flavored with aniseed
**an·isog·a·mous** \ˌa-(ˌ)nī-'sä-gə-məs\ *adjective* (1891)
**:** characterized by fusion of heterogamous gametes or of individuals that usually differ chiefly in size ⟨*anisogamous* reproduction⟩
— **an·isog·a·my** \-(ˌ)nī-'sä-gə-mē\ *noun*
**an·iso·me·tro·pia** \a-ˌnī-sə-mə-'trō-pē-ə\ *noun* [New Latin, from Greek *anisometros* of unequal measure (from *anis-* + *metron* measure) + New Latin *-opia* — more at MEASURE] (circa 1880)
**:** unequal refractive power in the two eyes
— **an·iso·me·tro·pic** \-'trä-pik, -'trō-\ *adjective*
**an·iso·trop·ic** \a-ˌnī-sə-'trä-pik\ *adjective* (1879)
**:** exhibiting properties with different values when measured in different directions ⟨an *anisotropic* crystal⟩
— **an·iso·trop·i·cal·ly** \-pi-k(ə-)lē\ *adverb*
— **an·isot·ro·py** \-(ˌ)nī-'sä-trə-pē\ *also* **an·isot·ro·pism** \-ˌpi-zəm\ *noun*
**an·ker·ite** \'aŋ-kə-ˌrīt\ *noun* [German *Ankerit*, from M. J. *Anker* (died 1843) Austrian mineralogist] (circa 1843)

**:** a dolomitic iron-containing mineral
**ankh** \'äŋk\ *noun* [Egyptian *'nḫ* live] (1888)
**:** a cross having a loop for its upper vertical arm and serving especially in ancient Egypt as an emblem of life
**an·kle** \'aŋ-kəl\ *noun* [Middle English *ankel*, from Old English *anclēow*; akin to Old High German *anchlāo* ankle] (before 12th century)

ankh

**1 :** the joint between the foot and the leg; *also* **:** the region of this joint
**2 :** the joint between the cannon bone and pastern (as in the horse)
**an·kle·bone** \'aŋ-kəl-ˌbōn, ˌaŋ-kəl-'\ *noun* (14th century)
**:** ²TALUS 1
**an·klet** \'aŋ-klət\ *noun* (1819)
**1 :** something (as an ornament) worn around the ankle
**2 :** a short sock reaching slightly above the ankle
**an·ky·lo·saur** \'aŋ-kə-lō-ˌsȯr\ *noun* [New Latin *Ankylosauria*, from *Ankylosaurus*] (1949)
**:** any of a suborder (Ankylosauria) of herbivorous Cretaceous dinosaurs having a long low-lying thickset body covered dorsally with bony plates
**an·ky·lo·sau·rus** \ˌaŋ-kə-lō-'sȯr-əs\ *noun* [New Latin, genus name, from Greek *ankylos* + *sauros* lizard] (1908)
**:** any of a North American genus (*Ankylosaurus*) of large ankylosaurs having a bony club at the end of the tail
**an·ky·lose** \'aŋ-ki-ˌlōs, -ˌlōz\ *verb* **-losed; -los·ing** [back-formation from *ankylosis*] (1787)
*transitive verb*
**:** to unite or stiffen by ankylosis
*intransitive verb*
**:** to undergo ankylosis
**an·ky·lo·sis** \ˌaŋ-ki-'lō-səs\ *noun, plural* **-lo·ses** \-ˌsēz\ [New Latin, from Greek *ankylōsis*, from *ankyloun* to make crooked, from *ankylos* crooked — more at ANGLE] (1713)
**1 :** stiffness or fixation of a joint by disease or surgery
**2 :** union of separate bones or hard parts to form a single bone or part
— **an·ky·lot·ic** \-'lä-tik\ *adjective*
**an·ky·lo·sto·mi·a·sis** \ˌaŋ-ki-lō-stə-'mī-ə-səs\ *variant of* ANCYLOSTOMIASIS
**an·la·ge** \'än-ˌlä-gə\ *noun, plural* **-gen** \-gən\ *also* **-ges** \-gəz\ [German, literally, act of laying on] (1892)
**:** the foundation of a subsequent development; *especially* **:** PRIMORDIUM
**an·na** \'ä-nə\ *noun* [Hindi *ānā*] (1708)
**1 :** a former monetary unit of Burma, India, and Pakistan equal to 1/16 rupee
**2 :** a coin representing one anna
**an·nal·ist** \'a-n°l-ist\ *noun* (circa 1611)
**:** a writer of annals **:** CHRONICLER
— **an·nal·is·tic** \ˌa-n°l-'is-tik\ *adjective*
**an·nals** \'a-n°lz\ *noun plural* [Latin *annales*, from plural of *annalis* yearly — more at ANNUAL] (1542)
**1 :** a record of events arranged in yearly sequence
**2 :** historical records **:** CHRONICLES
**3 :** records of the activities of an organization
**An·nam·ese** \ˌa-nə-'mēz, -'mēs\ *noun, plural* **Annamese** [*Annam*, region of Vietnam] (1826)
**1** *or* **An·nam·ite** \'a-nə-ˌmīt\ **:** a native or inhabitant of Annam
**2 :** VIETNAMESE 2
— **Annamese** *adjective*
— **Annamite** *adjective*
**an·nat·to** \ə-'nä-(ˌ)tō\ *noun* [Carib *annoto* tree producing annatto] (1629)
**:** a yellowish red dyestuff made from the pulp

around the seeds of a tropical tree (*Bixa orellana*, family Bixaceae); *also* **:** the tree that yields annatto
**an·neal** \ə-'nē(ə)l\ *verb* [Middle English *anelen* to set on fire, from Old English *onælan*, from *on* + *ælan* to set on fire, burn, from *āl* fire; akin to Old English *æled* fire, Old Norse *eldr*] (1664)
*transitive verb*
**1 a :** to heat and then cool (as steel or glass) usually for softening and making less brittle; *also* **:** to cool slowly usually in a furnace **b :** to heat and then cool (nucleic acid) in order to separate strands and induce combination at lower temperature especially with complementary strands of a different species
**2 :** STRENGTHEN, TOUGHEN
*intransitive verb*
**:** to be capable of combining with complementary nucleic acid by a process of heating and cooling
**an·ne·lid** \'a-n°l-əd, 'a-nə-ˌlid\ *noun* [ultimately from Latin *anellus* little ring — more at ANNULET] (1834)
**:** any of a phylum (Annelida) of usually elongated segmented coelomate invertebrates (as earthworms, various marine worms, and leeches)
— **annelid** *adjective*
— **an·nel·i·dan** \ə-'ne-lə-d°n, a-\ *adjective or noun*
¹**an·nex** \ə-'neks, 'a-ˌneks\ *transitive verb* [Middle English, from Middle French *annexer*, from Old French, from *annexe* joined, from Latin *annexus*, past participle of *annectere* to bind to, from *ad-* + *nectere* to bind] (14th century)
**1 :** to attach as a quality, consequence, or condition
**2** *archaic* **:** to join together materially **:** UNITE
**3 :** to add to something earlier, larger, or more important
**4 :** to incorporate (a country or other territory) within the domain of a state
**5 :** to obtain or take for oneself
— **an·nex·ation** \ˌa-ˌnek-'sā-shən\ *noun*
— **an·nex·ation·al** \-shnəl, -shə-n°l\ *adjective*
— **an·nex·ation·ist** \-sh(ə-)nist\ *noun*
²**an·nex** \'a-ˌneks, -niks\ *noun* (1501)
**:** something annexed as an expansion or supplement: as **a :** an added stipulation or statement **:** APPENDIX **b :** a subsidiary or supplementary structure **:** WING
**an·nexe** \'a-ˌneks, -niks\ *chiefly British variant of* ²ANNEX
**An·nie Oak·ley** \ˌa-nē-'ō-klē\ *noun, plural* **Annie Oakleys** [*Annie Oakley* (died 1926) American markswoman; from the resemblance of a punched pass to a playing card with bullet holes through the spots] (circa 1910)
**:** a free ticket
**an·ni·hi·late** \ə-'nī-ə-ˌlāt\ *verb* **-lat·ed; -lat·ing** [Late Latin *annihilatus*, past participle of *annihilare* to reduce to nothing, from Latin *ad-* + *nihil* nothing — more at NIL] (1525)
*transitive verb*
**1 a :** to cause to be of no effect **:** NULLIFY **b :** to destroy the substance or force of
**2 :** to regard as of no consequence
**3 :** to cause to cease to exist; *especially* **:** KILL
**4 a :** to destroy a considerable part of ⟨bombs *annihilated* the city⟩ **b :** to vanquish completely **:** ROUT ⟨*annihilated* the visitors 56–0⟩
*intransitive verb*
*of a particle and its antiparticle* **:** to vanish or cease to exist by coming together and changing into other forms of energy (as radiation or particles)
— **an·ni·hi·la·tion** \-ˌnī-ə-'lā-shən\ *noun*

\ə\ abut \°\ kitten \ər\ further \a\ ash \ā\ ace
\ä\ mop, mar \au̇\ out \ch\ chin \e\ bet \ē\ easy
\g\ go \i\ hit \ī\ ice \j\ job \ŋ\ sing \ō\ go
\ȯ\ law \ȯi\ boy \th\ thin \th\ the \ü\ loot \u̇\ foot
\y\ yet \zh\ vision *see also* Guide to Pronunciation

— **an·ni·hi·la·tor** \-,lā-tər\ *noun*
— **an·ni·hi·la·to·ry** \-'nī-ə-lə-,tōr-ē, -,tor-\ *adjective*

**an·ni·ver·sa·ry** \,a-nə-'vərs-rē, -'vər-sə-\ *noun, plural* **-ries** [Middle English *anniversarie*, from Medieval Latin *anniversarium*, from Latin, neuter of *anniversarius* returning annually, from *annus* year + *versus*, past participle of *vertere* to turn — more at ANNUAL, WORTH] (13th century)
**1 :** the annual recurrence of a date marking a notable event
**2 :** the celebration of an anniversary

**an·no Do·mi·ni** \,a-(,)nō-'dä-mə-nē, -'dō-, -,nī\ *adverb, often A capitalized* [Medieval Latin, in the year of the Lord] (1530)
— used to indicate that a time division falls within the Christian era

**an·no he·gi·rae** \-hi-'jī-(,)rē, -'he-jə-,rē\ *adverb, often A&H capitalized* [New Latin, in the year of the Hegira] (circa 1889)
— used to indicate that a time division falls within the Islamic era

**an·no·tate** \'a-nə-,tāt\ *verb* **-tat·ed; -tat·ing** [Latin *annotatus*, past participle of *annotare*, from *ad-* + *notare* to mark — more at NOTE] (1733)
*intransitive verb*
**:** to make or furnish critical or explanatory notes or comment
*transitive verb*
**:** to make or furnish annotations for (as a literary work or subject)
— **an·no·ta·tive** \-,tā-tiv\ *adjective*
— **an·no·ta·tor** \-,tā-tər\ *noun*

**an·no·ta·tion** \,a-nə-'tā-shən\ *noun* (15th century)
**1 :** a note added by way of comment or explanation
**2 :** the act of annotating

**an·nounce** \ə-'naún(t)s\ *verb* **-nounced; -nounc·ing** [Middle English, from Middle French *annoncer*, from Latin *annuntiare*, from *ad-* + *nuntiare* to report, from *nuntius* messenger] (15th century)
*transitive verb*
**1 :** to make known publicly **:** PROCLAIM ⟨*announced* the appointment⟩
**2 a :** to give notice of the arrival, presence, or readiness of ⟨*announce* dinner⟩ **b :** to indicate beforehand **:** FORETELL
**3 :** to serve as an announcer of
*intransitive verb*
**1 :** to serve as an announcer
**2 a :** to declare one's candidacy **b :** to declare oneself politically — used with *for* or *against*
**synonym** see DECLARE

**an·nounce·ment** \ə-'naún(t)-smənt\ *noun* (1798)
**1 :** the act of announcing or of being announced
**2 :** a public notification or declaration
**3 :** a piece of formal stationery designed for a social or business announcement

**an·nounc·er** \ə-'naún(t)-sər\ *noun* (circa 1611)
**:** one that announces: as **a :** a person who introduces television or radio programs, makes commercial announcements, or gives station identification **b :** a person who describes and comments on the action in a broadcast sports event

**an·noy** \ə-'nói\ *verb* [Middle English *anoien*, from Middle French *enuier*, from Late Latin *inodiare* to make loathsome, from Latin *in* + *odium* hatred — more at ODIUM] (13th century)
*transitive verb*
**1 :** to disturb or irritate especially by repeated acts
**2 :** to harass especially by quick brief attacks
*intransitive verb*
**:** to cause annoyance ☆
— **an·noy·er** *noun*

**an·noy·ance** \ə-'nói-ən(t)s\ *noun* (14th century)

**1 :** the act of annoying or of being annoyed
**2 :** the state or feeling of being annoyed **:** VEXATION
**3 :** a source of vexation or irritation **:** NUISANCE

**an·noy·ing** *adjective* (14th century)
**:** causing vexation **:** IRRITATING
— **an·noy·ing·ly** \-iŋ-lē\ *adverb*

¹**an·nu·al** \'an-yə(-wə)l\ *adjective* [Middle English, from Middle French & Late Latin; Middle French *annuel*, from Late Latin *annualis*, blend of Latin *annuus* yearly (from *annus* year) and Latin *annalis* yearly (from *annus* year); probably akin to Gothic *athnam* (dative plural) years, Sanskrit *atati* he walks, goes] (14th century)
**1 :** covering the period of a year ⟨*annual* rainfall⟩
**2 :** occurring or happening every year or once a year **:** YEARLY ⟨an *annual* reunion⟩
**3 :** completing the life cycle in one growing season
— **an·nu·al·ly** *adverb*

²**annual** *noun* (14th century)
**1 :** an event that occurs yearly
**2 :** a publication appearing yearly
**3 :** something that lasts one year or season; *specifically* **:** an annual plant

**an·nu·al·ize** \'an-yə(-wə)-,līz\ *transitive verb* **-ized; -iz·ing** (1918)
**:** to calculate or adjust to reflect a rate based on a full year ⟨quarterly returns yielding at an *annualized* rate of 7 percent⟩

**annual ring** *noun* (circa 1879)
**:** the layer of wood produced by a single year's growth of a woody plant

**an·nu·itant** \ə-'nü-ət-ənt, -'nyü-\ *noun* (1720)
**:** a beneficiary of an annuity

**an·nu·ity** \ə-'nü-ə-tē, -'nyü-\ *noun, plural* **-ities** [Middle English *annuite*, from Middle French *annuité*, from Medieval Latin *annuitat-, annuitas*, from Latin *annuus* yearly] (15th century)
**1 :** a sum of money payable yearly or at other regular intervals
**2 :** the right to receive an annuity
**3 :** a contract or agreement providing for the payment of an annuity

**an·nul** \ə-'nəl\ *transitive verb* **an·nulled; an·nul·ling** [Middle English *annullen*, from Middle French *annuller*, from Late Latin *annullare*, from Latin *ad-* + *nullus* not any — more at NULL] (15th century)
**1 :** to reduce to nothing **:** OBLITERATE
**2 :** to make ineffective or inoperative **:** NEUTRALIZE ⟨*annul* the drug's effect⟩
**3 :** to declare or make legally invalid or void ⟨wants the marriage *annulled*⟩
**synonym** see NULLIFY

**an·nu·lar** \'an-yə-lər\ *adjective* [Middle French or Medieval Latin; Middle French *annulaire*, from Medieval Latin *anularis*, from Latin *anulus*] (1571)
**:** of, relating to, or forming a ring ⟨an *annular* skin lesion⟩

**annular eclipse** *noun* (1771)
**:** an eclipse in which a thin outer ring of the sun's disk is not covered by the apparently smaller dark disk of the moon

**an·nu·late** \'an-yə-lət, -,lāt\ *adjective* (circa 1823)
**:** furnished with or composed of rings **:** RINGED

**an·nu·la·tion** \,an-yə-'lā-shən\ *noun* (1829)
**:** a ringlike anatomical structure

**an·nu·let** \'an-yə-lət\ *noun* [modification of Middle French *annelet*, diminutive of *anel*, from Latin *anellus*, diminutive of *anulus*] (1598)
**1 :** a little ring
**2 :** a small architectural molding or ridge forming a ring

**an·nul·ment** \ə-'nəl-mənt\ *noun* (15th century)
**1 :** the act of annulling **:** the state of being annulled

**2 :** a judicial pronouncement declaring a marriage invalid

**an·nu·lus** \'an-yə-ləs\ *noun, plural* **-li** \-,lī, -(,)lē\ *also* **-lus·es** [Medieval Latin, from Latin *anulus* finger ring, from *anus* ring — more at ANUS] (1563)
**1 :** RING
**2 :** a part, structure, or marking resembling a ring: as **a :** a line of cells around a fern sporangium that ruptures the sporangium by contracting **b :** a growth ring (as on the scale of a fish) that is used in estimating age

**an·nun·ci·ate** \ə-'nən(t)-sē-,āt\ *transitive verb* **-at·ed; -at·ing** (circa 1536)
**:** ANNOUNCE

**an·nun·ci·a·tion** \ə-,nən(t)-sē-'ā-shən\ *noun* [Middle English *annunciacioun*, from Middle French *anunciation*, from Late Latin *annuntiation-, annuntiatio*, from Latin *annuntiare* — more at ANNOUNCE] (14th century)
**1** *capitalized* **:** March 25 observed as a church festival in commemoration of the announcement of the Incarnation to the Virgin Mary
**2 :** the act of announcing or of being announced **:** ANNOUNCEMENT

**an·nun·ci·a·tor** \ə-'nən(t)-sē-,ā-tər\ *noun* (circa 1753)
**:** one that annunciates; *specifically* **:** a usually electrically controlled signal board or indicator
— **an·nun·ci·a·to·ry** \-sē-ə-,tōr-ē, -,tor-\ *adjective*

**an·nus mi·ra·bi·lis** \,a-nəs-mə-'rä-bə-ləs, ,ä-\ *noun, plural* **an·ni mi·ra·bi·les** \,a-,nī-mə-'rä-bə-,lēz, ,ä-(,)nē-mə-'rä-bə-,läs\ [New Latin, literally, wonderful year] (1660)
**:** a remarkable or notable year

**an·ode** \'a-,nōd\ *noun* [Greek *anodos* way up, from *ana-* + *hodos* way] (1834)
**1 :** the electrode of an electrochemical cell at which oxidation occurs: as **a :** the positive terminal of an electrolytic cell **b :** the negative terminal of a galvanic cell
**2 :** the electron-collecting electrode of an electron tube — compare CATHODE
— **an·od·ic** \a-'nä-dik\ *also* **an·od·al** \-'nō-d°l\ *adjective*
— **an·od·i·cal·ly** \-di-k(ə-)lē\ *also* **an·od·al·ly** \-d°l-ē\ *adverb*

**an·od·ize** \'a-nə-,dīz\ *transitive verb* **-ized; -iz·ing** (1931)
**:** to subject (a metal) to electrolytic action as the anode of a cell in order to coat with a protective or decorative film
— **an·od·iza·tion** \,a-,nō-də-'zā-shən, ,a-nə-\ *noun*

¹**an·o·dyne** \'a-nə-,dīn\ *adjective* [Latin *anodynos*, from Greek *anōdynos*, from *a-* + *odynē* pain; probably akin to Old English *etan* to eat] (1543)
**1 :** serving to assuage pain
**2 :** not likely to offend or arouse tensions **:** INNOCUOUS

²**anodyne** *noun* (circa 1550)
**1 :** something that soothes, calms, or comforts ⟨the *anodyne* of bridge, a comfortable book, or sport —Harrison Smith⟩

---

☆ **SYNONYMS**
**Annoy, vex, irk, bother** mean to upset a person's composure. ANNOY implies a wearing on the nerves by persistent petty unpleasantness ⟨their constant complaining *annoys* us⟩. VEX implies greater provocation and stronger disturbance and usually connotes anger but sometimes perplexity or anxiety ⟨*vexed* by her teenager's failure to pick up his room⟩. IRK stresses difficulty in enduring and the resulting weariness or impatience of spirit ⟨careless waste *irks* the boss⟩. BOTHER suggests interference with comfort or peace of mind ⟨don't *bother* me while I'm reading⟩. See in addition WORRY.

**2 :** a drug that allays pain

**anoint** \ə-'nȯint\ *transitive verb* [Middle English, from Middle French *enoint,* past participle of *enoindre,* from Latin *inunguere,* from *in-* + *unguere* to smear — more at OINTMENT] (14th century)
**1 :** to smear or rub with oil or an oily substance
**2 a :** to apply oil to as a sacred rite especially for consecration **b :** to choose by or as if by divine election; *also* **:** to designate as if by a ritual anointment
— **anoint·er** *noun*
— **anoint·ment** \-mənt\ *noun*

**anointing of the sick** (circa 1884)
**:** EXTREME UNCTION

**ano·le** \ə-'nō-lē\ *noun* [probably from French *anolis,* from Arawak of the Lesser Antilles] (circa 1753)
**:** any of a genus (*Anolis* of the family Iguanidae) of arboreal American lizards (as the American chameleon) that have a brightly colored dewlap and the ability to change color

**anom·a·lous** \ə-'nä-mə-ləs\ *adjective* [Late Latin *anomalus,* from Greek *anōmalos,* literally, uneven, from *a-* + *homalos* even, from *homos* same — more at SAME] (1655)
**1 :** inconsistent with or deviating from what is usual, normal, or expected **:** IRREGULAR, UNUSUAL
**2 a :** of uncertain nature or classification **b :** marked by incongruity or contradiction **:** PARADOXICAL
*synonym* see IRREGULAR
— **anom·a·lous·ly** *adverb*
— **anom·a·lous·ness** *noun*

**anom·a·ly** \ə-'nä-mə-lē\ *noun, plural* **-lies** (1603)
**1 :** the angular distance of a planet from its perihelion as seen from the sun
**2 :** deviation from the common rule **:** IRREGULARITY
**3 :** something different, abnormal, peculiar, or not easily classified

**an·o·mie** *also* **an·o·my** \'a-nə-mē\ *noun* [French *anomie,* from Middle French, from Greek *anomia* lawlessness, from *anomos* lawless, from *a-* + *nomos* law, from *nemein* to distribute — more at NIMBLE] (1933)
**:** social instability resulting from a breakdown of standards and values; *also* **:** personal unrest, alienation, and uncertainty that comes from a lack of purpose or ideals
— **ano·mic** \ə-'nä-mik, -'nō-\ *adjective*

**anon** \ə-'nän\ *adverb* [Middle English, from Old English *on ān,* from *on* in + *ān* one — more at ON, ONE] (before 12th century)
**1** *archaic* **:** at once **:** IMMEDIATELY
**2 :** SOON, PRESENTLY
**3 :** after a while **:** LATER

**an·o·nym** \'a-nə-ˌnim\ *noun* (1812)
**1 :** one who is anonymous
**2 :** PSEUDONYM

**an·o·nym·i·ty** \ˌa-nə-'ni-mə-tē\ *noun, plural* **-ties** (1820)
**1 :** the quality or state of being anonymous
**2 :** one that is anonymous

**anon·y·mous** \ə-'nä-nə-məs\ *adjective* [Late Latin *anonymus,* from Greek *anōnymos,* from *a-* + *onyma* name — more at NAME] (1631)
**1 :** not named or identified ⟨an *anonymous* author⟩ ⟨they wish to remain *anonymous*⟩
**2 :** of unknown authorship or origin ⟨an *anonymous* tip⟩
**3 :** lacking individuality, distinction, or recognizability ⟨the *anonymous* faces in the crowd⟩ ⟨the gray *anonymous* streets —William Styron⟩
— **anon·y·mous·ly** *adverb*
— **anon·y·mous·ness** *noun*

**anoph·e·les** \ə-'nä-fə-ˌlēz\ *noun* [New Latin, genus name, from Greek *anōphelēs* useless, from *a-* + *ophelos* advantage, help; akin to Greek *ophellein* to increase, Armenian *aweli* more] (1899)

**:** any of a genus (*Anopheles*) of mosquitoes that includes all mosquitoes which transmit malaria to humans
— **anoph·e·line** \-ˌlīn\ *adjective or noun*

**an·o·rak** \'a-nə-ˌrak\ *noun* [Danish, from Inuit (Greenland) *annoraaq*] (1922)
**:** a usually pullover hooded jacket long enough to cover the hips

**¹an·o·rec·tic** \ˌa-nə-'rek-tik\ *also* **an·o·ret·ic** \-'re-tik\ *adjective* [Greek *anorektos,* from *a-* + *oregein* to reach after — more at RIGHT] (circa 1894)
**1 a :** lacking appetite **b :** ANOREXIC 2
**2 :** causing loss of appetite

**²anorectic** *also* **anoretic** *noun* (circa 1957)
**1 :** an anorectic agent
**2 :** ANOREXIC

**an·orex·ia** \ˌa-nə-'rek-sē-ə, -'rek-shə\ *noun* [New Latin, from Greek, from *a-* + *orexis* appetite, from *oregein*] (1598)
**1 :** loss of appetite especially when prolonged
**2 :** ANOREXIA NERVOSA

**anorexia ner·vo·sa** \-(ˌ)nər-'vō-sə, -zə\ *noun* [New Latin, nervous anorexia] (1873)
**:** a serious disorder in eating behavior primarily of young women in their teens and early twenties that is characterized especially by a pathological fear of weight gain leading to faulty eating patterns, malnutrition, and usually excessive weight loss

**¹an·orex·ic** \ˌa-nə-'rek-sik\ *adjective* (circa 1907)
**1 :** ANORECTIC
**2 :** affected with or as if with anorexia nervosa

**²anorexic** *noun* (1912)
**:** a person affected with anorexia nervosa

**an·orex·i·gen·ic** \ˌa-nə-ˌrek-sə-'je-nik\ *adjective* (1948)
**:** ANORECTIC 2

**an·or·thite** \ə-'nȯr-ˌthīt\ *noun* [French, from *a-* + Greek *orthos* straight] (1833)
**:** a white, grayish, or reddish feldspar occurring in many igneous rocks
— **an·or·thit·ic** \ˌa-nȯr-'thi-tik\ *adjective*

**an·or·tho·site** \ə-'nȯr-thə-ˌsīt\ *noun* [French *anorthose,* a feldspar, from *a-* + Greek *orthos* — more at ORTH-] (1863)
**:** a granular plutonic igneous rock composed almost exclusively of a soda-lime feldspar (as labradorite)
— **an·or·tho·si·tic** \ə-ˌnȯr-thə-'si-tik\ *adjective*

**an·os·mia** \a-'näz-mē-ə\ *noun* [New Latin, from *a-* + Greek *osmē* smell — more at ODOR] (circa 1811)
**:** loss or impairment of the sense of smell
— **an·os·mic** \-mik\ *adjective*

**¹an·oth·er** \ə-'nə-thər *also* a- *or* ā-\ *adjective* (12th century)
**1 :** different or distinct from the one first considered ⟨the same scene viewed from *another* angle⟩
**2 :** some other ⟨do it *another* time⟩
**3 :** being one more in addition to one or more of the same kind ⟨have *another* piece of pie⟩

**²another** *pronoun* (13th century)
**1 :** an additional one of the same kind **:** one more
**2 :** one that is different from the first or present one
**3 :** one of a group of unspecified or indefinite things ⟨in one way or *another*⟩

**anoth·er-guess** \ə-'nə-thər-ˌges\ *adjective* [alteration of *anothergates,* from ¹*another* + *gate*] (1644)
*archaic* **:** of another sort

**an·ovu·la·to·ry** \(ˌ)an-'äv-yə-lə-ˌtōr-ē, -'ōv-, -ˌtȯr-\ *adjective* (1934)
**1 :** not involving or accompanied by ovulation ⟨*anovulatory* bleeding⟩
**2 :** suppressing ovulation

**an·ox·emia** \ˌa-ˌnäk-'sē-mē-ə\ *noun* [New Latin] (circa 1881)
**:** a condition of subnormal oxygenation of the arterial blood
— **an·ox·emic** \-mik\ *adjective*

**an·ox·ia** \a-'näk-sē-ə\ *noun* [New Latin] (1931)
**:** hypoxia especially of such severity as to result in permanent damage

**an·ox·ic** \(ˌ)a-'näk-sik\ *adjective* (1920)
**1 :** of, relating to, or affected with anoxia
**2 :** greatly deficient in oxygen **:** OXYGENLESS ⟨*anoxic* water⟩

**an·ser·ine** \'an(t)-sə-ˌrīn\ *adjective* [Latin *anserinus,* from *anser* goose — more at GOOSE] (circa 1828)
**:** of, relating to, or resembling a goose

**¹an·swer** \'an(t)-sər\ *noun* [Middle English, from Old English *andswaru* (akin to Old Norse *andsvar* answer); akin to Old English *and-* against, *swerian* to swear — more at ANTE-] (before 12th century)
**1 a :** something spoken or written in reply to a question **b :** a correct response
**2 :** a reply to a legal charge or suit **:** PLEA; *also* **:** DEFENSE
**3 :** something done in response or reaction ⟨his only *answer* was to walk out⟩
**4 :** a solution of a problem
**5 :** one that imitates, matches, or corresponds to another ⟨television's *answer* to the news magazines⟩

**²answer** *verb* **an·swered; an·swer·ing** \'an(t)s-riŋ, 'an(t)s-sə-\ (before 12th century)
*intransitive verb*
**1 :** to speak or write in reply
**2 a :** to be or make oneself responsible or accountable **b :** to make amends **:** ATONE
**3 :** to be in conformity or correspondence ⟨*answered* to the description⟩
**4 :** to act in response to an action performed elsewhere or by another
**5 :** to be adequate **:** SERVE
*transitive verb*
**1 a :** to speak or write in reply to **b :** to say or write by way of reply
**2 :** to reply in rebuttal, justification, or explanation
**3 a :** to correspond to ⟨*answers* the description⟩ **b :** to be adequate or usable for **:** FULFILL
**4** *obsolete* **:** to atone for
**5 :** to act in response to ⟨*answered* the call to arms⟩
**6 :** to offer a solution for; *especially* **:** SOLVE ☆
— **an·swer·er** \'an(t)-sər-ər\ *noun*

**an·swer·able** \'an(t)s-rə-bəl, 'an(t)-sə-\ *adjective* (1536)
**1** *archaic* **:** SUITABLE, ADEQUATE
**2 :** liable to be called to account **:** RESPONSIBLE
**3** *archaic* **:** CORRESPONDING, SIMILAR
**4 :** capable of being refuted
*synonym* see RESPONSIBLE

**answering machine** *noun* (1961)
**:** a machine that receives telephone calls by playing a recorded message and usually by recording messages from callers

---

☆ **SYNONYMS**
**Answer, respond, reply, rejoin, retort** mean to say, write, or do something in return. ANSWER implies the satisfying of a question, demand, call, or need ⟨*answered* all the questions⟩. RESPOND may suggest an immediate or quick reaction ⟨*responded* eagerly to a call for volunteers⟩. REPLY implies making a return commensurate with the original question or demand ⟨an invitation that requires you to *reply*⟩. REJOIN often implies sharpness or quickness in answering ⟨"who asked you?" she *rejoined*⟩. RETORT suggests responding to an explicit charge or criticism by way of retaliation ⟨he *retorted* to the attack with biting sarcasm⟩.

---

\ə\ abut \ᵊ\ kitten \ər\ **further** \a\ **ash** \ā\ **ace**
\ä\ **mop, mar** \au̇\ **out** \ch\ **chin** \e\ **bet** \ē\ **easy**
\g\ **go** \i\ **hit** \ī\ **ice** \j\ **job** \ŋ\ **sing** \ō\ **go**
\ȯ\ **law** \ȯi\ **boy** \th\ **thin** \t̲h̲\ **the** \ü\ **loot** \u̇\ **foot**
\y\ **yet** \zh\ **vision** *see also* Guide to Pronunciation

**answering service** *noun* (1941)
**:** a commercial service that answers telephone calls for its clients
**ant** \'ant\ *noun* [Middle English *ante, emete,* from Old English *æmette;* akin to Old High German *āmeiza* ant] (before 12th century)
**:** any of a family (Formicidae) of colonial hymenopterous insects with a complex social organization and various castes performing special duties
— **ants in one's pants :** impatience for action or activity **:** RESTLESSNESS
**ant-** — see ANTI-
**¹-ant** *noun suffix* [Middle English, from Old French, from *-ant,* present participle suffix, from Latin *-ant-, -ans,* present participle suffix of first conjugation, from *-a-* (stem vowel of first conjugation) + *-nt-, -ns,* present participle suffix; akin to Old English *-nde,* present participle suffix, Greek *-nt-, -n,* participle suffix]
**1 a :** one that performs (a specified action) **:** personal or impersonal agent ⟨claim*ant*⟩ ⟨cool*ant*⟩ **b :** thing that promotes (a specified action or process) ⟨expector*ant*⟩
**2 :** one connected with ⟨annuit*ant*⟩
**3 :** thing acted upon (in a specified manner) ⟨inhal*ant*⟩
**²-ant** *adjective suffix*
**1 :** performing (a specified action) or being (in a specified condition) ⟨somnambul*ant*⟩
**2 :** promoting (a specified action or process) ⟨expector*ant*⟩
**an·ta** \'an-tə\ *noun, plural* **antas** *or* **an·tae** \-ˌtē, -ˌtī\ [Latin; akin to Old Norse *ǫnd* anteroom] (1598)
**:** a pier produced by thickening a wall at its termination
**ant·ac·id** \(ˌ)ant-'a-səd, 'an-ˌta-\ *noun* (1732)
**:** an agent that counteracts or neutralizes acidity
— **antacid** *adjective*
**An·tae·an** \an-'tē-ən\ *adjective* [*Antaeus,* a giant overcome by Hercules] (1921)
**1 :** MAMMOTH
**2 :** having superhuman strength
**an·tag·o·nism** \an-'ta-gə-ˌni-zəm\ *noun* (circa 1828)
**1 a :** opposition of a conflicting force, tendency, or principle ⟨the *antagonism* of democracy to dictatorship⟩ **b :** actively expressed opposition or hostility ⟨*antagonism* between factions⟩
**2 :** opposition in physiological action; *especially* **:** interaction of two or more substances such that the action of any one of them on living cells or tissues is lessened
**synonym** see ENMITY
**an·tag·o·nist** \-nist\ *noun* (1594)
**1 :** one that contends with or opposes another **:** ADVERSARY, OPPONENT
**2 :** an agent of physiological antagonism: as **a :** a muscle that contracts with and limits the action of an agonist with which it is paired — called also *antagonistic muscle* **b :** a chemical that acts within the body to reduce the physiological activity of another chemical substance (as an opiate); *especially* **:** one that opposes the action on the nervous system of a drug or a substance occurring naturally in the body by combining with and blocking its nervous receptor — compare AGONIST 2b
**an·tag·o·nis·tic** \(ˌ)an-ˌta-gə-'nis-tik\ *adjective* (1632)
**:** marked by or resulting from antagonism
— **an·tag·o·nis·ti·cal·ly** \-ti-k(ə-)lē\ *adverb*
**an·tag·o·nize** \an-'ta-gə-ˌnīz\ *transitive verb* **-nized; -niz·ing** [Greek *antagōnizesthai,* from *anti-* + *agōnizesthai* to struggle, from *agōn* contest — more at AGONY] (circa 1742)
**1 :** to act in opposition to **:** COUNTERACT
**2 :** to incur or provoke the hostility of
**ant·arc·tic** \(ˌ)ant-'ärk-tik, -'är-tik\ *adjective,*

*often capitalized* [Middle English *antartik,* from Latin *antarcticus,* from Greek *antarktikos,* from *anti-* + *arktikos* arctic] (14th century)
**:** of or relating to the south pole or to the region near it
**antarctic circle** *noun, often A&C capitalized* (1556)
**:** the parallel of latitude that is approximately 66½ degrees south of the equator and that circumscribes the southern frigid zone
**An·tar·es** \an-'tar-(ˌ)ēz, -'ter-\ *noun* [Greek *Antarēs*]
**:** a giant red star of very low density that is the brightest star in Scorpio
**ant·bear** \'ant-ˌbar, -ˌber\ *noun* (circa 1889)
**:** AARDVARK
**ant cow** *noun* (1875)
**:** an aphid from which ants obtain honeydew
**¹an·te** \'an-tē\ *noun* [*ante-*] (1838)
**1 :** a poker stake usually put up before the deal to build the pot ⟨the dealer called for a dollar *ante*⟩
**2 :** COST, PRICE ⟨these improvements would raise the *ante*⟩
**²ante** *verb* **an·ted; an·te·ing** (1845)
*transitive verb*
**:** to put up (an ante); *also* **:** PAY, PRODUCE — often used with *up*
*intransitive verb*
**:** PAY UP — often used with *up*
**ante-** *prefix* [Middle English, from Latin, from *ante* before, in front of; akin to Old English *and-* against, Greek *anti* before, against — more at END]
**1 a :** prior **:** earlier ⟨*ante*date⟩ **b :** anterior **:** forward ⟨*ante*room⟩
**2 a :** prior to **:** earlier than ⟨*ante*diluvian⟩ **b :** in front of ⟨*ante*choir⟩
**ant·eat·er** \'ant-ˌē-tər\ *noun* (1764)
**:** any of several mammals that feed largely or entirely on ants or termites: as **a :** any of a family (Myrmecophagidae) of New World edentates with a long narrow snout, a long tongue, and large salivary glands that includes the giant anteater and tamandua **b :** PANGOLIN **c :** ECHIDNA **d :** AARDVARK
**an·te·bel·lum** \ˌan-ti-'be-ləm\ *adjective* [Latin *ante bellum* before the war] (circa 1847)
**:** existing before a war; *especially* **:** existing before the Civil War
**an·te·cede** \ˌan-tə-'sēd\ *transitive verb* **-ced·ed; -ced·ing** [Latin *antecedere*] (1624)
**:** PRECEDE
**an·te·ced·ence** \-'sē-d°n(t)s\ *noun* (1651)
**:** PRIORITY, PRECEDENCE
**¹an·te·ced·ent** \ˌan-tə-'sē-d°nt\ *noun* [Middle English, from Medieval Latin & Latin; Medieval Latin *antecedent-, antecedens,* from Latin, what precedes, from neuter of *antecedent-, antecedens,* present participle of *antecedere* to go before, from *ante-* + *cedere* to go] (14th century)
**1 :** a substantive word, phrase, or clause whose denotation is referred to by a pronoun (as *John* in "Mary saw John and called to him"); *broadly* **:** a word or phrase replaced by a substitute
**2 :** the conditional element in a proposition (as *if A* in "if A, then B")
**3 :** the first term of a mathematical ratio
**4 a :** a preceding event, condition, or cause **b** *plural* **:** the significant events, conditions, and traits of one's earlier life
**5 a :** PREDECESSOR; *especially* **:** a model or stimulus for later developments **b** *plural* **:** ANCESTORS, PARENTS
**²antecedent** *adjective* (14th century)
**:** PRIOR
**synonym** see PRECEDING
— **an·te·ced·ent·ly** *adverb*
**an·te·ces·sor** \ˌan-ti-'se-sər\ *noun* [Middle English *antecessour,* from Latin *antecessor* — more at ANCESTOR] (14th century)
**:** one that goes before **:** PREDECESSOR
**an·te·cham·ber** \'an-ti-ˌchām-bər\ *noun*

[French *antichambre,* from Middle French, from Italian *anti-* (from Latin *ante-*) + Middle French *chambre* room] (circa 1656)
**:** ANTEROOM
**an·te·chap·el** \-ˌcha-pəl\ *noun* (1703)
**:** a vestibule or anteroom to a chapel or church
**an·te·choir** \'an-ti-ˌkwī(-ə)r\ *noun* (circa 1889)
**:** a space enclosed or reserved for the clergy and choristers at the entrance to a choir
**¹an·te·date** \'an-ti-ˌdāt\ *noun* (15th century)
**:** a date assigned to an event or document earlier than the actual date of the event or document
**²an·te·date** \'an-ti-ˌdāt, ˌan-ti-'\ *transitive verb* (1572)
**1 a :** to date as of a time prior to that of execution **b :** to assign to a date prior to that of actual occurrence
**2** *archaic* **:** ANTICIPATE
**3 :** to precede in time
**an·te·di·lu·vi·an** \ˌan-ti-də-'lü-vē-ən, -ˌ(ˌ)dī-\ *adjective* [*ante-* + Latin *diluvium* flood — more at DELUGE] (1646)
**1 :** of or relating to the period before the flood described in the Bible
**2 :** made, evolved, or developed a long time ago ⟨an *antediluvian* automobile⟩
— **antediluvian** *noun*
**an·te·fix** \'an-ti-ˌfiks\ *noun, plural* **-fix·ae** \-ˌfik-ˌsē\ *or* **-fix·es** \-ˌfik-səz\ [Latin *antefixum,* from neuter of *antefixus,* past participle of *antefigere* to fasten before, from *ante-* + *figere* to fasten — more at FIX] (1832)
**:** an ornament at the eaves of a classical building concealing the ends of the joint tiles of the roof
**an·te·lope** \'an-t°l-ˌōp\ *noun, plural* **-lope** *or* **-lopes** [Middle English, fabulous heraldic beast, probably from Middle French *antelop* savage animal with sawlike horns, from Medieval Latin *anthalopus,* from Late Greek *antholop-, antholops*] (15th century)
**1 a :** any of various ruminant mammals (family Bovidae) chiefly of Africa and southwest Asia that differ from the true oxen especially in lighter racier build and horns directed upward and backward **b :** PRONGHORN
**2 :** leather from antelope hide
**an·te me·ri·di·em** \ˌan-ti-mə-'ri-dē-əm, -dē-ˌem\ *adjective* [Latin] (1563)
**:** being before noon — abbreviation *a.m.*
**an·te·mor·tem** \-'mȯr-təm\ *adjective* [Latin *ante mortem*] (1883)
**:** preceding death
**an·te·na·tal** \-'nā-t°l\ *adjective* (1817)
**:** PRENATAL ⟨*antenatal* diagnosis of birth defects⟩
— **an·te·na·tal·ly** \-ē\ *adverb*
**an·ten·na** \an-'te-nə\ *noun, plural* **-nae** \-(ˌ)nē\ *or* **-nas** [Medieval Latin, from Latin, sail yard] (1646)
**1** *plural* **-nae :** one of a pair of slender movable segmented sensory organs on the head of insects, myriapods, and crustaceans — see INSECT illustration
**2 :** a usually metallic device (as a rod or wire) for radiating or receiving radio waves
**3** *antennae plural* **:** a special sensitivity or receptiveness ⟨his political *antennae* proved to be shrewder than ever —Erich Segal⟩ ◆
— **an·ten·nal** \-'te-n°l\ *adjective*
**an·ten·nule** \an-'ten-(ˌ)yü(-ə)l\ *noun* (1845)
**:** a small antenna or similar appendage
— **an·ten·nu·lar** \-'ten-yə-lər\ *adjective*
**an·te·nup·tial** \ˌan-ti-'nəp-shəl, -chəl; ÷shə-wəl, ÷-chə-\ *adjective* (1818)
**:** PRENUPTIAL
**an·te·pen·di·um** \ˌan-ti-'pen-dē-əm\ *noun, plural* **-di·ums** *or* **-dia** \-dē-ə\ [Medieval Latin, from Latin *ante-* + *pendēre* to hang — more at PENDANT] (circa 1696)
**:** a hanging for the front of an altar, pulpit, or lectern
**an·te·pe·nult** \ˌan-ti-'pē-ˌnəlt, -pi-\ *also* **an·te·pen·ul·ti·ma** \-pi-'nəl-tə-mə\ *noun* [Late

*A* anta

Latin *antepaenultima*, feminine of *antepaenultimus* preceding the next to last, from Latin *ante-* + *paenultimus* penultimate] (1581)
: the third syllable of a word counting from the end (as *cu* in *accumulate*)
— **an·te·pen·ul·ti·mate** \-pi-'nəl-tə-mət\ *adjective or noun*

**ante–post** \'an-ti-,pōst\ *adjective* (1902)
*British* : relating to or being wagers on a horse race made especially before the day of the race

**an·te·ri·or** \an-'tir-ē-ər\ *adjective* [Latin, comparative of *ante* before — more at ANTE-] (1541)
**1 a** : situated before or toward the front **b** : situated near or toward the head or part most nearly corresponding to a head
**2** : coming before in time or development
*synonym* see PRECEDING
— **an·te·ri·or·ly** *adverb*

**an·te·room** \'an-ti-,rüm, -,rüm\ *noun* (1762)
: an outer room that leads to another room and that is often used as a waiting room

**anth-** — see ANTI-

**an·thel·min·tic** \,ant-,hel-'min-tik, ,an-,thel-\ *adjective* [*anti-* + Greek *helminth-, helmis* worm] (1684)
: expelling or destroying parasitic worms especially of the intestine
— **anthelmintic** *noun*

**an·them** \'an(t)-thəm\ *noun* [Middle English *antem*, from Old English *antefn*, from Late Latin *antiphona*, from Late Greek *antiphōna*, plural of *antiphōnon*, from Greek, neuter of *antiphōnos* responsive, from *anti-* + *phōnē* sound — more at BAN] (before 12th century)
**1 a** : a psalm or hymn sung antiphonally or responsively **b** : a sacred vocal composition with words usually from the Scriptures
**2** : a song or hymn of praise or gladness

**an·the·mi·on** \an-'thē-mē-ən\ *noun, plural* **-mia** \-mē-ə\ [Greek, from diminutive of *anthemon* flower, from *anthos* — more at ANTHOLOGY] (1865)
: a flat ornament of floral form (as in relief sculpture or in painting)

**an·ther** \'an(t)-thər\ *noun* [New Latin *anthera*, from Latin, medicine made from flowers, from Greek *anthēra*, from feminine of *anthēros* flowery, from *anthos*] (circa 1706)
: the part of a stamen that produces and contains pollen and is usually borne on a stalk
— see FLOWER illustration
— **an·ther·al** \-thə-rəl\ *adjective*

**an·ther·id·i·um** \,an(t)-thə-'ri-dē-əm\ *noun, plural* **-id·ia** \-dē-ə\ [New Latin, from *anthera*] (1854)
: the male reproductive organ of some cryptogamous plants
— **an·ther·id·i·al** \-dē-əl\ *adjective*

**an·the·sis** \an-'thē-səs\ *noun* [New Latin, from Greek *anthēsis* bloom, from *anthein* to flower, from *anthos*] (circa 1823)
: the action or period of opening of a flower

**ant·hill** \'ant-,hil\ *noun* (14th century)
: a mound of debris thrown up by ants or termites in digging their nest

**an·tho·cy·a·nin** \,an(t)-thə-'sī-ə-nən\ *also* **an·tho·cy·an** \-'sī-ən, -,an\ *noun* [Greek *anthos* + *kyanos* dark blue] (1839)
: any of various soluble glycoside pigments producing blue to red coloring in flowers and plants

**an·thol·o·gist** \an-'thä-lə-jist\ *noun* (1805)
: a compiler of an anthology

**an·thol·o·gize** \-,jīz\ *transitive verb* **-gized; -giz·ing** (1892)
: to compile, publish, or include in an anthology
— **an·thol·o·giz·er** \-,jī-zər\ *noun*

**an·thol·o·gy** \an-'thä-lə-jē\ *noun, plural* **-gies** [New Latin *anthologia* collection of epigrams, from Middle Greek, from Greek, flower gathering, from *anthos* flower + *logia* collecting, from *legein* to gather; akin to Sanskrit *andha* herb — more at LEGEND] (1640)
**1** : a collection of selected literary pieces or passages or works of art or music
**2** : ASSORTMENT 〈an *anthology* of threadbare clichés of . . . bistro cuisine —Jay Jacobs〉
— **an·tho·log·i·cal** \,an(t)-thə-'lä-ji-kəl\ *adjective*

**an·thoph·i·lous** \an-'thä-fə-ləs\ *adjective* [International Scientific Vocabulary, from Greek *anthos* + English *-philous*] (1883)
: feeding upon or living among flowers 〈*anthophilous* insects〉

**an·tho·phyl·lite** \,an(t)-thə-'fi-,līt, (,)an-'thä-fə-\ *noun* [German *Anthophyllit*, from New Latin *anthophyllum*, from Greek *anthos* + *phyllon* leaf — more at BLADE] (circa 1828)
: an orthorhombic mineral of the amphibole group that is essentially a silicate of magnesium and iron and is usually lamellar or fibrous and when fibrous is one of the less common forms of asbestos

**an·tho·zo·an** \,an(t)-thə-'zō-ən\ *noun* [ultimately from Greek *anthos* + *zōion* animal; akin to Greek *zōē* life — more at QUICK] (circa 1889)
: any of a class (Anthozoa) of marine coelenterates (as the corals and sea anemones) having polyps with radial partitions
— **anthozoan** *adjective*

**an·thra·cene** \'an(t)-thrə-,sēn\ *noun* (1863)
: a crystalline aromatic hydrocarbon $C_{14}H_{10}$ obtained from coal-tar distillation

**an·thra·cite** \'an(t)-thrə-,sīt\ *noun* [Greek *anthrakitis*, from *anthrak-, anthrax* coal] (1812)
: a hard natural coal of high luster differing from bituminous coal in containing little volatile matter and in burning very cleanly — called also *hard coal*
— **an·thra·cit·ic** \,an(t)-thrə-'si-tik\ *adjective*

**an·thrac·nose** \an-'thrak-,nōs\ *noun* [French, from Greek *anthrak-, anthrax* + *nosos* disease] (1886)
: any of numerous destructive plant diseases caused by imperfect fungi and characterized especially by necrotic lesions

**an·thra·ni·late** \an-'thra-nᵊl-,āt, ,an-thrə-'ni-,lāt\ *noun* (1921)
: a salt or ester of anthranilic acid

**an·thra·nil·ic acid** \,an(t)-thrə-'ni-lik-\ *noun* [International Scientific Vocabulary *anthracene* + *anil*ine] (1881)
: a crystalline acid $NH_2C_6H_4COOH$ used as an intermediate in the manufacture of dyes (as indigo), pharmaceuticals, and perfumes

**an·thra·qui·none** \,an(t)-thrə-kwi-'nōn, -'kwi-,nōn\ *noun* [probably from French, from *anthracene* + *quinone*] (1869)
: a yellow crystalline ketone $C_{14}H_8O_2$ often derived from anthracene and used especially in the manufacture of dyes

**an·thrax** \'an-,thraks\ *noun* [Middle English *antrax* carbuncle, from Latin *anthrax*, from Greek, coal, carbuncle] (1876)
: an infectious disease of warm-blooded animals (as cattle and sheep) caused by a spore-forming bacterium (*Bacillus anthracis*), transmissible to humans especially by the handling of infected products (as wool), and characterized by external ulcerating nodules or by lesions in the lungs

**anthro-** *or* **anthropo-** *combining form* [Latin *anthropo-*, from Greek *anthrōp-, anthrōpo-*, from *anthrōpos*]
: human being 〈*anthropo*genic〉

**an·throp·ic** \an-'thrä-pik\ *or* **an·throp·i·cal** \-pi-kəl\ *adjective* [Greek *anthrōpikos*, from *anthrōpos*] (circa 1806)
: of or relating to human beings or the period of their existence on earth

**anthropic principle** *noun* (1974)
: either of two principles in cosmology: **a** : conditions that are observed in the universe must allow the observer to exist — called also *weak anthropic principle* **b** : the universe must have properties that make inevitable the existence of intelligent life — called also *strong anthropic principle*

**an·thro·po·cen·tric** \,an(t)-thrə-pə-'sen-trik\ *adjective* (1863)
**1** : considering human beings as the most significant entity of the universe
**2** : interpreting or regarding the world in terms of human values and experiences
— **an·thro·po·cen·tri·cal·ly** \-tri-k(ə-)lē\ *adverb*
— **an·thro·po·cen·tric·i·ty** \-pō-(,)sen-'tri-sə-tē\ *noun*
— **an·thro·po·cen·trism** \-'sen-,tri-zəm\ *noun*

**an·thro·po·gen·ic** \-pə-'je-nik\ *adjective* (1923)
: of, relating to, or resulting from the influence of human beings on nature 〈*anthropogenic* pollutants〉

**an·thro·poid** \'an(t)-thrə-,pòid\ *noun* [Greek *anthrōpoeidēs* resembling a human, from *anthrōpos*] (1832)
**1** : APE 1b
**2** : a person resembling an ape 〈the howling *anthropoids* of the Hookworm Belt —H. L. Mencken〉
— **anthropoid** *adjective*

**anthropoid ape** *noun* (circa 1837)
: APE 1b

**an·thro·pol·o·gy** \,an(t)-thrə-'pä-lə-jē\ *noun* [New Latin *anthropologia*, from *anthrop-* + *-logia* -logy] (1593)
**1** : the science of human beings; *especially* : the study of human beings in relation to distribution, origin, classification, and relationship of races, physical character, environmental and social relations, and culture
**2** : theology dealing with the origin, nature, and destiny of human beings
— **an·thro·po·log·i·cal** \-pə-'lä-ji-kəl\ *adjective*
— **an·thro·po·log·i·cal·ly** \-ji-k(ə-)lē\ *adverb*
— **an·thro·pol·o·gist** \,an(t)-thrə-'pä-lə-jist\ *noun*

**an·thro·pom·e·try** \,an(t)-thrə-'pä-mə-trē\ *noun* [French *anthropométrie*, from *anthrop-* + *-métrie* -metry] (circa 1839)
: the study of human body measurements especially on a comparative basis
— **an·thro·po·met·ric** \-pə-'me-trik\ *adjective*

**an·thro·po·morph** \'an(t)-thrə-pə-,mòrf\ *noun* (1894)
: a stylized human figure (as in prehistoric art)

**an·thro·po·mor·phic** \,an(t)-thrə-pə-'mòr-fik\ *adjective* [Late Latin *anthropomorphus* of

---

◇ WORD HISTORY
**antenna** In Classical Latin *antenna* means "sail yard," the long spar tapered toward the ends that supports and spreads the head of a sail on a sailing vessel. The Greek word for a sail yard was *keraia*, a derivative of *keras*, meaning "horn." But *keraia* was also used for a number of other things that thrust outward, such as the projections of the hipbone or the spur of a mountain. Aristotle, in his *Historia Animalium* ("Natural History of Animals") used plural *keraiai* for the "horns" or feelers of insects. In a Latin translation of Aristotle's work made during the Renaissance, the word *antennae* appears for Greek *keraiai*. When scientific writings on insects began appearing in English in the 17th century, entomologists borrowed *antennae* as the word for those feelers.

---

\ə\ abut \ᵊ\ kitten \ər\ further \a\ ash \ā\ ace
\ä\ mop, mar \aù\ out \ch\ chin \e\ bet \ē\ easy
\g\ go \i\ hit \ī\ ice \j\ job \ŋ\ sing \ō\ go
\ò\ law \òi\ boy \th\ thin \ṯẖ\ the \ü\ loot \ù\ foot
\y\ yet \zh\ vision *see also* Guide to Pronunciation

human form, from Greek *anthrōpomorphos,* from *anthrōp-* + *-morphos* -morphous] (1827)
**1 :** described or thought of as having a human form or human attributes 〈*anthropomorphic* deities〉
**2 :** ascribing human characteristics to nonhuman things 〈*anthropomorphic* supernaturalism〉
— **an·thro·po·mor·phi·cal·ly** \-fi-k(ə-)lē\ *adverb*
**an·thro·po·mor·phism** \-,fi-zəm\ *noun* (1753)
**:** an interpretation of what is not human or personal in terms of human or personal characteristics **:** HUMANIZATION
— **an·thro·po·mor·phist** \-fist\ *noun*
**an·thro·po·mor·phize** \-,fīz\ *verb* **-phized; -phiz·ing** (1845)
*transitive verb*
**:** to attribute human form or personality to
*intransitive verb*
**:** to attribute human form or personality to things not human
— **an·thro·po·mor·phi·za·tion** \-,mȯr-fə-'zā-shən\ *noun*
**an·thro·po·pa·thism** \,an(t)-thrə-'pä-pə-,thi-zəm, -pō-'pa-,thi-\ *noun* [Late Greek *anthrōpopatheia* humanity, from Greek *anthrōpopathēs* having human feelings, from *anthrōp-* + *pathos* experience — more at PATHOS] (1847)
**:** the ascription of human feelings to something not human
**an·thro·poph·a·gous** \,an(t)-thrə-'pä-fə-gəs\ *adjective* (circa 1828)
**:** feeding on human flesh
— **an·thro·poph·a·gy** \-fə-jē\ *noun*
**an·thro·poph·a·gus** \-fə-gəs\ *noun, plural* **-a·gi** \-fə-,gī, -,jī, -,gē\ [Latin, from Greek *anthrōpophagos,* from *anthrōp-* + *-phagos* -phagous] (1552)
**:** MAN-EATER, CANNIBAL
**an·thro·pos·o·phy** \,an(t)-thrə-'pä-sə-fē\ *noun* (1916)
**:** a 20th century religious system growing out of theosophy and centering on human development
**an·thur·i·um** \an-'thu̇r-ē-əm, -'thyu̇r-\ *noun* [New Latin, from Greek *anthos* flower + *oura* tail — more at ANTHOLOGY, ASS] (circa 1839)
**:** any of a genus (*Anthurium*) of tropical American plants of the arum family with large often highly colored leaves, a cylindrical spadix, and a colored spathe
**¹an·ti** \'an-,tī, 'an-tē\ *noun, plural* **antis** [*anti-*] (1788)
**:** one that is opposed
**²anti** *adjective* (1857)
**:** OPPOSED
**³anti** *preposition* (1953)
**:** opposed to **:** AGAINST
**anti-** *or* **ant-** *or* **anth-** *prefix* [*anti-* from Middle English, from Middle French & Latin; Middle French, from Latin, against, from Greek, from *anti; ant-* from Middle English, from Latin, against, from Greek, from *anti; anth-* from Latin, against, from Greek, from *anti* — more at ANTE-]
**1 a :** of the same kind but situated opposite, exerting energy in the opposite direction, or pursuing an opposite policy 〈*anti*clinal〉 **b** **:** one that is opposite in kind to 〈*anti*climax〉
**2 a :** opposing or hostile to in opinion, sympathy, or practice 〈*anti*-Semite〉 **b :** opposing in effect or activity 〈*anti*acid〉
**3 :** serving to prevent, cure, or alleviate 〈*anti*anxiety〉
**4 :** combating or defending against 〈*anti*aircraft〉 〈*anti*missile〉

an·ti·ac·a·dem·ic
an·ti·ac·ne
an·ti·ad·min·is·tra·tion
an·ti·ag·gres·sion
an·ti·ag·ing
an·ti–AIDS
an·ti·al·co·hol
an·ti·al·co·hol·ism
an·ti·alien
an·ti·al·ler·gen·ic
an·ti·ane·mia
an·ti·apart·heid
an·ti·aph·ro·di·si·ac

an·ti·aris·to·crat·ic
an·ti·ar·thrit·ic
an·ti·ar·thri·tis
an·ti·as·sim·i·la·tion
an·ti·asth·ma
an·ti·au·thor·i·tar·i·an
an·ti·au·thor·i·tar·i·an·ism
an·ti·au·thor·i·ty
an·ti·back·lash
an·ti·bi·as
an·ti·bill·board
an·ti–Bol·she·vik
an·ti·boss
an·ti·bour·geois
an·ti·boy·cott
an·ti–Brit·ish
an·ti·bug
an·ti·bu·reau·crat·ic
an·ti·bur·glar
an·ti·bur·glary
an·ti·cak·ing
an·ti·cap·i·tal·ism
an·ti·cap·i·tal·ist
an·ti·car·cin·o·gen
an·ti·car·ci·no·gen·ic
an·ti·car·ies
an·ti–Cath·o·lic
an·ti–Ca·thol·i·cism
an·ti·cel·lu·lite
an·ti·cen·sor·ship
an·ti·cho·les·ter·ol
an·ti–Chris·tian
an·ti–Chris·tian·i·ty
an·ti·church
an·ti·cig·a·rette
an·ti·city
an·ti·clas·si·cal
an·ti·cling
an·ti·clot·ting
an·ti·cold
an·ti·col·li·sion
an·ti·co·lo·nial
an·ti·co·lo·nial·ism
an·ti·co·lo·nial·ist
an·ti·com·mer·cial
an·ti·com·mer·cial·ism
an·ti·com·mu·nism
an·ti·com·mu·nist
an·ti·con·glom·er·ate
an·ti·con·ser·va·tion
an·ti·con·ser·va·tion·ist
an·ti·con·sum·er
an·ti·con·ven·tion·al
an·ti·cor·po·rate
an·ti·cor·ro·sion
an·ti·cor·ro·sive
an·ti·cor·rup·tion
an·ti·coun·ter·feit·ing
an·ti·crack
an·ti·cre·ative
an·ti·crime
an·ti·cru·el·ty
an·ti·cult
an·ti·cul·tur·al
an·ti·dan·druff
an·ti–Dar·win·i·an
an·ti–Dar·win·ism
an·ti·def·a·ma·tion
an·ti·de·pres·sion
an·ti·de·seg·re·ga·tion
an·ti·de·sert·i·fi·ca·tion
an·ti·des·ic·cant
an·ti·de·vel·op·ment
an·ti·di·a·bet·ic
an·ti·di·ar·rhe·al
an·ti·di·lu·tion
an·ti·dis·crim·i·na·tion
an·ti·dog·mat·ic

an·ti·draft
an·ti·eco·nom·ic
an·ti·ed·u·ca·tion·al
an·ti·egal·i·tar·i·an
an·ti·elite
an·ti·elit·ism
an·ti·elit·ist
an·ti·emet·ic
an·ti–En·glish
an·ti·en·tro·pic
an·ti·ep·i·lep·sy
an·ti·ep·i·lep·tic
an·ti·erot·ic
an·ti·es·tab·lish·ment
an·ti·es·tro·gen
an·ti·evo·lu·tion
an·ti·evo·lu·tion·ary
an·ti·evo·lu·tion·ism
an·ti·evo·lu·tion·ist
an·ti·fam·i·ly
an·ti·fas·cism
an·ti·fas·cist
an·ti·fash·ion
an·ti·fash·ion·able
an·ti·fa·tigue
an·ti·fe·male
an·ti·fem·i·nine
an·ti·fem·i·nism
an·ti·fem·i·nist
an·ti·fil·i·bus·ter
an·ti·flu
an·ti·foam
an·ti·foam·ing
an·ti·fog·ging
an·ti·fore·clo·sure
an·ti·for·eign
an·ti·for·eign·er
an·ti·for·mal·ist
an·ti·fraud
an·ti–French
an·ti·fric·tion
an·ti·fur
an·ti·gam·bling
an·ti·gay
an·ti–Ger·man
an·ti·glare
an·ti·gov·ern·ment
an·ti·growth
an·ti·guer·ril·la
an·ti·gun
an·ti·her·pes
an·ti·hi·er·ar·chi·cal
an·ti·hi·jack
an·ti·his·tor·i·cal
an·ti·ho·mo·sex·u·al
an·ti·hu·man·ism
an·ti·hu·man·is·tic
an·ti·hu·man·i·tar·i·an
an·ti·hunt·er
an·ti·hunt·ing
an·ti·hys·ter·ic
an·ti·ic·ing
an·ti–ideo·log·i·cal
an·ti·im·pe·ri·al·ism
an·ti·im·pe·ri·al·ist
an·ti·in·cum·bent
an·ti·in·fec·tive
an·ti·in·fla·tion
an·ti·in·fla·tion·ary
an·ti·in·sti·tu·tion·al
an·ti·in·te·gra·tion
an·ti·in·tru·sion
an·ti·Ital·ian
an·ti·jam
an·ti·jam·ming
an·ti–Jap·a·nese
an·ti–Jew·ish
an·ti·kick·back
an·ti·knock
an·ti·la·bor
an·ti·leak
an·ti·lep·ro·sy
an·ti·lib·er·al
an·ti·lib·er·al·ism

an·ti·lib·er·tar·i·an
an·ti·lit·er·ate
an·ti·lit·ter
an·ti·lit·ter·ing
an·ti·log·i·cal
an·ti·lynch·ing
an·ti·ma·cho
an·ti·ma·lar·ia
an·ti·male
an·ti·man
an·ti·man·age·ment
an·ti·mar·i·jua·na
an·ti·mar·ket
an·ti·ma·te·ri·al·ism
an·ti·ma·te·ri·al·ist
an·ti·mech·a·nist
an·ti·merg·er
an·ti·met·a·bol·ic
an·ti·meta·phys·i·cal
an·ti·mil·i·ta·rism
an·ti·mil·i·ta·rist
an·ti·mil·i·tary
an·ti·mis·ce·ge·na·tion
an·ti·mis·sile
an·ti·mod·ern
an·ti·mod·ern·ist
an·ti·mo·nar·chi·cal
an·ti·mon·ar·chist
an·ti·mo·nop·o·list
an·ti·mo·nop·o·ly
an·ti·mos·qui·to
an·ti·mu·si·cal
an·ti·nar·ra·tive
an·ti·na·tion·al
an·ti·na·tion·al·ist
an·ti·nat·u·ral
an·ti·na·ture
an·ti·nau·sea
an·ti–Na·zi
an·ti–Ne·gro
an·ti·nep·o·tism
an·ti·noise
an·ti·obe·si·ty
an·ti·ob·scen·i·ty
an·ti·or·ga·ni·za·tion
an·ti·pa·pal
an·ti·par·ty
an·ti·pes·ti·cide
an·ti·pi·ra·cy
an·ti·plague
an·ti·plaque
an·ti·plea·sure
an·ti·poach·ing
an·ti·po·lice
an·ti·po·lit·i·cal
an·ti·pol·i·tics
an·ti·pop·u·lar
an·ti·porn
an·ti·por·no·graph·ic
an·ti·por·nog·ra·phy
an·ti·pot
an·ti·pov·er·ty
an·ti·pred·a·tor
an·ti·press
an·ti·prof·i·teer·ing
an·ti·pro·gres·sive
an·ti·pros·ti·tu·tion
an·ti·pru·rit·ic
an·ti·ra·bies
an·ti·rac·ism
an·ti·rac·ist
an·ti·rack·e·teer·ing
an·ti·ra·dar
an·ti·rad·i·cal
an·ti·rad·i·cal·ism
an·ti·rape
an·ti·ra·tio·nal
an·ti·ra·tio·nal·ism
an·ti·ra·tio·nal·ist
an·ti·ra·tio·nal·i·ty
an·ti·re·al·ism
an·ti·re·al·ist
an·ti·re·ces·sion
an·ti·re·ces·sion·ary
an·ti·red

an·ti·re·duc·tion·ism
an·ti·re·duc·tion·ist
an·ti·re·flec·tion
an·ti·re·flec·tive
an·ti·re·form
an·ti·reg·u·la·to·ry
an·ti·re·li·gion
an·ti·re·li·gious
an·ti·rev·o·lu·tion·ary
an·ti·ri·ot
an·ti·rit·u·al·ism
an·ti·rock
an·ti·roll
an·ti·ro·man·tic
an·ti·ro·man·ti·cism
an·ti·roy·al·ist
an·ti–Rus·sian
an·ti·rust
an·ti·sat·el·lite
an·ti·schizo·phre·nia
an·ti·schiz·o·phren·ic
an·ti·sci·ence
an·ti·sci·en·tif·ic
an·ti·se·cre·cy
an·ti·seg·re·ga·tion
an·ti·sei·zure
an·ti·sen·ti·men·tal
an·ti·sep·a·rat·ist
an·ti·sex
an·ti·sex·ist
an·ti·sex·u·al
an·ti·sex·u·al·i·ty
an·ti·shark
an·ti·ship
an·ti·shock
an·ti·shop·lift·ing
an·ti·skid
an·ti·slav·ery
an·ti·sleep
an·ti·slip
an·ti·smog
an·ti·smoke
an·ti·smok·er
an·ti·smok·ing
an·ti·smug·gling
an·ti·smut
an·ti·snob
an·ti·so·cial·ist
an·ti–So·vi·et
an·ti–So·vi·et·ism
an·ti·spec·u·la·tion
an·ti·spec·u·la·tive
an·ti·spend·ing
an·ti–Sta·lin·ist
an·ti·state
an·ti·stick
an·ti·sto·ry
an·ti·stress
an·ti·strike
an·ti·stu·dent
an·ti·sub·ma·rine
an·ti·sub·si·dy
an·ti·sub·ver·sion
an·ti·sub·ver·sive
an·ti·sui·cide
an·ti·syph·i·lit·ic
an·ti·take·over
an·ti·tank
an·ti·tar·nish
an·ti·tax
an·ti·tech·no·log·i·cal
an·ti·tech·nol·o·gy
an·ti·ter·ror·ism
an·ti·ter·ror·ist
an·ti·theft
an·ti·the·o·ret·i·cal
an·ti·to·bac·co
an·ti·to·tal·i·tar·i·an
an·ti·tra·di·tion·al
an·ti·tu·ber·cu·lar
an·ti·tu·ber·cu·lo·sis
an·ti·tu·ber·cu·lous
an·ti·tu·mor

**an·ti·tu·mor·al**
**an·ti·ty·phoid**
**an·ti·ul·cer**
**an·ti·un·em·ploy·
ment**
**an·ti·un·ion**
**an·ti·uni·ver·si·ty**
**an·ti·ur·ban**
**an·ti·vi·o·lence**
**an·ti·vi·ral**
**an·ti·vi·rus**

**an·ti·vivi·sec·tion**
**an·ti·vivi·sec·tion·ist**
**an·ti·war**
**an·ti·wear**
**an·ti·wel·fare**
**an·ti–West**
**an·ti–West·ern**
**an·ti·whal·ing**
**an·ti·wom·an**
**an·ti·wrin·kle**
**an·ti–Zi·on·ist**

**an·ti·abor·tion** \ˌan-tē-ə-'bȯr-shən, ˌan-ˌtī-\
*adjective* (1971)
**:** opposed to abortion ⟨*antiabortion* lobbyists⟩
— **an·ti·abor·tion·ist** \-sh(ə-)nist\ *noun*
**an·ti·air** \ˌan-tē-'ar, -'er, -ˌtī-\ *adjective* (1925)
**:** ANTIAIRCRAFT
¹**an·ti·air·craft** \-'ar-ˌkraft, -'er-\ *adjective*
(1914)
**:** designed for or concerned with defense
against air attack
²**antiaircraft** *noun* (1926)
**:** antiaircraft guns or their fire
**an·ti–Amer·i·can** \-ə-'mer-ə-kən, -'mər-,
-'mar-, -i-kən\ *adjective* (1773)
**:** opposed or hostile to the people or the government policies of the U.S.
— **an·ti–Amer·i·can·ism** \-kə-ˌni-zəm\
*noun*
**an·ti·anx·i·ety** \-(ˌ)aŋ-'zī-ə-tē\ *adjective*
(1962)
**:** tending to prevent or relieve anxiety ⟨*anti-
anxiety* drugs⟩
**an·ti·ar·rhyth·mic** \ˌan-tē-(ˌ)ā-'rith-mik, ˌan-
ˌtī-\ *adjective* (1954)
**:** tending to prevent or relieve cardiac arrhythmia ⟨an *antiarrhythmic* agent⟩
**an·ti·art** \-'ärt\ *noun* (1937)
**:** art based on premises antithetical to traditional or popular art forms; *specifically* **:** DADA
**an·ti·aux·in** \-'ȯk-sən\ *noun* (1949)
**:** a plant substance that opposes or suppresses
the natural effect of an auxin
**an·ti·bac·te·ri·al** \ˌan-ti-bak-'tir-ē-əl, ˌan-ˌtī-\
*adjective* (circa 1897)
**:** directed or effective against bacteria
— **antibacterial** *noun*
**an·ti·bal·lis·tic missile** \ˌan-ti-bə-'lis-tik-,
ˌan-ˌtī\ *noun* (circa 1959)
**:** a missile for intercepting and destroying ballistic missiles
**an·ti·bi·o·sis** \-bī-'ō-səs, -bē-\ *noun* [New
Latin] (1899)
**:** antagonistic association between organisms
to the detriment of one of them or between
one organism and a metabolic product of another
¹**an·ti·bi·ot·ic** \ˌan-ti-bī-'ä-tik, -ˌtī-; ˌan-ti-bē-\
*adjective* (1894)
**1 :** tending to prevent, inhibit, or destroy life
**2 :** of or relating to antibiosis or to antibiosis
— **an·ti·bi·ot·i·cal·ly** \-ti-k(ə-)lē\ *adverb*
²**antibiotic** *noun* (1943)
**:** a substance produced by or a semisynthetic
substance derived from a microorganism and
able in dilute solution to inhibit or kill another
microorganism
**an·ti·black** \-'blak\ *adjective* (1952)
**:** opposed or hostile to black people
— **an·ti·black·ism** \-'bla-ki-zəm\ *noun*
**an·ti·body** \'an-ti-ˌbä-dē\ *noun* (1900)
**:** any of a large number of proteins of high
molecular weight that are produced normally
by specialized B cells after stimulation by an
antigen and act specifically against the antigen
in an immune response, that are produced abnormally by some cancer cells, and that typically consist of four subunits including two
heavy chains and two light chains — called
also *immunoglobulin*
**an·ti·busi·ness** \ˌan-ti-'biz-nəs, ˌan-ˌtī-, -nəz\
*adjective* (1938)
**:** antagonistic toward business and especially
big business
**an·ti·bus·ing** \-'bə-siŋ\ *adjective* (circa 1969)

**:** opposed to the busing of schoolchildren ⟨*antibusing* parents⟩ ⟨*antibusing* campaign⟩
¹**an·tic** \'an-tik\ *noun* [Italian *antico* ancient
thing or person, from *antico* ancient, from Latin *antiquus* — more at ANTIQUE ] (1529)
**1 :** an attention-drawing often wildly playful
or funny act or action **:** CAPER ⟨childish *antics*⟩
**2** *archaic* **:** a performer of a grotesque or ludicrous part **:** BUFFOON ◆
²**antic** *adjective* (1548)
**1** *archaic* **:** GROTESQUE, BIZARRE
**2 a :** characterized by clownish extravagance
or absurdity **b :** whimsically gay **:** FROLICSOME
— **an·ti·cal·ly** \-ti-k(ə-)lē\ *adverb*
**an·ti·can·cer** \ˌan-ˌtī-'kan(t)-sər, ˌan-ti-\ *adjective* (1926)
**:** used against or tending to arrest cancer ⟨*anticancer* drugs⟩ ⟨*anticancer* activity⟩ ⟨antican-
cer effects⟩
**an·ti·cho·lin·er·gic** \-ˌkō-lə-'nər-jik\ *adjective* (1942)
**:** opposing or blocking the physiologic action
of acetylcholine
— **anticholinergic** *noun*
**an·ti·cho·lin·es·ter·ase** \-'nes-tə-ˌrās, -ˌrāz\
*noun* (1942)
**:** a substance (as neostigmine) that inhibits a
cholinesterase by combination with it
**An·ti·christ** \'an-ti-ˌkrīst, -ˌtī-\ *noun* [Middle
English *anticrist*, from Old English & Late
Latin; Old English *antecrist*, from Late Latin
*Antichristus*, from Greek *Antichristos*, from
*anti-* + *Christos* Christ] (before 12th century)
**1 :** one who denies or opposes Christ; *specifically* **:** a great antagonist expected to fill the
world with wickedness but to be conquered
forever by Christ at his second coming
**2 :** a false Christ
**an·tic·i·pant** \an-'ti-sə-pənt\ *adjective* (1626)
**:** EXPECTANT, ANTICIPATING — usually used
with *of*
— **anticipant** *noun*
**an·tic·i·pate** \an-'ti-sə-ˌpāt\ *verb* **-pat·ed;
-pat·ing** [Latin *anticipatus*, past participle of
*anticipare*, from *ante-* + *-cipare* (from *capere*
to take) — more at HEAVE] (1532)
*transitive verb*
**1 :** to give advance thought, discussion, or
treatment to
**2 :** to meet (an obligation) before a due date
**3 :** to foresee and deal with in advance **:** FORE-
STALL
**4 :** to use or expend in advance of actual possession
**5 :** to act before (another) often so as to check
or counter
**6 :** to look forward to as certain **:** EXPECT
*intransitive verb*
**:** to speak or write in knowledge or expectation of later matter
*synonym* see FORESEE, PREVENT
— **an·tic·i·pat·able** \-ˌpā-tə-bəl\ *adjective*
— **an·tic·i·pa·tor** \-ˌpā-tər\ *noun*
**an·tic·i·pa·tion** \(ˌ)an-ˌti-sə-'pā-shən\ *noun*
(14th century)
**1 a :** a prior action that takes into account or
forestalls a later action **b :** the act of looking
forward; *especially* **:** pleasurable expectation
**2 :** the use of money before it is available
**3 a :** visualization of a future event or state **b
:** an object or form that anticipates a later type
**4 :** the early sounding of one or more tones of
a succeeding chord to form a temporary dissonance — compare SUSPENSION
*synonym* see PROSPECT
**an·tic·i·pa·to·ry** \an-'ti-sə-pə-ˌtōr-ē, -ˌtȯr-\
*adjective* (1669)
**:** characterized by anticipation **:** ANTICIPATING
**an·ti·cler·i·cal** \ˌan-ti-'kler-i-kəl, ˌan-ˌtī-\ *adjective* (1845)
**:** opposed to clericalism or to the interference
or influence of the clergy in secular affairs
— **anticlerical** *noun*
— **an·ti·cler·i·cal·ism** \-kə-ˌli-zəm\ *noun*

**an·ti·cli·mac·tic** \-klī-'mak-tik, -klə-\ *also*
**an·ti·cli·mac·ti·cal** \-ti-kəl\ *adjective*
(1898)
**:** of, relating to, or marked by anticlimax
— **an·ti·cli·mac·ti·cal·ly** \-ti-k(ə-)lē\ *adverb*
**an·ti·cli·max** \-'klī-ˌmaks\ *noun* (1710)
**1 :** the usually sudden transition in discourse
from a significant idea to a trivial or ludicrous
idea; *also* **:** an instance of this transition
**2 :** an event (as at the end of a series) that is
strikingly less important than what has preceded it
**an·ti·cli·nal** \ˌan-ti-'klī-nᵊl\ *adjective* [*anti-* +
Greek *klinein* to lean — more at LEAN] (1882)
**:** occurring at right angles to the surface or circumference of a plant organ ⟨an *anticlinal* pattern of cell walls⟩
**an·ti·cline** \'an-ti-ˌklīn\ *noun* (circa 1861)
**:** an arch of stratified
rock in which the lay-
ers bend downward
in opposite directions
from the crest —
compare SYNCLINE

cross section of strata
showing anticline

**an·ti·clock·wise**
\ˌan-ti-'kläk-ˌwīz, ˌan-
ˌtī-\ *adjective or adverb* (1898)
*chiefly British* **:** COUNTERCLOCKWISE
**an·ti·co·ag·u·lant** \-kō-'a-gyə-lənt\ *noun*
(circa 1905)
**:** a substance that hinders the clotting of blood
— **anticoagulant** *adjective*
**an·ti·co·don** \-'kō-ˌdän\ *noun* (1965)
**:** a triplet of nucleotide bases in transfer RNA
that identifies the amino acid carried and binds
to a complementary codon in messenger RNA
during protein synthesis at a ribosome
**an·ti·com·pet·i·tive** \-kəm-'pe-tə-tiv\ *adjective* (1952)
**:** tending to reduce or discourage competition
**an·ti·con·vul·sant** \-kən-'vəl-sənt\ *also* **an-
ti·con·vul·sive** \-siv\ *adjective* (1734)
**:** used or tending to control or to prevent convulsions (as in epilepsy)
— **anticonvulsant** *also* **anticonvulsive**
*noun*
**an·ti·cy·clone** \ˌan-ti-'sī-ˌklōn\ *noun* (1877)
**1 :** a system of winds that rotates about a center of high atmospheric pressure clockwise in
the northern hemisphere and counterclockwise
in the southern, that usually advances at 20 to
30 miles (about 30 to 50 kilometers) per hour,
and that usually has a diameter of 1500 to
2500 miles (2400 to 4000 kilometers)
**2 :** HIGH 2
— **an·ti·cy·clon·ic** \-sī-'klä-nik\ *adjective*
**an·ti·dem·o·crat·ic** \ˌan-ti-ˌde-mə-'kra-tik,
ˌan-ˌtī-\ *adjective* (1837)
**:** opposed or hostile to the theories or policies
of democracy
¹**an·ti·de·pres·sant** \-di-'pre-sᵊnt\ *adjective*
(1961)

◇ WORD HISTORY
**antic** The fantastic mural paintings found
in the ruins of ancient Roman buildings were,
by reason of their age, *antichi*—"ancient
things"—to the Italians of the Renaissance.
In Renaissance England, on the other hand,
any similarly fantastic painting—of whatever
vintage—that showed strange combinations
of human, animal, and floral forms came to
be called *antike* or *anticke*, from the Italian
word for "ancient," *antico*. And any odd gesture or strange behavior reminiscent of such
artwork became an *antic*.

\ə\ abut \ᵊ\ kitten \ər\ further \a\ ash \ā\ ace
\ä\ mop, mar \aủ\ out \ch\ chin \e\ bet \ē\ easy
\g\ go \i\ hit \ī\ ice \j\ job \ŋ\ sing \ō\ go
\ȯ\ law \ȯi\ boy \th\ thin \th\ the \ü\ loot \ủ\ foot
\y\ yet \zh\ vision *see also* Guide to Pronunciation

**:** used or tending to relieve or prevent psychic depression

**²antidepressant** *noun* (1962)
**:** an antidepressant drug — compare TRICYCLIC ANTIDEPRESSANT

**an·ti·de·riv·a·tive** \-di-'ri-və-tiv\ *noun* (circa 1942)
**:** INDEFINITE INTEGRAL

**an·ti·di·uret·ic hormone** \,an-ti-,dī-yù-'re-tik-\ *noun* (1942)
**:** VASOPRESSIN

**an·ti·dot·al** \,an-ti-'dō-t°l\ *adjective* (1646)
**:** of, relating to, or acting as an antidote
— **an·ti·dot·al·ly** \-t°l-ē\ *adverb*

**an·ti·dote** \'an-ti-,dōt\ *noun* [Middle English *antidot,* from Latin *antidotum,* from Greek *antidotos,* from feminine of *antidotos* given as an antidote, from *antididonai* to give as an antidote, from *anti-* + *didonai* to give — more at DATE] (15th century)
**1 :** a remedy to counteract the effects of poison
**2 :** something that relieves, prevents, or counteracts ⟨an *antidote* to the mechanization of our society⟩
— **antidote** *transitive verb*

**an·ti·drom·ic** \,an-ti-'drä-mik\ *adjective* [*anti-* + Greek *dromos* racecourse, running — more at DROMEDARY] (circa 1927)
**:** proceeding or conducting in a direction opposite to the usual one — used especially of a nerve impulse or fiber
— **an·ti·drom·i·cal·ly** \-mi-k(ə-)lē\ *adverb*

**an·ti·drug** \'an-,tī-,drəg, ,an-tī-'\ *adjective* (1970)
**:** acting against or opposing illicit drugs or their use ⟨*antidrug* activist⟩ ⟨*antidrug* program⟩

**an·ti·dump·ing** \,an-ti-'dəm-piŋ, ,an-,tī-\ *adjective* (1915)
**:** designed to discourage the importation and sale of foreign goods at prices well below domestic prices ⟨*antidumping* tariffs⟩

**an·ti·elec·tron** \,an-tē-ə-'lek-,trän, ,an-,tī-\ *noun* (1931)
**:** POSITRON

**an·ti·fed·er·al·ist** \,an-ti-'fe-d(ə-)rə-list, ,an-,tī-\ *noun, often A&F capitalized* (1787)
**:** a member of the group that opposed the adoption of the U.S. Constitution

**an·ti·fer·ro·mag·net·ic** \-,fer-ō-mag-'ne-tik\ *adjective* (1936)
**:** FERRIMAGNETIC
— **an·ti·fer·ro·mag·net** \-'mag-nət\ *noun*
— **an·ti·fer·ro·mag·net·i·cal·ly** \-mag-'ne-ti-k(ə-)lē\ *adverb*
— **an·ti·fer·ro·mag·net·ism** \-'mag-nə-,ti-zəm\ *noun*

**an·ti·fer·til·i·ty** \-fər-'ti-lə-tē\ *adjective* (1953)
**:** capable of or tending to reduce or destroy fertility **:** CONTRACEPTIVE ⟨*antifertility* agents⟩

**an·ti·flu·o·ri·da·tion·ist** \-,flùr-ə-'dā-sh(ə-)nist, -,flōr-, -,flòr-\ *noun* (1961)
**:** a person opposed to the fluoridation of public water supplies

**an·ti·foul·ing** \-'faù-liŋ\ *adjective* (1895)
**:** intended to prevent fouling of underwater structures (as the bottoms of ships) ⟨*antifouling* paint⟩

**an·ti·freeze** \'an-ti-,frēz\ *noun* (1924)
**:** a substance added to a liquid (as the water in an automobile engine) to lower its freezing point

**an·ti·fun·gal** \,an-ti-'fəŋ-gəl, ,an-,tī-\ *adjective* (1945)
**:** destroying fungi; *also* **:** inhibiting the growth of fungi
— **antifungal** *noun*

**an·ti·gen** \'an-ti-jən, -,jen\ *noun* [German, from French *antigène,* from *anticorps* antibody + *-gène* -gen] (1908)
**:** a usually protein or carbohydrate substance (as a toxin or enzyme) capable of stimulating an immune response
— **an·ti·gen·ic** \,an-ti-'je-nik\ *adjective*

— **an·ti·gen·i·cal·ly** \-ni-k(ə-)lē\ *adverb*
— **an·ti·ge·nic·i·ty** \-jə-'ni-sə-tē\ *noun*

**antigenic determinant** *noun* (1950)
**:** EPITOPE

**an·ti·glob·u·lin** \,an-ti-'glä-byə-lən, ,an-,tī-\ *noun* (circa 1909)
**:** an antibody that combines with and precipitates globulin

**An·tig·o·ne** \an-'ti-gə-(,)nē\ *noun* [Greek *Antigonē*]
**:** a daughter of Oedipus and Jocasta who buries her brother Polynices' body against the order of her uncle Creon

**¹an·ti·grav·i·ty** \,an-ti-'gra-və-tē, ,an-,tī-\ *adjective* (1944)
**:** reducing, canceling, or protecting against the effect of gravity

**²antigravity** *noun* (1949)
**:** a hypothetical effect resulting from cancellation or reduction of a gravitational field

**an·ti·he·mo·phil·ic factor** \-,hē-mə-'fi-lik-\ *noun* (1947)
**:** FACTOR VIII

**an·ti·he·ro** \'an-ti-,hē-(,)rō, 'an-,tī-, -,hir-(,)ō\ *noun* (1714)
**:** a protagonist or notable figure who is conspicuously lacking in heroic qualities
— **an·ti·he·ro·ic** \,an-ti-hi-'rō-ik, ,an-,tī-\ *adjective*

**an·ti·her·o·ine** \,an-ti-'her-ə-wən, ,an-,tī-\ *noun* (1907)
**:** a female antihero

**an·ti·his·ta·mine** \-'his-tə-,mēn, -mən\ *noun* (1946)
**:** any of various compounds that counteract histamine in the body and that are used for treating allergic reactions (as hay fever) and cold symptoms
— **antihistamine** *adjective*
— **an·ti·his·ta·min·ic** \-,his-tə-'mi-nik\ *adjective or noun*

**an·ti·hu·man** \-'hyü-mən, -'yü-\ *adjective* (1854)
**1 :** acting or being against humanity
**2 :** reacting strongly with human antigens

**an·ti·hy·per·ten·sive** \-,hī-pər-'ten(t)-siv\ *noun* (circa 1957)
**:** a substance that is effective against high blood pressure
— **antihypertensive** *adjective*

**an·ti·id·io·type** \,an-tē-'i-dē-ə-,tīp, ,an-tī-\ *noun* (1975)
**:** an antibody that treats another antibody as an antigen and suppresses its immunoreactivity
— **an·ti·id·io·typ·ic** \-,i-dē-ə-'ti-pik\ *adjective*

**an·ti·in·flam·ma·to·ry** \-in-'fla-mə-,tōr-ē, -,tòr-\ *adjective* (circa 1957)
**:** counteracting inflammation
— **anti–inflammatory** *noun*

**an·ti·in·tel·lec·tu·al** \-,in-t°l-'ek-ch(ə-w)əl, -'ek-shwəl\ *adjective* (1936)
**:** opposing or hostile to intellectuals or to an intellectual view or approach
— **anti–intellectual** *noun*
— **an·ti·in·tel·lec·tu·al·ism** \-'ek-chə-(wə)-,li-zəm, -'ek-shwə-\ *noun*

**an·ti·leu·ke·mic** \-lü-'kē-mik\ *adjective* (1951)
**:** counteracting the effects of leukemia

**an·ti·life** \-'līf\ *adjective* (1929)
**:** antagonistic or antithetical to life or to normal human values

**an·ti·lock** \'an-,tī-,läk, 'an-ti-\ *adjective* (1974)
**:** being a braking system for a motor vehicle designed to keep the wheels from locking by electronically controlled pulsed application of the brake for each wheel

**an·ti·log** \'an-ti-,lòg, 'an-,tī-, -,läg\ *noun* (1910)
**:** ANTILOGARITHM

**an·ti·log·a·rithm** \,an-ti-'lò-gə-,ri-thəm, ,an-,tī-, -'lä-\ *noun* (1675)
**:** the number corresponding to a given logarithm

**an·ti·ma·cas·sar** \,an-ti-mə-'ka-sər\ *noun*

[*anti-* + *Macassar* (*oil*) (a hairdressing)] (1852)
**:** a cover to protect the back or arms of furniture

**an·ti·mag·net·ic** \,an-ti-mag-'ne-tik, ,an-,tī-\ *adjective* (1946)
*of a watch* **:** having a balance unit composed of alloys that will not remain magnetized

**an·ti·ma·lar·i·al** \-mə-'ler-ē-əl\ *adjective* (circa 1893)
**:** serving to prevent, check, or cure malaria
— **antimalarial** *noun*

**an·ti·mat·ter** \'an-ti-,ma-tər, 'an-,tī-\ *noun* (1950)
**:** matter composed of antiparticles

**an·ti·me·tab·o·lite** \,an-ti-mə-'ta-bə-,līt, ,an-,tī-\ *noun* (1945)
**:** a substance that replaces or inhibits an organism's utilization of a metabolite

**an·ti·mi·cro·bi·al** \,an-ti-mī-'krō-bē-əl\ *adjective* (circa 1910)
**:** destroying or inhibiting the growth of microorganisms
— **antimicrobial** *noun*

**an·ti·mis·sile missile** \,an-ti-'mi-səl-, ,an-,tī-; *chiefly British* ,an-ti-'mi-,sīl-\ *noun* (circa 1956)
**:** ANTIBALLISTIC MISSILE

**an·ti·mi·tot·ic** \,an-ti-mī-'tä-tik, ,an-,tī-\ *adjective* (1970)
**:** inhibiting or disrupting mitosis ⟨*antimitotic* agents⟩ ⟨*antimitotic* activity⟩
— **antimitotic** *noun*

**an·ti·mo·ni·al** \,an-tə-'mō-nē-əl\ *adjective* (1605)
**:** of, relating to, or containing antimony
— **antimonial** *noun*

**an·ti·mo·nide** \'an-ti-mə-,nīd\ *noun* (1863)
**:** a binary compound of antimony with a more positive element

**an·ti·mo·ny** \'an-tə-,mō-nē\ *noun* [Middle English *antimonie,* from Medieval Latin *antimonium*] (15th century)
**1 :** STIBNITE
**2 :** a trivalent and pentavalent metalloid element that is commonly metallic silvery white, crystalline, and brittle and that is used especially as a constituent of alloys and semiconductors — see ELEMENT table

**an·ti·my·cin A** \,an-ti-'mī-s°n-'ā\ *noun* [*anti-* + *-mycin*] (1949)
**:** a crystalline antibiotic $C_{28}H_{40}N_2O_9$ used especially as a fungicide, insecticide, and miticide — called also *antimycin*

**an·ti·neo·plas·tic** \,an-ti-,nē-ə-'plas-tik, ,an-,tī-\ *adjective* (1954)
**:** inhibiting or preventing the growth and spread of neoplasms or malignant cells

**an·ti·neu·tri·no** \-nü-'trē-(,)nō, -nyü-\ *noun* (1934)
**:** the antiparticle of the neutrino

**an·ti·neu·tron** \-'nü-,trän, -'nyü-\ *noun* (1942)
**:** the antiparticle of the neutron

**ant·ing** \'an-tiŋ\ *noun* (1936)
**:** bird behavior in which ants are rubbed on the feathers to obtain chemicals (as formic acid) from the ants

**an·ti·node** \'an-ti-,nōd, 'an-,tī-\ *noun* [International Scientific Vocabulary] (1882)
**:** a region of maximum amplitude situated between adjacent nodes in a vibrating body
— **an·ti·nod·al** \,an-ti-'nō-d°l, ,an-,tī-\ *adjective*

**an·ti·no·mi·an** \,an-ti-'nō-mē-ən\ *noun* [Medieval Latin *antinomus,* from Latin *anti-* + Greek *nomos* law] (1645)
**1 :** one who holds that under the gospel dispensation of grace the moral law is of no use or obligation because faith alone is necessary to salvation
**2 :** one who rejects a socially established morality
— **antinomian** *adjective*
— **an·ti·no·mi·an·ism** \-mē-ə-,ni-zəm\ *noun*

**an·ti·no·my** \an-'ti-nə-mē\ *noun, plural* **-mies** [German *Antinomie,* from Latin *antinomia* conflict of laws, from Greek, from *anti-* + *nomos* law — more at NIMBLE] (1592)
**1 :** a contradiction between two apparently equally valid principles or between inferences correctly drawn from such principles
**2 :** a fundamental and apparently unresolvable conflict or contradiction ⟨*antinomies* of beauty and evil, freedom and slavery —Stephen Holden⟩
— **an·ti·nom·ic** \,an-ti-'nä-mik\ *adjective*
**an·ti·nov·el** \'an-ti-,nä-vəl, 'an-,tī-\ *noun* (1958)
**:** a work of fiction that lacks most or all of the traditional features of the novel
— **an·ti·nov·el·ist** \-,näv-list, -,nä-və-\ *noun*
**an·ti·nu·cle·ar** \,an-ti-'nü-klē-ər, ,an-,tī-, -'nyü-, ÷-kyə-lər\ *adjective* (1958)
**1 :** tending to react with cell nuclei or their components (as DNA) ⟨*antinuclear* antibodies⟩
**2 :** opposing the use or production of nuclear power plants
**an·ti·nu·cle·on** \-'n(y)ü-klē-,än\ *noun* (1946)
**:** the antiparticle of a nucleon
**an·ti·nuke** \-'nük, -'nyük\ *adjective* (1975)
**:** ANTINUCLEAR 2
**an·ti·ox·i·dant** \,an-tē-'äk-sə-dənt, ,an-,tī-\ *noun* (1926)
**:** a substance that inhibits oxidation or reactions promoted by oxygen or peroxides
— **antioxidant** *adjective*
**an·ti·ozon·ant** \-'ō-(,)zō-nənt\ *noun* (1954)
**:** a substance that opposes ozonization or protects against it
**an·ti·par·al·lel** \,an-ti-'par-ə-,lel, ,an-,tī-, -ləl\ *adjective* (circa 1660)
**:** parallel but oppositely directed or oriented ⟨*antiparallel* electron spins⟩ ⟨two *antiparallel* chains of nucleotides comprise DNA⟩
**an·ti·par·a·sit·ic** \,an-ti-,par-ə-'si-tik, ,an-,tī-\ *adjective* (circa 1860)
**:** acting against parasites
**an·ti·par·ti·cle** \'an-ti-,pär-ti-kəl, 'an-,tī-\ *noun* (1934)
**:** a subatomic particle identical to another subatomic particle in mass but opposite to it in electric and magnetic properties (as sign of charge) that when brought together with its counterpart produces mutual annihilation; *especially* **:** a subatomic particle not found in ordinary matter
**an·ti·pas·to** \,an-ti-'pas-(,)tō, ,än-ti-, -'päs-\ *noun, plural* **-ti** \-(,)tē\ [Italian, from *anti-* (from Latin *ante-*) + *pasto* food, from Latin *pastus,* from *pascere* to feed — more at FOOD] (1590)
**:** any of various typically Italian hors d'oeuvres; *also* **:** a plate of these served especially as the first course of a meal
**an·ti·pa·thet·ic** \,an-ti-pə-'the-tik, (,)an-,ti-pə-\ *adjective* (1640)
**1 :** having a natural aversion; *also* **:** not sympathetic **:** HOSTILE
**2 :** arousing antipathy ⟨mountains . . . are *antipathetic* to me —Havelock Ellis⟩
— **an·ti·pa·thet·i·cal·ly** \-ti-k(ə-)lē\ *adverb*
**an·tip·a·thy** \an-'ti-pə-thē\ *noun, plural* **-thies** [Latin *antipathia,* from Greek *antipatheia,* from *antipathēs* of opposite feelings, from *anti-* + *pathos* experience — more at PATHOS] (1601)
**1** *obsolete* **:** opposition in feeling
**2 :** settled aversion or dislike **:** DISTASTE
**3 :** an object of aversion
**synonym** see ENMITY
**an·ti·per·son·nel** \,an-ti-,pər-s²n-'el, ,an-,tī-\ *adjective* (1939)
**:** designed for use against military personnel ⟨an *antipersonnel* mine⟩
**an·ti·per·spi·rant** \-'pər-sp(ə-)rənt\ *noun* (1943)
**:** a preparation used to check perspiration

**an·ti·phlo·gis·tic** \-flə-'jis-tik\ *adjective* (1769)
**:** ANTI-INFLAMMATORY
**an·ti·phon** \'an-tə-fən, -,fän\ *noun* [Middle English *antiphone,* from Middle French, from Late Latin *antiphona* — more at ANTHEM] (15th century)
**1 :** a psalm, anthem, or verse sung responsively
**2 :** a verse usually from Scripture said or sung before and after a canticle, psalm, or psalm verse as part of the liturgy
**¹an·tiph·o·nal** \an-'ti-fə-n²l\ *noun* (1537)
**:** ANTIPHONARY
**²antiphonal** *adjective* (1719)
**:** of, relating to, or suggesting an antiphon or antiphony
— **an·tiph·o·nal·ly** \-n²l-ē\ *adverb*
**an·tiph·o·nary** \an-'ti-fə-,ner-ē\ *noun, plural* **-nar·ies** (15th century)
**1 :** a book containing a collection of antiphons
**2 :** a book containing the choral parts of the Divine Office
**an·tiph·o·ny** \an-'ti-fə-nē\ *noun, plural* **-nies** (1592)
**:** responsive alternation between two groups especially of singers
**an·tiph·ra·sis** \an-'ti-frə-səs\ *noun, plural* **-ra·ses** \-,sēz\ [Late Latin, from Greek, from *anti-* + *phrasis* diction — more at PHRASE] (1533)
**:** the usually ironic or humorous use of words in senses opposite to the generally accepted meanings (as in "this giant of 3 feet 4 inches")
**¹an·tip·o·dal** \an-'ti-pə-d²l\ *adjective* (1646)
**1 :** of or relating to the antipodes; *specifically* **:** situated at the opposite side of the earth or moon ⟨an *antipodal* meridian⟩ ⟨an *antipodal* continent⟩
**2 :** diametrically opposite ⟨an *antipodal* point on a sphere⟩
**3 :** entirely opposed ⟨a system *antipodal* to democracy⟩
**²antipodal** *noun* (1919)
**:** any of three cells in the female gametophyte of most angiosperms that are grouped at the end of the embryo sac farthest from the micropyle — called also *antipodal cell*
**an·ti·pode** \'an-tə-,pōd\ *noun, plural* **an·tip·o·des** \an-'ti-pə-,dēz\ [Middle English *antipodes,* plural, persons dwelling at opposite points on the globe, from Latin, from Greek, from plural of *antipod-, antipous* with feet opposite, from *anti-* + *pod-, pous* foot — more at FOOT] (1549)
**1 :** the parts of the earth diametrically opposite — usually used in plural; often used of Australia and New Zealand
**2 :** the exact opposite or contrary
— **an·tip·o·de·an** \(,)an-,ti-pə-'dē-ən\ *adjective or noun*
**an·ti·po·et·ic** \,an-ti-pō-'e-tik, ,an-,tī-\ *adjective* (1847)
**:** of, relating to, or characterized by opposition to traditional poetic technique or style
**an·ti·pol·lu·tion** \-pə-'lü-shən\ *adjective* (1924)
**:** designed to prevent, reduce, or eliminate pollution ⟨*antipollution* laws⟩
— **antipollution** *noun*
**an·ti·pope** \'an-ti-,pōp\ *noun* [Middle English *antepope,* from Middle French *antipape,* from Medieval Latin *antipapa,* from *anti-* + *papa* pope] (15th century)
**:** one elected or claiming to be pope in opposition to the pope canonically chosen
**an·ti·pro·ton** \,an-ti-'prō-,tän, ,an-,tī-\ *noun* (1940)
**:** the antiparticle of the proton
**an·ti·psy·chot·ic** \,an-ti-sī-'kä-tik\ *noun* (1966)
**:** NEUROLEPTIC
— **antipsychotic** *adjective*
**an·ti·py·ret·ic** \-pī-'re-tik\ *noun* (circa 1681)
**:** an agent that reduces fever
— **antipyretic** *adjective*

**an·ti·py·rine** \-'pīr-,ēn\ *noun* [from *Antipyrine,* a trademark] (1884)
**:** an analgesic and antipyretic $C_{11}H_{12}N_2O$ formerly widely used but now largely replaced in oral use by less toxic substances (as aspirin)
**¹an·ti·quar·i·an** \,an-tə-'kwer-ē-ən\ *noun* (1610)
**:** one who collects or studies antiquities
**²antiquarian** *adjective* (1771)
**1 :** of or relating to antiquarians or antiquities
**2 :** dealing in old or rare books
— **an·ti·quar·i·an·ism** \-ē-ə-,ni-zəm\ *noun*
**an·ti·quark** \'an-ti-,kwärk, 'an-,tī-\ *noun* (1964)
**:** the antiparticle of the quark
**an·ti·quary** \'an-tə-,kwer-ē\ *noun, plural* **-quar·ies** (1586)
**:** ANTIQUARIAN
**an·ti·quate** \'an-tə-,kwāt\ *transitive verb* **-quat·ed; -quat·ing** [Late Latin *antiquátus,* past participle of *antiquare,* from Latin *antiquus*] (1596)
**:** to make old or obsolete
— **an·ti·qua·tion** \,an-tə-'kwā-shən\ *noun*
**an·ti·quat·ed** *adjective* (1623)
**1 :** OBSOLETE ⟨an *antiquated* calendar⟩
**2 :** outmoded or discredited by reason of age **:** being out of style or fashion ⟨*antiquated* methods of farming⟩
**3 :** advanced in age
**synonym** see OLD
**¹an·tique** \(,)an-'tēk\ *noun* (1530)
**1 :** a relic or object of ancient times
**2 a :** a work of art, piece of furniture, or decorative object made at an earlier period and according to various customs laws at least 100 years ago **b :** a manufactured product (as an automobile) from an earlier period
**²an·tique** \(,)an-'tēk, *in verse often* 'an-tik\ *adjective* [Middle French, from Latin *antiquus,* from *ante* before — more at ANTE-] (1534)
**1 :** existing since or belonging to earlier times **:** ANCIENT ⟨*antique* trade routes to the Orient⟩
**2 a :** being in the style or fashion of former times ⟨*antique* manners and graces⟩ **b :** made in or representative of the work of an earlier period ⟨*antique* mirrors⟩; *also* **:** being an antique
**3 :** selling or exhibiting antiques ⟨an *antique* show⟩
**synonym** see OLD
**³an·tique** \(,)an-'tēk\ *verb* **-tiqued; -tiqu·ing** (1923)
*transitive verb*
**:** to finish or refinish in antique style **:** give an appearance of age to
*intransitive verb*
**:** to shop around for antiques
— **an·tiqu·er** \an-'tē-kər\ *noun*
**an·tiq·ui·ty** \an-'ti-kwə-tē\ *noun, plural* **-ties** (13th century)
**1 :** ancient times; *especially* **:** those before the Middle Ages
**2 :** the quality of being ancient
**3** *plural* **a :** relics or monuments (as coins, statues, or buildings) of ancient times **b :** matters relating to the life or culture of ancient times
**4 :** the people of ancient times
**an·ti·ra·chit·ic** \,an-ti-rə-'ki-tik, ,an-,tī-\ *adjective* (circa 1860)
**:** used or tending to prevent the development of rickets ⟨an *antirachitic* vitamin⟩
**an·ti·re·jec·tion** \,an-ti-ri-'jek-shən, ,an-,tī-\ *adjective* (1968)
**:** used or tending to prevent organ transplant rejection ⟨*antirejection* drugs⟩ ⟨*antirejection* treatment⟩
**an·ti·rheu·mat·ic** \-rú-'ma-tik\ *adjective* (1817)

\ə\ abut \ᵊ\ kitten \ər\ further \a\ ash \ā\ ace
\ä\ mop, mar \aú\ out \ch\ chin \e\ bet \ē\ easy
\g\ go \i\ hit \ī\ ice \j\ job \ŋ\ sing \ō\ go
\ó\ law \ói\ boy \th\ thin \th\ the \ü\ loot \ú\ foot
\y\ yet \zh\ vision *see also* Guide to Pronunciation

: alleviating or preventing rheumatism ⟨*antirheumatic* therapy⟩ ⟨*antirheumatic* drugs⟩
— **antirheumatic** *noun*

**an·ti–roll bar** \'an-ˌtī-ˌrōl\ *noun* (1951)
: SWAY BAR

**an·tir·rhi·num** \ˌan-tə-'rī-nəm\ *noun* [New Latin, genus name, from Latin, snapdragon, from Greek *antirrhinon*, from *anti-* like (from *anti* against, equivalent to) + *rhin-*, *rhis* nose — more at ANTI-] (1548)
: SNAPDRAGON

**antis** *plural of* ANTI

**an·ti·scor·bu·tic** \ˌan-ti-skòr-'byü-tik, ˌan-ˌtī-\ *adjective* (1725)
: counteracting scurvy ⟨the *antiscorbutic* vitamin is vitamin C⟩
— **antiscorbutic** *noun*

**an·ti–Sem·i·tism** \ˌan-ti-'se-mə-ˌti-zəm, ˌan-ˌtī-\ *noun* (1882)
: hostility toward or discrimination against Jews as a religious, ethnic, or racial group
— **an·ti–Se·mit·ic** \-sə-'mi-tik\ *adjective*
— **an·ti–Sem·ite** \-'se-ˌmīt\ *noun*

**an·ti·sense** \'an-ˌtī-ˌsen(t)s, 'an-ti-\ *adjective* [*anti-* + non*sense*] (1984)
: having a complementary sequence to a segment of genetic material (as mRNA) and serving to inhibit gene function ⟨*antisense* nucleotides⟩ ⟨*antisense* RNA⟩ — compare MISSENSE, NONSENSE

**an·ti·sep·sis** \ˌan-tə-'sep-səs\ *noun* (1875)
: the inhibiting of the growth and multiplication of microorganisms by antiseptic means

¹**an·ti·sep·tic** \ˌan-tə-'sep-tik\ *adjective* [*anti-* + Greek *sēptikos* putrefying, septic] (1751)
**1 a** : opposing sepsis, putrefaction, or decay; *especially* : preventing or arresting the growth of microorganisms (as on living tissue) **b** : acting or protecting like an antiseptic **2** : relating to or characterized by the use of antiseptics **3 a** : scrupulously clean : ASEPTIC **b** : extremely neat or orderly; *especially* : neat to the point of being bare or uninteresting **c** : free from what is held to be contaminating **4** : coldly impersonal ⟨an *antiseptic* greeting⟩
— **an·ti·sep·ti·cal·ly** \-ti-k(ə-)lē\ *adverb*

²**antiseptic** *noun* (1751)
: a substance that checks the growth or action of microorganisms especially in or on living tissue; *also* : GERMICIDE

**an·ti·se·rum** \'an-ti-ˌsir-əm, 'an-ˌtī-, -ˌser-\ *noun* [International Scientific Vocabulary] (1901)
: a serum containing antibodies

**an·ti·so·cial** \ˌan-ti-'sō-shəl, ˌan-ˌtī-\ *adjective* (1797)
**1** : averse to the society of others : UNSOCIABLE **2** : hostile or harmful to organized society; *especially* : being or marked by behavior deviating sharply from the social norm
— **an·ti·so·cial·ly** \-shə-lē\ *adverb*

**an·ti·so·lar** \-'sō-lər\ *noun* (circa 1890)
: being or having a direction away from the sun ⟨the *antisolar* point⟩

**an·ti·spas·mod·ic** \-spaz-'mä-dik\ *adjective* (1763)
: capable of preventing or relieving spasms or convulsions
— **antispasmodic** *noun*

**an·ti·stat** \-'stat\ *or* **an·ti·stat·ic** \-'sta-tik\ *adjective* (1952)
: reducing, removing, or preventing the buildup of static electricity

**an·tis·tro·phe** \an-'tis-trə-(ˌ)fē\ *noun* [Late Latin, from Greek *antistrophē*, from *anti-* + *strophē* strophe] (circa 1550)
**1 a** : the repetition of words in reversed order **b** : the repetition of a word or phrase at the end of successive clauses **2 a** : a returning movement in Greek choral dance exactly answering to a previous strophe **b** : the part of a choral song delivered during the antistrophe
— **an·ti·stroph·ic** \ˌan-tə-'strä-fik\ *adjective*

— **an·ti·stroph·i·cal·ly** \-fi-k(ə-)lē\ *adverb*

**an·ti·sym·met·ric** \-sə-'me-trik\ *adjective* (1923)
: relating to or being a relation (as "is a subset of") that implies equality of any two quantities for which it holds in both directions ⟨the relation *R* is antisymmetric if *aRb* and *bRa* implies *a* = *b*⟩

**an·tith·e·sis** \an-'ti-thə-səs\ *noun, plural* **-e·ses** \-ˌsēz\ [Late Latin, from Greek, literally, opposition, from *antitithenai* to oppose, from *anti-* + *tithenai* to set — more at DO] (1529)
**1 a** (1) : the rhetorical contrast of ideas by means of parallel arrangements of words, clauses, or sentences (as in "action, not words" or "they promised freedom and provided slavery") (2) : OPPOSITION, CONTRAST ⟨the *antithesis* of prose and verse⟩ **b** (1) : the second of two opposing constituents of an antithesis (2) : the direct opposite **2** : the second stage of a dialectic process

**an·ti·thet·i·cal** \ˌan-tə-'the-ti-kəl\ *also* **an·ti·thet·ic** \-'the-tik\ *adjective* (1583)
**1** : constituting or marked by antithesis **2** : being in direct and unequivocal opposition
**synonym** see OPPOSITE
— **an·ti·thet·i·cal·ly** \-ti-k(ə-)lē\ *adverb*

**an·ti·throm·bin** \ˌan-ti-'thräm-bən, ˌan-ˌtī-\ *noun* (circa 1911)
: any of a group of substances that inhibit blood clotting by inactivating thrombin

**an·ti·thy·roid** \ˌan-ti-'thī-ˌròid\ *adjective* (1908)
: able to counteract excessive thyroid activity ⟨*antithyroid* drugs⟩

**an·ti·tox·ic** \-'täk-sik\ *adjective* (circa 1890)
**1** : counteracting toxins **2** : being or containing antitoxins ⟨*antitoxic* serum⟩

**an·ti·tox·in** \ˌan-ti-'täk-sən\ *noun* [International Scientific Vocabulary] (circa 1890)
: an antibody that is capable of neutralizing the specific toxin (as a specific causative agent of disease) that stimulated its production in the body and is produced in animals for medical purposes by injection of a toxin or toxoid with the resulting serum being used to counteract the toxin in other individuals; *also* : an antiserum containing antitoxins

**an·ti·trades** \'an-ti-ˌtrādz, 'an-ˌtī-\ *noun plural* (1875)
: the westerly winds above the trade winds

**an·ti·trust** \ˌan-ti-'trəst, ˌan-ˌtī-\ *adjective* (1890)
: of, relating to, or being legislation against or opposition to trusts or combinations; *specifically* : consisting of laws to protect trade and commerce from unlawful restraints and monopolies or unfair business practices

**an·ti·trust·er** \-'trəs-tər\ *noun* (1947)
: one who advocates or enforces antitrust provisions of the law

**an·ti·tus·sive** \-'tə-siv\ *noun* (circa 1909)
: a cough suppressant
— **antitussive** *adjective*

**an·ti–uto·pia** \ˌan-ti-yù-'tō-pē-ə, ˌan-ˌtī-\ *noun* (1966)
**1** : DYSTOPIA 1 **2** : a work describing an anti-utopia
— **an·ti–uto·pi·an** \-pē-ən\ *adjective or noun*

**an·ti·ven·in** \ˌan-ti-'ve-nən, ˌan-ˌtī-\ *noun* [International Scientific Vocabulary] (1895)
: an antitoxin to a venom; *also* : an antiserum containing such antitoxin

**an·ti·vi·ta·min** \'an-ti-ˌvī-tə-mən, *British usually* -ˌvi-\ *noun* (1927)
: a substance that makes a vitamin metabolically ineffective

**an·ti·white** \ˌan-ti-'hwīt, ˌan-ˌtī-, -'wīt\ *adjective* (1906)
: opposed or hostile to people belonging to a light-skinned race

**ant·ler** \'ant-lər\ *noun* [Middle English *aunteler*, from Middle French *antoillier*, from (as-

sumed) Vulgar Latin *anteoculare*, from neuter of *anteocularis* located before the eye, from Latin *ante-* + *oculus* eye — more at EYE] (14th century)
: one of the paired deciduous solid bone processes that arise from the frontal bone on the head of an animal of the deer family; *also* : a branch of an antler
— **ant·lered** \-lərd\ *adjective*

**ant lion** *noun* (1815)
: any of various neuropterous insects (as of the genus *Myrmeleon*) having a long-jawed larva that digs a conical pit in which it lies in wait to catch insects (as ants) on which it feeds

ant lion: *1* larva, *2* adult

**An·to·ni·an** \an-'tō-nē-ən\ *noun* [Latin *Antonius* Anthony] (circa 1907)
: a member of one of several monastic communities (as the Armenian Antonians) that follow a rule devised by Saint Anthony

**an·to·no·ma·sia** \ˌan-tə-nō-'mā-zh(ē-)ə, (ˌ)an-ˌtä-nə-\ *noun* [Latin, use of an epithet for a proper name, from Greek, from *antonomazein* to call by a new name, from *anti-* + *onomazein* to name, from *onoma* name — more at NAME] (circa 1550)
: the use of a proper name to designate a member of a class (as a *Solomon* for a *wise ruler*); *also* : use of an epithet or title in place of a proper name (as *the Bard* for *Shakespeare*)

**an·to·nym** \'an-tə-ˌnim\ *noun* (1870)
: a word of opposite meaning ⟨the usual *antonym* of *good* is *bad*⟩
— **an·to·nym·ic** \ˌan-tə-'ni-mik\ *adjective*
— **an·ton·y·mous** \an-'tä-nə-məs\ *adjective*
— **an·ton·y·my** \-mē\ *noun*

**an·tre** \'an-tər\ *noun* [French, from Latin *antrum*] (1604)
: CAVE 1

**an·trum** \'an-trəm\ *noun, plural* **an·tra** \-trə\ [Late Latin, from Latin, cave, from Greek *antron;* akin to Armenian *ayr* cave] (circa 1751)
: the cavity of a hollow organ or a sinus
— **an·tral** \-trəl\ *adjective*

**ant·sy** \'ant-sē\ *adjective* (1838)
**1** : impatient of restraint; *especially* : FIDGETY **2** : NERVOUS, APPREHENSIVE

**Anu·bis** \ə-'nü-bəs, -'nyü-\ *noun* [Latin, from Greek *Anoubis*, from Egyptian *inpw*]
: a jackal-headed god in Egyptian mythology who leads the dead to judgment

**an·uran** \ə-'nyùr-ən, a-, -'nùr-\ *adjective or noun* [ultimately from Greek *a-* + *oura* tail — more at ASS] (1900)
: any of an order (Anura) of amphibians comprising the frogs, toads, and tree toads all of which lack a tail in the adult stage and have long strong hind limbs suited to leaping and swimming
— **anuran** *adjective*

**an·uria** \ə-'nyùr-ē-ə, a-, -'nùr-\ *noun* [New Latin] (1838)
: absence or defective excretion of urine
— **an·uric** \-'nyùr-ik, -'nùr-\ *adjective*

**anus** \'ā-nəs\ *noun* [Latin, ring, anus; perhaps akin to Old Irish *ánne* ring] (15th century)
: the posterior opening of the alimentary canal

**an·vil** \'an-vəl\ *noun* [Middle English *anfilt*, from Old English; akin to Old High German *anafalz* anvil; akin to Latin *pellere* to beat — more at FELT] (before 12th century)
**1** : a heavy usually steel-faced iron block on which metal is shaped (as by hand hammering) **2** : INCUS

**anx·i·ety** \aŋ-'zī-ə-tē\ *noun, plural* **-eties** [Latin *anxietas*, from *anxius*] (circa 1525)

**1 a :** painful or apprehensive uneasiness of mind usually over an impending or anticipated ill **b :** fearful concern or interest **c :** a cause of anxiety
**2 :** an abnormal and overwhelming sense of apprehension and fear often marked by physiological signs (as sweating, tension, and increased pulse), by doubt concerning the reality and nature of the threat, and by self-doubt about one's capacity to cope with it
**synonym** see CARE

**an·xi·o·lyt·ic** \ˌaŋ-zē-ō-ˈli-tik, ˌaŋ(k)-sē-\ *noun* [anxiety + -o- + -lytic] (1965)
**:** a drug that relieves anxiety
**— anxiolytic** *adjective*

**anx·ious** \ˈaŋ(k)-shəs\ *adjective* [Latin *anxius;* akin to Latin *angere* to strangle, distress — more at ANGER] (circa 1616)
**1 :** characterized by extreme uneasiness of mind or brooding fear about some contingency **:** WORRIED
**2 :** characterized by, resulting from, or causing anxiety **:** WORRYING
**3 :** ardently or earnestly wishing □
**synonym** see EAGER
**— anx·ious·ly** *adverb*
**— anx·ious·ness** *noun*

**¹any** \ˈe-nē\ *adjective* [Middle English, from Old English *ǣnig;* akin to Old High German *einag* any, Old English *ān* one — more at ONE] (before 12th century)
**1 :** one or some indiscriminately of whatever kind: **a :** one or another taken at random ⟨ask *any* man you meet⟩ **b :** EVERY — used to indicate one selected without restriction ⟨*any* child would know that⟩
**2 :** one, some, or all indiscriminately of whatever quantity: **a :** one or more — used to indicate an undetermined number or amount ⟨have you *any* money⟩ **b :** ALL — used to indicate a maximum or whole ⟨needs *any* help he can get⟩ **c :** a or some without reference to quantity or extent ⟨grateful for *any* favor at all⟩
**3 a :** unmeasured or unlimited in amount, number, or extent ⟨*any* quantity you desire⟩ **b :** appreciably large or extended ⟨could not endure it *any* length of time⟩

**²any** *pronoun, singular or plural in construction* (before 12th century)
**1 :** any person or persons **:** ANYONE
**2 a :** any thing or things **b :** any part, quantity, or number

**³any** *adverb* (14th century)
**:** to any extent or degree **:** AT ALL ⟨was never *any* good⟩

**any·body** \-ˌbä-dē, -bə-\ *pronoun* (14th century)
**:** any person **:** ANYONE □

**any·how** \-ˌhau̇\ *adverb* (1690)
**1 a :** in any manner whatever **b :** in a haphazard manner
**2 a :** at any rate **b :** in any event

**any·more** \ˌe-nē-ˈmōr, -ˈmȯr\ *adverb* (14th century)
**1 :** any longer ⟨I was not moving *anymore* with my feet —Anaïs Nin⟩
**2 :** at the present time **:** NOW ⟨hardly a day passes without rain *anymore*⟩ □

**any·one** \ˈe-nē-(ˌ)wən\ *pronoun* (1536)
**:** any person at all
**usage** see ANYBODY

**any·place** \-ˌplās\ *adverb* (1916)
**:** in any place **:** ANYWHERE

**¹any·thing** \-ˌthiŋ\ *pronoun* (before 12th century)
**:** any thing whatever **:** any such thing

**²anything** *adverb* (before 12th century)
**:** AT ALL

**any·time** \ˈe-nē-ˌtīm\ *adverb* (1926)
**:** at any time whatever

**any·way** \-ˌwā\ *adverb* (13th century)
**1 :** ANYWISE
**2 :** in any case **:** ANYHOW

**any·ways** \-ˌwāz\ *adverb* (13th century)

**1 a** *archaic* **:** ANYWISE **b** *dialect* **:** to any degree at all
**2** *chiefly dialect* **:** ANYHOW, ANYWAY

**¹any·where** \-ˌ(h)wer, -ˌ(h)war, -(h)wər\ *adverb* (14th century)
**1 :** at, in, or to any place or point
**2 :** to any extent **:** AT ALL
**3 —** used as a function word to indicate limits of variation ⟨*anywhere* from 40 to 60 students⟩

**²anywhere** *noun* (1924)
**:** any place

**any·wheres** \-ˌ(h)werz, -ˌ(h)war̄z, -(h)wərz\ *adverb* (1775)
*chiefly dialect* **:** ANYWHERE

**any·wise** \ˈe-nē-ˌwīz\ *adverb* (13th century)
**:** in any way whatever **:** AT ALL

**An·zac** \ˈan-ˌzak\ *noun* [Australian and New Zealand Army Corps] (1915)
**:** a soldier from Australia or New Zealand

**A–OK** \ˌā-(ˌ)ō-ˈkā\ *adverb or adjective* (1959)
**:** very definitely OK

**A1** \ˈā-ˈwən\ *adjective* (1837)
**1 :** having the highest possible classification — used of a ship
**2 :** of the finest quality **:** FIRST-RATE

**ao·rist** \ˈā-ə-rəst, ˈe-ə-\ *noun* [Late Latin & Greek; Late Latin *aoristos,* from Greek, from *aoristos* undefined, from *a* + *horistos* definable, from *horizein* to define — more at HORIZON] (1581)
**:** an inflectional form of a verb typically denoting simple occurrence of an action without reference to its completeness, duration, or repetition
**— aorist** *or* **ao·ris·tic** \ˌā-ə-ˈris-tik, ˌe-ə-\ *adjective*
**— ao·ris·ti·cal·ly** \-ti-k(ə-)lē\ *adverb*

**aor·ta** \ā-ˈȯr-tə\ *noun, plural* **-tas** *or* **-tae** \-tē\ [New Latin, from Greek *aortē,* from *aeirein* to lift] (1543)
**:** the great arterial trunk that carries blood from the heart to be distributed by branch arteries through the body — see HEART illustration
**— aor·tic** \-ˈȯr-tik\ *adjective*

**aortic arch** *noun* (1903)
**:** one of the arterial branches in vertebrate embryos that exist in a series of pairs with one on each side of the embryo, connect the ventral arterial system lying anterior to the heart to the dorsal arterial system above the alimentary tract, and persist in adult fishes but are reduced or much modified in the adult of higher forms

**aor·tog·ra·phy** \ˌā-ȯr-ˈtä-grə-fē\ *noun* (circa 1935)
**:** arteriography of the aorta
**— aor·to·graph·ic** \(ˌ)ā-ˌȯr-tə-ˈgra-fik\ *adjective*

**aou·dad** \ˈau̇-ˌdad, ˈä-u̇-\ *noun* [French, from Berber *audad*] (1861)
**:** a wild bovine (*Ammotragus lervia*) of North Africa that is closely related to goats and sheep and has been introduced into the southwestern U.S.

**à ou·trance** \ˌä-ü-ˈträⁿs\ *adverb* [French] (1883)
**:** to the limit **:** UNSPARINGLY

**¹ap-** — see AD-
**²ap-** — see APO-

**apace** \ə-ˈpās\ *adverb* [Middle English, probably from Middle French *à pas* on step] (14th century)
**1 :** at a quick pace **:** SWIFTLY
**2 :** ABREAST — used with *of* or *with*

**Apache** \ə-ˈpa-chē, *in sense 3* ə-ˈpash\ *noun, plural* **Apache** *or* **Apach·es** \-ˈpa-chēz, -ˈpash, -ˈpa-shəz\ [American Spanish, perhaps from Zuni *ʔaʹpacu* Navajo, Apachean] (1745)
**1 :** a member of a group of American Indian peoples of the southwestern U.S.
**2 :** any of the Athabascan languages of the Apache people
**3** *not capitalized* [French, from *Apache*

Apache Indian] **a :** a member of a gang of criminals especially in Paris **b :** RUFFIAN
**— Apach·e·an** \ə-ˈpa-chē-ən\ *adjective or noun*

**ap·a·nage** *variant of* APPANAGE

**ap·a·re·jo** \ˌa-pə-ˈrā-(ˌ)(h)ō\ *noun, plural* **-jos** [American Spanish] (1844)
**:** a packsaddle of stuffed leather or canvas

**¹apart** \ə-ˈpärt\ *adverb* [Middle English, from Middle French *a part,* literally, to the side] (14th century)
**1 a :** at a little distance ⟨tried to keep *apart*

---

□ USAGE

**anxious** The opinion that *anxious* must not be used to mean "eager" was formed in the U.S. at the beginning of the 20th century. British commentators have largely ignored the problem—after all, sense 3 of *anxious* had been established in British English for 160 years before American commentators decided it must be wrong ⟨his manner was perhaps the more seductive, because he ne'er seem'd *anxious* to seduce —Lord Byron (1824)⟩. Of course, it was just as firmly established in American English too ⟨at any hour of the day or night, I have been *anxious* to improve the nick of time —Henry David Thoreau (1854)⟩. But the topic is still dear to the hearts of American commentators, few of whom notice that the use is standard.

**anybody** The indefinite pronouns *anybody* and *anyone* share with other indefinite pronouns the characteristic of taking a singular verb and, more often than not, a plural pronoun in reference. The use of the plural pronoun—*they, their, them*—has traditionally been disapproved by those who insist that agreement in number is more important than avoidance of gender-specific third-person singular pronouns. But use of the plural pronouns has long been established ⟨as *anybody* in their senses would have done —Jane Austen (1814)⟩ ⟨if *anybody* thinks that kings, nobles, or priests are good conservators of the public happiness send them here —Thomas Jefferson (letter from Paris, 1786)⟩ and increasing resistance to generic *he* seems to be easing their acceptance. Usage is still mixed ⟨I had never examined all the papers left by *anybody* after his death —Donald Winch⟩ ⟨isn't interested in serving lunch or having *anyone* get their own —Andy Rooney⟩.

**anymore** Although both *anymore* and *any more* are found in written use, in the 20th century *anymore* is the more common styling. *Anymore* is regularly used in negative ⟨no one can be natural *anymore* —May Sarton⟩, interrogative ⟨do you read much *anymore*?⟩, and conditional ⟨if you do that *anymore,* I'll leave⟩ contexts and in certain positive constructions ⟨the Washingtonian is too sophisticated to believe *anymore* in solutions —Russell Baker⟩. In many regions of the U.S. the use of *anymore* in sense 2 is quite common in positive constructions, especially in speech ⟨everybody's cool *anymore* —Bill White⟩ ⟨every time we leave the house *anymore,* I play a game called "Stump the Housebreaker" —Erma Bombeck⟩. The positive use appears to have been of Midland origin, but it is now reported to be widespread in all speech areas of the U.S. except New England.

---

\ə\ abut \ᵊ\ kitten \ər\ further \a\ ash \ā\ ace
\ä\ mop, mar \au̇\ out \ch\ chin \e\ bet \ē\ easy
\g\ go \i\ hit \ī\ ice \j\ job \ŋ\ sing \ō\ go
\ȯ\ law \ȯi\ boy \th\ thin \t͟h\ the \ü\ loot \u̇\ foot
\y\ yet \zh\ vision    *see also* Guide to Pronunciation

from the family squabbles) **b :** away from one another in space or time ⟨towns 20 miles *apart*⟩
**2 a :** as a separate unit **:** INDEPENDENTLY ⟨viewed *apart*, his arguments were unsound⟩ **b :** so as to separate one from another ⟨found it hard to tell the twins *apart*⟩
**3 :** excluded from consideration **:** ASIDE ⟨a few blemishes *apart*, the novel is excellent⟩
**4 :** in or into two or more parts **:** to pieces ⟨coming *apart* at the seams⟩

**²apart** *adjective* (1786)
**1 :** SEPARATE, ISOLATED
**2 :** holding different opinions **:** DIVIDED
— **apart·ness** *noun*

**apart from** *preposition* (1833)
**:** other than **:** BESIDES

**apart·heid** \ə-'pär-ˌtāt, -ˌtīt\ *noun* [Afrikaans, from Dutch, from *apart* apart + *-heid* -hood] (1947)
**1 :** racial segregation; *specifically* **:** a policy of segregation and political and economic discrimination against non-European groups in the Republic of South Africa
**2 :** SEPARATION, SEGREGATION ⟨I favor *apartheid* of smokers —L. E. Bellin⟩ ⟨sexual *apartheid*⟩

**apart·ment** \ə-'pärt-mənt\ *noun* [French *appartement*, from Italian *appartamento*] (1641)
**1 :** a room or set of rooms fitted especially with housekeeping facilities and usually leased as a dwelling
**2 :** a building containing several individual apartments
— **apart·men·tal** \ə-ˌpärt-'men-t³l\ *adjective*

**apartment hotel** *noun* (1909)
**:** a hotel containing apartments as well as accommodations for transients

**apartment house** *noun* (1874)
**:** a building containing separate residential apartments — called also *apartment building*

**ap·a·thet·ic** \ˌa-pə-'the-tik\ *adjective* (1744)
**1 :** having or showing little or no feeling or emotion **:** SPIRITLESS
**2 :** having little or no interest or concern **:** INDIFFERENT
*synonym* see IMPASSIVE
— **ap·a·thet·i·cal·ly** \-ti-k(ə-)lē\ *adverb*

**ap·a·thy** \'a-pə-thē\ *noun* [Greek *apatheia*, from *apathēs* without feeling, from *a-* + *pathos* emotion — more at PATHOS] (1603)
**1 :** lack of feeling or emotion **:** IMPASSIVENESS
**2 :** lack of interest or concern **:** INDIFFERENCE

**ap·a·tite** \'a-pə-ˌtīt\ *noun* [German *Apatit*, from Greek *apatē* deceit] (1803)
**:** any of a group of calcium phosphate minerals occurring variously as hexagonal crystals, as granular masses, or in fine-grained masses as the chief constituent of phosphate rock and of bones and teeth; *especially* **:** calcium phosphate fluoride

**apato·sau·rus** \ə-ˌpa-tə-'sòr-əs\ *noun* [New Latin, from Greek *apatē* + *sauros* lizard] (circa 1899)
**:** BRONTOSAURUS

**¹ape** \'āp\ *noun* [Middle English, from Old English *apa;* akin to Old High German *affo* ape] (before 12th century)
**1 a :** MONKEY; *especially* **:** one of the larger tailless or short-tailed Old World forms **b :** any of two families (Pongidae and Hylobatidae) of large tailless semierect primates (as the chimpanzee, gorilla, orangutan, or gibbon) — called also *anthropoid, anthropoid ape*
**2 a :** MIMIC **b :** a large uncouth person
— **ape·like** \'āp-ˌlīk\ *adjective*

**²ape** *transitive verb* **aped; ap·ing** (1632)
**:** to copy closely but often clumsily and ineptly
*synonym* see COPY
— **ap·er** *noun*

**³ape** *adjective* (circa 1955)
**:** being beyond restraint **:** CRAZY, WILD — usually used in the phrase *go ape*

**apeak** \ə-'pēk\ *adjective or adverb* [alteration of earlier *apike*, probably from French *à pic* vertically] (1596)
**:** being in a vertical position ⟨with oars *apeak*⟩

**ape–man** \'āp-ˌman, -'man\ *noun* (1879)
**:** a primate (as an australopithecine) intermediate in character between Homo sapiens and the higher apes

**aper·çu** \ä-per-sᵫ, ˌa-pər-'sü\ *noun, plural* **aperçus** \-sᵫ(z), -'süz\ [French, from *aperçu*, past participle of *apercevoir* to perceive, from Old French *aperceivre*, from *a-* (from Latin *ad-*) + *perceivre* to perceive — more at PERCEIVE] (1828)
**1 :** a brief survey or sketch **:** OUTLINE
**2 :** an immediate impression; *especially* **:** INSIGHT 2

**ape·ri·ent** \ə-'pir-ē-ənt\ *adjective* [Latin *aperient-, aperiens*, present participle of *aperire*] (1626)
**:** gently moving the bowels **:** LAXATIVE
— **aperient** *noun*

**ape·ri·od·ic** \ˌā-ˌpir-ē-'ä-dik\ *adjective* (1879)
**1 :** of irregular occurrence ⟨*aperiodic* floods⟩
**2 :** not having periodic vibrations **:** not oscillatory
— **ape·ri·od·i·cal·ly** \-di-k(ə-)lē\ *adverb*
— **ape·ri·o·dic·i·ty** \-ē-ə-'di-sə-tē\ *noun*

**aper·i·tif** \ə-ˌper-ə-'tēf, a-; ˌä-pər-(ə-)'tēf\ *noun* [French *apéritif* aperient, aperitif, from Middle French *aperitif*, adjective, aperient, from Medieval Latin *aperitivus*, irregular from Latin *aperire*] (1894)
**:** an alcoholic drink taken before a meal as an appetizer

**ap·er·ture** \'ap-ə(r)-ˌchùr, -chər, -ˌtyùr, -ˌtùr\ *noun* [Middle English, from Latin *apertura*, from *apertus*, past participle of *aperire* to open] (15th century)
**1 :** an opening or open space **:** HOLE
**2 a :** the opening in a photographic lens that admits the light **b :** the diameter of the stop in an optical system that determines the diameter of the bundle of rays traversing the instrument **c :** the diameter of the objective lens or mirror of a telescope

**apet·al·ous** \(ˌ)ā-'pe-t³l-əs\ *adjective* (circa 1706)
**:** having no petals

**apex** \'ā-ˌpeks\ *noun, plural* **apex·es** *or* **api·ces** \'ā-pə-ˌsēz, 'a-\ [Latin] (1601)
**1 a :** the uppermost point **:** VERTEX ⟨the *apex* of a mountain⟩ **b :** the narrowed or pointed end **:** TIP ⟨the *apex* of the tongue⟩
**2 :** the highest or culminating point ⟨the *apex* of his career⟩
*synonym* see SUMMIT

**Ap·gar score** \'ap-ˌgär-\ *noun* [Virginia *Apgar* (died 1974) American anesthesiologist] (1962)
**:** an index used to evaluate the condition of a newborn infant based on a rating of 0, 1, or 2 for each of the five characteristics of color, heart rate, response to stimulation of the sole of the foot, muscle tone, and respiration with 10 being a perfect score

**aphaer·e·sis** *or* **apher·e·sis** \ə-'fer-ə-səs\ *noun, plural* **-e·ses** \-ˌsēz\ [Late Latin, from Greek *aphairesis*, literally, taking off, from *aphairein* to take away, from *apo-* + *hairein* to take] (circa 1550)
**:** the loss of one or more sounds or letters at the beginning of a word (as in *round* for *around* and *coon* for *raccoon*)
— **aph·ae·ret·ic** \ˌa-fə-'re-tik\ *adjective*

**aph·a·nite** \'a-fə-ˌnīt\ *noun* [French, from Greek *aphanēs* invisible, from *a-* + *phainesthai* to appear — more at PHENOMENON] (circa 1828)
**:** a dark rock of such close texture that its separate grains are invisible to the naked eye
— **aph·a·nit·ic** \ˌa-fə-'ni-tik\ *adjective*

**apha·sia** \ə-'fā-zh(ē-)ə\ *noun* [New Latin, from Greek, from *a-* + *-phasia*] (1867)

**:** loss or impairment of the power to use or comprehend words usually resulting from brain damage
— **apha·sic** \-zik\ *noun or adjective*

**aph·e·lion** \a-'fēl-yən\ *noun, plural* **-elia** \-yə\ [New Latin, from *apo-* + Greek *hēlios* sun — more at SOLAR] (1656)
**:** the point in the path of a celestial body (as a planet) that is farthest from the sun — compare PERIHELION

**aphe·e·sis** \'a-fə-səs\ *noun, plural* **-e·ses** \-ˌsēz\ [New Latin, from Greek, release, from *aphienai* to let go, from *apo-* + *hienai* to send — more at JET] (1880)
**:** aphaeresis consisting of the loss of a short unaccented vowel (as in *lone* for *alone*)
— **aphet·ic** \ə-'fe-tik\ *adjective*
— **aphet·i·cal·ly** \-ti-k(ə-)lē\ *adverb*

**aphid** \'ā-fəd *also* 'a-fəd\ *noun* (1884)
**:** any of numerous very small sluggish homopterous insects (superfamily Aphidoidea) that suck the juices of plants

**aphid lion** *noun* (1949)
**:** any of several insect larvae (as a lacewing or ladybug larva) that feed on aphids — called also *aphis lion*

**aphis** \'ā-fəs *also* 'a-fəs\ *noun, plural* **aphi·des** \'ā-fə-ˌdēz, 'a-fə-\ [New Latin *Aphid-, Aphis*, genus name] (1771)
**:** any of a genus (*Aphis*) of aphids; *broadly* **:** APHID

**apho·nia** \(ˌ)ā-'fō-nē-ə\ *noun* [New Latin, from Greek *aphōnia*, from *aphōnos* voiceless, from *a-* + *phōnē* sound — more at BAN] (1778)
**:** loss of voice and of all but whispered speech
— **apho·nic** \-'fä-nik, -'fō-\ *adjective*

**aph·o·rism** \'a-fə-ˌri-zəm\ *noun* [Middle French *aphorisme*, from Late Latin *aphorismus*, from Greek *aphorismos* definition, aphorism, from *aphorizein* to define, from *apo-* + *horizein* to bound — more at HORIZON] (1528)
**1 :** a concise statement of a principle
**2 :** a terse formulation of a truth or sentiment **:** ADAGE
— **aph·o·rist** \-rist\ *noun*
— **aph·o·ris·tic** \ˌa-fə-'ris-tik\ *adjective*
— **aph·o·ris·ti·cal·ly** \-ti-k(ə-)lē\ *adverb*

**aph·o·rize** \'a-fə-ˌrīz\ *intransitive verb* **-rized; -riz·ing** (1669)
**:** to write or speak in or as if in aphorisms

**apho·tic** \(ˌ)ā-'fō-tik\ *adjective* (circa 1900)
**:** being the deep zone of an ocean or lake receiving too little light to permit photosynthesis

**aph·ro·di·si·ac** \ˌa-frə-'dē-zē-ˌak, -'di-zē-\ *noun* [Greek *aphrodisiakos* sexual, gem with aphrodisiac properties, from *aphrodisia* heterosexual pleasures, from neuter plural of *aphrodisios* of Aphrodite, from *Aphroditē*] (1719)
**1 :** an agent (as a food or drug) that arouses or is held to arouse sexual desire
**2 :** something that excites
— **aphrodisiac** *also* **aph·ro·di·si·a·cal** \ˌa-frə-di-'sī-ə-kəl, -'zī-\ *adjective*

**Aph·ro·di·te** \ˌa-frə-'dī-tē\ *noun* [Greek *Aphroditē*]
**:** the Greek goddess of love and beauty — compare VENUS

**api·ar·i·an** \ˌā-pē-'er-ē-ən\ *adjective* (1801)
**:** of or relating to beekeeping or bees

**api·a·rist** \'ā-pē-ə-rist, -pē-ˌer-ist\ *noun* (1816)
**:** BEEKEEPER

**api·ary** \'ā-pē-ˌer-ē\ *noun, plural* **-ar·ies** [Latin *apiarium*, from *apis* bee] (1654)
**:** a place where bees are kept; *especially* **:** a collection of hives or colonies of bees kept for their honey

**api·cal** \'ā-pi-kəl *also* 'a-pi-\ *adjective* [probably from New Latin *apicalis*, from Latin *apic-, apex*] (1828)
**1 :** of, relating to, or situated at an apex
**2 :** of, relating to, or formed with the tip of the tongue ⟨*n*, *l*, and *r* are *apical* consonants⟩
— **api·cal·ly** \-k(ə-)lē\ *adverb*

**apical dominance** *noun* (1947)

: inhibition of the growth of lateral buds by the terminal bud of a shoot

**api·cal meristem** *noun* (circa 1934)
: a meristem at the apex of a root or shoot that is responsible for increase in length

**apic·u·late** \ə-'pi-kyə-lət, -ˌā-\ *adjective* [New Latin *apiculus,* diminutive of Latin *apic-, apex*] (1830)
: ending abruptly in a small distinct point ⟨an *apiculate* leaf⟩

**api·cul·ture** \'ā-pə-ˌkəl-chər\ *noun* [probably from French, from Latin *apis* bee + French *culture*] (1864)
: the keeping of bees especially on a large scale
— **api·cul·tur·al** \ˌā-pə-'kəl-ch(ə-)rəl\ *adjective*
— **api·cul·tur·ist** \-ch(ə-)rist\ *noun*

**apiece** \ə-'pēs\ *adverb* (15th century)
: for each one : INDIVIDUALLY

**Apis** \'ā-pəs\ *noun* [Latin, from Greek, from Egyptian *ḥp*]
: a sacred bull worshiped by the ancient Egyptians

**ap·ish** \'ā-pish\ *adjective* (1532)
: resembling an ape: as **a** : extremely silly or affected **b** : given to slavish imitation
— **ap·ish·ly** *adverb*
— **ap·ish·ness** *noun*

**APL** \ˌā-(ˌ)pē-'el\ *noun* [*a programming language*] (1966)
: a computer programming language designed especially for the concise representation of algorithms

**ap·la·nat·ic** \ˌa-plə-'na-tik\ *adjective* [*a-* + Greek *planasthai* to wander — more at PLANET] (1794)
: free from or corrected for spherical aberration ⟨an *aplanatic* lens⟩

**aplas·tic anemia** \(ˌ)ā-'plas-tik-\ *noun* (1928)
: anemia that is characterized by defective function of the blood-forming organs (as the bone marrow) and is caused by toxic agents (as chemicals or X rays) or is idiopathic in origin

**¹aplen·ty** \ə-'plen-tē\ *adjective* (1830)
: being in plenty or abundance — used postpositively ⟨money *aplenty* for all his needs⟩

**²aplenty** *adverb* (1846)
**1** : in abundance : PLENTIFULLY
**2** : very much : EXTREMELY ⟨scared *aplenty*⟩

**ap·lite** \'a-ˌplīt\ *noun* [probably from German *Aplit,* from Greek *haploos* simple — more at HAPL-] (1879)
: a fine-grained light-colored granite consisting almost entirely of quartz and feldspar
— **ap·lit·ic** \a-'pli-tik\ *adjective*

**aplomb** \ə-'pläm, -'pləm\ *noun* [French, literally, perpendicularity, from Middle French, from *a plomb,* literally, according to the plummet] (1828)
: complete and confident composure or self-assurance : POISE
**synonym** see CONFIDENCE

**ap·nea** \'ap-nē-ə\ *noun* [New Latin, from *a-* + *-pnea*] (circa 1719)
**1** : transient cessation of respiration
**2** : ASPHYXIA
— **ap·ne·ic** \-nē-ik\ *adjective*

**ap·noea** *chiefly British variant of* APNEA

**apo-** *or* **ap-** *prefix* [Middle English, from Middle French & Latin; Middle French, from Latin, from Greek, from *apo* — more at OF]
**1** : away from : off ⟨*aphelion*⟩
**2** : detached : separate ⟨*apogamy*⟩
**3** : formed from : related to ⟨*apomorphine*⟩

**apoc·a·lypse** \ə-'pä-kə-ˌlips\ *noun* [Middle English, revelation, Revelation, from Late Latin *apocalypsis,* from Greek *apokalypsis,* from *apokalyptein* to uncover, from *apo-* + *kalyptein* to cover — more at HELL] (13th century)
**1 a** : one of the Jewish and Christian writings of 200 B.C. to A.D. 150 marked by pseudonymity, symbolic imagery, and the expectation of

an imminent cosmic cataclysm in which God destroys the ruling powers of evil and raises the righteous to life in a messianic kingdom **b** *capitalized* : REVELATION 3
**2 a** : something viewed as a prophetic revelation **b** : ARMAGEDDON

**apoc·a·lyp·tic** \ə-ˌpä-kə-'lip-tik\ *also* **apoc·a·lyp·ti·cal** \-ti-kəl\ *adjective* (1663)
**1** : of, relating to, or resembling an apocalypse
**2** : forecasting the ultimate destiny of the world : PROPHETIC
**3** : foreboding imminent disaster or final doom : TERRIBLE
**4** : wildly unrestrained : GRANDIOSE
**5** : ultimately decisive : CLIMACTIC
— **apoc·a·lyp·ti·cal·ly** \-ti-k(ə-)lē\ *adverb*

**apoc·a·lyp·ti·cism** \-tə-ˌsi-zəm\ *or* **apoc·a·lyp·tism** \ə-'pä-kə-ˌlip-ˌti-zəm\ *noun* (1884)
: apocalyptic expectation; *especially* : a doctrine concerning an imminent end of the world and an ensuing general resurrection and final judgment

**apoc·a·lyp·tist** \ə-'pä-kə-ˌlip-tist\ *noun* (1835)
: the writer of an apocalypse

**apo·chro·mat·ic** \ˌa-pə-krō-'ma-tik\ *adjective* [International Scientific Vocabulary] (1887)
: free from chromatic and spherical aberration ⟨an *apochromatic* lens⟩

**apoc·o·pe** \ə-'pä-kə-(ˌ)pē\ *noun* [Late Latin, from Greek *apokopē,* literally, cutting off, from *apokoptein* to cut off, from *apo-* + *koptein* to cut — more at CAPON] (circa 1550)
: the loss of one or more sounds or letters at the end of a word (as in *sing* from Old English *singan*)

**apo·crine** \'a-pə-krən, -ˌkrīn, -ˌkrēn\ *adjective* [International Scientific Vocabulary *apo-* + Greek *krinein* to separate — more at CERTAIN] (1926)
: producing a fluid secretion by pinching off one end of the secretory cell while leaving the rest intact ⟨an *apocrine* gland⟩; *also* : produced by an apocrine gland

**apoc·ry·pha** \ə-'pä-krə-fə\ *noun plural but singular or plural in construction* [Medieval Latin, from Late Latin, neuter plural of *apocryphus* secret, not canonical, from Greek *apokryphos* obscure, from *apokryptein* to hide away, from *apo-* + *kryptein* to hide — more at CRYPT] (14th century)
**1** : writings or statements of dubious authenticity
**2** *capitalized* **a** : books included in the Septuagint and Vulgate but excluded from the Jewish and Protestant canons of the Old Testament — see BIBLE table **b** : early Christian writings not included in the New Testament ◆

**apoc·ry·phal** \-fəl\ *adjective* (1590)
**1** : of doubtful authenticity : SPURIOUS
**2** *often capitalized* : of or resembling the Apocrypha
**synonym** see FICTITIOUS
— **apoc·ry·phal·ly** \-fə-lē\ *adverb*
— **apoc·ry·phal·ness** *noun*

**apo·dic·tic** \ˌa-pə-'dik-tik\ *also* **apo·deic·tic** \-'dīk-tik\ *adjective* [Latin *apodicticus,* from Greek *apodeiktikos,* from *apodeiknynai* to demonstrate, from *apo-* + *deiknynai* to show — more at DICTION] (circa 1645)
: expressing or of the nature of necessary truth or absolute certainty
— **apo·dic·ti·cal·ly** \-ti-k(ə-)lē\ *adverb*

**apod·o·sis** \ə-'pä-də-səs\ *noun, plural* **-o·ses** \-ˌsēz\ [New Latin, from Greek, from *apodidonai* to give back, deliver, from *apo-* + *didonai* to give — more at DATE] (circa 1638)
: the main clause of a conditional sentence — compare PROTASIS

**apo·en·zyme** \ˌa-pō-'en-ˌzīm\ *noun* [International Scientific Vocabulary] (1936)
: a protein that forms an active enzyme system

by combination with a coenzyme and determines the specificity of this system for a substrate

**apog·a·my** \ə-'pä-gə-mē\ *noun* [International Scientific Vocabulary] (circa 1878)
: development of a sporophyte from a gametophyte without fertilization
— **apog·a·mous** \ə-'pä-gə-məs\ *adjective*

**apo·gee** \'a-pə-(ˌ)jē\ *noun* [French *apogée,* from New Latin *apogaeum,* from Greek *apogaion,* from neuter of *apogeios, apogaios* far from the earth, from *apo-* + *gē, gaia* earth] (1594)

apogee 1

**1** : the point in the orbit of an object (as a satellite) orbiting the earth that is at the greatest distance from the center of the earth; *also* : the point farthest from a planet or a satellite (as the moon) reached by an object orbiting it — compare PERIGEE
**2** : the farthest or highest point : CULMINATION ⟨Aegean civilization reached its *apogee* in Crete⟩
— **apo·ge·an** \ˌa-pə-'jē-ən\ *adjective*

**apo·li·po·pro·tein** \ˌa-pō-ˌlī-pō-'prō-ˌtēn, -ˌli-, -ˌtē-ən\ *noun* (1970)
: a protein that combines with a lipid to form a lipoprotein

**apo·lit·i·cal** \ˌā-pə-'li-ti-kəl\ *adjective* (1935)
**1** : having no interest or involvement in political affairs; *also* : having an aversion to politics or political affairs
**2** : having no political significance
— **apo·lit·i·cal·ly** \-k(ə-)lē\ *adverb*

**Ap·ol·lin·i·an** \ˌa-pə-'li-nē-ən\ *adjective* (1924)
: APOLLONIAN

**Apol·lo** \ə-'pä-(ˌ)lō\ *noun* [Latin *Apollin-, Apollo,* from Greek *Apollōn*]
: the Greek and Roman god of sunlight, prophecy, music, and poetry

**Ap·ol·lo·ni·an** \ˌa-pə-'lō-nē-ən\ *adjective* (1663)
**1** : of, relating to, or resembling the god Apollo

---

◇ **WORD HISTORY**
**apocrypha** *Apocrypha* is the neuter plural form of the Late Latin adjective *apocryphus,* meaning "secret" or "uncanonical." Latin took the word from Greek *apokryphos,* meaning "hidden," which was a derivative of the verb *apokryptein* "to hide." The term *apocrypha* was used in reference to scriptural writings that were "hidden" from the general public. Such books were considered to contain esoteric knowledge accessible to only a small circle of believers. The non-initiates, on the other hand, considered these books to be of doubtful authenticity, or even heretical, so *apocrypha* began to be applied to spurious works. In his Latin translation of the Bible, called the Vulgate, St. Jerome designated as *apocrypha* those books of the Old Testament that were in the Septuagint (a Greek translation of pre-Christian times) but not in the Hebrew-language scriptures to which he had access. Although the Roman Church rejected Jerome's designation and accepted the books as authentic Holy Scripture, Jerome was supported by the German Protestant theologian Karlstadt in 1520. Martin Luther included them in his 1534 German Bible but in a supplement under the heading "Apocrypha."

---

\ə\ **abut** \ᵊ\ **kitten** \ər\ **further** \a\ **ash** \ā\ **ace**
\ä\ **mop, mar** \aů\ **out** \ch\ **chin** \e\ **bet** \ē\ **easy**
\g\ **go** \i\ **hit** \ī\ **ice** \j\ **job** \ŋ\ **sing** \ō\ **go**
\ȯ\ **law** \ȯi\ **boy** \th\ **thin** \t̸h\ **the** \ü\ **loot** \ů\ **foot**
\y\ **yet** \zh\ **vision** *see also* Guide to Pronunciation

**2 :** harmonious, measured, ordered, or balanced in character — compare DIONYSIAN

**Apol·lyon** \ə-'päl-yən, -'pä-lē-ən\ *noun* [Greek *Apollyōn*]
**:** the angel of the bottomless pit in the Book of Revelation

¹**apol·o·get·ic** \ə-,pä-lə-'je-tik\ *noun* (15th century)
**:** APOLOGETICS 1

²**apologetic** *adjective* [Greek *apologētikos*, from *apologeisthai* to defend, from *apo-* + *logos* speech] (1649)
**1 a :** offered in defense or vindication ⟨the *apologetic* writings of the early Christians⟩ **b :** offered by way of excuse or apology ⟨an *apologetic* smile⟩
**2 :** regretfully acknowledging fault or failure **:** CONTRITE ⟨was *apologetic* about his mistake⟩
— **apol·o·get·i·cal·ly** \-ti-k(ə-)lē\ *adverb*

**apol·o·get·ics** \-tiks\ *noun plural but singular or plural in construction* (circa 1733)
**1 :** systematic argumentative discourse in defense (as of a doctrine)
**2 :** a branch of theology devoted to the defense of the divine origin and authority of Christianity

**ap·o·lo·gia** \,a-pə-'lō-j(ē-)ə\ *noun* [Late Latin] (1784)
**:** a defense especially of one's opinions, position, or actions ⟨the finest *apologia* or explanation of what drives a man to devote his life to pure mathematics —*British Book News*⟩
**synonym** see APOLOGY

**apol·o·gise** *British variant of* APOLOGIZE

**apol·o·gist** \ə-'pä-lə-jist\ *noun* (1640)
**:** one who speaks or writes in defense of someone or something

**apol·o·gize** \-,jīz\ *intransitive verb* **-gized; -giz·ing** (1597)
**:** to make an apology
— **apol·o·giz·er** *noun*

**ap·o·logue** \'a-pə-,lȯg, -,läg\ *noun* [French, from Latin *apologus*, from Greek *apologos*, from *apo-* + *logos* speech, narrative] (circa 1555)
**:** an allegorical narrative usually intended to convey a moral

**apol·o·gy** \ə-'pä-lə-jē\ *noun, plural* **-gies** [Middle French or Late Latin; Middle French *apologie*, from Late Latin *apologia*, from Greek, from *apo-* + *logos* speech — more at LEGEND] (1533)
**1 a :** a formal justification **:** DEFENSE **b :** EXCUSE 2a
**2 :** an admission of error or discourtesy accompanied by an expression of regret
**3 :** a poor substitute **:** MAKESHIFT ☆

**apo·lune** \'a-pə-,lün\ *noun* [*apo-* + Latin *luna* moon — more at LUNAR] (circa 1968)
**:** the point in the path of a body orbiting the moon that is farthest from the center of the moon — compare PERILUNE

**apo·mict** \'a-pə-,mikt\ *noun* [probably back-formation from International Scientific Vocabulary *apomictic*, from *apo-* + Greek *mignynai* to mix — more at MIX] (circa 1938)
**:** one produced or reproducing by apomixis
— **apo·mic·tic** \,a-pə-'mik-tik\ *adjective*
— **apo·mic·ti·cal·ly** \-ti-k(ə-)lē\ *adverb*

**apo·mix·is** \,a-pə-'mik-səs\ *noun, plural* **-mix·es** \-,sēz\ [New Latin, from *apo-* + Greek *mixis* act of mixing, from *mignynai*] (1913)
**:** reproduction (as apogamy or parthenogenesis) involving specialized generative tissues but not dependent on fertilization

**apo·mor·phine** \,a-pə-'mȯr-,fēn\ *noun* [International Scientific Vocabulary] (1888)
**:** a crystalline morphine derivative $C_{17}H_{17}NO_2$ that is a dopamine agonist and is administered as the hydrochloride for its powerful emetic action

**apo·neu·ro·sis** \,a-pə-nu̇-'rō-səs, -nyu̇-\ *noun* [New Latin, from Greek *aponeurōsis*, from

*aponeurousthai* to pass into a tendon, from *apo-* + *neuron* sinew — more at NERVE] (1676)
**:** a broad flat sheet of dense fibrous collagenous connective tissue that covers, invests, and forms the terminations and attachments of various muscles
— **apo·neu·rot·ic** \-'rä-tik\ *adjective*

**ap·o·phthegm** \'a-pə-,them\ *variant of* APOTHEGM

**apo·phyl·lite** \,a-pə-'fi-,līt, ə-'pä-fə-,līt\ *noun* [French, from *apo-* + Greek *phyllon* leaf — more at BLADE] (1810)
**:** a mineral composed of a hydrous potassium calcium silicate that is related to the zeolites and is usually found in transparent square prisms or white or grayish masses

**apoph·y·sis** \ə-'pä-fə-səs\ *noun, plural* **-y·ses** \-,sēz\ [New Latin, from Greek, from *apo-* + *phyein* to bring forth — more at BE] (1646)
**:** an expanded or projecting part especially of an organism
— **apoph·y·se·al** \-,pä-fə-'sē-əl\ *adjective*

**ap·o·plec·tic** \,a-pə-'plek-tik\ *adjective* [French or Late Latin; French *apoplectique*, from Late Latin *apoplecticus*, from Greek *apoplēktikos*, from *apoplēssein*] (1611)
**1 :** of, relating to, or causing stroke
**2 :** affected with, inclined to, or showing symptoms of stroke
**3 :** of a kind to cause or apparently cause stroke ⟨an *apoplectic* rage⟩; *also* **:** greatly excited or angered
— **ap·o·plec·ti·cal·ly** \-ti-k(ə-)lē\ *adverb*

**ap·o·plexy** \'a-pə-,plek-sē\ *noun* [Middle English *apoplexie*, from Middle French & Late Latin; Middle French, from Late Latin *apoplexia*, from Greek *apoplēxia*, from *apoplēssein* to cripple by a stroke, from *apo-* + *plēssein* to strike — more at PLAINT] (15th century)
**:** STROKE 5

**aport** \ə-'pȯrt, -'pȯrt\ *adverb* (1627)
**:** on or toward the left side of a ship ⟨put the helm hard *aport*⟩

**apo·se·mat·ic** \,a-pə-si-'ma-tik\ *adjective* (1890)
**:** being conspicuous and serving to warn ⟨*aposematic* coloration⟩
— **apo·se·mat·i·cal·ly** \-ti-k(ə-)lē\ *adverb*

**ap·o·si·o·pe·sis** \,a-pə-,sī-ə-'pē-səs\ *noun, plural* **-pe·ses** \-,sēz\ [Late Latin, from Greek *aposiōpēsis*, from *aposiōpan* to be fully silent, from *apo-* + *siōpan* to be silent, from *siōpē* silence] (1578)
**:** the leaving of a thought incomplete usually by a sudden breaking off (as in "his behavior was—but I blush to mention that")
— **ap·o·si·o·pet·ic** \-'pe-tik\ *adjective*

**apos·po·ry** \'a-pə-,spȯr-ē, -,spȯr-; ə-'päs-pə-rē\ *noun* (1884)
**:** production of gametophytes directly from diploid cells of the sporophytes without spore formation (as in certain ferns and mosses)
— **apos·po·rous** \'a-pə-,spȯr-əs, -,spȯr-; ə-'päs-pə-rəs\ *adjective*

**apos·ta·sy** \ə-'päs-tə-sē\ *noun, plural* **-sies** [Middle English *apostasie*, from Late Latin *apostasia*, from Greek, literally, revolt, from *aphistasthai* to revolt, from *apo-* + *histasthai* to stand — more at STAND] (14th century)
**1 :** renunciation of a religious faith
**2 :** abandonment of a previous loyalty **:** DEFECTION

**apos·tate** \ə-'päs-,tāt, -tət\ *noun* (14th century)
**:** one who commits apostasy
— **apostate** *adjective*

**apos·ta·tise** *British variant of* APOSTATIZE

**apos·ta·tize** \ə-'päs-tə-,tīz\ *intransitive verb* **-tized; -tiz·ing** (1611)
**:** to commit apostasy

**a pos·te·ri·o·ri** \,ä-(,)pō-,stir-ē-'ōr-ē, -,ster-; ,ä-(,)pä-,stir-ē-'ōr-,ī, -(,)pō-, -'ȯr-ē; -'ȯr-\ *adjective* [Latin, literally, from the latter] (1588)

**1 :** INDUCTIVE
**2 :** relating to or derived by reasoning from observed facts — compare A PRIORI
— **a posteriori** *adverb*

**apos·tle** \ə-'pä-səl\ *noun* [Middle English, from Old French & Old English; Old French *apostle* & Old English *apostol*, both from Late Latin *apostolus*, from Greek *apostolos*, from *apostellein* to send away, from *apo-* + *stellein* to send] (before 12th century)
**1 :** one sent on a mission: as **a :** one of an authoritative New Testament group sent out to preach the gospel and made up especially of Christ's 12 original disciples and Paul **b :** the first prominent Christian missionary to a region or group
**2 a :** a person who initiates a great moral reform or who first advocates an important belief or system **b :** an ardent supporter **:** ADHERENT ⟨an *apostle* of liberty⟩
**3 :** the highest ecclesiastical official in some church organizations
**4 :** one of a Mormon administrative council of 12 men
— **apos·tle·ship** \-,ship\ *noun*

**Apostles' Creed** *noun* (circa 1658)
**:** a Christian statement of belief ascribed to the Twelve Apostles and used especially in public worship

**apos·to·late** \ə-'päs-tə-,lāt, -lət\ *noun* [Late Latin *apostolatus*, from *apostolus*] (14th century)
**1 :** the office or mission of an apostle
**2 :** an association of persons dedicated to the propagation of a religion or a doctrine

**ap·os·tol·ic** \,a-pə-'stä-lik\ *adjective* (13th century)
**1 a :** of or relating to an apostle **b :** of, relating to, or conforming to the teachings of the New Testament apostles
**2 a :** of or relating to a succession of spiritual authority from the apostles held (as by Roman Catholics, Anglicans, and Eastern Orthodox) to be perpetuated by successive ordinations of bishops and to be necessary for valid sacraments and orders **b :** PAPAL
— **apos·to·lic·i·ty** \,a-,päs-tə-'li-sə-tē\ *noun*

**apostolic delegate** *noun* (circa 1907)
**:** an ecclesiastical representative of the Holy See to the Catholic hierarchy of another country

**Apostolic Father** *noun* (1828)
**:** a church father of the first or second century A.D.

¹**apos·tro·phe** \ə-'päs-trə-(,)fē\ *noun* [Latin, from Greek *apostrophē*, literally, active of turning away, from *apostrephein* to turn away, from *apo-* + *strephein* to turn] (1533)

---

☆ SYNONYMS
**Apology, apologia, excuse, plea, pretext, alibi** mean matter offered in explanation or defense. APOLOGY usually applies to an expression of regret for a mistake or wrong with implied admission of guilt or fault and with or without reference to palliating circumstances ⟨said by way of *apology* that he would have met them if he could⟩. APOLOGIA implies not admission of guilt or regret but a desire to make clear the grounds for some course, belief, or position ⟨his speech was an *apologia* for his foreign policy⟩. EXCUSE implies an intent to avoid or remove blame or censure ⟨used illness as an *excuse* for missing the meeting⟩. PLEA stresses argument or appeal for understanding or sympathy or mercy ⟨her usual *plea* that she was nearsighted⟩. PRETEXT suggests subterfuge and the offering of false reasons or motives in excuse or explanation ⟨used any *pretext* to get out of work⟩. ALIBI implies a desire to shift blame or evade punishment and imputes plausibility rather than truth to the explanation offered ⟨his *alibi* failed to stand scrutiny⟩.

: the addressing of a usually absent person or a usually personified thing rhetorically ⟨Carlyle's "O Liberty, what things are done in thy name!" is an example of *apostrophe*⟩
— **ap·os·troph·ic** \ˌa-pə-'strä-fik\ *adjective*
**²apostrophe** *noun* [Middle French & Late Latin; Middle French, from Late Latin *apostrophus*, from Greek *apostrophos*, from *apostrophos* turned away, from *apostrephein*] (1727)
: a mark ' used to indicate the omission of letters or figures, the possessive case, or the plural of letters or figures
— **apostrophic** *adjective*
**apos·tro·phise** *British variant of* APOSTROPHIZE
**apos·tro·phize** \ə-'päs-trə-ˌfīz\ *verb* **-phized; -phiz·ing** (1718)
*transitive verb*
: to address by or in an apostrophe
*intransitive verb*
: to make use of apostrophe
**apothecaries' measure** *noun* (circa 1900)
: a system of liquid units of measure used chiefly by pharmacists
**apothecaries' weight** *noun* (1765)
: a system of weights used chiefly by pharmacists — see WEIGHT table
**apoth·e·cary** \ə-'pä-thə-ˌker-ē\ *noun, plural* **-car·ies** [Middle English *apothecarie*, from Medieval Latin *apothecarius*, from Late Latin, shopkeeper, from Latin *apotheca* storehouse, from Greek *apothēkē*, from *apotithenai* to put away, from *apo-* + *tithenai* to put — more at DO] (14th century)
**1** : one who prepares and sells drugs or compounds for medicinal purposes
**2** : PHARMACY
**apo·the·ci·um** \ˌa-pə-'thē-shē-əm, -sē-\ *noun, plural* **-cia** \-shē-ə, -sē-\ [New Latin, from Latin *apotheca*] (1830)
: a spore-bearing structure in many lichens and fungi consisting of a discoid or cupped body bearing asci on the exposed flat or concave surface
— **apo·the·cial** \-sh(ē-)əl, -sē-əl\ *adjective*
**ap·o·thegm** \'a-pə-ˌthem\ *noun* [Greek *apophthegmat-, apophthegma*, from *apophthengesthai* to speak out, from *apo-* + *phthengesthai* to utter] (circa 1587)
: a short, pithy, and instructive saying or formulation : APHORISM
— **ap·o·theg·mat·ic** \ˌa-pə-theg-'ma-tik\ *adjective*
**ap·o·them** \'a-pə-ˌthem\ *noun* [International Scientific Vocabulary *apo-* + *-them* (from Greek *thema* something laid down, theme)] (circa 1856)
: the perpendicular from the center of a regular polygon to one of the sides
**apo·the·o·sis** \ə-ˌpä-thē-'ō-səs, ˌa-pə-'thē-ə-səs\ *noun, plural* **-o·ses** \-ˌsēz\ [Late Latin, from Greek *apotheōsis*, from *apotheoun* to deify, from *apo-* + *theos* god] (circa 1580)
**1** : elevation to divine status : DEIFICATION
**2** : the perfect example : QUINTESSENCE ⟨this is the literary *apotheosis* of the shaggy dog story —Thomas Sutcliffe⟩
— **apo·the·o·size** \ˌa-pə-'thē-ə-ˌsīz, ə-'pä-thē-ə-\ *transitive verb*
**apo·tro·pa·ic** \ˌa-pə-trō-'pā-ik\ *adjective* [Greek *apotropaios*, from *apotrepein* to avert, from *apo-* + *trepein* to turn] (1883)
: designed to avert evil ⟨an *apotropaic* ritual⟩
— **apo·tro·pa·i·cal·ly** \-'pā-ə-k(ə)lē\ *adverb*
**Ap·pa·la·chian** \ˌa-pə-'lā-ch(ē-)ən, -'la-, -sh(ē-)ən\ *noun* (1888)
: a white native or resident of the Appalachian mountain area
**Appalachian dulcimer** *noun* (1962)
: DULCIMER 2
**ap·pall** *also* **ap·pal** \ə-'pol\ *verb* **ap·palled; ap·pall·ing** [Middle English, from Middle French *apalir*, from Old French, from *a-* (from Latin *ad-*) + *palir* to grow pale, from Latin

*pallescere*, inchoative of *pallēre* to be pale — more at FALLOW] (14th century)
*intransitive verb*
*obsolete* : WEAKEN, FAIL
*transitive verb*
: to overcome with consternation, shock, or dismay
**synonym** see DISMAY
**ap·pall·ing** *adjective* (1817)
: inspiring horror, dismay, or disgust ⟨living under *appalling* conditions⟩
— **ap·pall·ing·ly** *adverb*
**Ap·pa·loo·sa** \ˌa-pə-'lü-sə\ *noun* [origin unknown] (1947)
: any of a breed of rugged saddle horses developed in western North America and usually having a white or solid-colored coat with small spots

**Appaloosa**

**ap·pa·nage** \'a-pə-nij\ *noun* [French *apanage*, from Old French, from *apaner* to provide for a younger offspring, from Medieval Latin *appanare*, from Latin *ad-* + *panis* bread — more at FOOD] (1602)
**1 a** : a grant (as of land or revenue) made by a sovereign or a legislative body to a dependent member of the royal family or a principal vassal **b** : a property or privilege appropriated to or by a person as something due
**2** : a rightful endowment or adjunct
**ap·pa·rat** \'a-pə-ˌrat, ˌä-pə-'rät\ *noun* [Russian] (1941)
: APPARATUS 2
**ap·pa·rat·chik** \ˌä-pə-'rä(t)-chik\ *noun, plural* **-chiks** *also* **-chi·ki** \-chi-kē\ [Russian, from *apparat*] (1941)
**1** : a member of a Communist apparat
**2** : an official blindly devoted to superiors or to the organization
**ap·pa·ra·tus** \ˌa-pə-'ra-təs, -'rā-\ *noun, plural* **-tus·es** *or* **-tus** [Latin, from *apparare* to prepare, from *ad-* + *parare* to prepare — more at PARE] (circa 1628)
**1 a** : a set of materials or equipment designed for a particular use **b** : a group of anatomical or cytological parts functioning together ⟨mitotic *apparatus*⟩ **c** : an instrument or appliance designed for a specific operation
**2** : the functional processes by means of which a systematized activity is carried out: as **a** : the machinery of government **b** : the organization of a political party or an underground movement
**¹ap·par·el** \ə-'par-əl\ *transitive verb* **-eled** *or* **-elled; -el·ing** *or* **-el·ling** [Middle English *appareillen*, from Middle French *apareillier* to prepare, from (assumed) Vulgar Latin *appariculare*, from Latin *apparare*] (14th century)
**1** : to put clothes on : DRESS
**2** : ADORN, EMBELLISH
**²apparel** *noun* (14th century)
**1** : the equipment (as sails and rigging) of a ship
**2** : personal attire : CLOTHING
**3** : something that clothes or adorns ⟨the bright *apparel* of spring⟩
**ap·par·ent** \ə-'par-ənt, -'per-\ *adjective* [Middle English, from Middle French *aparent*, from Latin *apparent-, apparens*, present participle of *apparēre* to appear] (14th century)
**1** : open to view : VISIBLE
**2** : clear or manifest to the understanding
**3** : appearing as actual to the eye or mind
**4** : having an indefeasible right to succeed to a title or estate ▸
**5** : manifest to the senses or mind as real or true on the basis of evidence that may or may not be factually valid ⟨the air of spontaneity is perhaps more *apparent* than real —J. R. Sutherland⟩ ☆

— **ap·par·ent·ness** \-'par-ənt-nəs, -'per-\ *noun*
**ap·par·ent·ly** \-lē\ *adverb* (1566)
: it seems apparent ⟨the window had *apparently* been forced open⟩ ⟨*apparently*, we're supposed to wait here⟩
**apparent magnitude** *noun* (1875)
: the luminosity of a celestial body (as a star) as observed from the earth — compare ABSOLUTE MAGNITUDE
**apparent time** *noun* (1694)
: the time of day indicated by the hour angle of the sun or by a sundial
**ap·pa·ri·tion** \ˌa-pə-'ri-shən\ *noun* [Middle English *apparicioun*, from Late Latin *apparition-, apparitio* appearance, from Latin *apparēre*] (15th century)
**1 a** : an unusual or unexpected sight : PHENOMENON **b** : a ghostly figure
**2** : the act of becoming visible : APPEARANCE
— **ap·pa·ri·tion·al** \-'rish-nəl, -'ri-shə-nᵊl\ *adjective*
**ap·par·i·tor** \ə-'par-ə-tər\ *noun* [Latin, from *apparēre*] (15th century)
: an official formerly sent to carry out the orders of a magistrate, judge, or court
**¹ap·peal** \ə-'pē(ə)l\ *noun* (13th century)
**1** : a legal proceeding by which a case is brought before a higher court for review of the decision of a lower court
**2** : a criminal accusation
**3 a** : an application (as to a recognized authority) for corroboration, vindication, or decision **b** : an earnest plea : ENTREATY
**4** : the power of arousing a sympathetic response : ATTRACTION ⟨movies had a great *appeal* for him⟩
**²appeal** *verb* [Middle English *appelen* to accuse, appeal, from Middle French *apeler*, from Latin *appellare*, from *appellere* to drive to, from *ad-* + *pellere* to drive — more at FELT] (14th century)
*transitive verb*
**1** : to charge with a crime : ACCUSE
**2** : to take proceedings to have (a lower court's decision) reviewed in a higher court
*intransitive verb*
**1** : to take a lower court's decision to a higher court for review
**2** : to call upon another for corroboration, vindication, or decision
**3** : to make an earnest request
**4** : to arouse a sympathetic response
— **ap·peal·abil·i·ty** \-ˌpē-lə-'bi-lə-tē\ *noun*
— **ap·peal·able** \-'pē-lə-bəl\ *adjective*
— **ap·peal·er** *noun*

☆ **SYNONYMS**
**Apparent, illusory, seeming, ostensible** mean not actually being what appearance indicates. APPARENT suggests appearance to unaided senses that is not or may not be borne out by more rigorous examination or greater knowledge ⟨the *apparent* cause of the accident⟩. ILLUSORY implies a false impression based on deceptive resemblance or faulty observation, or influenced by emotions that prevent a clear view ⟨an *illusory* sense of security⟩. SEEMING implies a character in the thing observed that gives it the appearance, sometimes through intent, of something else ⟨the *seeming* simplicity of the story⟩. OSTENSIBLE suggests a discrepancy between an openly declared or naturally implied aim or reason and the true one ⟨the *ostensible* reason for their visit⟩. See in addition EVIDENT.

\ə\ abut \ᵊ\ kitten \ər\ further \a\ ash \ā\ ace
\ä\ mop, mar \aù\ out \ch\ chin \e\ bet \ē\ easy
\g\ go \i\ hit \ī\ ice \j\ job \ŋ\ sing \ō\ go
\ò\ law \òi\ boy \th\ thin \t͟h\ the \ü\ loot \ù\ foot
\y\ yet \zh\ vision    *see also* Guide to Pronunciation

**ap·peal·ing** \ə-'pē-liŋ\ *adjective* (1813)
**1 :** marked by earnest entreaty **:** IMPLORING
**2 :** having appeal **:** PLEASING
— **ap·peal·ing·ly** \-liŋ-lē\ *adverb*
**ap·pear** \ə-'pir\ *intransitive verb* [Middle English *apperen*, from Old French *aparoir*, from Latin *apparēre*, from *ad-* + *parēre* to show oneself] (13th century)
**1 a :** to be or come in sight ⟨the sun *appears* on the horizon⟩ **b :** to show up ⟨*appears* promptly at eight each day⟩
**2 :** to come formally before an authoritative body ⟨must *appear* in court today⟩
**3 :** to have an outward aspect **:** SEEM ⟨*appears* happy enough⟩
**4 :** to become evident or manifest ⟨there *appears* to be evidence to the contrary⟩
**5 :** to come into public view ⟨first *appeared* on a television variety show⟩ ⟨the book *appeared* in print a few years ago⟩
**6 :** to come into existence ⟨hominids *appeared* late in the evolutionary chain⟩
**ap·pear·ance** \ə-'pir-ən(t)s\ *noun* (14th century)
**1 a :** external show **:** SEMBLANCE ⟨although hostile, he preserved an *appearance* of neutrality⟩ **b :** outward aspect **:** LOOK ⟨had a fierce *appearance*⟩ **c** *plural* **:** outward indication ⟨trying to keep up *appearances*⟩
**2 a :** a sense impression or aspect of a thing ⟨the blue of distant hills is only an *appearance*⟩ **b :** the world of sensible phenomena
**3 a :** the act, action, or process of appearing **b :** the presentation of oneself in court as a party to an action often through the representation of an attorney
**4 a :** something that appears **:** PHENOMENON **b :** an instance of appearing **:** OCCURRENCE
**ap·pease** \ə-'pēz\ *transitive verb* **ap·peased; ap·peas·ing** [Middle English *appesen*, from Middle French *apaisier*, from *a-* (from Latin *ad-*) + *pais* peace — more at PEACE] (14th century)
**1 :** to bring to a state of peace or quiet **:** CALM
**2 :** to cause to subside **:** ALLAY ⟨*appeased* my hunger⟩
**3 :** PACIFY, CONCILIATE; *especially* **:** to buy off (an aggressor) by concessions usually at the sacrifice of principles
**synonym** see PACIFY
— **ap·peas·able** \-'pē-zə-bəl\ *adjective*
— **ap·pease·ment** \-'pēz-mənt\ *noun*
— **ap·peas·er** *noun*
¹**ap·pel·lant** \ə-'pe-lənt\ *adjective* (14th century)
**:** of or relating to an appeal **:** APPELLATE
²**appellant** *noun* (15th century)
**:** one that appeals; *specifically* **:** one that appeals from a judicial decision or decree
**ap·pel·late** \ə-'pe-lət\ *adjective* [Latin *appellatus*, past participle of *appellare*] (1768)
**:** of, relating to, or recognizing appeals; *specifically* **:** having the power to review the judgment of another tribunal ⟨an *appellate* court⟩
**ap·pel·la·tion** \,a-pə-'lā-shən\ *noun* (15th century)
**1 :** an identifying name or title **:** DESIGNATION
**2** *archaic* **:** the act of calling by a name
**3 :** a geographical name (as of a region, village or vineyard) under which a winegrower is authorized to identify and market wine
**ap·pel·la·tive** \ə-'pe-lə-tiv\ *adjective* (15th century)
**1 :** of or relating to a common noun
**2 :** of, relating to, or inclined to the giving of names
— **ap·pel·la·tive** *noun*
— **ap·pel·la·tive·ly** *adverb*
**ap·pel·lee** \,a-pə-'lē\ *noun* (1531)
**:** one against whom an appeal is taken
**ap·pend** \ə-'pend\ *transitive verb* [Middle English, from Middle French *appendre*, from Late Latin *appendere*, from Latin, to weigh, from *ad-* + *pendere* to weigh — more at PENDANT] (14th century)
**1 :** ATTACH, AFFIX

**2 :** to add as a supplement or appendix (as in a book)
**ap·pend·age** \ə-'pen-dij\ *noun* (1649)
**1 :** an adjunct to something larger or more important **:** APPURTENANCE
**2 :** a subordinate or derivative body part; *especially* **:** a limb or analogous part (as a seta)
**3 :** a dependent or subordinate person
**ap·pen·dant** \ə-'pen-dənt\ *adjective* (15th century)
**1 :** belonging as a right by prescription — used of annexed land in English law
**2 :** associated as an attendant circumstance
**3 :** attached as an appendage ⟨a seal *appendant* to a document⟩
— **appendant** *noun*
**ap·pen·dec·to·my** \,a-pən-'dek-tə-mē, ,a-,pen-\ *noun, plural* **-mies** [Latin *appendic-, appendix* + English *-ectomy*] (circa 1895)
**:** surgical removal of the vermiform appendix
**ap·pen·di·cec·to·my** \ə-,pen-də-'sek-tə-mē\ *noun, plural* **-mies** (1894)
*British* **:** APPENDECTOMY
**ap·pen·di·ci·tis** \ə-,pen-də-'sī-təs\ *noun* [New Latin] (1886)
**:** inflammation of the vermiform appendix
**ap·pen·dic·u·lar** \,a-pən-'di-kyə-lər\ *adjective* (1651)
**:** of or relating to an appendage and especially a limb ⟨the *appendicular* skeleton⟩
**ap·pen·dix** \ə-'pen-diks\ *noun, plural* **-dix·es** or **-di·ces** \-də-,sēz\ [Latin *appendic-, appendix*, from *appendere*] (1542)
**1 a :** APPENDAGE **b :** supplementary material usually attached at the end of a piece of writing
**2 :** a bodily outgrowth or process; *specifically* **:** VERMIFORM APPENDIX
**ap·per·ceive** \,a-pər-'sēv\ *transitive verb* **-ceived; -ceiv·ing** [French *apercevoir*] (1876)
**:** to have apperception of
**ap·per·cep·tion** \-'sep-shən\ *noun* [French *aperception*, from *apercevoir*, from Middle French *aperceivre*, from *a-* (from Latin *ad-*) + *perceivre* to perceive] (1753)
**1 :** introspective self-consciousness
**2 :** mental perception; *especially* **:** the process of understanding something perceived in terms of previous experience
— **ap·per·cep·tive** \-'sep-tiv\ *adjective*
**ap·per·tain** \,a-pər-'tān\ *intransitive verb* [Middle English *apperteinen*, from Middle French *apartenir*, from Late Latin *appertinēre*, from Latin *ad-* + *pertinēre* to belong — more at PERTAIN] (14th century)
**:** to belong or be connected as a rightful part or attribute **:** PERTAIN
**ap·pe·tence** \'a-pə-tən(t)s\ *noun* (1610)
**:** APPETENCY
**ap·pe·ten·cy** \-tən(t)-sē\ *noun, plural* **-cies** [Latin *appetentia*, from *appetent-, appetens*, present participle of *appetere*] (1631)
**:** a fixed and strong desire **:** APPETITE
— **ap·pe·tent** \-tənt\ *adjective*
**ap·pe·tis·er, ap·pe·tis·ing** *British variant of* APPETIZER, APPETIZING
**ap·pe·tite** \'a-pə-,tīt\ *noun* [Middle English *apetit*, from Middle French, from Latin *appetitus*, from *appetere* to strive after, from *ad-* + *petere* to go to — more at FEATHER] (14th century)
**1 :** any of the instinctive desires necessary to keep up organic life; *especially* **:** the desire to eat
**2 a :** an inherent craving ⟨an insatiable *appetite* for work⟩ **b :** TASTE, PREFERENCE ⟨the cultural *appetites* of the time —J. D. Hart⟩
— **ap·pe·ti·tive** \-,tī-tiv\ *adjective*
**ap·pe·tiz·er** \'a-pə-,tī-zər\ *noun* (1859)
**:** a food or drink that stimulates the appetite and is usually served before a meal
**ap·pe·tiz·ing** \-,tī-ziŋ\ *adjective* (1653)
**:** appealing to the appetite especially in appearance or aroma; *also* **:** appealing to one's taste ⟨an *appetizing* display of merchandise⟩

**synonym** see PALATABLE
— **ap·pe·tiz·ing·ly** \-ziŋ-lē\ *adverb*
**ap·plaud** \ə-'plȯd\ *verb* [Middle English, from Middle French or Latin; Middle French *applaudir*, from Latin *applaudere*, from *ad-* + *plaudere* to applaud] (15th century)
*intransitive verb*
**:** to express approval especially by clapping the hands
*transitive verb*
**1 :** to express approval of **:** PRAISE ⟨*applaud* her efforts to lose weight⟩
**2 :** to show approval of especially by clapping the hands
— **ap·plaud·able** \-'plȯ-də-bəl\ *adjective*
— **ap·plaud·ably** \-blē\ *adverb*
— **ap·plaud·er** *noun*
**ap·plause** \ə-'plȯz\ *noun* [Medieval Latin *applausus*, from Latin, beating of wings, from *applaudere*] (15th century)
**1 :** marked commendation **:** ACCLAIM ⟨the kind of *applause* every really creative writer wants —Robert Tallant⟩
**2 :** approval publicly expressed (as by clapping the hands)
**ap·ple** \'a-pəl\ *noun, often attributive* [Middle English *appel*, from Old English *æppel*; akin to Old High German *apful* apple, Old Irish *ubull*, Old Church Slavonic *ablŭko*] (before 12th century)
**1 :** the fleshy usually rounded and red, yellow, or green edible pome fruit of a tree (genus *Malus*) of the rose family; *also* **:** an apple tree
**2 :** a fruit or other vegetable production suggestive of an apple — compare OAK APPLE
— **apple of one's eye :** one that is highly cherished ⟨his daughter is the *apple of his eye*⟩
**apple butter** *noun* (circa 1774)
**:** a thick brown spread made by cooking apples with sugar and spices usually in cider
**ap·ple·cart** \-,kärt\ *noun* (1788)
**:** a plan, system, situation, or undertaking that may be disrupted or terminated ⟨upset the *applecart*⟩
**ap·ple–cheeked** \'a-pəl-,chēkt\ *adjective* (1864)
**:** having cheeks the color of red apples
**ap·ple·jack** \-,jak\ *noun* (1816)
**:** brandy distilled from hard cider; *also* **:** an alcoholic beverage traditionally made by freezing hard cider and siphoning off the concentrated liquor
**ap·ple–knock·er** \-,nä-kər\ *noun* (1919)
**:** RUSTIC
**apple maggot** *noun* (1867)
**:** a dipteran fly (*Rhagoletis pomonella*) whose larva burrows in and feeds especially on apples
**ap·ple–pie** \'a-pəl-'pī\ *adjective* (1780)
**1 :** EXCELLENT, PERFECT ⟨*apple-pie* order⟩
**2 :** of, relating to, or characterized by traditionally American values (as honesty or simplicity) ⟨is the epitome of *apple-pie* wholesomeness⟩
**ap·ple–pol·ish** \'a-pəl-,pä-lish\ *verb* [from the traditional practice of schoolchildren bringing a shiny apple as a gift to their teacher] (1935)
*intransitive verb*
**:** to attempt to ingratiate oneself **:** TOADY
*transitive verb*
**:** to curry favor with (as by flattery)
— **ap·ple–pol·ish·er** *noun*
**ap·ple·sauce** \-,sȯs\ *noun* (1739)
**1 :** a relish or dessert made of apples stewed to a pulp and sweetened
**2** *slang* **:** BUNKUM, NONSENSE
**apple scab** *noun* (circa 1899)
**:** a disease of apple trees caused by a fungus (*Venturia inaequalis*) producing dark blotches or lesions on the leaves, fruit, and sometimes the young twigs
**ap·pli·ance** \ə-'plī-ən(t)s\ *noun* (1561)
**1 :** an act of applying
**2 a :** a piece of equipment for adapting a tool or machine to a special purpose **:** ATTACHMENT

**b :** an instrument or device designed for a particular use; *specifically* **:** a household or office device (as a stove, fan, or refrigerator) operated by gas or electric current **c** *British* **:** FIRE ENGINE
**3** *obsolete* **:** COMPLIANCE
*synonym* see IMPLEMENT

**ap·pli·ca·ble** \'a-pli-kə-bəl *also* ə-'pli-kə-\ *adjective* (1660)
**:** capable of or suitable for being applied **:** APPROPRIATE ⟨statutes *applicable* to the case⟩
*synonym* see RELEVANT
— **ap·pli·ca·bil·i·ty** \ˌa-pli-kə-'bi-lə-tē *also* ə-ˌpli-kə-\ *noun*

**ap·pli·cant** \'a-pli-kənt\ *noun* (circa 1782)
**:** one who applies ⟨a job *applicant*⟩

**ap·pli·ca·tion** \ˌa-plə-'kā-shən\ *noun* [Middle English *applicacioun*, from Latin *application-, applicatio* inclination, from *applicare*] (15th century)
**1 :** an act of applying: **a** (1) **:** an act of putting to use ⟨*application* of new techniques⟩ (2) **:** a use to which something is put ⟨new *applications* for old remedies⟩ (3) **:** a program (as a word processor or a spreadsheet) that performs one of the important tasks for which a computer is used **b :** an act of administering or superposing ⟨*application* of paint to a house⟩ **c :** assiduous attention ⟨succeeds by *application* to her studies⟩
**2 a :** REQUEST, PETITION ⟨an *application* for financial aid⟩ **b :** a form used in making a request
**3 :** the practical inference to be derived from a discourse (as a moral tale)
**4 :** a medicated or protective layer or material ⟨an oily *application* for dry skin⟩
**5 :** capacity for practical use ⟨words of varied *application*⟩

**ap·pli·ca·tive** \'a-plə-ˌkā-tiv, ə-'pli-kə-\ *adjective* (1638)
**1 :** APPLICABLE, PRACTICAL
**2 :** put to use **:** APPLIED
— **ap·pli·ca·tive·ly** *adverb*

**ap·pli·ca·tor** \'a-plə-ˌkā-tər\ *noun* (1659)
**:** one that applies; *specifically* **:** a device for applying a substance (as medicine or polish)

**ap·pli·ca·to·ry** \'a-pli-kə-ˌtōr-ē, -ˌtòr-, ə-'pli-kə-\ *adjective* (1649)
**:** capable of being applied

**ap·plied** \ə-'plīd\ *adjective* (1656)
**1 :** put to practical use ⟨*applied* art⟩; *especially* **:** applying general principles to solve definite problems ⟨*applied* sciences⟩
**2 :** working in an applied science ⟨an *applied* physicist⟩

**¹ap·pli·qué** \ˌa-plə-'kā\ *noun* [French, past participle of *appliquer* to put on, from Latin *applicare*] (1801)
**:** a cutout decoration fastened to a larger piece of material

**²appliqué** *transitive verb* **-quéd; -qué·ing** (1881)
**:** to apply (as a decoration or ornament) to a larger surface **:** OVERLAY

**ap·ply** \ə-'plī\ *verb* **ap·plied; ap·ply·ing** [Middle English *applien*, from Middle French *aplier*, from Latin *applicare*, from *ad-* + *plicare* to fold — more at PLY] (14th century)
*transitive verb*
**1 a :** to put to use especially for some practical purpose ⟨*applies* pressure to get what he wants⟩ **b :** to bring into action ⟨*apply* the brakes⟩ **c :** to lay or spread on ⟨*apply* varnish⟩ **d :** to put into operation or effect ⟨*apply* a law⟩
**2 :** to employ diligently or with close attention ⟨should *apply* yourself to your work⟩
*intransitive verb*
**1 :** to have relevance or a valid connection ⟨this rule *applies* to freshmen only⟩
**2 :** to make an appeal or request especially in the form of a written application ⟨*apply* for a job⟩
— **ap·pli·er** \-'plī(-ə)r\ *noun*

**ap·pog·gia·tu·ra** \ə-ˌpä-jə-'tùr-ə\ *noun* [Italian, literally, support] (1753)

**:** an embellishing note or tone preceding an essential melodic note or tone and usually written as a note of smaller size

**ap·point** \ə-'pòint\ *verb* [Middle English, from Middle French *apointier* to arrange, from *a-* (from Latin *ad-*) + *point* point] (14th century)
*transitive verb*
**1 a :** to fix or set officially ⟨*appoint* a trial date⟩ **b :** to name officially ⟨will *appoint* her director of the program⟩ **c** *archaic* **:** ARRANGE **d :** to determine the disposition of (an estate) to someone by virtue of a power of appointment
**2 :** to provide with complete and usually appropriate or elegant furnishings or equipment
*intransitive verb*
**:** to exercise a power of appointment
*synonym* see FURNISH

**ap·poin·tee** \ə-ˌpòin-'tē, ˌa-\ *noun* (1768)
**1 :** one who is appointed
**2 :** one to whom an estate is appointed

**ap·point·ive** \ə-'pòin-tiv\ *adjective* (1881)
**:** of, relating to, or filled by appointment ⟨an *appointive* office⟩

**ap·point·ment** \ə-'pòint-mənt\ *noun* (15th century)
**1 a :** an act of appointing **:** DESIGNATION **b :** the designation by virtue of a vested power of a person to enjoy an estate
**2 :** an arrangement for a meeting **:** ENGAGEMENT
**3 :** EQUIPMENT, FURNISHINGS — usually used in plural
**4 :** a nonelective office or position ⟨holds an academic *appointment*⟩

**ap·por·tion** \ə-'pōr-shən, -'pòr-\ *transitive verb* **-tioned; -tion·ing** \-sh(ə-)niŋ\ [Middle French *apportionner*, from *a-* (from Latin *ad-*) + *portionner* to portion] (1574)
**:** to divide and share out according to a plan; *especially* **:** to make a proportionate division or distribution of
— **ap·por·tion·able** \-shə-nə-bəl\ *adjective*

**ap·por·tion·ment** \-shən-mənt\ *noun* (1579)
**:** an act or result of apportioning; *especially* **:** the apportioning of representatives or taxes among the states according to U.S. law

**ap·pose** \a-'pōz\ *transitive verb* **ap·posed; ap·pos·ing** [Middle French *aposer*, from Old French, from *a-* + *poser* to put — more at POSE] (1596)
**1** *archaic* **:** to put before **:** apply (one thing) to another
**2 :** to place in juxtaposition or proximity

**ap·po·site** \'a-pə-zət\ *adjective* [Latin *appositus*, from past participle of *apponere* to place near, from *ad-* + *ponere* to put — more at POSITION] (1621)
**:** highly pertinent or appropriate **:** APT
*synonym* see RELEVANT
— **ap·po·site·ly** *adverb*
— **ap·po·site·ness** *noun*

**ap·po·si·tion** \ˌa-pə-'zi-shən\ *noun* (15th century)
**1 a :** a grammatical construction in which two usually adjacent nouns having the same referent stand in the same syntactical relation to the rest of a sentence (as *the poet* and *Burns* in "a biography of the poet Burns") **b :** the relation of one of such a pair of nouns or noun equivalents to the other
**2 a :** an act or instance of apposing; *specifically* **:** the deposition of successive layers upon those already present (as in cell walls) **b :** the state of being apposed
— **ap·po·si·tion·al** \-'zish-nəl, -'zi-shə-nᵊl\ *adjective*

**ap·pos·i·tive** \ə-'pä-zə-tiv, a-\ *adjective* (1693)
**:** of, relating to, or standing in grammatical apposition
— **appositive** *noun*
— **ap·pos·i·tive·ly** *adverb*

**ap·prais·al** \ə-'prā-zəl\ *noun* (1817)

**:** an act or instance of appraising; *especially* **:** a valuation of property by the estimate of an authorized person

**ap·praise** \ə-'prāz\ *transitive verb* **appraised; ap·prais·ing** [Middle English *appreisen*, from Middle French *aprisier* to apprize] (15th century)
**1 :** to set a value on **:** estimate the amount of
**2 :** to evaluate the worth, significance, or status of; *especially* **:** to give an expert judgment of the value or merit of
*synonym* see ESTIMATE
— **ap·prais·ee** \ə-ˌprā-'zē\ *noun*
— **ap·praise·ment** \-'prāz-mənt\ *noun*
— **ap·prais·er** *noun*
— **ap·prais·ing·ly** \-'prā-ziŋ-lē\ *adverb*
— **ap·prais·ive** \-'prā-ziv\ *adjective*

**ap·pre·cia·ble** \ə-'prē-shə-bəl, -'pri-sh(ē-)ə-bəl\ *adjective* (1818)
**:** capable of being perceived or measured
*synonym* see PERCEPTIBLE
— **ap·pre·cia·bly** \-blē\ *adverb*

**ap·pre·ci·ate** \ə-'prē-shē-ˌāt, -'pri- *also* -'prē-sē-\ *verb* **-at·ed; -at·ing** [Late Latin *appretiatus*, past participle of *appretiare*, from Latin *ad-* + *pretium* price — more at PRICE] (1655)
*transitive verb*
**1 a :** to grasp the nature, worth, quality, or significance of ⟨*appreciate* the difference between right and wrong⟩ **b :** to value or admire highly ⟨*appreciates* our work⟩ **c :** to judge with heightened perception or understanding **:** be fully aware of ⟨must see it to *appreciate* it⟩ **d :** to recognize with gratitude ⟨certainly *appreciates* your kindness⟩
**2 :** to increase the value of
*intransitive verb*
**:** to increase in number or value ☆
— **ap·pre·ci·a·tor** \-ˌā-tər\ *noun*
— **ap·pre·cia·to·ry** \-'prē-shə-ˌtōr-ē, -'pri-shə-, -ˌtòr-\ *adjective*

**ap·pre·ci·a·tion** \ə-ˌprē-shē-'ā-shən, -ˌpri- *also* -ˌprē-sē-\ *noun* (1604)
**1 a :** JUDGMENT, EVALUATION; *especially* **:** a favorable critical estimate **b :** sensitive awareness; *especially* **:** recognition of aesthetic values **c :** an expression of admiration, approval, or gratitude
**2 :** increase in value

**ap·pre·cia·tive** \ə-'prē-shə-tiv, -'pri- *also* -'prē-shē-ˌā-\ *adjective* (circa 1698)
**:** having or showing appreciation
— **ap·pre·cia·tive·ly** *adverb*
— **ap·pre·cia·tive·ness** *noun*

**ap·pre·hend** \ˌa-pri-'hend\ *verb* [Middle English, from Latin *apprehendere*, literally, to seize, from *ad-* + *prehendere* to seize — more at GET] (15th century)
*transitive verb*
**1 :** ARREST, SEIZE ⟨*apprehend* a thief⟩

☆ SYNONYMS
**Appreciate, value, prize, treasure, cherish** mean to hold in high estimation. APPRECIATE often connotes sufficient understanding to enjoy or admire a thing's excellence ⟨*appreciates* fine wine⟩. VALUE implies rating a thing highly for its intrinsic worth ⟨*values* our friendship⟩. PRIZE implies taking a deep pride in something one possesses ⟨Americans *prize* their freedom⟩. TREASURE emphasizes jealously safeguarding something considered precious ⟨a *treasured* memento⟩. CHERISH implies a special love and care for something ⟨*cherishes* her children above all⟩. See in addition UNDERSTAND.

\ə\ **abut** \ᵊ\ **kitten** \ər\ **further** \a\ **ash** \ā\ **ace**
\ä\ **mop, mar** \aú\ **out** \ch\ **chin** \e\ **bet** \ē\ **easy**
\g\ **go** \i\ **hit** \ī\ **ice** \j\ **job** \ŋ\ **sing** \ō\ **go**
\ò\ **law** \òi\ **boy** \th\ **thin** \t͟h\ **the** \ü\ **loot** \ù\ **foot**
\y\ **yet** \zh\ **vision** *see also* Guide to Pronunciation

**2 a :** to become aware of **:** PERCEIVE **b :** to anticipate especially with anxiety, dread, or fear **3 :** to grasp with the understanding **:** recognize the meaning of
*intransitive verb*
**:** UNDERSTAND, GRASP
**ap·pre·hen·si·ble** \ˌa-pri-ˈhen(t)-sə-bəl\ *adjective* (circa 1631)
**:** capable of being apprehended
— **ap·pre·hen·si·bly** \-blē\ *adverb*
**ap·pre·hen·sion** \ˌa-pri-ˈhen(t)-shən\ *noun* [Middle English, from Late Latin *apprehension-, apprehensio,* from Latin *apprehendere*] (14th century)
**1 a :** the act or power of perceiving or comprehending ⟨a person of dull *apprehension*⟩ **b :** the result of apprehending mentally **:** CONCEPTION ⟨according to popular *apprehension*⟩
**2 :** seizure by legal process **:** ARREST
**3 :** suspicion or fear especially of future evil **:** FOREBODING
**ap·pre·hen·sive** \-ˈhen(t)-siv\ *adjective* (14th century)
**1 :** capable of apprehending or quick to do so **:** DISCERNING
**2 :** having apprehension **:** COGNIZANT
**3 :** viewing the future with anxiety or alarm
*synonym* see FEARFUL
— **ap·pre·hen·sive·ly** *adverb*
— **ap·pre·hen·sive·ness** *noun*
**¹ap·pren·tice** \ə-ˈpren-təs\ *noun* [Middle English *aprentis,* from Middle French, from Old French, from *aprendre* to learn, from Latin *apprendere, apprehendere*] (14th century)
**1 a :** one bound by indenture to serve another for a prescribed period with a view to learning an art or trade **b :** one who is learning by practical experience under skilled workers a trade, art, or calling
**2 :** an inexperienced person **:** NOVICE ⟨an *apprentice* in cooking⟩
— **ap·pren·tice·ship** \-tə(sh)-ˌship, -təs-ˌship\ *noun*
**²apprentice** *verb* **-ticed; -tic·ing** (1596)
*transitive verb*
**:** to set at work as an apprentice; *especially* **:** to bind to an apprenticeship by contract or indenture
*intransitive verb*
**:** to serve as an apprentice
**ap·pressed** \a-ˈprest\ *adjective* [Latin *appressus,* past participle of *apprimere* to press to, from *ad-* + *premere* to press — more at PRESS] (1791)
**:** pressed close to or lying flat against something ⟨leaves *appressed* against the stem⟩
**ap·pres·so·ri·um** \ˌa-pre-ˈsōr-ē-əm, -ˈsȯr-\ *noun, plural* **-ria** \-ē-ə\ [New Latin, from Latin *apprimere*] (1897)
**:** the flattened thickened tip of a hyphal branch by which some parasitic fungi are attached to their host
**ap·prise** \ə-ˈprīz\ *transitive verb* **ap·prised; ap·pris·ing** [French *appris,* past participle of *apprendre* to learn, teach, from Old French *aprendre*] (1694)
**:** to give notice to **:** TELL
*synonym* see INFORM
**ap·prize** \ə-ˈprīz\ *transitive verb* **ap·prized; ap·priz·ing** [Middle English *apprisen,* from Middle French *apriser,* from *a-* (from Latin *ad-*) + *prisier* to appraise — more at PRIZE] (14th century)
**:** VALUE, APPRECIATE
**¹ap·proach** \ə-ˈprōch\ *verb* [Middle English *approchen,* from Old French *aprochier,* from Late Latin *appropiare,* from Latin *ad-* + *prope* near; akin to Latin *pro* before — more at FOR] (13th century)
*transitive verb*
**1 a :** to draw closer to **:** NEAR **b :** to come very near to **:** be almost the same as ⟨its mathematics *approaches* mysticism —Theodore Sturgeon⟩ ⟨as the quantity *x approaches* zero⟩
**2 a :** to make advances to especially in order to create a desired result ⟨was *approached* by

several Broadway producers⟩ **b :** to take preliminary steps toward accomplishment or full knowledge or experience of ⟨*approach* the subject with an open mind⟩
*intransitive verb*
**1 :** to draw nearer
**2 :** to make an approach in golf
**²approach** *noun* (15th century)
**1 a :** an act or instance of approaching ⟨the *approach* of summer⟩ **b :** APPROXIMATION ⟨in this book he makes his closest *approach* to greatness⟩
**2 a :** the taking of preliminary steps toward a particular purpose ⟨experimenting with new lines of *approach*⟩ **b :** a particular manner of taking such steps ⟨a highly individual *approach* to language⟩
**3 :** a means of access **:** AVENUE
**4 a :** a golf shot from the fairway toward the green **b :** the steps taken by a bowler before he delivers the ball; *also* **:** the part of the alley behind the foul line from which the bowler delivers the ball
**5 :** the descent of an aircraft toward a landing place
**ap·proach·able** \ə-ˈprō-chə-bəl\ *adjective* (1571)
**:** capable of being approached **:** ACCESSIBLE; *specifically* **:** easy to meet or deal with
— **ap·proach·abil·i·ty** \-ˌprō-chə-ˈbi-lə-tē\ *noun*
**ap·pro·bate** \ˈa-prə-ˌbāt\ *transitive verb* **-bat·ed; -bat·ing** [Middle English, from Latin *approbatus,* past participle of *approbare* — more at APPROVE] (15th century)
**:** APPROVE, SANCTION
— **ap·pro·ba·to·ry** \ˈa-prə-bə-ˌtōr-ē, ə-ˈprō-bə-, -ˌtȯr-\ *adjective*
**ap·pro·ba·tion** \ˌa-prə-ˈbā-shən\ *noun* (14th century)
**1** *obsolete* **:** PROOF
**2 a :** an act of approving formally or officially **b :** COMMENDATION, PRAISE
**¹ap·pro·pri·ate** \ə-ˈprō-prē-ˌāt\ *transitive verb* **-at·ed; -at·ing** [Middle English, from Late Latin *appropriatus,* past participle of *appropriare,* from Latin *ad-* + *proprius* own] (15th century)
**1 :** to take exclusive possession of **:** ANNEX ⟨no one should *appropriate* a common benefit⟩
**2 :** to set apart for or assign to a particular purpose or use ⟨*appropriate* money for the research program⟩
**3 :** to take or make use of without authority or right
— **ap·pro·pri·a·ble** \-prē-ə-bəl\ *adjective*
— **ap·pro·pri·a·tor** \-prē-ˌā-tər\ *noun*
**²ap·pro·pri·ate** \ə-ˈprō-prē-ət\ *adjective* (15th century)
**:** especially suitable or compatible **:** FITTING
*synonym* see FIT
— **ap·pro·pri·ate·ly** *adverb*
— **ap·pro·pri·ate·ness** *noun*
**ap·pro·pri·a·tion** \ə-ˌprō-prē-ˈā-shən\ *noun* (14th century)
**1 :** an act or instance of appropriating
**2 :** something that has been appropriated; *specifically* **:** money set aside by formal action for a specific use
— **ap·pro·pri·a·tive** \-ˈprō-prē-ˌā-tiv\ *adjective*
**ap·prov·able** \ə-ˈprü-və-bəl\ *adjective* (15th century)
**:** capable or worthy of being approved
— **ap·prov·ably** \-blē\ *adverb*
**ap·prov·al** \ə-ˈprü-vəl\ *noun* (1616)
**:** an act or instance of approving **:** APPROBATION
— **on approval :** subject to a prospective buyer's acceptance or refusal ⟨stamps sent to collectors *on approval*⟩
**ap·prove** \ə-ˈprüv\ *verb* **ap·proved; ap·prov·ing** [Middle English, from Middle French *aprover,* from Latin *approbare,* from *ad-* + *probare* to prove — more at PROVE] (14th century)

*transitive verb*
**1** *obsolete* **:** PROVE, ATTEST
**2 :** to have or express a favorable opinion of ⟨couldn't *approve* such conduct⟩
**3 a :** to accept as satisfactory ⟨hopes she will *approve* the date of the meeting⟩ **b :** to give formal or official sanction to **:** RATIFY ⟨Congress *approved* the proposed budget⟩
*intransitive verb*
**:** to take a favorable view ⟨doesn't *approve* of fighting⟩
— **ap·prov·ing·ly** \-ˈprü-viŋ-lē\ *adverb*
**approved school** *noun* (1932)
*British* **:** a school for juvenile delinquents
**¹ap·prox·i·mate** \ə-ˈpräk-sə-mət\ *adjective* [Late Latin *approximatus,* past participle of *approximare* to come near, from Latin *ad-* + *proximare* to come near — more at PROXIMATE] (15th century)
**1 :** located close together ⟨*approximate* leaves⟩
**2 :** nearly correct or exact ⟨an *approximate* solution⟩
— **ap·prox·i·mate·ly** *adverb*
**²ap·prox·i·mate** \-ˌmāt\ *verb* **-mat·ed; -mat·ing** (15th century)
*transitive verb*
**1 a :** to bring near or close **b :** to bring ⟨cut edges of tissue⟩ together
**2 :** to come near to or be close to in position, value, or characteristics ⟨a child tries to *approximate* his parents' speech⟩
*intransitive verb*
**:** to come close — usually used with *to*
**ap·prox·i·ma·tion** \ə-ˌpräk-sə-ˈmā-shən\ *noun* (15th century)
**1 :** the act or process of drawing together
**2 :** the quality or state of being close or near ⟨an *approximation* to the truth⟩ ⟨an *approximation* of justice⟩
**3 :** something that is approximate; *especially* **:** a mathematical quantity that is close in value to but not the same as a desired quantity
— **ap·prox·i·ma·tive** \-ˈpräk-sə-ˌmā-tiv\ *adjective*
**ap·pur·te·nance** \ə-ˈpərt-nən(t)s, -ˈpər-tᵊn-ən(t)s\ *noun* (14th century)
**1 :** an incidental right ⟨as a right-of-way⟩ attached to a principal property right and passing in possession with it
**2 :** a subordinate part or adjunct ⟨the *appurtenance* of welcome is fashion and ceremony —Shakespeare⟩
**3** *plural* **:** accessory objects **:** APPARATUS
**ap·pur·te·nant** \ə-ˈpərt-nənt, -ˈpər-tᵊn-ənt\ *adjective* [Middle English *apertenant,* from Middle French, from Old French, present participle of *apartenir* to belong — more at APPERTAIN] (14th century)
**1 :** constituting a legal accompaniment
**2 :** AUXILIARY, ACCESSORY
— **appurtenant** *noun*
**aprax·ia** \(ˌ)ā-ˈprak-sē-ə\ *noun* [New Latin, from Greek, inaction, from *a-* + *praxis* action, from *prassein* to do — more at PRACTICAL] (circa 1881)
**:** loss or impairment of the ability to execute complex coordinated movements without impairment of the muscles or senses

☆ **SYNONYMS**
**Approve, endorse, sanction, accredit, certify** mean to have or express a favorable opinion of. APPROVE often implies no more than this but may suggest considerable esteem or admiration ⟨the parents *approve* of the marriage⟩. ENDORSE suggests an explicit statement of support ⟨publicly *endorsed* her for Senator⟩. SANCTION implies both approval and authorization ⟨the President *sanctioned* covert operations⟩. ACCREDIT and CERTIFY usually imply official endorsement attesting to conformity to set standards ⟨the board voted to *accredit* the college⟩ ⟨must be *certified* to teach⟩.

— **aprac·tic** \-'prak-tik\ *or* **aprax·ic** \-'prak-sik\ *adjective*

**après** \(,)ä-'prā, ,ä-,prā; 'a-,\ *preposition* [French *après-*, from *après* after] (1967)
**:** AFTER ⟨*après* tennis⟩ — usually used in combination ⟨*après*-theater party⟩

**après–ski** \,ä-,prä-'skē, ,a-\ *noun, often attributive* [French *après* after + *ski* ski, skiing] (1951)
**:** social activity (as at a ski lodge) after a day's skiing

**apri·cot** \'a-prə-,kät, 'ā-\ *noun, often attributive* [alteration of earlier *abrecock*, ultimately from Arabic *al-birqūq* the apricot, ultimately from Latin (*persicum*) *praecox*, literally, early ripening (peach) — more at PRECOCIOUS] (1551)
**1 a :** the oval orange-colored fruit of a temperate-zone tree (*Prunus armeniaca*) resembling the related peach and plum in flavor
**b :** a tree that bears apricots
**2 :** a variable color averaging a moderate orange ◆

**April** \'ā-prəl\ *noun* [Middle English, from Old French & Latin; Old French *avrill*, from Latin *Aprilis*] (before 12th century)
**:** the 4th month of the Gregorian calendar

**April fool** *noun* (1687)
**:** the butt of a joke or trick played on April Fools' Day; *also* **:** such a joke or trick

**April Fools' Day** *noun* (1854)
**:** April 1 characteristically marked by the playing of practical jokes

**a pri·o·ri** \,ä-prē-'ör-ē, ,a-; ,ä-(,)prī-'ör-,ī, -,prē-'ör-ē; -'ör-\ *adjective* [Latin, literally, from the former] (1652)
**1 a :** DEDUCTIVE **b :** relating to or derived by reasoning from self-evident propositions — compare A POSTERIORI **c :** presupposed by experience
**2 a :** being without examination or analysis **:** PRESUMPTIVE **b :** formed or conceived beforehand
— **a priori** *adverb*
— **apri·or·i·ty** \-'ör-ə-tē\ *noun*

**apron** \'ā-prən, -pərn\ *noun, often attributive* [Middle English, alteration (resulting from false division of *a napron*) of *napron*, from Middle French *naperon*, diminutive of *nape* cloth, modification of Latin *mappa* napkin] (15th century)
**1 :** a garment usually of cloth, plastic, or leather usually tied around the waist and used to protect clothing or adorn a costume
**2 :** something that suggests or resembles an apron in shape, position, or use: as **a :** the lower member under the sill of the interior casing of a window **b :** an upward or downward vertical extension of a bathroom fixture (as a sink or tub) **c :** an endless belt for carrying material **d :** an extensive fan-shaped deposit of detritus **e :** the part of the stage in front of the proscenium arch **f :** the area along the waterfront edge of a pier or wharf **g :** a shield (as of concrete or gravel) to protect against erosion (as of a waterway) by water **h :** the extensive paved part of an airport immediately adjacent to the terminal area or hangars ◆
— **aproned** \-prənd, -pərnd\ *adjective*

**apron string** *noun* (1542)
**:** the string of an apron — usually used in plural as a symbol of dominance or complete control ⟨though 40 years old he was still tied to his mother's *apron strings*⟩

¹**ap·ro·pos** \,a-prə-'pō, 'a-prə-,\ *adverb* [French *à propos*, literally, to the purpose] (1668)
**1 :** at an opportune time **:** SEASONABLY
**2 :** BY THE WAY

²**apropos** *adjective* (1686)
**:** being both relevant and opportune
*synonym* see RELEVANT

³**apropos** *preposition* (1910)
**:** APROPOS OF

**apropos of** *preposition* (1746)

**:** with regard to **:** CONCERNING

**apro·tic** \(,)ā-'prō-tik\ *adjective* [²a- + *proton* + ¹-*ic*] (1931)
*of a solvent* **:** incapable of acting as a proton donor

**apse** \'aps\ *noun* [Medieval Latin & Latin; Medieval Latin *apsis*, from Latin] (1822)
**1 :** APSIS 1
**2 :** a projecting part of a building (as a church) that is usually semicircular in plan and vaulted

**ap·si·dal** \'ap-sə-d°l\ *adjective* (1846)
**:** of or relating to an apse or apsis

**ap·sis** \'ap-səs\ *noun, plural* **ap·si·des** \-sə-,dēz\ [New Latin *apsid-, apsis*, from Latin, arch, orbit, from Greek *hapsid-, hapsis*, from *haptein* to fasten] (1658)
**1 :** the point in an astronomical orbit at which the distance of the body from the center of attraction is either greatest or least
**2 :** APSE 2

**apt** \'apt\ *adjective* [Middle English, from Latin *aptus*, literally, fastened, from past participle of *apere* to fasten; akin to Latin *apisci* to grasp, obtain, *apud* near, Hittite *hap-* to attach] (14th century)
**1 :** unusually fitted or qualified **:** READY ⟨proved an *apt* tool in the hands of the conspirators⟩
**2 a :** having a tendency **:** LIKELY ⟨plants *apt* to suffer from drought⟩ **b :** ordinarily disposed **:** INCLINED ⟨*apt* to accept what is plausible as true⟩
**3 :** suited to a purpose; *especially* **:** being to the point ⟨an *apt* quotation⟩
**4 :** keenly intelligent and responsive
*synonym* see FIT, QUICK
*usage* see LIABLE
— **apt·ly** \'ap(t)-lē\ *adverb*
— **apt·ness** \'ap(t)-nəs\ *noun*

**ap·ter·ous** \'ap-tə-rəs\ *adjective* [Greek *apteros*, from *a-* + *pteron* wing — more at FEATHER] (1775)
**:** lacking wings ⟨*apterous* insects⟩

**ap·ter·yx** \'ap-tə-riks\ *noun* [New Latin, from *a-* + Greek *pteryx* wing; akin to Greek *pteron*] (1813)
**:** KIWI

**ap·ti·tude** \'ap-tə-,tüd, -,tyüd\ *noun* [Middle English, from Medieval Latin *aptitudo*, from Late Latin, fitness, from Latin *aptus*] (15th century)
**1 a :** INCLINATION, TENDENCY **b :** a natural ability **:** TALENT
**2 :** capacity for learning **:** APTNESS
**3 :** general suitability
*synonym* see GIFT
— **ap·ti·tu·di·nal** \,ap-tə-'tü-d°n-əl, -'tyü-\ *adjective*
— **ap·ti·tu·di·nal·ly** *adverb*

**aptitude test** *noun* (1923)
**:** a standardized test designed to predict an individual's ability to learn certain skills

**ap·y·rase** \'a-pə-,rās, -,rāz\ *noun* [adenosine + *py*rophosphate + -*ase*] (1945)
**:** any of several enzymes that hydrolyze ATP with the liberation of phosphate and energy

**aqua** \'ä-kwə *also* 'a-\ *noun* [Latin — more at ISLAND] (14th century)
**1** *plural* **aquae** \'ä-,kwī *also* 'a-(,)kwē\ **:** WATER; *especially* **:** WATER 5a(2)
**2** *plural* **aquas :** a light greenish blue color

**aqua·cade** \'ä-kwə-,kād, 'a-\ *noun* [*Aquacade*, a water spectacle originally at Cleveland, Ohio] (1937)
**:** a water spectacle that consists usually of exhibitions of swimming and diving with musical accompaniment

**aqua·cul·ture** *also* **aqui·cul·ture** \'ä-kwə-,kəl-chər, 'a-\ *noun* [Latin *aqua* + English -*culture* (as in *agriculture*)] (1867)
**:** the cultivation of the natural produce of water (as fish or shellfish)
— **aqua·cul·tur·al** \,ä-kwə-'kəl-ch(ə-)rəl, ,a-\ *adjective*
— **aqua·cul·tur·ist** \-ch(ə-)rist\ *noun*

**aqua for·tis** \'ä-kwə-'för-təs, 'a-\ *noun* [New Latin *aqua fortis*, literally, strong water] (15th century)
**:** NITRIC ACID

**Aqua–Lung** \'ä-kwə-,ləŋ, 'a-\ *trademark*
— used for an underwater breathing apparatus

**aqua·ma·rine** \,ä-kwə-mə-'rēn, ,a-\ *noun* [New Latin *aqua marina*, from Latin, sea water] (1677)
**1 :** a transparent beryl that is blue, blue-green, or green in color
**2 :** a pale blue to light greenish blue

**aqua·naut** \'ä-kwə-,nöt, 'a-, -,nät\ *noun* [Latin *aqua* + English -*naut* (as in *aeronaut*)] (1881)
**:** a scuba diver who lives and operates both inside and outside an underwater shelter for an extended period

¹**aqua·plane** \'ä-kwə-,plān, 'a-\ *noun* (1914)
**:** a board towed behind a speeding motorboat and ridden by a person standing on it
— **aqua·plan·er** *noun*

²**aquaplane** *intransitive verb* (circa 1923)
**1 :** to ride on an aquaplane
**2** *British* **:** HYDROPLANE

**aqua re·gia** \-'rē-j(ē-)ə\ *noun* [New Latin, literally, royal water] (1610)
**:** a mixture of nitric and hydrochloric acids that dissolves gold or platinum

**aqua·relle** \,a-kwə-'rel, ,ä-\ *noun* [French,

---

◇ **WORD HISTORY**
**apricot** The apricot is native to China and was probably not introduced to the Mediterranean region before the first century B.C. We assume that the fruit which the Roman poet Martial called *persica praecocia*, literally, "early-ripening peaches," was the apricot. A Greek form of the second word in this phrase, *praikokion*, migrated to the eastern end of the Mediterranean, and when the Arabs entered this area in the early Middle Ages, they turned *praikokion* into *barqūq* or *birqūq*. In areas that they occupied, such as Sicily and the Iberian Peninsula, the Arabs revived apricot cultivation. Arabic *al-barqūq* "the apricot" entered Spanish as *albaricoque*, Portuguese as *albricoque*, and Catalan as *albercoc* or *abercoc*. The earliest English form of the word, *aprecock*, appears to be borrowed from French *abricot* (itself also from Iberian Romance). The change of *b* to *p* (notable also in German *Aprikose*) was perhaps by association with Latin *apricus* "sunny, warmed by sunshine."

**apron** In late Medieval French a diminutive form of *nape*, meaning "tablecloth," was *naperon*, which was usually used for a small cloth placed over a more elegant tablecloth to protect it from stains. This word appears in English of the 14th century as *napron*; like its French source, *napron* denoted a protective cloth, but one that was placed over clothing rather than on a table. Because in connected speech it is often difficult to tell where word boundaries fall, *a napron* was incorrectly understood as *an apron*. The new form *apron* had effectively replaced *napron* by the 17th century, completely obscuring the etymological relation of *apron* to *napkin*, the name for yet another kind of protective cloth. Curiously, the modern French word for "apron," *tablier*, has undergone a similar sense shift; originally a derivative of *table* "table," in Old French it meant "tablecloth."

---

\ə\ abut \°\ kitten \ər\ further \a\ ash \ā\ ace
\ä\ mop, mar \aù\ out \ch\ chin \e\ bet \ē\ easy
\g\ go \i\ hit \ī\ ice \j\ job \ŋ\ sing \ō\ go
\ò\ law \òi\ boy \th\ thin \t̲h̲\ the \ü\ loot \ù\ foot
\y\ yet \zh\ vision *see also* Guide to Pronunciation

from obsolete Italian *acquarella* (now *acquarello*), from *acqua* water, from Latin *aqua*] (1869)
: a drawing usually in transparent watercolor
— **aqua·rell·ist** \-'re-list\ *noun*
**Aquar·i·an** \ə-'kwar-ē-ən, -'kwer-\ *noun* (1911)
: AQUARIUS 2b
— **Aquarian** *adjective*
**aquar·ist** \ə-'kwar-ist, -'kwer-\ *noun* (circa 1893)
: a person who keeps or maintains an aquarium
**aquar·i·um** \ə-'kwar-ē-əm, -'kwer-\ *noun, plural* **-i·ums** *or* **-ia** \-ē-ə\ [probably alteration of *aquatic vivarium*] (circa 1847)
**1** : a container (as a glass tank) or an artificial pond in which living aquatic animals or plants are kept
**2** : an establishment where aquatic collections of living organisms are kept and exhibited
**Aquar·i·us** \-ē-əs\ *noun* [Latin (genitive *Aquarii*), literally, water carrier]
**1** : a constellation south of Pegasus pictured as a man pouring water
**2 a** : the 11th sign of the zodiac in astrology — see ZODIAC table **b** : one born under the sign of Aquarius
**¹aquat·ic** \ə-'kwä-tik, -'kwa-\ *adjective* (1642)
**1** : growing or living in or frequenting water ⟨*aquatic* mosquito larvae⟩
**2** : taking place in or on water ⟨*aquatic* sports⟩
— **aquat·i·cal·ly** \-ti-k(ə-)lē\ *adverb*
**²aquatic** *noun* (circa 1600)
**1** : an aquatic animal or plant
**2** *plural but singular or plural in construction* : water sports
**aqua·tint** \'a-kwə-,tint, 'ä-\ *noun* [Italian *acqua tinta* dyed water] (1782)
: a method of etching a printing plate so that tones similar to watercolor washes can be reproduced; *also* : a print made from a plate so etched
— **aquatint** *transitive verb*
— **aqua·tint·er** *noun*
— **aqua·tint·ist** \-,tin-tist\ *noun*
**aqua·vit** \'ä-kwə-,vēt\ *noun* [Swedish, Danish, & Norwegian *akvavit*, from Medieval Latin *aqua vitae*] (1890)
: a clear Scandinavian liquor flavored with caraway seeds
***word history*** see WHISKEY
**aqua vi·tae** \,a-kwə-'vī-tē, ,ä-\ *noun* [Middle English, from Medieval Latin, literally, water of life] (15th century)
: a strong alcoholic liquor (as brandy)
***word history*** see WHISKEY
**aq·ue·duct** \'a-kwə-,dəkt\ *noun* [Latin *aquaeductus*, from *aquae* (genitive of *aqua*) + *ductus* act of leading — more at DUCT] (1538)
**1 a** : a conduit for water; *especially* : one for carrying a large quantity of flowing water **b** : a structure for conveying a canal over a river or hollow
**2** : a canal or passage in a part or organ
**aque·ous** \'ā-kwē-əs, 'a-\ *adjective* [Medieval Latin *aqueus*, from Latin *aqua*] (1646)
**1 a** : of, relating to, or resembling water **b** : made from, with, or by water
**2** : of or relating to the aqueous humor
**aqueous humor** *noun* (1643)
: a transparent fluid occupying the space between the crystalline lens and the cornea of the eye
**aqui·fer** \'a-kwə-fər, 'ä-\ *noun* [New Latin, from Latin *aqua* + *-fer*] (1901)
: a water-bearing stratum of permeable rock, sand, or gravel
— **aquif·er·ous** \a-'kwi-fə-rəs, ä-\ *adjective*
**Aq·ui·la** \'a-kwə-lə *also* ə-'kwi-lə\ *noun* [Latin (genitive *Aquilae*), literally, eagle]
: a constellation in the northern hemisphere represented by the figure of an eagle
**aq·ui·le·gia** \,a-kwə-'lē-j(ē-)ə\ *noun* [New Latin] (1871)
: COLUMBINE

**aq·ui·line** \'a-kwə-,līn, -lən\ *adjective* [Latin *aquilinus*, from *aquila* eagle] (1646)
**1** : curving like an eagle's beak ⟨an *aquiline* nose⟩
**2** : of, relating to, or resembling an eagle
— **aq·ui·lin·i·ty** \,a-kwə-'li-nə-tē\ *noun*
**aquiv·er** \ə-'kwi-vər\ *adjective* (1883)
: marked by trembling or quivering ⟨all *aquiver* with excitement⟩
**ar** \'är\ *noun* [Middle English] (14th century)
: the letter *r*
**-ar** *adjective suffix* [Middle English, from Latin *-aris*, alteration of *-alis* -al]
: of or relating to ⟨molecu*lar*⟩ : being ⟨spectacu*lar*⟩ : resembling ⟨oracu*lar*⟩
**Ar·ab** \'ar-əb, 'er-; *dialect also* 'ā-,rab\ *noun* [Middle English, from Latin *Arabus, Arabs*, from Greek *Arab-, Araps*] (14th century)
**1 a** : a member of the Semitic people of the Arabian peninsula **b** : a member of an Arabic-speaking people
**2** : ARABIAN HORSE
— **Arab** *adjective*
**¹ar·a·besque** \,ar-ə-'besk\ *adjective* [French, from Italian *arabesco* Arabian in fashion, from *arabo* Arab, from Latin *Arabus*] (circa 1656)
: of, relating to, or being in the style of arabesque or an arabesque
**²arabesque** *noun* (1786)
**1** : an ornament or style that employs flower, foliage, or fruit and sometimes animal and figural outlines to produce an intricate pattern of interlaced lines
**2** : a posture in ballet in which the body is bent forward from the hip on one leg with one arm extended forward and the other arm and leg backward

arabesque 1

**3** : an elaborate or intricate pattern ⟨richly pierced by an *arabesque* of wormholes —John Chase⟩ ⟨as lawyers . . . perform their procedural *arabesques* —Daniel Okrent⟩
**¹Ara·bi·an** \ə-'rā-bē-ən\ *noun* (14th century)
**1** : a native or inhabitant of Arabia
**2** : ARABIAN HORSE
**²Arabian** *adjective* (14th century)
: ARABIC 1
**Arabian horse** *noun* (1737)
: any of a breed of swift compact horses developed in Arabia and usually having gray or chestnut silky hair
**¹Ar·a·bic** \'ar-ə-bik\ *noun* (14th century)
: a Semitic language originally of the Arabs of the Hejaz and Nejd that is now the prevailing speech of a wide region of southwestern Asia and northern Africa
**²Arabic** *adjective* (1526)
**1** : of, relating to, or characteristic of Arabia or the Arabs
**2** : of, relating to, or constituting Arabic
**3** : expressed in or utilizing Arabic numerals
**arab·i·ca** \ə-'ra-bə-kə\ *noun, often attributive* [New Latin, specific epithet of *Coffea arabica*, from Latin, feminine of *Arabicus* Arabian] (1922)
**1** : an evergreen shrub or tree (*Coffea arabica*) yielding seeds that produce a high-quality coffee and form a large portion of the coffee of commerce
**2** : the seeds of arabica
**Arabic alphabet** *noun* (1841)
: an alphabet of 28 letters derived from the Aramaic alphabet which is used for writing Arabic and also with adaptations for other languages of the Islamic world
**arab·i·cize** \ə-'ra-bə-,sīz\ *transitive verb* **-cized; -ciz·ing** *often capitalized* (1872)
**1** : to adapt (a language or elements of a language) to the phonetic or structural pattern of Arabic
**2** : ARABIZE 1

— **arab·i·ci·za·tion** \ə-,ra-bə-sə-'zā-shən\ *noun*
**Arabic numeral** *noun* (circa 1847)
: any of the number symbols 0, 1, 2, 3, 4, 5, 6, 7, 8, 9 — see NUMBER table
**arab·i·nose** \ə-'ra-bə-,nōs, -,nōz\ *noun* [International Scientific Vocabulary *arabin* (the solid principle in gum arabic, from *gum arabic* + ¹*-in*) + *-ose*] (circa 1884)
: a white crystalline aldose sugar $C_5H_{10}O_5$ occurring especially in vegetable gums
**ara·bi·no·side** \,ar-ə-'bi-nə-,sīd, ə-'ra-bə-nō-,sīd\ *noun* (1927)
: a glycoside that yields arabinose on hydrolysis
**Ar·ab·ise** *British variant of* ARABIZE
**Ar·ab·ism** \'ar-ə-,bi-zəm\ *noun* (1614)
**1** : a characteristic feature of Arabic occurring in another language
**2** : devotion to Arab interests, culture, aspirations, or ideals
**Ar·ab·ist** \'ar-ə-bist\ *noun* (1753)
**1** : a specialist in the Arabic language or in Arabic culture
**2** : a person who favors Arab interests and positions in international affairs
**Ar·ab·ize** \'ar-ə-,bīz\ *transitive verb* **-ized; -iz·ing** (1883)
**1 a** : to cause to acquire Arabic customs, manners, speech, or outlook **b** : to modify (a population) by intermarriage with Arabs
**2** : ARABICIZE 1
— **Ar·ab·i·za·tion** \,ar-ə-bə-'zā-shən\ *noun*
**¹ar·a·ble** \'ar-ə-bəl\ *adjective* [Middle French or Latin; Middle French, from Latin *arabilis*, from *arare* to plow; akin to Old English *erian* to plow, Greek *aroun*] (15th century)
**1** : fit for or used for the growing of crops
**2** *British* : engaged in, produced by, or being the cultivation of arable land
— **ar·a·bil·i·ty** \,ar-ə-'bi-lə-tē\ *noun*
**²arable** *noun* (1576)
*chiefly British* : land fit or used for the growing of crops; *also* : a plot of such land
**ar·a·chi·don·ic acid** \,ar-ə-kə-'dä-nik-\ *noun* [New Latin *Arachid-, Arachis* + English *-onic* (as in *gluconic acid*)] (1913)
: a liquid unsaturated fatty acid $C_{20}H_{32}O_2$ that occurs in most animal fats, is a precursor of prostaglandins, and is considered essential in animal nutrition
**ar·a·chis oil** \'ar-ə-kəs-\ *noun* [New Latin *Arachis*, genus that includes the peanut, from Greek *arakis*, diminutive of *arakos*, a legume] (circa 1889)
: PEANUT OIL
**arach·nid** \ə-'rak-nəd, -,nid\ *noun* [New Latin *Arachnida*, from Greek *arachnē* spider] (1869)
: any of a class (Arachnida) of arthropods comprising chiefly terrestrial invertebrates, including the spiders, scorpions, mites, and ticks, and having a segmented body divided into two regions of which the anterior bears four pairs of legs but no antennae
— **arachnid** *adjective*
**¹arach·noid** \ə-'rak-,nóid\ *adjective* (1789)
**1** : of or relating to a thin membrane of the brain and spinal cord that lies between the dura mater and the pia mater
**2** : covered with or composed of soft loose hairs or fibers
**²arachnoid** *noun* [New Latin *arachnoides*, from Greek *arachnoeidēs*, like a cobweb, from *arachnē* spider, spider's web] (circa 1847)
: an arachnoid membrane
**³arachnoid** *adjective* [New Latin *Arachn*ida + English *-oid*] (1852)
: resembling or related to the arachnids
**ar·a·go·nite** \ə-'ra-gə-,nīt, 'ar-ə-gə-\ *noun* [German *Aragonit*, from *Aragon*, Spain] (1803)
: a mineral similar to calcite in consisting of calcium carbonate but differing from calcite in its orthorhombic crystallization, greater density, and less distinct cleavage

— **ara·go·nit·ic** \ə-ˌra-gə-'ni-tik, ˌar-ə-gə-\ *adjective*

**ar·ak** *variant of* ARRACK

**Ar·a·mae·an** \ˌar-ə-'mē-ən\ *noun* [Latin *Aramaeus*, from Greek *Aramaios*, from Hebrew *'Ărām* Aram, ancient name for Syria] (1839)
**1** : ARAMAIC
**2** : a member of a Semitic people of the second millennium B.C. in Syria and Upper Mesopotamia
— **Aramaean** *adjective*

**Ar·a·ma·ic** \ˌar-ə-'mā-ik\ *noun* (1882)
: a Semitic language known since the ninth century B.C. as the speech of the Aramaeans and later used extensively in southwest Asia as a commercial and governmental language and adopted as their customary speech by various non-Aramaean peoples including the Jews after the Babylonian exile

**Aramaic alphabet** *noun* (1925)
**1** : an extinct North Semitic alphabet dating from the ninth century B.C. which was for several centuries the commercial alphabet of southwest Asia and the parent of other alphabets (as Syriac and Arabic)
**2** : the square Hebrew alphabet as distinguished from the early Hebrew alphabet

**ar·a·mid** \'ar-ə-məd, -ˌmid\ *noun* [*aromatic* poly*amide*] (1972)
: any of a group of lightweight but very strong heat-resistant synthetic aromatic polyamide materials that are fashioned into fibers, filaments, or sheets and used especially in textiles and plastics

**Arap·a·ho** *or* **Arap·a·hoe** \ə-'ra-pə-ˌhō\ *noun, plural* **-ho** *or* **-hos** *or* **-hoe** *or* **-hoes** (1812)
**1** : a member of an American Indian people of the plains region ranging from Saskatchewan and Manitoba to New Mexico and Texas
**2** : the Algonquian language of the Arapaho people

**Arau·ca·ni·an** \ə-ˌraù-'kä-nē-ən, ˌar-ˌȯ-'kä-\ *also* **Arau·can** \ə-'raù-kən\ *noun* [Spanish *araucano*, from *Arauco*, former province in Chile] (1809)
**1** : a member of a group of Indian peoples of south central Chile and adjacent regions of Argentina
**2** : the language of the Araucanian people that constitutes an independent language family
— **Araucanian** *adjective*

**ar·au·car·ia** \ˌar-ˌȯ-'kar-ē-ə\ *noun* [New Latin, from *Arauco*] (1809)
: any of a genus (*Araucaria* of the family Araucariaceae, the araucaria family) of South American or Australian coniferous trees that resemble pines and are often grown as ornamentals
— **ar·au·car·i·an** \-ē-ən\ *adjective*

**Ar·a·wak** \'ar-ə-ˌwäk, -ˌwak\ *noun, plural* **Arawak** *or* **Arawaks** (1769)
**1** : a member of an Indian people of the Arawakan group now living chiefly along the coast of Guyana
**2** : the language of the Arawak people

**Ar·a·wak·an** \ˌar-ə-'wä-kən, -'wa-\ *noun, plural* **Arawakan** *or* **Arawakans** (1901)
**1** : a member of a group of Indian peoples of South America and the West Indies
**2** : the language family of the Arawakan peoples

**arb** \'ärb\ *noun* (1979)
: ARBITRAGEUR

**ar·ba·lest** *or* **ar·ba·list** \'är-bə-list\ *noun* [Middle English *arblast*, from Old English, from Old French *arbaleste*, from Late Latin *arcuballista*, from Latin *arcus* bow + *ballista* — more at ARROW] (before 12th century)
: a crossbow especially of medieval times

**ar·bi·ter** \'är-bə-tər\ *noun* [Middle English *arbitre*, from Middle French, from Latin *arbitr-, arbiter*] (14th century)
**1** : a person with power to decide a dispute
: JUDGE

**2** : a person or agency having the power of deciding

**arbiter el·e·gan·ti·a·rum** \-ˌe-lə-ˌgan-shē-'ar-əm, -'er-\ *noun* [Latin, literally, arbiter of refinements] (1818)
: a person who prescribes, rules on, or is a recognized authority on matters of social behavior and taste

**ar·bi·tra·ble** \'är-bə-trə-bəl, är-'bi-\ *adjective* (1531)
: subject to decision by arbitration

**¹ar·bi·trage** \'är-bə-ˌträzh\ *noun* [French, from Middle French, arbitration, from Old French, from *arbitrer* to render judgment, from Latin *arbitrari*, from *arbitr-, arbiter*] (1875)
**1** : the nearly simultaneous purchase and sale of securities or foreign exchange in different markets in order to profit from price discrepancies
**2** : the purchase of the stock of a takeover target especially with a view to selling it profitably to the raider

**²arbitrage** *intransitive verb* **-traged; -traging** (1900)
: to engage in arbitrage

**ar·bi·tra·geur** \ˌär-bə-(ˌ)trä-'zhər\ *or* **ar·bi·trag·er** \'är-bə-ˌträ-zhər\ *noun* [French *arbitrageur*, from *arbitrage*] (1870)
: one that practices arbitrage

**ar·bi·tral** \'är-bə-trəl\ *adjective* (1609)
: of or relating to arbiters or arbitration

**ar·bit·ra·ment** \är-'bi-trə-mənt\ *noun* [Middle English, from Middle French *arbitrement*, from *arbitrer*] (15th century)
**1** *archaic* : the right or power of deciding
**2** : the settling of a dispute by an arbiter
**3** : the judgment given by an arbitrator

**ar·bi·trary** \'är-bə-ˌtrer-ē\ *adjective* (15th century)
**1** : depending on individual discretion (as of a judge) and not fixed by law ⟨the manner of punishment is *arbitrary*⟩
**2 a** : not restrained or limited in the exercise of power : ruling by absolute authority ⟨an *arbitrary* government⟩ **b** : marked by or resulting from the unrestrained and often tyrannical exercise of power ⟨protection from *arbitrary* arrest and detention⟩
**3 a** : based on or determined by individual preference or convenience rather than by necessity or the intrinsic nature of something ⟨an *arbitrary* standard⟩ ⟨take any *arbitrary* positive number⟩ ⟨*arbitrary* division of historical studies into watertight compartments —A. J. Toynbee⟩ **b** : existing or coming about seemingly at random or by chance or as a capricious and unreasonable act of will ⟨when a task is not seen in a meaningful context it is experienced as being *arbitrary* —Nehemiah Jordan⟩
— **ar·bi·trari·ly** \ˌär-bə-'trer-ə-lē\ *adverb*
— **ar·bi·trar·i·ness** \'är-bə-ˌtrer-ē-nəs\ *noun*

**ar·bi·trate** \'är-bə-ˌträt\ *verb* **-trat·ed; -trat·ing** (1592)
*transitive verb*
**1** *archaic* : DECIDE, DETERMINE
**2** : to act as arbiter upon
**3** : to submit or refer for decision to an arbiter ⟨agreed to *arbitrate* their differences⟩
*intransitive verb*
: to act as arbitrator
— **ar·bi·tra·tive** \-ˌträ-tiv\ *adjective*

**ar·bi·tra·tion** \ˌär-bə-'trä-shən\ *noun* (15th century)
: the action of arbitrating; *especially* : the hearing and determination of a case in controversy by an arbiter
— **ar·bi·tra·tion·al** \-sh(ə-)nəl\ *adjective*

**ar·bi·tra·tor** \'är-bə-ˌträ-tər\ *noun* (15th century)
: one that arbitrates : ARBITER

**¹ar·bor** \'är-bər\ *noun* [Middle English *erber* plot of grass, arbor, from Middle French *her-*

*bier* plot of grass, from *herbe* herb, grass] (14th century)
: a shelter of vines or branches or of latticework covered with climbing shrubs or vines

**²arbor** *noun* [Latin, tree, shaft] (1659)
**1** : a spindle or axle of a wheel
**2** : a main shaft or beam
**3** : a shaft on which a revolving cutting tool is mounted
**4** : a spindle on a cutting machine that holds the work to be cut

**arbor-** *or* **arbori-** *combining form* [Latin *arbor*]
: tree ⟨*arbori*culture⟩

**Arbor Day** *noun* [Latin *arbor* tree] (1872)
: a day designated for planting trees

**ar·bo·re·al** \är-'bōr-ē-əl, -'bȯr-\ *adjective* [Latin *arboreus* of a tree, from *arbor*] (circa 1667)
**1** : of, relating to, or resembling a tree
**2** : inhabiting or frequenting trees ⟨*arboreal* monkeys⟩
— **ar·bo·re·al·ly** \-ə-lē\ *adverb*

**ar·bo·re·ous** \-ē-əs\ *adjective* (1646)
: ARBOREAL ⟨an *arboreous* palm⟩

**ar·bo·res·cent** \ˌär-bə-'re-sᵊnt\ *adjective* (1675)
: resembling a tree in properties, growth, structure, or appearance
— **ar·bo·res·cence** \-sᵊn(t)s\ *noun*

**ar·bo·re·tum** \ˌär-bə-'rē-təm\ *noun, plural* **-retums** *or* **-re·ta** \-'rē-tə\ [New Latin, from Latin, plantation of trees, from *arbor*] (1838)
: a place where trees, shrubs, and herbaceous plants are cultivated for scientific and educational purposes

**ar·bor·i·cul·ture** \'är-bər-ə-ˌkəl-chər, är-'bȯr-ə-\ *noun* [*arbori-* + *-culture* (as in *agriculture*)] (1828)
: the cultivation of trees and shrubs especially for ornamental purposes
— **ar·bor·i·cul·tur·al** \ˌär-bər-ə-'kəl-chər-əl, är-ˌbȯr-ə-\ *adjective*

**ar·bor·ist** \'är-bə-rist\ *noun* (1578)
: a specialist in the care and maintenance of trees

**ar·bor·i·za·tion** \ˌär-bə-rə-'zā-shən\ *noun* (1794)
: formation of or into an arborescent figure or arrangement; *also* : such a figure or arrangement (as a dendritic process of a nerve cell)

**ar·bor·ize** \'är-bə-ˌrīz\ *intransitive verb* **-ized; -iz·ing** (1847)
: to branch freely and repeatedly

**ar·bor·vi·tae** \ˌär-bər-'vī-tē\ *noun* [New Latin *arbor vitae*, literally, tree of life] (1646)
: any of various evergreen trees and shrubs (especially genus *Thuja*) of the cypress family that usually have closely overlapping or compressed scale leaves and are often grown for ornament and in hedges

**ar·bour** *chiefly British variant of* ARBOR

**ar·bo·vi·rus** \ˌär-bə-'vī-rəs\ *noun* [*arthropod-borne virus*] (1957)
: any of various RNA viruses (as the causative agents of encephalitis, yellow fever, and dengue) transmitted by arthropods

**ar·bu·tus** \är-'byü-təs\ *noun* [New Latin, from Latin, strawberry tree] (1548)
**1** : any of a genus (*Arbutus*) of shrubs and trees of the heath family with white or pink flowers and red or orange berries
**2** : a creeping plant (*Epigaea repens*) of the heath family that occurs in eastern North America and bears fragrant pink or white flowers in early spring

**¹arc** \'ärk\ *noun* [Middle English *ark*, from Middle French *arc* bow, from Latin *arcus* bow, arch, arc — more at ARROW] (14th century)

\ə\ abut \ᵊ\ kitten \ər\ further \a\ ash \ā\ ace \ä\ mop, mar \aù\ out \ch\ chin \e\ bet \ē\ easy \g\ go \i\ hit \ī\ ice \j\ job \ŋ\ sing \ō\ go \ȯ\ law \ȯi\ boy \th\ thin \th\ the \ü\ loot \ù\ foot \y\ yet \zh\ vision *see also* Guide to Pronunciation

**1 :** the apparent path described above and below the horizon by a celestial body (as the sun)
**2 :** something arched or curved
**3 :** a sustained luminous discharge of electricity across a gap in a circuit or between electrodes; *also* **:** ARC LAMP
**4 :** a continuous portion (as of a circle or ellipse) of a curved line
**5 :** degree measurement on the circumference of a circle — used especially in the phrase *of arc* ⟨11 minutes 3 seconds of *arc*⟩

**²arc** *intransitive verb* **arced** \'ärkt\; **arc·ing** \'är-kiŋ\ (1893)
**1 :** to form an electric arc
**2 :** to follow an arc-shaped course ⟨the missile *arced* across the sky⟩

**³arc** *adjective* [*arc sine* arc or angle (corresponding to the) sine (of so many degrees)] (circa 1949)
**:** INVERSE 2 — used with the trigonometric functions and hyperbolic functions

**ar·cade** \är-'kād\ *noun* [French, from Italian *arcata*, from *arco* arch, from Latin *arcus*] (1725)
**1 :** a long arched building or gallery
**2 :** an arched covered passageway or avenue (as between shops)
**3 :** a series of arches with their columns or piers
**4 :** an amusement center having coin-operated games

**ar·cad·ed** \-'kā-dəd\ *adjective* (1805)
**:** having, formed in, or decorated with arches or arcades ⟨*arcaded* streets⟩ ⟨an *arcaded* bowl⟩

**ar·ca·dia** \är-'kā-dē-ə\ *noun, often capitalized* [*Arcadia*, region of ancient Greece frequently chosen as background for pastoral poetry] (circa 1890)
**:** a region or scene of simple pleasure and quiet

**ar·ca·di·an** \är-'kā-dē-ən\ *adjective, often capitalized* (1589)
**1 :** idyllically pastoral; *especially* **:** idyllically innocent, simple, or untroubled
**2 a :** of or relating to Arcadia or the Arcadians **b :** of or relating to Arcadian

**Ar·ca·di·an** \är-'kā-dē-ən\ *noun* (1590)
**1** *often not capitalized* **:** a person who lives a simple quiet life
**2 :** a native or inhabitant of Arcadia
**3 :** the dialect of ancient Greek used in Arcadia

**ar·cad·ing** \är-'kā-diŋ\ *noun* (1849)
**:** a series of arches or arcades used in the construction or decoration especially of a building

**Ar·ca·dy** \'är-kə-dē\ *noun* (14th century)
**:** ARCADIA

**ar·cane** \är-'kān\ *adjective* [Latin *arcanus*] (1547)
**:** known or knowable only to the initiate **:** SECRET ⟨the *arcane* rites of a mystery cult⟩; *broadly* **:** MYSTERIOUS, OBSCURE ⟨the technical consultant's *arcane* explanations⟩

**ar·ca·num** \är-'kā-nəm\ *noun, plural* **-na** \-nə\ [Latin, from neuter of *arcanus* secret, from *arca* chest — more at ARK] (15th century)
**1 :** mysterious knowledge, language, or information accessible only by the initiate — usually used in plural
**2 :** ELIXIR 1

**arc·co·sine** \(ˌ)är(k)-'kō-ˌsīn\ *noun* (circa 1884)
**:** the inverse function to the cosine ⟨if *y* is the cosine of θ, then θ is the *arccosine* of *y*⟩

**¹arch** \'ärch\ *noun* [Middle English *arche*, from Middle French, from (assumed) Vulgar Latin *arca*, from Latin *arcus* — more at ARROW] (14th century)
**1 :** a typically curved structural member spanning an opening and serving as a support (as for the wall or other weight above the opening)
**2 a :** something resembling an arch in form or function; *especially* **:** either of two vaulted portions of the bony structure of the foot that

impart elasticity to it **b :** a curvature having the form of an arch
**3 :** ARCHWAY

arch 1: *1* round: *imp* impost, *sp* springer, *v* voussoir, *k* keystone, *ext* extrados, *int* intrados; *2* horseshoe; *3* lancet; *4* ogee; *5* trefoil; *6* basket-handle; *7* Tudor

**²arch** (15th century)
*transitive verb*
**1 :** to cover or provide with an arch
**2 :** to form into an arch
*intransitive verb*
**1 :** to form an arch
**2 :** to take an arch-shaped course

**³arch** *adjective* ['arch-] (1547)
**1 :** PRINCIPAL, CHIEF ⟨your *arch* opponent⟩
**2 a :** MISCHIEVOUS, SAUCY **b :** marked by a deliberate and often forced irony, brashness, or impudence
— **arch·ly** *adverb*
— **arch·ness** *noun*

**¹arch-** *prefix* [Middle English *arche-*, *arch-*, from Old English & Old French; Old English *arce-*, from Late Latin *arch-* & Latin *archi-*; Old French *arch-*, from Late Latin *arch-* & Latin *archi-*, from Greek *arch-*, *archi-*, from *archein* to begin, rule; akin to Greek *archē* beginning, rule, *archos* ruler]
**1 :** chief **:** principal ⟨*arch*fiend⟩
**2 :** extreme **:** most fully embodying the qualities of the kind ⟨*arch*conservative⟩

**²arch-** — see ARCHI-

**¹-arch** *noun combining form* [Middle English *-arche*, from Old French & Late Latin & Latin; Old French *-arche*, from Late Latin *-archa*, from Latin *-arches*, *-archus*, from Greek *-archēs*, *-archos*, from *archein*]
**:** ruler **:** leader ⟨matri*arch*⟩

**²-arch** *adjective combining form* [probably from German, from Greek *archē* beginning]
**:** having ⟨such⟩ a point or ⟨so many⟩ points of origin ⟨end*arch*⟩

**archae-** *or* **archaeo-** *also* **archeo-** *combining form* [Greek *archaio-*, from *archaios* ancient, from *archē* beginning]
**:** ancient **:** primitive ⟨*archaeo*pteryx⟩ ⟨*Archeo*zoic⟩

**ar·chae·bac·te·ri·um** \ˌär-kē-ˌbak-'tir-ē-əm\ *noun* [New Latin] (1977)
**:** any of a class (Archaebacteria) or a separate kingdom (Archaebacteria) of primitive bacteria including methane-producing forms, some red halophilic forms, and others of harsh hot acidic environments

**ar·chaeo·as·tron·o·my** \ˌär-kē-(ˌ)ō-ə-'strä-nə-mē\ *noun* (1971)
**:** the study of the astronomy of ancient cultures

**ar·chae·ol·o·gy** *or* **ar·che·ol·o·gy** \ˌär-kē-'ä-lə-jē\ *noun* [French *archéologie*, from Late Latin *archaeologia* antiquarian lore, from Greek *archaiologia*, from *archaio-* + *-logia* -logy] (1837)
**1 :** the scientific study of material remains (as fossil relics, artifacts, and monuments) of past human life and activities
**2 :** remains of the culture of a people **:** ANTIQUITIES
— **ar·chae·o·log·i·cal** \ˌär-kē-ə-'lä-ji-kəl\ *adjective*
— **ar·chae·o·log·i·cal·ly** \-k(ə-)lē\ *adverb*
— **ar·chae·ol·o·gist** \ˌär-kē-'ä-lə-jist\ *noun*

**ar·chae·op·ter·yx** \ˌär-kē-'äp-tə-riks\ *noun*

[New Latin, from *archae-* + Greek *pteryx* wing; akin to Greek *pteron* wing — more at FEATHER] (1859)
**:** a primitive crow-sized bird (genus *Archaeopteryx*) of the Upper Jurassic period of Europe having reptilian characteristics (as teeth and a long bony tail)

**ar·cha·ic** \är-'kā-ik\ *adjective* [French or Greek; French *archaïque*, from Greek *archaïkos*, from *archaios*] (1832)
**1 :** having the characteristics of the language of the past and surviving chiefly in specialized uses
**2 :** of, relating to, or characteristic of an earlier or more primitive time **:** ANTIQUATED ⟨*archaic* legal traditions⟩
**3** *capitalized* **:** of or belonging to the early or formative phases of a culture or a period of artistic development; *especially* **:** of or belonging to the period leading up to the classical period of Greek culture
**4 :** surviving from an earlier period; *specifically* **:** typical of a previously dominant evolutionary stage
**5** *capitalized* **:** of or relating to the period from about 8000 B.C. to 1000 B.C. and the North American cultures of that time
**synonym** see OLD
— **ar·cha·i·cal·ly** \-i-k(ə-)lē\ *adverb*

**archaic smile** *noun* (1889)
**:** an expression that resembles a smile and is characteristic of early Greek sculpture

**ar·cha·ism** \'är-kē-ˌi-zəm, -(ˌ)kā-ˌi-\ *noun* [New Latin *archaïsmus*, from Greek *archaïsmos*, from *archaios*] (1643)
**1 :** the use of archaic diction or style
**2 :** an instance of archaic usage
**3 :** something archaic; *especially* **:** something (as a practice or custom) that is outmoded or old-fashioned
— **ar·cha·ist** \-ist\ *noun*
— **ar·cha·is·tic** \ˌär-kē-'is-tik, -(ˌ)kā-\ *adjective*
— **ar·cha·ize** \'är-kē-ˌīz, -(ˌ)kā-\ *verb*

**arch·an·gel** \'ärk-ˌān-jəl\ *noun* [Middle English, from Old French or Late Latin; Old French *archangele*, from Late Latin *archangelus*, from Greek *archangelos*, from *archi-* + *angelos* angel] (12th century)
**1 :** a chief angel
**2** *plural* **:** an order of angels — see CELESTIAL HIERARCHY
— **arch·an·gel·ic** \ˌär-(ˌ)kan-'je-lik\ *adjective*

**arch·bish·op** \(ˌ)ärch-'bi-shəp\ *noun* [Middle English, from Old English *arcebiscop*, from Late Latin *archiepiscopus*, from Late Greek *archiepiskopos*, from *archi-* + *episkopos* bishop — more at BISHOP] (before 12th century)
**:** a bishop at the head of an ecclesiastical province or one of equivalent honorary rank

**arch·bish·op·ric** \-shə-(ˌ)prik\ *noun* (before 12th century)
**1 :** the see or province over which an archbishop exercises authority
**2 :** the jurisdiction or office of an archbishop

**arch·con·ser·va·tive** \(ˌ)ärch-kən-'sər-və-tiv\ *noun* (1934)
**:** an extreme conservative
— **archconservative** *adjective*

**arch·dea·con** \(ˌ)ärch-'dē-kən\ *noun* [Middle English *archedeken*, from Old English *arcediacon*, from Late Latin *archidiaconus*, from Late Greek *archidiakonos*, from Greek *archi-* + *diakonos* deacon] (before 12th century)
**:** a clergyman having the duty of assisting a diocesan bishop in ceremonial functions or administrative work

**arch·dea·con·ry** \-kən-rē\ *noun, plural* **-ries** (1779)
**:** the district or residence of an archdeacon

**arch·di·o·cese** \(ˌ)ärch-'dī-ə-səs, -ˌsēz, -ˌsēs\ *noun, plural* **-ces·es** \-'dī-ə-ˌsēz, -ˌsē-zəz, -sə-səz, -sə-ˌsēz\ (1844)
**:** the diocese of an archbishop

— **arch·di·oc·e·san** \,ärch-dī-'ä-sə-sən\ *adjective*
**arch·du·cal** \(,)ärch-'dü-kəl, -'dyü-\ *adjective* [French *archiducal*, from *archiduc*] (1665)
: of or relating to an archduke or archduchy
**arch·duch·ess** \-'də-chəs\ *noun* [French *archiduchesse*, feminine of *archiduc* archduke, from Middle French *archeduc*] (1618)
**1** : the wife or widow of an archduke
**2** : a woman having in her own right a rank equal to that of an archduke
**arch·duchy** \-'də-chē\ *noun* [French *archiduché*, from Middle French *archeduché*, from *arche-* arch- + *duché* duchy] (1680)
: the territory of an archduke or archduchess
**arch·duke** \-'dük, -'dyük\ *noun* [Middle French *archeduc*, from *arche-* arch- + *duc* duke] (circa 1530)
**1** : a sovereign prince
**2** : a prince of the imperial family of Austria
— **arch·duke·dom** \-dəm\ *noun*
**Ar·che·an** *or* **Ar·chae·an** \är-'kē-ən\ *adjective* [Greek *archaios*] (1872)
**1** : of, relating to, or being the earliest eon of geological history or the corresponding system of rocks — see GEOLOGIC TIME table
**2** : PRECAMBRIAN
— **Archean** *noun*
**ar·che·go·ni·al** \,är-ki-'gō-nē-əl\ *adjective* (1865)
: of or relating to an archegonium; *also* : ARCHEGONIATE
¹**ar·che·go·ni·ate** \-nē-ət\ *adjective* (circa 1888)
: bearing archegonia
²**archegoniate** *noun* (circa 1903)
: a plant (as a moss, fern, horsetail, or club moss) that bears archegonia
**ar·che·go·ni·um** \-nē-əm\ *noun, plural* **-nia** \-nē-ə\ [New Latin, from Greek *archegonos* originator, from *archein* to begin + *gonos* procreation; akin to Greek *gignesthai* to be born — more at ARCH-, KIN] (1854)
: the flask-shaped female sex organ of bryophytes, lower vascular plants (as ferns), and some gymnosperms
**arch·en·e·my** \(,)ärch-'e-nə-mē\ *noun, plural* **-mies** (1550)
: a principal enemy
**arch·en·ter·on** \är-'ken-tə-,rän, -rən\ *noun* [New Latin] (1877)
: the cavity of a gastrula forming a primitive gut
**Ar·cheo·zo·ic** *also* **Ar·chaeo·zo·ic** \,är-kē-ə-'zō-ik\ *adjective* (1872)
: ARCHEAN 1
— **Archeozoic** *noun*
**ar·cher** \'är-chər\ *noun* [Middle English, from Old French, from Late Latin *arcarius*, alteration of *arcuarius*, from *arcuarius* of a bow, from Latin *arcus* bow — more at ARROW] (14th century)
**1** : a person who uses a bow and arrow
**2** *capitalized* : SAGITTARIUS
**ar·cher·fish** \'är-chər-,fish\ *noun* (circa 1889)
: a small East Indian fish (*Toxotes jaculator*) that catches insects by stunning them with water ejected from its mouth; *also* : any of various related fish of similar habits
**ar·chery** \'är-chə-rē\ *noun* (15th century)
**1** : the art, practice, or skill of shooting with bow and arrow
**2** : an archer's weapons
**3** : a body of archers
**ar·che·spo·ri·um** \,är-ki-'spōr-ē-əm, -'spȯr-\ *noun, plural* **-spo·ria** \-ē-ə\ [New Latin, from *arche-* (as in *archegonium*) + *-sporium* (from *spora* spore)] (circa 1889)
: the cell or group of cells from which spore mother cells develop
— **ar·che·spo·ri·al** \,är-ki-'spōr-ē-əl, -'spȯr-\ *adjective*
**ar·che·type** \'är-ki-,tīp\ *noun* [Latin *archetypum*, from Greek *archetypon*, from neuter of *archetypos* archetypal, from *archein* + *typos* type] (1545)

**1** : the original pattern or model of which all things of the same type are representations or copies : PROTOTYPE; *also* : a perfect example
**2** : IDEA 1a
**3** : an inherited idea or mode of thought in the psychology of C. G. Jung that is derived from the experience of the race and is present in the unconscious of the individual
— **ar·che·typ·al** \,är-ki-'tī-pəl\ *also* **ar·che·typ·i·cal** \-'ti-pi-kəl\ *adjective*
— **ar·che·typ·al·ly** \-pə-lē\ *adverb*
**arch·fiend** \(,)ärch-'fēnd\ *noun* (1667)
: a chief fiend; *especially* : SATAN
**archi-** *or* **arch-** *prefix* [French or Latin; French, from Latin, from Greek — more at ARCH-]
: primitive : original : primary 〈*arch*enteron〉
**ar·chi·di·ac·o·nal** \,är-ki-dī-'a-kə-n°l\ *adjective* [Late Latin *archidiaconus* archdeacon] (15th century)
: of or relating to an archdeacon
**ar·chi·epis·co·pal** \,är-kē-ə-'pis-kə-pəl\ *adjective* [Medieval Latin *archiepiscopalis*, from Late Latin *archiepiscopus* archbishop — more at ARCHBISHOP] (1611)
: of or relating to an archbishop
— **ar·chi·epis·co·pal·ly** \-p(ə-)lē\ *adverb*
**ar·chi·epis·co·pate** \-pət, -,pāt\ *noun* (1792)
: ARCHBISHOPRIC
**ar·chil** \'är-chəl\ *noun* [Middle English *orchell*] (15th century)
**1** : a violet dye obtained from lichens (genera *Roccella* and *Lecanora*)
**2** : a lichen that yields archil
**ar·chi·man·drite** \,är-kə-'man-,drīt\ *noun* [Late Latin *archimandrites*, from Late Greek *archimandritēs*, from Greek *archi-* + Late Greek *mandra* monastery, from Greek, fold, pen] (1591)
: a dignitary in an Eastern church ranking below a bishop; *specifically* : the superior of a large monastery or group of monasteries
**Ar·chi·me·des' screw** \,är-kə-'mē-dēz-\ *noun* [*Archimedes*] (circa 1859)
: a device made of a tube bent spirally around an axis or of a broad-threaded screw encased by a cylinder and used to raise water

**Archimedes' screw**

**ar·chi·pe·lag·ic** \,är-kə-pə-'la-jik, ,är-chə-\ *adjective* (1841)
: of, relating to, or located in an archipelago
**ar·chi·pel·a·go** \,är-kə-'pe-lə-,gō, ,är-chə-\ *noun, plural* **-goes** *or* **-gos** [*Archipelago* Aegean Sea, from Italian *Arcipelago*, literally, chief sea, from *arci-* (from Latin *archi-*) + Greek *pelagos* sea — more at PLAGAL] (1502)
**1** : an expanse of water with many scattered islands
**2** : a group of islands
**ar·chi·tect** \'är-kə-,tekt\ *noun* [Middle French *architecte*, from Latin *architectus*, from Greek *architektōn* master builder, from *archi-* + *tektōn* builder, carpenter — more at TECHNICAL] (1563)
**1** : a person who designs buildings and advises in their construction
**2** : a person who designs and guides a plan or undertaking 〈the *architect* of American foreign policy〉
**ar·chi·tec·ton·ic** \,är-kə-,tek-'tä-nik\ *adjective* [Latin *architectonicus*, from Greek *architektonikos*, from *architektōn*] (1645)
**1** : of, relating to, or according with the principles of architecture : ARCHITECTURAL
**2** : having an organized and unified structure that suggests an architectural design
— **ar·chi·tec·ton·i·cal·ly** \-ni-k(ə-)lē\ *adverb*
**ar·chi·tec·ton·ics** \-'tä-niks\ *noun plural but* 

*singular or plural in construction, also* **ar·chi·tec·ton·ic** \-nik\ (1660)
**1** : the science of architecture
**2 a** : the unifying structural design of something **b** : the system of structure
**ar·chi·tec·tur·al** \,är-kə-'tek-chə-rəl, -'tek-shrəl\ *adjective* (circa 1794)
**1** : of or relating to architecture : conforming to the rules of architecture
**2** : having or conceived of as having a single unified overall design, form, or structure
— **ar·chi·tec·tur·al·ly** *adverb*
**ar·chi·tec·ture** \'är-kə-,tek-chər\ *noun* (1555)
**1** : the art or science of building; *specifically* : the art or practice of designing and building structures and especially habitable ones
**2 a** : formation or construction as or as if as the result of conscious act 〈the *architecture* of the garden〉 **b** : a unifying or coherent form or structure 〈the novel lacks *architecture*〉
**3** : architectural product or work
**4** : a method or style of building
**5** : the manner in which the components of a computer or computer system are organized and integrated
**ar·chi·trave** \'är-kə-,trāv\ *noun* [Middle French, from Old Italian, from *archi-* + *trave* beam, from Latin *trab-, trabs* — more at THORP] (1563)
**1** : the lowest division of an entablature resting in classical architecture immediately on the capital of the column — see ENTABLATURE illustration
**2** : the molding around a rectangular opening (as a door)
**ar·chi·val** \är-'kī-vəl\ *adjective* (circa 1828)
: of, relating to, contained in, or constituting archives
¹**ar·chive** \'är-,kīv\ *noun* [French & Latin; French, from Latin *archivum*, from Greek *archeion* government house (in plural, official documents), from *archē* rule, government — more at ARCH-] (1603)
: a place in which public records or historical documents are preserved; *also* : the material preserved — often used in plural
²**archive** *transitive verb* **ar·chived; ar·chiv·ing** (1926)
: to file or collect (as records or documents) in or as if in an archive
**ar·chi·vist** \'är-kə-vist, -,kī-\ *noun* (1753)
: a person in charge of archives
**ar·chi·volt** \'är-kə-,vōlt\ *noun* [Italian *archivolto*, from Medieval Latin *archivoltum*] (circa 1731)
: an ornamental molding around an arch corresponding to an architrave
**ar·chon** \'är-,kän, -kən\ *noun* [Latin, from Greek *archōn*, from present participle of *archein*] (1579)
**1** : a chief magistrate in ancient Athens
**2** : a presiding officer
**ar·cho·saur** \'är-kə-,sȯr\ *noun* [New Latin *Archosauria*, from Greek *archōn* + *sauros* lizard] (1933)
: any of a subclass (Archosauria) of reptiles comprising the dinosaurs, pterosaurs, and crocodilians
— **ar·cho·sau·ri·an** \,är-kə-'sȯr-ē-ən\ *adjective*
**arch·priest** \(,)ärch-'prēst\ *noun* (14th century)
: a priest of preeminent rank
**arch·way** \'ärch-,wā\ *noun* (1802)
: a way or passage under an arch; *also* : an arch over a passage
**-archy** *noun combining form, plural* **-archies** [Middle English *-archie*, from Middle French, from Latin *-archia*, from Greek, from *archein* to rule — more at ARCH-]

: rule : government ⟨squire*archy*⟩

**arc lamp** *noun* (1882)
: an electric lamp that produces light by an arc made when a current passes between two incandescent electrodes surrounded by gas — called also *arc light*

**ar·co** \'är-(,)kō\ *adverb or adjective* [Italian, from *arco* bow, from Latin *arcus* — more at ARROW] (1806)
: with the bow — usually used as a direction in music for players of stringed instruments; compare PIZZICATO

**arc·sine** \(,)ärk-'sīn\ *noun* (circa 1909)
: the inverse function to the sine ⟨if *y* is the sine of θ, then θ is the *arcsine* of *y*⟩

**arc·tan·gent** \(,)ärk-'tan-jənt\ *noun* (circa 1909)
: the inverse function to the tangent ⟨if *y* is the tangent of θ, then θ is the *arctangent* of *y*⟩

¹**arc·tic** \'ärk-tik, 'är-tik\ *adjective* [Middle English *artik,* from Latin *arcticus,* from Greek *arktikos,* from *arktos* bear, Ursa Major, north; akin to Latin *ursus* bear, Sanskrit *ṛkṣa*] (14th century)
**1** *often capitalized* : of or relating to the north pole or the region near it
**2 a** : a bitter cold : FRIGID **b** : cold in temper or mood ⟨an *arctic* smile⟩
— **arc·ti·cal·ly** \-ti-k(ə-)lē\ *adverb*

²**arc·tic** \'är-tik, 'ärk-tik\ *noun* (1867)
: a rubber overshoe reaching to the ankle or above

**arctic char** *noun* (circa 1902)
: a Holarctic char (*Salvelinus alpinus*) of arctic waters occurring in freshwater or anadromous populations

**arctic circle** *noun, often A&C capitalized* (1834)
: the parallel of latitude that is approximately 66½ degrees north of the equator and that circumscribes the northern frigid zone

**arctic fox** *noun* (1772)
: a small migratory Holarctic fox (*Alopex lagopus*) especially of coastal arctic and alpine tundra

**arctic tern** *noun* (1844)
: a Holarctic tern (*Sterna paradisaea*) that breeds in arctic regions and migrates to southern Africa and South America

**Arc·tu·rus** \ärk-'tu̇r-əs, -'tyu̇r-\ *noun* [Latin, from Greek *Arktouros,* literally, bear watcher]
: a giant fixed star of the first magnitude in Boötes

**ar·cu·ate** \'är-kyə-wət, -,wāt\ *adjective* [Latin *arcuatus,* past participle of *arcuare* to bend like a bow, from *arcus* bow] (1626)
: curved like a bow ⟨an *arcuate* cloud⟩
— **ar·cu·ate·ly** *adverb*

**-ard** *also* **-art** *noun suffix* [Middle English, from Old French, of Germanic origin; akin to Old High German *-hart* (in personal names such as *Gērhart* Gerard), Old English *heard* hard]
: one that is characterized by performing some action, possessing some quality, or being associated with some thing especially conspicuously or excessively ⟨bragg*art*⟩ ⟨dull*ard*⟩ ⟨poll*ard*⟩

**ar·den·cy** \'är-d°n(t)-sē\ *noun* (1549)
: the quality or state of being ardent

**ar·dent** \'är-d°nt\ *adjective* [Middle English, from Middle French, from Latin *ardent-, ardens,* present participle of *ardēre* to burn, from *ardor*] (14th century)
**1** : characterized by warmth of feeling typically expressed in eager zealous support or activity
**2** : FIERY, HOT ⟨an *ardent* sun⟩
**3** : SHINING, GLOWING ⟨*ardent* eyes⟩
**synonym** *see* IMPASSIONED
— **ar·dent·ly** *adverb*

**ardent spirits** *noun plural* (1833)
: strong distilled liquors

**ar·dor** \'är-dər\ *noun* [Middle English *ardour,* from Middle French & Latin; Middle French, from Latin *ardor* burning, heat, ardor, from *aridus* dry — more at ARID] (14th century)

**1 a** : an often restless or transitory warmth of feeling ⟨the sudden *ardors* of youth⟩ **b** : extreme vigor or energy : INTENSITY **c** : ZEAL **d** : LOYALTY
**2** : sexual excitement
**synonym** *see* PASSION

**ar·dour** *chiefly British variant of* ARDOR

**ar·du·ous** \'är-jə-wəs, -dyu̇-wəs\ *adjective* [Latin *arduus* high, steep, difficult; akin to Old Irish *ard* high] (1538)
**1 a** : hard to accomplish or achieve : DIFFICULT ⟨years of *arduous* training⟩ **b** : marked by great labor or effort : STRENUOUS ⟨a life of *arduous* toil —A. C. Cole⟩
**2** : hard to climb : STEEP
**synonym** *see* HARD
— **ar·du·ous·ly** *adverb*
— **ar·du·ous·ness** *noun*

¹**are** [Middle English, from Old English *earun;* akin to Old Norse *eru, erum* are, Old English *is* is] *present 2d singular or present plural of* BE

²**are** \'ar, 'er, 'är\ *noun* [French, from Latin *area*] (circa 1819)
— *see* METRIC SYSTEM table

**ar·ea** \'ar-ē-ə, 'er-; 'ä-rē-ə\ *noun* [Latin, open space, threshing floor; perhaps akin to Latin *arēre* to be dry — more at ARID] (1538)
**1** : a level piece of ground
**2** : the surface included within a set of lines; *specifically* : the number of unit squares equal in measure to the surface — see METRIC SYSTEM table, WEIGHT table
**3** : the scope of a concept, operation, or activity : FIELD ⟨the whole *area* of foreign policy⟩
**4** : AREAWAY ⟨went down the steps into the *area* of a house —James Joyce⟩
**5** : a particular extent of space or surface or one serving a special function: as **a** : a part of the surface of the body **b** : a geographic region
**6** : a part of the cerebral cortex having a particular function
— **ar·e·al** \-ē-əl\ *adjective*
— **ar·e·al·ly** \-ə-lē\ *adverb*

**area code** *noun* (1961)
: a 3-digit number that identifies each telephone service area in a country (as the U.S. or Canada)

**ar·ea·way** \'ar-ē-ə-,wā, 'er-; 'ä-rē-\ *noun* (1899)
: a sunken space affording access, air, and light to a basement

**are·ca** \ə-'rē-kə, 'ar-i-kə\ *noun* [New Latin, from Portuguese, from Malayalam *aṭaykka*] (1510)
: any of several tropical Asian palms (*Areca* or related genera); *especially* : BETEL PALM

**arec·o·line** \ə-'re-kə-,lēn\ *noun* [International Scientific Vocabulary *areca* + ¹*-ol* + ²*-ine*] (1899)
: a toxic parasympathomimetic alkaloid $C_8H_{13}NO_2$ that is used as a veterinary anthelmintic and occurs naturally in betel nuts

**are·na** \ə-'rē-nə\ *noun* [Latin *harena, arena* sand, sandy place] (1600)
**1** : an area in a Roman amphitheater for gladiatorial combats
**2 a** : an enclosed area used for public entertainment **b** : a building containing an arena
**3 a** : a sphere of interest, activity, or competition ⟨the political *arena*⟩ **b** : a place or situation for controversy ⟨in the public *arena*⟩

**ar·e·na·ceous** \,ar-ə-'nā-shəs\ *adjective* [Latin *arenaceus,* from *arena*] (1646)
**1** : resembling, made of, or containing sand or sandy particles
**2** : growing in sandy places

**arena theater** *noun* (1943)
: THEATER-IN-THE-ROUND

**ar·e·nic·o·lous** \,ar-ə-'ni-kə-ləs\ *adjective* [Latin *arena* + English *-i-* + *-colous*] (circa 1859)
: living, burrowing, or growing in sand

**aren't** \'ärnt, 'är-ənt\ (1810)
**1** : are not
**2** : am not — used in questions

**ar·eo·cen·tric** \,ar-ē-ō-'sen-trik\ *adjective* [Greek *Areios* of Ares, from *Ares*] (1877)
: having or relating to the planet Mars as a center

**are·o·la** \ə-'rē-ə-lə\ *noun, plural* **-lae** \-,lē\ *or* **-las** [New Latin, from Latin, small open space, diminutive of *area*] (1664)
: a small area between things or about something; *especially* : a colored ring (as about the nipple, a vesicle, or a pustule)
— **are·o·lar** \-lər\ *adjective*
— **are·o·late** \-lət\ *adjective*

**ar·e·ole** \'ar-ē-,ōl\ *noun* (circa 1934)
: a small pit or cavity

**Ar·e·op·a·gite** \,ar-ē-'ä-pə-,gīt, -,jīt\ *noun* (14th century)
: a member of the Areopagus
— **Ar·e·op·a·git·ic** \-,ä-pə-'ji-tik\ *adjective*

**Ar·e·op·a·gus** \,ar-ē-'ä-pə-gəs\ *noun* [Latin, from Greek *Areios pagos,* from *Areios pagos* (literally, hill of Ares), a hill in Athens where the tribunal met] (1586)
: the supreme tribunal of Athens

**Ar·es** \'ar-(,)ēz, 'er-\ *noun* [Greek *Arēs*]
: the Greek god of war — compare MARS

**arête** \ə-'rāt\ *noun* [French, literally, fish bone, from Late Latin *arista,* from Latin, beard of grain] (1838)
: a sharp-crested ridge in rugged mountains

**Ar·e·thu·sa** \,ar-ə-'thü-zə, -'thyü-\ *noun* [Latin, from Greek *Arethousa*]
: a wood nymph who is changed into a spring while fleeing the advances of the river-god Alpheus

**ar·ga·li** \'är-gə-lē\ *noun* [Mongolian] (circa 1774)
: a large wild sheep (*Ovis ammon*) of Asia that is noted for its large horns

**Ar·gand diagram** \är-'gän-, -'gan-\ *noun* [Jean Robert *Argand* (died 1825) Swiss mathematician] (1908)
: a system of rectangular coordinates in which the complex number $x + iy$ is represented by the point whose coordinates are $x$ and $y$

**ar·gent** \'är-jənt\ *noun* [Middle English, from Middle French & Latin; Middle French, from Latin *argentum;* akin to Greek *argyros* silver, *argos* white, Sanskrit *rajata* whitish, silvery] (15th century)
**1** *archaic* : the metal silver; *also* : WHITENESS
**2** : the heraldic color silver or white
— **argent** *adjective*

**ar·gen·tif·er·ous** \,är-jən-'ti-f(ə-)rəs\ *adjective* (1801)
: containing silver

¹**ar·gen·tine** \'är-jən-,tīn, -,tēn\ *adjective* (15th century)
: SILVER, SILVERY

²**argentine** *noun* (1577)
: SILVER; *also* : any of various similar materials

**ar·gen·tite** \'är-jən-,tīt\ *noun* (circa 1837)
: native silver sulfide having a metallic luster and dark lead-gray color and constituting a valuable ore of silver

**ar·gil** \'är-jəl\ *noun* [Middle English, from Latin *argilla,* from Greek *argillos;* akin to Greek *argos* white] (14th century)
: CLAY; *especially* : POTTER'S CLAY

**ar·gil·la·ceous** \,är-jə-'lā-shəs\ *adjective* (circa 1731)
: of, relating to, or containing clay or clay minerals : CLAYEY

**ar·gil·lite** \'är-jə-,līt\ *noun* (1795)
: a compact argillaceous rock cemented by silica and having no slaty cleavage

**ar·gi·nase** \'är-jə-,nās, -,nāz\ *noun* [International Scientific Vocabulary] (1904)
: a crystalline enzyme that converts naturally occurring arginine into ornithine and urea

**ar·gi·nine** \'är-jə-,nēn\ *noun* [German *Arginin*] (1886)
: a crystalline basic amino acid $C_6H_{14}N_4O_2$ derived from guanidine

**Ar·give** \'är-ˌjīv, -ˌgīv\ *adjective* [Latin *Argivus*, from Greek *Argeios*, literally, of Argos, from *Argos* city-state of ancient Greece] (1598)
: of or relating to the Greeks or Greece and especially the Achaean city of Argos or the surrounding territory of Argolis
— **Argive** *noun*

**ar·gle-bar·gle** \ˌär-gəl-'bär-gəl\ *noun* [reduplication of Scots & English *argle,* alteration of *argue*] (1872)
*chiefly British* **:** ARGY-BARGY

**Ar·go** \'är-(ˌ)gō\ *noun* [Latin (genitive *Argus*), from Greek *Argō*]
: a large constellation in the southern hemisphere lying principally between Canis Major and the Southern Cross

**ar·gol** \'är-ˌgól\ *noun* [Middle English *argoile,* from Anglo-French *argoil*] (14th century)
: crude tartar deposited in wine casks during aging

**ar·gon** \'är-ˌgän\ *noun* [Greek, neuter of *argos* idle, lazy, from *a-* + *ergon* work; from its relative inertness — more at WORK] (1894)
: a colorless odorless inert gaseous element found in the air and in volcanic gases and used especially in welding, lasers, and electric bulbs — see ELEMENT table

**ar·go·naut** \'är-gə-ˌnót, -ˌnät\ *noun* [Latin *Argonautes,* from Greek *Argonautēs,* from *Argō,* ship in which the Argonauts sailed + *nautēs* sailor — more at NAUTICAL] (14th century)
**1 a** *capitalized* **:** any of a band of heroes sailing with Jason in quest of the Golden Fleece **b** **:** an adventurer engaged in a quest
**2 :** PAPER NAUTILUS

**ar·go·sy** \'är-gə-sē\ *noun, plural* **-sies** [modification of Italian *ragusea* Ragusan vessel, from *Ragusa,* Dalmatia (now Dubrovnik, Croatia)] (1587)
**1 :** a large ship; *especially* **:** a large merchant ship ⟨three of your *argosies* are . . . come to harbor —Shakespeare⟩
**2 :** a fleet of ships
**3 :** a rich supply ⟨an *argosy* of railway folklore —F. P. Donovan⟩

**ar·got** \'är-gət, -(ˌ)gō\ *noun* [French] (1860)
: an often more or less secret vocabulary and idiom peculiar to a particular group ⟨shoved into a taxi by a porter whose *argot* I couldn't understand —Allen Tate⟩

**ar·gu·able** \'är-gyü-ə-bəl\ *adjective* (circa 1611)
**1 :** open to argument, dispute, or question
**2 :** that can be plausibly or convincingly argued

**ar·gu·ably** \'är-gyü-(ə-)blē\ *adverb* (1890)
: it can be argued ⟨the word is *arguably* useful⟩ ⟨*arguably* the busiest airport in the world⟩

**ar·gue** \'är-(ˌ)gyü\ *verb* **ar·gued; ar·gu·ing** [Middle English, from Middle French *arguer* to accuse, reason & Latin *arguere* to demonstrate, prove; Middle French *arguer,* from Latin *argutare* to prate, frequentative of *arguere;* akin to Hittite *arkuwai-* to plead, respond] (14th century)
*intransitive verb*
**1 :** to give reasons for or against something **:** REASON
**2 :** to contend or disagree in words **:** DISPUTE
*transitive verb*
**1 :** to give evidence of **:** INDICATE
**2 :** to consider the pros and cons of **:** DISCUSS
**3 :** to prove or try to prove by giving reasons **:** MAINTAIN
**4 :** to persuade by giving reasons **:** INDUCE
**synonym** *see* DISCUSS
— **ar·gu·er** \-gyə-wər\ *noun*

**ar·gu·fy** \'är-gyə-ˌfī\ *verb* **-fied; -fy·ing** (1771)
*transitive verb*
**:** DISPUTE, DEBATE
*intransitive verb*
**:** WRANGLE
— **ar·gu·fi·er** \-ˌfī(-ə)r\ *noun*

**ar·gu·ment** \'är-gyə-mənt\ *noun* [Middle English, from Middle French, from Latin *argumentum,* from *arguere*] (14th century)
**1** *obsolete* **:** an outward sign **:** INDICATION
**2 a :** a reason given in proof or rebuttal **b** **:** discourse intended to persuade
**3 a :** the act or process of arguing **:** ARGUMENTATION **b :** a coherent series of statements leading from a premise to a conclusion **c** **:** QUARREL, DISAGREEMENT
**4 :** an abstract or summary especially of a literary work ⟨a later editor added an *argument* to the poem⟩
**5 :** the subject matter especially of a literary work
**6 a :** one of the independent variables upon whose value that of a function depends **b :** a substantive (as the direct object of a transitive verb) that is required by a predicate in grammar **c :** the angle assigned to a complex number when it is plotted in a complex plane using polar coordinates — called also *amplitude;* compare ABSOLUTE VALUE 2

**ar·gu·men·ta·tion** \ˌär-gyə-mən-'tā-shən, -ˌmen-\ *noun* (15th century)
**1 :** the act or process of forming reasons and of drawing conclusions and applying them to a case in discussion
**2 :** DEBATE, DISCUSSION

**ar·gu·men·ta·tive** \ˌär-gyə-'men-tə-tiv\ *also* **ar·gu·men·tive** \-'men-tiv\ *adjective* (15th century)
**1 :** characterized by argument **:** CONTROVERSIAL
**2 :** given to argument **:** DISPUTATIOUS
— **ar·gu·men·ta·tive·ly** *adverb*

**ar·gu·men·tum** \ˌär-gyə-'men-təm\ *noun, plural* **-men·ta** \-'men-tə\ [Latin] (1690)
**:** ARGUMENT 3b

**Ar·gus** \'är-gəs\ *noun* [Latin, from Greek *Argos*]
**1 :** a hundred-eyed monster of Greek mythology
**2 :** a watchful guardian

**Ar·gus—eyed** \'är-gəs-ˌīd\ *adjective* (1603)
: vigilantly observant

**ar·gy–bar·gy** \ˌär-jē-'bär-jē, ˌär-gē-'bär-gē\ *noun* [reduplication of Scots & English dialect *argy,* alteration of *argue*] (1887)
*chiefly British* **:** a lively discussion **:** ARGUMENT, DISPUTE

**ar·gyle** *also* **ar·gyll** \'är-ˌgī(ə)l, är-'\ *noun, often capitalized* [*Argyle, Argyll,* branch of the Scottish clan of Campbell, from whose tartan the design was adapted] (1899)
: a geometric knitting pattern of varicolored diamonds in solid and outline shapes on a single background color; *also* **:** a sock knit in this pattern

**ar·hat** \'är-(ˌ)hət\ *noun* [Sanskrit, from present participle of *arhati* he deserves; akin to Greek *alphein* to gain] (1870)
: a Buddhist who has reached the stage of enlightenment
— **ar·hat·ship** \-ˌship\ *noun*

**aria** \'är-ē-ə\ *noun* [Italian, literally, atmospheric air, modification of Latin *aer*] (circa 1724)
**1 :** AIR, MELODY, TUNE; *specifically* **:** an accompanied elaborate melody sung (as in an opera) by a single voice
**2 :** a striking solo performance (as in a movie)

**Ar·i·ad·ne** \ˌar-ē-'ad-nē\ *noun* [Latin, from Greek *Ariadnē*]
: a daughter of Minos who helps Theseus escape from the labyrinth

**¹Ar·i·an** \'ar-ē-ən, 'er-\ *adjective* (14th century)
: of or relating to Arius or his doctrines especially that the Son is not of the same substance as the Father but was created as an agent for creating the world
— **Ar·i·an·ism** \-ə-ˌni-zəm\ *noun*

**²Arian** *noun* (14th century)
: a supporter of Arian doctrines

**³Ar·i·an** \'er-ē-ən, 'ar-\ *noun* (1917)
**:** ARIES 2b

**-ar·i·an** *noun suffix* [Latin *-arius* -ary]
**1 :** believer ⟨necessit*arian*⟩ **:** advocate ⟨latitudin*arian*⟩
**2 :** producer ⟨disciplin*arian*⟩

**ari·bo·fla·vin·osis** \ˌā-ˌrī-bə-ˌflā-və-'nō-səs\ *noun* [New Latin] (1939)
: a deficiency disease due to inadequate intake of riboflavin and characterized by sores on the mouth

**ar·id** \'ar-əd\ *adjective* [French or Latin; French *aride,* from Latin *aridus,* from *arēre* to be dry; akin to Sanskrit *āsa* ash, Old English *asce*] (1652)
**1 :** excessively dry; *specifically* **:** having insufficient rainfall to support agriculture
**2 :** lacking in interest and life **:** JEJUNE
— **arid·i·ty** \ə-'ri-də-tē, a-\ *noun*
— **ar·id·ness** \'ar-əd-nəs\ *noun*

**Ar·i·el** \'ar-ē-əl, 'er-\ *noun*
: a prankish spirit in Shakespeare's *The Tempest*

**Ar·ies** \'er-ˌēz, 'ar-, -ē-ˌēz\ *noun* [Latin (genitive *Arietis*), literally, ram; perhaps akin to Greek *eriphos* kid, Old Irish *heirp* she-goat]
**1 :** a constellation between Pisces and Taurus pictured as a ram
**2 a :** the first sign of the zodiac in astrology — see ZODIAC table **b :** one born under the sign of Aries

**ari·et·ta** \ˌär-ē-'e-tə, ˌar-\ *noun* [Italian, diminutive of *aria*] (circa 1724)
: a short aria

**aright** \ə-'rīt\ *adverb* [Middle English, from Old English *ariht,* from *¹a-* + *riht* right] (before 12th century)
**:** RIGHT, CORRECTLY ⟨if I remember *aright*⟩

**Arik·a·ra** \ə-'ri-kə-rə\ *noun, plural* **Arikara** (1811)
**1 :** a member of an American Indian people of the Missouri River Valley in North Dakota
**2 :** the language of the Arikara

**ar·il** \'ar-əl\ *noun* [probably from New Latin *arillus,* from Medieval Latin, raisin, grape seed] (1794)
: an exterior covering or appendage of some seeds (as of the yew) that develops after fertilization as an outgrowth from the ovule stalk
— **ar·il·late** \'ar-ə-ˌlāt\ *adjective*

**ari·o·so** \ˌär-ē-'ō-(ˌ)sō, -(ˌ)zō\ *noun, plural* **-sos** *also* **-si** \-(ˌ)sē, -(ˌ)zē\ [Italian, from *aria*] (circa 1724)
: a musical passage or composition having a mixture of free recitative and metrical song

**arise** \ə-'rīz\ *intransitive verb* **arose** \-'rōz\; **aris·en** \-'ri-zᵊn\; **aris·ing** \-'rī-ziŋ\ [Middle English, from Old English *ārīsan,* from *ā-,* perfective prefix + *rīsan* to rise — more at ABIDE] (before 12th century)
**1 :** to get up **:** RISE
**2 a :** to originate from a source **b :** to come into being or to attention
**3 :** ASCEND
**synonym** *see* SPRING

**aris·ta** \ə-'ris-tə\ *noun, plural* **-tae** \-(ˌ)tē, -ˌtī\ *or* **-tas** [New Latin, from Latin, beard of grain] (1691)
: a bristlelike structure or appendage
— **aris·tate** \-ˌtāt\ *adjective*

**aris·to** \ə-'ris-(ˌ)tō\ *noun, plural* **-tos** [by shortening] (1864)
**:** ARISTOCRAT

**ar·is·toc·ra·cy** \ˌar-ə-'stä-krə-sē\ *noun, plural* **-cies** [Middle French & Late Latin; Middle French *aristocratie,* from Late Latin *aristocratia,* from Greek *aristokratia,* from *aristos* best + *-kratia* -cracy] (1561)
**1 :** government by the best individuals or by a small privileged class

---

\ə\ **abut**  \ᵊ\ **kitten**  \ər\ **further**  \a\ **ash**  \ā\ **ace**
\ä\ **mop, mar**  \au̇\ **out**  \ch\ **chin**  \e\ **bet**  \ē\ **easy**
\g\ **go**  \i\ **hit**  \ī\ **ice**  \j\ **job**  \ŋ\ **sing**  \ō\ **go**
\ȯ\ **law**  \ȯi\ **boy**  \th\ **thin**  \t͟h\ **the**  \ü\ **loot**  \u̇\ **foot**
\y\ **yet**  \zh\ **vision**     *see also* Guide to Pronunciation

**2 a :** a government in which power is vested in a minority consisting of those believed to be best qualified **b :** a state with such a government **3 :** a governing body or upper class usually made up of an hereditary nobility **4 :** the aggregate of those believed to be superior

**aris·to·crat** \ə-'ris-tə-ˌkrat, a-; 'ar-ə-stə-\ noun (1789)
**1 :** a member of an aristocracy; especially **:** NOBLE **2 a :** one who has the bearing and viewpoint typical of the aristocracy **b :** one who favors aristocracy **3 :** one believed to be superior of its kind ⟨the aristocrat of Southern resorts —Southern Living⟩

**aris·to·crat·ic** \ə-ˌris-tə-'kra-tik, (ˌ)a-ˌris-tə-, ˌar-ə-stə-\ adjective [Middle French aristocratique, from Medieval Latin aristocraticus, from Greek aristokratikos, from aristokratia] (1602)
**1 :** belonging to, having the qualities of, or favoring aristocracy **2 a :** socially exclusive ⟨an aristocratic neighborhood⟩ **b :** SNOBBISH
— **aris·to·crat·i·cal·ly** \-ti-k(ə-)lē\ adverb

**Ar·is·to·te·lian** also **Ar·is·to·te·lean** \ˌar-ə-stə-'tēl-yən\ adjective [Latin Aristoteles Aristotle, from Greek Aristotelēs] (1607)
**:** of or relating to the Greek philosopher Aristotle or his philosophy
— **Aristotelian** noun
— **Ar·is·to·te·lian·ism** \-yə-ˌni-zəm\ noun

**arith·me·tic** \ə-'rith-mə-ˌtik\ noun [Middle English arsmetrik, from Old French arismetique, from Latin arithmetica, from Greek arithmētikē, from feminine of arithmētikos arithmetical, from arithmein to count, from arithmos number; akin to Old English rīm number, and perhaps to Greek arariskein to fit] (15th century)
**1 a :** a branch of mathematics that deals usually with the nonnegative real numbers including sometimes the transfinite cardinals and with the application of the operations of addition, subtraction, multiplication, and division to them **b :** a treatise on arithmetic **2 :** COMPUTATION, CALCULATION
— **ar·ith·met·ic** \ˌar-ith-'me-tik\ or **ar·ith·met·i·cal** \-ti-kəl\ adjective
— **ar·ith·met·i·cal·ly** \-ti-k(ə-)lē\ adverb
— **arith·me·ti·cian** \ə-ˌrith-mə-'ti-shən\ noun

**arithmetic mean** noun (1767)
**:** a value that is computed by dividing the sum of a set of terms by the number of terms
**arithmetic progression** noun (1594)
**:** a progression (as 3, 5, 7, 9) in which the difference between any term and its predecessor is constant
**-arium** noun suffix, plural **-ariums** or **-aria** [Latin, from neuter of -arius -ary]
**:** thing or place relating to or connected with ⟨planetarium⟩
**ark** \'ärk\ noun [Middle English, from Old English arc, from Latin arca chest; akin to Latin arcēre to hold off, defend, Greek arkein, Hittite ḫark- to have, hold] (before 12th century)
**1 a :** a boat or ship held to resemble that in which Noah and his family were preserved from the Flood **b :** something that affords protection and safety **2 a :** the sacred chest representing to the Hebrews the presence of God among them **b :** a repository traditionally in or against the wall of a synagogue for the scrolls of the Torah
**ar·kose** \'är-ˌkōs, -ˌköz\ noun [French] (1839)
**:** a sandstone characterized by feldspar fragments that is derived from granite or gneiss which has disintegrated rapidly
— **ar·ko·sic** \(ˌ)är-'kō-sik, -zik\ adjective
**¹arm** \'ärm\ noun [Middle English, from Old English earm; akin to Latin armus shoulder, Sanskrit īrma arm] (before 12th century)

**1 :** a human upper limb; especially **:** the part between the shoulder and the wrist **2 :** something like or corresponding to an arm: as **a :** the forelimb of a vertebrate **b :** a limb of an invertebrate animal **c :** a branch or lateral shoot of a plant **d :** a slender part of a structure, machine, or an instrument projecting from a main part, axis, or fulcrum **e :** the end of a ship's yard; also **:** the part of an anchor from the crown to the fluke — see ANCHOR illustration **f :** any of the usually two parts of a chromosome lateral to the centromere **3 :** an inlet of water (as from the sea) **4 :** a narrow extension of a larger area, mass, or group **5 :** POWER, MIGHT ⟨the long arm of the law⟩ **6 :** a support (as on a chair) for the elbow and forearm **7 :** SLEEVE **8 :** the ability to throw or pitch a baseball well; also **:** a player having such ability **9 :** a functional division of a group, organization, institution, or activity ⟨the logistical arm of the air force⟩
— **arm·less** \'ärm-ləs\ adjective
— **arm·like** \-ˌlīk\ adjective
— **arm in arm :** with arms linked together ⟨walked down the street arm in arm⟩
**²arm** verb [Middle English armen, from Old French armer, from Latin armare, from arma weapons, tools; akin to Latin ars skill, Greek harmos joint, arariskein to fit] (12th century)
transitive verb
**1 :** to furnish or equip with weapons **2 :** to furnish with something that strengthens or protects **3 :** to fortify morally **4 :** to equip or ready for action or operation ⟨arm a bomb⟩
intransitive verb
**:** to prepare oneself for struggle or resistance
**³arm** noun, often attributive [Middle English armes (plural) weapons, from Old French, from Latin arma] (13th century)
**1 a :** a means (as a weapon) of offense or defense; especially **:** FIREARM **b :** a combat branch (as of an army) **c :** an organized branch of national defense (as the navy) **2** plural **a :** the hereditary heraldic devices of a family **b :** heraldic devices adopted by a government **3** plural **a :** active hostilities **:** WARFARE **b :** military service
— **up in arms :** aroused and ready to undertake hostilities
**ar·ma·da** \är-'mä-də, -'mā- also -'ma-\ noun [Spanish, from Medieval Latin armata army, fleet, from Latin, feminine of armatus, past participle of armare to arm, from arma] (1533)
**1 :** a fleet of warships **2 :** a large force or group usually of moving things ⟨an armada of fishing boats⟩
**ar·ma·dil·lo** \ˌär-mə-'di-(ˌ)lō\ noun, plural **-los** [Spanish, from diminutive of armado armed one, from Latin armatus] (1577)
**:** any of a family (Dasypodidae) of burrowing edentate mammals found from the southern U.S. to Argentina and having the body and head encased in an armor of small bony plates

armadillo

**Ar·ma·ged·don** \ˌär-mə-'ge-d³n\ noun [Greek Armageddōn, Harmagedōn, scene of the battle foretold in Revelation 16:14–16] (1534)
**1 a :** the site or time of a final and conclusive battle between the forces of good and evil **b :** the battle taking place at Armageddon **2 :** a usually vast decisive conflict or confrontation

**Ar·ma·gnac** \'är-mən-ˌyak\ noun [French, from Armagnac, region in southwest France] (1850)
**:** a brandy produced in the Gers department of France
**ar·ma·ment** \'är-mə-mənt also 'ärm-mənt\ noun [French armement, from Latin armamenta (plural) utensils, military or naval equipment, from armare] (1699)
**1 :** a military or naval force **2 a :** the aggregate of a nation's military strength **b :** WEAPONS, ARMS **3 :** the process of preparing for war
**ar·ma·men·tar·i·um** \ˌär-mə-ˌmen-'ter-ē-əm, -mən-\ noun, plural **-tar·ia** \-ē-ə\ [Latin, armory, from armamenta] (circa 1860)
**1 :** the equipment and methods used especially in medicine **2 :** matter available or utilized for an undertaking or field of activity ⟨a whole armamentarium of devices to create an illusion of real life —Kenneth Rexroth⟩
**arm and a leg** noun (1967)
**:** an exorbitant price
**ar·ma·ture** \'är-mə-ˌchùr, -chər, -ˌtyùr, -ˌtùr\ noun [Latin armatura armor, equipment, from armatus] (15th century)
**1 :** an organ or structure (as teeth or thorns) for offense or defense **2 a :** a piece of soft iron or steel that connects the poles of a magnet or of adjacent magnets **b :** a usually rotating part of an electric machine (as a generator or motor) which consists essentially of coils of wire around a metal core and in which electric current is induced or in which the input current interacts with a magnetic field to produce torque **c :** the movable part of an electromagnetic device (as a loudspeaker) **d :** a framework used by a sculptor to support a figure being modeled in a plastic material **e :** FRAMEWORK 1b ⟨the armature of the book derives from fourteenth century England —Stanley Kauffmann⟩
**arm·band** \'ärm-ˌband\ noun (1797)
**:** a band usually worn around the upper part of a sleeve for identification or in mourning
**¹arm·chair** \'ärm-ˌcher, -ˌchar\ noun (1633)
**:** a chair with armrests
**²armchair** adjective (1886)
**1 :** remote from direct dealing with problems **:** theoretical rather than practical ⟨armchair strategists⟩ **2 :** sharing vicariously in another's experiences ⟨an armchair traveler⟩
**¹armed** \'ärmd\ adjective (13th century)
**1 a :** furnished with weapons **b :** furnished with something that provides security, strength, or efficacy **2 :** marked by the maintenance of armed forces in readiness
**²armed** adjective (1606)
**:** having an arm or arms especially of a specified kind or number — usually used in combination ⟨long-armed⟩ ⟨two-armed⟩
**armed forces** noun plural (1943)
**:** the combined military, naval, and air forces of a nation — called also armed services
**Ar·me·nian** \är-'mē-nē-ən, -nyən\ noun (1537)
**1 :** a member of a people dwelling chiefly in Armenia and neighboring areas (as Turkey or Azerbaijan) **2 :** the Indo-European language of the Armenians — see INDO-EUROPEAN LANGUAGES table **3 :** a member of the Armenian church established by Saint Gregory the Illuminator that adheres to the decisions of the first three ecumenical councils
— **Armenian** adjective
**arm·ful** \'ärm-ˌfùl\ noun, plural **arm·fuls** \-ˌfùlz\ or **arms·ful** \'ärmz-ˌfùl\ (1579)
**:** as much as the arm or arms can hold
**arm·hole** \'ärm-ˌhōl\ noun (circa 1775)
**:** an opening for the arm in a garment
**ar·mi·ger** \'är-mi-jər\ noun [Medieval Latin,

from Latin, armor-bearer, from *armiger* bearing arms, from *arma* arms + *gerere* to carry] (1762)
**1** : SQUIRE
**2** : one entitled to bear heraldic arms
— **ar·mig·er·al** \är-'mi-jə-rəl\ *adjective*
**ar·mig·er·ous** \är-'mi-jər-əs\ *adjective* (circa 1731)
: bearing heraldic arms
**ar·mil·la·ry sphere** \'är-mə-ˌler-ē-, är-'mi-lə-rē-\ *noun* [French *sphère armillaire*, from Medieval Latin *armilla*, from Latin, bracelet, iron ring, from *armus* shoulder — more at ARM] (1664)
: an old astronomical instrument composed of rings showing the positions of important circles of the celestial sphere
**Ar·min·i·an** \är-'mi-nē-ən\ *adjective* (1618)
: of or relating to Arminius or his doctrines opposing the absolute predestination of strict Calvinism and maintaining the possibility of salvation for all
— **Arminian** *noun*
— **Ar·min·i·an·ism** \-nē-ə-ˌni-zəm\ *noun*
**ar·mi·stice** \'är-mə-stəs\ *noun* [French or New Latin; French, from New Latin *armistitium*, from Latin *arma* + *-stitium* (as in *solstitium* solstice)] (circa 1707)
: temporary suspension of hostilities by agreement between the opponents : TRUCE
**Armistice Day** *noun* [from the armistice terminating World War I on November 11, 1918] (1919)
: VETERANS DAY — used before the official adoption of *Veterans Day* in 1954
**arm·let** \'ärm-lət\ *noun* (1535)
**1** : a band (as of cloth or metal) worn around the upper arm
**2** : a small arm (as of the sea)
**arm·load** \'ärm-ˌlōd\ *noun* (1906)
: ARMFUL
**arm·lock** \-ˌläk\ *noun* (1905)
: HAMMERLOCK
**ar·moire** \ärm-'wär, *Southern also* 'är-mər\ *noun* [Middle French, from Old French *armaire*, from Latin *armarium*, from *arma*] (1571)
: a usually tall cupboard or wardrobe
**ar·mor** \'är-mər\ *noun* [Middle English *armure*, from Old French, from Latin *armatura* — more at ARMATURE] (13th century)
**1** : defensive covering for the body; *especially* : covering (as of metal) used in combat
**2** : a quality or circumstance that affords protection ⟨the *armor* of prosperity⟩
**3** : a protective outer layer (as of a ship, a plant or animal, or a cable)
**4** : armored forces and vehicles (as tanks)
— **armor** *transitive verb*
— **ar·mored** \-mərd\ *adjective*
— **ar·mor·less** \-mər-ləs\ *adjective*
**armored scale** *noun* (circa 1903)
: any of a family (Diaspididae) of scale insects having a firm covering of wax best developed in the female
**ar·mor·er** \'är-mər-ər\ *noun* (14th century)
**1** : one that makes armor or arms
**2** : one that repairs, assembles, and tests firearms
**ar·mo·ri·al** \är-'mōr-ē-əl, -'mȯr-\ *adjective* [*armory* (heraldry)] (1576)
: of, relating to, or bearing heraldic arms
— **ar·mo·ri·al·ly** \-ē-ə-lē\ *adverb*

armor 1:
*1 helmet, 2 gorget, 3 shoulder piece, 4 pallette, 5 breastplate, 6 brassard, 7 elbow piece, 8 skirt of tasses, 9 tuille, 10 gauntlet, 11 cuisse, 12 knee piece, 13 jambeau, 14 solleret*

**Ar·mor·i·can** \är-'mȯr-i-kən, -'mär-\ *or* **Ar·mor·ic** \-ik\ *noun* (circa 1645)
: a native or inhabitant of Armorica; *especially* : BRETON
— **Armorican** *or* **Armoric** *adjective*
**ar·mory** \'ärm-rē, 'är-mə-\ *noun, plural* **ar·mor·ies** (14th century)
**1 a** : a supply of arms for defense or attack **b** : a collection of available resources
**2** : a place where arms and military equipment are stored; *especially* : one used for training reserve military personnel
**3** : a place where arms are manufactured
**ar·mour, ar·moury** *chiefly British variant of* ARMOR, ARMORY
**arm·pit** \'ärm-ˌpit\ *noun* (14th century)
**1** : the hollow beneath the junction of the arm and shoulder
**2** : the least desirable place : PIT ⟨77th Street Station . . . was the *armpit* of detective duty —Joseph Wambaugh⟩
**arm·rest** \-ˌrest\ *noun* (circa 1889)
: a support for the arm
**arm's length** *noun* (circa 1909)
**1** : a distance discouraging personal contact or familiarity ⟨kept people at *arm's length*⟩
**2** : the condition or fact that the parties to a transaction are independent and on an equal footing
— **arm's–length** *adjective*
**arm–twist·ing** \-ˌtwis-tiŋ\ *noun* (1948)
: the use of direct personal pressure in order to achieve a desired end ⟨for all the *arm-twisting*, the . . . vote on the measure was unexpectedly tight —*Newsweek*⟩
— **arm–twist** \-ˌtwist\ *verb*
**arm wrestling** *noun* (1973)
: a form of wrestling in which two opponents sit face to face gripping usually their right hands, set corresponding elbows firmly on a surface (as a tabletop), and attempt to force each other's arm down — called also *Indian wrestling*
**ar·my** \'är-mē\ *noun, plural* **armies** [Middle English *armee*, from Middle French, from Medieval Latin *armata* — more at ARMADA] (14th century)
**1 a** : a large organized body of armed personnel trained for war especially on land **b** : a unit capable of independent action and consisting usually of a headquarters, two or more corps, and auxiliary troops **c** *often capitalized* : the complete military organization of a nation for land warfare
**2** : a great multitude ⟨an *army* of bicycles —Norm Fruchter⟩
**3** : a body of persons organized to advance a cause
**army ant** *noun* (1874)
: any of a subfamily (Dorylinae) of aggressive nomadic tropical ants that prey on insects and spiders
**ar·my·worm** \'är-mē-ˌwərm\ *noun* (1816)
: any of numerous moths whose larvae travel in multitudes from field to field destroying grass, grain, and other crops; *especially* : the common armyworm (*Pseudaletia unipuncta*) of the northern U.S.
**ar·ni·ca** \'är-ni-kə\ *noun* [New Latin] (circa 1753)
: any of a genus (*Arnica*) of composite herbs including some with bright yellow ray flowers
**ar·oid** \'ar-ˌȯid, 'er-\ *adjective* [New Latin *Arum*] (circa 1890)
: of or relating to the arum family
— **aroid** *noun*
**aroint** \ə-'rȯint\ *verb imperative* [origin unknown] (1605)
*archaic* : BEGONE ⟨*aroint* thee, witch —Shakespeare⟩
**aro·ma** \ə-'rō-mə\ *noun* [Middle English *aromat* spice, from Old French, from Latin *aromat-, aroma*, from Greek *arōmat-, arōma*] (1814)
**1 a** : a distinctive pervasive and usually pleasant or savory smell; *broadly* : ODOR **b** : the

odor of a wine imparted by the grapes from which it is made
**2** : a distinctive quality or atmosphere : FLAVOR ⟨the *aroma* of enjoyment —Stella D. Gibbons⟩
**synonym** see SMELL
**aro·ma·ther·a·py** \ə-ˌrō-mə-'ther-ə-pē\ *noun* [French *aromathérapie*, from Latin *aroma* + French *thérapie* therapy] (1969)
: massage of the body and especially of the face with a preparation of fragrant essential oils extracted from herbs, flowers, and fruits
— **aro·ma·ther·a·pist** \-pist\ *noun*
¹**ar·o·mat·ic** \ˌar-ə-'ma-tik\ *adjective* (14th century)
**1** : of, relating to, or having aroma: **a** : FRAGRANT **b** : having a strong smell **c** : having a distinctive quality
**2** : of an organic compound : characterized by increased chemical stability resulting from the delocalization of electrons in a ring system (as benzene) containing usually multiple conjugated double bonds — compare ALICYCLIC, ALIPHATIC
**synonym** see ODOROUS
— **ar·o·mat·i·cal·ly** \-ti-k(ə-)lē\ *adverb*
— **aro·ma·tic·i·ty** \ˌar-ə-mə-'ti-sə-tē, ə-ˌrō-mə-\ *noun*
²**aromatic** *noun* (15th century)
**1** : an aromatic plant or plant part; *especially* : an aromatic herb or spice
**2** : an aromatic organic compound
**aro·ma·tize** \ə-'rō-mə-ˌtīz\ *transitive verb* **-tized; -tiz·ing** (15th century)
**1** : to make aromatic : FLAVOR
**2** : to convert into one or more aromatic compounds
— **aro·ma·ti·za·tion** \-ˌrō-mə-tə-'zā-shən\ *noun*
**arose** *past of* ARISE
¹**around** \ə-'raund\ *adverb* [Middle English, from ¹*a-* + ²*round*] (14th century)
**1 a** : in a circle or in circumference ⟨the wheel goes *around*⟩ ⟨a tree five feet *around*⟩ **b** : in, along, or through a circuit ⟨the road goes *around* by the lake⟩
**2 a** : on all or various sides : in every or any direction ⟨papers lying *around*⟩ ⟨nothing for miles *around*⟩ **b** : in close from all sides so as to surround ⟨people crowded *around*⟩ **c** : in or near one's present place or situation ⟨wait *around* awhile⟩
**3 a** : here and there : from one place to another ⟨travels *around* on business⟩ **b** : to a particular place ⟨come *around* for dinner⟩
**4 a** : in rotation or succession ⟨another winter comes *around*⟩ **b** : from beginning to end : THROUGH ⟨mild the year *around*⟩ **c** : in order ⟨the other way *around*⟩
**5** : in or to an opposite direction or position ⟨turn *around*⟩
**6** : with some approach to exactness : APPROXIMATELY ⟨cost *around* $5⟩
²**around** *preposition* (14th century)
**1 a** : on all sides of **b** : so as to encircle or enclose ⟨seated *around* the table⟩ **c** : so as to avoid or get past : on or to another side of ⟨find a way *around* their objections⟩ ⟨went *around* the lake⟩ ⟨*around* the corner⟩ **d** : NEAR ⟨lives *around* Chicago⟩ ⟨*around* the turn of the century⟩
**2** : in all directions outward from ⟨look *around* you⟩
**3** : here and there in or throughout ⟨barnstorming *around* the country⟩
**4** : so as to have a center or basis in ⟨a society organized *around* kinship ties⟩
³**around** *adjective* (1849)
**1** : ABOUT 1 ⟨has been up and *around* for two days⟩

**2 :** being in existence, evidence, or circulation ⟨the most intelligent of the artists *around* today —R. M. Coates⟩
**— been around :** gone through many varied experiences **:** become worldly-wise
**around–the–clock** *adjective* (1943)
**:** being in effect, continuing, or lasting 24 hours a day **:** CONSTANT
**arouse** \ə-'raŭz\ *verb* **aroused; arous·ing** [*a-* (as in *arise*) + *rouse*] (1593)
*transitive verb*
**1 :** to awaken from sleep
**2 :** to rouse or stimulate to action or to physiological readiness for activity **:** EXCITE ⟨the book *aroused* debate⟩
*intransitive verb*
**:** to awake from sleep **:** STIR
**— arous·al** \ə-'raŭ-zəl\ *noun*
**ar·peg·gi·ate** \är-'pe-jē-ät\ *transitive verb* **-at·ed; -at·ing** (1953)
**:** to play (as a chord or passage) in arpeggio
**ar·peg·gio** \är-'pe-jē-ō, -'pe-jō\ *noun, plural* **-gios** [Italian, from *arpeggiare* to play on the harp, from *arpa* harp, of Germanic origin; akin to Old High German *harpha* harp] (circa 1724)
**1 :** production of the tones of a chord in succession and not simultaneously
**2 :** a chord played in arpeggio
**ar·pent** \är-'päⁿ\ *noun, plural* **ar·pents** \-'päⁿ(z)\ [Middle French] (1580)
**1 :** any of various old French units of land area; *especially* **:** one used in French sections of Canada and the U.S. equal to about 0.85 acre (0.34 hectare)
**2 :** a unit of length equal to one side of a square arpent
**ar·que·bus** \'är-kwi-(,)bəs, -kə-bəs\ *variant of* HARQUEBUS
**ar·rack** \'ar-ək, ə-'rak\ *noun* [Arabic *'araq* sweet juice, liquor] (1521)
**:** an Asian alcoholic beverage like rum that is distilled from a fermented mash of malted rice with toddy or molasses
**ar·raign** \ə-'rān\ *transitive verb* [Middle English *arreinen*, from Middle French *araisner*, from Old French, from *a-* (from Latin *ad-*) + *raisnier* to speak, from (assumed) Vulgar Latin *ratiōnare*, from Latin *ration-, ratio* reason — more at REASON] (14th century)
**1 :** to call (a defendant) before a court to answer to an indictment **:** CHARGE
**2 :** to accuse of wrong, inadequacy, or imperfection
**— ar·raign·ment** \-mənt\ *noun*
**ar·range** \ə-'rānj\ *verb* **-ranged; -rang·ing** [Middle English *arangen*, from Middle French *arangier*, from Old French, from *a-* + *rengier* to set in a row, from *reng* row — more at RANK] (1789)
*transitive verb*
**1 :** to make preparations for **:** PLAN ⟨*arranged* a reception for the visitor⟩
**2 :** to put into a proper order or into a correct or suitable sequence, relationship, or adjustment ⟨*arrange* flowers in a vase⟩ ⟨*arrange* cards alphabetically⟩
**3 a :** to adapt (a musical composition) by scoring for voices or instruments other than those for which originally written **b :** ORCHESTRATE
**4 :** to bring about an agreement or understanding concerning **:** SETTLE ⟨*arrange* an exchange of war prisoners⟩
*intransitive verb*
**1 :** to bring about an agreement or understanding ⟨*arranged* to have a table at the restaurant⟩
**2 :** to make preparations **:** PLAN ⟨*arranged* for a vacation with his family⟩
**synonym** see ORDER
**— ar·rang·er** \ə-'rān-jər\ *noun*
**ar·range·ment** \ə-'rānj-mənt\ *noun* (1690)
**1 a :** the state of being arranged **:** ORDER ⟨everything in neat *arrangement*⟩ **b :** the act of arranging ⟨the *arrangement* of the details was quickly accomplished⟩

**2 :** something arranged: as **a :** a preliminary measure **:** PREPARATION ⟨travel *arrangements*⟩
**b :** an adaptation of a musical composition by rescoring **c :** an informal agreement or settlement especially on personal, social, or political matters ⟨*arrangements* under the new regime⟩
**3 :** something made by arranging parts or things together ⟨a floral *arrangement*⟩
**ar·rant** \'ar-ənt\ *adjective* [alteration of *errant*] (1553)
**:** being notoriously without moderation **:** EXTREME ⟨we are *arrant* knaves, all; believe none of us —Shakespeare⟩
**— ar·rant·ly** *adverb*
**ar·ras** \'ar-əs\ *noun, plural* **arras** [Middle English, from *Arras*, France] (15th century)
**1 :** a tapestry of Flemish origin used especially for wall hangings and curtains
**2 :** a wall hanging or screen of tapestry
¹**ar·ray** \ə-'rā\ *transitive verb* [Middle English, from Old French *arayer*, from (assumed) Vulgar Latin *arredare*, from Latin *ad-* + a base of Germanic origin; akin to Gothic *garaiths* arranged — more at READY] (14th century)
**1 :** to dress or decorate especially in splendid or impressive attire **:** ADORN
**2 a :** to set or place in order **:** DRAW UP, MARSHAL **b :** to set or set forth in order (as a jury) for the trial of a cause
**— ar·ray·er** *noun*
²**array** *noun* (14th century)
**1 a :** a regular and imposing grouping or arrangement **:** ORDER ⟨lined up . . . in soldierly *array* —Donald Barthelme⟩ **b :** an orderly listing of jurors impaneled
**2 a :** CLOTHING, ATTIRE **b :** rich or beautiful apparel **:** FINERY
**3 :** a body of soldiers **:** MILITIA ⟨the baron and his feudal *array*⟩
**4 :** an imposing group **:** large number ⟨faced a whole *array* of problems⟩
**5 a** (1) **:** a number of mathematical elements arranged in rows and columns (2) **:** a data structure in which similar elements of data are arranged in a table **b :** a series of statistical data arranged in classes in order of magnitude
**6 :** a group of elements forming a complete unit ⟨an antenna *array*⟩
**ar·rear** \ə-'rir\ *noun* [Middle English *arrere* behind, backward, from Middle French, from (assumed) Vulgar Latin *ad retro* backward, from Latin *ad* to + *retro* backward, behind — more at AT, RETRO-] (1620)
**1 :** the state of being behind in the discharge of obligations — usually used in plural ⟨in *arrears* with the rent⟩
**2 a :** an unfinished duty — usually used in plural ⟨*arrears* of work that have piled up⟩ **b :** an unpaid and overdue debt — usually used in plural ⟨paying off the *arrears* of the past several months⟩
**ar·rear·age** \-ij\ *noun* (14th century)
**1 :** the condition of being in arrears
**2 :** something unpaid and overdue; *especially* **:** something unpaid and overdue
¹**ar·rest** \ə-'rest\ *transitive verb* [Middle English *aresten*, from Middle French *arester* to rest, arrest, from (assumed) Vulgar Latin *arrestare*, from Latin *ad-* + *restare* to remain — more at REST] (14th century)
**1 a :** to bring to a stop ⟨sickness *arrested* his activities⟩ **b :** CHECK, SLOW **c :** to make inactive ⟨an *arrested* tumor⟩
**2 :** SEIZE, CAPTURE; *specifically* **:** to take or keep in custody by authority of law
**3 :** to catch suddenly and engagingly
**— ar·rest·er** *or* **ar·res·tor** \-'res-tər\ *noun*
**— ar·rest·ment** \-'res(t)-mənt\ *noun*
²**arrest** *noun* (14th century)
**1 a :** the act of stopping **b :** the condition of being stopped or inactive
**2 :** the taking or detaining in custody by authority of law
**— under arrest :** in legal custody
**ar·res·tant** \ə-'res-tənt\ *noun* (1962)

**:** a substance that stimulates an insect to stop locomotion
**ar·rest·ee** \ə-,res-'tē\ *noun* (1944)
**:** one that is under arrest
**ar·rest·ing** \ə-'res-tiŋ\ *adjective* (1792)
**:** catching the attention **:** STRIKING, IMPRESSIVE
**— ar·rest·ing·ly** \-tiŋ-lē\ *adverb*
**ar·rhyth·mia** \ā-'rith-mē-ə\ *noun* [New Latin, from Greek, lack of rhythm, from *arrhythmos* unrhythmical, from *a-* + *rhythmos* rhythm] (circa 1860)
**:** an alteration in rhythm of the heartbeat either in time or force
**ar·rhyth·mic** \-mik\ *adjective* [Greek *arrhythmos*] (1853)
**:** lacking rhythm or regularity ⟨*arrhythmic* locomotor activity⟩
**ar·ri·ère–ban** \,ar-ē-,er-'bän, -'ban\ *noun* [French] (1523)
**:** a proclamation of a king (as of France) calling his vassals to arms; *also* **:** the body of vassals summoned
**ar·ri·ère–pen·sée** \-pän-'sā\ *noun* [French, from *arrière* in back + *pensée* thought] (1824)
**:** mental reservation
**ar·ris** \'ar-əs\ *noun, plural* **arris** *or* **ar·ris·es** [probably modification of Middle French *areste*, literally, fishbone, from Late Latin *arista* — more at ARÊTE] (1677)
**:** the sharp edge or salient angle formed by the meeting of two surfaces especially in moldings
**ar·riv·al** \ə-'rī-vəl\ *noun* (14th century)
**1 :** the act of arriving
**2 :** the attainment of an end or state
**3 :** one that has recently reached a destination
**ar·rive** \ə-'rīv\ *intransitive verb* **ar·rived; ar·riv·ing** [Middle English *ariven*, from Old French *ariver*, from (assumed) Vulgar Latin *arripare* to come to shore, from Latin *ad-* + *ripa* shore — more at RIVE] (13th century)
**1 a :** to reach a destination **b :** to make an appearance ⟨the guests have *arrived*⟩
**2 a** archaic **:** HAPPEN **b :** to be near in time **:** COME ⟨the moment has *arrived*⟩
**3 :** to achieve success
**— ar·riv·er** *noun*
**— arrive at :** to reach by effort or thought ⟨*arrived at* a decision⟩
**ar·ri·vé** \,ar-i-'vā\ *noun* [French, from past participle of *arriver* to arrive, from Old French *ariver*] (1925)
**:** one who has risen rapidly to success, power, or fame
**ar·ri·viste** \-'vēst\ *noun* [French, from *arriver*] (1901)
**:** one that is a new and uncertain arrival (as in social position or artistic endeavor)
**ar·ro·ba** \ə-'rō-bə\ *noun* [Spanish & Portuguese, from Arabic *ar-rub'*, literally, the quarter] (1555)
**1 :** an old Spanish unit of weight equal to about 25 pounds
**2 :** an old Portuguese unit of weight equal to about 32 pounds
**ar·ro·gance** \'ar-ə-gən(t)s\ *noun* (14th century)
**:** a feeling or an impression of superiority manifested in an overbearing manner or presumptuous claims
**ar·ro·gant** \-gənt\ *adjective* [Middle English, from Latin *arrogant-, arrogans*, present participle of *arrogare*] (14th century)
**1 :** exaggerating or disposed to exaggerate one's own worth or importance in an overbearing manner ⟨an *arrogant* official⟩
**2 :** proceeding from or characterized by arrogance ⟨*arrogant* manners⟩
**synonym** see PROUD
**— ar·ro·gant·ly** *adverb*
**ar·ro·gate** \-,gāt\ *transitive verb* **-gat·ed; -gat·ing** [Latin *arrogatus*, past participle of *arrogare*, from *ad-* + *rogare* to ask — more at RIGHT] (1537)
**1 a :** to claim or seize without justification **b :** to make undue claims to having **:** ASSUME

**2 :** to claim on behalf of another **:** ASCRIBE
— **ar·ro·ga·tion** \ˌar-ə-'gā-shən\ *noun*
**ar·ron·disse·ment** \ə-'rän-də-smənt, ˌar-ˌōⁿ-(ˌ)dē-'smäⁿ\ *noun* [French] (1807)
**1 :** an administrative district of some large French cities
**2 :** the largest division of a French department
¹**ar·row** \'ar-(ˌ)ō\ *noun* [Middle English *arwe*, from Old English; akin to Gothic *arhwazna* arrow, Latin *arcus* bow, arch, arc] (before 12th century)
**1 :** a missile weapon shot from a bow and usually having a slender shaft, a pointed head, and feathers at the butt
**2 :** something shaped like an arrow; *especially* **:** a mark (as on a map or signboard) to indicate direction

arrow 1

²**arrow** *intransitive verb* (1827)
**:** to move fast and straight like an arrow in flight **:** DART
**ar·row·head** \'ar-ō-ˌhed, 'ar-ə-\ *noun* (14th century)
**1 :** a wedge-shaped piercing tip usually fixed to an arrow
**2 :** something resembling an arrowhead

arrowhead 1

**3 :** any of a genus (*Sagittaria*) of marsh or aquatic plants of the water-plantain family with leaves shaped like arrowheads
**ar·row·root** \-ˌrüt, -ˌrut\ *noun* (1696)
**1 a :** any of a genus (*Maranta* of the family Marantaceae, the arrowroot family) of tropical American plants with tuberous roots; *especially* **:** one (*M. arundinacea*) whose roots yield an easily digested edible starch **b :** any of several plants (as coontie) that yield starch
**2 :** starch yielded by an arrowroot
**ar·row·wood** \-ˌwud\ *noun* (1709)
**:** any of several common viburnums (especially *Viburnum dentatum*) of the eastern U.S.
**ar·row·worm** \-ˌwərm\ *noun* (circa 1889)
**:** any of a phylum (Chaetognatha) of small planktonic wormlike marine organisms having curved bristles on either side of the head for seizing prey
**ar·rowy** \'ar-ə-wē\ *adjective* (1637)
**1 :** resembling or suggesting an arrow; *especially* **:** swiftly moving
**2 :** consisting of arrows
**ar·royo** \ə-'rȯi-(ˌ)ō, -ə\ *noun, plural* **-royos** [Spanish] (1843)
**1 :** a watercourse (as a creek) in an arid region
**2 :** a water-carved gully or channel
**ar·roz con po·llo** \ä-ˌrȯth-(ˌ)kȯn-'pōl-(ˌ)yō, -ˌpō-(ˌ)yō\ *noun* [Spanish, literally, rice with chicken] (1938)
**:** chicken cooked with rice and usually flavored with saffron
**arse** *variant of* ASS
**ar·se·nal** \'ärs-nəl, 'är-s°n-əl\ *noun* [Italian *arsenale*, ultimately from Arabic *dār ṣinā'ah* house of manufacture] (1555)
**1 a :** an establishment for the manufacture or storage of arms and military equipment **b :** a collection of weapons
**2 :** STORE, REPERTORY ⟨the team's *arsenal* of veteran players⟩
**ar·se·nate** \'ärs-nət, 'är-s°n-ət, -s°n-ˌāt\ *noun* (1800)
**:** a salt or ester of an arsenic acid

¹**ar·se·nic** \'ärs-nik, -s°n-ik\ *noun* [Middle English, yellow orpiment, from Middle French & Latin; Middle French, from Latin *arsenicum*, from Greek *arsenikon, arrhenikon*, from Syriac *zarnīg*, of Iranian origin; akin to Avestan *zaranya* gold, Sanskrit *hari* yellowish — more at YELLOW] (14th century)
**1 :** a trivalent and pentavalent solid poisonous element that is commonly metallic steel-gray, crystalline, and brittle — see ELEMENT table
**2 :** a poisonous trioxide $As_2O_3$ or $As_4O_6$ of arsenic used especially as an insecticide or weed killer — called also *arsenic trioxide*
²**ar·sen·ic** \är-'se-nik\ *adjective* (1801)
**:** of, relating to, or containing arsenic especially with a valence of five
**ar·sen·i·cal** \är-'se-ni-kəl\ *adjective* (1605)
**:** of, relating to, containing, or caused by arsenic ⟨*arsenical* poisoning⟩
— **arsenical** *noun*
**ar·se·nide** \'är-s°n-ˌīd\ *noun* (circa 1859)
**:** a binary compound of arsenic with a more positive element
**ar·se·ni·ous** \är-'sē-nē-əs\ *adjective* (1818)
**:** of, relating to, or containing arsenic especially when trivalent
**ar·se·nite** \'är-s°n-ˌīt\ *noun* (1800)
**:** a salt or ester of an arsenious acid
**ar·se·no·py·rite** \ˌär-s°n-ō-'pī-ˌrīt\ *noun* (1881)
**:** a mineral consisting of a combined sulfide and arsenide of iron occurring in prismatic orthorhombic crystals or in masses or grains
**ar·sine** \är-'sēn, 'är-ˌ\ *noun* [International Scientific Vocabulary, from *arsenic*] (1876)
**:** a colorless flammable extremely poisonous gas $AsH_3$ with an odor like garlic; *also* **:** a derivative of arsine
**ar·sis** \'är-səs\ *noun, plural* **ar·ses** \-ˌsēz\ [Late Latin & Greek; Late Latin, raising of the voice, accented part of foot, from Greek, upbeat, less important part of foot, literally, act of lifting, from *aeirein, airein* to lift] (14th century)
**1 a :** the lighter or shorter part of a poetic foot especially in quantitative verse **b :** the accented or longer part of a poetic foot especially in accentual verse
**2 :** the unaccented part of a musical measure — compare THESIS
**ar·son** \'är-s°n\ *noun* [Anglo-French *arsoun*, alteration of Old French *arsin* act of burning, from *ars*, past participle of *ardre* to burn, from Latin *ardēre* — more at ARDOR] (circa 1680)
**:** the willful or malicious burning of property (as a building) especially with criminal or fraudulent intent
— **ar·son·ist** \-ist\ *noun*
— **ar·son·ous** \-əs\ *adjective*
**ars·phen·a·mine** \ärs-'fe-nə-ˌmēn, -mən\ *noun* [International Scientific Vocabulary *arsenic* + *phenamine*] (1917)
**:** a light-yellow toxic hygroscopic powder $C_{12}Cl_2H_{14}As_2N_2O_2·2H_2O$ formerly used in the treatment especially of syphilis and yaws
¹**art** \'ärt, ərt\ [Middle English, from Old English *eart*; akin to Old Norse *est, ert* (thou) art, Old English *is* is] *archaic present 2d singular of* BE
²**art** \'ärt\ *noun* [Middle English, from Old French, from Latin *art-, ars* — more at ARM] (13th century)
**1 :** skill acquired by experience, study, or observation ⟨the *art* of making friends⟩
**2 a :** a branch of learning: (1) **:** one of the humanities (2) *plural* **:** LIBERAL ARTS **b** *archaic* **:** LEARNING, SCHOLARSHIP
**3 :** an occupation requiring knowledge or skill ⟨the *art* of organ building⟩
**4 a :** the conscious use of skill and creative imagination especially in the production of aesthetic objects; *also* **:** works so produced **b** (1) **:** FINE ARTS (2) **:** one of the fine arts (3) **:** a graphic art
**5 a** *archaic* **:** a skillful plan **b :** the quality or state of being artful

**6 :** decorative or illustrative elements in printed matter ☆
**-art** — see -ARD
**art de·co** \ˌärt-'de-ˌkō; ˌär(t)-dā-'kō, 'är(t)-'dā-(ˌ)kō\ *noun, often A&D capitalized* [French *Art Déco*, from *Exposition Internationale des Arts Décoratifs et Industriels Modernes,* an exposition of modern decorative and industrial arts held in Paris, France, in 1925] (1966)
**:** a popular design style of the 1920s and 1930s characterized especially by bold outlines, geometric and zigzag forms, and the use of new materials (as plastic)
**ar·te·fact** *chiefly British variant of* ARTIFACT
**ar·tel** \är-'tel; -'tel'\ *noun* [Russian *artel'*] (1884)
**:** a workers' or craftsmen's cooperative in Russia and later the U.S.S.R
**Ar·te·mis** \'är-tə-məs\ *noun* [Greek]
**:** a Greek moon goddess often portrayed as a virgin huntress — compare DIANA
**ar·te·mi·sia** \ˌär-tə-'mi-zh(ē-)ə, -zē-ə\ *noun* [New Latin, from Latin, artemisia, from Greek, wormwood] (14th century)
**:** any of a genus (*Artemisia*) of aromatic composite herbs and shrubs (as sagebrush) — compare WORMWOOD 1
**arteri-** *or* **arterio-** *combining form* [Greek *artēri-, artērio-,* from *artēria* artery]
**1 :** artery ⟨*arteriogram*⟩
**2 :** arterial and ⟨*arterio*venous⟩
¹**ar·te·ri·al** \är-'tir-ē-əl\ *adjective* (15th century)
**1 a :** of or relating to an artery **b :** relating to or being the bright red blood present in most arteries that has been oxygenated in lungs or gills
**2 :** of, relating to, or constituting through traffic
— **ar·te·ri·al·ly** \-ē-ə-lē\ *adverb*
²**arterial** *noun* (1932)
**:** a through street or highway
**ar·te·rio·gram** \är-'tir-ē-ə-ˌgram\ *noun* [International Scientific Vocabulary] (1929)
**:** a roentgenogram of an artery made by arteriography
**ar·te·ri·og·ra·phy** \är-ˌtir-ē-'ä-grə-fē\ *noun, plural* **-phies** [International Scientific Vocabulary] (1929)
**:** the roentgenographic visualization of an artery after injection of a radiopaque substance
— **ar·te·rio·graph·ic** \-ē-ə-'gra-fik\ *adjective*
**ar·te·ri·ole** \är-'tir-ē-ˌōl\ *noun* [French or New Latin; French *artériole,* probably from New Latin *arteriola,* diminutive of Latin *arteria*] (circa 1847)
**:** any of the small terminal twigs of an artery that ends in capillaries
— **ar·te·ri·o·lar** \-ˌtir-ē-'ō-lär, -lər\ *adjective*

---

☆ **SYNONYMS**
**Art, skill, cunning, artifice, craft** mean the faculty of executing well what one has devised. ART implies a personal, unanalyzable creative power ⟨the *art* of choosing the right word⟩. SKILL stresses technical knowledge and proficiency ⟨the *skill* of a glassblower⟩. CUNNING suggests ingenuity and subtlety in devising, inventing, or executing ⟨a mystery plotted with great *cunning*⟩. ARTIFICE suggests technical skill especially in imitating things in nature ⟨believed realism in film could be achieved only by *artifice*⟩. CRAFT may imply expertness in workmanship ⟨the *craft* of a master goldsmith⟩.

---

\ə\ abut \ᵊ\ kitten \ər\ further \a\ ash \ā\ ace
\ä\ mop, mar \au̇\ out \ch\ chin \e\ bet \ē\ easy
\g\ go \i\ hit \ī\ ice \j\ job \ŋ\ sing \ō\ go
\ȯ\ law \ȯi\ boy \th\ thin \th\ the \ü\ loot \u̇\ foot
\y\ yet \zh\ vision *see also* Guide to Pronunciation

**ar·te·rio·scle·ro·sis** \är-ˌtir-ē-ō-sklə-'rō-səs\ *noun* [New Latin] (1881)
: a chronic disease characterized by abnormal thickening and hardening of the arterial walls with resulting loss of elasticity
— **ar·te·rio·scle·rot·ic** \-'rä-tik\ *adjective or noun*

**ar·te·rio·ve·nous** \-'vē-nəs\ *adjective* [International Scientific Vocabulary] (circa 1880)
: of, relating to, or connecting the arteries and veins ⟨an *arteriovenous* fistula⟩

**ar·ter·i·tis** \ˌär-tə-'rī-təs\ *noun* [New Latin] (1836)
: arterial inflammation

**ar·tery** \'är-tə-rē, 'är-trē\ *noun, plural* **-ter·ies** [Middle English *arterie*, from Latin *arteria*, from Greek *artēria*; akin to Greek *aortē* aorta] (14th century)
**1** : any of the tubular branching muscular- and elastic-walled vessels that carry blood from the heart through the body
**2** : a channel (as a river or highway) of transportation or communication; *especially* : the main channel in a branching system

**ar·te·sian well** \är-'tē-zhən-\ *noun* [French *artésien*, literally, of Artois, from Old French, from *Arteis* Artois, France] (1842)
**1** : a well in which water is under pressure; *especially* : one in which the water flows to the surface naturally
**2** : a deep well

**art film** *noun* (1926)
: a motion picture produced as an artistic effort

**art form** *noun* (1868)
**1** : a recognized form (as a symphony) or medium (as sculpture) of artistic expression
**2** : an unconventional form or medium in which impulses regarded as artistic may be expressed ⟨describe pinball as a great American *art form* —Tom Buckley⟩

**art·ful** \'ärt-fəl\ *adjective* (1615)
**1** : performed with or showing art or skill ⟨an *artful* performance on the violin⟩
**2 a** : using or characterized by art and skill : DEXTEROUS ⟨an *artful* prose stylist⟩ **b** : adroit in attaining an end often by insinuating or indirect means : WILY ⟨an *artful* cross-examiner⟩
**3** : ARTIFICIAL ⟨trim walks and *artful* bowers —William Wordsworth⟩
*synonym* see SLY
— **art·ful·ly** \-fə-lē\ *adverb*
— **art·ful·ness** *noun*

**art glass** *noun* (1926)
: articles of glass designed primarily for decorative purposes; *especially* : novelty glassware

**art historical** *adjective* (1933)
: of or relating to the history of art
— **art historically** *adverb*

**art house** *noun* (1951)
: ART THEATER

**arthr-** *or* **arthro-** *combining form* [Latin, from Greek, from *arthron*; akin to Greek *arariskein* to fit — more at ARM]
: joint ⟨*arthr*opathy⟩

**ar·thral·gia** \är-'thral-j(ē-)ə\ *noun* [New Latin] (circa 1848)
: neuralgic pain in one or more joints
— **ar·thral·gic** \-jik\ *adjective*

**ar·thrit·ic** \är-'thri-tik\ *adjective* (14th century)
**1** : of, relating to, or affected with arthritis
**2** : being or showing effects associated with aging ⟨*arthritic* anxiety⟩
— **arthritic** *noun*
— **ar·thrit·i·cal·ly** \-ti-k(ə-)lē\ *adverb*

**ar·thri·tis** \är-'thrī-təs\ *noun, plural* **-thrit·i·des** \-'thri-tə-ˌdēz\ [Latin, from Greek, from *arthron*] (1543)
: inflammation of joints due to infectious, metabolic, or constitutional causes; *also* : a specific arthritic condition

**ar·throd·e·sis** \är-'thrä-də-səs\ *noun, plural* **-e·ses** \-ˌsēz\ [New Latin, from *arthr-* + Greek *desis* binding, from *dein* to bind] (circa 1901)
: the surgical immobilization of a joint so that the bones grow solidly together

**ar·throp·a·thy** \är-'thrä-pə-thē\ *noun, plural* **-thies** (circa 1860)
: a disease of a joint

**ar·thro·pod** \'är-thrə-ˌpäd\ *noun* [New Latin *Arthropoda*, from *arthr-* + Greek *pod-*, *pous* foot — more at FOOT] (1877)
: any of a phylum (Arthropoda) of invertebrate animals (as insects, arachnids, and crustaceans) that have a segmented body and jointed appendages, a usually chitinous exoskeleton molted at intervals, and a dorsal anterior brain connected to a ventral chain of ganglia
— **arthropod** *adjective*
— **ar·throp·o·dan** \är-'thrä-pə-dən\ *adjective*

**ar·thros·co·py** \är-'thräs-kə-pē\ *noun* (circa 1935)
: visual examination of the interior of a joint (as the knee) with a special surgical instrument; *also* : joint surgery using an arthroscope
— **ar·thro·scope** \'är-thrə-ˌskōp\ *noun*
— **ar·thro·scop·ic** \ˌär-thrə-'skä-pik\ *adjective*

**ar·thro·sis** \är-'thrō-səs\ *noun, plural* **-thro·ses** \-ˌsēz\ [New Latin, from Greek *arthrōsis* jointing, articulation, from *arthroun* to articulate, from *arthron*] (1634)
**1** : an articulation between bones
**2** : a degenerative disease of a joint

**ar·thro·spore** \'är-thrə-ˌspōr, -ˌspȯr\ *noun* (1895)
: OIDIUM 1b

**Ar·thur** \'är-thər\ *noun*
: a legendary king of the Britons whose story is based on traditions of a 6th century military leader

**Ar·thu·ri·an** \är-'thur-ē-ən, -'thyur-\ *adjective* (1612)
: of or relating to King Arthur and his court

**ar·ti·choke** \'är-tə-ˌchōk\ *noun* [Italian dialect *articiocco*, ultimately from Arabic *al-khurshūf* the artichoke] (1530)
**1** : a tall composite herb (*Cynara scolymus*) like a thistle with coarse pinnately incised leaves; *also* : its edible immature flower head which is cooked as a vegetable
**2** : JERUSALEM ARTICHOKE

**¹ar·ti·cle** \'är-ti-kəl\ *noun* [Middle English, from Old French, from Latin *articulus* joint, division, diminutive of *artus* joint, limb; akin to Greek *arariskein* to fit — more at ARM] (13th century)
**1 a** : a distinct often numbered section of a writing **b** : a separate clause **c** : a stipulation in a document (as a contract or a creed) **d** : a nonfictional prose composition usually forming an independent part of a publication (as a magazine)
**2** : an item of business : MATTER
**3** : any of a small set of words or affixes (as *a*, *an*, and *the*) used with nouns to limit or give definiteness to the application
**4** : a member of a class of things; *especially* : an item of goods ⟨*articles* of value⟩
**5** : a thing of a particular and distinctive kind ⟨the genuine *article*⟩

**²article** *transitive verb* **ar·ti·cled; ar·ti·cling** \-k(ə-)liŋ\ (1820)
: to bind by articles (as of apprenticeship)

**article of faith** (15th century)
: a basic belief

**ar·tic·u·la·ble** \är-'ti-kyə-lə-bəl\ *adjective* (1833)
: capable of being articulated

**ar·tic·u·la·cy** \är-'ti-kyə-lə-sē\ *noun* (1918)
*chiefly British* : the quality or state of being articulate

**ar·tic·u·lar** \är-'ti-kyə-lər\ *adjective* [Middle English *articuler*, from Latin *articularis*, from *articulus*] (15th century)
: of or relating to a joint ⟨*articular* cartilage⟩

**¹ar·tic·u·late** \är-'ti-kyə-lət\ *adjective* [Latin *articulatus* jointed, past participle of *articulare*, from *articulus*] (1586)
**1 a** : divided into syllables or words meaningfully arranged : INTELLIGIBLE **b** : able to speak **c** : expressing oneself readily, clearly, or effectively; *also* : expressed in this manner
**2 a** : consisting of segments united by joints : JOINTED ⟨*articulate* animals⟩ **b** : distinctly marked off
— **ar·tic·u·late·ly** *adverb*
— **ar·tic·u·late·ness** *noun*

**²ar·tic·u·late** \-ˌlāt\ *verb* **-lat·ed; -lat·ing** (1594)
*transitive verb*
**1 a** : to utter distinctly ⟨*articulating* each note in the musical phrase⟩ **b** : to give clear and effective utterance to : put into words ⟨*articulate* one's grievances⟩ **c** : to give definition to (as a shape or object) ⟨shades of gray were chosen to *articulate* different spaces —Carol Vogel⟩
**2 a** : to unite by means of a joint : JOINT **b** : to form or fit into a systematic whole ⟨*articulating* a program for all school grades⟩
*intransitive verb*
**1** : to utter articulate sounds
**2** : to become united or connected by or as if by a joint
— **ar·tic·u·la·tive** \-lə-tiv, -ˌlā-\ *adjective*
— **ar·tic·u·la·tor** \-ˌlā-tər\ *noun*

**ar·tic·u·lat·ed** \-ˌlā-təd\ *adjective* (1899)
*of a vehicle* : having a hinge or pivot connection especially to allow negotiation of sharp turns ⟨*articulated* lorry⟩ ⟨*articulated* bus⟩

**ar·tic·u·la·tion** \(ˌ)är-ˌti-kyə-'lā-shən\ *noun* (15th century)
**1 a** : a joint or juncture between bones or cartilages in the skeleton of a vertebrate **b** : a movable joint between rigid parts of an animal
**2 a** : the action or manner of jointing or interrelating **b** : the state of being jointed or interrelated
**3 a** : the act of giving utterance or expression **b** : the act or manner of articulating sounds **c** : an articulated utterance or sound; *specifically* : CONSONANT
**4** : OCCLUSION 1b

**ar·tic·u·la·to·ry** \är-'ti-kyə-lə-ˌtōr-ē, -ˌtȯr-\ *adjective* (1818)
: of or relating to articulation

**ar·ti·fact** \'är-ti-ˌfakt\ *noun* [Latin *arte* by skill (ablative of *art-*, *ars* skill) + *factum*, neuter of *factus*, past participle of *facere* to do — more at ARM, DO] (1821)
**1 a** : something created by humans usually for a practical purpose; *especially* : an object remaining from a particular period ⟨caves containing prehistoric *artifacts*⟩ **b** : something characteristic of or resulting from a human institution or activity ⟨self-consciousness . . . turns out to be an *artifact* of our education system —*Times Literary Supplement*⟩
**2** : a product of artificial character (as in a scientific test) due usually to extraneous (as human) agency
— **ar·ti·fac·tu·al** \ˌär-ti-'fak-chə(-wə)l, -'fak-shwəl\ *adjective*

**ar·ti·fice** \'är-tə-fəs\ *noun* [Middle French, from Latin *artificium*, from *artific-*, *artifex* artificer, from Latin *art-*, *ars* + *facere*] (circa 1604)
**1 a** : clever or artful skill : INGENUITY ⟨believing that characters had to be created from within rather than with *artifice* —Garson Kanin⟩ **b** : an ingenious device or expedient
**2 a** : an artful stratagem : TRICK **b** : false or insincere behavior ⟨social *artifice*⟩
*synonym* see TRICK, ART

**ar·ti·fi·cer** \är-'ti-fə-sər, 'är-tə-fə-sər\ *noun* (14th century)
**1** : a skilled or artistic worker or craftsman
**2** : one that makes or contrives : DEVISER ⟨had been the *artificer* of his own fortunes —*Times Literary Supplement*⟩

**ar·ti·fi·cial** \ˌär-tə-'fi-shᵊl\ *adjective* (14th century)

**1 :** humanly contrived often on a natural model **:** MAN-MADE ⟨an *artificial* limb⟩ ⟨*artificial* diamonds⟩
**2 a :** having existence in legal, economic, or political theory **b :** caused or produced by a human and especially social or political agency ⟨an *artificial* price advantage⟩ ⟨*artificial* barriers of discrimination —R. C. Weaver⟩
**3** *obsolete* **:** ARTFUL, CUNNING
**4 a :** lacking in natural or spontaneous quality ⟨an *artificial* smile⟩ ⟨an *artificial* excitement⟩ **b :** IMITATION, SHAM ⟨*artificial* flavor⟩
**5 :** based on differential morphological characters not necessarily indicative of natural relationships ⟨an *artificial* key for plant identification⟩
— **ar·ti·fi·ci·al·i·ty** \ˌär-tə-ˌfi-shē-'a-lə-tē\ *noun*
— **ar·ti·fi·cial·ly** \-'fi-sh°l-ē\ *adverb*
— **ar·ti·fi·cial·ness** \-'fi-shəl-nəs\ *noun*
**artificial horizon** *noun* (1920)
**:** a gyroscopic flight instrument designed to indicate aircraft attitude with respect to the true horizon
**artificial insemination** *noun* (1897)
**:** introduction of semen into the uterus or oviduct by other than natural means

artificial horizon (showing plane banking left): *a* miniature airplane, *b* horizon line

**artificial intelligence** *noun* (1956)
**1 :** the capability of a machine to imitate intelligent human behavior
**2 :** a branch of computer science dealing with the simulation of intelligent behavior in computers
**artificial respiration** *noun* (1852)
**:** the rhythmic forcing of air into and out of the lungs of a person whose breathing has stopped
**ar·til·ler·ist** \är-'ti-lə-rist\ *noun* (1781)
**:** GUNNER, ARTILLERYMAN
**ar·til·lery** \är-'ti-lər-ē, -'til-rē\ *noun, plural* **-ler·ies** [Middle English *artillerie,* from Middle French, from *artillier* to equip, arm, alteration of Old French *atillier,* from (assumed) Vulgar Latin *apticulare,* from Latin *aptare* to don, prepare, fit — more at ADAPT] (15th century)
**1 :** weapons (as bows, slings, and catapults) for discharging missiles
**2 a :** large bore crew-served mounted firearms (as guns, howitzers, and rockets) **:** ORDNANCE **b :** a branch of an army armed with artillery
**3 :** means of impressing, arguing, or persuading
**ar·til·lery·man** \-mən\ *noun* (1635)
**:** a soldier in the artillery
**ar·tio·dac·tyl** \ˌär-tē-ō-'dak-t°l\ *noun* [New Latin *Artiodactyla,* from Greek *artios* fitting, even-numbered + *daktylos* finger, toe; akin to Greek *arariskein* to fit — more at ARM] (circa 1879)
**:** any of an order (Artiodactyla) of ungulates (as the camel or pig) with an even number of functional toes on each foot
— **artiodactyl** *adjective*
**ar·ti·san** \'är-tə-zən, -sən, *chiefly British* ˌär-tə-'zan\ *noun* [Middle French, ultimately from Old Italian *artigiano,* from *arte* art, from Latin *art-, ars*] (1538)
**:** CRAFTSMAN
— **ar·ti·san·al** \-zə-n°l, -sə-, -'za-\ *adjective*
— **ar·ti·san·ship** \-ˌship\ *noun*
**art·ist** \'är-tist\ *noun* (circa 1507)
**1 a** *obsolete* **:** one skilled or versed in learned arts **b** *archaic* **:** PHYSICIAN **c** *archaic* **:** ARTISAN
**2 a :** one who professes and practices an imaginative art **b :** a person skilled in one of the fine arts
**3 :** a skilled performer; *especially* **:** ARTISTE

**4 :** one who is adept at something ⟨con *artist*⟩ ⟨strikeout *artist*⟩
**ar·tiste** \är-'tēst\ *noun* [French] (1823)
**:** a skilled adept public performer; *specifically* **:** a musical or theatrical entertainer
**ar·tis·tic** \är-'tis-tik\ *adjective* (circa 1753)
**1 :** of, relating to, or characteristic of art or artists ⟨*artistic* subjects⟩ ⟨an *artistic* success⟩
**2 :** showing imaginative skill in arrangement or execution ⟨*artistic* photography⟩
— **ar·tis·ti·cal·ly** \-ti-k(ə-)lē\ *adverb*
**art·ist·ry** \'är-tə-strē\ *noun* (1868)
**1 :** artistic quality of effect or workmanship ⟨the *artistry* of his novel⟩
**2 :** artistic ability ⟨the *artistry* of the violinist⟩ ⟨a lawyer's *artistry* in persuading juries⟩
**art·less** \'ärt-ləs\ *adjective* (1589)
**1 :** lacking art, knowledge, or skill **:** UNCULTURED
**2 a :** made without skill **:** CRUDE **b :** free from artificiality **:** NATURAL ⟨*artless* grace⟩
**3 :** free from guile or craft **:** sincerely simple
*synonym* see NATURAL
— **art·less·ly** *adverb*
— **art·less·ness** *noun*
**art mo·derne** \ˌär(t)-mō-'dern\ *noun, often A&M capitalized* [French — more at ART DECO] (1931)
**:** ART DECO
**art nou·veau** \ˌär(t)-nü-'vō\ *noun, often A&N capitalized* [French, literally, new art] (1908)
**:** a design style of late 19th century origin characterized especially by sinuous lines and foliate forms
**Arts and Crafts** *noun* (1888)
**:** a movement in European and American design during the late 19th and early 20th centuries promoting handcraftsmanship over industrial mass production
**art song** *noun* (1890)
**:** a usually through-composed lyric song with melody and accompaniment
**art·sy** \'ärt-sē\ *adjective* (1902)
**:** ARTY
**artsy–craftsy** \ˌärt-sē-'kraf(t)-sē\ *also* **arty–crafty** \ˌärt-ē-'kraf-tē\ *adjective* [from the phrase *arts and crafts*] (1902)
**:** ARTY
**art theater** *noun* (1923)
**:** a theater that specializes in the presentation of art films
**art·work** \'ärt-ˌwərk\ *noun* (1877)
**1 a :** an artistic production ⟨an 8-foot metal *artwork*⟩ **b :** artistic work ⟨*artwork* being sold on the sidewalk⟩
**2 a :** ART 6 **b :** material (as a drawing or photograph) prepared for reproduction in printed matter
**arty** \'är-tē\ *adjective* **art·i·er; -est** (1901)
**:** showily or pretentiously artistic ⟨*arty* lighting and photography⟩
— **art·i·ly** \'är-t°l-ē\ *adverb*
— **art·i·ness** \'är-tē-nəs\ *noun*
**aru·gu·la** \ə-'rü-gə-lə, -gyə-\ *noun* [probably from Italian dialect; akin to Italian dialect (Lombardy) *arigola* arugula, Italian *ruca* — more at ROCKET] (1967)
**:** a yellowish-flowered European herb (*Eruca vesicaria*) of the mustard family cultivated for its foliage which is used especially in salads — called also *garden rocket, rocket, rugola*
**ar·um** \'ar-əm, 'er-\ *noun* [New Latin, from Latin *arum,* from Greek *aron*] (14th century)
**:** any of a genus (*Arum* of the family Araceae, the arum family) of Old World plants having usually arrow-shaped leaves and a showy spathe partially enclosing a spadix; *broadly* **:** a plant of the arum family
**¹-ary** \US usually \ˌer-ē *when an unstressed syllable precedes,* ə-rē *or* rē *when a stressed syllable precedes; British usually* ə-rē *or* rē *in all cases*\ *noun suffix* [Middle English *-arie,* from Old French & Latin; Old French *-aire, -arie,* from Latin *-arius, -aria, -arium,* from *-arius,* adjective suffix]

**1 :** thing belonging to or connected with; *especially* **:** place of ⟨ov*ary*⟩
**2 :** person belonging to, connected with, or engaged in ⟨function*ary*⟩
**²-ary** *adjective suffix* [Middle English *-arie,* from Middle French & Latin; Middle French *-aire,* from Latin *-arius*]
**:** of, relating to, or connected with ⟨budget*ary*⟩
**¹Ary·an** \'ar-ē-ən, 'er-; 'är-yən\ *adjective* [Sanskrit *ārya* noble, belonging to the people speaking an Indo-European dialect who migrated into northern India] (1839)
**1 :** INDO-EUROPEAN
**2 a :** of or relating to a hypothetical ethnic type illustrated by or descended from early speakers of Indo-European languages **b :** NORDIC **c** — used in Nazism to designate a supposed master race of non-Jewish Caucasians having especially Nordic features
**3 :** of or relating to Indo-Iranian or its speakers
**²Aryan** *noun* (1851)
**1 :** INDO-EUROPEAN
**2 a :** NORDIC **b :** GENTILE
**ar·yl** \'ar-əl\ *adjective* [International Scientific Vocabulary *ar*omatic + *-yl*] (1906)
**:** having or being a univalent organic group (as phenyl) derived from an aromatic hydrocarbon by the removal of one hydrogen atom — often used in combination
**ar·y·te·noid** \ˌar-ə-'tē-ˌnȯid, ə-'ri-t°n-ˌȯid\ *adjective* [New Latin *arytaenoides,* from Greek *arytainoeidēs,* literally, ladle-shaped, from *arytaina* ladle] (circa 1751)
**1 :** relating to or being either of two small laryngeal cartilages to which the vocal cords are attached
**2 :** relating to or being either of a pair of small muscles or an unpaired muscle of the larynx
— **arytenoid** *noun*
**¹as** \əz, (ˌ)az\ *adverb* [Middle English, from Old English *eallswā* likewise, just as — more at ALSO] (before 12th century)
**1 :** to the same degree or amount ⟨*as* deaf as a post⟩ ⟨twice *as* long⟩
**2 :** for instance ⟨various trees, *as* oak or pine⟩
**3 :** when considered in a specified form or relation — usually used before a preposition or a participle ⟨my opinion *as* distinguished from his⟩
**²as** *conjunction* (12th century)
**1 :** AS IF ⟨looks *as* he had seen a ghost —S. T. Coleridge⟩
**2 :** in or to the same degree in which ⟨deaf *as* a post⟩ — usually used as a correlative after an adjective or adverb modified by adverbial *as* or *so* ⟨*as* cool *as* a cucumber⟩
**3 :** in the way or manner that ⟨do *as* I do⟩
**4 :** in accordance with what or the way in which ⟨quite good *as* boys go⟩
**5 :** WHILE, WHEN ⟨spilled the milk *as* she got up⟩
**6 :** regardless of the degree to which **:** THOUGH ⟨improbable *as* it seems, it's true⟩
**7 :** for the reason that **:** BECAUSE, SINCE ⟨stayed home *as* she had no car⟩
**8 :** that the result is ⟨so clearly guilty *as* to leave no doubt⟩
*usage* see LIKE
— **as is :** in the presently existing condition without modification ⟨bought the clock at an auction *as is*⟩
— **as it were :** as if it were so **:** in a manner of speaking
**³as** *pronoun* (12th century)
**1 :** THAT, WHO, WHICH — used after *same* or *such* ⟨in the same building *as* my brother⟩ ⟨tears such *as* angels weep —John Milton⟩ and chiefly dialect after a substantive not modified

\ə\ **abut** \°\ **kitten** \ər\ **further** \a\ **ash** \ā\ **ace**
\ä\ **mop, mar** \au̇\ **out** \ch\ **chin** \e\ **bet** \ē\ **easy**
\g\ **go** \i\ **hit** \ī\ **ice** \j\ **job** \ŋ\ **sing** \ō\ **go**
\ȯ\ **law** \ȯi\ **boy** \th\ **thin** \th̲\ **the** \ü\ **loot** \u̇\ **foot**
\y\ **yet** \zh\ **vision** *see also* Guide to Pronunciation

by *same* or *such* ⟨that kind of fruit *as* maids call medlars —Shakespeare⟩
**2 :** a fact that ⟨is a foreigner, *as* is evident from his accent⟩
**⁴as** *preposition* (13th century)
**1 a :** LIKE 2 ⟨all rose *as* one man⟩ **b :** LIKE 1a ⟨his face was *as* a mask —Max Beerbohm⟩
**2 :** in the capacity, character, condition, or role of ⟨works *as* an editor⟩
**⁵as** \'as\ *noun, plural* **as·ses** \'a-,sēz, 'a-səz\ [Latin] (1540)
**1 a :** a bronze coin of the ancient Roman republic **b :** a unit of value equivalent to an as coin
**2 :** LIBRA 2a
**as-** — see AD-
**asa·fet·i·da** *or* **asa·foe·ti·da** \,a-sə-'fe-tə-də, -'fē-; *Southern also* -'fi-tə-dē\ *noun* [Middle English *asafetida*, from Medieval Latin *asafoetida*, from Persian *azā* mastic + Latin *foetida*, feminine of *foetidus* fetid] (14th century)
**:** the fetid gum resin of various oriental plants (genus *Ferula*) of the carrot family formerly used in medicine as an antispasmodic and in folk medicine as a general prophylactic against disease
**asa·na** \'ä-sə-nə\ *noun* [Sanskrit *āsana* manner of sitting, from *āste* he sits; akin to Greek *hēsthai* to sit, Hittite *es*-] (circa 1934)
**:** any of various yogic postures
**Asan·te** \ə-'san-tē, -'sän-\ *noun, plural* **Asante** (1721)
**:** ASHANTI
**as·bes·tos** \as-'bes-təs, az-\ *noun* [Middle English *albestron* mineral supposed to be inextinguishable when set on fire, probably from Middle French, from Medieval Latin *asbeston*, alteration of Latin *asbestos*, from Greek, unslaked lime, from *asbestos* inextinguishable, from *a-* + *sbennynai* to quench] (1607)
**:** any of several minerals (as chrysotile) that readily separate into long flexible fibers, that have been implicated as causes of certain cancers, and that have been used especially formerly as fireproof insulating materials
**as·bes·to·sis** \,as-,bes-'tō-səs, ,az-\ *noun, plural* **-to·ses** \-,sēz\ (1927)
**:** a pneumoconiosis due to asbestos particles
**asc-** *or* **asco-** *combining form* [New Latin, from *ascus*]
**:** ascus ⟨*asco*carp⟩
**as·ca·ri·a·sis** \,as-kə-'rī-ə-səs\ *noun, plural* **-a·ses** \-,sēz\ [New Latin] (circa 1888)
**:** infestation with or disease caused by ascarids
**as·ca·rid** \'as-kə-rəd\ *noun* [ultimately from Late Latin *ascarid-, ascaris* intestinal worm, from Greek *askarid-, askaris*, probably by back-formation from *askarizein* to jump, throb, alteration of *skarizein*, from *skairein* to gambol] (circa 1890)
**:** any of a family (Ascaridae) of nematode worms that includes the common roundworm (*Ascaris lumbricoides*) parasitic in the human intestine
**as·ca·ris** \'as-kə-rəs\ *noun, plural* **as·car·i·des** \a-'skar-ə-,dēz\ (14th century)
**:** ASCARID
**as·cend** \ə-'send\ *verb* [Middle English, from Latin *ascendere*, from *ad-* + *scandere* to climb — more at SCAN] (14th century)
*intransitive verb*
**1 a :** to move upward **b :** to slope upward
**2 a :** to rise from a lower level or degree **b :** to go back in time or in order of genealogical succession
*transitive verb*
**1 :** to go or move up ⟨*ascend* a staircase⟩
**2 :** to succeed to : OCCUPY ⟨*ascend* the throne⟩
**— as·cend·able** *or* **as·cend·ible** \-'sen-də-bəl\ *adjective*
**as·cen·dance** *also* **as·cen·dence** \ə-'sen-dən(t)s\ *noun* (1742)
**:** ASCENDANCY
**as·cen·dan·cy** *also* **as·cen·den·cy** \ə-'sen-dən(t)-sē\ *noun* (1712)

**:** governing or controlling influence : DOMINATION
**¹as·cen·dant** *also* **as·cen·dent** \ə-'sen-dənt\ *noun* [Middle English *ascendent*, from Medieval Latin *ascendent-, ascendens*, from Latin, present participle of *ascendere*] (14th century)
**1 :** the point of the ecliptic or degree of the zodiac that rises above the eastern horizon at any moment
**2 :** a state or position of dominant power or importance
**3 :** a lineal or collateral relative in the ascending line
**²ascendant** *also* **ascendent** *adjective* (1591)
**1 a :** moving upward : RISING **b :** directed upward ⟨an *ascendant* stem⟩
**2 a :** SUPERIOR **b :** DOMINANT
**— as·cen·dant·ly** *adverb*
**as·cend·er** \ə-'sen-dər, 'a-\ *noun* (circa 1867)
**:** the part of a lowercase letter (as b) that rises above the main body of the letter; *also* : a letter that has such a part
**as·cend·ing** \ə-'sen-diŋ\ *adjective* (1599)
**1 a :** mounting or sloping upward **b :** rising or increasing to higher levels, values, or degrees ⟨*ascending* powers of *x*⟩
**2 :** rising upward usually from a more or less prostrate base or point of attachment
**as·cen·sion** \ə-'sen(t)-shən\ *noun* [Middle English, from Latin *ascension-, ascensio*, from *ascendere*] (14th century)
**:** the act or process of ascending
**as·cen·sion·al** \ə-'sench-nəl, ə-'sen(t)-shə-n°l\ *adjective* (1594)
**:** of or relating to ascension or ascent
**Ascension Day** *noun* (14th century)
**:** the Thursday 40 days after Easter observed in commemoration of Christ's ascension into Heaven
**as·cen·sive** \ə-'sen(t)-siv\ *adjective* (1646)
**:** rising or tending to rise
**as·cent** \ə-'sent, a-\ *noun* [irregular from *ascend*] (circa 1596)
**1 a :** the act of rising or mounting upward : CLIMB **b :** an upward slope or rising grade : ACCLIVITY **c :** the degree of elevation : INCLINATION, GRADIENT
**2 :** an advance in social status or reputation : PROGRESS
**3 :** a going back in time or upward in order of genealogical succession
**as·cer·tain** \,a-sər-'tān\ *transitive verb* [Middle English *acertainen*, from Middle French *acertainer*, from a- (from Latin *ad-*) + *certain*] (15th century)
**1** *archaic* **:** to make certain, exact, or precise
**2 :** to find out or learn with certainty
*synonym* see DISCOVER
**— as·cer·tain·able** \-'tā-nə-bəl\ *adjective*
**— as·cer·tain·ment** \-'tān-mənt\ *noun*
**as·ce·sis** \ə-'sē-səs\ *noun, plural* **-ce·ses** \-'sē-(,)sēz\ [Late Latin or Greek; Late Latin, from Greek *askēsis*, literally, exercise, from *askein*] (1873)
**:** SELF-DISCIPLINE, ASCETICISM
**as·cet·ic** \ə-'se-tik, a-\ *also* **as·cet·i·cal** \-ti-kəl\ *adjective* [Greek *askētikos*, literally, laborious, from *askētēs* one that exercises, hermit, from *askein* to work, exercise] (1646)
**1 :** practicing strict self-denial as a measure of personal and especially spiritual discipline
**2 :** austere in appearance, manner, or attitude
*synonym* see SEVERE
**— ascetic** *noun*
**— as·cet·i·cal·ly** \-ti-k(ə-)lē\ *adverb*
**— as·cet·i·cism** \-tə-,si-zəm\ *noun*
**as·cid·i·an** \ə-'si-dē-ən\ *noun* [New Latin *Ascidia*, group comprising tunicates, from *Ascidium*, genus name, from Greek *askidion*, diminutive of *askos* wineskin, bladder] (1856)
**:** any of a class (Ascidiacea) of solitary or colonial sessile tunicates that have an oral and an atrial siphon — called also *sea squirt*

**ASCII** \'as-(,)kē\ *noun* [American Standard Code for Information Interchange] (1963)
**:** a code for representing alphanumeric information
**as·ci·tes** \ə-'sī-tēz\ *noun, plural* **ascites** [Middle English *aschytes*, from Late Latin *ascites*, from Greek *askitēs*, from *askos*] (14th century)
**:** accumulation of serous fluid in the spaces between tissues and organs in the cavity of the abdomen
**— as·cit·ic** \-'si-tik\ *adjective*
**as·cle·pi·ad** \ə-'sklē-pē-əd, a-, -,ad\ *noun* [ultimately from Greek *asklēpiad-, asklēpias* swallowwort, from *Asklēpios*, Greek god of medicine] (1859)
**:** MILKWEED
**as·co·carp** \'as-kə-,kärp\ *noun* (circa 1887)
**:** the mature fruiting body of an ascomycetous fungus; *broadly* : such a body with its enclosed asci, spores, and paraphyses
**— as·co·car·pic** \,as-kə-'kär-pik\ *adjective*
**as·co·go·ni·um** \,as-kə-'gō-nē-əm\ *noun, plural* **-nia** \-nē-ə\ [New Latin] (1875)
**:** the female sex organ in ascomycetous fungi
**as·co·my·cete** \,as-kō-'mī-,sēt, -,mī-'sēt\ *noun* [ultimately from Greek *askos* + *mykēt-, mykēs* fungus; akin to Greek *myxa* mucus — more at MUCUS] (1875)
**:** any of a class (Ascomycetes) or subdivision (Ascomycotina) of higher fungi (as yeasts or molds) with septate hyphae and spores formed in asci
**— as·co·my·ce·tous** \-,mī-'sē-təs\ *adjective*
**ascor·bate** \ə-'skor-,bāt, -bət\ *noun* (1941)
**:** a salt of ascorbic acid
**ascor·bic acid** \ə-'skor-bik-\ *noun* [International Scientific Vocabulary a- + New Latin *scorbutus* scurvy — more at SCORBUTIC] (1933)
**:** VITAMIN C
**as·co·spore** \'as-kə-,spor, -,spor\ *noun* (1875)
**:** any of the spores contained in an ascus
**— as·co·spor·ic** \,as-kə-'spor-ik, -'spor-\ *adjective*
**as·cot** \'as-kət, -,kät\ *noun* [Ascot Heath, racetrack near Ascot, England] (1898)
**:** a broad neck scarf that is looped under the chin
**as·cribe** \ə-'skrīb\ *transitive verb* **as·cribed; as·crib·ing** [Middle English, from Latin *ascribere*, from *ad-* + *scribere* to write — more at SCRIBE] (15th century)
**:** to refer to a supposed cause, source, or author ☆
**— as·crib·able** \-'skrī-bə-bəl\ *adjective*
**ascribed** *adjective* (1972)
**:** acquired or assigned arbitrarily (as at birth) ⟨*ascribed* social status⟩
**as·crip·tion** \ə-'skrip-shən\ *noun* [Late Latin *ascription-, ascriptio*, from Latin, written addition, from *ascribere*] (1600)
**1 :** the act of ascribing : ATTRIBUTION

---

☆ SYNONYMS
**Ascribe, attribute, assign, impute, credit** mean to lay something to the account of a person or thing. ASCRIBE suggests an inferring or conjecturing of cause, quality, authorship ⟨forged paintings formerly *ascribed* to masters⟩. ATTRIBUTE suggests less tentativeness than ASCRIBE, less definiteness than ASSIGN ⟨*attributed* to Rembrandt but possibly done by an associate⟩. ASSIGN implies ascribing with certainty or after deliberation ⟨*assigned* the bones to the Cretaceous Period⟩. IMPUTE suggests ascribing something that brings discredit by way of accusation or blame ⟨tried to *impute* sinister motives to my actions⟩. CREDIT implies ascribing a thing or especially an action to a person or other thing as its agent, source, or explanation ⟨*credited* his teammates for his success⟩.

**2 :** arbitrary placement (as at birth) in a particular social status

**as·crip·tive** \ə-'skrip-tiv\ *adjective* (1650)
**:** relating to, marked by, or involving ascription

**as·cus** \'as-kəs\ *noun, plural* **as·ci** \'as-ˌkī, -ˌkē, 'a-ˌsī\ [New Latin, from Greek *askos* wineskin, bladder] (1830)
**:** the membranous oval or tubular spore case of an ascomycete

**as·dic** \'az-(ˌ)dik\ *noun* [from *asdics* underwater echo ranging, probably from *Anti-Submarine Division* (British Admiralty department 1916–18) + *-ics*] (1939)
*chiefly British* **:** SONAR
**word history** see SONAR

**-ase** *noun suffix* [French, from *diastase*]
**:** enzyme ⟨prote*ase*⟩

**asep·sis** \(ˌ)ā-'sep-səs, ə-\ *noun* [New Latin] (1892)
**1 :** the condition of being aseptic
**2 :** the methods of making or keeping aseptic

**asep·tic** \(ˌ)ā-'sep-tik, ə-\ *adjective* [International Scientific Vocabulary] (circa 1859)
**1 a :** preventing infection ⟨*aseptic* techniques⟩ **b :** free or freed from pathogenic microorganisms ⟨an *aseptic* operating room⟩
**2 :** lacking vitality, emotion, or warmth ⟨the bureaucrat's world is prim and proper and *aseptic* —R. M. Weaver⟩
— **asep·ti·cal·ly** \-ti-k(ə-)lē\ *adverb*

**asex·u·al** \(ˌ)ā-'sek-sh(ə-)wəl, -'sek-shəl\ *adjective* (1830)
**1 :** lacking sex or functional sex organs ⟨*asexual* plants⟩
**2 a :** involving or reproducing by reproductive processes (as cell division, spore formation, fission, or budding) that do not involve the union of individuals or germ cells ⟨*asexual* reproduction⟩ **b :** produced by asexual reproduction ⟨*asexual* spores⟩
**3 :** devoid of sexuality ⟨an *asexual* relationship⟩
— **asex·u·al·i·ty** \ˌā-ˌsek-shə-'wa-lə-tē\ *noun*
— **asex·u·al·ly** \(ˌ)ā-'sek-sh(ə-)wə-lē, -ˌsek-sh(ə-)lē\ *adverb*

**¹as far as** *conjunction* (14th century)
**:** to the extent or degree that ⟨is safe, *as far as* we know⟩ — often used in expressions like "as far as (something) goes" and "as far as (something) is concerned" to mean "with regard to (something)" ⟨we felt pretty safe *as far as* the fire was concerned —Mark Twain⟩ or in expressions like "as far as (someone) is concerned" to mean "in (someone's) opinion" ⟨*as far as* I'm concerned, it's a mistake⟩

**²as far as** *preposition* (1523)
**:** with regard to **:** CONCERNING ⟨neatly groomed and, *as far as* clothes, casual looking —*N.Y. Times*⟩ ⟨*as far as* being mentioned in the Ten Commandments, I think it is —Billy Graham⟩ — chiefly in oral use

**as for** *preposition* (1533)
**:** with regard to **:** CONCERNING ⟨*as for* the others, they'll arrive later⟩

**As·gard** \'as-ˌgärd, 'az-\ *noun* [Old Norse *āsgarthr*]
**:** the home of the Norse gods

**¹ash** \'ash\ *noun* [Middle English *asshe*, from Old English *æsc*; akin to Old High German *ask* ash, Latin *ornus* mountain ash] (before 12th century)
**1 :** any of a genus (*Fraxinus*) of trees of the olive family with pinnate leaves, thin furrowed bark, and gray branchlets
**2 :** the tough elastic wood of an ash
**3** [Old English *æsc*, name of the corresponding runic letter] **:** the ligature æ used in Old English and some phonetic alphabets to represent a low front vowel \a\

**²ash** *noun, often attributive* [Middle English *asshe*, from Old English *asce* — more at ARID] (before 12th century)
**1 :** something that symbolizes grief, repentance, or humiliation

**2 a :** the solid residue left when combustible material is thoroughly burned or is oxidized by chemical means **b :** fine particles of mineral matter from a volcanic vent
**3** *plural* **:** the remains of the dead human body after cremation or disintegration
**4** *plural* **:** deathly pallor ⟨the lip of *ashes* and the cheek of flame —Lord Byron⟩
**5** *plural* **:** RUINS
— **ash·less** \-ləs\ *adjective*

**³ash** *transitive verb* (1894)
**:** to convert into ash

**ashamed** \ə-'shāmd\ *adjective* [Middle English, from Old English *āscamod*, past participle of *āscamian* to shame, from *ā-* (perfective prefix) + *scamian* to shame — more at ABIDE, SHAME] (before 12th century)
**1 a :** feeling shame, guilt, or disgrace **b :** feeling inferior or unworthy
**2 :** restrained by anticipation of shame ⟨was *ashamed* to beg⟩
— **asham·ed·ly** \-'shā-məd-lē\ *adverb*

**Ashan·ti** \ə-'shan-tē, -'shän-\ *noun, plural* **Ashanti** or **Ashantis** [Twi *àsàntéꜜ*] (1721)
**1 :** a member of a people of southern Ghana
**2 :** the dialect of Akan spoken by the Ashanti people

**ash–blond** or **ash–blonde** \'ash-'bländ\ *adjective* (1903)
**:** pale or grayish blond ⟨*ash-blond* hair⟩

**Ash·can** \'ash-ˌkan\ *adjective* (1939)
**:** of or relating to a group of 20th century American painters who depicted city life realistically ⟨*Ashcan* school⟩

**ash can** *noun* (1899)
**1 :** a metal receptacle for refuse
**2** *slang* **:** DEPTH CHARGE

**¹ash·en** \'a-shən\ *adjective* (before 12th century)
**:** of, relating to, or made from ash wood

**²ashen** *adjective* (14th century)
**:** resembling ashes (as in color); *especially* **:** deadly pale ⟨a face *ashen* and haggard⟩

**Ash·er** \'a-shər\ *noun* [Hebrew *Āshēr*]
**:** a son of Jacob and the traditional eponymous ancestor of one of the tribes of Israel

**ash·fall** \'ash-ˌfȯl\ *noun* (1923)
**:** a deposit of volcanic ash

**Ash·ke·nazi** \ˌäsh-kə-'nä-zē, ˌash-kə-'na-\ *noun, plural* **-naz·im** \-'nä-zəm, -'na-\ [Late Hebrew *Ashkĕnāzī*, from *Ashkĕnāz*, medieval rabbinical name for Germany] (1839)
**:** a member of one of the two great divisions of Jews comprising the eastern European Yiddish-speaking Jews — compare SEPHARDI
— **Ash·ke·naz·ic** \-'nä-zik, -'na-\ *adjective*

**ash·lar** \'ash-lər\ *noun* [Middle English *asheler*, from Middle French *aisselier* traverse beam, from Old French, from *ais* board, from Latin *axis*, alteration of *assis*] (14th century)
**1 :** hewn or squared stone; *also* **:** masonry of such stone
**2 :** a thin squared and dressed stone for facing a wall of rubble or brick

**ashore** \ə-'shōr, -'shȯr\ *adverb* (1582)
**:** on or to the shore

**as how** *conjunction* (1771)
**:** THAT ⟨allowed *as how* she was glad to be here⟩

**ash·ram** \'äsh-rəm, -ˌräm; 'ash-ˌram\ *noun* [Sanskrit *āśrama*, from *śrama* religious exercise] (1917)
**1 :** a secluded dwelling of a Hindu sage; *also* **:** the group of disciples instructed there
**2 :** a religious retreat

**Ash·to·reth** \'ash-tə-ˌreth\ *noun* [Hebrew *'Ashtōreth*]
**:** ASTARTE

**ash·tray** \'ash-ˌtrā\ *noun* (1887)
**:** a receptacle for tobacco ashes and for cigar and cigarette butts

**Ashur** \'ä-ˌshùr\ *noun* [Akkadian *Ashūr*]
**:** the chief deity of the Assyrians

**Ash Wednesday** *noun* (14th century)
**:** the first day of Lent — see EASTER table

**ashy** \'a-shē\ *adjective* **ash·i·er; -est** (14th century)
**1 :** of or relating to ashes
**2 :** ASHEN

**Asi·a·go** \ˌä-zhē-'ä-(ˌ)gō, ˌä-sē-, -shē-\ *noun* [*Asiago*, town in Italy] (1938)
**:** a pungent hard yellow cheese of Italian origin suitable for grating

**¹Asian** \'ā-zhən *also* -shən\ *adjective* (1550)
**:** of, relating to, or characteristic of the continent of Asia or its people ◼

**²Asian** *noun* (circa 1890)
**:** a native or inhabitant of Asia

**Asian–Amer·i·can** \-ə-'mər-ə-kən\ *noun* (1974)
**:** an American of Asian descent
— **Asian–American** *adjective*

**Asian elephant** *noun* (1981)
**:** ELEPHANT 1b

**Asian influenza** *noun* (1957)
**:** influenza caused by a mutant strain of the influenza virus isolated during the 1957 epidemic in Asia — called also *Asian flu*

**Asi·at·ic** \ˌā-zhē-'a-tik, -zē-\ *adjective* (1602)
**:** ASIAN — sometimes taken to be offensive
— **Asiatic** *noun*
*usage* see ASIAN

**Asiatic cholera** *noun* (1831)
**:** cholera of Asian origin that is caused by virulent strains of the cholera vibrio (*Vibrio cholerae*)

**Asiatic elephant** *noun* (1930)
**:** ELEPHANT 1b

**¹aside** \ə-'sīd\ *adverb* (14th century)
**1 :** to or toward the side ⟨stepped *aside*⟩
**2 :** away from others or into privacy ⟨pulled him *aside*⟩
**3 :** out of the way especially for future use **:** AWAY ⟨putting *aside* savings⟩
**4 :** away from one's thought or consideration ⟨jesting *aside*⟩

**²aside** *preposition* (1592)
*obsolete* **:** BEYOND, PAST

**³aside** *noun* (circa 1751)
**1 :** an utterance meant to be inaudible to someone; *especially* **:** an actor's speech heard by the audience but supposedly not by other characters
**2 :** a straying from the theme **:** DIGRESSION

**aside from** *preposition* (1818)
**1 :** in addition to **:** BESIDES
**2 :** EXCEPT FOR

**as if** *conjunction* (13th century)
**1 :** as it would be if ⟨it was *as if* he had lost his last friend⟩
**2 :** as one would do if ⟨he ran *as if* ghosts were chasing him⟩
**3 :** THAT ⟨it seemed *as if* the day would never end⟩

**as·i·nine** \'a-sᵊn-ˌīn\ *adjective* [Latin *asininus*, from *asinus* ass] (15th century)
**1 :** marked by inexcusable failure to exercise

\ə\ **abut** \ᵊ\ **kitten** \ər\ **further** \a\ **ash** \ā\ **ace**
\ä\ **mop, mar** \aù\ **out** \ch\ **chin** \e\ **bet** \ē\ **easy**
\g\ **go** \i\ **hit** \ī\ **ice** \j\ **job** \ŋ\ **sing** \ō\ **go**
\ȯ\ **law** \ȯi\ **boy** \th\ **thin** \t͟h\ **the** \ü\ **loot** \ù\ **foot**
\y\ **yet** \zh\ **vision** *see also* Guide to Pronunciation

intelligence or sound judgment ⟨an *asinine* excuse⟩
**2 :** of, relating to, or resembling an ass
**synonym** see SIMPLE
— **as·i·nine·ly** *adverb*
— **as·i·nin·i·ty** \,a-sə-'ni-nə-tē\ *noun*
**ask** \'ask, 'åsk; *dialect* 'aks\ *verb* **asked** \'as(k)t, 'ås(k)t, 'ask; *dialect* 'akst\; **ask·ing** [Middle English, from Old English *āscian;* akin to Old High German *eiscōn* to ask, Lithuanian *eiškoti* to seek, Sanskrit *icchati* he seeks] (before 12th century)
*transitive verb*
**1 a :** to call on for an answer **b :** to put a question about **c :** SPEAK, UTTER ⟨*ask* a question⟩
**2 a :** to make a request of ⟨she *asked* her teacher for help⟩ **b :** to make a request for ⟨she *asked* help from her teacher⟩
**3 :** to call for **:** REQUIRE
**4 :** to set as a price ⟨*asked* $3000 for the car⟩
**5 :** INVITE
*intransitive verb*
**1 :** to seek information
**2 :** to make a request ⟨*asked* for food⟩
**3 :** LOOK — often used in the phrase *ask for trouble* ☆ ☆ ■
— **ask·er** *noun*
**askance** \ə-'skan(t)s\ *also* **askant** \-'skant\ *adverb* [origin unknown] (circa 1530)
**1 :** with a side-glance **:** OBLIQUELY
**2 :** with disapproval or distrust **:** SCORNFULLY
**as·ke·sis** \ə-'skē-səs\ *variant of* ASCESIS
**askew** \ə-'skyü\ *adverb or adjective* [probably from ¹*a-* + *skew*] (1573)
**:** out of line **:** AWRY ⟨the picture hung *askew*⟩
— **askew·ness** *noun*
**asking price** *noun* (1755)
**:** the price at which something is offered for sale
¹**aslant** \ə-'slant\ *adverb or adjective* (14th century)
**:** in a slanting direction **:** OBLIQUELY
²**aslant** *preposition* (1602)
**:** over or across in a slanting direction
¹**asleep** \ə-'slēp\ *adjective* [Middle English *aslepe,* from Old English *on slæpe*] (13th century)
**1 :** being in a state of sleep
**2 :** DEAD
**3 :** lacking sensation **:** NUMB
**4 a :** INACTIVE, DORMANT **b :** not alert **:** INDIFFERENT
²**asleep** *adverb* (13th century)
**1 :** into a state of sleep
**2 :** into the sleep of death
**3 :** into a state of inactivity, sluggishness, or indifference
**as long as** *conjunction* (15th century)
**1 :** provided that ⟨can do as they like *as long as* they have a B average⟩
**2 :** INASMUCH AS, SINCE ⟨*as long as* you're going, I'll go too⟩
**aslope** \ə-'slōp\ *adjective or adverb* (14th century)
**:** being in a sloping or slanting position or direction
**aso·cial** \(,)ā-'sō-shəl\ *adjective* (1883)
**:** not social: as **a :** rejecting or lacking the capacity for social interaction **b :** ANTISOCIAL
**as of** *preposition* (1900)
**:** ON, AT, FROM — used to indicate a time or date at which something begins or ends ⟨takes effect *as of* July 1⟩
¹**asp** \'asp\ *noun* [Middle English, from Old English *æspe*] (before 12th century)
**:** ASPEN
²**asp** *noun* [Middle English *aspis,* from Latin, from Greek] (14th century)
**:** a small venomous snake of Egypt usually held to be a cobra (*Naja haje*)
**as·par·a·gine** \ə-'spar-ə-,jēn\ *noun* [French, from Latin *asparagus*] (1813)
**:** a nonessential amino acid $C_4H_8N_2O_3$ that is an amide of aspartic acid

**as·par·a·gus** \ə-'spar-ə-gəs\ *noun, plural* **-gus** [New Latin, genus name, from Latin, asparagus plant, from Greek *asparagos;* perhaps akin to Greek *spargan* to swell] (1548)
**:** any of a genus (*Asparagus*) of Old World perennial plants of the lily family having much-branched stems, minute scalelike leaves, and narrow usually filiform branchlets that function as leaves; especially **:** one (*A. officinalis*) widely cultivated for its edible young shoots

asparagus

**as·par·tame** \'as-pər-,tām, ə-'spär-,tām\ *noun* [*aspartic* acid + *phenyl*alanine + *methyl* + *es*ter] (1972)
**:** a crystalline compound $C_{14}H_{18}N_2O_5$ that is a diamide synthesized from phenylalanine and aspartic acid and that is used as a low-calorie sweetener
**as·par·tate** \ə-'spär-,tāt\ *noun* (1863)
**:** a salt or ester of aspartic acid
**as·par·tic acid** \ə-'spär-tik-\ *noun* [International Scientific Vocabulary, irregular from Latin *asparagus*] (1863)
**:** a crystalline amino acid $C_4H_7NO_4$ found especially in plants
**as·pect** \'as-,pekt\ *noun* [Middle English, from Latin *aspectus,* from *aspicere* to look at, from *ad-* + *specere* to look — more at SPY] (14th century)
**1 a :** the position of planets or stars with respect to one another held by astrologers to influence human affairs; *also* **:** the apparent position (as conjunction) of a body in the solar system with respect to the sun **b :** a position facing a particular direction **:** EXPOSURE ⟨the house has a southern *aspect*⟩ **c :** the manner of presentation of a plane to a fluid through which it is moving or to a current
**2 a** (1) **:** appearance to the eye or mind (2) **:** a particular appearance of countenance **:** MIEN **b :** a particular status or phase in which something appears or may be regarded ⟨studied every *aspect* of the question⟩
**3** *archaic* **:** an act of looking **:** GAZE
**4 a :** the nature of the action of a verb as to its beginning, duration, completion, or repetition and without reference to its position in time **b :** a set of inflected verb forms that indicate aspect
— **as·pec·tu·al** \a-'spek-chə(-wə)l\ *adjective*
**aspect ratio** *noun* (1907)
**:** a ratio of one dimension to another: as **a :** the ratio of span to mean chord of an airfoil **b :** the ratio of the width of a television or motion-picture image to its height
**as·pen** \'as-pən\ *noun* [Middle English, of an aspen, from *asp* aspen, from Old English *æspe;* akin to Old High German *aspa* aspen, Russian *osina*] (1596)
**:** any of several poplars (especially *Populus tremula* of Europe and *P. tremuloides* and *P. grandidentata* of North America) with leaves that flutter in the lightest wind because of their flattened petioles
**as per** \'az-,pər\ *preposition* (1859)
**:** in accordance with **:** ACCORDING TO
— **as per usual :** as usual
**as·per·ges** \ə-'spər-(,)jēz\ *noun* [Latin, thou wilt sprinkle, from *aspergere*] (circa 1587)
**:** a ceremony of sprinkling altar and people with holy water
**as·per·gil·lo·sis** \,as-pər-(,)ji-'lō-səs\ *noun, plural* **-lo·ses** \-,sēz\ (1898)
**:** infection with or disease caused (as in poultry) by molds (genus *Aspergillus*)
**as·per·gil·lum** \,as-pər-'ji-ləm\ *noun, plural* **-la** \-lə\ *or* **-lums** [New Latin, from Latin *aspergere*] (1649)

**:** a brush or small perforated container with a handle that is used for sprinkling holy water in a liturgical service
**as·per·gil·lus** \-'ji-ləs\ *noun, plural* **-gil·li** \-'ji-,lī\ [New Latin, genus name, from *aspergillum*] (circa 1847)
**:** any of a genus (*Aspergillus*) of ascomycetous fungi with branched radiate sporophores including many common molds
**as·per·i·ty** \a-'sper-ə-tē, ə-\ *noun, plural* **-ties** [Middle English *asprete,* from Old French *aspreté,* from *aspre* rough, from Latin *asper,* from (assumed) Old Latin *absperos,* from *ab-* + *-speros;* akin to Sanskrit *apasphura* repelling, Latin *spernere* to spurn — more at SPURN] (13th century)
**1 :** RIGOR, SEVERITY
**2 a :** roughness of surface **:** UNEVENNESS; *also*

aspergillum

: a tiny projection from a surface **b** : roughness of sound
**3** : roughness of manner or of temper : HARSHNESS

**as·perse** \ə-'spərs, a-\ *transitive verb* **as·persed; as·pers·ing** [Latin *aspersus*, past participle of *aspergere*, from *ad-* + *spargere* to scatter — more at SPARK] (15th century)
**1** : SPRINKLE; *especially* : to sprinkle with holy water
**2** : to attack with evil reports or false or injurious charges
**synonym** see MALIGN

**as·per·sion** \ə-'spər-zhən, -shən\ *noun* (circa 1587)
**1** : a sprinkling with water especially in religious ceremonies
**2 a** : the act of calumniating **b** : a calumnious expression ⟨cast *aspersions* on her integrity⟩

**¹as·phalt** \'as-ˌfȯlt *also* 'ash-, *especially British* -ˌfalt\ *also* **as·phal·tum** \as-'fȯl-təm, *especially British* -'fal-\ *noun* [Middle English *aspalt*, from Late Latin *aspaltus*, from Greek *asphaltos*] (14th century)
**1** : a dark bituminous substance that is found in natural beds and is also obtained as a residue in petroleum refining and that consists chiefly of hydrocarbons
**2** : an asphaltic composition used for pavements and as a waterproof cement
— **as·phal·tic** \as-'fȯl-tik, *especially British* -'fal-\ *adjective*

**²asphalt** *transitive verb* (circa 1859)
: to cover with asphalt : PAVE 1

**as·phalt·ite** \'as-ˌfȯl-ˌtīt, *especially British* -ˌfal-\ *noun* (circa 1899)
: a native asphalt occurring in vein deposits below the surface of the ground

**asphalt jungle** *noun* (1920)
: a big city or a specified part of a big city

**as·pher·ic** \(ˌ)ā-'sfir-ik, -'sfer-\ *or* **as·pher·i·cal** \-i-kəl\ *adjective* (circa 1922)
: departing slightly from the spherical form especially in order to correct for spherical aberration ⟨an *aspheric* lens⟩

**as·pho·del** \'as-fə-ˌdel\ *noun* [Latin *asphodelus*, from Greek *asphodelos*] (1597)
: any of various Old World usually perennial herbs (especially genera *Asphodelus* and *Asphodeline*) of the lily family with flowers in usually long erect racemes

**as·phyx·ia** \as-'fik-sē-ə, əs-\ *noun* [New Latin, from Greek, stopping of the pulse, from *a-* + *sphyzein* to throb] (1778)
: a lack of oxygen or excess of carbon dioxide in the body that is usually caused by interruption of breathing and that causes unconsciousness

**as·phyx·i·ate** \-sē-ˌāt\ *verb* **-at·ed; -at·ing** (1836)
*transitive verb*
: to cause asphyxia in; *also* : to kill or make unconscious by inadequate oxygen, presence of noxious agents, or other obstruction to normal breathing
*intransitive verb*
: to become asphyxiated
— **as·phyx·i·a·tion** \-ˌfik-sē-'ā-shən\ *noun*

**¹as·pic** \'as-pik\ *noun* [Middle French, alteration of *aspe*, from Latin *aspis*] (1530)
*obsolete* : ²ASP

**²aspic** *noun* [French, literally, asp] (1789)
: a clear savory jelly (as of fish or meat stock) used as a garnish or to make a meat, fish, or vegetable mold

**as·pi·dis·tra** \ˌas-pə-'dis-trə\ *noun* [New Latin, irregular from Greek *aspid-, aspis* shield] (1822)
: an Asian plant (*Aspidistra elatior*) of the lily family that has large basal leaves and is often grown as a foliage plant

**¹as·pi·rant** \'as-p(ə-)rənt, ə-'spī-rənt\ *noun* (1738)
: one who aspires ⟨presidential *aspirants*⟩

**²aspirant** *adjective* (1814)

: seeking to attain a desired position or status
**¹as·pi·rate** \'as-p(ə-)rət\ *noun* (1617)
**1** : an independent sound \h\ or a character (as the letter *h*) representing it
**2** : a consonant having aspiration as its final component ⟨in English the \p\ of *pit* is an *aspirate*⟩
**3** : material removed by aspiration

**²as·pi·rate** \'as-pə-ˌrāt\ *transitive verb* **-rat·ed; -rat·ing** [Latin *aspiratus*, past participle of *aspirare*] (circa 1700)
**1** : to pronounce (a vowel or a consonant) with aspiration (sense 1a)
**2 a** : to draw by suction **b** : to remove (as blood) by aspiration **c** : to take into the lungs by aspiration

**as·pi·ra·tion** \ˌas-pə-'rā-shən\ *noun* (14th century)
**1 a** : audible breath that accompanies or comprises a speech sound **b** : the pronunciation or addition of an aspiration; *also* : the symbol of an aspiration
**2** : a drawing of something in, out, up, or through by or as if by suction: as **a** : the act of breathing and especially of breathing in **b** : the withdrawal of fluid or tissue from the body **c** : the taking of foreign matter into the lungs with the respiratory current
**3 a** : a strong desire to achieve something high or great **b** : an object of such desire
**synonym** see AMBITION
— **as·pi·ra·tion·al** \-'rā-sh(ə-)nəl\ *adjective*

**as·pi·ra·tor** \'as-pə-ˌrā-tər\ *noun* (1804)
: an apparatus for producing suction or moving or collecting materials by suction; *especially* : a hollow tubular instrument connected with a partial vacuum and used to remove fluid or tissue or foreign bodies from the body

**as·pire** \ə-'spīr\ *intransitive verb* **as·pired; as·pir·ing** [Middle English, from Middle French or Latin; Middle French *aspirer*, from Latin *aspirare*, literally, to breathe upon, from *ad-* + *spirare* to breathe] (14th century)
**1** : to seek to attain or accomplish a particular goal ⟨*aspired* to a career in medicine⟩
**2** : ASCEND, SOAR
— **as·pir·er** *noun*

**as·pi·rin** \'as-p(ə-)rən\ *noun, plural* **aspirin** *or* **aspirins** [International Scientific Vocabulary, from *acetyl* + *spiraeic* acid (former name of salicylic acid), from New Latin *Spiraea*, genus of shrubs — more at SPIREA] (1899)
**1** : a white crystalline derivative $C_9H_8O_4$ of salicylic acid used for relief of pain and fever
**2** : a tablet of aspirin

**as regards** *also* **as respects** *preposition* (1840)
: in regard to : with respect to

**¹ass** \'as\ *noun* [Middle English, from Old English *assa*, probably from Old Irish *asan*, from Latin *asinus*] (before 12th century)
**1** : any of several hardy gregarious African or Asian perissodactyl mammals (genus *Equus*) smaller than the horse and having long ears; *especially* : an African mammal (*E. asinus*) that is the ancestor of the donkey
**2** : a stupid, obstinate, or perverse person — often compounded with a preceding adjective ⟨don't be a smart-*ass*⟩; often considered vulgar

**²ass** \'as\ *or* **arse** \'as, 'ärs\ *noun* [Middle English *ars, ers*, from Old English *ærs, ears*; akin to Old High German & Old Norse *ars* buttocks, Greek *orrhos* buttocks, *oura* tail] (before 12th century)
**1 a** : BUTTOCKS — often used in emphatic reference to a specific person ⟨get your *ass* over here⟩ ⟨saved my *ass*⟩; often considered vulgar
**b** : ANUS — often considered vulgar
**2** : SEXUAL INTERCOURSE — usually considered vulgar

**³ass** *adverb* [²*ass*] (1955)
— used as a postpositive intensive especially with words of derogatory implication ⟨fancy-*ass*⟩; often considered vulgar

**as·sai** \ä-'sī\ *adverb* [Italian, from (assumed) Vulgar Latin *ad satis* enough — more at ASSET] (circa 1724)
: VERY — used with tempo direction in music ⟨allegro *assai*⟩

**as·sail** \ə-'sā(ə)l\ *transitive verb* [Middle English, from Old French *asaillir*, from (assumed) Vulgar Latin *assalire*, alteration of Latin *assilire* to leap upon, from *ad-* + *salire* to leap — more at SALLY] (13th century)
: to attack violently with blows or words
**synonym** see ATTACK
— **as·sail·able** \-'sā-lə-bəl\ *adjective*
— **as·sail·ant** \-'sā-lənt\ *noun*

**As·sam·ese** \ˌa-sə-'mēz, -'mēs\ *noun, plural* **Assamese** (1826)
**1** : a native or inhabitant of Assam, India
**2** : the Indo-Aryan language of Assam
— **Assamese** *adjective*

**as·sas·sin** \ə-'sa-sᵊn\ *noun* [Medieval Latin *assassinus*, from Arabic *ḥashshāshīn*, plural of *ḥashshāsh* one who smokes or chews hashish, from *hashish* hashish] (circa 1520)
**1** *capitalized* : one of a secret order of Muslims that at the time of the Crusades terrorized Christians and other enemies by secret murder committed under the influence of hashish
**2** : a person who commits murder; *especially* : one who murders a politically important person either for hire or from fanatical motives

**as·sas·si·nate** \ə-'sa-sᵊn-ˌāt\ *transitive verb* **-nat·ed; -nat·ing** (1607)
**1** : to injure or destroy unexpectedly and treacherously
**2** : to murder by sudden or secret attack usually for impersonal reasons
**synonym** see KILL
— **as·sas·si·na·tion** \-ˌsa-sᵊn-'ā-shən\ *noun*
— **as·sas·si·na·tor** \-'sa-sᵊn-ˌā-tər\ *noun*

**assassin bug** *noun* (1895)
: any of a family (Reduviidae) of bugs that are usually predatory on insects though some (as a conenose) suck the blood of mammals — called also *reduviid*

**¹as·sault** \ə-'sȯlt\ *noun* [Middle English *assaut*, from Old French, from (assumed) Vulgar Latin *assaltus*, from *assalire*] (14th century)
**1 a** : a violent physical or verbal attack **b** : a military attack usually involving direct combat with enemy forces **c** : a concerted effort (as to reach a goal or defeat an adversary)
**2 a** : a threat or attempt to inflict offensive physical contact or bodily harm on a person (as by lifting a fist in a threatening manner) that puts the person in immediate danger of or in apprehension of such harm or contact — compare BATTERY 1b **b** : RAPE

**²assault** (15th century)
*transitive verb*
**1** : to make an assault on
**2** : RAPE
*intransitive verb*
: to make an assault
**synonym** see ATTACK
— **as·sault·er** *noun*
— **as·saul·tive** \-'sȯl-tiv\ *adjective*
— **as·saul·tive·ly** *adverb*
— **as·saul·tive·ness** *noun*

**assault boat** *noun* (1941)
: a small portable boat used in an amphibious military attack or in land warfare for crossing rivers or lakes

**assault rifle** *noun* (1975)
: any of various automatic or semiautomatic rifles designed for military use with large capacity magazines

**¹as·say** \'a-ˌsā, a-'sā\ *noun* [Middle English, from Old French *essai, assai* test, effort — more at ESSAY] (14th century)

\ə\ abut \ᵊ\ kitten \ər\ further \a\ ash \ā\ ace \ä\ mop, mar \aȯ\ out \ch\ chin \e\ bet \ē\ easy \g\ go \i\ hit \ī\ ice \j\ job \ŋ\ sing \ō\ go \ȯ\ law \ȯi\ boy \th\ thin \th\ the \ü\ loot \ȯ\ foot \y\ yet \zh\ vision *see also* Guide to Pronunciation

**1** *archaic* **:** TRIAL, ATTEMPT
**2 :** examination and determination as to characteristics (as weight, measure, or quality)
**3 :** analysis (as of an ore or drug) to determine the presence, absence, or quantity of one or more components
**4 :** a substance to be assayed; *also* **:** the tabulated result of assaying
²**as·say** \a-'sā, 'a-,sā\ (14th century)
*transitive verb*
**1 :** TRY, ATTEMPT
**2 a :** to analyze (as an ore) for one or more specific components **b :** to judge the worth of **:** ESTIMATE
*intransitive verb*
**:** to prove up in an assay
— **as·say·er** *noun*
**assed** \'ast\ *adverb* (1932)
**:** ³ASS — used in combination ⟨smart-*assed*⟩; often considered vulgar
**as·se·gai** *or* **as·sa·gai** \'a-si-,gī\ *noun* [ultimately from Arabic *az-zaghāya* the assegai, from *al-* the + *zaghāya* assegai] (1600)
**:** a slender hardwood spear or light javelin usually tipped with iron and used in southern Africa
**as·sem·blage** \ə-'sem-blij, *for 3 also* ,a-,säm-'bläzh\ *noun* (1690)
**1 :** a collection of persons or things **:** GATHERING
**2 :** the act of assembling **:** the state of being assembled
**3 a :** an artistic composition made from scraps, junk, and odds and ends (as of paper, cloth, wood, stone, or metal) **b :** the art of making assemblages
**as·sem·blag·ist** \-bli-jist, -'blä-zhist\ *noun* (1965)
**:** an artist who specializes in assemblages
**as·sem·ble** \ə-'sem-bəl\ *verb* **as·sem·bled; as·sem·bling** \-b(ə-)liŋ\ [Middle English, from Old French *assembler*, from (assumed) Vulgar Latin *assimulare*, from Latin *ad-* + *simul* together — more at SAME] (13th century)
*transitive verb*
**1 :** to bring together (as in a particular place or for a particular purpose)
**2 :** to fit together the parts of
*intransitive verb*
**:** to meet together **:** CONVENE
*synonym* see GATHER
**as·sem·bler** \-b(ə-)lər\ *noun* (1635)
**1 :** one that assembles
**2 a :** a computer program that automatically converts instructions written in assembly language into machine language **b :** ASSEMBLY LANGUAGE
**as·sem·bly** \ə-'sem-blē\ *noun, plural* **-blies** [Middle English *assemblee*, from Middle French, from Old French, from *assembler*] (14th century)
**1 :** a company of persons gathered for deliberation and legislation, worship, or entertainment
**2** *capitalized* **:** a legislative body; *specifically* **:** the lower house of a legislature
**3 :** ASSEMBLAGE 1, 2
**4 :** a signal for troops to assemble or fall in
**5 a :** the fitting together of manufactured parts into a complete machine, structure, or unit of a machine **b :** a collection of parts so assembled
**6 :** the translation of assembly language to machine language by an assembler
**assembly language** *noun* (circa 1964)
**:** a programming language that consists of instructions that are mnemonic codes for corresponding machine language instructions
**assembly line** *noun* (1914)
**1 :** an arrangement of machines, equipment, and workers in which work passes from operation to operation in direct line until the product is assembled
**2 :** a process for turning out a finished product in a mechanically efficient manner ⟨academic *assembly lines*⟩

**as·sem·bly·man** \ə-'sem-blē-mən\ *noun* (1647)
**:** a member of an assembly
**Assembly of God** (1952)
**:** a congregation belonging to a Pentecostal body founded in the U.S. in 1914
**as·sem·bly·wom·an** \-,wu̇-mən\ *noun* (1969)
**:** a woman who is a member of an assembly
¹**as·sent** \ə-'sent, a-\ *intransitive verb* [Middle English, from Old French *assenter*, from Latin *assentari*, from *assentire*, from *ad-* + *sentire* to feel — more at SENSE] (14th century)
**:** to agree to something especially after thoughtful consideration **:** CONCUR ☆
— **as·sen·tor** *or* **as·sent·er** \-'sen-tər\ *noun*
²**assent** *noun* (14th century)
**:** an act of assenting **:** ACQUIESCENCE, AGREEMENT
**as·sen·ta·tion** \,a-s³n-'tā-shən, ,a-,sen-\ *noun* (15th century)
**:** ready assent especially when insincere or obsequious
**as·sert** \ə-'sərt, a-\ *transitive verb* [Latin *assertus*, past participle of *asserere*, from *ad-* + *serere* to join — more at SERIES] (circa 1604)
**1 :** to state or declare positively and often forcefully or aggressively
**2 a :** to demonstrate the existence of ⟨*assert* his manhood —James Joyce⟩ **b :** POSIT, POSTULATE ☆
— **assert oneself :** to compel recognition especially of one's rights
**as·sert·ed·ly** \ə-'sər-təd-lē, a-\ *adverb* (1937)
**:** by positive and usually unsubstantiated assertion **:** ALLEGEDLY
**as·ser·tion** \ə-'sər-shən, a-\ *noun* (15th century)
**:** the act of asserting; *also* **:** DECLARATION, AFFIRMATION
**as·ser·tive** \ə-'sər-tiv, a-\ *adjective* (circa 1619)
**1 :** disposed to or characterized by bold or confident assertion
**2 :** having a strong or distinctive flavor or aroma ⟨*assertive* wines⟩
*synonym* see AGGRESSIVE
— **as·ser·tive·ly** *adverb*
— **as·ser·tive·ness** *noun*
**assertiveness training** *noun* (1975)
**:** a method of training individuals to act in a bold self-confident manner
**asses** *plural of* AS *or of* ASS
**as·sess** \ə-'seṡ, a-\ *transitive verb* [Middle English, probably from Medieval Latin *assessus*, past participle of *assidēre*, from Latin, to sit beside, assist in the office of a judge — more at ASSIZE] (15th century)
**1 :** to determine the rate or amount of (as a tax)
**2 a :** to impose (as a tax) according to an established rate **b :** to subject to a tax, charge, or levy
**3 :** to make an official valuation of (property) for the purposes of taxation
**4 :** to determine the importance, size, or value of
**5 :** to charge (a player or team) with a foul or penalty
*synonym* see ESTIMATE
— **as·sess·able** \-'se-sə-bəl\ *adjective*
**as·sess·ment** \ə-'ses-mənt, a-\ *noun* (1534)
**1 :** the action or an instance of assessing **:** APPRAISAL
**2 :** the amount assessed
**as·ses·sor** \ə-'se-sər\ *noun* (14th century)
**1 :** an official who assists a judge or magistrate
**2 :** one that assesses; *especially* **:** an official who assesses property for taxation
**as·set** \'a-,set *also* -sət\ *noun* [back-formation from *assets*, singular, sufficient property to pay debts and legacies, from Anglo-French *asetz*, from Old French *assez* enough, from (assumed) Vulgar Latin *ad satis*, from Latin

*ad* to + *satis* enough — more at AT, SAD] (1531)
**1** *plural* **a :** the property of a deceased person subject by law to the payment of his or her debts and legacies **b :** the entire property of a person, association, corporation, or estate applicable or subject to the payment of debts
**2 :** ADVANTAGE, RESOURCE ⟨his wit is his chief *asset*⟩
**3 a :** an item of value owned **b** *plural* **:** the items on a balance sheet showing the book value of property owned
**as·sev·er·ate** \ə-'se-və-,rāt\ *transitive verb* **-at·ed; -at·ing** [Latin *asseveratus*, past participle of *asseverare*, from *ad-* + *severus* severe] (1791)
**:** to affirm or aver positively or earnestly
— **as·sev·er·a·tion** \-,se-və-'rā-shən\ *noun*
— **as·sev·er·a·tive** \-'se-və-,rā-tiv\ *adjective*
**ass·hole** \'as-,(h)ōl\ *noun* (14th century)
**1 :** ANUS — usually considered vulgar
**2 a :** a stupid, incompetent, or detestable person — usually considered vulgar **b :** a despicable place — usually used in the phrase *asshole of the universe*; usually considered vulgar
**as·si·du·i·ty** \,a-sə-'dü-ə-tē, -'dyü-\ *noun, plural* **-ities** (1596)
**1 :** the quality or state of being assiduous **:** DILIGENCE
**2 :** persistent personal attention — usually used in plural
**as·sid·u·ous** \ə-'sij-wəs, -'si-jə-\ *adjective* [Latin *assiduus*, from *assidēre*] (1660)
**:** marked by careful unremitting attention or persistent application ⟨an *assiduous* book collector⟩ ⟨tended her garden with *assiduous* attention⟩
*synonym* see BUSY
— **as·sid·u·ous·ly** *adverb*
— **as·sid·u·ous·ness** *noun*

---

☆ SYNONYMS
**Assent, consent, accede, acquiesce, agree, subscribe** mean to concur with what has been proposed. ASSENT implies an act involving the understanding or judgment and applies to propositions or opinions ⟨voters *assented* to the proposal⟩. CONSENT involves the will or feelings and indicates compliance with what is requested or desired ⟨*consented* to their daughter's going⟩. ACCEDE implies a yielding, often under pressure, of assent or consent ⟨officials *acceded* to the prisoners' demands⟩. ACQUIESCE implies tacit acceptance or forbearance of opposition ⟨*acquiesced* to his boss's wishes⟩. AGREE sometimes implies previous difference of opinion or attempts at persuasion ⟨finally *agreed* to come along⟩. SUBSCRIBE implies not only consent or assent but hearty approval and active support ⟨*subscribes* wholeheartedly to the idea⟩.

**Assert, declare, affirm, protest, avow** mean to state positively usually in anticipation of denial or objection. ASSERT implies stating confidently without need for proof or regard for evidence ⟨*asserted* that modern music is just noise⟩. DECLARE stresses open or public statement ⟨*declared* her support for the candidate⟩. AFFIRM implies conviction based on evidence, experience, or faith ⟨*affirmed* the existence of an afterlife⟩. PROTEST emphasizes affirming in the face of denial or doubt ⟨*protested* that he really had been misquoted⟩. AVOW stresses frank declaration and acknowledgment of personal responsibility for what is declared ⟨*avowed* that all investors would be repaid in full⟩. See in addition MAINTAIN.

¹**as·sign** \ə-'sīn\ *transitive verb* [Middle English, from Old French *assigner,* from Latin *assignare,* from *ad-* + *signare* to mark, from *signum* mark, sign] (13th century)
**1 :** to transfer (property) to another especially in trust or for the benefit of creditors
**2 a :** to appoint to a post or duty ⟨*assigned* them to light duty⟩ ⟨*assigned* me two clerks⟩ **b :** to appoint as a duty or task ⟨*assigns* 20 pages for homework⟩
**3 :** to fix or specify in correspondence or relationship ⟨*assign* counsel to the defendant⟩ ⟨*assign* a value to the variable⟩
**4 a :** to ascribe as a motive, reason, or cause especially after deliberation **b :** to consider to belong to (a specified period of time)
**synonym** see ASCRIBE
— **as·sign·abil·i·ty** \-,sī-nə-'bi-lə-tē\ *noun*
— **as·sign·able** \-'sī-nə-bəl\ *adjective*
— **as·sign·er** \ə-'sī-nər\ *or* **as·sign·or** \,a-sə-'nȯr, ,a-,sī-, ə-,sī-\ *noun*

²**assign** *noun* (15th century)
**:** ASSIGNEE 3 ⟨heirs and *assigns*⟩

**as·si·gnat** \,a-(,)sēn-'yä, 'a-sig-,nat\ *noun* [French, from Latin *assignatus,* past participle of *assignare*] (1790)
**:** a bill issued as currency by the French Revolutionary government (1789–96) on the security of expropriated lands

**as·sig·na·tion** \,a-sig-'nā-shən\ *noun* (15th century)
**1 :** the act of assigning or the assignment made
**2 :** an appointment of time and place for a meeting; *especially* **:** TRYST ⟨returned from an *assignation* with his mistress —W. B. Yeats⟩

**assigned risk** *noun* (1946)
**:** a poor risk (as an accident-prone motorist) that insurance companies would normally reject but are forced to insure by state law

**as·sign·ee** \,a-sə-'nē, ,a-,sī-, ə-,sī-\ *noun* (14th century)
**1 :** a person to whom an assignment is made
**2 :** a person appointed to act for another
**3 :** a person to whom a right or property is legally transferred

**as·sign·ment** \ə-'sīn-mənt\ *noun* (14th century)
**1 :** the act of assigning
**2 a :** a position, post, or office to which one is assigned **b :** a specified task or amount of work assigned or undertaken as if assigned by authority
**3 :** the transfer of property; *especially* **:** the transfer of property to be held in trust or to be used for the benefit of creditors
**synonym** see TASK

**as·sim·i·la·ble** \ə-'si-mə-lə-bəl\ *adjective* (1667)
**:** capable of being assimilated
— **as·sim·i·la·bil·i·ty** \-,si-mə-lə-'bi-lə-tē\ *noun*

¹**as·sim·i·late** \ə-'si-mə-,lāt\ *verb* **-lat·ed; -lat·ing** [Middle English, from Medieval Latin *assimilatus,* past participle of *assimilare,* from Latin *assimilare* to make similar, from *ad-* + *simulare* to make similar, simulate] (15th century)
*transitive verb*
**1 a :** to take in and appropriate as nourishment **:** absorb into the system **b :** to take into the mind and thoroughly comprehend
**2 a :** to make similar **b :** to alter by assimilation **c :** to absorb into the culture or mores of a population or group
**3 :** COMPARE, LIKEN
*intransitive verb*
**:** to become assimilated ∎
— **as·sim·i·la·tor** \-,lā-tər\ *noun*

²**as·sim·i·late** \-lət, -,lāt\ *noun* (1935)
**:** something that is assimilated

**as·sim·i·la·tion** \ə-,si-mə-'lā-shən\ *noun* (15th century)
**1 a :** an act, process, or instance of assimilating **b :** the state of being assimilated
**2 :** the incorporation or conversion of nutri-

ents into protoplasm that in animals follows digestion and absorption and in higher plants involves both photosynthesis and root absorption
**3 :** change of a sound in speech so that it becomes identical with or similar to a neighboring sound ⟨the usual *assimilation* of \z\ to \sh\ in the phrase *his shoe*⟩
**4 :** the process of receiving new facts or of responding to new situations in conformity with what is already available to consciousness

**as·sim·i·la·tion·ist** \-sh(ə-)nist\ *noun* (1899)
**:** a person who advocates a policy of assimilating differing racial or cultural groups
— **as·sim·i·la·tion·ism** \-shə-,ni-zəm\ *noun*
— **as·sim·i·la·tion·ist** *adjective*

**as·sim·i·la·tive** \ə-'si-mə-,lā-tiv, -lə-tiv\ *adjective* (14th century)
**:** of, relating to, or causing assimilation

**as·sim·i·la·to·ry** \ə-'si-mə-lə-,tȯr-ē, -,tȯr-\ *adjective* (circa 1847)
**:** ASSIMILATIVE

**As·sin·i·boin** *or* **As·sin·i·boine** \ə-'si-nə-,bȯin\ *noun, plural* **-boin** *or* **-boins** *or* **boine** *or* **-boines** [Ojibwa dialect *assini'pwa'n,* literally, stone Sioux] (1804)
**:** a member of an American Indian people originally of the area between the upper Missouri and middle Saskatchewan rivers

¹**as·sist** \ə-'sist\ *verb* [Middle French or Latin; Middle French *assister* to help, stand by, from Latin *assistere,* from *ad-* + *sistere* to cause to stand; akin to Latin *stare* to stand — more at STAND] (15th century)
*transitive verb*
**:** to give usually supplementary support or aid to
*intransitive verb*
**1 :** to give support or aid ⟨*assisted* at the stove⟩ ⟨another surgeon *assisted* on the operation⟩
**2 :** to be present as a spectator ⟨the ideal figures *assisting* at Italian holy scenes —Mary McCarthy⟩

²**assist** *noun* (1597)
**1 :** an act of assistance **:** AID
**2 :** the action (as a throw or pass) of a player who enables a teammate to make a putout or score a goal; *also* **:** official credit given for such an action
**3 :** a mechanical device that provides assistance

**as·sis·tance** \ə-'sis-tən(t)s\ *noun* (14th century)
**:** the act of assisting or the help supplied **:** AID ⟨financial and technical *assistance*⟩

**as·sis·tant** \-tənt\ *noun* (15th century)
**:** a person who assists **:** HELPER; *also* **:** a person holding an assistantship
— **assistant** *adjective*

**assistant professor** *noun* (1851)
**:** a member of a college or university faculty who ranks above an instructor and below an associate professor
— **assistant professorship** *noun*

**as·sis·tant·ship** \ə-'sis-tən(t)-,ship\ *noun* (1948)
**:** a paid appointment awarded annually to a qualified graduate student that requires part-time teaching, research, or residence hall duties

**as·size** \ə-'sīz\ *noun* [Middle English *assise,* from Old French, session, settlement, from *asseoir* to seat, from (assumed) Vulgar Latin *assedēre,* from Latin *assidēre* to sit beside, assist in the office of a judge, from *ad-* + *sedēre* to sit — more at SIT] (14th century)
**1 a :** a judicial inquest **b :** an action to be decided by such an inquest, the writ for instituting it, or the verdict or finding rendered by the jury
**2 a :** the former periodical sessions of the superior courts in English counties for trial of civil and criminal cases — usually used in

plural **b :** the time or place of holding such a court, the court itself, or a session of it — usually used in plural

¹**as·so·ci·ate** \ə-'sō-shē-,āt, -sē-\ *verb* **-at·ed; -at·ing** [Middle English *associat* associated, from Latin *associatus,* past participle of *associare* to unite, from *ad-* + *sociare* to join, from *socius* companion — more at SOCIAL] (14th century)
*transitive verb*
**1 :** to join as a partner, friend, or companion
**2** *obsolete* **:** to keep company with **:** ATTEND
**3 :** to join or connect together **:** COMBINE
**4 :** to bring together or into relationship in any of various intangible ways (as in memory or imagination)
*intransitive verb*
**1 :** to come or be together as partners, friends, or companions
**2 :** to combine or join with other parts **:** UNITE
**synonym** see JOIN

²**as·so·ci·ate** \ə-'sō-shē-ət, -sē-, -,āt, -shət\ *adjective* (14th century)
**1 :** closely connected (as in function or office) with another
**2 :** closely related especially in the mind
**3 :** having secondary or subordinate status ⟨*associate* membership in a society⟩

³**as·so·ci·ate** \*same as* ²\ *noun* (1533)
**1 :** one associated with another: as **a :** PARTNER, COLLEAGUE **b :** COMPANION, COMRADE
**2 a :** an entry-level member (as of a learned society, professional organization, or profession) **b :** EMPLOYEE, WORKER
**3** *often capitalized* **:** a degree conferred especially by a junior college ⟨*associate* in arts⟩
— **as·so·ci·ate·ship** \-,ship\ *noun*

**associate professor** *noun* (1822)
**:** a member of a college or university faculty who ranks above an assistant professor and below a professor
— **associate professorship** *noun*

**as·so·ci·a·tion** \ə-,sō-sē-'ā-shən, -shē-\ *noun* (1535)
**1 a :** the act of associating **b :** the state of being associated **:** COMBINATION, RELATIONSHIP
**2 :** an organization of persons having a common interest **:** SOCIETY
**3 :** something linked in memory or imagination with a thing or person
**4 :** the process of forming mental connections or bonds between sensations, ideas, or memories
**5 :** the aggregation of chemical species to form (as with hydrogen bonds) loosely bound complexes
**6 :** a major unit in ecological community organization characterized by essential uniformity and usually by two or more dominant species
— **as·so·ci·a·tion·al** \-sh(ə-)nʔl\ *adjective*

**association area** *noun* (circa 1909)
**:** an area of the cerebral cortex that functions in linking and coordinating the sensory and motor areas

**association football** *noun* (1873)
**:** SOCCER

**as·so·ci·a·tion·ism** \ə-,sō-sē-'ā-shə-,ni-zəm, -,sō-shē-\ *noun* (1875)
**:** a reductionist school of psychology that

☐ USAGE
**assimilate** When *assimilate* is followed by a preposition, transitive senses 2a and 2c commonly take *to* and *into* and less frequently *with;* 2b regularly takes *to;* sense 3 most often takes *to* and sometimes *with.* The most frequent prepositions used with the intransitive sense are *to* and *into.*

\ə\ abut \ᵊ\ kitten \ər\ further \a\ ash \ā\ ace \ä\ mop, mar \aù\ out \ch\ chin \e\ bet \ē\ easy \g\ go \i\ hit \ī\ ice \j\ job \ŋ\ sing \ō\ go \ȯ\ law \ȯi\ boy \th\ thin \t͟h\ the \ü\ loot \ù\ foot \y\ yet \zh\ vision *see also* Guide to Pronunciation

holds that the content of consciousness can be explained by the association and reassociation of irreducible sensory and perceptual elements — **as·so·ci·a·tion·ist** \-'ā-sh(ə-)nist\ *noun* — **as·so·ci·a·tion·is·tic** \-,ā-shə-'nis-tik\ *adjective*

**as·so·cia·tive** \ə-'sō-shē-,ā-tiv, -sē-, -shə-tiv\ *adjective* (1812)
**1 :** of or relating to association especially of ideas or images
**2 :** dependent on or acquired by association or learning
**3 :** of, having, or being the property of producing the same result no matter which pair of elements next to each other in a mathematical expression is used to perform a given operation first if the elements in the expression are listed in a fixed order ⟨addition is *associative* since $(a + b) + c = a + (b + c)$⟩ — **as·so·cia·tive·ly** *adverb* — **as·so·cia·tiv·i·ty** \-,sō-shē-ə-'ti-və-tē, -sē-, -shə-'ti-\ *noun*

**associative learning** *noun* (1957)
**:** a learning process in which discrete ideas and percepts become linked to one another

**associative neuron** *noun* (1935)
**:** a neuron that conveys impulses from one neuron to another

**as·soil** \ə-'sói(ə)l\ *transitive verb* [Middle English, from Old French *assoldre,* from Latin *absolvere* to absolve] (13th century)
**1** *archaic* **:** ABSOLVE, PARDON
**2** *archaic* **:** ACQUIT, CLEAR
**3** *archaic* **:** EXPIATE — **as·soil·ment** \-mənt\ *noun, archaic*

**as·so·nance** \'a-sə-nən(t)s\ *noun* [French, from Latin *assonare* to answer with the same sound, from *ad-* + *sonare* to sound, from *sonus* sound — more at SOUND] (1727)
**1 :** resemblance of sound in words or syllables
**2 a :** relatively close juxtaposition of similar sounds especially of vowels **b :** repetition of vowels without repetition of consonants (as in *stony* and *holy*) used as an alternative to rhyme in verse — **as·so·nant** \-nənt\ *adjective or noun* — **as·so·nant·al** \,a-sə-'nan-t°l\ *adjective*

**as soon as** *conjunction* (14th century)
**:** immediately at or shortly after the time that

**as·sort** \ə-'sòrt\ *verb* [Middle French *assortir,* from *a-* (from Latin *ad-*) + *sorte* sort] (15th century)
*transitive verb*
**1 :** to distribute into groups of a like kind **:** CLASSIFY
**2 :** to supply with an assortment (as of goods)
*intransitive verb*
**1 :** to agree in kind **:** HARMONIZE
**2 :** to keep company **:** ASSOCIATE — **as·sort·er** *noun*

**as·sor·ta·tive** \ə-'sòr-tə-tiv\ *adjective* (1897)
**:** being nonrandom mating based on like or unlike characteristics — **as·sor·ta·tive·ly** \-lē\ *adverb*

**as·sort·ed** \-'sòr-təd\ *adjective* (circa 1797)
**1 :** suited especially by nature or character ⟨an ill-*assorted* pair⟩
**2 :** consisting of various kinds ⟨*assorted* chocolates⟩

**as·sort·ment** \-'sòrt-mənt\ *noun* (1611)
**1 a :** the act of assorting **b :** the state of being assorted
**2 :** a collection of assorted things or persons

**as·suage** \ə-'swāj *also* -'swāzh *or* -'swäzh\ *transitive verb* **as·suaged; as·suag·ing** [Middle English *aswagen,* from Old French *assouagier,* from (assumed) Vulgar Latin *assuaviare,* from Latin *ad-* + *suavis* sweet — more at SWEET] (14th century)
**1 :** to lessen the intensity of (something that pains or distresses) **:** EASE
**2 :** PACIFY, QUIET
**3 :** to put an end to by satisfying **:** APPEASE, QUENCH
**synonym** *see* RELIEVE — **as·suage·ment** \-mənt\ *noun*

**as·sua·sive** \ə-'swā-siv, -ziv\ *adjective* (1708)
**:** SOOTHING, CALMING

**as·sume** \ə-'süm\ *transitive verb* **as·sumed; as·sum·ing** [Middle English, from Latin *assumere,* from *ad-* + *sumere* to take — more at CONSUME] (15th century)
**1 a :** to take up or in **:** RECEIVE **b :** to take into partnership, employment, or use
**2 a :** to take to or upon oneself **:** UNDERTAKE **b :** PUT ON, DON
**3 :** to take control of
**4 :** to pretend to have or be **:** FEIGN ⟨*assumed* an air of confidence in spite of her dismay⟩
**5 :** to take as granted or true **:** SUPPOSE
**6 :** to take over (the debts of another) as one's own ☆ — **as·sum·abil·i·ty** \-,sü-mə-'bi-lə-tē\ *noun* — **as·sum·able** \-'sü-mə-bəl\ *adjective* — **as·sum·ably** \-blē\ *adverb*

**as·sum·ing** *adjective* (1695)
**:** PRETENTIOUS, PRESUMPTUOUS

**as·sump·sit** \ə-'səm(p)-sət\ *noun* [New Latin, he undertook, from Latin *assumere* to undertake] (1590)
**1 :** an express or implied promise or contract not under seal on which an action may be brought
**2 a :** a former common-law action brought to recover damages alleged from the breach of an assumpsit **b :** an action to recover damages for breach of a contract

**as·sump·tion** \ə-'səm(p)-shən\ *noun* [Middle English, from Late Latin *assumption-, assumptio* taking up, from Latin *assumere*] (13th century)
**1 a :** the taking up of a person into heaven **b** *capitalized* **:** August 15 observed in commemoration of the Assumption of the Virgin Mary
**2 :** a taking to or upon oneself ⟨the *assumption* of a new position⟩
**3 :** the act of laying claim to or taking possession of something ⟨the *assumption* of power⟩
**4 :** ARROGANCE, PRETENSION
**5 a :** an assuming that something is true **b :** a fact or statement (as a proposition, axiom, postulate, or notion) taken for granted
**6 :** the taking over of another's debts

**as·sump·tive** \ə-'səm(p)-tiv\ *adjective* (1611)
**:** of, relating to, or based on assumption

**as·sur·ance** \ə-'shùr-ən(t)s\ *noun* (14th century)
**1 :** the act or action of assuring: as **a :** PLEDGE, GUARANTEE **b :** the act of conveying real property; *also* **:** the instrument by which it is conveyed **c** *chiefly British* **:** INSURANCE
**2 :** the state of being assured: as **a :** SECURITY **b :** a being certain in the mind ⟨the puritan's *assurance* of salvation⟩ **c :** confidence of mind or manner **:** easy freedom from self-doubt or uncertainty; *also* **:** excessive self-confidence **:** BRASHNESS, PRESUMPTION
**3 :** something that inspires or tends to inspire confidence ⟨gave repeated *assurances* of goodwill⟩
**synonym** *see* CONFIDENCE

**as·sure** \ə-'shùr\ *transitive verb* **as·sured; as·sur·ing** [Middle English, from Middle French *assurer,* from Medieval Latin *assecurare,* from Latin *ad-* + *securus* secure] (14th century)
**1 :** to make safe (as from risks or against overthrow) **:** INSURE
**2 :** to give confidence to ⟨and hereby we know that we are of the truth, and shall *assure* our hearts —1 John 3:19 (Authorized Version)⟩
**3 :** to make sure or certain **:** CONVINCE ⟨glancing back to *assure* himself no one was following⟩
**4 :** to inform positively ⟨I *assure* you that we will do better next time⟩
**5 :** to make certain the coming or attainment of **:** GUARANTEE ⟨worked hard to *assure* accuracy⟩
**synonym** *see* ENSURE

**¹as·sured** \ə-'shùrd\ *adjective* (15th century)
**1 :** characterized by certainty or security **:** GUARANTEED ⟨an *assured* market⟩
**2 a :** SELF-ASSURED **b :** SELF-SATISFIED
**3 :** satisfied as to the certainty or truth of a matter ⟨rest *assured* we got what we came for⟩ — **as·sured·ness** \-'shùr-əd-nəs, -'shùrd-\ *noun*

**²assured** *noun, plural* **assured** *or* **assureds** (1755)
**:** INSURED

**as·sured·ly** \ə-'shùr-əd-lē\ *adverb* (14th century)
**1 :** without a doubt **:** CERTAINLY
**2 :** in an assured manner **:** CONFIDENTLY

**as·sur·er** \ə-'shùr-ər\ *or* **as·sur·or** \ə-'shùr-ər, ə-,shùr-'òr\ *noun* (1607)
**:** one that assures **:** INSURER

**as·sur·gent** \ə-'sər-jənt\ *adjective* [Latin *assurgent-, assurgens,* present participle of *assurgere* to rise, from *ad-* + *surgere* to rise — more at SURGE] (1578)
**:** moving upward **:** RISING; *especially* **:** ASCENDANT 1b

**As·syr·i·an** \ə-'sir-ē-ən\ *noun* (15th century)
**1 :** a native or inhabitant of ancient Assyria
**2 :** the dialect of Akkadian spoken by the Assyrians — **Assyrian** *adjective*

**As·syr·i·ol·o·gy** \ə-,sir-ē-'ä-lə-jē\ *noun* (1828)
**:** the science or study of the history, language, and antiquities of ancient Assyria and Babylonia — **As·syr·i·o·log·i·cal** \-,sir-ē-ə-'lä-ji-kəl\ *adjective* — **As·syr·i·ol·o·gist** \-'ä-lə-jist\ *noun*

**-ast** *noun suffix* [Middle English, from Latin *-astes,* from Greek *-astēs,* from verbs in *-azein*]
**:** one connected with ⟨ecdysi*ast*⟩

**astar·board** \ə-'stär-bərd\ *adverb* (circa 1630)
**:** toward or on the starboard side of a ship ⟨put the helm hard *astarboard*⟩

**As·tar·te** \ə-'stär-tē\ *noun* [Latin, from Greek *Astartē*]
**:** the Phoenician goddess of fertility and of sexual love

**as·ta·tine** \'as-tə-,tēn\ *noun* [Greek *astatos* unsteady, from *a-* + *statos* standing, from *histanai* to cause to stand — more at STAND] (1947)
**:** a radioactive halogen element discovered by bombarding bismuth with alpha particles and also formed by radioactive decay — see ELEMENT table

**as·ter** \'as-tər\ *noun* (1664)
**1** [New Latin, from Latin, aster, from Greek *aster-, astēr* star, aster — more at STAR] **a** **:** any of various chiefly fall-blooming leafy-stemmed composite herbs (*Aster* and closely

---

related genera) with often showy heads containing disk flowers or both disk and ray flowers **b** : CHINA ASTER
**2** [New Latin, from Greek *aster-*, *astēr*] : a system of microtubules arranged radially about a centriole at either end of the mitotic or meiotic spindle
**-aster** *noun suffix* [Middle English, from Latin, suffix denoting partial resemblance]
: one that is inferior or not genuine ⟨criticaster⟩
**as·te·ria** \a-'stir-ē-ə\ *noun* [Latin, a precious stone, from Greek, feminine of *asterios* starry, from *aster-*, *astēr*] (1903)
: a gemstone cut to show asterism
**as·te·ri·at·ed** \-ē-ˌā-təd\ *adjective* [Greek *asterios*] (1816)
: exhibiting asterism ⟨*asteriated* sapphire⟩
**¹as·ter·isk** \'as-tə-ˌrisk, *especially in plural also* ÷-ˌrik\ *noun* [Middle English, *astarisc*, from Late Latin *asteriscus*, from Greek *asteriskos*, literally, little star, diminutive of *aster-*, *astēr*] (14th century)
: the character * used in printing or writing as a reference mark, as an indication of the omission of letters or words, to denote a hypothetical or unattested linguistic form, or for various arbitrary meanings
— **as·ter·isk·less** \-ləs\ *adjective*
**²asterisk** *transitive verb* (circa 1733)
: to mark with an asterisk : STAR
**as·ter·ism** \'as-tə-ˌri-zəm\ *noun* [Greek *asterismos*, from *asterizein* to arrange in constellations, from *aster-*, *astēr*] (1598)
**1 a** : CONSTELLATION **b** : a small group of stars
**2** : a star-shaped figure exhibited by some crystals by reflected light (as in a star sapphire) or by transmitted light (as in some mica)
**astern** \ə-'stərn\ *adverb or adjective* (1627)
**1** : behind a ship
**2** : at or toward the stern of a ship
**3** : STERNFOREMOST, BACKWARD
**¹as·ter·oid** \'as-tə-ˌrȯid\ *noun* [Greek *asteroeidēs* starlike, from *aster-*, *astēr*] (1802)
**1** : any of the small celestial bodies found especially between the orbits of Mars and Jupiter
**2** : STARFISH
— **as·ter·oi·dal** \ˌas-tə-'rȯi-d°l\ *adjective*
**²asteroid** *adjective* (1854)
**1** : resembling a star ⟨*asteroid* bodies in sporotrichosis⟩
**2** : of or resembling a starfish
**asteroid belt** *noun* (1952)
: the region of interplanetary space between the orbits of Mars and Jupiter in which most asteroids are found
**aster yellows** *noun plural* (1922)
: a widespread disease that affects more than 40 families of plants, is characterized especially by yellowing and dwarfing, and is caused by a mycoplasma transmitted by leafhoppers
**as·the·nia** \as-'thē-nē-ə\ *noun* [New Latin, from Greek *astheneia*, from *asthenēs* weak, from *a-* + *sthenos* strength] (1802)
: lack or loss of strength : DEBILITY
**as·then·ic** \as-'the-nik\ *adjective* (1789)
**1** : of, relating to, or exhibiting asthenia : WEAK
**2** : ECTOMORPHIC 2
**as·the·no·sphere** \as-'the-nə-ˌsfir\ *noun* [Greek *asthenēs* weak + English *-o-* + *sphere*] (1914)
: a hypothetical zone of a celestial body (as the earth) which lies beneath the lithosphere and within which the material is believed to yield readily to persistent stresses
— **as·the·no·spher·ic** \-ˌthe-nə-'sfir-ik, -'sfer-\ *adjective*
**asth·ma** \'az-mə, *British* 'as-\ *noun* [Middle English *asma*, from Medieval Latin, modification of Greek *asthma*] (14th century)
: a condition often of allergic origin that is marked by continuous or paroxysmal labored breathing accompanied by wheezing, by a

sense of constriction in the chest, and often by attacks of coughing or gasping
— **asth·mat·ic** \az-'ma-tik, *British* as-\ *adjective or noun*
— **asth·mat·i·cal·ly** \-ti-k(ə-)lē\ *adverb*
**as though** *conjunction* (13th century)
: AS IF
**as·tig·mat·ic** \ˌas-tig-'ma-tik\ *adjective* [*a-* + Greek *stigmat-*, *stigma* stigma] (1849)
**1** : affected with, relating to, or correcting astigmatism
**2** : showing incapacity for observation or discrimination ⟨an *astigmatic* fanaticism, a disregard for the facts —*N.Y. Herald Tribune*⟩
— **astigmatic** *noun*
**astig·ma·tism** \ə-'stig-mə-ˌti-zəm\ *noun* (1849)
**1** : a defect of an optical system (as a lens) causing rays from a point to fail to meet in a focal point resulting in a blurred and imperfect image
**2** : a defect of vision due to astigmatism of the refractive system of the eye and especially to corneal irregularity
**3** : distorted understanding suggestive of the blurred vision of an astigmatic person
**astil·be** \ə-'stil-(ˌ)bē\ *noun* [New Latin, from ²*a-* + Greek *stilbē*, feminine of *stilbos* sparkling]
: any of a genus (*Astilbe*) of chiefly Asian perennials of the saxifrage family having simple or usually compound leaves and widely cultivated for their panicles of white or red flowers
**astir** \ə-'stər\ *adjective* (1823)
**1** : exhibiting activity
**2** : being out of bed : UP
**As·ti Spu·man·te** \ˌäs-tē-spü-'män-(ˌ)tē, 'as-tē-, -spü-'man-\ *noun* [Italian, from *Asti*, Italy + Italian *spumante* effervescent, literally, foaming] (1908)
: a sweet sparkling white wine made in and around the village of Asti in Piedmont
**as to** *preposition* (14th century)
**1** : AS FOR, ABOUT ⟨at a loss *as to* how to explain the error⟩
**2** : ACCORDING TO, BY ⟨graded *as to* size and color⟩
**as·ton·ied** \ə-'stä-nēd\ *adjective* [Middle English, from past participle of *astonien*] (14th century)
**1** *archaic* : deprived briefly of the power to act : DAZED
**2** *archaic* : filled with consternation or dismay
**as·ton·ish** \ə-'stä-nish\ *transitive verb* [probably from earlier *astony* (from Middle English *astonen*, *astonien*, from Old French *estoner*, from — assumed — Vulgar Latin *extonare*, from Latin *ex-* + *tonare* to thunder) + *-ish* (as in *abolish*) — more at THUNDER] (1535)
**1** *obsolete* : to strike with sudden fear
**2** : to strike with sudden and usually great wonder or surprise
**synonym** see SURPRISE
**as·ton·ish·ing** \-ni-shiŋ\ *adjective* (1543)
: causing astonishment : SURPRISING
— **as·ton·ish·ing·ly** \-shiŋ-lē\ *adverb*
**as·ton·ish·ment** \ə-'stä-nish-mənt\ *noun* (circa 1586)
**1 a** : the state of being astonished **b** : CONSTERNATION **c** : AMAZEMENT
**2** : a cause of amazement or wonder
**¹as·tound** \ə-'staund\ *adjective* [Middle English *astoned*, from past participle of *astonen*] (14th century)
*archaic* : overwhelmed with astonishment or amazement : ASTOUNDED
**²astound** *transitive verb* (1634)
: to fill with bewilderment or wonder
**synonym** see SURPRISE
**as·tound·ing** \ə-'staun-diŋ\ *adjective* (1586)
: causing astonishment or amazement
— **as·tound·ing·ly** \-diŋ-lē\ *adverb*
**astr-** *or* **astro-** *combining form* [Middle English *astro-*, from Old French, from Latin *astr-*, *astro-*, from Greek, from *astron* — more at STAR]

: star : heavens : outer space : astronomical ⟨*astrophysics*⟩
**¹astrad·dle** \ə-'stra-d°l\ *adverb* (1703)
: on or above and extending onto both sides : ASTRIDE
**²astraddle** *preposition* (1935)
: with one leg on each side of : ASTRIDE
**as·tra·gal** \'as-tri-gəl\ *noun* [Latin *astragalus*, from Greek *astragalos* anklebone, molding; akin to Greek *astakos* lobster, *osteon* bone — more at OSSEOUS] (1563)
**1** : a narrow half-round molding
**2** : a projecting strip on the edge of a folding door
**as·tra·khan** \'as-trə-kən, -ˌkan\ *noun, often capitalized* [*Astrakhan*, Russia] (1766)
**1** : karakul of Russian origin
**2** : a cloth with a usually wool, curled, and looped pile resembling karakul
**as·tral** \'as-trəl\ *adjective* [Late Latin *astralis*, from Latin *astrum* star, from Greek *astron*] (1605)
**1** : of, relating to, or coming from the stars ⟨*astral* influences⟩ ⟨unusual *astral* occurrences⟩
**2** : of or relating to a mitotic or meiotic aster
**3** : of or consisting of a supersensible substance held in theosophy to be next above the tangible world in refinement
**4 a** : VISIONARY **b** : elevated in station or position : EXALTED
— **as·tral·ly** \-trə-lē\ *adverb*
**astray** \ə-'strā\ *adverb or adjective* [Middle English, from Middle French *estraié* wandering, from *estraier* to stray — more at STRAY] (14th century)
**1** : off the right path or route : STRAYING
**2** : in error : away from what is proper or desirable
**¹astride** \ə-'strīd\ *adverb* (1664)
**1** : with one leg on each side : astride a horse ⟨she rode *astride*, not sidesaddle⟩
**2** : with the legs stretched wide apart ⟨standing *astride*⟩
**²astride** *preposition* (1713)
**1** : on or above and with one leg on each side of
**2** : placed or lying on both sides of
**3** : extending over or across : SPANNING, BRIDGING
**as·trin·gen·cy** \ə-'strin-jən(t)-sē\ *noun* (1601)
: the quality or state of being astringent
**¹as·trin·gent** \-jənt\ *adjective* [probably from Middle French, from Latin *astringent-*, *astringens*, present participle of *astringere* to bind fast, from *ad-* + *stringere* to bind tight — more at STRAIN] (1541)
**1** : able to draw together the soft organic tissues : STYPTIC, PUCKERY ⟨*astringent* lotions⟩ ⟨an *astringent* fruit⟩
**2** : suggestive of an astringent effect upon tissue : rigidly severe : AUSTERE ⟨dry *astringent* comments⟩; *also* : PUNGENT, CAUSTIC
— **as·trin·gent·ly** *adverb*
**²astringent** *noun* (1626)
: an astringent agent or substance
**as·tro·bi·ol·o·gy** \ˌas-trō-(ˌ)bī-'ä-lə-jē\ *noun* (1955)
: EXOBIOLOGY
— **as·tro·bi·ol·o·gist** \-(ˌ)bī-'ä-lə-jist\ *noun*
**as·tro·cyte** \'as-trə-ˌsīt\ *noun* [International Scientific Vocabulary] (1898)
: a star-shaped cell (as of the neuroglia)
— **as·tro·cyt·ic** \ˌas-trə-'si-tik\ *adjective*

---

\ə\ abut \°\ kitten \ər\ further \a\ ash \ā\ ace \ä\ mop, mar \aú\ out \ch\ chin \e\ bet \ē\ easy \g\ go \i\ hit \ī\ ice \j\ job \ŋ\ sing \ō\ go \ò\ law \òi\ boy \th\ thin \t͟h\ the \ü\ loot \ú\ foot \y\ yet \zh\ vision *see also* Guide to Pronunciation

**as·tro·cy·to·ma** \,as-trə-sī-'tō-mə\ *noun, plural* **-mas** *or* **-ma·ta** \-mə-tə\ [New Latin] (circa 1923)
: a nerve-tissue tumor composed of astrocytes

**as·tro·dome** \'as-trə-,dōm\ *noun* [International Scientific Vocabulary] (1941)
: a transparent dome in the upper surface of an airplane from within which the navigator makes celestial observations

**as·tro·labe** \'as-trə-,lāb *also* -,lab\ *noun* [Middle English, from Middle French & Medieval Latin; Middle French, from Medieval Latin *astrolabium,* from Late Greek *astrolabion,* from Greek *astrolabos,* from *astr-* + *lambanein* to take — more at LATCH] (14th century)
: a compact instrument used to observe and calculate the position of celestial bodies before the invention of the sextant

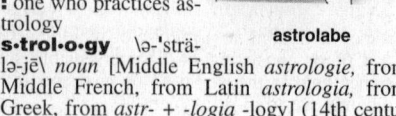

astrolabe

**as·trol·o·ger** \ə-'strä-lə-jər\ *noun* (14th century)
: one who practices astrology

**as·trol·o·gy** \ə-'strä-lə-jē\ *noun* [Middle English *astrologie,* from Middle French, from Latin *astrologia,* from Greek, from *astr-* + *-logia* -logy] (14th century)
**1** *archaic* : ASTRONOMY
**2** : the divination of the supposed influences of the stars and planets on human affairs and terrestrial events by their positions and aspects
— **as·tro·log·i·cal** \,as-trə-'lä-ji-kəl\ *adjective*
— **as·tro·log·i·cal·ly** \-k(ə-)lē\ *adverb*

**as·trom·e·try** \ə-'strä-mə-trē\ *noun* (circa 1859)
: a branch of astronomy that deals with measurements (as of positions and movements) of celestial bodies
— **as·tro·me·tric** \,as-trə-'me-trik\ *adjective*

**as·tro·naut** \'as-trə-,nȯt, -,nät\ *noun* [*astr-* + *-naut* (as in *aeronaut*)] (1929)
: a person who travels beyond the earth's atmosphere; *also* : a trainee for spaceflight

**as·tro·nau·tics** \,as-trə-'nȯ-tiks, -'nä-\ *noun plural but singular or plural in construction* (1928)
: the science of the construction and operation of vehicles for travel in space beyond the earth's atmosphere
— **as·tro·nau·tic** \-tik\ *or* **as·tro·nau·ti·cal** \-ti-kəl\ *adjective*
— **as·tro·nau·ti·cal·ly** \-ti-k(ə-)lē\ *adverb*

**as·tron·o·mer** \ə-'strä-nə-mər\ *noun* (14th century)
: one who is skilled in astronomy or who makes observations of celestial phenomena

**as·tro·nom·i·cal** \,as-trə-'nä-mi-kəl\ *also* **as·tro·nom·ic** \-mik\ *adjective* (1556)
**1** : of or relating to astronomy
**2** : enormously or inconceivably large or great ⟨*astronomical* numbers⟩
— **as·tro·nom·i·cal·ly** \-mi-k(ə-)lē\ *adverb*

**astronomical unit** *noun* (1903)
: a unit of length used in astronomy equal to the mean distance of the earth from the sun or about 93 million miles (150 million kilometers)

**as·tron·o·my** \ə-'strä-nə-mē\ *noun, plural* **-mies** [Middle English *astronomie,* from Old French, from Latin *astronomia,* from Greek, from *astr-* + *-nomia* -nomy] (13th century)
: the study of objects and matter outside the earth's atmosphere and of their physical and chemical properties

**as·tro·pho·tog·ra·phy** \,as-(,)trō-fə-'tä-grə-fē\ *noun* [International Scientific Vocabulary] (circa 1858)

: photography as used in astronomical investigations
— **as·tro·pho·to·graph** \-'fō-tə-,graf\ *noun*
— **as·tro·pho·tog·ra·pher** \-fə-'tä-grə-fər\ *noun*

**as·tro·phys·ics** \,as-trə-'fi-ziks\ *noun plural but singular or plural in construction* [International Scientific Vocabulary] (1890)
: a branch of astronomy dealing especially with the behavior, physical properties, and dynamic processes of celestial objects and phenomena
— **as·tro·phys·i·cal** \-zi-kəl\ *adjective*
— **as·tro·phys·i·cal·ly** \-zi-k(ə-)lē\ *adverb*
— **as·tro·phys·i·cist** \-'fi-zə-sist, -'fiz-sist\ *noun*

**as·tute** \ə-'stüt, a-, -'styüt\ *adjective* [Latin *astutus,* from *astus* craft] (circa 1611)
: having or showing shrewdness and perspicacity ⟨an *astute* observer⟩ ⟨*astute* remarks⟩; *also* : CRAFTY, WILY
**synonym** see SHREWD
— **as·tute·ly** *adverb*
— **as·tute·ness** *noun*

**As·ty·a·nax** \ə-'stī-ə-,naks\ *noun* [Greek]
: a son of Hector and Andromache hurled by the Greeks from the walls of Troy

**asun·der** \ə-'sən-dər\ *adverb or adjective* (14th century)
**1** : into parts ⟨torn *asunder*⟩
**2** : apart from each other in position ⟨wide *asunder*⟩

**aswarm** \ə-'swȯrm\ *adjective* (circa 1869)
: filled to overflowing : SWARMING ⟨streets *aswarm* with people⟩

**¹as well as** *conjunction* (15th century)
: and in addition : AND ⟨brave *as well as* loyal⟩

**²as well as** *preposition* (1589)
: in addition to : BESIDES ⟨the coach, *as well as* the team, is ready⟩

**aswirl** \ə-'swər(-ə)l\ *adjective* (1877)
: being in a swirl : SWIRLING

**aswoon** \ə-'swün\ *adjective* (14th century)
: being in a swoon : DAZED

**asy·lum** \ə-'sī-ləm\ *noun* [Middle English, from Latin, from Greek *asylon,* neuter of *asylos* inviolable, from *a-* + *sylon* right of seizure] (15th century)
**1** : an inviolable place of refuge and protection giving shelter to criminals and debtors : SANCTUARY
**2** : a place of retreat and security : SHELTER
**3 a** : the protection or inviolability afforded by an asylum : REFUGE **b** : protection from arrest and extradition given especially to political refugees by a nation or by an embassy or other agency enjoying diplomatic immunity
**4** : an institution for the care of the destitute or sick and especially the insane

**asym·met·ri·cal** \,ā-sə-'me-tri-kəl\ *or* **asym·met·ric** \-trik\ *adjective* [Greek *asymmetria* lack of proportion, from *asymmetros* ill-proportioned, from *a-* + *symmetros* symmetrical] (1690)
**1** : not symmetrical
**2** *usually* **asymmetric,** *of a carbon atom* : bonded to four different atoms or groups
— **asym·met·ri·cal·ly** \-tri-k(ə-)lē\ *adverb*
— **asym·me·try** \(,)ā-'si-mə-trē\ *noun*

**asymp·tom·at·ic** \,ā-,sim(p)-tə-'ma-tik\ *adjective* (1927)
: presenting no symptoms of disease
— **asymp·tom·at·i·cal·ly** \-ti-k(ə-)lē\ *adverb*

**as·ymp·tote** \'a-səm(p)-,tōt\ *noun* [probably from (assumed) New Latin *asymptotus,* from Greek *asymptōtos* not meeting, from *a-* + *sympiptein* to meet — more at SYMPTOM] (1656)
: a straight line associated with a curve such that as a point moves along an infinite branch of the curve the distance from the point to the line approaches zero and the slope of the curve at the point approaches the slope of the line

— **as·ymp·tot·ic** \,a-səm(p)-'tä-tik\ *adjective*
— **as·ymp·tot·i·cal·ly** \-ti-k(ə-)lē\ *adverb*

**asyn·ap·sis** \,ā-sə-'nap-səs\ *noun, plural* **-ap·ses** \-,sēz\ [New Latin ²*a-* + *synapsis*] (1930)
: failure of pairing of homologous chromosomes in meiosis

**asyn·chro·nous** \(,)ā-'siŋ-krə-nəs, -'sin-\ *adjective* (1748)

asymptotes to the hyperbola

**1** : not synchronous
**2** : of, used in, or being digital communication (as between computers) in which there is no timing requirement for transmission and in which the start of each character is individually signaled by the transmitting device
— **asyn·chro·nous·ly** *adverb*

**asyn·chro·ny** \-krə-nē\ *or* **asyn·chro·nism** \-krə-,ni-zəm\ *noun* (1875)
: the quality or state of being asynchronous : absence or lack of concurrence in time

**as·yn·det·ic** \,a-s°n-'de-tik\ *adjective* (circa 1864)
: marked by asyndeton
— **as·yn·det·i·cal·ly** \-ti-k(ə-)lē\ *adverb*

**asyn·de·ton** \ə-'sin-də-,tän, (,)ā-'sin-\ *noun, plural* **-tons** *or* **-ta** \-də-tə\ [Late Latin, from Greek, from neuter of *asyndetos* unconnected, from *a-* + *syndetos* bound together, from *syndein* to bind together, from *syn-* + *dein* to bind — more at DIADEM] (1555)
: omission of the conjunctions that ordinarily join coordinate words or clauses (as in "I came, I saw, I conquered")

**¹at** \ət, 'at\ *preposition* [Middle English, from Old English *æt;* akin to Old High German *az* at, Latin *ad*] (before 12th century)
**1** — used as a function word to indicate presence or occurrence in, on, or near ⟨staying *at* a hotel⟩ ⟨*at* a party⟩ ⟨sick *at* heart⟩
**2** — used as a function word to indicate the goal of an indicated or implied action or motion ⟨aim *at* the target⟩ ⟨creditors are *at* him again⟩
**3** — used as a function word to indicate that with which one is occupied or employed ⟨*at* work⟩ ⟨*at* the controls⟩ ⟨good *at* chess⟩
**4** — used as a function word to indicate situation in an active or passive state or condition ⟨*at* liberty⟩ ⟨*at* rest⟩
**5** — used as a function word to indicate the means, cause, or manner ⟨sold *at* auction⟩ ⟨laughed *at* my joke⟩ ⟨act *at* your own discretion⟩
**6 a** — used as a function word to indicate the rate, degree, or position in a scale or series ⟨the temperature *at* 90⟩ ⟨*at* first⟩ **b** — used as a function word to indicate age or position in time ⟨will retire *at* 65⟩

**²at** \'ät\ *noun, plural* **at** [Lao] (1955)
— see *kip* at MONEY table

**at-** — see AD-

**At·a·brine** \'a-tə-brən, -,brēn\ *trademark*
— used for quinacrine

**atac·tic** \(,)ā-'tak-tik\ *adjective* [International Scientific Vocabulary ²*a-* + *-tactic*] (1957)
: of, relating to, or being a polymer exhibiting no stereochemical regularity of structure ⟨*atactic* polypropylene⟩ — compare ISOTACTIC

**At·a·lan·ta** \,a-t°l-'an-tə\ *noun* [Latin, from Greek *Atalantē*]
: a fleet-footed huntress in Greek mythology who challenges her suitors to a race and is defeated by Hippomenes when she stops to pick up three golden apples he has dropped

**at all** *adverb* (14th century)
: in any way or respect : to the least extent or degree : under any circumstances ⟨doesn't smoke *at all*⟩

**at·a·man** \,a-tə-'man\ *noun* [Russian] (1835)
: HETMAN

**at·a·mas·co lily** \‚a-tə-'mas-(‚)kō-\ *noun* [Virginia Algonquian *attamusco*] (1743) : any of a genus (*Zephyranthes*) of American bulbous herbs of the amaryllis family with pink, white, or yellowish flowers; *especially* : one (*Z. atamasco*) of the southeastern U.S. with white flowers usually tinged with purple

**at·a·rac·tic** \‚a-tə-'rak-tik\ *or* **at·a·rax·ic** \-'rak-sik\ *noun* [ataractic from Greek *ataraktos* calm, from *a-* + *tarassein* to disturb; *ataraxic* from Greek *ataraxia* calmness, from *a-* + *tarassein*] (1955) : TRANQUILIZER 2
— **ataractic** *or* **ataraxic** *adjective*

**at·a·vism** \'a-tə-‚vi-zəm\ *noun* [French *atavisme*, from Latin *atavus* ancestor, from *at-* (probably akin to *atta* daddy) + *avus* grandfather — more at UNCLE] (1833) **1 a** : recurrence in an organism of a trait or character typical of an ancestral form and usually due to genetic recombination **b** : recurrence of or reversion to a past style, manner, outlook, or approach ⟨architectural *atavism*⟩ **2** : one that manifests atavism : THROWBACK
— **at·a·vis·tic** \‚a-tə-'vis-tik\ *adjective*
— **at·a·vis·ti·cal·ly** \-ti-k(ə-)lē\ *adverb*

**atax·ia** \ə-'tak-sē-ə, (‚)ā-\ *noun* [Greek, from *a-* + *tassein* to put in order] (1670) : an inability to coordinate voluntary muscular movements that is symptomatic of some nervous disorders
— **atax·ic** \-sik\ *adjective*

**at bat** *noun* (1884) : an official time at bat charged to a baseball batter except when he walks, sacrifices, is hit by a pitched ball, or is interfered with by the catcher ⟨three hits in five *at bats*⟩

**ate** *past of* EAT

**Ate** \'ä-tē, 'ā-(‚)tē; 'ä-‚tā\ *noun* [Greek *Atē*] : a Greek goddess personifying foolhardy and ruinous impulse

**¹-ate** *noun suffix* [Middle English *-at*, from Old French, from Latin *-atus, -atum,* masculine & neuter of *-atus,* past participle ending] **1** : one acted upon (in a specified way) ⟨distill*ate*⟩ **2** [New Latin *-atum,* from Latin] : chemical compound or complex anion derived from a (specified) compound or element ⟨phenol*ate*⟩; *especially* : salt or ester of an acid with a name ending in *-ic* and not beginning with *hydro-* ⟨borate⟩

**²-ate** *noun suffix* [Middle English *-at,* from Old French, from Latin *-atus,* from *-a-,* stem vowel of 1st conjugation + *-tus,* suffix of verbal nouns] **1** : office : function : rank : group of persons holding a (specified) office or rank or having a (specified) function ⟨vicar*ate*⟩ **2** : state : dominion : jurisdiction ⟨emir*ate*⟩ ⟨khan*ate*⟩

**³-ate** *adjective suffix* [Middle English *-at,* from Latin *-atus,* from past participle ending of 1st conjugation verbs, from *-a-,* stem vowel of 1st conjugation + *-tus,* past participle suffix — more at -ED] : marked by having ⟨craniate⟩

**⁴-ate** *verb suffix* [Middle English *-aten,* from Latin *-atus,* past participle ending] : act on (in a specified way) ⟨insul*ate*⟩ : cause to be modified or affected by ⟨camphor*ate*⟩ : cause to become ⟨activ*ate*⟩ : furnish with ⟨capacit*ate*⟩

**-ated** *adjective suffix* : ³-ATE ⟨pileat*ed*⟩

**at·el·ec·ta·sis** \‚a-tᵊl-'ek-tə-səs\ *noun, plural* **-ta·ses** \-‚sēz\ [New Latin, from Greek *atelēs* incomplete, defective (from *a-* ²a- + *telos* end) + *ektasis* extension, from *ekteinein* to stretch out, from *ex-* + *teinein* to stretch — more at TELOS, THIN] (1859) : collapse of the expanded lung; *also* : defective expansion of the pulmonary alveoli at birth

**ate·lier** \‚a-tᵊl-'yā\ *noun* [French, from Middle French *astelier* woodpile, from *astele* splinter,

from Late Latin *astella*, diminutive of Latin *astula*] (1699) **1** : an artist's or designer's studio or workroom **2** : WORKSHOP

**ate·moya** \‚ä-tə-'mói-ə, ‚a-\ *noun* [ates sweetsop (from Tagalog) + cheri*moya*] (1914) : a white-pulped tropical fruit of a tree that is a hybrid of the sweetsop and the cherimoya

**a tem·po** \ä-'tem-(‚)pō\ *adverb or adjective* [Italian] (circa 1740) : in time — used as a direction in music to return to the original tempo

**atem·po·ral** \(‚)ā-'tem-p(ə-)rəl\ *adjective* (1870) : independent of or unaffected by time : TIMELESS

**Ate·ri·an** \ə-'tir-ē-ən\ *adjective* [French *atérien,* from Bir el-*Ater* (Constantine), Algeria] (1928) : of or relating to a Paleolithic culture of northern Africa characterized by Mousterian features, tanged arrow points, and leaf-shaped spearheads

**Ath·a·bas·can** \‚a-thə-'bas-kən\ *or* **Ath·a·pas·kan** \-'pas-\ *also* **Ath·a·bas·kan** \-'bas-\ *or* **Ath·a·pas·can** \-'pas-\ *noun* [*Athabasca,* a Cree band, from Cree dialect *aδapaska·w,* name for the area east of Lake Athabasca, literally, (where) there are reeds one after another] (1846) **1** : a family of American Indian languages spoken primarily in western Canada, Alaska, and the U.S. Southwest **2** : a member of a people speaking an Athabascan language

**Ath·a·na·sian** \‚a-thə-'nā-zhən, -shən\ *adjective* (1586) : of or relating to Athanasius or his advocacy of the homoousian doctrine against Arianism

**Athanasian Creed** *noun* (1586) : a Christian creed originating in Europe about A.D. 400 and relating especially to the Trinity and Incarnation

**athe·ism** \'ā-thē-‚i-zəm\ *noun* [Middle French *athéisme,* from *athée* atheist, from Greek *atheos* godless, from *a-* + *theos* god] (1546) **1** *archaic* : UNGODLINESS, WICKEDNESS **2 a** : a disbelief in the existence of deity **b** : the doctrine that there is no deity

**athe·ist** \'ā-thē-ist\ *noun* (1571) : one who denies the existence of God
— **athe·is·tic** \‚ā-thē-'is-tik\ *or* **athe·is·ti·cal** \‚ā-thē-'is-ti-kəl\ *adjective*
— **athe·is·ti·cal·ly** \-ti-k(ə-)lē\ *adverb*

**ath·e·ling** \'a-thə-liŋ, 'a-thᵊl-\ *noun* [Middle English, from Old English *ætheling,* from *æthelu* nobility, akin to Old High German *adal* nobility] (before 12th century) : an Anglo-Saxon prince or nobleman; *especially* : the heir apparent or a prince of the royal family

**Athe·na** \ə-'thē-nə\ *or* **Athe·ne** \-nē\ *noun* [Latin *Athena,* from Greek *Athēnē*] : the Greek goddess of wisdom — compare MINERVA

**ath·e·nae·um** *or* **ath·e·ne·um** \‚a-thə-'nē-əm\ *noun* [Latin *Athenaeum,* a school in ancient Rome for the study of arts, from Greek *Athēnaion,* a temple of Athena, from *Athēnē*] (1799) **1** : a building or room in which books, periodicals, and newspapers are kept for use **2** : a literary or scientific association

**athe·o·ret·i·cal** \‚ā-‚thē-ə-'re-ti-kəl, -‚thi(-ə)r-'e-\ *adjective* (1969) : not based on or concerned with theory

**athero-** *combining form* [Greek *athēra*] : atheroma ⟨*athero*genic⟩

**ath·ero·gen·e·sis** \‚a-thə-rō-'je-nə-səs\ *noun* (1953) : the process of developing atheroma

**ath·ero·gen·ic** \-'je-nik\ *adjective* (1954) : relating to or producing degenerative changes in arterial walls ⟨*athero*genic diet⟩

**ath·er·o·ma** \‚a-thə-'rō-mə\ *noun* [New Latin

*atheromat-, atheroma,* from Latin, a tumor containing matter resembling gruel, from Greek *athērōma,* from *athēra* gruel] (1875) **1** : fatty degeneration of the inner coat of the arteries **2** : an abnormal fatty deposit in an artery
— **ath·er·o·ma·tous** \-'rō-mə-təs\ *adjective*

**ath·ero·scle·ro·sis** \‚a-thə-‚rō-sklə-'rō-səs\ *noun* [New Latin] (1910) : an arteriosclerosis characterized by atheromatous deposits in and fibrosis of the inner layer of the arteries
— **ath·ero·scle·rot·ic** \-sklə-'rä-tik\ *adjective*

**athirst** \ə-'thərst\ *adjective* [Middle English, from Old English *ofthyrst,* past participle of *ofthyrstan* to suffer from thirst, from *of* off, from + *thyrstan* to thirst — more at OF] (before 12th century) **1** *archaic* : THIRSTY **2** : having a strong eager desire ⟨I that for ever feel *athirst* for glory —John Keats⟩
*synonym* see EAGER

**ath·lete** \'ath-‚lēt, ÷'a-thə-‚lēt\ *noun* [Middle English, from Latin *athleta,* from Greek *athlētēs,* from *athlein* to contend for a prize, from *athlon* prize, contest] (15th century) : a person who is trained or skilled in exercises, sports, or games requiring physical strength, agility, or stamina

**athlete's foot** *noun* (1928) : ringworm of the feet

**ath·let·ic** \ath-'le-tik, ÷‚a-thə-'le-\ *adjective* (1636) **1** : of or relating to athletes or athletics **2** : characteristic of an athlete; *especially* : VIGOROUS, ACTIVE **3** : MESOMORPHIC **4** : used by athletes
— **ath·let·i·cal·ly** \-ti-k(ə-)lē\ *adverb*
— **ath·let·i·cism** \-'le-tə-‚si-zəm\ *noun*

**ath·let·ics** \ath-'le-tiks, ÷‚a-thə-'le-\ *noun plural but singular or plural in construction* (1727) **1** : exercises, sports, or games engaged in by athletes **2** : the practice or principles of athletic activities

**athletic supporter** *noun* (1927) : a supporter for the genitals worn by men participating in sports or strenuous activities

**at–home** \ət-'hōm\ *adjective* (1951) **1** : intended or suitable for one's home ⟨an *at-home* dress⟩ **2** : being or occurring at one's home ⟨*at-home* entertainment⟩

**at home** *noun* (1745) : a reception given at one's home

**-athon** *noun combining form* [marathon] : event or activity lasting a long time ⟨talka*thon*⟩

**ath·ro·cyte** \'a-thrə-‚sīt\ *noun* [Greek *athroos* together, collected + International Scientific Vocabulary *-cyte*] (1938) : a cell that has the ability to store up substances of an excretory nature

**¹athwart** \ə-'thwórt, nautical often -'thórt\ *preposition* (15th century) **1** : ACROSS **2** : in opposition to ⟨a procedure directly *athwart* the New England prejudices —R. G. Cole⟩

**²athwart** *adverb* (circa 1500) **1** : across especially in an oblique direction **2** : in opposition to the right or expected course ⟨and quite *athwart* goes all decorum —Shakespeare⟩

**athwart·ship** \-‚ship\ *adjective* (1879)

---

\ə\ abut \ᵊ\ kitten \ər\ further \a\ ash \ā\ ace \ä\ mop, mar \aú\ out \ch\ chin \e\ bet \ē\ easy \g\ go \i\ hit \ī\ ice \j\ job \ŋ\ sing \ō\ go \ó\ law \ói\ boy \th\ thin \th\ the \ü\ loot \ú\ foot \y\ yet \zh\ vision *see also* Guide to Pronunciation

: being across the ship from side to side ⟨*athwartship* and longitudinal framing⟩

**athwart·ships** \-,ships\ *adverb* (1718)
: across the ship from side to side

**atilt** \ə-'tilt\ *adverb or adjective* (1562)
**1** : in a tilted position
**2** : with lance in hand ⟨run *atilt* at death —Shakespeare⟩

**atin·gle** \ə-'tiŋ-gəl\ *adjective* (1855)
: tingling especially with excitement

**-ation** *noun suffix* [Middle English *-acioun,* from Old French *-ation,* from Latin *-ation-, -atio,* from *-a-,* stem vowel of 1st conjugation + *-tion-, -tio,* noun suffix]
: action or process ⟨flir*tation*⟩ : something connected with an action or process ⟨discolor*ation*⟩

**-ative** *adjective suffix* [Middle English, from Middle French *-atif,* from Latin *-ativus,* from *-atus* -ate + *-ivus* -ive]
: of, relating to, or connected with ⟨authorita*tive*⟩ : tending to ⟨talk*ative*⟩

**At·ka mackerel** \'at-kə-, 'ät-\ *noun* [Atka Island, Alaska] (1893)
: a greenling (*Pleurogrammus monopterygius*) of Alaska and adjacent regions valued as a food fish

¹**At·lan·te·an** \,at-,lan-'tē-ən, ət-'lan-tē-\ *adjective* (1667)
: of, relating to, or resembling Atlas : STRONG

²**Atlantean** *adjective* (circa 1828)
: of or relating to Atlantis

**At·lan·tic** \ət-'lan-tik, at-\ *adjective* (1601)
**1 a** : of, relating to, or found in, on, or near the Atlantic Ocean **b** : of, relating to, or found on or near the east coast of the U.S.
**2** : of or relating to the nations that border the Atlantic Ocean ⟨the *Atlantic* community⟩

**Atlantic croaker** *noun* (circa 1949)
: a small fish (*Micropogonias undulatus*) of the Gulf coast and the Atlantic coast — called also *hardhead*

**At·lan·ti·cism** \-'lan-tə-,si-zəm\ *noun* (1950)
: a policy of military cooperation between European powers and the U.S.
— **At·lan·ti·cist** \-sist\ *noun*

**Atlantic salmon** *noun* (1902)
: SALMON 1a

**Atlantic time** *noun* (circa 1909)
: the time of the fourth time zone west of Greenwich that includes the Canadian Maritime Provinces, Puerto Rico, and the Virgin Islands

**At·lan·tis** \ət-'lan-təs, at-\ *noun* [Latin, from Greek, from *Atlas*]
: a fabled island in the Atlantic that according to legend sank beneath the sea

**at·las** \'at-ləs\ *noun* [Latin *Atlant-, Atlas,* from Greek]
**1** *capitalized* : a Titan who for his part in the Titans' revolt against the gods is forced by Zeus to support the heavens on his shoulders
**2** *capitalized* : one who bears a heavy burden
**3 a** : a bound collection of maps often including illustrations, informative tables, or textual matter **b** : a bound collection of tables, charts, or plates
**4** : the first vertebra of the neck
**5** *plural usually* **at·lan·tes** \ət-'lan-(,)tēz, at-\ : a male figure used like a caryatid as a supporting column or pilaster — called also *telamon* ◆

atlas 5

**at·latl** \'ät-,lä-t°l\ *noun* [Nahuatl *ahtlatl*] (1871)
: a device for throwing a spear or dart that consists of a rod or board with a projection (as

a hook or thong) at the rear end to hold the weapon in place until released

**At·li** \'ät-lē\ *noun* [Old Norse]
: a king of the Huns figuring in Germanic legend and corresponding to the historical Attila

**at·man** \'ät-mən, -,män\ *noun, often capitalized* [Sanskrit *ātman,* literally, breath, soul; akin to Old English *ǣthm* breath] (1785)
**1** *Hinduism* : the innermost essence of each individual
**2** *Hinduism* : the supreme universal self : BRAHMA

**at·mom·e·ter** \at-'mä-mə-tər\ *noun* [Greek *atmos* + English *-meter*] (1815)
: an instrument for measuring the evaporating capacity of the air

**at·mo·sphere** \'at-mə-,sfir\ *noun* [New Latin *atmosphaera,* from Greek *atmos* vapor + Latin *sphaera* sphere] (1677)
**1 a** : the gaseous envelope of a celestial body (as a planet) **b** : the whole mass of air surrounding the earth
**2** : the air of a locality
**3** : a surrounding influence or environment ⟨an *atmosphere* of hostility⟩
**4** : a unit of pressure equal to the pressure of the air at sea level or approximately 14.7 pounds per square inch (101,325 pascals)
**5 a** : the overall aesthetic effect of a work of art **b** : a dominant aesthetic or emotional effect or appeal
— **at·mo·sphered** \-,sfird\ *adjective*

**at·mo·spher·ic** \,at-mə-'sfir-ik, -'sfer-\ *adjective* (1783)
**1 a** : of, relating to, or occurring in the atmosphere **b** : resembling the atmosphere : AIRY
**2** : having, marked by, or contributing aesthetic or emotional atmosphere
— **at·mo·spher·i·cal·ly** \-i-k(ə-)lē\ *adverb*

**at·mo·spher·ics** \-iks\ *noun plural* (1915)
**1** : audible disturbances produced in radio receiving apparatus by atmospheric electrical phenomena (as lightning); *also* : the electrical phenomena causing these disturbances
**2** : actions (as official statements) intended to create or suggest a particular atmosphere or mood in politics and especially international relations; *also* : the mood so created or suggested
**3** : realistic detail added (as to a literary work) to create a mood

**atoll** \'a-,tȯl, -,täl, -,tōl, 'ā-\ *noun* [Divehi (Indo-Aryan language of the Maldive Islands) *atolu*] (1625)
: a coral island consisting of a reef surrounding a lagoon

atoll

**at·om** \'a-təm\ *noun* [Middle English, from Latin *atomus,* from Greek *atomos,* from *atomos* indivisible, from *a-* + *temnein* to cut] (15th century)
**1** : one of the minute indivisible particles of which according to ancient materialism the universe is composed
**2** : a tiny particle : BIT
**3** : the smallest particle of an element that can exist either alone or in combination
**4** : the atom considered as a source of vast potential energy ◆

**atom·ic** \ə-'tä-mik\ *adjective* (1678)
**1 a** : of, relating to, or concerned with atoms ⟨*atomic* physics⟩ **b** : NUCLEAR 2 ⟨*atomic* energy⟩
**2 a** : marked by acceptance of the theory of atomism **b** : ATOMISTIC 2
**3** : MINUTE
**4** *of a chemical element* : existing in the state of separate atoms
— **atom·i·cal·ly** \-mi-k(ə-)lē\ *adverb*

**atomic bomb** *noun* (1914)

**1** : a bomb whose violent explosive power is due to the sudden release of energy resulting from the splitting of nuclei of a heavy chemical element (as plutonium or uranium) by neutrons in a very rapid chain reaction — called also *atom bomb*
**2** : a nuclear weapon (as a hydrogen bomb)

**atomic clock** *noun* (1938)
: a precision clock that depends for its operation on an electrical oscillator regulated by the natural vibration frequencies of an atomic system (as a beam of cesium atoms)

**atomic mass** *noun* (1898)
: the mass of an atom usually expressed in atomic mass units; *also* : ATOMIC WEIGHT

**atomic mass unit** *noun* (circa 1942)
: a unit of mass for expressing masses of atoms, molecules, or nuclear particles equal to $\frac{1}{12}$ the mass of a single atom of the most abundant carbon isotope $^{12}C$ — called also *dalton*

**atomic number** *noun* (1821)
: an experimentally determined number characteristic of a chemical element that represents the number of protons in the nucleus which in a neutral atom equals the number of electrons outside the nucleus and that determines the place of the element in the periodic table — see ELEMENT table

**atomic reactor** *or* **atomic pile** *noun* (1945)
: REACTOR 3b

**atomic theory** *noun* (circa 1847)
**1** : a theory of the nature of matter: all material substances are composed of minute particles or atoms of a comparatively small number of kinds and all the atoms of the same kind are uniform in size, weight, and other properties

---

◇ WORD HISTORY

**atlas** In Greek myth, the Titan Atlas, following the defeat of the Titans in a war with Zeus and the other gods, was punished by being forced to support the heavens on his shoulders. A representation of Atlas as a man bearing on his back the globe of the earth became a conventional title-page illustration in bound volumes of maps during the 16th century. In 1585, the Flemish mathematician and mapmaker Gerhardus Mercator initiated a series of map collections with a flowery Latin title that can be translated as *Atlas, or Cosmographical Reflections on the Edifice of the World and the Representation of its Form.* The word *atlas* eventually became the generic term for a book of maps in most languages of Europe, including English.

**atom** For ancient Greek thinkers, ideas about the nature of matter and motion, what we think of as physics, were inseparable from philosophical reflections about existence and plurality. On grounds that a modern physicist would consider philosophical rather than experimental, Leucippus and his better-known student Democritus decided that matter was not infinitely divisible, but rather consisted of particles of being separated by empty space. These particles of being that made up all things were called *atoma sōmata* "indivisible bodies." The later Greek word *atomos,* borrowed into Latin as *atomus* and into French as *atome,* was used in Epicurean philosophy. Long after ancient Greece and Rome the concept was taken up again by early experimental science in the 17th century. With the development of modern atomic chemistry in the 19th and 20th centuries, the atoms of Democritus proved real enough, though they were not indivisible after all, and the splitting of their nuclei was discovered to be the source of enormous energy.

**2 :** any of several theories of the structure of the atom; *especially* **:** one based on experimentation and theoretical considerations holding that the atom is composed essentially of a small positively charged comparatively heavy nucleus surrounded by a comparatively large arrangement of electrons

**atomic weight** *noun* (1820)
**:** the mass of one atom of an element; *specifically* **:** the average mass of an atom of an element as it occurs in nature that is expressed in atomic mass units — see ELEMENT table

**at·om·ise, at·om·is·er** *British variant of* AT-OMIZE, ATOMIZER

**at·om·ism** \'a-tə-ˌmi-zəm\ *noun* (1678)
**1 :** a doctrine that the physical or physical and mental universe is composed of simple indivisible minute particles
**2 :** INDIVIDUALISM 1
— **at·om·ist** \-mist\ *noun*

**at·om·is·tic** \ˌa-tə-'mis-tik\ *adjective* (1809)
**1 :** of or relating to atoms or atomism
**2 :** composed of many simple elements; *also* **:** characterized by or resulting from division into unconnected or antagonistic fragments ⟨an *atomistic* society⟩
— **at·om·is·ti·cal·ly** \-ti-k(ə-)lē\ *adverb*

**at·om·ize** \'a-tə-ˌmīz\ *transitive verb* **-ized; -iz·ing** (1845)
**1 :** to treat as made up of many discrete units
**2 :** to reduce to minute particles or to a fine spray
**3 :** DIVIDE, FRAGMENT
**4 :** to subject to attack by nuclear weapons
— **at·om·iza·tion** \ˌa-tə-mə-'zā-shən\ *noun*

**at·om·iz·er** \'a-tə-ˌmī-zər\ *noun* (1865)
**:** an instrument for atomizing usually a perfume, disinfectant, or medicament

**atom smasher** *noun* (1937)
**:** ACCELERATOR d

**at·o·my** \'a-tə-mē\ *noun, plural* **-mies** [irregular from Latin *atomi,* plural of *atomus* atom] (1591)
**:** a tiny particle **:** ATOM, MITE

**aton·al** \(ˌ)ā-'tō-nᵊl, (ˌ)a-\ *adjective* [²a- + tonal] (1922)
**:** marked by avoidance of traditional musical tonality; *especially* **:** organized without reference to key or tonal center and using the tones of the chromatic scale impartially
— **aton·al·ism** \-nᵊl-ˌi-zəm\ *noun*
— **aton·al·ist** \-ist\ *noun*
— **ato·nal·i·ty** \ˌā-tō-'na-lə-tē, ˌa-\ *noun*
— **aton·al·ly** \(ˌ)ā-'tō-nᵊl-ē, (ˌ)a-\ *adverb*

**atone** \ə-'tōn\ *verb* **atoned; aton·ing** [Middle English, to become reconciled, from *at on* in harmony, from *at + on* one] (1593)
*transitive verb*
**1** *obsolete* **:** RECONCILE
**2 :** to supply satisfaction for **:** EXPIATE
*intransitive verb*
**:** to make amends

**atone·ment** \ə-'tōn-mənt\ *noun* (1513)
**1** *obsolete* **:** RECONCILIATION
**2 :** the reconciliation of God and man through the sacrificial death of Jesus Christ
**3 :** reparation for an offense or injury **:** SATISFACTION
**4** *Christian Science* **:** the exemplifying of man's oneness with God

**aton·ic** \(ˌ)ā-'tä-nik, ə-\ *adjective* (1792)
**1 :** characterized by atony
**2 :** uttered without accent or stress

**at·o·ny** \'a-tᵊn-ē\ *noun* [Late Latin *atonia,* from Greek, from *atonos* without tone, from *a- + tonos* tone] (1693)
**:** lack of physiological tone especially of a contractile organ

**¹atop** \ə-'täp\ *preposition* (1655)
**:** on top of

**²atop** *adverb or adjective* (1658)
**:** on, to, or at the top

**at·o·py** \'a-tə-pē\ *noun* [Greek *atopia* uncommonness, from *atopos* out of the way, uncommon, from *a- + topos* place] (1923)
**:** a probably hereditary allergy characterized

by symptoms (as asthma, hay fever, or hives) produced upon exposure to the exciting antigen without inoculation
— **atop·ic** \(ˌ)ā-'tä-pik, -'tō-\ *adjective*

**-ator** *noun suffix* [Middle English *-atour,* from Old French & Latin; Old French, from Latin *-ator,* from *-a-,* stem vowel of 1st conjugation *+ -tor,* agent suffix]
**:** one that does ⟨totaliz*ator*⟩

**ATP** \ˌā-ˌtē-'pē\ *noun* [adenosine *tri*phosphate] (1939)
**:** a phosphorylated nucleoside $C_{10}H_{16}N_5O_{13}P_3$ of adenine that supplies energy for many biochemical cellular processes by undergoing enzymatic hydrolysis especially to ADP — called also *adenosine triphosphate*

**ATPase** \ˌā-ˌtē-'pē-ˌās, -ˌāz\ *noun* (1946)
**:** an enzyme that hydrolyzes ATP; *especially* **:** one that hydrolyzes ATP to ADP and inorganic phosphate

**at·ra·bil·ious** \ˌa-trə-'bil-yəs\ *adjective* [Latin *atra bilis* black bile] (1651)
**1 :** given to or marked by melancholy **:** GLOOMY
**2 :** ILL-NATURED, PEEVISH
— **at·ra·bil·ious·ness** *noun*

**at·ra·zine** \'a-trə-ˌzēn\ *noun* [perhaps from *amino + triazine*] (1962)
**:** a photosynthesis-inhibiting persistent herbicide $C_8H_{14}ClN_5$ used especially to kill annual weeds and quack grass

**atrem·ble** \ə-'trem-bəl\ *adjective* (1862)
**:** shaking involuntarily **:** TREMBLING ⟨he was white as death and all *atremble* —Robert Coover⟩

**atre·sia** \ə-'trē-zhə\ *noun* [New Latin, from ²a- + Greek *trēsis* perforation, from *tetrainein* to pierce — more at THROW] (circa 1807)
**1 :** absence or closure of a natural passage of the body
**2 :** absence or disappearance of an anatomical part (as an ovarian follicle) by degeneration

**Atreus** \'ā-ˌtrüs, -trē-əs\ *noun* [Greek]
**:** a king of Mycenae and father of Agamemnon and Menelaus

**atrial natriuretic factor** *noun* (1984)
**:** a peptide hormone secreted by the cardiac atria that stimulates natriuresis and diuresis and helps regulate blood pressure

**atrio·ven·tric·u·lar** \ˌā-trē-ō-ven-'tri-kyə-lər, -vən-\ *adjective* [New Latin *atrium* + English *ventricular*] (circa 1860)
**:** of, relating to, or located between an atrium and ventricle of the heart

**atrioventricular node** *noun* (circa 1934)
**:** a small mass of tissue in the right atrioventricular region of higher vertebrates through which impulses from the sinoatrial node are passed to the ventricles

**atrip** \ə-'trip\ *adjective* (1796)
*of an anchor* **:** AWEIGH

**atri·um** \'ā-trē-əm\ *noun, plural* **atria** \-trē-ə\ *also* **atri·ums** [Latin] (1577)
**1 :** the central room of a Roman house
**2** *plural usually* **atriums :** a rectangularly shaped open patio around which a house is built; *also* **:** a many-storied court in a building (as a hotel) usually with a skylight
**3** [New Latin, from Latin] **:** an anatomical cavity or passage; *especially* **:** the chamber or either of the chambers of the heart that receives blood from the veins and forces it into the ventricle or ventricles — see HEART illustration
— **atri·al** \-trē-əl\ *adjective*

**atro·cious** \ə-'trō-shəs\ *adjective* [Latin *atroc-, atrox* gloomy, atrocious, from *atr-, ater* black + *-oc-, -ox* (akin to Greek *ōps* eye) — more at EYE] (1669)
**1 :** extremely wicked, brutal, or cruel **:** BARBARIC
**2 :** APPALLING, HORRIFYING ⟨the *atrocious* weapons of modern war⟩
**3 a :** utterly revolting **:** ABOMINABLE ⟨*atrocious* working conditions⟩ **b :** of very poor quality ⟨*atrocious* handwriting⟩

— **atro·cious·ly** *adverb*
— **atro·cious·ness** *noun*

**atroc·i·ty** \ə-'trä-sə-tē\ *noun, plural* **-ties** (1534)
**1 :** the quality or state of being atrocious
**2 :** an atrocious act, object, or situation ⟨the . . . sufferings and *atrocities* of trench warfare —Aldous Huxley⟩

**at·ro·phy** \'a-trə-fē\ *noun, plural* **-phies** [Late Latin *atrophia,* from Greek, from *atrophos* ill fed, from *a- + trephein* to nourish] (1601)
**1 :** decrease in size or wasting away of a body part or tissue; *also* **:** arrested development or loss of a part or organ incidental to the normal development or life of an animal or plant
**2 :** a wasting away or progressive decline **:** DEGENERATION ⟨the *atrophy* of freedom⟩ ⟨was not a solitude of *atrophy,* of negation, but of perpetual flowering —Willa Cather⟩
— **atro·phic** \(ˌ)ā-'trō-fik\ *adjective*
— **atrophy** \'a-trə-fē, -ˌfī\ *verb*

**at·ro·pine** \'a-trə-ˌpēn\ *noun* [German *Atropin,* from New Latin *Atropa,* genus name of belladonna, from Greek *Atropos,* one of the three Fates] (1836)
**:** a racemic mixture of hyoscyamine obtained from any of various solanaceous plants (as belladonna) and used especially in the form of its sulfate for its anticholinergic effects (as pupil dilation or inhibition of smooth muscle spasms)

**att** *variant of* ²AT

**at·ta·boy** \'a-də-ˌbȯi\ *interjection* [probably alteration of *that's the boy*] (1909)
**—** used to express encouragement, approval, or admiration

**at·tach** \ə-'tach\ *verb* [Middle English, from Middle French *attacher,* from Old French *estachier,* from *estache* stake, of Germanic origin; akin to Old English *staca* stake] (14th century)
*transitive verb*
**1 :** to take by legal authority especially under a writ ⟨*attached* the property⟩
**2 a :** to bring (oneself) into an association **b :** to assign temporarily
**3 :** to bind by personal ties (as of affection or sympathy) ⟨was strongly *attached* to his family⟩
**4 :** to make fast (as by tying or gluing) ⟨*attach* a label to a package⟩
**5 :** to associate especially as a property **:** ATTRIBUTE ⟨*attached* great importance to public opinion polls⟩
*intransitive verb*
**:** to become attached **:** ADHERE
*synonym see* FASTEN
— **at·tach·able** \-'ta-chə-bəl\ *adjective*

**at·ta·ché** \ˌa-tə-'shā, ˌa-ˌta-, ə-ˌta-\ *noun* [French, past participle of *attacher*] (1829)
**1 :** a technical expert on the diplomatic staff of his country at a foreign capital ⟨a military *attaché*⟩
**2 :** ATTACHÉ CASE

**at·ta·ché case** \ˌa-ˌta-'shā-, ˌa-tə-; ə-'ta-(ˌ)shā-\ *noun* (1904)
**1 :** a small thin suitcase used especially for carrying business papers
**2 :** BRIEFCASE

**at·tached** \ə-'tacht\ *adjective* (1854)
**:** permanently fixed when adult ⟨*attached* barnacles⟩

**at·tach·ment** \ə-'tach-mənt\ *noun* (14th century)
**1 :** a seizure by legal process; *also* **:** the writ or precept commanding such seizure
**2 a :** the state of being personally attached **:** FIDELITY ⟨*attachment* to a cause⟩ **b :** affectionate regard ⟨a deep *attachment* to nature⟩

**3 :** a device attached to a machine or implement

**4 :** the physical connection by which one thing is attached to another

**5 :** the process of physically attaching

¹**at·tack** \ə-'tak\ verb [Middle French attaquer, from (assumed) Old Italian estaccare to attach, from stacca stake, of Germanic origin; akin to Old English staca] (1600)

transitive verb

**1 :** to set upon or work against forcefully

**2 :** to assail with unfriendly or bitter words

**3 :** to begin to affect or to act on injuriously

**4 :** to set to work on

**5 :** to threaten (a piece in chess) with immediate capture

intransitive verb

**:** to make an attack ☆

— **at·tack·er** noun

²**attack** noun (1661)

**1 :** the act of attacking with physical force or unfriendly words **:** ASSAULT

**2 :** a belligerent or antagonistic action

**3 a :** a fit of sickness; especially **:** an active episode of a chronic or recurrent disease **b :** a period of being strongly affected by something (as a desire or mood)

**4 a :** an offensive or scoring action ⟨won the game with an eight-hit attack⟩ **b :** offensive players or the positions taken up by them

**5 :** the setting to work on some undertaking ⟨made a new attack on the problem⟩

**6 :** the beginning of destructive action (as by a chemical agent)

**7 :** the act or manner of beginning a musical tone or phrase

**at·tack·man** \-ˌman\ noun (1940)

**:** a player (as in lacrosse) assigned to an offensive zone or position

**at·tain** \ə-'tān\ verb [Middle English atteynen, from Old French ataindre, from (assumed) Vulgar Latin attangere, alteration of Latin attingere, from ad- + tangere to touch — more at TANGENT] (14th century)

transitive verb

**1 :** to reach as an end **:** GAIN, ACHIEVE ⟨attain a goal⟩

**2 :** to come into possession of **:** OBTAIN ⟨he attained preferment over his fellows⟩

**3 :** to come to as the end of a progression or course of movement ⟨they attained the top of the hill⟩ ⟨attain a ripe old age⟩

intransitive verb

**:** to come or arrive by motion, growth, or effort — usually used with to

— **at·tain·abil·i·ty** \-ˌtā-nə-'bi-lə-tē\ noun

— **at·tain·able** \-'tā-nə-bəl\ adjective

**at·tain·der** \ə-'tān-dər\ noun [Middle English attaynder, from Middle French ataindre to accuse, attain] (15th century)

**1 :** extinction of the civil rights and capacities of a person upon sentence of death or outlawry usually after a conviction of treason

**2** obsolete **:** DISHONOR

**at·tain·ment** \ə-'tān-mənt\ noun (1549)

**1 :** the act of attaining **:** the condition of being attained

**2 :** something attained **:** ACCOMPLISHMENT ⟨scientific attainments⟩

¹**at·taint** \ə-'tānt\ transitive verb [Middle English attaynten, from Middle French ataint, past participle of ataindre] (14th century)

**1 :** to affect by attainder

**2 a :** INFECT, CORRUPT **b** archaic **:** TAINT, SULLY

**3** archaic **:** ACCUSE

²**attaint** noun (1592)

obsolete **:** a stain upon honor or purity **:** DISGRACE

**at·tar** \'a-tər, 'a-ˌtär\ noun [Persian 'aṭir perfumed, from Arabic, from 'iṭr perfume] (1798)

**:** a fragrant essential oil (as from rose petals); also **:** FRAGRANCE

¹**at·tempt** \ə-'tem(p)t\ transitive verb [Middle English, from Middle French & Latin; Middle French attempter, from Latin attemptare, from ad- + temptare to touch, try — more at TEMPT] (14th century)

**1 :** to make an effort to do, accomplish, solve, or effect ⟨attempted to swim the swollen river⟩

**2** archaic **:** TEMPT

**3** archaic **:** to try to subdue or take by force **:** ATTACK ☆

— **at·tempt·able** \-'tem(p)-tə-bəl\ adjective

²**attempt** noun (1534)

**1 a :** the act or an instance of attempting; especially **:** an unsuccessful effort **b :** something resulting from or representing an attempt ⟨surrounded by . . . a few attempts at rose bushes —Marian Engel⟩

**2 :** ATTACK, ASSAULT ⟨an attempt on the life of the president⟩

**at·tend** \ə-'tend\ verb [Middle English, from Old French atendre, from Latin attendere, literally, to stretch to, from ad- + tendere to stretch — more at THIN] (14th century)

transitive verb

**1 :** to pay attention to

**2 :** to look after **:** take charge of ⟨campsites . . . attended by park rangers —Jackson Rivers⟩

**3 a :** to go or stay with as a companion, nurse, or servant **b :** to visit professionally as a physician

**4** archaic **a :** to wait for **b :** to be in store for

**5 :** to be present with **:** ACCOMPANY

**6 :** to be present at **:** go to ⟨attend law school⟩

intransitive verb

**1 :** to apply oneself ⟨attend to your work⟩

**2 :** to apply the mind or pay attention **:** HEED

**3 a :** to be ready for service ⟨ministers who attend upon the king⟩ **b :** to be present

**4** obsolete **:** WAIT, STAY

**5 :** to direct one's attention **:** SEE ⟨I'll attend to that⟩

— **at·tend·er** noun

**at·ten·dance** \ə-'ten-dən(t)s\ noun (14th century)

**1 :** the act or fact of attending ⟨a physician in attendance⟩

**2 a :** the persons or number of persons attending ⟨daily attendance at the fair⟩ **b :** the number of times a person attends

**attendance officer** noun (1884)

**:** one employed by a public-school system to investigate the continued absences of pupils

¹**at·ten·dant** \ə-'ten-dənt\ noun (15th century)

**1 :** one who attends another to perform a service; especially **:** an employee who waits on customers

**2 :** something that accompanies **:** CONCOMITANT

**3 :** ATTENDEE

²**attendant** adjective (15th century)

**1 :** accompanying, waiting upon, or following in order to perform service ⟨Cherub and Seraph . . . attendant on their Lord —John Milton⟩

**2 :** accompanying or following as a consequence or result ⟨problems attendant upon pollution⟩

**at·tend·ee** \ə-ˌten-'dē, ˌa-\ noun (1937)

**:** a person who is present on a given occasion or at a given place ⟨attendees at a convention⟩

**at·tend·ing** \ə-'ten-diŋ\ adjective (circa 1923)

**:** serving as a physician on the staff of a teaching hospital ⟨attending surgeon⟩

**at·ten·tion** \ə-'ten(t)-shən; sense 4 often (ə-)ten(ch)-'hət\ noun [Middle English attencioun, from Latin attention-, attentio, from attendere] (14th century)

**1 a :** the act or state of attending especially through applying the mind to an object of sense or thought **b :** a condition of readiness for such attention involving especially a selective narrowing or focusing of consciousness and receptivity

**2 :** OBSERVATION, NOTICE; especially **:** consideration with a view to action ⟨a problem requiring prompt attention⟩

**3 a :** an act of civility or courtesy especially in courtship **b :** sympathetic consideration of the needs and wants of others **:** ATTENTIVENESS

**4 :** a position assumed by a soldier with heels together, body erect, arms at the sides, and eyes to the front — often used as a command

— **at·ten·tion·al** \-'ten(t)-sh(ə-)nəl\ adjective

**attention deficit disorder** noun (1980)

**:** a syndrome of learning and behavioral problems that is not caused by any serious underlying physical or mental disorder and is characterized especially by difficulty in sustaining attention, by impulsive behavior (as in speaking out of turn), and usually by excessive activity

**attention line** noun (1925)

**:** a line usually placed above the salutation in a business letter directing the letter to one specified

**attention span** noun (1934)

**:** the length of time during which an individual is able to concentrate or remain interested

**at·ten·tive** \ə-'ten-tiv\ adjective (14th century)

**1 :** MINDFUL, OBSERVANT ⟨attentive to what he is doing⟩

**2 :** heedful of the comfort of others **:** SOLICITOUS

**3 :** offering attentions in or as if in the role of a suitor

— **at·ten·tive·ly** adverb

— **at·ten·tive·ness** noun

¹**at·ten·u·ate** \ə-'ten-yə-ˌwāt\ verb **-at·ed; -at·ing** [Latin attenuatus, past participle of attenuare to make thin, from ad- + tenuis thin — more at THIN] (15th century)

transitive verb

**1 :** to make thin or slender

**2 :** to make thin in consistency **:** RAREFY

**3 :** to lessen the amount, force, magnitude, or value of **:** WEAKEN

**4 :** to reduce the severity, virulence, or vitality of

intransitive verb

**:** to become thin, fine, or less

— **at·ten·u·a·tion** \-ˌten-yə-'wā-shən\ noun

²**at·ten·u·ate** \ə-'ten-yə-wət\ adjective (15th century)

---

☆ **SYNONYMS**

**Attack, assail, assault, bombard, storm** mean to make an onslaught upon. ATTACK implies taking the initiative in a struggle ⟨plan to attack the town at dawn⟩. ASSAIL implies attempting to break down resistance by repeated blows or shots ⟨assailed the enemy with artillery fire⟩. ASSAULT suggests a direct attempt to overpower by suddenness and violence of onslaught ⟨commandos assaulted the building from all sides⟩. BOMBARD applies to attacking with bombs or shells ⟨bombarded the city nightly⟩. STORM implies attempting to break into a defended position ⟨preparing to storm the fortress⟩.

**Attempt, try, endeavor, essay, strive** mean to make an effort to accomplish an end. ATTEMPT stresses the initiation or beginning of an effort ⟨will attempt to photograph the rare bird⟩. TRY is often close to ATTEMPT but may stress effort or experiment made in the hope of testing or proving something ⟨tried to determine which was the better procedure⟩. ENDEAVOR heightens the implications of exertion and difficulty ⟨endeavored to find crash survivors in the mountains⟩. ESSAY implies difficulty but also suggests tentative trying or experimenting ⟨will essay a dramatic role for the first time⟩. STRIVE implies great exertion against great difficulty and specifically suggests persistent effort ⟨continues to strive for peace⟩.

**1 :** attenuated especially in thickness, density, or force
**2 :** tapering gradually usually to a long slender point ⟨*attenuate* leaves⟩
**at·ten·u·a·tor** \-yə-ˌwā-tər\ *noun* (1924)
**:** a device for attenuating; *especially* **:** one for reducing the amplitude of an electrical signal without appreciable distortion
**at·test** \ə-ˈtest\ *verb* [Middle French *attester,* from Latin *attestari,* from *ad-* + *testis* witness — more at TESTAMENT] (1596)
*transitive verb*
**1 a :** to affirm to be true or genuine; *specifically* **:** to authenticate by signing as a witness
**b :** to authenticate officially
**2 :** to establish or verify the usage of
**3 :** to be proof of **:** MANIFEST ⟨her record *attests* her integrity⟩
**4 :** to put on oath
*intransitive verb*
**:** to bear witness **:** TESTIFY ⟨*attest* to a belief⟩
**synonym** see CERTIFY
— **at·tes·ta·tion** \ˌa-ˌtes-ˈtā-shən, ˌa-tə-ˈstā-\ *noun*
— **at·test·er** \ə-ˈtes-tər\ *noun*
**at·tic** \ˈa-tik\ *noun* [French *attique,* from *attique* of Attica, from Latin *Atticus*] (circa 1696)
**1 :** a low story or wall above the main order of a facade in the classical styles
**2 :** a room behind an attic
**3 :** a room or a space immediately below the roof of a building **:** GARRET
**4 :** something resembling an attic (as in being used for storage) ◆
¹**At·tic** \ˈa-tik\ *adjective* [Latin *Atticus* of Attica, from Greek *Attikos,* from *Attikē* Attica, Greece] (1599)
**1 :** of, relating to, or having the characteristics of Athens or its ancient civilization
**2 :** marked by simplicity, purity, and refinement ⟨an *Attic* prose style⟩
²**Attic** *noun* (circa 1771)
**:** a dialect of ancient Greek originally used in Attica and later the literary language of the Greek-speaking world
**at·ti·cism** \ˈa-tə-ˌsi-zəm\ *noun, often capitalized* (1593)
**1 :** a witty or well-turned phrase
**2 :** a characteristic feature of Attic Greek occurring in another language or dialect
¹**at·tire** \ə-ˈtīr\ *transitive verb* **at·tired; at·tir·ing** [Middle English, from Old French *atirier,* from *a-* (from Latin *ad-*) + *tire* order, rank, of Germanic origin; akin to Old English *tīr* glory, ornament] (14th century)
**:** to put garments on **:** DRESS, ARRAY; *especially*
**:** to clothe in fancy or rich garments
²**attire** *noun* (14th century)
**1 :** DRESS, CLOTHES; *especially* **:** splendid or decorative clothing
**2 :** the antlers or antlers and scalp of a stag or buck
**at·ti·tude** \ˈa-tə-ˌtüd, -ˌtyüd\ *noun* [French, from Italian *attitudine,* literally, aptitude, from Late Latin *aptitudin-, aptitudo* fitness — more at APTITUDE] (1668)
**1 :** the arrangement of the parts of a body or figure **:** POSTURE
**2 :** a position assumed for a specific purpose ⟨a threatening *attitude*⟩
**3 :** a ballet position similar to the arabesque in which the raised leg is bent at the knee
**4 a :** a mental position with regard to a fact or state **b :** a feeling or emotion toward a fact or state
**5 :** the position of an aircraft or spacecraft determined by the relationship between its axes and a reference datum (as the horizon or a particular star)
**6 :** an organismic state of readiness to respond in a characteristic way to a stimulus (as an object, concept, or situation)
**7 a :** a negative or hostile state of mind **b :** a cocky or arrogant manner
**at·ti·tu·di·nal** \ˌa-tə-ˈtü-dᵊn-əl, -ˈtyü-\ *adjec-*

*tive* [*attitude* + *-inal* (as in *aptitudinal,* from Latin *aptitudin-, aptitudo*)] (1831)
**:** relating to, based on, or expressive of personal attitudes or feelings ⟨*attitudinal* judgment⟩
— **at·ti·tu·di·nal·ly** \-ə-lē\ *adverb*
**at·ti·tu·di·nise** *British variant of* ATTITUDINIZE
**at·ti·tu·di·nize** \ˌa-tə-ˈtü-dᵊn-ˌīz, -ˈtyü-\ *intransitive verb* **-nized; -niz·ing** (1784)
**:** to assume an affected mental attitude **:** POSE
**at·to-** \ˈa-(ˌ)tō\ *combining form* [International Scientific Vocabulary, from Danish or Norwegian *atten* eighteen, from Old Norse *āttjān;* akin to Old English *eahtatīene* eighteen]
**:** one quintillionth ($10^{-18}$) part of ⟨*attogram*⟩
**at·torn** \ə-ˈtərn\ *intransitive verb* [Middle English *attournen,* from Middle French *atorner,* from Old French, from *a-* (from Latin *ad-*) + *torner* to turn] (15th century)
**:** to agree to be tenant to a new owner or landlord of the same property
— **at·torn·ment** \-mənt\ *noun*
**at·tor·ney** \ə-ˈtər-nē\ *noun, plural* **-neys** [Middle English *attourney,* from Middle French *atorné,* past participle of *atorner*] (14th century)
**:** one who is legally appointed to transact business on another's behalf; *specifically* **:** a legal agent qualified to act for suitors and defendants in legal proceedings
— **at·tor·ney·ship** \-ˌship\ *noun*
**attorney–at–law** *noun, plural* **attorneys–at–law** (1768)
**:** a practitioner in a court of law who is legally qualified to prosecute and defend actions in such court on the retainer of clients
**attorney general** *noun, plural* **attorneys general** *or* **attorney generals** (1585)
**:** the chief law officer of a nation or state who represents the government in litigation and serves as its principal legal adviser
**at·tract** \ə-ˈtrakt\ *verb* [Middle English, from Latin *attractus,* past participle of *attrahere,* from *ad-* + *trahere* to pull, draw] (15th century)
*transitive verb*
**:** to cause to approach or adhere: as **a :** to pull to or draw toward oneself or itself ⟨a magnet *attracts* iron⟩ **b :** to draw by appeal to natural or excited interest, emotion, or aesthetic sense **:** ENTICE ⟨*attract* attention⟩
*intransitive verb*
**:** to exercise attraction ☆
— **at·trac·tor** \-ˈtrak-tər\ *noun*
**at·trac·tance** \-tən(t)s\ *noun* (1948)
**:** ATTRACTANCY
**at·trac·tan·cy** \ə-ˈtrak-tən(t)-sē\ *noun* (1948)
**:** the quality or capacity (as of a pheromone) of attracting
**at·trac·tant** \ə-ˈtrak-tənt\ *noun* (1920)
**:** a substance (as of a pheromone) that attracts insects or other animals
**at·trac·tion** \ə-ˈtrak-shən\ *noun* (14th century)
**1 a :** the act, process, or power of attracting **b :** personal charm
**2 :** the action or power of drawing forth a response **:** an attractive quality
**3 :** a force acting mutually between particles of matter, tending to draw them together, and resisting their separation
**4 :** something that attracts or is intended to attract people by appealing to their desires and tastes ⟨coming *attractions*⟩ ☆
**at·trac·tive** \ə-ˈtrak-tiv\ *adjective* (14th century)
**1 :** having or relating to the power to attract ⟨*attractive* forces between molecules⟩ ⟨an *attractive* offer⟩
**2 :** arousing interest or pleasure **:** CHARMING ⟨an *attractive* smile⟩
— **at·trac·tive·ly** *adverb*
— **at·trac·tive·ness** *noun*
¹**at·tri·bute** \ˈa-trə-ˌbyüt\ *noun* [Middle English, from Latin *attributus,* past participle of

*attribuere* to attribute, from *ad-* + *tribuere* to bestow — more at TRIBUTE] (14th century)
**1 :** an inherent characteristic; *also* **:** an accidental quality
**2 :** an object closely associated with or belonging to a specific person, thing, or office ⟨a scepter is the *attribute* of power⟩; *especially* **:** such an object used for identification in painting or sculpture
**3 :** a word ascribing a quality; *especially*
**:** ADJECTIVE
**synonym** see QUALITY
²**at·trib·ute** \ə-ˈtri-ˌbyüt, -byət\ *transitive verb* **-ut·ed; -ut·ing** (1530)

---

☆ **SYNONYMS**
**Attract, allure, charm, captivate, fascinate, enchant** mean to draw another by exerting a powerful influence. ATTRACT applies to any degree or kind of ability to exert influence over another ⟨students *attracted* by the school's locale⟩. ALLURE implies an enticing by what is fair, pleasing, or seductive ⟨an *alluring* smile⟩. CHARM implies the power of casting a spell over the person or thing affected and so compelling a response ⟨*charmed* by their hospitality⟩, but it may, like CAPTIVATE, suggest no more than evoking delight or admiration ⟨her performances *captivated* audiences⟩. FASCINATE suggests a magical influence and tends to stress the ineffectiveness of attempts to resist ⟨a story that continues to *fascinate* children⟩. ENCHANT is perhaps the strongest of these terms in stressing the appeal of the agent and the degree of delight evoked in the subject ⟨hopelessly *enchanted* by her beauty⟩.

**Attraction, affinity, sympathy** mean the relationship existing between things or persons that are naturally or involuntarily drawn together. ATTRACTION implies the possession by one thing of a quality that pulls another to it ⟨felt an *attraction* to danger⟩. AFFINITY implies a susceptibility or predisposition on the part of the one drawn ⟨an *affinity* for mathematics⟩. SYMPATHY implies a reciprocal or natural relation between two things that are both susceptible to the same influence ⟨two minds in *sympathy*⟩.

---

◇ **WORD HISTORY**
**attic** The ancient Greek city-state of Athens included the whole of the Attic peninsula, the region called Attica. Typical of the Attic or Athenian style of architecture is the use of pilasters, rectangular columns projecting from, but attached to, the wall. These take the place of the freestanding and usually rounded pillars common in other architectural styles. Occasionally the large columns and entablature that form the facade of a building are surmounted by a similar but smaller decorative structure, whose columns are usually pilasters, rather than pillars. Because this small upper order is in the Attic style, the French named it *attique.* The English borrowed the word as *attic,* and extended its meaning, originally in the phrases *attic story* and *attic floor,* to designate the top story of any building just under the roof. So a word that was once associated with an elegant architectural style now names what is usually no more than a lowly storage area.

---

\ə\ **abut** \ᵊ\ **kitten** \ər\ **further** \a\ **ash** \ā\ **ace**
\ä\ **mop, mar** \aů\ **out** \ch\ **chin** \e\ **bet** \ē\ **easy**
\g\ **go** \i\ **hit** \ī\ **ice** \j\ **job** \ŋ\ **sing** \ō\ **go**
\ò\ **law** \òi\ **boy** \th\ **thin** \t̲h̲\ **the** \ü\ **loot** \ů\ **foot**
\y\ **yet** \zh\ **vision** *see also* Guide to Pronunciation

**1 :** to explain by indicating a cause ⟨*attributed* his success to his coach⟩
**2 a :** to regard as a characteristic of a person or thing **b :** to reckon as made or originated in an indicated fashion ⟨*attributed* the invention to a Russian⟩ **c :** CLASSIFY, DESIGNATE
**synonym** see ASCRIBE
— **at·trib·ut·able** \-byü-tə-bəl, -byə-\ *adjective*

**at·tri·bu·tion** \,a-trə-'byü-shən\ *noun* (1651)
**1 :** the act of attributing; *especially* **:** the ascribing of a work (as of literature or art) to a particular author or artist
**2 :** an ascribed quality, character, or right
— **at·tri·bu·tion·al** \-sh(ə-)nəl\ *adjective*

**at·trib·u·tive** \ə-'tri-byə-tiv\ *adjective* (1606)
**1 :** relating to or of the nature of an attribute **:** ATTRIBUTING
**2 :** joined directly to a modified noun without a linking verb (as *city* in *city streets*)
— **attributive** *noun*
— **at·trib·u·tive·ly** *adverb*

**at·trit·ed** \ə-'trī-təd\ *adjective* (1760)
**:** worn by attrition

**at·tri·tion** \ə-'tri-shən, a-\ *noun* [Latin *attrition-, attritio,* from *atterere* to rub against, from *ad-* + *terere* to rub — more at THROW] (14th century)
**1** [Middle English *attricioun,* from Medieval Latin *attrition-, attritio,* from Latin] **:** sorrow for one's sins that arises from a motive other than that of the love of God
**2 :** the act of rubbing together **:** FRICTION; *also* **:** the act of wearing or grinding down by friction
**3 :** the act of weakening or exhausting by constant harassment, abuse, or attack
**4 :** a reduction in numbers usually as a result of resignation, retirement, or death
— **at·tri·tion·al** \-'tri-sh(ə-)nəl\ *adjective*

**at·tune** \ə-'tün, -'tyün\ *transitive verb* (1596)
**1 :** to bring into harmony **:** TUNE
**2 :** to make aware or responsive ⟨*attune* businesses to changing trends⟩
— **at·tune·ment** \-mənt\ *noun*

**atwit·ter** \ə-'twi-tər\ *adjective* (1833)
**:** nervously concerned **:** EXCITED ⟨gossips *atwitter* with speculation —*Time*⟩

**atyp·i·cal** \(,)ā-'ti-pi-kəl\ *adjective* (1885)
**:** not typical **:** IRREGULAR, UNUSUAL
— **atyp·i·cal·i·ty** \ā-,ti-pə-'ka-lə-tē\ *noun*
— **atyp·i·cal·ly** \(,)ā-'ti-pi-k(ə-)lē\ *adverb*

**au·bade** \ō-'bäd\ *noun* [French, from Middle French, from Old Provençal *aubada,* from *alba, auba* dawn, from (assumed) Vulgar Latin *alba,* from Latin, feminine of *albus* white — more at ALB] (circa 1678)
**1 :** a song or poem greeting the dawn
**2 a :** a morning love song **b :** a song or poem of lovers parting at dawn
**3 :** morning music — compare NOCTURNE

**au·berge** \ō-'berzh\ *noun* [French, from Middle French, of Germanic origin; akin to Old High German *heriberga* military quarters — more at HARBOR] (1599)
**:** INN 1a

**au·ber·gine** \'ō-bər-,zhēn\ *noun* [French, from Catalan *albergínia,* from Arabic *al-bādhinjān* the eggplant] (1794)
**1** *chiefly British* **:** EGGPLANT 1
**2 :** EGGPLANT 2

**¹au·burn** \'ö-bərn\ *adjective* [Middle English *auborne* blond, from Middle French, from Medieval Latin *alburnus* whitish, from Latin *alburnum* sapwood] (15th century)
**1 :** of the color auburn
**2 :** of a reddish brown color

**²auburn** *noun* (1613)
**:** a moderate brown

**Au·bus·son** \,ō-bə-'sōⁿ\ *noun* [*Aubusson,* town in France] (1851)
**:** a figured scenic tapestry used for wall hangings and upholstery; *also* **:** a rug woven to resemble Aubusson tapestry

**au cou·rant** \,ō-ku̇-'räⁿ\ *adjective* [French, literally, in the current] (1762)

**1 a :** fully informed **:** UP-TO-DATE **b :** FASHIONABLE, STYLISH
**2 :** fully familiar **:** CONVERSANT

**¹auc·tion** \'ȯk-shən\ *noun* [Latin *auction-, auctio,* from *augēre* to increase — more at EKE] (1595)
**1 :** a sale of property to the highest bidder
**2 :** the act or process of bidding in some card games

**²auction** *transitive verb* **auc·tioned; auc·tion·ing** \-sh(ə-)niŋ\ (circa 1798)
**:** to sell at auction ⟨*auctioned* off his library⟩

**auction bridge** *noun* (1908)
**:** a bridge game differing from contract bridge in that tricks made in excess of the contract are scored toward game

**auc·tion·eer** \,ȯk-shə-'nir\ *noun* (circa 1708)
**:** an agent who sells goods at auction

**auc·to·ri·al** \ȯk-'tōr-ē-əl, -'tȯr-\ *adjective* [Latin *auctor* author — more at AUTHOR] (1821)
**:** of or relating to an author

**au·da·cious** \ȯ-'dā-shəs\ *adjective* [Middle French *audacieux,* from *audace* boldness, from Latin *audacia,* from *audac-, audax* bold, from *audēre* to dare, from *avidus* eager — more at AVID] (1550)
**1 a :** intrepidly daring **:** ADVENTUROUS ⟨an *audacious* mountain climber⟩ **b :** recklessly bold **:** RASH
**2 :** contemptuous of law, religion, or decorum **:** INSOLENT
**3 :** marked by originality and verve
— **au·da·cious·ly** *adverb*
— **au·da·cious·ness** *noun*

**au·dac·i·ty** \ȯ-'da-sə-tē\ *noun, plural* **-ties** [Middle English *audacite,* from Latin *audac-, audax*] (15th century)
**1 :** the quality or state of being audacious: as
**a :** intrepid boldness **b :** bold or arrogant disregard of normal restraints
**2 :** an audacious act — usually used in plural
**synonym** see TEMERITY

**au·di·al** \'ȯ-dē-əl\ *adjective* [*audio* + ¹-*al*] (1966)
**:** of, relating to, or affecting the sense of hearing **:** AURAL

**¹au·di·ble** \'ȯ-də-bəl\ *adjective* [Late Latin *audibilis,* from Latin *audire* to hear; akin to Greek *aisthanesthai* to perceive, Sanskrit *āvis* evidently] (1529)
**:** heard or capable of being heard
— **au·di·bil·i·ty** \,ȯ-də-'bi-lə-tē\ *noun*
— **au·di·bly** \'ȯ-də-blē\ *adverb*

**²audible** *noun* (1962)
**:** a substitute offensive or defensive play called at the line of scrimmage in football

**au·di·ence** \'ȯ-dē-ən(t)s, 'ä-\ *noun* [Middle English, from Middle French, from Latin *audientia,* from *audient-, audiens,* present participle of *audire*] (14th century)
**1 :** the act or state of hearing
**2 a :** a formal hearing or interview ⟨an *audience* with the pope⟩ **b :** an opportunity of being heard ⟨I would succeed if I were once given *audience*⟩
**3 a :** a group of listeners or spectators **b :** a reading, viewing, or listening public
**4 :** a group of ardent admirers or devotees **:** FOLLOWING

**au·dile** \'ȯ-,dīl\ *adjective* [*aud*itory + -*ile* (as in *tactile*)] (1897)
**:** AUDITORY

**aud·ing** \'ȯ-diŋ\ *noun* [Latin *aud*ire + English ¹-*ing*] (circa 1949)
**:** the process of hearing, recognizing, and interpreting spoken language

**¹au·dio** \'ȯ-dē-,ō\ *adjective* [*audio-*] (1916)
**1 :** of or relating to acoustic, mechanical, or electrical frequencies corresponding to normally audible sound waves which are of frequencies approximately from 15 to 20,000 hertz
**2 a :** of or relating to sound or its reproduction and especially high-fidelity reproduction **b** **:** relating to or used in the transmission or re-

ception of sound — compare VIDEO **c :** of, relating to, or utilizing recorded sound

**²audio** *noun* (1934)
**1 :** an audio signal; *broadly* **:** SOUND
**2 :** the section of television or motion-picture equipment that deals with sound
**3 :** the transmission, reception, or reproduction of sound

**audio-** *combining form* [Latin *audire* to hear]
**1 :** hearing ⟨*audio*meter⟩
**2 :** sound ⟨*audio*phile⟩
**3 :** auditory and ⟨*audio*visual⟩

**au·dio–an·i·ma·tron·ic** \,ȯ-dē-ō-,a-nə-mə-'trä-nik\ *adjective* [from *Audio-Animatronics,* a trademark] (1964)
**:** being or consisting of a lifelike electromechanical figure of a person or animal that has synchronized movement and sound

**au·dio·cas·sette** \,ȯ-dē-(,)ō-kə-'set, -ka-\ *noun* (1971)
**:** an audiotape recording mounted in a cassette

**au·dio·gen·ic** \,ȯ-dē-ō-'je-nik\ *adjective* (1941)
**:** produced by frequencies corresponding to sound waves — used especially of epileptoid responses

**au·dio·gram** \'ȯ-dē-ō-,gram\ *noun* (1927)
**:** a graphic representation of the relation of vibration frequency and the minimum sound intensity for hearing

**au·dio–lin·gual** \,ȯ-dē-ō-'liŋ-gwəl *also* -gyə-wəl\ *adjective* (1960)
**:** involving a drill routine of listening and speaking in language learning

**au·di·ol·o·gy** \,ȯ-dē-'ä-lə-jē\ *noun* (1946)
**:** a branch of science dealing with hearing; *specifically* **:** therapy of individuals having impaired hearing
— **au·di·o·log·i·cal** \-ē-ə-'lä-ji-kəl\ *also* **au·di·o·log·ic** \-ē-ə-'lä-jik\ *adjective*
— **au·di·ol·o·gist** \-ē-'ä-lə-jist\ *noun*

**au·di·om·e·ter** \,ȯ-dē-'ä-mə-tər\ *noun* (1879)
**:** an instrument used in measuring the acuity of hearing
— **au·dio·met·ric** \-dē-ō-'me-trik\ *adjective*
— **au·di·om·e·try** \-dē-'ä-mə-trē\ *noun*

**au·dio·phile** \'ȯ-dē-ō-,fīl\ *noun* (1951)
**:** a person who is enthusiastic about high-fidelity sound reproduction

**au·dio·tape** \'ȯ-dē-ō-,tāp\ *noun* (1958)
**:** a tape recording of sound

**au·dio·vi·su·al** \,ȯ-dē-ō-(,)ō-'vi-zhə-wəl, -zhəl\ *adjective* (1937)
**1 :** designed to aid in learning or teaching by making use of both hearing and sight
**2 :** of or relating to both hearing and sight

**au·dio·vi·su·als** \-zhə-wəlz, -zhəlz\ *noun plural* (1955)
**:** audiovisual teaching materials (as filmstrips accompanied by recordings)

**¹au·dit** \'ȯ-dət\ *noun* [Middle English, from Latin *auditus* act of hearing, from *audire*] (15th century)
**1 a :** a formal examination of an organization's or individual's accounts or financial situation **b :** the final report of an audit
**2 :** a methodical examination and review
— **au·dit·able** \-di-tə-bəl\ *adjective*

**²audit** *transitive verb* (15th century)
**1 :** to perform an audit of or for ⟨*audit* the books⟩ ⟨*audit* the company⟩
**2 :** to attend (a course) without working for or expecting to receive formal credit

**¹au·di·tion** \ȯ-'di-shən\ *noun* [Middle French or Latin; Middle French, from Latin *audition-, auditio,* from *audire*] (1599)
**1 :** the power or sense of hearing
**2 :** the act of hearing; *especially* **:** a critical hearing ⟨an *audition* of new recordings⟩
**3 :** a trial performance to appraise an entertainer's merits

**²audition** *verb* **au·di·tioned; au·di·tion·ing** \-'di-sh(ə-)niŋ\ (1934)
*transitive verb*
**:** to test especially in an audition

*intransitive verb*
: to give a trial performance
**au·di·tor** \'ȯ-də-tər\ *noun* (14th century)
**1** : a person authorized to examine and verify accounts
**2** : one that hears or listens; *especially* : one that is a member of an audience
**3** : a person who audits a course of study
**4** : one who hears (as a court case) in the capacity of judge
**au·di·to·ri·um** \ȯ-də-'tȯr-ē-əm, -'tȯr-\ *noun, plural* **-riums** *or* **-ria** \-ē-ə\ [Latin, literally, lecture room] (circa 1751)
**1** : the part of a public building where an audience sits
**2** : a room, hall, or building used for public gatherings
**¹au·di·to·ry** \'ȯ-də-ˌtȯr-ē, -ˌtȯr\ *noun* [Middle English *auditorie,* from Latin *auditorium*] (14th century)
**1** *archaic* : AUDIENCE
**2** *archaic* : AUDITORIUM
**²au·di·to·ry** *adjective* [Late Latin *auditorius*] (1578)
: of, relating to, or experienced through hearing
— **au·di·to·ri·ly** *adverb*
**auditory nerve** *noun* (1724)
: either of the 8th pair of cranial nerves connecting the inner ear with the brain and transmitting impulses concerned with hearing and balance — see EAR illustration
**auditory tube** *noun* (1907)
: EUSTACHIAN TUBE
**audit trail** *noun* (1954)
: a record of a sequence of events (as actions performed by a computer) from which a history may be reconstructed
**Auf·klä·rung** \'au̇f-ˌkler-əŋ, -ˌu̇ŋ\ *noun* [German] (1842)
: ENLIGHTENMENT 2
**auf Wie·der·seh·en** \au̇f-'vē-dər-ˌzā(-ə)n\ *interjection* [German, literally, till seeing again] (1885)
— used to express farewell
**Au·ge·an** \ȯ-'jē-ən\ *adjective* [Latin *Augeas,* king of Elis, from Greek *Augeias;* from the legend that his stable, left neglected for 30 years, was finally cleaned by Hercules] (1599)
: extremely formidable or difficult and occasionally distasteful ⟨an *Augean* task⟩
**Augean stable** *noun* (1635)
: a condition or place marked by great accumulation of filth or corruption
**au·ger** \'ȯ-gər\ *noun* [Middle English, alteration (resulting from false division of *a nauger*) of *nauger,* from Old English *nafogār;* akin to Old High German *nabugēr* auger, Old English *nafu* nave, *gār* spear — more at NAVE, GORE] (before 12th century)
: any of various tools or devices having a helical shaft or member that are used for boring holes (as in wood, earth, or ice) or moving loose material (as snow) ◆

auger:
*1, 2 screw,*
*3 tapering*
*pod*

**Au·ger effect** \(ˌ)ō-'zhā-\ *noun* [Pierre V. *Auger* (born 1899) French physicist] (1931)
: a process in which an atom that has been ionized through the emission of an electron with energy in the X-ray range undergoes a transition in which a second electron is emitted rather than an X-ray photon — called also *Auger process*
**Auger electron** *noun* (1939)
: an electron emitted from an atom in the Auger effect
**Auger electron spectroscopy** *noun* (1970)
: an instrumental method for determining the chemical composition of a material's surface by bombardment with an electron beam to produce Auger electrons whose energy spectra are characteristic of their parent atoms — called also *Auger spectroscopy*

**¹aught** \'ȯt, 'ät\ *pronoun* [Middle English, from Old English *āwiht,* from *ā* ever + *wiht* creature, thing — more at AYE, WIGHT] (before 12th century)
**1** : ANYTHING
**2** : ALL, EVERYTHING ⟨for *aught* I care⟩ ⟨for *aught* we know⟩
**²aught** *adverb* (13th century)
*archaic* : AT ALL
**³aught** *noun* [alteration (resulting from false division of *a naught*) of naught] (1872)
**1** : ZERO, CIPHER
**2** *archaic* : NONENTITY, NOTHING
**au·gite** \'ȯ-ˌjīt\ *noun* [Latin *augites,* a precious stone, from Greek *augitēs*] (1804)
**1** : an aluminous usually black or dark green pyroxene that is found in igneous rocks
**2** : PYROXENE
— **au·git·ic** \ȯ-'ji-tik\ *adjective*
**¹aug·ment** \ȯg-'ment\ *verb* [Middle English, from Middle French *augmenter,* from Late Latin *augmentare,* from Latin *augmentum* increase, from *augēre* to increase — more at EKE] (14th century)
*transitive verb*
**1** : to make greater, more numerous, larger, or more intense ⟨the impact of the report was *augmented* by its timing⟩
**2** : to add an augment to
**3** : SUPPLEMENT ⟨*augmented* her scholarship by working nights⟩
*intransitive verb*
: to become augmented
**synonym** SEE INCREASE
— **aug·ment·er** *or* **aug·men·tor** \-'men-tər\ *noun*
**²aug·ment** \'ȯg-ˌment\ *noun* (circa 1771)
: a vowel prefixed or a lengthening of the initial vowel to mark past time especially in Greek and Sanskrit verbs
**aug·men·ta·tion** \ˌȯg-mən-'tā-shən, -ˌmen-\ *noun* (14th century)
**1 a** : the act or process of augmenting **b** : the state of being augmented
**2** : something that augments : ADDITION
**¹aug·men·ta·tive** \ȯg-'men-tə-tiv\ *adjective* (15th century)
**1** : able to augment
**2** : indicating large size and sometimes awkwardness or unattractiveness — used of words and affixes; compare DIMINUTIVE
**²augmentative** *noun* (1804)
: an augmentative word or affix
**aug·ment·ed** \ȯg-'men-təd\ *adjective* (1825)
*of a musical interval* : made one half step greater than major or perfect ⟨an *augmented* fifth⟩
**augmented matrix** *noun* (circa 1949)
: a matrix whose elements are the coefficients of a set of simultaneous linear equations with the constant terms of the equations entered in an added column
**au gra·tin** \ō-'grä-t°n, ȯ-, -'gra-\ *adjective* [French, literally, with the burnt scrapings from the pan] (1806)
: covered with bread crumbs or grated cheese and browned (as under a broiler)
**¹au·gur** \'ȯ-gər\ *noun* [Latin; akin to Latin *augēre*] (14th century)
**1** : an official diviner of ancient Rome
**2** : one held to foretell events by omens
**²augur** (1601)
*transitive verb*
**1** : to foretell especially from omens
**2** : to give promise of : PRESAGE ⟨higher pay *augurs* a better future⟩
*intransitive verb*
: to predict the future especially from omens
**au·gu·ry** \'ȯ-gyə-rē, -gə-\ *noun, plural* **-ries** (14th century)
**1** : divination from auspices or omens; *also* : an instance of this
**2** : OMEN, PORTENT
**au·gust** \ȯ-'gəst, 'ȯ-(ˌ)gəst\ *adjective* [Latin *augustus;* akin to Latin *augur*] (1664)
: marked by majestic dignity or grandeur

— **au·gust·ly** *adverb*
— **au·gust·ness** \ȯ-'gəs(t)-nəs, 'ȯ-(ˌ)gəs(t)-\ *noun*
**Au·gust** \'ȯ-gəst\ *noun* [Middle English, from Old English, from Latin *Augustus,* from *Augustus* Caesar] (before 12th century)
: the 8th month of the Gregorian calendar
**Au·gus·tan** \ȯ-'gəs-tən, ə-\ *adjective* (1704)
**1** : of, relating to, or characteristic of Augustus Caesar or his age
**2** : of, relating to, or characteristic of the neoclassical period in England
— **Augustan** *noun*
**¹Au·gus·tin·i·an** \ˌȯ-gə-'sti-nē-ən\ *noun* (1602)
**1** : a member of an Augustinian order; *specifically* : a friar of the Hermits of Saint Augustine founded in 1256 and devoted to educational, missionary, and parish work
**2** : a follower of Saint Augustine
**²Augustinian** *adjective* (1674)
**1** : of or relating to Saint Augustine or his doctrines
**2** : of or relating to any of several orders under a rule ascribed to Saint Augustine
— **Au·gus·tin·i·an·ism** \-nē-ə-ˌni-zəm\ *noun*
**au jus** \ō-'zhü(s), -'jüs; ō-zhœ\ *adjective* [French, literally, with juice] (circa 1919)
*of meat* : served in the juice obtained from roasting
**auk** \'ȯk\ *noun* [Norwegian or Icelandic *alk, alka,* from Old Norse *ālka*] (1674)
: any of several black-and-white short-necked diving seabirds (family Alcidae) that breed in colder parts of the northern hemisphere
**auk·let** \'ȯ-klət\ *noun* (1886)
: any of several small auks of the North Pacific coasts
**auld** \'ȯl(d), 'äl(d)\ *adjective* (14th century)
*chiefly Scottish* : OLD

**auk**

**auld lang syne** \ˌȯl(d)-,(l)aŋ-'zīn, ˌȯl(d)-\ *noun* [Scots, literally, old long ago] (1692)
: the good old times
**au na·tu·rel** \ˌō-ˌna-tə-'rel, -ˌna-chə-\ *adjective* [French] (1817)
**1** : cooked or served plainly
**2 a** : being in natural style or condition **b** : NUDE
**aunt** \'ant, 'änt\ *noun* [Middle English, from Old French *ante,* from Latin *amita;* akin to Old High German *amma* mother, nurse, Greek *amma* nurse] (14th century)

◇ **WORD HISTORY**
**auger** *Auger,* like *apron,* arose because it is hard to be sure of word boundaries in connected speech. *Auger* began its life in Old English as *nafogār,* a compound of *nafu* "nave of a wheel" and *gār* "spear," a "nave-spear" being the tool used to bore a hole through the hub of a wheel into which the axle could be inserted. By Middle English, *nafogār* had shrunk to *nauger,* obscuring the original sense of the compound. Already in Middle English, the combination of indefinite article and noun was spelled as both *an auger* and *a nauger,* an indication that younger generations of speakers who heard the word in connected speech were unsure whether it began with a consonant or a vowel. The form *auger* emerged as dominant in the 17th century.

\ə\ abut \ᵊ\ kitten \ər\ further \a\ ash \ā\ ace
\ä\ mop, mar \au̇\ out \ch\ chin \e\ bet \ē\ easy
\g\ go \i\ hit \ī\ ice \j\ job \ŋ\ sing \ō\ go
\ȯ\ law \ȯi\ boy \th\ thin \t͟h\ the \ü\ loot \u̇\ foot
\y\ yet \zh\ vision *see also* Guide to Pronunciation

**1 :** the sister of one's father or mother
**2 :** the wife of one's uncle
— **aunt·hood** \-ˌhu̇d\ *noun*
— **aunt·like** \-ˌlīk\ *adjective*
— **aunt·ly** *adjective*
**Aunt Sal·ly** \-'sa-lē\ *noun, plural* **Aunt Sallies** [*Aunt Sally*, name given to an effigy of a woman smoking a pipe set up as an amusement attraction at English fairs for patrons to throw missiles at] (1898)
*British* **:** an object of criticism or contention; *especially* **:** one that is set up to invite criticism or be easily refuted
**au pair** \ō-'par, -'per\ *noun, plural* **au pairs** \-'parz, -'perz\ [French, on even terms] (1960)
**:** a usually young foreign person who does domestic work for a family in return for room and board and the opportunity to learn the family's language
**au poivre** \ō-'pwäv(r°)\ *adjective* [French, with pepper] (?)
**:** prepared or served with a generous amount of usually coarsely ground black pepper ⟨steak *au poivre*⟩
**au·ra** \'ȯr-ə\ *noun* [Middle English, from Latin, puff of air, breeze, from Greek; probably akin to Greek *aēr* air] (1732)
**1 a :** a subtle sensory stimulus (as an aroma) **b :** a distinctive atmosphere surrounding a given source ⟨the place had an *aura* of mystery⟩
**2 :** a luminous radiation **:** NIMBUS
**3 :** a subjective sensation (as of lights) experienced before an attack of some disorders (as epilepsy or a migraine)
**4 :** an energy field that is held to emanate from a living being
**au·ral** \'ȯr-əl\ *adjective* [Latin *auris* ear — more at EAR] (1847)
**:** of or relating to the ear or to the sense of hearing
— **au·ral·ly** \-ə-lē\ *adverb*
**aurar** *plural of* EYRIR
**au·re·ate** \'ȯr-ē-ət\ *adjective* [Middle English *aureat*, from Medieval Latin *aureatus* decorated with gold, from Latin *aureus*] (15th century)
**1 :** of a golden color or brilliance
**2 :** marked by grandiloquent and rhetorical style
**au·re·ole** \'ȯr-ē-ˌōl\ *or* **au·re·o·la** \ȯ-'rē-ə-lə, ə-\ *noun* [Middle English *aureole* heavenly crown worn by saints, from Medieval Latin *aureola*, from Latin, feminine of *aureolus* golden, diminutive of *aureus*] (13th century)
**1 a :** a radiant light around the head or body of a representation of a sacred personage **b :** something resembling an aureole ⟨an *aureole* of hair⟩
**2 :** RADIANCE, AURA ⟨an *aureole* of youth and health⟩
**3 :** the luminous area surrounding the sun or other bright light when seen through thin cloud or mist **:** CORONA
**4 :** a ring-shaped zone around an igneous intrusion
— **aureole** *transitive verb*
**Au·reo·my·cin** \ˌȯr-ē-ō-'mī-sˀn\ *trademark*
— used for a preparation of the hydrochloride of chlortetracycline
**au·re·us** \'ȯr-ē-əs\ *noun, plural* **-rei** \-ē-ˌī\ [Latin, literally, golden, from *aurum* gold; akin to Old Prussian *ausis* gold] (1609)
**:** a gold coin of ancient Rome varying in weight from ⅛₀ to ⅟₇₀ libra
**au re·voir** \ˌō-rə-'vwär, ˌȯr-, *French* ȯr(-ə)-vwȧr\ *noun* [French, literally, till seeing again] (1694)
**:** GOOD-BYE — often used interjectionally
**au·ric** \'ȯr-ik\ *adjective* [Latin *aurum*] (circa 1828)
**:** of, relating to, or derived from gold
**au·ri·cle** \'ȯr-i-kəl\ *noun* [Latin *auricula*, from diminutive of *auris* ear — more at EAR] (15th century)
**1 a :** an atrium of a heart **b :** PINNA 2b **c :** an

anterior ear-shaped pouch in each atrium of the human heart
**2 :** an angular or ear-shaped lobe, process, or appendage
**au·ric·u·la** \ȯ-'ri-kyə-lə\ *noun* [New Latin, from Latin, external ear] (1655)
**:** a yellow-flowered Alpine primrose (*Primula auricula*)
**au·ric·u·lar** \ȯ-'ri-kyə-lər\ *adjective* (15th century)
**1 :** told privately ⟨an *auricular* confession⟩
**2 :** understood or recognized by the sense of hearing
**3 :** of, relating to, or using the ear or the sense of hearing
**4 :** of or relating to an auricle
**au·ric·u·late** \ȯ-'ri-kyə-lət\ *adjective* (1713)
**:** having auricles
**au·rif·er·ous** \ȯ-'ri-f(ə-)rəs\ *adjective* [Latin *aurifer*, from *aurum* + *-fer* -ferous] (1727)
**:** containing gold
**Au·ri·ga** \ȯ-'rī-gə\ *noun* [Latin, literally, charioteer]
**:** a constellation between Perseus and Gemini
**Au·ri·gna·cian** \ˌȯr-ēn-'yä-shən\ *adjective* [French *aurignacien*, from *Aurignac*, France] (1909)
**:** of or relating to an Upper Paleolithic culture marked by finely made artifacts of stone and bone, paintings, and engravings
**au·rochs** \'au̇r-ˌäks, 'ȯr-\ *noun, plural* **aurochs** [German, from Old High German *ūrohso*, from *ūro* aurochs + *ohso* ox; akin to Old English *ūr* aurochs — more at ox] (1766)
**1 :** an extinct large long-horned wild ox (*Bos primigenius*) of Europe that is the ancestor of domestic cattle
**2 :** WISENT
**au·ro·ra** \ə-'rȯr-ə, ȯ-, -'rȯr-\ *noun, plural* **auroras** *or* **au·ro·rae** \-(ˌ)ē\ [Latin — more at EAST] (14th century)
**1 :** DAWN
**2** *capitalized* **:** the Roman goddess of dawn — compare EOS
**3 :** a luminous phenomenon that consists of streamers or arches of light appearing in the upper atmosphere of a planet's magnetic polar regions and is caused by the emission of light from atoms excited by electrons accelerated along the planet's magnetic field lines
— **au·ro·ral** \-əl\ *adjective*
— **au·ro·re·an** \-ē-ən\ *adjective*
**aurora aus·tra·lis** \-ȯ-'strä-ləs, -ä-'strä-\ *noun* [New Latin, literally, southern dawn] (1741)
**:** an aurora that occurs in earth's southern hemisphere — called also *southern lights*
**aurora bo·re·al·is** \-ˌbȯr-ē-'a-ləs, -ˌbȯr-\ *noun* [New Latin, literally, northern dawn] (1717)
**:** an aurora that occurs in earth's northern hemisphere — called also *northern lights*
**aus·cul·tate** \'ȯ-skəl-ˌtāt\ *transitive verb* **-tat·ed; -tat·ing** [back-formation from *auscultation*] (circa 1860)
**:** to examine by auscultation
— **aus·cul·ta·to·ry** \ȯ-'skəl-tə-ˌtōr-ē, -ˌtȯr-\ *adjective*
**aus·cul·ta·tion** \ˌȯ-skəl-'tā-shən\ *noun* [Latin *auscultation-, auscultatio* act of listening, from *auscultare* to listen; akin to Latin *auris* ear — more at EAR] (circa 1828)
**:** the act of listening to sounds arising within organs (as the lungs) as an aid to diagnosis and treatment
**aus·land·er** \'au̇s-ˌlen-dər, -ˌlan-\ *noun* [German *Ausländer*] (1936)
**:** OUTSIDER, FOREIGNER
**aus·pice** \'ȯs-pəs\ *noun, plural* **aus·pic·es** \-pə-səz, -ˌsēz\ [Latin *auspicium*, from *auspic-, auspex* diviner by birds, from *avis* bird + *specere* to look, look at — more at AVIARY, SPY] (1533)
**1 :** observation by an augur especially of the flight and feeding of birds to discover omens

**2** *plural* **:** kindly patronage and guidance
**3 :** a prophetic sign; *especially* **:** a favorable sign
**aus·pi·cious** \ȯ-'spi-shəs\ *adjective* (1593)
**1 :** affording a favorable auspice **:** PROPITIOUS ⟨made an *auspicious* beginning⟩
**2 :** attended by good auspices **:** PROSPEROUS ⟨an *auspicious* year⟩
*synonym* see FAVORABLE
— **aus·pi·cious·ly** *adverb*
— **aus·pi·cious·ness** *noun*
**Aus·sie** \'ȯ-sē, 'ä-sē, *British & Australian usually* 'ȯ-zē\ *noun* [*Australian + -ie*] (1917)
**:** a native or inhabitant of Australia
**aus·ten·ite** \'ȯs-tə-ˌnīt, 'äs-\ *noun* [French, from Sir W. C. Roberts-*Austen* (died 1902) English metallurgist] (1902)
**:** a solid solution in iron of carbon and sometimes other solutes that occurs as a constituent of steel under certain conditions
— **aus·ten·it·ic** \ˌȯs-tə-'ni-tik, ˌäs-\ *adjective*
**aus·tere** \ȯ-'stir *also* -'ster\ *adjective* [Middle English, from Middle French, from Latin *austerus*, from Greek *austēros* harsh, severe; akin to Greek *hauos* dry — more at SERE] (14th century)
**1 a :** stern and cold in appearance or manner **b :** SOMBER, GRAVE ⟨an *austere* critic⟩
**2 :** morally strict **:** ASCETIC
**3 :** markedly simple or unadorned ⟨an *austere* office⟩ ⟨an *austere* style of writing⟩
**4 :** giving little or no scope for pleasure ⟨*austere* diets⟩
**5** *of a wine* **:** having the flavor of acid or tannin predominant over fruit flavors usually indicating a capacity for aging
*synonym* see SEVERE
— **aus·tere·ly** *adverb*
— **aus·tere·ness** *noun*
**aus·ter·i·ty** \ȯ-'ster-ə-tē *also* -'stir-\ *noun, plural* **-ties** (14th century)
**1 :** the quality or state of being austere
**2 a :** an austere act, manner, or attitude **b :** an ascetic practice
**3 :** enforced or extreme economy
¹**Austr-** *or* **Austro-** *combining form* [Latin, from *Austr-, Auster* south wind]
**:** south **:** southern ⟨*Austro*asiatic⟩
²**Austr-** *or* **Austro-** *combining form* [probably from New Latin, from *Austria*]
**:** Austrian and ⟨*Austro*-Hungarian⟩
¹**aus·tral** \'ȯs-trəl, 'äs-\ *adjective* [Middle English, from Latin *australis*, from *Austr-, Auster*] (14th century)
**1 :** of or relating to the Southern hemisphere
**2** *capitalized* **:** AUSTRALIAN
²**aus·tral** \au̇-'sträl\ *noun, plural* **aus·tral·es** \-'strä-lās\ *also* **australs** [Spanish] (1985)
**:** the basic monetary unit of Argentina 1985–91
**Aus·tra·lia Day** \ȯ-'sträl-yə-, ä-, ə-\ *noun* (1911)
**:** a national holiday in Australia commemorating the landing of the British at Sydney Cove in 1788 and observed on the Monday of or next following Jan. 26
¹**Aus·tra·lian** \ȯ-'sträl-yən, ä-, ə-\ *adjective* (1814)
**1 :** of, relating to, or characteristic of the continent or commonwealth of Australia, its inhabitants, or the languages spoken there
**2 :** of, relating to, or being a biogeographic region that comprises Australia, the islands north of it from Celebes eastward, Tasmania, New Zealand, and Polynesia
²**Australian** *noun* (1814)
**1 :** a native or inhabitant of the Australian commonwealth
**2 :** a group of about 200 languages spoken by the aboriginal inhabitants of Australia
**Australian ballot** *noun* (1888)
**:** an official ballot printed at public expense on which the names of all the candidates and proposals appear and which is distributed only at the polling place and marked in secret

**Australian cattle dog** *noun* (1926)
: any of a breed of medium-sized dogs that were developed in Australia to herd cattle and that have upright ears and a red or blue mottled coat

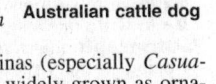

**Aus·tra·lian·ism** \ȯ-'strāl-yə-ˌni-zəm, -ä-, -ə-\ *noun* (1883)
: a characteristic feature of Australian English

**Australian cattle dog**

**Australian pine** *noun* (1919)
: any of several casuarinas (especially *Casuarina equisetifolia*) now widely grown as ornamentals in warm regions

**Australian Rules football** *noun* (1904)
: a game resembling rugby that is played between two teams of 18 players on a field 180–190 yards long that has four goalposts at each end

**Australian shepherd** *noun* (1964)
: any of a breed of bobtailed medium-sized dogs developed in America and often used in herding

**Australian terrier** *noun* (1903)
: any of a breed of small rather short-legged wirehaired terriers of Australian origin usually having a tan and blue or sandy coat

**Aus·tra·loid** \'ȯs-trə-ˌlȯid, 'äs-\ *adjective* [*Australi*a + English *-oid*] (1901)
*in some classifications* : of or relating

**Australian terrier**

to a racial group including the Australian aborigines and other peoples of southern Asia and Pacific islands
— **Australoid** *noun*

**aus·tra·lo·pith·e·cine** \ȯ-ˌstrā-lō-'pi-thə-ˌsīn, ä-; ˌȯs-trə-, ˌäs-\ *noun* [ultimately from Latin *australis* + Greek *pithēkos* ape] (1943)
: any of a genus (*Australopithecus*) of extinct southern and eastern African hominids that include gracile and robust forms with near-human dentition and a relatively small brain
— **australopithecine** *adjective*

**Austrian pine** *noun* (1858)
: a tall European pine (*Pinus nigra*) widely cultivated for ornament and having needles in clusters of two

**Aus·tro·asi·at·ic** \'ȯs-(ˌ)trō-ˌā-zhē-'a-tik, -zē-'a-, 'äs- *also* -ˌā-shē-\ *adjective* (1922)
: of, relating to, or constituting a family of languages of south and southeast Asia that includes Mon-Khmer and Munda as subfamilies

**Aus·tro·ne·sian** \ˌȯs-trə-'nē-zhən, ˌäs-, -shən\ *adjective* [*Austronesia*, islands of the southern Pacific] (1925)
: of, relating to, or constituting a family of languages spoken in the area extending from Madagascar eastward through the Malay Peninsula and Archipelago to Hawaii and Easter Island and including practically all the native languages of the Pacific islands with the exception of the Australian and Papuan languages

**aut-** *or* **auto-** *combining form* [Greek, from *autos* same, -self, self]
**1** : self : same one ⟨*autism*⟩ ⟨*auto*biography⟩
**2** : automatic : self-acting ⟨*autopilot*⟩

**au·ta·coid** \'ȯ-tə-ˌkȯid\ *noun* [*aut-* + Greek *akos* remedy; probably akin to Old Irish *ícc* cure] (1914)
: a physiologically active substance (as serotonin, bradykinin, or angiotensin) produced by and acting within the body

**au·tar·chic** \ȯ-'tär-kik\ *adjective* (1883)
: AUTARKIC
— **au·tar·chi·cal** \-ki-kəl\ *adjective*

**¹au·tar·chy** \'ȯ-ˌtär-kē\ *noun* [by alteration] (1617)
: AUTARKY

**²autarchy** *noun, plural* **-chies** [Greek *autarchia*, from *aut-* + *-archia* -archy] (1665)
: absolute sovereignty : AUTOCRACY

**au·tar·kic** \ȯ-'tär-kik\ *adjective* (1936)
: of, relating to, or marked by autarky
— **au·tar·ki·cal** \-ki-kəl\ *adjective*

**au·tar·ky** \'ȯ-ˌtär-kē\ *noun* [German *Autarkie*, from Greek *autarkeia*, from *autarkēs* self-sufficient, from *aut-* + *arkein* to defend, suffice — more at ARK] (1657)
**1** : SELF-SUFFICIENCY, INDEPENDENCE; *specifically* : national economic self-sufficiency and independence
**2** : a policy of establishing a self-sufficient and independent national economy

**aut·ecol·o·gy** \ˌȯ-ti-'kä-lə-jē, ˌȯt-ē-\ *noun* [International Scientific Vocabulary] (1910)
: ecology dealing with individual organisms or individual species of organisms
— **aut·eco·log·i·cal** \ˌȯt-ˌē-kə-'lä-ji-kəl, -ˌe-kə-\ *adjective*

**au·teur** \ō-'tər\ *noun* [French, originator, author, from Old French *autor*, from Latin *auctor* — more at AUTHOR] (1967)
: a film director whose practice accords with the auteur theory
— **au·teur·ist** \-ist\ *adjective or noun*

**au·teur theory** \ō-'tər-\ *noun* (1962)
: a view of filmmaking in which the director is considered the primary creative force in a motion picture

**au·then·tic** \ə-'then-tik, ȯ-\ *adjective* [Middle English *autentik*, from Middle French *autentique*, from Late Latin *authenticus*, from Greek *authentikos*, from *authentēs* perpetrator, master, from *aut-* + *-hentēs* (akin to Greek *anyein* to accomplish, Sanskrit *sanoti* he gains)] (14th century)
**1** *obsolete* : AUTHORITATIVE
**2 a** : worthy of acceptance or belief as conforming to or based on fact ⟨paints an *authentic* picture of our society⟩ **b** : conforming to an original so as to reproduce essential features ⟨an *authentic* reproduction of a colonial farmhouse⟩ **c** : made or done the same way as an original ⟨*authentic* Mexican fare⟩
**3** : not false or imitation : REAL, ACTUAL ⟨based on *authentic* documents⟩ ⟨an *authentic* cockney accent⟩
**4 a** *of a church mode* : ranging upward from the keynote — compare PLAGAL 1 **b** *of a cadence* : progressing from the dominant chord to the tonic — compare PLAGAL 2
**5** : true to one's own personality, spirit, or character ☆
— **au·then·ti·cal·ly** \-ti-k(ə-)lē\ *adverb*
— **au·then·tic·i·ty** \ˌȯ-ˌthen-'ti-sə-tē, -thən-\ *noun*

**au·then·ti·cate** \ə-'then-ti-ˌkāt, ȯ-\ *transitive verb* **-cat·ed; -cat·ing** (1653)
: to prove or serve to prove the authenticity of
*synonym* see CONFIRM
— **au·then·ti·ca·tion** \-ˌthen-ti-'kā-shən\ *noun*
— **au·then·ti·ca·tor** \-'then-ti-ˌkā-tər\ *noun*

**¹au·thor** \'ȯ-thər\ *noun* [Middle English *auctour*, from Old North French, from Latin *auctor* promoter, originator, author, from *augēre* to increase — more at EKE] (14th century)
**1 a** : one that originates or creates : SOURCE ⟨software *authors*⟩ ⟨the *author* of this crime⟩ **b** *capitalized* : GOD 1
**2** : the writer of a literary work (as a book)
— **au·tho·ri·al** \ȯ-'thȯr-ē-əl, -'thȯr-\ *adjective*

**²author** *transitive verb* (1596)
: to be the author of

**au·thor·ess** \'ȯ-th(ə-)rəs\ *noun* (15th century)
: a woman author

**au·tho·rise** *British variant of* AUTHORIZE

**au·thor·i·tar·i·an** \ȯ-ˌthär-ə-'ter-ē-ən, ə-, -ˌthȯr-\ *adjective* (1879)
**1** : of, relating to, or favoring blind submission to authority ⟨had *authoritarian* parents⟩
**2** : of, relating to, or favoring a concentration of power in a leader or an elite not constitutionally responsible to the people
— **authoritarian** *noun*
— **au·thor·i·tar·i·an·ism** \-ē-ə-ˌni-zəm\ *noun*

**au·thor·i·ta·tive** \ə-'thär-ə-ˌtā-tiv, ȯ-, -'thȯr-\ *adjective* (1605)
**1 a** : having or proceeding from authority : OFFICIAL ⟨*authoritative* church doctrine⟩ **b** : showing evident authority : DEFINITIVE ⟨a most *authoritative* literary critique⟩
**2** : DICTATORIAL 2
— **au·thor·i·ta·tive·ly** *adverb*
— **au·thor·i·ta·tive·ness** *noun*

**au·thor·i·ty** \ə-'thär-ə-tē, ȯ-, -'thȯr-\ *noun, plural* **-ties** [Middle English *auctorite*, from Old French *auctorité*, from Latin *auctoritat-*, *auctoritas* opinion, decision, power, from *auctor*] (13th century)
**1 a** (1) : a citation (as from a book or file) used in defense or support (2) : the source from which the citation is drawn **b** (1) : a conclusive statement or set of statements (as an official decision of a court) (2) : a decision taken as a precedent (3) : TESTIMONY **c** : an individual cited or appealed to as an expert
**2 a** : power to influence or command thought, opinion, or behavior **b** : freedom granted by one in authority : RIGHT
**3 a** : persons in command; *specifically* : GOVERNMENT **b** : a governmental agency or corporation to administer a revenue-producing public enterprise ⟨the transit *authority*⟩
**4 a** : GROUNDS, WARRANT ⟨had excellent *authority* for believing the claim⟩ **b** : convincing force ⟨lent *authority* to the performance⟩
*synonym* see INFLUENCE, POWER

**au·tho·ri·za·tion** \ˌȯ-th(ə-)rə-'zā-shən\ *noun* (15th century)
**1** : the act of authorizing
**2** : an instrument that authorizes : SANCTION

**au·tho·rize** \'ȯ-thə-ˌrīz\ *transitive verb* **-rized; -riz·ing** (14th century)
**1** : to establish by or as if by authority : SANCTION ⟨a custom *authorized* by time⟩
**2** : to invest especially with legal authority : EMPOWER ⟨*authorized* to act for her husband⟩
**3** *archaic* : JUSTIFY 1a
— **au·tho·riz·er** *noun*

**Authorized Version** *noun* (1824)
: a revision of the English Bishops' Bible carried out under James I, published in 1611, and widely used by Protestants — called also *King James Version*

**au·thor·ship** \'ȯ-thər-ˌship\ *noun* (1710)
**1** : the profession of writing

---

☆ **SYNONYMS**
**Authentic, genuine, bona fide** mean being actually and exactly what is claimed. AUTHENTIC implies being fully trustworthy as according with fact ⟨an *authentic* account of the perilous journey⟩; it can also stress painstaking or faithful imitation of an original ⟨an *authentic* reproduction⟩ ⟨*authentic* Vietnamese cuisine⟩. GENUINE implies actual character not counterfeited, imitated, or adulterated ⟨*genuine* piety⟩ ⟨*genuine* maple syrup⟩; it also connotes definite origin from a source ⟨a *genuine* Mark Twain autograph⟩. BONA FIDE implies good faith and sincerity of intention ⟨a *bona fide* offer for the stock⟩.

---

\ə\ abut \ᵊ\ kitten \ər\ further \a\ ash \ā\ ace \ä\ mop, mar \aú\ out \ch\ chin \e\ bet \ē\ easy \g\ go \i\ hit \ī\ ice \j\ job \ŋ\ sing \ō\ go \ȯ\ law \ȯi\ boy \th\ thin \th\ the \ü\ loot \ú\ foot \y\ yet \zh\ vision *see also* Guide to Pronunciation

**2 :** the source (as the author) of a piece of writing, music, or art
**3 :** the state or act of writing, creating, or causing

**au·tism** \'ȯ-,ti-zəm\ *noun* (1912)
**1 :** absorption in self-centered subjective mental activity (as daydreams, fantasies, delusions, and hallucinations) usually accompanied by marked withdrawal from reality
**2 :** a mental disorder originating in infancy that is characterized by self-absorption, inability to interact socially, repetitive behavior, and language dysfunction (as echolalia)
— **au·tis·tic** \ȯ-'tis-tik\ *adjective or noun*
— **au·tis·ti·cal·ly** \-ti-k(ə-)lē\ *adverb*
**au·to** \'ȯ-(,)tō, 'ä-\ *noun, plural* **autos** (1899)
**:** AUTOMOBILE
**auto-** — see AUT-
**au·to·an·ti·body** \,ȯ-(,)tō-'an-ti-,bä-dē\ *noun* (circa 1910)
**:** an antibody active against a tissue constituent of the individual producing it
**au·to·bahn** \'ȯ-tō-,bän, 'au̇-\ *noun* [German, from *Auto + Bahn* road] (1937)
**:** a German, Swiss, or Austrian expressway
**au·to·bi·og·ra·phy** \,ȯ-tə-bī-'ä-grə-fē, -bē-\ *noun* (1771)
**:** the biography of a person narrated by himself
— **au·to·bi·og·ra·pher** \-fər\ *noun*
— **au·to·bio·graph·i·cal** \-,bī-ə-'gra-fi-kəl\ *also* **au·to·bio·graph·ic** \-fik\ *adjective*
— **au·to·bio·graph·i·cal·ly** \-fi-k(ə-)lē\ *adverb*
**au·to·bus** \'ȯ-tō-,bəs\ *noun* [*auto + bus*] (1899)
**:** OMNIBUS 1
**au·to·cat·a·ly·sis** \,ȯ-tō-kə-'ta-lə-səs\ *noun, plural* **-y·ses** \-,sēz\ [New Latin] (1891)
**:** catalysis of a reaction by one of its products
— **au·to·cat·a·lyt·ic** \-,ka-tə-'li-tik\ *adjective*
— **au·to·cat·a·lyt·i·cal·ly** \-ti-k(ə-)lē\ *adverb*
**au·to·ceph·a·lous** \,ȯ-tō-'se-f(ə-)ləs\ *adjective* [Late Greek *autokephalos*, from Greek *aut- + kephalē* head — more at CEPHALIC] (1863)
**:** being independent of external and especially patriarchal authority — used especially of Eastern national churches
— **au·to·ceph·a·ly** \-fə-lē\ *noun*
**au·toch·thon** \ȯ-'täk-thən\ *noun, plural* **-thons** *or* **-tho·nes** \-thə-,nēz\ [Greek *autochthōn*, from *aut- + chthōn* earth — more at HUMBLE] (1590)
**:** one (as a person, plant, or animal) that is autochthonous
**au·toch·tho·nous** \ȯ-'täk-thə-nəs\ *adjective* (1805)
**1 :** INDIGENOUS, NATIVE ⟨an *autochthonous* people⟩
**2 :** formed or originating in the place where found ⟨*autochthonous* rock⟩ ⟨an *autochthonous* infection⟩
— **au·toch·tho·nous·ly** *adverb*
**¹au·to·clave** \'ȯ-tō-,klāv\ *noun* [French, from *aut- + * Latin *clavis* key — more at CLAVICLE] (1876)
**:** an apparatus in which special conditions (as high or low pressure or temperature) can be established for a variety of applications; *especially* **:** an apparatus (as for sterilizing) using superheated steam under high pressure
**²autoclave** *transitive verb* **-claved; -clav·ing** (1911)
**:** to treat in an autoclave
**au·to·cor·re·la·tion** \,ȯ-tō-,kȯr-ə-'lā-shən, -,kär-\ *noun* (1950)
**:** the correlation between paired values of a function of a mathematical or statistical variable taken at usually constant intervals that indicates the degree of periodicity of the function
**au·toc·ra·cy** \ȯ-'tä-krə-sē\ *noun, plural* **-cies** (1655)

**1 :** the authority or rule of an autocrat
**2 :** government in which one person possesses unlimited power
**3 :** a community or state governed by autocracy

**au·to·crat** \'ȯ-tə-,krat\ *noun* [French *autocrate,* from Greek *autokratēs* ruling by oneself, absolute, from *aut- + -kratēs* ruling — more at -CRAT] (1803)
**1 :** a person (as a monarch) ruling with unlimited authority
**2 :** one who has undisputed influence or power
**au·to·crat·ic** \,ȯ-tə-'kra-tik\ *also* **au·to·crat·i·cal** \-ti-kəl\ *adjective* (1823)
**1 :** of, relating to, or being an autocracy **:** ABSOLUTE ⟨an *autocratic* government⟩
**2 :** characteristic of or resembling an autocrat **:** DESPOTIC ⟨an *autocratic* ruler⟩
— **au·to·crat·i·cal·ly** \-ti-k(ə-)lē\ *adverb*
**au·to·cross** \'ȯ-tō-,krȯs, 'ä-tō-\ *noun* [*auto + * moto*cross*] (1963)
**:** an automobile gymkhana
**au·to·da·fé** \,au̇-tō-də-'fā, ,ȯ-tō-\ *noun, plural* **au·tos-da·fé** \-,tōz-də-\ [Portuguese *auto da fé,* literally, act of the faith] (1723)
**:** the ceremony accompanying the pronouncement of judgment by the Inquisition and followed by the execution of sentence by the secular authorities; *broadly* **:** the burning of a heretic
**au·to·di·dact** \,ȯ-tō-'dī-,dakt, -,dī-', -də-\ *noun* [Greek *autodidaktos* self-taught, from *aut- + didaktos* taught, from *didaskein* to teach] (1748)
**:** a self-taught person
— **au·to·di·dac·tic** \-,dī-'dak-tik, -də-\ *adjective*
**au·toe·cious** \ȯ-'tē-shəs\ *adjective* [*aut- + * Greek *oikia* house — more at VICINITY] (circa 1882)
**:** passing through all life stages on the same host ⟨*autoecious* rusts⟩
— **au·toe·cious·ly** *adverb*
— **au·toe·cism** \-'tē-,si-zəm\ *noun*
**au·to·er·o·tism** \,ȯ-tō-'er-ə-,ti-zəm\ *or* **au·to·erot·i·cism** \-i-'rä-tə-,si-zəm\ *noun* (1898)
**1 :** sexual feeling arising without known external stimulation
**2 :** sexual gratification obtained solely through stimulation by oneself of one's own body
— **au·to·erot·ic** \-i-'rä-tik\ *adjective*
**au·tog·a·my** \ȯ-'tä-gə-mē\ *noun* [International Scientific Vocabulary] (1877)
**:** SELF-FERTILIZATION: as **a :** pollination of a flower by its own pollen **b :** conjugation of two sister cells or sister nuclei of protozoans or fungi
— **au·tog·a·mous** \-məs\ *adjective*
**au·tog·e·nous** \ȯ-'tä-jə-nəs\ *also* **au·to·gen·ic** \,ȯ-tə-'je-nik\ *adjective* [Greek *autogenēs,* from *aut- + -genēs* born, produced — more at -GEN] (1846)
**1 :** produced independently of external influence or aid **:** ENDOGENOUS
**2 :** originating or derived from sources within the same individual ⟨an *autogenous* graft⟩ ⟨*autogenous* vaccine⟩
**3 :** not requiring a meal of blood to produce eggs ⟨*autogenous* mosquitoes⟩
— **au·tog·e·nous·ly** *adverb*
— **au·tog·e·ny** \ȯ-'tä-jə-nē\ *noun*
**au·to·gi·ro** *or* **au·to·gy·ro** \,ȯ-tō-'jīr-(,)ō\ *noun, plural* **-ros** [from *Autogiro,* a trademark] (1923)
**:** a rotary-wing aircraft that employs a propeller for forward motion and a freely rotating rotor for lift
**au·to·graft** \'ȯ-tō-,graft\ *noun* (circa 1913)

**autogiro**

**:** a tissue or organ that is transplanted from one part to another of the same body
— **autograft** *transitive verb*
**¹au·to·graph** \'ȯ-tə-,graf\ *noun* [Late Latin *autographum,* from Latin, neuter of *autographus* written with one's own hand, from Greek *autographos,* from *aut- + -graphos* written — more at -GRAPH] (circa 1644)
**:** something written or made with one's own hand: **a :** an original manuscript or work of art **b :** a person's handwritten signature
— **au·tog·ra·phy** \ȯ-'tä-grə-fē\ *noun*
**²autograph** *transitive verb* (1818)
**1 :** to write with one's own hand
**2 :** to write one's signature in or on
**³autograph** *adjective* (1832)
**:** being in the writer's own handwriting **:** not copied or duplicated ⟨an *autograph* letter⟩
**au·to·graph·ic** \,ȯ-tə-'gra-fik\ *adjective* (1810)
**1 :** of, relating to, or constituting an autograph
**2 a** *of an instrument* **:** SELF-RECORDING **b** *of a record* **:** recorded by a self-recording instrument
— **au·to·graph·i·cal·ly** \-fi-k(ə-)lē\ *adverb*
**Au·to·harp** \'ȯ-tō-,härp\ *trademark*
— used for a zither with button-controlled dampers for selected strings
**au·to·hyp·no·sis** \,ȯ-tō-hip-'nō-səs\ *noun* [New Latin] (1903)
**:** self-induced and usually automatic hypnosis
— **au·to·hyp·not·ic** \-'nä-tik\ *adjective*
**au·to·im·mune** \-im-'yün\ *adjective* (1952)
**:** of, relating to, or caused by autoantibodies or lymphocytes that attack molecules, cells, or tissues of the organism producing them ⟨*autoimmune* diseases⟩
— **au·to·im·mu·ni·ty** \-'yü-nə-tē\ *noun*
— **au·to·im·mu·ni·za·tion** \-,im-yə-nə-'zā-shən *also* -im-,yü-\ *noun*
**au·to·in·fec·tion** \-in-'fek-shən\ *noun* [International Scientific Vocabulary] (1903)
**:** reinfection with larvae produced by parasitic worms already in the body
**au·to·in·tox·i·ca·tion** \-in-,täk-sə-'kā-shən\ *noun* [International Scientific Vocabulary] (1887)
**:** a state of being poisoned by toxic substances produced within the body
**au·to·load·ing** \,ȯ-tō-'lō-diŋ\ *adjective* (1923)
**:** SEMIAUTOMATIC b
**au·tol·o·gous** \ȯ-'tä-lə-gəs\ *adjective* [*aut- + -ologous* (as in *homologous*)] (circa 1921)
**:** derived from the same individual ⟨*autologous* blood transfusion⟩
**au·tol·y·sate** \ȯ-'tä-lə-,sāt, -,zāt\ *also* **au·tol·y·zate** \-,zāt\ *noun* (1910)
**:** a product of autolysis
**au·to·lyse** *British variant of* AUTOLYZE
**au·tol·y·sis** \-lə-səs\ *noun* [New Latin] (1902)
**:** breakdown of all or part of a cell or tissue by self-produced enzymes
— **au·to·lyt·ic** \,ȯ-t⁰l-'i-tik\ *adjective*
**au·to·lyze** \'ȯ-tō-,līz\ *verb* **-lyzed; -lyzing** [back-formation from *autolysis*] (1903)
*intransitive verb*
**:** to undergo autolysis
*transitive verb*
**:** to subject to autolysis
**au·to·mak·er** \'ȯ-tō-,mā-kər, 'ä-tō-\ *noun* (circa 1905)
**:** a manufacturer of automobiles
**au·to·man** \'ȯ-tō-,man, 'ä-tō-\ *noun* (1952)
**:** AUTOMAKER
**Au·to·mat** \'ȯ-tə-,mat\ *service mark*
— used for a cafeteria in which food is obtained especially from vending machines
**au·to·mate** \'ȯ-tə-,māt\ *verb* **-mat·ed; -mat·ing** [back-formation from *automation*] (1952)
*transitive verb*
**1 :** to operate by automation
**2 :** to convert to largely automatic operation
**:** AUTOMATIZE

*intransitive verb*
: to undergo automation
— **au·to·mat·able** \-ˌmā-tə-bəl\ *adjective*
**automated teller machine** *noun* (1981)
: a computerized electronic machine that performs basic banking functions (as handling check deposits or issuing cash withdrawals) — called also *automatic teller, automatic teller machine*

**¹au·to·mat·ic** \ˌȯ-tə-'ma-tik\ *adjective* [Greek *automatos* self-acting, from *aut-* + *-matos* (akin to Latin *ment-, mens* mind) — more at MIND] (1748)
**1 a :** largely or wholly involuntary; *especially* : REFLEX 5 ⟨*automatic* blinking of the eyelids⟩ **b :** acting or done spontaneously or unconsciously **c :** done or produced as if by machine : MECHANICAL ⟨the answers were *automatic*⟩
**2 :** having a self-acting or self-regulating mechanism
**3** *of a firearm* **:** using either gas pressure or force of recoil and mechanical spring action for repeatedly ejecting the empty cartridge shell, introducing a new cartridge, and firing it
**synonym** see SPONTANEOUS
— **au·to·mat·i·cal·ly** \-ti-k(ə-)lē\ *adverb*
— **au·to·ma·tic·i·ty** \-mə-'ti-sə-tē, -ma-\ *noun*

**²automatic** *noun* (1902)
**1 :** a machine or apparatus that operates automatically: as **a :** an automatic firearm **b :** an automatic gear-shifting mechanism
**2 :** a semiautomatic firearm
**3 :** AUDIBLE

**automatic pilot** *noun* (1916)
**1 :** AUTOPILOT 1
**2 :** a state or condition in which activity or behavior is regulated automatically in a predetermined or instinctive manner ⟨would go on *automatic pilot* and repeat all his standard denunciations —G. J. Church⟩

**automatic writing** *noun* (1883)
: writing produced without conscious intention as if of telepathic or spiritualistic origin

**au·to·ma·tion** \ˌȯ-tə-'mā-shən\ *noun* [¹*automatic*] (circa 1948)
**1 :** the technique of making an apparatus, a process, or a system operate automatically
**2 :** the state of being operated automatically
**3 :** automatically controlled operation of an apparatus, process, or system by mechanical or electronic devices that take the place of human organs of observation, effort, and decision

**au·tom·a·tism** \ȯ-'tä-mə-ˌti-zəm\ *noun* [French *automatisme*, from *automate* automaton, from Latin *automaton*] (1838)
**1 a :** the quality or state of being automatic **b :** an automatic action
**2 :** the power or fact of moving or functioning without conscious control either independently of external stimuli (as in the beating of the heart) or under the influence of external stimuli (as in pupil dilation)
**3 :** a theory that views the body as a machine and consciousness as a noncontrolling adjunct of the body
**4 :** suspension of the conscious mind to release subconscious images ⟨*automatism* —the surrealist trend toward spontaneity and intuition —*Elle*⟩
— **au·tom·a·tist** \-'tä-mə-tist\ *noun or adjective*

**au·tom·a·tize** \ȯ-'tä-mə-ˌtīz\ *transitive verb* **-tized; -tiz·ing** [¹*automatic*] (1952)
: to make automatic
— **au·tom·a·ti·za·tion** \ȯ-ˌtä-mə-tə-'zā-shən, -ˌtī-'zā-\ *noun*

**au·tom·a·ton** \ȯ-'tä-mə-tən, -ˌtän\ *noun*, *plural* **-atons** *or* **-a·ta** \-mə-tə, -mə-ˌtä\ [Latin, from Greek, neuter of *automatos*] (1645)
**1 :** a mechanism that is relatively self-operating; *especially* : ROBOT
**2 :** a machine or control mechanism designed to follow automatically a predetermined sequence of operations or respond to encoded instructions
**3 :** an individual who acts in a mechanical fashion

**¹au·to·mo·bile** \'ȯ-tə-mō-ˌbēl, ˌȯ-tə-mō-'bē(ə)l, ˌȯ-tə-'mō-ˌbēl\ *adjective* [French, from *aut-* + *mobile*] (1883)
**:** AUTOMOTIVE

**²automobile** *noun* (circa 1889)
**:** a usually four-wheeled automotive vehicle designed for passenger transportation
— **automobile** *intransitive verb*
— **au·to·mo·bil·ist** \-'bē-list, -ˌbē-\ *noun*

**au·to·mo·bil·i·ty** \ˌȯ-tō-mə-'bi-lə-tē, -mō-\ *noun* (1903)
**:** the use of automobiles as the major means of transportation

**au·to·mor·phism** \ˌȯ-tə-'mȯr-ˌfi-zəm\ *noun* [*aut-* + *isomorphism*] (1903)
**:** an isomorphism of a set (as a group) with itself

**au·to·mo·tive** \ˌȯ-tə-'mō-tiv\ *adjective* (1898)
**1 :** of, relating to, or concerned with self-propelled vehicles or machines
**2 :** SELF-PROPELLED

**au·to·nom·ic** \ˌȯ-tə-'nä-mik\ *adjective* (1898)
**1 :** acting or occurring involuntarily ⟨*autonomic* reflexes⟩
**2 :** relating to, affecting, or controlled by the autonomic nervous system or its effects or activity ⟨*autonomic* drugs⟩
— **au·to·nom·i·cal·ly** \-mi-k(ə-)lē\ *adverb*

**autonomic nervous system** *noun* (1898)
**:** a part of the vertebrate nervous system that innervates smooth and cardiac muscle and glandular tissues and governs involuntary actions (as secretion and peristalsis) and that consists of the sympathetic nervous system and the parasympathetic nervous system

**au·ton·o·mist** \ȯ-'tä-nə-mist\ *noun* (1865)
**:** one who advocates autonomy

**au·ton·o·mous** \ȯ-'tä-nə-məs\ *adjective* [Greek *autonomos* independent, from *aut-* + *nomos* law — more at NIMBLE] (1800)
**1 :** of, relating to, or marked by autonomy
**2 a :** having the right or power of self-government **b :** undertaken or carried on without outside control : SELF-CONTAINED ⟨an *autonomous* school system⟩
**3 a :** existing or capable of existing independently ⟨an *autonomous* zooid⟩ **b :** responding, reacting, or developing independently of the whole ⟨an *autonomous* growth⟩
**4 :** controlled by the autonomic nervous system
**synonym** see FREE
— **au·ton·o·mous·ly** *adverb*

**au·ton·o·my** \-mē\ *noun*, *plural* **-mies** (circa 1623)
**1 :** the quality or state of being self-governing; *especially* **:** the right of self-government
**2 :** self-directing freedom and especially moral independence
**3 :** a self-governing state

**au·to·pi·lot** \'ȯ-tō-ˌpī-lət\ *noun* (1935)
**1 :** a device for automatically steering ships, aircraft, and spacecraft
**2 :** AUTOMATIC PILOT 2

**au·to·poly·ploid** \ˌȯ-tō-'pä-li-ˌplȯid\ *noun* (1930)
**:** an individual or strain whose chromosome complement consists of more than two complete copies of the genome of a single ancestral species
— **autopolyploid** *adjective*
— **au·to·poly·ploi·dy** \-ˌplȯi-dē\ *noun*

**au·top·sy** \'ȯ-ˌtäp-sē, 'ȯ-təp-\ *noun*, *plural* **-sies** [Greek *autopsia* act of seeing with one's own eyes, from *aut-* + *opsis* sight, appearance — more at OPTIC] (1678)
**1 :** an examination of a body after death to determine the cause of death or the character and extent of changes produced by disease
**2 :** a critical examination, evaluation, or assessment of someone or something past
— **autopsy** *transitive verb*

**au·to·ra·dio·gram** \ˌȯ-tō-'rā-dē-ə-ˌgram\ *noun* (1949)
**:** AUTORADIOGRAPH

**au·to·ra·dio·graph** \ˌȯ-tō-'rā-dē-ə-ˌgraf\ *noun* [International Scientific Vocabulary] (1903)
**:** an image produced on a photographic film or plate by the radiations from a radioactive substance in an object which is in close contact with the emulsion
— **au·to·ra·dio·graph·ic** \-ˌrā-dē-ə-'gra-fik\ *adjective*
— **au·to·ra·di·og·ra·phy** \-ˌrā-dē-'ä-grə-fē\ *noun*

**au·to·ro·ta·tion** \-rō-'tā-shən\ *noun* (1918)
**:** the turning of the rotor of an autogiro or a helicopter with the resulting lift caused solely by the aerodynamic forces induced by motion of the rotor along its flight path
— **au·to·ro·tate** \-'rō-ˌtāt\ *intransitive verb*

**au·to·route** \'ȯ-tō-ˌrüt, -ˌraut\ *noun* [French, from *automobile* + *route*] (1951)
**:** an expressway especially in France

**autos–da–fé** *plural of* AUTO-DA-FÉ

**au·to·sex·ing** \'ȯ-tō-ˌsek-siŋ\ *adjective* (1936)
**:** exhibiting different characters in the two sexes at birth or hatching

**au·to·some** \'ȯ-tə-ˌsōm\ *noun* (circa 1906)
**:** a chromosome other than a sex chromosome
— **au·to·so·mal** \ˌȯ-tə-'sō-məl\ *adjective*
— **au·to·so·mal·ly** \-mə-lē\ *adverb*

**au·to·stra·da** \ˌau-tō-'strä-də, ˌȯ-tō-\ *noun*, *plural* **-stradas** *or* **-stra·de** \-'strä-(ˌ)dā\ [Italian, from *automobile* + *strada* street, from Late Latin *strata* paved road — more at STREET] (1927)
**:** an expressway especially in Italy

**au·to·sug·ges·tion** \ˌȯ-tō-sə(g)-'jes-chən, -'jesh-\ *noun* [International Scientific Vocabulary] (1890)
**:** an influencing of one's own attitudes, behavior, or physical condition by mental processes other than conscious thought : SELF-HYPNOSIS
— **au·to·sug·gest** \-sə(g)-'jest\ *transitive verb*

**au·to·te·lic** \ˌȯ-tō-'te-lik, -'tē-\ *adjective* [Greek *autotelēs*, from *aut-* + *telos* end — more at TELOS] (circa 1901)
**:** having a purpose in and not apart from itself

**au·to·tet·ra·ploid** \ˌȯ-tō-'te-trə-ˌplȯid\ *noun* (1930)
**:** an individual or strain whose chromosome complement consists of four copies of a single genome due to doubling of an ancestral chromosome complement
— **autotetraploid** *adjective*
— **au·to·tet·ra·ploi·dy** \-ˌplȯi-dē\ *noun*

**au·tot·o·my** \ȯ-'tä-tə-mē\ *noun* [International Scientific Vocabulary] (1897)
**:** reflex separation of a part (as an appendage) from the body **:** division of the body into two or more pieces
— **au·tot·o·mous** \-məs\ *adjective*
— **au·tot·o·mize** \-ˌmīz\ *verb*

**au·to·trans·form·er** \ˌȯ-tō-tran(t)s-'fȯr-mər\ *noun* (1895)
**:** a transformer in which the primary and secondary coils have part or all of their turns in common

**au·to·trans·fu·sion** \ˌȯ-tō-tran(t)s-'fyü-zhən\ *noun* (circa 1923)
**:** return of autologous blood to the patient's own circulatory system

**au·to·troph** \'ȯ-tə-ˌtrōf, -ˌträf\ *noun* [German, from *autotroph*, adjective] (1938)
**:** an autotrophic organism

**au·to·tro·phic** \ˌȯ-tə-ˈtrō-fik\ *adjective* [probably from German *autotroph,* from Greek *autotrophos* supplying one's own food, from *aut-* + *trephein* to nourish] (circa 1900)
**1 :** needing only carbon dioxide or carbonates as a source of carbon and a simple inorganic nitrogen compound for metabolic synthesis
**2 :** not requiring a specified exogenous factor for normal metabolism
— **au·to·tro·phi·cal·ly** \-fi-k(ə-)lē\ *adverb*
— **au·tot·ro·phy** \ȯ-ˈtä-trə-fē\ *noun*
**au·to·wor·ker** \ˈȯ-tō-ˌwȯr-kər, ˈä-\ *noun* (1941)
**:** a person employed in the automobile manufacturing industry
**au·tox·i·da·tion** \ȯ-ˌtäk-sə-ˈdā-shən\ *noun* (1883)
**:** oxidation by direct combination with oxygen (as in air) at ordinary temperatures
**au·tumn** \ˈȯ-təm\ *noun* [Middle English *autumpne,* from Latin *autumnus*] (14th century)
**1 :** the season between summer and winter comprising in the northern hemisphere usually the months of September, October, and November or as reckoned astronomically extending from the September equinox to the December solstice — called also *fall*
**2 :** a period of maturity or incipient decline ⟨in the *autumn* of life⟩
— **au·tum·nal** \ȯ-ˈtəm-nəl\ *adjective*
— **au·tum·nal·ly** \-nə-lē\ *adverb*
**autumn crocus** *noun* (1885)
**:** an autumn-blooming colchicum (*Colchicum autumnale*)
**au·tun·ite** \ō-ˈtə-ˌnīt, ˈȯ-tᵊn-\ *noun* [*Autun,* town in France] (circa 1852)
**:** a radioactive lemon-yellow mineral occurring in tabular crystals with basal cleavage and in scales like mica
**aux·e·sis** \ȯg-ˈzē-səs, ȯk-ˈsē-\ *noun* [New Latin, from Greek *auxēsis* increase, growth, from *auxein* to increase — more at EKE] (circa 1848)
**:** GROWTH; *specifically* **:** increase of cell size without cell division
— **aux·et·ic** \-ˈze-tik, -ˈse-\ *adjective or noun*
**¹aux·il·ia·ry** \ȯg-ˈzil-yə-rē, -ˈzil-rē, -ˈzi-lə-\ *adjective* [Latin *auxiliaris,* from *auxilium* help; akin to Latin *augēre* to increase — more at EKE] (15th century)
**1 a :** offering or providing help **b :** functioning in a subsidiary capacity ⟨an *auxiliary* branch of the state university⟩
**2** *of a verb* **:** accompanying another verb and typically expressing person, number, mood, or tense
**3 a :** SUPPLEMENTARY **b :** constituting a reserve ⟨an *auxiliary* power plant⟩
**4 :** equipped with sails and a supplementary inboard engine
**²auxiliary** *noun, plural* **-ries** (1601)
**1 a :** an auxiliary person, group, or device; *specifically* **:** a member of a foreign force serving a nation at war **b :** a Roman Catholic titular bishop assisting a diocesan bishop and not having the right of succession — called also *auxiliary bishop*
**2 :** an auxiliary boat or ship
**3 :** an auxiliary verb
**aux·in** \ˈȯk-sən\ *noun* [International Scientific Vocabulary, from Greek *auxein*] (1934)
**1 :** any of various usually acidic organic substances that promote cell elongation in plant shoots and usually regulate other growth processes (as root initiation): as **a :** INDOLEACETIC ACID **b :** any of various synthetic substances (as 2,4-D) resembling indoleacetic acid in activity and used especially in research and agriculture
**2 :** PLANT HORMONE
— **aux·in·ic** \ȯk-ˈsi-nik\ *adjective*
**auxo·troph** \ˈȯk-sə-ˌtrȯf, -ˌträf\ *noun* (1950)
**:** an auxotrophic strain or individual

**auxo·tro·phic** \ˌȯk-sə-ˈtrō-fik\ *adjective* [Greek *auxein* to increase + *-o-* + English *-trophic*] (1944)
**:** requiring a specific growth substance beyond the minimum required for normal metabolism and reproduction by the parental or wild-type strain ⟨*auxotrophic* mutants of bacteria⟩
— **aux·ot·ro·phy** \ȯk-ˈsä-trə-fē\ *noun*
**¹avail** \ə-ˈvā(ə)l\ *verb* [Middle English, probably from *a-* (as in *abaten* to abate) + *vailen* to avail, from Old French *valoir* to be of worth, from Latin *valēre* — more at WIELD] (14th century)
*intransitive verb*
**:** to be of use or advantage **:** SERVE ⟨our best efforts did not *avail*⟩
*transitive verb*
**1 :** to be of use or advantage to **:** PROFIT
**2 :** to result in **:** bring about ⟨his efforts *availed* him nothing⟩
— **avail oneself of** *also* **avail of :** to make use of **:** take advantage of
**²avail** *noun* (15th century)
**1 :** advantage toward attainment of a goal or purpose **:** USE ⟨effort was of little *avail*⟩
**2** *plural* **:** profits or proceeds especially from a business or from the sale of property
**avail·abil·i·ty** \ə-ˌvā-lə-ˈbi-lə-tē\ *noun, plural* **-ties** (1803)
**1 :** the quality or state of being available
**2 :** an available person or thing
**avail·able** \ə-ˈvā-lə-bəl\ *adjective* (15th century)
**1** *archaic* **:** having a beneficial effect
**2 :** VALID — used of a legal plea or charge
**3 :** present or ready for immediate use
**4 :** ACCESSIBLE, OBTAINABLE ⟨articles *available* in any drugstore⟩
**5 :** qualified or willing to do something or to assume a responsibility ⟨*available* candidates⟩
**6 :** present in such chemical or physical form as to be usable (as by a plant) ⟨*available* nitrogen⟩ ⟨*available* water⟩
— **avail·able·ness** *noun*
— **avail·ably** \-blē\ *adverb*
**¹av·a·lanche** \ˈa-və-ˌlanch\ *noun* [French, from French dialect *lavantse, avalantse*] (1771)
**1 :** a large mass of snow, ice, earth, rock, or other material in swift motion down a mountainside or over a precipice
**2 :** a sudden great or overwhelming rush or accumulation of something ⟨office workers tied down with an *avalanche* of paperwork⟩
**3 :** a cumulative process in which photons or accelerated charge carriers produce additional photons or charge carriers through collisions (as with gas molecules)
**²avalanche** *verb* **-lanched; -lanch·ing** (1872)
*intransitive verb*
**:** to descend in an avalanche
*transitive verb*
**:** OVERWHELM, FLOOD
**Av·a·lon** \ˈa-və-ˌlän\ *noun*
**:** a paradise to which Arthur is carried after his death
**avant** \ˈä-ˌvän(t), ˈa-, -ˌvȯn(t), -ˌvōⁿ\ *adjective* [French *avant-* fore-, front, from *avant* before, from Latin *abante*] (1965)
**:** culturally or stylistically advanced **:** AVANT-GARDE ⟨*avant* jazz⟩
**¹avant–garde** \ˌä-ˌvän(t)-ˈgärd, ˌa-, ˌä-; ə-ˈvänt-; ˌa-ˌvōⁿ-, ˌa-ˌvȯn(t)-\ *noun* [French, vanguard] (1910)
**:** an intelligentsia that develops new or experimental concepts especially in the arts
— **avant–gard·ism** \-ˈgär-ˌdi-zəm\ *noun*
— **avant–gard·ist** \-ˈgär-dist\ *noun*
**²avant–garde** *adjective* (1925)
**:** of or relating to an avant-garde ⟨*avant-garde* writers⟩
**av·a·rice** \ˈa-və-rəs, ˈav-rəs\ *noun* [Middle English, from Old French, from Latin *avaritia,* from *avarus* avaricious, from *avēre* to crave — more at AVID] (14th century)

**:** excessive or insatiable desire for wealth or gain **:** GREEDINESS, CUPIDITY
**av·a·ri·cious** \ˌa-və-ˈri-shəs\ *adjective* (15th century)
**:** greedy of gain **:** excessively acquisitive especially in seeking to hoard riches
*synonym* see COVETOUS
— **av·a·ri·cious·ly** *adverb*
— **av·a·ri·cious·ness** *noun*
**avas·cu·lar** \(ˌ)ā-ˈvas-kyə-lər\ *adjective* (circa 1900)
**:** having few or no blood vessels ⟨*avascular* tissue⟩
— **avas·cu·lar·i·ty** \ˌā-ˌvas-kyə-ˈlar-ə-tē\ *noun*
**avast** \ə-ˈvast\ *verb imperative* [perhaps from Dutch *houd vast* hold fast] (1681)
— a nautical command to stop or cease
**av·a·tar** \ˈa-və-ˌtär\ *noun* [Sanskrit *avatāra* descent, from *avatarati* he descends, from *ava-* away + *tarati* he crosses over — more at UKASE, THROUGH] (1784)
**1 :** the incarnation of a Hindu deity (as Vishnu)
**2 a :** an incarnation in human form **b :** an embodiment (as of a concept or philosophy) often in a person
**3 :** a variant phase or version of a continuing basic entity
**avaunt** \ə-ˈvȯnt, -ˈvänt\ *adverb* [Middle English, from Middle French *avant,* from Latin *abante* forward, before, from *ab* from + *ante* before — more at OF, ANTE-] (15th century)
**:** AWAY, HENCE
**ave** \ˈä-(ˌ)vā\ *noun* [Middle English, from Latin, hail] (13th century)
**1 :** an expression of greeting or of leave-taking **:** HAIL, FAREWELL
**2** *often capitalized* **:** AVE MARIA
**avel·lan** \ə-ˈve-lən\ *or* **avel·lane** \ə-ˈve-ˌlān, ˈa-və-ˌlān\ *adjective* [Latin *abellana, avellana* filbert, from feminine of *Abellanus* of Abella, from *Abella,* ancient town in Italy] (1611)
*of a heraldic cross* **:** having the four arms shaped like conventionalized filberts — see CROSS illustration
**Ave Ma·ria** \ˌä-(ˌ)vā-mə-ˈrē-ə\ *noun* [Middle English, from Medieval Latin, hail, Mary] (13th century)
**:** HAIL MARY
**avenge** \ə-ˈvenj\ *transitive verb* **avenged; aveng·ing** [Middle English *avengen,* probably from *a-* (as in *abaten* to abate) + *vengen* to avenge, from Old French *vengier* — more at VENGEANCE] (14th century)
**1 :** to take vengeance for or on behalf of
**2 :** to exact satisfaction for (a wrong) by punishing the wrongdoer
— **aveng·er** *noun*
**av·ens** \ˈa-vənz\ *noun, plural* **avens** [Middle English *avence,* from Old French] (13th century)
**:** any of a genus (*Geum*) of perennial herbs of the rose family with white, purple, or yellow flowers
**av·en·tail** \ˈa-vən-ˌtāl\ *noun* [Middle English, modification of Old French *ventaille*] (14th century)
**:** VENTAIL
**aven·tu·rine** \ə-ˈven-chə-ˌrēn, -rən\ *noun* [French, from *aventure* chance — more at ADVENTURE] (1811)
**1 :** glass containing opaque sparkling particles of foreign material usually copper or chromic oxide
**2 :** a translucent quartz spangled throughout with scales of mica or other mineral
**av·e·nue** \ˈa-və-ˌnü, -ˌnyü\ *noun* [Middle French, from feminine of *avenu,* past participle of *avenir* to come to, from Latin *advenire* — more at ADVENTURE] (1600)
**1 :** a way of access **:** ROUTE
**2 :** a channel for pursuing a desired object ⟨*avenues* of communication⟩
**3 a** *chiefly British* **:** the principal walk or driveway to a house situated off a main road **b**

: a broad passageway bordered by trees
**4** : an often broad street or road

**aver** \ə-'vər\ *transitive verb* **averred; aver-ring** [Middle English *averren*, from Middle French *averer*, from Medieval Latin *adverare* to confirm as authentic, from Latin *ad-* + *verus* true — more at VERY] (15th century)
**1 a** : to verify or prove to be true in pleading a cause **b** : to allege or assert in pleading
**2** : to declare positively

**¹av·er·age** \'a-v(ə-)rij\ *noun* [from earlier *average* proportionally distributed charge for damage at sea, modification of Middle French *avarie* damage to ship or cargo, from Old Italian *avaria*, from Arabic *ʽawārīyah* damaged merchandise] (1735)
**1 a** : a single value (as a mean, mode, or median) that summarizes or represents the general significance of a set of unequal values **b** : MEAN 1b
**2 a** : an estimation of or approximation to an arithmetic mean **b** : a level (as of intelligence) typical of a group, class, or series ⟨above the *average*⟩
**3** : a ratio expressing the average performance especially of an athletic team or an athlete computed according to the number of opportunities for successful performance ☆
**— on average** *or* **on the average** : taking the typical example of the group under consideration ⟨prices have increased *on average* by five percent⟩

**²average** *adjective* (1770)
**1** : equaling an arithmetic mean
**2 a** : being about midway between extremes ⟨a man of *average* height⟩ **b** : not out of the ordinary : COMMON ⟨the *average* person⟩
**— av·er·age·ly** *adverb*
**— av·er·age·ness** *noun*

**³average** *verb* **av·er·aged; av·er·ag·ing** (1769)
*intransitive verb*
**1 a** : to be or come to an average ⟨the gain *averaged* out to 20 percent⟩ **b** : to have a medial value of ⟨a color *averaging* a pale purple⟩
**2** : to buy on a falling market or sell on a rising market additional shares or commodities so as to obtain a more favorable average price — usually used with *down* or *up*
*transitive verb*
**1** : to do, get, or have on the average or as an average sum or quantity ⟨*averages* 12 hours of work a day⟩
**2** : to find the arithmetic mean of (a series of unequal quantities)
**3 a** : to bring toward the average **b** : to divide among a number proportionately

**aver·ment** \ə-'vər-mənt\ *noun* (15th century)
**1** : the act of averring
**2** : something that is averred : AFFIRMATION

**averse** \ə-'vərs\ *adjective* [Latin *aversus*, past participle of *avertere*] (1597)
: having an active feeling of repugnance or distaste ⟨*averse* to strenuous exercise⟩
*synonym* see DISCLINED
*usage* see ADVERSE
**— averse·ly** *adverb*
**— averse·ness** *noun*

**aver·sion** \ə-'vər-zhən, -shən\ *noun* (1596)
**1** *obsolete* : the act of turning away
**2 a** : a feeling of repugnance toward something with a desire to avoid or turn from it ⟨regards drunkenness with *aversion*⟩ **b** : a settled dislike : ANTIPATHY ⟨expressed an *aversion* to parties⟩ **c** : a tendency to extinguish a behavior or to avoid a thing or situation and especially a usually pleasurable one because it is or has been associated with a noxious stimulus
**3** : one that is the object of aversion

**aversion therapy** *noun* (1946)
: therapy intended to change habits or antisocial behavior by inducing dislike for them through association with a noxious stimulus

**aver·sive** \ə-'vər-siv, -ziv\ *adjective* (1923)
: tending to avoid or causing avoidance of a noxious or punishing stimulus ⟨behavior modification by *aversive* stimulation⟩
**— aver·sive·ly** *adverb*
**— aver·sive·ness** *noun*

**avert** \ə-'vərt\ *transitive verb* [Middle English, from Middle French *avertir*, from Latin *avertere*, from *ab-* + *vertere* to turn — more at WORTH] (15th century)
**1** : to turn away or aside (as the eyes) in avoidance
**2** : to see coming and ward off : AVOID

**Aves·ta** \ə-'ves-tə\ *noun* [Middle Persian *Avastāk*, literally, original text] (1856)
: the book of the sacred writings of Zoroastrianism

**Aves·tan** \-tən\ *noun* (1856)
: an ancient Iranian language in which the sacred books of Zoroastrianism were written — see INDO-EUROPEAN LANGUAGES table
**— Avestan** *adjective*

**av·gas** \'av-,gas\ *noun* [*aviation gasoline*] (1943)
: gasoline for airplanes

**av·go·lem·o·no** \,äv-gō-'le-mə-(,)nō\ *noun* [New Greek *augolemono*, from *augo* egg + *lemoni* lemon] (1961)
: a soup or sauce made of chicken stock, rice, egg yolks, and lemon sauce

**avi·an** \'ā-vē-ən\ *adjective* [Latin *avis*] (1870)
: of, relating to, or derived from birds

**avi·ary** \'ā-vē-,er-ē\ *noun, plural* **-ar·ies** [Latin *aviarium*, from *avis* bird; akin to Greek *aetos* eagle] (1577)
: a place for keeping birds confined

**avi·ate** \'ā-vē-,āt, 'a-\ *intransitive verb* **-at·ed; -at·ing** [back-formation from *aviation*] (1887)
: to navigate the air (as in an airplane)

**avi·a·tion** \,ā-vē-'ā-shən, ,a-\ *noun, often attributive* [French, from Latin *avis*] (1866)
**1** : the operation of heavier-than-air aircraft
**2** : military airplanes
**3** : airplane manufacture, development, and design

**avi·a·tor** \'ā-vē-,ā-tər, 'a-\ *noun* (1887)
: the operator or pilot of an aircraft and especially an airplane

**aviator glasses** *noun plural* (1968)
: eyeglasses having a lightweight metal frame and relatively large usually tinted lenses

**avi·a·trix** \,ā-vē-'ā-triks, ,a-\ *noun, plural* **-trix·es** \-trik-səz\ *or* **-tri·ces** \-trə-,sēz\ (1910)
: a woman aviator

**avi·cul·ture** \'ā-və-,kəl-chər, 'a-\ *noun* [Latin *avis* + English *culture*] (circa 1879)
: the raising and care of birds and especially of wild birds in captivity
**— avi·cul·tur·ist** \,ā-və-'kəl-ch(ə-)rist, ,a-\ *noun*

**av·id** \'a-vəd\ *adjective* [French or Latin; French *avide*, from Latin *avidus*, from *avēre* to desire, crave; akin to Welsh *ewyllys* desire, Old Irish *con-oí* he protects] (1769)
**1** : desirous to the point of greed : urgently eager : GREEDY ⟨*avid* for publicity⟩
**2** : characterized by enthusiasm and vigorous pursuit ⟨*avid* readers⟩
*synonym* see EAGER
**— av·id·ly** *adverb*
**— av·id·ness** *noun*

**avi·din** \'a-və-dən\ *noun* [from its avidity for biotin] (1941)
: a protein found in egg white that inactivates biotin by combining with it

**avid·ity** \ə-'vi-də-tē, a-\ *noun, plural* **-ities** (15th century)
**1** : the quality or state of being avid: **a** : keen eagerness **b** : consuming greed
**2** : AFFINITY 2b(2)

**avi·fau·na** \,ā-və-'fo-nə, ,a-, -'fä-nə\ *noun* [New Latin, from Latin *avis* + New Latin *fauna*] (1874)
: the birds or the kinds of birds of a region, period, or environment
**— avi·fau·nal** \-'fo-n°l, -'fä-\ *adjective*

**avi·on·ics** \,ā-vē-'ä-niks, ,a-\ *noun plural* [*aviation electronics*] (1949)
: electronics designed for use in aerospace vehicles
**— avi·on·ic** \-nik\ *adjective*

**avir·u·lent** \(,)ā-'vir-(y)ə-lənt\ *adjective* [International Scientific Vocabulary] (circa 1900)
: not virulent — compare NONPATHOGENIC

**avi·ta·min·o·sis** \,ā-,vī-tə-mə-'nō-səs\ *noun, plural* **-o·ses** \-,sēz\ [New Latin] (1919)
: disease (as pellagra) resulting from a deficiency of one or more vitamins
**— avi·ta·min·ot·ic** \-mə-'nä-tik\ *adjective*

**A–V node** \,ā-'vē-, ,ä-,\ *noun* (1949)
: ATRIOVENTRICULAR NODE

**avo** \'a-(,)vü\ *noun, plural* **avos** [Portuguese, from *-avo* fractional part, from *-avo* ordinal suffix (as in *oitavo* eighth, from Latin *octavus*) — more at OCTAVE] (circa 1909)
— see *pataca* at MONEY table

**av·o·ca·do** \,ā-və-'kä-(,)dō, ,a-\ *noun, plural* **-dos** *also* **-does** [modification of Spanish *aguacate*, from Nahuatl *āhuacatl* avocado, testicle] (1697)
**1** : a pulpy green to purple nutty-flavored edible fruit of any of various tropical American trees (genus *Persea* especially *P. americana*) of the laurel family; *also* : a tree bearing avocados
**2** : a light yellowish green ◆

---

☆ **SYNONYMS**
**Average, mean, median, norm** mean something that represents a middle point. AVERAGE is exactly or approximately the quotient obtained by dividing the sum total of a set of figures by the number of figures ⟨scored an *average* of 85 on tests⟩. MEAN may be the simple average or it may represent value midway between two extremes ⟨a high of 70° and a low of 50° give a *mean* of 60°⟩. MEDIAN applies to the value that represents the point at which there are as many instances above as there are below ⟨*average* of a group of persons earning 3, 4, 5, 8, and 10 dollars a day is 6 dollars, whereas the *median* is 5 dollars⟩. NORM means the computed or estimated average of performance of a significantly large group, class, or grade ⟨scores about the *norm* for 5th grade arithmetic⟩.

---

◇ **WORD HISTORY**
**avocado** We owe the avocado, along with chocolate and the tomato, to pre-Columbian Middle America, and the words for these tasty items to Nahuatl, the language of several important Indian peoples, including the Aztecs, who lived in the area that is now Mexico City. The Nahuatl word for the avocado was *āhuacatl*, which also means "testicle"—one sense presumably being a metaphor for the other, though we do not know which came first. This word was borrowed into Spanish as *aguacate*, though by a peculiar twist of folk etymology some American Spanish speakers modified it to *abocado*, identical with *abocado* or *abogado* "advocate, lawyer." This modification eventually lost out to *aguacate* in almost all varieties of overseas Spanish, but not before it was borrowed into French (as *avocat*) and English (as *avocato* or *avocado*) in the late 17th century. Nahuatl *āhuacatl* also occurred in the compound *āhuacamōlli*, literally, "avocado sauce," borrowed into Spanish as *guacamole*, which American English borrowed several centuries later.

---

\ə\ abut \°\ kitten \ər\ further \a\ ash \ā\ ace
\ä\ mop, mar \aú\ out \ch\ chin \e\ bet \ē\ easy
\g\ go \i\ hit \ī\ ice \j\ job \ŋ\ sing \ō\ go
\ò\ law \òi\ boy \th\ thin \ th\ the \ü\ loot \ù\ foot
\y\ yet \zh\ vision    *see also* Guide to Pronunciation

**avocado pear** *noun* (1830)
*chiefly British* **:** AVOCADO 1

**av·o·ca·tion** \ˌa-və-'kā-shən\ *noun* [Latin *avocation-, avocatio*, from *avocare* to call away, from *ab-* + *vocare* to call, from *voc-, vox* voice — more at VOICE] (circa 1617)
**1** *archaic* **:** DIVERSION, DISTRACTION
**2 :** customary employment **:** VOCATION
**3 :** a subordinate occupation pursued in addition to one's vocation especially for enjoyment **:** HOBBY

**av·o·ca·tion·al** \ˌa-və-'kā-sh(ə-)nəl\ *adjective* (1921)
**1 :** of or relating to an avocation ⟨an *avocational* interest in sports⟩
**2 :** being such by avocation ⟨an *avocational* musician⟩
— **av·o·ca·tion·al·ly** \-sh(ə-)nə-lē\ *adverb*

**av·o·cet** \'a-və-ˌset\ *noun* [French & Italian; French *avocette*, from Italian *avocetta*] (1766)
**:** any of a genus (*Recurvirostra*) of rather large long-legged shorebirds with webbed feet and slender upward-curving bill

avocet

**Avo·ga·dro's num·ber** \ˌa-və-'gä-(ˌ)drōz-, ˌa-və-, -'ga-\ *noun* [Count Amedeo *Avogadro*] (1924)
**:** the number $6.023 \times 10^{23}$ indicating the number of atoms or molecules in a mole of any substance — called also *Avogadro number*

**avoid** \ə-'vȯid\ *transitive verb* [Middle English, from Middle French *esvuidier*, from *es-* (from Latin *ex-*) + *vuidier* to empty — more at VOID] (14th century)
**1 :** to make legally void **:** ANNUL ⟨*avoid* a plea⟩
**2** *obsolete* **:** VOID, EXPEL
**3 a :** to keep away from **:** SHUN **b :** to prevent the occurrence or effectiveness of **c :** to refrain from
**4** *archaic* **:** to depart or withdraw from **:** LEAVE
**synonym** see ESCAPE
— **avoid·able** \-'vȯi-də-bəl\ *adjective*
— **avoid·ably** \-blē\ *adverb*
— **avoid·er** *noun*

**avoid·ance** \ə-'vȯi-d°n(t)s\ *noun* (14th century)
**1** *obsolete* **a :** an action of emptying, vacating, or clearing away **b :** OUTLET
**2 :** ANNULMENT 1
**3 :** an act or practice of avoiding or withdrawing from something

**¹av·oir·du·pois** \ˌa-vər-də-'pȯiz, 'a-vər-də-ˌ\ *noun* [Middle English *avoir de pois* goods sold by weight, from Old French, literally, goods of weight] (15th century)
**1 :** AVOIRDUPOIS WEIGHT
**2 :** WEIGHT, HEAVINESS; *especially* **:** personal weight

**²avoirdupois** *adjective* (1755)
**:** expressed in avoirdupois weight ⟨one ounce *avoirdupois*⟩

**avoirdupois weight** *noun* (1619)
**:** the series of units of weight based on the pound of 16 ounces and the ounce of 16 drams — see WEIGHT table

**avouch** \ə-'vaùch\ *transitive verb* [Middle English, to cite as authority, from Middle French *avochier* to summon, from Latin *advocare* — more at ADVOCATE] (15th century)
**1 :** to declare as a matter of fact or as a thing that can be proved
**2 :** to vouch for **:** CORROBORATE
**3 a :** to acknowledge (as an act) as one's own **b :** CONFESS, AVOW

**avouch·ment** \-mənt\ *noun* (1574)
**:** an act of avouching **:** AVOWAL

**avow** \ə-'vaù\ *transitive verb* [Middle English, from Middle French *avouer*, from Latin *advocare*] (14th century)

**1 :** to declare assuredly
**2 :** to declare openly, bluntly, and without shame ⟨ever ready to *avow* his reactionary outlook⟩
**synonym** see ACKNOWLEDGE, ASSERT
— **avow·er** \-'vaù(-ə)r\ *noun*

**avow·al** \-'vaù(-ə)l\ *noun* (circa 1732)
**:** an open declaration or acknowledgment

**avow·ed·ly** \ə-'vaù-əd-lē\ *adverb* (1656)
**1 :** with open acknowledgment **:** FRANKLY ⟨an *avowedly* hostile review⟩
**2 :** by unsupported assertion or profession alone **:** ALLEGEDLY ⟨politicians remain skeptical of . . . *avowedly* democratic intentions —Jerry Kirshenbaum⟩

**avulse** \ə-'vəls\ *transitive verb* **avulsed; avuls·ing** [Latin *avulsus*, past participle of *avellere* to tear off, from *ab-* + *vellere* to pluck — more at VULNERABLE] (circa 1765)
**:** to separate by avulsion

**avul·sion** \ə-'vəl-shən\ *noun* (1622)
**:** a forcible separation or detachment: as **a :** a tearing away of a body part accidentally or surgically **b :** a sudden cutting off of land by flood, currents, or change in course of a body of water; *especially* **:** one separating land from one person's property and joining it to another's

**avun·cu·lar** \ə-'vən-kyə-lər\ *adjective* [Latin *avunculus* maternal uncle — more at UNCLE] (1831)
**1 :** of or relating to an uncle
**2 :** suggestive of an uncle especially in kindliness or geniality ⟨*avuncular* indulgence⟩
— **avun·cu·lar·i·ty** \ə-ˌvən-kyə-'la-rə-tē\ *noun*
— **avun·cu·lar·ly** \ə-'vən-kyə-lər-lē\ *adverb*

**aw** \'ȯ\ *interjection* (1852)
— used to express mild disappointment, gentle entreaty, or real or mock sympathy or sentiment

**await** \ə-'wāt\ *verb* [Middle English, from Old North French *awaitier*, from *a-* (from Latin *ad-*) + *waitier* to watch — more at WAIT] (13th century)
*transitive verb*
**1** *obsolete* **:** to lie in wait for
**2 a :** to wait for **b :** to remain in abeyance until ⟨a treaty *awaiting* ratification⟩
**3 :** to be in store for ⟨wonders what *awaits* him next⟩
*intransitive verb*
**1** *obsolete* **:** ATTEND
**2 :** to stay or be in waiting **:** WAIT
**3 :** to be in store

**¹awake** \ə-'wāk\ *verb* **awoke** \-'wōk\ *also* **awaked** \-'wākt\; **awo·ken** \-'wō-kən\ *or* **awaked** *also* **awoke; awak·ing** [Middle English *awaken* (from Old English *awacan, onwacan*, from *¹a-, on* + *wacan* to awake) & *awakien*, from Old English *awacian*, from *¹a-* + *wacian* to be awake — more at WAKE] (before 12th century)
*intransitive verb*
**1 :** to cease sleeping
**2 :** to become aroused or active again
**3 :** to become conscious or aware of something ⟨*awoke* to the possibilities⟩
*transitive verb*
**1 :** to arouse from sleep or a sleeplike state ⟨*awoken* by the storm⟩
**2 :** to make active **:** stir up ⟨*awoke* old memories⟩ ▪

**²awake** *adjective* (13th century)
**:** fully conscious, alert, and aware **:** not asleep
**synonym** see AWARE

**awak·en** \ə-'wā-kən\ *verb* **awak·ened; awak·en·ing** \-'wāk-niŋ, -'wā-kə-\ [Middle English, from Old English *awæcnian*, from *a-* + *wæcnian* to waken] (before 12th century)
**:** AWAKE
— **awak·en·er** \-'wāk-nər, -'wā-kə-\ *noun*

**¹award** \ə-'wȯrd\ *transitive verb* [Middle English, to decide, from Old North French *eswarder*, from *es-* (from Latin *ex-*) + *warder* to guard, of Germanic origin; akin to Old High German *wartēn* to watch — more at WARD] (14th century)
**1 :** to give by judicial decree or after careful consideration
**2 :** to confer or bestow as being deserved or merited or needed ⟨*award* scholarships to disadvantaged students⟩
**synonym** see GRANT
— **award·able** \-'wȯr-də-bəl\ *adjective*
— **award·ee** \-ˌwȯr-'dē\ *noun*
— **award·er** \-'wȯr-dər\ *noun*

**²award** *noun* (14th century)
**1 a :** a judgment or final decision; *especially* **:** the decision of arbitrators in a case submitted to them **b :** the document containing the decision of arbitrators
**2 :** something that is conferred or bestowed especially on the basis of merit or need

**aware** \ə-'war, -'wer\ *adjective* [Middle English *iwar*, from Old English *gewær*, from *ge-* (associative prefix) + *wær* wary — more at CO-, WARY] (before 12th century)
**1** *archaic* **:** WATCHFUL, WARY
**2 :** having or showing realization, perception, or knowledge ☆
— **aware·ness** *noun*

**awash** \ə-'wȯsh, -'wäsh\ *adjective* (1833)

---

☆ **SYNONYMS**
**Aware, cognizant, conscious, sensible, alive, awake** mean having knowledge of something. AWARE implies vigilance in observing or alertness in drawing inferences from what one experiences ⟨*aware* of changes in climate⟩. COGNIZANT implies having special or certain knowledge as from firsthand sources ⟨not fully *cognizant* of the facts⟩. CONSCIOUS implies that one is focusing one's attention on something or is even preoccupied by it ⟨*conscious* that my heart was pounding⟩. SENSIBLE implies direct or intuitive perceiving especially of intangibles or of emotional states or qualities ⟨*sensible* of a teacher's influence⟩. ALIVE adds to SENSIBLE the implication of acute sensitivity to something ⟨*alive* to the thrill of danger⟩. AWAKE implies that one has become alive to something and is on the alert ⟨a country always *awake* to the threat of invasion⟩.

---

□ **USAGE**
**awake** Our modern verb *awake* represents the amalgamation of two older verbs, one with regular verb parts and one with irregular parts. As a result, the modern verb has a mixture of regular and irregular parts whose status is still in flux. One old past participle, *awaken*, has become a separate verb. The past participle *awoken* is a curious case. It appears to have been formed from the past *awoke* and to have replaced an older past participle *awake*, now used only as an adjective. By the early 20th century, dictionary editors thought it had become obsolete, but it was staging a comeback under their very noses ⟨I was *awoken* by a very persistent lark —Robert Graves (1915)⟩ ⟨with eyes like sparks and his blood *awoken* —John Masefield (1919)⟩. It is likely that *awoken* is the prevailing past participle in British English today ⟨he had *awoken* early for once, rising before dawn —Salman Rushdie⟩. It appears also to be common in spoken American English—it appears in surveys—but we have little printed American evidence as yet. Here *awaked* prevails in print.

**1 a** : alternately covered and exposed by waves or tide **b** : washing about : AFLOAT **c** : covered with water : FLOODED
**2** : filled, covered, or completely overrun as if by a flood ⟨a movie *awash* in sentimentality⟩

**¹away** \ə-'wā\ *adverb* (before 12th century)
**1** : on the way : ALONG ⟨get *away* early⟩
**2** : from this or that place : HENCE, THENCE ⟨go *away*⟩
**3 a** : in a secure place or manner ⟨locked *away*⟩ **b** : in another direction ⟨look *away*⟩
**4** : out of existence : to an end ⟨echoes dying *away*⟩
**5** : from one's possession ⟨gave *away* a fortune⟩
**6** : steadily onward : UNINTERRUPTEDLY ⟨clocks ticking *away*⟩
**7** : by a long distance or interval : FAR ⟨*away* back in 1910⟩

**²away** *adjective* (14th century)
**1** : absent from a place : GONE ⟨*away* for the weekend⟩
**2** : distant in space or time ⟨a lake 10 miles *away*⟩ ⟨the season is two months *away*⟩
**3** : played on an opponent's grounds ⟨home and *away* games⟩
**4** *baseball* : OUT ⟨two *away* in the ninth⟩
— **away·ness** *noun*

**¹awe** \'ȯ\ *noun* [Middle English, from Old Norse *agi;* akin to Old English *ege* awe, Greek *achos* pain] (13th century)
**1** : an emotion variously combining dread, veneration, and wonder that is inspired by authority or by the sacred or sublime ⟨stood in *awe* of the king⟩ ⟨regard nature's wonders with *awe*⟩
**2** *archaic* **a** : DREAD, TERROR **b** : the power to inspire dread

**²awe** *transitive verb* **awed; aw·ing** (13th century)
: to inspire with awe

**aweary** \ə-'wir-ē\ *adjective* (1537)
*archaic* : being weary

**aweath·er** \ə-'we-thər\ *adverb* (1599)
: on or toward the weather or windward side — compare ALEE

**awed** \'ȯd\ *adjective* (1592)
: showing awe ⟨*awed* respect⟩

**aweigh** \ə-'wā\ *adjective* (1670)
: raised just clear of the bottom — used of an anchor

**awe·less** *or* **aw·less** \'ȯ-ləs\ *adjective* (14th century)
**1** : feeling no awe
**2** *obsolete* : inspiring no awe

**awe·some** \'ȯ-səm\ *adjective* (1598)
**1** : expressive of awe ⟨*awesome* tribute⟩
**2 a** : inspiring awe ⟨an *awesome* task⟩ **b** : TERRIFIC 2, 3; *especially* : EXTRAORDINARY
— **awe·some·ly** *adverb*
— **awe·some·ness** *noun*

**awe·struck** \-,strək\ *also* **awe·strick·en** \-,stri-kən\ *adjective* (1634)
: filled with awe

**¹aw·ful** \'ȯ-fəl\ *adjective* (13th century)
**1** : inspiring awe
**2** : filled with awe: as **a** *obsolete* : AFRAID, TERRIFIED **b** : deeply respectful or reverential
**3** : extremely disagreeable or objectionable
**4** : exceedingly great — used as an intensive ⟨an *awful* lot of money⟩ ☐
— **aw·ful·ly** \'ȯ-fə-lē, *especially as adverb of adjective senses 3 & 4* -flē\ *adverb*
— **aw·ful·ness** \-fəl-nəs\ *noun*

**²awful** *adverb* (1818)
: VERY, EXTREMELY ⟨*awful* tired⟩

**awhile** \ə-'hwī(ə)l, ə-'wī(ə)l\ *adverb* (before 12th century)
: for a while

**awhirl** \ə-'hwər(-ə)l, -'wər(-ə)l\ *adjective* (1883)
: being in a whirl

**awk·ward** \'ȯ-kwərd\ *adjective* [Middle English *awkeward* in the wrong direction, from *awke* turned the wrong way, from Old Norse

*ǫfugr;* akin to Old High German *abuh* turned the wrong way] (1530)
**1** *obsolete* : PERVERSE
**2** *archaic* : UNFAVORABLE, ADVERSE
**3 a** : lacking dexterity or skill (as in the use of hands) ⟨*awkward* with a needle and thread⟩ **b** : showing the result of a lack of expertness ⟨*awkward* pictures⟩
**4 a** : lacking ease or grace (as of movement or expression) **b** : lacking the right proportions, size, or harmony of parts : UNGAINLY
**5 a** : lacking social grace and assurance **b** : causing embarrassment ⟨an *awkward* moment⟩
**6** : not easy to handle or deal with : requiring great skill, ingenuity, or care ⟨an *awkward* load⟩ ⟨an *awkward* diplomatic situation⟩ ☆
— **awk·ward·ly** *adverb*
— **awk·ward·ness** *noun*

**awl** \'ȯl\ *noun* [Middle English *al,* from Old Norse *alr;* akin to Old High German *āla* awl, Sanskrit *ārā*] (before 12th century)
: a pointed tool for marking surfaces or piercing small holes (as in leather or wood)

**awls**

**awn** \'ȯn\ *noun* [Middle English, from Old English *agen,* from Old Norse *ǫgn;* akin to Old High German *agana* awn, Old English *ecg* edge — more at EDGE] (12th century)
: one of the slender bristles that terminate the glumes of the spikelet in some cereal and other grasses
— **awned** \'ȯnd\ *adjective*
— **awn·less** \'ȯn-ləs\ *adjective*

**aw·ning** \'ȯ-niŋ, 'ä-niŋ\ *noun* [origin unknown] (1624)
: a rooflike cover extending over or in front of a place (as over the deck or in front of a door or window) as a shelter
— **aw·ninged** \-niŋd\ *adjective*

**awoke** *past and past participle of* AWAKE
**awoken** *past participle of* AWAKE

**¹AWOL** \'ā-,wȯl, ,ā-,də-bəl-yü-,ō-'el\ *adjective or adverb, sometimes not capitalized* [absent without leave] (1919)
: ABSENT WITHOUT LEAVE; *broadly* : absent often without notice or permission ⟨the place looked as if its caretaker had been *AWOL* for some time —Daniel Ford⟩

**²AWOL** *noun, sometimes not capitalized* (1919)
: a person who is AWOL

**awry** \ə-'rī\ *adverb or adjective* (14th century)
**1** : in a turned or twisted position or direction : ASKEW
**2** : off the correct or expected course : AMISS

**aw–shucks** \'ȯ-,shəks\ *adjective* (1951)
: being or marked by an unsophisticated, self-conscious, or self-effacing manner

**¹ax** *or* **axe** \'aks\ *noun* [Middle English, from Old English *æcs;* akin to Old High German *ackus* ax, Latin *ascia,* Greek *axinē*] (before 12th century)
**1** : a cutting tool that consists of a heavy edged head fixed to a handle with the edge parallel to the handle and that is used especially for felling trees and chopping and splitting wood
**2** : a hammer with a sharp edge for dressing or spalling stone
**3** : abrupt removal (as from employment or from a budget) — sometimes used in the phrase *get the ax*
**4** : a musical instrument (as a guitar or a saxophone)
— **ax to grind** : an ulterior often selfish purpose to further

**²ax** *or* **axe** *transitive verb* **axed; ax·ing** (1679)
**1 a** : to shape, dress, or trim with an ax **b** : to chop, split, or sever with an ax

**2** : to remove abruptly (as from employment or from a budget)

**ax·el** \'ak-səl, 'äk-\ *noun, often capitalized* [*Axel* Paulsen (died 1938) Norwegian figure skater] (1930)
: a jump in figure skating from the outer forward edge of one skate with 1½ turns taken in the air and a return to the outer backward edge of the other skate

**axe·nic** \(,)ā-'ze-nik, -'zē-\ *adjective* [²a- + Greek *xenos* strange] (1942)
: free from other living organisms
— **axe·ni·cal·ly** \-ni-k(ə-)lē\ *adverb*

**ax·i·al** \'ak-sē-əl\ *adjective* (circa 1847)
**1** : of, relating to, or having the characteristics of an axis
**2 a** : situated around, in the direction of, on, or along an axis **b** : extending in a direction essentially perpendicular to the plane of a cyclic structure (as of cyclohexane) ⟨*axial* hydrogens⟩ — compare EQUATORIAL
— **ax·i·al·i·ty** \,ak-sē-'a-lə-tē\ *noun*
— **ax·i·al·ly** \'ak-sē-ə-lē\ *adverb*

**axial skeleton** *noun* (1872)
: the skeleton of the trunk and head

**ax·il** \'ak-səl, -,sil\ *noun* [New Latin *axilla,* from Latin] (1794)

---

---

---

\ə\ abut \ᵊ\ kitten \ər\ further \a\ ash \ā\ ace
\ä\ mop, mar \au̇\ out \ch\ chin \e\ bet \ē\ easy
\g\ go \i\ hit \ī\ ice \j\ job \ŋ\ sing \ō\ go
\ȯ\ law \ȯi\ boy \th\ thin \t͟h\ the \ü\ loot \u̇\ foot
\y\ yet \zh\ vision *see also* Guide to Pronunciation

: the angle between a branch or leaf and the axis from which it arises

**ax·il·la** \ag-'zi-lə, ak-'si-\ *noun, plural* **-lae** \-(,)lē, -,lī\ *or* **-las** [Latin, diminutive of *ala* wing, upper arm, armpit, axil — more at AISLE] (1616)
: the cavity beneath the junction of a forelimb and the body; *especially* : ARMPIT

**ax·il·lar** \ag-'zi-lər, ak-'si-, 'ag-zə-, 'ak-sə-, -,lär\ *noun* (1541)
: an axillary part (as a feather)

**¹ax·il·lary** \'ak-sə-,ler-ē\ *adjective* (1615)
**1** : of, relating to, or located near the axilla
**2** : situated in or growing from an axil ⟨*axillary* buds⟩

**²axillary** *noun, plural* **-lar·ies** (circa 1889)
: one of the feathers arising from the axilla and closing the space between the flight feathers and body of a flying bird

**ax·i·ol·o·gy** \,ak-sē-'ä-lə-jē\ *noun* [Greek *axios* + International Scientific Vocabulary *-logy*] (1908)
: the study of the nature, types, and criteria of values and of value judgments especially in ethics
— **ax·i·o·log·i·cal** \,ak-sē-ə-,lä-ji-kəl\ *adjective*
— **ax·i·o·log·i·cal·ly** \-ji-k(ə-)lē\ *adverb*

**ax·i·om** \'ak-sē-əm\ *noun* [Latin *axioma*, from Greek *axiōma*, literally, something worthy, from *axioun* to think worthy, from *axios* worth, worthy; akin to Greek *agein* to weigh, drive — more at AGENT] (15th century)
**1** : a maxim widely accepted on its intrinsic merit
**2** : a statement accepted as true as the basis for argument or inference : POSTULATE 1
**3** : an established rule or principle or a self-evident truth

**ax·i·om·at·ic** \,ak-sē-ə-'ma-tik\ *adjective* [Middle Greek *axiōmatikos*, from Greek, honorable, from *axiōmat-, axiōma*] (1797)
**1** : taken for granted : SELF-EVIDENT
**2** : based on or involving an axiom or system of axioms ⟨*axiomatic* set theory⟩
— **ax·i·om·at·i·cal·ly** \-ti-k(ə-)lē\ *adverb*

**ax·i·omat·isa·tion** *chiefly British variant of* AXIOMATIZATION

**ax·i·omat·iza·tion** \,ak-sē-ə-,ma-tə-'zā-shən, -sē-,ä-mə-tə-\ *noun* (1931)
: the act or process of reducing to a system of axioms
— **ax·i·om·a·tize** \-sē-'ä-mə-,tīz\ *transitive verb*

**axiom of choice** (1942)
: an axiom in set theory that is equivalent to Zorn's lemma: for every collection of nonempty sets there is a function which chooses an element from each set

**ax·ion** \'ak-sē-(,)än\ *noun* [*axial* + *²-on*] (1978)
: a hypothetical subatomic particle of low mass and energy that is postulated to exist because of certain properties of the strong force

**ax·is** \'ak-səs\ *noun, plural* **ax·es** \-,sēz\ [Latin, axis, axle; akin to Old English *eax* axis, axle, Greek *axōn*, Lithuanian *ašis*, Sanskrit *akṣa*] (14th century)
**1 a** : a straight line about which a body or a geometric figure rotates or may be supposed to rotate **b** : a straight line with respect to which a body or figure is symmetrical — called also *axis of symmetry* **c** : a straight line that bisects at right angles a system of parallel chords of a curve and divides the curve into two symmetrical parts **d** : one of the reference lines of a coordinate system
**2 a** : the second vertebra of the neck on which the head and first vertebra turn as on a pivot **b** : any of various central, fundamental, or axial parts
**3** : a plant stem
**4** : one of several imaginary lines assumed in describing the positions of the planes by which a crystal is bounded and the positions of atoms in the structure of the crystal

**5** : a main line of direction, motion, growth, or extension
**6 a** : an implied line in painting or sculpture through a composition to which elements in the composition are referred **b** : a line actually drawn and used as the basis of measurements in an architectural or other working drawing
**7** : any of three fixed lines of reference in an aircraft that run in the longitudinal, lateral, and vertical directions, are mutually perpendicular, and usually pass through the aircraft's center of gravity
**8** : PARTNERSHIP, ALLIANCE

**Axis** *adjective* (1938)
: of or relating to the three powers Germany, Italy, and Japan engaged against the Allied nations in World War II

**axi·sym·met·ric** \,ak-si-sə-'me-trik\ *also* **axi·sym·met·ri·cal** \-tri-kəl\ *adjective* [*axis* + *symmetric*] (1893)
: symmetric in respect to an axis
— **axi·sym·me·try** \-'si-mə-trē\ *noun*

**ax·le** \'ak-səl\ *noun* [Middle English *axel-* (as in *axeltre*)] (14th century)
**1 a** : a pin or shaft on or with which a wheel or pair of wheels revolves **b** (1) : a fixed bar or beam with bearings at its ends on which wheels (as of a cart) revolve (2) : the spindle of such a beam
**2** *archaic* : AXIS

**axle·tree** \-(,)trē\ *noun* [Middle English *axeltre*, from Old Norse *ǫxultrē*, from *ǫxull* axle + *trē* tree] (14th century)
: AXLE 1b(1)

**ax·man** \'ak-smən\ *noun* (1671)
: one who wields an ax

**Ax·min·ster** \'ak-,smin(t)-stər\ *noun* [*Axminster*, town in England] (1818)
: a machine-woven carpet with pile tufts inserted mechanically in a variety of textures and patterns

**ax·o·lotl** \'ak-sə-,lä-t°l\ *noun* [Nahuatl *āxōlōtl*] (circa 1768)
: any of several salamanders (genus *Ambystoma* especially *A. mexicanum* and *A. tigrinum*) of mountain lakes of Mexico and the western U.S. that ordinarily live and breed without metamorphosing

**ax·on** \'ak-,sän\ *also* **ax·one** \-,sōn\ *noun* [New Latin *axon*, from Greek *axōn*] (circa 1899)
: a usually long and single nerve-cell process that usually conducts impulses away from the cell body
— **ax·o·nal** \'ak-sə-n°l; ak-'sä-, -'sō-\ *adjective*

**ax·o·neme** \'ak-sə-,nēm\ *noun* [Greek *axōn* axis + *nēma* thread, from *nēn* to spin — more at NEEDLE] (1901)
: the fibrillar bundle of a flagellum or cilium that usually consists of nine pairs of microtubules arranged in a ring around a single central pair
— **ax·o·ne·mal** \,ak-sə-'nē-məl\ *adjective*

**ax·o·no·met·ric** \,ak-sə-nō-'me-trik\ *adjective* [Greek *axōn* axis + English *-metric*] (1908)
: being or prepared by the projection of objects on the drawing surface so that they appear inclined with three sides showing and with horizontal and vertical distances drawn to scale but diagonal and curved lines distorted ⟨an *axonometric* drawing⟩

**axo·plasm** \'ak-sə-,pla-zəm\ *noun* [*axon* + *-plasm*] (1900)
: the protoplasm of an axon
— **axo·plas·mic** \,ak-sə-'plaz-mik\ *adjective*

**ay** \'ī\ *interjection* [Middle French *aymi* ay me] (14th century)
— usually used with following *me* to express sorrow or regret

**ayah** \'ī-ə; 'ä-yə, -(,)yä\ *noun* [Hindi *āyā*, from Portuguese *aia*, from Latin *avia* grandmother] (1779)
: a nurse or maid native to India

**aya·hua·sca** \,ī-yə-'hwäs-kə, -'wäs-\ *noun* [American Spanish] (1949)
: an hallucinogenic beverage prepared from the bark of a South American vine (*Banisteriopsis caapi* of the family Malpighiaceae)

**aya·tol·lah** \,ī-ə-'tō-lə, -'tä-, -'tə-, 'ī-ə-,\ *noun* [Persian, literally, sign of God, from Arabic *āya* sign, miracle + *allāh* God] (1953)
: a religious leader among Shiite Muslims — used as a title of respect especially for one who is not an imam

**¹aye** *also* **ay** \'ā\ *adverb* [Middle English, from Old Norse *ei*; akin to Old English *ā* always, Latin *aevum* age, lifetime, Greek *aiōn* age] (13th century)
: ALWAYS, CONTINUALLY, EVER ⟨love that will *aye* endure —W. S. Gilbert⟩

**²aye** *also* **ay** \'ī\ *adverb* [perhaps from Middle English *ye, yie* — more at YEA] (1576)
: YES ⟨*aye, aye*, sir⟩

**³aye** *also* **ay** \'ī\ *noun, plural* **ayes** (1589)
: an affirmative vote or voter ⟨the *ayes* have it⟩

**aye–aye** \'ī-,ī\ *noun* [French, from Malagasy *aiay*] (circa 1781)
: a small primitive nocturnal forest-dwelling primate (*Daubentonia madagascariensis*) of northern Madagascar that has a round head, large eyes and ears, and long thin fingers

**ayin** \'ī-ən\ *noun* [Hebrew *'ayin*, literally, eye] (1823)
: the 16th letter of the Hebrew alphabet — see ALPHABET table

**Ay·ma·ra** \,ī-mə-'rä\ *noun, plural* **Aymara** *or* **Aymaras** [Spanish *aymará*] (1860)
**1** : a member of an Indian people of Bolivia and Peru
**2** : the language of the Aymara people

**Ayr·shire** \'ar-,shir, 'er-, -shər; 'ash-,ir\ *noun* [*Ayrshire*, Scotland] (1856)
: any of a breed of hardy dairy cattle originated in Ayr and usually marked with blotches of red or brown with white

**az-** *or* **azo-** *combining form* [International Scientific Vocabulary, from French *azote* nitrogen, from *a-* *²a-* + *-zote*, probably from Greek *zōtikos* maintaining life, from *zōē* life — more at QUICK]
: containing nitrogen especially as the bivalent group N=N ⟨*azine*⟩

**aza-** *or* **az-** *combining form* [International Scientific Vocabulary *az-* + *-a-*]
: containing nitrogen in place of carbon and usually the bivalent group NH for the group $CH_2$ or a single trivalent nitrogen atom for the group CH ⟨*azathioprine*⟩

**aza·lea** \ə-'zāl-yə\ *noun* [New Latin, genus name, from Greek, feminine of *azaleos* dry, from *azein* to parch, dry; akin to Hittite *ḫat-* to dry up and probably to Latin *ador* emmer] (1767)
: any of a subgenus (*Azalea*) of rhododendrons with funnel-shaped corollas and usually deciduous leaves including many species and hybrid forms cultivated as ornamentals

**aza·thi·o·prine** \,a-zə-'thī-ə-,prēn\ *noun* [*aza-* + *thi-* + *purine*] (1962)
: a purine antimetabolite $C_9H_7N_7O_2S$ used especially as an immunosuppressant

**Aza·zel** \ə-'zā-zəl, 'a-zə-,zel\ *noun* [Hebrew *'ăzāzēl*]
: an evil spirit of the wilderness to which a scapegoat was sent by the ancient Hebrews in a ritual of atonement

**azeo·trope** \'ā-zē-ə-,trōp\ *noun* [*²a-* + *zeo-* (from Greek *zein* to boil) + *-trope* something changed, from Greek *tropos* turn — more at YEAST, TROPE] (1938)
: a liquid mixture that is characterized by a constant minimum or maximum boiling point which is lower or higher than that of any of the components

**azide** \'ā-,zīd, 'a-\ *noun* (circa 1904)
: a compound containing the group $N_3$ combined with an element or radical

**az·i·do** \'a-zə-(,)dō\ *adjective* [International Scientific Vocabulary *azide* + *-o-*] (circa 1926)

: relating to or containing the univalent group N₃ — often used in combination

**az·i·do·thy·mi·dine** \ə-ˌzi-dō-ˈthī-mə-ˌdēn\ *noun* (1974)
: an antiviral drug $C_{10}H_{13}N_5O_4$ that inhibits replication of some retroviruses (as HIV) and is used to treat AIDS — called also *AZT, zidovudine*

**az·i·muth** \ˈaz-məth, ˈa-zə-\ *noun* [Middle English, from (assumed) Medieval Latin, from Arabic *as-sumūt* the azimuth, plural of *as-samt* the way] (14th century)
**1** : an arc of the horizon measured between a fixed point (as true north) and the vertical circle passing through the center of an object usually in astronomy and navigation clockwise from the north point through 360 degrees
**2** : horizontal direction expressed as the angular distance between the direction of a fixed point (as the observer's heading) and the direction of the object
— **az·i·muth·al** \ˌa-zə-ˈmə-thəl\ *adjective*
— **az·i·muth·al·ly** \-ˈmə-thə-lē\ *adverb*

**azimuthal equidistant projection** *noun* (1942)
: a map projection of the surface of the earth so centered at any given point that a straight line radiating from the center to any other point represents the shortest distance and can be measured to scale

**azine** \ˈā-ˌzēn, ˈa-\ *noun* (1887)
: a compound of the general formula RCH=NH=CHR or R₂C=NN=CR₂ formed by the action of hydrazine on aldehydes or ketones

**azo** \ˈā-(ˌ)zō, ˈa-\ *adjective* [*az-*] (circa 1879)
: relating to or containing the bivalent group N=N united at both ends to carbon

**azo dye** *noun* (1884)
: any of numerous dyes containing azo groups

**azo·ic** \(ˌ)ā-ˈzō-ik\ *adjective* [²*a-* + Greek *zōē* life — more at QUICK] (circa 1847)
: having no life; *especially* : of or relating to the part of geologic time that antedates life — compare ARCHEOZOIC

**azole** \ˈā-ˌzōl, ˈa-\ *noun* (circa 1899)
: any of numerous compounds characterized by a 5-membered ring containing at least one nitrogen atom

azimuthal equidistant projection, centered on Washington, D.C.: *1* London, *2* Algiers, *3* Moscow, *4* Rio de Janeiro, *5* Tokyo, *6* Auckland

**azon·al** \(ˌ)ā-ˈzō-nᵊl\ *adjective* (1938)
: of, relating to, or being a soil or a major group of soils lacking well-developed horizons often because of immaturity — compare INTRAZONAL, ZONAL

**azo·o·sper·mia** \(ˌ)ā-ˌzō-ə-ˈspər-mē-ə\ *noun* [New Latin, from Greek *azoos* lifeless (from *a-* ²*a-* + *zōē* life) + *sperma* semen, seed — more at SPERM] (circa 1881)
: absence of spermatozoa from the seminal fluid

**azo·te·mia** \ˌā-zō-ˈtē-mē-ə\ *noun* [International Scientific Vocabulary *azote* nitrogen + New Latin *-emia* — more at AZ-] (circa 1900)
: an excess of nitrogenous bodies in the blood as a result of kidney insufficiency — compare UREMIA
— **azo·te·mic** \-mik\ *adjective*

**az·oth** \ˈa-ˌzoth\ *noun* [Arabic *az-zāʾūq* the mercury] (15th century)
**1** : mercury regarded by alchemists as the first principle of metals
**2** : the universal remedy of Paracelsus

**azo·to·bac·ter** \ā-ˈzō-tə-ˌbak-tər\ *noun* [New Latin, genus name, from International Scientific Vocabulary *azote* + New Latin *bacterium*] (1910)
: any of a genus (*Azotobacter*) of large rod-shaped or spherical bacteria occurring in soil and sewage and fixing atmospheric nitrogen

**azo·tu·ria** \ˌā-zō-ˈtur̄-ē-ə, -ˈtyur̄-\ *noun* [International Scientific Vocabulary *azote* + New Latin *-uria*] (circa 1838)
: an abnormal condition of horses characterized by an excess of urea or other nitrogenous substances in the urine and muscle damage especially to the hindquarters

**AZT** \ˌā-(ˌ)zē-ˈtē\ *noun* (1985)
: AZIDOTHYMIDINE

**Az·tec** \ˈaz-ˌtek\ *noun* [Spanish *azteca*, from Nahuatl *aztēcah*, plural of *aztēcatl*] (1787)
**1 a** : a member of a Nahuatl-speaking people that founded the Mexican empire conquered by Cortes in 1519 **b** : a member of any people under Aztec influence
**2** : NAHUATL
— **Az·tec·an** \ˈaz-ˌte-kən, ˌaz-ˈte-\ *adjective*

**azure** \ˈa-zhər\ *noun* [Middle English *asur*, from Old French *azur*, probably from Old Spanish, modification of Arabic *lāzaward*, from Persian *lāzhuward*] (14th century)
**1** *archaic* : LAPIS LAZULI
**2 a** : the blue color of the clear sky **b** : the heraldic color blue
**3** : the unclouded sky
— **azure** *adjective*

**azur·ite** \ˈa-zhə-ˌrīt\ *noun* [French, from *azur* azure] (circa 1868)
**1** : a mineral that consists of blue basic carbonate of copper and is a copper ore
**2** : a semiprecious stone derived from azurite

**¹azy·gos** \ā-ˈzī-gəs\ *noun* [New Latin, from Greek, unyoked, from *a-* + *zygon* yoke — more at YOKE] (1646)
: an azygos anatomical part

**²azy·gos** *also* **azy·gous** \(ˌ)ā-ˈzī-gəs\ *adjective* (1681)
: not being one of a pair : SINGLE ⟨an *azygos* vein⟩

# B

B *is the second letter of the English alphabet and of most alphabets that are closely related to English. It came into these alphabets from the Latin, into the Latin (by way of Etruscan) from the Greek, and into the Greek from the Phoenician, where it was called* beth. B *usually represents the voiced bilabial stop, the consonant sound pronounced at the beginning of the English word* banana; *in a few English words it is silent, as in de*b*t and tom*b*. In related languages English* b *corresponds to German* b *(*Bru*der "brother"), Latin f (*frater *"brother,"* fero *"I bear"), Greek ph (*phe*ro "I bear"), and Sanskrit bh (*bharati *"he bears"). The small* b *developed from the capital form through the shrinking and eventual disappearance of the upper lobe, together with a reduction in the overall size of the letter.*

**b** \'bē\ *noun, plural* **b's** *or* **bs** \'bēz\ *often capitalized, often attributive* (before 12th century)
**1 a :** the 2d letter of the English alphabet **b :** a graphic representation of this letter **c :** a speech counterpart of orthographic *b*
**2 :** the 7th tone of a C-major scale
**3 :** a graphic device for reproducing the letter *b*
**4 :** one designated *b* especially as the 2d in order or class
**5 a :** a grade rating a student's work as good but short of excellent **b :** one graded or rated with a B
**6 :** something shaped like the letter B
**baa** \'ba, 'bä\ *intransitive verb* **baaed; baa-ing** [imitative] (circa 1586)
**:** to make the bleat of a sheep
— **baa** *noun*
**baal** \'bā(-ə)l\ *noun, plural* **baals** *or* **baa·lim** \'bā-(ə-)ləm, 'bä-ə-,lim\ *often capitalized* [Hebrew *ba'al* lord] (14th century)
**:** any of numerous Canaanite and Phoenician local deities
— **baal·ism** \'bā-(ə-),li-zəm\ *noun, often capitalized*
**baas** \'bäs\ *noun* [Afrikaans, from Dutch] (1785)
*South African* **:** BOSS, MASTER — used especially by nonwhites when speaking to or about Europeans in positions of authority
**ba·ba** \'bä-(,)bä, -bə\ *noun* [French, from Polish, literally, old woman] (1827)
**:** a rich cake soaked in a rum and sugar syrup
**ba·bas·su** \,bä-bə-'sü\ *noun* [Portuguese *babaçú*, from (assumed) Tupi *iwaβasu*, from Tupi *iwa* fruit + *βasu* large] (1917)
**:** a tall pinnate-leaved palm (*Orbignya barbosiana*) of Brazil with hard-shelled nuts yielding a valuable oil
**bab·bitt** \'ba-bət\ *noun* [Isaac *Babbitt* (died 1862) American inventor] (1900)
**:** an alloy used for lining bearings; *especially* **:** one containing tin, copper, and antimony — called also *babbitt metal*
— **bab·bitt·ed** \-bə-təd\ *adjective*
**Bab·bitt** \'ba-bət\ *noun* [George F. *Babbitt*, character in the novel *Babbitt* (1922) by Sinclair Lewis] (1923)
**:** a business or professional man who conforms unthinkingly to prevailing middle-class standards ◆
— **Bab·bitt·ry** \-bə-trē\ *noun*
— **Bab·bitty** \-tē\ *adjective*
**bab·ble** \'ba-bəl\ *verb* **bab·bled; bab·bling** \-b(ə-)liŋ\ [Middle English *babelen*, probably of imitative origin] (13th century)
*intransitive verb*
**1 a :** to talk enthusiastically or excessively **b :** to utter meaningless or unintelligible sounds
**2 :** to make sounds as though babbling
*transitive verb*
**1 :** to utter in an incoherently or meaninglessly repetitive manner

**2 :** to reveal by talk that is too free
— **babble** *noun*
— **bab·ble·ment** \-bəl-mənt\ *noun*
— **bab·bler** \-b(ə-)lər\ *noun*
**babe** \'bāb\ *noun* [Middle English, probably of imitative origin] (14th century)
**1 a :** INFANT, BABY **b** *slang* **:** GIRL, WOMAN
**2 :** a naive inexperienced person — used especially in the phrase *babe in the woods*
**Ba·bel** \'bā-bəl, 'ba-\ *noun* [Hebrew *Bābhel*, from Akkadian *bāb-ilu* gate of god]
**1 :** a city in Shinar where the building of a tower is held in Genesis to have been halted by the confusion of tongues
**2** *often not capitalized* **a :** a confusion of sounds or voices **b :** a scene of noise or confusion
**ba·be·sia** \bə-'bē-zh(ē-)ə\ *noun* [New Latin, from Victor *Babeş* (died 1926) Romanian bacteriologist] (1911)
**:** any of a genus (*Babesia*) of sporozoans parasitic in mammalian red blood cells (as in Texas fever) and transmitted by the bite of a tick — called also *piroplasm*
**bab·e·si·o·sis** \,ba-bə-'zī-ə-səs\ *noun* [New Latin] (1911)
**:** an infection with or disease caused by babesias
**Ba·bin·ski reflex** \bə-'bin-skē-\ *noun* [J.F.F. *Babinski* (died 1932) French neurologist] (1900)
**:** a reflex movement in which when the sole is tickled the big toe turns upward instead of downward and which is normal in infancy but indicates damage to the central nervous system (as in the pyramidal tracts) later in life — called also *Babinski sign, Ba·bin·ski's reflex* \-skēz\
**bab·i·ru·sa** \,ba-bə-'rü-sə, ,bä-\ *noun* [Malay, from *babi* pig + *rusa* deer] (1673)
**:** a large wild swine (*Babyrousa babyrussa*) of Indonesia
**ba·boon** \ba-'bün, *chiefly British* bə-\ *noun* [Middle English *babewin*, from Middle French *babouin*, from *baboue* grimace] (15th century)
**:** any of a genus (*Papio*) of large gregarious primates of Africa and southwestern Asia having a long square naked muzzle; *also* **:** any of several closely related primates
**ba·bu** *also* **ba·boo** \'bä-(,)bü\ *noun, often attributive* [Hindi *bābū*, literally, father] (1776)
**1 :** a Hindu gentleman — a form of address corresponding to *Mr.*
**2 a :** an Indian clerk who writes English **b :** an Indian having some education in English — often used disparagingly
**ba·bul** \bə-'bül\ *noun* [Persian *babūl*] (1780)
**:** an acacia tree (*Acacia nilotica* synonym *A. arabica*) widespread in India and northern Africa that yields gum arabic and tannins as well as fodder and timber

**ba·bush·ka** \bə-'büsh-kə, -'bùsh-\ *noun* [Russian, grandmother, diminutive of *baba* old woman] (1938)
**1 a :** a usually triangularly folded kerchief for the head **b :** a head covering resembling a babushka
**2 :** an elderly Russian woman

babushka 1a

**¹ba·by** \'bā-bē\ *noun, plural* **babies** [Middle English, from *babe*] (14th century)
**1 a** (1) **:** an extremely young child; *especially* **:** INFANT (2) **:** an extremely young animal **b :** the youngest of a group
**2 a :** one that is like a baby (as in behavior) **b :** something that is one's special responsibility, achievement, or interest
**3** *slang* **a :** GIRL, WOMAN — often used in address **b :** BOY, MAN — often used in address
**4 :** PERSON, THING ⟨is one tough *baby*⟩
— **ba·by·hood** \-bē-,hùd\ *noun*
— **ba·by·ish** \-ish\ *adjective*
**²baby** *adjective* (1591)
**1 :** of, relating to, or being a baby
**2 :** much smaller than the usual ⟨*baby* carrots⟩ ⟨a *baby* flattop⟩ ⟨take two *baby* steps⟩
**³baby** *transitive verb* **ba·bied; ba·by·ing** (1742)
**1 :** to tend to indulge with often excessive or inappropriate care and solicitude ⟨*babying* their only child⟩
**2 :** to operate or treat with care ⟨*baby* a new motor⟩ ⟨*babying* a sore knee⟩
*synonym* see INDULGE
**baby blue** *noun* (1889)
**:** a pale blue
**baby blue–eyes** \-'blü-,īz\ *noun plural but singular or plural in construction* (1887)
**:** a delicate blue-flowered California herb (*Nemophila menziesii*) of the waterleaf family
**baby boom** *noun* (1941)
**:** a marked rise in birthrate (as in the U.S. immediately following the end of World War II)
— **baby boomer** *noun*
**baby bust** *noun* (1971)
**:** a marked decline in birthrate
— **baby buster** *noun*
**baby carriage** *noun* (1866)
**:** a small four-wheeled carriage often with a folding top for pushing a baby around in — called also *baby buggy*
**baby grand** *noun* (circa 1903)
**:** a small grand piano
**Bab·y·lon** \'ba-bə-,län, -lən\ *noun* [*Babylon*, ancient city of Babylonia] (14th century)
**:** a city devoted to materialism and sensual pleasure

---

◇ **WORD HISTORY**
**Babbitt** *Babbitt* and *Babbittry* are words that sum up all the values, attitudes, and mores associated with the American middle class during the 1920's. Both derive from the protagonist of *Babbitt*, a satirical novel by Sinclair Lewis published in 1922. George F. Babbitt epitomizes the unimaginative and self-important businessmen that Lewis found typical of the provincial cities and towns of Middle America. A real estate agent by profession and a conformist by nature, Babbitt is a compulsive booster and joiner in his native Zenith, "The Zip City." Despite his evident prosperity and status in the community, he remains vaguely dissatisfied with his life. Although he makes tentative attempts at rebellion through brief encounters with artists, bohemians, and socialists and by having an extramarital affair, Babbitt finds his need for social acceptance greater than his desire for escape and he ends as he began.

**¹Bab·y·lo·nian** \,ba-bə-'lō-nyən, -nē-ən\ *noun* (1564)
**1** : a native or inhabitant of ancient Babylonia or Babylon
**2** : the form of the Akkadian language used in ancient Babylonia
**²Babylonian** *adjective* (1596)
**1** : of, relating to, or characteristic of Babylonia or Babylon, the Babylonians, or Babylonian
**2** : marked by luxury, extravagance, or the pursuit of sensual pleasure ⟨the *Babylonian* halls of the big hotel —G. K. Chesterton⟩ ⟨the *Babylonian* delights of the city⟩
**baby's breath** *noun* (circa 1890)
: GYPSOPHILA; *especially* : a perennial herb (*Gypsophila paniculata*) or an annual herb (*G. elegans*) commonly used in floral arrangements
**ba·by–sit** \'bā-bē-,sit\ *verb* **-sat** \-,sat\; **-sitting** [back-formation from *baby-sitter*] (1947)
*intransitive verb*
: to care for children usually during a short absence of the parents; *broadly* : to give care ⟨*baby-sit* for a neighbor's pets⟩
*transitive verb*
: to baby-sit for; *broadly* : MIND, TEND ⟨*baby-sit* house plants⟩ ⟨police *baby-sitting* a witness⟩
— **ba·by–sit·ter** *noun*
**baby talk** *noun* (1836)
**1 a** : the syntactically imperfect speech or phonetically modified forms used by small children learning to talk **b** : the consciously imperfect or altered speech used by adults in speaking to small children
**2** : oversimplified speech or writing
**baby tooth** *noun* (1939)
: MILK TOOTH
**bac·ca·lau·re·ate** \,ba-kə-'lȯr-ē-ət, -'lär-\ *noun* [Medieval Latin *baccalaureatus*, from *baccalaureus* bachelor, alteration of *baccalarius*] (circa 1649)
**1** : the degree of bachelor conferred by universities and colleges
**2 a** : a sermon to a graduating class **b** : the service at which this sermon is delivered
**bac·ca·rat** \,bä-kə-'rä, ,ba-\ *noun* [French *baccara*] (1865)
: a card game resembling chemin de fer in which three hands are dealt and players may bet either or both hands against the dealer's; *also* : a two-handed version in which players may bet on or against the dealer
**Bac·chae** \'ba-,kē, -,kī\ *noun plural* [Latin, from Greek *Bakchai*, from *Bakchos* Bacchus] (circa 1909)
**1** : the female attendants or priestesses of Bacchus
**2** : the women participating in the Bacchanalia
**¹bac·cha·nal** \'ba-kə-nᵊl, 'bä-; ,ba-kə-'nal, ,bä-kə-'näl\ *noun* [Latin, shrine of Bacchus, probably back-formation from *Bacchanalia*] (1550)
**1** : ORGY 2, 3
**2 a** : a devotee of Bacchus; *especially* : one who celebrates the Bacchanalia **b** : REVELER
**²bac·cha·nal** \'ba-kə-nᵊl\ *adjective* (1550)
: of, relating to, or suggestive of the Bacchanalia : BACCHANALIAN
**bac·cha·na·lia** \,ba-kə-'näl-yə, 'bä-\ *noun, plural* **bacchanalia** [Latin, from *Bacchus*] (1591)
**1** *plural, capitalized* : a Roman festival of Bacchus celebrated with dancing, song, and revelry
**2** : ORGY 2, 3
— **bac·cha·na·lian** \-'näl-yən\ *adjective or noun*
**bac·chant** \bə-'kant, -'känt; 'ba-kənt, 'bä-\ *noun, plural* **bacchants** *or* **bacchantes** \bə-'kants, -'känts, -'kan-tēz, -'kän-tēz\ [Latin *bacchant-, bacchans*, from present participle of *bacchari* to take part in the orgies of Bacchus] (1699)
: BACCHANAL
— **bacchant** *adjective*

**bac·chante** \bə-'kant, -'känt; -'kan-tē, -'kän-\ *noun* [French, from Latin *bacchant-, bacchans*] (1579)
: a priestess or female follower of Bacchus : MAENAD
**bac·chic** \'ba-kik, 'bä-\ *adjective, often capitalized* (1669)
: of, relating to, or suggestive of Bacchus or the Bacchanalia : BACCHANALIAN
**Bac·chus** \'ba-kəs, 'bä-\ *noun* [Latin, from Greek *Bakchos*]
: the Greek god of wine — called also *Dionysus*
**¹bach** \'bach\ *noun* (1855)
: BACHELOR 3a
**²bach** *intransitive verb* (1870)
: to live as a bachelor — often used with *it*
**³bach** *noun* [²*bach*] (1925)
*New Zealand* : a small house or weekend cottage
**¹bach·e·lor** \'bach-lər, 'ba-chə-\ *noun* [Middle English *bacheler*, from Old French] (14th century)
**1** : a young knight who follows the banner of another
**2** : a person who has received what is usually the lowest degree conferred by a four-year college, university, or professional school ⟨*bachelor* of arts⟩
**3 a** : an unmarried man **b** : a male animal (as a fur seal) without a mate during breeding time
— **bach·e·lor·dom** \-dəm\ *noun*
— **bach·e·lor·hood** \-,hu̇d\ *noun*
**²bachelor** *adjective* (1857)
**1** : suitable for or occupied by a single person ⟨a *bachelor* apartment⟩
**2** : UNMARRIED ⟨*bachelor* women⟩ ⟨*bachelor* parents⟩
**bach·e·lor·ette** \,bach-lə-'ret, ,ba-chə-\ *noun* (1938)
: a bachelor woman
**bachelor's button** *noun* (1847)
: a European composite (*Centaurea cyanus*) having flower heads with blue, pink, or white rays that is often cultivated in North America — called also *cornflower*
**ba·cil·la·ry** \'ba-sə-,ler-ē, bə-'si-lə-rē\ *or* **ba·cil·lar** \bə-'si-lər, 'ba-sə-lər\ *adjective* [Medieval Latin & New Latin *bacillus*] (1865)
**1** : shaped like a rod; *also* : consisting of small rods
**2** : of, relating to, or caused by bacilli
**ba·cil·lus** \bə-'si-ləs\ *noun, plural* **-li** \-,lī *also* -lē\ [New Latin, from Medieval Latin, small staff, rod, diminutive of Latin *baculus* staff, alteration of *baculum*] (circa 1879)
**1** : any of a genus (*Bacillus*) of aerobic rod-shaped gram-positive bacteria producing endospores that do not thicken the rod and including many saprophytes and some parasites (as *B. anthracis* of anthrax); *broadly* : a straight rod-shaped bacterium
**2** : BACTERIUM; *especially* : a disease-producing bacterium
**bac·i·tra·cin** \,ba-sə-'trā-sᵊn\ *noun* [New Latin *Bacillus subtilis* (species of bacillus producing the toxin) + Margaret *Tracy* (born about 1936) American child in whose tissues it was found] (1945)
: a toxic polypeptide antibiotic isolated from a bacillus (*Bacillus subtilis*) and usually used topically especially against gram-positive bacteria
**¹back** \'bak\ *noun* [Middle English, from Old English *bæc*; akin to Old High German *bah* back] (before 12th century)
**1 a** (1) : the rear part of the human body especially from the neck to the end of the spine (2) : the body considered as the wearer of clothes (3) : capacity for labor, effort, or endurance (4) : the back considered as the seat of one's awareness of duty or failings ⟨get off my *back*⟩ **b** : the part of a lower animal (as a quadruped) corresponding to the human back
**c** : SPINAL COLUMN **d** : BACKBONE 4

**2 a** : the side or surface opposite the front or face : the rear part; *also* : the farther or reverse side **b** : something at or on the back for support ⟨*back* of a chair⟩ **c** : a place away from the front ⟨sat in *back*⟩
**3** : a position in some games (as football or soccer) behind the front line of players; *also* : a player in this position
— **backed** \'bakt\ *adjective*
— **back·less** \'bak-ləs\ *adjective*
— **back of one's hand** *or* **back of the hand** : a show of contempt
— **back of one's mind** : the remote part of one's mind where thoughts and memories are stored to be drawn on
— **behind one's back** : without one's knowledge : in secret
— **in back of** : BEHIND
**²back** *adverb* (14th century)
**1 a** : to, toward, or at the rear **b** : in or into the past : backward in time; *also* : AGO **c** : to or at an angle off the vertical **d** (1) : under restraint (2) : in a delayed or retarded condition
**2 a** : to, toward, or in a place from which a person or thing came **b** : to or toward a former state **c** : in return or reply
**³back** *adjective* (15th century)
**1 a** : being at or in the back ⟨*back* door⟩ **b** : distant from a central or main area ⟨*back* roads⟩ **c** : articulated at or toward the back of the oral passage ⟨*back* vowels⟩
**2** : having returned or been returned
**3** : being in arrears : OVERDUE
**4** : moving or operating backward : REVERSE
**5** : not current ⟨*back* numbers of a magazine⟩
**6** : constituting the final 9 holes of an 18-hole golf course
**⁴back** (1548)
*transitive verb*
**1 a** : to support by material or moral assistance — usually used with *up* **b** : SUBSTANTIATE **c** : to assume financial responsibility for **d** : to provide musical accompaniment for — often used with *up*
**2 a** : to cause to go back or in reverse **b** : to articulate (a sound) with the tongue farther back
**3 a** : to furnish with a back **b** : to be at the back of
*intransitive verb*
**1** : to move backward — often used with *up*
**2** *of the wind* : to shift counterclockwise — compare VEER
**3** : to have the back in the direction of something
**synonym** see SUPPORT, RECEDE
— **back·er** \'ba-kər\ *noun*
— **back and fill 1** : to manage the sails of a ship so as to keep it clear of obstructions as it floats down with the current of a river or channel **2** : to take opposite positions alternately : SHILLY-SHALLY
— **back into** : to get into inadvertently ⟨*backed into* the antiques business⟩
**back·ache** \'bak-,āk\ *noun* (1601)
: a pain in the lower back
**back–and–forth** *noun* (1941)
: DISCUSSION 1, GIVE-AND-TAKE; *also* : EXCHANGE 1
**back and forth** *adverb* (1613)
: backward and forward; *also* : between two places or persons
**back away** *intransitive verb* (1919)
: to move away (as from a stand on an issue)
**back bacon** *noun* (1947)
*chiefly British* : CANADIAN BACON
**back·beat** \'bak-,bēt\ *noun* (1928)
: a steady pronounced rhythm stressing the second and fourth beats of a four-beat measure
**back·bench** *noun* (1874)

: a bench in a British legislature (as the House of Commons) occupied by rank-and-file members — compare FRONT BENCH

**— back·bench·er** \-'ben-chər\ *noun*

**back·bite** \-,bīt\ *verb* **-bit; -bit·ten; -bit·ing** (12th century)
*transitive verb*
: to say mean or spiteful things about
*intransitive verb*
: to backbite a person

**— back·bit·er** *noun*

**backbiting** \'bak-,bī-tiŋ\ *noun* (12th century)
: malicious comment about one not present

**back·block** \-,bläk\ *noun* (1870)
*Australian & New Zealand* : BOONDOCKS 2 — usually used in plural

**back·board** \-,bōrd, -,bȯrd\ *noun* (1761)
: a board placed at or serving as the back of something; *especially* : a rounded or rectangular board behind the basket on a basketball court which serves to keep missed shots from going out-of-bounds and from which the ball can be made to rebound into the basket

**back·bone** \-'bōn, -,bōn\ *noun* (14th century)
**1** : SPINAL COLUMN, SPINE
**2** : something that resembles a backbone: as **a** : a chief mountain ridge, range, or system **b** : the foundation or most substantial or sturdiest part of something **c** : the longest chain of atoms or groups of atoms in a usually long molecule (as a polymer or protein)
**3** : firm and resolute character
**4** : SPINE 1c

**back·break·ing** \-,brā-kiŋ\ *adjective* (1870)
: extremely tiring or demanding : OPPRESSIVE ⟨*backbreaking* labor⟩ ⟨*backbreaking* rents⟩

**— back·break·er** \-kər\ *noun*

**back burner** *noun* (1963)
: the condition of being out of active consideration or development — usually used in the phrase *on the back burner*

**back channel** *noun* (1975)
: a secret, unofficial, or irregular means of communication

**— back–channel** *adjective*

**back·chat** \'bak-,chat\ *noun* (1901)
**1** : BACK TALK
**2** : gossip or bantering conversation

**back–check** \-,chek\ *intransitive verb* (1937)
: to skate back toward one's own goal while closely defending against the offensive rushes of an opposing player in ice hockey

**— back–check·er** \-,che-kər\ *noun*

**back·cloth** \-,klȯth\ *noun* (1886)
*chiefly British* : BACKDROP

**back–coun·try** \-,kən-trē\ *noun, often attributive* (1746)
: a remote undeveloped rural area

**back·court** \-'kȯrt, -,kȯrt\ *noun* (1890)
**1** : the area near or nearest the back boundary lines or back wall of the playing area in a net or court game
**2** : a basketball team's defensive half of the court; *also* : the part of the offensive half of the court farthest from the goal
**3** : the basketball players who play the backcourt

**back·court·man** \-mən\ *noun* (1954)
: a guard on a basketball team

**¹back·cross** \'bak-,krȯs\ *transitive verb* (1904)
: to cross (a first-generation hybrid) with one of the parental types

**²backcross** *noun* (1918)
: a mating that involves backcrossing; *also*
: an individual produced by backcrossing

**back·date** \'bak-,dāt\ *transitive verb* (1944)
: to put a date earlier than the actual one on ⟨*backdate* a memo⟩; *also* : to make retroactive ⟨*backdate* pension rights⟩

**back dive** *noun* (circa 1934)
: a dive from a position facing the diving board

**back·door** \'bak-'dōr, -'dȯr\ *adjective* (1805)
: INDIRECT, DEVIOUS

**back down** *intransitive verb* (1849)

: to withdraw from a commitment or position

**back·drop** \'bak-,dräp\ *noun* (1913)
**1** : a painted cloth hung across the rear of a stage
**2** : BACKGROUND

**— backdrop** *transitive verb*

**back·field** \-,fēld\ *noun* (1920)
: the football players whose positions are behind the line of scrimmage; *also* : the positions themselves

**back·fill** \-,fil\ *noun* (1908)
*transitive verb*
: to refill (as an excavation) usually with excavated material
*intransitive verb*
: to backfill an excavation

**— backfill** *noun*

**¹back·fire** \-,fīr\ *noun* (1839)
**1** : a fire started to check an advancing fire by clearing an area
**2** : a loud noise caused by the improperly timed explosion of fuel mixture in the cylinder of an internal combustion engine

**²backfire** *intransitive verb* (1886)
**1** : to make or undergo a backfire
**2** : to have the reverse of the desired or expected effect

**back·fit** \'bak-,fit\ *transitive verb* (1967)
: RETROFIT

**— backfit** *noun*

**back·flow** \-,flō\ *noun* (1884)
: a flowing back or returning toward a source

**back–formation** *noun* (1889)
**1** : a word formed by subtraction of a real or supposed affix from an already existing longer word (as *burgle* from *burglar*)
**2** : the formation of back-formations

**back·gam·mon** \'bak-,ga-mən, bak-'\ *noun* [perhaps from ³*back* + Middle English *gamen, game* game] (circa 1645)
: a board game played with dice and counters in which players try to be the first to gather their pieces into one corner and then systematically remove them from the board

**¹back·ground** \'bak-,graúnd\ *noun, often attributive* (1672)
**1 a** : the scenery or ground behind something **b** : the part of a painting representing what lies behind objects in the foreground
**2** : an inconspicuous position
**3 a** : the conditions that form the setting within which something is experienced **b** (1) : the circumstances or events antecedent to a phenomenon or development (2) : information essential to understanding of a problem or situation **c** : the total of a person's experience, knowledge, and education
**4 a** : intrusive sound or radiation that interferes with received or recorded electronic signals **b** : a more or less steady level of noise above which the effect (as radioactivity) being measured by an apparatus (as a Geiger counter) is detected; *especially* : a somewhat steady level of radiation in the natural environment (as from cosmic rays) ☆

**²background** *transitive verb* (1768)
: to provide with background

**back·ground·er** \'bak-,graún-dər\ *noun* (1960)
: an off-the-record briefing for reporters

**background music** *noun* (1928)
: music to accompany the dialogue or action of a motion picture or radio or television drama

**background radiation** *noun* (1969)
: the microwave radiation pervading the universe that has the spectral energy distribution of a blackbody having a temperature of 2.7 K and that is the principle evidence supporting the big bang theory — called also *cosmic background radiation*

**¹back·hand** \'bak-,hand\ *noun* (1657)
**1 a** : a stroke (as in tennis) made with the back of the hand turned in the direction of movement; *also* : the side on which such

strokes are made **b** : a catch (as in baseball) made to the side of the body opposite the hand being used
**2** : handwriting whose strokes slant downward from left to right

**²backhand** *adjective* (1695)
: made with a backhand ⟨a *backhand* tennis stroke⟩

backhand 1a

**³backhand** *or* **back·hand·ed** \-'han-dəd\ *adverb* (1889)
: with a backhand

**⁴backhand** *transitive verb* (circa 1935)
: to do, hit, or catch backhand

**back·hand·ed** \'bak-'han-dəd\ *adjective* (1800)
**1** : INDIRECT, DEVIOUS; *especially* : SARCASTIC ⟨a *backhanded* compliment⟩
**2** : using or made with a backhand

**— back·hand·ed·ly** *adverb*

**back·hand·er** \-dər\ *noun* (1960)
*British* : BRIBE

**back·hoe** \-,hō\ *noun* (1928)
: an excavating machine having a bucket that is attached to a rigid bar hinged to a boom and that is drawn toward the machine in operation

**back·house** \-,haús\ *noun* (circa 1847)
: PRIVY 1a

**back·ing** \'ba-kiŋ\ *noun* (1793)
**1** : something forming a back
**2 a** : SUPPORT, AID **b** : endorsement especially of a warrant by a magistrate

**back judge** *noun* (circa 1966)
: a football official whose duties include keeping the game's official time and identifying eligible pass receivers

**back·land** \'bak-,land\ *noun* (1681)
: BACKCOUNTRY, HINTERLAND — usually used in plural

**back·lash** \'bak-,lash\ *noun* (1815)
**1 a** : a sudden violent backward movement or reaction **b** : the play between adjacent movable parts (as in a series of gears); *also* : the jar caused by this when the parts are put into action
**2** : a snarl in that part of a fishing line wound on the reel
**3** : a strong adverse reaction (as to a recent political or social development)

**— back·lash·er** *noun*

**back·light** \-,līt\ *noun* (circa 1846)
: illumination from behind; *also* : the source of such illumination

**— backlight** *transitive verb*

**back·list** \'bak-,list\ *noun* (1964)

☆ SYNONYMS
**Background, setting, environment, milieu, mise-en-scène** mean the place, time, and circumstances in which something occurs. BACKGROUND often refers to the circumstances or events that precede a phenomenon or development ⟨the shocking decision was part of the *background* of the riots⟩. SETTING suggests looking at real-life situations in literary or dramatic terms ⟨a militant reformer who was born into an unlikely social *setting*⟩. ENVIRONMENT applies to all the external factors that have a formative influence on one's physical, mental, or moral development ⟨the kind of *environment* that produces juvenile delinquents⟩. MILIEU applies especially to the physical and social surroundings of a person or group of persons ⟨an intellectual *milieu* conducive to artistic experimentation⟩. MISE-EN-SCENE strongly suggests the use of properties to achieve a particular atmosphere or theatrical effect ⟨a gothic thriller with a carefully crafted *mise-en-scène*⟩.

: a list of books kept in print as distinguished from books newly published

**¹back·log** \-ˌlȯg, -ˌläg\ *noun* (1684)
**1** : a large log at the back of a hearth fire
**2** : an accumulation of tasks unperformed or materials not processed

**²backlog** *verb* (1963)
: ACCUMULATE

**back matter** *noun* (1947)
: matter following the main text of a book

**back mutation** *noun* (1939)
: mutation of a previously mutated gene to its former condition

**back of** *preposition* (1694)
: BEHIND

**back of beyond** (1816)
: a remote place

**back off** *intransitive verb* (1938)
: BACK DOWN

**back–office** \ˈbak-ˌä-fəs, -ˌȯ-fəs\ *adjective* (1953)
: of or relating to the inner workings of a business or institution : INTERNAL ⟨*back-office* operations⟩

**back out** *intransitive verb* (1807)
: to withdraw especially from a commitment or contest

**¹back·pack** \ˈbak-ˌpak\ *noun* (1914)
**1 a** : a load carried on the back **b** : a camping pack (as of canvas or nylon) supported by a usually aluminum frame and carried on the back
**2** : a piece of equipment designed for use while being carried on the back

**²backpack** (1927)
*transitive verb*
: to carry (food or equipment) on the back especially in hiking
*intransitive verb*
: to hike with a backpack
— **back·pack·er** *noun*

**back·ped·al** \ˈbak-ˌpe-dᵊl\ *intransitive verb* (1901)
: to retreat or move backward

**back·rest** \-ˌrest\ *noun* (1859)
: a rest for the back

**back·room** \ˈbak-ˈrüm, -ˈrùm\ *adjective* (1940)
: made or operating in an inconspicuous way : BEHIND-THE-SCENES ⟨*backroom* deals⟩ ⟨a *backroom* politician⟩

**back room** *noun* (1592)
**1** : a room situated in the rear
**2** : the meeting place of a directing group that exercises its authority in an inconspicuous and indirect way

**back·saw** \ˈbak-ˌsȯ\ *noun* (circa 1877)
: a saw with a metal rib along its back

**back·scat·ter** \-ˌska-tər\ *or* **back·scat·ter·ing** \-tə-riŋ\ *noun* (1940)
: the scattering of radiation or particles in a direction opposite to that of the incident radiation due to reflection from particles of the medium traversed; *also* : the radiation or particles so reversed in direction
— **backscatter** *transitive verb*

**back–scratch·ing** \ˈbak-ˌskra-chiŋ\ *noun* (1924)
: the reciprocal exchange of favors, services, assistance, or praise

**back·seat** \-ˈsēt\ *noun* (1829)
**1** : a seat in the back (as of an automobile)
**2** : an inferior position ⟨won't take a *backseat* to anyone⟩

**back·set** \ˈbak-ˌset\ *noun* (1721)
: SETBACK

**back·side** \-ˌsīd\ *noun* (circa 1500)
: BUTTOCKS — often used in plural

**back·slap** \-ˌslap\ (1926)
*transitive verb*
: to display excessive or effusive goodwill for
*intransitive verb*
: to display excessive cordiality or goodwill
— **backslap** *noun*
— **back·slap·per** *noun*

**back·slide** \-ˌslīd\ *intransitive verb* **-slid** \-ˌslid\; **-slid** *or* **-slid·den** \-ˌsli-dᵊn\; **-slid·ing** \-ˌslī-diŋ\ (1581)
**1** : to lapse morally or in the practice of religion
**2** : to revert to a worse condition : RETROGRESS
— **back·slid·er** \-ˌslī-dər\ *noun*

**back·space** \-ˌspās\ *intransitive verb* (1911)
: to move back one space in a text with each depression of a key
— **backspace** *noun*

**back·spin** \-ˌspin\ *noun* (circa 1909)
: a backward rotary motion of a ball

**back·splash** \ˈbak-ˌsplash\ *noun* (1947)
: a vertical surface (as of tiles) designed to protect the wall behind a stove or countertop

**back·stab·bing** \-ˌsta-biŋ\ *noun* (1946)
: betrayal (as by a verbal attack against one not present) especially by a false friend
— **back·stab** \-ˌstab\ *verb*
— **back·stab·ber** \-ˌsta-bər\ *noun*

**¹back·stage** \ˈbak-ˌstāj\ *adjective* (1916)
**1** : of, relating to, or occurring in the area behind the proscenium and especially in the dressing rooms
**2** : of or relating to the private lives of theater people
**3** : of or relating to the inner working or operation (as of an organization)

**²backstage** \ˈbak-ˈstāj\ *adverb* (1923)
**1** : in or to a backstage area
**2** : in private : SECRETLY

**back·stairs** \-ˌstarz, -ˌsterz\ *adjective* (1663)
**1** : SECRET, FURTIVE ⟨*backstairs* political deals⟩
**2** : SORDID, SCANDALOUS ⟨*backstairs* gossip⟩

**back·stay** \-ˌstā\ *noun* (1626)
**1** : a stay extending from the mastheads to the side of a ship and slanting aft
**2** : a strengthening or supporting device at the back (as of a carriage or a shoe)

**back·stitch** \-ˌstich\ *noun* (1611)
: a stitch sewn one stitch length backward on the front side and two stitch lengths forward on the reverse side to form a solid line of stitching on both sides
— **backstitch** *verb*

**¹back·stop** \-ˌstäp\ *noun* (1851)
**1** : something at the back serving as a stop: as **a** : a screen or fence for keeping a ball from leaving the field of play **b** : a stop (as a pawl) that prevents a backward movement (as of a wheel)
**2** : a player (as the catcher) positioned behind the batter

**²backstop** *transitive verb* (1941)
**1** : SUPPORT, BOLSTER
**2** : to serve as a backstop to

**back·street** \ˈbak-ˌstrēt\ *noun* (15th century)
: a street away from the main thoroughfares

**back·stretch** \ˈbak-ˌstrech\ *noun* (1839)
: the side opposite the homestretch on a racecourse

**back·stroke** \-ˌstrōk\ *noun* (1879)
: a swimming stroke executed on the back and usually consisting of alternating circular arm pulls and a flutter kick

**back·swept** \-ˌswept\ *adjective* (circa 1918)
: swept or slanting backward

**back swimmer** *noun* (1862)
: an aquatic bug (family Notonectidae) that swims on its back

**back·swing** \ˈbak-ˌswiŋ\ *noun* (1899)
: the movement of a club, racket, bat, or arm backward to a position from which the forward or downward swing is made

**back·sword** \-ˌsōrd, -ˌsȯrd\ *noun* (1609)
: a single-edged sword

**back talk** *noun* (1858)
: impudent, insolent, or argumentative replies

**back–to–back** *adjective or adverb* (15th century)
**1** : facing in opposite directions and often touching
**2** : coming one after the other : CONSECUTIVE

**back·track** \ˈbak-ˌtrak\ *intransitive verb* (1904)

**1 a** : to retrace one's course **b** : to go back to an earlier point in a sequence
**2** : to reverse a position

**back·up** \-ˌəp\ *noun, often attributive* (1951)
**1 a** : one that serves as a substitute or support ⟨a *backup* plan⟩ **b** : musical accompaniment
**2** : an accumulation caused by a stoppage in the flow ⟨traffic *backup*⟩
**3** : the act or an instance of backing up a computer's hard disk

**back up** (1837)
*intransitive verb*
: to accumulate in a congested state ⟨traffic *backed up* for miles⟩
*transitive verb*
**1** : to move into a position behind (a teammate) in order to assist on a play
**2** : HOLD BACK 1
**3** : to make copies of the computer files on (a hard disk) to protect against loss of data

**¹back·ward** \ˈbak-wərd\ *or* **back·wards** \-wərdz\ *adverb* (14th century)
**1 a** : toward the back **b** : with the back foremost
**2 a** : in a reverse or contrary direction or way **b** : toward the past **c** : toward a worse state
— **bend over backward** *or* **lean over backward** : to make extreme efforts (as at concession)

**²backward** *adjective* (14th century)
**1 a** : directed or turned backward **b** : done or executed backward
**2** : DIFFIDENT, SHY
**3** : retarded in development
— **back·ward·ly** *adverb*
— **back·ward·ness** *noun*

**³backward** *noun* (1610)
: the part behind or past

**back·wash** \ˈbak-ˌwȯsh, -ˌwäsh\ *noun* (1876)
**1** : a backward flow or movement (as of water or air) produced especially by a propelling force; *also* : the fluid that is moving backward
**2** : CONSEQUENCE, AFTERMATH

**back·wa·ter** \-ˌwȯ-tər, -ˌwä-\ *noun* (1629)
**1 a** : water backed up in its course by an obstruction, an opposing current, or the tide **b** : a body of water (as an inlet or tributary) that is out of the main current of a larger body
**2** : an isolated or backward place or condition

**back·woods** \-ˈwùdz\ *noun plural but singular or plural in construction, often attributive* (1709)
**1** : wooded or partly cleared areas far from cities
**2** : a remote or culturally backward area
— **back·woodsy** \-ˈwùd-zē\ *adjective*

**back·woods·man** \ˌbak-ˈwùdz-mən, ˈbak-ˌ\ *noun* (1774)
: one who lives in the backwoods

**back·wrap** \-ˌrap\ *noun* (1951)
: a wraparound garment (as a skirt) that fastens in the back

**back·yard** \-ˈyärd\ *noun* (1659)
**1** : an area at the rear of a house
**2** : an area that is one's special domain

**ba·con** \ˈbā-kən\ *noun* [Middle English, from Middle French, of Germanic origin; akin to Old High German *bahho* side of bacon, *bah* back] (14th century)
: a side of a pig cured and smoked

**Ba·co·ni·an** \bā-ˈkō-nē-ən\ *adjective* (1812)
**1** : of, relating to, or characteristic of Francis Bacon or his doctrines
**2** : of or relating to those who believe that Francis Bacon wrote the works usually attributed to Shakespeare
— **Baconian** *noun*

**bac·ter·emia** \ˌbak-tə-ˈrē-mē-ə\ *noun* [New Latin, alteration of *bacteriemia*, from *bacteri-* + *-emia*] (circa 1890)

---

\ə\ abut \ᵊ\ kitten \ər\ further \a\ ash \ā\ ace
\ä\ mop, mar \aù\ out \ch\ chin \e\ bet \ē\ easy
\g\ go \i\ hit \ī\ ice \j\ job \ŋ\ sing \ō\ go
\ȯ\ law \ȯi\ boy \th\ thin \th̲\ the \ü\ loot \ù\ foot
\y\ yet \zh\ vision *see also* Guide to Pronunciation

: the usually transient presence of bacteria in the blood
— **bac·ter·emic** \-mik\ *adjective*
**bacteri-** *or* **bacterio-** *combining form* [New Latin *bacterium*]
: bacteria ⟨*bacterio*lysis⟩
**bac·te·ria** \bak-'tir-ē-ə\ *noun, plural* **-ri·as** [plural of *bacterium*] (1884)
: a group (as a genus, species, or strain) of bacteria — used chiefly in nontechnical writing and in news broadcasts ■
**bac·te·ri·al** \bak-'tir-ē-əl\ *adjective* (1871)
: of, relating to, or caused by bacteria ⟨*bacterial* infection⟩
— **bac·te·ri·al·ly** \-ə-lē\ *adverb*
**bac·te·ri·cid·al** \bak-,tir-ə-'sī-d°l\ *adjective* (1878)
: destroying bacteria
— **bac·te·ri·cid·al·ly** \-d°l-ē\ *adverb*
— **bac·te·ri·cide** \-'tir-ə-,sīd\ *noun*
**bac·ter·in** \'bak-tə-rən\ *noun* (circa 1912)
: a suspension of killed or attenuated bacteria for use as a vaccine
**bac·te·rio·chlo·ro·phyll** \bak-,tir-ē-ō-'klor-ə-,fil, -'klor-, -fəl\ *noun* (1938)
: a pyrrole derivative in photosynthetic bacteria related to the chlorophyll of higher plants
**bac·te·rio·cin** \bak-'tir-ē-ə-sən\ *noun* [International Scientific Vocabulary *bacteri-* + *-cin* (as in *colicin*)] (1954)
: an antibiotic (as colicin) produced by bacteria
**bac·te·ri·ol·o·gy** \(,)bak-,tir-ē-'ä-lə-jē\ *noun* [International Scientific Vocabulary] (1884)
**1** : a science that deals with bacteria and their relations to medicine, industry, and agriculture
**2** : bacterial life and phenomena
— **bac·te·ri·o·log·ic** \bak-,tir-ē-ə-'lä-jik\ *or* **bac·te·ri·o·log·i·cal** \-'lä-ji-kəl\ *adjective*
— **bac·te·ri·o·log·i·cal·ly** \-ji-k(ə-)lē\ *adverb*
— **bac·te·ri·ol·o·gist** \(,)bak-,tir-ē-'ä-lə-jist\ *noun*
**bac·te·ri·ol·y·sis** \(,)bak-,tir-ē-'ä-lə-səs\ *noun* [New Latin] (1900)
: destruction or lysis of bacterial cells
— **bac·te·ri·o·lyt·ic** \bak-,tir-ē-ə-'li-tik\ *adjective*
**bac·te·rio·phage** \bak-'tir-ē-ə-,fāj *also* -,fäzh\ *noun* [International Scientific Vocabulary] (1920)
: a virus that infects bacteria
— **bac·te·ri·oph·a·gy** \(,)bak-,tir-ē-'ä-fə-jē\ *noun*
**bac·te·rio·rho·dop·sin** \bak-,tir-ē-ə-rō-'däp-sin\ *noun* (1974)
: a purple-pigmented protein found in the outer membrane of a bacterium (*Halobacterium halobium*) that converts light energy into chemical energy in the synthesis of ATP
**bac·te·rio·sta·sis** \bak-,tir-ē-ō-'stā-səs\ *noun* [New Latin] (1920)
: inhibition of the growth of bacteria without destruction
**bac·te·rio·stat** \-'tir-ē-ō-,stat\ *noun* (1920)
: an agent that causes bacteriostasis
— **bac·te·rio·stat·ic** \-,tir-ē-ō-'sta-tik\ *adjective*
**bac·te·ri·um** \bak-'tir-ē-əm\ *noun, plural* **-ria** \-ē-ə\ [New Latin, from Greek *baktērion* staff] (circa 1849)
: any of a group (as Kingdom Procaryotae or Kingdom Monera) of prokaryotic unicellular round, spiral, or rod-shaped single-celled microorganisms that are often aggregated into colonies or motile by means of flagella, that live in soil, water, organic matter, or the bodies of plants and animals, and that are autotrophic, saprophytic, or parasitic in nutrition and important because of their biochemical effects and pathogenicity
**bac·te·ri·uria** \bak-,tir-ē-'yur-ē-ə\ *noun* [New Latin] (1900)
: the presence of bacteria in the urine

**bac·te·rize** \'bak-tə-,rīz\ *transitive verb* **-rized; -riz·ing** (1914)
: to subject to bacterial action
— **bac·te·ri·za·tion** \,bak-tə-rə-'zā-shən\ *noun*
**bac·te·roid** \'bak-tə-,roid\ *noun* (1878)
: an irregularly shaped bacterium (as a rhizobium) found especially in root nodules of legumes
**Bac·tri·an camel** \'bak-trē-ən-\ *noun* (1609)
: CAMEL 1b
**¹bad** \'bad\ *adjective* **worse** \'wərs\; **worst** \'wərst\ [Middle English] (14th century)
**1 a** : failing to reach an acceptable standard : POOR **b** : UNFAVORABLE ⟨make a *bad* impression⟩ **c** : not fresh : SPOILED ⟨*bad* fish⟩ **d** : not sound : DILAPIDATED ⟨the house was in *bad* condition⟩
**2 a** : morally objectionable **b** : MISCHIEVOUS, DISOBEDIENT
**3** : inadequate or unsuited to a purpose ⟨a *bad* plan⟩ ⟨*bad* lighting⟩
**4** : DISAGREEABLE, UNPLEASANT ⟨*bad* news⟩
**5 a** : INJURIOUS, HARMFUL **b** : SERIOUS, SEVERE ⟨in *bad* trouble⟩ ⟨a *bad* cough⟩
**6** : INCORRECT, FAULTY ⟨*bad* grammar⟩
**7 a** : suffering pain or distress ⟨felt generally *bad*⟩ **b** : UNHEALTHY, DISEASED ⟨*bad* teeth⟩
**8** : SORROWFUL, SORRY
**9** : INVALID, VOID ⟨a *bad* check⟩
**10 bad·der; bad·dest** *slang* **a** : GOOD, GREAT **b** : TOUGH, MEAN
— **bad·ness** *noun*
**²bad** *noun* (15th century)
**1** : something that is bad
**2** : an evil or unhappy state
**³bad** *adverb* (1681)
: BADLY
**¹bad-ass** \-,as\ *adjective* (1956)
: ready to cause or get into trouble : MEAN — often considered vulgar
**²badass** *noun* (1984)
: a person who is badass — often considered vulgar
**bad blood** *noun* (1825)
: ill feeling : BITTERNESS
**bad·die** *or* **bad·dy** \'ba-dē\ *noun, plural* **baddies** (1937)
: one that is bad; *especially* : an opponent of the hero (as in fiction or motion pictures)
**bade** *past and past participle of* BID
**badge** \'baj\ *noun* [Middle English *bage*, *bagge*] (14th century)
**1** : a device or token especially of membership in a society or group
**2** : a characteristic mark
**3** : an emblem awarded for a particular accomplishment
— **badge** *transitive verb*
**¹bad·ger** \'ba-jər\ *noun* [probably from *badge*; from the white mark on its forehead] (1523)
**1 a** : any of various burrowing mammals (especially *Taxidea taxus* and *Meles meles*) that are related to the weasels and are widely distributed in the northern hemisphere **b** : the pelt or fur of a badger
**2** *capitalized* : a native or resident of Wisconsin — used as a nickname
**²badger** *transitive verb* [from the sport of baiting badgers] (1794)
: to harass or annoy persistently
**synonym** see BAIT
**ba·di·nage** \,ba-d°n-'äzh\ *noun* [French] (circa 1658)
: playful repartee : BANTER
**bad·land** \'bad-,land\ *noun* (1851)
: a region marked by intricate erosional sculpturing, scanty vegetation, and fantastically formed hills — usually used in plural
**bad·ly** \'bad-lē\ *adverb* (14th century)
**1** : in a bad manner ⟨played *badly*⟩
**2** : to a great or intense degree ⟨want something *badly*⟩
*usage* see BAD

**bad·min·ton** \'bad-,min-t°n\ *noun* [*Badminton*, residence of the Duke of Beaufort, England] (1874)
: a court game played with light long-handled rackets and a shuttlecock volleyed over a net
**bad–mouth** \'bad-,mauth, -,mauth\ *transitive verb* (1942)
: to criticize severely
**bad news** *noun plural but singular in construction* (1930)
: one that is troublesome, unwelcome, or dangerous ⟨stay away from him, he's *bad news*⟩
**Bae·de·ker** \'bā-di-kər, 'be-\ *noun* [Karl *Baedeker* (died 1859) German publisher of guidebooks] (1924)
: GUIDEBOOK
**¹baf·fle** \'ba-fəl\ *transitive verb* **baf·fled; baf·fling** \-f(ə-)liŋ\ [probably alteration of Middle English (Scots) *bawchillen* to denounce, discredit publicly] (circa 1590)
**1** : to defeat or check (as a person) by confusing or puzzling : DISCONCERT
**2** : to check or break the force or flow of by or as if by a baffle
**synonym** see FRUSTRATE
— **baf·fle·ment** \-fəl-mənt\ *noun*
— **baf·fler** \-f(ə-)lər\ *noun*
— **baf·fling·ly** \'ba-fliŋ-lē\ *adverb*
**²baffle** *noun* (circa 1900)
: a device (as a plate, wall, or screen) to deflect, check, or regulate flow (as of a fluid, light, or sound)
— **baf·fled** \'ba-fəld\ *adjective*

**¹bag** \'bag *also* 'bȧg\ *noun* [Middle English *bagge*, from Old Norse *baggi*] (13th century)
**1 :** a usually flexible container that may be closed for holding, storing, or carrying something: as **a :** PURSE; *especially* **:** HANDBAG **b :** a bag for game **c :** SUITCASE
**2 :** something resembling a bag: as **a :** a pouched or pendulous bodily part or organ; *especially* **:** UDDER **b :** a puffed-out sag or bulge in cloth **c :** a square white stuffed canvas bag to mark a base in baseball
**3 :** the amount contained in a bag
**4 a :** a quantity of game taken; *also* **:** the maximum legal quantity of game **b :** an assortment or collection especially of nonmaterial things ⟨a *bag* of tricks⟩
**5 :** an unattractive woman
**6 :** something one likes or does regularly or well; *also* **:** one's characteristic way of doing things
— **in the bag :** SURE, CERTAIN ⟨her nomination was *in the bag*⟩
**²bag** *verb* **bagged; bag·ging** (15th century)
*intransitive verb*
**1 :** to swell out **:** BULGE
**2 :** to hang loosely
*transitive verb*
**1 :** to cause to swell
**2 :** to put into a bag
**3 a :** to take (animals) as game **b :** to get possession of especially by strategy or stealth **c :** CAPTURE, SEIZE **d :** to shoot down **:** DESTROY
*synonym* see CATCH
— **bag·ger** *noun*
**ba·gasse** \bə-'gas\ *noun* [French] (circa 1826)
**:** plant residue (as of sugarcane or grapes) left after a product (as juice) has been extracted
**bag·a·telle** \ˌbag-ə-'tel\ *noun* [French, from Italian *bagattella*] (1633)
**1 :** TRIFLE 1
**2 :** any of various games involving the rolling of balls into scoring areas
**3 :** a short literary or musical piece in light style
**ba·gel** \'bā-gəl\ *noun* [Yiddish *beygl*, from (assumed) Middle High German *böugel* ring, from Middle High German *bouc* ring, from Old High German *boug*; akin to Old English *bēag* ring, *būgan* to bend — more at BOW] (1932)
**:** a hard glazed doughnut-shaped roll
**bag·ful** \'bag-ˌfu̇l\ *noun* (15th century)
**1 :** as much or as many as a bag will hold
**2 :** a large number or amount ⟨had a *bagful* of tricks⟩
**¹bag·gage** \'ba-gij\ *noun* [Middle English *bagage*, from Middle French, from *bague* bundle] (15th century)
**1 :** suitcases, trunks, and personal belongings of travelers **:** LUGGAGE
**2 :** transportable equipment especially of a military force
**3 :** things (as objects, circumstances, or beliefs) that get in the way **:** IMPEDIMENTA
**²baggage** *noun* [probably modification of Middle French *bagasse*, from Old Provençal *bagassa*] (1594)
**1 :** a contemptible woman; *especially* **:** PROSTITUTE
**2 :** a young woman
**bag·ging** \'ba-giŋ\ *noun* (1732)
**:** material (as cloth) for bags
**bag·gy** \'ba-gē\ *adjective* **bag·gi·er; -est** (1831)
**:** loose, puffed out, or hanging like a bag ⟨*baggy* trousers⟩
— **bag·gi·ly** \'ba-gə-lē\ *adverb*
— **bag·gi·ness** \'ba-gē-nəs\ *noun*
**bag·house** \'bag-ˌhau̇s\ *noun* (1914)
**:** a device or facility in which particulates are removed from a stream of exhaust gases (as from a blast furnace) as the stream passes through a large cloth bag; *also* **:** the bag used to filter the gas stream
**bag lady** *noun* (1979)

**:** a homeless woman who roams the streets of a large city carrying her possessions in shopping bags
**bag·man** \'bag-mən\ *noun* (1765)
**1** *chiefly British* **:** TRAVELING SALESMAN
**2 :** a person who on behalf of another collects or distributes illicitly gained money
**ba·gnio** \'ban-(ˌ)yō\ *noun, plural* **bagnios** [Italian *bagno*, literally, public baths (from the Turks' use of Roman baths at Constantinople as prisons), from Latin *balneum*, from Greek *balaneion*] (1599)
**1** *obsolete* **:** PRISON
**2 :** BORDELLO
**bag of waters** (circa 1881)
**:** the double-walled fluid-filled sac that encloses and protects the fetus in the womb and that breaks releasing its fluid during the birth process
**bag·pipe** \'bag-ˌpīp\ *noun* (14th century)
**:** a wind instrument consisting of a reed melody pipe and from one to five drones with air supplied continuously either by a bag with valve-stopped mouth tube or by bellows — often used in plural
— **bag·pip·er** \-ˌpī-pər\ *noun*
**ba·guette** \ba-'get\ *noun* [French, literally, rod] (1926)
**1 :** a gem having the shape of a narrow rectangle; *also* **:** the shape itself
**2 :** a long thin loaf of French bread
**bag·wig** \'bag-ˌwig\ *noun* (1717)
**:** an 18th century wig with the back hair enclosed in a small silk bag

bagpipe

**bag·worm** \-ˌwərm\ *noun* (1862)
**:** any of a family (Psychidae) of moths with wingless females and plant-feeding larvae that live in a silk case covered with plant debris; *especially* **:** one (*Thyridopteryx ephemeraeformis*) often destructive to deciduous and evergreen trees of the eastern U.S.
**bah** \'bä, 'ba\ *interjection* (1600)
— used to express disdain or contempt
**Ba·ha'i** \bä-'hä-ē, -'hī\ *noun, plural* **Baha'is** [Persian *bahā'ī*, literally, of glory, from *bahā* glory] (1889)
**:** an adherent of a religious movement originating in Iran in the 19th century and emphasizing the spiritual unity of mankind
— **Baha'i** *adjective*
— **Ba·ha·ism** \-'hä-ˌi-zəm, -'hī-ˌi-\ *noun*
— **Ba·ha·ist** \-'hä-(ˌ)ist\ *noun*
**Ba·ha·sa In·do·ne·sia** \bə-ˌhä-sə-ˌin-də-'nē-zhə, -shə\ *noun* [Indonesian *bahasa indonésia*, literally, Indonesian language] (1952)
**:** INDONESIAN 2b
**Ba·hia grass** \bə-'hē-ə-\ *noun* [*Bahia*, state in Brazil] (circa 1927)
**:** a perennial tropical American grass (*Paspalum notatum*) used in the southern U.S. as a lawn grass
**baht** \'bät\ *noun, plural* **baht** *also* **bahts** [Thai *bàad*] (1828)
— see MONEY table
**¹bail** \'bā(ə)l\ *noun* [Middle English *baille*, from Middle French, bucket, from Medieval Latin *bajula* water vessel, from feminine of Latin *bajulus*] (14th century)
**:** a container used to remove water from a boat
**²bail** *transitive verb* (1613)
**1 :** to clear (water) from a boat by dipping and

throwing over the side — usually used with *out*
**2 :** to clear water from by dipping and throwing — usually used with *out*
— **bail·er** *noun*
**³bail** *noun* [Middle English, custody, bail, from Middle French, custody, from *baillier* to have in charge, deliver, from Medieval Latin *bajulare* to control, from Latin, to carry a load, from *bajulus* porter] (15th century)
**1 :** the temporary release of a prisoner in exchange for security given for the due appearance of the prisoner
**2 :** security given for the release of a prisoner on bail
**3 :** one who provides bail
**⁴bail** *transitive verb* (1548)
**1 :** to release under bail
**2 :** to procure the release of by giving bail — often used with *out*
**3 :** to help from a predicament — used with *out* ⟨*bailing* out impoverished countries⟩
— **bail·able** *adjective*
**⁵bail** *noun* [Middle English *beil, baile*, probably of Scandinavian origin; akin to Swedish *bygel* bow, hoop; akin to Old English *būgan* to bend — more at BOW] (15th century)
**1 a :** a supporting half hoop **b :** a hinged bar for holding paper against the platen of a typewriter
**2 :** a usually arched handle (as of a kettle or pail)
**⁶bail** *transitive verb* [Anglo-French *baillier*, from French] (1768)
**:** to deliver (personal property) in trust to another for a special purpose and for a limited period
**⁷bail** *noun* [perhaps from ⁵*bail*] (1844)
*chiefly British* **:** a device for confining or separating animals
**bail·ee** \bā-'lē\ *noun* (1528)
**:** the person to whom personal property is bailed
**bai·ley** \'bā-lē\ *noun, plural* **baileys** [Middle English *bailli*, palisade, bailey, from Old French *baille, balie*] (13th century)
**1 :** the outer wall of a castle or any of several walls surrounding the keep
**2 :** a courtyard within the external wall or between two outer walls of a castle
**bai·lie** \'bā-lē\ *noun* [Middle English] (14th century)
**1** *chiefly dialect* **:** BAILIFF
**2 :** a Scottish municipal magistrate corresponding to an English alderman
**bai·liff** \'bā-ləf\ *noun* [Middle English *baillif, bailie*, from Old French *baillif*, from *bail* custody, jurisdiction — more at BAIL] (14th century)
**1 a :** an official employed by a British sheriff to serve writs and make arrests and executions **b :** a minor officer of some U.S. courts usually serving as a messenger or usher
**2** *chiefly British* **:** one who manages an estate or farm
— **bai·liff·ship** \-ˌship\ *noun*
**bai·li·wick** \'bā-li-ˌwik\ *noun* [Middle English *baillifwik*, from *baillif* + *wik* dwelling place, village, from Old English *wīc*, from Latin *vicus* village — more at VICINITY] (15th century)
**1 :** the office or jurisdiction of a bailiff
**2 :** a special domain
**bail·ment** \'bā(ə)l-mənt\ *noun* (1554)
**:** the act of bailing a person or personal property
**bail·or** \bā-'lȯr, 'bā-lər\ *or* **bail·er** \'bā-lər\ *noun* (1602)

\ə\ abut \ᵊ\ kitten \ər\ further \a\ ash \ā\ ace
\ä\ mop, mar \au̇\ out \ch\ chin \e\ bet \ē\ easy
\g\ go \i\ hit \ī\ ice \j\ job \ŋ\ sing \ō\ go
\ȯ\ law \ȯi\ boy \th\ thin \th\ the \ü\ loot \u̇\ foot
\y\ yet \zh\ vision *see also* Guide to Pronunciation

: a person who delivers personal property to another in trust

**bail·out** \'bā-,laut\ *noun* (1951)
: a rescue (as of a corporation) from financial distress

**bail out** *intransitive verb* (1930)
**1** : to parachute from an aircraft
**2** : to abandon a harmful or difficult situation; *also* : LEAVE, DEPART

**bails·man** \'bā(ə)lz-mən\ *noun* (1862)
: one who gives bail for another

**bairn** \'barn, 'bern\ *noun* [Middle English *bern*, *barn*, from Old English *bearn* & Old Norse *barn*; akin to Old High German *barn* child] (before 12th century)
*chiefly Scottish* : CHILD

**¹bait** \'bāt\ *verb* [Middle English, from Old Norse *beita*; akin to Old English *bǣtan* to bait, *bītan* to bite] (13th century)
*transitive verb*
**1 a** : to persecute or exasperate with unjust, malicious, or persistent attacks **b** : TEASE
**2 a** : to harass (as a chained animal) with dogs usually for sport **b** : to attack by biting and tearing
**3 a** : to furnish with bait **b** : ENTICE, LURE
**4** : to give food and drink to (an animal) especially on the road
*intransitive verb*
*archaic* : to stop for food and rest when traveling ☆
— **bait·er** *noun*

**²bait** *noun* [Middle English, from Old Norse *beit* pasturage & *beita* food; akin to Old English *bītan* to bite] (14th century)
**1 a** : something used in luring especially to a hook or trap **b** : a poisonous material placed where it will be eaten by usually wild animals considered undesirable or deleterious
**2** : LURE, TEMPTATION

**bait and switch** *noun* (1967)
: a sales tactic in which a customer is attracted by the advertisement of a low-priced item but is then encouraged to buy a higher-priced one

**bai·za** \'bī-(,)zä\ *noun, plural* **baiza** *or* **bai·zas** [Arabic, from Hindi *paisā*] (1970)
— see *rial* at MONEY table

**baize** \'bāz\ *noun* [Middle French *baies*, plural of *baie* baize, from feminine of *bai* bay-colored] (1578)
: a coarse woolen or cotton fabric napped to imitate felt

**¹bake** \'bāk\ *verb* **baked; bak·ing** [Middle English, from Old English *bacan*; akin to Old High German *bahhan* to bake, Greek *phōgein* to roast] (before 12th century)
*transitive verb*
**1** : to cook (as food) by dry heat especially in an oven
**2** : to dry or harden by subjecting to heat
*intransitive verb*
**1** : to prepare food by baking it
**2** : to become baked
**3** : to become extremely hot
— **bak·er** *noun*

**²bake** *noun* (1565)
**1** : the act or process of baking
**2** : a social gathering at which a baked food is served
**3** : baked food ⟨a *bake* sale⟩

**Ba·ke·lite** \'bā-kə-,līt, -,klīt\ *trademark*
— used for any of various synthetic resins and plastics

**baker's dozen** *noun* (1596)
: THIRTEEN

**baker's yeast** *noun* (1854)
: a yeast (as *Saccharomyces cerevisiae*) used or suitable for use as leaven

**bak·ery** \'bā-k(ə-)rē\ *noun, plural* **-er·ies** (circa 1820)
: a place for baking or selling baked goods

**bake·shop** \'bāk-,shäp\ *noun* (1789)
: BAKERY

**baking powder** *noun* (1850)
: a powder used as a leavening agent in making baked goods (as quick breads) that con-

sists of a carbonate, an acid substance, and starch or flour

**baking soda** *noun* (1881)
: SODIUM BICARBONATE

**bak·la·va** \,bä-klə-'vä\ *noun* [Turkish] (1653)
: a dessert made of thin pastry, nuts, and honey

**bak·sheesh** \'bak-,shēsh, bak-'\ *noun* [Persian *bakhshīsh*, from *bakhshīdan* to give; akin to Greek *phagein* to eat, Sanskrit *bhajati* he allots] (1775)
: payment (as a tip or bribe) to expedite service

**BAL** \,bē-(,)ā-'el\ *noun* [British Anti-*L*ewisite] (1942)
: DIMERCAPROL

**Ba·laam** \'bā-ləm\ *noun* [Greek, from Hebrew *Bil'ām*]
: an Old Testament prophet who is reproached by the ass he is riding and rebuked by God's angel while on the way to meet with an enemy of Israel

**bal·a·cla·va** \,ba-lə-'klä-və, -'kla-\ *noun* [*Balaclava*, Crimea, where a battle of the Crimean War was fought] (1881)
: a knit cap for the head and neck — called also *balaclava helmet*

**bal·a·lai·ka** \,ba-lə-'lī-kə\ *noun* [Russian] (1788)
: a usually 3-stringed instrument of Russian origin with a triangular body played by plucking or strumming

**¹bal·ance** \'ba-lən(t)s\ *noun* [Middle English, from Old French, from (assumed) Vulgar Latin *bilancia*, from Late Latin *bilanc-*, *bilanx* having two scalepans, from Latin *bi-* + *lanc-*, *lanx* plate] (13th century)
**1** : an instrument for weighing: as **a** : a beam that is supported freely in the center and has two pans of equal weight suspended from its ends **b** : a device that uses the elasticity of a spiral spring for measuring weight or force **c** *capitalized* : LIBRA
**2** : a means of judging or deciding
**3** : a counterbalancing weight, force, or influence
**4** : an oscillating wheel operating with a hairspring to regulate the movement of a timepiece
**5 a** : stability produced by even distribution of weight on each side of the vertical axis **b** : equipoise between contrasting, opposing, or interacting elements **c** : equality between the totals of the two sides of an account
**6 a** : an aesthetically pleasing integration of elements **b** : the juxtaposition in writing of syntactically parallel constructions containing similar or contrasting ideas
**7 a** : physical equilibrium **b** : the ability to retain one's balance
**8 a** : weight or force of one side in excess of another **b** : something left over : REMAINDER **c** : an amount in excess especially on the credit side of an account
**9** : mental and emotional steadiness
— **bal·anced** \-lən(t)st\ *adjective*
— **in the balance** *or* **in balance** : with the fate or outcome about to be determined
— **on balance** : with all things considered

**²balance** *verb* **bal·anced; bal·anc·ing** (1588)
*transitive verb*
**1 a** (1) : to compute the difference between the debits and credits of (an account) (2) : to pay the amount due on : SETTLE **b** (1) : to arrange so that one set of elements exactly equals another ⟨*balance* a mathematical equa-

tion⟩ (2) : to complete (a chemical equation) so that the same number of atoms and electric charges of each kind appears on each side
**2 a** : COUNTERBALANCE, OFFSET **b** : to equal or equalize in weight, number, or proportion
**3** : to weigh in or as if in a balance
**4 a** : to bring to a state or position of equipoise **b** : to poise in or as if in balance **c** : to bring into harmony or proportion
*intransitive verb*
**1** : to become balanced or established in balance
**2** : to be an equal counterpoise
**3** : WAVER 1 ⟨*balances* and temporizes on matters that demand action⟩

**balance beam** *noun* (circa 1949)
**1** : a narrow wooden beam supported in a horizontal position approximately four feet above the floor and used for balancing feats in gymnastics
**2** : an event in gymnastics competition in which the balance beam is used

**balance of payments** (1844)
: a summary of the international transactions of a country or region over a period of time including commodity and service transactions, capital transactions, and gold movements

**balance of power** (1701)
: an equilibrium of power sufficient to discourage or prevent one nation or party from imposing its will on or interfering with the interests of another

**balance of trade** (1668)
: the difference in value over a period of time between a country's imports and exports

**bal·anc·er** \'ba-lən(t)-sər\ *noun* (15th century)
: one that balances; *specifically* : HALTERE

**balance sheet** *noun* (circa 1771)
: a statement of financial condition at a given date

**balance wheel** *noun* (1669)
**1** : a wheel that regulates or stabilizes the motion of a mechanism
**2** : a balancing or stabilizing force

**balancing act** *noun* (1954)
: an attempt to cope with several often conflicting factors or situations at the same time

**Ba·lante** \bə-'länt\ *noun, plural* **Balante** *or* **Balantes** [French, from Balante *Bulanda*] (circa 1895)
**1** : a member of a people of Senegal and Guinea-Bissau
**2** : the language of the Balante people

**bal·as** \'ba-ləs\ *noun* [Middle English, from Middle French *balais*, from Arabic *balakhsh*, from *Balakhshān*, ancient region of Afghanistan] (15th century)
: a ruby spinel of a pale rose-red or orange

**ba·la·ta** \bə-'lä-tə\ *noun* [Spanish, from Carib] (1860)
: a substance like gutta-percha that is the dried juice of tropical American trees (especially *Manilkara bidentata*) of the sapodilla family and is used especially in belting and golf balls; *also* : a tree yielding it

balalaika (image caption)

---

☆ SYNONYMS
**Bait, badger, heckle, hector, chivy, hound** mean to harass by efforts to break down. BAIT implies wanton cruelty or delight in persecuting a helpless victim ⟨*baited* the chained dog⟩. BADGER implies pestering so as to drive a person to confusion or frenzy ⟨*badgered* her father for a car⟩. HECKLE implies persistent annoying or belligerent interruptions of a speaker ⟨drunks *heckled* the stand-up comic⟩. HECTOR carries an implication of bullying and domineering ⟨football players *hectored* by their coach⟩. CHIVY suggests persecution by teasing or nagging ⟨*chivied* the new student mercilessly⟩. HOUND implies unrelenting pursuit and harassing ⟨*hounded* by creditors⟩.

**bal·boa** \bal-'bō-ə\ noun [Spanish, from Vasco Núñez de *Balboa*] (circa 1909)
— see MONEY table

**bal·brig·gan** \bal-'bri-gən\ noun [*Balbriggan*, town in Ireland] (1885)
: a knitted cotton fabric used especially for underwear or hosiery

**bal·co·ny** \'bal-kə-nē\ noun, plural **-nies** [Italian *balcone*, from Old Italian, large window, of Germanic origin; akin to Old High German *balko* beam — more at BALK] (1618)
**1** : a platform that projects from the wall of a building and is enclosed by a parapet or railing
**2** : an interior projecting gallery in a public building (as a theater)
— **bal·co·nied** \-nēd\ adjective

**¹bald** \'bȯld\ adjective [Middle English *balled*; probably akin to Danish *bældet* bald, Latin *fulica* coot, Greek *phalios* having a white spot] (14th century)
**1 a** : lacking a natural or usual covering (as of hair, vegetation, or nap) **b** : having little or no tread ⟨*bald* tires⟩
**2** : UNADORNED
**3** : UNDISGUISED, PALPABLE
**4** : marked with white
**synonym** see BARE
— **bald·ish** \'bȯl-dish\ adjective
— **bald·ly** \'bȯl(d)-lē\ adverb
— **bald·ness** \'bȯl(d)-nəs\ noun

**²bald** (1602)
*transitive verb*
: to make bald
*intransitive verb*
: to become bald

**bal·da·chin** \'bȯl-də-kən, 'bal-\ or **bal·da·chi·no** \ˌbal-də-'kē-(ˌ)nō, ˌbäl-\ noun, plural **baldachins** or **baldachinos** [Italian *baldacchino*, from *Baldacco* Baghdad, Iraq] (1537)
**1** : a cloth canopy fixed or carried over an important person or a sacred object
**2** : a rich embroidered fabric of silk and gold
**3** : an ornamental structure resembling a canopy used especially over an altar

**bald cypress** noun (1709)
**1** : either of two large swamp trees (*Taxodium distichum* and *T. ascendens* of the family Taxodiaceae, the bald cypress family) of the southern U.S. that are related to the sequoias
**2** : the hard red wood of bald cypress that is much used for shingles

**bald eagle** noun (1688)
: an eagle (*Haliaeetus leucocephalus*) of North America that is brown when young with white only on the undersides of the wings but in full adult plumage has white head and neck feathers and a white tail

**Bal·der** \'bȯl-dər\ noun [Old Norse *Baldr*]
: the son of Odin and Frigga and Norse god of light and peace slain through the trickery of Loki by a mistletoe sprig

**bald eagle**

**bal·der·dash** \'bȯl-dər-ˌdash\ noun [origin unknown] (1674)
: NONSENSE

**bald–faced** \'bȯl(d)-'fāst\ adjective (1943)
: BAREFACED

**bald·head** \'bȯld-ˌhed\ noun (1535)
: a bald-headed person

**balding** adjective (1938)
: getting bald ⟨bespectacled and *balding*⟩

**bald·pate** \'bȯl(d)-ˌpāt\ noun (1592)
**1** : BALDHEAD
**2** : a North American wigeon (*Anas americana*) with a large white patch on each wing and in the male a white crown

**bal·dric** \'bȯl-drik\ noun [Middle English *baudry*, *baudrik*, from Middle French *baudré*, from Old French *baldrei*] (14th century)
: an often ornamented belt worn over one shoulder to support a sword or bugle

**¹bale** \'bā(ə)l\ noun [Middle English, from Old English *bealu*; akin to Old High German *balo* evil, Old Church Slavonic *bolĭ* sick person] (before 12th century)
**1** : great evil
**2** : WOE, SORROW

**²bale** noun [Middle English, from Middle French, of Germanic origin; akin to Old High German *balla* ball] (14th century)
: a large bundle of goods; *specifically* : a large closely pressed package of merchandise bound and usually wrapped ⟨a *bale* of paper⟩ ⟨a *bale* of hay⟩

**³bale** transitive verb **baled; bal·ing** (1760)
: to make up into a bale
— **bal·er** noun

**ba·leen** \bə-'lēn, 'ba-ˌlēn\ noun [Middle English *baleine* whale, baleen, from Latin *balaena* whale; akin to Greek *phallaina* whale] (14th century)
: a horny substance found in two rows of plates from 2 to 12 feet long attached along the upper jaws of baleen whales

**baleen whale** noun (1874)
: any of a suborder (Mysticeti) of usually large whales lacking teeth but having baleen which is used to filter chiefly small marine crustaceans (as krill) out of large quantities of seawater

**bale·fire** \'bā(ə)l-ˌfīr\ noun [Middle English, from Old English *bǣlfȳr* funeral fire, from *bǣl* pyre + *fȳr* fire] (before 12th century)
: an outdoor fire often used as a signal fire

**bale·ful** \-fəl\ adjective (before 12th century)
**1** : deadly or pernicious in influence
**2** : foreboding evil : OMINOUS
**synonym** see SINISTER
— **bale·ful·ly** \-fə-lē\ adverb
— **bale·ful·ness** \-fəl-nəs\ noun

**Ba·li·nese** \ˌbä-li-'nēz, ˌba-, -'nēs\ noun [Dutch *Balinees*, from *Bali* island of Indonesia] (1967)
: any of a breed of slender long-haired cats that originated as a spontaneous mutation of the Siamese

**¹balk** \'bȯk\ noun [Middle English *balke*, from Old English *balca*; akin to Old High German *balko* beam, Latin *fulcire* to prop, Greek *phalanx* log, phalanx] (before 12th century)
**1** : a ridge of land left unplowed as a dividing line or through carelessness
**2** : BEAM, RAFTER
**3** : HINDRANCE, CHECK
**4 a** : the space behind the balkline on a billiard table **b** : any of the outside divisions made by the balklines
**5** : failure of a player to complete a motion; *especially* : an illegal motion of the pitcher in baseball while in position

**²balk** (15th century)
*transitive verb*
**1** *archaic* : to pass over or by
**2** : to check or stop by or as if by an obstacle : BLOCK
*intransitive verb*
**1** : to stop short and refuse to proceed
**2** : to refuse abruptly — used with *at*
**3** : to commit a balk in sports
**synonym** see FRUSTRATE
— **balk·er** noun

**bal·kan·ize** \'bȯl-kə-ˌnīz\ transitive verb **-ized; -iz·ing** often capitalized [*Balkan* Peninsula] (1919)

: to break up (as a region or group) into smaller and often hostile units
— **bal·kan·i·za·tion** \ˌbȯl-kə-nə-'zā-shən\ noun, often capitalized

**balk·line** \'bȯ-ˌklīn\ noun (1839)
**1** : a line across a billiard table near one end behind which the cue balls are placed in making opening shots
**2 a** : one of four lines parallel to the cushions of a billiard table dividing it into nine compartments **b** : a billiards game that sets restrictions in scoring caroms according to these lines

**balky** \'bȯ-kē\ adjective **balk·i·er; -est** (1847)
: refusing or likely to refuse to proceed, act, or function as directed or expected ⟨a *balky* mule⟩
**synonym** see CONTRARY
— **balk·i·ness** noun

**¹ball** \'bȯl\ noun, often attributive [Middle English *bal*, from Old Norse *bǫllr*; akin to Old English *bealluc* testis, Old High German *balla* ball, Old English *blāwan* to blow] (13th century)
**1** : a round or roundish body or mass: as **a** : a spherical or ovoid body used in a game or sport **b** : EARTH, GLOBE **c** : a spherical or conical projectile; *also* : projectiles used in firearms **d** : a roundish protuberant anatomic structure; *especially* : the rounded eminence at the base of the thumb or big toe
**2 a** : TESTIS — often considered vulgar **b** *plural* (1) : NONSENSE — often used interjectionally; often considered vulgar (2) : NERVE 3 — often considered vulgar
**3** : a game in which a ball is thrown, kicked, or struck; *also* : the quality of play in such a game
**4 a** : a pitch not swung at by the batter that fails to pass through the strike zone **b** : a hit or thrown ball in various games ⟨foul *ball*⟩
— **on the ball 1** : COMPETENT, KNOWLEDGEABLE, ALERT ⟨the other introductory essay . . . is much more *on the ball* —*Times Literary Supplement*⟩ ⟨keep *on the ball*⟩ **2** : of ability or competence ⟨if the teacher has something *on the ball*, the pupils won't squirm much —*New Yorker*⟩

**²ball** (1658)
*transitive verb*
**1** : to form or gather into a ball ⟨*balled* the paper into a wad⟩
**2** : to have sexual intercourse with — usually considered vulgar
*intransitive verb*
**1** : to form or gather into a ball
**2** : to engage in sexual intercourse — usually considered vulgar

**³ball** noun [French *bal*, from Old French, from *baller* to dance, from Late Latin *ballare*, from Greek *ballizein*] (circa 1639)
**1** : a large formal gathering for social dancing
**2** : a very pleasant experience : a good time ⟨had a *ball* on their vacation⟩

**bal·lad** \'ba-ləd\ noun [Middle English *balade*, ballade, song, from Middle French, from Old Provençal *balada* dance, song sung while dancing, from *balar* to dance, from Late Latin *ballare*] (14th century)
**1 a** : a narrative composition in rhythmic verse suitable for singing **b** : an art song accompanying a traditional ballad
**2** : a simple song : AIR
**3** : a popular song; *especially* : a slow romantic or sentimental song
— **bal·lad·ic** \bə-'la-dik, ba-\ adjective

**bal·lade** \bə-'läd, ba-\ noun [Middle English *balade*, from Middle French, ballad, ballade] (14th century)

\ə\ abut \ᵊ\ kitten \ər\ further \a\ ash \ā\ ace \ä\ mop, mar \aù\ out \ch\ chin \e\ bet \ē\ easy \g\ go \i\ hit \ī\ ice \j\ job \ŋ\ sing \ō\ go \ȯ\ law \ȯi\ boy \th\ thin \t̲h̲\ the \ü\ loot \ù\ foot \y\ yet \zh\ vision *see also* Guide to Pronunciation

**1 :** a fixed verse form consisting usually of three stanzas with recurrent rhymes, an envoi, and an identical refrain for each part
**2 :** a musical composition usually for piano suggesting the epic ballad
**bal·lad·eer** \ˌba-lə-'dir\ *noun* (1830)
**:** a singer of ballads
**bal·lad·ist** \'ba-lə-dist\ *noun* (1858)
**:** one who writes or sings ballads
**bal·lad·ry** \'ba-lə-drē\ *noun* (1596)
**1 :** the composing or performing of ballads
**2 :** BALLADS
**ballad stanza** *noun* (circa 1934)
**:** a stanza consisting of four lines with the first and third lines unrhymed iambic tetrameters and the second and fourth lines rhymed iambic trimeters
**ball–and–socket joint** *noun* (1809)
**1 :** a joint in which a ball moves within a socket so as to allow rotary motion in every direction within certain limits
**2 :** an articulation (as the hip joint) in which the rounded head of one bone fits into a cuplike cavity of the other and admits movement in any direction

ball-and-socket joint 1

¹**bal·last** \'ba-ləst\ *noun* [probably from Low German, of Scandinavian origin; akin to Danish & Swedish *barlast* ballast; perhaps akin to Old English *bær* bare & to Old English *hlæst* load, *hladan* to load — more at LADE] (1530)
**1 :** a heavy substance used to improve the stability and control the draft of a ship or the ascent of a balloon
**2 :** something that gives stability (as in character or conduct)
**3 :** gravel or broken stone laid in a railroad bed or used in making concrete
**4 :** a device used to provide the starting voltage or to stabilize the current in a circuit (as of a fluorescent lamp)
**— in ballast** *of a ship* **:** having only ballast for a load
²**ballast** *transitive verb* (1538)
**1 :** to steady or equip with or as if with ballast
**2 :** to fill in (as a railroad bed) with ballast
**ball bearing** *noun* (1883)
**:** a bearing in which the journal turns upon loose hardened steel balls that roll easily in a race; *also* **:** one of the balls in such a bearing
**ball boy** *noun* (1903)
**:** a male tennis court attendant who retrieves balls for the players
**ball·car·ri·er** \'bȯl-ˌkar-ē-ər\ *noun* (1935)
**:** the football player carrying the ball on an offensive play
**ball cock** *noun* (1790)
**:** an automatic valve whose opening and closing are controlled by a spherical float at the end of a lever
**ball control** *noun* (1928)
**:** an offensive strategy (as in football) in which a team tries to maintain possession of the ball for extended periods of time
**bal·le·ri·na** \ˌba-lə-'rē-nə\ *noun* [Italian, from *ballare* to dance, from Late Latin] (1815)
**:** a woman who is a ballet dancer **:** DANSEUSE
**bal·let** \'ba-ˌlā, ba-'\ *noun* [French, from Italian *balletto*, diminutive of *ballo* dance, from *ballare*] (1634)
**1 a :** a theatrical art form using dancing, music, and scenery to convey a story, theme, or atmosphere **b :** dancing in which conventional poses and steps are combined with light flowing figures (as leaps and turns)
**2 :** music for a ballet
**3 :** a group that performs ballets
**— bal·let·ic** \ba-'le-tik\ *adjective*
**bal·let·o·mane** \ba-'le-tə-ˌmān\ *noun* [*ballet* + *-o-* + *-mane* (from *mania*)] (1930)
**:** a devotee of ballet

**— bal·let·o·ma·nia** \-ˌle-tə-'mā-nē-ə, -nyə\ *noun*
**ball–flow·er** \'bȯl-ˌflau̇-(ə)r\ *noun* (1845)
**:** an architectural ornament consisting of a ball in the flower-shaped hollow of a circular mold
**ball game** *noun* (1848)
**1 :** a game played with a ball
**2 a :** a set of circumstances **:** SITUATION ⟨a whole new *ball game*⟩ **b :** CONTEST 1
**ball girl** *noun* (1926)
**:** a female tennis court attendant who retrieves balls for the players
**ball handler** *noun* (1948)
**:** a player who controls the ball in any of various games; *especially* **:** a player who is skilled at handling the ball (as in basketball)
**— ball·han·dling** *noun*
**bal·lis·ta** \bə-'lis-tə\ *noun, plural* **-tae** \-ˌtē\ [Latin, from (assumed) Greek *ballistēs*, from *ballein* to throw — more at DEVIL] (14th century)
**:** an ancient military engine often in the form of a crossbow for hurling large missiles
**bal·lis·tic** \bə-'lis-tik\ *adjective* [Latin *ballista*] (circa 1775)
**1 :** of or relating to ballistics or to a body in motion according to the laws of ballistics
**2 :** suddenly and extremely upset or angry **:** WILD — usually used with *go*
**— bal·lis·ti·cal·ly** \-ti-k(ə-)lē\ *adverb*
**ballistic missile** *noun* (1954)
**:** a missile guided in the ascent of a high-arch trajectory and freely falling in the descent
**bal·lis·tics** \bə-'lis-tiks\ *noun plural but singular or plural in construction* (circa 1753)
**1 a :** the science of the motion of projectiles in flight **b :** the flight characteristics of a projectile
**2 a :** the study of the processes within a firearm as it is fired **b :** the firing characteristics of a firearm or cartridge
**ball joint** *noun* (circa 1884)
**:** BALL-AND-SOCKET JOINT 1
**ball lightning** *noun* (1857)
**:** a rare form of lightning consisting of luminous balls that may move along solid objects or float in the air
**ball mill** *noun* (1903)
**:** a pulverizing machine consisting of a rotating drum which contains pebbles or metal balls as the grinding implements
**ball of fire** (circa 1900)
**:** a person of unusual energy, vitality, or drive
**ball of wax** (circa 1953)
**:** AFFAIR, CONCERN ⟨the whole *ball of wax*⟩
**bal·lon** \ba-'lō<sup>n</sup>\ *noun* [French, literally, balloon] (1830)
**:** lightness of movement that exaggerates the duration of a ballet dancer's jump
**bal·lo·net** \ˌba-lə-'nā\ *noun* [French *ballonnet*, diminutive of *ballon*] (1902)
**:** a compartment of variable volume within the interior of a balloon or airship used to control ascent and descent
¹**bal·loon** \bə-'lün\ *noun* [French *ballon* large football, balloon, from Italian dialect *ballone* large football, augmentative of *balla* ball, of Germanic origin] (1783)
**1 :** a nonporous bag of tough light material filled with heated air or a gas lighter than air so as to rise and float in the atmosphere
**2 :** an inflatable bag (as of rubber) usually used as a toy or for decoration
**3 :** the outline enclosing words spoken or thought by a figure especially in a cartoon
²**balloon** *adjective* (circa 1786)
**1 :** relating to, resembling, or suggesting a balloon ⟨a *balloon* sleeve⟩
**2 :** being or having a final installment that is much larger than preceding ones in a term or installment note
³**balloon** (1841)
*intransitive verb*
**1 :** to swell or puff out **:** EXPAND ⟨*ballooned* to 200 pounds⟩
**2 :** to ascend or travel in a balloon

**3 :** to increase rapidly
*transitive verb*
**:** INFLATE, INCREASE
**balloon angioplasty** *noun* (1980)
**:** dilatation of an atherosclerotically obstructed artery by the passage of a balloon catheter through the vessel to the area of disease where inflation of the catheter compresses the plaque against the vessel wall
**balloon catheter** *noun* (1961)
**:** a catheter with an inflatable tip that is used especially to measure blood pressure in a blood vessel or to expand a partly closed or obstructed bodily passage or tube (as a coronary artery)
**bal·loon·ing** \bə-'lü-niŋ\ *noun* (1784)
**:** the act or sport of riding in a balloon
**bal·loon·ist** \-nist\ *noun* (1784)
**:** a person who rides in a balloon
**balloon tire** *noun* (1923)
**:** a low-pressure pneumatic tire with a flexible carcass and large cross section designed to provide cushioning
**balloon vine** *noun* (1836)
**:** a tropical American vine (*Cardiospermum halicacabum*) of the soapberry family bearing large ornamental pods
¹**bal·lot** \'ba-lət\ *noun* [Italian *ballotta*, from Italian dialect, diminutive of *balla* ball] (1549)
**1 a :** a small ball used in secret voting **b :** a sheet of paper used to cast a secret vote
**2 a :** the action or system of secret voting **b :** the right to vote **c :** VOTE 1a
**3 :** the number of votes cast
**4 :** the drawing of lots ◆
²**ballot** *intransitive verb* (1580)
**:** to vote or decide by ballot
**— bal·lot·er** *noun*
**ballot box** *noun* (circa 1680)
**1 :** a box for receiving ballots
**2 :** BALLOT 2a
¹**ball–park** \'bȯl-ˌpärk\ *noun* (1899)
**1 :** a park in which ball games (as baseball) are played
**2 :** a range (as of prices or views) within which comparison or compromise is possible
**— in the ballpark :** approximately correct
²**ballpark** *adjective* [from the expression *in the ballpark*] (1967)
**:** approximately correct ⟨a *ballpark* figure⟩
**ball·play·er** \'bȯl-ˌplā-ər\ *noun* (1619)
**:** a person who plays ball; *especially* **:** a baseball player
**ball·point** \-ˌpȯint\ *noun* (1953)
**:** a pen having as the writing point a small rotating metal ball that inks itself by contact with an inner magazine
**ball·room** \'bȯl-ˌrüm, -ˌru̇m\ *noun* (1736)
**:** a large room used for dances

◇ WORD HISTORY
**ballot** Small objects have long been used as a means of tallying votes. In ancient Greece, a word for "pebble," *psēphos,* came to designate any voting token, and then to mean simply "vote," from the practice of dropping a pebble into one of two urns as decisions were made in public assemblies. (Today, the scientific study of elections is sometimes referred to as *psephology.*) In late medieval Venice, small balls were utilized in public lotteries and elections; one lottery involved the placement of gold and silver balls in urns on a pedestal, from which members of the Great Council would draw to determine nominating committees for state officeholders. In the Venetian form of Italian at that time, the word for "small ball" was *ballotta* (corresponding to Tuscan *pallottola*), which was extended to other tokens used in drawing lots and voting, such as scraps of linen or paper. Familiarity with Venetian electoral practices led to the adoption of the word in English.

**balls–up** \'bȯl-ˌzəp\ *noun* (1939)
*British* **:** FOUL-UP
**ball·sy** \'bȯl-zē\ *adjective* **ball·si·er; -est**
[¹*ball*] (1959)
**:** aggressively tough **:** GUTSY — sometimes
considered vulgar
**ball up** (1885)
*transitive verb*
**:** to make a mess of **:** CONFUSE, MUDDLE
*intransitive verb*
**:** to become badly muddled or confused
**ball valve** *noun* (1839)
**:** a valve in which a ball regulates the aperture
by its rise and fall due to fluid pressure, a
spring, or its own weight
**bally** \'ba-lē\ *adjective or adverb* [euphemism
for *bloody,* adjective, adverb] (1885)
*British* — used as an intensive
**bal·ly·hoo** \'ba-lē-ˌhü\ *noun, plural* **-hoos**
[origin unknown] (1901)
**1 :** a noisy attention-getting demonstration or
talk
**2 :** flamboyant, exaggerated, or sensational
advertising or propaganda
— **ballyhoo** *transitive verb*
**bal·ly·rag** \-ˌrag\ *variant of* BULLYRAG
**balm** \'bä(l)m, *New England also* 'bȧm\ *noun*
[Middle English *basme, baume,* from Old
French, from Latin *balsamum* balsam] (13th
century)
**1 :** a balsamic resin; *especially* **:** one from
small tropical evergreen trees (genus *Commiphora* of the family Burseraceae)
**2 :** an aromatic preparation (as a healing ointment)
**3 :** any of several aromatic plants of the mint
family; *especially* **:** LEMON BALM
**4 :** a spicy aromatic odor
**5 :** a soothing restorative agency
**bal·ma·caan** \ˌbal-mə-'kan, -'kän\ *noun* [*Bal-
macaan,* estate near Inverness, Scotland]
(1919)
**:** a loose single-breasted overcoat usually having raglan sleeves and a short turnover collar
**balm of Gil·e·ad** \-'gi-lē-əd\ [*Gilead,* region
of ancient Palestine known for its balm]
(1703)
**1 :** a small evergreen African and Asian tree
(*Commiphora meccanensis* of the family
Burseraceae) with aromatic leaves; *also* **:** a
fragrant oleoresin from this tree
**2 :** an agency that soothes, relieves, or heals
**3 :** either of two poplars: **a :** a hybrid northern
tree (*Populus gileadensis*) with broadly cordate leaves that are pubescent especially on
the underside **b :** BALSAM POPLAR
**bal·mor·al** \bal-'mȯr-əl, -'mär-\ *noun* [*Bal-
moral* Castle, Scotland] (1859)
**1 :** a laced boot or shoe
**2** *often capitalized* **:** a round flat cap with a
top projecting all around
**balmy** \'bä-mē, 'bȧl-mē, *New England also*
'bȧ-mē\ *adjective* **balm·i·er; -est** (15th century)
**1 a :** having the qualities of balm **:** SOOTHING **b**
**:** MILD
**2 :** CRAZY, FOOLISH
— **balm·i·ly** \-mə-lē\ *adverb*
— **balm·i·ness** \-mē-nəs\ *noun*
**bal·ne·ol·o·gy** \ˌbal-nē-'ä-lə-jē\ *noun* [Inter-
national Scientific Vocabulary, from Latin *balneum* bath — more at BAGNIO] (circa 1879)
**:** the science of the therapeutic use of baths
**¹ba·lo·ney** \bə-'lō-nē\ *variant of* BOLOGNA
**²baloney** *noun* [*bologna*] (1923)
**:** pretentious nonsense **:** BUNKUM — often
used as a generalized expression of disagreement
**bal·sa** \'bȯl-sə\ *noun* [Spanish] (circa 1600)
**1 :** a small raft or boat; *specifically* **:** one made
of tightly bundled reeds and used on Lake
Titicaca
**2 :** a tropical American tree (*Ochroma pyrami-
dale* synonym *O. lagopus*) of the silk-cotton
family with extremely light strong wood used
especially for floats; *also* **:** its wood

**bal·sam** \'bȯl-səm\ *noun* [Latin *balsamum,*
from Greek *balsamon,* probably of Semitic origin; akin to Hebrew *bāshām* balsam] (before
12th century)
**1 a :** an aromatic and usually oily and resinous substance flowing from various plants; *especially* **:** any of several resinous substances
containing benzoic or cinnamic acid and used
especially in medicine **b :** a preparation containing resinous substances and having a balsamic odor
**2 a :** a balsam-yielding tree; *especially* **:** BAL-
SAM FIR **b :** IMPATIENS; *especially* **:** a common
garden ornamental (*Impatiens balsamina*)
**3 :** BALM 5
— **bal·sam·ic** \bȯl-'sa-mik\ *adjective*
**balsam fir** *noun* (1805)
**:** a resinous American fir (*Abies balsamea*)
that is widely used for pulpwood and as a
Christmas tree and is the source of Canada
balsam
**balsamic vinegar** *noun* [translation of Italian *aceto balsamico,* literally, curative vine-
gar] (1982)
**:** an aged Italian vinegar made from the must
of white grapes
**balsam poplar** *noun* (1819)
**:** a North American poplar (*Populus balsam-
ifera*) that is often cultivated as a shade tree
and has buds thickly coated with an aromatic
resin — called also *balm of Gilead, tacama-
hac*
**Bal·ti** \'bəl-tē, 'bȯl-\ *noun* (1901)
**:** a Tibeto-Burman language of northern Kashmir
**Bal·tic** \'bȯl-tik\ *adjective* [Medieval Latin
(*mare*) *balticum* Baltic Sea] (circa 1590)
**1 :** of or relating to the Baltic Sea or to the
states of Lithuania, Latvia, and Estonia
**2 :** of or relating to a branch of the Indo-
European language family containing Latvian,
Lithuanian, and Old Prussian — see INDO-
EUROPEAN LANGUAGES table
**Bal·ti·more oriole** \'bȯl-tə-ˌmȯr-, -ˌmȯr-,
-mər-\ *noun* [George Calvert, Lord *Baltimore*]
(1808)
**:** a northern oriole (*Icterus galbula galbula*) of
the eastern and central U.S. and southern Canada in which the male has a solid black head
and the female usually has an olive brown
back and orange yellow underside
**Bal·to–Slav·ic** \ˌbȯl-(ˌ)tō-'slä-vik, -'sla-\ *noun*
(1896)
**:** a subgroup of Indo-European languages consisting of the Baltic and the Slavic branches
— see INDO-EUROPEAN LANGUAGES table
**Ba·lu·chi** \bə-'lü-chē\ *noun, plural* **Baluchis**
*also* **Baluchi** [Persian *Balūchī* of the Baluchis, from *Balūch, Baloch* Baluchi] (1616)
**1 :** a member of an Indo-Iranian people of
Baluchistan
**2 :** the Iranian language of the Baluchi people
**bal·us·ter** \'ba-lə-stər\ *noun* [French *balustre,*
from Italian *balaustro,* from *balaustra* wild
pomegranate flower, from Latin *balaustium,*
from Greek *balaustion;* from its shape] (1602)
**1 :** an object or vertical member (as the leg of
a table, a round in a chair back, or the stem of
a glass) having a vaselike or turned outline
**2 :** an upright often vase-shaped support for a
rail
**bal·us·trade** \'ba-lə-ˌsträd\ *noun* [French,
from Italian *balaustrata,* from *balaustro*]
(1644)
**1 :** a row of balusters topped by a rail
**2 :** a low parapet or barrier
— **bal·us·trad·ed** \-ˌsträ-dəd\ *adjective*
**bam** *noun* [imitative] (1930)
**:** a dull resounding noise (as of a hard blow or
impact) — often used interjectionally
**Bam·ba·ra** \bäm-'bär-ə\ *noun, plural* **Bambara** *or* **Bambaras** (1883)
**1 :** a member of an African people of the upper Niger
**2 :** a Mande language of the Bambara people

**bam·bi·no** \bam-'bē-(ˌ)nō, bäm-\ *noun, plural*
**-nos** *or* **-ni** \-(ˌ)nē\ [Italian, diminutive of
*bambo* child] (1722)
**1** *plural usually* **bambini :** a representation of
the infant Christ
**2 :** CHILD, BABY
**bam·boo** \(ˌ)bam-'bü, 'bam-ˌ\ *noun, plural*
**bamboos** *often attributive* [Malay *bambu*]
(1586)
**:** any of various
chiefly tropical
woody or arbores-
cent grasses (as of
the genera *Bam-
busa, Arundinaria,*
and *Dendrocala-
mus*) including
some with hollow
stems used for
building, furniture,
or utensils and
young shoots used
for food

bamboo

**bamboo curtain**
*noun, often B&C
capitalized* (1949)
**:** a political, mili-
tary, and ideologi-
cal barrier isolat-
ing an area of the
Orient
**bam·boo·zle** \bam-'bü-zəl\ *transitive verb*
**-boo·zled; -boo·zling** \-'büz-liŋ, -'bü-zə-\
[origin unknown] (1703)
**:** to deceive by underhanded methods **:** DUPE,
HOODWINK
— **bam·boo·zle·ment** \-'bü-zəl-mənt\
*noun*
**¹ban** \'ban\ *verb* **banned; ban·ning** [Middle
English *bannen* to summon, curse, from Old
English *bannan* to summon; akin to Old High
German *bannan* to command, Latin *fari* to
speak, Greek *phanai* to say, *phōnē* sound,
voice] (12th century)
*transitive verb*
**1** *archaic* **:** CURSE
**2 :** to prohibit especially by legal means ⟨*ban*
discrimination⟩; *also* **:** to prohibit the use, performance, or distribution of ⟨*ban* a book⟩ ⟨*ban*
a pesticide⟩
*intransitive verb*
**:** to utter curses or maledictions
**²ban** *noun* [Middle English, partly from *bannen* & partly from Old French *ban,* of Germanic origin; akin to Old High German *bannan* to command] (14th century)
**1 :** the summoning in feudal times of the
king's vassals for military service
**2 :** ANATHEMA, EXCOMMUNICATION
**3 :** MALEDICTION, CURSE
**4 :** legal or formal prohibition
**5 :** censure or condemnation especially
through social pressure
**³ban** \'bän\ *noun, plural* **ba·ni** \'bä-(ˌ)nē\ [Ro-
manian] (1880)
— see *leu* at MONEY table
**Ba·nach space** \'bä-ˌnäk-, -nək-\ *noun* [Ste-
fan *Banach* (died 1945) Polish mathematician]
(1949)
**:** a normed vector space for which the field of
multipliers comprises the real or complex
numbers and in which every Cauchy sequence
converges to a point in the space
**ba·nal** \bə-'nal, ba-, -'näl; bā-'nal; 'bā-n²l\ *adjective* [French, from Middle French, of compulsory feudal service, possessed in common,
commonplace, from *ban*] (1840)
**:** lacking originality, freshness, or novelty
**:** TRITE
**synonym** see INSIPID

— **ba·nal·i·ty** \bə-'na-lə-tē *also* bā- *or* ba-\ *noun*
— **ba·nal·ize** \bə-'na-,līz, ba-, -'nà-; bā-'na-; 'bā-n°l-,īz\ *transitive verb*
— **ba·nal·ly** \bə-'nal-lē, ba-, -'nàl-; bā-'nal-; 'bā-n°l-(l)ē\ *adverb*

**ba·nana** \bə-'na-nə, *especially British* -'nä-\ *noun, often attributive* [Spanish or Portuguese; Spanish, from Portuguese, of African origin; akin to Wolof *banäna* banana] (1597)
**1** : an elongated usually tapering tropical fruit with soft pulpy flesh enclosed in a soft usually yellow rind **2** : any of several widely cultivated perennial herbs (genus *Musa* of the family Musaceae, the banana family) bearing bananas in compact pendent bunches

**banana oil** *noun* (1926)
: a colorless liquid acetate $C_7H_{14}O_2$ of amyl alcohol that has a pleasant fruity odor and is used as a solvent and in the manufacture of artificial fruit essences

banana 2

**banana republic** *noun* (1935)
: a small dependent country usually of the tropics; *especially* : one run despotically

**ba·nan·as** \bə-'na-nəz, *especially British* -'nä-\ *adjective* (1968)
: CRAZY ⟨go *bananas*⟩ ⟨drives me *bananas*⟩
**word history** see NUTS

**banana seat** *noun* (1965)
: an elongated bicycle saddle

**bananas Fos·ter** \-'fòs-tər, -'fäs-\ *noun* [Richard *Foster*, friend of New Orleans restaurateur Owen E. Brennan, at whose restaurant the dish was first made] (1976)
: a dessert of bananas flamed (as with rum) and served with ice cream

**banana split** *noun* (1920)
: ice cream served on a banana sliced in half lengthwise and usually garnished with flavored syrups, fruits, nuts, and whipped cream

**ba·nau·sic** \bə-'nò-sik, -zik\ *adjective* [Greek *banausikos* of an artisan, nonintellectual, vulgar, from *banausos* artisan] (1845)
: relating to or concerned with earning a living — used pejoratively ⟨contempt for the *banausic* occupations —T. S. Eliot⟩; *also* : UTILITARIAN, PRACTICAL ⟨such mundane and *banausic* considerations as comfort and durability —G. B. Boyer⟩

**¹band** \'band\ *noun* [in senses 1 & 2, from Middle English *band, bond* something that constricts, from Old Norse *band;* akin to Old English *bindan* to bind; in other senses, from Middle English *bande* strip, from Middle French, from (assumed) Vulgar Latin *binda,* of Germanic origin; akin to Old High German *binta* fillet; akin to Old English *bindan* to bind, *bend* fetter] (12th century)
**1** : something that confines or constricts while allowing a degree of movement **2** : something that binds or restrains legally, morally, or spiritually **3** : a strip serving to join or hold things together: as **a** : BELT 2 **b** : a cord or strip across the back of a book to which the sections are sewn **4** : a thin flat encircling strip especially for binding: as **a** : a close-fitting strip that confines material at the waist, neck, or cuff of clothing **b** : a strip of cloth used to protect a newborn baby's navel — called also *bellyband* **c** : a ring of elastic **5 a** : a strip (as of living tissue or rock) or a stripe (as on an animal) differentiable (as by color, texture, or structure) from the adjacent

material or area **b** : a more or less well-defined range of wavelengths, frequencies, or energies **c** : RANGE 7a
**6** : a narrow strip serving chiefly as decoration: as **a** : a narrow strip of material applied as trimming to an article of dress **b** *plural* : a pair of strips hanging at the front of the neck as part of a clerical, legal, or academic dress **c** : a ring without raised portions
**7** : TRACK 1e(2)

**²band** (15th century)
*transitive verb*
**1** : to affix a band to or tie up with a band **2** : to finish or decorate with a band **3** : to gather together : UNITE ⟨*banded* themselves together for protection⟩
*intransitive verb*
: to unite for a common purpose — often used with *together* ⟨have *banded* together in hopes of attacking the blight that is common to them all —J. B. Conant⟩
— **band·er** *noun*

**³band** *noun* [Middle French *bande* troop, from Old Provençal *banda,* of Germanic origin; akin to Gothic *bandwo* sign, standard — more at BANNER] (15th century)
: a group of persons, animals, or things; *especially* : a group of musicians organized for ensemble playing and using chiefly woodwinds, brass, and percussion instruments — compare ORCHESTRA

**¹ban·dage** \'ban-dij\ *noun* [Middle French, from *bande*] (1599)
**1** : a strip of fabric used especially to dress and bind up wounds **2** : a flexible strip or band used to cover, strengthen, or compress something

**²bandage** *transitive verb* **ban·daged; ban·dag·ing** (1774)
: to bind, dress, or cover with a bandage

**Band–Aid** \'ban-'dād\ *trademark*
— used for a small adhesive strip with a gauze pad for covering minor wounds

**ban·dan·na** *or* **ban·dana** \ban-'da-nə\ *noun* [Hindi *bādhnū* tie-dyeing, cloth so dyed, from *bādhnā* to tie, from Sanskrit *badhnāti* he ties; akin to Old English *bindan*] (1741)
: a large often colorfully patterned handkerchief

**¹band·box** \'ban(d)-,bäks\ *noun* (1631)
**1** : a usually cylindrical box of paperboard or thin wood for holding light articles of attire **2** : a structure (as a baseball park) having relatively small interior dimensions

**²bandbox** *adjective* (1844)
: exquisitely neat, clean, or ordered as if just taken from a bandbox ⟨a *bandbox* perfection of appearance⟩
— **bandbox** *adverb*

**ban·deau** \ban-'dō\ *noun, plural* **ban·deaux** \-'dōz\ [French, diminutive of *bande*] (1706)
**1** : a fillet or band especially for the hair **2** : BRASSIERE; *also* : a band-shaped covering for the breasts

**band·ed** \'ban-dəd\ *adjective* (1787)
: having or marked with bands

**ban·de·ril·la** \,ban-də-'rē(l)-yə\ *noun* [Spanish, diminutive of *bandera* banner] (1797)
: a decorated barbed dart that the banderillero thrusts into the neck or shoulders of the bull in a bullfight

**ban·de·ril·le·ro** \,ban-də-(,)rē(l)-'yer-(,)ō\ *noun, plural* **-ros** [Spanish, from *banderilla*] (1797)
: one who thrusts in the banderillas in a bullfight

**ban·de·role** *or* **ban·de·rol** \'ban-də-,rōl\ *noun* [French *banderole,* from Italian *banderuola,* diminutive of *bandiera* banner, of Germanic origin; akin to Gothic *bandwo* sign] (1562)
**1** : a long narrow forked flag or streamer **2** : a long scroll bearing an inscription or a device

**ban·di·coot** \'ban-di-,küt\ *noun* [Telugu *pandikokku*] (1813)

**1** : any of several very large rats (genera *Bandicota* and *Nesokia*) of southern Asia destructive to crops **2** : any of a family (Peramelidae) of small insectivorous and herbivorous marsupial mammals of Australia, Tasmania, and New Guinea

**ban·dit** \'ban-dət\ *noun* [Italian *bandito,* from past participle of *bandire* to banish, of Germanic origin; akin to Old High German *bannan* to command — more at BAN] (1591)
**1** *plural also* **ban·dit·ti** \ban-'di-tē\ : an outlaw who lives by plunder; *especially* : a member of a band of marauders **2** : ROBBER **3** : an enemy plane
— **ban·dit·ry** \'ban-də-trē\ *noun*

**band·lead·er** \'band-,lē-dər\ *noun* (1894)
: the conductor of a band (as a dance band)

**band·mas·ter** \'ban(d)-,mas-tər\ *noun* (1858)
: BANDLEADER; *especially* : a conductor of a military or concert band

**ban·dog** \'ban-,dòg\ *noun* [Middle English *bandogge,* from *band* + *dogge* dog] (14th century)
: a dog kept tied to serve as a watchdog or because of its ferocity

**ban·do·lier** *or* **ban·do·leer** \,ban-də-'lir\ *noun* [Middle French *bandouliere,* ultimately from Old Spanish *bando* band, of Germanic origin; akin to Gothic *bandwo*] (circa 1577)
: a belt worn over the shoulder and across the breast often for the suspending or supporting of some article (as cartridges) or as a part of an official or ceremonial dress

**ban·dore** \'ban-,dōr, -,dòr\ *or* **ban·do·ra** \ban-'dōr-ə, -'dòr-\ *noun* [Spanish *bandurria* or Portuguese *bandurra,* from Late Latin *pandura* 3-stringed lute, from Greek *pandoura*] (1566)
: a bass stringed instrument resembling a guitar

**band–pass filter** \'ban(d)-,pas-\ *noun* (1926)
: a filter that transmits only frequencies within a selected band

**band saw** *noun* (circa 1864)
: a saw in the form of an endless steel belt running over pulleys; *also* : a power sawing machine using this device

**band shell** *noun* (1926)
: a bandstand having at the rear a sounding board shaped like a huge concave seashell

**bands·man** \'ban(d)z-mən\ *noun* (circa 1842)
: a member of a musical band

**band·stand** \'ban(d)-,stand\ *noun* (1859)
**1** : a usually roofed platform on which a band or orchestra performs outdoors **2** : a platform in a ballroom or nightclub on which musicians perform

**band·wag·on** \'band-,wa-gən\ *noun* (1855)
**1** : a usually ornate and high wagon for a band of musicians especially in a circus parade **2** : a popular party, faction, or cause that attracts growing support — often used in such phrases as *climb on the bandwagon* **3** : a current or fashionable trend

**band·width** \'band-,width\ *noun* (circa 1937)
**1** : a range within a band of wavelengths, frequencies, or energies; *especially* : a range of radio frequencies which is occupied by a modulated carrier wave, which is assigned to a service, or over which a device can operate **2** : the data transfer rate of an electronic communications system

**¹ban·dy** \'ban-dē\ *verb* **ban·died; ban·dy·ing** [probably from Middle French *bander* to be tight, to bandy, from *bande* strip — more at BAND] (1577)
*transitive verb*
**1** : to bat (as a tennis ball) to and fro **2 a** : to toss from side to side or pass about from one to another often in a careless or inappropriate manner **b** : EXCHANGE; *especially* : to exchange (words) argumentatively **c** : to discuss lightly or banteringly **d** : to use in a glib or offhand manner — often used with

about ⟨bandy these statistics about with considerable bravado —Richard Pollak⟩
**3** archaic **:** to band together
intransitive verb
**1** obsolete **:** CONTEND
**2** archaic **:** UNITE
**²bandy** noun [perhaps from Middle French bandé, past participle of bander] (1693)
**:** a game similar to hockey and believed to be its prototype
**³bandy** adjective [probably from bandy (hockey stick)] (1687)
**1** of legs **:** BOWED
**2 :** BOWLEGGED
— **ban·dy-legged** \'ban-dē-,legd\, ,ban-dē-'le-gəd, -'lā-\ adjective
**¹bane** \'bān\ noun [Middle English, from Old English bana; akin to Old High German bano death] (before 12th century)
**1 a** obsolete **:** KILLER, SLAYER **b :** POISON **c :** DEATH, DESTRUCTION ⟨to stop the way of those that seek my bane —Philip Sidney⟩ **d :** WOE
**2 :** a source of harm or ruin **:** CURSE ⟨national frontiers have been more of a bane than a boon for mankind —D. C. Thomson⟩
**²bane** transitive verb **baned; ban·ing** (1578)
obsolete **:** to kill especially with poison
**³bane** noun [Middle English (northern dialect) ban, from Old English bān] (before 12th century)
chiefly Scottish **:** BONE
**bane·ber·ry** \'bān-,ber-ē\ noun (1755)
**:** any of several perennial herbs (genus Actaea) of the buttercup family having acrid poisonous berries; also **:** one of the berries
**bane·ful** \'bān-fəl\ adjective (1579)
**1 :** productive of destruction or woe **:** seriously harmful ⟨a baneful influence⟩
**2** archaic **:** POISONOUS
**synonym** see PERNICIOUS
— **bane·ful·ly** \-fə-lē\ adverb
**¹bang** \'baŋ\ verb [probably of Scandinavian origin; akin to Icelandic banga to hammer] (circa 1550)
transitive verb
**1 :** to strike sharply **:** BUMP
**2 :** to knock, beat, or thrust vigorously often with a sharp noise
**3 :** to have sexual intercourse with — often considered vulgar
intransitive verb
**1 :** to strike with a sharp noise or thump
**2 :** to produce a sharp often metallic explosive or percussive noise or series of such noises
**²bang** noun (circa 1550)
**1 :** a resounding blow
**2 :** a sudden loud noise — often used interjectionally
**3 a :** a sudden striking effect **b :** a quick burst of energy ⟨start off with a bang⟩ **c :** THRILL ⟨I get a bang out of all this —W. H. Whyte⟩
— **bang for the buck** also **bang for one's buck :** value received from outlay or effort ⟨investment is yielding less bang for the buck —Fortune⟩
**³bang** adverb (1828)
**:** RIGHT, DIRECTLY ⟨ran bang up against more trouble⟩
**⁴bang** noun [probably short for bangtail (short tail)] (1878)
**:** a fringe of banged hair — usually used in plural
**⁵bang** transitive verb (1878)
**:** to cut (as front hair) short and squarely across
**ban·ga·lore torpedo** \'baŋ-gə-,lōr-, -,lȯr-\ noun [Bangalore, India] (1913)
**:** a metal tube that contains explosives and a firing mechanism and is used to cut barbed wire and detonate buried mines
**bang away** intransitive verb (circa 1889)
**1 :** to work with determined effort ⟨students banging away at their homework⟩

**2 :** to attack persistently ⟨police are going to keep banging away at you —Erle Stanley Gardner⟩
**bang·er** \'baŋ-ər\ noun (circa 1919)
**1** British **:** SAUSAGE
**2** British **:** FIRECRACKER
**3** British **:** JALOPY
**bang·kok** \'baŋ-,käk, baŋ-'\ noun [earlier bangkok, a fine straw, from Bangkok, Thailand] (1916)
**:** a hat woven of fine palm fiber in the Philippines
**ban·gle** \'baŋ-gəl\ noun [Hindi baṅglī] (1787)
**1 :** a stiff usually ornamental bracelet or anklet slipped or clasped on
**2 :** an ornamental disk that hangs loosely (as on a bracelet)
**bang on** adjective (1936)
chiefly British **:** exactly correct or appropriate
**Bang's disease** \'baŋz-\ noun [Bernhard L. F. Bang (died 1932) Danish veterinarian] (circa 1929)
**:** BRUCELLOSIS; specifically **:** contagious abortion of cattle caused by a brucella (Brucella abortus)
**bang·tail** \'baŋ-,tāl\ noun [bangtail (short tail)] (1921)
**:** RACEHORSE
**bang–up** \'baŋ-,əp\ adjective [³bang] (1810)
**:** FIRST-RATE, EXCELLENT ⟨a bang-up job⟩
**bang up** transitive verb [¹bang] (1920)
**:** to cause extensive damage to
**bani** plural of ³BAN
**ban·ish** \'ba-nish\ transitive verb [Middle English, from Middle French baniss-, stem of banir, of Germanic origin; akin to Old High German bannan to command — more at BAN] (14th century)
**1 :** to require by authority to leave a country
**2 :** to drive out or remove from a home or place of usual resort or continuance
**3 :** to clear away **:** DISPEL ⟨his discovery banishes anxiety —Stringfellow Barr⟩ ☆
— **ban·ish·er** noun
— **ban·ish·ment** \-nish-mənt\ noun
**ban·is·ter** \'ba-nəs-tər\ noun [alteration of baluster] (1667)
**1 :** BALUSTER 2
**2 a :** a handrail with its supporting posts **b :** HANDRAIL
— **ban·is·tered** \-tərd\ adjective
**ban·jax** \'ban-,jaks\ transitive verb [origin unknown] (1939)
chiefly Irish **:** DAMAGE, RUIN; also **:** SMASH
**ban·jo** \'ban-(,)jō\ noun, plural **banjos** also **banjoes** [probably of African origin; akin to Kimbundu mbanza, a similar instrument] (1739)
**:** a musical instrument with a drumlike body, a fretted neck, and usually four or five strings which may be plucked or strummed
— **ban·jo·ist** \-,jō-ist\ noun
**banjo clock** noun (1903)
**:** a pendulum clock whose shape suggests a banjo
**¹bank** \'baŋk\ noun [Middle English, probably of Scandinavian origin; akin to Old Norse bakki bank; akin to Old English benc bench — more at BENCH] (13th century)
**1 :** a mound, pile, or ridge raised above the surrounding level: as **a :** a piled-up mass of cloud or fog **b :** an undersea elevation rising especially from the continental shelf
**2 :** the rising ground bordering a lake, river, or sea or forming the edge of a cut or hollow
**3 a :** a steep slope (as of a hill) **b :** the lateral inward tilt of a surface along a curve or of a vehicle (as an airplane) when taking a curve
**4 :** a protective or cushioning rim or piece ◆
**²bank** (1590)

banjo

transitive verb
**1 a :** to raise a bank about **b :** to cover (as a fire) with fresh fuel and adjust the draft of air so as to keep in an inactive state **c :** to build a (curve) with the roadbed or track inclined laterally upward from the inside edge
**2 :** to heap or pile in a bank
**3 :** to drive (a ball in billiards) into a cushion
**4 :** to form or group in a tier
intransitive verb
**1 :** to rise in or form a bank — often used with up ⟨clouds would bank up about midday, and showers fall —William Beebe⟩
**2 a :** to incline an airplane laterally **b** (1) **:** to incline laterally (2) **:** to follow a curve or incline ⟨skiers banking around the turn⟩
**³bank** noun [Middle English, from Middle French or Old Italian; Middle French banque, from Old Italian banca, literally, bench, of Germanic origin; akin to Old English benc] (15th century)
**1 a :** an establishment for the custody, loan, exchange, or issue of money, for the extension of credit, and for facilitating the transmission of funds **b** obsolete **:** the table, counter, or place of business of a money changer
**2 :** a person conducting a gambling house or game; specifically **:** DEALER
**3 :** a supply of something held in reserve: as **a :** the fund of supplies (as money, chips, or pieces) held by the banker or dealer for use in a game **b :** a fund of pieces belonging to a game (as dominoes) from which the players draw
**4 :** a place where something is held available ⟨memory bank⟩; especially **:** a depot for the collection and storage of a biological product of human origin for medical use ⟨blood bank⟩
**⁴bank** (circa 1751)

☆ **SYNONYMS**
**Banish, exile, deport, transport** mean to remove by authority from a state or country. BANISH implies compulsory removal from a country not necessarily one's own ⟨banished for seditious activities⟩. EXILE may imply compulsory removal or an enforced or voluntary absence from one's own country ⟨a writer who exiled himself for political reasons⟩. DEPORT implies sending out of the country an alien who has illegally entered or whose presence is judged inimical to the public welfare ⟨illegal aliens will be deported⟩. TRANSPORT implies sending a convicted criminal to an overseas penal colony ⟨a convict who was transported to Australia⟩.

◇ **WORD HISTORY**
**bank** Long before the days of automatic teller machines, money transactions took place between individuals over a table or counter. The medieval Italian word for such a counter was banco. As the transactions of financial institutions became more complex than simple exchanges of money across a counter, especially in Italian cities such as Florence and Venice, the word banco was extended to the institution itself. Italian banking practices spread to the rest of Europe, and with them went the word banco, usually via the feminine variant banca—hence late medieval French banque and late Middle English banke. In Italian, banca, possibly influenced by the feminine gender of the French noun, has now largely supplanted banco in the sense "bank."

*intransitive verb*
**1 :** to manage a bank
**2 :** to deposit money or have an account in a bank
*transitive verb*
**:** to deposit in a bank
— **bank on :** to depend or rely on
⁵**bank** *noun* [Middle English *banc* bench, from Old French, of Germanic origin; akin to Old English *benc*] (1614)
**1 :** a group or series of objects arranged together in a row or a tier: as **a :** a set of elevators **b :** a row or tier of telephones
**2 :** one of the horizontal and usually secondary or lower divisions of a headline
**bank·able** \'baŋ-kə-bəl\ *adjective* (1818)
**1 :** acceptable to or at a bank
**2 :** sure to bring in a profit ⟨Hollywood's most *bankable* star —Sidney Sheldon⟩
— **bank·abil·i·ty** \ˌbaŋ-kə-'bi-lə-tē\ *noun*
**bank·book** \'baŋk-ˌbuk\ *noun* (1714)
**:** the depositor's book in which a bank records deposits and withdrawals — called also *passbook*
**bank·card** \-ˌkärd\ *noun* (1970)
**:** a credit card issued by a bank
**bank discount** *noun* (1841)
**:** the interest discounted in advance on a note and computed on the face value of the note
¹**bank·er** \'baŋ-kər\ *noun* (1534)
**1 :** one that engages in the business of banking
**2 :** the player who keeps the bank in various games
— **bank·er·ly** \-lē\ *adjective*
²**banker** *noun* (1666)
**:** a man or boat employed in the cod fishery on the Newfoundland banks
³**banker** *noun* (1677)
**:** a sculptor's or mason's workbench
**banker's acceptance** *noun* (circa 1924)
**:** a short-term credit instrument issued by an importer's bank that guarantees payment of an exporter's invoice
**bank holiday** *noun* (1871)
**1** *British* **:** LEGAL HOLIDAY
**2 :** a period when banks in general are closed often by government fiat
**bank·ing** *noun* (1735)
**:** the business of a bank or a banker
**bank money** *noun* (1904)
**:** a medium of exchange consisting chiefly of checks and drafts
**bank·note** \'baŋk-ˌnōt\ *noun* (1695)
**:** a promissory note issued by a bank payable to bearer on demand without interest and acceptable as money
¹**bank·roll** \'baŋ-ˌkrōl\ *noun* (1887)
**:** supply of money **:** FUNDS
²**bankroll** *transitive verb* (1928)
**:** to supply the capital for or pay the cost of (a business or project)
— **bank·roll·er** *noun*
¹**bank·rupt** \'baŋ-(ˌ)krəpt\ *noun* [modification of Middle French & Old Italian; Middle French *banqueroute* bankruptcy, from Old Italian *bancarotta*, from *banca* bank + *rotta* broken, from Latin *rupta*, feminine of *ruptus*, past participle of *rumpere* to break — more at BANK, REAVE] (1533)
**1 a :** a person who has done any of the acts that by law entitle his creditors to have his estate administered for their benefit **b :** a person judicially declared subject to having his estate administered under the bankrupt laws for the benefit of his creditors **c :** a person who becomes insolvent
**2 :** one who is destitute of a particular thing ⟨a moral *bankrupt*⟩
²**bankrupt** *adjective* (1570)
**1 a :** reduced to a state of financial ruin **:** IMPOVERISHED; *specifically* **:** legally declared a bankrupt ⟨the company went *bankrupt*⟩ **b :** of or relating to bankrupts or bankruptcy ⟨*bankrupt* laws⟩

**2 a :** BROKEN, RUINED ⟨a *bankrupt* professional career⟩ **b :** exhausted of valuable qualities **:** STERILE ⟨a *bankrupt* old culture⟩ **c :** DESTITUTE — used with *of* or *in* ⟨*bankrupt* of all merciful feelings⟩
³**bankrupt** *transitive verb* (1588)
**1 :** to reduce to bankruptcy
**2 :** IMPOVERISH ⟨defections had *bankrupted* the party of its brainpower⟩
**synonym** see DEPLETE
**bank·rupt·cy** \'baŋ-(ˌ)krəp(t)-sē\ *noun, plural* **-cies** (1700)
**1 :** the quality or state of being bankrupt
**2 :** utter failure or impoverishment
**bank shot** *noun* (1897)
**1 :** a shot in billiards and pool in which a player banks the cue ball or the object ball
**2 :** a shot in basketball played to rebound from the backboard into the basket
**bank·sia** \'baŋ(k)-sē-ə\ *noun* [New Latin, genus name, from Sir Joseph *Banks*] (1788)
**:** any of a genus (*Banksia*) of Australian evergreen trees or shrubs of the protea family with alternate leathery leaves and flowers in dense cylindrical heads
**bank·side** \'baŋk-ˌsīd\ *noun* (15th century)
**:** the slope of a bank especially of a stream
¹**ban·ner** \'ba-nər\ *noun* [Middle English *banere*, from Old French, of Germanic origin; akin to Gothic *bandwo* sign; probably akin to Greek *phainein* to show — more at FANCY] (13th century)
**1 a :** a piece of cloth attached by one edge to a staff and used by a leader (as a monarch or feudal lord) as his standard **b :** ²FLAG 1 **c :** an ensign displaying a distinctive or symbolic device or legend; *especially* **:** one presented as an award of honor or distinction
**2 :** a headline in large type running across a newspaper page
**3 :** a strip of cloth on which a sign is painted ⟨welcome *banners* stretched across the street⟩
**4 :** a name, slogan, or goal associated with a particular group or ideology ⟨the new *banner* is "community control" —F. M. Hechinger⟩ — often used with *under* ⟨every new administration arrives . . . under the *banner* of change —John Cogley⟩
²**banner** *adjective* (1840)
**1 :** prominent in support of a political party ⟨a *banner* Democratic county⟩
**2 :** distinguished from all others especially in excellence ⟨a *banner* year for business⟩
³**banner** *transitive verb* (1889)
**1 :** to furnish with a banner
**2 :** to print (as a news story) under a banner usually on the front page
¹**ban·ner·et** \'ba-nə-rət, ˌba-nə-'ret\ *noun, often capitalized* [Middle English *baneret*, from Old French, from *banere*] (14th century)
**:** a knight leading his vassals into the field under his own banner
²**banneret** *also* **ban·ner·ette** *noun* (14th century)
**:** a small banner
**ban·ne·rol** \'ba-nə-ˌrōl\ *noun* (1548)
**:** BANDEROLE
**bannister** *variant of* BANISTER
**ban·nock** \'ba-nək\ *noun* [Middle English *bannok*, from Old English *bannuc*] (before 12th century)
**1 :** a usually unleavened flat bread or biscuit made with oatmeal or barley meal
**2** *chiefly New England* **:** CORN BREAD; *especially* **:** a thin cake baked on a griddle
**banns** \'banz\ *noun plural* [plural of *bann*, from Middle English *bane, ban* proclamation, ban] (14th century)
**:** public announcement especially in church of a proposed marriage
¹**ban·quet** \'baŋ-kwət, 'ban- *also* -ˌkwet\ *noun* [Middle French, from Old Italian *banchetto*, from diminutive of *banca* bench, bank]·(15th century)

**1 :** a sumptuous feast; *especially* **:** an elaborate and often ceremonious meal for numerous people often in honor of a person ⟨a state *banquet*⟩
**2 :** a meal held in recognition of some occasion or achievement ⟨an awards *banquet*⟩
²**banquet** (circa 1500)
*intransitive verb*
**:** to partake of a banquet
*transitive verb*
**:** to treat with a banquet **:** FEAST
— **ban·quet·er** *noun*
**banquet room** *noun* (1837)
**:** a large room (as in a restaurant or hotel) suitable for banquets
**ban·quette** \baŋ-'ket, ban-, *1b is also* 'baŋ-kət\ *noun* [French, from Middle French, from Old Provençal *banqueta*, diminutive of *banc* bench, of Germanic origin; akin to Old English *benc* bench] (1629)
**1 a :** a raised way along the inside of a parapet or trench for gunners or guns **b** *Southern* **:** SIDEWALK
**2 a :** a long upholstered bench **b :** a sofa having one roll-over arm **c :** a built-in upholstered bench along a wall
**Ban·quo** \'baŋ-(ˌ)kwō, 'ban-\ *noun*
**:** a murdered Scottish thane in Shakespeare's *Macbeth* whose ghost appears to Macbeth
**ban·shee** \'ban-(ˌ)shē, ban-\ *noun* [Irish *bean sídhe* & Scottish Gaelic *bean sith*, literally, woman of fairyland] (1771)
**:** a female spirit in Gaelic folklore whose appearance or wailing warns a family that one of them will soon die
¹**ban·tam** \'ban-təm\ *noun* [*Bantam*, former residency in Java] (1749)
**1 :** any of numerous small domestic fowls that are often miniatures of members of the standard breeds
**2 :** a person of diminutive stature and often combative disposition
²**bantam** *adjective* (1782)
**1 :** SMALL, DIMINUTIVE
**2 :** pertly combative
**ban·tam·weight** \-ˌwāt\ *noun* (1884)
**:** a boxer in a weight division having a maximum limit of 118 pounds for professionals and 119 pounds for amateurs — compare FEATHERWEIGHT, FLYWEIGHT
**ban·teng** \'bän-ˌteŋ\ *noun* [Malay of Indonesia, from Javanese *banṭéng*] (1817)
**:** a wild ox (*Bos javanicus* synonym *B. banteng*) of southeastern Asia sometimes domesticated for use as a draft animal or for its meat
¹**ban·ter** \'ban-tər\ *verb* [origin unknown] (1676)
*transitive verb*
**1 :** to speak to or address in a witty and teasing manner
**2** *archaic* **:** DELUDE
**3** *chiefly Southern & Midland* **:** CHALLENGE
*intransitive verb*
**:** to speak or act playfully or wittily
— **ban·ter·er** \-tər-ər\ *noun*
— **ban·ter·ing·ly** \'ban-tə-riŋ-lē\ *adverb*
²**banter** *noun* (1690)
**:** good-natured and usually witty and animated joking
**bant·ling** \'bant-liŋ\ *noun* [perhaps modification of German *Bänkling* bastard, from *Bank* bench, from Old High German — more at BENCH] (1593)
**:** a very young child
**Ban·tu** \'ban-(ˌ)tü, 'bän-\ *noun, plural* **Bantu** *or* **Bantus** (1862)
**1 :** a family of Niger-Congo languages spoken in central and southern Africa
**2 :** a member of any of a group of African peoples who speak Bantu languages
**Ban·tu·stan** \ˌban-tù-'stan, ˌbän-tù-'stän\ *noun* [*Bantu* + *-stan* land (as in *Hindustan*)] (1949)
**:** any of several all-black enclaves in the Republic of South Africa that have a limited degree of self-government

**ban·yan** \'ban-yən\ *noun* [earlier *banyan* Gujarati trader, from Portuguese *banean*, probably from Tamil *vāṇiyan* trader, from Sanskrit *vāṇija;* from a tree of the species in Iran under which such traders conducted business] (1634)
**:** an East Indian fig tree (*Ficus benghalensis*) of the mulberry family with branches that send out shoots which grow down to the soil and root to form secondary trunks

**ban·zai** \(ˌ)bän-'zī, 'bän-ˌ\ *noun* [Japanese] (1893)
**:** a Japanese cheer or war cry

**banzai attack** *noun* (1944)
**:** a mass attack by Japanese soldiers in World War II; *also* **:** an all-out usually desperate attack

**banzai charge** *noun* (1944)
**1 :** BANZAI ATTACK
**2 :** a determined often reckless act

**bao·bab** \'baū-ˌbab, 'bā-ə-\ *noun* [New Latin *bahobab*] (1640)
**:** a broad-trunked Old World tropical tree (*Adansonia digitata*) of the silk-cotton family with an edible acid fruit resembling a gourd and bark used in making paper, cloth, and rope

**bap** \'bap\ *noun* [origin unknown] (circa 1575) *British* **:** a small bun or roll

**bap·ti·sia** \bap-'ti-zh(ē-)ə\ *noun* [New Latin, genus name, from Greek *baptisis* a dipping, from *baptein*] (circa 1868)
**:** any of a genus (*Baptisia*) of North American leguminous plants having showy papilionaceous flowers similar in form to those of the pea plant

**bap·tism** \'bap-ˌti-zəm, *especially Southern* 'bab-\ *noun* [Middle English *baptisme*] (14th century)
**1 a :** a Christian sacrament marked by ritual use of water and admitting the recipient to the Christian community **b :** a non-Christian rite using water for ritual purification **c** *Christian Science* **:** purification by or submergence in Spirit
**2 :** an act, experience, or ordeal by which one is purified, sanctified, initiated, or named
— **bap·tis·mal** \bap-'tiz-məl, *especially Southern* bab-\ *adjective*
— **bap·tis·mal·ly** \-mə-lē\ *adverb*

**baptismal name** *noun* (1869)
**:** a name given at christening or confirmation

**baptism of fire** (1857)
**1 :** an introductory or initial experience that is a severe ordeal; *specifically* **:** a soldier's first exposure to enemy fire
**2 :** a spiritual baptism by a gift of the Holy Spirit — often used in allusion to Acts 2:3–4; Matthew 3:11 (Revised Standard Version)

**bap·tist** \'bap-tist, *especially Southern* 'bab-\ *noun* (13th century)
**1 :** one that baptizes
**2** *capitalized* **:** a member or adherent of an evangelical Protestant denomination marked by congregational polity and baptism by immersion of believers only
— **Baptist** *adjective*

**bap·tis·tery** *or* **bap·tis·try** \'bap-tə-strē, *especially Southern* 'bab-\ *noun, plural* **-ter·ies** *or* **-tries** (14th century)
**:** a part of a church or formerly a separate building used for baptism

**bap·tize** *also* **bap·tise** \bap-'tīz, 'bap-ˌ, *especially Southern* bab- *or* 'bab-\ *verb* **bap·tized** *also* **bap·tised; bap·tiz·ing** *also* **bap·tis·ing** [Middle English, from Old French *baptiser*, from Late Latin *baptizare*, from Greek *baptizein* to dip, baptize, from *baptein* to dip, dye; akin to Old Norse *kvefja* to quench] (13th century)
*transitive verb*
**1 :** to administer baptism to
**2 a :** to purify or cleanse spiritually especially by a purging experience or ordeal **b :** INITIATE
**3 :** to give a name to (as at baptism) **:** CHRISTEN

*intransitive verb*
**:** to administer baptism
— **bap·tiz·er** *noun*

**¹bar** \'bär\ *noun, often attributive* [Middle English *barre*, from Middle French] (12th century)
**1 a :** a straight piece (as of wood or metal) that is longer than it is wide and has any of various uses (as for a lever, support, barrier, or fastening) **b :** a solid piece or block of material that is usually considerably longer than it is wide ⟨a *bar* of gold⟩ ⟨candy *bar*⟩ **c :** a usually rigid piece (as of wood or metal) longer than it is wide that is used as a handle or support; *especially* **:** a handrail used by ballet dancers to maintain balance while exercising
**2 :** something that obstructs or prevents passage, progress, or action: as **a :** the destruction of an action or claim in law; *also* **:** a plea or objection that effects such destruction **b :** an intangible or nonphysical impediment **c :** a submerged or partly submerged bank (as of sand) along a shore or in a river often obstructing navigation
**3 a** (1) **:** the railing in a courtroom that encloses the place about the judge where prisoners are stationed or where the business of the court is transacted in civil cases (2) **:** COURT, TRIBUNAL (3) **:** a particular system of courts (4) **:** an authority or tribunal that hands down judgment **b** (1) **:** the barrier in the English Inns of Court that formerly separated the seats of the benchers or readers from the body of the hall occupied by the students (2) **:** the whole body of barristers or lawyers qualified to practice in the courts of any jurisdiction (3) **:** the profession of barrister or lawyer
**4 :** a straight stripe, band, or line much longer than it is wide: as **a :** one of two or more horizontal stripes on a heraldic shield **b :** a metal or embroidered strip worn on a usually military uniform especially to indicate rank (as of a company officer) or service
**5 a :** a counter at which food or especially alcoholic beverages are served **b :** BARROOM **c :** SHOP 2b
**6 a :** a vertical line across the musical staff before the initial measure accent **b :** MEASURE
**7 :** a lace and embroidery joining covered with buttonhole stitch for connecting various parts of the pattern in needlepoint lace and cutwork
— **behind bars :** in jail

**²bar** *transitive verb* **barred; bar·ring** (13th century)
**1 a :** to fasten with a bar **b :** to place bars across to prevent ingress or egress
**2 :** to mark with bars **:** STRIPE
**3 a :** to confine or shut in by or as if by bars **b :** to set aside **:** RULE OUT **c :** to keep out **:** EXCLUDE
**4 a :** to interpose legal objection to or to the claim of **b :** PREVENT, FORBID

**³bar** *preposition* (1714)
**:** EXCEPT

**⁴bar** *noun* [German, from Greek *baros*] (1910)
**:** a unit of pressure equal to one million dynes per square centimeter

**bar-** *or* **baro-** *combining form* [Greek *baros;* akin to Greek *barys* heavy — more at GRIEVE]
**:** weight **:** pressure ⟨*barometer*⟩

**Bar·ab·bas** \bə-'ra-bəs\ *noun* [Greek, from Aramaic *Bar-abba*]
**:** a Jewish prisoner according to Matthew, Mark, and John released in preference to Christ at the demand of the multitude

**bar·a·thea** \ˌbar-ə-'thē-ə\ *noun* [from *Barathea*, a trademark] (1862)
**:** a fabric that has a broken rib weave and a pebbly texture and that is made of silk, worsted, or synthetic fiber or a combination of these

**¹barb** \'bärb\ *noun* [Middle English *barbe* barb, beard, from Middle French, from Latin *barba* — more at BEARD] (14th century)
**1 :** a medieval cloth headdress passing over or under the chin and covering the neck

**2 a :** a sharp projection extending backward (as from the point of an arrow or fishhook) and preventing easy extraction; *also* **:** a sharp projection with its point similarly oblique to something else **b :** a biting or pointedly critical remark or comment
**3 :** ²BARBEL
**4 :** any of the side branches of the shaft of a feather — see FEATHER illustration
**5 :** a plant hair or bristle ending in a hook

**²barb** *transitive verb* (1759)
**:** to furnish with a barb

**³barb** *noun* [French *barbe*, from Italian *barbero*, from *barbero* of Barbary, from *Barberia* Barbary, coastal region in Africa] (1636)
**:** any of a northern African breed of horses that are noted for speed and endurance and are related to Arabians

**⁴barb** *noun* (1967)
*slang* **:** BARBITURATE

**bar·bar·i·an** \bär-'ber-ē-ən, -'bar-\ *adjective* [Latin *barbarus*] (14th century)
**1 :** of or relating to a land, culture, or people alien and usually believed to be inferior to another land, culture, or people
**2 :** lacking refinement, learning, or artistic or literary culture
— **barbarian** *noun*
— **bar·bar·i·an·ism** \-ē-ə-ˌni-zəm\ *noun*

**bar·bar·ic** \bär-'bar-ik\ *adjective* (15th century)
**1 a :** of, relating to, or characteristic of barbarians **b :** possessing or characteristic of a cultural level more complex than primitive savagery but less sophisticated than advanced civilization
**2 a :** marked by a lack of restraint **:** WILD **:** having a bizarre, primitive, or unsophisticated quality
**3 :** BARBAROUS 3 ◆
— **bar·bar·i·cal·ly** \-i-k(ə-)lē\ *adverb*

**bar·ba·rism** \'bär-bə-ˌri-zəm\ *noun* (15th century)
**1 a :** a barbarian or barbarous social or intellectual condition **:** BACKWARDNESS **b :** the practice or display of barbarian acts, attitudes, or ideas
**2 :** an idea, act, or expression that in form or use offends against contemporary standards of good taste or acceptability

**bar·bar·i·ty** \bär-'bar-ə-tē\ *noun, plural* **-ties** (circa 1570)
**1 :** BARBARISM
**2 a :** barbarous cruelty **:** INHUMANITY **b :** an act or instance of such cruelty

**bar·ba·ri·za·tion** \ˌbär-bə-rə-'zā-shən\ *noun* (1822)

◇ **WORD HISTORY**
**barbaric** It is unfortunate that the ancient Greeks, in spite of their scientific curiosity and their distinction in the writing of history, left scant records of the languages spoken by peoples with whom they came into contact—languages now mostly lost forever to investigation. On the whole, the Greeks were not very interested in those who were not *Hellēnes*, "Greek-speakers." All non-Greek speakers were collectively *barbaroi*, a word that is onomatopoeic in origin, mimicking the babble-like sound of foreign speech to Greek ears. Especially after the Greeks' wars with the Persians, the *barbaroi* par excellence to the Greeks, the derivative *barbarikos* came to mean "violent" or "savage" in addition to simply "foreign." It is these senses we have inherited in the loanword *barbaric*.

\ə\ abut  \ᵊ\ kitten  \ər\ further  \a\ ash  \ā\ ace
\ä\ mop, mar  \aū\ out  \ch\ chin  \e\ bet  \ē\ easy
\g\ go  \i\ hit  \ī\ ice  \j\ job  \ŋ\ sing  \ō\ go
\ò\ law  \òi\ boy  \th\ thin  \th̲\ the  \ü\ loot  \u̇\ foot
\y\ yet  \zh\ vision   *see also* Guide to Pronunciation

: the act or process of barbarizing : the state of being barbarized

**bar·ba·rize** \'bär-bə-ˌrīz\ *verb* **-rized; -riz·ing** (1648)
*transitive verb*
: to make barbarian or barbarous
*intransitive verb*
: to become barbarous

**bar·ba·rous** \'bär-b(ə-)rəs\ *adjective* [Latin *barbarus*, from Greek *barbaros* foreign, ignorant] (15th century)
**1 a :** UNCIVILIZED **b :** lacking culture or refinement **:** PHILISTINE
**2 :** characterized by the occurrence of barbarisms
**3 :** mercilessly harsh or cruel
**synonym** see FIERCE
— **bar·ba·rous·ly** *adverb*
— **bar·ba·rous·ness** *noun*

**Bar·ba·ry ape** \'bär-b(ə-)rē-\ *noun* [*Barbary*, Africa] (1864)
: a tailless monkey (*Macaca sylvanus*) of northern Africa and Gibraltar

**Barbary Coast** *noun* (1880)
: a district or section of a city noted as a center of gambling, prostitution, and riotous nightlife

**Barbary sheep** *noun* (circa 1898)
: AOUDAD

**barbe** \'bärb\ *noun* [Middle English, from Middle French, literally, beard] (14th century)
: ¹BARB 1

**¹bar·be·cue** \'bär-bi-ˌkyü\ *transitive verb* **-cued; -cu·ing** (1690)
**1 :** to roast or broil on a rack over hot coals or on a revolving spit before or over a source of heat
**2 :** to cook in a highly seasoned vinegar sauce
— **bar·be·cu·er** *noun*

**²barbecue** *also* **bar·be·que** *noun* [American Spanish *barbacoa* framework for supporting meat over a fire, probably from Taino] (1709)
**1 :** a large animal (as a steer) roasted whole or split over an open fire or a fire in a pit; *also* **:** smaller pieces of barbecued meat
**2 :** a social gathering especially in the open air at which barbecued food is eaten
**3 :** an often portable fireplace over which meat and fish are roasted

**barbed** \'bärbd\ *adjective* (1611)
**1 :** having barbs
**2 :** characterized by pointed and biting criticism or sarcasm ⟨*barbed* witticisms⟩

**barbed wire** \'bärb(d)-'wīr, 'bäb(d)-\ *noun* (1881)
: twisted wires armed with barbs or sharp points — called also *barbwire*

**¹bar·bel** \'bär-bəl\ *noun* [Middle English, from Middle French, from (assumed) Vulgar Latin *barbellus*, diminutive of Latin *barbus* barbel, from *barba* beard — more at BEARD] (14th century)
: a European freshwater cyprinid fish (*Barbus barbus*) with four barbels on its upper jaw; *also* **:** any of various closely related fishes

**²barbel** *noun* [obsolete French, from Middle French, diminutive of *barbe* barb, beard] (1601)
: a slender tactile process on the lips of certain fishes (as catfishes)

**bar·bell** \'bär-ˌbel\ *noun* (1887)
: a bar with adjustable weighted disks attached to each end that is used for exercise and in weight lifting

**¹bar·ber** \'bär-bər\ *noun* [Middle English, from Middle French *barbeor*, from *barbe* beard — more at BARB] (14th century)
: one whose business is cutting and dressing hair, shaving and trimming beards, and performing related services

**²barber** *verb* **bar·bered; bar·ber·ing** \-b(ə-)riŋ\ (1606)
*transitive verb*
: to perform the services of a barber for
*intransitive verb*
: to perform the services of a barber

**bar·ber·ry** \'bär-ˌber-ē\ *noun* [Middle English *barbere*, from Middle French *barbarin*, from Arabic *barbārīs*] (14th century)
: any of a genus (*Berberis* of the family Berberidaceae, the barberry family) of shrubs usually having spines, yellow flowers, and oblong red berries

**¹bar·ber·shop** \'bär-bər-ˌshäp\ *noun* (1579)
: a barber's place of business

**²barbershop** *adjective* [from the old custom of men in barbershops forming quartets for impromptu singing of sentimental songs] (1910)
: of a style of unaccompanied group singing of popular songs usually marked by highly conventionalized close harmony

**bar·bet** \'bär-bət\ *noun* [probably from ¹*barb*] (1824)
: any of a family (Capitonidae) of nonpasserine tropical birds with a stout bill bearing bristles and usually swollen at the base

**bar·bette** \bär-'bet\ *noun* [French, diminutive of *barbe* headdress] (1772)
**1 :** a mound of earth or a protected platform from which guns fire over a parapet
**2 :** an armored structure protecting a gun turret on a warship

**bar·bi·can** \'bär-bi-kən\ *noun* [Middle English, from Middle French *barbacane*, from Medieval Latin *barbacana*] (13th century)
: an outer defensive work; *especially* **:** a tower at a gate or bridge

**bar·bi·cel** \'bär-bə-ˌsel\ *noun* [New Latin *barbicella*, diminutive of Latin *barba*] (1869)
: any of the small hook-bearing processes on a barbule of a feather — see FEATHER illustration

**bar·bi·tal** \'bär-bə-ˌtol\ *noun* [*barbit*uric + *-al* (as in *Veronal*, trademark for barbital)] (1919)
: a white crystalline addictive hypnotic $C_8H_{12}N_2O_3$ often administered in the form of its soluble sodium salt

**bar·bi·tone** \'bär-bə-ˌtōn\ *noun* [*barbit*uric + *-one*] (1914)
*British* **:** BARBITAL

**bar·bi·tu·rate** \bär-'bi-chə-rət, -ˌrāt; ˌbär-bə-'tyür-ət, -'tür-, -ˌāt\ *noun* (1928)
**1 :** a salt or ester of barbituric acid
**2 :** any of various derivatives of barbituric acid used especially as sedatives, hypnotics, and antispasmodics

**bar·bi·tu·ric acid** \ˌbär-bə-'t(y)ùr-ik-\ *noun* [part translation of German *Barbitursäure*, irregular from the name *Barbara* + International Scientific Vocabulary *uric* + German *Säure* acid] (1866)
: a synthetic crystalline acid $C_4H_4N_2O_3$ derived from pyrimidine

**Bar·bi·zon** \ˌbär-bə-'zōn, -'zän\ *adjective* [*Barbizon*, France] (1890)
: of, relating to, or being a school of mid-nineteenth century French landscape painters whose naturalistic canvases were based on direct observation of nature

**bar·bule** \'bär-(ˌ)byü(ə)l\ *noun* (1835)
: a minute barb; *especially* **:** one of the processes that fringe the barbs of a feather — see FEATHER illustration

**barb·wire** \'bärb-'wīr, 'bäb-\ *noun* (1880)
: BARBED WIRE

**bar car** *noun* (1945)
: CLUB CAR

**bar·ca·role** *or* **bar·ca·rolle** \'bär-kə-ˌrōl\ *noun* [French *barcarolle*, from Italian dialect (Venice) *barcarola*, from *barcarolo* gondolier, from *barca* bark, from Late Latin] (circa 1779)
**1 :** a Venetian boat song usually in ⁶/₈ or ¹²/₈ time characterized by the alternation of a strong and weak beat that suggests a rowing rhythm
**2 :** music imitating a barcarole

**Bar·ce·lo·na chair** \ˌbär-sə-'lō-nə-\ *noun* [*Barcelona*, Spain] (1970)
: an armless chair with leather-covered cushions on a stainless steel frame

**bar·chan** \(ˌ)bär-'kän, -'kän\ *noun* [Russian *barkhan*, from Kazakh] (1888)
: a moving crescent-shaped sand dune

**bar chart** *noun* (1914)
: BAR GRAPH

**bar code** *noun* (1963)
: a code consisting of a group of printed and variously patterned bars and spaces and sometimes numerals that is designed to be scanned and read into computer memory as identification for the object it labels

Barcelona chair

**¹bard** \'bärd\ *noun* [Middle English, from Scottish Gaelic & Irish] (15th century)
**1 a :** a tribal poet-singer skilled in composing and reciting verses on heroes and their deeds **b :** a composer, singer, or declaimer of epic or heroic verse
**2 :** POET
— **bard·ic** \'bär-dik\ *adjective*

**²bard** *or* **barde** \'bärd\ *noun* [Middle French *barde*, from Old Spanish *barda*, from Arabic *barda'ah*] (15th century)
: a piece of armor or ornament for a horse's neck, breast, or flank

**³bard** *transitive verb* (circa 1521)
**1 :** to furnish with bards
**2 :** to dress meat for cooking by covering with strips of fat

**bard·ol·a·ter** \bär-'dä-lə-tər\ *noun* [*Bard (of Avon)*, epithet of Shakespeare + *-o-* + *-later*] (1903)
: a person who idolizes Shakespeare
— **bard·ol·a·try** \-lə-trē\ *noun*

**Bar·do·li·no** \ˌbär-dºl-'ē-(ˌ)nō\ *noun, plural* **-nos** [*Bardolino*, village on Lake Garda, Italy] (1934)
: a light red Italian wine

**¹bare** \'bar, 'ber\ *adjective* **bar·er; bar·est** [Middle English, from Old English *bær;* akin to Old High German *bar* naked, Lithuanian *basas* barefoot] (before 12th century)
**1 a :** lacking a natural, usual, or appropriate covering **b** (1) **:** lacking clothing (2) *obsolete* **:** BAREHEADED **c :** UNARMED
**2 :** open to view **:** EXPOSED
**3 a :** unfurnished or scantily supplied **b :** DESTITUTE ⟨*bare* of all safeguards⟩
**4 a :** having nothing left over or added ⟨the *bare* necessities of life⟩ **b :** MERE ⟨a *bare* two hours away⟩ **c :** devoid of amplification or adornment
**5** *obsolete* **:** WORTHLESS ☆
— **bare·ness** *noun*

**²bare** *transitive verb* **bared; bar·ing** (before 12th century)
: to make or lay bare **:** UNCOVER

**³bare** *archaic past of* BEAR

**bare·back** \-ˌbak\ *or* **bare·backed** \-'bakt\ *adverb or adjective* (1562)
: on the bare back of a horse **:** without a saddle ⟨likes riding *bareback*⟩ ⟨*bareback* riding⟩

---

☆ **SYNONYMS**
**Bare, naked, nude, bald, barren** mean deprived of naturally or conventionally appropriate covering. BARE implies the removal of what is additional, superfluous, ornamental, or dispensable ⟨an apartment with *bare* walls⟩. NAKED suggests absence of protective or ornamental covering but may imply a state of nature, of destitution, or of defenselessness ⟨poor half-*naked* children⟩. NUDE applies especially to the unclothed human figure ⟨a *nude* model posing for art students⟩. BALD implies actual or seeming absence of natural covering and may suggest a conspicuous bareness ⟨a *bald* mountain peak⟩. BARREN often suggests aridity or impoverishment or sterility ⟨*barren* plains⟩.

**bare·boat** \-ˌbōt\ *noun* (circa 1949)
: a boat chartered without its crew
**bare bones** *noun plural* (1915)
: the barest essentials, facts, or elements
— **bare–bones** *adjective*
**bare·faced** \'bar-ˌfāst, 'ber-\ *adjective* (1590)
**1** : having the face uncovered: **a** : having no whiskers : BEARDLESS **b** : wearing no mask
**2 a** : OPEN, UNCONCEALED **b** : lacking scruples
— **bare·faced·ly** \-'fā-səd-lē, -'fāst-lē\ *adverb*
— **bare·faced·ness** \-'fā-səd-nəs, -'fās(t)-nəs\ *noun*
**bare·foot** \-ˌfůt\ *or* **bare·foot·ed** \-'fů-təd\ *adverb or adjective* (before 12th century)
: with the feet bare ⟨went *barefoot* most of the summer⟩ ⟨*barefoot* boy, with cheek of tan —J. G. Whittier⟩
**barefoot doctor** *noun* (1971)
: an auxiliary medical worker trained to provide basic health care in rural areas of China
**bare–hand·ed** \'bar-'han-dəd, 'ber-\ *adverb or adjective* (15th century)
**1** : without gloves
**2** : without tools or weapons ⟨fight an animal *bare-handed*⟩
**bare·head·ed** \-'he-dəd\ *adverb or adjective* (14th century)
: without a covering for the head ⟨went *bareheaded* in the hot sun⟩ ⟨a *bareheaded* boy who had lost his cap⟩
**bare–knuck·le** \-'nə-kəl\ *also* **bare–knuck·led** \-kəld\ *adjective or adverb* (1903)
**1** : not using boxing gloves ⟨champion *bare-knuckle* prizefighter of England —Dennis Craig⟩ ⟨when men fought *bare-knuckle*⟩
**2** : having a fierce unrelenting character ⟨*bare-knuckle* politics⟩
**bare·ly** *adverb* (before 12th century)
**1** : in a meager manner : PLAINLY ⟨a *barely* furnished room⟩
**2** : SCARCELY, HARDLY ⟨*barely* enough money for lunch⟩
**barf** \'bärf\ *intransitive verb* [origin unknown] (1957)
: VOMIT
**bar·fly** \'bär-ˌflī\ *noun* (1910)
: a person who spends much time in bars
**¹bar·gain** \'bär-gən\ *noun, often attributive* (14th century)
**1** : an agreement between parties settling what each gives or receives in a transaction between them or what course of action or policy each pursues in respect to the other
**2** : something acquired by or as if by bargaining; *especially* : an advantageous purchase
**3** : a transaction, situation, or event regarded in the light of its results
— **into the bargain** *also* **in the bargain**
: BESIDES ⟨tastes good and is good for you, *into the bargain*⟩
**²bargain** *verb* [Middle English, from Middle French *bargaignier*, probably of Germanic origin; akin to Old English *borgian* to borrow — more at BURY] (14th century)
*intransitive verb*
**1** : to negotiate over the terms of a purchase, agreement, or contract : HAGGLE
**2** : to come to terms : AGREE
*transitive verb*
**1** : to bring to a desired level by bargaining ⟨*bargain* a price down⟩
**2** : to sell or dispose of by bargaining
— **bar·gain·er** *noun*
— **bargain for** : EXPECT ⟨more work than I *bargained for*⟩
**bar·gain–base·ment** \'bär-gən-'bās-mənt\ *adjective* (1948)
**1** : of inferior quality or worth
**2** : markedly inexpensive ⟨*bargain-basement* rates⟩
**bargain basement** *noun* (1899)
: a section of a store (as the basement) where merchandise is sold at reduced prices

**¹barge** \'bärj\ *noun* [Middle English, from Middle French, from Late Latin *barca*] (14th century)
: any of various boats: as **a** : a roomy usually flat-bottomed boat used chiefly for the transport of goods on inland waterways and usually propelled by towing **b** : a large motorboat supplied to the flag officer of a flagship **c** : a roomy pleasure boat; *especially* : a boat of state elegantly furnished and decorated
**²barge** *verb* **barged; barg·ing** (1649)
*transitive verb*
: to carry by barge
*intransitive verb*
**1** : to move ponderously or clumsily
**2** : to thrust oneself heedlessly or unceremoniously ⟨*barged* into the meeting⟩
**barge·board** \'bärj-ˌbōrd, -ˌbȯrd\ *noun* [origin unknown] (1833)
: an often ornamented board that conceals roof timbers projecting over gables
**barg·ee** \bär-'jē\ *noun* (1666)
*British* : BARGEMAN
**bar·gel·lo** \bär-'je-(ˌ)lō\ *noun* [the *Bargello*, museum in Florence, Italy; from the use of this stitch in the upholstery of 17th century chairs at the Bargello] (circa 1924)
: a needlework stitch that produces a zigzag pattern
**barge·man** \'bärj-mən\ *noun* (14th century)
: the master or a deckhand of a barge
**bar graph** *noun* (1924)
: a graphic means of quantitative comparison by rectangles with lengths proportional to the measure of the data or things being compared — called also *bar chart*
**bar·hop** \'bär-ˌhäp\ *intransitive verb* (1947)
: to visit and drink at a series of bars in the course of an evening
**bar·ite** \'bar-ˌīt, 'ber-\ *noun* [Greek *barytēs* weight, from *barys*] (1868)
: barium sulfate occurring as a mineral
**¹bari·tone** \'bar-ə-ˌtōn\ *noun* [French *baryton* or Italian *baritono*, from Greek *barytonos* deep sounding, from *barys* heavy + *tonos* tone — more at GRIEVE] (1609)
**1** : a male singing voice of medium compass between bass and tenor; *also* : a person having this voice
**2** : a member of a family of instruments having a range between tenor and bass; *especially* : the baritone saxhorn or baritone saxophone
— **bari·ton·al** \ˌbar-ə-'tō-nᵊl\ *adjective*
**²baritone** *adjective* (1729)
: relating to or having the range or part of a baritone
**bar·i·um** \'bar-ē-əm, 'ber-\ *noun* [New Latin, from *bar-*] (1808)
: a silver-white malleable toxic bivalent metallic element of the alkaline-earth group that occurs only in combination — see ELEMENT table
**barium sulfate** *noun* (1903)
: a colorless crystalline insoluble compound $BaSO_4$ that is used as a pigment and extender, as a filler, and as a substance opaque to X rays in medical photography of the alimentary canal
**¹bark** \'bärk\ *verb* [Middle English *berken*, from Old English *beorcan;* akin to Old Norse *berkja* to bark, Lithuanian *burgėti* to growl] (before 12th century)
*intransitive verb*
**1 a** : to make the characteristic short loud cry of a dog **b** : to make a noise resembling a bark
**2** : to speak in a curt loud and usually angry tone : SNAP
*transitive verb*
**1** : to utter in a curt loud usually angry tone
**2** : to advertise by persistent outcry ⟨*barking* their wares⟩
— **bark up the wrong tree** : to proceed under a misapprehension; *also* : to misdirect one's efforts
**²bark** *noun* (before 12th century)

**1 a** : the sound made by a barking dog **b** : a similar sound
**2** : a short sharp peremptory tone of speech or utterance
— **bark·less** \'bär-kləs\ *adjective*
**³bark** *noun* [Middle English, from Old Norse *bark-, bọrkr;* akin to Middle Dutch & Middle Low German *borke* bark] (14th century)
**1** : the tough exterior covering of a woody root or stem; *specifically* : the tissues outside the cambium that include an inner layer especially of secondary phloem and an outer layer of periderm
**2** : CINCHONA 2
— **bark·less** \'bär-kləs\ *adjective*
**⁴bark** *transitive verb* (14th century)
**1** : to treat with an infusion of tanbark
**2 a** : to strip the bark from **b** : to rub off or abrade the skin of
**⁵bark** *noun* [Middle English, from Middle French *barque*, from Old Provençal *barca*, from Late Latin] (15th century)
**1 a** : a small sailing ship **b** : a sailing ship of three or more masts with the aftmost mast fore-and-aft rigged and the others square-rigged
**2** : a craft propelled by sails or oars
**bark beetle** *noun* (1862)
: any of numerous beetles (family Scolytidae) that bore under the bark of trees both as a larva and as an adult
**bar·keep** \'bär-ˌkēp\ *also* **bar·keep·er** \-ˌkē-pər\ *noun* (1712)
: BARTENDER
**bar·ken·tine** \'bär-kən-ˌtēn\ *noun* [⁵*bark* + *-entine*, alteration of *-antine* (as in *brigantine*)] (1693)
: a sailing ship of three or more masts with the foremast square-rigged and the others fore-and-aft rigged
**¹bark·er** \'bär-kər\ *noun* (14th century)
: one that barks; *especially* : a person who advertises by hawking at an entrance to a show
**²barker** *noun* (1611)
: one that removes or prepares bark
**barking deer** *noun* (1880)
: MUNTJAC
**barky** \'bär-kē\ *adjective* **bark·i·er; -est** (1590)
: covered with or resembling bark
**bar·ley** \'bär-lē\ *noun* [Middle English *barly*, from Old English *bærlic* of barley; akin to Old English *bere* barley, Latin *far* spelt] (before 12th century)
: a cereal grass (genus *Hordeum*, especially *H. vulgare*) having the flowers in dense spikes with long awns and three spikelets at each joint of the rachis; *also* : its seed used especially in malt beverages, breakfast foods, and stock feeds
**bar·ley–bree** \-ˌbrē\ *also* **bar·ley–broo** \-ˌbrü\ *noun* [barley + Scots *bree* or *broo* (bree)] (1724)
*chiefly Scottish* : WHISKY; *also* : MALT LIQUOR
**bar·ley·corn** \-ˌkȯrn\ *noun* (1500)
**1** : a grain of barley
**2** : an old unit of length equal to a third of an inch
**bar·low** \'bär-ˌlō\ *noun* [*Barlow*, family of 18th century English knife makers] (1884)
: a sturdy inexpensive jackknife
**barm** \'bärm\ *noun* [Middle English *berme*, from Old English *beorma;* akin to Latin *fermentum* yeast, *fervēre* to boil, Old Irish *berbaid* he boils] (before 12th century)
: yeast formed on fermenting malt liquors
**bar·maid** \'bär-ˌmād\ *noun* (circa 1658)
: a woman who serves liquor at a bar
**bar·man** \-mən\ *noun* (1837)
*chiefly British* : BARTENDER

\ə\ abut \ᵊ\ kitten \ər\ further \a\ ash \ā\ ace
\ä\ mop, mar \au̇\ out \ch\ chin \e\ bet \ē\ easy
\g\ go \i\ hit \ī\ ice \j\ job \ŋ\ sing \ō\ go
\ȯ\ law \ȯi\ boy \th\ thin \t͟h\ the \ü\ loot \u̇\ foot
\y\ yet \zh\ vision *see also* Guide to Pronunciation

**Bar·me·cid·al** \ˌbär-mə-'sī-dᵊl\ *or* **Bar·me·cide** \'bär-mə-ˌsīd\ *adjective* [*Barmecide*, a wealthy Persian, who, in a tale of *The Arabian Nights' Entertainments*, invited a beggar to a feast of imaginary food] (1842)
**:** providing only the illusion of abundance ⟨a *Barmecidal* feast⟩

¹**bar mitz·vah** \ˌbär-'mits-və\ *noun, often* **B&M** *capitalized* [Hebrew *bar miṣwāh*, literally, son of the (divine) law] (1816)
**1 :** a Jewish boy who reaches his 13th birthday and attains the age of religious duty and responsibility
**2 :** the initiatory ceremony recognizing a boy as a bar mitzvah

²**bar mitzvah** *transitive verb* **bar mitz·vahed; bar mitz·vah·ing** (1947)
**:** to administer the ceremony of bar mitzvah to

¹**barmy** \'bär-mē\ *adjective* **barm·i·er; -est** (15th century)
**:** full of froth or ferment

²**barmy** *adjective* **barm·i·er; -est** [alteration of *balmy*] (1892)
*chiefly British* **:** BALMY 2

**barn** \'bärn\ *noun* [Middle English *bern*, from Old English *bereærn*, from *bere* barley + *ærn* house, store] (before 12th century)
**1 a :** a usually large building for the storage of farm products or feed and usually for the housing of farm animals or farm equipment **b :** an unusually large and usually bare building ⟨a great *barn* of a hotel —W. A. White⟩
**2 :** a large building for the housing of a fleet of vehicles (as trolley cars or trucks) ◆
— **barn·like** \-ˌlīk\ *adjective*
— **barny** \'bär-nē\ *adjective*

**Bar·na·bas** \'bär-nə-bəs\ *noun* [Greek, from Aramaic *Barnebhū'āh*]
**:** a companion of the apostle Paul on his first missionary journey

**bar·na·cle** \'bär-ni-kəl\ *noun* [Middle English *barnakille*, alteration of *bernake, bernekke*] (15th century)
**1 :** BARNACLE GOOSE
**2** [from a popular belief that the goose grew from the crustacean] **:** any of numerous marine crustaceans (subclass Cirripedia) with feathery appendages for gathering food that are free-swimming as larvae but permanently fixed (as to rocks, boat hulls, or whales) as adults
— **bar·na·cled** \-kəld\ *adjective*

barnacle 2:
*1* peduncle, *2* cirri

**barnacle goose** *noun* (1768)
**:** a European goose (*Branta leucopsis*) that breeds in the arctic and is larger than the related brant

**barn burner** *noun* (circa 1960)
**:** one that arouses much interest or excitement ⟨the game should be a real *barn burner*⟩

**barn dance** *noun* (1831)
**:** an American social dance originally held in a barn and featuring several dance forms (as square dancing)

**barn lot** *noun* (1724)
*chiefly Southern & Midland* **:** BARNYARD

**barn owl** *noun* (1674)
**:** a widely distributed owl (*Tyto alba*) that has plumage mottled buff brown and gray above and chiefly white below, frequents barns and other buildings, and preys especially on rodents

**barn raising** *noun* (1856)
**:** a gathering for the purpose of erecting a barn — compare ³BEE

**barn·storm** \'bärn-ˌstȯrm\ (1883)
*intransitive verb*
**1 :** to tour through rural districts staging usually theatrical performances

**2 :** to travel from place to place making brief stops (as in a political campaign or a promotional tour)
**3 :** to pilot one's airplane in sight-seeing flights with passengers or in exhibition stunts in an unscheduled course especially in rural districts
*transitive verb*
**:** to travel across while barnstorming
— **barn·storm·er** *noun*

**barn swallow** *noun* (1851)
**:** a swallow (*Hirundo rustica*) that is widespread in the northern hemisphere, has a deeply forked tail, and often nests in or near buildings

¹**barn·yard** \-ˌyärd\ *noun* (14th century)
**:** a usually fenced area adjoining a barn

²**barnyard** *adjective* (1927)
**:** SMUTTY, EARTHY, SCATOLOGICAL ⟨*barnyard* humor⟩

**barnyard grass** *noun* (1843)
**:** a coarse annual panicled grass (*Echinochloa crusgalli*) that has flowers borne on only one side of the raceme and is nearly cosmopolitan as a weed in cultivated ground

**baro-** — see BAR-

**baro·gram** \'bar-ə-ˌgram\ *noun* [International Scientific Vocabulary] (1884)
**:** a barographic tracing

**baro·graph** \-ˌgraf\ *noun* [International Scientific Vocabulary] (circa 1864)
**:** a recording barometer
— **baro·graph·ic** \ˌbar-ə-'gra-fik\ *adjective*

**Ba·ro·lo** \bä-'rō-(ˌ)lō, bə-\ *noun, plural* **-los** [*Barolo*, village in the Piedmont region, Italy] (1875)
**:** a dry red Italian wine

**ba·rom·e·ter** \bə-'rä-mə-tər\ *noun* (circa 1666)
**1 :** an instrument for determining the pressure of the atmosphere and hence for assisting in forecasting weather and for determining altitude
**2 :** one that indicates fluctuations (as in public opinion)
**3 :** STANDARD 4 ⟨a *barometer* to measure high school talent —Jeff Fellenzer⟩
— **baro·met·ric** \ˌbar-ə-'me-trik\ *adjective*
— **baro·met·ri·cal·ly** \-tri-k(ə-)lē\ *adverb*
— **ba·rom·e·try** \bə-'rä-mə-trē\ *noun*

**barometric pressure** *noun* (1827)
**:** the pressure of the atmosphere usually expressed in terms of the height of a column of mercury

**bar·on** \'bar-ən\ *noun* [Middle English, from Old French, of Germanic origin; akin to Old High German *baro* freeman] (13th century)
**1 a :** one of a class of tenants holding his rights and title by military or other honorable service directly from a feudal superior (as a king) **b :** a lord of the realm **:** NOBLE, PEER
**2 a :** a member of the lowest grade of the peerage in Great Britain **b :** a nobleman on the continent of Europe of varying rank **c :** a member of the lowest order of nobility in Japan
**3 :** a joint of meat consisting of two sirloins or loins and legs not cut apart at the backbone ⟨a *baron* of beef⟩
**4 :** a man of great power or influence in some field of activity ⟨cattle *baron*⟩

**bar·on·age** \-ə-nij\ *noun* (13th century)
**:** the whole body of barons or peers **:** NOBILITY 2

**bar·on·ess** \'bar-ə-nəs, -ˌnes, *US also* ˌbar-ə-'nes\ *noun* (15th century)
**1 :** the wife or widow of a baron
**2 :** a woman who holds a baronial title in her own right

**bar·on·et** \'bar-ə-nət, *US also* ˌbar-ə-'net\ *noun* (1614)
**:** the holder of a rank of honor below a baron and above a knight

**bar·on·et·age** \'bar-ə-nə-(ˌ)tij, ˌbar-ə-'ne-tij\ *noun* (1760)
**1 :** BARONETCY

**2 :** the whole body of baronets

**bar·on·et·cy** \'bar-ə-nət-sē, ˌbar-ə-'net-sē\ *noun* (1795)
**:** the rank of a baronet

**ba·rong** \bə-'rȯŋ, -'räŋ\ *noun* [of Austronesian origin; akin to Malay *parang* knife] (1898)
**:** a thick-backed thin-edged knife or sword used by the Moros

**ba·ro·ni·al** \bə-'rō-nē-əl\ *adjective* (1767)
**1 :** of or relating to a baron or the baronage
**2 :** STATELY, AMPLE ⟨a *baronial* room⟩

**bar·ony** \'bar-ə-nē\ *noun, plural* **-on·ies** (14th century)
**1 :** the domain, rank, or dignity of a baron
**2 :** a vast private landholding
**3 :** a field of activity under the sway of an individual or a special group

¹**ba·roque** \bə-'rōk, ba-, -'räk, -'rȯk\ *adjective, often capitalized* [French, from Middle French *barroque* irregularly shaped (of a pearl), from Portuguese *barroco* irregularly shaped pearl] (1765)
**1 :** of, relating to, or having the characteristics of a style of artistic expression prevalent especially in the 17th century that is marked generally by use of complex forms, bold ornamentation, and the juxtaposition of contrasting elements often conveying a sense of drama, movement, and tension
**2 :** characterized by grotesqueness, extravagance, complexity, or flamboyance
**3 :** irregularly shaped — used of gems ⟨a *baroque* pearl⟩
— **ba·roque·ly** *adverb*

²**baroque** *noun, often capitalized* (1877)
**:** the baroque style or the period in which it flourished

**baro·re·cep·tor** \ˌbar-ō-ri-'sep-tər\ *also* **baro·cep·tor** \'bar-ō-ˌsep-tər\ *noun* (1948)
**:** a neural receptor (as of the arterial walls) sensitive to changes in pressure

**ba·rouche** \bə-'rüsh\ *noun* [German *Barutsche*, from Italian *biroccio*, ultimately from Late Latin *birotus* two-wheeled, from Latin *bi-* + *rota* wheel — more at ROLL] (1801)
**:** a four-wheeled carriage with a driver's seat high in front, two double seats inside facing each other, and a folding top over the back seat

**barque** \'bärk\, **bar·quen·tine** \'bär-kən-ˌtēn\ *variant of* BARK, BARKENTINE

**bar·quette** \bär-'ket\ *noun* [French, diminutive of *barque* bark (ship)] (circa 1949)
**:** a small boat-shaped pastry shell

¹**bar·rack** \'bar-ək, -ik\ *noun* [French *baraque* hut, from Catalan *barraca*] (1686)
**1 :** a building or set of buildings used especially for lodging soldiers in garrison
**2 a :** a structure resembling a shed or barn that provides temporary housing **b :** housing characterized by extreme plainness or dreary uniformity — usually used in plural in all senses

◇ WORD HISTORY

**barn** Some English words that are monosyllabic today were obvious compound words to the Anglo-Saxons. Such a word is *barn*, from Old English *berern*, a compound of *bere, bære* "barley" and *ærn* "house, building." Neither *bere* nor *ærn* have left many direct descendants in Modern English, though in Scotland *bear* survived into the 20th century as a word for barley, and *ærn* "house, building" is akin to Old Norse *rann* "house," which figures in English *ransack*. Already in late Old English the compound *berern* was reduced to *bern*, which by the end of the Middle English period had become *barn*. In England, unlike the United States, a barn is still principally a place for storing fodder, so "barley-house" is not too inappropriate. English cows are typically housed and milked in a separate structure, the *cowhouse* or *cowshed*.

²**barrack** *transitive verb* (1701)
: to lodge in barracks
³**barrack** *verb* [origin unknown] (1887)
*transitive verb*
*chiefly British* : to shout at derisively or sarcastically
*intransitive verb*
**1** *chiefly British* : ROOT, CHEER — usually used with *for*
**2** *chiefly British* : JEER, SCOFF
— **bar·rack·er** *noun*
**barracks bag** *noun* (1938)
: a fabric bag for carrying personal equipment; *especially* : DUFFEL BAG
**bar·ra·coon** \ˌbar-ə-ˈkün\ *noun* [Spanish *barracón*, augmentative of *barraca* hut, from Catalan] (1848)
: an enclosure or barracks formerly used for temporary confinement of slaves or convicts — often used in plural
**bar·ra·cou·ta** \ˌbar-ə-ˈkü-tə\ *noun* [modification of American Spanish *barracuda*] (1835)
: a large elongate marine fish (*Thyrsites atun* of the family Gempylidae) used for food
**bar·ra·cu·da** \ˌbar-ə-ˈkü-də\ *noun, plural* **-da** *or* **-das** [American Spanish] (1678)
**1** : any of a genus (*Sphyraena* of the family Sphyraenidae) of elongate predaceous often large fishes of warm seas that include fishes used for food as well as some forms regarded as toxic
**2** : one that uses aggressive, selfish, and sometimes unethical methods to obtain a goal especially in business
¹**bar·rage** \ˈbär-ij\ *noun* [French, from *barrer* to bar, from *barre* bar] (1859)
: a dam placed in a watercourse to increase the depth of water or to divert it into a channel for navigation or irrigation
²**bar·rage** \bə-ˈräzh, -ˈräj\ *noun* [French (*tir de*) *barrage* barrier fire] (1916)
**1** : artillery fire laid on a line close to friendly troops to screen and protect them
**2** : a vigorous or rapid outpouring or projection of many things at once 〈a *barrage* of protests〉
³**bar·rage** \bə-ˈräzh, -ˈräj\ *transitive verb* **barraged; bar·rag·ing** (1918)
: to deliver a barrage against
**barrage balloon** *noun* (circa 1920)
: a small captive balloon used to support wires or nets as protection against air attacks
**bar·ra·mun·di** \ˌbar-ə-ˈmən-dē\ *also* **bar·ra·mun·da** \-də\ *noun* [probably from an Australian aboriginal language of Queensland] (1864)
: any of several Australian fishes (especially *Lates calcarifer* of the family Centropomidae) used for food
**bar·ran·ca** \bə-ˈraŋ-kə\ *or* **bar·ran·co** \-(ˌ)kō\ *noun, plural* **-cas** *or* **-cos** [Spanish] (circa 1691)
**1** : a deep gully or arroyo with steep sides
**2** : a steep bank or bluff
**bar·ra·tor** *also* **bar·ra·ter** \ˈbar-ə-tər\ *noun* (15th century)
: one who engages in barratry
**bar·ra·try** \ˈbar-ə-trē\ *noun, plural* **-tries** [Middle English *barratrie*, from Middle French *baraterie* deception, from *barater* to deceive, exchange] (15th century)
**1** : the purchase or sale of office or preferment in church or state
**2** : an unlawful act or fraudulent breach of duty on the part of a master of a ship or of the mariners to the injury of the owner of the ship or cargo
**3** : the persistent incitement of litigation
**Barr body** \ˈbär-\ *noun* [Murray Llewellyn *Barr* (born 1908) Canadian anatomist] (1963)
: material of the inactivated X chromosome present in each of the female's somatic cells of most mammals used as a test of genetic femaleness (as in a fetus or an athlete) — called also *sex chromatin*

**barre** \ˈbär\ *noun* [French, from Medieval Latin *barra*] (1936)
: BAR 1c
**barred** \ˈbärd\ *adjective* (14th century)
: marked by or divided off by bars; *especially* : having alternate bands of different color 〈*barred* feather〉
**barred owl** *noun* (1811)
: a large American owl (*Strix varia*) with brown eyes and bars of dark brown on the breast
¹**bar·rel** \ˈbar-əl\ *noun* [Middle English *barel*, from Middle French *baril*] (14th century)
**1** : a round bulging vessel of greater length than breadth that is usually made of staves bound with hoops and has flat ends of equal diameter
**2 a** : the amount contained in a barrel; *especially* : the amount (as 31 gallons of fermented beverage or 42 gallons of petroleum) fixed for a certain commodity used as a unit of measure **b** : a great quantity
**3** : a drum or cylindrical part: as **a** : the discharging tube of a gun **b** : the cylindrical metal box enclosing the mainspring of a timepiece **c** : the part of a fountain pen or of a pencil containing the ink or lead **d** : a cylindrical or tapering housing containing the optical components of a photographic-lens system and the iris diaphragm **e** : TUMBLING BARREL **f** : the fuel outlet from the carburetor on a gasoline engine
**4** : the trunk of a quadruped
— **bar·reled** \-əld\ *adjective*
— **on the barrel** : asking for or granting no credit
— **over a barrel** : at a disadvantage : in an awkward position
²**barrel** *verb* **-reled** *or* **-relled; -rel·ing** *or* **-rel·ling** (15th century)
*transitive verb*
: to put or pack in a barrel
*intransitive verb*
: to move at a high speed or without hesitation
**bar·rel·age** \ˈbar-ə-lij\ *noun* (1890)
: amount (as of beer) in barrels
**barrel cactus** *noun* (1881)
: any of a genus (*Ferocactus*) of nearly globular deeply ribbed spiny cacti of Mexico and the adjacent U.S.

barrel cactus

**bar·rel–chest·ed** \ˈbar-əl-ˌches-təd\ *adjective* (1926)
: having a large rounded chest
**barrel cuff** *noun* (1926)
: an unfolded cuff (as on a shirt) usually fastened by a button
**bar·rel·ful** \ˈbar-əl-ˌful\ *noun, plural* **barrel·fuls** \-ˌfulz\ *or* **bar·rels·ful** \-əlz-ˌful\ (14th century)
**1** : as much or as many as a barrel will hold
**2** : a large number or amount
**bar·rel·head** \-ˌhed\ *noun* (1840)
: the flat end of a barrel
— **on the barrelhead** : asking for or granting no credit 〈paid cash *on the barrelhead*〉
**bar·rel·house** \-ˌhaus\ *noun* (1883)
**1** : a cheap drinking and usually dancing establishment
**2** : a strident, uninhibited, and forcefully rhythmic style of jazz or blues
**barrel organ** *noun* (1772)
: an instrument for producing music by the action of a revolving cylinder studded with pegs on a series of valves that admit air from a bellows to a set of pipes
**barrel racing** *noun* (1972)
: a rodeo event for women in which a mounted rider makes a series of sharp turns around three barrels in a cloverleaf pattern

— **barrel race** *noun*
— **barrel racer** *noun*
**barrel roll** *noun* (circa 1920)
: an airplane maneuver in which a complete revolution about the longitudinal axis is made
**barrel vault** *noun* (1849)
: a semicylindrical vault
— **bar·rel–vault·ed** \-ˌvol-təd\ *adjective*
¹**bar·ren** \ˈbar-ən\ *adjective* [Middle English *bareine*, from Old French *baraine*] (13th century)
**1** : not reproducing: as **a** : incapable of producing offspring — used especially of females or matings **b** : not yet or not recently pregnant **c** : habitually failing to fruit
**2** : not productive: as **a** : producing little or no vegetation : DESOLATE 〈*barren* deserts〉 **b** : producing inferior crops 〈*barren* soil〉 **c** : unproductive of results or gain : FRUITLESS 〈a *barren* scheme〉
**3** : DEVOID, LACKING — used with *of* 〈*barren* of excitement〉
**4** : lacking interest, information, or charm
**5** : DULL, UNRESPONSIVE
**synonym** see BARE
— **bar·ren·ly** *adverb*
— **bar·ren·ness** \-ə(n)-nəs\ *noun*
²**barren** *noun* (1651)
**1** *plural* : an extent of usually level land having an inferior growth of trees or little vegetation
**2** : a tract of barren land
**bar·rette** \bä-ˈret, bə-\ *noun* [French, diminutive of *barre* bar] (1901)
: a clip or bar for holding hair in place
¹**bar·ri·cade** \ˈbar-ə-ˌkād, ˌbar-ə-ˈ\ *transitive verb* **-cad·ed; -cad·ing** (1592)
**1** : to block off or stop up with a barricade
**2** : to prevent access to by means of a barricade
²**barricade** *noun* [French, from Middle French *barriquer* to barricade, from *barrique* barrel] (1642)
**1** : an obstruction or rampart thrown up across a way or passage to check the advance of the enemy
**2** : BARRIER 3, OBSTACLE
**3** *plural* : a field of combat or dispute
**bar·ri·ca·do** \ˌbar-ə-ˈkā-(ˌ)dō\ *noun, plural* **-does** [modification of Middle French *barricade*] (1590)
*archaic* : BARRICADE
— **barricado** *transitive verb, archaic*
**bar·ri·er** \ˈbar-ē-ər\ *noun* [Middle English *barrere*, from Middle French *barriere*, from *barre*] (14th century)
**1 a** : something material that blocks or is intended to block passage 〈highway *barriers*〉 〈a *barrier* contraceptive〉 **b** : a natural formation or structure that prevents or hinders movement or action 〈geographic *barriers* to species dissemination〉 〈*barrier* beaches〉 〈drugs that cross the placental *barrier*〉
**2** *plural often capitalized* : a medieval war game in which combatants fight on foot with a fence or railing between them
**3** : something immaterial that impedes or separates : OBSTACLE 〈behavioral *barriers*〉 〈trade *barriers*〉 〈a *barrier* to honest communication〉
**barrier island** *noun* (1943)
: a long broad sandy island lying parallel to a shore that is built up by the action of waves, currents, and winds and that protects the shore from the effects of the ocean
**barrier reef** *noun* (1805)
: a coral reef roughly parallel to a shore and separated from it by a lagoon
**bar·ring** \ˈbär-iŋ\ *preposition* (15th century)
: excluding by exception : EXCEPTING

\ə\ abut \ᵊ\ kitten \ər\ further \a\ ash \ā\ ace \ä\ mop, mar \au\ out \ch\ chin \e\ bet \ē\ easy \g\ go \i\ hit \ī\ ice \j\ job \ŋ\ sing \ō\ go \ȯ\ law \ȯi\ boy \th\ thin \t̲h̲\ the \ü\ loot \ u̇\ foot \y\ yet \zh\ vision *see also* Guide to Pronunciation

**bar·rio** \'bär-ē-ˌō, 'bar-\ *noun, plural* **-ri·os** [Spanish, from Arabic *barrī* of the open country, from *barr* outside, open country] (1841) **1** : a ward, quarter, or district of a city or town in Spanish-speaking countries **2** : a Spanish-speaking quarter or neighborhood in a city or town in the U.S. especially in the Southwest

**bar·ris·ter** \'bar-ə-stər\ *noun* [Middle English *barrester,* from *barre* bar + *-ster* (as in *legister* lawyer)] (15th century) : a counsel admitted to plead at the bar and undertake the public trial of causes in an English superior court — compare SOLICITOR

**bar·room** \'bär-ˌrüm, -ˌrùm\ *noun* (1797) : a room or establishment whose main feature is a bar for the sale of liquor

**¹bar·row** \'bar-(ˌ)ō\ *noun* [Middle English *bergh,* from Old English *beorg;* akin to Old High German *berg* mountain, Sanskrit *bṛhant* high] (before 12th century) **1** : MOUNTAIN, MOUND — used only in the names of hills in England **2** : a large mound of earth or stones over the remains of the dead : TUMULUS

**²barrow** *noun* [Middle English *barow,* from Old English *bearg;* akin to Old High German *barug* barrow] (before 12th century) : a male hog castrated before sexual maturity

**³barrow** *noun* [Middle English *barew,* from Old English *bearwe;* akin to Old English *beran* to carry — more at BEAR] (before 12th century) **1 a** : HANDBARROW **b** : WHEELBARROW **2** : a cart with a shallow box body, two wheels, and shafts for pushing it

**barrow boy** *noun* (1939) *British* : COSTERMONGER

**bar sinister** *noun* (1823) **1** : a heraldic charge held to be a mark of bastardy **2** : the fact or condition of being of illegitimate birth

**bar·tend·er** \'bär-ˌten-dər\ *noun* (1836) : one that serves liquor at a bar

**¹bar·ter** \'bär-tər\ *verb* [Middle English *bartren,* from Middle French *barater* to deceive, exchange] (15th century) *intransitive verb* : to trade by exchanging one commodity for another *transitive verb* : to trade or exchange by or as if by bartering — **bar·ter·er** \-tər-ər\ *noun*

**²barter** *noun* (15th century) **1** : the act or practice of carrying on trade by bartering **2** : the thing given in exchange in bartering

**Bar·tho·lin's gland** \'bär-thə-lənz-, 'bär-tᵊl-ənz-\ *noun* [Kaspar *Bartholin* (died 1738) Danish physician] (1901) : either of two oval racemose glands lying one to each side of the lower part of the vagina and secreting a lubricating mucus — compare COWPER'S GLAND

**bar·ti·zan** \'bär-tə-zən, ˌbär-tə-'zan\ *noun* [alteration of Middle English *bretasinge,* from *bretais* parapet — more at BRATTICE] (1808) : a small structure (as a turret) projecting from a building and serving especially for lookout or defense

**Ba·ruch** \bə-'rük, 'bär-ˌük\ *noun* [Late Latin, from Greek *Barouch,* from Hebrew *Bārūkh*] : a homiletic book included in the Roman Catholic canon of the Old Testament and in the Protestant Apocrypha — see BIBLE table

**bar·ware** \'bär-ˌwar, -ˌwer\ *noun* (1941) : glassware or utensils used in preparing and serving alcoholic beverages

**bary·on** \'bar-ē-ˌän\ *noun* [International Scientific Vocabulary *bary-* (from Greek *barys* heavy) + *²-on* — more at GRIEVE] (1953) : any of a group of elementary particles (as nucleons) that are subject to the strong force and are held to be a combination of three quarks

— **bary·on·ic** \ˌbar-ē-'ä-nik\ *adjective*

**bar·yte** \'bar-ˌīt, 'ber-\ *or* **ba·ry·tes** \bə-'rī-tēz\ *variant of* BARITE

**bary·tone** \'bar-ə-ˌtōn\ *variant of* BARITONE

**bas·al** \'bā-səl, -zəl\ *adjective* (1645) **1 a** : relating to, situated at, or forming the base **b** : arising from the base of a stem ⟨*basal* leaves⟩ **2 a** : of or relating to the foundation, base, or essence : FUNDAMENTAL **b** : of, relating to, or being essential for maintaining the fundamental vital activities of an organism : MINIMAL **c** : used for teaching beginners ⟨*basal* readers⟩ — **ba·sal·ly** *adverb*

**basal body** *noun* (1902) : a minute distinctively staining cell organelle found at the base of a flagellum or cilium and identical to a centriole in structure — called also *basal granule, kinetosome*

**basal cell** *noun* (circa 1903) : one of the innermost cells of the deeper epidermis of the skin

**basal ganglion** *noun* (circa 1889) : any of four deeply placed masses of gray matter (as the amygdala) in each cerebral hemisphere — called also *basal nucleus*

**basal metabolic rate** *noun* (1922) : the rate at which heat is given off by an organism at complete rest

**basal metabolism** *noun* (1913) : the turnover of energy in a fasting and resting organism using energy solely to maintain vital cellular activity, respiration, and circulation as measured by the basal metabolic rate

**ba·salt** \bə-'sòlt, 'bā-ˌ\ *noun* [Latin *basaltes,* manuscript variant of *basanites* touchstone, from Greek *basanitēs (lithos),* from *basanos* touchstone, from Egyptian *bḥnw*] (1601) : a dark gray to black dense to fine-grained igneous rock that consists of basic plagioclase, augite, and usually magnetite — **ba·sal·tic** \bə-'sòl-tik\ *adjective*

**bas·cule** \'bas-(ˌ)kyü(ə)l\ *noun* [French, seesaw] (1678) : an apparatus or structure (as a drawbridge) in which one end is counterbalanced by the other on the principle of the seesaw or by weights

**¹base** \'bās\ *noun, plural* **bas·es** \'bā-səz\ [Middle English, from Middle French, from Latin *basis,* from Greek, step, base, from *bainein* to go — more at COME] (13th century) **1 a** (1) : the lower part of a wall, pier, or column considered as a separate architectural feature (2) : the lower part of a complete architectural design **b** : the bottom of something considered as its support : FOUNDATION **c** (1) : a side or face of a geometrical figure from which an altitude can be constructed; *especially* : one on which the figure stands (2) : the length of a base **d** : that part of a bodily organ by which it is attached to another more central structure of the organism **2 a** : a main ingredient ⟨paint having a latex *base*⟩ **b** : a supporting or carrying ingredient (as of a medicine) **3 a** : the fundamental part of something : GROUNDWORK, BASIS **b** : the economic factors on which in Marxist theory all legal, social, and political relations are formed **4** : the lower part of a heraldic field **5 a** : the starting point or line for an action or undertaking **b** : a baseline in surveying **c** : a center or area of operations: as (1) : the place from which a military force draws supplies (2) : a place where military operations begin (3) : a permanent military installation **d** (1) : a number (as 5 in $5^{6.44}$ or $5^7$) that is raised to a power; *especially* : the number that when raised to a power equal to the logarithm of a

base of a column: *1* upper torus, *2* scotia, *3* lower torus, *4* plinth, *5* shaft, *6* fillets

number yields the number itself ⟨the logarithm of 100 to the *base* 10 is 2 since $10^2 = 100$⟩ (2) : a number equal to the number of units in a given digit's place that for a given system of writing numbers is required to give the numeral 1 in the next higher place ⟨the decimal system uses a *base* of 10⟩; *also* : such a system of writing numbers using an indicated base ⟨convert from *base* 10 to *base* 2⟩ (3) : a number that is multiplied by a rate or of which a percentage or fraction is calculated ⟨to find the interest on $90 at 10% multiply the *base* 90 by .10⟩ **e** : ROOT 6 **6 a** : the starting place or goal in various games **b** : any one of the four stations at the corners of a baseball infield **c** : a point to be considered ⟨his opening remarks touched every *base*⟩ **7 a** : any of various typically water-soluble and bitter tasting compounds that in solution have a pH greater than 7, are capable of reacting with an acid to form a salt, and are molecules or ions able to take up a proton from an acid or able to give up an unshared pair of electrons to an acid **b** : any of the five purine or pyrimidine bases of DNA and RNA that include cytosine, guanine, adenine, thymine, and uracil **8** : a price level at which a security previously actively declining in price resists further price decline **9** : the part of a transformational grammar that consists of rules and a lexicon and generates the deep structures of a language — **based** \'bāst\ *adjective* — **base·less** \'bā-sləs\ *adjective* — **off base 1** : WRONG, MISTAKEN **2** : UNAWARES

**²base** *transitive verb* **based; bas·ing** (1587) **1** : to make, form, or serve as a base for **2** : to find a base or basis for — usually used with *on* or *upon*

**³base** *adjective* [Middle English *bas,* from Middle French, from Medieval Latin *bassus* short, low] (14th century) **1** *archaic* : of little height **2** *obsolete* : low in place or position **3** *obsolete* : BASS **4** *archaic* : BASEBORN **5 a** : resembling a villein : SERVILE ⟨a *base* tenant⟩ **b** : held by villenage ⟨*base* tenure⟩ **6 a** : being of comparatively low value and having relatively inferior properties (as lack of resistance to corrosion) ⟨a *base* metal such as iron⟩ — compare NOBLE **b** : containing a larger than usual proportion of base metals ⟨*base* silver denarii⟩ **7 a** : lacking or indicating the lack of higher qualities of mind or spirit : IGNOBLE **b** : lacking higher values : DEGRADING ⟨a drab *base* way of life⟩ ☆ — **base·ly** *adverb* — **base·ness** *noun*

**base angle** *noun* (circa 1949) : either of the angles of a triangle that have one side in common with the base

**base·ball** \'bās-ˌbòl\ *noun, often attributive* (circa 1815) : a game played with a bat and ball between two teams of nine players each on a large field

☆ **SYNONYMS**
**Base, low, vile** mean deserving of contempt because of the absence of higher values. BASE stresses the ignoble and may suggest cruelty, treachery, greed, or grossness ⟨*base* motives⟩. LOW may connote crafty cunning, vulgarity, or immorality and regularly implies an outraging of one's sense of decency or propriety ⟨refused to listen to such *low* talk⟩. VILE, the strongest of these words, tends to suggest disgusting depravity or filth ⟨a *vile* remark⟩.

having four bases that mark the course a runner must take to score; *also* **:** the ball used in this game

**base·board** \-ˌbȯrd, -ˌbȯrd\ *noun* (1853)
**:** a board situated at or forming the base of something; *specifically* **:** a molding covering the joint of a wall and the adjoining floor

**base-born** \-ˈbȯrn\ *adjective* (1591)
**1 :** MEAN, IGNOBLE
**2 a :** of humble birth **b :** of illegitimate birth

**base burner** *noun* (1874)
**:** a stove in which the fuel is fed from a hopper as the lower layer is consumed

**base exchange** *noun* (circa 1956)
**:** a post exchange at a naval or air force base

**base hit** *noun* (1874)
**:** a hit in baseball that enables the batter to reach base safely without benefit of an error or fielder's choice

**base·line** \ˈbās-ˌlīn\ *noun, often attributive* (1750)
**1 :** a line serving as a basis; *especially* **:** one of known measure or position used (as in surveying or navigation) to calculate or locate something
**2 a :** either of the lines leading from home plate to first base and third base that are extended into the outfield as foul lines **b :** BASE PATH
**3 :** a boundary line at either end of a court (as in tennis or basketball)
**4 :** a set of critical observations or data used for comparison or a control
**5 :** a starting point ⟨the *baseline* of this discussion⟩

**base·lin·er** \ˈbās-ˌlī-nər\ *noun* (circa 1929)
**:** a tennis player who stays on or near the baseline and seldom moves to the net

**base·ment** \ˈbā-smənt\ *noun* [probably from ¹*base*] (1730)
**1 :** the part of a building that is wholly or partly below ground level
**2 :** the ground floor facade or interior in Renaissance architecture
**3 :** the lowest or fundamental part of something; *specifically* **:** the rocks underlying stratified rocks
**4** *chiefly New England* **:** a toilet or washroom especially in a school
— **base·ment·less** \-ləs\ *adjective*

**basement membrane** *noun* (1847)
**:** a thin membranous layer of connective tissue that separates a layer of epithelial cells from the underlying lamina propia

**ba·sen·ji** \bə-ˈsen-jē, -ˈzen-\ *noun* [probably from Lingala *basenji*, plural of *mosenji* native] (1933)
**:** any of a breed of small curly-tailed dogs of African origin that do not bark

**base on balls** *noun* (circa 1891)
**:** an advance to first base awarded a baseball player who during his turn at bat takes four pitches that are balls

**base pair** *noun* (1962)
**:** one of the pairs of chemical bases composed of a purine on one strand of DNA joined by hydrogen bonds to a pyrimidine on the other that hold together the two complementary strands much like the rungs of a ladder and include adenine linked to thymine or sometimes to uracil and guanine linked to cytosine

**base path** *noun* (1935)
**:** the area between the bases of a baseball field used by a base runner

**base pay** *noun* (1920)
**:** a rate or amount of pay for a standard work period, job, or position exclusive of additional payments or allowances

**base runner** *noun* (1867)
**:** a baseball player of the team at bat who is on base or is attempting to reach a base
— **base·run·ning** *noun*

**bases** *plural of* BASE *or of* BASIS

**¹bash** \ˈbash\ *verb* [origin unknown] (1750)

*transitive verb*
**1 :** to strike violently **:** HIT; *also* **:** to injure or damage by striking **:** SMASH — often used with *in*
**2 :** to attack physically or verbally ⟨media *bashing*⟩ ⟨celebrity *bashing*⟩
*intransitive verb*
**:** CRASH
— **bash·er** *noun*

**²bash** *noun* (1805)
**1 :** a forceful blow
**2 :** a festive social gathering **:** PARTY
**3 :** TRY, ATTEMPT ⟨have a *bash* at it⟩

**ba·shaw** \bə-ˈshȯ\ *variant of* PASHA

**bash·ful** \ˈbash-fəl\ *adjective* [obsolete *bash* (to be abashed)] (1548)
**1 :** socially shy or timid **:** DIFFIDENT, SELF-CONSCIOUS
**2 :** resulting from or typical of a bashful nature ⟨a *bashful* smile⟩
*synonym* see SHY
— **bash·ful·ly** \-fə-lē\ *adverb*
— **bash·ful·ness** \-fəl-nəs\ *noun*

**¹ba·sic** \ˈbā-sik *also* -zik\ *adjective* (1842)
**1 :** of, relating to, or forming the base or essence **:** FUNDAMENTAL
**2 :** constituting or serving as the basis or starting point
**3 a :** of, relating to, containing, or having the character of a chemical base **b :** having an alkaline reaction
**4 :** containing relatively little silica ⟨*basic* rocks⟩
**5 :** relating to, made by, used in, or being a process of making steel done in a furnace lined with basic material and under basic slag
— **ba·sic·i·ty** \bā-ˈsi-sə-tē\ *noun*

**²basic** *noun* (1926)
**1 :** something that is basic **:** FUNDAMENTAL ⟨get back to *basics*⟩
**2 :** BASIC TRAINING

**BA·SIC** \ˈbā-sik\ *noun* [*Beginner's All-purpose Symbolic Instruction Code*] (1964)
**:** a simplified language for programming a computer

**ba·si·cal·ly** \ˈbā-si-k(ə-)lē *also* -zi-\ *adverb* (1903)
**1 a :** at a basic level **:** in fundamental disposition or nature ⟨*basically* correct⟩ ⟨*basically*, they are simple people⟩ **b :** for the most part ⟨they *basically* play zone defense⟩
**2 :** in a basic manner **:** SIMPLY ⟨live *basically*⟩

**basic slag** *noun* (1888)
**:** a slag low in silica and high in base-forming oxides that is used in the basic process of steelmaking and that is subsequently useful as a fertilizer

**basic training** *noun* (1943)
**:** the initial period of training of a military recruit

**ba·sid·io·my·cete** \bə-ˌsi-dē-ō-ˈmī-ˌsēt, -ˌmī-ˈsēt\ *noun* [ultimately from New Latin *basidium* + Greek *mykēt-, mykēs* fungus; akin to Greek *myxa* mucus — more at MUCUS] (1899)
**:** any of a large class (Basidiomycetes) or subdivision (Basidiomycotina) of higher fungi having septate hyphae, bearing spores on a basidium, and including rusts, smuts, mushrooms, and puffballs
— **ba·sid·io·my·ce·tous** \-dē-ō-ˌmī-ˈsē-təs\ *adjective*

**ba·sid·io·spore** \bə-ˈsi-dē-ə-ˌspȯr, -ˌspȯr\ *noun* [New Latin *basidium* + English *-o-* + *spore*] (1859)
**:** a spore produced by a basidium

**ba·sid·i·um** \bə-ˈsi-dē-əm\ *noun, plural* **-ia** \-dē-ə\ [New Latin, from Latin *basis*] (1859)
**:** a structure on the fruiting body of a basidiomycete in which karyogamy occurs followed by meiosis to form usually four basidiospores

**ba·si·fy** \ˈbā-sə-ˌfī\ *transitive verb* **-fied; -fy·ing** (circa 1847)
**:** to convert into a base or make alkaline
— **ba·si·fi·ca·tion** \ˌbā-sə-fə-ˈkā-shən\ *noun*

**ba·sil** \ˈba-zəl, ˈbā-, -səl\ *noun* [Middle French *basile*, from Late Latin *basilicum*, from Greek *basilikon*, from neuter of *basilikos*] (15th century)
**1 :** any of several aromatic herbs (genus *Ocimum*) of the mint family; *especially* **:** SWEET BASIL
**2 :** the dried or fresh leaves of a basil used especially as a seasoning

**bas·i·lar** \ˈba-zə-lər, -sə-l\ *also* ˈbā-\ *adjective* [Middle French *basilaire*, irregular from *base*] (1541)
**:** of, relating to, or situated at the base

**basilar membrane** *noun* (1867)
**:** a membrane extending from the bony shelf of the cochlea to the outer wall and supporting the organ of Corti

**Ba·sil·i·an** \bə-ˈzi-lē-ən\ *noun* (1780)
**:** a member of the monastic order founded by Saint Basil in the 4th century in Cappadocia
— **Basilian** *adjective*

**ba·sil·i·ca** \bə-ˈsi-li-kə *also* -ˈzi-\ *noun* [Latin, from Greek *basilikē*, from feminine of *basilikos* royal, from *basileus* king] (1541)
**1 :** an oblong building ending in a semicircular apse used in ancient Rome especially for a court of justice and place of public assembly
**2 :** an early Christian church building consisting of nave and aisles with clerestory and a large high transept from which an apse projects
**3 :** a Roman Catholic church given ceremonial privileges
— **ba·sil·i·can** \-kən\ *adjective*

**bas·i·lisk** \ˈba-sə-ˌlisk, ˈba-zə-\ *noun* [Middle English, from Latin *basiliscus*, from Greek *basiliskos*, from diminutive of *basileus*] (14th century)
**1 :** a legendary reptile with fatal breath and glance
**2 :** any of several crested tropical American lizards (genus *Basiliscus*) related to the iguanas and noted for their ability to run on their hind legs
— **basilisk** *adjective*

**ba·sin** \ˈbā-sⁿn\ *noun* [Middle English, from Old French *bacin*, from Late Latin *bacchinon*] (13th century)
**1 a :** an open usually circular vessel with sloping or curving sides used typically for holding water for washing **b** *chiefly British* **:** a bowl used especially in cooking **c :** the quantity contained in a basin
**2 a :** a dock built in a tidal river or harbor **b :** an enclosed or partly enclosed water area
**3 a :** a large or small depression in the surface of the land or in the ocean floor **b :** the entire tract of country drained by a river and its tributaries **c :** a great depression in the surface of the lithosphere occupied by an ocean
**4 :** a broad area of the earth beneath which the strata dip usually from the sides toward the center
— **ba·sin·al** \-sⁿn-əl\ *adjective*
— **ba·sined** \-sⁿnd\ *adjective*
— **ba·sin·ful** \-ˌfůl\ *noun*

**bas·i·net** \ˌba-sə-ˈnet\ *noun* [Middle English *bacinet*, from Middle French, diminutive of Old French *bacin*] (14th century)
**:** a light often pointed steel helmet

**ba·sip·e·tal** \bā-ˈsi-pə-tⁿl, -ˈzi-\ *adjective* [Latin *basis* + *petere* to go toward — more at FEATHER] (1869)
**:** proceeding from the apex toward the base or from above downward ⟨*basipetal* maturation of an inflorescence⟩
— **ba·sip·e·tal·ly** \-tⁿl-ē\ *adverb*

**ba·sis** \ˈbā-səs\ *noun, plural* **ba·ses** \-ˌsēz\ [Latin — more at BASE] (14th century)

**1 :** the bottom of something considered as its foundation
**2 :** the principal component of something
**3 a :** something on which something else is established or based **b :** an underlying condition or state of affairs ⟨hired on a trial *basis*⟩ ⟨on a first-name *basis*⟩
**4 :** the basic principle
**5 :** a set of linearly independent vectors in a vector space such that any vector in the vector space can be expressed as a linear combination of them with appropriately chosen coefficients

**basis point** *noun* (1967)
**:** one hundredth of one percent in the yield of an investment

**bask** \'bask\ *verb* [Middle English, probably from Old Norse *bathask,* reflexive of *batha* to bathe; akin to Old English *bæth* bath] (14th century)
*intransitive verb*
**1 :** to lie in or expose oneself to a pleasant warmth or atmosphere
**2 :** to take pleasure or derive enjoyment
*transitive verb*
*obsolete* **:** to warm by continued exposure to heat

**bas·ket** \'bas-kit, *British also* 'bäs-\ *noun* [Middle English, probably from (assumed) Old North French *baskot;* akin to Old French *baschoue* wooden vessel; both from Latin *bascauda* kind of basin, of Celtic origin; akin to Middle Irish *basc* necklace — more at FASCIA] (14th century)
**1 a :** a receptacle made of interwoven material (as osiers) **b :** any of various lightweight usually wood containers **c :** the quantity contained in a basket
**2 :** something that resembles a basket especially in shape or use
**3 a :** a net open at the bottom and suspended from a metal ring that constitutes the goal in basketball **b :** a field goal in basketball
**4 a :** an aggregate of values (as of selected currencies) the average of which serves as a monetary standard **b :** a selection of financial instruments (as equities, futures, or options) the values of which reflect market fluctuations
**5 :** a ring around the lower end of a ski pole that keeps the pole from sinking too deep in snow
— **bas·ket·like** \-,līk\ *adjective*

**bas·ket·ball** \-,bȯl\ *noun, often attributive* (1892)
**:** a usually indoor court game between two teams of usually five players each who score by tossing an inflated ball through a raised goal; *also* **:** the ball used in this game

**basket case** *noun* (1919)
**1 :** a person who has all four limbs amputated
**2 :** one that is completely incapacitated, inoperative, or worn out (as from nervous tension)

**bas·ket·ful** \'bas-kit-,fu̇l\ *noun, plural* **bas·ket·fuls** \-,fu̇lz\ *also* **bas·kets·ful** \-kits-,fu̇l\ (14th century)
**:** as much or as many as a basket will hold; *also* **:** a considerable quantity

**basket hilt** *noun* (circa 1550)
**:** a hilt with a basket-shaped guard to protect the hand
— **bas·ket–hilt·ed** \,bas-kit-'hil-təd\ *adjective*

**Basket Maker** *noun* (1897)
**:** any of three stages of an ancient culture of the plateau area of southwestern U.S.; *also* **:** a member of the people who produced the Basket Maker culture

**basket–of–gold** *noun* (1930)
**:** a European perennial herb (*Aurinia saxatilis* synonym *Alyssum saxatile*) widely cultivated for its grayish foliage and yellow flowers

**bas·ket·ry** \'bas-ki-trē\ *noun, plural* **-ries** (1851)
**1 :** BASKETWORK
**2 :** the art or craft of making baskets or objects woven like baskets

**basket star** *noun* (circa 1923)
**:** any of various brittle stars (suborder Euryalina) with slender complexly branched interlacing arms

**basket weave** *noun* (circa 1915)
**:** a textile weave resembling the checkered pattern of a plaited basket; *also* **:** something resembling this weave

**bas·ket·work** \'bas-kit-,wərk\ *noun* (1769)
**:** objects produced by basketry

**bask·ing shark** \'bas-kiŋ-\ *noun* (circa 1769)
**:** a large plankton-feeding shark (*Cetorhinus maximus*) that has an oil-rich liver and sometimes attains a length of 40 feet (12 meters)

**bas·ma·ti rice** \,bäz-'mä-tē- *also* ,baz-\ *noun* [Hindi *bāsmatī* kind of rice, literally, something fragrant] (1845)
**:** a cultivated aromatic long-grain rice of South Asian origin — called also *basmati*

**bas mitz·vah** \bäs-'mits-və\ *noun, often B&M capitalized* [Hebrew *bath miṣwāh,* literally, daughter of the (divine) law] (1952)
**1 :** a Jewish girl who at about 13 years of age assumes religious responsibilities
**2 :** the initiatory ceremony recognizing a girl as a bas mitzvah

**ba·so·phil** \'bā-sə-,fil, -zə-\ *or* **ba·so·phile** \-,fīl\ *noun* (circa 1890)
**:** a basophilic substance or structure; *especially* **:** a leukocyte containing basophilic granules that is similar in function to a mast cell

**ba·so·phil·ia** \,bā-sə-'fi-lē-ə, -zə-\ *noun* [New Latin] (1905)
**1 :** tendency to stain with basic dyes
**2 :** an abnormal condition in which some tissue element has increased basophilia

**ba·so·phil·ic** \-'fi-lik\ *adjective* [International Scientific Vocabulary *base* + *-o-* + *-philic*] (circa 1894)
**:** staining readily with basic stains

**Ba·so·tho** \bä-'sō-,tō, -'sü-,tü\ *noun plural* (1895)
**:** a Bantu-speaking people of Lesotho

**Basque** \'bask\ *noun* [French, from Middle French, from Latin *Vasco*] (1835)
**1 :** a member of a people inhabiting the western Pyrenees on the Bay of Biscay
**2 :** the language of the Basques of unknown relationship
**3** *not capitalized* **:** a tight-fitting bodice for women
— **Basque** *adjective*

**bas–re·lief** \,bä-ri-'lēf, 'bä-ri-,\ *noun* [French, from *bas* low + *relief* raised work] (1667)
**:** sculptural relief in which the projection from the surrounding surface is slight and no part of the modeled form is undercut; *also* **:** sculpture executed in bas-relief

bas-relief

**¹bass** \'bas\ *noun, plural* **bass** *or* **bass·es** [Middle English *base,* *bærs,* from Old English *bærs;* akin to Old High German *bersich* perch] (before 12th century)
**:** any of numerous edible spiny-finned marine or freshwater fishes (especially families Centrarchidae, Serranidae, and Percichthyidae)

**²bass** \'bās\ *adjective* [Middle English *bas* base] (15th century)
**1 :** deep or grave in tone
**2 a :** of low pitch **b :** relating to or having the range or part of a bass

**³bass** \'bās\ *noun* (15th century)
**1 a :** the lowest voice part in a 4-part chorus **b :** the lower half of the whole vocal or instrumental tonal range — compare TREBLE **c :** the lowest adult male singing voice; *also* **:** a person having this voice **d :** a member of a family of instruments having the lowest range; *especially* **:** DOUBLE BASS
**2 :** a deep or grave tone **:** a low-pitched sound

**⁴bass** \'bas\ *noun* [alteration of *bast*] (1691)
**1 :** BASSWOOD 1
**2 :** a coarse tough fiber from palms

**bass clef** *noun* (circa 1771)
**1 :** a clef placing the F below middle C on the fourth line of the staff
**2 :** the bass staff

**bass drum** *noun* (1804)
**:** a large drum having two heads and giving a booming sound of low indefinite pitch — see DRUM illustration

**bas·set hound** \'ba-sət-\ *noun* [French *basset,* from Middle French, from *basset* short, from *bas* low — more at BASE] (1883)
**:** any of an old breed of short-legged hunting dogs of French origin having very long ears and crooked front legs — called also *bas·sett*

basset hound

**bass fiddle** *noun* (1951)
**:** DOUBLE BASS

**bass horn** *noun* (circa 1846)
**:** an obsolete wind instrument shaped like a bassoon but with a cup-shaped mouthpiece

**bas·si·net** \,ba-sə-'net\ *noun* [probably modification of French *barcelonnette,* diminutive of *berceau* cradle] (1854)
**1 :** a baby's basketlike bed (as of wickerwork or plastic) often with a hood over one end
**2 :** a perambulator that resembles a bassinet

**bass·ist** \'bā-sist\ *noun* (circa 1909)
**:** a person who plays an acoustic or electric bass

**bas·so** \'ba-(,)sō, 'bä-\ *noun, plural* **bassos** *or* **bas·si** \'bä-,sē\ [Italian, from Medieval Latin *bassus,* from *bassus* short, low] (circa 1724)
**1 :** a bass singer; *especially* **:** an operatic bass
**2 :** a low deep voice

**bas·soon** \bə-'sün, ba-\ *noun* [French *basson,* from Italian *bassone,* from *basso*] (1724)
**:** a double-reed woodwind instrument having a long U-shaped conical tube connected to the mouthpiece by a thin metal tube and a usual range two octaves lower than that of the oboe
— **bas·soon·ist** \-'sü-nist\ *noun*

**bas·so pro·fun·do** \,ba-(,)sō-prə-'fən-(,)dō, ,bä-, -'fün-\ *noun, plural* **basso profundos** [Italian, literally, deep bass] (1860)

bassoon

**:** a deep heavy bass voice with an exceptionally low range; *also* **:** a person having this voice

**bas·so–re·lie·vo** *also* **bas·so–ri·lie·vo** \,ba-(,)sō-ri-'lē-(,)vō, ,bä-(,)sō-rēl-'yä-(,)vō\ *noun* [Italian *bassorilievo,* from *basso* low + *rilievo* relief] (1644)
**:** BAS-RELIEF

**bass viol** *noun* (1590)
**1 :** VIOLA DA GAMBA
**2 :** DOUBLE BASS

**bass·wood** \'bas-,wu̇d\ *noun* (1670)
**1 :** any of several New World lindens; *especially* **:** LINDEN 1b
**2 :** the straight-grained white wood of a basswood

**bast** \'bast\ *noun* [Middle English, from Old English *bæst;* akin to Old High German & Old Norse *bast* bast] (before 12th century)
**1 :** PHLOEM
**2 :** BAST FIBER

**¹bas·tard** \'bas-tərd\ *noun* [Middle English, from Old French, probably of Germanic origin; akin to Old Frisian *bost* marriage, Old English *bindan* to bind] (14th century)
**1** : an illegitimate child
**2** : something that is spurious, irregular, inferior, or of questionable origin
**3 a** : an offensive or disagreeable person — used as a generalized term of abuse **b** : MAN, FELLOW
— **bas·tard·ly** *adjective*
**²bastard** *adjective* (14th century)
**1** : ILLEGITIMATE
**2** : of mixed or ill-conceived origin 〈known for coining *bastard* words〉
**3** : of abnormal shape or irregular size
**4** : of a kind similar to but inferior to or less typical than some standard 〈*bastard* measles〉
**5** : lacking genuineness or authority : FALSE
**bas·tard·ise** *British variant of* BASTARDIZE
**bas·tard·ize** \'bas-tər-,dīz\ *transitive verb* **-ized; -iz·ing** (1587)
**1** : to reduce from a higher to a lower state or condition : DEBASE
**2** : to declare or prove to be a bastard
**3** : to modify especially by introducing discordant or disparate elements
— **bas·tard·i·za·tion** \,bas-tər-də-'zā-shən\ *noun*
**bastard wing** *noun* (1772)
: ALULA
**bas·tardy** \'bas-tər-dē\ *noun, plural* **-tard·ies** (15th century)
**1** : the quality or state of being a bastard : ILLEGITIMACY
**2** : the begetting of an illegitimate child
**¹baste** \'bāst\ *transitive verb* **bast·ed; bast·ing** [Middle English, from Middle French *bastir*, of Germanic origin; akin to Old High German *besten* to patch, Old English *bǣst* bast] (15th century)
: to sew with long loose stitches in order to hold something in place temporarily
— **bas·ter** *noun*
**²baste** *transitive verb* **bast·ed; bast·ing** [Middle English *baisten*] (15th century)
: to moisten (as meat) at intervals with a liquid (as melted butter, fat, or pan drippings) especially during cooking
— **bast·er** *noun*
**³baste** *transitive verb* **bast·ed; bast·ing** [probably from Old Norse *beysta;* akin to Old English *bēatan* to beat] (1533)
**1** : to beat severely or soundly : THRASH
**2** : to scold vigorously : BERATE
**bast fiber** *noun* (circa 1885)
: a strong woody fiber obtained chiefly from the phloem of plants and used especially in cordage, matting, and fabrics
**bas·tille** *noun* \ba-'stē(ə)l\ [French *bastille*, from the *Bastille,* fortress in Paris, from Middle French *bastille,* modification of Old Provençal *bastida* fortified town, from *bastir* to build, of Germanic origin; akin to Old High German *besten* to patch] (1741)
: PRISON, JAIL
**Bastille Day** *noun* (1920)
: July 14 observed in France as a national holiday in commemoration of the fall of the Bastille in 1789
**¹bas·ti·na·do** \,bas-tə-'nā-(,)dō, -'nä-\ *or* **bas·ti·nade** \,bas-tə-'nād, -'näd\ *noun, plural* **-na·does** *or* **-nades** [Spanish *bastonada,* from *bastón* stick, from Late Latin *bastum*] (1572)
**1** : a blow with a stick or cudgel
**2 a** : a beating especially with a stick **b** : a punishment consisting of beating the soles of the feet with a stick
**3** : STICK, CUDGEL
**²bastinado** *transitive verb* **-doed; -do·ing** (1599)
: to subject to repeated blows
**¹bast·ing** \'bā-stiŋ\ *noun* (15th century)
**1** : the action of a sewer who bastes

**2 a** : the thread used in basting **b** : the stitching made by basting
**²basting** *noun* (1530)
**1** : the action of one that bastes food
**2** : the liquid used in basting
**³basting** *noun* (1590)
: a severe beating
**bas·tion** \'bas-chən\ *noun* [Middle French, from Old Italian *bastione,* augmentative of *bastia* fortress, derivative from dialect form of *bastire* to build, of Germanic origin; akin to Old High German *besten* to patch] (1562)
**1** : a projecting part of a fortification
**2** : a fortified area or position
**3** : something that is considered a stronghold : BULWARK
— **bas·tioned** \-chənd\ *adjective*
**Ba·su·to** \bə-'sü-(,)tō\ *noun, plural* **Basuto** *or* **Basutos** (1835)
: a member of the Basotho people
**¹bat** \'bat\ *noun* [Middle English, from Old English *batt*] (before 12th century)
**1** : a stout solid stick : CLUB
**2** : a sharp blow : STROKE
**3 a** : a usually wooden implement used for hitting the ball in various games **b** : a paddle used in various games (as table tennis) **c** : the short whip used by a jockey
**4 a** : BATSMAN **b** : a turn at batting — usually used in the phrase *at bat*
**5** : BATT
**6** *British* : rate of speed : GAIT
**7** : BINGE
— **off one's own bat** *chiefly British* : through one's own efforts
— **off the bat** : without delay : IMMEDIATELY
**²bat** *verb* **bat·ted; bat·ting** (15th century)
*transitive verb*
**1** : to strike or hit with or as if with a bat
**2 a** : to advance (a base runner) by batting **b** : to have a batting average of
**3** : to discuss at length : consider in detail
*intransitive verb*
**1 a** : to strike or hit a ball with a bat **b** : to take one's turn at bat
**2** : to wander aimlessly
**³bat** *noun* [alteration of Middle English *bakke,* probably of Scandinavian origin; akin to Old Swedish *nattbakka* bat] (1580)
: any of a widely distributed order (Chiroptera) of nocturnal usually frugivorous or insectivorous flying mammals that have wings formed from four elongated digits of the forelimb covered by a cutaneous membrane and that have adequate visual capabilities but often rely on echolocation
**⁴bat** *transitive verb* **bat·ted; bat·ting** [probably alteration of ²*bate*] (circa 1838)
: to wink especially in surprise or emotion 〈never *batted* an eye〉; *also* : FLUTTER 〈*batted* his eyelashes〉
**bat·boy** \'bat-,bȯi\ *noun* (circa 1925)
: a boy employed to look after the equipment (as bats) of a baseball team
**¹batch** \'bach\ *noun* [Middle English *bache;* akin to Old English *bacan* to bake] (15th century)
**1** : the quantity baked at one time : BAKING
**2 a** : the quantity of material prepared or required for one operation; *specifically* : a mixture of raw materials ready for fusion into glass **b** : the quantity produced at one operation **c** : a group of jobs (as programs) which are submitted for processing on a computer and whose results are obtained at a later time 〈*batch* processing〉 — compare TIME-SHARING
**3** : a quantity (as of persons or things) considered as a group
**²batch** *transitive verb* (1876)
: to bring together or process as a batch
— **batch·er** *noun*
**³batch** *variant of* BACH
**¹bate** \'bāt\ *verb* **bat·ed; bat·ing** [Middle English, short for *abaten* to abate] (14th century)

*transitive verb*
**1** : to reduce the force or intensity of : RESTRAIN 〈with *bated* breath〉
**2** : to take away : DEDUCT
**3** *archaic* : to lower especially in amount or estimation
**4** *archaic* : BLUNT
*intransitive verb*
*obsolete* : DIMINISH, DECREASE
**²bate** *intransitive verb* **bat·ed; bat·ing** [Middle English, from Middle French *batre* to beat, from Latin *battuere*] (14th century)
*of a falcon or hawk* : to attempt to fly off something (as a gauntlet) in fear
**bat–eared fox** \'bat-,ird-\ *noun* (1946)
: a large-eared yellowish gray fox (*Otocyon megalotis*) that inhabits arid unforested areas of eastern and southern Africa
**ba·teau** \ba-'tō\ *noun, plural* **ba·teaux** \-'tō(z)\ [Canadian French, from French, from Old French *batel,* from Old English *bāt* boat — more at BOAT] (1711)
: any of various small craft; *especially* : a flat-bottomed boat with raked bow and stern and flaring sides
**Bates·ian** \'bāt-sē-ən\ *adjective* [Henry Walter *Bates* (died 1892) English naturalist] (1896)
: characterized by or being mimicry involving resemblance of an innocuous species to another that is protected from predators by repellent qualities (as unpalatability) 〈*Batesian* mimic〉
**bat·fish** \'bat-,fish\ *noun* (1873)
: any of several fishes with winglike processes; *especially* : any of a family (Ogcocephalidae) of flattened pediculate fishes (as a common West Indian form *Ogcocephalus vespertillo*)
**bat·fowl** \-,faul\ *intransitive verb* (15th century)
: to catch birds at night by blinding them with a light and knocking them down with a stick or netting them

batfish

**¹bath** \'bath, 'bȧth\ *noun, plural* **baths** \'bathz, 'baths, 'bȧthz, 'bȧths\ [Middle English, from Old English *bæth;* akin to Old High German *bad* bath, Old High German *bāen* to warm] (before 12th century)
**1** : a washing or soaking (as in water or steam) of all or part of the body
**2 a** : water used for bathing **b** (1) : a contained liquid for a special purpose (2) : a receptacle holding the liquid **c** (1) : a medium for regulating the temperature of something placed in or on it (2) : a vessel containing this medium
**3 a** : BATHROOM **b** : a building containing an apartment or a series of rooms designed for bathing **c** : SPA — usually used in plural **d** *British* : SWIMMING POOL — often used in plural
**4 a** : the quality or state of being covered with a liquid **b** : FLOOD 3
**5** : BATHTUB
**6** : a financial setback : LOSS 〈took a *bath* in the market〉
**²bath** (15th century)
*transitive verb*
*British* : to give a bath to
*intransitive verb*
*British* : to take a bath
**³bath** *noun* [Hebrew] (14th century)

: an ancient Hebrew liquid measure corresponding to the ephah of dry measure

**bath chair** \'bath-, 'bȧth-\ *noun, often B capitalized* [*Bath*, England] (1823)
: a hooded and sometimes glassed wheeled chair used especially by invalids; *broadly*
: WHEELCHAIR

¹**bathe** \'bāth\ *verb* **bathed; bath·ing** [Middle English, from Old English *bathian;* akin to Old English *bæth* bath] (before 12th century)
*transitive verb*
**1 :** MOISTEN, WET
**2 :** to wash in a liquid (as water)
**3 :** to apply water or a liquid medicament to
**4 :** to flow along the edge of **:** LAVE
**5 :** to suffuse with or as if with light
*intransitive verb*
**1 :** to take a bath
**2 :** to go swimming
**3 :** to become immersed or absorbed
— **bath·er** \'bā-thər\ *noun*

²**bathe** *noun* (1831)
**1** *British* **:** ¹BATH 1
**2** *British* **:** SWIM, DIP

**ba·thet·ic** \bə-'the-tik\ *adjective* [*bathos* + *-etic* (as in *pathetic*)] (circa 1864)
: characterized by bathos
— **ba·thet·i·cal·ly** \-ti-k(ə-)lē\ *adverb*

**bath·house** \'bath-,haus, 'bȧth-\ *noun* (1705)
**1 :** a building equipped for bathing
**2 :** a building containing dressing rooms for bathers

**bathing beauty** *noun* (1920)
: a woman in a bathing suit who is a contestant in a beauty contest

**bathing suit** *noun* (1873)
: SWIMSUIT

**bath mat** *noun* (1895)
: a usually washable mat used in a bathroom

**bath·o·lith** \'ba-thə-,lith\ *noun* [Greek *bathos* depth + International Scientific Vocabulary *-lith*] (circa 1900)
: a great mass of intruded igneous rock that for the most part stopped in its rise a considerable distance below the surface
— **bath·o·lith·ic** \,ba-thə-'li-thik\ *adjective*

**ba·thos** \'bā-,thäs\ *noun* [Greek, literally, depth] (1727)
**1 a :** the sudden appearance of the commonplace in otherwise elevated matter or style **b**
**:** ANTICLIMAX
**2 :** exceptional commonplaceness **:** TRITENESS
**3 :** insincere or overdone pathos **:** SENTIMENTALISM

**bath·robe** \'bath-,rōb, 'bȧth-\ *noun* (1902)
: a loose often absorbent robe worn before and after bathing or as a dressing gown

**bath·room** \-,rüm, -,rum\ *noun* (1780)
**1 :** a room containing a bathtub or shower and usually a sink and toilet
**2 :** LAVATORY 2

**bath salts** *noun plural* (1907)
: a usually colored crystalline compound for perfuming and softening bathwater

**bath·tub** \-,təb\ *noun* (1869)
: a usually fixed tub for bathing

**bathtub gin** *noun* (1930)
: a homemade spirit concocted from raw alcohol, water, essences, and essential oils

**bath·wa·ter** \'bath-,wȯ-tər, 'bȧth-, -,wä-tər\ *noun* (14th century)
: water for a bath

**bathy-** *combining form* [International Scientific Vocabulary, from Greek, from *bathys* deep]
**1 :** deep **:** depth ⟨*bathy*al⟩
**2 :** deep-sea ⟨*bathy*sphere⟩

**bathy·al** \'ba-thē-əl\ *adjective* (1921)
: of or relating to the ocean depths or floor usually from 600 to 6000 feet (180 to 1800 meters)

**ba·thym·e·try** \bə-'thi-mə-trē\ *noun, plural* **-tries** [International Scientific Vocabulary] (circa 1859)
: the measurement of water depth at various places in a body of water; *also* **:** the information derived from such measurements

— **bathy·met·ric** \,ba-thi-'me-trik\ *also*
**bathy·met·ri·cal** \-tri-kəl\ *adjective*
— **bathy·met·ri·cal·ly** \-tri-k(ə-)lē\ *adverb*

**bathy·pe·lag·ic** \,ba-thi-pə-'la-jik\ *adjective* (circa 1900)
: of, relating to, or living in the ocean depths especially between 2000 and 12,000 feet (600 and 3600 meters)

**bathy·scaphe** \'ba-thi-,skaf, -,skāf\ *or* **bathy·scaph** \-,skaf\ *noun* [International Scientific Vocabulary *bathy-* + Greek *skaphē* light boat] (1947)
: a navigable submersible for deep-sea exploration having a spherical watertight cabin attached to its underside

**bathy·sphere** \-,sfir\ *noun* (1930)
: a strongly built steel diving sphere for deep-sea observation

**bathy·ther·mo·graph** \-'thər-mə-,graf\ *noun* (1938)
: an instrument designed to record water temperature as a function of depth

**ba·tik** \bə-'tēk, 'ba-tik\ *noun* [Javanese *batik*] (1880)
**1 :** a fabric printed by an Indonesian method of hand-printing textiles by coating with wax the parts not to be dyed; *also* **:** the method itself
**2 :** a design executed in batik

**bat·ing** \'bā-tiŋ\ *preposition* (1647)
: with the exception of **:** EXCEPTING

**ba·tiste** \bə-'tēst, ba-\ *noun* [French] (1697)
: a fine soft sheer fabric of plain weave made of various fibers

**bat·man** \'bat-mən\ *noun* [French *bât* packsaddle] (1755)
: an orderly of a British military officer

**bat mitz·vah** \bät-'mits-və\ *often B&M capitalized, variant of* BAS MITZVAH

**ba·ton** \bə-'tän, ba-, -'tōⁿ *also* 'ba-tᵊn\ *noun* [French *bâton*, from Old French *baston*, from Late Latin *bastum* stick] (1520)
**1 :** CUDGEL, TRUNCHEON; *specifically* **:** BILLY CLUB
**2 :** a staff borne as a symbol of office
**3 :** a narrow heraldic bend
**4 :** a slender rod with which a leader directs a band or orchestra
**5 :** a hollow cylinder carried by each member of a relay team and passed to the succeeding runner
**6 :** a hollow metal rod with a weighted bulb at one or both ends that is flourished or twirled by a drum major or drum majorette

**bat out** *transitive verb* (1941)
: to compose especially in a casual, careless, or hurried manner

**ba·tra·chi·an** \bə-'trā-kē-ən\ *noun* [ultimately from Greek *batrachos* frog] (circa 1828)
: AMPHIBIAN 1; *especially* **:** FROG, TOAD
— **batrachian** *adjective*

**bats** \'bats\ *adjective* (1919)
: BATTY 2

**bats·man** \'bat-smən\ *noun* (1756)
: a batter especially in cricket

**batt** \'bat\ *noun* (1871)
: BATTING 2; *also* **:** an often square piece of batting

**bat·tai·lous** \'ba-tᵊl-əs\ *adjective* [Middle English *battaillous*, from Middle French *battaillous*, from *bataille* battle] (14th century)
*archaic* **:** ready for battle **:** WARLIKE

**bat·ta·lia** \bə-'tāl-yə, -'tal-\ *noun* [Italian *battaglia*] (1569)
**1** *archaic* **:** order of battle
**2** *obsolete* **:** a large body of men in battle array

**bat·tal·ion** \bə-'tal-yən\ *noun* [Middle French *bataillon*, from Old Italian *battaglione*, augmentative of *battaglia* company of soldiers, battle, from Late Latin *battalia* combat — more at BATTLE] (1579)
**1 :** a considerable body of troops organized to act together **:** ARMY

**2 :** a military unit composed of a headquarters and two or more companies, batteries, or similar units
**3 :** a large group

**bat·teau** *variant of* BATEAU

**bat·te·ment** \,bat-'mäⁿ\ *noun* [French, from *battre* to beat, from Latin *battuere*] (1830)
: a ballet movement in which the foot is extended in any direction usually followed by a beat against the supporting foot

¹**bat·ten** \'ba-tᵊn\ *verb* **bat·tened; bat·ten·ing** \'bat-niŋ, 'ba-tᵊn-iŋ\ [probably from Old Norse *batna* to improve; akin to Old English *betera* better] (1591)
*intransitive verb*
**1 a :** to grow fat **b :** to feed gluttonously
**2 :** to grow prosperous especially at the expense of another — usually used with *on*
*transitive verb*
**:** FATTEN

²**batten** *noun* [alteration of Middle English *batent, bataunt* finished board, from Middle French *batant*, from present participle of *battre*] (1658)
**1 a** *British* **:** a piece of lumber used especially for flooring **b :** a thin narrow strip of lumber used especially to seal or reinforce a joint
**2 :** a strip, bar, or support resembling or used similarly to a batten

³**batten** *verb* **bat·tened; bat·ten·ing** \'bat-niŋ, 'ba-tᵊn-iŋ\ (1663)
*transitive verb*
**1 :** to furnish with battens
**2 :** to fasten with or as if with battens — often used with *down*
*intransitive verb*
**:** to make one secure by or as if by battens ⟨*battening* down for the hurricane⟩

¹**bat·ter** \'ba-tər\ *verb* [Middle English *bateren*, probably frequentative of *batten* to bat, from *bat*] (14th century)
*transitive verb*
**1 a :** to beat with successive blows so as to bruise, shatter, or demolish **b :** BOMBARD
**2 :** to subject to strong, overwhelming, or repeated attack
**3 :** to wear or damage by hard usage or blows ⟨a *battered* old hat⟩
*intransitive verb*
**:** to strike heavily and repeatedly **:** BEAT
**synonym** see MAIM

²**batter** *noun* [Middle English *bater*, probably from *bateren*] (14th century)
**1 a :** a mixture consisting chiefly of flour, egg, and milk or water and being thin enough to pour or drop from a spoon **b :** a mixture (as of flour and egg) used as a coating for food (as chicken) that is to be fried
**2 :** an instance of battering

³**batter** *transitive verb* (1973)
: to coat (food) with batter for frying

⁴**batter** *noun* [origin unknown] (1743)
: a receding upward slope of the outer face of a structure

⁵**batter** *transitive verb* (circa 1882)
: to give a receding upward slope to (as a wall)

⁶**batter** *noun* (1773)
: one that bats; *especially* **:** the player whose turn it is to bat

**battered child syndrome** *noun* (1962)
: the complex of physical injuries sustained by a grossly abused child

**bat·te·rie** \,ba-tə-'rē\ *noun* [French, literally, beating — more at BATTERY] (1712)
: a ballet movement consisting of beating together the feet or calves of the legs during a leap

**battering ram** *noun* (1593)
**1 :** a military siege engine consisting of a large wooden beam with a head of iron used in ancient times to beat down the walls of a besieged place
**2 :** a heavy metal bar with handles used (as by firefighters) to batter down doors and walls

**bat·tery** \'ba-t(ə-)rē\ *noun, plural* **-ter·ies** [Middle French *batterie*, from Old French, from *battre* to beat, from Latin *battuere*] (1531)
**1 a :** the act of battering or beating **b :** an offensive touching or use of force on a person without the person's consent — compare AS- SAULT 2a
**2 a :** a grouping of artillery pieces for tactical purposes **b :** the guns of a warship
**3 :** an artillery unit in the army equivalent to a company
**4 a :** a combination of apparatus for producing a single electrical effect **b :** a group of two or more cells connected together to furnish electric current; *also :* a single cell that furnishes electric current ⟨a flashlight *battery*⟩
**5 a :** a number of similar articles, items, or devices arranged, connected, or used together **:** SET, SERIES ⟨a *battery* of tests⟩ **b :** a usually impressive or imposing group **:** ARRAY
**6 :** the position of readiness of a gun for firing
**7 :** the pitcher and catcher of a baseball team
**bat·ting** \'ba-tiŋ\ *noun* (1773)
**1 a :** the action of one who bats **b :** the use of or ability with a bat
**2 :** layers or sheets of raw cotton or wool or of synthetic fibrous material used for lining quilts or for stuffing or packaging; *also :* a blanket of thermal insulation (as fiberglass)
**batting average** *noun* (1867)
**1 :** a ratio (as a rate per thousand) of base hits to official times at bat for a baseball player
**2 :** a record of achievement or accomplishment
**¹bat·tle** \'ba-tᵊl\ *noun, often attributive* [Middle English *batel*, from Old French *bataille* battle, fortifying tower, battalion, from Late Latin *battalia* combat, alteration of *battualia* fencing exercises, from Latin *battuere* to beat] (13th century)
**1** *archaic :* BATTALION
**2 :** a combat between two persons
**3 :** a general encounter between armies, ships of war, or aircraft
**4 :** an extended contest, struggle, or controversy
**²battle** *verb* **bat·tled; bat·tling** \'bat-liŋ, 'ba-tᵊl-iŋ\ (14th century)
*intransitive verb*
**1 :** to engage in battle **:** FIGHT
**2 :** to contend with full strength, vigor, skill, or resources **:** STRUGGLE
*transitive verb*
**1 :** to fight against
**2 :** to force (as one's way) by battling
— **bat·tler** \-lər, 'ba-tᵊl-ər\ *noun*
**³battle** *transitive verb* **bat·tled; bat·tling** [Middle English *batailen*, from Middle French *bataillier* to fortify, from Old French, from *bataille*] (14th century)
*archaic :* to fortify with battlements
**bat·tle–ax** \'ba-tᵊl-,aks\ *noun* (14th century)
**1 :** a broadax formerly used as a weapon of war
**2 :** a sharp-tongued domineering usually older woman
**battle cruiser** *noun* (1911)
**:** a large heavily armed warship that is lighter, faster, and more maneuverable than a battleship
**battle cry** *noun* (1814)
**:** WAR CRY
**battle fatigue** *noun* (1945)
**:** COMBAT FATIGUE
— **bat·tle–fa·tigued** *adjective*
**bat·tle·field** \'ba-tᵊl-,fēld\ *noun* (1812)
**1 :** a place where a battle is fought
**2 :** an area of conflict
**bat·tle·front** \-,frənt\ *noun* (1914)
**:** the military sector in which actual combat takes place
**bat·tle·ground** \-,graúnd\ *noun* (1815)
**:** BATTLEFIELD
**battle line** (1814)
**1 :** a line along which a battle is fought

**2 :** a line defining the positions of opposing groups in a conflict or controversy — usually used in plural ⟨*battle lines* were drawn over economic policies⟩
**bat·tle·ment** \'ba-tᵊl-mənt\ *noun* [Middle English *batelment*, from Middle French *bataille*] (14th century)
**:** a parapet with open spaces that surmounts a wall and is used for defense or decoration
— **bat·tle·ment·ed** \-,men-təd\ *adjective*

battlement:
1 crenellations,
2 merlons,
3 machicolations

**battle royal** *noun, plural* **battles royal** *or* **battle royals** (1672)
**1 a :** a fight participated in by more than two combatants; *especially :* one in which the last man in the ring or on his feet is declared the winner **b :** a violent struggle
**2 :** a heated dispute
**bat·tle·ship** \'ba-tᵊl-,ship\ *noun* [short for *line-of-battle ship*] (1794)
**:** a warship of the largest and most heavily armed and armored class
**bat·tle·wag·on** \-,wa-gən\ *noun* (circa 1927)
**:** BATTLESHIP
**bat·tu** \ba-'tü, -'tyü\ *adjective* [French, from past participle of *battre* to beat] (1947)
*of a ballet movement :* performed with a striking together of the legs
**bat·tue** \ba-'tü, -'tyü\ *noun* [French, from *battre* to beat] (1816)
**:** the beating of woods and bushes to flush game; *also :* a hunt in which this procedure is used
**bat·ty** \'ba-tē\ *adjective* **bat·ti·er; -est** (1590)
**1 :** of, relating to, or resembling a bat
**2 :** mentally unstable **:** CRAZY
— **bat·ti·ness** *noun*
**bau·ble** \'bȯ-bəl, 'bä-\ *noun* [Middle English *babel*, from Middle French] (14th century)
**1 :** TRINKET
**2 :** a fool's scepter
**3 :** TRIFLE
**Bau·cis** \'bȯ-səs\ *noun* [Latin, from Greek *Baukis*]
**:** the wife of Philemon
**baud** \'bȯd, 'bäd, *British* 'bōd\ *noun, plural* **baud** *also* **bauds** [*baud* (telegraphic transmission speed unit), from J. M. E. *Baudot* (died 1903) French inventor] (1931)
**:** a variable unit of data transmission speed (as one bit per second)
**Bau·haus** \'baú-,haús\ *adjective* [German *Bauhaus,* literally, architecture house, school founded by Walter Gropius] (1923)
**:** of, relating to, or influenced by a school of design noted especially for a program that synthesized technology, craftsmanship, and design aesthetics
**baulk** *chiefly British variant of* BALK
**Bau·mé** \bō-'mā\ *adjective* [Antoine *Baumé* (1877)]
**:** being, calibrated in accordance with, or according to either of two arbitrary hydrometer scales for liquids lighter than water or for liquids heavier than water that indicate specific gravity in degrees
**baum marten** \'baúm-,mär-tᵊn\ *noun* [part translation of German *Baummarder,* from *Baum* tree + *Marder* marten] (1909)
**:** the pelt or fur of the European marten (*Martes martes*)
**baux·ite** \'bȯk-,sīt, 'bäk-\ *noun* [French *bauxite,* from Les *Baux,* near Arles, France] (1861)
**:** an impure mixture of earthy hydrous aluminum oxides and hydroxides that is the principal source of aluminum
— **baux·it·ic** \bȯk-'si-tik, bäk-\ *adjective*
**Ba·var·i·an** \bə-'ver-ē-ən, -'var-\ *noun* (1638)
**1 :** a native or inhabitant of Bavaria

**2 :** the High German dialect of southern Bavaria and Austria
— **Bavarian** *adjective*
**Bavarian cream** *noun* (circa 1879)
**:** flavored custard or pureed fruit combined with gelatin and whipped cream
**baw·bee** \'bȯ-(,)bē, bȯ-'\ *noun* [probably from Alexander *Orrok,* laird of *Sillebawbe* (flourished 1538) Scottish master of the mint] (1542)
**1 :** any of various Scottish coins of small value
**2 :** an English halfpenny
**baw·cock** \'bȯ-,käk\ *noun* [French *beau coq,* from *beau* fine + *coq* fellow, cock] (1599)
*archaic :* a fine fellow
**bawd** \'bȯd\ *noun* [Middle English *bawde*] (14th century)
**1** *obsolete :* PANDER
**2 a :** one who keeps a house of prostitution **:** MADAM **b :** PROSTITUTE
**bawd·ry** \'bȯ-drē\ *noun* [Middle English *bawderie,* from *bawde*] (15th century)
**1** *obsolete :* UNCHASTITY
**2 :** suggestive, coarse, or obscene language
**¹bawdy** \'bȯ-dē\ *adjective* **bawd·i·er; -est** [*bawd*] (1513)
**1 :** OBSCENE, LEWD
**2 :** boisterously or humorously indecent
— **bawd·i·ly** \'bȯ-dᵊl-ē\ *adverb*
— **bawd·i·ness** \'bȯ-dē-nəs\ *noun*
**²bawdy** *noun* [probably from ¹*bawdy*] (1656)
**:** BAWDRY 2
**bawdy house** *noun* (1552)
**:** BORDELLO
**¹bawl** \'bȯl\ *verb* [Middle English, to bark, probably of Scandinavian origin; akin to Icelandic *baula* to low] (1570)
*intransitive verb*
**1 :** to cry out loudly and unrestrainedly **:** YELL, BELLOW
**2 :** to cry loudly **:** WAIL
*transitive verb*
**:** to cry out at the top of one's voice
— **bawl·er** *noun*
**²bawl** *noun* (1792)
**:** a loud prolonged cry **:** OUTCRY
**bawl out** *transitive verb* (1905)
**:** to reprimand loudly or severely
**¹bay** \'bā\ *adjective* [Middle English, from Middle French *bai,* from Latin *badius;* akin to Old Irish *buide* yellow] (14th century)
**:** reddish brown ⟨a *bay* mare⟩
**²bay** *noun* (1535)
**1 :** a bay-colored animal; *specifically :* a horse with a bay-colored body and black mane, tail, and points — compare CHESTNUT 4, ¹SORREL 1
**2 :** a reddish brown
**³bay** *noun* [Middle English, from Middle French *baee* opening, from Old French, from feminine of *baé,* past participle of *baer* to gape, yawn — more at ABEYANCE] (14th century)
**1 :** a principal compartment of the walls, roof, or other part of a building or of the whole building
**2 :** a main division of a structure
**3 :** any of various compartments or sections used for a special purpose (as in an airplane, spacecraft, or service station) ⟨bomb *bay*⟩ ⟨cargo *bay*⟩
**4 :** BAY WINDOW 1
**5 :** a support or housing for electronic equipment
**⁴bay** *verb* [Middle English *baien, abaien,* from Old French *abaiier,* of imitative origin] (14th century)
*intransitive verb*
**1 :** to bark with prolonged tones
**2 :** to cry out **:** SHOUT

\ə\ abut \ᵊ\ kitten \ər\ **further** \a\ **ash** \ā\ **ace**
\ä\ **mop, mar** \aú\ **out** \ch\ **chin** \e\ **bet** \ē\ **easy**
\g\ **go** \i\ **hit** \ī\ **ice** \j\ **job** \ŋ\ **sing** \ō\ **go**
\ȯ\ **law** \ȯi\ **boy** \th\ **thin** \th̲\ **the** \ü\ **loot** \ú\ **foot**
\y\ **yet** \zh\ **vision** *see also* Guide to Pronunciation

*transitive verb*
**1 :** to bark at
**2 :** to bring to bay
**3 :** to pursue with barking
**4 :** to utter in deep prolonged tones
⁵**bay** *noun* (14th century)
**1 :** a baying of dogs
**2 :** the position of one unable to retreat and forced to face danger ⟨brought his quarry to *bay*⟩
**3 :** the position of one checked ⟨police kept the rioters at *bay*⟩
⁶**bay** *noun, often attributive* [Middle English *baye,* from Middle French *baie*] (14th century)
**1 :** an inlet of the sea or other body of water usually smaller than a gulf
**2 :** a small body of water set off from the main body
**3 :** any of various terrestrial formations resembling a bay of the sea
⁷**bay** *noun* [Middle English, berry, from Middle French *baie,* from Latin *baca*] (15th century)
**1 a :** the European laurel (*Laurus nobilis*) **b :** any of several shrubs or trees (as of the genera *Magnolia, Pimenta,* and *Gordonia*) resembling the laurel
**2 a :** a garland or crown especially of laurel given as a prize for victory or excellence **b :** HONOR, FAME — usually used in plural
**ba·ya·dere** \'bī-ə-ˌdir, -ˌder\ *noun* [French *bayadère* professional female dancer in India] (1856)
**:** a fabric with horizontal stripes in strongly contrasted colors
**bay·ber·ry** \'bā-ˌber-ē\ *noun* (1687)
**1 :** any of several wax myrtles; *especially* **:** a hardy shrub (*Myrica pensylvanica*) of coastal eastern North America bearing dense clusters of small berries covered with grayish white wax
**2 :** the fruit of a bayberry
**Bayes·ian** \'bā-zē-ən, -zhən\ *adjective* (1961)
**:** being, relating to, or concerned with a theory (as of decision making or statistical inference) involving the application of Bayes' theorem and the use of probabilities based on prior knowledge and accumulated experience ⟨*Bayesian* probability models⟩
**Bayes' theorem** \'bāz-\ *noun* [Thomas *Bayes* (died 1761) English mathematician] (1939)
**:** a theorem about conditional probabilities: the probability that an event A occurs given that another event B has already occurred is equal to the probability that the event B occurs given that A has already occurred multiplied by the probability of occurrence of event A and divided by the probability of occurrence of event B
**bay leaf** *noun* (15th century)
**:** the dried leaf of the European laurel (*Laurus nobilis*) used in cooking
**bay·man** \'bā-mən, -ˌman\ *noun* (1641)
**:** a person and especially a fisherman who lives or works on or about a bay
¹**bay·o·net** \'bā-ə-nət, -ˌnet, ˌbā-ə-'net\ *noun* [French *baïonnette,* from *Bayonne,* France] (1704)
**:** a steel blade attached at the muzzle end of a shoulder arm (as a rifle) and used in hand-to-hand combat
²**bayonet** *verb* **-net·ed** *also* **-net·ted; -net·ing** *also* **-net·ting** (1858)
*transitive verb*
**1 :** to stab with a bayonet
**2 :** to compel or drive by or as if by the bayonet
*intransitive verb*
**:** to use a bayonet
**bay·ou** \'bī-(ˌ)ü, -(ˌ)ō\ *noun* [Louisiana French, from Choctaw *bayuk*] (1763)
**1 :** a creek, secondary watercourse, or minor river that is tributary to another body of water
**2 :** any of various usually marshy or sluggish bodies of water
**bay rum** *noun* (1840)

**:** a fragrant cosmetic and medicinal liquid distilled from the leaves of a West Indian bay tree (*Pimenta racemosa*) or usually prepared from essential oils, alcohol, and water
**Bay Stat·er** \'bā-ˌstā-tər\ *noun* (1845)
**:** a native or resident of Massachusetts — used as a nickname
**bay window** *noun* (15th century)
**1 :** a window or series of windows forming a bay in a room and projecting outward from the wall
**2 :** POTBELLY 1
**ba·zaar** \bə-'zär\ *noun* [Persian *bāzār*] (1612)
**1 :** an oriental market consisting of rows of shops or stalls selling miscellaneous goods
**2 a :** a place for the sale of goods **b :** DEPARTMENT STORE
**3 :** a fair for the sale of articles especially for charitable purposes
**ba·zoo·ka** \bə-'zü-kə\ *noun* [*bazooka* (a crude musical instrument made of pipes and a funnel)] (1943)
**:** a light portable antitank weapon consisting of an open-breech smoothbore firing tube that launches an armor-piercing rocket and is fired from the shoulder
**BB** \'bē-(ˌ)bē\ *noun* (1874)
**1 :** a shot pellet 0.18 inch in diameter for use in a shotgun cartridge
**2 :** a shot pellet 0.175 inch in diameter for use in an air gun
**BCD** \ˌbē-(ˌ)sē-'dē\ *noun* [binary coded decimal] (circa 1962)
**:** a computer code for representing alphanumeric information
**B cell** *noun* [bone-marrow-derived *cell*] (1968)
**:** any of the lymphocytes that have antibody molecules on the surface and comprise the antibody-secreting plasma cells when mature — called also *B lymphocyte; compare* T CELL
**BCG vaccine** \ˌbē-(ˌ)sē-'jē-\ *noun* [Bacillus Calmette-Guérin (an attenuated strain of tubercle bacilli), from Albert *Calmette* (died 1933) and Camille *Guérin* (died 1961) French bacteriologists] (1927)
**:** a vaccine prepared from a living attenuated strain of tubercle bacilli and used to vaccinate human beings against tuberculosis — called also *BCG*
**B complex** *noun* (1934)
**:** VITAMIN B COMPLEX
**BC soil** \'bē-'sē-\ *noun* (circa 1938)
**:** a soil whose profile has only B horizons and C horizons
**bdel·li·um** \'de-lē-əm\ *noun* [Middle English, from Latin, from Greek *bdellion*] (14th century)
**:** a gum resin similar to myrrh obtained from various trees (genus *Commiphora*) of the East Indies and Africa
**be** \'bē\ *verb, past 1st & 3d singular* **was** \'wəz, 'wäz\; *2d singular* **were** \'wər\; *plural* **were;** *past subjunctive* **were;** *past participle* **been** \'bin, *chiefly British* 'bēn\; *present participle* **be·ing** \'bē-(i)ŋ\; *present 1st singular* **am** \əm, 'am\; *2d singular* **are** \'är, ər\; *3d singular* **is** \'iz, əz\ *plural* **are;** *present subjunctive* **be** [Middle English, from Old English *bēon;* akin to Old High German *bim* am, Latin *fui* I have been, *futurus* about to be, *fieri* to become, be done, Greek *phynai* to be born, be by nature, *phyein* to produce] (before 12th century)
*intransitive verb*
**1 a :** to equal in meaning **:** have the same connotation as **:** SYMBOLIZE ⟨God *is* love⟩ ⟨January *is* the first month⟩ ⟨let *x be* 10⟩ **b :** to have identity with ⟨the first person I met *was* my brother⟩ **c :** to constitute the same class as **d :** to have a specified qualification or characterization ⟨the leaves *are* green⟩ **e :** to belong to the class of ⟨the fish *is* a trout⟩ — used regularly in senses 1a through 1e as the copula of simple predication
**2 a :** to have an objective existence **:** have reality or actuality **:** LIVE ⟨I think, therefore I *am*⟩

⟨once upon a time there *was* a knight⟩ **b :** to have, maintain, or occupy a place, situation, or position ⟨the book *is* on the table⟩ **c :** to remain unmolested, undisturbed, or uninterrupted — used only in infinitive form ⟨let him *be*⟩ **d :** to take place **:** OCCUR ⟨the concert *was* last night⟩ **e :** to come or go ⟨has already *been* and gone⟩ ⟨has never *been* to the circus⟩ **f** *archaic* **:** BELONG, BEFALL
*verbal auxiliary*
**1** — used with the past participle of transitive verbs as a passive-voice auxiliary ⟨the money *was* found⟩ ⟨the house is *being* built⟩
**2** — used as the auxiliary of the present participle in progressive tenses expressing continuous action ⟨he *is* reading⟩ ⟨I have *been* sleeping⟩
**3** — used with the past participle of some intransitive verbs as an auxiliary forming archaic perfect tenses ⟨Christ *is* risen from the dead —1 Corinthians 15:20 (Douay Version)⟩
**4** — used with the infinitive with *to* to express futurity, arrangement in advance, or obligation ⟨I *am* to interview him today⟩ ⟨she *was* to become famous⟩
**be-** *prefix* [Middle English, from Old English *bi-, be-;* akin to Old English *bī* by, near — more at BY]
**1 :** on **:** around **:** over ⟨*be*daub⟩ ⟨*be*smear⟩
**2 :** to a great or greater degree **:** thoroughly ⟨*be*fuddle⟩ ⟨*be*rate⟩
**3 :** excessively **:** ostentatiously — in intensive verbs formed from simple verbs ⟨*be*deck⟩ and in adjectives based on adjectives ending in -ed ⟨*be*ribboned⟩
**4 :** about **:** to **:** at **:** upon **:** against **:** across ⟨*be*stride⟩ ⟨*be*speak⟩
**5 :** make **:** cause to be **:** treat as ⟨*be*little⟩ ⟨*be*fool⟩ ⟨*be*friend⟩
**6 :** call or dub especially excessively ⟨*be*doctor⟩
**7 :** affect, afflict, treat, provide, or cover with especially excessively ⟨*be*devil⟩ ⟨*be*fog⟩
¹**beach** \'bēch\ *noun* [origin unknown] (1535)
**1 :** shore pebbles **:** SHINGLE
**2 a :** a shore of a body of water covered by sand, gravel, or larger rock fragments **b :** a seashore area
²**beach** *transitive verb* (1840)
**1 :** to run or drive ashore
**2 :** to strand on or as if on a beach
**beach ball** *noun* (1940)
**:** a large inflated ball for use at the beach
**beach-boy** \-ˌbȯi\ *noun* (1941)
**:** a male beach attendant (as at a club or hotel)
**beach buggy** *noun* (1943)
**:** DUNE BUGGY
**beach·comb·er** \'bēch-ˌkō-mər\ *noun* (1840)
**1 :** a white man living as a drifter or loafer especially on the islands of the South Pacific
**2 :** a person who searches along a shore (as for salable refuse or for seashells)
— **beach·comb** \-ˌkōm\ *verb*
**beach flea** *noun* (1843)
**:** any of numerous amphipod crustaceans (family Talitridae) living on ocean beaches and leaping like fleas
**beach·front** \'bēch-ˌfrənt\ *noun* (1921)
**:** a strip of land that fronts a beach
**beach·go·er** \-ˌgō-ər\ *noun* (1954)
**:** a person who frequently goes to the beach
**beach grass** *noun* (1681)
**:** any of several tough strongly rooted grasses that grow on exposed sandy shores; *especially* **:** any of a genus (*Ammophila*) of rhizomatous perennials widely planted to bind sandy slopes
**beach·head** \'bēch-ˌhed\ *noun* (1940)
**1 :** an area on a hostile shore occupied to secure further landing of troops and supplies
**2 :** FOOTHOLD
**beach pea** *noun* (1802)
**:** a wild pea (*Lathyrus japonicus* synonym *L. maritimus*) having tough roots and purple flowers that is found along sandy shores
**beach plum** *noun* (1784)

: a shrubby plum (*Prunus maritima*) having white flowers and growing along the northeastern coast of North America; *also* : its edible usually dark purple fruit that is used especially in preserves

**beach·side** \'bēch-,sīd\ *adjective* (1952)
: located at a beach

**beach·wear** \-,war, -,wer\ *noun* (1928)
: clothing for wear at a beach

**beachy** \'bē-chē\ *adjective* (1597)
: covered with pebbles or shingle

¹**bea·con** \'bē-kən\ *noun* [Middle English *beken*, from Old English *bēacen* sign; akin to Old High German *bouhhan* sign] (14th century)
**1** : a signal fire commonly on a hill, tower, or pole
**2 a** : a lighthouse or other signal for guidance **b** : a radio transmitter emitting signals for guidance of aircraft
**3** : a source of light or inspiration

²**beacon** (1821)
*transitive verb*
: to furnish with a beacon
*intransitive verb*
: to shine as a beacon

¹**bead** \'bēd\ *noun* [Middle English *bede* prayer, prayer bead, from Old English *bed*, *gebed* prayer; akin to Old English *biddan* to entreat, pray — more at BID] (before 12th century)
**1 a** *obsolete* : PRAYER — usually used in plural **b** *plural* : a series of prayers and meditations made with a rosary
**2** : a small piece of material pierced for threading on a string or wire (as in a rosary)
**3** *plural* **a** : ROSARY **b** : a necklace of beads or pearls
**4** : a small ball-shaped body: as **a** : a drop of sweat or blood **b** : a bubble formed in or on a beverage **c** : a small metal knob on a firearm used as a front sight **d** : a blob or a line of weld metal
**5** : a projecting rim, band, or molding ◆

²**bead** (1577)
*transitive verb*
**1** : to furnish, adorn, or cover with beads or beading
**2** : to string together like beads
*intransitive verb*
: to form into a bead

**bead·ing** *noun* (1845)
**1** : a beaded molding
**2** : material or a part or a piece consisting of a bead
**3** : an openwork trimming
**4** : BEADWORK

**bea·dle** \'bē-d°l\ *noun* [Middle English *bedel* messenger, from Old French *bydel*; akin to Old High German *butil* bailiff, Old English *bēodan* to command — more at BID] (1581)
: a minor parish official whose duties include ushering and preserving order at services and sometimes civil functions

**bead·roll** \'bēd-,rōl\ *noun* [from the reading in church of a list of names of persons for whom prayers are to be said] (1529)
**1** : a list of names : CATALOG
**2** : ROSARY

**beads·man** \'bēdz-mən\ *noun* (13th century)
*archaic* : one who prays for another

**bead·work** \'bēd-,wərk\ *noun* (1751)
**1** : ornamental work in beads
**2** : joinery beading

**beady** \'bē-dē\ *adjective* **bead·i·er; -est** (1826)
**1 a** : resembling beads **b** : small, round, and shiny with interest or greed ⟨*beady* eyes⟩
**2** : marked by bubbles or beads ⟨a *beady* liquor⟩
**— bead·i·ly** \'bē-də-lē\ *adverb*

**bea·gle** \'bē-gəl\ *noun* [Middle English *begle*] (15th century)
: any of a breed of small short-legged smooth-coated often black, white, and tan hounds

**beak** \'bēk\ *noun* [Middle English *bec*, from Old French, from Latin *beccus*, of Gaulish origin] (13th century)
**1 a** : the bill of a bird; *especially* : a strong short broad bill **b**
(1) : the elongated sucking mouth of some insects (as the true bugs) (2) : any of various rigid projecting mouth structures (as of a turtle) **c** : the human nose
**2** : a pointed structure or formation: **a** : a metal-pointed beam projecting from the bow especially of an ancient galley for piercing an enemy ship **b** : the spout of a vessel **c** : a continuous slight architectural projection ending in an arris — see MOLDING illustration **d** : a process suggesting the beak of a bird
**3** *chiefly British* **a** : MAGISTRATE **b** : HEADMASTER
**— beaked** \'bēkt\ *adjective*
**— beaky** \'bē-kē\ *adjective*

**beagle**

**beaked whale** *noun* (1877)
: any of a widely distributed family (Ziphiidae) of medium-sized toothed whales that have an elongated snout and a small dorsal fin

**beak·er** \'bē-kər\ *noun* [Middle English *biker*, from Old Norse *bikarr*, probably from Old Saxon *bikeri*, from Medieval Latin *bicarium*] (14th century)
**1** : a large drinking cup that has a wide mouth and is sometimes supported on a standard
**2** : a deep widemouthed thin-walled vessel usually with a lip for pouring that is used especially in science laboratories

**be-all and end-all** \'bē-,ò-lən-'(d)en-,dòl\ *noun* (1605)
**1** : prime cause : essential element
**2** : TOTALITY 1

¹**beam** \'bēm\ *noun* [Middle English *beem*, from Old English *bēam* tree, beam; akin to Old High German *boum* tree] (before 12th century)
**1 a** : a long piece of heavy often squared timber suitable for use in construction **b** : a wood or metal cylinder in a loom on which the warp is wound **c** : the part of a plow to which handles, standard, and coulter are attached **d** : the bar of a balance from which scales hang **e** : one of the principal horizontal supporting members (as of a building or ship) ⟨a steel *beam* supporting a floor⟩; *also* : BOOM, SPAR ⟨the *beam* of a crane⟩ **f** : the extreme width of a ship at the widest part **g** : an oscillating lever on a central axis receiving motion at one end from an engine piston rod and transmitting it at the other
**2 a** : a ray or shaft of light **b** : a collection of nearly parallel rays (as X rays) or a stream of particles (as electrons) **c** : a constant directional radio signal transmitted for the guidance of pilots; *also* : the course indicated by a radio beam
**3** : the main stem of a deer's antler
**4** : the width of the buttocks
**— on the beam 1** : following a guiding beam **2** : proceeding or operating correctly

²**beam** (15th century)
*transitive verb*
**1** : to emit in beams or as a beam
**2** : to support with beams
**3 a** : to aim and transmit (a broadcast) by directional antennas or by satellite **b** : to direct to a particular audience
*intransitive verb*
**1** : to send out beams of light
**2** : to smile with joy

**beam–ends** \'bēm-'en(d)z\ *noun plural* (1773)
: the ends of a ship's beams
**— on her beam–ends** : inclined so much on one side that the beams approach a vertical position

**beam·ish** \'bē-mish\ *adjective* (1870)
: beaming and bright with optimism, promise, or achievement
**— beam·ish·ly** *adverb*

**beam splitter** *noun* (1935)
: a mirror or prism or a combination of the two that is used to divide a beam of radiation into two or more parts

**beamy** \'bē-mē\ *adjective* (14th century)
**1** : emitting beams of light : RADIANT
**2** : broad in the beam ⟨a *beamy* cargo ship⟩

¹**bean** \'bēn\ *noun* [Middle English *bene*, from Old English *bēan*; akin to Old High German *bōna* bean] (before 12th century)
**1 a** : BROAD BEAN **b** : the seed of any of various erect or climbing leguminous plants (especially genera *Phaseolus*, *Dolichos*, and *Vigna*) other than the broad bean **c** : a plant bearing beans **d** : an immature bean pod used as a vegetable
**2 a** : a valueless item **b** *plural* : the least amount ⟨didn't know *beans* about it⟩
**3** : any of various seeds or fruits that resemble beans or bean pods; *also* : a plant producing these
**4 a** *plural* : EXUBERANCE — used in the phrase *full of beans* **b** *plural* : NONSENSE, BUNKUM — used in the phrase *full of beans*
**5** : HEAD, BRAIN
**6** : a protuberance on the upper mandible of waterfowl — see DUCK illustration

²**bean** *transitive verb* (1910)
: to strike (a person) on the head with an object

**bean·bag** \'bēn-,bag\ *noun* (1871)
**1** : a cloth bag partially filled typically with dried beans and used as a toy
**2** : any of various pellet-filled bags used as furniture (as a chair) or household articles (as an ashtray base)

**bean·ball** \-,bòl\ *noun* (circa 1905)
: a pitch thrown at a batter's head

**bean counter** *noun* (1975)
: a person involved in corporate financial decisions and especially one reluctant to spend money

**bean curd** *noun* (circa 1889)
: a soft vegetable cheese prepared by treating soybean milk with coagulants (as magnesium chloride or dilute acids) — called also *tofu*

**bean·ery** \'bēn-rē, 'bē-nə-\ *noun, plural* **-er·ies** (1887)
: RESTAURANT

**bean·ie** \'bē-nē\ *noun* (1940)
: a small round tight-fitting skullcap worn especially by schoolboys and college freshmen

◇ **WORD HISTORY**
**bead** Middle English *bede* developed from Old English *gebed*. Originally the word meant "a prayer." The number and order of a series of prayers were kept track of with the aid of what is today called a rosary, a string of variously sized small round balls. Because each of these balls stands for a particular prayer, the name *bede*, Modern English *bead*, was transferred to the balls themselves. Today *bead* is used to refer to any small piece of material pierced for threading on a string or wire. The sense is also extended to refer to any small, round object, such as a drop of sweat.

\ə\ abut \°\ kitten \ər\ further \a\ ash \ā\ ace
\ä\ mop, mar \aú\ out \ch\ chin \e\ bet \ē\ easy
\g\ go \i\ hit \ī\ ice \j\ job \ŋ\ sing \ō\ go
\ò\ law \òi\ boy \th\ thin \th\ the \ü\ loot \ú\ foot
\y\ yet \zh\ vision *see also* Guide to Pronunciation

**beano** \'bē-(,)nō\ *noun, plural* **beanos** [by alteration] (1935)
**:** BINGO
**bean·pole** \'bēn-,pō(ə)l\ *noun* (1798)
**1 :** a pole up which bean vines may climb
**2 :** a tall thin person
**bean sprouts** *noun plural* (1921)
**:** the sprouts of bean seeds especially of the mung bean used as a vegetable
¹**bear** \'bar, 'ber\ *noun, plural* **bears** *often attributive* [Middle English *bere,* from Old English *bera;* akin to Old English *brūn* brown — more at BROWN] (before 12th century)
**1** *or plural* **bear :** any of a family (Ursidae of the order Carnivora) of large heavy mammals of America and Eurasia that have long shaggy hair, rudimentary tails, and plantigrade feet and feed largely on fruit and insects as well as on flesh
**2 :** a surly, uncouth, or shambling person
**3** [probably from the proverb about *selling the bearskin before catching the bear*] **:** one that sells securities or commodities in expectation of a price decline — compare BULL
— **bear·like** \-,līk\ *adjective*
²**bear** *verb* **bore** \'bōr, 'bȯr\; **borne** \'bōrn, 'bȯrn\ *also* **born** \'bȯrn\; **bear·ing** [Middle English *beren* to carry, bring forth, from Old English *beran;* akin to Old High German *beran* to carry, Latin *ferre,* Greek *pherein*] (before 12th century)
*transitive verb*
**1 a :** to move while holding up and supporting **b :** to be equipped or furnished with **c :** BEHAVE, CONDUCT ⟨*bearing* himself well⟩ **d :** to have as a feature or characteristic **e :** to give as testimony ⟨*bear* false witness⟩ **f :** to have as an identification ⟨*bore* the name of John⟩ **g :** to hold in the mind **h :** DISSEMINATE **i :** LEAD, ESCORT **j :** RENDER, GIVE
**2 a :** to give birth to **b :** to produce as yield **c** (1) **:** to permit growth of (2) **:** CONTAIN ⟨oil-*bearing* shale⟩
**3 a :** to support the weight of **:** SUSTAIN **b :** to put up with especially without giving way ⟨couldn't *bear* the pain⟩ **c :** to call for as suitable or essential ⟨it *bears* watching⟩ **d :** to hold above, on top, or aloft **e :** to admit of **:** ALLOW **f :** ASSUME, ACCEPT
**4 :** THRUST, PRESS
*intransitive verb*
**1 :** to produce fruit **:** YIELD
**2 a :** to force one's way **b :** to extend in a direction indicated or implied **c :** to be situated **:** LIE **d :** to become directed **e :** to go or incline in an indicated direction
**3 :** to support a weight or strain — often used with *up*
**4 a :** to exert influence or force **b :** APPLY, PERTAIN ☆
— **bear a hand :** to join in and help out
— **bear arms 1 :** to carry or possess arms
**2 :** to serve as a soldier
— **bear fruit :** to come to satisfying fruition, production, or development
— **bear in mind :** to think of especially as a warning **:** REMEMBER
— **bear with :** to be indulgent, patient, or forbearing
**bear·able** \'bar-ə-bəl, 'ber-\ *adjective* (circa 1550)
**:** capable of being borne
— **bear·abil·i·ty** \,bar-ə-'bi-lə-tē, ,ber-\ *noun*
— **bear·ably** \-blē\ *adverb*
**bear·bait·ing** \'bar-,bā-tiŋ, 'ber-\ *noun* (14th century)
**:** the practice of setting dogs on a chained bear
**bear·ber·ry** \-,ber-ē\ *noun* (1625)
**:** a trailing evergreen plant (*Arctostaphylos uva-ursi*) of the heath family with astringent foliage and red berries
¹**beard** \'bird\ *noun* [Middle English *berd,* from Old English *beard;* akin to Old High German *bart* beard, Latin *barba*] (before 12th century)

**1 :** the hair that grows on a man's face often excluding the mustache
**2 :** a hairy or bristly appendage or tuft
**3 :** FRONT 7a
— **beard·ed** \'bir-dəd\ *adjective*
— **beard·ed·ness** *noun*
— **beard·less** \'bird-ləs\ *adjective*
²**beard** *transitive verb* (1525)
**1 :** to confront and oppose with boldness, resolution, and often effrontery **:** DEFY
**2 :** to furnish with a beard
**bearded collie** *noun* (1880)
**:** any of a breed of large working dogs of Scottish origin that have a long rough coat and drooping ears
**bearded iris** *noun* (1923)
**:** any of numerous wild or cultivated irises with a growth of short hairs on each fall
**bearded seal** *noun* (1913)
**:** a large arctic seal (*Erignathus barbatus*) with a tuft of long whiskers on each side of the muzzle
**bear down** (14th century)
*transitive verb*
**:** OVERCOME, OVERWHELM
*intransitive verb*
**:** to exert full strength and concentrated attention
— **bear down on 1 :** EMPHASIZE **2 :** to weigh heavily on **:** BURDEN
**beard·tongue** \'bird-,təŋ\ *noun* (1821)
**:** PENSTEMON
**bear·er** \'bar-ər, 'ber-\ *noun* (13th century)
**:** one that bears: as **a :** PORTER 1 **b :** a plant yielding fruit **c :** PALLBEARER **d :** one holding a check, draft, or other order for payment especially if marked payable to bearer
**bear grass** *noun* (1750)
**:** any of several plants (genera *Yucca, Nolina,* or *Xerophyllum*) of the lily or agave families chiefly of the southern and western U.S. with foliage resembling coarse blades of grass
**bear hug** *noun* (1921)
**:** a rough tight embrace
**bear·ing** *noun* (13th century)
**1 :** the manner in which one bears or comports oneself
**2 a :** the act, power, or time of bringing forth offspring or fruit **b :** a product of bearing **:** CROP
**3 a :** an object, surface, or point that supports **b :** a machine part in which another part (as a journal or pin) turns or slides
**4 :** a figure borne on a heraldic field
**5 :** PRESSURE, THRUST
**6 a :** the situation or horizontal direction of one point with respect to another or to the compass **b :** a determination of position **c** *plural* **:** comprehension of one's position, environment, or situation **d :** RELATION, CONNECTION; *also* **:** PURPORT
**7 :** the part of a structural member that rests on its supports ☆
**bearing rein** *noun* (1794)
**:** CHECKREIN 1
**bear·ish** \'bar-ish, 'ber-\ *adjective* (1744)
**1 :** resembling a bear in build or in roughness, gruffness, or surliness
**2 a :** marked by, tending to cause, or fearful of falling prices (as in a stock market) **b :** PESSIMISTIC
— **bear·ish·ly** *adverb*
— **bear·ish·ness** *noun*
**bé·ar·naise sauce** \,bā-är-'nāz-, -ər-; 'ber-\ *noun* [French *béarnaise,* feminine of *béarnais* of Béarn, France] (1877)
**:** a sauce of egg yolks and butter flavored with shallots, wine, vinegar, and seasonings
**bear out** *transitive verb* (15th century)
**:** CONFIRM, SUBSTANTIATE
**bear·skin** \'bar-,skin, 'ber-\ *noun* (1752)
**:** an article made of the skin of a bear; *especially* **:** a military hat made of the skin of a bear
**bear up** (13th century)
*transitive verb*

**:** SUPPORT, ENCOURAGE
*intransitive verb*
**:** to summon up courage, resolution, or strength ⟨*bearing up* under the strain⟩
**beast** \'bēst\ *noun* [Middle English *beste,* from Old French, from Latin *bestia*] (13th century)
**1 a :** a four-footed mammal as distinguished from a human being, a lower vertebrate, and an invertebrate **b :** a lower animal as distinguished from a human being **c :** an animal as distinguished from a plant **d :** an animal under human control
**2 :** a contemptible person
**3 :** something formidably difficult to control or deal with
**beast epic** *noun* (1889)
**:** a poem with epic conventions in which animals speak and act like human beings
**beast fable** *noun* (1865)
**:** a usually didactic prose or verse fable in which animals speak and act like human beings
**beast·ie** \'bē-stē\ *noun* (circa 1773)
**:** BEAST, ANIMAL, CRITTER
**beas·tings** *variant of* BEESTINGS
¹**beast·ly** \'bēst-lē\ *adjective* **beast·li·er; -est** (13th century)
**1 :** BESTIAL 1
**2 :** ABOMINABLE, DISAGREEABLE ⟨*beastly* weather⟩
— **beast·li·ness** *noun*
²**beastly** *adverb* (1865)
**:** VERY ⟨a *beastly* cold day⟩
**beast of burden** (1740)
**:** an animal employed to carry heavy loads or to perform other heavy work (as pulling a plow)
¹**beat** \'bēt\ *verb* **beat; beat·en** \'bē-t°n\ *or* **beat; beat·ing** [Middle English *beten,* from Old English *bēatan;* akin to Old High German *bōzan* to beat] (before 12th century)
*transitive verb*

---

☆ SYNONYMS
**Bear, suffer, endure, abide, tolerate, stand** mean to put up with something trying or painful. BEAR usually implies the power to sustain without flinching or breaking ⟨forced to *bear* a tragic loss⟩. SUFFER often suggests acceptance or passivity rather than courage or patience in bearing ⟨*suffering* many insults⟩. ENDURE implies continuing firm or resolute through trials and difficulties ⟨*endured* years of rejection⟩. ABIDE suggests acceptance without resistance or protest ⟨cannot *abide* their rudeness⟩. TOLERATE suggests overcoming or successfully controlling an impulse to resist, avoid, or resent something injurious or distasteful ⟨refused to *tolerate* such treatment⟩. STAND emphasizes more strongly the ability to bear without discomposure or flinching ⟨cannot *stand* teasing⟩.

**Bearing, deportment, demeanor, mien, manner, carriage** mean the outward manifestation of personality or attitude. BEARING is the most general of these words but now usually implies characteristic posture ⟨a woman of regal *bearing*⟩. DEPORTMENT suggests actions or behavior as formed by breeding or training ⟨your *deportment* was atrocious⟩. DEMEANOR suggests one's attitude toward others as expressed in outward behavior ⟨the haughty *demeanor* of the headwaiter⟩. MIEN is a literary term referring both to bearing and demeanor ⟨a *mien* of supreme self-satisfaction⟩. MANNER implies characteristic or customary way of moving and gesturing and addressing others ⟨the imperious *manner* of a man used to giving orders⟩. CARRIAGE applies chiefly to habitual posture in standing or walking ⟨the kind of *carriage* learned at boarding school⟩.

**1** : to strike repeatedly: **a** : to hit repeatedly so as to inflict pain — often used with *up* **b** : to walk on : TREAD **c** : to strike directly against forcefully and repeatedly : dash against **d** : to flap or thrash at vigorously **e** : to strike at in order to rouse game; *also* : to range over in or as if in quest of game **f** : to mix by stirring : WHIP — often used with *up* **g** : to strike repeatedly in order to produce music or a signal ⟨*beat* a drum⟩
**2 a** : to drive or force by blows **b** : to pound into a powder, paste, or pulp **c** : to make by repeated treading or driving over **d** (1) : to dislodge by repeated hitting (2) : to lodge securely by repeated striking **e** : to shape by beating ⟨*beat* swords into plowshares⟩; *especially* : to flatten thin by blows **f** : to sound or express especially by drumbeat
**3** : to cause to strike or flap repeatedly
**4 a** : OVERCOME, DEFEAT; *also* : SURPASS — often used with *out* **b** : to prevail despite ⟨*beat* the odds⟩ **c** : BEWILDER, BAFFLE **d** (1) : FATIGUE, EXHAUST (2) : to leave dispirited, irresolute, or hopeless **e** : CHEAT, SWINDLE
**5 a** (1) : to act ahead of usually so as to forestall (2) : to report a news item in advance of **b** : to come or arrive before **c** : CIRCUMVENT ⟨*beat* the system⟩ **d** : to outmaneuver (a defender) and get free **e** : to score against (a goalkeeper)
**6** : to indicate by beating ⟨*beat* the tempo⟩
*intransitive verb*
**1 a** : to become forcefully impelled : DASH **b** : to glare or strike with oppressive intensity **c** : to sustain distracting activity **d** : to beat a drum
**2 a** (1) : PULSATE, THROB (2) : TICK **b** : to sound upon being struck
**3 a** : to strike repeated blows **b** : to strike the air : FLAP **c** : to strike cover in order to rouse game; *also* : to range or scour for or as if for game
**4** : to progress with much difficulty
**5** : to sail to windward by a series of tacks
— **beat·a·ble** \'bē-tə-bəl\ *adjective*
— **beat about the bush** *or* **beat around the bush** : to fail or refuse to come to the point in discourse
— **beat a retreat** : to leave in haste
— **beat it 1** : to hurry away : SCRAM **2** : HURRY, RUSH
— **beat one's brains out** : to try intently to resolve something difficult by thinking
— **beat the bushes** : to search thoroughly through all possible areas
— **beat the drum** : to proclaim as meritorious or significant : publicize vigorously
— **beat the rap** : to escape or evade the penalties connected with an accusation or charge
— **beat up on** : to attack physically or verbally

²**beat** *noun* (1615)
**1 a** : a single stroke or blow especially in a series; *also* : PULSATION, TICK **b** : a sound produced by or as if by beating **c** : a driving impact or force
**2** : one swing of the pendulum or balance of a timepiece
**3 a** : a regularly traversed round ⟨the cop on the *beat*⟩ **b** : a group of news sources that a reporter covers regularly
**4 a** : a metrical or rhythmic stress in poetry or music or the rhythmic effect of these stresses **b** : the tempo indicated (as by a conductor) to a musical performer **c** : the pronounced rhythm that is the characteristic driving force in jazz or rock music; *also* : ²ROCK 2
**5 a** : one that excels ⟨I've never seen the *beat* of it⟩ **b** : the reporting of a news story ahead of competitors
**6** : DEADBEAT
**7 a** : an act of beating to windward **b** : one of the reaches so traversed : TACK

**8** : each of the pulsations of amplitude produced by the union of sound or radio waves or electric currents having different frequencies
**9** : an accented stroke (as of one leg or foot against the other) in dancing
— **beat·less** \-ləs\ *adjective*
³**beat** *adjective* [Middle English *beten, bete*, from past participle of *beten*] (1832)
**1 a** : being in a state of exhaustion : EXHAUSTED **b** : sapped of resolution or morale
**2** *often capitalized* : of, relating to, or being beatniks ⟨*beat* poets⟩
⁴**beat** *noun, often capitalized* (1957)
: BEATNIK
**beat·en** \'bē-t°n\ *adjective* (13th century)
**1** : hammered into a desired shape
**2** : much trodden and worn smooth; *also* : FAMILIAR ⟨a *beaten* path⟩
**3** : being in a state of exhaustion : EXHAUSTED
**beaten biscuit** *noun* (1876)
: a biscuit whose dough is lightened by beating and folding
**beat·er** \'bē-tər\ *noun* (14th century)
**1** : one that beats: as **a** : EGGBEATER **b** : a rotary blade attached to an electric mixer **c** : DRUMSTICK 1
**2** : one that strikes cover to rouse game
**be·atif·ic** \,bē-ə-'ti-fik\ *adjective* [Latin *beatificus* making happy, from *beatus* happy, from past participle of *beare* to bless; perhaps akin to Latin *bonus* good — more at BOUNTY] (1649)
**1** : of, possessing, or imparting beatitude
**2** : having a blissful appearance ⟨a *beatific* smile⟩
— **be·atif·i·cal·ly** \-fi-k(ə-)lē\ *adverb*
**beatific vision** *noun* (1639)
: the direct knowledge of God enjoyed by the blessed in heaven
**be·at·i·fy** \bē-'a-tə-,fī\ *transitive verb* **-fied; -fy·ing** [Middle French *beatifier*, from Late Latin *beatificare*, from Latin *beatus* + *facere* to make — more at DO] (1535)
**1** : to make supremely happy
**2** : to declare to have attained the blessedness of heaven and authorize the title "Blessed" and limited public religious honor
— **be·at·i·fi·ca·tion** \-,a-tə-fə-'kā-shən\ *noun*
**beat·ing** \'bē-tiŋ\ *noun* (13th century)
**1** : an act of striking with repeated blows so as to injure or damage; *also* : the injury or damage thus inflicted
**2** : PULSATION
**3** : DEFEAT, SETBACK
**beating reed** *noun* (1879)
: a reed in a musical instrument that vibrates against the edges of an air opening (as in a clarinet or organ pipe) to which it is attached — compare FREE REED
**be·at·i·tude** \bē-'a-tə-,tüd, -,tyüd\ *noun* [Latin *beatitudo*, from *beatus*] (15th century)
**1 a** : a state of utmost bliss **b** — used as a title for a primate especially of an Eastern church
**2** : any of the declarations made in the Sermon on the Mount (Matthew 5:3–12) beginning in the Authorized Version "Blessed are"
**beat·nik** \'bēt-nik\ *noun* [³*beat* + *-nik*] (1958)
: a person who rejects the mores of established society (as by dressing and behaving unconventionally) and indulges in exotic philosophizing and self-expression
**beat off** (15th century)
*transitive verb*
: REPEL
*intransitive verb*
: MASTURBATE — used of a male; usually considered vulgar
**beat out** *transitive verb* (1607)
**1** : to make or perform by or as if by beating
**2** : to mark or accompany by beating
**3** : to turn (a routine ground ball) into a hit in baseball by fast running to first base
**Be·atrice** \,bā-ä-'trē-(,)chā, 'bē-ə-trəs\ *noun* [Italian]

: a Florentine woman idealized in Dante's *Vita Nuova* and *Divina Commedia*
**beat–up** \'bēt-,əp, -'əp\ *adjective* (1946)
: DILAPIDATED, SHABBY
**beau** \'bō\ *noun, plural* **beaux** \'bōz\ *or* **beaus** [French, from *beau* beautiful, from Latin *bellus* pretty] (1684)
**1** : DANDY 1
**2** : BOYFRIEND 2
**Beau Brum·mell** \'bō-'brə-məl\ *noun* [nickname of G. B. *Brummell*] (1920)
: DANDY 1
**beau·coup** \'bō-(,)kü\ *adjective* [French] (1918)
*slang* : great in quantity or amount : MANY, MUCH ⟨spent *beaucoup* dollars⟩
**Beau·fort scale** \'bō-fərt-\ *noun* [Sir Francis *Beaufort*] (1858)
: a scale in which the force of the wind is indicated by numbers from 0 to 12
▶ The Beaufort scale table is on page 156.
**beau geste** \bō-'zhest\ *noun, plural* **beaux gestes** *or* **beau gestes** \bō-'zhest\ [French, literally, beautiful gesture] (1914)
**1** : a graceful or magnanimous gesture
**2** : an ingratiating conciliatory gesture
**beau ide·al** \,bō-ī-'dē(-ə)l, ,bō-,ē-dā-'äl\ *noun, plural* **beau ideals** [French *beau idéal* ideal beauty] (1809)
: the perfect type or model
**Beau·jo·lais** \,bō-zhō-'lā, -zhə-\ *noun, plural* **Beaujolais** [French, from *Beaujolais*, region of eastern France] (1863)
: a light fruity red burgundy wine made from the Gamay grape
**beau monde** \bō-'mänd, -mōⁿd\ *noun, plural* **beau mondes** \-'män(d)z\ *or* **beaux mondes** \bō-mōⁿd\ [French, literally, fine world] (1673)
: the world of high society and fashion
¹**beaut** \'byüt\ *noun* (1896)
: BEAUTY 4
²**beaut** *adjective* (1918)
*Australian & New Zealand* : EXCELLENT 2
**beau·te·ous** \'byü-tē-əs\ *adjective* [Middle English, from *beaute*] (15th century)
: BEAUTIFUL
— **beau·te·ous·ly** *adverb*
— **beau·te·ous·ness** *noun*
**beau·ti·cian** \byü-'ti-shən\ *noun* [*beauty* + *-ician*] (1924)
: COSMETOLOGIST
**beau·ti·ful** \'byü-ti-fəl\ *adjective* (15th century)
**1** : having qualities of beauty : exciting aesthetic pleasure
**2** : generally pleasing : EXCELLENT ☆

---

☆ **SYNONYMS**
**Beautiful, lovely, handsome, pretty, comely, fair** mean exciting sensuous or aesthetic pleasure. BEAUTIFUL applies to whatever excites the keenest of pleasure to the senses and stirs emotion through the senses ⟨*beautiful* mountain scenery⟩. LOVELY is close to BEAUTIFUL but applies to a narrower range of emotional excitation in suggesting the graceful, delicate, or exquisite ⟨a *lovely* melody⟩. HANDSOME suggests aesthetic pleasure due to proportion, symmetry, or elegance ⟨a *handsome* Georgian mansion⟩. PRETTY often applies to superficial or insubstantial attractiveness ⟨a painter of conventionally *pretty* scenes⟩. COMELY is like HANDSOME in suggesting what is coolly approved rather than emotionally responded to ⟨the *comely* grace of a dancer⟩. FAIR suggests beauty because of purity, flawlessness, or freshness ⟨*fair* of face⟩.

---

\ə\ **abut** \ᵊ\ **kitten** \ər\ **further** \a\ **ash** \ā\ **ace**
\ä\ **mop, mar** \au̇\ **out** \ch\ **chin** \e\ **bet** \ē\ **easy**
\g\ **go** \i\ **hit** \ī\ **ice** \j\ **job** \ŋ\ **sing** \ō\ **go**
\ȯ\ **law** \ȯi\ **boy** \th\ **thin** \t͟h\ **the** \ü\ **loot** \u̇\ **foot**
\y\ **yet** \zh\ **vision** *see also* Guide to Pronunciation

## BEAUFORT SCALE

| BEAUFORT NUMBER | NAME | WIND SPEED | | DESCRIPTION |
|---|---|---|---|---|
| | | MPH | KPH | |
| 0 | calm | <1 | <1 | calm; smoke rises vertically |
| 1 | light air | 1-3 | 1-5 | direction of wind shown by smoke but not by wind vanes |
| 2 | light breeze | 4-7 | 6-11 | wind felt on face; leaves rustle; wind vane moves |
| 3 | gentle breeze | 8-12 | 12-19 | leaves and small twigs in constant motion; wind extends light flag |
| 4 | moderate breeze | 13-18 | 20-28 | wind raises dust and loose paper; small branches move |
| 5 | fresh breeze | 19-24 | 29-38 | small-leaved trees begin to sway; crested wavelets form on inland waters |
| 6 | strong breeze | 25-31 | 39-49 | large branches move; overhead wires whistle; umbrellas difficult to control |
| 7 | moderate gale *or* near gale | 32-38 | 50-61 | whole trees sway; walking against wind is difficult |
| 8 | fresh gale *or* gale | 39-46 | 62-74 | twigs break off trees; moving cars veer |
| 9 | strong gale | 47-54 | 75-88 | slight structural damage occurs; shingles may blow away |
| 10 | whole gale *or* storm | 55-63 | 89-102 | trees uprooted; considerable structural damage occurs |
| 11 | storm *or* violent storm | 64-72 | 103-117 | widespread damage occurs |
| 12 | hurricane* | >72 | >117 | widespread damage occurs |

*The U.S. uses 74 statute mph as the speed criterion for a hurricane.

— **beau·ti·ful·ly** \-f(ə-)lē\ *adverb*
— **beau·ti·ful·ness** \-fəl-nəs\ *noun*
**beautiful people** *noun plural, often B&P capitalized* (1964)
: wealthy or famous people whose lifestyle is usually expensive and well-publicized
**beau·ti·fy** \'byü-tə-,fī\ *verb* **-fied; -fy·ing** (1526)
*transitive verb*
: to make beautiful or add beauty to
*intransitive verb*
: to grow beautiful
**synonym** see ADORN
— **beau·ti·fi·ca·tion** \byü-tə-fə-'kā-shən\ *noun*
— **beau·ti·fi·er** \'byü-tə-,fī(-ə)r\ *noun*
**beau·ty** \'byü-tē\ *noun, plural* **beauties** [Middle English *beaute,* from Old French *biauté,* from *bel, biau* beautiful, from Latin *bellus* pretty; akin to Latin *bonus* good — more at BOUNTY] (14th century)
**1** : the quality or aggregate of qualities in a person or thing that gives pleasure to the senses or pleasurably exalts the mind or spirit : LOVELINESS
**2** : a beautiful person or thing; *especially* : a beautiful woman
**3** : a particularly graceful, ornamental, or excellent quality
**4** : a brilliant, extreme, or egregious example or instance ⟨that mistake was a *beauty*⟩
**5** : a quantum characteristic that accounts for the existence and lifetime of the upsilon particle; *also* : a particle having this characteristic
**beauty bush** *noun* (1926)

: a Chinese shrub (*Kolkwitzia amabilis*) of the honeysuckle family with pinkish flowers and bristly fruit
**beauty contest** *noun* (1899)
**1** : an assemblage of girls or women at which judges select the most beautiful
**2** : a presidential primary election in which the popular vote does not determine the number of convention delegates a candidate receives
**beauty part** *noun* (1951)
: the most desirable or beneficial aspect of something
**beauty shop** *noun* (1901)
: an establishment or department where hairdressing, facials, and manicures are done — called also *beauty parlor, beauty salon*
**beauty spot** *noun* (1657)
**1** : ¹PATCH 2
**2** : NEVUS
¹**beaux arts** \bō-'zär\ *noun plural* [French *beaux-arts*] (1821)
: FINE ARTS
²**beaux arts** *adjective, often B&A capitalized* [French *École des Beaux-Arts* School of Fine Arts, in Paris] (1924)
: characterized by the use of historic forms, rich decorative detail, and a tendency toward monumental conception in architecture
¹**bea·ver** \'bē-vər\ *noun, plural* **beavers** [Middle English *bever,* from Old English *beofor;* akin to Old High German *bibar* beaver, and probably to Old English *brūn* brown — more at BROWN] (before 12th century)
**1** *or plural* **beaver a** : either of two large semiaquatic herbivorous rodents (*Castor canadensis* of North America and *C. fiber* of Eurasia) having webbed hind feet and a broad

flat scaly tail and constructing dams and partially submerged lodges **b** : the fur or pelt of the beaver
**2 a** : a hat made of beaver fur or a fabric imitation **b** : SILK HAT
**3** : a heavy fabric of felted wool or of cotton napped on both sides
**4** : the pudenda of a woman — usually considered vulgar
²**beaver** *noun* [Middle English *baviere,* from Middle French] (15th century)
**1** : a piece of armor protecting the lower part of the face
**2** : a helmet visor
³**beaver** *intransitive verb* (1946)
: to work energetically ⟨*beavering* away at the problem⟩
**bea·ver·board** \'bē-vər-,bōrd, -,bȯrd\ *noun* [from *Beaver Board,* a trademark] (1909)
: a fiberboard used for partitions and ceilings
**be·bop** \'bē-,bäp\ *noun* [imitative] (1944)
: ³BOP 1
— **be·bop·per** *noun*
**be·calm** \bi-'kä(l)m, *New England also* -'kȧm\ *transitive verb* (1582)
**1 a** : to keep motionless by lack of wind **b** : to stop the progress of ⟨an industry *becalmed* by decreasing demand⟩
**2** : to make calm : SOOTHE
**be·cause** \bi-'kȯz, -'kəz *also* -'kȯs\ *conjunction* [Middle English *because that, because,* from *by cause that*] (14th century)
**1** : for the reason that : SINCE ⟨rested *because* he was tired⟩
**2** : the fact that : THAT ⟨the reason I haven't been fired is *because* my boss hasn't got round to it yet —E. B. White⟩
**because of** *preposition* (14th century)
: by reason of : on account of
**bé·cha·mel** \,bā-shə-'mel\ *noun* [French *sauce béchamelle,* from Louis de *Béchamel* (died 1703) French courtier] (1796)
: a rich white sauce
**be·chance** \bi-'chan(t)s\ *verb* (1527)
*archaic* : BEFALL
**bêche–de–mer** \,besh-də-'mer, ,bāsh-\ *noun* [French, alteration of *biche de mer,* from Portuguese *bicho do mar,* literally, sea worm] (1783)
**1** *plural* **bêche–de–mer** *or* **bêches–de–mer** \,besh-də-, ,be-shəz-, ,bāsh-\ : TREPANG
**2** *B&M capitalized* : any of several English-based pidgins spoken on islands of the western Pacific
¹**beck** \'bek\ *noun* [Middle English *bek,* from Old Norse *bekkr;* akin to Old English *bæc* brook, Old High German *bah,* Lithuanian *bègti* to flee — more at PHOBIA] (14th century)
*British* : CREEK 2
²**beck** *transitive verb* [Middle English, alteration of *beknen*] (14th century)
*archaic* : BECKON
³**beck** *noun* (14th century)
**1** *chiefly Scottish* : BOW, CURTSY
**2 a** : a beckoning gesture **b** : SUMMONS, BIDDING
— **at one's beck and call** : ready to obey one's command immediately
**beck·et** \'be-kət\ *noun* [origin unknown] (circa 1769)
: a device for holding something in place: as **a** : a grommet or a loop of rope with a knot at one end to catch in an eye at the other **b** : a ring of rope or metal **c** : a loop of rope (as for a handle)
**beck·on** \'be-kən\ *verb* **beck·oned; beck·on·ing** [Middle English *beknen,* from Old English *bīecnan,* from *bēacen* sign — more at BEACON] (before 12th century)
*intransitive verb*

*B beaver 1*

**1 :** to summon or signal typically with a wave or nod
**2 :** to appear inviting **:** ATTRACT
*transitive verb*
**:** to beckon to
— **beckon** *noun*
**be·cloud** \bi-'klaud\ *transitive verb* (1598)
**1 :** to obscure with or as if with a cloud
**2 :** to prevent clear perception or realization of **:** MUDDLE ⟨prejudices that *becloud* his judgment⟩
**be·come** \bi-'kəm\ *verb* **-came** \-'kām\; **-come; -com·ing** [Middle English, to come to, become, from Old English *becuman*, from *be-* + *cuman* to come] (before 12th century)
*intransitive verb*
**1 a :** to come into existence **b :** to come to be ⟨*become* sick⟩
**2 :** to undergo change or development
*transitive verb*
**:** to suit or be suitable to ⟨seriousness *becoming* the occasion⟩ ⟨her clothes *become* her⟩
— **become of :** to happen to
**be·com·ing** \-'kə-miŋ\ *adjective* (15th century)
**:** SUITABLE. FITTING; *especially* **:** attractively suitable ⟨*becoming* modesty⟩
— **be·com·ing·ly** \-miŋ-lē\ *adverb*
¹**bed** \'bed\ *noun* [Middle English, from Old English *bedd*; akin to Old High German *betti* bed, Latin *fodere* to dig] (before 12th century)
**1 a :** a piece of furniture on or in which to lie and sleep **b** (1) **:** a place of sex relations (2) **:** marital relationship **c :** a place for sleeping **d :** SLEEP; *also* **:** a time for sleeping ⟨took a walk before *bed*⟩ **e** (1) **:** a mattress filled with soft material (2) **:** BEDSTEAD **f :** the equipment and services needed to care for one hospitalized patient or hotel guest
**2 :** a flat or level surface: as **a :** a plot of ground prepared for plants; *also* **:** the plants grown in such a plot **b :** the bottom of a body of water; *especially* **:** an area of sea bottom supporting a heavy growth of a particular organism ⟨an oyster *bed*⟩
**3 :** a supporting surface or structure **:** FOUNDATION
**4 :** LAYER, STRATUM
**5 a :** the place or material in which a block or brick is laid **b :** the lower surface of a brick, slate, or tile
**6 :** a mass or heap resembling a bed ⟨a *bed* of ashes⟩ ⟨served on a *bed* of lettuce⟩
— **in bed :** in the act of sexual intercourse
²**bed** *verb* **bed·ded; bed·ding** (before 12th century)
*intransitive verb*
**1 a :** to find or make sleeping accommodations **b :** to go to bed
**2 :** to form a layer
**3 :** to lie flat or flush
*transitive verb*
**1 a :** to furnish with a bed or bedding **:** settle in sleeping quarters — often used with *down* **b :** to put, take, or send to bed
**2 a :** EMBED **b :** to plant or arrange in beds **c :** BASE, ESTABLISH
**3 a :** to lay flat or in a layer **b :** to make a bed in or of
**4 :** to have sexual intercourse with — often used with *down*
**be·dab·ble** \bi-'da-bəl\ *transitive verb* (1590)
*archaic* **:** to wet or soil by dabbling
**bed–and–breakfast** *noun* (1910)
**:** an establishment (as an inn) offering lodging and breakfast
**be·daub** \bi-'dob, -'däb\ *transitive verb* (1558)
**1 :** to daub over **:** BESMEAR
**2 :** to ornament with vulgar excess
**be·daz·zle** \bi-'da-zəl\ *transitive verb* (1596)
**1 :** to confuse by a strong light **:** DAZZLE
**2 :** to impress forcefully **:** ENCHANT
— **be·daz·zle·ment** \-mənt\ *noun*
**bed board** *noun* (1946)
**:** a stiff thin wide board inserted usually between a bedspring and mattress especially to

give support to one's back or to protect a mattress from sagging springs
**bed·bug** \'bed-,bəg\ *noun* (1808)
**:** a wingless bloodsucking bug (*Cimex lectularius*) sometimes infesting houses and especially beds and feeding on human blood
**bed·cham·ber** \-,chām-bər\ *noun* (14th century)
**:** BEDROOM
**bed check** *noun* (1927)
**:** a night inspection to check the presence of persons (as soldiers) required by regulations to be in bed or in quarters
**bed·clothes** \'bed-,klō(th)z\ *noun plural* (14th century)
**:** the covering (as sheets and blankets) used on a bed
**bed·cov·er** \-,kə-vər\ *also* **bed·cov·er·ing** \-,kə-v(ə-)riŋ\ *noun* (circa 1656)
**1 :** BEDSPREAD
**2 :** BEDCLOTHES — usually used in plural
**bed·ded** \'be-dəd\ *adjective* (1788)
**:** having a bed or beds of a specified kind or number — used in combination ⟨a twin-*bedded* room⟩
**bed·der** \'be-dər\ *noun* (1803)
**1 :** one that makes up beds
**2 :** a bedding plant
¹**bed·ding** \'be-diŋ\ *noun* [Middle English, from Old English, from *bedd*] (before 12th century)
**1 :** BEDCLOTHES
**2 :** a bottom layer **:** FOUNDATION
**3 :** material to provide a bed for livestock
**4 :** STRATIFICATION
²**bedding** *adjective* [from gerund of ²*bed*] (1856)
**:** suitable for planting in large groups in flower beds to produce a mass display ⟨*bedding* plants⟩
**be·deck** \bi-'dek\ *transitive verb* (circa 1566)
**1 :** to clothe with finery **:** DECK
**2 :** DECORATE 2
**be·dev·il** \bi-'de-vəl\ *transitive verb* (1574)
**1 :** to possess with or as if with a devil
**2 :** to cause distress **:** TROUBLE
**3 :** to change for the worse **:** SPOIL
**4 :** to confuse utterly **:** BEWILDER
— **be·dev·il·ment** \-mənt\ *noun*
**be·dew** \bi-'dü, -'dyü\ *transitive verb* (14th century)
**:** to wet with or as if with dew
**bed·fast** \'bed-,fast\ *adjective* (1560)
**:** BEDRIDDEN
**bed·fel·low** \-,fe-(,)lō\ *noun* (15th century)
**1 :** one who shares a bed with another
**2 :** ASSOCIATE, ALLY ⟨political *bedfellows*⟩
**Bed·ford cord** \'bed-fərd-\ *noun* [perhaps from New *Bedford*, Massachusetts] (1862)
**:** a clothing fabric with lengthwise ribs that resembles corduroy; *also* **:** the weave used in making this fabric
**be·dight** \bi-'dīt\ *transitive verb* **be·dight·ed** *or* **bedight; be·dight·ing** (14th century)
*archaic* **:** EQUIP, ARRAY
**be·dim** \bi-'dim\ *transitive verb* (1583)
**1 :** to make less bright
**2 :** to make indistinct **:** OBSCURE
**Bed·i·vere** \'be-də-,vir\ *noun*
**:** a knight of the Round Table
**be·di·zen** \bi-'dī-z°n, -'di-\ *transitive verb* (1661)
**:** to dress or adorn gaudily
— **be·di·zen·ment** \-mənt\ *noun*
**bed·lam** \'bed-ləm\ *noun* [*Bedlam,* popular name for the Hospital of Saint Mary of Bethlehem, London, an insane asylum, from Middle English *Bedlem* Bethlehem] (1522)
**1** *obsolete* **:** MADMAN, LUNATIC
**2** *often capitalized* **:** a lunatic asylum
**3 :** a place, scene, or state of uproar and confusion ◆
— **bedlam** *adjective*
**bed·lam·ite** \'bed-lə-,mīt\ *noun* (1589)
**:** MADMAN, LUNATIC
— **bedlamite** *adjective*

**Bed·ling·ton terrier** \'bed-liŋ-tən-\ *noun* [*Bedlington,* England] (1867)
**:** a swift lightly built terrier of English origin with a long narrow head, arched back, and usually curly coat — called also *Bedlington*
**bed·mate** \'bed-,māt\ *noun* (1583)
**:** one who shares one's bed; *especially* **:** a sexual partner
**bed molding** *noun* (1703)
**:** the molding of a cornice below the corona and above the frieze; *also* **:** a molding below a deep projection
**bed of roses** (1648)
**:** a place or situation of agreeable ease
**bed·ou·in** *or* **bed·u·in** \'be-də-wən\ *noun, plural* **bedouin** *or* **bedouins** *or* **beduin** *or* **beduins** *often capitalized* [Middle English *Bedoyne,* from Middle French *bedoïn,* from Arabic *badawī* desert dweller] (15th century)
**:** a nomadic Arab of the Arabian, Syrian, or North African deserts
**bed·pan** \'bed-,pan\ *noun* (1678)
**:** a shallow vessel used by a bedridden person for urination or defecation
**bed·plate** \-,plāt\ *noun* (1850)
**:** a plate or framing used as a support
**bed·post** \-,pōst\ *noun* (1598)
**:** the usually turned or carved post of a bed
**be·drag·gle** \bi-'dra-gəl\ *transitive verb* (1727)
**:** to wet thoroughly
**be·drag·gled** \bi-'dra-gəld\ *adjective* (1824)
**1 :** left wet and limp by or as if by rain
**2 :** soiled and stained by or as if by trailing in mud
**3 :** DILAPIDATED ⟨*bedraggled* buildings⟩
**bed rest** *noun* (1944)
**:** confinement of a sick person to bed
**bed·rid·den** \'bed-,ri-d°n\ *also* **bed·rid** \-,rid\ *adjective* [alteration of Middle English *bedrede, bedreden,* from Old English *bedreda,* from *bedreda* one confined to bed, from *bedd* bed + *-rida, -reda,* from *rīdan* to ride] (before 12th century)
**:** confined (as by illness) to bed
¹**bed·rock** \-'räk, -,räk\ *noun* (1850)
**1 :** the solid rock underlying unconsolidated surface materials (as soil)
**2 a :** lowest point **:** NADIR **b :** BASIS
²**bed·rock** *adjective* (1896)
**:** solidly fundamental, basic, or reliable ⟨traditional *bedrock* values⟩ ⟨a *bedrock* constituency⟩
**bed·roll** \-,rōl\ *noun* (1910)
**:** bedding rolled up for carrying
¹**bed·room** \-,rüm, -,rum\ *noun* (1616)

◇ WORD HISTORY
**bedlam** In 1247 a house was founded in London for the religious order of St. Mary of Bethlehem. By 1330 this priory had become the Hospital of St. Mary of Bethlehem, and it was intended to serve the poor or homeless who where afflicted with any ailment. By 1405 the hospital, now under royal control, was being used, at least in part, as an asylum for the insane—the first such institution in England. Over time everyday speech telescoped *Bethlehem* into *Bedlam.* And over time Bedlam became proverbial for its wretched conditions and tumultuous commotion. By the latter part of the 17th century, the word *bedlam* had begun to be used generically for any lunatic asylum. At about the same time, the term was first applied metaphorically to a scene of wild uproar or confusion, its common meaning today.

\ə\ abut \ª\ kitten \ər\ **further** \a\ ash \ā\ ace
\ä\ mop, mar \au̇\ out \ch\ chin \e\ bet \ē\ easy
\g\ go \i\ hit \ī\ ice \j\ job \ŋ\ sing \ō\ go
\ȯ\ law \ȯi\ boy \th\ thin \t͟h\ the \ü\ loot \u̇\ foot
\y\ yet \zh\ vision *see also* Guide to Pronunciation

: a room furnished with a bed and intended primarily for sleeping
— **bed·roomed** \-,rümd, -,rümd\ *adjective*
²**bed·room** *adjective* (1915)
**1** : dealing with, suggestive of, or inviting sexual relations ⟨a *bedroom* farce⟩ ⟨*bedroom* eyes⟩
**2** : inhabited or used by commuters ⟨a *bedroom* community⟩
**bed·sheet** \'bed-,shēt\ *noun* (15th century)
: an oblong piece of usually cotton or linen cloth used as an article of bedding
¹**bed·side** \'bed-,sīd\ *noun* (14th century)
: the side of a bed : a place beside a bed
²**bedside** *adjective* (1837)
**1** : of, relating to, or conducted at the bedside ⟨a *bedside* diagnosis⟩
**2** : suitable for reading in bed ⟨a *bedside* book⟩
**bedside manner** *noun* (1869)
: the manner that a physician assumes toward patients
**bed·sit·ter** \'bed-,si-tər\ *noun* [*bed-sit*ting room + *-er* (as in *fresh*er freshman, *rugg*er rugby)] (1927)
*British* : a one-room apartment serving as both bedroom and sitting room — called also *bed-sit, bed-sitting-room*
**bed·sore** \'bed-,sōr, -,sȯr\ *noun* (1861)
: an ulceration of tissue deprived of adequate blood supply by prolonged pressure
**bed·spread** \-,spred\ *noun* (1845)
: a usually ornamental cloth cover for a bed
**bed·spring** \-,spriŋ\ *noun* (1897)
: a spring supporting a mattress
**bed·stead** \'bed-,sted\ *noun* [Middle English *bedstede*, from *bed* + *stede* stead, place — more at STEAD] (15th century)
: the framework of a bed
**bed·straw** \-,strȯ\ *noun* [from its use for mattresses] (1527)
: any of a genus (*Galium*) of herbs of the madder family having squarish stems, whorled leaves, and small flowers
**bed table** *noun* (1811)
**1** : an adjustable table used (as for eating or writing) by a person in bed
**2** : a small table beside a bed
**bed·time** \-,tīm\ *noun* (13th century)
: a time for going to bed
**bedtime story** *noun* (1899)
: a story read or recounted to someone (as a child) at bedtime
**be·du** \'be-(,)dü\ *noun, plural* **bedu** *often capitalized* [Arabic *badw* Bedouins, literally, desert] (1912)
: BEDOUIN
**bed warmer** *noun* (1922)
: a covered pan containing hot coals used to warm a bed
**bed·wet·ting** \-,we-tiŋ\ *noun* (1890)
: enuresis especially when occurring in bed during sleep
— **bed wetter** *noun*
¹**bee** \'bē\ *noun* [Middle English, from Old English *bēo;* akin to Old High German *bīa* bee, Old Irish *bech,* Lithuanian *bitis*] (before 12th century)
**1** : HONEYBEE; *broadly* : any of numerous insects (superfamily Apoidea) that differ from the related wasps especially in the heavier hairier body and in having sucking as well as chewing mouthparts, that feed on pollen and nectar, and that store both and often also honey
**2** : an eccentric notion : FANCY
— **bee·like** \-,līk\ *adjective*
— **bee in one's bonnet** : ¹BEE 2
²**bee** *noun* (14th century)
: the letter *b*
³**bee** *noun* [perhaps from English dialect *been* help given by neighbors, from Middle English *bene* prayer, boon, from Old English *bēn* prayer — more at BOON] (1769)
: a gathering of people for a specific purpose ⟨quilting *bee*⟩

**bee balm** *noun* (1840)
**1** : any of several monardas; *especially* : OSWEGO TEA
**2** : LEMON BALM
**bee-bee** *variant of* BB
**bee·bread** \'bē-,bred\ *noun* (1657)
: bitter yellowish brown pollen stored up in honeycomb cells and used mixed with honey by bees as food
**beech** \'bēch\ *noun, plural* **beech·es** *or* **beech** [Middle English *beche,* from Old English *bēce;* akin to Old English *bōc* beech, Old High German *buohha,* Latin *fagus,* Greek *phēgos* oak] (before 12th century)
: any of a genus (*Fagus* of the family Fagaceae, the beech family) of hardwood trees with smooth gray bark and small edible nuts; *also* : its wood
— **beech·en** \'bē-chən\ *adjective*
**beech·drops** \'bēch-,dräps\ *noun plural but singular or plural in construction* (1815)
: a plant (*Epifagus virginiana*) of the broomrape family parasitic on the roots of beeches
**beech·nut** \-,nət\ *noun* (1739)
: the nut of the beech
**bee–eat·er** \'bē-,ē-tər\ *noun* (1668)
: any of a family (Meropidae) of brightly colored slender-billed insectivorous chiefly tropical Old World birds
¹**beef** \'bēf\ *noun, plural* **beefs** \'bēfs\ *or* **beeves** \'bēvz\ [Middle English, from Old French *buef* ox, beef, from Latin *bov-, bos* head of cattle — more at COW] (14th century)
**1** : the flesh of an adult domestic bovine (as a steer or cow) used as food
**2 a** : an ox, cow, or bull in a full-grown or nearly full-grown state; *especially* : a steer or cow fattened for food ⟨quality Texas *beeves*⟩ ⟨a herd of good *beef*⟩ **b** : a dressed carcass of a beef animal
**3** : muscular flesh : BRAWN
**4** *plural* **beefs** : COMPLAINT
²**beef** (1860)
*transitive verb*
: to add substance, strength, or power to — usually used with *up* ⟨money to *beef* up its staff of professional economists —John Fischer⟩
*intransitive verb*
: COMPLAIN
**beef·a·lo** \'bē-fə-,lō\ *noun, plural* **-a·los** *or* **-a·loes** [blend of ¹*beef* and *buffalo*] (1973)
: any of a breed of beef cattle developed in the U.S. that is genetically ⅜ North American bison and ⅝ domestic bovine
**beef·cake** \'bēf-,kāk\ *noun* (1949)
: a usually photographic display of muscular male physiques; *also* : men of the type featured in such a display — compare CHEESECAKE
**beef cattle** *noun plural* (1758)
: cattle developed primarily for the efficient production of meat and marked by capacity for rapid growth, heavy well-fleshed body, and stocky build
**beef·eat·er** \'bē-,fē-tər\ *noun, often capitalized* (1671)
: a yeoman of the guard of an English monarch

beef 2b: *A wholesale cuts:* 1 shank, 2 round with rump and shank cut off, 3 rump, 4 sirloin, 5 short loin, 6 flank, 7 rib, 8 chuck, 9 plate, 10 brisket, 11 shank; *B retail cuts:* a heel pot roast, b round steak, c rump roast, d sirloin steak, e pinbone steak, f short ribs, g porterhouse, h T-bone, i club steak, j flank steak, k rib roast, l blade rib roast, m plate, n brisket, o crosscut shank, p arm pot roast, q boneless neck, r blade roast

**bee fly** *noun* (1852)
: any of a family (Bombyliidae) of dipteran flies many of which resemble bees
**beef·steak** \'bēf-,stāk\ *noun* (1711)
: a steak of beef usually from the hindquarter
**beefsteak tomato** *noun* (1968)
: a very large globe-shaped red tomato with dense flesh
**beef Stro·ga·noff** \-'strȯ-gə-,nȯf, -'strō-\ *noun* [Count Paul *Stroganoff,* 19th century Russian diplomat] (1932)
: beef sliced thin and cooked in a sour-cream sauce
**beef Wel·ling·ton** \-'we-liŋ-tən\ *noun* [probably from the name *Wellington*] (1965)
: a fillet of beef covered with pâté de foie gras and baked in a casing of pastry
**beef·wood** \'bēf-,wud\ *noun* (1805)
**1** : the hard heavy reddish wood of any of various chiefly tropical trees (as the Australian pine)
**2** : AUSTRALIAN PINE
**beefy** \'bē-fē\ *adjective* **beef·i·er; -est** (1743)
**1 a** : heavily and powerfully built **b** : SUBSTANTIAL, STURDY
**2** : full of beef
**bee·hive** \'bē-,hīv\ *noun* (14th century)
**1** : HIVE 1
**2** : something resembling a hive for bees: as **a** : a scene of crowded activity **b** : a woman's hairdo that is conical in shape
— **beehive** *adjective*
**beehive oven** *noun* (circa 1881)
: an arched oven used especially for baking food and formerly for coking coal
**bee·keep·er** \-,kē-pər\ *noun* (1817)
: a person who raises bees
— **bee·keep·ing** *noun*
¹**bee·line** \-,līn\ *noun* [from the belief that nectar-laden bees return to their hives in a direct line] (1830)
: a straight direct course
²**beeline** *intransitive verb* (1940)
: to go quickly in a straight direct course
**Beel·ze·bub** \bē-'el-zi-,bəb, 'bēl-zi-, 'bel-\ *noun* [*Beelzebub,* prince of devils, from Latin, from Greek *Beelzeboub,* from Hebrew *Ba'al zĕbhūbh,* a Philistine god, literally, lord of flies] (before 12th century)
**1** : DEVIL
**2** : a fallen angel in Milton's *Paradise Lost* ranking next to Satan
**been** *past participle of* BE
¹**beep** \'bēp\ *noun* [imitative] (1929)
: a short usually high-pitched sound (as from a horn or an electronic device) that serves as a signal or warning
²**beep** (1936)
*intransitive verb*
**1** : to sound a horn
**2** : to make a beep
*transitive verb*
: to cause (as a horn) to sound
**beep·er** \'bē-pər\ *noun* (1970)
: an electronic device that beeps to make contact with the person carrying it when it receives a special radio signal
**beer** \'bir\ *noun* [Middle English *ber,* from Old English *bēor;* akin to Old High German *bior* beer] (before 12th century)
**1** : an alcoholic beverage usually made from malted cereal grain (as barley), flavored with hops, and brewed by slow fermentation
**2** : a carbonated nonalcoholic or a fermented slightly alcoholic beverage with flavoring from roots or other plant parts ⟨birch *beer*⟩
**3** : fermented mash
**4** : a drink of beer
**beer and skittles** *noun plural but singular or plural in construction* (1857)
: a situation of ease ⟨won't be all *beer and skittles*⟩
**beery** \'bir-ē\ *adjective* **beer·i·er; -est** (1848)

**1 :** smelling or tasting of beer ⟨*beery* tavern⟩
**2 :** affected or caused by beer ⟨*beery* voices⟩
**bees·tings** \'bē-stiŋz\ *noun plural but singular or plural in construction* [Middle English *bestynge*, from Old English *bȳsting*, from *bēost* beestings; akin to Old High German *biost* beestings] (before 12th century)
**:** the colostrum especially of a cow
**bee-stung** \'bē-,stəŋ\ *adjective* (1933)
**:** having a red puffy appearance as if from being stung by a bee ⟨*bee-stung* lips⟩
**bees·wax** \'bēz-,waks\ *noun* (1676)
**:** WAX 1
**beet** \'bēt\ *noun* [Middle English *bete*, from Old English *bēte*, from Latin *beta*] (before 12th century)
**:** a biennial garden plant (*Beta vulgaris*) of the goosefoot family that has several cultivars (as Swiss chard and sugar beet) and possesses thick long-stalked edible leaves and swollen root used as a vegetable, as a source of sugar, or for forage; *also* **:** its root
**beet armyworm** *noun* (1902)
**:** an armyworm (*Spodoptera exigua*) that eats the foliage of beets, alfalfa, and vegetables
**¹bee·tle** \'bē-t°l\ *noun* [Middle English *betylle*, from Old English *bitula*; akin to *bītan* to bite] (before 12th century)
**1 :** any of an order (Coleoptera) of insects having four wings of which the outer pair are modified into stiff elytra that protect the inner pair when at rest
**2 :** any of various insects resembling a beetle
**²beetle** *intransitive verb* **bee·tled; bee·tling** \'bē-t°l-iŋ\ (circa 1919)
**:** to scurry like a beetle ⟨editors *beetled* around the office⟩
**³beetle** *noun* [Middle English *betel*, from Old English *bīetel*; akin to Old English *bēatan* to beat] (before 12th century)
**1 :** a heavy wooden hammering or ramming instrument
**2 :** a wooden pestle or bat for domestic tasks
**⁴beetle** *adjective* [Middle English *bitel-browed* having overhanging brows, probably from *betylle, bitel* beetle] (14th century)
**:** being prominent and overhanging ⟨*beetle* brows⟩
**⁵beetle** *intransitive verb* **bee·tled; bee·tling** \'bē-t°l-iŋ\ (1602)
**:** PROJECT, JUT ⟨to scale the *beetling* crags —R. L. Stevenson⟩
**beet leafhopper** *noun* (1919)
**:** a leafhopper (*Circulifer tenellus*) that transmits curly top virus to sugar beets and other garden plants
**bee tree** *noun* (1782)
**:** a hollow tree in which honeybees nest
**beet·root** \'bēt-,rüt\ *noun* (1579)
*chiefly British* **:** a beet grown for its edible usually red root; *also* **:** the root
**beeves** *plural of* BEEF
**bee·yard** \'bē-,yärd\ *noun* (15th century)
**:** APIARY
**be·fall** \bi-'fȯl\ *verb* **-fell** \-'fel\; **-fall·en** \-'fȯ-lən\ (13th century)
*intransitive verb*
**:** to happen especially as if by fate
*transitive verb*
**:** to happen to
**be·fit** \bi-'fit\ *transitive verb* **be·fit·ted; be·fit·ting** (15th century)
**:** to be proper or becoming to
**be·fit·ting** \-'fi-tiŋ\ *adjective* (1564)
**1 :** SUITABLE, APPROPRIATE
**2 :** PROPER, DECENT
— **be·fit·ting·ly** \-tiŋ-lē\ *adverb*
**be·fog** \bi-'fȯg, -'fäg\ *transitive verb* (1601)
**1 :** CONFUSE
**2 :** FOG, OBSCURE
**be·fool** \bi-'fül\ *transitive verb* (14th century)
**1 :** to make a fool of
**2 :** DELUDE, DECEIVE
**¹be·fore** \bi-'fȯr, -'fȯr\ *adverb or adjective* [Middle English, adverb & preposition, from

Old English *beforan*, from *be-* + *foran* before, from *fore*] (before 12th century)
**1 :** in advance **:** AHEAD ⟨marching on *before*⟩
**2 :** at an earlier time **:** PREVIOUSLY ⟨the night *before*⟩ ⟨knew her from *before*⟩
**²before** *preposition* (before 12th century)
**1 a** (1) **:** in front of (2) **:** in the presence of **b :** under the jurisdiction or consideration of ⟨the case *before* the court⟩ **c** (1) **:** at the disposal of (2) **:** in store for
**2 :** preceding in time **:** earlier than
**3 :** in a higher or more important position than ⟨put quantity *before* quality⟩
**³before** *conjunction* (13th century)
**1 a** (1) **:** earlier than the time that ⟨call me *before* you go⟩ (2) **:** sooner or quicker than ⟨I'll be done *before* you know it⟩ (3) **:** so that . . . do not ⟨get out of there *before* you get dirty⟩ **b :** until the time that ⟨miles to go *before* I sleep —Robert Frost⟩ **c** (1) **:** or else . . . not ⟨must be convicted *before* he can be removed from office⟩ (2) **:** or else ⟨get out of here *before* I call a cop⟩
**2 :** rather or sooner than ⟨would starve *before* he'd steal⟩
**be·fore·hand** \bi-'fȯr-,hand, -'fȯr-\ *adverb or adjective* (13th century)
**1 a :** in anticipation **b :** in advance
**2 :** ahead of time **b :** EARLY
**be·fore·time** \-,tīm\ *adverb* (14th century)
*archaic* **:** FORMERLY
**be·foul** \bi-'faù(ə)l\ *transitive verb* (before 12th century)
**:** to make foul with or as if with dirt
**be·friend** \bi-'frend\ *transitive verb* (1559)
**:** to act as a friend to
**be·fud·dle** \bi-'fə-d°l\ *transitive verb* (circa 1879)
**1 :** to muddle or stupefy with or as if with drink
**2 :** CONFUSE, PERPLEX
— **be·fud·dle·ment** \-mənt\ *noun*
**beg** \'beg\ *verb* **begged; beg·ging** [Middle English *beggen*] (13th century)
*transitive verb*
**1 :** to ask for as a charity
**2 a :** to ask earnestly for **:** ENTREAT **b :** to require as necessary or appropriate
**3 a :** EVADE, SIDESTEP ⟨*begged* the real problems⟩ **b :** to pass over or ignore by assuming to be established or settled ⟨*beg* the question⟩
*intransitive verb*
**1 :** to ask for alms
**2 :** to ask earnestly ⟨*begged* for mercy⟩ ☆
**be·get** \bi-'get\ *transitive verb* **-got** \-'gät\ *also* **-gat** \-'gat\; **-got·ten** \-'gä-t°n\ *or* **-got; -get·ting** [Middle English *begeten*, alteration of *beyeten*, from Old English *bigietan* — more at GET] (13th century)
**1 :** to procreate as the father **:** SIRE
**2 :** to produce especially as an effect or outgrowth
— **be·get·ter** *noun*
**¹beg·gar** \'be-gər\ *noun* [Middle English *beggere, beggare*, from *beggen* to beg + *-ere, -are* ²-er] (13th century)
**1 :** one that begs; *especially* **:** a person who lives by asking for gifts
**2 :** PAUPER
**3 :** FELLOW 4c
**²beggar** *transitive verb* **beg·gared; beg·gar·ing** \-gə-riŋ\ (15th century)
**1 :** to reduce to beggary
**2 :** to exceed the resources or abilities of **:** DEFY ⟨*beggars* description⟩
**beg·gar·ly** \'be-gər-lē\ *adjective* (1526)
**1 :** contemptibly mean, scant, petty, or paltry
**2 :** befitting or resembling a beggar; *especially* **:** marked by extreme poverty
— **beg·gar·li·ness** *noun*
**beg·gar's–lice** \'be-gərz-,līs\ *or* **beg·gar–lice** \-gər-,līs\ *noun plural but singular or plural in construction* (1837)
**:** any of various plants (as of the genera *Hackelia* and *Cynoglossum*) with prickly or adhesive fruits; *also* **:** one of these fruits

**beg·gar–ticks** *also* **beg·gar's–ticks** \-,tiks\ *noun plural but singular or plural in construction* (circa 1818)
**1 :** BUR MARIGOLD; *also* **:** its prickly achenes
**2 :** BEGGAR'S-LICE
**beg·gar·weed** \'be-gər-,wēd\ *noun* (circa 1809)
**1 :** any of various plants (as a knotgrass, spurrey, or dodder) that grow in waste ground
**2 :** any of several tick trefoils (genus *Desmodium*); *especially* **:** a West Indian forage plant (*D. tortuosum*) cultivated in the southern U.S.
**beg·gary** \'be-gə-rē\ *noun, plural* **-gar·ies** (14th century)
**1 :** POVERTY, PENURY
**2 :** the class of beggars
**3 :** the practice of begging
**be·gin** \bi-'gin\ *verb* **be·gan** \-'gan\; **be·gun** \-'gən\; **be·gin·ning** [Middle English *beginnen*, from Old English *beginnan*; akin to Old High German *biginnan* to begin, Old English *onginnan*] (before 12th century)
*intransitive verb*
**1 :** to do the first part of an action **:** go into the first part of a process **:** START
**2 a :** to come into existence **:** ARISE **b :** to have a starting point
**3 :** to do or succeed in the least degree ⟨I can't *begin* to tell you how pleased I am⟩
*transitive verb*
**1 :** to set about the activity of **:** START
**2 a :** to bring into being **:** FOUND **b :** ORIGINATE, INVENT ☆

---

☆ SYNONYMS
**Beg, entreat, beseech, implore, supplicate, adjure, importune** mean to ask urgently. BEG suggests earnestness or insistence especially in asking for a favor ⟨children *begging* to stay up late⟩. ENTREAT implies an effort to persuade or to overcome resistance ⟨*entreated* him to change his mind⟩. BESEECH implies great eagerness or anxiety ⟨I *beseech* you to have mercy⟩. IMPLORE adds to BESEECH a suggestion of greater urgency or anguished appeal ⟨*implored* her not to leave him⟩. SUPPLICATE suggests a posture of humility ⟨with bowed heads they *supplicated* their Lord⟩. ADJURE implies advising as well as pleading and suggests the invoking of something sacred ⟨in God's name I *adjure* you to cease⟩. IMPORTUNE suggests an annoying persistence in trying to break down resistance to a request ⟨*importuning* viewers for contributions⟩.

**Begin, commence, start, initiate, inaugurate, usher in** mean to take the first step in a course, process, or operation. BEGIN, START, and COMMENCE are often interchangeable. BEGIN, opposed to *end*, is the most general ⟨*begin* a trip⟩ ⟨*began* dancing⟩. START, opposed to *stop*, applies especially to first actions, steps, or stages ⟨the work *started* slowly⟩. COMMENCE can be more formal or bookish than BEGIN or START ⟨*commence* firing⟩ ⟨*commenced* a conversation⟩. INITIATE implies taking a first step in a process or series that is to continue ⟨*initiated* diplomatic contacts⟩. INAUGURATE suggests a beginning of some formality or notion of significance ⟨the discovery of penicillin *inaugurated* a new era in medicine⟩. USHER IN is somewhat less weighty than INAUGURATE ⟨*ushered in* a period of economic decline⟩.

---

\ə\ abut  \ᵊ\ kitten  \ər\ further  \a\ ash  \ā\ ace
\ä\ mop, mar  \aù\ out  \ch\ chin  \e\ bet  \ē\ easy
\g\ go  \i\ hit  \ī\ ice  \j\ job  \ŋ\ sing  \ō\ go
\ȯ\ law  \ȯi\ boy  \th\ thin  \t̲h̲\ the  \ü\ loot  \ù\ foot
\y\ yet  \zh\ vision  *see also* Guide to Pronunciation

**— to begin with :** as the first thing to be considered

**be·gin·ner** \bi-'gi-nər\ *noun* (14th century)
: one that begins something; *especially* : an inexperienced person

¹**be·gin·ning** \bi-'gi-niŋ\ *noun* (12th century)
**1 :** the point at which something begins **:** START
**2 :** the first part
**3 :** ORIGIN, SOURCE
**4 :** a rudimentary stage or early period — usually used in plural

²**beginning** *adjective* (1576)
**1 :** just starting out ⟨a *beginning* writer⟩
**2 a :** being first or the first part ⟨the *beginning* chapters⟩ **b :** INTRODUCTORY ⟨*beginning* chemistry⟩

**beginning rhyme** *noun* (1913)
**1 :** rhyme at the beginning of successive lines of verse
**2 :** ALLITERATION

**be·gird** \bi-'gərd\ *transitive verb* **-gird·ed** *or* **-girt** \-'gərt\; **-girt·ing** (before 12th century)
**1 :** GIRD 1a
**2 :** SURROUND, ENCOMPASS

**be·glam·our** *also* **be·glam·or** \bi-'gla-mər\ *transitive verb* (1822)
**:** to impress or deceive with glamour

**beg off** *intransitive verb* (1854)
**:** to ask to be excused from something
**— beg–off** \'beg-,óf\ *noun*

**be·gone** \bi-'gón *also* -'gän\ *intransitive verb* [Middle English, from *be gone* (imperative)] (14th century)
**:** to go away **:** DEPART — used especially in the imperative

**be·go·nia** \bi-'gōn-yə\ *noun* [New Latin, from Michel *Bégon* (died 1710) French governor of Santo Domingo] (1751)
**:** any of a large genus (*Begonia* of the family Begoniaceae, the begonia family) of tropical herbs and shrubs that have asymmetrical leaves and are widely cultivated as ornamentals

**be·gor·ra** \bi-'gór-ə, -'gär-\ *interjection* [euphemism for *by God*] (1839)
*Irish* — used as a mild oath

**be·grime** \bi-'grīm\ *transitive verb* **be·grimed; be·grim·ing** (circa 1553)
**1 :** to make dirty with grime
**2 :** SULLY, CORRUPT

**be·grudge** \bi-'grəj\ *transitive verb* (14th century)
**1 :** to give or concede reluctantly or with displeasure
**2 :** to look upon with disapproval
**— be·grudg·ing·ly** \-'grə-jiŋ-lē\ *adverb*

**be·guile** \bi-'gī(ə)l\ *verb* **be·guiled; be·guil·ing** (13th century)
*transitive verb*
**1 :** to lead by deception
**2 :** HOODWINK
**3 :** to while away especially by some agreeable occupation; *also* **:** DIVERT 2
**4 :** to engage the interest of by or as if by guile
*intransitive verb*
**:** to deceive by wiles
**synonym** see DECEIVE
**— be·guile·ment** \-'gī(ə)l-mənt\ *noun*
**— be·guil·er** \-'gī-lər\ *noun*
**— be·guil·ing·ly** \-'gī-liŋ-lē\ *adverb*

**be·guine** \bi-'gēn\ *noun* [American French *béguine*, from French *béguin* flirtation] (1935)
**:** a vigorous popular dance of the islands of Saint Lucia and Martinique that somewhat resembles the rumba

**Be·guine** \'bā-,gēn, bā-'\ *noun* [Middle French] (15th century)
**:** a member of one of various ascetic and philanthropic communities of women not under vows founded chiefly in the Netherlands in the 13th century

**be·gum** \'bā-gəm, 'bē-\ *noun* [Hindi *begam*] (1617)
**:** a Muslim woman of high rank (as in India or Pakistan)

**be·half** \bi-'haf, -'háf\ *noun* [Middle English, from *by* + *half* half, side] (14th century)
**:** INTEREST, BENEFIT; *also* **:** SUPPORT, DEFENSE ⟨argued in his *behalf*⟩
**— on behalf of** *or* **in behalf of :** in the interest of; *also* **:** as a representative of

**be·have** \bi-'hāv\ *verb* **be·haved; be·hav·ing** [Middle English *behaven*, from *be-* + *haven* to have, hold] (15th century)
*transitive verb*
**1 :** to manage the actions of (oneself) in a particular way
**2 :** to conduct (oneself) in a proper manner
*intransitive verb*
**1 :** to act, function, or react in a particular way
**2 :** to conduct oneself properly ☆
**— be·hav·er** *noun*

**be·hav·ior** \bi-'hā-vyər\ *noun* [alteration of Middle English *behavour*, from *behaven*] (15th century)
**1 a :** the manner of conducting oneself **b** **:** anything that an organism does involving action and response to stimulation **c :** the response of an individual, group, or species to its environment
**2 :** the way in which someone behaves; *also* **:** an instance of such behavior
**3 :** the way in which something functions or operates
**— be·hav·ior·al** \-vyə-rəl\ *adjective*
**— be·hav·ior·al·ly** \-rə-lē\ *adverb*

**behavioral science** *noun* (1951)
**:** a science (as psychology, sociology, or anthropology) that deals with human action and seeks to generalize about human behavior in society
**— behavioral scientist** *noun*

**be·hav·ior·ism** \bi-'hā-vyə-,ri-zəm\ *noun* (1913)
**:** a school of psychology that takes the objective evidence of behavior (as measured responses to stimuli) as the only concern of its research and the only basis of its theory without reference to conscious experience — compare INTROSPECTIONISM
**— be·hav·ior·ist** \-vyə-rist\ *adjective or noun*
**— be·hav·ior·is·tic** \-,hā-vyə-'ris-tik\ *adjective*

**behavior therapy** *noun* (1961)
**:** psychotherapy that emphasizes the application of the principles of learning to substitute desirable responses and behavior patterns for undesirable ones — called also *behavior modification*

**be·hav·iour** *chiefly British variant of* BEHAVIOR

**be·head** \bi-'hed\ *transitive verb* (before 12th century)
**:** to cut off the head of **:** DECAPITATE

**be·he·moth** \bi-'hē-məth, 'bē-ə-məth, -,mäth, -,móth\ *noun, often attributive* [Middle English, from Late Latin, from Hebrew *běhēmōth*] (14th century)
**1** *often capitalized* **:** a mighty animal described in Job 40:15–24 as an example of the power of God
**2 :** something of monstrous size or power

**be·hest** \bi-'hest\ *noun* [Middle English, promise, command, from Old English *behǣs* promise, from *behātan* to promise, from *be-* + *hātan* to command, promise — more at HIGHT] (12th century)
**1 :** an authoritative order **:** COMMAND
**2 :** an urgent prompting ⟨called at the *behest* of my friends⟩

¹**be·hind** \bi-'hīnd\ *adverb or adjective* [Middle English *behinde*, from Old English *behindan*, from *be-* + *hindan* from behind; akin to Old English *hinder* behind — more at HIND] (before 12th century)
**1 a :** in the place or situation that is being or has been departed from ⟨stay *behind*⟩ **b :** in, to, or toward the back ⟨look *behind*⟩ ⟨came from *behind*⟩ **c :** later in time ⟨can spring be far *behind*⟩
**2 a :** in a secondary or inferior position **b :** in arrears ⟨*behind* in the rent⟩ **c :** SLOW
**3** *archaic* **:** still to come

²**behind** *preposition* (before 12th century)
**1 a :** in or to a place or situation in back of or to the rear of ⟨look *behind* you⟩ ⟨put *behind* bars⟩ **b** — used as a function word to indicate something that screens an observer ⟨the sun went *behind* a cloud⟩ **c :** following in order ⟨marched *behind* the band⟩
**2** — used as a function word to indicate backwardness, delay, or deficiency ⟨*behind* the times⟩ ⟨*behind* schedule⟩ ⟨lagged *behind* last year's sales⟩
**3 a :** in the background of ⟨the conditions *behind* the strike⟩ **b :** out of the mind or consideration of ⟨put our troubles *behind* us⟩ **c :** beyond in depth or time ⟨the story *behind* the story⟩ ⟨go back *behind* Saint Augustine⟩
**4 a :** in support of **:** on the side of ⟨solidly *behind* the candidate⟩ **b** **:** with the support of ⟨won 1–0 *behind* brilliant pitching⟩

³**behind** *noun* [¹*behind*] (circa 1830)
**:** BUTTOCKS

**be·hind·hand** \bi-'hīnd-,hand\ *adjective* (1535)
**1 :** being in arrears
**2 a :** being in an inferior position **b :** being behind schedule

**behind–the–scenes** *adjective* (1711)
**1 :** being or working out of public view or in secret ⟨*behind-the-scenes* wrangling⟩ ⟨a *behind-the-scenes* player⟩
**2 :** revealing or reporting the hidden workings ⟨a *behind-the-scenes* account⟩ ⟨a *behind-the-scenes* glimpse⟩

**be·hold** \bi-'hōld\ *verb* **-held** \-'held\; **-hold·ing** [Middle English, to keep, behold, from Old English *behealdan*, from *be-* + *healdan* to hold] (before 12th century)

---

☆ **SYNONYMS**
**Behave, conduct, deport, comport, acquit** mean to act or to cause oneself to do something in a certain way. BEHAVE may apply to the meeting of a standard of what is proper or decorous ⟨the children *behaved* in church⟩. CONDUCT implies action or behavior that shows the extent of one's power to control or direct oneself ⟨*conducted* herself with unfailing good humor⟩. DEPORT implies behaving so as to show how far one conforms to conventional rules of discipline or propriety ⟨the hero *deported* himself in accord with the code of chivalry⟩. COMPORT suggests conduct measured by what is expected or required of one in a certain class or position ⟨*comported* themselves as gentlemen⟩. ACQUIT applies to action under stress that deserves praise or meets expectations ⟨*acquitted* herself well in her first assignment⟩.

---

□ **USAGE**
**behalf** A body of opinion favors *in* with the "interest, benefit" sense of *behalf* and *on* with the "support, defense" sense. This distinction has been observed by some writers but overall has never had a sound basis in actual usage. In current British use, *on behalf of* has replaced *in behalf (of)*; both are still used in American English, but the distinction is frequently not observed.

*transitive verb*
**1** **:** to perceive through sight or apprehension **:** SEE
**2** **:** to gaze upon **:** OBSERVE
*intransitive verb*
— used in the imperative especially to call attention
— **be·hold·er** *noun*
**be·hold·en** \bi-'hōl-dən\ *adjective* [Middle English, from past participle of *beholden*] (14th century)
**:** being under obligation for a favor or gift **:** INDEBTED ⟨I'm *beholden* to you⟩
**be·hoof** \bi-'hüf\ *noun* [Middle English *behof*, from Old English *behōf* profit, need; akin to Old English *hebban* to raise — more at HEAVE] (before 12th century)
**:** ADVANTAGE, PROFIT ⟨for his own *behoof*⟩
**be·hoove** \bi-'hüv\ *verb* **be·hooved; be·hoov·ing** [Middle English *behoven*, from Old English *behōfian*, from *behōf*] (before 12th century)
*transitive verb*
**:** to be necessary, proper, or advantageous for ⟨it *behooves* us to go⟩
*intransitive verb*
**:** to be necessary, fit, or proper
**be·hove** \bi-'hōv\ *chiefly British variant of* BEHOOVE
¹**beige** \'bāzh\ *noun* [French] (circa 1858)
**1** **:** cloth made of natural undyed wool
**2 a** **:** a variable color averaging light grayish yellowish brown **b** **:** a pale to grayish yellow
— **beigy** \'bā-zhē\ *adjective*
²**beige** *adjective* (1879)
**1** **:** of the color beige
**2** **:** VANILLA 2, VAPID
**bei·gnet** \,bān-'yā, ,ben-\ *noun* [American French & French; American French, from French, from Middle French *bignet*, from *buyne* bump, bruise] (1835)
**1** **:** FRITTER
**2** **:** a light square doughnut
¹**be·ing** \'bē-(i)ŋ\ *noun* (14th century)
**1 a** **:** the quality or state of having existence **b** (1) **:** something conceivable as existing (2) **:** something that actually exists (3) **:** the totality of existing things **c** **:** conscious existence **:** LIFE
**2** **:** the qualities that constitute an existent thing **:** ESSENCE; *especially* **:** PERSONALITY
**3** **:** a living thing; *especially* **:** PERSON
²**being** *adjective* [present participle of *be*] (14th century)
**:** PRESENT — used in the phrase *for the time being*
³**being** *conjunction* (1528)
*chiefly dialect* **:** SINCE, BECAUSE — usually used with *as, as how,* or *that* ■
**Be·ja** \'bā-jə\ *noun, plural* **Beja** (1819)
**1** **:** a member of a pastoral people living between the Nile and the Red Sea
**2** **:** the Cushitic language of the Beja people
**be·je·sus** *also* **be·jee·zus** \bi-'jē-zəs, -'jā-, -zəz\ *interjection* [alteration of *by Jesus*] (circa 1908)
— used as a mild oath; used as a noun for emphasis ⟨scares the *bejesus* out of me⟩
**be·jew·eled** *or* **be·jew·elled** \bi-'jü-əld, -'jüld *also* -'jú(ə)ld\ *adjective* (1557)
**:** ornamented with or as if with jewels
**bel** \'bel\ *noun* [Alexander Graham *Bell*] (1929)
**:** ten decibels
**be·la·bor** \bi-'lā-bər\ *transitive verb* (1596)
**1 a** **:** to attack verbally **b** **:** to beat soundly
**2** **:** to explain or insist on excessively ⟨*belabor* the obvious⟩
**be·la·bour** *chiefly British variant of* BELABOR
**be·lat·ed** \bi-'lā-təd\ *adjective* [past participle of *belate* (to make late)] (1670)
**1** **:** delayed beyond the usual time
**2** **:** existing or appearing past the normal or proper time

— **be·lat·ed·ly** *adverb*
— **be·lat·ed·ness** *noun*
**be·laud** \bi-'lòd\ *transitive verb* (circa 1849)
**:** to praise usually to excess
¹**be·lay** \bi-'lā\ *verb* [Middle English *beleggen* to beset, from Old English *belecgan*, from *be-* + *lecgan* to lay] (1548)
*transitive verb*
**1 a** **:** to secure (as a rope) by turns around a cleat, pin, or bitt **b** **:** to make fast
**2** **:** STOP
**3 a** **:** to secure (a person) at the end of a rope **b** **:** to secure (a rope) to a person or object
*intransitive verb*
**1** **:** to be made fast
**2** **:** STOP, QUIT — used in the imperative ⟨*belay* there⟩
**3** **:** to make a line fast by turns around a cleat, pin, or bitt
²**belay** *noun* (1908)
**1** **:** the securing of a person or a safety rope to an anchor point (as during mountain climbing); *also* **:** a method of so securing a person or rope
**2** **:** something (as a projection of rock) to which a person or rope is anchored
**bel can·to** \bel-'kän-(,)tō, -'kan-\ *noun* [Italian, literally, beautiful singing] (1894)
**:** operatic singing originating in 17th century and 18th century Italy and stressing ease, purity, and evenness of tone production and an agile and precise vocal technique
**belch** \'belch\ *verb* [Middle English, from Old English *bealcan*] (before 12th century)
*intransitive verb*
**1** **:** to expel gas suddenly from the stomach through the mouth
**2** **:** to erupt, explode, or detonate violently
**3** **:** to issue forth spasmodically **:** GUSH
*transitive verb*
**1** **:** to eject or emit violently
**2** **:** to expel (gas) from the stomach suddenly **:** ERUCT
— **belch** *noun*
**bel·dam** *or* **bel·dame** \'bel-dəm\ *noun* [Middle English *beldam* grandmother, from Middle French *bel* beautiful + Middle English *dam*] (1580)
**:** an old woman
**be·lea·guer** \bi-'lē-gər\ *transitive verb* **-guered; -guer·ing** \-g(ə-)riŋ\ [Dutch *belegeren*, from *be-* (akin to Old English *be-*) + *leger* camp; akin to Old High German *legar* bed — more at LAIR] (1587)
**1** **:** BESIEGE
**2** **:** TROUBLE, HARASS ⟨*beleaguered* parents⟩
— **be·lea·guer·ment** \-mənt\ *noun*
**bel·em·nite** \'be-ləm-,nīt\ *noun* [New Latin *belemnites*, from Greek *belemnon* dart; akin to Greek *ballein* to throw — more at DEVIL] (1646)
**:** any of a genus (*Belemnites*) of extinct cephalopods that had bullet-shaped internal shells and were especially abundant in the Mesozoic era
**bel·fry** \'bel-frē\ *noun, plural* **belfries** [Middle English *belfrey*, alteration of *berfrey,* from Middle French *berfrei* bell tower, siege tower, of Germanic origin (akin to Middle High German *bërvrit* siege tower); akin to Old High German *bergan* to shelter and to Old English *frith* peace, refuge — more at BURY] (15th century)
**1** **:** a bell tower; *especially* **:** one surmounting or attached to another structure
**2** **:** a room or framework for enclosing a bell
**3** **:** HEAD 2a ⟨batty in the *belfry*⟩ ◆
**Bel·gae** \'bel-,gī, -,jē\ *noun plural* [Latin, plural of *Belga*] (circa 1895)
**:** a people occupying parts of northern Gaul and Britain in Caesar's time
— **Bel·gic** \-jik\ *adjective*
**Bel·gian** \'bel-jən\ *noun* (circa 1623)
**1** **:** a native or inhabitant of Belgium

**2** **:** any of a breed of heavy muscular usually roan or chestnut draft horses developed in Belgium
— **Belgian** *adjective*
**Belgian endive** *noun* (1931)
**:** ENDIVE 2
**Belgian hare** *noun* (1900)
**:** any of a breed of slender chestnut-colored domestic rabbits
**Belgian Ma·li·nois** \-,ma-lən-'wä\ *noun* (1968)
**:** any of a breed of squarely built working dogs closely related to the Belgian sheepdog and having relatively short straight hair with a dense undercoat — called also *Malinois*
**Belgian sheepdog** *noun* (1929)
**:** any of a breed of hardy black dogs developed in Belgium especially for herding sheep
**Belgian Ter·vu·ren** \-(,)tər-'vyür-ən, -ter-\ *noun* [*Tervuren,* commune in Brabant, Belgium] (1964)
**:** any of a breed of working dogs closely related to the Belgian sheepdog but having abundant long straight fawn-colored hair with black tips
**Be·lial** \'bē-lē-əl, 'bēl-yəl\ *noun* [Greek, from Hebrew *bĕlīya'al* worthlessness] (13th century)

---

□ USAGE

**being**   If your own vocabulary does not include the conjunction *being* or its compound forms *being as, being as how,* and *being that,* you might well wonder at the wide coverage these terms receive in handbooks. The point that almost all of the handbooks miss is that this conjunction is dialectal. Like many words that have dwindled to regional use, *being* was once standard ⟨Sir John, you loiter here too long, *being* you are to take soldiers up in counties as you go —Shakespeare⟩ ⟨I am tired of Lives of Nelson, *being that* I never read any —Jane Austen⟩. *The Dictionary of American Regional English* reports that *being* and its compound forms still survive in the South, South Midland, and New England speech areas.

---

◇ WORD HISTORY

**belfry**   In our day *belfry* means bell tower; the first syllable appears to be a perfect match with *bell,* whatever *-fry* might mean. But in fact *belfry* does not derive from *bell,* and the original meaning of its medieval French source was not "bell tower," but rather "siege tower." A siege tower was a wheeled wooden structure that was pushed up to the walls of a besieged castle to provide both shelter and a base of attack for the besiegers. A Middle High German word for such a tower was *bercvrit,* which appears to be a compound of the verb *bergen* "to protect, conceal, shelter" and *vride* "peace, refuge," the presumed sense of the compound being "that which affords refuge." The ancient Germanic language that had the greatest influence on early French was Frankish, and the Frankish counterpart to such a word would have been *bergfrithu.* This word would have emerged in Old French as *berfroi,* for which we have evidence from the mid-12th century. In some dialects, *berfroi* underwent alteration to *belfroi,* and it is from an Anglo-French form of this word that Middle English borrowed *belfrey*—hence Modern English *belfry,* with its illusory suggestion of *bell.*

---

**1** — a biblical name of the devil or one of the fiends
**2** : one of the fallen angels in Milton's *Paradise Lost*
**be·lie** \bi-'lī\ *transitive verb* **-lied; -ly·ing** (before 12th century)
**1 a** : to give a false impression of **b** : to present an appearance not in agreement with
**2 a** : to show (something) to be false or wrong
**b** : to run counter to : CONTRADICT
**3** : DISGUISE 3
— **be·li·er** \-'lī(-ə)r\ *noun*
**be·lief** \bə-'lēf\ *noun* [Middle English *beleave*, probably alteration of Old English *gelēafa*, from *ge-*, associative prefix + *lēafa*; akin to Old English *lȳfan*] (12th century)
**1** : a state or habit of mind in which trust or confidence is placed in some person or thing
**2** : something believed; *especially* : a tenet or body of tenets held by a group
**3** : conviction of the truth of some statement or the reality of some being or phenomenon especially when based on examination of evidence ☆
**be·liev·able** \-'lē-və-bəl\ *adjective* (14th century)
: capable of being believed especially as within the range of known possibility or probability
— **be·liev·abil·i·ty** \-,lē-və-'bi-lə-tē\ *noun*
— **be·liev·ably** \-'lē-və-blē\ *adverb*
**be·lieve** \bə-'lēv\ *verb* **be·lieved; be·liev·ing** [Middle English *beleven*, from Old English *belēfan*, from *be-* + *lȳfan, lēfan* to allow, believe; akin to Old High German *gilouben* to believe, Old English *lēof* dear — more at LOVE] (before 12th century)
*intransitive verb*
**1 a** : to have a firm religious faith **b** : to accept as true, genuine, or real (ideals we *believe* in) (*believes* in ghosts)
**2** : to have a firm conviction as to the goodness, efficacy, or ability of something (*believe* in exercise)
**3** : to hold an opinion : THINK (I *believe* so)
*transitive verb*
**1 a** : to consider to be true or honest (*believe* the reports) (you wouldn't *believe* how long it took) **b** : to accept the word or evidence of (I *believe* you) (couldn't *believe* my ears)
**2** : to hold as an opinion : SUPPOSE (I *believe* it will rain soon)
— **be·liev·er** *noun*
— **not believe** : to be astounded at (I couldn*'t believe* my luck)
**be·like** \bi-'līk\ *adverb* (circa 1533) *archaic*
: most likely : PROBABLY
**be·lit·tle** \bi-'li-t³l\ *transitive verb* **-lit·tled; -lit·tling** \-'li-t³l-iŋ, -'lit-liŋ\ (1797)
**1** : to speak slightingly of : DISPARAGE (*belittles* her efforts)
**2** : to cause (a person or thing) to seem little or less
*synonym* see DECRY
— **be·lit·tle·ment** \-'li-t³l-mənt\ *noun*
— **be·lit·tler** \-'li-t³l-ər, -'lit-lər\ *noun*
**be·live** \bi-'līv\ *adverb* [Middle English *bilive* vigorously, from *by* + *live*, dative of *lif* life] (1594)
*Scottish* : in due time : BY AND BY
**¹bell** \'bel\ *noun* [Middle English *belle*, from Old English; perhaps akin to Old English *bellan* to roar — more at BELLOW] (before 12th century)
**1 a** : a hollow metallic device that gives off a reverberating sound when struck **b** : DOORBELL
**2 a** : the sounding of a bell as a signal **b** : a stroke of a bell (as on shipboard) to indicate the time; *also* : the time so indicated **c** : a half hour period of a watch on shipboard indicated by the strokes of a bell — see SHIP'S BELLS table below
**3** : something having the form of a bell: as **a** : the corolla of a flower **b** : the part of the capital of a column between the abacus and neck

molding **c** : the flared end of a wind instrument
**4 a** : a percussion instrument consisting of metal bars or tubes that when struck give out tones resembling bells — usually used in plural **b** : GLOCKENSPIEL

## SHIP'S BELLS

| NO. OF BELLS | HOUR (A.M. OR P.M.) | | |
|---|---|---|---|
| 1 | 12:30 | 4:30 | 8:30 |
| 2 | 1:00 | 5:00 | 9:00 |
| 3 | 1:30 | 5:30 | 9:30 |
| 4 | 2:00 | 6:00 | 10:00 |
| 5 | 2:30 | 6:30 | 10:30 |
| 6 | 3:00 | 7:00 | 11:00 |
| 7 | 3:30 | 7:30 | 11:30 |
| 8 | 4:00 | 8:00 | 12:00 |

**²bell** (14th century)
*transitive verb*
**1** : to provide with a bell
**2** : to flare the end of (as a tube) into the shape of a bell
*intransitive verb*
: to take the form of a bell : FLARE
— **bell the cat** : to do a daring or risky deed
**³bell** *intransitive verb* [Middle English, from Old English *bellan*] (before 12th century)
: to make a resonant bellowing or baying sound (the wild buck *bells* from ferny brake —Sir Walter Scott)
**⁴bell** *noun* (1862)
: BELLOW, ROAR
**bel·la·don·na** \,be-lə-'dä-nə\ *noun* [Italian, literally, beautiful lady] (1597)
**1** : an Old World poisonous plant (*Atropa belladonna*) of the nightshade family having purple or green bell-shaped flowers, glossy black berries, and root and leaves that yield atropine — called also *deadly nightshade*
**2** : a medicinal extract (as atropine) from the belladonna plant
**belladonna lily** *noun* (1734)
: AMARYLLIS
**bell-bird** \'bel-,bərd\ *noun* (1802)
: any of various birds (as of the genera *Procnias* and *Anthornis*) whose notes suggest the sound of a bell
**bell-bot·toms** \'bel-'bä-təmz\ *noun plural* (1898)
: pants with wide flaring bottoms
— **bell–bottom** *adjective*
**bell-boy** \'bel-,bȯi\ *noun* (1861)
: BELLHOP
**bell buoy** *noun* (1838)
: a buoy with a bell rung by the action of the waves
**bell captain** *noun* (1926)
: CAPTAIN 2c
**bell curve** *noun* [from the shape] (circa 1941)
: NORMAL CURVE
**belle** \'bel\ *noun* [French, from feminine of *beau* beautiful — more at BEAU] (1622)
: a popular and attractive girl or woman; *especially* : a girl or woman whose charm and beauty make her a favorite (the *belle* of the ball)
**Bel·leek** \bə-'lēk\ *noun* [*Belleek*, town in Northern Ireland] (1869)
: a very thin translucent porcelain with a lustrous pearly glaze produced in Ireland — called also *Belleek china, Belleek ware*
**belle epoque** or **belle époque** \'bel-ā-'pȯk\ *noun, often B&E capitalized* [French, literally, beautiful age] (1954)
: a period of high artistic or cultural development; *especially* : such a period in fin de siècle France
**Bel·ler·o·phon** \bə-'ler-ə-fən, -,fän\ *noun* [Latin, from Greek *Bellerophōn*]
: a legendary Greek hero noted for killing the Chimera

**belles let·tres** \bel-letr³\ *noun plural but singular in construction* [French, literally, fine letters] (1710)
: literature that is an end in itself and not merely informative; *specifically* : light, entertaining, and often sophisticated literature
**bel·le·trist** \bel-'le-trist\ *noun* [*belles lettres*] (1816)
: a writer of belles lettres
— **bel·le·tris·tic** \,be-lə-'tris-tik\ *adjective*
**bell-flow·er** \'bel-,flaū(-ə)r\ *noun* (1578)
: any of a genus (*Campanula* of the family Campanulaceae, the bellflower family) of widely cultivated herbs having alternate leaves and usually showy flowers
**bell-hop** \-,häp\ *noun* [short for *bell-hopper*] (1910)
: a hotel or club employee who escorts guests to rooms, assists them with luggage, and runs errands
**bel·li·cose** \'be-li-,kōs\ *adjective* [Middle English, from Latin *bellicosus*, from *bellicus* of war, from *bellum* war] (15th century)
: favoring or inclined to start quarrels or wars
*synonym* see BELLIGERENT
— **bel·li·cos·i·ty** \,be-li-'kä-sə-tē\ *noun*
**bel·lied** \'be-lēd\ *adjective* (15th century)
: having a belly of a specified kind — used in combination (a big-*bellied* man)
**bel·lig·er·ence** \bə-'lij-rən(t)s, -'li-jə-\ *noun* (1814)
: an aggressive or truculent attitude, atmosphere, or disposition
**bel·lig·er·en·cy** \-rən(t)-sē\ *noun* (1863)
**1** : the state of being at war or in conflict; *specifically* : the status of a legally recognized belligerent state or nation
**2** : BELLIGERENCE
**bel·lig·er·ent** \-rənt\ *adjective* [modification of Latin *belligerant-, belligerans*, present participle of *belligerare* to wage war, from *belliger* waging war, from *bellum* + *gerere* to wage] (1577)
**1** : waging war; *specifically* : belonging to or recognized as a state at war and protected by and subject to the laws of war
**2** : inclined to or exhibiting assertiveness, hostility, or combativeness ☆
— **belligerent** *noun*
— **bel·lig·er·ent·ly** *adverb*
**bell jar** *noun* (circa 1859)

---

☆ SYNONYMS

**Belief, faith, credence, credit** mean assent to the truth of something offered for acceptance. BELIEF may or may not imply certitude in the believer (my *belief* that I had caught all the errors). FAITH almost always implies certitude even where there is no evidence or proof (an unshakable *faith* in God). CREDENCE suggests intellectual assent without implying anything about grounds for assent (a theory now given *credence* by scientists). CREDIT may imply assent on grounds other than direct proof (gave full *credit* to the statement of a reputable witness). See in addition OPINION.

**Belligerent, bellicose, pugnacious, quarrelsome, contentious** mean having an aggressive or fighting attitude. BELLIGERENT implies being actually at war or engaged in hostilities (*belligerent* nations). BELLICOSE suggests a disposition to fight (a drunk in a *bellicose* mood). PUGNACIOUS suggests a disposition that takes pleasure in personal combat (a *pugnacious* thug). QUARRELSOME stresses an ill-natured readiness to fight without good cause (the heat made us all *quarrelsome*). CONTENTIOUS implies perverse and irritating fondness for arguing and quarreling (wearied by his *contentious* disposition).

: a bell-shaped usually glass vessel designed to cover objects or to contain gases or a vacuum

**bell–ly·ra** \'bel-'lī-rə\ *or* **bell lyre** \-,līr\ *noun* [*lyra* from Latin, lyre] (circa 1943)
: a glockenspiel mounted in a portable lyre-shaped frame and used especially in marching bands

**bell jar**

**bell·man** \'bel-mən\ *noun* (14th century)
**1** : a man (as a town crier) who rings a bell
**2** : BELLHOP

**bell metal** *noun* (1541)
: bronze that consists usually of three to four parts of copper to one of tin and that is used for making bells

**Bel·lo·na** \bə-'lō-nə\ *noun* [Latin]
: the Roman goddess of war

**bel·low** \'be-(,)lō\ *verb* [Middle English *belwen,* from Old English *bylgian;* akin to Old English & Old High German *bellan* to roar] (before 12th century)
*intransitive verb*
**1** : to make the loud deep hollow sound characteristic of a bull
**2** : to shout in a deep voice
*transitive verb*
: BAWL ⟨*bellows* the orders⟩
— **bellow** *noun*

**bel·lows** \'be-(,)lōz, -ləz\ *noun plural but singular or plural in construction* [Middle English *belu,* from Old English *belg* — more at BELLY] (before 12th century)
**1** : an instrument or machine that by alternate expansion and contraction draws in air through a valve or orifice and expels it through a tube; *also* : any of various other blowers
**2** : LUNGS
**3** : the pleated expansible part in a camera; *also* : a metallic or plastic flexible and expansible vessel

**bell pepper** *noun* (1707)
: SWEET PEPPER

**bell·pull** \'bel-,pul\ *noun* (1832)
: a handle or knob attached to a cord by which one rings a bell; *also* : the cord itself

**bell push** *noun* (1884)
: a button that is pushed to ring a bell

**bells and whistles** *noun plural* (1969)
: items or features that are useful or decorative but not essential : FRILLS

**bell–shaped** \'bel-,shāpt\ *adjective* (circa 1828)
**1** : shaped like a bell
**2** : relating to or being a normal curve or a normal distribution

**Bell's palsy** \'belz-\ *noun* [Sir Charles *Bell* (died 1842) Scottish anatomist] (circa 1860)
: paralysis of the facial nerve producing distortion on one side of the face

**bell tower** *noun* (1614)
: a tower that supports or shelters a bell

**bell·weth·er** \'bel-'we-thər, -,we-\ *noun* [Middle English, leading sheep of a flock, leader, from *belle* bell + *wether;* from the practice of belling the leader of a flock] (13th century)
: one that takes the lead or initiative : LEADER; *also* : an indicator of trends

**bell·wort** \'bel-,wərt, -,wȯrt\ *noun* (1784)
: any of a small genus (*Uvularia*) of herbs of the lily family with yellow drooping flowers

**¹bel·ly** \'be-lē\ *noun, plural* **bellies** [Middle English *bely* bellows, belly, from Old English *belg* bag, skin; akin to Old High German *balg* bag, skin, Old English *blāwan* to blow — more at BLOW] (before 12th century)
**1 a** : ABDOMEN 1; *also* : POTBELLY 1 **b** : the stomach and its adjuncts **c** : the undersurface of an animal's body; *also* : hide from this part
**d** : WOMB, UTERUS
**2** : an internal cavity : INTERIOR
**3** : appetite for food

**4** : a surface or object curved or rounded like a human belly
**5 a** : the enlarged fleshy body of a muscle **b** : the part of a sail that swells out when filled with wind
**6** : GUT 1a(2)

**²belly** *verb* **bel·lied; bel·ly·ing** (1606)
*transitive verb*
: to cause to swell or fill out
*intransitive verb*
**1** : SWELL, FILL
**2 a** : to slide or crawl on one's belly **b** : BELLY-LAND

**¹bel·ly·ache** \'be-lē-,āk\ *noun* (1552)
: pain in the abdomen and especially in the bowels : COLIC

**²bellyache** *intransitive verb* (1881)
: to complain whiningly or peevishly : find fault
— **bel·ly·ach·er** *noun*

**bel·ly·band** \'be-lē-,band\ *noun* (15th century)
: a band around or across the belly: as **a** : GIRTH 1 **b** : BAND 4b

**belly button** *noun* (circa 1877)
: the human navel

**belly dance** *noun* (1899)
: a usually solo dance emphasizing movements of the belly
— **belly dance** *intransitive verb*
— **belly dancer** *noun*

**belly flop** *noun* (1895)
: a dive (as into water or in coasting prone on a sled) in which the front of the body strikes flat against another surface — called also *belly flopper*
— **belly flop** *intransitive verb*

**bel·ly·ful** \'be-lē-,fu̇l\ *noun* (1535)
: an excessive amount ⟨a *bellyful* of advice⟩

**bel·ly–land** \-,land\ *intransitive verb* (1943)
: to land an airplane on its undersurface without use of landing gear
— **belly landing** *noun*

**belly laugh** *noun* (1921)
: a deep hearty laugh

**bel·ly–up** \-'əp\ *adjective* [from the floating position of a dead fish] (1939)
: hopelessly ruined or defeated; *especially* : BANKRUPT ⟨the business went *belly-up*⟩

**belly up** *intransitive verb* (1948)
: to move close or next to ⟨*bellied up* to the bar⟩

**be·long** \bi-'lȯṅ\ *verb* [Middle English *belongen,* from *be-* + *longen* to be suitable — more at LONG] (14th century)
*intransitive verb*
**1 a** : to be suitable, appropriate, or advantageous ⟨a dictionary *belongs* in every home⟩ **b** : to be in a proper situation ⟨a man of his ability *belongs* in teaching⟩
**2 a** : to be the property of a person or thing — used with *to* **b** : to be attached or bound by birth, allegiance, or dependency **c** : to be a member of a club, organization, or set
**3** : to be an attribute, part, adjunct, or function of a person or thing ⟨nuts and bolts *belong* to a car⟩
**4** : to be properly classified
*verbal auxiliary*
*chiefly Southern & southern Midland* : OUGHT, MUST

**be·long·ing** \-'lȯṅ-iṅ\ *noun* (1817)
**1** : POSSESSION — usually used in plural
**2** : close or intimate relationship ⟨a sense of *belonging*⟩
— **be·long·ing·ness** *noun*

**Belo·rus·sian** \,be-lō-'rə-shən, ,bye-\ *noun* (1943)
**1** : a native or inhabitant of Belorussia (Belarus)
**2** : the Slavic language of the Belorussians
— **Belorussian** *adjective*

**be·loved** \bi-'ləvd, -'lə-vəd\ *adjective* [Middle English, from past participle of *beloven* to love, from *be-* + *loven* to love] (14th century)
: dearly loved : dear to the heart
— **beloved** *noun*

**¹be·low** \bi-'lō\ *adverb* [Middle English *bilooghe,* from *bi* by + *looghe* ³low] (14th century)
**1** : in or to a lower place
**2 a** : on earth **b** : in or to Hades or hell
**3** : on or to a lower floor or deck
**4 a** : in, to, at, or by a lower rank or number **b** : below zero ⟨20 degrees *below*⟩
**5** : lower on the same page or on a following page
**6** : under the surface of the water

**²below** *preposition* (1575)
**1 a** : lower in place, rank, or value than : UNDER **b** : down river from **c** : south of
**2** : inferior to (as in rank)
**3** : not suitable to the rank of : BENEATH

**³below** *noun* (1697)
: something that is below

**⁴below** *adjective* (1916)
: written or discussed lower on the same page or on a following page

**be·low·decks** \bi-,lō-'deks; -'lō-,deks\ *adverb* (1909)
: inside or into the superstructure of a boat : down to a lower deck

**be·low·ground** \-'graúnd; -,graúnd\ *adjective* (1928)
: being under the ground

**Bel·shaz·zar** \bel-'sha-zər\ *noun* [Hebrew *Bēlshaṣṣar*]
: a son of Nebuchadnezzar and king of Babylon

**¹belt** \'belt\ *noun* [Middle English, from Old English; akin to Old High German *balz* belt; both from Latin *balteus* belt] (before 12th century)
**1 a** : a strip of flexible material worn especially around the waist **b** : a similar article worn as a corset or for protection or safety or as a symbol of distinction
**2** : a continuous band of tough flexible material for transmitting motion and power or conveying materials
**3** : an area characterized by some distinctive feature (as of culture, habitation, geology, or life forms); *especially* : one suited to a particular crop ⟨the corn *belt*⟩
**4** : BELTWAY
— **belt·ed** \'bel-təd\ *adjective*
— **belt·less** \'belt-ləs\ *adjective*
— **below the belt** : UNFAIR, UNFAIRLY
— **under one's belt** : in one's possession : as part of one's experience

**²belt** (14th century)
*transitive verb*
**1 a** : to encircle or fasten with a belt **b** : to strap on
**2 a** : to beat with or as if with a belt : THRASH **b** : STRIKE, HIT
**3** : to mark with a band
**4** : to sing in a forceful manner or style ⟨*belting* out popular songs⟩
*intransitive verb*
**1** : to move or act in a speedy, vigorous, or violent manner
**2** : to sing loudly
— **belt·er** \'bel-tər\ *noun*

**³belt** *noun* (1899)
**1** : a jarring blow : WHACK
**2** : DRINK ⟨a *belt* of gin⟩

**Bel·tane** \'bel-,tān, -tin\ *noun* [Middle English (Scots), 1st or 3rd of May, from Scottish Gaelic *bealltain*] (15th century)
: the Celtic May Day festival

**belted kingfisher** *noun* (1811)
: a North American kingfisher (*Ceryle alcyon* synonym *Megaceryle alcyon*) that is slate blue above and white below with a slate blue breast band and an additional chestnut-colored band in the female

\ə\ abut \ᵊ\ kitten \ər\ further \a\ ash \ā\ ace
\ä\ mop, mar \aú\ out \ch\ chin \e\ bet \ē\ easy
\g\ go \i\ hit \ī\ ice \j\ job \ṅ\ sing \ō\ go
\ȯ\ law \ȯi\ boy \th\ thin \th\ the \ü\ loot \ú\ foot
\y\ yet \zh\ vision    *see also* Guide to Pronunciation

**belt·ing** \'bel-tiŋ\ *noun* (1567)
**1** : BELTS
**2** : material for belts
**belt–tight·en·ing** \'belt-,tīt-niŋ, -,tī-t°n-iŋ\ *noun* (1937)
: a reduction in spending
**belt up** *intransitive verb* (1949)
*British* : SHUT UP
**belt·way** \'belt-,wā\ *noun* (circa 1952)
: a highway skirting an urban area — often used to refer specifically to the beltway around Washington D.C. especially as delimiting what is seen as an insular political and social world
**be·lu·ga** \bə-'lü-gə\ *noun* [Russian, from *belyĭ* white; akin to Greek *phalios* having a white spot — more at BALD] (1772)
**1 a** : a large white sturgeon (*Huso huso* synonym *Acipenser huso*) of the Black Sea, Caspian Sea, and their tributaries **b** : caviar processed from beluga roe
**2** [Russian *belukha*, from *belyĭ*] : WHITE WHALE
**bel·ve·dere** \'bel-və-,dir\ *noun* [Italian, literally, beautiful view] (1593)
: a structure (as a cupola or a summerhouse) designed to command a view
**be·ma** \'bē-mə\ *noun* [Late Latin & Late Greek; Late Latin, from Late Greek *bēma*, from Greek, step, tribunal, from *bainein* to go — more at COME] (1683)
**1** : the usually raised part of an Eastern church containing the altar
**2** : a raised platform in a synagogue from which the Pentateuch and the Prophets are read
**Bem·ba** \'bem-bə\ *noun, plural* **Bemba** *or* **Bembas** (1940)
**1** : a member of a primarily agricultural Bantu-speaking people of northeastern Zambia
**2** : a Bantu language of the Bemba people
**be·med·aled** *or* **be·med·alled** \bi-'me-d°ld\ *adjective* (1880)
: wearing or decorated with medals
**be·mire** \bi-'mīr\ *transitive verb* (circa 1532)
**1** : to soil with mud or dirt
**2** : to drag through or sink in mire
**be·moan** \bi-'mōn\ *transitive verb* (before 12th century)
**1** : to express deep grief or distress over
**2** : to regard with displeasure, disapproval, or regret
***synonym*** see DEPLORE
**be·mock** \bi-'mäk, -'mȯk\ *transitive verb* (1607)
*archaic* : MOCK
**be·muse** \bi-'myüz\ *transitive verb* (1735)
**1** : to make confused : BEWILDER
**2** : to occupy the attention of : ABSORB
— **be·mus·ed·ly** \-'myü-zəd-lē\ *adverb*
— **be·muse·ment** \-'myüz-mənt\ *noun*
**¹ben** \'ben\ *adverb* [Middle English, from Old English *binnan*, from *be-* + *innan* within, from within, from *in*] (before 12th century)
*Scottish* : WITHIN
**²ben** *preposition* (before 12th century)
*Scottish* : WITHIN
**³ben** *noun* (circa 1799)
*Scottish* : the inner room or parlor of a 2-room cottage
**Bence–Jones protein** \'ben(t)s-'jōnz-\ *noun* [Henry *Bence-Jones* (died 1873) English physician and chemist] (circa 1923)
: an immunoglobulin that is composed only of light chain polypeptides and that is found especially in the urine of persons affected with multiple myeloma
**¹bench** \'bench\ *noun* [Middle English, from Old English *benc*; akin to Old High German *bank* bench] (before 12th century)
**1 a** : a long seat for two or more persons **b** : a thwart in a boat **c** (1) : a seat on which the members of an athletic team await a turn or opportunity to play (2) : the reserve players on a team
**2 a** : the seat where a judge sits in court **b** : the place where justice is administered

: COURT **c** : the office or dignity of a judge **d** : the persons who sit as judges
**3 a** : the office or dignity of an official **b** : a seat for an official **c** : the officials occupying a bench
**4 a** : a long worktable; *also* : LABORATORY ⟨*bench* chemist⟩ ⟨*bench* test⟩ **b** : a table forming part of a machine
**5** : TERRACE, SHELF: as **a** : a former wave-cut shore of a sea or lake or floodplain of a river **b** : a shelf or ridge formed in working an open excavation on more than one level
**6** : a compartmented platform on which dogs or cats are kept at a show when not being judged
**²bench** (14th century)
*transitive verb*
**1** : to furnish with benches
**2 a** : to seat on a bench **b** (1) : to remove from or keep out of a game (2) : to remove from the starting lineup
**3** : to exhibit (dogs or cats) to the public on a bench
*intransitive verb*
: to form a bench by natural processes
**bench·er** \'ben-chər\ *noun* (15th century)
: one who sits on or presides at a bench
**bench·land** \'bench-,land\ *noun* (1857)
: BENCH 5a
**bench·mark** \'bench-,märk\ *noun* (circa 1842)
**1** *usually* **bench mark** : a mark on a permanent object indicating elevation and serving as a reference in topographical surveys and tidal observations
**2 a** : a point of reference from which measurements may be made **b** : something that serves as a standard by which others may be measured or judged **c** : a standardized problem or test that serves as a basis for evaluation or comparison (as of computer system performance)
**bench press** *noun* (1973)
: a press in weight lifting performed by a lifter lying on a bench
— **bench–press** *transitive verb*
**bench seat** *noun* (1975)
: a seat in an automotive vehicle that extends the full width of the passenger section
**bench·warm·er** \'bench-,wȯr-mər\ *noun* (1892)
: a reserve player on an athletic team
**bench warrant** *noun* (1696)
: a warrant issued by a presiding judge or by a court against a person guilty of contempt or indicted for a crime
**¹bend** \'bend\ *verb* **bent** \'bent\; **bend·ing** [Middle English, from Old English *bendan*; akin to Old English *bend* fetter — more at BAND] (before 12th century)
*transitive verb*
**1** : to constrain or strain to tension by curving ⟨*bend* a bow⟩
**2 a** : to turn or force from straight or even to curved or angular **b** : to force from a proper shape **c** : to force back to an original straight or even condition
**3** : FASTEN ⟨*bend* a sail to its yard⟩
**4 a** : to cause to turn from a straight course : DEFLECT **b** : to guide or turn toward : DIRECT **c** : INCLINE, DISPOSE **d** : to adapt to one's purpose : DISTORT ⟨*bend* the rules⟩
**5** : to direct strenuously or with interest : APPLY
**6** : to make submissive : SUBDUE
*intransitive verb*
**1** : to curve out of a straight line or position; *specifically* : to incline the body in token of submission
**2** : to apply oneself vigorously ⟨*bending* to their work⟩
**3** : INCLINE, TEND
**4** : to make concessions : COMPROMISE
— **bend·a·ble** \'ben-də-bəl\ *adjective*
— **bend one's ear** : to talk to someone at length

**²bend** *noun* (15th century)
**1** : the act or process of bending : the state of being bent
**2** : something that is bent: as **a** : a curved part of a stream or road **b** : ¹WALE 2 — usually used in plural
**3** *plural but singular or plural in construction* : a sometimes fatal disorder that is marked by neuralgic pains and paralysis, distress in breathing, and often collapse and that is caused by the release of gas bubbles (as of nitrogen) in tissue upon too rapid decrease in air pressure after a stay in a compressed atmosphere — usually used with *the*; called also *caisson disease, decompression sickness*; compare AEROEMBOLISM
— **around the bend** : MAD, CRAZY
**³bend** *noun* [Middle English, from Middle French *bende*, of Germanic origin; akin to Old High German *binta, bant* band — more at BAND] (15th century)
**1** : a diagonal band that runs from the dexter chief to the sinister base on a heraldic shield — compare BEND SINISTER
**2** [Middle English, band, from Old English *bend* fetter — more at BAND] : a knot by which one rope is fastened to another or to some object
**ben·day** \'ben-'dā\ *adjective, often capitalized* [*Benjamin Day* (died 1916) American printer] (1903)
: involving a process for adding shaded or tinted areas made up of dots for reproduction by line engraving
— **benday** *transitive verb*
**bend·er** \'ben-dər\ *noun* (15th century)
**1** : one that bends
**2** : SPREE
**bend sinister** *noun* (1612)
: a diagonal bend that runs from the sinister chief to the dexter base on a heraldic shield
**bendy** \'ben-dē\ *adjective* (1928)
: FLEXIBLE, PLIABLE ⟨a *bendy* mast⟩
**¹be·neath** \bi-'nēth\ *adverb* [Middle English *benethe*, from Old English *beneothan*, from *be-* + *neothan* below; akin to Old English *nithera* nether] (before 12th century)
**1** : in or to a lower position : BELOW
**2** : directly under : UNDERNEATH
**²beneath** *preposition* (before 12th century)
**1 a** : in or to a lower position than : BELOW **b** : directly under **c** : at the foot of
**2** : not suitable to the rank of : unworthy of
**3** : under the control, pressure, or influence of
**4** : concealed by : under the guise of ⟨a warm heart *beneath* a gruff manner⟩
**ben·e·dict** \'be-nə-,dikt\ *noun* [alteration of *Benedick*, character in Shakespeare's *Much Ado about Nothing*] (1821)
: a newly married man who has long been a bachelor
**Ben·e·dic·tine** \,be-nə-'dik-tən, -,tēn\ *noun* (15th century)
: a monk or a nun of one of the congregations following the rule of Saint Benedict and devoted especially to scholarship and liturgical worship
— **Benedictine** *adjective*
**bene·dic·tion** \,be-nə-'dik-shən\ *noun* [Middle English *benediccioun*, from Late Latin *benediction-, benedictio*, from *benedicere* to bless, from Latin, to speak well of, from *bene* well (akin to Latin *bonus* good) + *dicere* to say — more at BOUNTY, DICTION] (15th century)
**1** : the invocation of a blessing; *especially* : the short blessing with which public worship is concluded
**2** : something that promotes goodness or well-being
**3** *often capitalized* : a Roman Catholic or Anglo-Catholic devotion including the exposition of the eucharistic Host in the monstrance and the blessing of the people with it
**4** : an expression of good wishes
**bene·dic·to·ry** \-'dik-t(ə-)rē\ *adjective* (1710)

: of or expressing benediction

**Ben·e·dict's solution** \'be-nə-ˌdik(t)s-\ *noun* [Stanley Rossiter *Benedict* (died 1936) American chemist] (1921)

: a blue solution containing a carbonate, citrate, and sulfate which yields a red, yellow, or orange precipitate upon warming with a sugar (as glucose) that is a reducing agent

**Ben·e·dic·tus** \ˌbe-nə-'dik-təs\ *noun* [Late Latin, blessed, from past participle of *benedicere;* from its first word] (1552)

**1** : a canticle from Luke 1:68 beginning "Blessed be the Lord God of Israel"
**2** : a canticle from Matthew 21:9 beginning "Blessed is he that cometh in the name of the Lord"

**ben·e·fac·tion** \ˌbe-nə-'fak-shən\ *noun* [Late Latin *benefaction-, benefactio,* from Latin *bene facere* to do good to, from *bene* + *facere* to do — more at DO] (circa 1662)

**1** : the act of benefiting
**2** : a benefit conferred; *especially* : a charitable donation

**ben·e·fac·tor** \'be-nə-ˌfak-tər\ *noun* (15th century)

: one that confers a benefit; *especially* : one that makes a gift or bequest

**ben·e·fac·tress** \'be-nə-ˌfak-tris\ *noun* (1711)

: a woman who is a benefactor

**be·nef·ic** \bə-'ne-fik\ *adjective* [Latin *beneficus,* from *bene* + *facere*] (1641)

: BENEFICENT

**ben·e·fice** \'be-nə-fəs\ *noun* [Middle English, from Middle French, from Medieval Latin *beneficium,* from Latin, favor, promotion, from *beneficus*] (14th century)

**1** : an ecclesiastical office to which the revenue from an endowment is attached
**2** : a feudal estate in lands : FIEF
— **benefice** *transitive verb*

**be·nef·i·cence** \bə-'ne-fə-sən(t)s\ *noun* [Latin *beneficentia,* from *beneficus*] (15th century)

**1** : the quality or state of being beneficent
**2** : BENEFACTION

**be·nef·i·cent** \-sənt\ *adjective* [back-formation from *beneficence*] (1616)

**1** : doing or producing good; *especially* : performing acts of kindness and charity
**2** : BENEFICIAL
— **be·nef·i·cent·ly** *adverb*

**ben·e·fi·cial** \ˌbe-nə-'fi-shəl\ *adjective* [Latin *beneficium* favor, benefit] (15th century)

**1** : conferring benefits : conducive to personal or social well-being
**2** : receiving or entitling one to receive advantage, use, or benefit ⟨a *beneficial* legacy⟩
— **be·nef·i·cial·ly** \-'fi-shə-)lē\ *adverb*
— **ben·e·fi·cial·ness** *noun*

**ben·e·fi·cia·ry** \ˌbe-nə-'fi-shē-ˌer-ē, -'fi-sh(ə-)rē\ *noun, plural* **-ries** (1662)

**1** : one that benefits from something
**2 a** : the person designated to receive the income of a trust estate **b** : the person named (as in an insurance policy) to receive proceeds or benefits
— **beneficiary** *adjective*

**ben·e·fi·ci·a·tion** \ˌbe-nə-ˌfi-shē-'ā-shən\ *noun* (circa 1881)

: the treatment of raw material (as iron ore) to improve physical or chemical properties especially in preparation for smelting
— **ben·e·fi·ci·ate** \-'fi-shē-ˌāt\ *transitive verb*

**¹ben·e·fit** \'be-nə-ˌfit\ *noun* [Middle English, from Anglo-French *benfet,* from Latin *bene factum,* from neuter of *bene factus,* past participle of *bene facere*] (14th century)

**1** *archaic* : an act of kindness : BENEFACTION
**2 a** : something that promotes well-being : ADVANTAGE **b** : useful aid : HELP
**3 a** : financial help in time of sickness, old age, or unemployment **b** : a payment or service provided for under an annuity, pension plan, or insurance policy

**4** : an entertainment or social event to raise funds for a person or cause

**²benefit** *verb* **-fit·ed** \-ˌfi-təd\ *also* **-fit·ted; -fit·ing** *also* **-fit·ting** (15th century)
*transitive verb*
: to be useful or profitable to
*intransitive verb*
: to receive benefit
— **ben·e·fit·er** \-ˌfi-tər\ *noun*

**benefit of clergy** (15th century)

**1** : clerical exemption from trial in a civil court
**2** : the ministration or sanction of the church

**be·nev·o·lence** \bə-'nev-lən(t)s, -'ne-və-\ *noun* (14th century)

**1** : disposition to do good
**2 a** : an act of kindness **b** : a generous gift
**3** : a compulsory levy by certain English kings with no other authority than the claim of prerogative

**be·nev·o·lent** \-lənt\ *adjective* [Middle English, from Latin *benevolent-, benevolens,* from *bene* + *volent-, volens,* present participle of *velle* to wish — more at WILL] (15th century)

**1 a** : marked by or disposed to doing good ⟨a *benevolent* donor⟩ **b** : organized for the purpose of doing good ⟨a *benevolent* society⟩
**2** : marked by or suggestive of goodwill ⟨*benevolent* smiles⟩
— **be·nev·o·lent·ly** *adverb*
— **be·nev·o·lent·ness** *noun*

**Ben·gali** \ben-'gȯ-lē, beŋ-\ *noun* [Hindi *Baṅgālī,* from *Baṅgāl* Bengal] (1848)

**1** : a native or resident of Bengal
**2** : the modern Indo-Aryan language of Bengal
— **Bengali** *adjective*

**ben·ga·line** \'beŋ-gə-ˌlēn\ *noun* [French, from *Bengal*] (1884)

: a fabric with a crosswise rib made from textile fibers (as rayon, nylon, cotton, or wool) often in combination

**Ben·gal light** \'ben-ˌgȯl-, ˌbeŋ-, -ˌgäl-, -gəl-\ *noun* (1818)

: a usually blue light or flare used formerly especially for signaling and illumination

**Bengal tiger** *noun* (circa 1864)

: a tiger (*Panthera tigris tigris*) occurring especially in India

**be·night·ed** \bi-'nī-təd\ *adjective* (15th century)

**1** : overtaken by darkness or night
**2** : existing in a state of intellectual, moral, or social darkness : UNENLIGHTENED
— **be·night·ed·ly** *adverb*
— **be·night·ed·ness** *noun*

**be·nign** \bi-'nīn\ *adjective* [Middle English *benigne,* from Middle French, from Latin *benignus,* from *bene* + *gignere* to beget — more at KIN] (14th century)

**1** : of a gentle disposition : GRACIOUS ⟨a *benign* teacher⟩
**2 a** : showing kindness and gentleness ⟨*benign* faces⟩ **b** : FAVORABLE, WHOLESOME ⟨a *benign* climate⟩
**3 a** : of a mild type or character that does not threaten health or life ⟨a *benign* tumor⟩ **b** : having no significant effect : HARMLESS ⟨environmentally *benign*⟩
— **be·nig·ni·ty** \-'nig-nə-tē\ *noun*
— **be·nign·ly** \-'nīn-lē\ *adverb*

**be·nig·nan·cy** \bi-'nig-nən(t)-sē\ *noun* (1876)

: benignant quality

**be·nig·nant** \-nənt\ *adjective* [benign + -ant (as in *malignant*)] (circa 1782)

**1** : serenely mild and kindly : BENIGN
**2** : FAVORABLE, BENEFICIAL ⟨a *benignant* power⟩
— **be·nig·nant·ly** *adverb*

**benign neglect** *noun* (1970)

: an attitude or policy of ignoring an often undesirable situation that one is perceived to be responsible for dealing with

**ben·i·son** \'be-nə-sən, -zən\ *noun* [Middle English *beneson,* from Middle French *beneiçon,*

from Late Latin *benediction-, benedictio*] (14th century)

: BLESSING, BENEDICTION

**Ben·ja·min** \'ben-jə-mən\ *noun* [Hebrew *Binyāmīn*]

: a son of Jacob and the traditional eponymous ancestor of one of the tribes of Israel

**ben·ne** *also* **bene** \'be-nē\ *noun* [of African origin; akin to Malinke *běne* sesame] (1769)

: SESAME 1

**ben·ny** \'be-nē\ *noun, plural* **bennies** [*Benzedrine* + *-ie*] (1949)

*slang* : a tablet of amphetamine taken as a stimulant

**ben·o·myl** \'be-nə-ˌmil\ *noun* [*benz-* + *-o-* + *methyl*] (1969)

: a derivative $C_{14}H_{18}N_4O_3$ of carbamate and benzimidazole used especially as a systemic agricultural fungicide

**¹bent** \'bent\ *noun* [Middle English, grassy place, bent grass, from Old English *beonot-;* akin to Old High German *binuz* rush] (14th century)

**1** : unenclosed grassland
**2** (1) : a reedy grass (2) : a stalk of stiff coarse grass **b** : BENT GRASS

**²bent** *adjective* [Middle English, from past participle of *benden* to bend] (14th century)

**1** : changed by bending out of an originally straight or even condition ⟨*bent* twigs⟩
**2** : strongly inclined : DETERMINED ⟨was *bent* on going⟩
**3** *slang* **a** : different from the normal or usual **b** *chiefly British* : DISHONEST, CORRUPT

**³bent** *noun* [irregular from ¹*bend*] (1586)

**1 a** : a strong inclination or interest : BIAS **b** : a special inclination or capacity : TALENT
**2** : capacity of endurance
**3** : a transverse framework (as in a bridge) to carry lateral as well as vertical loads
**synonym** see GIFT

**bent grass** *noun* (1778)

: any of a genus (*Agrostis*) of grasses including important chiefly perennial and rhizomatous pasture and lawn grasses with fine velvety or wiry herbage

**Ben·tham·ism** \'ben(t)-thə-ˌmi-zəm\ *noun* (1829)

: the utilitarian philosophy of Jeremy Bentham and his followers
— **Ben·tham·ite** \-ˌmīt\ *noun or adjective*

**ben·thic** \'ben(t)-thik\ *adjective* [*benthos*] (1902)

**1** : of, relating to, or occurring at the bottom of a body of water
**2** : of, relating to, or occurring in the depths of the ocean

**ben·thon·ic** \ben-'thä-nik\ *adjective* [irregular from *benthos*] (1897)

: BENTHIC

**ben·thos** \'ben-ˌthäs\ *noun* [New Latin, from Greek, depth, deep sea; akin to Greek *bathys* deep] (1891)

: organisms that live on or in the bottom of a body of water

**ben·ton·ite** \'ben-tˀn-ˌīt\ *noun* [Fort *Benton,* Mont.] (1898)

: an absorptive and colloidal clay used especially as a sealing agent or carrier (as of drugs)
— **ben·ton·it·ic** \ˌben-tˀn-'i-tik\ *adjective*

**ben tro·va·to** \ˌben-trō-'vä-(ˌ)tō\ *adjective* [Italian, literally, well found] (1876)

: characteristic or appropriate even if not true ⟨the story is *ben trovato*⟩

**bent·wood** \'bent-ˌwu̇d\ *adjective* (1862)

: made of wood that is bent rather than cut into shape ⟨*bentwood* furniture⟩
— **bentwood** *noun*

\ə\ abut \ˀ\ kitten \ər\ further, \a\ ash \ā\ ace \ä\ mop, mar \au̇\ out \ch\ chin \e\ bet \ē\ easy \g\ go \i\ hit \ī\ ice \j\ job \ŋ\ sing \ō\ go \ȯ\ law \ȯi\ boy \th\ thin \t͟h\ the \ü\ loot \u̇\ foot \y\ yet \zh\ vision *see also* Guide to Pronunciation

**be·numb** \bi-'nəm\ *transitive verb* [Middle English *benomen*, from *benomen*, past participle of *benimen* to deprive, from Old English *beniman*, from *be-* + *niman* to take — more at NIMBLE] (14th century)
**1** : to make inactive : DEADEN
**2** : to make numb especially by cold

**benz-** *or* **benzo-** *combining form* [International Scientific Vocabulary, from *benzoin*]
: related to benzene or benzoic acid ⟨*benzophenone*⟩ ⟨*benzyl*⟩

**benz·al·de·hyde** \ben-'zal-də-,hīd\ *noun* [International Scientific Vocabulary] (1866)
: a colorless nontoxic aromatic liquid $C_6H_5CHO$ found in essential oils (as in peach kernels) and used in flavoring and perfumery, in pharmaceuticals, and in synthesis of dyes

**benz·an·thra·cene** \ben-'zan(t)-thrə-,sēn\ *noun* [International Scientific Vocabulary] (1938)
: a crystalline feebly carcinogenic cyclic hydrocarbon $C_{18}H_{12}$ that is found in small amounts in coal tar

**Ben·ze·drine** \'ben-zə-,drēn\ *trademark*
— used for amphetamine

**ben·zene** \'ben-,zēn, ben-'\ *noun* [International Scientific Vocabulary *benz-* + *-ene*] (circa 1872)
: a colorless volatile flammable toxic liquid aromatic hydrocarbon $C_6H_6$ used in organic synthesis, as a solvent, and as a motor fuel — called also *benzol*
— **ben·ze·noid** \'ben-zə-,nóid\ *adjective*

**benzene hexa·chlo·ride** \-,hek-sə-'klōr-,īd, -'klȯr-\ *noun* (1884)
: BHC

**benzene ring** *noun* (1877)
: a structural arrangement of atoms held to exist in benzene and other aromatic compounds and marked by six carbon atoms linked in a planar symmetrical hexagon with each carbon attached to hydrogen in benzene itself or to other atoms or groups in substituted benzenes — compare META- 4a, ORTH- 4b, PARA- 2b

**ben·zi·dine** \'ben-zə-,dēn\ *noun* [International Scientific Vocabulary *benz-* + *-idine*] (1878)
: a crystalline base $C_{12}H_{12}N_2$ prepared from nitrobenzene and used especially in making dyes

**benz·imid·azole** \,ben-,zi-mə-'da-,zōl, ,ben-zə-'mi-də-,zōl\ *noun* [International Scientific Vocabulary] (circa 1929)
: a crystalline base $C_7H_6N_2$ used especially to inhibit the growth of various viruses, parasitic worms, or fungi; *also* : one of its derivatives

**ben·zine** \'ben-,zēn, ben-'\ *noun* [German *Benzin*, from *benz-*] (1835)
: any of various volatile flammable petroleum distillates used especially as solvents or as motor fuels

**ben·zo·a·py·rene** \,ben-zō-,ā-'pīr-,ēn, -zō-,al-fə-\ *noun* [*benz-* + *-a-*, denoting attachment of the benzene substituent at carbon atoms 1 and 2 of the pyrene molecule + *pyrene*] (1950)
: a yellow crystalline carcinogenic hydrocarbon $C_{20}H_{12}$ found in coal tar — *a* often italicized and placed in parentheses or brackets or between hyphens

**ben·zo·ate** \'ben-zə-,wāt\ *noun* (1806)
: a salt or ester of benzoic acid

**ben·zo·caine** \'ben-zə-,kān\ *noun* [International Scientific Vocabulary *benz-* + *-caine*] (1922)
: a white crystalline ester $C_9H_{11}NO_2$ used as a local anesthetic

**ben·zo·di·az·e·pine** \,ben-zō-dī-'a-zə-,pēn\ *noun* [*benz-* + *di-* + *az-* + *-epine* (from *hepta-* + ²-*ine*)] (1934)
: any of a group of aromatic lipophilic amines (as diazepam and chlordiazepoxide) used especially as tranquilizers

**ben·zo·fu·ran** \,ben-zō-'fyùr-,an, -fyù-'ran\ *noun* (1946)

: a compound $C_8H_6O$ found in coal tar and polymerized with indene to form thermoplastic resins used especially in adhesives and printing inks

**ben·zo·ic acid** \ben-'zō-ik-\ *noun* [International Scientific Vocabulary, from *benzoin*] (1791)
: a white crystalline acid $C_7H_6O_2$ found naturally (as in benzoin or in cranberries) or made synthetically and used especially as a preservative of foods, in medicine, and in organic synthesis

**ben·zo·in** \'ben-zə-wən, -,wēn; -,zóin\ *noun* [Middle French *benjoin*, from Catalan *benjuí*, from Arabic *lubān jāwī*, literally, frankincense of Java] (1562)
**1** : a hard fragrant yellowish balsamic resin from trees (genus *Styrax*) of southeastern Asia used especially in medication, as a fixative in perfumes, and as incense
**2** : a white crystalline hydroxy ketone $C_{14}H_{12}O_2$ made from benzaldehyde

**ben·zol** \'ben-,zól, -,zōl\ *noun* [German, from *benz-* + *-ol*] (1838)
: BENZENE; *also* : a mixture of benzene and other aromatic hydrocarbons

**ben·zo·phe·none** \,ben-zō-fi-'nōn, -'fē-,nōn\ *noun* [International Scientific Vocabulary *benz-* + *phen-* + *-one*] (1885)
: a colorless crystalline ketone $C_{13}H_{10}O$ used chiefly in perfumery and sunscreens; *also* : a derivative of benzophenone

**ben·zo·yl** \'ben-zə-,wil, -,zóil\ *noun* [German, from *Benzoësäure* benzoic acid + Greek *hylē* matter, literally, wood] (circa 1855)
: the radical $C_6H_5CO$ of benzoic acid

**benzoyl peroxide** *noun* (1924)
: a white crystalline flammable compound $C_{14}H_{10}O_4$ used in bleaching and in medicine especially in the treatment of acne

**ben·zyl** \'ben-,zēl, -zəl\ *noun* [International Scientific Vocabulary *benz-* + *-yl*] (1869)
: a univalent radical $C_6H_5CH_2$ derived from toluene
— **ben·zyl·ic** \ben-'zi-lik\ *adjective*

**Be·o·wulf** \'bā-ə-,wùlf\ *noun*
: a legendary Geatish warrior and hero of the Old English poem *Beowulf*

**be·paint** \bi-'pānt\ *transitive verb* (circa 1555)
*archaic* : TINGE

**be·queath** \bi-'kwēth, -'kwēth\ *transitive verb* [Middle English *bequethen*, from Old English *becwethan*, from *be-* + *cwethan* to say — more at QUOTH] (before 12th century)
**1** : to give or leave by will — used especially of personal property
**2** : to hand down : TRANSMIT
— **be·queath·al** \-'kwē-thəl, -thəl\ *noun*

**be·quest** \bi-'kwest\ *noun* [Middle English, irregular from *bequethen*] (14th century)
**1** : the act of bequeathing
**2** : something bequeathed : LEGACY

**be·rate** \bi-'rāt\ *transitive verb* (1548)
: to scold or condemn vehemently and at length
**synonym** see SCOLD

**Ber·ber** \'bər-bər\ *noun* [Arabic *Barbar*] (1732)
**1** : a member of any of various peoples living in northern Africa west of Tripoli
**2 a** : a branch of the Afro-Asiatic language family comprising languages spoken by various peoples of northern Africa and the Sahara (as the Tuaregs and the Kabyles) **b** : any one of the Berber languages

**ber·ber·ine** \'bər-bə-,rēn\ *noun* [German *Berberin*, from New Latin *berberis*] (circa 1847)
: a bitter crystalline yellow alkaloid $C_{20}H_{19}NO_5$ obtained from the roots of various plants (as barberry) and used as a tonic in medicine

**ber·ber·is** \'bər-bər-əs\ *noun* [New Latin, the genus including barberry, alteration of Medieval Latin *barberis* barberry, from Arabic *barbāris*] (circa 1868)
: BARBERRY

**ber·ceuse** \ber-'sœz, -'süz\ *noun, plural* **ber·ceuses** \-'sœz; -'süz; -'sü-zəz\ [French] (1876)
**1** : LULLABY
**2** : a musical composition usually in ⁶/₈ time that resembles a lullaby

**be·reave** \bi-'rēv\ *transitive verb* **-reaved** *or* **-reft** \-'reft\; **-reav·ing** [Middle English *bereven*, from Old English *berēafian*, from *be-* + *rēafian* to rob — more at REAVE] (before 12th century)
**1** : to deprive of something — usually used with *of* ⟨madam, you have *bereft* me of all words —Shakespeare⟩
**2** : to take away (a valued or necessary possession) especially by force

**¹be·reaved** \bi-'rēvd\ *adjective* (1828)
: suffering the death of a loved one

**²bereaved** *noun, plural* **bereaved** (1943)
: one who is bereaved

**be·reave·ment** \bi-'rēv-mənt\ *noun* (circa 1731)
: the state or fact of being bereaved; *especially* : the loss of a loved one by death

**be·reft** \-'reft\ *adjective* (1586)
**1 a** : deprived or robbed of the possession or use of something — usually used with *of* ⟨both players are instantly *bereft* of their poise —A. E. Wier⟩ **b** : lacking something needed, wanted, or expected — used with *of* ⟨the book is . . . completely *bereft* of an index — *Times Literary Supplement*⟩
**2** : BEREAVED ⟨a *bereft* mother⟩

**be·ret** \bə-'rā\ *noun* [French *béret*, from Gascon *berret*, from Old Provençal, cap — more at BIRETTA] (1827)
: a visorless usually woolen cap with a tight headband and a soft full flat top

**berg** \'bərg\ *noun* (1823)
: ICEBERG

**ber·ga·mot** \'bər-gə-,mät\ *noun* [French *bergamote*, from Italian *bergamotta*, modification of Turkish *bey armudu*, literally, the bey's pear] (1696)
**1** : a pear-shaped orange (*Citrus aurantium bergamia*) having a rind which yields an essential oil used in perfumery; *also* : this oil
**2** : any of several mints (genus *Monarda*) — compare WILD BERGAMOT

**be·rib·boned** \bi-'ri-bənd\ *adjective* (1863)
: adorned with ribbons

**beri·beri** \,ber-ē-'ber-ē\ *noun* [Sinhalese *bæribæri*] (1703)
: a deficiency disease marked by inflammatory or degenerative changes of the nerves, digestive system, and heart and caused by a lack of or inability to assimilate thiamine

**Berke·le·ian** *or* **Berke·ley·an** \'bär-klē-ən, 'bər-; bär-', ,bər-\ *adjective* (1842)
: of, relating to, or suggestive of Bishop Berkeley or his system of philosophical idealism
— **Berkeleian** *noun*
— **Berke·le·ian·ism** \-ə-,ni-zəm\ *noun*

**berke·li·um** \'bər-klē-əm\ *noun* [New Latin, from *Berkeley*, Calif.] (1950)
: a radioactive metallic element produced by bombarding americium 241 with helium ions — see ELEMENT table

**Berk·shire** \'bərk-,shir, -shər\ *noun* [*Berkshire*, England] (1831)
: any of a breed of medium-sized black swine with white markings

**berm** \'bərm\ *noun* [French *berme*, from Dutch *berm* strip of ground along a dike; akin to Middle English *brimme* brim] (1729)
: a narrow shelf, path, or ledge typically at the top or bottom of a slope; *also* : a mound or wall of earth ⟨a landscaped *berm*⟩

**Ber·mu·da bag** \(,)bər-'myü-də-, *especially Southern* -'mü-də-\ *noun* [*Bermuda* islands, North Atlantic] (1979)
: a round or oval-shaped handbag with a wooden handle and removable cloth covers

**Bermuda grass** *noun* (1808)

: a creeping stoloniferous southern European grass (*Cynodon dactylon*) often used as a lawn and pasture grass

**Bermuda rig** *noun* (1853)
: a fore-and-aft rig marked by a triangular sail and a mast with an extreme rake

**Ber·mu·das** \(ˌ)bər-ˈmyü-dəz, *especially* *Southern* -ˈmü-dəz\ *noun plural* (1961)
: BERMUDA SHORTS

**Bermuda shorts** *noun plural* (1951)
: knee-length walking shorts

**Ber·nese mountain dog** \ˈbər-ˌnēz-, -ˌnēs-\ *noun* [*Bern*, Switzerland] (1935)
: any of a breed of large powerful long-coated black dogs of Swiss origin that have tan and white markings and were developed as draft animals

**Ber·noul·li's principle** \bər-ˈnü-lēz-, ˌber-ˌnü-ˈlē-\ *noun* [Daniel *Bernoulli* (died 1782) Swiss physicist] (1940)
: a principle in hydrodynamics: the pressure in a stream of fluid is reduced as the speed of the flow is increased

**Ber·noul·li trial** \bər-ˈnü-lē-, ˌber-ˌnü-ˈlē-\ *noun* [Jacques *Bernoulli* (died 1705) Swiss mathematician] (1951)
: one of the repetitions of a statistical experiment having two mutually exclusive outcomes with constant probability of occurrence

**ber·ried** \ˈber-ēd\ *adjective* (1794)
**1** : having or covered with berries ⟨*berried* shrub⟩
**2** : bearing eggs ⟨a *berried* lobster⟩

**¹ber·ry** \ˈber-ē\ *noun, plural* **berries** [Middle English *berye*, from Old English *berie;* akin to Old High German *beri* berry] (before 12th century)
**1 a** : a pulpy and usually edible fruit (as a strawberry, raspberry, or checkerberry) of small size irrespective of its structure **b** : a simple fruit (as a currant, grape, tomato, or banana) with a pulpy or fleshy pericarp **c** : the dry seed of some plants (as wheat)
**2** : an egg of a fish or lobster

**²berry** *intransitive verb* **ber·ried; ber·ry·ing** (circa 1780)
**1** : to bear or produce berries ⟨a *berrying* shrub⟩
**2** : to gather or seek berries

**ber·ry·like** \ˈber-ē-ˌlīk\ *adjective* (1864)
**1** : resembling a berry especially in size or structure
**2** : being small and rounded : COCCOID

**ber·seem** \(ˌ)bər-ˈsēm\ *noun* [Arabic *barsīm*, from Coptic *bersīm*] (circa 1902)
: a succulent clover (*Trifolium alexandrinum*) cultivated as a forage plant and green-manure crop especially in the alkaline soils of the Nile valley and in the southwestern U.S. — called also *Egyptian clover*

**¹ber·serk** \bə(r)-ˈsərk, ˌbər-, -ˈzərk; ˈbər-ˌ\ *or* **ber·serk·er** \-ˈsər-kər, -ˈzər-; ˈbər-ˌ\ *noun* [Old Norse *berserkr*, from *bjǫrn* bear + *serkr* shirt] (1818)
**1** : an ancient Scandinavian warrior frenzied in battle and held to be invulnerable
**2** : one whose actions are recklessly defiant ◆

**²berserk** *adjective* (1851)
: FRENZIED, CRAZED — usually used in the phrase *go berserk* ⟨sinister ravings of an imagination gone *berserk* —John Gruen⟩
— **berserk** *adverb*
— **ber·serk·ly** *adverb*

**¹berth** \ˈbərth\ *noun* [probably from ²*bear* + -*th*] (15th century)
**1 a** : sufficient distance for maneuvering a ship **b** : safe distance — used especially with *wide*
**2 a** : the place where a ship lies when at anchor or at a wharf **b** : a space for an automotive vehicle at rest ⟨a truck-loading *berth*⟩
**3** : a place to sit or sleep especially on a ship or vehicle : ACCOMMODATION
**4 a** : a billet on a ship **b** : JOB, POSITION, PLACE ⟨a starting *berth* on the team⟩

**²berth** (1667)

*transitive verb*
**1** : to bring into a berth
**2** : to allot a berth to
*intransitive verb*
: to come into a berth

**ber·tha** \ˈbər-thə\ *noun* [French *berthe*, from *Berthe* (Bertha) (died 783) queen of the Franks] (1842)
: a wide round collar covering the shoulders

**Ber·til·lon system** \ˈbər-tᵊl-ˌän-, ˈber-tē-ˌyōⁿ-\ *noun* [Alphonse *Bertillon* (died 1914) French criminologist] (1896)
: a system of identification of persons by a description based on anthropometric measurements, photographs, and notation of data (as markings, color, and thumb line impressions)

**ber·yl** \ˈber-əl\ *noun* [Middle English, from Middle French *beril*, from Latin *beryllus*, from Greek *bēryllos*, back-formation from *bēryllion* beryl, of Indo-Aryan origin; akin to Prakrit *verulia, veluriya* beryl] (13th century)
: a mineral consisting of a silicate of beryllium and aluminum of great hardness and occurring in green, bluish green, yellow, pink, or white hexagonal prisms

**be·ryl·li·um** \bə-ˈri-lē-əm\ *noun* [New Latin, from Greek *bēryllion*] (circa 1847)
: a steel-gray light strong brittle toxic bivalent metallic element used chiefly as a hardening agent in alloys — see ELEMENT table

**be·seech** \bi-ˈsēch\ *verb* **-seeched** *or* **-sought** \-ˈsȯt\; **-seech·ing** [Middle English *besechen*, from *be-* + *sechen* to seek] (12th century)
*transitive verb*
**1** : to beg for urgently or anxiously
**2** : to request earnestly : IMPLORE
*intransitive verb*
: to make supplication
**synonym** see BEG
— **be·seech·ing·ly** \-ˈsē-chiŋ-lē\ *adverb*

**be·seem** \bi-ˈsēm\ (13th century)
*intransitive verb*
*archaic* : to be fitting or becoming
*transitive verb*
*archaic* : to be suitable to : BEFIT

**be·set** \bi-ˈset, bē-\ *transitive verb* **-set; -set·ting** [Middle English *besetten*, from Old English *besettan*, from *be-* + *settan* to set] (before 12th century)
**1** : to set or stud with or as if with ornaments
**2** : TROUBLE, HARASS ⟨inflation *besets* the economy⟩
**3 a** : to set upon : ASSAIL ⟨the settlers were *beset* by savages⟩ **b** : to hem in : SURROUND
— **be·set·ment** \-mənt\ *noun*

**be·set·ting** *adjective* (1795)
: constantly present or attacking : OBSESSIVE

**be·shrew** \bi-ˈshrü, bē-, *especially* *Southern* -ˈsrü\ *transitive verb* (14th century)
*archaic* : CURSE

**¹be·side** \bi-ˈsīd\ *preposition* [Middle English, adverb & preposition, from Old English *be sīdan* at or to the side, from *be* at (from *bī*) + *sīdan*, dative & accusative of *sīde* side — more at BY] (13th century)
**1 a** : by the side of ⟨walk *beside* me⟩ **b** : in comparison with **c** : on a par with
**2** : BESIDES
**3** : not relevant to ⟨*beside* the point⟩
— **beside oneself** : in a state of extreme excitement

**²beside** *adverb* (14th century)
**1** *archaic* : NEARBY
**2** *archaic* : BESIDES

**¹be·sides** \bi-ˈsīdz\ *preposition* (14th century)
**1** : OTHER THAN, EXCEPT
**2** : together with

**²besides** *adverb* (1564)
**1** : as well : ALSO
**2** : MOREOVER, FURTHERMORE

**³besides** *adjective* (1954)
: ELSE

**be·siege** \bi-ˈsēj\ *transitive verb* **-sieged; -sieg·ing** (14th century)
**1** : to surround with armed forces

**2 a** : to press with requests : IMPORTUNE **b** : to cause worry or distress to : BESET ⟨doubts *besieged* him⟩
— **be·sieg·er** *noun*

**be·smear** \bi-ˈsmir\ *transitive verb* (before 12th century)
: SMEAR

**be·smirch** \bi-ˈsmərch\ *transitive verb* (1599)
: SULLY, SOIL

**be·som** \ˈbē-zəm\ *noun* [Middle English *beseme*, from Old English *besma;* akin to Old High German *besmo* broom] (before 12th century)
: BROOM 2; *especially* : one made of twigs

**besom pocket** *noun* [origin unknown] (1966)
: a pocket with a welted slit opening

**be·sot** \bi-ˈsät\ *transitive verb* **be·sot·ted; be·sot·ting** [*be-* + *sot* (to stultify)] (1581)
**1** : INFATUATE 2
**2** : to make dull or stupid; *especially* : to muddle with drunkenness

**be·spat·ter** \bi-ˈspa-tər\ *transitive verb* (1640)
: SPATTER

**be·speak** \bi-ˈspēk\ *transitive verb* **-spoke** \-ˈspōk\; **-spo·ken** \-ˈspō-kən\; **-speak·ing** (1536)
**1** : to hire, engage, or claim beforehand
**2** : to speak to especially with formality : ADDRESS
**3** : REQUEST ⟨*bespeak* a favor⟩
**4 a** : INDICATE, SIGNIFY ⟨her performance *bespeaks* considerable practice⟩ **b** : to show beforehand : FORETELL

**be·spec·ta·cled** \bi-ˈspek-(ˌ)ti-kəld\ *adjective* (1742)
: wearing spectacles

**be·spoke** \bi-ˈspōk\ *or* **be·spo·ken** \-ˈspō-kən\ *adjective* [past participle of *bespeak*] (1607)
**1 a** : CUSTOM-MADE **b** : dealing in or producing custom-made articles
**2** *dialect* : ENGAGED

**be·sprent** \bi-ˈsprent\ *adjective* [Middle English *bespreynt*, from past participle of *besprengen* to besprinkle, from Old English *besprengan*, from *be-* + *sprengan* to scatter; akin to Old English *springan* to spring] (14th century)
*archaic* : sprinkled over

---

◇ WORD HISTORY

**berserk** During the 19th century, the word *berserk* made a rapid linguistic trip from literary use as a noun—arising out of antiquarian interest in medieval Scandinavia—to colloquial use as an adjective. In Old Norse sagas, a *berserkr* was a man experiencing a sort of ecstatic frenzy called *berserksgangr*. The 13th century Icelandic author Snorri Sturluson describes men seized by *berserksgangr* as going into battle without coats of mail and gnawing the rims of their shields. They supposedly had the strength of bears or oxen, and were invulnerable to iron or fire. The word *berserkr* is a compound of *ber-*, presumed to mean "bear," and *sarkr* "shirt." Originally the "bear-shirt" probably referred to a man dressed in a mask or garment representing a bear who entered a trancelike state in which he magically assumed powers associated with the animal. By the time the legend of the *berserkr* had made its way into Norse saga, it was this ecstatic frenzy—not bear paraphernalia—that characterized him and that is still dimly reflected in English *berserk*.

---

\ə\ **abut** \ᵊ\ **kitten** \ər\ **further** \a\ **ash** \ā\ **ace** \ä\ **mop, mar** \au̇\ **out** \ch\ **chin** \e\ **bet** \ē\ **easy** \g\ **go** \i\ **hit** \ī\ **ice** \j\ **job** \ŋ\ **sing** \ō\ **go** \ȯ\ **law** \ȯi\ **boy** \th\ **thin** \t͟h\ **the** \ü\ **loot** \u̇\ **foot** \y\ **yet** \zh\ **vision** *see also* Guide to Pronunciation

**be·sprin·kle** \bi-'spriŋ-kəl\ *transitive verb* [Middle English *besprengeln*, frequentative of *besprengen*] (15th century)
**:** SPRINKLE
**Bes·sel function** \'be-səl-\ *noun* [Friedrich W. *Bessel* (died 1846) Prussian astronomer] (1872)
**:** one of a class of transcendental functions expressible as infinite series and occurring in the solution of the differential equation

$$x^2 \frac{d^2 y}{dx^2} + x \frac{dy}{dx} = (n^2 - x^2)y$$

**Bes·se·mer converter** \'be-sə-mər-\ *noun* (circa 1887)
**:** the furnace used in the Bessemer process
**Bessemer process** *noun* [Sir Henry *Bessemer*] (1875)
**:** a process of making steel from pig iron by burning out carbon and other impurities by means of a blast of air forced through the molten metal
**¹best** \'best\ *adjective, superlative of* GOOD [Middle English, from Old English *betst;* akin to Old English *bōt* remedy — more at BETTER] (before 12th century)
**1 :** excelling all others ⟨the *best* student⟩
**2 :** most productive of good or of advantage, utility, or satisfaction ⟨what is the *best* thing to do⟩
**3 :** MOST, LARGEST ⟨it rained for the *best* part of their vacation⟩
**²best** *adverb, superlative of* WELL (before 12th century)
**1 :** in the best way **:** to greatest advantage ⟨some things are *best* left unsaid⟩
**2 :** MOST ⟨those *best* able will provide needed support⟩
**³best** *noun, plural* **best** (before 12th century)
**1 :** the best state or part
**2 :** one that is best ⟨the *best* falls short⟩
**3 :** the greatest degree of good or excellence
**4 :** one's maximum effort ⟨do your *best*⟩
**5 :** best clothes ⟨Sunday *best*⟩
**— at best :** under the most favorable circumstances
**⁴best** *transitive verb* (1863)
**:** to get the better of **:** OUTDO
**⁵best** *verbal auxiliary* (1941)
**:** had best ⟨you *best* listen⟩
**best–ball** \'bes(t)-'bȯl\ *adjective* (1909)
**:** relating to or being a golf match in which one player competes against the best individual score of two or more players for each hole — compare FOUR-BALL
**best boy** *noun* (1937)
**:** the chief assistant to the gaffer in motion-picture or television production
**best–case** \'bes(t)-'kās\ *adjective* (1977)
**:** being, relating to, or based on a projection of future events that assumes only the best possible circumstances ⟨a *best-case* scenario⟩
**¹be·stead** *or* **be·sted** \bi-'sted\ *adjective* [Middle English *bested*, from *be-* + *sted*, past participle of *steden* to place, from *stede* place — more at STEAD] (14th century)
*archaic* **:** SITUATED
**²bestead** *transitive verb* **be·stead·ed; be·stead; be·stead·ing** [*be-* + *stead*] (1581)
**1** *archaic* **:** HELP
**2** *archaic* **:** to be useful to **:** AVAIL
**bes·tial** \'bes-chəl, 'besh-, 'bēs-, 'bēsh-\ *adjective* [Middle English, from Middle French, from Latin *bestialis*, from *bestia* beast] (14th century)
**1 a :** of or relating to beasts **b :** resembling a beast
**2 a :** lacking intelligence or reason **b :** marked by base or inhuman instincts or desires **:** BRUTAL
**synonym** see BRUTAL
**— bes·tial·ize** \-chə-‚līz\ *transitive verb*
**— bes·tial·ly** \-chə-lē\ *adverb*

**bes·ti·al·i·ty** \‚bes-chē-'a-lə-tē, ‚besh-, ‚bēs-, ‚bēsh-\ *noun, plural* **-ties** (14th century)
**1 :** the condition or status of a lower animal
**2 :** display or gratification of bestial traits or impulses
**3 :** sexual relations between a human being and a lower animal
**bes·ti·ary** \'bes-chē-‚er-ē, 'besh-, 'bēs-, 'bēsh-\ *noun, plural* **-ar·ies** [Medieval Latin *bestiarium*, from Latin, neuter of *bestiarius* of beasts, from *bestia*] (1840)
**1 :** a medieval allegorical or moralizing work on the appearance and habits of real or imaginary animals
**2 :** a collection of descriptions of real or imaginary animals
**be·stir** \bi-'stər\ *transitive verb* (14th century)
**:** to rouse to action **:** get going
**best man** *noun* (circa 1782)
**:** the principal groomsman at a wedding
**be·stow** \bi-'stō\ *transitive verb* [Middle English, from *be-* + *stowe* place — more at STOW] (14th century)
**1 :** to put to use **:** APPLY ⟨*bestowed* his spare time on study⟩
**2 :** to put in a particular or appropriate place **:** STOW
**3 :** to provide with quarters **:** PUT UP
**4 :** to convey as a gift — usually used with *on* or *upon*
**synonym** see GIVE
**— be·stow·al** \-'stō-əl\ *noun*
**be·strew** \bi-'strü\ *transitive verb* **-strewed; -strewed** *or* **-strewn** \-'strün\; **-strew·ing** (before 12th century)
**1 :** STREW
**2 :** to lie scattered over
**be·stride** \bi-'strīd\ *transitive verb* **-strode** \-'strōd\; **-strid·den** \-'strid-ᵊn\; **-strid·ing** \-'strī-diŋ\ (before 12th century)
**1 :** to ride, sit, or stand astride **:** STRADDLE
**2 :** to tower over **:** DOMINATE ⟨the bloated bureaucracy that *bestrides* us all —Edward Ney⟩
**3** *archaic* **:** to stride across
**best–sell·er** \'bes(t)-'se-lər\ *noun* (1889)
**:** an article (as a book) whose sales are among the highest of its class
**— best–sell·er·dom** \-dəm\ *noun*
**— best–sell·ing** \-'se-liŋ\ *adjective*
**¹bet** \'bet\ *noun* [origin unknown] (1592)
**1 a :** something that is laid, staked, or pledged typically between two parties on the outcome of a contest or a contingent issue **:** WAGER **b :** the act of giving such a pledge
**2 :** something to wager on
**3 :** a choice made by consideration of probabilities ⟨your best *bet* is the back road⟩
**²bet** *verb* **bet** *also* **bet·ted; bet·ting** (1597) *transitive verb*
**1 a :** to stake on the outcome of an issue or the performance of a contestant **b :** to be able to be sure that — usually used in the expression *you bet* ⟨you *bet* I'll be there⟩
**2 a :** to maintain with or as if with a bet **b :** to make a bet with **c :** to make a bet on
*intransitive verb*
**:** to lay a bet
**¹be·ta** \'bā-tə, *chiefly British* 'bē-\ *noun* [Middle English *betha*, from Latin *beta*, from Greek *bēta*, of Semitic origin; akin to Hebrew *bēth* beth] (14th century)
**1 :** the 2d letter of the Greek alphabet — see ALPHABET table
**2 :** BETA PARTICLE
**3 :** a measure of a stock's or a portfolio's volatility that is expressed numerically as deviation from the market's volatility taken as unity
**²beta** *adjective* (1899)
**:** second in position in the structure of an organic molecule from a particular group or atom ⟨*beta* substitution⟩ — often used in combination; symbol β
**be·ta–ad·ren·er·gic** \-‚a-drə-'nər-jik\ *adjective* (1965)
**:** of, relating to, or being a beta-receptor ⟨*beta-adrenergic* blocking action⟩

**be·ta–block·er** \-‚blä-kər\ *noun* (1968)
**:** any of a class of drugs (as propranolol) that slow heart action and increase coronary blood flow by blocking the activity of beta-receptors
**— be·ta–block·ing** \-kiŋ\ *adjective*
**be·ta–car·o·tene** \-'kar-ə-‚tēn\ *noun* (1938)
**:** an isomer of carotene found in dark green and dark yellow vegetables and fruits
**beta cell** *noun* (1926)
**:** any of the insulin-secreting pancreatic cells in the islets of Langerhans
**beta decay** *noun* (1934)
**:** a radioactive nuclear transformation governed by the weak force in which a nucleon (as a neutron) changes into the other type of nucleon (as a proton) with the emission of an electron or positron and a neutrino and which results in a change in the atomic number of the nucleus of +1 or −1
**be·ta–en·dor·phin** \-en-'dȯr-fən\ *noun* (1977)
**:** an endorphin of the pituitary gland having a much greater analgesic potency than morphine
**beta globulin** *noun* [International Scientific Vocabulary] (1945)
**:** any of several globulins of plasma or serum that have at alkaline pH electrophoretic mobilities intermediate between those of the alpha globulins and gamma globulins
**be·ta·ine** \'bē-tə-‚ēn\ *noun* [International Scientific Vocabulary, from Latin *beta* beet] (1879)
**:** a sweet crystalline quaternary ammonium salt $C_5H_{11}NO_2$ occurring especially in beet juice; *also* **:** its hydrate $C_5H_{13}NO_3$ or its hydrochloride $C_5H_{12}NO_2Cl$
**be·take** \bi-'tāk\ *transitive verb* **-took** \-'tůk\; **-tak·en** \-'tā-kən\; **-tak·ing** (14th century)
**1** *archaic* **:** COMMIT
**2 :** to cause (oneself) to go
**be·ta–lac·ta·mase** \-'lak-tə-‚mās, -‚māz\ *noun* [*lactam*, a cyclic amide (from International Scientific Vocabulary *lact-* + *amide*) + *-ase*] (1965)
**:** PENICILLINASE
**be·ta–ox·i·da·tion** \'bā-tə-‚äk-sə-'dā-shən\ *noun* (circa 1935)
**:** stepwise catabolism of fatty acids in which two-carbon fragments are successively removed from the carboxyl end of the chain
**beta particle** *noun* (1904)
**:** a high-speed electron; *specifically* **:** one emitted by a radioactive nucleus in beta decay
**beta ray** *noun* (1902)
**1 :** BETA PARTICLE
**2 :** a stream of beta particles — called also *beta radiation*
**be·ta–re·cep·tor** \'bā-tə-ri-'sep-tər\ *noun* (1948)
**:** any of a group of receptors postulated to exist on nerve cell membranes of the sympathetic nervous system to explain the specificity of certain adrenergic agents in affecting only some sympathetic activities (as vasodilation, increase in muscular contraction and beat of the heart, and relaxation of smooth muscle in the bronchi and intestine)
**be·ta–thal·as·se·mia** \-‚tha-lə-'sē-mē-ə\ *noun* (1962)
**:** thalassemia in which the longer hemoglobin chain is affected and which comprises Cooley's anemia in the homozygous condition and a less severe thalassemia in the heterozygous condition
**be·ta·tron** \'bā-tə-‚trän\ *noun* [International Scientific Vocabulary] (1941)
**:** an accelerator in which electrons are propelled by the inductive action of a rapidly varying magnetic field
**beta wave** *noun* (1936)
**:** an electrical rhythm of the brain with a frequency of 13 to 30 cycles per second that is associated with normal conscious waking experience — called also *beta, beta rhythm*
**be·tel** \'bē-tᵊl\ *noun* [Portuguese *bétele*, from Tamil *verrilai*] (1553)

: a climbing pepper (*Piper betle*) whose leaves are chewed together with betel nut and mineral lime as a stimulant masticatory especially by southeastern Asians

**Be·tel·geuse** \'bē-t'l-,jüs, 'be-, -,jüz\ *noun* [French *Bételgeuse*, from Arabic *bayt al-jawzā'* Gemini, literally, the house of the twins (confused with Orion & Betelgeuse)]
: a variable red giant star of the first magnitude near one shoulder of Orion

**betel nut** *noun* [from its being chewed with betel leaves] (1681)
: the astringent seed of the betel palm

**betel palm** *noun* (1875)
: an Asian pinnate-leaved palm (*Areca catechu*) that has an orange-colored drupe with an outer fibrous husk

**bête noire** \,bet-'nwär, ,bāt-\ *noun, plural* **bêtes noires** \,bet-'nwär(z), ,bāt-\ [French, literally, black beast] (1844)
: a person or thing strongly detested or avoided : BUGBEAR

**beth** \'bāth, 'bāt, 'bās\ *noun* [Hebrew *bēth*, from *bayith* house] (circa 1823)
: the 2d letter of the Hebrew alphabet — see ALPHABET table

**beth·el** \'be-thəl\ *noun* [Hebrew *bēth'ēl* house of God] (circa 1617)
**1** : a hallowed spot
**2 a** : a chapel for Nonconformists **b** : a place of worship for seamen

**be·think** \bi-'think\ *transitive verb* **-thought** \-'thȯt\; **-think·ing** (before 12th century)
**1 a** : REMEMBER, RECALL **b** : to cause (oneself) to be reminded
**2** : to cause (oneself) to consider

**be·tide** \bi-'tīd\ (12th century)
*intransitive verb*
: to happen especially as if by fate
*transitive verb*
: to happen to : BEFALL — used chiefly in the phrase *woe betide* ⟨woe *betide* our enemies⟩

**be·times** \bi-'tīmz\ *adverb* (13th century)
**1** : in good time : EARLY
**2** *archaic* : in a short time : SPEEDILY
**3** : at times : OCCASIONALLY

**bê·tise** \bā-'tēz\ *noun, plural* **bê·tises** \-'tēz\ [French] (1827)
**1** : an act of foolishness or stupidity
**2** : lack of good sense : STUPIDITY

**be·to·ken** \bi-'tō-kən\ *transitive verb* **-to·kened**; **-to·ken·ing** \-'tōk-niŋ, -'tō-kə-\ (15th century)
**1** : to typify beforehand : PRESAGE
**2** : to give evidence of : SHOW

**be·tray** \bi-'trā\ *verb* [Middle English, from *be-* + *trayen* to betray, from Old French *traïr*, from Latin *tradere* — more at TRAITOR] (13th century)
*transitive verb*
**1** : to lead astray; *especially* : SEDUCE
**2** : to deliver to an enemy by treachery
**3** : to fail or desert especially in time of need
**4 a** : to reveal unintentionally **b** : SHOW, INDICATE **c** : to disclose in violation of confidence
*intransitive verb*
: to prove false
**synonym** see REVEAL
— **be·tray·al** \-'trā-(ə)l\ *noun*
— **be·tray·er** \-'trā-ər\ *noun*

**be·troth** \bi-'trōth, -'trȯth\ *transitive verb* [Middle English, from *be-* + *trouthe* truth, troth] (14th century)
**1** : to promise to marry
**2** : to give in marriage

**be·troth·al** \-'trō-thəl, -'trȯ-, -thəl\ *noun* (1844)
**1** : the act of betrothing or fact of being betrothed
**2** : a mutual promise or contract for a future marriage

**be·trothed** \bi-'trōthd, -'trȯtht\ *noun* (1588)
: the person to whom one is betrothed

**bet·ta** \'be-tə\ *noun* [New Latin] (1927)
: any of a genus (*Betta*) of small brilliantly colored long-finned freshwater fishes of southeastern Asia; *especially* : SIAMESE FIGHTING FISH

**¹bet·ter** \'be-tər\ *adjective, comparative of* GOOD [Middle English *bettre*, from Old English *betera*; akin to Old English *bōt* remedy, Sanskrit *bhadra* fortunate] (before 12th century)
**1** : greater than half
**2** : improved in health or mental attitude
**3** : more attractive, favorable, or commendable
**4** : more advantageous or effective
**5** : improved in accuracy or performance

**²better** (before 12th century)
*transitive verb*
**1** : to make better: as **a** : to make more tolerable or acceptable ⟨trying to *better* the lot of slum dwellers⟩ **b** : to make more complete or perfect ⟨looked forward to *bettering* her acquaintance with the new neighbors⟩
**2** : to surpass in excellence : EXCEL
*intransitive verb*
: to become better
**synonym** see IMPROVE

**³better** *adverb, comparative of* WELL (12th century)
**1 a** : in a more excellent manner **b** : to greater advantage : PREFERABLY ⟨some things are *better* left unsaid⟩
**2 a** : to a higher or greater degree ⟨he knows the story *better* than you do⟩ **b** : MORE ⟨it is *better* than nine miles to the next town⟩

**⁴better** *noun* (12th century)
**1 a** : something better **b** : a superior especially in merit or rank
**2** : ADVANTAGE, VICTORY ⟨get the *better* of him⟩

**⁵better** *verbal auxiliary* (1831)
: had better ⟨you *better* hurry⟩

**bet·ter·ment** \'be-tər-mənt\ *noun* (1598)
**1** : a making or becoming better
**2** : an improvement that adds to the value of a property or facility

**better-off** \,be-tə-'rȯf\ *adjective* (circa 1859)
**1** : being in comfortable economic circumstances ⟨the *better-off* people live in the older section of town⟩
**2** : being in a more advantageous position

**betting shop** *noun* (1852)
*British* : a shop where bets are taken

**bet·tor** *or* **bet·ter** \'be-tər\ *noun* (1609)
: one that bets

**¹be·tween** \bi-'twēn\ *preposition* [Middle English *betwene*, preposition & adverb, from Old English *betwēonum*, from *be-* + *-twēonum* (dative plural) (akin to Gothic *tweihnai* two each); akin to Old English *twā* two] (before 12th century)
**1 a** : by the common action of : jointly engaging ⟨shared the work *between* the two of them⟩ ⟨talks *between* the three —*Time*⟩ **b** : in common to : shared by ⟨divided *between* his four grandchildren⟩
**2 a** : in the time, space, or interval that separates **b** : in intermediate relation to
**3 a** : from one to another of ⟨air service *between* Miami and Chicago⟩ **b** : serving to connect or unite in a relationship (as difference, likeness, or proportion) ⟨a one-to-one correspondence *between* sets⟩ **c** : setting apart ⟨the line *between* fact and fancy⟩
**4** : in point of comparison of ⟨not much to choose *between* the two coats⟩
**5** : in confidence restricted to ⟨a secret *between* you and me⟩ ▪

**²between** *adverb* (before 12th century)
: in an intermediate space or interval

**be·tween-brain** \-,brān\ *noun* (circa 1909)
: DIENCEPHALON

**be·tween·ness** \bi-'twēn-nəs\ *noun* (1892)
: the quality or state of being between two others in an ordered mathematical set

**be·tween·times** \bi-'twēn-,tīmz\ *adverb* (1907)

: at or during intervals

**be·tween·whiles** \-,hwīlz, -,wīlz\ *adverb* (1678)
: BETWEENTIMES

**be·twixt** \bi-'twikst\ *adverb or preposition* [Middle English, from Old English *betwux*, from *be-* + *-twux* (akin to Gothic *tweihnai*)] (before 12th century)
: BETWEEN

**betwixt and between** *adverb or adjective* (1832)

---

□ USAGE

**between** There is a persistent but unfounded notion that *between* can be used only of two items and that *among* must be used for more than two. *Between* has been used of more than two since Old English; it is especially appropriate to denote a one-to-one relationship, regardless of the number of items. It can be used when the number is unspecified ⟨economic cooperation *between* nations⟩, when more than two are enumerated ⟨*between* you and me and the lamppost⟩ ⟨partitioned *between* Austria, Prussia, and Russia —Nathaniel Benchley⟩, and even when only one item is mentioned (but repetition is implied) ⟨pausing *between* every sentence to rap the floor —George Eliot⟩. *Among* is more appropriate where the emphasis is on distribution rather than individual relationships ⟨discontent *among* the peasants⟩. When *among* is automatically chosen for more than two, English idiom may be strained ⟨a worthy book that nevertheless falls *among* many stools —John Simon⟩ ⟨the author alternates *among* mod slang, clichés and quotes from literary giants —A. H. Johnston⟩.

Grammarians and other commentators have been hard put to explain the occurrence of *I* where *me* would be expected as the proper form after this preposition: *between you and I.* The most common explanation put forward is hypercorrection—the use of an improper form in one expression on analogy with a proper use of the same form in another expression. In this instance it is supposed that many people taught to say "It is I" instead of "It is me" become intimidated by *me* and substitute *I* whenever they have a chance. On the surface of it, this seems to be a far-fetched explanation, and another point against it is that the phrase can be found as early as the end of the 16th century, when there were no schoolteachers harping on "It is I" ⟨an argument too deepe to be discussed *between you and I* —Thomas Deloney (1597)⟩ ⟨all debts are cleared *between you and I* —Shakespeare, *The Merchant of Venice* (1600)⟩. The most plausible explanation is that offered by the linguist Noam Chomsky, who in a 1986 book postulated that compound phrases like *you and I* are barriers to the assignment of case by verb or preposition, which means that pronouns may appear as nominative or objective or may even be reflexive—in our phrase, *I, me,* or *myself.* Chomsky's theory has the advantage of also accounting for other anomalies of pronoun case in compound subjects and objects of verbs. It is to be observed that the expected case—nominative in subject position, objective in object position—predominates, and that the others, while common, are much more likely to be found in speech than in writing.

---

\ə\ abut \ᵊ\ kitten \ər\ further \a\ ash \ā\ ace
\ä\ mop, mar \au̇\ out \ch\ chin \e\ bet \ē\ easy
\g\ go \i\ hit \ī\ ice \j\ job \ŋ\ sing \ō\ go
\ȯ\ law \ȯi\ boy \th\ thin \t̲h̲\ the \ü\ loot \u̇\ foot
\y\ yet \zh\ vision *see also* Guide to Pronunciation

: in a midway position : neither one thing nor the other

**Beu·lah** \'byü-lə\ *noun*
: an idyllic land near the end of life's journey in Bunyan's *Pilgrim's Progress*

**beurre blanc** \'bər-'blä<sup>n</sup>\ *noun* [French, literally, white butter] (1931)
: a hot butter sauce (as for fish) flavored with vinegar or lemon juice

**beurre ma·nié** \-män-'yā\ *noun* [French, literally, handled butter] (1939)
: flour and butter kneaded together used as a thickener in sauces

**beurre noir** \-'nwär\ *noun* [French, literally, black butter] (1856)
: butter heated until brown or black and often flavored with vinegar or lemon juice

**¹bev·el** \'be-vəl\ *adjective* (circa 1600)
: OBLIQUE, BEVELED

**²bevel** *noun* [(assumed) Middle French, from Old French *baïf* with open mouth, from *baer* to yawn — more at ABEYANCE] (1610)

bevel 2

**1** : an instrument consisting of two rules or arms jointed together and opening to any angle for drawing angles or adjusting surfaces to be cut at an angle
**2 a** : the angle that one surface or line makes with another when they are not at right angles **b** : the slant of such a surface or line
**3** : the part of printing type extending from face to shoulder

**³bevel** *verb* **-eled** *or* **-elled; -el·ing** *or* **-el·ling** \'bev-liŋ, 'be-və-\ (1677)
*transitive verb*
: to cut or shape to a bevel
*intransitive verb*
: INCLINE, SLANT

**bevel gear** *noun* (1833)
: either of a pair of toothed wheels whose working surfaces are inclined to nonparallel axes

bevel gears

**bev·er·age** \'bev-rij, 'be-və-\ *noun* [Middle English, from Middle French *bevrage*, from *beivre* to drink, from Latin *bibere* — more at POTABLE] (14th century)
: a drinkable liquid

**bevy** \'be-vē\ *noun, plural* **bev·ies** [Middle English *bevey*] (15th century)
**1** : a large group or collection ⟨a *bevy* of girls⟩
**2** : a group of animals and especially quail together

**be·wail** \bi-'wā(ə)l\ *transitive verb* (14th century)
**1** : to wail over
**2** : to express deep sorrow for usually by wailing and lamentation ⟨wringing her hands and *bewailing* her fate⟩
**synonym** see DEPLORE

**be·ware** \bi-'war, -'wer\ *verb* [Middle English *been war*, from *been* to be + *war* careful — more at BE, WARE] (14th century)
*intransitive verb*
: to be on one's guard ⟨*beware* of the dog⟩
*transitive verb*
**1** : to take care of ⟨*beware* your wallet⟩
**2** : to be wary of ⟨we must . . . *beware* the exceedingly tenuous generalization. —Matthew Lipman⟩

**be·whis·kered** \-'hwis-kərd, -'wis-\ *adjective* (1820)
: wearing whiskers

**be·wigged** \bi-'wigd\ *adjective* (1774)
: wearing a wig

**be·wil·der** \bi-'wil-dər\ *transitive verb* **-wildered; -wil·der·ing** \-d(ə-)riŋ\ (1684)
**1** : to cause to lose one's bearings
**2** : to perplex or confuse especially by a complexity, variety, or multitude of objects or considerations
**synonym** see PUZZLE
— **be·wil·dered·ly** *adverb*
— **be·wil·dered·ness** *noun*
— **be·wil·der·ing·ly** \-d(ə-)riŋ-lē\ *adverb*

**be·wil·der·ment** \-dər-mənt\ *noun* (1820)
**1** : the quality or state of being bewildered
**2** : a bewildering tangle or confusion

**be·witch** \bi-'wich\ (13th century)
*transitive verb*
**1 a** : to influence or affect especially injuriously by witchcraft **b** : to cast a spell over
**2** : to attract as if by the power of witchcraft : ENCHANT ⟨*bewitched* by her beauty⟩
*intransitive verb*
: to bewitch someone or something
— **be·witch·ery** \-'wi-ch(ə-)rē\ *noun*
— **be·witch·ing·ly** \-'wi-chiŋ-lē\ *adverb*

**be·witch·ment** \-'wich-mənt\ *noun* (1607)
**1 a** : the act or power of bewitching **b** : a spell that bewitches
**2** : the state of being bewitched

**be·wray** \bi-'rā\ *transitive verb* [Middle English, from *be-* + *wreyen* to accuse, from Old English *wrēgan;* akin to Old High German *ruogen* to accuse] (13th century)
*archaic* : DIVULGE, BETRAY

**bey** \'bā\ *noun* [Turkish, gentleman, chief] (1595)
**1 a** : a provincial governor in the Ottoman Empire **b** : the former native ruler of Tunis or Tunisia
**2** — used as a courtesy title in Turkey and Egypt

**¹be·yond** \bē-'änd\ *adverb* [Middle English, preposition & adverb, from Old English *begeondan*, from *be-* + *geondan* beyond, from *geond* yond — more at YOND] (before 12th century)
**1** : on or to the farther side : FARTHER
**2** : in addition : BESIDES

**²beyond** *preposition* (before 12th century)
**1** : on or to the farther side of : at a greater distance than
**2 a** : out of the reach or sphere of **b** : in a degree or amount surpassing **c** : out of the comprehension of
**3** : in addition to : BESIDES

**³beyond** *noun* (14th century)
**1** : something that lies beyond
**2** : something that lies outside the scope of ordinary experience; *specifically* : HEREAFTER

**be·zant** \'be-z<sup>ə</sup>nt, bə-'zant\ *noun* [Middle English *besant*, from Old French, from Medieval Latin *Byzantius* Byzantine, from *Byzantium*, ancient name of Istanbul] (13th century)
**1** : SOLIDUS 1
**2** : a flat disk used in architectural ornament

**be·zel** \'bē-zəl, 'be-\ *noun* [probably from dialect form of French *biseau* bezel, from Middle French] (circa 1616)
**1** : a rim that holds a transparent covering (as on a watch, clock, or headlight) or that is rotatable and has special markings (as on a watch)
**2** : the oblique side or face of a cut gem; *specifically* : the upper faceted portion of a brilliant projecting from the setting
**3** : a usually metal rim of a piece of jewelry in which an ornament (as a gem) is set

**be·zique** \bə-'zēk\ *noun* [French *bésique*] (1861)
: a card game similar to pinochle that is played with a pack of 64 cards

**be·zoar** \'bē-,zōr, -,zòr\ *noun* [Middle French, from Medieval Latin, from Arabic dialect *bezuwār*, from Arabic *bāzahr*, from Persian *pādzahr*, from *pād* protecting (against) + *zahr* poison] (1577)

: any of various calculi found chiefly in the gastrointestinal organs and formerly believed to possess magical properties — called also *bezoar stone*

**B-girl** *noun* [probably from *bar* + *girl*] (1936)
: a woman who entertains bar patrons and encourages them to spend freely

**BHA** \,bē-(,)āch-'ā\ *noun* [butylated hydroxyanisole] (1950)
: a phenolic antioxidant $C_{11}H_{16}O_2$ used especially to preserve fats and oils in food

**Bha·ga·vad Gi·ta** \,bä-gə-,väd-'gē-tə\ *noun* [Sanskrit *Bhagavadgītā*, literally, song of the blessed one (Krishna)] (circa 1785)
: a Hindu devotional work in poetic form

**bhak·ti** \'bək-tē\ *noun* [Sanskrit, literally, portion] (1832)
: devotion to a deity constituting a way to salvation in Hinduism

**bhang** \'baŋ, 'bäŋ\ *noun* [Hindi *bhā̃g*] (1563)
: HEMP 1a, c; *also* : the leaves and flowering tops of uncultivated hemp : CANNABIS — compare MARIJUANA, HASHISH

**bha·ral** \'bər-əl, 'bə-rəl\ *noun* [Hindi] (1838)
: a goatlike artiodactyl mammal (*Pseudois nayaur*) of the Himalayas and western China having a bluish-gray coat

**BHC** \,bē-,āch-'sē\ *noun* [benzene hexachloride] (1947)
**1** : any of several stereoisomeric chlorine derivatives $C_6H_6Cl_6$ of cyclohexane in which the chlorine atoms are all attached to different carbon atoms
**2** : LINDANE

**Bhoj·puri** \'bōj-,pur-ē, 'bäj-, -pə-rē\ *noun* [Hindi *bhojpurī*, from *Bhojpur*, village in Bihar] (1901)
: an Indo-Aryan language spoken in western Bihar and eastern Uttar Pradesh, India

**B horizon** *noun* (1938)
: a subsurface soil layer that is immediately beneath the A horizon from which it obtains organic matter chiefly by illuviation and is usually distinguished by less weathering

**BHT** \,bē-,āch-'tē\ *noun* [butylated hydroxytoluene] (1961)
: a phenolic antioxidant $C_{15}H_{24}O$ used especially to preserve fats and oils in food, cosmetics, and pharmaceuticals

**bi** \'bī\ *noun or adjective* (circa 1965)
: BISEXUAL

**¹bi-** *prefix* [Middle English, from Latin — more at TWI-]
**1 a** : two ⟨*bi*lateral⟩ **b** : coming or occurring every two ⟨*bi*centennial⟩ **c** : into two parts ⟨*bi*sect⟩
**2 a** : twice : doubly : on both sides ⟨*bi*convex⟩ **b** : coming or occurring two times ⟨*bi*annual⟩ — compare SEMI-
**3** : between, involving, or affecting two (specified) symmetrical parts ⟨*bi*labial⟩
**4 a** : containing one (specified) constituent in double the proportion of the other constituent or in double the ordinary proportion ⟨*bi*carbonate⟩ **b** : DI- 2 ⟨*bi*phenyl⟩ ◼

☐ USAGE
**bi-** Many people are puzzled about *bimonthly* and *biweekly*, which are often ambiguous because they are formed from both senses 1b and 2b of *bi-*. This ambiguity has been in existence for nearly a century and a half and cannot be eliminated by the dictionary. The chief difficulty is that many users of these words assume that others know exactly what they mean, and they do not bother to make their context clear. So if you need *bimonthly* or *biweekly*, you should leave some clues in your context to the sense of *bi-* you mean. And if you need the meaning "twice a," you can substitute *semi-* for *bi-*. *Biannual* and *biennial* are usually differentiated.

# BIBLE

| OLD TESTAMENT | | NEW TESTAMENT | PROTESTANT APOCRYPHA | JEWISH SCRIPTURE |
|---|---|---|---|---|
| ROMAN CATHOLIC CANON | PROTESTANT CANON | Matthew<br>Mark<br>Luke<br>John | 1 & 2 Esdras<br>Tobit<br>Judith | *Law*<br>Genesis<br>Exodus |
| Genesis | Genesis | Acts of the | Additions to | Leviticus |
| Exodus | Exodus | Apostles | Esther | Numbers |
| Leviticus | Leviticus | Romans | Wisdom of | Deuteronomy |
| Numbers | Numbers | 1 & 2 | Solomon | *Prophets* |
| Deuteronomy | Deuteronomy | Corinthians | Ecclesiasticus | Joshua |
| Joshua | Joshua | Galatians | or the Wisdom | Judges |
| Judges | Judges | Ephesians | of Jesus Son | 1 & 2 Samuel |
| Ruth | Ruth | Philippians | of Sirach | 1 & 2 Kings |
| 1 & 2 Samuel | 1 & 2 Samuel | Colossians | Baruch | Isaiah |
| 1 & 2 Kings | 1 & 2 Kings | 1 & 2 | Prayer of | Jeremiah |
| 1 & 2 Chronicles | 1 & 2 Chronicles | Thessalonians | Azariah and | Ezekiel |
| Ezra | Ezra | 1 & 2 Timothy | the Song of | Hosea |
| Nehemiah | Nehemiah | Titus | the Three Holy | Joel |
| Tobit | | Philemon | Children | Amos |
| Judith | | Hebrews | Susanna | Obadiah |
| Esther | Esther | James | Bel and the | Jonah |
| Job | Job | 1 & 2 Peter | Dragon | Micah |
| Psalms | Psalms | 1, 2, 3 John | The Prayer of | Nahum |
| Proverbs | Proverbs | Jude | Manasses | Habakkuk |
| Ecclesiastes | Ecclesiastes | Revelation *or* | 1 & 2 Maccabees | Zephaniah |
| Song of Songs | Song of Solomon | Apocalypse | | Haggai |
| Wisdom | | | | Zechariah |
| Sirach | | | | Malachi |
| Isaiah | Isaiah | | | *Hagiographa* |
| Jeremiah | Jeremiah | | | Psalms |
| Lamentations | Lamentations | | | Proverbs |
| Baruch | | | | Job |
| Ezekiel | Ezekiel | | | Song of Songs |
| Daniel | Daniel | | | Ruth |
| Hosea | Hosea | | | Lamentations |
| Joel | Joel | | | Ecclesiastes |
| Amos | Amos | | | Esther |
| Obadiah | Obadiah | | | Daniel |
| Jonah | Jonah | | | Ezra |
| Micah | Micah | | | Nehemiah |
| Nahum | Nahum | | | 1 & 2 Chronicles |
| Habakkuk | Habakkuk | | | |
| Zephaniah | Zephaniah | | | |
| Haggai | Haggai | | | |
| Zechariah | Zechariah | | | |
| Malachi | Malachi | | | |
| 1 & 2 Maccabees | | | | |

**²bi-** *or* **bio-** *combining form* [Greek, from *bios* mode of life — more at QUICK]
**:** life **:** living organisms or tissue ⟨*bio*luminescence⟩
**bi·aly** \bē-'a-lē\ *noun, plural* **bialys** [Yiddish, short for *bialystoker,* from *bialystoker* of Bialystok, city in Poland] (1965)
**:** a flat breakfast roll that has a depressed center and is usually covered with onion flakes
**bi·an·nu·al** \(,)bī-'an-yə(-wə)l\ *adjective* (1877)
**:** occurring twice a year; *sometimes* **:** BIENNIAL 1
    *usage* see BI-
— **bi·an·nu·al·ly** *adverb*
**¹bi·as** \'bī-əs\ *noun* [Middle French *biais*] (1530)
**1 :** a line diagonal to the grain of a fabric; *especially* **:** a line at a 45° angle to the selvage often utilized in the cutting of garments for smoother fit
**2 a :** a peculiarity in the shape of a bowl that causes it to swerve when rolled on the green **b :** the tendency of a bowl to swerve; *also* **:** the impulse causing this tendency **c :** the swerve of the bowl
**3 a :** BENT, TENDENCY **b :** an inclination of temperament or outlook; *especially* **:** a personal and sometimes unreasoned judgment **:** PREJUDICE **c :** an instance of such prejudice **d** (1) **:** deviation of the expected value of a statistical estimate from the quantity it estimates (2) **:** systematic error introduced into sampling or testing by selecting or encouraging one outcome or answer over others

**4 a :** a voltage applied to a device (as a transistor control electrode) to establish a reference level for operation **b :** a high-frequency voltage combined with an audio signal to reduce distortion in tape recording
**synonym** SEE PREDILECTION
— **on the bias :** ASKEW, OBLIQUELY
**²bias** *adjective* (1551)
**:** DIAGONAL, SLANTING — used chiefly of fabrics and their cut
— **bi·as·ness** *noun*
**³bias** *adverb* (1575)
**1 :** DIAGONALLY ⟨cut cloth *bias*⟩
**2** *obsolete* **:** AWRY
**⁴bias** *transitive verb* **bi·ased** *or* **bi·assed;** **bi·as·ing** *or* **bi·as·sing** (circa 1628)
**1 :** to give a settled and often prejudiced outlook to ⟨his background *biases* him against foreigners⟩
**2 :** to apply a slight negative or positive voltage to (as an electron-tube grid)
**synonym** SEE INCLINE
**bi·as–belt·ed tire** \'bī-əs-,bel-təd-\ *noun* (1968)
**:** a pneumatic tire with a belt (as of steel or fiberglass) around the tire under the tread and on top of the ply cords set diagonally to the center line of the tread
**bi·ased** *adjective* (1649)
**1 :** exhibiting or characterized by bias; *especially* **:** PREJUDICED
**2 :** tending to yield one outcome more frequently than others in a statistical experiment ⟨a *biased* coin⟩

**3 :** having an expected value different from the quantity or parameter estimated ⟨a *biased* estimate⟩
**bias–ply tire** \'bī-əs-,plī-\ *noun* (1968)
**:** a pneumatic tire having crossed layers of ply-cord set diagonally to the center line of the tread
**bias tape** *noun* (1926)
**:** a narrow strip of cloth cut on the bias, folded, and used for finishing or decorating clothing
**bi·ath·lete** \bī-'ath-,lēt\ *noun* [blend of *athlete* and *biathlon*] (1968)
**:** a competitor in a biathlon
**bi·ath·lon** \bī-'ath-lən, -,län\ *noun* [¹*bi-* + *-athlon* (as in *decathlon*)] (1958)
**:** a composite athletic contest consisting of cross-country skiing and rifle sharpshooting
**bi·ax·i·al** \(,)bī-'ak-sē-əl\ *adjective* (1854)
**:** having or relating to two axes or optic axes ⟨a *biaxial* crystal⟩
— **bi·ax·i·al·ly** \-ə-lē\ *adverb*
**¹bib** \'bib\ *verb* **bibbed; bib·bing** [Middle English *bibben*] (14th century)
**:** DRINK
**²bib** *noun* (1580)
**1 :** a cloth or plastic shield tied under the chin to protect the clothes
**2 :** the part of an apron or of overalls extending above the waist
**3 :** a patch of differently colored feathers or fur immediately below the bill or chin of a bird or mammal
— **bibbed** \'bibd\ *adjective*
— **bib·less** \'bib-ləs\ *adjective*
**bib and tucker** *noun* (1747)
**:** an outfit of clothing — usually used in the phrase *best bib and tucker*
**bib·ber** \'bi-bər\ *noun* (1536)
**:** a person who regularly drinks alcoholic beverages
— **bib·bery** \'bi-bə-rē\ *noun*
**Bibb lettuce** \'bib-\ *noun* [Major John *Bibb,* 19th century American grower] (1961)
**:** lettuce of a variety that has a small head and dark green color
**bib·cock** \'bib-,käk\ *also* **bibb cock** *noun* (circa 1853)
**:** a faucet having a bent-down nozzle
**bi·be·lot** \'bē-bə-,lō\ *noun, plural* **bibelots** \-,lō(z)\ [French] (1873)
**:** a small household ornament or decorative object **:** TRINKET
**bi·ble** \'bī-bəl\ *noun* [Middle English, from Old French, from Medieval Latin *biblia,* from Greek, plural of *biblion* book, diminutive of *byblos* papyrus, book, from *Byblos,* ancient Phoenician city from which papyrus was exported] (14th century)
**1** *capitalized* **a :** the sacred scriptures of Christians comprising the Old Testament and the New Testament **b :** the sacred scriptures of some other religion (as Judaism)
**2** *obsolete* **:** BOOK
**3** *capitalized* **:** a copy or an edition of the Bible
**4 :** a publication that is preeminent especially in authoritativeness or wide readership ⟨the fisherman's *bible*⟩ ⟨the *bible* of the entertainment industry⟩
**Bible Belt** *noun* (1925)
**:** an area chiefly in the southern U.S. believed to hold uncritical allegiance to the literal accuracy of the Bible; *broadly* **:** an area characterized by ardent religious fundamentalism
**Bible paper** *noun* (1903)
**:** INDIA PAPER 2
**Bi·ble–thump·er** \'bī-bəl-,thəm-pər\ *noun* (1937)

\ə\ abut \ᵊ\ kitten \ər\ further \a\ ash \ā\ ace \ä\ mop, mar \aů\ out \ch\ chin \e\ bet \ē\ easy \g\ go \i\ hit \ī\ ice \j\ job \ŋ\ sing \ō\ go \ȯ\ law \ȯi\ boy \th\ thin \th\ the \ü\ loot \ů\ foot \y\ yet \zh\ vision   *see also* Guide to Pronunciation

: an overzealous proponent of Christian fundamentalism
— **Bi·ble–thump·ing** \-piŋ\ *adjective*
**bibli-** *or* **biblio-** *combining form* [Middle French, from Latin, from Greek, from *biblion*]
: book ⟨*bibliology*⟩
**bib·li·cal** \'bi-bli-kəl\ *adjective* [Medieval Latin *biblicus*, from *biblia*] (circa 1775)
**1** : of, relating to, or being in accord with the Bible
**2** : suggestive of the Bible or Bible times
— **bib·li·cal·ly** \-k(ə-)lē\ *adverb*
**bib·li·cism** \'bi-blə-,si-zəm\ *noun, often capitalized* (1851)
: adherence to the letter of the Bible
— **bib·li·cist** \-lə-sist\ *noun, often capitalized*
**bib·li·og·ra·pher** \,bi-blē-'ä-grə-fər\ *noun* (1775)
**1** : an expert in bibliography
**2** : a compiler of bibliographies
**bib·li·og·ra·phy** \,bi-blē-'ä-grə-fē\ *noun, plural* **-phies** [probably from New Latin *bibliographia*, from Greek, the copying of books, from *bibli-* + *-graphia* -graphy] (1802)
**1** : the history, identification, or description of writings or publications
**2 a** : a list often with descriptive or critical notes of writings relating to a particular subject, period, or author **b** : a list of works written by an author or printed by a publishing house
**3** : the works or a list of the works referred to in a text or consulted by the author in its production
— **bib·lio·graph·ic** \,bi-blē-ə-'gra-fik\ *also* **bib·lio·graph·i·cal** \-fi-kəl\ *adjective*
— **bib·lio·graph·i·cal·ly** \-k(ə-)lē\ *adverb*
**bib·li·ol·a·ter** \,bi-blē-'ä-lə-tər\ *noun* (1847)
**1** : one having excessive reverence for the letter of the Bible
**2** : one overly devoted to books
— **bib·li·ol·a·trous** \-'ä-lə-trəs\ *adjective*
— **bib·li·ol·a·try** \-trē\ *noun*
**bib·li·ol·o·gy** \,bi-blē-'ä-lə-jē\ *noun* (1806)
**1** : the history and science of books as physical objects : BIBLIOGRAPHY
**2** *often capitalized* : the study of the theological doctrine of the Bible
**bib·lio·ma·nia** \,bi-blē-ə-'mā-nē-ə, -nyə\ *noun* [French *bibliomanie*, from *bibli-* + *manie* mania, from Late Latin *mania*] (1734)
: extreme preoccupation with collecting books
— **bib·lio·ma·ni·ac** \-nē-,ak\ *noun or adjective*
— **bib·lio·ma·ni·a·cal** \-lē-ō-mə-'nī-ə-kəl\ *adjective*
**bib·li·op·e·gy** \,bi-blē-'ä-pə-jē\ *noun* [ultimately from Greek *bibli-* + *pēgnynai* to fasten together — more at PACT] (circa 1859)
: the art of binding books
— **bib·li·o·pe·gic** \,bi-blē-ə-'pe-jik, -'pē-\ *adjective*
— **bib·li·op·e·gist** \,bi-blē-'ä-pə-jist\ *noun*
**bib·lio·phile** \'bi-blē-ə-,fīl\ *noun* [French, from *bibli-* + *-phile*] (1824)
: a lover of books especially for qualities of format; *also* : a book collector
— **bib·lio·phil·ic** \,bi-blē-ə-'fi-lik\ *adjective*
— **bib·li·oph·i·lism** \-'ä-fə-,li-zəm\ *noun*
— **bib·li·oph·i·ly** \-lē\ *noun*
**bib·li·o·pole** \'bi-blē-ə-,pōl\ *or* **bib·li·op·o·list** \,bi-blē-'ä-pə-list\ *noun* [Latin *bibliopola* bookseller, from Greek *bibliopōlēs*, from *bibli-* + *pōlein* to sell] (1775)
: a dealer especially in rare or curious books
**bib·lio·the·ca** \,bi-blē-ə-'thē-kə\ *noun, plural* **-cas** *or* **-cae** \-,sē, -,kē\ [Latin, from Greek *bibliothēkē*, from *bibli-* + *thēkē* case; akin to Greek *tithenai* to put, place — more at DO] (circa 1824)
**1** : a collection of books
**2** : a list of books
— **bib·lio·the·cal** \-'thē-kəl\ *adjective*
**bib·lio·ther·a·py** \,bi-blē-ə-'ther-ə-pē\ *noun* (1919)

: the use of reading materials for help in solving personal problems or for psychiatric therapy
**bib·li·ot·ics** \,bi-blē-'ä-tiks\ *noun plural but singular in construction* [*bibli-* + ¹*-otic* + *-ics*] (1901)
: the study of handwriting, documents, and writing materials especially for determining genuineness or authorship
— **bib·li·ot·ic** \-'tik\ *adjective*
— **bib·li·o·tist** \'bi-blē-ə-tist\ *noun*
**bib·u·lous** \'bi-byə-ləs\ *adjective* [Latin *bibulus*, from *bibere* to drink — more at POTABLE] (1675)
**1** : highly absorbent
**2 a** : fond of alcoholic beverages **b** : of, relating to, or marked by the consumption of alcoholic beverages
— **bib·u·lous·ly** *adverb*
— **bib·u·lous·ness** *noun*
**bi·cam·er·al** \(,)bī-'kam-rəl, -'ka-mə-\ *adjective* [¹*bi-* + Late Latin *camera* chamber — more at CHAMBER] (1856)
: having, consisting of, or based on two legislative chambers ⟨a *bicameral* legislature⟩
— **bi·cam·er·al·ism** \-rə-,li-zəm\ *noun*
**bi·carb** \(,)bī-'kärb, 'bī-,\ *noun* (1922)
: SODIUM BICARBONATE
**bi·car·bon·ate** \(,)bī-'kär-bə-,nāt, -nət\ *noun* [International Scientific Vocabulary] (1819)
: an acid carbonate
**bicarbonate of soda** (circa 1887)
: SODIUM BICARBONATE
**bi·cen·te·na·ry** \,bī-(,)sen-'te-nə-rē, (,)bī-'sen-t°n-,er-ē, ,bī-(,)sen-'tē-nə-rē\ *noun* (1872)
: BICENTENNIAL
— **bicentenary** *adjective*
**bi·cen·ten·ni·al** \,bī-(,)sen-'te-ne-əl\ *noun* (1883)
: a 200th anniversary or its celebration
— **bicentennial** *adjective*
**bi·ceps** \'bī-,seps\ *noun, plural* **biceps** *also* **bi·ceps·es** [New Latin *bicipit-, biceps*, from Latin, two-headed, from *bi-* + *capit-, caput* head — more at HEAD] (1650)
: a muscle having two heads: as **a** : the large flexor muscle of the front of the upper arm **b** : the large flexor muscle of the back of the upper leg
**biceps bra·chii** \-'brā-kē-,ī, -kē-,ē\ *noun* [New Latin, literally, biceps of the arm] (circa 1860)
: BICEPS a
**biceps fe·mo·ris** \-'fe-mə-rəs\ *noun* [New Latin, literally, biceps of the femur] (circa 1860)
: BICEPS b
**bi·chlo·ride of mercury** \(,)bī-'klōr-,īd-, -'klòr-\ [International Scientific Vocabulary] (1810)
: MERCURIC CHLORIDE
**bi·chon fri·se** \bē-,shō°-frē-'zā\ *noun, plural* **bi·chons fri·ses** \-,shō°-frē-'zā(z)\ [modification of French *bichon à poil frisé* curly-haired lapdog] (1966)
: any of a breed of small sturdy dogs of Mediterranean origin having a thick wavy white coat
**bi·chro·mate** \(,)bī-'krō-,māt, 'bī-krō-\ *noun* (1836)
: a dichromate especially of sodium or potassium
— **bi·chro·mat·ed** \-,mā-təd\ *adjective*
**bi·chrome** \'bī-,krōm\ *adjective* (1924)
: two-colored
**bi·cip·i·tal** \bī-'si-pə-t°l\ *adjective* (1646)
: of, relating to, or being a biceps
¹**bick·er** \'bi-kər\ *noun* [Middle English *biker*] (14th century)
**1** : petulant quarreling : ALTERCATION
**2** : a sound of or as if of bickering
²**bicker** *intransitive verb* **bick·ered; bick·er·ing** \-k(ə-)riŋ\ (15th century)
**1** : to engage in a petulant or petty quarrel
**2 a** : to move with a rapidly repeated noise ⟨a *bickering* stream⟩ **b** : QUIVER, FLICKER

— **bick·er·er** \-kə-rər\ *noun*
**bi·coast·al** \(,)bī-'kōs-təl\ *adjective* (1972)
: of or relating to or living or working on both the East and West coasts of the U.S.
**bi·col·ored** \'bī-,kə-lərd\ *or* **bi·col·or** \-lər\ *adjective* [Latin *bicolor*, from *bi-* + *color*] (circa 1843)
: two-colored
— **bicolor** *noun*
**bi·com·po·nent** \(,)bī-kəm-'pō-nənt, -käm-, -'käm-,\ *adjective* (1962)
: being a fiber made of two polymers having slightly different physical properties so that the fiber has a permanent crimp and fabrics made from it have inherent bulk and stretchability
**bi·con·cave** \(,)bī-(,)kän-'kāv, -'kän-,\ *adjective* (1833)
: concave on both sides
— **bi·con·cav·i·ty** \,bī-(,)kän-'ka-və-tē\ *noun*
**bi·con·di·tion·al** \,bī-kən-'dish-nəl, -'di-shə-\ *noun* (1940)
: a relation between two propositions that is true only when both propositions are simultaneously true or false
**bi·con·vex** \,bī-(,)kän-'veks, (,)bī-'kän-,\ *adjective* [International Scientific Vocabulary] (circa 1852)
: convex on both sides
— **bi·con·vex·i·ty** \,bī-kən-'vek-sə-tē, -(,)kän-\ *noun*
**bi·corne** \'bī-,kòrn\ *noun* [French, from Latin *bicornis* two-horned, from *bi-* + *cornu* horn — more at HORN] (1936)
: COCKED HAT 2
**bi·cul·tur·al** \(,)bī-'kəl-chər-əl\ *adjective* (1940)
: of, relating to, or including two distinct cultures ⟨*bicultural* education⟩
— **bi·cul·tur·al·ism** \-ə-,li-zəm\ *noun*
¹**bi·cus·pid** \(,)bī-'kəs-pəd\ *adjective* [New Latin *bicuspid-, bicuspis*, from *bi-* + Latin *cuspid-, cuspis* point] (circa 1839)
: having or ending in two points ⟨*bicuspid* teeth⟩
²**bicuspid** *noun* (1852)
: a human premolar tooth — see TOOTH illustration
**bicuspid valve** *noun* (circa 1903)
: a cardiac valve consisting of two triangular flaps which allow only unidirectional blood flow from the left atrium to the ventricle — called also *mitral valve*
¹**bi·cy·cle** \'bī-si-kəl, -,si- *also* -,sī-\ *noun* [French, from *bi-* + *-cycle* (as in *tricycle*)] (1868)
: a vehicle with two wheels tandem, a steering handle, a saddle seat, and pedals by which it is propelled; *also* : a stationary exercise machine that resembles such a vehicle
²**bicycle** *intransitive verb* **bi·cy·cled; bi·cy·cling** \-k(ə-)liŋ\ (1869)
: to ride a bicycle
— **bi·cy·cler** \-klər\ *noun*
— **bi·cy·clist** \-klist\ *noun*
**bi·cy·clic** \(,)bī-'sī-klik, -'si-\ *adjective* [International Scientific Vocabulary] (circa 1909)
**1** : consisting of or arranged in two cycles
**2** : containing two usually fused rings in the structure of the molecule
¹**bid** \'bid\ *verb* **bade** \'bad, 'bād\ *or* **bid; bid·den** \'bi-d°n\ *or* **bid** *also* **bade; bid·ding** [partly from Middle English *bidden*, from Old English *biddan*; akin to Old High German *bitten* to entreat, and perhaps to Sanskrit *bādhate* he presses; partly from Middle English *beden* to offer, command, from Old English *bēodan*; akin to Old High German *biotan* to offer, Greek *pynthanesthai* to examine, Sanskrit *bodhi* enlightenment] (before 12th century)
*transitive verb*
**1 a** *obsolete* : BESEECH, ENTREAT **b** : to issue an order to : TELL **c** : to request to come : INVITE
**2** : to give expression to ⟨*bade* a tearful farewell⟩

**3 a** : OFFER — usually used in the phrase *to bid defiance* **b** *past and past participle* **bid** (1) : to offer (a price) whether for payment or acceptance (2) : to make a bid of or in (a suit at cards)
*intransitive verb*
: to make a bid
**synonym** see COMMAND
— **bid·der** *noun*
— **bid fair** : to seem likely

²**bid** *noun* (1788)
**1 a** : the act of one who bids **b** : a statement of what one will give or take for something; *especially* : an offer of a price **c** : something offered as a bid
**2** : an opportunity to bid
**3** : INVITATION
**4 a** : an announcement of what a cardplayer proposes to undertake **b** : the amount of such a bid **c** : a biddable bridge hand
**5** : an attempt or effort to win, achieve, or attract ⟨a *bid* for reelection⟩

**bid·da·ble** \'bi-də-bəl\ *adjective* (circa 1768)
**1** : easily led, taught, or controlled : DOCILE
**2** : capable of being bid
— **bid·da·bil·i·ty** \,bi-də-'bi-lə-tē\ *noun*
— **bid·da·bly** \'bi-də-blē\ *adverb*

¹**bid·dy** \'bi-dē\ *noun, plural* **biddies** [perhaps imitative] (1601)
: HEN 1a; *also* : a young chicken

²**biddy** *noun, plural* **biddies** [diminutive of the name *Bridget*] (circa 1861)
**1** : a hired girl or cleaning woman
**2** : WOMAN; *especially* : an elderly woman — usually used disparagingly

**bide** \'bīd\ *verb* **bode** \'bōd\ *or* **bid·ed; bid·ed; bid·ing** [Middle English, from Old English *bīdan;* akin to Old High German *bītan* to wait, Latin *fidere* to trust, Greek *peithesthai* to believe] (before 12th century)
*transitive verb*
**1** *past usually* **bided** : to wait for — used chiefly in the phrase *bide one's time*
**2** *archaic* : WITHSTAND ⟨two men . . . might *bide* the winter storm —W. C. Bryant⟩
**3** *chiefly dialect* : to put up with : TOLERATE
*intransitive verb*
**1** : to continue in a state or condition
**2** : to wait awhile : TARRY
**3** : to continue in a place : SOJOURN
— **bid·er** *noun*

**bi·det** \bi-'dā\ *noun* [French, small horse, bidet, from Middle French, from *bider* to trot] (1766)
: a bathroom fixture used especially for bathing the external genitals and the posterior parts of the body

**bi·di·a·lec·tal·ism** \,bī-,dī-ə-'lek-t°l-,i-zəm\ *noun* (1958)
: facility in using two dialects of the same language; *also* : the teaching of Standard English to pupils who normally use a nonstandard dialect
— **bi·di·a·lec·tal** *adjective*

**bi·di·rec·tion·al** \,bī-də-'rek-shnəl, -dī-, -shə-n°l\ *adjective* (1928)
: involving, moving, or taking place in two usually opposite directions ⟨*bidirectional* flow⟩ ⟨*bidirectional* replication of DNA⟩
— **bi·di·rec·tion·al·ly** *adverb*

**bi·don·ville** \,bē-dōⁿ-'vē(ə)l\ *noun* [French, from *bidon* metal can or drum + *ville* city] (1952)
: a settlement of jerry-built dwellings on the outskirts of a city (as in France or North Africa)

**bid up** *transitive verb* (1864)
: to raise the price of (as property at auction) by a succession of offers

**Bie·der·mei·er** \'bē-dər-,mī-(ə)r\ *adjective* [after Gottlieb *Biedermeier,* satirical name for an uninspired German bourgeois] (1905)
: of a style of unostentatious furniture and interior decoration popular especially with the middle class in early 19th century Germany

**bi·en·ni·al** \(,)bī-'e-nē-əl\ *adjective* (1562)

**1** : occurring every two years
**2** : continuing or lasting for two years; *specifically* : growing vegetatively during the first year and fruiting and dying during the second
*usage* see BI-
— **biennial** *noun*
— **bi·en·ni·al·ly** \-ə-lē\ *adverb*

**bi·en·ni·um** \bī-'e-nē-əm\ *noun, plural* **-ni·ums** *or* **-nia** \-nē-ə\ [Latin, from *bi-* + *annus* year — more at ANNUAL] (1899)
: a period of two years

**bier** \'bir\ *noun* [Middle English *bere,* from Old English *bǣr;* akin to Old English *beran* to carry — more at BEAR] (before 12th century)
**1** *archaic* : a framework for carrying
**2** : a stand on which a corpse or coffin is placed; *also* : a coffin together with its stand

**bi·face** \'bī-,fās\ *noun* (1934)
: a bifacial stone tool

**bi·fa·cial** \(,)bī-'fā-shəl\ *adjective* (circa 1847)
: having opposite sides or faces worked on to form an edge for cutting or scraping
— **bi·fa·cial·ly** *adverb*

**biff** \'bif\ *noun* [probably imitative] (circa 1889)
: WHACK, BLOW
— **biff** *transitive verb*

**bi·fid** \'bī-,fid, -fəd\ *adjective* [Latin *bifidus,* from *bi-* + *-fidus* -fid] (1846)
: divided into two equal lobes or parts by a median cleft ⟨a *bifid* leaf⟩

**bi·fi·lar** \(,)bī-'fī-lər\ *adjective* [International Scientific Vocabulary *bi-* + Latin *filum* thread — more at FILE] (1846)
**1** : involving two threads or wires ⟨*bifilar* suspension of a pendulum⟩
**2** : involving a single thread or wire doubled back upon itself ⟨a *bifilar* resistor⟩
— **bi·fi·lar·ly** *adverb*

**bi·fla·gel·late** \(,)bī-'fla-jə-lət, -,lāt; -flə-'je-lət\ *adjective* (1856)
: having two flagella ⟨*biflagellate* gametes⟩

¹**bi·fo·cal** \'bī-,fō-kəl\ *adjective* [International Scientific Vocabulary] (1888)
**1** : having two focal lengths
**2** : having one part that corrects for near vision and one for distant vision ⟨a *bifocal* eyeglass lens⟩

²**bifocal** *noun* (1899)
**1** *plural* : eyeglasses with bifocal lenses
**2** : a bifocal glass or lens

**bi·func·tion·al** \(,)bī-'fəŋ(k)-shnəl, -shə-n°l\ *adjective* (1936)
: having two functions; *especially* : DIFUNCTIONAL

**bi·fur·cate** \'bī-(,)fər-,kāt, bī-'fər-\ *verb* **-cat·ed; -cat·ing** [Medieval Latin *bifurcatus,* past participle of *bifurcare,* from Latin *bifurcus* two-pronged, from *bi-* + *furca* fork] (1615)
*transitive verb*
: to cause to divide into two branches or parts
*intransitive verb*
: to divide into two branches or parts
— **bi·fur·cate** \(,)bī-'fər-kət, -,kāt; 'bī-(,)fər-,kāt\ *adjective*

**bi·fur·ca·tion** \,bī-(,)fər-'kā-shən\ *noun* (1615)
**1 a** : the point at which bifurcating occurs **b** : BRANCH
**2** : the act of bifurcating : the state of being bifurcated

¹**big** \'big\ *adjective* **big·ger; big·gest** [Middle English, perhaps of Scandinavian origin; akin to Norwegian dialect *bugge* important man] (14th century)
**1 a** *obsolete* : of great strength **b** : of great force ⟨a *big* storm⟩
**2 a** : large or great in dimensions, bulk, or extent ⟨a *big* house⟩; *also* : large or great in quantity, number, or amount ⟨a *big* fleet⟩ **b** : operating on a large scale ⟨*big* government⟩ **c** : CAPITAL 1
**3 a** : PREGNANT; *especially* : nearly ready to give birth **b** : full to bursting : SWELLING ⟨*big* with rage⟩ **c** *of the voice* : full and resonant

**4 a** : CHIEF, PREEMINENT ⟨the *big* issue of the campaign⟩ **b** : outstandingly worthy or able ⟨a truly *big* man⟩ **c** : of great importance or significance ⟨the *big* moment⟩ **d** : IMPOSING, PRETENTIOUS; *also* : marked by or given to boasting ⟨*big* talk⟩ **e** : MAGNANIMOUS, GENEROUS ⟨was *big* about it⟩
**5** : POPULAR ⟨soft drinks are very *big* in Mexico —Russ Leadabrand⟩
**6** : full-bodied and flavorful — used of wine
— **big·ly** *adverb*
— **big·ness** *noun*
— **big on** : strongly favoring or liking; *also* : noted for ⟨she is *big on* blushing —Arnold Hano⟩

²**big** *adverb* (1807)
**1** : in a loud or declamatory manner; *also* : in a boasting manner ⟨talk *big*⟩
**2 a** : to a large amount or extent ⟨won *big*⟩ ⟨lost *big*⟩ **b** : on a large scale ⟨think *big*⟩ ⟨worry *big*⟩
**3** : HARD ⟨hits her forehand *big*⟩

³**big** *noun* (1965)
: an individual or organization of outstanding importance or power; *especially* : MAJOR LEAGUE — usually used in plural ⟨playing in the *bigs*⟩

**big·a·mous** \'bi-gə-məs\ *adjective* (1864)
**1** : guilty of bigamy
**2** : involving bigamy
— **big·a·mous·ly** *adverb*

**big·a·my** \'bi-gə-mē\ *noun* [Middle English *bigamie,* from Medieval Latin *bigamia,* from Latin *bi-* + Late Latin *-gamia* -gamy] (13th century)
: the act of entering into a marriage with one person while still legally married to another
— **big·a·mist** \-mist\ *noun*

**bi·ga·rade** \,bē-gä-'räd\ *noun* [French, from Provençal *bigarrado,* from *bigarra* to variegate] (1703)
**1** : SOUR ORANGE
**2** : a brown sauce flavored with the juice and grated rind of oranges

**big band** *noun* (1926)
: a band that is larger than a combo and that usually features a mixture of ensemble playing and solo improvisation typical of jazz or swing

**big bang** *noun* (1950)
: the cosmic explosion that marked the beginning of the universe according to the big bang theory

**big bang theory** *noun* (1955)
: a theory in astronomy: the universe originated billions of years ago in an explosion from a single point of nearly infinite energy density
— compare STEADY STATE THEORY

**big beat** *noun, often both Bs capitalized* (1958)
: music (as rock) characterized by a heavy persistent beat

**Big Ben** \-'ben\ *noun* [Sir *Benjamin* Hall (died 1867) English Chief Commissioner of Works] (circa 1895)
**1** : a large bell in the clock tower of the Houses of Parliament in London
**2** : the tower that houses Big Ben; *also* : the clock in the tower

**big boy** *noun* (1926)
: BIG GUN — usually used in plural

**big brother** *noun* (1863)
**1** : an older brother
**2** : a man who befriends a delinquent or friendless boy
**3** *both Bs capitalized* [*Big Brother,* personification of the power of the state in *1984* (1949) by George Orwell] **a** : the leader of an authoritarian state or movement **b** : an all-powerful government or organization monitoring and

\ə\ abut \ᵊ\ kitten \ər\ further \a\ ash \ā\ ace
\ä\ mop, mar \au̇\ out \ch\ chin \e\ bet \ē\ easy
\g\ go \i\ hit \ī\ ice \j\ job \ŋ\ sing \ō\ go
\ȯ\ law \ȯi\ boy \th\ thin \t͟h\ the \ü\ loot \u̇\ foot
\y\ yet \zh\ vision *see also* Guide to Pronunciation

directing people's actions ⟨data banks that tell *Big Brother* all about us —Herbert Brucker⟩

**Big Broth·er·ism** \-'brə-thər-₁i-zəm\ *noun* (1950)
: authoritarian attempts at complete control (as of a person or a nation)

**big buck** *noun* (1970)
: a large sum of money — usually used in plural; usually hyphenated when attributive

**big business** *noun* (1905)
1 : an economic group consisting of large profit-making corporations especially with regard to their influence on social or political policy
2 : a very profitable enterprise

**big C** *noun, often B capitalized* (1968)
: CANCER 2

**big daddy** *noun, often B&D capitalized* (1958)
: one preeminent especially by reason of power, size, or seniority : one representing paternalistic authority

**big deal** *noun* (1949)
: something of special importance — sometimes used ironically as an interjection

**Big Dipper** *noun*
: the seven principal stars in the constellation of Ursa Major

**bi·gem·i·ny** \bī-'je-mə-nē\ *noun* [*bigeminal* (double, paired), from Late Latin *bigeminus*, from *bi-* + *geminus* twin] (circa 1923)
: the state of having a pulse characterized by two beats close together with a pause following each pair of beats
— **bi·gem·i·nal** \-mə-nªl\ *adjective*

**bi·ge·ner·ic** \₁bī-jə-'ner-ik\ *adjective* (1885)
: of, relating to, or involving two genera ⟨a *bigeneric* hybrid⟩

**big·eye** \'big-₁ī\ *noun* (circa 1889)
: either of two small widely distributed reddish to silvery bony fishes (*Priacanthus cruentatus* and *P. arenatus* of the family Priacanthidae) of tropical seas

**big·foot** \'big-₁fút\ *noun, often capitalized* [from the size of the footprints ascribed to it] (1958)
: SASQUATCH

**big game** *noun* (1864)
1 : large animals sought or taken by hunting or fishing for sport
2 : an important objective especially when involving risk

**big·ge·ty** *or* **big·gi·ty** \'bi-gə-tē\ *adjective* [*big* + *-ety* (as in *persnickety*)] (1880)
1 *Southern & Midland* : CONCEITED, VAIN
2 *Southern & Midland* : rudely self-important : IMPUDENT ⟨never acted *biggety* in court, but she would bow her head only so low —Claude Brown⟩

**big·gie** \'bi-gē\ *noun* (circa 1931)
: one that is big

**¹big·gin** *or* **big·ging** \'bi-gən\ *noun* [Middle English *bigging*, from *biggen* to dwell, from Old Norse *byggja*; akin to Old English *bēon* to be] (14th century)
*archaic* : BUILDING

**²biggin** *noun* [Middle French *beguin*] (1530)
*archaic* : CAP: **a** : a child's cap **b** : NIGHTCAP

**big·gish** \'bi-gish\ *adjective* (circa 1626)
: somewhat big

**big gun** *noun* (1834)
: one having preeminent status or power in a field

**big·head** \'big-₁hed\ *noun* (1805)
1 : any of several diseases of animals marked by swelling about the head
2 : an exaggerated opinion of one's importance — usually used with *the*
— **big·head·ed** \-'he-dəd\ *adjective*

**big·heart·ed** \-'här-təd\ *adjective* (1868)
: GENEROUS, CHARITABLE
— **big·heart·ed·ly** *adverb*
— **big·heart·ed·ness** *noun*

**big·horn sheep** \'big-₁hórn-\ *noun* (1838)

: a usually grayish brown wild sheep (*Ovis canadensis*) of mountainous and desert regions of western North America — called also *bighorn*

**big house** *noun, often B&H capitalized* (1916)
*slang* : PENITENTIARY

**bighorn sheep**

**bight** \'bīt\ *noun* [Middle English, from Old English *byht* bend, bay; akin to Old English *būgan* to bend — more at BOW] (15th century)
1 : a bend in a coast forming an open bay; *also* : a bay formed by such a bend
2 : a slack part or loop in a rope

**big league** *noun* (1899)
1 : MAJOR LEAGUE
2 : BIG TIME 2 — often used in plural
— **big–league** *adjective*
— **big leaguer** *noun*

**big lie** *noun, sometimes B&L capitalized* (1946)
: a deliberate gross distortion of the truth used especially as a propaganda tactic

**big-mouthed** \'big-₁maúthd, 'big-₁maútht, 'big-\ *adjective* (1642)
1 : having a large mouth
2 : LOUDMOUTHED

**big name** *noun* (1932)
: a performer or personage of top rank in popular recognition
— **big–name** *adjective*

**big·no·nia** \big-'nō-nē-ə\ *noun* [New Latin, genus name, from J. P. Bignon (died 1743) French royal librarian] (1785)
: any of a genus (*Bignonia*) of American and Japanese woody vines of the trumpet-creeper family with compound leaves and tubular flowers

**big·ot** \'bi-gət\ *noun* [Middle French, hypocrite, bigot] (1661)
: a person obstinately or intolerantly devoted to his or her own opinions and prejudices
— **big·ot·ed** \-gə-təd\ *adjective*
— **big·ot·ed·ly** *adverb*

**big·ot·ry** \'bi-gə-trē\ *noun, plural* **-ries** (circa 1674)
1 : the state of mind of a bigot
2 : acts or beliefs characteristic of a bigot

**big picture** *noun, often B&P capitalized* (circa 1960)
: the entire perspective on a situation or issue — used with *the*

**big shot** \'big-₁shät\ *noun* (1929)
: a person of consequence or prominence

**big stick** *noun* (1904)
: threat especially of military or political intervention

**big–tick·et** \'big-'ti-kət\ *adjective* (1945)
: having a high price

**big time** \-₁tīm\ *noun* (1910)
1 : a high-paying vaudeville circuit requiring only two performances a day
2 : the top rank of an activity or enterprise
— **big–time** *adjective*
— **big–tim·er** \-₁tī-mər\ *noun*

**big toe** *noun* (circa 1887)
: the innermost and largest toe of the foot

**big top** *noun* (1895)
1 : the main tent of a circus
2 : CIRCUS 2a, b, c

**big tree** *noun* (1853)
: a California evergreen (*Sequoiadendron giganteum*) of the bald cypress family that sometimes exceeds 270 feet (about 82 meters) in height — called also *giant sequoia, sequoia*

**big wheel** *noun* (1942)

: BIGWIG, BIG SHOT

**big·wig** \'big-₁wig\ *noun* (1703)
: an important person

**Bi·ha·ri** \bi-'här-ē\ *noun* (1882)
1 : a group of Indo-Aryan languages (as Bhojpuri) spoken in Bihar, India, and adjacent areas
2 **a** : a native or inhabitant of Bihar **b** : a Muslim born in Bihar who emigrated after the partition of India in 1947; *also* : a descendant of such a person

**bi·jec·tion** \(₁)bī-'jek-shən\ *noun* [¹*bi-* + *-jection* (as in *injection*)] (1966)
: a mathematical function that is a one-to-one and onto mapping — compare INJECTION, SURJECTION
— **bi·jec·tive** \-'jek-tiv\ *adjective*

**bi·jou** \'bē-₁zhü\ *noun, plural* **bijous** *or* **bi·joux** \-₁zhü(z)\ [French, from Breton *bizou* ring, from *biz* finger] (1668)
1 : a small dainty usually ornamental piece of delicate workmanship : JEWEL
2 : something delicate, elegant, or highly prized
— **bijou** *adjective*

**bi·jou·te·rie** \bi-'zhü-tə-(₁)rē\ *noun* [French, from *bijou*] (1815)
: a collection of trinkets or ornaments : JEWELS; *also* : DECORATION

**¹bike** \'bīk\ *noun* [Middle English] (14th century)
1 *chiefly Scottish* : a nest of wild bees, wasps, or hornets
2 *chiefly Scottish* : a crowd or swarm of people

**²bike** *noun* [by shortening & alteration] (1882)
1 : BICYCLE
2 : MOTORCYCLE
3 : MOTORBIKE

**³bike** *intransitive verb* **biked; bik·ing** (1895)
: to ride a bike

**bik·er** \'bī-kər\ *noun* (1883)
1 : BICYCLIST
2 : MOTORCYCLIST; *especially* : one who is a member of an organized gang

**bike·way** \'bīk-₁wā\ *noun* (1965)
: a thoroughfare for bicycles

**bik·ie** \'bī-kē\ *noun* [²*bike* + *-ie*] (1967)
: BIKER 2

**bi·ki·ni** \bə-'kē-nē\ *noun* [French, from *Bikini*, atoll of the Marshall islands] (1947)
1 **a** : a woman's scanty two-piece bathing suit **b** : a man's brief swimsuit
2 : a man's or woman's low-cut briefs ◆
— **bi·ki·nied** \-nēd\ *adjective*

**¹bi·la·bi·al** \(₁)bī-'lā-bē-əl\ *adjective* [International Scientific Vocabulary] (1894)
*of a consonant* : produced with both lips

**²bilabial** *noun* (1899)
: a bilabial consonant

**bi·la·bi·ate** \-bē-ət\ *adjective* (1794)
: having two lips ⟨a *bilabiate* corolla⟩

**bi·lat·er·al** \(₁)bī-'la-t(ə-)rəl\ *adjective* (1775)
1 : having two sides
2 : affecting reciprocally two nations or parties ⟨a *bilateral* treaty⟩ ⟨a *bilateral* trade agreement⟩
3 **a** : of, relating to, or affecting the right and left sides of the body or the right and left members of paired organs ⟨*bilateral* nephrectomy⟩ **b** : having bilateral symmetry
— **bi·lat·er·al·ism** \-t(ə-)rə-₁li-zəm\ *noun*
— **bi·lat·er·al·ly** *adverb*

**bilateral symmetry** *noun* (1860)
: symmetry in which similar anatomical parts are arranged on opposite sides of a median axis so that only one plane can divide the individual into essentially identical halves

**bi·lay·er** \'bī-₁lā-ər, -₁le(-ə)r\ *noun* (1963)
: a film or membrane with two molecular layers ⟨a *bilayer* of phospholipid molecules⟩
— **bilayer** *adjective*

**bil·ber·ry** \'bil-₁ber-ē\ *noun* [*bil-* (probably of Scandinavian origin; akin to Danish *bølle* whortleberry) + *berry*] (1577)

: any of several ericaceous shrubs (genus *Vaccinium*) that resemble blueberries but have flowers which arise solitary or in very small clusters from axillary buds; *also* : its sweet edible fruit

¹**bil·bo** \'bil-(,)bō\ *noun, plural* **bilboes** [perhaps from *Bilboa,* Spain] (1557)
: a long bar of iron with sliding shackles used to confine the feet of prisoners especially on shipboard

²**bilbo** *or* **bil·boa** \'bil-(,)bō\ *noun, plural* **bilboes** *or* **bilboas** [*Bilboa, Bilbao,* Spain] (1565)
: SWORD

**bil·dungs·ro·man** \'bil-dùn(k)s-rō-,män, -dùnz-\ *noun* [German, from *Bildung* education + *Roman* novel] (1910)
: a novel about the moral and psychological growth of the main character

**bile** \'bī(ə)l\ *noun* [Latin *bilis;* akin to Welsh *bustl* bile] (1547)
**1 a :** either of two humors associated in old physiology with irascibility and melancholy **b :** a yellow or greenish viscid alkaline fluid secreted by the liver and passed into the duodenum where it aids especially in the emulsification and absorption of fats
**2 :** inclination to anger

**bile acid** *noun* (circa 1881)
: any of several steroid acids (as cholic acid) of or derived from bile

**bile duct** *noun* (1774)
: a duct by which bile passes from the liver or gallbladder to the duodenum

**bile salt** *noun* (1881)
**1 :** a salt of bile acid
**2** *plural* : a dry mixture of the principal salts of the gall of the ox used as a liver stimulant and as a laxative

¹**bi·lev·el** \'bī-'le-vəl\ *adjective* (1960)
**1 :** having two levels of freight or passenger space
**2 :** divided vertically into two ground-floor levels

²**bi·level** \'bī-,\ *noun* (1966)
: a bi-level house

¹**bilge** \'bilj\ *noun* [probably modification of Middle French *boulge, bouge* leather bag, curved part — more at BUDGET] (1513)
**1 :** the bulging part of a cask or barrel
**2 a :** the part of the underwater body of a ship between the flat of the bottom and the vertical topsides **b :** the lowest point of a ship's inner hull
**3 :** stale or worthless remarks or ideas

²**bilge** *intransitive verb* **bilged; bilg·ing** (1728)
: to become damaged in the bilge

**bilge keel** *noun* (1850)
: a projection like a fin extending from the hull near the turn of the bilge on either side to check rolling

**bilge·wa·ter** \'bilj-,wò-tər, -,wä-\ *noun* (1706)
: water that collects in the bilge of a ship

**bil·har·zia** \bil-'här-zē-ə, -'härt-sē-\ *noun* [New Latin, genus name, from Theodor *Bilharz* (died 1862) German zoologist] (circa 1881)
**1 :** SCHISTOSOMIASIS
**2 :** SCHISTOSOME
— **bil·har·zi·al** \-zē-əl; -sē-\ *adjective*

**bil·har·zi·a·sis** \,bil-,här-'zī-ə-səs; -,härt-'sī-\ *noun, plural* **-a·ses** \-,sēz\ [New Latin] (circa 1900)
: SCHISTOSOMIASIS

**bil·i·ary** \'bi-lē-,er-ē\ *adjective* [French *biliare,* from Latin *bilis*] (1731)
: of, relating to, or conveying bile; *also* : affecting the bile-conveying structures

**bi·lin·ear** \(,)bī-'li-nē-ər\ *adjective* (1886)
: linear with respect to each of two mathematical variables; *specifically* : of or relating to an algebraic form each term of which involves one variable to the first degree from each of two sets of variables

**bi·lin·gual** \(,)bī-'lin-gwəl *also* -gyə-wəl\ *adjective* [Latin *bilinguis,* from *bi-* + *lingua* tongue — more at TONGUE] (1845)
**1 :** having or expressed in two languages
**2 :** using or able to use two languages especially with equal fluency
**3 :** of or relating to bilingual education
— **bilingual** *noun*
— **bi·lin·gual·ly** *adverb*

**bilingual education** *noun* (1972)
: education in an English-language school system in which minority students with little fluency in English are taught in their native language

**bi·lin·gual·ism** \-gwə-,li-zəm\ *noun* (1873)
: the ability to speak two languages : the frequent oral use of two languages

**bil·ious** \'bil-yəs\ *adjective* [Middle French *bilieux,* from Latin *biliosus,* from *bilis*] (1541)
**1 a :** of or relating to bile **b :** marked by or suffering from liver dysfunction and especially excessive secretion of bile **c :** appearing as if affected by a bilious disorder
**2 :** of or indicative of a peevish ill-natured disposition
— **bil·ious·ly** *adverb*
— **bil·ious·ness** *noun*

**bil·i·ru·bin** \,bi-li-'rü-bən, 'bi-li-,\ *noun* [Latin *bilis* + *ruber* red — more at RED] (1871)
: a reddish yellow water insoluble pigment occurring especially in bile and blood and causing jaundice if accumulated in excess

**bil·i·ver·din** \-'vər-d²n, -,vər-\ *noun* [Swedish, from Latin *bilis* + obsolete French *verd* green] (1845)
: a green pigment that occurs in bile and is an intermediate in the degradation of hemoglobin heme groups to bilirubin

¹**bilk** \'bilk\ *transitive verb* [perhaps alteration of ²*balk*] (1651)
**1 :** to block the free development of : FRUSTRATE ⟨fate *bilks* their hopes⟩
**2 a :** to cheat out of something valuable : DEFRAUD **b :** to evade payment of or to ⟨*bilks* his creditors⟩
**3 :** to slip away from : ELUDE ⟨*bilked* her pursuers⟩
— **bilk·er** *noun*

²**bilk** *noun* (1790)
: an untrustworthy tricky individual : CHEAT

¹**bill** \'bil\ *noun* [Middle English *bile,* from Old English; akin to Old English *bill*] (before 12th century)
**1 :** the jaws of a bird together with their horny covering
**2 :** a mouthpart (as the beak of a turtle) that resembles a bird's bill
**3 :** the point of an anchor fluke — see ANCHOR illustration
**4 :** the visor of a cap or hood

bill 1: *1* flamingo, *2* falcon, *3* pigeon, *4* thrush, *5* merganser, *6* toucan, *7* finch, *8* spoonbill, *9* pelican

²**bill** *intransitive verb* (1592)
**1 :** to touch and rub bill to bill
**2 :** to caress affectionately ⟨*billing* and cooing⟩

³**bill** *noun* [Middle English *bil,* from Old English *bill* sword; akin to Old High German *bill* pickax] (14th century)
**1 :** a weapon in use up to the 18th century that consists of a long staff ending in a hook-shaped blade
**2 :** BILLHOOK

⁴**bill** *noun* [Middle English, from Medieval Latin *billa* seal, alteration of *bulla,* from Latin *bulla* bubble, boss] (14th century)
**1 :** an itemized list or a statement of particulars (as a list of materials or of members of a ship's crew)
**2 :** a written document or note
**3** *obsolete* : a formal petition
**4 a :** an itemized account of the separate cost of goods sold, services performed, or work done : INVOICE **b :** an amount expended or owed **c :** a statement of charges for food or drink : CHECK
**5 a :** a written or printed advertisement posted or otherwise distributed to announce an event of interest to the public; *especially* : an announcement of a theatrical entertainment **b :** a programmed presentation (as a motion picture, play, or concert)
**6 :** a draft of a law presented to a legislature for enactment; *also* : the law itself ⟨the GI *bill*⟩
**7 :** a declaration in writing stating a wrong a complainant has suffered from a defendant or stating a breach of law by some person ⟨a *bill* of complaint⟩
**8 a :** a piece of paper money **b :** an individual or commercial note ⟨*bills* receivable⟩ **c** *slang* : one hundred dollars
— **fill the bill** *or* **fit the bill** : to be exactly what is needed : be suitable

⁵**bill** *transitive verb* (14th century)
**1 a :** to enter in an accounting system : prepare a bill of (charges) **b :** to submit a bill of charges to **c :** to enter (as freight) in a waybill **d :** to issue a bill of lading to or for
**2 :** to announce (as a performance) especially by posters or placards
**3 :** ADVERTISE, PROMOTE ⟨the book is *billed* as a "report" —P. G. Altbach⟩
— **bill·able** *adjective*

**bil·la·bong** \'bi-lə-,bòn, -,bän\ *noun* [Wiradhuri (Australian aboriginal language of central New South Wales) *bilabaŋ*] (1861)

\ə\ abut \ᵊ\ kitten \ər\ further \a\ ash \ā\ ace
\ä\ mop, mar \aù\ out \ch\ chin \e\ bet \ē\ easy
\g\ go \i\ hit \ī\ ice \j\ job \ŋ\ sing \ō\ go
\ò\ law \òi\ boy \th\ thin \th\ the \ü\ loot \ù\ foot
\y\ yet \zh\ vision *see also* Guide to Pronunciation

**1** *Australian* **a :** a blind channel leading out from a river **b :** a usually dry streambed that is filled seasonally
**2** *Australian* **:** a backwater forming a stagnant pool
**¹bill·board** \'bil-ˌbōrd, -ˌbȯrd\ *noun* (1851)
**:** a flat surface (as of a panel, wall, or fence) on which bills are posted; *specifically* **:** a large panel designed to carry outdoor advertising
**²billboard** *transitive verb* (1950)
**:** to promote by a conspicuous display on or as if on a billboard
**bill·bug** \'bil-ˌbəg\ *noun* [¹*bill* + *bug*] (1861)
**:** any of various weevils (as of the genus *Sphenophorus*) having larvae that eat the roots of cereal and other grasses
**billed** \'bild\ *adjective*
**:** having a bill of a specified kind — used in combination ⟨spoon-*billed*⟩
**bill·er** \'bi-lər\ *noun* (1920)
**:** one that bills; *especially* **:** one that makes out bills
**¹bil·let** \'bi-lət\ *noun* [Middle English *bylet*, from Middle French *billette*, diminutive of *bulle* document, from Medieval Latin *bulla*] (15th century)
**1** *archaic* **:** a brief letter **:** NOTE
**2 a :** an official order directing that a member of a military force be provided with board and lodging (as in a private home) **b :** quarters assigned by or as if by a billet
**3 :** POSITION, JOB ⟨a lucrative *billet*⟩
**²billet** *transitive verb* (1594)
**1 :** to assign lodging to (as soldiers) by or as if by a billet
**2 :** to serve with a billet ⟨*billet* a householder⟩
**³billet** *noun* [Middle English *bylet*, from Middle French *billete*, diminutive of *bille* log, of Celtic origin; akin to Old Irish *bile* landmark tree] (15th century)
**1 a :** a chunky piece of wood (as for firewood) **b** *obsolete* **:** CUDGEL
**2 a :** a bar of metal **b :** a piece of semifinished iron or steel nearly square in section made by rolling an ingot or bloom **c :** a section of nonferrous metal ingot hot-worked by forging, rolling, or extrusion **d :** a nonferrous casting suitable for rolling or extrusion
**bil·let-doux** \ˌbi-lē-'dü, ˌbi-(ˌ)lā-\ *noun, plural* **bil·lets-doux** \-'dü(z)\ [French *billet doux*, literally, sweet letter] (1673)
**:** a love letter
**bill·fish** \'bil-ˌfish\ *noun* (1782)
**:** a fish with long slender jaws; *especially* **:** any of a family (Istiophoridae) including marlins, spearfishes, and sailfishes
**bill·fold** \-ˌfōld\ *noun* [short for earlier *billfolder*] (1895)
**:** a folding pocketbook for paper money **:** WALLET
**bill·hook** \-ˌhu̇k\ *noun* (1611)
**:** a cutting or pruning tool with a hooked blade
**bil·liard** \'bil-yərd\ *noun* (1580)
**—** used as an attributive form of *billiards* ⟨*billiard* ball⟩
**bil·liards** \-yərdz\ *noun plural but singular in construction* [Middle French *billard* billiard cue, billiards, from *bille*] (1580)
**:** any of several games played on an oblong table by driving small balls against one another or into pockets with a cue; *specifically* **:** a game in which one scores by causing a cue ball to hit in succession two object balls — compare POOL
**bil·li-bi** *also* **bil·ly-bi** \'bi-lē-ˌbē, ˌbi-lē-'\ *noun* [French, alteration of *Billy B.*, perhaps from William B. Leeds, Jr. (died 1972) American industrialist] (1961)
**:** a soup of mussel stock, white wine, and cream served hot or cold
**bill·ing** \'bi-liŋ\ *noun* [⁵*bill*] (1875)
**1 :** advertising or public promotion (as of a product or personality); *also* **:** relative prominence of a name in such promotion ⟨got top *billing*⟩

**2 :** total amount of business or investments (as of an advertising agency) within a given period
**bil·lings·gate** \'bi-liŋz-ˌgāt, *British usually* -git\ *noun* [*Billingsgate,* old gate and fish market, London, England] (1652)
**:** coarsely abusive language ◆
**synonym** *see* ABUSE
**bil·lion** \'bi(l)-yən\ *noun* [French, from *bi-* + *-illion* (as in *million*)] (1834)
**1** — see NUMBER table
**2 :** a very large number
**— billion** *adjective*
**— bil·lionth** \-yən(t)th\ *adjective or noun*
**bil·lion·aire** \ˌbi(l)-yə-'nar, -'ner, 'bi(l)-yə-ˌ\ *noun* [*billion* + *-aire* (as in *millionaire*)] (1860)
**:** one whose wealth is estimated at a billion or more (as of dollars or pounds)
**bill of exchange** (1534)
**:** an unconditional written order from one person to another to pay a specified sum of money to a designated person
**bill of fare** (1636)
**1 :** MENU
**2 :** PROGRAM
**bill of goods** (1920)
**1 :** a consignment of merchandise
**2 :** something intentionally misrepresented **:** something passed off in a deception or fraud — often used in the phrase *sell a bill of goods*
**bill of health** (1644)
**1 :** a certificate given to the ship's master at the time of leaving port that indicates the state of health of a ship's company and of a port with regard to infectious diseases
**2 :** a usually favorable report following an examination or investigation ⟨gave the criticized textbook a clean *bill of health*⟩
**bill of indictment** (circa 1530)
**:** an indictment before it is found or ignored by the grand jury
**bill of lading** (1532)
**:** a receipt listing goods shipped that is signed by the agent of the owner of a ship or issued by a common carrier
**bill of particulars** (circa 1860)
**:** a detailed listing of charges or claims brought in a legal action or of a defendant's response or counterclaim
**bill of rights** *often B&R capitalized* (1798)
**:** a summary of fundamental rights and privileges guaranteed to a people against violation by the state — used especially of the first 10 amendments to the U.S. Constitution
**bill of sale** (1608)
**:** a formal instrument for the conveyance or transfer of title to goods and chattels
**bil·lon** \'bi-lən\ *noun* [French, from Middle French, from *bille* log — more at BILLET] (circa 1727)
**1 :** gold or silver heavily alloyed with a less valuable metal
**2 :** an alloy of silver containing more than 50 percent of copper by weight
**¹bil·low** \'bi-(ˌ)lō\ *noun* [Old Norse *bylgja;* akin to Old High German *balg* bag — more at BELLY] (1552)
**1 :** WAVE; *especially* **:** a great wave or surge of water
**2 :** a rolling mass (as of flame or smoke) that resembles a high wave
**— bil·lowy** \'bi-lə-wē\ *adjective*
**²billow** (1597)
*intransitive verb*
**1 :** to rise or roll in waves or surges
**2 :** to bulge or swell out (as through action of the wind)
*transitive verb*
**:** to cause to billow
**¹bil·ly** \'bi-lē\ *noun, plural* **billies** [Scots *billy-pot* cooking utensil] (1839)
*chiefly Australian & New Zealand* **:** a metal or enamelware pail or pot with a lid and wire bail — called also *billycan*

**²billy** *noun, plural* **billies** [probably from the name *Billy*] (1848)
**1 :** BILLY CLUB
**2 :** BILLY GOAT
**billy club** *noun* [²*billy*] (1949)
**:** a heavy usually wooden club; *specifically* **:** a police officer's club
**bil·ly·cock** \'bi-lē-ˌkäk\ *noun* [origin unknown] (1721)
*British* **:** DERBY 3
**billy goat** *noun* [from the name *Billy*] (1861)
**:** a male goat
**bi·lobed** \'bī-'lōbd\ *adjective* (1756)
**:** divided into two lobes ⟨a *bilobed* nucleus⟩
**bi·lo·ca·tion** \ˌbī-lō-'kā-shən\ *noun* (1858)
**:** the state of being or ability to be in two places at the same time
**bil·tong** \'bil-ˌtȯŋ, -ˌtäŋ\ *noun* [Afrikaans, from *bil* rump + *tong* tongue] (1815)
*chiefly South African* **:** jerked meat
**bi·man·u·al** \(ˌ)bī-'man-yə-wəl, -yəl\ *adjective* (circa 1889)
**:** done with or requiring the use of both hands
**— bi·man·u·al·ly** *adverb*
**bim·bo** \'bim-(ˌ)bō\ *noun, plural* **bimbos** [perhaps from Italian *bimbo* baby] (1919)
**1** *slang* **:** MAN, WOMAN — usually used disparagingly ⟨telling a thickheaded pitcher that the *bimbo* at the plate hasn't hit a curve in three seasons —Jay Stuller⟩ and especially of an attractive but empty-headed person ⟨we didn't want a blond *bimbo* in that role . . . we wanted her to be smart —Hugh Wilson⟩
**2** *slang* **:** TRAMP 1c ⟨evidence of how her hubby's been cheating on her with various *bimbos* —Dan Greenburg⟩
**bi·met·al** \'bī-ˌme-t°l\ *adjective* (1924)
**:** BIMETALLIC
**— bimetal** *noun*
**bi·me·tal·lic** \ˌbī-mə-'ta-lik\ *adjective* (1876)
**1 :** relating to, based on, or using bimetallism
**2 :** composed of two different metals — often used of devices having a part in which two metals that expand differently are bonded together
**— bimetallic** *noun*
**bi·met·al·lism** \(ˌ)bī-'me-t°l-ˌi-zəm\ *noun* [French *bimétallisme*, from *bi-* + *métal* metal] (1876)
**:** the use of two metals (as gold and silver) jointly as a monetary standard with both constituting legal tender at a predetermined ratio
**— bi·met·al·list** \-t°l-ist\ *noun*
**— bi·met·al·lis·tic** \ˌbī-ˌme-t°l-'is-tik\ *adjective*
**bi·mil·le·na·ry** \(ˌ)bī-'mi-lə-ˌner-ē, ˌbī-mə-'le-nə-rē\ *or* **bi·mil·len·ni·al** \ˌbī-mə-'le-nē-əl\ *noun* (1850)
**1 :** a period of 2000 years

◇ **WORD HISTORY**
**billingsgate** Billingsgate was one of two water gates in the wall of the city of London that from Britain's days as a Roman colony gave access to the River Thames. A marketplace developed in the vicinity of the gate, and in 1699, by government decree, it was devoted exclusively to the sale of fish. While Billingsgate was indeed renowned for its fish, it achieved an equal measure of fame for the coarse language that resounded through the stalls. The fishmongers, especially the women, enjoyed a reputation for unrestrained insult that was wittily inventive, vulgarly explicit, and vigorously conveyed. In the 18th century, *billingsgate* came to be used as a simple common noun meaning "abusive language." Today, about all that is left of Billingsgate is its lexical legacy. London's principal fish market was moved in 1982 to a modern warehouse on the Isle of Dogs, overlooking the West India Dock on the Thames.

**2 :** a 2000th anniversary
**— bimillenary** *adjective*
**bi·mod·al** \(ˌ)bī-'mō-dᵊl\ *adjective* (1903)
**:** having or relating to two modes; *especially*
**:** having or occurring with two statistical modes
**— bi·mo·dal·i·ty** \ˌbī-mō-'da-lə-tē\ *noun*
**bi·mo·lec·u·lar** \ˌbī-mə-'le-kyə-lər\ *adjective*
[International Scientific Vocabulary] (1899)
**1 :** relating to or formed from two molecules
**2 :** being two molecules thick 〈bimolecular lipid layers〉
**— bi·mo·lec·u·lar·ly** *adverb*
**¹bi·month·ly** \(ˌ)bī-'mən(t)th-lē\ *adjective* (1846)
**1 :** occurring every two months
**2 :** occurring twice a month **:** SEMIMONTHLY
*usage* see BI-
**²bimonthly** *adverb* (1864)
**1 :** once every two months
**2 :** twice a month
**³bimonthly** *noun* (circa 1890)
**:** a bimonthly publication
**bi·mor·phe·mic** \ˌbī-mȯr-'fē-mik\ *adjective* (1942)
**:** consisting of two morphemes
**¹bin** \'bin\ *noun* [Middle English *binn*, from Old English] (before 12th century)
**:** a box, frame, crib, or enclosed place used for storage
**²bin** *transitive verb* **binned; bin·ning** (1841)
**:** to put into a bin
**bin-** *prefix* [Middle English, from Late Latin, from Latin *bini* two by two; akin to Old English *twinn* twofold — more at TWIN]
**:** ¹BI- 〈*bin*aural〉
**¹bi·na·ry** \'bī-nə-rē, -ˌner-ē\ *noun, plural* **-ries** (15th century)
**:** something made of or based on two things or parts: as **a :** BINARY STAR **b :** a binary number system
**²binary** *adjective* [Late Latin *binarius*, from Latin *bini*] (1597)
**1 :** compounded or consisting of or marked by two things or parts
**2 a :** DUPLE — used of measure or rhythm **b :** having two musical subjects or two complementary sections
**3 a :** relating to, being, or belonging to a system of numbers having 2 as its base 〈the *binary* digits 0 and 1〉 **b :** involving a choice or condition of two alternatives (as on-off or yes-no)
**4 a :** composed of two chemical elements, an element and a radical that acts as an element, or two such radicals **b :** utilizing two harmless ingredients that upon combining form a lethal substance (as a gas) 〈*binary* weapon〉
**5 :** relating two logical or mathematical elements 〈*binary* operation〉
**binary fission** *noun* (1897)
**:** reproduction of a cell by division into two approximately equal parts 〈the *binary fission* of protozoans〉
**binary star** *noun* (circa 1847)
**:** a system of two stars that revolve around each other under their mutual gravitation — called also *binary system*
**bi·na·tion·al** \(ˌ)bī-'na-sh(ə-)nəl\ *adjective* (1888)
**:** of or relating to two nations 〈a *binational* board of directors〉
**bin·au·ral** \(ˌ)bī-'nȯr-əl, (ˌ)bi-\ *adjective* [International Scientific Vocabulary] (1861)
**1 :** of, relating to, or involving two or both ears
**2 :** of, relating to, or constituting sound reproduction involving the use of two separated microphones and two transmission channels to achieve a stereophonic effect
**— bin·au·ral·ly** \-ə-lē\ *adverb*
**¹bind** \'bīnd\ *verb* **bound** \'baůnd\; **bind·ing** [Middle English, from Old English *bindan*; akin to Old High German *bintan* to bind, Greek *peisma* cable, Sanskrit *badhnāti* he binds] (before 12th century)

*transitive verb*
**1 a :** to make secure by tying **b :** to confine, restrain, or restrict as if with bonds **c :** to put under an obligation 〈*binds* himself with an oath〉 **d :** to constrain with legal authority
**2 a :** to wrap around with something so as to enclose or cover **b :** BANDAGE
**3 :** to fasten round about
**4 :** to tie together (as stocks of wheat)
**5 a :** to cause to stick together **b :** to take up and hold (as by chemical forces) **:** combine with
**6 :** CONSTIPATE
**7 :** to make a firm commitment for 〈a handshake *binds* the deal〉
**8 :** to protect, strengthen, or decorate by a band or binding
**9 :** to apply the parts of the cover to (a book)
**10 :** to set at work as an apprentice **:** INDENTURE
**11 :** to cause or bring about an emotional attachment
**12 :** to fasten together
*intransitive verb*
**1 a :** to form a cohesive mass **b :** to combine or be taken up especially by chemical action 〈antibody *binds* to a specific antigen〉
**2 :** to hamper free movement or natural action
**3 :** to become hindered from free operation
**4 :** to exert a restraining or compelling effect 〈a promise that *binds*〉
**²bind** *noun* (before 12th century)
**1 a :** something that binds **b :** the act of binding **:** the state of being bound **c :** a place where binding occurs
**2 :** TIE 3
**3 :** a position or situation in which one is hampered, constrained, or prevented from free movement or action
**— in a bind :** in trouble
**bind·er** \'bīn-dər\ *noun* (before 12th century)
**1 :** a person or machine that binds something (as books)
**2 a :** something used in binding **b :** a usually detachable cover (as for holding sheets of paper)
**3 :** something (as tar or cement) that produces or promotes cohesion in loosely assembled substances
**4 :** a temporary insurance contract that provides coverage until the policy is issued
**5 :** something (as money) given in earnest; *also* **:** the agreement arrived at
**bind·ery** \'bīn-d(ə-)rē\ *noun, plural* **-er·ies** (1810)
**:** a place where books are bound
**¹bind·ing** \'bīn-diŋ\ *noun* (13th century)
**1 :** the action of one that binds
**2 :** a material or device used to bind: as **a :** the cover and materials that hold a book together **b :** a narrow fabric used to finish raw edges **c :** a set of ski fastenings for holding the boot firm on the ski
**²binding** *adjective* (14th century)
**1 :** that binds
**2 :** imposing an obligation
**— bind·ing·ly** \-diŋ-lē\ *adverb*
**— bind·ing·ness** *noun*
**binding energy** *noun* (1932)
**:** the energy required to break up a molecule, atom, or atomic nucleus completely into its constituent particles
**bin·dle stiff** \'bin-dᵊl-ˌstif\ *noun* [*bindle*, perhaps alteration of *bundle*] (1901)
**:** HOBO; *especially* **:** one who carries his clothes or bedding in a bundle
**bind off** *transitive verb* (circa 1939)
**:** to cast off in knitting
**bind over** *transitive verb* (1610)
**:** to put under a bond to do something (as to appear in court)
**bind·weed** \'bīnd-ˌwēd\ *noun* (1548)
**:** any of various twining plants (especially genus *Convolvulus* of the morning-glory family) that mat or interlace with plants among which they grow

**bine** \'bīn\ *noun* [alteration of ²*bind*] (1727)
**:** a twining stem or flexible shoot (as of the hop); *also* **:** a plant (as woodbine) whose shoots are bines
**Bi·net–Si·mon scale** \bi-ˌnā-sē-'mōⁿ-\ *noun* [Alfred *Binet* (died 1911) and Théodore *Simon* (died 1961) French psychologists] (1914)
**:** an intelligence test consisting originally of tasks graded from the level of the average 3-year-old to that of the average 12-year-old but later extended in range
**¹binge** \'binj\ *noun* [English dialect *binge* (to drink heavily)] (1854)
**1 a :** a drunken revel **:** SPREE **b :** an unrestrained and often excessive indulgence 〈a buying *binge*〉
**2 :** a social gathering **:** PARTY
**²binge** *intransitive verb* **binged; binge·ing** *or* **bing·ing** (1910)
**:** to go on a binge; *especially* **:** to go on an eating binge
**— bing·er** \'bin-jər\ *noun*
**¹bin·go** \'biŋ-(ˌ)gō\ *interjection* [alteration of *bing* (interjection suggestive of a ringing sound)] (1925)
**1 —** used to announce an unexpected event or instantaneous result
**2 —** used to announce a winning position in bingo
**²bingo** *noun, plural* **bingos** (1932)
**:** a game of chance played with cards having numbered squares corresponding to numbered balls drawn at random and won by covering five such squares in a row; *also* **:** a social gathering at which bingo is played
**bin·na·cle** \'bi-ni-kəl\ *noun* [alteration of Middle English *bitakle*, from Old Portuguese or Old Spanish; Old Portuguese *bitácola* & Old Spanish *bitácula*, from Latin *habitaculum* dwelling place, from *habitare* to inhabit — more at HABITATION] (1762)
**:** a housing for a ship's compass and a lamp
**¹bin·oc·u·lar** \bī-'nä-kyə-lər, bə-\ *adjective* (1738)
**:** of, relating to, using, or adapted to the use of both eyes 〈*binocular* vision〉
**— bin·oc·u·lar·i·ty** \(ˌ)bī-ˌnä-kyə-'lar-ə-tē, bə-\ *noun*
**— bin·oc·u·lar·ly** \bī-'nä-kyə-lər-lē, bə-\ *adverb*
**²bin·oc·u·lar** \bə-'nä-kyə-lər, bī-\ *noun* (1871)
**1 :** a binocular optical instrument
**2 :** a handheld optical instrument composed of two telescopes and a focusing device and usually having prisms to increase magnifying ability — usually used in plural
**bi·no·mi·al** \bī-'nō-mē-əl\ *noun* [New Latin *binomium*, from Medieval Latin, neuter of *binomius* having two names, alteration of Latin *binominis*, from *bi-* + *nomin-*, *nomen* name — more at NAME] (1557)
**1 :** a mathematical expression consisting of two terms connected by a plus sign or minus sign
**2 :** a biological species name consisting of two terms
**— binomial** *adjective*
**— bi·no·mi·al·ly** \-mē-ə-lē\ *adverb*
**binomial coefficient** *noun* (circa 1889)
**:** a coefficient of a term in the expansion of the binomial $(x + y)^n$ according to the binomial theorem
**binomial distribution** *noun* (1911)
**:** a probability function each of whose values gives the probability that an outcome will occur with constant probability of occurrence in a statistical experiment will occur a given number of times in a succession of repetitions of the experiment
**binomial nomenclature** *noun* (1880)

\ə\ abut \ᵊ\ kitten \ər\ further \a\ ash \ā\ ace
\ä\ mop, mar \aů\ out \ch\ chin \e\ bet \ē\ easy
\g\ go \i\ hit \ī\ ice \j\ job \ŋ\ sing \ō\ go
\ȯ\ law \ȯi\ boy \th\ thin \th̲\ the \ü\ loot \ů\ foot
\y\ yet \zh\ vision *see also* Guide to Pronunciation

: a system of nomenclature in which each species of animal or plant receives a name of two terms of which the first identifies the genus to which it belongs and the second the species itself

**binomial theorem** noun (1755)
: a theorem that specifies the expansion of a binomial of the form $(x + y)^n$ as the sum of $n + 1$ terms of which the general term is of the form

$$\frac{n!}{(n-k)!\,k!}\,x^{(n-k)}y^k$$

where $k$ takes on values from 0 to $n$

**bint** \'bint\ noun [Arabic, girl, daughter] (1855) British : GIRL, WOMAN

**bi·nu·cle·ate** \(ˌ)bī-'nü-klē-ət also -'nyü-\ also **bi·nu·cle·at·ed** \-klē-ˌā-təd\ adjective (1881)
: having two cellular nuclei ⟨binucleate hepatocytes⟩

**bio** \'bī-(ˌ)ō\ noun, plural **bi·os** (1947)
: a biography or biographical sketch

**bio-** — see BI-

**bio·acous·tics** \ˌbī-(ˌ)ō-ə-'kü-stiks\ noun plural but singular in construction (1957)
: a branch of science concerned with the production of sound by and its effects on living systems

**bio·ac·tive** \ˌbī-ō-'ak-tiv\ adjective (1965)
: having an effect on a living organism ⟨bioactive molecules⟩
— **bio·ac·tiv·i·ty** \-ak-'ti-və-tē\ noun

**bio·as·say** \ˌbī-(ˌ)ō-'a-ˌsā, -a-'sā\ noun (1912)
: determination of the relative strength of a substance (as a drug) by comparing its effect on a test organism with that of a standard preparation
— **bio·as·say** \-a-'sā, -'a-ˌsā\ transitive verb

**bio·avail·abil·i·ty** \-ə-ˌvā-lə-'bi-lə-tē\ noun (1971)
: the degree and rate at which a substance (as a drug) is absorbed into a living system or is made available at the site of physiological activity
— **bio·avail·able** \-'vā-lə-bəl\ adjective

**bio·ce·no·sis** or **bio·coe·no·sis** \ˌbī-ō-sə-'nō-səs\ noun, plural **-no·ses** \-ˌsēz\ [New Latin, from ²bi- + Greek koinōsis sharing, from koinos common] (1883)
: an ecological community especially when forming a self-regulating unit

**bio·chem·i·cal** \ˌbī-ō-'ke-mi-kəl\ adjective [International Scientific Vocabulary] (1851)
**1** : of or relating to biochemistry
**2** : characterized by, produced by, or involving chemical reactions in living organisms
— **biochemical** noun
— **bio·chem·i·cal·ly** \-k(ə-)lē\ adverb

**biochemical oxygen demand** noun (circa 1927)
: the oxygen used in meeting the metabolic needs of aerobic microorganisms in water rich in organic matter (as water polluted with sewage)

**bio·chem·is·try** \ˌbī-ō-'ke-mə-strē\ noun [International Scientific Vocabulary] (1881)
**1** : chemistry that deals with the chemical compounds and processes occurring in organisms
**2** : the chemical characteristics and reactions of a particular living system or biological substance (as chlorophyll) ⟨a change in the patient's biochemistry⟩
— **bio·chem·ist** \-mist\ noun

**bio·chip** \'bī-ō-ˌchip\ noun (1981)
: a hypothetical computer logic circuit or storage device in which the physical or chemical properties of large biological molecules (as proteins) are used to process information

**bio·cid·al** \ˌbī-ə-'sī-d°l\ adjective (1949)
: destructive to life

**bio·cide** \'bī-ə-ˌsīd\ noun (1947)

: a substance (as DDT) that is destructive to many different organisms

**bio·cli·mat·ic** \ˌbī-ō-klī-'ma-tik\ adjective (1918)
: of or relating to the relations of climate and living matter ⟨bioclimatic adaptations⟩

**bio·com·pat·i·bil·i·ty** \-kəm-ˌpa-tə-'bi-lə-tē\ noun (1971)
: compatibility with living tissue or a living system by not being toxic or injurious and not causing immunological rejection
— **bio·com·pat·i·ble** \-'pa-tə-bəl\ adjective

**bio·con·trol** \ˌbī-ō-kən-'trōl\ noun (1967)
: BIOLOGICAL CONTROL

**bio·con·ver·sion** \ˌbī-(ˌ)ō-kən-'vər-zhən, -shən\ noun (1960)
: the conversion of organic materials (as wastes) into an energy source (as methane) by processes (as fermentation) involving living organisms

**bio·de·grad·able** \-di-'grā-də-bəl\ adjective (1961)
: capable of being broken down especially into innocuous products by the action of living things (as microorganisms) ⟨biodegradable trash bags⟩
— **bio·de·grad·abil·i·ty** \-ˌgrā-də-'bi-lə-tē\ noun
— **bio·deg·ra·da·tion** \-ˌde-grə-'dā-shən\ noun
— **bio·de·grade** \-di-'grād\ verb

**bio·de·te·ri·o·ra·tion** \-di-ˌtir-ē-ə-'rā-shən\ noun (1953)
: the breakdown of materials by microbial action

**bio·di·ver·si·ty** \-də-'vər-sə-tē, -dī-\ noun (1986)
: biological diversity in an environment as indicated by numbers of different species of plants and animals

**bio·dy·nam·ic** \-di-'na-mik, -dī-\ adjective (1939)
: of or relating to a system of farming that uses only organic materials for fertilizing and soil conditioning

**bio·elec·tric** \-i-'lek-trik\ also **bio·elec·tri·cal** \-tri-kəl\ adjective (1918)
: of or relating to electric phenomena in animals and plants
— **bio·elec·tric·i·ty** \-ˌlek-'tri-sə-tē, -'tris-tē\ noun

**bio·en·er·get·ics** \-ˌe-nər-'je-tiks\ noun plural but singular in construction (1912)
**1** : the biology of energy transformations and energy exchanges (as in photosynthesis) within and between living things and their environments
**2** : a system of physical and psychological therapy that is held to increase well-being by releasing blocked physical and psychic energy
— **bio·en·er·get·ic** \-'je-tik\ adjective

**bio·en·gi·neer·ing** \-ˌen-jə-'nir-iŋ\ noun (circa 1954)
: biological or medical application of engineering principles or engineering equipment; broadly : BIOTECHNOLOGY 1
— **bio·en·gi·neer** \-'nir\ noun or transitive verb

**bio·eth·ics** \-'e-thiks\ noun plural but singular in construction (1971)
: a discipline dealing with the ethical implications of biological research and applications especially in medicine
— **bio·eth·i·cal** \-'e-thi-kəl\ adjective
— **bio·eth·i·cist** \-'e-thə-sist\ noun

**bio·feed·back** \-'fēd-ˌbak\ noun (1970)
: the technique of making unconscious or involuntary bodily processes (as heartbeats or brain waves) perceptible to the senses (as by the use of an oscilloscope) in order to manipulate them by conscious mental control

**bio·foul·ing** \-'faú-liŋ\ noun (1943)
: the gradual accumulation of waterborne organisms (as bacteria and protozoa) on the surfaces of engineering structures in water that

contributes to corrosion of the structures and to a decrease in the efficiency of moving parts

**bio·gas** \'bī-ō-ˌgas\ noun (1974)
: a mixture of methane and carbon dioxide produced by the bacterial decomposition of organic wastes and used as a fuel

**bio·gen·e·sis** \ˌbī-ō-'je-nə-səs\ noun [New Latin] (1870)
**1** : the development of life from preexisting life
**2** : a supposed tendency for stages in the evolutionary history of a race to briefly recur during the development and differentiation of an individual of that race
**3** : the synthesis of chemical compounds or structures in the living organism — compare BIOSYNTHESIS
— **bio·ge·net·ic** \-jə-'ne-tik\ adjective
— **bio·ge·net·i·cal·ly** \-ti-k(ə-)lē\ adverb

**biogenetic law** noun (1882)
: a theory of development much disputed in biology: an organism passes through successive stages resembling the series of ancestral types from which it has descended so that the ontogeny of the individual is a recapitulation of the phylogeny of the group

**bio·gen·ic** \-'je-nik\ also **bi·og·e·nous** \bī-'ä-jə-nəs\ adjective (1913)
: produced by living organisms ⟨biogenic methane formation⟩

**bio·geo·chem·i·cal** \-ˌjē-ə-'ke-mi-kəl\ noun (1938)
: of or relating to the partitioning and cycling of chemical elements and compounds between the living and nonliving parts of an ecosystem
— **bio·geo·chem·is·try** \-mə-strē\ noun

**bio·ge·og·ra·phy** \-jē-'ä-grə-fē\ noun [International Scientific Vocabulary] (1895)
: a science that deals with the geographical distribution of animals and plants
— **bio·ge·og·ra·pher** \-grə-fər\ noun
— **bio·geo·graph·ic** \-ˌjē-ə-'gra-fik\ or **bio·geo·graph·i·cal** \-fi-kəl\ adjective

**bi·og·ra·phee** \bī-ˌä-grə-'fē also bē-\ noun (1841)
: a person about whom a biography is written

**bi·og·ra·pher** \-'ä-grə-fər\ noun (1715)
: a writer of a biography

**bio·graph·i·cal** \ˌbī-ə-'gra-fi-kəl\ also **bio·graph·ic** \-fik\ adjective (1738)
**1** : of, relating to, or constituting biography
**2** : consisting of biographies ⟨a biographical dictionary⟩
**3** : relating to a list briefly identifying persons ⟨biographical notes⟩
— **bio·graph·i·cal·ly** \-fi-k(ə-)lē\ adverb

**bi·og·ra·phy** \bī-'ä-grə-fē also bē-\ noun, plural **-phies** [Late Greek biographia, from Greek bi- + -graphia -graphy] (1683)
**1** : a usually written history of a person's life
**2** : biographical writings as a whole
**3** : an account of the life of something (as an animal, a coin, or a building)

**bio·haz·ard** \'bī-ō-ˌha-zərd\ noun (1967)
: a biological agent or condition that constitutes a hazard to humans or the environment; also : a hazard posed by such an agent or condition

**bi·o·log·ic** \ˌbī-ə-'lä-jik\ or **bi·o·log·i·cal** \-ji-kəl\ noun (1921)
: a biological product used in medicine

**biological** also **biologic** adjective (1859)
**1** : of or relating to biology or to life and living processes
**2** : used in or produced by applied biology
**3** : related by direct genetic relationship rather than by adoption or marriage ⟨biological parents⟩
— **bi·o·log·i·cal·ly** \-ji-k(ə-)lē\ adverb

**biological clock** noun (1955)
: an inherent timing mechanism that is inferred to exist in some living systems (as a cell) in order to explain various cyclical behaviors and physiological processes

**biological control** noun (1923)

: reduction in numbers or elimination of pest organisms by interference with their ecology (as by the introduction of parasites or diseases)

**bi·o·log·i·cal oxygen demand** *noun* (1945)
: BIOCHEMICAL OXYGEN DEMAND

**bi·o·log·i·cal warfare** *noun* (1946)
: warfare involving the use of living organisms (as disease germs) or their toxic products as weapons; *also* : warfare involving the use of herbicides

**bi·ol·o·gism** \bī-'ä-lə-ˌji-zəm\ *noun* (1924)
: preoccupation with biological explanations in the analysis of social situations
— **bi·ol·o·gis·tic** \-ˌä-lə-'jis-tik\ *adjective*

**bi·ol·o·gy** \bī-'ä-lə-jē\ *noun* [German *Biologie*, from *bi-* + *-logie* -logy] (1819)
**1** : a branch of knowledge that deals with living organisms and vital processes
**2 a** : the plant and animal life of a region or environment **b** : the life processes especially of an organism or group; *broadly* : ECOLOGY
— **bi·ol·o·gist** \-jist\ *noun*

**bi·o·lu·mi·nes·cence** \ˌbī-ō-ˌlü-mə-'ne-sᵊn(t)s\ *noun* [International Scientific Vocabulary] (1916)
: the emission of light from living organisms; *also* : the light so produced
— **bi·o·lu·mi·nes·cent** \-sᵊnt\ *adjective*

**bio·mass** \'bī-ō-ˌmas\ *noun* (1934)
**1** : the amount of living matter (as in a unit area or volume of habitat)
**2** : plant materials and animal waste used especially as a source of fuel

**bio·ma·te·ri·al** \ˌbī-ō-mə-'tir-ē-əl\ *noun* (1966)
: material used for or suitable for use in prostheses that come in direct contact with living tissues

**bio·math·e·mat·ics** \-ˌma-thə-'ma-tiks, -math-'ma-\ *noun plural but usually singular in construction* (1923)
: mathematics of special use in biology and medicine
— **bio·math·e·mat·i·cal** \-ti-kəl\ *adjective*
— **bio·math·e·ma·ti·cian** \-ˌmath-mə-'ti-shən, -ˌma-thə-\ *noun*

**bi·ome** \'bī-ˌōm\ *noun* [²*bi-* + *-ome*] (1916)
: a major ecological community type (as tropical rain forest, grassland, or desert)

**bio·me·chan·ics** \'bī-ō-mə-'ka-niks\ *noun plural but singular or plural in construction* (circa 1933)
: the mechanics of biological and especially muscular activity (as in locomotion or exercise); *also* : the scientific study of this
— **bio·me·chan·i·cal** \-ni-kəl\ *adjective*
— **bio·me·chan·i·cal·ly** \-ni-k(ə-)lē\ *adverb*

**bio·med·i·cal** \ˌbī-ō-'me-di-kəl\ *adjective* (1955)
**1** : of or relating to biomedicine
**2** : of, relating to, or involving biological, medical, and physical science

**bio·med·i·cine** \-'me-də-sən, *British usually* -'med-sən\ *noun* (1947)
: medicine based on the application of the principles of the natural sciences and especially biology and biochemistry

**bio·me·te·o·rol·o·gy** \-ˌmē-tē-ə-'rä-lə-jē\ *noun* (1946)
: a science that deals with the relationship between living things and atmospheric phenomena
— **bio·me·te·o·ro·log·i·cal** \-rə-'lä-ji-kəl\ *adjective*

**bi·om·e·try** \bī-'ä-mə-trē\ *noun* [International Scientific Vocabulary] (1831)
: the statistical analysis of biological observations and phenomena
— **bio·met·ric** \ˌbī-ō-'me-trik\ *or* **bio·met·ri·cal** \-tri-kəl\ *adjective*
— **bio·me·tri·cian** \-mə-'tri-shən\ *noun*
— **bio·met·rics** \-'me-triks\ *noun plural but singular or plural in construction*

**bio·mol·e·cule** \ˌbī-ō-'mä-li-ˌkyü(ə)l\ *noun* (1901)
: an organic molecule and especially a macromolecule in living organisms
— **bio·mo·lec·u·lar** \-mə-'le-kyə-lər\ *adjective*

**bio·mor·phic** \ˌbī-ō-'mȯr-fik\ *adjective* (1895)
: resembling or suggesting the forms of living organisms ⟨*biomorphic* sculptures⟩ ⟨*biomorphic* images⟩

**bi·on·ic** \bī-'ä-nik\ *adjective* (1963)
**1** : of or relating to bionics
**2** : having normal biological capability or performance enhanced by or as if by electronic or electromechanical devices

**bi·on·ics** \bī-'ä-niks\ *noun plural but singular or plural in construction* [²*bi-* + *-onics* (as in *electronics*)] (1960)
: a science concerned with the application of data about the functioning of biological systems to the solution of engineering problems

**bi·o·nom·ics** \ˌbī-ə-'nä-miks\ *noun plural but singular or plural in construction* [*bionomic*, adjective, probably from French *bionomique*, from *bionomie* ecology, from *bi-* + *-nomie* -nomy] (1888)
: ECOLOGY
— **bi·o·nom·ic** \-mik\ *adjective*

**bio·phys·ics** \ˌbī-ō-'fi-ziks\ *noun plural but singular or plural in construction* (1892)
: a branch of science concerned with the application of physical principles and methods to biological problems
— **bio·phys·i·cal** \-zi-kəl\ *adjective*
— **bio·phys·i·cist** \-'fi-zə-sist, -'fiz-sist\ *noun*

**bio·pic** \'bī-(ˌ)ō-ˌpik\ *noun* [²*bi-* + ¹*pic*] (1951)
: a biographical movie

**bio·poly·mer** \ˌbī-ō-'pä-lə-mər\ *noun* (1961)
: a polymeric substance (as a protein or polysaccharide) formed in a biological system

**bi·op·sy** \'bī-ˌäp-sē\ *noun, plural* **-sies** [International Scientific Vocabulary ²*bi-* + *-opsy* (as in *autopsy*)] (1895)
: the removal and examination of tissue, cells, or fluids from the living body
— **biopsy** *transitive verb*

**bio·re·ac·tor** \ˌbī-ō-rē-'ak-tər\ *noun* (1974)
: a device or apparatus in which living organisms and especially bacteria synthesize useful substances (as interferon) or break down harmful ones (as in sewage)

**bio·rhythm** \'bī-ō-ˌri-thəm\ *noun* (1960)
: an inherent rhythm that appears to control or initiate various biological processes
— **bio·rhyth·mic** \-'rith-mik\ *adjective*

**bio·safe·ty** \ˌbī-ō-'sāf-tē\ *noun* (1977)
: safety with respect to the effects of biological research on humans and the environment

**bio·sci·ence** \-'sī-ən(t)s\ *noun* (1941)
: BIOLOGY 1; *also* : LIFE SCIENCE
— **bio·sci·en·tif·ic** \-ˌsī-ən-'ti-fik\ *adjective*
— **bio·sci·en·tist** \-'sī-ən-tist\ *noun*

**bio·sen·sor** \-'sen-ˌsȯr, -'sen(t)-sər\ *noun* (1962)
: a device that is sensitive to a physical or chemical stimulus (as heat or an ion) and transmits information about a life process

**-biosis** *noun combining form, plural* **-bioses** [New Latin, from Greek *biōsis*, from *bioun* to live, from *bios* life — more at QUICK]
: mode of life ⟨para*biosis*⟩

**bio·so·cial** \ˌbī-ō-'sō-shəl\ *adjective* (1897)
: of, relating to, or concerned with the interaction of the biological aspects and social relationships of living organisms ⟨*biosocial* science⟩
— **bio·so·cial·ly** \-'sōsh-lē, -'sō-shə-\ *adverb*

**bio·sphere** \'bī-ə-ˌsfir\ *noun* (1899)
**1** : the part of the world in which life can exist
**2** : living beings together with their environment
— **bio·spher·ic** \ˌbī-ə-'sfir-ik, -'sfer-\ *adjective*

**bio·sta·tis·tics** \ˌbī-ō-stə-'tis-tiks\ *noun plural but singular in construction* (1950)
: statistics applied to the analysis of biological data
— **bio·sta·tis·ti·cal** \-ti-kəl\ *adjective*
— **bio·stat·is·ti·cian** \-ˌsta-tə-'sti-shən\ *noun*

**bio·strati·graph·ic** \-ˌstra-tə-'gra-fik\ *adjective* (1947)
: of or relating to the branch of paleontology dealing with the conditions and order of deposition of sedimentary rocks
— **bio·stra·tig·ra·phy** \-strə-'ti-grə-fē\ *noun*

**bio·syn·the·sis** \-'sin(t)-thə-səs\ *noun* [New Latin] (1930)
: the production of a chemical compound by a living organism
— **bio·syn·thet·ic** \-sin-'the-tik\ *adjective*
— **bio·syn·thet·i·cal·ly** \-ti-k(ə-)lē\ *adverb*

**bio·sys·te·mat·ics** \-ˌsis-tə-'ma-tiks\ *noun plural but singular or plural in construction* (1945)
: experimental taxonomy especially as based on cytogenetics and genetics
— **bio·sys·te·mat·ic** \-tik\ *adjective*
— **bio·sys·tem·atist** \-'sis-tə-mə-tist, -ˌsis-'te-mə-\ *noun*

**bi·o·ta** \bī-'ō-tə\ *noun* [New Latin, from Greek *biotē* life; akin to Greek *bios*] (1901)
: the flora and fauna of a region

**bio·tech** \'bī-ō-ˌtek\ *noun* (1974)
: BIOTECHNOLOGY 1

**bio·tech·ni·cal** \ˌbī-ō-'tek-ni-kəl\ *adjective* (1938)
: of or relating to biotechnology

**bio·tech·nol·o·gy** \ˌbī-ō-tek-'nä-lə-jē\ *noun* (1941)
**1** : applied biological science (as bioengineering or recombinant DNA technology)
**2** : ERGONOMICS
— **bio·tech·no·log·i·cal** \-ˌtek-nə-'läj-i-kəl\ *adjective*
— **bio·tech·nol·o·gist** \-'nä-lə-jist\ *noun*

**bio·te·lem·e·try** \-tə-'le-mə-trē\ *noun* (1963)
: the remote detection and measurement of a human or animal function, activity, or condition
— **bio·tel·e·met·ric** \-ˌte-lə-'me-trik\ *adjective*

**bi·ot·ic** \bī-'ä-tik\ *adjective* [Greek *biōtikos*, from *bioun*] (1868)
: of or relating to life; *especially* : caused or produced by living beings ⟨*biotic* diversity⟩

**-biotic** *adjective combining form* [probably from New Latin *-bioticus*, from Greek *biōtikos*]
: having a (specified) mode of life ⟨endo*biotic*⟩

**biotic potential** *noun* (1935)
: the inherent capacity of an organism or species to reproduce and survive

**bi·o·tin** \'bī-ə-tən\ *noun* [International Scientific Vocabulary, from Greek *biotos* life, sustenance; akin to Greek *bios*] (1936)
: a colorless crystalline growth vitamin $C_{10}H_{16}N_2O_3S$ of the vitamin B complex found especially in yeast, liver, and egg yolk

**bi·o·tite** \'bī-ə-ˌtīt\ *noun* [German *Biotit*, from Jean B. *Biot* (died 1862) French mathematician] (1862)
: a generally black or dark green form of mica that is a constituent of crystalline rocks and consists of a silicate of iron, magnesium, potassium, and aluminum
— **bi·o·tit·ic** \ˌbī-ə-'ti-tik\ *adjective*

**bio·tope** \'bī-ə-ˌtōp\ *noun* [²*bi-* + Greek *topos* place] (1927)

: a region uniform in environmental conditions and in its populations of animals and plants for which it is the habitat

**bio·trans·for·ma·tion** \'bī-ō-,tran(t)s-fər-'mā-shən, -,fȯr-\ *noun* (1955)
: the transformation of chemical compounds within a living system

**bio·type** \-,tīp\ *noun* [International Scientific Vocabulary] (1906)
: the organisms sharing a specified genotype; *also* : the genotype shared or its distinguishing peculiarity
— **bio·typ·ic** \,bī-ə-'ti-pik\ *adjective*

**bi·pa·ren·tal** \,bī-pə-'ren-t°l\ *adjective* (1900)
: of, relating to, involving, or derived from two parents
— **bi·pa·ren·tal·ly** \-t°l-ē\ *adverb*

**bi·par·ti·san** \(,)bī-'pär-tə-zən, -sən, -,zan, *chiefly British* ,bī-,pär-tə-'zan\ *adjective* (circa 1909)
: of, relating to, or involving members of two parties ⟨a *bipartisan* commission⟩
— **bi·par·ti·san·ism** \-zə-,ni-zəm, -sə-\ *noun*
— **bi·par·ti·san·ship** \-zən-,ship, -sən-\ *noun*

**bi·par·tite** \(,)bī-'pär-,tīt\ *adjective* [Latin *bipartitus*, past participle of *bipartire* to divide in two, from *bi-* + *partire* to divide, from *part-, pars* part] (1574)
**1 a** : being in two parts **b** : having a correspondent part for each of two parties ⟨a *bipartite* contract⟩ **c** : shared by two ⟨a *bipartite* treaty⟩
**2** : divided into two parts almost to the base ⟨a *bipartite* leaf⟩
— **bi·par·tite·ly** *adverb*
— **bi·par·ti·tion** \,bī-(,)pär-'ti-shən\ *noun*

**bi·ped** \'bī-,ped\ *noun* [Latin *biped-, bipes*, from *bi-* + *ped-, pes* foot — more at FOOT] (1646)
: a two-footed animal
— **bi·ped·al** \(,)bī-'pe-d°l\ *adjective*
— **bi·ped·al·ly** \-ē\ *adverb*

**bi·ped·al·ism** \(,)bī-'pe-d°l-,i-zəm\ *noun* (1907)
: the condition of having two feet or of using only two feet for locomotion

**bi·pe·dal·i·ty** \,bī-pə-'da-lə-tē\ *noun* (1847)
: BIPEDALISM

**bi·phas·ic** \(,)bī-'fā-zik\ *adjective* (circa 1909)
: having two phases ⟨a *biphasic* immune response⟩

**bi·phe·nyl** \(,)bī-'fe-n°l, -'fē-\ *noun* [International Scientific Vocabulary] (circa 1923)
: a white crystalline hydrocarbon $C_6H_5 \cdot C_6H_5$ used especially as a heat-transfer medium

**bi·pin·nate** \-'pi-,nāt\ *adjective* (1794)
: twice pinnate
— **bi·pin·nate·ly** *adverb*

**bi·plane** \'bī-,plān\ *noun* (1874)
: an aircraft with two main supporting surfaces usually placed one above the other

**bi·pod** \'bī-,päd\ *noun* [*bi-* + *-pod* (as in *tripod*)] (1922)
: a two-legged support

**bi·po·lar** \(,)bī-'pō-lər\ *adjective* (1810)
**1** : having or marked by two mutually repellent forces or diametrically opposed natures or views
**2 a** : having or involving the use of two poles or polarities **b** : relating to, being, or using a transistor in which both electrons and holes are utilized as charge carriers
**3** : relating to, associated with, or occurring in both polar regions ⟨*bipolar* species of birds⟩
**4** : characterized by the alternation of manic and depressive states ⟨a *bipolar* affective disorder⟩
— **bi·po·lar·i·ty** \,bī-pō-'lar-ə-tē\ *noun*
— **bi·po·lar·iza·tion** \(,)bī-,pō-lə-rə-'zā-shən\ *noun*
— **bi·po·lar·ize** \(,)bī-'pō-lə-,rīz\ *transitive verb*

**bi·pro·pel·lant** \,bī-prə-'pe-lənt\ *noun* (1947)

: a rocket propellant consisting of separate fuel and oxidizer that come together only in a combustion chamber

**bi·pyr·a·mid** \(,)bī-'pir-ə-mid\ *noun* (1897)
: a crystal consisting of two identical pyramids base to base
— **bi·py·ra·mi·dal** \-pə-'ra-mə-d°l\ *adjective*

**bi·qua·drat·ic** \,bī-kwä-'dra-tik\ *adjective or noun* (1668)
: QUARTIC

**bi·ra·cial** \(,)bī-'rā-shəl\ *adjective* (1922)
: of, relating to, or involving members of two races
— **bi·ra·cial·ism** \-shə-,li-zəm\ *noun*

**bi·ra·di·al** \(,)bī-'rā-dē-əl\ *adjective* (circa 1909)
: having both bilateral and radial symmetry

**bi·ra·mous** \(,)bī-'rā-məs\ *adjective* (1877)
: having two branches

**¹birch** \'bərch\ *noun* [Middle English, from Old English *beorc;* akin to Old High German *birka* birch, Old English *beorht* bright, and probably to Latin *fraxinus* ash tree — more at BRIGHT] (before 12th century)
**1** : any of a genus (*Betula* of the family Betulaceae, the birch family) of monoecious deciduous usually short-lived trees or shrubs having simple petioled leaves and typically a layered membranous outer bark that peels readily
**2** : the hard pale close-grained wood of a birch
**3** : a birch rod or bundle of twigs for flogging
— **birch** *or* **birch·en** \'bər-chən\ *adjective*

**²birch** *transitive verb* (1830)
: to beat with or as if with a birch : WHIP

**Birch·er** \'bər-chər\ *noun* (1961)
: a member or adherent of the John Birch Society
— **Birch·ism** \'bər-,chi-zəm\ *noun*
— **Birch·ist** \-chist\ *or* **Birch·ite** \-,chīt\ *noun or adjective*

**¹bird** \'bərd\ *noun, often attributive* [Middle English, from Old English *bridd*] (before 12th century)
**1** *archaic* : the young of a feathered vertebrate
**2** : any of a class (Aves) of warm-blooded vertebrates distinguished by having the body more or less completely covered with feathers and the forelimbs modified as wings
**3** : a game bird
**4** : CLAY PIGEON
**5 a** : FELLOW **b** : a peculiar person **c** *chiefly British* : GIRL
**6** : SHUTTLECOCK
**7** *chiefly British* **a** : a hissing or jeering expressive of disapproval **b** : dismissal from employment
**8** : a thin piece of meat rolled up with stuffing and cooked
**9** : something (as an aircraft, rocket, or satellite) resembling a bird especially by flying or being aloft

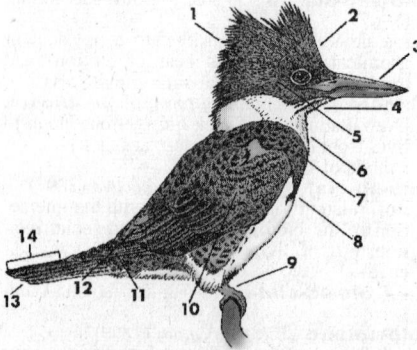

bird 2 (kingfisher): *1* crest, *2* crown, *3* bill, *4* throat, *5* auricular region, *6* breast, *7* scapulars, *8* abdomen, *9* tarsus, *10* upper wing coverts, *11* primaries, *12* secondaries, *13* rectrix, *14* tail

**10** : an obscene gesture of contempt made by pointing the middle finger upward while keeping the other fingers down — usually used with *the* — called also *finger*
— **bird·like** \-,līk\ *adjective*
— **for the birds** : WORTHLESS, RIDICULOUS

**²bird** *intransitive verb* (1918)
: to observe or identify wild birds in their natural environment

**bird·bath** \'bərd-,bath, -,bȧth\ *noun* (1895)
: a usually ornamental basin set up for birds to bathe in

**bird·brain** \-,brān\ *noun* (1943)
**1** : a stupid person
**2** : SCATTERBRAIN
— **bird·brained** \-,brānd\ *adjective*

**bird·cage** \-,kāj\ *noun* (15th century)
: a cage for confining birds

**bird·call** \-,kȯl\ *noun* (circa 1625)
**1** : a device for imitating the cry of a bird
**2** : the note or cry of a bird; *also* : a sound imitative of it

**bird colonel** *noun* [from the eagle serving as insignia for this rank] (circa 1947)
*slang* : COLONEL 1a

**bird–dog** \'bərd-,dȯg\ (1943)
*intransitive verb*
: to watch closely
*transitive verb*
: to seek out : FOLLOW, DETECT

**bird dog** *noun* (circa 1888)
**1** : a gundog trained to hunt or retrieve birds
**2 a** : one (as a canvasser or talent scout) who seeks out something for another **b** : one who steals another's date

**bird–dog·ging** \-,dȯ-gin\ *noun* (circa 1941)
**1** : the stealing of another's date (as at a party)
**2** : the action of one that bird-dogs

**bird·er** \'bər-dər\ *noun* (15th century)
**1** : a catcher or hunter of birds especially for market
**2** : a person who birds

**bird·house** \'bərd-,haùs\ *noun* (1870)
: an artificial nesting site for birds; *also* : AVIARY

**¹bird·ie** \'bər-dē\ *noun* (1792)
**1** : a little bird
**2** : a golf score of one stroke less than par on a hole — compare EAGLE

**²birdie** *transitive verb* **bird·ied; bird·ie·ing** (1948)
: to score a birdie on

**bird·lime** \'bərd-,līm\ *noun* (15th century)
**1** : a sticky substance usually made from the bark of a holly (*Ilex aquifolium*) that is smeared on twigs to snare small birds
**2** : something that ensnares
— **birdlime** *transitive verb*

**bird louse** *noun* (1826)
: BITING LOUSE

**bird·man** \'bərd-mən, *especially for 1 also* -,man\ *noun* (1697)
**1** : a person who deals with birds
**2** : a person who flies (as in an aircraft)

**bird–of–paradise** *noun* (circa 1884)
: an ornamental plant (*Strelitzia reginae* of the family Strelitziaceae) having scapes of orange or yellow and purple flowers with three sepals and three very irregular petals

**bird of paradise** (1638)
: any of numerous brilliantly colored plumed oscine birds (family Paradiseidae) of the New Guinea area

**bird of passage** (1728)
**1** : a migratory bird
**2** : a person who leads a wandering or unsettled life

**bird of prey** (14th century)
: a carnivorous bird (as a hawk, falcon, or vulture) that feeds wholly or chiefly on meat taken by hunting or on carrion

**bird pepper** *noun* (1696)
: a capsicum (*Capsicum annuum glabriusculum*) having very small oblong extremely pungent red fruits

**bird·seed** \'bərd-,sēd\ *noun* (1840)

: a mixture of seeds (as of hemp, millet, and sunflowers) used for feeding caged and wild birds

**¹bird's-eye** \'bərd-,zī\ *noun* (1597)
**1** : any of numerous plants with small bright-colored flowers; *especially* : a speedwell (*Veronica chamaedrys*)
**2 a** : an allover pattern for textiles consisting of a small diamond with a center dot **b** : a fabric woven with this pattern
**3** : a small spot in wood surrounded with an ellipse of concentric fibers

**²bird's-eye** *adjective* (1665)
**1** : marked with spots resembling birds' eyes
**2** : having or involving a bird's-eye view ⟨*bird's-eye* perspective⟩ ⟨a *bird's-eye* survey of the topic⟩

**bird's-eye view** *noun* (1762)
**1** : a view from a high angle as if seen by a bird in flight
**2** : an overall or cursory look at something

**bird's-foot trefoil** \'bərdz-,füt-\ *noun* (1833)
: a European legume (*Lotus corniculatus*) having claw-shaped pods and widely used especially in the U.S. as a forage and fodder plant or often planted along roadsides

**bird's-foot violet** *noun* (1839)
: a common violet (*Viola pedata*) of the eastern U.S. with deeply cleft leaves and pale blue to purple flattened flowers

**bird's-nest fern** \'bərdz-,nest-\ *noun* (1858)
: a large epiphytic spleenwort (*Asplenium nidus*) of tropical Asia and Polynesia that has large lance-shaped leaves and is often grown as a houseplant

**bird's nest soup** *noun* (1871)
: a soup made with the nests of small cave-nesting swifts (genus *Collocalia*) that build them using a glutinous secretion from their salivary glands

**bird-song** \'bərd-,sȯŋ\ *noun* (1896)
: the song of a bird

**bird-watch** \'bərd-,wäch\ *intransitive verb* [back-formation from *bird-watcher*] (1948)
: BIRD

**bird-watch-er** \-,wä-chər\ *noun* (1905)
: BIRDER 2

**bi-re-frin-gence** \,bī-ri-'frin-jən(t)s\ *noun* [International Scientific Vocabulary] (1898)
: the refraction of light in an anisotropic material (as calcite) in two slightly different directions to form two rays
— **bi-re-frin-gent** \-jənt\ *adjective*

**bi-reme** \'bī-,rēm\ *noun* [Latin *biremis*, from *bi-* + *remus* oar — more at ROW] (1662)
: a galley with two banks of oars used especially by the ancient Greeks and Phoenicians

**bi-ret-ta** \bə-'re-tə\ *noun* [Italian *berretta*, from Old Provençal *berret* cap, from Medieval Latin *birretum*, from Late Latin *birrus* cloak with a hood, perhaps of Celtic origin; akin to Middle Irish *berr* short] (1598)
: a square cap with three ridges on top worn by clergymen especially of the Roman Catholic Church

**birk** \'birk\ *noun* [Middle English *birch, birk*] (14th century)
*chiefly Scottish* : BIRCH

**birk-ie** \'bir-kē, 'bər-\ *noun* [origin unknown] (1724)
**1** *Scottish* : a lively smart assertive person
**2** *Scottish* : FELLOW, BOY

**biretta**

**¹birl** \'bər(-ə)l, *Scottish also* 'bir(-ə)l\ *intransitive verb* [Middle English from Old English *byrelian*; probably akin to Old English *beran* to carry — more at BEAR] (circa 1585)
*chiefly Scottish* : CAROUSE

**²birl** *verb* [perhaps imitative] (1790)
*transitive verb*
**1** : SPIN

**2** : to cause (a floating log) to rotate by treading
*intransitive verb*
: to progress by whirling
— **birl-er** \'bər-lər, 'bir-\ *noun*

**Bi-ro** \'bī-(,)rō\ *trademark*
— used for a ballpoint pen

**birr** \'bər, 'bir\ *noun, plural* **birr** [Arabic] (circa 1978)
— see MONEY table

**birse** \'birs, 'bərs\ *noun* [(assumed) Middle English *birst*, from Old English *byrst* — more at BRISTLE] (before 12th century)
**1** *chiefly Scottish* : a bristle or tuft of bristles
**2** *chiefly Scottish* : ANGER

**¹birth** \'bərth\ *noun, often attributive* [Middle English, from Old Norse *byrth*; akin to Old English *beran*] (13th century)
**1 a** : the emergence of a new individual from the body of its parent **b** : the act or process of bringing forth young from the womb
**2** : a state resulting from being born especially at a particular time or place ⟨a Southerner by *birth*⟩
**3 a** : LINEAGE, EXTRACTION ⟨marriage between equals in *birth*⟩ **b** : high or noble birth
**4 a** *archaic* : one that is born **b** : BEGINNING, START ⟨the *birth* of an idea⟩

**²birth** (1906)
*transitive verb*
**1** *chiefly dialect* : to bring forth
**2** : to give rise to : ORIGINATE
*intransitive verb*
: to bring forth a child or young

**birth canal** *noun* (1927)
: the channel formed by the cervix, vagina, and vulva through which the fetus passes during birth

**birth certificate** *noun* (1900)
: a copy of an official record of a person's date and place of birth and parentage

**birth control** *noun* (1914)
: control of the number of children born especially by preventing or lessening the frequency of conception : CONTRACEPTION

**birth-day** \'bərth-,dā\ *noun* (14th century)
**1 a** : the day of a person's birth **b** : a day of origin
**2** : an anniversary of a birth ⟨her 21st *birthday*⟩

**birthday suit** *noun* (1753)
: unclothed skin : NAKEDNESS

**birth defect** *noun* (1971)
: a physical or biochemical defect that is present at birth and may be inherited or environmentally induced

**birth-mark** \'bərth-,märk\ *noun* (1580)
: an unusual mark or blemish on the skin at birth : NEVUS

**birth pang** *noun* (circa 1887)
**1** : one of the regularly recurrent pains that are characteristic of childbirth — usually used in plural
**2** *plural* : disorder and distress incident especially to a major social change

**birth-place** \'bərth-,plās\ *noun* (1607)
: place of birth or origin

**birth-rate** \'bərth-,rāt\ *noun* (1859)
: the ratio between births and individuals in a specified population and time

**birth-right** \'bərth-,rīt\ *noun* (1535)
: a right, privilege, or possession to which a person is entitled by birth

**birth-root** \'bərth-,rüt, -,rút\ *noun* (1822)
: any of several trilliums with astringent roots used in folk medicine

**birth-stone** \'bərth-,stōn\ *noun* (1907)
: a gemstone associated symbolically with the month of one's birth

**birth-wort** \-,wərt, -,wȯrt\ *noun* (1551)
: any of several herbs or woody vines (genus *Aristolochia* of the family Aristolochiaceae, the birthwort family) with aromatic roots used in folk medicine to aid childbirth

**bis** \'bis\ *adverb* [Latin, from Old Latin *dvis*; akin to Old High German *zwiro* twice, Latin *duo* two — more at TWO] (1819)
**1** : AGAIN — used in music as a direction to repeat
**2** : TWICE

**Bi-sa-yan** \bə-'sī-ən\ *noun* [Bisayan *Bisayâ*] (1951)
**1** : a member of any of several peoples in the Visayan islands, Philippines
**2** : the group of Austronesian languages of the Bisayans

**bis-cuit** \'bis-kət\ *noun, plural* **biscuits** *also* **biscuit** [Middle English *bisquite*, from Middle French *bescuit*, from (*pain*) *bescuit* twice-cooked bread] (14th century)
**1 a** : any of various hard or crisp dry baked products: as (1) *British* : CRACKER 4 (2) *British* : COOKIE **b** : a small quick bread made from dough that has been rolled out and cut or dropped from a spoon
**2** : earthenware or porcelain after the first firing and before glazing
**3 a** : a light grayish yellowish brown **b** : a grayish yellow ◇

**bi-sect** \'bī-,sekt, bī-'\ *verb* [¹*bi-* + inter*sect*] (circa 1645)
*transitive verb*
: to divide into two usually equal parts
*intransitive verb*
: CROSS, INTERSECT
— **bi-sec-tion** \'bī-,sek-shən, bī-'\ *noun*
— **bi-sec-tion-al** \-shnəl, -shə-nᵊl\ *adjective*
— **bi-sec-tion-al-ly** *adverb*

**bi-sec-tor** \'bī-,sek-tər, bī-'\ *noun* (1864)
: one that bisects; *especially* : a straight line that bisects an angle or a line segment

**bi-sex-u-al** \(,)bī-'sek-sh(ə-)wəl, -shəl\ *adjective* (1824)
**1 a** : possessing characters of both sexes : HERMAPHRODITIC **b** : sexually oriented toward both sexes
**2** : of, relating to, or involving both sexes
— **bisexual** *noun*
— **bi-sex-u-al-i-ty** \,bī-,sek-shə-'wa-lə-tē\ *noun*
— **bi-sex-u-al-ly** \(,)bī-'sek-sh(ə-)wə-lē, -sh(ə-)lē\ *adverb*

**bish-op** \'bi-shəp\ *noun* [Middle English *bisshop*, from Old English *bisceop*, from Late Latin *episcopus*, from Greek *episkopos*, literally, overseer, from *epi-* + *skeptesthai* to look — more at SPY] (before 12th century)
**1** : one having spiritual or ecclesiastical supervision: as **a** : an Anglican, Eastern Orthodox, or Roman Catholic clergyman ranking above a

---

◇ **WORD HISTORY**

**biscuit** In earlier ages the preservation of food presented a greater problem than it does today, especially on long journeys. One approach was to preserve flat cakes of bread by baking them a second time in order to dry them out. In medieval French the result of this process was called *pain bescuit*, literally "twice-cooked bread." In the 14th century, the second element of this phrase was borrowed into English. The notion of cooking twice having been lost, *biscuit* came to be used to designate various hard or crisp, dry baked products. (This is the sense that now prevails in England, while Americans would say *cookie* or *cracker*.) Similarities in shape and size led to the use of *biscuit* as the name for a small quick bread made from dough that has been rolled out and cut, or dropped from a spoon.

---

priest, having authority to ordain and confirm, and typically governing a diocese **b** : any of various Protestant clerical officials who superintend other clergy **c** : a Mormon high priest presiding over a ward or over all other bishops and over the Aaronic priesthood
**2** : either of two pieces of each color in a set of chessmen having the power to move diagonally across any number of adjoining unoccupied squares
**3** : mulled port wine flavored with roasted oranges and cloves
**bish·op·ric** \'bi-shə-(,)prik\ *noun* [Middle English *bisshopriche*, from Old English *bisceoprīce*, from *bisceop* + *rīce* kingdom — more at RICH] (before 12th century)
**1** : DIOCESE
**2** : the office of bishop
**3** : the administrative body of a Mormon ward consisting of a bishop and two high priests as counselors
**Bishops' Bible** *noun* (1835)
: an officially commissioned English translation of the Bible published in 1568
**bis·muth** \'biz-məth\ *noun* [New Latin *bismuthum*, modification of German *Wismut*] (1668)
: a heavy brittle grayish white chiefly trivalent metallic element that is chemically like arsenic and antimony and that is used in alloys and pharmaceuticals — see ELEMENT table
— **bis·mu·thic** \biz-'mə-thik, -'myü-\ *adjective*
**bi·son** \'bī-s°n, -z°n\ *noun, plural* **bison** [Latin *bisont-, bison*, of Germanic origin; akin to Old High German *wisant* aurochs; akin to Old Prussian *wissambrs* aurochs] (1611)
: any of several large shaggy-maned usually gregarious recent or extinct bovine mammals (genus *Bison*) having a large head with short horns and heavy forequarters surmounted by a large fleshy hump: as **a** : WISENT **b** : BUFFALO 1c(1)
— **bi·son·tine** \-s°n-,tīn, -z°n-\ *adjective*
**¹bisque** \'bisk\ *noun* [French] (1647)
**1 a** : a thick cream soup made with shellfish or game **b** : a cream soup of pureed vegetables
**2** : ice cream containing powdered nuts or macaroons
**²bisque** *noun* [French] (circa 1656)
: odds allowed an inferior player: as **a** : a point taken when desired in a set of tennis **b** : an extra turn in croquet **c** : one or more strokes off a golf score
**³bisque** *noun* [by shortening & alteration] (1664)
: BISCUIT 2; *especially* : unglazed china that is not to be glazed but is hard-fired and vitreous
**bi·state** \'bī-,stāt\ *adjective* (1928)
: of or relating to two states
**bis·ter** *or* **bis·tre** \'bis-tər\ *noun* [French *bistre*] (circa 1751)
**1** : a yellowish brown to dark brown pigment used in art
**2** : a grayish to yellowish brown
— **bis·tered** \-tərd\ *adjective*
**bis·tort** \'bis-,tòrt, bis-'\ *noun* [Middle French *bistorte*, from (assumed) Medieval Latin *bistorta*, from Latin *bis* + *torta*, feminine of *tortus*, past participle of *torquēre* to twist — more at TORTURE] (1578)
: any of several polygonums; *especially* : a European herb (*Polygonum bistorta*) or a related American plant (*P. bistortoides*) with twisted roots used as astringents
**bis·tro** \'bēs-(,)trō, 'bis-\ *noun, plural* **bistros** [French] (1921)
**1** : a small or unpretentious restaurant
**2 a** : a small bar or tavern **b** : NIGHTCLUB
— **bis·tro·ic** \bēs-'trō-ik, bis-\ *adjective*
**bi·sul·fate** \(,)bī-'səl-,fāt\ *noun* (circa 1846)
: an acid sulfate
**bi·sul·fide** \-,fīd\ *noun* [International Scientific Vocabulary] (1863)
: DISULFIDE

**bi·sul·fite** \-,fīt\ *noun* [French, from *bi-* + *sulfite*] (circa 1846)
: an acid sulfite
**bi–swing** \'bī-'swiŋ\ *adjective* [¹*bi-* + *swing*; perhaps from the freedom of movement allowed by this jacket] (1968)
: made with a pleat or gusset at the back of the arms ⟨*bi-swing* jacket⟩
**¹bit** \'bit\ *noun* [Middle English *bitt*, from Old English *bite* act of biting; akin to Old English *bītan*] (14th century)
**1 a** (1) : the biting or cutting edge or part of a tool (2) : a replaceable part of a compound tool that actually performs the function (as drilling or boring) for which the whole tool is designed **b** *plural* : the jaws of tongs or pincers
**2** : something bitten or held with the teeth: **a** : the usually steel part of a bridle inserted in the mouth of a horse **b** : the rimmed mouth end on the stem of a pipe or cigar holder
**3** : something that curbs or restrains
**4** : the part of a key that enters the lock and acts on the bolt and tumblers
**²bit** *transitive verb* **bit·ted; bit·ting** (1583)
**1 a** : to put a bit in the mouth of (a horse) **b** : to control as if with a bit
**2** : to form a bit on (a key)
**³bit** *noun* [Middle English, from Old English *bita;* akin to Old English *bītan*] (before 12th century)
**1** : a small quantity of food; *especially* : a small delicacy
**2 a** : a small piece or quantity of some material thing **b** (1) : a small coin (2) : a unit of value equal to ⅛ of a dollar ⟨four *bits*⟩
**3** : something small or unimportant of its kind: as **a** : a brief period : WHILE **b** : an indefinite usually small degree, extent, or amount ⟨a *bit* of a rascal⟩ ⟨every *bit* as powerful⟩ **c** (1) : a small part usually with spoken lines in a theatrical performance (2) : a usually short theatrical routine ⟨a corny comedy *bit*⟩
**4** : the aggregate of items, situations, or activities appropriate to a given style, genre, or role ⟨rejected the whole *bit* about love-marriage-motherhood —Vance Packard⟩
— **a bit** : SOMEWHAT, RATHER ⟨the play was *a bit* dull⟩
— **a bit much** : a little more than one wants to endure
— **bit by bit** : by degrees : LITTLE BY LITTLE
**⁴bit** *noun* [*bi*nary dig*it*] (1948)
**1** : a unit of computer information equivalent to the result of a choice between two alternatives (as *yes* or *no*, *on* or *off*)
**2** : the physical representation of a bit by an electrical pulse, a magnetized spot, or a hole whose presence or absence indicates data
**bi·tar·trate** \(,)bī-'tär-,trāt\ *noun* [International Scientific Vocabulary] (1879)
: an acid tartrate
**¹bitch** \'bich\ *noun* [Middle English *bicche*, from Old English *bicce*] (before 12th century)
**1** : the female of the dog or some other carnivorous mammals
**2 a** : a lewd or immoral woman **b** : a malicious, spiteful, or domineering woman — sometimes used as a generalized term of abuse
**3** : something that is highly objectionable or unpleasant
**4** : COMPLAINT
**²bitch** (1823)
*transitive verb*
**1** : SPOIL, BOTCH ⟨I must have *bitched* up my life —Mavis Gallant⟩
**2** : CHEAT, DOUBLECROSS
**3** : to complain of or about
*intransitive verb*
: COMPLAIN
**bitch·ery** \'bi-chə-rē\ *noun, plural* **-er·ies** (1936)
: malicious, spiteful, or domineering behavior; *also* : an instance of such behavior
**bitch goddess** *noun* (1906)

: SUCCESS; *especially* : material or worldly success
**bitchy** \'bi-chē\ *adjective* **bitch·i·er; -est** (1937)
: characterized by malicious, spiteful, or arrogant behavior
— **bitch·i·ly** \'bi-chə-lē\ *adverb*
— **bitch·i·ness** \'bi-chē-nəs\ *noun*
**¹bite** \'bīt\ *verb* **bit** \'bit\; **bit·ten** \'bi-t°n\ *also* **bit; bit·ing** \'bī-tiŋ\ [Middle English, from Old English *bītan;* akin to Old High German *bīzan* to bite, Latin *findere* to split] (before 12th century)
*transitive verb*
**1 a** : to seize especially with teeth or jaws so as to enter, grip, or wound **b** : to wound, pierce, or sting especially with a fang or a proboscis
**2** : to cut or pierce with or as if with an edged weapon
**3** : to cause sharp pain or stinging discomfort to
**4** : to take hold of
**5** *archaic* : to take in : CHEAT
*intransitive verb*
**1** : to bite or have the habit of biting something
**2** *of a weapon or tool* : to cut, pierce, or take hold
**3** : to cause irritation or smarting
**4** : CORRODE
**5 a** *of fish* : to take a bait **b** : to respond so as to be caught (as by a trick)
**6** : to take or maintain a firm hold
— **bit·er** \'bī-tər\ *noun*
— **bite off more than one can chew** : to undertake more than one can perform
— **bite the bullet** : to enter with resignation upon a difficult or distressing course of action
— **bite the dust 1** : to fall dead especially in battle **2** : to suffer humiliation or defeat
— **bite the hand that feeds one** : to injure a benefactor maliciously
**²bite** *noun* (15th century)
**1** : the act or manner of biting
**2** : FOOD: as **a** : the amount of food taken at a bite : MORSEL **b** : a small amount of food : SNACK
**3** *archaic* **a** : CHEAT, TRICK **b** : SHARPER
**4** : a wound made by biting
**5** : the hold or grip by which friction is created or purchase is obtained
**6** : a surface that creates friction or is brought into contact with another for the purpose of obtaining a hold
**7 a** : a keen incisive quality **b** : a sharp penetrating effect
**8** : a single exposure of an etcher's plate to the corrosive action of acid
**9** : an amount taken usually in one operation for one purpose : CUT
**bite·wing** \'bīt-,wiŋ\ *noun* (1938)
: a dental X-ray film designed to show the crowns of the upper and lower teeth simultaneously
**bit·ing** \'bī-tiŋ\ *adjective* (14th century)
: having the power to bite ⟨a *biting* wind⟩; *especially* : able to grip and impress deeply ⟨the report is *biting* in its intolerance of deceit⟩
— **bit·ing·ly** \-tiŋ-lē\ *adverb*
**biting louse** *noun* (1896)
: any of numerous wingless insects (order Mallophaga) that are parasitic especially on birds — called also *bird louse*
**biting midge** *noun* (1945)
: any of a family (Ceratopogonidae) of tiny biting dipteran flies of which some are vectors of filarial worms
**bit·stock** \'bit-,stäk\ *noun* (circa 1887)
: BRACE 3
**bit·sy** \'bit-sē\ *adjective* [itsy-bitsy] (1905)
: TINY
**¹bitt** \'bit\ *noun* [perhaps from Old Norse *biti* beam; akin to Old English *bōt* boat] (14th century)

**1** : a post or pair of posts fixed on the deck of a ship for securing lines
**2** : BOLLARD 1
²**bitt** transitive verb (1769)
: to make (a cable) fast about a bitt
¹**bit·ter** \'bi-tər\ adjective [Middle English, from Old English biter; akin to Old High German bittar bitter, Old English bītan] (before 12th century)
**1 a** : being or inducing the one of the four basic taste sensations that is peculiarly acrid, astringent, or disagreeable and suggestive of an infusion of hops — compare SALT, SOUR, SWEET **b** : distasteful or distressing to the mind : GALLING ⟨a bitter sense of shame⟩
**2** : marked by intensity or severity: **a** : accompanied by severe pain or suffering ⟨a bitter death⟩ **b** : being relentlessly determined : VEHEMENT ⟨a bitter partisan⟩ **c** : exhibiting intense animosity ⟨bitter enemies⟩ **d** (1) : harshly reproachful ⟨bitter complaints⟩ (2) : marked by cynicism and rancor ⟨bitter contempt⟩ **e** : intensely unpleasant especially in coldness or rawness
**3** : expressive of severe pain, grief, or regret ⟨bitter tears⟩
— **bit·ter·ish** \'bi-tə-rish\ adjective
— **bit·ter·ly** adverb
— **bit·ter·ness** noun
²**bitter** noun (before 12th century)
**1** : bitter quality
**2 a** plural : a usually alcoholic solution of bitter and often aromatic plant products used especially in preparing mixed drinks or as a mild tonic **b** British : a very dry heavily hopped ale
³**bitter** transitive verb (12th century)
: to make bitter ⟨bittered ale⟩
⁴**bitter** adverb (1749)
: to a bitter degree ⟨it's bitter cold⟩
**bitter almond** noun (1632)
: an almond with a bitter taste that contains amygdalin; also : a tree (Prunus dulcis amara) producing bitter almonds
**bit·ter·brush** \'bi-tər-ˌbrəsh\ noun (1910)
: a much-branched silvery shrub (Purshia tridentata) of arid western North America that has 3-toothed leaves and yellow flowers and is valuable for forage
**bitter cress** noun (circa 1890)
: any of a genus (Cardamine) of cruciferous herbs that produce flat pods and wingless seeds
¹**bitter end** noun [probably from ²bitter end] (1849)
: the last extremity however painful or calamitous
— **bit·ter-end·er** \ˌbi-tər-'en-dər\ noun
²**bitter end** noun [bitter (a turn of cable around the bitts)] (circa 1862)
: the inboard end of a ship's anchoring cable
¹**bit·tern** \'bi-tərn\ noun [Middle English bitoure, from Middle French butor, from (assumed) Vulgar Latin butitaurus, from Latin buteo hawk + taurus bull] (1515)
: any of various small or medium-sized usually secretive herons (especially genera Botaurus and Ixobrychus)
²**bittern** noun [irregular from ¹bitter] (1682)
: the bitter water solution of salts that remains after sodium chloride has crystallized out of a brine
**bit·ter·root** \'bi-tə(r)-ˌrüt, -ˌrut\ noun (1838)
: a succulent herb (Lewisia rediviva) of mountainous slopes of western North America that has starchy roots and pink or white flowers
¹**bit·ter·sweet** \'bi-tər-ˌswēt\ noun (14th century)
**1** : something that is bittersweet; especially : pleasure alloyed with pain
**2 a** : a sprawling poisonous weedy nightshade (Solanum dulcamara) with purple flowers and oval reddish orange berries **b** : a North American woody climbing plant (Celastrus scandens) of the staff-tree family having clusters

of small greenish flowers succeeded by yellow capsules that open when ripe and disclose the scarlet aril
²**bittersweet** adjective (1611)
**1** : being at once bitter and sweet; especially : pleasant but including or marked by elements of suffering or regret ⟨a bittersweet ballad⟩
**2** : of or relating to a prepared chocolate containing little sugar
— **bit·ter·sweet·ly** adverb
— **bit·ter·sweet·ness** noun
**bit·ter·weed** \'bi-tər-ˌwēd\ noun (1819)
: any of several American plants containing a bitter substance: as **a** : HORSEWEED **b** : a sneezeweed (Helenium amarum synonym H. tenuifolium) **c** : an erect composite herb (Hymenoxys odorata) of the southwestern U.S. that has yellow terminal flowerheads and is poisonous to livestock
**bit·tock** \'bi-tək\ noun (circa 1802)
chiefly Scottish : a little bit
¹**bit·ty** \'bi-tē\ adjective (1892)
chiefly British : made up of or containing bits; especially : not cohesive or flowing
²**bitty** adjective (1905)
: SMALL, TINY ⟨a little bitty room⟩
**bi·tu·men** \bə-'tyü-mən, bī-, -'tü-, especially British also 'bit-yə-\ noun [Middle English bithumen mineral pitch, from Latin bitumin-, bitumen] (15th century)
**1** : an asphalt of Asia Minor used in ancient times as a cement and mortar
**2** : any of various mixtures of hydrocarbons (as tar) often together with their nonmetallic derivatives that occur naturally or are obtained as residues after heat-refining natural substances (as petroleum); specifically : such a mixture soluble in carbon disulfide
— **bi·tu·mi·ni·za·tion** \bə-ˌtyü-mə-nə-'zāshən, bī-, -ˌtü-\ noun
— **bi·tu·mi·nize** \-'tyü-mə-ˌnīz, -'tü-\ transitive verb
**bi·tu·mi·nous** \bə-'tyü-mə-nəs, bī-, -'tü-\ adjective (1620)
**1** : containing or impregnated with bitumen
**2** : of or relating to bituminous coal
**bituminous coal** noun (1827)
: a coal that when heated yields considerable volatile bituminous matter — called also soft coal
**bi·unique** \ˌbī-yü-'nēk\ adjective (1941)
: being a correspondence between two sets that is one-to-one in both directions
— **bi·unique·ness** noun
¹**bi·va·lent** \ˌ(ˌ)bī-'vā-lənt, 'bī-və-\ adjective (1869)
**1** : DIVALENT
**2** : associated in pairs in synapsis
²**bivalent** noun (circa 1934)
: a pair of synaptic chromosomes
¹**bi·valve** \'bī-ˌvalv\ adjective (1661)
: having a shell composed of two valves
²**bivalve** noun (1683)
: an animal (as a clam) with a 2-valved shell
**bi·var·i·ate** \ˌ(ˌ)bī-'ver-ē-ət, -'var-\ adjective (1920)
: of, relating to, or involving two variables ⟨a bivariate frequency distribution⟩
**biv·ouac** \'bi-və-ˌwak, 'biv-ˌwak\ noun [French, from Low German biwacht, from bi by + wacht guard] (circa 1702)
**1** : a usually temporary encampment under little or no shelter
**2 a** : encampment usually for a night **b** : temporary shelter or settlement
²**bivouac** intransitive verb **-ouacked; -ouack·ing** (1809)
: to make a bivouac : CAMP
¹**bi·week·ly** \ˌ(ˌ)bī-'wē-klē\ adjective (1832)
**1** : occurring twice a week
**2** : occurring every two weeks : FORTNIGHTLY
**usage** see BI-
— **biweekly** adverb
²**biweekly** noun (circa 1890)

**1** : a publication issued every two weeks
**2** : SEMIWEEKLY
**bi·year·ly** \ˌ(ˌ)bī-'yir-lē\ adjective (circa 1909)
**1** : BIANNUAL 1
**2** : BIENNIAL 1
**biz** \'biz\ noun (1862)
: BUSINESS
¹**bi·zarre** \bə-'zär\ adjective [French, from Italian bizzarro] (circa 1648)
: strikingly out of the ordinary: as **a** : odd, extravagant, or eccentric in style or mode **b** : involving sensational contrasts or incongruities
**synonym** see FANTASTIC
— **bi·zarre·ly** adverb
— **bi·zarre·ness** noun
²**bizarre** noun (circa 1753)
: a flower with atypical striped marking
**bi·zar·re·rie** \bi-ˌzär-ə-'rē\ noun [French] (1747)
**1** : a bizarre quality
**2** : something bizarre
**bi·zon·al** \ˌ(ˌ)bī-'zō-n°l\ adjective (1946)
: of or relating to the affairs of a zone governed or administered by two powers acting together
— **bi·zone** \'bī-ˌzōn\ noun
¹**blab** \'blab\ noun [Middle English blabbe; akin to Middle English blaberen] (14th century)
**1** archaic : one that blabs : TATTLETALE
**2** : idle or excessive talk : CHATTER
— **blab·by** \'bla-bē\ adjective
²**blab** verb **blabbed; blab·bing** (15th century)
intransitive verb
**1** : to talk idly or thoughtlessly : PRATTLE
**2** : to reveal a secret especially by indiscreet chatter
transitive verb
: to reveal especially without reserve or discretion ⟨blabbed the whole affair to the press⟩
¹**blab·ber** \'bla-bər\ verb **blab·bered; blab·ber·ing** \-b(ə-)riŋ\ [Middle English blaberen] (14th century)
intransitive verb
: to talk foolishly or excessively
transitive verb
: to say indiscreetly
²**blabber** noun (circa 1913)
: idle talk : BABBLE
³**blabber** noun [²blab] (1557)
: one that blabs
**blab·ber·mouth** \'bla-bər-ˌmauth\ noun (1936)
: a person who talks too much; especially : TATTLETALE
¹**black** \'blak\ adjective [Middle English blak, from Old English blæc; akin to Old High German blah black, and probably to Latin flagrare to burn, Greek phlegein] (before 12th century)
**1 a** : of the color black **b** (1) : very dark in color ⟨his face was black with rage⟩ (2) : having a very deep or low register ⟨a bass with a black voice⟩ (3) : HEAVY, SERIOUS ⟨the play was a black intrigue⟩
**2 a** : having dark skin, hair, and eyes : SWARTHY ⟨the black Irish⟩ **b** (1) often capitalized : of or relating to any of various population groups having dark pigmentation of the skin ⟨black Americans⟩ (2) : of or relating to the Afro-American people or their culture ⟨black literature⟩ ⟨a black college⟩ ⟨black pride⟩ ⟨black studies⟩ (3) : typical or representative of the most readily attended parts of black culture ⟨tried to play blacker jazz⟩
**3** : dressed in black
**4** : DIRTY, SOILED ⟨hands black with grime⟩

| | | | | | |
|---|---|---|---|---|---|
| \ə\ abut | \ᵊ\ kitten | \ər\ further | \a\ ash | \ā\ ace | |
| \ä\ mop, mar | \au̇\ out | \ch\ chin | \e\ bet | \ē\ easy | |
| \g\ go | \i\ hit | \ī\ ice | \j\ job | \ŋ\ sing | \ō\ go |
| \ȯ\ law | \ȯi\ boy | \th\ thin | \t̲h\ the | \ü\ loot | \u̇\ foot |
| \y\ yet | \zh\ vision | | see also Guide to Pronunciation | | |

**5 a :** characterized by the absence of light ⟨a *black* night⟩ **b :** reflecting or transmitting little or no light ⟨*black* water⟩ **c :** served without milk or cream ⟨*black* coffee⟩
**6 a :** thoroughly sinister or evil **:** WICKED ⟨a *black* deed⟩ **b :** indicative of condemnation or discredit ⟨got a *black* mark for being late⟩
**7 :** connected with or invoking the supernatural and especially the devil ⟨*black* magic⟩
**8 a :** very sad, gloomy, or calamitous ⟨*black* despair⟩ **b :** marked by the occurrence of disaster ⟨*black* Friday⟩
**9 :** characterized by hostility or angry discontent **:** SULLEN ⟨*black* resentment filled his heart⟩
**10** *chiefly British* **:** subject to boycott by trade-union members as employing or favoring nonunion workers or as operating under conditions considered unfair by the trade union
**11 a** *of propaganda* **:** conducted so as to appear to originate within an enemy country and designed to weaken enemy morale **b :** characterized by or connected with the use of black propaganda ⟨*black* radio⟩
**12 :** characterized by grim, distorted, or grotesque satire ⟨*black* humor⟩
**13 :** of or relating to covert intelligence operations ⟨*black* government programs⟩
— **black·ish** \'bla-kish\ *adjective*
— **black·ly** *adverb*
— **black·ness** *noun*
²**black** *noun* (before 12th century)
**1 :** a black pigment or dye; *especially* **:** one consisting largely of carbon
**2 :** the achromatic color of least lightness characteristically perceived to belong to objects that neither reflect nor transmit light
**3 :** something that is black: **a :** black clothing ⟨looks good in *black*⟩ **b :** a black animal (as a horse)
**4 a :** a person belonging to any of various population groups having dark pigmentation of the skin **b :** AFRO-AMERICAN
**5 :** the pieces of a dark color in a board game for two players (as chess)
**6 :** total or nearly total absence of light ⟨the *black* of night⟩
**7 :** the condition of making a profit — usually used with *the* ⟨operating in the *black*⟩; compare RED
³**black** (13th century)
*intransitive verb*
**:** to become black
*transitive verb*
**1 :** to make black
**2** *chiefly British* **:** to declare (as a business or industry) subject to boycott by trade-union members
**black alder** *noun* (1805)
**:** WINTERBERRY 1
**black·a·moor** \'bla-kə-ˌmùr\ *noun* [irregular from *black* + *Moor*] (1547)
**:** a dark-skinned person; *especially* **:** BLACK 4a
**black–and–blue** \ˌbla-kən-'blü\ *adjective* (14th century)
**:** darkly discolored from blood effused by bruising
**black–and–tan** \-kən-'tan\ *adjective* (1850)
**1 :** having a predominantly black color pattern with deep red or rusty tan on the feet, breeching, and cheek patches, above the eyes, and inside the ears
**2 :** favoring or practicing proportional representation of whites and blacks in politics
**3 :** frequented by both blacks and whites ⟨a *black-and-tan* bar⟩
**black and tan** *noun* (1870)
**1 :** a black-and-tan animal (as a dog)
**2** *chiefly British* **:** a drink consisting of a dark beer (as stout or porter) and ale or beer
**3** *B&T capitalized* [from the color of his uniform] **:** a recruit enlisted in England in 1920–21 for service in the Royal Irish Constabulary against the armed movement for Irish independence

**4 :** a member of a black-and-tan political organization (as in the southern U.S.) — compare LILY-WHITE
**black–and–tan coonhound** *noun* (1948)
**:** any of a breed of strong vigorous coonhounds of American origin with black-and-tan markings
**black–and–white** \ˌbla-kən-'hwīt, -'wīt\ *adjective* (1612)
**1 :** being in writing or print
**2 :** partly black and partly white in color
**3 :** executed in dark pigment on a light background or in light pigment on a dark ground ⟨a *black-and-white* drawing⟩
**4 :** MONOCHROME 2a ⟨*black-and-white* film⟩ ⟨*black-and-white* television⟩
**5 a :** sharply divided into good and evil **b :** evaluating or viewing things as either all good or all bad ⟨*black-and-white* morality⟩ **c :** sharply defined **:** CLEAR-CUT ⟨the truth is not always *black-and-white*⟩
**black and white** *noun* (1599)
**1 :** WRITING, PRINT
**2 :** a drawing or print done in black and white or in monochrome
**3 :** monochrome reproduction of visual images (as by photography or television)
**Black Angus** *noun* (1948)
**:** ANGUS
**black–a–vised** \'bla-kə-ˌvīst\ *adjective* [*black* + French *à vis* as to face] (circa 1758)
**:** having a dark complexion
¹**black·ball** \'blak-ˌból\ *transitive verb* (1770)
**1 :** to vote against; *especially* **:** to exclude from membership by casting a negative vote
**2 a :** to exclude socially **:** OSTRACIZE **b :** BOYCOTT
²**blackball** *noun* (circa 1847)
**1 :** a small black ball for use as a negative vote in a ballot box
**2 :** an adverse vote especially against admitting someone to membership in an organization
**black bass** *noun* (1815)
**:** any of a genus (*Micropterus*) of freshwater sunfishes native to eastern and central North America and including the largemouth bass and smallmouth bass
**black bean** *noun* (1792)
**1 :** a black kidney bean commonly used in Latin American cuisine
**2 :** a black soybean commonly used in oriental cuisine
**black bear** *noun* (1781)
**:** the common American bear (*Ursus americanus*) ranging in color from brown or typical black to white
**black beast** *noun* (1926)
**:** BÊTE NOIRE
¹**black belt** \'blak-ˌbelt\ *noun* (1870)
**1 :** an area characterized by rich black soil
**2** *often both Bs capitalized* **:** an area densely populated by blacks
²**black belt** *noun* (1954)
**:** one who holds the rating of expert in various arts of self-defense (as judo and karate); *also* **:** the rating itself
**black·ber·ry** \'blak-ˌber-ē\ *noun* (before 12th century)
**1 :** the usually black or dark purple juicy but seedy edible aggregate fruit of various brambles (genus *Rubus*) of the rose family
**2 :** a plant that bears blackberries
**black bile** *noun* (1797)
**:** a humor of medieval physiology believed to be secreted by the kidneys or spleen and to cause melancholy
**black birch** *noun* (1674)
**:** SWEET BIRCH
¹**black·bird** \'blak-ˌbərd\ *noun* (14th century)

**1 :** any of various birds of which the males are largely or entirely black: as **a :** a common thrush (*Turdus merula*) of Eurasia and northern Africa having an orange bill and eye rim **b :** any of several American birds (family Icteridae)
**2 :** a Pacific islander kidnapped for use as a plantation laborer
²**blackbird** *intransitive verb* (1894)
**:** to engage in the slave trade especially in the South Pacific
**black·bird·er** *noun* (1880)
**1 :** a person who blackbirds
**2 :** a ship used in blackbirding
**black·board** \'blak-ˌbórd, -ˌbòrd\ *noun* (1823)
**:** a hard smooth usually dark surface used especially in a classroom for writing or drawing on with chalk
**black·body** \'blak-'bä-dē\ *noun* (1710)
**:** an ideal body or surface that completely absorbs all radiant energy falling upon it with no reflection and that radiates at all frequencies with a spectral energy distribution dependent on its absolute temperature
**black book** *noun* (1592)
**:** a book containing a blacklist
**black box** *noun* (circa 1945)
**1 :** a usually complicated electronic device that functions and is packaged as a unit and whose internal mechanism is usually hidden from or mysterious to the user; *broadly* **:** anything that has mysterious or unknown internal functions or mechanisms
**2 :** a crashworthy device in aircraft for recording cockpit conversations and flight data
**black·cap** \'blak-ˌkap\ *noun* (1678)
**1 :** any of several birds with black heads or crowns: as **a :** a small European warbler (*Sylvia atricapilla*) with a black crown **b :** CHICKADEE
**2 :** BLACK RASPBERRY
**black–capped** \-'kapt\ *adjective* (1781)
*of a bird* **:** having the top of the head black
**black·cock** \-ˌkäk\ *noun* (15th century)
*chiefly British* **:** BLACK GROUSE; *specifically* **:** the male black grouse
**black cohosh** *noun* (1828)
**:** a bugbane (*Cimicifuga racemosa*) of the eastern U.S.
**black crappie** *noun* (circa 1827)
**:** a silvery black-mottled sunfish (*Pomoxis nigromaculatus*) of the Mississippi drainage and eastern U.S. having seven or eight protruding spines on the dorsal fins
**black–crowned night heron** \'blak-ˌkraúnd-\ *noun* (1844)
**:** a widely distributed night heron (*Nycticorax nycticorax*) having a black crown and back
**black damp** *noun* (1836)
**:** a carbon dioxide mixture occurring as a mine gas and incapable of supporting life or flame
**black death** *noun, often B&D capitalized* [from the black patches formed on the skin of its victims] (1780)
**1 :** PLAGUE 2b
**2 :** a severe epidemic of plague and especially bubonic plague that occurred in Asia and Europe in the 14th century
**black diamond** *noun* (1763)
**1 :** dense black hematite
**2** *plural* **:** COAL 3a
**3 :** ³CARBONADO
**black duck** *noun* (1637)
**:** any of several ducks that are dark in color; *especially* **:** a common brown duck (*Anas rubripes*) of eastern North America
**black dwarf** *noun, plural* **black dwarfs** (1945)
**:** a very small star that emits no detectable light
**black·en** \'bla-kən\ *verb* **black·ened**; **black·en·ing** \'blak-niŋ, 'bla-kə-\ (14th century)
*intransitive verb*

**black bear**

: to become dark or black ⟨the sky *blackens*⟩
*transitive verb*
**1 :** to make black
**2 :** DEFAME, SULLY
— **black·en·er** \'blak-nər, 'bla-kə-\ *noun*
**black·ened** \-kənd\ *adjective* (1984)
: coated with a mixture of cayenne pepper and spices and cooked in a frying pan over extremely high heat ⟨*blackened* redfish⟩
**Black English** *noun* (1969)
: a nonstandard variety of English spoken by some American blacks — called also *Black English vernacular*
**black·en·ing** \'blak-niŋ, 'bla-kə-\ *noun* (circa 1909)
: BLACKING
**black eye** *noun* (1604)
**1 :** a discoloration of the skin around the eye from bruising
**2 :** a bad reputation
**black–eyed pea** \'blak-ˌīd-\ *noun* (1728)
: COWPEA
**black–eyed Su·san** \-'sü-z°n\ *noun* (1892)
: either of two North American coneflowers (*Rudbeckia hirta* and *R. serotina*) having flower heads with deep yellow to orange rays and dark conical disks
**black·face** \'blak-ˌfās\ *noun* (1869)
: makeup applied to a performer playing a black person especially in a minstrel show; *also* : a performer wearing such makeup
**black·fish** \-ˌfish\ *noun* (1754)
**1 :** any of numerous dark-colored fishes: as **a** TAUTOG **b :** a small food fish (*Dallia pectoralis*) of Alaska and Siberia that is noted for its resistance to cold
**2 :** any of several small toothed whales (genus *Globicephala*) found in warm seas
**black–flag** \-'flag\ *transitive verb* (1963)
: to signal (a race-car driver) to go immediately to the pits
**black flag** *noun* (1720)
: a pirate's flag usually bearing a skull and crossbones
**black·fly** \'blak-ˌflī\ *noun, plural* **-flies** *or* **-fly** (1608)
: any of various small dark-colored insects; *especially* : any of a family (Simuliidae and especially genus *Simulium*) of bloodsucking dipteran flies whose larvae usually live in flowing streams
**Black·foot** \'blak-ˌfut\ *noun, plural* **Black-feet** *or* **Blackfoot** (1794)
**1 :** a member of an American Indian people of Montana, Alberta, and Saskatchewan
**2 :** the Algonquian language of the Blackfeet
**black–foot·ed albatross** \'blak-ˌfu-təd-\ *noun* (1839)
: an albatross (*Diomedea nigripes*) of the Pacific that is chiefly blackish with dusky bill and black feet and legs — called also *gooney*
**black–footed ferret** *noun* (1846)
: a rare weasel (*Mustela nigripes*) of western North American prairies having a yellow-ish coat, dark feet and facial mask, and a dark-tipped tail

**black-footed ferret**

**black gold** *noun* (1910)
: PETROLEUM
**black grouse** *noun* (1678)
: a large grouse (*Lyrurus tetrix*) of western Asia and Europe of which the male is black with white wing patches and the female is barred and mottled
**¹black·guard** \'bla-gərd, -ˌgärd; 'blak-ˌgärd\ *noun* (1535)
**1** *obsolete* : the kitchen servants of a household
**2 a :** a rude or unscrupulous person **b :** a person who uses foul or abusive language

— **black·guard·ism** \-gər-ˌdi-zəm, -ˌgär-\ *noun*
— **black·guard·ly** \-gərd-lē, -ˌgärd-\ *adjective or adverb*
**²blackguard** *transitive verb* (1823)
: to talk about or address in abusive terms
**black gum** *noun* (1709)
: a tupelo (*Nyssa sylvatica*) of the eastern U.S. with light and soft but tough wood
**black hand** *noun, often B&H capitalized* [*Black Hand*, a Sicilian and Italian-American secret society of the late 19th and 20th centuries] (1904)
: a lawless secret society engaged in criminal activities (as terrorism or extortion)
— **black·hand·er** \'blak-ˌhan-dər\ *noun*
**black·head** \'blak-ˌhed\ *noun* (circa 1837)
**1 :** a small plug of sebum blocking the duct of a sebaceous gland especially on the face
**2 :** a destructive disease of turkeys and related birds caused by a protozoan (*Histomonas meleagridis*) that invades the intestinal ceca and liver
**3 :** a larval clam or mussel attached to the skin or gills of a freshwater fish
**black·heart** \-ˌhärt\ *noun* (1909)
: a plant disease in which the central tissues blacken
**black hole** *noun* (1968)
**1 :** a hypothetical celestial object with a gravitational field so strong that light cannot escape from it which is believed to be created in the collapse of a very massive star
**2 :** something resembling a black hole: as **a** : something that consumes a resource continually ⟨a financial *black hole*⟩ **b :** an empty space : VOID
**black ice** *noun* (1961)
: a thin film of ice on paved surfaces (as roads) that is difficult to see
**black·ing** \'bla-kiŋ\ *noun* (1571)
: a substance (as a paste or polish) that is applied to an object to make it black
**¹black·jack** \-ˌjak\ *noun* (1591)
**1** [*black* + *jack* (vessel)] : a tankard for beer or ale usually of tar-coated leather
**2 :** SPHALERITE
**3 :** a hand weapon typically consisting of a piece of leather-enclosed metal with a strap or springy shaft for a handle
**4 :** an often scrubby oak (*Quercus marilandica*) chiefly of the southeastern U.S. — called also *blackjack oak*
**5 :** a card game the object of which is to be dealt cards having a higher count than those of the dealer up to but not exceeding 21 — called also *twenty-one, vingt-et-un*
**²blackjack** *transitive verb* (1905)
**1 :** to strike with a blackjack
**2 :** to coerce with threats or pressure
**black·land** \'blak-ˌland\ *noun* (1803)
**1 :** a heavy sticky black soil such as that covering large areas in Texas
**2** *plural* : a region of blackland
**black·lead** \'blak-ˌled\ *noun* (1583)
*chiefly British* : GRAPHITE 1
**black·leg** \'blak-ˌleg, -ˌlāg\ *noun* (circa 1722)
**1 :** a usually fatal toxemia especially of young cattle caused by a soil bacterium (*Clostridium chauvoei*)
**2 :** a cheating gambler : SWINDLER
**3** *chiefly British* : a worker hostile to trade unionism or acting in opposition to union policies : SCAB
**black letter** *noun* (circa 1644)
: a heavy angular condensed typeface used especially by the earliest European printers and based on handwriting used chiefly in the 13th to 15th centuries; *also* : this style of handwriting
**black light** *noun* (1927)

## mnopqrstuv

**black letter**

**1 :** invisible ultraviolet light
**2 :** a lamp that radiates black light
**black·light trap** \'blak-ˌlīt-\ *noun* (1961)
: a trap for insects that uses a form of black light perceptible to particular insects as an attractant
**¹black·list** \-ˌlist\ *noun* (circa 1619)
: a list of persons who are disapproved of or are to be punished or boycotted
**²blacklist** *transitive verb* (1718)
: to put on a blacklist
— **black·list·er** *noun*
**black locust** *noun* (1787)
: a tall tree (*Robinia pseudoacacia*) of eastern North America with pinnately compound leaves, drooping racemes of fragrant white flowers, and strong stiff wood
**black lung** *noun* (1837)
: pneumoconiosis caused by habitual inhalation of coal dust
**black·mail** \'blak-ˌmāl\ *noun* [*black* + ¹*mail*] (1552)
**1 :** a tribute anciently exacted on the Scottish border by freebooting chiefs for immunity from pillage
**2 a :** extortion or coercion by threats especially of public exposure or criminal prosecution **b :** the payment that is extorted
— **blackmail** *transitive verb*
— **black·mail·er** *noun*
**Black Ma·ria** \ˌblak-mə-'rī-ə\ *noun* (1847)
: PADDY WAGON
**black–mar·ket** (1943)
*intransitive verb*
: to buy or sell goods in the black market
*transitive verb*
: to sell in the black market
— **black marketer** *or* **black marke-teer** \-ˌmär-kə-'tir\ *noun*
**black market** *noun* (1931)
: illicit trade in goods or commodities in violation of official regulations; *also* : a place where such trade is carried on
**Black Mass** *noun* (1893)
: a travesty of the Christian mass ascribed to worshipers of Satan
**Black Muslim** *noun* (1960)
: a member of a chiefly black group that professes Islamic religious belief
**black nationalist** *noun, often B&N capitalized* (1963)
: a member of a group of militant blacks who advocate separatism from the whites and the formation of self-governing black communities
— **black nationalism** *noun, often B&N capitalized*
**black·out** \'blak-ˌaut\ *noun* (1913)
**1 a :** a turning off of the stage lighting to separate scenes in a play or end a play or skit; *also* : a skit that ends with a blackout **b :** a period of darkness enforced as a precaution against air raids **c :** a period of darkness (as in a city) caused by a failure of electrical power
**2 :** a transient dulling or loss of vision, consciousness, or memory ⟨an alcoholic *blackout*⟩
**3 a :** a wiping out : OBLITERATION **b :** a blotting out by censorship : SUPPRESSION ⟨a news *blackout*⟩
**4 :** a usually temporary loss of a radio signal
**5 :** the prohibition or restriction of the telecasting of a sports event
**black out** *noun* (1921)
*intransitive verb*
**1 :** to become enveloped in darkness

\ə\ abut \°\ kitten \ər\ further \a\ ash \ā\ ace \ä\ mop, mar \au̇\ out \ch\ chin \e\ bet \ē\ easy \g\ go \i\ hit \ī\ ice \j\ job \ŋ\ sing \ō\ go \ȯ\ law \ȯi\ boy \th\ thin \t͟h\ the \ü\ loot \u̇\ foot \y\ yet \zh\ vision *see also* Guide to Pronunciation

**2 :** to undergo a temporary loss of vision, consciousness, or memory
*transitive verb*
**1 :** to cause to black out ⟨*black out* the stage⟩
**2 :** to make inoperative (as by a power failure)
**3 a :** BLOT OUT, ERASE ⟨*blacked out* the event from his mind⟩ **b :** to suppress by censorship ⟨*black out* the news⟩
**4 :** to impose a blackout on
**Black Panther** *noun* (1965)
**:** a member of an organization of militant American blacks
**black pepper** *noun* (before 12th century)
**:** a spice that consists of the fruit of an East Indian plant (*Piper nigrum*) ground with the black husk still on
**black·poll** \'blak-,pōl\ *noun* (1783)
**:** a North American warbler (*Dendroica striata*) with the male having a black cap when in breeding plumage
**black powder** *noun* (circa 1909)
**:** an explosive mixture of potassium nitrate or sodium nitrate, charcoal, and sulfur used especially in fireworks and as a propellant in antique firearms — compare GUNPOWDER
**black power** *noun, often B&P capitalized* (1966)
**:** the mobilization of the political and economic power of American blacks especially to compel respect for their rights and improve their condition
**black pudding** *noun* (1568)
*chiefly British* **:** BLOOD SAUSAGE
**black racer** *noun* (1849)
**:** an American blacksnake (*Coluber constrictor constrictor*) common in the eastern U.S.
**black raspberry** *noun* (circa 1782)
**:** a raspberry (*Rubus occidentalis*) of eastern North America that has a purplish black fruit and is the source of several cultivated varieties — called also *blackcap*
**black rhinoceros** *noun* (1850)
**:** a rhinoceros (*Diceros bicornis*) of sub-Saharan Africa having a prehensile upper lip that protrudes in the middle — called also *black rhino*
**Black Rod** *noun* (circa 1607)
**:** the principal usher of the House of Lords
**black rot** *noun* (1849)
**:** a bacterial or fungal rot of plants marked by dark brown discoloration
**black sheep** *noun* (1792)
**:** a discreditable member of a respectable group
**Black·shirt** \'blak-,shərt\ *noun* (1922)
**:** a member of a fascist organization having a black shirt as a distinctive part of its uniform; *especially* **:** a member of the Italian Fascist party
**black·smith** \'blak-,smith\ *noun* [from a distinction between black metal (iron) and white metal (tin)] (15th century)
**:** a smith who forges iron
**— black·smith·ing** \-,smi-thiŋ\ *noun*
**black smoker** *noun* (1980)
**:** a vent in a geologically active region of the sea floor from which issues superheated water laden with minerals (as sulfide precipitates)
**black·snake** \-,snāk\ *noun* (1634)
**1 :** any of several snakes that are largely black or very dark in color; *especially* **:** either of two harmless snakes (*Coluber constrictor* and *Elaphe obsoleta*) of the U.S.
**2 :** a long tapering braided whip of rawhide or leather
**black spot** *noun* (circa 1889)
**:** any of several bacterial or fungal diseases of plants characterized by black spots or blotches especially on the leaves
**black·tail** \'blak-,tāl\ *noun* (1828)
**:** BLACK-TAILED DEER
**black–tailed deer** \'blak-,tāl(d)-\ *noun* (1806)

**:** MULE DEER; *specifically* **:** one of a subspecies (*Odocoileus hemionus columbianus*) especially of British Columbia, Oregon, and Washington
**black tea** *noun* (1789)
**:** tea that is dark in color from complete fermentation of the leaf before firing
**black·thorn** \'blak-,thȯrn\ *noun* (14th century)
**:** a European spiny plum (*Prunus spinosa*) with hard wood and small white flowers
**black–tie** *adjective* (1933)
**:** characterized by or requiring the wearing of semiformal evening clothes consisting of a usually black tie and tuxedo for men and a formal dress for women ⟨a *black-tie* dinner⟩ — compare WHITE-TIE
**black·top** \'blak-,täp\ *noun* (1931)
**:** a bituminous material used especially for surfacing roads; *also* **:** a surface paved with blacktop
**— blacktop** *transitive verb*
**Blackwall hitch** \'blak-,wȯl-\ *noun* [*Blackwall,* shipyard in London, England] (circa 1862)
**:** a hitch for securing a rope to a hook — see KNOT illustration
**black walnut** *noun* (1612)
**:** a walnut (*Juglans nigra*) of eastern North America with hard strong heavy dark brown wood and oily edible nuts; *also* **:** its wood or nut
**black·wa·ter** \'blak-,wȯ-tər, -,wä-\ *noun* (1800)
**:** any of several diseases (as blackwater fever) characterized by dark-colored urine
**blackwater fever** *noun* (1884)
**:** a febrile complication of repeated malarial attacks that is characterized especially by extensive kidney damage and urine discolored by heme from blood
**black widow** *noun* (1915)
**:** a venomous New World spider (*Latrodectus mactans*) the female of which is black with an hourglass-shaped red mark on the underside of the abdomen
**black·wood** \'blak-,wu̇d\ *noun* (1631)

**black widow**

**:** any of several hardwood trees (as the legumes *Acacia melanoxylon* and *Dalbergia latifolia*) or their dark-colored wood
**blad·der** \'bla-dər\ *noun* [Middle English, from Old English *blǣdre;* akin to Old High German *blātara* bladder, Old English *blāwan* to blow] (before 12th century)
**1 a :** a membranous sac in animals that serves as the receptacle of a liquid or contains gas; *especially* **:** URINARY BLADDER **b :** CYST 2b
**2 :** something (as the rubber bag inside a football) resembling a bladder
**— blad·der·like** \-,līk\ *adjective*
**bladder campion** *noun* (1817)
**:** an Old World campion (*Silene vulgaris* synonym *S. cucubalus*) with an inflated calyx introduced into temperate North America
**blad·der·nut** \'bla-dər-,nət\ *noun* (1578)
**:** any of a genus (*Staphylea* of the family Staphyleaceae, the bladdernut family) of ornamental shrubs or small trees with panicles of small white flowers followed by inflated capsules; *also* **:** one of the capsules
**bladder worm** *noun* (1858)
**:** a bladderlike larval tapeworm (as a cysticercus)
**blad·der·wort** \'bla-dər-,wərt, -,wȯrt\ *noun* (circa 1815)

**:** any of a genus (*Utricularia* of the family Lentibulariaceae, the bladderwort family) of chiefly aquatic plants with leaves usually having insect-trapping bladders
**bladder wrack** *noun* (1810)
**:** a common rockweed (*Fucus vesiculosus*) used in preparing kelp and as a manure
**blade** \'blād\ *noun* [Middle English, from Old English *blæd;* akin to Old High German *blat* leaf, Latin *folium*, Greek *phyllon*, Old English *blōwan* to blossom — more at BLOW] (before 12th century)
**1 a :** LEAF 1a(1); *especially* **:** the leaf of an herb or a grass **b :** the flat expanded part of a leaf as distinguished from the petiole
**2 :** something resembling the blade of a leaf: as **a :** the broad flattened part of an oar or paddle **b :** an arm of a screw propeller, electric fan, or steam turbine **c :** the broad flat or concave part of a machine (as a bulldozer or snowplow) that comes into contact with the material to be moved **d :** a broad flat body part; *specifically* **:** SCAPULA — used chiefly in naming cuts of meat **e :** the flat portion of the tongue immediately behind the tip; *also* **:** this portion together with the tip
**3 a :** the cutting part of an implement **b** (1) **:** SWORD (2) **:** SWORDSMAN (3) **:** a dashing lively man **c :** the runner of an ice skate
**— blade·like** \-,līk\ *adjective*
**blad·ed** \'blā-dəd\ *adjective* (1578)
**:** having blades — often used in combination ⟨five-*bladed* propeller⟩
**blae** \'blā\ *adjective* [Middle English *bla, blo,* from Old Norse *blār;* akin to Old High German *blāo* blue — more at BLUE] (13th century)
*chiefly Scottish* **:** dark blue or bluish gray
**blae·ber·ry** \'blā-,ber-ē, -,b(ə-)rē\ *noun* (15th century)
*chiefly Scottish* **:** WHORTLEBERRY 1
**¹blah** \'blä\ *noun* [imitative] (1918)
**1** *also* **blah–blah** \-,blä\ **:** silly or pretentious chatter or nonsense
**2** *plural* [perhaps influenced in meaning by *blasé*] **:** a feeling of boredom, lethargy, or general dissatisfaction
**²blah** *adjective* (1923)
**:** lacking interest **:** MEDIOCRE ⟨a *blah* winter day⟩
**blain** \'blān\ *noun* [Middle English, from Old English *blegen;* akin to Middle Low German *bleine* blain, Old English *blāwan* to blow] (before 12th century)
**:** an inflammatory swelling or sore
**blam·able** \'blā-mə-bəl\ *adjective* (14th century)
**:** deserving blame **:** REPREHENSIBLE
*synonym* see BLAMEWORTHY
**— blam·ably** \-blē\ *adverb*
**¹blame** \'blām\ *transitive verb* **blamed; blam·ing** [Middle English, from Old French *blamer*, from Late Latin *blasphemare* to blaspheme, from Greek *blasphēmein*] (13th century)
**1 :** to find fault with **:** CENSURE ⟨the right to praise or *blame* a literary work⟩
**2 a :** to hold responsible ⟨they *blame* me for everything⟩ **b :** to place responsibility for ⟨*blames* it on me⟩ ■
**— blam·er** *noun*
**— to blame :** at fault **:** RESPONSIBLE
**²blame** *noun* (13th century)
**1 :** an expression of disapproval or reproach **:** CENSURE
**2 a :** a state of being blameworthy **:** CULPABILITY **b** *archaic* **:** FAULT, SIN

☐ USAGE
**blame** Use of *blame* in sense 2b with *on* has occasionally been disparaged as wrong. Such disparagement is without basis; *blame on* occurs as frequently in carefully edited prose as *blame for*. Both forms are standard.

**3** : responsibility for something believed to deserve censure ⟨they must share the *blame*⟩
— **blame·less** \-ləs\ *adjective*
— **blame·less·ly** *adverb*
— **blame·less·ness** *noun*
**blame·ful** \'blām-fəl\ *adjective* (14th century)
: BLAMABLE
— **blame·ful·ly** \-fə-lē\ *adverb*
**blame·wor·thy** \-ˌwər-thē\ *adjective* (14th century)
: being at fault : deserving blame ☆
— **blame·wor·thi·ness** *noun*
**blanc fixe** \'blaŋk-'fiks\ *noun* [French, literally, fixed white] (1866)
: barium sulfate prepared as a heavy white powder and used especially as a filler in paper, rubber, and linoleum or as a pigment
**blanch** \'blanch\ *verb* [Middle English *blaunchen*, from Middle French *blanchir*, from Old French *blanche*, feminine of *blanc*, adjective, white — more at BLANK] (15th century)
*transitive verb*
: to take the color out of: as **a** : to bleach by excluding light ⟨*blanch* celery⟩ **b** : to scald or parboil in water or steam in order to remove the skin from, whiten, or stop enzymatic action in (as food for freezing) **c** : to make ashen or pale ⟨fear *blanches* the cheek⟩
*intransitive verb*
: to become white or pale
— **blanch·er** *noun*
**blanc·mange** \blə-'mänj, -'mä\n\zh\ *noun* [Middle English *blancmanger*, from Middle French *blanc manger*, literally, white food] (14th century)
: a usually sweetened and flavored dessert made from gelatinous or starchy ingredients and milk
**bland** \'bland\ *adjective* [Latin *blandus*] (1661)
**1 a** : smooth and soothing in manner or quality ⟨a *bland* smile⟩ **b** : exhibiting no personal concern or embarrassment : UNPERTURBED ⟨a *bland* confession of guilt⟩
**2 a** : not irritating, stimulating, or invigorating : SOOTHING **b** : DULL, INSIPID ⟨*bland* stories with little plot or action⟩
*synonym* see SUAVE
— **bland·ly** \'blan(d)-lē\ *adverb*
— **bland·ness** \'blan(d)-nəs\ *noun*
**blan·dish** \'blan-dish\ *verb* [Middle English, from Middle French *blandiss-*, stem of *blandir*, from Latin *blandiri*, from *blandus* mild, flattering] (14th century)
*transitive verb*
: to coax with flattery : CAJOLE
*intransitive verb*
: to act or speak in a flattering or coaxing manner
— **blan·dish·er** *noun*
**blan·dish·ment** \-dish-mənt\ *noun* (1591)
: something that tends to coax or cajole : ALLUREMENT — often used in plural
**¹blank** \'blaŋk\ *adjective* [Middle English, from Middle French *blanc* colorless, white, of Germanic origin; akin to Old High German *blanch* white; probably akin to Latin *flagrare* to burn — more at BLACK] (14th century)
**1** *archaic* : COLORLESS
**2 a** : appearing or causing to appear dazed, confounded, or nonplussed ⟨stared in *blank* dismay⟩ **b** : EXPRESSIONLESS ⟨a *blank* stare⟩
**3 a** : devoid of covering or content; *especially* : free from writing or marks ⟨*blank* paper⟩ **b** : having spaces to be filled in **c** : lacking interest, variety, or change ⟨*blank* hours⟩
**4** : ABSOLUTE, UNQUALIFIED ⟨a *blank* refusal⟩
**5** : UNFINISHED; *especially* : having a plain or unbroken surface where an opening is usual ⟨a *blank* key⟩ ⟨a *blank* arch⟩
*synonym* see EMPTY
— **blank·ly** *adverb*
— **blank·ness** *noun*
**²blank** *noun* (1554)
**1** *obsolete* : the bull's-eye of a target

**2 a** : an empty space (as on a paper) **b** : a paper with spaces for the entry of data ⟨an order *blank*⟩
**3 a** : a piece of material prepared to be made into something (as a key) by a further operation **b** : a cartridge loaded with propellant and a seal but no projectile
**4** : an empty or featureless place or space ⟨my mind was a *blank*⟩ **b** : a vacant or uneventful period ⟨a long *blank* in history⟩
**5** : a dash substituting for an omitted word
**³blank** (circa 1765)
*transitive verb*
**1 a** : OBSCURE, OBLITERATE ⟨*blank* out a line⟩ **b** : to stop access to : SEAL ⟨*blank* off a tunnel⟩
**2** : to keep (an opposing team) from scoring ⟨were *blanked* for eight innings⟩
*intransitive verb*
**1** : FADE — usually used with *out* ⟨the music *blanked* out⟩
**2** : to become confused or abstracted — often used with *out* ⟨his mind *blanked* out momentarily⟩
**blank check** *noun* (1884)
**1** : complete freedom of action or control : CARTE BLANCHE
**2** : a signed check with the amount unspecified
**¹blan·ket** \'blaŋ-kət\ *noun* [Middle English, from Old French *blankete*, from *blanc*] (14th century)
**1 a** : a large usually oblong piece of woven fabric used as a bed covering **b** : a similar piece of fabric used as a body covering (as for an animal) ⟨a horse *blanket*⟩
**2** : something that resembles a blanket ⟨a *blanket* of fog⟩ ⟨a *blanket* of gloom⟩
**3** : a rubber or plastic sheet on the cylinder in an offset press that transfers the image to the surface being printed
— **blan·ket·like** \-ˌlīk\ *adjective*
**²blanket** *transitive verb* (1605)
**1** : to cover with or as if with a blanket ⟨new grass *blankets* the slope⟩
**2 a** : to cover so as to obscure, interrupt, suppress, or extinguish ⟨*blanket* a fire with foam⟩ **b** : to apply or cause to apply to uniformly despite wide separation or diversity among the elements included ⟨freight rates that *blanket* a region⟩ **c** : to cause to be included ⟨automatically *blanketed* into the insurance program⟩
**³blanket** *adjective* (1886)
**1** : covering all members of a group or class ⟨a *blanket* wage increase⟩
**2** : effective or applicable in all instances
**blan·ket·flow·er** \'blaŋ-kət-ˌflau̇(-ə)r\ *noun* (1879)
: GAILLARDIA
**blanket stitch** *noun* (1880)
: a buttonhole stitch with spaces of variable width used on materials too thick to hem
— **blanket–stitch** *transitive verb*

**blanket stitch**

**blank verse** *noun* (1588)
: unrhymed verse; *specifically* : unrhymed iambic pentameter verse
**blan·quette** \blä\n-'ket\ *noun* [French, from Provençal *blanqueto*, from *blanc* white, of Germanic origin; akin to Old High German *blanch* white] (1727)
: a stew of light meat or seafood in a white sauce ⟨*blanquette* of veal⟩ ⟨*blanquette* of lobster⟩
**¹blare** \'blar, 'bler\ *verb* **blared; blar·ing** [Middle English *bleren*; akin to Middle Dutch *blēren* to shout] (15th century)
*intransitive verb*
: to sound loud and strident ⟨radios *blaring*⟩
*transitive verb*
**1** : to sound or utter raucously ⟨sat *blaring* the car horn⟩
**2** : to proclaim flamboyantly ⟨headlines *blared* his defeat⟩

**²blare** *noun* (1809)
**1** : a loud strident noise
**2** : dazzling often garish brilliance
**3** : FLAMBOYANCE
**blar·ney** \'blär-nē\ *noun* [*Blarney stone*, a stone in Blarney Castle, near Cork, Ireland, held to bestow skill in flattery on those who kiss it] (1796)
**1** : skillful flattery : BLANDISHMENT
**2** : NONSENSE, HUMBUG ◆
— **blarney** *verb*
**bla·sé** \blä-'zā\ *also* **bla·se** *adjective* [French] (1819)
**1** : apathetic to pleasure or excitement as a result of excessive indulgence or enjoyment : WORLD-WEARY
**2** : SOPHISTICATED, WORLDLY-WISE
**3** : UNCONCERNED
*synonym* see SOPHISTICATED
**blas·pheme** \blas-'fēm, 'blas-ˌ\ *verb* **blas·phemed; blas·phem·ing** [Middle English *blasfemen*, from Late Latin *blasphemare* — more at BLAME] (14th century)
*transitive verb*
**1** : to speak of or address with irreverence
**2** : REVILE, ABUSE
*intransitive verb*
: to utter blasphemy
— **blas·phem·er** \-'fē-mər; 'blas-ˌfē-mər, -fə-mər\ *noun*
**blas·phe·mous** \'blas-fə-məs\ *adjective* (15th century)
: impiously irreverent : PROFANE
— **blas·phe·mous·ly** *adverb*
— **blas·phe·mous·ness** *noun*
**blas·phe·my** \'blas-fə-mē\ *noun, plural* **-mies** (13th century)

---

☆ SYNONYMS
**Blameworthy, blamable, guilty, culpable** mean deserving reproach or punishment. BLAMEWORTHY and BLAMABLE apply to any degree of reprehensibility ⟨conduct adjudged *blameworthy*⟩ ⟨an accident for which no one is *blamable*⟩. GUILTY implies responsibility for or consciousness of crime, sin, or, at the least, grave error or misdoing ⟨*guilty* of a breach of etiquette⟩. CULPABLE is weaker than *guilty* and is likely to connote malfeasance or errors of ignorance, omission, or negligence ⟨*culpable* neglect⟩.

---

◇ WORD HISTORY
**blarney** *Blarney* is the name of a town, a stream, and especially a castle, built in 1446, in County Cork, Ireland. Embedded in the southern wall of the castle's keep is a block of limestone, known as the Blarney Stone. Legend has it that anyone who manages to kiss the Blarney Stone (its position makes it not easily accessible) will be blessed with the gift of flattery or cajolery. The tradition of making a pilgrimage to the castle to kiss the Blarney Stone is supposedly based on a particular event in the castle's history. The story goes that in 1602 the lord of the castle contrived an endless series of plausible excuses and expressions of flattery to forestall a promised surrender of the castle to attacking English forces until help could arrive. The lack of historical evidence for the story has failed to stifle the claim that anyone who kisses the stone will acquire comparable persuasive powers.

---

\ə\ abut \ᵊ\ kitten \ər\ further \a\ ash \ā\ ace
\ä\ mop, mar \au̇\ out \ch\ chin \e\ bet \ē\ easy
\g\ go \i\ hit \ī\ ice \j\ job \ŋ\ sing \ō\ go
\ȯ\ law \ȯi\ boy \th\ thin \t͟h\ the \ü\ loot \u̇\ foot
\y\ yet \zh\ vision *see also* Guide to Pronunciation

**1 a :** the act of insulting or showing contempt or lack of reverence for God **b :** the act of claiming the attributes of deity
**2 :** irreverence toward something considered sacred or inviolable

¹**blast** \'blast\ *noun* [Middle English, from Old English *blǣst;* akin to Old High German *blāst* blast, *blāsan* to blow, Old English *blāwan* — more at BLOW] (before 12th century)
**1 a :** a violent gust of wind **b :** the effect or accompaniment (as sleet) of such a gust
**2 :** the sound produced by an impulsion of air through a wind instrument or whistle
**3 :** something resembling a gust of wind: as **a :** a stream of air or gas forced through a hole **b :** a vehement outburst **c :** the continuous blowing to which a charge of ore or metal is subjected in a blast furnace
**4 a :** a sudden pernicious influence or effect ⟨the *blast* of a huge epidemic⟩ **b :** a disease of plants that causes the foliage or flowers to wither
**5 a :** an explosion or violent detonation **b :** the violent effect produced in the vicinity of an explosion that consists of a wave of increased atmospheric pressure followed by a wave of decreased atmospheric pressure
**6 :** SPEED, CAPACITY, OPERATION ⟨go full *blast*⟩ ⟨in full *blast*⟩
**7 :** an enjoyably exciting experience, occasion, or event; *especially* **:** PARTY

²**blast** (14th century)
*intransitive verb*
**1 :** BLARE ⟨music *blasting* from the radio⟩
**2 :** to make a vigorous attack
**3 a :** to use an explosive **b :** SHOOT
**4 :** to hit a golf ball out of a sand trap with explosive force
*transitive verb*
**1 a :** to injure by or as if by the action of wind **b :** BLIGHT
**2 a :** to shatter by or as if by an explosive **b :** to remove, open, or form by or as if by an explosive **c :** SHOOT
**3 :** to attack vigorously
**4 :** to cause to blast off ⟨will *blast* themselves from the moon's surface⟩
**5 :** to hit vigorously and effectively
— **blast·er** *noun*

**blast-** *or* **blasto-** *combining form* [German, from Greek, from *blastos*]
**:** bud : budding : germ ⟨*blasto*disc⟩ ⟨*blast*ula⟩

**-blast** \,blast\ *noun combining form* [New Latin *-blastus,* from Greek *blastos* bud, shoot, from *blastanein* to bud, sprout]
**:** formative unit especially of living matter
**:** germ : cell : cell layer ⟨epi*blast*⟩

**blast·ed** *adjective* (1552)
**1 :** damaged by or as if by an explosive, lightning, wind, or supernatural force ⟨upon this *blasted* heath —Shakespeare⟩ ⟨a *blasted* apple tree⟩
**2 :** DAMNED, DETESTABLE ⟨this *blasted* weather⟩

**blas·te·ma** \bla-'stē-mə\ *noun, plural* **-mas** *or* **-ma·ta** \-mə-tə\ [New Latin, from Greek *blastēma* offshoot, from *blastanein*] (circa 1823)
**:** a mass of living substance capable of growth and differentiation
— **blas·te·mal** \-məl\ *or* **blas·te·mat·ic** \,blas-tə-'ma-tik\ *adjective*

**blast furnace** *noun* (1706)
**:** a furnace in which combustion is forced by a current of air under pressure; *especially* **:** one for the reduction of iron ore

**-blastic** *adjective combining form* [International Scientific Vocabulary, from *-blast*]
**:** having (such or so many) buds, germs, cells, or cell layers ⟨diplo*blastic*⟩

**blast·ie** \'blas-tē\ *noun* [Scots *blast* to wither, from ²*blast*] (1787)
*Scottish* **:** an ugly little creature

**blast·ment** \'blas(t)-mənt\ *noun* (1602)
*archaic* **:** a blighting influence

**blas·to·coel** *or* **blas·to·coele** \'blas-tə-,sēl\ *noun* [International Scientific Vocabulary] (1877)
**:** the cavity of a blastula — see BLASTULA illustration
— **blas·to·coe·lic** \,blas-tə-'sē-lik\ *adjective*

**blas·to·cyst** \'blas-tə-,sist\ *noun* (circa 1881)
**:** the modified blastula of a placental mammal

**blas·to·derm** \-,dərm\ *noun* [German, from *blast-* + *-derm*] (circa 1843)
**:** a blastodisc after completion of cleavage and formation of the blastocoel

**blas·to·der·mic vesicle** \'blas-tə-,dər-mik-\ *noun* (circa 1860)
**:** BLASTOCYST

**blas·to·disc** \'blas-tə-,disk\ *noun* (circa 1881)
**:** the embryo-forming portion of an egg with discoidal cleavage usually appearing as a small disc on the upper surface of the yolk mass — see EGG illustration

**blast-off** \'blas-,tȯf\ *noun* (1951)
**:** a blasting off (as of a rocket)

**blast off** *intransitive verb* (1951)
**:** TAKE OFF 2d — used especially of rocket-propelled missiles and vehicles

**blas·to·mere** \'blas-tə-,mir\ *noun* [International Scientific Vocabulary] (1877)
**:** a cell produced during cleavage of a fertilized egg

**blas·to·my·co·sis** \,blas-tə-,mī-'kō-səs\ *noun* [New Latin, from *Blastomyces,* fungus genus, from *blast-* + Greek *mykēs* fungus; akin to Greek *myxa* mucus — more at MUCUS] (circa 1900)
**:** any of several fungal infections; *especially* **:** an infectious disease caused by a fungus (*Blastomyces dermtitides*) that affects especially the lungs and skin

**blas·to·pore** \'blas-tə-,pōr, -,pȯr\ *noun* (1880)
**:** the opening of the archenteron
— **blas·to·por·ic** \-'pōr-ik, -'pȯr-\ *adjective*

**blas·to·spore** \'blas-tə-,spōr, -,spȯr\ *noun* [*blast-* + *spore*] (circa 1923)
**:** a fungal spore produced by budding

**blas·tu·la** \'blas-chə-lə\ *noun, plural* **-las** *or* **-lae** \-,lē\ [New Latin, from Greek *blastos*] (1887)
**:** an early metazoan embryo typically having the form of a hollow fluid-filled rounded cavity bounded by a single layer of cells — compare GASTRULA, MORULA
— **blas·tu·la·tion** \,blas-chə-'lā-shən\ *noun*

**blat** \'blat\ *verb* **blat·ted; blat·ting** [perhaps alteration of *bleat*] (1846)
*intransitive verb*
**1 :** to cry like a calf or sheep **:** BLEAT
**2 a :** to make a raucous noise **b :** BLAB
*transitive verb*
**:** to utter loudly or foolishly **:** BLURT
— **blat** *noun*

**bla·tan·cy** \'blā-tᵊn(t)-sē\ *noun, plural* **-cies** (1610)
**1 :** the quality or state of being blatant
**2 :** something that is blatant

**bla·tant** \'blā-tᵊnt\ *adjective* [perhaps from Latin *blatire* to chatter] (circa 1656)
**1 :** noisy especially in a vulgar or offensive manner **:** CLAMOROUS
**2 :** completely obvious, conspicuous, or obtrusive especially in a crass or offensive manner **:** BRAZEN
*synonym* see VOCIFEROUS
— **bla·tant·ly** *adverb*

**blate** \'blāt\ *adjective* [Middle English] (1535)
*chiefly Scottish* **:** TIMID, SHEEPISH

¹**blath·er** \'bla-thər\ *intransitive verb* **blath·ered; blath·er·ing** \-th(ə-)riŋ\ [Old Norse

*blathra;* akin to Middle High German *blōdern* to chatter] (1524)
**:** to talk foolishly at length — often used with *on*
— **blath·er·er** \-thər-ər\ *noun*

²**blather** *noun* (1719)
**1 :** voluble nonsensical or inconsequential talk or writing
**2 :** STIR, COMMOTION

**blath·er·skite** \'bla-thər-,skīt\ *noun* [*blather* + Scots dialect *skate* a contemptible person] (circa 1650)
**1 :** a person who blathers a lot
**2 :** NONSENSE, BLATHER

**blat·ter** \'bla-tər\ *intransitive verb* [perhaps from Latin *blaterare* to chatter] (circa 1555)
*dialect* **:** to talk noisily and fast

**blaw** \'blȯ\ *verb* **blawed; blawn** \'blȯn\; **blaw·ing** \'blȯ(-)iŋ\ [Middle English (northern dialect) *blawen,* from Old English *blāwan*] (before 12th century)
*chiefly Scottish* **:** BLOW

**blax·ploi·ta·tion** \,blak-(,)splȯi-'tā-shən\ *noun* [blend of *blax-* (alteration of *blacks*) and *exploitation*] (1972)
**:** the exploitation of blacks by producers of black-oriented films

¹**blaze** \'blāz\ *noun* [Middle English *blase,* from Old English *blǣse* torch] (before 12th century)
**1 a :** an intensely burning fire **b :** intense direct light often accompanied by heat ⟨the *blaze* of TV lights⟩ **c :** an active burning; *especially* **:** a sudden bursting forth of flame
**2 :** something that resembles the blaze of a fire: as **a :** a dazzling display ⟨a *blaze* of color⟩ **b :** a sudden outburst ⟨a *blaze* of fury⟩ **c** *plural* **:** HELL ⟨go to *blazes*⟩ ⟨as hot as *blazes*⟩

²**blaze** *intransitive verb* **blazed; blaz·ing** (13th century)
**1 a :** to burn brightly ⟨the sun *blazed* overhead⟩ **b :** to flare up **:** FLAME ⟨inflation *blazed* up⟩
**2 :** to be conspicuously brilliant or resplendent ⟨fields *blazing* with flowers⟩
**3 :** to shoot rapidly and repeatedly — usually used with *away*

³**blaze** *transitive verb* **blazed; blaz·ing** [Middle English *blasen,* from Middle Dutch *blāsen* to blow; akin to Old High German *blāst* blast] (1541)
**:** to make public or conspicuous

⁴**blaze** *noun* [German *Blas,* from Old High German *plas;* akin to Old English *blǣse*] (1639)
**1 a :** a usually white stripe down the center of the face of an animal **b :** a white or gray streak in the hair of the head
**2 :** a trail marker; *especially* **:** a mark made on a tree by chipping off a piece of the bark

⁵**blaze** *transitive verb* **blazed; blaz·ing** (1750)
**1 :** to mark (as a trail) with blazes
**2 :** to lead in some direction or activity ⟨*blaze* new trails in education⟩

**blaz·er** \'blā-zər\ *noun* (circa 1635)
**1 :** one that blazes
**2 :** a sports jacket often with notched collar and patch pockets

**blaz·ing** *adjective* (1596)
**:** of outstanding power, speed, heat, or intensity ⟨*blazing* eyes⟩ ⟨a *blazing* fastball⟩ ⟨*blazing* gunfire⟩
— **blaz·ing·ly** *adverb*

**blazing star** *noun* (15th century)
**1** *archaic* **:** COMET
**2 :** any of various plants having conspicuous flower clusters or star-shaped flowers: as **a :** any of a genus (*Liatris*) of North American composite herbs with spikes of rosy-purple rayless flowers — called also *button snakeroot* **b :** any of several North American rough-

section of blastula:
*c* blastocoel,
*ma* macromere,
*mi* micromere,
*a* animal pole,
*v* vegetal pole

leaved herbs (genus *Mentzelia* of the family Losaceae)

**¹bla·zon** \'blā-z°n\ *noun* [Middle English *blason*, from Middle French] (14th century)
**1 a :** armorial bearings **:** COAT OF ARMS **b :** the proper description or representation of heraldic or armorial bearings
**2 :** ostentatious display

**²blazon** *transitive verb* **bla·zoned; blazon·ing** \'blāz-niŋ; 'blā-z°n-iŋ\ (1534)
**1 :** to publish widely **:** PROCLAIM
**2 a :** to describe (heraldic or armorial bearings) in technical terms **b :** to represent (armorial bearings) in drawing or engraving
**3 a :** DISPLAY **b :** DECK, ADORN ⟨the town was *blazoned* with flags⟩
**— bla·zon·er** \-nər; -z°n-ər\ *noun*
**— blazoning** *noun*

**bla·zon·ry** \'blā-z°n-rē\ *noun, plural* **-ries** (1622)
**1 a :** BLAZON 1b **b :** BLAZON 1a
**2 :** a dazzling display

**¹bleach** \'blēch\ *verb* [Middle English *blechen*, from Old English *blǣcean;* akin to Old English *blāc* pale; probably akin to Latin *flagrare* to burn — more at BLACK] (before 12th century)
*transitive verb*
**1 :** to remove color or stains from
**2 :** to make whiter or lighter especially by physical or chemical removal of color
*intransitive verb*
**:** to grow white or lose color
**— bleach·able** \'blē-chə-bəl\ *adjective*

**²bleach** *noun* (1887)
**1 :** the act or process of bleaching
**2 :** a preparation used in bleaching
**3 :** the degree of whiteness obtained by bleaching

**bleach·er** \'blē-chər\ *noun* (1550)
**1 :** one that bleaches or is used in bleaching
**2 :** a usually uncovered stand of tiered planks providing seating for spectators — usually used in plural
**— bleach·er·ite** \-chə-ˌrīt\ *noun*

**bleaching powder** *noun* (circa 1846)
**:** a white powder consisting chiefly of calcium hydroxide, calcium chloride, and calcium hypochlorite and used as a bleach, disinfectant, or deodorant

**bleak** \'blēk\ *adjective* [Middle English *bleke* pale; probably akin to Old English *blāc*] (1574)
**1 :** exposed and barren and often windswept
**2 :** COLD, RAW ⟨a *bleak* November evening⟩
**3 a :** lacking in warmth, life, or kindliness **:** GRIM **b :** not hopeful or encouraging **:** DEPRESSING ⟨a *bleak* outlook⟩ **c :** severely simple or austere
**— bleak·ish** \'blē-kish\ *adjective*
**— bleak·ly** *adverb*
**— bleak·ness** *noun*

**¹blear** \'blir\ *transitive verb* [Middle English *bleren*] (14th century)
**1 :** to make (the eyes) sore or watery
**2 :** DIM, BLUR

**²blear** *adjective* (14th century)
**1 :** dim with water or tears
**2 :** obscure to the view or imagination

**blear–eyed** \-ˌīd\ *adjective* (14th century)
**:** BLEARY-EYED

**bleary** \'blir-ē\ *adjective* (14th century)
**1** *of the eyes or vision* **:** dull or dimmed especially from fatigue or sleep
**2 :** poorly outlined or defined **:** DIM
**3 :** tired to the point of exhaustion
**— blear·i·ly** \'blir-ə-lē\ *adverb*
**— blear·i·ness** \'blir-ē-nəs\ *noun*

**bleary–eyed** \-ˌīd\ *adjective* (circa 1927)
**:** having the eyes dimmed and watery (as from fatigue, drink, or emotion)

**¹bleat** \'blēt, *Northern also* 'blat, *Southern usually* 'blāt\ *verb* [Middle English *bleten*, from Old English *blǣtan;* akin to Latin *flēre* to

weep, Old English *bellan* to roar — more at BELLOW] (before 12th century)
*intransitive verb*
**1 a :** to utter the natural cry of a sheep or goat or a similar sound **b :** WHIMPER
**2 a :** to talk complainingly or with a whine **b :** BLATHER
*transitive verb*
**:** to utter in a bleating manner
**— bleat·er** *noun*

**²bleat** *noun* (circa 1505)
**1 :** the cry of a sheep or goat or a similar sound
**2 :** a feeble outcry, protest, or complaint

**bleb** \'bleb\ *noun* [perhaps alteration of *blob*] (1607)
**1 :** a small blister
**2 :** BUBBLE; *also* **:** a small particle
**— bleb·by** \'ble-bē\ *adjective*

**¹bleed** \'blēd\ *verb* **bled** \'bled\; **bleed·ing** [Middle English *bleden*, from Old English *blēdan*, from *blōd* blood] (before 12th century)
*intransitive verb*
**1 a :** to emit or lose blood **b :** to sacrifice one's blood especially in battle
**2 :** to feel anguish, pain, or sympathy ⟨a heart that *bleeds* at a friend's misfortune⟩
**3 :** to escape by oozing or flowing (as from a wound)
**4 :** to give up some constituent (as sap or dye) by exuding or diffusing it
**5 a :** to pay out or give money **b :** to have money extorted
**6 :** to be printed so as to run off one or more edges of the page after trimming
*transitive verb*
**1 :** to remove or draw blood from
**2 :** to get or extort money from especially over a prolonged period
**3 :** to draw sap from (a tree)
**4 a :** to extract or let out some or all of a contained substance from ⟨*bleed* a brake line⟩ **b :** to extract or cause to escape from a container **c :** to diminish gradually — usually used with *off* ⟨a pilot *bleeding* off airspeed⟩
**5 :** to cause (as a printed illustration) to bleed
**— bleed white :** to drain of blood or resources

**²bleed** *noun* (circa 1937)
**:** printed matter (as an illustration) that bleeds; *also* **:** the part of a bleed trimmed off

**bleed·er** *noun* (1803)
**1 :** one that bleeds; *especially* **:** HEMOPHILIAC
**2** *British* **:** ROTTER; *also* **:** BLOKE

**bleed·ing** \'blē-diŋ, -d°n\ *adjective or adverb* (1858)
*chiefly British* **:** BLOODY — used as an intensive

**bleeding heart** *noun* (1691)
**1 :** a garden plant (*Dicentra spectabilis*) of the fumitory family with racemes of usually deep pink drooping heart-shaped flowers; *broadly* **:** any of several plants (genus *Dicentra*)
**2 :** a person who shows extravagant sympathy especially for an object of alleged persecution

**¹bleep** \'blēp\ *noun* [imitative] (1953)
**:** a short high-pitched sound (as from electronic equipment)

**²bleep** *transitive verb* (1968)
**:** BLIP

**³bleep** *interjection* (1970)
**—** used in place of an expletive

**¹blem·ish** \'ble-mish\ *transitive verb* [Middle English *blemisshen*, from Middle French *blesmiss-*, stem of *blesmir* to make pale, wound] (14th century)
**:** to spoil by a flaw

**²blemish** *noun* (1535)
**:** a noticeable imperfection; *especially* **:** one that seriously impairs appearance

**¹blench** \'blench\ *intransitive verb* [Middle English, to deceive, blench, from Old English *blencan* to deceive; akin to Old Norse *blekkja* to impose on] (13th century)

**:** to draw back or turn aside from lack of courage **:** FLINCH
*synonym* see RECOIL

**²blench** *verb* [alteration of *blanch*] (1813)
**:** BLEACH, WHITEN

**¹blend** \'blend\ *verb* **blend·ed** *also* **blent** \'blent\; **blend·ing** [Middle English, modification of Old Norse *blanda;* akin to Old English *blandan* to mix, Lithuanian *blandus* impure, cloudy] (14th century)
*transitive verb*
**1 :** MIX; *especially* **:** to combine or associate so that the separate constituents or the line of demarcation cannot be distinguished
**2 :** to prepare by thoroughly intermingling different varieties or grades
*intransitive verb*
**1 a :** to mingle intimately or unobtrusively **b :** to combine into an integrated whole
**2 :** to produce a harmonious effect
*synonym* see MIX

**²blend** *noun* (1883)
**1 :** something produced by blending: as **a :** a product prepared by blending **b :** a word (as *brunch*) produced by combining other words or parts of words
**2 :** a group of two or more consecutive consonants that begin a syllable

**blende** \'blend\ *noun* [German, from *blenden* to blind, from Old High German *blenten;* akin to Old English *blind*] (circa 1753)
**:** SPHALERITE

**blended whiskey** *noun* (1940)
**:** whiskey blended from two or more straight whiskeys or from whiskey and neutral spirits

**blend·er** \'blen-dər\ *noun* (circa 1798)
**:** one that blends; *especially* **:** an electric appliance for grinding or mixing ⟨a food *blender*⟩

**blending inheritance** *noun* (1922)
**:** the expression in offspring of phenotypic characters (as pink flower color from red and white parents) intermediate between those of the parents; *also* **:** inheritance in a now discarded theory in which the genetic material of offspring was held to be a uniform blend of that of the parents

**blen·ny** \'ble-nē\ *noun, plural* **blennies** [Latin *blennius*, a sea fish, from Greek *blennos*] (1774)
**:** any of numerous usually small and elongated marine fishes (especially families Blenniidae and Clinidae) including both scaled and scaleless forms

**blephar-** *or* **blepharo-** *combining form* [New Latin, from Greek, from *blepharon*]
**1 :** eyelid ⟨*blepharo*spasm⟩
**2 :** cilium **:** flagellum ⟨*blepharo*plast⟩

**bleph·a·ro·plast** \'ble-fə-rō-ˌplast\ *noun* (1897)
**:** a basal body especially of a flagellated cell

**bleph·a·ro·plas·ty** \-ˌplas-tē\ *noun* (circa 1881)
**:** plastic surgery on the eyelid especially to remove fatty or excess tissue

**bleph·a·ro·spasm** \-ˌspa-zəm\ *noun* (1872)
**:** spasmodic winking from involuntary contraction of the orbicular muscle of the eyelids

**bles·bok** \'bles-ˌbäk\ *noun* [Afrikaans, from *bles* blaze + *bok* male antelope] (1824)
**:** a South African antelope (*Damaliscus dorcas*) having a large white patch down the center of the face

**bless** \'bles\ *transitive verb* **blessed** \'blest\ *also* **blest** \'blest\; **bless·ing** [Middle English, from Old English *blētsian*, from *blōd* blood; from the use of blood in consecration] (before 12th century)
**1 :** to hallow or consecrate by religious rite or word
**2 :** to hallow with the sign of the cross

**3 :** to invoke divine care for ⟨*bless* your heart⟩
**4 a :** PRAISE, GLORIFY ⟨*bless* his holy name⟩ **b :** to speak well of **:** APPROVE
**5 :** to confer prosperity or happiness upon
**6** *archaic* **:** PROTECT, PRESERVE
**7 :** ENDOW, FAVOR ⟨*blessed* with athletic ability⟩

**bless·ed** \'ble-səd\ *also* **blest** \'blest\ *adjective* (before 12th century)
**1 a :** held in reverence **:** VENERATED ⟨the *blessed* saints⟩ **b :** honored in worship **:** HALLOWED ⟨the *blessed* Trinity⟩ **c :** BEATIFIC ⟨a *blessed* visitation⟩
**2 :** of or enjoying happiness; *specifically* **:** enjoying the bliss of heaven — used as a title for a beatified person
**3 :** bringing pleasure, contentment, or good fortune
**4 —** used as an intensive ⟨no one gave us a *blessed* penny —*Saturday Review*⟩
— **bless·ed·ly** *adverb*
— **bless·ed·ness** *noun*

**Bless·ed Sacrament** \'ble-səd-\ *noun* (15th century)
**:** the Communion elements; *specifically* **:** the consecrated host

**bless·ing** *noun* (before 12th century)
**1 a :** the act or words of one that blesses **b :** APPROVAL, ENCOURAGEMENT
**2 :** a thing conducive to happiness or welfare
**3 :** grace said at a meal

**bleth·er** \'ble-thər\ *variant of* BLATHER

**blew** *past of* BLOW

**¹blight** \'blīt\ *noun* [origin unknown] (1611)
**1 a :** a disease or injury of plants resulting in withering, cessation of growth, and death of parts without rotting **b :** an organism that causes blight
**2 :** something that frustrates plans or hopes
**3 :** something that impairs or destroys
**4 :** a deteriorated condition ⟨urban *blight*⟩

**²blight** (1695)
*transitive verb*
**1 :** to affect (as a plant) with blight
**2 :** to cause to deteriorate
*intransitive verb*
**:** to suffer from or become affected with blight

**blight·er** \'blī-tər\ *noun* (1822)
**1 :** one that blights
**2** *chiefly British* **a :** a disliked or contemptible person **b :** FELLOW, GUY

**blimp** \'blimp\ *noun* [imitative; perhaps from the sound made by striking the gas bag with the thumb] (1916)
**1 :** a nonrigid airship
**2** *capitalized* **:** COLONEL BLIMP

**blimp·ish** \'blim-pish\ *adjective, often capitalized* (1938)
**:** of, relating to, or suggesting a Colonel Blimp
— **blimp·ish·ly** *adverb*
— **blimp·ish·ness** *noun*

**blin** \'blin\ *noun, plural* **bli·ni** \'blē-nē, 'bli-; blə-'nē\ *or* **bli·nis** \'blē-nēz, 'bli-; blə-'nēz\ [Russian] (1888)
**:** a thin often buckwheat pancake usually filled (as with sour cream) and folded

**¹blind** \'blīnd\ *adjective* [Middle English, from Old English; akin to Old High German *blint* blind, Old English *blandan* to mix — more at BLEND] (before 12th century)
**1 a** (1) **:** SIGHTLESS (2) **:** having less than ⅒ of normal vision in the more efficient eye when refractive defects are fully corrected by lenses **b :** of or relating to sightless persons
**2 a :** unable or unwilling to discern or judge ⟨*blind* to a lover's faults⟩ **b :** UNQUESTIONING ⟨*blind* loyalty⟩ ⟨*blind* faith⟩
**3 a :** having no regard to rational discrimination, guidance, or restriction ⟨*blind* choice⟩ **b :** lacking a directing or controlling consciousness ⟨*blind* chance⟩ **c :** DRUNK
**4 :** made or done without sight of certain objects or knowledge of certain facts that could serve for guidance ⟨a *blind* taste test⟩; *especially* **:** performed solely by the aid of instruments within an airplane ⟨*blind* landing⟩

**5 :** DEFECTIVE: as **a :** lacking a growing point or producing leaves instead of flowers **b :** lacking a complete or legible address ⟨*blind* mail⟩
**6 a :** difficult to discern, make out, or discover **b :** hidden from sight **:** COVERED ⟨*blind* seam⟩
**7 :** having but one opening or outlet ⟨*blind* sockets⟩
**8 :** having no opening for light or passage **:** BLANK ⟨*blind* wall⟩
— **blind·ly** \'blīn(d)-lē\ *adverb*
— **blind·ness** \'blīn-nəs\ *noun*

**²blind** *transitive verb* (before 12th century)
**1 a :** to make blind **b :** DAZZLE
**2 a :** to withhold light from **b :** HIDE, CONCEAL
— **blind·ing·ly** \'blīn-diŋ-lē\ *adverb*

**³blind** *noun* (1702)
**1 :** something to hinder sight or keep out light: as **a :** a window shutter **b :** a roller window shade **c :** VENETIAN BLIND **d :** BLINDER
**2 :** a place of concealment; *especially* **:** a concealing enclosure from which one may shoot game or observe wildlife
**3 a :** something put forward for the purpose of misleading **:** SUBTERFUGE **b :** a person who acts as a decoy or distraction

**⁴blind** *adverb* (circa 1775)
**1 :** BLINDLY: as **a :** to the point of insensibility ⟨*blind* drunk⟩ **b :** without seeing outside an airplane ⟨fly *blind*⟩
**2 —** used as an intensive ⟨was robbed *blind*⟩

**blind alley** *noun* (1583)
**:** a fruitless or mistaken course or direction

**blind date** *noun* (1925)
**1 :** a date between two persons who have not previously met
**2 :** either participant in a blind date

**blind·er** \'blīn-dər\ *noun* (1809)
**1 :** either of two flaps on a horse's bridle to keep it from seeing objects at its sides
**2** *plural* **:** a limitation or obstruction to sight or discernment

**blind·fish** \'blīn(d)-,fish\ *noun* (1843)
**:** any of several small fishes with vestigial functionless eyes found usually in the waters of caves

**¹blind·fold** \-,fōld\ *transitive verb* [alteration of Middle English *blindfellen, blindfelden* to strike blind, blindfold, from *blind* + *fellen* to fell] (1599)
**1 :** to cover the eyes of with or as if with a bandage
**2 :** to hinder from seeing; *especially* **:** to keep from comprehension
— **blindfold** *adjective*

**²blindfold** *noun* (1880)
**1 :** a bandage for covering the eyes
**2 :** something that obscures mental or physical vision

**blind gut** *noun* (15th century)
**:** a digestive cavity open at only one end; *especially* **:** the cecum of the large intestine

**blind·man's buff** \'blīn(d)-'manz-\ *noun* (1600)
**:** a group game in which a blindfolded player tries to catch and identify another player — called also *blindman's bluff*

**blind pig** *noun* (1887)
**:** BLIND TIGER

**blind·side** \'blīn(d)-,sīd\ *transitive verb* (1968)
**1 :** to hit unexpectedly from or as if from the blind side
**2 :** to surprise unpleasantly

**blind side** *noun* (1606)
**1 :** the side away from which one is looking
**2 :** the side on which one that is blind in one eye cannot see

**blind spot** *noun* (1872)
**1 a :** the nearly circular light-colored area at the back of the retina where the optic nerve enters the eyeball and which is not sensitive to light — called also *optic disk;* see EYE illustration **b :** a portion of a field that cannot be seen or inspected with available equipment

**2 :** an area in which one fails to exercise judgment or discrimination

**blind tiger** *noun* (1857)
**:** a place that sells intoxicants illegally

**blind trust** *noun* (1969)
**:** an arrangement in which the financial holdings of a person in an influential position (as a government official) are placed in the control of a fiduciary in order to avoid a possible conflict of interest

**blind·worm** \'blīnd-,wərm\ *noun* (15th century)
**:** SLOWWORM

**¹blink** \'bliŋk\ *verb* [Middle English, to open one's eyes] (14th century)
*intransitive verb*
**1 a** *obsolete* **:** to look glancingly **:** PEEP **b :** to look with half-shut eyes **c :** to close and open the eyes involuntarily (as when dazzled)
**2 :** to shine dimly or intermittently
**3 a :** to look with too little concern **b :** to look with surprise or dismay
*transitive verb*
**1 a :** to cause to blink **b :** to remove (as tears) from the eye by blinking
**2 :** to deny recognition to

**²blink** *noun* (1594)
**1** *chiefly Scottish* **:** GLIMPSE, GLANCE
**2 :** GLIMMER, SPARKLE
**3 :** a usually involuntary shutting and opening of the eye
**4 :** ICEBLINK
— **on the blink :** in or into a disabled or useless condition

**¹blink·er** \'bliŋ-kər\ *noun* (1636)
**1 :** one that blinks; *especially* **:** a light that flashes off and on (as for the directing of traffic or the coded signaling of messages)
**2 a :** BLINDER 1 **b :** a cloth hood with shades projecting at the sides of the eye openings used on skittish racehorses — usually used in plural
**3** *plural* **:** BLINDER 2

**²blinker** *transitive verb* (1865)
**:** to put blinders on

**blink·ered** \'bliŋ-kərd\ *adjective* (1867)
**1 :** limited in scope or understanding **:** NARROW-MINDED
**2 :** fitted with blinders

**blin·tze** \'blin(t)-sə\ *or* **blintz** \'blin(t)s\ *noun* [Yiddish *blintse,* of Slavic origin; akin to Ukrainian *mlynets',* diminutive of *mlyn* pancake] (1903)
**:** a thin usually wheat-flour pancake folded to form a casing and then sautéed or baked

**¹blip** \'blip\ *noun* [imitative] (1945)
**1 :** a trace on an oscilloscope; *especially* **:** a spot on a radar screen
**2 :** a short crisp sound
**3 :** an interruption of the sound received in a radio or television program or occurring in a recording as a result of blipping
**4 :** a transient sharp movement up or down (as of a quantity commonly shown on a graph)

**²blip** *transitive verb* **blipped; blip·ping** (1968)
**:** to remove (recorded sound) from a recording so that there is an interruption of the sound in the reproduction ⟨a censor *blipped* the swearwords⟩

**bliss** \'blis\ *noun* [Middle English *blisse,* from Old English *bliss;* akin to Old English *blīthe* blithe] (before 12th century)
**1 :** complete happiness
**2 :** PARADISE, HEAVEN

**blissed–out** \'blist-'aut\ *adjective* (1973)
**:** being in a state of bliss **:** ECSTATIC

**bliss·ful** \'blis-fəl\ *adjective* (12th century)
**1 :** full of, marked by, or causing bliss
**2 :** happily benighted ⟨*blissful* ignorance⟩
— **bliss·ful·ly** \-fə-lē\ *adverb*
— **bliss·ful·ness** *noun*

**¹blis·ter** \'blis-tər\ *noun* [Middle English, modification of Old French or Middle Dutch;

Old French *blostre* leprous nodule, from Middle Dutch *bluyster* blister; akin to Old English *blǣst* blast] (14th century)
**1** : an elevation of the epidermis containing watery liquid
**2** : an enclosed raised spot (as in paint) resembling a blister
**3** : an agent that causes blistering
**4** : a disease of plants marked by large swollen patches on the leaves
**5** : any of various structures that bulge out (as a gunner's compartment on a bomber)
— **blis·tery** \-t(ə-)rē\ *adjective*
**²blister** *verb* **blis·tered; blis·ter·ing** \-t(ə-)riŋ\ (15th century)
*intransitive verb*
: to become affected with a blister
*transitive verb*
**1** : to raise a blister on
**2** : LAMBASTE 2
**blister beetle** *noun* (1816)
: a beetle (as the Spanish fly) used medicinally dried and powdered to raise blisters on the skin; *broadly* : any of a family (Meloidae) of soft-bodied beetles
**blister copper** *noun* (1861)
: metallic copper of a black blistered surface that is the product of converting copper matte and is about 98.5 to 99.5 percent pure
**blis·ter·ing** *adjective* (1562)
: extremely intense or severe
— **blistering** *adverb*
— **blis·ter·ing·ly** \-t(ə-)riŋ-lē\ *adverb*
**blister pack** *noun* (1955)
: a package holding and displaying merchandise in a clear plastic case sealed to a sheet of cardboard
**blister rust** *noun* (1916)
: any of several diseases of pines that are caused by rust fungi (genus *Cronartium*) in the aecial stage and that affect the sapwood and inner bark and produce blisters externally
**blithe** \'blīth, 'blīth\ *adjective* **blith·er; blith·est** \'Middle English, from Old English *blīthe*; akin to Old High German *blīdi* joyous] (before 12th century)
**1** : of a happy lighthearted character or disposition
**2** : lacking due thought or consideration : CASUAL, HEEDLESS ⟨*blithe* unconcern⟩
**synonym** see MERRY
— **blithe·ly** *adverb*
**blith·er** \'bli-thər\ *intransitive verb or noun* [by alteration] (1868)
: BLATHER
**blithe·some** \'blīth-səm, 'blīth-\ *adjective* (1724)
: GAY, MERRY
— **blithe·some·ly** *adverb*
**blitz** \'blits\ *noun* (circa 1939)
**1 a** : BLITZKRIEG 1 **b** (1) : an intensive aerial campaign (2) : AIR RAID
**2 a** : an intensive nonmilitary campaign : a sudden overwhelming bombardment ⟨an advertising *blitz*⟩ **b** : a rush of the passer by the defensive linebackers in football
— **blitz** *verb*
**blitz·krieg** \-ˌkrēg\ *noun* [German, from *Blitz* lightning + *Krieg* war] (1939)
**1** : war conducted with great speed and force; *specifically* : a violent surprise offensive by massed air forces and mechanized ground forces in close coordination
**2** : BLITZ 2a
**bliz·zard** \'bli-zərd\ *noun* [origin unknown] (1870)
**1** : a long severe snowstorm
**2** : an intensely strong cold wind filled with fine snow
**3** : an overwhelming rush or deluge ⟨the *blizzard* of mail at Christmas⟩ ◆
— **bliz·zardy** \'bli-zər-dē\ *also* **bliz·zard·ly** \-ˌzərd-lē\ *adjective*
**¹bloat** \'blōt\ *adjective* [alteration of Middle English *blout*] (14th century)
: BLOATED, PUFFY

**²bloat** (1677)
*transitive verb*
**1** : to make turgid or swollen
**2** : to fill to capacity or overflowing
*intransitive verb*
: SWELL
**³bloat** *noun* (1860)
**1** : one that is bloated
**2** : a flatulent digestive disturbance of domestic animals and especially cattle marked by abdominal bloating
**bloat·ed** *adjective* (1711)
**1** : being much larger than what is warranted ⟨a *bloated* estimate⟩
**2** : obnoxiously vain
**¹bloat·er** \'blō-tər\ *noun* [obsolete *bloat* (to cure)] (1832)
: a large fat herring or mackerel lightly salted and briefly smoked
**²bloater** *noun* [²*bloat*] (1896)
: a small but common cisco (*Coregonus hoyi*) of the Great Lakes
**¹blob** \'bläb\ *noun* [Middle English] (15th century)
**1 a** : a small drop or lump of something viscid or thick **b** : a daub or spot of color
**2** : something ill-defined or amorphous
**²blob** *transitive verb* **blobbed; blob·bing** (15th century)
: to mark with blobs : SPLOTCH
**bloc** \'bläk\ *noun* [French, literally, block] (1903)
**1 a** : a temporary combination of parties in a legislative assembly **b** : a group of legislators who act together for some common purpose irrespective of party lines
**2 a** : a combination of persons, groups, or nations forming a unit with a common interest or purpose **b** : a group of nations united by treaty or agreement for mutual support or joint action
**¹block** \'bläk\ *noun, often attributive* [Middle English *blok*, from Middle French *bloc*, from Middle Dutch *blok*; akin to Old High German *bloh* block] (14th century)
**1** : a compact usually solid piece of substantial material especially when worked or altered to serve a particular purpose: as **a** : the piece of wood on which the neck of a person condemned to be beheaded is laid for execution **b** : a mold or form on which articles are shaped or displayed **c** : a hollow rectangular building unit usually of artificial material **d** : a lightweight usually cubical and solid wooden or plastic building toy that is usually provided in sets **e** : the casting that contains the cylinders of an internal-combustion engine
**2 a** : OBSTACLE **b** : an obstruction of an opponent's play in sports; *especially* : a halting or impeding of the progress or movement of an opponent in football by use of the body **c** (1) : interruption of normal physiological function (as of a tissue or organ); *especially* : HEART BLOCK (2) : local anesthesia (as by injection) produced by interruption of the flow of impulses along a nerve **d** : interruption or cessation especially of train of thought by competing thoughts or psychological suppression
**3** *slang* : HEAD 1 ⟨threatened to knock his *block* off⟩
**4** : a wooden or metal case enclosing one or more pulleys and having a hook, eye, or strap by which it may be attached
**5** : a piece of material (as wood or linoleum) having on its surface a hand-cut design from which impressions are to be printed
**6 a** (1) : a usually rectangular space (as in a city) enclosed by streets and occupied by or intended for buildings (2) : the distance along one of the sides of such a block **b** (1) : a large building divided into separate functional units (2) : a line of row houses (3) : a distinctive part of a building or integrated group of buildings **c** : a short section of railroad track in the block system

**7** : a platform from which property is sold at auction
**8 a** : a quantity, number, or section of things dealt with as a unit **b** : BLOC 2
— **on the block** : for sale
**²block** (1580)
*transitive verb*
**1 a** : to make unsuitable for passage or progress by obstruction **b** *archaic* : BLOCKADE **c** : to hinder the passage, progress, or accomplishment of by or as if by interposing an obstruction **d** : to shut off from view ⟨forest canopy *blocking* the sun⟩ **e** : to interfere usually legitimately with (as an opponent) in various games or sports **f** : to prevent normal functioning of **g** : to restrict the exchange of (as currency or checks)
**2** : to mark or indicate the outline or chief lines of ⟨*block* out a design⟩ ⟨*block* in a sketched figure⟩
**3** : to shape on, with, or as if with a block ⟨*block* a hat⟩
**4** : to secure, support, or provide with a block
**5** : to work out or chart the movements of (as stage performers) — often used with *out*
**6** : to make (two or more lines of writing or type) flush at the left or at both left and right
*intransitive verb*
: to block an opponent in sports
**synonym** see HINDER
— **block·er** *noun*
**¹block·ade** \blä-'kād\ *transitive verb* **block·ad·ed; block·ad·ing** (1680)
**1** : to subject to a blockade
**2** : BLOCK, OBSTRUCT
— **block·ad·er** *noun*
**²blockade** *noun* (1693)
**1** : the isolation by a warring nation of an enemy area (as a harbor) by troops or warships to prevent passage of persons or supplies; *broadly* : a restrictive measure designed to obstruct the commerce and communications of an unfriendly nation
**2** : something that blocks
**3** : interruption of normal physiological function (as transmission of nerve impulses) of a tissue or organ
**block·ade–run·ner** \-'kād-ˌrə-nər\ *noun* (1863)
: a ship or person that runs through a blockade

\ə\ abut \ᵊ\ kitten \ər\ further \a\ ash \ā\ ace
\ä\ mop, mar \aù\ out \ch\ chin \e\ bet \ē\ easy
\g\ go \i\ hit \ī\ ice \j\ job \ŋ\ sing \ō\ go
\ò\ law \òi\ boy \th\ thin \th\ the \ü\ loot \ù\ foot
\y\ yet \zh\ vision *see also* Guide to Pronunciation

**— block·ade–run·ning** \-,rə-niŋ\ *noun*

**block·age** \'blä-kij\ *noun* (1874)
: an act or instance of obstructing : the state of being blocked ⟨a *blockage* in a coronary artery⟩

**block and tackle** *noun* (1838)
: pulley blocks with associated rope or cable for hoisting or hauling

**block·bust·er** \'bläk-,bəs-tər\ *noun* (1942)
**1** : a very large high-explosive bomb
**2** : one that is notably effective, successful, large, or violent
**3** : one who engages in blockbusting

**block·bust·ing** \-tiŋ\ *noun* (1954)
: profiteering by inducing property owners to sell hastily and often at a loss by appeals to fears of depressed values because of threatened minority encroachment and then reselling at inflated prices

**block diagram** *noun* (1944)
: a diagram (as of a system, process, or program) in which labeled figures (as rectangles) and interconnecting lines represent the relationship of parts

**blocked** \'bläkt\ *adjective* (1945)
: exhibiting or affected by a psychological block ⟨a *blocked* writer⟩

**block grant** *noun* (1900)
: an unrestricted federal grant

**block·head** \'bläk-,hed\ *noun* (1549)
: a stupid person

**block·house** \-,haůs\ *noun* (1512)
**1 a** : a structure of heavy timbers formerly used for military defense with sides loopholed and pierced for gunfire and often with a projecting upper story **b** : a small easily defended building for protection from enemy fire

blockhouse 1a

**2** : a building usually of reinforced concrete serving as an observation point for an operation likely to be accompanied by heat, blast, or radiation hazard

**block·ish** \'blä-kish\ *adjective* (1565)
: resembling a block

**block letter** *noun* (1908)
: an often hand-drawn simple capital letter composed of strokes of uniform thickness

**block party** *noun* (1941)
: an outdoor public party put on by the residents of a city block or neighborhood

**block plane** *noun* (circa 1884)
: a small plane made with the blade set at a lower pitch than other planes and used chiefly on end grains of wood

**block system** *noun* (1864)
: a system by which a railroad track is divided into short sections and trains are run by guidance signals

**blocky** \'blä-kē\ *adjective* **block·i·er; -est** (circa 1879)
**1** : resembling a block in form : CHUNKY
**2** : filled with or made up of blocks or patches

**bloke** \'blōk\ *noun* [origin unknown] (1851)
*chiefly British* : MAN, FELLOW

**¹blond** *or* **blonde** \'bländ\ *adjective* [Middle French *blond*, masculine, *blonde*, feminine] (15th century)
**1 a** : of a flaxen, golden, light auburn, or pale yellowish brown color ⟨*blond* hair⟩ **b** : of a pale white or rosy white color ⟨*blond* skin⟩ **c** : being a blond
**2 a** : of a light color **b** : of the color blond **c** : made light-colored by bleaching ⟨a table of *blond* walnut⟩
**— blond·ish** \'blän-dish\ *adjective*

**²blond** *or* **blonde** *noun* (1822)
**1** : a person having blond hair and usually a light complexion and blue or gray eyes
**2** : a light yellowish brown to dark grayish yellow

**¹blood** \'bləd\ *noun, often attributive* [Middle English, from Old English *blōd*; akin to Old High German *bluot* blood] (before 12th century)
**1 a** : the fluid that circulates in the heart, arteries, capillaries, and veins of a vertebrate animal carrying nourishment and oxygen to and bringing away waste products from all parts of the body **b** : a comparable fluid of an invertebrate **c** : a fluid resembling blood
**2** : the shedding of blood; *also* : the taking of life
**3 a** : LIFEBLOOD; *broadly* : LIFE **b** : human stock or lineage; *especially* : royal lineage ⟨a prince of the *blood*⟩ **c** : relationship by descent from a common ancestor : KINSHIP **d** : persons related through common descent : KINDRED **e** (1) : honorable or high birth or descent (2) : descent from parents of recognized breed or pedigree
**4 a** : blood regarded as the seat of the emotions : TEMPER **b** *obsolete* : LUST **c** : a showy foppish man : RAKE
**5** : PERSONNEL ⟨a company in need of new *blood*⟩
**6** : a black American male — used especially among blacks

**²blood** *transitive verb* (1633)
**1** *archaic* : BLEED 1
**2** : to stain or wet with blood
**3** : to expose (a hunting dog) to sight, scent, or taste of the blood of its prey
**4** : to give experience to ⟨troops *blooded* in battle⟩

**blood–and–guts** \'blə-dⁿ-'gəts\ *adjective* (1937)
: marked by great vigor, violence, or fierceness ⟨*blood-and-guts* competition⟩

**blood·bath** \'bləd-,bath, -,bȧth\ *noun* (1867)
: a great slaughter

**blood–brain barrier** \'bləd-'brān-\ *noun* (1944)
: a barrier created by the modification of brain capillaries (as by reduction in fenestration and formation of tight cell-to-cell contacts) that prevents many substances from leaving the blood and crossing the capillary walls into the brain tissues

**blood brother** *noun* (1890)
**1** : a brother by birth
**2** : one of two men pledged to mutual loyalty by a ceremonial use of each other's blood
**— blood brotherhood** *noun*

**blood cell** *noun* (1846)
: a cell normally present in blood

**blood count** *noun* (circa 1900)
: the determination of the blood cells in a definite volume of blood; *also* : the number of cells so determined

**blood·cur·dling** \'bləd-,kərd-liŋ, -,kər-dᵊl-iŋ\ *adjective* (1904)
: arousing fright or horror ⟨*bloodcurdling* screams⟩

**blood doping** *noun* (1973)
: a technique for temporarily improving athletic performance in which oxygen-carrying red blood cells from blood previously withdrawn from an athlete are reinjected just before an event — called also *blood packing*

**blood·ed** \'blə-dəd\ *adjective* (1595)
**1** : having blood of a specified kind — used in combination ⟨cold-*blooded*⟩
**2** : being entirely or largely purebred ⟨a herd of *blooded* stock⟩

**blood feud** *noun* (1858)
: a feud between different clans or families

**blood fluke** *noun* (1872)
: SCHISTOSOME

**blood group** *noun* (1916)
: one of the classes (as those designated A, B, AB, or O) into which individuals or their blood can be separated on the basis of the presence or absence of specific antigens in the blood — called also *blood type*

**blood·guilt** \'bləd-,gilt\ *noun* (1593)
: guilt resulting from bloodshed

**— blood·guilt·i·ness** \-,gil-tē-nəs\ *noun*
**— blood·guilty** \-tē\ *adjective*

**blood·hound** \'bləd-,haůnd\ *noun* (14th century)
**1** : any of a breed of large powerful hounds of European origin remarkable for acuteness of smell
**2** : a person keen in pursuit

bloodhound 1

**blood·less** \'bləd-ləs\ *adjective* (before 12th century)
**1** : deficient in or free from blood
**2** : not accompanied by loss or shedding of blood ⟨a *bloodless* victory⟩
**3** : lacking in spirit or vitality
**4** : lacking in human feeling ⟨*bloodless* statistics⟩
**— blood·less·ly** *adverb*
**— blood·less·ness** *noun*

**blood·let·ting** \-,le-tiŋ\ *noun* (13th century)
**1** : PHLEBOTOMY
**2** : BLOODSHED
**3** : elimination of personnel or resources

**blood·line** \-,līn\ *noun* (circa 1909)
: a sequence of direct ancestors especially in a pedigree; *also* : FAMILY, STRAIN

**blood·mo·bile** \-mō-,bēl\ *noun* (1948)
: an automotive vehicle staffed and equipped for collecting blood from donors

**blood money** *noun* (1535)
**1** : money obtained at the cost of another's life
**2** : money paid by a manslayer or members of his family, clan, or tribe to the next of kin of a person killed by him

**blood orange** *noun* (1855)
: a cultivated sweet orange having fruit with usually red pulp; *also* : its fruit

**blood platelet** *noun* (1898)
: one of the minute protoplasmic disks of vertebrate blood that assist in blood clotting

**blood poisoning** *noun* (1863)
: SEPTICEMIA

**blood pressure** *noun* (1874)
: pressure that is exerted by the blood upon the walls of the blood vessels and especially arteries and that varies with the muscular efficiency of the heart, the blood volume and viscosity, the age and health of the individual, and the state of the vascular wall

**blood·red** \'bləd-'red\ *adjective* (before 12th century)
: having the color of blood

**blood·root** \-,rüt, -,růt\ *noun* (1722)
: a plant (*Sanguinaria canadensis*) of the poppy family having a red root and sap and bearing a solitary lobed leaf and white flower in early spring — called also *sanguinaria*

**blood sausage** *noun* (1868)
: very dark sausage containing a large proportion of blood — called also *blood pudding*

**blood serum** *noun* (circa 1909)
: blood from which the fibrin and suspended material (as cells) have been removed

**blood·shed** \'bləd-,shed\ *noun* (15th century)
**1** : the shedding of blood
**2** : the taking of life : SLAUGHTER

**blood·shot** \-,shät\ *adjective* (1552)
*of an eye* : inflamed to redness

**blood sport** *noun* (1895)
: a sport or contest (as hunting or cockfighting) involving bloodshed

**blood·stain** \-,stān\ *noun* (1820)
: a discoloration caused by blood

**blood·stained** \-,stānd\ *adjective* (1596)
**1** : stained with blood
**2** : involved with slaughter ⟨a *bloodstained* chronicle of war⟩

**blood·stock** \-,stäk\ *noun* (1830)
: horses of Thoroughbred breeding

**blood·stone** \-ˌstōn\ *noun* (1551)
: a green chalcedony sprinkled with red spots resembling blood — called also *heliotrope*

**blood·stream** \-ˌstrēm\ *noun* (1873)
**1** : the flowing blood in a circulatory system
**2** : a mainstream of power or vitality ⟨introduce into the economic *bloodstream* a large amount of money —*Harper's*⟩

**blood·suck·er** \-ˌsə-kər\ *noun* (14th century)
**1** : an animal that sucks blood; *especially* : LEECH
**2** : a person who sponges or preys on another
— **blood·suck·ing** \-kiŋ\ *adjective*

**blood sugar** *noun* (1918)
: the glucose in the blood; *also* : its concentration (as in milligrams per 100 milliliters)

**blood test** *noun* (1912)
: a test of the blood; *especially* : a serologic test for the presence of substances indicative of disease (as syphilis) or disease-causing agents (as HIV)

**blood·thirsty** \ˈbləd-ˌthər-stē\ *adjective* (1535)
: eager for or marked by the shedding of blood, violence, or killing
— **blood·thirst·i·ly** \-stə-lē\ *adverb*
— **blood·thirst·i·ness** \-stē-nəs\ *noun*

**blood–typ·ing** \-ˌtī-piŋ\ *noun* (1926)
: the action or process of determining an individual's blood group

**blood vessel** *noun* (1694)
: any of the vessels through which blood circulates in the body

**blood·worm** \ˈbləd-ˌwərm\ *noun* (1714)
**1** : any of various reddish annelid worms (as of genera *Glycera* or *Tubifex*) often used as bait
**2** : any of several strongyle worms (genus *Strongylus*) that are parasitic in the large intestine of horses

**¹bloody** \ˈblə-dē\ *adjective* **blood·i·er; -est** (before 12th century)
**1 a** : containing or made up of blood **b** : of or contained in the blood
**2** : smeared or stained with blood
**3** : accompanied by or involving bloodshed; *especially* : marked by great slaughter
**4 a** : MURDEROUS **b** : MERCILESS, CRUEL
**5** : BLOODRED
**6** — used as an intensive; sometimes considered vulgar ☆
— **blood·i·ly** \ˈblə-dᵊl-ē\ *adverb*
— **blood·i·ness** \ˈblə-dē-nəs\ *noun*

**²bloody** *transitive verb* **blood·ied; bloody·ing** (1530)
: to make bloody or bloodred

**³bloody** *adverb* (1676)
— used as an intensive; sometimes considered vulgar

**Bloody Mary** *noun, plural* **Bloody Marys** [probably from *Bloody Mary,* appellation of Mary I of England] (1947)
: a cocktail consisting essentially of vodka and usually spiced tomato juice

**bloody–mind·ed** \ˌblə-dē-ˈmīn-dəd\ *adjective* (1584)
**1** : inclined towards violence or bloodshed
**2** *chiefly British* : stubbornly contrary or obstructive : CANTANKEROUS
— **bloody–mind·ed·ness** *noun*

**bloody murder** *adverb* (1925)
: in a loud and violent manner ⟨ran off, screaming *bloody murder*⟩; *also* : in vehement protest ⟨screaming *bloody murder* over the pay cut⟩

**bloody shirt** *noun* (1874)
: something intended to stir up or revive partisan animosity — usually used in the phrase *wave the bloody shirt*

**¹bloom** \ˈblüm\ *noun* [Middle English *blome* lump of metal, from Old English *blōma*] (before 12th century)
**1** : a mass of wrought iron from the forge or puddling furnace
**2** : a bar of iron or steel hammered or rolled from an ingot

**²bloom** *noun* [Middle English *blome,* from Old Norse *blōm;* akin to Old English *blōwan* to blossom — more at BLOW] (13th century)
**1 a** : FLOWER **b** : the flowering state ⟨the roses in *bloom*⟩ **c** : a period of flowering ⟨the spring *bloom*⟩ **d** : an excessive growth of plankton
**2 a** : a state or time of beauty, freshness, and vigor **b** : a state or time of high development or achievement ⟨a career in full *bloom*⟩
**3** : a surface coating or appearance: as **a** : a delicate powdery coating on some fruits and leaves **b** : a rosy appearance of the cheeks; *broadly* : an outward evidence of freshness or healthy vigor **c** : a cloudiness on a film of varnish or lacquer **d** : a grayish discoloration on chocolate **e** : glare caused by an object reflecting too much light into a television camera

**³bloom** (13th century)
*intransitive verb*
**1 a** : to produce or yield flowers **b** : to support abundant plant life ⟨make the desert *bloom*⟩
**2 a** (1) : to mature into achievement of one's potential (2) : to flourish in youthful beauty, freshness or excellence **b** : to shine out : GLOW
**3** : to appear or occur unexpectedly or in remarkable quantity or degree
**4** : to become densely populated with microorganisms and especially plankton — used of bodies of water
*transitive verb*
**1** *obsolete* : to cause to bloom
**2** : to give bloom to

**¹bloom·er** \ˈblü-mər\ *noun* (circa 1736)
**1** : a plant that blooms
**2** : a person who reaches full competence or maturity
**3** [*blooming*] : a stupid blunder

**²bloo·mer** \ˈblü-mər\ *noun* [Amelia *Bloomer*] (1851)
**1** : a costume for women consisting of a skirt over long loose trousers gathered closely about the ankles
**2** *plural* **a** : full loose trousers gathered at the knee formerly worn by women for athletics **b** : underpants of similar design worn chiefly by girls and women ◆

**bloom·ing** \ˈblü-mən, -miŋ\ *adjective or adverb* [probably euphemism for *bloody*] (1882)
*chiefly British* — used as a generalized intensive ⟨*blooming* fool⟩

**bloomy** \ˈblü-mē\ *adjective* (1593)
**1** : full of bloom
**2** : covered with bloom ⟨*bloomy* plums⟩
**3** : showing freshness or vitality ⟨all the *bloomy* flush of life is fled —Oliver Goldsmith⟩

**bloop** \ˈblüp\ *noun* [back-formation from *blooper*] (1967)
: BLOOPER 1a
— **bloop** *transitive verb*

**bloop·er** \ˈblü-pər\ *noun* [*bloop* (an unpleasant sound)] (1937)
**1 a** : a fly ball hit barely beyond a baseball infield **b** : a high baseball pitch lobbed to the batter
**2** : an embarrassing public blunder

**¹blos·som** \ˈblä-səm\ *noun* [Middle English *blosme,* from Old English *blōstm;* akin to Old English *blōwan*] (before 12th century)
**1 a** : the flower of a seed plant; *also* : the mass of such flowers on a single plant **b** : the state of bearing flowers
**2** : a peak period or stage of development
— **blos·somy** \-sə-mē\ *adjective*

**²blossom** *intransitive verb* (before 12th century)
**1** : BLOOM
**2 a** : to come into one's own : DEVELOP ⟨a *blossoming* talent⟩ **b** : to become evident : make an appearance

**¹blot** \ˈblät\ *noun* [Middle English] (14th century)
**1** : a soiling or disfiguring mark : SPOT
**2** : a mark of reproach : moral flaw

**3** : a usually nitrocellulose sheet that contains spots of immobilized macromolecules (as of DNA, RNA, or protein) or their fragments and is used to identify specific components of the spots by applying a molecular probe (as a complementary nucleic acid or a radioactively labeled antibody)

**²blot** *verb* **blot·ted; blot·ting** (15th century)
*transitive verb*
**1** : to spot, stain, or spatter with a discoloring substance
**2** *obsolete* : MAR; *especially* : to stain with infamy
**3 a** : to dry (as writing) with an absorbing agent **b** : to remove with absorbing material ⟨*blotting* up spilled water⟩
*intransitive verb*
**1** : to make a blot
**2** : to become marked with a blot

**³blot** *noun* [origin unknown] (1595)
**1** : a lone backgammon man exposed to capture
**2** *archaic* : a weak or exposed point

**¹blotch** \ˈbläch\ *transitive verb* (1604)
: to mark or mar with blotches

**²blotch** *noun* [perhaps blend of ¹*blot* and ³*botch*] (1669)
**1** : IMPERFECTION, BLEMISH
**2** : a spot or mark (as of color or ink) especially when large or irregular
— **blotch·i·ly** \ˈblä-chə-lē\ *adverb*
— **blotchy** \ˈblä-chē\ *adjective*

---

☆ **SYNONYMS**

**Bloody, sanguinary, gory** mean affected by or involving the shedding of blood. BLOODY is applied especially to things that are actually covered with blood or are made up of blood ⟨*bloody* hands⟩. SANGUINARY applies especially to something attended by, or someone inclined to, bloodshed ⟨the Civil War was America's most *sanguinary* conflict⟩. GORY suggests a profusion of blood and slaughter ⟨exceptionally *gory,* even for a horror movie⟩.

---

◇ **WORD HISTORY**

**bloomer** *Bloomers* are named after a small-town feminist who unwittingly sparked a fashion revolution. A resident of Seneca Falls, New York—the site of a historic women's rights convention in 1848—Amelia Jenks Bloomer (1818–1894) was a feminist long before the cause was popular or the term even invented. A newspaper journalist already writing about various women's issues, she became involved with the right of women to liberate themselves from traditional clothing in 1849, when she defended the wearing of pantalets by the actress Fanny Kemble. The following year she rushed to the defense of visiting feminists who appeared in Seneca Falls wearing full Turkish pantaloons under a shortened skirt. Her articles attracted the attention of newspapers in New York City and elsewhere, and soon a fad of national proportions developed. Correspondents from all over solicited her for patterns and information about the new attire, which was first known in 1851 as the "Bloomer Costume" and immediately shortened to *bloomer* or *bloomers*. Bloomer herself wore the new attire exclusively for the next several years. Aided by their suitability for women's bicycling, bloomers remained fashionable for the rest of the 19th century.

---

\ə\ abut \ᵊ\ kitten \ər\ further \a\ ash \ā\ ace \ä\ mop, mar \aú\ out \ch\ chin \e\ bet \ē\ easy \g\ go \i\ hit \ī\ ice \j\ job \ŋ\ sing \ō\ go \ò\ law \òi\ boy \th\ thin \th\ the \ü\ loot \ú\ foot \y\ yet \zh\ vision *see also* Guide to Pronunciation

**blot out** *transitive verb* (1530)
**1 :** to make obscure, insignificant, or inconsequential
**2 :** WIPE OUT, DESTROY
**blot·ter** \'blä-tər\ *noun* (1591)
**1 :** a piece of blotting paper
**2 :** a book in which entries (as of transactions or occurrences) are made temporarily pending their transfer to permanent record books ⟨police *blotter*⟩
**blotting paper** *noun* (15th century)
**:** a spongy unsized paper for absorbing ink
**blot·to** \'blä-(ˌ)tō\ *adjective* [probably irregular from ²*blot*] (1917)
**:** DRUNK 1a
**¹blouse** \'blaus *also* 'blauz\ *noun, plural* **blous·es** \'blau-səz, -zəz\ [French] (1828)
**1 a :** a long loose overgarment that resembles a shirt or smock and is worn especially by workmen, artists, and peasants **b :** the jacket of a uniform
**2 :** a usually loose-fitting garment especially for women that covers the body from the neck to the waist
**— blousy** \'blau-sē, -zē\ *adjective*
**²blouse** \'blaus, 'blauz\ *verb* **bloused; blous·ing** (1904)
*intransitive verb*
**:** to fall in a fold ⟨coats that *blouse* above the hip⟩
*transitive verb*
**:** to cause to blouse ⟨trousers are *bloused* over the boots⟩
**blou·son** \'blau-ˌsän, 'blü-ˌzän\ *noun* [French, from *blouse*] (1904)
**:** a garment (as a dress) having a close waistband with blousing of material over it
**¹blow** \'blō\ *verb* **blew** \'blü\; **blown** \'blōn\; **blow·ing** [Middle English, from Old English *blāwan;* akin to Old High German *blāen* to blow, Latin *flare*, Greek *phallos* penis] (before 12th century)
*intransitive verb*
**1** *of air* **:** to move with speed or force
**2 :** to send forth a current of air or other gas
**3 a :** to make a sound by or as if by blowing **b** *of a wind instrument* **:** SOUND
**4 a :** BOAST **b :** to talk windily
**5 a :** PANT, GASP ⟨the horse *blew* heavily⟩ **b** *of a cetacean* **:** to eject moisture-laden air from the lungs through the blowhole
**6 :** to move or be carried by or as if by wind ⟨just *blew* into town⟩
**7** *of an electric fuse* **:** to melt when overloaded — often used with *out*
**8** *of a tire* **:** to release the contained air through a spontaneous rupture — usually used with *out*
*transitive verb*
**1 a :** to set (gas or vapor) in motion **b :** to act on with a current of gas or vapor
**2 :** to play or sound on (a wind instrument)
**3 a :** to spread by report **b** *past participle* **blowed** \'blōd\ **:** DAMN ⟨*blow* the expense⟩ ⟨I'm *blowed* if I know⟩
**4 a :** to drive with a current of gas or vapor **b :** to clear of contents by forcible passage of a current of air **c :** to project (a gesture or sound made with the mouth) by blowing ⟨*blew* him a kiss⟩
**5 a :** to distend with or as if with gas **b :** to produce or shape by the action of blown or injected air ⟨*blowing* bubbles⟩ ⟨*blowing* glass⟩
**6** *of insects* **:** to deposit eggs or larvae on or in
**7 :** to shatter, burst, or destroy by explosion
**8 a :** to put out of breath with exertion **b :** to let (as a horse) pause to catch the breath
**9 a :** to expend (as money) extravagantly ⟨*blew* $50 on lunch⟩ **b :** to treat with unusual expenditure ⟨I'll *blow* you to a steak⟩
**10 :** to cause (a fuse) to blow
**11 :** to rupture by too much pressure ⟨*blew* a gasket⟩
**12 :** to foul up hopelessly ⟨*blew* her lines⟩ ⟨*blew* his chance⟩
**13 :** to leave hurriedly ⟨*blew* town⟩

**14 :** to propel with great force or speed ⟨*blew* a fastball by the batter⟩
**— blow hot and cold :** to be favorable at one moment and adverse the next
**— blow off steam :** to release pent-up emotions
**— blow one's cool :** to lose one's composure
**— blow one's cover :** to reveal one's real identity
**— blow one's mind :** to overwhelm one with wonder or bafflement
**— blow one's top** *or* **blow one's stack**
**1 :** to become violently angry **2 :** to go crazy
**— blow smoke :** to speak idly, misleadingly, or boastfully
**— blow the whistle :** to call public or official attention to something (as a wrongdoing) kept secret — usually used with *on*
**²blow** *noun* (1660)
**1 :** a blowing of wind especially when strong or violent
**2 :** BRAG, BOASTING
**3 :** an act or instance of blowing
**4 a :** the time during which air is forced through molten metal to refine it **b :** the quantity of metal refined during that time
**5** *slang* **:** COCAINE
**³blow** *intransitive verb* **blew** \'blü\; **blown** \'blōn\; **blow·ing** [Middle English, from Old English *blōwan;* akin to Old High German *bluoen* to bloom, Latin *flōrēre* to bloom, *flor-, flos* flower] (before 12th century)
**:** FLOWER, BLOOM
**⁴blow** *noun* (1710)
**1 :** BLOSSOMS
**2 :** ²BLOOM 1b ⟨lilacs in full *blow*⟩
**⁵blow** *noun* [Middle English (northern dialect) *blaw;* probably akin to Old High German *bliuwan* to beat] (15th century)
**1 :** a forcible stroke delivered with a part of the body or with an instrument
**2 :** a hostile act or state **:** COMBAT ⟨come to *blows*⟩
**3 :** a forcible or sudden act or effort **:** ASSAULT
**4 :** an unfortunate or calamitous happening ⟨failure to land the job came as a *blow*⟩
**blow away** *transitive verb* (1776)
**1 :** to kill by gunfire **:** shoot dead
**2 :** to dissipate or remove as if with a current of air ⟨their doubts were *blown away*⟩
**3 :** to impress very strongly and usually favorably
**4 :** to defeat soundly ⟨*blew* their rivals *away* in the first game⟩
**blow·by** \'blō-ˌbī\ *noun* (1926)
**:** leakage of combustion gases between a piston and the cylinder wall into the crankcase in an automobile
**blow-by-blow** \'blō-bī-'blō, -bə-\ *adjective* (1933)
**:** minutely detailed ⟨a *blow-by-blow* account⟩
**blow·down** \'blō-ˌdaun\ *noun* (1895)
**:** an instance of trees being blown down by the wind; *also* **:** a tree blown down
**blow-dried** \'blō-ˌdrīd\ *adjective* (1976)
**:** having blow-dried hair; *also* **:** being or appearing well-groomed but superficial or vacuous
**blow-dry** \-ˌdrī\ (1966)
*transitive verb*
**:** to dry and usually style (hair) with a blow-dryer
*intransitive verb*
**:** to dry hair with a blow-dryer
**— blow-dry** *noun*
**blow-dryer** \-ˌdrī-(-ə)r\ *noun* (1976)
**:** a handheld hair dryer
**blow·er** \'blō-(-ə)r\ *noun* (before 12th century)
**1 :** one that blows
**2 :** a device for producing a current of air or gas
**3 :** BRAGGART
**4** *British* **:** TELEPHONE
**blow·fish** \'blō-ˌfish\ *noun* (circa 1893)
**:** PUFFER 2a

**blow·fly** \-ˌflī\ *noun* (1821)
**:** any of a family (Calliphoridae) of dipteran flies (as the bluebottle or screwworm) that deposit their eggs especially on meat or in wounds
**blow·gun** \-ˌgən\ *noun* (1864)
**:** a tube through which a projectile (as a dart) may be impelled by the force of the breath
**blow·hard** \-ˌhärd\ *noun* (1857)
**:** BRAGGART
**blow·hole** \-ˌhōl\ *noun* (1691)
**1 :** a hole in metal caused by a bubble of gas captured during solidification
**2 :** a nostril in the top of the head of a cetacean and especially a whale
**blow in** *intransitive verb* (1895)
**:** to arrive casually or unexpectedly
**blow job** *noun* (1956)
**:** an act of fellatio — usually considered vulgar
**blown** \'blōn\ *adjective* [Middle English *blowen*, from past participle of *blowen* to blow] (14th century)
**1 a :** SWOLLEN **b :** affected with bloat
**2 :** being out of breath
**blow off** *transitive verb* (1987)
**1 :** to refuse to take notice of, honor, or deal with **:** IGNORE ⟨decided to *blow off* two billion viewers —Harry Homburg⟩
**2 :** to fail to attend or show up for ⟨*blew off* an official dinner⟩
**blow·out** \'blō-ˌaut\ *noun* (1824)
**1 :** a festive social affair
**2 :** a bursting of a container (as a tire) by pressure of the contents on a weak spot
**3 :** an uncontrolled eruption of an oil or gas well
**4 :** an easy or one-sided victory
**blow out** (14th century)
*transitive verb*
**1 :** to extinguish by a gust
**2 :** to dissipate (itself) by blowing — used of storms
**3 :** to defeat easily
*intransitive verb*
**1 :** to become extinguished by a gust
**2 :** to erupt out of control — used of an oil or gas well
**blow over** *intransitive verb* (1617)
**:** to pass away without effect
**blow·pipe** \'blō-ˌpīp\ *noun* (1685)
**1 :** a small tubular instrument for directing a jet of air or other gas into a flame so as to concentrate and increase the heat
**2 :** BLOWGUN
**3 :** a tubular instrument used for revealing or cleaning a bodily cavity by forcing air into it
**4 :** a long metal tube on the end of which a glassmaker gathers a quantity of molten glass and through which he blows to expand and shape it
**blow·sy** *also* **blow·zy** \'blau-zē\ *adjective* [English dialect *blowse, blowze* wench] (circa 1770)
**1 :** having a sloppy appearance or aspect **:** FROWSY
**2 :** being coarse and ruddy of complexion
**blow·torch** \'blō-ˌtorch\ *noun* (1897)
**:** a small burner having a device to intensify combustion by means of a blast of air or oxygen, usually including a fuel tank pressurized by a hand pump, and used especially in plumbing
**blow·up** \'blō-ˌəp\ *noun* (1807)
**:** a blowing up: as **a :** EXPLOSION **b :** an outburst of temper **c :** a photographic enlargement
**blow up** (1536)
*transitive verb*
**1 :** to build up or tout to an unreasonable extent ⟨advertisers *blowing up* their products⟩
**2 :** to rend apart, shatter, or destroy by explosion
**3 :** to fill up with a gas (as air) ⟨*blow up* a balloon⟩
**4 :** to make a photographic enlargement of

**5 :** to bring into existence by blowing of wind ⟨it may *blow up* a storm⟩
*intransitive verb*
**1 a :** EXPLODE **b :** to be disrupted or destroyed (as by explosion) **c :** to lose self-control; *especially* : to become violently angry
**2 :** to become or come into being by or as if by blowing of wind
**3 a :** to become filled with a gas (as air) **b :** to become expanded to unreasonable proportions
**blowy** \'blō-ē\ *adjective* (1830)
**1 :** WINDY ⟨a *blowy* March day⟩
**2 :** readily blown about ⟨*blowy* desert sand⟩
**BLT** *noun* (1952)
: a bacon, lettuce, and tomato sandwich
**blub** \'bləb\ *intransitive verb* **blubbed; blubbing** (1804)
*chiefly British* : BLUBBER
**¹blub·ber** \'blə-bər\ *verb* **blub·bered; blub·ber·ing** \'blə-b(ə-)riŋ\ [Middle English *blubren* to make a bubbling sound, from *bluber*] (15th century)
*intransitive verb*
: to weep noisily
*transitive verb*
**1 :** to swell, distort, or wet with weeping
**2 :** to utter while weeping
**²blubber** *noun* [Middle English *bluber* bubble, foam, probably of imitative origin] (15th century)
**1 a :** the fat of whales and other large marine mammals **b :** excessive fat on the body
**2 :** the action of blubbering
**³blubber** *adjective* (1667)
: puffed out : THICK ⟨*blubber* lips⟩
**blub·bery** \'blə-b(ə-)rē\ *adjective* (1791)
**1 :** having or characterized by blubber
**2 :** puffed out : THICK
**blu·cher** \'blü-chər *also* -kər\ *noun* [G. L. von *Blücher*] (1831)
: a shoe having the tongue and vamp cut in one piece and the quarters lapped over the vamp and laced together for closing
**¹blud·geon** \'blə-jən\ *noun* [origin unknown] (circa 1730)
**1 :** a short stick that usually has one thick or loaded end and is used as a weapon
**2 :** something used to attack or bully ⟨the *bludgeon* of satire⟩
**²bludgeon** *transitive verb* (1868)
**1 :** to hit with heavy impact
**2 :** to overcome by aggressive argument
**blud·ger** \'blə-jər\ *noun* [probably contraction of *bludgeoner* pimp, from ¹*bludgeon*] (1939)
*chiefly Australian & New Zealand* : LOAFER, SHIRKER
**¹blue** \'blü\ *adjective* **blu·er; blu·est** [Middle English, from Old French *blou*, of Germanic origin; akin to Old High German *blāo* blue; akin to Latin *flavus* yellow] (13th century)
**1 :** of the color blue
**2 a :** BLUISH **b :** discolored by or as if by bruising ⟨*blue* with cold⟩ **c :** bluish gray ⟨*blue* cat⟩
**3 a :** low in spirits : MELANCHOLY **b :** marked by low spirits : DEPRESSING ⟨a *blue* funk⟩ ⟨things looked *blue*⟩
**4 :** wearing blue
**5** *of a woman* : LEARNED, INTELLECTUAL
**6 :** PURITANICAL
**7 a :** PROFANE, INDECENT ⟨*blue* movie⟩ **b :** OFF-COLOR, RISQUÉ ⟨*blue* jokes⟩
**8 :** of, relating to, or used in blues ⟨a *blue* song⟩
— **blue·ly** *adverb*
— **blue·ness** *noun*
— **blue in the face** : extremely exasperated
**²blue** *noun* (13th century)
**1 :** a color whose hue is that of the clear sky or that of the portion of the color spectrum lying between green and violet
**2 a :** a pigment or dye that colors blue **b :** BLUING
**3 a :** blue clothing or cloth **b** *plural* : a blue costume or uniform

**4 a :** a Union soldier in the Civil War **b :** the Union army
**5 a** (1) : SKY (2) : the far distance **b :** SEA
**6 :** a blue object
**7 :** BLUESTOCKING
**8 :** any of numerous small chiefly blue butterflies (family Lycaenidae)
**9 :** BLUEFISH
**10 :** BLUE CHEESE
— **out of the blue** : without advance notice : UNEXPECTEDLY ⟨the job offer came *out of the blue*⟩
**³blue** *verb* **blued; blue·ing** *or* **blu·ing** (1606)
*transitive verb*
: to make blue
*intransitive verb*
: to turn blue
**blue baby** *noun* (circa 1899)
: an infant with a bluish tint usually from a congenital heart defect in which mingling of venous and arterial blood occurs
**blue·beard** \'blü-ˌbird\ *noun, often capitalized* [*Bluebeard*, a fairy-tale character] (1822)
: a man who marries and kills one wife after another
**blue·bell** \-ˌbel\ *noun* (1578)
**1 :** any of various bellflowers; *especially* : HAREBELL
**2 :** any of various plants bearing blue bell-shaped flowers: as **a :** a European herb (*Endymion nonscriptus* synonym *Scilla nonscripta*) of the lily family having scapose racemes of drooping bell-shaped flowers — called also *wild hyacinth* **b** *plural* : a glabrous erect eastern U.S. herb (*Mertensia virginica*) of the borage family with entire leaves and showy blue flowers pink in the bud — called also *Virginia bluebells*
**blue·ber·ry** \'blü-ˌber-ē, -b(ə-)rē\ *noun* (1709)
: the edible blue or blackish berry of any of several plants (genus *Vaccinium*) of the heath family; *also* : a low or tall shrub producing these berries
**blue·bird** \-ˌbərd\ *noun* (1688)
: any of several small North American thrushes (genus *Sialia*) that are blue above and reddish brown or pale blue below
**blue blood** *noun* (1834)
**1** \'blü-ˈbləd\ : membership in a noble or socially prominent family
**2** \-ˌbləd\ : a member of a noble or socially prominent family
— **blue–blood·ed** \-ˈblə-dəd\ *adjective*
**blue·bon·net** \'blü-ˌbä-nət\ *noun* (1682)
**1 a :** a wide flat round cap of blue wool formerly worn in Scotland **b :** one that wears such a cap; *specifically* : SCOT
**2 :** either of two low-growing annual lupines (*Lupinus subcarnosus* or *Latin texensis*) of Texas with silky foliage and blue flowers
**blue book** *noun* (1836)
**1 :** a register especially of socially prominent persons
**2 :** a book of specialized information often published under government auspices
**3 :** a blue-covered booklet used for writing examinations
**4 :** a periodically issued price list (as of used cars)
**blue·bot·tle** \'blü-ˌbä-t³l\ *noun* (15th century)
**1 :** BACHELOR'S BUTTON
**2 :** any of several blowflies (genus *Calliphora*) that have the abdomen or the whole body iridescent blue in color and that make a loud buzzing noise in flight
**blue catfish** *noun* (1835)
: a large bluish catfish (*Ictalurus furcatus*) of the Mississippi valley that may weigh over 100 pounds (45 kilograms)
**blue cheese** *noun* (1925)
: cheese having veins of greenish blue mold
**blue chip** *noun* (1929)
**1 a :** a stock issue of high investment quality that usually pertains to a substantial well-established company and enjoys public confi-

dence in its worth and stability **b :** a consistently successful and profitable venture or enterprise
**2 a :** an outstandingly worthwhile or valuable property or asset **b :** an athlete rated as excellent or as an excellent prospect
— **blue–chip** *adjective*
**blue–chip·per** \'blü-ˌchi-pər\ *noun* (1968)
: BLUE CHIP 2b
**blue·coat** \'blü-ˌkōt\ *noun* (1593)
: a person who wears a blue coat: as **a :** a Union soldier during the Civil War **b :** POLICE OFFICER
**blue cohosh** *noun* (1821)
: a perennial herb (*Caulophyllum thalictroides*) of the barberry family that has greenish yellow or purplish flowers and large blue berrylike fruits
**blue–col·lar** \'blü-ˈkä-lər\ *adjective* (1946)
: of, relating to, or constituting the class of wage earners whose duties call for the wearing of work clothes or protective clothing — compare WHITE-COLLAR
**blue crab** *noun* (1883)
: a large bluish green edible crab (*Callinectes sapidus*) of the Atlantic and Gulf coasts

**blue crab**

**blue curls** *noun plural but singular or plural in construction* (1817)
: any of several mints (genus *Trichostema*) with irregular blue flowers
**blue devils** *noun plural* (1781)
: low spirits : DESPONDENCY
**blue–eyed** \'blü-ˌīd\ *adjective* (1610)
**1 :** having blue eyes
**2 :** performed by whites ⟨*blue-eyed* soul⟩; *also* : WHITE ⟨a *blue-eyed* soul singer⟩
**blue–eyed grass** *noun* (1784)
: any of several herbs (genus *Sisyrinchium*) of the iris family with grasslike foliage and blue flowers
**blue–fin tuna** \'blü-ˌfin-\ *noun* (1922)
: a very large tuna (*Thunnus thynnus*) that is an important food and game fish — called also *bluefin*
**blue·fish** \-ˌfish\ *noun* (circa 1622)
**1 :** an active food and game marine fish (*Pomatomus saltatrix*) that is bluish above with silvery sides
**2 :** any of various dark or bluish fishes (as the pollack)
**blue flag** *noun* (1784)
: a blue-flowered iris; *especially* : a common iris (*Iris versicolor*) of the eastern U.S. with a root formerly used medicinally
**blue flu** *noun* [from the color of a police uniform] (1970)
: a sick-out staged by police officers
**blue·gill** \'blü-ˌgil\ *noun* (1881)
: a common sunfish (*Lepomis macrochirus*) of the eastern and central U.S. sought for food and sport
**blue·grass** \-ˌgras\ *noun* (1751)
**1 :** any of several grasses (genus *Poa*) of which some have bluish green culms; *especially* : KENTUCKY BLUEGRASS
**2** [from the *Blue Grass Boys*, performing group, from *Bluegrass state*, nickname of Kentucky] : country music played on unamplified stringed instruments (as banjo, fiddle, guitar, and mandolin) and characterized by free improvisation and close usually high-pitched harmony
**blue–green alga** \'blü-ˈgrēn-\ *noun* (1899)

: any of a group of photosynthetic microorganisms now usually classified as bacteria (division Cyanobacteria) or sometimes as plants (division Cyanophyta) — called also *blue-green bacterium, cyanobacterium*

**blue gum** *noun* (1799)
: any of several Australian trees (genus *Eucalyptus*) that yield valuable timber

**blue heron** *noun* (circa 1730)
: either of two herons with bluish or slaty plumage; *especially* : GREAT BLUE HERON

**blue·jack·et** \-ˌja-kət\ *noun* (1830)
: an enlisted man in the navy : SAILOR

**blue jay** \-ˌjā\ *noun* (1709)
: a crested bright blue North American jay (*Cyanocitta cristata*)

**blue jeans** *noun plural* (1901)
: pants usually made of blue denim
— **blue–jeaned** \-ˌjēnd\ *adjective*

**blue law** *noun* (1781)
**1** : one of numerous extremely rigorous laws designed to regulate morals and conduct in colonial New England
**2** : a statute regulating work, commerce, and amusements on Sundays

**blue line** *noun* (1937)
: either of two blue lines that divide an ice-hockey rink into three equal zones and that separate the offensive and defensive zones from the center-ice neutral zone

**blue mold** *noun* (1664)
: any of various fungi (genus *Penicillium*) that produce blue or blue-green surface growths

**blue moon** *noun* (1821)
: a very long period of time ⟨such people happen along only once in a *blue moon* — *Saturday Review*⟩

**blue·nose** \'blü-ˌnōz\ *noun* (1903)
: a person who advocates a rigorous moral code

**blue note** *noun* [from its frequent use in blues music] (1919)
: a variable microtonal lowering of the third, seventh, and occasionally fifth degrees of the major scale

**blue–pen·cil** \'blü-'pen(t)-səl\ *transitive verb* (1888)
: to edit especially by shortening or deletion
— **blue penciller** *noun*

**blue pencil** *noun* (1893)
: a writing instrument used for editing; *also*
: the act or practice of blue-penciling

**blue pe·ter** \-'pē-tər\ *noun* [probably from the name *Peter*] (1823)
: a blue signal flag with a white square in the center used to indicate that a merchant vessel is ready to sail

**blue pike** *noun* (1842)
: a grayish-blue walleye categorized as either a morph or a subspecies (*Stizostedion vitreum glaucum*)

**blue plate** *adjective* (1926)
: being a main course usually offered at a special price in a restaurant ⟨a *blue plate* luncheon⟩

**blue·point** \'blü-ˌpȯint\ *noun* [*Blue Point*, Long Island] (1789)
: a small oyster (*Crassostrea virginica*) typically from the south shore of Long Island

**blue point** \-ˌpȯint\ *adjective* (1944)
*of a domestic cat* : having a bluish cream body coat with dark gray points
— **blue point** *noun*

**blue·print** \-ˌprint\ *noun* (1886)
**1** : a photographic print in white on a bright blue ground or blue on a white ground used especially for copying maps, mechanical drawings, and architects' plans
**2** : something resembling a blueprint; *especially* : a detailed plan or program of action ⟨a *blueprint* for victory⟩
— **blueprint** *transitive verb*

**blue racer** *noun* (1886)
: a blue or greenish blue blacksnake (*Coluber constrictor* subspecies) occurring from Michigan and Wisconsin to Texas

**blue–ribbon** *adjective* (1926)
: of outstanding quality; *especially* : consisting of individuals selected for quality, reputation, or authority ⟨a *blue-ribbon* committee⟩ ⟨a *blue-ribbon* jury⟩

**blue ribbon** *noun* (1651)
**1** : an honor or award gained for preeminence
**2** : a blue ribbon awarded as an honor (as to the first-place winner in a competition)

**blues** \'blüz\ *noun plural but singular or plural in construction* [*blue devils*] (1741)
**1** : low spirits : MELANCHOLY
**2** : a song often of lamentation characterized by usually 12-bar phrases, 3-line stanzas in which the words of the second line usually repeat those of the first, and continual occurrence of blue notes in melody and harmony
**3** : jazz or popular music using harmonic and phrase structures of blues

**blue shark** *noun* (circa 1672)
: a chiefly pelagic shark (*Prionace glauca*) found in all tropical and temperate seas that occasionally attacks humans

**blue sheep** *noun* (1911)
: BHARAL

**blue·shift** \'blü-'shift\ *noun* (1951)
: the displacement of the spectrum of an approaching celestial body toward shorter wavelengths
— **blue·shift·ed** *adjective*

**blue–sky** \'blü-'skī\ *adjective* (1906)
**1** : having little or no value ⟨*blue-sky* stock⟩
**2** : not grounded in the realities of the present : VISIONARY ⟨*blue-sky* thinking⟩

**blue–sky law** *noun* (1912)
: a law providing for the regulation of the sale of securities (as stock)

**blues·man** \'blüz-mən\ *noun* (1966)
: a man who plays or sings the blues

**blue spruce** *noun* (1884)
: a spruce (*Picea pungens*) of the Rocky Mountains having sharp usually bluish gray needles and often planted as an ornamental

**blue·stem** \'blü-ˌstem\ *noun* (circa 1862)
**1** : a tall North American grass (*Andropogon gerardii* synonym *A. furcatus*) that has smooth bluish leaf sheaths and slender spikes borne in pairs or clusters and is used for hay and forage
**2** : LITTLE BLUESTEM

**blue·stock·ing** \-ˌstä-kiŋ\ *noun* [*Bluestocking* society, 18th century literary clubs] (1790)
: a woman having intellectual or literary interests ◆

**blue·stone** \-ˌstōn\ *noun* (1709)
: a building stone of bluish gray color

**blue streak** *noun* (1830)
**1** : something that moves very fast
**2** : a constant stream of words ⟨talked a *blue streak*⟩

**blue·sy** \'blü-zē\ *adjective* **blues·i·er; -est** (1946)
: resembling, characteristic of, or suited to the blues

**blu·et** \'blü-ət\ *noun* [probably from ¹*blue*] (circa 1821)
: a North American plant (*Hedyotis caerulea* synonym *Houstonia caerulea*) of the madder family having tufted stems and bluish or white flowers with yellow centers

**blue·tick** \-ˌtik\ *noun* (1945)
: any of a breed of tricolor coonhounds of American origin having the white areas of the coat heavily ticked with black

**blue·tongue** \'blü-ˌtəŋ\ *noun* (1863)
: a serious virus disease especially of sheep characterized by hyperemia, cyanosis, and punctate hemorrhages and by swelling and sloughing of the epithelium especially about the mouth and tongue

**blue vitriol** *noun* (1728)
: a hydrated copper sulfate $CuSO_4 \cdot 5H_2O$

**blue water** *noun* (1582)
: the open sea
— **blue–wa·ter** \'blü-ˌwȯ-tər, -ˌwä-\ *adjective*

**blue·weed** \'blü-ˌwēd\ *noun* (circa 1837)
**1** : VIPER'S BUGLOSS
**2** : a small weedy sunflower (*Helianthus ciliaris*) of the southwestern U.S. with blue-green or gray-green foliage

**blue whale** *noun* (1851)
: a very large baleen whale (*Balaenoptera musculus* synonym *Sibbaldus musculus*) that may reach a weight of 150 tons (135 metric tons)

blue whale

and a length of 100 feet (30 meters) and is generally considered the largest living animal

**bluey** \'blü-ē\ *noun* [from the blue blanket commonly used to wrap the bundle] (1877) *Australian* : a swagman's bundle of personal effects; *also* : a bag of clothing carried in travel

¹**bluff** \'bləf\ *adjective* [obsolete Dutch *blaf* flat; akin to Middle Low German *blaff* smooth] (1627)
**1 a** : having a broad flattened front **b** : rising steeply with a broad flat or rounded front
**2** : good-naturedly frank and outspoken ☆

---

☆ **SYNONYMS**
**Bluff, blunt, brusque, curt, crusty, gruff** mean abrupt and unceremonious in speech and manner. BLUFF connotes good-natured outspokenness and unconventionality ⟨a *bluff* manner⟩. BLUNT suggests directness of expression in disregard of others' feelings ⟨a *blunt* appraisal⟩. BRUSQUE applies to a sharpness or ungraciousness ⟨a *brusque* response⟩. CURT implies disconcerting shortness or rude conciseness ⟨a *curt* command⟩. CRUSTY suggests a harsh or surly manner sometimes concealing an inner kindliness ⟨a *crusty* exterior⟩. GRUFF suggests a hoarse or husky speech which may imply bad temper but more often implies embarrassment or shyness ⟨puts on a *gruff* pose⟩.

---

◇ **WORD HISTORY**
**bluestocking** The origin of *bluestocking* goes back to the mid-18th century, to a circle of English ladies who decided to replace their social evenings of cardplaying and idle chatter to which tradition had confined them, with more intellectual pursuits. Taking the literary salons of Paris as their model, they decided to hold discussions at which illustrious men of letters would be the honored guests. On one occasion, they invited the English botanist and sometime poet Benjamin Stillingfleet. A poor scholar who lacked fancy clothes, including the black silk stockings customarily worn to such high-society events, he felt obliged to decline the invitation, until he was assured that his everyday clothes, including his blue worsted stockings, would be quite acceptable. Thus attired, Stillingfleet became a popular fixture at the evening conversations and was dubbed "blue stockings." As it was then considered unseemly for women to aspire to learning, the circle presided over by Stillingfleet acquired the derisive nickname the "Blue Stocking Society." Rather defiantly, the members of the group embraced the intended put-down, adopting the name *Bluestocking*, or its French equivalent *Bas Bleu*. By the early 19th century, any woman with intellectual interests was called, often derogatorily still, a *bluestocking*.

— **bluff·ly** *adverb*
— **bluff·ness** *noun*

²**bluff** *noun* (1666)
: a high steep bank : CLIFF

³**bluff** *verb* [probably from Dutch *bluffen* to boast, play a kind of card game] (1839)
*transitive verb*
**1 a :** to deter or frighten by pretense or a mere show of strength **b :** DECEIVE **c :** FEIGN ⟨the catcher *bluffed* a throw to first⟩
**2 :** to deceive (an opponent) in cards by a bold bet on an inferior hand
*intransitive verb*
: to bluff someone : act deceptively
— **bluff·er** *noun*

⁴**bluff** *noun* (1845)
**1 a :** an act or instance of bluffing **b :** the practice of bluffing
**2 :** one who bluffs

**blu·ing** *or* **blue·ing** \'blü-iŋ\ *noun* (1669)
: a preparation used in laundering to counteract yellowing of white fabrics

**blu·ish** \'blü-ish\ *adjective* (14th century)
: somewhat blue : having a tinge of blue
— **blu·ish·ness** *noun*

¹**blun·der** \'blən-dər\ *verb* **blun·dered; blun·der·ing** \-d(ə-)riŋ\ [Middle English *blundren*] (14th century)
*intransitive verb*
**1 :** to move unsteadily or confusedly
**2 :** to make a mistake through stupidity, ignorance, or carelessness
*transitive verb*
**1 :** to utter stupidly, confusedly, or thoughtlessly
**2 :** to make a stupid, careless, or thoughtless mistake in
— **blun·der·er** \-dər-ər\ *noun*
— **blun·der·ing·ly** \-d(ə-)riŋ-lē\ *adverb*

²**blunder** *noun* (circa 1706)
: a gross error or mistake resulting usually from stupidity, ignorance, or carelessness
**synonym** see ERROR

**blun·der·buss** \'blən-dər-,bəs\ *noun* [by folk etymology from obsolete Dutch *donderbus,* from Dutch *donder* thunder + obsolete Dutch *bus* gun] (1654)
**1 :** a muzzle-loading firearm with a short barrel and flaring muzzle to facilitate loading

**blunderbuss 1**
**2 :** a blundering person

¹**blunt** \'blənt\ *adjective* [Middle English] (13th century)
**1 a :** slow or deficient in feeling : INSENSITIVE **b :** obtuse in understanding or discernment : DULL
**2 :** having an edge or point that is not sharp
**3 a :** abrupt in speech or manner **b :** being straight to the point : DIRECT
**synonym** see DULL, BLUFF
— **blunt·ly** *adverb*
— **blunt·ness** *noun*

²**blunt** (14th century)
*transitive verb*
: to make less sharp or definite
*intransitive verb*
: to become blunt

¹**blur** \'blər\ *noun* [perhaps akin to Middle English *bleren* to blear] (1548)
**1 :** a smear or stain that obscures
**2 :** something vaguely or indistinctly perceived; *especially* : something moving or occurring too quickly to be clearly perceived

²**blur** *verb* **blurred; blur·ring** (1581)
*transitive verb*
**1 :** to obscure or blemish by smearing
**2 :** SULLY
**3 :** to make dim, indistinct, or vague in outline or character
**4 :** to make cloudy or confused

*intransitive verb*
**1 :** to make blurs
**2 :** to become vague or indistinct
— **blur·ring·ly** \'blər-iŋ-lē\ *adverb*

¹**blurb** \'blərb\ *noun* [coined by Gelett Burgess] (1914)
: a short publicity notice (as on a book jacket)

²**blurb** *transitive verb* (1915)
: to describe or praise in a blurb

**blur·ry** \'blər-ē\ *adjective* **blur·ri·er; -est** (1884)
: marked by blurring
— **blur·ri·ly** \'blər-ə-lē\ *adverb*
— **blur·ri·ness** \'blər-ē-nəs\ *noun*

**blurt** \'blərt\ *transitive verb* [probably imitative] (1573)
: to utter abruptly and impulsively — usually used with *out*
— **blurt·er** *noun*

¹**blush** \'bləsh\ *noun* [Middle English, probably from *blusshen*] (14th century)
**1 :** outward appearance : VIEW ⟨at first *blush*⟩
**2 :** a reddening of the face especially from shame, modesty, or confusion
**3 :** a red or rosy tint
— **blush·ful** \-fəl\ *adjective*

²**blush** *intransitive verb* [Middle English *blusshen,* from Old English *blyscan* to redden; akin to Old English *blȳsa* flame, Old High German *bluhhen* to burn brightly] (15th century)
**1 :** to become red in the face especially from shame, modesty, or confusion
**2 :** to feel shame or embarrassment
**3 :** to have a rosy or fresh color : BLOOM
— **blush·ing·ly** \'blə-shiŋ-lē\ *adverb*

**blush·er** \'blə-shər\ *noun* (1665)
**1 :** one that blushes
**2 :** a cosmetic applied to the face to give a usually pink color or to accent the cheekbones

**blush wine** *noun* (1985)
: any of various pinkish table wines

¹**blus·ter** \'bləs-tər\ *verb* **blus·tered; blus·ter·ing** \-t(ə-)riŋ\ [Middle English *blustren,* probably from Middle Low German *blüsteren*] (15th century)
*intransitive verb*
**1 :** to talk or act with noisy swaggering threats
**2 a :** to blow in stormy noisy gusts **b :** to be windy and boisterous
*transitive verb*
**1 :** to utter with noisy self-assertiveness
**2 :** to drive or force by blustering
— **blus·ter·er** \-tər-ər\ *noun*
— **blus·ter·ing·ly** \-t(ə-)riŋ-lē\ *adverb*

²**bluster** *noun* (1583)
**1 :** a violent boisterous blowing
**2 :** violent commotion
**3 :** loudly boastful or threatening speech
— **blus·ter·ous** \-t(ə-)rəs\ *adjective*
— **blus·tery** \-t(ə-)rē\ *adjective*

**B lymphocyte** *noun* (1971)
: B CELL

**B movie** *noun* (1948)
: a cheaply produced motion picture

**boa** \'bō-ə\ *noun* [Latin, a water snake] (14th century)
**1 :** a large snake (as the boa constrictor, anaconda, or python) that kills by constriction
**2 :** a long fluffy scarf of fur, feathers, or delicate fabric

**boa constrictor** *noun* (1809)
: a tropical American boa (*Constrictor constrictor* synonym *Boa constrictor*) that is light brown barred or mottled with darker brown and reaches a length of 10 feet (3 meters) or more; *broadly* : BOA 1

**boar** \'bōr, 'bȯr\ *noun* [Middle English *bor,* from Old English *bār;* akin to Old High German & Old Saxon *bēr* boar] (before 12th century)
**1 a :** an uncastrated male swine **b :** the male of any of several mammals (as a guinea pig or raccoon)
**2 :** WILD BOAR

— **boar·ish** \-ish\ *adjective*

¹**board** \'bōrd, 'bȯrd\ *noun* [Middle English *bord* piece of sawed lumber, border, ship's side, from Old English; akin to Old High German *bort* ship's side] (before 12th century)
**1** *obsolete* : BORDER, EDGE
**2 :** the side of a ship
**3 a :** a piece of sawed lumber of little thickness and a length greatly exceeding its width **b** *plural* : STAGE 2a(2)
**4 a** *archaic* : TABLE 3a **b :** a table spread with a meal **c :** daily meals especially when furnished for pay **d :** a table at which a council or magistrates sit **e** (1) : a group of persons having managerial, supervisory, investigatory, or advisory powers ⟨*board* of directors⟩ ⟨*board* of examiners⟩ (2) : an examination given by an examining board — often used in plural ⟨pass the medical *boards*⟩ **f :** LEAGUE, ASSOCIATION **g** (1) : the exposed hands of all the players in a stud poker game (2) : an exposed dummy hand in bridge
**5 a :** a flat usually rectangular piece of material (as wood) designed for a special purpose: as (1) : SPRINGBOARD 1 (2) : SURFBOARD **b :** BACKBOARD; *also* : a rebound in basketball **c :** a surface, frame, or device for posting notices **d :** BLACKBOARD **e :** SWITCHBOARD
**6 a :** PAPERBOARD **b :** the stiff foundation piece for the side of a book cover
**7 :** a securities or commodities exchange
**8** *plural* : the low wooden wall enclosing a hockey rink
**9 :** a sheet of insulating material carrying circuit elements and terminals so that it can be inserted in an electronic apparatus (as a computer)
— **board·like** \-,līk\ *adjective*
— **across the board :** so as to include or affect all classes or categories ⟨cut spending *across the board*⟩; *also* : in all areas or respects ⟨considered an average player *across the board*⟩
— **on board :** ABOARD

²**board** (15th century)
*transitive verb*
**1** *archaic* : to come up against or alongside (a ship) usually to attack
**2 :** ACCOST, ADDRESS

\ə\ abut \ᵊ\ kitten \ər\ further \a\ ash \ā\ ace \ä\ mop, mar \aù\ out \ch\ chin \e\ bet \ē\ easy \g\ go \i\ hit \ī\ ice \j\ job \ŋ\ sing \ō\ go \ȯ\ law \ȯi\ boy \th\ thin \t͟h\ the \ü\ loot \ù\ foot \y\ yet \zh\ vision    *see also* Guide to Pronunciation

**3 a :** to go aboard (as a ship, train, airplane, or bus) **b :** to put aboard ⟨an airliner *boarding* passengers⟩
**4 :** to cover with boards ⟨*board* up a window⟩
**5 :** to provide with regular meals and often also lodging usually for compensation
**6 :** to check with a board check
*intransitive verb*
**:** to take one's meals usually as a paying customer
**board check** *noun* (circa 1936)
**:** a body check of an opposing player against the rink boards in ice hockey
**board·er** \'bōr-dər, 'bór-\ *noun* (1530)
**:** one that boards; *especially* **:** one that is provided with regular meals or regular meals and lodging
**board foot** *noun* (1896)
**:** a unit of quantity for lumber equal to the volume of a board 12 × 12 × 1 inches — abbreviation **bd ft**
**board game** *noun* (1934)
**:** a game of strategy (as checkers, chess, or backgammon) played by moving pieces on a board
**board·ing·house** \'bōr-diŋ-,haús, 'bór-\ *noun* (1728)
**:** a lodging house at which meals are provided
**boarding school** *noun* (1677)
**:** a school at which meals and lodging are provided
**board·man** \'bōrd-,man, 'bórd-, *especially for* 2 -mən\ *noun* (circa 1923)
**1 :** a member of a board
**2 :** one who works at a board
**board of trade** (1780)
**1** *B&T capitalized* **:** a British governmental department concerned with commerce and industry
**2 :** a commodities exchange
**board·room** \'bōrd-,rüm, 'bórd-, -,rúm\ *noun* (1836)
**:** a room that is designated for meetings of a board
**board·sail·ing** \-,sā-liŋ\ *noun* (1980)
**:** WINDSURFING
— **board·sail·or** \-,sā-lər\ *noun*
**board·walk** \-,wók\ *noun* (1872)
**1 :** a walk constructed of planking
**2 :** a walk constructed along a beach
**boart** \'bōrt, 'bórt\ *variant of* BORT
**¹boast** \'bōst\ *noun* [Middle English *boost*] (14th century)
**1 :** the act or an instance of boasting **:** BRAG
**2 :** a cause for pride
— **boast·ful** \'bōst-fəl\ *adjective*
— **boast·ful·ly** \-fə-lē\ *adverb*
— **boast·ful·ness** *noun*
**²boast** (14th century)
*intransitive verb*
**1 :** to puff oneself up in speech **:** speak vaingloriously
**2** *archaic* **:** GLORY, EXULT
*transitive verb*
**1 :** to speak of or assert with excessive pride
**2 a :** to possess and often call attention to (something that is a source of pride) ⟨*boasts* a new stadium⟩ **b :** HAVE, CONTAIN ⟨a room *boasting* no more than a desk and a chair⟩ ☆
— **boast·er** *noun*
**³boast** *transitive verb* [origin unknown] (1823)
**:** to shape (stone) roughly in sculpture and stonecutting as a preliminary to finer work
**¹boat** \'bōt\ *noun* [Middle English *boot*, from Old English *bāt*; akin to Old Norse *beit* boat] (before 12th century)
**1 a :** a small vessel for travel on water **b :** SHIP
**2 :** a boat-shaped container, utensil, or device ⟨a gravy *boat*⟩ ⟨a laboratory *boat*⟩
— **boat·ful** \-,fúl\ *noun*
— **boat·like** \-,līk\ *adjective*
— **in the same boat :** in the same situation or predicament
**²boat** (1613)
*transitive verb*

**:** to place in or bring into a boat
*intransitive verb*
**:** to go by boat
**boat·build·er** \-,bil-dər\ *noun* (1679)
**:** one that builds boats
— **boat·build·ing** \-,bil-diŋ\ *noun*
**boat·er** \'bō-tər\ *noun* (1605)
**1 :** one who travels in a boat
**2 :** a stiff hat usually made of braided straw with a brim, hatband, and flat crown
**boat hook** *noun* (circa 1611)
**:** a pole-handled hook with a point or knob on the back used especially to pull or push a boat, raft, or log into place
**boat·house** \-,haús\ *noun* (1722)
**:** a building to house and protect boats
**boat·load** \'bōt-,lōd\ *noun* (1680)
**1 :** a load that fills a boat
**2 :** an indefinitely large number ⟨a *boatload* of money⟩
**boat·man** \'bōt-mən\ *noun* (14th century)
**:** a man who works on, deals in, or operates boats
**boat people** *noun plural* (1977)
**:** refugees fleeing by boat
**boat·swain** \'bō-sᵊn\ *noun* [Middle English *bootswein*, from *boot* boat + *swein* boy, servant — more at SWAIN] (14th century)
**1 :** a petty officer on a merchant ship having charge of hull maintenance and related work
**2 :** a naval warrant officer in charge of the hull and all related equipment
**boat train** *noun* (1884)
**:** an express train for transporting passengers between a port and a city
**boat·yard** \'bōt-,yärd\ *noun* (1847)
**:** a yard where boats are built, repaired, and stored and often sold or rented
**¹bob** \'bäb\ *verb* **bobbed; bob·bing** [Middle English *boben*] (13th century)
*transitive verb*
**1 :** to strike with a quick light blow **:** RAP
**2 :** to move up and down in a short quick movement ⟨*bob* the head⟩
**3 :** to polish with a bob **:** BUFF
*intransitive verb*
**1 a :** to move up and down briefly or repeatedly ⟨a cork *bobbed* in the water⟩ **b :** to emerge, arise, or appear suddenly or unexpectedly ⟨the question *bobbed* up again⟩
**2 :** to nod or curtsy briefly
**3 :** to try to seize a suspended or floating object with the teeth ⟨*bob* for apples⟩
**²bob** *noun* (1550)
**1 a :** a short quick down-and-up motion **b** *Scottish* **:** any of several folk dances
**2** *obsolete* **:** a blow or tap especially with the fist
**3 a :** a modification of the order in change ringing **b :** a method of change ringing using a bob
**4 :** a small polishing wheel of solid felt or leather with rounded edges
**³bob** *transitive verb* **bobbed; bob·bing** [Middle English *bobben*, from Middle French *bober*] (14th century)
**1** *obsolete* **:** DECEIVE, CHEAT
**2** *obsolete* **:** to take by fraud **:** FILCH
**⁴bob** *noun* [Middle English *bobbe*] (14th century)
**1 a** (1) **:** BUNCH, CLUSTER (2) *Scottish* **:** NOSEGAY **b :** a knob, knot, twist, or curl especially of ribbons, yarn, or hair **c :** a short haircut on a woman or child
**2 :** FLOAT 2a
**3 :** a hanging ball or weight (as on a plumb line)
**4 :** TRIFLE 1
**⁵bob** *transitive verb* **bobbed; bob·bing** (1675)
**1 :** to cut shorter **:** CROP ⟨*bob* a horse's tail⟩
**2 :** to cut (hair) in the style of a bob
**⁶bob** *noun, plural* **bob** [perhaps from the name *Bob*] (1789)
*slang British* **:** SHILLING
**⁷bob** *noun* (1856)

**:** BOBSLED
**¹bob·ber** \'bä-bər\ *noun* (1593)
**:** one that bobs
**²bobber** *noun* (1904)
**:** a person who rides or races on a bobsled
**bob·bery** \'bä-b(ə-)rē\ *noun, plural* **-ber·ies** [Hindi *bāp re*, literally, oh father!] (1803)
**:** HUBBUB
**bob·bin** \'bä-bən\ *noun* [origin unknown] (1530)
**1 a :** a cylinder or spindle on which yarn or thread is wound (as in a sewing machine) **b :** any of various small round devices on which threads are wound for working handmade lace **c :** a coil of insulated wire or the reel it is wound on
**2 :** a cotton cord formerly used by dressmakers for piping
**bob·bi·net** \'bä-bə-,net\ *noun* [blend of *bobbin* and *net*] (1814)
**:** a machine-made net of cotton, silk, or nylon usually with hexagonal mesh
**¹bob·ble** \'bä-bəl\ *verb* **bob·bled; bob·bling** \-b(ə-)liŋ\ [frequentative of ¹*bob*] (1812)
**1 :** ¹BOB
**2 :** FUMBLE
**²bobble** *noun* (1880)
**1 :** a repeated bobbing movement
**2 :** a small ball of fabric; *especially* **:** one in a series used on an edging ⟨curtains with *bobbles*⟩
**3 :** ERROR, MISTAKE; *especially* **:** a mishandling of the ball in baseball or football
**bob·by** \'bä-bē\ *noun, plural* **bobbies** [*Bobby*, nickname for *Robert*, after Sir *Robert* Peel, who organized the London police force] (1844)
*British* **:** POLICE OFFICER
**bobby pin** *noun* [perhaps from ⁴*bob*] (1932)
**:** a flat wire hairpin with prongs that press close together
**bobby socks** *or* **bobby sox** *noun plural* [perhaps from *bobby* pin] (1943)
**:** girls' socks reaching above the ankle
**bob·by–sox·er** \-,säk-sər\ *noun* (1944)
**:** an adolescent girl
**bob·cat** \'bäb-,kat\ *noun* [⁴*bob*; from the stubby tail] (1888)
**:** a common North American lynx (*Lynx rufus*) variably reddish in base color with dark markings

bobcat

**bo·beche** \bō-'besh, -'bäsh\ *noun* [French *bobèche*] (circa 1897)
**:** a usually glass collar on a candle socket to catch drippings or on a candlestick or chandelier to hold suspended glass prisms
**bob·o·link** \'bä-bə-,liŋk\ *noun* [imitative] (circa 1801)

---

☆ **SYNONYMS**
**Boast, brag, vaunt, crow** mean to express pride in oneself or one's accomplishments. BOAST often suggests ostentation and exaggeration ⟨*boasts* of every trivial success⟩, but it may imply a claiming with proper and justifiable pride ⟨the town *boasts* one of the best museums in the area⟩. BRAG suggests crudity and artlessness in glorifying oneself ⟨*bragging* of their exploits⟩. VAUNT usually connotes more pomp and bombast than BOAST and less crudity or naïveté than BRAG ⟨*vaunted* his country's military might⟩. CROW usually implies exultant boasting or bragging ⟨*crowed* after winning the championship⟩.

: an American migratory songbird (*Dolichonyx oryzivorus*) with the breeding male chiefly black

**bob·sled** \'bäb-ˌsled\ *noun* [perhaps from ⁴*bob*] (1839)
**1 :** a short sled usually used as one of a pair joined by a coupling
**2 :** a large usually metal sled used in racing and equipped with two pairs of runners in tandem, a long seat for two or more people, a steering wheel, and a hand brake
— **bobsled** *intransitive verb*
— **bob·sled·der** *noun*

**bob·sled·ding** \-ˌsle-diŋ\ *noun* (1883)
: the act, skill, or sport of riding or racing on a bobsled

**bob·stay** \'bäb-ˌstā\ *noun* [probably from ²*bob*] (1758)
: a stay to hold a ship's bowsprit down

**bob·tail** \'bäb-ˌtāl\ *noun* [⁴*bob*] (1605)
**1 a :** a bobbed tail **b :** a horse, dog, or cat with a bobbed or very short tail; *especially* : OLD ENGLISH SHEEPDOG
**2 :** something curtailed
— **bobtail** *or* **bob·tailed** \-ˌtāld\ *adjective*

**bob veal** \'bäb-\ *noun* [English dialect *bob* young calf] (1855)
: the veal of a very young or unborn calf

**bob·white** \'bäb-ˈhwīt, -ˈwīt\ *noun* [imitative] (1819)
: any of a genus (*Colinus*) of quail; *especially* : a popular game bird (*C. virginianus*) of the eastern and central U.S.

**bo·cac·cio** \bə-ˈkä-chē-ˌō, -chō\ *noun* [perhaps modification of Spanish *bocacha*, augmentative of *boca* mouth] (circa 1890)
: a large rockfish (*Sebastes paucispinis*) of the Pacific coast locally important as a market fish

**boc·cie** *or* **boc·ci** *or* **boc·ce** \'bä-chē\ *noun* [Italian *bocce*, plural of *boccia* ball, from (assumed) Vulgar Latin *bottia* boss] (1926)
: a game of Italian origin similar to lawn bowling played on a long narrow usually dirt court

**bock** \'bäk\ *noun* [German, short for *Bockbier*, by shortening & alteration from *Einbecker Bier*, literally, beer from Einbeck, from *Einbeck*, Germany] (1856)
: a heavy dark rich beer usually sold in the early spring

**bod** \'bäd\ *noun* (1933)
**1** *British* : FELLOW, GUY
**2 :** BODY

**bo·da·cious** \bō-ˈdā-shəs\ *adjective* [probably blend of *bold* and *audacious*] (1845)
**1** *Southern & Midland* : OUTRIGHT, UNMISTAKABLE
**2 :** REMARKABLE, NOTEWORTHY ⟨the *bodacious* 1974 comedy —*People*⟩
— **bo·da·cious·ly** *adverb*

¹**bode** \'bōd\ *transitive verb* **bod·ed; bod·ing** [Middle English, from Old English *bodian*; akin to Old English *bēodan* to proclaim — more at BID] (before 12th century)
**1** *archaic* : to announce beforehand : FORETELL
**2 :** to indicate by signs : PRESAGE ⟨this controversy . . . will *bode* ill for both of us —A. H. Lowe⟩

²**bode** *past of* BIDE

**bo·de·ga** \bō-ˈdā-gə\ *noun* [Spanish, from Latin *apotheca* storehouse — more at APOTHECARY] (1846)
**1 :** a storehouse for maturing wine
**2 a :** WINESHOP **b** (1) : ¹BAR 5a (2) : BARROOM
**3 :** a store specializing in Hispanic groceries

**bode·ment** \'bōd-mənt\ *noun* (1605)
**1 :** OMEN, FOREBODING
**2 :** PREDICTION, PROPHECY

**bo·dhi·satt·va** *or* **bod·dhi·satt·va** \ˌbō-di-ˈsət-və, -ˈsät-\ *noun* [Sanskrit *bodhisattva* one whose essence is enlightenment, from *bodhi* enlightenment + *sattva* being — more at BID] (1828)
: a being that compassionately refrains from entering nirvana in order to save others and is worshiped as a deity in Mahayana Buddhism

**bodh·ran** \'bȯ-(ˌ)rän, -rən\ *noun* [Irish *bodhrán*] (1972)
: an Irish goatskin drum

**bod·ice** \'bä-dəs\ *noun* [alteration of *bodies*, plural of ¹*body*] (circa 1567)
**1 :** the upper part of a woman's dress
**2** *archaic* : CORSET, STAYS ◆

**bodice ripper** *noun* (1980)
: a historical or Gothic romance typically featuring scenes in which the heroine is subjected to sexual violence

**bod·ied** \'bä-dēd\ *adjective* (circa 1547)
: having a body of a specified kind — used in combination ⟨full-*bodied*⟩ ⟨glass-*bodied*⟩

**bodi·less** \'bä-di-ləs, 'bä-dᵊl-əs\ *adjective* (14th century)
: having no body

¹**bodi·ly** \'bä-dᵊl-ē\ *adjective* (14th century)
**1 :** having a body : PHYSICAL
**2 :** of or relating to the body ⟨*bodily* comfort⟩ ⟨*bodily* organs⟩

²**bodily** *adverb* (14th century)
**1 :** in the flesh
**2 :** as a whole : ALTOGETHER

**bod·ing** \'bō-diŋ\ *noun* (13th century)
: FOREBODING

**bod·kin** \'bäd-kən\ *noun* [Middle English *bodekin*] (14th century)
**1 a :** DAGGER, STILETTO **b :** a sharp slender instrument for making holes in cloth **c :** an ornamental hairpin shaped like a stiletto
**2 :** a blunt needle with a large eye for drawing tape or ribbon through a loop or hem

¹**body** \'bä-dē\ *noun, plural* **bod·ies** [Middle English, from Old English *bodig*; akin to Old High German *boteh* corpse] (before 12th century)
**1 a :** the main part of a plant or animal body especially as distinguished from limbs and head : TRUNK **b :** the main, central, or principal part: as (1) : the nave of a church (2) : the bed or box of a vehicle on or in which the load is placed (3) : the enclosed or partly enclosed part of an automobile
**2 a :** the organized physical substance of an animal or plant either living or dead: as (1) : the material part or nature of a human being (2) : the dead organism : CORPSE **b :** a human being : PERSON
**3 a :** a mass of matter distinct from other masses ⟨a *body* of water⟩ ⟨a celestial *body*⟩ **b** : something that embodies or gives concrete reality to a thing; *also* : a sensible object in physical space **c :** AGGREGATE, QUANTITY ⟨a *body* of evidence⟩
**4 a :** the part of a garment covering the body or trunk **b :** the main part of a literary or journalistic work : TEXT 2b **c :** the sound box or pipe of a musical instrument
**5 :** a group of persons or things: as **a :** a fighting unit : FORCE **b :** a group of individuals organized for some purpose ⟨a legislative *body*⟩
**6 a :** fullness and richness of flavor (as of wine) **b :** VISCOSITY, CONSISTENCY — used especially of oils and grease **c :** compactness or firmness of texture **d :** fullness or resonance of a musical tone

²**body** *transitive verb* **bod·ied; body·ing** (15th century)
**1 :** to give form or shape to : EMBODY
**2 :** REPRESENT, SYMBOLIZE — usually used with *forth*

**body bag** *noun* (1954)
: a large zippered usually rubber bag in which a human corpse is placed especially for transportation

**body blow** *noun* (1792)
**1 :** a blow to the body
**2 :** a damaging or deeply felt blow ⟨an economic *body blow*⟩

**body·build·ing** \-ˌbil-diŋ\ *noun* (1904)
: the developing of the body through exercise and diet; *specifically* : the developing of the physique for competitive exhibition
— **body·build·er** *noun*

**body cavity** *noun* (1875)

: a cavity in an animal body; *specifically* : COELOM

**body–cen·tered** \'bä-dē-ˌsen-tərd\ *adjective* (1921)
: relating to or being a crystal space lattice in which each cubic unit cell has an atom at its center and at each vertex — compare FACE-CENTERED

**body check** *noun* (1892)
: a blocking of an opposing player with the body (as in ice hockey or lacrosse)
— **body–check** \'bä-dē-ˌchek\ *transitive verb*

**body clock** *noun* (1968)
: the internal mechanisms that schedule periodic bodily functions and activities — usually not used technically

**body corporate** *noun* (15th century)
: CORPORATION

**body count** *noun* (1967)
**1 :** a count of the bodies of killed enemy soldiers
**2 :** the number of persons involved in a particular activity

**body English** *noun* (1908)
: bodily motions made in a usually unconscious effort to influence the progress of a propelled object (as a ball)

**body·guard** \'bä-dē-ˌgärd\ *noun* (circa 1735)
: a usually armed attendant or group of attendants whose duty is to protect a person

**body language** *noun* (1926)
: the gestures, movements, and mannerisms by which a person or animal communicates with others

**body louse** *noun* (1575)
: a louse feeding primarily on the body; *especially* : a sucking louse (*Pediculus humanus humanus*) feeding on the body and living in the clothing of humans — called also *cootie*

**body mechanics** *noun plural but singular or plural in construction* (circa 1970)
: systematic exercises designed especially to develop coordination, endurance, and poise

**body politic** *noun* (15th century)
**1 :** a group of persons politically organized under a single governmental authority
**2** *archaic* : CORPORATION 2
**3 :** a people considered as a collective unit

**body shirt** *noun* (1967)
**1 :** a close-fitting shirt or blouse
**2 :** a woman's close-fitting top made with a sewn-in or snapped crotch

**body shop** *noun* (1954)

◇ WORD HISTORY
**bodice** The word *bodice* was originally identical with *bodies*, the plural of *body*. In the 16th century, *body* was used for one half of a corsetlike undergarment worn originally by both women and men. The front and back halves together were called "a pair of bodies." In the 14th century, a tendency had begun to pronounce plural -*s* after a vowel sound as \z\, but in the 16th century this rule was not absolute. It was with the \s\ sound that *bodies* in "a pair of bodies" froze, as speakers lost the sense that *bodies* in reference to a corset had any connection with the plural of *body*. Like all other words ending in a vowel *body* came to form its plural exclusively with a final \z\ sound. By 1679 "a pair of bodies" was being spelled "a pair of bodice," and even when still spelled *bodies* it began to be used as a singular noun rather than a plural. By that time it frequently had its modern sense "the upper part of a woman's dress."

: a shop where automotive bodies are made or repaired

**body snatcher** *noun* (1812)
: one that steals corpses from graves

**body stocking** *noun* (1965)
: a sheer close-fitting one-piece garment for the torso that often has sleeves and legs

**body·suit** \'bä-dē-,süt\ *noun* (1970)
: a close-fitting one-piece garment for the torso

**body·surf** \'bä-dē-,sərf\ *intransitive verb* (1943)
: to ride on a wave without a surfboard by planing on the chest and stomach
— **body·surf·er** *noun*

**body wall** *noun* (1888)
: the external surface of the animal body consisting of ectoderm and mesoderm and enclosing the body cavity

**body·work** \'bä-dē-,wərk\ *noun* (1908)
**1** : a vehicle body
**2** : the act or process of making or repairing vehicle bodies
**3** : therapeutic touching or manipulation of the body by using specialized techniques

**boehm·ite** \'bā-,mīt, 'bə(r)-\ *noun* [German *Böhmit*, from J. *Böhm* (Boehm), 20th century German scientist] (circa 1929)
: a mineral consisting of an orthorhombic form of aluminum oxide and hydroxide AlO(OH) found in bauxite

**Boer** \'bōr, 'bör, 'bùr\ *noun* [Dutch, literally, farmer — more at BOOR] (1834)
: a South African of Dutch or Huguenot descent

**¹boff** \'bäf\ *transitive verb* [from *boff* blow, punch, perhaps imitative] (1937)
: to have sexual intercourse with — sometimes considered vulgar

**²boff** *or* **bof·fo** \'bä-(,)fō\ *noun, plural* **boffs** *or* **boffos** [perhaps from *box office*] (1946)
**1** : a hearty laugh
**2** : a gag or line that produces a hearty laugh
**3** : something that is conspicuously successful
: HIT

**bof·fin** \'bä-fən\ *noun* [origin unknown] (1945)
*chiefly British* : a scientific expert; *especially*
: one involved in technological research

**bof·fo** \'bä-(,)fō\ *adjective* (1949)
: extremely successful : SENSATIONAL

**bof·fo·la** \bä-'fō-lə\ *noun* [irregular from *boff*] (1946)
: BOFF

**Bo·fors gun** \'bō-,förz-, 'bü-\ *noun* [*Bofors*, munition works in Sweden] (1939)
: a double-barreled automatic antiaircraft gun

**¹bog** \'bäg, 'bòg\ *noun* [Middle English (Scots), from Scottish Gaelic & Irish *bog-* (as in *bogluachair* bulrushes), from *bog* marshy, literally, soft, from Middle Irish *bocc;* probably akin to Old English *būgan* to bend — more at BOW] (14th century)
: wet spongy ground; *especially* : a poorly drained usually acid area rich in accumulated plant material, frequently surrounding a body of open water, and having a characteristic flora (as of sedges, heaths, and sphagnum)
— **bog·gy** \'bä-gē, 'bò-\ *adjective*

**²bog** *verb* **bogged; bog·ging** (1599)
*transitive verb*
: to cause to sink into or as if into a bog : IMPEDE, MIRE — usually used with *down*
*intransitive verb*
: to become impeded or stuck — usually used with *down*

**bog asphodel** *noun* (1857)
: either of two bog herbs (*Narthecium ossifragum* of Europe and *N. americanum* of the U.S.) of the lily family

**¹bo·gey** *also* **bo·gie** *or* **bo·gy** *noun, plural* **bogeys** *also* **bogies** [probably alteration of *bogle*] (1857)
**1** \'bù-gē, 'bō-, 'bü-\ : SPECTER, PHANTOM
**2** \'bō-gē *also* 'bù- *or* 'bü-\ : a source of fear, perplexity, or harassment

**3** \'bō-gē\ **a** *chiefly British* : an average golfer's score used as a standard for a particular hole or course **b** : one stroke over par on a hole in golf
**4** \'bō-gē\ : a numerical standard of performance set up as a mark to be aimed at in competition
**5** \'bō-gē\ : an unidentified aircraft; *especially* : one not positively identified as friendly and so assumed to be hostile

**²bo·gey** \'bō-gē\ *transitive verb* **bo·geyed; bo·gey·ing** (1948)
: to shoot (a hole in golf) in one over par

**bo·gey·man** *also* **bo·gy·man** \'bù-gē-,man, 'bō-, 'bü-, 'bù-gər-\ *noun* (circa 1890)
**1** : a monstrous imaginary figure used in threatening children
**2** : a terrifying or dreaded person or thing
: BUGBEAR

**bog·gle** \'bä-gəl\ *verb* **bog·gled; bog·gling** \-g(ə-)liŋ\ [perhaps from *bogle*] (1598)
*intransitive verb*
**1** : to start with fright or amazement : be overwhelmed (the mind *boggles* at the research needed)
**2** : to hesitate because of doubt, fear, or scruples
*transitive verb*
**1** : MISHANDLE, BUNGLE
**2** : to overwhelm with wonder or bewilderment
— **boggle** *noun*

**bo·gie** *also* **bo·gey** \'bō-gē\ *noun, plural* **bo·gies** *also* **bogeys** [origin unknown] (1835)
**1** : a low strongly built cart
**2 a** *chiefly British* : a swiveling railway truck **b** : the driving-wheel assembly consisting of the rear four wheels of a 6-wheel automotive truck
**3** : a small supporting or aligning wheel (as on the inside perimeter of a tank tread)

**bo·gle** \'bō-gəl\ *also* **bog·gle** \'bä-gəl\ *noun* [origin unknown] (circa 1505)
*dialect British* : GOBLIN, SPECTER; *also* : an object of fear or loathing

**Bo·go·mil** *also* **Bo·go·mile** \,bə-gə-'mē(ə)l\ *noun* [Middle Greek *Bogomilos*, from *Bogomilos* Bogomil, 10th century Bulgarian priest, founder of the sect] (1841)
: a member of a medieval Bulgarian sect holding that God has two sons, the rebellious Satan and the obedient Jesus

**bo·gus** \'bō-gəs\ *adjective* [*bogus* (a machine for making counterfeit money)] (1825)
: not genuine : COUNTERFEIT, SHAM

**bo·hea** \bō-'hē\ *noun, often capitalized* [Chinese (Fujian) *Bú-î*, hills in China where it was grown] (1701)
: a black tea

**bo·he·mia** \bō-'hē-mē-ə\ *noun, often capitalized* [translation of French *bohème*] (1861)
: a community of bohemians : the world of bohemians

**Bo·he·mi·an** \-mē-ən\ *noun* (1603)
**1 a** : a native or inhabitant of Bohemia **b** : the group of Czech dialects used in Bohemia
**2** *often not capitalized* **a** : VAGABOND, WANDERER; *especially* : GYPSY **b** : a person (as a writer or an artist) living an unconventional life usually in a colony with others
— **bohemian** *adjective, often capitalized*

**Bohemian Brethren** *noun plural* (circa 1862)
: a Christian body originating in Bohemia in 1467 and forming a parent body of the Moravian Church

**bo·he·mi·an·ism** \bō-'hē-mē-ə-,ni-zəm\ *noun, often capitalized* (1861)
: the unconventional way of life of bohemians

**Bohr effect** \'bōr-, 'bòr-\ *noun* [Christian *Bohr* (died 1911) Danish physiologist] (1939)
: the decrease in the oxygen affinity of a respiratory pigment (as hemoglobin) in response to decreased blood pH resulting from increased carbon dioxide concentration in the blood

**Bohr theory** *noun* [Niels *Bohr*] (1922)

: a theory in early quantum physics: an atom consists of a positively charged nucleus about which revolves one or more electrons of quantized energy

**bo·hunk** \'bō-,həŋk\ *noun* [*Bohemian* + *Hunk* person of central European descent, by shortening & alteration of *Hungarian*] (circa 1903)
: a person of central European descent or birth — usually used disparagingly

**¹boil** \'bòi(ə)l\ *verb* [Middle English, from Old French *boillir,* from Latin *bullire* to bubble, from *bulla* bubble] (13th century)
*intransitive verb*
**1 a** : to come to the boiling point **b** : to generate bubbles of vapor when heated — used of a liquid **c** : to cook in boiling water
**2** : to become agitated like boiling water
: SEETHE
**3** : to be moved, excited, or stirred up (made his blood *boil*)
**4 a** : to rush headlong **b** : to burst forth
: ERUPT (water *boiling* from a spring)
**5** : to undergo the action of a boiling liquid
*transitive verb*
**1** : to subject to the action of a boiling liquid
**2** : to heat to the boiling point
**3** : to form or separate (as sugar or salt) by boiling
— **boil·able** \'bòi-lə-bəl\ *adjective*

**²boil** *noun* [Middle English, alteration of *bile,* from Old English *bȳl;* akin to Old High German *pūlla* bladder] (15th century)
: a localized swelling and inflammation of the skin resulting from infection in a skin gland, having a hard central core, and forming pus

**³boil** *noun* (15th century)
**1** : the act or state of boiling
**2** : a swirling upheaval (as of water)

**boil down** (1845)
*transitive verb*
**1** : to reduce in bulk by boiling
**2** : CONDENSE, SUMMARIZE (boil down a report)
*intransitive verb*
**1** : to undergo reduction in bulk by boiling
**2 a** : to be equivalent in summary : AMOUNT (his speech *boiled down* to a plea for more money) **b** : to reduce ultimately (your choices *boil down* to three)

**boil·er** \'bòi-lər\ *noun* (circa 1540)
**1** : one that boils
**2 a** : a vessel used for boiling **b** : the part of a steam generator in which water is converted into steam and which consists usually of metal shells and tubes **c** : a tank in which water is heated or hot water is stored

**boil·er·mak·er** \'bòi-lər-,mā-kər\ *noun* (1865)
**1** : a worker who makes, assembles, or repairs boilers
**2** : whiskey with a beer chaser

**boil·er·plate** \-,plāt\ *noun* (1897)
**1** : syndicated material supplied especially to weekly newspapers in matrix or plate form
**2 a** : standardized text **b** : formulaic or hackneyed language (bureaucratic *boilerplate*)

**boiler room** *noun* (1903)
**1** : a room in which a boiler is located
**2** : a room equipped with telephones used for making high-pressure usually fraudulent sales pitches

**boil·er·suit** \-,süt\ *noun* (1928)
: COVERALL

**¹boil·ing** \'bòi-liŋ\ *adjective* (14th century)
**1 a** : heated to the boiling point **b** : TORRID (a *boiling* sun)
**2** : intensely agitated (a *boiling* sea) (*boiling* with anger)

**²boiling** *adverb* (1607)
: to an extreme degree : VERY (*boiling* mad) (*boiling* hot)

**boiling point** *noun* (1773)
**1** : the temperature at which a liquid boils
**2 a** : the point at which a person becomes uncontrollably angry **b** : the point of crisis
: HEAD 17b (matters had reached the *boiling point*)

**boil over** *intransitive verb* (15th century)
**1 :** to overflow while boiling or during boiling
**2 :** to become so incensed as to lose one's temper
**bois d'arc** \'bō-ˌdä(r)k, *dialect also* 'bwä-, 'bȯr-\ *noun, plural* **bois d'arcs** *or* **bois d'arc** [American French, literally, bow wood] (1805)
**:** OSAGE ORANGE; *also* **:** its wood
**bois·ter·ous** \'bȯi-st(ə-)rəs\ *adjective* [Middle English *boistous* rough] (14th century)
**1** *obsolete* **a :** COARSE **b :** DURABLE, STRONG **c :** MASSIVE
**2 a :** noisily turbulent **:** ROWDY **b :** marked by or expressive of exuberance and high spirits
**3 :** STORMY, TUMULTUOUS
**synonym** see VOCIFEROUS
— **bois·ter·ous·ly** *adverb*
— **bois·ter·ous·ness** *noun*
**boîte** \'bwät\ *noun* [French, literally, box] (1922)
**:** NIGHTCLUB
**bok choy** \'bäk-'chȯi\ *noun* [Chinese (Guangdong) *baahk-choi*, literally, white vegetable] (1938)
**:** a Chinese cabbage (*Brassica chinensis*) forming an open head with long white stalks and green leaves
**Bok·mål** \'bük-ˌmȯl, 'bōk-\ *noun* [Norwegian, literally, book language] (1931)
**:** a literary form of Norwegian developed by the gradual reform of written Danish — compare NYNORSK
**bo·la** \'bō-lə\ *or* **bo·las** \-ləs\ *noun, plural* **bo·las** \-ləz\ *also* **bo·las·es** [American Spanish *bolas*, from Spanish *bola* ball] (1818)
**:** a cord with weights attached to the ends for throwing at and entangling an animal

**bola**

¹**bold** \'bōld\ *adjective* [Middle English, from Old English *beald*; akin to Old High German *bald* bold] (before 12th century)
**1 a :** fearless before danger **:** INTREPID **b :** showing or requiring a fearless daring spirit ⟨a *bold* plan⟩
**2 :** IMPUDENT, PRESUMPTUOUS
**3** *obsolete* **:** ASSURED, CONFIDENT
**4 :** SHEER, STEEP ⟨*bold* cliffs⟩
**5 :** ADVENTUROUS, FREE ⟨a *bold* thinker⟩
**6 :** standing out prominently
**7 :** being or set in boldface
— **bold·ly** \'bōl(d)-lē\ *adverb*
— **bold·ness** \'bōl(d)-nəs\ *noun*
²**bold** *noun* (circa 1871)
**:** BOLDFACE
**bold·face** \'bōl(d)-ˌfās\ *noun* (circa 1889)
**:** a heavy-faced type; *also* **:** printing in boldface
**bold-faced** \'bōl(d)-'fāst\ *adjective* (1591)
**1 :** bold in manner or conduct **:** IMPUDENT
**2** *usually* **bold·faced :** being or set in boldface
**bole** \'bōl\ *noun* [Middle English, from Old Norse *bolr*] (14th century)
**:** TRUNK 1a
**bo·le·ro** \bə-'ler-(ˌ)ō\ *noun, plural* **-ros** [Spanish] (1787)
**1 :** a Spanish dance characterized by sharp turns, stamping of the feet, and sudden pauses in a position with one arm arched over the head; *also* **:** music in ¾ time for a bolero
**2 :** a loose waist-length jacket open at the front
**bo·lete** \bō-'lēt\ *noun* [New Latin *Boletus*] (1914)
**:** any of a family (Boletaceae) of fleshy stalked pore fungi that usually grow on the ground in wooded areas; *especially* **:** BOLETUS
**bo·le·tus** \bō-'lē-təs\ *noun, plural* **-tus** *or* **-ti** \-ˌlē-ˌtī\ [New Latin, genus name, from Latin, mushroom] (1601)

**:** any of a genus (*Boletus*) of boletes (as a cèpe) some of which are poisonous and others edible
**bo·lide** \'bō-ˌlīd, -lid\ *noun* [French, from Latin *bolid-, bolis*, from Greek, from *bolē* throw, stroke] (1852)
**:** a large meteor **:** FIREBALL; *especially* **:** one that explodes
**bo·li·var** \bə-'lē-ˌvär, 'bä-lə-vər\ *noun, plural* **-va·res** \ˌbä-lə-'vär-ˌās, ˌbō-li-\ *or* **-vars** [American Spanish *bolívar*, from Simón *Bolívar*] (circa 1895)
— see MONEY table
**bo·li·vi·a·no** \bə-ˌli-vē-'ä-(ˌ)nō\ *noun, plural* **-nos** [American Spanish] (circa 1872)
— see MONEY table
**boll** \'bōl\ *noun* [Middle English] (15th century)
**:** the pod or capsule of a plant (as cotton)
**bol·lard** \'bä-lərd, *British also* -ˌlärd\ *noun* [perhaps from *bole*] (circa 1775)
**1 :** a post of metal or wood on a wharf around which to fasten mooring lines
**2 :** BITT 1
**3** *chiefly British* **:** any of a series of short posts set at intervals to delimit an area (as a traffic island) or to exclude vehicles
**bol·lix** \'bä-liks\ *transitive verb* [alteration of *ballocks*, plural of *ballock* (testis), from Middle English, from Old English *bealluc* — more at BALL] (1937)
**:** to throw into disorder; *also* **:** BUNGLE — usually used with *up*
— **bollix** *noun*
**boll weevil** *noun* (1895)
**:** a grayish weevil (*Anthonomus grandis*) that infests the cotton plant and feeds on the squares and bolls
**boll·worm** \'bōl-ˌwərm\ *noun* (1847)
**:** CORN EARWORM; *also* **:** any of several other moths or their immature stages that feed on cotton bolls as larvae
**bo·lo** \'bō-(ˌ)lō\ *noun, plural* **bolos** [Philippine Spanish] (circa 1900)
**:** a long heavy single-edged knife of Philippine origin used to cut vegetation and as a weapon
**bo·lo·gna** \bə-'lō-nē *also* -nyə, -nə\ *noun* [short for *Bologna sausage*, from *Bologna*, Italy] (1596)
**:** a large smoked sausage of beef, veal, and pork; *also* **:** a sausage made (as of turkey) to resemble bologna
**bo·lom·e·ter** \bō-'lä-mə-tər\ *noun* [Greek *bolē* stroke, beam of light (from *ballein* to throw) + English *-o- + -meter* — more at DEVIL] (1881)
**:** a very sensitive thermometer whose electrical resistance varies with temperature and which is used in the detection and measurement of feeble thermal radiation and is especially adapted to the study of infrared spectra
— **bo·lo·met·ric** \ˌbō-lə-'me-trik\ *adjective*
— **bo·lo·met·ri·cal·ly** \-tri-k(ə-)lē\ *adverb*
**bo·lo·ney** \bə-'lō-nē\ *variant of* BALONEY
**bo·lo tie** \'bō-lō-\ *or* **bo·la tie** \-lə-\ *noun* [probably from *bola*] (1964)
**:** a cord fastened around the neck with an ornamental clasp and worn as a necktie
**Bol·she·vik** \'bōl-shə-ˌvik, 'bȯl-, 'bäl-, -ˌvēk\ *noun, plural* **Bolsheviks** *also* **Bol·she·vi·ki** \ˌbōl-shə-'vi-kē, ˌbȯl-, ˌbäl-, -'vē-kē\ [Russian *bol'shevik*, from *bol'shiĭ* greater] (1917)
**1 :** a member of the extremist wing of the Russian Social Democratic party that seized power in Russia by the Revolution of November 1917
**2 :** COMMUNIST 3
— **Bolshevik** *adjective*
**bol·she·vism** \'bōl-shə-ˌvi-zəm, 'bȯl-, 'bäl-\ *noun, often capitalized* (1917)
**1 :** the doctrine or program of the Bolsheviks advocating violent overthrow of capitalism
**2 :** Russian communism
**Bol·she·vist** \-vist\ *noun or adjective* (1917)
**:** BOLSHEVIK

**bol·she·vize** \-ˌvīz\ *transitive verb* **-vized; -viz·ing** (1919)
**:** to make Bolshevist
— **Bol·she·vi·za·tion** \ˌbōl-shə-və-'zā-shən, ˌbȯl-, ˌbäl-\ *noun*
**bol·shie** *or* **bol·shy** \'bōl-shē, 'bȯl-, 'bäl-\ *noun or adjective, often capitalized* [by shortening & alteration] (1918)
**:** BOLSHEVIK
¹**bol·ster** \'bōl-stər\ *noun* [Middle English, from Old English; akin to Old English *belg* bag — more at BELLY] (before 12th century)
**1 :** a long pillow or cushion
**2 :** a structural part designed to eliminate friction or provide support or bearing
²**bolster** *transitive verb* **bol·stered; bol·ster·ing** \-st(ə-)riŋ\ (1508)
**1 :** to support with or as if with a bolster **:** REINFORCE
**2 :** to give a boost to ⟨news that *bolstered* his spirits⟩
— **bol·ster·er** \-stər-ər\ *noun*
¹**bolt** \'bōlt\ *noun* [Middle English, from Old English; akin to Old High German *bolz* crossbow bolt, and perhaps to Lithuanian *beldėti* to beat] (before 12th century)
**1 a :** a shaft or missile designed to be shot from a crossbow or catapult; *especially* **:** a short stout usually blunt-headed arrow

**bolt 4**

**b :** a lightning stroke; *also* **:** THUNDERBOLT
**2 a :** a wood or metal bar or rod used to fasten a door **b :** the part of a lock that is shot or withdrawn by the key
**3 :** a roll of cloth or wallpaper of specified length
**4 :** a metal rod or pin for fastening objects together that usually has a head at one end and a screw thread at the other and is secured by a nut
**5 a :** a block of timber to be sawed or cut **b :** a short round section of a log
**6 :** a metal cylinder that drives the cartridge into the chamber of a firearm, locks the breech, and usually contains the firing pin and extractor
²**bolt** (13th century)
*intransitive verb*
**1 :** to move suddenly or nervously **:** START
**2 :** to move rapidly **:** DASH
**3 a :** to dart off or away **:** FLEE **b :** to break away from control or a set course
**4 :** to break away from or oppose one's previous affiliation (as with a political party or candidate)
**5 :** to produce seed prematurely
*transitive verb*
**1 a** *archaic* **:** SHOOT, DISCHARGE **b :** FLUSH, START ⟨*bolt* rabbits⟩
**2 :** to say impulsively **:** BLURT
**3 :** to secure with a bolt
**4 :** to attach or fasten with bolts
**5 :** to swallow hastily or without chewing
**6 :** to break away from or refuse to support (as a political party)
³**bolt** *adverb* (14th century)
**1 :** in an erect or straight-backed position **:** RIGIDLY ⟨sat *bolt* upright⟩
**2** *archaic* **:** DIRECTLY, STRAIGHT
⁴**bolt** *noun* (1550)
**:** the act or an instance of bolting

---

\ə\ **abut** \ᵊ\ **kitten** \ər\ **further** \a\ **ash** \ā\ **ace**
\ä\ **mop, mar** \au̇\ **out** \ch\ **chin** \e\ **bet** \ē\ **easy**
\g\ **go** \i\ **hit** \ī\ **ice** \j\ **job** \ŋ\ **sing** \ō\ **go**
\ȯ\ **law** \ȯi\ **boy** \th\ **thin** \t̷h\ **the** \ü\ **loot** \u̇\ **foot**
\y\ **yet** \zh\ **vision**    *see also* Guide to Pronunciation

**⁵bolt** *transitive verb* [Middle English *bulten,* from Old French *buleter,* modification of Middle High German *biuteln* to sift, from *biutel* bag, from Old High German *būtil*] (13th century)
**1 :** to sift (as flour) usually through fine-meshed cloth
**2** *archaic* **:** SIFT 2
**bolt–ac·tion** \'bōlt-'ak-shən\ *adjective* (1896) *of a firearm* **:** loaded by means of a manually operated bolt
**bolt·er** \'bōl-tər\ *noun* (circa 1699)
**:** one that bolts: as **a :** a horse given to running away **b :** a voter who bolts from a political party
**bolt–hole** \'bōlt-,hōl\ *noun* (circa 1851) *chiefly British* **:** a place of escape or refuge
**bolt·rope** \'bōlt-,rōp\ *noun* (circa 1626)
**:** a strong rope stitched to the edges of a sail to strengthen it
**bo·lus** \'bō-ləs\ *noun* [Late Latin, from Greek *bōlos* lump] (1562)
**:** a rounded mass: as **a :** a large pill **b :** a soft mass of chewed food
**¹bomb** \'bäm\ *noun* [French *bombe,* from Italian *bomba,* probably from Latin *bombus* deep hollow sound, from Greek *bombos,* of imitative origin] (1684)
**1 a :** an explosive device fused to detonate under specified conditions **b :** ATOMIC BOMB; *also* **:** nuclear weapons in general — usually used with *the*
**2 :** a vessel for compressed gases: as **a :** a pressure vessel for conducting chemical experiments **b :** a container for an aerosol **:** SPRAY CAN
**3 :** a rounded mass of lava exploded from a volcano
**4 :** a lead-lined container for radioactive material
**5 :** FAILURE, FLOP ⟨the play was a *bomb*⟩
**6** *British* **:** a large sum of money
**7** *British* **:** a great success **:** HIT
**8 :** a long pass in football
**²bomb** (1688)
*transitive verb*
**1 :** to attack with or as if with bombs **:** BOMBARD
**2 :** to defeat decisively
*intransitive verb*
**1 :** to fall flat **:** FAIL
**2** *slang* **:** to move rapidly ⟨*bombed* down the hill⟩
**— bomb·ing** *noun*
**¹bom·bard** \'bäm-,bärd\ *noun* [Middle English *bombarde,* from Middle French, probably from Latin *bombus*] (15th century)
**:** a late medieval cannon used to hurl large stones
**²bom·bard** \bäm-'bärd *also* bəm-\ *transitive verb* (1686)
**1 :** to attack especially with artillery or bombers
**2 :** to assail vigorously or persistently (as with questions)
**3 :** to subject to the impact of rapidly moving particles (as electrons)
**synonym** see ATTACK
**— bom·bard·ment** \-mənt\ *noun*
**bom·bar·dier** \,bäm-bə-'dir, -bər-\ *noun* (1560)
**1 a** *archaic* **:** ARTILLERYMAN **b :** a noncommissioned officer in the British artillery
**2 :** a bomber-crew member who releases the bombs
**bom·bar·don** \'bäm-bər-,dōn, bäm-'bär-d°n\ *noun* [French, from Italian *bombardone*] (1856)
**1 :** a bass tuba
**2 :** the bass member of the shawm family
**bom·bast** \'bäm-,bast\ *noun* [Middle English *bombast* cotton padding, from Middle French *bombace,* from Medieval Latin *bombac-, bombax* cotton, alteration of Latin *bombyc-, bom-*

*byx* silkworm, silk, from Greek *bombyk-, bombyx*] (1589)
**:** pretentious inflated speech or writing
**bom·bas·tic** \bäm-'bas-tik\ *adjective* (1704)
**:** marked by or given to bombast **:** POMPOUS, OVERBLOWN
**— bom·bas·ti·cal·ly** \-ti-k(ə-)lē\ *adverb*
**bom·ba·zine** \,bäm-bə-'zēn\ *noun* [Middle French *bombasin,* from Medieval Latin *bombacinum, bombycinum* silken texture, from Latin, neuter of *bombycinus* of silk, from *bombyc-, bombyx*] (1572)
**1 :** a twilled fabric with silk warp and worsted filling
**2 :** a silk fabric in twill weave dyed black
**bombe** \'bäm, 'bōⁿ(m)b\ *noun* [French, literally, bomb] (1892)
**:** a frozen dessert usually containing ice cream and formed in layers in a mold
**bom·bé** *or* **bom·be** \(,)bäm-'bā, (,)bōⁿ-\ *adjective* [French, from *bombe*] (1904)
**:** having outward curving lines — usually used of furniture
**bombed** \'bämd\ *adjective* (1959)
**:** affected by alcohol or drugs **:** DRUNK, HIGH
**bomb·er** \'bä-mər\ *noun* (1915)
**1 :** one that bombs; *specifically* **:** an airplane designed for bombing
**2 :** BOMBER JACKET
**bomber jacket** *noun* (1952)
**:** a zippered usually leather jacket with front pockets and knitted cuffs and waistband
**bom·bi·nate** \'bäm-bə-,nāt\ *intransitive verb* **-nat·ed; -nat·ing** [New Latin *bombinatus,* past participle of *bombinare,* alteration of Latin *bombilare,* from *bombus*] (1880)
**:** BUZZ, DRONE
**— bom·bi·na·tion** \,bäm-bə-'nā-shən\ *noun*
**bomb·proof** \'bäm-,prüf\ *adjective* (1702)
**:** safe from the force of bombs
**bomb·shell** \'bäm-,shel\ *noun* (1708)
**1 :** BOMB 1a
**2 :** one that is stunning, amazing, or devastating ⟨the book was a political *bombshell*⟩
**bomb·sight** \-,sīt\ *noun* (1917)
**:** a sighting device for aiming bombs
**bo·na fi·des** \'bō-nə-,fīd, 'bä-; ,bō-nə-'fī-dē, -'fī-də\ *adjective* [Latin, literally, in good faith] (1788)
**1 :** made in good faith without fraud or deceit ⟨a *bona fide* offer to buy a farm⟩
**2 :** made with earnest intent **:** SINCERE
**3 :** neither specious nor counterfeit **:** GENUINE
**synonym** see AUTHENTIC
**bo·na fi·des** \,bō-nə-'fī-,dēz, ÷'bō-nə-,fīdz\ *noun* [Latin, literally, good faith] (1798)
**1 :** good faith **:** SINCERITY
**2 :** the fact of being genuine — often plural in construction
**3 :** evidence of one's good faith or genuineness — often plural in construction
**4 :** evidence of one's qualifications or achievements — often plural in construction
**bo·nan·za** \bə-'nan-zə\ *noun* [Spanish, literally, calm sea, from Medieval Latin *bonacia,* alteration of Latin *malacia,* from Greek *malakia,* literally, softness, from *malakos* soft] (1844)
**1 :** an exceptionally large and rich mineral deposit (as of an ore, precious metal, or petroleum)
**2 a :** something that is very valuable, profitable, or rewarding ⟨a box-office *bonanza*⟩ **b :** an extremely large amount ⟨expected a *bonanza* of sympathy⟩
**Bo·na·part·ism** \'bō-nə-,pär-,ti-zəm\ *noun* (1815)
**1 :** support of the French emperors Napoleon I, Napoleon III, or their dynasty
**2 :** a political movement associated chiefly with authoritarian rule usually by a military leader ostensibly supported by a popular mandate
**— Bo·na·part·ist** \-,pär-tist\ *noun or adjective*

**bon·bon** \'bän-,bän\ *noun* [French, reduplication of *bon* good, from Latin *bonus* — more at BOUNTY] (1796)
**:** a candy with chocolate or fondant coating and fondant center that sometimes contains fruits and nuts
**¹bond** \'bänd\ *noun* [Middle English *band, bond* — more at BAND] (12th century)
**1 :** something that binds or restrains **:** FETTER
**2 :** a binding agreement **:** COVENANT
**3 a :** a band or cord used to tie something **b :** a material or device for binding **c :** an attractive force that holds together the atoms, ions, or groups of atoms in a molecule or crystal **:** an adhesive, cementing material, or fusible ingredient that combines, unites, or strengthens
**4 :** a uniting or binding element or force **:** TIE ⟨the *bonds* of friendship⟩
**5 a :** an obligation made binding by a money forfeit; *also* **:** the amount of the money guarantee **b :** one who acts as bail or surety **c :** an interest-bearing certificate of public or private indebtedness **d :** an insurance agreement pledging surety for financial loss caused to another by the act or default of a third person or by some contingency over which the third person may have no control
**6 :** the systematic lapping of brick in a wall
**7 :** the state of goods made, stored, or transported under the care of bonded agencies until the duties or taxes on them are paid
**8 :** a 100-proof straight whiskey aged at least four years under government supervision before being bottled — called also *bonded whiskey*
**9 :** BOND PAPER
**²bond** (1677)
*transitive verb*
**1 :** to lap (as brick) for solidity of construction
**2 a :** to secure payment of duties and taxes on (goods) by giving a bond **b :** to convert into a debt secured by bonds **c :** to provide a bond for or cause to provide such a bond ⟨*bond* an employee⟩
**3 a :** to cause to adhere firmly **b :** to embed in a matrix **c :** to hold together in a molecule or crystal by chemical bonds
*intransitive verb*
**:** to hold together or solidify by or as if by means of a bond or binder
**— bond·able** \'bän-də-bəl\ *adjective*
**— bond·er** *noun*
**³bond** *adjective* [Middle English *bonde,* from *bonde* peasant, serf, from Old English *bōnda* householder, from Old Norse *bōndi*] (14th century)
*archaic* **:** bound in slavery
**bond·age** \'bän-dij\ *noun* (14th century)
**1 :** the tenure or service of a villein, serf, or slave
**2 :** a state of being bound usually by compulsion (as of law or mastery): as **a :** CAPTIVITY, SERFDOM **b :** servitude or subjugation to a controlling person or force ⟨young people in *bondage* to drugs⟩
**bond·ed** \'bän-dəd\ *adjective* (1945)
**:** composed of two or more layers of the same or different fabrics held together by an adhesive ⟨*bonded* jersey⟩
**bond·hold·er** \'bänd-,hōl-dər\ *noun* (1823)
**:** one that holds a government or corporation bond
**bond·ing** *noun* (1976)
**1 :** the formation of a close personal relationship (as between a mother and child) especially through frequent or constant association
**2 :** the attaching of a material (as porcelain) to a tooth surface especially for cosmetic purposes
**bond·maid** \'bän(d)-,mād\ *noun* (1526)
*archaic* **:** a female bond servant
**bond·man** \'bän(d)-mən\ *noun* (13th century)
**:** SLAVE, SERF
**bond paper** *noun* (circa 1877)

**:** a durable paper originally used for documents

**bond servant** *noun* (15th century)
**:** one bound to service without wages; *also* **:** SLAVE

¹**bonds·man** \'bän(d)z-mən\ *noun* (1713)
**:** one who assumes the responsibility of a bond **:** SURETY

²**bondsman** *noun* (1735)
**:** BONDMAN

**bond·stone** \'bän(d)-ˌstōn\ *noun* (circa 1845)
**:** a stone long enough to extend through the full thickness of a wall to bind it together

**bond·wom·an** \'bän-ˌdwù-mən\ *noun* (14th century)
**:** a female slave

¹**bone** \'bōn\ *noun, often attributive* [Middle English *bon,* from Old English *bān;* akin to Old High German & Old Norse *bein* bone, and perhaps to Old Irish *benaid* he hews] (before 12th century)
**1 a :** one of the hard parts of the skeleton of a vertebrate **b :** any of various hard animal substances or structures (as baleen or ivory) akin to or resembling bone **c :** the hard largely calcareous connective tissue of which the adult skeleton of most vertebrates is chiefly composed
**2 a :** ESSENCE, CORE ⟨cut costs to the *bone*⟩ ⟨a liberal to the *bone*⟩ **b :** the most deeply ingrained part **:** HEART — usually used in plural ⟨knew in his *bones* that it was wrong⟩
**3** *plural* **a** (1) **:** SKELETON (2) **:** BODY ⟨rested my weary *bones*⟩ (3) **:** CORPSE ⟨inter a person's *bones*⟩ **b :** the basic design or framework (as of a play or novel)
**4 :** MATTER, SUBJECT ⟨a *bone* of contention⟩
**5 a** *plural* **:** thin bars of bone, ivory, or wood held in pairs between the fingers and used to produce musical rhythms **b :** a strip of whalebone or steel used to stiffen a corset or dress **c** *plural* **:** DICE
**6 :** something that is designed to placate **:** SOP
**7 :** a light beige
— **boned** \'bōnd\ *adjective*
— **bone·less** \'bōn-ləs\ *adjective*
— **bone to pick :** a matter to argue or complain about

²**bone** *verb* **boned; bon·ing** (15th century)
*transitive verb*
**1 :** to remove the bones from ⟨*bone* a fish⟩
**2 :** to provide (a garment) with stays
*intransitive verb*
**:** to study hard **:** GRIND ⟨*bone* through medical school⟩

³**bone** *adverb* (circa 1825)
**:** EXTREMELY, VERY ⟨*bone* tired⟩; *also* **:** TOTALLY

**bone ash** *noun* (1622)
**:** the white porous residue chiefly of tribasic calcium phosphate from bones calcined in air used especially in making pottery and glass and in cleaning jewelry

**bone black** *noun* (1815)
**:** the black residue chiefly of tribasic calcium phosphate and carbon from bones calcined in closed vessels used especially as a pigment or as a decolorizing adsorbent in sugar manufacturing — called also *bone char*

**bone china** *noun* (circa 1895)
**:** translucent white china made with bone ash or calcium phosphate and characterized by whiteness

**bone–dry** \'bōn-'drī\ *adjective* (circa 1825)
**1 :** very dry
**2 :** DRY 5

**bone·fish** \'bōn-ˌfish\ *noun* (1884)
**1 :** a slender silvery small-scaled fish (*Albula vulpes*) that is a notable sport and food fish of warm seas
**2 :** LADYFISH 2
— **bone·fish·ing** *noun*

¹**bone·head** \-ˌhed\ *noun* (1909)
**:** a stupid person **:** NUMSKULL
— **bone·head·ed** \-'he-dəd\ *adjective*
— **bone·head·ed·ness** *noun*

²**bonehead** *adjective* (1915)

**:** being a college course for students lacking fundamental skills ⟨teaches *bonehead* English⟩

**bone·meal** \'bōn-ˌmē(ə)l\ *noun* (1850)
**:** crushed or ground bone used especially as fertilizer or feed

**bon·er** \'bō-nər\ *noun* (circa 1899)
**1 :** one that bones
**2 :** HOWLER 2

**bone·set** \'bōn-ˌset\ *noun* (1764)
**:** any of several composite herbs (genus *Eupatorium*); *especially* **:** a perennial (*E. perfoliatum*) with opposite perfoliate leaves and white-rayed flower heads used in folk medicine

**bone·set·ter** \-ˌse-tər\ *noun* (15th century)
**:** a person who sets broken or dislocated bones usually without being a licensed physician

**bone up** *intransitive verb* (1887)
**1 :** to try to master necessary information quickly **:** CRAM ⟨*bone up* for the exam⟩
**2 :** to renew one's skill or refresh one's memory ⟨*boned up* on the speech just before giving it⟩

**bone·yard** \-ˌyärd\ *noun* (1866)
**1 :** CEMETERY
**2 :** a place where worn-out or damaged objects (as cars) are collected to await disposal

**bon·fire** \'bän-ˌfīr\ *noun* [Middle English *bonefire* a fire of bones, from *bon* bone + *fire*] (15th century)
**:** a large fire built in the open air

¹**bong** \'bäŋ, 'bóŋ\ *noun* [imitative] (1860)
**:** the deep resonant sound especially of a bell
— **bong** *verb*

²**bong** *noun* [Thai *bhaung³*] (1971)
**:** a simple water pipe consisting of a bottle or vertical tube partially filled with a liquid (as water or liqueur) and a smaller offset tube ending in a bowl

¹**bon·go** \'bäŋ-(ˌ)gō, 'bóŋ-\ *noun, plural* **bongos** *also* **bongoes** [American Spanish *bongó*] (1920)
**:** one of a pair of small connected drums of different sizes and pitches played with the hands
— **bon·go·ist** \-ˌgō-ist\ *noun*

²**bongo** *noun, plural* **bongo** *or* **bongos** [probably from Kele (Bantu language of Gabon)] (1861)
**:** an African antelope (*Tragelaphus euryceros* synonym *Boocerus euryceros*) that is chestnut-red with narrow white vertical stripes and is found in forests from Sierra Leone to Kenya

**bon·ho·mie** \ˌbä-nə-'mē, ˌbō-\ *noun* [French *bonhomie,* from *bonhomme* good-natured man, from *bon* good + *homme* man] (1779)
**:** good-natured easy friendliness
— **bon·ho·mous** \'bä-nə-məs\ *adjective*

**bon·i·face** \'bä-nə-fas, -ˌfās\ *noun* [*Boniface,* innkeeper in *The Beaux' Stratagem* (1707) by George Farquhar] (1803)
**:** the proprietor of a hotel, nightclub, or restaurant

**bo·ni·to** \bə-'nē-(ˌ)tō, -'nē-tə\ *noun, plural* **-tos** *or* **-to** [Spanish, from *bonito* pretty, diminutive of *bueno* good, from Latin *bonus*] (circa 1565)
**:** any of several scombroid fishes (especially genera *Sarda* and *Euthynnus*) intermediate between the smaller mackerels and the larger tunas

**bon·kers** \'bäŋ-kərz, 'bóŋ-\ *adjective* [perhaps from *bonk* to hit, bang + *-ers* (as in *crackers*)] (circa 1948)
**:** CRAZY, MAD ⟨if I don't work, I go *bonkers* —Zoe Caldwell⟩
**word history** *see* NUTS

**bon mot** \bōⁿ-'mō\ *noun, plural* **bons mots** \bōⁿ-'mō(z)\ *or* **bon mots** \-'mō(z)\ [French, literally, good word] (circa 1730)
**:** a clever remark **:** WITTICISM

**bonne** \'bón\ *noun* [French, from feminine of *bon*] (1771)
**:** a French nursemaid or maidservant

¹**bon·net** \'bä-nət\ *noun* [Middle English *bonet,* from Middle French, probably of German-

ic origin; akin to Old Saxon *gibund* bundle, Old English *bindan* to bind] (14th century)
**1 a** (1) *chiefly Scottish* **:** a man's or boy's cap (2) **:** a brimless Scotch cap of seamless woolen fabric — compare TAM-O'-SHANTER **2 b :** a cloth or straw hat tied under the chin and worn by women and children
**2 a** *British* **:** an automobile hood **b :** a metal covering or cowl (as for a fireplace, valve chamber, or ventilator)

²**bonnet** *transitive verb* (1858)
**:** to provide with or dress in a bonnet

**bon·ny** *also* **bon·nie** \'bä-nē\ *adjective* **bon·ni·er; -est** [Middle English *bonie,* from Middle French *bon* good, from Latin *bonus*] (15th century)
*chiefly British* **:** ATTRACTIVE, FAIR; *also* **:** FINE, EXCELLENT
— **bon·ni·ly** \'bä-nə-lē\ *adverb*

**bon·ny·clab·ber** \'bä-nē-ˌkla-bər\ *noun* [Irish *bainne clabair,* from *bainne* milk + *clabair,* genitive of *clabar* sour thick milk] (1616)
*Northern & Midland* **:** CLABBER

**bon·sai** \(ˌ)bōn-'sī, 'bōn-ˌ, 'bän-, *also* 'bän-ˌzī\ *noun, plural* **bonsai** [Japanese, literally, tray planting] (1900)
**:** a potted plant (as a tree) dwarfed and trained to an artistic shape by special methods of culture; *also* **:** the art of growing such a plant

bonsai

**bon·spiel** \'bän-ˌspēl\ *noun* [perhaps from Dutch *bond* league + *spel* game] (circa 1772)
**:** a match or tournament between curling clubs

**bon ton** \(ˌ)bän-'tän, 'bän-ˌ\ *noun* [French, literally, good tone] (1747)
**1 a :** fashionable manner or style **b :** the fashionable or proper thing
**2 :** high society

**bo·nus** \'bō-nəs\ *noun* [Latin, literally, good — more at BOUNTY] (1773)
**:** something in addition to what is expected or strictly due: as **a :** money or an equivalent given in addition to an employee's usual compensation **b :** a premium (as of stock) given by a corporation to a purchaser of its securities, to a promoter, or to an employee **c :** a government payment to war veterans **d :** a sum in excess of salary given an athlete for signing with a team

**bon vi·vant** \ˌbän-vē-'vänt, ˌbōⁿ-vē-'väⁿ\ *noun, plural* **bons vivants** \ˌbän-vē-'vän(t)s, ˌbōⁿ-vē-'väⁿ(z)\ *or* **bon vivants** \*same*\ [French, literally, good liver] (circa 1695)
**:** a person having cultivated, refined, and sociable tastes especially in respect to food and drink

**bon voy·age** \ˌbōⁿ-ˌvói-'äzh, ˌbän-; ˌbōⁿ-ˌvwī-'äzh, -ˌvwä-'yäzh\ *noun* [French, literally, good journey!] (15th century)
**:** FAREWELL — often used interjectionally

**bony** *also* **bon·ey** \'bō-nē\ *adjective* **bon·i·er; -est** (14th century)
**1 a :** consisting of bone **b :** resembling bone
**2 a :** full of bones ⟨a *bony* piece of fish⟩ **b :** having prominent bones ⟨a rugged *bony* face⟩
**3 a :** SKINNY, SCRAWNY **b :** BARREN, LEAN

**bony fish** *noun* (circa 1890)
**:** any of a major taxon (class Osteichthyes or superclass Teleostomi) comprising fishes (as a sturgeon, salmon, marlin, or ocean sunfish)

with a bony rather than a cartilaginous skeleton — called also *teleost;* compare CARTILAGINOUS FISH, JAWLESS FISH

**bonze** \'bänz\ *noun* [Middle French, from Portuguese *bonzo,* from Japanese *bonsō*] (1588) : a Buddhist monk

¹**boo** \'bü\ *interjection* [Middle English *bo*] (15th century) — used to express contempt or disapproval or to startle or frighten

²**boo** *noun, plural* **boos** (1575)
**1 :** a shout of disapproval or contempt
**2 :** any sound at all — usually used in negative constructions ⟨never said *boo*⟩

³**boo** (1884)
*intransitive verb*
**:** to deride especially by uttering *boo*
*transitive verb*
**:** to express disapproval of by booing ⟨the crowd *booed* the referee⟩

⁴**boo** *noun* [origin unknown] (circa 1959)
**:** MARIJUANA

¹**boob** \'büb\ *noun* [short for ¹*booby*] (1909)
**1 :** a stupid awkward person **:** SIMPLETON
**2 :** BOOR, PHILISTINE
— **boob·ish** \'bü-bish\ *adjective*

²**boob** *noun* [³*boob*] (1934)
*British* **:** MISTAKE, BLUNDER

³**boob** *intransitive verb* [¹*boob*] (1935)
*British* **:** GOOF 2

⁴**boob** *noun* [short for ²*booby*] (1945)
**:** BREAST — sometimes considered vulgar

**boob·oi·sie** \,büb-,wä-'zē\ *noun* [blend of ¹*boob* and *bourgeoisie*] (1922)
**:** the general public regarded as consisting of boobs

**boo–boo** \'bü-(,)bü\ *noun, plural* **boo-boos** [probably baby-talk alteration of *boohoo,* imitation of the sound of weeping] (1953)
**1 :** a usually trivial injury (as a bruise or scratch) — used especially by or of a child
**2 :** MISTAKE, BLUNDER

**boob tube** *noun* (1966)
**:** TELEVISION — used with *the*

¹**boo·by** \'bü-bē\ *noun, plural* **boobies** [modification of Spanish *bobo,* from Latin *balbus* stammering, probably of imitative origin] (circa 1603)
**1 :** an awkward foolish person **:** DOPE
**2 :** any of several tropical seabirds (family Sulidae, especially genus *Sula*)

²**boo·by** \'bü-bē, 'bü-\ *noun, plural* **boobies** [alteration of *bubby*] (1934)
**:** BREAST — sometimes considered vulgar

**booby hatch** *noun* (1840)
**1 :** a raised framework with a sliding cover over a small hatch on a ship
**2 :** an insane asylum

**booby prize** *noun* (1889)
**1 :** an award for the poorest performance in a game or competition
**2 :** an acknowledgment of notable inferiority

**booby trap** *noun* (1850)
**1 :** a trap for the unwary or unsuspecting **:** PITFALL
**2 :** a concealed explosive device contrived to go off when some harmless-looking object is touched
— **boo·by–trap** *transitive verb*

**boo·dle** \'bü-d³l\ *noun* [Dutch *boedel* estate, lot, from Middle Dutch; akin to Old Norse *būth* booth] (1833)
**1 :** a collection or lot of persons **:** CABOODLE
**2 a :** bribe money **b :** a large amount especially of money

**boog·er** \'bu̇-gər, 'bü-\ *noun* [alteration of English dialect *buggard, boggart,* from ¹*bug* + *-ard*] (1866)
**1 :** BOGEYMAN
**2 :** a piece of dried nasal mucus

**boo·gey·man** \'bu̇-gē-,man, 'bü-\ *also* **boog·er·man** \'bu̇-gər-, 'bü-\ *noun* [by alteration] (circa 1850)
**:** BOGEYMAN

¹**boo·gie** \'bu̇-gē, 'bü-\ *noun* (1929)
**1 :** BOOGIE-WOOGIE

**2 :** earthy and strongly rhythmic rock music conducive to dancing; *also* **:** a period of or occasion for dancing to this music

²**boogie** *also* **boo·gy** *or* **boo·gey** \'bu̇-gē, 'bü-\ *intransitive verb* **boo·gied** *also* **boo·geyed; boo·gy·ing** *also* **boo·gey·ing** (1930)
**1 :** to dance to rock music; *also* **:** REVEL, PARTY
**2 a :** to move quickly **b :** to get going

**boo·gie–woo·gie** \,bu̇-gē-'wu̇-gē, ,bü-gē-'wü-gē\ *noun* [origin unknown] (1928)
**:** a percussive style of playing blues on the piano characterized by a steady rhythmic ground bass of eighth notes in quadruple time and a series of improvised melodic variations

¹**book** \'bu̇k\ *noun* [Middle English, from Old English *bōc;* akin to Old High German *buoh* book, Gothic *boka* letter] (before 12th century)
**1 a :** a set of written sheets of skin or paper or tablets of wood or ivory **b :** a set of written, printed, or blank sheets bound together into a volume **c :** a long written or printed literary composition **d :** a major division of a treatise or literary work **e :** a record of a business's financial transactions or financial condition — often used in plural ⟨the *books* show a profit⟩
**2** *capitalized* **:** BIBLE 1
**3 :** something that yields knowledge or understanding ⟨the great *book* of nature⟩ ⟨her face was an open *book*⟩
**4 a :** the total available knowledge and experience that can be brought to bear on a task or problem ⟨tried every trick in the *book*⟩ ⟨the *book* on him is that he can't hit a curveball⟩ **b :** the standards or authority relevant in a situation ⟨run by the *book*⟩
**5 a :** all the charges that can be made against an accused person ⟨threw the *book* at him⟩ **b :** a position from which one must answer for certain acts **:** ACCOUNT ⟨bring criminals to *book*⟩
**6 a :** LIBRETTO **b :** the script of a play **c :** a book of arrangements for a musician or dance orchestra **:** musical repertory
**7 :** a packet of items bound together like a book ⟨a *book* of stamps⟩ ⟨a *book* of matches⟩
**8 a :** BOOKMAKER **b :** the bets registered by a bookmaker; *also* **:** the business or activity of giving odds and taking bets
**9 :** the number of tricks a cardplayer or side must win before any trick can have scoring value
— **book·ful** \'bu̇k-,fu̇l\ *noun*
— **in one's book :** in one's own opinion
— **in one's good books :** in favor with one
— **one for the book :** an act or occurrence worth noting
— **on the books :** on the records

²**book** *adjective* (13th century)
**1 :** derived from books and not from practical experience ⟨*book* learning⟩
**2 :** shown by books of account ⟨*book* assets⟩

³**book** (1807)
*transitive verb*
**1 a :** to register (as a name) for some future activity or condition (as to engage transportation or reserve lodgings) ⟨*booked* to sail on Monday⟩ **b :** to schedule engagements for ⟨*book* the band for a week⟩ **c :** to set aside time for **d :** to reserve in advance ⟨*book* two seats at the theater⟩ ⟨were all *booked* up⟩
**2 a :** to enter charges against in a police register **b** *chiefly British* **:** to charge (as a soccer player) with an infraction of the rules
*intransitive verb*
**1 :** to make a reservation ⟨*book* through your travel agent⟩
**2** *chiefly British* **:** to register in a hotel — usually used with *in*
— **book·able** \'bu̇-kə-bəl\ *adjective, chiefly British*
— **book·er** *noun*

**book·bind·ing** \'bu̇k-,bīn-diŋ\ *noun* (1771)
**1 :** the art or trade of binding books

**2 :** the binding of a book
— **book·bind·er** \-,bīn-dər\ *noun*
— **book·bind·ery** \-d(ə-)rē\ *noun*

**book·case** \-,kās\ *noun* (1726)
**:** a piece of furniture consisting of shelves to hold books

**book club** *noun* (1905)
**:** an organization that ships selected books to members usually on a regular schedule and often at discount prices

**book·end** \-,end\ *noun* (1907)
**:** a support placed at the end of a row of books

**book·ie** \'bu̇k-ē\ *noun* [by shortening & alteration] (1885)
**:** BOOKMAKER 2

**book·ing** \'bu̇-kiŋ\ *noun* (1881)
**1 :** the act of one that books
**2 :** an engagement or scheduled performance
**3 :** RESERVATION 1c

**booking office** *noun* (circa 1837)
*chiefly British* **:** a ticket office; *especially* **:** one in a railroad station

**book·ish** \'bu̇-kish\ *adjective* (1567)
**1 a :** of or relating to books **b :** fond of books and reading
**2 a :** inclined to rely on book knowledge **b** *of words* **:** literary and formal as opposed to colloquial and informal **c :** given to literary or scholarly pursuits; *also* **:** affectedly learned
— **book·ish·ly** *adverb*
— **book·ish·ness** *noun*

**book·keep·er** \'bu̇k-,kē-pər\ *noun* (1555)
**:** one who records the accounts or transactions of a business
— **book·keep·ing** \-piŋ\ *noun*

**book·let** \'bu̇k-lət\ *noun* (1859)
**:** a little book; *especially* **:** PAMPHLET

**book louse** *noun* (1867)
**:** any of various tiny usually wingless insects (order Psocoptera) that feed on organic matter; *especially* **:** an insect (as *Liposcelis divinatorius*) injurious especially to books

**book lung** *noun* (1879)
**:** a saccular breathing organ in many arachnids containing thin folds of membrane arranged like the leaves of a book

**book·mak·er** \'bu̇k-,mā-kər\ *noun* (1515)
**1 :** a printer, binder, or designer of books
**2 :** one who determines odds and receives and pays off bets
— **book·mak·ing** \-kiŋ\ *noun*

**book·man** \-mən\ *noun* (1583)
**1 :** one who has a love of books and especially of reading
**2 :** one who is involved in the writing, publishing, or selling of books

**book·mark** \-,märk\ *or* **book·mark·er** \-,mär-kər\ *noun* (1838)
**:** a marker for finding a place in a book

**book–match** \-,mach\ *transitive verb* (1942)
**:** to match the grains of (as two sheets of veneer) so that one sheet seems to be the mirrored image of the other

**book·mo·bile** \'bu̇k-mō-,bēl\ *noun* (1926)
**:** a truck that serves as a traveling library

**Book of Common Prayer** (1549)
**:** the service book of the Anglican Communion

**book off** *intransitive verb* (1971)
*Canadian* **:** to notify an employer that one is not reporting for work (as because of sickness)

**book·plate** \'bu̇k-,plāt\ *noun* (1791)
**:** a book owner's identification label that is usually pasted to the inside front cover of a book

**book·sell·er** \'bu̇k-,se-lər\ *noun* (15th century)
**:** one who sells books; *especially* **:** the proprietor of a bookstore
— **book·sell·ing** \-,se-liŋ\ *noun*

**book·shelf** \-,shelf\ *noun* (1818)
**:** an open shelf for holding books

**book·shop** \-,shäp\ *noun* (1862)
**:** BOOKSTORE

**book·stall** \-,stȯl\ *noun* (1800)
**1 :** a stall where books are sold

**2** *chiefly British* : NEWSSTAND
**book·store** \-,stor, -,stor\ *noun* (circa 1763)
: a place of business where books are the main item offered for sale — called also *bookshop*
**book value** *noun* (1899)
: the value of something as shown on bookkeeping records as distinguished from market value: **a** : the value of an asset equal to cost less depreciation **b** : the value of a corporation's capital stock equal to its book value less its liabilities
**book·worm** \'bùk-,wərm\ *noun* (1592)
: a person unusually devoted to reading and study
**Bool·ean** \'bü-lē-ən\ *adjective* [George *Boole* (died 1864) English mathematician] (1851)
: of, relating to, or being a logical combinatorial system (as Boolean algebra) that represents symbolically relationships (as those implied by the logical operators AND, OR, and NOT) between entities (as sets, propositions, or on-off computer circuit elements) (*Boolean* expression) (*Boolean* search strategy for information retrieval)
**Boolean algebra** *noun* (1889)
: a set that is closed under two commutative binary operations and that can be described by any of various systems of postulates all of which can be deduced from the postulates that an identity element exists for each operation, that each operation is distributive over the other, and that for every element in the set there is another element which when combined with the first under one of the operations yields the identity element of the other operation
**¹boom** \'büm\ *verb* [imitative] (15th century)
*intransitive verb*
**1** : to make a deep hollow sound
**2 a** : to increase in importance or esteem **b** : to experience a sudden rapid growth and expansion usually with an increase in prices (business was *booming*) **c** : to develop rapidly in population and importance (California *boomed* when gold was discovered there)
*transitive verb*
**1** : to cause to resound — often used with *out* (his voice *booms* out the lyrics)
**2** : to cause a rapid growth or increase in : BOOST
**²boom** *noun* (circa 1500)
**1** : a booming sound or cry
**2** : a rapid expansion or increase: as **a** : a general movement in support of a candidate for office **b** : rapid settlement and development of a town or district **c** : a rapid widespread expansion of economic activity
**³boom** *noun* [Dutch, tree, beam; akin to Old High German *boum* tree — more at BEAM] (1627)
**1** : a long spar used to extend the foot of a sail
**2 a** : a chain cable or line of connected floating timbers extended across a river, lake, or harbor (as to obstruct passage or catch floating objects) **b** : a temporary floating barrier used to contain an oil spill
**3 a** : a long beam projecting from the mast of a derrick to support or guide cargo **b** : a long more or less horizontal supporting arm or brace (as for holding a microphone or for supporting an antenna)
**4** : a spar or outrigger connecting the tail surfaces and the main supporting structure of an aircraft
**boom box** *noun* (1981)
: a large portable radio and often tape player with two attached speakers
**boom·er** *noun* (1880)
**1** : one that booms
**2** : one that joins a rush of settlers to a boom area
**3** : a transient worker (as a bridge builder)
**boo·mer·ang** \'bü-mə-,raŋ\ *noun* [Dharuk (Australian aboriginal language of the Port Jackson area) *bumarin*ʸ] (1825)
**1** : a bent or angular throwing club typically flat on one side and rounded on the other so

that it soars or curves in flight; *especially* : one designed to return near the thrower
**2** : an act or utterance that backfires on its originator
**— boomerang** *intransitive verb*
**boom·let** \'büm-lət\ *noun* (1880)
: a small boom; *specifically* : a sudden increase in business activity (a stock market *boomlet*)
**boom·town** \'büm-,taùn\ *noun* (1896)
: a town enjoying a business and population boom
**boomy** \'bü-mē\ *adjective* **boom·i·er; -est** (1888)
**1** : of, relating to, or characterized by an economic boom
**2** : having an excessive accentuation on the tones of lower pitch in reproduced sound
**¹boon** \'bün\ *noun* [Middle English, from Old Norse *bōn* petition; akin to Old English *bēn* prayer, *bannan* to summon — more at BAN] (12th century)
**1** : BENEFIT, FAVOR; *especially* : one that is given in answer to a request
**2** : a timely benefit : BLESSING
**²boon** *adjective* [Middle English *bon*, from Middle French, good — more at BONNY] (14th century)
**1** *archaic* : FAVORABLE
**2** : CONVIVIAL (a *boon* companion)
**boon·docks** \'bün-,däks\ *noun plural* [Tagalog *bundok* mountain] (circa 1909)
**1** : rough country filled with dense brush
**2** : a rural area : STICKS
**boon·dog·gle** \'bün-,dä-gəl, -,do-\ *noun* [coined by Robert H. Link (died 1957) American scoutmaster] (1929)
**1** : a braided cord worn by Boy Scouts as a neckerchief slide, hatband, or ornament
**2** : a wasteful or impractical project or activity often involving graft ◆
**— boondoggle** *intransitive verb*
**— boon·dog·gler** \-g(ə-)lər\ *noun*
**boon·ies** \'bü-nēz\ *noun plural* (1956)
*slang* : BOONDOCKS 2
**boor** \'bùr\ *noun* [Dutch *boer*; akin to Old English *būan* to dwell — more at BOWER] (1551)
**1** : PEASANT
**2** : a rude or insensitive person
**boor·ish** \'bùr-ish\ *adjective* (1562)
: resembling or befitting a boor (as in crude insensitivity) ☆
**— boor·ish·ly** *adverb*
**— boor·ish·ness** *noun*
**¹boost** \'büst\ *verb* [origin unknown] (circa 1815)
*transitive verb*
**1** : to push or shove up from below
**2** : INCREASE, RAISE (plans to *boost* production) (an extra holiday to *boost* morale)
**3** : to promote the cause or interests of : PLUG (a campaign to *boost* the new fashions)
**4** : to raise the voltage of or across (an electric circuit)
**5** *slang* : STEAL, SHOPLIFT
*intransitive verb*
*slang* : SHOPLIFT
**synonym** see LIFT
**²boost** *noun* (1825)
**1** : a push upward
**2** : an act that brings help or encouragement : ASSIST
**3** : an increase in amount
**boost·er** \'bü-stər\ *noun* (1890)
: one that boosts: as **a** : an enthusiastic supporter **b** : an auxiliary device for increasing force, power, pressure, or effectiveness **c** *slang* : SHOPLIFTER **d** : a radio-frequency amplifier for a radio or television receiving set **e** : the first stage of a multistage rocket providing thrust for the launching and the initial part of the flight **f** : a substance that increases the effectiveness of a medicament; *especially* : BOOSTER SHOT

**boost·er·ism** \-stə-,ri-zəm\ *noun* (circa 1913)
: the activities and attitudes characteristic of boosters
**booster shot** *noun* (1944)
: a supplementary dose of an immunizing agent — called also *booster, booster dose*
**¹boot** \'bùt\ *noun* [Middle English, from Old English *bōt* remedy; akin to Old English *betera* better] (before 12th century)
**1** *archaic* : DELIVERANCE
**2** *chiefly dialect* : something to equalize a trade
**3** *obsolete* : AVAIL
**— to boot** : BESIDES
**²boot** *verb* (15th century)
*archaic* : AVAIL, PROFIT
**³boot** *noun* [Middle English, from Middle French *bote*] (14th century)
**1** : a fitted covering (as of leather or rubber) for the foot and usually reaching above the ankle
**2** : an instrument of torture used to crush the leg and foot
**3** : something that resembles or is likened to a boot; *especially* : an enclosing or protective casing or sheath (as for a rifle or over an electrical or mechanical connection)
**4** : a navy or marine corps recruit undergoing basic training

☆ SYNONYMS
**Boorish, churlish, loutish, clownish** mean uncouth in manners or appearance. BOORISH implies rudeness of manner due to insensitiveness to others' feelings and unwillingness to be agreeable (a drunk's *boorish* behavior). CHURLISH suggests surliness, unresponsiveness, and ungraciousness (*churlish* remarks). LOUTISH implies bodily awkwardness together with stupidity (a *loutish* oaf). CLOWNISH suggests ill-bred awkwardness, ignorance or stupidity, ungainliness, and often a propensity for absurd antics (an adolescent's *clownish* conduct).

◇ WORD HISTORY
**boondoggle** *Boondoggle* is one of those colorful concoctions that, like *hornswoggle* or *sockdolager*, seem redolent of the 19th century American frontier. It is, in fact, a 20th century coinage, although there is an outdoorsy connection. At the World Jamboree of Scouts in England in 1929, Robert H. Link, usually identified as a scoutmaster from Rochester, N.Y., dubbed a plaited lanyard—a standard item of Boy Scout handicraft—a *boondoggle*. So designated, the lanyard was presented to the Prince of Wales at the Jamboree. Owing to the public nature of the presentation, the term spread through scouting circles. In the fall of 1929 the British magazine *Punch* discussed the word in a report on the presentation of a boondoggle to Lord Baden-Powell, the founder of the Boy Scouts. In 1935, during a municipal hearing in New York City, *boondoggle* was used by a government employee to describe the handicrafts, apparently of dubious value, that he was teaching to people on relief. The appearance of the word in news reports of the hearing did much to popularize it. Soon opponents of President Roosevelt's New Deal were using it to refer to any government project whose major or sole achievement was the expenditure of public funds.

\ə\ **abut** \ʰ\ **kitten** \ər\ **further** \a\ **ash** \ā\ **ace**
\ä\ **mop, mar** \aù\ **out** \ch\ **chin** \e\ **bet** \ē\ **easy**
\g\ **go** \i\ **hit** \ī\ **ice** \j\ **job** \ŋ\ **sing** \ō\ **go**
\ò\ **law** \òi\ **boy** \th\ **thin** \th\ **the** \ü\ **loot** \ù\ **foot**
\y\ **yet** \zh\ **vision** *see also* Guide to Pronunciation

**5** *British* **:** an automobile trunk

**6 a :** a kick with the foot **b :** summary dismissal — used with *the* **c :** momentary pleasure or enjoyment **:** BANG ⟨got a big *boot* out of the joke⟩

**7 :** a sheath enclosing the inflorescence

**⁴boot** (15th century)
*transitive verb*
**1 :** to put boots on

**2 a :** KICK **b :** to eject or discharge summarily — often used with *out* ⟨was *booted* out of office⟩

**3 :** to make an error on (a grounder in baseball); *broadly* **:** BOTCH

**4 :** to ride (a horse) in a race ⟨*booted* home three winners⟩

**5** [²*bootstrap*] **a :** to load (a program) into a computer from a disk **b :** to start or ready for use especially by booting a program ⟨*boot* a microcomputer⟩ — often used with *up*
*intransitive verb*
**:** to become loaded into a computer's memory from a disk ⟨the program *boots* automatically⟩

— **boot·able** \'bü-tə-bəl\ *adjective*

**⁵boot** *noun* [¹*boot*] (1593)
*archaic* **:** BOOTY, PLUNDER

**boot·black** \'büt-,blak\ *noun* (1817)
**:** one who shines shoes

**boot camp** *noun* (circa 1942)
**:** a navy or marine corps camp for basic training

**boot·ed** \'bü-təd\ *adjective* (1552)
**:** wearing boots

**boo·tee** *or* **boo·tie** \bü-'tē, *of infants' footwear* 'bü-tē\ *noun* (1799)
**:** a usually ankle-length boot, slipper, or sock; *especially* **:** an infant's knitted or crocheted sock

**Bo·ö·tes** \bō-'ō-tēz\ *noun* [Latin (genitive *Boötis*), from Greek *Boōtēs*, literally, plowman, from *bous* head of cattle — more at COW]
**:** a northern constellation containing the bright star Arcturus

**booth** \'büth, *especially British* 'büth\ *noun*, *plural* **booths** \'büthz, 'büths\ [Middle English *bothe*, of Scandinavian origin; akin to Old Norse *būth* booth; akin to Old English *būan* to dwell — more at BOWER] (13th century)
**1 :** a temporary shelter for livestock or field workers

**2 a :** a stall or stand (as at a fair) for the sale or exhibition of goods **b** (1) **:** a small enclosure affording privacy for one person at a time ⟨a telephone *booth*⟩ ⟨polling *booth*⟩ (2) **:** a small enclosure that isolates its occupant especially from patrons or customers ⟨a ticket *booth*⟩ (3) **:** an isolated enclosure used in sound recording or in broadcasting ⟨a radio *booth*⟩ **c :** a restaurant seating arrangement consisting of a table between two high-back benches

**boot·jack** \'büt-,jak\ *noun* (circa 1841)
**:** a device (as with a V-shaped notch) used for pulling off boots

**boot·lace** \-,lās\ *noun* (circa 1887)
*British* **:** SHOELACE

**¹boot·leg** \-,leg, -,lāg\ *noun* (1634)
**1 :** the upper part of a boot

**2 :** something bootlegged; *specifically*
**:** MOONSHINE

**3 :** a football play in which the quarterback fakes a handoff, hides the ball against his hip, and rolls out — compare DRAW 8

— **bootleg** *adjective*

**²bootleg** (1900)
*transitive verb*
**1 a :** to carry (alcoholic liquor) on one's person illegally **b :** to manufacture, sell, or transport for sale (alcoholic liquor) illegally

**2 a :** to produce, reproduce, or distribute illicitly or without authorization **b :** SMUGGLE
*intransitive verb*
**1 :** to engage in bootlegging

**2 :** to run a bootleg play in football

— **boot·leg·ger** *noun*

**boot·less** \'büt-ləs\ *adjective* (1559)
**:** USELESS, UNPROFITABLE

— **boot·less·ly** *adverb*

— **boot·less·ness** *noun*

**boot·lick** \-,lik\ (1845)
*transitive verb*
**:** to try to gain favor with through a servile or obsequious manner
*intransitive verb*
**:** to act obsequiously

— **boot·lick·er** *noun*

**boots** \'büts\ *noun plural but singular or plural in construction* [from plural of ³*boot*] (circa 1837)
*British* **:** a servant who shines shoes especially in a hotel

**¹boot·strap** \'büt-,strap\ *noun* (1913)
**1** *plural* **:** unaided efforts — often used in the phrase *by one's own bootstraps*

**2 :** a looped strap sewed at the side or the rear top of a boot to help in pulling it on

**²bootstrap** *adjective* (1926)
**1 :** designed to function independently of outside direction **:** capable of using one internal function or process to control another ⟨a *bootstrap* operation to load a computer⟩

**2 :** carried out with minimum resources or advantages **:** SELF-RELIANT ⟨the city recovered from the flood by the *bootstrap* method⟩

**³bootstrap** *transitive verb* (1951)
**:** to promote or develop by initiative and effort with little or no assistance ⟨*bootstrapped* herself to the top⟩

**boo·ty** \'bü-tē\ *noun, plural* **booties** [modification of Middle French *butin*, from Middle Low German *būte* exchange] (15th century)
**1 :** plunder taken (as in war); *especially* **:** plunder taken on land as distinguished from prizes taken at sea

**2 :** a rich gain or prize
*synonym* see SPOIL

**¹booze** \'büz\ *intransitive verb* **boozed; booz·ing** [Middle English *bousen*, from Middle Dutch *būsen*] (14th century)
**:** to drink intoxicating liquor especially to excess — often used in the phrase *booze it up*

**²booze** *noun* (14th century)
**:** intoxicating drink; *especially* **:** hard liquor

— **booz·i·ly** \-zə-lē\ *adverb*

— **boozy** \-zē\ *adjective*

**booz·er** \'bü-zər\ *noun* (circa 1819)
**1 :** a person who boozes **:** DRUNK

**2** *British* **:** a drinking place **:** PUB

**¹bop** \'bäp\ *transitive verb* **bopped; bop·ping** [imitative] (1931)
**:** HIT, SOCK

**²bop** *noun* (1947)
**:** a blow (as with the fist or a club) that strikes a person

**³bop** *noun* [short for *bebop*] (1947)
**1 :** jazz characterized by harmonic complexity, convoluted melodic lines, and constant shifting of accent and often played at very rapid tempos

**2 :** JIVE 2

— **bop·per** *noun*

**⁴bop** *intransitive verb* **bopped; bop·ping** (1952)
**1 :** to go quickly or unceremoniously **:** POP ⟨*bop* into the corner store⟩ — often used with *off*

**2 :** to dance or shuffle along to or as if to bop music

**bo·peep** \(,)bō-'pēp\ *noun* [¹*boo* + ³*peep*] (1528)
**:** PEEKABOO

**bo·ra** \'bōr-ə, 'bòr-\ *noun* [Italian, from Italian dialect (Trieste), from Latin *boreas*] (1864)
**:** a violent cold northerly wind of the Adriatic

**bo·rac·ic acid** \bə-'ras-ik-\ *noun* [Medieval Latin *borac-, borax* borax] (1801)
**:** BORIC ACID

**bor·age** \'bòr-ij, 'bär-\ *noun* [Middle English, from Old French *bourage*] (14th century)
**:** a coarse hairy blue-flowered European herb (*Borago officinalis* of the family Boraginaceae, the borage family) used medicinally and in salads

**bo·rane** \'bōr-,ān, 'bòr-\ *noun* [International Scientific Vocabulary, from *boron*] (1916)
**1 :** a compound of boron and hydrogen; *specifically* **:** a compound $BH_3$ known only in the form of its derivatives

**2 :** a derivative of borane

**bo·rate** \-,āt\ *noun* (1816)
**:** a salt or ester of a boric acid

**bo·rat·ed** \-,ā-təd\ *adjective* (circa 1901)
**:** mixed or impregnated with borax or boric acid

**¹bo·rax** \'bōr-,aks, 'bòr-, -əks\ *noun* [Middle English *boras*, from Middle French, from Medieval Latin *borac-, borax*, from Arabic *būraq*, from Persian *būrah*] (14th century)
**:** a white crystalline compound that consists of a hydrated sodium borate $Na_2B_4O_7 \cdot 10H_2O$, that occurs as a mineral or is prepared from other minerals, and that is used especially as a flux, cleansing agent, and water softener, as a preservative, and as a fireproofing agent

**²borax** *noun* [origin unknown] (1932)
**:** cheap shoddy merchandise

**Bo·ra·zon** \'bōr-ə-,zän, 'bòr-\ *trademark*
— used for a boron nitride abrasive

**bor·bo·ryg·mus** \,bòr-bə-'rig-məs\ *noun, plural* **-mi** \-,mī\ [New Latin, from Greek *borborygmos*, from *borboryzein* to rumble] (circa 1796)
**:** intestinal rumbling caused by moving gas

**Bor·deaux** \bòr-'dō\ *noun, plural* **Bordeaux** \-'dōz\ *often not capitalized* (circa 1570)
**1 :** white or red wine of the Bordeaux region of France

**2 :** CLARET 2

**bor·deaux mixture** \bòr-'dō-, 'bòr-,\ *noun, often B capitalized* (1892)
**:** a fungicide made by reaction of copper sulfate, lime, and water

**bor·de·laise sauce** \'bòr-d°l-'āz-\ *noun, often B capitalized* [French *bordelaise*, feminine of *bordelais* of Bordeaux] (1902)
**:** a sauce consisting of stock thickened with roux and flavored typically with red wine and shallots

**bor·del·lo** \bòr-'de-(,)lō\ *noun, plural* **-los** [Italian, from Old French *bordel*, from *borde* hut, of Germanic origin; akin to Old English *bord* board] (1593)
**:** a building in which prostitutes are available

**¹bor·der** \'bòr-dər\ *noun* [Middle English *bordure*, from Middle French, from Old French, from *border* to border, from *bort* border, of Germanic origin; akin to Old English *bord*] (14th century)
**1 :** an outer part or edge

**2 :** an ornamental design at the edge of a fabric or rug

**3 :** a narrow bed of planted ground along the edge of a garden or walk ⟨a *border* of tulips⟩

**4 :** BOUNDARY ⟨crossed the *border* into Italy⟩

**5 :** a plain or decorative margin around printed matter

— **bor·dered** \-dərd\ *adjective*

**²border** *verb* **bor·dered; bor·der·ing** \'bòr-d(ə-)riŋ\ (14th century)
*transitive verb*
**1 :** to put a border on

**2 :** to touch at the edge or boundary **:** BOUND ⟨*borders* the city on the south⟩
*intransitive verb*
**1 :** to lie on the border ⟨the U.S. *borders* on Canada⟩

**2 :** to approach the nature of a specified thing **:** VERGE ⟨*borders* on the ridiculous⟩

— **bor·der·er** \-dər-ər\ *noun*

*bootjack*

**Border collie** *noun* (1941)
: any of a breed of medium-sized sheepdogs of British origin noted for their herding abilities

**bor·de·reau** \ˌbȯr-də-ˈrō\ *noun, plural* **-reaux** \-ˈrō(z)\ [French, from Middle French *bordrel,* probably from *bord* border, from Old French *bort*] (circa 1858)
: a detailed note or memorandum of account; *especially* : one containing an enumeration of documents

**bor·der·land** \ˈbȯr-dər-ˌland\ *noun* (1813)
**1 a** : territory at or near a border **b** : FRINGE 3a ⟨lives on the *borderland* of society⟩
**2** : a vague intermediate state or region ⟨the *borderland* between fantasy and reality⟩

¹**bor·der·line** \-ˌlīn\ *adjective* (1907)
**1** : being in an intermediate position or state : not fully classifiable as one thing or its opposite; *especially* : not quite up to what is usual, standard, or expected ⟨*borderline* intelligence⟩
**2** : situated at or near a border
— **borderline** *noun*

²**borderline** *adverb* (1925)
: ALMOST, NEARLY ⟨*borderline* tacky⟩ ⟨*borderline* suicidal⟩

**Border terrier** *noun* (1894)
: any of a breed of small terriers of British origin having a harsh dense coat and close undercoat

**bor·dure** \ˈbȯr-jər\ *noun* [Middle English] (14th century)
: a border on a heraldic shield

¹**bore** \ˈbȯr, ˈbȯr\ *verb* **bored; bor·ing** [Middle English, from Old English *borian;* akin to Old High German *borōn* to bore, Latin *forare* to bore, *ferire* to strike] (before 12th century)
*transitive verb*
**1** : to pierce with a turning or twisting movement of a tool
**2** : to make (as a cylindrical hole) by boring or digging away material ⟨*bored* a tunnel⟩
*intransitive verb*
**1 a** : to make a hole by or as if by boring **b** : to sink a mine shaft or well
**2** : to make one's way steadily especially against resistance ⟨we *bored* through the jostling crowd⟩

²**bore** *noun* (14th century)
**1 a** : a usually cylindrical hole made by or as if by boring **b** *chiefly Australian & New Zealand* : a borehole drilled especially to make an artesian well
**2 a** : the long usually cylindrical hollow part of something (as a tube or gun barrel) **b** : the inner surface of a hollow cylindrical object
**3** : the size of a bore: as **a** : the interior diameter of a gun barrel; *specifically, chiefly British* : GAUGE 1a(2) **b** : the diameter of an engine cylinder

³**bore** *past of* BEAR

⁴**bore** *noun* [(assumed) Middle English *bore* wave, from Old Norse *bāra*] (1601)
: a tidal flood with a high abrupt front

⁵**bore** *noun* [origin unknown] (1766)
: one that causes boredom: as **a** : a tiresome person **b** : something that is devoid of interest

⁶**bore** *transitive verb* **bored; bor·ing** (1768)
: to cause to feel boredom

**bo·re·al** \ˈbȯr-ē-əl\ *adjective* [Middle English *boriall,* from Late Latin *borealis,* from Latin *boreas* north wind, north, from Greek, from *Boreas*] (15th century)
**1** : of, relating to, or located in northern regions ⟨*boreal* waters⟩
**2** : of, relating to, or comprising the northern biotic area characterized especially by dominance of coniferous forests

**Bo·re·as** \-ē-əs\ *noun* [Latin, from Greek]
**1** : the Greek god of the north wind
**2** : the north wind personified

**bore·dom** \ˈbȯr-dəm, ˈbȯr-\ *noun* (1852)
: the state of being weary and restless through lack of interest

**bo·reen** \bȯr-ˈēn, bȯr-\ *noun* [Irish *bóthrín,* diminutive of *bóthar* road] (1836)
*Irish* : a narrow country lane

**bore·hole** \ˈbȯr-ˌhōl, ˈbȯr-\ *noun* (1708)
: a hole bored or drilled in the earth: as **a** : an exploratory well **b** *chiefly British* : a small-diameter well drilled especially to obtain water

**bor·er** \ˈbȯr-ər, ˈbȯr-\ *noun* (14th century)
**1** : a tool used for boring
**2 a** : SHIPWORM **b** : an insect that bores in the woody parts of plants

**bore·scope** \ˈbȯr-ˌskōp, ˈbȯr-\ *noun* (1941)
: an optical device (as a prism or optical fiber) used to inspect an inaccessible space (as an engine cylinder)

**boric acid** *noun* [*boron*] (1869)
: a white crystalline acid $H_3BO_3$ obtained from its salts and used especially as a weak antiseptic and fire-retardant

**bo·ride** \ˈbȯr-ˌīd, ˈbȯr-\ *noun* (1863)
: a binary compound of boron with a more electropositive element or radical

**bor·ing** \ˈbȯr-iŋ, ˈbȯr-\ *adjective* (1840)
: causing boredom : TIRESOME
— **bor·ing·ly** \-iŋ-lē\ *adverb*
— **bor·ing·ness** *noun*

**born** \ˈbȯrn\ *adjective* [Middle English, from Old English *boren,* past participle of *beran* to carry — more at BEAR] (before 12th century)
**1 a** : brought forth by or as if by birth **b** : NATIVE — usually used in combination ⟨American-*born*⟩ **c** : deriving or resulting from — usually used in combination ⟨poverty-*born* crime⟩
**2 a** : having from birth specified qualities ⟨a *born* leader⟩ **b** : being in specified circumstances from birth ⟨nobly *born*⟩ ⟨*born* to wealth⟩
**3** : destined from or as if from birth ⟨*born* to succeed⟩

**born–again** *adjective* [from the verse "Except a man be *born again,* he cannot see the Kingdom of God" (John 3:3 Authorized Version)] (1961)
**1** : of, relating to, or being a usually Christian person who has made a renewed or confirmed commitment of faith especially after an intense religious experience
**2** : having returned to or newly adopted an activity, a conviction, or a persona especially with a proselytizing zeal ⟨a *born-again* conservative⟩

¹**borne** \ˈbȯrn, ˈbȯrn\ *past participle of* BEAR

²**borne** *adjective* [*borne*] (circa 1559)
: transported or transmitted by — used in combination ⟨soil*borne*⟩ ⟨air*borne*⟩

**bor·ne·ol** \ˈbȯr-nē-ˌȯl, -ˌōl\ *noun* [International Scientific Vocabulary, from *Borneo,* island of Indonesia] (1876)
: a crystalline cyclic alcohol $C_{10}H_{17}OH$ that occurs in two enantiomeric forms, is found in essential oils, and is used especially in perfumery

**born·ite** \ˈbȯr-ˌnīt\ *noun* [German *Bornit,* from Ignaz von *Born* (died 1791) Austrian mineralogist] (circa 1847)
: a brittle metallic-looking mineral that consists of a sulfide of copper and iron and is a valuable copper ore

**boro-** *combining form*
: boron ⟨*boro*silicate⟩

**bo·ro·hy·dride** \ˌbȯr-ō-ˈhī-ˌdrīd, ˌbȯr-\ *noun* (1940)
: the anion $BH_4^-$ of boron and hydrogen that is used especially as a reducing agent and as a source of hydrogen atoms; *also* : any of various compounds (as of metals) containing the borohydride anion

**bo·ron** \ˈbȯr-ˌän, ˈbȯr-\ *noun* [*borax* + *-on* (as in *carbon*)] (1812)
: a trivalent metalloid element found in nature only in combination and used in metallurgy and in composite structural materials — see ELEMENT table
— **bo·ron·ic** \bȯr-ˈä-nik, bȯr-\ *adjective*

**boron carbide** *noun* (circa 1909)
: a refractory shiny black crystalline compound $B_4C$ that is one of the hardest known materials and is used especially in abrasives and as a structural reinforcing material

**bo·ro·sil·i·cate** \ˌbȯr-ō-ˈsi-lə-ˌkāt, ˌbȯr-, -ˈsi-li-kət\ *noun* [International Scientific Vocabulary] (1817)
**1** : a silicate containing boron in the anion and occurring naturally
**2** : BOROSILICATE GLASS

**borosilicate glass** *noun* (1933)
: a silicate glass that is composed of at least five percent oxide of boron and is used especially in heat-resistant glassware

**bor·ough** \ˈbər-(ˌ)ō, ˈbə-ˌrō\ *noun* [Middle English *burgh,* from Old English *burg* fortified town; akin to Old High German *burg* fortified place, and probably to Old English *beorg* hill — more at BARROW] (before 12th century)
**1 a** : a medieval fortified group of houses forming a town with special duties and privileges **b** : a town or urban constituency in Great Britain that sends a member to Parliament **c** : an urban area in Great Britain incorporated for purposes of self-government
**2 a** : a municipal corporation proper in some states (as New Jersey and Minnesota) corresponding to the incorporated town or village of the other states **b** : one of the five constituent political divisions of New York City
**3** : a civil division of the state of Alaska corresponding to a county in most other states

**borough English** *noun* (14th century)
: a custom formerly existing in parts of England by which the lands of an intestate descended to the youngest son

**borough hall** *noun* (1939)
: the chief administrative building of a borough

**bor·row** \ˈbär-(ˌ)ō, ˈbȯr-\ *verb* [Middle English *borwen,* from Old English *borgian;* akin to Old English *beorgan* to preserve — more at BURY] (before 12th century)
*transitive verb*
**1 a** : to receive with the implied or expressed intention of returning the same or an equivalent ⟨*borrow* a book⟩ ⟨*borrowed* a dollar⟩ **b** : to borrow (money) with the intention of returning the same plus interest
**2 a** : to appropriate for one's own use ⟨*borrow* a metaphor⟩ **b** : DERIVE, ADOPT
**3** : to take (one) from a digit of the minuend in arithmetical subtraction in order to add as 10 to the digit holding the next lower place
**4** : to adopt into one language from another
**5** *dialect* : LEND
*intransitive verb*
: to borrow something
— **bor·row·er** \-ə-wər\ *noun*
— **borrow trouble** : to do something unnecessarily that may result in adverse reaction or repercussions

**bor·rowed time** *noun* (1898)
: an uncertain and usually uncontrolled postponement of something inevitable — used with *living on*

**bor·row·ing** \ˈbär-ə-wiŋ, ˈbȯr-\ *noun* (circa 1630)
: something borrowed; *especially* : a word or phrase adopted from one language into another

**borrow pit** *noun* (1893)
: an excavated area where material has been dug for use as fill at another location

**Bors** \ˈbȯrz\ *noun* [Middle English, from Middle French *Bohort*]
: a knight of the Round Table and nephew of Lancelot

---

\ə\ abut \ᵊ\ kitten \ər\ further \a\ ash \ā\ ace
\ä\ mop, mar \au̇\ out \ch\ chin \e\ bet \ē\ easy
\g\ go \i\ hit \ī\ ice \j\ job \ŋ\ sing \ō\ go
\ȯ\ law \ȯi\ boy \th\ thin \t͟h\ the \ü\ loot \u̇\ foot
\y\ yet \zh\ vision    *see also* Guide to Pronunciation

**borscht** *or* **borsch** \'bȯrsh(t)\ *noun* [Yiddish *borsht* & Ukrainian & Russian *borshch*] (1829)
**:** a soup made primarily of beets and served hot or cold often with sour cream

**borscht belt** *also* **borsch belt** *noun* (1938)
**:** BORSCHT CIRCUIT

**borscht circuit** *or* **borsch circuit** *noun, often B&C capitalized* [from the popularity of borscht on menus of the resorts] (1938)
**:** the theaters and nightclubs associated with the Jewish summer resorts in the Catskills

**Bor·stal** \'bȯr-st°l\ *noun* [*Borstal*, English village where the first such institution was set up] (1907)
*British* **:** REFORMATORY

**bort** \'bȯrt\ *noun* [probably from Dutch *boort*] (1622)
**:** imperfectly crystallized diamond or diamond fragments used as an abrasive

**bor·zoi** \'bȯr-,zȯi\ *noun* [Russian *borzoĭ*, from *borzoĭ* swift] (1887)
**:** any of a breed of large long-haired dogs of greyhound type developed in Russia especially for pursuing wolves — called also *Russian wolfhound*

**bos·cage** *also* **bosk·age** \'bäs-kij\ *noun* [Middle English *boskage*, from Middle French *boscage*, from Old French, from *bois, bosc* forest, of Germanic origin; akin to Old High German *busk* forest, bush] (14th century)
**:** a growth of trees or shrubs **:** THICKET

**bosh** \'bäsh\ *noun* [Turkish *boş* empty] (1834)
**:** foolish talk or activity **:** NONSENSE — often used interjectionally

**bosk** *or* **bosque** \'bäsk\ *noun* [probably back-formation from *bosky*] (1814)
**:** a small wooded area

**bosky** \'bäs-kē\ *adjective* [English dialect *bosk* bush, from Middle English *bush, bosk*] (1593)
**1 :** having abundant trees or shrubs
**2 :** of or relating to a woods

**bo·s'n** *or* **bo'·s'n** *or* **bo·sun** *or* **bo'·sun** \'bō-s°n\ *variant of* BOATSWAIN

**¹bos·om** \'bu̇-zəm *also* 'bü-\ *noun* [Middle English, from Old English *bōsm*; akin to Old High German *buosam* bosom] (before 12th century)
**1 a :** the human chest and especially the front part of the chest ⟨hugged the child to his *bosom*⟩ **b :** a woman's breasts regarded especially as a single feature ⟨a woman with an ample *bosom*⟩; *also* **:** BREAST
**2 a :** the chest conceived of as the seat of the emotions and intimate feelings ⟨a story you will take to your *bosom*⟩ **b :** the security and intimacy of or like that of being hugged to someone's bosom ⟨lived in the *bosom* of her family⟩
**3 :** the part of a garment that covers the chest or the breasts

**²bosom** *adjective* (1590)
**:** CLOSE, INTIMATE ⟨*bosom* friends⟩

**³bosom** *transitive verb* (1605)
**1 :** EMBRACE
**2 :** to enclose or carry in the bosom

**bos·omed** \-zəmd\ *adjective* (1603)
**:** having a bosom of a specified kind — used in combination ⟨full-*bosomed*⟩

**bos·omy** \'bu̇-zə-mē *also* 'bü-\ *adjective* (1860)
**1 :** swelling upward or outward ⟨*bosomy* hills⟩
**2 :** having prominent breasts

**bo·son** \'bō-,sän, -,zän\ *noun* [Satyendranath *Bose* (died 1974) Indian physicist + English ²-*on*] (1947)
**:** a particle (as a photon or meson) whose spin is zero or an integral number — compare FERMION

**bos·quet** \'bäs-kət\ *noun* [French, from Italian *boschetto*, diminutive of *bosco* forest, of Germanic origin; akin to Old High German *busk* forest, bush] (circa 1737)
**:** THICKET

**¹boss** \'bäs, 'bȯs\ *noun* [Middle English *boce*, from Middle French, from (assumed) Vulgar Latin *bottia*] (14th century)
**1 a :** a protuberant part or body ⟨a *boss* of granite⟩ ⟨a *boss* on an animal's horn⟩
**b :** a raised ornamentation
**: STUD c :** an ornamental projecting block used in architecture
**2 :** a soft pad used in ceramics and glassmaking
**3 :** the hub of a propeller

boss 1c

**²boss** *transitive verb* (15th century)
**1 :** to ornament with bosses **:** EMBOSS
**2 :** to treat (as the surface of porcelain) with a boss

**³boss** *noun* [Dutch *baas* master] (1679)
**1 :** a person who exercises control or authority; *specifically* **:** one who directs or supervises workers
**2 :** a politician who controls votes in a party organization or dictates appointments or legislative measures ◆
**— boss·dom** \-dəm\ *noun*
**— boss·ism** \'bä-,si-zəm, 'bȯ-\ *noun*

**⁴boss** \'bȯs\ *adjective* (1836)
*slang* **:** EXCELLENT, FIRST-RATE

**⁵boss** \'bȯs\ *transitive verb* (1856)
**1 :** to act as boss of
**2 :** to give usually arbitrary orders to — usually used with *around*

**⁶boss** \'bȯs, 'bäs\ *noun* [English dialect, young cow] (1790)
**:** COW, CALF

**bos·sa no·va** \,bä-sə-'nō-və\ *noun* [Portuguese, literally, new trend] (1962)
**1 :** popular music of Brazilian origin that is rhythmically related to the samba but with complex harmonies and improvised jazzlike passages
**2 :** a dance performed to bossa nova music

**boss man** *noun* (1934)
**:** ³BOSS

**¹bossy** \'bä-sē, 'bȯ-\ *adjective* (1543)
**1 :** marked by a swelling or roundness
**2 :** marked by bosses **:** STUDDED

**²bossy** \'bȯ-sē, 'bä-\ *noun, plural* **boss·ies** (1843)
**:** COW, CALF

**³bossy** \'bȯ-sē, 'bä-\ *adjective* **boss·i·er; -est** (1882)
**:** inclined to domineer **:** DICTATORIAL
**— boss·i·ness** *noun*

**Bos·ton** \'bȯs-tən\ *noun* [French, from *Boston*, Mass.] (1800)
**1 :** a variation of whist played with two decks of cards
**2** [*Boston*, Mass.] **:** a dance somewhat like a waltz

**Boston cream pie** *noun* (circa 1933)
**:** a round cake that is split and filled with a custard or cream filling and usually frosted with chocolate

**Boston fern** *noun* (circa 1900)
**:** a luxuriant fern (*Nephrolepis exaltata bostoniensis*) often with drooping much-divided fronds

**Boston ivy** *noun* (circa 1900)
**:** a woody Asian vine (*Parthenocissus tricuspidata*) of the grape family typically having 3-lobed leaves

**Boston rocker** *noun* (1856)
**:** a wooden rocking chair with a high spindle back, a decorative top panel, and a seat and arms that curve down at the front

**Boston terrier** *noun* (1894)
**:** any of a breed of small smooth-coated terriers originating as a cross of the bulldog and bullterrier and being

Boston rocker

brindled or black with white markings — called also *Boston bull*

**Bos·well** \'bäz-,wel, -wəl\ *noun* [James *Boswell*] (1858)
**:** a person who records in detail the life of a usually famous contemporary
**— Bos·well·ian** \bäz-'we-lē-ən\ *adjective*
**— Bos·well·ize** \'bäz-wə-,līz, -,we-\ *verb*

**bot** *also* **bott** \'bät\ *noun* [Middle English; akin to Dutch lever*bot* liver fluke] (15th century)
**:** the larva of a botfly; *especially* **:** one infesting the horse

**bo·ta** \'bō-tə\ *noun* [Spanish, from Late Latin *buttis* cask] (1832)
**:** a leather bottle (as for wine)

**bo·tan·i·ca** \bə-'ta-ni-kə\ *noun* [American Spanish *botánica*, from feminine of Spanish *botánico* botanical] (1969)
**:** a shop that deals in herbs and charms used especially by adherents of Santeria

**¹bo·tan·i·cal** \bə-'ta-ni-kəl\ *adjective* [French *botanique*, from Greek *botanikos* of herbs, from *botanē* pasture, herb, from *boskein* to feed, graze; probably akin to Lithuanian *guotas* flock] (1658)
**1 :** of or relating to plants or botany
**2 :** derived from plants
**3 :** SPECIES ⟨*botanical* tulips⟩
**— bo·tan·i·cal·ly** \-k(ə-)lē\ *adverb*

**²botanical** *noun* (circa 1926)
**:** a plant part or extract used especially in skin and hair care products

**botanical garden** *noun* (1785)
**:** a garden often with greenhouses for the culture, study, and exhibition of special plants — called also *botanic garden* \bə-'ta-nik-\

**bot·an·ise** *British variant of* BOTANIZE

**bot·a·nist** \'bä-t°n-ist, 'bät-nist\ *noun* (circa 1682)
**:** a specialist in botany or in a branch of botany

**bot·a·nize** \-t°n-,īz\ *verb* **-nized; -niz·ing** (1767)
*intransitive verb*
**:** to collect plants for botanical investigation; *also* **:** to study plants especially on a field trip
*transitive verb*
**:** to explore for botanical purposes

**bot·a·ny** \'bä-t°n-ē, 'bät-nē\ *noun, plural* **-nies** [*botanic* botanical + ²-*y*] (1696)
**1 :** a branch of biology dealing with plant life
**2 a :** plant life **b :** the properties and life phenomena exhibited by a plant, plant type, or plant group
**3 :** a botanical treatise or study; *especially* **:** a particular system of botany

**¹botch** \'bäch\ *noun* [Middle English *boche*, from Old North French, from (assumed) Vulgar Latin *bottia* boss] (14th century)
**:** an inflammatory sore

**²botch** *transitive verb* [Middle English *boc-chen*] (1530)
**1 :** to foul up hopelessly — often used with *up*
**2 :** to put together in a makeshift way
— **botch·er** *noun*
**³botch** *noun* (1605)
**1 :** something that is botched **: MESS**
**2 : PATCHWORK, HODGEPODGE**
— **botchy** \'bä-chē\ *adjective*
**bot·fly** \'bät-ˌflī\ *noun* (1819)
**:** any of various stout dipteran flies (family Oestridae) with larvae parasitic in cavities or tissues of various mammals including humans
**¹both** \'bōth\ *pronoun, plural in construction* [Middle English *bothe*, from Old Norse *bāthir*; akin to Old High German *beide* both] (12th century)
**:** the one as well as the other ⟨*both* of us⟩ ⟨we are *both* well⟩ ⟨$1000 fine or 30 days in jail, or *both*⟩
**²both** *conjunction* (12th century)
— used as a function word to indicate and stress the inclusion of each of two or more things specified by coordinated words, phrases, or clauses ⟨prized *both* for its beauty and for its utility⟩ ⟨he prayeth well, who loveth well *both* man and bird and beast —S. T. Coleridge⟩
**³both** *adjective* (13th century)
**:** being the two **:** affecting or involving the one and the other ⟨*both* feet⟩ ⟨*both* his eyes⟩ ⟨*both* these armies⟩
**¹both·er** \'bä-thər\ *verb* **both·ered; both·er·ing** \'bäth-riŋ, 'bä-thə-\ [origin unknown] (circa 1745)
*transitive verb*
**1 :** to annoy especially by petty provocation **: IRK**
**2 :** to intrude upon **: PESTER**
**3 :** to cause to be anxious or concerned — often used interjectionally
*intransitive verb*
**1 :** to become concerned
**2 :** to take pains **:** take the trouble
**synonym** see ANNOY
**²bother** *noun* (1834)
**1 a :** a state of petty discomfort, annoyance, or worry **b :** something that causes petty annoyance or worry
**2 : FUSS**
**both·er·a·tion** \ˌbä-thə-'rā-shən\ *noun* (1797)
**1 :** the act of bothering **:** the state of being bothered
**2 :** something that bothers — often used interjectionally
**both·er·some** \'bä-thər-səm\ *adjective* (1834)
**:** causing bother **: VEXING**
**bo·thy** \'bä-thē, 'bō-\ *noun* [Scots, probably from obsolete Scots *both* booth] (1771)
*chiefly Scottish* **: HUT**
**bot·o·née** *or* **bot·on·née** \ˌbä-t°n-'ā\ *adjective* [Middle French *botonné*] (15th century)
*of a heraldic cross* **:** having a cluster of three balls or knobs at the end of each arm — see CROSS illustration
**bo tree** \'bō-\ *noun* [Sinhalese *bō*, from Sanskrit *bodhi* enlightenment; from Buddha receiving enlightenment under this tree — more at BID] (1862)
**: PIPAL**
**bot·ry·oi·dal** \ˌbä-trē-'ȯi-d°l\ *adjective* [Greek *botryoeidēs*, from *botrys* bunch of grapes] (1816)
**:** having the form of a bunch of grapes ⟨*botryoidal* garnets⟩
**bo·try·tis** \bō-'trī-təs\ *noun* [New Latin, from Greek *botrys*] (1900)
**:** any of a genus (*Botrytis*) of imperfect fungi having botryoidal conidia and including several serious plant pathogens
**¹bot·tle** \'bä-t°l\ *noun, often attributive* [Middle English *botel*, from Middle French *bouteille*, from Medieval Latin *butticula*, di-

minutive of Late Latin *buttis* cask] (14th century)
**1 a :** a rigid or semirigid container typically of glass or plastic having a comparatively narrow neck or mouth and usually no handle **b :** a usually bottle-shaped container made of skin for storing a liquid
**2 :** the quantity held by a bottle
**3 a :** intoxicating drink **:** the practice of drinking **b :** liquid food (as milk) used in place of mother's milk
— **bot·tle·ful** \-ˌfùl\ *noun*
**²bottle** *transitive verb* **bot·tled; bot·tling** \'bä-t°l-iŋ, 'bät-liŋ\ (1600)
**1 :** to confine as if in a bottle **: RESTRAIN** — usually used with *up* ⟨*bottling* up their anger⟩
**2 :** to put into a bottle
— **bot·tler** \'bä-t°l-ər, 'bät-lər\ *noun*
**bot·tle·brush** \'bä-t°l-ˌbrəsh\ *noun* [from the shape of the flowers] (circa 1841)
**:** any of a genus (*Callistemon*) of Australian trees and shrubs of the myrtle family widely cultivated in warm regions especially for their spikes of brightly colored flowers
**bottle club** *noun* (1943)
**:** a club serving patrons previously purchased or reserved alcoholic drinks after normal legal closing hours
**bottled gas** *noun* (1930)
**:** gas under pressure in portable cylinders
**bot·tle-feed** \'bä-t°l-ˌfēd\ *transitive verb* **-fed; -feed·ing** (circa 1865)
**:** to feed (as an infant) with a bottle
**bottle gourd** *noun* (circa 1828)
**:** a common cultivated gourd (*Lagenaria siceraria*) with a variably shaped fruit that is sometimes used as a container
**bottle green** *noun* (1804)
**:** a dark green
**¹bot·tle·neck** \'bä-t°l-ˌnek\ *adjective* (1896)
**: NARROW** ⟨*bottleneck* harbors⟩
**²bottleneck** *noun* (1907)
**1 a :** a narrow route **b :** a point of traffic congestion
**2 a :** a condition or situation that retards or halts free movement and progress **b : IMPASSE**
**3 :** a style of guitar playing in which glissando effects are produced by sliding an object (as a knife blade or the neck of a bottle) along the strings
**³bottleneck** *transitive verb* (1933)
**:** to slow or halt by causing a bottleneck
**bot·tle-nosed dolphin** \'bä-t°l-ˌnōz-\ *noun* (circa 1909)
**:** a relatively small stout-bodied chiefly gray toothed whale (*Tursiops truncatus*) with a prominent beak and falcate dorsal fin
**bottlenose dolphin** *noun* (1940)
**: BOTTLE-NOSED DOLPHIN**
**bot·tling** \'bä-t°l-iŋ, 'bät-liŋ\ *noun* (1954)
**:** a beverage and especially a wine that is bottled at a particular time
**¹bot·tom** \'bä-təm\ *noun* [Middle English *botme*, from Old English *botm;* akin to Old High German *bodam* bottom, Latin *fundus*, Greek *pythmēn*] (before 12th century)
**1 a :** the underside of something **b :** a surface (as the seat of a chair) designed to support something resting on it **c :** the posterior end of the trunk **: BUTTOCKS, RUMP**
**2 :** the surface on which a body of water lies
**3 a :** the part of a ship's hull lying below the water **b : BOAT, SHIP**
**4 a :** the lowest part or place **b :** the remotest or inmost point **c :** the lowest or last place in point of precedence ⟨started work at the *bottom*⟩ **d :** the pants of pajamas — usually used in plural **e :** the last half of an inning of baseball **f :** the bass or baritone instruments of a band
**5 : BOTTOMLAND** — usually used in plural
**6 : BASIS, SOURCE**
**7 :** capacity (as of a horse) to endure strain

**8 :** a foundation color applied to textile fibers before dyeing
— **bot·tomed** \-təmd\ *adjective*
— **at bottom :** REALLY, BASICALLY
**²bottom** (1544)
*transitive verb*
**1 :** to furnish with a bottom
**2 :** to provide a foundation for
**3 :** to bring to the bottom
**4 :** to get to the bottom of **: FATHOM**
*intransitive verb*
**1 :** to become based
**2 :** to reach the bottom
**3 :** to reach a low point before rebounding — usually used with *out*
— **bot·tom·er** *noun*
**³bottom** *adjective* (1561)
**1 :** of, relating to, or situated at the bottom ⟨*bottom* rock⟩
**2 :** frequenting the bottom ⟨*bottom* fish⟩
**3 :** having a quantum characteristic that accounts for the existence and lifetime of upsilon particles and that has a value of zero for most known particles ⟨*bottom* quark⟩
**bot·tom·land** \'bä-təm-ˌland\ *noun* (1728)
**:** low-lying land along a watercourse
**bot·tom·less** \-ləs\ *adjective* (14th century)
**1 :** having no bottom ⟨a *bottomless* chair⟩
**2 a :** extremely deep **b :** impossible to comprehend **: UNFATHOMABLE** ⟨a *bottomless* mystery⟩ **c : BOUNDLESS, UNLIMITED**
**3 a** [from the absence of lower as well as upper garments] **: NUDE** ⟨*bottomless* dancers⟩ **b :** featuring nude entertainers
— **bot·tom·less·ly** *adverb*
— **bot·tom·less·ness** *noun*
**bottom-line** \'bä-təm-ˌlīn\ *adjective* (1972)
**1 :** concerned only with cost or profits
**2 : PRAGMATIC, REALISTIC**
**bottom line** *noun* (1967)
**1 a :** the essential or salient point **: CRUX b :** the primary or most important consideration
**2 a :** the line at the bottom of a financial report that shows the net profit or loss **b :** financial considerations (as cost or profit or loss) **c :** the final result **: OUTCOME, UPSHOT**
**bot·tom·most** \'bä-tə(m)-ˌmōst\ *adjective* (1861)
**1 a :** situated at the very bottom **: LOWEST, DEEPEST b : LAST** ⟨the *bottommost* part of the day —Alfred Kazin⟩
**2 :** most basic ⟨the *bottommost* problems facing the world⟩
**bottom round** *noun* (1923)
**:** meat (as steak) from the outer part of a round of beef
**bot·u·lin** \'bä-chə-lən\ *noun* [probably from New Latin *botulinum*] (circa 1900)
**:** a neurotoxin formed by botulinum and causing botulism
**bot·u·li·num** \ˌbä-chə-'lī-nəm\ *also* **bot·u·li·nus** \-nəs\ *noun* [New Latin, from Latin *botulus* sausage] (1902)
**:** a spore-forming bacterium (*Clostridium botulinum*) that secretes botulin
— **bot·u·li·nal** \-'lī-n°l\ *adjective*
**bot·u·lism** \'bä-chə-ˌli-zəm\ *noun* (1887)
**:** an acute paralytic disease caused by botulin especially in food
**bou·bou** \'bü-ˌbü\ *noun* [French, from Malinke *bubu*] (1961)
**:** a long flowing garment worn in parts of Africa
**bou·chée** \bü-'shā\ *noun* [French, literally, mouthful, from Old French *buchiee*, from (assumed) Vulgar Latin *buccata*, from Latin *bucca* cheek, mouth] (1846)
**:** a small patty shell usually containing a creamed filling

---

\ə\ **abut** \°\ **kitten** \ər\ **further** \a\ **ash** \ā\ **ace**
\ä\ **mop, mar** \aù\ **out** \ch\ **chin** \e\ **bet** \ē\ **easy**
\g\ **go** \i\ **hit** \ī\ **ice** \j\ **job** \ŋ\ **sing** \ō\ **go**
\ȯ\ **law** \ȯi\ **boy** \th\ **thin** \t͟h\ **the** \ü\ **loot** \ù\ **foot**
\y\ **yet** \zh\ **vision** *see also* **Guide to Pronunciation**

**bou·clé** or **bou·cle** \bü-ʹklā\ noun [French bouclé curly, from past participle of boucler to curl, from bocle buckle, curl] (1895)
**1 :** an uneven yarn of three plies one of which forms loops at intervals
**2 :** a fabric of bouclé yarn
**bou·doir** \ʹbü-ˌdwär, ʹbu̇-, ˌbü-ʹ, ˌbu̇-ʹ\ noun [French, from bouder to pout] (1781)
**:** a woman's dressing room, bedroom, or private sitting room
**bouf·fant** \bü-ʹfänt, ʹbü-ˌ\ adjective [French, from Middle French, from present participle of bouffer to puff] (1880)
**:** puffed out ⟨bouffant hairdos⟩ ⟨a bouffant veil⟩
**bou·gain·vil·lea** also **bou·gain·vil·laea** \ˌbü-gən-ʹvil-yə, ˌbō-, ˌbu̇-, -ʹvē-ə\ noun [New Latin, from Louis Antoine de Bougainville] (1881)
**:** any of a genus (Bougainvillaea) of the four-o'clock family of ornamental tropical American woody vines with brilliant purple or red floral bracts
**bough** \ʹbau̇\ noun [Middle English, shoulder, bough, from Old English bōg; akin to Old High German buog shoulder, Greek pēchys forearm] (before 12th century)
**:** a branch of a tree; especially **:** a main branch
**— boughed** \ʹbau̇d\ adjective
**¹bought** \ʹbȯt\ past and past participle of BUY
**²bought** adjective [past participle of buy] (1599)
**:** STORE 2 ⟨bought clothes⟩
**bought·en** \ʹbȯ-tʰn\ adjective [bought + -en (as in forgotten)] (1793)
chiefly dialect **:** BOUGHT ⟨the only boughten carpet in the region —H. W. Thompson⟩
**bou·gie** \ʹbü-ˌzhē, -ˌjē\ noun [French, from Bougie, seaport in Algeria] (1755)
**1 :** a wax candle
**2 a :** a tapering cylindrical instrument for introduction into a tubular passage of the body **b**
**:** SUPPOSITORY
**bouil·la·baisse** \ˌbü-yə-ʹbäs, -ʹbāz, ʹbü-yə-ˌ, -ˌbäz\ noun [French] (1855)
**1 :** a highly seasoned fish stew made with at least two kinds of fish
**2 :** POTPOURRI
**bouil·lon** \ʹbu̇l-ˌyän, ʹbu̇l-; ʹbu̇l-yən; ʹbü-ˌyō°\ noun [French, from Old French boillon, from boillir to boil] (circa 1656)
**:** a clear seasoned soup made usually from lean beef; broadly **:** BROTH
**bouillon cube** noun (circa 1922)
**:** a cube of evaporated meat extract
**boul·der** \ʹbōl-dər\ noun [short for boulder stone, from Middle English bulder ston, part translation of a word of Scandinavian origin; akin to Swedish dialect bullersten large stone in a stream, from buller noise + sten stone] (1617)
**:** a detached and rounded or much-worn mass of rock
**— boul·dered** \-dərd\ adjective
**— boul·dery** \-d(ə-)rē\ adjective
**¹bou·le** \ʹbü-(ˌ)lē, bü-ʹlā\ noun [Greek boulē, literally, will, from boulesthai to wish] (1846)
**:** a legislative council of ancient Greece consisting first of an aristocratic advisory body and later of a representative senate
**²boule** \ʹbül\ noun [French, ball — more at BOWL] (1918)
**:** a pear-shaped synthetically formed mass (as of sapphire) with the atomic structure of a single crystal
**bou·le·vard** \ʹbu̇-lə-ˌvärd, ʹbü- also ʹbə-\ noun [French, modification of Middle Dutch bolwerc bulwark] (1769)
**:** a broad often landscaped thoroughfare ◆
**bou·le·vard·ier** \ˌbu̇-lə-ˌvär-ʹdyā, ˌbü-, -ʹdir\ noun [French, from boulevard] (1879)
**:** a frequenter of the Parisian boulevards; broadly **:** MAN-ABOUT-TOWN
**bou·le·ver·se·ment** \bül-ver-sə-mä°\ noun [French] (1782)
**1 :** REVERSAL

**2 :** a violent disturbance **:** DISORDER
**boulle** \ʹbül, ʹbyü(ə)l\ noun [André Charles Boulle (died 1732) French cabinetmaker] (1823)
**:** inlaid decoration of tortoiseshell, yellow metal, and white metal in cabinetwork
**¹bounce** \ʹbau̇n(t)s\ verb **bounced; bounc·ing** [Middle English bounsen] (13th century)
transitive verb
**1** obsolete **:** BEAT, BUMP
**2 :** to cause to rebound ⟨bounce a ball⟩
**3 a :** DISMISS, FIRE **b :** to expel precipitately from a place
**4 :** to issue (a check) drawn on an account with insufficient funds
**5 :** to present (as an idea) to another person to elicit comments or to gain approval — usually used with off
intransitive verb
**1 :** to rebound after striking a surface (as the ground)
**2 :** to recover from a blow or a defeat quickly — usually used with back
**3 :** to be returned by a bank because of insufficient funds in a checking account ⟨his checks bounce⟩
**4 a :** to leap suddenly **:** BOUND **b :** to walk with springing steps
**5 :** to hit a baseball so that it hits the ground before it reaches an infielder
**²bounce** noun (1523)
**1 a :** a sudden leap or bound **b :** REBOUND
**2 :** BLUSTER
**3 :** VERVE, LIVELINESS
**bounc·er** \ʹbau̇n(t)-sər\ noun (1865)
**:** one that bounces; especially **:** a person employed to restrain or eject disorderly persons
**bounc·ing** \-siŋ\ adjective (circa 1563)
**1 :** LIVELY, ANIMATED
**2 :** enjoying good health **:** ROBUST
**— bounc·ing·ly** \-siŋ-lē\ adverb
**bouncing bet** \-ʹbet\ noun, often cap 2nd B capitalized [from Bet, nickname for Elizabeth] (circa 1818)
**:** a European perennial herb (Saponaria officinalis) of the pink family that is widely naturalized in the U.S. and has pink or white flowers and leaves which yield a detergent when bruised
**bouncy** \ʹbau̇n(t)-sē\ adjective **bounc·i·er; -est** (1921)
**1 :** BUOYANT, EXUBERANT
**2 :** RESILIENT
**3 :** marked by or producing bounces
**— bounc·i·ly** \-sə-lē\ adverb
**¹bound** \ʹbau̇nd\ adjective [Middle English boun, from Old Norse būinn, past participle of būa to dwell, prepare; akin to Old High German būan to dwell — more at BOWER] (13th century)
**1** archaic **:** READY
**2 :** intending to go **:** GOING ⟨bound for home⟩ ⟨college-bound⟩
**²bound** noun [Middle English, from Old French bodne, from Medieval Latin bodina] (13th century)
**1 a :** a limiting line **:** BOUNDARY — usually used in plural **b :** something that limits or restrains ⟨beyond the bounds of decency⟩
**2** usually plural **a :** BORDERLAND **b :** the land within certain bounds
**3 :** a number greater than or equal to every number in a set (as the range of a function); also **:** a number less than or equal to every number in a set
**³bound** past and past participle of BIND
**⁴bound** transitive verb (14th century)
**1 :** to set limits or bounds to **:** CONFINE
**2 :** to form the boundary of **:** ENCLOSE
**3 :** to name the boundaries of
**⁵bound** adjective [Middle English bounden, from past participle of binden to bind] (14th century)
**1 :** placed under legal or moral restraint or obligation **:** OBLIGED ⟨duty-bound⟩

**2 a :** fastened by or as if by a band **:** CONFINED ⟨desk-bound⟩ **b :** very likely **:** SURE ⟨bound to rain soon⟩
**3 :** made costive **:** CONSTIPATED
**4** of a book **:** secured to the covers by cords, tapes, or glue
**5 :** DETERMINED, RESOLVED
**6 :** held in chemical or physical combination
**7 :** always occurring in combination with another linguistic form ⟨un- in unknown and -er in speaker are bound forms⟩ — compare FREE 11d
**⁶bound** noun [Middle French bond, from bondir to leap, from (assumed) Vulgar Latin bombitire to hum, from Latin bombus deep hollow sound — more at BOMB] (circa 1553)
**1 :** LEAP, JUMP
**2 :** the action of rebounding **:** BOUNCE
**⁷bound** intransitive verb (1592)
**1 :** to move by leaping
**2 :** REBOUND, BOUNCE
**bound·ary** \ʹbau̇n-d(ə-)rē\ noun, plural **-aries** (1626)
**:** something (as a line, point, or plane) that indicates or fixes a limit or extent
**boundary layer** noun (1921)
**:** a region of retarded fluid near the surface of a body which moves through a fluid or past which a fluid moves
**bound·ed·ness** \ʹbau̇n-dəd-nəs\ noun (1674)
**:** the quality or state of being bounded
**bound·en** \ʹbau̇n-dən\ adjective [Middle English] (14th century)
**1** archaic **:** being under obligation **:** BEHOLDEN
**2 :** made obligatory **:** BINDING ⟨our bounden duty⟩
**bound·er** \-dər\ noun (1505)
**1 :** one that bounds
**2 :** a man of objectionable social behavior **:** CAD
**— bound·er·ish** \-d(ə-)rish\ adjective
**bound·less** \ʹbau̇n(d)-ləs\ adjective (1592)
**:** having no boundaries **:** VAST
**— bound·less·ly** adverb
**— bound·less·ness** noun
**bound up** adjective (1611)
**:** closely involved or associated — usually used with with
**boun·te·ous** \ʹbau̇n-tē-əs\ adjective [Middle English bountevous, from Middle French bontif kind, from Old French, from bonté] (14th century)
**1 :** giving or disposed to give freely

**2 :** liberally bestowed
— **boun·te·ous·ly** *adverb*
— **boun·te·ous·ness** *noun*
**boun·tied** \'baùn-tēd\ *adjective* (1788)
**1 :** having the benefit of a bounty
**2 :** rewarded or rewardable by a bounty
**boun·ti·ful** \'baùn-ti-fəl\ *adjective* (1508)
**1 :** liberal in bestowing gifts or favors
**2 :** given or provided abundantly ⟨a *bountiful* harvest⟩
*synonym* see LIBERAL
— **boun·ti·ful·ly** \-f(ə-)lē\ *adverb*
— **boun·ti·ful·ness** \-fəl-nəs\ *noun*
**boun·ty** \'baùn-tē\ *noun, plural* **bounties**
[Middle English *bounte* goodness, from Old French *bonté*, from Latin *bonitat-, bonitas*, from *bonus* good, from Old Latin *duenos*; akin to Sanskrit *duva* reverence, favor] (13th century)
**1 :** something that is given generously
**2 :** liberality in giving **:** GENEROSITY
**3 :** yield especially of a crop
**4 :** a reward, premium, or subsidy especially when offered or given by a government: as **a :** an extra allowance to induce entry into the armed services **b :** a grant to encourage an industry **c :** a payment to encourage the destruction of noxious animals **d :** a payment for the capture of or assistance in the capture of an outlaw
**bounty hunter** *noun* (1930)
**1 :** one that tracks down and captures outlaws for whom a reward is offered
**2 :** one that hunts predatory animals for the reward offered
**bou·quet** \bō-'kā, bü-\ *noun* [French, from Middle French, thicket, from Old North French *bosquet*, from Old French *bosc* forest — more at BOSCAGE] (circa 1718)
**1 a :** flowers picked and fastened together in a bunch **:** NOSEGAY **b :** MEDLEY ⟨*bouquet* of songs⟩
**2 :** COMPLIMENT
**3 a :** a distinctive and characteristic fragrance (as of wine) **b :** a subtle aroma or quality (as of an artistic performance)
**bou·quet gar·ni** \-gär-'nē\ *noun, plural* **bouquets gar·nis** \-'kā(z)-gär-'nē\ [French, literally, garnished bouquet] (circa 1852)
**:** an herb mixture that is either tied together or enclosed in a porous container and is cooked with a dish but removed before serving
**bour·bon** \'bùr-bən, 'bōr-, 'bor-; *usually* 'bər- *in sense 3*\ *noun* [*Bourbon*, seigniory in France] (1600)
**1** *capitalized* **:** a member of a French family founded in 1272 to which belong the rulers of France from 1589 to 1793 and from 1814 to 1830, of Spain from 1700 to 1808, from 1814 to 1868, from 1875 to 1931, and from 1975, of Naples from 1735 to 1805, and of the Two Sicilies from 1815 to 1860
**2** [*Bourbon* (now Réunion), French island in the Indian Ocean] **:** a rose (*Rosa borboniana*) of compact upright growth with shining leaves, prickly branches, and clustered flowers
**3** [*Bourbon* county, Kentucky] **:** a whiskey distilled from a mash made up of not less than 51 percent corn plus malt and rye — compare CORN WHISKEY
**4** *often capitalized* **:** a person who clings obstinately to old social and political ideas; *specifically* **:** an extremely conservative member of the U.S. Democratic party usually from the South
— **bour·bon·ism** \-bə-ˌni-zəm\ *noun, often capitalized*
**bourg** \'bùr(g)\ *noun* [Middle English, from Middle French, from Old French *borc*, from Latin *burgus* fortified place, of Germanic origin; akin to Old High German *burg* fortified place — more at BOROUGH] (12th century)
**:** TOWN, VILLAGE: as **a :** one neighboring a castle **b :** a market town

**¹bour·geois** \'bùrzh-ˌwä *also* 'bùzh- *or* 'büzh- *or* bùrzh-'\ *adjective* [Middle French, from Old French *borjois*, from *borc*] (circa 1565)
**1 :** of, relating to, or characteristic of the townsman or of the social middle class
**2 :** marked by a concern for material interests and respectability and a tendency toward mediocrity
**3 :** dominated by commercial and industrial interests **:** CAPITALISTIC
— **bour·geois·i·fi·ca·tion** \ˌbù(r)zh-ˌwä-zə-fə-'kā-shən\ *noun*
— **bour·geois·i·fy** \ˌbù(r)zh-'wä-zə-ˌfī\ *verb*
**²bourgeois** *noun, plural* **bourgeois** \-ˌwä(z), -'wä(z)\ (circa 1674)
**1 a :** BURGHER **b :** a middle-class person
**2 :** a person with social behavior and political views held to be influenced by private-property interest **:** CAPITALIST
**3** *plural* **:** BOURGEOISIE
**bour·geoise** \'bùrzh-ˌwäz *also* 'bùzh- *or* 'büzh- *or* bùrzh-'\ *noun* [French, feminine of *bourgeois*] (1794)
**:** a woman of the middle class
**bour·geoi·sie** \ˌbù(r)zh-ˌwä-'zē\ *noun* [French, from *bourgeois*] (1707)
**1 :** MIDDLE CLASS
**2 :** a social order dominated by bourgeois
**bour·geon** \'bər-jən\ *variant of* BURGEON
**bour·gui·gnonne** \ˌbùr-gēn-'yòn\ *or* **bour·gui·gnon** \-'yō[n]\ *adjective, often capitalized* [French, from *Bourgogne* Burgundy, region in France] (circa 1919)
**:** prepared or served in the manner of Burgundy (as with a sauce made with red wine) ⟨beef *bourguignonne*⟩
**bourn** *or* **bourne** \'bōrn, 'bòrn, 'bùrn\ *noun* [Middle English *burn, bourne* — more at BURN] (12th century)
**:** STREAM, BROOK
**bourne** *also* **bourn** *noun* [Middle French *bourne*, from Old French *bodne* — more at BOUND] (1523)
**1 :** BOUNDARY, LIMIT
**2 :** GOAL, DESTINATION
**bour·rée** \bù-'rā, 'bü-\ *noun* [French] (1706)
**1 :** a 17th century French dance usually in quick duple time; *also* **:** a musical composition with the rhythm of this dance
**2 :** PAS DE BOURRÉE
**bour·ride** \bù-'rēd, bə-\ *noun* [French, from Provençal *bourrido*, alteration of *boulido* something boiled, from *bouli* to boil, from Latin *bullire* — more at BOIL] (circa 1919)
**:** a fish stew similar to bouillabaisse that is usually thickened with egg yolks and strongly flavored with garlic
**bourse** \'bùrs\ *noun* [Middle French, literally, purse, from Medieval Latin *bursa* — more at PURSE] (1597)
**1 :** EXCHANGE 5a; *specifically* **:** a European stock exchange
**2 :** a sale of numismatic or philatelic items on tables (as at a convention)
**bouse** *variant of* BOWSE
**bou·stro·phe·don** \ˌbü-strə-'fē-ˌdän, -d[n]n\ *noun* [Greek *boustrophēdon*, adverb, literally, turning like oxen in plowing, from *bous* ox, cow + *strephein* to turn — more at COW] (1699)
**:** the writing of alternate lines in opposite directions (as from left to right and from right to left)
— **boustrophedon** *adjective or adverb*
— **bou·stro·phe·don·ic** \-fē-'dä-nik\ *adjective*
**bout** \'baùt\ *noun* [English dialect, a trip going and returning in plowing, from Middle English *bought* bend] (1575)
**:** a spell of activity: as **a :** an athletic match (as of boxing) **b :** OUTBREAK, ATTACK ⟨a *bout* of lumbago⟩ **c :** SESSION
**bou·tique** \bü-'tēk\ *noun, often attributive* [French, shop, probably from Old Provençal *botica*, ultimately from Greek *apothēkē* storehouse — more at APOTHECARY] (1767)

**1 a :** a small fashionable specialty shop or business **b :** a small shop within a large department store
**2 :** a small company that offers highly specialized services ⟨an independent investment *boutique*⟩
**bou·ton·niere** \ˌbü-t[n]n-'ir, ˌbü-tən-'yer\ *noun* [French *boutonnière* buttonhole, from Middle French, from *bouton* button] (circa 1867)
**:** a flower or bouquet worn in a buttonhole
**Bou·vi·er des Flan·dres** \ˌbü-vē-ˌā-də-'fländərz, -'flä[n]dr[ə]\ *noun* [French, literally, cowherd of Flanders] (1929)
**:** any of a breed of large powerfully built rough-coated dogs of Belgian origin used especially for herding and in guard work — called also *Bouvier*

**Bouvier des Flandres**

**bou·zou·ki** \bü-'zü-kē\ *noun, plural* **-kis** *also* **-kia** \-kē-ə\ [New Greek *mpouzouki*] (1952)
**:** a long-necked stringed instrument of Greek origin that resembles a mandolin
**bo·vid** \'bō-vid\ *noun* [New Latin *Bovidae*, from *Bov-, Bos*, type genus, from Latin *bov-, bos*] (1939)
**:** any of a family (Bovidae) of ruminants that have hollow unbranched permanently attached horns present in both sexes and that include antelopes, oxen, sheep, and goats
**¹bo·vine** \'bō-ˌvīn, -ˌvēn\ *adjective* [Late Latin *bovinus*, from Latin *bov-, bos* ox, cow — more at COW] (1817)
**1 :** of, relating to, or resembling bovines and especially the ox or cow
**2 :** having qualities (as placidity or dullness) characteristic of oxen or cows
— **bo·vine·ly** *adverb*
— **bo·vin·i·ty** \bō-'vi-nə-tē\ *noun*
**²bovine** *noun* (1865)
**:** any of a subfamily (Bovinae) of bovids including oxen, bison, buffalo, and their close relatives
**¹bow** \'baù\ *verb* [Middle English, from Old English *būgan*; akin to Old High German *biogan* to bend, Sanskrit *bhujati* he bends] (before 12th century)
*intransitive verb*
**1 :** to cease from competition or resistance **:** SUBMIT, YIELD ⟨refusing to *bow* to the inevitable —John O'Hara⟩; *also* **:** to suffer defeat ⟨*bowed* to the champion⟩
**2 :** to bend the head, body, or knee in reverence, submission, or shame
**3 :** to incline the head or body in salutation or assent or to acknowledge applause
*transitive verb*
**1 :** to cause to incline
**2 :** to incline (as the head) especially in respect or submission
**3 :** to crush with a heavy burden
**4 a :** to express by bowing **b :** to usher in or out with a bow
**²bow** *noun* (circa 1656)
**:** a bending of the head or body in respect, submission, assent, or salutation; *also* **:** a show of respect or submission
**³bow** \'bō\ *noun* [Middle English *bowe*, from Old English *boga*; akin to Old English *būgan*] (before 12th century)
**1 a :** something bent into a simple curve **:** BEND, ARCH **b :** RAINBOW

**2 :** a weapon that is made of a strip of flexible material (as wood) with a cord connecting the two ends and holding the strip bent and that is used to propel an arrow
**3 :** ARCHER
**4 a :** a metal ring or loop forming a handle (as of a key) **b :** a knot formed by doubling a ribbon or string into two or more loops **c :** BOW TIE **d :** a frame for the lenses of eyeglasses; *also :* the sidepiece of the frame passing over the ear
**5 a :** a wooden rod with horsehairs stretched from end to end used in playing an instrument of the viol or violin family **b :** a stroke of such a bow

**⁴bow** \'bō\ (before 12th century)
*intransitive verb*
**1 :** to bend into a curve
**2 :** to play a stringed musical instrument with a bow
*transitive verb*
**1 :** to cause to bend into a curve
**2 :** to play (a stringed instrument) with a bow

**⁵bow** \'baú\ *noun* [Middle English *bowe, bowgh,* probably from Middle Dutch *boech* bow, shoulder; akin to Old English *bōg* bough] (15th century)
**1 :** the forward part of a ship
**2 :** ²BOWMAN

**Bow bells** \'bō-\ *noun plural* (1600)
**:** the bells of the Church of Saint Mary-le-Bow in London

**bowd·ler·ise** *British variant of* BOWDLERIZE

**bowd·ler·ize** \'bōd-lə-ˌrīz, 'baúd-\ *transitive verb* **-ized; -iz·ing** [Thomas *Bowdler* (died 1825) English editor] (1836)
**1 :** to expurgate (as a book) by omitting or modifying parts considered vulgar
**2 :** to modify by abridging, simplifying, or distorting in style or content ◆
— **bowd·ler·iza·tion** \ˌbōd-lə-rə-'zā-shən, ˌbaúd-\ *noun*
— **bowd·ler·iz·er** *noun*

**¹bowed** \'baúd\ *adjective* [past participle of ¹*bow*] (14th century)
**1 :** bent downward and forward ⟨listened with *bowed* heads⟩
**2 :** having the back and head inclined

**²bowed** \'bōd\ *adjective* [partly from ³*bow* + *-ed;* partly from past participle of ⁴*bow*] (15th century)
**:** furnished with or shaped like a bow

**bow·el** \'baú(-ə)l\ *noun* [Middle English, from Middle French *boel,* from Medieval Latin *botellus,* from Latin, diminutive of *botulus* sausage] (14th century)
**1 :** INTESTINE, GUT; *also :* one of the divisions of the intestines — usually used in plural except in medical use ⟨the large *bowel*⟩ ⟨move your *bowels*⟩
**2** *archaic* **:** the seat of pity, tenderness, or courage — usually used in plural
**3** *plural* **:** the interior parts; *especially :* the deep or remote parts ⟨*bowels* of the earth⟩
— **bow·el·less** \'baú(-ə)l-ləs\ *adjective*

**¹bow·er** \'baú(-ə)r\ *noun* [Middle English *bour* dwelling, from Old English *būr;* akin to Old English & Old High German *būan* to dwell, Old English *bēon* to be — more at BE] (before 12th century)
**1 :** an attractive dwelling or retreat
**2 :** a lady's private apartment in a medieval hall or castle
**3 :** a shelter (as in a garden) made with tree boughs or vines twined together **:** ARBOR
— **bow·ery** \-ē\ *adjective*

**²bower** *transitive verb* (1592)
**:** EMBOWER, ENCLOSE

**³bower** *noun* (1652)
**:** an anchor carried at the bow of a ship

**bow·er·bird** \'baú(-ə)r-ˌbərd\ *noun* (1845)
**:** any of a family (Ptilonorhynchidae) of passerine birds of the Australian region in which the male builds a chamber or passage arched over with twigs and grasses, often adorned with

bright-colored objects, and used especially to attract the female

**bow·ery** \'baú(-ə)r-ē\ *noun, plural* **-er·ies** [Dutch *bouwerij,* from *bouwer* farmer, from *bouwen* to till; akin to Old High German *būan* to dwell] (1650)
**1 :** a colonial Dutch plantation or farm
**2** [*Bowery,* street in New York City] **:** a city district known for cheap bars and derelicts

**bow·fin** \'bō-ˌfin\ *noun* (1845)
**:** a predaceous dull-green iridescent North American freshwater fish (*Amia calva*) that is the only surviving member of an order (Amiiformes) dating back to the Jurassic

**bow·front** \-ˌfrənt\ *adjective* (1925)
**1 :** having an outward curving front ⟨*bowfront* furniture⟩
**2 :** having a bow window in front ⟨*bowfront* houses⟩

**bow·head whale** \-ˌhed-\ *noun* (1887)
**:** a baleen whale (*Balaena mysticetus*) of arctic and subarctic seas — called also *bowhead*

**bow·ie knife** \'bü-ē-, 'bō-\ *noun* [James *Bowie*] (1836)
**:** a stout single-edged hunting knife with part of the back edge curved concavely to a point and sharpened

**bow·ing** \'bō-iŋ\ *noun* (1838)
**:** the technique or manner of managing the bow in playing a stringed musical instrument

**bow·knot** \'bō-ˌnät\ *noun* (1547)
**:** a knot with decorative loops

**¹bowl** \'bōl\ *noun* [Middle English *bolle,* from Old English *bolla;* akin to Old High German *bolla* blister] (before 12th century)
**1 :** a concave usually hemispherical vessel often used for holding liquids; *especially :* a drinking vessel (as for wine)
**2 :** the contents of a bowl
**3 :** a bowl-shaped or concave part: as **a :** the hollow of a spoon or tobacco pipe **b :** the receptacle of a toilet
**4 :** a natural formation or geographical region shaped like a bowl **b :** a bowl-shaped structure; *especially :* an athletic stadium
**5 :** a postseason football game between specially invited teams
— **bowled** \'bōld\ *adjective*
— **bowl·ful** \-ˌfúl\ *noun*

**²bowl** *noun* [Middle English *boule,* from Middle French, from Latin *bulla* bubble] (15th century)
**1 a :** a ball (as of lignum vitae) weighted or shaped to give it a bias when rolled in lawn bowling **b** *plural but singular in construction* **:** LAWN BOWLING
**2 :** a delivery of the ball in bowling
**3 :** a cylindrical roller or drum (as for a mechanical device)

**³bowl** (15th century)
*intransitive verb*
**1 a :** to participate in a game of bowling **b :** to roll a ball in bowling
**2 :** to travel smoothly and rapidly (as in a wheeled vehicle)
*transitive verb*
**1 a :** to roll (a ball) in bowling **b** (1) **:** to complete by bowling ⟨*bowl* a string⟩ (2) **:** to score by bowling ⟨*bowls* 150⟩
**2 :** to strike with a swiftly moving object
**3 :** to overwhelm with surprise

**bowl·der** *variant of* BOULDER

**bow·leg** \'bō-ˌleg, -ˌlāg, 'bō-\ *noun* (circa 1864)
**:** a leg bowed outward at or below the knee
— **bow·legged** \'bō-ˌle-gəd, -ˌlā-; -ˌlegd, -ˌlāgd\ *adjective*

**¹bowl·er** \'bō-lər\ *noun* (circa 1500)
**:** a person who bowls; *specifically :* the player that delivers the ball to the batsman in cricket

**²bowl·er** \'bō-lər\ *noun* [*Bowler,* 19th century family of English hatters] (1861)
**:** DERBY 3

**bow·line** \'bō-lən, -ˌlīn\ *noun* [Middle English *bouline,* perhaps from *bowe* bow + *line*] (13th century)

**1 :** a rope used to keep the weather edge of a square sail taut forward
**2 :** a knot used to form a loop that neither slips nor jams — see KNOT illustration

**bowl·ing** \'bō-liŋ\ *noun* (1535)
**:** any of several games in which balls are rolled on a green or down an alley at an object or group of objects

**bowl over** *transitive verb* (1867)
**1 :** to take unawares.
**2 :** ¹IMPRESS 2

**¹bow·man** \'bō-mən\ *noun* (13th century)
**:** ARCHER 1

**²bow·man** \'baú-mən\ *noun* (1829)
**:** a boatman, oarsman, or paddler stationed in the front of a boat

**Bow·man's capsule** \'bō-mənz-\ *noun* [Sir William *Bowman* (died 1892) English surgeon] (circa 1860)
**:** a thin membranous double-walled capsule surrounding the glomerulus of a vertebrate nephron

**bow out** *intransitive verb* (1942)
**:** RETIRE, WITHDRAW

**bow saw** \'bō-\ *noun* (1677)
**:** a saw having a narrow blade held under tension by a light bow-shaped frame

**bowse** \'baúz\ *verb* **bowsed; bows·ing** [origin unknown] (1593)
*transitive verb*
**:** to haul by means of a tackle
*intransitive verb*
**:** to bowse something

**bow shock** \'baú-\ *noun* (1950)
**:** the shock wave formed by the collision of a stellar wind with another medium (as the magnetosphere of a planet)

**bow·sprit** \'baú-ˌsprit, *British usually* 'bō-\ *noun* [Middle English *bouspret,* probably from Middle Low German *bōchsprēt,* from *bōch* bow + *sprēt* pole] (13th century)
**:** a large spar projecting forward from the stem of a ship

**bow·string** \'bō-ˌstriŋ\ *noun* (14th century)
**:** a waxed or sized cord joining the ends of a shooting bow

**bowstring hemp** *noun* (circa 1858)
**:** any of various Asian and African sansevierias; *also :* its soft tough leaf fiber used especially in cordage

**bow tie** \'bō-\ *noun* (1897)
**:** a short necktie tied in a bowknot

**bow window** \'bō-\ *noun* (1753)
**:** a usually curved bay window

---

◇ WORD HISTORY

**bowdlerize** Editors of books typically languish in obscurity, while authors bask in fame. Few editors have ever gained the public attention achieved by Thomas Bowdler (1754–1825). Born near Bath, England, and trained as a physician, Bowdler engaged in mostly nonmedical pursuits from the 1780s onward. His travels through Europe led to his first foray into publishing, a report warning English tourists against the uncleanliness of watering places in France. Expanding the scope of his interest in purification, he next tackled works of literature. His first effort was *The Family Shakespeare* (1818), the title page of which promised that "those words and expressions are omitted which cannot with propriety be read aloud in a family." Although Bowdler's edition met with adverse critical reaction, it pleased the 19th century public. Bowdler then went on to expurgate Gibbon's *History of the Decline and Fall of the Roman Empire* of all passages of "an irreligious or immoral tendency." A decade after his death Bowdler's name had become synonymous with censorship on moral grounds, and by 1836 *bowdlerize* was used to describe the expurgation of literary works.

**bow·wow** \'bau̇-ˌwau̇, bau̇-'\ *noun* [imitative] (1576)
**1** : the bark of a dog; *also* : DOG
**2** : noisy clamor
**3** : arrogant dogmatic manner
**bow·yer** \'bō-yər\ *noun* [Middle English *bowyere*] (14th century)
: a person who makes shooting bows
**¹box** \'bäks\ *noun, plural* **box** *or* **box·es** [Middle English, from Old English, from Latin *buxus*, from Greek *pyxos*] (before 12th century)
: an evergreen shrub or small tree (genus *Buxus* of the family Buxaceae, the box family) with opposite entire leaves and capsular fruits; *especially* : a widely cultivated shrub (*B. sempervirens*) used for hedges, borders, and topiary figures
**²box** *noun* [Middle English, from Old English, from Late Latin *buxis*, from Greek *pyxis*, from *pyxos* box tree] (before 12th century)
**1** : a rigid typically rectangular container with or without a cover ⟨a cigar *box*⟩: as **a** : an open cargo container of a vehicle **b** : COFFIN
**2** : the contents of a box especially as a measure of quantity
**3** : a box or boxlike container and its contents: as **a** *British* : a gift in a box **b** : an automobile transmission **c** : TELEVISION **d** : a signaling apparatus ⟨alarm *box*⟩ **e** : a usually self-contained piece of electronic equipment **f** : BOOM BOX
**4** : an often small space, compartment, or enclosure: as **a** : an enclosed group of seats for spectators (as in a theater or stadium) **b** : a driver's seat on a carriage or coach **c** : a cell for holding mail **d** *British* : BOX STALL **e** : PENALTY BOX
**5** : a usually rectangular space that is frequently outlined or demarcated on a surface: as **a** : any of six spaces on a baseball diamond where the batter, coaches, pitcher, and catcher stand **b** : a space on a page for printed matter or in which to make a mark
**6** : PREDICAMENT, FIX
**7** : a cubical building
— **box·ful** \-ˌfu̇l\ *noun*
— **box·like** \-ˌlīk\ *adjective*
**³box** *transitive verb* (15th century)
**1** : to enclose in or as if in a box
**2** : to hem in (as an opponent) — usually used with *in*, *out*, or *up* ⟨*boxed* out the opposing tackle⟩
**⁴box** *noun* [Middle English] (14th century)
: a punch or slap especially on the ear
**⁵box** (1519)
*transitive verb*
**1** : to hit (as the ears) with the hand
**2** : to engage in boxing with
*intransitive verb*
: to fight with the fists : engage in boxing
**⁶box** *transitive verb* [probably from Spanish *bojar* to circumnavigate, from Catalan *vogir* to turn, from Latin *volvere* to roll — more at VOLUBLE] (1753)
: to name the 32 points of (the compass) in their order — used figuratively in the phrase *box the compass* to describe making a complete reversal
**box·board** \'bäks-ˌbōrd, -ˌbȯrd\ *noun* (1841)
: paperboard used for making boxes and cartons
**box camera** *noun* (1902)
: a box-shaped camera with a simple lens and rotary shutter
**¹box·car** \'bäks-ˌkär\ *noun* (1856)
: a roofed freight car usually with sliding doors in the sides
**²boxcar** *adjective* [from the high numbers stenciled on the sides of boxcars] (1944)
: very large ⟨the judge awarded her a *boxcar* figure⟩
**box coat** *noun* (1822)
**1** : a heavy overcoat formerly worn for driving
**2** : a loose coat usually fitted at the shoulders
**box elder** *noun* (1787)

: a North American maple (*Acer negundo*) with compound leaves
**¹box·er** \'bäk-sər\ *noun* (1742)
**1** : a person who engages in the sport of boxing
**2** *plural* : SHORT 4b
**²boxer** *noun* (1871)
: one that makes boxes or packs things in boxes
**³boxer** *noun* [German, from English ¹*boxer*] (circa 1904)
: a compact medium-sized short-haired usually fawn or brindled dog of a breed originating in Germany
**Box·er** \'bäk-sər\ *noun* [approximate translation of Chinese (Beijing) *yìhé juǎn*, literally, righteous harmonious fist] (1899)
: a member of a Chinese secret society that in 1900 attempted by violence to drive foreigners out of China and to force Chinese converts to renounce Christianity
**boxer shorts** *noun plural* (1944)
: SHORT 4b
**¹box·ing** \'bäk-siŋ\ *noun* (1607)
**1** : an act of enclosing in a box
**2** : a boxlike enclosure : CASING
**3** : material used for boxes and casings
**²boxing** *noun* (1711)
: the art of attack and defense with the fists practiced as a sport
**Boxing Day** *noun* (1833)
: the first weekday after Christmas observed as a legal holiday in parts of the Commonwealth and marked by the giving of Christmas boxes to service workers (as postal workers)
**boxing glove** *noun* (1875)
: one of a pair of leather mittens heavily padded on the back and worn in boxing
**box kite** *noun* (1897)
: a tailless kite consisting of two or more open-ended connected boxes
**box lunch** *noun* (1950)
: a lunch packed in a container (as a box)
**box office** *noun* (1786)
**1 a** : an office (as in a theater) where tickets of admission are sold **b** : income from ticket sales (as for a film)
**2** : the ability or power (as of a show) to attract ticket buyers; *also* : something that enhances that ability ⟨any publicity is good *box office*⟩

box kite

**box pleat** *noun* (1883)
: a pleat made by forming two folded edges one facing right and the other left
**box score** *noun* [from its arrangement in a newspaper box] (1913)
: a printed score of a game (as baseball) giving the names and positions of the players and a record of the play arranged in tabular form; *broadly* : total count : SUMMARY
**box seat** *noun* (1849)
**1** : ²BOX 4b
**2 a** : a seat in a box (as in a theater or grandstand) **b** : a position favorable for viewing something
**box social** *noun* (1928)
: a fund-raising affair at which box lunches are auctioned to the highest bidder
**box spring** *noun* (1895)
: a bedspring that consists of spiral springs attached to a foundation and enclosed in a cloth-covered frame
**box stall** *noun* (1885)
: an individual enclosure within a barn or stable in which an animal may move about freely without a restraining device
**box·thorn** \'bäks-ˌthȯrn\ *noun* (1678)
: MATRIMONY VINE
**box turtle** *noun* (circa 1804)
: any of several North American land turtles (genus *Terrapene*) capable of withdrawing into its shell and closing it by hinged joints

in the lower half — called also *box tortoise*
**box·wood** \'bäks-ˌwu̇d\ *noun* (1652)
**1** : the very close-grained heavy tough hard wood of the box (*Buxus*); *also* : a wood of similar properties
**2** : a plant producing boxwood
**boxy** \'bäk-sē\ *adjective* **box·i·er; -est** (circa 1861)
: resembling a box
— **box·i·ness** *noun*

box turtle

**boy** \'bȯi\ *noun, often attributive* [Middle English] (13th century)
**1** : a male servant — sometimes taken to be offensive
**2 a** : a male child from birth to puberty **b** : SON **c** : an immature male : YOUTH **d** : SWEETHEART, BEAU
**3 a** : one native to a given place ⟨local *boy*⟩ **b** : FELLOW, PERSON ⟨the *boys* at the office⟩ **c** — used interjectionally to express intensity of feeling ⟨*boy*, what a game⟩
— **boy·hood** \-ˌhu̇d\ *noun*
— **boy·ish** \-ish\ *adjective*
— **boy·ish·ly** *adverb*
— **boy·ish·ness** *noun*
**bo·yar** *also* **bo·yard** \bō-'yär\ *noun* [Russian *boyarin*] (1591)
: a member of a Russian aristocratic order next in rank below the ruling princes until its abolition by Peter the Great
**boy·chick** \'bȯi-ˌchik\ *noun* [American Yiddish *boytshik*, from English *boy* + Yiddish *-tshik*, diminutive suffix] (circa 1951)
: a young man : BOY
**boy·cott** \'bȯi-ˌkät\ *transitive verb* [Charles C. Boycott (died 1897) English land agent in Ireland who was ostracized for refusing to reduce rents] (1880)
: to engage in a concerted refusal to have dealings with (as a person, store, or organization) usually to express disapproval or to force acceptance of certain conditions ◆

◇ WORD HISTORY
**boycott** In September 1880 the recently formed Irish National Land League, which grew out of unrest following an agricultural depression in Ireland during the late 1870s, initiated a campaign against the eviction of tenants unable to pay their rents. Charles S. Boycott, a retired English army captain who rented a farm in County Mayo and worked as an agent for an absentee landlord, became the first victim of the Land League's campaign. When the landlord's tenants refused to pay their rents unless they received a 25 percent abatement, Boycott attempted to serve eviction notices. As a result, he was ostracized by the community, his laborers and servants quit, and the crops on his farm began to rot. His plight became well-known through press coverage and Boycott's own letters to *The Times* in London. A force of fifty volunteers from Ulster was raised and sent to Mayo to harvest his crops, guarded by nearly a thousand troops and police. The newly popular tactic of shunning a person to assert a grievance needed a name and Boycott's name was at hand. The Land League was banned by Parliament in 1881, but the word *boycott*, noun and verb, is still part of English.

\ə\ abut \ᵊ\ kitten \ər\ further \a\ ash \ā\ ace
\ä\ mop, mar \au̇\ out \ch\ chin \e\ bet \ē\ easy
\g\ go \i\ hit \ī\ ice \j\ job \ŋ\ sing \ō\ go
\ȯ\ law \ȯi\ boy \th\ thin \t͟h\ the \ü\ loot \u̇\ foot
\y\ yet \zh\ vision *see also* Guide to Pronunciation

— **boycott** *noun*

— **boy·cott·er** *noun*

**boy·friend** \'bȯi-ˌfrend\ *noun* (1896)

**1 :** a male friend

**2 :** a frequent or regular male companion of a girl or woman

**3 :** a male lover

**Boyle's law** \'bȯilz-\ *noun* [Robert *Boyle*] (circa 1860)

**:** a statement in physics: the volume of a gas at constant temperature varies inversely with the pressure exerted on it

**boyo** \'bȯi-(ˌ)ō\ *noun, plural* **boy·os** [*boy* + ¹*-o*] (circa 1870)

*Irish* **:** BOY, LAD

**Boy Scout** *noun* (1909)

**1 :** a member of any of various national scouting programs (as the Boy Scouts of America) for boys usually 11 to 17 years of age

**2 :** a person whose values or actions are characteristic of a Boy Scout

**boy·sen·ber·ry** \'bȯi-zⁿn-ˌber-ē, -sⁿn-, -zⁿm-\ *noun* [Rudolph *Boysen* (died 1950) American horticulturist + English *berry*] (1935)

**:** a large bramble fruit with a raspberry flavor; *also* **:** the trailing hybrid bramble yielding this fruit and developed by crossing several blackberries and raspberries

**boy wonder** *noun* (1946)

**:** a young man of noteworthy achievements

**bo·zo** \'bō-(ˌ)zō\ *noun, plural* **bozos** [origin unknown] (1920)

**:** a foolish or incompetent person

**B picture** *noun* (circa 1937)

**:** B MOVIE

**bra** \'brä\ *noun* (1936)

**:** BRASSIERE

— **bra·less** *adjective*

**brab·ble** \'bra-bəl\ *intransitive verb* **brab·bled; brab·bling** \-b(ə-)liŋ\ [perhaps from Middle Dutch *brabbelen,* of imitative origin] (circa 1530)

**:** SQUABBLE

— **brabble** *noun*

¹**brace** \'brās\ *verb* **braced; brac·ing** [Middle English, from Middle French *bracier* to embrace, from *brace*] (14th century)

*transitive verb*

**1** *archaic* **:** to fasten tightly **:** BIND

**2 a :** to prepare for use by making taut **b :** PREPARE, STEEL ⟨*brace* yourself for the shock⟩ **c :** INVIGORATE, FRESHEN

**3 :** to turn (a sail yard) by means of a brace

**4 a :** to furnish or support with a brace ⟨heavily *braced* against the wind⟩ **b :** to make stronger **:** REINFORCE

**5 :** to put or plant firmly ⟨*braces* his foot in the stirrup⟩

**6 :** to waylay especially with demands or questions

*intransitive verb*

**1 :** to take heart — used with *up*

**2 :** to get ready (as for an attack)

²**brace** *noun, plural* **brac·es** [Middle English, clasp, pair, from Middle French, two arms, from Latin *bracchia,* plural of *bracchium* arm, from Greek *brachiōn,* from comparative of *brachys* short — more at BRIEF] (14th century)

**1 :** something (as a clasp) that connects or fastens

**2** *or plural* **brace :** two of a kind **:** PAIR ⟨several *brace* of quail⟩

**3 :** a crank-shaped instrument for turning a bit

**4 :** something that transmits, directs, resists, or supports weight or pressure: as **a :** a diagonal piece of structural material that serves to strengthen something (as a framework) **b :** a rope rove through a block at the end of a ship's yard to swing it horizontally **c** *plural* **:** SUSPENDERS **d :** an appliance for supporting a body part **e** *plural* **:** dental appliances used to exert pressure to straighten misaligned teeth

**5 a :** one of two marks { } used to connect words or items to be considered together **b :** one of these marks connecting two or more musical staffs carrying parts to be performed simultaneously **c :** BRACKET 3a

**6 :** a position of rigid attention

**7 :** something that arouses energy or strengthens morale

**brace·let** \'brās-lət\ *noun* [Middle English, from Middle French, diminutive of *bras* arm, from Latin *bracchium*] (15th century)

**1 :** an ornamental band or chain worn around the wrist

**2 :** something (as handcuffs) resembling a bracelet

¹**bra·cer** \'brā-sər\ *noun* [Middle English, from Middle French *braciere,* from Old French, from *braz* arm, from Latin *bracchium*] (14th century)

**:** an arm or wrist protector especially for use by an archer

²**brac·er** \'brā-sər\ *noun* (1579)

**1 :** one that braces, binds, or makes firm

**2 :** a drink (as of liquor) taken as a stimulant

**bra·ce·ro** \brä-'ser-(ˌ)ō\ *noun, plural* **-ros** [Spanish, laborer, from *brazo* arm, from Latin *bracchium*] (1920)

**:** a Mexican laborer admitted to the U.S. especially for seasonal contract labor in agriculture — compare WETBACK

**brace root** *noun* (1892)

**:** PROP ROOT

**brachi-** *or* **brachio-** *combining form* [Latin *bracchium, brachium*]

**1 :** arm ⟨*brachia*l⟩

**2 :** brachial and ⟨*brachio*cephalic⟩

**bra·chi·al** \'brā-kē-əl\ *adjective* (1578)

**:** of, relating to, or situated in the arm or an armlike process ⟨the *brachial* artery of the upper arm⟩

**brachial plexus** *noun* (circa 1860)

**:** a network of nerves lying mostly in the armpit and supplying nerves to the chest, shoulder, and arm

**bra·chi·ate** \'brā-kē-ˌāt\ *intransitive verb* **-at·ed; -at·ing** (1932)

**:** to progress by swinging from one hold to another by the arms ⟨a *brachiating* gibbon⟩

— **bra·chi·a·tion** \ˌbrā-kē-'ā-shən\ *noun*

— **bra·chi·a·tor** \'brā-kē-ˌā-tər\ *noun*

**bra·chio·ce·phal·ic artery** \ˌbrā-kē-(ˌ)ō-sə-'fa-lik-\ *noun* (circa 1839)

**:** a short artery that arises from the arch of the aorta and divides into the carotid and subclavian arteries of the right side — called also *innominate artery*

**brachiocephalic vein** *noun* (circa 1852)

**:** either of two large veins that occur one on each side of the neck, receive blood from the head and neck, and unite to form the superior vena cava — called also *innominate vein*

**bra·chio·pod** \'brā-kē-ə-ˌpäd\ *noun* [ultimately from Latin *bracchium* + Greek *pod-, pous* foot — more at FOOT] (1836)

**:** any of a phylum (Brachiopoda) of marine invertebrates with bivalve shells within which is a pair of arms bearing tentacles by which a current of water is made to bring microscopic food to the mouth

— **brachiopod** *adjective*

**brachy-** *combining form* [Greek, from *brachys* — more at BRIEF]

**:** short ⟨*brachy*cephalic⟩

**brachy·ce·phal·ic** \ˌbra-ki-sə-'fa-lik\ *adjective* [New Latin *brachycephalus,* from Greek *brachy-* + *kephalē* head — more at CEPHALIC] (circa 1852)

**:** short-headed or broad-headed with a cephalic index of over 80

— **brachy·ceph·a·ly** \-'se-fə-lē\ *noun*

**bra·chyp·ter·ous** \bra-'kip-tə-rəs\ *adjective* [Greek *brachypteros,* from *brachy-* + *pteron* wing — more at FEATHER] (circa 1847)

**:** having rudimentary or abnormally small wings ⟨*brachypterous* insects⟩

**brac·ing** \'brā-siŋ\ *adjective* (1750)

**:** giving strength, vigor, or freshness ⟨a *bracing* breeze⟩

— **brac·ing·ly** *adverb*

**bra·ci·o·la** \ˌbrä-chē-'ō-lə, -'chō-lə\ *or* **bra·ci·o·le** \-'ō-,lä\ *noun* [Italian, literally, slice of meat roasted over coals, from *brace* live coals, probably of Germanic origin; akin to Swedish *brasa* fire] (circa 1945)

**:** a thin slice of meat wrapped around a seasoned filling and often cooked in wine

**brack·en** \'bra-kən\ *noun* [Middle English *braken,* probably of Scandinavian origin; akin to Old Swedish *brækne* fern] (14th century)

**1 :** a large coarse fern; *especially* **:** a nearly cosmopolitan brake (*Pteridium aquilinum*) found in most tropical and temperate regions

**2 :** a growth of brakes

¹**brack·et** \'bra-kət\ *noun* [perhaps from Middle French *braguette* codpiece, from diminutive of *brague* breeches, from Old Provençal *braga,* from Latin *braca,* of Celtic origin — more at BREECH] (1580)

**1 :** an overhanging member that projects from a structure (as a wall) and is usually designed to support a vertical load or to strengthen an angle

**2 :** a fixture (as for holding a lamp) projecting from a wall or column

**3 a :** one of a pair of marks [ ] used in writing and printing to enclose matter or in mathematics and logic as signs of aggregation — called also *square bracket* **b :** one of the pair of marks ⟨ ⟩ used to enclose matter — called also *angle bracket* **c :** PARENTHESIS 3 **d :** BRACE 5b

**4 :** a section of a continuously numbered or graded series (as age ranges or income levels)

²**bracket** *transitive verb* (circa 1847)

**1 a :** to place within or as if within brackets ⟨editorial comments are *bracketed*⟩ ⟨news stories *bracketed* by commercials⟩ **b :** to eliminate from consideration ⟨*bracket* off politics⟩ **c :** to extend around so as to encompass **:** INCLUDE ⟨test pressures . . . which *bracket* virtually the entire range of passenger-car tire pressures —*Consumer Reports*⟩

**2 :** to furnish or fasten with brackets

**3 :** to put in the same category or group ⟨*bracketed* in a tie for third⟩

**4 a :** to get the range on (a target) by firing over and short ⟨there were mortar rounds *bracketing* the area —Ed Bradley⟩ **b :** to establish the limits of ⟨*bracketed* the problem neatly⟩ **c :** to take photographs at more than one exposure in order to ensure that the desired exposure is obtained

**bracket creep** *noun* (1980)

**:** movement into a higher tax bracket as a result of income rises intended to offset the effects of inflation

**brack·et·ed** *adjective* (1885)

*of a serif* **:** joined to the stroke by a curved line

**bracket fungus** *noun* (1899)

**:** a basidiomycete that forms shelflike sporophores

**brack·ish** \'bra-kish\ *adjective* [Dutch *brac* salty; akin to Middle Low German *brac* salty] (1538)

**1 :** somewhat salty ⟨*brackish* water⟩

**2 a :** not appealing to the taste ⟨*brackish* tea⟩ **b :** REPULSIVE

— **brack·ish·ness** *noun*

**brac·o·nid** \'bra-kə-(ˌ)nid\ *noun* [ultimately from Greek *brachys*] (circa 1893)

**:** any of a large family (Braconidae) of ichneumon flies

— **braconid** *adjective*

**bract** \'brakt\ *noun* [New Latin *bractea,* from Latin, thin metal plate] (1770)

**1** : a leaf from the axil of which a flower or floral axis arises
**2** : a leaf borne on a floral axis; *especially* : one subtending a flower or flower cluster
— **brac·te·al** \'brak-tē-əl\ *adjective*
— **brac·te·ate** \-tē-ət, -ˌāt\ *adjective*
— **bract·ed** \-təd\ *adjective*
**brac·te·ole** \'brak-tē-ˌōl\ *noun* [New Latin *bracteola,* from Latin, diminutive of *bractea*] (circa 1828)
: a small bract especially on a floral axis
¹**brad** \'brad\ *noun* [Middle English, from Old Norse *broddr* spike; perhaps akin to Old English *byrst* bristle — more at BRISTLE] (13th century)
**1** : a thin nail of the same thickness throughout but tapering in width and having a slight projection at the top of one side instead of a head
**2** : a slender wire nail with a small barrel-shaped head
²**brad** *transitive verb* **brad·ded; brad·ding** (1794)
: to fasten with brads
**brad·awl** \'brad-ˌól\ *noun* (1823)
: an awl with chisel edge used to make holes for brads or screws
**brady-** *combining form* [Greek *bradys*]
: slow ⟨*brady*kinin⟩
**bra·dy·car·dia** \ˌbrā-di-'kär-dē-ə *also* ˌbra-\ *noun* [New Latin] (circa 1890)
: relatively slow heart action — compare TACHYCARDIA
**bra·dy·ki·nin** \-'kī-nən\ *noun* (1949)
: a kinin that is formed locally in injured tissue, acts in vasodilation of small arterioles, is considered to play a part in inflammatory processes, and is composed of a chain of nine amino-acid residues
**brae** \'brā\ *noun* [Middle English *bra,* from Old Norse *brā* eyelid; akin to Old English *brǣw* eyebrow, and probably to Old English *bregdan* to move quickly — more at BRAID] (13th century)
*chiefly Scottish* : a hillside especially along a river
¹**brag** \'brag\ *noun* [Middle English] (14th century)
**1** : a pompous or boastful statement
**2** : arrogant talk or manner : COCKINESS
**3** : BRAGGART
²**brag** *verb* **bragged; brag·ging** (14th century)
*intransitive verb*
: to talk boastfully : engage in self-glorification
*transitive verb*
: to assert boastfully
**synonym** see BOAST
— **brag·ger** \'bra-gər\ *noun*
— **brag·gy** \'bra-gē\ *adjective*
³**brag** *adjective* **brag·ger; brag·gest** (1836)
: FIRST-RATE
**brag·ga·do·cio** \ˌbra-gə-'dō-sē-ˌō, -shē-, -chē-, -(ˌ)shō, -(ˌ)chō\ *noun, plural* **-cios** [*Braggadochio,* personification of boasting in *Faerie Queene* by Edmund Spenser] (1594)
**1** : BRAGGART
**2 a** : empty boasting **b** : arrogant pretension : COCKINESS
**brag·gart** \'bra-gərt\ *noun* (circa 1577)
: a loud arrogant boaster
— **braggart** *adjective*
¹**Brah·ma** \'brä-mə\ *noun* [Sanskrit *brahman*] (1690)
**1** : the creator god of the Hindu sacred triad — compare SIVA, VISHNU
**2** : the ultimate ground of all being in Hinduism
²**Brah·ma** \'brā-mə, 'brä-, 'bra-\ *noun* (1938)
: BRAHMAN 2
**Brah·man** or **Brah·min** \'brä-mən; *2 is* 'brā-, 'brä-, 'bra-\ *noun* [Middle English *Bragman* inhabitant of India, from Latin *Bracmanus,* from Greek *Brachman,* from Sanskrit *brāhmaṇa* of the Brahman caste, from *brāhmaṇa* Brahman] (15th century)

**1 a** : a Hindu of the highest caste traditionally assigned to the priesthood **b** : ¹BRAHMA 2
**2** : any of an Indian breed of humped cattle : ZEBU; *especially* : a large vigorous heat-resistant and tick-resistant usually silvery gray animal developed in the southern U.S. from the zebu
**3** *usually Brahmin* : a person of high social standing and cultivated intellect and taste ⟨Boston *Brahmins*⟩
— **Brah·man·ic** \brä-'ma-nik\ *or* **Brah·man·i·cal** \-ni-kəl\ *adjective*
**Brah·man·ism** \'brä-mə-ˌni-zəm\ *noun* (1816)
: orthodox Hinduism adhering to the pantheism of the Vedas and to the ancient sacrifices and family ceremonies
¹**braid** \'brād\ *transitive verb* [Middle English *breyden* to move suddenly, snatch, plait, from Old English *bregdan;* akin to Old High German *brettan* to draw (a sword)] (before 12th century)
**1 a** : to make from braids ⟨*braid* a rug⟩ **b** : to form (three or more strands) into a braid
**2** : to do up (the hair) by interweaving three or more strands
**3** : MIX, INTERMINGLE ⟨*braid* fact with fiction⟩
**4** : to ornament especially with ribbon or braid
— **braid·er** *noun*
²**braid** *noun* (1530)
**1 a** : a length of braided hair **b** : a cord or ribbon having usually three or more component strands forming a regular diagonal pattern down its length; *especially* : a narrow fabric of intertwined threads used especially for trimming
**2** : high-ranking naval officers
**braid·ed** *adjective* (15th century)
**1 a** : made by intertwining three or more strands **b** : ornamented with braid
**2** : forming an interlacing network of channels ⟨a *braided* river⟩
**braid·ing** \'brā-diŋ\ *noun* (15th century)
: something made of braided material
¹**brail** \'brā(ə)l\ *noun* [Middle English *brayle,* from Anglo-French *braiel,* from Old French, strap] (15th century)
**1** : a rope fastened to the leech of a sail and used for hauling the sail up or in
**2** : a dip net with which fish are hauled aboard a boat from a purse seine or trap
²**brail** *transitive verb* (1625)
**1** : to take in (a sail) by the brails
**2** : to hoist (fish) by means of a brail
**braille** \'brā(ə)l\ *noun, often capitalized* [Louis *Braille*] (1853)
: a system of writing for the blind that uses characters made up of raised dots ◆
— **braille** *transitive verb*
— **braill·ist** \'brā-list\ *noun*

| | a | b | c | d | e | f | g | h | i | j |
|---|---|---|---|---|---|---|---|---|---|---|
| | 1 | 2 | 3 | 4 | 5 | 6 | 7 | 8 | 9 | 0 |

| k | l | m | n | o | p | q | r | s | t |
|---|---|---|---|---|---|---|---|---|---|

| u | v | w | x | y | z | | | Capital Sign | Numeral Sign |
|---|---|---|---|---|---|---|---|---|---|

**braille alphabet**

**braille·writ·er** \-ˌrī-tər\ *noun, often capitalized* (1942)
: a machine for writing braille
¹**brain** \'brān\ *noun* [Middle English, from Old English *brægen;* akin to Middle Low German *bregen* brain, and perhaps to Greek *brechmos* front part of the head] (before 12th century)
**1 a** : the portion of the vertebrate central nervous system that constitutes the organ of thought and neural coordination, includes all the higher nervous centers receiving stimuli from the sense organs and interpreting and

correlating them to formulate the motor impulses, is made up of neurons and supporting and nutritive structures, is enclosed within the skull, and is continuous with the spinal cord through the foramen magnum **b** : a nervous center in invertebrates comparable in position and function to the vertebrate brain

**brain 1a:** *1* cerebral hemisphere, *2* corpus callosum, *3* ventricle, *4* fornix, *5* thalamus, *6* pituitary gland, *7* pons, *8* medulla oblongata, *9* spinal cord, *10* cerebellum, *11* midbrain

**2 a** (1) : INTELLECT, MIND ⟨has a clever *brain*⟩ (2) : intellectual endowment : INTELLIGENCE — often used in plural ⟨plenty of *brains* in that family⟩
**b** (1) : a very intelligent or intellectual person (2) : the chief planner of an organization or enterprise — usually used in plural
**3** : something that performs the functions of a brain; *especially* : an automatic device (as a computer) for control or computation
²**brain** *transitive verb* (14th century)
**1** : to kill by smashing the skull
**2** : to hit on the head
**brain·case** \'brān-ˌkās\ *noun* (1741)
: the cranium enclosing the brain
**brain·child** \-ˌchīld\ *noun* (1631)
: a product of one's creative imagination
**brain coral** *noun* (circa 1711)
: a massive reef-building coral (as genus *Maeandra*) having the surface covered by ridges and furrows
**brain death** *noun* (1964)
: final cessation of activity in the central nervous system especially as indicated by a flat electroencephalogram for a predetermined length of time
— **brain-dead** *adjective*
**brain drain** *noun* (1963)
: the departure of educated or professional people from one country, economic sector, or field for another usually for better pay or living conditions
**brained** \'brānd\ *adjective* (15th century)
: having a brain of a specified kind — used in combination ⟨feather*brained*⟩
**brain hormone** *noun* (1957)
: a hormone that is secreted by neurosecretory cells of the insect brain and that stimulates the prothoracic glands to secrete ecdysone
**brain·ish** \'brā-nish\ *adjective* (circa 1530)

◇ **WORD HISTORY**
**braille** The system of writing known as *braille* is named after its principal inventor, the Frenchman Louis Braille (1809–1852). Blinded at the age of three in an accident, Braille entered the Institution Nationale des Jeunes Aveugles (National Institute for Blind Children) in Paris in 1819. While there he became interested in a writing system developed by Charles Barbier in which messages were encoded in dots embossed on cardboard. Braille worked out an adaptation using a six-dot code and a simple instrument for producing the dots. He published treatises on his system in 1829 and 1837.

\ə\ abut \ᵊ\ kitten \ər\ further \a\ ash \ā\ ace
\ä\ mop, mar \aú\ out \ch\ chin \e\ bet \ē\ easy
\g\ go \i\ hit \ī\ ice \j\ job \ŋ\ sing \ō\ go
\ó\ law \ói\ boy \th\ thin \th\ the \ü\ loot \ú\ foot
\y\ yet \zh\ vision *see also* Guide to Pronunciation

*archaic* **:** IMPETUOUS, HOTHEADED ⟨and in this *brainish* apprehension kills the unseen good old man —Shakespeare⟩

**brain·less** \'brān-ləs\ *adjective* (15th century) **:** devoid of intelligence **:** STUPID
— **brain·less·ly** *adverb*
— **brain·less·ness** *noun*

**brain·pan** \'brān-ˌpan\ *noun* (14th century) **:** BRAINCASE

**brain–pick·ing** \-ˌpi-kiŋ\ *noun* (1954) **:** the act of gathering information from another's mind
— **brain–pick·er** \-kər\ *noun*

**brain·pow·er** \-ˌpau̇(-ə)r\ *noun* (1878) **1 :** intellectual ability **2 :** people with developed intellectual ability

**brain·sick** \-ˌsik\ *adjective* (15th century) **1 :** mentally disordered **2 :** arising from mental disorder ⟨a *brainsick* frenzy⟩
— **brain·sick·ly** *adverb*

**brain stem** *noun* (1879) **:** the part of the brain composed of the mesencephalon, pons, and medulla oblongata and connecting the spinal cord with the forebrain and cerebrum

**brain·storm** \-ˌstȯrm\ *noun* (circa 1894) **1 :** a violent transient fit of insanity **2 a :** a sudden bright idea **b :** a harebrained idea

**brain·storm·ing** \-ˌstȯr-miŋ\ *noun* (circa 1955) **:** a group problem-solving technique that involves the spontaneous contribution of ideas from all members of the group
— **brain·storm** *verb*
— **brain·storm·er** *noun*

**brains trust** *noun* (1934) *chiefly British* **:** BRAIN TRUST

**brain·teas·er** \-ˌtē-zər\ *noun* (1923) **:** something (as a puzzle) that demands mental effort and acuity for its solution

**brain trust** *noun* (1910) **:** a group of official or unofficial advisers concerned especially with planning and strategy
— **brain trust·er** \-ˌtrəs-tər\ *noun*

**brain·wash·ing** \'brān-ˌwȯ-shiŋ, -ˌwä-\ *noun* [translation of Chinese (Beijing) *xǐnǎo*] (1950) **1 :** a forcible indoctrination to induce someone to give up basic political, social, or religious beliefs and attitudes and to accept contrasting regimented ideas **2 :** persuasion by propaganda or salesmanship
— **brain·wash** *transitive verb*
— **brainwash** *noun*
— **brain·wash·er** *noun*

**brain wave** *noun* (1890) **1 :** BRAINSTORM 2a **2 a :** rhythmic fluctuations of voltage between parts of the brain resulting in the flow of an electric current **b :** a current produced by brain waves

**brainy** \'brā-nē\ *adjective* **brain·i·er; -est** (1874) **:** having or showing a well-developed intellect **:** INTELLIGENT
— **brain·i·ness** *noun*

**¹braise** \'brāz\ *transitive verb* **braised; brais·ing** [French *braiser*, from *braise* live coals, from Old French *breze*, probably of Germanic origin; akin to Swedish *brasa* fire] (1797) **:** to cook slowly in fat and little moisture in a closed pot

**²braise** *noun* (circa 1885) **:** an item of braised food

**¹brake** \'brāk\ *archaic past of* BREAK

**²brake** *noun* [Middle English, fern, probably back-formation from *braken* bracken] (14th century) **:** the common bracken fern (*Pteridium aquilinum*)

**³brake** *noun* [Middle English, from Middle Low German; akin to Old English *brecan* to break] (15th century)

**1 :** a toothed instrument or machine for separating out the fiber of flax or hemp by breaking up the woody parts **2 :** a machine for bending, flanging, folding, and forming sheet metal

**⁴brake** *noun* [Middle English *-brake*] (1563) **:** rough or marshy land overgrown usually with one kind of plant
— **braky** \'brā-kē\ *adjective*

**⁵brake** *noun* [perhaps from obsolete *brake* bridle] (circa 1782) **1 :** a device for arresting or preventing the motion of a mechanism usually by means of friction **2 :** something used to slow down or stop movement or activity ⟨use interest rates as a *brake* on spending⟩
— **brake·less** \'brā-kləs\ *adjective*

**⁶brake** *verb* **braked; brak·ing** (1868) *transitive verb* **:** to retard or stop by a brake *intransitive verb* **1 :** to operate or manage a brake; *especially* **:** to apply the brake on a vehicle **2 :** to become checked by a brake

**brake·man** \'brāk-mən\ *noun* (1833) **1 :** a freight or passenger train crew member who inspects the train and assists the conductor **2 :** the end man on a bobsled team who operates the brake

**bram·ble** \'bram-bəl\ *noun* [Middle English *brembel*, from Old English *brēmel*; akin to Old English *brōm* broom] (before 12th century) **:** any of a genus (*Rubus*) of usually prickly shrubs of the rose family including the raspberries and blackberries; *broadly* **:** a rough prickly shrub or vine
— **bram·bly** \-b(ə-)lē\ *adjective*

**bran** \'bran\ *noun* [Middle English, from Middle French] (14th century) **:** the edible broken seed coats of cereal grain separated from the flour or meal by sifting or bolting

**¹branch** \'branch\ *noun, often attributive* [Middle English, from Middle French *branche*, from Late Latin *branca* paw] (14th century) **1 :** a natural subdivision of a plant stem; *especially* **:** a secondary shoot or stem (as a bough) arising from a main axis (as of a tree) **2 :** something that extends from or enters into a main body or source: as **a** (1) **:** a stream that flows into another usually larger stream **:** TRIBUTARY (2) *Southern & Midland* **:** CREEK 2 **b :** a side road or way **c :** a slender projection (as the tine of an antler) **d :** a distinctive part of a mathematical curve **e :** a part of a computer program executed as a result of a program decision **3 :** a part of a complex body: as **a :** a division of a family descending from a particular ancestor **b :** an area of knowledge that may be considered apart from related areas ⟨pathology is a *branch* of medicine⟩ **c** (1) **:** a division of an organization (2) **:** a separate but dependent part of a central organization ⟨the neighborhood *branch* of the city library⟩ **d :** a language group less inclusive than a family ⟨the Germanic *branch* of the Indo-European language family⟩
— **branched** \'brancht\ *adjective*
— **branch·less** \'branch-ləs\ *adjective*
— **branchy** \'bran-chē\ *adjective*

**²branch** (14th century) *intransitive verb* **1 :** to put forth branches **:** RAMIFY **2 :** to spring out (as from a main stem) **:** DIVERGE **3 :** to be an outgrowth — used with *from* ⟨poetry that *branched* from religious prose⟩ **4 :** to extend activities — usually used with *out* ⟨the business is *branching* out⟩ **5 :** to follow one of two or more branches (as in a computer program)

*transitive verb* **1 :** to ornament with designs of branches **2 :** to divide up **:** SECTION

**bran·chi·al** \'braŋ-kē-əl\ *adjective* [Greek *branchia* gills] (1801) **:** of, relating to, or supplying the gills or associated structures or their embryonic precursors

**bran·chio·pod** \'braŋ-kē-ə-ˌpäd\ *noun* [ultimately from Greek *branchia* gills + *pod-, pous* foot — more at FOOT] (1836) **:** any of a group (Branchiopoda) of small usually freshwater crustaceans (as fairy shrimp or water fleas) with usually many pairs of setae-bearing appendages
— **branchiopod** *adjective*

**branch·let** \'branch-lət\ *noun* (circa 1731) **:** a small usually terminal branch

**branch·line** \-ˌlīn\ *noun* (1846) **:** a secondary line usually of a railroad

**branch water** *noun* [¹*branch* (creek)] (1835) **:** plain water ⟨bourbon and *branch* water⟩

**¹brand** \'brand\ *noun* [Middle English, torch, sword, from Old English; akin to Old English *bærnan* to burn] (before 12th century) **1 a :** a charred piece of wood **b :** FIREBRAND 1 **c :** something (as lightning) that resembles a firebrand **2 :** SWORD **3 a** (1) **:** a mark made by burning with a hot iron to attest manufacture or quality or to designate ownership (2) **:** a printed mark made for similar purposes **:** TRADEMARK **b** (1) **:** a mark put on criminals with a hot iron (2) **:** a mark of disgrace **:** STIGMA ⟨the *brand* of poverty⟩ **4 a :** a class of goods identified by name as the product of a single firm or manufacturer **:** MAKE **b :** a characteristic or distinctive kind ⟨a lively *brand* of theater⟩ **5 :** a tool used to produce a brand

**²brand** *transitive verb* (15th century) **1 :** to mark with a brand **2 :** to mark with disapproval **:** STIGMATIZE **3 :** to impress indelibly ⟨*brand* the lesson on his mind⟩
— **brand·er** *noun*

**brand·ed** \'bran-dəd\ *adjective* (1897) **:** having a brand name ⟨*branded* products⟩

**¹bran·dish** \'bran-dish\ *transitive verb* [Middle English *braundisshen*, from Middle French *brandiss-*, stem of *brandir*, from Old French, from *brand* sword, of Germanic origin; akin to Old English *brand*] (14th century) **1 :** to shake or wave (as a weapon) menacingly **2 :** to exhibit in an ostentatious or aggressive manner
**synonym** see SWING

**²brandish** *noun* (1599) **:** an act or instance of brandishing

**brand-name** \'bran(d)-ˌnām\ *adjective* (1949) **1 :** of or relating to a trade name ⟨*brand-name* products⟩ **2 :** having a reputation and a loyal following ⟨*brand-name* authors⟩

**brand name** *noun* (1922) **:** TRADE NAME 1b

**brand-new** \-ˈnü, -ˈnyü\ *adjective* [¹*brand*] (circa 1570) **:** conspicuously new and unused; *also* **:** recently introduced ⟨a *brand-new* executive officer⟩

**¹bran·dy** \'bran-dē\ *noun, plural* **brandies** [short for *brandywine*, from Dutch *brandewijn*, from Middle Dutch *brantwijn*, from *brant* distilled + *wijn* wine] (1657) **:** an alcoholic beverage distilled from wine or fermented fruit juice

**²brandy** *transitive verb* **bran·died; bran·dy·ing** (circa 1848) **:** to flavor, blend, or preserve with brandy

**Bran·gus** \'braŋ-gəs\ *trademark* — used for polled solid black beef cattle of a breed developed from a Brahman-Angus cross

**bran·ni·gan** \'bra-ni-gən\ *noun* [probably from the name *Brannigan*] (1927) **1 :** a drinking spree **2 :** SQUABBLE

**brant** \'brant\ *noun, plural* **brant** *or* **brants** [Middle English *brand gos*] (14th century)
**:** any of several wild geese (especially genus *Branta*); *especially* **:** a small black-necked goose (*Branta bernicla*) about the size of a mallard

¹**brash** \'brash\ *adjective* [origin unknown] (1566)
**1 :** BRITTLE ⟨*brash* wood⟩
**2 a :** heedless of the consequences **:** AUDACIOUS ⟨the *brashest* bush pilot of them all⟩ **b :** done in haste without regard for consequences **:** RASH ⟨*brash* acts⟩
**3 a :** full of fresh raw vitality ⟨a *brash* frontier town⟩ **b :** uninhibitedly energetic or demonstrative **:** BUMPTIOUS ⟨a *brash* comedian⟩
**4 a :** lacking restraint and discernment **:** TACTLESS ⟨*brash* remarks⟩ **b :** aggressively self-assertive **:** IMPUDENT ⟨*brash* to the point of arrogance⟩
**5 :** piercingly sharp **:** HARSH ⟨a *brash* squeal of brakes⟩
**6 :** marked by vivid contrast **:** BOLD ⟨*brash* colors⟩
— **brash·ly** *adverb*
— **brash·ness** *noun*

²**brash** *noun* [obsolete English *brash* to breach a wall] (1787)
**:** a mass of fragments (as of ice)

**brass** \'bras\ *noun* [Middle English *bras*, from Old English *bræs*; akin to Middle Low German *bras* metal] (before 12th century)
**1 :** an alloy consisting essentially of copper and zinc in variable proportions
**2 a :** the brass instruments of an orchestra or band — often used in plural **b :** a usually brass memorial tablet **c :** bright metal fittings, utensils, or ornaments **d :** empty cartridge shells
**3 :** brazen self-assurance **:** GALL
**4** *singular or plural in construction* **a :** high-ranking members of the military **b :** persons in high positions (as in a business or the government)
— **brass** *adjective*

**bras·sard** \brə-'särd, 'bra-\ *noun* [French *brassard*, from Middle French *brassal*, from Old Italian *bracciale*, from *braccio* arm, from Latin *bracchium* — more at BRACE] (1830)
**1 :** armor for protecting the arm — see ARMOR illustration
**2 :** a cloth band worn around the upper arm usually bearing an identifying mark

**brass band** *noun* (1834)
**:** a band consisting chiefly or solely of brass and percussion instruments

**brass·bound** \'bras-,baúnd, -'baúnd\ *adjective* (1867)
**1 :** having trim made of brass or a metal resembling brass
**2 a** (1) **:** tradition-bound and opinionated (2) **:** making no concessions **:** INFLEXIBLE **b :** BRAZEN, PRESUMPTUOUS

**brass collar Democrat** *noun* (1951)
**:** a conservative Democrat especially in the south who votes the straight Democratic ticket

**bras·se·rie** \,bras-'rē, ,bra-sə-\ *noun* [French, literally, brewery, from Middle French *brasser* to brew, from Old French *bracier*, from (assumed) Vulgar Latin *braciare*, of Celtic origin; akin to Welsh *brag* malt] (1864)
**:** an informal usually French restaurant serving simple hearty food

**brass hat** *noun* [from the gold braid worn on the cap] (1893)
**:** a member of the brass

**bras·si·ca** \'bra-si-kə\ *noun* [New Latin, genus name, from Latin, cabbage] (1832)
**:** any of a large genus (*Brassica*) of Old World temperate zone herbs (as cabbages) of the mustard family with beaked cylindrical pods

**bras·siere** \brə-'zir *also* ,bra-sē-'er\ *noun* [obsolete French *brassière* bodice, from Old French *braciere* arm protector, from *bras* arm — more at BRACELET] (1911)
**:** a woman's undergarment to cover and support the breasts

**brass instrument** *noun* (1854)
**:** any of a group of wind instruments (as a French horn, trombone, trumpet, or tuba) that is usually characterized by a long cylindrical or conical metal tube commonly curved two or more times and ending in a flared bell, that produces tones by the vibrations of the player's lips against a usually cup-shaped mouthpiece, and that usually has valves or a slide by which the player may produce all the tones within the instrument's range

**brass knuckles** *noun plural but singular or plural in construction* (1855)
**:** KNUCKLE 4

**brass ring** *noun* (1950)
**:** a rich opportunity **:** PRIZE

**brass tacks** *noun plural* (1897)
**:** details of immediate practical importance — usually used in the phrase *get down to brass tacks*

**brassy** \'bra-sē\ *adjective* **brass·i·er; -est** (1576)
**1 a :** being shamelessly bold **b :** OBSTREPEROUS
**2 :** resembling brass especially in color
**3 :** resembling the sound of a brass instrument
— **brass·i·ly** \'bra-sə-lē\ *adverb*
— **brass·i·ness** \'bra-sē-nəs\ *noun*

**brat** \'brat\ *noun* [perhaps from English dialect *brat* (coarse garment)] (circa 1505)
**1 a :** CHILD; *specifically* **:** an ill-mannered annoying child **b :** an ill-mannered immature person
**2 :** the son or daughter of a career military person
— **brat·ti·ness** \'bra-tē-nəs\ *noun*
— **brat·tish** \'bra-tish\ *adjective*
— **brat·ty** \-tē\ *adjective*

**brat·tice** \'bra-təs, 'bra-tish\ *noun* [Middle English *bretais* parapet, from Old French *bretesche*, from Medieval Latin *breteschia*] (circa 1846)
**:** an often temporary partition of planks or cloth used especially to control mine ventilation
— **brattice** *transitive verb*

¹**brat·tle** \'bra-tᵊl\ *noun* [probably imitative] (circa 1500)
*chiefly Scottish* **:** CLATTER, SCAMPER

²**brattle** *intransitive verb* **brat·tled; brat·tling** (1513)
*chiefly Scottish* **:** to make a clattering or rattling sound

**brat·wurst** \'brät-(,)wərst *also* 'brat- *also* -,vú(r)st; *sometimes* -,vüsht\ *noun* [German, from Old High German *brātwurst*, from *brāt* meat without waste + *wurst* sausage] (circa 1888)
**:** fresh pork sausage for frying

**braun·schweig·er** \'braún-,shwī-gər, -,shvī-*also* 'brän-\ *noun* [German *Braunschweiger* (*Wurst*), literally, Brunswick sausage] (1934)
**:** smoked liverwurst

**bra·va** \'brä-(,)vä, brä-'vä\ *noun* [Italian, feminine of *bravo*] (1803)
**:** BRAVO — used interjectionally in applauding a woman

**bra·va·do** \brə-'vä-(,)dō\ *noun, plural* **-does** *or* **-dos** [Middle French *bravade* & Old Spanish *bravata*, from Old Italian *bravata*, from *bravare* to challenge, show off, from *bravo*] (circa 1580)
**1 a :** blustering swaggering conduct **b :** a pretense of bravery
**2 :** the quality or state of being foolhardy

¹**brave** \'brāv\ *adjective* **brav·er; brav·est** [Middle French, from Old Italian & Old Spanish *bravo* courageous, wild, probably from Latin *barbarus* barbarous] (15th century)
**1 :** having courage **:** DAUNTLESS
**2 :** making a fine show **:** COLORFUL ⟨*brave* banners flying in the wind⟩
**3 :** EXCELLENT, SPLENDID ⟨the *brave* fire I soon had going —J. F. Dobie⟩

— **brave·ly** *adverb*

²**brave** *verb* **braved; brav·ing** (1546)
*transitive verb*
**1 :** to face or endure with courage
**2** *obsolete* **:** to make showy
*intransitive verb*
*archaic* **:** to make a brave show
— **brav·er** *noun*

³**brave** *noun* (1590)
**1** *archaic* **:** BRAVADO
**2 :** one who is brave; *specifically* **:** an American Indian warrior
**3** *archaic* **:** BULLY, ASSASSIN

**brave new world** *noun* [from the dystopian novel *Brave New World* (1932) by Aldous Huxley] (1933)
**:** a future world, situation, or development; *also* **:** a recent development or recently changed situation

**brav·ery** \'brāv-rē, 'brā-və-\ *noun, plural* **-er·ies** (1548)
**1 :** the quality or state of being brave **:** COURAGE
**2 a :** fine clothes **b :** showy display

¹**bra·vo** \'brä-(,)vō\ *noun, plural* **bravos** *or* **bravoes** [Italian, from *bravo* brave] (1597)
**:** VILLAIN, DESPERADO; *especially* **:** a hired assassin

²**bra·vo** \'brä-(,)vō, brä-'vō\ *noun, plural* **bravos** (1761)
**:** a shout of approval — often used interjectionally in applauding a performance

³**bra·vo** \*see* ²\ *transitive verb* **bra·voed; bra·vo·ing** (1831)
**:** to applaud by shouts of *bravo*

**Bra·vo** \'brä-(,)vō\ (1952)
— a communications code word for the letter *b*

¹**bra·vu·ra** \brə-'vyúr-ə, brä-, -'vúr-\ *noun* [Italian, literally, bravery, from *bravare*] (1757)
**1 :** a musical passage requiring exceptional agility and technical skill in execution
**2 :** a florid brilliant style
**3 :** a show of daring or brilliance

²**bravura** *adjective* (1920)
**1 :** marked by an ostentatious display of skill
**2 :** ORNATE, SHOWY

**braw** \'brò, 'brä\ *adjective* [modification of Middle French *brave*] (circa 1565)
**1** *chiefly Scottish* **:** GOOD, FINE
**2** *chiefly Scottish* **:** well dressed

¹**brawl** \'bròl\ *intransitive verb* [Middle English] (14th century)
**1 :** to quarrel or fight noisily **:** WRANGLE
**2 :** to make a loud confused noise
— **brawl·er** *noun*

²**brawl** *noun* (15th century)
**1 :** a noisy quarrel or fight
**2 :** a loud tumultuous noise

**brawly** \'brò-lē\ *adjective* **brawl·i·er; -est** (1940)
**1 :** inclined to brawl
**2 :** characterized by brawls or brawling

**brawn** \'brón\ *noun* [Middle English, from Middle French *braon* muscle, of Germanic origin; akin to Old English *brǣd* flesh] (13th century)
**1 a** *British* **:** the flesh of a boar **b :** HEADCHEESE
**2 a :** full strong muscles **b :** muscular strength

**brawny** \'brò-nē\ *adjective* **brawn·i·er; -est** (1599)
**1 :** MUSCULAR; *also* **:** STRONG, POWERFUL
**2 :** being swollen and hard ⟨a *brawny* infected foot⟩
— **brawn·i·ly** \-nə-lē\ *adverb*
— **brawn·i·ness** \-nē-nəs\ *noun*

\ə\ abut \ᵊ\ kitten \ər\ further \a\ ash \ā\ ace \ä\ mop, mar \aú\ out \ch\ chin \e\ bet \ē\ easy \g\ go \i\ hit \ī\ ice \j\ job \ŋ\ sing \ō\ go \ò\ law \ói\ boy \th\ thin \t̲h̲\ the \ü\ loot \ú\ foot \y\ yet \zh\ vision *see also* Guide to Pronunciation

**¹bray** \'brā\ *verb* [Middle English, from Middle French *braire* to cry, from (assumed) Vulgar Latin *bragere*, of Celtic origin; akin to Old Irish *braigid* he breaks wind] (14th century)
*intransitive verb*
: to utter the characteristic loud harsh cry of a donkey; *also* : to utter a sound like a donkey's
*transitive verb*
: to utter or play loudly, harshly, or discordantly
— **bray** *noun*

**²bray** *transitive verb* [Middle English, from Anglo-French *braier*, from Old French *breier*, of Germanic origin; akin to Old High German *brehhan* to break — more at BREAK] (14th century)
**1** : to crush or grind fine ⟨*bray* seeds in a mortar⟩
**2** : to spread thin ⟨*bray* printing ink⟩
**bray·er** \'brā-ər\ *noun* (1688)
: a printer's hand inking roller
**¹braze** \'brāz\ *transitive verb* **brazed; brazing** [irregular from *brass*] (1602)
*archaic* : HARDEN
**²braze** *transitive verb* **brazed; braz·ing** [French *braser*, from Old French, to burn, from *breze* hot coals — more at BRAISE] (1677)
: to solder with a nonferrous alloy that melts at a lower temperature than that of the metals being joined
— **braz·er** *noun*
**¹bra·zen** \'brā-zᵊn\ *adjective* [Middle English *brasen*, from Old English *bræsen*, from *bræs* brass] (before 12th century)
**1** : made of brass
**2 a** : sounding harsh and loud like struck brass **b** : of the color of polished brass
**3** : marked by contemptuous boldness
— **bra·zen·ly** *adverb*
— **bra·zen·ness** \'brā-zᵊn-(n)əs\ *noun*
**²brazen** *transitive verb* **bra·zened; brazen·ing** \'brāz-niŋ, 'brā-zᵊn-iŋ\ (circa 1555)
: to face with defiance or impudence — usually used in the phrase *brazen it out*
**bra·zen–faced** \'brā-zᵊn-ˌfāst\ *adjective* (1571)
: marked by insolence and bold disrespect ⟨*brazen-faced* assertions⟩
**¹bra·zier** \'brā-zhər\ *noun* [Middle English *brasier*, from *bras* brass] (14th century)
: one that works in brass
**²brazier** *noun* [French *brasier*, from Old French, fire of hot coals, from *breze*] (circa 1690)
**1** : a pan for holding burning coals
**2** : a utensil in which food is exposed to heat through a wire grill
**Bra·zil nut** \brə-'zil-\ *noun* [*Brazil*, South America] (1830)
: a tall South American tree (*Bertholletia excelsa* of the family Lecythidaceae) that bears large globular capsules each containing several closely packed roughly triangular oily edible nuts; *also* : its nut
**bra·zil·wood** \brə-'zil-ˌwùd\ *noun* [Spanish *brasil*, from *brasa* live coals (from the wood's color), probably of Germanic origin; akin to Swedish *brasa* fire] (1559)
: the heavy wood of any of various tropical leguminous trees (especially genus *Caesalpinia*) that is used as red and purple dyewood and in cabinetwork
**¹breach** \'brēch\ *noun* [Middle English *breche*, from Old English *bræc* act of breaking; akin to Old English *brecan* to break] (before 12th century)
**1** : infraction or violation of a law, obligation, tie, or standard
**2 a** : a broken, ruptured, or torn condition or area **b** : a gap (as in a wall) made by battering
**3 a** : a break in accustomed friendly relations
**b** : a temporary gap in continuity : HIATUS
**4** : a leap especially of a whale out of water
**²breach** (1547)

*transitive verb*
**1** : to make a breach in
**2** : BREAK, VIOLATE ⟨*breach* an agreement⟩
*intransitive verb*
: to leap out of water ⟨a whale *breaching*⟩
**breach of promise** (1590)
: violation of a promise especially to marry
**¹bread** \'bred\ *noun* [Middle English *breed*, from Old English *brēad*; akin to Old High German *brōt* bread, Old English *brēowan* to brew] (before 12th century)
**1** : a usually baked and leavened food made of a mixture whose basic constituent is flour or meal
**2** : FOOD, SUSTENANCE ⟨our daily *bread*⟩
**3 a** : LIVELIHOOD ⟨earns his *bread* as a laborer⟩
**b** *slang* : MONEY
— **bready** \'bre-dē\ *adjective*
— **bread upon the waters** : resources risked or charitable deeds performed without expectation of return
**²bread** *transitive verb* (1629)
: to cover with bread crumbs ⟨a *breaded* pork chop⟩
**bread–and–butter** *adjective* (circa 1837)
**1 a** : being as basic as the earning of one's livelihood ⟨*bread-and-butter* issues⟩ **b** : that can be depended on ⟨our *bread-and-butter* repertoire⟩
**2** : sent or given as thanks for hospitality ⟨a *bread-and-butter* letter⟩
**bread and butter** *noun* (1732)
: a means of sustenance or livelihood
**bread and circuses** *noun plural* [translation of Latin *panis et circenses*] (1914)
: a palliative offered especially to avert potential discontent
**bread·bas·ket** \'bred-ˌbas-kət\ *noun* (1753)
**1** *slang* : STOMACH
**2** : a major cereal-producing region
**¹bread·board** \'bred-ˌbōrd, -ˌbòrd\ *noun* (1857)
**1** : a board on which dough is kneaded or bread cut
**2** : a board on which components are mounted for breadboarding
**²breadboard** *transitive verb* (1956)
: to make an experimental arrangement of (as an electronic circuit or a mechanical system) to test feasibility
**bread·fruit** \'bred-ˌfrüt\ *noun* (1697)
: a round starchy usually seedless fruit that resembles bread in color and texture when baked; *also* : a tall tropical evergreen tree (*Artocarpus altilis*) of the mulberry family that bears this fruit
**bread·line** \-ˌlīn\ *noun* (1900)
: a line of people waiting to receive free bread
**bread mold** *noun* (1914)
: any of various molds found especially on bread; *especially* : a rhizopus (*Rhizopus nigricans* synonym *R. stolonifer*)
**bread·stuff** \-ˌstəf\ *noun* (1793)
**1** : a cereal product (as grain or flour)
**2** : BREAD
**breadth** \'bretth, 'bredth, ÷'breth\ *noun* [obsolete English *brede* breadth (from Middle English, from Old English *brǣdu*, from *brād* broad) + *-th* (as in *length*)] (15th century)
**1** : distance from side to side : WIDTH
**2** : something of full width
**3 a** : comprehensive quality : SCOPE ⟨*breadth* of his learning⟩ **b** : liberality of views or taste ⟨*breadth* of mind⟩
— **breadth·wise** \-ˌwīz\ *adverb or adjective*
**bread·win·ner** \'bred-ˌwi-nər\ *noun* (1818)
**1** : a means (as a tool or craft) of livelihood
**2** : a member of a family whose wages supply its livelihood
— **bread·win·ning** \-ˌwi-niŋ\ *noun*
**¹break** \'brāk\ *verb* **broke** \'brōk\; **bro·ken** \'brō-kən\; **break·ing** [Middle English *breken*, from Old English *brecan*; akin to Old High German *brehhan* to break, Latin *frangere*] (before 12th century)

*transitive verb*
**1 a** : to separate into parts with suddenness or violence **b** : FRACTURE ⟨*break* an arm⟩ **c** : RUPTURE ⟨*break* the skin⟩ **d** : to cut into and turn over the surface of ⟨*break* the soil⟩ **e** : to render inoperable ⟨*broke* his watch⟩
**2 a** : VIOLATE, TRANSGRESS ⟨*break* the law⟩ ⟨*break* a promise⟩ **b** : to invalidate (a will) by action at law
**3 a** *archaic* : to force entry into **b** : to burst and force a way through ⟨*break* the sound barrier⟩ ⟨*break* a racial barrier⟩ **c** : to escape by force from ⟨*break* jail⟩ **d** : to make or effect by cutting, forcing, or pressing through ⟨*break* a trail through the woods⟩
**4** : to disrupt the order or compactness of ⟨*break* ranks⟩
**5** : to make ineffective as a binding force ⟨*break* the spell⟩
**6 a** : to defeat utterly and end as an effective force : DESTROY **b** : to crush the spirit of **c** : to make tractable or submissive: as (1) *past participle often* **broke** : to train (an animal) to adjust to the service or convenience of humans ⟨a halter-*broke* horse⟩ (2) : INURE, ACCUSTOM **d** : to exhaust in health, strength, or capacity
**7 a** : to stop or bring to an end suddenly : HALT ⟨*break* a deadlock⟩ **b** : INTERRUPT, SUSPEND ⟨*break* the silence with a cry⟩ **c** : to open and bring about suspension of operation ⟨*break* an electric circuit⟩ **d** : to destroy unity or completeness of ⟨*break* a dining room set by buying a chair⟩ **e** : to change the appearance of uniformity of ⟨a dormer *breaks* the level roof⟩ **f** : to split the surface of ⟨fish *breaking* water⟩ **g** : to cause to discontinue a habit ⟨tried to *break* him of smoking⟩
**8 a** : to make known : TELL ⟨*break* the bad news gently⟩ **b** : to bring to attention or prominence initially ⟨radio stations *breaking* new musicians⟩ ⟨*break* a news story⟩
**9 a** : to ruin financially **b** : to reduce in rank
**10 a** : to split into smaller units, parts, or processes : DIVIDE **b** (1) : to give or get the equivalent of (a bill) in smaller denominations (2) : to use as the denomination in paying a bill ⟨didn't want to *break* a $20 bill⟩ — often used with *into*, *up*, or *down*
**11 a** : to check the speed, force, or intensity of ⟨the bushes will *break* his fall⟩ ⟨without *breaking* her stride⟩ **b** : to cause failure and discontinuance of (a strike) by measures outside bargaining processes
**12** : to cause a sudden significant decrease in the price, value, or volume of ⟨news likely to *break* the market sharply⟩
**13 a** : EXCEED, SURPASS ⟨*break* the record⟩ **b** : to score less than (a specified total) ⟨golfer trying to *break* 90⟩ **c** : to win against (an opponent's service) in a racket game
**14** : to open the action of (a breechloader)
**15 a** : to find an explanation or solution for : SOLVE ⟨the detective will *break* the case⟩ **b** : to discover the essentials of (a code or cipher system)
**16** : to demonstrate the falsity of ⟨*break* an alibi⟩
**17** : to ruin the prospects of ⟨could make or *break* her career⟩
**18** : to produce visibly ⟨barely *breaks* a sweat⟩
*intransitive verb*
**1 a** : to escape with sudden forceful effort — often used with *out* ⟨*break* out of jail⟩ **b** : to come into being by or as if by bursting forth ⟨day was *breaking*⟩ **c** : to effect a penetration ⟨*break* through security lines⟩ **d** : to emerge through the surface of the water **e** : to start abruptly ⟨when the storm *broke*⟩ **f** : to become known or published ⟨when the news *broke*⟩ **g** : to make a sudden dash ⟨*break* for cover⟩ **h** : to separate after a clinch in boxing
**2 a** : to come apart or split into pieces : BURST, SHATTER **b** : to open spontaneously or by pressure from within ⟨his boil finally *broke*⟩ **c** *of a wave* : to curl over and fall apart in surf or foam

**3 :** to interrupt one's activity or occupation for a brief period ⟨*break* for lunch⟩
**4 :** to alter sharply in tone, pitch, or intensity ⟨a voice *breaking* with emotion⟩
**5 :** to become fair **:** CLEAR ⟨when the weather *breaks*⟩
**6 :** to make the opening shot of a game of pool
**7 :** to end a relationship, connection, or agreement — usually used with *with*
**8 :** to give way in disorderly retreat
**9 a :** to swerve suddenly **b :** to curve, drop, or rise sharply ⟨a pitch that *breaks* away from the batter⟩
**10 a :** to fail in health, strength, vitality, resolve, or control ⟨may *break* under questioning⟩ — often used with *down* **b :** to become inoperative because of damage, wear, or strain
**11 :** to fail to keep a prescribed gait — used of a horse
**12 :** to undergo a sudden significant decrease in price, value, or volume ⟨transportation stocks may *break* sharply⟩
**13 :** HAPPEN, DEVELOP ⟨for the team to succeed, everything has to *break* right⟩
**14 :** to win against an opponent's service in a racket game
**15 a :** to divide into classes, categories, or types — usually used with *into* and often with *down* ⟨the topic *breaks* down into three questions⟩ **b :** to fold, bend, lift, or come apart at a seam, groove, or joint **c** *of cream* **:** to separate during churning into liquid and fat
— **break a leg** — used to wish good luck especially to a performer
— **break bread :** to dine together
— **break camp :** to pack up gear and leave a camp or campsite
— **break cover** *also* **break covert :** to start from a covert or lair
— **break even :** to achieve a balance; *especially* **:** to operate a business or enterprise without either loss or profit
— **break ground 1 :** to begin construction — usually used with *for* **2** *or* **break new ground :** to make or show discoveries **:** PIONEER
— **break into 1 :** to begin with or as if with a sudden throwing off of restraint ⟨*broke into* tears⟩ ⟨face *breaking into* a smile⟩ ⟨the horse *breaks into* a gallop⟩ **2 :** to make entry or entrance ⟨*broke into* the house⟩ ⟨*break into* show business⟩ **3 :** INTERRUPT ⟨*break into* a TV program with a news flash⟩
— **break one's heart :** to crush emotionally with sorrow
— **break one's wrists :** to turn the wrists as part of the swing of a club or bat
— **break ranks** *also* **break rank :** to differ in opinion or action from one's peers; often used with *with*
— **break the back of :** to subdue the main force of ⟨*break the back of* inflation⟩
— **break the ice 1 :** to make a beginning **2 :** to get through the first difficulties in starting a conversation or discussion
— **break wind :** to expel gas from the intestine

**²break** *noun* (14th century)
**1 a :** an act or action of breaking **b :** the opening shot in a game of pool or billiards
**2 a :** a condition produced by or as if by breaking **:** GAP ⟨a *break* in the clouds⟩ **b :** a gap in an otherwise continuous electric circuit
**3 :** the action or act of breaking in, out, or forth ⟨at *break* of day⟩ ⟨a jail *break*⟩
**4 :** a place or situation at which a break occurs; *especially* **:** the place at which a word is divided especially at the end of a line of print or writing
**5 :** an interruption in continuity ⟨a *break* in the weather⟩: as **a :** a notable change of subject matter, attitude, or treatment **b** (1) **:** an abrupt, significant, or noteworthy change or interruption in a continuous process, trend, or surface

(2) **:** a respite from work, school, or duty ⟨coffee *break*⟩ ⟨spring *break*⟩ (3) **:** a planned interruption in a radio or television program ⟨a *break* for the commercial⟩ **c :** deviation of a pitched baseball from a straight line **d** *mining* **:** FAULT, DISLOCATION **e :** failure of a horse to maintain the prescribed gait **f :** an abrupt change in musical or vocal pitch or quality **g :** the action or an instance of breaking service in a racket game **h :** a usually solo instrumental passage in jazz, folk, or popular music
**6 a :** DASH, RUSH ⟨a base runner making a *break* for home⟩ **b :** FAST BREAK
**7 :** a sudden and abrupt decline of prices or values
**8 a :** the start of a race **b :** the act of separating after a clinch in boxing
**9 a :** a stroke of luck and especially of good luck ⟨a bad *break*⟩ ⟨got the *breaks*⟩ **b :** a favorable or opportune situation **:** CHANCE ⟨waiting for a big *break* in show business⟩ **c :** favorable consideration or treatment ⟨a tax *break*⟩ ⟨a *break* on the price⟩
**10 a :** a rupture in previously agreeable relations ⟨a *break* between the two countries⟩ **b :** an abrupt split or difference with something previously adhered to or followed ⟨a sharp *break* with tradition⟩
**11 :** BREAKDOWN 1c ⟨suffered a mental *break*⟩

**break·able** \ˈbrā-kə-bəl\ *adjective* (1570)
**:** capable of being broken
— **breakable** *noun*

**break·age** \ˈbrā-kij\ *noun* (1813)
**1 a :** the action or an instance of breaking **b :** a quantity broken
**2 :** loss due to things broken

**¹break·away** \ˈbrā-kə-ˌwā\ *noun* (1881)
**1 a :** one that breaks away **b :** a departure from or rejection of (as a group or tradition)
**2 a :** a play (as in hockey) in which an offensive player breaks free of the defenders and rushes toward the goal **b :** a sudden acceleration by one or more bicyclists pulling away from the pack in a race
**3 :** an object made to shatter or collapse under pressure or impact

**²breakaway** *adjective* (1927)
**1 :** favoring independence from an affiliation **:** SECEDING ⟨a *breakaway* faction formed a new party⟩
**2 :** made to break, shatter, or bend easily ⟨*breakaway* road signs for highway safety⟩

**break away** *intransitive verb* (1535)
**1 :** to detach oneself especially from a group **:** get away
**2 :** to depart from former or accustomed ways
**3 :** to pull away with a burst of speed

**break·bone fever** \ˈbrāk-ˈbōn-\ *noun* (circa 1860)
**:** DENGUE

**break dancing** *noun* [perhaps from ²*break* (solo passage)] (1983)
**:** dancing in which solo dancers perform acrobatics that involve touching various parts of the body (as the back or head) to the ground
— **break–dance** \ˈbrāk-ˌdan(t)s\ *verb*
— **break–danc·er** \-ˌdan(t)-sər\ *noun*

**break·down** \ˈbrāk-ˌdaún\ *noun* (1832)
**1 :** the action or result of breaking down: as **a :** a failure to function **b :** failure to progress or have effect **:** DISINTEGRATION ⟨a *breakdown* of negotiations⟩ **c :** a physical, mental, or nervous collapse **d :** the process of decomposing **e :** division into categories **:** CLASSIFICATION; *also* **:** an account analyzed into categories
**2 :** a fast shuffling dance; *also* **:** music for such a dance

**break down** (14th century)
*transitive verb*
**1 a :** to cause to fall or collapse by breaking or shattering **b :** to make ineffective ⟨*break down* legal barriers⟩
**2 a :** to divide into parts or categories **b :** to separate (as a chemical compound) into sim-

pler substances **:** DECOMPOSE **c :** to take apart especially for storage or shipment and for later reassembling
*intransitive verb*
**1 a :** to stop functioning because of breakage or wear **b :** to become inoperative or ineffective **:** FAIL ⟨negotiations *broke down*⟩
**2** *of horses* **:** to tear or strain the tendons of the lower leg
**3 a :** to be susceptible to or undergo analysis or subdivision ⟨the statistics *break down* like this⟩ **b :** to undergo decomposition
*synonym* see ANALYZE

**¹break·er** \ˈbrā-kər\ *noun* (12th century)
**1 a :** one that breaks **b :** a machine or plant for breaking rocks or coal **c :** one who breaks up ships or cars for salvage
**2 :** a wave breaking into foam (as against the shore)
**3 :** a strip of fabric under the tread of a tire for extra protection of the carcass

**²brea·ker** \ˈbrā-kər\ *noun* [by folk etymology from Spanish *barrica*] (1833)
**:** a small water cask

**break·even** \ˈbrāk-ˈē-vən\ *noun* (1958)
**:** the point at which cost and income are equal and there is neither profit nor loss; *also* **:** a financial result reflecting neither profit nor loss

**break–even** \ˈbrāk-ˈē-vən\ *adjective* (1931)
**:** having equal cost and income

**break·fast** \ˈbrek-fəst\ *noun* (15th century)
**1 :** the first meal of the day especially when taken in the morning
**2 :** the food prepared for a breakfast ⟨eat your *breakfast*⟩
— **breakfast** *verb*
— **break·fast·er** *noun*

**break·front** \ˈbrāk-ˌfrənt\ *noun* (1928)
**:** a large cabinet or bookcase whose center section projects beyond the flanking end sections

**break–in** \ˈbrā-ˌkin\ *noun* (1856)
**1 :** the act or action of breaking in ⟨a rash of *break-ins* at the new apartment house⟩
**2 :** a performance or a series of performances serving as a trial run
**3 :** an initial period of operation during which working parts begin to function efficiently

**breakfront**

**break in** (circa 1552)
*intransitive verb*
**1 :** to enter a house or building by force
**2 a :** INTRUDE ⟨*break in* upon his privacy⟩ **b :** to interrupt a conversation
**3 :** to start in an activity or enterprise ⟨*breaking in* as a cub reporter⟩
*transitive verb*
**1 :** to accustom to a certain activity or occurrence ⟨*break in* the new clerk⟩
**2 :** to overcome the stiffness or newness of

**breaking and entering** *noun* (1797)
**:** the act of forcing or otherwise gaining unlawful passage into and entering another's building

**breaking point** *noun* (1908)
**1 :** the point at which a person gives way under stress
**2 :** the point at which a situation becomes critical

**break·neck** \ˈbrāk-ˈnek\ *adjective* (1562)
**:** very fast or dangerous ⟨*breakneck* speed⟩

**break off** (14th century)

*intransitive verb*
**:** to stop abruptly ⟨*break off* in the middle of a sentence⟩
*transitive verb*
**:** DISCONTINUE ⟨*break off* diplomatic relations⟩
**break·out** \'brā-ˌkaut\ *noun* (1820)
**:** a violent or forceful break from a restraining condition or situation; *especially* **:** a military attack to break from encirclement
**break out** (before 12th century)
*intransitive verb*
**1 :** to develop or emerge with suddenness or force ⟨fire *broke out*⟩ ⟨a riot *broke out*⟩
**2 a :** to become covered ⟨*break out* in a sweat⟩ **b :** to become affected with a skin eruption
**3 :** to make a break from a restraining condition or situation ⟨*broke out* of a slump⟩
*transitive verb*
**1 a :** to make ready for action or use ⟨*break out* the tents and make camp⟩ **b :** to produce for consumption ⟨*break out* a bottle⟩
**2 :** to display flying and unfurled
**3 :** to separate from a mass of data ⟨*break out* newsstand sales⟩
**break·through** \'brāk-ˌthrü\ *noun, often attributive* (1918)
**1 :** an offensive thrust that penetrates and carries beyond a defensive line in warfare
**2 :** an act or instance of breaking through an obstruction
**3 a :** a sudden advance especially in knowledge or technique ⟨a medical *breakthrough*⟩ **b :** a person's first notable success
**break through** *intransitive verb* (1955)
**:** to make a breakthrough
**break·up** \'brā-ˌkəp\ *noun* (1794)
**1 :** an act or instance of breaking up
**2 :** the breaking, melting, and loosening of ice in the spring
**break up** (15th century)
*intransitive verb*
**1 a :** to cease to exist as a unified whole **:** DISPERSE ⟨their partnership *broke up*⟩ **b :** to end a romance
**2 :** to lose morale, composure, or resolution; *especially* **:** to become abandoned to laughter ⟨*breaks up* completely, laughing himself into a coughing fit —Gene Williams⟩
*transitive verb*
**1 :** to break into pieces
**2 :** to bring to an end ⟨*broke up* the fight⟩
**3 :** to do away with **:** DESTROY ⟨*break up* a monopoly⟩
**4 :** to disrupt the continuity or flow of ⟨*break up* a dull routine⟩
**5 :** DECOMPOSE ⟨*break up* a chemical⟩
**6 :** to cause to laugh heartily ⟨that joke *breaks me up*⟩
**breakup value** *noun* (1902)
**:** the value especially of shares of stock of a corporation liquidating its assets
**break·wa·ter** \'brāk-ˌwȯ-tər, -ˌwä-\ *noun* (circa 1769)
**:** an offshore structure (as a wall) protecting a harbor or beach from the force of waves
**¹bream** \'brim, 'brēm\ *noun, plural* **bream** *or* **breams** [Middle English *breme*, from Middle French, of Germanic origin; akin to Old High German *brahsima* bream, Middle High German *brehen* to shine] (14th century)
**1 :** a European freshwater cyprinid fish (*Abramis brama*); *broadly* **:** any of various related fishes
**2 a :** a porgy or related fish (family Sparidae) **b :** any of various freshwater sunfishes (*Lepomis* and related genera); *especially* **:** BLUEGILL
**²bream** \'brēm\ *transitive verb* [probably from Dutch *brem* furze] (1626)
**:** to clean (a ship's bottom) by heating and scraping
**¹breast** \'brest\ *noun* [Middle English *brest*, from Old English *brēost*; akin to Old High German *brust* breast, Old Irish *brú* belly, Russian *bryukho*] (before 12th century)
**1 :** either of the pair of mammary glands extending from the front of the chest in pubes-

cent and adult human females and some other mammals; *also* **:** either of the analogous but rudimentary organs of the male chest especially when enlarged
**2 a :** the fore or ventral part of the body between the neck and the abdomen **b :** the part of an article of clothing covering the breast
**3 :** the seat of emotion and thought **:** BOSOM
**4 a :** something (as a front, swelling, or curving part) resembling a breast **b :** FACE 6
— **breast·ed** \'bres-təd\ *adjective*
**²breast** *transitive verb* (1599)
**1 :** to contend with resolutely **:** CONFRONT ⟨*breasting* the waves⟩
**2** *chiefly British* **:** CLIMB, ASCEND
**3 :** to thrust the chest against ⟨the sprinter *breasted* the tape⟩
**breast–beat·ing** \'bres(t)-ˌbē-tiŋ\ *noun* (1940)
**:** noisy demonstrative protestation (as of grief, anger, or self-recrimination)
**breast·bone** \'bres(t)-ˌbōn\ *noun* (before 12th century)
**:** STERNUM
**breast drill** *noun* (1865)
**:** a portable drill with a plate that is pressed by the breast in forcing the drill against the work
**breast–feed** \'brest-ˌfēd\ *transitive verb* (1903)
**:** to feed (a baby) from a mother's breast rather than from a bottle
**breast·plate** \'bres(t)-ˌplāt\ *noun* (14th century)
**1 :** a usually metal plate worn as defensive armor for the breast — see ARMOR illustration
**2 :** a vestment worn in ancient times by a Jewish high priest and set with 12 gems bearing the names of the tribes of Israel
**3 :** a piece against which a worker's breast is pressed in operating a tool (as a breast drill)
**breast·stroke** \'bres(t)-ˌstrōk\ *noun* (1867)
**:** a swimming stroke executed in a prone position by coordinating a kick in which the legs are brought forward with the knees together and the feet are turned outward and whipped back with a glide and a backward sweeping movement of the arms
— **breast·strok·er** \-ˌstrō-kər\ *noun*
**breast·work** \'brest-ˌwərk\ *noun* (1642)
**:** a temporary fortification
**breath** \'breth\ *noun* [Middle English *breth*, from Old English *brǣth*; akin to Old High German *brādam* breath, and perhaps to Old English *beorma* yeast — more at BARM] (before 12th century)
**1 a :** air filled with a fragrance or odor **b :** a slight indication **:** SUGGESTION ⟨the faintest *breath* of scandal⟩
**2 a :** the faculty of breathing ⟨recovering his *breath* after the race⟩ **b :** an act of breathing ⟨fought to the last *breath*⟩ **c :** opportunity or time to breathe **:** RESPITE
**3 :** a slight breeze
**4 a :** air inhaled and exhaled in breathing ⟨bad *breath*⟩ **b :** something (as moisture on a cold surface) produced by breath or breathing **c :** INHALATION
**5 :** a spoken sound **:** UTTERANCE
**6 :** SPIRIT, ANIMATION
— **in one breath** *or* **in the same breath :** almost simultaneously
— **out of breath :** breathing very rapidly (as from strenuous exercise)
**breath·able** \'brē-thə-bəl\ *adjective* (circa 1731)
**1 :** suitable for breathing ⟨*breathable* air⟩
**2 :** allowing air to pass through **:** POROUS ⟨a *breathable* synthetic fabric⟩
— **breath·abil·i·ty** \ˌbrē-thə-'bi-lə-tē\ *noun*
**Breath·a·ly·zer** \'bre-thə-ˌlī-zər\ *trademark*
— used for a device that is used to determine the alcohol content of a breath sample
**breathe** \'brēth\ *verb* **breathed; breathing** [Middle English *brethen*, from *breth*] (14th century)

*intransitive verb*
**1 a :** to draw air into and expel it from the lungs **:** RESPIRE; *broadly* **:** to take in oxygen and give out carbon dioxide through natural processes **b :** to inhale and exhale freely
**2 :** LIVE
**3 a** *obsolete* **:** to emit a fragrance or aura **b :** to become perceptible **:** be expressed ⟨a personality that *breathes* and that distinguishes his work —Bennett Schiff⟩
**4 :** to pause and rest before continuing
**5 :** to blow softly
**6 :** to feel free of restraint ⟨needs room to *breathe*⟩
**7** *of wine* **:** to develop flavor and bouquet by exposure to air
**8 a :** to permit passage of air or vapor ⟨a fabric that *breathes*⟩ **b** *of an internal-combustion engine* **:** to use air to support combustion
*transitive verb*
**1 a :** to send out by exhaling **b :** to instill by or as if by breathing ⟨*breathe* new life into the movement⟩
**2 :** to give rest from exertion to
**3 :** to take in in breathing ⟨*breathe* the scent of pines⟩
**4 :** to inhale and exhale ⟨*breathe* air⟩
**5 a :** UTTER, EXPRESS ⟨don't *breathe* a word of it to anyone⟩ **b :** to make manifest **:** EVINCE ⟨the novel *breathes* despair⟩
— **breathe down one's neck 1 :** to threaten especially in attack or pursuit **2 :** to keep one under close or constant surveillance ⟨parents always *breathing down his neck*⟩
— **breathe easily** *or* **breathe freely :** to enjoy relief (as from pressure or danger)
**breathed** \'bretht\ *adjective* (1555)
**1 :** having breath especially of a specified kind — usually used in combination ⟨sweet-*breathed*⟩
**2 :** VOICELESS 2
**breath·er** \'brē-thər\ *noun* (14th century)
**1 :** one that breathes
**2 :** a break in activity for rest or relief
**3 :** a small vent in an otherwise airtight enclosure
**breath·ing** \'brē-thiŋ\ *noun* (1746)
**:** either of the marks ʽ and ʼ used in writing Greek to indicate aspiration or its absence
**breathing space** *noun* (1650)
**:** some time in which to recover, get organized, or get going — called also *breathing room*, *breathing spell*
**breath·less** \'breth-ləs\ *adjective* (14th century)
**1 a :** not breathing **b :** DEAD
**2 a :** panting or gasping for breath **b :** leaving one breathless **:** very rapid or strenuous ⟨go at a *breathless* pace⟩ **c :** holding one's breath from emotion ⟨*breathless* in anticipation⟩ **d :** marked by or as if by a holding of one's breath **:** INTENSE, GRIPPING ⟨*breathless* tension⟩
**3 :** oppressive because of no fresh air or breeze
— **breath·less·ly** *adverb*
— **breath·less·ness** *noun*
**breath·tak·ing** \'breth-ˌtā-kiŋ\ *adjective* (1880)
**1 :** making one out of breath
**2 a :** EXCITING, THRILLING ⟨a *breathtaking* stock car race⟩ **b :** very great **:** ASTONISHING ⟨his *breathtaking* ignorance⟩
— **breath·tak·ing·ly** \-kiŋ-lē\ *adverb*
**breathy** \'bre-thē\ *adjective* **breath·i·er; -est** (1883)
**:** characterized or accompanied by or as if by the audible passage of breath
— **breath·i·ly** \-thə-lē\ *adverb*
— **breath·i·ness** \-thē-nəs\ *noun*
**brec·cia** \'bre-ch(ē-)ə\ *noun* [Italian] (1774)
**:** a rock consisting of sharp fragments embedded in a fine-grained matrix (as sand or clay)
**brec·ci·ate** \'bre-chē-ˌāt\ *transitive verb* **-at·ed; -at·ing** (1772)
**1 :** to form (rock) into breccia
**2 :** to break (rock) into fragments

— **brec·ci·a·tion** \bre-chē-'ā-shən\ *noun*

**brede** \'brēd\ *noun* [variant of *braid*] (1640)
*archaic* : EMBROIDERY

**bred-in-the-bone** \'bre-dᵊn-ṯẖ-ə-,bōn\ *adjective* (15th century)
**1** : DEEP-ROOTED ⟨*bred-in-the-bone* honesty⟩
**2** : INVETERATE ⟨a *bred-in-the-bone* gambler⟩

**breech** \'brēch\ *noun* [Middle English, breeches, from Old English *brēc*, plural of *brōc* leg covering; akin to Old High German *bruoh* breeches, Latin *brāca* pants] (before 12th century)
**1** *plural* \'bri-chəz *also* 'brē-\ **a** : short pants covering the hips and thighs and fitting snugly at the lower edges at or just below the knee **b** : PANTS
**2 a** : the hind end of the body : BUTTOCKS **b** : BREECH PRESENTATION; *also* : a fetus that is presented breech first
**3** : the part of a firearm at the rear of the barrel
**word history** see SILLY

**breech·block** \'brēch-,bläk\ *noun* (1881)
: the block in breech-loading firearms that closes the rear of the barrel against the force of the charge and prevents gases from escaping

**breech·cloth** \'brēch-,klȯth, 'brich-\ *noun* (1793)
: LOINCLOTH

**breech·clout** \-,klaut\ *noun* (1757)
: LOINCLOTH

**breech·es buoy** \'brē-chəz- *also* 'bri-\ *noun* (1880)
: a canvas seat in the form of breeches hung from a life buoy running on a hawser and used to haul persons from one ship to another or from ship to shore especially in rescue operations

**breech·ing** \'brē-chiŋ, 'bri-\ *noun* (circa 1524)
**1** : the part of a harness that passes around the rump of a draft animal
**2** : the short coarse wool on the rump and hind legs of a sheep or goat; *also* : the hair on the corresponding part of a dog

**breech·load·er** \'brēch-,lō-dər\ *noun* (1858)
: a firearm that loads at the breech
— **breech–load·ing** \-'lō-diŋ\ *adjective*

**breech presentation** *noun* (1811)
: presentation of the fetus in which the breech is the first part to appear at the uterine cervix

¹**breed** \'brēd\ *verb* bred \'bred\; **breed·ing** [Middle English *breden*, from Old English *brēdan*; akin to Old English *brōd* brood] (before 12th century)
*transitive verb*
**1** : to produce (offspring) by hatching or gestation
**2 a** : BEGET 1 **b** : PRODUCE, ENGENDER ⟨despair often *breeds* violence⟩
**3** : to propagate (plants or animals) sexually and usually under controlled conditions ⟨*bred* several strains of corn together to produce a superior variety⟩
**4 a** : BRING UP, NURTURE ⟨born and *bred* in the country⟩ **b** : to inculcate by training ⟨*breed* good manners into one's children⟩
**5 a** : ⁴MATE 3 **b** : to mate with : INSEMINATE **c** : IMPREGNATE 2
**6** : to produce (a fissionable element) by bombarding a nonfissionable element with neutrons from a radioactive element
*intransitive verb*
**1 a** : to produce offspring by sexual union **b** : COPULATE, MATE
**2** : to propagate animals or plants

²**breed** *noun* (1553)
**1** : a group of animals or plants presumably related by descent from common ancestors and visibly similar in most characters; *especially* : such a group differentiated from the wild type under domestication
**2** : a number of persons of the same stock
**3** : CLASS, KIND ⟨a new *breed* of athlete⟩

**breed·er** \'brē-dər\ *noun* (1531)
: one that breeds: as **a** : an animal or plant kept for propagation **b** : one engaged in the breeding of a specified organism **c** : a nuclear reactor designed to produce more fissionable material than it uses as fuel — called also *breeder reactor*

**breed·ing** *noun* (14th century)
**1** : the action or process of bearing or generating
**2** : ANCESTRY
**3 a** *archaic* : EDUCATION ⟨she had her *breeding* at my father's charge —Shakespeare⟩ **b** : training in or observance of the proprieties
**4** : the sexual propagation of plants or animals

**breeding ground** *noun* (1856)
**1** : the place to which animals go to breed
**2** : a place or set of circumstances suitable for or favorable to growth and development ⟨hurricane *breeding grounds*⟩

**breeks** \'brēks, 'briks\ *noun plural* [Middle English (northern dialect) *breke*, from Old English *brēc*] (14th century)
*chiefly Scottish* : BREECHES

¹**breeze** \'brēz\ *noun* [probably from Spanish *brisa* northeast wind] (1626)
**1 a** : a light gentle wind **b** : a wind of from 4 to 31 miles (6 to 50 kilometers) an hour
**2** : something easily done : CINCH
— **breeze·less** \-ləs\ *adjective*
— **in a breeze** : EASILY

²**breeze** *intransitive verb* breezed; breez·ing (1907)
**1** : to move swiftly and airily ⟨*breezed* past the protesters⟩
**2** : to make progress quickly and easily ⟨*breezed* through the exam⟩ ⟨*breezed* to victory⟩

³**breeze** *noun* [probably modification of French *braise* cinders — more at BRAISE] (1726)
: residue from the making of coke or charcoal

**breeze·way** \'brēz-,wā\ *noun* (1931)
: a roofed often open passage connecting two buildings (as a house and garage) or halves of a building

**breezy** \'brē-zē\ *adjective* breez·i·er; -est (1718)
**1** : swept by breezes
**2 a** : briskly informal **b** : AIRY, NONCHALANT
— **breez·i·ly** \-zə-lē\ *adverb*
— **breez·i·ness** \-zē-nəs\ *noun*

**breg·ma** \'breg-mə\ *noun, plural* -ma·ta \-mə-tə\ [New Latin *bregmat-, bregma*, from Late Latin *bregmat-, bregma*, from Greek; akin to Greek *brechmos* front part of the head — more at BRAIN] (1578)
: the point of junction of the coronal and sagittal sutures of the skull

**brems·strah·lung** \'brem(p)-,shträ-ləŋ\ *noun* [German, literally, decelerated radiation] (1939)
: the electromagnetic radiation produced by the sudden retardation of a charged particle in an intense electric field (as of an atomic nucleus); *also* : the process that produces such radiation

**brent goose** \'brent-\ *noun* (1570)
*chiefly British* : BRANT

**breth·ren** \'breth-rən; 'bre-ṯẖ-, -ṯẖərn\ *plural of* BROTHER (before 12th century)
— used chiefly in formal or solemn address or in referring to the members of a profession, society, or sect

**Brethren** *noun plural* (1822)
: members of various sects originating chiefly in 18th century German Pietism; *especially* : DUNKERS

**Bret·on** \'bre-tᵊn\ *noun* [French, from Medieval Latin *Briton-, Brito*, from Latin, Briton] (1653)
**1** : a native or inhabitant of Brittany
**2** : the Celtic language of the Breton people
— **Breton** *adjective*

**breve** \'brēv, 'brev\ *noun* [Latin, neuter of *brevis* brief — more at BRIEF] (15th century)
**1** : a note equivalent to two whole notes
**2** : a curved mark ˘ used to indicate a short vowel or a short or unstressed syllable

¹**brevet** \bri-'vet, *chiefly British* 'bre-vit\ *noun* [Middle English, an official message, from Middle French, from Old French, diminutive of *brief* letter — more at BRIEF] (1689)
: a commission giving a military officer higher nominal rank than that for which pay is received

²**brevet** *transitive verb* bre·vet·ted *or* brev·et·ed; bre·vet·ting *or* brev·et·ing (1824)
: to confer rank upon by brevet

**bre·via·ry** \'brē-və-rē, -vyə-, -vē-,er-ē *also* 'bre-\ *noun, plural* -ries [Middle English *breviarie*, from Medieval Latin *breviarium*, from Latin, summary, from *brevis*] (15th century)
**1** *often capitalized* **a** : a book containing the prayers, hymns, psalms, and readings for the canonical hours **b** : DIVINE OFFICE
**2** [Latin *breviarium*] : a brief summary : ABRIDGMENT

**brev·i·ty** \'bre-və-tē\ *noun, plural* -ties [Latin *brevitas*, from *brevis*] (15th century)
: shortness of duration; *especially* : shortness or conciseness of expression

¹**brew** \'brü\ *verb* [Middle English, from Old English *brēowan*; akin to Latin *fervēre* to boil — more at BARM] (before 12th century)
*transitive verb*
**1** : to prepare (as beer or ale) by steeping, boiling, and fermentation or by infusion and fermentation
**2 a** : to bring about : FOMENT ⟨*brew* trouble⟩ **b** : CONTRIVE, PLOT
**3** : to prepare (as tea) by infusion in hot water
*intransitive verb*
**1** : to brew beer or ale
**2** : to be in the process of formation ⟨a storm is *brewing* in the east⟩
— **brew·er** \'brü-ər, 'brü(-ə)r\ *noun*

²**brew** *noun* (circa 1510)
**1 a** : a brewed beverage (as beer) **b** : a serving of a brewed beverage ⟨quaff a few *brews*⟩ **c** : something produced by or as if by brewing
**2** : the process of brewing

**brew·age** \'brü-ij\ *noun* (1542)
: BREW 1a, 2

**brewer's yeast** *noun* (1871)
: a yeast used or suitable for use in brewing; *specifically* : the dried pulverized cells of such a yeast (*Saccharomyces cerevisiae*) used especially as a source of B-complex vitamins

**brew·ery** \'brü-ə-rē, 'brü(-ə)r-ē\ *noun, plural* -er·ies (1658)
: a plant where malt liquors are produced

¹**bri·ar** \'brī(-ə)r\ *variant of* BRIER

²**briar** *noun* (1882)
: a tobacco pipe made from the root or stem of a brier

**bri·ard** \brē-'är(d)\ *noun* [French, from *Brie*, district in France] (circa 1929)
: any of an old French breed of large long-coated sheepdogs

¹**bribe** \'brīb\ *noun* [Middle English, something stolen, from Middle French, bread given to a beggar] (15th century)
**1** : money or favor given or promised in order to influence the judgment or conduct of a person in a position of trust
**2** : something that serves to induce or influence

²**bribe** *verb* bribed; brib·ing (1528)
*transitive verb*
: to induce or influence by or as if by bribery
*intransitive verb*
: to practice bribery
— **brib·able** \'brī-bə-bəl\ *adjective*
— **brib·ee** \,brī-'bē\ *noun*

| | | |
|---|---|---|
| \ə\ abut | \ᵊ\ kitten | \ər\ further | \a\ ash | \ā\ ace |
| \ä\ mop, mar | \au̇\ out | \ch\ chin | \e\ bet | \ē\ easy |
| \g\ go | \i\ hit | \ī\ ice | \j\ job | \ŋ\ sing | \ō\ go |
| \ȯ\ law | \ȯi\ boy | \th\ thin | \ṯẖ\ the | \ü\ loot | \u̇\ foot |
| \y\ yet | \zh\ vision | *see also* Guide to Pronunciation |

**— brib·er** noun

**brib·ery** \'brī-b(ə-)rē\ noun, plural **-er·ies** (1549)
: the act or practice of giving or taking a bribe

**bric–a–brac** \'bri-kə-,brak\ noun, plural **bric–a–brac** [French bric-à-brac] (1840)
**1** : a miscellaneous collection of small articles commonly of ornamental or sentimental value
: CURIOS
**2** : something suggesting bric-a-brac especially in extraneous decorative quality

¹**brick** \'brik\ noun, often attributive [Middle English bryke, from Middle French brique, from Middle Dutch bricke] (15th century)
**1** plural **bricks** or **brick** : a handy-sized unit of building or paving material typically being rectangular and about 2¼ × 3¾ × 8 inches (57 × 95 × 203 millimeters) and of moist clay hardened by heat
**2** : a good-hearted person
**3** : a rectangular compressed mass (as of ice cream)
**4** : a semisoft cheese with numerous small holes, smooth texture, and often mild flavor
**5** : GAFFE, BLUNDER — used especially in the phrase drop a brick

²**brick** transitive verb (1592)
: to close, face, or pave with bricks — usually used with up, in, or over

**brick·bat** \'brik-,bat\ noun [brick + ¹bat (lump, fragment)] (circa 1587)
**1** : a fragment of a hard material (as a brick); especially : one used as a missile
**2** : an uncomplimentary remark

**brick·field** \-,fēld\ noun (1801)
British : BRICKYARD

**brick·lay·er** \'brik-,lā-ər, -,le(-ə)r\ noun (15th century)
: a person who lays brick
**— brick·lay·ing** \-,lā-iŋ\ noun

**brick·le** \'bri-kəl\ adjective [Middle English brekyl] (13th century)
dialect : BRITTLE

**brick red** noun (1810)
: a moderate reddish brown

**brick·work** \'brik-,wərk\ noun (1580)
: work of or with bricks and mortar

**brick·yard** \-,yärd\ noun (1731)
: a place where bricks are made

**bri·co·lage** \,brē-kō-'läzh, ,bri-\ noun [French, from bricoler to putter about] (1966)
: construction or something constructed by using whatever comes to hand

¹**brid·al** \'brī-d°l\ noun [Middle English bridale, from Old English brȳdealu, from brȳd + ealu ale — more at ALE] (before 12th century)
: a marriage festival or ceremony ◆

²**bridal** adjective (13th century)
**1** : of or relating to a bride or a wedding : NUPTIAL
**2** : intended for a newly married couple ⟨a bridal suite⟩

**bridal wreath** noun (circa 1889)
: a spirea (Spiraea prunifolia) widely grown for its umbels of small white flowers borne in spring

**bride** \'brīd\ noun [Middle English, from Old English brȳd; akin to Old High German brūt bride] (before 12th century)
: a woman just married or about to be married

**bride·groom** \'brīd-,grüm, -,grùm\ noun [Middle English (Scots) brydegrome, by folk etymology from Middle English bridegome, from Old English brȳdguma, from brȳd + guma man; akin to Old High German brūtgomo bridegroom — more at HOMAGE] (14th century)
: a man just married or about to be married

**bride–price** \'brīd-,prīs\ noun (1876)
: a payment given by or in behalf of a prospective husband to the bride's family in many cultures

**brides·maid** \'brīdz-,mād\ noun (1552)
**1** : a woman attendant of a bride
**2** : one that finishes just behind the winner

**bride·well** \'brīd-,wel, -wəl\ noun [Bridewell, London jail] (circa 1593)
: PRISON

¹**bridge** \'brij\ noun [Middle English brigge, from Old English brycg; akin to Old High German brucka bridge, Old Church Slavonic brŭvŭno beam] (before 12th century)
**1 a** : a structure carrying a pathway or roadway over a depression or obstacle **b** : a time, place, or means of connection or transition
**2** : something resembling a bridge in form or function: as **a** : the upper bony part of the nose; also : the part of a pair of glasses that rests upon it **b** : a piece raising the strings of a musical instrument — see VIOLIN illustration **c** : the forward part of a ship's superstructure from which the ship is navigated **d** : GANTRY **2b e** : the hand as a rest for a billiards or pool cue; also : a device used as a cue rest
**3 a** : a musical passage linking two sections of a composition **b** : a partial denture anchored to adjacent teeth **c** : a connection (as an atom or group of atoms) that joins two different parts of a molecule (as opposite sides of a ring)
**4** : an electrical instrument or network for measuring or comparing resistances, inductances, capacitances, or impedances by comparing the ratio of two opposing voltages to a known ratio
**— bridge·less** \-ləs\ adjective

bridge 1a: 1 simple truss, 2 steel arch, 3 continuous truss, 4 cantilever, 5 suspension

²**bridge** transitive verb **bridged; bridg·ing** (before 12th century)
**1** : to make a bridge over or across ⟨bridge the gap⟩; also : to join by a bridge
**2** : to provide with a bridge
**— bridge·able** \'bri-jə-bəl\ adjective

³**bridge** noun [alteration of earlier biritch, of unknown origin] (circa 1897)
: any of various card games for usually four players in two partnerships that bid for the right to declare a trump suit, seek to win tricks equal to the final bid, and play with the hand of declarer's partner exposed and played by declarer; especially : CONTRACT BRIDGE

**bridge·head** \-,hed\ noun (1812)
**1 a** : a fortification protecting the end of a bridge nearest an enemy **b** : an area around the end of a bridge
**2** : an advanced position seized in hostile territory

**bridge·work** \-,wərk\ noun (1883)
: dental bridges

¹**bri·dle** \'brī-d°l\ noun [Middle English bridel, from Old English brīdel; akin to Old English bregdan to move quickly — more at BRAID] (before 12th century)
**1** : the headgear with which a horse is governed and which carries a bit and reins
**2** : a length of line or cable attached to two parts of something to spread the force of a pull; especially : rigging on a kite for attaching line
**3** : CURB, RESTRAINT ⟨set a bridle on his power⟩

²**bridle** verb **bri·dled; bri·dling** \'brīd-liŋ, 'brī-d°l-iŋ\ (before 12th century)
transitive verb
**1** : to put a bridle on

**2** : to restrain, check, or control with or as if with a bridle ⟨bridle your tongue⟩
intransitive verb
: to show hostility or resentment (as to an affront to one's pride or dignity) especially by drawing back the head and chin
**synonym** see RESTRAIN

**bridle path** noun (1811)
: a trail suitable for horseback riding

**Brie** \'brē\ noun [French, from Brie, district in France] (1876)
: a soft surface-ripened cheese with a whitish rind and a pale yellow interior

¹**brief** \'brēf\ adjective [Middle English bref, breve, from Middle French brief, from Latin brevis; akin to Old High German murg short, Greek brachys] (14th century)
**1** : short in duration, extent, or length
**2 a** : CONCISE **b** : CURT, ABRUPT
**— brief·ness** noun

²**brief** noun [Middle English bref, from Middle French, from Medieval Latin brevis, from Late Latin, summary, from Latin brevis, adjective] (14th century)
**1** : an official letter or mandate; especially : a papal letter less formal than a bull
**2 a** : a concise article **b** : SYNOPSIS, SUMMARY **c** : a concise statement of a client's case made out for the instruction of counsel in a trial at law
**3** : an outline of an argument; especially : a formal outline especially in law that sets forth the main contentions with supporting statements or evidence
**4** plural : short snug pants or underpants
**— in brief** : in a few words : BRIEFLY

³**brief** transitive verb (15th century)
**1** : to make an abstract or abridgment of
**2 a** : to give final precise instructions to **b** : to coach thoroughly in advance **c** : to give essential information to
**— brief·er** noun

**brief·case** \'brēf-,kās\ noun (1917)
: a flat flexible case for carrying papers or books

**brief·ing** \'brē-fiŋ\ noun (1910)
: an act or instance of giving precise instructions or essential information

**brief·less** \'brē-fləs\ adjective (1824)
: having no legal clients

**brief·ly** \'brē-flē\ adverb (14th century)
**1 a** : in a brief way **b** : in brief
**2** : for a short time

¹**bri·er** \'brī-(ə)r\ noun [Middle English brere, from Old English brēr] (before 12th century)

◇ WORD HISTORY
**bridal** A secondary sense of Old English ealu, the ancestor of Modern English ale, was "feast, banquet," at which the drinking of ale was a prominent if not the main activity. The Middle and Modern English descendants of ealu preserved this sense, at least into the 19th century, especially in compounds of which the first element named the occasion for the feast. There was the leet-ale, held before a session of the leet (a kind of court), the Whitsunale, a parish festival held at Whitsuntide, and, incongruous as it may seem, the church-ale, a benefit at which ale brewed from malt provided to a parish would be sold to raise money for church upkeep. The oldest and most institutionalized such "ale" was the bride-ale, or wedding feast, attested in Old English as brydealu. It seems that already in Middle English the ale half of the compound had lost its secondary stress, becoming \əl\ or \ələ\. This ending was subsequently associated both with the noun suffix -al of espousal and funeral and with the adjective suffix -al of nuptial, parental, and autumnal. By the 18th century, bridal was perceived primarily as an adjective, which is its most common use today.

: a plant (as of the genera *Rosa, Rubus,* and *Smilax*) with a woody and thorny or prickly stem; *also* : a mass or twig of these
— **bri·ery** \'brī(-ə)r-ē\ *adjective*

²**brier** *noun* [French *bruyère* heath, from Middle French *bruiere,* from (assumed) Vulgar Latin *brucaria,* from Late Latin *brucus* heather, of Celtic origin; akin to Old Irish *froech* heather; akin to Greek *ereikē* heather] (1868)
: a heath (*Erica arborea*) of southern Europe whose roots and knotted stems are used for making briar tobacco pipes

¹**brig** \'brig\ *noun* [short for *brigantine*] (1712)
: a 2-masted square-rigged ship

²**brig** *noun* [probably from ¹*brig*] (1852)
**1** : a place (as on a ship) for temporary confinement of offenders in the U.S. Navy

brig

**2** : GUARDHOUSE, PRISON

¹**bri·gade** \bri-'gād\ *noun* [French, from Italian *brigata,* from *brigare*] (1637)
**1 a** : a large body of troops **b** : a tactical and administrative unit composed of a headquarters, one or more units of infantry or armor, and supporting units
**2** : a group of people organized for special activity

²**brigade** *transitive verb* **bri·gad·ed; bri·gad·ing** (1781)
: to form or unite into a brigade

**brig·a·dier** *noun* \,bri-gə-'dir\ [French, from *brigade*] (1678)
**1** : an officer in the British army commanding a brigade and ranking immediately below a major general
**2** : BRIGADIER GENERAL

**brigadier general** *noun* (1690)
: a commissioned officer in the army, air force, or marine corps who ranks above a colonel and whose insignia is one star

**Brig·a·doon** \,bri-gə-'dün\ *noun* [from *Brigadoon,* village in the musical *Brigadoon* (1947) by A. J. Lerner and F. Loewe] (1968)
: a place that is idyllic, unaffected by time, or remote from reality

**brig·and** \'bri-gənd\ *noun* [Middle English *brigaunt,* from Middle French *brigand,* from Old Italian *brigante,* from *brigare* to fight, from *briga* strife, of Celtic origin; akin to Old Irish *bríg* strength] (14th century)
: one who lives by plunder usually as a member of a band : BANDIT
— **brig·and·age** \-gən-dij\ *noun*

**brig·an·dine** \'bri-gən-,dēn\ *noun* [Middle English, from Middle French, from *brigand*] (15th century)
: medieval body armor of scales or plates

**brig·an·tine** \'bri-gən-,tēn\ *noun* [Middle French *brigantin,* from Old Italian *brigantino,* from *brigante*] (1525)
: a 2-masted sailing ship that is square-rigged except for a fore-and-aft mainsail

¹**bright** \'brīt\ *adjective* [Middle English, from Old English *beorht;* akin to Old High German *beraht* bright, Sanskrit *bhrājate* it shines] (before 12th century)
**1 a** : radiating or reflecting light : SHINING, SPARKLING ⟨*bright* lights⟩ ⟨*bright* eyes⟩ **b** : SUNNY ⟨a *bright* day⟩; *also* : radiant with happiness ⟨*bright* smiling faces⟩ ⟨*bright* moments⟩
**2** : ILLUSTRIOUS, GLORIOUS ⟨*brightest* star of the opera⟩
**3** : BEAUTIFUL
**4** : of high saturation or brilliance ⟨*bright* colors⟩

**5 a** : LIVELY, CHEERFUL ⟨be *bright* and jovial among your guests —Shakespeare⟩ **b** : INTELLIGENT, CLEVER ⟨a *bright* idea⟩ ⟨*bright* children⟩
**6** : AUSPICIOUS, PROMISING ⟨*bright* prospects for the future⟩ ☆
— **bright** *adverb*
— **bright·ly** *adverb*

²**bright** *noun* (1969)
: a bright color — usually used in plural ⟨rich earth tones and crisp *brights* —Patricia Peterson⟩

**bright·en** \'brī-t°n\ *verb* **bright·ened; bright·en·ing** \'brīt-niŋ, 'brī-t°n-iŋ\ (14th century)
*intransitive verb*
: to become bright or brighter
*transitive verb*
: to make bright or brighter
— **bright·en·er** \'brīt-nər, 'brī-t°n-ər\ *noun*

**bright·ness** *noun* (before 12th century)
**1 a** : the quality or state of being bright; *also* : an instance of such a quality or state **b** : LUMINANCE
**2** : the attribute of light-source colors by which emitted light is ordered continuously from light to dark in correlation with its intensity — compare HUE 2c, ¹LIGHTNESS 2, SATURATION 4

**Bright's disease** \'brīts-\ *noun* [Richard *Bright* (died 1858) English physician] (1831)
: any of several kidney diseases marked especially by albumin in the urine

**bright·work** \'brīt-,wərk\ *noun* (1841)
: polished or plated metalwork

**brill** \'bril\ *noun, plural* **brill** [Middle English *brell*] (15th century)
: a European flatfish (*Scophthalmus rhombus* synonym *Bothus rhombus* of the family Bothidae); *broadly* : TURBOT

**bril·liance** \'bril-yən(t)s\ *noun* (1755)
: the quality or state of being brilliant

**bril·lian·cy** \-yən(t)-sē\ *noun, plural* **-cies** (1747)
**1** : BRILLIANCE
**2** : an instance of brilliance

¹**bril·liant** \'bril-yənt\ *adjective* [French *brillant,* present participle of *briller* to shine, from Italian *brillare*] (circa 1681)
**1** : very bright : GLITTERING ⟨a *brilliant* light⟩
**2 a** : STRIKING, DISTINCTIVE ⟨a *brilliant* example⟩ **b** : distinguished by unusual mental keenness or alertness
**synonym** see BRIGHT
— **bril·liant·ly** *adverb*

²**brilliant** *noun* (1690)
: a gem (as a diamond) cut in a particular form with numerous facets so as to have special brilliance

**bril·lian·tine** \'bril-yən-,tēn\ *noun* (1873)
**1** : a light lustrous fabric that is similar to alpaca and is woven usually with a cotton warp and mohair or worsted filling
**2** : a preparation for making hair glossy

¹**brim** \'brim\ *noun* [Middle English *brimme;* akin to Middle High German *brem* edge] (13th century)
**1 a** (1) : an upper or outer margin : VERGE (2) *archaic* : the upper surface of a body of water **b** : the edge or rim of a hollow vessel, a natural depression, or a cavity
**2** : the projecting rim of a hat
— **brim·less** \-ləs\ *adjective*

²**brim** *verb* **brimmed; brim·ming** (1611)
*transitive verb*
: to fill to the brim
*intransitive verb*
**1** : to be or become full often to overflowing
**2** : to reach or overflow a brim

**brim·ful** \'brim-'fúl, -,fúl\ *adjective* (circa 1530)
: full to the brim : ready to overflow

**brimmed** \'brimd\ *adjective* (1606)
: having a brim of a specified nature — used in combination ⟨a wide-*brimmed* hat⟩

**brim·mer** \'bri-mər\ *noun* (1663)

: a brimming cup or glass

**brim·stone** \'brim-,stōn\ *noun* [Middle English *brinston,* probably from *birnen* to burn + *ston* stone] (12th century)
: SULFUR

**brind·ed** \'brin-dəd\ *adjective* [Middle English *brended*] (15th century)
*archaic* : BRINDLED

**brin·dle** \'brin-d°l\ *noun* [*brindle,* adjective] (1696)
**1** : a brindled color
**2** : a brindled animal

**brin·dled** \-d°ld\ *or* **brindle** *adjective* [alteration of *brindled*] (1679)
: having obscure dark streaks or flecks on a gray or tawny ground

¹**brine** \'brīn\ *noun* [Middle English, from Old English *brȳne;* akin to Middle Dutch *brīne* brine] (before 12th century)
**1 a** : water saturated or strongly impregnated with common salt **b** : a strong saline solution (as of calcium chloride)
**2** : the water of a sea or salt lake

²**brine** *transitive verb* **brined; brin·ing** (1552)
: to treat (as by steeping) with brine
— **brin·er** *noun*

**Bri·nell hardness** \brə-'nel-\ *noun* [Johann A. *Brinell* (died 1925) Swedish engineer] (1915)
: the hardness of a metal or alloy measured by hydraulically pressing a hard ball under a standard load into the specimen

**Brinell hardness number** *noun* (1915)
: a number expressing Brinell hardness and denoting the load applied in testing in kilograms divided by the spherical area of indentation produced in the specimen in square millimeters — called also *Brinell number*

**brine shrimp** *noun* (1836)
: any of a genus (*Artemia*) of branchiopod crustaceans that can exist in strongly saline environments

**bring** \'briŋ\ *verb* **brought** \'brot\; **bring·ing** \'briŋ-iŋ\ [Middle English, from Old English *bringan;* akin to Old High German *bringan* to bring, Welsh *he*brwng to accompany] (before 12th century)
*transitive verb*
**1 a** : to convey, lead, carry, or cause to come along with one toward the place from which the action is being regarded **b** : to cause to be, act, or move in a special way: as (1) : ATTRACT ⟨her screams *brought* the neighbors⟩ (2) : PERSUADE, INDUCE (3) : FORCE, COMPEL (4) : to cause to come into a particular state or condition ⟨*bring* water to a boil⟩ **c** *dialect* : ESCORT, ACCOMPANY
**2** : to cause to exist or occur: as **a** : to be the occasion of ⟨winter *brings* snow⟩ **b** : to result in **c** : INSTITUTE ⟨*bring* legal action⟩ **d** : ADDUCE ⟨*bring* an argument⟩
**3** : PREFER ⟨*bring* charges⟩
**4** : to procure in exchange : sell for

---

☆ **SYNONYMS**
**Bright, brilliant, radiant, luminous, lustrous** mean shining or glowing with light. BRIGHT implies emitting or reflecting a high degree of light. BRILLIANT implies intense often sparkling brightness. RADIANT stresses the emission or seeming emission of rays of light. LUMINOUS implies emission of steady, suffused, glowing light by reflection or in surrounding darkness. LUSTROUS stresses an even, rich light from a surface that reflects brightly without sparkling or glittering.

---

\ə\ abut \°\ kitten \ər\ further \a\ ash \ā\ ace \ä\ mop, mar \aú\ out \ch\ chin \e\ bet \ē\ easy \g\ go \i\ hit \ī\ ice \j\ job \ŋ\ sing \ō\ go \ò\ law \òi\ boy \th\ thin \th\ the \ü\ loot \ú\ foot \y\ yet \zh\ vision *see also* Guide to Pronunciation

*intransitive verb*
*chiefly Midland* : YIELD, PRODUCE ■
— **bring·er** *noun*
— **bring forth 1 :** BEAR ⟨*brought forth* fruit⟩
**2 :** to give birth to : PRODUCE **3 :** ADDUCE
⟨*bring forth* persuasive arguments⟩
— **bring forward 1 :** to produce to view
: INTRODUCE ⟨*brought* new evidence *forward*⟩
**2 :** to carry (a total) forward
— **bring home :** to make unmistakably
clear
— **bring to account 1 :** to bring to book
**2 :** REPRIMAND
— **bring to bear :** to use with effect ⟨*bring*
pressure *to bear*⟩
— **bring to book :** to compel to give an account
— **bring to light :** DISCLOSE, REVEAL
— **bring to mind :** RECALL
— **bring to terms :** to compel to agree, assent, or submit
— **bring up the rear :** to come last or behind
**bring about** *transitive verb* (14th century)
: to cause to take place : EFFECT
**bring around** *transitive verb* (1862)
**1 :** to restore to consciousness : REVIVE
**2 :** PERSUADE
**bring·down** \'briŋ-ˌdaun\ *noun* (circa 1944)
: COMEDOWN, LETDOWN
**bring down** *transitive verb* (14th century)
**1 :** to cause to fall by or as if by shooting
**2 :** to carry (a total) forward
— **bring down the house :** to win the
enthusiastic approval of the audience
**bring in** *transitive verb* (14th century)
**1 :** INCLUDE, INTRODUCE
**2 :** to produce as profit or return ⟨each sale
*brought in* $5⟩
**3 :** to enable (a base runner) to reach home
plate by hitting the ball
**4 :** to report to a court ⟨the jury *brought in* a
verdict⟩
**5 a :** to cause (as an oil well) to be productive
**b :** to win tricks with the cards of (a long suit)
in bridge
**6 :** EARN ⟨*brings in* a good salary⟩
**bring off** *transitive verb* (1606)
**1 :** to cause to escape : RESCUE
**2 :** to carry to a successful conclusion
: ACHIEVE, ACCOMPLISH
**bring on** *transitive verb* (1602)
: to cause to appear or occur
**bring out** *transitive verb* (1605)
**1 a :** to make apparent **b :** to effectively develop (as a quality)
**2 a :** to present to the public **b :** to introduce
formally to society
**3 :** UTTER
**bring to** *transitive verb* (1753)
**1 :** to cause (a boat) to lie to or come to a
standstill
**2 :** to restore to consciousness : REVIVE
**bring up** (14th century)
*transitive verb*
**1 :** to bring (a person) to maturity through nurturing care and education
**2 :** to cause to stop suddenly
**3 :** to bring to attention : INTRODUCE
**4 :** VOMIT
*intransitive verb*
: to stop suddenly
**brink** \'briŋk\ *noun* [Middle English, of Scandinavian origin; akin to Old Norse *brekka*
slope; akin to Middle Dutch *brink* grassland]
(13th century)
**1 :** EDGE; *especially* : the edge at the top of a
steep place
**2 :** a bank especially of a river
**3 :** the point of onset : VERGE ⟨on the *brink* of
war⟩
**4 :** the threshold of danger
**brink·man·ship** \'briŋk-mən-ˌship\ *also*
**brinks·man·ship** \'briŋ(k)s-mən-\ *noun*
(1956)

: the art or practice of pushing a dangerous situation or confrontation to the limit of safety
especially to force a desired outcome
*word history* see GAMESMANSHIP
**briny** \'brī-nē\ *adjective* **brin·i·er; -est**
(1590)
: of, relating to, or resembling brine or the sea
: SALTY
— **brin·i·ness** *noun*
**brio** \'brē-(ˌ)ō\ *noun* [Italian] (1734)
: enthusiastic vigor : VIVACITY, VERVE
**bri·oche** \brē-'ōsh, -'ösh\ *noun* [French, from
Middle French dialect, from *brier* to knead, of
Germanic origin; akin to Old High German
*brehhan* to break — more at BREAK] (1826)
: light slightly sweet bread made with a rich
yeast dough
**bri·o·lette** \ˌbrē-ə-'let\ *noun* [French] (1865)
: an oval or pear-shaped gemstone cut in triangular facets
**bri·quette** *or* **bri·quet** \bri-'ket\ *noun*
[French *briquette*, diminutive of *brique* brick]
(1883)
: a compacted often brick-shaped mass of usually fine material ⟨a charcoal *briquette*⟩
— **briquette** *transitive verb*
**bri·sance** \bri-'zän(t)s, -'zäⁿs\ *noun* [French,
from *brisant,* present participle of *briser* to
break, from Old French *brisier,* of Celtic origin; akin to Old Irish *brisid* he breaks; perhaps
akin to Latin *fricare* to rub — more at FRIC-
TION] (1915)
: the shattering or crushing effect of an explosive
— **bri·sant** \-'zänt, -'zäⁿ\ *adjective*
**¹brisk** \'brisk\ *adjective* [probably modification
of Middle French *brusque*] (1560)
**1 :** keenly alert : LIVELY
**2 a :** pleasingly tangy ⟨*brisk* tea⟩ **b :** FRESH, IN-
VIGORATING ⟨*brisk* weather⟩
**3 :** sharp in tone or manner
**4 :** ENERGETIC, QUICK ⟨a *brisk* pace⟩
— **brisk·ly** *adverb*
— **brisk·ness** *noun*
**²brisk** (1628)
*transitive verb*
: to make brisk
*intransitive verb*
: to become brisk — usually used with *up*
⟨business *brisked* up⟩
**bris·ket** \'bris-kət\ *noun* [Middle English *brus-
ket;* akin to Old English *brēost* breast] (14th
century)
: the breast or lower chest of a quadruped
animal; *also* : a cut of beef from the brisket
— see BEEF illustration
**bris·ling** \'briz-liŋ, 'bris-\ *noun* [Norwegian
*brisling,* from Low German *bretling,* from *bret*
broad; akin to Old English *brād* broad] (circa
1868)
: SPRAT 1a
**¹bris·tle** \'bris-əl\ *noun* [Middle English *bris-
til,* from *brust* bristle, from Old English *byrst;*
akin to Old High German *burst* bristle, and
perhaps to Latin *fastigium* top] (14th century)
: a short stiff coarse hair or filament
— **bris·tle·like** \'bris-ə-ˌlīk\ *adjective*
**²bristle** *verb* **bris·tled; bris·tling** \'bris-liŋ,
'bris-ə-\ (15th century)
*transitive verb*
**1 :** to furnish with bristles
**2 :** to make bristly : RUFFLE
*intransitive verb*
**1 a :** to rise and stand stiffly erect ⟨quills *bristling*⟩ **b :** to raise the bristles (as in anger)
**2 :** to take on an aggressive attitude or appearance (as in response to a slight)
**3 a :** to be full of or covered with especially
something suggestive of bristles ⟨roofs *bristled* with chimneys⟩ **b :** to be full of something
specified ⟨book *bristles* with detail and irony
—W. J. Broad⟩
**bris·tle·cone pine** \'bris-əl-ˌkōn-\ *noun*
(1894)

: either of two pines
(*Pinus longaeva*
and *P. aristata*) of
the western U.S.
that include the old-
est living trees
**bris·tle·tail** \-ˌtāl\
*noun* (1706)
: any of an order
(Thysanura) of
wingless insects
with two or three
slender caudal bris-
tles

**bristlecone pine**

**bris·tly** \'bris-lē, 'bri-sə-\ *adjective* **bris·tli·
er; -est** (circa 1591)
**1 a :** consisting of or resembling bristles **b**
: thickly set with bristles
**2 :** inclined to or exhibiting aggressiveness or
anger
**bris·tol board** \'bris-tᵊl-\ *noun* [*Bristol,* En-
gland] (1809)
: a paperboard with a smooth surface suitable
especially for artwork — called also *bristol*
**Bristol fashion** *adjective* [*Bristol,* England]
(1823)
: being in good order : SHIPSHAPE
**brit** *also* **britt** \'brit\ *noun* [perhaps from Cornish *brȳthel* mackerel] (1851)
: minute marine animals (as crustaceans and
pteropods) on which right whales feed
**Brit** \'brit\ *noun* (1901)
: BRITON 2
**Bri·tan·nia metal** \bri-'tan-yə-, -'ta-nē-ə-\
*noun* [*Britannia,* poetic name for Great Britain, from Latin] (1817)
: a silver-white alloy largely of tin, antimony,
and copper that is similar to pewter
**Bri·tan·nic** \bri-'ta-nik\ *adjective* (1641)
: BRITISH
**britch·es** \'bri-chəz\ *noun plural* [alteration of
*breeches*] (circa 1803)
: BREECHES, TROUSERS
**Brith Mi·lah** \'brit-mē-'lä, 'brith-, 'bris-, -'mē-
(ˌ)lä\ *noun* [Late Hebrew *bĕrīth mīlāh* covenant of circumcision] (circa 1902)
: the Jewish rite of circumcision
**Brit·i·cism** \'bri-tə-ˌsi-zəm\ *noun* [*Brit*ish +
*-icism* (as in *gallicism*)] (1868)
: a characteristic feature of British English

**Brit·ish** \'bri-tish\ noun [Middle English Bruttische of Britain, from Old English Brettisc, from Brettas Britons, of Celtic origin; akin to Welsh Brython Briton] (13th century)
**1 a :** the Celtic language of the ancient Britons **b :** BRITISH ENGLISH
**2** plural in construction **:** the people of Great Britain or the Commonwealth
— **British** adjective
— **Brit·ish·ism** \'bri-ti-,shi-zəm\ noun
— **Brit·ish·ness** noun
**British English** noun (1869)
**:** the native language of most inhabitants of England; especially **:** English characteristic of England and clearly distinguishable from that used elsewhere (as in the U.S. or Australia)
**Brit·ish·er** \'bri-ti-shər\ noun (1829)
**:** BRITON 2
**British thermal unit** noun (1876)
**:** the quantity of heat required to raise the temperature of one pound of water one degree Fahrenheit at a specified temperature (as 39°F)
**Brit·on** \'bri-t°n\ noun [Middle English Breton, from Middle French & Latin; Middle French, from Latin Britton-, Britto, of Celtic origin; akin to Welsh Brython] (13th century)
**1 :** a member of one of the peoples inhabiting Britain prior to the Anglo-Saxon invasions
**2 :** a native or subject of Great Britain; especially **:** ENGLISHMAN
**Brit·ta·ny** \'bri-t°n-ē\ noun, plural **Brittanys** also **Brittanies** [Brittany, region in France] (1967)
**:** any of a breed of medium-sized pointing spaniels of French origin — called also Brittany spaniel
¹**brit·tle** \'bri-t°l\ adjective **brit·tler** \'brit-lər, 'bri-t°l-ər\; **brit·tlest** \-ləst, -t°l-əst\ [Middle English britil; akin to Old English brēotan to break, Old Norse brjōta] (14th century)
**1 a :** easily broken, cracked, or snapped ⟨brittle clay⟩ ⟨brittle glass⟩ **b :** easily disrupted, overthrown, or damaged **:** FRAIL ⟨a brittle friendship⟩
**2 a :** PERISHABLE, MORTAL **b :** TRANSITORY, EVANESCENT
**3 :** easily hurt or offended **:** SENSITIVE ⟨a brittle personality⟩
**4 :** SHARP ⟨brittle staccato of snare drums⟩
**5 :** lacking warmth, depth, or generosity of spirit ⟨a brittle selfish person⟩
**6 :** affected with or being a form of diabetes characterized by large and unpredictable fluctuations in blood glucose level
**synonym** see FRAGILE
— **brit·tle·ly** \'bri-t°l-(l)ē\ adverb
— **brit·tle·ness** \'bri-t°l-nəs\ noun
²**brittle** noun (1913)
**:** a candy made with caramelized sugar and nuts spread in thin sheets ⟨peanut brittle⟩
**brittle star** noun (1843)
**:** any of a subclass or class (Ophiuroidea) of echinoderms that have slender flexible arms distinct from the central disk
**Brit·ton·ic** \bri-'tä-nik\ adjective [Latin Britton-, Britto Briton] (1923)
**:** BRYTHONIC
**Brix** \'briks\ adjective (1897)
**:** of or relating to a Brix scale
**Brix scale** noun [Adolf F. Brix (died 1870) Austrian scientist] (1897)
**:** a hydrometer scale for sugar solutions so graduated that its readings at a specified temperature represent percentages by weight of sugar in the solution — called also Brix
**bro** \'brō\ noun, plural **bros** [by alteration] (1838)
**1 :** BROTHER 1
**2 :** SOUL BROTHER — often used informally as a term of address
¹**broach** \'brōch\ noun [Middle English broche, from Middle French, from (assumed) Vulgar Latin brocca, from Latin, feminine of broccus projecting] (13th century)
**1 :** BROOCH

**2 :** any of various pointed or tapered tools, implements, or parts: as **a :** a spit for roasting meat **b :** a tool for tapping casks **c :** a cutting tool for removing material from metal or plastic to shape an outside surface or a hole
²**broach** (15th century)
transitive verb
**1 a :** to pierce (as a cask) in order to draw the contents; also **:** to open for the first time **b :** to open up or break into (as a mine or stores)
**2 :** to shape or enlarge (a hole) with a broach
**3 a :** to make known for the first time **b :** to open up (a subject) for discussion
intransitive verb
**:** to break the surface from below
**synonym** see EXPRESS
— **broach·er** noun
³**broach** intransitive verb [perhaps from ²broach] (1705)
**:** to veer or yaw dangerously so as to lie broadside to the waves — often used with to
¹**broad** \'brod\ adjective [Middle English brood, from Old English brād; akin to Old High German breit broad] (before 12th century)
**1 a :** having ample extent from side to side or between limits ⟨broad shoulders⟩ **b :** having a specified extension from side to side ⟨made the path 10 feet broad⟩
**2 :** extending far and wide **:** SPACIOUS ⟨the broad plains⟩
**3 a :** OPEN, FULL ⟨broad daylight⟩ **b :** PLAIN, OBVIOUS ⟨a broad hint⟩
**4 :** dialectal especially in pronunciation
**5 :** marked by lack of restraint, delicacy, or subtlety: **a** obsolete **:** OUTSPOKEN **b :** COARSE, RISQUÉ ⟨broad humor⟩
**6** of a vowel **:** OPEN — used specifically of a pronounced as in father
**7 a :** LIBERAL, TOLERANT ⟨broad views⟩ **b :** widely applicable or applied **:** GENERAL
**8 :** relating to the main or essential points ⟨broad outlines⟩ ☆
— **broad·ly** adverb
— **broad·ness** noun
²**broad** adverb (before 12th century)
**:** in a broad manner **:** FULLY
³**broad** noun (1659)
**1** British **:** an expansion of a river — often used in plural
**2** slang **:** WOMAN
**broad arrow** noun (14th century)
**1 :** an arrow with a flat barbed head
**2** British **:** a mark shaped like a broad arrow that identifies government property including clothing formerly worn by convicts
**broad·ax** or **broad·axe** \'brō-,daks\ noun (before 12th century)
**:** a large ax with a broad blade
**broad·band** \'brod-,band\ adjective (1956)
**1 :** operating at, responsive to, or comprising a wide band of frequencies ⟨a broadband radio antenna⟩
**2 :** of, relating to, or being a communications network in which a frequency range is divided into multiple independent channels for simultaneous transmission of signals (as voice, data, or video)
**broad bean** noun (1783)
**:** the large flat edible seed of an Old World upright vetch (Vicia faba); also **:** this plant widely grown for its seeds and as fodder
**broad–brush** \'brod-,brəsh\ adjective (1967)
**:** GENERAL, NONSPECIFIC
¹**broad·cast** \'brod-,kast\ adjective (1767)
**1 :** cast or scattered in all directions
**2 :** made public by means of radio or television
**3 :** of or relating to radio or television broadcasting
²**broadcast** verb **broadcast** also **broad·cast·ed; broad·cast·ing** (1813)
transitive verb
**1 :** to scatter or sow (as seed) broadcast
**2 :** to make widely known

**3 :** to transmit or make public by means of radio or television
intransitive verb
**1 :** to transmit a broadcast
**2 :** to speak or perform on a broadcast program
— **broad·cast·er** noun
³**broadcast** adverb (1814)
**:** to or over a broad area
⁴**broadcast** noun (1922)
**1 :** the act of transmitting sound or images by radio or television
**2 :** a single radio or television program
**Broad Church** adjective (1853)
**:** of or relating to a liberal party in the Anglican communion especially in the later 19th century
**broad·cloth** \'brod-,klȯth\ noun (15th century)
**1 :** a twilled napped woolen or worsted fabric with smooth lustrous face and dense texture
**2 :** a fabric usually of cotton, silk, or rayon made in plain and rib weaves with soft semigloss finish
**broad·en** \'brod-°n\ verb **broad·ened; broad·en·ing** \'brod-niŋ, 'bro-d°n-iŋ\ (1726)
transitive verb
**:** to make broader
intransitive verb
**:** to become broad
**broad–gauge** \'brod-'gāj\ or **broad–gauged** \-'gājd\ adjective (1858)
**1 :** wide in area or scope ⟨a broad-gauge effort⟩
**2 :** comprehensive in outlook, range, or capability ⟨a broad-gauge statesman⟩
**broad gauge** noun (1844)
**:** a railroad gauge wider than standard gauge
**broad jump** noun (1872)
**:** LONG JUMP
— **broad jumper** noun
**broad–leaved** \-'lēvd\ or **broad–leaf** \-'lēf\ also **broad–leafed** \-'lēft\ adjective (1552)
**1 :** having broad leaves; specifically **:** having leaves that are not needles
**2 :** composed of broad-leaved plants ⟨broad-leaved forests⟩
¹**broad·loom** \-,lüm\ adjective (1925)
**:** woven on a wide loom; also **:** so woven in solid color
²**broadloom** noun (1926)
**:** a broadloom carpet
**broad–mind·ed** \'brod-'mīn-dəd, -,mīn-\ adjective (1882)
**1 :** tolerant of varied views
**2 :** inclined to condone minor departures from conventional behavior
— **broad–mind·ed·ly** adverb
— **broad–mind·ed·ness** noun
**broad·scale** \-,skā(ə)l\ adjective (1939)
**:** broad in extent, range, or effect
**broad·sheet** \-,shēt\ noun (1705)
**1 :** BROADSIDE 1

☆ **SYNONYMS**
**Broad, wide, deep** mean having horizontal extent. BROAD and WIDE apply to a surface measured or viewed from side to side ⟨a broad avenue⟩. WIDE is more common when units of measurement are mentioned ⟨rugs eight feet wide⟩ or applied to unfilled space between limits ⟨a wide doorway⟩. BROAD is preferred when full horizontal extent is considered ⟨broad shoulders⟩. DEEP may indicate horizontal extent away from the observer or from a front or peripheral point ⟨a deep cupboard⟩ ⟨deep woods⟩.

\ə\ **abut** \ᵊ\ **kitten** \ər\ **further** \a\ **ash** \ā\ **ace** \ä\ **mop, mar** \au̇\ **out** \ch\ **chin** \e\ **bet** \ē\ **easy** \g\ **go** \i\ **hit** \ī\ **ice** \j\ **job** \ŋ\ **sing** \ō\ **go** \ȯ\ **law** \ȯi\ **boy** \th\ **thin** \t͟h\ **the** \ü\ **loot** \u̇\ **foot** \y\ **yet** \zh\ **vision** see also Guide to Pronunciation

**2** *British* : a newspaper with full-size pages as distinguished from a tabloid

**¹broad·side** \-ˌsīd\ *noun* (1575)
**1 a** (1) : a sizable sheet of paper printed on one side (2) : a sheet printed on one or both sides and folded **b** : something (as a ballad) printed on a broadside
**2** *archaic* : the side of a ship above the waterline
**3 a** : all the guns on one side of a ship; *also* : their simultaneous discharge **b** : a volley of abuse or denunciation
**4** : a broad or unbroken surface

**²broadside** *adjective* (1646)
: directed or placed broadside ⟨a *broadside* attack⟩

**³broadside** *adverb* (1870)
**1 a** : with the side forward or toward a given point : SIDEWAYS ⟨turned *broadside*⟩ **b** : directly from the side ⟨the car was hit *broadside*⟩
**2** : in one volley
**3** : at random

**⁴broadside** *transitive verb* (1981)
: to hit broadside ⟨the car was *broadsided*⟩

**broad–spectrum** *adjective* (1952)
: effective against a wide range of organisms (as insects or bacteria) ⟨*broad-spectrum* antibiotic⟩

**broad·sword** \'brȯd-ˌsȯrd, -ˌsȯrd\ *noun* (before 12th century)
: a large heavy sword with a broad blade for cutting rather than thrusting

**broad·tail** \-ˌtāl\ *noun* (1892)
**1** : KARAKUL 1
**2** : the fur or skin of a very young or premature karakul lamb having a flat and wavy appearance resembling moiré silk

**Broad·way** \'brȯd-ˌwā, -ˈwā\ *noun* [*Broadway*, street in New York City] (1835)
: the New York commercial theater and amusement world; *specifically* : playhouses located in the area between the Avenue of the Americas and Ninth Avenue and from W. 41st Street to W. 53d Street
— **Broadway** *adjective*
— **Broad·way·ite** \-ˌīt\ *noun*

**Brob·ding·nag·ian** \ˌbräb-diŋ-'na-gē-ən, -dig-'na-\ *adjective* [*Brobdingnag*, imaginary land of giants in *Gulliver's Travels*, by Jonathan Swift] (1728)
: marked by tremendous size
— **Brobdingnagian** *noun*

**bro·cade** \brō-ˈkād\ *noun* [Spanish *brocado*, from Catalan *brocat*, from Italian *broccato*, from *broccare* to spur, brocade, from *brocco* small nail, from Latin *broccus* projecting] (1588)
**1** : a rich oriental silk fabric with raised patterns in gold and silver
**2** : a fabric characterized by raised designs
— **brocade** *transitive verb*
— **bro·cad·ed** *adjective*

**Bro·ca's area** \'brō-kəz-\ *noun* [Paul P. *Broca* (died 1880) French surgeon] (circa 1898)
: a brain center associated with the motor control of speech and usually located in the left side of the frontal lobe

**broc·a·telle** \ˌbrä-kə-'tel\ *noun* [French, from Italian *broccatello*, diminutive of *broccato*] (1669)
: a stiff decorating fabric with patterns in high relief

**broc·co·li** \'brä-kə-lē, 'brä-klē\ *noun* [Italian, plural of *broccolo* flowering top of a cabbage, diminutive of *brocco* small nail, sprout] (1699)
**1** *chiefly British* : a large hardy cauliflower
**2 a** : either of two garden vegetable plants closely related to the cabbage: (1) : one with a thick central stem and a compact head of dense usually green florets that is classified with the cauliflower (2) : one (*Brassica oleracea italica*) with slender stems and usually green or purple florets not arranged in a central head **b** : the stems and immature florets of broccoli used as food

**broccoli rabe** \-ˌräb\ *noun* [perhaps modification of Italian *broccoli di rapa*, literally, flowering tops of the turnip] (1976)
: a garden brassica (*Brassica rapa ruvo*) that is related to the turnip and produces edible leafy branching stalks and compact clusters of yellow florets — called also *broccoli raab* \-ˌräb, -ˌrab\, *rapini*

**bro·chette** \brō-'shet\ *noun* [French, from Old French *brochete*, from *broche* pointed tool — more at BROACH] (15th century)
: SKEWER; *also* : food broiled on a skewer

**bro·chure** \brō-'shu̇r, *British especially* 'brō-\ *noun* [French, from *brocher* to sew, from Middle French, to prick, from Old French *brochier*, from *broche*] (1748)
: PAMPHLET, BOOKLET; *especially* : one containing descriptive or advertising material

**brock** \'bräk\ *noun* [Middle English, from Old English *broc*, of Celtic origin; akin to Welsh *broch* badger] (before 12th century)
*British* : BADGER

**brock·age** \'brä-kij\ *noun* [English dialect *brock* rubbish + English *-age*] (1879)
: an imperfectly minted coin

**brock·et** \'brä-kət\ *noun* [Middle English *broket*, from Old North French *broquard*; akin to Old French *broche* tine of an antler, pointed tool — more at BROACH] (1837)
: any of several small deer (genus *Mazama*) of Central and South America with unbranched antlers

**bro·gan** \'brō-gən, -ˌgan; brō-'gan\ *noun* [Irish *brógán*, diminutive of *bróg*] (1835)
: a heavy shoe; *especially* : a coarse work shoe reaching to the ankle

**¹brogue** \'brōg\ *noun* [Irish *bróg* & Scottish Gaelic *bròg*, from Middle Irish *bróc*, probably from Old Norse *brōk* leg covering; akin to Old English *brōc* leg covering — more at BREECH] (1586)
**1** : a stout coarse shoe worn formerly in Ireland and the Scottish Highlands
**2** : a heavy shoe often with a hobnailed sole : BROGAN
**3** : a stout oxford shoe with perforations and usually a wing tip

**²brogue** *noun* [Irish *barróg* accent, speech impediment, literally, wrestling hold, tight grip] (1705)
: a dialect or regional pronunciation; *especially* : an Irish accent

**broi·der** \'brȯi-dər\ *transitive verb* [Middle English *broideren*, modification of Middle French *broder* — more at EMBROIDER] (14th century)
: EMBROIDER
— **broi·dery** \'brȯi-d(ə-)rē\ *noun*

**¹broil** \'brȯi(-ə)l\ *verb* [Middle English, from Middle French *bruler* to burn, modification of Latin *ustulare* to singe, from *urere* to burn] (14th century)
*transitive verb*
: to cook by direct exposure to radiant heat : GRILL
*intransitive verb*
: to be subjected to great or oppressive heat ⟨*broiling* in the sun⟩

**²broil** *noun* (1583)
: the act or state of broiling

**³broil** *verb* [Middle English, from Middle French *brouiller* to mix, broil, from Old French *brooilier*, from *breu* broth, of Germanic origin; akin to Old High German *brod* broth — more at BROTH] (15th century)
*intransitive verb*
: BRAWL
*transitive verb*
: EMBROIL

**⁴broil** *noun* (1525)
: a noisy disturbance : TUMULT; *especially* : BRAWL ⟨a tavern row . . . widens into a general *broil* —J. R. Green⟩

**broil·er** \'brȯi-lər\ *noun* (14th century)
**1** : one that broils

**2** : a bird fit for broiling; *especially* : a young chicken of up to 2½ pounds (1.14 kilograms) dressed weight

**¹broke** \'brōk\ *past of* BREAK

**²broke** *adjective* [Middle English, alteration of *broken*] (1710)
: PENNILESS

**bro·ken** \'brō-kən\ *adjective* [Middle English, from Old English *brocen*, from past participle of *brecan* to break] (13th century)
**1** : violently separated into parts : SHATTERED
**2** : damaged or altered by breaking: as **a** : having undergone or been subjected to fracture ⟨a *broken* leg⟩ **b** *of land surfaces* : being irregular, interrupted, or full of obstacles **c** : violated by transgression ⟨a *broken* promise⟩ **d** : DISCONTINUOUS, INTERRUPTED **e** : disrupted by change **f** *of a flower* : having an irregular, streaked, or blotched pattern especially from virus infection
**3 a** : made weak or infirm **b** : subdued completely : CRUSHED ⟨a *broken* spirit⟩ **c** : BANKRUPT **d** : reduced in rank
**4 a** : cut off : DISCONNECTED **b** : imperfectly spoken or written ⟨*broken* English⟩
**5** : not complete or full
**6** : disunited by divorce, separation, or desertion of one parent ⟨children from *broken* homes⟩ ⟨a *broken* family⟩
— **bro·ken·ly** *adverb*
— **bro·ken·ness** \-kə(n)-nəs\ *noun*

**broken–down** *adjective* (1817)
: WORN-OUT, DEBILITATED

**bro·ken–field** \-ˌfēld\ *adjective* (1923)
: characterized by quick changes in direction to avoid widely scattered tacklers ⟨a halfback known for *broken-field* running⟩

**bro·ken·heart·ed** \-'här-təd\ *adjective* (1526)
: overcome by grief or despair

**bro·ken–wind·ed** \-'win-dəd\ *adjective* (1580)
: affected with or as if with heaves

**bro·ker** \'brō-kər\ *noun* [Middle English, negotiator, from Anglo-French *brocour*] (14th century)
**1** : one who acts as an intermediary: as **a** : an agent who arranges marriages **b** : an agent who negotiates contracts of purchase and sale (as of real estate, commodities, or securities)
**2** : POWER BROKER
— **broker** *verb*
— **bro·ker·ing** \'brō-k(ə-)riŋ\ *noun*

**bro·ker·age** \'brō-k(ə-)rij\ *noun* (15th century)
**1** : the business or establishment of a broker
**2** : a broker's fee or commission

**bro·kered** \-kərd\ *adjective* (1967)
: arranged or controlled by power brokers ⟨a *brokered* political convention⟩

**bro·king** \-kiŋ\ *noun* (1569)
*chiefly British* : the business of a broker : BROKERAGE

**brol·ly** \'brä-lē\ *noun, plural* **brollies** [by shortening & alteration] (circa 1874)
*chiefly British* : UMBRELLA

**brom-** *or* **bromo-** *combining form* [probably from French *brome*, from Greek *brōmos* bad smell]
: bromine ⟨*brom*ide⟩

**bro·mate** \'brō-ˌmāt\ *noun* (circa 1836)
: a salt of bromic acid

**brome–grass** \'brōm-ˌgras\ *noun* [New Latin *Bromus*, from Latin *bromos* oats, from Greek] (circa 1791)
: any of a large genus (*Bromus*) of tall grasses often having drooping spikelets

**bro·me·lain** \'brō-mə-lən, -ˌlān\ *also* **bro·me·lin** \'brō-mə-lən, brō-'mē-\ *noun* [*bromelain* by alteration of *bromelin*, from New Latin *Bromelia*] (1894)
: a protease obtained especially from the pineapple

**bro·me·li·ad** \brō-'mē-lē-ˌad\ *noun* [New Latin *Bromelia*, genus of tropical American plants, from Olaf *Bromelius* (died 1705) Swedish botanist] (1866)

**:** any of a family (Bromeliaceae) of chiefly tropical American usually epiphytic herbaceous plants including the pineapple, Spanish moss, and various ornamentals

**bro·mic acid** \'brō-mik-\ *noun* (1828)
**:** an unstable strongly oxidizing acid HBrO₃ known only in solution or in the form of its salts

**bro·mide** \'brō-ˌmīd\ *noun* (1836)
**1 :** a binary compound of bromine with another element or a radical including some (as potassium bromide) used as sedatives
**2 a :** a commonplace or tiresome person **:** BORE **b :** a commonplace or hackneyed statement or notion

**bro·mid·ic** \brō-'mi-dik\ *adjective* (1906)
**:** lacking in originality **:** TRITE

**bro·mi·nate** \'brō-mə-ˌnāt\ *transitive verb* **-nat·ed; -nat·ing** (1873)
**:** to treat or cause to combine with bromine or a compound of bromine
— **bro·mi·na·tion** \ˌbrō-mə-'nā-shən\ *noun*

**bro·mine** \'brō-ˌmēn\ *noun* [French *brome* bromine + English ²-*ine*] (1827)
**:** a nonmetallic halogen element that is isolated as a deep red corrosive toxic volatile liquid of disagreeable odor — see ELEMENT table

**bro·mo** \'brō-(ˌ)mō\ *noun, plural* **bromos** [*brom-*] (1923)
**:** a dose of a proprietary effervescent headache remedy and antacid

**bro·mo·crip·tine** \ˌbrō-mō-'krip-ˌtēn, -tən\ *noun* [by shortening & alteration from *bromoergocryptine,* from *brom-* + *ergocryptine,* an ergot derivative, from *ergo-* + Greek *kryptos* hidden — more at CRYPT] (1975)
**:** a polypeptide ergot derivative C₃₂H₄₀Br-N₅O₅ that mimics the activity of dopamine in inhibiting prolactin secretion

**bro·mo·ura·cil** \ˌbrō-mō-'yür-ə-ˌsil, -səl\ *noun* (1960)
**:** a mutagenic uracil derivative C₄H₃N₂O₂Br that is an analogue of thymine and pairs readily with adenine and sometimes with guanine

**brom·thy·mol blue** \ˌbrōm-'thī-ˌmȯl-\ *noun* (1920)
**:** a dye derived from thymol that is an acid-base indicator — called also *bro·mo·thy·mol blue* \ˌbrō-mō-'thī-ˌmȯl-\

**bronc** \'bräŋk\ *noun* [short for *bronco*] (1893)
**:** an unbroken or imperfectly broken range horse of western North America; *broadly*
**:** MUSTANG

**bronch-** *or* **broncho-** *combining form* [Late Latin, from Greek, from *bronchos* windpipe]
**:** bronchial tube **:** bronchial ⟨*bronch*itis⟩

**bronchi-** *or* **bronchio-** *combining form* [New Latin, from *bronchia,* plural, branches of the bronchi, from Late Latin, from Greek, diminutive of *bronchos*]
**:** bronchial tubes ⟨*bronchi*ectasis⟩

**bron·chi·al** \'bräŋ-kē-əl\ *adjective* (circa 1735)
**:** of or relating to the bronchi or their ramifications in the lungs
— **bron·chi·al·ly** \-kē-ə-lē\ *adverb*

**bronchial asthma** *noun* (circa 1881)
**:** asthma resulting from spasmodic contraction of bronchial muscles

**bronchial tube** *noun* (1847)
**:** a primary bronchus or any of its branches

**bron·chi·ec·ta·sis** \ˌbräŋ-kē-'ek-tə-səs\ *noun* [New Latin, from *bronchi-* + Greek *ektasis* extension — more at ATELECTASIS] (circa 1860)
**:** a chronic dilatation of bronchi or bronchioles

**bron·chi·ole** \'bräŋ-kē-ˌōl\ *noun* [New Latin *bronchiolum,* diminutive of *bronchia*] (circa 1860)
**:** a minute thin-walled branch of a bronchus
— **bron·chi·o·lar** \ˌbräŋ-kē-'ō-lər\ *adjective*

**bron·chi·tis** \brän-'kī-təs, bräŋ-\ *noun* [New Latin] (1808)
**:** acute or chronic inflammation of the bronchial tubes; *also* **:** a disease marked by this
— **bron·chit·ic** \-'ki-tik\ *adjective*

**bron·cho·di·la·tor** \ˌbrän-(ˌ)kō-dī-'lā-tər, -'dī-,\ *noun* (1903)
**:** a drug that relaxes bronchial muscle resulting in expansion of the bronchial air passages
— **bronchodilator** *adjective*

**bron·cho·gen·ic** \ˌbräŋ-kə-'je-nik\ *adjective* (1927)
**:** of, relating to, or arising in or by way of the air passages of the lungs ⟨*bronchogenic* carcinoma⟩

**bron·cho·pneu·mo·nia** \ˌbräŋ-(ˌ)kō-nu̇-'mō-nyə, -nyu̇-\ *noun* [New Latin] (1858)
**:** pneumonia involving many relatively small areas of lung tissue

**bron·cho·scope** \'bräŋ-kə-ˌskōp\ *noun* [International Scientific Vocabulary] (1899)
**:** a tubular illuminated instrument used for inspecting or passing instruments into the bronchi
— **bron·cho·scop·ic** \ˌbräŋ-kə-'skä-pik\ *adjective*
— **bron·chos·co·pist** \brän-'käs-kə-pist, bräŋ-\ *noun*
— **bron·chos·co·py** \-pē\ *noun*

**bron·cho·spasm** \'bräŋ-kə-ˌspa-zəm\ *noun* (circa 1901)
**:** constriction of the air passages of the lung (as in asthma) by spasmodic contraction of the bronchial muscles
— **bron·cho·spas·tic** \ˌbräŋ-kə-'spas-tik\ *adjective*

**bron·chus** \'bräŋ-kəs\ *noun, plural* **bron·chi** \'bräŋ-ˌkī, -ˌkē\ [New Latin, from Greek *bronchos*] (circa 1706)
**:** either of the two primary divisions of the trachea that lead respectively into the right and the left lung; *broadly* **:** BRONCHIAL TUBE

**bron·co** *also* **bron·cho** \'bräŋ-(ˌ)kō\ *noun, plural* **broncos** *also* **bronchos** [Mexican Spanish, from Spanish, literally, rough, wild] (1850)
**:** BRONC

**bron·co·bust·er** \-ˌbəs-tər\ *noun* (1887)
**:** one who breaks wild horses to the saddle

**bron·to·sau·rus** \ˌbrän-tə-'sȯr-əs\ *also* **bron·to·saur** \'brän-tə-ˌsȯr\ *noun* [New Latin, from Greek *brontē* thunder + *sauros* lizard; akin to Greek *bremein* to roar] (1905)
**:** any of a genus (*Apatosaurus* synonym *Brontosaurus*) of large sauropod dinosaurs of the Jurassic — called also *apatosaurus* ◆

**Bronx cheer** \'bräŋ(k)s-\ *noun* [*Bronx,* borough of New York City] (1929)
**:** RASPBERRY 2

**¹bronze** \'bränz\ *transitive verb* **bronzed; bronz·ing** (1645)
**:** to give the appearance of bronze to ⟨a *bronzed* sculpture⟩; *also* **:** TAN 2
— **bronz·er** *noun*

**²bronze** *noun, often attributive* [French, from Italian *bronzo*] (1739)
**1 a :** an alloy of copper and tin and sometimes other elements **b :** any of various copper-base alloys with little or no tin
**2 :** a sculpture or artifact of bronze
**3 :** a moderate yellowish brown
— **bronzy** \'brän-zē\ *adjective*

**Bronze Age** *noun* (1865)
**:** the period of ancient human culture characterized by the use of bronze that began between 4000 and 3000 B.C. and ended with the advent of the Iron Age

**Bronze Star Medal** *noun* (1944)
**:** a U.S. military decoration awarded for heroic or meritorious service not involving aerial flights

**bronz·ing** *noun* (1868)
**:** a bronze coloring or discoloration (as of leaves)

**brooch** \'brōch *also* 'brüch\ *noun* [Middle English *broche* pointed tool, brooch — more at BROACH] (13th century)
**:** an ornament that is held by a pin or clasp and is worn at or near the neck

**¹brood** \'brüd\ *noun* [Middle English, from Old English *brōd;* akin to Old English *beorma* yeast — more at BARM] (before 12th century)
**1 :** the young of an animal or a family of young; *especially* **:** the young (as of a bird or insect) hatched or cared for at one time
**2 :** a group having a common nature or origin

**²brood** *adjective* (15th century)
**:** kept for breeding ⟨a *brood* flock⟩

**³brood** (15th century)
*transitive verb*
**1 a :** to sit on or incubate (eggs) **b :** to produce by or as if by incubation **:** HATCH
**2** *of a bird* **:** to cover (young) with the wings
**3 :** to think anxiously or gloomily about **:** PONDER
*intransitive verb*
**1 a** *of a bird* **:** to brood eggs or young **b :** to sit quietly and thoughtfully **:** MEDITATE
**2 :** HOVER, LOOM
**3 a :** to dwell gloomily on a subject **:** WORRY **b :** to be in a state of depression
— **brood·ing·ly** \'brü-diŋ-lē\ *adverb*

**brood·er** \'brü-dər\ *noun* (1599)
**1 :** one that broods
**2 :** a heated structure used for raising young fowl

**brood·mare** \'brüd-ˌmar, -ˌmer\ *noun* (1821)
**:** a mare kept for breeding

**broody** \'brü-dē\ *adjective* (1523)
**1 :** being in a state of readiness to brood eggs that is characterized by cessation of laying and by marked changes in behavior and physiology ⟨a *broody* hen⟩
**2 :** given or conducive to introspection **:** CONTEMPLATIVE, MOODY
— **brood·i·ness** *noun*

**¹brook** \'bru̇k\ *noun* [Middle English, from Old English *brōc;* akin to Old High German *bruoh* marshy ground] (before 12th century)
**:** CREEK 2

**²brook** *transitive verb* [Middle English *brouken* to use, enjoy, from Old English *brūcan;* akin to Old High German *brūhhan* to use, Latin *frui* to enjoy] (15th century)
**:** to stand for **:** TOLERATE ⟨he would *brook* no interference with his plans⟩

**brook·ie** \'bru̇-kē\ *noun* (1933)
**:** BROOK TROUT

**brook·ite** \'bru̇-ˌkīt\ *noun* [Henry J. *Brooke* (died 1857) English mineralogist] (1825)

---

◇ **WORD HISTORY**
**brontosaurus** Although it has been ousted in scientific nomenclature, the word *brontosaurus* is part of the vocabulary of all dinosaur aficionados. *Brontosaurus*—according to a literal translation of its Greek elements, "thunder lizard"—was the name given by American paleontologist Edward Drinker Cope (1840–97) to a genus of gigantic sauropods whose fossilized bones he had unearthed while affiliated with the U.S. Geological Survey in the 1870s. Unbeknownst to Cope, the same sauropod had already been discovered by his archrival, Othniel Charles Marsh (1831–99), who named the animal *Apatosaurus* "deceptive lizard." Not until the specimens were studied in museums years later was it discovered that *Brontosaurus* and *Apatosaurus* were one and the same. Biologists' rules of classification are strict and clear: the first name given to a new species is the correct one. By the time the mistake was discovered, however, *Brontosaurus* was firmly entrenched not just in scientific literature but in the public imagination as well.

---

\ə\ **abut** \ᵊ\ **kitten** \ər\ **further** \a\ **ash** \ā\ **ace**
\ä\ **mop, mar** \au̇\ **out** \ch\ **chin** \e\ **bet** \ē\ **easy**
\g\ **go** \i\ **hit** \ī\ **ice** \j\ **job** \ŋ\ **sing** \ō\ **go**
\ȯ\ **law** \ȯi\ **boy** \th\ **thin** \t̲h̲\ **the** \ü\ **loot** \u̇\ **foot**
\y\ **yet** \zh\ **vision**    *see also* Guide to Pronunciation

: titanium dioxide TiO$_2$ occurring as a mineral in orthorhombic crystals commonly translucent brown or opaque brown to black

**brook·let** \'brůk-klət\ *noun* (1813)
: a small brook

**Brook·lyn·ese** \,brů-klə-'nēz, -'nēs\ *noun* [*Brooklyn*, borough of New York City] (1939)
: the vernacular speech of greater New York City and environs

**brook trout** *noun* (1836)
: the common speckled cold-water char (*Salvelinus fontinalis*) of North America

**¹broom** \'brüm, 'brům\ *noun* [Middle English, from Old English *brōm;* akin to Old High German *brāmo* bramble] (before 12th century)
**1** : any of various leguminous shrubs (especially genera *Cytisus* and *Genista*) with long slender branches, small leaves, and usually showy yellow flowers; *especially* : SCOTCH BROOM
**2** : a bundle of firm stiff twigs or fibers bound together on a long handle for sweeping and brushing

**²broom** *transitive verb* (1838)
**1** : to sweep with or as if with a broom
**2** : to finish (as a concrete surface) by means of a broom

**broom·ball** \-,ból\ *noun* (1933)
: a variation of ice hockey played on ice without skates and with brooms and a soccer ball used instead of sticks and a puck
— **broom·ball·er** \-,bó-lər\ *noun*

**broom·corn** \-,kórn\ *noun* (circa 1782)
: any of several tall cultivated sorghums having stiff-branched panicles used in brooms and brushes

**broom·rape** \-,rāp\ *noun* (1578)
: any of a genus (*Orobanche* of the family Orobanchaceae, the broomrape family) of herbs that have leaves modified to scales and that grow as parasites on the roots of other plants

**broom·stick** \-,stik\ *noun* (1683)
: the long thin handle of a broom

**brose** \'brōz\ *noun* [perhaps alteration of Scots *bruis* broth, from Middle English *brewes,* from Old French *broez,* nominative singular of *broet,* diminutive of *breu* broth — more at BROIL] (1515)
: a chiefly Scottish dish made with a boiling liquid and meal

**broth** \'bróth\ *noun, plural* **broths** \'bróths, 'bróthz\ [Middle English, from Old English; akin to Old High German *brod* broth, Old English *brēowan* to brew] (before 12th century)
**1** : liquid in which meat, fish, cereal grains, or vegetables have been cooked : STOCK
**2** : a fluid culture medium

**broth·el** \'brä-thəl, 'bró- *also* -thəl\ *noun* [Middle English, worthless fellow, prostitute, from *brothen,* past participle of *brethen* to waste away, go to ruin, from Old English *brēothan* to waste away; akin to Old English *brēotan* to break — more at BRITTLE] (circa 1593)
: BORDELLO

**broth·er** \'brə-thər\ *noun, plural* **brothers** *also* **breth·ren** \'breth-rən; 'bre-thə-rən, -thərn\ [Middle English, from Old English *brōthor;* akin to Old High German *bruodar* brother, Latin *frater,* Greek *phratēr* member of the same clan] (before 12th century)
**1** : a male who has the same parents as another or one parent in common with another
**2** : one related to another by common ties or interests
**3** : a fellow member — used as a title for ministers in some evangelical denominations
**4** : one of a type similar to another
**5 a** : KINSMAN **b** : one who shares with another a common national or racial origin; *especially* : SOUL BROTHER
**6 a** *capitalized* : a member of a congregation of men not in holy orders and usually in hospital or school work **b** : a member of a men's religious order who is not preparing for or is not ready for holy orders ⟨a lay *brother*⟩

**broth·er·hood** \'brə-thər-,hůd\ *noun* [Middle English *brotherhede, brotherhod,* alteration of *brotherrede,* from Old English *brōthorrǣden,* from *brōthor* + *rǣden* condition — more at KINDRED] (14th century)
**1** : the quality or state of being brothers
**2** : FELLOWSHIP, ALLIANCE
**3** : an association (as a labor union) for a particular purpose
**4** : the whole body of persons engaged in a business or profession

**broth·er–in–law** \'brəth-rən-,ló, 'brə-thə-; 'brə-thərn-\ *noun, plural* **broth·ers–in–law** \'brə-thər-zən-\ (14th century)
**1** : the brother of one's spouse
**2 a** : the husband of one's sister **b** : the husband of one's spouse's sister

**broth·er·ly** \'brə-thər-lē\ *adjective* (before 12th century)
**1** : of or relating to brothers
**2** : natural or becoming to brothers : AFFECTIONATE ⟨*brotherly* love⟩
— **broth·er·li·ness** *noun*
— **brotherly** *adverb*

**brougham** \'brü-(ə)m, 'brō(-ə)m\ *noun* [Henry Peter *Brougham,* Baron Brougham and Vaux (died 1868) Scottish jurist] (1851)
: a light closed horse-drawn carriage with the driver outside in front

**brought** *past and past participle of* BRING

**brou·ha·ha** \'brü-,hä-,hä, ,brü-,hä-'hä, brü-'hä-,hä\ *noun* [French] (1890)
: HUBBUB, UPROAR

**¹brow** \'brau\ *noun* [Middle English, from Old English *brū;* akin to Old Norse *brūn* eyebrow, Greek *ophrys,* Sanskrit *bhrū*] (before 12th century)
**1 a** : EYEBROW **b** : FOREHEAD
**2** : the projecting upper part or margin of a steep place
**3** : EXPRESSION, MIEN

**²brow** *noun* [perhaps from Danish or Swedish *brother* bridge; akin to Old English *brycg* bridge] (1867)
: GANGPLANK

**brow·beat** \'brau-,bēt\ *transitive verb* **-beat; -beat·en** \-'bē-t°n\ *or* **-beat; -beat·ing** (1581)
: to intimidate or disconcert by a stern manner or arrogant speech : BULLY
**synonym** see INTIMIDATE

**browed** \'braud\ *adjective* (15th century)
: having brows of a specified nature — used in combination ⟨smooth-*browed*⟩

**¹brown** \'braun\ *adjective* [Middle English *broun,* from Old English *brūn;* akin to Old High German *brūn* brown, Greek *phrynē* toad] (before 12th century)
: of the color brown; *especially* : of dark or tanned complexion

**²brown** *noun* (13th century)
**1** : any of a group of colors between red and yellow in hue, of medium to low lightness, and of moderate to low saturation
**2** : a brown-skinned person
— **brown·ish** \'brau-nish\ *adjective*
— **browny** \-nē\ *adjective*

**³brown** (14th century)
*intransitive verb*
: to become brown
*transitive verb*
: to make brown

**brown alga** *noun* (circa 1899)
: any of a division (Phaeophyta) of variable mostly marine algae with chlorophyll masked by brown pigment

**brown bagging** *noun* (1959)
**1** : the practice of carrying (as to work) one's lunch usually in a brown paper bag
**2** : the practice of carrying a bottle of liquor into a restaurant or club where setups are available
— **brown–bag** \'braun-,bag\ *verb or adjective*
— **brown bagger** *noun*

**brown bear** *noun* (1805)

: any of several bears predominantly brown in color that are sometimes considered a single species (*Ursus arctos*) including the grizzly bear and that formerly inhabited western North America from the barrens of Alaska to northern Mexico and much of Europe and Asia but are now much restricted in range

**brown Bet·ty** \-'be-tē\ *noun* (1864)
: a baked pudding of apples, bread crumbs, and spices

**brown bread** \-,bred\ *noun* (14th century)
**1** : bread made of whole wheat flour
**2** : a dark brown steamed bread made usually of cornmeal, white or whole wheat flours, molasses, soda, and milk or water

**brown coal** *noun* (circa 1828)
: LIGNITE

**brown dwarf** *noun* (1978)
: a celestial object that is much smaller than a normal star and has insufficient mass for nuclear fusion to begin but that is hot enough to radiate energy especially at infrared wavelengths

**brown earth** *noun* (1932)
: any of a group of intrazonal soils developed in temperate humid regions under deciduous forests and characterized by a dark brown mull horizon that grades through lighter colored soil into parent material

**brown–eyed Su·san** \'brau-,nīd-'sü-z°n\ *noun* [*brown-eyed* + *Susan* (as in *black-eyed Susan*)] (1896)
: a dark-centered coneflower (*Rudbeckia triloba*) of eastern North America often having tripartite lower leaves

**brown fat** *noun* (1951)
: a mammalian heat-producing tissue occurring especially in human newborns and in hibernators — called also *brown adipose tissue*

**Brown·ian motion** \'brau-nē-ən-\ *noun* [Robert *Brown* (died 1858) Scottish botanist] (circa 1889)
: a random movement of microscopic particles suspended in liquids or gases resulting from the impact of molecules of the fluid surrounding the particles — called also *Brownian movement*

**brown·ie** \'brau-nē\ *noun* [¹*brown*] (circa 1500)
**1** : a legendary good-natured elf that performs helpful services at night
**2** *capitalized* : a member of a program of the Girl Scouts for girls in the first through third grades in school
**3** : a small square or rectangle of rich usually chocolate cake often containing nuts

**brownie point** *noun, often B capitalized* (circa 1962)
: a credit regarded as earned especially by currying favor (as with a superior)

**Brow·ning automatic rifle** \'brau-niŋ-\ *noun* [John M. *Browning* (died 1926) American designer of firearms] (1920)
: a .30 caliber gas-operated air-cooled magazine-fed automatic rifle often provided with a rest for the barrel

**Browning machine gun** *noun* (1918)
: a .30 or .50 caliber recoil-operated air- or water-cooled machine gun fed by a cartridge belt

**brown lung** *noun* (1969)
: BYSSINOSIS

**brown·nose** \'brau(n)-,nōz\ *transitive verb* [from the implication that servility is equivalent to kissing the hinder parts of the person from whom advancement is sought] (circa 1939) *slang*
: to ingratiate oneself with : curry favor with
— **brownnose** *noun*
— **brown·nos·er** *noun*

**brown·out** \'brau-,naut\ *noun* [*brown* + *black-out*] (1942)
: a period of reduced voltage of electricity caused especially by high demand and resulting in subnormal illumination

**brown pelican** *noun* (1823)

: a pelican (*Pelecanus occidentalis*) of American coasts that has a brown body and a chiefly white or white with yellow head

**brown rat** *noun* (1826)
: a common domestic rat (*Rattus norvegicus*) that has been introduced worldwide — called also *Norway rat*

**brown recluse spider** *noun* (1964)
: a venomous spider (*Loxosceles reclusa*) of the U.S. that has a violin-shaped mark on the cephalothorax and produces a dangerous cytotoxin

**brown rice** *noun* (1916)
: hulled but unpolished rice that retains most of the bran layers, endosperm, and germ

**brown rot** *noun* (1894)
: a disease of stone fruits caused by fungi (genus *Monilinia*, especially *M. fructicola*)

**brown sauce** *noun* (1878)
: a sauce consisting typically of stock thickened with flour browned in fat

**brown·shirt** \'braún-,shərt\ *noun, often capitalized* (1932)
: NAZI; *especially* : STORM TROOPER

**brown·stone** \-,stōn\ *noun* (1858)
**1** : a reddish brown sandstone used for building
**2** : a dwelling faced with brownstone

**brown study** *noun* (1532)
: a state of serious absorption or abstraction

**brown sugar** *noun* (1704)
: soft sugar whose crystals are covered by a film of refined dark syrup

**Brown Swiss** *noun* (1902)
: any of a breed of large hardy brown dairy cattle originating in Switzerland

**brown–tail moth** \'braún-,tāl-\ *noun* (1782)
: a tussock moth (*Euproctis chrysorrhoea*) introduced in the U.S. and having larvae which feed on foliage and are irritating to the skin

**brown trout** *noun* (1886)
: a speckled European trout (*Salmo trutta*) widely introduced as a game fish

**brow·ridge** \'braú-,rij\ *noun* (1898)
: a prominence of the frontal bone above the eye caused by the projection of the frontal air sinuses

**¹browse** \'braúz\ *verb* **browsed; browsing** (15th century)
*transitive verb*
**1 a** : to consume as browse **b** : GRAZE
**2** : to look over casually : SKIM
*intransitive verb*
**1 a** : to feed on or as if on browse **b** : GRAZE
**2 a** : to skim through a book reading at random passages that catch the eye **b** : to look over or through an aggregate of things casually especially in search of something of interest
— **brows·er** *noun*

**²browse** *noun* [probably modification of Middle French *brouts*, plural of *brout* sprout, from Old French *brost*, of Germanic origin; akin to Old Saxon *brustian* to sprout, and perhaps to Old English *brēost* breast] (1523)
**1** : tender shoots, twigs, and leaves of trees and shrubs used by animals for food
**2** : an act or instance of browsing

**bru·cel·la** \brü-'se-lə\ *noun, plural* **-cel·lae** \-'se-(,)lē\ *or* **-cel·las** [New Latin, from Sir David *Bruce*] (1930)
: any of a genus (*Brucella*) of nonmotile pleomorphic bacteria that cause disease in humans and domestic animals

**bru·cel·lo·sis** \,brü-sə-'lō-səs\ *noun, plural* **-lo·ses** \-,sēz\ [New Latin] (1930)
: infection or disease caused by brucellae

**bru·cine** \'brü-,sēn\ *noun* [probably from French, from New Latin *Brucea* (genus name of *Brucea antidysenterica*, a shrub)] (1823)
: a poisonous alkaloid $C_{23}H_{26}N_2O_4$ found with strychnine especially in nux vomica

**bru·in** \'brü-ən\ *noun* [Middle Dutch, name of the bear in *Reynard the Fox*] (15th century)
: BEAR 1

**¹bruise** \'brüz\ *verb* **bruised; bruis·ing** [Middle English *brusen, brisen*, from Middle

French & Old English; Middle French *bruisier* to break, of Celtic origin; akin to Old Irish *bruid* he shatters; Old English *brȳsan* to bruise; akin to Old Irish *bruid*, Latin *frustum* piece] (14th century)
*transitive verb*
**1 a** *archaic* : DISABLE **b** : BATTER, DENT
**2** : to inflict a bruise on : CONTUSE
**3** : to break down (as leaves or berries) by pounding : CRUSH
**4** : WOUND, INJURE; *especially* : to inflict psychological hurt on
*intransitive verb*
**1** : to inflict a bruise
**2** : to undergo bruising

**²bruise** *noun* (1541)
**1 a** : an injury involving rupture of small blood vessels and discoloration without a break in the overlying skin : CONTUSION **b** : a similar injury to plant tissue
**2** : ABRASION, SCRATCH
**3** : an injury especially to the feelings

**bruis·er** \'brü-zər\ *noun* (1744)
: a big husky man

**¹bruit** *noun* [Middle English, from Middle French, from Old French, noise] (15th century)
**1** \'brüt\ *archaic* **a** : NOISE, DIN **b** : REPORT, RUMOR
**2** \'brü-ē\ [French, literally, noise] : any of several generally abnormal sounds heard on auscultation

**²bruit** \'brüt\ *transitive verb* (15th century)
: to noise abroad : REPORT

**bru·mal** \'brü-məl\ *adjective* [Latin *brumalis*, from *bruma* winter] (1513)
*archaic* : indicative of or occurring in the winter

**brum·by** \'brəm-bē\ *noun, plural* **brumbies** [origin unknown] (1880)
*Australian* : a wild or unbroken horse

**brume** \'brüm\ *noun* [French, mist, winter, from Old Provençal *bruma*, from Latin, winter solstice, winter; akin to Latin *brevis* short — more at BRIEF] (1808)
: MIST, FOG
— **bru·mous** \'brü-məs\ *adjective*

**brum·ma·gem** \'brə-mi-jəm\ *adjective* [alteration of *Birmingham*, England, the source in the 17th century of counterfeit groats] (1637)
**1** : SPURIOUS; *also* : cheaply showy : TAWDRY
— **brummagem** *noun*

**brunch** \'brənch\ *noun* [*breakfast* + l*unch*] (1896)
: a meal usually taken late in the morning that combines a late breakfast and an early lunch

**¹bru·net** *or* **bru·nette** \brü-'net\ *noun* (circa 1539)
: a person having brown or black hair and usually a relatively dark complexion

**²brunet** *or* **brunette** *adjective* [French *brunet*, masculine, *brunette*, feminine, brownish, from Old French, from *brun* brown, from Medieval Latin *brunus*, of Germanic origin; akin to Old High German *brūn* brown] (1752)
**1** : being a brunet
**2** : of a dark-brown or black color ⟨*brunet* hair⟩

**Brun·hild** \'brün-,hilt\ *noun* [German]
: a queen in Germanic legend won by Siegfried for Gunther

**bru·ni·zem** \'brü-nə-,zem\ *noun* [*bruni-* (from Medieval Latin *brunus* brown) + *-zem* earth (as in *chernozem*)] (1953)
: any of a zonal group of deep dark prairie soils developed from loess

**Bruns·wick stew** \'brənz-(,)wik-\ *noun* [*Brunswick* county, Va.] (1856)
: a stew made of vegetables and usually two meats (as chicken and squirrel)

**brunt** \'brənt\ *noun* [Middle English] (15th century)
**1** : the principal force, shock, or stress (as of an attack)
**2** : the greater part : BURDEN

**¹brush** \'brəsh\ *noun* [Middle English *brusch*, from Middle French *broce*] (14th century)
**1** : BRUSHWOOD
**2 a** : scrub vegetation **b** : land covered with scrub vegetation

**²brush** *noun* [Middle English *brusshe*, from Middle French *broisse*, from Old French *broce*] (14th century)
**1** : a device composed of bristles typically set into a handle and used especially for sweeping, smoothing, scrubbing, or painting
**2** : something resembling a brush: as **a** : a bushy tail **b** : a feather tuft worn on a hat
**3** : an electrical conductor that makes sliding contact between a stationary and a moving part (as of a generator or a motor)
**4 a** : an act of brushing **b** : a quick light touch or momentary contact in passing

**³brush** *transitive verb* (15th century)
**1 a** : to apply a brush to **b** : to apply with a brush
**2 a** : to remove with passing strokes (as of a brush) **b** : to dispose of in an offhand way : DISMISS ⟨*brushed* him off⟩
**3** : to pass lightly over or across : touch gently against in passing
— **brush·er** *noun*

**⁴brush** *noun* [Middle English *brusche* rush, hostile collision, from *bruschen*] (14th century)
: a brief encounter or skirmish ⟨a *brush* with disaster⟩ ⟨a *brush* with the law⟩

**⁵brush** *intransitive verb* [Middle English *bruschen* to rush, from Middle French *brosser* to dash through underbrush, from *broce*] (1674)
: to move lightly or heedlessly ⟨*brushed* past the well-wishers waiting to greet him⟩

**brush·abil·i·ty** \,brə-shə-'bi-lə-tē\ *noun* (1936)
: ease of application with a brush ⟨*brushability* of a paint⟩

**brush·back** \'brəsh-,bak\ *noun* (1954)
: a fastball intentionally thrown near the batter's head or body in baseball
— **brush back** *transitive verb*

**brush border** *noun* (1903)
: a stria of microvilli on the plasma membrane of an epithelial cell (as in a kidney tubule) that is specialized for absorption

**brush cut** *noun* (1945)
: CREW CUT

**brush discharge** *noun* (1849)
: a faintly luminous relatively slow electrical discharge having no spark

**brushed** \'brəsht\ *adjective* (1926)
**1** : finished with a nap ⟨a *brushed* fabric⟩
**2** : polished but not shiny ⟨*brushed* aluminum⟩

**brush·fire** \'brəsh-,fīr\ *adjective* [*brush fire* (a fire involving brush but not full-sized trees)] (1954)
: involving mobilization only on a small and local scale ⟨*brushfire* border wars⟩

**brush·land** \-,land\ *noun* (1853)
: an area covered with brush growth

**brush·off** \-,òf\ *noun* (1941)
: a quietly curt or disdainful dismissal

**brush up** (circa 1600)
*transitive verb*
**1** : to improve or polish as if by brushing
**2** : to renew one's skill in ⟨*brush up* your Spanish⟩
*intransitive verb*
: to refresh one's memory : renew one's skill ⟨*brush up* on math⟩
— **brush-up** \'brəsh-,əp\ *noun*

**brush·wood** \'brəsh-,wúd\ *noun* (circa 1613)
**1** : wood of small branches especially when cut or broken
**2** : a thicket of shrubs and small trees

**brush·work** \-,wərk\ *noun* (1868)

\ə\ abut \ə\ kitten \ər\ further \a\ ash \ā\ ace
\ä\ mop, mar \aú\ out \ch\ chin \e\ bet \ē\ easy
\g\ go \i\ hit \ī\ ice \j\ job \ŋ\ sing \ō\ go
\ò\ law \ói\ boy \th\ thin \th\ the \ü\ loot \ú\ foot
\y\ yet \zh\ vision *see also* Guide to Pronunciation

: work done with a brush (as in painting); *especially* : the characteristic work of an artist using a brush

**¹brushy** \'brə-shē\ *adjective* **brush·i·er; -est** (1658)
: covered with or abounding in brush or brushwood ⟨*brushy* hills⟩ ⟨a *brushy* habitat⟩

**²brushy** *adjective* **brush·i·er; -est** (1673)
: SHAGGY, ROUGH ⟨a *brushy* moustache⟩

**brusque** *also* **brusk** \'brəsk\ *adjective* [French *brusque*, from Italian *brusco*, from Medieval Latin *bruscus* butcher's-broom (plant with bristly twigs)] (1651)
**1** : markedly short and abrupt
**2** : blunt in manner or speech often to the point of ungracious harshness
*synonym* see BLUFF
— **brusque·ly** *adverb*
— **brusque·ness** *noun*

**brus·que·rie** \,brəs-kə-'rē\ *noun* [French, from *brusque*] (1752)
: abruptness of manner

**Brus·sels carpet** \'brə-səlz-\ *noun* [*Brussels*, Belgium] (1799)
: a carpet made of colored worsted yarns first fixed in a foundation web of strong linen thread and then drawn up in loops to form the pattern

**Brussels griffon** *noun* (1904)
: any of a breed of short-faced compact rough- or smooth-coated toy dogs of Belgian origin — called also *griffon*

**Brussels lace** *noun* (1748)
**1** : any of various fine needlepoint or bobbin laces with floral designs first made in or near Brussels
**2** : a machine-made net of hexagonal mesh

**brus·sels sprout** \'brə-səl-\ *noun, often B capitalized* (1796)
**1** *plural* : a plant (*Brassica oleracea gemmifera*) of the mustard family that bears small edible green heads on its stem
**2** : any of the edible green heads borne on brussels sprouts — usually used in plural

**brut** \'brüt, 'brœt\ *adjective* [French, literally, rough] (1891)
*of champagne* : very dry; *specifically* : being the driest made by the producer

**bru·tal** \'brüt-ᵊl\ *adjective* [Middle English, from Middle French or Medieval Latin; Middle French, from Medieval Latin *brutalis*, from Latin *brutus*] (15th century)
**1** *archaic* : typical of beasts : ANIMAL
**2** : befitting a brute: as **a** : grossly ruthless or unfeeling ⟨a *brutal* slander⟩ **b** : CRUEL, COLD-BLOODED ⟨a *brutal* attack⟩ **c** : HARSH, SEVERE ⟨*brutal* weather⟩ **d** : unpleasantly accurate and incisive ⟨the *brutal* truth⟩ ☆
— **bru·tal·ly** \-t̷ᵊl-ē\ *adverb*

**bru·tal·ise** *British variant of* BRUTALIZE

**bru·tal·i·ty** \brü-'ta-lə-tē\ *noun, plural* **-ties** (1549)
**1** : the quality or state of being brutal
**2** : a brutal act or course of action

**bru·tal·ize** \'brüt-ᵊl-ˌīz\ *transitive verb* **-ized; -iz·ing** (circa 1704)
**1** : to make brutal, unfeeling, or inhuman ⟨people *brutalized* by poverty and disease⟩
**2** : to treat brutally ⟨an accord not to *brutalize* prisoners of war⟩
— **bru·tal·iza·tion** \,brü-t̷ᵊl-ə-'zā-shən\ *noun*

**¹brute** \'brüt\ *adjective* [Middle English, from Middle French *brut* rough, from Latin *brutus*

**Brussels griffon**

**brussels sprout 1**

brutish, literally, heavy; akin to Latin *gravis* heavy — more at GRIEVE] (15th century)
**1** : of or relating to beasts ⟨the ways of the *brute* world⟩
**2** : INANIMATE 1a
**3** : characteristic of an animal in quality, action, or instinct: as **a** : CRUEL, SAVAGE ⟨*brute* violence⟩ **b** : not working by reason ⟨*brute* instinct⟩
**4** : purely physical ⟨*brute* strength⟩
**5** : unrelievedly harsh ⟨*brute* facts⟩ ⟨*brute* necessity⟩

**²brute** *noun* (1611)
**1** : BEAST
**2** : a brutal person

**brut·ish** \'brü-tish\ *adjective* (1534)
**1** : befitting beasts ⟨lived a short and *brutish* life as a slave⟩
**2 a** : strongly and grossly sensual ⟨*brutish* gluttony⟩ **b** : showing little intelligence or sensibility ⟨a *brutish* lack of understanding⟩
*synonym* see BRUTAL
— **brut·ish·ly** *adverb*
— **brut·ish·ness** *noun*

**brux·ism** \'brək-ˌsi-zəm\ *noun* [irregular from Greek *brychein* to gnash the teeth + English *-ism*] (circa 1940)
: the habit of unconsciously gritting or grinding the teeth especially in situations of stress or during sleep

**Bryn·hild** \'brin-ˌhild\ *noun* [Old Norse *Brynhildr*]
: a Valkyrie who is waked from an enchanted sleep by Sigurd and later has him killed when he forgets her

**bry·ol·o·gy** \brī-'ä-lə-jē\ *noun* [Greek *bryon* moss (akin to Greek *bryein* to grow luxuriantly) + International Scientific Vocabulary *-logy*] (circa 1859)
**1** : moss life or biology
**2** : a branch of botany that deals with the bryophytes
— **bry·o·log·i·cal** \brī-ə-'lä-ji-kəl\ *adjective*
— **bry·ol·o·gist** \brī-'ä-lə-jist\ *noun*

**bry·o·ny** \'brī-ə-nē\ *noun, plural* **-nies** [Middle English, from Latin *bryonia*, from Greek *bryōnia*; akin to Greek *bryein*] (14th century)
: any of a genus (*Bryonia*) of tendril-bearing vines of the gourd family with large leaves and red or black fruit

**bryo·phyl·lum** \ˌbrī-ə-'fi-ləm\ *noun* [New Latin, from Greek *bryon* + *phyllon* leaf — more at BLADE] (circa 1868)
: any of various kalanchoes; *especially* : a succulent kalanchoe (*Kalanchoe pinnata*) often grown as a foliage plant that propagates new plants from its leaves

**bryo·phyte** \'brī-ə-ˌfīt\ *noun* [ultimately from Greek *bryon* + *phyton* plant; akin to Greek *phyein* to bring forth — more at BE] (1878)
: any of a division (Bryophyta) of nonflowering plants comprising the mosses, liverworts, and hornworts
— **bryo·phyt·ic** \ˌbrī-ə-'fi-tik\ *adjective*

**bryo·zo·an** \ˌbrī-ə-'zō-ən\ *noun* [New Latin *Bryozoa*, from Greek *bryon* + New Latin *-zoa*] (circa 1864)
: any of a phylum (Bryozoa) of aquatic mostly marine invertebrate animals that reproduce by budding and usually form permanently attached branched or mossy colonies
— **bryozoan** *adjective*

**¹Bry·thon·ic** \bri-'thä-nik\ *adjective* (1884)
: of, relating to, or characteristic of the division of the Celtic languages that includes Welsh, Cornish, and Breton

**²Brythonic** *noun* (1884)
: the Brythonic branch of the Celtic languages
— see INDO-EUROPEAN LANGUAGES table

**Bt** \'bē-'tē\ *noun* [New Latin *Bacillus thuringiensis*, species name, literally, Thuringian bacillus] (1971)
: an insecticide composed of a bacterium (*Bacillus thuringiensis*) pathogenic especially for lepidopteran larvae; *also* : the bacterium itself

**bub** \'bəb\ *noun* [probably short for *bubby* little boy] (1839)
: FELLOW, BUDDY — used in informal address ⟨come on, *bub*, get moving⟩

**¹bub·ble** \'bə-bəl\ *noun, often attributive* [Middle English *bobel*] (14th century)
**1** : a small globule typically hollow and light: as **a** : a small body of gas within a liquid **b** : a thin film of liquid inflated with air or gas **c** : a globule in a transparent solid **d** : something (as a plastic or inflatable structure) that is hemispherical or semicylindrical
**2 a** : something that lacks firmness, solidity, or reality **b** : a delusive scheme
**3** : a sound like that of bubbling
**4** : MAGNETIC BUBBLE

**²bubble** *verb* **bub·bled; bub·bling** \'bə-b(ə-)liŋ\ (15th century)
*intransitive verb*
**1 a** : to form or produce bubbles **b** : to rise in or as if in bubbles — usually used with *up*
**2** : to flow with a gurgling sound ⟨a brook *bubbling* over rocks⟩
**3 a** : to become lively or effervescent ⟨*bubbling* with good humor⟩ **b** : to speak in a lively and fluent manner
*transitive verb*
**1** : to utter (as words) effervescently
**2** : to cause to bubble

**bubble and squeak** *noun* (circa 1785)
: a British dish consisting of usually leftover potatoes, greens (as cabbage), and sometimes meat fried together

**bubble chamber** *noun* (1953)
: a chamber of superheated liquid in which the path of an ionizing particle is made visible by a string of vapor bubbles

**bub·ble·gum** \'bə-bəl-ˌgəm\ *adjective* (1969)
: appealing to or characteristic of preteens or adolescents ⟨*bubblegum* music⟩

**bubble gum** *noun* (1937)
**1** : a chewing gum that can be blown into large bubbles
**2** *usually* **bub·ble·gum** \'bə-bəl-ˌgəm\ : rock music characterized by simple repetitive phrasings and intended especially for young teenagers

**bub·ble·head** \'bə-bəl-ˌhed\ *noun* (1949)
: a foolish or stupid person
— **bub·ble·head·ed** \-ˌhe-dəd\ *adjective*

**bubble memory** *noun* (1969)
: a computer memory that uses magnetic bubbles to store information

**bub·bler** \'bə-b(ə-)lər\ *noun* (1914)
**1** : a drinking fountain from which a stream of water bubbles upward
**2** : one that bubbles

**¹bub·bly** \'bə-b(ə-)lē\ *adjective* **bub·bli·er; -est** (1599)
**1** : full of bubbles : EFFERVESCENT ⟨a *bubbly* bottle of pop⟩
**2** : full of or showing good spirits : LIVELY, EFFUSIVE
**3** : resembling a bubble ⟨a *bubbly* dome⟩

**²bubbly** *noun* (1920)
: CHAMPAGNE

**bub·by** \'bə-bē\ *noun, plural* **bubbies** [probably of imitative origin] (1686)

---

☆ **SYNONYMS**
**Brutal, brutish, bestial, feral** mean characteristic of an animal in nature, action, or instinct. BRUTAL applies to people, their acts, or their words and suggests a lack of intelligence, feeling, or humanity ⟨a senseless and *brutal* war⟩. BRUTISH stresses likeness to an animal in low intelligence, in base appetites, and in behavior based on instinct ⟨*brutish* stupidity⟩. BESTIAL suggests a state of degradation unworthy of man and fit only for beasts ⟨*bestial* depravity⟩. FERAL suggests the savagery or ferocity of wild animals ⟨the struggle to survive unleashed their *feral* impulses⟩.

: BREAST 1 — sometimes considered vulgar

**bu·bo** \'byü-(,)bō, 'bü-\ *noun, plural* **buboes** [Medieval Latin *bubon-, bubo,* from Greek *boubōn*] (14th century)
: an inflammatory swelling of a lymph gland especially in the groin
— **bu·bon·ic** \byü-'bä-nik, bü-\ *adjective*

**bubonic plague** *noun* (1885)
: plague caused by a bacterium (*Yersinia pestis*) and characterized especially by the formation of buboes

**buc·cal** \'bə-kəl\ *adjective* [Latin *bucca* cheek] (circa 1771)
**1** : of, relating to, near, involving, or supplying a cheek ⟨the *buccal* surface of a tooth⟩ ⟨the *buccal* branch of the facial nerve⟩
**2** : of, relating to, involving, or lying in the mouth ⟨the *buccal* cavity⟩
— **buc·cal·ly** *adverb*

**buc·ca·neer** \,bə-kə-'nir\ *noun* [French *boucanier*] (circa 1690)
**1** : any of the freebooters preying on Spanish ships and settlements especially in the West Indies in the 17th century; *broadly* : PIRATE
**2** : an unscrupulous adventurer especially in politics or business ◆
— **buccaneer** *intransitive verb*
— **buc·ca·neer·ish** \-ish\ *adjective*

**buc·ci·na·tor** \'bək-sə-,nā-tər\ *noun* [New Latin, from Latin *bucinator* trumpeter, from *bucinare* to sound on the trumpet, from *bucina* trumpet, from *bov-, bos* cow + *canere* to sing, play — more at COW, CHANT] (1671)
: a thin broad muscle forming the wall of the cheek

**¹buck** \'bək\ *noun, plural* **bucks** [Middle English, from Old English *bucca* stag, he-goat; akin to Old High German *boc* he-goat, Middle Irish *bocc*] (before 12th century)
**1** *or plural* **buck** : a male animal; *especially* : a male deer or antelope
**2 a** : a male human being : MAN **b** : a dashing fellow : DANDY
**3** *or plural* **buck** : ANTELOPE
**4 a** : BUCKSKIN; *also* : an article (as a shoe) made of buckskin **b** (1) : DOLLAR 3b (2) : a sum of money especially to be gained ⟨make a quick *buck*⟩; *also* : MONEY — usually used in plural
**5** [short for *sawbuck* sawhorse] **a** : a supporting rack or frame **b** : a short thick leather-covered block for gymnastic vaulting

**²buck** (1750)
*transitive verb*
**1 a** *archaic* : ¹BUTT **b** : OPPOSE, RESIST ⟨*bucking* the system⟩
**2** : to throw (as a rider) by bucking
**3** : to charge into (as the opponent's line in football)
**4 a** : to pass especially from one person to another **b** : to move or load (as heavy objects) especially with mechanical equipment
*intransitive verb*
**1** *of a horse or mule* : to spring into the air with the back arched
**2** : to charge against something (as an obstruction)
**3 a** : to move or react jerkily **b** : to refuse assent : BALK
**4** : to strive for advancement sometimes without regard to ethical behavior ⟨*bucking* for a promotion⟩
— **buck·er** *noun*

**³buck** *noun* (circa 1877)
: an act or instance of bucking

**⁴buck** *noun* [short for earlier *buckhorn knife*] (1865)
**1** : an object formerly used in poker to mark the next player to deal; *broadly* : a token used as a mark or reminder
**2** : RESPONSIBILITY — used especially in the phrases *pass the buck* and *the buck stops here*

**⁵buck** *adjective* [probably from ¹*buck*] (1918)
: of the lowest grade within a military category ⟨*buck* private⟩

**⁶buck** *adverb* [origin unknown] (1928)

: STARK ⟨*buck* naked⟩

**buck–and–wing** \,bə-kᵊn-'wiŋ\ *noun* (1895)
: a solo tap dance with sharp foot accents, springs, leg flings, and heel clicks

**buck·a·roo** *also* **buck·er·oo** \,bə-kə-'rü, 'bə-kə-,\ *noun, plural* **-aroos** *also* **-eroos** [by folk etymology from Spanish *vaquero,* from *vaca* cow, from Latin *vacca* — more at VACCINE] (1827)
**1** : COWBOY
**2** : BRONCOBUSTER

**buck·bean** \'bək-,bēn\ *noun* (1578)
: a plant (*Menyanthes trifoliata* of the family Menyanthaceae) growing in bogs and having racemes of white or purplish flowers

**buck·board** \-,bōrd, -,bórd\ *noun* [obsolete English *buck* body of a wagon + English *board*] (1839)
: a four-wheeled vehicle with a floor made of long springy boards

**buckboard**

**¹buck·et** \'bə-kət\ *noun* [Middle English, from Anglo-French *buket,* from Old English *būc* pitcher, belly; akin to Old High German *būh* belly] (13th century)
**1** : a typically cylindrical vessel for catching, holding, or carrying liquids or solids
**2** : something resembling a bucket: as **a** : the scoop of an excavating machine **b** : one of the receptacles on the rim of a waterwheel **c** : one of the cups of an endless-belt conveyor **d** : one of the vanes of a turbine rotor
**3** : BUCKETFUL
**4** : BUCKET SEAT
**5** : BASKET 3b

**²bucket** (1649)
*transitive verb*
**1** : to draw or lift in buckets
**2** *British* : to ride (a horse) hard **b** : to drive hurriedly or roughly
**3** : to deal with in a bucket shop
*intransitive verb*
**1** : HUSTLE, HURRY
**2 a** : to move about haphazardly or irresponsibly **b** : to move roughly or jerkily

**bucket brigade** *noun* (1911)
: a chain of persons acting to put out a fire by passing buckets of water from hand to hand

**buck·et·ful** \'bə-kət-,ful\ *noun, plural* **buck·etfuls** \-,fulz\ *or* **buck·ets·ful** \-kəts-,ful\ (circa 1563)
: as much as a bucket will hold; *broadly* : a large quantity

**bucket seat** *noun* (1908)
: a low separate seat for one person (as in an automobile or an airplane)

**bucket shop** *noun* (1875)
**1** : a saloon in which liquor was formerly sold from or dispensed in open containers (as buckets or pitchers)
**2 a** : a gambling establishment that formerly used market fluctuations (as in securities or commodities) as a basis for gaming **b** : a dishonest brokerage firm; *especially* : one that formerly failed to execute customers' margin orders in expectation of making a profit from market fluctuations adverse to the customers' interests

**buck·eye** \'bə-,kī\ *noun* (1763)
**1** : a shrub or tree (genus *Aesculus*) of the horse-chestnut family; *also* : its large nutlike seed
**2** *capitalized* : a native or resident of Ohio — used as a nickname

**buck fever** *noun* (1841)
: nervous excitement of an inexperienced hunter at the sight of game

**¹buck·le** \'bə-kəl\ *noun* [Middle English *bocle,* from Middle French, boss of a shield, buckle, from Latin *buccula,* diminutive of *bucca* cheek] (14th century)

**1** : a fastening for two loose ends that is attached to one and holds the other by a catch
**2** : an ornamental device that suggests a buckle
**3** *archaic* : a crisp curl

**²buckle** *verb* **buck·led; buck·ling** \'bə-k(ə-)liŋ\ (14th century)
*transitive verb*
**1** : to fasten with a buckle
**2** : to prepare with vigor
**3** : to cause to bend, give way, or crumple
*intransitive verb*
**1** : to become fastened with a buckle
**2** : to apply oneself with vigor ⟨*buckles* down to the job⟩
**3** : to bend, heave, warp, or kink usually under the influence of some external agency ⟨wheat *buckling* in the wind⟩
**4** : COLLAPSE ⟨the props *buckled* under the strain⟩
**5** : to give way : YIELD ⟨he *buckled* under pressure⟩

**³buckle** *noun* (circa 1876)
**1** : a product of buckling
**2** : a coffee cake baked with berries and a crumbly topping ⟨blueberry *buckle*⟩

**¹buck·ler** \'bə-klər\ *noun* [Middle English *bocler,* from Middle French, shield with a boss, from *bocle*] (13th century)
**1 a** : a small round shield held by a handle at arm's length **b** : a shield worn on the left arm
**2** : one that shields and protects

**²buckler** *transitive verb* (1590)
: to shield or defend with a buckler

**buckle up** *intransitive verb* (1976)
: to fasten one's seat belt

**buck·min·ster·ful·ler·ene** \,bək-(,)min-stər-,fu-lə-'rēn\ *noun* [R. *Buckminster Fuller*] (1985)
: a spherical fullerene $C_{60}$ that is an extremely stable form of pure carbon, consists of interconnected pentagons and hexagons suggestive of the geometry of a geodesic dome, and is believed to be a major constituent of soot

**bucko** \'bə-(,)kō\ *noun, plural* **buck·oes** (1883)
**1** : a person who is domineering and bullying : SWAGGERER

\ə\ abut \ᵊ\ kitten \ər\ further \a\ ash \ā\ ace \ä\ mop, mar \au\ out \ch\ chin \e\ bet \ē\ easy \g\ go \i\ hit \ī\ ice \j\ job \ŋ\ sing \ō\ go \ò\ law \òi\ boy \th\ thin \t͟h\ the \ü\ loot \ù\ foot \y\ yet \zh\ vision *see also* Guide to Pronunciation

**2** *chiefly Irish* **:** young fellow **:** LAD
**buck passer** *noun* (1920)
**:** a person who habitually passes the buck
— **buck·pass·ing** \'bək-ˌpa-siŋ\ *noun*
¹**buck·ram** \'bə-krəm\ *noun* [Middle English *bukeram*, from Old French *boquerant*, from Old Provençal *bocaran*, probably from *Bokhara*, city of central Asia] (15th century)
**1 :** a stiff-finished heavily sized fabric of cotton or linen used for interlinings in garments, for stiffening in millinery, and in bookbinding
**2** *archaic* **:** STIFFNESS, RIGIDITY
²**buckram** *adjective* (circa 1589)
**:** suggesting buckram especially in stiffness
³**buckram** *transitive verb* (1783)
**1 :** to give strength or stiffness to (as with buckram)
**2** *archaic* **:** to make pretentious
**Buck Rogers** \'bək-'rä-jərz\ *adjective* [*Buck Rogers*, hero of a science-fiction comic strip created by Phil Nowlan] (1941)
**:** marked by futuristic and high-tech qualities
**:** suggestive of science fiction
**buck·saw** \'bək-ˌsȯ\ *noun* (1856)
**:** a saw set in a usually H-shaped frame for sawing wood
**buck·shee** \'bək-(ˌ)shē, ˌbək-'\ *noun* [Hindi *bakhśīś*, from Persian *bakhshīsh* — more at BAKSHEESH] (circa 1760)
**1** *British* **:** something extra obtained free; *especially* **:** extra rations
**2** *British* **:** WINDFALL, GRATUITY
¹**buck·shot** \'bək-ˌshät\ *noun* (1775)
**:** lead shot that is from .24 to .33 inch (about 6.1 to 8.4 millimeters) in diameter
²**buckshot** *adjective* (1941)
**:** SCATTERSHOT
**buck·skin** \-ˌskin\ *noun, often attributive* (14th century)
**1 a :** the skin of a buck **b :** a soft pliable usually suede-finished leather
**2 a** *plural* **:** buckskin breeches **b** *archaic* **:** a person dressed in buckskin; *especially* **:** an early American backwoodsman
**3 :** a horse of a light yellowish dun color with black mane and tail
**buck·skinned** \-ˌskind\ *adjective* (1829)
**:** dressed in buckskin
**buck·tail** \-ˌtāl\ *noun* (1911)
**:** an angler's lure made typically of hairs from the tail of a deer
**buck·thorn** \-ˌthȯrn\ *noun* (1578)
**1 :** any of a genus (*Rhamnus* of the family Rhamnaceae, the buckthorn family) of often thorny trees or shrubs some of which yield purgatives or pigments
**2 :** a tree (*Bumelia lycioides*) of the sapodilla family of the southern U.S.
**buck·tooth** \-ˈtüth\ *noun* (1753)
**:** a large projecting front tooth
— **buck·toothed** \-ˌtütht\ *adjective*
**buck up** *verb* [²*buck*] (1844)
*intransitive verb*
**:** to become encouraged
*transitive verb*
**1 :** IMPROVE, SMARTEN
**2 :** to raise the morale of
**buck·wheat** \'bək-ˌhwēt, -ˌwēt\ *noun* [Dutch *boekweit*, from Middle Dutch *boecweit*, from *boec-* (akin to Old High German *buohha* beech tree) + *weit* wheat — more at BEECH] (1548)
**1 :** any of a genus (*Fagopyrum* of the family Polygonaceae, the buckwheat family) of herbs with alternate leaves, clusters of apetalous pinkish white flowers, and triangular seeds; *especially* **:** either of two plants (*F. esculentum* and *F. tartaricum*) cultivated for their edible seeds
**2 :** the seed of a buckwheat used as a cereal grain
**bucky·ball** \'bə-kē-ˌbȯl\ *noun* [R. *Buck*minster Fuller + ⁴-*y*] (1985)
**:** a molecule of buckminsterfullerene
**bu·col·ic** \byü-'kä-lik\ *adjective* [Latin *bucolicus*, from Greek *boukolikos*, from *boukolos*

cowherd, from *bous* head of cattle + -*kolos* (akin to Latin *colere* to cultivate) — more at COW, WHEEL] (circa 1609)
**1 :** of or relating to shepherds or herdsmen **:** PASTORAL
**2 :** relating to or typical of rural life ⟨picnicked in a pleasant *bucolic* setting⟩
— **bu·col·i·cal·ly** \-li-k(ə-)lē\ *adverb*
¹**bud** \'bəd\ *noun* [Middle English *budde*] (14th century)
**1 :** a small lateral or terminal protuberance on the stem of a plant that may develop into a flower, leaf, or shoot
**2 :** something not yet mature or at full development: as **a :** an incompletely opened flower **b :** CHILD, YOUTH **c :** an outgrowth of an organism that differentiates into a new individual **:** GEMMA; *also* **:** PRIMORDIUM
— **in the bud :** in an early stage of development ⟨nipped the rebellion *in the bud*⟩
²**bud** *verb* **bud·ded; bud·ding** (14th century)
*intransitive verb*
**1** *of a plant* **a :** to set or put forth buds **b :** to commence growth from buds
**2 :** to grow or develop as if from a bud
**3 :** to reproduce asexually especially by the pinching off of a small part of the parent
*transitive verb*
**1 :** to produce or develop from buds
**2 :** to cause (as a plant) to bud
**3 :** to insert a bud from a plant of one kind into an opening in the bark of (a plant of another kind) usually in order to propagate a desired variety
— **bud·der** *noun*
**Bud·dha** \'bü-də, 'bu̇-\ *noun* [Sanskrit, enlightened; akin to Sanskrit *bodhi* enlightenment — more at BID] (1681)
**1 :** a person who has attained Buddhahood
**2 :** a representation of Gautama Buddha
**Bud·dha·hood** \-ˌhu̇d\ *noun* (1837)
**:** a state of perfect enlightenment sought in Buddhism
**Bud·dhism** \'bü-ˌdi-zəm, 'bu̇-\ *noun* (1801)
**:** a religion of eastern and central Asia growing out of the teaching of Gautama Buddha that suffering is inherent in life and that one can be liberated from it by mental and moral self-purification
— **Bud·dhist** \'bü-dist, 'bu̇-\ *noun or adjective*
— **Bud·dhis·tic** \bü-'dis-tik, bu̇-\ *adjective*
**bud·ding** \'bə-diŋ\ *adjective* (1581)
**:** being in an early stage of development ⟨*budding* novelists⟩
**bud·dle** \'bə-dᵊl\ *noun* [origin unknown] (circa 1532)
**:** an apparatus on which crushed ore is concentrated by washing
**bud·dle·ia** \'bəd-lē-ə, ˌbəd-'lē-\ *noun* [New Latin, genus name, from Adam *Buddle* (died 1715) English botanist] (1791)
**:** any of a genus (*Buddleia* of the family Loganiaceae) of shrubs or trees of warm regions with showy terminal clusters of usually yellow or violet flowers
¹**bud·dy** \'bə-dē\ *noun, plural* **buddies** [probably baby talk alteration of *brother*] (1850)
**1 a :** COMPANION, PARTNER **b :** FRIEND 1
**2 :** FELLOW — used especially in informal address
²**buddy** *intransitive verb* **bud·died; bud·dy·ing** (1918)
**:** to become friendly — usually used with *up* or *with*
³**buddy** *adjective* (1976)
**:** featuring a friendship or partnership between the two main usually male characters ⟨a *buddy* movie⟩
**bud·dy–bud·dy** \ˌbə-dē-'bə-dē\ *adjective* (1951)
**:** familiarly friendly
**buddy system** *noun* (1942)

**:** an arrangement in which two individuals are paired (as for mutual safety in a hazardous situation)
¹**budge** \'bəj\ *noun* [Middle English *bugee*, from Anglo-French *bogee*] (14th century)
**:** a fur formerly prepared from lambskin dressed with the wool outward
²**budge** *verb* **budged; budg·ing** [Middle French *bouger*, from (assumed) Vulgar Latin *bullicare*, from Latin *bullire* to boil — more at BOIL] (1590)
*intransitive verb*
**1 :** MOVE, SHIFT ⟨the mule wouldn't *budge*⟩
**2 :** to give way **:** YIELD ⟨wouldn't *budge* on the issue⟩
*transitive verb*
**:** to cause to move or change
³**budge** *adjective* [origin unknown] (1634)
*archaic* **:** POMPOUS, SOLEMN
**bud·ger·i·gar** \'bə-jə-rē-ˌgär\ *noun* [modification of Yuwaalaraay (Australian aboriginal language of northern New South Wales) *gijirrigaa*] (1840)
**:** a small Australian parrot (*Melopsittacus undulatus*) usually light green with black and yellow markings in the wild but bred under domestication in many colors
¹**bud·get** \'bə-jət\ *noun* [Middle English *bowgett*, from Middle French *bougette*, diminutive of *bouge* leather bag, from Latin *bulga*, of Celtic origin; akin to Middle Irish *bolg* bag; akin to Old English *belg* bag — more at BELLY] (15th century)
**1** *chiefly dialect* **:** a usually leather pouch, wallet, or pack; *also* **:** its contents
**2 :** STOCK, SUPPLY
**3 :** a quantity (as of energy or water) involved in, available for, or assignable to a particular situation; *also* **:** an account of gains and losses of such a quantity
**4 a :** a statement of the financial position of an administration for a definite period of time based on estimates of expenditures during the period and proposals for financing them **b :** a plan for the coordination of resources and expenditures **c :** the amount of money that is available for, required for, or assigned to a particular purpose ◆
— **bud·get·ary** \'bə-jə-ˌter-ē\ *adjective*
²**budget** (1618)
*transitive verb*
**1 a :** to put or allow for in a budget **b :** to require to adhere to a budget

◇ **WORD HISTORY**
**budget** Some loanwords have had a more successful career in the language that took them than in the one that gave them; on occasion this had led to reborrowing by the donor. Such a word is *budget*, borrowed from medieval French *bougette* "leather bag" and recorded in later Middle English as *bowgett*. The French word was a diminutive of *bouge* "travel bag, chest, sack." In French, both *bouge* and *bougette* became largely obsolete or historical in reference by the 18th century, at least in their original senses. Middle English *bowgett*, on the other hand, emerged in Early Modern English as *budget*. From its first sense "satchel," *budget* came to denote the contents of a satchel, especially a bundle of letters or papers—a semantic shift identical to that of ²*mail*. In the 18th century British Parliament, the Chancellor of the Exchequer was said "to open the budget" when he presented the government's estimates of revenues and expenditures for the following year. By the 19th century, any public or private estimation of a similar nature could be called a *budget*. The usefulness of this word and the influence of English parliamentary institutions led to the adoption of *budget* in a number of European languages, including French.

**2 a :** to allocate funds for in a budget ⟨*budget* a new hospital⟩ **b :** to plan or provide for the use of in detail ⟨*budgeting* manpower⟩
*intransitive verb*
**:** to put oneself on a budget ⟨*budgeting* for a vacation⟩
**³budget** *adjective* (1941)
**:** suitable for one on a budget **:** INEXPENSIVE
**bud·ge·teer** \ˌbə-jə-'tir\ *also* **bud·get·er** \'bə-jə-tər\ *noun* (circa 1845)
**1 :** one who prepares a budget
**2 :** one who is restricted to a budget
**bud·gie** \'bə-jē\ *noun* [by shortening and alteration] (1935)
**:** BUDGERIGAR
**bud scale** *noun* (circa 1880)
**:** one of the leaves resembling scales that form the sheath of a plant bud
**bud·worm** \'bəd-ˌwərm\ *noun* (1849)
**:** a moth larva that feeds on the buds of plants — compare SPRUCE BUDWORM
**¹buff** \'bəf\ *noun* [Middle French *buffle* wild ox, from Old Italian *bufalo*] (1580)
**1 :** a garment (as a uniform) made of buff leather
**2 :** the state of being nude ⟨sunbathing in the *buff*⟩
**3 a :** a moderate orange yellow **b :** a light to moderate yellow
**4 :** a device having a soft absorbent surface (as of cloth) by which polishing material is applied
**5** [earlier *buff* an enthusiast about going to fires; perhaps from the buff overcoats worn by volunteer firefighters in New York City *about* 1820] **:** FAN, ENTHUSIAST
**²buff** *adjective* (circa 1771)
**:** of the color buff
**³buff** *transitive verb* (1885)
**1 :** POLISH, SHINE ⟨waxed and *buffed* the floor⟩
**2 :** to give a velvety surface to ⟨leather⟩
**¹buf·fa·lo** \'bə-fə-ˌlō\ *noun, plural* **-lo** *or* **-loes** *also* **-los** *often attributive* [Italian *bufalo* & Spanish *búfalo*, from Late Latin *bufalus*, alteration of Latin *bubalus*, from Greek *boubalos* African gazelle] (1562)
**1 :** any of several wild bovids: as **a :** WATER BUFFALO **b :** CAPE BUFFALO **c** (1) **:** any of a genus (*Bison*) of bovids; *especially* **:** a large shaggy-maned North American bovid (*B. bison*) that has short horns

buffalo 1c(1)

and heavy forequarters with a large muscular hump and that was formerly abundant on the central and western plains — compare WISENT (2) **:** the flesh of the buffalo used as food
**2 :** any of several suckers (genus *Ictiobus*) found mostly in the Mississippi valley — called also *buffalofish*
**²buffalo** *transitive verb* **-loed; -lo·ing** (circa 1896)
**:** BEWILDER, BAFFLE
**buf·fa·lo·ber·ry** \-ˌber-ē\ *noun* (1805)
**:** either of two western U.S. shrubs (*Shepherdia argentea* and *S. canadensis*) of the oleaster family with silvery foliage; *also* **:** their edible scarlet berry
**buffalo gourd** *noun* (circa 1928)
**:** a perennial cucurbit (*Cucurbita foetidissima*) of arid lands of the central and southwest U.S. and Mexico with a large starchy taproot and seeds rich in an oil suitable after processing for use in cooking or as fuel
**buffalo grass** *noun* (1784)

**:** a low-growing grass (*Buchloë dactyloides*) of former feeding grounds of the American buffalo; *also* **:** GRAMA
**buffalo plaid** *noun* (1979)
**:** a broad checkered plaid pattern usually of two colors
**¹buff·er** \'bə-fər\ *noun, often attributive* [*buff*, verb, to react like a soft body when struck] (1835)
**1 :** any of various devices or pieces of material for reducing shock or damage due to contact
**2 :** a means or device used as a cushion against the shock of fluctuations in business or financial activity
**3 :** something that serves as a protective barrier: as **a :** BUFFER STATE **b :** a person who shields another especially from annoying routine matters **c :** MEDIATOR 1
**4 :** a substance capable in solution of neutralizing both acids and bases and thereby maintaining the original acidity or basicity of the solution; *also* **:** a solution containing such a substance
**5 :** a temporary storage unit (as in a computer); *especially* **:** one that accepts information at one rate and delivers it at another
**— buff·ered** \-fərd\ *adjective*
**²buffer** *transitive verb* **buff·ered; buff·er·ing** \-f(ə-)riŋ\ (1894)
**1 :** to lessen the shock of **:** CUSHION
**2 :** to treat (as a solution or its acidity) with a buffer; *also* **:** to prepare (aspirin) with an antacid
**3 :** to collect (as data) in a buffer
**³buffer** *noun* (1854)
**:** one that buffs
**buffer state** *noun* (1883)
**:** a usually neutral state lying between two larger potentially rival powers
**buffer zone** *noun* (1908)
**:** a neutral area separating conflicting forces; *broadly* **:** an area designed to separate
**¹buf·fet** \'bə-fət\ *noun* [Middle English, from Old French, diminutive of *buffe* blow] (13th century)
**1 :** a blow especially with the hand
**2 :** something that strikes with telling force
**²buffet** (13th century)
*transitive verb*
**1 :** to strike sharply especially with the hand **:** CUFF
**2 :** to strike repeatedly **:** BATTER ⟨the waves *buffeted* the shore⟩
**3 :** to drive, force, move, or attack by or as if by repeated blows
*intransitive verb*
**:** to make one's way especially under difficult conditions
**³buf·fet** \(ˌ)bə-'fā, bü-', *British especially* 'bü-ˌ\ *noun* [French] (1718)
**1 :** SIDEBOARD
**2 a :** a counter for refreshments **b** *chiefly British* **:** a restaurant operated as a public convenience (as in a railway station) **c :** a meal set out on a buffet or table for ready access and informal service
**⁴buf·fet** \*same as* ³\ *adjective* (1898)
**:** served informally (as from a buffet)
**buffing wheel** *noun* (circa 1889)
**:** a wheel covered with polishing material
**buff leather** *noun* (1580)
**:** a strong supple oil-tanned leather produced chiefly from cattle hides
**buf·fle·head** \'bə-fəl-ˌhed\ *noun* [archaic English *buffle* buffalo + English *head*] (1731)
**:** a small North American diving duck (*Bucephala albeola*)
**buf·fo** \'bü-(ˌ)fō\ *noun, plural* **buf·fi** \-(ˌ)fē\ *or* **buffos** [Italian, from *buffone*] (1764)
**:** CLOWN, BUFFOON; *specifically* **:** a male singer of comic roles in opera
**buf·foon** \(ˌ)bə-'fün\ *noun* [Middle French *bouffon*, from Old Italian *buffone*] (1585)
**1 :** a ludicrous figure **:** CLOWN

**2 :** a gross and usually ill-educated or stupid person
**— buf·foon·ish** \-'fü-nish\ *adjective*
**buf·foon·ery** \-'fü-nə-rē, -'fün-rē\ *noun, plural* **-er·ies** (1621)
**:** foolish or playful behavior or practice
**¹bug** \'bəg\ *noun* [Middle English *bugge* scarecrow; akin to Norwegian dialect *bugge* important man] (14th century)
*obsolete* **:** BOGEY, BUGBEAR
**²bug** *noun* [origin unknown] (1622)
**1 a :** an insect or other creeping or crawling invertebrate **b :** any of several insects commonly considered obnoxious: as (1) **:** BEDBUG (2) **:** COCKROACH (3) **:** HEAD LOUSE **c :** any of an order (Hemiptera and especially its suborder Heteroptera) of insects that have sucking mouthparts, forewings thickened at the base, and incomplete metamorphosis and are often economic pests — called also *true bug*
**2 :** an unexpected defect, fault, flaw, or imperfection
**3 a :** a germ or microorganism especially when causing disease **b :** an unspecified or nonspecific sickness usually presumed due to a bug
**4 :** a sudden enthusiasm
**5 :** ENTHUSIAST ⟨a camera *bug*⟩
**6 :** a prominent person
**7 :** a concealed listening device
**8** [from its designation by an asterisk on race programs] **:** a weight allowance given apprentice jockeys
**³bug** *transitive verb* **bugged; bug·ging** (1949)
**1 :** BOTHER, ANNOY ⟨don't *bug* me with petty details⟩
**2 :** to plant a concealed microphone in
**⁴bug** *verb* **bugged; bug·ging** [probably from ²*bug*] (1877)
*intransitive verb*
*of the eyes* **:** PROTRUDE, BULGE — often used with *out*
*transitive verb*
**:** to cause to bug ⟨his eyes were *bugged* with horror⟩
**bug·a·boo** \'bə-gə-ˌbü\ *noun, plural* **-boos** [origin unknown] (1740)
**1 :** an imaginary object of fear
**2 :** BUGBEAR 2; *also* **:** something that causes fear or distress out of proportion to its importance
**bug·bane** \'bəg-ˌbān\ *noun* (1804)
**:** any of several perennial herbs (genus *Cimicifuga*) of the buttercup family; *especially* **:** BLACK COHOSH
**bug·bear** \-ˌbar, -ˌber\ *noun* (1581)
**1 :** an imaginary goblin or specter used to excite fear
**2 a :** an object or source of dread **b :** a continuing source of irritation **:** PROBLEM
**bug·eye** \-ˌī\ *noun* (1881)
**:** a small boat with a flat bottom, a centerboard, and two raked masts
**bug·eyed** \-ˌīd\ *adjective* (1922)
**:** having the eyes bulging (as with astonishment)
**¹bug·ger** \'bə-gər, 'bu-gər\ *noun* [Middle English *bougre* heretic, from Middle French, from Medieval Latin *Bulgarus*, literally, Bulgarian; from the association of Bulgaria with the Bogomils, who were accused of sodomy] (1555)
**1 :** SODOMITE
**2 a :** a worthless person **:** RASCAL **b :** FELLOW, CHAP
**3 :** a small or annoying thing ⟨put down my keys and now I can't find the *buggers*⟩
**²bug·ger** \'bə-gər\ *transitive verb* (1598)

---

\ə\ abut \ᵊ\ kitten \ər\ further \a\ ash \ā\ ace \ä\ mop, mar \aù\ out \ch\ chin \e\ bet \ē\ easy \g\ go \i\ hit \ī\ ice \j\ job \ŋ\ sing \ō\ go \ò\ law \òi\ boy \th\ thin \th\ the \ü\ loot \ù\ foot \y\ yet \zh\ vision    *see also* Guide to Pronunciation

**1 :** to commit sodomy with — usually considered vulgar
**2 :** DAMN
³**bugger** *noun* (1955)
**:** a person who plants electronic bugs
**bugger all** *noun* (circa 1937)
*slang British* **:** NOTHING
**bugger off** *intransitive verb* (1922)
*slang British* **:** LEAVE, DEPART
**bug·ger·y** \'bə-gə-rē\ *noun* (1514)
**:** SODOMY
¹**bug·gy** \'bə-gē\ *adjective* **bug·gi·er; -est** (1714)
**:** infested with bugs
²**buggy** *noun, plural* **buggies** [origin unknown] (1773)
**1 :** a light one-horse carriage made with two wheels in England and with four wheels in the U.S.
**2 :** a small cart or truck for short transportations of heavy materials
**3 :** BABY CARRIAGE
¹**bug·house** \'bəg-,haus\ *adjective* (1895)
**:** mentally deranged **:** CRAZY
²**bughouse** *noun* (1902)
**:** an insane asylum
¹**bu·gle** \'byü-gəl\ *noun* [Middle English, from Old French, from Late Latin *bugula*] (13th century)
**:** any of a genus (*Ajuga*) of plants of the mint family; *especially* **:** a European annual (*A. reptans*) that has spikes of blue flowers and is naturalized in the U.S.
²**bugle** *noun* [Middle English, buffalo, instrument made of buffalo horn, bugle, from Middle French, from Latin *buculus*, diminutive of *bos* head of cattle — more at COW] (14th century)
**:** a valveless brass instrument that resembles a trumpet and is used especially for military calls

**bugle**

³**bugle** *intransitive verb* **bu·gled; bu·gling** \-g(ə-)liŋ\ (1884)
**1 :** to sound a bugle
**2 :** to utter the characteristic rutting call of the bull elk
⁴**bugle** *noun* [perhaps from ²*bugle*] (1579)
**:** a small cylindrical bead of glass or plastic used for trimming especially on women's clothing
**bu·gler** \'byü-glər\ *noun* (1838)
**:** a person who sounds a bugle
**bu·gle·weed** \'byü-gəl-,wēd\ *noun* (circa 1818)
**1 :** any of a genus (*Lycopus*) of mints; *especially* **:** one (*Latin virginicus*) that is mildly narcotic and astringent
**2 :** ¹BUGLE
**bu·gloss** \'byü-,gläs, -,glòs\ *noun* [Middle French *buglosse*, from Latin *buglossa*, irregular from Greek *bouglōssos*, from *bous* head of cattle + *glōssa* tongue — more at COW, GLOSS] (14th century)
**:** any of several coarse hairy plants (genera *Anchusa, Lycopsis,* and *Echium*) of the borage family — compare VIPER'S BUGLOSS
**bug off** *intransitive verb* [probably short for *bugger off*] (1971)
**:** LEAVE, DEPART — usually used as a command
**buhl** \'bül, 'byü(ə)l\ *variant of* BOULLE
**buhr·stone** \'bər-,stōn\ *noun* [probably from *burr* + *stone*] (1690)
**1 :** a siliceous rock used for millstones
**2 :** a millstone cut from buhrstone
¹**build** \'bild\ *verb* **built** \'bilt\; **build·ing** [Middle English *bilden*, from Old English *byldan;* akin to Old English *būan* to dwell — more at BOWER] (before 12th century)
*transitive verb*
**1 :** to form by ordering and uniting materials by gradual means into a composite whole **:** CONSTRUCT
**2 :** to cause to be constructed
**3 :** to develop according to a systematic plan, by a definite process, or on a particular base
**4 :** INCREASE, ENLARGE
*intransitive verb*
**1 :** to engage in building
**2 a :** to progress toward a peak (as of intensity) ⟨*build* to a climax⟩ **b :** to develop in extent ⟨a crowd *building*⟩
— **build a fire under :** to stimulate to vigorous action
— **build into :** to make an integral part of ⟨*build* quality *into* the product⟩
— **build on :** to use as a foundation ⟨*building on* past experience⟩
²**build** *noun* (1667)
**:** form or mode of structure **:** MAKE; *especially* **:** bodily conformation of a person or lower animal
**build·able** \'bil-də-bəl\ *adjective* (1927)
**:** suitable for building ⟨*buildable* land⟩
**build·ed** *archaic past of* BUILD
**build·er** \'bil-dər\ *noun* (13th century)
**1 :** one that builds; *especially* **:** one that contracts to build and supervises building operations
**2 :** a substance added to or used with detergents to increase their cleansing action
**build in** *transitive verb* (1933)
**:** to make an integral part of something
**build·ing** \'bil-diŋ\ *noun* (14th century)
**1 :** a usually roofed and walled structure built for permanent use (as for a dwelling)
**2 :** the art or business of assembling materials into a structure
**building block** *noun* (1846)
**:** a unit of construction or composition
**build-up** \'bil-,dəp\ *noun* (1926)
**1 :** something produced by building up ⟨fluid *buildup* in the lungs⟩
**2 :** the act or process of building up
**build up** (1611)
*transitive verb*
**1 :** to develop gradually by increments ⟨*building up* endurance⟩ ⟨*built up* a library⟩
**2 :** to promote the health, strength, esteem, or reputation of
*intransitive verb*
**:** to accumulate or develop appreciably
— **build·er-up·per** \'bil-dər-'ə-pər\ *noun*
**built** \'bilt\ *adjective* (1621)
**:** formed as to physique or bodily contours ⟨slimly *built*⟩; *especially* **:** well or attractively formed
¹**built-in** \'bilt-'in\ *adjective* (1898)
**1 :** forming an integral part of a structure; *especially* **:** constructed as or in a recess in a wall
**2 :** INHERENT
²**built-in** \-,in\ *noun* (1930)
**:** a built-in piece of furniture
**built-up** \'bilt-'əp\ *adjective* (1829)
**1 :** made of several sections or layers fastened together
**2 :** covered with buildings
**buird·ly** \'bür(d)-lē\ *adjective* [probably alteration of *burly*] (1773)
*Scottish* **:** STURDY
**bulb** \'bəlb\ *noun* [Latin *bulbus,* from Greek *bolbos* bulbous plant] (circa 1601)
**1 a :** a resting stage of a plant (as the lily, onion, hyacinth, or tulip) that is usually formed underground and consists of a short stem base bearing one or more buds

**bulb 1a: *1* hyacinth, *2* onion, *3* tulip, *4* lily**

enclosed in overlapping membranous or fleshy leaves **b :** a fleshy structure (as a tuber or corm) resembling a bulb in appearance **c :** a plant having or developing from a bulb
**2 :** a bulb-shaped part; *specifically* **:** a glass envelope enclosing the light source of an electric lamp or such an envelope together with the light source it encloses
**3 :** a rounded or swollen anatomical structure
**4 :** a camera setting that indicates that the shutter can be opened by pressing on the release and closed by ending the pressure
— **bulbed** \'bəlbd\ *adjective*
**bul·bar** \'bəl-bər, -,bär\ *adjective* (1878)
**:** of or relating to a bulb; *specifically* **:** involving the medulla oblongata
**bul·bil** \'bəl-bəl, -,bil\ *noun* [French *bulbille,* diminutive of *bulbe* bulb, from Latin *bulbus*] (1831)
**:** BULBLET
**bulb·let** \'bəl-blət\ *noun* (1842)
**:** a small or secondary bulb; *especially* **:** an aerial deciduous bud produced in a leaf axil or replacing the flowers and capable when separated of producing a new plant
**bul·bo·ure·thral gland** \,bəl-(,)bō-yù-'rē-thrəl-\ *noun* [Latin *bulbus* bulb + English *urethral*] (circa 1903)
**:** COWPER'S GLAND
**bul·bous** \'bəl-bəs\ *adjective* (1578)
**1 :** having a bulb **:** growing from or bearing bulbs
**2 :** resembling a bulb especially in roundness ⟨a *bulbous* nose⟩
— **bul·bous·ly** *adverb*
**bul·bul** \'bùl-,bùl\ *noun* [Persian, from Arabic] (1665)
**1 :** a Persian songbird frequently mentioned in poetry that is probably a nightingale (*Erithacus megarhynchos*)
**2 :** any of a group of gregarious passerine birds (family Pycnonotidae) of Asia and Africa
**Bul·gar** \'bəl-,gär, 'bùl-\ *noun* [Medieval Latin *Bulgarus*] (1591)
**:** BULGARIAN
**Bul·gar·i·an** \,bəl-'gar-ē-ən, bùl-, -'ger-\ *noun* (1555)
**1 :** a native or inhabitant of Bulgaria
**2 :** the Slavic language of the Bulgarians
— **Bulgarian** *adjective*
¹**bulge** \'bəlj *also* 'bùlj\ *verb* **bulged; bulging** (15th century)
*transitive verb*
**:** to cause to bulge
*intransitive verb*
**1** *archaic* **:** BILGE
**2 a :** to jut out **:** SWELL **b :** to bend outward **c :** to become swollen or protuberant
**3 :** to be filled to overflowing
²**bulge** *noun* [Middle French *boulge, bouge* leather bag, curved part — more at BUDGET] (1622)
**1 :** BILGE 1, 2
**2 :** a protuberant or swollen part or place
**3 :** ADVANTAGE, UPPER HAND
**4 :** sudden expansion
*synonym* SEE PROJECTION
— **bulgy** \'bəl-jē *also* 'bùl-\ *adjective*
**bul·gur** \'bəl-gər, 'bùl-\ *noun* [Turkish] (1926)
**:** parched cracked wheat
**bu·lim·ia** \bü-'lē-mē-ə, byü-, -'li-\ *noun* [New Latin, from Greek *boulimia* great hunger, from *bou-,* augmentative prefix (from *bous* head of cattle) + *limos* hunger — more at COW] (14th century)
**1 :** an abnormal and constant craving for food
**2 :** a serious eating disorder that occurs chiefly in females, is characterized by compulsive overeating usually followed by self-induced vomiting or laxative or diuretic abuse, and is often accompanied by guilt and depression
— **bu·lim·ic** \-'lē-mik, -'li-\ *adjective or noun*

¹**bulk** \'bəlk *also* 'bûlk\ *noun* [Middle English, heap, bulk, from Old Norse *bulki* cargo] (15th century)
**1 a :** spatial dimension : MAGNITUDE **b :** material that forms a mass in the intestine; *especially* : FIBER 1d
**2 a :** BODY; *especially* : a large or corpulent human body **b :** an organized structure especially when viewed primarily as a mass of material **c :** a ponderous shapeless mass
**3 :** the main or greater part ☆
— **in bulk 1 :** not divided into parts or packaged in separate units **2 :** in large quantities
²**bulk** (1540)
*transitive verb*
**1 :** to cause to swell or bulge : STUFF
**2 :** to gather into a mass or aggregate
*intransitive verb*
**1 :** SWELL, EXPAND
**2 :** to appear as a factor : LOOM ⟨a consideration that *bulks* large in everyone's thinking⟩
³**bulk** *adjective* (1693)
**1 :** being in bulk ⟨*bulk* cement⟩
**2 :** of or relating to materials in bulk
**bulk·head** \'bəlk-,hed, 'bəl-,ked\ *noun* [*bulk* structure projecting from a building + *head*] (15th century)
**1 :** an upright partition separating compartments
**2 :** a structure or partition to resist pressure or to shut off water, fire, or gas
**3 :** a retaining wall along a waterfront
**4 :** a projecting framework with a sloping door giving access to a cellar stairway or a shaft
**bulk up** (1981)
*intransitive verb*
**:** to gain weight especially by becoming more muscular
*transitive verb*
**:** to cause to bulk up
**bulky** \'bəl-kē *also* 'bûl-\ *adjective* **bulk·i·er; -est** (15th century)
**1 a :** having bulk **b** (1) : large of its kind (2) : CORPULENT
**2 :** having great volume in proportion to weight ⟨a *bulky* knit sweater⟩
— **bulk·i·ly** \-kə-lē\ *adverb*
— **bulk·i·ness** \-kē-nəs\ *noun*
¹**bull** \'bûl, 'bəl\ *noun* [Middle English *bule*, from Old English *bula;* akin to Old Norse *boli* bull] (before 12th century)
**1 a :** a male bovine; *especially* : an adult uncastrated male ox **b :** a usually adult male of various large animals (as elephants, whales, or seals)
**2 :** one who buys securities or commodities in expectation of a price rise or who acts to effect such a rise — compare BEAR
**3 :** one that resembles a bull (as in brawny physique)
**4 :** BULLDOG
**5** *slang* : POLICE OFFICER, DETECTIVE
**6** *capitalized* : TAURUS
²**bull** *adjective* (13th century)
**1 a :** of or relating to a bull **b :** MALE **c :** suggestive of a bull
**2 :** large of its kind
³**bull** (1884)
*intransitive verb*
**:** to advance forcefully
*transitive verb*
**1 :** to act on with violence
**2 :** FORCE ⟨*bulled* his way through the crowd⟩
⁴**bull** *noun* [Middle English *bulle*, from Medieval Latin *bulla*, from Latin, bubble, amulet] (14th century)
**1 :** a solemn papal letter sealed with a bulla or with a red-ink imprint of the device on the bulla
**2 :** EDICT, DECREE
⁵**bull** (1609)
*transitive verb*
*slang* : to fool especially by fast boastful talk
*intransitive verb*
*slang* : to engage in idle and boastful talk

⁶**bull** *noun* [perhaps from obsolete *bull* to mock] (1640)
**1 :** a grotesque blunder in language
**2** *slang* : empty boastful talk
**3** *slang* : NONSENSE 2
**bul·la** \'bû-lə\ *noun, plural* **bul·lae** \'bû-,lē, -,lī\ (14th century)
**1** [Medieval Latin] : the round usually lead seal attached to a papal bull
**2** [New Latin, from Latin] : a hollow thin-walled rounded bony prominence
**3 :** a large vesicle or blister
**bul·lace** \'bû-ləs\ *noun* [Middle English *bolace*, from Middle French *beloce*, from Medieval Latin *bolluca*] (14th century)
**:** a European plum (*Prunus domestica insititia*) with small ovoid fruit in clusters
**bull-bait·ing** \'bûl-,bā-tiŋ, 'bəl-\ *noun* (circa 1580)
**:** the former practice of baiting bulls with dogs
**bull-bat** \'bûl-,bat, 'bəl-\ *noun* (1838)
**:** NIGHTHAWK 1a
¹**bull·dog** \'bûl-,dòg *also* 'bəl-\ *noun* (circa 1500)
**1 :** any of a breed of compact muscular short-haired dogs having widely separated forelegs and an undershot lower jaw that were developed in England to fight bulls
**2 :** a handgun with a thick usually short barrel
**3 :** a proctor's attendant at an English university
²**bulldog** *adjective* (1855)
**:** suggestive of a bulldog ⟨*bulldog* tenacity⟩
³**bulldog** *transitive verb* (1907)
**:** to throw (a steer) by seizing the horns and twisting the neck
— **bull·dog·ger** *noun*
— **bull·dog·ging** *noun*
**bull·doze** \'bûl-,dōz *also* 'bəl-\ *verb* [perhaps from ¹*bull* + alteration of *dose*] (1876)
*transitive verb*
**1 :** to coerce or restrain by threats : BULLY
**2 :** to move, clear, gouge out, or level off by pushing with or as if with a bulldozer
**3 :** to force insensitively or ruthlessly ⟨*bulldozed* the program through the legislature⟩
*intransitive verb*
**1 :** to operate a bulldozer
**2 :** to force one's way like a bulldozer
*synonym* see INTIMIDATE
**bull·doz·er** \-,dō-zər\ *noun* (1876)
**1 :** one that bulldozes
**2 :** a tractor-driven machine usually having a broad blunt horizontal blade for moving earth (as in road building)
**bull dyke** *noun* (circa 1942)
**:** an aggressively masculine lesbian — often used disparagingly
**bul·let** \'bû-lət *also* 'bə-\ *noun, often attributive* [Middle French *boulette* small ball & *boulet* missile, diminutives of *boule* ball — more at BOWL] (1579)
**1 :** a round or elongated missile (as of lead) to be fired from a firearm; *broadly* : CARTRIDGE 1a
**2 a :** something resembling a bullet (as in curved form) **b :** a large dot placed in printed matter to call attention to a particular passage
**3 :** a very fast and accurately thrown ball
— **bul·let·ed** \-lə-təd\ *adjective*
— **bul·let-proof** \-lə-,prüf\ *adjective*
¹**bul·le·tin** \'bû-lə-t³n *also* 'bə-\ *noun* [French, from Middle French, from *bullette* seal, notice, diminutive of *bulle* seal, from Medieval Latin *bulla*] (1765)
**1 :** a brief public notice issuing usually from an authoritative source; *specifically* : a brief news item intended for immediate publication or broadcast
**2 :** PERIODICAL; *especially* : the organ of an institution or association
²**bulletin** *transitive verb* (1838)
**:** to make public by bulletin
**bulletin board** *noun* (1831)

**1 :** a board for posting notices (as at a school)
**2 :** a program on a computer system that allows users to read and write public notices and is accessed usually by modem
**bullet train** *noun* (1966)
**:** a high-speed passenger train especially of Japan
**bull fiddle** *noun* (1880)
**:** DOUBLE BASS
— **bull fiddler** *noun*
**bull·fight** \'bûl-,fīt *also* 'bəl-\ *noun* (1788)
**:** a spectacle in which men ceremonially fight with and in Hispanic tradition kill bulls in an arena for public entertainment
— **bull·fight·er** \-,fī-tər\ *noun*
**bull·fight·ing** \-tiŋ\ *noun* (circa 1753)
**:** the action involved in a bullfight
**bull·finch** \'bûl-,finch *also* 'bəl-\ *noun* (circa 1570)
**:** a European finch (*Pyrrhula pyrrhula*) having in the male rosy red underparts, blue-gray back, and black cap, chin, tail, and wings; *also* : any of several other finches
**bull·frog** \-,fròg, -,fräg\ *noun* (1698)
**:** a heavy-bodied deep-voiced frog (*Rana catesbeiana*) of the eastern U.S. and southern Canada that has been introduced elsewhere
**bull·head** \-,hed\ *noun* (15th century)
**:** any of various large-headed fishes (as a sculpin); *especially* : any of several common freshwater catfishes (genus *Ameiurus* sometimes included in the genus *Ictalurus*) of the U.S.
**bull·head·ed** \-'he-dəd\ *adjective* (1818)
**:** stupidly stubborn : HEADSTRONG
— **bull·head·ed·ly** *adverb*
— **bull·head·ed·ness** *noun*
**bull·horn** \-,hòrn\ *noun* (1942)
**1 :** a loudspeaker on a naval ship
**2 :** a handheld combined microphone and loudspeaker
**bul·lion** \'bûl-yən, -,yän\ *noun* [Middle English, from Anglo-French, mint] (14th century)
**1 a :** gold or silver considered as so much metal; *specifically* : uncoined gold or silver in bars or ingots **b :** metal in the mass ⟨lead *bullion*⟩
**2 :** lace, braid, or fringe of gold or silver threads
**bull·ish** \'bû-lish *also* 'bə-\ *adjective* (1566)
**1 :** suggestive of a bull (as in brawniness)
**2 a :** marked by, tending to cause, or hopeful of rising prices (as in a stock market) **b :** optimistic about something's or someone's prospects
— **bull·ish·ly** *adverb*
— **bull·ish·ness** *noun*
**bull·mas·tiff** \'bûl-'mas-təf *also* 'bəl-\ *noun* (1871)
**:** any of a breed of large powerful dogs developed by crossing bulldogs with mastiffs
**Bull Moose** *noun* [*bull moose*, emblem of the Progressive party of 1912] (1912)
**:** a follower of Theodore Roosevelt in the U.S. presidential campaign of 1912

---

☆ **SYNONYMS**
**Bulk, mass, volume** mean the aggregate that forms a body or unit. BULK implies an aggregate that is impressively large, heavy, or numerous (the darkened *bulk* of the skyscrapers). MASS suggests an aggregate made by piling together things of the same kind ⟨a *mass* of boulders⟩. VOLUME applies to an aggregate without shape or outline and capable of flowing or fluctuating ⟨a tremendous *volume* of water⟩.

---

\ə\ abut  \ᵊ\ kitten  \ər\ further  \a\ ash  \ā\ ace
\ä\ mop, mar  \aû\ out  \ch\ chin  \e\ bet  \ē\ easy
\g\ go  \i\ hit  \ī\ ice  \j\ job  \ŋ\ sing  \ō\ go
\ò\ law  \òi\ boy  \th\ thin  \th\ the  \ü\ loot  \û\ foot
\y\ yet  \zh\ vision  *see also* Guide to Pronunciation

**Bull Moos·er** \-'mü-sər\ *noun* (1912)
: BULL MOOSE
**bull neck** *noun* (1830)
: a thick short powerful neck
— **bull·necked** \'bùl-'nekt *also* 'bəl-\ *adjective*
**bull·ock** \'bù-lək *also* 'bə-\ *noun* (before 12th century)
**1** : a young bull
**2** : a castrated bull : STEER
— **bull·ocky** \-lə-kē\ *adjective*
**bul·lous** \'bù-ləs\ *adjective* (1833)
: resembling or characterized by bullae : VESICULAR ⟨*bullous* lesions⟩
**bull pen** *noun* (1809)
**1** : a large cell where prisoners are detained until brought into court
**2 a** : a place on a baseball field where pitchers warm up before they start pitching **b** : the relief pitchers of a baseball team
**3** : an open work area not divided into offices
**bull·ring** \'bùl-,riŋ\ *noun* (1802)
: an arena for bullfights
**bull session** *noun* [[6]*bull*] (1920)
: an informal discursive group discussion
**bull's-eye** \'bùl-,zī *also* 'bəl-\ *noun, plural* **bull's-eyes** (1825)
**1** : a very hard globular candy
**2** : a circular piece of glass with a lump in the middle formed at the end of a glassblower's pipe
**3 a** : the center of a target; *also* : something central or crucial **b** : a shot that hits the bull's-eye; *broadly* : something that precisely attains a desired end
**4** : a simple lens of short focal distance; *also* : a lantern with such a lens
**bull's-eye window** *noun* (1926)
: a circular window; *also* : a window made up of glassblower's bull's-eyes
[1]**bull·shit** \'bùl-,shit *also* 'bəl-\ *noun* [[1]*bull* & [6]*bull*] (circa 1915)
: NONSENSE; *especially* : foolish insolent talk — usually considered vulgar
[2]**bullshit** (circa 1942)
*intransitive verb*
**1** : to talk foolishly, boastfully, or idly — usually considered vulgar
**2** : to engage in a discursive discussion — usually considered vulgar
*transitive verb*
: to talk nonsense to especially with the intention of deceiving or misleading — usually considered vulgar
**bull·shot** \-,shät\ *noun* (1964)
: a drink made of vodka and bouillon
**bull snake** *noun* (1784)
: any of several large harmless North American snakes (genus *Pituophis*) that feed chiefly on rodents — called also *gopher snake, pine snake*
**bull·ter·ri·er** \'bùl-'ter-ē-ər *also* 'bəl-\ *noun* [*bull*dog + *terrier*] (1848)
: any of a breed of short-haired terriers originated in England by crossing the bulldog with terriers
**bull thistle** *noun* (1863)
: a European thistle (*Cirsium vulgare*) with rather large heads and prickly leaves that is naturalized as a weed in the U.S.
**bull tongue** *noun* (1831)
: a wide blade attached to a cultivator or plow to stir the soil, kill weeds, or mark furrows
**bull·whip** \'bùl-,(h)wip *also* 'bəl-\ *noun* (1852)
: a rawhide whip with a very long plaited lash
[1]**bul·ly** \'bù-lē, 'bə-\ *noun, plural* **bullies** [probably modification of Dutch *boel* lover, from Middle High German *buole*] (1538)
**1** *archaic* **a** : SWEETHEART **b** : a fine chap
**2 a** : a blustering browbeating person; *especially* : one habitually cruel to others who are weaker **b** : PIMP
**3** : a hired ruffian
[2]**bully** *adjective* (1681)
**1** : EXCELLENT, FIRST-RATE — often used in interjectional expressions ⟨*bully* for you⟩

**2** : resembling or characteristic of a bully
[3]**bully** *verb* **bul·lied; bul·ly·ing** (1710)
*transitive verb*
**1** : to treat abusively
**2** : to affect by means of force or coercion
*intransitive verb*
: to use browbeating language or behavior : BLUSTER
*synonym* see INTIMIDATE
[4]**bully** *noun* [probably modification of French (*bœuf*) *boulli* boiled beef] (1753)
: pickled or canned usually corned beef
**bul·ly-boy** \'bù-lē-,bói, 'bə-\ *noun* (1925)
: a swaggering tough
**bully pulpit** *noun* (1976)
: a prominent public position (as a political office) that provides an opportunity for expounding one's views; *also* : such an opportunity
**bul·ly·rag** \-,rag\ *transitive verb* [origin unknown] (circa 1790)
**1** : to intimidate by bullying
**2** : to vex by teasing : BADGER
**bul·rush** *also* **bull·rush** \'bùl-,rəsh\ *noun* [Middle English *bulrysche*] (15th century)
: any of several large rushes or sedges growing in wetlands: as **a** : any of a genus of annual or perennial sedges (*Scirpus*, especially *S. lacustris*) that bear solitary or much-clustered spikelets containing perfect flowers with a perianth of six bristles **b** *British* : either of two cattails (*Typha latifolia* and *T. angustifolia*) **c** : PAPYRUS
[1]**bul·wark** \'bùl-(,)wərk, -,wórk; 'bəl-(,)wərk; *sense 3 also* 'bə-,läk\ *noun* [Middle English *bulwerke*, from Middle Dutch *bolwerc*, from Middle High German, from *bole* plank + *werc* work] (15th century)
**1 a** : a solid wall-like structure raised for defense : RAMPART **b** : BREAKWATER, SEAWALL
**2** : a strong support or protection
**3** : the side of a ship above the upper deck — usually used in plural
*word history* see BOULEVARD
[2]**bulwark** *transitive verb* (15th century)
: to fortify or safeguard with a bulwark
[1]**bum** \'bəm\ *noun* [Middle English *bom*] (14th century)
*chiefly British* : BUTTOCKS — sometimes considered vulgar
[2]**bum** *adjective* [perhaps from [4]*bum*] (1859)
**1 a** : of poor quality or nature : INVALID, INFERIOR ⟨*bum* advice⟩ ⟨a *bum* check⟩ **b** : acutely disagreeable ⟨a *bum* trip⟩
**2** : not functioning because of damage or injury : DISABLED ⟨a *bum* knee⟩
[3]**bum** *verb* **bummed; bum·ming** [probably back-formation from [1]*bummer*] (1863)
*intransitive verb*
**1** : LOAF
**2** : to spend time unemployed and often wandering — often used with *around*
*transitive verb*
: to obtain by begging : CADGE
[4]**bum** *noun* [probably short for *bummer*] (1864)
**1 a** : one who sponges off others and avoids work **b** : one who performs a function poorly ⟨called the umpire a *bum*⟩ **c** : one who devotes his time to a recreational activity ⟨a beach *bum*⟩ ⟨ski *bums*⟩
**2** : VAGRANT, TRAMP
— **on the bum** : with no settled residence or means of support
[5]**bum** *noun* [probably from [3]*bum*] (1871)
: a drinking spree : BENDER
**bum·ber·shoot** \'bəm-bər-,shüt\ *noun* [*bumber*- (alteration of *umbr*- in *umbrella*) + *-shoot* (alteration of *-chute* in *parachute*)] (circa 1896)
: UMBRELLA
[1]**bum·ble** \'bəm-bəl\ *intransitive verb* **bumbled; bum·bling** \-b(ə-)liŋ\ [Middle English *bomblen* to boom, of imitative origin] (15th century)
**1** : BUZZ

**2** : DRONE, RUMBLE
[2]**bumble** *verb* **bumbled; bumbling** [perhaps alteration of *bungle*] (1532)
*intransitive verb*
**1** : BLUNDER; *specifically* : to speak ineptly in a stuttering and faltering manner
**2** : to proceed unsteadily : STUMBLE
*transitive verb*
: BUNGLE
— **bum·bler** \-b(ə-)lər\ *noun*
— **bum·bling·ly** \-b(ə-)liŋ-lē\ *adverb*
**bum·ble·bee** \'bəm-bəl-,bē\ *noun* (1530)
: any of numerous large robust hairy social bees (genus *Bombus*)
**bum·boat** \'bəm-,bōt\ *noun* [probably from Low German *bumboot*, from *bum* tree + *boot* boat] (1769)
: a boat that brings provisions and commodities for sale to larger ships in port or offshore
**bumf** *also* **bumph** \'bəm(p)f\ *noun* [from *bumf* toilet paper, short for *bumfodder*, from [1]*bum* + *fodder*] (circa 1889)
*chiefly British* : PAPERWORK
**bummed** \'bəmd\ *adjective* [probably back-formation from [2]*bummer*] (1971)
: DISAPPOINTED, DEPRESSED — usually used with *out*
[1]**bum·mer** \'bə-mər\ *noun* [probably modification of German *Bummler* loafer, from *bummeln* to dangle, loaf] (1855)
: one that bums
[2]**bummer** *noun* [[2]*bum* + [2]*-er*] (1967)
**1** : an unpleasant experience (as a bad reaction to a hallucinogenic drug)
**2** : FAILURE, FLOP
[1]**bump** \'bəmp\ *noun* [probably imitative of the sound of a blow] (1592)
**1** : a relatively abrupt convexity or protuberance on a surface: as **a** : a swelling of tissue **b** : a cranial protuberance
**2 a** : a sudden forceful blow, impact, or jolt **b** : DEMOTION
**3** : an act of thrusting the hips forward in an erotic manner
[2]**bump** (1611)
*transitive verb*
**1** : to strike or knock with force or violence
**2** : to collide with
**3 a** (1) : to dislodge with a jolt (2) : to subject to a scalar change ⟨rates being *bumped* up⟩ **b** : to oust usually by virtue of seniority or priority ⟨was *bumped* from the flight⟩
*intransitive verb*
**1** : to knock against something with a forceful jolt
**2** : to proceed in or as if in a series of bumps
**3** : to encounter something that is an obstacle or hindrance ⟨*bumped* up against a chair⟩
— **bump into** : to encounter especially by chance
[1]**bum·per** \'bəm-pər\ *noun* [probably from *bump* to bulge] (1676)
**1** : a brimming cup or glass
**2** : something unusually large
[2]**bumper** *adjective* (1885)
**1** : unusually large ⟨a *bumper* crop⟩
**2** : BANNER 2
[3]**bump·er** \'bəm-pər\ *noun* (1839)
**1** : a device for absorbing shock or preventing damage (as in collision); *specifically* : a usually metal bar at either end of an automobile
**2** : one that bumps
**bumper car** *noun* (1959)
: a small electric car made to be driven around in an enclosure and to be bumped into others (as at an amusement park)
**bumper sticker** *noun* (1967)
: a strip of adhesive paper or plastic bearing a printed message and designed to be stuck on a vehicle's bumper
**bumper-to-bumper** *adjective* (1951)
: marked by long closed lines of cars
[1]**bump·kin** \'bəm(p)-kən\ *noun* [perhaps from Flemish *bommekijn* small cask, from Middle Dutch, from *bomme* cask] (1570)
: an awkward and unsophisticated rustic

— **bump·kin·ish** \-kə-nish\ *adjective*

— **bump·kin·ly** \-kən-lē\ *adjective*

²**bump·kin** *or* **bum·kin** \'bəm(p)-kən\ *noun* [probably from Flemish *boomken,* diminutive of *boom* tree] (circa 1632)
: a spar projecting from a ship especially at the stern

**bump off** *transitive verb* (1910)
: to murder casually or cold-bloodedly

**bump·tious** \'bəm(p)-shəs\ *adjective* [¹*bump* + *-tious* (as in *fractious*)] (1803)
: presumptuously, obtusely, and often noisily self-assertive : OBTRUSIVE

— **bump·tious·ly** *adverb*

— **bump·tious·ness** *noun*

**bumpy** \'bəm-pē\ *adjective* **bump·i·er; -est** (1865)
**1** : having or covered with bumps ⟨a *bumpy* road⟩ ⟨*bumpy* skin⟩
**2 a** : marked by bumps or jolts ⟨a *bumpy* ride⟩ **b** : marked by or full of difficulties ⟨a *bumpy* relationship⟩

— **bump·i·ly** \-pə-lē\ *adverb*

— **bump·i·ness** \-pē-nəs\ *noun*

**bum's rush** \'bəmz-\ *noun* (1922)
: forcible eviction or dismissal

¹**bun** \'bən\ *noun* [Middle English *bunne*] (14th century)
**1** : a sweet or plain small bread; *especially* : a round roll
**2** : a knot of hair shaped like a bun
**3** *plural* : BUTTOCKS

²**bun** *noun* [perhaps from ¹*bun*] (1901)
: LOAD 4

**Bu·na** \'byü-nə, 'bü-\ *trademark*
— used for any of several rubbers made by polymerization or copolymerization of butadiene

¹**bunch** \'bənch\ *noun* [Middle English *bunche*] (14th century)
**1** : PROTUBERANCE, SWELLING
**2 a** : a number of things of the same kind ⟨a *bunch* of grapes⟩ **b** : GROUP 2a ⟨a *bunch* of friends⟩ **c** : a considerable amount : LOT ⟨a *bunch* of money⟩

— **bunch·i·ly** \'bən-chə-lē\ *adverb*

— **bunchy** \-chē\ *adjective*

²**bunch** (14th century)
*intransitive verb*
**1** : SWELL, PROTRUDE
**2** : to form a group or cluster — often used with *up*
*transitive verb*
: to form into a bunch

**bunch·ber·ry** \'bənch-,ber-ē\ *noun* (1845)
: a creeping perennial herb (*Cornus canadensis*) of the dogwood family that has whorled leaves and white floral bracts and bears red berries in capitate cymes

**bunch·grass** \-,gras\ *noun* (1839)
: any of several grasses (as of the genus *Andropogon*) especially of the western U.S. that grow in tufts

**bun·co** *or* **bun·ko** \'bəŋ-(,)kō\ *noun, plural* **buncos** *or* **bunkos** [perhaps alteration of Spanish *banca* bench, banking, bank in gambling, from Italian — more at BANK] (1872)
: a swindling game or scheme

— **bunco** *transitive verb*

¹**bund** \'bənd\ *noun* [Hindi *band,* from Persian] (1810)
**1** : an embankment used especially in India to control the flow of water
**2** : an embanked thoroughfare along a river or the sea especially in the Far East

²**bund** \'bund, 'bənd, 'bunt\ *noun, often capitalized* [Yiddish *bund* & German *Bund,* from Middle High German *bunt;* akin to Old English *byndel*] (1850)
: a political association: as **a** : a Jewish socialist organization founded in czarist Russia in 1897 **b** : a pro-Nazi German-American organization of the 1930s

— **bund·ist** \'bun-dist, 'bən-\ *noun, often capitalized*

¹**bun·dle** \'bən-d°l\ *noun* [Middle English *bundel,* from Middle Dutch; akin to Old English *byndel* bundle, *bindan* to bind] (14th century)
**1 a** : a group of things fastened together for convenient handling **b** : PACKAGE, PARCEL **c** : a considerable number : LOT **d** : a sizable sum of money **e** : a person embodying a specified quality or characteristic ⟨a *bundle* of energy⟩
**2 a** : a small band of mostly parallel fibers (as of nerve or muscle) **b** : VASCULAR BUNDLE

²**bundle** *verb* **bun·dled; bun·dling** \'bən(d)-liŋ, 'bən-d°l-iŋ\ (circa 1628)
*transitive verb*
**1** : to make into a bundle or package : WRAP
**2** : to hustle or hurry unceremoniously ⟨*bundled* the children off to school⟩
**3** : to include (a product or service) with a related product for sale at a single price ⟨software is *bundled* with computer hardware⟩
*intransitive verb*
**1** : HURRY, HUSTLE
**2** : to practice bundling

— **bun·dler** \-lər, -d°l-ər\ *noun*

**bundle up** (1918)
*transitive verb*
: to dress (someone) warmly
*intransitive verb*
: to dress warmly

**bun·dling** \'bən(d)-liŋ, 'bən-d°l-iŋ\ *noun* (1781)
: a former custom of an unmarried couple's occupying the same bed without undressing especially during courtship

¹**bung** \'bəŋ\ *noun* [Middle English, from Middle Dutch *bonne, bonghe*] (15th century)
**1** : the stopper especially in the bunghole of a cask; *also* : BUNGHOLE
**2** : the cecum or anus especially of a slaughtered animal

²**bung** *transitive verb* (1589)
**1** : to plug with or as if with a bung
**2** *British* : THROW, TOSS ⟨*bung* a spanner into the works —P. G. Wodehouse⟩

**bun·ga·low** \'bəŋ-gə-,lō\ *noun* [Hindi *baṅglā,* literally, (house) in the Bengal style] (1676)
: a usually one-storied house with a low-pitched roof

**bun·gee cord** \'bən-jē-\ *noun* [origin unknown] (1948)
: an elasticized cord used especially as a fastening or shock-absorbing device — called also *bungee*

**bung·hole** \'bəŋ-,hōl\ *noun* (1571)
: a hole for emptying or filling a cask

**bun·gle** \'bəŋ-gəl\ *verb* **bun·gled; bun·gling** \-g(ə-)liŋ\ [perhaps of Scandinavian origin; akin to Icelandic *banga* to hammer] (1549)
*intransitive verb*
: to act or work clumsily and awkwardly
*transitive verb*
: MISHANDLE, BOTCH

— **bungle** *noun*

— **bun·gler** \-g(ə-)lər\ *noun*

— **bun·gling·ly** \-g(ə-)liŋ-lē\ *adverb*

**bun·gle·some** \-gəl-səm\ *adjective* (circa 1889)
: AWKWARD, CLUMSY

**bung up** *transitive verb* (1951)
: BATTER

**bun·ion** \'bən-yən\ *noun* [probably alteration of *bunny* swelling] (circa 1718)
: an inflamed swelling of the small sac on the first joint of the big toe

¹**bunk** \'bəŋk\ *noun* [probably short for *bunker*] (1758)
**1 a** : BUNK BED **b** : a built-in bed (as on a ship) that is often one of a tier of berths **c** : a sleeping place
**2** : a feeding trough for farm animals and especially cattle

²**bunk** (1840)
*intransitive verb*
: to occupy a bunk or bed : stay the night ⟨*bunked* with a friend for the night⟩

*transitive verb*
: to provide with a bunk or bed

³**bunk** *noun* (1900)
: BUNKUM, NONSENSE

⁴**bunk** *noun* [origin unknown] (circa 1870)
*British* : a hurried departure or escape — usually used in the phrase *do a bunk*

**bunk bed** *noun* (1924)
: one of two single beds usually placed one above the other

¹**bun·ker** \'bəŋ-kər\ *noun* [Scots *bonker* chest, box] (1839)
**1** : a bin or compartment for storage; *especially* : one on shipboard for the ship's fuel
**2 a** : a protective embankment or dugout; *especially* : a fortified chamber mostly below ground often built of reinforced concrete and provided with embrasures **b** : a sand trap or embankment constituting a hazard on a golf course

— **bun·kered** \-kərd\ *adjective*

²**bunker** *verb* **bun·kered; bun·ker·ing** \-k(ə-)riŋ\ (1891)
*intransitive verb*
: to fill a ship's bunker with coal or oil
*transitive verb*
**1** : to place or store in a bunker
**2** : to hit (a golf ball or shot) into a bunker

**bunker mentality** *noun* (1976)
: a state of mind especially among members of a group that is characterized by chauvinistic defensiveness and self-righteous intolerance of criticism

**bunk·house** \'bəŋk-,haủs\ *noun* (1876)
: a rough simple building providing sleeping quarters

**bun·kum** *or* **bun·combe** \'bəŋ-kəm\ *noun* [*Buncombe* county, N.C.; from a remark made by its congressman, who defended an irrelevant speech by claiming that he was speaking to Buncombe] (1845)
: insincere or foolish talk : NONSENSE ◆

**bun·ny** \'bə-nē\ *noun, plural* **bunnies** [English dialect *bun* rabbit] (circa 1690)
**1** : RABBIT; *especially* : a young rabbit
**2** : a desirable young woman

**Bun·ra·ku** \bün-'rä-(,)kü\ *noun* [Japanese] (1920)

---

◇ WORD HISTORY
**bunkum** The word *bunkum* or *buncombe* "nonsense" first occurs in 1828 in the phrase *talk to bunkum,* alluding to overly long congressional speeches given to a nearly empty chamber. According to a tale that has become part of American political folklore, this phrase originated around 1820, when Felix Walker (1753–1828), a U.S. Congressman who represented a district in North Carolina that included Buncombe County, persisted in delivering an exceptionally wearisome speech to the Sixteenth Congress, despite the objections of his impatient colleagues. In self-defense Walker explained that he had done what his constituents expected of him, which was "to make a speech for Buncombe." Whatever the veracity of this story, *bunkum* has remained thoroughly entrenched in American English. The noun *bunk,* recorded in 1893 in the sense "something fraudulent" and in 1900 alluding to nonsensical talk, is probably short for *bunkum,* though it has very likely been influenced by *bunco* (or *bunko*), a word that developed in the late 19th century in reference to rigged games of chance.

---

\ə\ abut \ᵊ\ kitten \ər\ further \a\ ash \ā\ ace
\ä\ mop, mar \aủ\ out \ch\ chin \e\ bet \ē\ easy
\g\ go \i\ hit \ī\ ice \j\ job \ŋ\ sing \ō\ go
\ó\ law \ói\ boy \th\ thin \t̲h̲\ the \ü\ loot \ủ\ foot
\y\ yet \zh\ vision *see also* Guide to Pronunciation

: Japanese puppet theater featuring large costumed wooden puppets, puppeteers who are onstage, and a chanter who speaks all the lines

**Bun·sen burner** \'bən(t)-sən-\ *noun* [Robert Welsh *Bunsen*] (circa 1888)
: a gas burner consisting typically of a straight tube with small holes at the bottom where air enters and mixes with the gas to produce an intensely hot blue flame

**¹bunt** \'bənt\ *noun* [perhaps from Low German, bundle, from Middle Low German; akin to Old English *byndel* bundle] (circa 1582)
**1 a** : the middle part of a square sail **b** : the part of a furled sail gathered up in a bunch at the center of the yard
**2** : the bagging part of a fishing net

**²bunt** *verb* [alteration of *butt*] (1584)
*transitive verb*
**1** : to strike or push with or as if with the head : BUTT
**2** : to push or tap (a baseball) lightly without swinging the bat
*intransitive verb*
: to bunt a baseball
— **bunt·er** *noun*

**³bunt** *noun* (1767)
**1** : an act or instance of bunting
**2** : a bunted ball

**⁴bunt** *noun* [origin unknown] (circa 1790)
: a destructive covered smut of wheat caused by a fungus (*Tilletia foetida* or *T. caries*)

**¹bun·ting** \'bən-tiŋ\ *noun* [Middle English] (14th century)
: any of various stout-billed passerine birds (family Emberizidae) included with some of the finches — compare INDIGO BUNTING

**²bunting** *noun* [perhaps from English dialect *bunt* (to sift)] (1711)
**1** : a lightweight loosely woven fabric used chiefly for flags and festive decorations
**2 a** : FLAGS **b** : decorations especially in the colors of the national flag

**³bunting** *noun* [term of endearment in the nursery rhyme "Bye, baby bunting"] (1922)
: an infant's hooded sleeping bag made of napped fabric

**bunt·line** \'bənt-,līn, -lən\ *noun* (1627)
: one of the lines attached to the foot of a square sail to haul the sail up to the yard for furling

**Bun·yan·esque** \,bən-yə-'nesk\ *adjective* (1888)
**1** [John *Bunyan*] : of, relating to, or suggestive of the allegorical writings of John Bunyan
**2** [Paul *Bunyan*, legendary giant lumberjack of U.S. & Canada] **a** : of, relating to, or suggestive of the tales of Paul Bunyan **b** : of fantastically large size

**¹buoy** \'bü-ē, 'bȯi\ *noun* [Middle English *boye*, probably from Middle Dutch *boeye*; akin to Old High German *bouhhan* sign — more at BEACON] (13th century)
**1** : FLOAT 2; *especially* : a floating object moored to the bottom to mark a channel or something (as a shoal) lying under the water
**2** : LIFE BUOY

**²buoy** (1596)
*transitive verb*
**1** : to mark by or as if by a buoy
**2 a** : to keep afloat **b** : SUPPORT, UPLIFT 〈an economy *buoyed* by the dramatic postwar growth of industry —*Time*〉
**3** : to raise the spirits of — usually used with *up* 〈hope *buoys* him up〉
*intransitive verb*
: FLOAT — usually used with *up*

**buoy·ance** \'bȯi-ən(t)s, 'bü-yən(t)s\ *noun* (1821)
: BUOYANCY

**buoy·an·cy** \'bȯi-ən(t)-sē, 'bü-yən(t)-\ *noun* (1713)

**1 a** : the tendency of a body to float or to rise when submerged in a fluid **b** : the power of a fluid to exert an upward force on a body placed in it; *also* : the upward force exerted
**2** : the ability to recover quickly from depression or discouragement : RESILIENCE

**buoy·ant** \'bȯi-ənt, 'bü-yənt\ *adjective* (1578)
: having buoyancy: as **a** : capable of floating **b** : CHEERFUL, GAY **c** : capable of recovering : having positive indications 〈a *buoyant* economy〉
— **buoy·ant·ly** *adverb*

**bup·pie** \'bə-pē\ *noun* [¹*b*lack + *yuppie*] (1984)
: a college-educated black adult who is employed in a well-paying profession and who lives or works in or near a large city

**bur** *variant of* BURR

**Bur·ber·ry** \'bər-b(ə-)rē, 'bər-,ber-ē\ *trademark*
— used for various fabrics used especially for coats for outdoor wear

**¹bur·ble** \'bər-bəl\ *intransitive verb* **bur·bled; bur·bling** \-b(ə-)liŋ\ [Middle English] (14th century)
**1** : BUBBLE
**2** : BABBLE, PRATTLE
— **bur·bler** \-b(ə-)lər\ *noun*

**²burble** *noun* (1898)
**1** : PRATTLE
**2** : the breaking up of the streamline flow of air about a body (as an airplane wing)
— **bur·bly** \-b(ə-)lē\ *adjective*

**bur·bot** \'bər-bət\ *noun, plural* **burbot** *also* **burbots** [Middle English *borbot*, from Middle French *bourbote*, from *bourbeter* to burrow in the mud] (14th century)
: a Holarctic freshwater fish (*Lota lota*) of the cod family having barbels on the nose and chin

**burbs** \'bərbz\ *noun plural* (1971)
: SUBURBS

**¹bur·den** \'bər-dᵊn\ *noun* [Middle English, from Old English *byrthen*; akin to Old English *beran* to carry — more at BEAR] (before 12th century)
**1 a** : something that is carried : LOAD **b** : DUTY, RESPONSIBILITY
**2** : something oppressive or worrisome
**3 a** : the bearing of a load — usually used in the phrase *beast of burden* **b** : capacity for carrying cargo 〈a ship of a hundred tons *burden*〉
**4** : the amount of a deleterious parasite, growth, or substance present in a human or animal body 〈worm *burden*〉 〈cancer *burden*〉

**²burden** *transitive verb* **bur·dened; bur·den·ing** \'bərd-niŋ, 'bər-dᵊn-iŋ\ (1541)
: LOAD, OPPRESS 〈I will not *burden* you with a lengthy account〉

**³burden** *noun* [Middle English *burdoun*, from Middle French *bourdon* a drone bass, of imitative origin] (14th century)
**1** *archaic* : a bass or accompanying part
**2 a** : CHORUS, REFRAIN **b** : a central topic : THEME

**burden of proof** (1593)
: the duty of proving a disputed assertion or charge

**bur·den·some** \'bər-dᵊn-səm\ *adjective* (1578)
: imposing or constituting a burden : OPPRESSIVE 〈*burdensome* restrictions〉
**synonym** SEE ONEROUS

**bur·dock** \'bər-,däk\ *noun* (15th century)
: any of a genus (*Arctium*) of coarse composite herbs bearing globular flower heads with prickly bracts

**bu·reau** \'byu̇r-(,)ō\ *noun, plural* **bureaus** *also* **bu·reaux** \-(,)ōz\ [French, desk, cloth covering for desks, from Old French *burel* woolen cloth, from (assumed) Old French *bure*, from Late Latin *burra* shaggy cloth] (1699)
**1 a** *British* : WRITING DESK; *especially* : one having drawers and a slant top **b** : a low chest of drawers for use in a bedroom

**2 a** : a specialized administrative unit; *especially* : a subdivision of an executive department of a government **b** : a branch of a newspaper, newsmagazine, or wire service in an important news center **c** : a usually commercial agency that serves as an intermediary especially for exchanging information or coordinating activities 〈credit *bureau*〉

**bu·reau·cra·cy** \byu̇-'rä-krə-sē\ *noun, plural* **-cies** [French *bureaucratie*, from *bureau* + *-cratie* -cracy] (1818)
**1 a** : a body of nonelective government officials **b** : an administrative policy-making group
**2** : government characterized by specialization of functions, adherence to fixed rules, and a hierarchy of authority
**3** : a system of administration marked by officialism, red tape, and proliferation

**bu·reau·crat** \'byu̇r-ə-,krat\ *noun* (1842)
: a member of a bureaucracy

**bu·reau·crat·ese** \,byu̇r-ə-(,)kra-'tēz, -'tēs\ *noun* (1949)
: a style of language held to be characteristic of bureaucrats and marked by the prevalence of abstractions, jargon, euphemisms, and circumlocutions

**bu·reau·crat·ic** \,byu̇r-ə-'kra-tik\ *adjective* (1836)
: of, relating to, or having the characteristics of a bureaucracy or a bureaucrat 〈*bureaucratic* government〉
— **bu·reau·crat·i·cal·ly** \-ti-k(ə-)lē\ *adverb*

**bu·reau·cra·tise** *British variant of* BUREAUCRATIZE

**bu·reau·crat·ism** \'byu̇r-ə-(,)kra-,ti-zəm\ *noun* (1880)
: a bureaucratic system : BUREAUCRACY

**bu·reau·cra·tize** \byu̇-'rä-krə-,tīz\ *transitive verb* **-tized; -tiz·ing** (1892)
: to make bureaucratic
— **bu·reau·cra·ti·za·tion** \-,rä-krə-tə-'zā-shən\ *noun*

**bu·rette** *or* **bu·ret** \byu̇-'ret\ *noun* [Middle French, cruet, from *buire* pitcher, perhaps of Germanic origin; akin to Old English *būr* storehouse, dwelling — more at BOWER] (1836)
: a graduated glass tube with a small aperture and stopcock for delivering measured quantities of liquid or for measuring the liquid or gas received or discharged

**burg** \'bərg\ *noun* [Old English — more at BOROUGH] (1753)
**1** : an ancient or medieval fortress or walled town
**2** [German *Burg*] : CITY, TOWN

**bur·gage** \'bər-gij\ *noun* [Middle English, property held by burgage tenure, from Middle French *bourgage*, from Old French, from *bourg, borc* town — more at BOURG] (15th century)
: a tenure by which real property in England and Scotland was held under the king or a lord for a yearly rent or for watching and warding

**bur·gee** \,bər-'jē, 'bər-,\ *noun* [perhaps from French dialect *bourgeais* shipowner] (1750)
**1** : a swallow-tailed flag used especially by ships for signals or identification
**2** : the usually triangular identifying flag of a yacht club

**bur·geon** \'bər-jən\ *intransitive verb* [Middle English *burjonen*, from *burjon* bud, from Old French, from (assumed) Vulgar Latin *burrion-, burrio*, from Late Latin *burra* fluff, shaggy cloth] (14th century)
**1 a** : to send forth new growth (as buds or branches) : SPROUT **b** : BLOOM
**2** : to grow and expand rapidly : FLOURISH

**bur·ger** \'bər-gər\ *noun* (1939)
**1** : HAMBURGER
**2** : a sandwich similar to a hamburger — often used in combination 〈tofu *burger*〉

buoy 1

**bur·gess** \'bər-jəs\ *noun* [Middle English *burgeis*, from Old French *borjois*, from *borc*] (13th century)
**1 a** : a citizen of a British borough **b** : a representative of a borough, corporate town, or university in the British Parliament
**2** : a representative in the popular branch of the legislature of colonial Maryland and Virginia

**burgh** \'bər-(,)ō, 'bə-(,)rō\ *noun* [Middle English — more at BOROUGH] (12th century)
: BOROUGH; *specifically* : an incorporated town in Scotland having local jurisdiction of certain services
— **burgh·al** \'bər-gəl\ *adjective*

**bur·gher** \'bər-gər\ *noun* (13th century)
**1** : an inhabitant of a borough or a town
**2** : a member of the middle class : a prosperous solid citizen

**bur·glar** \'bər-glər *also* -gə-lər\ *noun* [Anglo-French *burgler*, from Medieval Latin *burglator*, probably alteration of *burgator*, from *burgare* to commit burglary] (1541)
: one who commits burglary

**bur·glar·ize** \'bər-glə-,rīz *also* 'bər-gə-lə-\ *verb* **-ized; -iz·ing** (1871)
*transitive verb*
**1** : to break into and steal from
**2** : to commit burglary against
*intransitive verb*
: to commit burglary

**bur·glar·proof** \'bər-glər-,prüf\ *adjective* (1856)
: protected against or designed to afford protection against burglary

**bur·glary** \'bər-glə-rē *also* -gə-lə-rē *also* -gəl-rē\ *noun, plural* **-glar·ies** (circa 1523)
: the act of breaking and entering a dwelling at night to commit a felony (as theft); *broadly* : the entering of a building with the intent to commit a crime
— **bur·glar·i·ous** \,bər-'glar-ē-əs, -'gler-\ *adjective*
— **bur·glar·i·ous·ly** *adverb*

**bur·gle** \'bər-gəl\ *transitive verb* **bur·gled; bur·gling** \-g(ə-)liŋ\ [back-formation from *burglar*] (1870)
: BURGLARIZE

**bur·go·mas·ter** \'bər-gə-,mas-tər\ *noun* [part modification, part translation of Dutch *burgemeester*, from *burg* town + *meester* master] (1592)
: the chief magistrate of a town in some European countries : MAYOR

**bur·go·net** \'bər-gə-nət, ,bər-gə-'net\ *noun* [modification of Middle French *bourguignotte*] (circa 1587)
: a helmet of either of two 16th century styles

**bur·goo** \'bər-,gü, (,)bər-'\ *noun, plural* **bur·goos** [origin unknown] (1700)
**1** : oatmeal gruel
**2** : hardtack and molasses cooked together
**3 a** : a stew or thick soup of meat and vegetables originally served at outdoor gatherings **b** : a picnic at which burgoo is served

**bur·gun·dy** \'bər-gən-dē\ *noun, plural* **-dies** [*Burgundy*, region in France] (1668)
**1** *often capitalized* : a red or white unblended wine from Burgundy; *also* : a blended red wine produced elsewhere (as California)
**2** : a reddish purple color

**buri·al** \'ber-ē-əl *also* 'bər-\ *noun, often attributive* [Middle English *beriel, berial*, back-formation from *beriels* (taken as a plural), from Old English *byrgels*; akin to Old Saxon *burgisli* tomb, Old English *byrgan* to bury — more at BURY] (13th century)
**1** : GRAVE, TOMB
**2** : the act or process of burying

**buri·er** \'ber-ē-ər *also* 'bər-\ *noun* (before 12th century)
: one that buries

**bu·rin** \'byùr-ən, 'bər-\ *noun* [French] (1662)
**1** : an engraver's steel cutting tool having the blade ground obliquely to a sharp point
**2** : a prehistoric flint tool with a beveled point

**burke** \'bərk\ *transitive verb* **burked; burk·ing** [from *burke* to suffocate, from William *Burke* (died 1829) Irish criminal executed for smothering victims to sell their bodies for dissection] (1840)
**1** : to suppress quietly or indirectly ⟨*burke* an inquiry⟩
**2** : BYPASS, AVOID ⟨*burke* an issue⟩

**Bur·kitt's lymphoma** \'bər-kəts-\ *also* **Bur·kitt lymphoma** \-kət-\ *noun* [Denis Parsons *Burkitt* (died 1993) British surgeon] (1963)
: a malignant lymphoma that occurs especially in children of central Africa and is associated with Epstein-Barr virus

**burl** \'bər(-ə)l\ *noun* [Middle English *burle*, from (assumed) Middle French *bourle* tuft of wool, from (assumed) Vulgar Latin *burrula*, diminutive of Late Latin *burra* shaggy cloth] (15th century)
**1** : a knot or lump in thread or cloth
**2 a** : a hard woody often flattened hemispherical outgrowth on a tree **b** : veneer made from burls

**bur·la·de·ro** \,bùr-lə-'der-(,)ō, ,bər-\ *noun, plural* **-ros** [Spanish, from *burlar* to make fun of, elude, from *burla* joke] (1938)
: a wooden shield near the wall in a bullring for bullfighters to take shelter behind if pursued

**bur·lap** \'bər-,lap\ *noun* [origin unknown] (circa 1696)
**1** : a coarse heavy plain-woven fabric usually of jute or hemp used for bagging and wrapping and in furniture and linoleum manufacture
**2** : a lightweight material resembling burlap used in interior decoration or for clothing

**burled** \'bər(-ə)ld\ *adjective* (1924)
: having a distorted grain due to burls

**¹bur·lesque** \(,)bər-'lesk\ *noun* [*burlesque*, adjective, comic, droll, from French, from Italian *burlesco*, from *burla* joke, from Spanish] (1667)
**1** : a literary or dramatic work that seeks to ridicule by means of grotesque exaggeration or comic imitation
**2** : mockery usually by caricature
**3** : theatrical entertainment of a broadly humorous often earthy character consisting of short turns, comic skits, and sometimes striptease acts
**synonym** see CARICATURE
— **burlesque** *adjective*
— **bur·lesque·ly** *adverb*

**²burlesque** *verb* **bur·lesqued; bur·lesqu·ing** (1676)
*transitive verb*
: to imitate in a humorous or derisive manner : MOCK
*intransitive verb*
: to employ burlesque
— **bur·lesqu·er** *noun*

**bur·ley** \'bər-lē\ *noun, often capitalized* [probably from the name *Burley*] (1881)
: a thin-bodied air-cured tobacco grown mainly in Kentucky

**bur·ly** \'bər-lē\ *adjective* **bur·li·er; -est** [Middle English] (13th century)
**1** : strongly and heavily built : HUSKY
**2** : heartily direct and frank : BLUFF, FORTHRIGHT ⟨an evocative story less *burly* than the real thing but entertaining —E. A. Weeks⟩
— **bur·li·ly** \-lə-lē\ *adverb*
— **bur·li·ness** \-lē-nəs\ *noun*

**bur marigold** *noun* (circa 1818)
: any of a genus (*Bidens*) of coarse composite herbs with prickly flattened achenes that adhere to clothing

**Bur·mese** \,bər-'mēz, -'mēs\ *noun, plural* **Burmese** (1824)
**1** : a native or inhabitant of Burma (Myanmar)
**2** : the Tibeto-Burman language of the Burmese people
**3** : any of a U.S.-developed breed of slender shorthaired cats having gold eyes and a usually dark brown coat

— **Burmese** *adjective*

**¹burn** \'bərn\ *noun* [Middle English, from Old English; akin to Old High German *brunno* spring of water] (before 12th century)
*British* : CREEK 2

**²burn** \'bərn\ *verb* **burned** \'bərnd, 'bərnt\ *or* **burnt** \'bərnt\; **burn·ing** [Middle English *birnen*, from Old English *byrnan*, intransitive verb, *bærnan*, transitive verb; akin to Old High German *brinnan* to burn] (before 12th century)
*intransitive verb*
**1 a** : to consume fuel and give off heat, light, and gases ⟨a small fire *burns* on the hearth⟩ **b** : to undergo combustion; *also* : to undergo nuclear fission or nuclear fusion **c** : to contain a fire ⟨a little stove *burning* in the corner⟩ **d** : to give off light : SHINE, GLOW ⟨a light *burning* in the window⟩
**2 a** : to be hot ⟨the *burning* sand⟩ **b** : to produce or undergo discomfort or pain ⟨ears *burning* from the cold⟩ **c** : to become emotionally excited or agitated: as (1) : to yearn ardently ⟨*burning* to tell the story⟩ (2) : to be or become very angry or disgusted ⟨the remark made him *burn*⟩
**3 a** : to undergo alteration or destruction by the action of fire or heat ⟨the house *burned* down⟩ ⟨the potatoes *burned* to a crisp⟩ **b** : to die in the electric chair
**4** : to force or make a way by or as if by burning ⟨her words *burned* into his heart⟩
**5** : to receive sunburn ⟨she *burns* easily⟩
*transitive verb*
**1 a** : to cause to undergo combustion; *especially* : to destroy by fire ⟨*burned* the trash⟩ **b** : to use as fuel ⟨this furnace *burns* gas⟩ **c** : to use up : CONSUME ⟨*burn* calories⟩
**2 a** : to transform by exposure to heat or fire ⟨*burn* clay to bricks⟩ **b** : to produce by burning ⟨*burned* a hole in his sleeve⟩
**3 a** : to injure or damage by or as if by exposure to fire, heat, or radiation : SCORCH ⟨*burned* his hand⟩ **b** : to execute by burning ⟨*burned* heretics at the stake⟩; *also* : ELECTROCUTE
**4 a** : IRRITATE, ANNOY — often used with *up* ⟨really *burns* me up⟩ **b** : to take advantage of: as (1) : DECEIVE, CHEAT — often used in passive (2) : OUTDO, BEAT ⟨*burned* the defense with a touchdown pass⟩
— **burn·able** \'bər-nə-bəl\ *adjective*
— **burn one's bridges** *also* **burn one's boats** : to cut off all means of retreat
— **burn one's ears** : to rebuke strongly
— **burn the candle at both ends** : to use one's resources or energies to excess
— **burn the midnight oil** : to work or study far into the night

**³burn** *noun* (1594)
**1** : an act, process, instance, or result of burning: as **a** : injury or damage resulting from exposure to fire, heat, caustics, electricity, or certain radiations **b** : a burned area ⟨a *burn* on the tabletop⟩ **c** : an abrasion (as of the skin) having the appearance of a burn ⟨rope *burns*⟩ **d** : a burning sensation ⟨the *burn* of iodine on a cut⟩
**2** : the firing of a spacecraft rocket engine in flight
**3** : ANGER; *especially* : increasing fury — used chiefly in the phrase *slow burn*

**burned–out** \'bərn-'daùt, 'bərnt-'aùt\ *or* **burnt–out** \'bərnt-'aùt\ *adjective* (1837)
: WORN-OUT; *also* : EXHAUSTED

**burn·er** \'bər-nər\ *noun* (14th century)
: one that burns; *especially* : the part of a fuel-burning or heat-producing device (as a furnace or stove) where the flame or heat is produced

**bur·net** \(,)bər-'net, 'bər-nət\ *noun* [Middle English, from Middle French *burnete*, from *brun* brown — more at BRUNET] (14th century)

---

: any of a genus (*Sanguisorba*) of herbs of the rose family with odd-pinnate stipulate leaves and spikes of apetalous flowers

**burn–in** \'bər-ˌnin\ *noun* (1966)
: the continuous operation of a device (as a computer) as a test for defects or failure prior to putting it to use

**burn in** *transitive verb* (circa 1939)
: to increase the density of (portions of a photographic print) during enlarging by giving extra exposure

**burn·ing** \'bər-niŋ\ *adjective* (before 12th century)
**1 a** : being on fire **b** : ARDENT, INTENSE ⟨*burning* enthusiasm⟩
**2 a** : affecting with or as if with heat ⟨a *burning* fever⟩ **b** : resembling that produced by a burn ⟨a *burning* sensation on the tongue⟩
**3** : of fundamental importance : URGENT ⟨one of the *burning* issues of our time⟩
— **burn·ing·ly** \-niŋ-lē\ *adverb*

**burning bush** *noun* (1785)
: any of several plants associated with fire (as by redness): as **a** : ²WAHOO **b** : SUMMER CYPRESS

**burning ghat** *noun* (1877)
: a level space at the head of a ghat for cremation

**¹bur·nish** \'bər-nish\ *transitive verb* [Middle English *burnischen*, from Middle French *bruniss-*, stem of *brunir*, literally, to make brown, from *brun*] (14th century)
**1 a** : to make shiny or lustrous especially by rubbing **b** : POLISH 3
**2** : to rub (a material) with a tool for compacting or smoothing or for turning an edge
— **bur·nish·er** *noun*
— **bur·nish·ing** *adjective or noun*

**²burnish** *noun* (circa 1647)
: LUSTER, GLOSS

**burn off** (circa 1925)
*intransitive verb*
: to be dissipated by the sun's warmth ⟨waiting for the fog to *burn off*⟩
*transitive verb*
: to cause to burn off

**bur·noose** *or* **bur·nous** \(ˌ)bər-'nüs\ *noun* [French *burnous*, from Arabic *burnus*] (1695)
: a one-piece hooded cloak worn by Arabs and Berbers
— **bur·noosed** \-'nüst\ *adjective*

**burn·out** \'bər-ˌnaut\ *noun* (1940)
**1** : the cessation of operation of a jet or rocket engine; *also* : the point at which burnout occurs
**2 a** : exhaustion of physical or emotional strength or motivation usually as a result of prolonged stress or frustration **b** : a person suffering from burnout
**3** : a person showing the results of drug abuse

**burn out** (1710)
*transitive verb*
**1** : to drive out or destroy the property of by fire
**2** : to cause to fail, wear out, or become exhausted especially from overwork or overuse
*intransitive verb*
: to suffer burnout

**burn·sides** \'bərn-ˌsīdz\ *noun plural* [Ambrose E. *Burnside*] (1875)
: SIDE-WHISKERS; *especially* : full muttonchop whiskers

**word history** see SIDEBURNS

**¹burp** \'bərp\ *noun* [imitative] (circa 1932)
: BELCH

**²burp** (circa 1932)
*intransitive verb*
: BELCH
*transitive verb*
: to help (a baby) expel gas from the stomach especially by patting or rubbing the back

**burp gun** *noun* (1944)
: a small submachine gun

**¹burr** \'bər\ *noun* [Middle English *burre*; akin to Old English *byrst* bristle — more at BRISTLE] (14th century)

**1** *usually* **bur a** : a rough or prickly envelope of a fruit **b** : a plant that bears burs
**2 a** : something that sticks or clings ⟨a *burr* in the throat⟩ **b** : HANGER-ON
**3** : an irregular rounded mass; *especially* : a tree burl
**4** : a thin ridge or area of roughness produced in cutting or shaping metal
**5 a** : a trilled uvular \r\ as used by some speakers of English especially in northern England and in Scotland **b** : a tongue-point trill that is the usual Scottish \r\
**6 a** : a small rotary cutting tool **b** *usually* **bur** : a bit used on a dental drill
**7** : a rough humming sound : WHIR
— **burred** \'bərd\ *adjective*

**²burr** (1798)
*intransitive verb*
**1** : to speak with a burr
**2** : to make a whirring sound
*transitive verb*
**1** : to pronounce with a burr
**2 a** : to form into a projecting edge **b** : to remove burrs from
— **burr·er** *noun*

**bur reed** *noun* (1597)
: any of a genus (*Sparganium* of the family Sparganiaceæ) of plants with globose fruits resembling burs

**bur·ri·to** \bə-'rē-(ˌ)tō\ *noun, plural* **-tos** [American Spanish, from Spanish, little donkey, diminutive of *burro*] (1934)
: a flour tortilla rolled or folded around a filling (as of meat, beans, or cheese) and usually baked

**bur·ro** \'bər-(ˌ)ō, 'bur-; 'bə-(ˌ)rō\ *noun, plural* **burros** [Spanish, irregular from *borrico*, from Late Latin *burricus* small horse] (1800)
: DONKEY; *especially* : a small one used as a pack animal

**¹bur·row** \'bər-(ˌ)ō; 'bə-(ˌ)rō\ *noun* [Middle English *borow*] (13th century)
: a hole or excavation in the ground made by an animal (as a rabbit) for shelter and habitation

**²burrow** (1602)
*transitive verb*
**1** *archaic* : to hide in or as if in a burrow
**2 a** : to construct by tunneling **b** : to penetrate by means of a burrow
**3** : to make a motion suggestive of burrowing with : NESTLE ⟨*burrows* her hand into mine⟩
*intransitive verb*
**1** : to conceal oneself in or as if in a burrow
**2 a** : to make a burrow **b** : to progress by or as if by digging
**3** : to make a motion suggestive of burrowing : SNUGGLE, NESTLE ⟨*burrowed* against his back for warmth⟩
— **bur·row·er** *noun*

**burrstone** *variant of* BUHRSTONE

**bur·ry** \'bər-ē\ *adjective* **bur·ri·er; -est** (15th century)
**1** : containing burs
**2** : PRICKLY
**3** *of speech* : characterized by a burr

**bur·sa** \'bər-sə\ *noun, plural* **bur·sas** \-səz\ *or* **bur·sae** \-ˌsē, -ˌsī\ *noun* [New Latin, from Medieval Latin, bag, purse — more at PURSE] (1803)
: a bodily pouch or sac: as **a** : a small serous sac between a tendon and a bone **b** : BURSA OF FABRICIUS
— **bur·sal** \-səl\ *adjective*

**bursa of Fa·bri·cius** \-fə-'brē-sh(ē-)əs, -'bri-, -s(ē-)əs\ [Johan C. *Fabricius* (died 1808) Danish entomologist] (1945)
: a lymphoid organ that opens into the cloaca of birds and functions in B cell production

**bur·sar** \'bər-sər, -ˌsär\ *noun* [Medieval Latin *bursarius*, from *bursa*] (13th century)
: an officer (as of a monastery or college) in charge of funds : TREASURER

**bur·sa·ry** \'bər-sə-rē, 'bərs-rē\ *noun, plural* **-ries** [Medieval Latin *bursaria*, from *bursa*] (1695)

**1** : the treasury of a college or monastery
**2** *British* : a monetary grant to a needy student : SCHOLARSHIP

**burse** \'bərs\ *noun* [Middle French *bourse*, from Medieval Latin *bursa*] (15th century)
**1 a** : PURSE **b** : a square cloth case used to carry the corporal in a Communion service
**2** *obsolete* : EXCHANGE, BOURSE

**bur·si·tis** \(ˌ)bər-'sī-təs\ *noun* [New Latin, from *bursa*] (1857)
: inflammation of a bursa especially of the shoulder or elbow

**¹burst** \'bərst\ *verb* **burst** *also* **burst·ed; burst·ing** [Middle English *bersten*, from Old English *berstan*; akin to Old High German *brestan* to burst] (before 12th century)
*intransitive verb*
**1** : to break open, apart, or into pieces usually from impact or from pressure from within
**2 a** : to give way from an excess of emotion ⟨my heart will *burst*⟩ **b** : to give vent suddenly to a repressed emotion ⟨*burst* into tears⟩ ⟨*burst* out laughing⟩
**3 a** : to emerge or spring suddenly ⟨*burst* out of the house⟩ ⟨*burst* onto the scene⟩ **b** : LAUNCH, PLUNGE ⟨*burst* into song⟩
**4** : to be filled to the breaking point ⟨*bursting* with excitement⟩ ⟨a crate *bursting* with fruit⟩
*transitive verb*
**1** : to cause to burst
**2** : to force open (as a door) by strong or vigorous action
**3** : to produce by or as if by bursting
— **burst at the seams** : to be larger, fuller, or more crowded than could reasonably have been anticipated

**²burst** *noun* (1610)
**1 a** : a sudden outbreak; *especially* : a vehement outburst (as of emotion) **b** : EXPLOSION, ERUPTION **c** : a sudden intense effort ⟨a *burst* of speed⟩ **d** : the duration of fire in one engagement of the mechanism of an automatic firearm
**2** : an act of bursting
**3** : a result of bursting; *especially* : a visible puff accompanying the explosion of a shell

**burst·er** \'bərs-tər\ *noun* (1611)
**1** : one that bursts
**2** : the celestial source of an outburst of radiation (as X rays)

**bur·then** \'bər-thən\ *variant of* BURDEN

**bur·weed** \'bər-ˌwēd\ *noun* (circa 1783)
: any of various plants (as a cocklebur or burdock) having burry fruit

**bury** \'ber-ē *also* 'bər-\ *transitive verb* **bur·ied; bury·ing** [Middle English *burien*, from Old English *byrgan*; akin to Old High German *bergan* to shelter, Russian *berech'* to spare] (before 12th century)
**1** : to dispose of by depositing in or as if in the earth; *especially* : to inter with funeral ceremonies
**2 a** : to conceal by or as if by covering with earth **b** : to cover from view ⟨*buried* her face in her hands⟩
**3 a** : to have done with ⟨*burying* their differences⟩ **b** : to conceal in obscurity ⟨*buried* the retraction among the classified ads⟩ **c** : SUBMERGE, ENGROSS — usually used with *in* ⟨*buried* himself in his books⟩
**4** : to put (a playing card) out of play by placing it in or under the dealer's pack
**5** : to succeed emphatically or impressively in making (a shot) ⟨*bury* a jumper⟩
**6** : to defeat overwhelmingly
**synonym** see HIDE
— **bury the hatchet** : to settle a disagreement : become reconciled

**¹bus** \'bəs\ *noun, plural* **bus·es** *or* **bus·ses** *often attributive* [short for *omnibus*] (circa 1909)
**1 a** : a large motor vehicle designed to carry passengers usually along a fixed route according to a schedule **b** : AUTOMOBILE
**2** : a small hand truck

**3 a :** BUS BAR **b :** a set of parallel conductors in a computer system that forms a main transmission path

**4 :** a spacecraft or missile that carries one or more detachable devices (as warheads) ◆

²**bus** *verb* **bused** *or* **bussed; bus·ing** *or* **bus·sing** (circa 1909)
*intransitive verb*
**1 :** to travel by bus
**2 :** to work as a busboy
*transitive verb*
**1 :** to transport by bus
**2 a :** CLEAR 4d ⟨*bus* dishes⟩ **b :** to remove dirty dishes from ⟨*bus* tables⟩

**bus bar** *noun* (1893)
**:** a conductor or an assembly of conductors for collecting electric currents and distributing them to outgoing feeders

**bus·boy** \'bəs-ˌbȯi\ *noun* [*omnibus* busboy] (1913)
**:** a waiter's assistant; *specifically* **:** one who removes dirty dishes and resets tables in a restaurant

**bus·by** \'bəz-bē\ *noun, plural* **busbies** [probably from the name *Busby*] (1853)
**1 :** a military full-dress fur hat with a pendent bag on one side usually of the color of regimental facings
**2 :** the bearskin worn by British guardsmen — not used by the guardsmen themselves

¹**bush** \'bush\ *noun, often attributive* [Middle English; akin to Old High German *busc* forest] (14th century)
**1 a :** SHRUB; *especially* **:** a low densely branched shrub **b :** a close thicket of shrubs suggesting a single plant
**2 :** a large uncleared or sparsely settled area (as in Australia) usually scrub-covered or forested **:** WILDERNESS — usually used with *the*
**3 a** *archaic* **:** a bunch of ivy formerly hung outside a tavern to indicate wine for sale **b** *obsolete* **:** TAVERN **c :** ADVERTISING ⟨good wine needs no *bush* —Shakespeare⟩
**4 :** a bushy tuft or mass ⟨a *bush* of hair⟩; *especially* **:** ²BRUSH 2a
**5 :** MINOR LEAGUE — usually used in plural

²**bush** (15th century)
*transitive verb*
**:** to support, mark, or protect with bushes
*intransitive verb*
**:** to extend like a bush **:** resemble a bush

³**bush** *adjective* (1595)
**1 :** having a low-growing compact bushy habit — used especially of cultivated beans ⟨*bush* snap beans⟩
**2 :** serving, occurring in, or used in the bush ⟨*bush* planes⟩

⁴**bush** *noun* [Dutch *bus* bushing, box, from Middle Dutch *busse* box, from Late Latin *buxis* — more at BOX] (1566)
*chiefly British* **:** BUSHING

⁵**bush** *adjective* [short for *bush-league*] (1970)
**:** falling below acceptable standards **:** UNPROFESSIONAL ⟨*bush* behavior⟩

**bush baby** *noun* (1901)
**:** GALAGO

**bush basil** *noun* (1597)
**:** a sweet basil of a cultivar with small leaves

**bush·buck** \'bush-ˌbək\ *noun, plural* **bush·buck** *or* **bushbucks** [translation of Afrikaans *bosbok*] (1852)
**:** a small African striped antelope (*Tragelaphus scriptus*) especially of sub-Saharan forests that has spirally twisted horns

**bush clover** *noun* (circa 1818)
**:** any of several usually shrubby lespedezas

¹**bushed** \'busht\ *adjective* (14th century)
**1 :** covered with or as if with a bushy growth
**2** *chiefly Australian* **a :** lost especially in the bush **b :** PERPLEXED 1, CONFUSED

**3 :** TIRED, EXHAUSTED

²**bushed** *adjective* (1907)
**:** having a bushing

¹**bush·el** \'bu-shəl\ *noun* [Middle English *busshel*, from Old French *boissel*, from (assumed) Old French *boisse* one sixth of a bushel, of Celtic origin; akin to Middle Irish *boss* breadth of the hand] (14th century)
**1 :** any of various units of dry capacity — see WEIGHT table
**2 :** a container holding a bushel
**3 :** a large quantity **:** LOTS ⟨makes *bushels* of money⟩

²**bushel** *verb* **bush·eled; bush·el·ing** \-sh(ə-)liŋ\ [probably from German *bosseln* to do poor work, to patch; akin to Old English *bēatan* to beat] (circa 1877)
**:** REPAIR, RENOVATE
— **bush·el·er** \-sh(ə-)lər\ *noun*

**bush-fire** \'bush-ˌfīr\ *noun* (1832)
*Australian* **:** an uncontrolled fire in a bush area

**Bu·shi·do** \'bu-shi-ˌdō, 'bü-\ *noun* [Japanese *bushidō*] (1898)
**:** a feudal-military Japanese code of chivalry valuing honor above life

**bush·ing** \'bu-shiŋ\ *noun* (1839)
**1 :** a usually removable cylindrical lining for an opening (as of a mechanical part) used to limit the size of the opening, resist abrasion, or serve as a guide
**2 :** an electrically insulating lining for a hole to protect a through conductor

**bush jacket** *noun* [from its use in rough country] (circa 1939)
**:** a long cotton jacket resembling a shirt and having four patch pockets and a belt

**bush·land** \'bush-ˌland\ *noun* (1827)
**:** ¹BUSH 2

**bush–league** *adjective* (1914)
**:** being of an inferior class or group of its kind

**bush league** *noun* (1909)
**:** MINOR LEAGUE
— **bush leaguer** *noun*

**bush·man** \'bush-mən\ *noun* (1785)
**1** *capitalized* [modification of obsolete Afrikaans *boschjesman*, from *boschje* (diminutive of *bosch* forest) + Afrikaans *man*] **a :** a member of a group of short-statured peoples of southern Africa who traditionally live by hunting and foraging **b :** the Khoisan languages spoken by these people
**2 a :** WOODSMAN **b** *chiefly Australian* **:** a person who lives in the bush

**bush·mas·ter** \-ˌmas-tər\ *noun* (1826)
**:** a tropical American pit viper (*Lachesis mutus*) that is the largest New World venomous snake

**bush·pig** \-ˌpig\ *noun* (1840)
**:** a wild usually reddish to black pig (*Potamochoerus porcus*) of forests and scrubland of sub-Saharan Africa and Madagascar that has much facial hair, long pointed ears, and a light-colored mane along the top of the neck and back

**bush pilot** *noun* (1936)
**:** a pilot who flies a small plane into remote areas

**bush·rang·er** \-ˌrān-jər\ *noun* (1801)
**1** *Australian* **:** an outlaw living in the bush
**2 :** FRONTIERSMAN, WOODSMAN
— **bush·rang·ing** \-jiŋ\ *noun*

**bush shirt** *noun* [from its use in rough country] (1909)
**:** a usually loose-fitting cotton shirt with patch pockets

**bush·tit** \-ˌtit\ *noun* (circa 1889)
**:** a small gray titmouse (*Psaltriparus minimus*) of western North America with light underparts that occurs in several geographic forms sometimes placed in separate species

**bush·whack** \'bush-ˌhwak, -ˌwak\ *verb* [back-formation from *bushwhacker*] (1866)

*transitive verb*
**:** AMBUSH; *broadly* **:** to attack suddenly **:** ASSAULT
*intransitive verb*
**:** to clear a path through thick woods especially by chopping down bushes and low branches
— **bush·whack·er** *noun*

**bushy** \'bu-shē\ *adjective* **bush·i·er; -est** (14th century)
**1 :** full of or overgrown with bushes
**2 :** resembling a bush; *especially* **:** being thick and spreading
— **bush·i·ly** \'bu-shə-lē\ *adverb*
— **bush·i·ness** \'bu-shē-nəs\ *noun*

**busi·ness** \'biz-nəs, -nəz, *Southern also* 'bid-\ *noun, often attributive* (14th century)
**1** *archaic* **:** purposeful activity **:** BUSYNESS
**2 a :** ROLE, FUNCTION ⟨how the human mind went about its *business* of learning —H. A. Overstreet⟩ **b :** an immediate task or objective **:** MISSION ⟨what is your *business* here⟩ **c :** a particular field of endeavor ⟨the best in the *business*⟩
**3 a :** a usually commercial or mercantile activity engaged in as a means of livelihood **:** TRADE, LINE ⟨in the restaurant *business*⟩ **b :** a commercial or sometimes an industrial enterprise; *also* **:** such enterprises ⟨the *business* district⟩ **c :** usually economic dealings **:** PATRONAGE ⟨took their *business* elsewhere⟩
**4 :** AFFAIR, MATTER ⟨the whole *business* got out of hand⟩ ⟨*business* as usual⟩
**5 :** CREATION, CONCOCTION
**6 :** movement or action (as lighting a cigarette) by an actor intended especially to establish atmosphere, reveal character, or explain a situation — called also *stage business*
**7 a :** personal concern ⟨none of your *business*⟩ **b :** RIGHT ⟨you have no *business* speaking to me that way⟩
**8 a :** serious activity requiring time and effort and usually the avoidance of distractions ⟨got down to *business*⟩ ⟨she means *business*⟩ **b :** maximum effort
**9 a :** a damaging assault **b :** REBUKE, TONGUE-LASHING ⟨gave him the *business* for staying out so late⟩ **c :** DOUBLE CROSS

---

◇ WORD HISTORY

**bus** In 1828 a new era in public transportation dawned when horse-drawn boxes on wheels seating fourteen people on facing benches began to run regular routes in Paris. They were christened with the name *omnibus,* taken to be short for *voitures omnibus* "vehicles (open) to all"; *omnibus,* the dative of Latin *omnes* "everybody, all," summed up in one word their general accessibility. An earlier transport line of the same kind had operated in the city of Nantes, and according to one tradition the name *omnibus* occurred to the proprietors because the line terminated at the shop of a certain M. Omnes, who used the slogan *Omnes Omnibus.* In 1829 a horse-drawn line patterned after the French *omnibus* opened in London with the vehicles bearing the same name. By 1832 Londoners had clipped *omnibus* to *bus.* As the vehicles became self-propelled, first by steam and then by internal-combustion engines, the coinage *autobus* appeared, in English by 1899 and in French by 1907. *Bus* and *autobus* have since become international words, current over much of the world and in a number of languages.

---

busby 1

\ə\ abut \ᵊ\ kitten \ər\ further \a\ ash \ā\ ace
\ä\ mop, mar \au̇\ out \ch\ chin \e\ bet \ē\ easy
\g\ go \i\ hit \ī\ ice \j\ job \ŋ\ sing \ō\ go
\ȯ\ law \ȯi\ boy \th\ thin \t͟h\ the \ü\ loot \u̇\ foot
\y\ yet \zh\ vision *see also* Guide to Pronunciation

**10 :** a bowel movement — used especially of pets ☆

**business administration** *noun* (circa 1911)
**:** a program of studies in a college or university providing general knowledge of business principles and practices

**business card** *noun* (1840)
**:** a small card bearing information (as name and address) about a business or business representative

**business cycle** *noun* (1919)
**:** a cycle of economic activity usually consisting of recession, recovery, growth, and decline

**business end** *noun* (1878)
**:** the end with, from, or through which a thing's function is fulfilled ⟨the *business end* of a revolver⟩

**busi·ness·like** \'biz-nəs-,līk, -nəz-\ *adjective* (1791)
**1 :** exhibiting qualities believed to be advantageous in business
**2 :** SERIOUS, PURPOSEFUL

**busi·ness·man** \-,man, -mən\ *noun* (1826)
**:** a man who transacts business; *especially* **:** a business executive

**busi·ness·peo·ple** \-,pē-pəl\ *noun plural* (1865)
**:** persons active in business

**busi·ness·per·son** \-,pər-sᵊn\ *noun* (1974)
**:** a businessman or businesswoman

**business suit** *noun* (1870)
**:** a man's suit consisting of matching coat and trousers and sometimes a vest

**busi·ness·wom·an** \-,wu̇-mən\ *noun* (1844)
**:** a woman who transacts business; *especially* **:** a female business executive

**bus·ing** *or* **bus·sing** \'bə-siŋ\ *noun* (1923)
**:** the act of transporting by bus; *specifically* **:** the transporting of children to a school outside their residential area as a means of establishing racial balance in that school

**busk·er** \'bəs-kər\ *noun* [*busk,* probably from Italian *buscare* to procure, gain, from Spanish *buscar* to look for] (1857)
*chiefly British* **:** a person who entertains especially by playing music on the street
**— busk** \'bəsk\ *intransitive verb*

**bus·kin** \'bəs-kən\ *noun* [probably modification of Middle French *brozequin*] (1503)
**1 :** a laced boot reaching halfway or more to the knee
**2 a :** COTHURNUS 1 **b :** TRAGEDY; *especially* **:** tragedy resembling that of ancient Greek drama

**bus·load** \'bəs-,lōd\ *noun* (1938)
**:** a load that fills a bus ⟨*busloads* of tourists⟩

**bus·man's holiday** \'bəs-mənz-\ *noun* (1893)
**:** a holiday spent in following or observing the practice of one's usual occupation

**buss** \'bəs\ *noun* [perhaps alteration of Middle English *bassen* to kiss] (1570)
**:** KISS
**— buss** *transitive verb*

**¹bust** \'bəst\ *noun* [French *buste,* from Italian *busto,* from Latin *bustum* tomb] (1645)
**1 :** a sculptured representation of the upper part of the human figure including the head and neck and usually part of the shoulders and breast
**2 :** the upper part of the human torso between neck and waist; *especially* **:** the breasts of a woman

**²bust** *verb* **bust·ed** *also* **bust; bust·ing** [alteration of *burst*] (1806)
*transitive verb*
**1 a :** to break or smash especially with force; *also* **:** to make inoperative ⟨*busted* my watch⟩ **b :** to bring an end to **:** BREAK UP ⟨helped *bust* trusts —*Newsweek*⟩ — often used with *up* ⟨better not try to *bust* up his happy marriage —*Forbes*⟩ **c :** to ruin financially **d :** EXHAUST, WEAR OUT — used in phrases like *bust one's butt* to describe making a strenuous effort
**2 :** TAME ⟨bronco *busting*⟩

**3 :** DEMOTE
**4** *slang* **a :** ARREST ⟨*busted* for carrying guns —Saul Gottlieb⟩ **b :** RAID ⟨*busted* the apartment⟩
**5 :** HIT, SLUG
*intransitive verb*
**1 :** to go broke
**2 a :** BURST ⟨laughing fit to *bust*⟩ **b :** BREAK DOWN
**3 a :** to lose at cards by exceeding a limit (as the count of 21 in blackjack) **b :** to fail to complete a straight or flush in poker

**³bust** *noun* (1840)
**1 a :** SPREE **b :** a hearty drinking session ⟨a beer *bust*⟩
**2 a :** a complete failure **:** FLOP **b :** a business depression
**3 :** PUNCH, SOCK
**4** *slang* **a :** a police raid **b :** ARREST 2

**⁴bust** *or* **bust·ed** \'bəs-təd\ *adjective* (1837)
**:** BANKRUPT, BROKE ⟨go *bust*⟩

**bus·tard** \'bəs-tərd\ *noun* [Middle English, modification of Middle French *bistarde,* from Old Italian *bistarda,* from Latin *avis tarda,* literally, slow bird] (15th century)
**:** any of a family (Otididae) of large chiefly terrestrial Old World and Australian game birds

**bust·er** \'bəs-tər\ *noun* (1848)
**1** *chiefly Australian* **:** a sudden violent wind often coming from the south
**2 a :** an unusually sturdy child **b** *often capitalized* **:** FELLOW — usually used as a noun of address ⟨hey *buster,* come here⟩
**3 :** one that breaks, breaks up, or eliminates something ⟨crime *busters*⟩: as **a :** PLOW **b** [short for *broncobuster*] **:** a person who breaks horses
**4 :** a bad fall

**bus·tier** \,büs-tē-'ā, ,bəs-, -'tyā\ *noun* [French, from *buste*] (1979)
**:** a tight-fitting often strapless top worn as a brassiere or outer garment

**¹bus·tle** \'bə-səl\ *intransitive verb* **bus·tled; bus·tling** \'bəs-liŋ, 'bə-sə-\ [probably alteration of obsolete *buskle* to prepare, frequentative of *busk,* from Old Norse *būask* to prepare oneself] (1580)
**1 :** to move briskly and often ostentatiously
**2 :** to be busily astir **:** TEEM
**— bustling** *adjective*
**— bus·tling·ly** \-liŋ-lē\ *adverb*

**²bustle** *noun* (1634)
**:** noisy, energetic, and often obtrusive activity ⟨the hustle and *bustle* of the big city⟩

**³bustle** *noun* [origin unknown] (1786)
**:** a pad or framework expanding and supporting the fullness and drapery of the back of a woman's skirt or dress; *also* **:** the drapery so supported

**bust·line** \'bəs(t)-,līn\ *noun* (1926)
**1 :** an arbitrary line encircling the fullest part of the bust
**2 :** body circumference at the bust

**busty** \'bəs-tē\ *adjective* **bust·i·er; -est** (1944)
**:** having a large bust

**bu·sul·fan** \byü-'səl-fən\ *noun* [butane + sulfonyl] (circa 1958)
**:** an antineoplastic agent $C_6H_{14}O_6S_2$ used in the treatment of chronic myelogenous leukemia

**¹busy** \'bi-zē\ *adjective* **busi·er; -est** [Middle English *bisy,* from Old English *bisig;* akin to Middle Dutch & Middle Low German *be-sich* busy] (before 12th century)
**1 a :** engaged in action **:** OCCUPIED **b :** being in use ⟨found the telephone *busy*⟩
**2 :** full of activity **:** BUSTLING ⟨a *busy* seaport⟩
**3 :** foolishly or intrusively active **:** MEDDLING
**4 :** full of distracting detail ⟨a *busy* design⟩ ☆
**— busi·ly** \'bi-zə-lē\ *adverb*
**— busy·ness** \'bi-zē-nəs\ *noun*

**²busy** *verb* **bus·ied; busy·ing** (before 12th century)
*transitive verb*

**:** to make busy **:** OCCUPY
*intransitive verb*
**:** BUSTLE ⟨small boats *busied* to and fro —Quentin Crewe⟩

**busy·body** \'bi-zē-,bä-dē\ *noun* (1526)
**:** an officious or inquisitive person

**busy·work** \-,wərk\ *noun* (1910)
**:** work that usually appears productive or of intrinsic value but actually only keeps one occupied

**¹but** \'bət\ *conjunction* [Middle English, from Old English *būtan,* preposition & conjugation, outside, without, except, except that; akin to Old High German *būzan* without, except; akin to Old English *be* by, *ūt* out — more at BY, OUT] (before 12th century)
**1 a :** except for the fact ⟨would have protested *but* that he was afraid⟩ **b :** THAT — used after a negative ⟨there is no doubt *but* he won⟩ **c :** without the concomitant that ⟨it never rains *but* it pours⟩ **d :** if not **:** UNLESS **e :** THAN ⟨no sooner started *but* it stopped⟩ — not often in formal use
**2 a :** on the contrary **:** on the other hand **:** NOTWITHSTANDING — used to connect coordinate elements ⟨he was called *but* he did not answer⟩ ⟨not peace *but* a sword⟩ **b :** YET ⟨poor *but* proud⟩ **c :** with the exception of — used before a word often taken to be the subject of a clause ⟨none *but* the brave deserves the fair —John Dryden⟩
**— but what :** that . . . not — used to indicate possibility or uncertainty ⟨I don't know *but what* I will go⟩

**²but** *preposition* (before 12th century)
**1 a :** with the exception of **:** BARRING ⟨no one there *but* me⟩ — compare ¹BUT 2c **b :** other than ⟨this letter is nothing *but* an insult⟩
**2** *Scottish* **a :** WITHOUT, LACKING **b :** OUTSIDE

**³but** *adverb* (12th century)
**1 :** ONLY, MERELY ⟨he is *but* a child⟩
**2** *Scottish* **:** OUTSIDE
**3 :** to the contrary ⟨who knows *but* that she may succeed⟩
**4** — used as an intensive ⟨get there *but* fast⟩

**⁴but** *pronoun* (1556)
**:** that not **:** who not ⟨nobody *but* has his fault —Shakespeare⟩

**⁵but** *noun* [Scots *but,* adjective (outer)] (1724)

---

☆ SYNONYMS
**Business, commerce, trade, industry, traffic** mean activity concerned with the supplying and distribution of commodities. BUSINESS may be an inclusive term but specifically designates the activities of those engaged in the purchase or sale of commodities or in related financial transactions. COMMERCE and TRADE imply the exchange and transportation of commodities. INDUSTRY applies to the producing of commodities, especially by manufacturing or processing, usually on a large scale. TRAFFIC applies to the operation and functioning of public carriers of goods and persons. See in addition WORK.

**Busy, industrious, diligent, assiduous, sedulous** mean actively engaged or occupied. BUSY chiefly stresses activity as opposed to idleness or leisure ⟨too *busy* to spend time with the children⟩. INDUSTRIOUS implies characteristic or habitual devotion to work ⟨*industrious* employees⟩. DILIGENT suggests earnest application to some specific object or pursuit ⟨very *diligent* in her pursuit of a degree⟩. ASSIDUOUS stresses careful and unremitting application ⟨*assiduous* practice⟩. SEDULOUS implies painstaking and persevering application ⟨a *sedulous* investigation of the murder⟩.

*Scottish* **:** the kitchen or living quarters of a 2-room cottage

**bu·ta·di·ene** \,byü-tə-'dī-,ēn, -,dī-'\ *noun* [International Scientific Vocabulary *butane* + *di-* + *-ene*] (1900)
**:** a flammable gaseous open chain hydrocarbon $C_4H_6$ used in making synthetic rubbers

**bu·tane** \'byü-,tān\ *noun* [International Scientific Vocabulary *butyric* + *-ane*] (1875)
**:** either of two isomeric flammable gaseous alkanes $C_4H_{10}$ obtained usually from petroleum or natural gas and used as fuels

**bu·ta·nol** \'byü-t°n-,ȯl, -,ōl, -,ȯl\ *noun* (1894)
**:** either of two flammable four-carbon alcohols $C_4H_9OH$ derived from normal butane

**butch** \'bu̇ch\ *adjective* [probably from *Butch,* male nickname] (1941)
**1 :** very masculine in appearance or manner
**2 :** playing the male role in a homosexual relationship

**¹butch·er** \'bu̇-chər\ *noun* [Middle English *bocher,* from Old French *bouchier,* from *bouc* he-goat, probably of Celtic origin; akin to Middle Irish *bocc* he-goat — more at BUCK] (13th century)
**1 a :** a person who slaughters animals or dresses their flesh **b :** a dealer in meat
**2 :** one that kills ruthlessly or brutally
**3 :** one that bungles or botches
**4 :** a vendor especially on trains or in theaters

**²butcher** *transitive verb* **butch·ered; butch·er·ing** \'bu̇ch-riŋ, 'bu̇-chə-\ (1562)
**1 :** to slaughter and dress for market ⟨*butcher* hogs⟩
**2 :** to kill in a barbarous manner
**3 :** BOTCH ⟨*butchered* the play⟩

**butch·er-bird** \'bu̇-chər-,bərd\ *noun* (1668)
**:** any of various shrikes

**butcher block** *noun* (1967)
**:** a block made with thick strips of usually laminated hardwood
— **butcher-block** *adjective*

**butch·er·ly** \'bu̇-chər-lē\ *adjective* (1513)
**:** resembling a butcher **:** SAVAGE

**butcher paper** *noun* (1944)
**:** heavy brown or white paper used especially for wrapping meats

**butch·ery** \'bu̇ch-rē, 'bu̇-chə-\ *noun, plural* **-er·ies** (14th century)
**1** *chiefly British* **:** SLAUGHTERHOUSE
**2 :** the preparation of meat for sale
**3 :** cruel and ruthless slaughter of human beings
**4 :** BOTCH

**bute** \'byüt\ *noun* (1968)
**:** PHENYLBUTAZONE

**bu·tene** \'byü-,tēn\ *noun* [International Scientific Vocabulary *butyl* + *-ene*] (1885)
**:** a normal butylene

**bu·teo** \'byü-tē-,ō\ *noun, plural* **-te·os** [New Latin, genus name, from Latin, a hawk] (1940)
**:** any of a genus (*Buteo*) of hawks with broad rounded wings, relatively short tails, and soaring flight

**but for** *preposition* (12th century)
**:** EXCEPT FOR

**but·ler** \'bət-lər\ *noun* [Middle English *buteler,* from Old French *bouteillier* bottle bearer, from *bouteille* bottle — more at BOTTLE] (13th century)
**1 :** a manservant having charge of the wines and liquors
**2 :** the chief male servant of a household who has charge of other employees, receives guests, directs the serving of meals, and performs various personal services

**butler's pantry** *noun* (1816)
**:** a service room between kitchen and dining room

**¹butt** \'bət\ *verb* [Middle English, from Old French *boter,* of Germanic origin; akin to Old High German *bōzan* to beat — more at BEAT] (13th century)

*intransitive verb*
**:** to thrust or push head foremost **:** strike with the head or horns
*transitive verb*
**:** to strike or shove with the head or horns

**²butt** *noun* (1647)
**:** a blow or thrust usually with the head or horns

**³butt** *noun* [Middle English, from Middle French *botte,* from Old Provençal *bota,* from Late Latin *buttis*] (14th century)
**1 :** a large cask especially for wine, beer, or water
**2 :** any of various units of liquid capacity; *especially* **:** a measure equal to 108 imperial gallons (491 liters)

**⁴butt** *noun* [Middle English, partly from Middle French *but* target, end, of Germanic origin; akin to Old Norse *būtr* log, Low German *butt* blunt; partly from Middle French *bute* backstop, from *but* target] (14th century)
**1 a :** a backstop (as a mound or bank) for catching missiles shot at a target **b :** TARGET **c** *plural* **:** RANGE 5c **d :** a blind for shooting birds
**2 a** *obsolete* **:** LIMIT, BOUND **b** *archaic* **:** GOAL ⟨here is my journey's end, here is my *butt* —Shakespeare⟩
**3 :** an object of abuse or ridicule **:** VICTIM ⟨the *butt* of all their jokes⟩

**⁵butt** *noun* [Middle English; probably akin to Middle English *buttok* buttock, Low German *butt* blunt] (15th century)
**1 :** BUTTOCKS — often used as a euphemism for *ass* in idiomatic expressions ⟨get your *butt* over here⟩ ⟨kick *butt*⟩ ⟨saved our *butts*⟩
**2 :** the large or thicker end part of something: **a :** a lean upper cut of the pork shoulder **b :** the base of a plant from which the roots spring **c :** the thicker or handle end of a tool or weapon
**3 :** an unused remainder
**4 :** the part of a hide or skin corresponding to the animal's back and sides

**⁶butt** *verb* [partly from ⁴*butt,* partly from ⁵*butt*] (1785)
*intransitive verb*
**:** ABUT — used with *on* or *against*
*transitive verb*
**1 :** to place end to end or side to side without overlapping
**2 :** to trim or square off (as a log) at the end
**3 :** to reduce (as a cigarette) to a butt by stubbing or stamping

**butte** \'byüt\ *noun* [French, knoll, from Middle French *bute*] (1805)
**:** an isolated hill or mountain with steep or precipitous sides usually having a smaller summit area than a mesa

**¹but·ter** \'bə-tər\ *noun* [Middle English, from Old English *butere,* from Latin *butyrum,* from Greek *boutyron,* from *bous* cow + *tyros* cheese; akin to Avestan *tūiri-* curds — more at COW] (before 12th century)
**1 :** a solid emulsion of fat globules, air, and water made by churning milk or cream and used as food
**2 :** a buttery substance: as **a :** any of various fatty oils remaining nearly solid at ordinary temperatures **b :** a creamy food spread; *especially* **:** one made of ground roasted nuts ⟨peanut *butter*⟩
**3 :** FLATTERY
— **but·ter·less** \-ləs\ *adjective*

**²butter** *transitive verb* (15th century)
**:** to spread with or as if with butter

**but·ter-and-eggs** \,bə-tər-°n-'egz, -'āgz\ *noun plural but singular or plural in construction* (1776)
**:** a common Eurasian perennial herb (*Linaria vulgaris*) of the snapdragon family that has showy yellow and orange flowers and is naturalized in much of North America — called also *toadflax*

**but·ter·ball** \'bə-tər-,bȯl\ *noun* (1813)
**1 :** BUFFLEHEAD
**2 :** a chubby person

**butter bean** *noun* (circa 1819)
**1 :** LIMA BEAN: as **a** *chiefly Southern & Midland* **:** a large dried lima bean **b :** SIEVA BEAN
**2 :** WAX BEAN
**3 :** a green shell bean especially as opposed to a snap bean

**butter clam** *noun* (1936)
**:** either of two clams (*Saxidomus nuttallii* and *S. giganteus*) of the Pacific coast of North America

**but·ter·cup** \'bə-tər-,kəp\ *noun* (1777)
**:** any of a genus (*Ranunculus* of the family Ranunculaceae, the buttercup family) of herbs with yellow or white flowers and alternate leaves

**but·ter·fat** \-,fat\ *noun* (1889)
**:** the natural fat of milk and chief constituent of butter consisting essentially of a mixture of glycerides (as those derived from butyric, capric, caproic, and caprylic acids)

**but·ter·fin·gered** \-,fiŋ-gərd\ *adjective* (1615)
**:** apt to let things fall or slip through the fingers **:** CARELESS
— **but·ter·fin·gers** \-gərz\ *noun plural but singular or plural in construction*

**but·ter·fish** \-,fish\ *noun* (1674)
**:** any of numerous bony fishes (especially family Stromateidae) with a slippery coating of mucus

**¹but·ter·fly** \-,flī\ *noun, often attributive* (before 12th century)
**1 :** any of numerous slender-bodied diurnal insects (order Lepidoptera) with broad often brightly colored wings
**2 :** something that resembles or suggests a butterfly; *especially* **:** a person chiefly occupied with the pursuit of pleasure
**3 :** a swimming stroke executed in a prone position by moving both arms in a circular motion while kicking both legs up and down
**4** *plural* **:** a feeling of hollowness or queasiness caused especially by emotional or nervous tension or anxious anticipation

**²butterfly** *transitive verb* **-flied; -fly·ing** (1954)
**:** to split almost entirely and spread apart ⟨a *butterflied* steak⟩ ⟨*butterflied* shrimp⟩

**butterfly bush** *noun* (1924)
**:** BUDDLEIA

**butterfly chair** *noun* (1953)
**:** a chair for lounging consisting of a cloth sling supported by a frame of metal tubing or bars

**but·ter·fly·er** \'bə-tər-,flī-(-ə)r\ *noun* (1967)
**:** a swimmer who specializes in the butterfly

**butterfly chair**

**butterfly fish** *noun* (1740)
**1 :** any of a family (Chaetodontidae) of small brilliantly colored spiny-finned fishes of tropical seas with a narrow deep body and scaled fins
**2 :** a small brown freshwater fish (*Pantodon buchholzi* of the family Pantodontidae) of western Africa that has elongate winglike pectoral fins

**butterfly valve** *noun* (1846)
**1 :** a valve consisting of two semicircular clappers hinged to a cross rib that permits fluid flow in only one direction
**2 :** a damper or valve in a pipe consisting of a disk turning on a diametral axis

**butterfly weed** *noun* (1816)
**:** an orange-flowered showy milkweed (*Asclepias tuberosa*) of eastern temperate North America

---

\ə\ abut \ə\ kitten \ər\ further \a\ ash \ā\ ace
\ä\ mop, mar \au̇\ out \ch\ chin \e\ bet \ē\ easy
\g\ go \i\ hit \ī\ ice \j\ job \ŋ\ sing \ō\ go
\ȯ\ law \ȯi\ boy \th\ thin \th\ the \ü\ loot \u̇\ foot
\y\ yet \zh\ vision *see also* Guide to Pronunciation

**but·ter·milk** \'bə-tər-,milk\ *noun* (15th century)
**1** : the liquid left after butter has been churned from milk or cream
**2** : cultured milk made by the addition of suitable bacteria to sweet milk
**but·ter·nut** \-,nət\ *noun* (1741)
**1** : an eastern North American tree of the walnut family with sweet egg-shaped nuts and light brown wood — called also *white walnut*
**2 a** : a light yellowish brown **b** *plural* : homespun overalls dyed brown with a butternut extract **c** : a soldier or partisan of the Confederacy during the Civil War
**butternut squash** *noun* (1945)
: a smooth somewhat bottle-shaped buff-colored winter squash with usually orange flesh
**but·ter·scotch** \-,skäch\ *noun* (1855)
**1** : a candy made from brown sugar, butter, corn syrup, and water; *also* : the flavor of such candy
**2** : a moderate yellowish brown
**butter up** *transitive verb* (1819)
: to charm or beguile with lavish flattery or praise
**but·ter·weed** \'bə-tər-,wēd\ *noun* (circa 1845)
: any of several plants having yellow flowers or smooth soft foliage: as **a** : HORSEWEED 1 **b** : a North American groundsel (*Senecio glabellus*)
**but·ter·wort** \-,wərt, -,wȯrt\ *noun* (1597)
: any of a genus (*Pinguicula*) of herbs of the bladderwort family with fleshy leaves that produce a viscid secretion serving to capture and digest insects
¹**but·tery** \'bə-tə-rē, 'bə-trē\ *noun, plural* **-ter·ies** [Middle English *boterie*, from Middle French, from *botte* cask, butt — more at BUTT] (14th century)
**1** : a storeroom for liquors
**2 a** *chiefly dialect* : PANTRY **b** : a room (as in an English college) stocking provisions for sale to students
²**but·tery** \'bə-tə-rē\ *adjective* (14th century)
**1 a** : having the qualities of butter **b** : containing or spread with butter
**2** : marked by flattery
**butt hinge** *noun* (1815)
: a hinge usually mortised flush into the edge of a door and its jamb
**butt in** *intransitive verb* (1900)
: to meddle in the affairs of others : INTERFERE
**butt·in·sky** *also* **butt·in·ski** \bə-'din-skē\ *noun, plural* **-skies** [*butt in* + *-sky, -ski* (last element in Slavic surnames)] (1902)
: a person given to butting in : a troublesome meddler
**butt joint** *noun* (1823)
: a joint made by fastening the parts together end-to-end without overlap and often with reinforcement
**but·tock** \'bə-tək *also* -,täk\ *noun* [Middle English *buttok* — more at BUTT] (14th century)
**1** : the back of a hip that forms one of the fleshy parts on which a person sits
**2** *plural* **a** : the seat of the body **b** : RUMP
¹**but·ton** \'bə-t°n\ *noun, often attributive* [Middle English *boton*, from Middle French, from Old French, from *boter* to thrust — more at BUTT] (14th century)
**1 a** : a small knob or disk secured to an article (as of clothing) and used as a fastener by passing it through a buttonhole or loop **b** : a usually circular metal or plastic badge bearing a stamped design or printed slogan ⟨campaign *button*⟩
**2** : something that resembles a button: as **a** : any of various parts or growths of a plant or of an animal: as (1) : an immature whole mushroom (2) : the terminal segment of a rattlesnake's rattle **b** : a small globule of metal remaining after fusion (as in assaying) **c** : a guard on the tip of a fencing foil

**3** : PUSH BUTTON
**4** : the point of the chin especially as a target for a knockout blow
— **but·ton·less** \-ləs\ *adjective*
— **on the button** ⟨arrived at noon *on the button*⟩; *also* : exactly on target : on the nose ⟨the estimate was right *on the button*⟩
²**button** *verb* **but·toned; but·ton·ing** \'bət-niŋ, 'bə-t°n-iŋ\ (14th century)
*transitive verb*
**1** : to furnish or decorate with buttons
**2 a** : to pass (a button) through a buttonhole or loop **b** : to close or fasten with buttons — often used with *up* ⟨*button* up your overcoat⟩
**3 a** : to close (the lips) to prevent speech ⟨*button* your lip⟩ **b** : to close or seal tightly — usually used with *up* ⟨*button* up the house for winter⟩
*intransitive verb*
: to have buttons for fastening ⟨this dress *buttons* at the back⟩
— **but·ton·er** \'bət-nər, 'bə-t°n-ər\ *noun*
**but·ton·ball** \'bə-t°n-,bȯl\ *noun* (1821)
: ²PLANE
**but·ton·bush** \-,bu̇sh\ *noun* (1754)
: a North American shrub (*Cephalanthus occidentalis*) of the madder family with globular flower heads
¹**but·ton–down** \-,dau̇n\ *adjective* (1934)
**1 a** *of a collar* : having the ends fastened to the garment with buttons **b** *of a garment* : having a button-down collar
**2** *also* **but·toned–down** \-t°n-,dau̇n\ : conservatively traditional or conventional; *especially* : adhering to conventional ideals in dress and behavior ⟨*button-down* businessmen⟩
²**button–down** *noun* (1952)
: a shirt with a button-down collar
**but·toned–up** \'bə-tən-'dəp\ *adjective* (1936)
: coldly reserved or standoffish
¹**but·ton·hole** \'bə-t°n-,hōl\ *noun* (1561)
**1** : a slit or loop through which a button is passed
**2** *chiefly British* : BOUTONNIERE
²**buttonhole** *transitive verb* (1828)
**1** : to furnish with buttonholes
**2** : to work with buttonhole stitch
— **but·ton·hol·er** \-,hō-lər\ *noun*
³**buttonhole** *transitive verb* [alteration of *buttonhold*] (1862)
: to detain in conversation by or as if by holding on to the outer garments of
**buttonhole stitch** *noun* (circa 1885)
: a closely worked loop stitch used to make a firm edge (as on a buttonhole)
**but·ton·hook** \'bə-t°n-,hu̇k\ *noun* (1870)
**1** : a hook for drawing small buttons through buttonholes
**2** : an offensive play in football in which the pass receiver runs straight downfield and then abruptly cuts back toward the line of scrimmage
— **buttonhook** *intransitive verb*
**button man** *noun* [perhaps from *buttons* bellhop] (1966)
: a low-ranking member of a criminal underworld organization
**button mushroom** *noun* (1865)
: a small cultivated mushroom (*Agaricus bisporus* synonym A. *brunnescens*)
**button quail** *noun* (1885)
: any of a family (Turnicidae) of small terrestrial Old World birds that resemble quails and have only three toes on a foot with the hind toe being absent
**button snakeroot** *noun* (1775)
**1** : BLAZING STAR 2a
**2** : any of several usually prickly herbs (genus *Eryngium*) of the carrot family
**but·ton·wood** \'bə-t°n-,wu̇d\ *noun* (1674)
: ²PLANE
¹**but·tress** \'bə-trəs\ *noun* [Middle English *butres*, from Middle French *bouterez*, from

Old French *boterez*, from *boter* — more at BUTT] (14th century).
**1** : a projecting structure of masonry or wood for supporting or giving stability to a wall or building
**2** : something that resembles a buttress: as **a** : a projecting part of a mountain or hill **b** : a horny protuberance on a horse's hoof at the heel — see HOOF illustration **c** : the broadened base of a tree trunk or a thickened vertical part of it
**3** : something that supports or strengthens ⟨a *buttress* of the cause of peace⟩
— **but·tressed** \-trəst\ *adjective*
²**buttress** *transitive verb* (14th century)
: to furnish or shore up with a buttress; *also* : SUPPORT, STRENGTHEN ⟨arguments *buttressed* by solid facts⟩
**butt shaft** *noun* (1588)
: a target arrow without a barb
**butt·stock** \'bət-,stäk\ *noun* (circa 1909)
: the stock of a firearm in the rear of the breech mechanism
**butt weld** *noun* (circa 1864)
: a butt joint made by welding
— **butt–weld** *transitive verb*
**but·ty** \'bə-tē\ *noun, plural* **butties** [origin unknown] (circa 1790)
*chiefly British* : a fellow worker : CHUM, PARTNER
**bu·tut** \bü-'tüt\ *noun, plural* **bututs** *or* **butut** [Wolof] (1972)
— see *dalasi* at MONEY table
**bu·tyl** \'byü-t°l\ *noun* [International Scientific Vocabulary *butyric* + *-yl*] (1869)
: any of four isomeric univalent radicals $C_4H_9$ derived from butanes
**butyl alcohol** *noun* (circa 1871)
: any of four flammable alcohols $C_4H_9OH$ (as butanol) used in organic synthesis and as solvents
**bu·tyl·at·ed** \'byü-t°l-,ā-təd\ *adjective* (1942)
: combined with the butyl group
— **bu·tyl·a·tion** \,byü-t°l-'ā-shən\ *noun*
**butylated hy·droxy·an·i·sole** \-(,)hī-,dräk-sē-'a-nə-,sōl\ *noun* [*hydroxy* + *anise* + *-ole*] (1950)
: BHA
**butylated hy·droxy·tol·u·ene** \-'täl-yə-,wēn\ *noun* (1961)
: BHT
**bu·tyl·ene** \'byü-t°l-,ēn\ *noun* (1877)
: any of three isomeric hydrocarbons $C_4H_8$ of the ethylene series obtained usually by cracking petroleum
**butyl rubber** *noun* (1940)
: any of a class of synthetic rubbers that are made by copolymerizing isobutylene with a small amount usually of isoprene at low temperature
**butyr-** *or* **butyro-** *combining form* [International Scientific Vocabulary, from *butyric*]
: butyric ⟨*butyr*aldehyde⟩
**bu·tyr·al·de·hyde** \,byü-tə-'ral-də-,hīd\ *noun* [International Scientific Vocabulary] (circa 1885)
: either of two aldehydes $C_4H_8O$ used especially in making synthetic resins
**bu·ty·rate** \'byü-tə-,rāt\ *noun* (1873)
: a salt or ester of butyric acid
**bu·tyr·ic** \byü-'tir-ik\ *adjective* [French *butyrique*, from Latin *butyrum* butter — more at BUTTER] (1854)
: relating to or producing butyric acid ⟨*butyric* fermentation⟩
**butyric acid** *noun* (1826)
: either of two isomeric fatty acids $C_4H_8O_2$; *especially* : an acid of unpleasant odor normally found in perspiration and rancid butter
**bu·ty·ro·phe·none** \,byü-tə-(,)rō-fə-'nōn\ *noun* [*butyr-* + *phen-* + *-one*] (1970)
: any of a class of neuroleptic drugs (as haloperidol) used especially in the treatment of schizophrenia
**bux·om** \'bək-səm\ *adjective* [Middle English *buxsum*, from (assumed) Old English *būhsum*;

akin to Old English *būgan* to bend — more at BOW] (12th century)
**1** *obsolete* **a :** OBEDIENT, TRACTABLE **b :** offering little resistance **:** FLEXIBLE, PLIANT ⟨wing silently the *buxom* air —John Milton⟩
**2** *archaic* **:** full of gaiety **:** BLITHE
**3 :** vigorously or healthily plump; *specifically* **:** full-bosomed
— **bux·om·ly** *adverb*
— **bux·om·ness** *noun*
¹**buy** \'bī\ *verb* **bought** \'bȯt\; **buy·ing** [Middle English *byen*, from Old English *bycgan*; akin to Gothic *bugjan* to buy] (before 12th century)
*transitive verb*
**1 :** to acquire possession, ownership, or rights to the use or services of by payment especially of money **:** PURCHASE
**2 a :** to obtain in exchange for something often at a sacrifice ⟨they *bought* peace with their freedom⟩ **b :** REDEEM 6
**3 :** BRIBE, HIRE
**4 :** to be the purchasing equivalent of ⟨the dollar *buys* less today than it used to⟩
**5 :** ACCEPT, BELIEVE ⟨I don't *buy* that hooey⟩
*intransitive verb*
**:** to make a purchase
— **buy·er** \'bī-(-ə)r\ *noun*
— **buy it** *or* **buy the farm :** to get killed **:** DIE
— **buy time :** to delay an imminent action or decision **:** STALL
²**buy** *noun* (1879)
**1 :** something of value at a favorable price; *especially* **:** BARGAIN ⟨it's a real *buy* at that price⟩
**2 :** an act of buying **:** PURCHASE
**buy·back** \'bī-,bak\ *noun* (1974)
**:** the act or an instance of buying something back; *especially* **:** the repurchase by a corporation of shares of its own common stock on the open market
**buyer's market** *noun* (1926)
**:** a market in which goods are plentiful, buyers have a wide range of choice, and prices tend to be low — compare SELLER'S MARKET
**buy off** *transitive verb* (1629)
**1 :** to induce to refrain (as from prosecution) by a payment or other consideration
**2 :** to free (as from military service) by payment
**buy·out** \'bī-,au̇t\ *noun* (1971)
**:** an act or instance of buying out
**buy out** *transitive verb* (1644)
**1 :** to purchase the share or interest of
**2 :** to purchase the entire stock-in-trade and the goodwill of (a business)
**buy up** *transitive verb* (circa 1534)
**1 :** to buy freely or extensively
**2 :** to buy the entire available supply of
¹**buzz** \'bəz\ *verb* [Middle English *bussen*, of imitative origin] (14th century)
*intransitive verb*
**1 :** to make a low continuous humming sound like that of a bee
**2 a :** MURMUR, WHISPER **b :** to be filled with a confused murmur ⟨the room *buzzed* with excitement⟩
**3 :** to make a signal with a buzzer
**4 :** to go quickly **:** HURRY ⟨*buzzed* around town in a sports car⟩; *also* **:** SCRAM — usually used with *off*
*transitive verb*
**1 :** to utter covertly by or as if by whispering
**2 :** to cause to buzz
**3 :** to fly fast and close to ⟨planes *buzz* the crowd⟩
**4 :** to summon or signal with a buzzer
**5** *dialect English* **:** to drink to the last drop ⟨get some more port whilst I *buzz* this bottle —W. M. Thackeray⟩
²**buzz** *noun* (1605)
**1 :** a persistent vibratory sound
**2 a :** RUMOR, GOSSIP **b :** a confused murmur **c :** a flurry of activity **d :** FAD, CRAZE
**3 :** a signal conveyed by buzzer; *specifically* **:** a telephone call

**4 :** HIGH 4
**buz·zard** \'bə-zərd\ *noun* [Middle English *busard*, from Old French, alteration of *buison*, from Latin *buteon-, buteo* hawk] (14th century)
**1** *chiefly British* **:** BUTEO
**2 :** any of various usually large birds of prey (as the turkey vulture)
**3 :** a contemptible or rapacious person
**buzz bomb** *noun* (1944)
**:** an unguided jet-propelled missile used by the Germans against England in World War II
**buzz cut** *noun* (1983)
**:** CREW CUT
**buzz·er** \'bə-zər\ *noun* (1606)
**1 :** one that buzzes; *specifically* **:** an electric signaling device that makes a buzzing sound
**2 :** the sound of a buzzer
**buzz saw** *noun* (1858)
**:** CIRCULAR SAW
**buzz·word** \'bəz-,wərd\ *noun* (1946)
**1 :** an important-sounding usually technical word or phrase often of little meaning used chiefly to impress laymen
**2 :** a voguish word or phrase — called also *buzz phrase*
**BVD** \,bē-(,)vē-'dē\ *trademark*
— used for underwear
**B vitamin** *noun* (1920)
**:** any vitamin of the vitamin B complex
**bwa·na** \'bwä-nə\ *noun* [Swahili, from Arabic *abūna* our father] (1878)
**:** MASTER, BOSS
¹**by** \'bī, *before consonants also* bə\ *preposition* [Middle English, preposition & adverb, from Old English, preposition, *be, bī;* akin to Old High German *bī* by, near, Latin *ambi-* on both sides, around, Greek *amphi*] (before 12th century)
**1 :** in proximity to **:** NEAR ⟨standing *by* the window⟩
**2 a :** through or through the medium of **:** VIA ⟨enter *by* the door⟩ **b :** in the direction of **:** TOWARD ⟨north *by* east⟩ **c :** into the vicinity of and beyond **:** PAST ⟨went right *by* him⟩
**3 a :** during the course of ⟨studied *by* night⟩ **b :** not later than ⟨*by* 2 p.m.⟩
**4 a :** through the agency or instrumentality of ⟨*by* force⟩ **b :** born or begot of **c :** sired or borne by
**5 :** with the witness or sanction of ⟨swear *by* all that is holy⟩
**6 a :** in conformity with ⟨acted *by* the rules⟩ **b :** ACCORDING TO ⟨called her *by* name⟩
**7 a :** on behalf of ⟨did right *by* his children⟩ **b :** with respect to ⟨a lawyer *by* profession⟩
**8 a :** in or to the amount or extent of ⟨win *by* a nose⟩ **b** *chiefly Scottish* **:** in comparison with **:** BESIDE
**9** — used as a function word to indicate successive units or increments ⟨little *by* little⟩ ⟨walk two *by* two⟩
**10** — used as a function word in multiplication, in division, and in measurements ⟨divide *a by b*⟩ ⟨multiply 10 *by* 4⟩ ⟨a room 15 feet *by* 20 feet⟩
**11 :** in the opinion of ⟨okay *by* me⟩
— **by the by** *or* **by the bye :** INCIDENTALLY 2
²**by** \'bī\ *adverb* (before 12th century)
**1 a :** close at hand **:** NEAR **b :** at or to another's home ⟨stop *by*⟩
**2 :** PAST ⟨saw him go *by*⟩
**3 :** ASIDE, AWAY
³**by** *or* **bye** \'bī\ *adjective* (14th century)
**1 :** being off the main route **:** SIDE
**2 :** INCIDENTAL
⁴**by** *or* **bye** \'bī\ *noun, plural* **byes** \'bīz\ (1567)
**:** something of secondary importance **:** a side issue
⁵**by** *or* **bye** \'bī\ *interjection* [short for *goodbye*] (1709)
— used to express farewell; often used with following *now*
**by-and-by** \,bī-ən-'bī\ *noun* (1591)
**:** a future time or occasion

**by and by** *adverb* (1526)
**:** before long **:** SOON
**by and large** *adverb* (1706)
**:** on the whole **:** in general
**by-blow** \'bī-,blō\ *noun* (1594)
**1 :** an indirect blow
**2 :** an illegitimate child
**bye** \'bī\ *noun* [alteration of ²*by*] (1883)
**:** the position of a participant in a tournament who advances to the next round without playing
¹**bye-bye** *or* **by-by** \'bī-,bī, bī-'bī\ *interjection* [baby-talk reduplication of *goodbye*] (circa 1736)
— used to express farewell
²**bye-bye** *or* **by-by** \'bī-,bī\ *adverb* (1917)
**:** out especially for a walk or ride — used with the verb *go*
³**bye-bye** *or* **by-by** \'bī-,bī\ *noun* (1867)
**:** BED, SLEEP ⟨lie down . . . and go to *bye-bye* —Rudyard Kipling⟩
⁴**bye-bye** *or* **by-by** \'bī-,bī\ *adverb* (1920)
**:** to bed or sleep — used with the verb *go*
**by-elec·tion** *also* **bye-election** \'bī-ə-,lek-shən\ *noun* (1880)
**:** a special election held between regular elections in order to fill a vacancy
**by·gone** \'bī-,gȯn *also* -,gän\ *adjective* (15th century)
**:** gone by **:** PAST; *especially* **:** OUTMODED
— **bygone** *noun*
**by·law** *or* **bye-law** \'bī-,lȯ\ *noun* [Middle English *bilawe*, probably from (assumed) Old Norse *bȳlǫg*, from Old Norse *bȳr* town + *lǫg* law] (14th century)
**1 :** a rule adopted by an organization chiefly for the government of its members and the regulation of its affairs
**2 :** a local ordinance
¹**by-line** \'bī-,līn\ *noun* (1916)
**1 :** a secondary line **:** SIDELINE
**2 :** a line at the beginning of a news story, magazine article, or book giving the writer's name
²**byline** *transitive verb* (1938)
**:** to write (an article) under a byline
— **by·lin·er** \-,lī-nər\ *noun*
**by·name** \'bī-,nām\ *noun* (14th century)
**1 :** a secondary name
**2 :** NICKNAME
¹**by·pass** \'bī-,pas\ *noun* (1848)
**1 :** a passage to one side; *especially* **:** a deflected route usually around a town
**2 a :** a channel carrying a fluid around a part and back to the main stream **b** (1) **:** SHUNT 1b (2) **:** SHUNT 1c; *also* **:** a surgical procedure for the establishment of a shunt ⟨have a coronary *bypass*⟩
²**bypass** *transitive verb* (1886)
**1 a :** to avoid by means of a bypass **b :** to cause to follow a bypass
**2 a :** to neglect or ignore usually intentionally **b :** CIRCUMVENT
**by·past** \'bī-,past\ *adjective* (15th century)
**:** BYGONE
**by·path** \-,path, -,pȧth\ *noun* (14th century)
**:** BYWAY
**by·play** \-,plā\ *noun* (1812)
**:** action engaged in on the side while the main action proceeds (as during a dramatic production)
**by-prod·uct** \-,prä-(,)dəkt\ *noun* (1857)
**1 :** something produced in a usually industrial or biological process in addition to the principal product
**2 :** a secondary and sometimes unexpected or unintended result ⟨unpleasant *by-products* of civilization⟩
**byre** \'bīr\ *noun* [Middle English, from Old English *bȳre;* akin to Old English *būr* dwelling

---

\ə\ abut \ᵊ\ kitten \ər\ further \a\ ash \ā\ ace
\ä\ mop, mar \au̇\ out \ch\ chin \e\ bet \ē\ easy
\g\ go \i\ hit \ī\ ice \j\ job \ŋ\ sing \ō\ go
\ȯ\ law \ȯi\ boy \th\ thin \th̲\ the \ü\ loot \u̇\ foot
\y\ yet \zh\ vision *see also* Guide to Pronunciation

— more at BOWER] (before 12th century)
*chiefly British* **:** a cow barn

**by·road** \'bī-ˌrōd\ *noun* (1673)
**:** BYWAY

**bys·si·no·sis** \ˌbi-sə-'nō-səs\ *noun, plural*
**-no·ses** \-ˌsēz\ [New Latin, from Latin *byssi-
nus* of fine linen, from Greek *byssinos,* from
*byssos*] (1881)
**:** an occupational respiratory disease associated with inhalation of cotton, flax, or hemp
dust and characterized initially by chest tightness, shortness of breath, and cough and eventually by irreversible lung disease

**bys·sus** \'bi-səs\ *noun, plural* **bys·sus·es** *or*
**bys·si** \-ˌsī, -(ˌ)sē\ [Middle English *bissus,*
from Latin *byssus,* from Greek *byssos* flax, of
Semitic origin; akin to Hebrew *būṣ* linen
cloth] (14th century)
**1 :** a fine probably linen cloth of ancient times
**2** [New Latin, from Latin] **:** a tuft of long
tough filaments by which some bivalve mollusks (as mussels) adhere to a surface

**by·stand·er** \'bī-ˌstan-dər\ *noun* (circa 1619)
**:** one present but not taking part in a situation
or event **:** a chance spectator

**by·street** \-ˌstrēt\ *noun* (1672)
**:** a street off a main thoroughfare

**byte** \'bīt\ *noun* [perhaps alteration of ²*bite*]
(1959)
**:** a group of eight binary digits processed as a
unit by a computer and used especially to represent an alphanumeric character — compare WORD 2c

**by·way** \'bī-ˌwā\ *noun* (14th century)
**1 :** a little traveled side road
**2 :** a secondary or little known aspect or field
⟨meandering more and more in the fascinating
*byways* of learning —*Times Literary Supplement*⟩

**by·word** \-ˌwərd\ *noun* (before 12th century)
**1 :** a proverbial saying **:** PROVERB
**2 a :** one that personifies a type **b :** one that is
noteworthy or notorious
**3 :** EPITHET
**4 :** a frequently used word or phrase

**by–your–leave** \ˌbī-yər-'lēv\ *noun* (1914)
**:** a request for permission ⟨imposed . . . without so much as a *by-your-leave* —J. L.
Granatstein⟩

**¹Byz·an·tine** \'bi-zᵊn-ˌtēn, 'bī-, -ˌtīn; bə-'zan-ˌ,
bī-'\ *adjective* (1794)
**1 :** of, relating to, or characteristic of the ancient city of Byzantium
**2 :** of, relating to, or having the characteristics
of a style of architecture developed in the
Byzantine Empire especially in the 5th and 6th
centuries featuring the dome carried on pen-
dentives over a square and incrustation with
marble veneering and with colored mosaics on
grounds of gold
**3 :** of or relating to the churches using a traditional Greek rite and subject to Eastern canon
law
**4** *often not capitalized* **a :** of, relating to, or
characterized by a devious and usually surreptitious manner of operation ⟨a *Byzantine* power struggle⟩ **b :** intricately involved **:** LABYRIN-
THINE ⟨rules of *Byzantine* complexity⟩

**²Byzantine** *noun* (1836)
**:** a native or inhabitant of Byzantium

**By·zan·tin·ist** \bi-'zan-ti-nist, bī-\ *noun*
(1892)
**:** a student of Byzantine culture

**C** *is the third letter of the English alphabet and of most alphabets closely related to that of English. It came through the Latin from the Etruscan and there from the Greek, which took it from the Phoenician; it has the alphabetic position, but not the pronunciation, of Greek* gamma *and Phoenician* gimel. *In Phoenician and Greek,* C *represented the sound of* g *in* go. *Etruscan assigned* C *the value of* k, *since its speakers did not use the* g *sound. Latin, on the other hand, had both sound values, and so the Romans invented a new letter* G *for the value* g, *while keeping* C *for the value* k. C *retains the* k *pronunciation in modern English before* a, o, u, *or a consonant other than* h, *and has taken on the pronunciation of* s *before* e, i, *or* y. *The small form of* c *emerged through a simple reduction in the size of the capital form.*

---

**c** \\'sē\\ *noun, plural* **c's** *or* **cs** \\'sēz\\ *often capitalized, often attributive*
**1 a :** the 3rd letter of the English alphabet **b :** a graphic representation of this letter **c :** a speech counterpart of orthographic *c*
**2 a :** one hundred — see NUMBER table **b** *slang :* a sum of $100
**3 :** the keynote of a C-major scale
**4 :** a graphic device for reproducing the letter *c*
**5 :** one designated *c* especially as the 3rd in order or class
**6 a :** a grade rating a student's work as fair or mediocre in quality **b :** one graded or rated with a C
**7 :** something shaped like the letter C
**8 :** a structured programming language designed to produce a compact and efficient translation of a program into machine language
**ca'** \\'kȯ, 'kä\\ *Scottish variant of* CALL
¹**cab** \\'kab, 'käb\\ *noun* [Hebrew *qabh*] (1535)
**:** an ancient Hebrew unit of capacity equal to about two quarts (2.2 liters)
²**cab** \\'kab\\ *noun* [short for *cabriolet*] (1827)
**1 a** (1) **:** CABRIOLET (2) **:** a similar light closed carriage (as a hansom) **b :** a carriage for hire
**2 :** TAXICAB
**3** [short for *cabin*] **a :** the part of a locomotive that houses the engineer and operating controls **b :** a comparable shelter (as on a truck) housing operating controls
¹**ca·bal** \\kə-'bäl, -'bal\\ *noun* [French *cabale* cabala, intrigue, cabal, from Medieval Latin *cabbala* cabala, from Late Hebrew *qabbālāh*, literally, received (lore)] (1614)
**:** the artifices and intrigues of a group of persons secretly united to bring about an overturn or usurpation especially in public affairs; *also*
**:** a group engaged in such artifices and intrigues
**synonym** *see* PLOT
²**cabal** *intransitive verb* **ca·balled; ca·balling** (1680)
**:** to unite in or form a cabal
**ca·ba·la** *or* **cab·ba·la** *or* **cab·ba·lah** \\kə-'bä-lə, 'ka-bə-lə\\ *noun, often capitalized* [Medieval Latin *cabbala*] (1521)
**1 :** a medieval and modern system of Jewish theosophy, mysticism, and thaumaturgy marked by belief in creation through emanation and a cipher method of interpreting Scripture
**2 a :** a traditional, esoteric, occult, or secret matter **b :** esoteric doctrine or mysterious art
— **cab·a·lism** \\'ka-bə-ˌli-zəm, 'ka-\\ *noun*
— **cab·a·lis·tic** \\ˌka-bə-'lis-tik, ˌka-\\ *adjective*
**ca·ba·let·ta** \\ˌka-ba-'le-tə, ˌkä-\\ *noun* [Italian] (1842)
**1 :** an operatic song in simple popular style characterized by a uniform rhythm

**2 :** the lively bravura concluding section of an extended aria or duet
¹**ca·ba·list** \\kə-'bä-list, 'ka-bə-\\ *noun* (circa 1533)
**1** *often capitalized* **:** a student, interpreter, or devotee of the Jewish cabala
**2 :** one skilled in esoteric doctrine or mysterious art
²**ca·bal·ist** \\kə-'ba-list, -'bä-\\ *noun* (1569)
**:** a member of a cabal
**ca·bal·le·ro** \\ˌka-bə-'ler-(ˌ)ō, -bə(l)-'yer-\\ *noun, plural* **-ros** [Spanish, from Late Latin *caballarius* hostler — more at CAVALIER] (1749)
**1 :** KNIGHT, CAVALIER
**2** *chiefly Southwest* **:** HORSEMAN
**ca·bana** \\kə-'ban-yə, -'ba-nə\\ *noun* [Spanish *cabaña*, literally, hut, from Medieval Latin *capanna*] (1890)
**1 :** a shelter resembling a cabin usually with an open side facing a beach or swimming pool
**2 :** a lightweight structure with living facilities
**cab·a·ret** \\ˌka-bə-'rā, 'ka-bə-ˌ\\ *noun* [French, from Old North French] (1655)
**1** *archaic* **:** a shop selling wines and liquors
**2 a :** a restaurant serving liquor and providing entertainment (as by singers or dancers) **:** NIGHTCLUB **b :** the show provided at a cabaret
¹**cab·bage** \\'ka-bij\\ *noun, often attributive* [Middle English *caboche*, from Old North French, head] (15th century)
**1 :** a leafy garden plant (*Brassica oleracea capitata*) of European origin with a short stem and a dense globular head of usually green leaves that is used as a vegetable
**2** *slang* **:** PAPER MONEY, BANKNOTES ◆
²**cabbage** *noun* [perhaps by folk etymology from Middle French *cabas* cheating, theft] (1663)
*British* **:** pieces of cloth left in cutting out garments and traditionally kept by tailors as perquisites
³**cabbage** *transitive verb* **cab·baged; cab·bag·ing** (1712)
**:** STEAL, FILCH
**cabbage butterfly** *noun* (1816)
**:** any of several largely white butterflies (family Pieridae) whose green larvae are cabbageworms; *especially* **:** a small cosmopolitan butterfly (*Pieris rapae* synonym *Artogeia rapae*) that is a pest on cabbage — called also *cabbage white*
**cabbage looper** *noun* (circa 1902)
**:** a noctuid moth (*Trichoplusia ni*) having pale green white-striped larvae that feed on cruciferous plants (as the cabbage)
**cabbage palm** *noun* (circa 1784)

**:** a palm with terminal buds eaten as a vegetable
**cabbage palmetto** *noun* (1802)
**:** a cabbage palm (*Sabal palmetto*) with fan-shaped leaves that is native to coastal southeastern U.S. and the Bahamas
**cabbage rose** *noun* (1795)
**:** a fragrant garden rose (*Rosa centifolia*) with upright branches and large pink flowers
**cab·bage·worm** \\'ka-bij-ˌwərm\\ *noun* (1688)
**:** an insect larva (as of a cabbage butterfly) that feeds on cabbages
**cab·bie** *or* **cab·by** \\'ka-bē\\ *noun, plural* **cabbies** (1859)
**:** CABDRIVER
**cab·driv·er** \\'kab-ˌdrī-vər\\ *noun* (1830)
**:** a driver of a cab
**ca·ber** \\'kā-bər, 'kä-\\ *noun* [Scottish Gaelic *cabar*] (1505)
**:** POLE; *especially* **:** a young tree trunk used for tossing as a trial of strength in a Scottish sport
**cab·er·net sau·vi·gnon** \\ˌka-bər-'nä-sō-vē-'nyōⁿ\\ *noun, often C&S capitalized* [French] (1941)
**:** a dry red wine made from a single widely cultivated variety of black grape — called also *cabernet*
¹**cab·in** \\'ka-bən\\ *noun* [Middle English *cabane*, from Middle French, from Old Provençal *cabana* hut, from Medieval Latin *capanna*] (14th century)
**1 a** (1) **:** a private room on a ship or boat (2) **:** a compartment below deck on a boat used for living accommodations **b :** the passenger or cargo compartment of a vehicle (as an airplane or automobile) **c :** the crew compartment of an exploratory vehicle (as a spacecraft)
**2 :** a small one-story dwelling usually of simple construction
**3** *chiefly British* **:** CAB 3
²**cabin** (1586)
*intransitive verb*
**:** to live in or as if in a cabin
*transitive verb*
**:** CONFINE
**cabin boy** *noun* (1726)
**:** a boy working as servant on a ship
**cabin car** *noun* (1879)
**:** CABOOSE
**cabin class** *noun* (1929)
**:** a class of accommodations on a passenger ship superior to tourist class and inferior to first class

---

◇ WORD HISTORY
**cabbage** Old French *caboce* was a jocular word for "head," probably similar in this respect to the English word *noggin*. The form of the word in the dialects of Normandy and Picardy was *caboche,* which spread to the French of the Paris region and retains some currency in Modern French. The origin of *caboce* and *caboche* is not entirely clear, though the second syllable appears to be *boce* "boss, protuberance." While *caboche* has remained limited to very colloquial uses in French, the medieval French word found its way into later Middle English in the sense "head of cabbage." In English it has become the everyday word for the vegetable that the French call *chou.* Middle English *caboche* emerged as *cabage* in Early Modern English, through the same change of a final \\ch\\ sound to \\j\\ in an unstressed syllable that is evident in *knowledge* (Middle English *knowleche*) and *sausage* (Middle English *sawsiche*).

---

cabbage butterfly:
*1* larva, *2* adult

**cabin cruiser** *noun* (1921)
: CRUISER 1b

¹**cab·i·net** \'kab-nit, 'ka-bə-\ *noun* [Middle French, small room, diminutive of Old North French *cabine* gambling house] (circa 1550)
**1 a :** a case or cupboard usually having doors and shelves **b :** a collection of specimens especially of biological or numismatic interest **c :** CONSOLE 4a **d :** a chamber having temperature and humidity controls and used especially for incubating biological samples
**2 a** *archaic* **:** a small room providing seclusion **b :** a small exhibition room in a museum
**3 a** *archaic* (1) **:** the private room serving as council chamber of the chief councillors or ministers of a sovereign (2) **:** the consultations and actions of these councillors **b** (1) *often capitalized* **:** a body of advisers of a head of state (2) **:** a similar advisory council of a governor of a state or a mayor **c** *British* **:** a meeting of a cabinet

²**cabinet** *adjective* (1631)
**1 :** of or relating to a governmental cabinet
**2 :** suitable by reason of size for a small room or by reason of attractiveness or perfection for preservation and display in a cabinet
**3 a :** used or adapted for cabinetmaking **b :** done or used by a cabinetmaker

**cab·i·net·mak·er** \-,mā-kər\ *noun* (1681)
: a skilled woodworker who makes fine furniture
— **cab·i·net·mak·ing** \-,mā-kiŋ\ *noun*

**cab·i·net·ry** \'kab-ni-trē, 'ka-bə-\ *noun* (1926)
**:** CABINETWORK; *also* **:** CABINETS ⟨kitchen *cabinetry*⟩

**cab·i·net·work** \-,wərk\ *noun* (1732)
**:** finished woodwork made by a cabinetmaker

**cabin fever** *noun* (1918)
: extreme irritability and restlessness from living in isolation or a confined indoor area for a prolonged time

¹**ca·ble** \'kā-bəl\ *noun, often attributive* [Middle English, from Old North French, from Medieval Latin *capulum* lasso, from Latin *capere* to take — more at HEAVE] (13th century)
**1 a :** a strong rope especially of 10 inches (25 centimeters) or more in circumference **b :** a cable-laid rope **c :** a wire rope or metal chain of great tensile strength **d :** a wire or wire rope by which force is exerted to control or operate a mechanism
**2 :** CABLE LENGTH
**3 a :** an assembly of electrical conductors insulated from each other but laid up together usually by being twisted around a central core **b :** CABLEGRAM; *also* **:** a radio message or telegram
**4 :** something resembling or fashioned like a cable ⟨a fiber-optic *cable*⟩
**5 :** CABLE TELEVISION

²**cable** *verb* **ca·bled; ca·bling** \'kā-b(ə-)liŋ\ (circa 1500)
*transitive verb*
**1 :** to fasten with or as if with a cable
**2 :** to provide with cables
**3 :** to telegraph by submarine cable
**4 :** to make into a cable or into a form resembling a cable
*intransitive verb*
**:** to communicate by a submarine cable

**cable car** *noun* (1887)
**:** a vehicle moved by an endless cable: **a :** one suspended from an overhead cable **b :** one that moves along tracks

**ca·ble·gram** \'kā-bəl-,gram\ *noun* (1868)
**:** a message sent by a submarine telegraph cable

**ca·ble–laid** \'kā-bəl-'lād\ *adjective* (1723)
**:** composed of three ropes laid together left-handed with each containing three strands twisted together

**cable length** *noun* (1555)
**:** a maritime unit of length variously reckoned as 100 fathoms, 120 fathoms, or 608 feet

**cable television** *noun* (1965)
**:** a system of television reception in which signals from distant stations are picked up by a master antenna and sent by cable to the individual receivers of paying subscribers — called also *cable TV*

**ca·ble·way** \'kā-bəl-,wā\ *noun* (1899)
**:** a suspended cable used as a track along which carriers can be pulled

**cab·man** \'kab-mən\ *noun* (1834)
**:** CABDRIVER

**cab·o·chon** \'ka-bə-,shän\ *noun* [Middle French, diminutive of Old North French *caboche* head] (1578)
**:** a gem or bead cut in convex form and highly polished but not faceted; *also* **:** this style of cutting
— **cabochon** *adverb*

**ca·boo·dle** \kə-'bü-d°l\ *noun* [probably from *ca-* (intensive prefix) + *boodle*] (circa 1848)
**:** COLLECTION, LOT ⟨sell the whole *caboodle*⟩

**ca·boose** \kə-'büs\ *noun* [probably from Dutch *kabuis*, from Middle Low German *kabūse*] (1769)
**1 :** a ship's galley
**2 :** a freight-train car attached usually to the rear mainly for the use of the train crew
**3 :** one that follows or brings up the rear

**cab·o·tage** \'ka-bə-,täzh\ *noun* [French, from *caboter* to sail along the coast] (1831)
**1 :** trade or transport in coastal waters or airspace or between two points within a country
**2 :** the right to engage in cabotage

**ca·bret·ta** \kə-'bre-tə\ *noun* [modification of Portuguese and Spanish *cabra* goat] (1926)
**:** a light soft leather from skins of hairy sheep

**ca·bril·la** \kə-'brē-ə, -'bri-lə\ *noun* [Spanish, diminutive of *cabra* goat, from Latin *capra* she-goat, feminine of *caper* he-goat — more at CAPRIOLE] (1859)
**:** any of various sea basses (especially of the genera *Epinephelus* and *Paralabrax*) of the Mediterranean, the California coast, and the warmer parts of the western Atlantic

**cab·ri·ole** \'ka-brē-,ōl\ *noun* [French, caper] (circa 1797)
**1 :** a ballet leap in which one leg is extended in midair and the other struck against it
**2 :** a curved furniture leg ending in an ornamental foot

**cab·ri·o·let** \,ka-brē-ə-'lā\ *noun* [French, from diminutive of *cabriole* caper, alteration of Middle French *capriole*] (1763)
**1 :** a light 2-wheeled one-horse carriage with a folding leather hood, a large apron, and upward-curving shafts
**2 :** a convertible coupe

**cab·stand** \'kab-,stand\ *noun* (1848)
**:** a place where cabs await hire

**cac-** *or* **caco-** *combining form* [New Latin, from Greek *kak-, kako-,* from *kakos* bad]
**:** bad ⟨*caco*graphy⟩

**ca' can·ny** \kȯ-'ka-nē\ *noun* [Scots, verb, to proceed cautiously, from *ca'* (call) + *canny* careful] (1886)
*British* **:** SLOWDOWN
— **ca' canny** *intransitive verb, British*

**ca·cao** \kə-'kaü, kə-'kā-(,)ō\ *noun, plural* **ca·caos** [Spanish, from Nahuatl *cacahuatl* cacao beans] (1555)
**1 :** the dried partly fermented fatty seeds of a South American evergreen tree (*Theobroma cacao* of the family Sterculiaceae) that are used in making cocoa, chocolate, and cocoa butter — called also *cacao bean, cocoa bean*
**2 :** a tree having small yellowish flowers followed by fleshy pods with many seeds that bears cacao

**cacao butter** *variant of* COCOA BUTTER

**cac·cia·to·re** \,kä-chə-'tȯr-ē, -'tȯr-\ *adjective* [Italian, from *cacciatore* hunter] (1942)
**:** cooked with tomatoes and herbs and sometimes wine ⟨chicken *cacciatore*⟩

**cach·a·lot** \'ka-shə-,lät, -,lō\ *noun* [French] (1747)
**:** SPERM WHALE

¹**cache** \'kash\ *noun* [French, from *cacher* to press, hide, from (assumed) Vulgar Latin *coacticare* to press together, from Latin *coactare* to compel, frequentative of *cogere* to compel — more at COGENT] (1797)
**1 a :** a hiding place especially for concealing and preserving provisions or implements **b :** a secure place of storage
**2 :** something hidden or stored in a cache
**3 :** a computer memory with very short access time used for storage of frequently used instructions or data — called also *cache memory*

²**cache** *transitive verb* **cached; cach·ing** (1805)
**:** to place, hide, or store in a cache

**ca·chec·tic** \kə-'kek-tik, ka-\ *adjective* [French *cachectique*, from Latin *cachecticus*, from Greek *kachektikos*, from *kak-* + *echein*] (1634)
**:** affected by cachexia

**cache·pot** \'kash-,pät, 'kash-,pō, 'ka-shə-\ *noun* [French, from *cacher* to hide + *pot* pot] (1872)
**:** an ornamental receptacle to hold and usually to conceal a flowerpot

**ca·chet** \ka-'shā\ *noun* [French, from *cacher*] (circa 1639)
**1 a :** a seal used especially as a mark of official approval **b :** an indication of approval carrying great prestige
**2 a :** a characteristic feature or quality conferring prestige **b :** PRESTIGE ⟨being rich . . . doesn't have the *cachet* it used to —Truman Capote⟩
**3 :** a medicinal preparation for swallowing consisting of a case usually of rice-flour paste enclosing a medicine
**4 a :** a design or inscription on an envelope to commemorate a postal or philatelic event **b :** an advertisement forming part of a postage meter impression **c :** a motto or slogan included in a postal cancellation

**ca·chex·ia** \kə-'kek-sē-ə, ka-\ *noun* [Late Latin *cachexia*, from Greek *kachexia* bad condition, from *kak-* cac- + *hexis* condition, from *echein* to have, be disposed — more at SCHEME] (1541)
**:** general physical wasting and malnutrition usually associated with chronic disease

**cach·in·nate** \'ka-kə-,nāt\ *intransitive verb* **-nat·ed; -nat·ing** [Latin *cachinnatus*, past participle of *cachinnare*, of imitative origin] (1824)
**:** to laugh loudly or immoderately
— **cach·in·na·tion** \,ka-kə-'nā-shən\ *noun*

**ca·chou** \ka-'shü, 'ka-\ *noun* [French, from Portuguese *cachu*, from Malayalam *kāccu*] (circa 1879)
**:** a pill or pastille used to sweeten the breath

**ca·cique** \kə-'sēk\ *noun* [Spanish, from Taino, chief] (1555)
**1 :** a native Indian chief in areas dominated primarily by a Spanish culture
**2 :** a local political boss in Spain and Latin America
— **ca·ciqu·ism** \-'sē-,ki-zəm\ *noun*

**cack·le** \'ka-kəl\ *intransitive verb* **cack·led; cack·ling** \-k(ə-)liŋ\ [Middle English *cakelen*, of imitative origin] (13th century)
**1 :** to make the sharp broken noise or cry characteristic of a hen especially after laying
**2 :** to laugh especially in a harsh or sharp manner
**3 :** CHATTER
— **cackle** *noun*
— **cack·ler** \-k(ə-)lər\ *noun*

**caco·de·mon** \,ka-kə-'dē-mən\ *noun* [Greek *kakodaimōn*, from *kak-* cac- + *daimōn* spirit] (1594)
**:** DEMON
— **caco·de·mon·ic** \-di-'mä-nik\ *adjective*

**cacodylic acid** \,ka-kə-'di-lik-\ *noun* [German *Kakodyl* the radical As(CH₃)₂, from Greek *kakōdēs* foul-smelling, from *kak-* +

-ōdēs (akin to Greek *ozein* to smell) — more at ODOR] (1850)
**:** a toxic crystalline compound of arsenic C₂H₇AsO₂ used especially as an herbicide

**caco·ë·thes** \ˌka-kə-'wē-(ˌ)thēz\ *noun* [Latin, from Greek *kakoēthes* wickedness, from neuter of *kakoēthēs* malignant, from *kak-* cac- + *ēthos* character — more at SIB] (circa 1587)
**:** an insatiable desire **:** MANIA

**ca·cog·ra·phy** \ka-'kä-grə-fē\ *noun* (1580)
**1 :** bad spelling — compare ORTHOGRAPHY
**2 :** bad handwriting — compare CALLIGRAPHY
— **caco·graph·i·cal** \ˌka-kə-'gra-fi-kəl\ *adjective*

**cac·o·mis·tle** \'ka-kə-ˌmi-səl, ˌka-kə-'mis(t)-lē\ *noun* [Mexican Spanish, from Nahuatl *tlahcomiztli*, from *tlahco* half + *miztli* mountain lion] (1869)
**:** RINGTAIL 2

**ca·coph·o·nous** \ka-'kä-fə-nəs, -'kō- *also* -'ka-\ *adjective* [Greek *kakophōnos*, from *kak-* + *phōnē* voice, sound — more at BAN] (1797)
**:** marked by cacophony **:** harsh-sounding
— **ca·coph·o·nous·ly** *adverb*

**ca·coph·o·ny** \-nē\ *noun, plural* **-nies** (circa 1656)
**:** harsh or discordant sound **:** DISSONANCE 2; *specifically* **:** harshness in the sound of words or phrases

**cac·tus** \'kak-təs\ *noun, plural* **cac·ti** \-ˌtī, -(ˌ)tē\ *or* **cac·tus·es** *also* **cactus** [New Latin, genus name, from Latin, cardoon, from Greek *kaktos*] (1767)
**:** any of a family (Cactaceae, the cactus family) of plants that have succulent stems and branches with scales or spines instead of leaves and are found especially in dry areas (as deserts)

**ca·cu·mi·nal** \ka-'kyü-mə-n°l, kə-\ *adjective* [International Scientific Vocabulary, from Latin *cacumin-, cacumen* top, point] (1862)
**:** RETROFLEX 2

**cad** \'kad\ *noun* [English dialect, unskilled assistant, short for Scots *caddie*] (1833)
**1 :** an omnibus conductor
**2 :** a man who acts with deliberate disregard for another's feelings or rights

**ca·das·tral** \kə-'das-trəl\ *adjective* (1858)
**1 :** of or relating to a cadastre
**2 :** showing or recording property boundaries, subdivision lines, buildings, and related details
— **ca·das·tral·ly** \-trə-lē\ *adverb*

**ca·das·tre** \kə-'das-tər\ *noun* [French, from Italian *catastro*, from Old Italian *catastico*, from Late Greek *katastichon* notebook, from Greek *kata* by + *stichos* row, line — more at CATA-, DISTICH] (1804)
**:** an official register of the quantity, value, and ownership of real estate used in apportioning taxes

**ca·dav·er** \kə-'da-vər\ *noun* [Latin, from *cadere* to fall] (circa 1500)
**:** a dead body; *especially* **:** one intended for dissection
— **ca·dav·er·ic** \-'dav-rik, -'da-və-\ *adjective*

**ca·dav·er·ine** \kə-'da-və-ˌrēn\ *noun* (1887)
**:** a syrupy colorless poisonous ptomaine C₅H₁₄N₂ formed by decarboxylation of lysine especially in putrefaction of flesh

**ca·dav·er·ous** \kə-'dav-rəs, -'da-vər-əs\ *adjective* (1627)
**1 a :** of or relating to a corpse **b :** suggestive of corpses or tombs
**2 a :** PALLID, LIVID **b :** GAUNT, EMACIATED
— **ca·dav·er·ous·ly** *adverb*

**cad·die** *or* **cad·dy** \'ka-dē\ *noun, plural* **caddies** [French *cadet* military cadet] (circa 1730)
**1** *Scottish* **:** one that waits about for odd jobs
**2 a :** one who assists a golfer especially by carrying the clubs **b :** a wheeled device for conveying things not readily carried by hand
— **caddie** *or* **caddy** *intransitive verb*

---

**¹cad·dis** *also* **cad·dice** \'ka-dəs\ *noun* [Middle English *cadas* cotton wool, probably from Middle French *cadaz*, from Old Provençal *cadarz*] (1530)
**:** worsted yarn; *specifically* **:** a worsted ribbon or binding formerly used for garters and girdles

**²caddis** *noun* (1651)
**:** CADDISWORM

**caddis fly** *noun* (1787)
**:** any of an order (Trichoptera) of insects with four membranous wings, vestigial mouthparts, slender many-jointed antennae, and aquatic larvae — compare CADDISWORM

**cad·dish** \'ka-dish\ *adjective* (1868)
**:** of, relating to, or resembling a cad
— **cad·dish·ly** *adverb*
— **cad·dish·ness** *noun*

**cad·dis·worm** \'ka-dəs-ˌwərm\ *noun* [probably alteration of obsolete *codworm*; from the case or tube in which it lives] (1622)
**:** the larva of a caddis fly that lives in and carries around a silken case covered with bits of debris

**Cad·do** \'ka-(ˌ)dō\ *noun, plural* **Caddo** *or* **Caddos** (1805)
**:** a member of a group of American Indian peoples of Louisiana, Arkansas, and eastern Texas

**cad·dy** \'ka-dē\ *noun, plural* **caddies** [Malay *kati* catty] (1792)
**1 :** a small box, can, or chest used especially to keep tea in
**2 :** a container or device for storing or holding objects when they are not in use

**caddisworm**

**cade** \'kād\ *adjective* [English dialect *cade* pet lamb, from Middle English *cad*] (1551)
**:** left by its mother and reared by hand **:** PET ⟨a *cade* lamb⟩

**-cade** *noun combining form* [cavalcade]
**:** procession ⟨motorcade⟩

**ca·delle** \kə-'del\ *noun* [French, from Provençal *cadello*, from Latin *catella*, feminine of *catellus* little dog, diminutive of *catulus* young animal] (circa 1861)
**:** a small cosmopolitan black beetle (*Tenebroides mauritanicus*) destructive to stored grain

**ca·dence** \'kā-d°n(t)s\ *noun* [Middle English, from Old Italian *cadenza*, from *cadere* to fall, from Latin — more at CHANCE] (14th century)
**1 a :** a rhythmic sequence or flow of sounds in language **b :** the beat, time, or measure of rhythmical motion or activity
**2 a :** a falling inflection of the voice **b :** a concluding and usually falling strain; *specifically* **:** a musical chord sequence moving to a harmonic close or point of rest and giving the sense of harmonic completion
**3 :** the modulated and rhythmic recurrence of a sound especially in nature
— **ca·denced** \-d°n(t)st\ *adjective*
— **ca·den·tial** \kā-'den(t)-shəl\ *adjective*

**ca·den·cy** \'kā-d°n(t)-sē\ *noun, plural* **-cies** (1627)
**:** CADENCE

**ca·dent** \'kā-d°nt\ *adjective* [Latin *cadent-, cadens*, present participle of *cadere*] (1605)
**1** *archaic* **:** being in the process of falling ⟨with *cadent* tears fret channels in her cheeks —Shakespeare⟩
**2 :** having rhythmic cadence

**ca·den·za** \kə-'den-zə\ *noun* [Italian, cadence, cadenza] (1836)
**1 :** a parenthetical flourish in an aria or other solo piece commonly just before a final or other important cadence
**2 :** a technically brilliant sometimes improvised solo passage toward the close of a concerto

---

**3 :** an exceptionally brilliant part of an artistic work

**cade oil** \'kād-\ *noun* [cade juniper, from Middle French, from Old Provençal, from Medieval Latin *catanus*] (1880)
**:** JUNIPER TAR

**ca·det** \kə-'det\ *noun, often attributive* [French, from Gascon *capdet* chief, from Late Latin *capitellum*, diminutive of Latin *capit-, caput* head — more at HEAD] (1610)
**1 a :** a younger brother or son **b :** youngest son **c :** a younger branch of a family or a member of it
**2 :** one in training for a military or naval commission; *especially* **:** a student in a service academy
**3** *slang* **:** PIMP ◆
— **ca·det·ship** \-ˌship\ *noun*

**Ca·dette** \kə-'det\ *noun* [from *cadet*] (1963)
**:** a member of a program of the Girl Scouts for girls in the sixth through ninth grades in school

**cadge** \'kaj\ *verb* **cadged; cadg·ing** [back-formation from Scots *cadger* carrier, huckster, from Middle English *cadgear*] (circa 1812)
**:** BEG, SPONGE
— **cadg·er** *noun*

**cad·mi·um** \'kad-mē-əm\ *noun* [New Latin, from Latin *cadmia* zinc oxide, from Greek *kadmeia*, literally, Theban (earth), from feminine of *kadmeios* Theban, from *Kadmos*; from the occurrence of its ores together with zinc oxide] (1822)
**:** a bluish white malleable ductile toxic bivalent metallic element used especially in protective platings and in bearing metals — see ELEMENT table

**cadmium sulfide** *noun* (circa 1893)
**:** a yellow-brown poisonous salt CdS used especially in electronic parts, in photoelectric cells, and in medicine

**Cad·mus** \'kad-məs\ *noun* [Latin, from Greek *Kadmos*]
**:** the legendary founder of Thebes

**cad·re** \'ka-ˌdrā, 'kä-, -ˌdrē; *especially British* 'kä-də(r), 'kā-, -drə\ *noun* [French, from Italian *quadro*, from Latin *quadrum* square — more at QUARREL] (1830)

---

\ə\ abut \°\ kitten \ər\ further \a\ ash \ā\ ace
\ä\ mop, mar \aù\ out \ch\ chin \e\ bet \ē\ easy
\g\ go \i\ hit \ī\ ice \j\ job \ŋ\ sing \ō\ go
\ò\ law \òi\ boy \th\ thin \th\ the \ü\ loot \ù\ foot
\y\ yet \zh\ vision    *see also* Guide to Pronunciation

**1 :** FRAME, FRAMEWORK
**2 :** a nucleus or core group especially of trained personnel able to assume control and to train others; *broadly* **:** a group of people having some unifying relationship ⟨a *cadre* of lawyers⟩
**3 :** a cell of indoctrinated leaders active in promoting the interests of a revolutionary party
**4 :** a member of a cadre
**ca·du·ceus** \kə-'dü-sē-əs, -'dyü-, -shəs\ *noun, plural* **-cei** \-sē-ī\ [Latin, modification of Greek *karykeion,* from *karyx, kēryx* herald; akin to Sanskrit *kāru* singer] (1588)
**1 :** the symbolic staff of a herald; *specifically* **:** a representation of a staff with two entwined snakes and two wings at the top
**2 :** an insignia bearing a caduceus and symbolizing a physician
**ca·du·ci·ty** \kə-'dü-sə-tē, -'dyü-\ *noun* [French *caducité,* from *caduc* transitory, from Latin *caducus*] (1769)
**1 :** SENILITY
**2 :** the quality of being transitory or perishable
**ca·du·cous** \kə-'dü-kəs, -'dyü-\ *adjective* [Latin *caducus* tending to fall, transitory, from *cadere* to fall — more at CHANCE] (1808)
**:** falling off easily or before the usual time — used especially of floral organs
**cae·cal, cae·cum** *variant of* CECAL, CECUM
**cae·ci·lian** \si-'sil-yən, -'sēl-, -'si-lē-ən\ *noun* [ultimately from Latin *caecilia* slowworm, from *caecus* blind] (circa 1879)
**:** any of an order (Gymnophiona) of chiefly tropical burrowing amphibians resembling worms
— **caecilian** *adjective*
**Caer·phil·ly** \kär-'fi-lē\ *noun* [*Caerphilly,* urban district in Wales] (circa 1893)
**:** a mild white friable cheese of Welsh origin
**Cae·sar** \'sē-zər\ *noun* [Gaius Julius *Caesar*] (1567)
**1 :** any of the Roman emperors succeeding Augustus Caesar — used as a title
**2 a** *often not capitalized* **:** a powerful ruler: (1) **:** EMPEROR (2) **:** AUTOCRAT, DICTATOR **b** [from the reference in Matthew 22:21] **:** the civil power **:** temporal ruler
— **Cae·sar·e·an** *or* **Cae·sar·i·an** \si-'zar-ē-ən, -zer-\ *adjective*
**cae·sar·e·an** *also* **cae·sar·i·an** *variant of* CESAREAN
**Cae·sar·ism** \'sē-zə-,ri-zəm\ *noun* (1857)
**:** imperial authority or system **:** political absolutism **:** DICTATORSHIP
— **Cae·sar·ist** \-zə-rist\ *noun*
**Caesar salad** *noun* [*Caesar*'s, restaurant in Tijuana, Mexico] (1950)
**:** a tossed salad usually made of romaine, garlic, anchovies, and croutons and dressed with olive oil, coddled egg, lemon juice, and grated cheese
**cae·si·um** *chiefly British variant of* CESIUM
**caes·pi·tose** \'ses-pə-,tōs\ *adjective* [New Latin *caespitosus,* from Latin *caespit-, cáespes* turf] (1830)
**1 :** growing in clusters or tufts
**2 :** forming a dense turf
**cae·su·ra** \si-'zyùr-ə, -'zhùr-\ *noun, plural* **-suras** *or* **-su·rae** \-'zyùr-(,)ē, -'zhùr-\ [Late Latin, from Latin, act of cutting, from *caedere* to cut] (1556)
**1** *in modern prosody* **:** a usually rhetorical break in the flow of sound in the middle of a line of verse
**2** *Greek & Latin prosody* **:** a break in the flow of sound in a verse caused by the ending of a word within a foot
**3 :** BREAK, INTERRUPTION
**4 :** a pause marking a rhythmic point of division in a melody
— **cae·su·ral** \-'zyùr-əl, -'zhùr-\ *adjective*
**ca·fé** *also* **ca·fe** \ka-'fā, kə-\ *noun, often attributive* [French *café* coffee, café, from Turkish *kahve* — more at COFFEE] (1802)

**1 :** a usually small and informal establishment serving various refreshments (as coffee); *broadly* **:** RESTAURANT
**2 :** BARROOM
**3 :** CABARET, NIGHTCLUB
**ca·fé au lait** \(,)ka-'fā-ō-'lā\ *noun* [French, coffee with milk] (1763)
**1 :** coffee with usually hot milk in about equal parts
**2 :** the color of coffee with milk
**ca·fé noir** \-'nwär\ *noun* [French, black coffee] (1841)
**:** coffee without milk or cream; *also* **:** DEMITASSE
**café society** *noun* (1937)
**:** society of persons who are regular patrons of fashionable cafés
**¹caf·e·te·ria** \,ka-fə-'tir-ē-ə\ *noun* [American Spanish *cafetería* coffeehouse, from *cafetera* coffee maker, from French *cafetière,* from *café*] (1894)
**:** a restaurant in which the customers serve themselves or are served at a counter and take the food to tables to eat ◆
**²cafeteria** *adjective* (1951)
**:** providing a selection from which a choice may be made ⟨*cafeteria* benefit plan⟩ ⟨a *cafeteria* curriculum⟩
**caf·e·to·ri·um** \-'tōr-ē-əm, -'tòr-\ *noun* [blend of *cafeteria* and *auditorium*] (1952)
**:** a large room (as in a school building) designed for use both as a cafeteria and an auditorium
**caff** \'kaf\ *noun* (1931)
*British* **:** CAFÉ 1
**caf·feine** \ka-'fēn, 'ka-,\ *noun* [German *Kaffein,* from *Kaffee* coffee, from French *café*] (circa 1823)
**:** a bitter alkaloid $C_8H_{10}N_4O_2$ found especially in coffee, tea, and kola nuts and used medicinally as a stimulant and diuretic
**caf·fe lat·te** \'kä-(,)fā-'lä-(,)tā\ *noun* [Italian *caffelatte,* short for *caffè e latte* coffee and milk] (1927)
**:** espresso mixed with hot or steamed milk
**caf·tan** \'kaf-(,)tan\ *noun* [Russian *kaftan,* from Turkish, from Persian *qaftān*] (1591)
**:** a usually cotton or silk ankle-length garment with long sleeves that is common throughout the Levant
**¹cage** \'kāj\ *noun* [Middle English, from Old French, from Latin *cavea* cavity, cage, from *cavus* hollow — more at CAVE] (13th century)
**1 :** a box or enclosure having some openwork for confining or carrying animals (as birds)
**2 a :** a barred cell for confining prisoners **b :** a fenced area for prisoners of war
**3 :** a framework serving as support ⟨the steel *cage* of a skyscraper⟩
**4 a :** an enclosure resembling a cage in form or purpose ⟨a cashier's *cage*⟩ **b :** an arrangement of atoms or molecules so bonded as to enclose a space in which another atom or ion (as of a metal) can reside
**5 a :** a screen placed behind home plate to stop baseballs during batting practice **b :** a goal consisting of posts or a frame with a net attached (as in ice hockey)
**6 :** a large building containing an area for practicing outdoor sports and often adapted for indoor events
— **cage·ful** \-,fùl\ *noun*
**²cage** *transitive verb* **caged; cag·ing** (1577)
**1 :** to confine or keep in or as if in a cage
**2 :** to drive (as a puck) into a cage and score a goal
**cage·ling** \'kāj-liŋ\ *noun* (1859)
**:** a caged bird
**ca·gey** *also* **ca·gy** \'kā-jē\ *adjective* **ca·gi·er; -est** [origin unknown] (circa 1893)
**1 :** hesitant about committing oneself
**2 a :** wary of being trapped or deceived **:** SHREWD ⟨a *cagey* consumer⟩ **b :** marked by cleverness ⟨a *cagey* reply⟩
— **ca·gi·ly** \-jə-lē\ *adverb*

— **ca·gi·ness** *also* **ca·gey·ness** \-jē-nəs\ *noun*
**ca·hier** \kä-'yā, kī-'ā\ *noun* [French, from Middle French *quaer, caier* quire — more at QUIRE] (1789)
**:** a report or memorial concerning policy especially of a parliamentary body
**ca·hoot** \kə-'hüt\ *noun* [perhaps from French *cahute* cabin, hut] (1829)
**:** PARTNERSHIP, LEAGUE — usually used in plural ⟨they're in *cahoots*⟩
**ca·how** \kə-'haú\ *noun* [imitative] (1615)
**:** a dark-colored petrel (*Pterodroma cahow*) formerly abundant in Bermuda but now nearly extinct
**cai·man** \'kā-mən; kā-'man, kī-\ *noun* [Spanish *caimán,* probably from Carib *cayman*] (1577)
**:** any of several Central and South American crocodilians (genera *Caiman, Melanosuchus,* and *Paleosuchus*) similar to alligators
**Cain** \'kān\ *noun* [Hebrew *Qayin*]
**:** the brother and murderer of Abel
**-caine** *noun combining form* [German *-kain,* from *kokain* cocaine]
**:** synthetic alkaloid anesthetic ⟨procaine⟩
**ca·ique** \kä-'ēk, 'kīk\ *noun* [French, from Turkish *kayık*] (1625)
**1 :** a light skiff used on the Bosporus
**2 :** a Levantine sailing vessel
**caird** \'kerd\ *noun* [Scottish Gaelic *ceard* craftsman; akin to Greek *kerdos* profit] (1663)
*Scottish* **:** a traveling tinker; *also* **:** TRAMP, GYPSY
**cairn** \'karn, 'kern\ *noun* [Middle English (Scots) *carne,* from Scottish Gaelic *carn;* akin to Old Irish & Welsh *carn* cairn] (15th century)
**:** a heap of stones piled up as a memorial or as a landmark
— **cairned** \'karnd, 'kernd\ *adjective*
**cairn·gorm** \'karn-,górm, 'kern-\ *noun* [*Cairngorm,* mountain in Scotland] (1794)
**:** a yellow or smoky-brown crystalline quartz
**cairn terrier** *noun* [from its use in hunting among cairns] (1910)
**:** any of a breed of small compactly built hard-coated terriers of Scottish origin
**cais·son** \'kā-,sän, -s°n, *British also* kə-'sün\ *noun* [French, from Middle French, from Old

Provençal, from *caissa* chest, from Latin *capsa* — more at CASE] (circa 1702)
**1 a :** a chest to hold ammunition **b :** a usually 2-wheeled vehicle for artillery ammunition attachable to a horse-drawn limber; *also :* a limber with its attached caisson

caisson 1b

**2 a :** a watertight chamber used in construction work under water or as a foundation **b :** a hollow floating box or a boat used as a floodgate for a dock or basin
**3 :** COFFER 3
**caisson disease** *noun* (1873)
: ²BEND 3
**cai·tiff** \'kā-təf\ *adjective* [Middle English *caitif*, from Old North French, captive, vile, from Latin *captivus* captive] (14th century)
: being base, cowardly, or despicable
— **caitiff** *noun*
**caj·e·put** \'ka-jə-pət, -ˌpút\ *noun* [Malay *kayu putih*, from *kayu* wood, tree + *putih* white] (1832)
: an Australian and southeast Asian tree (*Melaleuca quinquenervia* synonym *M. leucadendron*) of the myrtle family that yields a pungent medicinal oil and has been introduced into Florida
**ca·jole** \kə-'jōl\ *transitive verb* **ca·joled; ca·jol·ing** [French *cajoler*] (1645)
**1 :** to persuade with flattery or gentle urging especially in the face of reluctance : COAX ⟨had to *cajole* them into going⟩
**2 :** to deceive with soothing words or false promises
— **ca·jole·ment** \-'jōl-mənt\ *noun*
— **ca·jol·er** *noun*
— **ca·jol·ery** \-'jō-lə-rē\ *noun*
**¹Ca·jun** *also* **Ca·jan** \'kā-jən\ *noun* [alteration of *Acadian*] (1868)
: a Louisianian descended from French-speaking immigrants from Acadia
**²Cajun** *adjective* (1885)
**1 :** of, relating to, or characteristic of the Cajuns
**2 :** of, relating to, or prepared in a style of cooking originating among the Cajuns and characterized by the use of hot seasonings (as cayenne pepper)
**¹cake** \'kāk\ *noun* [Middle English, from Old Norse *kaka;* akin to Old High German *kuocho* cake] (13th century)
**1 a :** a breadlike food made from a dough or batter that is usually fried or baked in small flat shapes and is often unleavened **b :** a sweet baked food made from a dough or thick batter usually containing flour and sugar and often shortening, eggs, and a raising agent (as baking powder) **c :** a flattened usually round mass of food that is baked or fried ⟨a fish *cake*⟩
**2 a :** a block of compacted or congealed matter ⟨a *cake* of ice⟩ **b :** a hard or brittle layer or deposit
— **cak·ey** \'kā-kē\ *adjective*
**²cake** *verb* **caked; cak·ing** (1607)
*transitive verb*
**1 :** ENCRUST ⟨*caked* with dust⟩
**2 :** to fill (a space) with a packed mass
*intransitive verb*
: to form or harden into a mass
**cake·walk** \'kāk-ˌwók\ *noun* (1879)
**1 :** a black American entertainment having a cake as prize for the most accomplished steps and figures in walking
**2 :** a stage dance developed from walking steps and figures typically involving a high prance with backward tilt
**3 a :** a one-sided contest **b :** an easy task
— **cakewalk** *intransitive verb*
— **cake·walk·er** *noun*

**Cal·a·bar bean** \'ka-lə-ˌbär-\ *noun* [*Calabar*, Nigeria] (circa 1876)
: the dark brown highly poisonous seed of a tropical African woody vine (*Physostigma venenosum*) that is used as a source of physostigmine and as an ordeal poison in native witchcraft trials
**cal·a·bash** \'ka-lə-ˌbash\ *noun* [French & Spanish; French *calebasse* gourd, from Spanish *calabaza*] (1596)
**1 :** a tropical American tree (*Crescentia cujete*) of the trumpet-creeper family; *also :* its hard globose fruit
**2 :** GOURD; *especially :* one whose hard shell is used for a utensil
**3 :** a utensil (as a bottle or dipper) made from the shell of a calabash
**cal·a·boose** \'ka-lə-ˌbüs\ *noun* [Spanish *calabozo* dungeon] (1792)
: JAIL; *especially :* a local jail
**ca·la·di·um** \kə-'lā-dē-əm\ *noun* [New Latin, genus name, from Malay *kěladi*, an aroid plant] (circa 1845)
: any of a genus (*Caladium*, especially *C. bicolor*) of tropical American plants of the arum family widely cultivated for their showy variably colored leaves
**cal·a·man·der** \'ka-lə-ˌman-dər, ˌka-lə-'\ *noun* [probably from Dutch *kalamanderhout* calamander wood] (1804)
: the hazel-brown black-striped wood of a southeast Asian tree (genus *Diospyros*, especially *D. quaesita*) that is used in furniture manufacturing
**cal·a·mari** \ˌkä-lə-'mär-ē, 'ka-lə-ˌmer-ē\ *noun* [Italian, plural of *calamaro, calamaio*, from Medieval Latin *calamarium* ink pot, from Latin *calamus;* from the inky substance the squid secretes] (circa 1961)
: squid used as food
**cal·a·mary** \'ka-lə-ˌmer-ē\ *noun, plural* **-mar·ies** [Medieval Latin *calamarium*] (1567)
: SQUID
**cal·a·mine** \'ka-lə-ˌmīn, -mən\ *noun* [Middle English *calamyn* ore of zinc, from Medieval Latin *calamina*, alteration of Latin *cadmia* — more at CADMIUM] (15th century)
: a mixture of zinc oxide with a small amount of ferric oxide used in lotions, liniments, and ointments
**cal·a·mint** \'ka-lə-ˌmint\ *noun* [Middle English *calament*, from Old French, from Medieval Latin *calamentum*, from Greek *kalaminthē*] (14th century)
: any of a genus (*Satureja*, especially *S. calamintha*) of mints
**cal·a·mite** \'ka-lə-ˌmīt\ *noun* [New Latin *Calamites*, genus of fossil plants, from Latin *calamus*] (1837)
: a Paleozoic fossil plant (especially genus *Calamites*) resembling a giant horsetail
**ca·lam·i·tous** \kə-'la-mə-təs\ *adjective* (1545)
: being, causing, or accompanied by calamity
— **ca·lam·i·tous·ly** *adverb*
**ca·lam·i·ty** \kə-'la-mə-tē\ *noun, plural* **-ties** [Middle English *calamytey*, from Middle French *calamité*, from Latin *calamitat-, calamitas;* perhaps akin to Latin *clades* destruction] (15th century)
**1 :** a state of deep distress or misery caused by major misfortune or loss
**2 :** an extraordinarily grave event marked by great loss and lasting distress and affliction
**cal·a·mon·din** \ˌka-lə-'män-dən\ *noun* [Tagalog *kalamunding*] (circa 1928)
: a small hybrid citrus tree (*Citrofortunella mitis* synonym *Citrus mitis*); *also :* its tart fruit
**cal·a·mus** \'ka-lə-məs\ *noun, plural* **-mi** \-ˌmī, -ˌmē\ [Latin, reed, reed pen, from Greek *kalamos* — more at HAULM] (14th century)
**1 a :** SWEET FLAG **b :** the aromatic peeled and dried rhizome of the sweet flag that is the source of a carcinogenic essential oil
**2 :** the hollow basal portion of a feather below the vane : QUILL

**ca·lash** \kə-'lash\ *noun* [French *calèche*, from German *Kalesche*, from Czech *kolesa* wheels, carriage; akin to Greek *kyklos* wheel — more at WHEEL] (1679)
**1 a :** a light small-wheeled 4-passenger carriage with a folding top **b :** CALÈCHE 1b
**2 :** a large hood worn by women in the 18th century
**calc-** *or* **calci-** *combining form* [Latin *calc-, calx* lime — more at CHALK]
: calcium : calcium salt ⟨*calcic*⟩ ⟨*calcify*⟩
**cal·ca·ne·al** \kal-'kā-nē-əl\ *adjective* (circa 1849)
: relating to the heel or calcaneus
**cal·ca·ne·um** \-nē-əm\ *noun, plural* **-nea** \-nē-ə\ [Latin, heel — more at CALK] (circa 1751)
: CALCANEUS
**cal·ca·ne·us** \-nē-əs\ *noun, plural* **-nei** \-nē-ˌī\ [Late Latin, heel, alteration of Latin *calcaneum*] (circa 1925)
: a tarsal bone that in humans is the great bone of the heel
**cal·car·e·ous** \kal-'kar-ē-əs, -'ker-\ *adjective* [Latin *calcarius* of lime, from *calc-, calx*] (1677)
**1 a :** resembling calcite or calcium carbonate especially in hardness **b :** consisting of or containing calcium carbonate; *also :* containing calcium
**2 :** growing on limestone or in soil impregnated with lime
— **cal·car·e·ous·ly** *adverb*
**calces** *plural of* CALX
**cal·cic** \'kal-sik\ *adjective* (1871)
: derived from or containing calcium or lime
: rich in calcium
**cal·ci·cole** \'kal-sə-ˌkōl\ *noun* [French, calcicolous, from *calc-* + *-cole* -colous] (1882)
: a plant normally growing on calcareous soils
— **cal·cic·o·lous** \kal-'si-kə-ləs\ *adjective*
**cal·cif·er·ol** \kal-'si-fə-ˌról, -ˌrōl\ *noun* [*calciferous* + *ergosterol*] (1931)
: an alcohol $C_{28}H_{43}OH$ usually prepared by irradiation of ergosterol and used as a dietary supplement in nutrition and medicinally in the control of rickets and related disorders — called also *vitamin* $D_2$
**cal·cif·er·ous** \kal-'si-f(ə-)rəs\ *adjective* (1799)
: producing or containing calcium carbonate
**cal·cif·ic** \kal-'si-fik\ *adjective* [*calcify*] (1861)
: involving or caused by calcification ⟨*calcific* lesions⟩
**cal·ci·fuge** \'kal-sə-ˌfyüj\ *noun* [French, calcifugous, from *calc-* + Latin *fugere* to flee — more at FUGITIVE] (1926)
: a plant not normally growing on calcareous soils
— **calcifuge** *also* **cal·cif·u·gous** \kal-'si-fyə-gəs\ *adjective*
**cal·ci·fy** \'kal-sə-ˌfī\ *verb* **-fied; -fy·ing** (1854)
*transitive verb*
**1 :** to make calcareous by deposit of calcium salts
**2 :** to make inflexible or unchangeable
*intransitive verb*
**1 :** to become calcareous
**2 :** to become inflexible and changeless : HARDEN
— **cal·ci·fi·ca·tion** \ˌkal-sə-fə-'kā-shən\ *noun*
**cal·ci·mine** \'kal-sə-ˌmīn\ *noun* [alteration of *kalsomine*, of unknown origin] (circa 1859)
: a white or tinted wash of glue, whiting or zinc white, and water that is used especially on plastered surfaces
— **calcimine** *transitive verb*

**cal·ci·na·tion** \,kal-sə-'nā-shən\ noun (14th century)
: the act or process of calcining : the state of being calcined

**¹cal·cine** \kal-'sīn, 'kal-,\ verb **cal·cined; cal·cin·ing** [Middle English calcenen, from Medieval Latin calcinare, from Late Latin calcina lime, from Latin calc-, calx] (14th century)
transitive verb
: to heat (as inorganic materials) to a high temperature but without fusing in order to drive off volatile matter or to effect changes (as oxidation or pulverization)
intransitive verb
: to undergo calcination

**²cal·cine** \'kal-,sīn\ noun (circa 1909)
: a product (as a metal oxide) of calcination or roasting

**cal·ci·no·sis** \,kal-sə-'nō-səs\ noun, plural **-no·ses** \-,sēz\ [New Latin, irregular (influenced by International Scientific Vocabulary calcine) from calc- + -osis] (circa 1929)
: the abnormal deposition of calcium salts in a part or tissue of the body

**cal·cite** \'kal-,sīt\ noun (1849)
: a mineral $CaCO_3$ consisting of calcium carbonate crystallized in hexagonal form and including common limestone, chalk, and marble — compare ARAGONITE
— **cal·cit·ic** \kal-'si-tik\ adjective

**cal·ci·to·nin** \,kal-sə-'tō-nən\ noun [calci- + -tonin (as in serotonin)] (1961)
: a polypeptide hormone especially from the thyroid gland that tends to lower the level of calcium in the blood plasma — called also thyrocalcitonin

**cal·ci·um** \'kal-sē-əm\ noun, often attributive [New Latin, from Latin calc-, calx lime] (1808)
: a silver-white bivalent metallic element of the alkaline-earth group occurring only in combination — see ELEMENT table

**calcium carbide** noun (circa 1888)
: a usually dark gray crystalline compound $CaC_2$ used especially for the generation of acetylene and for making calcium cyanamide

**calcium carbonate** noun (1873)
: a compound $CaCO_3$ found in nature as calcite and aragonite and in plant ashes, bones, and shells and used in making lime and portland cement and as a gastric antacid

**calcium channel blocker** noun (1982)
: any of a class of drugs that prevent or slow the influx of calcium ions into smooth muscle cells and are used to treat some forms of angina pectoris and some cardiac arrhythmias

**calcium chloride** noun (circa 1885)
: a white deliquescent salt $CaCl_2$ used in its anhydrous state as a drying and dehumidifying agent and in a hydrated state for controlling dust and ice on roads

**calcium cyanamide** noun (circa 1893)
: a compound $CaCN_2$ used as a fertilizer and a weed killer and as a source of other nitrogen compounds

**calcium gluconate** noun (1884)
: a white powdery salt $CaC_{12}H_{22}O_{14}$ used especially to supplement bodily calcium stores

**calcium hydroxide** noun (circa 1889)
: a white crystalline strong alkali $Ca(OH)_2$ that is used especially to make mortar and plaster and to soften water

**calcium hypochlorite** noun (circa 1889)
: a white powder $CaCl_2O_2$ used especially as a bleaching agent and disinfectant

**calcium oxalate** noun (1919)
: a crystalline salt $CaC_2O_4$ normally deposited in many plant cells and in animals sometimes excreted in urine or retained in the form of urinary calculi

**calcium oxide** noun (circa 1885)
: a caustic solid $CaO$ that is white when pure and that is the chief constituent of lime

**calcium phosphate** noun (1869)
: any of various phosphates of calcium: as **a** : the phosphate $CaH_4P_2O_8$ used as a fertilizer and in baking powder **b** : the phosphate $CaHPO_4$ used in pharmaceutical preparations and animal feeds **c** : the phosphate $Ca_3P_2O_8$ used as a fertilizer **d** : the naturally occurring phosphate $Ca_5(F,Cl,OH,\frac{1}{2}CO_3)(PO_4)_3$ that contains other elements or radicals and is the chief constituent of phosphate rock, bones, and teeth

**calcium silicate** noun (circa 1888)
: any of several silicates of calicum used especially in construction materials (as portland cement)

**calcium sulfate** noun (circa 1885)
: a white salt $CaSO_4$ that occurs especially as anhydrite, gypsum, and plaster of paris and that in hydrated form is used as a building material and in anhydrous form is used as a drying agent

**cal·cu·la·ble** \'kal-kyə-lə-bəl\ adjective (circa 1734)
**1** : subject to or ascertainable by calculation
**2** : that may be counted on : DEPENDABLE

**cal·cu·late** \'kal-kyə-,lāt\ verb **-lat·ed; -lat·ing** [Latin calculatus, past participle of calculare, from calculus pebble (used in reckoning), perhaps irregular diminutive of calc-, calx lime — more at CHALK] (1570)
transitive verb
**1 a** : to determine by mathematical processes **b** : to reckon by exercise of practical judgment : ESTIMATE **c** : to solve or probe the meaning of : FIGURE OUT ⟨trying to calculate his expression —Hugh MacLennan⟩
**2** : to design or adapt for a purpose
**3 a** : to judge to be true or probable **b** : INTEND ⟨I calculate to do it or perish in the attempt —Mark Twain⟩
intransitive verb
**1 a** : to make a calculation **b** : to forecast consequences
**2** : COUNT, RELY

**cal·cu·lat·ed** \-,lā-təd\ adjective (1722)
**1** : APT, LIKELY
**2 a** : worked out by mathematical calculation **b** : engaged in, undertaken, or displayed after reckoning or estimating the statistical probability of success or failure ⟨a calculated risk⟩
**3 a** : planned or contrived to accomplish a purpose **b** : DELIBERATE, INTENDED
— **cal·cu·lat·ed·ly** adverb
— **cal·cu·lat·ed·ness** noun

**cal·cu·lat·ing** \-,lā-tiŋ\ adjective (1710)
**1** : making calculations ⟨calculating machine⟩
**2** : marked by prudent analysis or by shrewd consideration of self-interest : SCHEMING
— **cal·cu·lat·ing·ly** \-tiŋ-lē\ adverb

**cal·cu·la·tion** \,kal-kyə-'lā-shən\ noun (14th century)
**1 a** : the process or an act of calculating **b** : the result of an act of calculating
**2 a** : studied care in analyzing or planning **b** : cold heartless planning to promote self-interest
— **cal·cu·la·tion·al** \-'lāsh-nəl, -'lā-shə-nᵊl\ adjective

**cal·cu·la·tor** \'kal-kyə-,lā-tər\ noun (14th century)
: one that calculates: as **a** : a usually electronic device for performing mathematical calculations **b** : a person who operates a calculator

**cal·cu·lous** \'kal-kyə-ləs\ adjective (1605)
: caused or characterized by a calculus or calculi

**cal·cu·lus** \-ləs\ noun, plural **-li** \-,lī, -,lē\ also **-lus·es** [Latin, stone (used in reckoning)] (1666)
**1 a** : a method of computation or calculation in a special notation (as of logic or symbolic logic) **b** : the mathematical methods comprising differential and integral calculus
**2** : CALCULATION
**3 a** : a concretion usually of mineral salts around organic material found especially in hollow organs or ducts **b** : TARTAR 2

**4** : a system or arrangement of intricate or interrelated parts ◆

**calculus of variations** (1837)
: a branch of mathematics concerned with applying the methods of calculus to finding the maxima and minima of a function which depends for its values on another function or a curve

**cal·de·ra** \kal-'der-ə, kȯl-, -'dir-\ noun [Spanish, literally, caldron, from Late Latin caldaria — more at CAULDRON] (1691)
: a volcanic crater that has a diameter many times that of the vent and is formed by collapse of the central part of a volcano or by explosions of extraordinary violence

**cal·dron** variant of CAULDRON

**ca·lèche** or **ca·leche** \kə-'lesh, -'lash\ noun [French calèche — more at CALASH] (1666)
**1 a** : CALASH 1a **b** : a 2-wheeled horse-drawn vehicle with a driver's seat on the splashboard used in Quebec
**2** : CALASH 2

**cal·e·fac·to·ry** \,ka-lə-'fak-t(ə-)rē\ noun, plural **-ries** [Medieval Latin calefactorium, from Latin calefacere to warm — more at CHAFE] (circa 1681)
: a monastery room warmed and used as a sitting room

**¹cal·en·dar** \'ka-lən-dər\ noun [Middle English calender, from Anglo-French and Medieval Latin; Anglo-French calender, from Medieval Latin kalendarium, from Latin, moneylender's account book, from kalendae calends] (13th century)
**1** : a system for fixing the beginning, length, and divisions of the civil year and arranging days and longer divisions of time (as weeks and months) in a definite order — see MONTH table
**2** : a tabular register of days according to a system usually covering one year and referring the days of each month to the days of the week
**3** : an orderly list: as **a** : a list of cases to be tried in court **b** : a list of bills or other items reported out of committee for consideration by a legislative assembly **c** : a list or schedule of planned events or activities giving dates and details
**4** British : a university catalog

**²calendar** transitive verb **-dared; -dar·ing** \-d(ə-)riŋ\ (15th century)
: to enter in a calendar

**calendar year** noun (circa 1909)
**1** : a period of a year beginning and ending with the dates that are conventionally accepted as marking the beginning and end of a numbered year
**2** : a period of time equal in length to that of the year in the calendar conventionally in use

**¹cal·en·der** \'ka-lən-dər\ transitive verb **-dered; -der·ing** \-d(ə-)riŋ\ [Middle French calandrer, from calandre machine for calendering, from (assumed) Vulgar Latin colendra

◇ **WORD HISTORY**
**calculus** In Latin calculus meant "pebble." Because the Romans used pebbles to do addition and subtraction on a counting board, the word became associated with computation, and the phrase ponere calculos, literally, "to place pebbles" meant figuratively "to perform a computation." Latin and Late Latin derivatives from calculus include calculator "person versed in arithmetic" and calculare "to reckon" (hence English calculate). Calculus itself has been borrowed into English as a medical term to refer to concretions of matter in the body such as kidney and bladder stones—a sense first found in Medieval Latin and a straightforward extension of the meaning "pebble"—and to refer to systems of mathematical computations such as differential and integral calculus.

cylinder, modification of Greek *kylindros* — more at CYLINDER] (1513)
**:** to press (as cloth, rubber, or paper) between rollers or plates in order to smooth and glaze or to thin into sheets
— **cal·en·der·er** \-dər-ər\ *noun*
²**calender** *noun* (1688)
**:** a machine for calendering something
³**calender** *noun* [Persian *qalandar*, from Arabic, from Persian *kalandar* uncouth man] (1621)
**:** a member of a Sufic order of wandering mendicant dervishes
**ca·len·dri·cal** \kə-'len-dri-kəl, ka-\ *also* **ca·len·dric** \-drik\ *adjective* (circa 1843)
**:** of, relating to, characteristic of, or used in a calendar
**cal·ends** \'ka-lən(d)z, 'kā-\ *noun plural but singular or plural in construction* [Middle English *kalendes*, from Latin *kalendae, calendae*] (14th century)
**:** the first day of the ancient Roman month from which days were counted backward to the ides
**ca·len·du·la** \kə-'len-jə-lə, -dyů-lə\ *noun* [New Latin, genus name, from Medieval Latin, from Latin *calendae* calends] (1789)
**:** any of a small genus (*Calendula*) of yellow-rayed composite herbs of temperate regions
**cal·en·ture** \'ka-lən-chůr\ *noun* [Spanish *calentura*, from *calentar* to heat, from Latin *calent-, calens*, present participle of *calēre* to be warm — more at LEE] (1593)
**:** a fever formerly supposed to affect sailors in the tropics
¹**calf** \'kaf, 'kȧf, *dialect also* 'kȧf\ *noun, plural* **calves** \'kavz, 'kȧvz, 'kȧvz\ *also* **calfs** *often attributive* [Middle English, from Old English *cealf*; akin to Old High German *kalb* calf] (before 12th century)
**1 a :** the young of the domestic cow; *also* **:** that of a closely related mammal (as a bison) **b :** the young of various large animals (as the elephant or whale)
**2** *plural* **calfs :** the hide of the domestic calf; *especially* **:** CALFSKIN
**3 :** an awkward or silly youth
— **calf·like** \'kaf-,līk, 'kȧf-, *dialect also* 'kȧf-\ *adjective*
— **in calf :** PREGNANT — used of a cow
²**calf** *noun, plural* **calves** \'kavz, 'kȧvz\ [Middle English, from Old Norse *kȧlfi*] (14th century)
**:** the fleshy back part of the leg below the knee
**calf–love** \-,ləv\ *noun* (1823)
**:** PUPPY LOVE
**calf's–foot jelly** \'kavz-,fůt-, 'kafs-, 'kȧvz-, 'kȧfs- *also* 'kȧvz-\ *noun* (1775)
**:** jelly made from gelatin obtained by boiling calves' feet
**calf·skin** \'kaf-,skin, 'kȧf- *also* 'kȧf-\ *noun* (15th century)
**:** leather made of the skin of a calf
**Cal·gon** \'kal-,gän\ *trademark*
— used for a water softener
**Cal·i·ban** \'ka-lə-,ban\ *noun*
**:** a savage and deformed slave in Shakespeare's *The Tempest*
**cal·i·ber** *or* **cal·i·bre** \'ka-lə-bər, *British also* kə-'lē-\ *noun* [Middle French *calibre*, from Old Italian *calibro*, from Arabic *qālib* shoemaker's last] (1567)
**1 a :** degree of mental capacity or moral quality **b :** degree of excellence or importance
**2 a :** the diameter of a bullet or other projectile **b :** the diameter of a bore of a gun usually expressed in hundredths or thousandths of an inch and typically written as a decimal fraction ⟨.32 *caliber*⟩
**3 :** the diameter of a round body; *especially* **:** the internal diameter of a hollow cylinder
**cal·i·brate** \'ka-lə-,brāt\ *transitive verb* **-brat·ed; -brat·ing** (circa 1864)
**1 :** to ascertain the caliber of (as a thermometer tube)

**2 :** to determine, rectify, or mark the graduations of (as a thermometer tube)
**3 :** to standardize (as a measuring instrument) by determining the deviation from a standard so as to ascertain the proper correction factors
**4 :** to adjust precisely for a particular function
— **cal·i·bra·tor** \-,brā-tər\ *noun*
**cal·i·bra·tion** \,ka-lə-'brā-shən\ *noun* (circa 1859)
**1 :** the act or process of calibrating **:** the state of being calibrated
**2 :** a set of graduations to indicate values or positions — usually used in plural ⟨*calibrations* on a gauge⟩
**ca·li·che** \kə-'lē-chē\ *noun* [American Spanish, from Spanish, flake of lime, from *cal* lime, from Latin *calx* — more at CHALK] (circa 1858)
**1 :** the nitrate-bearing gravel or rock of the sodium nitrate deposits of Chile and Peru
**2 :** a crust of calcium carbonate that forms on the stony soil of arid regions
**cal·i·co** \'ka-li-,kō\ *noun, plural* **-coes** *or* **-cos** [*Calicut,* India] (1578)
**1 a :** cotton cloth imported from India **b** *British* **:** a plain white cotton fabric that is heavier than muslin **c :** any of various cheap cotton fabrics with figured patterns
**2 :** a blotched or spotted animal; *especially* **:** one that is predominantly white with red and black patches
— **calico** *adjective*
**calico bass** *noun* (circa 1882)
**:** BLACK CRAPPIE
**calico bush** *noun* (1814)
**:** MOUNTAIN LAUREL
**Cal·i·for·nia condor** \,ka-lə-'fȯr-nyə-\ *noun* [*California,* state of U.S.] (circa 1889)
**:** a large nearly extinct vulture (*Gymnogyps californianus*) found most recently in the mountains of southern California that is related to the condor of South America
**California laurel** *noun* (1871)
**:** an evergreen Pacific coast tree (*Umbellularia californica*) of the laurel family with small umbellate flowers
**California pop·py** *noun* (1891)
**:** any of a genus (*Eschscholzia*) of herbs of the poppy family; *especially* **:** one (*E. californica*) widely cultivated for its usually yellow or orange flowers
**Cal·i·for·nio** \,ka-lə-'fȯr-nē-,ō\ *noun, plural* **-nios** [Spanish, from *California*] (1923)
**:** one of the original Spanish colonists of California or their descendants
**cal·i·for·ni·um** \,ka-lə-'fȯr-nē-əm\ *noun* [New Latin, from *California,* U.S.] (1950)
**:** a radioactive element discovered by bombarding curium 242 with alpha particles — see ELEMENT table
**ca·lig·i·nous** \kə-'li-jə-nəs\ *adjective* [Middle French or Latin; Middle French *caligineux*, from Latin *caliginosus*, from *caligin-, caligo* darkness] (1548)
**:** MISTY, DARK
¹**cal·i·per** \'ka-lə-pər\ *noun* [alteration of *caliber*] (1588)
**1 a :** any of various measuring instruments having two usually adjustable arms, legs, or jaws used especially to measure diameter or thickness — usually used in plural ⟨a pair of *calipers*⟩ **b :** a device consisting of two plates lined with a frictional material that press

against the sides of a rotating wheel or disc in certain brake systems
**2 :** thickness especially of paper, paperboard, or a tree
²**caliper** *transitive verb* **-pered; -per·ing** \-p(ə-)riŋ\ (1876)
**:** to measure by or as if by calipers
**ca·liph** *or* **ca·lif** \'kā-ləf, 'ka-\ *noun* [Middle English *caliphe*, from Middle French *calife*, from Arabic *khalīfah* successor] (14th century)
**:** a successor of Muhammad as temporal and spiritual head of Islam — used as a title
— **ca·liph·al** \-lə-fəl\ *adjective*
**ca·liph·ate** \-lə-,fāt, -fət\ *noun* (1614)
**:** the office or dominion of a caliph
**cal·is·then·ic** \,ka-ləs-'the-nik\ *adjective* (1827)
**:** of or relating to calisthenics
**cal·is·then·ics** \-niks\ *noun plural but singular or plural in construction* [Greek *kalos* beautiful + *sthenos* strength] (1827)
**1 :** systematic rhythmic bodily exercises performed usually without apparatus
**2** *usually singular in construction* **:** the art or practice of calisthenics
**ca·lix** \'kā-liks, 'ka-\ *noun, plural* **ca·li·ces** \'kā-lə-,sēz, 'ka-\ [Latin *calic-, calix* — more at CHALICE] (1698)
**:** CUP
¹**calk** \'kȯk\, **calk·er** \'kȯ-kər\ *variant of* CAULK, CAULKER
²**calk** \'kȯk\ *noun* [probably alteration of *calkin,* from Middle English *kakun,* from Middle Dutch or Old North French; Middle Dutch *calcoen* horse's hoof, from Old North French *calcain* heel, from Latin *calcaneum,* from *calc-, calx* heel] (1587)
**:** a tapered piece projecting downward on the shoe of a horse to prevent slipping; *also* **:** a similar device worn on the sole of a shoe
³**calk** *transitive verb* (1624)
**1 :** to furnish with calks
**2 :** to wound with a calk
¹**call** \'kȯl\ *verb* [Middle English, from Old Norse *kalla;* akin to Old English *hildecalla* battle herald, Old High German *kallōn* to talk loudly, Old Church Slavonic *glasŭ* voice] (before 12th century)
*intransitive verb*
**1 a :** to speak in a loud distinct voice so as to be heard at a distance **:** SHOUT ⟨*call* for help⟩ **b :** to make a request or demand ⟨*call* for an investigation⟩ **c** *of an animal* **:** to utter a characteristic note or cry **d :** to get or try to get into communication by telephone — often used with *up* **e :** to make a demand in card games (as for a particular card or for a show of hands) **f :** to give the calls for a square dance
**2 :** to make a brief visit ⟨*called* to pay his respects⟩ ⟨*called* on a friend⟩
*transitive verb*
**1 a** (1) **:** to utter in a loud distinct voice — often used with *out* ⟨*call* out a number⟩ (2) **:** to announce or read loudly or authoritatively ⟨*call* the roll⟩ ⟨*call* off a row of figures⟩ **b** (1) **:** to command or request to come or be present ⟨*called* to testify⟩ (2) **:** to cause to come **:** BRING ⟨*calls* to mind an old saying⟩ **c :** to summon to a particular activity, employment, or office ⟨was *called* to active duty⟩ **d :** to invite or command to meet **:** CONVOKE ⟨*call* a meeting⟩ **e :** to rouse from sleep or summon to get up **f** (1) **:** to give the order for **:** bring into action ⟨*call* a strike against the company⟩ ⟨*call* a pitchout⟩ (2) **:** to manage by giving the signals or orders ⟨that catcher *calls* a good game⟩

California condor

\ə\ abut \ᵊ\ kitten \ər\ further \a\ ash \ā\ ace
\ä\ mop, mar \au̇\ out \ch\ chin \e\ bet \ē\ easy
\g\ go \i\ hit \ī\ ice \j\ job \ŋ\ sing \ō\ go
\ȯ\ law \ȯi\ boy \th\ thin \ṯh\ the \ü\ loot \u̇\ foot
\y\ yet \zh\ vision *see also* Guide to Pronunciation

**g** (1) **:** to make a demand in bridge for (a card or suit) (2) **:** to require (a player) to show the hand in poker by making an equal bet (3) **:** to challenge to make good on a statement (4) **:** to charge with or censure for an offense ⟨deserves to be *called* on that⟩ **h :** to attract (as game) by imitating the characteristic cry **i :** to halt (as a baseball game) because of unsuitable conditions **j :** to rule on the status of (as a pitched ball or a player's action) ⟨*call* balls and strikes⟩ ⟨*call* a base runner safe⟩ **k :** to give the calls for (a square dance) — often used with *off* **l** (1) **:** to demand payment of especially by formal notice ⟨*call* a loan⟩ (2) **:** to demand presentation of (as a bond or option) for redemption **m** (1) **:** to get or try to get in communication with by telephone (2) **:** to generate signals for (a telephone number) in order to reach the party to whom the number is assigned ⟨*call* 911⟩ (3) **:** to make a signal to in order to transmit a message ⟨*call* the flagship⟩ **2 a :** to speak of or address by a specified name **:** give a name to ⟨*call* her Kitty⟩ **b** (1) **:** to regard or characterize as of a certain kind **:** CONSIDER ⟨can hardly be *called* generous⟩ (2) **:** to estimate or consider for purposes of an estimate or for convenience ⟨*call* it an even dollar⟩ **c** (1) **:** to describe correctly in advance of or without knowledge of the event **:** PREDICT (2) **:** to name or specify in advance ⟨*call* the toss of a coin⟩ **3 :** to temporarily transfer control of computer processing to (as a subroutine or procedure)
**synonym** see SUMMON
— **call a spade a spade :** to speak frankly
— **call for 1 :** to come (as at one's house) to get ⟨I'll *call for* you after dinner⟩ **2 :** to require as necessary or appropriate ⟨the job *calls for* typing skills⟩ ⟨the design *calls for* three windows⟩
— **call forth :** ELICIT, EVOKE ⟨these events *call forth* great emotions⟩
— **call in question** *or* **call into question :** to cast doubt upon
— **call it a day :** to stop for the remainder of the day or for the present whatever one has been doing
— **call it quits :** to call it a day **:** QUIT
— **call names :** to address or speak of a person or thing contemptuously or offensively
— **call on 1 :** to call upon **2 :** to elicit a response from (as a student) ⟨the teacher *called on* her first⟩
— **call one's bluff :** to challenge in order to expose an empty pretense or threat
— **call the shots :** to be in charge or control **:** determine the policy or procedure
— **call the tune :** to call the shots
— **call time :** to ask for or grant a time-out
— **call to account :** to hold responsible **:** REPRIMAND
— **call upon 1 :** REQUIRE, OBLIGE ⟨may be *called upon* to do several jobs⟩ **2 :** to make a demand on **:** depend on ⟨universities are *called upon* to produce trained professionals⟩
**²call** *noun* (14th century)
**1 a :** an act of calling with the voice **:** SHOUT **b :** an imitation of the cry of a bird or other animal made to attract it **c :** an instrument used for calling ⟨a duck *call*⟩ **d :** the cry of an animal (as a bird)
**2 a :** a request or command to come or assemble **b :** a summons or signal on a drum, bugle, or pipe **c :** admission to the bar as a barrister **d :** an invitation to become the minister of a church or to accept a professional appointment **e :** a divine vocation or strong inner prompting to a particular course of action **f :** a summoning of actors to rehearsal ⟨the *call* is for 11 o'clock⟩ **g :** the attraction or appeal of a particular activity, condition, or place ⟨the *call* of the wild⟩ **h :** an order specifying the number of men to be inducted into the armed services during a specified period **i :** the selection of a play in football

**3 a :** DEMAND, CLAIM **b :** NEED, JUSTIFICATION **c :** a demand for payment of money **d :** an option to buy a specified amount of a security (as stock) or commodity (as wheat) at a fixed price at or within a specified time — compare PUT 2 **e :** an instance of asking for something **:** REQUEST ⟨many *calls* for Christmas stories⟩
**4 :** ROLL CALL
**5 :** a short usually formal visit
**6 :** the name or thing called ⟨the *call* was heads⟩
**7 :** the act of calling in a card game
**8 :** the act of calling on the telephone
**9 :** a direction or a succession of directions for a square dance rhythmically called to the dancers
**10 :** a decision or ruling made by an official of a sports contest; *also* **:** DECISION 1 ⟨a tough *call* to make⟩
**11 :** a temporary transfer of control of computer processing to a particular set of instructions (as a subroutine or procedure)
— **at call** *or* **on call 1 a :** available for use **:** at the service of ⟨thousands of men *at* his *call*⟩ **b :** ready to respond to a summons or command ⟨a doctor *on call*⟩ **2 :** subject to demand for payment or return without previous notice ⟨money lent *at call*⟩
— **within call :** within hearing or reach of a summons **:** subject to summons
**call·a·ble** \'kȯ-lə-bəl\ *adjective* (1826)
**:** capable of being called; *specifically* **:** subject to a demand for presentation for payment ⟨*callable* bond⟩
**cal·la lily** \'ka-lə-\ *noun* [New Latin, genus name, modification of Greek *kallaia* rooster's wattles] (1870)
**:** any of several herbs (genus *Zantedeschia*) of the arum family; *especially* **:** a house or greenhouse plant (*Z. aethiopica*) with a white showy spathe and yellow spadix — called also *calla*
**cal·la·loo** \ˌka-lə-'lü, 'ka-lə-ˌ\ *noun* [American Spanish *calalú* plant of the genus *Xanthosoma* whose leaves are used as greens] (1892)
**:** a soup or stew made with greens, onions, and crabmeat
**cal·lant** \'ka-lənt, 'kä-\ *noun* [Dutch or Old North French; Dutch *kalant* customer, fellow, from Old North French *calland* customer, from Latin *calent-, calens*, present participle of *calēre* to be warm — more at LEE] (circa 1592)
*chiefly Scottish* **:** BOY, LAD
**call·back** \'kȯl-ˌbak\ *noun* (1926)
**1 :** a return call
**2 a :** RECALL 5 **b :** a recall of an employee to work after a layoff **c :** a second or additional audition for a theatrical part
**call–board** \-ˌbȯrd, -ˌbȯrd\ *noun* (1886)
**:** BULLETIN BOARD 1
**call box** *noun* (1885)
**1** *British* **:** a public telephone booth
**2 :** a telephone usually located on the side of a road for reporting emergencies (as fires or automobile breakdowns)
**call·boy** \'kȯl-ˌbȯi\ *noun* (1794)
**:** BELLHOP, PAGE
**call down** *transitive verb* (1810)
**1 :** to cause or entreat to descend ⟨*call down* a blessing⟩
**2 :** REPRIMAND ⟨*called* me *down* for being late⟩
**called strike** *noun* (1887)
**:** a pitched baseball not struck at by the batter that passes through the strike zone
**¹cal·ler** \'kä-lər\ *adjective* [Middle English *callour*] (14th century)
**1** *Scottish* **:** FRESH
**2** *Scottish* **:** COOL
**²call·er** \'kȯ-lər\ *noun* (15th century)
**:** one that calls
**cal·let** \'ka-lət\ *noun* [perhaps from Middle French *caillette* frivolous person, from *Caillette* (flourished 1500) French court fool] (15th century)
*chiefly Scottish* **:** PROSTITUTE

**call girl** *noun* (circa 1940)
**:** a prostitute with whom an appointment may be made by telephone
**call house** *noun* (1929)
**:** a house or apartment where call girls may be procured
**cal·lig·ra·pher** \kə-'li-grə-fər\ *noun* (1753)
**1 :** a professional copyist or engrosser
**2 :** one who writes a beautiful hand
**3 :** PENMAN ⟨a fair *calligrapher*⟩
**cal·lig·ra·phist** \-fist\ *noun* (1816)
**:** CALLIGRAPHER
**cal·lig·ra·phy** \-fē\ *noun* [French or Greek; French *calligraphie*, from Greek *kalligraphia*, from *kalli-* beautiful (from *kallos* beauty) + *-graphia* -graphy] (1604)
**1 a :** artistic, stylized, or elegant handwriting or lettering **b :** the art of producing such writing
**2 :** PENMANSHIP
**3 :** an ornamental line in drawing or painting
— **cal·li·graph·ic** \ˌka-lə-'gra-fik\ *adjective*
— **cal·li·graph·i·cal·ly** \-fi-k(ə-)lē\ *adverb*
**call–in** \'kȯl-ˌin\ *adjective* (1967)
**:** allowing listeners to engage in broadcast telephone conversations with the host or a guest ⟨a *call-in* show⟩
**call in** (1597)
*transitive verb*
**1 :** to order to return or to be returned: as **a :** to withdraw from an advanced position ⟨*call in* the outposts⟩ **b :** to withdraw from circulation ⟨*call in* bank notes and issue new ones⟩
**2 :** to summon to one's aid or for consultation ⟨*call in* a mediator⟩
**3 :** to deliver (a message) by telephone ⟨*call in* an order for pizza⟩
*intransitive verb*
**:** to communicate with a person by telephone
— **call in sick :** to report by telephone that one will be absent because of illness
**call·ing** \'kȯ-liŋ\ *noun* (14th century)
**1 :** a strong inner impulse toward a particular course of action especially when accompanied by conviction of divine influence
**2 :** the vocation or profession in which one customarily engages
**3 :** the characteristic cry of a female cat in heat; *also* **:** the period of heat
**synonym** see WORK
**calling card** *noun* (1896)
**1 :** VISITING CARD
**2 :** a sign or evidence that someone or something is or has been present; *broadly* **:** an identifying mark
**cal·li·ope** \kə-'lī-ə-(ˌ)pē, in sense 2 also 'ka-lē-ˌōp\ *noun* [Latin, from Greek *Kalliopē*]
**1** *capitalized* **:** the Greek Muse of heroic poetry
**2 :** a keyboard musical instrument resembling an organ and consisting of a series of whistles sounded by steam or compressed air
**cal·li·per** *chiefly British variant of* CALIPER
**cal·li·pyg·ian** \ˌka-lə-'pi-j(ē-)ən\ *or* **cal·li·py·gous** \-'pī-gəs\ *adjective* [Greek *kallipygos*, from *kalli-* + *pygē* buttocks] (circa 1800)
**:** having shapely buttocks
**Cal·lis·to** \kə-'lis-(ˌ)tō\ *noun* [Latin, from Greek *Kallistō*]
**:** a nymph loved by Zeus, changed into a she-bear by Hera, and subsequently changed into the Great Bear constellation
**cal·li·thump** \'ka-li-ˌthəmp\ *noun* [back-formation from *callithumpian*, adjective, alteration of English dialect *gallithumpian* disturber of order at elections in 18th century] (1856)
**:** a noisy boisterous band or parade
— **cal·li·thump·ian** \ˌka-lə-'thəm-pē-ən\ *adjective*
**call letters** *noun plural* (1913)
**:** CALL SIGN
**call loan** *noun* (1852)
**:** a loan payable at the discretion of the borrower or on demand of the lender
**call number** *noun* (1876)

: a combination of characters assigned to a library book to indicate its place on a shelf

**call off** *transitive verb* (1633)
**1** : to draw away : DIVERT ⟨her attention was *called off* by a new arrival⟩
**2** : CANCEL ⟨*call* the trip *off*⟩

**call of nature** (1763)
: the need to urinate or defecate

**cal·los·i·ty** \ka-'lä-sə-tē, kə-\ *noun, plural* **-ties** (1578)
**1** : the quality or state of being callous: as **a** : marked or abnormal hardness and thickness **b** : lack of feeling or capacity for emotion
**2** : CALLUS 1

**¹cal·lous** \'ka-ləs\ *adjective* [Middle French *calleux*, from Latin *callosus*, from *callum, callus* callous skin] (15th century)
**1 a** : being hardened and thickened **b** : having calluses
**2 a** : feeling no emotion **b** : feeling no sympathy for others
— **cal·lous·ly** *adverb*
— **cal·lous·ness** *noun*

**²callous** *transitive verb* (1834)
: to make callous

**call out** *transitive verb* (15th century)
**1** : to summon into action ⟨*call out* troops⟩
**2** : to challenge to a duel
**3** : to order on strike ⟨*call out* the workers⟩

**cal·low** \'ka-(,)lō\ *adjective* [Middle English *calu* bald, from Old English; akin to Old High German *kalo* bald, Old Church Slavonic *golŭ* bare] (1580)
: lacking adult sophistication : IMMATURE ⟨*callow* youth⟩
— **cal·low·ness** \'ka-lō-nəs, -lə-nəs\ *noun*

**call sign** *noun* (1919)
: the combination of identifying letters or letters and numbers assigned to an operator, office, activity, or station for use in communication (as in the address of a message sent by radio)

**call slip** *noun* (1881)
: a form filled out by a library patron for a desired book

**call to quarters** (circa 1918)
: a bugle call usually shortly before taps that summons soldiers to their quarters

**call–up** \'kȯ-,ləp\ *noun* (1940)
: an order to report for military service

**call up** *transitive verb* (1632)
**1** : to bring to mind : EVOKE
**2** : to summon before an authority
**3** : to summon together (as for a united effort) ⟨*call up* all his forces for the attack⟩
**4** : to summon for active military duty
**5** : to bring forward for consideration or action
**6** : to retrieve from the memory of a computer especially for display and user interaction

**¹cal·lus** \'ka-ləs\ *noun* [Latin] (1563)
**1** : a thickening of or a hard thickened area on skin or bark
**2** : a mass of exudate and connective tissue that forms around a break in a bone and is converted into bone in healing
**3** : soft tissue that forms over a wounded or cut plant surface

**²callus** (1864)
*intransitive verb*
: to form callus
*transitive verb*
: to cause callus to form on

**call–waiting** *noun* (1986)
: a telephone service that signals (as by a click) to the user when an incoming call is received during a call in progress

**¹calm** \'käm, 'kälm, 'kam, 'kȯ(l)m, *New England also* 'käm\ *noun* [Middle English *calme*, from Middle French, from Old Italian *calma*, from Late Latin *cauma* heat, from Greek *kauma*, from *kaiein* to burn] (14th century)
**1 a** : a period or condition of freedom from storms, high winds, or rough activity of water

**b** : complete absence of wind or presence of wind having a speed no greater than one mile (1.6 kilometers) per hour — see BEAUFORT SCALE table
**2** : a state of tranquillity

**²calm** (14th century)
*intransitive verb*
: to become calm — usually used with *down*
*transitive verb*
: to make calm — often used with *down*

**³calm** *adjective* (14th century)
**1** : marked by calm : STILL ⟨a *calm* sea⟩
**2** : free from agitation, excitement, or disturbance ⟨a *calm* manner⟩ ☆
— **calm·ly** *adverb*
— **calm·ness** *noun*

**calm·ative** \'kä-mə-tiv, 'käl-, *also* 'kä-, 'kȯ(l)-, 'ka-\ *noun or adjective* [²calm + -ative (as in *sedative*)] (1870)
: SEDATIVE

**cal·mod·u·lin** \(,)kal-'mä-jə-lin, -dyü-lin\ *noun* [calcium + modulate + ¹-in] (1979)
: a calcium-binding protein that regulates cellular metabolic processes (as the contraction of muscle fibers) by modifying the activity of calcium-sensitive enzymes

**ca·ló** \kə-'lō\ *noun* [Spanish, argot, speech of Spanish Gypsies, from Romany *kalo* Gypsy, literally, black, from Sanskrit *kāla*] (circa 1948)
: any of several Spanish argots; *especially* : an argot used by Chicano youths in cities of the U.S. Southwest

**cal·o·mel** \'ka-lə-məl, -,mel\ *noun* [probably from (assumed) New Latin *calomelas*, from Greek *kalos* beautiful + *melas* black — more at MELAN-] (1676)
: a white tasteless compound $Hg_2Cl_2$ used especially as a fungicide and insecticide and occasionally in medicine as a purgative — called also *mercurous chloride*

**¹ca·lo·ric** \kə-'lȯr-ik, -'lōr-\ *noun* [French *calorique*, from Latin *calor*] (1792)
**1** : a supposed form of matter formerly held responsible for the phenomena of heat and combustion
**2** *archaic* : HEAT

**²caloric** *adjective* (circa 1828)
**1** : of or relating to heat
**2** : of or relating to calories
— **ca·lo·ri·cal·ly** \kə-'lȯr-i-k(ə-)lē, -'lōr-\ *adverb*

**cal·o·rie** *also* **cal·o·ry** \'ka-lə-rē, 'kal-rē\ *noun, plural* **-ries** [French *calorie*, from Latin *calor* heat, from *calēre* to be warm — more at LEE] (1866)
**1 a** : the amount of heat required at a pressure of one atmosphere to raise the temperature of one gram of water one degree Celsius that is equal to about 4.19 joules — called also *gram calorie, small calorie*; abbreviation *cal* **b** : the amount of heat required to raise the temperature of one kilogram of water one degree Celsius : 1000 gram calories or 3.968 Btu — called also *large calorie*; abbreviation *Cal*
**2 a** : a unit equivalent to the large calorie expressing heat-producing or energy-producing value in food when oxidized in the body **b** : an amount of food having an energy-producing value of one large calorie

**cal·o·rif·ic** \,ka-lə-'ri-fik\ *adjective* [French or Latin; French *calorifique*, from Latin *calorificus*, from *calor*] (1812)
**1** : CALORIC
**2** : of or relating to heat production

**cal·o·rim·e·ter** \,ka-lə-'ri-mə-tər\ *noun* [International Scientific Vocabulary, from Latin *calor*] (1794)
: any of several apparatuses for measuring quantities of absorbed or evolved heat or for determining specific heats
— **ca·lo·ri·met·ric** \,ka-lə-rə-'me-trik; kə-,lȯr-ə-, -,lōr-\ *adjective*
— **ca·lo·ri·met·ri·cal·ly** \-tri-k(ə-)lē\ *adverb*
— **cal·o·rim·e·try** \,ka-lə-'ri-mə-trē\ *noun*

**ca·lotte** \kə-'lät\ *noun* [French] (1632)
: SKULLCAP 1; *especially* : ZUCCHETTO

**cal·o·type** \'ka-lə-,tīp\ *noun* [Greek *kalos* beautiful + -type (as in *daguerreotype*)] (1845)
: a photographic process by which a large number of prints could be produced from a paper negative; *also* : a positive print so made

**cal·pac** *or* **cal·pack** \'kal-,pak, kal-'\ *noun* [Turkish *kalpak*] (1598)
: a high-crowned cap worn in Turkey, Iran, and neighboring countries

**calque** \'kalk\ *noun* [French, literally, copy, from *calquer* to trace, from Italian *calcare* to trample, trace, from Latin, to trample — more at CAULK] (1937)
: LOAN TRANSLATION

**cal·trop** \'kal-trəp, 'kȯl-\ *also* **cal·throp** \-thrəp\ *noun* [Middle English *caltrappe*, alteration of *calketrappe* star thistle, from Old English *calcatrippe*, from Medieval Latin *calcatrippa*] (15th century)
**1 a** *plural but singular or plural in construction* : STAR THISTLE 1 **b** : PUNCTURE VINE; *also* : any of various related herbs (genera *Tribulus* and *Kallstroemia*) of the same family (Zygophyllaceae, the caltrop family)
**2** : a device with four metal points so arranged that when any three are on the ground the fourth projects upward as a hazard to the hooves of horses or to pneumatic tires

**cal·u·met** \'kal-yə-,met, -mət\ *noun* [American French, from French dialect, pipe stem, from Late Latin *calamellus*, diminutive of Latin *calamus* reed — more at CALAMUS] (1673)
: a highly ornamented ceremonial pipe of the American Indians

**calumet**

**ca·lum·ni·ate** \kə-'ləm-nē-,āt\ *transitive verb* **-at·ed; -at·ing** (1554)
**1** : to utter maliciously false statements, charges, or imputations about
**2** : to injure the reputation of by calumny
*synonym* see MALIGN
— **ca·lum·ni·a·tion** \-,ləm-nē-'ā-shən\ *noun*
— **ca·lum·ni·a·tor** \-'ləm-nē-,ā-tər\ *noun*

**cal·um·ny** \'ka-ləm-nē *also* 'kal-yəm-\ *noun, plural* **-nies** [Middle French & Latin; Middle French *calomnie*, from Latin *calumnia*, from *calvi* to deceive; perhaps akin to Old English *hōlian* to slander, Greek *kēlein* to beguile] (15th century)

---

☆ **SYNONYMS**
**Calm, tranquil, serene, placid, peaceful** mean quiet and free from disturbance. CALM often implies a contrast with a foregoing or nearby state of agitation or violence ⟨the protests ended, and the streets were *calm* again⟩. TRANQUIL suggests a very deep quietude or composure ⟨the *tranquil* beauty of a formal garden⟩. SERENE stresses an unclouded and lofty tranquillity ⟨watched the sunset of a *serene* summer's evening⟩. PLACID suggests an undisturbed appearance and often implies a degree of complacency ⟨remained *placid* despite the criticism⟩. PEACEFUL implies a state of repose in contrast with or following strife or turmoil ⟨grown *peaceful* in old age⟩.

---

\ə\ abut \ᵊ\ kitten \ər\ further \a\ ash \ā\ ace
\ä\ mop, mar \au̇\ out \ch\ chin \e\ bet \ē\ easy
\g\ go \i\ hit \ī\ ice \j\ job \ŋ\ sing \ō\ go
\ȯ\ law \ȯi\ boy \th\ thin \t͟h\ the \ü\ loot \u̇\ foot
\y\ yet \zh\ vision *see also* Guide to Pronunciation

**1 :** a misrepresentation intended to blacken another's reputation
**2 :** the act of uttering false charges or misrepresentations maliciously calculated to damage another's reputation
— **ca·lum·ni·ous** \kə-'ləm-nē-əs\ *adjective*
— **ca·lum·ni·ous·ly** *adverb*
**cal·u·tron** \'kal-yə-ˌträn\ *noun* [*Cal*ifornia *U*niversity cyclo*tron*] (1945)
**:** an electromagnetic apparatus for separating isotopes according to their masses
**cal·va·dos** \ˌkal-və-'dōs, 'kál-\ *noun, often capitalized* [French, from *Calvados,* department in Normandy, France] (1906)
**:** an applejack made in Calvados
**cal·var·i·um** \kal-'var-ē-əm, -'ver-\ *noun, plural -ia* \-ē-ə\ [New Latin, from Latin *calvaria* skull, from *calvus* bald; probably akin to Sanskrit *kulva* bald] (14th century)
**:** the portion of a skull including the braincase and excluding the lower jaw or lower jaw and facial portion
**cal·va·ry** \'kal-v(ə-)rē\ *noun, plural -ries* [*Calvary,* the hill near Jerusalem where Jesus was crucified] (1738)
**1 :** an open-air representation of the crucifixion of Jesus
**2 :** an experience of usually intense mental suffering
**Calvary cross** *noun* (1826)
**:** a Latin cross usually mounted on three steps
— see CROSS illustration
**calve** \'kav, 'káv\ *verb* **calved; calv·ing** [Middle English, from Old English *cealfian,* from *cealf* calf] (before 12th century)
*intransitive verb*
**1 :** to give birth to a calf; *also* **:** to produce offspring
**2** *of an ice mass* **:** to separate or break so that a part becomes detached
*transitive verb*
**1 :** to produce by birth
**2** *of an ice mass* **:** to let become detached
**calves** *plural of* CALF
**Cal·vin cycle** \'kal-vən-\ *noun* [Melvin *Calvin*] (1957)
**:** the cycle of enzyme-catalyzed dark reactions of photosynthesis that occurs in the chloroplasts of plants and in many bacteria and that involves the fixation of carbon dioxide and the formation of a six-carbon sugar
**Cal·vin·ism** \'kal-və-ˌni-zəm\ *noun* [John *Calvin*] (circa 1570)
**:** the theological system of Calvin and his followers marked by strong emphasis on the sovereignty of God, the depravity of mankind, and the doctrine of predestination
— **Cal·vin·ist** \-və-nist\ *noun or adjective*
— **Cal·vin·is·tic** \ˌkal-və-'nis-tik\ *adjective*
— **Cal·vin·is·ti·cal·ly** \-ti-k(ə-)lē\ *adverb*
**calx** \'kalks\ *noun, plural* **calx·es** *or* **cal·ces** \'kal-ˌsēz\ [Middle English *cals,* from Latin *calx* lime — more at CHALK] (15th century)
**:** the crumbly residue left when a metal or mineral has been subjected to calcination or combustion
**¹ca·lyp·so** \kə-'lip-(ˌ)sō\ *noun* [Latin, from Greek *Kalypsō*]
**1** *capitalized* **:** a sea nymph in Homer's *Odyssey* who keeps Odysseus seven years on the island of Ogygia
**2** *plural* **calypsos** [New Latin, genus name, probably from Latin] **:** a bulbous bog orchid (*Calypso bulbosa*) of northern regions bearing a single white to purple flower
**²calypso** *noun, plural* **-sos** *or* **-soes** [origin unknown] (1934)
**:** a style of music originating in the West Indies, marked by lively duple meter, and having lyrics that are often improvised and usually satirize local personalities and events; *also* **:** a song in this style
— **ca·lyp·so·ni·an** \kə-ˌlip-'sō-nē-ən, ˌka-(ˌ)lip-\ *noun or adjective*

**ca·lyp·tra** \kə-'lip-trə\ *noun* [New Latin, from Greek *kalyptra* veil, from *kalyptein* to cover — more at HELL] (circa 1753)
**:** a hoodlike structure in a plant; *especially* **:** haploid tissue forming a membranous hood over the capsule in a moss
**ca·lyx** \'kā-liks *also* 'ka-\ *noun, plural* **ca·lyx·es** *or* **ca·ly·ces** \'kā-lə-ˌsēz *also* 'ka-\ [Latin *calyc-, calyx,* from Greek *kalyx* — more at CHALICE] (1693)
**1 :** the usually green outer whorl of a flower consisting of sepals
**2 :** a cuplike animal structure (as the body wall of a crinoid or a division of the kidney pelvis)
**cal·zo·ne** \kal-'zōn, -'zō-nē, -'zō-nā; käl-'zò-nā\ *noun, plural* **calzone** *or* **calzones** [Italian, from *calzone* (singular of *calzoni* pants), augmentative of *calza* stocking, from Medieval Latin *calcea,* from Latin *calceus* shoe, from *calc-, calx* heel] (circa 1950)
**:** a baked or fried turnover of pizza dough stuffed with various fillings usually including cheese
**cam** \'kam\ *noun* [perhaps from French *came,* from German *Kamm,* literally, comb, from Old High German *kamb*] (1777)
**:** a rotating or sliding piece in a mechanical linkage used especially in transforming rotary motion into linear motion or vice versa
**ca·ma·ra·de·rie** \ˌkäm-'rä-d(ə-)rē, ˌkam-, ˌkä-mə-, ˌka-, -'ra-\ *noun* [French, from *camarade* comrade] (1840)
**:** a spirit of friendly good-fellowship
**cam·a·ril·la** \ˌka-mə-'ri-lə, -'rē-ə\ *noun* [Spanish, literally, small room] (1839)
**:** a group of unofficial often secret and scheming advisers; *also* **:** CABAL
**cam·as** *also* **cam·ass** \'ka-məs\ *noun* [Chinook Jargon *kamass*] (1805)
**:** any of a genus (*Camassia* especially *C. quamash*) of plants of the lily family chiefly of the western U.S. with edible bulbs — compare DEATH CAMAS
**¹cam·ber** \'kam-bər\ *verb* **cam·bered; cam·ber·ing** \-b(ə-)riŋ\ [French *cambrer,* from Middle French *cambre* curved, from Latin *camur*] (1627)
*intransitive verb*
**:** to curve upward in the middle
*transitive verb*
**1 :** to arch slightly
**2 :** to impart camber to
**²camber** *noun* (1823)
**1 :** a slight convexity, arching, or curvature (as of a beam, deck, or road)
**2 :** the convexity of the curve of an airfoil from the leading edge to the trailing edge
**3 :** a setting of the wheels of an automotive vehicle closer together at the bottom than at the top
**cam·bi·um** \'kam-bē-əm\ *noun, plural* **-bi·ums** *or* **-bia** \-bē-ə\ [New Latin, from Medieval Latin, exchange, from Latin *cambire* to exchange — more at CHANGE] (1671)
**:** a thin formative layer between the xylem and phloem of most vascular plants that gives rise to new cells and is responsible for secondary growth
— **cam·bi·al** \-bē-əl\ *adjective*
**Cam·bo·di·an** \kam-'bō-dē-ən\ *noun* (1770)
**1 :** a native or inhabitant of Cambodia
**2 :** KHMER 2
— **Cambodian** *adjective*
**Cam·bri·an** \'kam-brē-ən, 'kām-\ *adjective* [Medieval Latin *Cambria* Wales, from Middle Welsh *Cymry* Wales, Welshmen] (circa 1656)
**1 :** WELSH
**2 :** of, relating to, or being the earliest geologic period of the Paleozoic era or the corresponding system of rocks marked by fossils of every great animal type except the vertebrates — see GEOLOGIC TIME table
— **Cambrian** *noun*

**cam·bric** \'kām-brik\ *noun* [obsolete Flemish *Kameryk* Cambrai, city of France] (1530)
**1 :** a fine thin white linen fabric
**2 :** a cotton fabric that resembles cambric
**cambric tea** *noun* (1888)
**:** a hot drink of water, milk, sugar, and often a small amount of tea
**cam·cord·er** \'kam-ˌkór-dər\ *noun* [*cam*era + re*corder*] (1982)
**:** a small portable combined video camera and videocassette recorder
**¹came** *past of* COME
**²came** \'kām\ *noun* [origin unknown] (1688)
**:** a slender grooved lead rod used to hold together panes of glass especially in a stained-glass window
**cam·el** \'ka-məl\ *noun* [Middle English, from Old English & Old North French, from Latin *camelus,* from Greek *kamēlos,* of Semitic origin; akin to Hebrew *gāmāl* camel] (before 12th century)

camel 1: *1* dromedary, *2* Bactrian camel

**1 :** either of two large ruminant mammals (genus *Camelus*) used as draft and saddle animals in desert regions especially of Africa and Asia: **a :** the one-humped camel (*C. dromedarius*) extant only as a domestic or feral animal — called also *dromedary* **b :** the two-humped camel (*C. bactrianus* synonym *C. ferus*) of Chinese Turkestan and Mongolia — called also *Bactrian camel*
**2 :** a watertight structure used especially to lift submerged ships
**3 :** a light yellowish brown
**cam·el·back** \'kam-əl-ˌbak\ *noun* (1860)
**:** the back of a camel
**cam·el·eer** \ˌka-mə-'lir\ *noun* (1808)
**:** a camel driver
**camel hair** *also* **camel's hair** *noun* (14th century)
**1 :** the hair of the camel or a substitute for it (as hair from squirrels' tails)
**2 :** cloth made of camel hair or a mixture of camel hair and wool usually light tan and of soft silky texture
**ca·mel·lia** \kə-'mēl-yə\ *noun* [New Latin *Camellia,* from *Camellus* (Georg Josef Kamel died 1706) Moravian Jesuit missionary)] (circa 1753)
**:** any of a genus (*Camellia*) of shrubs or trees of the tea family; *especially* **:** an ornamental greenhouse shrub (*C. japonica*) with glossy leaves and roselike flowers
**cam·el·o·pard** \kə-'me-lə-ˌpärd\ *noun* [Late Latin *camelopardus,* alteration of Latin *camelopardalis,* from Greek *kamēlopardalis,* from *kamēlos* + *pardalis* leopard] (14th century)
**1** *archaic* **:** GIRAFFE
**2** *capitalized* **:** CAMELOPARDALIS
**Ca·mel·o·par·da·lis** \kə-ˌme-lə-'pär-dəl-əs\ *noun* [Latin (genitive *Camelopardalis*), camelopard]
**:** a northern constellation between Cassiopeia and Ursa Major
**Cam·e·lot** \'ka-mə-ˌlät\ *noun*
**1 :** the site of King Arthur's palace and court
**2 :** a time, place, or atmosphere of idyllic happiness
**Cam·em·bert** \'ka-məm-ˌber\ *noun* [French, from *Camembert,* Normandy, France] (1878)
**:** a soft surface-ripened cheese with a thin grayish white rind and a yellow interior
**cam·eo** \'ka-mē-ˌō\ *noun, plural* **-eos** [Middle English *camew,* from Middle French *camau, kamaheu*] (15th century)
**1 a :** a gem carved in relief; *especially* **:** a small piece of sculpture on a stone or shell cut

in relief in one layer with another contrasting layer serving as background **b :** a small medallion with a profiled head in relief
**2 :** a carving or sculpture made in the manner of a cameo
**3 :** a usually brief literary or filmic piece that brings into delicate or sharp relief the character of a person, place, or event
**4 :** a small theatrical role usually performed by a well-known actor and often limited to a single scene; *broadly* **:** any brief appearance
— **cameo** *adjective*
— **cameo** *transitive verb*
**cam·era** \'kam-rə, 'ka-mər-ə\ *noun* [Late Latin, room — more at CHAMBER] (1712)
**1 :** the treasury department of the papal curia
**2 a :** CAMERA OBSCURA **b :** a device that consists of a lightproof chamber with an aperture fitted with a lens and a shutter through which the image of an object is projected onto a surface for recording (as on film) or for translation into electrical impulses (as for television broadcast)
— **on camera :** before a live television camera
**cam·era lu·ci·da** \-'lü-sə-də\ *noun* [New Latin, literally, light chamber] (1831)
**:** an instrument that by means of a prism or mirrors and often a microscope causes a virtual image of an object to appear as if projected upon a plane surface so that an outline may be traced
**cam·era·man** \-ˌman, -mən\ *noun* (1908)
**:** a person who operates a camera (as for motion pictures or television)
**cam·era ob·scu·ra** \-ˌäb-'skyùr-ə\ *noun* [New Latin, literally, dark chamber] (1725)
**:** a darkened enclosure having an aperture usually provided with a lens through which light from external objects enters to form an image of the objects on the opposite surface
**cam·era·per·son** \-ˌpər-sˀn\ *noun* (1976)
**:** a cameraman or camerawoman
**cam·era·wom·an** \-ˌwù-mən\ *noun* (1971)
**:** a woman who operates a camera
**cam·er·len·go** \ˌka-mər-'leŋ-(ˌ)gō\ *noun, plural* **-gos** [Italian *camarlingo*] (1625)
**:** a cardinal who heads the Apostolic Camera
**ca·mion** \kà-'myōⁿ\ *noun* [French] (1911)
**:** MOTORTRUCK; *also* **:** BUS
**cam·i·sa·do** \ˌka-mə-'sä-(ˌ)dō, -'sä-\ *noun, plural* **-does** [probably from obsolete Spanish *camisada*] (1548)
*archaic* **:** an attack by night
**ca·mise** \kə-'mēz, -'mēs\ *noun* [Arabic *qamīṣ*, perhaps from Late Latin *camisia*] (1812)
**:** a light loose long-sleeved shirt, gown, or tunic
**cam·i·sole** \'ka-mə-ˌsōl\ *noun* [French, from Provençal *camisolla*, diminutive of *camisa* shirt, from Late Latin *camisia*] (1795)
**1 :** a short negligee jacket for women
**2 :** a short sleeveless garment for women
**cam·let** \'kam-lət\ *noun* [Middle English *cameloit*, from Middle French *camelot*, from Arabic *khamlat* woolen plush] (15th century)
**1 a :** a medieval Asian fabric of camel hair or angora wool **b :** a European fabric of silk and wool **c :** a fine lustrous woolen
**2 :** a garment made of camlet
**camomile** *variant of* CHAMOMILE
**ca·mor·ra** \kə-'mór-ə, -'mär-\ *noun* [Italian] (1865)
**:** a group of persons united for dishonest or dishonorable ends; *especially* **:** a secret organization formed about 1820 at Naples, Italy
**ca·mor·ris·ta** \ˌkä-mó-'rē-stə\ *noun, plural* **-ti** \-(ˌ)stē\ [Italian, from *camorra*] (1897)
**:** a member of a camorra
**¹cam·ou·flage** \'ka-mə-ˌfläzh, -ˌfläj\ *noun* [French, from *camoufler* to disguise] (1917)
**1 :** the disguising especially of military equipment or installations with paint, nets, or foliage; *also* **:** the disguise so applied

**2 a :** concealment by means of disguise **b** **:** behavior or artifice designed to deceive or hide
— **cam·ou·flag·ic** \ˌka-mə-'flä-zhik, -jik\ *adjective*
**²camouflage** *verb* **-flaged; -flag·ing** (1917)
*transitive verb*
**:** to conceal or disguise by camouflage
*intransitive verb*
**:** to practice camouflage
— **cam·ou·flage·able** \'ka-mə-ˌflä-zhə-bəl, -jə-bəl\ *adjective*
**³camouflage** *adjective* (1945)
**:** made in colors or patterns typical of camouflage ⟨a *camouflage* jacket⟩
**¹camp** \'kamp\ *noun, often attributive* [Middle French, probably from Old North French or Old Provençal, from Latin *campus* plain, field] (1528)
**1 a :** a place usually away from urban areas where tents or simple buildings (as cabins) are erected for shelter or for temporary residence (as for laborers, prisoners, or vacationers) ⟨migrant labor *camp*⟩ **b :** a group of tents, cabins, or huts ⟨fishing *camps* along the river⟩ **c :** a settlement newly sprung up in a lumbering or mining region **d :** a place usually in the country for recreation or instruction during the summer ⟨goes to *camp* every July⟩ ⟨computer *camp*⟩ ⟨football *camp*⟩
**2 a :** a body of persons encamped **b** (1) **:** a group of persons; *especially* **:** a group engaged in promoting or defending a theory, doctrine, position, or person (2) **:** an ideological position
**3 :** military service or life
**²camp** (1543)
*intransitive verb*
**1 :** to make camp or occupy a camp
**2 :** to live temporarily in a camp or outdoors — often used with *out*
**3 :** to take up one's quarters **:** LODGE
**4 :** to take up one's position **:** settle down
*transitive verb*
**:** to put into a camp; *also* **:** ACCOMMODATE
**³camp** *noun* [origin unknown] (circa 1909)
**1 :** exaggerated effeminate mannerisms exhibited especially by homosexuals
**2 :** a homosexual displaying camp
**3 :** something so outrageously artificial, affected, inappropriate, or out-of-date as to be considered amusing
**4 :** something self-consciously exaggerated or theatrical
— **camp·i·ly** \'kam-pə-lē\ *adverb*
— **camp·i·ness** \-pē-nəs\ *noun*
— **campy** \'kam-pē\ *adjective*
**⁴camp** *adjective* (1909)
**:** of, relating to, being, or displaying camp ⟨*camp* send-ups of the songs of the fifties and sixties —John Elsom⟩
**⁵camp** *intransitive verb* (1925)
**:** to engage in camp **:** exhibit the qualities of camp ⟨he . . . was *camping*, hands on hips, with a quick eye to notice every man who passed by —R. M. McAlmon⟩
**¹cam·paign** \(ˌ)kam-'pān\ *noun* [French *campagne*, probably from Italian *campagna* level country, campaign, from Late Latin *campania* level country, from Latin, the level country around Naples] (circa 1656)
**1 :** a connected series of military operations forming a distinct phase of a war
**2 :** a connected series of operations designed to bring about a particular result ⟨election *campaign*⟩
**²campaign** *intransitive verb* (1701)
**:** to go on, engage in, or conduct a campaign
— **cam·paign·er** *noun*
**cam·pa·ni·le** \ˌkam-pə-'nē-lē, ˌkäm-, -(ˌ)lā, *especially of US structures also* -'nē(ə)l\ *noun, plural* **-ni·les** *or* **-ni·li** \-'nē-lē\ [Italian, from *campana* bell, from Late Latin] (1640)
**:** a usually freestanding bell tower
**cam·pa·nol·o·gist** \ˌkam-pə-'nä-lə-jist\ *noun* (1857)

**:** one that practices or is skilled in campanology
**cam·pa·nol·o·gy** \-jē\ *noun* [New Latin *campanologia*, from Late Latin *campana* + New Latin -*o*- + -*logia* -logy] (circa 1823)
**:** the art of bell ringing
**cam·pan·u·la** \kam-'pan-yə-lə\ *noun* [New Latin, diminutive of Late Latin *campana*] (1664)
**:** any of a genus (*Campanula*) of bellflowers
**cam·pan·u·late** \-lət, -ˌlāt\ *adjective* [New Latin *campanula* bell-shaped part, diminutive of Late Latin *campana*] (1668)
**:** shaped like a bell ⟨*campanulate* flower⟩
**Camp·bell·ite** \'ka-mə-ˌlīt *also* 'kam-bə-\ *noun* [Alexander *Campbell*] (1830)
**:** DISCIPLE 2 — often taken to be offensive
**camp·craft** \'kamp-ˌkraft\ *noun* (circa 1893)
**:** skill and practice in the activities relating to camping
**camp·er** \'kam-pər\ *noun* (1856)
**1 :** one that camps
**2 :** a portable dwelling (as a specially equipped trailer or automotive vehicle) for use during casual travel and camping
**cam·pe·si·no** \ˌkam-pə-'sē-(ˌ)nō\ *noun, plural* **-nos** [Spanish, from *campo* field, country, from Latin *campus* field] (1898)
**:** a native of a Latin-American rural area; *especially* **:** a Latin-American Indian farmer or farm laborer
**cam·pes·tral** \kam-'pes-trəl\ *adjective* [Latin *campestr-*, *campester*, from *campus*] (circa 1750)
**:** of or relating to fields or open country **:** RURAL
**camp·fire** \'kamp-ˌfīr\ *noun* (1675)
**:** a fire built outdoors (as at a camp or a picnic)
**Camp Fire girl** *noun* [from *Camp Fire Girls*, Inc., former name of Camp Fire, Inc.] (1912)
**:** a girl who is a member of a national organization of young people from ages 5 to 18
**camp follower** *noun* (1810)
**1 :** a civilian who follows a military unit to attend or exploit military personnel; *specifically* **:** PROSTITUTE
**2 :** a disciple or follower who is not of the main body of members or adherents; *especially* **:** a politician who joins the party or movement solely for personal gain
**camp·ground** \'kamp-ˌgraùnd\ *noun* (1805)
**:** the area or place (as a field or grove) used for a camp, for camping, or for a camp meeting
**cam·phene** \'kam-ˌfēn\ *noun* (circa 1847)
**:** any of several terpenes related to camphor; *especially* **:** a colorless crystalline terpene $C_{10}H_{16}$ used in insecticides
**cam·phor** \'kam(p)-fər\ *noun* [Middle English *caumfre*, from Anglo-French, from Medieval Latin *camphora*, from Arabic *kāfūr*, from Malay *kapur*] (14th century)
**:** a tough gummy volatile aromatic crystalline compound $C_{10}H_{16}O$ obtained especially from the wood and bark of the camphor tree and used as a liniment and mild topical analgesic in medicine, as a plasticizer, and as an insect repellent; *also* **:** any of several similar compounds (as some terpene alcohols and ketones)
— **cam·pho·ra·ceous** \ˌkam(p)-fə-'rā-shəs\ *adjective*
**cam·phor·ate** \'kam(p)-fə-ˌrāt\ *transitive verb* **-at·ed; -at·ing** (1641)
**:** to impregnate or treat with camphor
**camphor tree** *noun* (1607)
**:** a large Asian evergreen tree (*Cinnamomum camphora*) of the laurel family grown in warm regions

\ə\ abut \ᵊ\ kitten \ər\ further \a\ ash \ā\ ace \ä\ mop, mar \aù\ out \ch\ chin \e\ bet \ē\ easy \g\ go \i\ hit \ī\ ice \j\ job \ŋ\ sing \ō\ go \ò\ law \òi\ boy \th\ thin \th̷\ the \ü\ loot \ù\ foot \y\ yet \zh\ vision *see also* Guide to Pronunciation

**cam·pi·on** \'kam-pē-ən\ *noun* [probably from obsolete *campion* (champion)] (1576)
**:** any of various plants (genera *Lychnis* and *Silene*) of the pink family
**camp meeting** *noun* (1803)
**:** a series of evangelistic meetings usually held outdoors and attended by persons who often camp nearby
**cam·po** \'kam-(ˌ)pō, 'käm-\ *noun, plural* **campos** [American Spanish, from Spanish, field, from Latin *campus*] (1863)
**:** a grassland plain in South America with scattered perennial herbs
**cam·po·ree** \ˌkam-pə-'rē\ *noun* [*camp* + jam*bor*ee] (1927)
**:** a gathering of Boy Scouts or Girl Scouts from a given geographic area
**camp shirt** *noun* (1979)
**:** a woman's shirt having a notched collar and often patch pockets
**camp·site** \'kamp-ˌsīt\ *noun* (1910)
**:** a place suitable for or used as the site of a camp
**cam·pus** \'kam-pəs\ *noun, often attributive* [Latin, plain] (1774)
**1 :** the grounds and buildings of a university, college, or school
**2 :** a university, college, or school viewed as an academic, social, or spiritual entity
**3 :** grounds that resemble a campus ⟨hospital *campus*⟩ ⟨landscaped corporate *campus*⟩
**cam·py·lo·bac·ter** \ˌkam-pi-lō-'bak-tər, kam-ˌpi-lə-\ *noun* [New Latin, from Greek *kampylos* bent + New Latin *bacterium;* akin to Greek *kampē* bend — more at GAMBIT] (1964)
**:** any of a genus (*Campylobacter*) of spirally curved motile gram-negative rod-shaped bacteria of which some are pathogenic in domestic animals and humans
**cam·py·lot·ro·pous** \ˌkam-pi-'lä-trə-pəs\ *adjective* [Greek *kampylos* + International Scientific Vocabulary *-tropous* -tropous] (1835)
**:** having the ovule curved
**cam·shaft** \'kam-ˌshaft\ *noun* (circa 1877)
**:** a shaft to which a cam is fastened or of which a cam forms an integral part
**cam wheel** *noun* (circa 1853)
**:** a wheel set or shaped to act as a cam
**¹can** \kən, 'kan\ *verb, past* **couid** \kəd, 'kud\ *pres singular & plural* **can** [Middle English (1st & 3d singular present indicative), from Old English; akin to Old High German *kan* (1st & 3d singular present indicative) know, am able, Old English *cnāwan* to know — more at KNOW] (before 12th century)
*transitive verb*
**1** *obsolete* **:** KNOW, UNDERSTAND
**2** *archaic* **:** to be able to do, make, or accomplish
*intransitive verb*
*archaic* **:** to have knowledge or skill
*verbal auxiliary*
**1 a :** know how to ⟨she *can* read⟩ **b :** be physically or mentally able to ⟨he *can* lift 200 pounds⟩ **c** — used to indicate possibility ⟨do you think he *can* still be alive⟩ ⟨those things *can* happen⟩; sometimes used interchangeably with *may* **d :** be permitted by conscience or feeling to ⟨*can* hardly blame her⟩ **e :** be made possible or probable by circumstances to ⟨he *can* hardly have meant that⟩ **f :** be inherently able or designed to ⟨everything that money *can* buy⟩ **g :** be logically or axiologically able to ⟨2 + 2 *can* also be written 3 + 1⟩ **h :** be enabled by law, agreement, or custom to
**2 :** have permission to — used interchangeably with *may* ⟨you *can* go now if you like⟩ ■
**²can** \'kan\ *noun* [Middle English *canne*, from Old English; akin to Old High German *channa*] (before 12th century)
**1 :** a usually cylindrical receptacle: **a :** a vessel for holding liquids; *specifically* **:** a drinking vessel **b :** a usually metal typically cylindrical receptacle usually with an open top, often with a removable cover, and sometimes

with a spout or side handles (as for holding milk or trash) **c :** a container (as of tinplate) in which products (as perishable foods) are hermetically sealed for preservation until use **d :** a jar for packing or preserving fruit or vegetables
**2 :** JAIL
**3 a :** TOILET **b :** BATHROOM 1
**4 :** BUTTOCKS
**5 :** DESTROYER 2
**6** *slang* **:** an ounce of marijuana
— **can·ful** \'kan-ˌful\ *noun*
— **in the can** *of a film or videotape* **:** completed and ready for release
**³can** \'kan\ *transitive verb* **canned; can·ning** (1861)
**1 a :** to put in a can **:** preserve by sealing in airtight cans or jars **b :** to hit (a golf shot) into the cup **c :** to hit (a shot) in basketball
**2 :** to discharge from employment
**3** *slang* **:** to put a stop or end to
— **can·ner** *noun*
**Ca·naan·ite** \'kā-nə-ˌnīt\ *noun* [Greek *Kananītēs,* from *Kanaan* Canaan, from Hebrew *Kena'an*] (1535)
**:** a member of a Semitic people inhabiting ancient Palestine and Phoenicia from about 3000 B.C.
— **Canaanite** *adjective*
**Can·a·da balsam** \'ka-nə-də-\ *noun* [Canada, country in North America] (1811)
**:** a viscid yellowish to greenish oleoresin exudate of the balsam fir (*Abies balsmea*) that solidifies to a transparent mass and is used as a transparent cement especially in microscopy
**Canada Day** *noun* (1950)
**:** July 1 observed as a legal holiday in commemoration of the proclamation of dominion status in 1867
**Canada goose** *noun* (1731)
**:** the common wild goose (*Branta canadensis*) of North America that is chiefly gray and brownish with black head and neck and a white patch running from the sides of the head under the throat

**Canada goose**

**Canada thistle** *noun* (1799)
**:** a European thistle (*Cirsium arvense*) with pinkish purple or white flowers naturalized as a weed in North America
**Ca·na·di·an** \kə-'nā-dē-ən\ *noun* (1568)
**:** a native or inhabitant of Canada
— **Canadian** *adjective*
**Canadian bacon** *noun* (circa 1934)
**:** bacon cut from the loin that has little fat and is cut into round or oblong slices
**Canadian football** *noun* (1944)
**:** a game resembling American football that is played on a turfed field between two teams of 12 players each
**Canadian French** *noun* (1816)
**:** the language of the French Canadians
**Canadian lynx** *or* **Canada lynx** *noun* (1840)
**:** LYNX c
**ca·naille** \kə-'nī, -'nā(ə)l\ *noun* [French, from Italian *canaglia,* from *cane* dog, from Latin *canis* — more at HOUND] (1661)
**1 :** RABBLE, RIFFRAFF
**2 :** PROLETARIAN
**¹ca·nal** \kə-'nal\ *noun* [Middle English, from Latin *canalis* pipe, channel, from *canna* reed — more at CANE] (15th century)
**1 :** a tubular anatomical passage or channel **:** DUCT
**2 :** CHANNEL, WATERCOURSE
**3 :** an artificial waterway for navigation or for draining or irrigating land

**4 :** any of various faint narrow lines on the planet Mars seen through telescopes and once thought by some to be canals built by Martians
**²canal** *transitive verb* **-nalled** *or* **-naled; -nal·ling** *or* **-nal·ing** (1819)
**:** to construct a canal through or across
**can·a·lic·u·lus** \ˌka-nə-'li-kyə-ləs\ *noun, plural* **-li** \-ˌlī, -ˌlē\ [Latin, diminutive of *canalis*] (1854)
**:** a minute canal in a bodily structure
— **can·a·lic·u·lar** \-lər\ *adjective*
**can·a·li·za·tion** \ˌka-nᵊl-ə-'zā-shən\ *noun* (1844)
**1 :** an act or instance of canalizing
**2 :** a system of channels
**can·a·lize** \'ka-nᵊl-ˌīz\ *verb* **-lized; -liz·ing** (1860)
*transitive verb*
**1 a :** to provide with a canal or channel **b :** to make into or similar to a canal
**2 :** to provide with an outlet; *especially* **:** to direct into preferred channels
*intransitive verb*
**1 :** to flow in or into a channel
**2 :** to establish new channels
**can·a·pé** \'ka-nə-pē, -ˌpā\ *noun* [French, literally, sofa, from Medieval Latin *canopeum, canapeum* mosquito net — more at CANOPY] (1890)
**:** an appetizer consisting of a piece of bread or toast or a cracker topped with a savory spread (as caviar or cheese) — compare HORS D'OEUVRE ◆
**ca·nard** \kə-'närd *also* -'när\ *noun* [French, literally, duck; in sense 1, from Middle French *vendre des canards à moitié* to cheat, literally, to half-sell ducks] (circa 1859)

---

**1 :** a false or unfounded report or story; *especially* **:** a fabricated report
**2 :** an airplane with horizontal stabilizing and control surfaces in front of supporting surfaces; *also* **:** a small airfoil in front of the wing of an aircraft that increases the aircraft's stability ◆

**ca·nary** \kə-'ner-ē\ *noun, plural* **ca·nar·ies** [Middle French *canarie*, from Old Spanish *canario*, from *Islas Canarias* Canary Islands] (1592)
**1 :** a lively 16th century court dance
**2 :** a Canary Islands usually sweet wine similar to Madeira
**3 :** a small finch (*Serinus canarius*) of the Canary Islands that is usually greenish to yellow and is kept as a cage bird and singer
**4** *slang* **:** INFORMER 2
**canary seed** *noun* (1597)
**:** seed of a Canary Islands grass (*Phalaris canariensis*) used as food for cage birds
**canary yellow** *noun* (circa 1865)
**:** a light to a moderate or vivid yellow
**ca·nas·ta** \kə-'nas-tə\ *noun* [Spanish, literally, basket] (1948)
**1 :** a form of rummy using two full decks in which players or partnerships try to meld groups of three or more cards of the same rank and score bonuses for 7-card melds
**2 :** a meld of seven cards of the same rank in canasta
**can·can** \'kan-ˌkan\ *noun* [French] (1848)
**:** a woman's dance of French origin characterized by high kicking usually while holding up the front of a full ruffled skirt
**¹can·cel** \'kan(t)-səl\ *verb* **-celed** *or* **-celled; -cel·ing** *or* **-cel·ling** \-s(ə-)liŋ\ [Middle English *cancellen*, from Middle French *canceller*, from Late Latin *cancellare*, from Latin, to make like a lattice, from *cancelli* (plural), diminutive of *cancer* lattice, probably alteration of *carcer* prison] (14th century)
*transitive verb*
**1 a :** to destroy the force, effectiveness, or validity of **:** ANNUL ⟨*cancel* a magazine subscription⟩ ⟨a *canceled* check⟩ **b :** to bring to nothingness **:** DESTROY **c :** to match in force or effect **:** OFFSET — often used with *out* ⟨his irritability *canceled* out his natural kindness —Osbert Sitwell⟩ **d :** to call off usually without expectation of conducting or performing at a later time ⟨*cancel* a football game⟩
**2 a :** to mark or strike out for deletion **b :** OMIT, DELETE
**3 a :** to remove (a common divisor) from numerator and denominator **b :** to remove (equivalents) on opposite sides of an equation or account
**4 :** to deface (a postage or revenue stamp) especially with a set of ink lines so as to invalidate for reuse
*intransitive verb*
**:** to neutralize each other's strength or effect **:** COUNTERBALANCE
— **can·cel·able** *or* **can·cel·la·ble** \-s(ə-)lə-bəl\ *adjective*
— **can·cel·er** *or* **can·cel·ler** \-s(ə-)lər\ *noun*
**²cancel** *noun* (1806)
**1 :** CANCELLATION
**2 a :** a deleted part or passage **b** (1) **:** a leaf containing matter to be deleted (2) **:** a new leaf or slip substituted for matter already printed
**can·cel·la·tion** *also* **can·cel·ation** \ˌkan(t)-sə-'lā-shən\ *noun* (1535)
**1 :** the act or an instance of canceling
**2 :** a released accommodation
**3 :** a mark made to cancel something (as a postage stamp)
**can·cel·lous** \kan-'se-ləs, 'kan(t)-sə-ləs\ *adjective* [New Latin *cancelli* intersecting osseous plates and bars in cancellous bone, from Latin, lattice] (circa 1839)
*of bone* **:** having a porous structure

**can·cer** \'kan(t)-sər\ *noun* [Middle English, from Latin (genitive *Cancri*), literally, crab; akin to Greek *karkinos* crab, cancer]
**1** *capitalized* **a :** a northern zodiacal constellation between Gemini and Leo **b** (1) **:** the 4th sign of the zodiac in astrology — see ZODIAC table (2) **:** one born under the sign of Cancer
**2** [Latin, crab, cancer] **a :** a malignant tumor of potentially unlimited growth that expands locally by invasion and systemically by metastasis **b :** an abnormal bodily state marked by such tumors
**3 :** something evil or malignant that spreads destructively ⟨the *cancer* of hidden resentment —Irish Digest⟩
**4 a :** an enlarged tumorlike plant growth (as that of crown gall) **b :** a plant disease marked by such growths
**word history** see RANKLE
— **can·cer·ous** \'kan(t)s-rəs, 'kan(t)-sə-\ *adjective*
— **can·cer·ous·ly** *adverb*
**Can·cer·ian** \kan-'ser-ē-ən, -'sir-\ *noun* (1911)
**:** CANCER 1b(2)
**can·de·la** \kan-'dē-lə, -'de-, -'dā-; 'kan-də-lə\ *noun* [Latin, candle] (1949)
**:** the base unit of luminous intensity in the International System of Units that is equal to the luminous intensity in a given direction of a source which emits monochromatic radiation of frequency $540 \times 10^{12}$ hertz and has a radiant intensity in that direction of $\frac{1}{683}$ watt per unit solid angle — called also *candle*; abbreviation cd
**can·de·la·bra** \ˌkan-də-'lä-brə sometimes -'la-\ *noun* [alteration of Latin *candelabrum*, from *candela*] (1815)
**:** a branched candlestick or lamp with several lights
**can·de·la·brum** \-brəm\ *noun, plural* **-bra** \-brə\ *also* **-brums** [Latin] (1811)
**:** CANDELABRA
**can·dent** \'kan-dənt\ *adjective* [Latin *candent-, candens*, present participle of *candēre*] (1577)
**:** glowing from or as if from great heat
**can·des·cence** \kan-'de-sᵊn(t)s\ *noun* (circa 1864)
**:** a candescent state **:** glowing whiteness
**can·des·cent** \-sᵊnt\ *adjective* [Latin *candescent-, candescens*, present participle of *candescere*, inchoative of *candēre*] (1824)
**:** glowing or dazzling from or as if from great heat
**can·did** \'kan-dəd\ *adjective* [French & Latin; French *candide*, from Latin *candidus* bright, white, from *candēre* to shine, glow; akin to Welsh *can* white, Sanskrit *candati* it shines] (1630)
**1 :** WHITE ⟨*candid* flames⟩
**2 :** free from bias, prejudice, or malice **:** FAIR ⟨a *candid* observer⟩
**3 :** marked by honest sincere expression **b :** indicating or suggesting sincere honesty and absence of deception **c :** disposed to criticize severely **:** BLUNT
**4 :** relating to photography of subjects acting naturally or spontaneously without being posed
**synonym** see FRANK
— **can·did·ly** *adverb*
— **can·did·ness** *noun*
**can·di·da** \'kan-də-də\ *noun* [New Latin, genus name, from Latin, feminine of *candidus*] (1939)
**:** any of a genus (*Candida*) of parasitic imperfect fungi that resemble yeasts and occur especially in the mouth, vagina, and intestinal tract and that are usually benign but can become pathogenic; *especially* **:** one (*C. albicans*) causing thrush

**can·di·da·cy** \'kan-də-də-sē, 'ka-nə-\ *noun, plural* **-cies** (1864)
**:** the state of being a candidate
**can·di·date** \'kan-də-ˌdāt, 'ka-nə-, -dət\ *noun* [Latin *candidatus*, from *candidatus* clothed in white, from *candidus* white; from the white toga worn by candidates for office in ancient Rome] (1600)
**1 a :** one that aspires to or is nominated or qualified for an office, membership, or award **b :** one likely or suited to undergo or be chosen for something specified ⟨a *candidate* for surgery⟩
**2 :** a student in the process of meeting final requirements for a degree ◆
**can·di·da·ture** \'kan-də-də-ˌchu̇r, 'ka-nə-, -chər\ *noun* (1851)
*chiefly British* **:** CANDIDACY
**candid camera** *noun* (1929)
**:** a camera used to record subjects in a natural, spontaneous, or unposed manner; *also* **:** something likened to a camera used in such a manner
— **candid–camera** *adjective*
**can·di·di·a·sis** \ˌkan-də-'dī-ə-səs\ *noun, plural* **-a·ses** \-ˌsēz\ [New Latin] (1951)
**:** infection with or disease caused by a candida — called also *moniliasis*
**can·died** \'kan-dēd\ *adjective* (circa 1606)
**1 :** encrusted or coated with sugar
**2 :** baked with sugar or syrup until translucent
**¹can·dle** \'kan-dᵊl\ *noun* [Middle English *candel*, from Old English, from Latin *candela*, from *candēre*] (before 12th century)
**1 :** a usually molded or dipped mass of wax or tallow containing a wick that may be burned (as to give light, heat, or scent or for celebration or votive purposes)
**2 :** something resembling a candle in shape or use ⟨a sulfur *candle* for fumigating⟩

candelabra

◇ **WORD HISTORY**
**canard** In 16th century France, *vendre des canards à moitié*, which means literally "to half-sell ducks," was a colorful way of saying "to cheat." Unfortunately, no one knows just what was meant by this expression; it probably alludes to an incident in some story widely known at the time that has not survived. At any rate, *canard* in the sense of "duck" came to stand for any hoax, especially a made-up report. And French *canard*, in this sense, was borrowed into English.

**candidate** A person campaigning for public office in ancient Rome traditionally wore a toga that had been whitened with chalk when he greeted voters in the Forum. Whatever the original significance of the whitening might have been, it apparently came to be regarded as a form of electioneering, and according to the historian Livy it was banned by the Senate as early as 432 B.C. As with later curbs on soliciting votes, however, the ban was habitually disregarded, and office seekers wore white togas for some time after the Caesars had replaced the Roman Republic. The Latin word for an office seeker was *candidatus*, from an adjective of the same form meaning "wearing white," itself a derivative of *candidus* "white, bright." In the 16th and 17th centuries, the word *candidatus* was borrowed into French (as *candidat*), German (as *Kandidat*), and English, denoting aspirants either to a political office or to some academic degree.

\ə\ **abut** \ᵊ\ **kitten** \ər\ **further** \a\ **ash** \ā\ **ace**
\ä\ **mop, mar** \au̇\ **out** \ch\ **chin** \e\ **bet** \ē\ **easy**
\g\ **go** \i\ **hit** \ī\ **ice** \j\ **job** \ŋ\ **sing** \ō\ **go**
\ȯ\ **law** \ȯi\ **boy** \th\ **thin** \th\ **the** \ü\ **loot** \u̇\ **foot**
\y\ **yet** \zh\ **vision** *see also* Guide to Pronunciation

**3 :** required effort, expense, or trouble — usually used in the phrase *not worth the candle*
**4 :** CANDELA

**²candle** *transitive verb* **can·dled; can·dling** \'kan(d)-liŋ, 'kan-d°l-iŋ\ (1879)
**:** to examine by holding between the eye and a light; *especially* **:** to test (eggs) in this way for staleness, blood clots, fertility, and growth
— **can·dler** \'kan(d)-lər, 'kan-d°l-ər\ *noun*

**can·dle·ber·ry** \'kan-d°l-ˌber-ē\ *noun* (circa 1730)
**:** a wax myrtle (*Myrica cerifera*); *also* **:** a bayberry (*Myrica pensylvanica*)

**can·dle·fish** \-ˌfish\ *noun* (1881)
**:** EULACHON

**can·dle·hold·er** \-ˌhōl-dər\ *noun* (1932)
**:** CANDLESTICK

**can·dle·light** \'kan-d°l-ˌ(l)īt\ *noun* (before 12th century)
**1 a :** the light of a candle **b :** a soft artificial light
**2 :** the time for lighting candles **:** TWILIGHT

**can·dle·light·er** \-ˌ(l)ī-tər\ *noun* (15th century)
**1 :** one who lights the candles for a ceremony
**2 :** a long-handled implement with a taper and a snuffer that is used for the ceremonial lighting and extinguishing of candles

**can·dle·lit** \-ˌ(l)it\ *or* **can·dle·light·ed** \-ˌ(l)ī-təd\ *adjective* (1917)
**:** illuminated by candlelight ⟨a *candlelit* dinner⟩

**Can·dle·mas** \'kan-d°l-məs\ *noun* [Middle English *candelmasse*, from Old English *candelmæsse*, from *candel* + *mæsse* mass, feast; from the candles blessed and carried in celebration of the feast] (before 12th century)
**:** February 2 observed as a church festival in commemoration of the presentation of Christ in the temple and the purification of the Virgin Mary

**can·dle·nut** \-ˌnət\ *noun* (circa 1836)
**:** the oily seed of a tropical tree (*Aleurites moluccana*) of the spurge family used locally to make candles and commercially as a source of oil; *also* **:** this tree

**can·dle·pin** \-ˌpin\ *noun* (1901)
**1 :** a slender bowling pin tapering toward top and bottom
**2** *plural but singular in construction* **:** a bowling game using candlepins and a smaller ball than that used in tenpins

**can·dle·pow·er** \-ˌpaů(-ə)r\ *noun* (1877)
**:** luminous intensity expressed in candelas; *also* **:** CANDELA

**can·dle·snuff·er** \-ˌsnə-fər\ *noun* (1552)
**:** an implement for snuffing candles that consists of a small hollow cone attached to a handle

**can·dle·stick** \-ˌstik\ *noun* (before 12th century)
**:** a holder with a socket for a candle

**can·dle·wick** \-ˌwik\ *noun* (before 12th century)
**1 :** the wick of a candle
**2 :** a soft cotton embroidery yarn; *also* **:** embroidery made with this yarn usually in tufts

**can·dle·wood** \-ˌwůd\ *noun* (1712)
**1 :** any of several trees or shrubs (as ocotillo) chiefly of resinous character
**2 :** slivers of resinous wood burned for light

**can-do** \'kan-ˈdü\ *adjective* (1945)
**:** characterized by eager willingness to accept and meet challenges ⟨a *can-do* attitude⟩

**can·dor** \'kan-dər, -ˌdȯr\ *noun* [French & Latin; French *candeur*, from Latin *candor*, from *candēre* — more at CANDID] (14th century)
**1 a :** WHITENESS, BRILLIANCE **b** *obsolete* **:** unstained purity
**2 :** freedom from prejudice or malice **:** FAIRNESS
**3** *archaic* **:** KINDLINESS
**4 :** unreserved, honest, or sincere expression **:** FORTHRIGHTNESS ⟨the *candor* with which he

acknowledged a weakness in his own case —Aldous Huxley⟩

**can·dour** \'kan-dər\ *chiefly British variant of* CANDOR

**¹can·dy** \'kan-dē\ *noun, plural* **candies** [Middle English *sugre candy*, part translation of Middle French *sucre candi*, part translation of Old Italian *zucchero candi*, from *zucchero* sugar + Arabic *qandī* candied, from *qand* cane sugar] (15th century)
**1 :** crystallized sugar formed by boiling down sugar syrup
**2 a :** a confection made with sugar and often flavoring and filling **b :** a piece of such confection
— **candy** *adjective*

**²candy** *verb* **can·died; can·dy·ing** (1533)
*transitive verb*
**1 :** to encrust in or coat with sugar; *specifically* **:** to cook (as fruit or fruit peel) in a heavy syrup until glazed
**2 :** to make attractive **:** SWEETEN
**3 :** to crystallize into sugar
*intransitive verb*
**:** to become coated or encrusted with sugar crystals **:** become crystallized into sugar

**candy floss** *noun* (1951)
**1** *British* **:** COTTON CANDY
**2** *usually* **candyfloss** *British* **:** something attractive but insubstantial

**candy striper** *noun* [from the striped uniform worn suggesting the stripes on some sticks of candy] (1963)
**:** a teenage volunteer worker at a hospital

**can·dy·tuft** \'kan-dē-ˌtəft\ *noun* [*Candy*, alteration of *Candia* Crete, Greek island + English *tuft*] (1664)
**:** any of a genus (*Iberis*) of plants of the mustard family cultivated for their white, pink, or purple flowers

**¹cane** \'kān\ *noun* [Middle English, from Middle French, from Old Provençal *cana*, from Latin *canna*, from Greek *kanna*, from Semitic origin; akin to Arabic *qanāh* hollow stick, reed] (14th century)
**1 a** (1) **:** a hollow or pithy and usually slender and flexible jointed stem (as of a reed) (2) **:** any of various slender woody stems; *especially* **:** an elongated flowering or fruiting stem (as of a rose) usually arising directly from the ground **b :** any of various tall woody grasses or reeds: as (1) **:** any of a genus (*Arundinaria*) of coarse grasses (2) **:** SUGARCANE (3) **:** SORGHUM
**2 :** cane dressed for use: as **a :** a cane walking stick; *broadly* **:** WALKING STICK **b :** a cane or rod for flogging **c :** RATTAN; *especially* **:** split rattan for wickerwork or basketwork
**3 :** a tiny glass rod used in decorative glasswork (as in millefiori and paperweights)

**²cane** *transitive verb* **caned; can·ing** (circa 1667)
**1 :** to beat with a cane ⟨he sat in a professor's chair and *caned* sophomores for blowing spitballs —H. L. Mencken⟩
**2 :** to weave or furnish with cane ⟨*cane* the seat of a chair⟩

**cane·brake** \'kān-ˌbrāk\ *noun* (1769)
**:** a thicket of cane

**can·er** \'kā-nər\ *noun* (1868)
**:** one that canes chairs

**ca·nes·cent** \kə-ˈne-s°nt, ka-\ *adjective* [Latin *canescent-, canescens*, present participle of *canescere*, inchoative of *canēre* to be gray, be white, from *canus* white, hoary — more at HARE] (circa 1828)
**:** growing white, whitish, or hoary; *especially* **:** having a fine grayish white pubescence ⟨*canescent* leaves⟩

**cane sugar** *noun* (1841)
**:** sugar from sugarcane

**cane·ware** \'kān-ˌwar, -ˌwer\ *noun* [from its color] (1878)
**:** a buff or yellowish stoneware

**ca·nic·o·la fever** \kə-ˈni-kə-lə-\ *noun* [New Latin *canicola*, from Latin *canis* dog + *-cola* inhabitant — more at HOUND, -COLOUS] (1943)
**:** an acute disease in humans and dogs characterized by gastroenteritis and mild jaundice and caused by a spirochete (*Leptospira canicola*)

**ca·nic·u·lar** \kə-ˈni-kyə-lər\ *adjective* [Middle English *caniculer* of the star Sirius, from Late Latin *canicularis*, from Latin *Canicula* Sirius, diminutive of *canis*] (12th century)
**:** of or relating to the dog days

**ca·nid** \'ka-nəd, 'kā-\ *noun* [New Latin *Canidae*, from *Canis*, type genus, from Latin *canis*] (circa 1889)
**:** any of a family (Canidae) of carnivorous animals that includes the wolves, jackals, foxes, coyote, and the domestic dog

**¹ca·nine** \'kā-ˌnīn, *British also* 'ka-\ *noun* (15th century)
**1** [Middle English, from Latin (*dens*) *caninus* canine tooth] **:** a conical pointed tooth; *especially* **:** one situated between the lateral incisor and the first premolar — see TOOTH illustration
**2 :** CANID; *also* **:** DOG 1a

**²canine** *adjective* [Latin *caninus*, from *canis* dog — more at HOUND] (1607)
**1 :** of or resembling that of a dog ⟨*canine* loyalty⟩
**2 :** of or relating to dogs or to the family (Canidae) including the canids

**Ca·nis Ma·jor** \ˌkā-nəs-ˈmā-jər, ˌka-\ *noun* [Latin (genitive *Canis Majoris*), literally, greater dog]
**:** a constellation to the southeast of Orion containing Sirius

**Canis Mi·nor** \-ˈmī-nər\ *noun* [Latin (genitive *Canis Minoris*), literally, lesser dog]
**:** a constellation to the east of Orion containing Procyon

**can·is·ter** *also* **can·nis·ter** \'ka-nə-stər\ *noun* [Latin *canistrum* basket, from Greek *kanastron* wicker basket, from *kanna* reed — more at CANE] (1711)
**1 :** an often cylindrical container for holding a usually specified object or substance ⟨a film *canister*⟩
**2 :** encased shot for close-range artillery fire
**3 :** a perforated metal box for gas masks with material to adsorb, filter, or detoxify airborne poisons and irritants

**¹can·ker** \'kaŋ-kər\ *noun* [Middle English, from Old North French *cancre*, from Latin *cancer* crab, cancer] (13th century)
**1 a** (1) **:** an erosive or spreading sore (2) **:** an area of necrosis in a plant; *also* **:** a plant disease characterized by cankers **b :** any of various disorders of animals marked by chronic inflammatory changes
**2** *archaic* **:** a caterpillar destructive to plants
**3** *chiefly dialect* **:** RUST 1
**4 :** a source of corruption or debasement
**5** *chiefly dialect* **:** DOG ROSE
— **can·ker·ous** \'kaŋ-k(ə-)rəs\ *adjective*

**²canker** *verb* **can·kered; can·ker·ing** \'kaŋ-k(ə-)riŋ\ (14th century)
*transitive verb*
**1** *obsolete* **:** to infect with a spreading sore
**2 :** to corrupt the spirit of
*intransitive verb*
**1 :** to become infested with canker
**2 :** to become corrupted

**canker sore** *noun* (circa 1909)
**:** a small painful ulcer especially of the mouth

**can·ker·worm** \'kaŋ-kər-ˌwərm\ *noun* (1530)
**:** either of two geometrid moths (*Alsophila pometaria* and *Paleacrita vernata*) and especially their larvae which are serious pests of fruit and shade trees

**can·na** \'ka-nə\ *noun* [New Latin, genus name, from Latin, reed — more at CANE] (1664)
**:** any of a genus (*Canna* of the family Cannaceae) of tropical herbs with simple stems, large leaves, and a terminal raceme of irregular flowers

**can·na·bi·noid** \kə-'na-bə-ˌnȯid\ *noun* [Latin *cannabis* + ¹*-in* + ¹*-oid*] (1970)
**:** any of various chemical constituents (as THC or cannabinol) of cannabis or marijuana

**can·na·bi·nol** \-ˌnȯl, -ˌnōl\ *noun* [Latin *cannabis* + ¹*-in* + ¹*-ol*] (1896)
**:** a physiologically inactive crystalline cannabinoid $C_{21}H_{26}O_2$

**can·na·bis** \'ka-nə-bəs\ *noun* [Latin, hemp, from Greek *kannabis;* akin to Old English *hænep* hemp] (1783)
**1 :** HEMP 1a
**2 :** any of the preparations (as marijuana or hashish) or chemicals (as THC) that are derived from the hemp and are psychoactive

**canned** \'kand\ *adjective* (1904)
**1 a :** prepared or recorded in advance; *especially* **:** prepared in standardized form for nonspecific use or wide distribution ⟨*canned* laughter⟩ ⟨*canned* music⟩ ⟨*canned* speeches⟩ **b :** lacking originality or individuality as if mass-produced ⟨*canned* sales pitch⟩
**2** *slang* **:** DRUNK 1a

**can·nel coal** \'ka-nᵊl-\ *noun* [probably from English dialect *cannel* candle, from Middle English *candel*] (1610)
**:** a bituminous coal containing much volatile matter that burns brightly

**can·nel·lo·ni** \ˌka-nə-'lō-nē\ *noun plural but singular or plural in construction* [Italian, plural of *cannellone*, augmentative of *cannello* segment of cane stalk, from *canna*] (1906)
**:** boiled tube-shaped or rolled pasta filled with a meat, fish, cheese, or vegetable mixture and baked in a sauce

**can·nery** \'ka-nə-rē\ *noun, plural* **-ner·ies** (1870)
**:** a factory for the canning of foods

**can·ni·bal** \'ka-nə-bəl\ *noun* [New Latin *Canibalis* Carib, from Spanish *Caníbal*, from Taino *Caniba*, of Cariban origin; akin to Carib *kariʔna* Carib, person] (1553)
**:** one that eats the flesh of its own kind ◆

**can·ni·bal·ise** *British variant of* CANNIBALIZE

**can·ni·bal·ism** \'ka-nə-bə-ˌli-zəm\ *noun* (1796)
**1 :** the usually ritualistic eating of human flesh by a human being
**2 :** the eating of the flesh of an animal by another animal of the same kind
**3 :** an act of cannibalizing something
**— can·ni·bal·is·tic** \ˌka-nə-bə-'lis-tik\ *adjective*

**can·ni·bal·ize** \'ka-nə-bə-ˌlīz\ *verb* **-ized; -iz·ing** (1943)
*transitive verb*
**1 a :** to take salvageable parts from (as a disabled machine) for use in building or repairing another machine **b :** to make use of (a part taken from one thing) in building or repairing something else
**2 :** to deprive of an essential part or element in creating or sustaining another facility or enterprise ⟨the energy system has begun *cannibalizing* the economic system it is supposed to fuel —Barry Commoner⟩
**3 :** to use or draw on material of (as another writer or an earlier work) ⟨a volume . . . that not only *cannibalizes* previous publications but is intended itself to be *cannibalized* —R. M. Adams⟩
**4 :** to take (sales) away from an existing product by selling or being sold as a similar but new product usually from the same manufacturer; *also* **:** to affect (as an existing product) adversely by cannibalizing sales
*intransitive verb*
**1 :** to practice cannibalism
**2 :** to cannibalize one unit for the sake of another of the same kind
**— can·ni·bal·i·za·tion** \ˌka-nə-bə-lə-'zā-shən\ *noun*

**can·ni·kin** \'ka-ni-kən\ *noun* [probably from obsolete Dutch *kanneken*, from Middle Dutch *canneken*, diminutive of *canne* can; akin to Old English *canne* can] (1570)
**:** a small can or drinking vessel

**can·no·li** \kə-'nō-lē, ka-\ *noun plural but singular or plural in construction* [Italian, plural of *cannolo* small tube, diminutive of *canna*] (1943)
**:** a deep-fried tube of pastry filled with sweetened and flavored ricotta cheese

**¹can·non** \'ka-nən\ *noun, plural* **cannons** *or* **cannon** [Middle French *canon*, from Italian *cannone*, literally, large tube, augmentative of *canna* reed, tube, from Latin, cane, reed — more at CANE] (15th century)
**1** *plural usually* **cannon a :** a large heavy gun usually mounted on a carriage **b :** a heavy-caliber automatic aircraft gun firing explosive shells
**2** *or* **can·on :** the projecting part of a bell by which it is hung **:** EAR
**3 :** the part of the leg in which the cannon bone is found

**²cannon** (1691)
*intransitive verb*
**:** to discharge cannon
*transitive verb*
**:** CANNONADE

**¹can·non·ade** \ˌka-nə-'nād\ *noun* (1562)
**1 :** a heavy fire of artillery
**2 :** an attack (as with words) likened to artillery fire **:** BOMBARDMENT

**²cannonade** *verb* **-ad·ed; -ad·ing** (circa 1670)
*transitive verb*
**:** to attack with or as if with artillery
*intransitive verb*
**:** to deliver artillery fire

**¹can·non·ball** \'ka-nən-ˌbȯl\ *noun* (1663)
**1 :** a usually round solid missile made for firing from a cannon
**2 :** a jump into water made with the arms holding the knees tight against the chest
**3 :** a hard flat tennis service
**4 :** an express train

**²cannonball** *intransitive verb* (1951)
**:** to travel with great speed

**cannon bone** *noun* [French *canon*, literally, cannon] (1834)
**:** a bone in hoofed mammals that extends from the knee or hock to the fetlock

**can·non·eer** \ˌka-nə-'nir\ *noun* (1562)
**:** an artillery gunner

**cannon fodder** *noun* (circa 1891)
**:** soldiers regarded or treated as expendable in battle

**can·non·ry** \'ka-nən-rē\ *noun, plural* **-ries** (circa 1840)
**:** a battery of cannons or cannon fire

**can·not** \'ka-(ˌ)nät; kə-'nät, ka-\ (15th century)
**:** can not
**— cannot but** *or* **cannot help but** *also* **cannot help :** to be unable to do otherwise than

**can·nu·la** \'kan-yə-lə\ *noun, plural* **-las** *or* **-lae** \-ˌlē, -ˌlī\ [New Latin, from Latin, diminutive of *canna* reed — more at CANE] (1684)
**:** a small tube for insertion into a body cavity or into a duct or vessel

**can·nu·lar** \'kan-yə-lər\ *adjective* (1823)
**:** TUBULAR

**¹can·ny** \'ka-nē\ *adjective* **can·ni·er; -est** [¹*can*] (1596)
**1 :** CLEVER, SHREWD; *also* **:** PRUDENT
**2** *chiefly Scottish* **a :** CAREFUL, STEADY; *also* **:** RESTRAINED **b :** QUIET, SNUG ⟨then *canny*, in some cozy place, they close the day —Robert Burns⟩
**— can·ni·ly** \'ka-nᵊl-ē\ *adverb*
**— can·ni·ness** \'ka-nē-nəs\ *noun*

**²canny** *adverb* (circa 1796)
*Scottish* **:** in a canny manner **:** CAREFULLY

**¹ca·noe** \kə-'nü\ *noun* [French, from New Latin *canoa*, from Spanish, from Arawakan, of Cariban origin; akin to Carib *kanaːwa* canoe] (1555)
**:** a light narrow boat with both ends sharp that is usually propelled by paddling

**²canoe** *verb* **ca·noed; ca·noe·ing** (1794)
*transitive verb*
**:** to transport in a canoe; *also* **:** to travel by canoe down (a river)
*intransitive verb*
**:** to go or travel in a canoe
**— ca·noe·able** \-ə-bəl\ *adjective*
**— ca·noe·ist** *noun*

**can of worms** (1962)
**:** PANDORA'S BOX

**ca·no·la** \kə-'nō-lə\ *noun* [*Can*ada *o*il—*l*ow *a*cid] (1979)
**1 :** a rape plant of an improved variety having seeds that are low in erucic acid and are the source of canola oil
**2 :** CANOLA OIL

**canola oil** *noun* (1986)
**:** an edible vegetable oil obtained from the seeds of canola that is high in monounsaturated fatty acids

**¹can·on** \'ka-nən\ *noun* [Middle English, from Old English, from Late Latin, from Latin, ruler, rule, model, standard, from Greek *kanōn*] (before 12th century)
**1 a :** a regulation or dogma decreed by a church council **b :** a provision of canon law
**2** [Middle English, probably from Old French, from Late Latin, from Latin, model] **:** the most solemn and unvarying part of the Mass including the consecration of the bread and wine
**3** [Middle English, from Late Latin, from Latin, standard] **a :** an authoritative list of books accepted as Holy Scripture **b :** the authentic works of a writer **c :** a sanctioned or accepted group or body of related works ⟨the *canon* of great literature⟩
**4 a :** an accepted principle or rule **b :** a criterion or standard of judgment **c :** a body of principles, rules, standards, or norms
**5** [Late Greek *kanōn*, from Greek, model] **:** a contrapuntal musical composition in two or more voice parts in which the melody is imitated exactly and completely by the successive voices though not always at the same pitch
**synonym** see LAW

**²canon** *noun* [Middle English *canoun*, from Anglo-French *canunie*, from Late Latin *canonicus* one living under a rule, from Latin, according to rule, from Greek *kanonikos*, from *kanōn*] (13th century)

◇ **WORD HISTORY**
**cannibal** On Christopher Columbus's first voyage to the New World, the mainly Arawakan-speaking peoples whom he encountered in Cuba and Hispaniola told him about a people living to their east, who periodically raided them and whom they greatly feared. In his log Columbus recorded a number of phonetically similar names for this people, including *canibales* and *caribes*. The Spanish court historian Petrus Martyr wrote a Latin account of Columbus's discoveries, first printed in 1516, that used these two words and widely disseminated them throughout Europe. In Petrus Martyr's words, "the inhabitants of these lands assert that the *Canibales* or *Caribes* are eaters of human flesh." Subsequently, the meaning of the two words diverged. *Caribes* was applied to the Carib-speaking peoples of the Lesser Antilles and northern South America who were so feared by the Arawakans; it is ultimately the base of the word *Caribbean*. *Canibales*, on the other hand, passed into English as *cannibal* and became a generic word for any creature that eats the flesh of its own kind.

\ə\ abut \ᵊ\ kitten \ər\ further \a\ ash \ā\ ace
\ä\ mop, mar \aů\ out \ch\ chin \e\ bet \ē\ easy
\g\ go \i\ hit \ī\ ice \j\ job \ŋ\ sing \ō\ go
\ȯ\ law \ȯi\ boy \th\ thin \th\ the \ü\ loot \ů\ foot
\y\ yet \zh\ vision *see also* Guide to Pronunciation

**1 :** a clergyman belonging to the chapter or the staff of a cathedral or collegiate church
**2 :** CANON REGULAR

**ca·ñon** \'kan-yən\ *variant of* CANYON

**can·on·ess** \'ka-nə-nəs\ *noun* (1682)
**1 :** a woman living in community under a religious rule but not under a perpetual vow
**2 :** a member of a Roman Catholic congregation of women corresponding to canons regular

**ca·non·ic** \kə-'nä-nik\ *adjective* (15th century)
**1 :** CANONICAL
**2 :** of or relating to musical canon

**ca·non·i·cal** \-ni-kəl\ *adjective* (15th century)
**1 :** of, relating to, or forming a canon
**2 :** conforming to a general rule or acceptable procedure **:** ORTHODOX
**3 :** of or relating to a clergyman who is a canon
**4 :** reduced to the canonical form ⟨a *canonical* matrix⟩
— **ca·non·i·cal·ly** \-k(ə-)lē\ *adverb*

**canonical form** *noun* (1851)
**:** the simplest form of something; *specifically*
**:** the form of a square matrix that has zero elements everywhere except along the principal diagonal

**canonical hour** *noun* (15th century)
**1 :** a time of day canonically appointed for an office of devotion
**2 :** one of the daily offices of devotion that compose the Divine Office and include matins with lauds, prime, terce, sext, none, vespers, and compline

**ca·non·i·cals** \kə-'nä-ni-kəlz\ *noun plural* (1748)
**:** the vestments prescribed by canon for an officiating clergyman

**can·on·ic·i·ty** \,ka-nə-'ni-sə-tē\ *noun* (1797)
**:** the quality or state of being canonical

**can·on·ist** \'ka-nə-nist\ *noun* (1542)
**:** a specialist in canon law

**can·on·ize** \'ka-nə-,nīz\ *transitive verb* **can·on·ized** \-,nīzd; *in* "Hamlet" *usually* kə-'nä-,nīzd\; **can·on·iz·ing** [Middle English, from Medieval Latin *canonizare*, from Late Latin *canon* catalog of saints, from Latin, standard] (14th century)
**1 :** to declare (a deceased person) an officially recognized saint
**2 :** to make canonical
**3 :** to sanction by ecclesiastical authority
**4 :** to attribute authoritative sanction or approval to
**5 :** to treat as illustrious, preeminent, or sacred
— **can·on·i·za·tion** \,ka-nə-nə-'zā-shən\ *noun*

**canon law** *noun* (1552)
**:** the usually codified law governing a church

**canon lawyer** *noun* (circa 1859)
**:** CANONIST

**canon regular** *noun, plural* **canons regular** (14th century)
**:** a member of one of several Roman Catholic religious institutes of regular priests living in community under a usually Augustinian rule

**can·on·ry** \'ka-nən-rē\ *noun, plural* **-ries** (15th century)
**:** the office of a canon; *also* **:** the endowment that financially supports a canon

**ca·no·pic jar** \kə-'nō-pik-, -'nä-\ *noun* [*Canopus*, Egypt] (1893)
**:** a jar in which the ancient Egyptians preserved the viscera of a deceased person usually for burial with the mummy

**Ca·no·pus** \kə-'nō-pəs\ *noun* [Latin, from Greek *Kanōpos*]
**:** a star of the first magnitude in the constellation Carina not visible north of 37° latitude

**¹can·o·py** \'ka-nə-pē\ *noun, plural* **-pies** [Middle En-

canopic jar

glish *canope*, from Medieval Latin *canopeum* mosquito net, from Latin *conopeum*, from Greek *kōnōpion*, from *kōnōps* mosquito] (14th century)
**1 a :** a cloth covering suspended over a bed **b** **:** a cover (as of cloth) fixed or carried above a person of high rank or a sacred object **:** BALDACHIN **c :** a protective covering: as (1) **:** the uppermost spreading branchy layer of a forest (2) **:** AWNING, MARQUEE
**2 :** an ornamental rooflike structure
**3 a :** the transparent enclosure over an airplane cockpit **b :** the fabric part of a parachute that catches the air
*word history* see CANAPÉ

**²canopy** *transitive verb* **-pied; -py·ing** (1599)
**:** to cover with or as if with a canopy

**ca·no·rous** \kə-'nōr-əs, -'nȯr-; 'ka-nə-rəs\ *adjective* [Latin *canorus*, from *canor* melody, from *canere* to sing — more at CHANT] (1646)
**:** pleasant sounding **:** MELODIOUS
— **ca·no·rous·ly** *adverb*
— **ca·no·rous·ness** *noun*

**canst** \kən(t)st, 'kan(t)st\ *archaic present 2d singular of* CAN

**¹cant** \'kant\ *adjective* [Middle English, probably from (assumed) Middle Low German *kant*] (14th century)
*dialect English* **:** LIVELY, LUSTY

**²cant** (circa 1543)
*transitive verb*
**1 :** to give a cant or oblique edge to **:** BEVEL
**2 :** to set at an angle **:** TILT
**3** *chiefly British* **:** to throw with a lurch
*intransitive verb*
**1 :** to pitch to one side **:** LEAN
**2 :** SLOPE

**³cant** *noun* [Middle English *cante* edge, probably from Middle Dutch or Old North French; Middle Dutch, edge, corner, from Old North French, from Latin *canthus, cantus* iron tire, perhaps of Celtic origin; akin to Welsh *cant* rim; perhaps akin to Greek *kanthos* corner of the eye] (1603)
**1** *obsolete* **:** CORNER, NICHE
**2 :** an external angle (as of a building)
**3 :** a log with one or more squared sides
**4 a :** an oblique or slanting surface **b :** INCLINATION, SLOPE

**⁴cant** *adjective* (1663)
**1 :** having canted corners or sides
**2 :** INCLINED 2

**⁵cant** *intransitive verb* [probably from Old North French *canter* to tell, literally, to sing, from Latin *cantare* — more at CHANT] (1567)
**1 :** to talk or beg in a whining or singsong manner
**2 :** to speak in cant or jargon
**3 :** to talk hypocritically

**⁶cant** *noun* (1640)
**1 :** affected singsong or whining speech
**2 a :** the private language of the underworld **b** *obsolete* **:** the phraseology peculiar to a religious class or sect **c :** JARGON 2
**3 :** a set or stock phrase
**4 :** the expression or repetition of conventional or trite opinions or sentiments; *especially* **:** the insincere use of pious words

**can't** \'kant, 'känt, 'kant, *especially Southern* 'känt\ (circa 1652)
**:** can not

**Can·tab** \'kan-,tab\ *noun* [by shortening] (1750)
**:** CANTABRIGIAN

**can·ta·bi·le** \kän-'tä-bi-,lā, -lē\ *adverb or adjective* [Italian, from Late Latin *cantabilis* worthy to be sung, from Latin *cantare*] (circa 1724)
**:** in a singing manner — often used as a direction in music

**Can·ta·brig·i·an** \,kan-tə-'bri-j(ē-)ən\ *noun* [Medieval Latin *Cantabrigia* Cambridge] (circa 1540)
**1 :** a student or graduate of Cambridge University

**2 :** a native or resident of Cambridge, Mass.
— **Cantabrigian** *adjective*

**can·ta·la** \kan-'tä-lə\ *noun* [New Latin, specific epithet of *Agave cantala*, perhaps from Sanskrit *kaṇṭala* babul, from *kaṇṭa* thorn] (1911)
**:** a hard fiber produced from the leaves of an agave (*Agave cantala*)

**can·ta·loupe** *also* **can·ta·loup** \'kant-ᵊl-,ōp *also* -,üp\ *noun* [*Cantalupo*, former papal villa near Rome, Italy] (1739)
**1 :** a muskmelon (*Cucumis melo reticulatus*) having a rind with netted tracery and reddish orange flesh
**2 :** any of several muskmelons resembling the cantaloupe; *broadly* **:** MUSKMELON

**can·tan·ker·ous** \kan-'taŋ-k(ə-)rəs, kən-\ *adjective* [perhaps irregular from obsolete *contack* (contention)] (1772)
**:** difficult or irritating to deal with
— **can·tan·ker·ous·ly** *adverb*
— **can·tan·ker·ous·ness** *noun*

**can·ta·ta** \kən-'tä-tə\ *noun* [Italian, from Latin, from feminine of *cantatus*, past participle of *cantare*] (1724)
**:** a composition for one or more voices usually comprising solos, duets, recitatives, and choruses and sung to an instrumental accompaniment

**can·ta·trice** \,kän-tə-'trē-(,)chā, ,kä ⁿ-tə-'trēs\ *noun, plural* **-trices** \-'trē-(,)chāz, -'trēs, -'trē-səz\ *or* **-tri·ci** \,kän-tə-'trē-(,)chē\ [Italian & French, from Italian, from Late Latin *cantatric-, cantatrix*, feminine of Latin *cantator* singer, from *cantare*] (1803)
**:** a woman who is a singer; *especially* **:** an opera singer

**cant dog** *noun* [³*cant*] (1850)
**:** PEAVEY

**can·teen** \kan-'tēn\ *noun* [French *cantine* bottle case, sutler's shop, from Italian *cantina* wine cellar, probably from *canto* corner, from Latin *canthus* iron tire — more at CANT] (1737)
**1 a :** a portable chest with compartments for carrying bottles or for cooking and eating utensils **b :** a flask for carrying liquids (as on a hike) **c :** MESS KIT **d** *British* **:** a chest for storing flatware
**2 a :** a bar at a military post or camp **b :** a general store at a military post **:** EXCHANGE **c** **:** an establishment that serves as an informal social club (as for soldiers or a community's teenagers) **d :** a small cafeteria or snack bar

**¹cant·er** \'kant-ər\ *noun* (1609)
**:** one that uses cant: as **a :** BEGGAR, VAGABOND **b :** a user of professional or religious cant

**²can·ter** \'kan-tər\ *verb* [short for obsolete *canterbury*, noun (canter), from *Canterbury*, England; from the supposed gait of pilgrims riding to Canterbury] (1706)
*intransitive verb*
**1 :** to move at or as if at a canter **:** LOPE
**2 :** to ride a horse at a canter ◆

*transitive verb*
: to cause to go at a canter

**³can·ter** *noun* (1755)
**1** : a 3-beat gait resembling but smoother and slower than the gallop
**2** : a ride at a canter

**Can·ter·bury bell** \'kan-tə(r)-ˌber-ē-, -ˌb(ə-)rē-\ *noun* [*Canterbury*, England] (1578)
: any of several bellflowers (as *Campanula medium*) cultivated for their showy flowers

**can·thar·i·din** \kan-'thar-ə-d°n, -'ther-\ *noun* (1819)
: a bitter crystalline compound $C_{10}H_{12}O_4$ that is the active blister-producing ingredient of cantharides

**can·tha·ris** \'kan(t)-thə-rəs\ *noun, plural* **can·thar·i·des** \kan-'thar-ə-ˌdēz\ [Middle English & Latin; Middle English *cantharide*, from Latin *cantharid-, cantharis*, from Greek *kantharid-, kantharis*] (14th century)
**1** : SPANISH FLY 1
**2** *plural but singular or plural in construction* : a preparation of dried beetles (as Spanish flies) used in medicine as a counterirritant and formerly as an aphrodisiac

**can·tha·xan·thin** \ˌkan(t)-thə-'zan-ˌthin\ *noun* [International Scientific Vocabulary *cantha-* (from New Latin *Cantharellus cinnabarinus*, mushroom species from which it was obtained) + *xanth-* + ¹-*in*] (circa 1951)
: a carotenoid $C_{40}H_{52}O_2$ used especially as a color additive for food

**cant hook** *noun* [³*cant*] (circa 1848)
: a lumberman's lever that has a pivoting hooked arm and a blunt often toothed metal cap at one end — compare PEAVEY

**can·thus** \'kan(t)-thəs\ *noun, plural* **can·thi** \'kan-ˌthī, -ˌthē\ [Late Latin, from Greek *kanthos* — more at CANT] (1646)
: either of the angles formed by the meeting of an eye's upper and lower eyelids

**can·ti·cle** \'kan-ti-kəl\ *noun* [Middle English, from Latin *canticulum*, diminutive of *canticum* song, from *cantus*, past participle of *canere*] (13th century)
: SONG; *specifically* : one of several liturgical songs (as the Magnificat) taken from the Bible

**Canticle of Canticles** (circa 1934)
: SONG OF SOLOMON

**Canticles** *noun plural but singular in construction* (15th century)
: SONG OF SOLOMON

**can·ti·le·na** \ˌkan-tə-'lā-nə, -'lē-\ *noun* [Italian, from Latin, song, from *cantus*] (circa 1740)
: a vocal or instrumental passage of sustained lyricism

**¹can·ti·le·ver** \'kan-tə-ˌlē-vər, -ˌle-\ *noun* [perhaps from ³*cant* + -*i*- + *lever*] (1667)
: a projecting beam or member supported at only one end: as **a** : a bracket-shaped member supporting a balcony or a cornice **b** : either of the two beams or trusses that project from piers toward each other and that when joined directly or by a suspended connecting member form a span of a cantilever bridge — see BRIDGE illustration

**²cantilever** (1902)
*transitive verb*
**1** : to support by a cantilever ⟨a *cantilevered* shelf⟩
**2** : to build as a cantilever
*intransitive verb*
: to project as a cantilever

**can·til·late** \'kan-t°l-ˌāt\ *transitive verb* **-lat·ed; -lat·ing** [Latin *cantilatus*, past participle of *cantilare* to sing, perhaps from *cantilena*] (circa 1828)
: to recite with musical tones
— **can·til·la·tion** \ˌkan-t°l-'ā-shən\ *noun*

**can·ti·na** \kan-'tē-nə\ *noun* [American Spanish, from Spanish, canteen, from Italian, wine cellar — more at CANTEEN] (1844)
**1** *Southwest* : a pouch or bag at the pommel of a saddle
**2** *Southwest* : a small barroom : SALOON

**cant·ing** \'kan-tiŋ\ *adjective* [⁵*cant*] (1663)
: affectedly pious or righteous

**can·tle** \'kan-t°l\ *noun* [Middle English *cantel*, from Old North French, diminutive of *can* edge, corner — more at CANT] (14th century)
**1** : a segment cut off or out of something : PART, PORTION
**2** : the upward projecting rear part of a saddle

**can·to** \'kan-(ˌ)tō\ *noun, plural* **cantos** [Italian, from Latin *cantus* song, from *canere* to sing — more at CHANT] (1590)
: one of the major divisions of a long poem

**¹can·ton** \'kan-t°n, -ˌtän\ *noun* [Middle French, from Italian *cantone*, from *canto* corner, from Latin *canthus* iron tire — more at CANT] (1522)
: a small territorial division of a country: as **a** : one of the states of the Swiss confederation **b** : a division of a French arrondissement

**²canton** *noun* [Middle French, from Old Provençal, from *cant* edge, corner, from Latin *canthus*] (1572)
**1** *obsolete* : DIVISION, SECTION
**2** : the top inner quarter of a flag
**3** : the dexter chief region of a heraldic field
— **can·ton·al** \'kan-t°n-əl, kan-'tä-n°l\ *adjective*

**Can·ton·ese** \ˌkan-t°n-'ēz, -'ēs\ *noun, plural* **Cantonese** (1857)
**1** : a native or inhabitant of Canton, China
**2** : the dialect of Chinese spoken in and around Canton
**3** : a style of Chinese cooking that is typically based on mild spices
— **Cantonese** *adjective*

**can·ton flannel** \'kan-ˌtän-, -t°n-\ *noun, often* *C capitalized* [*Canton*, China] (circa 1879)
: FLANNEL 1c

**can·ton·ment** \kan-'tōn-mənt, -'tän- *also* -'tün-\ *noun* (1756)
**1** : usually temporary quarters for troops
**2** : a permanent military station in India

**Can·ton ware** \'kan-ˌtän-\ *noun* (circa 1902)
: ceramic ware exported from China especially during the 18th and 19th centuries by way of Canton and including blue-and-white and enameled porcelain and various ornamented stonewares

**can·tor** \'kan-tər\ *noun* [Latin, singer, from *canere* to sing] (1538)
**1** : a choir leader : PRECENTOR
**2** : a synagogue official who sings or chants liturgical music and leads the congregation in prayer
— **can·to·ri·al** \kan-'tōr-ē-əl, -'tór-\ *adjective*

**can·trip** \'kan-trəp\ *noun* [probably alteration of *caltrop*] (1719)
**1** *chiefly Scottish* : a witch's trick : SPELL
**2** *chiefly British* : HOCUS-POCUS 2

**can·tus** \'kan-təs\ *noun, plural* **can·tus** \'kan-təs, 'kan-ˌtüs\ (1590)
**1** : CANTUS FIRMUS
**2** : the principal melody or voice

**cantus fir·mus** \-'fir-məs, -'fər-\ *noun* [Medieval Latin, literally, fixed song] (1847)
**1** : the plainsong or simple Gregorian melody originally sung in unison and prescribed as to form and use by ecclesiastical tradition
**2** : a melodic theme or subject; *especially* : one for contrapuntal treatment

**canty** \'kan-tē\ *adjective* [¹*cant*] (1720)
*dialect British* : CHEERFUL, SPRIGHTLY

**Ca·nuck** \kə-'nək *sometimes* -'nùk\ *noun* [origin unknown] (1835)
: a Canadian and especially a French Canadian

**¹can·vas** *also* **can·vass** \'kan-vəs\ *noun* [Middle English *canevas*, from Old North French, from (assumed) Vulgar Latin *cannabaceus* hempen, from Latin *cannabis* hemp — more at CANNABIS] (13th century)
**1** : a firm closely woven cloth usually of linen, hemp, or cotton used for clothing and formerly much used for tents and sails
**2** : a set of sails : SAIL

**3** : a piece of canvas used for a particular purpose
**4** : TENT; *also* : a group of tents
**5 a** : a piece of cloth backed or framed as a surface for a painting; *also* : the painting on such a surface **b** : the background, setting, or scope of an historical or fictional account or narrative
**6** : a coarse cloth so woven as to form regular meshes for working with the needle
**7** : the canvas-covered floor of a boxing or wrestling ring
— **can·vas·like** \-vəs-ˌlīk\ *adjective*

**²canvas** *transitive verb* **-vased** *or* **-vassed; -vas·ing** *or* **-vass·ing** (1556)
: to cover, line, or furnish with canvas

**can·vas·back** \'kan-vəs-ˌbak\ *noun* (1782)
: a North American wild duck (*Aythya valisineria*) that has a reddish brown head, black breast, and whitish body and is characterized especially by the elongate sloping profile of the bill and head

**¹can·vass** *also* **can·vas** \'kan-vəs\ (1508)
*transitive verb*
**1** *obsolete* : to toss in a canvas sheet in sport or punishment
**2 a** : to examine in detail; *specifically* : to examine (votes) officially for authenticity **b** : DISCUSS, DEBATE
**3** : to go through (a district) or go to (persons) in order to solicit orders or political support or to determine opinions or sentiments
*intransitive verb*
: to seek orders or votes : SOLICIT
— **can·vass·er** *also* **can·vas·er** *noun*

**²canvass** *also* **canvas** *noun* (circa 1611)
: the act or an instance of canvassing; *especially* : a personal solicitation of votes or survey of public opinion

**can·yon** \'kan-yən\ *noun* [American Spanish *cañón*, probably alteration of obsolete Spanish *callón*, augmentative of *calle* street, from Latin *callis* footpath] (1837)
: a deep narrow valley with steep sides and often with a stream flowing through it

**can·zo·ne** \kan-'zō-nē, känt-'sō-(ˌ)nā\ *noun, plural* **-nes** \-nēz, -(ˌ)nāz\ *or* **-ni** \-nē\ [Italian, from Latin *cantion-, cantio* song, from *canere* to sing — more at CHANT] (1589)
**1** : a medieval Italian or Provençal lyric poem
**2** : the musical setting of a canzone

**can·zo·net** \ˌkan-zə-'net\ *noun* [Italian *canzonetta*, diminutive of *canzone*] (1588)
**1** : a light usually strophic song
**2** : a part-song resembling but less elaborate than a madrigal

**caou·tchouc** \'kaù-ˌchúk, -ˌchük, -ˌchü\ *noun* [French, from obsolete Spanish *cauchuc* (now *caucho*), from Quechua *kawchu*] (1775)
: ¹RUBBER 2a

**¹cap** \'kap\ *noun, often attributive* [Middle English *cappe*, from Old English *cæppe*, from Late Latin *cappa* head covering, cloak] (before 12th century)
**1 a** : a head covering especially with a visor and no brim **b** : a distinctive head covering emblematic of a position or office: as (1) : a cardinal's biretta (2) : MORTARBOARD
**2** : a natural cover or top: as **a** : an overlying rock layer that is usually hard to penetrate **b** (1) : PILEUS (2) : CALYPTRA **c** : the top of a bird's head or a patch of distinctively colored feathers in this area
**3 a** : something that serves as a cover or protection especially for a tip, knob, or end ⟨a bottle *cap*⟩ **b** : a fitting for closing the end of a tube (as a water pipe or electric conduit) **c** *British* : CERVICAL CAP
**4** : an overlaying or covering structure

**5 :** a paper or metal container holding an explosive charge (as for a toy pistol)
**6 :** an upper limit (as on expenditures) **:** CEILING
**7 :** the symbol ∩ indicating the intersection of two sets — compare CUP 9
**8 :** a cluster of molecules or chemical groups bound to one end or a region of a cell, virus, or molecule
**— cap in hand :** in a respectful, humble, or sometimes fearful manner
**²cap** verb **capped; cap·ping** (15th century)
*transitive verb*
**1 a :** to provide or protect with a cap **b :** to give a cap to as a symbol of honor, rank, or achievement
**2 :** to form a cap over **:** CROWN ⟨the mountains were *capped* with mist —John Buchan⟩
**3 a :** to follow with something more noticeable or more significant **:** OUTDO **b :** CLIMAX
**4 :** to form a chemical cap on
*intransitive verb*
**:** to form or produce a chemical cap
**ca·pa·bil·i·ty** \ˌkā-pə-'bi-lə-tē\ *noun, plural* **-ties** (1587)
**1 :** the quality or state of being capable; *also* **:** ABILITY
**2 :** a feature or faculty capable of development **:** POTENTIALITY
**3 :** the facility or potential for an indicated use or deployment ⟨the *capability* of a metal to be fused⟩ ⟨nuclear *capability*⟩
**ca·pa·ble** \'kā-pə-bəl, *in rapid speech* 'kāp-bəl\ *adjective* [Middle French or Late Latin; Middle French *capable*, from Late Latin *capabilis*, irregular from Latin *capere* to take — more at HEAVE] (1579)
**1 :** SUSCEPTIBLE ⟨a remark *capable* of being misunderstood⟩
**2** *obsolete* **:** COMPREHENSIVE
**3 :** having attributes (as physical or mental power) required for performance or accomplishment ⟨is *capable* of intense concentration⟩
**4 :** having traits conducive to or features permitting ⟨this woman is *capable* of murder by violence —Robert Graves⟩ ⟨an outer coat of light color *capable* of reflecting solar heat —Current Biography⟩
**5 :** having legal right to own, enjoy, or perform
**6 :** having general efficiency and ability
**— ca·pa·ble·ness** \'kā-pə-bəl-nəs\ *noun*
**— ca·pa·bly** \-pə-blē\ *adverb*
**ca·pa·cious** \kə-'pā-shəs\ *adjective* [Latin *capac-, capax* capacious, capable, from Latin *capere*] (1614)
**:** containing or capable of containing a great deal
*synonym* see SPACIOUS
**— ca·pa·cious·ly** *adverb*
**— ca·pa·cious·ness** *noun*
**ca·pac·i·tance** \kə-'pa-sə-tən(t)s\ *noun* [*capacity*] (1893)
**1 a :** the property of an electric nonconductor that permits the storage of energy as a result of the separation of charge that occurs when opposite surfaces of the nonconductor are maintained at a difference of potential **b :** the measure of this property that is equal to the ratio of the charge on either surface to the potential difference between the surfaces
**2 :** a part of a circuit or network that possesses capacitance
**— ca·pac·i·tive** \-'pa-sə-tiv\ *adjective*
**— ca·pac·i·tive·ly** *adverb*
**ca·pac·i·tate** \kə-'pa-sə-ˌtāt\ *transitive verb* **-tat·ed; -tat·ing** (1657)
**1** *archaic* **:** to make capable
**2 :** to cause (sperm) to undergo capacitation
**ca·pac·i·ta·tion** \kə-ˌpa-sə-'tā-shən\ *noun* (1951)
**:** the change undergone by sperm in the female reproductive tract that enables them to penetrate and fertilize an egg
**ca·pac·i·tor** \kə-'pa-sə-tər\ *noun* (1925)

**:** a device giving capacitance and usually consisting of conducting plates or foils separated by thin layers of dielectric (as air or mica) with the plates on opposite sides of the dielectric layers oppositely charged by a source of voltage and the electrical energy of the charged system stored in the polarized dielectric
**¹ca·pac·i·ty** \kə-'pa-sə-tē, -'pas-tē\ *noun, plural* **-ties** [Middle English *capacite*, from Middle French *capacité*, from Latin *capacitat-, capacitas*, from *capac-, capax*] (15th century)
**1 :** legal competency or fitness
**2 a :** the potential or suitability for holding, storing, or accommodating **b :** the maximum amount or number that can be contained or accommodated ⟨a jug with a one-gallon *capacity*⟩ ⟨the auditorium was filled to *capacity*⟩ — see METRIC SYSTEM table, WEIGHT table
**3 a :** an individual's mental or physical ability **:** APTITUDE, SKILL **b :** the faculty or potential for treating, experiencing, or appreciating ⟨*capacity* for love⟩
**4 :** DUTY, POSITION, ROLE ⟨will be happy to serve in any *capacity*⟩
**5 :** the facility or power to produce, perform, or deploy **:** CAPABILITY ⟨a plan to double the factory's *capacity*⟩; *also* **:** maximum output ⟨industries running at three-quarter *capacity*⟩
**6 a :** CAPACITANCE **b :** the quantity of electricity that a battery can deliver under specified conditions
**²capacity** *adjective* (1897)
**:** equaling maximum capacity ⟨a *capacity* crowd⟩
**cap–a–pie** *or* **cap–à–pie** \ˌka-pə-'pē, -'pā\ *adverb* [Middle French (de) *cap a pé* from head to foot] (1523)
**:** from head to foot ⟨armed *cap-a-pie* for battle⟩
**¹ca·par·i·son** \kə-'par-ə-sən\ *noun* [Middle French *caparaçon*, from Old Spanish *caparazón*] (1579)
**1 a :** an ornamental covering for a horse **b :** decorative trappings and harness
**2 :** rich clothing **:** ADORNMENT
**²caparison** *transitive verb* (1594)
**:** to provide with or as if with a rich ornamental covering **:** ADORN
**¹cape** \'kāp\ *noun, often attributive* [Middle English *cap*, from Middle French, from Old Provençal, from Latin *caput* head — more at HEAD] (14th century)
**1 :** a point or extension of land jutting out into water as a peninsula or as a projecting point
**2** *often capitalized* **:** CAPE COD COTTAGE
**²cape** *noun* [probably from Spanish *capa* cloak, from Late Latin *cappa* head covering, cloak] (circa 1578)
**1 :** a sleeveless outer garment or part of a garment that fits closely at the neck and hangs loosely over the shoulders
**2 :** the short feathers covering the shoulders of a fowl — see DUCK illustration
**Cape buffalo** \'kāp-\ *noun* [*Cape* of Good Hope, Africa] (circa 1890)
**:** the large reddish brown to black wild buffalo (*Syncerus caffer*) of sub-Saharan Africa — called also *African buffalo*
**Cape Cod cottage** \(')kāp-'käd-\ *noun* [*Cape Cod*, Mass.] (1916)
**:** a compact rectangular dwelling of one or one-and-a-half stories usually with a central chimney and steep gable roof
**Cape gooseberry** *noun* (1833)
**:** any of several ground-cherries (especially *Physalis peruviana*) bearing edible acid berries; *also* **:** its berry
**Cape Horn·er** \ˌkāp-'hȯr-nər\ *noun* (1840)
**:** a ship that voyages around Cape Horn
**cape·let** \'kāp-lət\ *noun* (1912)
**:** a small cape usually covering the shoulders
**cap·e·lin** \'ka-p(ə-)lən\ *noun* [Canadian French *capelan*, from French, codfish, from Old Provençal, chaplain, codfish, from Medi-

eval Latin *cappellanus* chaplain — more at CHAPLAIN] (1620)
**:** a small northern sea fish (*Mallotus villosus*) related to the smelts
**Ca·pel·la** \kə-'pe-lə\ *noun* [Latin, literally, she-goat, from *caper* he-goat — more at CAPRIOLE]
**:** a star of the first magnitude in Auriga
**¹ca·per** \'kā-pər\ *noun* [back-formation from earlier *capers* (taken as a plural), from Middle English *caperis*, from Latin *capparis*, from Greek *kapparis*] (14th century)
**1 :** any of a genus (*Capparis* of the family Capparidaceae, the caper family) of low prickly shrubs of the Mediterranean region; *especially* **:** one (*C. spinosa*) cultivated for its buds
**2 :** one of the greenish flower buds or young berries of the caper pickled and used as a seasoning or garnish
**²caper** *intransitive verb* **ca·pered; ca·per·ing** \-p(ə-)riŋ\ [probably by shortening & alteration from *capriole*] (1588)
**:** to leap or prance about in a playful manner
**³caper** *noun* (1592)
**1 :** a frolicsome leap
**2 :** a capricious escapade **:** PRANK
**3 :** an illegal or questionable act; *especially* **:** THEFT
**cap·er·cail·lie** \ˌka-pər-'kā-lē, -'kāl-yē\ *or* **cap·er·cail·zie** \-'kāl-zē\ *noun, plural* **-caillie** *or* **-cailzies** *also* **-caillies** *or* **-cailzie** [Scottish Gaelic *capalcoille*, literally, horse of the woods] (1536)
**:** the largest Old World grouse (*Tetrao urogallus*)
**cape·skin** \'kāp-ˌskin\ *noun* [*Cape* of Good Hope, Africa] (1919)
**:** a light flexible leather made from sheepskins with the natural grain retained and used especially for gloves and garments
**Ca·pe·tian** \kə-'pē-shən\ *adjective* [Hugh *Capet*] (1836)
**:** of or relating to the French royal house that ruled from 987 to 1328
**— Capetian** *noun*
**cape·work** \'kāp-ˌwərk\ *noun* (1926)
**:** the art of the bullfighter in working a bull with the cape
**cap·ful** \'kap-ˌfůl\ *noun* (1873)
**:** as much as a cap will hold ⟨a *capful* of detergent⟩
**capful of wind** (1719)
**:** a sudden light breeze
**ca·pi·as** \'kā-pē-əs\ *noun* [Middle English, from Latin, literally, you should seize, from *capere* to take — more at HEAVE] (15th century)
**:** an arrest warrant
**cap·il·lar·i·ty** \ˌka-pə-'lar-ə-tē\ *noun, plural* **-ties** (1830)
**1 :** the property or state of being capillary
**2 :** the action by which the surface of a liquid where it is in contact with a solid (as in a capillary tube) is elevated or depressed depending on the relative attraction of the molecules of the liquid for each other and for those of the solid
**¹cap·il·lary** \'ka-pə-ˌler-ē, *British usually* kə-'pi-lə-rē\ *adjective* [French or Latin; French *capillaire*, from Latin *capillaris*, from *capillus* hair] (14th century)
**1 a :** resembling a hair especially in slender elongated form ⟨*capillary* leaves⟩ **b :** having a very small bore ⟨a *capillary* tube⟩
**2 :** involving, held by, or resulting from surface tension ⟨*capillary* water in the soil⟩
**3 :** of or relating to capillaries or capillarity
**²capillary** *noun, plural* **-lar·ies** (1667)
**:** a capillary tube; *especially* **:** any of the smallest blood vessels connecting arterioles with venules and forming networks throughout the body
**capillary attraction** *noun* (1813)
**:** the force of adhesion between a solid and a liquid in capillarity

**¹cap·i·tal** \'ka-pə-t⁰l, 'kap-t⁰l\ *noun* [Middle English, modification of Old North French *capitel*, from Late Latin *capitellum* small head, top of column, diminutive of Latin *capit-, caput* head — more at HEAD] (13th century)
: the uppermost member of a column or pilaster crowning the shaft and taking the weight of the entablature — see COLUMN illustration

**²capital** *adjective* [Middle English, from Latin *capitalis*, from *capit-, caput*] (14th century)
**1** *of a letter* : of or conforming to the series A, B, C, etc. rather than a, b, c, etc.
**2 a** : punishable by death ⟨a *capital* crime⟩ **b** : involving execution ⟨*capital* punishment⟩ **c** : most serious ⟨a *capital* error⟩
**3 a** : chief in importance or influence ⟨*capital* ships⟩ ⟨the *capital* importance of criticism in the work of creation itself —T. S. Eliot⟩ **b** : being the seat of government
**4** : of or relating to capital; *especially* : relating to or being assets that add to the long-term net worth of a corporation ⟨*capital* improvements⟩
**5** : EXCELLENT ⟨a *capital* book⟩

**³capital** *noun* [French or Italian; French, from Italian *capitale*, from *capitale*, adjective, chief, principal, from Latin *capitalis*] (circa 1639)
**1 a** (1) : a stock of accumulated goods especially at a specified time and in contrast to income received during a specified period; *also* : the value of these accumulated goods (2) : accumulated goods devoted to the production of other goods (3) : accumulated possessions calculated to bring in income **b** (1) : net worth (2) : CAPITAL STOCK **c** : persons holding capital **d** : ADVANTAGE, GAIN ⟨make *capital* of the situation⟩
**2** [²*capital*] **a** : a capital letter; *especially* : an initial capital letter **b** : a letter belonging to a style of alphabet modeled on the style customarily used in inscriptions
**3** [²*capital*] **a** : a city serving as a seat of government **b** : a city preeminent in some special activity ⟨the fashion *capital*⟩

**capital gain** *noun* (1921)
: the increase in value of an asset (as stock or real estate) between the time it is bought and the time it is sold

**capital goods** *noun plural* (1896)
: ³CAPITAL 1a(1), 1a(2)

**capital–intensive** *adjective* (1959)
: having a high capital cost per unit of output; *especially* : requiring greater expenditure in the form of capital than of labor

**cap·i·tal·ise** *British variant of* CAPITALIZE

**cap·i·tal·ism** \'ka-pə-t⁰l-,iz-əm, 'kap-t⁰l-, *British also* kə-'pi-t⁰l-\ *noun* (1877)
: an economic system characterized by private or corporate ownership of capital goods, by investments that are determined by private decision, and by prices, production, and the distribution of goods that are determined mainly by competition in a free market

**¹cap·i·tal·ist** \-ist\ *noun* (1792)
**1** : a person who has capital especially invested in business; *broadly* : a person of wealth : PLUTOCRAT
**2** : a person who favors capitalism

**²capitalist** *or* **cap·i·tal·is·tic** \,ka-pə-t⁰l-'is-tik, ,kap-t⁰l-, *British also* kə-,pi-t⁰l-\ *adjective* (1845)
**1** : owning capital ⟨the *capitalist* class⟩
**2 a** : practicing or advocating capitalism ⟨*capitalist* nations⟩ **b** : marked by capitalism ⟨*capitalist* period of history⟩
— **cap·i·tal·is·ti·cal·ly** \-ti-k(ə-)lē\ *adverb*

**cap·i·tal·i·za·tion** \,ka-pə-t⁰l-ə-'zā-shən, ,kap-t⁰l-, *British also* kə-,pi-t⁰l-\ *noun* (1860)
**1 a** : the act or process of capitalizing **b** : a sum resulting from a process of capitalizing **c** : the total liabilities of a business including both ownership capital and borrowed capital **d**

: the total par value or the stated value of no-par issues of authorized capital stock
**2** : the use of a capital letter in writing or printing

**cap·i·tal·ize** \'ka-pə-t⁰l-,īz, 'kap-t⁰l-, *British also* kə-'pi-t⁰l-\ *verb* **-ized; -iz·ing** (1764)
*transitive verb*
**1** : to write or print with an initial capital or in capitals
**2 a** : to convert into capital ⟨*capitalize* the company's reserve fund⟩ **b** : to treat as capital rather than as an expense
**3 a** : to compute the present value of (an income extended over a period of time) **b** : to convert (a periodic payment) into an equivalent capital sum ⟨*capitalized* annuities⟩
**4** : to supply capital for
*intransitive verb*
: to gain by turning something to advantage : PROFIT ⟨*capitalize* on an opponent's mistake⟩

**cap·i·tal·ly** \'ka-pə-t⁰l-ē, 'kap-t⁰l-\ *adverb* (1619)
**1** : in a manner involving capital punishment
**2** : in a capital manner : EXCELLENTLY

**capital stock** *noun* (1709)
**1** : the outstanding shares of a joint-stock company considered as an aggregate
**2** : CAPITALIZATION 1d
**3** : the ownership element of a corporation divided into shares and represented by certificates

**cap·i·tate** \'ka-pə-,tāt\ *adjective* [Latin *capitatus* headed, from *capit-, caput* head] (1661)
**1** : forming a head
**2** : abruptly enlarged and globose

**cap·i·ta·tion** \,ka-pə-'tā-shən\ *noun* [Late Latin *capitation-, capitatio* poll tax, from Latin *capit-, caput*] (1641)
**1** : a direct uniform tax imposed on each head or person : POLL TAX
**2** : a uniform per capita payment or fee

**cap·i·tol** \'ka-pə-t⁰l, 'kap-t⁰l\ *noun* [Latin *Capitolium*, temple of Jupiter at Rome on the Capitoline hill] (1699)
**1 a** : a building in which a state legislative body meets **b** : a group of buildings in which the functions of state government are carried out
**2** *capitalized* : the building in which the U.S. Congress meets at Washington

**Capitol Hill** *noun* [*Capitol Hill*, Washington, site of the U.S. Capitol] (1943)
: the legislative branch of the U.S. government

**Cap·i·to·line** \'ka-pə-t⁰l-,īn, *British usually* kə-'pi-tə-,līn\ *adjective* [Latin *capitolinus*, from *Capitolium*] (1667)
: of or relating to the smallest of the seven hills of ancient Rome, the temple on it, or the gods worshiped there

**ca·pit·u·lar** \kə-'pi-chə-lər\ *adjective* [Medieval Latin *capitularis*, from *capitulum*] (circa 1525)
: of or relating to an ecclesiastical chapter

**ca·pit·u·lary** \-,ler-ē\ *noun, plural* **-lar·ies** [Medieval Latin *capitulare*, literally, document divided into sections, from Late Latin *capitulum* section, chapter — more at CHAPTER] (1650)
: a civil or ecclesiastical ordinance; *also* : a collection of ordinances

**ca·pit·u·late** \kə-'pi-chə-,lāt\ *intransitive verb* **-lat·ed; -lat·ing** [Medieval Latin *capitulatus*, past participle of *capitulare* to distinguish by heads or chapters, from Late Latin *capitulum*] (1537)
**1** *archaic* : PARLEY, NEGOTIATE
**2 a** : to surrender often after negotiation of terms **b** : to cease resisting : ACQUIESCE
**synonym** see YIELD

**ca·pit·u·la·tion** \kə-,pi-chə-'lā-shən\ *noun* (1535)
**1** : a set of terms or articles constituting an agreement between governments
**2 a** : the act of surrendering or yielding **b** : the terms of surrender

**ca·pit·u·lum** \kə-'pi-chə-ləm\ *noun, plural* **-la** \-lə\ [New Latin, from Latin, small head — more at CHAPTER] (circa 1755)
**1** : a rounded protuberance of an anatomical part (as a bone)
**2** : a racemose inflorescence (as of the button-bush) with the axis shortened and dilated to form a rounded or flattened cluster of sessile flowers — see INFLORESCENCE illustration

**Cap·lets** \'ka-pləts\ *trademark*
— used for capsule-shaped medicinal tablets

**¹ca·po** \'kä-(,)pō\ *noun, plural* **capos** [short for *capotasto*, from Italian, literally, head of fingerboard] (1926)
: a movable bar attached to the fingerboard of a fretted instrument to uniformly raise the pitch of all the strings

**²ca·po** \'kä-(,)pō, 'ka-\ *noun, plural* **capos** [Italian, head, chief, from Latin *caput*] (circa 1959)
: the head of a branch of a crime syndicate

**ca·pon** \'kā-,pän, -pən\ *noun* [Middle English, from Old English *capūn*, probably from Old North French *capon*, from Latin *capon-, capo*; akin to Lithuanian *kapoti* to mince, Greek *koptein* to cut] (before 12th century)
: a castrated male chicken

**ca·po·na·ta** \,kä-pə-'nä-tə\ *noun* [Italian, from Italian dialect (Sicily) *capunata*, perhaps from *capuni* capon, from Latin *capon-, capo*] (1951)
: a relish of chopped eggplant and assorted vegetables

**ca·pote** \kə-'pōt\ *noun* [French, from *cape* cloak, from Late Latin *cappa*] (1799)
: a usually long and hooded cloak or overcoat

**cap·pel·let·ti** \,ka-pə-'le-tē\ *noun plural but singular or plural in construction* [Italian, plural of *cappelletto*, diminutive of *cappello* hat, from Medieval Latin *cappellus* cap, diminutive of Late Latin *cappa* head covering — more at CAP] (1945)
: pasta in the form of little peaked hats filled with a savory mixture

**cap·per** \'ka-pər\ *noun* (1587)
**1** : one that caps: as **a** : a device that fits caps on bottles **b** : FINALE, CLIMAX, CLINCHER
**2** : a lure or decoy especially in an illicit or questionable activity : SHILL

**cap·ping** \'ka-piŋ\ *noun* (14th century)
: something that caps

**cap·puc·ci·no** \,ka-pə-'chē-(,)nō, ,kä-pú-\ *noun* [Italian, literally, Capuchin; from the likeness of its color to that of a Capuchin's habit] (1948)
: espresso coffee mixed with frothed hot milk or cream and often flavored with cinnamon

**cap·ric acid** \'ka-prik-\ *noun* [International Scientific Vocabulary, from Latin *capr-, caper* goat; from its odor — more at CAPRIOLE] (1836)
: a fatty acid $C_{10}H_{20}O_2$ found in fats and oils and used in flavors and perfumes

**ca·pric·cio** \kə-'prē-ch(ē-,)ō\ *noun, plural* **-cios** [Italian] (1601)
**1** : FANCY, WHIMSY
**2** : CAPER, PRANK
**3** : an instrumental piece in free form usually lively in tempo and brilliant in style

**ca·price** \kə-'prēs\ *noun* [French, from Italian *capriccio* caprice, shudder, perhaps from *capo* head (from Latin *caput*) + *riccio* hedgehog, from Latin *ericius* — more at HEAD, URCHIN] (1667)
**1 a** : a sudden, impulsive, and seemingly unmotivated notion or action **b** : a sudden usually unpredictable condition, change, or series of changes ⟨the *caprices* of the weather⟩
**2** : a disposition to do things impulsively

\ə\ abut \⁰\ kitten \ər\ further \a\ ash \ā\ ace
\ä\ mop, mar \aú\ out \ch\ chin \e\ bet \ē\ easy
\g\ go \i\ hit \ī\ ice \j\ job \ŋ\ sing \ō\ go
\o\ law \oi\ boy \th\ thin \th\ the \ü\ loot \u\ foot
\y\ yet \zh\ vision    *see also* Guide to Pronunciation

**3 :** CAPRICCIO 3 ☆

**ca·pri·cious** \kə-'pri-shəs, -'prē-\ *adjective* (1601)
**:** governed or characterized by caprice **:** IMPULSIVE, UNPREDICTABLE
**synonym** see INCONSTANT
— **ca·pri·cious·ly** *adverb*
— **ca·pri·cious·ness** *noun*
**Cap·ri·corn** \'ka-pri-ˌkȯrn\ *noun* [Middle English *Capricorne*, from Latin *Capricornus* (genitive *Capricorni*), from *caper* goat + *cornu* horn — more at HORN]
**1 :** a southern zodiacal constellation between Sagittarius and Aquarius
**2 a :** the 10th sign of the zodiac in astrology — see ZODIAC table **b :** one born under the sign of Capricorn
**cap·ri·fi·ca·tion** \ˌka-prə-fə-'kā-shən\ *noun* [Latin *caprification-, caprificatio*, from *caprificare* to pollinate by caprification, from *caprificus*] (1601)
**:** artificial pollination of figs that usually bear only pistillate flowers by hanging male flowering branches of the caprifig in the trees to facilitate pollen transfer by a wasp
**cap·ri·fig** \'ka-prə-ˌfig\ *noun* [Middle English *caprifige*, part translation of Latin *caprificus*, from *capr-, caper* goat + *ficus* fig — more at FIG] (15th century)
**:** a wild fig (*Ficus carica sylvestris*) of southern Europe and Asia Minor used for caprification of the edible fig; *also* **:** its fruit
**cap·rine** \'ka-ˌprīn\ *adjective* [Latin *caprinus*, from *capr-, caper*] (15th century)
**:** of, relating to, or being a goat ⟨*caprine* serum⟩ ⟨the *caprine* family⟩
**cap·ri·ole** \'ka-prē-ˌōl\ *noun* [Middle French or Old Italian; Middle French *capriole*, from Old Italian *capriola*, from *capriolo* roebuck, from Latin *capreolus* goat, roebuck, from *capr-, caper* he-goat; akin to Old English *hæfer* goat, Greek *kapros* wild boar] (1594)
**1 :** a playful leap **:** CAPER
**2** *of a trained horse* **:** a vertical leap with a backward kick of the hind legs at the height of the leap
— **capriole** *intransitive verb*
**ca·pri pants** \kə-'prē-\ *noun plural, often C capitalized* [*Capri*, Italy] (circa 1956)
**:** close-fitting women's pants that end above the ankle — called also *capris*
**cap·rock** \'kap-ˌräk\ *noun* (1867)
**:** CAP 2a
**ca·pro·ic acid** \kə-ˌprō-ik-\ *noun* [International Scientific Vocabulary, from Latin *capr-, caper*] (circa 1847)
**:** a liquid fatty acid $C_6H_{12}O_2$ that is found as a glycerol ester in fats and oils or made synthetically and used in pharmaceuticals and flavors
**cap·ro·lac·tam** \ˌka-prō-'lak-ˌtam\ *noun* [*caproic* acid + *lactone* + *amide*] (1944)
**:** a white crystalline cyclic amide $C_6H_{11}NO$ used especially in making one type of nylon
**ca·pryl·ic acid** \kə-'pri-lik-\ *noun* [International Scientific Vocabulary *capryl*, a radical contained in it] (1845)
**:** a fatty acid $C_8H_{16}O_2$ of rancid odor occurring in fats and oils and used in perfumes
**cap·sa·i·cin** \kap-'sā-ə-sən\ *noun* [irregular from New Latin *Capsicum*] (circa 1890)
**:** a colorless irritant phenolic amide $C_{18}H_{27}NO_3$ that is found in various capsicums and that gives hot peppers their hotness
**Cap·si·an** \'kap-sē-ən\ *adjective* [French *capsien*, from Latin *Capsa* Gafsa, Tunisia] (1915)
**:** of or relating to a Paleolithic culture of northern Africa and southern Europe
**cap·si·cum** \'kap-si-kəm\ *noun* [New Latin, perhaps from Latin *capsa*] (1588)
**1 :** any of a genus (*Capsicum*) of tropical herbs and shrubs of the nightshade family widely cultivated for their many-seeded usually fleshy-walled berries — called also *pepper*

**2 :** the dried ripe fruit of some capsicums (as *C. frutescens*) used as a gastric and intestinal stimulant
**cap·sid** \'kap-səd\ *noun* [French *capside*, from Latin *capsa* case + French *-ide* ²-id] (1960)
**:** the outer protein shell of a virus particle
**cap·size** \'kap-ˌsīz, kap-'\ *verb* **cap·sized; cap·siz·ing** [perhaps from Spanish *capuzar* or Catalan *cabussar* to thrust (the head) underwater] (1788)
*transitive verb*
**:** to cause to overturn ⟨*capsize* a canoe⟩
*intransitive verb*
**:** to become upset or overturned **:** TURN OVER ⟨the canoe *capsized*⟩
**cap sleeve** *noun* (1926)
**:** a very short sleeve (as on a dress) that hangs over the edge of the shoulder without extending along the underside of the arm
**cap·stan** \'kap-stən, -ˌstan\ *noun* [Middle English, probably from Middle French *cabestant*] (14th century)
**1 :** a machine for moving or raising heavy weights that consists of a vertical drum which can be rotated and around which cable is turned
**2 :** a rotating shaft that drives tape at a constant speed in a recorder
**cap·stone** \'kap-ˌstōn\ *noun* [¹*cap*] (14th century)
**1 :** a coping stone **:** COPING
**2 :** the high point **:** crowning achievement
**cap·su·lar** \'kap-sə-lər\ *adjective* (circa 1730)
**1 :** of, relating to, or resembling a capsule
**2 :** CAPSULATED
**cap·su·lat·ed** \-ˌlā-təd\ *adjective* (1668)
**:** enclosed in a capsule
**¹cap·sule** \'kap-səl, -(ˌ)sül *also* -ˌsyü(ə)l\ *noun* [French, from Latin *capsula*, diminutive of *capsa* box — more at CASE] (circa 1693)
**1 a :** a membrane or sac enclosing a body part **b :** either of two layers of white matter in the cerebrum
**2 :** a closed receptacle containing spores or seeds: as **a :** a dry dehiscent usually many-seeded fruit composed of two or more carpels **b :** the spore case of a moss
**3 :** a shell usually of gelatin for packaging something (as a drug or vitamins); *also* **:** a usually medicinal or nutritional preparation for oral use consisting of the shell and its contents
**4 :** an often polysaccharide envelope surrounding a microorganism
**5 :** an extremely brief condensation **:** OUTLINE, SURVEY
**6 a :** a compact often sealed and detachable container or compartment **b :** a small pressurized compartment or vehicle (as for space flight or emergency escape)
**²capsule** *transitive verb* **cap·suled; cap·sul·ing** (1859)
**1 :** to equip with or enclose in a capsule
**2 :** to condense into or devise in a compact form
**³capsule** *adjective* (1938)
**1 :** extremely brief
**2 :** small and very compact
**cap·sul·ize** \'kap-sə-ˌlīz\ *transitive verb* **-ized; -iz·ing** (1945)
**:** CAPSULE
**¹cap·tain** \'kap-tən *also* 'kap-ᵊm\ *noun* [Middle English *capitane*, from Middle French *capitain*, from Late Latin *capitaneus*, adjective & noun, chief, from Latin *capit-, caput* head — more at HEAD] (14th century)
**1 a** (1) **:** a military leader **:** the commander of a unit or a body of troops (2) **:** a subordinate officer commanding under a sovereign or general (3) **:** a commissioned officer in the army, air force, or marine corps ranking above a first lieutenant and below a major **b :** a naval officer who is master or commander of a ship; *especially* **:** a commissioned officer in the navy ranking above a commander and below a commodore and in the coast guard ranking above a

commander and below a rear admiral **c :** a senior pilot who commands the crew of an airplane **d :** an officer in a police department or fire department in charge of a unit (as a precinct or company) and usually ranking above a lieutenant and below a chief
**2 :** one who leads or supervises: as **a :** a leader of a sports team or side **b :** HEADWAITER **c :** a person in charge of hotel bellhops — called also *bell captain*
**3 :** a person of importance or influence in a field ⟨*captains* of industry⟩
— **cap·tain·cy** \'kap-tən-sē\ *noun*
— **cap·tain·ship** \-ˌship\ *noun*
**²captain** *transitive verb* (1598)
**:** to be captain of **:** LEAD ⟨*captained* the football team⟩
**captain's chair** *noun* (1946)
**:** an armchair with a saddle seat and a low curved back with vertical spindles
**captain's mast** *noun* (1941)
**:** MAST 3
**cap·tan** \'kap-ˌtan\ *noun* [short for *mercaptan*] (1952)
**:** a fungicide $C_9H_8Cl_3NO_2S$ used on agricultural crops
**¹cap·tion** \'kap-shən\ *noun* [Middle English *capcioun*, from Latin *caption-, captio* act of taking, from *capere* to take — more at HEAVE] (1670)
**1 :** the part of a legal document that shows where, when, and by what authority it was taken, found, or executed
**2 a :** the heading especially of an article or document **:** TITLE **b :** the explanatory comment or designation accompanying a pictorial illustration **c :** a motion-picture subtitle
— **cap·tion·less** \-ləs\ *adjective*
**²caption** *transitive verb* **cap·tioned; cap·tion·ing** \-sh(ə-)niŋ\ (1901)
**:** to furnish with a caption
**cap·tious** \'kap-shəs\ *adjective* [Middle English *capcious*, from Middle French or Latin; Middle French *captieux*, from Latin *captiosus*, from *captio*] (14th century)
**1 :** marked by an often ill-natured inclination to stress faults and raise objections
**2 :** calculated to confuse, entrap, or entangle in argument
**synonym** see CRITICAL
— **cap·tious·ly** *adverb*
— **cap·tious·ness** *noun*
**cap·ti·vate** \'kap-tə-ˌvāt\ *transitive verb* **-vat·ed; -vat·ing** (circa 1555)
**1** *archaic* **:** SEIZE, CAPTURE
**2 :** to influence and dominate by some special charm, art, or trait and with an irresistible appeal
**synonym** see ATTRACT
— **cap·ti·va·tion** \ˌkap-tə-'vā-shən\ *noun*
— **cap·ti·va·tor** \'kap-tə-ˌvā-tər\ *noun*
**cap·tive** \'kap-tiv\ *adjective* [Middle English, from Latin *captivus*, from *captus*, past participle of *capere*] (14th century)
**1 a :** taken and held as or as if a prisoner of war **b :** kept within bounds **:** CONFINED
**2 :** held under control of another but having the appearance of independence; *especially* **:** owned or controlled by another concern and

---

☆ **SYNONYMS**

**Caprice, whim, vagary, crotchet** mean an irrational or unpredictable idea or desire. CAPRICE stresses lack of apparent motivation and suggests willfulness ⟨by sheer *caprice* she quit her job⟩. WHIM implies a fantastic, capricious turn of mind or inclination ⟨an odd antique that was bought on a *whim*⟩. VAGARY stresses the erratic, irresponsible character of the notion or desire ⟨recently he had been prone to strange *vagaries*⟩. CROTCHET implies an eccentric opinion or preference ⟨a serious scientist equally known for his bizarre *crotchets*⟩.

operated for its needs rather than for an open market ⟨a *captive* mine⟩
**3** : being such involuntarily because of a situation that makes free choice or departure difficult ⟨the airline passengers were a *captive* audience⟩
— **captive** *noun*
**cap·tiv·i·ty** \kap-'ti-və-tē\ *noun* (14th century)
**1** : the state of being captive ⟨some birds thrive in *captivity*⟩
**2** *obsolete* : a group of captives
**cap·to·pril** \'kap-tə-,pril\ *noun* [mer*captan* + *-o-* + *proline* + *-il*, alteration of *-yl*] (1978)
: an antihypertensive drug $C_9H_{15}NO_3S$ that is an ACE inhibitor
**cap·tor** \'kap-tər, -,tȯr\ *noun* [Late Latin, from Latin *capere*] (circa 1688)
: one that has captured a person or thing
¹**cap·ture** \'kap-chər, -shər\ *noun* [Middle French, from Latin *captura*, from *captus*] (circa 1542)
**1** : an act or instance of capturing: as **a** : an act of catching, winning, or gaining control by force, stratagem, or guile **b** : a move in a board game (as chess or checkers) that gains an opponent's piece **c** : the absorption by an atom, nucleus, or particle of a subatomic particle that often results in subsequent emission of radiation or in fission **d** : the act of recording in a permanent file ⟨data *capture*⟩
**2** : one that has been taken (as a prize ship)
²**capture** *transitive verb* **cap·tured; cap·tur·ing** \'kap-chə-riŋ, 'kap-shriŋ\ (1795)
**1 a** : to take captive; *also* : to gain control of especially by force ⟨*capture* a city⟩ **b** : to gain or win especially through effort ⟨*captured* 60% of the vote⟩
**2** : to emphasize, represent, or preserve (as a scene, mood, or quality) in a more or less permanent form ⟨at any such moment as a photograph might *capture* —C. E. Montague⟩
**3** : to captivate and hold the interest of
**4** : to take according to the rules of a game
**5** : to bring about the capture of (a subatomic particle)
**6** : to record in a permanent file (as in a computer)
**synonym** see CATCH
**capture the flag** *noun* (circa 1925)
: a game in which players on each of two teams seek to capture the other team's flag and return it to their side without being captured and imprisoned
**ca·puche** \kə-'püch, -'püsh\ *noun* [Middle French, from Italian *cappuccio*, from *cappa* cloak, from Late Latin] (circa 1600)
: HOOD; *especially* : the cowl of a Capuchin friar
**ca·pu·chin** \'ka-pyə-shən, -pə-, *especially for 3 also* kə-'pyü-, -'pü-\ *noun* [Middle French, from Old Italian *cappuccino*, from *cappuccio*; from his cowl] (1589)
**1** *capitalized* : a member of the Order of Friars Minor Capuchin forming since 1529 an austere branch of the first order of Saint Francis of Assisi engaged in missionary work and preaching
**2** : a hooded cloak for women
**3** : any of a genus (*Cebus*) of South American monkeys; *especially* : one (*C. capucinus*) with the hair on its crown resembling a monk's cowl
**Cap·u·let** \'ka-pyə-lət\ *noun*
: the family of Juliet in Shakespeare's *Romeo and Juliet*
**cap·y·bara** \,ka-pi-'bar-ə, -'bär-\ *noun* [Portuguese *capibara*, from Tupi] (1774)
: a tailless largely aquatic South American rodent (*Hydrochaerus hydrochaeris*) often exceeding four feet (1.2 meters) in length
**car** \'kär, *dialect also* 'kȯr, 'kyär\ *noun* [Middle English *carre*, from Anglo-French, from Latin *carra*, plural of *carrum*, alteration of *carrus*, of Celtic origin; akin to Old Irish & Middle Welsh *carr* vehicle; akin to Latin *currere* to run] (14th century)

**1** : a vehicle moving on wheels: as **a** *archaic* : CARRIAGE, CHARIOT **b** : a vehicle designed to move on rails (as of a railroad) **c** : AUTOMOBILE
**2** : the passenger compartment of an elevator
**3** : the part of an airship or balloon that carries the passengers and cargo
**ca·ra·bao** \,kar-ə-'bau̇, ,kär-\ *noun, plural* **-bao** *or* **-baos** [Philippine Spanish, from Bisayan of Samar and Leyte *karabáw*] (1900)
: WATER BUFFALO
**ca·ra·bid** \'kar-ə-bəd, kə-'ra-bəd\ *noun* [ultimately from Greek *karabos* horned beetle] (1880)
: GROUND BEETLE
**car·a·bi·neer** *or* **car·a·bi·nier** \,kar-ə-bə-'nir\ *noun* [French *carabinier*, from *carabine* carbine] (1672)
: a cavalry soldier armed with a carbine
**car·a·bi·ner** \,kar-ə-'bē-nər\ *noun* [German *Karabiner*, short for *Karabinerhaken*, literally, carabineer's hook] (1920)
: an oblong metal ring with one spring-hinged side that is used especially in mountain climbing as a connector and to hold a freely running rope
**ca·ra·bi·ne·ro** \,kar-ə-bə-'ner-(,)ō, ,kär-\ *noun, plural* **-ros** [Spanish, from *carabina* carbine, from French *carabine*] (1845)
**1** : a member of a Spanish national police force serving especially as frontier guards
**2** : a customs or coast guard officer in the Philippines
**ca·ra·bi·nie·re** \,kar-ə-bən-'yer-(,)ā, ,kär-\ *noun, plural* **-nie·ri** \-'yer-ē\ [Italian, from French *carabinier*] (1847)
: a member of the Italian national police force
**car·a·cal** \'kar-ə-,kal\ *noun* [French, from Turkish *karakulak*, from *kara* black + *kulak* ear] (1760)
: a long-legged reddish brown nocturnal cat (*Felis caracal* synonym *Lynx caracal*) of savannas in Africa and parts of Asia that has long pointed ears with a tuft of black hairs at the tip
**ca·ra·ca·ra** \,kar-ə-'kar-ə, -ə-kə-'rä\ *noun* [Spanish *caracara* & Portuguese *caracará*, from Tupi *caracará*] (1838)
: any of various large long-legged mostly South American hawks classified with the falcons
**car·a·cole** \'kar-ə-,kōl\ *noun* [French, from Spanish *caracol* snail, spiral stair, caracole] (1614)
: a half turn to right or left executed by a mounted horse
— **caracole** *verb*
**car·a·cul** \'kar-ə-kəl\ *noun* [alteration of *karakul*] (1894)
: the pelt of a karakul lamb after the curl begins to loosen
**ca·rafe** \kə-'raf, -'räf\ *noun* [French, from Italian *caraffa*, from Arabic *gharrāfah*] (1786)
: a bottle with a flaring lip used to hold beverages and especially wine
**car·am·bo·la** \,kar-əm-'bō-lə\ *noun* [Portuguese, from Marathi *karambal*, from Sanskrit *karmaphala*] (1598)
**1** : a five-angled green to yellow tropical fruit of star-shaped cross section — called also *starfruit*
**2** : a tropical tree (*Averrhoa carambola*) of the wood-sorrel family widely cultivated for carambolas
**car·a·mel** \'kär-məl; 'kar-ə-məl, -,mel\ *noun* [French, from Spanish *caramelo*, from Portuguese, icicle, caramel, from Late Latin *calamellus* small reed — more at SHAWM] (1725)
**1** : an amorphous brittle brown and somewhat bitter substance obtained by heating sugar and used as a coloring and flavoring agent

**2** : a firm chewy usually caramel-flavored candy
**car·a·mel·ise** *British variant of* CARAMELIZE
**car·a·mel·ize** \-mə-,līz\ *verb* **-ized; -iz·ing** (1842)
*transitive verb*
: to change (as sugar) into caramel
*intransitive verb*
: to change to caramel
**ca·ran·gid** \kə-'ran-jəd, -'raŋ-gəd\ *adjective* [ultimately from French *carangue* shad, horse mackerel, from Spanish *caranga*] (1931)
: of or relating to a large family (Carangidae of the order Perciformes) of marine spiny-finned bony fishes including important food fishes
— **carangid** *noun*
**car·a·pace** \'kar-ə-,pās\ *noun* [French, from Spanish *carapacho*] (1836)
**1** : a bony or chitinous case or shield covering the back or part of the back of an animal (as a turtle or crab)
**2** : a protective, decorative, or disguising shell ⟨the *carapace* of reserve he built around himself —M. M. Mintz⟩
¹**carat** *variant of* KARAT
²**car·at** \'kar-ət\ *noun* [Middle English, from Middle French, from Italian *carato*, from Arabic *qīrāṭ* bean pod, a small weight, from Greek *keration* carob bean, a small weight, from diminutive of *kerat-, keras* horn — more at HORN] (1555)
: a unit of weight for precious stones equal to 200 milligrams
¹**car·a·van** \'kar-ə-,van\ *noun* [Italian *caravana*, from Persian *kārwān*] (1588)
**1 a** : a company of travelers on a journey through desert or hostile regions; *also* : a train of pack animals **b** : a group of vehicles traveling together in a file
**2 a** : a covered wagon or motor vehicle equipped as traveling living quarters **b** *British* : TRAILER 3b
²**caravan** *intransitive verb* **-vanned** *or* **-vaned; -van·ning** *or* **-van·ing** (1885)
: to travel in a caravan
**car·a·van·ner** *or* **car·a·van·er** \-,va-nər\ *noun* (1909)
**1** : one that travels in a caravan
**2** *British* : one who goes camping with a trailer
**car·a·van·sa·ry** \,kar-ə-'van(t)-sə-rē\ *or* **car·a·van·se·rai** \-sə-,rī\ *noun, plural* **-ries** *or* **-rais** *or* **-rai** [Persian *kārwānsarāī*, from *kārwān* caravan + *sarāī* palace, inn] (1599)
**1** : an inn surrounding a court in eastern countries where caravans rest at night
**2** : HOTEL, INN
**car·a·vel** \'kar-ə-,vel, -vəl\ *noun* [Middle French *caravelle*, from Old Portuguese *caravela*] (1527)
: any of several sailing ships; *specifically* : a small 15th and 16th century ship that has broad bows, high narrow poop, and usually three masts with lateen or both square and lateen sails

**car·a·way** \'kar-ə-,wā\ *noun* [Middle English, probably from Medieval Latin *carvi*, from Arabic *karawyā*, from Greek *karon*] (13th century)

*caravel*

**1 :** a biennial usually white-flowered aromatic herb (*Carum carvi*) of the carrot family
**2 :** the pungent fruit of the caraway used in seasoning and medicine — called also *caraway seed*

**¹carb** \'kärb\ *noun* (circa 1942)
*slang :* CARBURETOR

**²carb** \'kärb\ *or* **car·bo** \'kär-(₁)bō\ *noun* (1965)
**:** CARBOHYDRATE; *also :* a high-carbohydrate food — usually used in plural

**carb-** *or* **carbo-** *combining form* [French, from *carbone*]
**:** carbon **:** carbonic **:** carbonyl **:** carboxyl ⟨*carb*ide⟩ ⟨*carbo*hydrate⟩

**car·ba·chol** \'kär-bə-ˌkól, -ˌkōl\ *noun* [*car*bamic acid + *chol*ine] (circa 1940)
**:** a synthetic parasympathomimetic drug $C_6H_{15}ClN_2O_2$ that is used in veterinary medicine and topically in glaucoma

**car·ba·mate** \'kär-bə-ˌmāt, kär-'ba-ˌmāt\ *noun* (1888)
**:** a salt or ester of carbamic acid; *especially* **:** one that is a synthetic organic insecticide

**car·bam·ic** \(ˌ)kär-'ba-mik-\ *noun* [International Scientific Vocabulary *carbam*ide + ¹*-ic*] (1869)
**:** an acid $CH_3NO_2$ known in the form of salts and esters that is a half amide of carbonic acid

**car·bam·ide** \'kär-bə-ˌmīd, kär-'ba-məd\ *noun* [International Scientific Vocabulary *carb-* + *amide*] (1865)
**:** UREA

**carb·ami·no** \ˌkär-bə-'mē-(ˌ)nō\ *adjective* (1922)
**:** relating to any carbamic acid derivative formed by reaction of carbon dioxide with an amino acid or a protein (as hemoglobin)

**carb·an·ion** \kär-'ba-ˌnī-ən, -ˌnī-ˌän\ *noun* (1933)
**:** an organic ion carrying a negative charge on a carbon atom — compare CARBONIUM ION

**car·barn** \'kär-ˌbärn\ *noun* (1880)
**:** a building that houses the cars of a street railway or the buses of a bus system

**car·ba·ryl** \'kär-bə-ˌril\ *noun* [*carb*amate + *aryl*] (1963)
**:** a carbamate insecticide $C_{12}H_{11}NO_2$ effective especially against numerous crop, forage, and forest pests

**car·ba·zole** \'kär-bə-ˌzōl\ *noun* [International Scientific Vocabulary *carb-* + *az-* + *-ole*] (1887)
**:** a crystalline slightly basic cyclic compound $C_{12}H_9N$ found in anthracene and used in making dyes

**car·bide** \'kär-ˌbīd\ *noun* [International Scientific Vocabulary] (circa 1865)
**1 :** a binary compound of carbon with a more electropositive element; *especially* **:** CALCIUM CARBIDE
**2 :** a very hard material made of carbon and one or more heavy metals

**car·bine** \'kär-ˌbēn, -ˌbīn\ *noun* [French *carabine*, from Middle French *carabin* carabineer] (1605)
**1 :** a short-barreled lightweight firearm originally used by cavalry
**2 :** a light short-barreled repeating rifle that is used as a supplementary military arm or for hunting in dense brush

**car·bi·nol** \'kär-bə-ˌnól, -ˌnōl\ *noun* [International Scientific Vocabulary, from obsolete German *Karbin* methyl, from German *karb-* carb-] (circa 1885)
**:** METHANOL; *also :* an alcohol derived from it

**car·bo·cy·clic** \ˌkär-bō-'sī-klik, -'si-\ *adjective* [International Scientific Vocabulary] (1899)
**:** being or having an organic ring composed of carbon atoms

**car·bo·hy·drase** \ˌkär-bō-'hī-ˌdrās, -bə-, -ˌdrāz\ *noun* [International Scientific Vocabulary] (1910)

**:** any of a group of enzymes (as amylase) that promote hydrolysis or synthesis of a carbohydrate (as a disaccharide)

**car·bo·hy·drate** \-ˌdrāt, -drət\ *noun* (circa 1869)
**:** any of various neutral compounds of carbon, hydrogen, and oxygen (as sugars, starches, and celluloses) most of which are formed by green plants and which constitute a major class of animal foods

**car·bol·ic** \kär-'bä-lik\ *noun* (1884)
**:** PHENOL 1

**carbolic acid** *noun* [International Scientific Vocabulary *carb-* + Latin *oleum* oil — more at OIL] (circa 1859)
**:** PHENOL 1

**car bomb** *noun* (1973)
**:** an explosive device concealed in an automobile for use as a weapon of terrorism

**car·bon** \'kär-bən\ *noun, often attributive* [French *carbone*, from Latin *carbon-, carbo* ember, charcoal] (1789)
**1 :** a nonmetallic chiefly tetravalent element found native (as in the diamond and graphite) or as a constituent of coal, petroleum, and asphalt, of limestone and other carbonates, and of organic compounds or obtained artificially in varying degrees of purity especially as carbon black, lampblack, activated carbon, charcoal, and coke — see ELEMENT table
**2 :** a carbon rod used in an arc lamp
**3 a :** a sheet of carbon paper **b :** CARBON COPY

**car·bo·na·ceous** \ˌkär-bə-'nā-shəs\ *adjective* (1791)
**1 :** rich in carbon
**2 :** relating to, containing, or composed of carbon

**¹car·bo·na·do** \ˌkär-bə-'nā-(ˌ)dō, -'nä-\ *noun, plural* **-dos** *or* **-does** [Spanish *carbonada*] (1586)
*archaic :* a piece of meat scored before grilling

**²carbonado** *transitive verb* (1599)
**1** *archaic :* to make a carbonado of
**2** *archaic :* CUT, SLASH

**³carbonado** *noun, plural* **-dos** [Portuguese, literally, carbonated] (1853)
**:** an impure opaque dark-colored fine-grained aggregate of diamond particles valuable for its superior toughness

**car·bo·nara** \ˌkär-bə-'när-ə\ *noun* [Italian dialect (*alla*) *carbonara*, literally, in the manner of a charcoal maker] (1963)
**:** a dish of hot pasta into which other ingredients (as eggs, bacon or ham, and grated cheese) have been mixed — often used as a postpositive modifier ⟨spaghetti *carbonara*⟩

**¹car·bon·ate** \'kär-bə-ˌnāt, -nət\ *noun* (1794)
**:** a salt or ester of carbonic acid

**²car·bon·ate** \-ˌnāt\ *transitive verb* **-at·ed; -at·ing** (1805)
**1 :** to convert into a carbonate
**2 :** to combine or impregnate with carbon dioxide ⟨*carbonated* beverages⟩
— **car·bon·ation** \ˌkär-bə-'nā-shən\ *noun*

**carbon black** *noun* (circa 1889)
**:** any of various colloidal black substances consisting wholly or principally of carbon obtained usually as soot and used especially in tires and as pigments

**carbon copy** *noun* (1895)
**1 :** a copy made by carbon paper
**2 :** DUPLICATE

**carbon cycle** *noun* (1912)
**1 :** the cycle of carbon in the earth's ecosystems in which carbon dioxide is fixed by photosynthetic organisms to form organic nutrients and is ultimately restored to the inorganic state by respiration and protoplasmic decay
**2 :** a cycle of thermonuclear reactions in which four hydrogen atoms synthesize into a helium atom by the catalytic action of carbon with the release of nuclear energy and which is held to be the source of most of the energy radiated by the sun and stars

**carbon dating** *noun* (1951)

**:** the determination of the age of old material (as an archaeological or paleontological specimen) by means of the content of carbon 14
— **carbon–date** \'kär-bən-'dāt\ *transitive verb*

**carbon dioxide** *noun* (1873)
**:** a heavy colorless gas $CO_2$ that does not support combustion, dissolves in water to form carbonic acid, is formed especially in animal respiration and in the decay or combustion of animal and vegetable matter, is absorbed from the air by plants in photosynthesis, and is used in the carbonation of beverages

**carbon disulfide** *noun* (1869)
**:** a colorless flammable poisonous liquid $CS_2$ used as a solvent for rubber and as an insect fumigant — called also *carbon bisulfide*

**carbon fiber** *noun* (1960)
**:** a very strong lightweight synthetic fiber made especially by carbonizing acrylic fiber at high temperatures

**carbon 14** \*see* FOURTEEN\ *noun* (1936)
**:** a heavy radioactive isotope of carbon of mass number 14 used especially in tracer studies and in dating archaeological and geological materials

**car·bon·ic** \kär-'bä-nik\ *adjective* (1791)
**:** of, relating to, or derived from carbon, carbonic acid, or carbon dioxide

**carbonic acid** *noun* (1791)
**:** a weak dibasic acid $H_2CO_3$ known only in solution that reacts with bases to form carbonates

**carbonic acid gas** *noun* (circa 1880)
**:** CARBON DIOXIDE

**carbonic an·hy·drase** \-an-'hī-ˌdrās, -ˌdrāz\ *noun* [*anhydrous* + *-ase;* from its promotion of dehydration] (1932)
**:** a zinc-containing enzyme that occurs in living tissues (as red blood cells) and aids carbon-dioxide transport from the tissues and its release from the blood in the lungs by catalyzing the reversible hydration of carbon dioxide to carbonic acid

**car·bon·if·er·ous** \ˌkär-bə-'ni-f(ə-)rəs\ *adjective* (1799)
**1 :** producing or containing carbon or coal
**2** *capitalized :* of, relating to, or being the period of the Paleozoic era between the Devonian and the Permian or the corresponding system of rocks that includes coal beds — see GEOLOGIC TIME table
— **Carboniferous** *noun*

**car·bo·ni·um ion** \kär-'bō-nē-əm-\ *noun* [*carb-* + *-onium*] (1942)
**:** an organic ion carrying a positive charge on a carbon atom — compare CARBANION

**car·bon·iza·tion** \ˌkär-bə-nə-'zā-shən\ *noun* (1804)
**:** the process of carbonizing; *especially* **:** DESTRUCTIVE DISTILLATION

**car·bon·ize** \'kär-bə-ˌnīz\ *verb* **-ized; -iz·ing** (1806)
*transitive verb*
**1 :** to convert into carbon or a carbonic residue
**2 :** CARBURIZE 1
*intransitive verb*
**:** to become carbonized **:** CHAR

**car·bon·less** \'kär-bən-ləs\ *adjective* (1850)
**1 :** being without carbon
**2 :** being or composed of paper that makes multiple copies without intervening layers of carbon paper ⟨*carbonless* forms⟩

**carbon monoxide** *noun* (1873)
**:** a colorless odorless very toxic gas CO that burns to carbon dioxide with a blue flame and is formed as a product of the incomplete combustion of carbon

**car·bon·nade** *also* **car·bo·nade** \ˌkär-bə-'näd\ *noun* [French, literally, dish of grilled meat, from Italian *carbonata*, from *carbone* charcoal, coal, from Latin *carbon-, carbo*] (1877)
**:** a beef stew cooked in beer

**carbon paper** *noun* (1895)
: a thin paper faced with a waxy pigmented coating so that when placed between two sheets of paper the pressure of writing or typing on the top sheet causes transfer of pigment to the bottom sheet

**carbon steel** *noun* (1903)
: a strong hard steel that derives its physical properties from the presence of carbon and is used in hand tools and kitchen utensils

**carbon tetrachloride** *noun* (1866)
: a colorless nonflammable toxic liquid $CCl_4$ that has an odor resembling that of chloroform and is used as a solvent and a refrigerant

**carbon 13** \-thir-'tēn, -'thir-ˌtēn\ *noun* (1939)
: an isotope of carbon of mass number 13 that constitutes about $1/70$ of natural carbon and is used as a tracer especially in spectroscopy utilizing nuclear magnetic resonance

**carbon 12** \-'twelv\ *noun* (1946)
: an isotope of carbon of mass number 12 that is the most abundant carbon isotope and is used as a standard for measurements of atomic weight

**car·bon·yl** \'kär-bə-ˌnil, -ˌnēl\ *noun* (1869)
**1** : an organic functional group —CO— occurring in aldehydes, ketones, carboxylic acids, esters, and their derivatives
**2** : a coordination complex involving the neutral radical CO ⟨chromium *carbonyl*⟩
— **car·bon·yl·ic** \ˌkär-bə-'ni-lik\ *adjective*
**car·bon·yl·a·tion** \(ˌ)kär-ˌbä-nə-'lā-shən\ *noun* (1946)
: the synthesis of a carbonyl compound especially by a reaction involving carbon monoxide

**Car·bo·run·dum** \ˌkär-bə-'rən-dəm\ *trademark*
— used for various abrasives

**carboxy-** *or* **carbox-** *combining form*
: carboxyl ⟨*carboxy*peptidase⟩

**car·box·yl** \kär-'bäk-səl\ *noun* [International Scientific Vocabulary] (1869)
: a univalent radical COOH typical of organic acids — called also *carboxyl group*
— **car·box·yl·ic** \ˌkär-(ˌ)bäk-'si-lik\ *adjective*

**car·box·yl·ase** \kär-'bäk-sə-ˌlās, -ˌlāz\ *noun* [International Scientific Vocabulary] (1911)
: an enzyme that catalyzes decarboxylation or carboxylation

**¹car·box·yl·ate** \-ˌlāt, -lət\ *noun* (1927)
: a salt or ester of a carboxylic acid

**²car·box·yl·ate** \-ˌlāt\ *transitive verb* **-at·ed; -at·ing** (circa 1928)
: to introduce carboxyl or carbon dioxide into (a compound) with formation of a carboxylic acid
— **car·box·yl·a·tion** \(ˌ)kär-ˌbäk-sə-'lā-shən\ *noun*

**carboxylic acid** *noun* (1902)
: an organic acid (as acetic acid) containing one or more carboxyl groups

**car·boxy·meth·yl·cel·lu·lose** \kär-ˌbäk-sē-ˌme-thəl-'sel-yə-ˌlōs, -ˌlōz\ *noun* (1947)
: an acid ether derivative of cellulose that in the form of its sodium salt is used as a thickening, emulsifying, and stabilizing agent and as a bulk laxative in medicine

**car·boxy·pep·ti·dase** \-'pep-tə-ˌdās, -ˌdāz\ *noun* (1937)
: an enzyme that hydrolyzes peptides and especially polypeptides by splitting off sequentially the amino acids at the end of the peptide chain which contain free carboxyl groups

**car·boy** \'kär-ˌbói\ *noun* [Persian *qarāba,* from Arabic *qarrābah* demijohn] (1753)
: a large container for liquids

**car·bun·cle** \'kär-ˌbəŋ-kəl\ *noun* [Middle English, from Old French, from Latin *carbunculus* small coal, carbuncle, diminutive of *carbon-, carbo* charcoal, ember] (13th century)
**1 a** *obsolete* : any of several red precious stones **b** : the garnet cut cabochon

**2** : a painful local purulent inflammation of the skin and deeper tissues with multiple openings for the discharge of pus and usually necrosis and sloughing of dead tissue
— **car·bun·cled** \-kəld\ *adjective*
— **car·bun·cu·lar** \kär-'bəŋ-kyə-lər\ *adjective*

**car·bu·ret·ed** \'kär-bə-ˌrā-təd, -byə-, *especially by chemists* -ˌre-təd\ *adjective* [back-formation from *carburetor*] (1972)
: equipped with a carburetor ⟨a *carbureted* engine⟩

**car·bu·re·tion** \ˌkär-bə-'rā-shən, -byə-\ *noun* [*carburet* to combine chemically with carbon, from obsolete *carburet* carbide] (1896)
: the process of mixing (as in a carburetor) the vapor of a flammable hydrocarbon (as gasoline) with air to form an explosive mixture especially for use in an internal-combustion engine

**car·bu·re·tor** \'kär-bə-ˌrā-tər, -byə-\ *noun* (1896)
: an apparatus for supplying an internal combustion engine with an explosive mixture of vaporized fuel and air

**car·bu·ret·tor** *also* **car·bu·ret·ter** \ˌkär-byə-'re-tər, 'kär-byə-ˌ\ *chiefly British variant of* CARBURETOR

**car·bu·rise** *British variant of* CARBURIZE

**car·bu·rize** \'kär-bə-ˌrīz, -byə-\ *transitive verb* **-rized; -riz·ing** [obsolete *carburet* carbide] (circa 1889)
: to combine or impregnate (as metal) with carbon
— **car·bu·ri·za·tion** \ˌkär-bə-rə-'zā-shən, -byə-\ *noun*

**car·ca·net** \'kär-kə-nət\ *noun* [Middle French *carcan*] (circa 1530)
*archaic* : an ornamental necklace, chain, collar, or headband

**car·case** \'kär-kəs\ *British variant of* CARCASS

**car·cass** \'kär-kəs\ *noun* [Middle English *carcays,* from Middle French *carcasse,* from Old French *carcois*] (14th century)
**1** : a dead body : CORPSE; *especially* : the dressed body of a meat animal
**2** : the living, material, or physical body
**3** : the decaying or worthless remains of a structure ⟨the *carcass* of an abandoned automobile⟩
**4** : the underlying structure or frame of something (as of a piece of furniture)

**carcin-** *or* **carcino-** *combining form* [Greek *karkin-, karkino-,* from *karkinos* ulcerous sore, literally, crab — more at CANCER]
: tumor : cancer ⟨*carcino*genic⟩

**car·ci·no·em·bry·on·ic antigen** \ˌkär-s°n-ō-ˌem-brē-'ä-nik-\ *noun* (1967)
: a glycoprotein present in fetal gut tissues during the first two trimesters of pregnancy and in peripheral blood of patients with some forms of cancer

**car·cin·o·gen** \kär-'si-nə-jən, 'kär-s°n-ə-ˌjen\ *noun* (1853)
: a substance or agent producing or inciting cancer
— **car·ci·no·gen·ic** \ˌkär-s°n-ō-'je-nik\ *adjective*
— **car·ci·no·ge·nic·i·ty** \-jə-'ni-sə-tē\ *noun*

**car·ci·no·gen·e·sis** \ˌkär-s°n-ō-'je-nə-sis\ *noun* (circa 1923)
: the production of cancer

**car·ci·noid** \'kär-s°n-ˌóid\ *noun* (1925)
: a benign or malignant tumor arising especially from the mucosa of the gastrointestinal tract

**car·ci·no·ma** \ˌkär-s°n-'ō-mə\ *noun, plural* **-mas** *or* **-ma·ta** \-mə-tə\ [Latin, from Greek *karkinōma* cancer, from *karkinos*] (circa 1751)
: a malignant tumor of epithelial origin
— **car·ci·no·ma·tous** \-'ō-mə-təs\ *adjective*
**car·ci·no·ma·to·sis** \-ˌō-mə-'tō-səs\ *noun* [New Latin, from Latin *carcinomat-, carcinoma*] (1903)

: a condition in which multiple carcinomas develop simultaneously usually after dissemination from a primary source

**car·ci·no·sar·co·ma** \ˌkär-s°n-ō-(ˌ)sär-'kō-mə\ *noun, plural* **-mas** *or* **-ma·ta** \-mə-tə\ (circa 1919)
: a malignant tumor combining elements of carcinoma and sarcoma

**car coat** *noun* (1958)
: a three-quarter-length overcoat

**¹card** \'kärd\ *transitive verb* (14th century)
: to cleanse, disentangle, and collect together (as fibers) by the use of cards preparatory to spinning
— **card·er** *noun*

**²card** *noun* [Middle English *carde,* from Middle French, from Late Latin *cardus* thistle, from Latin *carduus* — more at CHARD] (15th century)
**1** : an instrument or machine for carding fibers that consists usually of bent wire teeth set closely in rows in a thick piece of leather fastened to a back
**2** : an implement for raising a nap on cloth

**³card** *noun* [Middle English *carde,* modification of Middle French *carte,* probably from Old Italian *carta,* literally, leaf of paper, from Latin *charta* leaf of papyrus, from Greek *chartēs*] (15th century)
**1** : PLAYING CARD
**2** *plural but singular or plural in construction* **a** : a game played with cards **b** : card playing
**3** : something compared to a valuable playing card in one's hand
**4** : a usually clownishly amusing person : WAG
**5** : COMPASS CARD
**6 a** : a flat stiff usually small and rectangular piece of material (as paper, paperboard, or plastic) usually bearing information: as (1) : POSTCARD (2) : VISITING CARD (3) : CREDIT CARD (4) : one bearing a picture (as of a baseball player) on one side and usually statistical data on the other (5) : one on which computer information is stored (as in the form of punched holes or magnetic encoding) (6) : one bearing electronic circuit components for insertion into a larger electronic device (as a computer) **b** : PROGRAM; *especially* : a sports program **c** (1) : a wine list (2) : MENU **d** : GREETING CARD ⟨a birthday *card*⟩
— **in the cards** *also* **on the cards** : INEVITABLE

**⁴card** *transitive verb* (1884)
**1** : to place or fasten on or by means of a card
**2** : to provide with a card
**3** : to list or record on a card
**4** : SCORE
**5** : to ask for identification (as in a bar)

**car·da·mom** \'kär-də-məm, -ˌmäm\ *noun* [Latin *cardamomum,* from Greek *kardamōmon,* blend of *kardamon* peppergrass and *amōmon,* an Indian spice plant] (1553)
: the aromatic capsular fruit of an East Indian herb (*Elettaria cardamomum*) of the ginger family with seeds used as a spice or condiment and in medicine; *also* : this plant

**¹card·board** \'kärd-ˌbōrd, -ˌbord\ *noun* (1848)
: PAPERBOARD

**²cardboard** *adjective* (1893)
**1 a** : made of or as if of cardboard **b** : FLAT, TWO-DIMENSIONAL
**2** : UNREAL, STEREOTYPED ⟨a play with *cardboard* characters⟩

**card–car·ry·ing** \'kärd-ˌkar-ē-iŋ\ *adjective* [from the assumption that such a person carries an identification card] (1948)
**1** : being a full-fledged member especially of a Communist party
**2** : being strongly identified with a group (as of people with a common interest) ⟨*card-*

*carrying* members of the ecology movement
—Richard Neuhaus⟩

**card catalog** *noun* (1854)
: a catalog (as of books) in which the entries
are arranged systematically on cards

**card·hold·er** \'kärd-ˌhōl-dər\ *noun* (1909)
: one who possesses a card and especially a
credit card

**cardi-** *or* **cardio-** *combining form* [Greek
*kardi-, kardio-,* from *kardia* — more at
HEART]
: heart : cardiac : cardiac and ⟨*cardio*gram⟩
⟨*cardio*vascular⟩

**car·dia** \'kär-dē-ə\ *noun, plural* **-di·ae** \-dē-ˌē\
*or* **-dias** [New Latin, from Greek *kardia*
heart, upper orifice of the stomach] (1782)
: the opening of the esophagus into the stomach; *also* : the part of the stomach adjoining
this opening

**-cardia** *noun combining form* [New Latin,
from Greek *kardia*]
: heart action or location (of a specified type)
⟨tachy*cardia*⟩

¹**car·di·ac** \'kär-dē-ˌak\ *adjective* [Latin *car-
diacus,* from Greek *kardiakos,* from *kardia*]
(1601)
**1 a** : of, relating to, situated near, or acting on
the heart **b** : of or relating to the cardia of the
stomach
**2** : of, relating to, or affected with heart disease

²**cardiac** *noun* (circa 1929)
: a person with heart disease

**cardiac muscle** *noun* (circa 1881)
: the principal muscle tissue of the vertebrate
heart made up of striated fibers that appear to
be separated from each other under the electron microscope but that function in long-term
rhythmic contraction as if in protoplasmic
continuity

**car·di·gan** \'kär-di-gən\ *noun* [James Thomas
Brudenell, 7th Earl of *Cardigan* (died 1868)
English soldier] (1868)
: a usually collarless sweater or jacket that
opens the full length of the center front ◆

**Cardigan Welsh corgi** *noun* [*Cardigan,*
former county in Wales] (1935)
: a Welsh corgi with rounded ears, slightly
bowed forelegs, and long tail — called also
*Cardigan;* see WELSH CORGI illustration

¹**car·di·nal** \'kärd-nəl, 'kär-dᵊn-əl\ *noun* [Mid-
dle English, from Medieval Latin *cardinalis,*
from Late Latin *cardinalis,* adjective] (12th
century)
**1** : a high ecclesiastical official of the Roman
Catholic Church who ranks next below the
pope and is appointed by him to assist him as
a member of the college of cardinals
**2** : CARDINAL NUMBER — usually used in plural
**3** : a woman's short hooded cloak originally
of scarlet cloth
**4** [from its color, resembling that of the cardinal's robes] : a crested finch (*Cardinalis cardinalis*) of the eastern U.S. and adjacent Canada, the southwestern U.S., and Mexico to
Belize which has a black face and heavy red
bill in both sexes and is nearly completely red
in the male
— **car·di·nal·ship** \-ˌship\ *noun*

²**cardinal** *adjective* [Middle English, from
Late Latin *cardinalis,* from Latin, serving as a
hinge, from *cardin-, cardo* hinge] (14th century)
: of basic importance : MAIN, CHIEF, PRIMARY
**synonym** see ESSENTIAL
— **car·di·nal·ly** *adverb*

**car·di·nal·ate** \'kärd-nə-lət, 'kär-dᵊn-əl-et,
-ˌlāt\ *noun* (1645)
: the office, rank, or dignity of a cardinal

**cardinal flower** *noun* (1698)
: a North American lobelia (*Lobelia cardinalis*) that bears a spike of brilliant red flowers

**car·di·nal·i·ty** \ˌkär-dᵊn-'a-lə-tē\ *noun, plural*
**-ties** [¹*cardinal* + *-ity*] (1935)
: the number of elements in a given mathematical set

**cardinal number** *noun* (1591)
**1** : a number (as 1, 5, 15) that is used in simple counting and that indicates how many elements there are in an assemblage — see NUM-
BER table
**2** : the property that a mathematical set has in
common with all sets that can be put in one-
to-one correspondence with it

**cardinal point** *noun* (1755)
: one of the four principal compass points
north, south, east, and west

**cardinal virtue** *noun* (14th century)
**1** : one of the four classically defined natural virtues prudence, justice, temperance, or fortitude
**2** : a quality designated as a major virtue

**car·dio·gen·ic** \ˌkär-dē-ō-'je-nik\ *adjective*
(circa 1923)
: originating in the heart : caused by a cardiac
condition ⟨*cardiogenic* shock⟩

**car·dio·gram** \'kär-dē-ə-ˌgram\ *noun* [Interna-
tional Scientific Vocabulary] (1876)
: the curve or tracing made by a cardiograph

**car·dio·graph** \-ˌgraf\ *noun* [International
Scientific Vocabulary] (1870)
: an instrument that registers graphically
movements of the heart
— **car·dio·graph·ic** \ˌkär-dē-ə-'gra-fik\
*adjective*
— **car·di·og·ra·phy** \ˌkär-dē-'ä-grə-fē\
*noun*

**car·di·oid** \'kär-dē-ˌóid\ *noun* (1753)
: a heart-
shaped curve
that is traced
by a point on
the circum-
ference of a
circle rolling
completely
around an
equal fixed
circle and has
the general
equation ρ =
$a(1 + \cos\theta)$ in
polar co-
ordinates

cardioid: *ABP* fixed circle; *PCD*
first position of rolling circle;
*P* tracing point; *PM* diameter
through *P*; *P₁, P₂, P₃, P₄* various
positions of *P*; *P₁M₁, P₂M₂, P₃M₃,
P₄M₄* various positions of *PM*

**car·di·ol·o·gy** \ˌkär-dē-'ä-lə-jē\
*noun* [Inter-
national Sci-
entific Vocabulary] (1847)
: the study of the heart and its action and diseases
— **car·di·o·log·i·cal** \-dē-ə-'lä-ji-kəl\ *adjective*
— **car·di·ol·o·gist** \-dē-'ä-lə-jist\ *noun*

**car·dio·my·op·a·thy** \'kär-dē-ō-(ˌ)mī-'ä-
pə-thē\ *noun, plural* **-thies** (1961)
: a typically chronic disorder of heart muscle
that may involve hypertrophy and obstructive
damage to the heart

**car·di·op·a·thy** \ˌkär-dē-'ä-pə-thē\ *noun, plural* **-thies** (1885)
: any disease of the heart

**car·dio·pul·mo·nary** \ˌkär-dē-ō-'púl-mə-
ˌner-ē, -'pəl-\ *adjective* (circa 1881)
: of or relating to the heart and lungs

**cardiopulmonary resuscitation** *noun*
(1972)
: a procedure designed to restore normal
breathing after cardiac arrest that includes the
clearance of air passages to the lungs, mouth-
to-mouth method of artificial respiration, and
heart massage by the exertion of pressure on
the chest

**car·dio·re·spi·ra·to·ry** \ˌkär-dē-ō-'res-
p(ə-)rə-ˌtōr-ē, -ri-'spī-rə-, -ˌtór-\ *adjective* (1892)
: of or relating to the heart and the respiratory
system

**car·dio·tho·rac·ic** \-thə-'ra-sik\ *adjective*
(1962)
: relating to or involving the heart and chest

**car·dio·ton·ic** \-'tä-nik\ *adjective* (1927)
: tending to increase the tonus of heart muscle
— **cardiotonic** *noun*

**car·dio·vas·cu·lar** \-'vas-kyə-lər\ *adjective*
[International Scientific Vocabulary] (1879)
: of, relating to, or involving the heart and
blood vessels

**-cardium** *noun combining form, plural*
**-cardia** [New Latin, from Greek *kardia*]
: heart ⟨epi*cardium*⟩

**car·doon** \kär-'dün\ *noun* [French *cardon,*
from Late Latin *cardon-, cardo* thistle, from
*cardus,* from Latin *carduus* thistle, cardoon]
(1611)
: a large perennial plant (*Cynara cardunculus*)
related to the artichoke and cultivated for its
edible root and petioles; *also* : the root and
petioles

**card·play·er** \'kärd-ˌplā-ər\ *noun* (1589)
: one that plays cards

**card·sharp·er** \-ˌshär-pər\ *or* **card·sharp**
\-ˌshärp\ *noun* (1859)
: one who habitually cheats at cards

¹**care** \'ker, 'kar\ *noun* [Middle English, from
Old English *caru;* akin to Old High German
*kara* lament, Latin *garrire* to chatter] (before
12th century)
**1** : suffering of mind : GRIEF
**2 a** : a disquieted state of mixed uncertainty,
apprehension, and responsibility **b** : a cause
for such anxiety
**3 a** : painstaking or watchful attention **b**
: MAINTENANCE ⟨floor-*care* products⟩
**4** : regard coming from desire or esteem
**5** : CHARGE, SUPERVISION ⟨under a doctor's
*care*⟩
**6** : a person or thing that is an object of attention, anxiety, or solicitude ☆

²**care** *verb* **cared; car·ing** (before 12th century)
*intransitive verb*
**1 a** : to feel trouble or anxiety **b** : to feel interest or concern ⟨*care* about freedom⟩
**2** : to give care ⟨*care* for the sick⟩
**3 a** : to have a liking, fondness, or taste ⟨don't
*care* for your attitude⟩ **b** : to have an inclination ⟨would you *care* for some pie⟩
*transitive verb*
**1** : to be concerned about or to the extent of
**2** : WISH ⟨if you *care* to go⟩ ▪
— **car·er** *noun*
— **care less** : not to care — used positively and negatively with the same meaning
⟨I could *care less* what happens⟩ ⟨I couldn't
*care less* what happens⟩

¹**ca·reen** \kə-'rēn\ *verb* [from *carine* side of a
ship, from Middle French, submerged part of a

hull, from Latin *carina* hull, half of a nutshell; perhaps akin to Greek *karyon* nut] (circa 1583)
*transitive verb*
**1** : to put (a ship or boat) on a beach especially in order to clean, caulk, or repair the hull
**2** : to cause to heel over
*intransitive verb*
**1 a** : to careen a boat **b** : to undergo this process
**2** : to heel over
**3** : to sway from side to side : LURCH ⟨a *careening* carriage being pulled wildly . . . by a team of runaway horses —J. P. Getty⟩
**4** : CAREER
²**careen** *noun* (1712)
*archaic* : the act or process of careening : the state of being careened
¹**ca·reer** \kə-'rir\ *noun* [Middle French *carrière*, from Old Provençal *carriera* street, from Medieval Latin *carraria* road for vehicles, from Latin *carrus* car] (1580)
**1 a** : speed in a course ⟨ran at full *career*⟩ **b** : COURSE, PASSAGE
**2** : ENCOUNTER, CHARGE
**3** : a field for or pursuit of consecutive progressive achievement especially in public, professional, or business life ⟨Washington's *career* as a soldier⟩
**4** : a profession for which one trains and which is undertaken as a permanent calling ⟨a *career* diplomat⟩
²**career** *intransitive verb* (1647)
: to go at top speed especially in a headlong manner ⟨a car *careered* off the road⟩
**ca·reer·ism** \-ˌi-zəm\ *noun* (1933)
: the policy or practice of advancing one's career often at the cost of one's integrity
— **ca·reer·ist** \-ist\ *noun*
**care·free** \'ker-ˌfrē, 'kar-\ *adjective* (1795)
: free from care: as **a** : having no worries or troubles **b** : IRRESPONSIBLE ⟨is *carefree* with his money⟩
**care·ful** \-fəl\ *adjective* **care·ful·ler; care·ful·lest** (before 12th century)
**1** *archaic* **a** : SOLICITOUS, ANXIOUS **b** : filling with care or solicitude
**2** : exercising or taking care
**3 a** : marked by attentive concern and solicitude **b** : marked by wary caution or prudence ⟨be very *careful* with knives⟩ **c** : marked by painstaking effort to avoid errors or omissions — often used with *of* or an infinitive ⟨*careful* of money⟩ ⟨*careful* to adjust the machine⟩ ☆
— **care·ful·ly** \-f(ə-)lē\ *adverb*
— **care·ful·ness** \-fəl-nəs\ *noun*
**care·giv·er** \-ˌgi-vər\ *noun* (1975)
: a person who provides direct care (as for children or the chronically ill)
— **care·giv·ing** \-ˌgi-viŋ\ *noun*
**care·less** \-ləs\ *adjective* (before 12th century)
**1 a** : free from care : UNTROUBLED ⟨*careless* days⟩ **b** : INDIFFERENT, UNCONCERNED ⟨*careless* of the consequences⟩
**2** : not taking care
**3** : not showing or receiving care: **a** : NEGLIGENT, SLOVENLY ⟨*careless* writing⟩ **b** : UNSTUDIED, SPONTANEOUS ⟨*careless* grace⟩ **c** *obsolete* : UNVALUED, DISREGARDED
— **care·less·ly** *adverb*
— **care·less·ness** *noun*
¹**ca·ress** \kə-'res\ *noun* [French *caresse*, from Italian *carezza*, from *caro* dear, from Latin *carus* — more at CHARITY] (circa 1611)
**1** : an act or expression of kindness or affection : ENDEARMENT
**2 a** : a light stroking, rubbing, or patting **b** : KISS
— **ca·res·sive** \-'re-siv\ *adjective*
— **ca·res·sive·ly** *adverb*
²**caress** *transitive verb* (1658)
**1** : to treat with tokens of fondness, affection, or kindness : CHERISH

**2 a** : to touch or stroke lightly in a loving or endearing manner **b** : to touch or affect as if with a caress ⟨echoes that *caress* the ear⟩
— **ca·ress·er** *noun*
— **ca·ress·ing·ly** \kə-'re-siŋ-lē\ *adverb*
**car·et** \'kar-ət\ *noun* [Latin, there is lacking, from *carēre* to lack, be without] (1681)
: a wedge-shaped mark made on written or printed matter to indicate the place where something is to be inserted
**care·tak·er** \'ker-ˌtā-kər, 'kar-\ *noun* (1858)
**1** : one that gives physical or emotional care and support ⟨served as *caretaker* to the younger children⟩
**2** : one that takes care of the house or land of an owner who may be absent
**3** : one temporarily fulfilling the function of office ⟨a *caretaker* government⟩
— **care·take** \-ˌtāk\ *verb*
— **care·tak·ing** *noun*
**care·worn** \-ˌwȯrn, -ˌwȯrn\ *adjective* (1828)
: showing the effect of grief or anxiety ⟨a *careworn* face⟩
**car·fare** \'kär-ˌfar, -ˌfer\ *noun* (1870)
: passenger fare (as on a bus)
**car·ful** \'kär-ˌfu̇l\ *noun* (1832)
: as much or as many as a car will hold
**car·go** \'kär-(ˌ)gō\ *noun, plural* **cargoes** *or* **cargos** [Spanish, load, charge, from *cargar* to load, from Late Latin *carricare* — more at CHARGE] (1657)
: the goods or merchandise conveyed in a ship, airplane, or vehicle : FREIGHT
**cargo cult** *noun* (1949)
: any of various Melanesian religious groups characterized by the belief that material wealth (as money or manufactured goods) can be obtained through ritual worship
**cargo pocket** *noun* (1974)
: a large pocket usually with a flap and a pleat
**car·hop** \'kär-ˌhäp\ *noun* [*car* + *-hop* (as in *bellhop*)] (1937)
: one who serves customers at a drive-in restaurant
**Car·ib** \'kar-əb\ *noun* [New Latin *Caribes* (plural), from Spanish *Caribe*, of Cariban origin — more at CANNIBAL] (1555)
**1** : a member of an Indian people of northern South America and the Lesser Antilles
**2** : the language of the Caribs
**Car·i·ban** \'kar-ə-bən, kə-'rē-bən\ *noun* (1901)
**1** : a member of a group of Indian peoples of South America and the Lesser Antilles
**2** : the language family comprising the languages of the Cariban peoples
**Ca·rib·be·an** \ˌkar-ə-'bē-ən, kə-'ri-bē-ən\ *adjective* [New Latin *Caribbaeus*, from *Caribes*] (1777)
: of or relating to the Caribs, the eastern and southern West Indies, or the Caribbean Sea ▪
**ca·ri·be** \kə-'rē-bē\ *noun* [American Spanish, from Spanish, Carib, cannibal] (1868)
: PIRANHA
**car·i·bou** \'kar-ə-ˌbü\ *noun, plural* **-bou** *or* **-bous** [Canadian French, from Micmac *γalipu*] (circa 1665)
: a large gregarious deer (*Rangifer tarandus*) of Holarctic taiga and tundra that usually has palmate antlers in both sexes — used especially for one of the New World; called also *reindeer*

**caribou**

¹**car·i·ca·ture** \'kar-i-kə-ˌchu̇r, -ˌchər, -ˌtyu̇r, -ˌtu̇r\ *noun* [Italian *caricatura*, literally, act of loading, from

*caricare* to load, from Late Latin *carricare*] (1712)
**1** : exaggeration by means of often ludicrous distortion of parts or characteristics
**2** : a representation especially in literature or art that has the qualities of caricature

---

☆ SYNONYMS
**Care, concern, solicitude, anxiety, worry** mean a troubled or engrossed state of mind or the thing that causes this. CARE implies oppression of the mind weighed down by responsibility or disquieted by apprehension ⟨a face worn by years of *care*⟩. CONCERN implies a troubled state of mind because of personal interest, relation, or affection ⟨crimes caused *concern* in the neighborhood⟩. SOLICITUDE implies great concern and connotes either thoughtful or hovering attentiveness toward another ⟨acted with typical maternal *solicitude*⟩. ANXIETY stresses anguished uncertainty or fear of misfortune or failure ⟨plagued by *anxiety* and self-doubt⟩. WORRY suggests fretting over matters that may or may not be real cause for anxiety ⟨financial *worries*⟩.

**Careful, meticulous, scrupulous, punctilious** mean showing close attention to detail. CAREFUL implies attentiveness and cautiousness in avoiding mistakes ⟨a *careful* worker⟩. METICULOUS may imply either commendable extreme carefulness or a hampering finicky caution over small points ⟨*meticulous* scholarship⟩. SCRUPULOUS applies to what is proper or fitting or ethical ⟨*scrupulous* honesty⟩. PUNCTILIOUS implies minute, even excessive attention to fine points ⟨*punctilious* observance of ritual⟩.

---

□ USAGE
**care** The idiom *care less* is used with *could* in both positive and negative constructions. The positive form of this idiom, *could care less*, is apparently about 20 years younger than the negative, and it has been disparaged by some critics as illogical and worse. It is, as several commentators have pointed out, intended to be sarcastic. No one knows just how it started. It would be nice to account for it as a development from a form of the negative phrase in which the negative element is separated from the rest of the phrase ⟨none of these writers *could care less* about the "tradition of the novel" —Alfred Kazin⟩. But we do not have enough evidence to make a persuasive case. While *could care less* may be superior in speech for purposes of sarcasm, it is hard to be obviously sarcastic in print. Consequently most writers, faced with putting the words on paper, choose the clearer *couldn't care less*.

**Caribbean** The two pronunciations of *Caribbean* are equally popular, and one can sometimes hear the same speaker switch between the two variants in the course of a conversation. The variant \kə-'ri-bē-ən\ is the newer one and seems to have taken hold in the first half of the twentieth century. The fact that it is a newer variant in no way means that it is less acceptable than the variant \ˌkar-ə-'bē-ən\.

---

\ə\ **abut** \ᵊ\ **kitten** \ər\ **further** \a\ **ash** \ā\ **ace**
\ä\ **mop, mar** \au̇\ **out** \ch\ **chin** \e\ **bet** \ē\ **easy**
\g\ **go** \i\ **hit** \ī\ **ice** \j\ **job** \ŋ\ **sing** \ō\ **go**
\ȯ\ **law** \ȯi\ **boy** \th\ **thin** \t̲h̲\ **the** \ü\ **loot** \u̇\ **foot**
\y\ **yet** \zh\ **vision**    *see also* Guide to Pronunciation

**3 :** a distortion so gross as to seem like caricature ☆

— **car·i·ca·tur·al** \,kar-i-kə-'chúr-əl, -'chór-, -'tyúr-, -'túr-\ *adjective*

— **car·i·ca·tur·ist** \'kar-i-kə-,chúr-ist, -,chər-, -,tyúr-, -,túr-\ *noun*

²**caricature** *transitive verb* **-tured; -tur·ing** (circa 1771)
**:** to make or draw a caricature of **:** represent in caricature ⟨the portrait *caricatured* its subject⟩

**car·ies** \'kar-ēz, 'ker-\ *noun, plural* **caries** [Latin, decay; akin to Old Irish ara-*chrinn* it decays] (1634)
**:** a progressive destruction of bone or tooth; *especially* **:** tooth decay

**car·il·lon** \'kar-ə-,län, -lən; 'kar-ē-,än, -,ön; kə-'ril-yən\ *noun* [French, alteration of Old French *quarregnon,* modification of Late Latin *quaternio-, quaternio* set of four — more at QUATERNION] (1775)
**1 a :** a set of fixed chromatically tuned bells sounded by hammers controlled from a keyboard **b :** an electronic instrument imitating a carillon
**2 :** a composition for the carillon

**car·il·lon·neur** \,kar-ə-lə-'nər, ,kar-ē-ə-'nər, kə-,ril-yə-'nər\ *noun* [French, from *carillon*] (1772)
**:** a carillon player

**ca·ri·na** \kə-'rī-nə, -'rē-\ *noun, plural* **-nas** or **-nae** \-'rī-,nē, -'rē-,nī\ [New Latin, from Latin, hull, keel — more at CAREEN] (circa 1704)
**1 :** a keel-shaped anatomical part, ridge, or process
**2** *capitalized* **:** a constellation in the southern hemisphere lying near the Southern Cross

**car·i·nate** \'kar-ə-,nāt, -nət\ or **car·i·nat·ed** \-,nā-təd\ *adjective* (1781)
**:** having or shaped like a keel or carina

**ca·ri·o·ca** \,kar-ē-'ō-kə\ *noun* [Brazilian Portuguese] (1830)
**1** *capitalized* **:** a native or resident of Rio de Janeiro
**2 a :** a variation of the samba **b :** the music for this dance

**car·i·o·gen·ic** \,kar-ē-ə-'je-nik, ,ker-, -'jē-\ *adjective* [*caries* + -*o*- + -*genic*] (1930)
**:** producing or promoting the development of tooth decay ⟨*cariogenic* foods⟩

**car·i·ous** \'kar-ē-əs, 'ker-\ *adjective* [Latin *cariosus,* from *caries*] (1676)
**:** affected with caries

**car·jack·ing** \'kär-,ja-kiŋ\ *noun* [*car* + hi*jack* + -*ing*] (1991)
**:** the theft of an automobile from its driver by force or intimidation

— **car·jack·er** *noun*

**cark·ing** \'kär-kiŋ\ *adjective* [Middle English, from *carken,* literally, to load, burden, from Old North French *carquier,* from Late Latin *carricare*] (circa 1565)
**:** BURDENSOME, ANNOYING

**carl** or **carle** \'kär(-ə)l\ *noun* [Middle English, from Old English -*carl,* from Old Norse *karl* man, carl — more at CHURL] (before 12th century)
**1 :** a man of the common people
**2** *chiefly dialect* **:** CHURL, BOOR

**car·line** or **car·lin** \'kär-lən\ *noun* [Middle English *kerling,* from Old Norse, from *karl* man] (14th century)
*chiefly Scottish* **:** WOMAN; *especially* **:** an old woman

**Car·list** \'kär-list\ *noun* [Spanish *carlista,* from Don *Carlos*] (1830)
**:** a supporter of Don Carlos or his successors as having rightful title to the Spanish throne

— **Carlist** *adjective*

**car·load** \'kär-'lōd, -,lōd\ *noun* (1854)
**1 :** a load that fills a car
**2 :** the minimum number of tons required for shipping at carload rates

**carload rate** *noun* (1906)
**:** a rate for large shipments lower than that

quoted for less-than-carload lots of the same class

**Car·lo·vin·gian** \,kär-lə-'vin-j(ē-)ən\ *adjective* [French *carlovingien,* from Medieval Latin *Carlus* Charles + French -*ovingien* (as in *mérovingien* Merovingian)] (1781)
**:** CAROLINGIAN

**car·ma·gnole** \'kär-mən-,yōl\ *noun* [French] (1793)
**1 :** a lively song popular at the time of the first French Revolution
**2 :** a street dance in a meandering course to the tune of the carmagnole

**car·mak·er** \'kär-,mā-kər\ *noun* (1954)
**:** an automobile manufacturer

**Car·mel·ite** \'kär-mə-,līt\ *noun* [Middle English, from Medieval Latin *carmelita,* from *Carmel* Mount Carmel, Palestine] (15th century)
**:** a member of the Roman Catholic mendicant Order of Our Lady of Mount Carmel founded in the 12th century

— **Carmelite** *adjective*

**car·mi·na·tive** \kär-'mi-nə-tiv, 'kär-mə-,nā-\ *adjective* [French *carminatif,* from Latin *carminatus,* past participle of *carminare* to card, from (assumed) Latin *carmin-, carmen* card, from Latin *carrere* to card; akin to Lithuanian *karšti* to card] (15th century)
**:** expelling gas from the alimentary canal so as to relieve colic or griping

— **carminative** *noun*

**car·mine** \'kär-mən, -,mīn\ *noun* [French *carmin,* from Medieval Latin *carminium,* irregular from Arabic *qirmiz* kermes + Latin *minium* cinnabar] (1712)
**1 :** a rich crimson or scarlet lake made from cochineal
**2 :** a vivid red

**car·nage** \'kär-nij\ *noun* [French, from Medieval Latin *carnaticum* tribute consisting of animals or meat, from Latin *carn-, caro*] (circa 1656)
**1 :** the flesh of slain animals or men
**2 :** great and bloody slaughter (as in battle)

**car·nal** \'kär-nᵊl\ *adjective* [Middle English, from Old North French or Late Latin; Old North French, from Late Latin *carnalis,* from Latin *carn-, caro* flesh; akin to Greek *keirein* to cut — more at SHEAR] (14th century)
**1 a :** relating or given to crude bodily pleasures and appetites **b :** marked by sexuality
**2 :** BODILY, CORPOREAL
**3 a :** TEMPORAL **b :** WORLDLY ☆

— **car·nal·i·ty** \kär-'na-lə-tē\ *noun*

— **car·nal·ly** \'kär-nᵊl-ē\ *adverb*

**car·nall·ite** \'kär-nᵊl-,īt\ *noun* [German *Carnallit,* from Rudolf von *Carnall* (died 1874) German mining engineer] (1876)
**:** a mineral consisting of hydrous potassium-magnesium chloride that is an important source of potassium

**car·nas·si·al** \kär-'na-sē-əl\ *adjective* [French *carnassier* carnivorous, ultimately from Latin *carn-, caro*] (circa 1852)
**:** of, relating to, or being teeth of a carnivore often larger and longer than adjacent teeth and adapted for cutting rather than tearing

— **carnassial** *noun*

**car·na·tion** \kär-'nā-shən\ *noun* [Middle French, from Old Italian *carnagione,* from *carne* flesh, from Latin *carn-, caro*] (circa 1535)
**1 a** (1) **:** the variable color of human flesh (2) **:** a pale to grayish yellow **b :** a moderate red
**2 :** a plant of any of numerous often cultivated and usually double-flowered varieties or subspecies of an Old World pink (*Dianthus caryophyllus*) originally flesh-colored but now found in many color variations

**car·nau·ba** \kär-'nò-bə, -'naü-; ,kär-nə-'ü-bə\ *noun* [Portuguese] (1866)
**:** a fan-leaved palm (*Copernicia prunifera* synonym *C. cerifera*) of Brazil that has an edible root and yields a useful leaf fiber and carnauba wax

**carnauba wax** *noun* (1854)
**:** a hard brittle high-melting wax obtained from the leaves of the carnauba palm and used chiefly in polishes

**car·ne·lian** \kär-'nēl-yən\ *noun* [alteration of *cornelian,* from Middle English *corneline,* from Middle French, perhaps from *cornelle* cornel] (1695)
**:** a hard tough chalcedony that has a reddish color and is used in jewelry

**car·ni·tine** \'kär-nə-,tēn\ *noun* [International Scientific Vocabulary, from Latin *carn-, caro*] (circa 1922)
**:** a quaternary ammonium compound $C_7H_{15}$-$NO_3$ that is present especially in vertebrate muscle and is involved in the transfer of fatty acids across mitochondrial membranes

**car·ni·val** \'kär-nə-vəl\ *noun* [Italian *carnevale,* alteration of earlier *carnelevare,* literally, removal of meat, from *carne* flesh (from Latin *carn-, caro*) + *levare* to remove, from Latin, to raise] (1549)
**1 :** a season or festival of merrymaking before Lent
**2 a :** an instance of merrymaking, feasting, or masquerading **b :** an instance of riotous excess ⟨a *carnival* of violence⟩
**3 a :** a traveling enterprise offering amusements **b :** an organized program of entertainment or exhibition **:** FESTIVAL ⟨a winter *carnival*⟩ ◆

**car·niv·o·ra** \kär-'ni-və-rə\ *noun plural* [Latin, neuter plural of *carnivorus*] (1830)
**:** carnivorous mammals

**car·ni·vore** \'kär-nə-,vōr, -,vòr\ *noun* [ultimately from Latin *carnivorus*] (1840)
**1 :** a carnivorous animal; *especially* **:** any of an order (Carnivora) of flesh-eating mammals
**2 :** a carnivorous plant

**car·niv·o·rous** \kär-'ni-v(ə-)rəs\ *adjective* [Latin *carnivorus,* from *carn-, caro* + -*vorus* -vorous] (1592)
**1 :** subsisting or feeding on animal tissues
**2** *of a plant* **:** subsisting on nutrients obtained from the breakdown of animal protoplasm
**3 :** of or relating to the carnivores
**4 :** RAPACIOUS

— **car·niv·o·rous·ly** *adverb*

— **car·niv·o·rous·ness** *noun*

---

☆ **SYNONYMS**

**Caricature, burlesque, parody, travesty** mean a comic or grotesque imitation. CARICATURE implies ludicrous exaggeration of the characteristic features of a subject ⟨*caricatures* of politicians in cartoons⟩. BURLESQUE implies mockery especially through giving a serious or lofty subject a frivolous treatment ⟨a nightclub *burlesque* of a trial in court⟩. PARODY applies especially to treatment of a trivial or ludicrous subject in the exactly imitated style of a well-known author or work ⟨a witty *parody* of a popular novel⟩. TRAVESTY implies that the subject remains unchanged but that the style is extravagant or absurd ⟨this production is a *travesty* of the opera⟩.

**Carnal, fleshly, sensual, animal** mean having a relation to the body. CARNAL may mean only this but more often connotes derogatorily an action or manifestation of a person's lower nature ⟨a slave to *carnal* desires⟩. FLESHLY is less derogatory than CARNAL ⟨a saint who had experienced *fleshly* temptations⟩. SENSUAL may apply to any gratification of a bodily desire or pleasure but commonly implies sexual appetite with absence of the spiritual or intellectual ⟨fleshpots providing *sensual* delights⟩. ANIMAL stresses the physical as distinguished from the rational nature of a person ⟨led a mindless *animal* existence⟩.

**car·no·tite** \'kär-nə-ˌtīt\ *noun* [French, from M. A. *Carnot* (died 1920) French inspector general of mines] (1899)
**:** a mineral consisting of a hydrous radioactive vanadate of uranium and potassium that is a source of radium and uranium
**car·ny** *or* **car·ney** *or* **car·nie** \'kär-nē\ *noun, plural* **carnies** *or* **carneys** *often attributive* (circa 1933)
**1 :** CARNIVAL 3a
**2 :** a person who works with a carnival
**car·ob** \'kar-əb\ *noun* [Middle French *carobe,* from Medieval Latin *carrubium,* from Arabic *kharrūbah*] (1548)
**1 :** a Mediterranean evergreen leguminous tree (*Ceratonia siliqua*) with racemose red flowers
**2 :** a carob pod or its sweet pulp having a flavor similar to that of chocolate
**ca·roche** \kə-'rōch, -'rōsh\ *noun* [Middle French *carroche,* from Old Italian *carroccio,* augmentative of *carro* car, from Latin *carrus*] (1591)
**:** a luxurious horse-drawn carriage
**¹car·ol** \'kar-əl\ *noun* [Middle English *carole,* from Middle French, modification of Late Latin *choraula* choral song, from Latin, choral accompanist, from Greek *choraulēs,* from *choros* chorus + *aulein* to play a reed instrument, from *aulos,* a reed instrument — more at ALVEOLUS] (14th century)
**1 :** an old round dance with singing
**2 :** a song of joy or mirth ⟨the *carol* of a bird —Lord Byron⟩
**3 :** a popular song or ballad of religious joy ◆
**²carol** *verb* **-oled** *or* **-olled; -ol·ing** *or* **-ol·ling** (14th century)
*intransitive verb*
**1 :** to sing especially in a joyful manner
**2 :** to sing carols; *specifically* **:** to go about outdoors in a group singing Christmas carols
*transitive verb*
**1 :** to praise in or as if in song
**2 :** to sing especially in a cheerful manner **:** WARBLE
— **car·ol·er** *or* **car·ol·ler** \-ə-lər\ *noun*
**Car·o·line** \'kar-ə-ˌlīn, -lən\ *or* **Car·o·le·an** \ˌkar-ə-'lē-ən\ *adjective* [New Latin *carolinus,* from Medieval Latin *Carolus* Charles] (1652)
**:** of or relating to Charles — used especially with reference to Charles I and Charles II of England
**Car·o·lin·gi·an** \ˌkar-ə-'lin-j(ē-)ən\ *adjective* [French *carolingien,* from Medieval Latin *Karolingi* Carolingians, from *Karolus* Charlemagne + *-ingi* (as in *Merovingi* Merovingians)] (1881)
**:** of or relating to a Frankish dynasty dating from about A.D. 613 and including among its members the rulers of France from 751 to 987, of Germany from 752 to 911, and of Italy from 774 to 961
— **Carolingian** *noun*
**¹car·om** \'kar-əm\ *noun* [by shortening & alteration from obsolete *carambole,* from Spanish *carambola*] (1779)
**1 a :** a shot in billiards in which the cue ball strikes each of two object balls **b :** a shot in pool in which an object ball strikes another ball before falling into a pocket — compare COMBINATION SHOT
**2 :** a rebounding especially at an angle
**²carom** *intransitive verb* (1860)
**1 :** to strike and rebound **:** GLANCE ⟨the car *caromed* off a tree⟩
**2 :** to make a carom
**3 :** to proceed by or as if by caroms
**car·o·tene** \'kar-ə-ˌtēn\ *noun* [International Scientific Vocabulary, from Late Latin *carota* carrot] (1861)
**:** any of several orange or red crystalline hydrocarbon pigments $C_{40}H_{56}$ that occur in the chromoplasts of plants and in the fatty tissues of plant-eating animals and are convertible to vitamin A
**ca·rot·en·oid** *also* **ca·rot·in·oid** \kə-'rä-t³n-ˌoid\ *noun* (1911)

**:** any of various usually yellow to red pigments (as carotenes) found widely in plants and animals and characterized chemically by a long aliphatic polyene chain composed of eight isoprene units
— **carotenoid** *adjective*
**ca·rot·id** \kə-'rä-təd\ *adjective* [French or Greek; French *carotide,* from Greek *karōtides* carotid arteries, from *karoun* to stupefy; akin to Greek *kara* head — more at CEREBRAL] (1543)
**:** of, relating to, or being the chief artery or pair of arteries that pass up the neck and supply the head
— **carotid** *noun*
**carotid body** *noun* (1940)
**:** a small body of vascular tissue that adjoins the carotid sinus, functions as a chemoreceptor sensitive to change in the oxygen content of blood, and mediates reflex changes in respiratory activity
**carotid sinus** *noun* (circa 1923)
**:** a small but richly innervated arterial enlargement that is located near the point in the neck where either carotid artery divides to form its main branches and that functions in the regulation of heart rate and blood pressure
**ca·rous·al** \kə-'rau-zəl\ *noun* (1765)
**:** CAROUSE 2
**¹ca·rouse** \kə-'rauz\ *noun* [Middle French *carrousse,* from *carous,* adverb, all out (in *boire carous* to empty the cup), from German *gar aus*] (1559)
**1** *archaic* **:** a large draft of liquor **:** TOAST
**2 :** a drunken revel
**²carouse** *verb* **ca·roused; ca·rous·ing** (1567)
*intransitive verb*
**1 :** to drink liquor deeply or freely
**2 :** to take part in a carouse **:** engage in dissolute behavior
*transitive verb*
*obsolete* **:** to drink up **:** QUAFF
— **ca·rous·er** *noun*
**car·ou·sel** \ˌkar-ə-'sel *also* -'zel; 'kar-ə-ˌ\ *noun* [French *carrousel,* from Italian *carosello*] (1650)
**1 :** a tournament or exhibition in which horsemen execute evolutions
**2 a :** MERRY-GO-ROUND **b :** a circular conveyer ⟨the luggage *carousel* at the airport⟩ **c :** a revolving case used for storage or display
**¹carp** \'kärp\ *intransitive verb* [Middle English, of Scandinavian origin; akin to Icelandic *karpa* to dispute] (14th century)
**:** to find fault or complain querulously
— **carp·er** *noun*
**²carp** *noun* (1904)
**:** COMPLAINT
**³carp** *noun, plural* **carp** *or* **carps** [Middle English *carpe,* from Middle French, from Late Latin *carpa,* probably of Germanic origin; akin to Old High German *karpfo* carp] (15th century)
**1 :** a large variable Asian soft-finned freshwater cyprinid fish (*Cyprinus carpio*) of sluggish waters that is often raised for food and has been widely introduced into U.S. waters; *also* **:** any of various related fishes
**2 :** a fish (as the European sea bream) resembling a carp
**carp-** *or* **carpo-** *combining form* [French & New Latin, from Greek *karp-, karpo-,* from *karpos* — more at HARVEST]
**:** fruit ⟨*carpo*gonium⟩
**-carp** *noun combining form* [New Latin *-carpium,* from Greek *-karpion,* from *karpos*]
**:** part of a fruit ⟨meso*carp*⟩ **:** fruit ⟨schizo*carp*⟩
**car·pac·cio** \kär-'pä-ch(ē-)ō\ *noun* [Vittore *Carpaccio;* from the prominent use of red in his painting] (1969)
**:** thinly sliced raw meat or fish served with a sauce — often used as a postpositive modifier ⟨beef *carpaccio*⟩
**¹car·pal** \'kär-pəl\ *adjective* [New Latin *carpalis,* from *carpus*] (1743)
**:** relating to the carpus

**²carpal** *noun* (1855)
**:** a carpal element or bone
**carpal tunnel syndrome** *noun* (1954)
**:** a condition caused by compression of a nerve where it passes through the wrist into the hand and characterized especially by weakness, pain, and disturbances of sensation in the hand
**car park** *noun* (1926)
*chiefly British* **:** PARKING LOT
**car·pe di·em** \ˌkär-pe-'dē-ˌem, -'dī-, -əm\ *noun* [Latin, literally, pluck the day] (1817)
**:** the enjoyment of the pleasures of the moment without concern for the future
**car·pel** \'kär-pəl\ *noun* [New Latin *carpellum,* from Greek *karpos* fruit] (1835)
**:** one of the ovule-bearing structures in an angiosperm that comprises the innermost whorl of a flower — compare PISTIL
— **car·pel·lary** \-pə-ˌler-ē\ *adjective*
— **car·pel·late** \-ˌlāt, -lət\ *adjective*
**¹car·pen·ter** \'kär-pən-tər, 'kärp-³m-tər\ *noun* [Middle English, from Old North French *carpentier,* from Latin *carpentarius* carriage maker, from *carpentum* carriage, of Celtic origin; akin to Old Irish *carpat* chariot, *carr* vehicle — more at CAR] (14th century)
**:** a worker who builds or repairs wooden structures or their structural parts

---

◇ WORD HISTORY

**carnival** In Roman Catholic countries, Lent has traditionally been a period of abstinence from meat, and the days immediately before Lent a time of unrestrained indulgence and merrymaking that ended on the eve of Ash Wednesday. A pattern common to a number of European languages was to apply the name for the very beginning of Lent, the end of meat-eating, to the preceding festive period. In Italian dialects, the word for this period was a compound formed from descendants of Latin *carn-* "meat" and any of several verbs marking removal or cessation. Examples of such compounds are Tuscan *carnasciale,* ultimately from Latin *carn-* plus *laxare* "to let go," and, in the dialect of the area around Rome, *carnevale,* ultimately from Latin *carn-* plus *levare* "to raise, remove." The splendor of pre-Lenten festivities held in Rome during the Renaissance led to the adoption of *carnevale* into other languages of Europe in the 16th century, including French and English.

**carol** In medieval England and France, the word *carole* referred to a courtly dance that could be either processional or circular, one in which the musical accompaniment was provided by the dancers' own singing. The original choreography of such dances has not survived, nor are there any extant musical or literary texts from the 14th century or earlier that are explicitly given this name. It appears, though, that the leader of the dance sang verses to which the other dancers responded with a refrain. In any event, the Middle English word *carole* is applied in the 15th century to a kind of popular song with a refrain that both begins the song and is repeated after each stanza. Because these songs were often about events of the Nativity, the word *carol* has become closely associated with the Christmas season. Now it may refer not only to traditional compositions of medieval date but also to comparatively modern stanzaic hymns such as "Joy to the World" or "Hark the Herald Angels Sing."

---

\ə\ **abut** \³\ **kitten** \ər\ **further** \a\ **ash** \ā\ **ace**
\ä\ **mop, mar** \au\ **out** \ch\ **chin** \e\ **bet** \ē\ **easy**
\g\ **go** \i\ **hit** \ī\ **ice** \j\ **job** \ŋ\ **sing** \ō\ **go**
\ȯ\ **law** \ȯi\ **boy** \th\ **thin** \th\ **the** \ü\ **loot** \u̇\ **foot**
\y\ **yet** \zh\ **vision** *see also* Guide to Pronunciation

**²car·pen·ter** *verb* **-tered; -ter·ing** \-t(ə-)riŋ\ (circa 1815)
*intransitive verb*
**:** to follow the trade of a carpenter ⟨*carpentered* when he was young⟩
*transitive verb*
**1 :** to make by or as if by carpentry
**2 :** to put together often in a mechanical manner ⟨*carpentered* many television scripts⟩

**carpenter ant** *noun* (1883)
**:** an ant (especially genus *Camponotus*) that gnaws galleries especially in dead or decayed wood

**carpenter bee** *noun* (1838)
**:** any of various solitary bees (genera *Xylocopa* and *Ceratina*) that nest in wood

**car·pen·try** \-trē\ *noun* (14th century)
**1 :** the art or trade of a carpenter; *specifically* **:** the art of shaping and assembling structural woodwork
**2 :** timberwork constructed by a carpenter
**3 :** the form or manner of putting together the parts (as of a literary or musical composition)

**car·pet** \'kär-pət\ *noun* [Middle English, from Middle French *carpite*, from Old Italian *carpita*, from *carpire* to pluck, modification of Latin *carpere* to pluck — more at HARVEST] (15th century)
**1 :** a heavy often tufted fabric used as a floor covering; *also* **:** a floor covering made of this fabric
**2 :** a surface resembling or suggesting a carpet
— **carpet** *transitive verb*
— **on the carpet :** before an authority for censure or reproof

**¹car·pet·bag** \-,bag\ *noun* (1830)
**:** a traveler's bag made of carpet and widely used in the U.S. in the 19th century

**²carpetbag** *or* **car·pet·bag·ging** \-,ba-giŋ\ *adjective* (1870)
**:** of, relating to, or characteristic of carpetbaggers ⟨a *carpetbag* government⟩

**car·pet·bag·ger** \-,ba-gər\ *noun* [from their carrying all their belongings in carpetbags] (1868)
**1 :** a Northerner in the South after the American Civil War usually seeking private gain under the reconstruction governments
**2 :** OUTSIDER; *especially* **:** a nonresident or new resident who meddles in politics
— **car·pet·bag·gery** \-,ba-g(ə-)rē\ *noun*

**carpetbag steak** *noun* (1958)
**:** a thick piece of steak in which a pocket is cut and stuffed (as with oysters)

**carpet beetle** *noun* (1889)
**:** any of several small dermestid beetles (genera *Anthrenus* and *Attagenus*) whose larvae are destructive especially to woolen goods

**carpet bombing** *noun* (1944)
**:** the dropping of large numbers of bombs so as to cause uniform devastation over a given area
— **carpet bomb** *verb*

**car·pet·ing** \'kär-pə-tiŋ\ *noun* (1758)
**:** material for carpets; *also* **:** CARPETS

**car·pet·weed** \'kär-pət-,wēd\ *noun* (1784)
**:** a North American mat-forming weed (*Mollugo verticillata* of the family Aizoaceae, the carpetweed family)

**-carpic** *adjective combining form* [probably from New Latin *-carpicus*, from Greek *karpos* fruit]
**:** -CARPOUS ⟨mono*carpic*⟩

**carp·ing** \'kär-piŋ\ *adjective* (1581)
**:** marked by or inclined to querulous and often perverse criticism
**synonym** see CRITICAL
— **carp·ing·ly** \-piŋ-lē\ *adverb*

**car·po·go·ni·um** \,kär-pə-'gō-nē-əm\ *noun*, *plural* **-nia** \-nē-ə\ [New Latin] (1882)
**:** the flask-shaped egg-bearing portion of the female reproductive branch in some thallophytes (as red algae)
— **car·po·go·ni·al** \-nē-əl\ *adjective*

**car·pool** \'kär-,pü(ə)l\ *intransitive verb* (1962)
**:** to participate in a car pool
— **car·pool·er** *noun*

**car pool** *noun* (1942)
**:** an arrangement in which a group of people commute together by car; *also* **:** the group entering into such an arrangement

**car·po·phore** \'kär-pə-,fōr, -,fòr\ *noun* [probably from New Latin *carpophorum*, from *carp-* + *-phorum* -phore] (circa 1859)
**1 :** the stalk of a fungal fruiting body; *also* **:** the entire fruiting body
**2 :** a slender prolongation of a floral axis from which the carpels are suspended

**car·port** \'kär-,pōrt, -,pòrt\ *noun* (1939)
**:** an open-sided automobile shelter by the side of a building

**car·po·spore** \'kär-pə-,spōr, -,spòr\ *noun* (1881)
**:** a diploid spore of a red alga

**-carpous** *adjective combining form* [New Latin *-carpus*, from Greek *-karpos*, from *karpos* fruit — more at HARVEST]
**:** having (such) fruit or (so many) fruits ⟨syn*carpous*⟩
— **-carpy** *noun combining form*

**car·pus** \'kär-pəs\ *noun*, *plural* **car·pi** \-,pī, -,(,)pē\ [New Latin, from Greek *karpos* — more at WHARF] (1679)
**1 :** WRIST 1
**2 :** the bones of the wrist

**carr** \'kä(r)\ *noun* [Middle English *ker*, of Scandinavian origin; akin to Old Norse *kjarr* underbrush] (14th century)
*chiefly British* **:** ¹FEN

**car·rack** \'kar-ək, -ik\ *noun* [Middle English *carrake*, from Middle French *caraque*, from Old Spanish *carraca*, from Arabic *qarāqīr*, plural of *qurqūr* merchant ship] (14th century)
**:** a beamy sailing ship especially of the 15th and 16th centuries

**car·ra·geen** *also* **car·ra·gheen** \'kar-ə-,gēn\ *noun* [*Carragheen*, near Waterford, Ireland] (1829)
**1 :** IRISH MOSS 2
**2 :** CARRAGEENAN

**car·ra·geen·an** *or* **car·ra·geen·in** \,kar-ə-'gē-nən\ *noun* [*carrageen* + ³-*an* or ¹-*in*] (circa 1889)
**:** a colloid extracted from various red algae and especially Irish moss and used especially as a stabilizing or thickening agent

**car·re·four** \,kar-ə-'fùr\ *noun* [Middle French, from Late Latin *quadrifurcum*, neuter of *quadrifurcus* having four forks, from Latin *quadri-* + *furca* fork] (15th century)
**1 :** CROSSROADS
**2 :** SQUARE, PLAZA ⟨the farmers . . . preferred the open *carrefour* for their transactions —Thomas Hardy⟩

**car·rel** \'kar-əl\ *noun* [alteration of Middle English *caroll*, from Medieval Latin *carola*, perhaps from *carola* round dance, something circular, from Late Latin *choraula* choral song — more at CAROL] (1593)
**:** a table that is often partitioned or enclosed and is used for individual study especially in a library

**car·riage** \'kar-ij\ *noun* [Middle English *cariage*, from Old North French, from *carier* to transport in a vehicle — more at CARRY] (14th century)
**1 :** the act of carrying
**2 a** *archaic* **:** DEPORTMENT **b :** manner of bearing the body **:** POSTURE
**3** *archaic* **:** MANAGEMENT
**4** *chiefly British* **:** the price or expense of carrying
**5** *obsolete* **:** BURDEN, LOAD
**6 a :** a wheeled vehicle; *especially* **:** a horse-drawn vehicle designed for private use and comfort **b** *British* **:** a railway passenger coach
**7 :** a wheeled support carrying a burden
**8** *obsolete* **:** IMPORT, SENSE
**9** *obsolete* **:** a hanger for a sword
**10 :** a movable part of a machine for supporting some other movable object or part ⟨a typewriter *carriage*⟩
**synonym** see BEARING

**carriage trade** *noun* (circa 1909)
**:** trade from well-to-do or upper-class people; *also* **:** well-to-do people

**car·riage·way** \'kar-ij-,wā\ *noun* (1800)
*British* **:** a road used by vehicular traffic
**:** HIGHWAY

**car·rick bend** \'kar-ik-\ *noun* [probably from obsolete English *carrick* carrack, from Middle English *carrake, carryk*] (1819)
**:** a knot used to join the ends of two large ropes — see KNOT illustration

**car·ri·er** \'kar-ē-ər\ *noun* (14th century)
**1 :** one that carries **:** BEARER, MESSENGER
**2 a :** an individual or organization engaged in transporting passengers or goods for hire **b :** a transportation line carrying mail between post offices **c :** a postal employee who delivers or collects mail **d :** one that delivers newspapers **e :** an entity (as a hole or an electron) capable of carrying an electric charge
**3 a :** a container for carrying **b :** a device or machine that carries **:** CONVEYER
**4 :** AIRCRAFT CARRIER
**5 a :** a bearer and transmitter of a causative agent of an infectious disease; *especially* **:** one who carries the causative agent of a disease (as typhoid fever) systemically but is immune to it **b :** an individual (as one heterozygous for a recessive) having a specified gene that is not expressed or only weakly expressed in its phenotype
**6 a :** a usually inactive accessory substance **:** VEHICLE ⟨a *carrier* for a drug or an insecticide⟩ **b :** a substance (as a catalyst) by whose agency some element or group is transferred from one compound to another
**7 a :** an electromagnetic wave or alternating current whose modulations are used as signals in radio, telephonic, or telegraphic transmission **b :** a telecommunication company
**8 :** an organization acting as an insurer

**carrier pigeon** *noun* (1647)
**1 :** a pigeon used to carry messages; *especially* **:** HOMING PIGEON
**2 :** any of a breed of large long-bodied show pigeons

**car·ri·on** \'kar-ē-ən\ *noun* [Middle English *caroine*, from Anglo-French, from (assumed) Vulgar Latin *caronia*, irregular from Latin *carn-, caro* flesh — more at CARNAL] (14th century)
**:** dead and putrefying flesh; *also* **:** flesh unfit for food

**carrion crow** *noun* (1528)
**:** a uniformly black crow (*Corvus corone corone*) occurring in much of western Europe

**car·ron·ade** \,kar-ə-'nād\ *noun* [*Carron*, Scotland] (1779)
**:** a short-barreled gun of the late 18th and 19th centuries that fired large shot at short range and was used especially on warships

**car·rot** \'kar-ət\ *noun* [Middle French *carotte*, from Late Latin *carota*, from Greek *karōton*] (1533)
**1 :** a biennial herb (*Daucus carota* of the family Umbelliferae, the carrot family) with a usually orange spindle-shaped edible root; *also* **:** its root
**2 :** a reward or advantage offered especially as an inducement

**car·rot-and-stick** \,kar-ət-ᵊn-'stik\ *adjective* [from the traditional alternatives of driving a donkey on by either holding out a carrot or whipping it with a stick] (1951)
**:** characterized by the use of both reward and punishment to induce cooperation ⟨*carrot-and-stick* foreign policy⟩

**car·rot·top** \'kar-ə(t)-,täp\ *noun* (circa 1902)
**:** REDHEAD 1
— **car·rot·topped** \-,täpt\ *adjective*

**car·roty** \'kar-ə-tē\ *adjective* (1696)
**:** resembling carrots in color ⟨*carroty* hair⟩

**car·rou·sel** *variant of* CAROUSEL

**¹car·ry** \'kar-ē, 'ker-\ *verb* **car·ried; car·ry·ing** [Middle English *carien*, from Old North French *carier* to transport in a vehicle, from

*car* vehicle, from Latin *carrus* — more at CAR] (14th century)
*transitive verb*
**1** : to move while supporting : TRANSPORT ⟨her legs refused to *carry* her further —Ellen Glasgow⟩
**2** : to convey by direct communication ⟨*carry* tales about a friend⟩
**3** *chiefly dialect* : CONDUCT, ESCORT
**4** : to influence by mental or emotional appeal : SWAY
**5** : to get possession or control of : CAPTURE ⟨*carried* off the prize⟩
**6** : to transfer from one place (as a column) to another ⟨*carry* a number in adding⟩
**7** : to contain and direct the course of ⟨the drain *carries* sewage⟩
**8 a** : to wear or have on one's person **b** : to bear upon or within one ⟨is *carrying* an unborn child⟩
**9 a** : to have or bear especially as a mark, attribute, or property ⟨*carry* a scar⟩ **b** : IMPLY, INVOLVE ⟨the crime *carried* a heavy penalty⟩
**10** : to hold or comport (as one's person) in a specified manner
**11** : to sustain the weight or burden of ⟨pillars *carry* an arch⟩
**12** : to bear as a crop
**13** : to sing with reasonable correctness of pitch ⟨*carry* a tune⟩
**14 a** : to keep in stock for sale **b** : to provide sustenance for ⟨land *carrying* 10 head of cattle⟩ **c** : to have or maintain on a list or record ⟨*carry* a person on a payroll⟩
**15** : to be chiefly or solely responsible for the success, effectiveness, or continuation of ⟨a player capable of *carrying* a team⟩
**16** : to prolong in space, time, or degree ⟨*carry* a principle too far⟩
**17 a** : to gain victory for; *especially* : to secure the adoption or passage of **b** : to win a majority of votes in (as a legislative body or a state)
**18** : to present for public consumption ⟨newspapers *carry* weather reports⟩ ⟨channel 9 will *carry* the game⟩
**19 a** : to bear the charges of holding or having (as stocks or merchandise) from one time to another **b** : to keep on one's books as a debtor ⟨a merchant *carries* a customer⟩
**20** : to hold to and follow after (as a scent)
**21** : to hoist and maintain (a sail) in use
**22** : to pass over (as a hazard) at a single stroke in golf ⟨*carry* a bunker⟩
**23** : to propel and control (a puck or ball) along a playing surface
*intransitive verb*
**1** : to act as a bearer
**2 a** : to reach or penetrate to a distance ⟨voices *carry* well⟩ ⟨fly balls don't *carry* well in cold air⟩ **b** : to convey itself to a reader or audience
**3** : to undergo or admit of carriage in a specified way
**4** *of a hunting dog* : to keep and follow the scent
**5** : to win adoption ⟨the motion *carried* by a vote of 71–25⟩
— **carry a torch** *or* **carry the torch 1** : CRUSADE **2** : to be in love especially without reciprocation : cherish a longing or devotion ⟨still *carrying a torch* for a former lover⟩
— **carry the ball** : to perform or assume the chief role : bear the major portion of work or responsibility
— **carry the day** : WIN, PREVAIL
**²carry** *noun, plural* **car·ries** (1858)
**1** : carrying power; *especially* : the range of a gun or projectile or of a struck or thrown ball
**2 a** : PORTAGE **b** : the act or method of carrying ⟨fireman's *carry*⟩ **c** : the act of rushing with the ball in football ⟨averaged four yards per *carry*⟩
**3** : the position assumed by a color-bearer with the flag or guidon held in position for marching

**4** : a quantity that is transferred in addition from one number place to the adjacent one of higher place value
**car·ry·all** \'kar-ē-ˌȯl, 'ker-\ *noun* (1714)
**1** [by folk etymology from French *carriole*, from Old Provençal *carriola*, ultimately from Latin *carrus* car] **a** : a light covered carriage for four or more persons **b** : a passenger automobile used as a small bus
**2** [¹*carry* + ³*all*] : a capacious bag or carrying case
**carry away** *transitive verb* (1570)
**1** : to arouse to a high and often excessive degree of emotion or enthusiasm
**2** : CARRY OFF 1
**car·ry·back** \'kar-ē-ˌbak, 'ker-\ *noun* (1942) : a loss sustained or a portion of a credit not used in a given period that may be deducted from taxable income of a prior period
**car·ry·cot** \-ˌkät\ *noun* (1943)
*British* : a portable bed for an infant
**car·ry·for·ward** \'kar-ē-'for-wərd, 'ker-, -ˌfȯr-, *Southern also* -'fär-, -ˌfär\ *noun* (1898) : CARRYOVER
**carrying capacity** *noun* (1921) : the population (as of deer) that an area will support without undergoing deterioration
**carrying charge** *noun* (1914)
**1** : expense incident to ownership or use of property
**2** : a charge added to the price of merchandise sold on the installment plan
**car·ry·ing-on** \ˌkar-ē-iŋ-'ȯn, ˌker-, -'än\ *noun, plural* **carryings-on** (1663) : foolish, excited, or improper behavior; *also* : an instance of such behavior
**carry off** *transitive verb* (circa 1680)
**1** : to cause the death of ⟨the plague *carried off* thousands⟩
**2** : to perform or manage successfully : BRING OFF ⟨tried to look suave but couldn't *carry* it *off*⟩
**¹car·ry-on** \'kar-ē-ˌȯn, 'ker-, -ˌän\ *noun* (1890)
**1** *British* : CARRYING-ON
**2** : a piece of luggage suitable for being carried aboard an airplane by a passenger
**²carry-on** *adjective* (1967) : carried or suitable for being carried aboard ⟨*carry-on* baggage⟩
**carry on** (1644)
*transitive verb* : to continue doing, pursuing, or operating ⟨*carry on* research⟩ ⟨*carried on* the business⟩
*intransitive verb*
**1** : to behave or speak in a foolish, excited, or improper manner ⟨embarrassed by the way he *carries on*⟩
**2** : to continue especially in spite of hindrance or discouragement
**car·ry·out** \'kar-ē-ˌaut, 'ker-\ *noun* (1964)
**1** : prepared food packaged to be consumed away from its place of sale
**2** : an establishment selling carryout
— **carryout** *adjective*
**carry out** *transitive verb* (1605)
**1** : to put into execution ⟨*carry out* a plan⟩
**2** : to bring to a successful issue : COMPLETE, ACCOMPLISH ⟨you will be paid when you have *carried out* the assignment⟩
**3** : to continue to an end or stopping point
**car·ry·over** \'kar-ē-ˌō-vər, 'ker-\ *noun* (1894)
**1** : the act or process of carrying over
**2** : something retained or carried over
**carry over** (1745)
*transitive verb*
**1 a** : to transfer (an amount) to the next column, page, or book relating to the same account **b** : to hold over (as goods) for another time or season
**2** : to deduct (a loss or an unused credit) from taxable income of a later period
*intransitive verb* : to persist from one stage or sphere of activity to another
**carry through** (1605)
*transitive verb*

: CARRY OUT
*intransitive verb*
: PERSIST, SURVIVE ⟨feelings that *carry through* to the present⟩
**car·sick** \'kär-ˌsik\ *adjective* (1908) : affected with motion sickness especially in an automobile
— **car sickness** *noun*
**¹cart** \'kärt\ *noun* [Middle English, probably from Old Norse *kartr;* akin to Old English *cræt* cart] (13th century)
**1** : a heavy usually horse-drawn 2-wheeled vehicle used for farming or transporting freight
**2** : a lightweight 2-wheeled vehicle drawn by a horse, pony, or dog
**3** : a small wheeled vehicle
**²cart** *transitive verb* (14th century)
**1** : to carry or convey in or as if in a cart ⟨*cart* the kids to and from school —L. S. Gannett⟩
**2** : to take or drag away without ceremony or by force — usually used with *off* ⟨they *carted* him off to jail⟩
— **cart·er** *noun*
**cart·age** \'kär-tij\ *noun* (15th century) : the action of or rate charged for carting
**carte blanche** \'kärt-'blä[n]sh, -'blänch\ *noun, plural* **cartes blanches** \'kärt(s)-\ [French, literally, blank document] (1754) : full discretionary power ⟨was given *carte blanche* to furnish the house⟩
**carte du jour** \ˌkärt-də-'zhur\ *noun, plural* **cartes du jour** \ˌkärt(s)-\ [French, literally, card of the day] (1936) : MENU
**car·tel** \kär-'tel\ *noun* [French, letter of defiance, from Old Italian *cartello,* literally, placard, from *carta* leaf of paper — more at CARD] (1692)
**1** : a written agreement between belligerent nations
**2** : a combination of independent commercial or industrial enterprises designed to limit competition or fix prices
**3** : a combination of political groups for common action ◆

\ə\ **abut** \ᵊ\ **kitten** \ər\ **further** \a\ **ash** \ā\ **ace**
\ä\ **mop, mar** \au̇\ **out** \ch\ **chin** \e\ **bet** \ē\ **easy**
\g\ **go** \i\ **hit** \ī\ **ice** \j\ **job** \ŋ\ **sing** \ō\ **go**
\ȯ\ **law** \ȯi\ **boy** \th\ **thin** \t͟h\ **the** \ü\ **loot** \u̇\ **foot**
\y\ **yet** \zh\ **vision** *see also* Guide to Pronunciation

**car·tel·ise** British variant of CARTELIZE

**car·tel·ize** \'kär-tə-,līz\ transitive verb **-ized; -iz·ing** (1915)
: to bring under the control of a cartel
— **car·tel·i·za·tion** \,kär-tə-lə-'zā-shən\ noun

**Car·te·sian** \kär-'tē-zhən\ adjective [New Latin cartesianus, from Cartesius Descartes] (1656)
: of or relating to René Descartes or his philosophy ◆
— **Cartesian** noun
— **Car·te·sian·ism** \-zhə-,ni-zəm\ noun

**Cartesian coordinate** noun (circa 1888)
**1 :** either of two coordinates that locate a point on a plane and measure its distance from either of two intersecting straight-line axes along a line parallel to the other axis
**2 :** any of three coordinates that locate a point in space and measure its distance from any of three intersecting coordinate planes measured parallel to that one of three straight-line axes that is the intersection of the other two planes

**Cartesian plane** noun (1960)
: a plane whose points are labeled with Cartesian coordinates

**Cartesian product** noun (1958)
: a set that is constructed from two given sets and comprises all pairs of elements such that the first element of the pair is from the first set and the second is from the second set

**Car·thu·sian** \kär-'thü-zhən, -'thyü-\ noun [Medieval Latin Cartusiensis, from Cartusia Chartreuse, motherhouse of the Carthusian order, near Grenoble, France] (1526)
: a member of an ascetic contemplative religious order founded by Saint Bruno in 1084
— **Carthusian** adjective

**car·ti·lage** \'kär-t°l-ij, 'kärt-lij\ noun [Latin cartilagin-, cartilago] (15th century)
**1 :** a usually translucent somewhat elastic tissue that composes most of the skeleton of vertebrate embryos and except for a small number of structures (as some joints, respiratory passages, and the external ear) is replaced by bone during ossification in the higher vertebrates
**2 :** a part or structure composed of cartilage

**car·ti·lag·i·nous** \,kär-tə-'la-jə-nəs\ adjective (14th century)
: composed of, relating to, or resembling cartilage

**cartilaginous fish** noun (1695)
: any of a class (Chondrichthyes) of fishes (as a shark, ray, or chimaera) having the skeleton wholly or largely composed of cartilage — compare BONY FISH, JAWLESS FISH

**cart·load** \'kärt-,lōd, -,lŏd\ noun (14th century)
: as much as a cart will hold

**car·tog·ra·pher** \kär-'tä-grə-fər\ noun (circa 1847)
: one that makes maps

**car·tog·ra·phy** \-fē\ noun [French cartographie, from carte card, map + -graphie -graphy — more at CARD] (circa 1847)
: the science or art of making maps
— **car·to·graph·ic** \,kär-tə-'gra-fik\ also **car·to·graph·i·cal** \-fi-kəl\ adjective
— **car·to·graph·i·cal·ly** \-fi-k(ə-)lē\ adverb

**¹car·ton** \'kär-t°n\ noun [French, from Italian cartone pasteboard] (circa 1859)
: a box or container usually made of paperboard and often of corrugated paperboard

**²carton** (1921)
transitive verb
: to pack or enclose in a carton
intransitive verb
: to shape cartons from paperboard sheets

**car·toon** \kär-'tün\ noun, often attributive [Italian cartone pasteboard, cartoon, augmentative of carta leaf of paper — more at CARD] (1671)

**1 :** a preparatory design, drawing, or painting (as for a fresco)
**2 a :** a drawing intended as satire, caricature, or humor ⟨a political cartoon⟩ **b :** COMIC STRIP
**3 :** ANIMATED CARTOON
**4 :** a ludicrously simplistic, unrealistic, or one-dimensional portrayal or version ⟨the film's villain is an entertaining cartoon⟩
— **cartoon** verb
— **car·toon·ing** noun
— **car·toon·ish** \-'tü-nish\ adjective
— **car·toon·ish·ly** adverb
— **car·toon·ist** \-'tü-nist\ noun
— **car·toon·like** \-'tün-,līk\ adjective
— **car·toony** \-'tü-nē\ adjective

**car·top** \'kär-,täp\ adjective (1946)
: suitable in size and weight for carrying on top of an automobile ⟨a cartop fishing boat⟩
— **car·top·per** \-,tä-pər\ noun

**car·touche** also **car·touch** \kär-'tüsh\ noun [French cartouche, from Italian cartoccio, from carta] (1611)
**1 :** a gun cartridge with a paper case
**2 :** an ornate or ornamental frame
**3 :** an oval or oblong figure (as on ancient Egyptian monuments) enclosing a sovereign's name

**car·tridge** \'kär-trij, dialect 'ka-trij\ noun [alteration of earlier cartage, modification of Middle French cartouche] (1579)
: a case or container that holds a substance, device, or material which is difficult, troublesome, or awkward to handle and that usually can be easily changed: as **a :** a tube (as of metal) containing a complete charge for a firearm and usually an initiating device (as a primer) **b :** a case containing an explosive charge for blasting **c :** an often cylindrical container for insertion into a larger mechanism or apparatus **d :** CASSETTE 2 **e :** a small case that contains a phonograph needle and transducer and is attached to a tonearm **f :** a case containing a reel of magnetic tape arranged for insertion into a recorder or player **g :** a removable case containing a magnetic tape or one or more disks and used as a computer storage medium **h :** a case for holding printed circuit chips containing a computer program ⟨a video-game cartridge⟩

**cartridge belt** noun (1874)
**1 :** a belt having a series of loops for holding cartridges
**2 :** a belt worn around the waist and designed for carrying various attachable equipment (as a cartridge case, canteen, or compass)

**car·tu·lary** \'kär-chə-,ler-ē\ noun, plural **-lar·ies** [Medieval Latin chartularium, from chartula charter — more at CHARTER] (1541)
: a collection of charters; especially : a book holding copies of the charters and title deeds of an estate

**¹cart·wheel** \'kärt-,hwēl, -,wēl\ noun (1855)
**1 :** a large coin (as a silver dollar)
**2 :** a lateral handspring with arms and legs extended

**²cartwheel** intransitive verb (1917)
: to move like a turning wheel; specifically : to perform cartwheels
— **cart·wheel·er** noun

**car·un·cle** \'kar-,əŋ-kəl, kə-'rəŋ-\ noun [obsolete French caruncule, from Latin caruncula little piece of flesh, diminutive of caro flesh — more at CARNAL] (1615)
**1 :** a naked fleshy outgrowth (as a bird's wattle)
**2 :** an outgrowth on a seed adjacent to the micropyle

**car·va·crol** \'kär-və-,król, -,krōl\ noun [International Scientific Vocabulary, from New Latin carvi (specific epithet of Carum carvi caraway) + Latin acr-, acer sharp — more at CARAWAY, EDGE] (1854)
: a liquid phenol $C_{10}H_{14}O$ found in essential oils of various mints (as thyme) and used as a fungicide and disinfectant

**carve** \'kärv\ verb **carved; carv·ing** [Middle English kerven, from Old English ceorfan; akin to Old High German kerban to notch, Greek graphein to scratch, write] (before 12th century)
transitive verb
**1 :** to cut with care or precision ⟨carved fretwork⟩
**2 :** to make or get by or as if by cutting — often used with out ⟨carve out a career⟩
**3 :** to cut into pieces or slices ⟨carved the turkey⟩
intransitive verb
**1 :** to cut up and serve meat
**2 :** to work as a sculptor or engraver
— **carv·er** noun

**car·vel–built** \'kär-vəl-,bilt, -,vel-\ adjective [probably from Dutch karveel-, from karveel caravel, from Middle French carvelle] (1798)
: built with the planks meeting flush at the seams

**carv·en** \'kär-vən\ adjective (14th century)
: wrought or ornamented by carving

**carv·ing** \'kär-viŋ\ noun (13th century)
**1 :** the act or art of one who carves
**2 :** a carved object, design, or figure

**car wash** noun (1956)
: an area or structure equipped with facilities for washing automobiles

**cary-** or **caryo-** — see KARY-

**cary·at·id** \,kar-ē-'a-təd, 'kar-ē-ə-,tid\ noun, plural **-ids** or **-i·des** \,kar-ē-'a-tə-,dēz\ [Latin caryatides, plural, from Greek karyatides priestesses of Artemis at Caryae, caryatids, from Karyai Caryae in Laconia] (1563)
: a draped female figure supporting an entablature

caryatid

**cary·op·sis** \,kar-ē-'äp-səs\ noun, plural **-op·ses** \-,sēz\ also **-si·des** \-sə-,dēz\ [New Latin] (1830)
: a small one-seeded dry indehiscent fruit (as of Indian corn or wheat) in which the fruit and seed fuse in a single grain

**ca·sa** \'kä-sə\ noun [Spanish & Italian, from Latin, cottage] (1844)
chiefly Southwest : DWELLING

**ca·sa·ba** \kə-'sä-bə\ noun [Kasaba (now Turgutlu), Turkey] (1889)
: any of several winter melons with yellow rind and sweet flesh

**Ca·sa·no·va** \,ka-zə-'nō-və, ,ka-sə-\ noun [Giacomo Girolamo Casanova] (1888)
**:** LOVER; especially : a man who is a promiscuous and unscrupulous lover

**Cas·bah** \'kaz-,bä, 'käz-\ noun [French, from Arabic dialect qaṣbah] (1944)
**1 :** a North African castle or fortress
**2 :** the native section of a North African city

**cas·ca·bel** \'kas-kə-,bel\ noun [Spanish, literally, small bell] (1639)
**1 :** a projection behind the breech of a muzzle-loading cannon

---

◇ WORD HISTORY

**Cartesian** That the derivative adjective for the French philosopher and mathematician René Descartes should be Cartesian might seem puzzling at first. The explanation lies in the fact that Descartes lived and wrote in the 17th century, when Latin was the international language of science and letters. Descartes' name was Latinized as Renatus Cartesius, and so Cartesian became the word for things relating to him and his work.

**2 :** a small hollow perforated spherical bell enclosing a loose pellet

**¹cas·cade** \(ˌ)kas-'kād\ *noun* [French, from Italian *cascata,* from *cascare* to fall, from (assumed) Vulgar Latin *casicare,* from Latin *casus* fall] (1641)
**1 :** a steep usually small fall of water; *especially* **:** one of a series
**2 a :** something arranged or occurring in a series or in a succession of stages so that each stage derives from or acts upon the product of the preceding ⟨blood clotting involves a biochemical *cascade*⟩ **b :** a fall of material (as lace) that hangs in a zigzag line
**3 :** something falling or rushing forth in quantity ⟨a *cascade* of sound⟩ ⟨a *cascade* of events⟩

**²cascade** *verb* **cas·cad·ed; cas·cad·ing** (1702)
*intransitive verb*
**:** to fall, pour, or rush in or as if in a cascade
*transitive verb*
**1 :** to cause to fall like a cascade
**2 :** to connect in a cascade arrangement

**cas·cara** \ka-'skar-ə\ *noun* [Spanish *cáscara* husk, bark, probably from *cascar* to crack, break, from (assumed) Vulgar Latin *quassicare* to shake, from Latin *quassare* — more at QUASH] (1879)
**1 :** CASCARA BUCKTHORN
**2 :** CASCARA SAGRADA

**cascara buckthorn** *noun* (circa 1900)
**:** a buckthorn (*Rhamnus purshiana*) of the Pacific coast of the U.S. yielding cascara sagrada

**cascara sa·gra·da** \-sə-'grä-də\ *noun* [American Spanish *cáscara sagrada,* literally, sacred bark] (1885)
**:** the dried bark of cascara buckthorn used as a laxative

**cas·ca·ril·la** \ˌkas-kə-'ri-lə, -'rē-ə\ *noun* [Spanish, diminutive of *cáscara*] (1686)
**:** the aromatic bark of a West Indian shrub (*Croton eluteria*) of the spurge family used for making incense and as a tonic; *also* **:** this shrub

**¹case** \'kās\ *noun* [Middle English *cas,* from Old French, from Latin *casus* fall, chance, from *cadere* to fall — more at CHANCE] (13th century)
**1 a :** a set of circumstances or conditions ⟨is the statement true in all three *cases*⟩ **b** (1) **:** a situation requiring investigation or action (as by the police) (2) **:** the object of investigation or consideration
**2 :** CONDITION; *specifically* **:** condition of body or mind
**3** [Middle English *cas,* from Middle French, from Latin *casus,* translation of Greek *ptōsis,* literally, fall] **a :** an inflectional form of a noun, pronoun, or adjective indicating its grammatical relation to other words **b :** such a relation whether indicated by inflection or not
**4 :** what actually exists or happens **:** FACT
**5 a :** a suit or action in law or equity **b** (1) **:** the evidence supporting a conclusion or judgment (2) **:** ARGUMENT; *especially* **:** a convincing argument
**6 a :** an instance of disease or injury; *also* **:** PATIENT **b :** an instance that directs attention to a situation or exhibits it in action **:** EXAMPLE **c :** a peculiar person **:** CHARACTER
**7 :** oneself considered as an object of harassment ⟨get off my *case*⟩
**synonym** see INSTANCE
**— in any case :** without regard to or in spite of other considerations **:** whatever else is done or is the case ⟨war is inevitable *in any case*⟩ ⟨*in any case* the report will be made public next month⟩
**— in case :** as a precaution ⟨took an umbrella, just *in case*⟩
**— in case of :** in the event of ⟨*in case of* trouble, yell⟩

**²case** *noun* [Middle English *cas,* from Old North French *casse,* from Latin *capsa* chest, case, probably from *capere* to take — more at HEAVE] (14th century)
**1 a :** a box or receptacle for holding something **b :** a box together with its contents **c :** SET; *specifically* **:** PAIR
**2 a :** an outer covering or housing ⟨a pastry *case*⟩ **b :** a tube into which the components of a round of ammunition are loaded
**3 :** a divided tray for holding printing type
**4 :** the frame of a door or window **:** CASING

**³case** *transitive verb* **cased; cas·ing** (1575)
**1 :** to enclose in or cover with or as if with a case **:** ENCASE
**2 :** to line (as a well) with supporting material (as metal pipe)
**3 :** to inspect or study especially with intent to rob

**ca·se·ation** \ˌkā-sē-'ā-shən\ *noun* [Latin *caseus* cheese] (1866)
**:** necrosis with conversion of damaged tissue into a soft cheesy substance
**— ca·se·ate** \'kā-sē-ˌāt\ *intransitive verb*

**case·bear·er** \'kās-ˌbar-ər, -ˌber-\ *noun* (circa 1889)
**:** an insect larva that forms a protective case (as of silk)

**case·book** \-ˌbu̇k\ *noun* (1762)
**1 :** a book containing records of illustrative cases that is used for reference and instruction (as in law or medicine)
**2 :** a compilation of primary and secondary documents relating to a central topic together with scholarly comment, exercises, and study aids that is designed to serve as a sourcebook for short papers (as in a writing course) or as a point of departure for a research paper

**cased glass** \'kāst-\ *noun* (1849)
**:** glass consisting of two or more fused layers of different colors often decorated by cutting so that the inner layers show through — called also *case glass*

**case goods** *noun plural* (1922)
**1 :** furniture (as bureaus or bookcases) that provides interior storage space; *also* **:** dining-room and bedroom furniture sold as sets
**2 :** products often sold by the case

**case-hard·en** \'kās-ˌhär-d°n\ *transitive verb* (1677)
**1 :** to harden (a ferrous alloy) so that the surface layer is harder than the interior
**2 :** to make callous or insensible
**— case-hard·ened** *adjective*

**case history** *noun* (1894)
**:** a record of history, environment, and relevant details of a case especially for use in analysis or illustration

**ca·sein** \'kā-ˌsēn, kā-'\ *noun* [probably from French *caséine,* from Latin *caseus*] (1841)
**:** a phosphoprotein of milk: as **a :** one that is precipitated from milk by heating with an acid or by the action of lactic acid in souring and is used in making paints and adhesives **b :** one that is produced when milk is curdled by rennet, is the chief constituent of cheese, and is used in making plastics

**ca·sein·ate** \kā-'sē-ˌnāt, 'kā-si-ˌnāt\ *noun* (1904)
**:** a compound of casein with a metal (as calcium or sodium)

**case in point** (1965)
**:** an illustrative, relevant, or pertinent case

**case knife** *noun* (1704)
**1 :** SHEATH KNIFE
**2 :** a table knife

**case law** *noun* (1861)
**:** law established by judicial decision in cases

**case·load** \'kās-ˌlōd\ *noun* (1938)
**:** the number of cases handled (as by a court or clinic) usually in a particular period

**case·mate** \'kās-ˌmāt\ *noun* [Middle French, from Old Italian *casamatta*] (1575)
**:** a fortified position or chamber or an armored enclosure on a warship from which guns are fired through embrasures

**case·ment** \'kās-mənt\ *noun* [Middle English, hollow molding, probably from Old North French *encassement* frame, from *encasser* to enchase, frame, from *en-* + *casse*] (15th century)
**:** a window sash that opens on hinges at the side; *also* **:** a window with such a sash

**ca·se·ous** \'kā-sē-əs\ *adjective* [Latin *caseus* cheese] (1661)
**:** marked by caseation; *also* **:** CHEESY

**ca·sern** *or* **ca·serne** \kə-'zərn\ *noun* [French *caserne*] (1696)
**:** a military barracks in a garrison town

**case study** *noun* (1875)
**1 :** an intensive analysis of an individual unit (as a person or community) stressing developmental factors in relation to environment
**2 :** CASE HISTORY

**case system** *noun* (circa 1889)
**:** a system of teaching law in which instruction is chiefly on the basis of leading or selected cases as primary authorities instead of from textbooks

**case·work** \'kās-ˌwərk\ *noun* (1886)
**:** social work involving direct consideration of the problems, needs, and adjustments of the individual case (as a person or family)
**— case·work·er** \-ˌwər-kər\ *noun*

**¹cash** \'kash\ *noun* [modification of Middle French or Old Italian; Middle French *casse* money box, from Old Italian *cassa,* from Latin *capsa* chest — more at CASE] (1596)
**1 :** ready money
**2 :** money or its equivalent (as a check) paid for goods or services at the time of purchase or delivery
**— cash·less** \-ləs\ *adjective*

**²cash** *adjective* (1622)
**:** being a method of accounting that includes as income only what has been received in cash and as expenses only those paid in cash

**³cash** *transitive verb* (1811)
**1 :** to pay or obtain cash for ⟨*cash* a check⟩
**2 :** to lead and win a bridge trick with (a card that is the highest remaining card of its suit)
**— cash·able** \'ka-shə-bəl\ *adjective*

**⁴cash** *noun, plural* **cash** [Portuguese *caixa,* from Tamil *kācu,* a small copper coin, from Sanskrit *karṣa,* a weight of gold or silver] (1598)
**1 :** any of various coins of small value in China and southern India; *especially* **:** a Chinese coin with a square hole in the center
**2 :** a unit of value equivalent to one cash

**¹cash-and-car·ry** \ˌka-shᵊn-'kar-ē, -'ker-\ *adjective* (1917)
**:** sold or provided for cash and usually without delivery service

**²cash-and-carry** *noun* (1921)
**:** the policy of selling on a cash-and-carry basis

**cash bar** *noun* (1968)
**:** a bar (as at a reception) at which drinks are sold — compare OPEN BAR

**cash·book** \'kash-ˌbu̇k\ *noun* (1622)
**:** a book in which record is kept of all cash receipts and disbursements

**cash cow** *noun* (1979)
**:** a consistently profitable business, property, or product whose profits are used to finance a company's investments in other areas

**cash crop** *noun* (1868)
**:** a readily salable crop (as cotton or tobacco) produced or gathered primarily for market

**cash discount** *noun* (1917)
**:** a discount granted in consideration of immediate payment or payment within a prescribed time

**cash·ew** \'ka-(ˌ)shü, kə-'shü\ *noun* [Portuguese *acajú, cajú,* from Tupi *acajú*] (1598)

\ə\ **abut** \ᵊ\ **kitten** \ər\ **further** \a\ **ash** \ā\ **ace**
\ä\ **mop, mar** \au̇\ **out** \ch\ **chin** \e\ **bet** \ē\ **easy**
\g\ **go** \i\ **hit** \ī\ **ice** \j\ **job** \ŋ\ **sing** \ō\ **go**
\ȯ\ **law** \ȯi\ **boy** \th\ **thin** \tẖ\ **the** \ü\ **loot** \u̇\ **foot**
\y\ **yet** \zh\ **vision** *see also* Guide to Pronunciation

: a tropical American tree (*Anacardium occidentale* of the family Anacardiaceae, the cashew family) grown for a phenolic oil and the edible kernel of its nut and for a gum from its stem; *also* : CASHEW NUT

**cashew nut** *noun* (1796)
: the kidney-shaped kernel of the fruit of the cashew that is edible when roasted

**cash flow** *noun* (1954)
**1** : a measure of an organization's liquidity that usually consists of net income after taxes plus noncash charges (as depreciation) against income
**2** : a flow of cash; *especially* : one that provides liquidity

¹**ca·shier** \ka-'shir, kə-\ *transitive verb* [Dutch *casseren,* from Middle French *casser* to discharge, annul — more at QUASH] (1592)
**1** : to dismiss from service; *especially* : to dismiss dishonorably
**2** : REJECT, DISCARD

²**cash·ier** \(,)ka-'shir\ *noun* [Dutch or Middle French; Dutch *kassier,* from Middle French *cassier,* from *casse* money box] (1596)
: one that has charge of money: as **a** : a high officer in a bank or trust company responsible for moneys received and expended **b** : one who collects and records payments

**cashier's check** *noun* (1867)
: a check drawn by a bank on its own funds and signed by the cashier

**cash in** (1888)
*transitive verb*
: to obtain cash for ⟨*cashed in* the bonds⟩
*intransitive verb*
**1 a** : to retire from a gambling game **b** : to settle accounts and withdraw from an involvement (as a business deal)
**2** : to obtain advantage or financial profit — often used with *on* ⟨*cash in* on a best-seller⟩

**cash·mere** \'kazh-,mir, 'kash-\ *noun* [*Cashmere* (Kashmir)] (1684)
**1** : fine wool from the undercoat of the cashmere goat; *also* : a yarn of this wool
**2** : a soft twilled fabric made originally from cashmere

**cashmere goat** *noun* (circa 1890)
: an Indian goat raised especially for its undercoat of fine soft wool that constitutes the cashmere wool of commerce

**cash register** *noun* (1879)
: a business machine that usually has a money drawer, indicates the amount of each sale, and records the amount of money received and often automatically makes change

**cas·ing** \'kā-siŋ\ *noun* (1791)
**1** : something that encases : material for encasing: as **a** : an enclosing frame especially around a door or window opening **b** : a metal pipe used to case a well **c** : ⁴TIRE 2 **d** : a membranous case for processed meat
**2** : a space formed between two parallel lines of stitching through at least two layers of cloth into which something (as a rod or string) may be inserted

**ca·si·no** \kə-'sē-(,)nō\ *noun, plural* **-nos** [Italian, from *casa* house, from Latin, cottage] (1744)
**1** : a building or room used for social amusements; *specifically* : one used for gambling
**2** *also* **cas·si·no** : a card game in which cards are won by matching or combining cards in a hand with those exposed on the table
**3** : SUMMERHOUSE 2

**ca·si·ta** \kə-'sē-tə\ *noun* [Spanish, diminutive of *casa*] (1923)
: a small house

**cask** \'kask\ *noun* [Middle English *caske,* perhaps from Middle French *casque* helmet, from Spanish *casco* potsherd, skull, helmet] (15th century)
**1** : a barrel-shaped vessel of staves, headings, and hoops usually for liquids

**2** : a cask and its contents; *also* : the quantity contained in a cask

**cas·ket** \'kas-kət\ *noun* [Middle English, perhaps modification of Middle French *cassette*] (15th century)
**1** : a small chest or box (as for jewels)
**2** : a usually fancy coffin
— **casket** *transitive verb*

**casque** \'kask\ *noun* [Middle French — more at CASK] (1580)
**1** : a piece of armor for the head : HELMET
**2** : an anatomic structure suggestive of a helmet

**Cas·san·dra** \kə-'san-drə, -'sän-\ *noun* [Latin, from Greek *Kassandra*]
**1** : a daughter of Priam endowed with the gift of prophecy but fated never to be believed
**2** : one that predicts misfortune or disaster

**cas·sa·va** \kə-'sä-və\ *noun* [Spanish *cazabe* cassava bread, from Taino *caçábi*] (1555)
: any of several plants (genus *Manihot* and especially *M. esculenta*) of the spurge family grown in the tropics for their fleshy edible rootstocks which yield a nutritious starch; *also* : the rootstock

**cas·se·role** \'ka-sə-,rōl *also* 'ka-zə-\ *noun* [French, saucepan, from Middle French, diminutive of *casse* ladle, dripping pan, from Old Provençal *cassa,* probably ultimately from Greek *kyathos* ladle] (1708)
**1** : a dish in which food may be baked and served
**2** : food cooked and served in a casserole
**3** : a deep round usually porcelain dish with a handle used for heating substances in the laboratory

**cas·sette** *also* **ca·sette** \kə-'set, ka-\ *noun* [French, from Middle French, diminutive of Old North French *casse* case] (1793)
**1** : CASKET 1
**2** : a usually flat case or container that is used especially in a device or machine, that holds something which is difficult, troublesome, or awkward to handle, and that can be easily loaded or unloaded: as **a** : a lightproof magazine for holding film or plates for use in a camera **b** : a plastic cartridge containing magnetic tape with the tape on one reel passing to the other

**cas·sia** \'ka-shə\ *noun* [Middle English, from Old English, from Latin, from Greek *kassia,* of Semitic origin; akin to Hebrew *qĕṣī'āh* cassia] (before 12th century)
**1** : a coarse cinnamon bark (as from *Cinnamomum cassia*)
**2** : any of a genus (*Cassia*) of leguminous herbs, shrubs, and trees of warm regions

**cas·si·mere** \'ka-zə-,mir, 'ka-sə-\ *noun* [obsolete *Cassimere* (Kashmir)] (1774)
: a closely woven smooth twilled usually wool fabric (as for suits)

**Cas·si·ni division** \kə-'sē-nē-\ *noun* [Gian Domenico *Cassini* (died 1712) Italian astronomer] (circa 1909)
: the dark region between the two brightest rings of Saturn — called also *Cassini's division*

**Cas·si·o·pe·ia** \,ka-sē-ə-'pē-ə\ *noun* [Latin, from Greek *Kassiopeia*]
**1** : the wife of King Cepheus who gives birth to Andromeda and is later changed into a constellation
**2** [Latin (genitive *Cassiopeiae*), from Greek *Kassiopeia*] : a northern constellation between Andromeda and Cepheus

**cas·sis** \kə-'sēs\ *noun* [French, literally, black currants, perhaps from Latin *cassia*] (1899)
: a liqueur made from black currants

**cas·sit·er·ite** \kə-'si-tə-,rīt\ *noun* [French *cassitérite,* from Greek *kassiteros* tin] (1858)
: a brown or black mineral that consists of tin dioxide and is the chief source of metallic tin

**cas·sock** \'ka-sək\ *noun* [Middle French *casaque*] (1631)
: a close-fitting ankle-length garment worn especially in Roman Catholic and Anglican

churches by the clergy and by laymen assisting in services

**cas·sou·let** \,ka-sə-'lā\ *noun* [French, from Provençal, literally, earthenware dish, diminutive of *cassolo* dish, diminutive of *casso* ladle, from Old Provençal *cassa*] (circa 1929)
: a casserole of white beans baked with herbs and meat (as pork, lamb, and goose or duck)

**cas·so·wary** \'ka-sə-,wer-ē\ *noun, plural* **-war·ies** [Malay *kĕsuari,* from an Austronesian language of the Moluccas] (1611)

cassock

: any of a genus (*Casuarius*) of large ratite birds chiefly of New Guinea and northern Australia that have a horny casque on the head and are closely related to the emu

¹**cast** \'kast\ *verb* **cast; cast·ing** [Middle English, from Old Norse *kasta;* akin to Old Norse *kǫs* heap] (13th century)
*transitive verb*
**1 a** : to cause to move or send forth by throwing ⟨*cast* a fishing lure⟩ ⟨*cast* dice⟩ **b** : DIRECT ⟨*cast* a glance⟩ **c** (1) : to put forth ⟨the fire *casts* a warm glow⟩ (2) : to place as if by throwing ⟨*cast* doubt on their reliability⟩ **d** : to deposit (a ballot) formally **e** (1) : to throw off or away ⟨the horse *cast* a shoe⟩ (2) : to get rid of : DISCARD ⟨*cast* off all restraint⟩ (3) : SHED, MOLT (4) : to bring forth; *especially* : to give birth to prematurely **f** : to throw to the ground especially in wrestling **g** : to build by throwing up earth
**2 a** : to perform arithmetical operations on : ADD (2) : to calculate by means of astrology **b** *archaic* : DECIDE, INTEND
**3 a** : to dispose or arrange into parts or into a suitable form or order **b** (1) : to assign the parts of (a dramatic production) to actors (2) : to assign (as an actor) to a role or part
**4 a** : to give a shape to (a substance) by pouring in liquid or plastic form into a mold and letting harden without pressure ⟨*cast* steel⟩ **b** : to form by this process
**5** : TURN ⟨*cast* the scale slightly⟩
**6** : to make (a knot or stitch) by looping or catching up
**7** : TWIST, WARP ⟨a beam *cast* by age⟩
*intransitive verb*
**1** : to throw something; *specifically* : to throw out a lure with a fishing rod
**2** *dialect British* : VOMIT
**3** *dialect English* : to bear fruit : YIELD
**4 a** : to perform addition **b** *obsolete* : ESTIMATE, CONJECTURE
**5** : WARP
**6** : to range over land in search of a trail — used of hunting dogs or trackers
**7** : VEER
**synonym** see DISCARD, THROW
— **cast·abil·i·ty** \,kas-tə-'bi-lə-tē\ *noun*
— **cast·able** \'kas-tə-bəl\ *adjective*
— **cast lots** : to draw lots to determine a matter by chance

²**cast** *noun* (14th century)
**1 a** : an act of casting **b** : something that happens as a result of chance **c** : a throw of dice **d** : a throw of a line (as a fishing line) or net
**2 a** : the form in which a thing is constructed **b** (1) : the set of actors in a dramatic production (2) : a set (as in a narrative) of characters or persons **c** : the arrangement of draperies in a painting
**3** : the distance to which a thing can be thrown; *specifically* : the distance a bow can shoot
**4 a** : a turning of the eye in a particular direction; *also* : EXPRESSION ⟨this freakish, elfish *cast* came into the child's eye —Nathaniel Hawthorne⟩ **b** : a slight strabismus
**5** : something that is thrown or the quantity thrown; *especially, British* : the leader of a fishing line

**6 a :** something that is formed by casting in a mold or form: as (1) **:** a reproduction (as of a statue) in metal or plaster **:** CASTING (2) **:** a fossil reproduction of the details of a natural object by mineral infiltration **b :** an impression taken from an object with a liquid or plastic substance **:** MOLD **c :** a rigid dressing of gauze impregnated with plaster of paris for immobilizing a diseased or broken part
**7 :** FORECAST, CONJECTURE
**8 a :** an overspread of a color or modification of the appearance of a substance by a trace of some added hue **:** SHADE ⟨gray with a greenish *cast*⟩ **b :** TINGE, SUGGESTION
**9 a :** a ride on one's way in a vehicle **:** LIFT **b** *Scottish* **:** HELP, ASSISTANCE
**10 a :** SHAPE, APPEARANCE ⟨the delicate *cast* of her features⟩ **b :** characteristic quality ⟨his father's conservative *cast* of mind⟩
**11 :** something that is shed, ejected, or thrown out or off: as **a :** the excrement of an earthworm **b :** a mass of soft matter formed in cavities of diseased organs and discharged from the body **c :** the skin of an insect
**12 :** the ranging in search of a trail by a dog, hunting pack, or tracker
**cast about** (1575)
*intransitive verb*
**:** to look around **:** SEEK ⟨*cast about* for a seat⟩
*transitive verb*
**:** to lay plans concerning **:** CONTRIVE ⟨*cast about* how he was to go⟩
**cas·ta·net** \ˌkas-tə-'net\ *noun* [Spanish *castañeta,* from *castaña* chestnut, from Latin *castanea* — more at CHESTNUT] (circa 1647)
**:** a percussion instrument used especially by dancers that consists of two small shells of hard wood, ivory, or plastic usually fastened to the thumb and clicked together by the other fingers — usually used in plural

castanets

**cast around** *intransitive verb* (1946)
**:** CAST ABOUT
**cast·away** \'kas-tə-ˌwā\ *adjective* (1534)
**1 :** thrown away **:** REJECTED
**2 a :** cast adrift or ashore as a survivor of a shipwreck **b :** thrown out or left without friends or resources
— **castaway** *noun*
**cast down** *adjective* (14th century)
**:** DOWNCAST
**caste** \'kast *also* 'käst\ *noun* [Portuguese *casta,* literally, race, lineage, from feminine of *casto* pure, chaste, from Latin *castus*] (1613)
**1 :** one of the hereditary social classes in Hinduism that restrict the occupation of their members and their association with the members of other castes
**2 a :** a division of society based on differences of wealth, inherited rank or privilege, profession, or occupation **b :** the position conferred by caste standing **:** PRESTIGE
**3 :** a system of rigid social stratification characterized by hereditary status, endogamy, and social barriers sanctioned by custom, law, or religion
**4 :** a specialized form (as the worker of an ant or bee) of a polymorphic social insect that carries out a particular function in the colony
— **caste·ism** \'kas-ˌti-zəm\ *noun*
**cas·tel·lan** \'kas-tə-lən\ *noun* [Middle English *castelleyn,* from Old North French *castelain,* from Latin *castellanus* occupant of a castle, from *castellanus* of a castle, from *castellum* castle] (14th century)
**:** a governor or warden of a castle or fort
**cas·tel·lat·ed** \'kas-tə-ˌlā-təd\ *adjective* [Medieval Latin *castellatus,* past participle of *castellare* to fortify, from Latin *castellum*] (1679)
**1 :** having battlements like a castle
**2 :** having or supporting a castle

**cast·er** \'kas-tər\ *noun* (14th century)
**1 :** one that casts; *especially* **:** a machine that casts type
**2** *or* **cas·tor** \-tər\ **a :** a usually silver table vessel with a perforated top for sprinkling a seasoning (as sugar or spice) **b :** a usually revolving metal stand bearing condiment containers (as cruets, mustard pot, and often shakers) for table use **:** a cruet stand
**3 :** any of a set of wheels or rotating balls mounted in a swivel frame and used for the support and movement of furniture, trucks, and portable equipment
**4 :** the slight usually backward tilt of the upper end of the kingbolt of an automobile for giving directional stability to the front wheels
**cas·ti·gate** \'kas-tə-ˌgāt\ *transitive verb* **-gat·ed; -gat·ing** [Latin *castigatus,* past participle of *castigare* — more at CHASTEN] (1607)
**:** to subject to severe punishment, reproof, or criticism
**synonym** see PUNISH
— **cas·ti·ga·tion** \ˌkas-tə-'gā-shən\ *noun*
— **cas·ti·ga·tor** \'kas-tə-ˌgā-tər\ *noun*
**cas·tile soap** \ˌ(ˌ)kas-'tēl-\ *noun, often C capitalized* [Middle English *castell sope,* from *Castell* Castile] (15th century)
**:** a fine hard bland soap made from olive oil and sodium hydroxide; *also* **:** any of various similar soaps
**Cas·til·ian** \ka-'stil-yən\ *noun* (1796)
**1 :** a native or inhabitant of Castile; *broadly* **:** SPANIARD
**2 a :** the dialect of Castile **b :** the official and literary language of Spain based on this dialect
— **Castilian** *adjective*
**cast·ing** *noun* (14th century)
**1 :** something (as excrement) that is cast out or off
**2 :** the act of one that casts: as **a :** the throwing of a fishing line by means of a rod and reel **b :** the assignment of parts and duties to actors or performers
**3 :** something cast in a mold
**casting director** *noun* (1922)
**:** a person who supervises the casting of dramatic productions (as films and plays)
**casting vote** *noun* (1678)
**:** a deciding vote cast by a presiding officer to break a tie
**cast–iron** *adjective* (1692)
**1 :** made of cast iron
**2 :** resembling cast iron: as **a :** capable of withstanding great strain ⟨a *cast-iron* stomach⟩ **b :** not admitting change, adaptation, or exception **:** RIGID ⟨a *cast-iron* will⟩
**cast iron** *noun* (1664)
**:** a commercial alloy of iron, carbon, and silicon that is cast in a mold and is hard, brittle, nonmalleable, and incapable of being hammer-welded but more easily fusible than steel
**¹cas·tle** \'ka-səl\ *noun* [Middle English *castel,* from Old English, from Old North French, from Latin *castellum* fortress, castle, diminutive of *castrum* fortified place; perhaps akin to Latin *castrare* to castrate] (before 12th century)
**1 a :** a large fortified building or set of buildings **b :** a massive or imposing house
**2 :** a retreat safe against intrusion or invasion
**3 :** ³ROOK
**²castle** *verb* **cas·tled; cas·tling** \'kas-(ə-)liŋ\ (1587)
*transitive verb*
**1 :** to establish in a castle
**2 :** to move (the chess king) in castling
*intransitive verb*
**:** to move a chess king two squares toward a rook and in the same move the rook to the square next past the king
**cas·tled** \'ka-səld\ *adjective* (1789)
**:** CASTELLATED
**castle in the air** (1580)
**:** an impracticable project **:** DAYDREAM — called also *castle in Spain*

**cast–off** \'kas-ˌtof\ *adjective* (1746)
**:** thrown away or aside
— **cast·off** *noun*
**cast off** (1602)
*transitive verb*
**1 :** LOOSE ⟨*cast off* a hunting dog⟩
**2 :** UNFASTEN ⟨*cast off* a boat⟩
**3 :** to remove (a stitch) from a knitting needle in such a way as to prevent unraveling
*intransitive verb*
**1 :** to unfasten or untie a boat or a line
**2 :** to turn one's partner in a square dance and pass around the outside of the set and back
**3 :** to finish a knitted fabric by casting off all stitches
**cast on** *transitive verb* (1840)
**:** to place (stitches) on a knitting needle for beginning or enlarging knitted work
**cas·tor** \'kas-tər\ *noun* [Middle English, from Latin, from Greek *kastōr,* from *Kastōr* Castor] (14th century)
**1 :** BEAVER 1a
**2 :** CASTOREUM
**3 :** a beaver hat
**Cas·tor** \'kas-tər\ *noun* [Latin, from Greek *Kastōr*]
**1 :** one of the Dioscuri
**2 :** the more northern of the two bright stars in Gemini
**castor bean** *noun* (1819)
**:** the very poisonous seed of the castor-oil plant; *also* **:** CASTOR-OIL PLANT
**cas·to·re·um** \ka-'stōr-ē-əm, -'stȯr-\ *noun* [Middle English *castorium,* from Latin *castoreum,* from *castor*] (14th century)
**:** a bitter strong-smelling creamy orange-brown substance that consists of the dried perineal glands of the beaver and their secretion and is used especially by perfumers — called also *castor*
**castor oil** *noun* [probably from its former use as a substitute for castoreum in medicine] (1746)
**:** a pale viscous fatty oil from castor beans used especially as a cathartic and as a lubricant and plasticizer
**castor–oil plant** *noun* (1836)
**:** a tropical Old World herb (*Ricinus communis*) widely grown as an ornamental or for its oil-rich castor beans
**castor sugar** *or* **caster sugar** *noun* [*caster*] (1855)
*chiefly British* **:** finely granulated white sugar
**cast out** *transitive verb* (13th century)
**:** to drive out **:** EXPEL
**cas·trate** \'kas-ˌtrāt\ *transitive verb* **cas·trat·ed; cas·trat·ing** [Latin *castratus,* past participle of *castrare;* akin to Greek *keazein* to split, Sanskrit *śasati* he slaughters] (1609)
**1 a :** to deprive of the testes **:** GELD **b :** to deprive of the ovaries **:** SPAY
**2 :** to render impotent or deprive of vitality especially by psychological means
— **castrate** *noun*
— **cas·tra·tion** \kas-'trā-shən\ *noun*
— **cas·tra·tor** \-,trā-tər\ *noun*
— **cas·tra·to·ry** \'kas-trə-,tōr-ē, -,tȯr-\ *adjective*
**cas·tra·to** \ka-'strä-(,)tō, kə-\ *noun, plural* **-ti** \-tē\ [Italian, from past participle of *castrare* to castrate, from Latin] (1763)
**:** a singer castrated before puberty to preserve the soprano or contralto range of his voice
**Cas·tro·ism** \'kas-(,)trō-,i-zəm\ *noun* (1960)
**:** the political, economic, and social principles and policies of Fidel Castro
— **Cas·tro·ite** \-,īt\ *noun*
**¹ca·su·al** \'kazh-wəl, 'ka-zhə-wəl, 'ka-zhəl\ *adjective* [Middle English, from Middle French & Late Latin; Middle French *casuel,*

\ə\ abut \ᵊ\ kitten \ər\ further \a\ ash \ā\ ace
\ä\ mop, mar \au̇\ out \ch\ chin \e\ bet \ē\ easy
\g\ go \i\ hit \ī\ ice \j\ job \ŋ\ sing \ō\ go
\ȯ\ law \ȯi\ boy \th\ thin \t̲h\ the \ü\ loot \u̇\ foot
\y\ yet \zh\ vision *see also* Guide to Pronunciation

from Late Latin *casualis*, from Latin *casus* fall, chance — more at CASE] (14th century)
**1 :** subject to, resulting from, or occurring by chance
**2 a :** occurring without regularity **:** OCCASIONAL **b :** employed for irregular periods
**3 a :** feeling or showing little concern **:** NONCHALANT **b** (1) **:** INFORMAL, NATURAL (2) **:** designed for informal use
**synonym** see ACCIDENTAL, RANDOM
— **ca·su·al·ly** *adverb*
— **ca·su·al·ness** *noun*
**²casual** *noun* (circa 1852)
**1 :** a casual or migratory worker
**2 :** an officer or enlisted man awaiting assignment or transportation to a unit
**ca·su·al·ty** \'ka-zhəl-tē, 'kazh-wəl-, 'ka-zhə-wəl-\ *noun, plural* **-ties** (15th century)
**1** *archaic* **:** CHANCE, FORTUNE ⟨losses that befall them by mere *casualty* —Sir Walter Raleigh⟩
**2 :** serious or fatal accident **:** DISASTER
**3 a :** a military person lost through death, wounds, injury, sickness, internment, or capture or through being missing in action **b :** a person or thing injured, lost, or destroyed **:** VICTIM ⟨the ex-senator was a *casualty* of the last election⟩
**casual water** *noun* (1899)
**:** a temporary accumulation of water not forming a regular hazard of a golf course
**ca·su·a·ri·na** \ˌka-zhə-(wə-)'rē-nə\ *noun* [New Latin, genus name, from Malay (*pohon*) *kĕsuari*, literally, cassowary tree; from the resemblance of its twigs to cassowary feathers] (1806)
**:** any of a genus (*Casuarina* of the family Casuarinaceae) of dicotyledonous chiefly Australian trees which have whorls of scalelike leaves and jointed stems resembling horsetails and some of which yield a heavy hard wood
**ca·su·ist** \'ka-zhü-ist, 'kazh-wist\ *noun* [probably from Spanish *casuista*, from Latin *casus* fall, chance — more at CASE] (1609)
**:** one skilled in or given to casuistry
— **ca·su·is·tic** \ˌka-zhə-'wis-tik\ *or* **ca·su·is·ti·cal** \-ti-kəl\ *adjective*
**ca·su·ist·ry** \'kazh-wə-strē, 'ka-zhə-\ *noun, plural* **-ries** (1725)
**1 :** a resolving of specific cases of conscience, duty, or conduct through interpretation of ethical principles or religious doctrine
**2 :** specious argument **:** RATIONALIZATION
**ca·sus bel·li** \'kä-səs-'be-ˌlē, 'kä-səs-'be-ˌlī\ *noun, plural* **ca·sus belli** \'kä-ˌsüs-, 'kä-ˌsüs-\ [New Latin, occasion of war] (1849)
**:** an event or action that justifies or allegedly justifies a war or conflict
**¹cat** \'kat\ *noun, often attributive* [Middle English, from Old English *catt*, probably from Late Latin *cattus, catta* cat] (before 12th century)
**1 a :** a carnivorous mammal (*Felis catus*) long domesticated as a pet and for catching rats and mice **b :** any of a family (Felidae) of carnivorous usually solitary and nocturnal mammals (as the domestic cat, lion, tiger, leopard, jaguar, cougar, wildcat, lynx, and cheetah)
**2 :** a malicious woman
**3 :** a strong tackle used to hoist an anchor to the cathead of a ship
**4 a :** CATBOAT **b :** CATAMARAN
**5 :** CAT-O'-NINE-TAILS
**6 :** CATFISH
**7 a :** a player or devotee of jazz **b :** GUY
**²cat** *verb* **cat·ted; cat·ting** (1769)
*transitive verb*
**:** to bring (an anchor) up to the cathead
*intransitive verb*
**:** to search for a sexual mate — often used with *around*
**Cat** \'kat\ *trademark*
— used for a Caterpillar tractor
**cata-** *or* **cat-** *or* **cath-** *prefix* [Greek *kata-, kat-, kath-*, from *kata* down, in accordance with, by; akin to Old Welsh *cant* with, Hittite *katta*]

**:** down ⟨*cation*⟩ ⟨*cathode*⟩
**ca·tab·o·lism** \kə-'ta-bə-ˌli-zəm\ *noun* [Greek *katabolē* throwing down, from *kataballein* to throw down, from *kata-* + *ballein* to throw — more at DEVIL] (1876)
**:** destructive metabolism involving the release of energy and resulting in the breakdown of complex materials within the organism — compare ANABOLISM
— **cat·a·bol·ic** \ˌka-tə-'bä-lik\ *adjective*
— **cat·a·bol·i·cal·ly** \-li-k(ə-)lē\ *adverb*
**ca·tab·o·lite** \-ˌlīt\ *noun* (circa 1909)
**:** a product of catabolism
**ca·tab·o·lize** \-ˌlīz\ *verb* **-lized; -liz·ing** (circa 1926)
*transitive verb*
**:** to subject to catabolism
*intransitive verb*
**:** to undergo catabolism
**cat·a·chre·sis** \ˌka-tə-'krē-səs\ *noun, plural* **-chre·ses** \-ˌsēz\ [Latin, from Greek *katachrēsis* misuse, from *katachrēsthai* to use up, misuse, from *kata-* + *chrēsthai* to use] (1553)
**1 :** use of the wrong word for the context
**2 :** use of a forced and especially paradoxical figure of speech (as *blind mouths*)
— **cat·a·chres·tic** \-'kres-tik\ *or* **cat·a·chres·ti·cal** \-ti-kəl\ *adjective*
— **cat·a·chres·ti·cal·ly** \-ti-k(ə-)lē\ *adverb*
**cat·a·clysm** \'ka-tə-ˌkli-zəm\ *noun* [French *cataclysme*, from Latin *cataclysmos*, from Greek *kataklysmos*, from *kataklyzein* to inundate, from *kata-* + *klyzein* to wash — more at CLYSTER] (1637)
**1 :** FLOOD, DELUGE
**2 :** CATASTROPHE 3a
**3 :** a momentous and violent event marked by overwhelming upheaval and demolition; *broadly* **:** an event that brings great changes
— **cat·a·clys·mal** \ˌka-tə-'kliz-məl\ *or* **cat·a·clys·mic** \-mik\ *adjective*
— **cat·a·clys·mi·cal·ly** \-mi-k(ə-)lē\ *adverb*
**cat·a·comb** \'ka-tə-ˌkōm\ *noun* [Middle French *catacombe*, probably from Old Italian *catacomba*, from Late Latin *catacumbae*, plural] (15th century)
**1 :** a subterranean cemetery of galleries with recesses for tombs — usually used in plural
**2 :** something resembling a catacomb: as a **:** an underground passageway or group of passageways **b :** a complex set of interrelated things ⟨the endless *catacombs* of formal education —Kingman Brewster, Jr.⟩
**cata·di·op·tric** \ˌka-tə-dī-'äp-trik\ *adjective* (1723)
**:** belonging to, produced by, or involving both the reflection and the refraction of light
**ca·tad·ro·mous** \kə-'ta-drə-məs\ *adjective* [probably from New Latin *catadromus*, from *cata-* + *-dromus* -dromous] (1880)
**:** living in fresh water and going to the sea to spawn ⟨*catadromous* eels⟩ — compare ANADROMOUS
**cat·a·falque** \'ka-tə-ˌfo(l)k, -ˌfalk\ *noun* [Italian *catafalco*, from (assumed) Vulgar Latin *catafalicum* scaffold, from *cata-* + Latin *fala* siege tower] (1641)
**1 :** an ornamental structure sometimes used in funerals for the lying in state of the body
**2 :** a pall-covered coffin-shaped structure used at requiem masses celebrated after burial
**Cat·a·lan** \'ka-tə-lən, -ˌlan\ *noun* [Spanish *catalán*] (15th century)
**1 :** a native or inhabitant of Catalonia
**2 :** the Romance language of Catalonia, Valencia, Andorra, and the Balearic islands
— **Catalan** *adjective*
**cat·a·lase** \'ka-tə-ˌlās, -ˌlāz\ *noun* [*catalysis*] (1901)
**:** a red crystalline enzyme that consists of a protein complex with hematin groups and catalyzes the decomposition of hydrogen peroxide into water and oxygen
— **cat·a·lat·ic** \ˌka-tə-'la-tik\ *adjective*

**cat·a·lec·tic** \ˌka-tə-'lek-tik\ *adjective* [Late Latin *catalecticus*, from Greek *katalēktikos*, from *katalēgein* to leave off, from *kata-* + *lēgein* to stop — more at SLACK] (1589)
**:** lacking a syllable at the end or ending in an incomplete foot
— **catalectic** *noun*
**cat·a·lep·sy** \'ka-tə-ˌlep-sē\ *noun, plural* **-sies** [Middle English *catalempsi*, from Medieval Latin *catalepsia*, from Late Latin *catalepsis*, from Greek *katalēpsis*, literally, act of seizing, from *katalambanein* to seize, from *kata-* + *lambanein* to take — more at LATCH] (14th century)
**:** a condition of suspended animation and loss of voluntary motion in which the limbs remain in whatever position they are placed
— **cat·a·lep·tic** \ˌka-tə-'lep-tik\ *adjective or noun*
— **cat·a·lep·ti·cal·ly** \-ti-k(ə-)lē\ *adverb*
**cat·a·lex·is** \ˌka-tə-'lek-səs\ *noun, plural* **-lex·es** \-ˌsēz\ [New Latin, from Greek *katalēxis* close, cadence, from *katalēgein*] (1830)
**:** omission or incompleteness usually in the last foot of a line in metrical verse
**¹cat·a·log** *or* **cat·a·logue** \'ka-tə-ˌlog, -ˌläg\ *noun* [Middle English *cateloge*, from Middle French *catalogue*, from Late Latin *catalogus*, from Greek *katalogos*, from *katalegein* to list, enumerate, from *kata-* + *legein* to gather, speak — more at LEGEND] (15th century)
**1 :** LIST, REGISTER
**2 a :** a complete enumeration of items arranged systematically with descriptive details **b :** a pamphlet or book that contains such a list **c :** material in such a list
**²catalog** *or* **catalogue** *verb* **-loged** *or* **-logued; -log·ing** *or* **-logu·ing** (1598)
*transitive verb*
**1 :** to make a catalog of
**2 a :** to enter in a catalog **b :** to classify (as books or information) descriptively
*intransitive verb*
**1 :** to make or work on a catalog
**2 :** to become listed in a catalog at a specified price ⟨this stamp *catalogs* at $2⟩
— **cat·a·log·er** *or* **cat·a·logu·er** *noun*
**catalogue rai·son·né** \-ˌrā-zⁿ-'ā\ *noun, plural* **cat·a·logues rai·son·nés** \-ˌlog(z)-ˌrā-zⁿ-'ā\ [French, literally, reasoned catalog] (1784)
**:** a systematic annotated catalog; *especially* **:** a critical bibliography
**ca·tal·pa** \kə-'tal-pə, -'tol-\ *noun* [Creek *katalpa*, from *iká* head + *talpa* wing] (circa 1730)
**:** any of a genus (*Catalpa*) of American and Asian trees of the trumpet-creeper family with pale showy flowers in terminal clusters
**ca·tal·y·sis** \kə-'ta-lə-səs\ *noun, plural* **-y·ses** \-ˌsēz\ [Greek *katalysis* dissolution, from *katalyein* to dissolve, from *kata-* + *lyein* to dissolve, release — more at LOSE] (1836)
**1 :** a modification and especially increase in the rate of a chemical reaction induced by material unchanged chemically at the end of the reaction
**2 :** a reaction between two or more persons or forces precipitated by a separate agent ⟨a representative list of questions . . . valuable for the *catalysis* of class discussions —B. S. Meyer & D. B. Anderson⟩
**cat·a·lyst** \'ka-tᵊl-əst\ *noun* (1902)
**1 :** a substance (as an enzyme) that enables a chemical reaction to proceed at a usually faster rate or under different conditions (as at a lower temperature) than otherwise possible
**2 :** an agent that provokes or speeds significant change or action
**cat·a·lyt·ic** \ˌka-tᵊl-'i-tik\ *adjective* (1836)
**:** causing, involving, or relating to catalysis
— **cat·a·lyt·i·cal·ly** \-'li-ti-k(ə-)lē\ *adverb*
**catalytic converter** *noun* (1964)

: an automobile exhaust-system component containing a catalyst that causes decomposition of harmful gases into mostly harmless products (as water and carbon dioxide)

**catalytic cracker** *noun* (1947)
: the unit in a petroleum refinery in which cracking is carried out in the presence of a catalyst

**cat·a·lyze** \'ka-tə-ˌlīz\ *transitive verb* **-lyzed; -lyz·ing** (1902)
**1** : to bring about the catalysis of (a chemical reaction)
**2** : BRING ABOUT, INSPIRE
**3** : to alter significantly by catalysis ⟨innovations in basic chemical theory that have *catalyzed* the field —*Newsweek*⟩
— **cat·a·lyz·er** *noun*

**cat·a·ma·ran** \ˌka-tə-mə-ˈran, ˈka-tə-mə-ˌran\ *noun* [Tamil *kaṭṭumaram*, from *kaṭṭu* to tie + *maram* tree, wood] (1673)
: a vessel (as a sailboat) with twin hulls and usually a deck or superstructure connecting the hulls

**cat·a·me·nia** \ˌka-tə-ˈmē-nē-ə\ *noun plural* [New Latin, from Greek *katamēnia*, from neuter plural of *katamēnios* monthly, from *kata* by + *mēn* month — more at CATA-, MOON] (1750)
: MENSES
— **cat·a·me·ni·al** \-nē-əl\ *adjective*

**cat·a·mite** \'ka-tə-ˌmīt\ *noun* [Latin *catamitus*, from *Catamitus* Ganymede, from Etruscan *Catmite*, from Greek *Ganymēdēs*] (1593)
: a boy kept by a pederast

**cat·a·mount** \'ka-tə-ˌmaůnt\ *noun* [short for *cat-a-mountain*] (1664)
: any of various wild cats: as **a** : COUGAR **b** : LYNX

**cat–a–moun·tain** \ˌka-tə-ˈmaůn-tᵊn\ *noun* [Middle English *cat of the mountaine*] (15th century)
: any of various wild cats

**cat and mouse** *noun* (1887)
: behavior like that of a cat with a mouse: as **a** : the act of toying with or tormenting something before destroying it **b** : a contrived action involving constant pursuit, near captures, and repeated escapes ⟨played a game of *cat and mouse* with the police⟩; *broadly* : an evasive action

**ca·taph·o·ra** \kə-ˈta-fə-rə\ *noun* [*cata-* + *anaphora*] (1976)
: the use of a grammatical substitute (as a pronoun) that has the same reference as a following word or phrase

**cat·a·pho·re·sis** \ˌka-tə-fə-ˈrē-səs\ *noun, plural* **-re·ses** \-ˌsēz\ [New Latin] (1889)
: ELECTROPHORESIS
— **cat·a·pho·ret·ic** \-ˈre-tik\ *adjective*
— **cat·a·pho·ret·i·cal·ly** \-ti-k(ə-)lē\ *adverb*

**cat·a·phor·ic** \ˌka-tə-ˈför-ik\ *adjective* (1968)
: of or relating to cataphora; *especially* : being a word or phrase (as a pronoun) that takes its reference from a following word or phrase (as *her* in *before her Jane saw nothing but desert*) — compare ANAPHORIC

**cat·a·plasm** \'ka-tə-ˌpla-zəm\ *noun* [Middle French *cataplasme*, from Latin *cataplasma*, from Greek *kataplasma*, from *kataplassein* to plaster over, from *kata-* + *plassein* to mold — more at PLASTER] (1541)
: POULTICE

**cat·a·plexy** \'ka-tə-ˌplek-sē\ *noun, plural* **-plex·ies** \-sēz\ [German *Kataplexie*, from Greek *kataplēxis*, from *kataplēssein* to strike down, terrify, from *kata-* + *plēssein* to strike — more at PLAINT] (1883)
: sudden loss of muscle power following a strong emotional stimulus

**¹cat·a·pult** \'ka-tə-ˌpəlt, -ˌpůlt\ *noun* [Middle French or Latin; Middle French *catapulte*, from Latin *catapulta*, from Greek *katapaltēs*, from *kata-* + *pallein* to hurl] (1577)
**1** : an ancient military device for hurling missiles

**2** : a device for launching an airplane at flying speed (as from an aircraft carrier)

**catapult 1**

**²catapult** (1848)
*transitive verb*
: to throw or launch by or as if by a catapult
*intransitive verb*
: to become catapulted

**cat·a·ract** \'ka-tə-ˌrakt\ *noun* [Latin *cataracta* waterfall, portcullis, from Greek *kataraktēs*, from *katarassein* to dash down, from *kata-* + *arassein* to strike, dash] (14th century)
**1** [Middle English, from Middle French or Medieval Latin; Middle French *cataracte*, from Medieval Latin *cataracta*, from Latin, portcullis] : a clouding of the lens of the eye or of its surrounding transparent membrane that obstructs the passage of light
**2 a** *obsolete* : WATERSPOUT **b** : WATERFALL; *especially* : a large one over a precipice **c** : steep rapids in a river **d** : DOWNPOUR, FLOOD ⟨*cataracts* of rain⟩ ⟨*cataracts* of information⟩
— **cat·a·rac·tous** \ˌka-tə-ˈrak-təs\ *adjective*

**ca·tarrh** \kə-ˈtär\ *noun* [Middle French or Late Latin; Middle French *catarrhe*, from Late Latin *catarrhus*, from Greek *katarrhous*, from *katarrhein* to flow down, from *kata-* + *rhein* to flow — more at STREAM] (15th century)
: inflammation of a mucous membrane; *especially* : one chronically affecting the human nose and air passages
— **ca·tarrh·al** \-əl\ *adjective*
— **ca·tarrh·al·ly** \-ə-lē\ *adverb*

**cat·ar·rhine** \'ka-tə-ˌrīn\ *adjective* [New Latin *Catarrhina*, from Greek *katarrhina*, neuter plural of *katarrhin* hook-nosed, from *kata-* + *rhin-, rhis* nose] (1863)
: of, relating to, or being any of a division (Catarrhina) of primates comprising the Old World monkeys, higher apes, and hominids that have the nostrils close together and directed downward, 32 teeth, and the tail when present never prehensile
— **catarrhine** *noun*

**ca·tas·tro·phe** \kə-ˈtas-trə-(ˌ)fē\ *noun* [Greek *katastrophē*, from *katastrephein* to overturn, from *kata-* + *strephein* to turn] (1540)
**1** : the final event of the dramatic action especially of a tragedy
**2** : a momentous tragic event ranging from extreme misfortune to utter overthrow or ruin
**3 a** : a violent and sudden change in a feature of the earth **b** : a violent usually destructive natural event (as a supernova)
**4** : utter failure : FIASCO ◆
— **cat·a·stroph·ic** \ˌka-tə-ˈsträ-fik\ *adjective*
— **cat·a·stroph·i·cal·ly** \-fi-k(ə-)lē\ *adverb*

**catastrophe theory** *noun* (1976)
: mathematical theory and conjecture that uses topology to explain events (as an earthquake or a stock market crash) characterized by major abrupt changes

**ca·tas·tro·phism** \kə-ˈtas-trə-ˌfi-zəm\ *noun* (1869)
: a geological doctrine that changes in the earth's crust have in the past been brought about suddenly by physical forces operating in ways that cannot be observed today — compare UNIFORMITARIANISM
— **ca·tas·tro·phist** \-fist\ *noun*

**cat·a·to·nia** \ˌka-tə-ˈtō-nē-ə\ *noun* [New Latin, from German *katatonie*, from *kata-* cata- + New Latin *-tonia*] (circa 1891)

: catatonic schizophrenia

**cat·a·ton·ic** \-ˈtä-nik\ *adjective* (1904)
**1** : of, relating to, being, resembling, or affected by schizophrenia characterized especially by a marked psychomotor disturbance that may involve stupor or mutism, negativism, rigidity, purposeless excitement, and inappropriate or bizarre posturing
**2** : characterized by a marked lack of movement, activity, or expression
— **catatonic** *noun*
— **cat·a·ton·i·cal·ly** \-ni-k(ə-)lē\ *adverb*

**Ca·taw·ba** \kə-ˈtȯ-bə\ *noun* (1715)
**1** *plural* **Catawba** *or* **Catawbas** : a member of an American Indian people of North Carolina and South Carolina
**2** : the language of the Catawba people
**3** : any of various wines produced from a pale red native American grape

**cat·bird** \'kat-ˌbərd\ *noun* (1709)
: an American songbird (*Dumetella carolinensis*) that is dark gray in color with a black cap and reddish coverts under the tail and is related to the mockingbird

**catbird seat** *noun* (1942)
: a position of great prominence or advantage

**cat·boat** \'kat-ˌbōt\ *noun* (1878)
: a sailboat having a cat rig and usually a centerboard and being of light draft and broad beam

**cat·bri·er** \-ˌbrī(-ə)r\ *noun* (1839)
: any of a genus (*Smilax*) of dioecious often prickly climbing plants of the lily family

**cat burglar** *noun* (1907)
: a burglar who is adept at entering and leaving the burglarized place without attracting notice

**catboat**

**cat·call** \-ˌkȯl\ *noun* (1749)
: a loud or raucous cry made especially to express disapproval (as at a sports event)
— **catcall** *verb*

**¹catch** \'kach, 'kech\ *verb* **caught** \'kȯt *also* 'kät\; **catch·ing** [Middle English *cacchen*, from Old North French *cachier* to hunt, from (assumed) Vulgar Latin *captiare*, alteration of Latin *captare* to chase, frequentative of *capere* to take — more at HEAVE] (13th century)
*transitive verb*

◇ WORD HISTORY
**catastrophe** The Greek noun *katastrophē* meant "end, conclusion," especially one not desired; as a derivative of the verb *katastrephein* "to overturn, ruin, undo," it might more literally be translated "undoing." The word aptly fit the finale of a classical tragedy, which normally ended with the complete ruin of the central character. English *catastrophe*, borrowed from Greek in the 16th century, first denoted the dénouement of a play, comic or tragic. Later its scope was extended beyond drama to any kind of final event in a series, though usually an event of an unhappy nature, better matching the original sense of the Greek word. Since the 18th century, the meaning "unfortunate event" has prevailed over "conclusion," so that *catastrophe* is now nearly synonymous with *disaster*.

\ə\ abut \ᵊ\ kitten \ər\ further \a\ ash \ā\ ace
\ä\ mop, mar \aů\ out \ch\ chin \e\ bet \ē\ easy
\g\ go \i\ hit \ī\ ice \j\ job \ŋ\ sing \ō\ go
\ȯ\ law \ȯi\ boy \th\ thin \t͟h\ the \ü\ loot \ů\ foot
\y\ yet \zh\ vision    *see also* Guide to Pronunciation

**1 a :** to capture or seize especially after pursuit **b :** to take or entangle in or as if in a snare **c :** DECEIVE **d :** to discover unexpectedly : FIND ⟨*caught* in the act⟩ **e :** to check (oneself) suddenly or momentarily **f :** to become suddenly aware of ⟨*caught* me looking at him⟩
**2 a :** to take hold of : SEIZE **b :** to affect suddenly **c :** INTERCEPT **d :** to avail oneself of : TAKE **e :** to obtain through effort : GET **f :** to get entangled ⟨*catch* a sleeve on a nail⟩
**3 :** to become affected by: as **a :** CONTRACT ⟨*catch* a cold⟩ **b :** to respond sympathetically to the point of being imbued with ⟨*catch* the spirit of an occasion⟩ **c :** to be struck by **d :** to be subjected to : RECEIVE ⟨*catch* hell⟩
**4 a :** to seize and hold firmly **b :** FASTEN
**5 :** to take or get usually momentarily or quickly ⟨*catch* a glimpse of a friend⟩ ⟨*catch* a nap⟩
**6 a :** OVERTAKE **b :** to get aboard in time ⟨*catch* the bus⟩
**7 :** to attract and hold : ARREST, ENGAGE ⟨*caught* my attention⟩ ⟨*caught* her eye⟩
**8 :** to make contact with : STRIKE
**9 a :** to grasp by the senses or the mind ⟨you *catch* what I mean?⟩ ⟨didn't *catch* the name⟩ **b :** to apprehend and fix by artistic means
**10 a :** SEE, WATCH ⟨*catch* a game on TV⟩ **b :** to listen to
**11 :** to serve as a catcher for in baseball
**12 :** to meet with socially ⟨*catch* you later⟩
*intransitive verb*
**1 :** to grasp hastily or try to grasp
**2 :** to become caught
**3 :** to catch fire
**4** *of a crop* **:** to come up and become established
**5 :** to play the position of catcher on a baseball team
**6 :** KICK OVER ☆
— **catch·able** \'ka-chə-bəl, 'ke-\ *adjective*
— **catch a crab :** to fail to raise an oar clear of the water on recovery of a stroke
— **catch dead :** willing to be publicly exposed — used in negative constructions ⟨wouldn't be *caught dead* in that shirt⟩
— **catch fire 1 :** to become ignited **2 :** to become fired with enthusiasm **3 :** to increase greatly in scope, popularity, interest, or effectiveness ⟨this stock has not *caught fire*—yet —*Forbes*⟩
— **catch it :** to incur blame, reprimand, or punishment
— **catch one's breath :** to rest long enough to restore normal breathing; *broadly* : to rest after a period of intense activity
²**catch** *noun* (15th century)
**1 :** something caught; *especially* : the total quantity caught at one time ⟨a large *catch* of fish⟩
**2 a :** the act, action, or fact of catching **b :** a game in which a ball is thrown and caught
**3 :** something that checks or holds immovable ⟨a safety *catch*⟩
**4 :** one worth catching especially as a spouse
**5 :** a round for three or more unaccompanied usually male voices often with suggestive or obscene lyrics
**6 :** FRAGMENT, SNATCH
**7 :** a concealed difficulty or complication ⟨there must be a *catch*⟩
**8 :** the germination of a field crop to such an extent that replanting is unnecessary
**catch·all** \'ka-,chȯl, 'ke-\ *noun, often attributive* (1838)
**:** something that holds or includes odds and ends or a wide variety of things
**catch–as–catch–can** *adjective* (1764)
**:** using any available means or method : UNPLANNED ⟨a *catch-as-catch-can* existence begging and running errands —*Time*⟩
**catch·er** \'ka-chər, 'ke-\ *noun* (15th century)
**:** one that catches; *specifically* : a baseball player positioned behind home plate
**catch·fly** \'kach-,flī, 'kech-\ *noun* (1597)

**:** any of various plants (as of the genera *Lychnis* and *Silene*) of the pink family often with viscid stems
**catch·ing** *adjective* (1590)
**1 :** INFECTIOUS, CONTAGIOUS ⟨the flu is *catching*⟩ ⟨his spirit is *catching*⟩
**2 :** CATCHY, ALLURING
**catch·ment** \'kach-mənt, 'kech-\ *noun* (1847)
**1 :** something that catches water; *also* : the amount of water caught
**2 :** the action of catching water
**catchment area** *noun* (1940)
**:** the geographical area served by an institution
**catch on** *intransitive verb* (1883)
**1 :** to become aware : LEARN; *also* : UNDERSTAND ⟨didn't *catch on* to what was going on⟩
**2 :** to become popular ⟨this idea has already *caught on*⟩
**catch out** *transitive verb* (1816)
**:** to detect in error or wrongdoing ⟨delighting to *catch out* his literary victims in error —John Clive⟩
**catch·pen·ny** \'kach-,pe-nē, 'kech-\ *adjective* (1748)
**:** using sensationalism or cheapness for appeal ⟨a *catchpenny* newspaper⟩
**catch·phrase** \-,frāz\ *noun* (circa 1850)
**:** an expression that has caught on and is used repeatedly
**catch·pole** *or* **catch·poll** \-,pōl\ *noun* [Middle English *cacchepol*, from Old English *cæcepol*, from (assumed) Old North French *cachepol*, literally, chicken chaser, from Old North French *cachier* + *pol* chicken, from Latin *pullus* — more at CATCH, PULLET] (before 12th century)
**:** a sheriff's deputy; *especially* : one who makes arrests for failure to pay a debt
**catch–22** \-,twen-tē-'tü\ *noun, plural* **catch–22's** *or* **catch–22s** *often capitalized* [from *Catch-22*, paradoxical rule in the novel *Catch-22* (1961) by Joseph Heller] (1961)
**1 :** a problematic situation for which the only solution is denied by a circumstance inherent in the problem or by a rule ⟨the show-business *catch-22*—no work unless you have an agent, no agent unless you've worked —Mary Murphy⟩; *also* : the circumstance or rule that denies a solution
**2 a :** an illogical, unreasonable, or senseless situation **b :** a measure or policy whose effect is the opposite of what was intended **c :** a situation presenting two equally undesirable alternatives
**3 :** a hidden difficulty or means of entrapment : CATCH
**catch–up** \'ke-chəp, 'ka-; 'kat-səp\ *variant of* KETCHUP
¹**catch–up** \'kach-,əp, 'kech-\ *adjective* (1945)
**:** intended to catch up to a theoretical norm or a competitor's accomplishments
²**catch–up** *noun* (1948)
**:** the act or fact of catching up or trying to catch up (as with a norm or competitor) ⟨had to play *catch-up*⟩; *also* : an increase intended to achieve catch-up
**catch up** (14th century)
*transitive verb*
**1 a :** to pick up often abruptly ⟨the thief *caught* the purse *up* and ran⟩ **b :** ENSNARE, ENTANGLE ⟨education has been *caught up* in a stultifying mythology —N. M. Pusey⟩ **c :** ENTHRALL ⟨the . . . public was *caught up* in the car's magic —D. A. Jedlicka⟩
**2 :** to provide with the latest information ⟨*catch* me *up* on the news⟩
*intransitive verb*
**1 a :** to travel fast enough to overtake an advance party **b :** to reach a state of parity or of being able to cope ⟨kids left behind in preschool may never *catch up*⟩
**2 :** to bring about arrest for illicit activities ⟨the police *caught up* with the thieves⟩

**3 a :** to complete or compensate for something belatedly ⟨*catch up* on lost sleep⟩ **b :** to acquire belated information ⟨*catch up* on the news⟩
**catch·word** \'kach-,wərd, 'kech-\ *noun* (circa 1736)
**1 a :** a word under the right-hand side of the last line on a book page that repeats the first word on the following page **b :** GUIDE WORD
**2 :** a word or expression repeated until it becomes representative of a party, school, or point of view
**catchy** \'ka-chē, 'ke-chē\ *adjective* **catch·i·er; -est** (1831)
**1 :** tending to catch the interest or attention ⟨a *catchy* title⟩
**2 :** FITFUL, IRREGULAR ⟨*catchy* breathing⟩
**3 :** TRICKY ⟨a *catchy* question⟩
**cat·claw** \'kat-,klȯ\ *noun* (1898)
**:** a yellow-flowered spiny acacia (*Acacia greggi*) of the southwestern U.S. and Mexico
**cat distemper** *noun* (circa 1950)
**:** PANLEUKOPENIA
**cate** \'kāt\ *noun* [Middle English, article of purchased food, short for *acate*, from Old North French *acat* purchase, from *acater* to buy, from (assumed) Vulgar Latin *accaptare*, from Latin *acceptare* to accept] (15th century)
*archaic* **:** a dainty or choice food
**cat·e·che·sis** \,ka-tə-'kē-səs\ *noun, plural* **-che·ses** \-,sēz\ [Late Latin, from Greek *katēchēsis*, from *katēchein* to teach] (1753)
**:** oral instruction of catechumens
— **cat·e·chet·i·cal** \-'ke-ti-kəl\ *adjective*
**cat·e·chin** \'ka-tə-,kin\ *noun* [International Scientific Vocabulary *catechu* + ¹-*in*] (1853)
**:** a crystalline compound $C_{15}H_{14}O_6$ or its derivatives related chemically to the flavones and used in dyeing and tanning
**cat·e·chism** \'ka-tə-,ki-zəm\ *noun* (1502)
**1 :** oral instruction
**2 :** a manual for catechizing; *specifically* : a summary of religious doctrine often in the form of questions and answers
**3 a :** a set of formal questions put as a test **b :** something resembling a catechism especially in being a rote response or formulaic statement
— **cat·e·chis·mal** \,ka-tə-'kiz-məl\ *adjective*
— **cat·e·chis·tic** \-'kis-tik\ *adjective*
**cat·e·chist** \'ka-tə-kist\ *noun* (circa 1563)
**:** one that catechizes: as **a :** a teacher of catechumens **b :** a native in a missionary district who does Christian teaching
**cat·e·chize** \'ka-tə-,kīz\ *transitive verb* **-chized; -chiz·ing** [Late Latin *catechizare*, from Greek *katēchein* to teach, literally, to din into, from *kata-* cata- + *ēchein* to resound, from *ēchē* sound — more at ECHO] (15th century)
**1 :** to instruct systematically especially by questions, answers, and explanations and cor-

rections; *specifically* **:** to give religious instruction in such a manner
**2 :** to question systematically or searchingly
— **cat·e·chi·za·tion** \,ka-ti-kə-'zā-shən\ *noun*
— **cat·e·chiz·er** \'ka-tə-,kī-zər\ *noun*
**cat·e·chol** \'ka-tə-,kȯl, -,kōl\ *noun* (1880)
**1 :** CATECHIN
**2 :** PYROCATECHOL
**cat·e·chol·amine** \,ka-tə-'kō-lə-,mēn, -'kȯ-\ *noun* (1954)
**:** any of various amines (as epinephrine, norepinephrine, and dopamine) that function as hormones or neurotransmitters or both
**cat·e·chol·amin·er·gic** \-,kō-lə-mē-'nər-jik, -,kȯ-, -mi-\ *adjective* (1970)
**:** involving, liberating, or mediated by catecholamine
**cat·e·chu** \'ka-tə-,chü, -,shü\ *noun* [probably modification of Malay *kachu*, of Dravidian origin; akin to Tamil & Kannada *kācu* catechu] (1683)
**:** any of several dry, earthy, or resinous astringent substances obtained from tropical plants of Asia: as **a :** an extract of the heartwood of an East Indian acacia (*Acacia catechu*) **b :** GAMBIER
**cat·e·chu·men** \,ka-tə-'kyü-mən\ *noun* [Middle English *cathecumyn*, from Middle French *cathecumine*, from Late Latin *catechumenus*, from Greek *katēchoumenos*, present passive participle of *katēchein*] (15th century)
**1 :** a convert to Christianity receiving training in doctrine and discipline before baptism
**2 :** one receiving instruction in the basic doctrines of Christianity before admission to communicant membership in a church
**cat·e·gor·i·cal** \,ka-tə-'gȯr-i-kəl, -'gär-\ *also* **cat·e·gor·ic** \-ik\ *adjective* [Late Latin *categoricus*, from Greek *katēgorikos*, from *katēgoria*] (1588)
**1 :** ABSOLUTE, UNQUALIFIED 〈a *categorical* denial〉
**2 a :** of, relating to, or constituting a category **b :** involving, according with, or considered with respect to specific categories
— **cat·e·gor·i·cal·ly** \-i-k(ə-)lē\ *adverb*
**categorical imperative** *noun* (1827)
**:** a moral obligation or command that is unconditionally and universally binding
**cat·e·go·rise** *British variant of* CATEGORIZE
**cat·e·go·rize** \'ka-ti-gə-,rīz\ *transitive verb* **-rized; -riz·ing** (1705)
**:** to put into a category **:** CLASSIFY
— **cat·e·go·ri·za·tion** \,ka-ti-gə-rə-'zā-shən\ *noun*
**cat·e·go·ry** \'ka-tə-,gōr-ē, -,gȯr-\ *noun, plural* **-ries** [Late Latin *categoria*, from Greek *katēgoria* predication, category, from *katēgorein* to accuse, affirm, predicate, from *kata-* + *agora* public assembly, from *ageirein* to gather] (1588)
**1 :** any of several fundamental and distinct classes to which entities or concepts belong
**2 :** a division within a system of classification
**ca·te·na** \kə-'tē-nə\ *noun, plural* **-nae** \-(,)nē\ *or* **-nas** [Medieval Latin, from Latin, chain] (1641)
**:** a connected series of related things
**cat·e·nary** \'ka-tə-,ner-ē, *especially British* kə-'tē-nə-rē\ *noun, plural* **-nar·ies** [New Latin *catenaria*, from Latin, feminine of *catenarius* of a chain, from *catena*] (1788)
**1 :** the curve assumed by a cord of uniform density and cross section that is perfectly flexible but not capable of being stretched and that hangs freely from two fixed points
**2 :** something in the form of a catenary
— **catenary** *adjective*
**cat·e·nate** \'ka-tə-,nāt\ *transitive verb* **-nat·ed; -nat·ing** [Latin *catenatus*, past participle of *catenare*, from *catena*] (circa 1623)
**:** to connect in a series **:** LINK
— **cat·e·na·tion** \,ka-tə-'nā-shən\ *noun*
**ca·ter** \'kā-tər\ *verb* [obsolete *cater* buyer of provisions, from Middle English *catour*, short

for *acatour*, from Anglo-French, from Old North French *acater* to buy — more at CATE] (1600)
*intransitive verb*
**1 :** to provide a supply of food
**2 :** to supply what is required or desired 〈*catering* to middle-class tastes〉
*transitive verb*
**:** to provide food and service for 〈*catered* the banquet〉
— **ca·ter·er** \-tər-ər\ *noun*
**cat·er·an** \'ka-tə-rən\ *noun* [Middle English *ketharan*, probably from Scottish Gaelic *ceathairneach* freebooter, robber] (14th century)
**:** a former military irregular or brigand of the Scottish Highlands
**cat·er·cor·ner** \'ka-tē-,kȯr-nər, 'ka-tə-, 'ki-tē-\ *also* **cat·er·cor·nered** \-nərd\ *adverb or adjective* [obsolete *cater* four + *corner*] (1838)
**:** in a diagonal or oblique position **:** on a diagonal or oblique line 〈the house stood *catercorner* across the square〉
**ca·ter–cous·in** \'kā-tər-,kə-z°n\ *noun* [perhaps from obsolete *cater* buyer of provisions] (1519)
**:** an intimate friend
**cat·er·pil·lar** \'ka-tə(r)-,pi-lər\ *noun, often attributive* [Middle English *catyrpel*, from Old North French *catepelose*, literally, hairy cat] (15th century)
**:** the elongated wormlike larva of a butterfly or moth; *also* **:** any of various similar larvae ◆
**Caterpillar** *trademark*
— used for a tractor made for use on rough or soft ground and moved on two endless metal belts
**cat·er·waul** \'ka-tər-,wȯl\ *intransitive verb* [Middle English *caterwawen*] (14th century)
**1 :** to make a harsh cry
**2 :** to quarrel noisily
— **caterwaul** *noun*
**cat·fac·ing** \'kat-,fā-siŋ\ *noun* (1940)
**:** a disfigurement or malformation of fruit suggesting a cat's face in appearance
**cat·fight** \-,fīt\ *noun* (1919)
**:** an intense fight or argument between two women
**cat·fish** \-,fish\ *noun* (1612)
**:** any of an order (Siluriformes) of chiefly freshwater stout-bodied scaleless bony fishes having long tactile barbels

**catfish**

**cat·gut** \-,gət\ *noun* (1599)
**:** a tough cord made usually from sheep intestines
**cath-** — see CATA-
**Cath·ar** \'ka-,thär\ *noun, plural* **Cath·a·ri** \'ka-thə-,rī, -,rē\ *or* **Cathars** [Late Latin *cathari* (plural), from Late Greek *katharoi*, from Greek, plural of *katharos* pure] (1637)
**:** a member of one of various ascetic and dualistic Christian sects especially of the later Middle Ages teaching that matter is evil and professing faith in an angelic Christ who did not really undergo human birth or death
— **Cath·a·rism** \'ka-thə-,ri-zəm\ *noun*
— **Cath·a·rist** \-rist\ *or* **Cath·a·ris·tic** \,ka-thə-'ris-tik\ *adjective*
**ca·thar·sis** \kə-'thär-səs\ *noun, plural* **ca·thar·ses** \-,sēz\ [New Latin, from Greek *katharsis*, from *kathairein* to cleanse, purge, from *katharos*] (circa 1775)
**1 :** PURGATION
**2 a :** purification or purgation of the emotions (as pity and fear) primarily through art **b :** a purification or purgation that brings about spiritual renewal or release from tension

**3 :** elimination of a complex by bringing it to consciousness and affording it expression
¹**ca·thar·tic** \kə-'thär-tik\ *adjective* [Late Latin or Greek; Late Latin *catharticus*, from Greek *kathartikos*, from *kathairein*] (1612)
**:** of, relating to, or producing catharsis
²**cathartic** *noun* (1651)
**:** a cathartic medicine **:** PURGATIVE
**cat·head** \'kat-,hed\ *noun* (1626)
**:** a projecting piece of timber or iron near the bow of a ship to which the anchor is hoisted and secured
**ca·thect** \kə-'thekt, ka-\ *transitive verb* [back-formation from *cathectic*] (1925)
**:** to invest with mental or emotional energy
**ca·thec·tic** \kə-'thek-tik, ka-\ *adjective* [New Latin *cathexis*] (1927)
**:** of, relating to, or invested with mental or emotional energy
**ca·the·dra** \kə-'thē-drə\ *noun* [Latin, chair — more at CHAIR] (circa 1797)
**:** a bishop's official throne
¹**ca·the·dral** \kə-'thē-drəl\ *adjective* (14th century)
**1 :** of, relating to, or containing a cathedra
**2 :** emanating from a chair of authority
**3 :** suggestive of a cathedral
²**cathedral** *noun* (1587)
**1 :** a church that is the official seat of a diocesan bishop
**2 :** something that resembles or suggests a cathedral
**ca·thep·sin** \kə-'thep-sən\ *noun* [Greek *kathepsein* to digest (from *kata-* cata- + *hepsein* to boil) + English ²-*in*] (1929)
**:** any of several intracellular proteases of animal tissue that aid in autolysis
**Cath·er·ine wheel** \,ka-th(ə-)rin-\ *noun* [Saint *Catherine* of Alexandria (died about 307) Christian martyr] (1584)
**1 :** a wheel with spikes projecting from the rim
**2 :** PINWHEEL 1
**3 :** CARTWHEEL 2
**cath·e·ter** \'ka-thə-tər, 'kath-tər\ *noun* [Late Latin, from Greek *kathetēr*, from *kathienai* to send down, from *kata-* cata- + *hienai* to send — more at JET] (1601)
**:** a tubular medical device for insertion into canals, vessels, passageways, or body cavities usually to permit injection or withdrawal of fluids or to keep a passage open
**cath·e·ter·i·za·tion** \,ka-thə-tə-rə-'zā-shən, ,kath-tə-rə-\ *noun* (circa 1852)
**:** the use of or introduction of a catheter (as in or into the bladder, trachea, or heart)

---

◇ WORD HISTORY
**caterpillar** *Caterpillar*, our common word for a butterfly or moth larva, first appeared in a 15th century English-Latin dictionary as *catirpel*. It was presumably altered from the medieval form of a word which emerges in the modern French dialect of Normandy as *catepeleuse* or *carpeleuse* and which then meant literally "hairy cat." (Similar applications of a name for a furry animal to fuzzy larvae are English *woolly bear* and French *chenille* "caterpillar," descended from Latin *canicula* "little dog.") In the 16th century, *caterpil* is replaced by *catirpiller*, probably influenced by the now obsolete word *piller* "pillager, looter," a not inappropriate association in view of the destructive habits of some insects. The spelling *caterpillar*, which much less appropriately suggests *pillar*, was adopted by the 18th century lexicographer Samuel Johnson and has since remained standard.

---

— **cath·e·ter·ize** \'ka-thə-tə-ˌrīz, 'kath-tə-\ *transitive verb*

**ca·thex·is** \kə-'thek-səs, ka-\ *noun, plural* **ca·thex·es** \-ˌsēz\ [New Latin (intended as translation of German *Besetzung*), from Greek *kathexis* holding, from *katechein* to hold fast, occupy, from *kata-* + *echein* to have, hold — more at SCHEME] (1922)
**:** investment of mental or emotional energy in a person, object, or idea

**cath·ode** \'ka-ˌthōd\ *noun* [Greek *kathodos* way down, from *kata-* + *hodos* way] (1834)
**1 :** the electrode of an electrochemical cell at which reduction occurs: **a :** the negative terminal of an electrolytic cell **b :** the positive terminal of a galvanic cell
**2 :** the electron-emitting electrode of an electron tube — compare ANODE
— **cath·od·al** \'ka-ˌthō-dᵊl\ *adjective*
— **cath·od·al·ly** *adverb*
— **ca·thod·ic** \ka-'thä-dik, -'thō-\ *adjective*
— **ca·thod·i·cal·ly** \-di-k(ə-)lē\ *adverb*
**cathode ray** *noun* (1880)
**1** *plural* **:** the high-speed electrons emitted in a stream from the heated cathode of a vacuum tube
**2 :** a stream of electrons emitted from the cathode of a vacuum tube — usually used in plural
**cathode–ray tube** *noun* (1905)
**:** a vacuum tube in which a beam of electrons is projected on a fluorescent screen to produce a luminous spot at a point on the screen determined by the effect on the electron beam of a variable magnetic field within the tube
**cathod·ic protection** *noun* (1930)
**:** the prevention of electrolytic corrosion of a usually metallic structure (as a pipeline) by causing it to act as the cathode rather than as the anode of an electrochemical cell
**cath·o·lic** \'kath-lik, 'ka-thə-\ *adjective* [Middle French & Late Latin; Middle French *catholique*, from Late Latin *catholicus*, from Greek *katholikos* universal, general, from *katholou* in general, from *kata* by + *holos* whole — more at CATA-, SAFE] (14th century)
**1 a** *often capitalized* **:** of, relating to, or forming the church universal **b** *often capitalized* **:** of, relating to, or forming the ancient undivided Christian church or a church claiming historical continuity from it **c** *capitalized* **:** ROMAN CATHOLIC
**2 :** COMPREHENSIVE, UNIVERSAL; *especially* **:** broad in sympathies, tastes, or interests
— **ca·thol·i·cal·ly** \kə-'thä-li-k(ə-)lē\ *adverb*
— **ca·thol·i·cize** \-'thä-lə-ˌsīz\ *verb*
**Cath·o·lic** \'kath-lik, 'ka-thə-\ *noun* (15th century)
**1 :** a person who belongs to the universal Christian church
**2 :** a member of a Catholic church; *especially* **:** ROMAN CATHOLIC
**Catholic Apostolic** *adjective* (1888)
**:** of or relating to a Christian sect founded in 19th century England in anticipation of Christ's second coming
**ca·thol·i·cate** \kə-'thò-lə-ˌkāt, -kət\ *noun* (1850)
**:** the jurisdiction of a catholicos
**Catholic Epistles** *noun plural* (1582)
**:** the five New Testament letters including James, I and II Peter, I John, and Jude addressed to the early Christian churches at large
**Ca·thol·i·cism** \kə-'thä-lə-ˌsi-zəm\ *noun* (circa 1617)
**1 :** ROMAN CATHOLICISM
**2 :** the faith, practice, or system of Catholic Christianity
**cath·o·lic·i·ty** \ˌka-thə-'li-sə-tē, ˌkath-'li-\ *noun, plural* **-ties** (1704)
**1** *capitalized* **:** the character of being in conformity with a Catholic church

**2 a :** liberality of sentiments or views ⟨*catholicity* of viewpoint —W. V. O'Connor⟩ **b :** UNIVERSALITY **c :** comprehensive range ⟨*catholicity* of topics⟩
**ca·thol·i·con** \kə-'thä-lə-ˌkän\ *noun* [Middle English, from Medieval Latin, from Greek *katholikon*, neuter of *katholikos*] (15th century)
**:** CURE-ALL, PANACEA
**ca·thol·i·cos** \kə-'thò-li-kòs\ *noun, plural* **-i·cos·es** \-kò-saz\ *or* **-i·coi** \-'thò-lə-ˌkói\ *often capitalized* [Late Greek *katholikos*, from Greek, general] (1878)
**:** a primate of certain Eastern churches and especially of the Armenian or of the Nestorian church
**cat·house** \'kat-ˌhaùs\ *noun* (1931)
**:** BORDELLO
**cat·ion** \'kat-ˌī-ən, 'ka-(ˌ)tī-ən\ *noun* [Greek *kation*, neuter of *katiōn*, present participle of *katienai* to go down, from *kata-* cata- + *ienai* to go — more at ISSUE] (1834)
**:** the ion in an electrolyzed solution that migrates to the cathode; *broadly* **:** a positively charged ion
**cat·ion·ic** \ˌkat-(ˌ)ī-'ä-nik, ˌka-(ˌ)tī-\ *adjective* (circa 1920)
**1 :** of, relating to, or being a cation
**2 :** characterized by an active and especially surface-active cation ⟨a *cationic* dye⟩
— **cat·ion·i·cal·ly** \-ni-k(ə-)lē\ *adverb*
**cat·kin** \'kat-kən\ *noun* [from its resemblance to a cat's tail] (1578)
**:** a spicate inflorescence (as of the willow, birch, or oak) bearing scaly bracts and unisexual usually apetalous flowers — called also *ament*
**cat·like** \'kat-ˌlīk\ *adjective* (1600)
**:** resembling a cat; *especially* **:** STEALTHY ⟨with *catlike* tread, upon our prey we steal —W. S. Gilbert⟩
**cat·mint** \-ˌmint\ *noun* (13th century)
**:** CATNIP
**cat·nap** \-ˌnap\ *noun* (1823)
**:** a very short light nap
— **catnap** *intransitive verb*
**cat·nap·per** *also* **cat·nap·er** \'kat-ˌna-pər\ *noun* [¹*cat* + *-napper* (as in *kidnapper*)] (1942)
**:** one that steals cats usually to sell them for research
**cat·nip** \-ˌnip\ *noun* [¹*cat* + obsolete *nep* catnip, from Middle English, from Old English *nepte*, from Latin *nepeta*] (1712)
**1 :** a strong-scented mint (*Nepeta cataria*) that has whorls of small pale flowers in terminal spikes and contains a substance attractive to cats
**2 :** something very attractive
**cat–o'–nine–tails** \ˌka-tə-'nīn-ˌtālz\ *noun, plural* **cat–o'–nine–tails** [from the resemblance of its scars to the scratches of a cat] (1665)
**:** a whip made of usually nine knotted lines or cords fastened to a handle
**ca·top·tric** \kə-'täp-trik\ *adjective* [Greek *katoptrikos*, from *katoptron* mirror, from *katopsesthai* to be going to observe, from *kata-* + *opsesthai* to be going to see — more at OPTIC] (circa 1774)
**:** being or using a mirror to focus light
**cat rig** *noun* (1867)
**:** a rig consisting of a single mast far forward carrying a single large sail extended by a boom
— **cat–rigged** \'kat-ˌrigd\ *adjective*
**cats and dogs** *adverb* (1738)
**:** in great quantities **:** very hard ⟨it was raining *cats and dogs*⟩
**CAT scan** \'kat-\ *noun* [computerized *a*xial *t*omography] (1975)
**:** an image made by computed tomography
— **CAT scanning** *noun*
**CAT scanner** *noun* (1975)

**:** a medical instrument consisting of integrated X-ray and computing equipment and used for computed tomography

**cat's cradle** *noun* (1768)

**cat's cradle 1**

**1 :** a game in which a string looped in a pattern like a cradle on the fingers of one person's hands is transferred to the hands of another so as to form a different figure
**2 :** something that is intricate, complicated, or elaborate ⟨a *cat's cradle* of red tape⟩
**cat scratch disease** *noun* (1952)
**:** an illness characterized by swelling of the lymph glands, fever, and chills and assumed to be caused by a bacterium transmitted especially by a cat scratch — called also *cat scratch fever*
**cat's–eye** \'kat-ˌsī\ *noun, plural* **cat's–eyes** (circa 1599)
**1 :** any of various gems (as a chrysoberyl or a chalcedony) exhibiting opalescent reflections from within
**2 :** a marble with eyelike concentric circles
**cat's meow** *noun* (1926)
**:** a highly admired person or thing
**cat's–paw** \'kats-ˌpò\ *noun, plural* **cat's–paws** (circa 1769)
**1 :** a light air that ruffles the surface of the water in irregular patches during a calm
**2** [from the fable of the monkey that used a cat's paw to draw chestnuts from the fire] **:** one used by another as a tool **:** DUPE
**3 :** a hitch formed with two eyes for attaching a line to a hook — see KNOT illustration
**cat·sup** *variant of* KETCHUP
**cat·tail** \'kat-ˌtāl\ *noun* (1548)
**:** any of a genus (*Typha* of the family Typhaceae, the cattail family) of tall reedy marsh plants with brown furry fruiting spikes; *especially* **:** a plant (*Typha latifolia*) with long flat leaves used especially for making mats and chair seats
**cat·tery** \'ka-tə-rē\ *noun, plural* **-ter·ies** (circa 1843)
**:** an establishment for the breeding and boarding of cats
**cat·tle** \'ka-tᵊl\ *noun plural* [Middle English *catel*, from Old North French, personal property, from Medieval Latin *capitale*, from Latin, neuter of *capitalis* of the head — more at CAPITAL] (14th century)
**1 :** domesticated quadrupeds held as property or raised for use; *specifically* **:** bovine animals on a farm or ranch
**2 :** human beings especially en masse
**cattle call** *noun* (1952)
**:** a mass audition (as of actors)
**cattle egret** *noun* (circa 1899)
**:** a small Old World white egret (*Bubulcus ibis*) introduced into the New World and having a yellow bill and in the breeding season buff on the crown, breast, and back
**cattle grub** *noun* (1926)
**:** either of two warble flies (genus *Hypoderma*) especially in the larval stage: **a :** COMMON CATTLE GRUB **b :** a related warble fly (*H. bovis*)
**cat·tle·man** \-mən, -ˌman\ *noun* (1864)
**:** one who tends or raises cattle
**cattle tick** *noun* (1869)
**:** either of two ixodid ticks (*Boophilus annulatus* and *B. microplus*) that infest cattle and transmit the protozoan which causes Texas fever
**cat·tle·ya** \'kat-lē-ə; kat-'lā-ə, -'lē-\ *noun* [New Latin, from William *Cattley* (died 1832) English patron of botany] (1828)
**:** any of a genus (*Cattleya*) of tropical American epiphytic orchids with showy hooded flowers
**¹cat·ty** \'ka-tē\ *noun, plural* **catties** [Malay *kati*] (1598)

: any of various units of weight of China and southeast Asia varying around 1⅓ pounds (about 600 grams); *also* : a standard Chinese unit equal to 1.1023 pounds (500 grams)

²**catty** *adjective* **cat·ti·er; -est** (1886)
**1** : resembling a cat; *especially* : slyly spiteful : MALICIOUS
**2** : of or relating to a cat
— **cat·ti·ly** \'ka-t°l-ē\ *adverb*
— **cat·ti·ness** \'ka-tē-nəs\ *noun*

**cat·ty–cor·ner** *or* **cat·ty–cor·nered** *variant of* CATERCORNER

**cat·walk** \'kat-ˌwȯk\ *noun* (1885)
: a narrow walkway (as along a bridge)

**Cau·ca·sian** \kȯ-'kā-zhən, kä- *also* -'ka-zhən\ *adjective* (1807)
**1** : of or relating to the Caucasus or its inhabitants
**2 a** : of or relating to the white race of humankind as classified according to physical features **b** : of or relating to the white race as defined by law specifically as composed of persons of European, North African, or southwest Asian ancestry
— **Caucasian** *noun*
— **Cau·ca·soid** \'kȯ-kə-ˌsȯid\ *adjective or noun*

**Cau·chy sequence** \kō-'shē-, 'kō-shē-\ *noun* [Augustin-Louis *Cauchy* (died 1857) French mathematician] (circa 1949)
: a sequence of elements in a metric space such that for any positive number no matter how small there exists a term in the sequence for which the distance between any two terms beyond this term is less than the arbitrarily small number

¹**cau·cus** \'kȯ-kəs\ *noun* [origin unknown] (1763)
: a closed meeting of a group of persons belonging to the same political party or faction usually to select candidates or to decide on policy; *also* : a group of people united to promote an agreed-upon cause

²**caucus** *intransitive verb* (1788)
: to meet in or hold a caucus

**cau·dad** \'kȯ-ˌdad\ *adverb* [Latin *cauda*] (1889)
: toward the tail or posterior end

**cau·dal** \'kȯ-d°l\ *adjective* [New Latin *caudalis*, from Latin *cauda* tail] (1661)
**1** : of, relating to, or being a tail
**2** : situated in or directed toward the hind part of the body
— **cau·dal·ly** \-d°l-ē\ *adverb*

**cau·date** \'kȯ-ˌdāt\ *adjective* (1600)
: having a tail or a taillike appendage

**caudate nucleus** *noun* (circa 1903)
: the most medial of the four basal ganglia in each cerebral hemisphere — called also *caudate*

**cau·dex** \'kȯ-ˌdeks\ *noun, plural* **cau·di·ces** \'kȯ-də-ˌsēz\ *or* **cau·dex·es** [Latin, tree trunk or stem] (circa 1797)
**1** : the stem of a palm or tree fern
**2** : the woody base of a perennial plant

**cau·di·llis·mo** \ˌkaü-thē-'yēz-(ˌ)mō, -thēl-'yēz-\ *noun* [Spanish, from *caudillo*] (1927)
: the doctrine or practice of a caudillo

**cau·di·llo** \kaü-'thē-(ˌ)yō, -'thēl-(ˌ)yō\ *noun, plural* **-llos** [Spanish, from Late Latin *capitellum* small head — more at CADET] (1852)
: a Spanish or Latin-American military dictator

**cau·dle** \'kȯ-d°l\ *noun* [Middle English *caudel*, from Old North French, from *caut* warm, from Latin *calidus* — more at CAULDRON] (14th century)
: a drink (as for invalids) usually of warm ale or wine mixed with bread or gruel, eggs, sugar, and spices

¹**caught** \'kȯt\ *past and past participle of* CATCH

²**caught** *adjective* (1858)
: PREGNANT — often used in the phrase *get caught*

**caul** \'kȯl\ *noun* [Middle English *calle*, from Middle French *cale*] (14th century)
**1** : the large fatty omentum covering the intestines (as of a cow, sheep, or pig)
**2** : the inner fetal membrane of higher vertebrates especially when covering the head at birth

**caul·dron** \'kȯl-drən\ *noun* [Middle English, alteration of *cauderon*, from Old North French, diminutive of *caudiere*, from Late Latin *caldaria*, from feminine of Latin *caldarius* used for hot water, from *calidus* warm, from *calēre* to be warm — more at LEE] (14th century)
**1** : a large kettle or boiler
**2** : something resembling a boiling cauldron ⟨a *cauldron* of intense emotions⟩

**cau·li·flow·er** \'kȯ-li-ˌflaü(-ə)r, 'kä-\ *noun, often attributive* [Italian *cavolfiore*, from *cavolo* cabbage (from Late Latin *caulus*, from Latin *caulis* stem, cabbage) + *fiore* flower, from Latin *flor-, flos* — more at COLE, BLOW] (1597)
: a garden plant (*Brassica oleracea botrytis*) related to the cabbage and grown for its compact edible head of usually white undeveloped flowers; *also* : its flower cluster used as a vegetable

**cauliflower ear** *noun* (1909)
: an ear deformed from injury and excessive growth of reparative tissue

**cau·li·flow·er·et** \ˌkȯ-li-ˌflaü(-ə)-'ret, ˌkä-\ *noun* (1946)
: a bite-size piece of cauliflower

**cau·line** \'kȯ-ˌlīn\ *adjective* [probably from New Latin *caulinus*, from Latin *caulis*] (1756)
: of, relating to, or growing on a stem and especially on the upper part

¹**caulk** \'kȯk\ *transitive verb* [Middle English *caulken*, from Old North French *cauquer* to trample, from Latin *calcare*, from *calc-, calx* heel] (15th century)
: to stop up and make tight against leakage (as a boat or its seams, the cracks in a window frame, or the joints of a pipe)
— **caulk·er** *noun*

²**caulk** *also* **caulk·ing** \'kȯ-kiŋ\ *noun* (1954)
: material used to caulk

³**caulk** *variant of* ²CALK

**caus·al** \'kȯ-zəl\ *adjective* (circa 1530)
**1** : expressing or indicating cause : CAUSATIVE ⟨a *causal* clause introduced by *since*⟩
**2** : of, relating to, or constituting a cause ⟨the *causal* agent of a disease⟩
**3** : involving causation or a cause ⟨the relationship . . . was not one of *causal* antecedence so much as one of analogous growth —H. O. Taylor⟩
**4** : arising from a cause ⟨a *causal* development⟩
— **caus·al·ly** \-zə-lē\ *adverb*

**cau·sal·gia** \kȯ-'zal-j(ē-)ə, -'sal-\ *noun* [New Latin, from Greek *kausos* fever (from *kaiein* to burn) + New Latin *-algia*] (1872)
: a constant usually burning pain resulting from injury to a peripheral nerve
— **cau·sal·gic** \-jik\ *adjective*

**cau·sal·i·ty** \kȯ-'za-lə-tē\ *noun, plural* **-ties** (1603)
**1** : a causal quality or agency
**2** : the relation between a cause and its effect or between regularly correlated events or phenomena

**cau·sa·tion** \kȯ-'zā-shən\ *noun* (1615)
**1 a** : the act or process of causing **b** : the act or agency which produces an effect
**2** : CAUSALITY

**caus·a·tive** \'kȯ-zə-tiv\ *adjective* (15th century)
**1** : effective or operating as a cause or agent ⟨*causative* bacteria of cholera⟩
**2** : expressing causation; *specifically* : being a linguistic form that indicates that the subject causes an act to be performed or a condition to come into being
— **causative** *noun*
— **caus·a·tive·ly** *adverb*

¹**cause** \'kȯz\ *noun* [Middle English, from Old French, from Latin *causa*] (13th century)
**1 a** : a reason for an action or condition : MOTIVE **b** : something that brings about an effect or a result **c** : a person or thing that is the occasion of an action or state; *especially* : an agent that brings something about **d** : sufficient reason ⟨discharged for *cause*⟩
**2 a** : a ground of legal action **b** : CASE
**3** : a matter or question to be decided
**4 a** : a principle or movement militantly defended or supported **b** : a charitable undertaking ⟨for a good *cause*⟩
— **cause·less** \-ləs\ *adjective*

²**cause** *transitive verb* **caused; caus·ing** (14th century)
**1** : to serve as a cause or occasion of : MAKE
**2** : to effect by command, authority, or force
— **caus·er** *noun*

'**cause** \'kȯz, 'kəz\ *conjunction* (15th century)
: BECAUSE

**cause cé·lè·bre** *also* **cause ce·le·bre** \ˌkȯz-sə-'leb, -'le-brə, ˌkōz-, -'lebrᵊ\ *noun, plural* **causes cé·lè·bres** *also* **causes celebres** \same\ [French, literally, celebrated case] (1763)
**1** : a legal case that excites widespread interest
**2** : a notorious person, thing, incident, or episode

**cau·se·rie** \ˌkōz-'rē, ˌkō-zə-\ *noun* [French, from *causer* to chat, from Latin *causari* to plead, discuss, from *causa*] (1827)
**1** : an informal conversation : CHAT
**2** : a short informal essay

**cause·way** \'kȯz-ˌwā\ *noun* [Middle English *cauciwey*, from *cauci* + *wey* way] (15th century)
**1** : a raised way across wet ground or water
**2** : HIGHWAY; *especially* : one of ancient Roman construction in Britain
— **causeway** *transitive verb*

**cau·sey** \'kȯ-zē\ *noun, plural* **causeys** [Middle English *cauci*, from Old North French *caucie*, from Medieval Latin *calciata* paved highway, probably from Latin *calc-, calx* limestone — more at CHALK] (14th century)
**1** : CAUSEWAY 1
**2** *obsolete* : CAUSEWAY 2

¹**caus·tic** \'kȯs-tik\ *adjective* [Latin *causticus*, from Greek *kaustikos*, from *kaiein* to burn] (14th century)
**1** : capable of destroying or eating away by chemical action : CORROSIVE
**2** : marked by incisive sarcasm
**3** : relating to or being the surface or curve of a caustic ☆
— **caus·ti·cal·ly** \-ti-k(ə-)lē\ *adverb*
— **caus·tic·i·ty** \kȯ-'sti-sə-tē\ *noun*

²**caustic** *noun* (15th century)
**1** : a caustic agent: as **a** : a substance that burns or destroys organic tissue by chemical action **b** : SODIUM HYDROXIDE
**2** : the envelope of rays emanating from a point and reflected or refracted by a curved surface

**caustic potash** *noun* (1869)
: POTASSIUM HYDROXIDE

---

☆ SYNONYMS
**Caustic, mordant, acrid, scathing** mean stingingly incisive. CAUSTIC suggests a biting wit ⟨*caustic* comments⟩. MORDANT suggests a wit that is used with deadly effectiveness ⟨*mordant* reviews of the play⟩. ACRID implies bitterness and often malevolence ⟨*acrid* invective⟩. SCATHING implies indignant attacks delivered with fierce severity ⟨a *scathing* satire⟩.

---

\ə\ abut \ᵊ\ kitten \ər\ further \a\ ash \ā\ ace
\ä\ mop, mar \aü\ out \ch\ chin \e\ bet \ē\ easy
\g\ go \i\ hit \ī\ ice \j\ job \ŋ\ sing \ō\ go
\ȯ\ law \ȯi\ boy \th\ thin \t̠h̠\ the \ü\ loot \ü\ foot
\y\ yet \zh\ vision     *see also* Guide to Pronunciation

**caustic soda** *noun* (1876)
: SODIUM HYDROXIDE

**cau·ter·ize** \'kò-tə-ˌrīz\ *transitive verb* **-ized;**
**-iz·ing** (14th century)
**1** : to sear with a cautery or caustic
**2** : to make insensible : DEADEN ⟨must oust the feeling, or *cauterize* it —Robert Craft⟩
— **cau·ter·iza·tion** \ˌkò-tə-rə-'zā-shən\ *noun*

**cau·tery** \'kò-tə-rē\ *noun, plural* **-ter·ies**
[Latin *cauterium*, from Greek *kautērion* branding iron, from *kaiein*] (14th century)
**1** : the act or effect of cauterizing : CAUTERIZATION
**2** : an agent (as a hot iron or caustic) used to burn, sear, or destroy tissue

**¹cau·tion** \'kò-shən\ *noun* [Latin *caution-,* *cautio* precaution, from *cavēre* to be on one's guard — more at HEAR] (1596)
**1** : WARNING, ADMONISHMENT
**2** : PRECAUTION
**3** : prudent forethought to minimize risk
**4** : one that astonishes or commands attention ⟨some shoes you see . . . these days are a *caution* —Esquire⟩
— **cau·tion·ary** \-shə-ˌner-ē\ *adjective*

**²caution** *transitive verb* **cau·tioned; cau·tion·ing** \'kò-sh(ə-)niŋ\ (1683)
: to advise caution to

**cau·tious** \'kò-shəs\ *adjective* (circa 1640)
: marked by or given to caution ☆
— **cau·tious·ly** *adverb*
— **cau·tious·ness** *noun*

**cav·al·cade** \ˌka-vəl-'kād, 'ka-vəl-ˌ\ *noun*
[French, ride on horseback, from Old Italian *cavalcata*, from *cavalcare* to go on horseback, from Late Latin *caballicare*, from Latin *caballus* horse; akin to Greek *kaballeion* horse, Middle Irish *capall* workhorse] (1644)
**1 a** : a procession of riders or carriages **b** : a procession of vehicles or ships
**2** : a dramatic sequence or procession : SERIES

**¹cav·a·lier** \ˌka-və-'lir\ *noun* [Middle French, from Old Italian *cavaliere*, from Old Provençal *cavalier*, from Late Latin *caballarius* horseman, from Latin *caballus*] (1589)
**1** : a gentleman trained in arms and horsemanship
**2** : a mounted soldier : KNIGHT
**3** *capitalized* : an adherent of Charles I of England
**4** : GALLANT

**²cavalier** *adjective* (circa 1641)
**1** : DEBONAIR
**2** : marked by or given to offhand and often disdainful dismissal of important matters
**3 a** *capitalized* : of or relating to the party of Charles I of England in his struggles with the Puritans and Parliament **b** : ARISTOCRATIC **c** *capitalized* : of or relating to the English Cavalier poets of the mid-17th century
— **ca·va·lier·ism** \-ˌi-zəm\ *noun*
— **cav·a·lier·ly** *adverb*

**cavalier King Charles spaniel** \-'chär(-ə)lz-\ *noun* [¹*cavalier* + *King Charles spaniel*, a breed of toy spaniel, from *Charles* II of England] (1969)
: any of a breed of toy spaniels with a tapered muzzle and a long silky coat

**ca·val·la** \kə-'va-lə\ *noun, plural* **-la** *or* **-las**
[Spanish *caballa*, a fish, from Late Latin, mare, feminine of Latin *caballus*] (1624)
**1** *also* **ca·val·ly** \-'va-lē\ : any of various carangid fishes (especially genus *Caranx*)
**2** : CERO

**cav·al·let·ti** *also* **cav·a·let·ti** \ˌka-və-'le-tē\ *noun plural but singular or plural in construction* [Italian, plural of *cavalletto* trestle, diminutive of *cavallo* horse, from Latin *caballus*] (1950)
: a series of timber jumps that are adjustable in height for schooling horses

**cav·al·ry** \'ka-vəl-rē, ÷'kal-və-rē\ *noun, plural*
**-ries** [Italian *cavalleria* cavalry, chivalry, from *cavaliere*] (1546)
**1 a** : an army component mounted on horseback **b** : an army component moving in motor vehicles or helicopters and assigned to combat missions that require great mobility
**2** : HORSEMEN ⟨a thousand *cavalry* in flight⟩

**cav·al·ry·man** \-rē-mən, -ˌman\ *noun* (1860)
: a cavalry soldier

**cavalry twill** *noun* (1942)
: TRICOTINE

**cav·a·ti·na** \ˌka-və-'tē-nə, ˌkä-\ *noun* [Italian, from *cavata* production of sound from an instrument, extraction, from *cavare* to dig out, from Latin, to make hollow, from *cavus*] (1813)
**1** : an operatic solo simpler and briefer than an aria
**2** : a songlike instrumental piece or movement

**¹cave** \'kāv\ *noun* [Middle English, from Old French, from Latin *cava*, from *cavus* hollow; akin to Greek *koilos* hollow, and probably to Greek *kyein* to be pregnant — more at CYME] (13th century)
**1** : a natural underground chamber or series of chambers open to the surface
**2** : a usually underground chamber for storage ⟨a wine *cave*⟩; *also* : the articles stored there

**²cave** *verb* **caved; cav·ing** (15th century)
*transitive verb*
: to form a cave in or under : HOLLOW, UNDERMINE
*intransitive verb*
: to explore caves especially as a sport or hobby
— **cav·er** \'kā-vər\ *noun*

**³cave** \'kāv\ *verb* **caved; cav·ing** [probably alteration of *calve*] (1513)
*intransitive verb*
**1** : to fall in or down especially from being undermined — usually used with *in*
**2** : to cease to resist : SUBMIT — usually used with *in*
*transitive verb*
: to cause to fall or collapse — usually used with *in*

**ca·ve·at** \'ka-vē-ˌät, -ˌat; 'kä-vē-ˌät; 'kā-vē-ˌat\ *noun* [Latin, let him beware, from *cavēre* — more at HEAR] (1533)
**1 a** : a warning enjoining one from certain acts or practices **b** : an explanation to prevent misinterpretation
**2** : a legal warning to a judicial officer to suspend a proceeding until the opposition has a hearing

**caveat emp·tor** \-'em(p)-tər, -ˌtòr\ *noun*
[New Latin, let the buyer beware] (1523)
: a principle in commerce: without a warranty the buyer takes the risk

**cave dweller** *noun* (1865)
**1** : one (as a prehistoric man) that dwells in a cave
**2** : one that lives in a city apartment building

**cave–in** \'kā-ˌvin\ *noun* (1860)
**1** : the action of caving in
**2** : a place where earth has caved in

**cave·man** \'kāv-ˌman\ *noun* (1865)
**1** : a cave dweller especially of the Stone Age
**2** : a man who acts in a rough or crude manner

**¹cav·ern** \'ka-vərn *also* -vrən\ *noun* [Middle English *caverne*, from Middle French, from Latin *caverna*, from *cavus*] (14th century)
: CAVE; *especially* : one of large or indefinite extent

**²cavern** *transitive verb* (circa 1630)
**1** : to place in or as if in a cavern
**2** : to form a cavern of : HOLLOW — used with *out*

**cav·er·nic·o·lous** \ˌka-vər-'ni-kə-ləs\ *adjective* (circa 1889)
: inhabiting caves

**cav·ern·ous** \'ka-vər-nəs\ *adjective* (15th century)
**1 a** : having caverns or cavities **b** *of animal tissue* : composed largely of vascular sinuses and capable of dilating with blood to bring about the erection of a body part
**2** : constituting or suggesting a cavern

— **cav·ern·ous·ly** *adverb*

**ca·vet·to** \kə-'ve-(ˌ)tō, kä-\ *noun, plural* **-ti**
\-tē\ [Italian, from *cavo* hollow, from Latin *cavus*] (1664)
: a concave molding having a curve that approximates a quarter circle — see MOLDING illustration

**cav·i·ar** *or* **cav·i·are** \'ka-vē-ˌär *also* 'kä-\ *noun* [earlier *cavery, caviarie,* from obsolete Italian *caviari,* plural of *caviaro,* from Turkish *havyar*] (circa 1560)
**1** : processed salted roe of large fish (as sturgeon)
**2** : something considered too delicate or lofty for mass appreciation — usually used in the phrase *caviar to the general*
**3** : something considered the best of its kind ⟨the *caviar* of porcelain⟩

**cav·il** \'ka-vəl\ *verb* **-iled** *or* **-illed; -il·ing** *or* **-il·ling** \'ka-və-liŋ, 'kav-liŋ\ [Latin *cavillari* to jest, cavil, from *cavilla* raillery; akin to Latin *calvi* to deceive — more at CALUMNY] (1542)
*intransitive verb*
: to raise trivial and frivolous objection
*transitive verb*
: to raise trivial objections to
— **cavil** *noun*
— **cav·il·er** *or* **cav·il·ler** \'ka-və-lər, 'kav-lər\ *noun*

**cav·ing** \'kā-viŋ\ *noun* (1932)
: the sport of exploring caves : SPELUNKING

**cav·i·tary** \'ka-və-ˌter-ē\ *adjective* (1835)
: of, relating to, or characterized by bodily cavitation ⟨*cavitary* tuberculosis⟩ ⟨*cavitary* lesions⟩

**cav·i·tate** \'ka-və-ˌtāt\ *verb* **-tat·ed; -tat·ing** (1909)
*intransitive verb*
: to form cavities or bubbles
*transitive verb*
: to cavitate in

**cav·i·ta·tion** \ˌka-və-'tā-shən\ *noun* [*cavity* + *-ation*] (1895)
: the process of cavitating: as **a** : the formation of partial vacuums in a liquid by a swiftly moving solid body (as a propeller) or by high-intensity sound waves; *also* : the pitting and wearing away of solid surfaces (as of metal or concrete) as a result of the collapse of these vacuums in surrounding liquid **b** : the formation of cavities in an organ or tissue especially in disease

**cav·i·ty** \'ka-və-tē\ *noun, plural* **-ties** [Middle French *cavité,* from Late Latin *cavitas,* from Latin *cavus*] (1541)
**1** : an unfilled space within a mass; *especially* : a hollowed-out space
**2** : an area of decay in a tooth : CARIES

**ca·vort** \kə-'vòrt\ *intransitive verb* [perhaps alteration of *curvet*] (1794)
**1** : PRANCE
**2** : to engage in extravagant behavior

**ca·vy** \'kā-vē\ *noun, plural* **cavies** [New Latin *Cavia,* genus name, from obsolete Portuguese *çavía* (now *savía*), from Tupi *sawiya* rat] (1796)

---

☆ **SYNONYMS**
**Cautious, circumspect, wary, chary**
mean prudently watchful and discreet in the face of danger or risk. CAUTIOUS implies the exercise of forethought usually prompted by fear of danger ⟨a *cautious* driver⟩. CIRCUMSPECT suggests less fear and stresses the surveying of all possible consequences before acting or deciding ⟨*circumspect* in his business dealings⟩. WARY emphasizes suspiciousness and alertness in watching for danger and cunning in escaping it ⟨keeps a *wary* eye on the competition⟩. CHARY implies a cautious reluctance to give, act, or speak freely ⟨*chary* of signing papers without having read them first⟩.

**:** any of several short-tailed rough-haired South American rodents (family Caviidae); *especially* **:** GUINEA PIG

**caw** \'kȯ\ *intransitive verb* [imitative] (1589)
**:** to utter the harsh raucous natural call of the crow or a similar cry
— **caw** *noun*

**cay** \'kē, 'kā\ *noun* [Spanish *cayo* — more at KEY] (1707)
**:** a low island or reef of sand or coral

**cay·enne pepper** \(,)kī-'en-, (,)kā-; 'kī-, 'kā-,\ *noun* [by folk etymology from earlier *cayan,* modification of Tupi *kyinha*] (1756)
**1 :** a pungent condiment consisting of the ground dried fruits or seeds of hot peppers
**2 :** HOT PEPPER; *especially* **:** a cultivated pepper with very long twisted pungent red fruits
**3 :** the fruit of a cayenne pepper

**cay·man** *variant of* CAIMAN

**Ca·yu·ga** \kā-'yü-gə, kī-\ *noun, plural* **Cayuga** *or* **Cayugas** (1744)
**1 :** a member of an American Indian people of New York
**2 :** the Iroquoian language of the Cayuga people

**Cay·use** \'kī-,yüs, kī-'\ *noun, plural* **Cayuse** *or* **Cayuses** (1825)
**1 :** a member of an American Indian people of Oregon and Washington
**2** *plural* **cayuses,** *not capitalized, West* **:** a native range horse

**CB** \,sē-'bē\ *noun* (1959)
**:** CITIZENS BAND; *also* **:** the radio transmitting and receiving set used for citizens-band communications

**CBer** \(,)sē-'bē-ər, -'bir\ *noun* (1959)
**:** one that operates a CB radio

**CCD** \,sē-(,)sē-'dē\ *noun* (1973)
**:** CHARGE-COUPLED DEVICE

**C-clamp** \'sē-,klamp\ *noun* (1926)
**:** a C-shaped general-purpose clamp

**C clef** *noun* (1596)
**:** a movable clef indicating middle C by its placement on one of the lines of the staff

**CD** \,sē-'dē\ *noun* (1979)
**:** COMPACT DISC

**CD4** \,sē-(,)dē-'fōr, -'fȯr\ *noun* [cluster of *d*ifferentiation] (1985)
**:** a large glycoprotein that is found on the surface of T4 cells and is the receptor for HIV

**cDNA** \'sē-,dē-(,)en-'ā, ,sē-\ *noun* [complementary] (1973)
**:** a strand of DNA that is complementary to a given messenger RNA and that serves as a template for production of the messenger RNA in the presence of reverse transcriptase

**CD-ROM** \,sē-,dē-'räm\ *noun* [compact *d*isc *r*ead-*o*nly *m*emory] (1983)
**:** a compact disc containing data that can be read by a computer

**ce·a·no·thus** \,sē-ə-'nō-thəs\ *noun* [New Latin, from Greek *keanōthos,* a thistle] (1785)
**:** any of a genus (*Ceanothus*) of American vines, shrubs, and small trees of the buckthorn family having the calyx disk adherent to the ovary

**¹cease** \'sēs\ *verb* **ceased; ceas·ing** [Middle English *cesen,* from Middle French *cesser,* from Latin *cessare* to hold back, be remiss, frequentative of *cedere*] (14th century)
*transitive verb*
**:** to cause to come to an end especially gradually **:** no longer continue
*intransitive verb*
**1 a :** to come to an end **b :** to bring an activity or action to an end **:** DISCONTINUE
**2** *obsolete* **:** to become extinct **:** DIE OUT
**synonym** see STOP

**²cease** *noun* (14th century)
**:** CESSATION — usually used with *without*

**cease and desist order** *noun* (1926)
**:** an order from an administrative agency to refrain from a method of competition or a labor practice found by the agency to be unfair

**cease–fire** \'sēs-'fīr\ *noun* (1859)
**1 :** a military order to cease firing

**2 :** a suspension of active hostilities

**cease·less** \'sēs-ləs\ *adjective* (1586)
**:** continuing without cease **:** CONSTANT
— **cease·less·ly** *adverb*
— **cease·less·ness** *noun*

**ce·cro·pia moth** \si-'krō-pē-ə-\ *noun* [New Latin *cecropia,* from Latin, feminine of *Cecropius* Athenian, from Greek *Kekropios,* from *Kekrops* Cecrops, legendary king of Athens] (1885)
**:** a large North American saturniid moth (*Hyalophora cecropia*) that is brown with red, white, and black markings

**ce·cum** \'sē-kəm\ *noun, plural* **ce·ca** \-kə\ [New Latin, from Latin *intestinum caecum,* literally, blind intestine] (circa 1721)
**:** a cavity open at one end (as the blind end of a duct); *especially* **:** the blind pouch at the beginning of the large intestine into which the ileum opens from one side and which is continuous with the colon
— **ce·cal** \-kəl\ *adjective*
— **ce·cal·ly** \-kə-lē\ *adverb*

**ce·dar** \'sē-dər\ *noun* [Middle English *cedre,* from Old French, from Latin *cedrus,* from Greek *kedros*] (14th century)
**1 a :** any of a genus (*Cedrus*) of usually tall coniferous trees (as the cedar of Lebanon or the deodar) of the pine family noted for their fragrant durable wood **b :** any of numerous coniferous trees (as of the genera *Juniperus, Chamaecyparis,* or *Thuja*) that resemble the true cedars especially in the fragrance and durability of their wood
**2 :** the wood of a cedar

**ce·dar-ap·ple rust** \'sē-dər-'a-pəl-\ *noun* (1946)
**:** a gall-producing disease especially of the apple caused by a rust fungus (*Gymnosporangium juniperi-virginianae*) that completes the first part of its life cycle on the common red cedar (*Juniperus virginiana*) and the second on the leaves and fruit of the apple

**ce·dar·bird** \-,bərd\ *noun* (1883)
**:** CEDAR WAXWING

**ce·darn** \'sē-dərn\ *adjective* (1634)
*archaic* **:** made of or suggestive of cedar

**cedar of Leb·a·non** \-'leb-nän, -'le-bə-, -nən\ (14th century)
**:** a long-lived cedar (*Cedrus libani*) native to Asia Minor with short fascicled leaves and erect cones

**cedar waxwing** *noun* (circa 1844)
**:** a brown gregarious American waxwing (*Bombycilla cedrorum*) with a yellow band on the tip of the tail and a pale yellow belly

**ce·dar·wood** \'sē-dər-,wùd\ *noun* (14th century)
**:** the wood of a cedar that is especially repellent to insects

**cede** \'sēd\ *transitive verb* **ced·ed; ced·ing** [French or Latin; French *céder,* from Latin *cedere* to go, withdraw, yield] (1754)
**1 :** to yield or grant typically by treaty
**2 :** ASSIGN, TRANSFER
— **ced·er** *noun*

**ce·di** \'sā-dē\ *noun* [Twi *sedi* cowry] (1965)
— see MONEY table

**ce·dil·la** \si-'di-lə\ *noun* [Spanish, the obsolete letter ç (actually a medieval form of the letter z), cedilla, from diminutive of *ceda, zeda* the letter *z,* from Late Latin *zeta* — more at ZED] (1599)
**:** the diacritical mark ¸ placed under a letter (as ç in French) to indicate an alteration or modification of its usual phonetic value (as in the French word *façade*)

**cee** \'sē\ *noun* (1542)
**:** the letter *c*

**cei·ba** \'sā-bə\ *noun* [Spanish] (1790)
**1 :** a massive tropical tree (*Ceiba pentandra*) of the silk-cotton family with large pods filled with seeds invested with a silky floss that yields the fiber kapok
**2 :** KAPOK

**ceil** \'sē(ə)l\ *transitive verb* [Middle English *celen,* from Medieval Latin *celare, caelare,* perhaps from Latin *caelare* to carve, from *caelum* chisel; akin to Latin *caedere* to cut] (15th century)
**1 :** to furnish (as a wooden ship) with a lining
**2 :** to furnish with a ceiling

**ceil·ing** \'sē-liŋ\ *noun* [Middle English *celing,* from *celen*] (1535)
**1 a :** the overhead inside lining of a room **b :** material used to ceil a wall or roof of a room
**2 :** something thought of as an overhanging shelter or a lofty canopy ⟨a *ceiling* of stars⟩
**3 a :** the height above the ground from which prominent objects on the ground can be seen and identified **b :** the height above the ground of the base of the lowest layer of clouds when over half of the sky is obscured
**4 a :** ABSOLUTE CEILING **b :** SERVICE CEILING
**5 :** an upper usually prescribed limit ⟨a *ceiling* on prices, rents, and wages⟩
— **ceil·inged** \-liŋd\ *adjective*

**ceil·om·e·ter** \sē-'lä-mə-tər\ *noun* [*ceil*ing + *-o-* + *-meter*] (1943)
**:** a photoelectric instrument for determining by triangulation the height of the cloud ceiling above the earth

**cein·ture** \saⁿ(n)-'tyùr, -'tùr, 'san-chər\ *noun* [Middle English *seynture,* from Middle French *ceinture,* from Latin *cinctura* — more at CINCTURE] (15th century)
**:** a belt or sash for the waist

**cel** *also* **cell** \'sel\ *noun* [short for *celluloid*] (1938)
**:** a transparent sheet of celluloid on which objects are drawn or painted in the making of animated cartoons

**cel·a·don** \'se-lə-,dän, -lə-dⁿn\ *noun* [French *céladon*] (circa 1768)
**1 :** a grayish yellow green
**2 :** a ceramic glaze originated in China that is greenish in color; *also* **:** an article with a celadon glaze

**cel·an·dine** \'se-lən-,dīn, -,dēn\ *noun* [Middle English *celidoine,* from Middle French, from Latin *chelidonia,* from feminine of *chelidonius* of the swallow, from Greek *chelidonios,* from *chelidon-, chelidōn* swallow] (12th century)
**1 :** a yellow-flowered Eurasian biennial herb (*Chelidonium majus*) of the poppy family naturalized in the eastern U.S.
**2 :** LESSER CELANDINE

**-cele** *noun combining form* [Middle French, from Latin, from Greek *kēlē;* akin to Old English *hēala* hernia]
**:** tumor **:** hernia ⟨varico*cele*⟩

**ce·leb** \sə-'leb\ *noun* (circa 1912)
**:** CELEBRITY 2

**cel·e·brant** \'se-lə-brənt\ *noun* (1839)
**:** one who celebrates; *specifically* **:** the priest officiating at the Eucharist

**cel·e·brate** \'se-lə-,brāt\ *verb* **-brat·ed; -brat·ing** [Latin *celebratus,* past participle of *celebrare* to frequent, celebrate, from *celebr-, celeber* much frequented, famous; perhaps akin to Latin *celer*] (15th century)
*transitive verb*
**1 :** to perform (a sacrament or solemn ceremony) publicly and with appropriate rites ⟨*celebrate* the mass⟩
**2 a :** to honor (as a holiday) by solemn ceremonies or by refraining from ordinary business **b :** to mark (as an anniversary) by festivities or other deviation from routine
**3 :** to hold up or play up for public notice ⟨her poetry *celebrates* the glory of nature⟩
*intransitive verb*
**1 :** to observe a holiday, perform a religious ceremony, or take part in a festival

\ə\ abut \ᵊ\ kitten \ər\ further \a\ ash \ā\ ace
\ä\ mop, mar \aù\ out \ch\ chin \e\ bet \ē\ easy
\g\ go \i\ hit \ī\ ice \j\ job \ŋ\ sing \ō\ go
\ȯ\ law \ȯi\ boy \th\ thin \t͟h\ the \ü\ loot \ù\ foot
\y\ yet \zh\ vision *see also* Guide to Pronunciation

**2** : to observe a notable occasion with festivities
**synonym** see KEEP
— **cel·e·bra·tion** \,se-lə-'brā-shən\ noun
— **cel·e·bra·tor** \'se-lə-,brā-tər\ noun
— **cel·e·bra·to·ry** \-brə-,tōr-ē, -,tór-; ,se-lə-'brā-\ adjective
**cel·e·brat·ed** adjective (circa 1669)
: widely known and often referred to
**synonym** see FAMOUS
— **cel·e·brat·ed·ness** noun
**ce·leb·ri·ty** \sə-'le-brə-tē\ noun, plural **-ties** (14th century)
**1** : the state of being celebrated
**2** : a celebrated person
**ce·le·ri·ac** \sə-'ler-ē-,ak, -'lir-\ noun [irregular from celery] (1743)
: a celery (Apium graveolens rapaceum) grown for its knobby edible root — called also celery root
**ce·ler·i·ty** \sə-'ler-ə-tē\ noun [Middle English celerite, from Middle French, from Latin celeritat-, celeritas, from celer swift — more at HOLD] (15th century)
: rapidity of motion or action
**cel·ery** \'se-lə-rē, 'sel-rē\ noun, plural **-er·ies** [obsolete French celeris, from Italian dialect seleri, plural of selero, modification of Late Latin selinon, from Greek] (1664)
: a European herb (Apium graveolens) of the carrot family; specifically : one of a cultivated variety (A. graveolens dulce) with leafstalks eaten raw or cooked
**celery cabbage** noun (1930)
: CHINESE CABBAGE b
**ce·les·ta** \sə-'les-tə, chə-\ or **ce·leste** \sə-'lest, chə-\ noun [French célesta, alteration of céleste, literally, heavenly, from Latin caelestis] (1899)
: a keyboard instrument with hammers that strike steel plates producing a tone similar to that of a glockenspiel
**¹ce·les·tial** \sə-'les-chəl, -'lesh-, -'les-tē-əl\ adjective [Middle English, from Middle French, from Latin caelestis celestial, from caelum sky] (14th century)
**1** : of, relating to, or suggesting heaven or divinity
**2** : of or relating to the sky or visible heavens ⟨the sun, moon, and stars are celestial bodies⟩
**3 a** : ETHEREAL, OTHERWORLDLY **b** : OLYMPIAN, SUPREME
**4** capitalized [Celestial Empire, old name for China] : of or relating to China or the Chinese
— **ce·les·tial·ly** \-chə-lē, -tē-ə-lē\ adverb
**²celestial** noun (1573)
**1** : a heavenly or mythical being
**2** capitalized : CHINESE 1a
**celestial equator** noun (1875)
: the great circle on the celestial sphere midway between the celestial poles
**celestial globe** noun (circa 1771)
: a globe depicting the celestial bodies
**celestial hierarchy** noun (1883)
: a traditional hierarchy of angels ranked from lowest to highest into the following nine orders: angels, archangels, principalities, powers, virtues, dominions, thrones, cherubim, and seraphim
**celestial marriage** noun (1919)
: a special order of Mormon marriage solemnized in a Mormon temple and held to be binding for a future life as well as the present one
**celestial navigation** noun (1939)
: navigation by observation of the positions of celestial bodies
**celestial pole** noun (1868)
: either of the two points on the celestial sphere around which the diurnal rotation of the stars appears to take place
**celestial sphere** noun (1879)
: an imaginary sphere of infinite radius against which the celestial bodies appear to be projected and of which the apparent dome of the visible sky forms half

**ce·les·tite** \'se-ləs-,tīt, sə-'les-,tīt\ noun [German Zölestin, from Latin caelestis] (1854)
: a usually white mineral consisting of the sulfate of strontium
**ce·li·ac** \'sē-lē-,ak\ adjective [Latin coeliacus, from Greek koiliakos, from koilia cavity, from koilos hollow — more at CAVE] (1662)
: of or relating to the abdominal cavity
**celiac disease** noun (1911)
: a chronic nutritional disorder especially in young children that is characterized by defective digestion and utilization of fats and often by abdominal distention, diarrhea, and fatty stools
**cel·i·ba·cy** \'se-lə-bə-sē\ noun (1663)
**1** : the state of not being married
**2 a** : abstention from sexual intercourse **b** : abstention by vow from marriage
**cel·i·bate** \'se-lə-bət\ noun [Latin caelibatus, from caelib-, caelebs unmarried] (circa 1847)
: a person who lives in celibacy
— **celibate** adjective
**cell** \'sel\ noun [Middle English, from Old English, religious house and Old French celle hermit's cell, from Latin cella small room; akin to Latin celare to conceal — more at HELL] (12th century)
**1** : a small religious house dependent on a monastery or convent
**2 a** : a one-room dwelling occupied by a solitary person (as a hermit) **b** : a single room (as in a convent or prison) usually for one person
**3** : a small compartment, cavity, or bounded space: as **a** : one of the compartments of a honeycomb **b** : a membranous area bounded by veins in the wing of an insect
**4** : a small usually microscopic mass of protoplasm bounded externally by a semipermeable membrane, usually including one or more nuclei and various other organelles with their products, capable alone or interacting with other cells of performing all the fundamental functions of life, and forming the smallest structural unit of living matter capable of functioning independently
**5 a** (1) : a receptacle (as a cup or jar) containing electrodes and an electrolyte either for generating electricity by chemical action or for use in electrolysis (2) : FUEL CELL **b** : a single unit in a device for converting radiant energy into electrical energy or for varying the intensity of an electrical current in accordance with radiation
**6** : a unit in a statistical array (as a spreadsheet) formed by the intersection of a column and a row
**7** : the basic and usually smallest unit of an organization or movement ⟨a communist cell⟩
**8** : a portion of the atmosphere that behaves as a unit
**9** : any of the small sections of a geographic area of a cellular telephone system

cell 4 (schematic): A plant, B animal; 1 cell wall, 2 middle lamella, 3 plasma membrane, 4 mitochondrion, 5 vacuole, 6 Golgi apparatus, 7 cytoplasm, 8 nuclear membrane, 9 nucleolus, 10 nucleus, 11 chromatin, 12 endoplasmic reticulum with associated ribosomes, 13 chloroplast, 14 centriole, 15 lysosome

**¹cel·lar** \'se-lər\ noun [Middle English celer, from Anglo-French, from Latin cellarium storeroom, from cella] (13th century)
**1 a** : BASEMENT; also : a covered excavation **b** : the lowest grade or rank; especially : the lowest place in the standings (as of an athletic league)
**2** : a stock of wines
**²cellar** transitive verb (1677)
: to put into a cellar (as for storage)
**cel·lar·age** \'se-lə-rij\ noun (1602)
: cellar space especially for storage
**cel·lar·er** \'se-lər-ər\ noun [Middle English celerer, from Old French, from Late Latin cellariarius, from Latin cellarium] (13th century)
: an official (as in a monastery) in charge of provisions
**cel·lar·ette** or **cel·lar·et** \,se-lə-'ret\ noun (circa 1807)
: a case or sideboard for holding bottles of wine or liquor
**cell body** noun (1878)
: the nucleus-containing central part of a neuron exclusive of its axons and dendrites
**cell cycle** noun (1961)
: the complete series of events from one cell division to the next — compare $G_1$ PHASE, $G_2$ PHASE, M PHASE, S PHASE
**cell division** noun (1882)
: the process by which cells multiply involving both nuclear and cytoplasmic division — compare MEIOSIS, MITOSIS
**celled** \'seld\ adjective
: having (such or so many) cells — used in combination ⟨single-celled organisms⟩
**cell–me·di·at·ed** \'sel-'mē-dē-,ā-təd\ adjective (1967)
: relating to or being the part of immunity or the immune response that is mediated primarily by T cells
**cell membrane** noun (1870)
: PLASMA MEMBRANE
**cel·lo** \'che-(,)lō\ noun, plural **cello** also **cel·li** \-lē\ [short for violoncello] (circa 1876)
: the bass member of the violin family tuned an octave below the viola
— **cel·list** \'che-list\ noun
**cel·lo·bi·ose** \,se-lə-'bī-,ōs, -,ōz\ noun [International Scientific Vocabulary cellulose + -o- + biose disaccharide, from ¹bi- + ²-ose] (1902)
: a faintly sweet disaccharide $C_{12}H_{22}O_{11}$ obtained by partial hydrolysis of cellulose
**cel·loi·din** \se-'lói-d°n\ noun [cellulose + ¹-oid + ¹-in] (1883)
: a purified pyroxylin used chiefly in microscopy
**cel·lo·phane** \'se-lə-,fān\ noun [French, from cellulose + -phane (as in diaphane diaphanous, from Medieval Latin diaphanus)] (1912)
: regenerated cellulose in thin transparent sheets used especially for packaging
**cell plate** noun (1882)
: a disk formed in the phragmoplast of a dividing plant cell that eventually forms the middle lamella of the wall between the daughter cells
**cell sap** noun (circa 1889)
**1** : the liquid contents of a plant cell vacuole
**2** : CYTOSOL
**cell theory** noun (circa 1890)
: a theory in biology that includes one or both of the statements that the cell is the fundamental structural and functional unit of living matter and that the organism is composed of autonomous cells with its properties being the sum of those of its cells
**cel·lu·lar** \'sel-yə-lər\ adjective [New Latin cellularis, from cellula living cell, from Latin, diminutive of cella small room] (circa 1739)
**1** : of, relating to, or consisting of cells
**2** : containing cavities : having a porous texture ⟨cellular rocks⟩
**3** : of, relating to, or being a radiotelephone

system in which a geographical area (as a city) is divided into small sections each served by a transmitter of limited range so that any available radio channel can be used in different parts of the area simultaneously

— **cel·lu·lar·i·ty** \,sel-yə-'lar-ə-tē\ *noun*
**cel·lu·lase** \'sel-yə-,lās, -,lāz\ *noun* [International Scientific Vocabulary] (1903)
: an enzyme that hydrolyzes cellulose
**cel·lule** \'sel-(,)yü(ə)l\ *noun* [Latin *cellula*] (circa 1693)
: a small cell
**cel·lu·lite** \'sel-yə-,līt, -,lēt\ *noun* [French, literally, accumulation of subcutaneous fat, cellulitis, from *cellule* cell + *-ite* -itis] (1968)
: lumpy fat found in the thighs, hips, and buttocks of some women
**cel·lu·li·tis** \,sel-yə-'lī-təs\ *noun* [New Latin, from *cellula*] (1861)
: diffuse and especially subcutaneous inflammation of connective tissue
**cel·lu·loid** \'sel-yə-,lȯid\ *noun* [from *Celluloid*, a trademark] (1871)
**1** : a tough flammable thermoplastic composed essentially of cellulose nitrate and camphor
**2** : a motion-picture film ⟨a work . . . making its third appearance on *celluloid* —John McCarten⟩
— **celluloid** *adjective*
**cel·lu·lo·lyt·ic** \,sel-yə-lō-'li-tik\ *adjective* [*cellulose* + *-o-* + *-lytic*] (1943)
: hydrolyzing or having the capacity to hydrolyze cellulose
**cel·lu·lose** \'sel-yə-,lōs, -,lōz\ *noun* [French, from *cellule* living cell, from New Latin *cellula*] (1848)
: a polysaccharide $(C_6H_{10}O_5)_x$ of glucose units that constitutes the chief part of the cell walls of plants, occurs naturally in such fibrous products as cotton and kapok, and is the raw material of many manufactured goods (as paper, rayon, and cellophane)
**cellulose acetate** *noun* (1895)
: any of several compounds insoluble in water that are formed especially by the action of acetic acid, anhydride of acetic acid, and sulfuric acid on cellulose and are used for making textile fibers, packaging sheets, photographic films, and varnishes
**cellulose nitrate** *noun* (1880)
: NITROCELLULOSE
**cel·lu·los·ic** \,sel-yə-'lō-sik, -zik\ *adjective* (1881)
: of, relating to, or made from cellulose
— **cellulosic** *noun*
**cell wall** *noun* (circa 1849)
: the usually rigid nonliving permeable wall that surrounds the plasma membrane and encloses and supports the cells of most plants, bacteria, fungi, and algae — see CELL illustration
**Cel·si·us** \'sel-sē-əs, -shəs\ *adjective* [Anders Celsius] (circa 1850)
: relating to, conforming to, or having the international thermometric scale on which the interval between the triple point of water and the boiling point of water is divided into 99.99 degrees with 0.01° representing the triple point and 100° the boiling point ⟨10° *Celsius*⟩ — abbreviation *C*; compare CENTIGRADE ◆
**celt** \'selt\ *noun* [Late Latin *celtis* chisel] (1715)
: a prehistoric stone or metal implement shaped like a chisel or ax head
**Celt** \'kelt, 'selt\ *noun* [Latin *Celtae*, plural, from Greek *Keltoi*] (1550)
**1** : a member of a division of the early Indo-European peoples distributed from the British Isles and Spain to Asia Minor
**2** : a modern Gael, Highland Scot, Irishman, Welshman, Cornishman, or Breton
**¹Celt·ic** \'kel-tik, 'sel-\ *adjective* (1590)
: of, relating to, or characteristic of the Celts or their languages

**²Celtic** *noun* (1739)
: a group of Indo-European languages usually subdivided into Brythonic and Goidelic and now largely confined to Brittany, Wales, western Ireland, and the Scottish Highlands — see INDO-EUROPEAN LANGUAGES table
**Celtic cross** *noun* (1873)
: a cross having essentially the form of a Latin cross with a ring about the intersection of the crossbar and upright shaft — see CROSS illustration
**Celt·i·cist** \'kel-tə-sist, 'sel-\ *noun* (1912)
: a specialist in Celtic languages or cultures
**cem·ba·lo** \'chem-bə-,lō\ *noun, plural* **-ba·li** \-(,)lē\ *or* **-balos** [Italian] (circa 1801)
: HARPSICHORD
**¹ce·ment** \si-'ment *also* 'sē-ment\ *noun* [Middle English *sement*, from Middle French *ciment*, from Latin *caementum* stone chips used in making mortar, from *caedere* to cut] (14th century)
**1 a** : a powder of alumina, silica, lime, iron oxide, and magnesium oxide burned together in a kiln and finely pulverized and used as an ingredient of mortar and concrete; *also* : any mixture used for a similar purpose **b** : CONCRETE
**2** : a binding element or agency: as **a** : a substance to make objects adhere to each other **b** : something serving to unite firmly ⟨justice is the *cement* that holds a political community together —R. M. Hutchins⟩
**3** : CEMENTUM
**4** : a plastic composition made especially of zinc or silica for filling dental cavities
**5** : the fine-grained groundmass or glass of a porphyry
**²cement** (14th century)
*transitive verb*
**1** : to unite or make firm by or as if by cement
**2** : to overlay with concrete
*intransitive verb*
: to become cemented
— **ce·ment·er** *noun*
**ce·men·ta·tion** \,sē-,men-'tā-shən\ *noun* (1594)
**1** : a process of surrounding a solid with a powder and heating the whole so that the solid is changed by chemical combination with the powder
**2** : the act or process of cementing : the state of being cemented
**ce·men·tite** \si-'men-,tīt\ *noun* [¹*cement*] (1888)
: a hard brittle iron carbide $Fe_3C$ that occurs in steel, cast iron, and iron-carbon alloys
**ce·men·ti·tious** \,sē-,men-'ti-shəs\ *adjective* (circa 1828)
: having the properties of cement
**ce·men·tum** \si-'men-təm\ *noun* [New Latin, from Latin *caementum*] (1842)
: a specialized external bony layer covering the dentin of the part of a tooth normally within the gum — see TOOTH illustration
**cem·e·tery** \'se-mə-,ter-ē\ *noun, plural* **-ter·ies** [Middle English *cimitery*, from Middle French *cimitere*, from Late Latin *coemeterium*, from Greek *koimētērion* sleeping chamber, burial place, from *koiman* to put to sleep; akin to Greek *keisthai* to lie, Sanskrit *śete* he lies] (15th century)
: a burial ground
**cen·a·cle** \'se-ni-kəl\ *noun* [Late Latin *cenaculum* the room where Christ and his disciples had the Last Supper, from Latin, top story, probably from *cena* dinner] (1889)
: a retreat house; *especially* : one for Roman Catholic women directed by nuns of the Society of Our Lady of the Cenacle
**-cene** *adjective combining form* [Greek *kainos* new, recent — more at RECENT]
: recent — in names of geologic periods ⟨*Eocene*⟩
**cen·o·bite** \'se-nə-,bīt, *especially British* 'sē-\ *noun* [Late Latin *coenobita*, from *coenobium* monastery, from Late Greek *koinobion*, ulti-

mately from Greek *koin-* coen- + *bios* life — more at QUICK] (circa 1500)
: a member of a religious group living together in a monastic community
— **cen·o·bit·ic** \,se-nə-'bi-tik, ,sē-\ *adjective*
**ce·no·spe·cies** \'sē-nə-,spē-(,)shēz, 'se-, -(,)sēz\ *noun* [*coen-* + *species*] (1922)
: a group of related biological taxonomic units capable by reason of closely related genotypes of essentially free gene interchange
**ceno·taph** \'se-nə-,taf, -,täf\ *noun* [French *cénotaphe*, from Latin *cenotaphium*, from Greek *kenotaphion*, from *kenos* empty + *taphos* tomb] (1603)
: a tomb or a monument erected in honor of a person or group of persons whose remains are elsewhere
**ce·no·te** \si-'nō-tē\ *noun* [Mexican Spanish, from Yucatec *ts'onot*] (1841)
: a deep sinkhole in limestone with a pool at the bottom that is found especially in Yucatán
**Ce·no·zo·ic** \,sē-nə-'zō-ik, ,se-\ *adjective* [Greek *kainos* + English *-zoic*] (1854)
: of, relating to, or being an era of geological history that extends from the beginning of the Tertiary period to the present time and is marked by a rapid evolution of mammals and birds and of angiosperms and especially grasses and by little change in the invertebrates; *also* : relating to the corresponding system of rocks — see GEOLOGIC TIME table
— **Cenozoic** *noun*
**cense** \'sen(t)s\ *transitive verb* **censed; cens·ing** [Middle English, probably short for *encensen* to incense, from Middle French *encenser*, from Late Latin *incensare*, from *incensum* incense] (14th century)
: to perfume especially with a censer
**cen·ser** \'sen(t)-sər\ *noun* (13th century)
: a vessel for burning incense; *especially* : a covered incense burner swung on chains in a religious ritual
**¹cen·sor** \'sen(t)-sər\ *noun* [Latin, from *censēre* to give as one's opinion, assess; perhaps akin to Sanskrit *śaṃsati* he praises] (1531)
**1** : one of two magistrates of early Rome acting as census takers, assessors, and inspectors of morals and conduct
**2** : one who supervises conduct and morals: as **a** : an official who examines materials (as publications or films) for objectionable matter **b** : an official (as in time of war) who reads communications (as letters) and deletes material considered sensitive or harmful

censer

---

◇ WORD HISTORY
**Celsius** The Celsius scale is named after the Swedish astronomer Anders Celsius (1701–44), whose astronomical work is now largely forgotten. Although he was not the first to propose a temperature metric of 100 degrees, Celsius' observations on the usefulness of the freezing and boiling points of water as thermometric constants, published in 1742, were influential. Celsius chose 0° as the boiling point and 100° as the freezing point, but in 1747 the Swedes reversed the order. The Swedish 100-degree system gained widespread scientific acceptance in the 19th century.

---

**3 :** a hypothetical psychic agency that represses unacceptable notions before they reach consciousness
— **cen·so·ri·al** \sen-'sōr-ē-əl, -'sòr-\ *adjective*

²**censor** *transitive verb* **cen·sored; cen·sor·ing** \'sen(t)-sə-riŋ, 'sen(t)s-riŋ\ (1882)
**:** to examine in order to suppress or delete anything considered objectionable

**cen·so·ri·ous** \sen-'sōr-ē-əs, -'sòr-\ *adjective* [Latin *censorius* of a censor, from *censor*] (1536)
**:** marked by or given to censure
*synonym* see CRITICAL
— **cen·so·ri·ous·ly** *adverb*
— **cen·so·ri·ous·ness** *noun*

**cen·sor·ship** \'sen(t)-sər-,ship\ *noun* (circa 1591)
**1 a :** the institution, system, or practice of censoring **b :** the actions or practices of censors; *especially* **:** censorial control exercised repressively
**2 :** the office, power, or term of a Roman censor
**3 :** exclusion from consciousness by the psychic censor

**cen·sur·able** \'sen(t)-sh(ə-)rə-bəl\ *adjective* (1634)
**:** deserving or open to censure

¹**cen·sure** \'sen(t)-shər\ *noun* [Latin *censura*, from *censēre*] (14th century)
**1 :** a judgment involving condemnation
**2** *archaic* **:** OPINION, JUDGMENT
**3 :** the act of blaming or condemning sternly
**4 :** an official reprimand

²**censure** *transitive verb* **cen·sured; cen·sur·ing** \'sen(t)-sh(ə-)riŋ\ (1587)
**1** *obsolete* **:** ESTIMATE, JUDGE
**2 :** to find fault with and criticize as blameworthy
*synonym* see CRITICIZE
— **cen·sur·er** \'sen(t)-shər-ər\ *noun*

**cen·sus** \'sen(t)-səs\ *noun* [Latin, from *censēre*] (1634)
**1 :** a count of the population and a property evaluation in early Rome
**2 :** a usually complete enumeration of a population; *specifically* **:** a periodic governmental enumeration of population
**3 :** COUNT, TALLY
— **census** *transitive verb*

**cent** \'sent\ *noun* [Middle French, hundred, from Latin *centum* — more at HUNDRED] (1782)
**1 :** a monetary unit equal to ¹/₁₀₀ of a basic unit of value — see *birr, dollar, gulden, leone, lilangeni, lira, pound, rand, rupee, shilling* at MONEY table
**2 :** a coin, token, or note representing one cent
**3 :** the fen of the People's Republic of China

**cen·tal** \'sen-t⁸l\ *noun* [Latin *centum* + English *-al* (as in *quintal*)] (1870)
*chiefly British* **:** HUNDREDWEIGHT 1

**cen·taur** \'sen-,tòr\ *noun* [Middle English, from Latin *Centaurus*, from Greek *Kentauros*] (14th century)
**:** any of a race of creatures fabled to be half man and half horse and to live in the mountains of Thessaly

**cen·tau·rea** \sen-'tòr-ē-ə\ *noun* [New Latin, genus name, from Medieval Latin] (circa 1829)
**:** any of a large genus (*Centaurea*) of composite herbs (as knapweed) including several cultivated for their showy heads of tubular florets

**Cen·tau·rus** \-'tòr-əs\ *noun* [Latin (genitive *Centauri*)]
**:** a southern constellation between the Southern Cross and Hydra

**cen·tau·ry** \'sen-,tòr-ē\ *noun, plural* **-ries** [Middle English *centaure*, from Middle French *centaurée*, from Medieval Latin *centaurea*, from Latin *centaureum*, from Greek *kentaureion*, from *Kentauros*] (14th century)

**1 :** any of a genus (*Centaurium*) of low herbs of the gentian family; *especially* **:** an Old World herb (*C. umbellatum*) formerly used as a tonic
**2 :** an herb (*Sabatia angularis*) of the eastern U.S. closely related to centaury

¹**cen·ta·vo** \sen-'tä-(,)vō\ *noun, plural* **-vos** [Spanish, literally, hundredth, from *ciento* hundred, from Latin *centum*] (1883)
— see *boliviano, colón, cordoba, lempira, peso, quetzal, sol, sucre* at MONEY table

²**cen·ta·vo** \-'tä-(,)vü, -(,)vō\ *noun, plural* **-vos** [Portuguese, from Spanish] (1920)
— see *escudo, metical* at MONEY table

**cen·te·nar·i·an** \,sen-tə-'ner-ē-ən\ *noun* (circa 1841)
**:** one that is 100 years old or older
— **centenarian** *adjective*

**cen·te·na·ry** \sen-'te-nə-rē, 'sen-tə-,ner-ē, *especially British* sen-'tē-nə-rē\ *noun, plural* **-ries** [Late Latin *centenarium*, from Latin *centenarius* of a hundred, from *centeni* one hundred each, from *centum* hundred — more at HUNDRED] (1788)
**:** CENTENNIAL
— **centenary** *adjective*

**cen·ten·ni·al** \sen-'te-nē-əl\ *noun* [Latin *centum* + English *-ennial* (as in *biennial*)] (1876)
**:** a 100th anniversary or its celebration
— **centennial** *adjective*
— **cen·ten·ni·al·ly** \-ə-lē\ *adverb*

¹**cen·ter** \'sen-tər, 'se-nər\ *noun* [Middle English *centre*, from Middle French, from Latin *centrum*, from Greek *kentron* sharp point, center of a circle, from *kentein* to prick; probably akin to Old High German *hantag* pointed] (14th century)
**1 a :** the point around which a circle or sphere is described; *broadly* **:** a point that is related to a geometrical figure in such a way that for any point on the figure there is another point on the figure such that a straight line joining the two points is bisected by the original point — called also *center of symmetry* **b :** the center of the circle inscribed in a regular polygon
**2 a :** a point, area, person, or thing that is most important or pivotal in relation to an indicated activity, interest, or condition ⟨a railroad *center*⟩ ⟨the *center* of the controversy⟩ **b :** a source from which something originates ⟨a propaganda *center*⟩ **c :** a group of nerve cells having a common function ⟨respiratory *center*⟩ **d :** a region of concentrated population ⟨an urban *center*⟩ **e :** a facility providing a place for a particular activity or service ⟨a day-care *center*⟩
**3 a :** the middle part (as of the forehead or a stage) **b** *often capitalized* (1) **:** a grouping of political figures holding moderate views especially between those of conservatives and liberals (2) **:** the views of such politicians (3) **:** the adherents of such views
**4 a :** a player occupying a middle position on a team: as (1) **:** the football player in the middle of a line who passes the ball between his legs to a back to start a down (2) **:** the usually tallest player on a basketball team who usually plays near the basket **b :** CENTER FIELD
**5 a :** either of two tapered rods which support work in a lathe or grinding machine and about or with which the work revolves **b :** a conical recess in the end of work (as a shaft) for receiving such a center
— **cen·ter·less** \-ləs\ *adjective*

²**center** *verb* **cen·tered; cen·ter·ing** \'sen-t(ə-)riŋ, 'se-nər-iŋ\ (1610)
*transitive verb*
**1 :** to place or fix at or around a center or central area or position ⟨*center* the picture on the wall⟩
**2 :** to give a central focus or basis ⟨*centers* her hopes on her son⟩ ⟨the plot was *centered* on espionage⟩
**3 :** to adjust (as lenses) so that the axes coincide

**4 a :** to pass (a ball or puck) from either side toward the middle of the playing area **b :** to hand or pass (a football) backward between one's legs to a back to start a down
*intransitive verb*
**:** to have a specified center **:** FOCUS ■

**cen·ter·board** \'sen-tər-,bòrd, 'se-nər-, -,bòrd\ *noun* (1867)
**:** a retractable keel used especially in sailboats

**cen·tered** \'sen-tərd, 'se-nərd\ *adjective* (circa 1893)
**1 :** having a center — often used in combination ⟨a dark-*centered* coneflower⟩
**2 :** having a center of curvature — often used in combination ⟨a 3-*centered* arch⟩
**3 :** emotionally stable and secure
— **cen·tered·ness** \-nəs\ *noun*

**center field** *noun* (1857)
**1 :** the position of the player for defending center field
**2 :** the part of the baseball outfield between right and left field
— **center fielder** *noun*

**cen·ter·fold** \'sen-tər-,fōld, 'se-nər-\ *noun* (1952)
**1 :** a foldout that is the center spread of a magazine
**2 :** a picture (as of a nude) on a centerfold; *also* **:** a model featured in such a picture

**cen·ter·line** \-'līn, -,līn\ *noun* (1807)
**:** a real or imaginary line that is equidistant from the surface or sides of something

**center of curvature** (circa 1856)
**:** the center of the circle whose center lies on the concave side of a curve on the normal to a given point of the curve and whose radius is equal to the radius of curvature at that point

**center of gravity** (1659)
**1 :** CENTER OF MASS
**2 :** the point at which the entire weight of a body may be considered as concentrated so that if supported at this point the body would remain in equilibrium in any position
**3 :** CENTER 2a

**center of mass** (1879)
**:** the point in a body or system of bodies at which the whole mass may be considered as concentrated

**cen·ter·piece** \-,pēs\ *noun* (1803)
**1 :** an object occupying a central position; *especially* **:** an adornment in the center of a table
**2 :** one that is of central importance or interest in a larger whole

**center punch** *noun* (1879)
**:** a hand punch consisting of a short steel bar with a hardened conical point at one end used for marking the centers of holes to be drilled

**center stage** *noun* (1954)
**1 :** the central part of a theatrical stage
**2 :** a central or highly prominent position
— **center stage** *adjective or adverb*

**cen·tes·i·mal** \sen-'te-sə-məl\ *adjective* [Latin *centesimus* hundredth, from *centum*] (1809)
**:** marked by or relating to division into hundredths

¹**cen·tes·i·mo** \chen-'te-zə-,mō\ *noun, plural* **-mi** \-(,)mē\ [Italian] (1851)

---

□ **USAGE**
**center** The intransitive verb *center* is most commonly used with the prepositions *in, on, at,* and *around. At* appears to be favored in mathematical contexts; the others are found in a broad range of contexts. *Center around,* a standard idiom, has often been objected to as illogical. The logic on which the objections are based is irrelevant, since *center around* is an idiom and idioms have their own logic. *Center on* is currently more common in edited prose, and *revolve around* and similar verbs are available if you want to avoid *center around.*

— see *lira* at MONEY table

**²cen·tes·i·mo** \sen-'te-sə-,mō\ *noun, plural* **-mos** [Spanish *centésimo*] (circa 1883)
— see *balboa, peso* at MONEY table

**centi-** *combining form* [French & Latin; French, hundredth, from Latin, hundred, from *centum* — more at HUNDRED]
**1 :** hundred ⟨*centi*pede⟩
**2 :** hundredth part ⟨*centi*meter⟩

**cen·ti·grade** \'sen-tə-,grād, 'sän-\ *adjective* [French, from Latin *centi-* hundred + French *grade*] (1801)
**:** relating to, conforming to, or having a thermometric scale on which the interval between the freezing point of water and the boiling point of water is divided into 100 degrees with 0° representing the freezing point and 100° the boiling point ⟨10° *centigrade*⟩ — abbreviation *C*; compare CELSIUS

**cen·ti·gram** \-,gram\ *noun* (1801)
— see METRIC SYSTEM table

**cen·ti·li·ter** \'sen-ti-,lē-tər, 'sän-\ *noun* (1801)
— see METRIC SYSTEM table

**cen·til·lion** \sen-'til-yən\ *noun, often attributive* [Latin *centum* + English *-illion* (as in *million*)] (circa 1889)
— see NUMBER table

**cen·time** \'sän-,tēm, 'sen-\ *noun* [French, from *cent* hundred, from Latin *centum*] (1801)
— see *dinar, dirham, franc, gourde* at MONEY table

**cen·ti·me·ter** \'sen-tə-,mē-tər, 'sän-\ *noun* (1801)
— see METRIC SYSTEM table

**centimeter–gram–second** *adjective* (1875)
**:** of, relating to, or being a system of units based on the centimeter as the unit of length, the gram as the unit of mass, and the second as the unit of time — abbreviation *cgs*

**cen·ti·mo** \'sen-tə-,mō\ *noun, plural* **-mos** [Spanish *céntimo*] (1899)
— see *bolivar, colon, dobra, guarani, peseta* at MONEY table

**cen·ti·mor·gan** \'sen-tə-,mòr-gən, 'sän-\ *noun* (1919)
**:** a genetic unit equivalent to ¹/₁₀₀ of a morgan

**cen·ti·pede** \'sen-tə-,pēd\ *noun* [Latin *centipeda*, from *centi-* + *ped-, pes* foot — more at FOOT] (1601)
**:** any of a class (Chilopoda) of long flattened many-segmented predaceous arthropods with each segment bearing one pair of legs of which the foremost pair is modified into poison fangs

**cent·ner** \'sent-nər\ *noun* [probably from Low German] (1683)
**:** any of various units of weight used especially in Europe and usually equal to about 110 pounds (about 50 kilograms)

**cen·to** \'sen-(,)tō\ *noun, plural* **cen·to·nes** \sen-'tō-(,)nēz\ [Late Latin, from Latin, patchwork garment; perhaps akin to Sanskrit *kanthā* patched garment] (1605)
**:** a literary work made up of parts from other works

**centr-** *or* **centri-** *or* **centro-** *combining form* [Greek *kentr-, kentro-*, from *kentron* center — more at CENTER]
**:** center ⟨*centr*ifugal⟩ ⟨*centr*oid⟩

**centra** *plural of* CENTRUM

**¹cen·tral** \'sen-trəl\ *adjective* [Latin *centralis*, from *centrum* center] (1647)
**1 :** containing or constituting a center
**2 :** of cardinal importance **:** ESSENTIAL, PRINCIPAL ⟨the *central* character of the novel⟩
**3 a :** situated at, in, or near the center **b :** easily accessible from outlying districts ⟨a *central* location for the new theater⟩
**4 a :** centrally placed and superseding separate scattered units ⟨*central* heating⟩ **b :** controlling or directing local or branch activities ⟨the *central* committee⟩
**5 :** holding to a middle between extremes **:** MODERATE

**6 :** of, relating to, or comprising the brain and spinal cord; *also* **:** originating within the central nervous system ⟨*central* deafness⟩
— **cen·tral·ly** \-trə-lē\ *adverb*

**²central** *noun* (1889)
**1 :** a telephone exchange or operator
**2 :** a central office or bureau usually controlling others ⟨weather *central*⟩

**central angle** *noun* (1904)
**:** an angle formed by two radii of a circle

**central bank** *noun* (1922)
**:** a national bank that operates to establish monetary and fiscal policy and to control the money supply and interest rate
— **central banker** *noun*

**central casting** *noun* (1957)
**:** the department of a movie studio responsible for casting actors — usually used figuratively ⟨a politician right out of *central casting*⟩

**central city** *noun* (1950)
**:** a city that constitutes the densely populated center of a metropolitan area

**cen·tral·ise** *British variant of* CENTRALIZE

**cen·tral·ism** \'sen-trə-,li-zəm\ *noun* (1831)
**:** the concentration of power and control in the central authority of an organization (as a political or educational system) — compare FEDERALISM
— **cen·tral·ist** \-list\ *noun or adjective*
— **cen·tral·is·tic** \,sen-trə-'lis-tik\ *adjective*

**cen·tral·i·ty** \sen-'tra-lə-tē\ *noun, plural* **-ties** (1647)
**1 :** the quality or state of being central
**2 :** central situation
**3 :** tendency to remain in or at the center

**cen·tral·ize** \'sen-trə-,līz\ *verb* **-ized; -iz·ing** (1800)
*intransitive verb*
**:** to form a center **:** cluster around a center
*transitive verb*
**1 :** to bring to a center **:** CONSOLIDATE ⟨*centralize* all the data in one file⟩
**2 :** to concentrate by placing power and authority in a center or central organization
— **cen·tral·i·za·tion** \,sen-trə-lə-'zā-shən\ *noun*
— **cen·tral·iz·er** \'sen-trə-,lī-zər\ *noun*

**central limit theorem** *noun* (1951)
**:** any of several fundamental theorems of probability and statistics that state the conditions under which the distribution of a sum of independent random variables is approximated by the normal distribution; *especially* **:** one which is much applied in sampling and which states that the distribution of a mean of a sample from a population with finite variance is approximated by the normal distribution as the number in the sample becomes large

**central nervous system** *noun* (circa 1907)
**:** the part of the nervous system which in vertebrates consists of the brain and spinal cord, to which sensory impulses are transmitted and from which motor impulses pass out, and which coordinates the activity of the entire nervous system — compare AUTONOMIC NERVOUS SYSTEM

**central processing unit** *noun* (1961)
**:** PROCESSOR 2a(2) — abbreviation *cpu*

**central tendency** *noun* (circa 1928)
**:** the degree of clustering of the values of a statistical distribution that is usually measured by the arithmetic mean, mode, or median

**central time** *noun, often C capitalized* (1883)
**:** the time of the 6th time zone west of Greenwich that includes the central U.S. — see TIME ZONE illustration

**cen·tre** *chiefly British variant of* CENTER

**cen·tric** \'sen-trik\ *adjective* [Greek *kentrikos* of the center, from *kentron*] (circa 1590)
**1 :** located in or at a center **:** CENTRAL ⟨a *centric* point⟩
**2 :** concentrated about or directed to a center ⟨a *centric* activity⟩
**3 :** of, relating to, or having a centromere

**4 :** of, relating to, or resembling an order (Centrales) of radially symmetrical diatoms
— **cen·tri·cal·ly** \-tri-k(ə-)lē\ *adverb*
— **cen·tric·i·ty** \sen-'tri-sə-tē\ *noun*

**-centric** *adjective combining form* [Medieval Latin *-centricus*, from Latin *centrum* center]
**1 :** having (such) a center or (such or so many) centers ⟨poly*centric*⟩
**2 :** having (something specified) as its center ⟨helio*centric*⟩

**¹cen·trif·u·gal** \sen-'tri-fyə-gəl, -'tri-fi-, *especially British* ,sen-tri-'fyü-gəl\ *adjective* [New Latin *centrifugus*, from *centr-* + Latin *fugere* to flee — more at FUGITIVE] (circa 1721)
**1 :** proceeding or acting in a direction away from a center or axis
**2 :** using or acting by centrifugal force ⟨a *centrifugal* pump⟩
**3 :** EFFERENT
**4 :** tending away from centralization **:** SEPARATIST ⟨*centrifugal* tendencies in modern society⟩
— **cen·trif·u·gal·ly** \-gə-lē\ *adverb*

**²centrifugal** *noun* (1866)
**:** a centrifugal machine or a drum in such a machine

**centrifugal force** *noun* (circa 1721)
**1 :** the force that tends to impel a thing or parts of a thing outward from a center of rotation
**2 :** the force that an object moving along a circular path exerts on the body constraining the object and that acts outwardly away from the center of rotation ⟨a stone whirled on a string exerts *centrifugal force* on the string⟩

**cen·tri·fu·ga·tion** \,sen-trə-fyù-'gā-shən, -f(y)ə-\ *noun* (1903)
**:** the process of centrifuging

**¹cen·tri·fuge** \'sen-trə-,fyüj\ *noun* [French, from *centrifuge* centrifugal, from New Latin *centrifugus*] (1887)
**:** a machine using centrifugal force for separating substances of different densities, for removing moisture, or for simulating gravitational effects

**²centrifuge** *transitive verb* **-fuged; -fug·ing** (circa 1895)
**:** to subject to centrifugal action especially in a centrifuge

**cen·tri·ole** \'sen-trē-,ōl\ *noun* [German *Zentriol*, from *Zentrum* center] (circa 1896)
**:** one of a pair of cellular organelles that occur especially in animals, are adjacent to the nucleus, function in the formation of the spindle apparatus during cell division, and consist of a cylinder with nine microtubules arranged peripherally in a circle — see CELL illustration

**cen·trip·e·tal** \sen-'tri-pə-t°l\ *adjective* [New Latin *centripetus*, from *centr-* + Latin *petere* to go to, seek — more at FEATHER] (1709)
**1 :** proceeding or acting in a direction toward a center or axis
**2 :** AFFERENT
**3 :** tending toward centralization **:** UNIFYING
— **cen·trip·e·tal·ly** \-t°l-ē\ *adverb*

**centripetal force** *noun* (1709)
**:** the force that is necessary to keep an object moving in a circular path and that is directed inward toward the center of rotation ⟨a string on the end of which a stone is whirled about exerts *centripetal force* on the stone⟩

**cen·trist** \'sen-trist\ *noun* (1872)
**1 :** *often capitalized* **:** a member of a center party
**2 :** one who holds moderate views
— **cen·trism** \-,tri-zəm\ *noun*
— **centrist** *adjective*

**cen·troid** \'sen-,tròid\ *noun* (1882)
**1 :** CENTER OF MASS

\ə\ abut \ᵊ\ kitten \ər\ further \a\ ash \ā\ ace
\ä\ mop, mar \aù\ out \ch\ chin \e\ bet \ē\ easy
\g\ go \i\ hit \ī\ ice \j\ job \ŋ\ sing \ō\ go
\ò\ law \òi\ boy \th\ thin \th\ the \ü\ loot \ù\ foot
\y\ yet \zh\ vision *see also* Guide to Pronunciation

**2 :** a point whose coordinates are the averages of the corresponding coordinates of a given set of points and which for a given planar or three-dimensional figure (as a triangle or sphere) corresponds to the center of mass of a thin plate of uniform thickness and consistency or a body of uniform consistency having the same boundary

**cen·tro·mere** \'sen-trə-,mir\ *noun* [International Scientific Vocabulary] (circa 1925)
**:** the point or region on a chromosome to which the spindle attaches during mitosis and meiosis
— **cen·tro·mer·ic** \,sen-trə-'mir-ik, -'mer-\ *adjective*

**cen·tro·some** \'sen-trə-,sōm\ *noun* [International Scientific Vocabulary] (1889)
**1 :** CENTRIOLE
**2 :** the centriole-containing region of clear cytoplasm adjacent to the cell nucleus

**cen·tro·sym·met·ric** \,sen-trə-sə-'me-trik\ *adjective* (circa 1909)
**:** symmetric with respect to a central point ⟨*centrosymmetric* molecules⟩ ⟨a *centrosymmetric* curve⟩

**cen·trum** \'sen-trəm\ *noun, plural* **centrums** *or* **cen·tra** \-trə\ [Latin — more at CENTER] (1854)
**1 :** CENTER
**2 :** the body of a vertebra ventral to the neural arch

**cen·tum** \'ken-təm, -,tùm\ *adjective* [Latin, hundred; from the fact that its initial sound (a velar stop) is the representative of an Indo-European palatal stop — more at HUNDRED] (1901)
**:** of, relating to, or constituting an Indo-European language group in which the palatal stops did not in prehistoric times become palatal or alveolar fricatives — compare SATEM

**cen·tu·ri·on** \sen-'chùr-ē-ən, -'tyùr-, -'tùr-\ *noun* [Middle English, from Middle French & Latin; Middle French, from Latin *centurion-, centurio,* from *centuria*] (13th century)
**:** an officer commanding a Roman century

**cen·tu·ry** \'sen(t)-sh(ə-)rē\ *noun, plural* **-ries** [Latin *centuria,* irregular from *centum* hundred] (1533)
**1 :** a subdivision of the Roman legion
**2 :** a group, sequence, or series of 100 like things
**3 :** a period of 100 years especially of the Christian era or of the preceding period of human history
**4 :** a race over a hundred units (as yards or miles)

**century plant** *noun* (1764)
**:** a Mexican agave (*Agave americana*) that takes many years to mature, flowers only once, and then dies

**CEO** \,sē-(,)ē-'ō\ *noun* [chief executive officer] (1975)
**:** the executive with the chief decision-making authority in an organization or business

**ceorl** \'chā-,ôrl\ *noun* [Old English — more at CHURL] (before 12th century)
**:** a freeman of the lowest rank in Anglo-Saxon England

**cèpe** *or* **cepe** \'sēp, sep\ *also* **cep** \'sep\ *noun* [French, from Gascon *cep* tree trunk, mushroom, from Latin *cippus* stake, post] (1865)
**:** a wild edible boletus mushroom (especially *Boletus edulis*)

**cephal-** *or* **cephalo-** *combining form* [Latin, from Greek *kephal-, kephalo-,* from *kephalē*]
**:** head ⟨*cephal*ad⟩ ⟨*cephalo*pod⟩

**ceph·a·lad** \'se-fə-,lad\ *adverb* (1887)
**:** toward the head or anterior end of the body

**ceph·a·lex·in** \,se-fə-'lek-sən\ *noun* [*cepha*losporin + *-ex-* (of unknown origin) + [1]*-in*] (1967)
**:** a semisynthetic cephalosporin $C_{16}H_{17}N_3O_4S$ with a spectrum of antibiotic activity similar to the penicillins

**ce·phal·ic** \sə-'fa-lik\ *adjective* [Middle French *céphalique,* from Latin *cephalicus,*

from Greek *kephalikos,* from *kephalē* head; akin to Old High German *gebal* skull, Old Norse *gafl* gable, Tocharian A *śpāl* head] (1599)
**1 :** of or relating to the head
**2 :** directed toward or situated on or in or near the head
— **ce·phal·i·cal·ly** \-li-k(ə-)lē\ *adverb*

**cephalic index** *noun* (1866)
**:** the ratio multiplied by 100 of the maximum breadth from side to side of the head to its maximum length from front to back in living individuals — compare CRANIAL INDEX

**ceph·a·lin** \'ke-fə-lən, 'se-\ *noun* [International Scientific Vocabulary] (circa 1899)
**:** PHOSPHATIDYLETHANOLAMINE

**ceph·a·li·za·tion** \,se-fə-lə-'zā-shən\ *noun* (1864)
**:** a tendency in the evolution of organisms to concentrate the sensory and neural organs in an anterior head

**ceph·a·lom·e·try** \,se-fə-'lä-mə-trē\ *noun* [International Scientific Vocabulary] (circa 1889)
**:** the science of measuring the head in living individuals — compare CRANIOMETRY
— **ceph·a·lo·met·ric** \-lō-'me-trik\ *adjective*

**ceph·a·lo·pod** \'se-fə-lə-,päd\ *noun* [ultimately from *cephal-* + Greek *pod-, pous* foot — more at FOOT] (1826)
**:** any of a class (Cephalopoda) of marine mollusks including the squids, cuttlefishes, and octopuses that move by expelling water from a tubular siphon under the head and that have a group of muscular usually sucker-bearing arms around the front of the head, highly developed eyes, and usually a sac containing ink which is ejected for defense or concealment
— **cephalopod** *adjective*

**ceph·a·lor·i·dine** \,se-fə-'lòr-ə-,dēn, -'lär-\ *noun* [probably from *cephalo*sporin + *-idine*] (1965)
**:** a semisynthetic broad-spectrum antibiotic $C_{19}H_{17}N_3O_4S_2$ derived from cephalosporin

**ceph·a·lo·spo·rin** \,se-fə-lə-'spòr-ən, -'spòr-\ *noun* [*Cephalosporium,* genus of fungi + [1]*-in*] (1951)
**:** any of several antibiotics produced by an imperfect fungus (genus *Cephalosporium*)

**ceph·a·lo·thin** \'se-fə-lə-thən, -,thin\ *noun* [*cephalo*sporin + *thi-* + [1]*-in*] (1962)
**:** a semisynthetic broad-spectrum antibiotic derived from cephalosporin and used as the sodium salt $C_{16}H_{15}N_2NaO_6S_2$

**ceph·a·lo·tho·rax** \,se-fə-lə-'thòr-,aks, -'thòr-\ *noun* [International Scientific Vocabulary] (1835)
**:** the united head and thorax of an arachnid or higher crustacean

**Ce·phe·id** \'se-f(ē-)id, 'sē-\ *noun* [International Scientific Vocabulary, from *Cepheus*] (circa 1903)
**:** any of a class of pulsating stars whose very regular light variations are related directly to their intrinsic luminosities and whose apparent luminosities are used to estimate distances in astronomy

**Ce·pheus** \'sē-,fyüs, 'sē-fē-əs, 'se-\ *noun* [Latin (genitive *Cephei*), from Greek *Kēpheus*]
**:** a constellation between Cygnus and the north pole

**[1]ce·ram·ic** \sə-'ra-mik, *especially British* kə-\ *adjective* [Greek *keramikos,* from *keramos* potter's clay, pottery] (1850)
**:** of or relating to the manufacture of any product (as earthenware, porcelain, or brick) made essentially from a nonmetallic mineral (as clay) by firing at a high temperature; *also* **:** of or relating to such a product

**[2]ceramic** *noun* (1859)
**1** *plural but singular in construction* **:** the art or process of making ceramic articles
**2 :** a product of ceramic manufacture

**ce·ra·mist** \sə-'ra-mist, 'ser-ə-\ *or* **ce·ram·i·cist** \sə-'ra-mə-sist\ *noun* (1855)

**:** one who engages in ceramics

**ce·ras·tes** \sə-'ras-(,)tēz\ *noun* [Middle English, from Latin, from Greek *kerastēs,* literally, horned, from *keras* horn] (14th century)
**:** a venomous viper (*Cerastes cornutus*) of the Near East having a horny process over each eye — called also *horned viper*

**ce·rate** \'sir-,āt\ *noun* [Middle English, from Latin *ceratum* wax salve, from *cera* wax — more at CERUMEN] (15th century)
**:** an unctuous preparation for external use consisting of wax or resin or spermaceti mixed with oil, lard, and medicinal ingredients

**cer·a·top·sian** \,ser-ə-'täp-sē-ən\ *noun* [New Latin *Ceratopsia,* from *Ceratops,* a genus, from Greek *kerat-, keras* horn + *ōps* facehorn, eye] (1909)
**:** any of a suborder (Ceratopsia) of ornithischian dinosaurs of the Late Cretaceous having horns, a sharp horny beak, and a bony frill projecting backward from the skull
— **ceratopsian** *adjective*

**Cer·ber·us** \'sər-b(ə-)rəs\ *noun* [Latin, from Greek *Kerberos*]
**:** a 3-headed dog that in Greek mythology guards the entrance to Hades
— **Cer·ber·e·an** \,sər-bə-'rē-ən\ *adjective*

**-cerque** *adjective combining form* [French *-cerque,* from Greek *kerkos* tail]
**:** -tailed ⟨homo*cercal*⟩

**cer·car·ia** \(,)sər-'kar-ē-ə, -'ker-\ *noun, plural* **-i·ae** \-ē-,ē\ [New Latin, from Greek *kerkos*] (circa 1871)
**:** a usually tadpole-shaped larval trematode worm that develops in a molluscan host from a redia
— **cer·car·i·al** \-ē-əl\ *adjective*

**cer·cus** \'sər-kəs\ *noun, plural* **cer·ci** \'sər-,sī, -,kī\ [New Latin, from Greek *kerkos*] (1826)
**:** either of a pair of simple or segmented appendages at the posterior end of various arthropods that usually act as sensory organs

**[1]cere** \'sir\ *transitive verb* **cered; cer·ing** [Middle English, to wax, from Middle French *cirer,* from Latin *cerare,* from *cera*] (15th century)
**:** to wrap in or as if in a cerecloth

**[2]cere** *noun* [Middle English *sere,* from Middle French *cere,* from Medieval Latin *cera,* from Latin, wax] (15th century)
**:** a usually waxy protuberance or enlarged area at the base of the bill of a bird

**[1]ce·re·al** \'sir-ē-əl\ *adjective* [French or Latin; French *céréale,* from Latin *cerealis* of Ceres, of grain, from *Ceres*] (1818)
**:** relating to grain or to the plants that produce it; *also* **:** made of grain

**[2]cereal** *noun* (1832)
**1 :** a plant (as a grass) yielding starchy grain suitable for food; *also* **:** its grain
**2 :** a prepared foodstuff of grain

**cereal leaf beetle** *noun* (1962)
**:** a small reddish brown black-headed Old World chrysomelid beetle (*Oulema melanopus*) that feeds on cereal grasses and is a serious threat to U.S. grain crops

**cer·e·bel·lum** \,ser-ə-'be-ləm\ *noun, plural* **-bellums** *or* **-bel·la** \-'be-lə\ [Medieval Latin, from Latin, diminutive of *cerebrum*] (1543)
**:** a large dorsally projecting part of the brain concerned especially with the coordination of muscles and the maintenance of bodily equilibrium, situated between the brain stem and the back of the cerebrum, and formed in humans of two lateral lobes and a median lobe — see BRAIN illustration
— **cer·e·bel·lar** \-'be-lər\ *adjective*

**cerebr-** *or* **cerebro-** *combining form* [*cerebrum*]
**1 :** brain **:** cerebrum ⟨*cerebr*ation⟩
**2 :** cerebral and ⟨*cerebro*spinal⟩

**ce·re·bral** \sə-'rē-brəl, 'ser-ə-\ *adjective* [French *cérébral,* from Latin *cerebrum* brain; akin to Old High German *hirni* brain, Greek

*kara* head, *keras* horn, Sanskrit *śiras* head — more at HORN] (1816)
**1 a :** of or relating to the brain or the intellect **b :** of, relating to, or being the cerebrum **2 a :** appealing to intellectual appreciation ⟨*cerebral* drama⟩ **b :** primarily intellectual in nature ⟨a *cerebral* society⟩
— **ce·re·bral·ly** \-brə-lē\ *adverb*
**cerebral cortex** *noun* (1926)
: the surface layer of gray matter of the cerebrum that functions chiefly in coordination of sensory and motor information
**cerebral hemisphere** *noun* (1816)
: either of the two hollow convoluted lateral halves of the cerebrum — see BRAIN illustration
**cerebral palsy** *noun* (1889)
: a disability resulting from damage to the brain before, during, or shortly after birth and outwardly manifested by muscular incoordination and speech disturbances — compare SPASTIC PARALYSIS
— **cerebral–palsied** *adjective*
**cer·e·brate** \'ser-ə-ˌbrāt\ *intransitive verb* **-brat·ed; -brat·ing** [back-formation from *cerebration,* from *cerebrum*] (1915)
: to use the mind : THINK
— **cer·e·bra·tion** \ˌser-ə-'brā-shən\ *noun*
**ce·re·bro·side** \'ser-ə-brə-ˌsīd, sə-'rē-\ *noun* [*cerebrose* galactose] (1883)
: any of various lipids found especially in nerve tissue
**ce·re·bro·spi·nal** \sə-ˌrē-brō-'spī-n°l, ˌser-ə-brō-\ *adjective* (1826)
: of or relating to the brain and spinal cord or to these together with the cranial and spinal nerves that innervate voluntary muscles
**cerebrospinal fluid** *noun* (circa 1889)
: a liquid that is comparable to serum, is secreted from the blood into the lateral ventricles of the brain, and serves chiefly to maintain uniform pressure within the brain and spinal cord
**cerebrospinal meningitis** *noun* (1889)
: inflammation of the meninges of both brain and spinal cord; *specifically* : an infectious epidemic and often fatal meningitis caused by the meningococcus
**ce·re·bro·vas·cu·lar** \sə-ˌrē-brō-'vas-kyə-lər, ˌser-ə-brō-\ *adjective* (1935)
: of or involving the cerebrum and the blood vessels supplying it
**ce·re·brum** \sə-'rē-brəm, 'ser-ə-brəm\ *noun,* *plural* **-brums** *or* **-bra** \-brə\ [Latin] (1615)
**1 :** BRAIN 1a
**2 :** an enlarged anterior or upper part of the brain; *especially* : the expanded anterior portion of the brain that in higher mammals overlies the rest of the brain, consists of cerebral hemispheres and connecting structures, and is considered to be the seat of conscious mental processes : TELENCEPHALON
**cere·cloth** \'sir-ˌklȯth\ *noun* [alteration of earlier *cered cloth* (waxed cloth)] (1553)
: cloth treated with melted wax or gummy matter and formerly used especially for wrapping a dead body
**cere·ment** \'ser-ə-mənt, 'sir-mənt\ *noun* (1602)
: a shroud for the dead; *especially* : CERECLOTH — usually used in plural
**¹cer·e·mo·ni·al** \ˌser-ə-'mō-nē-əl\ *adjective* (14th century)
: marked by, involved in, or belonging to ceremony : stressing careful attention to form and detail ☆
— **cer·e·mo·ni·al·ism** \-ə-ˌli·zəm\ *noun*
— **cer·e·mo·ni·al·ist** \-ə-list\ *noun*
— **cer·e·mo·ni·al·ly** \-ə-lē\ *adverb*
**²ceremonial** *noun* (14th century)
: a ceremonial act, action, or system
**cer·e·mo·ni·ous** \ˌser-ə-'mō-nē-əs\ *adjective* (1553)
**1 :** devoted to forms and ceremony : PUNCTILIOUS
**2 :** of, relating to, or constituting a ceremony

**3 :** according to formal usage or prescribed procedures
**4 :** marked by ceremony
*synonym* see CEREMONIAL
— **cer·e·mo·ni·ous·ly** *adverb*
— **cer·e·mo·ni·ous·ness** *noun*
**cer·e·mo·ny** \'ser-ə-ˌmō-nē\ *noun,* *plural* **-nies** [Middle English *ceremonie,* from Middle French *cérémonie,* from Latin *caerimonia*] (14th century)
**1 :** a formal act or series of acts prescribed by ritual, protocol, or convention ⟨the marriage *ceremony*⟩
**2 a :** a conventional act of politeness or etiquette ⟨the *ceremony* of introduction⟩ **b :** an action performed only formally with no deep significance **c :** a routine action performed with elaborate pomp
**3 a :** prescribed procedures : USAGES ⟨the *ceremony* attending an inauguration⟩ **b :** observance of an established code of civility or politeness ⟨opened the door without *ceremony* and strode in⟩
**Ce·ren·kov radiation** \chə-'reŋ-kȯf-, chər-'yeŋ-\ *noun* [P. A. *Cherenkov*] (1939)
: light produced by charged particles (as electrons) traversing a transparent medium at a speed greater than that of light in the same medium — called also *Cerenkov light*
**Ce·res** \'sir-(ˌ)ēz\ *noun* [Latin]
: the Roman goddess of agriculture — compare DEMETER
**ce·re·us** \'sir-ē-əs\ *noun* [New Latin, genus name, from Latin, wax candle, from *cera* wax — more at CERUMEN] (1730)
: any of various cacti (as of the genus *Cereus*) of the western U.S. and tropical America
**ce·ric** \'sir-ik, 'ser-\ *adjective* (circa 1879)
: of, relating to, or containing cerium especially with a valence of four
**ce·rise** \sə-'rēs, -'rēz\ *noun* [French, literally, cherry, from Late Latin *ceresia* — more at CHERRY] (1844)
: a moderate red
**ce·ri·um** \'sir-ē-əm\ *noun* [New Latin, from *Ceres*] (1804)
: a malleable ductile metallic element that is the most abundant of the rare-earth group — see ELEMENT table
**cer·met** \'sər-ˌmet\ *noun* [*cer*amic + *met*al] (1948)
: a composite structural material of a heat-resistant compound (as titanium carbide) and a metal (as nickel) used especially for turbine blades
**cero** \'ser-(ˌ)ō\ *noun,* *plural* **cero** *or* **ceros** [modification of Spanish *sierra* saw, cero] (1884)
: either of two large food and sport fishes (*Scomberomorus regalis* and *S. cavalla* of the warmer parts of the western Atlantic
**ce·rous** \'sir-əs\ *adjective* (circa 1872)
: of, relating to, or containing cerium especially with a valence of three
**¹cer·tain** \'sər-t°n\ *adjective* [Middle English, from Old French, from (assumed) Vulgar Latin *certanus,* from Latin *certus,* from past participle of *cernere* to sift, discern, decide; akin to Greek *krinein* to separate, decide, judge, Old Irish *criathar* sieve] (13th century)
**1 :** FIXED, SETTLED ⟨a *certain* percentage of the profit⟩
**2 :** of a specific but unspecified character, quantity, or degree ⟨the house has a *certain* charm⟩
**3 a :** DEPENDABLE, RELIABLE ⟨a *certain* remedy for the disease⟩ **b :** known or proved to be true : INDISPUTABLE ⟨it is *certain* that we exist⟩
**4 a :** INEVITABLE ⟨the *certain* advance of age⟩ **b :** incapable of failing : DESTINED — used with a following infinitive ⟨she is *certain* to do well⟩
**5 :** assured in mind or action
*synonym* see SURE
— **for certain** : as a certainty : ASSUREDLY

**²certain** *pronoun, plural in construction* (15th century)
: certain ones
**cer·tain·ly** \-lē\ *adverb* (14th century)
**1 :** in a manner that is certain : with certainty
**2 :** it is certain that : ASSUREDLY
**cer·tain·ty** \'sər-t°n-tē\ *noun, plural* **-ties** (14th century)
**1 :** something that is certain
**2 :** the quality or state of being certain especially on the basis of evidence ☆
**cer·tes** \'sər-tēz, 'sərts\ *adverb* [Middle English, from Old French, from *cert* certain, from Latin *certus*] (13th century)
*archaic* : in truth : CERTAINLY
**¹cer·tif·i·cate** \(ˌ)sər-'ti-fi-kət\ *noun* [Middle English *certificat,* from Middle French, from Medieval Latin *certificatum,* from Late Latin, neuter of *certificatus,* past participle of *certificare* to certify] (15th century)
**1 :** a document containing a certified statement especially as to the truth of something; *specifically* : a document certifying that one has fulfilled the requirements of and may practice in a field
**2 :** something serving the same end as a certificate
**3 :** a document evidencing ownership or debt ⟨a *certificate* of deposit⟩
**²cer·tif·i·cate** \-'ti-fə-ˌkāt\ *transitive verb* **-cat·ed; -cat·ing** (1883)
: to testify to or authorize by a certificate; *especially* : to recognize as having met special qualifications (as of a governmental agency or professional board) within a field
— **cer·tif·i·ca·to·ry** \-'ti-fi-kə-ˌtōr-ē, -ˌtȯr-\ *adjective*
**cer·ti·fi·ca·tion** \ˌsər-tə-fə-'kā-shən\ *noun* (15th century)
**1 :** the act of certifying : the state of being certified
**2 :** a certified statement
**certification mark** *noun* (1947)

---

☆ **SYNONYMS**

**Ceremonial, ceremonious, formal, conventional** mean marked by attention to or adhering strictly to prescribed forms. CEREMONIAL and CEREMONIOUS both imply strict attention to what is prescribed by custom or by ritual, but CEREMONIAL applies to things that are associated with ceremonies ⟨a *ceremonial* offering⟩, CEREMONIOUS to persons given to ceremony or to acts attended by ceremony ⟨made his *ceremonious* entrance⟩. FORMAL applies both to things prescribed by and to persons obedient to custom and may suggest stiff, restrained, or old-fashioned behavior ⟨a *formal* report⟩ ⟨the headmaster's *formal* manner⟩. CONVENTIONAL implies accord with general custom and usage ⟨*conventional* courtesy⟩ and may suggest a stodgy lack of originality or independence ⟨*conventional* fiction⟩.

**Certainty, certitude, conviction** mean a state of being free from doubt. CERTAINTY and CERTITUDE are very close; CERTAINTY may stress the existence of objective proof ⟨claims that cannot be confirmed with scientific *certainty*⟩, while CERTITUDE may emphasize a faith in something not needing or not capable of proof ⟨believes with *certitude* in an afterlife⟩. CONVICTION applies especially to belief strongly held by an individual ⟨holds firm *convictions* on every issue⟩.

---

\ə\ abut \°\ kitten \ər\ further \a\ ash \ā\ ace
\ä\ mop, mar \au̇\ out \ch\ chin \e\ bet \ē\ easy
\g\ go \i\ hit \ī\ ice \j\ job \ŋ\ sing \ō\ go
\ȯ\ law \ȯi\ boy \th\ thin \th\ the \ü\ loot \u̇\ foot
\y\ yet \zh\ vision *see also* Guide to Pronunciation

: a mark or device used to identify a product or service that has been certified to conform to a particular set of standards

**certified mail** *noun* (1955)
: first class mail for which proof of delivery is secured but no indemnity value is claimed

**certified milk** *noun* (1899)
: milk produced in dairies that operate under the rules and regulations of an authorized medical milk commission

**certified public accountant** *noun* (1896)
: an accountant who has met the requirements of a state law and has been granted a certificate

**cer·ti·fy** \'sər-tə-ˌfī\ *transitive verb* **-fied; -fy-ing** [Middle English *certifien*, from Middle French *certifier*, from Late Latin *certificare*, from Latin *certus* certain — more at CERTAIN] (14th century)
**1 :** to attest authoritatively: as **a :** CONFIRM **b :** to present in formal communication **c :** to attest as being true or as represented or as meeting a standard **d :** to attest officially to the insanity of
**2 :** to inform with certainty **:** ASSURE
**3 :** to guarantee (a personal check) as to signature and amount by so indicating on the face
**4 :** CERTIFICATE, LICENSE ☆
— **cer·ti·fi·able** \-ˌfī-ə-bəl\ *adjective*
— **cer·ti·fi·ably** \-blē\ *adverb*
— **cer·ti·fi·er** \-ˌfī(-ə)r\ *noun* See in addition APPROVE.

**cer·tio·ra·ri** \ˌsər-sh(ē-)ə-ˈrar-ē, -ˈrär-ē\ *noun* [Middle English, from Latin, literally, to be informed; from the use of the word in the writ] (15th century)
: a writ of superior court to call up the records of an inferior court or a body acting in a quasi-judicial capacity

**cer·ti·tude** \'sər-tə-ˌtüd *also* -ˌtyüd\ *noun* [Middle English, from Late Latin *certitudo*, from Latin *certus*] (15th century)
**1 :** the state of being or feeling certain
**2 :** certainty of act or event
**synonym** see CERTAINTY

**ce·ru·le·an** \sə-ˈrü-lē-ən\ *adjective* [Latin *caeruleus* dark blue] (1667)
: resembling the blue of the sky

**ce·ru·lo·plas·min** \sə-ˌrü-lō-ˈplaz-mən\ *noun* [International Scientific Vocabulary *cerulo-* (from Latin *caeruleus*) + *plasma* + $^1$*-in*] (circa 1952)
: a blue copper-binding serum alpha globulin with enzymatic activity

**ce·ru·men** \sə-ˈrü-mən\ *noun* [New Latin, irregular from Latin *cera* wax; akin to Greek *kēros* wax] (1741)
: the yellow waxy secretion from the glands of the external ear — called also *earwax*
— **ce·ru·mi·nous** \-mə-nəs\ *adjective*

**ce·ruse** \sə-ˈrüs, 'sir-ˌüs\ *noun* [Middle English, from Middle French *céruse*, from Latin *cerussa*] (14th century)
**1 :** white lead as a pigment
**2 :** a cosmetic containing white lead

**ce·rus·site** \sə-ˈrə-ˌsīt\ *noun* [German *Zerussit*, from Latin *cerussa*] (1850)
: a mineral that consists of lead carbonate occurring in colorless transparent crystals and also in massive form and is a source of white lead

**cer·ve·lat** \'sər-və-ˌlat, -ˌlä\ *noun* [obsolete French (now *cervelas*)] (1613)
: smoked sausage made from a combination of pork and beef

**cer·vi·cal** \'sər-vi-kəl\ *adjective* (1681)
: of or relating to a neck or cervix

**cervical cap** *noun* (1923)
: a contraceptive device in the form of a thimble-shaped molded cap that fits over the uterine cervix and blocks sperm from entering the uterus

**cer·vi·ci·tis** \ˌsər-və-ˈsī-təs\ *noun* [New Latin] (1889)
: inflammation of the uterine cervix

**cer·vine** \'sər-ˌvīn\ *adjective* [Latin *cervinus* of a deer, from *cervus* stag, deer — more at HART] (circa 1828)
: of, relating to, or resembling deer

**cer·vix** \'sər-viks\ *noun, plural* **cer·vi·ces** \'sər-və-ˌsēz, (ˌ)sər-ˈvī-(ˌ)sēz\ *or* **cer·vix·es** [Latin *cervic-, cervix*] (15th century)
**1 :** NECK; *especially* **:** the back part of the neck
**2 :** a constricted portion of an organ or part; *especially* **:** the narrow outer end of the uterus

**ce·sar·e·an** *also* **ce·sar·i·an** \si-ˈzar-ē-ən, -ˈzer-\ *noun* (circa 1903)
: CESAREAN SECTION
— **cesarean** *also* **cesarian** *adjective*

**cesarean section** *also* **cesarian section** *noun* [from the belief that Julius Caesar was born this way] (1615)
: surgical incision of the walls of the abdomen and uterus for delivery of offspring ◆

**ce·si·um** \'sē-zē-əm *also* -zhē-\ *noun* [New Latin, from Latin *caesius* bluish gray] (1861)
: a silver-white soft ductile element of the alkali metal group that is the most electropositive element known and that is used especially in photoelectric cells — see ELEMENT table

**cesium 133** *noun* (1966)
: an isotope of cesium used especially in atomic clocks and one of whose atomic transitions is used as a scientific time standard

**cess** \'ses\ *noun* [probably short for *success*] (1830)
*chiefly Irish* **:** LUCK — usually used in the phrase *bad cess to you*

**ces·sa·tion** \se-ˈsā-shən\ *noun* [Middle English *cessacioun*, from Middle French *cessation*, from Latin *cessation-, cessatio* delay, idleness, from *cessare* to delay, be idle — more at CEASE] (14th century)
: a temporary or final ceasing (as of action)
**:** STOP

**ces·sion** \'se-shən\ *noun* [Middle English, from Middle French, from Latin *cession-, cessio*, from *cedere* to withdraw — more at CEDE] (15th century)
: a yielding to another **:** CONCESSION

**cess·pit** \'ses-ˌpit\ *noun* [*cesspool* + *pit*] (1777)
: a pit for the disposal of refuse (as sewage)

**cess·pool** \-ˌpü(ə)l\ *noun* [by folk etymology from Middle English *suspiral* vent, cesspool, from Middle French *souspirail* ventilator, from *souspirer* to sigh, from Latin *suspirare*, literally, to draw a long breath — more at SUSPIRE] (1782)
: an underground reservoir for liquid waste (as household sewage)

**ces·ta** \'ses-tə\ *noun* [Spanish, literally, basket, from Latin *cista* box, basket] (circa 1902)
: a narrow curved wicker basket used to catch and propel the ball in jai alai

**ces·tode** \'ses-ˌtōd\ *noun* [New Latin *Cestoda*, taxonomic group comprising tapeworms, ultimately from Greek *kestos* girdle] (circa 1890)
: TAPEWORM
— **cestode** *adjective*

**¹ces·tus** \'ses-təs\ *noun, plural* **ces·ti** \-ˌtī\ [Latin, girdle, belt, from Greek *kestos*, from *kestos* stitched, from *kentein* to prick — more at CENTER] (1557)
: a woman's belt; *especially* **:** a symbolic one worn by a bride

*cesta*

**²cestus** *noun* [Latin *cestus, caestus*] (circa 1720)
: a hand covering of leather bands often loaded with lead or iron and used by boxers in ancient Rome

**ce·su·ra** *variant of* CAESURA

**ce·ta·cean** \si-ˈtā-shən\ *noun* [ultimately from Latin *cetus* whale, from Greek *kētos*] (1836)
: any of an order (Cetacea) of aquatic mostly marine mammals that include the whales, dolphins, porpoises, and related forms and that have a torpedo-shaped nearly hairless body, paddle-shaped forelimbs but no hind limbs, one or two nares opening externally at the top of the head, and a horizontally flattened tail used for locomotion
— **cetacean** *adjective*
— **ce·ta·ceous** \-shəs\ *adjective*

**ce·tane** \'sē-ˌtān\ *noun* [from *cetyl*, the radical $C_{16}H_{33}$] (1871)
: a colorless oily hydrocarbon $C_{16}H_{34}$ found in petroleum

**cetane number** *noun* (1935)
: a measure of the ignition value of a diesel fuel that represents the percentage by volume of cetane in a mixture of liquid methylnaphthalene that gives the same ignition lag as the oil being tested — called also *cetane rating*; compare OCTANE NUMBER

**ce·te·ris pa·ri·bus** \ˈkā-tər-əs-ˈpar-ə-bəs, 'ke-, 'se-\ *adverb* [New Latin, other things being equal] (1601)
: if all other relevant things, factors, or elements remain unaltered

**ce·tol·o·gy** \sē-ˈtä-lə-jē\ *noun* [Latin *cetus* whale] (circa 1828)
: a branch of zoology dealing with the cetaceans
— **ce·tol·o·gist** \-jist\ *noun*

**Ce·tus** \'sē-təs\ *noun* [Latin (genitive *Ceti*), literally, whale]
: an equatorial constellation south of Pisces and Aries

---

☆ **SYNONYMS**
**Certify, attest, witness, vouch** mean to testify to the truth or genuineness of something. CERTIFY usually applies to a written statement, especially one carrying a signature or seal ⟨*certified* that the candidate had met all requirements⟩. ATTEST applies to oral or written testimony usually from experts or witnesses ⟨*attested* to the authenticity of the document⟩. WITNESS applies to the subscribing of one's own name to a document as evidence of its genuineness ⟨*witnessed* the signing of the will⟩. VOUCH applies to one who testifies as a competent authority or a reliable person ⟨willing to *vouch* for her integrity⟩.

---

◇ **WORD HISTORY**
**cesarean section** The name *Caesar* is a cognomen, a nickname given to one member of a Roman clan and borne by his descendants as a kind of surname. No one knows who the original Caesar was, but his descendants within his clan, the Julii, continued to use his cognomen and formed a major branch of the clan. According to a legend related by the Roman naturalist Pliny, the first Caesar was so called because he was cut from the womb of his mother ( *a caeso matris utero*), *Caesar* supposedly being a derivative of the verb *caedere* "to cut." This etymology is dubious, but the name *Caesar* has continued to be associated with surgery to remove a child that cannot be delivered naturally. In recent centuries, it has been widely believed that the most famous bearer of the cognomen, the politician and general Gaius Julius Caesar (100–44 B.C.), was delivered by cesarean section, but there is no authority for this notion in ancient sources. Moreover, Julius Caesar's mother lived long after his birth, an unlikely outcome if she had undergone such an operation, which few women could have survived in those days.

**ce·tyl alcohol** \'sē-t°l-\ *noun* [International Scientific Vocabulary *cet-* (from Latin *cetus* whale) + *-yl;* from its occurrence in spermaceti] (1873)
**:** a waxy crystalline alcohol $C_{16}H_{34}O$ obtained by the saponification of spermaceti or the hydrogenation of palmitic acid and used especially in pharmaceutical and cosmetic preparations and in making detergents

**ce·vi·che** \sə-'vē-(,)chä, -chē\ *variant of* SEVICHE

**Cha·blis** \sha-'blē, shə-, shä-; 'sha-(,)blē\ *noun, plural* **Cha·blis** \-'blēz, -(,)blēz\ [French, from *Chablis,* town in France] (1668)
**1 :** a dry sharp white burgundy wine
**2 :** a semidry soft white California wine

**cha-cha** \'chä-(,)chä\ *noun* [American Spanish *cha-cha-cha*] (1954)
**:** a fast rhythmic ballroom dance of Latin-American origin with a basic pattern of three steps and a shuffle

**chac·ma baboon** \'chäk-mə-\ *noun* [Khoikhoi] (circa 1909)
**:** a large dusky baboon (*Papio ursinus*) of southern African savannas — called also *chacma*

**cha·conne** \shä-'kòn, sha-, -'kän, -'kən\ *noun* [French & Spanish; French *chaconne,* from Spanish *chacona*] (1685)
**1 :** an old Spanish dance tune of Latin American origin
**2 :** a musical composition in moderate triple time typically consisting of variations on a repeated succession of chords

**chad** \'chad\ *noun* [origin unknown] (1947)
**:** small pieces of paper or cardboard produced in punching paper tape or data cards; *also* **:** a piece of chad
— **chad·less** \-ləs\ *adjective*

**Chad·ic** \'cha-dik\ *or* **Chad** \'chad\ *noun* (circa 1950)
**:** a subfamily of the Afro-Asiatic language family comprising numerous languages of northern Nigeria, northern Cameroon, and Chad
— **Chadic** *adjective*

**cha·dor** \'chə-dər, 'chä-\ *noun* [Hindi & Persian; Hindi *caddar,* from Persian *chaddar, chādar*] (1614)
**:** a large cloth worn as a combination head covering, veil, and shawl usually by Muslim women especially in Iran

**chae·ta** \'kē-tə\ *noun, plural* **chae·tae** \'kē-,tē\ [New Latin, from Greek *chaitē* long flowing hair] (circa 1866)
**:** BRISTLE, SETA
— **chae·tal** \'kē-t°l\ *adjective*

**chae·to·gnath** \'kē-,täg-,nath, -tə(g)-\ *noun* [New Latin *Chaetognatha,* class or phylum name, ultimately from Greek *chaitē* + *gnathos* jaw — more at -GNATHOUS] (circa 1889)
**:** ARROWWORM
— **chaetognath** *adjective*

**¹chafe** \'chāf\ *verb* **chafed; chaf·ing** [Middle English *chaufen* to warm, from Middle French *chaufer,* from (assumed) Vulgar Latin *calfare,* alteration of Latin *calefacere,* from *calēre* to be warm + *facere* to make — more at LEE, DO] (14th century)
*transitive verb*
**1 :** IRRITATE, VEX
**2 :** to warm by rubbing especially with the hands
**3 a :** to rub so as to wear away **:** ABRADE (the boat *chafed* its sides against the dock) **b :** to make sore by or as if by rubbing
*intransitive verb*
**1 :** to feel irritation or discontent **:** FRET (*chafes* at his restrictive desk job)
**2 :** to rub and thereby cause wear or irritation

**²chafe** *noun* (1551)
**1 :** a state of vexation **:** RAGE
**2 :** injury or wear caused by friction; *also* **:** FRICTION, RUBBING

**cha·fer** \'chā-fər\ *noun* [Middle English *cheafer,* from Old English *ceafor;* probably akin to Old English *ceafl* jowl — more at JOWL] (before 12th century)
**:** any of various scarab beetles (as a cockchafer) that feed on leaves and flowers and whose larvae feed on plant roots

**¹chaff** \'chaf\ *noun* [Middle English *chaf,* from Old English *ceaf;* akin to Old High German *cheva* husk] (before 12th century)
**1 :** the seed coverings and other debris separated from the seed in threshing grain
**2 :** something comparatively worthless
**3 :** the scales borne on the receptacle among the florets in the heads of many composite plants
**4 :** material (as strips of foil or clusters of fine wires) ejected into the air for reflecting radar waves (as for confusing an enemy's radar detection or for tracking a descending spacecraft)
— **chaffy** \'cha-fē\ *adjective*

**²chaff** *noun* [probably from ¹*chaff*] (1821)
**:** light jesting talk **:** BANTER

**³chaff** (1827)
*transitive verb*
**:** to tease good-naturedly
*intransitive verb*
**:** JEST, BANTER

**¹chaf·fer** \'cha-fər\ *noun* [Middle English *chaffare,* from *chep* trade + *fare* journey — more at CHEAP, FARE] (13th century)
*archaic* **:** a haggling about price

**²chaffer** *verb* **chaf·fered; chaf·fer·ing** \'cha-f(ə-)riŋ\ (14th century)
*intransitive verb*
**1 :** HAGGLE
**2** *British* **:** to exchange small talk **:** CHATTER
*transitive verb*
**1 :** EXCHANGE, BARTER
**2 :** to bargain for
— **chaf·fer·er** \-fər-ər\ *noun*

**chaf·finch** \'cha-(,)finch\ *noun* [Middle English, from Old English *ceaffinc,* from *ceaf* + *finc* finch] (before 12th century)
**:** a common European finch (*Fringilla coelebs*) of which the male has a pinkish-brown breast

**chaf·ing dish** \'chā-fiŋ-\ *noun* [Middle English *chafing,* present participle of *chaufen, chafen* to warm] (15th century)
**:** a utensil for cooking or keeping food warm especially at the table

**Cha·gas' disease** \'shä-gəs-, -gə-səz-\ *noun* [Carlos *Chagas* (died 1934) Brazilian physician] (1912)
**:** a tropical American disease that is caused by a trypanosome (*Trypanosoma cruzi*) and is marked by prolonged high fever, edema, and enlargement of the spleen, liver, and lymph nodes

**¹cha·grin** \shə-'grin\ *noun* [French, from *chagrin* sad] (circa 1681)
**:** disquietude or distress of mind caused by humiliation, disappointment, or failure

**²chagrin** *transitive verb* **cha·grined** \-'grind\; **cha·grin·ing** \-'gri-niŋ\ (1733)
**:** to vex or unsettle by disappointing or humiliating

**¹chain** \'chān\ *noun, often attributive* [Middle English *cheyne,* from Middle French *chaeine,* from Latin *catena*] (14th century)
**1 a :** a series of usually metal links or rings connected to or fitted into one another and used for various purposes (as support, restraint, transmission of mechanical power, or measurement) **b :** a series of links used or worn as an ornament or insignia **c (1) :** a measuring instrument of 100 links used in surveying **(2) :** a unit of length equal to 66 feet (20 meters)
**2 :** something that confines, restrains, or secures
**3 a :** a series of things linked, connected, or associated together (a *chain* of events) **b :** a group of enterprises or institutions of the same kind or function usually under a single ownership, management, or control (fast-food *chains*) **c :** a number of atoms or chemical groups united like links in a chain

**²chain** *transitive verb* (14th century)
**1 :** to obstruct or protect by a chain
**2 :** to fasten, bind, or connect with or as if with a chain; *also* **:** FETTER

**chaî·né** \shā-'nā\ *noun* [French, from past participle of *chaîner* to chain] (1897)
**:** a series of short usually fast turns by which a ballet dancer moves across the stage

**chain gang** *noun* (1834)
**:** a gang of convicts chained together especially as an outside working party

**chain letter** *noun* (1905)
**:** a letter sent to several persons with a request that each send copies of the letter to an equal number of persons

**chain–link fence** *noun* (circa 1927)
**:** a fence of heavy steel wire woven to form a diamond-shaped mesh

**chain mail** *noun* (1822)
**:** flexible armor of interlinked metal rings

**chain of command** *noun* (1898)
**:** a series of executive positions in order of authority (a military *chain of command*)

**chain pickerel** *noun* [from the markings resembling chains on the sides] (1887)
**:** a large greenish black pickerel (*Esox niger*) with dark markings along the sides that is common in quiet waters of eastern North America

**chain reaction** *noun* (circa 1902)
**1 a :** a series of events so related to each other that each one initiates the next **b :** a number of events triggered by the same initial event
**2 :** a self-sustaining chemical or nuclear reaction yielding energy or products that cause further reactions of the same kind
— **chain–re·act** \,chān-rē-'akt\ *intransitive verb*

**chain rule** *noun* (circa 1847)
**:** a mathematical rule concerning the differentiation of a function of a function (as $f\,[u(x)]$) by which under suitable conditions of continuity and differentiability one function is differentiated with respect to the second function considered as an independent variable and then the second function is differentiated with respect to its independent variable

**chain saw** *noun* (1944)
**:** a portable power saw that has teeth linked together to form an endless chain
— **chain–saw** \'chān-,sò\ *transitive verb*

**chain–smoke** \'chān-'smōk\ (1930)
*intransitive verb*
**:** to smoke especially cigarettes continually
*transitive verb*
**:** to smoke (as cigarettes) almost without interruption
— **chain–smok·er** \-,smō-kər\ *noun*

**chain stitch** *noun* (1820)
**1 :** an ornamental stitch like chain links
**2 :** a machine stitch forming a chain on the underside of the work

**chain store** *noun* (1910)
**:** one of numerous usually retail stores having the same ownership and selling the same lines of goods

**chain-wheel** \'chān-,hwēl, -,wēl\ *noun* (1845)
**:** SPROCKET 1

**¹chair** \'cher, 'char\ *noun* [Middle English *chaiere,* from Old French, from Latin *cathedra,* from Greek *kathedra,* from *kata-* cata- + *hedra* seat — more at SIT] (13th century)
**1 a :** a seat typically having four legs and a back for one person **b :** ELECTRIC CHAIR — used with *the*

**2 a :** an official seat or a seat of authority, state, or dignity **b :** an office or position of authority or dignity **c :** PROFESSORSHIP ⟨holds a university *chair*⟩ **d :** CHAIRMAN 1
**3 :** a sedan chair
**4 :** a position of employment usually of one occupying a chair or desk; *specifically* **:** the position of a player in an orchestra or band
**5 :** any of various devices that hold up or support
*usage* see CHAIRMAN
**²chair** *transitive verb* (1552)
**1 :** to install in office
**2** *chiefly British* **:** to carry on the shoulders in acclaim ⟨we *chaired* you through the market place —A. E. Housman⟩
**3 :** to preside as chairman of
**chair car** *noun* (1880)
**1 :** a railroad car having pairs of chairs with individually adjustable backs on each side of the aisle
**2 :** PARLOR CAR
**chair·lift** \'cher-,lift, 'char-\ *noun* (1940)
**:** a motor-driven conveyor consisting of a series of seats suspended from a cable and used for transporting skiers or sightseers up or down a long slope or mountainside
**¹chair·man** \-mən\ *noun* (1650)
**1 a :** the presiding officer of a meeting or an organization or committee **b :** the administrative officer of a department of instruction (as in a college)
**2 :** a carrier of a sedan chair ▪
**— chair·man·ship** \-,ship\ *noun*
**²chairman** *transitive verb* **-maned** *or* **-manned; -man·ing** *or* **-man·ning** (1888)
**:** CHAIR 3
**chair·per·son** \-,pər-sᵊn\ *noun* (1971)
**:** CHAIRMAN 1
*usage* see CHAIRMAN
**chair·wom·an** \-,wu̇-mən\ *noun* (1685)
**:** a woman who acts as chairman
*usage* see CHAIRMAN
**chaise** \'shāz\ *noun* [French, chair, chaise, alteration of Old French *chaiere*] (1701)
**1 :** any of various light horse-drawn vehicles: as **a :** a two-wheeled carriage for one or two persons with a folding top **b :** POST CHAISE
**2 :** CHAISE LONGUE
**chaise longue** \'shāz-'lȯṅ\ *noun, plural* **chaise longues** *also* **chaises longues** \'shāz-'lȯṅ(z)\ [French, literally, long chair] (1800)
**:** a long reclining chair
**chaise lounge** \'shāz-'laȯnj, 'chās-\ *noun* [by folk etymology from French *chaise longue*] (circa 1906)
**:** CHAISE LONGUE
**chak·ra** \'chä-krə, 'shä-, 'chə-\ *noun* [Sanskrit *cakra,* literally, wheel — more at WHEEL] (1888)
**:** any of several points of physical or spiritual energy in the human body according to yoga philosophy
**cha·la·za** \kə-'lā-zə, -'la-\ *noun, plural* **-zae** \-,zē\ *or* **-zas** [New Latin, from Greek, hailstone] (circa 1704)
**1 :** either of two spiral bands in the white of a bird's egg that extend from the yolk and attach to opposite ends of the lining membrane — see EGG illustration
**2 :** the basal part of a plant ovule where the nucellus is fused to the surrounding integument and to which the funiculus is usually attached
**— cha·la·zal** \-'lā-zəl, -'la-\ *adjective*
**Chal·ce·do·ni·an** \,kal-sə-'dō-nē-ən\ *adjective* (1788)
**:** of or relating to Chalcedon or the ecumenical council held there in A.D. 451 declaring Monophysitism heretical
**— Chalcedonian** *noun*
**chal·ce·do·ny** \kal-'se-dᵊn-ē, chal-; 'kal-sə-,dō-nē, 'chal-, -,dä-\ *noun, plural* **-nies** [Middle English *calcedonie,* a precious stone, from

Late Latin *chalcedonius,* from Greek *Chalkē-dōn* Chalcedon] (13th century)
**:** a translucent quartz that is commonly pale blue or gray with nearly waxlike luster
**— chal·ce·don·ic** \,kal-sə-'dä-nik\ *adjective*
**chal·cid** \'kal-səd\ *noun* [ultimately from Greek *chalkos* copper, bronze] (1893)
**:** any of a large superfamily (Chalcidoidea) of mostly minute hymenopterous insects parasitic in the larval state on the larvae or pupae of other insects
**— chalcid** *adjective*
**chal·co·cite** \'kal-kə-,sīt\ *noun* [alteration of *chalcosine,* from French, irregular from Greek *chalkos*] (1868)
**:** a black or gray lustrous metallic mineral that consists of a sulfide of copper and is an important copper ore
**chal·co·gen** \'kal-kə-jən\ *noun* [International Scientific Vocabulary *chalk-* bronze, ore (from Greek *chalkos*) + *-gen;* from the occurrence of oxygen and sulfur in many ores] (circa 1961)
**:** any of the elements oxygen, sulfur, selenium, and tellurium
**chal·co·gen·ide** \-jə-,nīd\ *noun* (1945)
**:** a binary compound of a chalcogen with a more electropositive element or radical
**chal·co·py·rite** \,kal-kə-'pī-,rīt\ *noun* [New Latin *chalcopyrites,* from Greek *chalkos* + Latin *pyrites*] (1835)
**:** a yellow mineral consisting of copper-iron sulfide and constituting an important ore of copper
**Chal·da·ic** \kal-'dā-ik, kȯl-, käl-\ *adjective or noun* (1662)
**:** CHALDEAN
**Chal·de·an** \kal-'dē-ən, kȯl-, käl-\ *noun* [Latin *Chaldaeus* Chaldean, astrologer, from Greek *Chaldaios,* from *Chaldaia* Chaldea, region of ancient Babylonia] (1581)
**1 a :** a member of an ancient Semitic people that became dominant in Babylonia **b :** the Semitic language of the Chaldeans
**2 :** a person versed in the occult arts
**— Chaldean** *adjective*
**Chal·dee** \'kal-,dē, 'kȯl-, 'käl-\ *noun* [Middle English *Caldey,* probably from Middle French *chaldée,* from Latin *Chaldaeus*] (14th century)
**1 :** CHALDEAN 1a
**2 :** the Aramaic vernacular that was the original language of some parts of the Bible
**chal·dron** \'chȯl-drən, 'chäl-\ *noun* [Middle French *chauderon,* from *chaudere* pot, from Late Latin *caldaria* — more at CAULDRON] (1615)
**:** any of various old units of measure varying from 32 to 72 imperial bushels
**cha·let** \sha-'lā, 'sha-(,)lā\ *noun* [French] (1782)
**1 :** a remote herdsman's hut in the Alps
**2 a :** a Swiss dwelling with unconcealed structural members and a wide overhang at the front and sides **b :** a cottage or house in chalet style

**chalet 2a**

**chal·ice** \'cha-ləs\ *noun* [Middle English, from Anglo-French, from Latin *calic-, calix;* akin to Greek *kalyx* calyx] (14th century)
**1 :** a drinking cup **:** GOBLET; *especially* **:** the eucharistic cup
**2 :** the cup-shaped interior of a flower
**¹chalk** \'chȯk\ *noun* [Middle English, from Old English *cealc,* from Latin *calc-, calx* lime; akin to Greek *chalix* pebble] (before 12th century)
**1 a :** a soft white, gray, or buff limestone composed chiefly of the shells of foraminifers **b :** chalk or a material resembling chalk especially when used in the form of a crayon

**2 a :** a mark made with chalk **b** *British* **:** a point scored in a game
**— chalky** \'chȯ-kē\ *adjective*
**²chalk** (1580)
*transitive verb*
**1 :** to write or draw with chalk
**2 :** to rub or mark with chalk
**3 a :** to delineate roughly **:** SKETCH ⟨*chalk* out a plan of attack⟩ **b :** to set down or add up with or as if with chalk **:** RECORD — usually used with *up* ⟨*chalk* up a victory⟩
*intransitive verb*
**:** to become chalky
**chalk·board** \'chȯk-,bōrd, -,bȯrd\ *noun* (1936)
**:** BLACKBOARD
**chalk talk** \'chȯk-,tȯk\ *noun* (1881)
**:** a talk or lecture illustrated at a blackboard
**chalk up** *transitive verb* (1826)
**1 :** ASCRIBE, CREDIT
**2 :** ATTAIN, ACHIEVE ⟨*chalk up* a record score for the season⟩
**chal·lah** *also* **chal·la** \'kä-lə, 'hä-\ *noun* [Yiddish *khale,* from Hebrew *ḥallāh*] (1927)
**:** egg-rich yeast-leavened bread that is usually braided or twisted before baking and is traditionally eaten by Jews on the Sabbath and holidays
**¹chal·lenge** \'cha-lənj\ *verb* **chal·lenged; chal·leng·ing** [Middle English *chalengen* to accuse, from Old French *chalengier,* from Latin *calumniari* to accuse falsely, from *calumnia* calumny] (13th century)
*transitive verb*
**1 :** to demand as due or deserved **:** REQUIRE ⟨an event that *challenges* explanation⟩
**2 :** to order to halt and prove identity ⟨the sentry *challenged* the stranger⟩
**3 :** to dispute especially as being unjust, invalid, or outmoded **:** IMPUGN ⟨new data that *challenges* old assumptions⟩
**4 :** to question formally the legality or legal qualifications of
**5 a :** to confront or defy boldly **:** DARE **b :** to call out to duel or combat **c :** to invite into competition
**6 :** to arouse or stimulate especially by presenting with difficulties
**7 :** to administer a physiological and especially an immunologic challenge to (an organism or cell)
*intransitive verb*
**1 :** to make or present a challenge

**2 :** to take legal exception
— **chal·leng·er** *noun*
²**challenge** *noun* (14th century)
**1 a :** a summons that is often threatening, provocative, stimulating, or inciting; *specifically*
**:** a summons to a duel to answer an affront **b**
**:** an invitation to compete in a sport
**2 a :** a calling to account or into question **:** PROTEST **b :** an exception taken to a juror before he is sworn **c :** a sentry's command to halt and prove identity **d :** a questioning of the right or validity of a vote or voter
**3 :** a stimulating task or problem ⟨looking for new *challenges*⟩
**4 :** the process of provoking or testing physiological activity by exposure to a specific substance; *especially* **:** a test of immunity by exposure to an antigen
**chal·leng·ing** \-lən-jiŋ\ *adjective* (1842)
**1 :** arousing competitive interest, thought, or action ⟨a *challenging* course of study⟩
**2 :** invitingly provocative **:** FASCINATING ⟨a *challenging* personality⟩
— **chal·leng·ing·ly** \-jiŋ-lē\ *adverb*
**chal·lis** \'sha-lē\ *noun, plural* **chal·lises** \'sha-lēz\ [probably from the name *Challis*] (circa 1837)
**:** a lightweight soft clothing fabric made of cotton, wool, or synthetic yarns
**cha·lone** \'kā-,lōn, 'ka-\ *noun* [Greek *chalōn*, present participle of *chalan* to slacken] (1914)
**:** an internal secretion that is held to inhibit mitosis in a specific tissue — compare HORMONE
¹**cha·ly·be·ate** \kə-'lē-bē-ət, -'li-\ *adjective* [probably from New Latin *chalybeatus*, irregular from Latin *chalybs* steel, from Greek *chalyb-, chalyps*, from *Chalybes*, ancient people in Asia Minor] (1634)
**:** impregnated with salts of iron; *also* **:** having a taste due to iron ⟨*chalybeate* springs⟩
²**chalybeate** *noun* (1667)
**:** a chalybeate liquid or medicine
**cham** \'kam\ *variant of* KHAN
**cham·ae·phyte** \'ka-mi-,fīt\ *noun* [Greek *chamai* on the ground + English *-phyte* — more at HUMBLE] (1913)
**:** a perennial plant that bears its perennating buds just above the surface of the soil
¹**cham·ber** \'chām-bər\ *noun* [Middle English *chambre*, from Old French, from Late Latin *camera*, from Latin, arched roof, from Greek *kamara* vault] (13th century)
**1 :** ROOM; *especially* **:** BEDROOM
**2 :** a natural or artificial enclosed space or cavity
**3 a :** a hall for the meetings of a deliberative, legislative, or judicial body ⟨the senate *chamber*⟩ **b :** a room where a judge transacts business — usually used in plural **c :** the reception room of a person of rank or authority
**4 a :** a legislative or judicial body; *especially* **:** either of the houses of a bicameral legislature **b :** a voluntary board or council
**5 a :** the part of the bore of a gun that holds the charge **b :** a compartment in the cartridge cylinder of a revolver
— **cham·bered** \-bərd\ *adjective*
²**chamber** *transitive verb* **cham·bered; cham·ber·ing** \-b(ə-)riŋ\ (1575)
**1 :** to place in or as if in a chamber **:** HOUSE
**2 :** to serve as a chamber for; *especially* **:** to accommodate in the chamber of a firearm
³**chamber** *adjective* (1706)
**:** being, relating to, or performing chamber music
**chambered nautilus** *noun* (1858)
**:** NAUTILUS 1
**cham·ber·lain** \'chām-bər-lən\ *noun* [Middle English, from Old French *chamberlayn*, of Germanic origin; akin to Old High German *chamarling* chamberlain, from *chamara* chamber, from Late Latin *camera*] (13th century)
**1 :** an attendant on a sovereign or lord in his bedchamber

**2 a :** a chief officer in the household of a king or nobleman **b :** TREASURER
**3 :** an often honorary papal attendant; *specifically* **:** a priest having a rank of honor below domestic prelate
**cham·ber·maid** \-,mād\ *noun* (1587)
**:** a maid who makes beds and does general cleaning of bedrooms (as in a hotel)
**chamber music** *noun* (circa 1789)
**:** music and especially instrumental ensemble music intended for performance in a private room or small auditorium and usually having one performer for each part
**chamber of commerce** (1797)
**:** an association of businessmen to promote commercial and industrial interests in the community
**chamber of horrors** (1849)
**:** a place in which macabre or horrible objects are exhibited; *also* **:** a collection of such exhibits
**chamber orchestra** *noun* (circa 1927)
**:** a small orchestra usually with one player for each part
**chamber pot** *noun* (1540)
**:** a bedroom vessel for urination and defecation
**cham·bray** \'sham-,brā, -brē\ *noun* [irregular from *Cambrai*, France] (1814)
**:** a lightweight clothing fabric with colored warp and white filling yarns
**cha·me·leon** \kə-'mēl-yən\ *noun, often attributive* [Middle English *camelion*, from Middle French, from Latin *chamaeleon*, from Greek *chamaileōn*, from *chamai* on the ground + *leōn* lion — more at HUMBLE] (14th century)
**1 :** any of a family (Chamaeleontidae) of chiefly arboreal Old World lizards with prehensile tail, independently movable eyeballs, and unusual ability to change the color of the skin
**2 a :** a person given to often expedient or facile change in ideas or character **b :** one that is subject to quick or frequent change especially in appearance
**3 :** AMERICAN CHAMELEON
— **cha·me·le·on·ic** \-,mē-lē-'ä-nik\ *adjective*
— **cha·me·leon·like** \-līk\ *adjective*
¹**cham·fer** \'cham(p)-fər, 'cham-pər\ *transitive verb* **cham·fered; cham·fer·ing** \-f(ə-)riŋ, -p(ə-)riŋ\ [back-formation from *chamfering*, alteration of Middle French *chanfreint*, from past participle of *chanfraindre* to bevel, from *chant* edge (from Latin *canthus* iron tire) + *fraindre* to break, from Latin *frangere* — more at CANT, BREAK] (circa 1573)
**1 :** to cut a furrow in (as a column) **:** GROOVE
**2 :** to make a chamfer on **:** BEVEL
²**chamfer** *noun* (circa 1847)
**:** a beveled edge
**cham·fron** \'sham-frən, 'cham-\ *noun* [Middle English *shamfron*, from Middle French *chanfrein*] (15th century)
**:** the headpiece of a horse's bard
**cham·ois** \'sha-mē, *sense 1 also* sham-'wä\ *noun, plural* **cham·ois** *also* **cham·oix** \*sense 1* 'sha-mē(z) *or* sham-'wä(z), *senses 2 & 3* 'sha-mēz\ [Middle French, from Late Latin *camox*] (1560)
**1 :** a small goatlike antelope (*Rupicapra rupicapra*) of mountainous regions from southern Europe to the Caucasus
**2** *also* **cham·my** *or* **sham·my** \'sha-mē\ **:** a soft pliant leather prepared from the skin of the chamois or from sheepskin
**3 :** a cotton fabric made in imitation of chamois leather
**cham·o·mile** \'ka-mə-,mīl, -,mēl\ *noun* [Middle English *camemille*, from Medieval Latin *camomilla*, modification of Latin *chamaemelon*, from Greek *chamaimēlon*, from *chamai + mēlon* apple] (13th century)
**1 :** a composite herb (*Chamaemelum nobile* synonym *Anthemis nobilis*) of Europe and

North Africa with strong-scented foliage and flower heads that contain a bitter medicinal substance
**2 :** any of several composite plants (genera *Matricaria* and *Anthemis*) related to chamomile; *especially* **:** a Eurasian herb (*M. recutita* synonym *M. chamomilla*) naturalized in North America

chamomile

¹**champ** \'champ, 'chämp, 'chômp\ *verb* [perhaps imitative] (14th century)
*transitive verb*
**1 :** CHOMP
**2 :** MASH, TRAMPLE
*intransitive verb*
**1 :** to make biting or gnashing movements
**2 :** to show impatience of delay or restraint — usually used in the phrase *champing at the bit* ⟨he was *champing* at the bit to begin⟩
²**champ** \'champ\ *noun* (1868)
**:** CHAMPION
**cham·pac** *or* **cham·pak** \'cham-,pak, 'chəm-(,)pək\ *noun* [Hindi & Sanskrit; Hindi *campak*, from Sanskrit *campaka*] (circa 1770)
**:** an Asian tree (*Michelia champaca*) of the magnolia family with yellow flowers
**cham·pagne** \sham-'pān\ *noun* [French, from *Champagne*, France] (1664)
**1 :** a white sparkling wine made in the old province of Champagne, France; *also* **:** a similar wine made elsewhere
**2 :** a pale orange yellow to light grayish yellowish brown
**cham·paign** \sham-'pān\ *noun* [Middle English *champaine*, from Middle French *champagne*, from Late Latin *campania* — more at CAMPAIGN] (15th century)
**1 :** an expanse of level open country **:** PLAIN
**2** *archaic* **:** BATTLEFIELD
— **champaign** *adjective*
**cham·pers** \'sham-pərz\ *noun plural but singular in construction* [by alteration] (1955)
*British* **:** CHAMPAGNE 1
**cham·per·ty** \'cham-pər-tē\ *noun* [Middle English *champartie*, from Middle French *champart* field rent, from *champ* field (from Latin *campus*) + *part* portion — more at PART] (15th century)
**:** a proceeding by which a person not a party in a suit bargains to aid in or carry on its prosecution or defense in consideration of a share of the matter in suit
— **cham·per·tous** \-pər-təs\ *adjective*
**cham·pi·gnon** \(,)sham-pē-'nyōn, (,)shäm-'nyōⁿ; sham-'pin-yən, cham-\ *noun* [French, from Middle French, alteration of *champigneul*, ultimately from Late Latin *campania*] (1670)
**:** an edible fungus; *especially* **:** MEADOW MUSHROOM
¹**cham·pi·on** \'cham-pē-ən\ *noun* [Middle English, from Old French, from Medieval Latin *campion-, campio*, of West Germanic origin; akin to Old English *cempa* warrior] (13th century)
**1 :** WARRIOR, FIGHTER
**2 :** a militant advocate or defender ⟨a *champion* of civil rights⟩
**3 :** one that does battle for another's rights or honor ⟨God will raise me up a *champion* —Sir Walter Scott⟩
**4 :** a winner of first prize or first place in competition; *also* **:** one who shows marked superiority ⟨a *champion* at selling⟩
²**champion** *transitive verb* (1605)
**1** *archaic* **:** CHALLENGE, DEFY

\ə\ abut \ə⟩\ kitten \ər\ further \a\ ash \ā\ ace
\ä\ mop, mar \aù\ out \ch\ chin \e\ bet \ē\ easy
\g\ go \i\ hit \ī\ ice \j\ job \ŋ\ sing \ō\ go
\ò\ law \òi\ boy \th\ thin \th\ the \ü\ loot \ù\ foot
\y\ yet \zh\ vision *see also* Guide to Pronunciation

**2** : to protect or fight for as a champion

**3** : to act as militant supporter of : UPHOLD, ADVOCATE ⟨always *champions* the cause of the underdog⟩

*synonym* see SUPPORT

**cham·pi·on·ship** \-ˌship\ *noun* (1825)
**1** : designation as champion
**2** : the act of championing : DEFENSE ⟨his *championship* of freedom of speech⟩
**3** : a contest held to determine a champion

**champ·le·vé** \ˌshäⁿl(-ə)-ˈvā\ *adjective* [French] (1856)
: of, relating to, or being a style of enamel decoration in which the enamel is applied and fired in cells depressed (as by incising) into a metal background — compare CLOISONNÉ
— **champlevé** *noun*

**¹chance** \ˈchan(t)s\ *noun* [Middle English, from Old French, from (assumed) Vulgar Latin *cadentia* fall, from Latin *cadent-, cadens,* present participle of *cadere* to fall; perhaps akin to Sanskrit *śad-* to fall off] (14th century)
**1 a** : something that happens unpredictably without discernible human intention or observable cause **b** : the assumed impersonal purposeless determiner of unaccountable happenings : LUCK **c** : the fortuitous or incalculable element in existence : CONTINGENCY
**2** : a situation favoring some purpose : OPPORTUNITY ⟨needed a *chance* to relax⟩
**3** : a fielding opportunity in baseball
**4 a** : the possibility of a particular outcome in an uncertain situation; *also* : the degree of likelihood of such an outcome ⟨a small *chance* of success⟩ **b** *plural* : the more likely indications ⟨*chances* are he's already gone⟩
**5 a** : RISK ⟨not taking any *chances*⟩ **b** : a raffle ticket
— **chance** *adjective*
— **by chance** : in the haphazard course of events ⟨they met *by chance*⟩

**²chance** *verb* **chanced; chanc·ing** (14th century)
*intransitive verb*
**1 a** : to take place or come about by chance : HAPPEN **b** : to be found by chance **c** : to have the good or bad luck ⟨we *chanced* to meet⟩
**2** : to come or light by chance
*transitive verb*
**1** : to leave the outcome of to chance
**2** : to accept the hazard of : RISK
— **chance one's arm** *British* : to take a risk

**chance·ful** \ˈchan(t)s-fəl\ *adjective* (1594)
**1** *archaic* : CASUAL
**2** : EVENTFUL

**chan·cel** \ˈchan(t)-səl\ *noun* [Middle English, from Middle French, from Late Latin *cancellus* lattice, from Latin *cancelli* from the latticework enclosing it — more at CANCEL] (14th century)
: the part of a church containing the altar and seats for the clergy and choir

**chan·cel·lery** *or* **chan·cel·lory** \ˈchan(t)-s(ə-)lə-rē, -səl-rē\ *noun, plural* **-ler·ies** *or* **-lor·ies** (14th century)
**1 a** : the position, court, or department of a chancellor **b** : the building or room where a chancellor has his office
**2** : the office of secretary of the court of a person high in authority
**3** : the office or staff of an embassy or consulate

**chan·cel·lor** \ˈchan(t)-s(ə-)lər\ *noun* [Middle English *chanceler,* from Old French *chancelier,* from Late Latin *cancellarius* doorkeeper, secretary, from *cancellus*] (14th century)
**1 a** : the secretary of a nobleman, prince, or king **b** : the lord chancellor of Great Britain **c** *British* : the chief secretary of an embassy **d** : a Roman Catholic priest heading the office in which diocesan business is transacted and recorded

**2 a** : the titular head of a British university **b** (1) : a university president (2) : the chief executive officer in some state systems of higher education
**3 a** : a lay legal officer or adviser of an Anglican diocese **b** : a judge in a court of chancery or equity in various states of the U.S.
**4** : the chief minister of state in some European countries
— **chan·cel·lor·ship** \-ˌship\ *noun*

**chancellor of the exchequer** *often* C&E capitalized (1672)
: a member of the British cabinet in charge of the public income and expenditure

**chance–med·ley** \ˈchan(t)s-ˈmed-lē\ *noun* [Anglo-French *chance medlée* mingled chance] (15th century)
**1** : accidental homicide not entirely without fault of the killer but without evil intent
**2** : haphazard action : CONFUSION

**chan·cery** \ˈchan(t)-sə-rē, ˈchan(t)s-rē\ *noun, plural* **-cer·ies** [Middle English *chancerie,* alteration of *chancellerie* chancellery, from Old French, from *chancelier*] (14th century)
**1** *capitalized* : a high court of equity in England and Wales with common-law functions and jurisdiction over causes in equity **b** : a court of equity in the American judicial system **c** : the principles and practice of judicial equity
**2** : a record office for public archives or those of ecclesiastical, legal, or diplomatic proceedings
**3 a** : a chancellor's court or office or the building in which it is located **b** : the office in which the business of a Roman Catholic diocese is transacted and recorded **c** : the office of an embassy : CHANCELLERY 3
— **in chancery 1** : in litigation in a court of chancery; *also* : under the superintendence of the lord chancellor ⟨a ward *in chancery*⟩ **2** : in a hopeless predicament

**chan·cre** \ˈshaŋ-kər\ *noun* [French, from Latin *cancer*] (circa 1605)
: a primary sore or ulcer at the site of entry of a pathogen (as in tularemia); *especially* : the initial lesion of syphilis
— **chan·crous** \-k(ə-)rəs\ *adjective*

**chan·croid** \ˈshaŋ-ˌkroid\ *noun* (1861)
: a venereal disease caused by a hemophilic bacterium (*Hemophilus ducreyi*) and characterized by chancres unlike those of syphilis in lacking firm indurated margins — called also *soft chancre*
— **chan·croi·dal** \shaŋ-ˈkroi-dᵊl\ *adjective*

**chancy** \ˈchan(t)-sē\ *adjective* **chanc·i·er; -est** (1513)
**1** *Scottish* : bringing good luck : AUSPICIOUS
**2** : uncertain in outcome or prospect : RISKY
**3** : occurring by chance : HAPHAZARD
— **chanc·i·ness** *noun*

**chan·de·lier** \ˌshan-də-ˈlir\ *noun* [French, literally, candlestick, modification of Latin *candelabrum*] (1736)
: a branched often ornate lighting fixture suspended from a ceiling
— **chan·de·liered** \-ˈlird\ *adjective*

**chan·delle** \shan-ˈdel, shäⁿ-\ *noun* [French, literally, candle] (1918)
: an abrupt climbing turn of an airplane in which the momentum of the plane is used to attain a higher rate of climb
— **chandelle** *intransitive verb*

**chan·dler** \ˈchan(d)-lər\ *noun* [Middle English *chandeler,* from Middle French *chandelier,* from Old French, from *chandelle* candle, from Latin *candela*] (14th century)
**1** : a maker or seller of tallow or wax candles and usually soap

**2** : a retail dealer in provisions and supplies or equipment of a specified kind ⟨a yacht *chandler*⟩

**chan·dlery** \-lə-rē\ *noun, plural* **-dler·ies** (15th century)
**1** : a place where candles are kept
**2** : the business of a chandler
**3** : the commodities sold by a chandler

**¹change** \ˈchānj\ *verb* **changed; chang·ing** [Middle English, from Old French *changier,* from Latin *cambiare* to exchange, probably of Celtic origin; akin to Old Irish *camm* crooked] (13th century)
*transitive verb*
**1 a** : to make different in some particular : ALTER ⟨never bothered to *change* the will⟩ **b** : to make radically different : TRANSFORM ⟨can't *change* human nature⟩ **c** : to give a different position, course, or direction to
**2 a** : to replace with another ⟨let's *change* the subject⟩ **b** : to make a shift from one to another : SWITCH ⟨always *changes* sides in an argument⟩ **c** : to exchange for an equivalent sum or comparable item **d** : to undergo a modification of ⟨foliage *changing* color⟩ **e** : to put fresh clothes or covering on ⟨*change* a bed⟩
*intransitive verb*
**1** : to become different ⟨her mood *changes* every hour⟩
**2** *of the moon* : to pass from one phase to another
**3** : to shift one's means of conveyance : TRANSFER ⟨on the bus trip he had to *change* twice⟩
**4** *of the voice* : to shift to lower register : BREAK
**5** : to undergo transformation, transition, or substitution ⟨winter *changed* to spring⟩
**6** : to put on different clothes
**7** : EXCHANGE, SWITCH ⟨neither liked his seat so they *changed* with each other⟩ ☆
— **chang·er** *noun*
— **change hands** : to pass from the possession of one owner to that of another ⟨money *changes hands* many times⟩

**²change** *noun* (13th century)
**1** : the act, process, or result of changing: as a : ALTERATION ⟨a *change* in the weather⟩ **b** : TRANSFORMATION ⟨a time of vast social *change*⟩ ⟨going through *changes*⟩ **c** : SUBSTITUTION ⟨a *change* of scenery⟩ **d** : the passage of the moon from one monthly revolution to another; *also* : the passage of the moon from one phase to another
**2** : a fresh set of clothes
**3** *British* : EXCHANGE 5a
**4 a** : money in small denominations received in exchange for an equivalent sum in larger denominations **b** : money returned when a payment exceeds the amount due **c** : coins especially of low denominations ⟨a pocketful of *change*⟩ **d** : a negligible additional amount ⟨only six minutes and *change* left in the game⟩
**5** : an order in which a set of bells is struck in change ringing
**6** : CHANGE-UP

chandelier

☆ **SYNONYMS**
**Change, alter, vary, modify** mean to make or become different. CHANGE implies making either an essential difference often amounting to a loss of original identity or a substitution of one thing for another ⟨*changed* the shirt for a larger size⟩. ALTER implies a difference in some particular respect without suggesting loss of identity ⟨slightly *altered* the original design⟩. VARY stresses a breaking away from sameness, duplication, or exact repetition ⟨*vary* your daily routine⟩. MODIFY suggests a difference that limits, restricts, or adapts to a new purpose ⟨*modified* the building for use by the handicapped⟩.

**change·able** \'chān-jə-bəl\ *adjective* (13th century)
**:** capable of change: as **a :** able or apt to vary ⟨*changeable* weather⟩ **b :** subject to change **:** ALTERABLE **c :** FICKLE **d :** IRIDESCENT
— **change·abil·i·ty** \,chān-jə-'bi-lə-tē\ *noun*
— **change·able·ness** \'chān-jə-bəl-nəs\ *noun*
— **change·ably** \-blē\ *adverb*
**change·ful** \'chānj-fəl\ *adjective* (1591)
**:** notably variable **:** UNCERTAIN
— **change·ful·ly** \-fə-lē\ *adverb*
— **change·ful·ness** *noun*
**change·less** \'chānj-ləs\ *adjective* (1580)
**:** marked by the absence of change **:** CONSTANT
— **change·less·ly** *adverb*
— **change·less·ness** *noun*
**change·ling** \'chānj-liŋ\ *noun* (1537)
**1** *archaic* **:** TURNCOAT
**2 :** a child secretly exchanged for another in infancy
**3** *archaic* **:** IMBECILE
— **changeling** *adjective*
**change off** *intransitive verb* (1873)
**1 :** to alternate with another at doing an act
**2 :** to alternate between two different acts or instruments or between an action and a rest period
**change of heart** (circa 1828)
**:** a reversal in position or attitude
**change of life** (1834)
**:** ²CLIMACTERIC 2
**change of pace** (1912)
**1 :** CHANGE-UP
**2 :** an interruption of continuity by a shift to a different activity
**change·over** \'chān-,jō-vər\ *noun* (1907)
**1 :** CONVERSION, TRANSITION
**2 :** a pause in a tennis match during which the players change sides of the court
**change ringing** *noun* (1872)
**:** the art or practice of ringing a set of tuned bells (as in the bell tower of a church) in continually varying order
**change–up** \'chān-,jəp\ *noun* (1949)
**:** a slow pitch in baseball thrown with the same motion as a fastball in order to deceive the batter
**¹chan·nel** \'cha-n°l\ *noun* [Middle English *chanel*, from Middle French, from Latin *canalis* channel — more at CANAL] (14th century)
**1 a :** the bed where a natural stream of water runs **b :** the deeper part of a river, harbor, or strait **c :** a strait or narrow sea between two close landmasses **d :** a means of communication or expression: as (1) **:** a path along which information (as data or music) in the form of an electrical signal passes (2) *plural* **:** a fixed or official course of communication ⟨went through established military *channels* with his grievances⟩ **e :** a way, course, or direction of thought or action ⟨new *channels* of exploration⟩ **f :** a band of frequencies of sufficient width for a single radio or television communication **g :** CHANNELER
**2 a :** a usually tubular enclosed passage **:** CONDUIT **b :** a passage created in a selectively permeable membrane by a conformational change in membrane proteins
**3 :** a long gutter, groove, or furrow
**4 :** a metal bar of flattened U-shaped section
**²channel** *transitive verb* **-neled** *or* **-nelled; -nel·ing** *or* **-nel·ling** (15th century)
**1 a :** to form, cut, or wear a channel in **b :** to make a groove in ⟨*channel* a chair leg⟩
**2 :** to convey or direct into or through a channel ⟨*channel* his energy into constructive activities⟩
**3 :** to serve as a channeler or intermediary for
**³channel** *noun* [alteration of *chainwale*, from ¹*chain* + ¹*wale*] (1769)
**:** one of the flat ledges of heavy plank or metal bolted edgewise to the outside of a ship to increase the spread of the shrouds
**channel bass** *noun* (1887)

**:** a large coppery drum (*Sciaenops ocellatus*) chiefly of the Atlantic coast of North America that has a black spot at the base of the tail and is an important game and food fish — called also *red drum, redfish*
**channel catfish** *noun* (1820)
**:** a large black-spotted catfish (*Ictalurus punctatus*) that is an important freshwater food fish of the U.S. and Canada — called also *channel cat*
**chan·nel·er** \'cha-n°l-ər\ *noun* (1987)
**:** a person who conveys thoughts or energy from a source believed to be outside the person's body or conscious mind; *specifically* **:** one who speaks for nonphysical beings or spirits
**chan·nel·ize** \'cha-n°l-,īz\ *transitive verb* **-ized; -iz·ing** (1609)
**1 :** CHANNEL 1, 2
**2 :** to straighten by means of a channel ⟨*channelize* a stream⟩
— **chan·nel·i·za·tion** \,cha-n°l-ə-'zā-shən\ *noun*
**channel surfing** *noun* (1990)
**:** the act or practice of scanning through television programs usually by use of a remote control to find something of interest
— **channel surf** *intransitive verb*
— **channel surfer** *noun*
**chan·son** \shän-'sō�against\ *noun, plural* **chan·sons** \-'sō against(z)\ [French, from Latin *cantion-, cantio*, from *canere*] (1602)
**:** SONG; *specifically* **:** a music-hall or cabaret song
**chanson de geste** \-də-'zhest\ *noun, plural* **chansons de geste** \*same*\ [French, literally, song of heroic deeds] (1868)
**:** any of several Old French epic poems of the 11th to the 13th centuries
**chan·son·nier** \,shä against-sō-'nyā\ *noun* [French, from *chanson*] (1887)
**:** a writer or singer of chansons; *especially* **:** a cabaret singer
**¹chant** \'chant\ *verb* [Middle English *chaunten*, from Middle French *chanter*, from Latin *cantare*, frequentative of *canere* to sing; akin to Old English *hana* rooster, Old Irish *canid* he sings] (14th century)
*intransitive verb*
**1 :** to make melodic sounds with the voice; *especially* **:** to sing a chant
**2 :** to recite in a monotonous repetitive tone
*transitive verb*
**1 :** to utter as in chanting
**2 :** to celebrate or praise in song or chant
**²chant** *noun* (1671)
**1 :** SONG
**2 a :** PLAINSONG **b :** a rhythmic monotonous utterance or song **c :** a composition for chanting
**chant·er** \'chan-tər\ *noun* (14th century)
**1 :** one that chants: **a :** CHORISTER **b :** CANTOR
**2 :** the chief singer in a chantry
**3 :** the reed pipe of a bagpipe with finger holes on which the melody is played
**chan·te·relle** \,shan-tə-'rel, ,shän-\ *noun* [French] (1775)
**:** a fragrant edible mushroom (*Cantharellus cibarius*) of rich yellow color
**chan·teuse** \shan-'tüz, shä against-'tə(r)z\ *noun, plural* **chan·teuses** \-'tüz, -'tü-zəz, -'tə(r)z, -'tə(r)-zəz\ [French, feminine of *chanteur* singer, from *chanter*] (1888)
**:** a woman who is a concert or nightclub singer
**chan·tey** *or* **chan·ty** \'shan-tē, 'chan-\ *noun, plural* **chanteys** *or* **chanties** [modification of French *chanter*] (1856)
**:** a song sung by sailors in rhythm with their work
**chan·ti·cleer** \,chan-tə-'klir, ,shan-\ *noun* [Middle English *Chantecleer*, rooster in verse narratives, from Old French *Chantecler*, rooster in the *Roman de Renart*] (14th century)
**:** ROOSTER

**Chan·til·ly lace** \shan-'ti-lē-\ *noun* [*Chantilly*, France] (1848)
**:** a delicate silk, linen, or synthetic lace having a six-sided mesh ground and a floral or scrolled design — called also *Chantilly*
**chan·try** \'chan-trē\ *noun, plural* **chantries** [Middle English *chanterie*, from Middle French, singing, from *chanter*] (14th century)
**1 :** an endowment for the chanting of masses commonly for the founder
**2 :** a chapel endowed by a chantry
**Cha·nu·kah** \'kä-nə-kə, 'hä-\ *variant of* HANUKKAH
**cha·os** \'kā-,äs\ *noun* [Latin, from Greek — more at GUM] (15th century)
**1** *obsolete* **:** CHASM, ABYSS
**2 a** *often capitalized* **:** a state of things in which chance is supreme; *especially* **:** the confused unorganized state of primordial matter before the creation of distinct forms — compare COSMOS **b :** the inherent unpredictability in the behavior of a natural system (as the atmosphere, boiling water, or the beating heart)
**3 a :** a state of utter confusion **b :** a confused mass or mixture ⟨a *chaos* of television antennas⟩
— **cha·ot·ic** \kā-'ä-tik\ *adjective*
— **cha·ot·i·cal·ly** \-ti-k(ə-)lē\ *adverb*
**¹chap** \'chap\ *noun* (14th century)
**:** a crack in or a sore roughening of the skin caused by exposure to wind or cold
**²chap** *verb* **chapped; chap·ping** [Middle English *chappen*; akin to Middle Dutch *cappen* to cut down] (15th century)
*intransitive verb*
**:** to open in cracks, slits, or chinks; *also* **:** to become cracked, roughened, or reddened especially by the action of wind or cold ⟨hands often *chap* in winter⟩
*transitive verb*
**:** to cause to chap ⟨wind-*chapped* lips⟩
**³chap** \'chäp, 'chap\ *noun* [origin unknown] (1555)
**1 a :** the fleshy covering of a jaw; *also* **:** JAW — usually used in plural ⟨a wolf's *chaps*⟩
**2 :** the forepart of the face — usually used in plural
**⁴chap** *noun* [short for *chapman*] (1716)
**1 :** FELLOW 4c
**2** *Southern & Midland* **:** BABY, CHILD
**chap·a·ra·jos** *or* **chap·a·re·jos** \,sha-pə-'rä-(,)ōs, -'rä-\ *noun plural* [modification of Mexican Spanish *chaparreras*, from *chaparro*] (1887)
**:** CHAPS
**chap·ar·ral** \,sha-pə-'ral, -'rel\ *noun* [Spanish, from *chaparro* dwarf evergreen oak, from Basque *txapar*] (1845)
**1 :** a thicket of dwarf evergreen oaks; *broadly* **:** a dense impenetrable thicket of shrubs or dwarf trees
**2 :** an ecological community composed of shrubby plants adapted to dry summers and moist winters that occurs especially in southern California
**chaparral cock** *noun* (1853)
**:** ROADRUNNER — called also *chaparral bird*
**cha·pa·ti** *also* **chap·pa·ti** \chə-'pä-tē\ *noun, plural* **chapatis** *also* **chappatis** [Hindi *capātī*] (1810)
**:** a round flat unleavened bread of India that is usually made of whole wheat flour and cooked on a griddle
**chap·book** \'chap-,buk\ *noun* [*chapman* + *book*] (1798)
**:** a small book containing ballads, poems, tales, or tracts

---

\ə\ abut \ʾ\ kitten \ər\ further \a\ ash \ā\ ace
\ä\ mop, mar \aú\ out \ch\ chin \e\ bet \ē\ easy
\g\ go \i\ hit \ī\ ice \j\ job \ŋ\ sing \ō\ go
\ò\ law \òi\ boy \th\ thin \th\ the \ü\ loot \ú\ foot
\y\ yet \zh\ vision    *see also* Guide to Pronunciation

**chape** \'chāp, 'chap\ *noun* [Middle English, scabbard, from Middle French, cape, from Late Latin *cappa*] (14th century)
: the metal mounting or trimming of a scabbard or sheath

**cha·peau** \sha-'pō, shə-\ *noun, plural* **cha·peaus** \-'pōz\ *or* **cha·peaux** \-'pō(z)\ [Middle French, from Old French *chapel* — more at CHAPLET] (1523)
: HAT

**chap·el** \'cha-pəl\ *noun* [Middle English, from Old French *chapele*, from Medieval Latin *cappella*, from diminutive of Late Latin *cappa* cloak; from the cloak of Saint Martin of Tours preserved as a sacred relic in a chapel built for that purpose] (13th century)
**1** : a subordinate or private place of worship: as **a** : a place of worship serving a residence or institution **b** : a small house of worship usually associated with a main church **c** : a room or recess in a church for meditation and prayer or small religious services
**2** : a place of worship used by a Christian group other than an established church
**3** : a choir of singers belonging to a chapel
**4** : a chapel service or assembly at a school or college
**5** : an association of the employees in a printing office
**6 a** : FUNERAL HOME **b** : a room for funeral services in a funeral home ◆

**chapel of ease** (1538)
: a chapel or dependent church built to accommodate an expanding parish

**¹chap·er·on** *or* **chap·er·one** \'sha-pə-,rōn\ *noun* [French *chaperon*, literally, hood, from Middle French, head covering, from *chape*] (1720)
**1** : a person (as a matron) who for propriety accompanies one or more young unmarried women in public or in mixed company
**2** : an older person who accompanies young people at a social gathering to ensure proper behavior; *broadly* : one delegated to ensure proper behavior

**²chaperon** *or* **chaperone** *verb* **-oned; -on·ing** (1796)
*transitive verb*
**1** : ESCORT
**2** : to act as chaperon to or for
*intransitive verb*
: to act as a chaperon
— **chap·er·on·age** \-,rō-nij\ *noun*

**chap·fall·en** \'chap-,fȯ-lən, 'chäp-\ *adjective* (1598)
**1** : having the lower jaw hanging loosely
**2** : cast down in spirit : DEPRESSED

**chap·i·ter** \'cha-pə-tər\ *noun* [Middle English *chapitre*, from Middle French, alteration of Old French *chapitle*, from Latin *capitulum*, literally, little head] (15th century)
: the capital of a column

**chap·lain** \'cha-plən\ *noun* [Middle English *chapelain*, from Old French, from Medieval Latin *cappellanus*, from *cappella*] (14th century)
**1** : a clergyman in charge of a chapel
**2** : a clergyman officially attached to a branch of the military, to an institution, or to a family or court
**3** : a person chosen to conduct religious exercises (as at a meeting of a club or society)
**4** : a clergyman appointed to assist a bishop (as at a liturgical function)
— **chap·lain·cy** \-sē\ *noun*

**chap·let** \'chap-lət\ *noun* [Middle English *chapelet*, from Middle French, from Old French, diminutive of *chapel* hat, garland, from Medieval Latin *cappellus* head covering, from Late Latin *cappa*] (14th century)
**1** : a wreath to be worn on the head
**2 a** : a string of beads **b** : a part of a rosary comprising five decades
**3** : a small molding carved with small decorative forms
— **chap·let·ed** \-lə-təd\ *adjective*

**chap·man** \'chap-mən\ *noun* [Middle English, from Old English *cēapman*, from *cēap* trade + *man* — more at CHEAP] (before 12th century)
**1** *archaic* : MERCHANT, TRADER
**2** *British* : PEDDLER

**chaps** \'shaps, 'chaps\ *noun plural* [modification of Mexican Spanish *chaparreras*] (1844)
: leather leggings joined by a belt or lacing, often having flared outer flaps, and worn over the trousers (as by western ranch hands)

**chap·ter** \'chap-tər\ *noun* [Middle English *chapitre*, from Old French, from Late Latin *capitulum* division of a book & Medieval Latin, meeting place of canons, from Latin, diminutive of *capit-, caput* head — more at HEAD] (13th century)
**1 a** : a main division of a book **b** : something resembling a chapter in being a significant specified unit ⟨a new *chapter* in my life⟩
**2 a** : a regular meeting of the canons of a cathedral or collegiate church or of the members of a religious house **b** : the body of canons of a cathedral or collegiate church
**3** : a local branch of an organization

chaps

**chapter and verse** *noun* (1628)
**1** : the exact reference or source of information or justification for an assertion ⟨clinched their arguments by citing *chapter and verse* —J. M. Burns⟩
**2** : full precise information or detail ⟨can give *chapter and verse* on the effects of diverting defense spending —Horace Sutton⟩
— **chapter and verse** *adverb*

**¹char** \'chär\ *noun, plural* **char** *or* **chars** [origin unknown] (1662)
: any of a genus (*Salvelinus*) of small-scaled trouts with light-colored spots

**²char** *verb* **charred; char·ring** [*charcoal*] (1679)
*transitive verb*
**1** : to convert to charcoal or carbon usually by heat : BURN
**2** : to burn slightly or partly : SCORCH ⟨the fire *charred* the beams⟩
*intransitive verb*
: to become charred

**³char** *noun* (1879)
: a charred substance : CHARCOAL; *specifically*
: a combustible residue remaining after the destructive distillation of coal

**⁴char** *intransitive verb* **charred; char·ring** [*charwoman*] (1732)
: to work as a cleaning woman

**⁵char** *noun* [by shortening] (1906)
*British* : CHARWOMAN

**char·a·banc** \'shar-ə-,baŋ, -,bäŋ\ *noun* [French *char à bancs*, literally, wagon with benches] (1914)
*British* : a sight-seeing motor coach

**char·a·cin** \'kar-ə-sən\ *noun* [ultimately from Greek *charak-, charax* pointed stake, a fish] (1882)
: any of a family (Characidae) of usually small brightly colored tropical freshwater fishes that includes many aquarium fishes
— **characin** *adjective*

**¹char·ac·ter** \'kar-ik-tər\ *noun* [Middle English *caracter*, from Middle French *caractère*, from Latin *character* mark, distinctive quality, from Greek *charaktēr*, from *charassein* to scratch, engrave; perhaps akin to Lithuanian *žeyti* to scratch] (14th century)
**1 a** : a conventionalized graphic device placed on an object as an indication of ownership, origin, or relationship **b** : a graphic symbol (as a hieroglyph or alphabet letter) used in writing or printing **c** : a magical or astrological emblem **d** : ALPHABET **e** (1) : WRITING, PRINTING (2) : style of writing or printing (3) : CIPHER **f** : a symbol (as a letter or number) that repre-

sents information; *also* : a representation of such a character that may be accepted by a computer
**2 a** : one of the attributes or features that make up and distinguish an individual **b** (1) : a feature used to separate distinguishable things into categories; *also* : a group or kind so separated ⟨advertising of a very primitive *character*⟩ (2) : the detectable expression of the action of a gene or group of genes (3) : the aggregate of distinctive qualities characteristic of a breed, strain, or type ⟨a wine of great *character*⟩ **c** : the complex of mental and ethical traits marking and often individualizing a person, group, or nation **d** : main or essential nature especially as strongly marked and serving to distinguish ⟨excess sewage gradually changed the *character* of the lake⟩
**3** : POSITION, CAPACITY ⟨his *character* as a town official⟩
**4** : REFERENCE 4b
**5** : REPUTATION
**6** : moral excellence and firmness ⟨a man of sound *character*⟩
**7 a** : a person marked by notable or conspicuous traits ⟨quite a *character*⟩ **b** : one of the persons of a drama or novel **c** : the personality or part which an actor recreates **d** : characterization especially in drama or fiction **e** : PERSON, INDIVIDUAL ⟨some *character* just stole her purse⟩
**8** : a short literary sketch of the qualities of a social type
**synonym** see DISPOSITION, QUALITY, TYPE
— **char·ac·ter·less** \-ləs\ *adjective*
— **in character** : in accord with a person's usual qualities or traits
— **out of character** : not in accord with a person's usual qualities or traits

**²character** *transitive verb* (1591)
**1** *archaic* : ENGRAVE, INSCRIBE
**2 a** *archaic* : REPRESENT, PORTRAY **b** : CHARACTERIZE

**³character** *adjective* (1893)
**1** : capable of portraying an unusual or eccentric personality often markedly different from the player ⟨a *character* actor⟩
**2** : requiring the qualities of a character actor ⟨a *character* role⟩

**character assassination** *noun* (1949)
: the slandering of a person usually with the intention of destroying public confidence in that person

**char·ac·ter·ful** \'kar-ik-tər-fəl\ *adjective* (1901)
**1** : markedly expressive of character ⟨a *characterful* face⟩

◇ WORD HISTORY
**chapel**  One harsh winter while he was a youthful soldier in the Roman army, St. Martin of Tours (ca. 316–397) is said to have divided his military cloak in half with his sword, giving one part to a naked pauper at the gate of Amiens and keeping the other part for himself. After his death, a cloak supposedly belonging to the saint, to which his demonstration of charity gave special significance, was preserved as a relic by Frankish kings. In early Medieval Latin documents, St. Martin's cloak was referred to as *capella* or *cappella*, a diminutive of Late Latin *cappa*, also meaning "cloak." The meaning of *capella* was eventually expanded to include not only the cloak, but the entire royal treasury of saints' relics, and then the rooms in the royal palace set aside for private worship, where the relics were kept. By the early 9th century, *capella* could refer to any private place of worship. *Chapelle*, the vernacular form of *capella* in the medieval French of the Paris region, is first attested about 1100, and it had been borrowed into English by the early 13th century.

**2 :** marked by character ⟨a *characterful* decision⟩

**¹char·ac·ter·is·tic** \,kar-ik-tə-'ris-tik\ *noun* (1664)
**1 :** a distinguishing trait, quality, or property
**2 :** the integral part of a common logarithm
**3 :** the smallest positive integer *n* which for an operation in a ring or field yields 0 when any element is used *n* times with the operation
**²characteristic** *adjective* (1665)
**:** revealing, distinguishing, or typical of an individual character ☆
— **char·ac·ter·is·ti·cal·ly** \-ti-k(ə-)lē\ *adverb*
**characteristic equation** *noun* (circa 1925)
**:** an equation in which the characteristic polynomial of a matrix is set equal to 0
**characteristic polynomial** *noun* (circa 1957)
**:** the determinant of a square matrix in which an arbitrary variable (as *x*) is subtracted from each of the elements along the principal diagonal
**characteristic root** *noun* (circa 1957)
**:** EIGENVALUE
**characteristic value** *noun* (1956)
**:** EIGENVALUE
**characteristic vector** *noun* (1957)
**:** EIGENVECTOR
**char·ac·ter·iza·tion** \,kar-ik-t(ə-)rə-'zā-shən\ *noun* (1814)
**:** the act of characterizing; *especially* **:** the artistic representation (as in fiction or drama) of human character or motives
**char·ac·ter·ize** \'kar-ik-tə-,rīz\ *transitive verb* **-ized; -iz·ing** (1633)
**1 :** to describe the character or quality of ⟨*characterizes* him as ambitious⟩
**2 :** to be a characteristic of **:** DISTINGUISH ⟨an era *characterized* by greed⟩
**char·ac·ter·olog·i·cal** \,kar-ik-t(ə-)rə-'lä-ji-kəl\ *adjective* [*characterology* study of character] (1916)
**:** of, relating to, or based on character or the study of character including its development and its differences in different individuals
— **char·ac·ter·olog·i·cal·ly** \-'lä-ji-k(ə-)lē\ *adverb*
**character witness** *noun* (1952)
**:** a person who gives evidence in a legal action concerning the reputation, conduct, and moral nature of a party
**char·ac·tery** \'kar-ik-t(ə-)rē, kə-'rak-\ *noun, plural* **-ter·ies** (1598)
**:** a system of written letters or symbols used in the expression of thought
**cha·rade** \shə-'rād, -'räd\ *noun* [French, from Provençal *charrado* chat, from *charrá* to chat, chatter] (1776)
**1 :** a word represented in riddling verse or by picture, tableau, or dramatic action
**2 :** *plural* **:** a game in which some of the players try to guess a word or phrase from the actions of another player who may not speak
**3 :** an empty or deceptive act or pretense ⟨his concern was a *charade*⟩
**cha·ras** \'chär-əs\ *noun* [Hindi *caras*] (circa 1860)
**:** HASHISH
**char·broil** \'chär-,broi(ə)l\ *transitive verb* (1968)
**:** to broil on a rack over hot charcoal
— **char·broil·er** \-,broi-lər\ *noun*
**¹char·coal** \'chär-,kōl\ *noun* [Middle English *charcole*] (14th century)
**1 :** a dark or black porous carbon prepared from vegetable or animal substances (as from wood by charring in a kiln from which air is excluded)
**2 a :** a piece or pencil of fine charcoal used in drawing **b :** a charcoal drawing
**3 :** a dark gray
**²charcoal** *transitive verb* (1965)
**:** CHARBROIL
**char·cu·te·rie** \(,)shär-,kü-tə-'rē\ *noun* [French, literally, pork-butcher's shop, from

Middle French *chaircuiterie*, from *chaircutier* pork butcher, from *chair cuite* cooked meat] (circa 1858)
**:** a delicatessen specializing in dressed meats and meat dishes; *also* **:** the products sold in such a shop
**chard** \'chärd\ *noun* [modification of French *carde*, from Provençal *cardo*, from Latin *carduus* thistle, cardoon] (1664)
**:** SWISS CHARD
**char·don·nay** \,shär-dᵊn-'ā\ *noun, often capitalized* [French] (circa 1941)
**:** a dry white table wine of Chablis type
**chare** \'char, 'cher\ *or* **char** \'chär\ *noun* [Middle English *char* turn, piece of work, from Old English *cierr*; akin to Old English *cierran* to turn] (before 12th century)
**:** CHORE
**¹charge** \'chärj\ *noun* [Middle English, from Old French, from *chargier*] (13th century)
**1 a** *obsolete* **:** a material load or weight **b :** a figure borne on a heraldic field
**2 a :** the quantity that an apparatus is intended to receive and fitted to hold **b :** a store or accumulation of impelling force ⟨the deeply emotional *charge* of the drama⟩ **c :** a definite quantity of electricity; *especially* **:** an excess or deficiency of electrons in a body **d :** THRILL, KICK ⟨got a *charge* out of the game⟩
**3 a :** OBLIGATION, REQUIREMENT **b :** MANAGEMENT, SUPERVISION ⟨has *charge* of the home office⟩ **c :** the ecclesiastical jurisdiction (as a parish) committed to a clergyman **d :** a person or thing committed to the care of another
**4 a :** INSTRUCTION, COMMAND **b :** instruction in points of law given by a court to a jury
**5 a :** EXPENSE, COST ⟨gave the banquet at his own *charge*⟩ **b :** the price demanded for something ⟨no admission *charge*⟩ **c :** a debit to an account ⟨the purchase was a *charge*⟩ **d :** the record of a loan (as of a book from a library) **e** *British* **:** an interest in property granted as security for a loan
**6 a :** a formal assertion of illegality ⟨a *charge* of murder⟩ **b :** a statement of complaint or hostile criticism ⟨denied the *charges* of nepotism that were leveled against him⟩
**7 :** a violent rush forward (as to attack)
— **in charge :** having control or custody of something ⟨he is *in charge* of the training program⟩
**²charge** *verb* **charged; charg·ing** [Middle English, from Old French *chargier*, from Late Latin *carricare*, from Latin *carrus* wheeled vehicle — more at CAR] (14th century)
*transitive verb*
**1 a** *archaic* **:** to lay or put a load on or in **:** LOAD **b** (1) **:** to place a charge (as of powder) in (2) **:** to load or fill to capacity **c** (1) **:** to restore the active materials in (a storage battery) by the passage of a direct current through in the opposite direction to that of discharge (2) **:** to give an electric charge to ⟨*charge* a capacitor⟩ **d** (1) **:** to assume as a heraldic bearing (2) **:** to place a heraldic bearing on **e :** to fill or furnish fully ⟨the music is *charged* with excitement⟩
**2 a :** to impose a task or responsibility on ⟨*charge* him with the job of finding a new meeting place⟩ **b :** to command, instruct, or exhort with authority ⟨I *charge* you not to go⟩ **c** *of a judge* **:** to give a charge to (a jury)
**3 a :** to make an assertion against especially by ascribing guilt or blame ⟨*charges* him with armed robbery⟩ ⟨they were *charged* as being instigators⟩ **b :** to place the guilt or blame for ⟨*charge* her failure to negligence⟩ **c :** to assert as an accusation ⟨*charges* that he distorted the data⟩
**4 a :** to bring (a weapon) into position for attack **:** LEVEL ⟨*charge* a lance⟩ **b :** to rush against **:** ATTACK; *also* **:** to rush into (an opponent) usually illegally in various sports
**5 a** (1) **:** to impose a financial burden on ⟨*charge* his estate with debts incurred⟩ (2) **:** to

impose or record as financial obligation ⟨*charge* debts to an estate⟩ **b** (1) **:** to fix or ask as fee or payment ⟨*charges* $50 for an office visit⟩ (2) **:** to ask payment of (a person) ⟨*charge* a client for expenses⟩ **c :** to record (an item) as an expense, debt, obligation, or liability ⟨*charged* a new sofa⟩
*intransitive verb*
**1 :** to rush forward in or as if in assault **:** ATTACK; *also* **:** to charge an opponent in sports
**2 :** to ask or set a price ⟨do you *charge* for this service?⟩
**3 :** to charge an item to an account ⟨*charge* now, pay later⟩
*synonym* see COMMAND
**charge·able** \'chär-jə-bəl\ *adjective* (14th century)
**1** *archaic* **:** financially burdensome **:** EXPENSIVE
**2 :** liable to be charged: as **a :** liable to be accused or held responsible **b :** suitable to be charged to a particular account **c :** qualified to be made a charge on the county or parish
**charge account** *noun* (1903)
**:** a customer's account with a creditor (as a merchant) to which the purchase of goods is charged
**charge card** *noun* (1950)
**:** CREDIT CARD
**charge–coupled device** *noun* (1971)
**:** a semiconductor device that is used especially as an optical sensor and that stores charge and transfers it sequentially to an amplifier and detector — called also *CCD*
**charged** \'chärjd\ *adjective* (1934)
**1 :** possessing or showing strong emotion ⟨attacked the author in a highly *charged* review⟩
**2 :** capable of arousing strong emotion ⟨a politically *charged* subject⟩
**char·gé d'af·faires** \(,)shär-,zhā-də-'far, -'fer\ *noun, plural* **char·gés d'affaires** \-,zhā-də-, -,zhāz-də-\ [French, literally, one charged with affairs] (1767)
**1 :** a subordinate diplomat who substitutes for an absent ambassador or minister
**2 :** a diplomat inferior in rank to an ambassador or minister who heads a mission when no ambassador or minister is assigned
**charge·hand** \'chärj-,hand\ *noun* (1916)
*British* **:** FOREMAN
**charge off** *transitive verb* (circa 1923)
**:** to treat as a loss or expense
— **charge–off** \'chärj-,óf\ *noun*
**charge of quarters** (circa 1918)
**:** an enlisted man designated to handle administrative matters in his unit especially after duty hours — abbreviation *CQ*

---

☆ **SYNONYMS**
**Characteristic, individual, peculiar, distinctive** mean indicating a special quality or identity. CHARACTERISTIC applies to something that distinguishes or identifies a person or thing or class ⟨responded with her *characteristic* wit⟩. INDIVIDUAL stresses qualities that distinguish one from all other members of the same kind or class ⟨a highly *individual* writing style⟩. PECULIAR applies to qualities possessed only by a particular individual or class or kind and stresses rarity or uniqueness ⟨an eccentricity that is *peculiar* to the British⟩. DISTINCTIVE indicates qualities distinguishing and uncommon and often superior or praiseworthy ⟨a *distinctive* aura of grace and elegance⟩.

---

\ə\ **abut** \ᵊ\ **kitten** \ər\ **further** \a\ **ash** \ā\ **ace**
\ä\ **mop, mar** \au̇\ **out** \ch\ **chin** \e\ **bet** \ē\ **easy**
\g\ **go** \i\ **hit** \ī\ **ice** \j\ **job** \ŋ\ **sing** \ō\ **go**
\ȯ\ **law** \ȯi\ **boy** \th\ **thin** \t͟h\ **the** \ü\ **loot** \u̇\ **foot**
\y\ **yet** \zh\ **vision** *see also* Guide to Pronunciation

**¹char·ger** \'chär-jər\ *noun* [Middle English *chargeour*; akin to Middle English *chargen* to charge] (14th century)
**:** a large flat dish or platter

**²charg·er** *noun* (1539)
**1 :** one that charges: as **a :** an appliance for holding or inserting a charge of powder or shot in a gun **b :** a cartridge clip **c :** a device for charging storage batteries
**2 :** a horse for battle or parade

**char·i·ness** \'char-ē-nəs, 'cher-\ *noun* (1571)
**1 :** the quality or state of being chary **:** CAUTION
**2 :** carefully preserved state **:** INTEGRITY

**¹char·i·ot** \'char-ē-ət\ *noun* [Middle English, from Middle French, from Old French, from *char* wheeled vehicle, from Latin *carrus* — more at CAR] (14th century)
**1 :** a light four-wheeled pleasure or state carriage
**2 :** a two-wheeled horse-drawn battle car of ancient times used also in processions and races

**²chariot** (1550)
*intransitive verb*
**:** to drive or ride in or as if in a chariot
*transitive verb*
**:** to carry in or as if in a chariot

**char·i·ot·eer** \,char-ē-ə-'tir\ *noun* (14th century)
**1 :** one who drives a chariot
**2** *capitalized* **:** AURIGA

**cha·ris·ma** \kə-'riz-mə\ *also* **char·ism** \'kar-,i-zəm\ *noun, plural* **cha·ris·ma·ta** \kə-'riz-mə-tə, ,kər-iz-'mä-tə\ *also* **charisms** [Greek *charisma* favor, gift, from *charizesthai* to favor, from *charis* grace; akin to Greek *chairein* to rejoice — more at YEARN] (circa 1641)
**1 :** an extraordinary power (as of healing) given a Christian by the Holy Spirit for the good of the church
**2 a :** a personal magic of leadership arousing special popular loyalty or enthusiasm for a public figure (as a political leader) **b :** a special magnetic charm or appeal ⟨the *charisma* of a popular actor⟩

**¹char·is·mat·ic** \,kar-əz-'ma-tik\ *adjective* [*charisma*] (circa 1868)
**1 :** of, relating to, or constituting charisma
**2 :** having, exhibiting, or based on charisma ⟨*charismatic* sects⟩ ⟨*charismatic* leader⟩

**²charismatic** *noun* (1951)
**:** a member of a charismatic religious group or movement

**char·i·ta·ble** \'char-ə-tə-bəl\ *adjective* (14th century)
**1 :** full of love for and goodwill toward others **:** BENEVOLENT
**2 a :** liberal in benefactions to the needy **:** GENEROUS **b :** of or relating to charity ⟨*charitable* institutions⟩
**3 :** merciful or kind in judging others **:** LENIENT
— **char·i·ta·ble·ness** *noun*
— **char·i·ta·bly** \-blē\ *adverb*

**char·i·ty** \'char-ə-tē\ *noun, plural* **-ties** [Middle English *charite*, from Old French *charité*, from Late Latin *caritat-, caritas* Christian love, from Latin, dearness, from *carus* dear; akin to Old Irish *carae* friend, Sanskrit *kāma* love] (13th century)
**1 :** benevolent goodwill toward or love of humanity
**2 a :** generosity and helpfulness especially toward the needy or suffering; *also* **:** aid given to those in need **b :** an institution engaged in relief of the poor **c :** public provision for the relief of the needy
**3 a :** a gift for public benevolent purposes **b :** an institution (as a hospital) founded by such a gift
**4 :** lenient judgment of others
*synonym* SEE MERCY

**cha·ri·va·ri** \,shi-və-'rē, 'shi-və-,\ *noun* [French, perhaps from Late Latin *caribaria* headache, from Greek *karēbaria*, from *kara*,

*karē* head + *barys* heavy — more at CEREBRAL, GRIEVE] (circa 1681)
**:** SHIVAREE

**char·la·tan** \'shär-lə-tən\ *noun* [Italian *ciarlatano*, alteration of *cerretano*, literally, inhabitant of Cerreto, from *Cerreto*, Italy] (1618)
**1 :** QUACK 2 ⟨*charlatans* killing their patients with empirical procedures⟩
**2 :** one making usually showy pretenses to knowledge or ability **:** FRAUD, FAKER ◆
— **char·la·tan·ism** \-tə-,ni-zəm\ *noun*
— **char·la·tan·ry** \-rē\ *noun*

**Charles's Wain** \'chärlz-'wān, ,chärl-zəz-\ *noun* [*Charlemagne*]
**:** BIG DIPPER

**Charles·ton** \'chärl-stən\ *noun* [*Charleston*, S. C.] (1925)
**:** a lively ballroom dance in which the knees are twisted in and out and the heels are swung sharply outward on each step

**char·ley horse** \'chär-lē-,hòrs\ *noun* [from *Charley*, nickname for *Charles*] (1888)
**:** a muscular pain, cramping, or stiffness especially of the quadriceps that results from a strain or bruise

**char·lie** *also* **char·ley** \'chär-lē\ *noun, often capitalized* [from the name *Charlie*] (circa 1946)
*British* **:** FOOL

**Char·lie** \'chär-lē\ [from the name *Charlie*] (1946)
— a communications code word for the letter *c*

**char·lock** \'chär-,läk, -lək\ *noun* [Middle English *cherlok*, from Old English *cerlic*] (before 12th century)
**:** a mustard (*Brassica kaber*) that is a common weed in grainfields — called also *wild mustard*

**char·lotte** \'shär-lət\ *noun* [French] (1796)
**:** a dessert consisting of a filling (as of fruit, whipped cream, or custard) layered with or placed in a mold lined with strips of bread, ladyfingers, or biscuits

**char·lotte russe** \'shär-lət-'rüs\ *noun* [French, literally, Russian charlotte] (circa 1845)
**:** a charlotte made with sponge cake or ladyfingers and a whipped-cream or custard-gelatin filling

**¹charm** \'chärm\ *noun* [Middle English *charme*, from Middle French, from Latin *carmen* song, from *canere* to sing — more at CHANT] (14th century)
**1 a :** the chanting or reciting of a magic spell **:** INCANTATION **b :** a practice or expression believed to have magic power
**2 :** something worn about the person to ward off evil or ensure good fortune **:** AMULET
**3 a :** a trait that fascinates, allures, or delights **b :** a physical grace or attraction — used in plural **c :** compelling attractiveness ⟨the island possessed great *charm*⟩
**4 :** a small ornament worn on a bracelet or chain
**5 :** a quantum characteristic of subatomic particles that accounts for the unexpectedly long lifetime of the J/psi particle, explains difficulties in the theory of the weak force, is conserved in interactions involving electromagnetism or the strong force, and has a value of zero for most known particles
— **charm·less** \-ləs\ *adjective*

**²charm** (14th century)
*transitive verb*
**1 a :** to affect by or as if by magic **:** COMPEL **b :** to please, soothe, or delight by compelling attraction ⟨*charms* customers with his suave manner⟩
**2 :** to endow with or as if with supernatural powers by means of charms; *also* **:** to protect by or as if by spells, charms, or supernatural influences
**3 :** to control (an animal) typically by charms (as the playing of music) ⟨*charm* a snake⟩
*intransitive verb*

**1 :** to practice magic and enchantment
**2 :** to have the effect of a charm **:** FASCINATE
*synonym* SEE ATTRACT
— **charm·er** \'chär-mər\ *noun*

**charmed** \'chärmd\ *adjective* (1964)
**:** having the quantum characteristic of charm ⟨a *charmed* antiquark⟩

**charmed circle** *noun* (1898)
**:** a group marked by exclusiveness

**char·meuse** \(,)shär-'müz, -'müs, -'myüz, -'mə(r)z\ *noun* [French, feminine of *charmeur* charmer, from *charmer* to charm] (1907)
**:** a fine semilustrous crepe in satin weave

**charm·ing** \'chär-min\ *adjective* (1663)
**:** extremely pleasing or delightful **:** ENTRANCING
— **charm·ing·ly** \-min-lē\ *adverb*

**char·nel** \'chär-n²l\ *noun* [Middle English, from Middle French, from Medieval Latin *carnale*, from Late Latin, neuter of *carnalis* of the flesh — more at CARNAL] (14th century)
**:** a building or chamber in which bodies or bones are deposited — called also *charnel house*
— **charnel** *adjective*

**Cha·ro·lais** \,shar-ə-'lā\ *noun* [*Charolais*, district in eastern France] (1893)
**:** any of a breed of large white cattle developed in France and used primarily for beef and crossbreeding

**Char·on** \'kar-ən, 'ker-, -än\ *noun* [Latin, from Greek *Charōn*]
**:** a son of Erebus who in Greek mythology ferries the souls of the dead over the Styx

**char·poy** \'chär-,pòi\ *noun, plural* **charpoys** [Hindi *cārpāī*] (1845)
**:** a bed used especially in India consisting of a frame strung with tapes or light rope

**charr** \'chär\ *variant of* ¹CHAR

**¹chart** \'chärt\ *noun* [Middle French *charte*, from Latin *charta* piece of papyrus, document — more at CARD] (1571)
**1 :** MAP: as a **:** an outline map exhibiting something (as climatic or magnetic variations) in its geographical aspects **b :** a map for the use of navigators
**2 a :** a sheet giving information in tabular form **b :** GRAPH **c :** DIAGRAM **d :** a sheet of paper ruled and graduated for use in a recording instrument **e :** a listing by rank (as of sales) — usually used in plural ⟨number one on the *charts* —Tim Cahill⟩
**3 :** a musical arrangement; *also* **:** a part in such an arrangement

**²chart** (1842)
*transitive verb*
**1 :** to lay out a plan for
**2 :** to make a map or chart of

◇ WORD HISTORY
**charlatan** There was a wide gap in medieval Italy between the handful of learned physicians who had studied medicine at the great schools of Salerno or Bologna and the average peasant who knew only simple folk remedies. This gap was filled by a large group of pretenders to medical skills, who would perform surgery on demand and traveled from one market town to another advertising cures of dubious efficacy. For reasons now oscbure, the region of Umbria in central Italy was particularly noted as the home of itinerant medicine-peddlers, and the Italian word *cerretano*, which literally meant an inhabitant of Cerreto, a town in eastern Umbria, became an epithet for a quack physician. *Cerretano* was blended with the verb *ciarlare* "to chatter," alluding to the patter of the medicine seller, to form *ciarlatano*, in use by the end of the 15th century. *Ciarlatano* was borrowed into French as *charlatan* and hence into English, where it was in use by the early 17th century.

*intransitive verb*
**:** to be ranked on a chart ⟨the song *charted* for three months⟩
**¹char·ter** \'chär-tər\ *noun* [Middle English *chartre*, from Old French, from Medieval Latin *chartula*, from Latin, diminutive of *charta*] (13th century)
**1 :** a written instrument or contract (as a deed) executed in due form
**2 a :** a grant or guarantee of rights, franchises, or privileges from the sovereign power of a state or country **b :** a written instrument that creates and defines the franchises of a city, educational institution, or corporation **c :** CONSTITUTION
**3 :** a written instrument from the authorities of a society creating a lodge or branch
**4 :** a special privilege, immunity, or exemption
**5 :** a mercantile lease of a ship or some principal part of it
**6 :** a charter travel arrangement
**²charter** *transitive verb* (15th century)
**1 a :** to establish, enable, or convey by charter **b** *British* **:** CERTIFY ⟨a *chartered* mechanical engineer⟩
**2 :** to hire, rent, or lease for usually exclusive and temporary use ⟨*chartered* a boat for deep-sea fishing⟩
**synonym** see HIRE
— **char·ter·er** \-tər-ər\ *noun*
**³charter** *adjective* (1922)
**:** of, relating to, or being a travel arrangement in which transportation (as a bus or plane) is hired by and for one specific group of people ⟨a *charter* flight⟩
**chartered accountant** *noun* (1855)
*British* **:** a member of a chartered institute of accountants
**charter member** *noun* (circa 1909)
**:** an original member of a group (as a society or corporation)
— **charter membership** *noun*
**Char·tism** \'chär-ˌti-zəm\ *noun* [Medieval Latin *charta* charter, from Latin, document] (1839)
**:** the principles and practices of a body of 19th century English political reformers advocating better social and industrial conditions for the working classes
— **Char·tist** \'chär-tist\ *noun or adjective*
**chart·ist** \'chär-tist\ *noun* (1919)
**1 :** an analyst of market action whose predictions of market courses are based on study of graphic presentations of past market performance
**2 :** CARTOGRAPHER
**char·treuse** \shär-'trüz, -'trüs\ *noun* [*Chartreuse*] (1884)
**:** a variable color averaging a brilliant yellow green
**Chartreuse** *trademark*
— used for a usually green or yellow liqueur
**char·tu·lary** \'kär-chə-ˌler-ē\ *noun, plural* **-lar·ies** [Medieval Latin *chartularium*] (1571)
**:** CARTULARY
**char·wom·an** \'chär-ˌwu̇-mən\ *noun* [*chare* + *woman*] (1596)
**:** a cleaning woman especially in a large building
**chary** \'char-ē, 'cher-\ *adjective* **chari·er; -est** [Middle English, sorrowful, dear, from Old English *cearig* sorrowful, from *caru* sorrow — more at CARE] (15th century)
**1** *archaic* **:** DEAR, TREASURED
**2 :** discreetly cautious: as **a :** hesitant and vigilant about dangers and risks **b :** slow to grant, accept, or expend ⟨a person very *chary* of compliments⟩
**synonym** see CAUTIOUS
— **chari·ly** \'char-ə-lē, 'cher-\ *adverb*
**Cha·ryb·dis** \kə-'rib-dəs *also* shə- *or* chə-\ *noun* [Latin, from Greek]

**:** a whirlpool off the coast of Sicily personified in Greek mythology as a female monster — compare SCYLLA
**¹chase** \'chās\ *noun* (13th century)
**1 a :** the hunting of wild animals — used with *the* **b :** the act of chasing **:** PURSUIT **c :** an earnest or frenzied seeking after something desired
**2 :** something pursued **:** QUARRY
**3 :** a tract of unenclosed land used as a game preserve
**4 :** STEEPLECHASE 1
**5 :** a sequence (as in a movie) in which the characters pursue one another
**²chase** *verb* **chased; chas·ing** [Middle English, from Middle French *chasser*, from (assumed) Vulgar Latin *captiare* — more at CATCH] (14th century)
*transitive verb*
**1 a :** to follow rapidly **:** PURSUE **b :** HUNT **c :** to follow regularly or persistently with the intention of attracting or alluring
**2** *obsolete* **:** HARASS
**3 :** to seek out — often used with *down* ⟨detectives *chasing* down clues⟩
**4 :** to cause to depart or flee **:** DRIVE ⟨*chase* the dog out of the garden⟩
**5 :** to cause the removal of (a baseball pitcher) by a batting rally
*intransitive verb*
**1 :** to chase an animal, person, or thing ⟨*chase* after material possessions⟩
**2 :** RUSH, HASTEN ⟨*chased* all over town looking for a place to stay⟩ ☆
**³chase** *transitive verb* **chased; chas·ing** [Middle English *chassen*, modification of Middle French *enchasser* to set] (15th century)
**1 a :** to ornament (metal) by indenting with a hammer and tools without a cutting edge **b :** to make by such indentation **c :** to set with gems
**2 a :** GROOVE, INDENT **b :** to cut (a thread) with a chaser
**⁴chase** *noun* [French *chas* eye of a needle, from Late Latin *capsus* enclosed space, alteration of Latin *capsa* box — more at CASE] (1611)
**1 :** GROOVE, FURROW
**2 :** the bore of a cannon
**3 a :** TRENCH **b :** a channel (as in a wall) for something to lie in or pass through
**⁵chase** *noun* [probably from French *châsse* frame, reliquary, from Middle French *chasse*, from Latin *capsa*] (1612)
**:** a rectangular steel or iron frame in which letterpress matter is locked (as for printing)
**¹chas·er** \'chā-sər\ *noun* (13th century)
**1 :** one that chases
**2 :** a mild drink (as beer) taken after hard liquor
**²chaser** *noun* (1707)
**1 :** a skilled worker who produces ornamental chasing
**2 :** a tool for cutting screw threads
**Cha·sid** *or* **Chas·sid** \'hä-səd, 'kä-\ *noun, plural* **Cha·si·dim** *or* **Chas·si·dim** \'hä-sə-dəm, kä-'sē-\ *variant of* HASID
**chasm** \'ka-zəm\ *noun* [Latin *chasma*, from Greek; akin to Latin *hiare* to yawn — more at YAWN] (1596)
**1 :** a deep cleft in the surface of a planet (as the earth) **:** GORGE
**2 :** a marked division, separation, or difference ⟨a political *chasm* between the two countries⟩
**¹chas·sé** \sha-'sā\ *intransitive verb* **chas·séd; chas·sé·ing** (1803)
**1 :** to make a chassé
**2 :** SASHAY
**²chassé** *noun* [French, from past participle of *chasser* to chase] (1828)
**:** a sliding dance step resembling the galop
**chasse·pot** \'shas-ˌpō, 'sha-sə-\ *noun* [French, from Antoine A. *Chassepot* (died 1905) French inventor] (1869)
**:** a bolt-action rifle firing a paper cartridge

**chas·seur** \sha-'sər\ *noun* [French, from Middle French *chasser*] (1795)
**1 :** HUNTER, HUNTSMAN
**2 :** one of a body of light cavalry or infantry trained for rapid maneuvering
**3 :** a liveried attendant **:** FOOTMAN
**chas·sis** \'cha-sē, 'sha-sē *also* 'cha-səs\ *noun, plural* **chas·sis** \-sēz\ [French *châssis*, from Middle French *chaciz*, from *chasse*] (circa 1864)
**:** the supporting frame of a structure (as an automobile or television); *also* **:** the frame and working parts (as of an automobile or electronic device) exclusive of the body or housing
**chaste** \'chāst\ *adjective* **chast·er; chast·est** [Middle English, from Old French, from Latin *castus* pure] (13th century)
**1 :** innocent of unlawful sexual intercourse
**2 :** CELIBATE
**3 :** pure in thought and act **:** MODEST
**4 a :** severely simple in design or execution **:** AUSTERE ⟨*chaste* classicism⟩ **b :** CLEAN, SPOTLESS ☆
— **chaste·ly** *adverb*
— **chaste·ness** \'chās(t)-nəs\ *noun*
**chas·ten** \'chā-sⁿn\ *transitive verb* **chas·tened; chas·ten·ing** \'chās-niŋ, 'chā-sⁿn-iŋ\ [alteration of obsolete English *chaste* to chasten, from Middle English, from Old French *chastier*, from Latin *castigare*, from *castus* + *-igare* (from *agere* to drive) — more at ACTIVE] (13th century)
**1 :** to correct by punishment or suffering **:** DISCIPLINE; *also* **:** PURIFY
**2 a :** to prune (as a work or style of art) of excess, pretense, or falsity **:** REFINE **b :** to cause to be more humble or restrained **:** SUBDUE
**synonym** see PUNISH
— **chas·ten·er** \'chās-nər, 'chā-sⁿn-ər\ *noun*
**chas·tise** \(ˌ)chas-'tīz\ *transitive verb* **chas·tised; chas·tis·ing** [Middle English *chastisen*, alteration of *chasten*] (14th century)
**1 :** to inflict punishment on (as by whipping)
**2 :** to censure severely **:** CASTIGATE

☆ **SYNONYMS**
**Chase, pursue, follow, trail** mean to go after or on the track of something or someone. CHASE implies going swiftly after and trying to overtake something fleeing or running ⟨a dog *chasing* a cat⟩. PURSUE suggests a continuing effort to overtake, reach, or attain ⟨*pursued* the criminal through narrow streets⟩. FOLLOW puts less emphasis upon speed or intent to overtake ⟨friends *followed* me home in their car⟩. TRAIL may stress a following of tracks or traces rather than a visible object ⟨*trail* deer⟩ ⟨*trailed* a suspect across the country⟩.

**Chaste, pure, modest, decent** mean free from all taint of what is lewd or salacious. CHASTE primarily implies a refraining from acts or even thoughts or desires that are not virginal or not sanctioned by marriage vows ⟨they maintained *chaste* relations⟩. PURE differs from CHASTE in implying innocence and absence of temptation rather than control of one's impulses and actions ⟨the *pure* of heart⟩. MODEST and DECENT apply especially to deportment and dress as outward signs of inward chastity or purity ⟨preferred more *modest* swimsuits⟩ ⟨*decent* people didn't go to such movies⟩.

\ə\ abut \ᵊ\ kitten \ər\ further \a\ ash \ā\ ace
\ä\ mop, mar \au̇\ out \ch\ chin \e\ bet \ē\ easy
\g\ go \i\ hit \ī\ ice \j\ job \ŋ\ sing \ō\ go
\ȯ\ law \ȯi\ boy \th\ thin \th\ the \ü\ loot \u̇\ foot
\y\ yet \zh\ vision *see also* Guide to Pronunciation

**3** *archaic* **:** CHASTEN 2
**synonym** see PUNISH
— **chas·tise·ment** \(ˌ)chas-'tīz-mənt *also* 'chas-təz-\ *noun*
— **chas·tis·er** \(ˌ)chas-'tī-zər\ *noun*
**chas·ti·ty** \'chas-tə-tē\ *noun* (13th century)
**1 :** the quality or state of being chaste: as **a :** abstention from unlawful sexual intercourse **b :** abstention from all sexual intercourse **c :** purity in conduct and intention **d :** restraint and simplicity in design or expression **2 :** personal integrity
**chastity belt** *noun* (1931)
**:** a belt device (as of medieval times) designed to prevent sexual intercourse on the part of the woman wearing it
**cha·su·ble** \'cha-zə-bəl, -zhə-, -sə-\ *noun* [Middle French, from Late Latin *casubla* hooded garment] (14th century)
**:** a sleeveless outer vestment worn by the officiating priest at mass

chasuble: *1* Gothic, *2* fiddleback

¹**chat** \'chat\ *verb* **chat·ted; chat·ting** [Middle English *chatten*, short for *chatteren*] (15th century)
*intransitive verb*
**1 :** CHATTER, PRATTLE
**2 :** to talk in an informal or familiar manner
*transitive verb*
*chiefly British* **:** to talk to; *especially* **:** to talk lightly, glibly, or flirtatiously with — often used with *up*
²**chat** *noun* (1530)
**1 :** idle small talk **:** CHATTER
**2 :** light familiar talk; *especially* **:** CONVERSATION
**3** [imitative] **:** any of several songbirds (as of the genera *Saxicola, Granatellus,* or *Icteria*)
**châ·teau** \sha-'tō\ *noun, plural* **châ·teaus** \-'tōz\ *or* **châ·teaux** \-'tō(z)\ [French, from Latin *castellum* castle] (1739)
**1 :** a feudal castle or fortress in France
**2 :** a large country house **:** MANSION
**3 :** a French vineyard estate
**cha·teau·bri·and** \(ˌ)sha-ˌtō-brē-'äⁿ\ *noun, often capitalized* [François René de *Chateaubriand*] (1877)
**:** a large tenderloin steak usually grilled or broiled and served with a sauce (as béarnaise)
**chat·e·lain** \'sha-tᵊl-ˌān\ *noun* [Middle French *châtelain,* from Latin *castellanus* occupant of a castle] (15th century)
**:** CASTELLAN
**chat·e·laine** \'sha-tᵊl-ˌān\ *noun* [French *châtelaine,* feminine of *châtelain*] (1845)
**1 a :** the wife of a castellan **:** the mistress of a château **b :** the mistress of a household or of a large establishment
**2 :** a clasp or hook for a watch, purse, or bunch of keys
**cha·toy·ance** \shə-'tȯi-ən(t)s\ *noun* (1910)
**:** CHATOYANCY
**cha·toy·an·cy** \-ən(t)-sē\ *noun* (1894)
**:** the quality or state of being chatoyant
¹**cha·toy·ant** \shə-'tȯi-ənt\ *adjective* [French, from present participle of *chatoyer* to shine like a cat's eyes] (1816)
**:** having a changeable luster or color with an undulating narrow band of white light ⟨*chatoyant* gem⟩
²**chatoyant** *noun* (circa 1828)
**:** a chatoyant gem
**chat show** *noun* (1969)
*British* **:** TALK SHOW
**chat·tel** \'cha-tᵊl\ *noun* [Middle English *chatel* property, from Middle French, from Medieval Latin *capitale* — more at CATTLE] (14th century)

**1 :** an item of tangible movable or immovable property except real estate, freehold, and things (as buildings) connected with real property
**2 :** SLAVE, BONDSMAN
¹**chat·ter** \'cha-tər\ *verb* [Middle English *chatteren,* of imitative origin] (13th century)
*intransitive verb*
**1 :** to utter rapid short sounds suggestive of language but inarticulate and indistinct ⟨squirrels *chattered* angrily⟩ ⟨a *chattering* stream⟩
**2 :** to talk idly, incessantly, or fast **:** JABBER
**3 a :** to click repeatedly or uncontrollably ⟨teeth *chattering* with cold⟩ ⟨machine guns *chattering*⟩ **b :** to vibrate rapidly especially as a consequence of repeated sticking and slipping ⟨*chattering* brakes⟩
*transitive verb*
**:** to utter rapidly, idly, or indistinctly
— **chat·ter·er** *noun*
²**chatter** *noun* (13th century)
**1 :** the action or sound of chattering
**2 :** idle talk **:** PRATTLE
**chat·ter·box** \'cha-tər-ˌbäks\ *noun* (1774)
**:** one who engages in much idle talk
**chatter mark** *noun* (1888)
**1 :** a fine undulation formed on the surface of work by a chattering tool
**2 :** one of a series of short curved cracks on a glaciated rock surface transverse to the glacial striae
**chat·ty** \'cha-tē\ *adjective* **chat·ti·er; -est** (circa 1762)
**1 :** fond of chatting **:** TALKATIVE ⟨a *chatty* neighbor⟩
**2 :** having the style and manner of light familiar conversation ⟨a *chatty* letter⟩
— **chat·ti·ly** \'cha-tᵊl-ē\ *adverb*
— **chat·ti·ness** \'cha-tē-nəs\ *noun*
¹**chauf·feur** \'shō-fər, shō-'\ *noun* [French, literally, stoker, from *chauffer* to heat, from Middle French *chaufer* — more at CHAFE] (1899)
**1 :** a person employed to drive a motor vehicle
**2 :** one that transports others by operating a motor vehicle ◆
²**chauffeur** *verb* **chauf·feured; chauf·feur·ing** \'shō-f(ə-)riŋ, shō-'fər-iŋ\ (1917)
*intransitive verb*
**:** to do the work of a chauffeur
*transitive verb*
**1 :** to transport in the manner of a chauffeur ⟨*chauffeurs* the children to school⟩
**2 :** to operate (as an automobile) as chauffeur
**chaul·moo·gra** \chȯl-'mü-grə\ *noun* [Bengali *cālmugrā*] (circa 1815)
**:** any of several East Indian trees (family Flacourtiaceae) that yield an acrid oil used especially formerly in treating leprosy and skin diseases
**chaunt** \'chȯnt, 'chänt\, **chaunt·er** *variant of* CHANT, CHANTER
**chaus·sure** \shō-'sœr\ *noun, plural* **chaussures** \*same*\ [Middle English *chaucer,* from Middle French *chaussure,* from *chausser* to put on footwear, from Latin *calceare,* from *calceus* shoe — more at CALZONE] (14th century)
**1 :** FOOTGEAR
**2** *plural* **:** SHOES
**chau·tau·qua** \shə-'tȯ-kwə\ *noun, often capitalized* [*Chautauqua* Lake] (1873)
**:** an institution that flourished in the late 19th and early 20th centuries providing popular education combined with entertainment in the form of lectures, concerts, and plays often presented outdoors or in a tent
**chau·vin·ism** \'shō-və-ˌni-zəm\ *noun* [French *chauvinisme,* from Nicolas *Chauvin,* character noted for his excessive patriotism and devotion to Napoleon in Théodore and Hippolyte Cogniard's play *La Cocarde tricolore* (1831)] (1870)
**1 :** excessive or blind patriotism — compare JINGOISM

**2 :** undue partiality or attachment to a group or place to which one belongs or has belonged
**3 :** an attitude of superiority toward members of the opposite sex; *also* **:** behavior expressive of such an attitude
— **chau·vin·ist** \-və-nist\ *noun or adjective*
— **chau·vin·is·tic** \ˌshō-və-'nis-tik\ *adjective*
— **chau·vin·is·ti·cal·ly** \-ti-k(ə-)lē\ *adverb*
¹**chaw** \'chȯ\ *verb* [by alteration] (1506)
**:** CHEW
²**chaw** *noun* (1709)
**:** a chew especially of tobacco
**chaw·ba·con** \'chȯ-ˌbā-kən\ *noun* [¹*chaw* + *bacon*] (1537)
**:** BUMPKIN, HICK
**cha·yo·te** \chī-'yō-tē, chē-, -(ˌ)tā\ *noun* [Spanish, from Nahuatl *chayohtli*] (1887)
**:** the pear-shaped fruit of a West Indian annual vine (*Sechium edule*) of the gourd family that is widely cultivated as a vegetable; *also* **:** the plant — called also *mirliton*
¹**cheap** \'chēp\ *noun* [Middle English *chep,* from Old English *cēap* trade; akin to Old High German *kouf* trade; both from Latin *caupo* tradesman] (before 12th century)
*obsolete* **:** BARGAIN
— **on the cheap :** at minimum expense
**:** CHEAPLY
²**cheap** *adjective* (1509)
**1 a :** purchasable below the going price or the real value **b :** charging or obtainable at a low price **c :** depreciated in value (as by currency inflation) ⟨*cheap* dollars⟩
**2 :** gained with little effort ⟨a *cheap* victory⟩
**3 a :** of inferior quality or worth **:** TAWDRY, SLEAZY **b :** contemptible because of lack of any fine, lofty, or redeeming qualities **c :** STINGY
**4 a :** yielding small satisfaction **b :** paying or able to pay less than going prices
**5** *of money* **:** obtainable at a low rate of interest
— **cheap** *adverb*
— **cheap·ish** \'chē-pish\ *adjective*
— **cheap·ish·ly** *adverb*
— **cheap·ly** \'chē-plē\ *adverb*
— **cheap·ness** *noun*
**cheap·en** \'chē-pən\ *verb* **cheap·ened; cheap·en·ing** \'chēp-niŋ, 'chē-pə-\ (1574)
*transitive verb*
**1** [obsolete English *cheap* to price, bid for] *archaic* **a :** to ask the price of **b :** to bid or bargain for
**2 a :** to make cheap in price or value **b :** to lower in general esteem **c :** to make tawdry, vulgar, or inferior
*intransitive verb*
**:** to become cheap
**cheap·ie** \'chē-pē\ *noun* (circa 1898)
**:** one that is cheap; *especially* **:** an inexpensively produced motion picture

◇ WORD HISTORY
**chauffeur** *Chauffeur* in French means literally "stoker," a person who maintains the fire that powers the steam engine of a locomotive or ship. In the 1890s, *chauffeur* also began to be used for the driver of an automobile, who in effect stoked the engine mechanically with the accelerator. Earlier, the compound *chauffeur-mécanicien* "stoker-engineer" was applied to someone who both stoked an engine and ran it, and it is possible that *chauffeur* in the sense "driver" is actually short for *chauffeur-mécanicien.* In any case, the French word has had a successful career in a number of other European languages, from Spanish *chófer* to Russian *shofyor,* usually denoting a professional driver of a motor vehicle. In English, *chauffeur* often refers to someone who is hired to drive a passenger car.

**— cheapie** *adjective*
**¹cheap·jack** \'chēp-,jak\ *noun* [*cheap* + the name *Jack*] (1851)
**1 :** a haggling huckster
**2 :** a dealer in cheap merchandise
**²cheapjack** *adjective* (1865)
**1 :** being inferior, cheap, or worthless ⟨*cheapjack* movie companies⟩
**2 :** unscrupulously opportunistic ⟨*cheapjack* speculators⟩
**cheapo** \'chē-(,)pō\ *adjective* (1972)
**:** CHEAP
**cheap shot** *noun* (1971)
**1 :** an act of deliberate roughness against a defenseless opponent especially in a contact sport
**2 :** a critical statement that takes unfair advantage of a known weakness of the target
**cheap·skate** \'chēp-,skāt\ *noun* (1896)
**:** a miserly or stingy person; *especially* **:** one who tries to avoid paying a fair share of costs or expenses
**¹cheat** \'chēt\ (1590)
*transitive verb*
**1 :** to deprive of something valuable by the use of deceit or fraud
**2 :** to influence or lead by deceit, trick, or artifice
**3 :** to elude or thwart by or as if by outwitting ⟨*cheat* death⟩
*intransitive verb*
**1 a :** to practice fraud or trickery **b :** to violate rules dishonestly (as at cards or on an examination)
**2 :** to be sexually unfaithful — usually used with *on* ☆
**— cheat·er** *noun*
**²cheat** *noun* [earlier *cheat* forfeited property, from Middle English *chet* escheat, short for *eschete* — more at ESCHEAT] (1631)
**1 :** the act or an instance of fraudulently deceiving **:** DECEPTION, FRAUD
**2 :** one that cheats **:** PRETENDER, DECEIVER
**3 :** any of several grasses; *especially* **:** the common chess (*Bromus secalinus*)
**4 :** the obtaining of property from another by an intentional active distortion of the truth
**¹check** \'chek\ *noun* [Middle English *chek*, from Middle French *eschec*, from Arabic *shāh*, from Persian, literally, king; akin to Greek *ktasthai* to acquire, Sanskrit *kṣatra* dominion] (15th century)
**1 :** exposure of a chess king to an attack from which he must be protected or moved to safety
**2 a :** a sudden stoppage of a forward course or progress **:** ARREST **b :** a checking of an opposing player (as in ice hockey)
**3 :** a sudden pause or break in a progression
**4** *archaic* **:** REPRIMAND, REBUKE
**5 :** one that arrests, limits, or restrains **:** RESTRAINT ⟨against all *checks*, rebukes, and manners, I must advance —Shakespeare⟩
**6 a :** a standard for testing and evaluation **:** CRITERION **b :** EXAMINATION **c :** INSPECTION, INVESTIGATION ⟨a loyalty *check* on government employees⟩ **d :** the act of testing or verifying; *also* **:** the sample or unit used for testing or verifying
**7 :** a written order directing a bank to pay money as instructed **:** DRAFT
**8 a :** a ticket or token showing ownership or identity or indicating payment made ⟨a baggage *check*⟩ **b :** a counter in various games **c :** a slip indicating the amount due **:** BILL
**9** [Middle English *chek*, short for *cheker* checker] **a :** a pattern in squares that resembles a checkerboard **b :** a fabric woven or printed with such a design
**10 :** a mark typically √ placed beside an item to show it has been noted, examined, or verified
**11 :** CRACK, BREAK
**— check·less** \'che-kləs\ *adjective*
**— in check :** under restraint or control
**²check** (14th century)
*transitive verb*

**1 :** to put (a chess king) in check
**2** *chiefly dialect* **:** REBUKE, REPRIMAND
**3 a :** to slow or bring to a stop **:** BRAKE ⟨hastily *checked* the impulse⟩ **b :** to block the progress of (as a hockey player)
**4 a :** to restrain or diminish the action or force of **:** CONTROL **b :** to slack or ease off and then belay again (as a rope)
**5 a :** to compare with a source, original, or authority **:** VERIFY **b :** to inspect, examine, or look at appraisingly — usually used with *out* or *over* ⟨*checking* out new cars⟩ **c :** to mark with a check as examined, verified, or satisfactory — often used with *off* ⟨*checked* off each item⟩
**6 a :** to consign (as luggage) to a common carrier from which one has purchased a passenger ticket ⟨*checked* our bags before boarding⟩ **b :** to ship or accept for shipment under such a consignment
**7 :** to mark into squares **:** CHECKER
**8 :** to leave or accept for safekeeping in a checkroom
**9 :** to make checks or chinks **:** cause to crack ⟨the sun *checks* timber⟩
*intransitive verb*
**1 a :** *of a dog* **:** to stop in a chase especially when scent is lost **b :** to halt through caution, uncertainty, or fear **:** STOP
**2 a :** to investigate conditions ⟨*checked* on the passengers' safety⟩ **b :** to prove to be consistent or truthful ⟨the description *checks* with the photograph⟩ — often used with *out* ⟨the story *checked* out⟩
**3 :** to draw a check on a bank
**4 :** to waive the right to initiate the betting in a round of poker
**5 :** CRACK, SPLIT
**synonym** see RESTRAIN
**— check into 1 :** to check in at ⟨*check into* a hotel⟩ **2 :** INVESTIGATE
**— check up on :** INVESTIGATE
**check·able** *adjective* (1877)
**1 :** capable of being checked ⟨a *checkable* story⟩
**2 :** held in or being a bank account on which checks can be drawn ⟨*checkable* deposits⟩
**check·book** \'chek-,bu̇k\ *noun* (circa 1846)
**:** a book containing blank checks to be drawn on a bank
**checkbook journalism** *noun* (1975)
**:** the practice of paying someone for a news story and especially for granting an interview
**¹check·er** \'che-kər\ *noun* [Middle English *cheker*, from Middle French *eschequier*, from *eschec*] (14th century)
**1** *archaic* **:** CHESSBOARD
**2 :** a square or spot resembling the markings of a checkerboard
**3** [singular of *checkers*] **:** a piece in checkers
**²checker** *transitive verb* **check·ered; check·er·ing** \'che-k(ə-)riŋ\ (15th century)
**1 a :** to variegate with different colors or shades **b :** to vary with contrasting elements or situations ⟨had a *checkered* career⟩
**2 :** to mark into squares
**³checker** *noun* (1535)
**1 :** one that checks ⟨a fact *checker*⟩ ⟨spelling *checker*⟩
**2 :** an employee who checks out purchases in a self-service store
**check·er·ber·ry** \'che-kər-,ber-ē\ *noun* [*checker* wild service tree + *berry*] (1776)
**1 :** the spicy red berrylike fruit of an American wintergreen (*Gaultheria procumbens*)
**2 :** a plant producing checkerberries
**check·er·board** \-,bōrd, -,bȯrd\ *noun* (1775)
**1 :** a board used in various games (as checkers) with usually 64 squares in 2 alternating colors
**2 :** something that has a pattern or arrangement like a checkerboard
**check·ers** \'che-kərz\ *noun plural but singular in construction* (1712)
**:** a checkerboard game for 2 players each with 12 pieces

**check–in** \'che-,kin\ *noun* (1927)
**:** an act or instance of checking in
**check in** (1918)
*intransitive verb*
**1 :** to register at a hotel
**2 :** to report one's presence or arrival ⟨*check in* at a convention⟩
*transitive verb*
**:** to satisfy all requirements in returning ⟨*check in* the equipment after using⟩
**checking account** *noun* (circa 1909)
**:** a bank account against which the depositor can draw checks
**check·list** \'chek-,list\ *noun* (1853)
**:** a list of things to be checked or done ⟨a pilot's *checklist* before takeoff⟩; *also* **:** a comprehensive list ⟨a *checklist* of bird species⟩
**check mark** *noun* (1917)
**:** CHECK 10
**— check·mark** *transitive verb*
**¹check·mate** \'chek-,māt\ *transitive verb* [Middle English *chekmaten*, from *chekmate*, interjection used to announce checkmate, from Middle French *eschec mat*, from Arabic *shāh māt*, from Persian, literally, the king is left unable to escape] (14th century)
**1 :** to arrest, thwart, or counter completely
**2 :** to check (a chess opponent's king) so that escape is impossible
**²checkmate** *noun* (15th century)
**1 a :** the act of checkmating **b :** the situation of a checkmated king
**2 :** a complete check
**check·off** \'che-,kȯf\ *noun* (1911)
**1 a :** the deduction of union dues from a worker's paycheck by the employer **b :** designation on an income tax return of a small amount of money to be applied to a special fund (as for financing political campaigns)
**2 :** AUTOMATIC 2
**check off** (1839)
*transitive verb*
**1 :** to eliminate from further consideration
**2 :** to deduct (union dues) from a worker's paycheck
*intransitive verb*
**:** to change a play at the line of scrimmage in football by calling an automatic
**check·out** \'che-,kau̇t\ *noun* (1933)
**1 :** the action or an instance of checking out
**2 :** the time at which a lodger must vacate a room (as in a hotel) or be charged for retaining it
**3 :** a counter or area in a store where goods are checked out
**4 a :** the action of examining and testing something for performance, suitability, or readiness **b :** the action of familiarizing oneself with the operation of a mechanical thing (as an airplane)
**check out** (1921)
*intransitive verb*

---

☆ SYNONYMS
**Cheat, cozen, defraud, swindle** mean to get something by dishonesty or deception. CHEAT suggests using trickery that escapes observation ⟨*cheated* me out of a dollar⟩. COZEN implies artful persuading or flattering to attain a thing or a purpose ⟨always able to *cozen* her grandfather out of a few dollars⟩. DEFRAUD stresses depriving one of his or her rights and usually connotes deliberate perversion of the truth ⟨*defrauded* of her inheritance by an unscrupulous lawyer⟩. SWINDLE implies large-scale cheating by misrepresentation or abuse of confidence ⟨*swindled* of their savings by con artists⟩.

---

\ə\ abut \ᵊ\ kitten \ər\ **further** \a\ ash \ā\ ace
\ä\ mop, mar \au̇\ **out** \ch\ **chin** \e\ bet \ē\ **easy**
\g\ go \i\ hit \ī\ **ice** \j\ **job** \ŋ\ **sing** \ō\ go
\ȯ\ **law** \ȯi\ **boy** \th\ **thin** \t̲h̲\ **the** \ü\ **loot** \u̇\ **foot**
\y\ **yet** \zh\ **vision** *see also* Guide to Pronunciation

: to vacate and pay for one's lodging (as at a hotel)
*transitive verb*
**1** : to satisfy all requirements in taking away ⟨*checked out* a library book⟩
**2 a** : to itemize and total the cost of and receive payment for (outgoing merchandise) especially in a self-service store **b** : to have the cost totaled and pay for (purchases) at a checkout
**check·point** \'chek-ˌpóint\ *noun* (1926)
: a point at which a check is performed ⟨vehicles were inspected at various *checkpoints*⟩
**check·rein** \-ˌrān\ *noun* (circa 1809)
**1** : a short rein looped over a hook on the saddle of a harness to prevent a horse from lowering its head
**2** : a branch rein connecting the driving rein of one horse of a pair with the bit of the other
**check·room** \-ˌrüm, -ˌrùm\ *noun* (1900)
: a room at which baggage, parcels, or clothing is checked
**check·up** \'che-ˌkəp\ *noun* (1921)
: EXAMINATION; *especially* : a general physical examination
**check valve** *noun* (circa 1877)
: a valve that permits flow in one direction only
**ched·dar** \'che-dər\ *noun, often capitalized* [*Cheddar*, England] (circa 1661)
: a hard white, yellow, or orange smooth-textured cheese with a flavor that ranges from mild to strong as the cheese matures — called also *cheddar cheese*
**che·der** \'kā-dər, 'ke-\ *variant of* HEDER
**chee·cha·ko** \chē-'chä-(ˌ)kō, -'chȯ- *also* -'cha-\ *noun, plural* **-kos** [Chinook Jargon, from *chee* new (from Lower Chinook *čxi* right away) + *chako* come, from Nootka *čokʷa* come, imperative] (1897)
: TENDERFOOT 1 — used chiefly in Alaska
¹**cheek** \'chēk\ *noun* [Middle English *cheke*, from Old English *cēace*; akin to Middle Low German *kāke* jawbone] (before 12th century)
**1** : the fleshy side of the face below the eye and above and to the side of the mouth; *broadly* : the lateral aspect of the head
**2** : something suggestive of the human cheek in position or form; *especially* : one of two laterally paired parts
**3** : insolent boldness and self-assurance
**4** : BUTTOCK 1
*synonym* see TEMERITY
— **cheek·ful** \-ˌfùl\ *noun*
²**cheek** *transitive verb* (1840)
*chiefly British* : to speak rudely or impudently to
**cheek·bone** \'chēk-ˌbōn\ *noun* (circa 1775)
: the prominence below the eye that is formed by the zygomatic bone; *also* : ZYGOMATIC BONE
**cheek by jowl** *adverb* (1577)
: SIDE BY SIDE
**cheeked** \'chēkt\ *adjective* (1592)
: having cheeks of a specified nature — used in combination ⟨rosy-*cheeked*⟩
**cheek tooth** *noun* (14th century)
: any of the molar or premolar teeth
**cheeky** \'chē-kē\ *adjective* **cheek·i·er; -est** (1859)
: having or showing cheek : IMPUDENT
— **cheek·i·ly** \-kə-lē\ *adverb*
— **cheek·i·ness** \-kē-nəs\ *noun*
**cheep** \'chēp\ *intransitive verb* [imitative] (1513)
**1** : to utter faint shrill sounds : PEEP
**2** : to utter a single word or sound
— **cheep** *noun*
¹**cheer** \'chir\ *noun* [Middle English *chere* face, cheer, from Old French, face, from Medieval Latin *cara*, probably from Greek *kara* head, face — more at CEREBRAL] (13th century)
**1 a** *obsolete* : FACE **b** *archaic* : facial expression
**2** : state of mind or heart : SPIRIT ⟨be of good cheer —Matthew 9:2 (Authorized Version)⟩

**3** : lightness of mind and feeling : ANIMATION, GAIETY
**4** : hospitable entertainment : WELCOME
**5** : food and drink for a feast : FARE
**6** : something that gladdens ⟨words of *cheer*⟩
**7** : a shout of applause or encouragement
²**cheer** (14th century)
*transitive verb*
**1 a** : to instill with hope or courage : COMFORT — usually used with *up* **b** : to make glad or happy — usually used with *up*
**2** : to urge on or encourage especially by shouts ⟨*cheered* the team on⟩
**3** : to applaud with shouts
*intransitive verb*
**1** *obsolete* : to be mentally or emotionally disposed
**2** : to grow or be cheerful : REJOICE — usually used with *up*
**3** : to utter a shout of applause or triumph
— **cheer·er** *noun*
**cheer·ful** \'chir-fəl\ *adjective* (15th century)
**1 a** : full of good spirits : MERRY **b** : UNGRUDGING ⟨*cheerful* obedience⟩
**2** : conducive to cheer : likely to dispel gloom or worry ⟨sunny *cheerful* room⟩
— **cheer·ful·ly** \-f(ə-)lē\ *adverb*
— **cheer·ful·ness** \-fəl-nəs\ *noun*
**cheer·io** \ˌchir-ē-'ō\ *interjection* [*cheery* + *-o*] (1910)
*chiefly British* — usually used as a farewell and sometimes as a greeting or toast
**cheer·lead·er** \'chir-ˌlē-dər\ *noun* (1903)
: one that calls for and directs organized cheering (as at a football game)
— **cheer·lead** \-ˌlēd\ *transitive verb*
**cheer·less** \-ləs\ *adjective* (1579)
: lacking qualities that cheer : BLEAK, JOYLESS ⟨a *cheerless* room⟩
— **cheer·less·ly** *adverb*
— **cheer·less·ness** *noun*
**cheers** \'chirz\ *interjection* (1919)
— used as a toast
**cheery** \'chir-ē\ *adjective* **cheer·i·er; -est** (15th century)
**1** : marked by cheerfulness or good spirits
**2** : causing or suggesting cheerfulness
— **cheer·i·ly** \'chir-ə-lē\ *adverb*
— **cheer·i·ness** \'chir-ē-nəs\ *noun*
¹**cheese** \'chēz\ *noun, often attributive* [Middle English *chese*, from Old English *cēse*, from Latin *caseus* cheese] (before 12th century)
**1 a** : a food consisting of the coagulated, compressed, and usually ripened curd of milk separated from the whey **b** : an often cylindrical cake of this food
**2** : something resembling cheese in shape or consistency
²**cheese** *transitive verb* **cheesed; cheesing** [origin unknown] (circa 1811)
: to put an end to : STOP
— **cheese it** — used in the imperative as a warning of danger ⟨*cheese it*, the cops⟩
³**cheese** *noun* [perhaps from Urdu *chīz* thing] (1920)
*slang* : someone important
**cheese·burg·er** \'chēz-ˌbər-gər\ *noun* [*cheese* + ham*burger*] (circa 1938)
: a hamburger topped with a slice of cheese
**cheese·cake** \-ˌkāk\ *noun* (15th century)
**1** : a dessert consisting of a creamy filling usually containing cheese baked in a pastry or pressed-crumb shell
**2** : a photographic display of shapely and scantily clothed female figures — compare BEEFCAKE
**cheese·cloth** \-ˌklȯth\ *noun* [from its use in the making of cheese] (14th century)
: a very lightweight unsized cotton gauze
**cheese·par·ing** \-ˌpar-iŋ, -ˌper-\ *noun* (1597)
**1** : something worthless or insignificant
**2** : miserly economizing
— **cheeseparing** *adjective*
**cheesy** \'chē-zē\ *adjective* **chees·i·er; -est** (14th century)

**1 a** : resembling or suggesting cheese especially in consistency or odor **b** : containing cheese
**2** : SHABBY 3c, CHEAP
— **chees·i·ness** *noun*
**chee·tah** \'chē-tə\ *noun, plural* **cheetahs** *also* **cheetah** [Hindi *cītā* leopard, from Sanskrit *citraka*, from *citra* bright, variegated; akin to Old High German *heitar* bright — more at -HOOD] (1610)
: a long-legged spotted swift-moving African and formerly Asian cat (*Acinonyx jubatus*) about the size of a small leopard that has blunt nonretractile claws and is often trained to run down game

cheetah

**chef** \'shef\ *noun* [French, short for *chef de cuisine* head of the kitchen] (1826)
**1** : a skilled cook who manages the kitchen (as of a restaurant)
**2** : COOK
— **chef** *intransitive verb*
— **chef·dom** \-dəm\ *noun*
**chef d'oeu·vre** \shā-'dœvrᵊ, (ˌ)shā-'də(r)v\ *noun, plural* **chefs d'oeuvre** \-'dœvrᵊ, -'də(r)v(z)\ [French *chef-d'oeuvre*, literally, leading work] (1619)
: a masterpiece especially in art or literature
**che·la** \'kē-lə\ *noun, plural* **che·lae** \-(ˌ)lē\ [New Latin, from Greek *chēlē* claw] (1646)
: a pincerlike organ or claw borne by a limb of a crustacean or arachnid
¹**che·late** \'kē-ˌlāt *also* 'chē-\ *adjective* (1826)
**1** : resembling or having chelae
**2** : of, relating to, or being a chelate
²**chelate** *verb* **che·lat·ed; che·lat·ing** (1922)
*transitive verb*
: to combine with (a metal) so as to form a chelate ring
*intransitive verb*
: to react so as to form a chelate ring
— **che·lat·able** \-ˌlā-tə-bəl\ *adjective*
— **che·la·tion** \kē-'lā-shən *also* chē-\ *noun*
— **che·la·tor** \-ˌlā-tər\ *noun*
³**chelate** *noun* (1943)
: a compound having a ring structure that usually contains a metal ion held by coordinate bonds
**che·lic·era** \ki-'li-sə-rə\ *noun, plural* **-er·ae** \-ˌrē\ [New Latin, from French *chélicère*, from Greek *chēlē* + *keras* horn — more at HORN] (1835)
: one of the anterior pair of appendages of an arachnid often specialized as fangs
— **che·lic·er·al** \-sə-rəl\ *adjective*
**che·li·ped** \'kē-lə-ˌped\ *noun* [Greek *chēlē* claw + English *-i-* + *-ped*] (1869)
: one of the pair of legs that bears the large chelae in decapod crustaceans
**Chel·le·an** *or* **Chel·li·an** \'she-lē-ən\ *adjective* [French *chelléen*, from *Chelles*, France] (1893)
: ABBEVILLIAN
**che·lo·ni·an** \ki-'lō-nē-ən\ *noun* [Greek *chelōnē* tortoise] (1828)
: TURTLE
— **chelonian** *adjective*
**chem-** *or* **chemo-** *also* **chemi-** *combining form* [New Latin, from Late Greek *chēmeia* alchemy — more at ALCHEMY]
**1** : chemical : chemistry ⟨*chemo*taxis⟩
**2** : chemically ⟨*chemi*sorb⟩
**chem·ic** \'ke-mik\ *adjective* [New Latin *chimicus* alchemist, from Medieval Latin *alchimicus*, from *alchimia* alchemy] (1576)
**1** *archaic* : ALCHEMIC
**2** : CHEMICAL
¹**chem·i·cal** \'ke-mi-kəl\ *adjective* (1576)

**1 :** of, relating to, used in, or produced by chemistry
**2 a :** acting or operated or produced by chemicals **b :** detectable by chemical means
— **chem·i·cal·ly** \-mi-k(ə-)lē\ *adverb*
²**chemical** *noun* (1747)
**:** a substance obtained by a chemical process or used for producing a chemical effect
**chemical engineering** *noun* (1888)
**:** engineering dealing with the industrial application of chemistry
**chemical warfare** *noun* (1917)
**:** tactical warfare using incendiary mixtures, smokes, or irritant, burning, poisonous, or asphyxiating gases
**chemical weapon** *noun* (1980)
**:** a weapon used in chemical warfare
**chemi·lu·mi·nes·cence** \,ke-mē-,lü-mə-'ne-s°n(t)s, ,kē-\ *noun* [International Scientific Vocabulary] (1889)
**:** luminescence (as bioluminescence) due to chemical reaction
— **chemi·lu·mi·nes·cent** \-'ne-s°nt\ *adjective*
**che·min de fer** \shə-,man-də-'fer\ *noun, plural* **che·mins de fer** \*same*\ [French, literally, railroad] (1891)
**:** a card game in which two hands are dealt, any number of players may bet against the dealer, and the winning hand is the one that comes closer to but does not exceed a count of nine on two or three cards
**chemi·os·mot·ic** \,ke-mē-äz-'mä-tik, ,kē-\ *adjective* (1966)
**:** relating to or being a hypothesis that seeks to explain the mechanism of ATP formation in oxidative phosphorylation by mitochondria and chloroplasts without recourse to the formation of high-energy intermediates by postulating the formation of an energy gradient of hydrogen ions across the organelle membranes that results in the reversible movement of hydrogen ions to the outside and is generated by electron transport or the activity of electron carriers
**che·mise** \shə-'mēz, *sometimes* -'mēs\ *noun* [Middle English, from Old French, shirt, from Late Latin *camisia*] (13th century)
**1 :** a woman's one-piece undergarment
**2 :** a loose straight-hanging dress
**chem·i·sette** \,she-mi-'zet\ *noun* [French, diminutive of *chemise*] (1807)
**:** a woman's garment; *especially* **:** one (as of lace) to fill the open front of a dress
**chem·i·sorb** \'ke-mi-,sórb, 'kē-, -,zórb\ *transitive verb* [*chem-* + *-sorb* (as in *adsorb*)] (1935)
**:** to take up and hold usually irreversibly by chemical forces
— **chem·i·sorp·tion** \,ke-mi-'sórp-shən, ,kē-, -'zórp-\ *noun*
**chem·ist** \'ke-mist\ *noun* [New Latin *chimista*, short for Medieval Latin *alchimista*] (1562)
**1 a** *obsolete* **:** ALCHEMIST **b :** one trained in chemistry
**2** *British* **:** PHARMACIST
**chem·is·try** \'ke-mə-strē\ *noun, plural* **-tries** (1646)
**1 :** a science that deals with the composition, structure, and properties of substances and with the transformations that they undergo
**2 a :** the composition and chemical properties of a substance ⟨the *chemistry* of iron⟩ **b :** chemical processes and phenomena (as of an organism) ⟨blood *chemistry*⟩
**3 :** a strong mutual attraction, attachment, or sympathy ⟨they have a special *chemistry*⟩
**che·mo** \'kē-(,)mō\ *noun* (1982)
**:** CHEMOTHERAPY
**che·mo·au·to·tro·phic** \,kē-mō-,ó-tə-'trō-fik *also* ,ke-\ *adjective* (1945)
**:** being autotrophic and oxidizing an inorganic compound as a source of energy ⟨*chemoautotrophic* bacteria⟩

— **che·mo·au·tot·ro·phy** \-ó-'tä-trə-fē\ *noun*
**che·mo·pro·phy·lax·is** \-,prō-fə-'lak-səs *also* -,prä-fə-\ *noun* (1936)
**:** the prevention of infectious disease by the use of chemical agents
— **che·mo·pro·phy·lac·tic** \-'lak-tik\ *adjective*
**che·mo·re·cep·tion** \-ri-'sep-shən\ *noun* [International Scientific Vocabulary] (1919)
**:** the physiological reception of chemical stimuli
— **che·mo·re·cep·tive** \-'sep-tiv\ *adjective*
**che·mo·re·cep·tor** \-ri-'sep-tər\ *noun* [International Scientific Vocabulary] (1906)
**:** a sense organ (as a taste bud) responding to chemical stimuli
**che·mo·sur·gery** \,kē-mō-'sərj-rē, -'sər-jə-rē\ *noun* (circa 1944)
**:** chemical removal of diseased or unwanted tissue
— **che·mo·sur·gi·cal** \-'sər-ji-kəl\ *adjective*
**che·mo·syn·the·sis** \-'sin(t)-thə-səs\ *noun* [New Latin] (1901)
**:** synthesis of organic compounds (as in living cells) by energy derived from chemical reactions
— **che·mo·syn·thet·ic** \-sin-'the-tik\ *adjective*
**che·mo·tac·tic** \-'tak-tik\ *adjective* (1893)
**:** involving, inducing, or exhibiting chemotaxis
— **che·mo·tac·ti·cal·ly** \-ti-k(ə-)lē\ *adverb*
**che·mo·tax·is** \-'tak-səs\ *noun* [New Latin] (circa 1887)
**:** orientation or movement of an organism or cell in relation to chemical agents
**che·mo·tax·on·o·my** \-(,)tak-'sä-nə-mē\ *noun* (1963)
**:** the classification of plants and animals based on similarities and differences in biochemical composition
— **che·mo·tax·o·nom·ic** \-,tak-sə-'nä-mik\ *adjective*
— **che·mo·tax·on·o·mist** \-(,)tak-'sä-nə-mist\ *noun*
**che·mo·ther·a·peu·tic** \-,ther-ə-'pyü-tik\ *adjective* (1907)
**:** of, relating to, or used in chemotherapy
— **chemotherapeutic** *noun*
— **che·mo·ther·a·peu·ti·cal·ly** \-ti-k(ə-)lē\ *adverb*
**che·mo·ther·a·py** \-'ther-ə-pē\ *noun* [International Scientific Vocabulary] (1910)
**:** the use of chemical agents in the treatment or control of disease or mental illness
— **che·mo·ther·a·pist** \-pist\ *noun*
**che·mot·ro·pism** \ki-'mä-trə-,pi-zəm, ke-\ *noun* [International Scientific Vocabulary] (1897)
**:** orientation of cells or organisms in relation to chemical stimuli
**che·nille** \shə-'nē(ə)l\ *noun* [French, literally, caterpillar, from Latin *canicula*, diminutive of *canis* dog; from its hairy appearance — more at HOUND] (circa 1739)
**1 :** a wool, cotton, silk, or rayon yarn with protruding pile; *also* **:** a pile-face fabric with a filling of this yarn
**2 :** an imitation of chenille yarn or fabric
**che·no·pod** \'kē-nə-,päd, 'ke-\ *noun* [ultimately from Greek *chēn* goose + *podion*, diminutive of *pod-, pous* foot — more at GOOSE, FOOT] (1555)
**:** any plant of the goosefoot family
**cheong·sam** \'chòŋ-,säm\ *noun* [Chinese (Guangdong) *chèuhng-sāam*, literally, long gown] (1952)
**:** an oriental dress with a slit skirt and a mandarin collar
**cheque** \'chek\ *chiefly British variant of* ¹CHECK 7

**che·quer** \'che-kər\ *chiefly British variant of* CHECKER
**cher·i·moya** \,cher-ə-'mói-ə, ,chir-\ *noun* [Spanish *chirimoya*] (1736)
**:** a round, oblong, or heart-shaped fruit with a pitted rind that is borne by a widely cultivated tropical American tree (*Annona cherimola*) of the custard-apple family; *also* **:** this tree
**cher·ish** \'cher-ish\ *transitive verb* [Middle English *cherisshen*, from Middle French *cheriss-*, stem of *cherir* to cherish, from Old French, from *chier* dear, from Latin *carus* — more at CHARITY] (14th century)
**1 a :** to hold dear **:** feel or show affection for **b :** to keep or cultivate with care and affection
**2 :** to entertain or harbor in the mind deeply and resolutely ⟨still *cherishes* that memory⟩
*synonym* see APPRECIATE
— **cher·ish·able** \-i-shə-bəl\ *adjective*
— **cher·ish·er** \-i-shər\ *noun*
**cher·no·zem** \,cher-nə-'zyòm, -'zem\ *noun* [Russian, from *chërnyĭ* black + *zemlya* earth] (1841)
**:** any of a group of dark-colored zonal soils with a deep rich humus horizon found in regions (as the grasslands of central North America) of temperate to cool climate
— **cher·no·zem·ic** \-'zyò-mik, -'ze-\ *adjective*
**Cher·o·kee** \'cher-ə-(,)kē\ *noun, plural* **Cherokee** *or* **Cherokees** [probably from Creek *tciloki* people of a different speech] (1674)
**1 :** a member of an American Indian people originally of Tennessee and North Carolina
**2 :** the language of the Cherokee people
**Cherokee rose** *noun* (1823)
**:** a Chinese climbing rose (*Rosa laevigata*) with a fragrant white blossom
**che·root** \shə-'rüt, chə-\ *noun* [Tamil *curuṭṭu*, literally, roll] (circa 1679)
**:** a cigar cut square at both ends
**cher·ry** \'cher-ē\ *noun, plural* **cherries** [Middle English *chery*, from Old North French *cherise* (taken as a plural), from Late Latin *ceresia*, from Latin *cerasus* cherry tree, from Greek *kerasos*] (14th century)
**1 a :** any of numerous trees and shrubs (genus *Prunus*) of the rose family that bear pale yellow to deep red or blackish smooth-skinned drupes enclosing a smooth seed and that include some cultivated for their fruits or ornamental flowers — compare SWEET CHERRY **b :** the fruit of a cherry **c :** the wood of a cherry
**2 :** a variable color averaging a moderate red
**3 a :** HYMEN **b :** VIRGINITY
*word history* see SHERRY
— **cher·ry·like** \-,līk\ *adjective*
**cherry bomb** *noun* (1953)
**:** a powerful globular red firecracker
**cherry picker** *noun* (circa 1944)
**:** a traveling crane equipped for holding a passenger at the end of the boom
**cher·ry·stone** \'cher-ē-,stōn\ *noun* (1880)
**:** a small quahog
**cherry tomato** *noun* (1847)
**:** a small globose red or orange tomato borne in long dense clusters; *also* **:** a plant (*Lycopersicon lypersicum cerasiforme*) bearing cherry tomatoes
**chert** \'chərt, 'chat\ *noun* [origin unknown] (1679)
**:** a rock resembling flint and consisting essentially of a large amount of fibrous chalcedony with smaller amounts of cryptocrystalline quartz and amorphous silica
— **cherty** \'chər-tē, 'cha-\ *adjective*
**cher·ub** \'cher-əb\ *noun, plural usually* **cher·u·bim** \'cher-ə-,bim, 'ker- *also* 'cher-yə-\ [Latin, from Greek *cheroub*, from Hebrew *kĕrūbh*] (13th century)

**1** *plural* **:** an order of angels — see CELESTIAL HIERARCHY
**2** *plural usually* **cherubs a :** a beautiful usually winged child in painting and sculpture **b :** an innocent-looking usually chubby and rosy person
— **che·ru·bic** \chə-'rü-bik *also* 'cher-ə-\ *adjective*
— **che·ru·bi·cal·ly** \-bi-k(ə-)lē\ *adverb*
— **cher·ub·like** \'cher-əb-,līk\ *adjective*

**cher·vil** \'chər-vəl\ *noun* [Middle English *cherville*, from Old English *cerfille*, from Latin *caerefolium*, modification of (assumed) Greek *chairephyllon*, from *chairein* to rejoice + *phyllon* leaf — more at YEARN, BLADE] (before 12th century)
**:** an aromatic herb (*Anthriscus cerefolium*) of the carrot family with divided leaves that are often used in soups and salads; *also* **:** any of several related plants

**Ches·a·peake Bay retriever** \'che-sə-,pēk-'bā-\ *noun* (1891)
**:** any of a breed of large brown sporting dogs developed in Maryland and having a dense oily water-shedding coat

**Chesh·ire cat** \'che-shər-\ *noun* [*Cheshire*, England] (1866)
**:** a broadly grinning cat in Lewis Carroll's *Alice's Adventures in Wonderland*

**Cheshire cheese** *noun* (1597)
**:** a cheese similar to cheddar made chiefly in Cheshire, England

**¹chess** \'ches\ *noun* [Middle English *ches*, from Middle French *esches*, accusative plural of *eschec* check at chess — more at CHECK] (14th century)
**:** a game for 2 players each of whom moves 16 pieces according to fixed rules across a checkerboard and tries to checkmate the opponent's king

**²chess** *noun* [origin unknown] (1736)
**:** a weedy annual bromegrass (*Bromus secalinus*) widely distributed as a weed especially in grain; *broadly* **:** any of several weedy bromegrasses

chessboard with chess pieces arranged as at the beginning of a game

**chess·board** \'ches-,bōrd, -,bord\ *noun* (15th century)
**:** a checkerboard used in the game of chess

**chess·man** \-,man, -mən\ *noun* (15th century)
**:** any of the pieces used in chess

**chess pie** *noun* [perhaps alteration of *chest*] (1932)
**:** a pie or tart with a filling made especially of eggs, butter, and sugar

**chest** \'chest\ *noun* [Middle English, from Old English *cest, cist* chest, box, from Latin *cista*, from Greek *kistē* basket, hamper] (before 12th century)
**1 a :** a container for storage or shipping; *especially* **:** a box with a lid used especially for the safekeeping of belongings **b :** a cupboard used especially for the storing of medicines or first-aid supplies
**2 :** the place where money of a public institution is kept **:** TREASURY; *also* **:** the fund so kept
**3 a :** THORAX; *especially* **:** the human thorax ⟨a pain in the *chest*⟩ **b :** BREAST 2a ⟨a hairy *chest*⟩
— **chest·ful** \-,fúl\ *noun*

**chest·ed** \'ches-təd\ *adjective* (1662)
**:** having a chest of a specified kind — used in combination ⟨flat-*chested*⟩

**ches·ter·field** \'ches-tər-,fēld\ *noun* [from a 19th century Earl of *Chesterfield*] (1852)
**1 :** a single-breasted or double-breasted semi-fitted overcoat with velvet collar

**2 :** a davenport usually with upright armrests

**Ches·ter White** \'ches-tər-\ *noun* [*Chester* County, Pa.] (1856)
**:** any of a breed of large white swine

**¹chest·nut** \'ches(t)-(,)nət\ *noun* [Middle English *chasteine, chesten* chestnut tree, from Middle French *chastaigne*, from Latin *castanea*, from Greek *kastanea*] (14th century)
**1 a :** any of a genus (*Castanea*) of trees or shrubs of the beech family; *especially* **:** an American tree (*C. dentata*) that was formerly a dominant or codominant member of many deciduous forests of the eastern U.S. but has now been largely eliminated by the chestnut blight and seldom grows beyond the shrub or sapling stage **b :** the edible nut of a chestnut **c :** the wood of a chestnut
**2 :** a grayish to reddish brown
**3 :** HORSE CHESTNUT
**4 :** a chestnut-colored animal; *specifically* **:** a horse having a body color of any shade of pure or reddish brown with mane, tail, and points of the same or a lighter shade — compare ²BAY 1, ¹SORREL 1
**5 :** a callosity on the inner side of the leg of the horse — see HORSE illustration
**6 a :** an old joke or story **b :** something (as a musical piece or a saying) repeated to the point of staleness

**²chestnut** *adjective* (1555)
**1 :** of the color chestnut
**2 :** of, relating to, or resembling a chestnut

**chestnut blight** *noun* (circa 1909)
**:** a destructive disease of the American chestnut marked by cankers of the bark and cambium and caused by an imported fungus (*Endothia parasitica* synonym *Cryphonectria parasitica*)

**chestnut oak** *noun* (1703)
**:** any of several oaks having oblong to lanceolate leaves with crenate or serrate edges: as
**a :** CHINQUAPIN OAK **b :** a medium-sized oak (*Quercus prinus*) of eastern North America with large acorns and leaves that are shiny yellow-green above and paler below

**chest of drawers** (1649)
**:** a piece of furniture designed to contain a set of drawers (as for holding clothing)

**chesty** \'ches-tē\ *adjective* **chest·i·er; -est** (1899)
**1 :** proudly or arrogantly self-assertive
**2 :** marked by a large or well-developed chest

**chet·rum** \'chē-trəm, 'che-\ *noun, plural* **chetrums** *or* **chetrum** [Tibetan] (1973)
— see *ngultrum* at MONEY table

**che·val–de–frise** \shə-,val-də-'frēz\ *noun, plural* **che·vaux–de–frise** \shə-,vō-\ [French, literally, horse from Friesland] (1668)
**1 :** a defense consisting of a timber or an iron barrel covered with projecting spikes and often strung with barbed wire
**2 :** a protecting line (as of spikes) on top of a wall — usually used in plural

**che·val glass** \shə-'val-\ *noun* [French *cheval* horse, support] (1828)
**:** a full-length mirror in a frame in which it may be tilted

**che·va·lier** \,she-və-'lir, *especially for 1b & 2 also* shə-'val-,yā\ *noun* [Middle English, from Middle French, from Late Latin *caballarius* horseman — more at CAVALIER] (14th century)
**1 a :** CAVALIER 2 **b :** a member of any of various orders of knighthood or of merit (as the Legion of Honor)
**2 a :** a member of the lowest rank of French nobility **b :** a cadet of the French nobility
**3 :** a chivalrous man

**che·ve·lure** \shəv-lⁱr\ *noun* [French, from Late Latin *capillatura*, from Latin *capillatus* having long hair, from *capillus* hair] (15th century)
**:** a head of hair

**chev·i·ot** \'she-vē-ət, *especially British* 'che-\ *noun, often capitalized* (1815)
**1 :** any of a breed of hardy hornless relatively small sheep that are a source of quality mutton and have their origin in the Cheviot hills
**2 a :** a fabric of cheviot wool **b :** a heavy rough napped plain or twill fabric of coarse wool or worsted **c :** a sturdy soft-finished plain or twill cotton shirting

**chèvre** \'shev(rᵉ), 'shev-rə\ *noun* [French, literally, goat, from Old French *chievre*, from Latin *capra* she-goat, from *caper* he-goat — more at CAPRIOLE] (1950)
**:** GOAT CHEESE

**chev·ron** \'shev-rən\ *noun* [Middle English, from Middle French, rafter, chevron, from (assumed) Vulgar Latin *caprion-, caprio* rafter; akin to Latin *caper* goat] (14th century)
**:** a figure, pattern, or object having the shape of a V or an inverted V: as **a** *or* **chev·er·on** \'shev-rən, 'she-və-\ **:** a heraldic charge consisting of two diagonal stripes meeting at an angle usually with the point up **b :** a sleeve badge that usually consists of one or more chevron-shaped stripes that indicates the wearer's rank and service (as in the armed forces)

chevrons b: *1* marine staff sergeant, *2* air force staff sergeant, *3* army staff sergeant

**¹chew** \'chü\ *verb* [Middle English *chewen*, from Old English *cēowan*; akin to Old High German *kiuwan* to chew, Russian *zhevat'*] (before 12th century)
*transitive verb*
**:** to crush, grind, or gnaw (as food) with or as if with the teeth **:** MASTICATE
*intransitive verb*
**:** to chew something; *specifically* **:** to chew tobacco
— **chew·able** \-ə-bəl\ *adjective*
— **chew·er** *noun*
— **chewy** \'chü-ē\ *adjective*
— **chew the rag** *or* **chew the fat** *slang* **:** to make friendly familiar conversation **:** CHAT

**²chew** *noun* (13th century)
**1 :** the act of chewing
**2 :** something for chewing

**chewing gum** *noun* (1850)
**:** a sweetened and flavored insoluble plastic material (as a preparation of chicle) used for chewing

**che·wink** \chi-'wiŋk\ *noun* [imitative] (1793)
**:** TOWHEE 1

**chew out** *transitive verb* (1943)
**:** REPRIMAND, BAWL OUT

**chew over** *transitive verb* (1939)
**:** to meditate on **:** think about reflectively

**Chey·enne** \shī-'an, -'en\ *noun, plural* **Cheyenne** *or* **Cheyennes** [Canadian French, from Dakota *šahíyena*] (1778)
**1 :** a member of an American Indian people of the western plains of the U.S.
**2 :** the Algonquian language of the Cheyenne people

**chez** \'shā\ *preposition* [French, from Latin *casae* at home, locative of *casa* cottage] (1740)
**:** at or in the home or business place of

**chi** \'kī, 'kē\ *noun* [Greek *chei, chi*] (15th century)
**:** the 22nd letter of the Greek alphabet — see ALPHABET table

**Chi·a·ni·na** \,kē-ə-'nē-nə\ *noun, plural* **Chianina** *or* **Chianinas** [Italian, from feminine of *chianino* of the *Chiani* River valley, Italy] (1914)
**:** any of a breed of tall white cattle of Italian origin noted especially for producing lean meat

**Chi·an·ti** \kē-'än-tē, -'an-\ *noun* [Italian, from the *Chianti* region, Italy] (1833)
**:** a dry usually red wine from the Tuscany region of Italy; *also* **:** a similar wine made elsewhere

**chiar·oscu·rist** \kē-,är-ə-'skyu̇r-ist, kē-,ar-, -'sku̇r-\ *noun* (circa 1798)
**:** an artist who specializes in chiaroscuro
**chiar·oscu·ro** \-'skyu̇r-(,)ō, -'sku̇r-\ *noun, plural* **-ros** [Italian, from *chiaro* clear, light + *oscuro* obscure, dark] (1686)
**1 :** pictorial representation in terms of light and shade without regard to color
**2 a :** the arrangement or treatment of light and dark parts in a pictorial work of art **b :** the interplay or contrast of dissimilar qualities (as of mood or character)
**3 :** a 16th century woodcut technique involving the use of several blocks to print different tones of the same color; *also* **:** a print made by this technique
**4 :** the interplay of light and shadow on or as if on a surface
**5 :** the quality of being veiled or partly in shadow
**chi·asm** \'kī-,a-zᵊm, 'kē-\ *noun* [New Latin *chiasma*] (1870)
**:** CHIASMA 1
**chi·as·ma** \kī-'az-mə, kē-\ *noun, plural* **-ma·ta** \-mə-tə\ [New Latin, X-shaped configuration, from Greek, crosspiece, from *chiazein* to mark with a chi, from *chi* (x)] (1839)
**1 :** an anatomical intersection or decussation — compare OPTIC CHIASMA
**2 :** a cross-shaped configuration of paired chromatids visible in the diplotene of meiotic prophase and considered the cytological equivalent of genetic crossing-over — **chi·as·mat·ic** \,kī-əz-'ma-tik, ,kē-\ *adjective*
**chi·as·mus** \kī-'az-məs, kē-\ *noun* [New Latin, from Greek *chiasmos*, from *chiazein* to mark with a chi] (1871)
**:** an inverted relationship between the syntactic elements of parallel phrases (as in Goldsmith's *to stop too fearful, and too faint to go*)
**chiaus** \'chau̇s, 'chau̇sh\ *noun* [Turkish *çavuş*] (1595)
**:** a Turkish messenger or sergeant
**Chib·cha** \'chib-(,)chä\ *noun, plural* **Chibcha** *or* **Chibchas** [Spanish] (1814)
**1 :** a member of an Indian people of central Colombia
**2 :** the extinct language of the Chibcha people
**Chib·chan** \-chən\ *adjective* (1902)
**:** of, relating to, or constituting a language family of Colombia and Central America
**chi·bouk** *or* **chi·bouque** \chə-'bük, shə-\ *noun* [French *chibouque*, from Turkish *çubuk*] (1813)
**:** a long-stemmed Turkish tobacco pipe with a clay bowl
**¹chic** \'shēk\ *noun* [French] (1856)
**1 :** smart elegance and sophistication especially of dress or manner **:** STYLE ⟨wears her clothes with superb *chic*⟩
**2 :** a distinctive mode of dress or manner associated with a fashionable lifestyle, ideology, or pursuit
**²chic** *adjective* (1865)
**1 :** cleverly stylish **:** SMART ⟨the woman who is *chic* adapts fashion to her own personality —Elizabeth L. Post⟩
**2 :** currently fashionable ⟨a *chic* restaurant⟩
— **chic·ly** *adverb*
— **chic·ness** *noun*
**Chi·ca·na** \chi-'kä-nə *also* shi-\ *noun* [Mexican Spanish, feminine of *chicano*] (1967)
**:** an American woman or girl of Mexican descent
— **Chicana** *adjective*
**¹chi·cane** \shi-'kān, chi-\ *verb* **chi·caned; chi·can·ing** [French *chicaner*, from Middle French, to quibble, prevent justice] (circa 1672)
*intransitive verb*
**:** to use chicanery ⟨a wretch he had taught to lie and *chicane* —George Meredith⟩
*transitive verb*
**:** TRICK, CHEAT
**²chicane** *noun* (1686)

**1 :** CHICANERY
**2 a :** an obstacle on a racecourse **b :** a series of tight turns in opposite directions in an otherwise straight stretch of a road-racing course
**3 :** the absence of trumps in a hand of cards
**chi·ca·nery** \-'kān-rē, -'kā-nə-\ *noun, plural* **-ner·ies** (1609)
**1 :** deception by artful subterfuge or sophistry **:** TRICKERY
**2 :** a piece of sharp practice (as at law) **:** TRICK
**Chi·ca·no** \chi-'kä-(,)nō *also* shi-\ *noun, plural* **-nos** [Mexican Spanish, alteration of Spanish *mexicano* Mexican] (1947)
**:** an American of Mexican descent
— **Chicano** *adjective*
**¹chi·chi** \'shē-(,)shē *also* 'chē-(,)chē\ *noun* [French] (1908)
**1 :** frilly or elaborate ornamentation
**2 :** AFFECTATION, PRECIOSITY
**3 :** CHIC
**²chichi** *adjective* (1926)
**1 :** elaborately ornamented **:** SHOWY, FRILLY ⟨a *chichi* dress⟩
**2 :** ARTY, PRECIOUS ⟨*chichi* poetry⟩
**3 :** CHIC, FASHIONABLE ⟨a *chichi* nightclub⟩
**chick** \'chik\ *noun* [Middle English *chyke*, alteration of *chiken*] (15th century)
**1 a :** a domestic chicken; *especially* **:** one newly hatched **b :** the young of any bird
**2 :** CHILD
**3** *slang* **:** a young woman
**chick·a·dee** \'chi-kə-(,)dē\ *noun* [imitative] (1838)
**:** any of several crestless American titmice (genus *Parus*) usually with the crown of the head sharply demarked and darker than the body
**chick·a·ree** \'chi-kə-,rē\ *noun* [imitative] (1829)
**:** RED SQUIRREL; *also* **:** a related squirrel (*Tamiasciurus douglasii*) of forests from southwestern British Columbia to central California
**Chick·a·saw** \'chi-kə-,so̊\ *noun, plural* **Chickasaw** *or* **Chickasaws** (1674)
**1 :** a member of an American Indian people of Mississippi and Alabama
**2 :** a dialect of Choctaw spoken by the Chickasaw
**¹chick·en** \'chi-kᵊn, *sometimes* -kᵊŋ\ *noun* [Middle English *chiken*, from Old English *cicen* young chicken; akin to Old English *cocc* cock] (14th century)
**1 a :** the common domestic fowl (*Gallus gallus*) especially when young; *also* **:** its flesh used as food — compare JUNGLE FOWL **b :** any of various birds or their young
**2 :** a young woman
**3 a :** COWARD **b :** any of various contests in which the participants risk personal safety in order to see which one will give up first
**4** [short for *chickenshit*] *slang* **:** petty details
**5 :** a young male homosexual
**²chicken** *adjective* (1941)
**1 a :** SCARED **b :** TIMID, COWARDLY
**2** *slang* **a :** insistent on petty details of duty or discipline **b :** PETTY, UNIMPORTANT
**³chicken** *intransitive verb* **chick·ened; chick·en·ing** \'chi-kᵊn-iŋ, 'chik-niŋ\ (1943)
**:** to lose one's nerve — usually used with *out* ⟨seemed to exhibit courage, manliness, and conviction when others *chickened* out —J. R. Seeley⟩
**chicken–and–egg** *adjective* [from the proverbial question "which came first, the chicken or the egg?"] (1959)
**:** of, relating to, or being a cause-and-effect dilemma
**chicken colonel** *noun* [from the eagle serving as insignia of the rank] (1947)
*slang* **:** COLONEL 1a
**chicken feed** *noun* (1836)
*slang* **:** a paltry sum (as in profits or wages)
**chick·en–fried steak** \'chi-kᵊn-'frīd-\ *noun* (1952)

**:** steak coated with batter, fried, and served with gravy
**chicken hawk** *noun* (1827)
**:** a hawk that preys or is believed to prey on chickens
**chick·en·heart·ed** \'chi-kən-,här-təd\ *adjective* (1681)
**:** TIMID, COWARDLY
**chick·en–liv·ered** \-,li-vərd\ *adjective* (1872)
**:** FAINTHEARTED, COWARDLY
**chicken pox** *noun* (circa 1738)
**:** an acute contagious disease especially of children marked by low-grade fever and formation of vesicles and caused by a herpesvirus — compare HERPES ZOSTER
**¹chick·en·shit** \'chi-kᵊn-,shit\ *noun* (1947)
**1 :** the petty details of a duty or discipline — usually considered vulgar
**2 :** COWARD, CHICKEN — usually considered vulgar
**²chickenshit** *adjective* (1951)
**1 :** PETTY, INSIGNIFICANT — usually considered vulgar
**2 :** lacking courage, manliness, or effectiveness — usually considered vulgar
**chicken snake** *noun* (1709)
**:** RAT SNAKE
**chicken wire** *noun* [from its use for making enclosures for chickens] (circa 1904)
**:** a light galvanized wire netting of hexagonal mesh
**chick·pea** \'chik-,pē\ *noun* [alteration of *chich pea*, from Middle English *chiche*, from Middle French, from Latin *cicer*] (circa 1722)
**:** an Asian leguminous herb (*Cicer arietinum*) cultivated for its short pods with one or two seeds; *also* **:** its seed
**chick·weed** \-,wēd\ *noun* (14th century)
**:** any of various low-growing small-leaved weedy plants of the pink family (especially genera *Cerastium* and *Stellaria*); *especially* **:** a cosmopolitan weed (*Stelleria media*) naturalized in the U.S. from Eurasia
**chi·cle** \'chi-kəl, 'chi-klē\ *noun* [American Spanish, from Nahuatl *tzictli*] (circa 1889)
**:** a gum from the latex of the sapodilla used as the chief ingredient of chewing gum
**chic·o·ry** *also* **chick·o·ry** \'chi-k(ə-)rē\ *noun, plural* **-ries** [Middle English *cicoree*, from Middle French *cichorée*, *chicorée*, from Latin *cichoreum*, from Greek *kichoreia*] (15th century)
**1 :** a thick-rooted usually blue-flowered European perennial composite herb (*Cichorium intybus*) widely grown for its roots and as a salad plant — compare ENDIVE 2, RADICCHIO
**2 :** the dried ground roasted root of chicory used to flavor or adulterate coffee
**chide** \'chīd\ *verb* **chid** \'chid\ *or* **chid·ed** \'chī-dəd\; **chid** *or* **chid·den** \'chi-dᵊn\ *or* **chided; chid·ing** \'chī-diŋ\ [Middle English, from Old English *cīdan* to quarrel, chide, from *cīd* strife] (before 12th century)
*intransitive verb*
**:** to speak out in angry or displeased rebuke
*transitive verb*
**:** to voice disapproval to **:** reproach in a usually mild and constructive manner **:** SCOLD
*synonym* see REPROVE
**¹chief** \'chēf\ *adjective* (14th century)
**1 :** accorded highest rank or office ⟨*chief* librarian⟩
**2 :** of greatest importance or influence ⟨the *chief* reasons⟩
**²chief** *adverb* (14th century)
*archaic* **:** CHIEFLY
**³chief** *noun* [Middle English, from Middle French, head, chief, from Latin *caput* head — more at HEAD] (15th century)

\ə\ abut \ᵊ\ kitten \ər\ further \a\ ash \ā\ ace
\ä\ mop, mar \au̇\ out \ch\ chin \e\ bet \ē\ easy
\g\ go \i\ hit \ī\ ice \j\ job \ŋ\ sing \ō\ go
\o̊\ law \o̊i\ boy \th\ thin \th\ the \ü\ loot \u̇\ foot
\y\ yet \zh\ vision *see also* Guide to Pronunciation

**1 :** the upper part of a heraldic field
**2 :** the head of a body of persons or an organization **:** LEADER ⟨*chief* of police⟩
**3 :** the principal or most valuable part
— **chief·dom** \-dəm\ *noun*
— **chief·ship** \-,ship\ *noun*
— **in chief :** in the chief position or place — often used in titles ⟨commander *in chief*⟩

**chief executive** *noun* (1833)
**:** a principal executive officer: as **a :** the president of a republic **b :** the governor of a state

**chief justice** *noun* (1534)
**:** the presiding or principal judge of a court of justice

**¹chief·ly** \'chē-flē\ *adverb* (14th century)
**1 :** most importantly **:** PRINCIPALLY, ESPECIALLY
**2 :** for the most part **:** MOSTLY, MAINLY

**²chiefly** *adjective* (1870)
**:** of or relating to a chief ⟨*chiefly* duties⟩

**chief master sergeant** *noun* (1959)
**:** a noncommissioned officer in the air force ranking above a senior master sergeant

**chief master sergeant of the air force** (circa 1961)
**:** the ranking noncommissioned officer in the air force serving as adviser to the chief of staff

**chief of naval operations** (1915)
**:** the commanding officer of the navy and a member of the Joint Chiefs of Staff

**chief of staff** (circa 1881)
**1 :** the ranking officer of a staff in the armed forces serving as principal adviser to a commander
**2 :** the commanding officer of the army or air force and a member of the Joint Chiefs of Staff

**chief of state** (1950)
**:** the formal head of a national state as distinguished from the head of the government

**chief petty officer** *noun* (circa 1887)
**:** an enlisted man in the navy or coast guard ranking above a petty officer first class and below a senior chief petty officer

**chief·tain** \'chēf-tən\ *noun* [Middle English *chieftaine*, from Middle French *chevetain*, from Late Latin *capitaneus* chief — more at CAPTAIN] (14th century)
**:** a chief especially of a band, tribe, or clan
— **chief·tain·ship** \-,ship\ *noun*

**chief·tain·cy** \-sē\ *noun, plural* **-cies** (1788)
**1 :** the rank, dignity, office, or rule of a chieftain
**2 :** a region or a people ruled by a chief **:** CHIEFDOM

**chief warrant officer** *noun* (1956)
**:** a warrant officer of senior rank in the armed forces; *also* **:** a commissioned officer in the navy or coast guard ranking below an ensign

**chiel** \'chē(ə)l\ *or* **chield** \'chē(ə)ld\ *noun* [Middle English (Scots) *cheld*, alteration of Middle English *child* child] (1728)
*chiefly Scottish* **:** FELLOW, LAD

**chiff·chaff** \'chif-,chaf\ *noun* [imitative] (1780)
**:** a small grayish European warbler (*Phylloscopus collybita*)

**¹chif·fon** \shi-'fän, 'shi-,\ *noun* [French, literally, rag, from *chiffe* old rag, alteration of Middle French *chipe*, from Middle English *chip* chip] (1765)
**1 :** an ornamental addition (as a knot of ribbons) to a woman's dress
**2 :** a sheer fabric especially of silk

**²chiffon** *adjective* (1903)
**1 :** resembling chiffon in sheerness or softness
**2 :** having a light delicate texture achieved usually by adding whipped egg whites or whipped gelatin ⟨lemon *chiffon* pie⟩

**chif·fo·nade** \,shi-fə-'näd, -'näd\ *noun* [French *chiffonnade*, from *chiffonner* to crumple, from *chiffon*] (1877)
**:** shredded or finely cut vegetables used especially as a garnish

**chif·fo·nier** \,shi-fə-'nir\ *noun* [French *chiffonnier*, from *chiffon*] (1765)

**:** a high narrow chest of drawers

**chif·fo·robe** \'shi-fə-,rōb\ *noun* [*chiffon*ier + ward*robe*] (1908)
**:** a combination of wardrobe and chest of drawers

**chig·ger** \'chi-gər, 'ji-\ *noun* (1756)
**1 :** CHIGOE 1
**2** [alteration of *²jigger*] **:** a 6-legged mite larva (family Trombiculidae) that sucks the blood of vertebrates and causes intense irritation

**chifforobe**

**chi·gnon** \'shēn-,yän *also* -,yòn\ *noun* [French, from Middle French *chaignon* chain, collar, nape] (1783)
**:** a knot of hair that is worn at the back of the head and especially at the nape of the neck

**chi·goe** \'chi-(,)gō, 'chē-\ *noun* [Carib *chico*] (1691)
**1 :** a tropical flea (*Tunga penetrans*) of which the fertile female causes great discomfort by burrowing under the skin
**2 :** CHIGGER 2

**Chi·hua·hua** \chə-'wä-(,)wä, shə-, -wə\ *noun* [Mexican Spanish, from *Chihuahua*, Mexico] (1858)
**:** any of a breed of very small round-headed dogs that occur in short-coated and long-coated varieties

**chil·blain** \'chil-,blān\ *noun* [¹*chill*] (1547)
**:** an inflammatory swelling or sore caused by exposure (as of the feet or hands) to cold

**Chihuahua**

**child** \'chī(ə)ld\ *noun, plural* **chil·dren** \'chil-drən, -dərn\ *often attributive* [Middle English, from Old English *cild*; akin to Gothic *kilthei* womb, and perhaps to Sanskrit *jathara* belly] (before 12th century)
**1 a :** an unborn or recently born person **b** *dialect* **:** a female infant
**2 a :** a young person especially between infancy and youth **b :** a childlike or childish person **c :** a person not yet of age
**3** *usually* **childe** \'chī(ə)ld\ *archaic* **:** a youth of noble birth
**4 a :** a son or daughter of human parents **b :** DESCENDANT
**5 :** one strongly influenced by another or by a place or state of affairs
**6 :** PRODUCT, RESULT ⟨barbed wire . . . is truly a *child* of the plains —W. P. Webb⟩
— **child·less** \'chī(ə)ld-ləs\ *adjective*
— **child·less·ness** *noun*
— **with child :** PREGNANT

**child·bear·ing** \'chīl(d)-,bar-iŋ, -,ber-\ *adjective* (14th century)
**:** of or relating to the process of conceiving, being pregnant with, and giving birth to children ⟨women of *childbearing* age⟩
— **childbearing** *noun*

**child·bed** \-,bed\ *noun* (13th century)
**:** the condition of a woman in childbirth

**childbed fever** *noun* (1928)
**:** PUERPERAL FEVER

**child·birth** \'chīl(d)-,bərth\ *noun* (15th century)
**:** PARTURITION

**child·hood** \'chīld-,hùd\ *noun* (before 12th century)
**1 :** the state or period of being a child
**2 :** the early period in the development of something

**child·ish** \'chīl-dish\ *adjective* (before 12th century)

**1 :** of, relating to, or befitting a child or childhood
**2 a :** marked by or suggestive of immaturity and lack of poise ⟨a *childish* spiteful remark⟩ **b :** lacking complexity **:** SIMPLE ⟨it's a *childish* device, but it works⟩ **c :** deteriorated with age especially in mind **:** SENILE
— **child·ish·ly** *adverb*
— **child·ish·ness** *noun*

**child·like** \'chī(ə)l(d)-,līk\ *adjective* (1586)
**:** of, relating to, or resembling a child or childhood; *especially* **:** marked by innocence, trust, and ingenuousness
— **child·like·ness** *noun*

**child·ly** \'chī(ə)l(d)-lē\ *adjective* (before 12th century)
**:** CHILDLIKE

**child·proof** \'chīl(d)-,prüf\ *adjective* (1956)
**:** designed to prevent tampering or opening by children ⟨*childproof* pill bottles⟩

**child's play** *noun* (14th century)
**1 :** an extremely simple task or act
**2 :** something that is insignificant ⟨his injury was *child's play* compared with the damage he inflicted⟩

**Chile saltpeter** \'chi-lē-, 'chē-(,)lā-\ *noun* [*Chile*, South America] (circa 1909)
**:** sodium nitrate especially occurring naturally (as in caliche)

**chili** *or* **chile** *or* **chil·li** \'chi-lē\ *noun, plural* **chil·ies** *or* **chil·es** *or* **chil·lies** [Spanish *chile*, from Nahuatl *chīlli*] (1604)
**1 a :** HOT PEPPER **b** *usually* chilli, *chiefly British* **:** a pepper whether hot or sweet
**2 a :** a thick sauce of meat and chilies **b :** CHILI CON CARNE

**chil·i·ad** \'ki-lē-,ad, -əd\ *noun* [Late Latin *chiliad-, chilias*, from Greek, from *chilioi* thousand] (1598)
**1 :** a group of 1000
**2 :** MILLENNIUM 2a

**chil·i·asm** \'ki-lē-,a-z³m\ *noun* [New Latin *chiliasmus*, from Late Latin *chiliastes* one that believes in chiliasm, from *chilias*] (1610)
**:** MILLENARIANISM
— **chil·i·ast** \-lē-,ast, -lē-əst\ *noun*
— **chil·i·as·tic** \,ki-lē-'as-tik\ *adjective*

**chili con car·ne** \,chi-lē-,kän-'kär-nē, -kən-\ *noun* [American Spanish *chile con carne* chili with meat] (1857)
**:** a spiced stew of ground beef and minced chilies or chili powder usually with beans

**chili dog** *noun* (1969)
**:** a hot dog topped with chili

**chili powder** *noun* (1938)
**:** a condiment made with chilies ground to a powder

**chili sauce** *noun* (1880)
**:** a spiced tomato sauce usually made with red and green peppers

**¹chill** \'chil\ *noun* [Middle English *chile* chill, frost, from Old English *ciele*; akin to Old English *ceald* cold] (before 12th century)
**1 a :** a sensation of cold accompanied by shivering **b :** a disagreeable sensation of coldness
**2 :** a moderate but disagreeable degree of cold
**3 :** a check to enthusiasm or warmth of feeling ⟨felt the *chill* of his opponent's stare⟩

**²chill** *adjective* (14th century)
**1 a :** moderately cold **b :** COLD, RAW
**2 :** affected by cold ⟨*chill* travelers⟩
**3 :** DISTANT, FORMAL ⟨a *chill* reception⟩
**4 :** DEPRESSING, DISPIRITING ⟨*chill* penury —Thomas Gray⟩
— **chill·ness** *noun*

**³chill** (14th century)
*intransitive verb*
**1 a :** to become cold **b :** to shiver or quake with or as if with cold
**2 :** to become taken with a chill
*transitive verb*
**1 a :** to make cold or chilly **b :** to make cool especially without freezing
**2 :** to affect as if with cold **:** DISPIRIT, DISCOURAGE ⟨were *chilled* by the drab austerity —William Attwood⟩

— **chill·ing·ly** \'chi-liŋ-lē\ *adverb*
**chill·er** \'chi-lər\ *noun* (1798)
**1** : one that chills
**2** : an eerie or frightening story of murder, violence, or the supernatural
**chill factor** *noun* (1965)
: WINDCHILL
**chill out** *intransitive verb* (1983) *slang*
: to calm down : go easy : RELAX — often used in the imperative
**chil·lum** \'chi-ləm\ *noun* [Hindi *cilam,* from Persian *chilam*] (1781)
**1** : the part of a water pipe that contains the substance (as tobacco or hashish) which is smoked; *also* : a quantity of a substance thus smoked
**2** : a funnel-shaped clay pipe for smoking
**chilly** \'chi-lē\ *adjective* **chill·i·er; -est** (1570)
**1** : noticeably cold : CHILLING
**2** : unpleasantly affected by cold
**3** : lacking warmth of feeling
**4** : tending to arouse fear or apprehension ⟨*chilly* suspicions⟩
— **chill·i·ly** \'chi-lə-lē\ *adverb*
— **chill·i·ness** \'chi-lē-nəs\ *noun*
¹**chi·mae·ra** \kī-'mir-ə, kə-\ *variant of* CHIMERA
²**chimaera** *noun* [New Latin, genus name, from Latin, chimera] (1804)
: any of a family (Chimaeridae) of marine cartilaginous fishes with a tapering or threadlike tail and usually no anal fin
**chi·mae·ric, chi·mae·rism** *British variant of* CHIMERIC, CHIMERISM
¹**chime** \'chīm\ *noun* [Middle English *chimbe,* from Old English *cimb-;* akin to Middle Dutch *kimme* edge of a cask] (14th century)
: the edge or rim of a cask or drum
²**chime** *verb* **chimed; chim·ing** (14th century)
*intransitive verb*
**1 a** : to make a musical and especially a harmonious sound **b** : to make the sounds of a chime
**2** : to be or act in accord ⟨the music and the mood *chimed* well together⟩
*transitive verb*
**1** : to cause to sound musically by striking
**2** : to produce by chiming
**3** : to call or indicate by chiming ⟨the clock *chimed* midnight⟩
**4** : to utter repetitively : DIN 2
— **chim·er** *noun*
³**chime** *noun* [Middle English, cymbal, from Middle French *chimbe,* from Old French, from Latin *cymbalum* cymbal] (15th century)
**1** : an apparatus for chiming a bell or set of bells
**2 a** : a musically tuned set of bells **b** : one of a set of objects giving a bell-like sound when struck
**3 a** : the sound of a set of bells — usually used in plural **b** : a musical sound suggesting that of bells
**4** : ACCORD, HARMONY ⟨such happy *chime* of fact and theory —Henry Maudsley⟩
**chime in** (1681)
*intransitive verb*
**1** : to combine harmoniously ⟨the artist's illustrations *chime in* perfectly with the text —Book Production⟩
**2** : to break into a conversation or discussion especially to express an opinion
*transitive verb*
: to remark while chiming in
**chi·me·ra** \kī-'mir-ə, kə-\ *noun* [Latin *chimaera,* from Greek *chimaira* she-goat, chimera; akin to Old Norse *gymbr* yearling ewe, Greek *cheimōn* winter — more at HIBERNATE]
**1 a** *cap* : a fire-breathing she-monster in Greek mythology having a lion's head, a goat's body, and a serpent's tail **b** : an imaginary monster compounded of incongruous parts

**2** : an illusion or fabrication of the mind; *especially* : an unrealizable dream ⟨a fancy, a *chimera* in my brain, troubles me in my prayer —John Donne⟩
**3** : an individual, organ, or part consisting of tissues of diverse genetic constitution
**chi·mere** \shə-'mir, chə-\ *noun* [Middle English *chemer, chemeyr*] (14th century)
: a loose sleeveless robe worn by Anglican bishops over the rochet
**chi·me·ric** \kī-'mir-ik, kə-, -'mer-\ *adjective* (1973)
: relating to, derived from, or being a genetic chimera or its genetic material ⟨a *chimeric* cat⟩
**chi·me·ri·cal** \kī-'mer-i-kəl, kə-, -'mir-\ *also* **chi·me·ric** \-ik\ *adjective* [*chimera*] (1638)
**1** : existing only as the product of unchecked imagination : fantastically visionary or improbable
**2** : given to fantastic schemes
**synonym** see IMAGINARY
— **chi·me·ri·cal·ly** \-i-k(ə-)lē\ *adverb*
**chi·me·rism** \kī-'mir-,i-zəm, kə-; 'kī-mə-,ri-\ *noun* (1961)
: the state of being a genetic chimera
**chi·mi·chan·ga** \,chi-mē-'chän-gə\ *noun* [Mexican Spanish, trinket] (1982)
: a tortilla wrapped around a filling (as of meat) and deep-fried
**chim·ney** \'chim-nē\ *noun, plural* **chimneys** [Middle English, from Middle French *cheminée,* from Late Latin *caminata,* from Latin *caminus* furnace, fireplace, from Greek *kaminos;* perhaps akin to Greek *kamara* vault] (14th century)
**1** *dialect* : FIREPLACE, HEARTH
**2** : a vertical structure incorporated into a building and enclosing a flue or flues that carry off smoke; *especially* : the part of such a structure extending above a roof
**3** : SMOKESTACK
**4** : a tube usually of glass placed around a flame (as of a lamp)
**5** : something resembling a chimney: as **a** : a narrow cleft in rock **b** : a tall column of rock on the ocean floor that is formed by the precipitation of minerals from superheated water issuing through a vent in the earth's crust and rising through the column of rock
— **chim·ney·like** \-,līk\ *adjective*
**chim·ney·piece** \'chim-nē-,pēs\ *noun* (1680)
: an ornamental construction over and around a fireplace that includes the mantel
**chimney pot** *noun* (circa 1806)
: a usually earthenware pipe placed at the top of a chimney
**chimney sweep** *noun* (1727)
: a person whose occupation is cleaning soot from chimney flues — called also *chimney sweeper*
**chimney swift** *noun* (1849)
: a small sooty-gray swift (*Chaetura pelagica*) with long narrow wings that often builds its nest inside an unused chimney — called also *chimney swallow*
**chimp** \'chimp *sometimes* 'shimp\ *noun* (1877)
: CHIMPANZEE
**chim·pan·zee** \(,)chim-,pan-'zē, -pən-'zē, -'pan-zē *sometimes* (,)shim-\ *noun* [Kongo dialect *chimpenzi*] (1738)
: an anthropoid ape (*Pan troglodytes*) of equatorial Africa that is smaller and more arboreal than the gorilla — compare PYGMY CHIMPANZEE
¹**chin** \'chin\ *noun* [Middle English, from Old English *cinn;* akin to Old High German *kinni* chin, Latin *gena* cheek, Greek *genys* jaw, cheek] (before 12th century)

**1** : the lower portion of the face lying below the lower lip and including the prominence of the lower jaw
**2** : the surface beneath or between the branches of the lower jaw
— **chin·less** \-ləs\ *adjective*
²**chin** *verb* **chinned; chin·ning** (1869)
*transitive verb*
**1** : to bring to or hold with the chin ⟨*chin* a violin⟩
**2** : to raise (oneself) while hanging by the hands until the chin is level with the support
*intransitive verb*
*slang* : to talk idly
**chi·na** \'chī-nə\ *noun* [Persian *chīnī* Chinese porcelain] (1579)
**1** : PORCELAIN; *also* : vitreous porcelain wares (as dishes, vases, or ornaments) for domestic use
**2** : earthenware or porcelain tableware
**China aster** *noun* (1794)
: a common annual garden aster (*Callistephus chinensis*) native to northern China that occurs in many showy forms
**chi·na·ber·ry** \'chī-nə-,ber-ē, *Southern also* 'chä-nē-,ber-ē\ *noun* (1890)
: a small Asian tree (*Melia azedarach*) of the mahogany family naturalized in the southern U.S. where it is widely planted for shade or ornament
**china clay** *noun* (1840)
: KAOLIN
**china closet** *noun* (1771)
: a cabinet or cupboard for the storage or display of household china
**Chi·na·man** \'chī-nə-mən\ *noun* (1849)
: a native of China : CHINESE — often taken to be offensive
**China rose** *noun* (circa 1731)
: any of numerous garden roses derived from a shrubby Chinese rose (*Rosa chinensis*)
**China Syndrome** *noun* [from the notion that the molten reactor contents could theoretically sink through the earth to reach China] (1970)
: MELTDOWN 1
**Chi·na·town** \'chī-nə-,taůn\ *noun* (1857)
: the Chinese quarter of a city
**China tree** *noun* (1819)
: CHINABERRY
**chi·na·ware** \'chī-nə-,war, -,wer\ *noun* (1634)
: tableware made of china
**chin·bone** \'chin-,bōn\ *noun* (before 12th century)
: MANDIBLE; *especially* : the median anterior part of the human mandible
**chinch** \'chinch\ *noun* [Spanish *chinche,* from Latin *cimic-, cimex*] (1616)
: BEDBUG
**chinch bug** *noun* (1785)
: a small black-and-white bug (*Blissus leucopterus*) very destructive to cereal grasses
**chin·che·rin·chee** \,chin-chə-ri(n)-'chē, ,chin-kə-\ *noun, plural* **chincherinchee** *or* **chincherinchees** [Afrikaans *tjienkerientjee*] (1904)
: a southern African perennial bulbous herb (*Ornithogalum thyrsoides*) of the lily family with spikes of white to golden-yellow blossoms
**chin·chil·la** \chin-'chi-lə\ *noun* [Spanish] (1604)
**1** : either of two small South American rodents (*Chinchilla laniger* and *C. brevicaudata*) of the high Andes that are the size of large squirrels, have very soft pearly gray fur, and are extensively bred in captivity; *also* : the fur of a chinchilla

chimpanzee

chinchilla

\ə\ abut \ᵊ\ kitten \ər\ further \a\ ash \ā\ ace \ä\ mop, mar \aů\ out \ch\ chin \e\ bet \ē\ easy \g\ go \i\ hit \ī\ ice \j\ job \ŋ\ sing \ō\ go \ȯ\ law \ȯi\ boy \th\ thin \th\ the \ü\ loot \ů\ foot \y\ yet \zh\ vision   *see also* Guide to Pronunciation

**2 :** a heavy twilled woolen coating

**¹chine** \'chīn\ *noun* [Middle English, from Middle French *eschine*, of Germanic origin; akin to Old High German *scina* shinbone, needle — more at SHIN] (14th century)
**1 :** BACKBONE, SPINE; *also* **:** a cut of meat including all or part of the backbone
**2 :** the intersection of the bottom and the sides of a flat or V-bottomed boat

**²chine** *transitive verb* **chined; chin·ing** (circa 1611)
**:** to cut through the backbone of (as in butchering)

**Chi·nese** \chī-'nēz, -'nēs\ *noun, plural* **Chinese** (1606)
**1 a :** a native or inhabitant of China **b :** a person of Chinese descent
**2 :** a group of related languages used by the people of China that are often mutually unintelligible in their spoken form but share a single system of writing and that constitute a branch of the Sino-Tibetan language family; *especially* **:** MANDARIN
**— Chinese** *adjective*

**Chinese boxes** *noun plural* (1829)
**1 :** a set of boxes graduated in size so that each fits into the next larger one
**2 :** something that resembles a set of Chinese boxes especially in complexity

**Chinese cabbage** *noun* (1842)
**:** either of two Asian brassicas now grown in the U.S. and widely used as greens: **a :** BOK CHOY **b :** one (*Brassica rapa pekinensis*) that forms elongate more or less solid cylindrical heads and has pale green or cream-colored leaves

**Chinese checkers** *noun plural but singular or plural in construction* (1938)
**:** a game in which each player seeks to be the first to transfer a set of marbles from a home point to the opposite point of a pitted 6-pointed star by single moves or jumps

**Chinese chestnut** *noun* (circa 1909)
**:** an Asian chestnut (*Castanea mollissima*) that is resistant to chestnut blight

**Chinese copy** *noun* (1920)
**:** an exact imitation or duplicate that includes defects as well as desired qualities

**Chinese crested** *noun* (1976)
**:** any of a breed of hairless or coated dogs with a plumed tail and a crest of hair on the head

**Chinese gooseberry** *noun* (1925)
**:** a subtropical vine (*Actinidia chinensis* of the family Actinidiaceae) that bears kiwifruit; *also* **:** KIWIFRUIT

**Chinese lantern** *noun* (1825)
**:** a collapsible translucent covering for a light

**Chinese parsley** *noun* (circa 1953)
**:** CILANTRO

**Chinese puzzle** *noun* (circa 1815)
**1 :** an intricate or ingenious puzzle
**2 :** something intricate and obscure

**Chinese restaurant syndrome** *noun* (1968)
**:** a group of symptoms (as numbness of the neck, arms, and back with headache, dizziness, and palpitations) that is held to affect susceptible persons eating food and especially Chinese food heavily seasoned with monosodium glutamate

**chinese shar–pei** *noun* (1975)
**:** SHAR-PEI

**Chinese wall** *noun* [*Chinese Wall*, a defensive wall built in the 3d century B.C. between China and Mongolia] (1900)
**:** a strong barrier; *especially* **:** a serious obstacle to understanding

**Chinese white** *noun* (circa 1884)
**:** ZINC WHITE

**Ching** *or* **Ch'ing** \'chiŋ\ *noun* [Chinese (Beijing) *Qīng*] (1795)
**:** a Manchu dynasty in China dated 1644–1912 and the last imperial dynasty

**¹chink** \'chiŋk\ *noun* [probably alteration of Middle English *chine* crack, fissure] (1535)

**1 :** a small cleft, slit, or fissure ⟨a *chink* in the curtain⟩
**2 :** a weak spot that may leave one vulnerable
**3 :** a narrow beam of light shining through a chink

**²chink** *transitive verb* (1748)
**:** to fill the chinks of (as by caulking) ⟨*chink* a log cabin⟩

**³chink** *noun* [imitative] (1573)
**1** *archaic* **:** COIN, MONEY
**2 :** a short sharp sound

**⁴chink** (1589)
*intransitive verb*
**:** to make a slight sharp metallic sound
*transitive verb*
**:** to cause to make a chink

**Chink** \'chiŋk\ *noun or adjective* [perhaps alteration of *Chinese*] (1887)
**:** CHINESE — usually taken to be offensive

**chi·no** \'chē-(ˌ)nō, 'shē-\ *noun, plural* **chinos** [origin unknown] (1943)
**1 :** a usually khaki cotton or synthetic-fiber twill of the type used for military uniforms
**2** *plural* **:** an article of clothing made of chino

**chi·noi·se·rie** \shēn-'wäz-rē, -'wä-zə-; ˌshēn-ˌwäz-'rē, -, wä-zə-\ *noun* [French, from *chinois* Chinese, from *Chine* China] (1883)
**:** a style in art (as in decoration) reflecting Chinese qualities or motifs; *also* **:** an object or decoration in this style

**Chi·nook** \shə-'nùk, chə-, -'nük\ *noun, plural* **Chinook** *or* **Chinooks** [Lower Chehalis (Salishan language of western Washington) *činúk*, name of a Chinook village] (1805)
**1 :** a member of an American Indian people of the north shore of the Columbia River at its mouth
**2 :** a Chinookan language of the Chinook and other nearby peoples
**3** *often not capitalized* **a :** a warm moist southwest wind of the coast from Oregon northward **b :** a warm dry wind that descends the eastern slopes of the Rocky Mountains
**4** *not capitalized* **:** CHINOOK SALMON

**Chi·nook·an** \-'nù-kən, -'nü-\ *noun* (circa 1890)
**:** an American Indian language family of Washington and Oregon
**— Chinookan** *adjective*

**Chinook jargon** *noun, often J capitalized* (1840)
**:** a pidgin language based on Chinook and other Indian languages, French, and English and formerly used as a lingua franca in the northwestern U.S. and on the Pacific coast of Canada and Alaska

**chinook salmon** *noun* (1851)
**:** a large commercially important Pacific salmon (*Oncorhynchus tshawytscha*) with red flesh that occurs in the northern Pacific Ocean — called also *king salmon*

**chin·qua·pin** *or* **chin·ka·pin** \'chiŋ-ki-ˌpin\ *noun* [probably modification of Virginia Algonquian *chechinquamin* chinquapin nut] (1612)
**1 :** the edible nut of a chinquapin
**2 :** any of several trees (genera *Castanea* and *Castanopsis*); *especially* **:** a dwarf chestnut (*Castanea pumila*) of the U.S.

**chinquapin oak** *noun* (1785)
**:** either of two chestnut oaks (*Quercus muhlenbergii* and *Q. prinoides*) of the eastern U.S.

**chintz** \'chin(t)s\ *noun* [earlier *chints*, plural of *chint*, from Hindi *chīṭ*] (1614)
**1 :** a printed calico from India
**2 :** a usually glazed printed cotton fabric

**chintzy** \'chin(t)-sē\ *adjective* **chintz·i·er; -est** (1851)
**1 :** decorated with or as if with chintz
**2 a :** GAUDY, CHEAP ⟨*chintzy* toys⟩ **b :** STINGY

**chin–up** \'chi-(ˌ)nəp\ *noun* (1954)
**:** the act or an instance of chinning oneself especially as a conditioning exercise

**chin–wag** \'chin-ˌwag\ *noun* (1879)
*slang* **:** CONVERSATION, CHAT

**chi·o·no·doxa** \ˌkī-ə-nō-'däk-sə, ˌkī-ˌä-nə-\ *noun* [New Latin, genus name, from Greek *chion-, chiōn* snow (akin to Greek *cheimōn* winter) + *doxa* glory — more at HIBERNATE, DOXOLOGY] (1879)
**:** GLORY-OF-THE-SNOW

**¹chip** \'chip\ *noun* [Middle English; akin to Old English *-cippian*] (14th century)
**1 a :** a small usually thin and flat piece (as of wood or stone) cut, struck, or flaked off **b** (1) **:** a small thin slice of food; *especially* **:** POTATO CHIP (2) **:** FRENCH FRY
**2 :** something small, worthless, or trivial
**3 a :** one of the counters used as a token for money in poker and other games **b** *plural* **:** MONEY — used especially in the phrase *in the chips* **c :** something valuable that can be used for advantage in negotiation or trade ⟨a bargaining *chip*⟩
**4 :** a piece of dried dung — usually used in combination ⟨cow *chip*⟩
**5 :** a flaw left after a chip is removed
**6 a :** INTEGRATED CIRCUIT **b :** a small wafer of semiconductor material that forms the base for an integrated circuit
**7 :** CHIP SHOT
**— chip off the old block :** a child that resembles his or her parent
**— chip on one's shoulder :** a challenging or belligerent attitude

**²chip** *verb* **chipped; chip·ping** [Middle English *chippen*, from Old English *-cippian* (as in *forcippian* to cut off); akin to Old English *cipp* beam, Old High German *chipfa* stave] (15th century)
*transitive verb*
**1 a :** to cut or hew with an edged tool **b** (1) **:** to cut or break (a small piece) from something (2) **:** to cut or break a fragment from (3) **:** to cut into chips ⟨*chip* a tree stump⟩
**2** *British* **:** CHAFF, BANTER
**3 :** to hit (a return in tennis) with backspin
*intransitive verb*
**1 :** to break off in small pieces
**2 :** to play a chip shot

**chip·board** \'chip-ˌbōrd, -ˌbòrd\ *noun* (1919)
**:** a paperboard usually made entirely from wastepaper

**chip in** (1861)
*intransitive verb*
**1 :** CONTRIBUTE ⟨everyone *chipped in* for the gift⟩
**2** *chiefly British* **:** CHIME IN 2
*transitive verb*
**:** CONTRIBUTE

**chip·munk** \'chip-ˌməŋk\ *noun* [alteration of earlier *chitmunk*, probably from Ojibwa *ačitamoˀnˀ* red squirrel] (1832)
**:** any of a genus (*Tamias*) of small striped North American and Asian rodents of the squirrel family

**chipped beef** \'chip(t)-\ *noun* (1859)
**:** smoked dried beef sliced thin

**Chip·pen·dale** \'chi-pən-ˌdāl\ *adjective* [Thomas *Chippendale*] (1876)
**:** of or relating to an 18th century English furniture style characterized by graceful outline and often ornate rococo ornamentation

**¹chip·per** \'chi-pər\ *noun* (1513)
**:** one that chips

**²chipper** *adjective* [perhaps alteration of English dialect *kipper* (lively)] (1838)
**:** SPRIGHTLY

**Chip·pe·wa** \'chi-pə-ˌwò, -ˌwä, -ˌwā, -wə\ *noun, plural* **Chippewa** *or* **Chippewas** (1671)
**:** OJIBWA

**chip·ping sparrow** \'chi-piŋ-\ *noun* [*chip* to cheep] (1791)
**:** a small gray-breasted North American sparrow (*Spizella passerina*) with a black line through the eye, a white line above it, and in breeding plumage a reddish patch on the top of the head

**chip·py** \'chi-pē\ *adjective* **chip·pi·er; -est** [*chip* on one's shoulder] (1898)

**:** aggressively belligerent ⟨a *chippy* hockey player⟩; *also* **:** marked by much fighting ⟨a *chippy* game⟩

**chip shot** *noun* (1909)
**:** a short usually low approach shot in golf that lofts the ball to the green and allows it to roll

**chir-** *or* **chiro-** *combining form* [Latin, from Greek *cheir-, cheiro-,* from *cheir;* akin to Hittite *keššar* hand]
**:** hand ⟨*chiropractic*⟩

**chi·ral** \'kī-rəl\ *adjective* [*chir-* + [1]*-al*] (1894)
**:** of or relating to a molecule that is not superimposable on its mirror image
— **chi·ral·i·ty** \kī-'ra-lə-tē, kə-\ *noun*

**chiral center** *noun* (1970)
**:** an atom especially in an organic molecule that has four different atoms or groups attached to it

**Chi–Rho** \'kī-'rō, 'kē-\ *noun, plural* **Chi–Rhos** [*chi* + *rho*] (1868)
**:** a Christian monogram and symbol formed from the first two letters X and P of the Greek word for *Christ* — called also *Christogram*

**Chir·i·ca·hua** \,chir-ə-'kä-wə\ *noun, plural* **Chiricahua** *or* **Chiricahuas** (1885)
**:** a member of an Apache people of Arizona

**chir·i·moya** *variant of* CHERIMOYA

**chirk** \'chərk\ *verb* [Middle English *charken, chirken* to creak, chirp, from Old English *cearcian* to creak, chirp, from Old English *cracian* to crack] (1843)
**:** CHEER ⟨play with her and *chirk* her up a little —Harriet B. Stowe⟩

**chi·rog·ra·phy** \kī-'rä-grə-fē\ *noun* (1654)
**1 :** HANDWRITING, PENMANSHIP
**2 :** CALLIGRAPHY 1
— **chi·rog·ra·pher** \-fər\ *noun*
— **chi·ro·graph·ic** \,kī-rə-'gra-fik\ *or* **chi·ro·graph·i·cal** \-fi-kəl\ *adjective*

**chi·ro·man·cy** \'kī-rə-,man(t)-sē\ *noun* [probably from Middle French *chiromancie,* from Medieval Latin *chiromantia,* from Greek *cheir-* chir- + *-manteia* -mancy] (circa 1528)
**:** PALMISTRY
— **chi·ro·man·cer** \-,man(t)-sər\ *noun*

**chi·ron·o·mid** \kī-'rä-nə-məd\ *noun* [ultimately from Greek *cheironomos* one who gestures with his hands] (1915)
**:** any of a family (Chironomidae) of midges that lack piercing mouthparts
— **chironomid** *adjective*

**chi·rop·o·dy** \kə-'rä-pə-dē, shə-* also* kī-\ *noun* [*chir-* + *pod-;* from its original concern with both hands and feet] (1886)
**:** PODIATRY
— **chi·rop·o·dist** \-dist\ *noun*

**chi·ro·prac·tic** \'kī-rə-,prak-tik, ,kī-rə-'\ *noun* [*chir-* + Greek *praktikos* practical, operative — more at PRACTICAL] (1898)
**:** a system of therapy which holds that disease results from a lack of normal nerve function and which employs manipulation and specific adjustment of body structures (as the spinal column)
— **chi·ro·prac·tor** \-tər\ *noun*

**chi·rop·ter·an** \kī-'räp-tə-rən\ *noun* [ultimately from Greek *cheir* hand + *pteron* wing — more at FEATHER] (1835)
**:** [3]BAT

**chirp** \'chərp\ *noun* [imitative] (circa 1755)
**:** the characteristic short sharp sound especially of a small bird or insect
— **chirp** *intransitive verb*

**chirpy** \'chər-pē\ *adjective* **chirp·i·er; -est** (1837)
**1 :** cheerfully lively ⟨a *chirpy* manner⟩
**2 a :** making chirps **b :** suggestive of chirping ⟨a *chirpy* voice⟩
— **chirp·i·ly** \-pə-lē\ *adverb*

**chirr** \'chər\ *noun* [imitative] (circa 1600)
**:** the short vibrant or trilled sound characteristic of an insect (as a grasshopper or cicada)
— **chirr** *intransitive verb*

**chir·rup** \'chər-əp, 'chir-\ *noun* [imitative] (1788)
**:** CHIRP

— **chirrup** *intransitive verb*

**chir·ru·py** \'chər-ə-pē, 'chir-\ *adjective* (1874)
**:** CHIRPY

**chi·rur·geon** \kī-'rər-jən\ *noun* [Middle English *cirurgian,* from Old French *cirurgien,* from *cirurgie* surgery] (13th century)
*archaic* **:** SURGEON

[1]**chis·el** \'chi-zəl\ *noun* [Middle English, from Old North French, from (assumed) Vulgar Latin *cisellum,* alteration of *caesellum,* from Latin *caesus,* past participle of *caedere* to cut] (14th century)
**:** a metal tool with a sharpened edge at one end used to chip, carve, or cut into a solid material (as wood, stone, or metal)

[2]**chisel** *verb* **-eled** *or* **-elled; -el·ing** *or* **-el·ling** \'chi-zəl-iŋ, 'chiz-liŋ\ (1509)
*transitive verb*
**1 :** to cut or work with or as if with a chisel
**2 :** to employ shrewd or unfair practices on in order to obtain one's end; *also* **:** to obtain by such practices ⟨*chisel* a job⟩
*intransitive verb*
**1 :** to work with or as if with a chisel
**2 a :** to employ shrewd or unfair practices **b :** to thrust oneself **:** INTRUDE ⟨*chisel* in on a racket⟩
— **chis·el·er** *or* **chis·el·ler** \'chi-zəl-ər, 'chiz-lər\ *noun*

**chis·eled** *or* **chis·elled** \'chi-zəld\ *adjective* (1821)
**:** formed or crafted as if with a chisel ⟨*chiseled* good looks⟩ ⟨a *chiseled* essay⟩

**chi–square** \'kī-'skwar, -'skwer\ *noun, often attributive* (circa 1934)
**:** a statistic that is a sum of terms each of which is a quotient obtained by dividing the square of the difference between the observed and theoretical values of a quantity by the theoretical value

**chi–square distribution** *noun* (circa 1956)
**:** a probability density function that gives the distribution of the sum of the squares of a number of independent random variables each with a normal distribution with zero mean and unit variance, that has the property that the sum of two or more random variables with such a distribution also has one, and that is widely used in testing statistical hypotheses especially about the theoretical and observed values of a quantity and about population variances and standard deviations

[1]**chit** \'chit\ *noun* [Middle English *chitte* kitten, cub] (circa 1624)
**1 :** CHILD
**2 :** a pert young woman

[2]**chit** *noun* [Hindi *ciṭṭhī*] (1757)
**1 :** a short letter or note; *especially* **:** a signed voucher of a small debt (as for food)
**2 :** a small slip of paper with writing on it

**chit·chat** \'chit-,chat\ *noun* [reduplication of *chat*] (1710)
**:** SMALL TALK, GOSSIP
— **chitchat** *intransitive verb*

**chi·tin** \'kī-tⁿn\ *noun* [French *chitine,* from Greek *chitōn*] (circa 1839)
**:** a horny polysaccharide that forms part of the hard outer integument especially of insects, arachnids, and crustaceans
— **chi·tin·ous** \'kī-tⁿn-əs, 'kīt-nəs\ *adjective*

**chi·ton** \'kī-tⁿn, 'kī-,tän\ *noun* [New Latin, genus name, from Greek *chitōn* tunic, of Semitic origin; akin to Hebrew *kuttōneth* tunic] (1816)
**1 :** any of a class (Polyplacophora) of elongated bilaterally symmetrical marine mollusks with a dorsal shell of calcareous plates
**2** [Greek *chitōn*] **:** the basic garment of ancient Greece worn usually knee-length by men and full-length by women

**chit·ter** \'chi-tər\ *intransitive verb* [Middle English *chiteren,* probably of imitative origin] (13th century)
**:** TWITTER, CHIRP; *also* **:** CHATTER

**chit·ter·lings** *or* **chit·lins** \'chit-lənz\ *noun plural* [Middle English *chiterling*] (13th century)

**:** the intestines of hogs especially when prepared as food

**chi·val·ric** \shə-'val-rik\ *adjective* (1797)
**:** relating to chivalry **:** CHIVALROUS

**chiv·al·rous** \'shi-vəl-rəs\ *adjective* (14th century)
**1 :** VALIANT
**2 :** of, relating to, or characteristic of chivalry and knight-errantry
**3 a :** marked by honor, generosity, and courtesy **b :** marked by gracious courtesy and high-minded consideration especially to women
*synonym* see CIVIL
— **chiv·al·rous·ly** *adverb*
— **chiv·al·rous·ness** *noun*

**chiv·al·ry** \'shi-vəl-rē\ *noun, plural* **-ries** [Middle English *chivalrie,* from Middle French *chevalerie,* from *chevalier* knight — more at CHEVALIER] (14th century)
**1 :** mounted men-at-arms
**2** *archaic* **a :** martial valor **b :** knightly skill
**3 :** gallant or distinguished gentlemen
**4 :** the system, spirit, or customs of medieval knighthood
**5 :** the qualities of the ideal knight **:** chivalrous conduct

**chive** \'chīv\ *noun* [Middle English, from Old North French, from Latin *cepa* onion] (14th century)
**:** a perennial plant (*Allium schoenoprasum*) related to the onion and having slender leaves used as a seasoning — usually used in plural

**chivy** *or* **chiv·vy** \'chi-vē\ *transitive verb* **chiv·ied** *or* **chiv·vied; chiv·y·ing** *or* **chiv·vy·ing** [*chivy,* noun (chase, hunt), probably from English dialect *Chevy Chase* chase, confusion, from the name of a ballad describing the battle of Otterburn (1388)] (1918)
**1 :** to tease or annoy with persistent petty attacks
**2 :** to move or obtain by small maneuvers
*synonym* see BAIT

**chla·myd·ia** \klə-'mi-dē-ə\ *noun, plural* **-i·ae** \-dē-,ē\ [New Latin, from Greek *chlamyd-, chlamys*] (1966)
**1 :** any of a genus (*Chlamydia,* family Chlamydiaceae) of spherical gram-negative intracellular bacteria; *especially* **:** one (*C. trachomatis*) that causes or is associated with various diseases of the eye and urogenital tract including trachoma, lymphogranuloma venereum, cervicitis, and some forms of urethritis
**2 :** a disease or infection caused by chlamydiae
— **chla·myd·i·al** \-dē-əl\ *adjective*

**chla·mydo·spore** \klə-'mi-də-,spōr, -,spor\ *noun* [Latin *chlamyd-, chlamys* + International Scientific Vocabulary *spore*] (1884)
**:** a thick-walled usually resting fungal spore

**chla·mys** \'kla-məs, 'klā-\ *noun, plural* **chla·mys·es** *or* **chla·my·des** \-mə-,dēz\ [Latin *chlamyd-, chlamys,* from Greek] (1699)
**:** a short oblong mantle worn by young men of ancient Greece

**Chloe** \'klō-ē\ *noun* [Latin, from Greek *Chloē*]
**:** a lover of Daphnis in a Greek pastoral romance

**chlor-** *or* **chloro-** *combining form* [New Latin, from Greek, from *chlōros* greenish yellow — more at YELLOW]
**1 :** green ⟨*chlor*ine⟩ ⟨*chlor*osis⟩
**2 :** chlorine **:** containing chlorine ⟨*chloro*prene⟩

chlamys

**chlor·ac·ne** \klō-'rak-nē, klȯ-\ *noun* (circa 1928)
**:** a skin eruption resembling acne and resulting from exposure to chlorine or its compounds
**chlo·ral** \'klōr-əl, 'klȯr-\ *noun* [French, from *chlor-* + *al*cool alcohol] (1838)
**1 :** a pungent colorless oily aldehyde $CCl_3CHO$ used in making DDT and chloral hydrate
**2 :** CHLORAL HYDRATE
**chloral hydrate** *noun* (1874)
**:** a bitter white crystalline drug $C_2H_3Cl_3O_2$ used as a hypnotic and sedative or in knockout drops
**chlo·ral·ose** \'klōr-ə-,lōs, 'klȯr-, -,lōz\ *noun* (1893)
**:** a bitter crystalline compound $C_8H_{11}Cl_3O_6$ used especially to anesthetize animals
— **chlo·ral·osed** \-,lōst, -,lōzd\ *adjective*
**chlo·ra·mine** \'klōr-ə-,mēn, 'klȯr-\ *noun* [International Scientific Vocabulary] (1893)
**:** any of various compounds containing nitrogen and chlorine
**chlor·am·phen·i·col** \,klōr-,am-'fe-ni-,kȯl, ,klȯr-, -,kōl\ *noun* [*chlor-* + *amide* + *phen-* + *nitr-* + *glycol*] (1949)
**:** a broad-spectrum antibiotic $C_{11}H_{12}Cl_2N_2O_5$ isolated from cultures of a soil actinomycete (*Streptomyces venezuelae*) or prepared synthetically
**chlo·rate** \'klōr-,āt, 'klȯr-\ *noun* (1823)
**:** a salt containing the anion $ClO_3^-$ ⟨*chlorate* of potassium⟩
**chlor·dane** \'klȯr-,dān\ *noun* [*chlor-* + in*dane* ($C_9H_{10}$)] (1947)
**:** a highly chlorinated viscous volatile liquid insecticide $C_{10}H_6Cl_8$
**chlor·di·az·epox·ide** \,klōr-dī-,a-zə-'päk-,sīd, ,klȯr-\ *noun* [*chlor-* + *di-* + *az-* + *epoxide*] (1961)
**:** a benzodiazepine $C_{16}H_{14}ClN_3O$ related to diazepam and used in the form of its hydrochloride especially as a tranquilizer and in the treatment of alcoholism
**chlo·rel·la** \klə-'re-lə\ *noun* [New Latin, genus name, from Greek *chlōros*] (1904)
**:** any of a genus (*Chlorella*) of unicellular green algae
**chlor·en·chy·ma** \klōr-'eŋ-kə-mə, klȯr-\ *noun* (1894)
**:** chlorophyll-containing parenchyma of plants
**chlo·ride** \'klōr-,īd, 'klȯr-\ *noun* [German *Chlorid*, from *chlor-* + *-id* -ide] (1812)
**1 :** a compound of chlorine with another element or group; *especially* **:** a salt or ester of hydrochloric acid
**2 :** a univalent anion consisting of one atom of chlorine
**chloride of lime** (1826)
**:** BLEACHING POWDER
**chlo·ri·nate** \'klōr-ə-,nāt, 'klȯr-\ *transitive verb* **-nat·ed; -nat·ing** (1856)
**:** to treat or combine with chlorine or a chlorine compound
— **chlo·ri·na·tion** \,klōr-ə-'nā-shən, ,klȯr-\ *noun*
— **chlo·ri·na·tor** \'klōr-ə-,nā-tər, 'klȯr-\ *noun*
**chlorinated lime** *noun* (1876)
**:** BLEACHING POWDER
**chlo·rine** \'klōr-,ēn, 'klȯr-, -ən\ *noun* (1810)
**:** a halogen element that is isolated as a heavy greenish yellow gas of pungent odor and is used especially as a bleach, oxidizing agent, and disinfectant in water purification — see ELEMENT table
**chlo·rin·i·ty** \klō-'ri-nə-tē, klȯ-\ *noun* (circa 1931)
**:** a measure of the concentration of halides in one kilogram of seawater
**¹chlo·rite** \'klōr-,īt, 'klȯr-\ *noun* [German *Chlorit*, from Latin *chloritis*, a green stone, from Greek *chlōritis*, from *chlōros*] (1794)
**:** any of a group of monoclinic usually green minerals associated with and resembling the micas

— **chlo·rit·ic** \klō-'ri-tik, klȯ-\ *adjective*
**²chlorite** *noun* [probably from French, from *chlor-*] (1853)
**:** a salt containing the anion $ClO_2^-$ ⟨*chlorite* of sodium⟩
**chloro-** — see CHLOR-
**chlo·ro·ben·zene** \,klōr-ō-'ben-,zēn, ,klȯr-, -ben-'\ *noun* [International Scientific Vocabulary] (circa 1889)
**:** a colorless flammable volatile toxic liquid $C_6H_5Cl$ used in organic synthesis (as of DDT) and as a solvent
**chlo·ro·fluo·ro·car·bon** \,klōr-ō-,flȯr-ō-'kär-bən, ,klȯr-, -,flu̇r-, -,flȯr-\ *noun* (1949)
**:** any of several simple gaseous compounds that contain carbon, chlorine, fluorine, and sometimes hydrogen, that are used as refrigerants, cleaning solvents, and aerosol propellants and in the manufacture of plastic foams, and that are suspected to be a major cause of stratospheric ozone depletion — abbreviation *CFC*
**chlo·ro·fluo·ro·meth·ane** \-'me-,thān, *British usually* -'mē-\ *noun* (1965)
**:** a chlorofluorocarbon derived from methane
**¹chlo·ro·form** \'klōr-ə-,fȯrm, 'klȯr-\ *noun* [French *chloroforme*, from *chlor-* + *formyle* formyl; from its having been regarded as a trichloride of this group] (1838)
**:** a colorless volatile heavy toxic liquid $CHCl_3$ with an ether odor used especially as a solvent or as a veterinary anesthetic
**²chloroform** *transitive verb* (1848)
**:** to treat with or as if with chloroform especially so as to produce anesthesia, insensibility, or death
**chlo·ro·gen·ic acid** \,klōr-ə-'je-nik-, ,klȯr-\ *noun* (circa 1889)
**:** a crystalline acid $C_{16}H_{18}O_9$ occurring in various plant parts (as coffee beans)
**chlo·ro·hy·drin** \,klōr-ə-'hī-drən, ,klȯr-\ *noun* [International Scientific Vocabulary *chlor-* + *hydr-* + *¹-in*] (circa 1890)
**:** any of various organic compounds derived from diols or polyhydroxy alcohols by substitution of chlorine for part of the hydroxyl groups
**Chlo·ro·my·ce·tin** \,klōr-ō-mī-'sē-t°n, ,klȯr-\ *trademark*
— used for chloramphenicol
**chlo·ro·phyll** \'klōr-ə-,fil, 'klȯr-, -fəl\ *noun* [French *chlorophylle*, from *chlor-* + Greek *phyllon* leaf — more at BLADE] (1819)
**1 :** the green photosynthetic pigment found chiefly in the chloroplasts of plants and occurring especially as a blue-black ester $C_{55}H_{72}MgN_4O_5$ or a dark green ester $C_{55}H_{70}MgN_4O_6$ — called also respectively *chlorophyll a, chlorophyll b*
**2 :** a waxy green chlorophyll-containing substance extracted from green plants and used as a coloring agent or deodorant
— **chlo·ro·phyl·lous** \,klōr-ə-'fi-ləs, ,klȯr-\ *adjective*
**chlo·ro·pic·rin** \,klōr-ə-'pi-krən, ,klȯr-\ *noun* [German *Chlorpikrin*, from *chlor-* + Greek *pikros* sharp — more at PAINT] (circa 1889)
**:** a colorless liquid $CCl_3NO_2$ that causes tears and vomiting and is used especially as a soil fumigant
**chlo·ro·plast** \'klōr-ə-,plast, 'klȯr-\ *noun* [International Scientific Vocabulary] (1887)
**:** a plastid that contains chlorophyll and is the site of photosynthesis — see CELL illustration
— **chlo·ro·plas·tic** \,klōr-ə-'plas-tik, ,klȯr-\ *adjective*
**chlo·ro·prene** \-,prēn\ *noun* [*chlor-* + iso*prene*] (1931)
**:** a colorless liquid $C_4H_5Cl$ used especially in making neoprene by polymerization
**chlo·ro·quine** \'klōr-ə-,kwēn, 'klȯr-\ *noun* [*chlor-* + *quinoline*] (1946)
**:** an antimalarial drug $C_{18}H_{26}ClN_3$ administered as the bitter crystalline diphosphate
**chlo·ro·sis** \klə-'rō-səs\ *noun* (1678)

**1 :** an iron-deficiency anemia especially of adolescent girls that may impart a greenish tint to the skin — called also *greensickness*
**2 :** a diseased condition in green plants marked by yellowing or blanching
— **chlo·rot·ic** \-'rä-tik\ *adjective*
**chlo·ro·thi·a·zide** \,klōr-ō-'thī-ə-,zīd, ,klȯr-, -zəd\ *noun* (1957)
**:** a thiazide diuretic $C_7H_6ClN_3O_4S_2$ used especially to treat edema and to increase the effectiveness of antihypertensive drugs
**chlor·prom·a·zine** \klōr-'prä-mə-,zēn, klȯr-\ *noun* [*chlor-* + *propyl* + *methyl* + *azine*] (1952)
**:** a phenothiazine $C_{17}H_{19}ClN_2S$ used as a tranquilizer especially in the form of its hydrochloride to suppress the more flagrant symptoms of psychotic disorders (as in schizophrenia)
**chlor·prop·amide** \-'prä-pə-,mīd, -'prō-\ *noun* [*chlor-* + *propane* + *amide*] (1960)
**:** a sulfonylurea drug $C_{10}H_{13}ClN_2O_3S$ used orally to reduce blood sugar in the treatment of mild diabetes
**chlor·tet·ra·cy·cline** \,klōr-,te-trə-'sī-,klēn, ,klȯr-\ *noun* (1953)
**:** a yellow crystalline broad-spectrum antibiotic $C_{22}H_{23}ClN_2O_8$ that is produced by a soil actinomycete (*Streptomyces aureofaciens*) and is sometimes used in animal feeds to stimulate growth
**cho·ano·cyte** \kō-'a-nə-,sīt\ *noun* [International Scientific Vocabulary *choan-* funnel-shaped (from Greek *choanē* funnel) + *-cyte*] (1888)
**:** COLLAR CELL
**¹chock** \'chäk\ *noun* [origin unknown] (1769)
**1 :** a wedge or block for steadying a body (as a cask) and holding it motionless, for filling in an unwanted space, or for blocking the movement of a wheel
**2 :** a heavy metal casting (as on the bow or stern of a ship) with two short horn-shaped arms curving inward between which ropes or hawsers may pass for mooring or towing
**²chock** *adverb* (1834)
**:** as close or as completely as possible
**³chock** *transitive verb* (1854)
**:** to stop or make fast with or as if with chocks
**¹chock·a·block** \'chä-kə-,bläk\ *adverb* (1850)
**:** CHOCK ⟨*chockablock* full⟩
**²chockablock** *adjective* (circa 1890)
**1 :** brought close together
**2 :** very full
**chock–full** *or* **chock·ful** \'chək-,fu̇l, 'chäk-, -,fu̇l\ *adjective* [Middle English *chokkefull*, probably from *choken* to choke + *full*] (15th century)
**:** full to the limit
**choc·o·hol·ic** \,chä-kə-'hȯ-lik, ,chȯ-, -'hä-\ *noun* [*chocolate* + *-oholic* (as in *alcoholic*)] (1968)
**:** a person who craves or compulsively consumes chocolate
**choc·o·late** \'chä-k(ə)lət, 'chȯ-\ *noun* [Spanish, from Nahuatl *chocolātl*] (1604)
**1 :** a beverage made by mixing chocolate with water or milk
**2 :** a food prepared from ground roasted cacao beans
**3 :** a small candy with a center (as a fondant) and a chocolate coating
**4 :** a brownish gray
— **chocolate** *adjective*
**chocolate–box** *adjective* [from the pictures formerly commonly seen on boxes of chocolates] (1901)
**:** superficially pretty or sentimental
**choc·o·la·tier** \,chä-k(ə-)lə-'tir, ,chȯ-\ *noun* [French, from *chocolat* chocolate] (1888)
**:** a maker or seller of chocolate candy
**choc·o·laty** *or* **choc·o·lat·ey** \'chä-k(ə-)lə-tē, 'chȯ-\ *adjective* (1926)
**:** made of or like chocolate; *also* **:** having a rich chocolate flavor

**Choc·taw** \'chäk-(,)tȯ\ *noun, plural* **Choc-taw** *or* **Choctaws** [Choctaw *čahta*] (1722)
**1 :** a member of an American Indian people of Mississippi, Alabama, and Louisiana
**2 :** the language of the Choctaw and Chickasaw people

¹**choice** \'chȯis\ *noun* [Middle English *chois*, from Old French, from *choisir* to choose, of Germanic origin; akin to Old High German *kiosan* to choose — more at CHOOSE] (13th century)
**1 :** the act of choosing **:** SELECTION
**2 :** power of choosing **:** OPTION
**3 a :** the best part **:** CREAM **b :** a person or thing chosen
**4 :** a sufficient number and variety to choose among
**5 :** care in selecting
**6 :** a grade of meat between prime and good
**— of choice :** to be preferred ☆

²**choice** *adjective* **choic·er; choic·est** (14th century)
**1 :** worthy of being chosen
**2 :** selected with care
**3 a :** of high quality **b :** of a grade between prime and good ⟨*choice* meat⟩ ☆
**— choice·ly** *adverb*
**— choice·ness** *noun*

¹**choir** \'kwī(-ə)r\ *noun* [Middle English *quer*, from Middle French *cuer*, from Medieval Latin *chorus*, from Latin, chorus — more at CHORUS] (14th century)
**1 :** an organized company of singers (as in a church service)
**2 :** a group of instruments of the same class ⟨a brass *choir*⟩
**3 :** an organized group of persons or things
**4 :** a division of angels
**5 :** the part of a church occupied by the singers or by the clergy; *also* **:** the part of a church where the services are performed
**6 :** a group organized for ensemble speaking

²**choir** *intransitive verb* (1596)
**:** to sing or sound in chorus or concert

**choir·boy** \'kwī(-ə)r-,bȯi\ *noun* (1837)
**:** a boy member of a choir

**choir loft** *noun* (1929)
**:** a gallery occupied by a church choir

**choir·mas·ter** \-,mas-tər\ *noun* (1860)
**:** the director of a choir (as in a church)

¹**choke** \'chōk\ *verb* **choked; chok·ing** [Middle English, alteration of *achoken*, from Old English *ācēocian*, from *ā-*, perfective prefix + *cēoce, cēace* jaw, cheek — more at ABIDE, CHEEK] (14th century)
*transitive verb*
**1 :** to check normal breathing of by compressing or obstructing the trachea or by poisoning or adulterating available air
**2 a :** to check the growth, development, or activity of ⟨the flowers were *choked* by the weeds⟩ **b :** to obstruct by filling up or clogging ⟨leaves *choked* the drain⟩ **c :** to fill completely **:** JAM ⟨roads *choked* with traffic⟩
**3 :** to enrich the fuel mixture of (a motor) by partially shutting off the air intake of the carburetor
**4 :** to grip (as a baseball bat) some distance from the end of the handle
*intransitive verb*
**1 :** to become choked in breathing
**2 a :** to become obstructed or checked **b :** to become or feel constricted in the throat (as from strong emotion) — usually used with *up* ⟨*choked* up and couldn't finish the speech⟩
**3 :** to shorten one's grip especially on the handle of a bat — usually used with *up*
**4 :** to lose one's composure and fail to perform effectively in a critical situation

²**choke** *noun* (1736)
**1 :** the filamentous inedible center of an artichoke head; *broadly* **:** an artichoke head
**2 :** something that obstructs passage or flow: as **a :** a valve for choking a gasoline engine **b :** a constriction in an outlet (as of an oil well) that restricts flow **c :** REACTOR 2 **d :** a constric-

tion (as a narrowing of the barrel or an attachment) at the muzzle of a shotgun that serves to limit the spread of shot
**3 :** the act of choking

**choke·ber·ry** \-,ber-ē\ *noun* (1778)
**:** a small berrylike astringent fruit; *also* **:** any of a genus (*Aronia*) of shrubs of the rose family bearing chokeberries

**choke chain** *noun* (1955)
**:** a collar that may be tightened as a noose and that is used especially in training and controlling powerful or stubborn dogs — called also **choke collar**

**choke·cher·ry** \'chōk-,cher-ē\ *noun* (1784)
**:** an American wild cherry (*Prunus virginiana*) with bitter or astringent red to black edible fruit; *also* **:** this fruit

**choke coil** *noun* (circa 1896)
**:** REACTOR 2

**choke off** *transitive verb* (1818)
**:** to bring to a stop or an end as if by choking

**choke point** *noun* (1944)
**:** a strategic narrow route providing passage through or to another region

**chok·er** \'chō-kər\ *noun* (circa 1552)
**1 :** one that chokes
**2 :** something (as a collar or necklace) worn closely about the throat or neck

**chok·ing** \'chō-kiŋ\ *adjective* (1562)
**1 :** producing the feeling of strangulation ⟨a *choking* cloud of smog⟩
**2 :** indistinct in utterance — used especially of a person's voice ⟨a low *choking* laugh⟩
**— chok·ing·ly** \-kiŋ-lē\ *adverb*

**choky** \'chō-kē\ *adjective* (1579)
**:** tending to cause choking or to become choked

**chol-** *or* **chole-** *or* **cholo-** *combining form* [Greek *chol-, cholē-, cholo-*, from *cholē, cholos* — more at GALL]
**:** bile **:** gall ⟨*chol*ate⟩

**chol·an·gi·og·ra·phy** \kə-,lan-jē-'ä-grə-fē, (,)kō-\ *noun* (1936)
**:** radiographic visualization of the bile ducts after injection of a radiopaque substance
**— chol·an·gio·graph·ic** \-jē-ə-'gra-fik\ *adjective*
**— chol·an·gio·gram** \-'lan-jē-ə-,gram\ *noun*

**cho·late** \'kō-,lāt\ *noun* (circa 1846)
**:** a salt or ester of cholic acid

**cho·le·cal·cif·er·ol** \,kō-lə-(,)kal-'si-fə-,ròl, -,rōl\ *noun* [International Scientific Vocabulary] (1955)
**:** a sterol $C_{27}H_{43}OH$ that is a natural form of vitamin D found especially in fish, egg yolks, and fish-liver oils and is formed in the skin on exposure to sunlight or ultraviolet rays — called also *vitamin D₃*

**cho·le·cys·tec·to·my** \-(,)sis-'tek-tə-mē\ *noun, plural* **-mies** [New Latin *cholecystis* gallbladder (from *chol-* + Greek *kystis* bladder) + International Scientific Vocabulary *-ectomy* — more at CYST] (1885)
**:** surgical excision of the gallbladder
**— cho·le·cys·tec·to·mized** \-,mīzd\ *adjective*

**cho·le·cys·ti·tis** \-(,)sis-'tī-təs\ *noun* [New Latin, from *cholecystis*] (1866)
**:** inflammation of the gallbladder

**cho·le·cys·to·ki·nin** \-,sis-tə-'kī-nən\ *noun* [New Latin *cholecystis* + English *-o-* + *kinin*] (circa 1929)
**:** a hormone secreted especially by the duodenal mucosa that regulates the emptying of the gallbladder and secretion of enzymes by the pancreas and that has been found in the brain — called also *cholecystokinin-pancreozymin, pancreozymin*

**cho·le·li·thi·a·sis** \,kō-lə-li-'thī-ə-səs\ *noun* [New Latin] (circa 1860)
**:** production of gallstones; *also* **:** the resulting abnormal condition

**cho·ler** \'kä-lər, 'kō-\ *noun* [Middle English *coler*, from Middle French *colere*, from Latin *cholera* cholera, from Greek] (14th century)

**1 a** *archaic* **:** YELLOW BILE **b** *obsolete* **:** BILE 1a
**2** *obsolete* **:** the quality or state of being bilious
**3 :** ready disposition to irritation **:** IRASCIBILITY; *also* **:** ANGER

**chol·era** \'kä-lə-rə\ *noun* [Latin] (1601)
**:** any of several diseases of humans and domestic animals usually marked by severe gastrointestinal symptoms; *especially* **:** an acute diarrheal disease caused by an enterotoxin produced by a comma-shaped gram-negative bacillus (*Vibrio cholerae* synonym *V. comma*) when it is present in large numbers in the proximal part of the human small intestine ◆

---

☆ **SYNONYMS**
**Choice, option, alternative, preference, selection, election** mean the act or opportunity of choosing or the thing chosen. CHOICE suggests the opportunity or privilege of choosing freely ⟨freedom of *choice*⟩. OPTION implies a power to choose that is specifically granted or guaranteed ⟨the *option* of paying now or later⟩. ALTERNATIVE implies a necessity to choose one and reject another possibility ⟨equally attractive *alternatives*⟩. PREFERENCE suggests the guidance of choice by one's judgment or predilections ⟨a *preference* for cool weather⟩. SELECTION implies a wide range of choice ⟨a varied *selection* of furniture⟩. ELECTION implies an end or purpose which requires exercise of judgment ⟨a tax return forces certain *elections* on you⟩.

**Choice, exquisite, elegant, rare, delicate, dainty** mean having qualities that appeal to a cultivated taste. CHOICE stresses preeminence in quality or kind ⟨*choice* fabric⟩. EXQUISITE implies a perfection in workmanship or design that appeals only to very sensitive taste ⟨an *exquisite* gold bracelet⟩. ELEGANT applies to what is rich and luxurious but restrained by good taste ⟨a sumptuous but *elegant* dining room⟩. RARE suggests an uncommon excellence ⟨*rare* beauty⟩. DELICATE implies exquisiteness, subtlety, and fragility ⟨*delicate* craftsmanship⟩. DAINTY sometimes carries an additional suggestion of smallness and of appeal to the eye or palate ⟨*dainty* sandwiches⟩.

---

◇ **WORD HISTORY**
**cholera** The word *cholera* now usually denotes Asiatic cholera, a still dreaded disease that typically assumes epidemic proportions when a concentrated population, such as that of a city or refugee camp, draws its drinking water from a source contaminated by fecal matter. Nineteenth-century medicine also recognized other forms of cholera ("summer cholera" or "European cholera") that manifested the same symptoms—vomiting and diarrhea—but in milder form. The antiquity of severe gastrointestinal disorders is evidenced by the word *cholera* itself, which is part of the medical vocabulary inherited by us from the ancient Greeks. Classical authors were divided on whether the Greek word was a derivative of *cholē* "bile" or *cholades* "intestines." In Late Latin, *cholera*, by association with Greek *cholē*, was used in the sense "bile." Through the medieval theory of humors, one of which was yellow bile (the fiery humor), it gave us English *choler* and *choleric*. See in addition HUMOR.

---

\ə\ abut \ᵊ\ kitten \ər\ further \a\ ash \ā\ ace
\ä\ mop, mar \aù\ out \ch\ chin \e\ bet \ē\ easy
\g\ go \i\ hit \ī\ ice \j\ job \ŋ\ sing \ō\ go
\ò\ law \òi\ boy \th\ thin \t̲h̲\ the \ü\ loot \ù\ foot
\y\ yet \zh\ vision *see also* Guide to Pronunciation

**chol·era mor·bus** \-'mȯr-bəs, *dialect* -'mä(r)-; *dialect* 'kä-lē-\ *noun* [New Latin, literally, the disease cholera] (1673)
**:** gastrointestinal illness characterized by griping, diarrhea, and sometimes vomiting — not used technically

**cho·ler·ic** \'kä-lə-rik, kə-'ler-ik\ *adjective* (1583)
**1 :** easily moved to often unreasonable or excessive anger **:** hot-tempered
**2 :** ANGRY, IRATE
— **cho·ler·i·cal·ly** \-ri-k(ə-)lē, -i-k(ə-)lē\ *adverb*

**cho·le·sta·sis** \ˌkō-lə-'stā-səs\ *noun, plural* **-sta·ses** \-ˌsēz\ [New Latin] (circa 1935)
**:** a checking or failure of bile flow
— **cho·le·stat·ic** \-'sta-tik\ *adjective*

**cho·le·ster·ic** \ˌkō-lə-'ster-ik, kə-'les-tə-rik\ *adjective* [*cholesteric* relating to cholesterol, from French *cholesterique*] (1942)
**:** of, relating to, or being the phase of a liquid crystal characterized by arrangement of molecules in layers with the long molecular axes parallel to one another in the plane of each layer and incrementally displaced in successive layers to give helical stacking — compare NEMATIC, SMECTIC

**cho·les·ter·ol** \kə-'les-tə-ˌrōl, -ˌrȯl\ *noun* [International Scientific Vocabulary, from *chol-* + Greek *stereos* solid] (1894)
**:** a steroid alcohol $C_{27}H_{45}OH$ that is present in animal cells and body fluids, regulates membrane fluidity, and functions as a precursor molecule in various metabolic pathways and as a constituent of LDL may cause arteriosclerosis

**cho·le·styr·amine** \(ˌ)kō-ˌles-tə-'ra-ˌmēn, kə-; ˌkō-lə-'stir-ə-ˌmēn\ *noun* [*chol-* + *styrene* + *amine*] (circa 1962)
**:** a strongly basic synthetic resin that forms insoluble complexes with bile acids and has been used to lower cholesterol levels in hypercholesterolemic patients

**cho·lic acid** \'kō-lik-\ *noun* [Greek *cholikos* bilious, from *cholē*] (1846)
**:** a crystalline bile acid $C_{24}H_{40}O_5$

**cho·line** \'kō-ˌlēn\ *noun* [International Scientific Vocabulary] (circa 1871)
**:** a base $C_5H_{15}NO_2$ that occurs as a component of phospholipids especially in animals, is a precursor of acetylcholine, and is essential to liver function

**cho·lin·er·gic** \ˌkō-lə-'nər-jik\ *adjective* [International Scientific Vocabulary] (1934)
**1 :** liberating, activated by, or involving acetylcholine ⟨*cholinergic* nerve fiber⟩ ⟨*cholinergic* functions⟩
**2 :** resembling acetylcholine especially in physiologic action ⟨a *cholinergic* drug⟩
— **cho·lin·er·gi·cal·ly** \-ji-k(ə-)lē\ *adverb*

**cho·lin·es·ter·ase** \ˌkō-lə-'nes-tə-ˌrās, -ˌrāz\ *noun* (1932)
**1 :** ACETYLCHOLINESTERASE
**2 :** an enzyme that hydrolyzes choline esters and that is found especially in blood plasma — called also *pseudocholinesterase*

**chol·la** \'chȯi-yə\ *noun* [Mexican Spanish, from Spanish, head] (1846)
**:** any of numerous shrubby opuntias chiefly of the southwestern U.S. and Mexico that have needlelike spines partly enclosed in a papery sheath and cylindrical joints

**chomp** \'chämp, 'chȯmp\ *verb* [alteration of *champ*] (circa 1847)
*intransitive verb*
**:** to chew or bite on something
*transitive verb*
**:** to chew or bite on

cholla

**chon** \'chän\ *noun, plural* **chon** [Korean *chŏn*]
— see *won* at MONEY table

**chon·dri·o·some** \'kän-drē-ə-ˌsōm\ *noun* [Greek *chondrion*, diminutive of *chondros* grain + International Scientific Vocabulary *-some*] (1910)
**:** MITOCHONDRION

**chon·drite** \'kän-ˌdrīt\ *noun* [International Scientific Vocabulary, from Greek *chondros*] (1883)
**:** a meteoric stone characterized by the presence of chondrules
— **chon·drit·ic** \kän-'dri-tik\ *adjective*

**chon·dro·cra·ni·um** \ˌkän-drō-'krā-nē-əm\ *noun* [Greek *chondros* grain, cartilage] (1875)
**:** the cartilaginous parts of an embryonic cranium; *also* **:** the part of the adult skull derived therefrom

**chon·droi·tin** \kän-'drȯi-tᵊn, -'drō-ə-tᵊn\ *noun* [International Scientific Vocabulary *chondroit*ic acid, an acid found in cartilage + ¹-*in*] (1895)
**:** a mucopolysaccharide occurring in sulfated form in various animal tissues (as cartilage)

**chon·drule** \'kän-(ˌ)drül\ *noun* [Greek *chondros* grain] (circa 1889)
**:** a rounded granule of cosmic origin often found embedded in meteoric stones and sometimes free in marine sediments

**chook** \'chu̇k\ *noun* [imitative] (1880)
*Australian & New Zealand* **:** CHICKEN 1

**choose** \'chüz\ *verb* **chose** \'chōz\; **cho·sen** \'chō-zᵊn\; **choos·ing** \'chü-ziŋ\ [Middle English *chosen*, from Old English *cēosan*; akin to Old High German *kiosan* to choose, Latin *gustare* to taste] (before 12th century)
*transitive verb*
**1 a :** to select freely and after consideration ⟨*choose* a career⟩ **b :** to decide on especially by vote **:** ELECT ⟨*chose* her as captain⟩
**2 a :** to have a preference for ⟨*choose* one car over another⟩ **b :** DECIDE ⟨*chose* to go by train⟩
*intransitive verb*
**1 :** to make a selection
**2 :** to take an alternative — used after *cannot* and usually followed by *but* ⟨when earth is so kind, men cannot *choose* but be happy —J. A. Froude⟩
— **choos·er** \'chü-zər\ *noun*

**choose up** (1910)
*transitive verb*
**:** to form (sides) especially for a game by having opposing captains choose their players
*intransitive verb*
**:** to form sides for a game ⟨let's *choose up* and play ball⟩

**choosy** *or* **choos·ey** \'chü-zē\ *adjective* **choos·i·er; -est** (1862)
**:** fastidiously selective **:** PARTICULAR

**¹chop** \'chäp\ *verb* **chopped; chop·ping** [Middle English *chappen, choppen* — more at CHAP] (14th century)
*transitive verb*
**1 a :** to cut into or sever usually by repeated blows of a sharp instrument **b :** to cut into pieces — often used with *up* **c :** to weed and thin out (young cotton) **d :** to cut as if by chopping ⟨*chop* prices⟩ ⟨a bridge *chops* the lake in two⟩
**2 :** to strike (as a ball) with a short quick downward stroke
**3 :** to subject to the action of a chopper ⟨*chop* a beam of light⟩
*intransitive verb*
**1 :** to make a quick stroke or repeated strokes with or as if with a sharp instrument (as an ax)
**2** *archaic* **:** to move or act suddenly or violently

**²chop** *noun* (14th century)
**1 a :** a forceful usually slanting blow with or as if with an ax or cleaver **b :** a sharp downward blow or stroke
**2 :** a small cut of meat often including part of a rib — see LAMB illustration
**3 :** a mark made by or as if by chopping
**4 :** material that has been chopped up

**5 a :** a short abrupt motion (as of a wave) **b :** a stretch of choppy sea
**6 :** CHOPPER 6
**7** *chiefly British* **:** AX 3

**³chop** *intransitive verb* **chopped; chop·ping** [Middle English *chappen, choppen* to barter, from Old English *cēapian*] (1540)
**1 :** to change direction
**2 :** to veer with or as if with wind
— **chop logic :** to argue with sophistical reasoning and minute distinctions

**⁴chop** *noun* [Hindi *chāp* stamp] (1614)
**1 a :** a seal or official stamp or its impression **b :** a license validated by a seal
**2 a :** a mark on goods or coins to indicate nature or quality **b :** a kind, brand, or lot of goods bearing the same chop **c :** QUALITY, GRADE ⟨of the first *chop*⟩

**chop–chop** \'chäp-'chäp, 'chäp-'\ *adverb* [Chinese Pidgin English, reduplication of *chop* fast] (1834)
**:** without delay **:** QUICKLY

**chop·fall·en** \'chäp-ˌfȯ-lən\ *variant of* CHAPFALLEN

**chop·house** \'chäp-ˌhau̇s\ *noun* (circa 1690)
**:** RESTAURANT

**cho·pine** \shä-'pēn, chä-\ *noun* [Middle French *chapin*, from Old Spanish] (1577)
**:** a woman's shoe of the 16th and 17th centuries with a very high sole designed to increase stature and protect the feet from mud and dirt

**chop·log·ic** \'chäp-ˌlä-jik\ *noun* [obsolete *chop* to exchange, trade, from Middle English *choppen* to barter] (1533)
**:** involved and often specious argumentation
— **choplogic** *adjective*

**chop mark** *noun* (1949)
**:** an indentation made on a coin to attest weight, silver content, or legality
— **chop–marked** \'chäp-ˌmärkt\ *adjective*

**chopped liver** *noun* (1980)
*slang* **:** one that is insignificant or not worth considering

**¹chop·per** \'chä-pər\ *noun* (1552)
**1 :** one that chops
**2** *plural, slang* **:** TEETH
**3 :** a device that interrupts an electric current or a beam of radiation (as light) at short regular intervals
**4 :** MACHINE GUN
**5 :** HELICOPTER
**6 :** a high-bouncing batted baseball
**7 :** a customized motorcycle

**²chopper** *verb* (1955)
**:** HELICOPTER

**chop·pi·ness** \'chä-pē-nəs\ *noun* (1881)
**:** the quality or state of being choppy

**chopping block** *noun* (1703)
**:** a wooden block on which material (as meat, wood, or vegetables) is cut, split, or diced

**¹chop·py** \'chä-pē\ *adjective* **chop·pi·er; -est** [²*chop*] (1605)
**1 :** being roughened **:** CHAPPED
**2 :** rough with small waves
**3 a :** interrupted by ups and downs ⟨*choppy* country⟩ **b :** JERKY ⟨short *choppy* strides⟩ **c :** DISCONNECTED ⟨*choppy* writing⟩
— **chop·pi·ly** \'chä-pə-lē\ *adverb*

**²choppy** *adjective* **chop·pi·er; -est** [³*chop*] (1865)
**:** CHANGEABLE, VARIABLE ⟨a *choppy* wind⟩

**chops** \'chäps\ *noun plural* [alteration of ³*chap*] (1589)
**1 :** JAW
**2 a :** MOUTH **b :** the fleshy covering of the jaws ⟨a dog licking its *chops*⟩
**3** *slang* **:** EMBOUCHURE; *broadly* **:** the technical facility of a musical performer

**chop shop** *noun* (1977)
**:** a place where stolen automobiles are stripped of salable parts

**chop·stick** \'chäp-ˌstik\ *noun* [Chinese Pidgin English *chop* fast + English *stick*] (1699)

: one of a pair of slender sticks held between thumb and fingers and used chiefly in oriental countries to lift food to the mouth

**chop su·ey** \ˌchäp-'sü-ē\ *noun, plural* **chop sueys** [Chinese (Guangdong) *jaahp-seui* odds and ends, from *jaahp* miscellaneous + *seui* bits] (1888)

**chopsticks**

: a dish prepared chiefly from bean sprouts, bamboo shoots, water chestnuts, onions, mushrooms, and meat or fish and served with rice and soy sauce

**cho·ra·gus** \kə-'rā-gəs\ *or* **cho·re·gus** \-'rē-, -'rā-\ *noun* [Latin & Greek; Latin *choragus*, from Greek *choragos*, *chorēgos*, from *choros* chorus + *agein* to lead — more at AGENT] (1625)
**1** : the leader of a chorus or choir; *broadly* : the leader of any group or movement
**2** : a leader of a dramatic chorus in ancient Greece
— **cho·rag·ic** \-'ra-jik\ *adjective*

**cho·ral** \'kōr-əl, 'kȯr-\ *adjective* [French or Medieval Latin; French *choral*, from Medieval Latin *choralis*, from Latin *chorus*] (1587)
**1** : of or relating to a chorus or choir ⟨a *choral* group⟩
**2** : sung or designed for singing by a choir ⟨a *choral* arrangement⟩
— **cho·ral·ly** \-ə-lē\ *adverb*

**cho·rale** \kə-'ral, -'räl\ *noun* [German *Choral*, short for *Choralgesang* choral song] (1841)
**1** : a hymn or psalm sung to a traditional or composed melody in church; *also* : a harmonization of a chorale melody ⟨a Bach *chorale*⟩
**2** : CHORUS, CHOIR

**chorale prelude** *noun* (circa 1924)
: a composition usually for organ based on a chorale

¹**chord** \'kȯrd\ *noun* [alteration of Middle English *cord*, short for *accord*] (1608)
: three or more musical tones sounded simultaneously

²**chord** (14th century)
*intransitive verb*
**1** : ACCORD
**2** : to play chords especially on a stringed instrument
*transitive verb*
**1** : to make chords on
**2** : HARMONIZE

³**chord** *noun* [alteration of ¹*cord*] (1543)
**1** : CORD 3a
**2** : a straight line segment joining and included between two points on a circle; *broadly* : a straight line joining two points on a curve
**3** : an individual emotion or disposition ⟨struck a responsive *chord*⟩
**4** : either of the two outside members of a truss connected and braced by the web members
**5** : the straight line distance joining the leading and trailing edges of an airfoil

**chord·al** \'kȯr-dᵊl\ *adjective* (1848)
**1** : of, relating to, or suggesting a chord
**2** : relating to music characterized more by harmony than by counterpoint

**chor·da·meso·derm** \ˌkȯr-də-'me-zə-ˌdərm *also* -'me-sə-\ *noun* [New Latin *chorda* cord + English *mesoderm*] (1939)
: the portion of the embryonic mesoderm that forms notochord and related structures and induces the formation of neural structures
— **chor·da·meso·der·mal** \-ˌme-zə-'dər-məl, -ˌme-sə-\ *adjective*

**chor·date** \'kȯr-ˌdāt, -dət\ *noun* [ultimately from Latin *chorda* cord] (1897)
: any of a phylum (Chordata) of animals having at least at some stage of development a notochord, dorsally situated central nervous system, and gill clefts and including the vertebrates, lancelets, and tunicates
— **chordate** *adjective*

**chore** \'chōr, 'chȯr\ *noun* [alteration of *chare*] (1746)
**1** *plural* : the regular or daily light work of a household or farm
**2** : a routine task or job
**3** : a difficult or disagreeable task
*synonym* see TASK

**cho·rea** \kə-'rē-ə\ *noun* [New Latin, from Latin, dance, from Greek *choreia*, from *choros* chorus] (1804)
: a nervous disorder (as of humans or dogs) marked by spasmodic movements of limbs and facial muscles and by incoordination
— **cho·re·ic** \-'rē-ik\ *adjective*

**cho·re·i·form** \kə-'rē-ə-ˌfȯrm\ *adjective* [International Scientific Vocabulary] (circa 1899)
: resembling chorea ⟨*choreiform* convulsions⟩

**cho·reo·graph** \'kōr-ē-ə-ˌgraf, 'kȯr-\ (1943)
*transitive verb*
**1** : to compose the choreography of
**2** : to arrange or direct the movements, progress, or details of
*intransitive verb*
: to engage in choreography
— **cho·re·og·ra·pher** \ˌkōr-ē-'ä-grə-fər, ˌkȯr-\ *noun*

**cho·re·og·ra·phy** \ˌkōr-ē-'ä-grə-fē, ˌkȯr-\ *noun, plural* **-phies** [French *chorégraphie*, from Greek *choreia* + French *-graphie* -graphy] (circa 1789)
**1** : the art of symbolically representing dancing
**2 a** : the composition and arrangement of dances especially for ballet **b** : a composition created by this art
**3** : something resembling choreography ⟨a snail-paced *choreography* of delicate high diplomacy —Wolfgang Saxon⟩
— **cho·reo·graph·ic** \ˌkōr-ē-ə-'gra-fik, ˌkȯr-\ *adjective*
— **cho·reo·graph·i·cal·ly** \-fi-k(ə-)lē\ *adverb*

**cho·ric** \'kōr-ik, 'kȯr-, 'kär-\ *adjective* (1830)
: of, relating to, or being in the style of a chorus and especially a Greek chorus

**cho·rine** \'kōr-ˌēn, 'kȯr-\ *noun* [*chorus* + *-ine*, feminine noun suffix (as in *Pauline*)] (1922)
: CHORUS GIRL

**cho·rio·al·lan·to·is** \ˌkōr-ē-(ˌ)ō-ə-'lan-tə-wəs, ˌkȯr-\ *noun* [New Latin, from Greek *chorion* + New Latin *allantois*] (1933)
: a vascular fetal membrane composed of the fused chorion and adjacent wall of the allantois that in the hen's egg is used as a living culture medium for viruses and for tissues — called also *chorioallantoic membrane*
— **cho·rio·al·lan·to·ic** \-ˌa-lən-'tō-ik\ *adjective*

**cho·rio·car·ci·no·ma** \-ˌkär-sᵊn-'ō-mə\ *noun* [New Latin, from *chorion* + *carcinoma*] (1901)
: a malignant tumor developing in the uterus from the trophoblast and rarely in the testes from a neoplasm

**cho·ri·on** \'kōr-ē-ˌän, 'kȯr-\ *noun* [New Latin, from Greek] (1545)
: the highly vascular outer embryonic membrane of reptiles, birds, and mammals that in placental mammals is associated with the allantois in the formation of the placenta

**cho·ri·on·ic** \ˌkōr-ē-'ä-nik, ˌkȯr-\ *adjective* (1892)
**1** : of, relating to, or being part of the chorion ⟨*chorionic* villi⟩
**2** : secreted or produced by chorionic or related tissue (as in the placenta or a choriocarcinoma) ⟨human *chorionic* gonadotropin⟩

**cho·ris·ter** \'kōr-ə-stər, 'kȯr-, 'kär-\ *noun* [Middle English *querister*, from Anglo-French *cueristre*, from Medieval Latin *chorista*, from Latin *chorus*] (14th century)
**1** : a singer in a choir; *specifically* : CHOIRBOY

**2** : the leader of a church choir

**cho·ri·zo** \chə-'rē-(ˌ)zō, -(ˌ)sō\ *noun, plural* **-zos** [Spanish] (1846)
: a pork sausage highly seasoned especially with chili powder and garlic

**C horizon** *noun* (1935)
: the soil layer lying beneath the B horizon and consisting essentially of more or less weathered parent rock

**cho·rog·ra·phy** \kə-'rä-grə-fē\ *noun* [Latin *chorographia*, from Greek *chōrographia*, from *chōros* place + *-graphia* -graphy] (1559)
**1** : the art of describing or mapping a region or district
**2** : a description or map of a region; *also* : the physical conformation and features of such a region
— **cho·rog·ra·pher** \-grə-fər\ *noun*
— **cho·ro·graph·ic** \ˌkȯr-ə-'gra-fik, ˌkär-\ *adjective*

**cho·roid** \'kōr-ˌȯid, 'kȯr-\ *also* **cho·ri·oid** \'kōr-ē-ˌȯid, 'kȯr-\ *noun* [New Latin *choroides* resembling the chorion, from Greek *chorioeidēs*, from *chorion* chorion] (1683)
: a vascular membrane containing large branched pigmented cells that lies between the retina and the sclera of the vertebrate eye — called also *choroid coat*; see EYE illustration
— **choroid** *or* **cho·roi·dal** \kə-'rȯi-dᵊl\ *adjective*

**chor·tle** \'chȯr-tᵊl\ *verb* **chor·tled; chor·tling** \'chȯrt-liŋ, 'chȯr-tᵊl-iŋ\ [probably blend of *chuckle* and *snort*] (1872)
*intransitive verb*
**1** : to sing or chant exultantly ⟨he *chortled* in his joy —Lewis Carroll⟩
**2** : to laugh or chuckle especially in satisfaction or exultation
*transitive verb*
: to say or sing with a chortling intonation
— **chortle** *noun*
— **chor·tler** \'chȯrt-lər, 'chȯr-tᵊl-ər\ *noun*

¹**cho·rus** \'kōr-əs, 'kȯr-\ *noun* [Latin, ring dance, chorus, from Greek *choros*] (1586)
**1 a** : a company of singers and dancers in Athenian drama participating in or commenting on the action; *also* : a similar company in later plays **b** : a character in Elizabethan drama who speaks the prologue and epilogue and comments on the action **c** : an organized company of singers who sing in concert : CHOIR; *especially* : a body of singers who sing the choral parts of a work (as in opera) **d** : a group of dancers and singers supporting the featured players in a musical comedy or revue
**2 a** : a part of a song or hymn recurring at intervals **b** : the part of a drama sung or spoken by the chorus **c** : a composition to be sung by a number of voices in concert **d** : the main part of a popular song; *also* : a jazz variation on a melodic theme
**3 a** : something performed, sung, or uttered simultaneously or unanimously by a number of persons or animals ⟨a *chorus* of boos⟩ ⟨that eternal *chorus* of: "Are we there yet?" from the back seat —Sheila More⟩ **b** : sounds so uttered ⟨visitors are taken to the woods by car to hear the mournful *choruses* of howling wolves —Bob Gaines⟩
— **in chorus** : in unison

²**chorus** *transitive verb* (1826)
: to sing or utter in chorus

**chorus boy** *noun* (1943)
: a young man who sings or dances in the chorus of a theatrical production (as a musical or revue)

**chorus girl** *noun* (1894)

\ə\ abut \ᵊ\ kitten \ər\ further \a\ ash \ā\ ace
\ä\ mop, mar \aù\ out \ch\ chin \e\ bet \ē\ easy
\g\ go \i\ hit \ī\ ice \j\ job \ŋ\ sing \ō\ go
\ȯ\ law \ȯi\ boy \th\ thin \t̶h̶\ the \ü\ loot \ù\ foot
\y\ yet \zh\ vision *see also* Guide to Pronunciation

**:** a young woman who sings or dances in the chorus of a theatrical production (as a musical or revue)

**¹chose** *past of* CHOOSE

**²chose** \'shōz\ *noun* [French, from Latin *causa* cause, reason] (1670)
**:** a piece of personal property **:** THING

**¹cho·sen** \'chō-z³n\ *noun, plural* **chosen** (13th century)
**:** one who is the object of choice or of divine favor **:** an elect person

**²chosen** *adjective* [Middle English, from past participle of *chosen* to choose] (14th century)
**1 :** ELECT
**2 :** selected or marked for favor or special privilege ⟨a *chosen* few⟩

**Chou** \'jō\ *noun* [Chinese (Beijing) *Zhōu*] (1771)
**:** a Chinese dynasty traditionally dated 1122 to about 256 B.C. and marked by the development of the philosophical schools of Confucius, Mencius, Lao-tzu, and Mo Ti

**chough** \'chəf\ *noun* [Middle English] (13th century)
**:** either of two Old World birds (*Pyrrhocorax pyrrhocorax* and *P. graculus*) that are related to the crows and have red legs and glossy blue-black plumage

**¹chouse** \'chaús\ *transitive verb* **choused; chous·ing** [perhaps from Turkish *çavuş* doorkeeper, messenger] (1708)
**:** CHEAT, TRICK

**²chouse** *transitive verb* **choused; chous·ing** [origin unknown] (1904)
*West* **:** to drive or herd roughly

**¹chow** \'chaú\ *noun* [short for *chowchow*] (1856)
**:** FOOD, VICTUALS

**²chow** *intransitive verb* (1917)
**:** EAT — often used with *down*

**³chow** *noun* [by shortening] (1889)
**:** CHOW CHOW

**chow-chow** \'chaú-,chaú\ *noun* [Chinese Pidgin English *chowchow* food] (1850)
**1 :** a Chinese preserve of ginger, fruits, and peels in heavy syrup
**2 :** a relish of chopped mixed pickles in mustard sauce

**chow chow** \'chaú-,chaú\ *noun, often both Cs capitalized* [perhaps from *chow-chow* Chinese person, from Chinese Pidgin English *chowchow* food] (1886)
**:** any of a breed of heavy-coated blocky dogs of Chinese origin having a broad head and muzzle, a distinctive blue-black tongue and black-lined mouth, and either a long dense coat with a full ruff or a short smooth coat — called also *chow*

**chow chow**

**¹chow·der** \'chaú-dər\ *transitive verb* (1732)
**:** to make chowder of

**²chowder** *noun* [French *chaudière* kettle, contents of a kettle, from Late Latin *caldaria* — more at CAULDRON] (1751)
**:** a soup or stew of seafood (as clams or fish) usually made with milk or tomatoes, salt pork, onions, and other vegetables (as potatoes); *also* **:** a soup resembling chowder ⟨corn *chowder*⟩

**chow·der·head** \-,hed\ *noun* [alteration of dialect *jolterhead* blockhead] (1833)
**:** DOLT, BLOCKHEAD

**— chow·der·head·ed** \'chaú-dər-,he-dəd\ *adjective*

**chow·hound** \'chaú-,haúnd\ *noun* (1942)
**:** one fond of eating

**chow line** *noun* (1919)
**:** a line of people waiting to be served food

**chow mein** \'chaú-'mān\ *noun* [Chinese (Guangdong) *cháau-mihn* fried noodles] (1903)
**:** a seasoned stew of shredded or diced meat, mushrooms, and vegetables that is usually served with fried noodles

**chres·tom·a·thy** \kre-'stä-mə-thē\ *noun, plural* **-thies** [New Latin *chrestomathia*, from Greek *chrēstomatheia*, from *chrēstos* useful + *manthanein* to learn — more at MATHEMATICAL] (1832)
**1 :** a selection of passages compiled as an aid to learning a language
**2 :** a volume of selected passages or stories of an author

**chrism** \'kri-zəm\ *noun* [Middle English *crisme*, from Old English *crisma*, from Late Latin *chrisma*, from Greek, ointment, from *chriein* to anoint] (before 12th century)
**:** consecrated oil used in Greek and Latin churches especially in baptism, chrismation, confirmation, and ordination

**chris·ma·tion** \kriz-'mā-shən\ *noun* [Medieval Latin *chrismation-, chrismatio* anointment with chrism, from Late Latin *chrismare* to anoint with chrism, from *chrisma*] (1642)
**:** a confirmatory sacrament of the Eastern Orthodox Church in which a baptized member is anointed with chrism

**chris·mon** \'kriz-,män\ *noun, plural* **chris·ma** \-mə\ *or* **chrismons** [Medieval Latin, from Latin *Chris*tus Christ + Late Latin *mono*gramma monogram] (1872)
**:** CHI-RHO

**chris·om** \'kri-zəm\ *noun* [Middle English *crisom*, short for *crisom cloth*, from *crisom* chrism + *cloth*] (13th century)
**:** a white cloth or robe put on a person at baptism as a symbol of innocence

**chrisom child** *noun* (1593)
**:** a child that dies in its first month

**Christ** \'krīst\ *noun* [Middle English *Crist*, from Old English, from Latin *Christus*, from Greek *Christos*, literally, anointed, from *chriein*] (before 12th century)
**1 :** MESSIAH
**2 :** JESUS
**3 :** an ideal type of humanity
**4** *Christian Science* **:** the ideal truth that comes as a divine manifestation of God to destroy incarnate error
**— Christ·like** \-,līk\ *adjective*
**— Christ·ly** \-lē\ *adjective*

**chris·ten** \'kri-s³n\ *transitive verb* **christened; chris·ten·ing** \'kris-niŋ, 'kri-s³n-iŋ\ [Middle English *cristnen*, from Old English *cristnian*, from *cristen* Christian, from Latin *christianus*] (before 12th century)
**1 a :** BAPTIZE **b :** to name at baptism
**2 :** to name or dedicate (as a ship) by a ceremony suggestive of baptism
**3 :** NAME
**4 :** to use for the first time

**Chris·ten·dom** \'kri-s³n-dəm\ *noun* [Middle English *cristendom*, from Old English *cristendōm*, from *cristen*] (before 12th century)
**1 :** CHRISTIANITY 1
**2 :** the part of the world in which Christianity prevails

**chris·ten·ing** *noun* (14th century)
**:** the ceremony of baptizing and naming a child

**¹Chris·tian** \'kris-chən, 'krish-\ *noun* [Latin *christianus*, adjective & noun, from Greek *christianos*, from *Christos*] (1526)
**1 a :** one who professes belief in the teachings of Jesus Christ **b** (1) **:** DISCIPLE 2 (2) **:** a member of one of the Churches of Christ separating from the Disciples of Christ in 1906 (3) **:** a member of the Christian denomination having part in the union of the United Church of Christ concluded in 1961
**2 :** the hero in Bunyan's *Pilgrim's Progress*

**²Christian** *adjective* (1553)

**1 a :** of or relating to Christianity ⟨*Christian* scriptures⟩ **b :** based on or conforming with Christianity ⟨*Christian* ethics⟩
**2 a :** of or relating to a Christian ⟨*Christian* responsibilities⟩ **b :** professing Christianity ⟨a *Christian* affirmation⟩
**3 :** commendably decent or generous ⟨has a very *Christian* concern for others⟩
**— Chris·tian·ly** *adjective or adverb*

**Christian Brother** *noun* (1883)
**:** a member of the Roman Catholic institute of Brothers of the Christian Schools founded by Saint John Baptist de la Salle in France in 1684 and dedicated to education

**Christian era** *noun* (1657)
**:** the period dating from the birth of Christ

**chris·ti·a·nia** \,kris-chē-'a-nē-ə, ,krish-, ,kris-tē-, -'ä-nē-ə\ *noun* [*Christiania*, former name of Oslo, Norway] (1905)
**:** CHRISTIE

**Chris·tian·i·ty** \,kris-chē-'a-nə-tē, ,krish-, -'cha-nə-, ,kris-tē-'a-\ *noun* (14th century)
**1 :** the religion derived from Jesus Christ, based on the Bible as sacred scripture, and professed by Eastern, Roman Catholic, and Protestant bodies
**2 :** conformity to the Christian religion
**3 :** CHRISTENDOM 2

**Chris·tian·ize** \'kris-chə-,nīz, 'krish-\ *transitive verb* **-ized; -iz·ing** (1593)
**:** to make Christian
**— Chris·tian·i·za·tion** \,kris-chə-nə-'zā-shən, ,krish-\ *noun*
**— Chris·tian·iz·er** \'kris-chə-,nī-zər, 'krish-\ *noun*

**Christian name** *noun* (1549)
**:** GIVEN NAME

**Christian Science** *noun* (circa 1867)
**:** a religion founded by Mary Baker Eddy in 1866 that was organized under the official name of the Church of Christ, Scientist, that derives its teachings from the Scriptures as understood by its adherents, and that includes a practice of spiritual healing based on the teaching that cause and effect are mental and that sin, sickness, and death will be destroyed by a full understanding of the divine principle of Jesus's teaching and healing
**— Christian Scientist** *noun*

**chris·tie** *or* **chris·ty** \'kris-tē\ *noun, plural* **christies** [by shortening & alteration from *christiania*] (1925)
**:** a skiing turn used for altering the direction of hill descent or for stopping and executed usually at high speed by shifting the body weight forward and skidding into a turn with parallel skis

**Christ·mas** \'kris-məs\ *noun, often attributive* [Middle English *Christemasse*, from Old English *Cristes mæsse*, literally, Christ's mass] (before 12th century)
**1 :** a Christian feast on December 25 or among some Eastern Orthodox on January 7 that commemorates the birth of Christ and is usually observed as a legal holiday
**2 :** CHRISTMASTIDE
**— Christ·mas·sy** *or* **Christ·masy** \-mə-sē\ *adjective*

**Christmas cactus** *noun* [from its annual blooming around Christmastime] (circa 1900)
**:** a branching Brazilian cactus (*Schlumbergera truncata* synonym *Zygocactus truncatus*) with flat stems, joints with margins having one to several blunt teeth, and showy usually red, pink, white, or violet zygomorphic flowers — called also *crab cactus*

**Christmas card** *noun* (1883)
**:** a greeting card sent at Christmas

**Christmas club** *noun* (circa 1925)
**:** a savings account in which regular deposits are made throughout the year to provide money for Christmas shopping

**Christmas fern** *noun* (1878)
**:** a North American evergreen fern (*Polystichum acrostichoides*)

**Christmas rose** *noun* (1688)

: a European evergreen herb (*Helleborus niger*) of the buttercup family that has usually white flowers produced in winter

**Christ·mas·tide** \'kris-məs-ˌtīd\ *noun* (1626)
: the festival season from Christmas Eve till after New Year's Day or especially in England till Epiphany

**Christ·mas·time** \-ˌtīm\ *noun* (1837)
: the Christmas season

**Christmas tree** *noun* (1835)
**1** : a usually evergreen tree decorated at Christmas
**2** : an oil-well control device consisting of an assembly of fittings placed at the top of the well

**Chris·to·cen·tric** \ˌkris-tə-'sen-trik, ˌkrīs-\ *adjective* [Greek *Christos* Christ + English *-centric*] (1873)
: centering theologically on Christ

**Chris·to·gram** \'kris-tə-ˌgram, 'krīs-\ *noun* [Greek *Christos* + English *-gram*] (1900)
: a graphic symbol of Christ; *especially* : CHI-RHO

**Chris·tol·o·gy** \kris-'tä-lə-jē, krīs-\ *noun, plural* **-gies** [Greek *Christos* + English *-logy*] (1673)
: theological interpretation of the person and work of Christ
— **Chris·to·log·i·cal** \ˌkris-tə-'lä-ji-kəl, 'krīs-\ *adjective*

**Christ's–thorn** \'krīs(ts)-ˌthòrn\ *or* **Christ–thorn** \'krīs(t)-\ *noun* (1562)
: any of several prickly or thorny shrubs (as the shrub *Paliurus spina-christi* or the jujube *Ziziphus jujuba*)

**chrom-** *or* **chromo-** *combining form* [International Scientific Vocabulary, from Greek *chrōma* color]
**1** : chromium ⟨*chromize*⟩
**2 a** : color : colored ⟨*chromo*lithograph⟩ **b** : pigment ⟨*chromogen*⟩

**chro·ma** \'krō-mə\ *noun* [Greek *chrōma*] (circa 1889)
**1** : SATURATION 4a
**2** : a quality of color combining hue and saturation

**chro·maf·fin** \'krō-mə-fən\ *adjective* [International Scientific Vocabulary *chrom-* + Latin *affinis* bordering on, related — more at AFFINITY] (1903)
: staining deeply with chromium salts ⟨*chromaffin* cells of the adrenal medulla⟩

**chromat-** *or* **chromato-** *combining form* [Greek *chrōmat-*, *chrōma*]
**1** : color ⟨*chromat*id⟩
**2** : chromatin ⟨*chromato*lysis⟩

**chro·mate** \'krō-ˌmāt\ *noun* [French, from Greek *chrōma*] (1819)
: a salt of chromic acid

**¹chro·mat·ic** \krō-'ma-tik\ *noun* (1708)
: ACCIDENTAL 2

**²chromatic** *adjective* [Greek *chrōmatikos*, from *chrōmat-*, *chrōma* skin, color, modified tone; akin to Greek *chrōs* color] (circa 1798)
**1 a** : of or relating to color or color phenomena or sensations **b** : highly colored
**2** : of or relating to chroma
**3 a** : of, relating to, or giving all the tones of the chromatic scale **b** : characterized by frequent use of accidentals
— **chro·mat·i·cal·ly** \-ti-k(ə-)lē\ *adverb*
— **chro·mat·i·cism** \-'ma-tə-ˌsi-zəm\ *noun*

**chromatic aberration** *noun* (1831)
: aberration caused by the differences in refraction of the colored rays of the spectrum

**chro·ma·tic·i·ty** \ˌkrō-mə-'ti-sə-tē\ *noun* (1922)
: the quality of color characterized by its dominant or complementary wavelength and purity taken together

**chro·mat·ics** \krō-'ma-tiks\ *noun plural but singular in construction* (circa 1790)
: the branch of colorimetry that deals with hue and saturation

**chromatic scale** *noun* (circa 1789)
: a musical scale consisting entirely of half steps

**chro·ma·tid** \'krō-mə-təd\ *noun* (1900)
: one of the usually paired and parallel strands of a duplicated chromosome joined by a single centromere

**chro·ma·tin** \'krō-mə-tən\ *noun* (1882)
: a complex of nucleic acid and basic proteins (as histone) in eukaryotic cells that is usually dispersed in the interphase nucleus and condensed into chromosomes in mitosis and meiosis — compare EUCHROMATIN, HETEROCHROMATIN; see CELL illustration
— **chro·ma·tin·ic** \ˌkrō-mə-'ti-nik\ *adjective*

**chro·mato·gram** \krō-'ma-tə-ˌgram, krə-\ *noun* (1922)
**1** : the pattern formed on the adsorbent medium by the layers of components separated by chromatography
**2** : a time-based graphic record (as of concentration of eluted materials) of a chromatographic separation

**chro·mato·graph** \krō-'ma-tə-ˌgraf, krə-\ *noun* (1946)
: an instrument for performing chromatographic separations and producing chromatograms
— **chromatograph** *verb*
— **chro·ma·tog·ra·pher** \ˌkrō-mə-tə-'tä-grə-fər\ *noun*

**chro·ma·tog·ra·phy** \ˌkrō-mə-tə-'tä-grə-fē\ *noun* (1937)
: a process in which a chemical mixture carried by a liquid or gas is separated into components as a result of differential distribution of the solutes as they flow around or over a stationary liquid or solid phase
— **chro·mato·graph·ic** \krō-ˌma-tə-'gra-fik, krə-\ *adjective*
— **chro·mato·graph·i·cal·ly** \-fi-k(ə-)lē\ *adverb*

**chro·ma·tol·y·sis** \ˌkrō-mə-'tä-lə-səs\ *noun* [New Latin] (1901)
: the dissolution and breaking up of chromophil material (as chromatin) of a cell and especially a nerve cell
— **chro·mato·lyt·ic** \krō-ˌma-tə-'li-tik, krə-\ *adjective*

**chro·mato·phore** \krō-'ma-tə-ˌfōr, krə-, -ˌfòr\ *noun* [International Scientific Vocabulary] (circa 1859)
**1** : a pigment-bearing cell; *especially* : one of the cells of an animal integument capable of causing integumentary color changes by expanding or contracting
**2** : the organelle of photosynthesis in blue-green algae and photosynthetic bacteria; *broadly* : CHROMOPLAST, CHLOROPLAST

**¹chrome** \'krōm\ *noun* [French, from Greek *chrōma*] (1800)
**1 a** : CHROMIUM **b** : a chromium pigment
**2** : something plated with an alloy of chromium

**²chrome** *transitive verb* **chromed; chroming** (1876)
**1** : to treat with a compound of chromium (as in dyeing)
**2** : CHROMIZE

**-chrome** \ˌkrōm\ *noun combining form or adjective combining form* [Medieval Latin *-chromat-*, *-chroma* colored thing, from Greek *chrōmat-*, *chrōma*]
**1** : colored thing ⟨helio*chrome*⟩
**2** : coloring matter ⟨uro*chrome*⟩

**chrome green** *noun* (circa 1859)
: any of various brilliant green pigments containing or consisting of chromium compounds

**chrome yellow** *noun* (1819)
: a yellow pigment consisting essentially of neutral lead chromate $PbCrO_4$

**chro·mic** \'krō-mik\ *adjective* (circa 1828)
: of, relating to, or derived from chromium especially with a valence of three

**chromic acid** *noun* (1800)

: an acid $H_2CrO_4$ analogous to sulfuric acid but known only in solution and especially in the form of its salts

**chro·mi·nance** \'krō-mə-nən(t)s\ *noun* [*chrom-* + lum*inance*] (1952)
: the difference between a color and a chosen reference color of the same luminous intensity in color television

**chro·mite** \'krō-ˌmīt\ *noun* [German *Chromit*, from *chrom-*] (1840)
**1** : a mineral that consists of an oxide of iron and chromium
**2** : an oxide of bivalent chromium

**chro·mi·um** \'krō-mē-əm\ *noun* [New Latin, from French *chrome*] (1807)
: a blue-white metallic element found naturally only in combination and used especially in alloys and in electroplating — see ELEMENT table

**chro·mize** \'krō-ˌmīz\ *transitive verb* **chromized; chro·miz·ing** (1939)
: to treat (metal) with chromium in order to form a protective surface alloy

**chro·mo** \'krō-(ˌ)mō\ *noun, plural* **chromos** (1869)
: CHROMOLITHOGRAPH

**chro·mo·cen·ter** \'krō-mə-ˌsen-tər\ *noun* (1926)
: a densely staining aggregation of heterochromatic regions in the nucleus of some cells

**chro·mo·dy·nam·ics** \ˌkrō-mə-dī-'na-miks\ *noun plural but singular in construction* (1976)
: QUANTUM CHROMODYNAMICS

**chro·mo·gen** \'krō-mə-jən\ *noun* [International Scientific Vocabulary] (1858)
**1** : a precursor of a biochemical pigment
**2** : a pigment-producing microorganism

**chro·mo·gen·ic** \ˌkrō-mə-'je-nik\ *adjective* (1884)
**1** : of or relating to a chromogen
**2** : being a process of photographic film development in which silver halides activate precursors of chemical dyes that form the final image while the silver is removed; *also* : being a film developed by this process

**chro·mo·litho·graph** \ˌkrō-mə-'li-thə-ˌgraf\ *noun* (1860)
: a picture printed in colors from a series of lithographic stones or plates
— **chromolithograph** *transitive verb*
— **chro·mo·litho·graph·ic** \-ˌli-thə-'gra-fik\ *adjective*
— **chro·mo·li·thog·raph·er** \-li-'thä-grə-fər\ *noun*
— **chro·mo·li·thog·ra·phy** \-grə-fē\ *noun*

**chro·mo·mere** \'krō-mə-ˌmir\ *noun* [International Scientific Vocabulary] (1896)
: one of the small bead-shaped and heavily staining masses of coiled chromatin that are linearly arranged along the chromosome
— **chro·mo·mer·ic** \ˌkrō-mə-'mer-ik, -'mir-\ *adjective*

**chro·mo·ne·ma** \ˌkrō-mə-'nē-mə\ *noun, plural* **-ne·ma·ta** \-'nē-mə-tə\ [New Latin, from *chrom-* + Greek *nēmat-*, *nēma* thread — more at NEMAT-] (circa 1925)
: the coiled filamentous core of a chromatid
— **chro·mo·ne·mat·ic** \-ni-'ma-tik\ *adjective*

**chro·mo·phil** \'krō-mə-ˌfil\ *adjective* [International Scientific Vocabulary] (1899)
: staining readily with dyes

**chro·mo·phobe** \-ˌfōb\ *adjective* (circa 1909)
: resisting staining with dyes

**chro·mo·phore** \'krō-mə-ˌfōr, -ˌfòr\ *noun* [International Scientific Vocabulary] (1879)
: a chemical group (as an azo group) that absorbs light at a specific frequency and so im-

parts color to a molecule; *also* **:** a colored chemical compound
— **chro·mo·phor·ic** \ˌkrō-mə-ˈfȯr-ik, -ˈfär-\ *adjective*
**chro·mo·plast** \ˈkrō-mə-ˌplast\ *noun* [International Scientific Vocabulary] (1900)
**:** a colored plastid usually containing red or yellow pigment (as carotene)
**chro·mo·pro·tein** \ˌkro-mə-ˈprō-ˌtēn, -ˈprō-tē-ən\ *noun* (1924)
**:** any of various proteins (as hemoglobins, carotenoids, or flavoproteins) having a pigment as a prosthetic group
**chro·mo·some** \ˈkrō-mə-ˌsōm, -ˌzōm\ *noun* [International Scientific Vocabulary] (1889)
**:** one of the linear or sometimes circular DNA-containing bodies of viruses, prokaryotic organisms, and the cell nucleus of eukaryotic organisms that contain most or all of the genes of the individual — compare CHROMATIN
— **chro·mo·som·al** \ˌkrō-mə-ˈsō-məl, -ˈzō-\ *adjective*
— **chro·mo·som·al·ly** \-mə-lē\ *adverb*
**chromosome number** *noun* (1910)
**:** the usually constant number of chromosomes characteristic of a particular kind of animal or plant
**chro·mo·sphere** \ˈkrō-mə-ˌsfir\ *noun* (1868)
**:** the region of the atmosphere of a star (as the sun) between the star's photosphere and its corona
— **chro·mo·spher·ic** \ˌkrō-mə-ˈsfir-ik, -ˈsfer-\ *adjective*
**chro·mous** \ˈkrō-məs\ *adjective* (1840)
**:** of, relating to, or derived from chromium especially with a valence of two
**chron-** *or* **chrono-** *combining form* [Greek, from *chronos*]
**:** time ⟨*chrono*gram⟩
**chron·ax·ie** *also* **chron·axy** \ˈkrō-ˌnak-sē, ˈkrä-\ *noun* [French *chronaxie*, from *chron-* + Greek *axia* value, from *axios* worthy — more at AXIOM] (1917)
**:** the minimum time required for excitation of a structure (as a nerve cell) by a constant electric current of twice the threshold voltage
**chron·ic** \ˈkrä-nik\ *adjective* [French *chronique*, from Greek *chronikos* of time, from *chronos*] (1601)
**1 a :** marked by long duration or frequent recurrence **:** not acute ⟨*chronic* indigestion⟩ ⟨*chronic* experiments⟩ **b :** suffering from a chronic disease ⟨the special needs of *chronic* patients⟩
**2 a :** always present or encountered; *especially* **:** constantly vexing, weakening, or troubling ⟨*chronic* petty warfare⟩ **b :** being such habitually ⟨a *chronic* grumbler⟩
**synonym** see INVETERATE
— **chronic** *noun*
— **chron·i·cal·ly** \-ni-k(ə-)lē\ *adverb*
— **chro·nic·i·ty** \krä-ˈni-sə-tē, krō-\ *noun*
¹**chron·i·cle** \ˈkrä-ni-kəl\ *noun* [Middle English *cronicle*, from Anglo-French, alteration of Old French *chronique*, from Latin *chronica*, from Greek *chronika*, from neuter plural of *chronikos*] (14th century)
**1 :** a usually continuous historical account of events arranged in order of time without analysis or interpretation
**2 :** NARRATIVE
²**chronicle** *transitive verb* **-cled; -cling** \-k(ə-)liŋ\ (15th century)
**1 :** to record in or as if in a chronicle
**2 :** LIST, DESCRIBE
— **chron·i·cler** \-k(ə-)lər\ *noun*
**chronicle play** *noun* (1902)
**:** a play with a theme from history consisting usually of rather loosely connected episodes chronologically arranged
**Chron·i·cles** \ˈkrä-ni-kəlz\ *noun plural but singular in construction*
**:** either of two historical books of canonical Jewish and Christian Scripture — called also *Paralipomenon;* see BIBLE table

**chro·no·bi·ol·o·gy** \ˌkrä-nō-bī-ˈä-lə-jē, ˌkrō-\ *noun* (1972)
**:** the study of biological rhythms
— **chro·no·bi·o·log·ic** \-bī-ə-ˈlä-jik\ *or* **chro·no·bi·o·log·i·cal** \-ji-kəl\ *adjective*
— **chro·no·bi·o·lo·gist** \-bī-ˈä-lə-jist\ *noun*
**chro·no·gram** \ˈkrä-nə-ˌgram, ˈkrō-\ *noun* (1621)
**:** an inscription, sentence, or phrase in which certain letters express a date or epoch
**chro·no·graph** \ˈkrä-nə-ˌgraf, ˈkrō-\ *noun* (1868)
**:** an instrument for measuring and recording time intervals: as **a :** an instrument having a revolving drum on which a stylus makes marks **b :** STOPWATCH; *also* **:** a watch incorporating the functions of a stopwatch **c :** an instrument for measuring the time of flight of projectiles
— **chro·no·graph·ic** \ˌkrä-nə-ˈgra-fik, ˌkrō-\ *adjective*
— **chro·nog·ra·phy** \krə-ˈnä-grə-fē\ *noun*
**chro·nol·o·ger** \krə-ˈnä-lə-jər\ *noun* (circa 1572)
**:** CHRONOLOGIST
**chro·no·log·i·cal** \ˌkrä-nə-ˈlä-ji-kəl, ˌkrō-\ *also* **chro·no·log·ic** \-jik\ *adjective* (1614)
**:** of, relating to, or arranged in or according to the order of time ⟨*chronological* tables of American history⟩; *also* **:** reckoned in units of time ⟨*chronological* age⟩
— **chro·no·log·i·cal·ly** \-ji-k(ə-)lē\ *adverb*
**chro·nol·o·gist** \krə-ˈnä-lə-jist\ *noun* (1611)
**:** an expert in chronology
**chro·nol·o·gy** \-jē\ *noun, plural* **-gies** [New Latin *chronologia*, from *chron-* + *-logia* -logy] (1593)
**1 :** the science that deals with measuring time by regular divisions and that assigns to events their proper dates
**2 :** a chronological table, list, or account
**3 :** an arrangement (as of events) in order of occurrence ⟨reconstruct the *chronology* of the trip⟩
**chro·nom·e·ter** \krə-ˈnä-mə-tər\ *noun* (circa 1735)
**:** TIMEPIECE; *especially* **:** one designed to keep time with great accuracy
**chro·no·met·ric** \ˌkrä-nə-ˈme-trik, ˌkrō-\ *also* **chro·no·met·ri·cal** \-tri-kəl\ *adjective* (1830)
**:** of or relating to a chronometer or chronometry
— **chro·no·met·ri·cal·ly** \-tri-k(ə-)lē\ *adverb*
**chro·nom·e·try** \krə-ˈnä-mə-trē\ *noun* (1833)
**:** the measuring of time
**chro·no·ther·a·py** \ˌkrä-nō-ˈther-ə-pē, ˌkrō-\ *noun* (1973)
**:** treatment of a sleep disorder (as insomnia) by changing sleeping and waking times in an attempt to reset the patient's biological clock
**chrys-** *or* **chryso-** *combining form* [Greek, from *chrysos*]
**:** gold **:** yellow ⟨*chrys*arobin⟩
**chrys·a·lid** \ˈkri-sə-ləd\ *noun* (1777)
**:** CHRYSALIS
— **chrysalid** *adjective*
**chrys·a·lis** \ˈkri-sə-ləs\ *noun, plural* **chrys·al·i·des** \kri-ˈsa-lə-ˌdēz\ *or* **chrys·a·lis·es** [Latin *chrysallid-, chrysallis* gold-colored pupa of butterflies, from Greek, from *chrysos* gold, of Semitic origin; akin to Hebrew *ḥārūṣ* gold] (1601)
**1 :** a pupa of a butterfly; *broadly* **:** an insect pupa
**2 :** a protecting covering **:** a sheltered state or stage of being or growth ⟨a budding writer could not emerge from his *chrysalis* too soon —William Du Bois⟩
**chry·san·the·mum** \kri-ˈsan(t)-thə-məm *also* -ˈzan(t)-\ *noun* [Latin, from Greek *chrysanthemon*, from *chrys-* + *anthemon* flower; akin to Greek *anthos* flower] (1551)

**1 :** any of various composite plants (genus *Chrysanthemum*) including weeds, ornamentals grown for their brightly colored often double flower heads, and others important as sources of medicinals and insecticides
**2 :** a flower head of an ornamental chrysanthemum
**chrys·a·ro·bin** \ˌkri-sə-ˈrō-bən\ *noun* [*chrys-* + ar*aroba*, powder found in the wood of a Brazilian tree (*Andira araroba*) + ¹*-in*] (1887)

**chrysanthemum 2**

**:** a powder derived from the wood of a tropical tree used to treat skin diseases
**Chry·se·is** \krī-ˈsē-əs\ *noun* [Latin, from Greek *Chrysēis*]
**:** a daughter of a priest of Apollo in the *Iliad* narrative taken at Troy by Agamemnon but later restored to her father
**chryso·ber·yl** \ˈkri-sə-ˌber-əl\ *noun* [Latin *chrysoberyllus*, from Greek *chrysobēryllos*, from *chrys-* + *bēryllos* beryl] (1661)
**1** *obsolete* **:** a yellowish beryl
**2 :** a usually yellow or pale green mineral consisting of beryllium aluminum oxide with a little iron and sometimes used as a gem
**chrys·o·lite** \ˈkri-sə-ˌlīt\ *noun* [Middle English *crisolite*, from Middle French, from Latin *chrysolithus*, from Greek, from *chrys-* + *-lithos* -lite] (13th century)
**:** OLIVINE
**chrys·o·me·lid** \kri-sə-ˈme-ləd, -ˈmē-\ *noun* [ultimately from Greek *chrysomēlolonthē* golden cockchafer] (circa 1904)
**:** any of a large family (Chrysomelidae) of small, usually oval and smooth, shining, and brightly colored beetles (as the Colorado potato beetle)
— **chrysomelid** *adjective*
**chryso·phyte** \ˈkri-sə-ˌfīt\ *noun* [ultimately from Greek *chrysos* + *phyton* plant — more at PHYT-] (1959)
**:** GOLDEN-BROWN ALGA
**chrys·o·prase** \ˈkri-sə-ˌpräz\ *noun* [alteration of Middle English *crisopace*, from Old French, from Latin *chrysoprasus*, from Greek *chrysoprasos*, from *chrys-* + *prason* leek; akin to Latin *porrum* leek] (1646)
**:** an apple-green chalcedony valued as a gem
**chrys·o·tile** \-ˌtīl\ *noun* [German *Chrysotil*, from *chrys-* + *-til* fiber, from Greek *tillein* to pluck] (1850)
**:** a mineral consisting of a fibrous silky serpentine and constituting a kind of asbestos
**chthon·ic** \ˈthä-nik\ *also* **chtho·ni·an** \ˈthō-nē-ən\ *adjective* [Greek *chthon-, chthōn* earth — more at HUMBLE] (1882)
**:** of or relating to the underworld **:** INFERNAL ⟨*chthonic* deities⟩
**chub** \ˈchəb\ *noun, plural* **chub** *or* **chubs** [Middle English *chubbe*] (15th century)
**1 :** any of numerous freshwater cyprinid fishes (as of the genera *Gila* and *Nocomis*)
**2 :** any of several marine or freshwater fishes that are not cyprinids
**chub·bi·ly** \ˈchə-bə-lē\ *adverb* (1909)
**:** in the manner of one that is chubby
**chub·by** \ˈchə-bē\ *adjective* **chub·bi·er; -est** [*chub*] (1722)
**:** PLUMP ⟨a *chubby* boy⟩
— **chub·bi·ness** \ˈchə-bē-nəs\ *noun*
¹**chuck** \ˈchək\ *verb* [Middle English *chukken*, of imitative origin] (14th century)
**:** CLUCK
²**chuck** *noun* [perhaps from *chuck* chicken] (1595)
— used as an endearment
³**chuck** *transitive verb* [origin unknown] (1583)
**1 :** PAT, TAP
**2 a :** TOSS **b :** DISCARD ⟨*chucked* his old shirt⟩ **c :** DISMISS, OUST — used especially with *out* ⟨was *chucked* out of office⟩

**3 :** to have done with ⟨*chucked* his job⟩ ⟨*chuck* it all and retire⟩

**⁴chuck** *noun* (1611)
**1 :** a pat or nudge under the chin
**2 :** an abrupt movement or toss

**⁵chuck** *noun* [English dialect *chuck* lump] (1723)
**1 :** a cut of beef that includes most of the neck, the parts about the shoulder blade, and those about the first three ribs — see BEEF illustration
**2** *chiefly West* **:** FOOD
**3 :** an attachment for holding a workpiece or tool in a machine (as a drill or lathe)

**chuck·hole** \'chək-ˌhōl\ *noun* [perhaps from ³*chuck* + *hole*] (1836)
**:** a hole or rut in a road **:** POTHOLE

**chuck·le** \'chə-kᵊl\ *intransitive verb* **chuck·led; chuck·ling** [probably frequentative of ¹*chuck*] (1803)
**1 :** to laugh inwardly or quietly
**2 :** to make a continuous gentle sound resembling suppressed mirth ⟨the clear bright water *chuckled* over gravel —B. A. Williams⟩
— **chuckle** *noun*
— **chuck·le·some** \-səm\ *adjective*
— **chuck·ling·ly** \-iŋ-lē\ *adverb*

**chuck·le·head** \'chə-kᵊl-ˌhed\ *noun* [*chuckle* lumpish + *head*] (1748)
**:** BLOCKHEAD
— **chuck·le·head·ed** \-ˌhe-dəd\ *adjective*

**chuck wagon** *noun* [⁵*chuck*] (1890)
**:** a wagon carrying supplies and provisions for cooking (as on a ranch)

**chuck·wal·la** \'chək-ˌwä-lə\ *or* **chuck·a·wal·la** \'chə-kə-ˌwä-lə\ *noun* [American Spanish *chacahuala*, from Cahuilla (Uto-Aztecan language of southeast California) *čáxwal*] (1893)
**:** a large herbivorous lizard (*Sauromalus obesus* of the family Iguanidae) of desert regions of the southwestern U.S.

**chuck–will's–wid·ow** \ˌchək-ˌwilz-'wi-(ˌ)dō\ *noun* [imitative] (1791)
**:** a nightjar (*Caprimulgus carolinensis*) of the southern U.S.

chuckwalla

**¹chuff** \'chəf\ *noun* [Middle English *chuffe*] (15th century)
**:** BOOR, CHURL

**²chuff** *intransitive verb* [imitative] (1914)
**:** to produce noisy exhaust or exhalations **:** proceed or operate with chuffs ⟨the *chuffing* and snorting of switch engines —Paul Gallico⟩

**³chuff** *noun* (1915)
**:** the sound of noisy exhaust or exhalations

**chuffed** \'chəft\ *adjective* [English dialect *chuff* pleased, puffed with fat] (1957)
*British* **:** PROUD, SATISFIED

**chuf·fy** \'chə-fē\ *adjective* **chuf·fi·er; -est** [English dialect *chuff* puffed with fat] (1611)
**:** FAT, CHUBBY

**¹chug** \'chəg\ *noun* [imitative] (1866)
**:** a dull explosive sound made by or as if by a laboring engine

**²chug** *intransitive verb* **chugged; chug·ging** (1896)
**:** to move or go with or as if with chugs ⟨a locomotive *chugging* along⟩
— **chug·ger** *noun*

**³chug** *transitive verb* **chugged; chug·ging** (circa 1969)
**:** CHUGALUG

**chug·a·lug** \'chə-gə-ˌləg\ *verb* **-lugged; -lug·ging** [imitative] (1956)
*transitive verb*
**:** to drink a container of (as beer) without pause; *also* **:** GUZZLE

*intransitive verb*
**:** to drink a container (as of beer) without pause

**chu·kar** \'chə-kər *also* chə-'kär\ *noun* [Hindi *cakor*] (1814)
**:** a grayish brown Eurasian partridge (*Alectoris chukar*) introduced as a game bird into arid mountainous regions of the western U.S. — called also *chukar partridge*

**chuk·ka** \'chə-kə\ *noun* [*chukka*, alteration of *chukker*; from a similar polo player's boot] (1948)
**:** a usually ankle-length leather boot with two or three pairs of eyelets or a buckle and strap

**chuk·ker** \'chə-kər\ *also* **chuk·ka** \'chə-kə\ *noun* [Hindi *cakkar* circular course, from Sanskrit *cakra* wheel, circle — more at WHEEL] (1898)
**:** a playing period of a polo game

**¹chum** \'chəm\ *noun* [perhaps by shortening & alteration from *chamber fellow* roommate] (1684)
**:** a close friend **:** PAL
— **chum·ship** \-ˌship\ *noun*

**²chum** *intransitive verb* **chummed; chum·ming** (1730)
**1 :** to room together
**2 a :** to be a close friend **b :** to show affable friendliness

**³chum** *noun* [origin unknown] (1857)
**:** animal or vegetable matter (as chopped fish or corn) thrown overboard to attract fish

**⁴chum** *verb* **chummed; chum·ming** (1857)
*transitive verb*
**:** to attract with chum
*intransitive verb*
**:** to throw chum overboard to attract fish

**⁵chum** *noun* [Chinook Jargon *cəm* spotted, striped, from Lower Chinook *c̓ə́m* variegated] (1902)
**:** CHUM SALMON

**Chu·mash** \'chü-ˌmash\ *noun* (1891)
**:** a member of an American Indian people of southwestern California

**chum·my** \'chə-mē\ *adjective* **chum·mi·er; -est** (1884)
**:** INTIMATE, SOCIABLE
— **chum·mi·ly** \'chə-mə-lē\ *adverb*
— **chum·mi·ness** \'chə-mē-nəs\ *noun*

**chump** \'chəmp\ *noun* [perhaps blend of *chunk* and *lump*] (1883)
**:** FOOL, DUPE

**chump change** *noun* (circa 1968)
**:** a relatively small or insignificant amount of money

**chum salmon** *noun* [⁵*chum*] (1907)
**:** a salmon (*Oncorhynchus keta*) of the northern Pacific — called also *chum*

**¹chunk** \'chəŋk\ *noun* [perhaps alteration of *chuck* short piece of wood] (1691)
**1 :** a short thick piece or lump (as of wood or coal)
**2 :** a large noteworthy quantity ⟨bet a sizable *chunk* of money on the race⟩
**3 :** a strong thickset horse usually smaller than a draft horse

**²chunk** *intransitive verb* [imitative] (1890)
**:** to make a dull plunging or explosive sound ⟨the rhythmic *chunking* of thrown quoits —John Updike⟩

**chunky** \'chəŋ-kē\ *adjective* **chunk·i·er; -est** (1751)
**1 :** short and thick or broad; *especially* **:** STOCKY
**2 :** filled with chunks ⟨*chunky* peanut butter⟩
— **chunk·i·ly** \-kə-lē\ *adverb*

**chun·ter** \'chən-tər\ *intransitive verb* [probably of imitative origin] (1599)
*British* **:** to talk in a low inarticulate way
**:** MUTTER

**¹church** \'chərch\ *noun* [Middle English *chirche*, from Old English *cirice*, ultimately from Late Greek *kyriakon*, from Greek, neuter of *kyriakos* of the lord, from *kyrios* lord, mas-

ter; akin to Sanskrit *śūra* hero, warrior] (before 12th century)
**1 :** a building for public and especially Christian worship
**2 :** the clergy or officialdom of a religious body
**3 :** a body or organization of religious believers: **a :** the whole body of Christians **b :** DENOMINATION **c :** CONGREGATION
**4 :** a public divine worship ⟨goes to *church* every Sunday⟩
**5 :** the clerical profession ⟨considered the *church* as a possible career⟩

**²church** *adjective* (before 12th century)
**1 :** of or relating to a church ⟨*church* government⟩
**2** *chiefly British* **:** of or relating to the established church

**³church** *transitive verb* (14th century)
**:** to bring to church to receive one of its rites

**churched** \'chərcht\ *adjective* (14th century)
**:** affiliated with a church

**church father** *noun* (1856)
**:** FATHER 4

**church·go·er** \'chərch-ˌgō(-ə)r\ *noun* (1687)
**:** one who habitually attends church
— **church·go·ing** \-ˌgō-iŋ, -ˌgȯ(-)iŋ\ *adjective or noun*

**church·i·an·i·ty** \ˌchər-chē-'a-nə-tē\ *noun* [*church* + *-ianity* (as in *Christianity*)] (1837)
**:** the usually excessive or sectarian attachment to the practices and interests of a particular church

**church·ing** *noun* (15th century)
**:** the administration or reception of a rite of the church; *specifically* **:** a ceremony in some churches by which women after childbirth are received in the church with prayers, blessings, and thanksgiving

**church key** *noun* (circa 1953)
**:** an implement with a triangular pointed head at one end for piercing the tops of cans and often with a rounded head at the other end for opening bottles

**church·less** \'chərch-ləs\ *adjective* (1641)
**:** not affiliated with a church

**church·ly** \'chərch-lē\ *adjective* (before 12th century)
**1 :** of or relating to a church
**2 :** suitable to or suggestive of a church
**3 :** adhering to a church
**4 :** CHURCHY 1
— **church·li·ness** *noun*

**church·man** \'chərch-mən\ *noun* (14th century)
**1 :** CLERGYMAN
**2 :** a member of a church

**church·man·ship** \-mən-ˌship\ *noun* (circa 1680)
**:** the attitude, belief, or practice of a churchman

**church mode** *noun* (circa 1864)
**:** one of eight scales prevalent in medieval music each utilizing a different pattern of intervals and beginning on a different tone

**Church of England** (1534)
**:** the established episcopal church of England

**church register** *noun* (1846)
**:** a parish register of baptisms, marriages, and deaths

**church school** *noun* (1862)
**1 :** a school providing a general education but supported by a particular church in contrast to a public school or a nondenominational private school
**2 :** an organization of officers, teachers, and pupils for purposes of moral and religious education under the supervision of a local church

**Church Slavonic** *noun* (1850)
**:** any of several Slavic literary and liturgical languages that continue Old Church Slavonic

\ə\ **abut** \ᵊ\ **kitten** \ər\ **further** \a\ **ash** \ā\ **ace**
\ä\ **mop, mar** \au̇\ **out** \ch\ **chin** \e\ **bet** \ē\ **easy**
\g\ **go** \i\ **hit** \ī\ **ice** \j\ **job** \ŋ\ **sing** \ō\ **go**
\ȯ\ **law** \ȯi\ **boy** \th\ **thin** \t̶h̶\ **the** \ü\ **loot** \u̇\ **foot**
\y\ **yet** \zh\ **vision**    *see also* Guide to Pronunciation

but vary regionally under influence of vernacular languages

**church·war·den** \'chərch-ˌwȯr-d°n\ *noun* (15th century)
**1** : one of two lay parish officers in Anglican churches with responsibility especially for parish property and alms
**2** : a long-stemmed clay pipe

**church·wom·an** \-ˌwu̇-mən\ *noun* (1722)
: a woman who is a member of a church

**churchy** \'chər-chē\ *adjective* (1843)
**1** : marked by strict conformity or zealous adherence to the forms or beliefs of a church
**2** : of or suggestive of a church or church services

**church·yard** \'chərch-ˌyärd\ *noun* (12th century)
: a yard that belongs to a church and is often used as a burial ground

**churl** \'chər(-ə)l\ *noun* [Middle English, from Old English *ceorl* man, ceorl; akin to Old Norse *karl* man, husband] (before 12th century)
**1** : CEORL
**2** : a medieval peasant
**3** : RUSTIC, COUNTRYMAN
**4 a** : a rude ill-bred person **b** : a stingy morose person

**churl·ish** \'chər-lish\ *adjective* (before 12th century)
**1** : of, resembling, or characteristic of a churl : VULGAR
**2** : marked by a lack of civility or graciousness : SURLY
**3** : difficult to work with or deal with : INTRACTABLE ⟨*churlish* soil⟩
**synonym** see BOORISH
— **churl·ish·ly** *adverb*
— **churl·ish·ness** *noun*

**¹churn** \'chərn\ *noun* [Middle English *chyrne*, from Old English *cyrin;* akin to Old Norse *kjarni* churn] (before 12th century)
: a vessel for making butter in which milk or cream is agitated in order to separate the oily globules from the watery medium

**²churn** (15th century)
*transitive verb*
**1** : to agitate (milk or cream) in a churn in order to make butter
**2 a** : to stir or agitate violently ⟨an old sternwheeler *churning* the muddy river⟩ **b** : to make (as foam) by so doing
**3** : to make (the account of a client) excessively active by frequent purchases and sales primarily in order to generate commissions
*intransitive verb*
**1** : to work a churn
**2 a** : to produce or be in violent motion **b** : to proceed by means of rotating members (as wheels)

**churn out** *transitive verb* (1912)
: to produce mechanically or copiously : GRIND OUT ⟨the usual pap which has been *churned out* about this superstar —W. S. Murphy⟩

**churr** \'chər\ *intransitive verb* [imitative] (1555)
: to make a vibrant or whirring noise like that made by some insects (as the cockchafer) or some birds (as the partridge)
— **churr** *noun*

**chur·ri·gue·resque** \ˌchu̇r-i-gə-'resk\ *adjective, often capitalized* [Spanish *churrigueresco,* from José *Churriguera* (died 1725) Spanish architect] (1845)
: of or relating to a Spanish baroque architectural style characterized by elaborate surface decoration or its Latin-American adaptation

**¹chute** \'shüt\ *noun* [French, from Old French, from *cheoir* to fall, from Latin *cadere* — more at CHANCE] (1805)
**1 a** : FALL 6b **b** : a quick descent (as in a river) : RAPID
**2** : an inclined plane, sloping channel, or passage down or through which things may pass : SLIDE
**3** : PARACHUTE

**²chute** *verb* **chut·ed; chut·ing** (1884)
*transitive verb*
: to convey by a chute
*intransitive verb*
**1** : to go in or as if in a chute
**2** : to utilize a chute (as by passing ore down it)

**chut·ist** \'shü-tist\ *noun* (1920)
: PARACHUTIST

**chut·ney** \'chət-nē\ *noun, plural* **chutneys** [Hindi *caṭnī*] (1813)
: a thick sauce of Indian origin that contains fruits, vinegar, sugar, and spices and is used as a condiment

**chutz·pah** *also* **chutz·pa** \'hu̇t-spə, 'ku̇t-, -(ˌ)spä\ *noun* [Yiddish *khutspe,* from Late Hebrew *ḥuṣpāh*] (1892)
: supreme self-confidence : NERVE, GALL
**synonym** see TEMERITY

**chyle** \'kī(ə)l\ *noun* [Late Latin *chylus,* from Greek *chylos* juice, chyle; akin to Greek *chein* to pour — more at FOUND] (1541)
: lymph that is milky from emulsified fats, characteristically present in the lacteals, and most apparent during intestinal absorption of fats
— **chy·lous** \'kī-ləs\ *adjective*

**chy·lo·mi·cron** \ˌkī-lō-'mī-ˌkrän\ *noun* [Greek *chylos* + *mikron,* neuter of *mikros* small — more at MICRO-] (1921)
: a microscopic lipid particle common in the blood during fat digestion and assimilation

**chyme** \'kīm\ *noun* [New Latin *chymus,* from Late Latin, chyle, from Greek *chymos* juice; akin to Greek *chein*] (1607)
: the semifluid mass of partly digested food expelled by the stomach into the duodenum

**chy·mo·tryp·sin** \ˌkī-mō-'trip-sən\ *noun* [*chyme* + *-o-* + *trypsin*] (1933)
: a protease that hydrolyzes peptide bonds and is formed in the intestine from chymotrypsinogen
— **chy·mo·tryp·tic** \-tik\ *adjective*

**chy·mo·tryp·sin·o·gen** \-ˌtrip-'si-nə-jən\ *noun* (1933)
: a zymogen that is secreted by the pancreas and is converted by trypsin to chymotrypsin

**ciao** \'chau̇\ *interjection* [Italian, from Italian dialect, literally, (I am your) slave, from Medieval Latin *sclavus* — more at SLAVE] (1929)
— used conventionally as an utterance at meeting or parting

**ci·bo·ri·um** \sə-'bōr-ē-əm, -'bȯr-\ *noun, plural* **-ria** \-ē-ə\ [Medieval Latin, from Latin, cup, from Greek *kibōrion*] (1651)
**1** : a goblet-shaped vessel for holding eucharistic bread
**2** : BALDACHIN; *specifically* : a freestanding vaulted canopy supported by four columns over a high altar

**ci·ca·da** \sə-'kā-də, -'kä-\ or **sī-'kā-\** *noun, plural* **-das** *also* **-dae** \-'kā-(ˌ)dē, -'kä-\ [New Latin, genus name, from Latin, cicada] (14th century)
: any of a family (Cicadidae) of homopterous insects which have a stout body, wide blunt head, and large transparent wings and the males of which produce a loud buzzing noise usually by stridulation

**ci·ca·la** \sə-'kä-lə\ *noun* [Italian, from Medieval Latin, alteration of Latin *cicada*] (1820)
: CICADA

**cic·a·tri·cial** \ˌsi-kə-'tri-shəl\ *adjective* (1881)
: of or relating to a cicatrix

**cic·a·trix** \'si-kə-ˌtriks, sə-'kā-triks\ *noun, plural* **cic·a·tri·ces** \ˌsi-kə-'trī-(ˌ)sēz, sə-'kā-trə-ˌsēz\ [Latin *cicatric-, cicatrix*] (1641)
**1** : a scar resulting from formation and contraction of fibrous tissue in a wound
**2** : a mark resembling a scar especially when caused by the previous attachment of an organ or part (as a leaf)

**cic·a·tri·za·tion** \ˌsi-kə-trə-'zā-shən\ *noun* (15th century)
: scar formation at the site of a healing wound
— **cic·a·trize** \'si-kə-ˌtrīz\ *transitive verb*

**ci·ce·ro·ne** \ˌsi-sə-'rō-nē, ˌchē-chə-\ *noun, plural* **-ni** \-(ˌ)nē\ [Italian, from *Cicerone* Cicero] (1726)
: a guide who conducts sightseers

**cich·lid** \'si-kləd\ *noun* [ultimately from Greek *kichlē* thrush, a kind of wrasse; perhaps akin to Greek *chelidōn* swallow] (1884)
: any of a family (Cichlidae) of mostly tropical spiny-finned usually freshwater fishes including several kept in tropical aquariums
— **cichlid** *adjective*

**ci·cis·beo** \ˌchē-chəz-'bā-(ˌ)ō\ *noun, plural* **-bei** \-'bā-ˌē\ [Italian] (1718)
: LOVER, GALLANT
— **ci·cis·be·ism** \-'bā-ˌi-zəm\ *noun*

**-cidal** *adjective combining form* [Late Latin *-cidalis,* from Latin *-cida*]
: killing : having power to kill ⟨insecti*cidal*⟩

**-cide** *noun combining form* [Middle French, from Latin *-cida,* from *caedere* to cut, kill]
**1** : killer ⟨insecti*cide*⟩
**2** [Middle French, from Latin *-cidium,* from *caedere*] : killing ⟨sui*cide*⟩

**ci·der** \'sī-dər\ *noun* [Middle English *sidre,* from Middle French, from Late Latin *sicera* strong drink, from Greek *sikera,* from Hebrew *shēkhār*] (13th century)
**1** : fermented apple juice often made sparkling by carbonation or fermentation in a sealed container
**2** : the expressed juice of fruit (as apples) used as a beverage or for making other products (as applejack)

**cider vinegar** *noun* (1851)
: vinegar made from fermented cider

**ci·de·vant** \ˌsē-də-'väⁿ\ *adjective* [French, literally, formerly] (1790)
: FORMER

**ci·gar** \si-'gär\ *noun* [Spanish *cigarro*] (1730)
: a small roll of tobacco leaf for smoking

**cig·a·rette** *also* **cig·a·ret** \ˌsi-gə-'ret, 'si-gə-ˌ\ *noun* [French *cigarette,* diminutive of *cigare* cigar, from Spanish *cigarro*] (1835)
: a slender roll of cut tobacco enclosed in paper and meant to be smoked; *also* : a similar roll of another substance (as marijuana)

**cig·a·ril·lo** \ˌsi-gə-'ri-(ˌ)lō, -'rē-(ˌ)yō\ *noun, plural* **-los** [Spanish *cigarrillo* cigarette, diminutive of *cigarro* cigar] (1832)
**1** : a very small cigar
**2** : a cigarette wrapped in tobacco rather than paper

**ci·gua·te·ra** \ˌsē-gwə-'ter-ə, ˌsi-\ *noun* [American Spanish, from *ciguato* person ill with ciguatera, perhaps from *cigua* sea snail] (1862)
: poisoning caused by the ingestion of various normally edible tropical fish in whose flesh a toxic substance has accumulated

**ci·lan·tro** \si-'län-(ˌ)trō, -'lan-\ *noun* [Spanish, coriander, from Medieval Latin *celiandrum,* alteration of Latin *coriandrum* — more at CORIANDER] (1903)
: leaves of coriander used as a flavoring or garnish; *also* : CORIANDER 1

**cil·i·ary** \'si-lē-ˌer-ē\ *adjective* (1691)
**1** : of or relating to cilia
**2** : of, relating to, or being the annular suspension of the lens of the eye

**cil·i·ate** \'si-lē-ət, -lē-ˌāt\ *noun* (1916)
: any of a phylum or subphylum (Ciliophora) of ciliated protozoans (as paramecia)

**cil·i·at·ed** \'si-lē-ˌā-təd\ *or* **cil·i·ate** \-lē-ət, -lē-ˌāt\ *adjective* (1753)
: possessing cilia ⟨*ciliated* epithelial cells⟩ ⟨leaves with *ciliate* petioles⟩
— **cil·i·a·tion** \ˌsi-lē-'ā-shən\ *noun*

**cil·i·um** \'si-lē-əm\ *noun, plural* **cil·ia** \-lē-ə\ [New Latin, from Latin, eyelid; akin to Latin *celare* to conceal — more at HELL] (1794)
**1** : a minute short hairlike process often forming part of a fringe; *especially* : one on a cell that is capable of lashing movement and serves especially in free unicellular organisms to produce locomotion or in higher forms a current of fluid

**2 :** EYELASH

**ci·met·i·dine** \sī-'me-tə-ˌdēn\ *noun* [*ci*- (alteration of *cyan*-) + *methyl* + -*idine*] (1975)
**:** a histamine analogue C$_{10}$H$_{16}$N$_6$S used especially in the treatment of duodenal ulcers

**¹Cim·me·ri·an** \sə-'mir-ē-ən\ *adjective* (1580)
**:** very dark or gloomy ⟨under ebon shades . . . in dark *Cimmerian* desert ever dwell —John Milton⟩

**²Cimmerian** *noun* [Latin *Cimmerii*, a mythical people, from Greek *Kimmerioi*] (1584)
**:** any of a mythical people described by Homer as dwelling in a remote realm of mist and gloom

**¹cinch** \'sinch\ *noun* [Spanish *cincha*, from Latin *cingula* girdle, girth, from *cingere*] (1859)
**1 :** a girth for a pack or saddle
**2 :** a tight grip
**3 a :** a thing done with ease **b :** a certainty to happen

**²cinch** (1866)
*transitive verb*
**1 :** to put a cinch on
**2 :** to make certain **:** ASSURE
*intransitive verb*
**:** to tighten the cinch — often used with *up*

**cin·cho·na** \siŋ-'kō-nə, sin-'chō-\ *noun* [New Latin, genus name, from the countess of *Chinchón* (died 1641) wife of the Peruvian viceroy] (1786)
**1 :** any of a genus (*Cinchona*) of South American trees and shrubs of the madder family
**2 :** the dried bark of a cinchona (as *C. ledgeriana*) containing alkaloids (as quinine) and formerly used as a specific in malaria

**cin·cho·nine** \'siŋ-kə-ˌnēn, 'sin-chə-\ *noun* (1825)
**:** a bitter white crystalline alkaloid C$_{19}$H$_{22}$N$_2$O found especially in cinchona bark and used like quinine

**cin·cho·nism** \'siŋ-kə-ˌni-zəm, 'sin-chə-\ *noun* (1857)
**:** a disorder due to excessive or prolonged use of cinchona or its alkaloids and marked by temporary deafness, ringing in the ears, headache, dizziness, and rash

**cinc·ture** \'siŋ(k)-chər\ *noun* [Latin *cinctura* girdle, from *cinctus*, past participle of *cingere* to gird; probably akin to Sanskrit *kāñcī* girdle] (1600)
**1 :** the act of encircling
**2 a :** an encircling area **b :** GIRDLE, BELT; *especially* **:** a cord or sash of cloth worn around an ecclesiastical vestment (as an alb) or the habit of a religious

**cin·der** \'sin-dər\ *noun* [Middle English *sinder*, from Old English; akin to Old High German *sintar* dross, slag, Serbo-Croatian *sedra* calcium carbonate] (before 12th century)
**1 :** the slag from a metal furnace **:** DROSS
**2 a** *plural* **:** ASHES **b :** a fragment of ash
**3 a :** a partly burned combustible in which fire is extinct **b :** a hot coal without flame **c :** a partly burned coal capable of further burning without flame
**4 :** a fragment of lava from an erupting volcano
— **cin·dery** \-d(ə-)rē\ *adjective*

**cinder block** *noun* (1926)
**:** a hollow rectangular building block made of cement and coal cinders

**cinder cone** *noun* (1849)
**:** a conical hill formed by the accumulation of volcanic debris around a vent

**Cin·der·el·la** \ˌsin-də-'re-lə\ *noun* [after *Cinderella*, fairy-tale heroine who is used as a drudge by her stepmother but ends up married to a prince] (1840)
**:** one resembling the fairy-tale Cinderella: as **a** **:** one suffering undeserved neglect **b :** one suddenly lifted from obscurity to honor or significance

**cine** \'si-nē\ *noun* [probably from French *ciné*, short for *cinéma* cinema] (1920)
**:** MOTION PICTURE

**cine·ast** \'si-nē-ˌast, -nē-əst\ *or* **cine·aste** \-ˌast\ *or* **ciné·aste** \-ˌast\ *noun* [French *cinéaste*, from *ciné* + -*aste* (as in *enthousiaste* enthusiast)] (1926)
**:** a devotee of motion pictures; *also* **:** MOVIEMAKER

**cin·e·ma** \'si-nə-mə, *British also* -ˌmä\ *noun* [short for *cinematograph*] (1909)
**1 a :** MOTION PICTURE — usually used attributively **b :** a motion-picture theater
**2 a :** MOVIES; *especially* **:** the film industry **b :** the art or technique of making motion pictures

**cin·e·ma·go·er** \-ˌgō(-ə)r\ *noun* (1920)
**:** MOVIEGOER

**cin·e·ma·theque** \ˌsi-nə-mə-'tek\ *noun* [French *cinémathèque* film library, from *cinéma* + -*thèque* (as in *bibliothèque* library)] (1966)
**:** a small movie house specializing in avant-garde films

**cin·e·mat·ic** \ˌsi-nə-'ma-tik\ *adjective* (1916)
**1 :** of, relating to, suggestive of, or suitable for motion pictures or the filming of motion pictures ⟨*cinematic* principles and techniques⟩
**2 :** filmed and presented as a motion picture ⟨*cinematic* fantasies⟩
— **cin·e·mat·i·cal·ly** \-'ma-ti-k(ə-)lē\ *adverb*

**cin·e·ma·tize** \'si-nə-mə-ˌtīz\ *transitive verb* **-tized; -tiz·ing** (1916)
**:** to make a motion picture of (as a novel) **:** adapt for motion pictures

**cin·e·mat·o·graph** \ˌsi-nə-'ma-tə-ˌgraf\ *noun* [French *cinématographe*, from Greek *kinēmat*-, *kinēma* movement (from *kinein* to move) + French -*o*- + -*graphe* -graph — more at -KINESIS] (1896)
*chiefly British* **:** a motion-picture camera, projector, theater, or show

**cin·e·ma·tog·ra·pher** \ˌsi-nə-mə-'tä-grə-fər\ *noun* (1897)
**1 :** a motion-picture cameraman
**2 :** a motion-picture projectionist

**cin·e·ma·tog·ra·phy** \ˌsi-nə-mə-'tä-grə-fē\ *noun* (1897)
**:** the art or science of motion-picture photography
— **cin·e·mat·o·graph·ic** \-ˌma-tə-'gra-fik\ *adjective*
— **cin·e·mat·o·graph·i·cal·ly** \-fi-k(ə-)lē\ *adverb*

**ci·ne·ma ve·ri·té** \'si-nə-mə-ˌver-i-'tā; si-nā-'mä-ve-rē-'tā\ *noun* [French *cinéma-vérité*, literally, cinema-truth, translation of Russian *kinopravda*] (1963)
**:** the art or technique of filming a motion picture so as to convey candid realism

**cin·e·ole** \'si-nē-ˌōl\ *noun* [International Scientific Vocabulary, by transposition from New Latin *oleum cinae* wormseed oil] (1885)
**:** a liquid C$_{10}$H$_{18}$O with a camphor odor contained in many essential oils (as of eucalyptus) and used especially as an expectorant and flavoring agent — called also *eucalyptol*

**cin·er·ar·ia** \ˌsi-nə-'rer-ē-ə, -'rar-\ *noun* [New Latin, from Latin, feminine of *cinerarius* of ashes, from *ciner*-, *cinis* ashes — more at INCINERATE] (1597)
**:** any of several garden or potted plants derived from a perennial composite herb (*Senecio cruentus*) of the Canary Islands and having heart-shaped leaves and clusters of bright flower heads

**cin·er·ar·i·um** \-ē-əm\ *noun, plural* **-ia** \-ē-ə\ [Latin, from *ciner*-, *cinis*] (1880)
**:** a place to receive the ashes of the cremated dead
— **cin·er·ary** \'si-nə-ˌrer-ē\ *adjective*

**ci·ne·re·ous** \sə-'nir-ē-əs\ *adjective* [Latin *cinereus*, from *ciner*-, *cinis*] (1661)
**1 :** gray tinged with black
**2 :** resembling or consisting of ashes

**cin·er·in** \'si-nə-rən\ *noun* [Latin *ciner*-, *cinis*] (1948)
**:** either of two oily liquid esters C$_{20}$H$_{28}$O$_3$ and

C$_{21}$H$_{28}$O$_5$ occurring especially in the flowers of pyrethrum and possessing insecticidal properties

**cin·gu·lum** \'siŋ-gyə-ləm\ *noun, plural* **-la** \-lə\ [New Latin, from Latin, girdle, from *cingere* to gird — more at CINCTURE] (1845)
**:** an anatomical band or encircling ridge
— **cin·gu·late** \-lət\ *adjective*

**cin·na·bar** \'si-nə-ˌbär\ *noun* [Middle English *cynabare*, from Middle French & Latin; Middle French *cenobre*, from Latin *cinnabaris*, from Greek *kinnabari*, of non-Indo-European origin; akin to Arabic *zinjafr* cinnabar] (14th century)
**1 :** artificial red mercuric sulfide used especially as a pigment
**2 :** native red mercuric sulfide HgS that is the only important ore of mercury
— **cin·na·bar·ine** \-bə-ˌrīn, -ˌbär-in\ *adjective*

**cinnabar moth** *noun* (circa 1893)
**:** a European moth (*Tyria jacobeae*) that has been introduced into the western U.S. in attempts to control the tansy ragwort on which its larvae feed — called also *cinnabar*

**cin·nam·ic acid** \sə-'na-mik-\ *noun* [French *cinnamique* of cinnamon, from *cinname* cinnamon, from Latin *cinnamomum*] (circa 1864)
**:** a white crystalline odorless acid C$_9$H$_8$O$_2$ found especially in cinnamon oil and storax

**cin·na·mon** \'si-nə-mən\ *noun, often attributive* [Middle English *cynamone*, from Latin *cinnamomum*, *cinnamon*, from Greek *kinnamōmon*, *kinnamon*, of non-Indo-European origin; akin to Hebrew *qinnāmōn* cinnamon] (14th century)
**1 a :** any of several Asian trees (genus *Cinnamomum*) of the laurel family **b :** an aromatic spice prepared from the dried inner bark of a cinnamon (especially *C. zeylanicum*); *also* **:** the bark
**2 :** a light yellowish brown

**cinnamon fern** *noun* (1818)
**:** a large fern (*Osmunda cinnamomea*) with cinnamon-colored spore-bearing fronds shorter than and separate from the green foliage fronds

**cinnamon stone** *noun* (1805)
**:** ESSONITE

**cin·quain** \'siŋ-ˌkān, 'saŋ-\ *noun* [French, from *cinq* five, from Latin *quinque* — more at FIVE] (1882)
**:** a 5-line stanza

**cin·que·cen·tist** \ˌchiŋ-kwi-'chen-tist\ *noun* (1871)
**:** an Italian of the cinquecento; *especially* **:** a poet or artist of this period

**cin·que·cen·to** \ˌchiŋ-kwi-'chen-(ˌ)tō\ *noun* [Italian, literally, five hundred, from *cinque* five (from Latin *quinque*) + *cento* hundred, from Latin *centum* — more at HUNDRED] (1760)
**:** the 16th century especially in Italian art and literature

**cinque·foil** \'siŋk-ˌfȯil, 'saŋk-\ *noun* [Middle English *sink foil*, from Middle French *cincfoille*, from Latin *quinquefolium*, from *quinque* five + *folium* leaf — more at BLADE] (14th century)
**1 :** any of a genus (*Potentilla*) of herbs and shrubs of the rose family with 5-lobed leaves and 5-petaled flowers — called also *potentilla*
**2 :** a design enclosed by five joined foils

**cinquefoil 2**

**ciop·pi·no** \chə-'pē-(ˌ)nō\ *noun* [perhaps from Italian dialect] (1936)
**:** a dish of fish and shellfish cooked usually with tomatoes, wine, spices, and herbs

---

\ə\ **abut** \ᵊ\ **kitten** \ər\ **further** \a\ **ash** \ā\ **ace**
\ä\ **mop, mar** \au̇\ **out** \ch\ **chin** \e\ **bet** \ē\ **easy**
\g\ **go** \i\ **hit** \ī\ **ice** \j\ **job** \ŋ\ **sing** \ō\ **go**
\ȯ\ **law** \ȯi\ **boy** \th\ **thin** \th\ **the** \ü\ **loot** \u̇\ **foot**
\y\ **yet** \zh\ **vision** *see also* Guide to Pronunciation

**¹ci·pher** \'sī-fər\ *noun, often attributive* [Middle English, from Middle French *cifre,* from Medieval Latin *cifra,* from Arabic *ṣifr* empty, cipher, zero] (14th century)
**1 a :** ZERO 1a **b :** one that has no weight, worth, or influence **:** NONENTITY
**2 a :** a method of transforming a text in order to conceal its meaning — compare CODE 3b **b :** a message in code
**3 :** ARABIC NUMERAL
**4 :** a combination of symbolic letters; *especially* **:** the interwoven initials of a name

**²cipher** *verb* **ci·phered; ci·pher·ing** \-f(ə-)riŋ\ (circa 1530)
*intransitive verb*
**:** to use figures in a mathematical process
*transitive verb*
**1 :** ENCIPHER
**2 :** to compute arithmetically

**ci·pher·text** \'sī-fər-ˌtekst\ *noun* (1939)
**:** the enciphered form of a text or of its elements — compare PLAINTEXT

**cir·ca** \'sər-kə\ *preposition* [Latin, from *circum* around — more at CIRCUM-] (1861)
**:** at, in, or of approximately — used especially with dates ⟨born *circa* 1600⟩

**cir·ca·di·an** \sər-'kā-dē-ən\ *adjective* [Latin *circa* about + *dies* day + English ²-*an* — more at DEITY] (1959)
**:** being, having, characterized by, or occurring in approximately 24-hour periods or cycles (as of biological activity or function) ⟨*circadian* rhythms in activity⟩

**Cir·cas·sian** \(ˌ)sər-'ka-sh(ē-)ən\ *noun* [*Circassia,* region of the Caucasus] (1555)
**1 :** a member of a group of peoples of the northwestern Caucasus
**2 :** the language of the Circassian peoples
— **Circassian** *adjective*

**Circassian walnut** *noun* (1914)
**:** the light brown irregularly black-veined wood of the English walnut much used for veneer and cabinetwork

**Cir·ce** \'sər-(ˌ)sē\ *noun* [Latin, from Greek *Kirkē*]
**:** a sorceress who changes Odysseus' men into swine but is forced by Odysseus to change them back

**cir·ci·nate** \'sər-s°n-ˌāt\ *adjective* [Latin *circinatus,* past participle of *circinare* to round, from *circinus* pair of compasses, from *circus*] (1830)
**:** ROUNDED, COILED; *especially* **:** rolled in the form of a flat coil with the apex as a center ⟨*circinate* fern fronds unfolding⟩
— **cir·ci·nate·ly** *adverb*

**¹cir·cle** \'sər-kəl\ *noun, often attributive* [Middle English *cercle,* from Old French, from Latin *circulus,* diminutive of *circus* circle, circus, from or akin to Greek *krikos, kirkos* ring; akin to Old English *hring* ring — more at RING] (14th century)
**1 a :** RING, HALO **b :** a closed plane curve every point of which is equidistant from a fixed point within the curve **c :** the plane surface bounded by such a curve
**2 :** the orbit of a celestial body
**3 :** something in the form of a circle or section of a circle: as **a :** DIADEM **b :** an instrument of astronomical observation the graduated limb of which consists of an entire circle **c :** a balcony or tier of seats in a theater **d :** a circle formed on the surface of a sphere by the intersection of a plane that passes through it

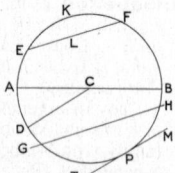
**circle 1b:** *AB* diameter; *C* center; *CD, CA, CB* radii; *EKF* arc on chord *EF; EFKL* (area) segment on chord *EF; ACD* (area) sector; *GH* secant; *TPM* tangent at point *P; EKFBPDA* circumference

⟨*circle* of latitude⟩ **e :** ROTARY 2
**4 :** an area of action or influence **:** REALM
**5 a :** CYCLE, ROUND ⟨the wheel has come full circle⟩ **b :** fallacious reasoning in which something to be demonstrated is covertly assumed
**6 :** a group of persons sharing a common interest or revolving about a common center ⟨the sewing *circle* of her church⟩ ⟨family *circle*⟩ ⟨the gossip of court *circles*⟩
**7 :** a territorial or administrative division or district
**8 :** a curving side street

**²circle** *verb* **cir·cled; cir·cling** \-k(ə-)liŋ\ (14th century)
*transitive verb*
**1 :** to enclose in or as if in a circle
**2 :** to move or revolve around
*intransitive verb*
**1 a :** to move in or as if in a circle **b :** CIRCULATE
**2 :** to describe or extend in a circle
— **cir·cler** \-k(ə-)lər\ *noun*

**circle graph** *noun* (1928)
**:** PIE CHART

**cir·clet** \'sər-klət\ *noun* (15th century)
**:** a little circle; *especially* **:** a circular ornament

**¹cir·cuit** \'sər-kət\ *noun, often attributive* [Middle English, from Middle French *circuite,* from Latin *circuitus,* from *circumire, circuire* to go around, from *circum-* + *ire* to go — more at ISSUE] (14th century)
**1 a :** a usually circular line encompassing an area **b :** the space enclosed within such a line
**2 a :** a course around a periphery **b :** a circuitous or indirect route
**3 a :** a regular tour (as by a traveling judge or preacher) around an assigned district or territory **b :** the route traveled **c :** a group of church congregations ministered to by one pastor
**4 a :** the complete path of an electric current including usually the source of electric energy **:** HOOKUP **c :** a two-way communication path between points (as in a computer)
**5 a :** an association of similar groups **:** LEAGUE **b :** a number or series of public outlets (as theaters, radio shows, or arenas) offering the same kind of presentation **c :** a number of similar social gatherings ⟨cocktail *circuit*⟩
— **cir·cuit·al** \-kə-t°l\ *adjective*

**²circuit** (15th century)
*transitive verb*
**:** to make a circuit about
*intransitive verb*
**:** to make a circuit

**circuit board** *noun* (1948)
**:** BOARD 9

**circuit breaker** *noun* (1872)
**:** a switch that automatically interrupts an electric circuit under an infrequent abnormal condition

**circuit court** *noun* (1708)
**:** a court that sits at two or more places within one judicial district

**circuit judge** *noun* (1801)
**:** a judge who holds a circuit court

**cir·cu·i·tous** \(ˌ)sər-'kyü-ə-təs\ *adjective* [perhaps from Medieval Latin *circuitosus,* from Latin *circuitus*] (1664)
**1 :** having a circular or winding course ⟨a *circuitous* route⟩
**2 :** not being forthright or direct in language or action
— **cir·cu·i·tous·ly** *adverb*
— **cir·cu·i·tous·ness** *noun*

**circuit rider** *noun* (1837)
**:** a clergyman assigned to a circuit especially in a rural area

**cir·cuit·ry** \'sər-kə-trē\ *noun, plural* **-ries** (1946)
**1 :** the detailed plan or arrangement of an electric circuit
**2 :** the components of an electric circuit

**cir·cu·ity** \(ˌ)sər-'kyü-ə-tē\ *noun, plural* **-ities** [*circuitous*] (circa 1626)
**:** lack of straightforwardness **:** INDIRECTION

**¹cir·cu·lar** \'sər-kyə-lər\ *adjective* [Middle English *circuler,* from Middle French, from Late Latin *circularis,* from Latin *circulus* circle] (15th century)
**1 a :** having the form of a circle **:** ROUND **b :** moving in or describing a circle or spiral
**2 a :** of or relating to a circle or its mathematical properties ⟨a *circular* arc⟩ **b :** having a circular base or bases ⟨a *circular* cylinder⟩
**3 :** CIRCUITOUS, INDIRECT
**4 :** marked by or moving in a cycle
**5 :** being or involving reasoning that uses in the argument or proof a conclusion to be proved or one of its unproved consequences
**6 :** intended for circulation
— **cir·cu·lar·i·ty** \ˌsər-kyə-'lar-ə-tē\ *noun*
— **cir·cu·lar·ly** \'sər-kyə-lər-lē\ *adverb*
— **cir·cu·lar·ness** *noun*

**²circular** *noun* (1789)
**:** a paper (as a leaflet) intended for wide distribution

**circular dichroism** *noun* (circa 1961)
**1 :** the property (as of an optically active medium) of unequal absorption of right and left plane-polarized light so that the emergent light is elliptically polarized
**2 :** a spectroscopic technique that makes use of circular dichroism

**circular file** *noun* (1967)
**:** WASTEBASKET

**circular function** *noun* (1884)
**:** TRIGONOMETRIC FUNCTION

**cir·cu·lar·ise** *British variant of* CIRCULARIZE

**cir·cu·lar·ize** \'sər-kyə-lə-ˌrīz\ *transitive verb* **-ized; -iz·ing** (1848)
**1 a :** to send circulars to **b :** to poll by questionnaire
**2 :** PUBLICIZE
— **cir·cu·lar·i·za·tion** \ˌsər-kyə-lər-ə-'zā-shən\ *noun*

**circular saw** *noun* (1817)
**:** a power saw with a circular cutting blade; *also* **:** the blade itself

**cir·cu·late** \'sər-kyə-ˌlāt\ *verb* **-lat·ed; -lat·ing** [Latin *circulatus,* past participle of *circulare,* from *circulus*] (circa 1650)
*intransitive verb*
**1 :** to move in a circle, circuit, or orbit; *especially* **:** to follow a course that returns to the starting point ⟨blood *circulates* through the body⟩
**2 :** to pass from person to person or place to place: as **a :** to flow without obstruction **b :** to become well-known or widespread ⟨rumors *circulated* through the town⟩ **c :** to go from group to group at a social gathering **d :** to come into the hands of readers; *specifically* **:** to become sold or distributed
*transitive verb*
**:** to cause to circulate
— **cir·cu·lat·able** \-ˌlā-tə-bəl\ *adjective*
— **cir·cu·la·tive** \-ˌlā-tiv\ *adjective*
— **cir·cu·la·tor** \-ˌlā-tər\ *noun*

**circulating decimal** *noun* (1768)
**:** REPEATING DECIMAL

**cir·cu·la·tion** \ˌsər-kyə-'lā-shən\ *noun* (1654)
**1 :** orderly movement through a circuit; *especially* **:** the movement of blood through the vessels of the body induced by the pumping action of the heart
**2 :** FLOW
**3 a :** passage or transmission from person to person or place to place; *especially* **:** the interchange of currency ⟨coins in *circulation*⟩ **b :** the extent of dissemination: as (1) **:** the average number of copies of a publication sold over a given period (2) **:** the total number of items borrowed from a library

**cir·cu·la·to·ry** \'sər-kyə-lə-ˌtōr-ē, -ˌtȯr-\ *adjective* (1605)
**:** of or relating to circulation or the circulatory system ⟨*circulatory* failure⟩

**circulatory system** *noun* (1862)

**circum-** : the system of blood, blood vessels, lymphatics, and heart concerned with the circulation of the blood and lymph
**circum-** *prefix* [Old French or Latin; Old French, from Latin, from *circum*, from *circus* circle — more at CIRCLE]
: around : about ⟨*circum*polar⟩

**cir·cum·am·bi·ent** \ˌsər-kˈm-'am-bē-ənt\ *adjective* [Late Latin *circumambient-, circumambiens*, present participle of *circumambire* to surround in a circle, from Latin *circum-* + *ambire* to go around — more at AMBIENT] (1633)
: being on all sides : ENCOMPASSING
— **cir·cum·am·bi·ent·ly** *adverb*

**cir·cum·am·bu·late** \-'am-byə-ˌlāt\ *transitive verb* **-lat·ed; -lat·ing** [Late Latin *circumambulatus*, past participle of *circumambulare*, from Latin *circum-* + *ambulare* to walk] (circa 1656)
: to circle on foot especially ritualistically
— **cir·cum·am·bu·la·tion** \-ˌam-byə-'lā-shən\ *noun*

**cir·cum·cen·ter** \'sər-kˈm-ˌsen-tər\ *noun* (circa 1889)
: the point at which the perpendicular bisectors of the sides of a triangle intersect and which is equidistant from the three vertices

**cir·cum·cir·cle** \-ˌsər-kəl\ *noun* (1885)
: a circle which passes through all the vertices of a polygon (as a triangle)

**cir·cum·cise** \'sər-kˈm-ˌsīz\ *transitive verb* **-cised; -cis·ing** [Middle English, from Latin *circumcisus*, past participle of *circumcidere*, from *circum-* + *caedere* to cut] (13th century)
: to cut off the prepuce of (a male) or the clitoris of (a female)
— **cir·cum·cis·er** *noun*

**cir·cum·ci·sion** \ˌsər-kˈm-'si-zhən, 'sər-kˈm-ˌ\ *noun* (12th century)
**1 a :** the act of circumcising; *especially* : a Jewish rite performed on male infants as a sign of inclusion in the Jewish religious community **b :** the condition of being circumcised
**2** *capitalized* : January 1 observed as a church festival in commemoration of the circumcision of Jesus

**cir·cum·fer·ence** \sə(r)-'kəm(p)-fərn(t)s, -f(ə-)rən(t)s\ *noun* [Middle English, from Middle French, from Latin *circumferentia*, from *circumferre* to carry around, from *circum-* + *ferre* to carry — more at BEAR] (14th century)
**1 :** the perimeter of a circle
**2 :** the external boundary or surface of a figure or object : PERIPHERY
— **cir·cum·fer·en·tial** \-ˌkəm(p)-fə-'ren(t)-shəl\ *adjective*

**¹cir·cum·flex** \'sər-kˈm-ˌfleks\ *adjective* [Latin *circumflexus*, past participle of *circumflectere* to bend around, mark with a circumflex, from *circum-* + *flectere* to bend] (circa 1577)
**1 :** characterized by the pitch, quantity, or quality indicated by a circumflex
**2 :** marked with a circumflex

**²circumflex** *noun* (1609)
: a mark ˆ, ˜, or ˜ originally used in Greek over long vowels to indicate a rising-falling tone and in other languages to mark length, contraction, or a particular vowel quality

**cir·cum·flu·ent** \(ˌ)sər-'kəm-flü-ənt\ *adjective* [from Latin *circumfluent-, circumfluens*, present participle of *circumfluere* to flow around, from *circum-* + *fluere* to flow — more at FLUID] (1577)
: flowing round or surrounding in the manner of a fluid
— **cir·cum·flu·ous** \(ˌ)sər-'kəm-flü-əs\ *adjective*

**cir·cum·fuse** \ˌsər-kˈm-'fyüz\ *transitive verb* **-fused; -fus·ing** [Latin *circumfusus*, past participle of *circumfundere* to pour around, from *circum-* + *fundere* to pour — more at FOUND] (1605)
: SURROUND, ENVELOP
— **cir·cum·fu·sion** \-'fyü-zhən\ *noun*

**cir·cum·ja·cent** \ˌsər-kˈm-'jā-sˈnt\ *adjective* [Latin *circumjacent-, circumjacens*, present participle of *circumjacēre* to lie around, from *circum-* + *jacēre* to lie — more at ADJACENT] (15th century)
: lying adjacent on all sides : SURROUNDING

**cir·cum·lo·cu·tion** \ˌsər-kˈm-lō-'kyü-shən\ *noun* [Latin *circumlocution-, circumlocutio*, from *circum-* + *locutio* speech, from *loqui* to speak] (15th century)
**1 :** the use of an unnecessarily large number of words to express an idea
**2 :** evasion in speech
— **cir·cum·loc·u·to·ry** \-'lä-kyə-ˌtōr-ē, -ˌtȯr-\ *adjective*

**cir·cum·lu·nar** \ˌsər-kəm-'lü-nər\ *adjective* (circa 1909)
: revolving about or surrounding the moon

**cir·cum·nav·i·gate** \-'na-və-ˌgāt\ *transitive verb* [Latin *circumnavigatus*, past participle of *circumnavigare* to sail around, from *circum-* + *navigare* to navigate] (1634)
: to go completely around (as the earth) especially by water; *also* : to go around instead of through : BYPASS ⟨*circumnavigate* a congested area⟩
— **cir·cum·nav·i·ga·tion** \-ˌna-və-'gā-shən\ *noun*
— **cir·cum·nav·i·ga·tor** \-'na-və-ˌgā-tər\ *noun*

**cir·cum·po·lar** \ˌsər-kˈm-'pō-lər\ *adjective* (1686)
**1 :** continually visible above the horizon ⟨a *circumpolar* star⟩
**2 :** surrounding or found in the vicinity of a terrestrial pole

**cir·cum·scis·sile** \-'si-səl, -ˌsīl\ *adjective* [Latin *circumscissus*, past participle of *circumscindere* to tear around, from *circum-* + *scindere* to cut, split — more at SHED] (1835)
: dehiscing by fissure around the capsule of the fruit

**cir·cum·scribe** \'sər-kˈm-ˌskrīb\ *transitive verb* [Latin *circumscribere*, from *circum-* + *scribere* to write, draw — more at SCRIBE] (1835)
**1 a :** to constrict the range or activity of definitely and clearly **b :** to define or mark off carefully
**2 a :** to draw a line around **b :** to surround by or as if by a boundary
**3 :** to construct or be constructed around (a geometrical figure) so as to touch as many points as possible
*synonym* see LIMIT

**cir·cum·scrip·tion** \ˌsər-kˈm-'skrip-shən\ *noun* [Latin *circumscription-, circumscriptio*, from *circumscribere*] (1531)
**1 :** the act of circumscribing : the state of being circumscribed: as **a :** DEFINITION, DELIMITATION **b :** LIMITATION
**2 :** something that circumscribes: as **a :** LIMIT, BOUNDARY **b :** RESTRICTION
**3 :** a circumscribed area or district

**cir·cum·spect** \'sər-kˈm-ˌspekt\ *adjective* [Middle English, from Middle French or Latin; Middle French *circonspect*, from Latin *circumspectus*, from past participle of *circumspicere* to look around, be cautious, from *circum-* + *specere* to look — more at SPY] (15th century)
: careful to consider all circumstances and possible consequences : PRUDENT
*synonym* see CAUTIOUS
— **cir·cum·spec·tion** \ˌsər-kˈm-'spek-shən\ *noun*
— **cir·cum·spect·ly** \'sər-kˈm-ˌspek(t)-lē\ *adverb*

**cir·cum·stance** \'sər-kˈm-ˌstan(t)s, -stən(t)s\ *noun* [Middle English, from Old French, from Latin *circumstantia*, from *circumstant-, circumstans*, present participle of *circumstare* to stand around, from *circum-* + *stare* to stand — more at STAND] (13th century)
**1 a :** a condition, fact, or event accompanying, conditioning, or determining another : an essential or inevitable concomitant ⟨the weather is a *circumstance* to be taken into consideration⟩ **b :** a subordinate or accessory fact or detail ⟨cost is a minor *circumstance* in this case⟩ **c :** a piece of evidence that indicates the probability or improbability of an event (as a crime) ⟨the *circumstance* of the missing weapon told against him⟩ ⟨the *circumstances* suggest murder⟩
**2 a :** the sum of essential and environmental factors (as of an event or situation) ⟨constant and rapid change in economic *circumstance* —G. M. Trevelyan⟩ **b :** state of affairs : EVENTUALITY ⟨open rebellion was a rare *circumstance*⟩ — often used in plural ⟨a victim of *circumstances*⟩ **c** *plural* : situation with regard to wealth ⟨he was in easy *circumstances*⟩
**3 :** attendant formalities and ceremonial ⟨pride, pomp, and *circumstance* of glorious war —Shakespeare⟩
**4 :** an event that constitutes a detail (as of a narrative or course of events) ⟨considering each *circumstance* in turn⟩
*synonym* see OCCURRENCE

**cir·cum·stanced** \-ˌstan(t)st, -stən(t)st\ *adjective* (circa 1611)
: placed in particular circumstances especially in regard to property or income

**cir·cum·stan·tial** \ˌsər-kˈm-'stan(t)-shəl\ *adjective* (1600)
**1 :** belonging to, consisting in, or dependent on circumstances
**2 :** pertinent but not essential : INCIDENTAL
**3 :** marked by careful attention to detail : abounding in factual details ⟨a *circumstantial* account of the fight⟩
**4 :** CEREMONIAL ☆
— **cir·cum·stan·ti·al·i·ty** \-ˌstan(t)-shē-'a-lə-tē\ *noun*
— **cir·cum·stan·tial·ly** \-'stan(t)-sh(ə-)lē\ *adverb*

**circumstantial evidence** *noun* (1736)
: evidence that tends to prove a fact by proving other events or circumstances which afford a basis for a reasonable inference of the occurrence of the fact at issue

**cir·cum·stan·ti·ate** \ˌsər-kˈm-'stan(t)-shē-ˌāt\ *transitive verb* **-at·ed; -at·ing** (circa 1652)
: to supply with circumstantial evidence or support

**cir·cum·stel·lar** \ˌsər-kˈm-'ste-lər\ *adjective* (1951)
: surrounding or occurring in the vicinity of a star

**¹cir·cum·val·late** \-'va-ˌlāt\ *transitive verb* **-lat·ed; -lat·ing** [Latin *circumvallatus*, past participle of *circumvallare* to surround with siege works, from *circum-* + *vallum* rampart — more at WALL] (circa 1798)
: to surround by or as if by a rampart
— **cir·cum·val·la·tion** \-ˌva-'lā-shən\ *noun*

**²cir·cum·val·late** \-'va-ˌlāt, -'va-lət\ *adjective* (circa 1852)

---

☆ **SYNONYMS**
**Circumstantial, minute, particular, detailed** mean dealing with a matter fully and usually point by point. CIRCUMSTANTIAL implies fullness of detail that fixes something described in time and space ⟨a *circumstantial* account of our visit⟩. MINUTE implies close and searching attention to the smallest details ⟨a *minute* examination of a fossil⟩. PARTICULAR implies a precise attention to every detail ⟨a *particular* description of the scene of the crime⟩. DETAILED stresses abundance or completeness of detail ⟨a *detailed* analysis of the event⟩.

---

\ə\ **abut** \ˈ\ **kitten** \ər\ **further** \a\ **ash** \ā\ **ace** \ä\ **mop, mar** \au̇\ **out** \ch\ **chin** \e\ **bet** \ē\ **easy** \g\ **go** \i\ **hit** \ī\ **ice** \j\ **job** \ŋ\ **sing** \ō\ **go** \o̊\ **law** \o̊i\ **boy** \th\ **thin** \t̲h̲\ **the** \ü\ **loot** \u̇\ **foot** \y\ **yet** \zh\ **vision** *see also* Guide to Pronunciation

: being any of approximately 12 large papillae near the back of the tongue each of which is surrounded with a marginal sulcus and supplied with taste buds responsive especially to bitter flavors

**cir·cum·vent** \ˌsər-kᵊm-'vent\ *transitive verb* [Latin *circumventus*, past participle of *circumvenire*, from *circum-* + *venire* to come — more at COME] (1539)
**1 a :** to hem in **b :** to make a circuit around
**2 :** to manage to get around especially by ingenuity or stratagem ⟨the setup *circumvented* the red tape —Lynne McTaggart⟩
— **cir·cum·ven·tion** \-'ven(t)-shən\ *noun*
**cir·cum·vo·lu·tion** \ˌsər-kəm-və-'lü-shən, ˌsər-kᵊm-vō-\ *noun* [Middle English *circumvolucioun*, from Medieval Latin *circumvolution-, circumvolutio*, from Latin *circumvolvere* to revolve, from *circum-* + *volvere* to roll — more at VOLUBLE] (15th century)
: an act or instance of turning around an axis
**cir·cus** \'sər-kəs\ *noun, often attributive* [Latin, circle, circus — more at CIRCLE] (14th century)
**1 a :** a large arena enclosed by tiers of seats on three or all four sides and used especially for sports or spectacles (as athletic contests, exhibitions of horsemanship, or in ancient times chariot racing) **b :** a public spectacle
**2 a :** an arena often covered by a tent and used for variety shows usually including feats of physical skill, wild animal acts, and performances by clowns **b :** a circus performance **c :** the physical plant, livestock, and personnel of such a circus **d :** something suggestive of a circus (as in frenzied activity, sensationalism, theatricality, or razzle-dazzle)
**3 a** *obsolete* **:** CIRCLE, RING **b** *British* **:** a usually circular area at an intersection of streets
— **cir·cusy** \-kə-sē\ *adjective*
**circus catch** *noun* (1893)
: a catch (as in baseball or football) requiring an extraordinary or spectacular effort
**ci·ré** *also* **ci·re** \sə-'rā, sē-\ *noun* [French, from past participle of *cirer* to wax, from *cire* wax, from Latin *cera* — more at CERUMEN] (1921)
**1 :** a highly glazed finish for fabrics usually achieved by applying wax to the fabric
**2 :** a fabric or garment with a ciré finish
**cirque** \'sərk\ *noun* [French, from Latin *circus*] (1601)
**1** *archaic* **:** CIRCUS
**2 :** CIRCLE, CIRCLET
**3 :** a deep steep-walled basin on a mountain usually forming the blunt end of a valley
**cir·rho·sis** \sə-'rō-səs\ *noun, plural* **-rho·ses** \-ˌsēz\ [New Latin, from Greek *kirrhos* orange-colored; akin to Old English *hār* gray — more at HOAR] (circa 1847)

*cirque 3*

: widespread disruption of normal liver structure by fibrosis and the formation of regenerative nodules that is caused by any of various chronic progressive conditions affecting the liver (as long term alcohol abuse or hepatitis)
— **cir·rhot·ic** \-'rä-tik\ *adjective or noun*
**cirro-** *combining form* [New Latin *cirrus*]
: cirrus ⟨*cirro*stratus⟩
**cir·ro·cu·mu·lus** \ˌsir-ō-'kyü-myə-ləs\ *noun* [New Latin] (circa 1803)
: a cloud form of small white rounded masses at a high altitude usually in regular groupings forming a mackerel sky — see CLOUD illustration
**cir·ro·stra·tus** \ˌsir-ō-'strā-təs, -'stra-\ *noun* [New Latin] (circa 1803)
: a fairly uniform layer of high stratus darker than cirrus — see CLOUD illustration
**cir·rus** \'sir-əs\ *noun, plural* **cir·ri** \'sir-ˌī\ [New Latin, from Latin, curl] (1708)
**1 :** TENDRIL

**2 :** a slender usually flexible animal appendage: as **a :** an arm of a barnacle **b :** a filament of a crinoid **c :** a fused group of cilia functioning like a limb on some protozoans **d :** the male copulatory organ of various invertebrate animals
**3 :** a wispy white cloud usually of minute ice crystals formed at altitudes of 20,000 to 40,000 feet (6,000 to 12,000 meters) — see CLOUD illustration
**cis** \'sis\ *adjective* [Latin, literally, on this side] (1888)
: characterized by having certain atoms or groups of atoms on the same side of the longitudinal axis of a double bond or of the plane of a ring in a molecule
**cis-** *prefix* [Latin, from *cis* — more at HE]
**1 :** on this side ⟨*cis*lunar⟩
**2** *usually italic* **:** cis ⟨*cis*-dichloroethylene⟩ — compare TRANS- 2b
**cis·al·pine** \(ˌ)sis-'al-ˌpīn\ *adjective* (1542)
: situated on the south side of the Alps ⟨*Cisalpine* Gaul⟩ — compare TRANSALPINE
**cis·co** \'sis-(ˌ)kō\ *noun, plural* **ciscoes** [short for Canadian French *ciscoette*] (1848)
: any of various whitefishes (genus *Coregonus*); *especially* **:** LAKE HERRING
**cis·lu·nar** \(ˌ)sis-'lü-nər\ *adjective* (circa 1877)
: lying between the earth and the moon or the moon's orbit ⟨*cislunar* space⟩
**cis·plat·in** \(ˌ)sis-'pla-tᵊn\ *noun* [*cis-* + *platinum*] (1977)
: a platinum-containing antineoplastic drug $Cl_2H_6N_2Pt$ used especially in the treatment of testicular and ovarian tumors and advanced bladder cancer
**cis–plat·i·num** \-'plat-nəm, -'pla-tᵊn-əm\ *noun* (1977)
: CISPLATIN
**cissy** *British variant of* SISSY
**cist** \'sist, 'kist\ *noun* [Welsh, chest, from Latin *cista*] (1804)
: a neolithic or Bronze Age burial chamber typically lined with stone
**Cis·ter·cian** \sis-'tər-shən\ *noun* [Medieval Latin *Cistercium* Cîteaux] (1611)
: a member of a monastic order founded by Saint Robert of Molesme in 1098 at Cîteaux, France, under Benedictine rule
— **Cistercian** *adjective*
**cis·tern** \'sis-tərn\ *noun* [Middle English, from Old French *cisterne*, from Latin *cisterna*, from *cista* box, chest — more at CHEST] (13th century)
**1 :** an artificial reservoir (as an underground tank) for storing liquids and especially water (as rainwater)
**2 :** a large usually silver vessel formerly used (as in cooling wine) at the dining table
**3 :** a fluid-containing sac or cavity in an organism
**cis·ter·na** \sis-'tər-nə\ *noun, plural* **-nae** \-ˌnē\ [New Latin, from Latin, reservoir] (circa 1860)
: CISTERN 3: as **a :** one of the large spaces under the arachnoid membrane **b :** one of the interconnected flattened vesicles comprising the part of the endoplasmic reticulum that is studded with ribosomes
— **cis·ter·nal** \-nəl\ *adjective*
**cis·tron** \'sis-ˌträn\ *noun* [*cis-* + *trans-* + ²-*on*] (1957)
: a segment of DNA that is equivalent to a gene and that specifies a single functional unit (as a protein or enzyme)
— **cis·tron·ic** \sis-'trä-nik\ *adjective*
**cit·a·del** \'si-tə-dᵊl, -ˌdel\ *noun* [Middle French *citadelle*, from Old Italian *cittadella*, diminutive of *cittade* city, from Medieval Latin *civitat-, civitas* — more at CITY] (1562)
**1 :** a fortress that commands a city
**2 :** STRONGHOLD
**ci·ta·tion** \sī-'tā-shən\ *noun* (13th century)
**1 :** an official summons to appear (as before a court)

**2 a :** an act of quoting; *especially* **:** the citing of a previously settled case at law **b :** EXCERPT, QUOTE
**3 :** MENTION: as **a :** a formal statement of the achievements of a person receiving an academic honor **b :** specific reference in a military dispatch to meritorious performance of duty
*synonym* see ENCOMIUM
— **ci·ta·tion·al** \-shnəl, -shə-nᵊl\ *adjective*
**cite** \'sīt\ *transitive verb* **cit·ed; cit·ing** [Middle French *citer* to cite, summon, from Latin *citare* to put in motion, rouse, summon, from frequentative of *ciēre* to stir, move — more at -KINESIS] (15th century)
**1 :** to call upon officially or authoritatively to appear (as before a court)
**2 :** to quote by way of example, authority, or proof
**3 a :** to refer to; *especially* **:** to mention formally in commendation or praise **b :** to name in a citation
**4 :** to bring forward or call to another's attention especially as an example, proof, or precedent
*synonym* see SUMMON
— **cit·able** \'sī-tə-bəl\ *adjective*
**cith·a·ra** \'si-thə-rə, 'ki-\ *variant of* KITHARA
**cith·er** \'si-thər, -thər\ *noun* [French *cithare*, from Latin *cithara* kithara, from Greek *kithara*] (1606)
: CITTERN
**cit·ied** \'si-tēd\ *adjective* (1612)
: occupied by cities
**cit·i·fied** \'si-ti-ˌfīd\ *adjective* (1828)
: of, relating to, or characteristic of a sophisticated urban style of living — often used disparagingly
**cit·i·fy** \-ˌfī\ *transitive verb* **-fied; -fy·ing** (1828)
: URBANIZE
— **cit·i·fi·ca·tion** \ˌsi-tə-fi-'kā-shən\ *noun*
**cit·i·zen** \'si-tə-zən *also* -sən\ *noun* [Middle English *citizein*, from Anglo-French *citezein*, alteration of Old French *citeien*, from *cité* city] (14th century)
**1 :** an inhabitant of a city or town; *especially* **:** one entitled to the rights and privileges of a freeman
**2 a :** a member of a state **b :** a native or naturalized person who owes allegiance to a government and is entitled to protection from it
**3 :** a civilian as distinguished from a specialized servant of the state ☆
— **cit·i·zen·ly** \-zən-lē *also* -sən-\ *adjective*
**cit·i·zen·ess** \-zə-nəs *also* -sə-\ *noun* (1796)
: a female citizen
**cit·i·zen·ry** \-zən-rē *also* -sən-\ *noun, plural* **-ries** (1819)
: a whole body of citizens
**citizen's arrest** *noun* (1941)
: an arrest made not by a law officer but by a citizen who derives authority from the fact of being a citizen
**citizens band** *noun* (1948)
: a range of radio-wave frequencies that in the U.S. is allocated officially for private radio communications
**cit·i·zen·ship** \'si-tə-zən-ˌship\ *noun* (1611)

☆ SYNONYMS
**Citizen, subject, national** mean a person owing allegiance to and entitled to the protection of a sovereign state. CITIZEN is preferred for one owing allegiance to a state in which sovereign power is retained by the people and sharing in the political rights of those people ⟨the rights of a free *citizen*⟩. SUBJECT implies allegiance to a personal sovereign such as a monarch ⟨the king's *subjects*⟩. NATIONAL designates one who may claim the protection of a state and applies especially to one living or traveling outside that state ⟨American *nationals* working in the Middle East⟩.

**1 :** the status of being a citizen
**2 a :** membership in a community (as a college) **b :** the quality of an individual's response to membership in a community

**citr-** *or* **citri-** *or* **citro-** *combining form* [New Latin, from *Citrus*, genus name]
**1 :** citrus ⟨*citriculture*⟩
**2 :** citric acid ⟨*citrate*⟩

**cit·ral** \'si-ˌtral\ *noun* [International Scientific Vocabulary] (1891)
**:** an unsaturated liquid isomeric aldehyde $C_{10}H_{16}O$ of many essential oils that has a strong lemon odor and is used especially in perfumery and as a flavoring

**cit·rate** \'si-ˌtrāt\ *noun* [International Scientific Vocabulary] (1794)
**:** a salt or ester of citric acid

**cit·ric acid** \'si-trik-\ *noun* [International Scientific Vocabulary] (1813)
**:** a tricarboxylic acid $C_6H_8O_7$ occurring in cellular metabolism, obtained especially from lemon and lime juices or by fermentation of sugars, and used as a flavoring

**citric acid cycle** *noun* (1942)
**:** KREBS CYCLE

**cit·ri·cul·ture** \'si-trə-ˌkəl-chər\ *noun* (1916)
**:** the cultivation of citrus fruits
— **cit·ri·cul·tur·ist** \ˌsi-trə-'kəl-ch(ə-)rist\ *noun*

**¹cit·rine** \'si-ˌtrīn\ *adjective* [Middle English, from Middle French *citrin*, from Medieval Latin *citrinus*, from Latin *citrus* citron tree] (14th century)
**:** resembling a citron or lemon especially in color

**²ci·trine** \si-'trēn\ *noun* (1748)
**:** a semiprecious yellow stone resembling topaz formed by heating a black quartz in order to change its color

**ci·tri·nin** \si-'trī-nən\ *noun* [New Latin *citrinum*, specific epithet of *Penicillium citrinum*] (1931)
**:** a toxic antibiotic $C_{13}H_{14}O_5$ that is produced especially by a penicillium (*Penicillium citrinum*) and an aspergillus (*Aspergillus niveus*) and is effective against some gram-positive bacteria

**cit·ron** \'si-trən\ *noun* [Middle English, from Middle French, modification of Latin *citrus*] (15th century)
**1 a :** a citrus fruit resembling a lemon but larger with little pulp and a very thick rind **b :** a small shrubby tree (*Citrus medica*) that produces citrons and is cultivated in tropical regions **c :** the preserved rind of the citron used especially in cakes and puddings
**2 :** a small hard-fleshed watermelon used especially in pickles and preserves

**cit·ro·nel·la** \ˌsi-trə-'ne-lə\ *noun* [New Latin, from French *citronnelle* lemon balm, from *citron*] (circa 1858)
**:** a fragrant grass (*Cymbopogon nardus*) of southern Asia that yields an oil used in perfumery and as an insect repellent; *also* **:** its oil

**cit·ro·nel·lal** \-'ne-ˌlal\ *noun* [International Scientific Vocabulary, from New Latin *citronella*] (1893)
**:** a lemon-odored aldehyde $C_{10}H_{18}O$ that is derived especially from citronella oil and is used in perfumery and as an insect repellent

**cit·ro·nel·lol** \-'ne-ˌlȯl, -ˌlōl\ *noun* [International Scientific Vocabulary, from New Latin *citronella*] (1872)
**:** an unsaturated liquid alcohol $C_{10}H_{20}O$ with a roselike odor that is found in two optically active forms in many essential oils (as rose oil) and is used in perfumery and soaps

**ci·trov·o·rum factor** \sə-'trä-və-rəm-\ *noun* [New Latin *citrovorum*, specific epithet of *Leuconostoc citrovorum*, bacterium that requires this form of folic acid] (1948)
**:** a metabolically active form of folic acid that has been used in cancer therapy to protect normal cells against methotrexate

**cit·rul·line** \'si-trə-ˌlēn\ *noun* [International Scientific Vocabulary, from New Latin *Citrullus*, genus name of the watermelon] (1930)
**:** a crystalline amino acid $C_6H_{13}N_3O_3$ formed especially as an intermediate in the conversion of ornithine to arginine in the living system

**cit·rus** \'si-trəs\ *noun, plural* **citrus** *or* **cit·rus·es** *often attributive* [New Latin, genus name, from Latin] (1825)
**:** any of a group of often thorny trees and shrubs (*Citrus* and related genera) of the rue family grown in warm regions for their edible fruit (as the orange or lemon) with firm usually thick rind and pulpy flesh; *also* **:** the fruit
— **cit·rusy** \'si-trə-sē\ *adjective*

**citrus canker** *noun* (1916)
**:** a destructive disease of citrus caused by a bacterium (*Xanthomonas campestris citri*) that produces lesions on the leaves, twigs, and fruits

**citrus red mite** *noun* (1935)
**:** a relatively large mite (*Panonychus citri*) that is a destructive pest on the foliage of citrus

**cit·tern** \'si-tərn\ *also* **cith·ern** \'si-thərn, -thərn\ *or* **cith·ren** \'si-thrən\ *noun* [blend of *cither* and *gittern*] (1566)
**:** a Renaissance stringed instrument like a guitar with a flat pear-shaped body

**city** \'si-tē\ *noun, plural* **cit·ies** *often attributive* [Middle English *citie* large or small town, from Old French *cité*, from Medieval Latin *civitat-, civitas*, from Latin, citizenship, state, city of Rome, from *civis* citizen — more at HIND] (13th century)
**1 a :** an inhabited place of greater size, population, or importance than a town or village **b :** an incorporated British town usually of major size or importance having the status of an episcopal see **c** *capitalized* **(1) :** the financial district of London **(2) :** the influential financial interests of the British economy **d :** a usually large or important municipality in the U.S. governed under a charter granted by the state **e :** an incorporated municipal unit of the highest class in Canada
**2 :** CITY-STATE
**3 :** the people of a city
**4** *slang* — used with a preceding adjective or noun naming an abundant or quintessential feature or quality ⟨the movie was shoot-out *city*⟩

**city clerk** *noun* (1919)
**:** a public officer charged with recording the official proceedings and vital statistics of a city

**city council** *noun* (1789)
**:** the legislative body of a city

**city editor** *noun* (1834)
**:** a newspaper editor usually in charge of local news and staff assignments

**city father** *noun* (1845)
**:** a member (as an alderman or councilman) of the governing body of a city

**city hall** *noun* (1675)
**1 :** the chief administrative building of a city
**2 a :** a municipal government **b :** city officialdom or bureaucracy ⟨you can't fight *city hall*⟩

**city manager** *noun* (1913)
**:** an official employed by an elected council to direct the administration of a city government

**city planning** *noun* (1912)
**:** the drawing up of an organized arrangement (as of streets, parks, and business and residential areas) of a city
— **city planner** *noun*

**city room** *noun* (1919)
**:** the department where local news is handled in a newspaper editorial office

**city·scape** \'si-tē-ˌskāp\ *noun* (1856)
**1 :** a city viewed as a scene
**2 :** an artistic representation of a city

**city slicker** *noun* (1924)
**:** SLICKER 2b

**city-state** \'si-tē-ˌstāt *also* -'stāt\ *noun* (1893)
**:** an autonomous state consisting of a city and surrounding territory

**city·wide** \'si-tē-ˌwīd\ *adjective* (1961)
**:** including all parts of a city

**civ·et** \'si-vət\ *noun* [Middle French *civette*, from Old Italian *zibetto*, from Arabic *zabād* civet perfume] (1532)
**1 :** any of various Old World carnivorous mammals (family Viverridae) with long bodies, short legs, and a usually long tail
**2 :** a thick yellowish musky-odored substance found in a pouch near the sexual organs of the civet (especially genera *Civettictis, Viverra*, and *Viverricula*) and used in perfume

civet

**civet cat** *noun* (1607)
**1 :** CIVET 1
**2 :** RINGTAIL 2
**3 :** any of the small spotted skunks (genus *Spilogale*) of western North America

**civ·ic** \'si-vik\ *adjective* [Latin *civicus*, from *civis* citizen] (circa 1656)
**:** of or relating to a citizen, a city, citizenship, or civil affairs
— **civ·i·cal·ly** \'si-vi-k(ə-)lē\ *adverb*

**civ·ic-mind·ed** \ˌsi-vik-'mīn-dəd\ *adjective* (1947)
**:** disposed to look after civic needs and interests
— **civ·ic-mind·ed·ness** *noun*

**civ·ics** \'si-viks\ *noun plural but singular or plural in construction* (1886)
**:** a social science dealing with the rights and duties of citizens

**civ·il** \'si-vəl\ *adjective* [Middle English, from Middle French, from Latin *civilis*, from *civis*] (14th century)
**1 a :** of or relating to citizens **b :** of or relating to the state or its citizenry
**2 a :** CIVILIZED ⟨*civil* society⟩ **b :** adequate in courtesy and politeness **:** MANNERLY
**3 a :** of, relating to, or based on civil law **b :** relating to private rights and to remedies sought by action or suit distinct from criminal proceedings **c :** established by law
**4 :** of, relating to, or involving the general public, their activities, needs, or ways, or civic affairs as distinguished from special (as military or religious) affairs
**5** *of time* **:** based on the mean sun and legally recognized for use in ordinary affairs ☆

☆ **SYNONYMS**
**Civil, polite, courteous, gallant, chivalrous** mean observant of the forms required by good breeding. CIVIL often suggests little more than the avoidance of overt rudeness ⟨owed the questioner a *civil* reply⟩. POLITE commonly implies polish of speech and manners and sometimes suggests an absence of cordiality ⟨if you can't be pleasant, at least be *polite*⟩. COURTEOUS implies more actively considerate or dignified politeness ⟨clerks who were unfailingly *courteous* to customers⟩. GALLANT and CHIVALROUS imply courteous attentiveness especially to women. GALLANT suggests spirited and dashing behavior and ornate expressions of courtesy ⟨a *gallant* suitor of the old school⟩. CHIVALROUS suggests high-minded and self-sacrificing behavior ⟨a *chivalrous* display of duty⟩.

\ə\ abut \ᵊ\ kitten \ər\ further \a\ ash \ā\ ace
\ä\ mop, mar \aú\ out \ch\ chin \e\ bet \ē\ easy
\g\ go \i\ hit \ī\ ice \j\ job \ŋ\ sing \ō\ go
\ȯ\ law \ȯi\ boy \th\ thin \t̲h̲\ the \ü\ loot \ú\ foot
\y\ yet \zh\ vision *see also* Guide to Pronunciation

**civil death** *noun* (1767)
: the status of a living person equivalent in its legal consequences to natural death; *specifically* : deprivation of civil rights

**civil defense** *noun* (1939)
: the system of protective measures and emergency relief activities conducted by civilians in case of hostile attack, sabotage, or natural disaster

**civil disobedience** *noun* (1866)
: refusal to obey governmental demands or commands especially as a nonviolent and usually collective means of forcing concessions from the government

**civil engineer** *noun* (circa 1792)
: an engineer whose training or occupation is in the design and construction especially of public works (as roads or harbors)
— **civil engineering** *noun*

**ci·vil·ian** \sə-'vil-yən *also* -'vi-yən\ *noun* (14th century)
**1** : a specialist in Roman or modern civil law
**2 a** : one not on active duty in a military, police, or fire-fighting force **b** : OUTSIDER 1
— **civilian** *adjective*

**ci·vil·ian·ize** \-yə-,nīz\ *transitive verb* **-ized; -iz·ing** (1870)
: to convert from military to civilian status or control
— **ci·vil·ian·i·za·tion** \-,vil-yə-nə-'zā-shən\ *noun*

**civ·i·li·sa·tion, civ·i·lise** *chiefly British variant of* CIVILIZATION, CIVILIZE

**ci·vil·i·ty** \sə-'vi-lə-tē\ *noun, plural* **-ties** (1533)
**1** *archaic* : training in the humanities
**2 a** : COURTESY, POLITENESS **b** : a polite act or expression

**civ·i·li·za·tion** \,si-və-lə-'zā-shən\ *noun* (1772)
**1 a** : a relatively high level of cultural and technological development; *specifically* : the stage of cultural development at which writing and the keeping of written records is attained **b** : the culture characteristic of a particular time or place
**2** : the process of becoming civilized
**3 a** : refinement of thought, manners, or taste **b** : a situation of urban comfort
— **civ·i·li·za·tion·al** \-shnəl, -shə-nəl\ *adjective*

**civ·i·lize** \'si-və-,līz\ *verb* **-lized; -liz·ing** (1601)
*transitive verb*
**1** : to cause to develop out of a primitive state; *especially* : to bring to a technically advanced and rationally ordered stage of cultural development
**2 a** : EDUCATE, REFINE **b** : SOCIALIZE 1
*intransitive verb*
: to acquire the customs and amenities of a civil community
— **civ·i·liz·er** *noun*

**civilized** *adjective* (1611)
: characteristic of a state of civilization ⟨*civilized* society⟩; *especially* : characterized by taste, refinement, or restraint ⟨a *civilized* way to spend the evening⟩

**civil law** *noun, often C&L capitalized* (14th century)
**1** : Roman law especially as set forth in the Justinian code
**2** : the body of private law developed from Roman law and used in Louisiana and in many countries outside the English-speaking world
**3** : the law established by a nation or state for its own jurisdiction
**4** : the law of civil or private rights

**civil liberty** *noun* (1644)
: freedom from arbitrary governmental interference (as with the right of free speech) specifically by denial of governmental power and in the U.S. especially as guaranteed by the Bill of Rights — usually used in plural

— **civil libertarian** *noun or adjective*

**civ·il·ly** \'si-və(l)-lē\ *adverb* (15th century)
**1** : in terms of civil rights, law, or matters ⟨*civilly* dead⟩
**2** : in a civil manner : POLITELY

**civil marriage** *noun* (circa 1889)
: a marriage performed by a magistrate

**civil rights** *noun plural* (1721)
: the nonpolitical rights of a citizen; *especially* : the rights of personal liberty guaranteed to U.S. citizens by the 13th and 14th amendments to the Constitution and by acts of Congress

**civil servant** *noun* (1800)
**1** : a member of a civil service
**2** : a member of the administrative staff of an international agency (as the United Nations)

**civil service** *noun* (circa 1785)
: the administrative service of a government or international agency exclusive of the armed forces; *especially* : one in which appointments are determined by competitive examination

**civil war** *noun* (15th century)
: a war between opposing groups of citizens of the same country

**Civ·i·tan** \'si-və-,tan\ *noun* [*Civitan* (*Club*)] (1926)
: a member of a major national and international service club

**civ·vy** *also* **civ·ie** \'si-vē\ *noun, plural* **civ·vies** *also* **civies** (circa 1889)
**1** *plural* : civilian clothes as distinguished from a particular uniform (as of the military)
**2** : CIVILIAN

**civvy street** *noun, often C&S capitalized* (1943)
*British* : civilian life

**¹clab·ber** \'kla-bər\ *noun* [short for *bonnyclabber*] (1634)
*chiefly dialect* : sour milk that has thickened or curdled

**²clabber** *intransitive verb* (circa 1879)
*chiefly dialect* : CURDLE

**clach·an** \'kla-kən\ *noun* [Middle English, from Scottish Gaelic] (15th century)
*Scottish & Irish* : HAMLET

**¹clack** \'klak\ *verb* [Middle English, of imitative origin] (13th century)
*intransitive verb*
**1** : CHATTER, PRATTLE
**2** : to make an abrupt striking sound or series of sounds
**3** *of fowl* : CACKLE, CLUCK
*transitive verb*
**1** : to cause to make a clatter
**2** : to produce with a chattering sound; *specifically* : BLAB
— **clack·er** *noun*

**²clack** *noun* (15th century)
**1 a** : rapid continuous talk : CHATTER **b** : TONGUE
**2** *archaic* : an object (as a valve) that produces clapping or rattling noises usually in regular rapid sequence
**3** : a sound of clacking ⟨the *clack* of a typewriter⟩

**Clac·to·ni·an** \klak-'tō-nē-ən\ *adjective* [*Clacton*-on-Sea, England] (1932)
: of or relating to a Lower Paleolithic culture usually characterized by stone flakes with a half cone at the point of striking

**¹clad** \'klad\ *past and past participle of* CLOTHE

**²clad** *adjective* [Middle English, past participle of *clothen* to clothe] (14th century)
**1** : being covered or clothed ⟨ivy-*clad* buildings⟩
**2** *of a coin* : consisting of outer layers of one metal bonded to a core of a different metal

**³clad** *transitive verb* **clad; clad·ding** (1939)
: SHEATHE, FACE; *specifically* : to cover (a metal) with another metal by bonding

**⁴clad** *noun* (1941)
**1 a** : a composite material formed by cladding
**b** : a clad coin

**2** : CLADDING; *specifically* : the outer layer of a clad coin

**clad-** *or* **clado-** *combining form* [New Latin, from Greek *klad-, klado-,* from *klados* branch, shoot of a tree; akin to Old English *holt* woods — more at HOLT]
: slip : sprout ⟨*clado*phyll⟩

**clad·ding** \'kla-diŋ\ *noun* (1936)
: something that covers or overlays; *specifically* : metal coating bonded to a metal core

**clade** \'klād\ *noun* [Greek *klados*] (1911)
: a group of biological taxa (as species) that includes all descendants of one common ancestor

**cla·dis·tics** \klə-'dis-tiks, kla-\ *noun plural but singular in construction* (1965)
: a system of biological taxonomy that defines taxa uniquely by shared characteristics not found in ancestral groups and uses inferred evolutionary relationships to arrange taxa in a branching hierarchy such that all members of a given taxon have the same ancestors
— **cla·dist** \'kla-dist\ *noun*
— **cla·dis·tic** \-'dis-tik\ *adjective*
— **cla·dis·ti·cal·ly** \-ti-k(ə-)lē\ *adverb*

**cla·doc·er·an** \klə-'dä-sə-rən\ *noun* [New Latin *Cladocera*, from *clad-* + Greek *keras* horn — more at HORN] (1909)
: any of an order (Cladocera) of minute chiefly freshwater branchiopod crustaceans that includes the water fleas

**clad·ode** \'kla-,dōd\ *noun* [New Latin *cladodium,* from Greek *klados*] (1870)
: CLADOPHYLL
— **cla·do·di·al** \kla-'dō-dē-əl\ *adjective*

**clad·o·gen·e·sis** \,kla-də-'je-nə-səs\ *noun* (1953)
: evolutionary change characterized by treelike branching of taxa — compare ANAGENESIS
— **clad·o·ge·net·ic** \,kla-dō-jə-'ne-tik\ *adjective*
— **clad·o·ge·net·i·cal·ly** \-ti-k(ə-)lē\ *adverb*

**clad·o·gram** \'kla-də-,gram\ *noun* (1966)
: a branching diagrammatic tree used in cladistic classification to illustrate phylogenetic relationships

**clad·o·phyll** \'kla-də-,fil\ *noun* (1879)
: a flattened photosynthetic branch assuming the form of and closely resembling an ordinary foliage leaf

**¹claim** \'klām\ *transitive verb* [Middle English, from Middle French *clamer,* from Latin *clamare* to cry out, shout; akin to Latin *calare* to call — more at LOW] (14th century)
**1 a** : to ask for especially as a right ⟨*claimed* the inheritance⟩ **b** : to call for : REQUIRE ⟨this matter *claims* our attention⟩ **c** : TAKE 16b ⟨the accident *claimed* her life⟩
**2** : to take as the rightful owner ⟨went to *claim* their bags at the station⟩
**3 a** : to assert in the face of possible contradiction : MAINTAIN ⟨*claimed* that he'd been cheated⟩ **b** : to claim to have ⟨organization . . . which *claims* 11,000 . . . members —*Rolling Stone*⟩ **c** : to assert to be rightfully one's own ⟨*claimed* responsibility for the attack⟩
*synonym* see DEMAND
— **claim·able** \'klā-mə-bəl\ *adjective*

**²claim** *noun* (14th century)
**1** : a demand for something due or believed to be due ⟨insurance *claim*⟩
**2 a** : a right to something; *specifically* : a title to a debt, privilege, or other thing in the possession of another **b** : an assertion open to challenge ⟨a *claim* of authenticity⟩
**3** : something that is claimed; *especially* : a tract of land staked out

**claim·ant** \'klā-mənt\ *noun* (15th century)
: one that asserts a right or title ⟨a *claimant* to an estate⟩

**claim·er** \'klā-mər\ *noun* (15th century)
**1** : one that claims

**2 :** a horse running in a claiming race
**claiming race** *noun* (1935)
: a horse race in which each entry is offered for sale for a specified price that must be deposited before the race

**clair·au·di·ence** \klar-'ȯ-dē-ən(t)s, kler-, -'ä-\ *noun* [*clair-* (as in *clairvoyance*) + *audience* (act of hearing)] (1864)
: the power or faculty of hearing something not present to the ear but regarded as having objective reality
— **clair·au·di·ent** \-ənt\ *adjective*
— **clair·au·di·ent·ly** *adverb*

**clair·voy·ance** \klar-'vȯi-ən(t)s, kler-\ *noun* (1840)
**1 :** the power or faculty of discerning objects not present to the senses
**2 :** ability to perceive matters beyond the range of ordinary perception **:** PENETRATION

**¹clair·voy·ant** \-ənt\ *adjective* [French, from *clair* clear (from Latin *clarus*) + *voyant*, present participle of *voir* to see, from Latin *vidēre* — more at WIT] (1671)
**1 :** unusually perceptive **:** DISCERNING
**2 :** of or relating to clairvoyance
— **clair·voy·ant·ly** *adverb*

**²clairvoyant** *noun* (1851)
: one having the power of clairvoyance

**¹clam** \'klam\ *noun* [Middle English, from Old English *clamm* bond, fetter; akin to Old High German *klamma* constriction, Latin *glomus* ball] (before 12th century)
: CLAMP, CLASP

**²clam** *noun, often attributive* [¹*clam;* from the clamping action of the shells] (circa 1520)
**1 a :** any of numerous edible marine bivalve mollusks living in sand or mud **b :** a freshwater mussel
**2 :** a stolid or closemouthed person
**3 :** CLAMSHELL
**4 :** DOLLAR 3

**³clam** *intransitive verb* **clammed; clam·ming** (1636)
: to gather clams especially by digging
— **clam·mer** \'kla-mər\ *noun*

**cla·mant** \'klā-mənt, 'kla-\ *adjective* [Latin *clamant-, clamans,* present participle of *clamare* to cry out] (1639)
**1 :** CLAMOROUS, BLATANT
**2 :** demanding attention **:** URGENT
— **cla·mant·ly** *adverb*

**clam·bake** \'klam-,bāk\ *noun* (1835)
**1 a :** an outdoor party; *especially* **:** a seashore outing where food is usually cooked on heated rocks covered by seaweed **b :** the food served at a clambake
**2 :** a gathering characterized by noisy sociability; *especially* **:** a political rally

**clam·ber** \'klam-bər, 'kla-mər\ *intransitive verb* **clam·bered; clam·ber·ing** \'klamb(ə-)riŋ, 'klam-riŋ, 'kla-mər-iŋ\ [Middle English *clambren;* akin to Old English *climban* to climb] (14th century)
: to climb awkwardly (as by scrambling) ⟨*clambered* over the rocks⟩
— **clam·ber·er** \-bər-ər, -mər-ər\ *noun*

**clam·my** \'kla-mē\ *adjective* **clam·mi·er; -est** [Middle English, probably from *clammen* to smear, stick, from Old English *clǣman;* akin to Old English *clǣg* clay] (14th century)
**1 :** being damp, soft, sticky, and usually cool ⟨a *clammy* and intensely cold mist —Charles Dickens⟩
**2 :** lacking normal human warmth ⟨the *clammy* atmosphere of an institution⟩
— **clam·mi·ly** \'kla-mə-lē\ *adverb*
— **clam·mi·ness** \'kla-mē-nəs\ *noun*

**¹clam·or** \'kla-mər\ *noun* [Middle English,

from Middle French *clamour,* from Latin *clamor,* from *clamare* to cry out — more at CLAIM] (14th century)
**1 a :** noisy shouting **b :** a loud continuous noise
**2 :** insistent public expression (as of support or protest) ⟨a *clamor* against increased taxes⟩

**²clamor** *verb* **clam·ored; clam·or·ing** \'klam-riŋ, 'kla-mər-iŋ\ (14th century)
*intransitive verb*
**1 :** to make a din
**2 :** to become loudly insistent ⟨*clamored* for his impeachment⟩
*transitive verb*
**1 :** to utter or proclaim insistently and noisily
**2 :** to influence by means of clamor

**³clamor** *transitive verb* [origin unknown] (1611)
*obsolete* **:** SILENCE

**clam·or·ous** \'klam-rəs, 'kla-mər-əs\ *adjective* (15th century)
**1 :** marked by confused din or outcry **:** TUMULTUOUS ⟨the busy *clamorous* market⟩
**2 :** noisily insistent
**synonym** see VOCIFEROUS
— **clam·or·ous·ly** *adverb*
— **clam·or·ous·ness** *noun*

**clam·our** \'kla-mər\ *chiefly British variant of* CLAMOR

**¹clamp** \'klamp\ *noun* [Middle English, probably from (assumed) Middle Dutch *klampe;* akin to Old English *clamm* bond, fetter — more at CLAM] (14th century)
**1 :** a device designed to bind or constrict or to press two or more parts together so as to hold them firmly
**2 :** any of various instruments or appliances having parts brought together for holding or compressing something

**²clamp** *transitive verb* (circa 1696)
**1 :** to fasten with or as if with a clamp
**2 a :** to place by decree **:** IMPOSE — often used with *on* ⟨*clamped* on a curfew after the riots⟩ **b :** to hold tightly

**clamp·down** \'klamp-,daùn\ *noun* (1940)
: the act or action of making regulations and restrictions more stringent ⟨a *clampdown* on charge accounts, bank loans, and other inflationary influences —*Time*⟩

**clamp down** *intransitive verb* (1940)
: to impose restrictions **:** CRACK DOWN ⟨the police are *clamping* down on speeders⟩

**clams casino** *noun plural but singular or plural in construction, often 2d C capitalized* (1952)
: clams on the half shell usually topped with green pepper and baked or broiled

**clam·shell** \'klam-,shel\ *noun* (circa 1520)
**1 :** the shell of a clam
**2 a :** a bucket or grapple (as on a dredge) having two hinged jaws **b :** an excavating machine having a clamshell **c :** either of a pair of doors (as in an airplane tail) that open out and away from each other

**clam up** *intransitive verb* (1916)
: to become silent

**clam worm** *noun* (1885)
: any of several large burrowing polychaete worms (as a nereid) often used as bait

**clan** \'klan\ *noun* [Middle English, from Scottish Gaelic *clann* offspring, clan, from Old Irish *cland* plant, offspring, from Latin *planta* plant] (15th century)
**1 a :** a Celtic group especially in the Scottish Highlands comprising a number of households whose heads claim descent from a common ancestor **b :** a group of people tracing descent from a common ancestor
**2 :** a group united by a common interest or common characteristics

**clan·des·tine** \klan-'des-tən *also* -,tīn *or* -,tēn *or* 'klan-dəs-\ *adjective* [Middle French or Latin; Middle French *clandestin,* from Latin *clan-*

*destinus,* from *clam* secretly; akin to Latin *celare* to hide — more at HELL] (1566)
: marked by, held in, or conducted with secrecy **:** SURREPTITIOUS
**synonym** see SECRET
— **clan·des·tine·ly** *adverb*
— **clan·des·tine·ness** *noun*
— **clan·des·tin·i·ty** \,klan-də-'sti-nə-tē, -des-'ti-\ *noun*

**¹clang** \'klaŋ\ *verb* [Latin *clangere;* akin to Greek *klazein* to scream, bark, Old English *hliehhan* to laugh] (1576)
*intransitive verb*
**1 a :** to make a loud metallic ringing sound ⟨anvils *clanged*⟩ **b :** to go with a clang
**2 :** to utter the characteristic harsh cry of a bird
*transitive verb*
: to cause to clang ⟨*clang* a bell⟩

**²clang** *noun* (1596)
**1 :** a loud ringing metallic sound ⟨the *clang* of a fire alarm⟩
**2 :** a harsh cry of a bird (as a crane or goose)

**clang·er** \'klaŋ-ər\ *noun* (1948)
*British* **:** a conspicuous blunder — often used in the phrase *drop a clanger*

**¹clan·gor** \'klaŋ-ər *also* -gər\ *noun* [Latin *clangor,* from *clangere*] (1593)
: a resounding clang or medley of clangs ⟨the *clangor* of hammers⟩
— **clan·gor·ous** \-(g)ə-rəs\ *adjective*
— **clan·gor·ous·ly** *adverb*

**²clangor** *intransitive verb* (1837)
: to make a clangor

**clan·gour** \'klaŋ-ər, -gər\ *chiefly British variant of* CLANGOR

**¹clank** \'klaŋk\ *verb* [probably imitative] (1656)
*intransitive verb*
**1 :** to make a clank or series of clanks ⟨the radiator hissed and *clanked*⟩
**2 :** to go with or as if with a clank ⟨tanks *clanking* through the streets⟩
*transitive verb*
: to cause to clank
— **clank·ing·ly** \'klaŋ-kiŋ-lē\ *adverb*

**²clank** *noun* (1656)
: a sharp brief metallic ringing sound

**clan·nish** \'kla-nish\ *adjective* (1776)
**1 :** of or relating to a clan
**2 :** tending to associate only with a select group of similar background or status
— **clan·nish·ly** *adverb*
— **clan·nish·ness** *noun*

**clans·man** \'klanz-mən\ *noun* (1810)
: a member of a clan

**¹clap** \'klap\ *verb* **clapped** *also* **clapt; clap·ping** [Middle English *clappen,* from Old English *clæppan* to throb; akin to Old High German *klaphōn* to beat] (14th century)
*transitive verb*
**1 :** to strike (as two flat hard surfaces) together so as to produce a sharp percussive noise
**2 a :** to strike (the hands) together repeatedly usually in applause **b :** APPLAUD
**3 :** to strike with the flat of the hand in a friendly way ⟨*clapped* his friend on the shoulder⟩
**4 :** to place, put, or set especially energetically ⟨*clap* him into jail⟩ ⟨since I first *clapped* eyes on it⟩
**5 :** to improvise hastily
*intransitive verb*
**1 :** to produce a percussive sound; *especially* **:** SLAM
**2 :** to go abruptly or briskly
**3 :** APPLAUD

**²clap** *noun* (13th century)
**1 :** a device that makes a clapping noise

clam 1a: *a* incurrent orifice, *b* siphon, *c* excurrent orifice, *d* mantle, *e* shell, *f* foot

\ə\ abut \ᵊ\ kitten \ər\ further \a\ ash \ā\ ace
\ä\ mop, mar \aù\ out \ch\ chin \e\ bet \ē\ easy
\g\ go \i\ hit \ī\ ice \j\ job \ŋ\ sing \ō\ go
\ȯ\ law \ȯi\ boy \th\ thin \t͟h\ the \ü\ loot \ù\ foot
\y\ yet \zh\ vision *see also* Guide to Pronunciation

**2** *obsolete* **:** a sudden stroke of fortune and especially ill fortune
**3 :** a loud percussive noise; *specifically* **:** a sudden crash of thunder
**4 a :** a sudden blow **b :** a friendly slap
**5 :** the sound of clapping hands; *especially* **:** APPLAUSE

**³clap** *noun* [Middle French *clapoir* bubo] (1587)
**:** GONORRHEA — often used with *the*

**clap·board** \'kla-bərd; 'kla(p)-,bōrd, -,bȯrd\ *noun* [part translation of Dutch *klaphout* stave wood] (circa 1520)
**1** *archaic* **:** a size of board for making staves and wainscoting
**2 :** a narrow board usually thicker at one edge than the other used for siding
**3** \'klap-,bōrd, -,bȯrd\ **:** a pair of hinged boards one of which has a slate with data identifying a piece of film and which are banged together in front of a motion-picture camera at the start of a take to facilitate editing — called also *clapper board*
— **clapboard** *transitive verb*

**clapped–out** \,klapt-'aút\ *adjective* (1946)
*British* **:** WORN-OUT; *also* **:** TIRED

**clap·per** \'kla-pər\ *noun* (14th century)
**:** one that claps: as **a :** the tongue of a bell **b :** a mechanical device that makes noise especially by the banging of one part against another **c :** a person who applauds

**clap·per·claw** \'kla-pər-,klȯ\ *transitive verb* [perhaps from *clapper* + *claw* (verb)] (1590)
**1** *dialect English* **:** to claw with the nails
**2** *dialect English* **:** SCOLD, REVILE

**¹clap·trap** \'klap-,trap\ *noun* [²*clap;* from its attempt to win applause] (1799)
**:** pretentious nonsense **:** TRASH

**²claptrap** *adjective* (1815)
**:** characterized by or suggestive of claptrap; *especially* **:** of a cheap showy nature ⟨*claptrap* sentiment⟩

**claque** \'klak\ *noun* [French, from *claquer* to clap, of imitative origin] (1864)
**1 :** a group hired to applaud at a performance
**2 :** a group of sycophants

**cla·queur** \kla-'kər\ *noun* [French, from *claquer* to clap] (1837)
**:** a member of a claque

**clar·et** \'klar-ət\ *noun* [Middle English, from Middle French (*vin*) *claret* clear wine, from *claret* clear, from *cler* clear] (1707)
**1 :** a red Bordeaux wine; *also* **:** a similar wine produced elsewhere
**2 :** a dark purplish red
— **claret** *adjective*

**clar·i·fy** \'klar-ə-,fī\ *verb* **-fied; -fy·ing** [Middle English *clarifien,* from Middle French *clarifier,* from Late Latin *clarificare,* from Latin *clarus* clear — more at CLEAR] (14th century)
*transitive verb*
**1 :** to make (as a liquid) clear or pure usually by freeing from suspended matter
**2 :** to free of confusion
**3 :** to make understandable
*intransitive verb*
**:** to become clear
— **clar·i·fi·ca·tion** \,klar-ə-fə-'kā-shən\ *noun*
— **clar·i·fi·er** \'klar-ə-,fī-(ə)r\ *noun*

**clar·i·net** \,klar-ə-'net, 'klar-ə-nət\ *noun* [French *clarinette,* probably ultimately from Medieval Latin *clarion-, clario*] (1796)
**:** a single-reed woodwind instrument having a cylindrical tube with a moderately flared bell and a usual range from D below middle C upward for 3½ octaves
— **clar·i·net·ist** *or* **clar·i·net·tist** \,klar-ə-'ne-tist\ *noun*

**¹clar·i·on** \'klar-ē-ən\ *noun* [Middle English, from Middle French & Medieval Latin; Middle French *clairon,* from Medieval Latin *clarion-, clario,* from Latin *clarus*] (14th century)

**1 :** a medieval trumpet with clear shrill tones
**2 :** the sound of or as if of a clarion

**²clarion** *adjective* (1841)
**:** brilliantly clear ⟨her *clarion* top notes⟩; *also* **:** loud and clear ⟨a *clarion* call to action⟩

**clar·i·ty** \'klar-ə-tē\ *noun* [Middle English *clarite,* from Latin *claritat-, claritas,* from *clarus*] (1616)
**:** the quality or state of being clear **:** LUCIDITY

**clark·ia** \'klär-kē-ə\ *noun* [New Latin, from William *Clark*] (1827)
**:** any of a genus (*Clarkia*) of showy annual herbs of the evening-primrose family that are native to the Pacific slope of North America and southwestern South America

**cla·ro** \'klär-(,)ō\ *noun, plural* **claros** [Spanish, from *claro* light, from Latin *clarus*] (1891)
**:** a light-colored usually mild cigar

**clary** \'klar-ē, 'kler-\ *noun, plural* **clar·ies** [Middle English *clarie,* from Middle French *sclaree,* from Medieval Latin *sclareia*] (14th century)
**:** an aromatic mint (*Salvia sclarea*) of southern Europe that is widely cultivated especially as an ornamental

**¹clash** \'klash\ *verb* [imitative] (circa 1500)
*intransitive verb*
**1 :** to make a clash ⟨cymbals *clashed*⟩
**2 :** to come into conflict ⟨where ignorant armies *clash* by night —Matthew Arnold⟩; *also* **:** to be incompatible ⟨the colors *clashed*⟩
*transitive verb*
**:** to cause to clash
— **clash·er** *noun*

**²clash** *noun* (1513)
**1 :** a noisy usually metallic sound of collision
**2 a :** a hostile encounter **:** SKIRMISH **b :** a sharp conflict ⟨a *clash* of opinions⟩

**¹clasp** \'klasp\ *noun* [Middle English *claspe*] (14th century)
**1 a :** a device (as a hook) for holding objects or parts together **b :** a device (as a bar) attached to a military medal to indicate an additional award of the medal or the action or service for which it was awarded
**2 :** a holding or enveloping with or as if with the hands or arms

**²clasp** *transitive verb* (14th century)
**1 :** to fasten with or as if with a clasp ⟨a robe *clasped* with a brooch⟩
**2 :** to enclose and hold with the arms; *specifically* **:** EMBRACE
**3 :** to seize with or as if with the hand **:** GRASP

**clasp·er** \'klas-pər\ *noun* (circa 1847)
**:** a male copulatory structure: **a :** one of a pair of external anal processes of an insect that are used to grasp a female **b :** one of a pair of organs that are extensions of the pelvic fins of cartilaginous fishes

**clasp knife** *noun* (circa 1755)
**:** POCKETKNIFE; *especially* **:** a large one-bladed folding knife having a catch to hold the blade open

**¹class** \'klas\ *noun, often attributive* [French *classe,* from Latin *classis* group called to military service, fleet, class; perhaps akin to Latin *calare* to call — more at LOW] (1602)
**1 a :** a body of students meeting regularly to study the same subject **b :** the period during which such a body meets **c :** a course of instruction **d :** a body of students or alumni whose year of graduation is the same
**2 a :** a group sharing the same economic or social status ⟨the working *class*⟩ **b :** social rank; *especially* **:** high social rank **c :** high quality **:** ELEGANCE
**3 :** a group, set, or kind sharing common attributes: as **a :** a major category in biological taxonomy ranking above the order and below the phylum or division **b :** a collection of adjacent and discrete or continuous values of a random variable **c :** SET 21
**4 :** a division or rating based on grade or quality

**5 :** the best of its kind ⟨the *class* of the league⟩

**²class** *transitive verb* (1705)
**:** CLASSIFY

**class act** *noun* (1976)
**:** an example of outstanding quality or prestige

**class action** *noun* (1952)
**:** a legal action undertaken by one or more plaintiffs on behalf of themselves and all other persons having an identical interest in the alleged wrong

**class–conscious** *adjective* (1903)
**1 :** actively aware of one's common status with others in a particular economic or social level of society
**2 :** believing in class struggle
— **class consciousness** *noun*

**¹clas·sic** \'kla-sik\ *adjective* [French or Latin; French *classique,* from Latin *classicus* of the highest class of Roman citizens, of the first rank, from *classis*] (circa 1604)
**1 a :** serving as a standard of excellence **:** of recognized value **b :** TRADITIONAL, ENDURING **c :** characterized by simple tailored lines in fashion year after year ⟨a *classic* suit⟩
**2 :** of or relating to the ancient Greeks and Romans or their culture **:** CLASSICAL
**3 a :** historically memorable **b :** noted because of special literary or historical associations ⟨Paris is the *classic* refuge of expatriates⟩
**4 a :** AUTHENTIC, AUTHORITATIVE **b :** TYPICAL ⟨a *classic* example of chicanery⟩
**5** *capitalized* **:** of or relating to the period of highest development of Mesoamerican and especially Mayan culture about A.D. 300–900

**²classic** *noun* (1711)
**1 :** a literary work of ancient Greece or Rome
**2 a :** a work of enduring excellence; *also* **:** its author **b :** an authoritative source
**3 :** a typical or perfect example
**4 :** a traditional event ⟨a football *classic*⟩

**clas·si·cal** \'kla-si-kəl\ *adjective* [Latin *classicus*] (1599)
**1 :** STANDARD, CLASSIC
**2 a :** of or relating to the ancient Greek and Roman world and especially to its literature, art, architecture, or ideals **b :** versed in the classics
**3 a :** of or relating to music of the late 18th and early 19th centuries characterized by an emphasis on balance, clarity, and moderation **b :** of, relating to, or being music in the educated European tradition that includes such forms as art song, chamber music, opera, and symphony as distinguished from folk or popular music or jazz
**4 a :** AUTHORITATIVE, TRADITIONAL **b** (1) **:** of or relating to a form or system considered of first significance in earlier times ⟨*classical* Mendelian genetics⟩ (2) **:** not involving relativity, wave mechanics, or quantum theory ⟨*classical* physics⟩ **c :** conforming to a pattern of usage sanctioned by a body of literature rather than by everyday speech
**5 :** concerned with or giving instruction in the humanities, the fine arts, and the broad aspects of science ⟨a *classical* curriculum⟩

**classical conditioning** *noun* (1949)
**:** conditioning in which the conditioned stimulus (as the sound of a bell) is paired with and precedes the unconditioned stimulus (as the sight of food) until the conditioned stimulus alone is sufficient to elicit the response (as salivation in a dog) — compare OPERANT CONDITIONING

**clas·si·cal·i·ty** \,kla-sə-'ka-lə-tē\ *noun* (1819)
**1 :** the quality or state of being classic
**2 :** classical scholarship

**clas·si·cal·ly** \'kla-si-k(ə-)lē\ *adverb* (1772)
**1 :** in a classic or classical manner ⟨*classically* exact forms of the dance⟩ ⟨*classically* trained⟩
**2 a :** in classic or traditional circumstances **:** TYPICALLY ⟨*classically,* the whole fish is stuffed⟩ **b :** as a classic example ⟨*classically* bad writing⟩

**clas·si·cism** \'kla-sə-ˌsi-zəm\ *noun* (1830)
**1 a :** the principles or style embodied in the literature, art, or architecture of ancient Greece and Rome **b :** classical scholarship **c :** a classical idiom or expression
**2 :** adherence to traditional standards (as of simplicity, restraint, and proportion) that are universally and enduringly valid
**clas·si·cist** \-sist\ *noun* (1830)
**1 :** an advocate or follower of classicism
**2 :** a classical scholar
— **clas·si·cis·tic** \ˌkla-sə-'sis-tik\ *adjective*
**clas·si·cize** \'kla-sə-ˌsīz\ *verb* **-cized; -ciz·ing** (1854)
*transitive verb*
**:** to make classic or classical
*intransitive verb*
**:** to follow classic style
**clas·si·co** \'kla-si-(ˌ)kō\ *adjective* [Italian, from Latin *classicus*] (1968)
**:** produced in a delimited area of Italy known for its standards of quality ⟨Chianti *classico*⟩
**clas·si·fi·ca·tion** \ˌkla-sə-fə-'kā-shən\ *noun* (1790)
**1 :** the act or process of classifying
**2 a :** systematic arrangement in groups or categories according to established criteria; *specifically* **:** TAXONOMY **b :** CLASS, CATEGORY
— **clas·si·fi·ca·to·ry** \'kla-sə-fi-kə-ˌtōr-ē, kla-'si-fə-, -ˌtȯr-; 'kla-sə-fə-ˌkā-tə-rē\ *adjective* .
**clas·si·fied** \'kla-sə-ˌfīd\ *adjective* (1889)
**1 :** divided into classes or placed in a class ⟨*classified* ads⟩
**2 :** withheld from general circulation for reasons of national security ⟨*classified* information⟩
**clas·si·fi·er** \'kla-sə-ˌfī(-ə)r\ *noun* (1819)
**1 :** one that classifies; *specifically* **:** a machine for sorting out the constituents of a substance (as ore)
**2 :** a word or morpheme used with numerals or with nouns designating countable or measurable objects
**clas·si·fy** \'kla-sə-ˌfī\ *transitive verb* **-fied; -fy·ing** (1799)
**1 :** to arrange in classes ⟨*classifying* books according to subject matter⟩
**2 :** to assign (as a document) to a category
— **clas·si·fi·able** \ˌkla-sə-'fī-ə-bəl\ *adjective*
**class interval** *noun* (1929)
**:** CLASS 3b; *also* **:** its numerical width
**clas·sis** \'kla-sis\ *noun, plural* **clas·ses** \'kla-ˌsēz\ [New Latin, from Latin, class] (1593)
**1 :** a governing body in some Reformed churches (as in the former Reformed Church in the U.S.) corresponding to a presbytery
**2 :** the district governed by a classis
**class·ism** \'kla-ˌsi-zəm\ *noun* (1842)
**:** prejudice or discrimination based on class
— **class·ist** \'kla-sist\ *adjective*
**class·less** \'klas-ləs\ *adjective* (1878)
**1 :** belonging to no particular social class
**2 :** free from distinctions of social class ⟨a *classless* society⟩
— **class·less·ness** *noun*
**class·mate** \-ˌmāt\ *noun* (1713)
**:** a member of the same class in a school or college
**class·room** \-ˌrüm, -ˌrum\ *noun* (1870)
**:** a place where classes meet
**classy** \'kla-sē\ *adjective* **class·i·er; -est** (1891)
**:** ELEGANT, STYLISH ⟨a *classy* clientele⟩; *also* **:** notably superior ⟨a *classy* outfielder⟩
— **class·i·ness** *noun*
**clast** \'klast\ *noun* [Greek *klastos* broken, from *klan* to break; perhaps akin to Latin *clades* disaster] (1952)
**:** a fragment of rock
**clas·tic** \'klas-tik\ *adjective* [International Scientific Vocabulary] (1877)
**:** made up of fragments of preexisting rocks ⟨a *clastic* sediment⟩

— **clastic** *noun*
**clath·rate** \'kla-ˌthrāt\ *adjective* [Latin *clathratus*, furnished with a lattice, from *clathri* (plural) lattice, from Greek *klēithron* bar, from *kleiein* to close — more at CLAVICLE] (1906)
**:** relating to or being a compound formed by the inclusion of molecules of one kind in cavities of the crystal lattice of another
— **clathrate** *noun*
¹**clat·ter** \'kla-tər\ *verb* [Middle English *clatren*, from (assumed) Old English *clatrian*; of imitative origin] (13th century)
*intransitive verb*
**1 :** to make a rattling sound ⟨the dishes *clattered* on the shelf⟩
**2 :** to talk noisily or rapidly
**3 :** to move or go with a clatter ⟨*clattered* down the stairs⟩
*transitive verb*
**:** to cause to clatter
— **clat·ter·er** \-tər-ər\ *noun*
— **clat·ter·ing·ly** \'kla-tə-riŋ-lē\ *adverb*
²**clatter** *noun* (14th century)
**1 :** a rattling sound (as of hard bodies striking together) ⟨the *clatter* of pots and pans⟩
**2 :** COMMOTION ⟨the midday *clatter* of the business district⟩
**3 :** noisy chatter
— **clat·tery** \'kla-tə-rē\ *adjective*
**clau·di·ca·tion** \ˌklȯ-də-'kā-shən\ *noun* [Latin *claudication-, claudicatio*, from *claudicare* to limp, from *claudus* lame] (15th century)
**:** the quality or state of being lame **:** LIMPING
**claus·al** \'klȯ-zəl\ *adjective* (1904)
**:** relating to or of the nature of a clause
**clause** \'klȯz\ *noun* [Middle English, from Old French, from Medieval Latin *clausa* close of a rhetorical period, from Latin, feminine of *clausus*, past participle of *claudere* to close — more at CLOSE] (13th century)
**1 :** a group of words containing a subject and predicate and functioning as a member of a complex or compound sentence
**2 :** a separate section of a discourse or writing; *specifically* **:** a distinct article in a formal document
**claus·tral** \'klȯs-trəl\ *adjective* [Middle English, from Medieval Latin *claustralis*, from *claustrum* cloister, from Latin, bar, bolt, confining space, from *claudere*] (15th century)
**:** CLOISTRAL
**claus·tro·pho·bia** \ˌklȯs-trə-'fō-bē-ə\ *noun* [New Latin, from Latin *claustrum* + New Latin *-phobia*] (1879)
**:** abnormal dread of being in closed or narrow spaces
— **claus·tro·phobe** \'klȯs-trə-ˌfōb\ *noun*
**claus·tro·pho·bic** \ˌklȯs-trə-'fō-bik\ *adjective* (circa 1889)
**1 :** affected with or inclined to claustrophobia
**2 :** inducing or suggesting claustrophobia
— **claus·tro·pho·bi·cal·ly** \-bi-k(ə-)lē\ *adverb*
**claus·trum** \'klȯs-trəm, 'klaus-\ *noun, plural* **claus·tra** \-trə\ [New Latin, from Latin, bar] (1848)
**:** the one of the four basal ganglia in each cerebral hemisphere that consists of a thin lamina of gray matter separated from the lenticular nucleus by a layer of white matter
**cla·vate** \'klā-ˌvāt\ *adjective* [New Latin *clavatus*, from Latin *clava* club, from *clavus* nail, knot in wood] (1813)
**:** gradually thickening near the distal end
**:** shaped like a club
¹**clave** *past of* CLEAVE
²**clave** \'klä-(ˌ)vā, 'kläv\ *noun* [American Spanish, from Spanish, keystone, clef, from Latin *clavis*] (1928)
**:** one of a pair of cylindrical hardwood sticks that are used as a percussion instrument
**cla·ver** \'klā-vər\ *intransitive verb* [probably of Celtic origin; akin to Scottish Gaelic *clabaire* babbler] (circa 1605)
*chiefly Scottish* **:** PRATE, GOSSIP
— **claver** *noun, chiefly Scottish*

**clav·i·chord** \'kla-və-ˌkȯrd\ *noun* [Medieval Latin *clavichordium*, from Latin *clavis* key + *chorda* string — more at CORD] (15th century)
**:** an early keyboard instrument having strings struck by tangents attached directly to the key ends
— **clav·i·chord·ist** \-ˌkȯr-dist\ *noun*
**clav·i·cle** \'kla-vi-kəl\ *noun* [French *clavicule*, from New Latin *clavicula*, from Latin, diminutive of Latin *clavis*; akin to Greek *kleid-, kleis* key, *kleiein* to close] (1615)
**:** a bone of the vertebrate pectoral girdle typically serving to link the scapula and sternum — called also *collarbone*
— **cla·vic·u·lar** \kla-'vi-kyə-lər, klə-\ *adjective*
**cla·vier** \klə-'vir; 'klā-vē-ər, 'kla-\ *noun* [French, from Old French, key bearer, from Latin *clavis*] (1708)
**1 :** the keyboard of a musical instrument
**2** [German *Klavier*, from French *clavier*] **:** an early keyboard instrument
— **cla·vier·ist** \klə-'vir-ist; 'klā-vē-ə-rist, 'kla-\ *noun*
— **cla·vier·is·tic** \klə-ˌvi-'ris-tik; ˌklā-vē-ə-'ris-tik, ˌkla-\ *adjective*
¹**claw** \'klȯ\ *noun, often attributive* [Middle English *clawe*, from Old English *clawu* hoof, claw; akin to Old Norse *klō* claw, and probably to Old English *cliewen* ball — more at CLEW] (before 12th century)
**1 :** a sharp usually slender and curved nail on the toe of an animal
**2 :** any of various sharp curved processes especially at the end of a limb (as of an insect); *also* **:** a limb ending in such a process
**3 :** one of the pincerlike organs terminating some limbs of various arthropods (as a lobster or scorpion)
**4 :** something that resembles a claw; *specifically* **:** the forked end of a tool (as a hammer)
— **clawed** \'klȯd\ *adjective*
— **claw·like** \-ˌlīk\ *adjective*
²**claw** (before 12th century)
*transitive verb*
**:** to rake, seize, dig, or progress with or as if with claws
*intransitive verb*
**:** to scrape, scratch, dig, or pull with or as if with claws
**claw back** *transitive verb* (1953)
*chiefly British* **:** to get back (as money) by strenuous or forceful means (as taxation)
— **claw·back** \'klȯ-ˌbak\ *noun*
**claw·ham·mer** \'klȯ-ˌha-mər\ *adjective* (1964)
**:** of or relating to a style of banjo playing using the thumb and one or more fingers picking or strumming in a downward direction
**claw hammer** *noun* (circa 1769)
**1 :** a hammer with one end of the head forked for pulling out nails
**2 :** TAILCOAT
**clay** \'klā\ *noun, often attributive* [Middle English, from Old English *clǣg*; akin to Old High German *klīwa* bran, Latin *gluten* glue, Middle Greek *glia*] (before 12th century)
**1 a :** an earthy material that is plastic when moist but hard when fired, that is composed mainly of fine particles of hydrous aluminum silicates and other minerals, and that is used for brick, tile, and pottery; *specifically* **:** soil composed chiefly of this material having particles less than a specified size **b :** EARTH, MUD
**2 a :** a substance that resembles clay in plasticity and is used for modeling **b :** the human body as distinguished from the spirit **c :** fundamental nature or character ⟨the common *clay*⟩

\ə\ **abut** \ᵊ\ **kitten** \ər\ **further** \a\ **ash** \ā\ **ace**
\ä\ **mop, mar** \au̇\ **out** \ch\ **chin** \e\ **bet** \ē\ **easy**
\g\ **go** \i\ **hit** \ī\ **ice** \j\ **job** \ŋ\ **sing** \ō\ **go**
\ȯ\ **law** \ȯi\ **boy** \th\ **thin** \t̲h̲\ **the** \ü\ **loot** \u̇\ **foot**
\y\ **yet** \zh\ **vision** *see also* Guide to Pronunciation

**3 :** CLAY COURT
— **clay·ey** \'klā-ē\ *adjective*
— **clay·ish** \'klā-ish\ *adjective*
— **clay·like** \-ˌlīk\ *adjective*
**clay·bank** \'klā-ˌbaŋk\ *noun* (1851)
: a horse of yellowish color
**clay court** *noun* (1885)
: a tennis court with a clay surface or a synthetic surface that resembles clay
**clay loam** *noun* (circa 1889)
: a loam containing from 20 to 30 percent clay
**clay mineral** *noun* (1947)
: any of a group of hydrous silicates of aluminum and sometimes other metals formed chiefly in weathering processes and occurring especially in clay and shale
**clay·more** \'klā-ˌmōr, -ˌmȯr\ *noun* [Scottish Gaelic *claidheamh mór*, literally, great sword] (1772)
: a large 2-edged sword formerly used by Scottish Highlanders; *also* : their basket-hilted broadsword
**claymore mine** *noun* [perhaps from *claymore*] (1961)
: a usually electrically fired land mine that contains steel fragments which are discharged in a predetermined direction
**clay·pan** \-ˌpan\ *noun* (1837)
**1 :** hardpan consisting mainly of clay
**2** *Australian* : a shallow depression in which water collects after rain
**clay pigeon** *noun* (1888)
: a saucer-shaped target usually made of baked clay or limestone and pitch and thrown from a trap in skeet and trapshooting
**clay·ware** \'klā-ˌwar, -ˌwer\ *noun* (1896)
: articles made of fired clay
**¹clean** \'klēn\ *adjective* [Middle English *clene*, from Old English *clǣne*; akin to Old High German *kleini* delicate, dainty] (before 12th century)
**1 a :** free from dirt or pollution ⟨changed to *clean* clothes⟩ ⟨*clean* solar energy⟩ **b :** free from contamination or disease **c :** free or relatively free from radioactivity ⟨a *clean* atomic explosion⟩
**2 a :** UNADULTERATED, PURE ⟨the *clean* thrill of one's first flight⟩ **b** *of a precious stone* : having no interior flaws visible **c :** free from growth that hinders tillage
**3 a :** free from moral corruption or sinister connections of any kind ⟨a candidate with a *clean* record⟩ **b :** free from offensive treatment of sexual subjects and from the use of obscenity ⟨a *clean* joke⟩ **c :** observing the rules : FAIR ⟨a *clean* fight⟩
**4 :** ceremonially or spiritually pure ⟨and all who are *clean* may eat flesh —Leviticus 7:19 (Revised Standard Version)⟩
**5 a :** THOROUGH, COMPLETE ⟨a *clean* break with the past⟩ **b :** deftly executed : SKILLFUL ⟨*clean* ballet technique⟩ **c :** hit beyond the reach of an opponent ⟨a *clean* single to center⟩
**6 a :** relatively free from error or blemish : CLEAR; *specifically* : LEGIBLE ⟨*clean* copy⟩ **b :** UNENCUMBERED ⟨*clean* bill of sale⟩
**7 a :** characterized by clarity and precision : TRIM ⟨a *clean* prose style⟩ ⟨architecture with *clean* almost austere lines⟩ **b :** EVEN, SMOOTH ⟨a *clean* edge⟩ ⟨a sharp blow causing a *clean* break⟩ **c :** free from impedances to smooth flow ⟨a *clean* use of water or air⟩ ⟨a *clean* airplane⟩ ⟨a ship with a *clean* bottom⟩
**8 a :** EMPTY ⟨the ship returned with a *clean* hold⟩ **b :** free from drug addiction **c** *slang* : having no contraband (as weapons or drugs) in one's possession
**9 :** habitually neat
— **clean·ness** \'klēn-nəs\ *noun*
**²clean** *adverb* (before 12th century)
**1 a :** so as to clean ⟨a new broom sweeps *clean*⟩ **b :** in a clean manner ⟨play the game *clean*⟩
**2 :** all the way : COMPLETELY ⟨the bullet went *clean* through his arm⟩

**³clean** (15th century)
*transitive verb*
**1 a :** to make clean: as (1) : to rid of dirt, impurities, or extraneous matter (2) : to rid of corruption ⟨vowing to *clean* up city hall⟩ **b :** REMOVE, ERADICATE — usually used with *up* or *off* ⟨*clean* up that mess⟩
**2 a :** STRIP, EMPTY ⟨a tree *cleaned* of fruit⟩ **b :** to remove the entrails from ⟨*clean* fish⟩ **c :** to deprive of money or possessions — often used with *out* ⟨they *cleaned* him out completely⟩
*intransitive verb*
: to undergo or perform a process of cleaning ⟨*clean* up before dinner⟩
— **clean·abil·i·ty** \ˌklē-nə-'bi-lə-tē\ *noun*
— **clean·able** \'klē-nə-bəl\ *adjective*
— **clean house 1 :** to clean a house and its furniture **2 :** to make sweeping reforms or changes (as of personnel)
— **clean one's clock :** to beat one badly in a fight or competition
— **clean up one's act :** to behave in a more acceptable manner
**⁴clean** *noun* (circa 1889)
: an act of cleaning dirt especially from the surface of something
**clean and jerk** *noun* (1939)
: a lift in weight lifting in which the weight is raised to shoulder height, held momentarily, and then quickly thrust overhead usually with a lunge or a spring from the legs — compare PRESS, SNATCH
**clean–cut** \'klēn-'kət\ *adjective* (1843)
**1 :** cut so that the surface or edge is smooth and even
**2 :** sharply defined
**3 :** of wholesome appearance
**clean·er** \'klē-nər\ *noun* (circa 1792)
**1 a :** one whose work is cleaning **b :** DRY CLEANER
**2 :** a preparation for cleaning
**3 :** an implement or machine for cleaning
**clean·hand·ed** \'klēn-'han-dəd\ *adjective* (1728)
: innocent of wrongdoing
**clean–limbed** \'klēn-'limd\ *adjective* (15th century)
: well proportioned : TRIM ⟨*clean-limbed* youths⟩
**¹clean·ly** \'klēn-lē\ *adverb* (13th century)
: in a clean manner
**²clean·ly** \'klen-lē\ *adjective* **clean·li·er; -est** (circa 1500)
**1 :** careful to keep clean : FASTIDIOUS
**2 :** habitually kept clean
— **clean·li·ness** *noun*
**clean room** \'klēn-ˌrüm, -ˌrùm\ *noun* (1963)
: a room for the manufacture or assembly of objects (as precision parts) that is maintained at a high level of cleanliness by special means
**cleanse** \'klenz\ *verb* **cleansed; cleansing** [Middle English *clensen*, from Old English *clǣnsian* to purify, from *clǣne* clean] (before 12th century)
: CLEAN; *especially* : to rid of impurities by or as if by washing
**cleans·er** \'klen-zər\ *noun* (before 12th century)
**1 :** one that cleanses
**2 :** a preparation (as a scouring powder or a skin cream) used for cleaning
**¹clean·up** \'klē-ˌnəp\ *noun* (1872)
**1 :** an act or instance of cleaning
**2 :** an exceptionally large profit : KILLING
**²cleanup** *adjective* (1937)
: being in the fourth position in the batting order of a baseball team ⟨a *cleanup* hitter⟩
— **cleanup** *adverb*
**clean up** *intransitive verb* (1920)
: to make a spectacular profit in a business enterprise or a killing in speculation or gambling
**¹clear** \'klir\ *adjective* [Middle English *clere*, from Old French *cler*, from Latin *clarus* clear,

bright; akin to Latin *calare* to call — more at LOW] (13th century)
**1 a :** BRIGHT, LUMINOUS **b :** CLOUDLESS; *specifically* : less than one-tenth covered ⟨a *clear* sky⟩ **c :** free from mist, haze, or dust ⟨a *clear* day⟩ **d :** UNTROUBLED, SERENE ⟨a *clear* gaze⟩
**2 :** CLEAN, PURE: as **a :** free from blemishes **b :** easily seen through : TRANSPARENT **c :** free from abnormal sounds on auscultation
**3 a :** easily heard **b :** easily visible : PLAIN **c :** free from obscurity or ambiguity : easily understood : UNMISTAKABLE
**4 a :** capable of sharp discernment : KEEN **b :** free from doubt : SURE
**5 :** free from guile or guilt : INNOCENT
**6 :** unhampered by restriction or limitation: as **a :** unencumbered by debts or charges **b :** NET ⟨a *clear* profit⟩ **c :** UNQUALIFIED, ABSOLUTE **d :** free from obstruction **e :** emptied of contents or cargo **f :** free from entanglement **g :** BARE, DENUDED ☆ ☆
— **clear·ness** *noun*
**²clear** *adverb* (14th century)
**1 :** in a clear manner ⟨to cry loud and *clear*⟩
**2 :** all the way ⟨drove *clear* across the state⟩
**³clear** (14th century)
*transitive verb*
**1 a :** to make clear or translucent **b :** to free from pollution or cloudiness
**2 :** to free from accusation or blame : EXONERATE, VINDICATE ⟨the opportunity to *clear* himself⟩
**3 a :** to give insight to : ENLIGHTEN **b :** to make intelligible : EXPLAIN ⟨*clear* up the mystery⟩
**4 a :** to free from what obstructs or is unneeded: as (1) : OPEN 1b ⟨*clear* a path⟩ (2) : to remove unwanted growth or items from ⟨*clear* the land of timber⟩ (3) : to rid or make a rasping noise as if ridding (the throat) of phlegm (4) : to erase stored or displayed data from (as a computer or calculator) **b :** to empty of occupants ⟨*clear* the room⟩ **c :** DISENTANGLE ⟨*clear* a fishing line⟩ **d :** to remove from an area or place ⟨*clear* the dishes from the table⟩ **e :** TRANSMIT, DISPATCH
**5 a :** to submit for approval ⟨*clear* it with me first⟩ **b :** AUTHORIZE, APPROVE ⟨*cleared* the article for publication⟩: as (1) : to certify as trustworthy ⟨*clear* a person for classified information⟩ (2) : to permit (an aircraft) to proceed usually with a specified action
**6 a :** to free from obligation or encumbrance **b :** SETTLE, DISCHARGE ⟨*clear* an account⟩ **c** (1) : to free (a ship or shipment) by payment of duties or harbor fees (2) : to pass through (customs) **d :** to gain without deduction : NET ⟨*clear* a profit⟩ **e :** to put through a clearinghouse

---

**7 a :** to go over, under, or by without touching **b :** PASS ⟨the bill *cleared* the legislature⟩ *intransitive verb* **1 a :** to become clear ⟨it *cleared* up quickly after the rain⟩ **b :** to go away : VANISH ⟨the symptoms *cleared* gradually⟩ **c :** SELL **2 a :** to obtain permission to discharge cargo **b :** to conform to regulations or pay requisite fees prior to leaving port **3 :** to pass through a clearinghouse **4 :** to go to an authority (as for approval) before becoming effective — **clear·able** \'klir-ə-bəl\ *adjective* — **clear·er** \'klir-ər\ *noun* — **clear the air** *also* **clear the atmosphere :** to remove elements of hostility, tension, confusion, or uncertainty ⟨had a long meeting to *clear the air*⟩ — **clear the decks :** to make sweeping preparations for action

⁴**clear** *noun* (1674) **1 :** a clear space or part **2 :** a high arcing shot over an opponent's head in badminton — **in the clear 1 :** in inside measurement **2 :** free from guilt or suspicion **3 :** in plaintext **:** not in code or cipher ⟨a message sent *in the clear*⟩

**clear–air turbulence** *noun* (1955) **:** sudden severe turbulence occurring in cloudless regions that causes violent jarring or buffeting of aircraft

**clear·ance** \'klir-ən(t)s\ *noun* (1540) **1 :** an act or process of clearing: as **a :** the removal of buildings from an area (as a city slum) **b :** the act of clearing a ship at the customhouse; *also* **:** the papers showing that a ship has cleared **c :** the offsetting of checks and other claims among banks through a clearinghouse **d :** certification as clear of objection **:** AUTHORIZATION ⟨security *clearance*⟩ **e :** a sale to clear out stock **f :** authorization for an aircraft to proceed especially with a specified action ⟨*clearance* to land⟩ **2 :** the distance by which one object clears another or the clear space between them **3 :** the volume of blood or plasma that could be freed of a specified constituent in a specified time (usually one minute) by its excretion into the urine through the kidneys — called also *renal clearance*

¹**clear–cut** \'klir-'kət\ *adjective* (1855) **1 :** sharply outlined : DISTINCT **2 :** free from ambiguity or uncertainty : UNAMBIGUOUS

²**clear–cut** \-,kət\ *noun* (circa 1958) **:** an area of forest which has been clear-cut; *also* **:** CLEAR-CUTTING

**clear–cut·ting** \-,kə-tiŋ\ *noun* (1922) **:** removal of all the trees in a stand of timber — **clear–cut** *verb*

**clear–eyed** \'klir-,īd\ *adjective* (1530) **:** CLEAR-SIGHTED

**clear·head·ed** \-,he-dəd\ *adjective* (1709) **1 :** having a clear understanding : PERCEPTIVE **2 :** able to think clearly — **clear·head·ed·ly** *adverb* — **clear·head·ed·ness** *noun*

**clear·ing** \'klir-iŋ\ *noun* (14th century) **1 :** the act or process of making or becoming clear **2 :** a tract of land cleared of wood and brush **3 a :** a method of exchanging and offsetting commercial papers or accounts with cash settlement only of the balances due after the clearing **b** *plural* **:** the gross amount of balances so adjusted

**clear·ing·house** \-,haüs\ *noun* (1832) **1 :** an establishment maintained by banks for settling mutual claims and accounts **2 :** a central agency for the collection, classification, and distribution especially of information; *broadly* **:** an informal channel for distributing information or assistance

**clear·ly** \'klir-lē\ *adverb* (14th century) **1 :** in a clear manner ⟨speaking *clearly*⟩

**2 :** it is clear ⟨*clearly*, a new approach is needed⟩ **usage** see HOPEFULLY

**clear out** (1792) *intransitive verb* **:** DEPART *transitive verb* **:** to drive out or away usually forcibly

**clear–sight·ed** \'klir-,sī-təd\ *adjective* (1586) **1 :** having clear vision **2 :** DISCERNING — **clear–sight·ed·ly** *adverb* — **clear–sight·ed·ness** *noun*

**clear·sto·ry** *variant of* CLERESTORY

**clear·wing** \-,wiŋ\ *noun* (1868) **:** a moth (as of the families Aegeriidae or Sphingidae) having the wings largely transparent and devoid of scales

¹**cleat** \'klēt\ *noun* [Middle English *clete* wedge, from (assumed) Old English *clēat*; akin to Middle High German *klōz* lump — more at CLOUT] (14th century) **1 a :** a wedge-shaped piece fastened to or projecting from something and serving as a support or check **b :** a wooden or metal fitting usually with two projecting horns around which a rope may be made fast **2 a :** a strip fastened across something to give strength or hold in position **b** (1) **:** a projecting piece (as on the bottom of a shoe) that furnishes a grip (2) *plural* **:** shoes equipped with cleats

²**cleat** *transitive verb* (1794) **1 :** to secure to or by a cleat **2 :** to provide with a cleat

**cleav·able** \'klē-və-bəl\ *adjective* (circa 1864) **:** capable of being split

**cleav·age** \'klē-vij\ *noun* (1816) **1 a :** the quality of a crystallized substance or rock of splitting along definite planes; *also* **:** the occurrence of such splitting **b :** a fragment (as of a diamond) obtained by splitting **2 :** the action of cleaving : the state of being cleft **3 :** the series of synchronized mitotic cell divisions of the fertilized egg that results in the formation of the blastomeres and changes the single-celled zygote into a multicellular embryo; *also* **:** one of these cell divisions **4 :** the splitting of a molecule into simpler molecules **5 :** the depression between a woman's breasts especially when made visible by the wearing of a low-cut dress

¹**cleave** \'klēv\ *intransitive verb* **cleaved** \'klēvd\ *or* **clove** \'klōv\ *also* **clave** \'klāv\; **cleaved; cleav·ing** [Middle English *clevien*, from Old English *clifian*; akin to Old High German *kleben* to stick] (before 12th century) **:** to adhere firmly and closely or loyally and unwaveringly **synonym** see STICK

²**cleave** *verb* **cleaved** \'klēvd\ *also* **cleft** \'kleft\ *or* **clove** \'klōv\; **cleaved** *also* **cleft** *or* **clo·ven** \'klō-vən\; **cleav·ing** [Middle English *cleven*, from Old English *clēofan*; akin to Old Norse *kljūfa* to split, Latin *glubere* to peel, Greek *glyphein* to carve] (before 12th century) *transitive verb* **1 :** to divide by or as if by a cutting blow **:** SPLIT **2 :** to separate into distinct parts and especially into groups having divergent views **3 :** to subject to chemical cleavage ⟨a protein *cleaved* by an enzyme⟩ *intransitive verb* **1 :** to split especially along the grain **2 :** to penetrate or pass through something by or as if by cutting **synonym** see TEAR

**cleav·er** \'klē-vər\ *noun* (15th century) **1 :** one that cleaves; *especially* **:** a butcher's implement for cutting animal carcasses into joints or pieces

**2 :** a prehistoric stone tool having a sharp edge at one end

**cleav·ers** \'klē-vərz\ *noun plural but singular or plural in construction* [Middle English *clivre*, alteration of Old English *clife* burdock, cleavers; akin to Old English *clifian*] (14th century) **:** an annual bedstraw (*Galium aparine*) that has numerous stalked white flowers, stems covered with curved prickles, and whorls of bristle-tipped leaves; *also* **:** any of several related plants

**cleek** \'klēk\ *noun* [Middle English (northern) *cleke*, from *cleken* to clutch] (15th century) *chiefly Scottish* **:** a large hook (as for a pot over a fire)

**clef** \'klef\ *noun* [French, literally, key, from Latin *clavis* — more at CLAVICLE] (circa 1577) **:** a sign placed at the beginning of a musical staff to determine the pitch of the notes

¹**cleft** \'kleft\ *noun* [Middle English *clift*, from Old English *geclyft*; akin to Old English *clēofan* to cleave] (14th century) **1 :** a space or opening made by or as if by splitting : FISSURE **2 :** a usually V-shaped indented formation : a hollow between ridges or protuberances ⟨the anal *cleft* of the human body⟩

²**cleft** *adjective* [Middle English, from past participle of *cleven*] (14th century) **:** partially split or divided; *specifically* **:** divided about halfway to the midrib ⟨a *cleft* leaf⟩

clef: *1* treble clef, *2* bass clef

**cleft lip** *noun* (circa 1946) **:** HARELIP

**cleft palate** *noun* (1847) **:** congenital fissure of the roof of the mouth

**clei·do·ic** \klī-'dō-ik\ *adjective* [Greek *kleidoun* to fasten, lock in, from *kleid-, kleis* key — more at CLAVICLE] (1931) *of an egg* **:** enclosed in a relatively impervious shell which reduces free exchange with the environment

**cleis·tog·a·mous** \klī-'stä-gə-məs\ *also* **cleis·to·gam·ic** \,klī-stə-'ga-mik\ *adjective* [Greek *kleistos* closed (from *kleiein* to close) + International Scientific Vocabulary -*gamous* — more at CLAVICLE] (1874) **:** characterized by or being small inconspicuous closed self-pollinating flowers additional to and often more fruitful than showier ones on the same plant ⟨violets are *cleistogamous*⟩ — **cleis·tog·a·mous·ly** \klī-'stä-gə-məs-lē\ *adverb* — **cleis·tog·a·my** \-'stä-gə-mē\ *noun*

**cle·ma·tis** \'kle-mə-təs; kli-'ma-təs, -'mä-\ *noun* [New Latin, genus name, from Latin, from Greek *klēmatis* brushwood, clematis, from *klēmat-, klēma* twig, from *klan* to break — more at CLAST] (1578) **:** any of a genus (*Clematis*) of vines or herbs of the buttercup family having three leaflets on each leaf and usually white, red, pink, or purple flowers

**clem·en·cy** \'kle-mən(t)-sē\ *noun, plural* **-cies** (15th century) **1 a :** disposition to be merciful and especially to moderate the severity of punishment due **b :** an act or instance of leniency **2 :** pleasant mildness of weather **synonym** see MERCY

**clem·ent** \'kle-mənt\ *adjective* [Middle English, from Latin *clement-, clemens*] (15th century)

\ə\ abut \ᵊ\ kitten \ər\ further \a\ ash \ā\ ace \ä\ mop, mar \aü\ out \ch\ chin \e\ bet \ē\ easy \g\ go \i\ hit \ī\ ice \j\ job \ŋ\ sing \ō\ go \o\ law \oi\ boy \th\ thin \t͟h\ the \ü\ loot \u̇\ foot \y\ yet \zh\ vision *see also* Guide to Pronunciation

**1 :** inclined to be merciful **:** LENIENT ⟨a *clement* judge⟩
**2 :** MILD ⟨*clement* weather for November⟩
— **clem·ent·ly** *adverb*
**clench** \'klench\ *transitive verb* [Middle English, from Old English *-clencan;* akin to Old English *clingan* to cling] (13th century)
**1 :** CLINCH 2
**2 :** to hold fast **:** CLUTCH ⟨*clenched* the arms of the chair⟩
**3 :** to set or close tightly ⟨*clench* one's teeth⟩ ⟨*clench* one's fists⟩
— **clench** *noun*

**clepe** \'klep\ *transitive verb* **cleped** \'klept\; **yclept** \i-'klept\ *also* **cleped** *or* **ycleped** \i-'klept\; **clep·ing** \'kle-piŋ\ [Middle English, from Old English *clipian* to speak, call; akin to Old Frisian *kleppa* to ring] (before 12th century)
*archaic* **:** NAME, CALL
**clep·sy·dra** \'klep-sə-drə\ *noun, plural* **-dras** *or* **-drae** \-ˌdrē, -ˌdrī\ [Latin, from Greek *klepsydra,* from *kleptein* to steal + *hydōr* water — more at KLEPT-, WATER] (1646)
**:** WATER CLOCK
**clere·sto·ry** \'klir-ˌstōr-ē, -ˌstȯr-, -st(ə-)rē\ *noun* [Middle English, from *clere* clear + *story*] (15th century)
**1 :** an outside wall of a room or building that rises above an adjoining roof and contains windows
**2 :** GALLERY
**cler·gy** \'klər-jē\ *noun, plural* **cler·gies** [Middle English *clergie,* from Old French, from *clerc* clergyman] (13th century)
**1 :** a group ordained to perform pastoral or sacerdotal functions in a Christian church
**2 :** the official or sacerdotal class of a non-Christian religion

clerestory 1

**cler·gy·man** \-mən\ *noun* (1577)
**:** a member of the clergy
**cler·gy·wom·an** \-ˌwu̇-mən\ *noun* (1673)
**:** a woman who is a member of the clergy
**cler·ic** \'kler-ik\ *noun* [Late Latin *clericus*] (1621)
**:** a member of the clergy
**¹cler·i·cal** \'kler-i-kəl\ *adjective* (1592)
**1 :** of, relating to, or characteristic of the clergy
**2 :** of or relating to a clerk
— **cler·i·cal·ly** \-i-k(ə-)lē\ *adverb*
**²clerical** *noun* (1605)
**1 :** a member of the clergy
**2 :** CLERICALIST
**3 :** CLERK
**4** *plural* **:** clerical garments
**clerical collar** *noun* (1948)
**:** a narrow stiffly upright white collar worn buttoned at the back of the neck by members of the clergy
**cler·i·cal·ism** \'kler-i-kə-ˌli-zəm\ *noun* (1864)
**:** a policy of maintaining or increasing the power of a religious hierarchy
**cler·i·cal·ist** \-list\ *noun* (1881)
**:** one that favors maintained or increased ecclesiastical power and influence
**cler·i·hew** \'kler-i-ˌhyü\ *noun* [Edmund *Clerihew* Bentley (died 1956) English writer] (1928)
**:** a light verse quatrain rhyming *aabb* and usually dealing with a person named in the initial rhyme
**cler·i·sy** \'kler-ə-sē\ *noun* [German *Klerisei* clergy, from Medieval Latin *clericia,* from Late Latin *clericus* cleric] (1818)

**:** INTELLIGENTSIA
**¹clerk** \'klərk, *British usually* 'klärk\ *noun* [Middle English, from Old French *clerc* & Old English *clerc, clerc,* both from Late Latin *clericus,* from Late Greek *klērikos,* from Greek *klēros* lot, inheritance (in allusion to Deuteronomy 18:2), stick of wood; akin to Greek *klan* to break — more at CLAST] (before 12th century)
**1 :** CLERIC
**2** *archaic* **:** SCHOLAR
**3 a :** an official responsible (as to a government agency) for correspondence, records, and accounts and vested with specified powers or authority (as to issue writs or other processes as ordered by a court) ⟨city *clerk*⟩ **b :** one employed to keep records or accounts or to perform general office work **c :** one who works at a sales or service counter
— **clerk·ship** \-ˌship\ *noun*
**²clerk** *intransitive verb* (1551)
**:** to act or work as a clerk
**clerk·ly** \'klər-klē, *British usually* 'klär-\ *adjective* (15th century)
**1 :** of, relating to, or characteristic of a clerk
**2** *archaic* **:** SCHOLARLY
— **clerkly** *adverb*
**Cleve·land bay** \'klēv-lənd-\ *noun* [*Cleveland,* district in Yorkshire, England] (1796)
**:** a large strong horse of a breed of English origin that is uniformly bay with black legs, mane, and tail
**clev·er** \'kle-vər\ *adjective* [Middle English *cliver,* perhaps of Scandinavian origin; akin to Danish dialect *kløver* alert, skillful] (circa 1595)
**1 a :** skillful or adroit in using the hands or body **:** NIMBLE **b :** mentally quick and resourceful but often lacking in depth and soundness
**2 :** marked by wit or ingenuity
**3** *dialect* **a :** GOOD **b :** easy to use or handle ☆
— **clev·er·ish** \-v(ə-)rish\ *adjective*
— **clev·er·ly** \-vər-lē\ *adverb*
— **clev·er·ness** \-vər-nəs\ *noun*
**clev·is** \'kle-vəs\ *noun* [earlier *clevi,* perhaps of Scandinavian origin; akin to Old Norse *kljufa* to split — more at CLEAVE] (1592)
**:** SHACKLE 3
**¹clew** \'klü\ *noun* [Middle English *clewe,* from Old English *cliwen;* akin to Old High German *kliuwa* ball, Sanskrit *glau* lump] (before 12th century)
**1 :** a ball of thread, yarn, or cord
**2 :** CLUE
**3 a :** a lower corner or only the after corner of a sail **b :** a metal loop attached to the lower corner of a sail **c** *plural* **:** a combination of lines by which a hammock is suspended
**²clew** *transitive verb* (15th century)
**1 :** to roll into a ball
**2 :** CLUE
**3 :** to haul (a sail) up or down by ropes through the clews
**cli·ché** *also* **cli·che** \klē-'shā, 'klē-ˌ, kli-'\ *noun* [French, literally, printer's stereotype, from past participle of *clicher* to stereotype, of imitative origin] (1892)
**1 :** a trite phrase or expression; *also* **:** the idea expressed by it
**2 :** a hackneyed theme, characterization, or situation
**3 :** something (as a menu item) that has become overly familiar or commonplace ◆
— **cliché** *adjective*
**cli·chéd** \-'shād\ *adjective* (1928)
**1 :** marked by or abounding in clichés
**2 :** HACKNEYED
**¹click** \'klik\ *verb* [probably imitative] (1581)
*transitive verb*
**:** to strike, move, or produce with a click ⟨*clicked* his heels together⟩
*intransitive verb*
**1 :** to make a click
**2 a :** to fit or agree exactly **b :** to fit together

**:** hit it off ⟨they did not *click* as friends⟩ **c :** to function smoothly **d :** SUCCEED ⟨a movie that *clicks*⟩
**²click** *noun* (1611)
**1 a :** a slight sharp noise **b :** a speech sound in some languages made by enclosing air between two stop articulations of the tongue, enlarging the enclosure to rarefy the air, and suddenly opening the enclosure
**2 :** DETENT
**click beetle** *noun* (circa 1864)
**:** any of a family (Elateridae) of beetles able to right themselves with a click when inverted by flexing the articulation between the prothorax and mesothorax
**click stop** *noun* (1950)
**:** a turnable control device (as for a camera diaphragm opening) that engages with a definite click at specific settings
**cli·ent** \'klī-ənt\ *noun* [Middle English, from Middle French & Latin; Middle French *client,* from Latin *client-, cliens;* perhaps akin to Latin *clinare* to lean — more at LEAN] (14th century)
**1 :** one that is under the protection of another **:** DEPENDENT
**2 a :** a person who engages the professional advice or services of another ⟨a lawyer's *clients*⟩ **b :** CUSTOMER ⟨hotel *clients*⟩ **c :** a person served by or utilizing the services of a social agency ⟨a welfare *client*⟩
**3 :** CLIENT STATE
— **cli·ent·age** \-ən-tij\ *noun*
— **cli·en·tal** \klī-'en-t°l, 'klī-ən-\ *adjective*
— **cli·ent·less** \'klī-ənt-ləs\ *adjective*
**cli·en·tele** \ˌklī-ən-'tel, ˌklē-ən- *also* ˌklē-ˌän-\ *noun* [French *clientèle,* from Latin *clientela,* from *client-, cliens*] (circa 1587)
**:** a body of clients ⟨a shop that caters to an exclusive *clientele*⟩
**client state** *noun* (1918)
**:** a country that is economically, politically, or militarily dependent on another country
**cliff** \'klif\ *noun* [Middle English *clif,* from Old English; akin to Old High German *klep*] (before 12th century)
**:** a very steep, vertical, or overhanging face of rock, earth, or ice **:** PRECIPICE

☆ SYNONYMS
**Clever, adroit, cunning, ingenious**
mean having or showing practical wit or skill in contriving. CLEVER stresses physical or mental quickness, deftness, or great aptitude ⟨a person *clever* with horses⟩. ADROIT often implies a skillful use of expedients to achieve one's purpose in spite of difficulties ⟨an *adroit* negotiator⟩. CUNNING implies great skill in constructing or creating ⟨a filmmaker *cunning* in his use of special effects⟩. INGENIOUS suggests the power of inventing or discovering a new way of accomplishing something ⟨an *ingenious* software engineer⟩. See in addition INTELLIGENT.

◇ WORD HISTORY
**cliché** *Cliché* is the French word for a stereotype, a duplicate printing plate cast from a mold or a matrix of composed type. The production of such plates became standard in 19th century printing to save wear on type and permit longer press runs. Passing from printers' jargon to the world of letters, *cliché* was applied to a turn of phrase or metaphor that through repeated use loses its effectiveness and becomes the mark of unimaginative writing. The word *stereotype* itself, from French *stéréotype,* has undergone a similar shift in sense, and now usually refers to a conventional mental image of a person or thing that is passed about without critical reappraisal.

— **cliffy** \'kli-fē\ *adjective*
**cliff dweller** *noun* (1881)
**1** *often C&D capitalized* **a :** a member of a prehistoric American Indian people of the southwestern U.S. who built their homes on rock ledges or in the natural recesses of canyon walls and cliffs **b :** a member of any cliff-dwelling people
**2 :** a resident of a large usually metropolitan apartment building
— **cliff dwelling** *noun*
**cliff–hang** \'klif-ˌhaŋ\ *intransitive verb* [back-formation from *cliff-hanger*] (1946)
**:** to await the outcome of a suspenseful situation
**cliff–hang·er** \-ˌhaŋ-ər\ *noun* (circa 1937)
**1 :** an adventure serial or melodrama; *especially* **:** one presented in installments each ending in suspense
**2 :** a contest whose outcome is in doubt up to the very end; *broadly* **:** a suspenseful situation
— **cliff–hang·ing** \-iŋ\ *adjective*
**cliff swallow** *noun* (1825)
**:** a colonial swallow (*Petrochelidon pyrrhonota*) of the New World with a pale buff rump and dark throat patch that builds mud nests like jugs especially under eaves and on cliffs
**¹cli·mac·ter·ic** \klī-'mak-t(ə-)rik; ˌklī-ˌmak-'ter-ik, -'tir-\ *adjective* [Latin *climactericus*, from Greek *klimakterikos*, from *klimakter* critical point, literally, rung of a ladder, from *klimak-, klimax* ladder] (1582)
**1 :** constituting or relating to a climacteric
**2 :** CRITICAL, CRUCIAL
**²climacteric** *noun* (circa 1630)
**1 :** a major turning point or critical stage
**2 :** MENOPAUSE; *also* **:** a corresponding period in the male usually occurring with less well-defined physiological and psychological changes
**3 :** the marked and sudden rise in the respiratory rate of fruit just prior to full ripening
**cli·mac·tic** \klī-'mak-tik, klə-\ *adjective* (1872)
**:** of, relating to, or constituting a climax
— **cli·mac·ti·cal·ly** \-ti-k(ə-)lē\ *adverb*
**cli·mate** \'klī-mət\ *noun* [Middle English *climat*, from Middle French, from Late Latin *climat-, clima*, from Greek *klimat-, klima* inclination, latitude, climate, from *klinein* to lean — more at LEAN] (14th century)
**1 :** a region of the earth having specified climatic conditions
**2 a :** the average course or condition of the weather at a place usually over a period of years as exhibited by temperature, wind velocity, and precipitation **b :** the prevailing set of conditions (as of temperature and humidity) indoors ⟨a *climate*-controlled office⟩
**3 :** the prevailing influence or environmental conditions characterizing a group or period **:** ATMOSPHERE ⟨a *climate* of fear⟩
**cli·mat·ic** \klī-'ma-tik, klə-\ *adjective* (circa 1828)
**1 :** of or relating to climate
**2 :** resulting from or influenced by the climate rather than the soil ⟨forests that had reverted to the *climatic* type⟩ — compare EDAPHIC 2
— **cli·mat·i·cal·ly** \-ti-k(ə-)lē\ *adverb*
**climatic climax** *noun* (circa 1928)
**:** the one of the ecological climaxes possible in a particular climatic area whose stability is directly due to the influence of climate — compare EDAPHIC CLIMAX
**cli·ma·tol·o·gy** \ˌklī-mə-'tä-lə-jē\ *noun* (1843)
**:** the science that deals with climates and their phenomena
— **cli·ma·to·log·i·cal** \ˌklī-mə-tə-'lä-ji-kəl\ *adjective*
— **cli·ma·to·log·i·cal·ly** \-k(ə-)lē\ *adverb*
— **cli·ma·tol·o·gist** \-mə-'tä-lə-jist\ *noun*
**¹cli·max** \'klī-ˌmaks\ *noun* [Latin, from Greek *klimax* ladder, from *klinein* to lean] (circa 1550)

**1 :** a figure of speech in which a series of phrases or sentences is arranged in ascending order of rhetorical forcefulness
**2 a :** the highest point **:** CULMINATION **b :** the point of highest dramatic tension or a major turning point in the action (as of a play) **c :** ORGASM **d :** MENOPAUSE
**3 :** a relatively stable ecological stage or community especially of plants that is achieved through successful adjustment to an environment; *especially* **:** the final stage in ecological succession
**synonym** see SUMMIT
— **cli·max·less** *adjective*
**²climax** (1835)
*transitive verb*
**:** to bring to a climax ⟨*climaxed* his boxing career with a knockout⟩
*intransitive verb*
**:** to come to a climax ⟨a riot *climaxing* in the destruction of several houses⟩
**¹climb** \'klīm\ *verb* [Middle English, from Old English *climban;* probably akin to Old English *clifian* to adhere — more at CLEAVE] (before 12th century)
*intransitive verb*
**1 a :** to go upward with gradual or continuous progress **:** RISE, ASCEND **b :** to increase gradually **c :** to slope upward
**2 a :** to go upward or raise oneself especially by grasping or clutching with the hands ⟨*climbed* upon her father's knee⟩ **b** *of a plant* **:** to ascend in growth (as by twining)
**3 :** to go about or down usually by grasping or holding with the hands ⟨*climb* down the ladder⟩
**4 :** to get into or out of clothing usually with some haste or effort ⟨the firemen *climbed* into their clothes⟩
*transitive verb*
**1 :** to go upward on or along, to the top of, or over ⟨*climb* a hill⟩
**2 :** to draw or pull oneself up, over, or to the top of by using hands and feet ⟨children *climbing* the tree⟩
**3 :** to grow up or over
— **climb·able** \'klī-mə-bəl\ *adjective*
**²climb** *noun* (circa 1587)
**1 :** a place where climbing is necessary to progress
**2 :** the act or an instance of climbing **:** RISE, ASCENT
**climb·er** \'klī-mər\ *noun* (15th century)
**1 a :** one that climbs or helps in climbing **b :** a vine or twining plant (as a rose or sweet pea) that readily grows up a support or over other plants
**2 :** one who attempts to gain a superior social or business position
**climbing iron** *noun* (1857)
**:** a steel framework with spikes attached that may be affixed to one's boots for climbing (as a pole or tree)
**clime** \'klīm\ *noun* [Late Latin *clima*] (14th century)
**:** CLIMATE ⟨traveled to warmer *climes*⟩
**-cline** *adjective combining form* [International Scientific Vocabulary, from Greek *klinein* to lean — more at LEAN]
**:** sloping ⟨iso*clinal*⟩
**¹clinch** \'klinch\ *verb* [probably alteration of *clench*] (1542)
*transitive verb*
**1 :** CLENCH 3
**2 a :** to turn over or flatten the protruding pointed end of (a driven nail); *also* **:** to treat (as a screw, bolt, or rivet) in a similar way **b :** to fasten in this way
**3 :** to make final or irrefutable **:** SETTLE ⟨that *clinched* the argument⟩ **b :** to secure conclusively **:** WIN
*intransitive verb*
**1 :** to hold an opponent (as in boxing) at close quarters with one or both arms

**2 :** to hold fast or firmly
— **clinch·ing·ly** \'klin-chiŋ-lē\ *adverb*
**²clinch** *noun* (1659)
**1 :** a fastening by means of a clinched nail, rivet, or bolt; *also* **:** the clinched part of a nail, rivet, or bolt
**2** *archaic* **:** PUN
**3 :** an act or instance of clinching in boxing
**4 :** EMBRACE
**clinch·er** \'klin-chər\ *noun* (1737)
**:** one that clinches: as **a :** a decisive fact, argument, act, or remark ⟨the expense was the *clincher* that persuaded us to give up the enterprise⟩ **b :** a tire with flanged beads fitting into the wheel rim
**cline** \'klīn\ *noun* [Greek *klinein*] (1938)
**:** a gradient of morphological or physiological change in a group of related organisms usually along a line of environmental or geographic transition
— **clin·al** \'klī-nᵊl\ *adjective*
— **clin·al·ly** \-nᵊl-ē\ *adverb*
**-cline** *noun combining form* [back-formation from *-clinal*]
**:** slope ⟨mono*cline*⟩
**¹cling** \'kliŋ\ *intransitive verb* **clung** \'kləŋ\; **cling·ing** [Middle English, from Old English *clingan;* akin to Old High German *klunga* tangled ball of thread] (before 12th century)
**1 a :** to hold together **b :** to adhere as if glued firmly **c :** to hold or hold on tightly or tenaciously
**2 a :** to have a strong emotional attachment or dependence **b :** to remain or linger as if resisting complete dissipation or dispersal ⟨the odor *clung* to the room for hours⟩
**synonym** see STICK
— **cling·er** \'kliŋ-ər\ *noun*
— **clingy** \'kliŋ-ē\ *adjective*
**²cling** *noun* (circa 1625)
**:** an act or instance of clinging **:** ADHERENCE
**cling·stone** \'kliŋ-ˌstōn\ *noun* (1705)
**:** any of various stone fruits (as some peaches or plums) with flesh that adheres strongly to the pit
**clin·ic** \'kli-nik\ *noun* [French *clinique*, from Greek *klinikē* medical practice at the sickbed, from feminine of *klīnikos* of a bed, from *klinē* bed, from *klinein* to lean, recline — more at LEAN] (circa 1843)
**1 :** a class of medical instruction in which patients are examined and discussed
**2 :** a group meeting devoted to the analysis and solution of concrete problems or to the acquiring of specific skills or knowledge ⟨writing *clinics*⟩ ⟨golf *clinics*⟩
**3 a :** a facility (as of a hospital) for diagnosis and treatment of outpatients **b :** a group practice in which several physicians work cooperatively
**-clinic** *adjective combining form* [International Scientific Vocabulary, from Greek *klinein*]
**1 :** inclining **:** dipping
**2 :** having (so many) oblique intersections of the axes ⟨mono*clinic*⟩ ⟨tri*clinic*⟩
**clin·i·cal** \'kli-ni-kəl\ *adjective* (circa 1780)
**1 :** of, relating to, or conducted in or as if in a clinic: as **a :** involving direct observation of the patient **b :** diagnosable by or based on clinical observation
**2 :** analytical or coolly dispassionate ⟨a *clinical* attitude⟩
— **clin·i·cal·ly** \-k(ə-)lē\ *adverb*
**clinical thermometer** *noun* (1878)
**:** a thermometer for measuring body temperature that has a constriction in the tube where the column of liquid breaks when the temperature drops from its maximum and that continues to indicate the maximum temperature by

---

\ə\ **abut** \ᵊ\ **kitten** \ər\ **further** \a\ **ash** \ā\ **ace**
\ä\ **mop, mar** \au̇\ **out** \ch\ **chin** \e\ **bet** \ē\ **easy**
\g\ **go** \i\ **hit** \ī\ **ice** \j\ **job** \ŋ\ **sing** \ō\ **go**
\ȯ\ **law** \ȯi\ **boy** \th\ **thin** \t̲h̲\ **the** \ü\ **loot** \u̇\ **foot**
\y\ **yet** \zh\ **vision**    *see also* Guide to Pronunciation

the part of the column above the constriction until reset by shaking

**cli·ni·cian** \kli-'ni-shən\ *noun* (1875)
**1 :** a person qualified in the clinical practice of medicine, psychiatry, or psychology as distinguished from one specializing in laboratory or research techniques or in theory
**2 :** a person who conducts a clinic

**clin·i·co·path·o·log·ic** \,kli-ni-(,)kō-,pa-thə-'lä-jik\ *or* **clin·i·co·path·o·log·i·cal** \-'lä-ji-kəl\ *adjective* [*clinical*] (1898)
**:** relating to or concerned both with the signs and symptoms directly observable by the physician and with the results of laboratory examination
— **clin·i·co·path·o·log·i·cal·ly** \-ji-k(ə-)lē\ *adverb*

**¹clink** \'kliŋk\ *verb* [Middle English, of imitative origin] (14th century)
*intransitive verb*
**:** to give out a slight sharp short metallic sound
*transitive verb*
**:** to cause to clink

**²clink** *noun* (15th century)
**:** a clinking sound

**³clink** *noun* [probably from *Clink,* a prison in Southwark, London, England] (1515)
**1** *slang* **:** a prison cell
**2** *slang* **:** JAIL, PRISON

**¹clin·ker** \'kliŋ-kər\ *noun* [alteration of earlier *klinćard* a hard yellowish Dutch brick] (1641)
**1 :** a brick that has been burned too much in the kiln
**2 :** stony matter fused together **:** SLAG

**²clink·er** \'kliŋ-kər\ *noun* [¹*clink*] (1733)
**1** *British* **:** something first-rate
**2 a :** a wrong note **b :** a serious mistake or error **:** BONER **c :** an utter failure **:** FLOP **d :** something of poor quality

**clink·er–built** \-,bilt\ *adjective* [*clinker,* noun, *clinch*] (1769)
**:** having the external planks or plates overlapping like the clapboards on a house ⟨a *clinker-built* boat⟩

**clink·ety–clank** \'kliŋ-kə-tē-'klaŋk\ *noun* [imitative] (1901)
**:** a repeated usually rhythmic clanking sound ⟨the *clinkety-clank* of a loose tire chain⟩

**cli·nom·e·ter** \klī-'nä-mə-tər\ *noun* [Greek *klinein* to lean] (1811)
**:** any of various instruments for measuring angles of elevation or inclination

**-clinous** *adjective combining form* [probably from New Latin *-clinus,* from Greek *klinē* bed — more at CLINIC]
**:** having the androecium and gynoecium in a (single or different) flower or (two separate) flowers ⟨di*clinous*⟩

**¹clin·quant** \'kliŋ-kənt, klaⁿ-'käⁿ\ *adjective* [Middle French, from present participle of *clinquer* to glitter, literally, to clink, of imitative origin] (1591)
**:** glittering with gold or tinsel

**²clinquant** *noun* [French, from *clinquant,* adjective] (1682)
**:** TINSEL

**clin·to·nia** \klin-'tō-nē-ə\ *noun* [New Latin, genus name, from DeWitt *Clinton*] (1843)
**:** any of a genus (*Clintonia*) of herbs of the lily family with yellow or white flowers

**Clio** \'klī-(,)ō, 'klē-\ *noun* [Latin, from Greek *Kleiō*]
**1 :** the Greek Muse of history
**2** *plural* **Cli·os :** a statuette awarded annually by a professional organization for notable achievement in radio and television commercials

**clio·met·rics** \,klī-ə-'me-triks\ *noun plural but singular in construction* [*Clio* + *-metrics* (as in *econometrics*)] (1966)
**:** the application of methods developed in other fields (as economics, statistics, and data processing) to the study of history
— **clio·met·ric** \-trik\ *adjective*
— **clio·met·ri·cian** \-me-'tri-shən\ *noun*

**¹clip** \'klip\ *transitive verb* **clipped; clip·ping** [Middle English *clippen,* from Old English *clyppan;* akin to Old High German *klāftra* fathom, Lithuanian *globti* to embrace] (before 12th century)
**1 :** ENCOMPASS
**2 a :** to hold in a tight grip **:** CLUTCH **b :** to clasp or fasten with a clip

**²clip** *noun* (15th century)
**1 :** any of various devices that grip, clasp, or hook
**2 :** a device to hold cartridges for charging the magazines of some rifles; *also* **:** a magazine from which ammunition is fed into the chamber of a firearm
**3 :** a piece of jewelry held in position by a clip

**³clip** *verb* **clipped; clip·ping** [Middle English *clippen,* from Old Norse *klippa*] (13th century)
*transitive verb*
**1 a :** to cut or cut off with or as if with shears ⟨*clip* a dog's hair⟩ ⟨*clip* an hour off traveling time⟩ **b :** to cut off the distal or outer part of **c** (1) **:** ³EXCISE (2) **:** to cut items out of (as a newspaper)
**2 a :** CURTAIL, DIMINISH **b :** to abbreviate in speech or writing
**3 :** HIT, PUNCH
**4 :** to illegally block (an opposing player) in football
**5 :** to take money from unfairly or dishonestly especially by overcharging ⟨the nightclub *clipped* the tourist for $200⟩
*intransitive verb*
**1 :** to clip something
**2 :** to travel or pass rapidly
**3 :** to clip an opposing player in football

**⁴clip** *noun* (15th century)
**1 a** *plural, Scottish* **:** SHEARS **b :** a 2-bladed instrument for cutting especially the nails
**2 :** something that is clipped: as **a :** the product of a single shearing (as of sheep) **b :** a crop of wool of a sheep, a flock, or a region **c :** a section of filmed or videotaped material **d :** a clipping especially from a newspaper
**3 :** an act of clipping
**4 :** a sharp blow
**5 :** RATE 4a ⟨continues at a brisk *clip*⟩
**6 :** a single instance or occasion **:** TIME ⟨he charged $10 a *clip*⟩ — often used in the phrase *at a clip* ⟨trained 1000 workers at a *clip*⟩

**clip·board** \'klip-,bōrd, -,bórd\ *noun* (1896)
**:** a small writing board with a clip at the top for holding papers

**clip–clop** \'klip-,kläp\ *noun* [imitative] (1884)
**:** the sound made by or as if by a horse walking on a hard surface
— **clip–clop** *intransitive verb*

**clip joint** *noun* (1933)
**1** *slang* **:** a place of public entertainment (as a nightclub) that makes a practice of defrauding patrons (as by overcharging)
**2** *slang* **:** a business that makes a practice of overcharging

**clip–on** \'kli-,pòn, -,pän\ *adjective* (1909)
**:** of or relating to something that attaches with a clip ⟨a *clip-on* tie⟩ ⟨*clip-on* earrings⟩
— **clip–on** *noun*

**clip·per** \'kli-pər\ *noun* (14th century)
**1 :** one that clips something
**2 :** an implement for clipping especially hair, fingernails, or toenails — usually used in plural
**3 a :** one that moves swiftly **b :** a fast sailing ship; *especially* **:** one with long slender lines, an overhanging bow, tall masts, and a large sail area

**clip·ping** \'kli-piŋ\ *noun* (15th century)
**:** something that is clipped off or out of something; *especially* **:** an item clipped from a publication

**clip·sheet** \'klip-,shēt\ *noun* (1926)
**:** a sheet of newspaper material issued by an organization for clipping and reprinting

**clique** \'klēk, 'klik\ *noun* [French] (1711)

**:** a narrow exclusive circle or group of persons; *especially* **:** one held together by common interests, views, or purposes
— **cliqu·ey** *also* **cliquy** \'klē-kē, 'kli-\ *adjective*
— **cliqu·ish** \'kli-kish\ *adjective*
— **cliqu·ish·ly** *adverb*
— **cliqu·ish·ness** *noun*

**cli·tel·lum** \klī-'te-ləm\ *noun, plural* **-la** \-lə\ [New Latin, modification of Latin *clitellae* packsaddle] (1839)
**:** a thickened glandular section of the body wall of some annelids that secretes a viscid sac in which the eggs are deposited

**clit·ic** \'kli-tik\ *noun* [en*clitic* or pro*clitic*] (1946)
**:** a word that is treated in pronunciation as forming a part of a neighboring word and that is often unaccented or contracted

**clit·o·ri·dec·to·my** \,kli-tə-ri-'dek-tə-mē\ *also* **clit·o·rec·to·my** \,kli-tə-'rek-tə-mē\ *noun, plural* **-mies** (1866)
**:** excision of all or part of the clitoris

**clit·o·ris** \'kli-tə-rəs, kli-'tór-əs\ *noun, plural* **clit·o·ri·des** \kli-'tór-ə-,dēz\ [New Latin, from Greek *kleitoris*] (1615)
**:** a small erectile organ at the anterior or ventral part of the vulva homologous to the penis
— **clit·o·ral** \'kli-tə-rəl\ *or* **clit·or·ic** \kli-'tór-ik, -'tär-\ *adjective*

**clo·a·ca** \klō-'ā-kə\ *noun, plural* **-a·cae** \-,kē, -,sē\ [Latin; akin to Greek *klyzein* to wash — more at CLYSTER] (1599)
**1 :** ³SEWER
**2** [New Latin, from Latin] **:** the common chamber into which the intestinal, urinary, and generative canals discharge in birds, reptiles, amphibians, and many fishes; *also* **:** a comparable chamber of an invertebrate
— **clo·a·cal** \-'ā-kəl\ *adjective*

**¹cloak** \'klōk\ *noun* [Middle English *cloke,* from Old North French *cloque* bell, cloak, from Medieval Latin *clocca* bell; from its shape] (13th century)
**1 :** a loose outer garment
**2 :** something that conceals **:** PRETENSE, DISGUISE

**²cloak** *transitive verb* (1509)
**:** to cover or hide with or as if with a cloak
**synonym** see DISGUISE

**cloak–and–dagger** *adjective* (1860)
**:** dealing in or suggestive of melodramatic intrigue and action usually involving secret agents and espionage
— **cloak–and–dagger** *noun*

**cloak·room** \'klōk-,rüm, -,rùm\ *noun* (circa 1852)
**1 a :** a room in which outdoor clothing may be placed during one's stay **b :** a room or cubicle where garments, parcels, and luggage may be checked for temporary safekeeping
**2 :** an anteroom of a legislative chamber where members may relax and confer with colleagues
**3** *British* **:** LAVATORY 2

**¹clob·ber** \'klä-bər\ *noun* [origin unknown] (1879)
*slang British* **:** CLOTHES 1

**²clobber** *transitive verb* **clob·bered; clob·ber·ing** \-b(ə-)riŋ\ [origin unknown] (circa 1943)
**1 :** to pound mercilessly; *also* **:** to hit with force **:** SMASH
**2 :** to defeat overwhelmingly

**clo·chard** \klō-'shär\ *noun* [French, from *clocher* to limp, from (assumed) Vulgar Latin *cloppicare,* from Late Latin *cloppus* lame] (1937)
**:** TRAMP, VAGRANT

**cloche** \'klōsh\ *noun* [French, literally, bell, from Medieval Latin *clocca*] (1882)
**1 :** a transparent plant cover used outdoors especially for protection against cold
**2 :** a woman's small close-fitting hat usually with deep rounded crown and very narrow brim

**¹clock** \'kläk\ *noun, often attributive* [Middle English *clok*, from Middle Dutch *clocke* bell, clock, from Old North French or Medieval Latin; Old North French *cloque* bell, from Medieval Latin *clocca*, of Celtic origin; akin to Middle Irish *clocc* bell] (14th century)
**1 :** a device other than a watch for indicating or measuring time commonly by means of hands moving on a dial; *broadly* **:** any periodic system by which time is measured
**2 :** a registering device usually with a dial; *specifically* **:** ODOMETER
**3 :** TIME CLOCK
**4 :** a synchronizing device (as in a computer) that produces pulses at regular intervals
**5 :** BIOLOGICAL CLOCK
**— around the clock** *also* **round the clock 1 :** continuously for 24 hours **:** day and night without cessation **2 :** without relaxation and heedless of time
**— kill the clock** *or* **run out the clock :** to use up as much as possible of the playing time remaining in a game (as football) while retaining possession of the ball or puck especially to protect a lead
**²clock** (1883)
*transitive verb*
**1 :** to time with a stopwatch or by an electric timing device
**2 :** to register on a mechanical recording device ⟨wind velocities were *clocked* at 80 miles per hour⟩
**3 :** to hit hard
**4** *chiefly British* **:** ATTAIN, REALIZE — usually used with *up* ⟨just *clocked* up a million . . . paperback sales —*Punch*⟩
*intransitive verb*
**:** to register on a time sheet or time clock **:** PUNCH — used with *in, out, on, off* ⟨he *clocked* in late⟩
**— clock·er** *noun*
**³clock** *noun* [perhaps from ¹*clock*] (1530)
**:** an ornamental figure on the ankle or side of a stocking or sock
**clock·like** \'kläk-ˌlīk\ *adjective* (circa 1770)
**:** unusually regular, undeviating, and precise ⟨does his job with *clocklike* efficiency⟩
**clock radio** *noun* (1949)
**:** a combination clock and radio device in which the clock can be set to turn on the radio at a designated time
**clock–watch·er** \-ˌwä-chər\ *noun* (1911)
**:** a person (as a worker or student) who keeps close watch on the passage of time
**— clock–watch·ing** \-chiŋ\ *noun*
**clock·wise** \'kläk-ˌwīz\ *adverb* (1888)
**:** in the direction in which the hands of a clock rotate as viewed from in front or as if standing on a clock face
**— clockwise** *adjective*
**clock·work** \-ˌwərk\ *noun* (1628)
**1 :** the inner workings of something
**2 :** the machinery (as springs and a train of gears) that run a clock; *also* **:** a similar mechanism running a mechanical device (as a toy)
**3 :** the precision, regularity, or absence of variation associated with a clock or clockwork ⟨a *clockwork* operation⟩ ⟨the planning went like *clockwork*⟩
**clod** \'kläd\ *noun* [Middle English *clodde*, from Old English *clod-* (in *clodhamer* fieldfare)] (15th century)
**1 a :** a lump or mass especially of earth or clay **b :** SOIL, EARTH
**2 :** OAF, DOLT
**— clod·dish** \'klä-dish\ *adjective*
**— clod·dish·ness** *noun*
**— clod·dy** \'klä-dē\ *adjective*
**clod·hop·per** \'kläd-ˌhä-pər\ *noun* (1721)
**1 :** a clumsy and uncouth rustic
**2 :** a large heavy work shoe or boot
**clod·hop·ping** \-ˌhä-piŋ\ *adjective* (1843)
**:** BOORISH, RUDE
**clod·poll** *or* **clod·pole** \'kläd-ˌpōl\ *noun* (1601)

**:** BLOCKHEAD
**clo·fi·brate** \klō-'fī-ˌbrāt, -'fi-\ *noun* [perhaps from *chlor-* + *fibr-* + ¹*-ate*] (1964)
**:** a compound $C_{12}H_{15}ClO_3$ used especially to lower abnormally high concentrations of fats and cholesterol in the blood
**¹clog** \'kläg, 'klóg\ *noun* [Middle English *clogge* short thick piece of wood] (14th century)
**1 a :** a weight attached especially to an animal to hinder motion **b :** something that shackles or impedes **:** ENCUMBRANCE 1
**2 :** a shoe, sandal, or overshoe having a thick typically wooden sole
**²clog** *verb* **clogged; clog·ging** (1526)
*transitive verb*
**1 a :** to impede with a clog **:** HINDER **b :** to halt or retard the progress, operation, or growth of **:** ENCUMBER ⟨restraints that have been *clogging* the market —T. W. Arnold⟩
**2 :** to fill beyond capacity **:** OVERLOAD ⟨cars *clogged* the main street⟩ ⟨a speech *clogged* with clichés⟩
*intransitive verb*
**1 :** to become filled with extraneous matter
**2 :** to unite in a mass **:** CLOT
**3 :** to dance a clog dance
**synonym** see HAMPER
**— clog·ger** \'klä-gər, 'kló-\ *noun*
**clog dance** *noun* (1869)
**:** a dance in which the performer wears clogs and beats out a clattering rhythm on the floor
**— clog dancer** *noun*
**— clog dancing** *noun*
**cloi·son·né** *also* **cloi·son·ne** \ˌklói-zə-'nā, ˌklwä-\ *adjective* [French, from past participle of *cloisonner* to partition] (1863)
**:** of, relating to, or being a style of enamel decoration in which the enamel is applied and fired in raised cells (as of soldered wires) on a usually metal background — compare CHAMPLEVÉ
**— cloisonné** *noun*
**¹clois·ter** \'klói-stər\ *noun* [Middle English *cloistre*, from Old French, from Medieval Latin *claustrum*, from Latin, bar, bolt, from *claudere* to close — more at CLOSE] (13th century)
**1 a :** a monastic establishment **b :** an area within a monastery or convent to which the religious are normally restricted **c :** monastic life **d :** a place or state of seclusion

**cloister 2**

**2 :** a covered passage on the side of a court usually having one side walled and the other an open arcade or colonnade
**²cloister** *transitive verb* **clois·tered; clois·ter·ing** \-st(ə-)riŋ\ (1581)
**1 :** to seclude from the world in or as if in a cloister ⟨a scientist who *cloisters* herself in a laboratory⟩
**2 :** to surround with a cloister ⟨*cloistered* gardens⟩
**clois·tered** \'klói-stərd\ *adjective* (1581)
**1 :** being or living in or as if in a cloister
**2 :** providing shelter from contact with the outside world ⟨the *cloistered* atmosphere of a small college⟩
**clois·tral** \'klói-strəl\ *adjective* (1605)
**:** of, relating to, or suggestive of a cloister
**clois·tress** \'klói-strəs\ *noun* (1601)
*obsolete* **:** NUN
**clo·mi·phene** \'klō-mə-ˌfēn\ *noun* [*chlor-* + *amine* + *-phene* (from *phenyl*)] (1963)
**:** a synthetic drug $C_{26}H_{28}ClNO$ used in the form of its citrate to induce ovulation
**clomp** \'klämp, 'klómp, 'klɑmp\ *intransitive verb* [by alteration] (1829)

**:** CLUMP 1
**¹clone** \'klōn\ *noun* [Greek *klōn* twig, slip; akin to Greek *klan* to break — more at CLAST] (1903)
**1 a :** the aggregate of the asexually produced progeny of an individual; *also* **:** a group of replicas of all or part of a macromolecule (as DNA or an antibody) **b :** an individual grown from a single somatic cell of its parent and genetically identical to it
**2 :** one that appears to be a copy of an original form ⟨a *clone* of a personal computer⟩
**— clon·al** \'klō-n°l\ *adjective*
**— clon·al·ly** \-n°l-ē\ *adverb*
**²clone** *verb* **cloned; clon·ing** (circa 1948)
*transitive verb*
**1 :** to propagate a clone from
**2 :** to make a copy of
*intransitive verb*
**:** to produce a clone
**clo·ni·dine** \'klä-nə-ˌdēn, 'klō-, -ˌdīn\ *noun* [*chlor-* + *aniline* + *imide* + ²*-ine*] (1970)
**:** an antihypertensive drug $C_9H_9Cl_2N_3$ used to treat essential hypertension, to prevent migraine headache, and to diminish withdrawal symptoms
**clonk** \'kläŋk, 'klóŋk\ *verb* [imitative] (1930)
*intransitive verb*
**:** to make a dull hollow thumping sound
*transitive verb*
**:** to cause to clonk
**— clonk** *noun*
**clo·nus** \'klō-nəs\ *noun* [New Latin, from Greek *klonos* agitation — more at HOLD] (1817)
**:** a rapid succession of alternating contractions and partial relaxations of a muscle occurring in some nervous diseases
**— clon·ic** \'klä-nik\ *adjective*
**— clo·nic·i·ty** \klō-'ni-sə-tē, klä-\ *noun*
**cloot** \'klüt\ *noun* [probably of Scandinavian origin; akin to Old Norse *klō* claw — more at CLAW] (1725)
**1** *Scottish* **:** a cloven hoof
**2** *plural, capitalized, Scottish* **:** CLOOTIE
**Cloot·ie** \'klü-tē\ *noun* [diminutive of *cloot*] *chiefly Scottish* — used as a name of the devil
**clop** \'kläp\ *noun* [imitative] (1899)
**:** a sound made by or as if by a hoof or wooden shoe against the pavement
**— clop** *intransitive verb*
**clop–clop** \'kläp-ˌkläp\ *noun* (1901)
**:** a sound of rhythmically repeated clops
**— clop–clop** *intransitive verb*
**clo·que** *also* **clo·qué** \klō-'kā, 'klō-ˌ\ *noun* [French *cloqué*, from past participle of *cloquer* to become blistered, from French dialect (Picard) *cloque* bell, bubble, from Medieval Latin *clocca* bell — more at CLOCK] (1936)
**1 :** a fabric with an embossed design
**2 :** a fabric especially of piqué with small woven figures
**¹close** \'klōz\ *verb* **closed; clos·ing** [Middle English, from Old French *clos-*, stem of *clore*, from Latin *claudere* to shut, close; perhaps akin to Greek *kleiein* to close — more at CLAVICLE] (13th century)
*transitive verb*
**1 a :** to move so as to bar passage through something ⟨*close* the gate⟩ **b :** to block against entry or passage ⟨*close* a street⟩ **c :** to deny access to ⟨the city *closed* the beach⟩ **d :** SCREEN, EXCLUDE ⟨*close* a view⟩ **e :** to suspend or stop the operations of ⟨*close* school⟩ — often used with *down*
**2** *archaic* **:** ENCLOSE, CONTAIN
**3 a :** to bring to an end or period ⟨*close* an account⟩ **b :** to conclude discussion or negotiation about ⟨the question is *closed*⟩; *also* **:** to

consummate by performing something previously agreed ⟨*close* a transfer of real estate title⟩ **c :** to terminate access to (a computer file) **4 a :** to bring or bind together the parts or edges of ⟨a *closed* book⟩ **b :** to fill up (as an opening) **c :** to make complete by circling or enveloping or by making continuous ⟨*close* a circuit⟩ **d :** to reduce to nil ⟨*closed* the distance to the lead racer⟩
*intransitive verb*
**1 a :** to contract, fold, swing, or slide so as to leave no opening ⟨the door *closed* quietly⟩ **b :** to cease operation ⟨the factory *closed* down⟩ ⟨the stores *close* at 9 p.m.⟩
**2 a :** to draw near ⟨the ship was *closing* with the island⟩ **b :** to engage in a struggle at close quarters : GRAPPLE ⟨*close* with the enemy⟩
**3 a :** to come together : MEET **b :** to draw the free foot up to the supporting foot in dancing **4 :** to enter into or complete an agreement **5 :** to come to an end or period **6 :** to reduce a gap ⟨*closed* to within two points⟩ ☆
— **clos·able** *or* **close·able** \'klō-zə-bəl\ *adjective*
— **clos·er** *noun*
— **close one's doors 1 :** to refuse admission ⟨the nation *closed its doors* to immigrants⟩ **2 :** to go out of business
— **close one's eyes to :** to ignore deliberately
— **close ranks :** to unite in a concerted stand especially to meet a challenge
— **close the door :** to be uncompromisingly obstructive ⟨*closed the door* to further negotiation⟩

**²close** \'klōz\ *noun* (14th century)
**1 a :** a coming or bringing to a conclusion ⟨at the *close* of the party⟩ **b :** a conclusion or end in time or existence : CESSATION ⟨the decade drew to a *close*⟩ **c :** the concluding passage (as of a speech or play)
**2 :** the conclusion of a musical strain or period : CADENCE
**3** *archaic* **:** a hostile encounter
**4 :** the movement of the free foot in dancing toward or into contact with the supporting foot

**³close** \'klōs, *U.S. also* 'klōz\ *noun* [Middle English *clos,* literally, enclosure, from Old French *clos,* from Latin *clausum,* from neuter of *clausus,* past participle] (13th century)
**1 a :** an enclosed area **b** *chiefly British* **:** the precinct of a cathedral
**2** *chiefly British* **a :** a narrow passage leading from a street to a court and the houses within or to the common stairway of tenements **b :** a road closed at one end

**⁴close** \'klōs\ *adjective* **clos·er; clos·est** [Middle English *clos,* from Middle French, from Latin *clausus,* past participle of *claudere*] (14th century)
**1 :** having no openings : CLOSED
**2 a :** confined or carefully guarded ⟨*close* arrest⟩ **b** (1) *of a vowel* **:** HIGH 13 (2) **:** formed with the tongue in a higher position than for the other vowel of a pair
**3 :** restricted to a privileged class
**4 a :** SECLUDED, SECRET **b :** SECRETIVE ⟨she could tell us something if she would . . . but she was as *close* as wax —A. Conan Doyle⟩
**5 :** STRICT, RIGOROUS ⟨keep *close* watch⟩
**6 :** hot and stuffy
**7 :** not generous in giving or spending : TIGHT
**8 :** having little space between items or units ⟨a *close* weave⟩
**9 a :** fitting tightly or exactly **b :** very short or near to the surface ⟨a *close* haircut⟩
**10 :** being near in time, space, effect, or degree
**11 :** INTIMATE, FAMILIAR
**12 a :** ACCURATE, PRECISE ⟨a *close* study⟩ **b :** marked by fidelity to an original ⟨a *close* copy of an old master⟩ **c :** TERSE, COMPACT
**13 :** decided or won by a narrow margin ⟨a *close* baseball game⟩
**14 :** difficult to obtain ⟨money is *close*⟩

**15** *of punctuation* **:** characterized by liberal use especially of commas
**synonym** see STINGY
— **close·ly** *adverb*
— **close·ness** *noun*
— **close to home :** within one's personal interests so that one is strongly affected ⟨the speaker's remarks hit *close to home*⟩
— **close to the vest :** in a reserved or cautious manner

**⁵close** \'klōs\ *adverb* (15th century)
**:** in a close position or manner

**close call** \'klōs-\ *noun* (1881)
**:** a narrow escape

**close corporation** \'klōs-\ *noun* (circa 1902)
**:** a corporation whose stock is not publicly traded but held by a few persons (as those in management)

**close–cropped** \'klōs-,kräpt\ *adjective* (circa 1893)
**1 :** clipped short
**2 :** having the hair clipped short

**closed** \'klōzd\ *adjective* (13th century)
**1 a :** not open **b :** ENCLOSED **c :** composed entirely of closed tubes or vessels ⟨a *closed* circulatory system⟩
**2 a :** forming a self-contained unit allowing no additions ⟨*closed* association⟩ **b** (1) **:** traced by a moving point that returns to an arbitrary starting point ⟨*closed* curve⟩; *also* **:** so formed that every plane section is a closed curve ⟨*closed* surface⟩ (2) **:** characterized by mathematical elements that when subjected to an operation produce only elements of the same set ⟨the set of whole numbers is *closed* under addition and multiplication⟩ (3) **:** containing all the limit points of every possible subset ⟨a *closed* interval contains its endpoints⟩ **c :** characterized by continuous return and reuse of the working substance ⟨a *closed* cooling system⟩ **d** *of a racecourse* **:** having the same starting and finishing point
**3 a :** confined to a few ⟨*closed* membership⟩ **b :** excluding participation of outsiders or witnesses **:** conducted in strict secrecy **c :** rigidly excluding outside influence ⟨a *closed* mind⟩
**4 :** ending in a consonant ⟨*closed* syllable⟩

**closed book** *noun* (1913)
**:** something beyond comprehension : ENIGMA

**closed–cap·tioned** \'klōz(d)-'kap-shənd\ *adjective* (1980)
*of a television program* **:** broadcast with captions that appear only on the screen of a receiver equipped with a decoder

**closed–cir·cuit** \-'sər-kət\ *adjective* (1949)
**:** used in, shown on, or being a television installation in which the signal is transmitted by wire to a limited number of receivers

**closed corporation** *noun* (1924)
**:** CLOSE CORPORATION

**closed couplet** *noun* (1910)
**:** a rhymed couplet in which the sense is complete

**closed–door** \'klōz(d)-'dōr, -'dȯr\ *adjective* (1950)
**:** barring public and press ⟨a *closed-door* session of the investigating committee⟩

**closed–end** \'klōzd-'end\ *adjective* (circa 1938)
**:** having a fixed capitalization of shares that are traded on the market at prices determined by the operation of the law of supply and demand ⟨a *closed-end* investment company⟩ — compare OPEN-END

**closed loop** *noun* (1951)
**:** an automatic control system for an operation or process in which feedback in a closed path or group of paths acts to maintain output at a desired level

**close·down** \'klōz-,daủn\ *noun* (1889)
**:** an instance of suspending or stopping operations

**closed shop** *noun* (1904)
**:** an establishment in which the employer by agreement hires only union members in good standing

**closed stance** *noun* (circa 1934)
**:** a stance (as in golf) in which the forward foot is closer to the line of play than the back foot — compare OPEN STANCE

**close·fist·ed** \'klōs-,fis-təd\ *adjective* (1608)
**:** STINGY, TIGHTFISTED

**close–grained** \-,gränd\ *adjective* (1754)
**:** having a compacted smooth texture; especially **:** having narrow annual rings or small wood elements

**close–hauled** \-'hȯld\ *adjective* (1769)
**:** having the sails set for sailing as nearly against the wind as the vessel will go

**close–in** \'klōs-'in\ *adjective* (1945)
**:** near a center of activity and especially a city ⟨*close-in* suburbs⟩

**close in** \'klōz-\ (14th century)
*transitive verb*
**1 :** to encircle closely and isolate
**2 :** to enshroud to such an extent as to preclude entrance or exit ⟨the airport was *closed in* by the storm⟩
*intransitive verb*
**1 :** to gather in close all around with an oppressing or isolating effect ⟨despair *closed in* on her⟩
**2 :** to approach to close quarters especially for an attack, raid, or arrest ⟨the police *closed in*⟩
**3 :** to grow dark ⟨the short November day was already *closing in* —Ellen Glasgow⟩

**close–knit** \'klōs-'nit\ *adjective* (1926)
**:** bound together by intimate social or cultural ties or by close economic or political ties ⟨*close-knit* families⟩

**closely held** *adjective* (1946)
**:** having most stock shares and voting rights in the hands of a few ⟨a *closely held* business⟩

**close–mouthed** \'klōs-'maủthd, -'maủtht\ *adjective* (1881)
**:** cautious in speaking **:** UNCOMMUNICATIVE; *also* **:** SECRETIVE

**close order** *noun* (circa 1797)
**:** an arrangement of troops in a typical marching formation

**close–out** \'klō-,zaủt\ *noun* (1925)
**1 :** a clearing out by a sale usually at reduced prices of the whole remaining stock (as of a business)
**2 :** an article offered or bought at a closeout

**close out** \'klōz-\ (14th century)
*transitive verb*
**1 a :** EXCLUDE **b :** PRECLUDE ⟨*close out* his chances⟩
**2 a :** to dispose of a whole stock of by sale **b :** to dispose of (a business) **c :** SELL ⟨*closed out* his share of the business⟩ **d :** to put (an account) in order for disposal or transfer
**3 a :** to bring to an often rapid or abrupt conclusion **b :** to discontinue operation of
*intransitive verb*
**1 :** to sell out a business
**2 :** to buy or sell securities or commodities in order to terminate an account

---

☆ **SYNONYMS**
**Close, end, conclude, finish, complete, terminate** mean to bring or come to a stopping point or limit. CLOSE usually implies that something has been in some way open as well as unfinished ⟨*close* a debate⟩. END conveys a strong sense of finality ⟨*ended* his life⟩. CONCLUDE may imply a formal closing (as of a meeting) ⟨the service *concluded* with a blessing⟩. FINISH may stress completion of a final step in a process ⟨after it is painted, the house will be *finished*⟩. COMPLETE implies the removal of all deficiencies or a successful finishing of what has been undertaken ⟨the resolving of this last issue *completes* the agreement⟩. TERMINATE implies the setting of a limit in time or space ⟨your employment *terminates* after three months⟩.

**close quarters** \'klōs-\ *noun plural* (1809)
: immediate contact or close range ⟨fought at *close quarters*⟩

**close shave** \'klōs-, 'klōsh-\ *noun* (1834)
: a narrow escape

**close·stool** \'klōs-ˌstül\ *noun* (15th century)
: a stool holding a chamber pot

**¹clos·et** \'klä-zət, 'klȯ-\ *noun* [Middle English, from Middle French, diminutive of *clos* enclosure — more at CLOSE] (14th century)
**1 a :** an apartment or small room for privacy **b :** a monarch's or official's private chamber
**2 :** a cabinet or recess for especially china, household utensils, or clothing
**3 :** a place of retreat or privacy
**4 :** WATER CLOSET
**5 :** a state or condition of secrecy, privacy, or obscurity ⟨came out of the *closet*⟩
— **clos·et·ful** \-ˌfu̇l\ *noun*

**²closet** *transitive verb* (1595)
**1 :** to shut up in or as if in a closet
**2 :** to take into a closet for a secret interview

**³closet** *adjective* (circa 1615)
**1 :** closely private
**2 :** working in or suited to the closet as the place of seclusion or study : THEORETICAL
**3 :** being so in private ⟨a *closet* racist⟩

**closet drama** *noun* (1922)
: drama suited primarily for reading rather than production

**closet queen** *noun* (1967)
: one who secretly engages in homosexual activities while leading an ostensibly heterosexual life — often used disparagingly

**¹close–up** \'klō-ˌsəp\ *noun* (1913)
**1 :** a photograph or movie shot taken at close range
**2 :** an intimate view or examination of something

**²close–up** \ˌklō-'səp\ *adverb or adjective* (1926)
: at close range

**clos·ing** \'klō-ziŋ\ *noun* (1596)
**1 :** a concluding part (as of a speech)
**2 :** a closable gap (as in an article of clothing)
**3 :** a meeting of parties to a real-estate deal for formally transferring title

**clos·trid·i·um** \klä-'stri-dē-əm\ *noun, plural* **-ia** \-dē-ə\ [New Latin, genus name, from Greek *klōstēr* spindle, from *klōthein* to spin] (1884)
: any of a genus (*Clostridium*) of spore-forming mostly anaerobic soil or intestinal bacteria — compare BOTULINUM
— **clos·trid·i·al** \-dē-əl\ *adjective*

**clo·sure** \'klō-zhər\ *noun* [Middle English, from Middle French, from Latin *clausura*, from *clausus*, past participle of *claudere* to close — more at CLOSE] (14th century)
**1** *archaic* **:** means of enclosing : ENCLOSURE
**2 :** an act of closing : the condition of being closed ⟨*closure* of the eyelids⟩
**3 :** something that closes ⟨pocket with zipper *closure*⟩
**4** [translation of French *clôture*] **:** CLOTURE
**5 :** the property that a number system or a set has when it is mathematically closed under an operation
**6 :** a set that contains a given set together with all the limit points of the given set

**¹clot** \'klät\ *noun* [Middle English, from Old English *clott*; akin to Middle High German *klōz* lump, ball — more at CLOUT] (before 12th century)
**1 :** a portion of a substance cleaving together in a thick nondescript mass (as of clay or gum)
**2 a :** a roundish viscous lump formed by coagulation of a portion of liquid or by melting **b :** a coagulated mass produced by clotting of blood
**3** *British* **:** BLOCKHEAD
**4 :** CLUSTER, GROUP ⟨a *clot* of spectators⟩

**²clot** *verb* **clot·ted; clot·ting** (15th century)
*intransitive verb*
**1 :** to become a clot : form clots

**2 :** to undergo a sequence of complex chemical and physical reactions that results in conversion of fluid blood into a coagulated mass : COAGULATE
*transitive verb*
**1 :** to cause to form into or as if into a clot
**2 :** to fill with clots

**cloth** \'klȯth\ *noun, plural* **cloths** \'klȯthz, 'klȯths\ *often attributive* [Middle English, from Old English *clāth* cloth, garment; akin to Middle High German *kleit* garment] (before 12th century)
**1 a :** a pliable material made usually by weaving, felting, or knitting natural or synthetic fibers and filaments **b :** a similar material (as of glass)
**2 :** a piece of cloth adapted for a particular purpose; *especially* **:** TABLECLOTH
**3 a :** a distinctive dress of a profession or calling **b :** the dress of the clergy; *also* **:** CLERGY

**cloth·bound** \-ˌbau̇nd\ *adjective* (1860)
*of a book* **:** bound in stiff boards covered with cloth

**clothe** \'klōth\ *transitive verb* **clothed** *or* **clad** \'klad\; **cloth·ing** [Middle English, from Old English *clāthian*, from *clāth*] (before 12th century)
**1 a :** to cover with or as if with cloth or clothing **:** DRESS **b :** to provide with clothes
**2 :** to express or enhance by suitably significant language **:** COUCH ⟨treaties *clothed* in stately phraseology⟩
**3 :** to endow especially with power or a quality

**clothes** \'klōz also 'klōthz\ *noun plural, often attributive* [Middle English, from Old English *clāthas*, plural of *clāth*] (before 12th century)
**1 :** CLOTHING
**2 :** BEDCLOTHES
**3 :** all the cloth articles of personal and household use that can be washed

**clothes·horse** \-ˌhȯrs\ *noun* (1775)
**1 :** a frame on which to hang clothes
**2 :** a conspicuously dressy person

**¹clothes·line** \-ˌlīn\ *noun* (1830)
: a line (as of cord) on which clothes may be hung to dry

**²clothesline** *transitive verb* (1964)
: to knock down (a football player) by catching by the neck with an outstretched arm

**clothes moth** *noun* (1753)
: any of several small yellowish or buff-colored moths (especially *Tinea pellionella* and *Tineola bisselliella* of the family Tineidae) whose larvae eat wool, fur, or feathers

**clothes–peg** \'klōz-ˌpeg also 'klōthz-\ *noun* (1825)
*British* **:** CLOTHESPIN

**clothes·pin** \-ˌpin\ *noun* (1846)
: a forked piece of wood or plastic or a small spring clamp used for fastening clothes on a clothesline

**clothes·press** \-ˌpres\ *noun* (1713)
: a receptacle for clothes

**cloth·ier** \'klōth-yər, 'klō-thē-ər\ *noun* [Middle English, alteration of *clother*, from *cloth*] (14th century)
: one who makes or sells clothing

**cloth·ing** \'klō-thiŋ\ *noun* (13th century)
: garments in general; *also* **:** COVERING

**cloth yard** *noun* (15th century)
: a yard especially for measuring cloth; *specifically* **:** a unit of 37 inches equal to the Scottish ell and used also as a length for arrows

**clotted cream** *noun* (1878)
: a thick cream made chiefly in England by slowly heating whole milk on which the cream has been allowed to rise and then skimming the cooled cream from the top — called also *Devonshire cream*

**clo·ture** \'klō-chər\ *noun* [French *clôture*, literally, closure, alteration of Middle French *closure*] (1871)
: the closing or limitation of debate in a legislative body especially by calling for a vote
— **cloture** *transitive verb*

**¹cloud** \'klau̇d\ *noun, often attributive* [Middle English, rock, cloud, from Old English *clūd*; perhaps akin to Greek *gloutos* buttock] (14th century)
**1 :** a visible mass of particles of condensed vapor (as water or ice) suspended in the atmosphere of a planet (as the earth) or moon
**2 :** something resembling or suggesting a cloud: as **a :** a light filmy, puffy, or billowy mass seeming to float in the air ⟨a *cloud* of blond hair⟩ ⟨a ship under a *cloud* of sail⟩ **b** (1) **:** a usually visible mass of minute particles suspended in the air or a gas (2) **:** an aggregation of usually obscuring matter especially in interstellar space (3) **:** an aggregate of charged particles (as electrons) **c :** a great crowd or multitude **:** SWARM ⟨*clouds* of mosquitoes⟩
**3 :** something that has a dark, lowering, or threatening aspect ⟨*clouds* of war⟩ ⟨a *cloud* of suspicion⟩
**4 :** something that obscures or blemishes ⟨a *cloud* of ambiguity⟩
**5 :** a dark or opaque vein or spot (as in marble or a precious stone)

**²cloud** (1562)
*intransitive verb*
**1 :** to grow cloudy — usually used with *over* or *up* ⟨*clouded* over before the storm⟩
**2 a** *of facial features* **:** to become troubled, apprehensive, or distressed in appearance **b :** to become blurry, dubious, or ominous — often used with *over*
**3 :** to billow up in the form of a cloud
*transitive verb*
**1 a :** to envelop or hide with or as if with a cloud ⟨smog *clouded* our view⟩ **b :** to make opaque especially by condensation of moisture **c :** to make murky especially with smoke or mist
**2 :** to make unclear or confused ⟨*cloud* the issue⟩
**3 :** TAINT, SULLY ⟨a *clouded* reputation⟩
**4 :** to cast gloom over

**cloud·ber·ry** \'klau̇d-ˌber-ē\ *noun* (1597)
: a creeping herbaceous raspberry (*Rubus chamaemorus*) of north temperate regions; *also* **:** its pale amber-colored edible fruit

**cloud·burst** \-ˌbərst\ *noun* (1869)
**1 :** a sudden copious rainfall
**2 :** DELUGE 2

**cloud chamber** *noun* (1897)
: a vessel containing air saturated with water vapor whose sudden expansion reveals the passage of an ionizing particle by a trail of visible droplets

**cloud–cuck·oo–land** \ˌklau̇d-'kü-(ˌ)kü-ˌland, -'kü-\ *noun* [translation of Greek *nephelokokkygia*] (1899)
: a realm of fantasy or of whimsical or foolish behavior

**cloud·ed leopard** \'klau̇d-dəd-\ *noun* (1910)
: a medium-sized cat (*Neofelis nebulosa*) that occurs from Nepal to southeast China and Indonesia and is grayish to yellowish with darker irregular rings, ovals, and rosettes

**cloud forest** *noun* (1922)
: a wet tropical mountain forest at an altitude

cloud 1: *1* cirrus,
*2* cirrostratus,
*3* cirrocumulus,
*4* altostratus,
*5* altocumulus,
*6* stratocumulus,
*7* nimbostratus,
*8* cumulus,
*9* cumulonimbus,
*10* stratus

---

usually between 3000 and 8000 feet (1000 and 2500 meters) that is characterized by a profusion of epiphytes and the presence of clouds even in the dry season

**cloud·land** \'klaud-ˌland\ *noun* (1817)
**1** : the region of the clouds
**2** : the realm of visionary speculation or poetic imagination

**cloud·less** \-ləs\ *adjective* (14th century)
: free from clouds : CLEAR
— **cloud·less·ly** *adverb*
— **cloud·less·ness** *noun*

**cloud·let** \'klaud-lət\ *noun* (1788)
: a small cloud

**cloud nine** *noun* (1959)
: a feeling of well-being or elation — usually used with *on*

**cloud·scape** \'klaud-ˌskāp\ *noun* (1880)
: a view or pictorial representation of a cloud formation

**cloud street** *noun* (1943)
: a row of cumulus clouds

**cloudy** \'klaud-ē\ *adjective* **cloud·i·er; -est** (14th century)
**1** : of, relating to, or resembling cloud
**2** : darkened by gloom or anxiety
**3 a** : overcast with clouds **b** : having a cloudy sky
**4** : obscure in meaning ⟨*cloudy* issues⟩; *also* : uncertain as to fact or outcome ⟨a *cloudy* future⟩
**5** : dimmed or dulled as if by clouds ⟨a *cloudy* mirror⟩
**6** : uneven in color or texture
**7** : having visible material in suspension : MURKY
— **cloud·i·ly** \'klaud-ᵊl-ē\ *adverb*
— **cloud·i·ness** \'klaud-ē-nəs\ *noun*

**¹clout** \'klaut\ *noun* [Middle English, from Old English *clūt;* akin to Middle High German *klōz* lump, Russian *gluda*] (before 12th century)
**1** *dialect chiefly British* : a piece of cloth or leather : RAG
**2** : a blow especially with the hand; *also* : a hard hit in baseball
**3** : a white cloth on a stake or frame used as a target in archery
**4** : PULL, INFLUENCE ⟨political *clout*⟩

**²clout** *transitive verb* (14th century)
**1** : to cover or patch with a clout
**2** : to hit forcefully

**¹clove** \'klōv\ *noun* [Middle English, from Old English *clufu;* akin to Old English *clēofan* to cleave] (before 12th century)
: one of the small bulbs (as in garlic) developed in the axils of the scales of a large bulb

**²clove** *past of* CLEAVE

**³clove** \'klōv\ *noun* [alteration of Middle English *clowe,* from Old French *clou (de girofle),* literally, nail of clove, from Latin *clavus* nail] (13th century)
: the dried flower bud of a tropical tree (*Syzygium aromaticum* synonym *Eugenia aromatica*) of the myrtle family that is used as a spice and is the source of an oil; *also* : this tree

**clove hitch** \'klōv-\ *noun* [Middle English *cloven, clove* divided, from past participle of *clevien* to cleave] (circa 1769)
: a knot securing a rope temporarily to an object (as a post or spar) and consisting of a turn around the object, over the standing part, around the object again, and under the last turn — see KNOT illustration

**clo·ven** \'klō-vən\ *past participle of* CLEAVE
**cloven foot** *noun* (13th century)
: CLOVEN HOOF
— **clo·ven–foot·ed** \'klō-vən-ˌfu̇-təd\ *adjective*

**cloven hoof** *noun* (1870)
**1** : a foot (as of a sheep) divided into two parts at its distal extremity
**2** [from the traditional representation of Satan as cloven-hoofed] : the sign of devilish character

— **clo·ven–hoofed** \'klō-vən-ˌhu̇ft, -ˌhüft, -ˌhu̇vd, -ˌhüvd\ *adjective*

**clove pink** *noun* (circa 1855)
: CARNATION 2

**clo·ver** \'klō-vər\ *noun* [Middle English, from Old English *clāfre;* akin to Old High German *klēo* clover] (before 12th century)
**1** : any of a genus (*Trifolium*) of low leguminous herbs having trifoliolate leaves and flowers in dense heads and including many that are valuable for forage and attractive to bees
**2** : any of various leguminous plants (as of the genera *Melilotus, Lespedeza,* or *Medicago*) other than the clovers (genus *Trifolium*)
— **in clover** *or* **in the clover** : in prosperity or in pleasant circumstances

**¹clo·ver·leaf** \-ˌlēf\ *adjective* (1917)
: resembling a clover leaf in shape

**²cloverleaf** *noun, plural* **-leafs** \-ˌlēfs\ *or* **-leaves** \-ˌlēvz\ (1931)
: an interchange between two major highways that allows traffic to change from one to the other without requiring any left turns or crossings and that from above resembles a four-leaf clover

cloverleaf

**Clo·vis** \'klō-vəs\ *adjective* [*Clovis,* New Mexico] (1956)
: of or relating to a widely distributed prehistoric culture of North America characterized by leaf-shaped flint projectile points having fluted sides

**¹clown** \'klaun\ *noun* [probably of Low German origin; akin to Frisian *klönne* clumsy fellow, Old English *clyne* lump of metal] (1563)
**1** : FARMER, COUNTRYMAN
**2** : a rude ill-bred person : BOOR
**3 a** : a fool, jester, or comedian in an entertainment (as a play); *specifically* : a grotesquely dressed comedy performer in a circus **b** : a person who habitually plays the buffoon **c** : JOKER 1b

**²clown** *intransitive verb* (1599)
: to act as or like a clown

**clown·ery** \'klaun-ə-rē\ *noun, plural* **-er·ies** (1589)
: clownish behavior or an instance of clownishness : BUFFOONERY

**clown·ish** \'klaun-nish\ *adjective* (circa 1570)
: resembling or befitting a clown (as in ignorance and lack of sophistication)
synonym see BOORISH
— **clown·ish·ly** *adverb*
— **clown·ish·ness** *noun*

**clox·a·cil·lin** \ˌkläk-sə-'si-lən\ *noun* [*chlor-* + *oxacillin*] (1963)
: a semisynthetic oral penicillin $C_{19}H_{17}Cl-N_3NaO_5S$ effective especially against staphylococci which secrete penicillinase

**cloy** \'klȯi\ *verb* [alteration of Middle English *acloien* to lame, from Middle French *encloer* to drive in a nail, from Medieval Latin *inclavare,* from Latin *in + clavus* nail] (1528)
*transitive verb*
: to surfeit with an excess usually of something originally pleasing
*intransitive verb*
: to cause surfeit
synonym see SATIATE

**cloy·ing** \'klȯi-iŋ, 'klȯin\ *adjective* (1594)
: disgusting or distasteful by reason of excess ⟨*cloying* sweetness⟩; *also* : excessively sweet or sentimental ⟨a *cloying* romantic comedy⟩
— **cloy·ing·ly** *adverb*

**cloze** \'klōz\ *adjective* [by shortening & alteration from *closure*] (1953)
: of, relating to, or being a test of reading

comprehension that involves having the person being tested supply words which have been systematically deleted from a text

**¹club** \'kləb\ *noun, often attributive* [Middle English *clubbe,* from Old Norse *klubba;* akin to Old High German *kolbo* club] (13th century)
**1 a** : a heavy usually tapering staff especially of wood wielded as a weapon **b** : a stick or bat used to hit a ball in any of various games **c** : something resembling a club
**2 a** : a playing card marked with a stylized figure of a black clover **b** *plural but singular or plural in construction* : the suit comprising cards marked with clubs
**3 a** : an association of persons for some common object usually jointly supported and meeting periodically; *also* : a group identified by some common characteristic ⟨nations in the nuclear *club*⟩ **b** : the meeting place of a club **c** : an association of persons participating in a plan by which they agree to make regular payments or purchases in order to secure some advantage **d** : NIGHTCLUB **e** : an athletic association or team
— **club·bish** \'klə-bish\ *adjective*

**²club** *verb* **clubbed; club·bing** (1593)
*transitive verb*
**1 a** : to beat or strike with or as if with a club **b** : to gather into a club-shaped mass ⟨*clubbed* her hair⟩
**2 a** : to unite or combine for a common cause **b** : to contribute to a common fund
*intransitive verb*
**1** : to form a club : COMBINE
**2** : to pay a share of a common expense

**club·ba·ble** *also* **club·able** \'klə-bə-bəl\ *adjective* (1783)
: SOCIABLE

**clubbed** \'kləbd\ *adjective* (14th century)
: shaped like a club ⟨*clubbed* antennae⟩

**club·ber** \'klə-bər\ *noun* (1633)
: a member of a club

**club·by** \'klə-bē\ *adjective* **club·bi·er; -est** (1859)
: characteristic of a club or club members: as **a** : displaying friendliness especially to other members of the same social group : SOCIABLE **b** : open only to qualified or approved persons : SELECT, ELITE
— **club·bi·ness** *noun*

**club car** *noun* (1886)
: a railroad passenger car with facilities for serving refreshments and drinks — called also *bar car, lounge car*

**club chair** *noun* (1919)
: a deep low thickly upholstered easy chair often with rather low back and heavy sides and arms

**club cheese** *noun* (1916)
: a process cheese made by grinding cheddar and other cheeses usually with added condiments and seasoning

**club·foot** \'kləb-ˌfu̇t\ *noun* (1538)
: a misshapen foot twisted out of position from birth; *also* : this deformity
— **club·foot·ed** \-ˌfu̇-təd\ *adjective*

**club fungus** *noun* (1899)
: any of a family (Clavariaceae) of basidiomycetes with a simple or branched often club-shaped sporophore

**club·house** \'kləb-ˌhau̇s\ *noun* (1818)
**1** : a house occupied by a club or used for club activities
**2** : locker rooms used by an athletic team

**club·man** \'kləb-mən, -ˌman\ *noun* (1851)
: a usually wealthy man given to club life

**club moss** *noun* (1597)
: any of an order (Lycopodiales) of primitive vascular plants (as ground pine) often with the sporangia borne in club-shaped strobili

**club·root** \'kləb-ˌrüt, -ˌru̇t\ *noun* (1846)
: a disease of cruciferous plants and especially of cabbage caused by a slime mold (*Plasmodiophora brassicae*) producing swellings or distortions of the root

**club sandwich** *noun* (1903)
**:** a sandwich of three slices of bread with two layers of meat (as turkey) and lettuce, tomato, and mayonnaise

**club soda** *noun* (1942)
**:** SODA WATER 2a

**club steak** *noun* (1915)
**:** a small steak cut from the end of the short loin — see BEEF illustration

**¹cluck** \'klək\ *verb* [imitative] (15th century)
*intransitive verb*
**1 :** to make a cluck
**2 :** to make a clicking sound with the tongue
**3 :** to express interest or concern ⟨critics *clucked* over the new developments⟩
*transitive verb*
**1 :** to call with a cluck
**2 :** to express with interest or concern

**²cluck** *noun* (1703)
**1 :** the characteristic sound made by a hen especially in calling her chicks
**2 :** a stupid or naive person

**¹clue** \'klü\ *noun* [alteration of *clew*] (1596)
**:** something that guides through an intricate procedure or maze of difficulties; *specifically* **:** a piece of evidence that leads one toward the solution of a problem ◆

**²clue** *transitive verb* **clued; clue·ing** *or* **clu·ing** (1663)
**1 :** to provide with a clue
**2 :** to give reliable information to ⟨*clue* me in on how it happened⟩

**clue·less** \'klü-ləs\ *adjective* (1862)
**1 :** providing no clue
**2 :** completely or hopelessly bewildered, unaware, ignorant, or foolish

**clum·ber spaniel** \'kləm-bər-\ *noun, often C capitalized* [*Clumber,* estate in Nottinghamshire, England] (1883)
**:** any of a breed of large massive heavyset spaniels with a dense silky largely white coat

**¹clump** \'kləmp\ *noun* [probably from Low German *klump*] (circa 1586)
**1 :** a group of things clustered together ⟨a *clump* of bushes⟩
**2 :** a compact mass
**3 :** a heavy tramping sound
— **clumpy** \'kləm-pē\ *adjective*

**²clump** (1665)
*intransitive verb*
**1 :** to walk or move clumsily and noisily
**2 :** to form clumps
*transitive verb*
**:** to arrange in or cause to form clumps ⟨the serum *clumps* the bacteria⟩

**clum·sy** \'kləm-zē\ *adjective* **clum·si·er; -est** [probably from obsolete English *clumse* benumbed with cold] (circa 1598)
**1 a :** lacking dexterity, nimbleness, or grace ⟨*clumsy* fingers⟩ **b :** lacking tact or subtlety ⟨a *clumsy* joke⟩
**2 :** awkward or inefficient in use or construction **:** UNWIELDY
*synonym* see AWKWARD
— **clum·si·ly** \-zə-lē\ *adverb*
— **clum·si·ness** \-zē-nəs\ *noun*

**clung** *past and past participle of* CLING

**¹clunk** \'kləŋk\ *verb* [imitative] (circa 1796)
*intransitive verb*
**1 :** to make a clunk
**2 :** to hit something with a clunk
*transitive verb*
**:** to strike or hit with a clunk

**²clunk** *noun* (1823)
**1 :** a blow or the sound of a blow **:** THUMP
**2 :** a dull or stupid person

**clunk·er** \'kləŋ-kər\ *noun* (1943)
**1 :** an old or badly working piece of machinery; *especially* **:** a dilapidated automobile
**2 :** someone or something notably unsuccessful

**clunky** \'kləŋ-kē\ *adjective* **clunk·i·er; -est** (1968)
**:** clumsy in style, form, or execution ⟨a *clunky* thriller⟩ ⟨*clunky* earrings⟩

**clu·pe·id** \'klü-pē-əd\ *noun* [ultimately from Latin *clupea,* a small river fish] (1880)
**:** any of a large family (Clupeidae) of soft-finned bony fishes (as herrings) that have a laterally compressed body and a forked tail and usually occur in schools
— **clupeid** *adjective*

**¹clus·ter** \'kləs-tər\ *noun* [Middle English, from Old English *clyster;* akin to Old English *clott* clot] (before 12th century)
**:** a number of similar individuals that occur together: as **a :** two or more consecutive consonants or vowels in a segment of speech **b :** a group of buildings and especially houses built close together on a sizable tract in order to preserve open spaces larger than the individual yard for common recreation **c :** an aggregation of stars or galaxies that appear close together in the sky and are gravitationally associated
— **clus·tery** \-t(ə-)rē\ *adjective*

**²cluster** *verb* **clus·tered; clus·ter·ing** \-t(ə-)riŋ\ (14th century)
*transitive verb*
**1 :** to collect into a cluster ⟨*cluster* the tents together⟩
**2 :** to furnish with clusters
*intransitive verb*
**:** to grow, assemble, or occur in a cluster

**cluster analysis** *noun* (1948)
**:** a statistical classification technique for discovering whether the individuals of a population fall into different groups by making quantitative comparisons of multiple characteristics

**cluster bomb** *noun* (1967)
**:** an aircraft-dropped canister of small fragmentation bombs

**cluster headache** *noun* (1953)
**:** a headache that is characterized by severe pain in the eye or temple and tends to recur in a series of attacks

**¹clutch** \'kləch\ *verb* [Middle English *clucchen,* from Old English *clyccan*] (before 12th century)
*transitive verb*
**1 :** to grasp or hold with or as if with the hand or claws usually strongly, tightly, or suddenly
**2** *obsolete* **:** CLENCH
*intransitive verb*
**1 :** to seek to grasp and hold
**2 :** to operate an automobile clutch
*synonym* see TAKE

**²clutch** *noun* (13th century)
**1 a :** the claws or a hand in the act of grasping or seizing firmly **b :** an often cruel or unrelenting control, power, or possession ⟨the fell *clutch* of circumstance —W. E. Henley⟩ **c :** the act of grasping, holding, or restraining
**2 a :** a coupling used to connect and disconnect a driving and a driven part of a mechanism **b :** a lever (as a pedal) operating such a clutch
**3 :** a tight or critical situation **:** PINCH ⟨come through in the *clutch*⟩
**4 :** CLUTCH BAG

**³clutch** *adjective* (1944)
**1 :** made or done in a crucial situation ⟨a *clutch* hit⟩
**2 :** successful in a crucial situation ⟨a *clutch* pitcher⟩

**⁴clutch** *noun* [alteration of dialect English *cletch* hatching, brood] (1721)
**1 :** a nest of eggs or a brood of chicks
**2 :** GROUP, BUNCH

**clutch bag** *noun* (1949)
**:** a woman's small usually strapless handbag

**¹clut·ter** \'klə-tər\ *verb* [Middle English *clotteren* to clot, from *clot*] (1556)
*intransitive verb*
*chiefly dialect* **:** to run in disorder
*transitive verb*
**:** to fill or cover with scattered or disordered things that impede movement or reduce effectiveness — often used with *up*

**²clutter** *noun* (1649)
**1 a :** a crowded or confused mass or collection **b :** things that clutter a place

**2 :** interfering radar echoes caused by reflection from objects (as on the ground) other than the target
**3** *chiefly dialect* **:** DISTURBANCE, HUBBUB

**Clyde** \'klīd\ *noun* (1894)
**:** CLYDESDALE

**Clydes·dale** \'klīdz-,dāl\ *noun* (1786)
**:** a heavy draft horse with feathering on the legs of a breed originally from Clydesdale, Scotland

**clyp·e·us** \'kli-pē-əs\ *noun, plural* **clyp·ei** \-pē-,ī, -pē,ē\ [New Latin, from Latin, round shield] (1834)
**:** a plate on the anterior median aspect of an insect's head

**clys·ter** \'klis-tər\ *noun* [Middle English, from Middle French or Latin; Middle French *clistere,* from Latin *clyster,* from Greek *klystēr,* from *klyzein* to wash out; akin to Welsh *clir* pure, Old English *hlūtor* clean] (14th century)
**:** ENEMA

**Cly·tem·nes·tra** \,klī-təm-'nes-trə\ *noun* [Latin, from Greek *Klytaimnēstra*]
**:** the wife and murderess of Agamemnon

**cni·dar·i·an** \nī-'dar-ē-ən, -'der-\ *noun* [ultimately from New Latin *cnida* nematocyst, from Greek *knidē* nettle] (circa 1909)
**:** COELENTERATE
— **cnidarian** *adjective*

**co-** *prefix* [Middle English, from Latin, from *com-;* akin to Old English *ge-,* perfective and collective prefix, Old Irish *com-* with]
**1 :** with **:** together **:** joint **:** jointly ⟨*co*exist⟩ ⟨*co*heir⟩
**2 :** in or to the same degree ⟨*co*extensive⟩
**3 a :** one that is associated in an action with another **:** fellow **:** partner ⟨*co*author⟩ ⟨*co*worker⟩ **b :** having a usually lesser share in duty or responsibility **:** alternate **:** deputy ⟨*co*pilot⟩
**4 :** of, relating to, or constituting the complement of an angle ⟨*co*sine⟩ ⟨*co*declination⟩

| | |
|---|---|
| co·act | co·chair·per·son |
| co·ac·tive | co·chair·wom·an |
| co·ac·tor | co·cham·pi·on |
| co·ad·min·is·tra·tion | co·com·pos·er |
| co·an·chor | co·con·spir·a·tor |
| co·au·thor | co·coun·sel |
| co·au·thor·ship | co·cre·ate |
| co·cap·tain | co·cre·ator |
| co·cat·a·lyst | co·cul·ti·vate |
| co·chair | co·cul·ti·va·tion |
| co·chair·man | co·cul·ture |

\ə\ abut \ə\ kitten \ər\ further \a\ ash \ā\ ace
\ä\ mop, mar \au̇\ out \ch\ chin \e\ bet \ē\ easy
\g\ go \i\ hit \ī\ ice \j\ job \ŋ\ sing \ō\ go
\ȯ\ law \ȯi\ boy \th\ thin \th\ the \ü\ loot \u̇\ foot
\y\ yet \zh\ vision *see also* Guide to Pronunciation

co·cu·ra·tor
co·de·fen·dant
co·de·sign
co·de·vel·op
co·de·vel·op·er
co·di·rect
co·di·rec·tion
co·di·rec·tor
co·dis·cov·er
co·dis·cov·er·er
co·drive
co·driv·er
co·ed·it
co·ed·i·tor
co·eter·nal
co·ex·ec·u·tor
co·fa·vor·ite
co·fea·ture
co·fi·nance
co·found
co·found·er
co·head
co·heir
co·heir·ess
co·hold·er
co·host
co·host·ess
co·in·vent
co·in·ven·tor
co·in·ves·ti·ga·tor
co·in·ves·tor
co·join
co·lead
co·lead·er
co·man·age
co·man·age·ment
co·man·ag·er
co·mem·ber
co·nom·i·nee
co·oc·cur
co·oc·cur·rence

co—oc·cur·rent
co—of·fi·cial
co—or·ga·niz·er
co—own
co—own·er
co—own·er·ship
co—part·ner
co—part·ner·ship
co—pre·sent
co—pres·i·dent
co—prince
co—prin·ci·pal
co—pris·on·er
co—pro·cess·ing
co—pro·duce
co—pro·duc·er
co—pro·duc·tion
co—pro·mot·er
co—pro·pri·etor
co—pros·per·i·ty
co—pub·lish
co—pub·lish·er
co—re·cip·i·ent
co—re·search·er
co—res·i·dent
co—res·i·den·tial
co—rul·er
co—script
co—spon·sor
co—spon·sor·ship
co—star
co—sur·fac·tant
co—ten·ant
co—trans·duce
co—trans·duc·tion
co—trans·fer
co—trans·port
co—trust·ee
co—win·ner
co—work·er
co—write

**co·ac·er·vate** \kō-'a-sər-ˌvāt\ *noun* [Latin *coacervatus,* past participle of *coacervare* to heap up, from *co-* + *acervus* heap] (1929) : an aggregate of colloidal droplets held together by electrostatic attractive forces — **co·acer·vate** \ˌkō-ə-'sər-vət\ *adjective* — **co·ac·er·va·tion** \(ˌ)kō-ˌa-sər-'vā-shən\ *noun*

¹**coach** \'kōch\ *noun, often attributive* [Middle English *coche,* from Middle French, from German *Kutsche,* from Hungarian *kocsi (szekér),* literally, wagon from *Kocs,* Hungary] (1556) **1 a :** a large usually closed four-wheeled horse-drawn carriage having doors in the sides and an elevated seat in front for the driver **b :** a railroad passenger car intended primarily for day travel **c :** BUS 1a **d :** TRAILER 3b **e :** a two-door enclosed automobile **f :** a class of passenger air transportation at a lower fare than first class **2** [from the concept that the tutor conveys the student through his examinations] **a :** a private tutor **b :** one who instructs or trains a performer or a team of performers; *specifically :* one who instructs players in the fundamentals of a competitive sport and directs team strategy ⟨football *coach*⟩

²**coach** (1630) *intransitive verb* **1 :** to go in a coach **2 :** to instruct, direct, or prompt as a coach *transitive verb* **1 :** to train intensively (as by instruction and demonstration) ⟨*coach* pupils⟩ **2 :** to act as coach of ⟨*coach* tennis⟩ ⟨*coach* a team⟩ — **coach·able** \'kō-chə-bəl\ *adjective* — **coach·er** *noun*

**coach dog** *noun* (1840) **:** DALMATIAN

**coach·man** \'kōch-mən\ *noun* (1579) **:** a man who drives a coach or carriage

**coach·work** \-ˌwərk\ *noun* (1906) **:** an automobile body **:** BODYWORK

**co·ac·tion** \-'ak-shən\ *noun* (1625) **1 :** joint action **2 :** the interaction between individuals or kinds (as species) in an ecological community

**co·adapt·ed** \ˌkō-ə-'dap-təd\ *adjective* (1836) **:** mutually adapted especially by natural selection ⟨*coadapted* gene complexes⟩ — **co·ad·ap·ta·tion** \ˌkō-ˌa-ˌdap-'tā-shən, -dəp-'\ *noun*

**co·ad·ju·tor** \ˌkō-ə-'jü-tər, kō-'a-jə-tər\ *noun* [Middle English *coadjutour,* from Middle French *coadjuteur,* from Late Latin *coadjutor,* from Latin *co-* + *adjutor* helper, from *adjuvare* to help — more at AID] (15th century) **1 :** one who works together with another **:** ASSISTANT **2 :** a bishop assisting a diocesan bishop and often having the right of succession — **coadjutor** *adjective*

**co·ad·ju·trix** \ˌkō-ə-'jü-triks, kō-'a-jə-(ˌ)triks\ *noun, plural* **co·ad·ju·tri·ces** \ˌkō-ə-'jü-trə-ˌsēz, (ˌ)kō-ˌa-jə-'trī-(ˌ)sēz\ [New Latin, feminine of *coadjutor*] (1646) **:** a female coadjutor

**co·ag·u·lant** \kō-'a-gyə-lənt\ *noun* (1770) **:** something that produces coagulation

**co·ag·u·lase** \kō-'a-gyə-ˌlās, -ˌlāz\ *noun* (1914) **:** any of several enzymes that cause coagulation (as of blood)

¹**co·ag·u·late** \-lət, -ˌlāt\ *adjective* (14th century) *archaic* **:** being clotted or congealed

²**co·ag·u·late** \kō-'a-gyə-ˌlāt\ *verb* **-lat·ed; -lat·ing** [Latin *coagulatus,* past participle of *coagulare* to curdle, from *coagulum* curdling agent, from *cogere* to drive together — more at COGENT] (15th century) *transitive verb* **1 :** to cause to become viscous or thickened into a coherent mass **:** CURDLE, CLOT **2 :** to gather together or form into a mass or group *intransitive verb* **:** to become coagulated — **co·ag·u·la·bil·i·ty** \kō-ˌa-gyə-lə-'bi-lə-tē\ *noun* — **co·ag·u·la·ble** \-'a-gyə-lə-bəl\ *adjective* — **co·ag·u·la·tion** \-'lā-shən\ *noun*

**co·ag·u·lum** \kō-'a-gyə-ləm\ *noun, plural* **-u·la** \-lə\ *or* **-ulums** [Latin] (1658) **:** a coagulated mass or substance **:** CLOT

¹**coal** \'kōl\ *noun, often attributive* [Middle English *col,* from Old English; akin to Old High German & Old Norse *kol* burning ember, Middle Irish *gúal* coal] (before 12th century) **1 :** a piece of glowing carbon or charred wood **:** EMBER **2 :** CHARCOAL 1 **3 a :** a black or brownish black solid combustible substance formed by the partial decomposition of vegetable matter without free access of air and under the influence of moisture and often increased pressure and temperature that is widely used as a natural fuel **b** *plural, British* **:** pieces or a quantity of the fuel broken up for burning

²**coal** (1602) *transitive verb* **1 :** to burn to charcoal **:** CHAR **2 :** to supply with coal *intransitive verb* **:** to take in coal

**co·a·lesce** \ˌkō-ə-'les\ *verb* **co·a·lesced; co·a·lesc·ing** [Latin *coalescere,* from *co-* + *alescere* to grow — more at OLD] (circa 1656) *intransitive verb* **1 :** to grow together **2 a :** to unite into a whole **:** FUSE ⟨separate townships have *coalesced* into a single, sprawling colony —Donald Gould⟩ **b :** to unite for a common end **:** join forces ⟨people with different points of view *coalesce* into opposing factions —I. L. Horowitz⟩ **3 :** to arise from the combination of distinct elements ⟨an organized and a popular resis-

tance immediately *coalesced* —C. C. Menges⟩ *transitive verb* **:** to cause to unite ⟨sometimes a book *coalesces* a public into a mass market —Walter Meade⟩ **synonym** see MIX — **co·a·les·cence** \-'le-s°n(t)s\ *noun* — **co·a·les·cent** \-s°nt\ *adjective*

**coal·field** \'kōl-ˌfēld\ *noun* (1813) **:** a region rich in coal deposits

**coal·fish** \-ˌfish\ *noun* (1603) **:** any of several blackish or dark-backed fishes (as a pollack, cobia, or sablefish)

**coal gas** *noun* (1809) **:** gas made from coal: as **a :** the mixture of gases thrown off by burning coal **b :** gas made by carbonizing bituminous coal in retorts and used for heating and lighting

**coal·hole** \'kōl-ˌhōl\ *noun* (circa 1662) **1** *British* **:** a compartment for storing coal **2 :** a hole for coal (as an opening in a sidewalk leading to a coal bin)

**coal·i·fi·ca·tion** \ˌkō-lə-fə-'kā-shən\ *noun* (1911) **:** a process in which vegetable matter becomes converted into coal of increasingly higher rank with anthracite as the final product — **coal·i·fy** \'kō-lə-ˌfī\ *transitive verb*

**co·a·li·tion** \ˌkō-ə-'li-shən\ *noun* [French, from Latin *coalescere*] (1612) **1 a :** the act of coalescing **:** UNION **b :** a body formed by the coalescing of originally distinct elements **:** COMBINATION **2 :** a temporary alliance of distinct parties, persons, or states for joint action — **co·a·li·tion·ist** \-'li-sh(ə-)nist\ *noun*

**coal measures** *noun plural* (1832) **:** beds of coal with the associated rocks

**coal oil** *noun* (1858) **1 :** petroleum or a refined oil prepared from it **2 :** KEROSENE

**coal seam** *noun* (1849) **:** a bed of coal usually thick enough to be profitably mined

**coal tar** *noun* (1785) **:** tar obtained by distillation of bituminous coal and used especially in making dyes and drugs

**coam·ing** \'kō-miŋ\ *noun* [probably irregular from *comb*] (1611) **:** a raised frame (as around a hatchway in the deck of a ship) to keep out water

**co·apt** \kō-'apt\ *transitive verb* [Late Latin *coaptare,* from Latin *co-* + *aptus* fastened, fit — more at APT] (1570) **:** to fit together and make fast — **co·ap·ta·tion** \(ˌ)kō-ˌap-'tā-shən\ *noun*

**co·arc·ta·tion** \(ˌ)kō-ˌärk-'tā-shən\ *noun* (1545) **:** a stricture or narrowing especially of a canal or vessel (as the aorta)

**coarse** \'kōrs, 'kȯrs\ *adjective* **coars·er; coars·est** [Middle English *cors,* perhaps from *course,* noun] (14th century) **1 :** of ordinary or inferior quality or value **:** COMMON **2 a** (1) **:** composed of relatively large parts or particles ⟨*coarse* sand⟩ (2) **:** loose or rough in texture ⟨*coarse* cloth⟩ **b :** adjusted or designed for heavy, fast, or less delicate work ⟨a *coarse* saw with large teeth⟩ **c :** not precise or detailed with respect to adjustment or discrimination **3 :** crude or unrefined in taste, manners, or language **4 :** harsh, raucous, or rough in tone **5** *chiefly British* **:** of or relating to coarse fish ⟨*coarse* fishing⟩ ☆ — **coarse·ly** *adverb* — **coarse·ness** *noun*

**coarse fish** *noun* (1886) **1** *chiefly British* **:** a freshwater fish other than a salmonid **2 :** ROUGH FISH

**coarse–grained** \'kōrs-ˌgrānd, 'kȯrs-\ *adjective* (circa 1774)

**1 :** having a coarse grain
**2 :** CRUDE
**coars·en** \'kōr-s°n, 'kȯr-\ *verb* **coars·ened;**
  **coars·en·ing** (1805)
*transitive verb*
**:** to make coarse
*intransitive verb*
**:** to become coarse
**¹coast** \'kōst\ *noun* [Middle English *cost,* from
Middle French *coste,* from Latin *costa* rib,
side; akin to Old Church Slavonic *kostĭ* bone]
(14th century)
  **1 :** the land near a shore **:** SEASHORE
  **2** *obsolete* **:** BORDER, FRONTIER
  **3 a :** a hill or slope suited to coasting **b :** a
slide down a slope (as on a sled)
  **4** *often capitalized* **:** the Pacific coast of the
U.S.
  **5 :** the immediate area of view — used in the
phrase *the coast is clear*
  — **coast·al** \'kōs-t°l\ *adjective*
  — **coast·wise** \'kōst-,wīz\ *adverb or adjective*
  — **from coast to coast :** across an entire
nation or continent
**²coast** (14th century)
*transitive verb*
  **1** *obsolete* **:** to move along or past the side of
  **:** SKIRT
  **2 :** to sail along the shore of
*intransitive verb*
  **1 a** *archaic* **:** to travel on land along a coast or
along or past the side of something **b :** to sail
along the shore
  **2 a :** to slide, run, or glide downhill by the
force of gravity **b :** to move along without or
as if without further application of propulsive
power (as by momentum or gravity) **c :** to
proceed easily without special application of
effort or concern ⟨*coasted* through school⟩
**coast·er** \'kōs-tər\ *noun* (1574)
  **1 :** one that coasts: as **a :** a person engaged in
coastal traffic or commerce **b :** a ship sailing
along a coast or engaged in trade between
ports of the same country
  **2 :** a resident of a seacoast
  **3 a :** a tray or decanter stand usually of silver
and sometimes on wheels **b :** a shallow container or a plate or mat to protect a surface
  **4 a :** a small vehicle (as a sled or wagon) used
in coasting **b :** ROLLER COASTER
**coaster brake** *noun* (1899)
  **:** a brake in the hub of the rear wheel of a bicycle operated by reverse pressure on the pedals
**coaster wagon** *noun* (1911)
  **:** a child's toy wagon often used for coasting
**coast guard** *noun* (1833)
  **1 :** a military or naval force employed in
guarding a coast or responsible for the safety,
order, and operation of maritime traffic in
neighboring waters
  **2** *usually* **coast·guard** *chiefly British*
  **:** COASTGUARDSMAN
**coast·guards·man** \'kōs(t)-,gärdz-mən\ *or*
  **coast·guard·man** \-,gärd-mən\ *noun* (circa
1891)
  **:** a member of a coast guard
**coast·land** \-,land\ *noun* (1852)
  **:** land bordering the sea
**coast·line** \-,līn\ *noun* (circa 1859)
  **1 :** a line that forms the boundary between the
land and the ocean or a lake
  **2 :** the outline of a coast
**coast redwood** *noun* (circa 1897)
  **:** REDWOOD 3a
**coast–to–coast** \'kōs-tə-'kōst\ *adjective*
(1911)
  **:** extending or airing across an entire nation or
continent
**coast·ward** \'kōs-twərd\ *or* **coast·wards**
\-twərdz\ *adverb* (1853)
  **:** toward the coast
  — **coastward** *adjective*
**¹coat** \'kōt\ *noun, often attributive* [Middle

English *cote,* from Middle French, of Germanic origin; akin to Old High German *kozza*
coarse wool mantle] (14th century)
  **1 a :** an outer garment worn on the upper
body and varying in length and style according to fashion and use **b :** something resembling a coat
  **2 :** the external growth on an animal
  **3 :** a layer of one substance covering another
⟨a *coat* of paint⟩
  — **coat·ed** \'kō-təd\ *adjective*
  — **coat·less** *adjective*
**²coat** *transitive verb* (14th century)
  **1 :** to cover with a coat
  **2 :** to cover or spread with a finishing, protecting, or enclosing layer
  — **coat·er** *noun*
**coat·dress** \'kōt-,dres\ *noun* (1854)
  **:** a dress styled like a coat usually with a front
buttoning from neckline to hemline
**coat hanger** *noun* (1895)
  **:** a device which is shaped like the outline of a
person's shoulders and over which garments
may be hung
**co·a·ti** \kə-'wä-tē, kwä-'tē\ *noun* [Portuguese
*coati,* from Tupi] (1676)
  **:** either of two
tropical American
mammals (*Nasua
nasua* and *N. nel-
soni*) related to
the raccoon but
with a longer
body and tail and
a long flexible
snout
**co·a·ti·mun·di**
\kə-,wä-ti-'mən-
dē, ,kwä-, -'mùn-\
*noun* [Tupi] (1676)
  **:** COATI

coati

**coat·ing** \'kō-tiŋ\ *noun* (1768)
  **1 :** cloth for coats
  **2 :** COAT, COVERING
**coat of arms** [Middle English *cote of armes,*
translation of Middle French *cote d'armes*]
(14th century)
  **1 :** a tabard or surcoat embroidered with armorial bearings
  **2 a :** the particular heraldic bearings (as of a
person) usually depicted on an escutcheon often with accompanying adjuncts (as a crest,
motto, and supporters) **b :** a similar symbolic
emblem
**coat of mail** (15th century)
  **:** a garment of metal scales or chain mail worn
as armor
**coat·rack** \'kōt-,rak\ *noun* (1915)
  **:** a stand or rack fitted with pegs, hooks, or
hangers and used for the temporary storage of
garments
**coat·room** \-,rüm, -,rùm\ *noun* (1870)
  **:** CLOAKROOM
**coat·tail** \'kōt-,tāl\ *noun* (circa 1600)
  **1 :** the rear flap of a man's coat
  **2** *plural* **:** the skirts of a dress coat, cutaway,
or frock coat
  **3** *plural* **:** the influence or pulling power of a
popular movement or candidate ⟨congressmen
riding into office on the president's *coattails*⟩
**¹coax** \'kōks\ *transitive verb* [earlier *cokes,*
from *cokes* simpleton] (1589)
  **1** *obsolete* **:** FONDLE, PET
  **2 :** to influence or gently urge by caressing or
flattering **:** WHEEDLE
  **3 :** to draw, gain, or persuade by means of
gentle urging or flattery
  **4 :** to manipulate with great perseverance and
usually with considerable effort toward a desired state or activity ⟨*coax* a fire to burn⟩
**²co·ax** \'kō-,aks\ *noun* (1949)
  **:** COAXIAL CABLE
**co·ax·i·al** \(,)kō-'ak-sē-əl\ *adjective* (1881)
  **1 :** having coincident axes

  **2 :** mounted on concentric shafts
  — **co·ax·i·al·ly** \-sē-ə-lē\ *adverb*
**coaxial cable** *noun* (1936)
  **:** a transmission line that consists of a tube of
electrically conducting material surrounding a
central conductor held in place by insulators
and that is used to transmit telegraph, telephone, and television signals of high frequency — called also *coax cable*
**cob** \'käb\ *noun* [Middle English *cobbe* leader]
(15th century)
  **1 :** a male swan
  **2** *dialect English* **:** a rounded mass, lump, or
heap
  **3 :** a crudely struck old Spanish coin of irregular shape
  **4 :** CORNCOB 1
  **5 :** a stocky short-legged riding horse
  — **cob·by** \'kä-bē\ *adjective*
**co·bal·a·min** \kō-'ba-lə-mən\ *noun* [*cobal*t +
vit*amin*] (1956)
  **:** VITAMIN B$_{12}$
**co·balt** \'kō-,bȯlt\ *noun* [German *Kobalt,* alteration of *Kobold,* literally, goblin, from Middle
High German *kobolt;* from its occurrence in
silver ore, believed to be due to goblins]
(1683)
  **1 :** a tough lustrous silver-white magnetic metallic element that is related to and occurs with
iron and nickel and is used especially in alloys
  — see ELEMENT table
  **2 :** COBALT BLUE 2 ◆

---

☆ **SYNONYMS**
**Coarse, vulgar, gross, obscene, rib-
ald** mean offensive to good taste or morals.
COARSE implies roughness, rudeness, or
crudeness of spirit, behavior, or language
⟨found the *coarse* humor of coworkers offen-
sive⟩. VULGAR often implies boorishness or
ill-breeding ⟨a loud *vulgar* belch⟩. GROSS implies extreme coarseness and insensitiveness ⟨*gross* eating habits⟩. OBSCENE applies
to anything strongly repulsive to the sense of
decency and propriety especially in sexual
matters ⟨*obscene* language not allowed on
the air⟩. RIBALD applies to what is amusingly
or picturesquely vulgar or irreverent or mildly
indecent ⟨entertained the campers with *ribald*
folk songs⟩.

---

◇ **WORD HISTORY**
**cobalt**   The metallic element cobalt ultimately draws its name from folklore. In Middle High German, *kobolt* denoted a usually
helpful household elf that engaged in nasty
pranks only when it was offended. Later the
more malicious side of the spirit came to the
forefront, and early Modern German *Kobold*
was extended in sense to cover a variety of
goblins inhabiting fields and mountains. The
variant *Kobolt* in the 16th century was applied by German miners to ores containing
the metal cobalt, which they considered to be
worthless. This application was based on the
superstition that mountain goblins had
spoiled adjacent silver ores, or had stolen
the silver within the ore. The metal itself in
relatively pure form was not produced and
described until the 18th century, when German *Kobalt,* with its first letter influenced by
New Latin *cobaltum,* became part of the international language of science.

---

\ə\ abut \°\ kitten \ər\ further \a\ ash \ā\ ace
\ä\ mop, mar \aù\ out \ch\ chin \e\ bet \ē\ easy
\g\ go \i\ hit \ī\ ice \j\ job \ŋ\ sing \ō\ go
\ȯ\ law \ȯi\ boy \th\ thin \<u>th</u>\ the \ü\ loot \ù\ foot
\y\ yet \zh\ vision    *see also* Guide to Pronunciation

**cobalt blue** *noun* (1835)
**1 :** a greenish blue pigment consisting essentially of cobalt oxide and alumina
**2 :** a strong greenish blue
**cobalt chloride** *noun* (1885)
**:** a chloride of cobalt; *especially* **:** the dichloride $CoCl_2$ that is blue when dehydrated, turns red in the presence of moisture, and is used to indicate humidity
**co·bal·tic** \kō-'bȯl-tik\ *adjective* (1782)
**:** of, relating to, or containing cobalt especially with a valence of three
**co·balt·ite** \'kō-,bȯl-,tīt, kō-'\ *or* **co·balt·ine** \-,tēn\ *noun* [*cobaltite,* alteration of *cobaltine,* from French, from *cobalt*] (1868)
**:** a mineral consisting of a grayish to silver-white cobalt sulfur arsenide used in making smalt
**co·bal·tous** \kō-'bȯl-təs\ *adjective* (1863)
**:** of, relating to, or containing cobalt especially with a valence of two
**cobalt 60** *noun* (1946)
**:** a heavy radioactive isotope of cobalt of the mass number 60 produced in nuclear reactors and used as a source of gamma rays (as for radiotherapy)
**cob·ber** \'kȯ-bər\ *noun* [origin unknown] (1893)
*Australian & New Zealand* **:** BUDDY
¹**cob·ble** \'kä-bəl\ *transitive verb* **cob·bled; cob·bling** \-b(ə-)liŋ\ [Middle English *coblen,* perhaps back-formation from *cobelere* cobbler] (15th century)
**1** *chiefly British* **:** to mend or patch coarsely
**2 :** REPAIR, MAKE ⟨*cobble* shoes⟩
**3 :** to make or put together roughly or hastily — often used with *together* or *up*
²**cobble** *noun* (1600)
**1 :** COBBLESTONE
**2** *plural, chiefly British* **:** lump coal about the size of small cobblestones
**cobbled** *adjective* (1853)
**:** paved with cobblestones
**cob·bler** \'kä-blər\ *noun* [Middle English *cobelere*] (13th century)
**1 :** a mender or maker of shoes and often of other leather goods
**2** *archaic* **:** a clumsy workman
**3 :** a tall iced drink consisting usually of wine, rum, or whiskey and sugar garnished with mint or a slice of lemon or orange
**4 :** a deep-dish fruit dessert with a thick top crust
**cob·ble·stone** \'kä-bəl-,stōn\ *noun* [Middle English, from *cobble-* (probably from *cob*) + *stone*] (15th century)
**:** a naturally rounded stone larger than a pebble and smaller than a boulder; *especially* **:** such a stone used in paving a street or in construction
— **cob·ble·stoned** \-,stōnd\ *adjective*
**cob·by** \'kä-bē\ *adjective* **cob·bi·er; -est** (1883)
**:** STOCKY ⟨a *cobby* horse⟩
**co·bel·lig·er·ent** \,kō-bə-'lij-rənt, -'li-jə-\ *noun* (1813)
**:** a country fighting with another power against a common enemy
— **cobelligerent** *adjective*
**co·bia** \'kō-bē-ə\ *noun* [origin unknown] (circa 1873)
**:** a large bony fish (*Rachycentron canadum* of the family Rachycentridae) of warm seas that is a food and sport fish
**co·ble** \'kō-bəl\ *noun* [Middle English] (14th century)
**:** a flat-bottomed boat propelled chiefly by oars and used in Scotland and northern England especially for fishing
**cob·nut** \'käb-,nət\ *noun* (1580)
**:** the fruit of a European hazel (*Corylus avellana grandis*); *also* **:** the plant bearing this fruit
**CO·BOL** *or* **Co·bol** \'kō-,bȯl\ *noun* [*co*mmon *b*usiness *o*riented *l*anguage] (1960)

**:** a computer programming language designed for business applications
**co·bra** \'kō-brə\ *noun* [Portuguese *cobra (de capello),* literally, hooded snake, from Latin *colubra* snake] (1802)
**:** any of several venomous Asian and African elapid snakes (genera *Naja* and *Ophiophagus*) that when excited expand the skin of the neck into a hood by movement of the anterior ribs; *also* **:** any of several related African snakes
**cob·web** \'käb-,web\ *noun* [Middle English *coppeweb,* from *coppe* spider (from Old English *ātorcoppe*) + *web;* akin to Middle Dutch *coppe* spider] (14th century)
**1 a :** the network spread by a spider **:** SPIDERWEB **b :** tangles of the silken threads of a cobweb usually covered with accumulated dirt and dust
**2 :** something that entangles, obscures, or confuses ⟨a *cobweb* of law and politics⟩
— **cob·webbed** \-,webd\ *adjective*
— **cob·web·by** \-,we-bē\ *adjective*
**co·ca** \'kō-kə\ *noun* [Spanish, from Quechua *kuka*] (1577)
**1 :** any of several South American shrubs (genus *Erythroxylon,* family Erythroxylaceae); *especially* **:** one (*E. coca*) that is the primary source of cocaine
**2 :** dried leaves of a coca (especially *Erythroxylon coca*) containing alkaloids including cocaine
**co·caine** \kō-'kān, 'kō-,\ *noun* (1874)
**:** a bitter crystalline alkaloid $C_{17}H_{21}NO_4$ obtained from coca leaves that is used medically as a topical anesthetic and illicitly for its euphoric effects and that may result in a compulsive psychological need
**co·cain·ize** \kō-'kā-,nīz\ *transitive verb* **-ized; -iz·ing** (1887)
**:** to treat or anesthetize with cocaine
— **co·cain·i·za·tion** \-,kā-nə-'zā-shən\ *noun*
**co·car·box·yl·ase** \,kō-kär-'bäk-sə-,lās, -,lāz\ *noun* (1932)
**:** a coenzyme $C_{12}H_{19}ClN_4O_7P_2S \cdot H_2O$ that is a pyrophosphate of thiamine and is important in metabolic reactions (as decarboxylation in the Krebs cycle)
**co·car·cin·o·gen** \,kō-kär-'si-nə-jən, kō-'kär-sⁿ-ə-,jen\ *noun* (1938)
**:** an agent that aggravates the carcinogenic effects of another substance
— **co·car·cin·o·gen·ic** \,kō-,kär-sⁿ-ō-'je-nik\ *adjective*
**coc·cid** \'käk-səd\ *noun* [New Latin *Coccus,* genus of scales, from Greek *kokkos* grain, kermes] (circa 1889)
**:** SCALE INSECT
**coc·cid·i·oi·do·my·co·sis** \(,)käk-,si-dē-,ȯi-dō-(,)mī-'kō-səs\ *noun* [New Latin, from *Coccidioides,* genus of fungi (from *coccidium*) + *mycosis*] (1937)
**:** a disease especially of humans and domestic animals caused by a fungus (*Coccidioides immitis*) and marked especially by fever and pulmonary symptoms
**coc·cid·i·o·sis** \(,)käk-,si-dē-'ō-səs\ *noun, plural* **-o·ses** \-,sēz\ [New Latin] (1892)
**:** infestation with or disease caused by coccidia
**coc·cid·i·um** \käk-'si-dē-əm\ *noun, plural* **-ia** \-dē-ə\ [New Latin, diminutive of *coccus*] (circa 1879)
**:** any of an order (Coccidia) of protozoans usually parasitic in the digestive epithelium of vertebrates
**coc·coid** \'kä-,kȯid\ *adjective* (1893)
**:** of, relating to, or resembling a coccus **:** GLOBULAR 1a(1)
— **coccoid** *noun*
**coc·cus** \'kä-kəs\ *noun, plural* **coc·ci** \'kä-,kī, -,kē; 'käk-,sī, -,sē\ [New Latin, from Greek *kokkos*] (1888)
**:** a spherical bacterium
— **coc·cal** \'kä-kəl\ *adjective*

**-coccus** *noun combining form, plural* **-cocci** [New Latin]
**:** berry-shaped microorganism ⟨micro*coccus*⟩
**coc·cy·geal** \käk-'si-j(ē-)əl\ *adjective* [Medieval Latin *coccygeus* of the coccyx, from Greek *kokkyk-, kokkyx*] (1836)
**:** of or relating to the coccyx
**coc·cyx** \'käk-siks\ *noun, plural* **coc·cy·ges** \'käk-sə-,jēz\ *also* **coc·cyx·es** \'käk-sik-səz\ [New Latin, from Greek *kokkyx* cuckoo, coccyx; from its resemblance to a cuckoo's beak] (1615)
**:** a small bone that articulates with the sacrum and that usually consists of four fused vertebrae which form the terminus of the spinal column in humans and tailless apes
**Co·chin** \'kō-chin\ *noun* [*Cochin* China, part of French Indochina] (1853)
**:** any of an Asian breed of large domestic fowl with thick plumage, small wings and tail, and densely feathered legs and feet — called also *Cochin China*
**co·chi·neal** \'kä-chə-,nēl, 'kō-\ *noun* [Middle French & Spanish; Middle French *cochenille,* from Old Spanish *cochinilla* cochineal insect] (1582)
**1 :** a red dye consisting of the dried bodies of female cochineal insects
**2 :** COCHINEAL INSECT
**cochineal insect** *noun* (1801)
**:** a small red cactus-feeding scale insect (*Dactylopius coccus*) the females of which are the source of cochineal
**co·chlea** \'kō-klē-ə, 'kä-klē-\ *noun, plural* **co·chle·as** *or* **co·chle·ae** \-klē-,ē, -,ī\ [New Latin, from Latin, snail, snail shell, from Greek *kochlias,* from *kochlos* snail; probably akin to Greek *konchē* mussel] (1688)
**:** a division of the bony labyrinth of the inner ear of higher vertebrates that is usually coiled like a snail shell and is the seat of the hearing organ — see EAR illustration
— **co·chle·ar** \'kō-klē-ər, 'kä-\ *adjective*
¹**cock** \'käk\ *noun* [Middle English *cok,* from Old English *cocc,* of imitative origin] (before 12th century)
**1 a :** the adult male of the domestic fowl (*Gallus gallus*) **b :** the male of birds other than the domestic fowl **c :** WOODCOCK **d** *archaic* **:** the crowing of a cock; *also* **:** COCKCROW **e :** WEATHERCOCK
**2 :** a device (as a faucet or valve) for regulating the flow of a liquid
**3 a :** a chief person **:** LEADER **b :** a person of spirit and often of a certain swagger or arrogance
**4 a :** the hammer in the lock of a firearm **b :** the cocked position of the hammer
**5 :** PENIS — usually considered vulgar
— **cock of the walk :** one that dominates a group or situation especially overbearingly
²**cock** (1575)
*intransitive verb*
**1 :** STRUT, SWAGGER
**2 :** to turn, tip, or stick up
**3 :** to position the hammer of a firearm for firing
*transitive verb*
**1 a :** to draw the hammer of (a firearm) back and set for firing; *also* **:** to set (the trigger) for firing **b :** to draw or bend back in preparation for throwing or hitting **c :** to set a mechanism (as a camera shutter) for tripping
**2 a :** to set erect **b :** to turn, tip, or tilt usually to one side
**3 :** to turn up (as a hat brim)
— **cock a snook** *also* **cock snooks :** to thumb the nose
³**cock** *noun* (1717)
**:** TILT, SLANT ⟨*cock* of the head⟩
⁴**cock** *noun* [Middle English *cok,* of Scandinavian origin] (14th century)
**:** a small pile (as of hay)
⁵**cock** *transitive verb* (14th century)
**:** to put (as hay) into cocks
**cock·ade** \kä-'kād\ *noun* [modification of

French *cocarde*, from feminine of *cocard* vain, from *coq* cock, from Old French *coc*, of imitative origin] (1709)
: an ornament (as a rosette) usually worn on a hat as a badge
— **cock·ad·ed** \-'kā-dəd\ *adjective*

**cock–a–hoop** \ˌkä-kə-'hüp, -'hùp\ *adjective* [from the phrase *to set cock a hoop* to be festive] (1663)
**1** : triumphantly boastful : EXULTING
**2** : AWRY

**Cock·aigne** \kä-'kān\ *noun* [Middle English *cokaygne*, from Middle French (*pais de*) *cocaigne* land of plenty) (13th century)
: an imaginary land of great luxury and ease

**cock–a–leek·ie** \ˌkä-ki-'lē-kē\ *noun* [alteration of *cockie* (diminutive of *[1]cock*) + *leekie*, diminutive of *leek*] (1737)
: a soup made of chicken and leeks

**cock·a·lo·rum** \ˌkä-kə-'lōr-əm, -'lor-\ *noun*, *plural* **-rums** [probably modification of obsolete Flemish *kockeloeren* to crow, of imitative origin] (circa 1715)
**1** : a boastful and self-important person
**2** : LEAPFROG
**3** : boastful talk

**cock·a·ma·my** *or* **cock·a·ma·mie** \ˌkä-kə-'mā-mē\ *adjective* [perhaps alteration of *decalcomania*] (1960)
: RIDICULOUS, INCREDIBLE ⟨of all the *cockamamy* excuses I ever heard —Leo Rosten⟩

**cock–and–bull story** \'kä-kən-'bùl-\ *noun* (1795)
: an incredible story told as true

**cock·a·poo** \'kä-kə-ˌpü\ *noun* [alteration of *cocker* (*spaniel*) + *poo*dle] (1970)
: a dog that is a cross between a cocker spaniel and a poodle

**cock·a·tiel** \ˌkäk-ə-ˌtē(ə)l\ *noun* [Dutch *kaketielje*, from Portuguese *cacatilha*, from *cacatua* cockatoo] (1877)
: a crested small gray Australian parrot (*Nymphicus hollandicus*) with a yellow head

**cock·a·too** \'kä-kə-ˌtü\ *noun*, *plural* **-toos** [Dutch *kaketoe*, from Malay *kakatua*] (1634)
: any of various large noisy chiefly Australasian crested parrots (family Cacatuidae and especially genus *Cacatua*)

**cock·a·trice** \'kä-kə-trəs, -ˌtrīs\ *noun* [Middle English *cocatrice*, from Middle French *cocatris* ichneumon, cockatrice, from Medieval Latin *cocatric-, cocatrix* ichneumon] (14th century)
: a legendary serpent that is hatched by a reptile from a cock's egg and that has a deadly glance

**cockatoo**

**cock·boat** \'käk-ˌbōt\ *noun* (15th century)
: a small boat; *especially* : one used as a tender to a larger boat

**cock·cha·fer** \'käk-ˌchā-fər\ *noun* [*[1]cock* + *chafer*] (1712)
: a large European beetle (*Melolontha melolontha*) destructive to vegetation as an adult and to roots as a larva; *also* : any of various related beetles

**cock·crow** \'käk-ˌkrō\ *noun* (13th century)
: DAWN

**cocked hat** \'käkt-\ *noun* (1673)
**1** : a hat with brim turned up to give a 3-cornered appearance
**2** : a hat with brim turned up on two sides and worn either front to back or sideways

**[1]cock·er** \'kä-kər\ *transitive verb* [Middle English *cokeren*] (15th century)
: INDULGE, PAMPER

**[2]cocker** *noun* (1689)
: a keeper or handler of fighting cocks
**[3]cocker** *noun* (circa 1811)
: COCKER SPANIEL

**cock·er·el** \'kä-k(ə-)rəl\ *noun* [Middle English *cokerelle*, from Middle French dialect *kokerel*, diminutive of Old French *coc*] (15th century)
: a young male of the domestic fowl (*Gallus gallus*)

**cock·er spaniel** \'kä-kər-\ *noun* [*cocking* woodcock hunting] (1840)
**1** : ENGLISH COCKER SPANIEL
**2** : any of a breed of spaniels developed in the U.S. from the English cocker spaniel that are smaller in size and have a shorter muzzle and longer thicker coat

**cock·eye** \'käk-'ī, -ˌī\ *noun* (circa 1825)
: a squinting eye

**cock·eyed** \'käk-ˌīd\ *adjective* (1821)
**1** : having a cockeye
**2 a** : ASKEW, AWRY **b** : slightly crazy : TOPSY-TURVY ⟨a *cockeyed* scheme⟩ **c** : DRUNK 1a
— **cock·eyed·ly** \'käk-ˌī(-ə)d-lē\ *adverb*
— **cock·eyed·ness** \-ˌīd-nəs\ *noun*

**cock·fight** \'käk-ˌfīt\ *noun* (circa 1566)
: a contest in which gamecocks usually fitted with metal spurs are pitted against each other
— **cock·fight·ing** \-ˌfī-tiŋ\ *adjective or noun*

**cock·horse** \'käk-ˌhòrs\ *noun* [perhaps from *cock*, adjective, (male) + *horse*] (circa 1541)
: ROCKING HORSE

**[1]cock·le** \'kä-kəl\ *noun* [Middle English, from Old English *coccel*] (before 12th century)
: any of several weedy plants of the pink family; *especially* : CORN COCKLE

**[2]cockle** *noun* [Middle English *cokille*, from Middle French *coquille* shell, modification of Latin *conchylia*, plural of *conchylium*, from Greek *konchylion*, from *konchē* conch] (14th century)
**1** : any of various chiefly marine bivalve mollusks (family Cardiidae) having a shell with convex radially ribbed valves; *especially* : a common edible European bivalve (*Cerastoderma edule* synonym *Cardium edule*)
**2** : COCKLESHELL

**[3]cockle** *noun* [Middle English *kokell*, ultimately from Middle French *coquillé* wavy or rounded like a shell, from *coquille*] (15th century)
: PUCKER, WRINKLE
— **cockle** *verb*

**cock·le·bur** \'kä-kəl-ˌbər, 'kə-\ *noun* (1804)
: any of a genus (*Xanthium*) of prickly-fruited composite plants; *also* : one of its stiff-spined fruits

**cock·le·shell** \'kä-kəl-ˌshel\ *noun* (15th century)
**1 a** : the shell or one of the shell valves of a cockle **b** : a shell (as a scallop shell) suggesting a cockleshell
**2** : a light flimsy boat

**cockleshell 1a**

**cockles of the heart** [perhaps from *[2]cockle*] (1671)
: the core of one's being
— usually used in the phrase *warm the cockles of the heart*

**cock·loft** \'käk-ˌlòft\ *noun* [probably from *[1]cock*] (1589)
: a small garret

**cock·ney** \'käk-nē\ *noun*, *plural* **cockneys** [Middle English *cokeney*, literally, cocks' egg, from *coken* (genitive plural of *cok* cock) + *ey* egg, from Old English *ǣg*] (14th century)
**1** *obsolete* **a** : a spoiled child **b** : a squeamish woman
**2** *often capitalized* **a** : a native of London and especially of the East End of London **b** : the dialect of London or of the East End of London
— **cockney** *adjective*
— **cock·ney·fy** \'käk-ni-ˌfī\ *transitive verb*
— **cock·ney·ish** \-nē-ish\ *adjective*

— **cock·ney·ism** \-ˌi-zəm\ *noun*

**cock·pit** \'käk-ˌpit\ *noun* (1587)
**1 a** : a pit or enclosure for cockfights **b** : a place noted for especially bloody, violent, or long-continued conflict
**2** *obsolete* : the pit of a theater
**3** : a compartment in a sailing warship used as quarters for junior officers and for treatment of the wounded in an engagement
**4** : a space or compartment in a usually small vehicle (as a boat, airplane, or automobile) from which it is steered, piloted, or driven — see AIRPLANE illustration

**cock·roach** \'käk-ˌrōch\ *noun* [by folk etymology from Spanish *cucaracha* cockroach, from *cuca* caterpillar] (1623)
: any of an order or suborder (Blattodea synonym Blattaria) of chiefly nocturnal insects including some that are domestic pests

**cocks·comb** \'käks-ˌkōm\ *noun* (1542)
**1** : COXCOMB
**2** : a garden plant (*Celosia cristata*) of the amaranth family grown for its flowers

**cocks·foot** \-ˌfùt\ *noun* (1697)
: ORCHARD GRASS

**cock·shut** \'käk-ˌshət\ *noun* [from the time poultry are shut in to rest] (1598)
*dialect English* : evening twilight

**cock·shy** \-ˌshī\ *noun*, *plural* **cockshies** [*[1]cock* + *shy*] (1836)
**1 a** : a throw at an object set up as a mark **b** : a mark or target so set up
**2** : an object or person taken as a butt (as of criticism)

**cock·suck·er** \-ˌsə-kər\ *noun* (circa 1891)
: one who performs fellatio — usually considered obscene; often used as a generalized term of abuse

**cock·sure** \'käk-'shùr\ *adjective* [probably from *[1]cock* + *sure*] (1672)
**1** : feeling perfect assurance sometimes on inadequate grounds
**2** : marked by overconfidence or presumptuousness : COCKY
**synonym** SEE SURE
— **cock·sure·ly** *adverb*
— **cock·sure·ness** *noun*

**[1]cock·tail** \'käk-ˌtāl\ *noun* [probably from *[1]cock* + *tail*] (1806)
**1 a** : an iced drink of wine or distilled liquor mixed with flavoring ingredients **b** : something resembling or suggesting such a drink **c** : a solution of agents taken or used together especially for medical treatment or diagnosis
**2** : an appetizer served as a first course at a meal

**[2]cocktail** *adjective* (1865)
**1** : of, relating to, or set aside for cocktails ⟨*cocktail* hour⟩
**2** : designed for semiformal wear ⟨*cocktail* dress⟩

**[3]cocktail** *noun* [*[1]cock* + *tail*] (1808)
: a horse with its tail docked

**cocktail glass** *noun* (1907)
: a bell-shaped drinking glass usually having a foot and stem and holding about three ounces (90 milliliters)

**cocktail lounge** *noun* (1939)
: a public room (as in a hotel, club, or restaurant) where cocktails and other drinks are served

**cocktail party** *noun* (1928)
: an informal or semiformal party or gathering at which cocktails are served

**cocktail table** *noun* (1946)
: COFFEE TABLE

**cock·up** \'kä-ˌkəp\ *noun* (circa 1948)
*British* : MESS 3b

**cocky** \'kä-kē\ *adjective* **cock·i·er; -est** (1768)

**1** : boldly or brashly self-confident
**2** : JAUNTY
— **cock·i·ly** \'kä-kə-lē\ *adverb*
— **cock·i·ness** \'kä-kē-nəs\ *noun*
**co·co** \'kō-(,)kō\ *noun, plural* **cocos** [Spanish *coco* & Portuguese *côco* bogeyman, grimace, coconut] (1555)
: the coconut palm; *also* : its fruit
**co·coa** \'kō-(,)kō\ *noun* [modification of Spanish *cacao*] (1788)
**1 a** : powdered ground roasted cacao beans from which a portion of the fat has been removed **b** : a beverage prepared by heating cocoa with water or milk
**2** : CACAO 2
**3** : a medium brown color
**cocoa bean** *noun* (1855)
: CACAO 1
**cocoa butter** *noun* (1872)
: a pale vegetable fat with a low melting point obtained from cacao beans
**co·co·nut** \'kō-kə-(,)nət\ *noun* (1613)
**1** : the drupaceous fruit of the coconut palm whose outer fibrous husk yields coir and whose nut contains thick edible meat and coconut milk
**2** : the edible meat of the coconut
**coconut crab** *noun* (circa 1889)
: a large edible coconut-eating burrowing land crab (*Birgus latro*) widely distributed about islands of the tropical Indian and Pacific Oceans
**coconut oil** *noun* (1838)
: a fatty oil or semisolid fat extracted from fresh coconuts and used especially in making soaps and food products
**coconut palm** *noun* (1852)
: a tall pinnate-leaved coconut-bearing palm (*Cocos nucifera*) that grows along tropical coasts
**¹co·coon** \kə-'kün\ *noun* [French *cocon*, from Provençal *coucoun*, from *coco* shell, probably from Latin *coccum* kermes (thought to be a gall or berry), from Greek *kokkos* berry, kermes] (1699)
**1 a** : an envelope often largely of silk which an insect larva forms about itself and in which it passes the pupa stage **b** : any of various other protective coverings produced by animals
**2 a** : a covering suggesting a cocoon **b** : a protective covering placed or sprayed over military or naval equipment in storage
**²cocoon** *transitive verb* (1881)
: to wrap or envelop in or as if in a cocoon
**co·coon·ing** \-'kü-niŋ\ *noun* (1987)
: the practice of spending leisure time at home in preference to going out
**co·cotte** \kō-kót\ *noun, plural* **cocottes** \-kót(s)\ [French] (1867)
**1** : PROSTITUTE
**2** : a shallow individual baking dish usually with one or two handles
**co·co·yam** \'kō-(,)kō-yam\ *noun* [probably *coco* + *yam*] (1922)
**1** : TARO
**2** : YAUTIA
**co·cur·ric·u·lar** \,kō-kə-'ri-kyə-lər\ *adjective* (1949)
: being outside of but usually complementing the regular curriculum
**cod** \'käd\ *noun, plural* **cod** *also* **cods** [Middle English] (14th century)
**1** : any of various bottom-dwelling fishes (family Gadidae, the cod family) that usually occur in cold marine waters and often have barbels and three dorsal fins: as **a** : one (*Gadus morhua*) of the North Atlantic that is an important food fish **b** : one (*Gadus macrocephalus*) of the Pacific Ocean
**2** : any of various bony fishes resembling the true cods
**co·da** \'kō-də\ *noun* [Italian, literally, tail, from Latin *cauda*] (circa 1753)
**1 a** : a concluding musical section that is formally distinct from the main structure **b** : a concluding part of a literary or dramatic work

**2** : something that serves to round out, conclude, or summarize yet has its own interest
**cod·dle** \'kä-d°l\ *transitive verb* **cod·dled; cod·dling** \'käd-liŋ, 'kä-d°l-iŋ\ [perhaps from *caudle*] (1598)
**1** : to cook (as eggs) in liquid slowly and gently just below the boiling point
**2** : to treat with extreme care : PAMPER
— **cod·dler** \'käd-lər, 'kä-d°l-ər\ *noun*
**¹code** \'kōd\ *noun* [Middle English, from Middle French, from Latin *caudex, codex* trunk of a tree, document formed originally from wooden tablets] (14th century)
**1** : a systematic statement of a body of law; *especially* : one given statutory force
**2** : a system of principles or rules ⟨moral *code*⟩
**3 a** : a system of signals or symbols for communication **b** : a system of symbols (as letters or numbers) used to represent assigned and often secret meanings
**4** : GENETIC CODE
**5** : a set of instructions for a computer
— **code·less** \-ləs\ *adjective*
**²code** *verb* **cod·ed; cod·ing** (1815)
*transitive verb*
: to put in or into the form or symbols of a code
*intransitive verb*
: to specify the genetic code ⟨a gene that *codes* for a protein⟩
— **cod·able** \'kō-də-bəl\ *adjective*
— **cod·er** *noun*
**code·book** *noun* (1884)
: a book containing an alphabetical list of words or expressions with their code equivalents
**co·deine** \'kō-,dēn\ *noun* [French *codéine*, from Greek *kōdeia* poppyhead] (1881)
: a morphine derivative $C_{18}H_{21}NO_3 \cdot H_2O$ that is found in opium, is weaker in action than morphine, and is used especially in cough remedies
**code name** *noun* (1919)
: a designation having a secret meaning
— **code–name** \'kōd-,nām\ *transitive verb*
**co·de·pen·dence** \,kō-di-'pen-dən(t)s\ *noun* (1989)
: CODEPENDENCY
**co·de·pen·den·cy** \-dən(t)-sē\ *noun* (1987)
: a psychological condition or a relationship in which a person is controlled or manipulated by another who is affected with a pathological condition (as an addiction to alcohol or heroin)
— **co·de·pen·dent** \-dənt\ *noun or adjective*
**co·de·ter·mi·na·tion** \,kō-di-,tər-mə-'nā-shən\ *noun* (1949)
: the participation of labor with management in determining business policy
**code word** *noun* (1884)
**1** : CODE NAME
**2** : EUPHEMISM
**co·dex** \'kō-,deks\ *noun, plural* **co·di·ces** \'kō-də-,sēz, 'kä-\ [Latin] (1670)
: a manuscript book especially of Scripture, classics, or ancient annals
**cod·fish** \'käd-,fish\ *noun* (14th century)
: COD; *also* : its flesh used as food
**cod·ger** \'kä-jər\ *noun* [probably alteration of *cadger*] (1756)
: an often mildly eccentric and usually elderly fellow ⟨old *codger*⟩
**cod·i·cil** \'kä-də-səl, -,sil\ *noun* [Middle French *codicille*, from Latin *codicillus*, diminutive of *codic-, codex*] (15th century)
**1** : a legal instrument made to modify an earlier will
**2** : APPENDIX, SUPPLEMENT
— **cod·i·cil·la·ry** \,kä-də-'si-lə-rē\ *adjective*
**co·di·col·o·gy** \,kō-də-'kä-lə-jē, ,kä-\ *noun* [Latin *codic-, codex* + *-o-* + English *-logy*] (1953)
: the study of manuscripts as cultural artifacts for historical purposes

— **co·di·co·log·i·cal** \-kə-'lä-ji-kəl\ *adjective*
**cod·i·fy** \'kä-də-,fī, 'kō-\ *transitive verb* **-fied; -fy·ing** (circa 1800)
**1** : to reduce to a code
**2 a** : SYSTEMATIZE **b** : CLASSIFY
— **cod·i·fi·abil·i·ty** \,kä-də-,fī-ə-'bi-lə-tē, ,kō-\ *noun*
— **cod·i·fi·ca·tion** \-fə-'kā-shən\ *noun*
**¹cod·ling** \'käd-liŋ\ *noun* (13th century)
**1** : a young cod
**2** : any of several hakes (especially genus *Urophycis*)
**²cod·ling** \'käd-liŋ\ *or* **cod·lin** \-lən\ *noun* [alteration of Middle English *querdlyng*] (15th century)
: a small immature apple; *also* : any of several elongated greenish English cooking apples
**codling moth** *noun* (1747)
: a small tortricid moth (*Cydia pomonella*) having larvae that live in apples, pears, quinces, and English walnuts
**cod–liver oil** *noun* (1783)
: an oil obtained from the liver of the cod and closely related fishes and used as a source of vitamins A and D
**co·dom·i·nant** \,kō-'dä-mə-nənt, -'däm-nənt\ *adjective* (circa 1900)
**1 a** : forming part of the main canopy of a forest ⟨*codominant* trees⟩ **b** : sharing in the controlling influence of a biotic community
**2** : being fully expressed in the heterozygous condition ⟨*codominant* alleles⟩
— **codominant** *noun*
**co·don** \'kō-,dän\ *noun* [¹*code* + ²*-on*] (1963)
: a specific sequence of three consecutive nucleotides that is part of the genetic code and that specifies a particular amino acid in a protein or starts or stops protein synthesis
**cod·piece** \'käd-,pēs\ *noun* [Middle English *codpese*, from *cod* bag, scrotum (from Old English *codd*) + *pese* piece] (15th century)
: a flap or bag concealing an opening in the front of men's breeches especially in the 15th and 16th centuries
**cods·wal·lop** \'kódz-,wä-ləp, 'kädz-\ *noun* [origin unknown] (1963)
*British* : NONSENSE
**¹co·ed** \'kō-(,)ed\ *adjective* (1889)
**1** : of or relating to a coed
**2** : of or relating to coeducation
**3** : open to or used by both men and women
**²coed** *noun* [short for *coeducational student*] (circa 1893)
: a student and especially a female student in a coeducational institution
**co·edi·tion** \,kō-ə-'di-shən\ *noun* (1964)
: an edition of a book published simultaneously by more than one publisher usually in different countries and in different languages
**co·ed·u·ca·tion** \(,)kō-,e-jə-'kā-shən\ *noun* (1852)
: the education of students of both sexes at the same institution
— **co·ed·u·ca·tion·al** \-shnəl, -shə-n°l\ *adjective*
— **co·ed·u·ca·tion·al·ly** *adverb*
**co·ef·fi·cient** \,kō-ə-'fi-shənt\ *noun* [New Latin *coefficient-, coefficiens*, from Latin *co-* + *efficient-, efficiens* efficient] (circa 1715)
**1** : any of the factors of a product considered in relation to a specific factor; *especially* : a constant factor of a term as distinguished from a variable
**2 a** : a number that serves as a measure of some property or characteristic (as of a substance, device, or process) ⟨*coefficient* of expansion of a metal⟩ **b** : MEASURE
**coefficient of correlation** (1896)
: CORRELATION COEFFICIENT
**coefficient of viscosity** (1866)
: VISCOSITY 3
**coe·la·canth** \'sē-lə-,kan(t)th\ *noun* [ultimately from Greek *koilos* hollow + *akantha* spine — more at CAVE] (1857)

: any of an order (Coelacanthiformes) of lobe-finned fishes known chiefly from Paleozoic and Mesozoic fossils

**coelacanth**

**-coele** or **-coel** noun combining form [probably from New Latin -coela, from neuter plural of -coelus hollow, concave, from Greek -koilos, from koilos]
: cavity : chamber : ventricle ⟨blastocoel⟩ ⟨enterocoele⟩

**coe·len·ter·ate** \si-'len-tə-,rāt, -rət\ noun [ultimately from Greek koilos + enteron intestine — more at INTER-] (1872)
: any of a phylum (Cnidaria synonym Coelenterata) of radially symmetrical invertebrate animals including the corals, sea anemones, jellyfishes, and hydroids — called also cnidarian
— **coelenterate** adjective

**coe·len·ter·on** \-,rän, -rən\ noun, plural **-tera** \-rə\ [New Latin, from Greek koilos + enteron] (1893)
: the internal cavity of a coelenterate

**coe·li·ac** \'sē-lē-,ak\ variant of CELIAC

**coe·lom** \'sē-ləm\ noun, plural **coeloms** or **coe·lo·ma·ta** \si-'lō-mə-tə\ [German, from Greek koilōma cavity, from koilos] (1878)
: the usually epithelium-lined space between the body wall and the digestive tract of metazoans above the lower worms
— **coe·lo·mate** \'sē-lə-,māt\ adjective or noun
— **coe·lo·mic** \si-'lä-mik, -'lō-\ adjective

**coen-** or **coeno-** combining form [New Latin, from Greek koin-, koino-, from koinos]
: common : general ⟨coenocyte⟩

**coe·no·bite** \'sē-nə-,bīt\ variant of CENOBITE

**coe·no·cyte** \'sē-nə-,sīt\ noun [International Scientific Vocabulary] (1897)
**1 a** : a multinucleate mass of protoplasm resulting from repeated nuclear division unaccompanied by cell fission **b** : an organism consisting of such a structure
**2** : SYNCYTIUM 1
— **coe·no·cyt·ic** \,sē-nə-'si-tik\ adjective

**coe·nu·rus** \si-'nùr-əs, -'nyùr-\ noun, plural **-nu·ri** \-,ī\ [New Latin, from coen- + Greek oura tail] (1876)
: a complex tapeworm larva consisting of a sac from the inner wall of which numerous scolices develop

**co·en·zyme** \(,)kō-'en-,zīm\ noun (1908)
: a thermostable nonprotein compound that forms the active portion of an enzyme system after combination with an apoenzyme
— **co·en·zy·mat·ic** \(,)kō-,en-zə-'ma-tik, -(,)zī-\ adjective
— **co·en·zy·mat·i·cal·ly** \-ti-k(ə-)lē\ adverb

**coenzyme A** noun (1949)
: a coenzyme $C_{21}H_{36}N_7O_{16}P_3S$ that occurs in all living cells and is essential to the metabolism of carbohydrates, fats, and some amino acids — compare ACETYL COENZYME A

**coenzyme Q** noun (1958)
: UBIQUINONE

**co·equal** \(,)kō-'ē-kwəl\ adjective (14th century)
: equal with one another
— **coequal** noun
— **co·equal·i·ty** \,kō-ē-'kwä-lə-tē\ noun
— **co·equal·ly** \(,)kō-'ē-kwə-lē\ adverb

**co·erce** \kō-'ərs\ transitive verb **co·erced**; **co·erc·ing** [Latin coercēre, from co- + arcēre to shut up, enclose — more at ARK] (15th century)
**1** : to restrain or dominate by force ⟨religion in the past has tried to coerce the irreligious —W. R. Inge⟩
**2** : to compel to an act or choice
**3** : to bring about by force or threat ⟨coerce

the compliance of the rest of the community —Scott Buchanan⟩
**synonym** see FORCE
— **co·erc·ible** \-'ər-sə-bəl\ adjective

**co·er·cion** \-'ər-zhən, -shən\ noun (15th century)
: the act, process, or power of coercing

**co·er·cive** \-'ər-siv\ adjective (circa 1600)
: serving or intended to coerce
— **co·er·cive·ly** adverb
— **co·er·cive·ness** noun

**coercive force** noun (1827)
: the opposing magnetic intensity that must be applied to a magnetized material to remove the residual magnetism

**co·er·civ·i·ty** \,kō-,ər-'si-və-tē\ noun (1898)
: the property of a material determined by the value of the coercive force when the material has been magnetized to saturation

**co·e·ta·ne·ous** \,kō-ə-'tā-nē-əs\ adjective [Latin coaetaneus, from co- + aetas age — more at AGE] (1608)
: COEVAL

**co·e·val** \kō-'ē-vəl\ adjective [Latin coaevus, from co- + aevum age, lifetime — more at AYE] (circa 1662)
: of the same or equal age, antiquity, or duration
**synonym** see CONTEMPORARY
— **coeval** noun
— **co·e·val·i·ty** \,kō-(,)ē-'va-lə-tē\ noun

**co·evo·lu·tion** \,kō-,e-və-'lü-shən also -,ē-və-\ noun (1965)
: evolution involving successive changes in two or more ecologically interdependent species (as of a plant and its pollinators) that affect their interactions
— **co·evo·lu·tion·ary** \-shə-,ner-ē\ adjective
— **co·evolve** \,kō-i-'välv, -'vòlv\ intransitive verb

**co·ex·ist** \,kō-ig-'zist\ intransitive verb (1667)
**1** : to exist together or at the same time
**2** : to live in peace with each other especially as a matter of policy
— **co·ex·is·tence** \-'zis-tən(t)s\ noun
— **co·ex·is·tent** \-tənt\ adjective

**co·ex·ten·sive** \,kō-ik-'sten(t)-siv\ adjective (1771)
: having the same spatial or temporal scope or boundaries
— **co·ex·ten·sive·ly** adverb

**co·fac·tor** \'kō-,fak-tər\ noun (circa 1909)
**1** : the signed minor of an element of a square matrix or of a determinant with the sign positive if the sum of the column number and row number of the element is even and with the sign negative if it is odd
**2** : a substance that acts with another substance to bring about certain effects; especially : COENZYME

**cof·fee** \'kò-fē, 'kä-\ noun, often attributive [Italian & Turkish; Italian caffè, from Turkish kahve, from Arabic qahwa] (1598)
**1 a** : a beverage made by percolation, infusion, or decoction from the roasted and ground seeds of a coffee plant **b** : any of several Old World tropical plants (genus Coffea and especially C. arabica and C. canephora) of the madder family that are widely cultivated in warm regions for their seeds from which coffee is prepared **c** : coffee seeds especially roasted and often ground — compare ARABICA, ROBUSTA **d** : a dehydrated product made from brewed coffee (instant coffee); also : a beverage made from this
**2** : a cup of coffee ⟨two coffees⟩
**3** : COFFEE HOUR

**coffee 1b**

**coffee break** noun (1951)
: a short period for rest and refreshments

**coffee cake** noun (1879)
: a sweet rich bread often with added fruit, nuts, and spices that is sometimes glazed after baking

**coffee hour** noun (1952)
**1** : a usually fixed occasion of informal meeting and chatting at which refreshments are served
**2** : COFFEE BREAK

**cof·fee·house** \-,haùs\ noun (1612)
: an establishment that sells coffee and usually other refreshments and that commonly serves as an informal club for its regular customers

**coffee klatch** also **cof·fee–klatsch** \-,klach, -,kläch, -,klòch\ noun [part translation of German Kaffeeklatsch] (1895)
: KAFFEEKLATSCH

**cof·fee·mak·er** \-,mā-kər\ noun (1930)
: a utensil or appliance in which coffee is brewed

**coffee mill** noun (1691)
: a mill for grinding coffee beans

**cof·fee·pot** \-,pät\ noun (1704)
: a pot for brewing and serving coffee

**coffee ring** noun (1924)
: coffee cake in the shape of a ring

**coffee roll** noun (1945)
: a sweet roll

**coffee room** noun (1712)
: a room where refreshments are served

**coffee royal** noun (1921)
: a drink of black coffee and a liquor

**coffee shop** noun (1836)
: a small restaurant

**coffee–table** adjective (1962)
: of, relating to, or being an article (as a book or magazine) intended for display (as on a coffee table)

**coffee table** noun (1877)
: a low table customarily placed in front of a sofa — called also cocktail table

**coffee tree** noun (1741)
**1** : a tree (as arabica) that produces coffee
**2** : KENTUCKY COFFEE TREE

**¹cof·fer** \'kò-fər, 'kä-\ noun [Middle English coffre, from Old French, from Latin cophinus basket, from Greek kophinos] (13th century)
**1** : CHEST, BOX; especially : STRONGBOX
**2** : TREASURY — usually used in plural
**3** : a recessed panel in a vault, ceiling, or soffit

**²coffer** transitive verb (14th century)
**1** : to store or hoard up in a coffer
**2** : to form (as a ceiling) with recessed panels

**cof·fer·dam** \-,dam\ noun (1736)
**1** : a watertight enclosure from which water is pumped to expose the bottom of a body of water and permit construction (as of a pier)
**2** : a watertight structure for making repairs below the waterline of a ship

**¹cof·fin** \'kò-fən\ noun [Middle English, basket, receptacle, from Middle French cofin, from Latin cophinus] (1525)
: a box or chest for burying a corpse

**²coffin** transitive verb (1564)
: to enclose in or as if in a coffin

**coffin bone** noun (circa 1720)
: the principal bone enclosed within the hoof of a horse — called also pedal bone

**coffin corner** noun (1940)
: one of the corners formed by a goal line and a sideline on a football field into which a punt is often aimed so that it may go out of bounds close to the defender's goal line

**coffin nail** noun (1888)
slang : CIGARETTE

**cof·fle** \'kò-fəl, 'kä-\ noun [Arabic qāfila caravan] (1799)

\ə\ abut \ᵊ\ kitten \ər\ further \a\ ash \ā\ ace
\ä\ mop, mar \aù\ out \ch\ chin \e\ bet \ē\ easy
\g\ go \i\ hit \ī\ ice \j\ job \ŋ\ sing \ō\ go
\ò\ law \òi\ boy \th\ thin \t͟h\ the \ü\ loot \ù\ foot
\y\ yet \zh\ vision     see also Guide to Pronunciation

**:** a train of slaves or animals fastened together

**co·func·tion** \'kō-ˌfəŋ(k)-shən\ *noun* (1909)
**:** a trigonometric function whose value for the complement of an angle is equal to the value of a given trigonometric function of the angle itself (the sine is the *cofunction* of the cosine)

**¹cog** \'käg\ *noun* [Middle English *cogge*, of Scandinavian origin; akin to Norwegian *kug* cog] (13th century)
**1 :** a tooth on the rim of a wheel or gear
**2 :** a subordinate but vital person or part
— **cogged** \'kägd\ *adjective*

**²cog** *verb* **cogged; cog·ging** [obsolete *cog* a trick] (1532)
*intransitive verb*
**1** *obsolete* **:** to cheat in throwing dice
**2** *obsolete* **:** DECEIVE
**3** *obsolete* **:** to use venal flattery
*transitive verb*
**1 :** to direct the fall of (dice) fraudulently
**2** *obsolete* **:** WHEEDLE

**³cog** *transitive verb* **cogged; cog·ging** [probably alteration of *cock* to cog] (1823)
**:** to connect (as timbers or joists) by means of mortises and tenons

**⁴cog** *noun* (circa 1858)
**:** a tenon on a beam or timber

**co·gen·cy** \'kō-jən(t)-sē\ *noun* (1667)
**:** the quality or state of being cogent

**co·gen·e·ra·tion** \ˌkō-ˌje-nə-'rā-shən\ *noun* (1978)
**:** the production of electricity using waste heat (as in steam) from an industrial process or the use of steam from electric power generation as a source of heat
— **co·gen·er·a·tor** \-'je-nə-ˌrā-tər\ *noun*

**co·gent** \'kō-jənt\ *adjective* [Latin *cogent-, cogens,* present participle of *cogere* to drive together, collect, from *co-* + *agere* to drive — more at AGENT] (1659)
**1 :** having power to compel or constrain ⟨*cogent* forces⟩
**2 a :** appealing forcibly to the mind or reason **:** CONVINCING ⟨*cogent* evidence⟩ **b :** PERTINENT, RELEVANT ⟨a *cogent* analysis of a problem⟩
*synonym* see VALID
— **co·gent·ly** *adverb*

**cog·i·ta·ble** \'kä-jə-tə-bəl\ *adjective* (15th century)
**:** CONCEIVABLE, THINKABLE

**cog·i·tate** \'kä-jə-ˌtāt\ *verb* **-tat·ed; -tat·ing** [Latin *cogitatus,* past participle of *cogitare* to think, think about, from *co-* + *agitare* to drive, agitate] (circa 1587)
*transitive verb*
**:** to ponder or meditate on usually intently
*intransitive verb*
**:** to meditate deeply or intently
*synonym* see THINK

**cog·i·ta·tion** \ˌkä-jə-'tā-shən\ *noun* (13th century)
**1 a :** the act of cogitating **:** MEDITATION **b :** the capacity to think or reflect
**2 :** a single thought

**cog·i·ta·tive** \'kä-jə-ˌtā-tiv\ *adjective* (15th century)
**1 :** of or relating to cogitation
**2 :** capable of or given to cogitation

**co·gi·to** \'kä-gi-ˌtō, 'kō-, 'kä-ji-\ *noun* [New Latin *cogito, ergo sum,* literally, I think, therefore I am, principle stated by René Descartes] (1838)
**1 :** the philosophic principle that one's existence is demonstrated by the fact that one thinks
**2 :** the intellectual processes of the self or ego

**co·gnac** \'kōn-ˌyak *also* 'kȯn- *or* 'kän-\ *noun* [French, from *Cognac,* France] (1755)
**:** a brandy from the departments of Charente and Charente-Maritime distilled from white wine

**¹cog·nate** \'käg-ˌnāt\ *adjective* [Latin *cognatus,* from *co-* + *gnatus, natus,* past participle of *nasci* to be born; akin to Latin *gignere* to beget — more at KIN] (circa 1645)

**1 :** of the same or similar nature **:** generically alike
**2 :** related by blood; *also* **:** related on the mother's side
**3 a :** related by descent from the same ancestral language **b** *of a word or morpheme* **:** related by derivation, borrowing, or descent **c** *of a substantive* **:** related to a verb usually by derivation and serving as its object to reinforce the meaning
— **cog·nate·ly** *adverb*

**²cognate** *noun* (1754)
**:** one that is cognate with another

**cog·na·tion** \käg-'nā-shən\ *noun* (14th century)
**:** cognate relationship

**cog·ni·tion** \käg-'ni-shən\ *noun* [Middle English *cognicioun,* from Latin *cognition-, cognitio,* from *cognoscere* to become acquainted with, know, from *co-* + *gnoscere* to come to know — more at KNOW] (15th century)
**:** the act or process of knowing including both awareness and judgment; *also* **:** a product of this act
— **cog·ni·tion·al** \-'nish-nəl, -'ni-shə-nᵊl\ *adjective*

**cog·ni·tive** \'käg-nə-tiv\ *adjective* (1586)
**1 :** of, relating to, or involving cognition ⟨the *cognitive* elements of perception —C. H. Hamburg⟩
**2 :** based on or capable of being reduced to empirical factual knowledge
— **cog·ni·tive·ly** *adverb*

**cognitive dissonance** *noun* (1957)
**:** psychological conflict resulting from incongruous beliefs and attitudes held simultaneously

**cognitive science** *noun* (1976)
**:** an interdisciplinary science that draws on many fields (as psychology, artificial intelligence, linguistics, and philosophy) in developing theories about human perception, thinking, and learning

**cog·ni·za·ble** \'käg-nə-zə-bəl, käg-'nī-\ *adjective* (1678)
**1 :** capable of being known
**2 :** capable of being judicially heard and determined
— **cog·ni·za·bly** \-blē\ *adverb*

**cog·ni·zance** \'käg-nə-zən(t)s\ *noun* [Middle English *conisaunce,* from Middle French *conoissance,* from *conoistre* to know, from Latin *cognoscere*] (14th century)
**1 :** a distinguishing mark or emblem (as a heraldic bearing)
**2 a :** KNOWLEDGE, AWARENESS ⟨had no *cognizance* of the situation⟩ **b :** NOTICE, ACKNOWLEDGMENT ⟨take *cognizance* of their achievement⟩
**3 :** JURISDICTION, RESPONSIBILITY

**cog·ni·zant** \-zənt\ *adjective* (1820)
**:** knowledgeable of something especially through personal experience; *also* **:** MINDFUL
*synonym* see AWARE

**cog·nize** \käg-'nīz, 'käg-ˌ\ *transitive verb* **cog·nized; cog·niz·ing** [back-formation from *cognizance*] (circa 1837)
**:** KNOW, UNDERSTAND
— **cog·niz·er** *noun*

**cog·no·men** \käg-'nō-mən, 'käg-nə-\ *noun, plural* **cognomens** *or* **cog·no·mi·na** \käg-'nä-mə-nə, -'nō-\ [Latin, irregular from *co-* + *nomen* name — more at NAME] (1809)
**1 :** SURNAME; *especially* **:** the third of usually three names borne by a male citizen of ancient Rome
**2 :** NAME; *especially* **:** a distinguishing nickname or epithet
— **cog·nom·i·nal** \käg-'nä-mə-nᵊl\ *adjective*

**co·gno·scen·te** \ˌkän-yə-'shen-tē, ˌkäg-nə-, -'sen-\ *noun, plural* **-scen·ti** \-tē\ [obsolete Italian (now *conoscente*), from *cognoscente,* adjective, wise, from Latin *cognoscent-, cognoscens,* present participle of *cognoscere*] (1776)

**:** a person who is especially knowledgeable in a subject **:** CONNOISSEUR

**cog·nos·ci·ble** \käg-'nä-sə-bəl\ *adjective* [Late Latin *cognoscibilis,* from Latin *cognoscere*] (circa 1644)
**:** COGNIZABLE, KNOWABLE

**co·gon** \kō-'gōn\ *noun* [Spanish *cogón,* from Tagalog & Bisayan *kugon*] (1898)
**:** any of several coarse tall grasses (genus *Imperata*) used especially in the Philippines for thatching

**cog railway** *noun* (1896)
**:** a steep mountain railroad that has a rail with cogs engaged by a cogwheel on the locomotive to ensure traction

**cog·wheel** \'käg-ˌhwēl, -ˌwēl\ *noun* (14th century)
**:** a wheel with cogs **:** GEAR 6a(2)

**co·hab·it** \(ˌ)kō-'ha-bət\ *intransitive verb* [Late Latin *cohabitare,* from Latin *co-* + *habitare* to inhabit, from frequentative of *habēre* to have — more at GIVE] (circa 1530)
**1 :** to live together as or as if a married couple
**2 a :** to live together or in company ⟨buffaloes *cohabiting* with crossbred cows —*Biological Abstracts*⟩ **b :** to exist together ⟨two strains in his philosophy . . . *cohabit* in each of his major works —Justus Buchler⟩
— **co·hab·i·tant** \-bə-tənt\ *noun*
— **co·hab·i·ta·tion** \(ˌ)kō-ˌha-bə-'tā-shən\ *noun*

**co·here** \kō-'hir\ *verb* **co·hered; co·her·ing** [Latin *cohaerēre,* from *co-* + *haerēre* to stick] (1598)
*intransitive verb*
**1 a :** to hold together firmly as parts of the same mass; *broadly* **:** STICK, ADHERE **b :** to display cohesion of plant parts
**2 :** to hold together as a mass of parts that cohere
**3 a :** to become united in principles, relationships, or interests **b :** to be logically or aesthetically consistent
*transitive verb*
**:** to cause (parts or components) to cohere
*synonym* see STICK

**co·her·ence** \kō-'hir-ən(t)s, -'her-\ *noun* (1580)
**1 :** the quality or state of cohering: as **a :** systematic or logical connection or consistency **b :** integration of diverse elements, relationships, or values
**2 :** the property of being coherent

**co·her·en·cy** \kō-'hir-ən(t)-sē, -'her-\ *noun, plural* **-cies** (1630)
**:** COHERENCE

**co·her·ent** \-ənt\ *adjective* [Middle French or Latin; Middle French *cohérent,* from Latin *cohaerent-, cohaerens,* present participle of *cohaerēre*] (circa 1555)
**1 a :** logically or aesthetically ordered or integrated **:** CONSISTENT ⟨*coherent* style⟩ ⟨a *coherent* argument⟩ **b :** having clarity or intelligibility **:** UNDERSTANDABLE ⟨a *coherent* person⟩ ⟨a *coherent* passage⟩
**2 :** having the quality of cohering; *especially* **:** COHESIVE, COORDINATED ⟨a *coherent* plan for action⟩
**3 a :** relating to or composed of waves having a constant difference in phase ⟨*coherent* light⟩ **b :** producing coherent light ⟨a *coherent* source⟩
— **co·her·ent·ly** *adverb*

**co·her·er** \kō-'hir-ər\ *noun* (1894)
**:** a radio detector in which an imperfectly conducting contact between pieces of conductive material loosely resting against each other is materially improved in conductance by the passage of high-frequency current

**co·he·sion** \kō-'hē-zhən\ *noun* [Latin *cohaesus,* past participle of *cohaerēre*] (1660)
**1 :** the act or state of sticking together tightly; *especially* **:** UNITY ⟨the lack of *cohesion* in the Party —*Times Literary Supplement*⟩
**2 :** union between similar plant parts or organs

**3 :** molecular attraction by which the particles of a body are united throughout the mass
— **co·he·sion·less** \-ləs\ *adjective*
**co·he·sive** \kō-'hē-siv, -ziv\ *adjective* (circa 1731)
**:** exhibiting or producing cohesion or coherence ⟨a *cohesive* social unit⟩ ⟨*cohesive* soils⟩
— **co·he·sive·ly** *adverb*
— **co·he·sive·ness** *noun*
**co·ho** \'kō-(,)hō\ *noun, plural* **cohos** *or* **coho** [Halkomelem (Salishan language of southwest British Columbia) *k^wə́x^wəθ*] (1869)
**:** a rather small Pacific salmon (*Oncorhynchus kisutch*) that has light-colored flesh and is native to both coasts of the North Pacific and is stocked in the Great Lakes
**co·ho·mol·o·gy** \(,)kō-hō-'mä-lə-jē\ *noun* (circa 1959)
**:** a part of the theory of topology in which groups are used to study the properties of topological spaces and which is related in a complementary way to homology theory — called also *cohomology theory*
— **co·ho·mo·log·i·cal** \-,hō-mə-'lä-ji-kəl, -,hä-\ *adjective*
**co·hort** \'kō-,hort\ *noun* [Middle French & Latin; Middle French *cohorte*, from Latin *cohort-, cohors* — more at COURT] (15th century)
**1 a :** one of 10 divisions of an ancient Roman legion **b :** a group of warriors or soldiers **c :** BAND, GROUP **d :** a group of individuals having a statistical factor (as age or class membership) in common in a demographic study ⟨a *cohort* of premedical students⟩
**2 :** COMPANION, COLLEAGUE ⟨a few of their . . . *cohorts* decided to form a company —Burt Hochberg⟩ ▫
**co·hosh** \'kō-,häsh\ *noun* [Eastern Abenaki *kk^wàhas*] (1789)
**:** any of several American medicinal or poisonous plants: as **a :** BLACK COHOSH **b :** BLUE COHOSH **c :** BANEBERRY
**¹coif** \'koif, *in sense 2 also* 'kwäf\ *noun* [Middle English *coife*, from Middle French, from Late Latin *cofea*] (14th century)
**1 :** a close-fitting cap: as **a :** a hoodlike cap worn under a veil by nuns **b :** a protective usually metal skullcap formerly worn under a hood of mail **c :** a white cap formerly worn by English lawyers and especially by serjeants-at-law; *also* **:** the order or rank of a serjeant-at-law
**2 :** COIFFURE
**²coif** \'koif, 'kwäf\ *transitive verb* **coiffed** *or* **coifed; coiff·ing** *or* **coif·ing** (15th century)
**1 :** to cover or dress with or as if with a coif
**2 :** to arrange (hair) by brushing, combing, or curling
**coif·feur** \kwä-'fər\ *noun* [French, from *coiffer*] (1847)
**:** a man who is a hairdresser
**coif·feuse** \kwä-'fə(r)z, -'fyüz, -'füz\ *noun* [French, feminine of *coiffeur*] (1870)
**:** a woman who is a hairdresser
**coif·fure** \kwä-'fyür\ *noun* [French, from *coiffer* to cover with a coif, arrange (hair), from *coife*] (circa 1631)
**:** a style or manner of arranging the hair
**coif·fured** \-'fyürd\ *adjective* (1907)
**1 :** being dressed ⟨beautifully *coiffured* hair⟩
**2 :** having the hair brushed, combed, and curled ⟨stylishly *coiffured* women⟩
**coign of van·tage** \,koi-nə-'van-tij\ [*coign*, earlier spelling of ¹*coin* (corner)] (1605)
**:** an advantageous position
**¹coil** \'koi(ə)l\ *noun* [origin unknown] (1567)
**1 :** TURMOIL
**2 :** TROUBLE; *also* **:** everyday cares and worries ⟨when we have shuffled off this mortal *coil* —Shakespeare⟩
**²coil** *verb* [French *coillir, cuillir* to gather — more at CULL] (1611)
*transitive verb*

**1 :** to wind into rings or spirals
**2 :** to roll or twist into a shape resembling a coil
*intransitive verb*
**1 :** to move in a circular or spiral course
**2 :** to form or lie in a coil
— **coil·abil·i·ty** \,koi-lə-'bi-lə-tē\ *noun*
**³coil** *noun* (1627)
**1 a** (1) **:** a series of loops (2) **:** SPIRAL **b :** a single loop of such a coil
**2 a :** a number of turns of wire wound around a core (as of iron) to create a magnetic field for an electromagnet or an induction coil **b :** INDUCTION COIL
**3 :** a series of connected pipes in rows, layers, or windings
**4 :** a roll of postage stamps; *also* **:** a stamp from such a roll
**¹coin** \'koin\ *noun* [Middle English, from Middle French, wedge, corner, from Latin *cuneus* wedge] (14th century)
**1** *archaic* **a :** CORNER, CORNERSTONE, QUOIN **b :** WEDGE
**2 a :** a usually flat piece of metal issued by governmental authority as money **b :** metal money **c :** something resembling a coin especially in shape
**3 :** something used as if it were money (as in verbal or intellectual exchange) ⟨perhaps wisecracks . . . are respectable literary *coin* in the U.S. —*Times Literary Supplement*⟩ ⟨would repay him with the full *coin* of his mind —Ian Fleming⟩
**4 :** something having two different and usually opposing sides — usually used in the phrase *the other side of the coin*
**5 :** MONEY ⟨I'm in it for the *coin* —Sinclair Lewis⟩
**²coin** *transitive verb* (14th century)
**1 a :** to make (a coin) especially by stamping **b :** to convert (metal) into coins
**2 :** CREATE, INVENT ⟨*coin* a phrase⟩
— **coin·er** \'koi-nər\ *noun*
— **coin money :** to get rich quickly
**³coin** *adjective* (circa 1566)
**1 :** of or relating to coins
**2 :** operated by coins
**coin·age** \'koi-nij\ *noun* (14th century)
**1 :** the act or process of coining
**2 a :** COINS **b :** something (as a word) made up or invented
**co·in·cide** \,kō-ən-'sīd, 'kō-ən-,\ *intransitive verb* **-cid·ed; -cid·ing** [Medieval Latin *coincidere*, from Latin *co-* + *incidere* to fall on, from *in-* + *cadere* to fall — more at CHANCE] (1719)
**1 a :** to occupy the same place in space or time **b :** to occupy exactly corresponding or equivalent positions on a scale or in a series
**2 :** to correspond in nature, character, or function
**3 :** to be in accord or agreement **:** CONCUR
*synonym see* AGREE
**co·in·ci·dence** \kō-'in(t)-sə-dən(t)s, -sə-,den(t)s\ *noun* (1605)
**1 :** the act or condition of coinciding **:** CORRESPONDENCE
**2 :** the occurrence of events that happen at the same time by accident but seem to have some connection; *also* **:** any of these occurrences
**co·in·ci·dent** \-sə-dənt, -,dent\ *adjective* [French *coïncident*, from Medieval Latin *coincident-, coincidens*, present participle of *coincidere*] (circa 1587)
**1 :** of similar nature **:** HARMONIOUS ⟨a theory *coincident* with the facts⟩
**2 :** occupying the same space or time ⟨*coincident* events⟩
*synonym see* CONTEMPORARY
— **co·in·ci·dent·ly** \-sə-dənt-lē, -,dent-; (,)kō-,in(t)-sə-'dent-lē\ *adverb*
**co·in·ci·den·tal** \(,)kō-,in(t)-sə-'den-t°l\ *adjective* (circa 1800)
**1 :** resulting from a coincidence
**2 :** occurring or existing at the same time

— **co·in·ci·den·tal·ly** \-'dent-lē, -'den-t°l-ē\ *adverb*
**coin-op** \'koin-,näp\ *noun* (1961)
**:** a self-service laundry where the machines are operated by coins
**co·in·sur·ance** \,kō-ən-'shur-ən(t)s *also* -'in-,\ *noun* (circa 1889)
**1 :** joint assumption of risk (as by two underwriters) with another
**2 :** insurance (as fire insurance) in which the insured is obligated to maintain coverage on a risk at a stipulated percentage of its total value or in the event of loss suffer a penalty in proportion to the deficiency
**co·in·sure** \,kō-ən-'shur\ *transitive verb* (circa 1899)
**:** to insure jointly
— **co·in·sur·er** *noun*
**coir** \'koi(-ə)r\ *noun* [Tamil *kayiru* rope] (1582)
**:** a stiff coarse fiber from the outer husk of a coconut
**cois·trel** \'koi-strəl\ *noun* [Middle French *coustillier* soldier carrying a short sword, from *coustille* short sword, from Latin *cultellus* knife — more at CUTLASS] (1581)
*archaic* **:** a mean fellow **:** VARLET
**co·i·tion** \kō-'i-shən\ *noun* [Late Latin, from Latin *coition-, coitio* a coming together, from *coire* to come together, from *co-* + *ire* to go — more at ISSUE] (1615)
**:** COITUS
— **co·i·tion·al** \-'ish-nəl, -'i-shə-n°l\ *adjective*
**co·i·tus** \'kō-ə-təs, kō-'ē-, 'koi-təs\ *noun* [Latin, from *coire*] (1855)
**:** physical union of male and female genitalia accompanied by rhythmic movements usually leading to the ejaculation of semen from the

□ **USAGE**

**cohort** Sense 2 is an American development with a curious history. The first extension of the meaning of *cohort* was from the Roman army to other armies ⟨the Assyrian came down like the wolf on the fold, and his *cohorts* were gleaming in purple and gold —Lord Byron⟩. Then the word was extended to any group or band ⟨Harry, with a loyal *cohort* of adherents, forcibly barred his entrance —S. N. Behrman⟩. This sense could also be used in the plural ⟨Dr. Mossadegh and his *cohorts* nationalized the British-owned oil concession in southern Iran — *N. Y. Times*⟩. On reflection, it would seem clear that these cohorts are large and probably organized bands, but the word can easily be read as meaning "followers." Some uses could seem even more ambiguous ⟨as Carrie Nation and her *cohorts* swarmed forward and pounded the panels —Herbert Asbury⟩. Here evidently a mob scene is being described, a far cry from the disciplined Roman army units. And again *cohorts* can readily be interpreted as "friends, followers." It is presumably from uses like these that our sense 2 developed ⟨formulated a second constitution which virtually restricted the suffrage to the freedmen and their white *cohorts* —*Dictionary of American History*⟩ ⟨had left, accompanied by two of his *cohorts* —Mary McCarthy⟩. Sense 2 was becoming established in the 1940s, and ten years or so later some critics began to notice it disapprovingly. Disapproval came too late, though, for by then the sense was established as standard—at least in American English—and it is standard now.

\ə\ abut \°\ kitten \ər\ further \a\ ash \ā\ ace
\ä\ mop, mar \au̇\ out \ch\ chin \e\ bet \ē\ easy
\g\ go \i\ hit \ī\ ice \j\ job \ŋ\ sing \ō\ go
\ȯ\ law \oi\ boy \th\ thin \th\ the \ü\ loot \u̇\ foot
\y\ yet \zh\ vision *see also* Guide to Pronunciation

penis into the female reproductive tract; *also*
: INTERCOURSE 3 — compare ORGASM
— **co·i·tal** \-t°l\ *adjective*
— **co·i·tal·ly** \-t°l-ē\ *adverb*
**coitus in·ter·rup·tus** \-,in-tə-'rəp-təs\ *noun*
[New Latin, interrupted coitus] (1900)
: coitus in which the penis is withdrawn prior
to ejaculation to prevent the deposit of sperm
into the vagina
**¹coke** \'kōk\ *noun* [perhaps from dialect *coke,
colk* core, from Middle English; akin to Swedish *kälk* pith] (1669)
: the residue of coal left after destructive distillation and used as fuel; *also* : a similar residue left by other materials (as petroleum) distilled to dryness
**²coke** *verb* **coked; cok·ing** (1763)
*transitive verb*
: to change into coke
*intransitive verb*
: to become coke or like coke
**³coke** *noun* [by shortening & alteration] (circa
1903)
: COCAINE
**Coke** \'kōk\ *trademark*
— used for a cola drink
**coke·head** \'kō-ked, 'kōk-,hed\ *noun* (circa
1927)
: a person who uses cocaine compulsively
**col** \'käl\ *noun* [French, from Middle French,
neck, from Latin *collum*] (1853)
: SADDLE 3
**¹col-** — see COM-
**²col-** *or* **coli-** *or* **colo-** *combining form* [New
Latin, from Latin *colon*]
**1** : colon ⟨*coli*tis⟩ ⟨*colo*stomy⟩
**2** [New Latin *Escherichia coli*, species of colon bacillus] : colon bacillus ⟨*coli*form⟩
**¹cola** *plural of* COLON
**²co·la** \'kō-lə\ *noun* [from *Coca-Cola*, a trade-
mark] (1920)
: a carbonated soft drink colored usually with
caramel and flavored usually with extracts
from kola nuts
**col·an·der** \'käl-ən-dər, 'kəl-\ *noun* [Middle
English *colyndore*, probably modification of
Old Provençal *colador*, from Medieval Latin
*colatorium*, from Latin *colare* to sieve, from
*colum* sieve] (14th century)
: a perforated utensil for washing or draining
food
**co·lat·i·tude** \(,)kō-'la-tə-,tüd, -,tyüd\ *noun*
(1790)
: the complement of the latitude
**Col·by** \'kōl-bē\ *noun* [probably from the name
*Colby*] (1942)
: a moist mild cheese similar to cheddar
**col·can·non** \käl-'ka-nən\ *noun* [Irish *cál
ceannan*, literally, white-headed cabbage] (circa 1785)
: potatoes and cabbage boiled and mashed together with butter and seasoning
**col·chi·cine** \'käl-chə-,sēn, 'käl-kə-\ *noun*
(circa 1847)
: a poisonous alkaloid $C_{22}H_{25}NO_6$ that inhibits
mitosis, is extracted from the corms or seeds
of the autumn crocus (*Colchicum autumnale*),
and is used especially in the treatment of gout
and to produce polyploidy in plants
**col·chi·cum** \'käl-chi-kəm, 'käl-ki-\ *noun*
[New Latin, genus name, from Latin, a kind of
plant with a poisonous root, from Greek
*kolchikon*, literally, product of Colchis] (1597)
**1** : any of a genus (*Colchicum*) of Old World
corm-producing herbs of the lily family with
flowers that resemble crocuses
**2** : the dried corm or dried seeds of autumn
crocus containing colchicine, possessing emetic, diuretic, and cathartic action, and used to
treat gout
**¹cold** \'kōld\ *adjective* [Middle English, from
Old English *ceald, cald*; akin to Old High
German *kalt* cold, Latin *gelu* frost, *gelare* to
freeze] (before 12th century)
**1 a** : having or being a temperature that is uncomfortably low for humans ⟨it is *cold* outside

today⟩ **b** : having a relatively low temperature
or one lower than normal or expected ⟨the
bath water has gotten *cold*⟩ **c** : not heated: as
(1) *of food* : served without heating especially
after initial cooking or processing ⟨*cold* cereal⟩
⟨*cold* roast beef⟩ (2) : served chilled or with
ice ⟨a *cold* drink⟩ (3) : involving processing
without the use of heat ⟨*cold* working of steel⟩
**2 a** : marked by a lack of the warmth of normal human emotion, friendliness, or compassion ⟨got a *cold* reception⟩; *also* : not moved
to enthusiasm ⟨the movie leaves me *cold*⟩ **b**
: not colored or affected by personal feeling or
bias : DETACHED, INDIFFERENT ⟨*cold* chronicles
recorded by an outsider —Andrew Sarris⟩;
*also* : IMPERSONAL, OBJECTIVE ⟨*cold* facts⟩ ⟨*cold*
reality⟩ **c** : marked by sure familiarity : PAT
⟨had her lines *cold* weeks before opening
night⟩
**3** : conveying the impression of being cold: as
**a** : DEPRESSING, GLOOMY ⟨*cold* gray skies⟩ **b**
: COOL 6a
**4 a** : marked by the loss of normal body heat
⟨*cold* hands⟩; *especially* : DEAD **b** : giving the
appearance of being dead **b** : UNCONSCIOUS
⟨passed out *cold*⟩
**5 a** : having lost freshness or vividness
: STALE ⟨dogs trying to pick up a *cold* scent⟩ **b**
: far off the mark : not close to finding or
solving — used especially in children's
games **c** : marked by poor or unlucky performance ⟨the team's shooting turned *cold* in the
second half⟩ **d** : not prepared or suitably
warmed up
— **cold·ish** \'kōl-dish\ *adjective*
— **cold·ly** \'kōl(d)-lē\ *adverb*
— **cold·ness** \'kōl(d)-nəs\ *noun*
— **in cold blood** : with premeditation : DE-
LIBERATELY
**²cold** *noun* (13th century)
**1** : bodily sensation produced by loss or lack
of heat
**2** : a condition of low temperature; *especially*
: cold weather
**3** : a bodily disorder popularly associated with
chilling; *specifically* : COMMON COLD
— **out in the cold** : deprived of benefits
given others ⟨the plan benefits management
but leaves labor *out in the cold*⟩
**³cold** *adverb* (1889)
**1** : with utter finality : ABSOLUTELY, COMPLETE-
LY ⟨turned down *cold*⟩; *also* : ABRUPTLY
⟨stopped them *cold*⟩
**2 a** : without introduction or advance notice **b**
: without preparation or warm-up
**cold–blood·ed** \'kōl(d)-'blə-dəd\ *adjective*
(1595)
**1 a** : done or acting without consideration,
compunction, or clemency ⟨*cold-blooded* mur-
der⟩ **b** : MATTER-OF-FACT, EMOTIONLESS ⟨a *cold-
blooded* assessment⟩
**2** : having cold blood; *specifically* : having a
body temperature not internally regulated but
approximating that of the environment
**3** *or* **cold-blood** \-'bləd\ : of mixed or inferi-
or breeding
**4** : noticeably sensitive to cold
— **cold–blood·ed·ly** *adverb*
— **cold–blood·ed·ness** *noun*
**cold call** *noun* (1966)
: a telephone call soliciting business made directly to a potential customer without prior
contact or without a lead
— **cold–call** *verb*
**cold cash** *noun* (1925)
: money in hand
**cold chisel** *noun* (1699)
: a chisel made of tool steel of a strength,
shape, and temper suitable for chipping or cutting cold metal
**cold·cock** \'kōl(d)-'käk, ,kōl(d)-\ *transitive
verb* [perhaps ²*cock*] (circa 1927)
: to knock unconscious
**cold comfort** *noun* (14th century)
: quite limited sympathy, consolation, or encouragement

**cold cream** *noun* (1709)
: a soothing and cleansing cosmetic
**cold cuts** *noun plural* (1945)
: sliced assorted cold cooked meats
**cold duck** *noun* [translation of German *Kalte
Ente*] (1969)
: a beverage that consists of a blend of sparkling burgundy and champagne
**cold–eyed** \'kōl-'dīd, -,dīd\ *adjective* (1950)
: cold in manner or appearance; *especially*
: coolly dispassionate ⟨*cold-eyed* analysis⟩
**cold feet** *noun plural* (1893)
: apprehension or doubt strong enough to prevent a planned course of action
**cold fish** *noun* (1924)
: a cold aloof person
**cold frame** *noun* (1851)
: a usually
glass- or plastic-
covered frame
without artificial
heat used to
protect plants
and seedlings
outdoors

cold frame

**cold front** *noun*
(1921)
: an advancing edge of a cold air mass
**cold·heart·ed** \'kōld-'här-təd\ *adjective*
(1606)
: marked by lack of sympathy, interest, or sensitivity
— **cold·heart·ed·ly** *adverb*
— **cold·heart·ed·ness** *noun*
**cold shoulder** *noun* (1816)
: intentionally cold or unsympathetic treatment
— **cold–shoulder** *transitive verb*
**cold sore** *noun* (circa 1889)
: a group of blisters appearing about or within
the mouth and caused by a herpes simplex virus
**cold storage** *noun* (1877)
**1** : storage (as of food) in a cold place for
preservation
**2** : a condition of being held or continued
without being acted on : ABEYANCE
**cold store** *noun* (1895)
: a building for cold storage
**cold sweat** *noun* (1706)
: concurrent perspiration and chill usually associated with fear, pain, or shock
**¹cold turkey** *noun* (1921)
**1** : abrupt complete cessation of the use of an
addictive drug; *also* : the symptoms experienced by a person undergoing withdrawal
from a drug
**2** : unrelieved blunt language or procedure
**3** : a cold aloof person
— **cold turkey** *transitive verb*
**²cold turkey** *adverb* (1941)
: without a period of gradual adjustment, adaptation, or withdrawal : all at once ⟨quit
smoking *cold turkey*⟩
**cold type** *noun* (1949)
: composition or typesetting (as photocomposition) done without the casting of metal; *specifically* : such composition produced directly
on paper by a typewriter mechanism
**cold war** *noun* (1945)
**1** : a conflict over ideological differences carried on by methods short of sustained overt
military action and usually without breaking
off diplomatic relations; *specifically*, *often
C&W capitalized* : the ideological conflict between the U.S. and the U.S.S.R — compare
HOT WAR
**2** : a condition of rivalry, mistrust, and often
open hostility short of violence especially between power groups (as labor and management)
**cold warrior** *noun* (1949)
: one that supports or is engaged in a cold
war
**cold–water** *adjective* (1942)
: having only running water without heat or
utility services provided ⟨a *cold-water* flat⟩

**cold water** *noun* (1808)
**:** depreciation of something as being ill-advised, unwarranted, or worthless ⟨threw *cold water* on our hopes⟩

**cold wave** *noun* (1876)
**1 :** an unusually large and rapid drop in temperature over a short period of time (as 24 hours)
**2 :** a permanent wave set by a chemical preparation without the use of heat

**cole** \'kōl\ *noun* [Middle English, from Old English *cāl*, from Latin *caulis* stem, cabbage; akin to Greek *kaulos* stem, Latvian *kauls*] (before 12th century)
**:** any of several brassicas; *especially* **:** any of various crop plants (as broccoli, kale, brussels sprouts, cabbage, cauliflower, and kohlrabi) derived from the same wild ancestor (*Brassica oleracea*)

**cole·man·ite** \'kōl-mə-ˌnīt\ *noun* [William T. *Coleman* (died 1893) American businessman and mine owner] (1884)
**:** a mineral consisting of a hydrous calcium borate occurring in brilliant colorless or white massive monoclinic crystals

**co·le·op·tera** \ˌkō-lē-'äp-tə-rə\ *noun plural* [New Latin, ultimately from Greek *koleon* sheath + *pteron* wing — more at FEATHER] (1873)
**:** insects that are beetles
— **co·le·op·ter·ist** \-tə-rist\ *noun*
— **co·le·op·ter·ous** \-tə-rəs\ *adjective*

**co·le·op·ter·an** \-tə-rən\ *noun* (circa 1847)
**:** ¹BEETLE 1
— **coleopteran** *adjective*

**co·le·op·tile** \-'äp-tᵊl\ *noun* [New Latin *coleoptilum*, from Greek *koleon* + *ptilon* down; akin to Greek *pteron*] (circa 1866)
**:** the first leaf of a monocotyledon forming a protective sheath about the plumule

**co·le·o·rhi·za** \ˌkō-lē-ə-'rī-zə\ *noun, plural* **-zae** \-(ˌ)zē\ [New Latin, from Greek *koleon* + New Latin *-rhiza*] (circa 1866)
**:** the sheath investing the hypocotyl in some monocotyledonous plants through which the roots burst

**cole·slaw** \'kōl-ˌslo\ *noun* [Dutch *koolsla*, from *kool* cabbage + *sla* salad] (1794)
**:** a salad made of raw sliced or chopped cabbage

**co·le·us** \'kō-lē-əs\ *noun* [New Latin, genus name, from Greek *koleos, koleon* sheath] (1885)
**:** any of a large genus (*Coleus*) of herbs of the mint family

**cole·wort** \'kōl-ˌwərt, -ˌwort\ *noun* (14th century)
**:** COLE; *especially* **:** one (as kale) that forms no head

**coli-** — see COL-

**¹col·ic** \'kä-lik\ *noun* [Middle English, from Middle French *colique*, from Late Latin *colicus* colicky, from Greek *kōlikos*, from *kōlon*, alteration of *kolon* colon] (15th century)
**:** a paroxysm of acute abdominal pain localized in a hollow organ and often caused by spasm, obstruction, or twisting

**²colic** *adjective* (15th century)
**:** of or relating to colic **:** COLICKY ⟨*colic* crying⟩

**³co·lic** \'kō-lik, 'kä-\ *adjective* (1615)
**:** of or relating to the colon ⟨*colic* lymph nodes⟩

**co·li·cin** \'kō-lə-sən\ *also* **co·li·cine** \-ˌsēn\ *noun* [French *colicine*, from *col-* + *-cine* (as in *streptomycine* streptomycin)] (1946)
**:** any of various antibacterial substances that are produced by strains of intestinal bacteria (as of *Escherichia coli*) having a specific plasmid and that often act to inhibit macromolecular synthesis in related strains

**col·icky** \'kä-li-kē\ *adjective* (1742)
**1 :** relating to or associated with colic ⟨*colicky* pain⟩
**2 :** suffering from colic ⟨*colicky* babies⟩

**col·ic·root** \'kä-lik-ˌrüt, -ˌrut\ *noun* (1833)
**:** any of several plants having roots used in folk medicine to treat colic; *especially* **:** either of two bitter herbs (*Aletris farinosa* and *A. aurea*) of the lily family

**co·li·form** \'kō-lə-ˌform, 'kä-\ *adjective* (1906)
**:** relating to, resembling, or being the colon bacillus
— **coliform** *noun*

**co·lin·ear** \(ˌ)kō-'li-nē-ər\ *adjective* (1927)
**1 :** COLLINEAR
**2 :** having corresponding parts arranged in the same linear order ⟨a gene and the protein it determines are *colinear*⟩
— **co·lin·ear·i·ty** \(ˌ)kō-ˌli-nē-'ar-ə-tē\ *noun*

**co·li·phage** \'kō-lə-ˌfāj, -ˌfäzh\ *noun* (1944)
**:** any bacteriophage active against the colon bacillus

**col·i·se·um** \ˌkä-lə-'sē-əm\ *noun* [Medieval Latin *Colosseum, Colisseum*] (circa 1715)
**1** *capitalized* **:** COLOSSEUM 1
**2 :** a large sports stadium or building designed like the Colosseum for public entertainments

**co·lis·tin** \kə-'lis-tən, kō-\ *noun* [New Latin *colistinus*, specific epithet of the bacterium producing it] (1951)
**:** a polymyxin produced by a bacterium (*Bacillus polymyxa* variety *colistinus*) from Japanese soil

**co·li·tis** \kō-'lī-təs, kə-\ *noun* (circa 1860)
**:** inflammation of the colon

**coll-** *or* **collo-** *combining form* [New Latin, from Greek *koll-, kollo-*, from *kolla* — more at PROTOCOL]
**1 :** glue ⟨*coll*enchyma⟩
**2 :** colloid ⟨*collo*type⟩

**col·lab·o·rate** \kə-'la-bə-ˌrāt\ *intransitive verb* **-rat·ed; -rat·ing** [Late Latin *collaboratus*, past participle of *collaborare* to labor together, from Latin *com-* + *laborare* to labor] (1871)
**1 :** to work jointly with others or together especially in an intellectual endeavor
**2 :** to cooperate with or willingly assist an enemy of one's country and especially an occupying force
**3 :** to cooperate with an agency or instrumentality with which one is not immediately connected
— **col·lab·o·ra·tion** \-ˌla-bə-'rā-shən\ *noun*
— **col·lab·o·ra·tive** \-'la-bə-ˌrā-tiv, -b(ə-)rə-\ *adjective or noun*
— **col·lab·o·ra·tive·ly** \-lē\ *adverb*
— **col·lab·o·ra·tor** \-'la-bə-ˌrā-tər\ *noun*

**col·lab·o·ra·tion·ism** \kə-ˌla-bə-'rā-shə-ˌni-zəm\ *noun* (1923)
**:** the advocacy or practice of collaboration with an enemy
— **col·lab·o·ra·tion·ist** \-sh(ə-)nist\ *adjective or noun*

**col·lage** \kə-'läzh, ko-, kō-\ *noun* [French, literally, gluing, from *coller* to glue, from *colle* glue, from (assumed) Vulgar Latin *colla*, from Greek *kolla*] (1919)
**1 :** an artistic composition made of various materials (as paper, cloth, or wood) glued on a surface
**2 :** the art of making collages
**3 :** an assembly of diverse fragments ⟨a *collage* of ideas⟩
**4 :** a work (as a film) having disparate scenes in rapid succession without transitions
— **collage** *transitive verb*
— **col·lag·ist** \-'lä-zhist\ *noun*

**col·la·gen** \'kä-lə-jən\ *noun* [Greek *kolla* + International Scientific Vocabulary *-gen*] (circa 1865)
**:** an insoluble fibrous protein that occurs in vertebrates as the chief constituent of connective tissue fibrils and in bones and yields gelatin and glue on prolonged heating with water
— **col·lag·e·nous** \kə-'la-jə-nəs\ *adjective*

**col·la·ge·nase** \kə-'la-jə-ˌnās, 'kä-lə-jə-, -ˌnāz\ *noun* (1926)
**:** any of a group of proteolytic enzymes that decompose collagen and gelatin

**¹col·lapse** \kə-'laps\ *verb* **col·lapsed; col-**
**laps·ing** [Latin *collapsus*, past participle of *collabi*, from *com-* + *labi* to fall, slide — more at SLEEP] (1732)
*intransitive verb*
**1 :** to fall or shrink together abruptly and completely **:** fall into a jumbled or flattened mass through the force of external pressure ⟨a blood vessel that *collapsed*⟩
**2 :** to break down completely **:** DISINTEGRATE ⟨his case had *collapsed* in a mass of legal wreckage —Erle Stanley Gardner⟩
**3 :** to cave or fall in or give way
**4 :** to suddenly lose force, significance, effectiveness, or worth
**5 :** to break down in vital energy, stamina, or self-control through exhaustion or disease; *especially* **:** to fall helpless or unconscious
**6 :** to fold down into a more compact shape ⟨a chair that *collapses*⟩
*transitive verb*
**:** to cause to collapse
— **col·laps·ibil·i·ty** \-ˌlap-sə-'bi-lə-tē\ *noun*
— **col·laps·ible** \-'lap-sə-bəl\ *adjective*

**²collapse** *noun* (1801)
**1 a :** a breakdown in vital energy, strength, or stamina **b :** a state of extreme prostration and physical depression (as from circulatory failure or great loss of body fluids) **c :** an airless state of all or part of a lung originating spontaneously or induced surgically
**2 :** the act or action of collapsing ⟨the cutting of many tent ropes, the *collapse* of the canvas —Rudyard Kipling⟩
**3 :** a sudden failure **:** BREAKDOWN, RUIN
**4 :** a sudden loss of force, value, or effect ⟨the *collapse* of respect for ancient law and custom —L. S. B. Leakey⟩

**¹col·lar** \'kä-lər\ *noun* [Middle English *coler*, from Old French, from Latin *collare*, from *collum* neck; akin to Old English *heals* neck, and probably to Old English *hwēol* wheel — more at WHEEL] (14th century)
**1 :** a band, strip, or chain worn around the neck: as **a :** a band that serves to finish or decorate the neckline of a garment **b :** a short necklace **c :** a band placed about the neck of an animal **d :** a part of the harness of draft animals fitted over the shoulders and taking strain when a load is drawn **e :** an indication of control **:** a token of subservience **f :** a protective or supportive device (as a brace or cast) worn around the neck **g :** CLERICAL COLLAR
**2 :** something resembling a collar in shape or use (as a ring or round flange to restrain motion or hold something in place)
**3 :** any of various animal structures or markings similar to a collar
**4 :** an act of collaring **:** ARREST, CAPTURE
— **col·lared** \-lərd\ *adjective*
— **col·lar·less** \-lər-ləs\ *adjective*

**²collar** *transitive verb* (1613)
**1 a :** to seize by the collar or neck **b :** ARREST, GRAB **c :** to get control of **:** PREEMPT ⟨we can *collar* nearly the whole of this market —Roald Dahl⟩ **d :** to stop and detain in unwilling conversation
**2 :** to put a collar on

**col·lar·bone** \'kä-lər-ˌbōn\ *noun* (15th century)
**:** CLAVICLE

**collar cell** *noun* (circa 1889)
**:** a flagellated endodermal cell that lines the cavity of a sponge and has a contractile protoplasmic cup surrounding the flagellum — called also *choanocyte*

**col·lard** \'kä-lərd\ *noun* [alteration of *colewort*] (1755)

\ə\ abut \ᵊ\ kitten \ər\ further \a\ ash \ā\ ace
\ä\ mop, mar \aů\ out \ch\ chin \e\ bet \ē\ easy
\g\ go \i\ hit \ī\ ice \j\ job \ŋ\ sing \ō\ go
\o\ law \oi\ boy \th\ thin \th\ the \ü\ loot \ů\ foot
\y\ yet \zh\ vision *see also* Guide to Pronunciation

: a stalked smooth-leaved kale — usually used in plural

**col·late** \kə-'lāt, kä-, kō-; 'kä-,, 'kō-,\ *transitive verb* **col·lat·ed; col·lat·ing** [back-formation from *collation*] (1612)
**1 a :** to compare critically **b :** to collect, compare carefully in order to verify, and often to integrate or arrange in order
**2** [Latin *collatus*, past participle] : to institute (a cleric) to a benefice
**3 a :** to verify the order of (printed sheets) **b :** to assemble in proper order; *especially* **:** to assemble (as printed sheets) in order for binding
**synonym** see COMPARE
— **col·la·tor** \-'lā-tər, -,lā-\ *noun*

**¹col·lat·er·al** \kə-'la-t(ə-)rəl\ *adjective* [Middle English, probably from Middle French, from Medieval Latin *collateralis,* from Latin *com-* + *lateralis* lateral] (14th century)
**1 a :** accompanying as secondary or subordinate **:** CONCOMITANT ⟨digress into *collateral* matters⟩ **b :** INDIRECT **c :** serving to support or reinforce **:** ANCILLARY
**2 :** belonging to the same ancestral stock but not in a direct line of descent — compare LINEAL 3a
**3 :** parallel, coordinate, or corresponding in position, order, time, or significance ⟨*collateral* states like Athens and Sparta⟩
**4 a :** of, relating to, or being collateral used as security (as for payment of a debt or performance of a contract) **b :** secured by collateral
— **col·lat·er·al·i·ty** \-,la-tə-'ra-lə-tē\ *noun*
— **col·lat·er·al·ly** \-'la-t(ə-)rə-lē\ *adverb*

**²collateral** *noun* (1691)
**1 :** a collateral relative
**2 :** property (as securities) pledged by a borrower to protect the interests of the lender
**3 :** a branch of a bodily part (as a vein)

**col·lat·er·al·ize** \kə-'la-t(ə-)rə-,līz\ *transitive verb* **-ized; -iz·ing** (1941)
**1 :** to make (a loan) secure with collateral
**2 :** to use (as securities) for collateral

**col·la·tion** \kə-'lā-shən, kä-, kō-\ *noun* (14th century)
**1** [Middle English, from Medieval Latin *collation-, collatio,* from Late Latin, conference, from Latin, bringing together, comparison, from *conferre* (past participle *collatus*) to bring together — more at CONFER, TOLERATE]
**a :** a light meal allowed on fast days in place of lunch or supper **b :** a light meal
**2** [Middle English, from Latin *collation-, collatio*] : the act, process, or result of collating

**col·league** \'kä-(,)lēg\ *noun* [Middle French *collegue,* from Latin *collega,* from *com-* + *legare* to depute — more at LEGATE] (circa 1533)
**:** an associate in a profession or in a civil or ecclesiastical office
— **col·league·ship** \-,ship\ *noun*

**¹col·lect** \'kä-likt *also* -,lekt\ *noun* [Middle English *collecte,* from Old French, from Medieval Latin *collecta* (short for *oratio ad collectam* prayer upon assembly), from Late Latin, assembly, from Latin, assemblage, from feminine of *collectus*] (13th century)
**1 :** a short prayer comprising an invocation, petition, and conclusion; *specifically, often capitalized* **:** one preceding the eucharistic Epistle and varying with the day
**2 :** COLLECTION

**²col·lect** \kə-'lekt\ *verb* [Latin *collectus,* past participle of *colligere* to collect, from *com-* + *legere* to gather — more at LEGEND] (1563)
*transitive verb*
**1 a :** to bring together into one body or place **b :** to gather or exact from a number of persons or sources ⟨*collect* taxes⟩
**2 :** INFER, DEDUCE
**3 :** to gain or regain control of ⟨*collect* his thoughts⟩
**4 :** to claim as due and receive payment for
**5 :** to get and bring with one; *specifically*

**:** PICK UP ⟨went to *collect* her at the train station⟩
*intransitive verb*
**1 :** to come together in a band, group, or mass **:** GATHER
**2 a :** to collect objects **b :** to receive payment ⟨*collecting* on the insurance⟩
**synonym** see GATHER

**³col·lect** \kə-'lekt\ *adverb or adjective* (1893)
**:** to be paid for by the receiver

**col·lec·ta·nea** \,kä-,lek-'tā-nē-ə\ *noun plural* [Latin, neuter plural of *collectaneus* collected, from *collectus,* past participle] (1791)
**:** collected writings; *also* **:** literary items forming a collection

**col·lect·ed** \kə-'lek-təd\ *adjective* (1610)
**1 :** possessed of calmness and composure often through concentrated effort
**2 :** gathered together ⟨the *collected* works of Scott⟩
**3** *of a horse's gait* **:** performed slowly and restrainedly with the animal's center of gravity toward the hindquarters — compare EXTENDED
**synonym** see COOL
— **col·lect·ed·ly** *adverb*
— **col·lect·ed·ness** *noun*

**¹col·lect·ible** *or* **col·lect·able** \kə-'lek-tə-bəl\ *adjective* (1660)
**1 :** suitable for being collected
**2 :** due for present payment **:** PAYABLE

**²collectible** *or* **collectable** *noun* (1953)
**:** an object that is collected by fanciers; *especially* **:** one other than such traditionally collectible items as art, stamps, coins, and antiques

**col·lec·tion** \kə-'lek-shən\ *noun* (14th century)
**1 :** the act or process of collecting
**2 a :** something collected; *especially* **:** an accumulation of objects gathered for study, comparison, or exhibition or as a hobby **b :** GROUP, AGGREGATE **c :** a set of apparel designed for sale usually in a particular season

**¹col·lec·tive** \kə-'lek-tiv\ *adjective* (15th century)
**1 :** denoting a number of persons or things considered as one group or whole ⟨*flock* is a *collective* word⟩
**2 a :** formed by collecting **:** AGGREGATED **b** *of a fruit* **:** MULTIPLE
**3 a :** of, relating to, or being a group of individuals **b :** involving all members of a group as distinct from its individuals
**4 :** marked by similarity among or with the members of a group
**5 :** collectivized or characterized by collectivism
**6 :** shared or assumed by all members of the group ⟨*collective* responsibility⟩
— **col·lec·tive·ly** *adverb*

**²collective** *noun* (1655)
**1 :** a collective body **:** GROUP
**2 :** a cooperative unit or organization; *specifically* **:** COLLECTIVE FARM

**collective bargaining** *noun* (1891)
**:** negotiation between an employer and a labor union usually on wages, hours, and working conditions

**collective farm** *noun* (1925)
**:** a farm especially in a communist country formed from many small holdings collected into a single unit for joint operation under governmental supervision

**collective mark** *noun* (1938)
**:** a trademark or a service mark of a group (as a cooperative association)

**collective security** *noun* (1934)
**:** the maintenance by common action of the security of all members of an association of nations

**collective unconscious** *noun* (1917)
**:** the genetically determined part of the unconscious that especially in the psychoanalytic theory of C. G. Jung occurs in all the members of a people or race

**col·lec·tiv·ise** *chiefly British variant of* COLLECTIVIZE

**col·lec·tiv·ism** \kə-'lek-ti-,vi-zəm\ *noun* (1857)
**:** a political or economic theory advocating collective control especially over production and distribution; *also* **:** a system marked by such control
— **col·lec·tiv·ist** \-vist\ *adjective or noun*
— **col·lec·tiv·is·tic** \-,lek-ti-'vis-tik\ *adjective*
— **col·lec·tiv·is·ti·cal·ly** \-ti-k(ə-)lē\ *adverb*

**col·lec·tiv·i·ty** \kə-,lek-'ti-və-tē, ,kä-\ *noun, plural* **-ties** (1862)
**1 :** the quality or state of being collective
**2 :** a collective whole; *especially* **:** the people as a body

**col·lec·tiv·ize** \kə-'lek-ti-,vīz\ *transitive verb* **-ized; -iz·ing** (1893)
**:** to organize by collectivism
— **col·lec·tiv·i·za·tion** \kə-,lek-ti-və-'zā-shən\ *noun*

**col·lec·tor** \kə-'lek-tər\ *noun* (14th century)
**:** one that collects: as **a :** an official who collects funds or moneys **b :** a person who makes a collection ⟨stamp *collector*⟩ **c :** an object or device that collects ⟨the statuette was a dust *collector*⟩ **d :** SOLAR COLLECTOR
— **col·lec·tor·ship** \-,ship\ *noun*

**collector's item** *noun* (1932)
**:** an item whose rarity or excellence makes it especially worth collecting; *broadly* **:** COLLECTIBLE

**col·leen** \kä-'lēn, 'kä-,\ *noun* [Irish *cailín*] (1828)
**:** an Irish girl

**col·lege** \'kä-lij\ *noun, often attributive* [Middle English, from Middle French, from Latin *collegium* society, from *collega* colleague — more at COLLEAGUE] (14th century)
**1 :** a body of clergy living together and supported by a foundation
**2 :** a building used for an educational or religious purpose
**3 a :** a self-governing constituent body of a university offering living quarters and instruction but not granting degrees ⟨Balliol and Magdalen *Colleges* at Oxford⟩ **b :** a preparatory or high school **c :** an independent institution of higher learning offering a course of general studies leading to a bachelor's degree **d :** a part of a university offering a specialized group of courses **e :** an institution offering instruction usually in a professional, vocational, or technical field ⟨business *college*⟩
**4 :** COMPANY, GROUP; *specifically* **:** an organized body of persons engaged in a common pursuit or having common interests or duties
**5 a :** a group of persons considered by law to be a unit **b :** a body of electors — compare ELECTORAL COLLEGE
**6 :** the faculty, students, or administration of a college

**College Board** *service mark*
— used for administration of tests of aptitude and achievement considered by some colleges in determining admission and placement of students

**college try** *noun* [from the phrase "give it the old *college try*"] (1947)
**:** a zealous all-out effort

**col·le·gial** \kə-'lē-j(ē-)əl, *especially for 2a also* -'lē-gē-əl\ *adjective* (14th century)
**1 :** COLLEGIATE 2
**2 a :** marked by power or authority vested equally in each of a number of colleagues **b :** characterized by equal sharing of authority especially by Roman Catholic bishops
**3 :** marked by camaraderie among colleagues
— **col·le·gial·ly** *adverb*

**col·le·gi·al·i·ty** \-,lē-jē-'a-lə-tē, -,lē-gē-\ *noun* (1887)
**:** the relationship of colleagues; *specifically* **:** the participation of bishops in the govern-

ment of the Roman Catholic Church in collaboration with the pope

**col·le·gian** \kə-'lē-j(ē-)ən\ *noun* (15th century)
: a student or recent graduate of a college

**col·le·giate** \kə-'lē-jət, -jē-ət\ *adjective* [Medieval Latin *collegiatus*, from Latin *collegium*] (15th century)
**1** : of or relating to a collegiate church
**2** : of, relating to, or comprising a college
**3** : COLLEGIAL 2
**4** : designed for or characteristic of college students
— **col·le·giate·ly** *adverb*

**collegiate church** *noun* (15th century)
**1** : a church other than a cathedral that has a chapter of canons
**2** : a church or corporate group of churches under the joint pastorate of two or more ministers

**col·le·gi·um** \kə-'le-gē-əm, -'lā-\ *noun, plural* **-gia** \-gē-ə\ *or* **-giums** [modification of Russian *kollegiya*, from Latin *collegium*] (1917)
: a group in which each member has approximately equal power and authority

**col·lem·bo·lan** \kə-'lem-bə-lən\ *noun* [ultimately from *coll-* + Greek *embolos* wedge, stopper — more at EMBOLUS] (1873)
: SPRINGTAIL
— **collembolan** *or* **col·lem·bo·lous** \-ləs\ *adjective*

**col·len·chy·ma** \kə-'leŋ-kə-mə, kä-\ *noun* [New Latin] (1857)
: a plant tissue that consists of living usually elongated cells with unevenly thickened walls and acts as support especially in areas of primary growth — compare SCLERENCHYMA
— **col·len·chy·ma·tous** \,kä-lən-'ki-mə-təs, -'kī-\ *adjective*

**col·let** \'kä-lət\ *noun* [Middle French, diminutive of *col* collar, from Latin *collum* neck — more at COLLAR] (1528)
: a metal band, collar, ferrule, or flange: as **a** : a casing or socket for holding a tool (as a drill bit) **b** : a circle or flange in which a gem is set

**col·le·te·ri·al gland** \,kä-lə-'tir-ē-əl, -'ter-\ *noun* [New Latin *colleterium* colleterial gland, irregular from Greek *kollan* to glue — more at PROTOCOL] (1870)
: a gland in female insects that secretes a cement by which the eggs are glued together or attached to an external object

**col·lide** \kə-'līd\ *intransitive verb* **col·lid·ed; col·lid·ing** [Latin *collidere*, from *com-* + *laedere* to injure by striking] (1700)
**1** : to come together with solid or direct impact
**2** : CLASH

**col·lid·er** \kə-'lī-dər\ *noun* (1980)
: a particle accelerator in which two beams of particles moving in opposite directions are made to collide

**col·lie** \'kä-lē\ *noun* [probably from English dialect *colly* black] (circa 1651)
: any of a breed of large dogs developed in Scotland that occur in rough-coated and smooth-coated varieties

**col·lier** \'käl-yər\ *noun* [Middle English *colier*, from *col* coal] (13th century)
**1** : one that produces charcoal

collie

**2** : a coal miner
**3** : a ship for transporting coal

**col·liery** \'käl-yə-rē\ *noun, plural* **-lier·ies** (1635)
: a coal mine and its connected buildings

**col·lie-shang·ie** \'kä-lē-,shaŋ-ē, 'kə-\ *noun* [perhaps from *collie* + *shang* kind of meal] (1737)
*Scottish* : SQUABBLE, BRAWL

**col·li·gate** \'kä-lə-gāt\ *verb* **-gat·ed; -gat·ing** [Latin *colligatus*, past participle of *colligare*, from *com-* + *ligare* to tie — more at LIGATURE] (1545)
*transitive verb*
**1** : to bind, unite, or group together
**2** : to subsume (isolated facts) under a general concept
*intransitive verb*
: to be or become a member of a group or unit
— **col·li·ga·tion** \,kä-lə-'gā-shən\ *noun*

**col·li·ga·tive** \'kä-lə-,gā-tiv, kə-'li-gə-\ *adjective* (1901)
: depending on the number of particles (as molecules) and not on the nature of the particles (pressure is a *colligative* property)

**col·li·mate** \'kä-lə-,māt\ *transitive verb* **-mat·ed; -mat·ing** [Latin *collimatus*, past participle of *collimare*, manuscript variant of *collineare* to make straight, from *com-* + *linea* line] (1878)
: to make (as light rays) parallel
— **col·li·ma·tion** \,kä-lə-'mā-shən\ *noun*

**col·li·ma·tor** \'kä-lə-,mā-tər\ *noun* (1865)
**1** : a device for producing a beam of parallel rays (as of light) or for forming an infinitely distant virtual image that can be viewed without parallax
**2** : a device for obtaining a beam (as of particles) of limited cross section

**col·lin·ear** \kə-'li-nē-ər, kä-\ *adjective* [International Scientific Vocabulary] (1863)
**1** : lying on or passing through the same straight line
**2** : having axes lying end to end in a straight line (*collinear* antenna elements)
— **col·lin·ear·i·ty** \-,li-nē-'ar-ə-tē\ *noun*

**col·lins** \'kä-lənz\ *noun* [probably from the name *Collins*] (circa 1887)
: a tall iced drink of soda water, sugar, lemon or lime juice, and liquor (as gin)

**col·li·sion** \kə-'li-zhən\ *noun* [Middle English, from Latin *collision-, collisio*, from *collidere*] (15th century)
**1** : an act or instance of colliding : CLASH
**2** : an encounter between particles (as atoms or molecules) resulting in exchange or transformation of energy
— **col·li·sion·al** \-'lizh-nəl, -'li-zhə-nəl\ *adjective*
— **col·li·sion·al·ly** *adverb*

**collision course** *noun* (1944)
: a course (as of moving bodies or antithetical philosophies) that will result in collision or conflict if continued unaltered

**collo-** — see COLL-

**col·lo·cate** \'kä-lə-,kāt\ *verb* **-cat·ed; -cat·ing** [Latin *collocatus*, past participle of *collocare*, from *com-* + *locare* to place, from *locus* place — more at STALL] (1513)
*transitive verb*
: to set or arrange in a place or position; *especially* : to set side by side
*intransitive verb*
: to occur in conjunction with something

**col·lo·ca·tion** \,kä-lə-'kā-shən\ *noun* (1605)
: the act or result of placing or arranging together; *specifically* : a noticeable arrangement or conjoining of linguistic elements (as words)
— **col·lo·ca·tion·al** \-shnəl, -shə-nᵊl\ *adjective*

**col·lo·di·on** \kə-'lō-dē-ən\ *noun* [modification of New Latin *collodium*, from Greek *kollōdēs* glutinous, from *kolla* glue — more at PROTOCOL] (1851)

: a viscous solution of pyroxylin used especially as a coating for wounds or for photographic films

**col·logue** \kə-'lōg\ *intransitive verb* **col·logued; col·logu·ing** [origin unknown] (1646)
**1** *dialect* : INTRIGUE, CONSPIRE
**2** : to talk privately : CONFER

**col·loid** \'kä-,lóid\ *noun* [International Scientific Vocabulary *coll-* + *-oid*] (circa 1852)
**1** : a gelatinous or mucinous substance found in tissues in disease (as in the thyroid) or normally
**2 a** : a substance that consists of particles dispersed throughout another substance which are too small for resolution with an ordinary light microscope but are incapable of passing through a semipermeable membrane **b** : a mixture consisting of a colloid together with the medium in which it is dispersed (smoke is a *colloid*)
— **col·loi·dal** \kə-'lói-dᵊl, kä-\ *adjective*
— **col·loi·dal·ly** *adverb*

**col·lop** \'kä-ləp\ *noun* [Middle English] (14th century)
**1** : a small piece or slice especially of meat
**2** : a fold of fat flesh

**col·lo·qui·al** \kə-'lō-kwē-əl\ *adjective* (1751)
**1** : of or relating to conversation : CONVERSATIONAL
**2 a** : used in or characteristic of familiar and informal conversation; *also* : unacceptably informal **b** : using conversational style
— **colloquial** *noun*
— **col·lo·qui·al·i·ty** \-,lō-kwē-'a-lə-tē\ *noun*
— **col·lo·qui·al·ly** \-'lō-kwē-ə-lē\ *adverb*

**col·lo·qui·al·ism** \-'lō-kwē-ə-,li-zəm\ *noun* (1810)
**1 a** : a colloquial expression **b** : a local or regional dialect expression
**2** : colloquial style

**col·lo·quist** \'kä-lə-kwist\ *noun* (1792)
: SPEAKER

**col·lo·qui·um** \kə-'lō-kwē-əm\ *noun, plural* **-qui·ums** *or* **-quia** \-kwē-ə\ [Latin, colloquy] (1844)
: a usually academic meeting at which specialists deliver addresses on a topic or on related topics and then answer questions relating to them

**col·lo·quy** \'kä-lə-kwē\ *noun, plural* **-quies** [Latin *colloquium*, from *colloqui* to converse, from *com-* + *loqui* to speak] (15th century)
**1** : CONVERSATION, DIALOGUE
**2** : a high-level serious discussion : CONFERENCE

**col·lo·type** \'kä-lə-,tīp\ *noun* [International Scientific Vocabulary] (1883)
**1** : a photomechanical process for making prints directly from a hardened film of gelatin or other colloid that has ink-receptive and ink-repellent parts
**2** : a print made by collotype

**col·lude** \kə-'lüd\ *intransitive verb* **col·lud·ed; col·lud·ing** [Latin *colludere*, from *com-* + *ludere* to play, from *ludus* game — more at LUDICROUS] (1535)
: CONSPIRE, PLOT

**col·lu·sion** \kə-'lü-zhən\ *noun* [Middle English, from Middle French, from Latin *collusion-, collusio*, from *colludere*] (14th century)
: secret agreement or cooperation especially for an illegal or deceitful purpose
— **col·lu·sive** \-'lü-siv, -ziv\ *adjective*
— **col·lu·sive·ly** *adverb*

**col·lu·vi·um** \kə-'lü-vē-əm\ *noun, plural* **-via** \-vē-ə\ *or* **-vi·ums** [New Latin, from Medieval Latin, offscourings, alteration of Latin

*colluvies,* from *colluere* to wash, from *com-* + *lavere* to wash — more at LYE] (circa 1936)
**:** rock detritus and soil accumulated at the foot of a slope
— **col·lu·vi·al** \-vē-əl\ *adjective*

**col·ly** \'kä-lē\ *transitive verb* **col·lied; col·ly·ing** [alteration of Middle English *colwen,* from (assumed) Old English *colgian,* from Old English *col* coal] (1590)
*dialect chiefly British* **:** to blacken with or as if with soot

**col·lyr·i·um** \kə-'lir-ē-əm\ *noun, plural* **-ia** \-ē-ə\ *or* **-i·ums** [Middle English *collirium,* from Latin *collyrium,* from Greek *kollyrion* pessary, eye salve, from diminutive of *kollyra* roll of bread] (14th century)
**:** EYEWASH 1

**col·ly·wob·bles** \'kä-lē-,wä-bəlz\ *noun plural but singular or plural in construction* [perhaps by folk etymology from New Latin *cholera morbus,* literally, the disease cholera] (circa 1823)
**:** BELLYACHE

**colo-** — see COL-

**col·o·bus monkey** \'kä-lə-bəs-\ *noun* [New Latin *colobus,* from Greek *kolobos* docked, mutilated, from *kolos* docked; probably akin to Greek *klan* to break — more at CLAST] (1889)
**:** any of various long-tailed African monkeys (genus *Colobus* and related genera) — called also **colobus**

**co·lo·cate** \(,)kō-'lō-,kāt, -lō-'kāt\ *transitive verb* (1965)
**:** to locate together; *especially* **:** to place two or more units close together so as to share common facilities

**col·o·cynth** \'kä-lə-,sin(t)th\ *noun* [Latin *colocynthis,* from Greek *kolokynthis*] (1543)
**:** a Mediterranean and African herbaceous vine (*Citrullus colocynthis*) related to the watermelon; *also* **:** its spongy fruit from which a powerful cathartic is prepared

**co·log·a·rithm** \(,)kō-'lô-gə-,ri-thəm, -'lä-\ *noun* (1881)
**:** the logarithm of the reciprocal of a number

**co·logne** \kə-'lōn\ *noun* [*Cologne,* Germany] (1814)
**1 :** a perfumed liquid composed of alcohol and fragrant oils
**2 :** a cream or paste of cologne sometimes formed into a semisolid stick
— **co·logned** \-'lōnd\ *adjective*

**¹co·lon** \'kō-lən\ *noun, plural* **colons** *or* **co·la** \-lə\ [Middle English, from Latin, from Greek *kolon*] (14th century)
**:** the part of the large intestine that extends from the cecum to the rectum
— **co·lon·ic** \kō-'lä-nik, kə-\ *adjective*

**²colon** *noun, plural* **colons** *or* **co·la** \-lə\ [Latin, part of a poem, from Greek *kōlon* limb, part of a strophe] (circa 1550)
**1** *plural* **cola :** a rhythmical unit of an utterance; *specifically, in Greek or Latin verse* **:** a system or series of from two to not more than six feet having a principal accent and forming part of a line
**2** *plural* **colons a :** a punctuation mark **:** used chiefly to direct attention to matter (as a list, explanation, or quotation) that follows **b :** the sign **:** used between the parts of a numerical expression of time in hours and minutes (as in 1:15) or in hours, minutes, and seconds (as in 8:25:30), in a bibliographical reference (as in *Nation* 130:20), in a ratio where it is usually read as "to" (as in 4:1 read "four to one"), or in a proportion where it is usually read as "is to" or when doubled as "as" (as in 2:1::8:4 read "two is to one as eight is to four")

**³co·lon** \kō-'lōn, kə-'lōn\ *noun* [French, from Latin *colonus*] (1888)
**:** a colonial farmer or plantation owner

**co·lón** *also* **co·lone** \kə-'lōn\ *noun, plural* **co·lo·nes** \-'lō-,nās\ [Spanish *colón,* from

Cristóbal *Colón* Christopher Columbus] (1916)
— see MONEY table

**colon bacillus** *noun* (circa 1909)
**:** any of various bacilli (especially genera *Escherichia* and *Aerobacter*) that are normally commensal in vertebrate intestines; *especially* **:** one (*E. coli*) used extensively in genetic research

**col·o·nel** \'kər-n°l\ *noun* [alteration of *coronel,* from Middle French, modification of Old Italian *colonnello* column of soldiers, colonel, diminutive of *colonna* column, from Latin *columna*] (1548)
**1 a :** a commissioned officer in the army, air force, or marine corps ranking above a lieutenant colonel and below a brigadier general **b :** LIEUTENANT COLONEL
**2 :** a minor titular official of a state especially in southern or midland U.S. — used as an honorific title ◆
— **col·o·nel·cy** \-n°l-sē\ *noun*

**Colonel Blimp** \-'blimp\ *noun* [*Colonel Blimp,* cartoon character created by David Low] (1937)
**:** a pompous person with out-of-date or ultraconservative views; *broadly* **:** REACTIONARY
— **Colonel Blimp·ism** \-'blim-,pi-zəm\ *noun*

**¹co·lo·nial** \kə-'lō-nē-əl, -nyəl\ *adjective* (1776)
**1 :** of, relating to, or characteristic of a colony
**2** *often capitalized* **:** of or relating to the original 13 colonies forming the United States: as **a :** made or prevailing in America during the colonial period ⟨*colonial* architecture⟩ **b :** adapted from or reminiscent of an American colonial mode of design ⟨*colonial* furniture⟩
**3 :** forming or existing in a colony ⟨*colonial* organisms⟩
**4 :** possessing or composed of colonies ⟨a *colonial* empire⟩
— **co·lo·nial·ize** \-nē-ə-,līz, -nyə-,līz\ *transitive verb*
— **co·lo·nial·ly** *adverb*
— **co·lo·nial·ness** *noun*

**²colonial** *noun* (1798)
**1 :** a member or inhabitant of a colony
**2 a :** a product made for use in a colony **b :** a product (as a house) exhibiting colonial style

**co·lo·nial·ism** \kə-'lō-nē-ə-,li-zəm, -nyə-,li-\ *noun* (1853)
**1 :** the quality or state of being colonial
**2 :** something characteristic of a colony
**3 a :** control by one power over a dependent area or people **b :** a policy advocating or based on such control
— **co·lo·nial·ist** \-list\ *noun or adjective*
— **co·lo·nial·is·tic** \-,lō-nē-ə-'lis-tik, -nyə-'lis-\ *adjective*

**¹co·lon·ic** \kō-'lä-nik, kə-\ *adjective* (circa 1885)
**:** of or relating to the colon of the intestine

**²colonic** *noun* (1939)
**:** irrigation of the colon **:** ENEMA

**col·o·ni·sa·tion, col·o·nise** *British variant of* COLONIZATION, COLONIZE

**col·o·nist** \'kä-lə-nist\ *noun* (1701)
**1 :** a member or inhabitant of a colony
**2 :** one that colonizes or settles in a new country

**col·o·ni·za·tion** \,kä-lə-nə-'zā-shən\ *noun* (1770)
**:** an act or instance of colonizing
— **col·o·ni·za·tion·ist** \-sh(ə-)nist\ *noun*

**col·o·nize** \'kä-lə-,nīz\ *verb* **-nized; -niz·ing** (1622)
*transitive verb*
**1 a :** to establish a colony in or on or of **b :** to establish a colony
**2 :** to send illegal or irregularly qualified voters into ⟨*colonizing* doubtful districts⟩
**3 :** to infiltrate with usually subversive militants for propaganda and strategy reasons ⟨*colonize* industries⟩

*intransitive verb*
**:** to make or establish a colony **:** SETTLE
— **col·o·niz·er** *noun*

**col·on·nade** \,kä-lə-'nād\ *noun* [French, from Italian *colonnato,* from *colonna* column] (1718)
**:** a series of columns set at regular intervals and usually supporting the base of a roof structure
— **col·on·nad·ed** \-'nā-dəd\ *adjective*

**co·lo·nus** \kə-'lō-nəs\ *noun, plural* **-ni** \-,nī, -(,)nē\ [Latin, literally, farmer] (1888)
**:** a free-born serf in the later Roman Empire who could sometimes own property but who was bound to the land and obliged to pay a rent usually in produce

**col·o·ny** \'kä-lə-nē\ *noun, plural* **-nies** [Middle English *colonie,* from Middle French & Latin; Middle French, from Latin *colonia,* from *colonus* farmer, colonist, from *colere* to cultivate — more at WHEEL] (14th century)
**1 a :** a body of people living in a new territory but retaining ties with the parent state **b :** the territory inhabited by such a body
**2 :** a distinguishable localized population within a species ⟨*colony* of termites⟩
**3 a :** a circumscribed mass of microorganisms usually growing in or on a solid medium **b :** the aggregation of zooids of a compound animal
**4 a :** a group of individuals or things with common characteristics or interests situated in close association ⟨an artist *colony*⟩ **b :** the section occupied by such a group
**5 :** a group of persons institutionalized away from others ⟨a leper *colony*⟩ ⟨a penal *colony*⟩; *also* **:** the land or buildings occupied by such a group

**colony–stimulating factor** *noun* (1969)
**:** any of several glycoproteins that promote the differentiation of stem cells especially into blood granulocytes and macrophages and that stimulate their proliferation into colonies in culture

**col·o·phon** \'kä-lə-fən, -,fän\ *noun* [Latin, from Greek *kolophōn* summit, finishing touch; perhaps akin to Latin *culmen* top — more at HILL] (1774)
**1 :** an inscription placed at the end of a book or manuscript usually with facts relative to its production
**2 :** an identifying device used by a printer or a publisher

**co·lo·pho·ny** \kə-'lä-fə-nē, 'kä-lə-,fō-\ *noun, plural* **-nies** [Middle English *colophonie,* ultimately from Greek *Kolophōn* Colophon, an Ionian city] (14th century)
**:** ROSIN

**¹col·or** \'kə-lər\ *noun, often attributive* [Middle English *colour,* from Old French, from Latin

◇ WORD HISTORY
**colonel** The pronunciation of *colonel* as if it were spelled *kernel* is one of the more striking oddities of the English vocabulary. The source of this discrepancy was not sheer contrariness, for at one time a spelling *coronel* existed to match the pronunciation with \r\ and a pronunciation \'kəl-n°l\ existed to match the spelling *colonel.* For a time both forms competed, with *colonel* holding the ground long enough for this spelling to become standard. Later the pronunciation with \r\ made a resurgence and finally won the day, but a corresponding spelling change to *r* never took place. Both *coronel* and *colonel* were borrowed from 16th century French; the French form *coronel* resulted from a phonetic change called dissimilation, by which one of two identical or similar sounds in the same word changes to a contrasting sound. In this case the first \l\ became \r\.

color; akin to Latin *celare* to conceal — more at HELL] (13th century)
**1 a :** a phenomenon of light (as red, brown, pink, or gray) or visual perception that enables one to differentiate otherwise identical objects **b :** the aspect of objects and light sources that may be described in terms of hue, lightness, and saturation for objects and hue, brightness, and saturation for light sources **c :** a hue as contrasted with black, white, or gray
**2 a :** an outward often deceptive show : AP-PEARANCE ⟨his story has the *color* of truth⟩ **b :** a legal claim to or appearance of a right, authority, or office **c :** a pretense offered as justification : PRETEXT ⟨she could have drawn from the Versailles treaty the *color* of legality for any action she chose —*Yale Review*⟩ **d :** an appearance of authenticity : PLAUSIBILITY ⟨lending *color* to this notion⟩
**3 :** complexion tint: **a :** the tint characteristic of good health **b :** BLUSH
**4 a :** vividness or variety of effects of language **b :** LOCAL COLOR
**5 a :** an identifying badge, pennant, or flag — usually used in plural ⟨a ship sailing under Swedish *colors*⟩ **b :** colored clothing distinguishing one as a member of a particular group or representative of a particular person or thing — usually used in plural ⟨a jockey wearing the *colors* of the stable⟩
**6 a** *plural* **:** position as to a question or course of action : STAND ⟨the USSR changed neither its *colors* nor its stripes during all of this —Norman Mailer⟩ **b :** CHARACTER, NATURE — usually used in plural ⟨showed himself in his true *colors*⟩
**7 a :** the use or combination of colors **b :** two or more hues employed in a medium of presentation ⟨movies in *color*⟩ ⟨*color* television⟩
**8** *plural* **a :** a naval or nautical salute to a flag being hoisted or lowered **b :** ARMED FORCES
**9 :** VITALITY, INTEREST ⟨the play had a good deal of *color* to it⟩
**10 :** something used to give color : PIGMENT
**11 :** tonal quality in music ⟨the *color* and richness of the cello⟩
**12 :** skin pigmentation especially other than white characteristic of race ⟨a person of *color*⟩
**13 :** a small particle of gold in a gold miner's pan after washing
**14 :** analysis of game action or strategy, statistics and background information on participants, and other anecdotes provided by a sportscaster to give variety and interest to the broadcast of a game or contest
**15 :** a hypothetical property of quarks that differentiates each type into three forms having a distinct role in binding quarks together
— **col·or·ism** \-lə-ˌri-zəm\ *noun*
²**color** (14th century)
*transitive verb*
**1 a :** to give color to **b :** to change the color of (as by dyeing, staining, or painting)
**2 :** to change as if by dyeing or painting: as **a :** MISREPRESENT, DISTORT **b :** GLOSS, EXCUSE ⟨*color* a lie⟩ **c :** INFLUENCE ⟨the lives of most of us have been *colored* by politics —Christine Weston⟩
**3 :** CHARACTERIZE, LABEL ⟨call it progress; *color* it inevitable with shades of job security —C. E. Price⟩
*intransitive verb*
**:** to take on color; *specifically* **:** BLUSH
— **col·or·er** \'kə-lər-ər\ *noun*
**col·or·able** \'kə-lə-rə-bəl, 'kəl-rə-\ *adjective* (14th century)
**1 :** seemingly valid or genuine
**2 :** intended to deceive : COUNTERFEIT
— **col·or·ably** \-blē\ *adverb*
**Col·o·ra·do blue spruce** \ˌkä-lə-'ra-dō-, -'rä-\ *noun* [*Colorado*, state of the U.S.] (1897)
**:** BLUE SPRUCE

**Colorado potato beetle** *noun* (1868)
**:** a black-and-yellow striped beetle (*Leptinotarsa decemlineata*) that feeds on the leaves of the potato — called also *potato beetle, potato bug*

Colorado potato beetle

**col·or·ant** \'kə-lə-rənt\ *noun* (1884)
**:** a substance used for coloring a material : DYE, PIGMENT
**col·or·a·tion** \ˌkə-lə-'rā-shən\ *noun* (1617)
**1 a :** the state of being colored ⟨the dark *coloration* of his skin⟩ **b :** use or choice of colors (as by an artist) **c :** arrangement of colors ⟨the *coloration* of a butterfly's wing⟩
**2 a :** characteristic quality ⟨the newspapers . . . took on the former *coloration* of the magazine —L. B. Seltzer⟩ **b :** aspect suggesting an attitude : PERSUASION ⟨the chameleon talent for taking on the intellectual *coloration* of whatever idea he happened to fasten onto —Budd Schulberg⟩
**3 :** subtle variation of intensity or quality of tone ⟨a wide range of *coloration* from the orchestra⟩
**col·or·a·tu·ra** \ˌkə-lə-rə-'tur-ə, -'tyur-\ *noun* [obsolete Italian, literally, coloring, from Late Latin, from Latin *coloratus*, past participle of *colorare* to color, from *color*] (circa 1740)
**1 :** elaborate embellishment in vocal music; *broadly* **:** music with ornate figuration
**2 :** a soprano with a light agile voice specializing in coloratura
**color bar** *noun* (1913)
**:** a barrier preventing colored persons from participating with whites in various activities — called also *color line*
**col·or–bear·er** \'kə-lər-ˌbar-ər, -ˌber-\ *noun* (circa 1891)
**:** one that carries a color or standard especially in a military parade or drill
**col·or–blind** \-ˌblīnd\ *adjective* (1854)
**1 :** affected with partial or total inability to distinguish one or more chromatic colors
**2 :** INSENSITIVE, OBLIVIOUS
**3 :** not recognizing differences of race ⟨tried to get the welfare establishment . . . to abandon its *color-blind* policy —D. P. Moynihan⟩; *especially* **:** free from racial prejudice ⟨a white man with an invisible black skin in a *color-blind* community —James Farmer⟩
— **color blindness** *noun*
**col·or·bred** \-ˌbred\ *adjective* (1948)
**:** selectively bred for the development of particular colors ⟨pure *colorbred* dogs⟩
**co·lo·rec·tal** \ˌkō-lō-'rek-t°l\ *adjective* (1962)
**:** relating to or affecting the colon and rectum ⟨*colorectal* cancer⟩
¹**col·ored** \'kə-lərd\ *adjective* (14th century)
**1 :** having color
**2 a :** COLORFUL **b :** marked by exaggeration or bias
**3 a :** of a race other than the white; *especially* **:** BLACK 2b — sometimes taken to be offensive **b :** of mixed race — sometimes taken to be offensive
**4 :** of or relating to colored persons — sometimes taken to be offensive
²**colored** *noun, plural* **colored** or **coloreds** *often capitalized* (1916)
**:** a colored person — sometimes taken to be offensive
**col·or·fast** \'kə-lər-ˌfast\ *adjective* (1926)
**:** having color that retains its original hue without fading or running
— **col·or·fast·ness** \-ˌfas(t)-nəs\ *noun*
**col·or–field** \-ˌfē(ə)ld\ *noun, often attributive* (1964)
**:** abstract painting in which color is emphasized and form and surface are correspondingly de-emphasized
**color filter** *noun* (1900)
**:** FILTER 3b
**col·or·ful** \'kə-lər-fəl\ *adjective* (1889)

**1 :** having striking colors
**2 :** full of variety or interest
— **col·or·ful·ly** \-f(ə-)lē\ *adverb*
— **col·or·ful·ness** \-fəl-nəs\ *noun*
**color guard** *noun* (circa 1823)
**:** an honor guard for the colors of an organization
**col·or·if·ic** \ˌkə-lə-'ri-fik\ *adjective* (1676)
**:** capable of communicating color
**col·or·im·e·ter** \ˌkə-lə-'ri-mə-tər\ *noun* [International Scientific Vocabulary] (circa 1872)
**:** an instrument or device for determining and specifying colors; *specifically* **:** one used for chemical analysis by comparison of a liquid's color with standard colors
— **col·or·i·met·ric** \ˌkə-lə-rə-'me-trik\ *adjective*
— **col·or·i·met·ri·cal·ly** \-tri-k(ə-)lē\ *adverb*
— **col·or·im·e·try** \ˌkə-lə-'ri-mə-trē\ *noun*
**col·or·ing** \'kə-lə-riŋ\ *noun* (14th century)
**1 a :** the act of applying colors **b :** something that produces color or color effects **c** (1) **:** the effect produced by applying or combining colors (2) **:** natural color (3) **:** COMPLEXION, COLORATION **d :** change of appearance (as by adding color)
**2 :** INFLUENCE, BIAS
**3 :** COLOR 4
**4 :** TIMBRE, QUALITY
**col·or·ist** \'kə-lə-rist\ *noun* (1686)
**:** one that colors or deals with color
— **col·or·is·tic** \ˌkə-lə-'ris-tik\ *adjective*
— **col·or·is·ti·cal·ly** \-ti-k(ə-)lē\ *adverb*
**col·or·ize** \'kə-lə-ˌrīz\ *transitive verb* **-ized; -iz·ing** (1979)
**:** to add color to (a black-and-white film) by means of a computer
— **col·or·i·za·tion** \ˌkə-lə-rə-'zā-shən\ *noun*
**col·or·less** \'kə-lər-ləs\ *adjective* (14th century)
**:** lacking color: as **a :** PALLID, BLANCHED **b :** DULL, UNINTERESTING
— **col·or·less·ly** *adverb*
— **col·or·less·ness** *noun*
**col·or·man** \-ˌman\ *noun* (1973)
**:** a sportscaster who provides color
**color phase** *noun* (1927)
**1 :** a seasonally variant pelage color
**2 a :** a genetic variant manifested by the occurrence of a skin or pelage color unlike the wild type of the animal group in which it appears **b :** an individual marked by such a variant
**col·or·point shorthair** \'kə-lər-ˌpȯint-\ *noun* (1974)
**:** any of a breed of domestic cats of Siamese type and coat pattern but occurring in different colors — called also *colorpoint*
**color temperature** *noun* (1916)
**:** the temperature at which a blackbody emits radiant energy competent to evoke a color the same as that evoked by radiant energy from a given source (as a lamp)
**color wheel** *noun* (circa 1893)
**:** a circular diagram of the spectrum used to show the relationships between the colors
**co·los·sal** \kə-'lä-səl\ *adjective* (1712)
**1 :** of, relating to, or resembling a colossus
**2 :** of a bulk, extent, power, or effect approaching or suggesting the stupendous or incredible
**3 :** of an exceptional or astonishing degree
**synonym** see ENORMOUS
— **co·los·sal·ly** \-sə-lē\ *adverb*
**col·os·se·um** \ˌkä-lə-'sē-əm\ *noun* [Medieval Latin, from Latin, neuter of *colosseus* colossal, from *colossus*] (circa 1715)

**1** *capitalized* **:** an amphitheater built in Rome in the first century A.D.
**2 :** COLISEUM 2
**Co·los·sians** \kə-'lä-shənz *also* -shē-ənz, -sē-\ *noun plural but singular in construction*
**:** a letter written by Saint Paul to the Christians of Colossae and included as a book in the New Testament — see BIBLE table
**co·los·sus** \kə-'lä-səs\ *noun, plural* **co·los·si** \-'lä-ˌsī\ [Latin, from Greek *kolossos*] (14th century)
**1 :** a statue of gigantic size and proportions
**2 :** one that resembles a colossus in size or scope
**co·los·to·my** \kə-'läs-tə-mē\ *noun, plural* **-mies** [International Scientific Vocabulary *2col-* + *-stomy*] (1888)
**:** surgical formation of an artificial anus
**co·los·trum** \kə-'läs-trəm\ *noun* [Latin, beestings] (1577)
**:** milk secreted for a few days after parturition and characterized by high protein and antibody content
— **co·los·tral** \-trəl\ *adjective*
**col·our** \'kə-lər\ *chiefly British variant of* COLOR
**-colous** *adjective combining form* [Latin *-cola* inhabitant; akin to Latin *colere* to inhabit — more at WHEEL]
**:** living or growing in or on ⟨areni*colous*⟩
**col·por·tage** \'käl-ˌpōr-tij, -ˌpȯr-; ˌkäl-pōr-'täzh, -pȯr-\ *noun* (circa 1846)
**:** a colporteur's work
**col·por·teur** \'käl-ˌpōr-tər, -ˌpȯr-; ˌkäl-pōr-'tər, -ˌpȯr-\ *noun* [French, alteration of Middle French *comporteur*, from *comporter* to bear, peddle] (1796)
**:** a peddler of religious books
**colt** \'kōlt\ *noun* [Middle English, from Old English; akin to Swedish dialect *kult* half-grown pig] (before 12th century)
**1 a :** FOAL **b :** a young male horse that is either sexually immature or has not attained an arbitrarily designated age
**2 :** a young untried person
**colt·ish** \'kōl-tish\ *adjective* (14th century)
**1 a :** not subjected to discipline **b :** FRISKY, PLAYFUL
**2 :** of, relating to, or resembling a colt
— **colt·ish·ly** *adverb*
— **colt·ish·ness** *noun*
**colts·foot** \'kōlts-ˌfut\ *noun, plural* **colts·foots** (14th century)
**:** any of various plants with large rounded leaves resembling the foot of a colt; *especially* **:** a perennial composite herb (*Tussilago farfara*) with yellow flower heads appearing before the leaves
**col·u·brid** \'käl-yə-brəd, 'kä-lə-\ *noun* [ultimately from Latin *colubra* snake] (1887)
**:** any of a large cosmopolitan family (Colubridae) of chiefly nonvenomous snakes
— **colubrid** *adjective*
**col·u·brine** \-ˌbrīn\ *adjective* (circa 1528)
**1 :** of, relating to, or resembling a snake
**2 :** of or relating to colubrids **:** COLUBRID
**co·lu·go** \kə-'lü-(ˌ)gō\ *noun, plural* **-gos** [perhaps from a language of the Philippines] (circa 1890)
**:** FLYING LEMUR
**col·um·bar·i·um** \ˌkä-ləm-'bar-ē-əm, -'ber-\ *noun, plural* **-ia** \-ē-ə\ [Latin, literally, dovecote, from *columba* dove] (1846)
**1 :** a structure of vaults lined with recesses for cinerary urns
**2 :** a recess in a columbarium
**Co·lum·bia** \kə-'ləm-bē-ə\ *noun* [New Latin, from Christopher *Columbus*] (1775)
**:** the United States
**Co·lum·bi·an** \-bē-ən\ *adjective* (1757)
**:** of or relating to the United States or to Christopher Columbus
**col·um·bine** \'kä-ləm-ˌbīn\ *noun* [Middle English, from Medieval Latin *columbina*, from Latin, feminine of *columbinus* like a dove, from *columba* dove; akin to Old High German

*holuntar* elder tree, Greek *kolymbos* a small grebe, *kelainos* black] (14th century)
**:** any of a genus (*Aquilegia*) of plants of the buttercup family with irregular showy spurred flowers: as **a :** a red-flowered plant (*A. canadensis*) of eastern North America **b :** a blue-flowered plant (*A. caerulea*) of the Rocky Mountains
**Col·um·bine** \-ˌbīn, -ˌbēn\ *noun* [Italian *Colombina*]
**:** the saucy sweetheart of Harlequin in comedy and pantomime

**columbine a**

**col·um·bite** \kə-'ləm-ˌbīt, 'kä-ləm-\ *noun* [New Latin *columbium*] (1805)
**:** a black mineral consisting mostly of iron and niobium
**col·um·bi·um** \kə-'ləm-bē-əm\ *noun* [New Latin, from *Columbia*] (1801)
**:** NIOBIUM
**Co·lum·bus Day** \kə-'ləm-bəs-\ *noun* (1893)
**1 :** October 12 formerly observed as a legal holiday in many states of the U.S. in commemoration of the landing of Columbus in the Bahamas in 1492
**2 :** the second Monday in October observed as a legal holiday in many states of the U.S.
**col·u·mel·la** \ˌkäl-yə-'me-lə\ *noun, plural* **-mel·lae** \-'me-(ˌ)lē, -ˌlī\ [New Latin, from Latin, diminutive of *columna*] (circa 1755)
**1 :** the central column or axis of a spiral univalve shell
**2 :** the axis of the capsule in mosses and in some liverworts
**3 a :** the bony or partly cartilaginous rod connecting the tympanic membrane with the internal ear in birds and in many reptiles and amphibians **b :** the bony central axis of the cochlea
**4 :** the central sterile portion of the sporangium in various fungi (*Mucor* and related genera)
— **col·u·mel·lar** \-'me-lər\ *adjective*
**col·umn** \'kä-ləm *also* 'käl-yəm\ *noun* [Middle English *columne*, from Middle French *colomne*, from Latin *columna*, from *columen* top; akin to Latin *collis* hill — more at HILL] (15th century)
**1 a :** a vertical arrangement of items printed or written on a page **b :** one of two or more vertical sections of a printed page separated by a rule or blank space **c :** an accumulation arranged vertically **:** STACK **d :** one in a usually regular series of newspaper or magazine articles ⟨gossip *column*⟩
**2 :** a supporting pillar; *especially* **:** one consisting of a usually round shaft, a capital, and a base
**3 a :** something resembling a column in form, position, or function ⟨a *column* of water⟩ **b :** a tube or cylinder in which a chromatographic separation takes place
**4 :** a long row (as of soldiers)
**5 :** one of the vertical lines of elements of a determinant or matrix
— **col·umned** \-ləmd, -yəmd\ *adjective*
**col·um·nar** \kə-'ləm-nər\ *adjective* (1728)
**1 :** of, relating to, resembling, or characterized by columns
**2 :** of, relating to, being, or composed of tall

narrow somewhat cylindrical or prismatic epithelial cells
**co·lum·ni·a·tion** \kə-ˌləm-nē-'ā-shən\ *noun* [probably from *intercolumniation*] (1664)
**:** the employment or the arrangement of columns in a structure
**col·um·nist** \'kä-ləm-nist, -lə-mist *also* 'käl-yəm-nist, -yə-mist\ *noun* (1920)
**:** one who writes a newspaper or magazine column
— **col·um·nis·tic** \ˌkä-ləm-'nis-tik *also* ˌkäl-yəm-\ *adjective*
**col·za** \'käl-zə, 'kōl-\ *noun* [French, from Dutch *koolzaad*, from Middle Dutch *coolsaet*, from *coole* cabbage + *saet* seed] (1712)
**1 :** any of several coles; *especially* **:** one (as rape) producing seed used as a source of oil
**2 :** RAPESEED
**com-** *or* **col-** *or* **con-** *prefix* [Middle English, from Old French, from Latin, with, together, thoroughly — more at CO-]
**:** with **:** together **:** jointly — usually *com-* before *b*, *p*, or *m* ⟨*com*mingle⟩, *col-* before *l* ⟨*col*linear⟩, and *con-* before other sounds ⟨*con*centrate⟩
**¹co·ma** \'kō-mə\ *noun* [New Latin, from Greek *kōma* deep sleep] (1646)
**1 :** a state of profound unconsciousness caused by disease, injury, or poison
**2 :** a state of mental or physical sluggishness **:** TORPOR
**²coma** *noun, plural* **co·mae** \-ˌmē, -ˌmī\ [Latin, hair, from Greek *komē*] (1669)
**1 :** a tufted bunch (as of branches, bracts, or seed hairs)
**2 :** the head of a comet usually containing a nucleus
**3 :** an optical aberration in which the image of a point source is a comet-shaped blur
— **co·mat·ic** \kō-'ma-tik\ *adjective*
**Co·ma Ber·e·ni·ces** \'kō-mə-ˌber-ə-'nī-(ˌ)sēz\ *noun* [Latin (genitive *Comae Berenices*), literally, Berenice's hair]
**:** a constellation north of Virgo and between Boötes and Leo
**co·mak·er** \(ˌ)kō-'mā-kər\ *noun* (circa 1934)
**:** one that participates in an agreement; *specifically* **:** one who stands to meet a financial obligation in the event of the maker's default
**Co·man·che** \kə-'man-chē\ *noun, plural* **Comanche** *or* **Comanches** [American Spanish, from Southern Paiute *kimmancin^wi* Shoshones, strangers] (1806)
**1 :** a member of an American Indian people ranging from Wyoming and Nebraska south into New Mexico and northwestern Texas
**2 :** the Uto-Aztecan language of the Comanche people
**co·mate** \(ˌ)kō-'māt, 'kō-ˌ\ *noun* (1576)
**:** COMPANION
**co·ma·tose** \'kō-mə-ˌtōs, 'kä-\ *adjective* [French *comateux*, from Greek *kōmat-, kōma*] (1755)
**1 :** of, resembling, or affected with coma
**2 :** characterized by lethargic inertness **:** TORPID ⟨a *comatose* economy⟩
**¹comb** \'kōm\ *noun* [Middle English, from Old English *camb*; akin to Old High German *kamb* comb, Greek *gomphos* tooth] (before 12th century)
**1 a :** a toothed instrument used especially for adjusting, cleaning, or confining hair **b :** a structure resembling such a comb; *especially* **:** any of several toothed devices used in handling or ordering textile fibers **c :** CURRYCOMB
**2 a :** a fleshy crest on the head of the domestic fowl and other gallinaceous birds **b :** something (as the ridge of a roof) resembling the comb of a cock
**3 :** HONEYCOMB
— **combed** \'kōmd\ *adjective*
— **comb·like** \'kōm-ˌlīk\ *adjective*
**²comb** (14th century)
*transitive verb*

---

*Column 2 diagram labels:*
CORNICE
FRIEZE — ENTABLATURE
ARCHITRAVE
CAPITAL
SHAFT — COLUMN
BASE
PEDESTAL

**column 2**

**1 :** to draw a comb through for the purpose of arranging or cleaning **2 :** to pass across with a scraping or raking action **3 a :** to eliminate (as with a comb) by a thorough going-over **b :** to search or examine systematically **4 :** to use in a combing action
*intransitive verb* **1** *of a wave or its crest* **:** to roll over or break into foam **2 :** to make a thorough search ⟨*comb* through the classified ads⟩

¹**com·bat** \'käm-ˌbat\ *noun* (1546) **1 :** a fight or contest between individuals or groups **2 :** CONFLICT, CONTROVERSY **3 :** active fighting in a war **:** ACTION ⟨casualties suffered in *combat*⟩

²**com·bat** \kəm-'bat, 'käm-\ *verb* **-bat·ed** *or* **-bat·ted; -bat·ing** *or* **-bat·ting** [Middle French *combattre,* from (assumed) Vulgar Latin *combattere,* from Latin *com-* + *battuere* to beat] (1564) *intransitive verb* **:** to engage in combat **:** FIGHT *transitive verb* **1 :** to fight with **:** BATTLE **2 :** to struggle against; *especially* **:** to strive to reduce or eliminate ⟨*combat* pollution⟩ **synonym** see OPPOSE

³**com·bat** \'käm-ˌbat\ *adjective* (1825) **1 :** relating to combat ⟨*combat* missions⟩ **2 :** designed or destined for combat ⟨*combat* boots⟩ ⟨*combat* troops⟩

**com·bat·ant** \kəm-'ba-t²nt *also* 'käm-bə-tənt\ *noun* (15th century) **:** one that is engaged in or ready to engage in combat
— **combatant** *adjective*

**combat fatigue** *noun* (1943) **:** a traumatic psychoneurotic reaction or an acute psychotic reaction occurring under conditions (as wartime combat) that cause intense stress — called also *battle fatigue*

**com·bat·ive** \kəm-'ba-tiv\ *adjective* (circa 1834) **:** marked by eagerness to fight or contend
— **com·bat·ive·ly** *adverb*
— **com·bat·ive·ness** *noun*

**combe** \'küm, 'kōm\ *noun* [Middle English *coumbe, cumbe,* from Old English *cumb,* of Celtic origin; akin to Welsh *cwm* valley] (before 12th century) **1** *British* **:** a deep narrow valley **2** *British* **:** a valley or basin on the flank of a hill

**comb·er** \'kō-mər\ *noun* (circa 1682) **1 :** one that combs **2 :** a long curling wave of the sea

**com·bi·na·tion** \ˌkäm-bə-'nā-shən\ *noun, often attributive* (14th century) **1 a :** a result or product of combining; *especially* **:** an alliance of individuals, corporations, or states united to achieve a social, political, or economic end **b :** two or more persons working as a team **2 :** an ordered sequence: as **a :** a sequence of letters or numbers chosen in setting a lock; *also* **:** the mechanism operating or moved by the sequence **b :** a rapid sequence of punches in boxing **c :** any subset of a set considered without regard to order within the subset **3 :** any of various one-piece undergarments for the upper and lower parts of the body — usually used in plural **4 :** an instrument designed to perform two or more tasks **5 a :** the act or process of combining; *especially* **:** that of uniting to form a chemical compound **b :** the quality or state of being combined
— **com·bi·na·tion·al** \-shnəl, -shə-n°l\ *adjective*

**combination shot** *noun* (circa 1909) **:** a shot in pool in which a ball is pocketed by an object ball

**com·bi·na·tive** \'käm-bə-ˌnā-tiv, kəm-'bī-nə-\ *adjective* (1855) **1 :** tending or able to combine **2 :** resulting from combination

**com·bi·na·to·ri·al** \ˌkäm-bə-nə-'tōr-ē-əl, kəm-ˌbī-nə-, -(ˌ)bi-, -'tòr-\ *adjective* (1818) **1 :** of, relating to, or involving combinations **2 :** of or relating to the arrangement of, operation on, and selection of discrete mathematical elements belonging to finite sets or making up geometric configurations
— **com·bi·na·to·ri·al·ly** \-ē-ə-lē\ *adverb*

**com·bi·na·tor·ics** \-'tòr-iks, -'tär-\ *noun plural but singular in construction* (1951) **:** combinatorial mathematics

**com·bi·na·to·ry** \kəm-'bī-nə-ˌtōr-ē, -ˌtòr-\ *adjective* (1647) **:** COMBINATIVE

¹**com·bine** \kəm-'bīn\ *verb* **com·bined; com·bin·ing** [Middle English, from Middle French *combiner,* from Late Latin *combinare,* from Latin *com-* + *bini* two by two — more at BIN-] (15th century) *transitive verb* **1 a :** to bring into such close relationship as to obscure individual characters **:** MERGE **b :** to cause to unite into a chemical compound **c :** to unite into a single number or expression ⟨*combine* fractions and simplify⟩ **2 :** INTERMIX, BLEND **3 :** to possess in combination *intransitive verb* **1 a :** to become one **b :** to unite to form a chemical compound **2 :** to act together **synonym** see JOIN
— **com·bin·able** \-'bī-nə-bəl\ *adjective*
— **com·bin·er** *noun*

²**com·bine** \'käm-ˌbīn\ *noun* (1886) **1 :** a combination especially of business or political interests **2 :** a harvesting machine that heads, threshes, and cleans grain while moving over a field

³**com·bine** \'käm-ˌbīn\ *verb* **com·bined; com·bin·ing** (1926) *transitive verb* **:** to harvest with a combine *intransitive verb* **:** to combine a crop

**comb·ing** \'kō-miŋ\ *variant of* COAMING

**comb·ings** \'kō-miŋz\ *noun plural* (1656) **:** loose hair removed by a comb

**combing wool** *noun* (1757) **:** long-staple strong-fibered wool found suitable for combing and used especially in the manufacture of worsteds

**combining form** *noun* (1884) **:** a linguistic form that occurs only in compounds or derivatives and can be distinguished descriptively from an affix by its ability to occur as one immediate constituent of a form whose only other immediate constituent is an affix (as *cephal-* in *cephalic*) or by its being an allomorph of a morpheme having another allomorph that may occur alone or can be distinguished historically from an affix by the fact that it is borrowed from another language in which it is descriptively a word or a combining form

**comb jelly** *noun* (circa 1889) **:** CTENOPHORE

**com·bo** \'käm-(ˌ)bō\ *noun, plural* **combos** [*combination* + ¹-*o*] (1924) **1 :** a usually small jazz or dance band **2 :** COMBINATION

**com·bust** \kəm-'bəst\ *verb* [Latin *combustus,* past participle of *comburere* to burn up, irregular from *com-* + *urere* to burn — more at EMBER] (15th century) **:** BURN

**com·bus·ti·ble** \kəm-'bəs-tə-bəl\ *adjective* (1529) **1 :** capable of combustion **2 :** easily excited
— **com·bus·ti·bil·i·ty** \-ˌbəs-tə-'bi-lə-tē\ *noun*

— **combustible** *noun*
— **com·bus·ti·bly** \-'bəs-tə-blē\ *adverb*

**com·bus·tion** \kəm-'bəs-chən\ *noun* (15th century) **1 :** an act or instance of burning **2 :** a usually rapid chemical process (as oxidation) that produces heat and usually light; *also* **:** a slower oxidation (as in the body) **3 :** violent agitation **:** TUMULT
— **com·bus·tive** \-'bəs-tiv\ *adjective*

**com·bus·tor** \-'bəs-tər\ *noun* (1945) **:** a chamber (as in a gas turbine or a jet engine) in which combustion occurs — called also *combustion chamber*

¹**come** \'kəm\ *verb* **came** \'kām\; **come; com·ing** \'kə-miŋ\ [Middle English, from Old English *cuman;* akin to Old High German *queman* to come, Latin *venire,* Greek *bainein* to walk, go] (before 12th century) *intransitive verb* **1 a :** to move toward something **:** APPROACH ⟨*come* here⟩ **b :** to move or journey to a vicinity with a specified purpose ⟨*come* see us⟩ ⟨*come* and see what's going on⟩ **c** (1) **:** to reach a particular station in a series ⟨now we *come* to the section on health⟩ (2) **:** to arrive in due course ⟨the time has *come*⟩ **d** (1) **:** to approach in kind or quality ⟨this *comes* near perfection⟩ (2) **:** to reach a condition or conclusion ⟨*came* to regard him as a friend⟩ ⟨*come* to think of it, you may be right⟩ **e** (1) **:** to advance toward accomplishment ⟨learning new ways doesn't *come* easy⟩ ⟨the job is *coming* nicely⟩ (2) **:** to advance in a particular manner ⟨*come* running when I call⟩ (3) **:** to advance, rise, or improve in rank or condition ⟨has *come* a long way⟩ **f :** to get along **:** FARE — often used with *along* **g :** EXTEND ⟨her dress *came* to her ankles⟩ **2 a** (1) **:** to arrive at a particular place, end, result, or conclusion ⟨*came* to his senses⟩ ⟨*come* untied⟩ (2) **:** AMOUNT ⟨the taxes on it *come* to more than it's worth⟩ **b** (1) **:** to appear to the mind ⟨the answer *came* to them⟩ (2) **:** to appear on a scene **:** make an appearance ⟨children *come* equipped to learn any language⟩ **c** (1) **:** HAPPEN, OCCUR ⟨no harm will *come* to you⟩ (2) **:** to come to pass **:** take place — used in the subjunctive with inverted subject and verb to express the particular time or occasion ⟨*come* spring the days will be longer⟩ **d :** ORIGINATE, ARISE ⟨wine *comes* from grapes⟩ ⟨*come* of sturdy stock⟩ **e :** to enter or assume a condition ⟨artillery *came* into action⟩ **f :** to fall within a field of view or a range of application ⟨this *comes* within the terms of the treaty⟩ **g :** to issue forth ⟨a sob *came* from her throat⟩ **h :** to take form ⟨churn the butter *comes*⟩ **i :** to be available ⟨this model *comes* in several sizes⟩ ⟨as good as they *come*⟩ **j :** to experience orgasm — often considered vulgar **3 :** to fall to a person in a division or inheritance of property **4** *obsolete* **:** to become moved favorably **:** RELENT **5 :** to turn out to be ⟨good clothes *come* high⟩ **6 :** BECOME ⟨a dream that *came* true⟩ *transitive verb* **1 :** to approach or be near (an age) ⟨a child *coming* eight years old⟩ **2 :** to take on the aspect of ⟨*come* the stern parent⟩
— **come a cropper :** to fail completely
— **come clean :** to tell the whole story **:** CONFESS
— **come into :** to acquire as a possession or achievement ⟨*come into* a fortune⟩
— **come into one's own :** to achieve one's potential; *also* **:** to gain recognition

**— come of age :** to reach maturity
**— come off it :** to cease foolish or pretentious talk or behavior
**— come over :** to seize suddenly and strangely ⟨what's *come over* you⟩
**— come to :** to be a question of ⟨when it *comes to* pitching horseshoes, he's the champ⟩
**— come to grips with :** to meet or deal with firmly, frankly, or straightforwardly ⟨*come to grips with* the unemployment problem⟩
**— come to oneself :** to get hold of oneself **:** regain self-control
**— come to pass :** HAPPEN
**— come to terms 1 :** to reach an agreement — often used with *with* **2 :** to become adjusted especially emotionally or intellectually — usually used with *with* ⟨*come to terms* with modern life⟩

**²come** *noun* (1923)
**1 :** SEMEN — often considered vulgar
**2 :** ORGASM — often considered vulgar

**come about** *intransitive verb* (14th century)
**1 :** HAPPEN
**2 :** to change direction ⟨the wind has *come about* into the north⟩
**3 :** to shift to a new tack

**come across** *intransitive verb* (1910)
**1 :** to give over or furnish something demanded; *especially* **:** to pay over money
**2 :** to produce an impression ⟨*comes across* as a good speaker⟩
**3 :** COME THROUGH 2

**come along** *intransitive verb* (1694)
**1 :** to accompany someone who leads the way ⟨asked me to *come along* on the trip⟩
**2 :** to make progress ⟨work is *coming along* well⟩
**3 :** to make an appearance ⟨won't just marry the first man that *comes along*⟩

**come around** *intransitive verb* (1934)
**1 :** COME ROUND
**2 :** MENSTRUATE

**come·back** \'kəm-ˌbak\ *noun* (1889)
**1 a :** a sharp or witty reply **:** RETORT **b :** a cause for complaint
**2 :** a return to a former position or condition (as of success or prosperity) **:** RECOVERY, REVIVAL ⟨staging his ultimate *comeback* from self-imposed exile —Howard Mandel⟩

**come back** *intransitive verb* (1850)
**1 :** to return to life or vitality
**2 :** to return to memory ⟨it's all *coming back* to me now⟩
**3 :** REPLY, RETORT
**4 :** to regain a former favorable condition or position

**come by** (1863)
*intransitive verb*
**:** to make a visit
*transitive verb*
**:** to get possession of **:** ACQUIRE ⟨a good job is hard to *come by*⟩

**co·me·di·an** \kə-'mē-dē-ən\ *noun* (1581)
**1** *archaic* **a :** a writer of comedies **b :** an actor who plays comic roles
**2 :** a comical individual; *specifically* **:** a professional entertainer who uses any of various physical or verbal means to be amusing

**co·me·dic** \-'mē-dik\ *adjective* (1639)
**1 :** of or relating to comedy
**2 :** COMICAL 2
**— co·me·dic·al·ly** \-di-k(ə-)lē\ *adverb*

**co·me·di·enne** \-ˌmē-dē-'en\ *noun* [French *comédienne*, feminine of *comédien* comedian, from *comédie*] (circa 1859)
**:** a woman who is a comedian

**com·e·do** \'kä-mə-ˌdō\ *noun, plural* **com·e·do·nes** \ˌkä-mə-'dō-(ˌ)nēz\ [New Latin, from Latin, glutton, from *comedere* to eat — more at COMESTIBLE] (1866)
**:** BLACKHEAD 1

**come·down** \'kəm-ˌdaùn\ *noun* (1840)
**:** a descent in rank or dignity

**come down** *intransitive verb* (1711)
**1 a :** to pass by tradition ⟨a story that has

*come down* from medieval times⟩ **b :** to pass from a usually high source ⟨word *came down* that the strike was over⟩
**2 a :** to reduce itself **:** AMOUNT ⟨it *comes down* to this⟩ **b :** to deal with a subject directly ⟨when you *come down* to it, we all depend on others⟩
**3 :** to lose or fall in estate or condition ⟨has *come down* in the world⟩
**4 :** to place oneself in opposition ⟨*came down* hard on gambling⟩
**5 :** to become ill ⟨*came down* with measles⟩
**6 :** COME OUT 2

**com·e·dy** \'kä-mə-dē\ *noun, plural* **-dies** [Middle English, from Middle French *comedie*, from Latin *comoedia*, from Greek *kōmōidia*, from *kōmos* revel + *aeidein* to sing — more at ODE] (14th century)
**1 a :** a medieval narrative that ends happily ⟨Dante's Divine *Comedy*⟩ **b :** a literary work written in a comic style or treating a comic theme
**2 a :** a drama of light and amusing character and typically with a happy ending **b :** the genre of dramatic literature dealing with the comic or with the serious in a light or satirical manner — compare TRAGEDY
**3 :** a ludicrous or farcical event or series of events
**4 a :** the comic element ⟨the *comedy* of many life situations⟩ **b :** humorous entertainment ⟨nightclub *comedy*⟩

**comedy drama** *noun* (1885)
**:** serious drama that is interspersed with comedy

**comedy of manners** (1822)
**:** comedy that satirically portrays the manners and fashions of a particular class or set

**come-hith·er** \(ˌ)kəm-'hi-thər, (ˌ)kə-'mi-\ *adjective* (1925)
**:** sexually provocative ⟨that *come-hither* look in your eyes⟩

**come in** *intransitive verb* (14th century)
**1 a :** to arrive on a scene ⟨new models *coming in*⟩ **b :** to become available ⟨data began *coming in*⟩
**2 :** to place among those finishing ⟨*came in* last⟩
**3 a :** to function in an indicated manner ⟨*come in* handy⟩ **b** *of a telecommunications signal* **:** to be received ⟨*came in* loud and clear⟩
**4 :** to assume a role or function ⟨that's where you *come in*⟩
**5 :** to attain maturity, fruitfulness, or production
**— come in for :** to become subject to ⟨*coming in for* increasing criticism⟩

**come·ly** \'kəm-lē *also* 'kōm- *or* 'käm-\ *adjective* **come·li·er; -est** [Middle English *comly*, alteration of Old English *cȳmlic* glorious, from *cȳme* lively, fine; akin to Old High German *kūmig* weak] (13th century)
**1 :** pleasurably conforming to notions of good appearance, suitability, or proportion
**2 :** having a pleasing appearance **:** not homely or plain
*synonym* see BEAUTIFUL
**— come·li·ness** *noun*

**come off** (1596)
*intransitive verb*
**1 a :** to acquit oneself **:** FARE ⟨*came off* well in the contest⟩ **b :** APPEAR, SEEM
**2 :** SUCCEED ⟨a television series that never *came off* —TV Guide⟩
**3 :** HAPPEN, OCCUR
*transitive verb*
**:** to have recently completed or recovered from ⟨*coming off* a good year⟩ ⟨*coming off* an injury⟩

**come-on** \'kə-ˌmón, -ˌmän\ *noun* (1902)
**1 :** something (as an advertising promotion) intended to entice or allure
**2 :** a usually sexual advance

**come on** *intransitive verb* (15th century)

**1 a :** to advance by degrees ⟨darkness *came on*⟩ **b :** to begin by degrees ⟨rain *came on* toward noon⟩
**2 a :** PLEASE — used in cajoling or pleading **b** — used interjectionally to express astonishment, incredulity, or recognition of a put-on
**3 :** to project an indicated personal image ⟨*comes on* as a conservative⟩
**4 :** to show sexual interest in someone; *also* **:** to make sexual advances ⟨tried to *come on* to her⟩

**come out** *intransitive verb* (13th century)
**1 a :** to come into public view **:** make a public appearance ⟨a new magazine has *come out*⟩ **b :** to become evident ⟨his pride *came out* in his refusal to accept help⟩
**2 :** to declare oneself especially in public utterance ⟨*came out* in favor of the proposal⟩
**3 :** to turn out in an outcome **:** end up ⟨everything *came out* all right⟩
**4 :** to make a debut
**5 :** to openly declare one's homosexuality
**— com·ing-out** \ˌkə-miŋ-'aùt\ *adjective*
**— come out with 1 :** to give expression to ⟨*came out with* a new proposal⟩ **2 :** PUBLISH

**come-out·er** \(ˌ)kə-'maù-tər\ *noun* (1840)
**1 :** a person who withdraws from something established (as a religious body)
**2 :** a person who advocates political reform

**come over** *intransitive verb* (1576)
**1 a :** to change from one side (as of a controversy) to the other **b :** to visit casually **:** DROP IN ⟨*come over* whenever you like⟩
**2** *British* **:** BECOME

**com·er** \'kə-mər\ *noun* (14th century)
**1 :** one that comes or arrives ⟨all *comers*⟩
**2 :** one making rapid progress or showing promise

**come round** *intransitive verb* (1818)
**1 :** to change direction
**2 :** to return to a former condition; *especially* **:** COME TO 1
**3 :** to accede to a particular opinion or course of action ⟨knew you'd *come round* to our side eventually⟩

**¹co·mes·ti·ble** \kə-'mes-tə-bəl\ *adjective* [Middle French, from Medieval Latin *comestibilis*, from Latin *comestus*, past participle of *comedere* to eat, from *com-* + *edere* to eat — more at EAT] (15th century)
**:** EDIBLE

**²comestible** *noun* (1837)
**:** FOOD — usually used in plural

**com·et** \'kä-mət\ *noun* [Middle English *comete*, from Old English *cometa*, from Latin, from Greek *komētēs*, literally, long-haired, from *koman* to wear long hair, from *komē* hair] (before 12th century)
**:** a celestial body that consists of a fuzzy head usually surrounding a bright nucleus, that has a usually highly eccentric orbit, and that often when in the part of its orbit near the sun develops a long tail which points away from the sun
**— com·e·tary** \-mə-ˌter-ē\ *adjective*
**— co·met·ic** \kə-'me-tik, kä-\ *adjective*

**come through** *intransitive verb* (1914)
**1 :** to do what is needed or expected ⟨*came through* in the clutch⟩
**2 :** to become communicated

**come to** *intransitive verb* (circa 1572)
**1 :** to recover consciousness
**2 a :** to bring a ship's head nearer the wind **:** LUFF **b :** to come to anchor or to a stop

**come up** *intransitive verb* (14th century)
**1 :** RISE 6
**2 :** to come near **:** make an approach ⟨*came up* and introduced himself⟩
**3 :** to rise in rank or status ⟨an officer who *came up* from the ranks⟩
**4 a :** to come to attention or consideration ⟨the question never *came up*⟩ **b :** to occur in the course of time ⟨any problem that may *come up*⟩
**5 :** to turn out to be ⟨the coin *came up* tails⟩
**— come up with :** to produce especially in

dealing with a problem or challenge ⟨*came up with* a solution⟩

**come·up·pance** \(ˌ)kə-'mə-pən(t)s\ *noun* [*come up* + *-ance*] (1859)
: a deserved rebuke or penalty **:** DESERTS

**com·fit** \'kəm(p)-fət, 'käm(p)-\ *noun* [Middle English *confit,* from Middle French, from past participle of *confire* to prepare, from Latin *conficere,* from *com-* + *facere* to make — more at DO] (14th century)
: a candy consisting of a piece of fruit, a root (as licorice), a nut, or a seed coated and preserved with sugar

¹**com·fort** \'kəm(p)-fərt\ *transitive verb* [Middle English, from Old French *conforter,* from Late Latin *confortare* to strengthen greatly, from Latin *com-* + *fortis* strong] (13th century)
**1 :** to give strength and hope to **:** CHEER
**2 :** to ease the grief or trouble of **:** CONSOLE
— **com·fort·ing·ly** \-fər-tiŋ-lē\ *adverb*

²**comfort** *noun* (13th century)
**1 :** strengthening aid: **a :** ASSISTANCE, SUPPORT ⟨accused of giving aid and *comfort* to the enemy⟩ **b :** consolation in time of trouble or worry **:** SOLACE
**2 a :** a feeling of relief or encouragement **b :** contented well-being
**3 :** a satisfying or enjoyable experience
**4 :** one that gives or brings comfort ⟨all the *comforts* of home⟩
— **com·fort·less** \-ləs\ *adjective*

**com·fort·able** \'kəm(p)(f)-tə(r)-bəl, 'kəm(p)-fə(r)-tə-bəl, 'kəm-fə(r)-bəl\ *adjective* (1769)
**1 a :** affording or enjoying contentment and security ⟨a *comfortable* income⟩ **b :** affording or enjoying physical comfort ⟨a *comfortable* chair⟩ ⟨was too *comfortable* to move⟩
**2 a :** free from vexation or doubt ⟨*comfortable* assumptions⟩ **b :** free from stress or tension ⟨a *comfortable* routine⟩ ☆
— **com·fort·able·ness** *noun*
— **com·fort·ably** \-blē\ *adverb*

**com·fort·er** \'kəm(p)-fə(r)-tər\ *noun* (14th century)
**1 a** *capitalized* **:** HOLY SPIRIT **b :** one that gives comfort
**2 a :** a long narrow usually knitted neck scarf **b :** a thick bed covering made of two layers of cloth containing a filling (as down)

**comfort station** *noun* (circa 1913)
**:** REST ROOM

**com·frey** \'kəm(p)-frē\ *noun, plural* **comfreys** [Middle English *cumfirie,* from Old French, from Latin *conferva* a water plant, from *confervēre* to grow together (of bones), from *com-* + *fervēre* to boil — more at BARM] (13th century)
**:** any of a genus (*Symphytum*) of perennial herbs of the borage family with coarse hairy entire leaves and flowers in one-sided racemes

**com·fy** \'kəm(p)-fē\ *adjective* [by shortening & alteration] (1829)
**:** COMFORTABLE

¹**com·ic** \'kä-mik\ *adjective* [Latin *comicus,* from Greek *kōmikos,* from *kōmos* revel] (1576)
**1 :** of, relating to, or marked by comedy
**2 :** causing laughter or amusement **:** FUNNY
**3 :** of or relating to comic strips
**synonym** see LAUGHABLE

²**comic** *noun* (1581)
**1 :** COMEDIAN
**2 :** the comic element
**3 a :** COMIC STRIP **b :** COMIC BOOK **c** *plural* **:** the part of a newspaper devoted to comic strips

**com·i·cal** \'kä-mi-kəl\ *adjective* (15th century)
**1** *obsolete* **:** of or relating to comedy
**2 :** causing laughter especially because of a startlingly or unexpectedly humorous impact
**synonym** see LAUGHABLE
— **com·i·cal·i·ty** \ˌkä-mi-'ka-lə-tē\ *noun*
— **com·i·cal·ly** \'kä-mi-k(ə-)lē\ *adverb*

**comic book** *noun* (1941)
**:** a magazine containing sequences of comic strips

**comic–opera** *adjective* (1906)
**:** not to be taken seriously ⟨a *comic-opera* regime⟩

**comic opera** *noun* (1762)
**:** opera of a humorous character with a happy ending and usually some spoken dialogue

**comic relief** *noun* (1875)
**:** a relief from the emotional tension of a drama that is provided by the interposition of a comic episode or element

**comic strip** *noun* (1920)
**:** a group of cartoons in narrative sequence

¹**com·ing** \'kə-miŋ\ *noun* (13th century)
**:** an act or instance of arriving

²**coming** *adjective* (15th century)
**1 :** immediately due in sequence or development ⟨in the *coming* year⟩
**2 :** gaining importance

**co·min·gle** \kə-'miŋ-gəl\ *transitive verb* (1602)
**:** COMMINGLE

**coming–of–age** *noun* (1916)
**:** the attainment of prominence, respectability, recognition, or maturity

**Com·in·tern** \'kä-mən-ˌtərn\ *noun* [Russian *Komintern,* from *Kommunisticheskiĭ International* Communist International] (1923)
**:** the Communist International established in 1919 and dissolved in 1943

**co·mi·tia** \kə-'mi-sh(ē-)ə\ *noun, plural* **comitia** [Latin, plural of *comitium,* from *com-* + *-it-* (akin to *ire* to go) — more at ISSUE] (1600)
**:** any of several public assemblies of the people in ancient Rome for legislative, judicial, and electoral purposes
— **co·mi·tial** \-'mi-shəl\ *adjective*

**co·mi·ty** \'kä-mə-tē, 'kō-\ *noun, plural* **-ties** [Latin *comitat-, comitas,* from *comis* courteous, probably from Old Latin *cosmis,* from *com-* + *-smis* (akin to Sanskrit *smayate* he smiles) — more at SMILE] (1543)
**1 a :** friendly social atmosphere **:** social harmony ⟨group activities promoting *comity*⟩ **b :** a loose widespread community based on common social institutions ⟨the *comity* of civilization⟩ **c :** COMITY OF NATIONS **d :** the informal and voluntary recognition by courts of one jurisdiction of the laws and judicial decisions of another
**2 :** avoidance of proselytizing members of another religious denomination

**comity of nations** (1862)
**1 :** the courtesy and friendship of nations marked especially by mutual recognition of executive, legislative, and judicial acts
**2 :** the group of nations practicing international comity

**com·ma** \'kä-mə\ *noun* [Late Latin, from Latin, part of a sentence, from Greek *komma* segment, clause, from *koptein* to cut — more at CAPON] (1554)
**1 :** a punctuation mark , used especially as a mark of separation within the sentence
**2 :** PAUSE, INTERVAL
**3 :** any of several nymphalid butterflies (genus *Polygonia*) with a silvery comma-shaped mark on the underside of the hind wings

**comma fault** *noun* (circa 1934)
**:** COMMA SPLICE

¹**com·mand** \kə-'mand\ *verb* [Middle English *comanden,* from Middle French *comander,* from (assumed) Vulgar Latin *commandare,* alteration of Latin *commendare* to commit to one's charge — more at COMMEND] (14th century)
*transitive verb*
**1 :** to direct authoritatively **:** ORDER
**2 :** to exercise a dominating influence over **:** have command of: as **a :** to have at one's immediate disposal **b :** to demand or receive as one's due ⟨*commands* a high fee⟩ **c :** to overlook or dominate from or as if from a strategic

position **d :** to have military command of as senior officer
**3** *obsolete* **:** to order or request to be given
*intransitive verb*
**1 :** to have or exercise direct authority **:** GOVERN
**2 :** to give orders
**3 :** to be commander
**4 :** to dominate as if from an elevated place ☆
— **com·mand·able** \-'man-də-bəl\ *adjective*

²**command** *noun* (15th century)
**1 a :** an order given **b :** a signal that actuates a device (as a control mechanism in a spacecraft or one step in a computer); *also* **:** the activation of a device by means of such a signal
**2 a :** the ability to control **:** MASTERY **b :** the authority or right to command ⟨the officer in *command*⟩ **c** (1) **:** the power to dominate (2) **:** scope of vision **d :** facility in use ⟨a good *command* of French⟩
**3 :** the act of commanding
**4 :** the personnel, area, or organization under a commander; *specifically* **:** a unit of the U.S. Air Force higher than an air force
**5 :** a position of highest usually military authority
**synonym** see POWER

³**command** *adjective* (1826)
**:** done on command or request ⟨a *command* performance⟩

**com·man·dant** \'kä-mən-ˌdänt, -ˌdant\ *noun* (1687)
**:** COMMANDING OFFICER

---

☆ **SYNONYMS**

**Comfortable, cozy, snug, easy, restful** mean enjoying or providing a position of contentment and security. COMFORTABLE applies to anything that encourages serenity, well-being, or complacency as well as physical ease ⟨started feeling *comfortable* in our new surroundings⟩. COZY suggests warmth, shelter, assured ease, and friendliness ⟨a *cozy* neighborhood coffee shop⟩. SNUG suggests having just enough space for comfort and safety but no more ⟨a *snug* little cottage⟩. EASY implies relief from or absence of anything likely to cause physical or mental discomfort or constraint ⟨living in *easy* circumstances⟩. RESTFUL applies to whatever induces or contributes to rest or relaxation ⟨a quiet *restful* vacation⟩.

**Command, order, bid, enjoin, direct, instruct, charge** mean to issue orders. COMMAND and ORDER imply authority and usually some degree of formality and impersonality. COMMAND stresses official exercise of authority ⟨a general *commanding* troops⟩. ORDER may suggest peremptory or arbitrary exercise ⟨*ordered* his employees about like slaves⟩. BID suggests giving orders peremptorily (as to children or servants) ⟨she *bade* him be seated⟩. ENJOIN implies giving an order or direction authoritatively and urgently and often with admonition or solicitude ⟨a sign *enjoining* patrons to be quiet⟩. DIRECT and INSTRUCT both connote expectation of obedience and usually concern specific points of procedure or method, INSTRUCT sometimes implying greater explicitness or formality ⟨*directed* her assistant to hold all calls⟩ ⟨the judge *instructed* the jury to ignore the remark⟩. CHARGE adds to ENJOIN an implication of imposing as a duty or responsibility ⟨*charged* by the President with a secret mission⟩.

---

\ə\ abut \ᵊ\ kitten \ər\ further \a\ ash \ā\ ace
\ä\ mop, mar \aü\ out \ch\ chin \e\ bet \ē\ easy
\g\ go \i\ hit \ī\ ice \j\ job \ŋ\ sing \ō\ go
\ȯ\ law \ȯi\ boy \th\ thin \th\ the \ü\ loot \ u\ foot
\y\ yet \zh\ vision    *see also* Guide to Pronunciation

**command car** *noun* (1941)
: an open armored car designed especially for military reconnaissance and capable of traveling over rough terrain

**com·man·deer** \ˌkä-mən-'dir\ *transitive verb* [Afrikaans *kommandeer*, from French *commander* to command, from Old French *comander*] (1881)
**1 a :** to compel to perform military service **b :** to seize for military purposes
**2 :** to take arbitrary or forcible possession of

**com·mand·er** \kə-'man-dər\ *noun* (14th century)
**1 :** one in an official position of command or control: as **a :** COMMANDING OFFICER **b :** the presiding officer of a society or organization
**2 :** a commissioned officer in the navy or coast guard ranking above a lieutenant commander and below a captain
**— com·mand·er·ship** \-ˌship\ *noun*

**commander in chief** (1654)
: one who holds the supreme command of an armed force

**com·mand·ery** \kə-'man-d(ə-)rē\ *noun, plural* **-er·ies** (15th century)
**1 :** a district under the control of a commander of an order of knights
**2 :** an assembly or lodge in a secret order

**com·mand·ing** \kə-'man-diŋ\ *adjective* (1591)
**1 :** drawing attention or priority ⟨a *commanding* presence⟩
**2 :** difficult to overcome ⟨a *commanding* lead⟩
**— com·mand·ing·ly** \-diŋ-lē\ *adverb*

**commanding officer** *noun* (1720)
: an officer in command; *especially* : an officer in the armed forces in command of an organization or installation

**com·mand·ment** \kə-'man(d)-mənt\ *noun* (13th century)
**1 :** the act or power of commanding
**2 :** something that is commanded; *especially* : one of the biblical Ten Commandments

**command module** *noun* (1962)
: a space vehicle module designed to carry the crew, the chief communication equipment, and the equipment for reentry

**com·man·do** \kə-'man-(ˌ)dō\ *noun, plural* **-dos** *or* **-does** [Afrikaans *kommando*, from Dutch *commando* command, from Spanish *comando*, from *comandar* to command, from Late Latin *commandare*] (1884)
**1** *South African* **a :** a military unit or command of the Boers **b :** a raiding expedition
**2 a :** a military unit trained and organized as shock troops especially for hit-and-run raids into enemy territory **b :** a member of such a unit

**command post** *noun* (circa 1918)
: a post at which the commander of a unit in the field receives orders and exercises command

**command sergeant major** *noun* (1967)
: a noncommissioned officer in the army ranking above a first sergeant

**comma splice** *noun* (1924)
: the careless or unjustified use of a comma between coordinate main clauses not connected by a conjunction (as in "nobody goes there anymore, it's boring")

**com·me·dia del·l'ar·te** \kə-ˌmā-dē-ə-(ˌ)del-'är-tē, kə-ˌme-\ *noun* [Italian, literally, comedy of art] (1877)
: Italian comedy of the 16th to 18th centuries improvised from standardized situations and stock characters

**comme il faut** \ˌkə-mē(l)-'fō\ *adjective* [French, literally, as it should be] (1756)
: conforming to accepted standards : PROPER

**com·mem·o·rate** \kə-'me-mə-ˌrāt\ *transitive verb* **-rat·ed; -rat·ing** [Latin *commemoratus*, past participle of *commemorare*, from *com-* + *memorare* to remind of, from *memor* mindful — more at MEMORY] (1599)
**1 :** to call to remembrance

**2 :** to mark by some ceremony or observation : OBSERVE
**3 :** to serve as a memorial of ⟨a plaque that *commemorates* the battle⟩
**synonym** see KEEP
**— com·mem·o·ra·tor** \-ˌrā-tər\ *noun*

**com·mem·o·ra·tion** \kə-ˌme-mə-'rā-shən\ *noun* (14th century)
**1 :** the act of commemorating
**2 :** something that commemorates

**com·mem·o·ra·tive** \kə-'mem-rə-tiv, -'me-mə-; -'me-mə-ˌrā-tiv\ *adjective* (1612)
: intended as a commemoration; *especially* : issued in limited quantities for a relatively short period in commemoration of a person, place, or event ⟨a *commemorative* stamp⟩
**— commemorative** *noun*
**— com·mem·o·ra·tive·ly** *adverb*

**com·mence** \kə-'men(t)s\ *verb* **com·menced; com·menc·ing** [Middle English *comencen*, from Middle French *comencer*, from (assumed) Vulgar Latin *cominitiare*, from Latin *com-* + Late Latin *initiare* to begin, from Latin, to initiate] (14th century)
*transitive verb*
: to enter upon : BEGIN ⟨*commence* proceedings⟩
*intransitive verb*
**1 :** to have or make a beginning : START
**2** *chiefly British* : to begin to be or to act as
**3** *chiefly British* : to take a degree at a university
**synonym** see BEGIN
**— com·menc·er** *noun*

**com·mence·ment** \kəm-'men(t)s-mənt\ *noun* (13th century)
**1 :** an act, instance, or time of commencing
**2 a :** the ceremonies or the day for conferring degrees or diplomas **b :** the period of activities at this time

**com·mend** \kə-'mend\ *verb* [Middle English, from Latin *commendare*, from *com-* + *mandare* to entrust — more at MANDATE] (14th century)
*transitive verb*
**1 :** to entrust for care or preservation
**2 :** to recommend as worthy of confidence or notice
**3 :** to mention with approbation : PRAISE
*intransitive verb*
: to commend or serve as a commendation of something
**— com·mend·able** \-'men-də-bəl\ *adjective*
**— com·mend·ably** \-blē\ *adverb*
**— com·mend·er** *noun*

**com·men·da·tion** \ˌkä-mən-'dā-shən, -ˌmen-\ *noun* (14th century)
**1 a :** an act of commending **b :** something (as a formal citation) that commends
**2** *archaic* : COMPLIMENT

**com·men·da·to·ry** \kə-'men-də-ˌtōr-ē, -ˌtȯr-\ *adjective* (1555)
: serving to commend

**com·men·sal** \kə-'men(t)-səl\ *adjective* [Middle English, from Medieval Latin *commensalis*, from Latin *com-* + Late Latin *mensalis* of the table, from Latin *mensa* table] (1877)
: of, relating to, or living in a state of commensalism
**— commensal** *noun*
**— com·men·sal·ly** \-sə-lē\ *adverb*

**com·men·sal·ism** \-sə-ˌli-zəm\ *noun* (1870)
: a relation between two kinds of organisms in which one obtains food or other benefits from the other without damaging or benefiting it

**com·men·su·ra·ble** \kə-'men(t)s-rə-bəl, -'men(t)sh-; -'men(t)-sə-, -shə-\ *adjective* (1557)
**1 :** having a common measure; *specifically* : divisible by a common unit an integral number of times
**2 :** COMMENSURATE 2
**— com·men·su·ra·bil·i·ty** \-ˌmen(t)s-rə-'bi-lə-tē, -ˌmen(t)sh-; -ˌmen(t)-sə-, -shə-\ *noun*

**— com·men·su·ra·bly** \-'men(t)s-rə-blē, -'men(t)sh-; -'men(t)-sə-, -shə-\ *adverb*

**com·men·su·rate** \kə-'men(t)s-rət, -'men(t)sh-; -'men(t)-sə-, -shə-\ *adjective* [Late Latin *commensuratus*, from Latin *com-* + Late Latin *mensuratus*, past participle of *mensurare* to measure, from Latin *mensura* measure — more at MEASURE] (1641)
**1 :** equal in measure or extent : COEXTENSIVE ⟨lived a life *commensurate* with the early years of the republic⟩
**2 :** corresponding in size, extent, amount, or degree : PROPORTIONATE ⟨was given a job *commensurate* with her abilities⟩
**3 :** COMMENSURABLE 1
**— com·men·su·rate·ly** *adverb*
**— com·men·su·ra·tion** \-ˌmen(t)s-sə-'rā-shən, -shə-\ *noun*

**¹com·ment** \'kä-ˌment\ *noun* [Middle English, from Late Latin *commentum*, from Latin, invention, from neuter of *commentus*, past participle of *comminisci* to invent, from *com-* + *-minisci* (akin to *ment-, mens* mind) — more at MIND] (14th century)
**1 :** COMMENTARY
**2 :** a note explaining, illustrating, or criticizing the meaning of a writing
**3 a :** an observation or remark expressing an opinion or attitude **b :** a judgment expressed indirectly

**²comment** (15th century)
*transitive verb*
: to make a comment on ⟨the discovery . . . is hardly *commented* by the press —*Nation*⟩
*intransitive verb*
: to explain or interpret something by comment ⟨*commenting* on recent developments⟩

**com·men·ta·ry** \'kä-mən-ˌter-ē\ *noun, plural* **-tar·ies** (15th century)
**1 a :** an explanatory treatise — usually used in plural **b :** a record of events usually written by a participant — usually used in plural
**2 a :** a systematic series of explanations or interpretations (as of a writing) **b :** COMMENT 2
**3 a :** something that serves for illustration or explanation ⟨the dark, airless apartments and sunless factories . . . are a sad *commentary* upon our civilization —H. A. Overstreet⟩ **b :** an expression of opinion

**com·men·tate** \'kä-mən-ˌtāt\ *verb* **-tat·ed; -tat·ing** [back-formation from *commentator*] (1794)
*transitive verb*
: to give a commentary on
*intransitive verb*
: to comment in a usually expository or interpretive manner; *also* : to act as a commentator

**com·men·ta·tor** \-ˌtā-tər\ *noun* (14th century)
: one who gives a commentary; *especially* : one who reports and discusses news on radio or television

**¹com·merce** \'kä-(ˌ)mərs\ *noun* [Middle French, from Latin *commercium*, from *com-* + *merc-, merx* merchandise] (1537)
**1 :** social intercourse : interchange of ideas, opinions, or sentiments
**2 :** the exchange or buying and selling of commodities on a large scale involving transportation from place to place
**3 :** SEXUAL INTERCOURSE
**synonym** see BUSINESS

**²com·merce** \'kä-mərs, kə-'mərs\ *intransitive verb* **com·merced; com·merc·ing** (1596)
*archaic* : COMMUNE

**¹com·mer·cial** \kə-'mər-shəl\ *adjective* (1598)
**1 a** (1) : occupied with or engaged in commerce or work intended for commerce ⟨a *commercial* artist⟩ (2) : of or relating to commerce ⟨*commercial* regulations⟩ (3) : characteristic of commerce ⟨*commercial* weights⟩ (4) : suitable, adequate, or prepared for commerce ⟨found oil in *commercial* quantities⟩ **b** (1) : being of an average or inferior quality ⟨*commercial* oxalic

acid⟩ ⟨show-quality versus *commercial* cattle⟩ (2) **:** producing artistic work of low standards for quick market success
**2 a :** viewed with regard to profit ⟨a *commercial* success⟩ **b :** designed for a large market
**3 :** emphasizing skills and subjects useful in business
**4 :** supported by advertisers ⟨*commercial* TV⟩
— **com·mer·ci·al·i·ty** \kə-ˌmər-shē-'a-lə-tē\ *noun*
— **com·mer·cial·ly** \-'mər-sh(ə-)lē\ *adverb*
²**commercial** *noun* (1935)
**:** an advertisement broadcast on radio or television

**commercial bank** *noun* (1910)
**:** a bank organized chiefly to handle the everyday financial transactions of businesses (as through demand deposit accounts and short-term commercial loans)

**com·mer·cial·ise** *British variant of* COMMERCIALIZE

**com·mer·cial·ism** \kə-'mər-shə-ˌli-zəm\ *noun* (1849)
**1 :** commercial spirit, institutions, or methods
**2 :** excessive emphasis on profit
— **com·mer·cial·ist** \-'mər-sh(ə-)list\ *noun*
— **com·mer·cial·is·tic** \-ˌmər-shə-'lis-tik\ *adjective*

**com·mer·cial·ize** \kə-'mər-shə-ˌlīz\ *transitive verb* **-ized; -iz·ing** (1830)
**1 a :** to manage on a business basis for profit **b :** to develop commerce in
**2 :** to exploit for profit ⟨*commercialize* Christmas⟩
**3 :** to debase in quality for more profit
— **com·mer·cial·i·za·tion** \-ˌmər-sh(ə-)lə-'zā-shən\ *noun*

**commercial paper** *noun* (1836)
**:** short-term unsecured discounted paper usually sold by one company to another for immediate cash needs

**commercial traveler** *noun* (1807)
**:** TRAVELING SALESMAN

**com·mie** \'kä-mē\ *noun, often capitalized* [by shortening & alteration] (1940)
**:** COMMUNIST

**com·mi·na·tion** \ˌkä-mə-'nā-shən\ *noun* [Middle English, from Middle French or Latin; Middle French, from Latin *commination-, comminatio*, from *comminari* to threaten, from *com-* + *minari* to threaten — more at MOUNT] (15th century)
**:** DENUNCIATION
— **com·mi·na·to·ry** \'kä-mə-nə-ˌtōr-ē, -ˌtȯr-; kə-'mi-nə-, -'mī-\ *adjective*

**com·min·gle** \kə-'miŋ-gəl, kä-\ (circa 1626) *transitive verb*
**1 :** to blend thoroughly into a harmonious whole
**2 :** to combine (funds or properties) into a common fund or stock
*intransitive verb*
**:** to become commingled
**synonym** see MIX

**com·mi·nute** \'kä-mə-ˌnüt, -ˌnyüt\ *transitive verb* **-nut·ed; -nut·ing** [Latin *comminutus*, past participle of *comminuere*, from *com-* + *minuere* to lessen — more at MINOR] (1626)
**:** to reduce to minute particles **:** PULVERIZE
— **com·mi·nu·tion** \ˌkä-mə-'nü-shən, -'nyü-\ *noun*

**com·mis·er·ate** \kə-'mi-zə-ˌrāt\ *verb* **-at·ed; -at·ing** [Latin *commiseratus*, past participle of *commiserari*, from *com-* + *miserari* to pity, from *miser* wretched] (1599)
*intransitive verb*
**:** to feel or express sympathy **:** CONDOLE ⟨*commiserates* with them on their loss⟩
*transitive verb*
**:** to feel or express sorrow or compassion for
— **com·mis·er·at·ing·ly** *adverb*
— **com·mis·er·a·tion** \-ˌmi-zə-'rā-shən\ *noun*
— **com·mis·er·a·tive** \-'mi-zə-ˌrā-tiv\ *adjective*

**com·mis·sar** \'kä-mə-ˌsär\ *noun* [Russian *komissar*, from German *Kommissar*, from Medieval Latin *commissarius*] (1918)
**1 a :** a Communist party official assigned to a military unit to teach party principles and policies and to ensure party loyalty **b :** one that attempts to control public opinion or its expression
**2 :** the head of a government department in the U.S.S.R. until 1946
— **com·mis·sar·i·al** \ˌkä-mə-'sär-ē-əl, -'ser-\ *adjective*

**com·mis·sar·i·at** \ˌkä-mə-'ser-ē-ət, -'sär-, *especially for 3* -'sär-\ *noun* [New Latin *commissariatus*, from Medieval Latin *commissarius*] (1779)
**1 :** a system for supplying an army with food
**2 :** food supplies
**3** [Russian *komissariat*, from German *Kommissariat*, from New Latin *commissariatus*] **:** a government department in the U.S.S.R. until 1946
**4 :** a board of commissioners

**com·mis·sary** \'kä-mə-ˌser-ē\ *noun, plural* **-sar·ies** [Middle English *commissarie*, from Medieval Latin *commissarius*, from Latin *commissus*, past participle of *committere*] (14th century)
**1 :** one delegated by a superior to execute a duty or an office
**2 a :** a store for equipment and provisions; *especially* **:** a supermarket for military personnel **b :** food supplies **c :** a lunchroom especially in a motion-picture studio

¹**com·mis·sion** \kə-'mi-shən\ *noun* [Middle English, from Middle French, from Latin *commission-, commissio* act of bringing together, from *committere*] (14th century)
**1 a :** a formal written warrant granting the power to perform various acts or duties **b :** a certificate conferring military rank and authority; *also* **:** the rank and authority so conferred
**2 :** an authorization or command to act in a prescribed manner or to perform prescribed acts **:** CHARGE
**3 a :** authority to act for, in behalf of, or in place of another **b :** a task or matter entrusted to one as an agent for another
**4 a :** a group of persons directed to perform some duty **b :** a government agency having administrative, legislative, or judicial powers **c :** a city council having legislative and executive functions
**5 :** an act of committing something
**6 :** a fee paid to an agent or employee for transacting a piece of business or performing a service; *especially* **:** a percentage of the money received from a total paid to the agent responsible for the business
**7 :** an act of entrusting or giving authority
— **in commission** *or* **into commission 1 :** under the authority of commissioners **2** *of a ship* **:** ready for active service **3 :** in use or in condition for use
— **on commission :** with commission serving as partial or full pay for work done
— **out of commission 1 :** out of active service or use **2 :** out of working order

²**commission** *transitive verb* **-mis·sioned; -mis·sion·ing** \-'mi-sh(ə-)niŋ\ (circa 1661)
**1 :** to furnish with a commission: as **a :** to confer a formal commission on ⟨was *commissioned* lieutenant⟩ **b :** to appoint or assign to a task or function ⟨was *commissioned* to do the biography⟩
**2 :** to order to be made ⟨*commissioned* a portrait⟩
**3 :** to put (a ship) in commission

**com·mis·sion·aire** \kə-ˌmi-shə-'nar, -'ner\ *noun* [French *commissionnaire*, from *commission*] (1641)
*chiefly British* **:** a uniformed attendant

**commissioned officer** *noun* (15th century)

**:** an officer of the armed forces holding by a commission a rank of second lieutenant or ensign or above

**com·mis·sion·er** \kə-'mi-sh(ə-)nər\ *noun* (15th century)
**:** a person with a commission: as **a :** a member of a commission **b :** the representative of the governmental authority in a district, province, or other unit often having both judicial and administrative powers **c :** the officer in charge of a department or bureau of the public service **d :** the administrative head of a professional sport
— **com·mis·sion·er·ship** \-ˌship\ *noun*

**commission merchant** *noun* (1796)
**:** BROKER 1b

**commission plan** *noun* (1919)
**:** a method of municipal government under which a small elective commission exercises both executive and legislative powers and each commissioner directly administers one or more municipal departments

**com·mis·sure** \'kä-mə-ˌshu̇r\ *noun* [Middle English, from Middle French or Latin; Middle French, from Latin *commissura* a joining, from *commissus*, past participle] (15th century)
**1 :** a point or line of union or junction especially between two anatomical parts (as adjacent heart valves)
**2 :** a connecting band of nerve tissue in the brain or spinal cord
— **com·mis·sur·al** \ˌkä-mə-'shu̇r-əl\ *adjective*

**com·mit** \kə-'mit\ *verb* **com·mit·ted; com·mit·ting** [Middle English *committen*, from Latin *committere* to connect, entrust, from *com-* + *mittere* to send] (14th century)
*transitive verb*
**1 a :** to put into charge or trust **:** ENTRUST **b :** to place in a prison or mental institution **c :** to consign or record for preservation ⟨*commit* it to memory⟩ **d :** to put into a place for disposal or safekeeping **e :** to refer (as a legislative bill) to a committee for consideration and report
**2 :** to carry into action deliberately **:** PERPETRATE ⟨*commit* a crime⟩
**3 a :** OBLIGATE, BIND **b :** to pledge or assign to some particular course or use ⟨*commit* all troops to the attack⟩ **c :** to reveal the views of ⟨refused to *commit* himself on the issue⟩
*intransitive verb*
**1** *obsolete* **:** to perpetrate an offense
**2 :** to obligate or pledge oneself ☆
— **com·mit·ta·ble** \-'mi-tə-bəl\ *adjective*

---

☆ **SYNONYMS**
**Commit, entrust, confide, consign, relegate** mean to assign to a person or place for a definite purpose. COMMIT may express the general idea of delivering into another's charge or the special sense of transferring to a superior power or to a special place of custody ⟨*committed* the felon to prison⟩. ENTRUST implies committing with trust and confidence ⟨the president is *entrusted* with broad powers⟩. CONFIDE implies entrusting with great assurance or reliance ⟨*confided* complete control of my affairs to my attorney⟩. CONSIGN suggests removing from one's control with formality or finality ⟨*consigned* the damaging notes to the fire⟩. RELEGATE implies a consigning to a particular class or sphere often with a suggestion of getting rid of ⟨*relegated* to an obscure position in the company⟩.

---

\ə\ abut \ᵊ\ kitten \ər\ further \a\ ash \ā\ ace
\ä\ mop, mar \au̇\ out \ch\ chin \e\ bet \ē\ easy
\g\ go \i\ hit \ī\ ice \j\ job \ŋ\ sing \ō\ go
\ȯ\ law \ȯi\ boy \th\ thin \t̲h̲\ the \ü\ loot \u̇\ foot
\y\ yet \zh\ vision *see also* Guide to Pronunciation

**com·mit·ment** \kə-'mit-mənt\ *noun* (1621)
**1 a :** an act of committing to a charge or trust; as (1) **:** a consignment to a penal or mental institution (2) **:** an act of referring a matter to a legislative committee **b :** MITTIMUS
**2 a :** an agreement or pledge to do something in the future; *especially* **:** an engagement to assume a financial obligation at a future date **b :** something pledged **c :** the state or an instance of being obligated or emotionally impelled ⟨a *commitment* to a cause⟩

**com·mit·tal** \kə-'mi-t°l\ *noun* (1818)
**:** COMMITMENT, CONSIGNMENT

**com·mit·tee** \kə-'mi-tē, *sense 1 also* ,kä-mi-'tē\ *noun* (15th century)
**1** *archaic* **:** a person to whom a charge or trust is committed
**2 a :** a body of persons delegated to consider, investigate, take action on, or report on some matter; *especially* **:** a group of fellow legislators chosen by a legislative body to give consideration to legislative matters **b :** a self-constituted organization for the promotion of a common object

**com·mit·tee·man** \kə-'mi-tē-mən, -,man\ *noun* (1654)
**1 :** a member of a committee
**2 :** a party leader of a ward or precinct

**committee of the whole** (1775)
**:** the whole membership of a legislative house sitting as a committee and operating under informal rules

**com·mit·tee·wom·an** \-,wu̇-mən\ *noun* (1853)
**1 :** a woman who is a member of a committee
**2 :** a woman who is a party leader of a ward or precinct

**com·mix** \kə-'miks, kä-\ *verb* [back-formation from Middle English *comixt* blended, from Latin *commixtus*, past participle of *commiscēre* to mix together, from *com-* + *miscēre* to mix — more at MIX] (15th century)
*transitive verb*
**:** MINGLE, BLEND
*intransitive verb*
**:** to become mingled or blended

**com·mix·ture** \-chər\ *noun* [Latin *commixtura*, from *commixtus*] (1592)
**1 :** the act or process of mixing **:** the state of being mixed
**2 :** COMPOUND, MIXTURE

**com·mode** \kə-'mōd\ *noun* [French, from *commode*, adjective, suitable, convenient, from Latin *commodus*, from *com-* + *modus* measure — more at METE] (1688)
**1 :** a woman's ornate cap popular in the late 17th and early 18th centuries
**2 a :** a low chest of drawers **b :** a movable washstand with a cupboard underneath **c :** a boxlike structure holding a chamber pot under an open seat; *also* **:** CHAMBER POT **d :** TOILET 3b

**com·mod·i·fy** \kə-'mä-də-,fī\ *transitive verb* **-fied; -fy·ing** (1982)
**:** to turn (as an intrinsic value or a work of art) into a commodity
**— com·mod·i·fi·ca·tion** \-,mä-də-fə-'kā-shən\ *noun*

**com·mo·di·ous** \kə-'mō-dē-əs\ *adjective* [Middle English, useful, from Middle French *commodieux*, from Medieval Latin *commodiosus*, irregular from Latin *commodum* convenience, from neuter of *commodus*] (15th century)
**1 :** comfortably or conveniently spacious **:** ROOMY ⟨a *commodious* closet⟩
**2** *archaic* **:** HANDY, SERVICEABLE
**synonym** see SPACIOUS
**— com·mo·di·ous·ly** *adverb*
**— com·mo·di·ous·ness** *noun*

**com·mod·i·ty** \kə-'mä-də-tē\ *noun, plural*

**commode 1**

**-ties** [Middle English *commoditee*, from Middle French *commodité*, from Latin *commoditat-, commoditas*, from *commodus*] (15th century)
**1 :** an economic good: as **a :** a product of agriculture or mining **b :** an article of commerce especially when delivered for shipment ⟨*commodities* futures⟩ **c :** a mass-produced unspecialized product ⟨*commodity* chemicals⟩ ⟨*commodity* memory chips⟩
**2 a :** something useful or valued ⟨that valuable *commodity* patience⟩ **b :** CONVENIENCE, ADVANTAGE
**3** *obsolete* **:** QUANTITY, LOT

**com·mo·dore** \'kä-mə-,dōr, -,dȯr\ *noun* [probably modification of Dutch *commandeur* commander, from French, from Old French *comandeor*, from *comander* to command] (1695)
**1 a :** a captain in the navy in command of a squadron **b :** a commissioned officer in the navy formerly ranking above captain and below rear admiral and having an insignia of one star
**2 :** the ranking officer commanding a body of merchant ships
**3 :** the chief officer of a yacht club or boating association

¹**com·mon** \'kä-mən\ *adjective* [Middle English *commun*, from Old French, from Latin *communis* — more at MEAN] (13th century)
**1 a :** of or relating to a community at large **:** PUBLIC ⟨work for the *common* good⟩ **b :** known to the community ⟨*common* nuisances⟩
**2 a :** belonging to or shared by two or more individuals or things or by all members of a group ⟨a *common* friend⟩ ⟨buried in a *common* grave⟩ **b :** belonging equally to two or more mathematical entities ⟨triangles with a *common* base⟩ **c :** having two or more branches ⟨*common* carotid artery⟩
**3 a :** occurring or appearing frequently **:** FAMILIAR ⟨a *common* sight⟩ **b :** of the best known kind **c :** VERNACULAR 2 ⟨*common* names⟩
**4 a :** WIDESPREAD, GENERAL ⟨*common* knowledge⟩ **b :** characterized by a lack of privilege or special status ⟨*common* people⟩ **c :** just satisfying accustomed criteria **:** ELEMENTARY ⟨*common* decency⟩
**5 a :** falling below ordinary standards **:** SECOND-RATE **b :** lacking refinement **:** COARSE
**6 :** denoting nominal relations by a single linguistic form that in a more highly inflected language might be denoted by two or more different forms ⟨*common* gender⟩ ⟨*common* case⟩
**7 :** of, relating to, or being common stock ☆
**— com·mon·ly** *adverb*
**— com·mon·ness** \-mən-nəs\ *noun*

²**common** *noun* (14th century)
**1** *plural* **:** the common people
**2** *plural but singular in construction* **:** a dining hall
**3** *plural but singular or plural in construction, often capitalized* **a :** the political group or estate comprising the commoners **b :** the parliamentary representatives of the commoners **c :** HOUSE OF COMMONS
**4 :** the legal right of taking a profit in another's land in common with the owner or others
**5 :** a piece of land subject to common use: as **a :** undivided land used especially for pasture **b :** a public open area in a municipality
**6 a :** a religious service suitable for any of various festivals **b :** ORDINARY 2
**7 :** COMMON STOCK
**— in common :** shared together

**com·mon·age** \'kä-mə-nij\ *noun* (1649)
**1 :** community land
**2 :** COMMONALTY 1a(2)

**com·mon·al·i·ty** \,kä-mə-'na-lə-tē\ *noun, plural* **-ties** [Middle English *communalite* commonwealth, alteration of *communalte*] (1582)
**1 :** the common people

**2 a :** possession of common features or attributes **:** COMMONNESS **b :** a common feature or attribute

**com·mon·al·ty** \'kä-mə-n°l-tē\ *noun, plural* **-ties** [Middle English *communalte*, from Middle French *comunalté*, from *comunal* communal] (14th century)
**1 a** (1) **:** the common people (2) **:** the political estate formed by the common people **b :** a usage or practice common to members of a group
**2 :** a general group or body

**common carrier** *noun* (15th century)
**:** a business or agency that is available to the public for transportation of persons, goods, or messages

**common cattle grub** *noun* (1947)
**:** a cattle grub (*Hypoderma lineatum*) which is found throughout the U.S. and whose larva is particularly destructive to cattle

**common cold** *noun* (1786)
**:** an acute virus disease of the upper respiratory tract marked by inflammation of the mucous membranes of the nose, throat, eyes, and eustachian tubes and by a watery then purulent discharge

**common denominator** *noun* (1594)
**1 :** a common multiple of the denominators of a number of fractions
**2 :** a common trait or theme

**common difference** *noun* (circa 1891)
**:** the difference between two consecutive terms of an arithmetic progression

**common divisor** *noun* (circa 1847)
**:** a number or expression that divides two or more numbers or expressions without remainder — called also *common factor*

**com·mon·er** \'kä-mə-nər\ *noun* (14th century)
**1 a :** one of the common people **b :** one who is not of noble rank
**2 :** a student (as at Oxford) who pays for his own board

**Common Era** *noun* (circa 1889)
**:** CHRISTIAN ERA

**common fraction** *noun* (circa 1897)
**:** a fraction in which the numerator and denominator are both integers and are separated by a horizontal or slanted line — compare DECIMAL FRACTION

**common ground** *noun* (1874)
**:** a basis of mutual interest or agreement

**common–law** *adjective* (1848)
**1 :** of, relating to, or based on the common law
**2 :** relating to or based on a common-law marriage

**common law** *noun* (14th century)
**:** the body of law developed in England prima-

---

☆ **SYNONYMS**
**Common, ordinary, plain, familiar, popular, vulgar** mean generally met with and not in any way special, strange, or unusual. COMMON implies usual everyday quality or frequency of occurrence ⟨a *common* error⟩ ⟨lacked *common* honesty⟩ and may additionally suggest inferiority or coarseness ⟨*common* manners⟩. ORDINARY stresses conformance in quality or kind with the regular order of things ⟨an *ordinary* pleasant summer day⟩ ⟨a very *ordinary* sort of man⟩. PLAIN is likely to suggest homely simplicity ⟨*plain* hard-working people⟩. FAMILIAR stresses the fact of being generally known and easily recognized ⟨a *familiar* melody⟩. POPULAR applies to what is accepted by or prevalent among people in general sometimes in contrast to upper classes or special groups ⟨a writer of *popular* romances⟩. VULGAR, otherwise similar to POPULAR, is likely to carry derogatory connotations (as of inferiority or coarseness) ⟨souvenirs designed to appeal to the *vulgar* taste⟩.

rily from judicial decisions based on custom and precedent, unwritten in statute or code, and constituting the basis of the English legal system and of the system in all of the U.S. except Louisiana

**common-law marriage** *noun* (1900)
**1 :** a marriage recognized in some jurisdictions and based on the parties' agreement to consider themselves married and sometimes also on their cohabitation
**2 :** the cohabitation of a couple even when it does not constitute a legal marriage

**common logarithm** *noun* (circa 1903)
**:** a logarithm whose base is 10

**common market** *noun* (1952)
**:** an economic association (as of nations) formed to remove trade barriers among its members

**common measure** *noun* (1922)
**:** a meter consisting chiefly of iambic lines of 7 accents each arranged in rhymed pairs usually printed in 4-line stanzas — called also *common meter*

**common multiple** *noun* (circa 1890)
**:** a multiple of each of two or more numbers or expressions ⟨90 is a *common multiple* of 6 and 10⟩

**common noun** *noun* (circa 1864)
**:** a noun that may occur with limiting modifiers (as *a* or *an*, *some*, *every*, and *my*) and that designates any one of a class of beings or things

**common or garden** *adjective* (1892)
*chiefly British* **:** ORDINARY

**¹com·mon·place** \'kä-mən-ˌplās\ *noun* [translation of Latin *locus communis* widely applicable argument, translation of Greek *koinos topos*] (1561)
**1** *archaic* **:** a striking passage entered in a commonplace book
**2 a :** an obvious or trite comment **:** TRUISM **b** **:** something commonly found

**²commonplace** *adjective* (1609)
**:** commonly found **:** ORDINARY, UNREMARKABLE
— **com·mon·place·ness** *noun*

**commonplace book** *noun* (1578)
**:** a book of memorabilia

**common pleas** *noun plural* (1531)
**1** *singular in construction* **:** COURT OF COMMON PLEAS
**2 a :** actions over which the English crown did not exercise exclusive jurisdiction **b :** civil actions between English subjects

**common ratio** *noun* (1875)
**:** the ratio of each term of a geometric progression to the term preceding it

**common room** *noun* (1683)
**1 :** a lounge available to all members of a residential community
**2 :** a room in a college for faculty use

**common salt** *noun* (1676)
**:** SALT 1a

**common school** *noun* (circa 1657)
**:** a free public school

**common sense** *noun* (1535)
**1 :** the unreflective opinions of ordinary people
**2 :** sound and prudent but often unsophisticated judgment
**synonym** see SENSE
— **com·mon-sense** \'kä-mən-'sen(t)s\ *adjective*
— **com·mon-sen·si·ble** \-'sen(t)-sə-bəl\ *adjective*
— **com·mon-sen·si·cal** \-'sen(t)-si-kəl\ *adjective*
— **com·mon-sen·si·cal·ly** \-si-k(ə-)lē\ *adverb*

**common situs picketing** *noun* (1965)
**:** the picketing of an entire construction site by a trade union having a grievance with only a single subcontractor working there

**common stock** *noun* (1888)
**:** capital stock other than preferred stock

**common time** *noun* (1674)

**:** a musical meter marked by four beats per measure with the quarter note receiving a single beat

**common touch** *noun* (1944)
**:** the gift of appealing to or arousing the sympathetic interest of the common people

**com·mon·weal** \'kä-mən-ˌwēl\ *noun* (14th century)
**1** *archaic* **:** COMMONWEALTH
**2 :** the general welfare

**com·mon·wealth** \-ˌwelth *also* -ˌweltth\ *noun* (15th century)
**1** *archaic* **:** COMMONWEAL 2
**2 :** a nation, state, or other political unit: as **a** **:** one founded on law and united by compact or tacit agreement of the people for the common good **b :** one in which supreme authority is vested in the people **c :** REPUBLIC
**3** *capitalized* **a :** the English state from the death of Charles I in 1649 to the Restoration in 1660 **b :** PROTECTORATE 1b
**4 :** a state of the U.S. — used officially of Kentucky, Massachusetts, Pennsylvania, and Virginia
**5** *capitalized* **:** a federal union of constituent states — used officially of Australia
**6** *often capitalized* **:** an association of self-governing autonomous states more or less loosely associated in a common allegiance (as to the British crown)
**7** *often capitalized* **:** a political unit having local autonomy but voluntarily united with the U.S. — used officially of Puerto Rico and of the Northern Mariana Islands

**Commonwealth Day** *noun* (1959)
**:** May 24 observed in parts of the Commonwealth of Nations as the anniversary of Queen Victoria's birthday

**common year** *noun* (circa 1909)
**:** a calendar year containing no intercalary period

**com·mo·tion** \kə-'mō-shən\ *noun* [Middle English, from Middle French, from Latin *commotion-, commotio*, from *commovēre*] (15th century)
**1 :** a condition of civil unrest or insurrection
**2 :** steady or recurrent motion
**3 :** mental excitement or confusion
**4 a :** an agitated disturbance **:** TO-DO **b :** noisy confusion **:** AGITATION

**com·move** \kə-'müv, kä-\ *transitive verb*
**com·moved; com·mov·ing** [Middle English *commoeven*, from Middle French *commuev-*, present stem of *commovoir*, from Latin *commovēre*, from *com-* + *movēre* to move] (14th century)
**1 :** to move violently **:** AGITATE
**2 :** to rouse intense feeling in **:** excite to passion

**com·mu·nal** \kə-'myü-n°l, 'käm-yə-n°l\ *adjective* [French, from Late Latin *communalis*, from Latin *communis*] (1811)
**1 :** of or relating to one or more communes
**2 :** of or relating to a community
**3 a :** characterized by collective ownership and use of property **b :** participated in, shared, or used in common by members of a group or community
**4 :** of, relating to, or based on racial or cultural groups
— **com·mu·nal·ize** \kə-'myü-n°l-ˌīz, 'käm-yə-\ *transitive verb*
— **com·mu·nal·ly** *adverb*

**com·mu·nal·ism** \-n°l-ˌi-zəm\ *noun* (1871)
**1 :** social organization on a communal basis
**2 :** loyalty to a sociopolitical grouping based on religious or ethnic affiliation
— **com·mu·nal·ist** \-n°l-ist\ *noun or adjective*

**com·mu·nal·i·ty** \ˌkäm-yü-'na-lə-tē\ *noun, plural* **-ties** (1901)
**1 :** communal state or character
**2 :** a feeling of group solidarity

**com·mu·nard** \ˌkäm-yù-'när(d)\ *noun* [French] (1874)

**1** *capitalized* **:** one who supported or participated in the Commune of Paris in 1871
**2 :** a person who lives in a commune

**¹com·mune** \kə-'myün\ *verb* **com·muned; com·mun·ing** [Middle English, to converse, administer Communion, from Middle French *comunier* to converse, administer or receive Communion, from Late Latin *communicare*, from Latin] (15th century)
*transitive verb*
*obsolete* **:** TALK OVER, DISCUSS ⟨have more to commune —Shakespeare⟩
*intransitive verb*
**1 :** to receive Communion
**2 :** to communicate intimately ⟨*commune* with nature⟩

**²com·mune** \'käm-ˌyün; kə-'myün, kä-\ *noun* [French, alteration of Middle French *comugne*, from Medieval Latin *communia*, from Latin, neuter plural of *communis*] (1673)
**1 :** the smallest administrative district of many countries especially in Europe
**2 :** COMMONALTY 1a
**3 :** COMMUNITY: as **a :** a medieval usually municipal corporation **b** (1) **:** MIR (2) **:** an often rural community organized on a communal basis

**com·mu·ni·ca·ble** \kə-'myü-ni-kə-bəl\ *adjective* (1534)
**1 :** capable of being communicated **:** TRANSMITTABLE ⟨*communicable* disease⟩
**2 :** COMMUNICATIVE
— **com·mu·ni·ca·bil·i·ty** \-ˌmyü-ni-kə-'bi-lə-tē\ *noun*
— **com·mu·ni·ca·ble·ness** \-'myü-ni-kə-bəl-nəs\ *noun*
— **com·mu·ni·ca·bly** \-blē\ *adverb*

**com·mu·ni·cant** \-'myü-ni-kənt\ *noun* (1552)
**1 :** a church member entitled to receive Communion; *broadly* **:** a member of a fellowship
**2 :** one that communicates; *specifically* **:** INFORMANT
— **communicant** *adjective*

**com·mu·ni·cate** \kə-'myü-nə-ˌkāt\ *verb* **-cat·ed; -cat·ing** [Latin *communicatus*, past participle of *communicare* to impart, participate, from *communis* common — more at MEAN] (1526)
*transitive verb*
**1** *archaic* **:** SHARE
**2 a :** to convey knowledge of or information about **:** make known ⟨*communicate* a story⟩ **b** **:** to reveal by clear signs ⟨his fear *communicated* itself to his friends⟩
**3 :** to cause to pass from one to another ⟨some diseases are easily *communicated*⟩
*intransitive verb*
**1 :** to receive Communion
**2 :** to transmit information, thought, or feeling so that it is satisfactorily received or understood
**3 :** to open into each other **:** CONNECT ⟨the rooms *communicate*⟩
— **com·mu·ni·ca·tee** \-ˌmyü-ni-kə-'tē\ *noun*
— **com·mu·ni·ca·tor** \-'myü-nə-ˌkā-tər\ *noun*

**com·mu·ni·ca·tion** \kə-ˌmyü-nə-'kā-shən\ *noun* (14th century)
**1 :** an act or instance of transmitting
**2 a :** information communicated **b :** a verbal or written message
**3 a :** a process by which information is exchanged between individuals through a common system of symbols, signs, or behavior ⟨the function of pheromones in insect *communication*⟩; *also* **:** exchange of information **b** **:** personal rapport ⟨a lack of *communication* between old and young persons⟩
**4** *plural* **a :** a system (as of telephones) for

communicating **b :** a system of routes for moving troops, supplies, and vehicles **c :** personnel engaged in communicating
**5** *plural but singular or plural in construction* **a :** a technique for expressing ideas effectively (as in speech) **b :** the technology of the transmission of information (as by print or telecommunication)
— **com·mu·ni·ca·tion·al** \-shnəl, -shən°l\ *adjective*
**com·mu·ni·ca·tive** \kə-'myü-nə-ˌkā-tiv, -ni-kə-tiv\ *adjective* (14th century)
**1 :** tending to communicate : TALKATIVE
**2 :** of or relating to communication
— **com·mu·ni·ca·tive·ly** *adverb*
— **com·mu·ni·ca·tive·ness** *noun*
**com·mu·ni·ca·to·ry** \kə-'myü-ni-kə-ˌtōr-ē, -ˌtȯr-\ *adjective* (1646)
**1 :** designed to communicate information ⟨*communicatory* letters⟩
**2 :** COMMUNICATIVE 2
**com·mu·nion** \kə-'myü-nyən\ *noun* [Middle English, from Latin *communion-, communio* mutual participation, from *communis*] (14th century)
**1 :** an act or instance of sharing
**2 a** *capitalized* **:** a Christian sacrament in which consecrated bread and wine are consumed as memorials of Christ's death or as symbols for the realization of a spiritual union between Christ and communicant or as the body and blood of Christ **b :** the act of receiving Communion **c** *capitalized* **:** the part of a Communion service in which the sacrament is received
**3 :** intimate fellowship or rapport : COMMUNICATION
**4 :** a body of Christians having a common faith and discipline ⟨the Anglican *communion*⟩
**com·mu·ni·qué** \kə-'myü-nə-ˌkā, -ˌmyü-nə-'\ *noun* [French, from past participle of *communiquer* to communicate, from Latin *communicare*] (1852)
**:** BULLETIN 1
**com·mu·nise** *British variant of* COMMUNIZE
**com·mu·nism** \'käm-yə-ˌni-zəm\ *noun* [French *communisme*, from *commun* common] (1840)
**1 a :** a theory advocating elimination of private property **b :** a system in which goods are owned in common and are available to all as needed
**2** *capitalized* **a :** a doctrine based on revolutionary Marxian socialism and Marxism-Leninism that was the official ideology of the U.S.S.R. **b :** a totalitarian system of government in which a single authoritarian party controls state-owned means of production **c :** a final stage of society in Marxist theory in which the state has withered away and economic goods are distributed equitably **d :** communist systems collectively
**com·mu·nist** \'käm-yə-nist\ *noun* (1840)
**1 :** an adherent or advocate of communism
**2** *capitalized* **:** COMMUNARD
**3 a** *capitalized* **:** a member of a Communist party or movement **b** *often capitalized* **:** an adherent or advocate of a Communist government, party, or movement
**4** *often capitalized* **:** one held to engage in leftwing, subversive, or revolutionary activities
— **communist** *adjective, often capitalized*
— **com·mu·nis·tic** \ˌkäm-yə-'nis-tik\ *adjective, often capitalized*
— **com·mu·nis·ti·cal·ly** \-ti-k(ə-)lē\ *adverb*
**com·mu·ni·tar·i·an** \kə-ˌmyü-nə-'ter-ē-ən\ *adjective* (circa 1909)
**:** of or relating to social organization in small cooperative partially collectivist communities
— **communitarian** *noun*
— **com·mu·ni·tar·i·an·ism** \-ē-ə-ˌni-zəm\ *noun*
**com·mu·ni·ty** \kə-'myü-nə-tē\ *noun, plural* **-ties** *often attributive* [Middle English *comunete*, from Middle French *comuneté*, from Lat-

in *communitat-, communitas*, from *communis*] (14th century)
**1 :** a unified body of individuals: as **a :** STATE, COMMONWEALTH **b :** the people with common interests living in a particular area; *broadly* **:** the area itself ⟨the problems of a large *community*⟩ **c :** an interacting population of various kinds of individuals (as species) in a common location **d :** a group of people with a common characteristic or interest living together within a larger society ⟨a *community* of retired persons⟩ **e :** a group linked by a common policy **f :** a body of persons or nations having a common history or common social, economic, and political interests ⟨the international *community*⟩ **g :** a body of persons of common and especially professional interests scattered through a larger society ⟨the academic *community*⟩
**2 :** society at large
**3 a :** joint ownership or participation ⟨*community* of goods⟩ **b :** common character : LIKENESS ⟨*community* of interests⟩ **c :** social activity : FELLOWSHIP **d :** a social state or condition
**community antenna television** *noun* (1953)
**:** CABLE TELEVISION
**community center** *noun* (1915)
**:** a building or group of buildings for a community's educational and recreational activities
**community chest** *noun* (1919)
**:** a general fund accumulated from individual subscriptions to defray demands on a community for charity and social welfare
**community college** *noun* (1948)
**:** a 2-year government-supported college that offers an associate degree
**community property** *noun* (circa 1925)
**:** property held jointly by husband and wife
**com·mu·nize** \'käm-yə-ˌnīz\ *transitive verb* **-nized; -niz·ing** [back-formation from *communization*] (1888)
**1 a :** to make common **b :** to make into state-owned property
**2 :** to subject to Communist principles of organization
— **com·mu·ni·za·tion** \ˌkäm-yə-nə-'zā-shən\ *noun*
**com·mu·tate** \'käm-yə-ˌtāt\ *transitive verb* **-tat·ed; -tat·ing** [back-formation from *commutation*] (1893)
**:** to reverse every other half cycle of (an alternating current) so as to form a unidirectional current
**com·mu·ta·tion** \ˌkäm-yə-'tā-shən\ *noun* [Middle English, from Middle French, from Latin *commutation-, commutatio*, from *commutare*] (15th century)
**1 :** EXCHANGE, TRADE
**2 :** REPLACEMENT; *specifically* **:** a substitution of one form of payment or charge for another
**3 :** a change of a legal penalty or punishment to a lesser one
**4 :** an act or process of commuting
**5 :** the action of commutating
**commutation ticket** *noun* (1848)
**:** a transportation ticket sold for a fixed number of trips over the same route during a limited period
**com·mu·ta·tive** \kə-'myü-tə-tiv, 'käm-yə-ˌtā-tiv\ *adjective* (1612)
**1 :** of, relating to, or showing commutation
**2 :** of, relating to, having, or being the property that a given mathematical operation and set have when the result obtained using any two elements of the set with the operation does not differ with the order in which the elements are used ⟨a *commutative* group⟩ ⟨addition of the positive integers is *commutative*⟩
**com·mu·ta·tiv·i·ty** \kə-ˌmyü-tə-'ti-və-tē, ˌkäm-yə-tə-\ *noun* (1929)
**:** the property of being commutative ⟨the *commutativity* of a mathematical operation⟩
**com·mu·ta·tor** \'käm-yə-ˌtā-tər\ *noun* (1880)
**1 :** a series of bars or segments so connected

to armature coils of a generator or motor that rotation of the armature will in conjunction with fixed brushes result in unidirectional current output in the case of a generator and in the reversal of the current into the coils in the case of a motor
**2 :** an element of a mathematical group that when used to multiply the product of two given elements either on the right side or on the left side but not necessarily on both sides yields the product of the two given elements in reverse order
¹**com·mute** \kə-'myüt\ *verb* **com·mut·ed; com·mut·ing** [Latin *commutare* to change, exchange, from *com-* + *mutare* to change — more at MUTABLE] (15th century)
*transitive verb*
**1 a :** CHANGE, ALTER **b :** to give in exchange for another : EXCHANGE
**2 :** to convert (as a payment) into another form
**3 :** to exchange (a penalty) for another less severe
**4 :** COMMUTATE
*intransitive verb*
**1 :** MAKE UP, COMPENSATE
**2 :** to pay in gross
**3 :** to travel back and forth regularly (as between a suburb and a city)
**4 :** to yield the same mathematical result regardless of order — used of two elements undergoing an operation or of two operations on elements
— **com·mut·able** \-'myü-tə-bəl\ *adjective*
²**commute** *noun* (1954)
**1 :** an act or an instance of commuting
**2 :** the distance covered in commuting
**com·mut·er** \kə-'myü-tər\ *noun* (circa 1859)
**1 :** a person who commutes (as between a suburb and a city)
**2 :** a small airline that carries passengers relatively short distances on a regular schedule
**co·mo·no·mer** \(ˌ)kō-'mä-nə-mər, -'mō-\ *noun* [*co-* + *monomer*] (1945)
**:** one of the constituents of a copolymer
¹**comp** \'kämp\ *noun* [short for *complimentary*] (1887)
**:** a complimentary ticket; *broadly* **:** something provided free of charge
²**comp** \'kȯmp, 'kämp\ *intransitive verb* [short for *accompany*] (1949)
**:** to punctuate and support a jazz solo with irregularly spaced chords
¹**com·pact** \kəm-'pakt, käm-', 'käm-ˌ\ *adjective* [Middle English, firmly put together, from Latin *compactus*, from past participle of *compingere* to put together, from *com-* + *pangere* to fasten — more at PACT] (14th century)
**1 :** predominantly formed or filled : COMPOSED, MADE
**2 a :** having a dense structure or parts or units closely packed or joined ⟨a *compact* woolen⟩ ⟨*compact* bone⟩ **b :** not diffuse or verbose ⟨a *compact* statement⟩ **c :** occupying a small volume by reason of efficient use of space ⟨a *compact* camera⟩ ⟨a *compact* formation of troops⟩ **d :** short-bodied, solid, and without excess flesh
**3 :** being a topological space and especially a metric space with the property that for any collection of open sets which contains it there is a subset of the collection with a finite number of elements which also contains it
— **com·pact·ly** \-'pak(t)-lē, -ˌpak(t)-\ *adverb*
— **com·pact·ness** \-'pak(t)-nəs, -ˌpak(t)-\ *noun*
²**compact** (15th century)
*transitive verb*
**1 :** to make up by connecting or combining : COMPOSE
**2 a :** to knit or draw together : COMBINE **b :** to press together : COMPRESS
*intransitive verb*
**:** to become compacted

— **com·pact·ible** \-'pak-tə-bəl, -,pak-\ *adjective*

— **com·pac·tor** *also* **com·pact·er** \-'pak-tər, -,pak-\ *noun*

**³com·pact** \'käm-,pakt\ *noun* (1601)
: something that is compact or compacted: **a** : a small cosmetic case (as for compressed powder) **b** : an automobile smaller than an intermediate but larger than a subcompact

**⁴com·pact** \'käm-,pakt\ *noun* [Latin *compactum*, from neuter of *compactus*, past participle of *compacisci* to make an agreement, from *com-* + *pacisci* to contract — more at PACT] (1591)
: an agreement or covenant between two or more parties

**com·pact disc** \'käm-,pakt-\ *noun* (1979)
: a small plastic optical disc usually containing recorded music or computer data

**com·pac·tion** \kəm-'pak-shən, käm-\ *noun* (14th century)
: the act or process of compacting : the state of being compacted

**¹com·pan·ion** \kəm-'pan-yən\ *noun* [Middle English *compainoun*, from Old French *compagnon*, from Late Latin *companion-*, *companio*, from Latin *com-* + *panis* bread, food — more at FOOD] (13th century)
**1** : one that accompanies another : COMRADE, ASSOCIATE; *also* : one that keeps company with another
**2** *obsolete* : RASCAL
**3 a** : one that is closely connected with something similar **b** : one employed to live with and serve another ◆

**²companion** (1622)
*transitive verb*
: ACCOMPANY
*intransitive verb*
: to keep company

**³companion** *noun* [by folk etymology from Dutch *kampanje* poop deck] (1762)
**1** : a hood covering at the top of a companionway
**2** : COMPANIONWAY

**com·pan·ion·able** \kəm-'pan-yə-nə-bəl\ *adjective* (14th century)
: marked by, conducive to, or suggestive of companionship : SOCIABLE
— **com·pan·ion·abil·i·ty** \-,pan-yə-nə-'bi-lə-tē\ *noun*
— **com·pan·ion·able·ness** *noun*
— **com·pan·ion·ably** \-'pan-yə-nə-blē\ *adverb*

**com·pan·ion·ate** \kəm-'pan-yə-nət\ *adjective* (1926)
: relating to or having the manner of companions; *specifically* : harmoniously or suitably accompanying

**companion cell** *noun* (1887)
: a living nucleated cell that is closely associated in origin, position, and probably function with a cell making up part of a sieve tube of a vascular plant

**companion piece** *noun* (1844)
: a work (as of literature) that is associated with and complements another

**com·pan·ion·ship** \kəm-'pan-yən-,ship\ *noun* (1548)
: the fellowship existing among companions : COMPANY

**com·pan·ion·way** \-yən-,wā\ *noun* [³companion] (1840)
: a ship's stairway from one deck to another

**¹com·pa·ny** \'kəmp-nē, 'kəm-pə-\ *noun*, plural **-nies** *often attributive* [Middle English *companie*, from Old French *compagnie*, from *compain* companion, from Late Latin *companio*] (13th century)
**1 a** : association with another : FELLOWSHIP ⟨enjoy a person's *company*⟩ **b** : COMPANIONS, ASSOCIATES ⟨know a person by the *company* she keeps⟩ **c** : VISITORS, GUESTS ⟨having *company* for dinner⟩

**2 a** : a group of persons or things ⟨a *company* of horsemen⟩ **b** : a body of soldiers; *especially* : a unit (as of infantry) consisting usually of a headquarters and two or more platoons **c** : an organization of performing artists **d** : the officers and crew of a ship **e** : a fire-fighting unit
**3 a** : a chartered commercial organization or medieval trade guild **b** : an association of persons for carrying on a commercial or industrial enterprise **c** : those members of a partnership firm whose names do not appear in the firm name ⟨John Doe and *Company*⟩

**²company** *verb* **-nied; -ny·ing** (14th century)
*transitive verb*
: ACCOMPANY ⟨may . . . fair winds *company* your safe return —John Masefield⟩
*intransitive verb*
: ASSOCIATE

**company man** *noun* (circa 1921)
: a worker who acquiesces in company policy without complaint

**company officer** *noun* (1844)
: a commissioned officer in the army, air force, or marine corps of the rank of captain, first lieutenant, or second lieutenant — called also *company grade officer*; compare FIELD OFFICER, GENERAL OFFICER

**company town** *noun* (1927)
: a community that is dependent on one firm for all or most of the necessary services or functions of town life (as employment, housing, and stores)

**company union** *noun* (1917)
: an unaffiliated labor union of the employees of a single firm; *especially* : one dominated by the employer

**com·pa·ra·bil·i·ty** \,käm-p(ə-)rə-'bi-lə-tē, ÷kəm-,par-ə-\ *noun* (1843)
: the quality or state of being comparable

**com·pa·ra·ble** \'käm-p(ə-)rə-bəl, ÷kəm-'par-ə-bəl\ *adjective* (15th century)
**1** : capable of or suitable for comparison
**2** : SIMILAR, LIKE ⟨fabrics of *comparable* quality⟩
— **com·pa·ra·ble·ness** *noun*
— **com·pa·ra·bly** \-blē\ *adverb*

**comparable worth** *noun* (1983)
: the concept that women and men should receive equal pay for jobs calling for comparable skill and responsibility

**com·pa·ra·tist** \kəm-'par-ə-tist\ *noun* [*comparative* + *-ist*] (1933)
: one that uses a comparative method (as in the study of literature)

**¹com·par·a·tive** \kəm-'par-ə-tiv\ *adjective* (15th century)
**1** : of, relating to, or constituting the degree of comparison in a language that denotes increase in the quality, quantity, or relation expressed by an adjective or adverb
**2** : considered as if in comparison to something else as a standard not quite attained : RELATIVE ⟨a *comparative* stranger⟩
**3** : characterized by systematic comparison especially of likenesses and dissimilarities ⟨*comparative* anatomy⟩
— **com·par·a·tive·ly** *adverb*
— **com·par·a·tive·ness** *noun*

**²comparative** *noun* (15th century)
**1 a** : one that compares with another especially on equal footing : RIVAL **b** : one that makes witty or mocking comparisons
**2** : the comparative degree or form in a language

**com·par·a·tiv·ist** \kəm-'par-ə-ti-vist\ *noun* (1887)
: COMPARATIST

**com·par·a·tor** \kəm-'par-ə-tər\ *noun* (1883)
: a device for comparing something with a similar thing or with a standard measure

**¹com·pare** \kəm-'par, -'per\ *verb* **compared; com·par·ing** [Middle English, from Middle French *comparer*, from Latin *comparare* to couple, compare, from *compara* like, from *com-* + *par* equal] (14th century)

*transitive verb*
**1** : to represent as similar : LIKEN ⟨shall I *compare* thee to a summer's day? —Shakespeare⟩
**2 a** : to examine the character or qualities of especially in order to discover resemblances or differences ⟨*compare* your responses with the answers⟩ **b** : to view in relation to ⟨tall *compared* to me⟩
**3** : to inflect or modify (an adjective or adverb) according to the degrees of comparison
*intransitive verb*
**1** : to bear being compared
**2** : to make comparisons
**3** : to be equal or alike ⟨nothing *compares* to you⟩ ☆ ■

**²compare** *noun* (1589)
: the possibility of comparing ⟨beauty beyond *compare*⟩; *also* : something with which to be compared ⟨a city without *compare*⟩

---

☆ **SYNONYMS**
**Compare, contrast, collate** mean to set side by side in order to show differences and likenesses. COMPARE implies an aim of showing relative values or excellences by bringing out characteristic qualities whether similar or divergent ⟨*compared* the convention facilities of the two cities⟩. CONTRAST implies an emphasis on differences ⟨*contrasted* the computerized system with the old filing cards⟩. COLLATE implies minute and critical inspection in order to note points of agreement or divergence ⟨data from districts around the country will be *collated*⟩.

---

☐ **USAGE**
**compare**   A great many authors of handbooks and other commentators are eager to point out the difference between *compare to* and *compare with*. Their basic rule is easy enough: use *to* with *transitive verb* sense 1 and use *with* with *transitive verb* sense 2a. But in the less tidy world of actual usage these rules state only broad tendencies: more writers use *to* than *with* for sense 1; somewhat more writers use *with* than *to* for sense 2a. When *compared* is used as a detached participle, *to* and *with* are used with about equal frequency ⟨you always seemed so firm to me *compared* to myself —E. B. White⟩ ⟨*compared* with the fables, my own work is insignificant —Marianne Moore⟩. Sense 2b is unnoticed by the commentators, who probably include it within 2a; it takes either *to* or *with*. Intransitive senses use both prepositions.

---

◇ **WORD HISTORY**
**companion**   *Companion* descends ultimately from Late Latin *companio*, formed from Latin *com-* "with" and *panis* "bread," and so literally means "a person with whom one shares bread, a messmate." The word in all likelihood arose in the soldier's Latin of the declining Roman Empire and is a loan translation from a word in an early Germanic language such as Gothic *gahlaiba*, formed from *ga-* "with" and *hlaifs* "bread." The Roman army of that time recruited many troops from the Goths and other Germanic peoples who lived on the borders of the Empire. In the 4th century A.D. translation of the Bible into Gothic, *gahlaifa* renders Greek *synstratiōtēs*, literally, "fellow-soldier."

---

\ə\ abut \ᵊ\ kitten \ər\ further \a\ ash \ā\ ace
\ä\ mop, mar \aú\ out \ch\ chin \e\ bet \ē\ easy
\g\ go \i\ hit \ī\ ice \j\ job \ŋ\ sing \ō\ go
\ò\ law \òi\ boy \th\ thin \t͟h\ the \ü\ loot \ú\ foot
\y\ yet \zh\ vision   *see also* Guide to Pronunciation

**com·par·i·son** \kəm-'par-ə-sən\ *noun* [Middle English, from Middle French *comparaison*, from Latin *comparation-*, *comparatio*, from *comparare*] (14th century)
**1** : the act or process of comparing: as **a** : the representing of one thing or person as similar to or like another **b** : an examination of two or more items to establish similarities and dissimilarities
**2** : identity of features : SIMILARITY ⟨several points of *comparison* between the two⟩
**3** : the modification of an adjective or adverb to denote different levels of quality, quantity, or relation

**comparison shop** *intransitive verb* (1970)
: to compare prices (as of competing brands) in order to find the best value

¹**com·part·ment** \kəm-'pärt-mənt\ *noun* [Middle French *compartiment*, from Italian *compartimento*, from *compartire* to mark out in parts, from Late Latin *compartiri* to share out, from Latin *com-* + *partiri* to share, from *part-*, *pars* part, share] (circa 1578)
**1** : a separate division or section
**2** : one of the parts into which an enclosed space is divided
— **com·part·men·tal** \kəm-,pärt-'men-t³l, ,käm-\ *adjective*

²**com·part·ment** \-,ment, -mənt\ *transitive verb* (1918)
: COMPARTMENTALIZE

**com·part·men·tal·ise** *British variant of* COMPARTMENTALIZE

**com·part·men·tal·ize** \kəm-,pärt-'men-t³l-,īz, ,käm-\ *transitive verb* **-ized; -iz·ing** (1925)
: to separate into isolated compartments or categories
— **com·part·men·tal·i·za·tion** \-,men-t³l-ə-'zā-shən\ *noun*

**com·part·men·ta·tion** \kəm-,pärt-mən-'tā-shən, ,men-\ *noun* (1926)
: division into separate sections or units

¹**com·pass** \'kəm-pəs *also* 'käm-\ *transitive verb* [Middle English, from Old French *compasser* to measure, from (assumed) Vulgar Latin *compassare* to pace off, from Latin *com-* + *passus* pace] (14th century)
**1** : to devise or contrive often with craft or skill
**2** : ENCOMPASS
**3 a** : BRING ABOUT, ACHIEVE **b** : to get into one's possession or power : OBTAIN
**4** : COMPREHEND
— **com·pass·able** \-pə-sə-bəl\ *adjective*

²**compass** *noun* (14th century)
**1 a** : BOUNDARY, CIRCUMFERENCE ⟨within the *compass* of the city walls⟩ **b** : a circumscribed space ⟨within the narrow *compass* of 21 pages —V. L. Parrington⟩ **c** : RANGE, SCOPE ⟨the *compass* of a voice⟩
**2** : a curved or roundabout course ⟨a *compass* of seven days' journey —2 Kings 3:9 (Authorized Version)⟩
**3 a** : a device for determining directions by means of a magnetic needle or group of needles turning freely on a pivot and pointing to the magnetic north **b** : any of various nonmagnetic devices that indicate direction **c** : an instrument for describing circles or transferring measurements that consists of two pointed branches joined at the top by a pivot — usually used in plural; called also *pair of compasses*
**4** : DIRECTION 6c
**synonym** see RANGE

compass 3a

³**compass** *adjective* (1523)
: forming a curve : CURVED ⟨a *compass* timber⟩

**compass card** *noun* (circa 1859)
: the circular card attached to the needles of a mariner's compass on which are marked the

32 points of the compass and the 360° of the circle

**com·pas·sion** \kəm-'pa-shən\ *noun* [Middle English, from Middle French or Late Latin; Middle French, from Late Latin *compassion-*, *compassio*, from *compati* to sympathize, from Latin *com-* + *pati* to bear, suffer — more at PATIENT] (14th century)
: sympathetic consciousness of others' distress together with a desire to alleviate it
**synonym** see PITY
— **com·pas·sion·less** \-ləs\ *adjective*

¹**com·pas·sion·ate** \kəm-'pa-sh(ə-)nət\ *adjective* (1587)
**1** : having or showing compassion : SYMPATHETIC
**2** : granted because of unusual distressing circumstances affecting an individual — used of some military privileges (as leave)
— **com·pas·sion·ate·ly** *adverb*
— **com·pas·sion·ate·ness** *noun*

²**com·pas·sion·ate** \-'pa-shə-,nāt\ *transitive verb* **-at·ed; -at·ing** (1592)
: PITY

**compass plant** *noun* (1848)
: a coarse yellow-flowered composite plant (*Silphium laciniatum*) with large pinnatifid leaves that occurs in prairies and along roadsides and railroad tracks of the central U.S.

**compass rose** *noun* (circa 1891)
: a circle graduated to degrees or quarters and printed on a chart to show direction

**com·pat·i·ble** \kəm-'pa-tə-bəl\ *adjective* [Middle English, from Middle French, from Medieval Latin *compatibilis*, literally, sympathetic, from Late Latin *compati*] (15th century)
**1** : capable of existing together in harmony ⟨*compatible* theories⟩
**2** : capable of cross-fertilizing freely or uniting vegetatively
**3** : capable of forming a homogeneous mixture that neither separates nor is altered by chemical interaction
**4** : capable of being used in transfusion or grafting without immunological reaction (as agglutination or tissue rejection)
**5** : designed to work with another device or system without modification; *especially* : being a computer designed to operate in the same manner and use the same software as another computer
— **com·pat·i·bil·i·ty** \-,pa-tə-'bi-lə-tē\ *noun*
— **compatible** *noun*
— **com·pat·i·ble·ness** \-'pa-tə-bəl-nəs\ *noun*
— **com·pat·i·bly** \-blē\ *adverb*

**com·pa·tri·ot** \kəm-'pā-trē-ət, käm-, -trē-,ät, *chiefly British* -'pa-\ *noun* [French *compatriote*, from Late Latin *compatriota*, from Latin *com-* + Late Latin *patriota* fellow countryman — more at PATRIOT] (1611)
**1** : a person born, residing, or holding citizenship in the same country as another
**2** : COMPEER, COLLEAGUE
— **com·pa·tri·ot·ic** \kəm-,pā-trē-'ä-tik, ,käm-, *chiefly British* -,pa-\ *adjective*

¹**com·peer** \'käm-,pir, käm-', kəm-'\ *noun* [Middle English, from Old French *compere*, literally, godfather, from Medieval Latin *compater*, from Latin *com-* + *pater* father — more at FATHER] (13th century)
: COMPANION

²**compeer** *noun* [Middle English *compere*, from Old French, from Latin *compar*,

**compass card**

from *compar*, adjective, like — more at COMPARE] (15th century)
: EQUAL, PEER
— **compeer** *transitive verb*, *obsolete*

**com·pel** \kəm-'pel\ *transitive verb* **com·pelled; com·pel·ling** [Middle English *compellen*, from Middle French *compellir*, from Latin *compellere*, from *com-* + *pellere* to drive — more at FELT] (14th century)
**1** : to drive or urge forcefully or irresistibly
**2** : to cause to do or occur by overwhelming pressure
**3** *archaic* : to drive together
**synonym** see FORCE
— **com·pel·la·ble** \-'pe-lə-bəl\ *adjective*

**com·pel·la·tion** \,käm-pə-'lā-shən, -,pe-\ *noun* [Latin *compellation-*, *compellatio*, from *compellare* to address, from *com-* + *-pellare* (as in *appellare* to accost, appeal to)] (1603)
**1** : an act or action of addressing someone
**2** : APPELLATION 1

**com·pel·ling** \kəm-'pe-liŋ\ *adjective* (1606)
: that compels: as **a** : FORCEFUL ⟨a *compelling* personality⟩ **b** : demanding attention ⟨for *compelling* reasons⟩ **c** : CONVINCING ⟨no *compelling* evidence⟩
— **com·pel·ling·ly** *adverb*

**com·pend** \'käm-,pend\ *noun* [Medieval Latin *compendium*] (1596)
: COMPENDIUM

**com·pen·di·ous** \kəm-'pen-dē-əs\ *adjective* (14th century)
: marked by brief expression of a comprehensive matter : concise and comprehensive; *also* : COMPREHENSIVE ▪
**synonym** see CONCISE
— **com·pen·di·ous·ly** *adverb*
— **com·pen·di·ous·ness** *noun*

**com·pen·di·um** \kəm-'pen-dē-əm\ *noun, plural* **-di·ums** *or* **-dia** \-dē-ə\ [Medieval Latin, from Latin, saving, shortcut, from *compendere* to weigh together, from *com-* + *pendere* to weigh — more at PENDANT] (1589)
**1** : a brief summary of a larger work or of a field of knowledge : ABSTRACT
**2 a** : a list of a number of items **b** : COLLECTION, COMPILATION

**com·pen·sa·ble** \kəm-'pen(t)-sə-bəl\ *adjective* (1661)

---

☐ USAGE
**compendious** Noah Webster's *A Compendious Dictionary of the English Language* defines 37,000 words in 355 pages; he intended its vocabulary to be larger than that of Samuel Johnson's large two-volume dictionary. Webster's *compendious* meant "comprehensive and concise." And "comprehensive and concise" is how most dictionaries have since defined the word. This sense is still in use ⟨gives a *compendious* summary in an appendix —S. Schoenbaum⟩ ⟨newest effort to reap from the *compendious* "news magazine" format —George V. Higgins⟩. But users of the language have never been slaves to dictionaries. Some writers have stressed the notion of conciseness ⟨shall I teach you a *compendious* method of courtship, that will give you no trouble whatever? —Thomas Love Peacock⟩. But often the reader cannot tell if conciseness is intended along with comprehensiveness ⟨a *compendious* volume of thousands of articles about meter —Dennis Taylor⟩ and so a use stressing comprehensiveness has developed ⟨it is doubtful that even the most *compendious* traditional or teaching grammar notes such simple facts —Noam Chomsky⟩ ⟨what must be one of the most *compendious* collections of jackknives in the known universe —Jay Jacobs⟩. Both the original and the merely "comprehensive" senses are in current reputable use.

: that is to be or can be compensated ⟨a *compensable* job-related injury⟩
— **com·pen·sa·bil·i·ty** \kəm-ˌpen(t)-sə-'bi-lə-tē, ˌkäm-\ *noun*
**com·pen·sate** \'käm-pən-ˌsāt, -ˌpen-\ *verb* **-sat·ed; -sat·ing** [Latin *compensatus*, past participle of *compensare*, frequentative of *compendere*] (1646)
*transitive verb*
**1** : to be equivalent to : COUNTERBALANCE
**2** : to make an appropriate and usually counterbalancing payment to
**3 a** : to provide with means of counteracting variation **b** : to neutralize the effect of (variations)
*intransitive verb*
**1** : to supply an equivalent — used with *for*
**2** : to offset an error, defect, or undesired effect
**3** : to undergo or engage in psychological or physiological compensation
**synonym** see PAY
— **com·pen·sa·tive** \'käm-pən-ˌsā-tiv, -ˌpen-; kəm-'pen(t)-sə-\ *adjective*
— **com·pen·sa·tor** \'käm-pən-ˌsā-tər, -ˌpen-\ *noun*
— **com·pen·sa·to·ry** \kəm-'pen(t)-sə-ˌtōr-ē, -ˌtȯr-\ *adjective*
**com·pen·sa·tion** \ˌkäm-pən-'sā-shən, -ˌpen-\ *noun* (14th century)
**1 a** : the act of compensating : the state of being compensated **b** : correction of an organic defect or loss by hypertrophy or by increased functioning of another organ or unimpaired parts of the same organ **c** : a psychological mechanism by which feelings of inferiority, frustration, or failure in one field are counterbalanced by achievement in another
**2 a** (1) : something that constitutes an equivalent or recompense ⟨age has its *compensations*⟩ (2) : payment to unemployed or injured workers or their dependents **b** : PAYMENT, REMUNERATION
— **com·pen·sa·tion·al** \-shnəl, -shə-n°l\ *adjective*
**compensatory education** *noun* (1965)
: educational programs intended to make up for experiences (as cultural) lacked by disadvantaged children
¹**com·pere** *or* **com·père** \'käm-ˌper\ *noun* [French *compère*, literally, godfather — more at COMPEER] (1914)
*chiefly British* : the master of ceremonies of an entertainment (as a television program)
²**compere** *or* **compère** *verb* **com·pered** *or* **com·pèred; com·per·ing** *or* **com·pèr·ing** (1933)
*transitive verb*
*chiefly British* : to act as compere for
*intransitive verb*
*chiefly British* : to act as a compere
**com·pete** \kəm-'pēt\ *intransitive verb* **com·pet·ed; com·pet·ing** [Late Latin *competere* to seek together, from Latin, to come together, agree, be suitable, from *com-* + *petere* to go to, seek — more at FEATHER] (1620)
: to strive consciously or unconsciously for an objective (as position, profit, or a prize) : be in a state of rivalry
**com·pe·tence** \'käm-pə-tən(t)s\ *noun* (1632)
**1** : a sufficiency of means for the necessities and conveniences of life ⟨provided his family with a comfortable *competence* —Rex Ingamells⟩
**2** : the quality or state of being competent: as **a** : the properties of an embryonic field that enable it to respond in a characteristic manner to an organizer **b** : readiness of bacteria to undergo genetic transformation
**3** : the knowledge that enables a person to speak and understand a language — compare PERFORMANCE
**com·pe·ten·cy** \-pə-tən(t)-sē\ *noun, plural* **-cies** (1596)
: COMPETENCE

**com·pe·tent** \'käm-pə-tənt\ *adjective* [Middle English, suitable, from Middle French & Latin; Middle French, from Latin *competent-, competens,* from present participle of *competere*] (15th century)
**1** : proper or rightly pertinent
**2** : having requisite or adequate ability or qualities : FIT ⟨a *competent* teacher⟩ ⟨a *competent* piece of work⟩
**3** : legally qualified or adequate ⟨a *competent* witness⟩
**4** : having the capacity to function or develop in a particular way; *specifically* : having the capacity to respond (as by producing an antibody) to an antigenic determinant ⟨immunologically *competent* cells⟩
**synonym** see SUFFICIENT
— **com·pe·tent·ly** *adverb*
**com·pe·ti·tion** \ˌkäm-pə-'ti-shən\ *noun* [Late Latin *competition-, competitio,* from Latin *competere*] (1605)
**1** : the act or process of competing : RIVALRY: as **a** : the effort of two or more parties acting independently to secure the business of a third party by offering the most favorable terms **b** : active demand by two or more organisms or kinds of organisms for some environmental resource in short supply
**2** : a contest between rivals; *also* : one's competitors ⟨faced tough *competition*⟩
**com·pet·i·tive** \kəm-'pe-tə-tiv\ *adjective* (1829)
**1** : relating to, characterized by, or based on competition ⟨*competitive* sports⟩
**2** : inclined, desiring, or suited to compete ⟨a *competitive* personality⟩ ⟨salary benefits must be *competitive* —M. S. Eisenhower⟩
**3** : depending for effectiveness on the relative concentration of two or more substances ⟨*competitive* inhibition of an enzyme⟩
— **com·pet·i·tive·ly** *adverb*
— **com·pet·i·tive·ness** *noun*
**com·pet·i·tor** \kəm-'pe-tə-tər\ *noun* (1534)
: one that competes: as **a** : RIVAL **b** : one selling or buying goods or services in the same market as another **c** : an organism that lives in competition with another
**com·pi·la·tion** \ˌkäm-pə-'lā-shən *also* -ˌpī-\ *noun* (15th century)
**1** : the act or process of compiling
**2** : something compiled
**com·pile** \kəm-'pī(ə)l\ *transitive verb* **com·piled; com·pil·ing** [Middle English, from Middle French *compiler,* from Latin *compilare* to plunder] (14th century)
**1** : to compose out of materials from other documents
**2** : to collect and edit into a volume
**3** : to run (as a program) through a compiler
**4** : to build up gradually ⟨*compiled* a record of four wins and two losses⟩
**com·pil·er** \kəm-'pī-lər\ *noun* (14th century)
**1** : one that compiles
**2** : a computer program that translates an entire set of instructions written in a higher-level symbolic language (as Pascal) into machine language before the instructions can be executed
**com·pla·cence** \kəm-'plā-s°n(t)s\ *noun* (15th century)
**1** : calm or secure satisfaction with oneself or one's lot : SELF-SATISFACTION
**2** *obsolete* : COMPLAISANCE
**3** : UNCONCERN
**com·pla·cen·cy** \-s°n(t)-sē\ *noun, plural* **-cies** (1650)
**1** : COMPLACENCE; *especially* : self-satisfaction accompanied by unawareness of actual dangers or deficiencies
**2** : an instance of complacency
**com·pla·cent** \kəm-'plā-s°nt\ *adjective* [Latin *complacent-, complacens,* present participle of *complacēre* to please greatly, from *com-* + *placēre* to please — more at PLEASE] (1767)
**1** : SELF-SATISFIED ⟨a *complacent* smile⟩
**2** : COMPLAISANT 1

**3** : UNCONCERNED
— **com·pla·cent·ly** *adverb*
**com·plain** \kəm-'plān\ *intransitive verb* [Middle English *compleynen,* from Middle French *complaindre,* from (assumed) Vulgar Latin *complangere,* from Latin *com-* + *plangere* to lament — more at PLAINT] (14th century)
**1** : to express grief, pain, or discontent
**2** : to make a formal accusation or charge
— **com·plain·er** *noun*
— **com·plain·ing·ly** \-'plā-niŋ-lē\ *adverb*
**com·plain·ant** \kəm-'plā-nənt\ *noun* (15th century)
: the party who makes the complaint in a legal action or proceeding
**com·plaint** \kəm-'plānt\ *noun* [Middle English *compleynte,* from Middle French *complainte,* from Old French, from *complaindre*] (14th century)
**1** : expression of grief, pain, or dissatisfaction
**2 a** : something that is the cause or subject of protest or outcry **b** : a bodily ailment or disease
**3** : a formal allegation against a party
**com·plai·sance** \kəm-'plā-s°n(t)s, -z°n(t)s; ˌkäm-plā-'zan(t)s, -plə-, -'zän(t)s\ *noun* (1651)
: disposition to please or comply : AFFABILITY
**com·plai·sant** \-s°nt, -z°nt, -'zant, -'zänt\ *adjective* [French, from Middle French, from present participle of *complaire* to gratify, acquiesce, from Latin *complacēre*] (1647)
**1** : marked by an inclination to please or oblige
**2** : tending to consent to others' wishes
**synonym** see AMIABLE
— **com·plai·sant·ly** *adverb*
**com·pleat** \kəm-'plēt\ *adjective* [archaic variant of *complete* in *The Compleat Angler* (1653) by Izaak Walton] (1526)
: COMPLETE 3
**com·plect·ed** \kəm-'plek-təd\ *adjective* [irregular from *complexion*] (1806)
: having a specified facial complexion ⟨a tall, thin man, fairly dark *complected* —E. J. Kahn⟩ ◻
¹**com·ple·ment** \'käm-plə-mənt\ *noun* [Middle English, from Latin *complementum,* from *complēre* to fill up, complete, from *com-* + *plēre* to fill — more at FULL] (14th century)
**1 a** : something that fills up, completes, or makes perfect **b** : the quantity or number required to make a thing complete ⟨the usual *complement* of eyes and ears —Francis Parkman⟩; *especially* : the whole force or personnel of a ship **c** : one of two mutually completing parts : COUNTERPART
**2 a** : the angle or arc that when added to a given angle or arc equals a right angle in measure **b** : the set of all elements that do not belong to a given set and are contained in a particular mathematical set containing the given

\ə\ abut \°\ kitten \ər\ further \a\ ash \ā\ ace
\ä\ mop, mar \au̇\ out \ch\ chin \e\ bet \ē\ easy
\g\ go \i\ hit \ī\ ice \j\ job \ŋ\ sing \ō\ go
\o̅\ law \o̅i\ boy \th\ thin \th̶\ the \ü\ loot \u̇\ foot
\y\ yet \zh\ vision *see also* Guide to Pronunciation

set **c** : a number that when added to another number of the same sign yields zero if the significant digit farthest to the left is discarded — used especially in assembly language programming
**3** : the musical interval required with a given interval to complete the octave
**4** : an added word or expression by which a predication is made complete (as *president* in "they elected him president" and *beautiful* in "he thought her beautiful")
**5** : the thermolabile group of proteins in normal blood serum and plasma that in combination with antibodies causes the destruction especially of particulate antigens (as bacteria and foreign blood corpuscles)

complement 2a:
*ACB* right angle, *ACD* complement of *DCB* (and vice versa), *AD* complement of *DB* (and vice versa)

²**com·ple·ment** \-,ment\ (1602)
*intransitive verb*
*obsolete* : to exchange formal courtesies
*transitive verb*
**1** : to be complementary to
**2** *obsolete* : COMPLIMENT
**com·ple·men·tal** \,käm-plə-'men-t°l\ *adjective* (1597)
**1** : relating to or being a complement
**2** *obsolete* : CEREMONIOUS, COMPLIMENTARY
**com·ple·men·tar·i·ty** \,käm-plə-(,)men-'tar-ə-tē, -mən-\ *noun* (1911)
: the quality or state of being complementary
**com·ple·men·ta·ry** \,käm-plə-'men-t(ə-)rē\ *adjective* (1829)
**1** : relating to or constituting one of a pair of contrasting colors that produce a neutral color when combined in suitable proportions
**2** : serving to fill out or complete
**3** : mutually supplying each other's lack
**4** : being complements of each other ⟨*complementary* acute angles⟩
**5** : characterized by the capacity for precise pairing of purine and pyrimidine bases between strands of DNA and sometimes RNA such that the structure of one strand determines the other
— **com·ple·men·ta·ri·ly** \-'men-t(ə-)rə-lē, -(,)men-'ter-ə-lē\ *adverb*
— **com·ple·men·ta·ri·ness** \-'men-t(ə-)rē-nəs\ *noun*
— **complementary** *noun*
**com·ple·men·ta·tion** \,käm-plə-(,)men-'tā-shən, -mən-\ *noun* (1942)
**1** : the operation of determining the complement of a mathematical set
**2** : production of normal phenotype in an individual heterozygous for two closely related mutations with one on each homologous chromosome and at a slightly different position
**complement fixation** *noun* (1906)
: the process of binding serum complement to the product formed by the union of an antibody and the antigen for which it is specific that occurs when complement is added to a suitable mixture of such an antibody and antigen
**complement–fixation test** *noun* (1911)
: a diagnostic test for the presence of a particular antibody in the serum of a patient that involves inactivation of the complement in the serum, addition of measured amounts of the antigen for which the antibody is specific and of foreign complement, and detection of the presence or absence of complement fixation by the addition of a suitable indicator system — compare WASSERMANN TEST
**com·ple·men·ti·zer** \'käm-plə-mən-,tī-zər, -(,)men-\ *noun* (1965)
: a function word or morpheme that combines with a clause or verbal phrase to form a subordinate clause

¹**com·plete** \kəm-'plēt\ *adjective* **com·plet·er; -est** [Middle English *complet,* from Middle French, from Latin *completus,* from past participle of *complēre*] (14th century)
**1 a** : having all necessary parts, elements, or steps ⟨*complete* diet⟩ **b** : having all four sets of floral organs **c** *of a subject or predicate* : including modifiers, complements, or objects
**2** : brought to an end : CONCLUDED ⟨a *complete* period of time⟩
**3** : highly proficient ⟨a *complete* artist⟩
**4 a** : fully carried out : THOROUGH ⟨a *complete* renovation⟩ **b** : TOTAL, ABSOLUTE ⟨*complete* silence⟩
**5** *of insect metamorphosis* : characterized by the occurrence of a pupal stage between the motile immature stages and the adult — compare INCOMPLETE 1b
**6** *of a metric space* : having the property that every Cauchy sequence of elements converges to a limit in the space
*synonym* see FULL
— **com·plete·ly** *adverb*
— **com·plete·ness** *noun*
— **com·ple·tive** \-'plē-tiv\ *adjective*
— **complete with** : made complete by the inclusion of ⟨a birthday cake *complete with* candles⟩
²**complete** *transitive verb* **com·plet·ed; com·plet·ing** (15th century)
**1** : to bring to an end and especially into a perfected state ⟨*complete* a painting⟩
**2 a** : to make whole or perfect ⟨its song *completes* the charm of this bird⟩ **b** : to mark the end of ⟨a rousing chorus *completes* the show⟩ **c** : EXECUTE, FULFILL ⟨*complete* a contract⟩
**3** : to carry out (a forward pass) successfully
*synonym* see CLOSE
**complete fertilizer** *noun* (1900)
: a fertilizer that contains the three chief plant nutrients nitrogen, phosphoric acid, and potash
**com·ple·tion** \kəm-'plē-shən\ *noun* (1657)
**1** : the act or process of completing
**2** : the quality or state of being complete
**3** : a completed forward pass in football
¹**com·plex** \'käm-,pleks\ *noun* [Late Latin *complexus* totality, from Latin, embrace, from *complecti*] (1643)
**1** : a whole made up of complicated or interrelated parts ⟨a *complex* of university buildings⟩ ⟨a *complex* of welfare programs⟩ ⟨the military-industrial *complex*⟩
**2 a** : a group of culture traits relating to a single activity (as hunting), process (as use of flint), or culture unit **b** (1) : a group of repressed desires and memories that exerts a dominating influence upon the personality (2) : an exaggerated reaction to a subject or situation **c** : a group of obviously related units of which the degree and nature of the relationship is imperfectly known
**3** : a chemical association of two or more species (as ions or molecules) joined usually by weak electrostatic bonds rather than covalent bonds
²**com·plex** \käm-'pleks, kəm-', 'käm-,\ *adjective* [Latin *complexus,* past participle of *complecti* to embrace, comprise ⟨a multitude of objects⟩, from *com-* + *plectere* to braid — more at PLY] (circa 1652)
**1 a** : composed of two or more parts : COMPOSITE **b** (1) *of a word* : having a bound form as one or more of its immediate constituents ⟨*unmanly* is a *complex* word⟩ (2) *of a sentence* : consisting of a main clause and one or more subordinate clauses
**2** : hard to separate, analyze, or solve
**3** : of, concerned with, being, or containing complex numbers ⟨a *complex* root⟩ ⟨*complex* analysis⟩ ☆
— **com·plex·ly** *adverb*
— **com·plex·ness** *noun*
³**com·plex** \*same as* ²\ *transitive verb* (1658)
**1** : to make complex or into a complex

**2** : CHELATE
— **com·plex·a·tion** \,käm-,plek-'sā-shən, kəm-\ *noun*
**complex fraction** *noun* (1827)
: a fraction with a fraction or mixed number in the numerator or denominator or both — compare SIMPLE FRACTION
**com·plex·i·fy** \käm-'plek-sə-,fī, kəm-\ *verb* **-fied; -fy·ing** (1830)
*transitive verb*
: to make complex
*intransitive verb*
: to become complex
**com·plex·ion** \kəm-'plek-shən\ *noun* [Middle English, from Middle French, from Medieval Latin *complexion-, complexio,* from Latin, combination, from *complecti*] (14th century)
**1** : the combination of the hot, cold, moist, and dry qualities held in medieval physiology to determine the quality of a body
**2 a** : an individual complex of ways of thinking or feeling **b** : a complex of attitudes and inclinations
**3** : the hue or appearance of the skin and especially of the face ⟨a dark *complexion*⟩
**4** : overall aspect or character ⟨by changing the *complexion* of the legislative branch —Trevor Armbrister⟩
— **com·plex·ion·al** \-shnəl, -shə-n°l\ *adjective*
— **com·plex·ioned** \-shənd\ *adjective*
**com·plex·i·ty** \kəm-'plek-sə-tē, käm-\ *noun, plural* **-ties** (1685)
**1** : the quality or state of being complex
**2** : something complex
**complex number** *noun* (1860)
: a number of the form $a + b\sqrt{-1}$ where $a$ and $b$ are real numbers
**complex plane** *noun* (circa 1909)
: a plane whose points are identified by means of complex numbers; *especially* : ARGAND DIAGRAM
**com·pli·ance** \kəm-'plī-ən(t)s\ *noun* (1647)
**1 a** : the act or process of complying to a desire, demand, or proposal or to coercion **b** : conformity in fulfilling official requirements
**2** : a disposition to yield to others
**3** : the ability of an object to yield elastically when a force is applied : FLEXIBILITY
**com·pli·an·cy** \-ən(t)-sē\ *noun* (1643)
: COMPLIANCE
**com·pli·ant** \-ənt\ *adjective* (1642)
: ready or disposed to comply : SUBMISSIVE
— **com·pli·ant·ly** *adverb*
**com·pli·ca·cy** \'käm-pli-kə-sē\ *noun, plural* **-cies** [²*complicate*] (circa 1828)
**1** : the quality or state of being complicated
**2** : something that is complicated
¹**com·pli·cate** \'käm-plə-,kāt\ *transitive verb* **-cat·ed; -cat·ing** (1621)
**1** : to combine especially in an involved or inextricable manner
**2** : to make complex or difficult
**3** : INVOLVE; *especially* : to cause to be more

---

☆ **SYNONYMS**
**Complex, complicated, intricate, involved, knotty** mean having confusingly interrelated parts. COMPLEX suggests the unavoidable result of a necessary combining and does not imply a fault or failure ⟨a *complex* recipe⟩. COMPLICATED applies to what offers great difficulty in understanding, solving, or explaining ⟨*complicated* legal procedures⟩. INTRICATE suggests such interlacing of parts as to make it nearly impossible to follow or grasp them separately ⟨an *intricate* web of deceit⟩. INVOLVED implies extreme complication and often disorder ⟨a rambling, *involved* explanation⟩. KNOTTY suggests complication and entanglement that make solution or understanding improbable ⟨*knotty* ethical questions⟩.

complex or severe ⟨a virus disease *complicated* by bacterial infection⟩
**²com·pli·cate** \-pli-kət\ *adjective* [Latin *complicatus,* past participle of *complicare* to fold together, from *com-* + *plicare* to fold — more at PLY] (1638)
**1** : COMPLEX, INTRICATE
**2** : CONDUPLICATE
**com·pli·cat·ed** \'käm-plə-ˌkā-təd\ *adjective* (1656)
**1** : consisting of parts intricately combined
**2** : difficult to analyze, understand, or explain
**synonym** see COMPLEX
— **com·pli·cat·ed·ly** *adverb*
— **com·pli·cat·ed·ness** *noun*
**com·pli·ca·tion** \ˌkäm-plə-'kā-shən\ *noun* (15th century)
**1 a** : COMPLEXITY, INTRICACY; *especially* : a situation or a detail of character complicating the main thread of a plot **b** : a making difficult, involved, or intricate **c** : a complex or intricate feature or element **d** : a difficult factor or issue often appearing unexpectedly and changing existing plans, methods, or attitudes
**2** : a secondary disease or condition developing in the course of a primary disease or condition
**com·plice** \'käm-pləs, 'kəm-\ *noun* [Middle English, from Middle French, from Late Latin *complic-, complex,* from Latin, closely connected, from *complicare*] (15th century)
*archaic* : ASSOCIATE
**com·plic·it** \kəm-'pli-sət\ *adjective* (1973)
: having complicity
**com·plic·it·ous** \-'pli-sə-təs\ *adjective* (1860)
: COMPLICIT
**com·plic·i·ty** \kəm-'pli-s(ə-)tē\ *noun, plural* **-ties** (circa 1656)
**1** : association or participation in or as if in a wrongful act
**2** : an instance of complicity
**com·pli·er** \-'plī(-ə)r\ *noun* (1660)
: one that complies
**¹com·pli·ment** \'käm-plə-mənt\ *noun* [French, from Italian *complimento,* from Spanish *cumplimiento,* from *cumplir* to be courteous — more at COMPLY] (1654)
**1 a** : an expression of esteem, respect, affection, or admiration; *especially* : an admiring remark **b** : formal and respectful recognition : HONOR
**2** *plural* : best wishes : REGARDS ⟨accept my *compliments*⟩ ⟨*compliments* of the season⟩
**²com·pli·ment** \-ˌment\ *transitive verb* (1735)
**1** : to pay a compliment to
**2** : to present with a token of esteem
**com·pli·men·ta·ry** \ˌkäm-plə-'men-t(ə-)rē\ *adjective* (1716)
**1 a** : expressing or containing a compliment **b** : FAVORABLE ⟨the novel received *complimentary* reviews⟩
**2** : given free as a courtesy or favor ⟨*complimentary* tickets⟩
— **com·pli·men·ta·ri·ly** \-'men-t(ə-)rə-lē, -(ˌ)men-'ter-ə-lē\ *adverb*
**complimentary close** *noun* (1919)
: the words (as *sincerely yours*) that conventionally come immediately before the signature of a letter and express the sender's regard for the receiver — called also *complimentary closing*
**com·pline** \'käm-plən, -ˌplīn\ *noun, often capitalized* [Middle English *compline, complie,* from Old French *complie,* modification of Late Latin *completa,* from Latin, feminine of *completus* complete] (13th century)
: the seventh and last of the canonical hours
**¹com·plot** \'käm-ˌplät\ *noun* [Middle French *complot* crowd, plot] (1577)
*archaic* : PLOT, CONSPIRACY
**²com·plot** \kəm-'plät, käm-\ *verb* (1579)
*archaic* : PLOT
**com·ply** \kəm-'plī\ *intransitive verb* **complied; com·ply·ing** [Italian *complire,* from Spanish *cumplir* to complete, perform what is

due, be courteous, modification of Latin *complēre* to complete] (1602)
**1** *obsolete* : to be ceremoniously courteous
**2** : to conform or adapt one's actions to another's wishes, to a rule, or to necessity
**com·po** \'käm-(ˌ)pō\ *noun, plural* **compos** [short for *composition*] (1823)
: any of various composition materials
**¹com·po·nent** \kəm-'pō-nənt, 'käm-ˌ, käm-'\ *noun* [Latin *component-, componens,* present participle of *componere* to put together — more at COMPOUND] (1645)
**1** : a constituent part : INGREDIENT
**2 a** : any one of the vector terms added to form a vector sum or resultant **b** : a coordinate of a vector; *also* : either member of an ordered pair of numbers
**synonym** see ELEMENT
— **com·po·nen·tial** \ˌkäm-pə-'nen(t)-shəl\ *adjective*
**²component** *adjective* (1664)
: serving or helping to constitute : CONSTITUENT
**¹com·port** \kəm-'pōrt, -'port\ *verb* [Middle French *comporter* to bear, conduct, from Latin *comportare* to bring together, from *com-* + *portare* to carry — more at FARE] (1589)
*intransitive verb*
: to be fitting : ACCORD ⟨actions that *comport* with policy⟩
*transitive verb*
: BEHAVE; *especially* : to behave in a manner conformable to what is right, proper, or expected ⟨*comported* himself well in the crisis⟩
**synonym** see BEHAVE
— **com·port·ment** \-mənt\ *noun*
**²com·port** \'käm-ˌpōrt, -ˌport\ *noun* (1771)
: COMPOTE 2
**com·pose** \kəm-'pōz\ *verb* **com·posed; com·pos·ing** [Middle English, from Middle French *composer,* from Latin *componere* (perfect indicative *composui*) — more at COMPOUND] (15th century)
*transitive verb*
**1 a** : to form by putting together : FASHION ⟨a committee *composed* of three representatives —*Current Biography*⟩ **b** : to form the substance of : CONSTITUTE ⟨*composed* of many ingredients⟩ **c** : to produce (as columns or pages of type) by composition
**2 a** : to create by mental or artistic labor : PRODUCE ⟨*compose* a sonnet⟩ **b** (1) : to formulate and write (a piece of music) (2) : to compose music for
**3** : to deal with or act on so as to reduce to a minimum ⟨*compose* their differences⟩
**4** : to arrange in proper or orderly form
**5** : to free from agitation : CALM, SETTLE ⟨*composed* himself⟩
*intransitive verb*
: to practice composition
**com·posed** \-'pōzd\ *adjective* (1607)
: free from agitation : CALM; *especially* : SELF-POSSESSED
**synonym** see COOL
— **com·pos·ed·ly** \-'pō-zəd-lē\ *adverb*
— **com·pos·ed·ness** \-'pō-zəd-nəs\ *noun*
**com·pos·er** \kəm-'pō-zər\ *noun* (1597)
: one that composes; *especially* : a person who writes music
**composing room** *noun* (1737)
: the department in a printing office where typesetting and related operations are performed
**composing stick** *noun* (1679)
: a tray with an adjustable slide that a compositor holds in one hand and sets type into with the other
**¹com·pos·ite**
\käm-'pä-zət, kəm-', *especially British* 'käm-pə-zit\ *adjective* [Latin *com-*

*positus,* past participle of *componere*] (1563)
**1** : made up of distinct parts: as **a** *capitalized* : relating to or being a modification of the Corinthian order combining angular Ionic volutes with the acanthus-circled bell of the Corinthian **b** : of or relating to a very large family (Compositae) of dicotyledonous herbs, shrubs, and trees often considered to be the most highly evolved plants and characterized by florets arranged in dense heads that resemble single flowers **c** : factorable into two or more prime factors other than 1 and itself ⟨8 is a positive *composite* integer⟩
**2** : combining the typical or essential characteristics of individuals making up a group ⟨the *composite* man called the Poet —Richard Poirier⟩
**3** *of a statistical hypothesis* : specifying a range of values for one or more statistical parameters — compare SIMPLE 10
— **com·pos·ite·ly** *adverb*
**²composite** *noun* (1656)
**1** : something composite : COMPOUND
**2** : a composite plant
**3** : COMPOSITE FUNCTION
**4** : a solid material which is composed of two or more substances having different physical characteristics and in which each substance retains its identity while contributing desirable properties to the whole; *especially* : a structural material made of plastic within which a fibrous material (as silicon carbide) is embedded
**³composite** *transitive verb* **-it·ed; -it·ing** (1923)
: to make composite or into something composite ⟨*composited* four soil samples⟩
**composite function** *noun* (1965)
: a function whose values are found from two given functions by applying one function to an independent variable and then applying the second function to the result and whose domain consists of those values of the independent variable for which the result yielded by the first function lies in the domain of the second
**com·po·si·tion** \ˌkäm-pə-'zi-shən\ *noun* [Middle English *composicioun,* from Middle French *composition,* from Latin *composition-, compositio,* from *componere*] (14th century)
**1 a** : the act or process of composing; *specifically* : arrangement into specific proportion or relation and especially into artistic form **b** (1) : the arrangement of type for printing ⟨hand *composition*⟩ (2) : the production of type or typographic characters (as in photocomposition) arranged for printing
**2 a** : the manner in which something is composed **b** : general makeup ⟨the changing ethnic *composition* of the city —Leonard Buder⟩ **c** : the qualitative and quantitative makeup of a chemical compound
**3** : mutual settlement or agreement
**4** : a product of mixing or combining various elements or ingredients
**5** : an intellectual creation: as **a** : a piece of writing; *especially* : a school exercise in the form of a brief essay **b** : a written piece of music especially of considerable size and complexity
**6** : the quality or state of being compound
**7** : the operation of forming a composite function; *also* : COMPOSITE FUNCTION
— **com·po·si·tion·al** \-'zish-nəl, -'zi-shə-n°l\ *adjective*
— **com·po·si·tion·al·ly** *adverb*
**com·pos·i·tor** \kəm-'pä-zə-tər\ *noun* (1569)
: one who sets type

composing stick

**com·pos men·tis** \'käm-pəs-'men-təs\ *adjective* [Latin, literally, having mastery of one's mind] (1616)
: of sound mind, memory, and understanding

**¹com·post** \'käm-ˌpōst, *especially British* -ˌpäst\ *noun* [Middle French, from Medieval Latin *compostum,* from Latin, neuter of *compositus, compostus,* past participle of *componere*] (1587)
**1** : a mixture that consists largely of decayed organic matter and is used for fertilizing and conditioning land
**2** : MIXTURE, COMPOUND

**²compost** *transitive verb* (1829)
: to convert (as plant debris) to compost

**com·po·sure** \kəm-'pō-zhər\ *noun* (1647)
: a calmness or repose especially of mind, bearing, or appearance : SELF-POSSESSION
*synonym* see EQUANIMITY

**com·pote** \'käm-ˌpōt\ *noun* [French, from Old French *composte,* from Latin *composta,* feminine of *compostus,* past participle] (1693)
**1** : a dessert of fruit cooked in syrup
**2** : a bowl of glass, porcelain, or metal usually with a base and stem from which compotes, fruits, nuts, or sweets are served

**¹com·pound** \käm-'paund, kəm-', 'käm-,\ *verb* [Middle English *compounen,* from Middle French *compondre,* from Latin *componere,* from *com-* + *ponere* to put — more at POSITION] (14th century)
*transitive verb*
**1** : to put together (parts) so as to form a whole ⟨COMBINE ⟨*compound* ingredients⟩
**2** : to form by combining parts ⟨*compound* a medicine⟩
**3 a** : to settle amicably : adjust by agreement **b** : to agree for a consideration not to prosecute (an offense) ⟨*compound* a felony⟩
**4 a** : to pay (interest) on both the accrued interest and the principal **b** : to add to : AUGMENT ⟨we *compounded* our error in later policy —Robert Lekachman⟩
*intransitive verb*
**1** : to become joined in a compound
**2** : to come to terms of agreement
— **com·pound·able** \-'paun-də-bəl, -ˌpaun-\ *adjective*
— **com·pound·er** *noun*

**²com·pound** \'käm-ˌpaund, käm-', kəm-'\ *adjective* [Middle English *compouned,* past participle of *compounen*] (14th century)
**1** : composed of or resulting from union of separate elements, ingredients, or parts: as **a** : composed of united similar elements especially of a kind usually independent ⟨a *compound* plant ovary⟩ **b** : having the blade divided to the midrib and forming two or more leaflets on a common axis ⟨a *compound* leaf⟩
**2** : involving or used in a combination
**3 a** *of a word* : constituting a compound **b** *of a sentence* : having two or more main clauses

**³com·pound** \'käm-ˌpaund\ *noun* (1530)
**1 a** : a word consisting of components that are words (as *rowboat, high school, devil-may-care*) **b** : a word (as *anthropology, kilocycle, builder*) consisting of any of various combinations of words, combining forms, or affixes
**2** : something formed by a union of elements or parts; *especially* : a distinct substance formed by chemical union of two or more ingredients in definite proportion by weight

**⁴com·pound** \'käm-ˌpaund\ *noun* [by folk etymology from Malay *kampung* group of buildings, village] (1679)
: a fenced or walled-in area containing a group of buildings and especially residences

**compound–complex** *adjective* (1923)
*of a sentence* : having two or more main clauses and one or more subordinate clauses

**compound eye** *noun* (1836)
: an eye (as of an insect) made up of many separate visual units

**compound fracture** *noun* (1543)

: a bone fracture resulting in an open wound through which bone fragments usually protrude

**compound interest** *noun* (1660)
: interest computed on the sum of an original principal and accrued interest

**compound microscope** *noun* (circa 1859)
: a microscope consisting of an objective and an eyepiece mounted in a drawtube

**compound number** *noun* (15th century)
: a number (as 2 feet 5 in.) involving different denominations or more than one unit

**com·pra·dor** *or* **com·pra·dore** \ˌkäm-prə-'dōr, -'dȯr\ *noun* [Portuguese *comprador,* literally, buyer] (1840)
**1** : a Chinese agent engaged by a foreign establishment in China to have charge of its Chinese employees and to act as an intermediary in business affairs
**2** : INTERMEDIARY

**com·pre·hend** \ˌkäm-pri-'hend\ *transitive verb* [Middle English, from Latin *comprehendere,* from *com-* + *prehendere* to grasp — more at GET] (14th century)
**1** : to grasp the nature, significance, or meaning of
**2** : to contain or hold within a total scope, significance, or amount ⟨philosophy's scope *comprehends* the truth of everything which man may understand —H. O. Taylor⟩
**3** : to include by construction or implication ⟨does not prudence *comprehend* all the virtues? —Thomas B. Silver⟩
*synonym* see UNDERSTAND, INCLUDE
— **com·pre·hend·ible** \-'hen-də-bəl\ *adjective*

**com·pre·hen·si·ble** \-'hen(t)-sə-bəl\ *adjective* (1598)
: capable of being comprehended : INTELLIGIBLE
— **com·pre·hen·si·bil·i·ty** \-ˌhen(t)-sə-'bi-lə-tē\ *noun*
— **com·pre·hen·si·ble·ness** \-'hen(t)-sə-bəl-nəs\ *noun*
— **com·pre·hen·si·bly** \-blē\ *adverb*

**com·pre·hen·sion** \ˌkäm-pri-'hen(t)-shən\ *noun* [Middle French & Latin; Middle French, from Latin *comprehension-, comprehensio,* from *comprehendere* to understand, comprise] (15th century)
**1 a** : the act or action of grasping with the intellect : UNDERSTANDING **b** : knowledge gained by comprehending **c** : the capacity for understanding fully
**2 a** : the act or process of comprising **b** : the faculty or capability of including : COMPREHENSIVENESS
**3** : CONNOTATION 3

**com·pre·hen·sive** \-'hen(t)-siv\ *adjective* (1614)
**1** : covering completely or broadly : INCLUSIVE ⟨*comprehensive* examinations⟩ ⟨*comprehensive* insurance⟩
**2** : having or exhibiting wide mental grasp ⟨*comprehensive* knowledge⟩
— **com·pre·hen·sive·ly** *adverb*
— **com·pre·hen·sive·ness** *noun*

**¹com·press** \kəm-'pres\ *verb* [Middle English, from Late Latin *compressare* to press hard, frequentative of Latin *comprimere* to compress, from *com-* + *premere* to press — more at PRESS] (14th century)
*transitive verb*
**1** : to press or squeeze together
**2** : to reduce in size or volume as if by squeezing
*intransitive verb*
: to undergo compression
*synonym* see CONTRACT

**²com·press** \'käm-ˌpres\ *noun* [Middle French *compresse,* from *compresser* to compress, from Late Latin *compressare*] (1599)
**1** : a folded cloth or pad applied so as to press upon a body part

**2** : a machine for compressing

**com·pressed** \kəm-'prest *also* 'käm-,\ *adjective* (14th century)
**1** : pressed together : reduced in size or volume (as by pressure)
**2** : flattened as though subjected to compression: **a** : flattened laterally ⟨petioles *compressed*⟩ **b** : narrow from side to side and deep in a dorsoventral direction
— **com·pressed·ly** \kəm-'prest-lē, -'pre-səd-lē\ *adverb*

**compressed air** *noun* (1669)
: air under pressure greater than that of the atmosphere

**com·press·ible** \kəm-'pre-sə-bəl\ *adjective* (circa 1691)
: capable of being compressed
— **com·press·ibil·i·ty** \-ˌpre-sə-'bi-lə-tē\ *noun*

**com·pres·sion** \kəm-'pre-shən\ *noun* (15th century)
**1 a** : the act, process, or result of compressing **b** : the state of being compressed
**2** : the process of compressing the fuel mixture in a cylinder of an internal combustion engine (as in an automobile)
**3** : a much compressed fossil plant
— **com·pres·sion·al** \-'presh-nəl, -'pre-shə-nᵊl\ *adjective*

**compressional wave** *noun* (1887)
: a longitudinal wave (as a sound wave) propagated by the elastic compression of the medium — called also *compression wave*

**com·pres·sive** \kəm-'pre-siv\ *adjective* (1572)
**1** : of or relating to compression
**2** : tending to compress
— **com·pres·sive·ly** *adverb*

**com·pres·sor** \-'pre-sər\ *noun* (1839)
: one that compresses: as **a** : a muscle that compresses a part **b** : a machine that compresses gases

**com·prise** \kəm-'prīz\ *transitive verb* **com·prised; com·pris·ing** [Middle English, from Middle French *compris,* past participle of *comprendre,* from Latin *comprehendere*] (15th century)
**1** : to include especially within a particular scope ⟨civilization as Lenin used the term would then certainly have *comprised* the changes that are now associated in our minds with "developed" rather than "developing" states —*Times Literary Supplement*⟩
**2** : to be made up of ⟨a vast installation, *comprising* fifty buildings —Jane Jacobs⟩
**3** : COMPOSE, CONSTITUTE ⟨a misconception as to what *comprises* a literary generation —William Styron⟩ ⟨about 8 percent of our military forces are *comprised* of women —Jimmy Carter⟩ ▢

**¹com·pro·mise** \'käm-prə-ˌmīz\ *noun* [Middle English, mutual promise to abide by an arbiter's decision, from Middle French *compromis,* from Latin *compromissum,* from neuter of *compromissus,* past participle of *compromittere* to promise mutually, from *com-* + *promittere* to promise — more at PROMISE] (15th century)
**1 a** : settlement of differences by arbitration or by consent reached by mutual concessions **b** : something intermediate between or blending qualities of two different things
**2** : a concession to something derogatory or prejudicial ⟨a *compromise* of principles⟩

**²compromise** *verb* **-mised; -mis·ing** (1598)
*transitive verb*
**1** *obsolete* : to bind by mutual agreement
**2** : to adjust or settle by mutual concessions
**3 a** : to expose to suspicion, discredit, or mischief **b** : to reveal or expose to an unauthorized person and especially to an enemy ⟨confidential information was *compromised*⟩ **c** : to cause the impairment of ⟨a *compromised* immune system⟩ ⟨a seriously *compromised* patient⟩

*intransitive verb*
**1 a :** to come to agreement by mutual concession **b :** to find or follow a way between extremes
**2 :** to make a shameful or disreputable concession ⟨wouldn't *compromise* with their principles⟩
— **com·pro·mis·er** *noun*
**compt** \'kaünt, 'käm(p)t\ *archaic variant of* COUNT
**comp·trol·ler** \kən-'trō-lər, 'käm(p)-, käm(p)-\ *noun* [Middle English, alteration of *conterroller* controller] (15th century)
**1 :** a royal-household official who examines and supervises expenditures
**2 :** a public official who audits government accounts and sometimes certifies expenditures
**3 :** CONTROLLER 1c
— **comp·trol·ler·ship** \-,ship\ *noun*
**com·pul·sion** \kəm-'pəl-shən\ *noun* [Middle English, from Middle French or Late Latin; Middle French, from Late Latin *compulsion-, compulsio*, from Latin *compellere* to compel] (15th century)
**1 a :** an act of compelling : the state of being compelled **b :** a force that compels
**2 :** an irresistible impulse to perform an irrational act
**com·pul·sive** \-'pəl-siv\ *adjective* (1588)
**1 :** having power to compel
**2 :** of, relating to, caused by, or suggestive of psychological compulsion or obsession ⟨*compulsive* actions⟩
— **com·pul·sive·ly** *adverb*
— **com·pul·sive·ness** *noun*
— **com·pul·siv·i·ty** \kəm-,pəl-'si-və-tē, ,käm-\ *noun*
**com·pul·so·ry** \kəm-'pəls-rē, -'pəl-sə-\ *adjective* (1581)
**1 :** MANDATORY, ENFORCED
**2 :** COERCIVE, COMPELLING
— **com·pul·so·ri·ly** \-rə-lē\ *adverb*
**com·punc·tion** \kəm-'pəŋ(k)-shən\ *noun* [Middle English *compunccioun*, from Middle French *componction*, from Late Latin *compunction-, compunctio*, from Latin *compungere* to prick hard, sting, from *com-* + *pungere* to prick — more at PUNGENT] (14th century)
**1 a :** anxiety arising from awareness of guilt ⟨*compunctions* of conscience⟩ **b :** distress of mind over an anticipated action or result ⟨showed no *compunction* in planning devilish engines of . . . destruction —Havelock Ellis⟩
**2 :** a twinge of misgiving : SCRUPLE ⟨cheated without *compunction*⟩ ◆
**synonym** see PENITENCE, QUALM
— **com·punc·tious** \-shəs\ *adjective*
**com·pur·ga·tion** \,käm-(,)pər-'gā-shən\ *noun* [Late Latin *compurgation-, compurgatio*, from Latin *compurgare* to clear completely, from *com-* + *purgare* to purge] (circa 1658)
**:** the clearing of an accused person by oaths of others who swear to the veracity or innocence of the accused
**com·pur·ga·tor** \'käm-(,)pər-,gā-tər\ *noun* (1533)
**:** one that under oath vouches for the character or conduct of an accused person
**com·put·able** \kəm-'pyü-tə-bəl\ *adjective* (1646)
**:** capable of being computed
— **com·put·abil·i·ty** \-,pyü-tə-'bi-lə-tē\ *noun*
**com·pu·ta·tion** \,käm-pyù-'tā-shən\ *noun* (15th century)
**1 a :** the act or action of computing : CALCULATION **b :** the use or operation of a computer
**2 :** a system of reckoning
**3 :** an amount computed
— **com·pu·ta·tion·al** \-shnəl, -shə-nᵊl\ *adjective*
— **com·pu·ta·tion·al·ly** *adverb*
**com·pute** \kəm-'pyüt\ *verb* **com·put·ed; com·put·ing** [Latin *computare* — more at COUNT] (1616)

*transitive verb*
**:** to determine especially by mathematical means ⟨*compute* your income tax⟩; *also* **:** to determine or calculate by means of a computer
*intransitive verb*
**1 :** to make calculation : RECKON
**2 :** to use a computer
**computed tomography** *noun* (1975)
**:** radiography in which a three-dimensional image of a body structure is constructed by computer from a series of plane cross-sectional images made along an axis — called also *computed axial tomography, computerized axial tomography, computerized tomography*
**com·put·er** \kəm-'pyü-tər\ *noun, often attributive* (1646)
**:** one that computes; *specifically* **:** a programmable electronic device that can store, retrieve, and process data
— **com·put·er·dom** \-dəm\ *noun*
— **com·put·er·less** \-ləs\ *adjective*
— **com·put·er·like** \-,līk\ *adjective*
**com·put·er·ese** \-,pyü-tə-'rēz, -'rēs\ *noun* (circa 1960)
**:** jargon used by computer technologists
**com·put·er·ise** *chiefly British variant of* COMPUTERIZE
**com·put·er·ist** \kəm-'pyü-tə-rist\ *noun* (1973)
**:** a person who uses or operates a computer
**com·put·er·ize** \kəm-'pyü-tə-,rīz\ *transitive verb* **-ized; -iz·ing** (1957)
**1 :** to carry out, control, or produce by means of a computer
**2 :** to equip with computers
**3 a :** to store in a computer **b :** to put in a form that a computer can use
— **com·put·er·iz·able** \-,pyü-tə-'rī-zə-bəl\ *adjective*
— **com·put·er·i·za·tion** \-,pyü-tə-rə-'zā-shən\ *noun*
**com·put·er·nik** \kəm-'pyü-tər-,nik\ *noun* (1968)
**:** a computer enthusiast or expert
**com·put·er·phobe** \-,fōb\ *noun* (1976)
**:** a person who experiences anxiety about computers and especially about their use
— **com·put·er·pho·bia** \-,pyü-tər-'fō-bē-ə\ *noun*
— **com·put·er·pho·bic** \-'fō-bik\ *adjective*
**com·rade** \'käm-,rad, -rəd, *especially British* -,räd\ *noun* [Middle French *camarade* group sleeping in one room, roommate, companion, from Old Spanish *camarada*, from *cámara* room, from Late Latin *camera, camara* — more at CHAMBER] (1544)
**1 a :** an intimate friend or associate : COMPANION **b :** a fellow soldier
**2** [from its use as a form of address by communists] **:** COMMUNIST ◆
— **com·rade·li·ness** \-lē-nəs\ *noun*
— **com·rade·ly** *adjective*
— **com·rade·ship** \-,ship\ *noun*
**com·rad·ery** \'käm-,ra-d(ə-)rē, -rə-drē, -,räd(ə-)rē\ *noun* (1879)
**:** CAMARADERIE
**Comsat** \'käm-,sat\ *service mark*
— used for communications services involving an artificial satellite
**Com·stock·ery** \'käm-,stä-kə-rē *also* 'kəm-\ *noun* [Anthony *Comstock* + English *-ery*] (1905)
**1 :** strict censorship of materials considered obscene
**2 :** censorious opposition to alleged immorality (as in literature)
**Com·stock·ian** \käm-'stä-kē-ən *also* ,kəm-\ *adjective* (1921)
**:** of or relating to Comstockery
**com·symp** \'käm-,simp\ *noun* [communist + *sympathizer*] (circa 1961)
**:** a person sympathetic to communist causes — usually used disparagingly

**Comt·ian** *or* **Comt·ean** \'käm(p)-tē-ən, 'kōⁿ(n)-tē-\ *adjective* (1846)
**:** of or relating to Auguste Comte or his doctrines
— **Comt·ism** \'käm(p)-,ti-zəm, 'kōⁿ(n)-\ *noun*
— **Comt·ist** \'käm(p)-tist, 'kōⁿ(n)-\ *adjective or noun*
¹**con** \'kän\ *transitive verb* **conned; con·ning** [Middle English *connen* to know, learn, study, alteration of *cunnen* to know, infinitive of *can* — more at CAN] (13th century)
**1 :** to commit to memory
**2 :** to study or examine closely
²**con** *variant of* CONN
³**con** *adverb* [Middle English, short for *contra*] (15th century)
**:** on the negative side **:** in opposition ⟨so much has been written pro and *con*⟩
⁴**con** *noun* (1589)
**1 :** an argument or evidence in opposition
**2 :** the negative position or one holding it ⟨an appraisal of the pros and *cons*⟩

---

---

\ə\ **abut** \ᵊ\ **kitten** \ər\ **further** \a\ **ash** \ā\ **ace**
\ä\ **mop, mar** \aù\ **out** \ch\ **chin** \e\ **bet** \ē\ **easy**
\g\ **go** \i\ **hit** \ī\ **ice** \j\ **job** \ŋ\ **sing** \ō\ **go**
\ò\ **law** \òi\ **boy** \th\ **thin** \t͟h\ **the** \ü\ **loot** \ù\ **foot**
\y\ **yet** \zh\ **vision** *see also* Guide to Pronunciation

**⁵con** *adjective* [by shortening] (1889)
**:** CONFIDENCE

**⁶con** *transitive verb* **conned; con·ning** (1896)
**1 :** SWINDLE
**2 :** MANIPULATE 2b
**3 :** PERSUADE, CAJOLE

**⁷con** *noun* (1901)
**:** something (as a ruse) used deceptively to gain another's confidence; *also* **:** a confidence game **:** SWINDLE

**⁸con** *noun* [by shortening] (1893)
**:** CONVICT

**⁹con** *noun* [short for *consumption*] (1915)
*slang* **:** a destructive disease of the lungs; *especially* **:** TUBERCULOSIS

**con-** — see COM-

**con amo·re** \ˌkän-ə-'mȯr-ē, ˌkȯn-ə-'mȯr-(ˌ)ā, -'mȯr-\ *adverb* [Italian] (1739)
**1 :** with love, devotion, or zest
**2 :** in a tender manner — used as a direction in music

**con ani·ma** \kän-'ä-nə-ˌmä, kōn-'ä-ni-\ *adverb* [Italian, literally, with spirit] (circa 1906)
**:** in a spirited manner — used as a direction in music

**co·na·tion** \kō-'nā-shən\ *noun* [Latin *conation-, conatio* act of attempting, from *conari* to attempt — more at DEACON] (circa 1837)
**:** an inclination (as an instinct, a drive, a wish, or a craving) to act purposefully **:** IMPULSE 3
— **co·na·tive** \'kō-nə-tiv, 'kä-, 'kō-ˌnā-\ *adjective*

**con brio** \kän-'brē-(ˌ)ō, kōn-\ *adverb* [Italian, literally, with vigor] (circa 1889)
**:** in a vigorous or brisk manner — used as a direction in music

**con·ca·nav·a·lin** \ˌkän-kə-'na-və-lən\ *noun* [*com-* + *canavalin*, a noncrystalline globulin found in the jack bean, from New Latin *Canavalia*, genus name of the jack bean] (1917)
**:** either of two crystalline globulins occurring in the jack bean; *especially* **:** one that is a potent hemagglutinin

**¹con·cat·e·nate** \kän-'ka-tə-nət, kən-\ *adjective* [Middle English, from Late Latin *concatenatus*, past participle of *concatenare* to link together, from Latin *com-* + *catena* chain] (15th century)
**:** linked together

**²concatenate** \-ˌnāt\ *transitive verb* **-nat·ed; -nat·ing** (1598)
**:** to link together in a series or chain
— **con·cat·e·na·tion** \(ˌ)kän-ˌka-tə-'nā-shən, kən-\ *noun*

**¹con·cave** \kän-'kāv, 'kän-ˌ\ *adjective* [Middle English, from Middle French, from Latin *concavus*, from *com-* + *cavus* hollow — more at CAVE] (15th century)
**1 :** hollowed or rounded inward like the inside of a bowl
**2 :** arched in **:** curving in — used of the side of a curve or surface on which neighboring normals to the curve or surface converge and on which lies the chord joining two neighboring points of the curve or surface

**²con·cave** \'kän-ˌkāv\ *noun* (1552)
**:** a concave line or surface

**con·cav·i·ty** \kän-'ka-və-tē\ *noun, plural* **-ties** (15th century)
**1 :** a concave line, surface, or space **:** HOLLOW
**2 :** the quality or state of being concave

**con·ca·vo–con·vex** \kän-ˌkā-vō-kän-'veks; 'kän-, kän-ˌ\ *adjective* (1676)
**1 :** concave on one side and convex on the other
**2 :** having the concave side curved more than the convex ⟨a *concavo-convex* lens⟩

**con·ceal** \kən-'sē(ə)l\ *transitive verb* [Middle English *concelen*, from Middle French *conceler*, from Latin *concelare*, from *com-* + *celare* to hide — more at HELL] (14th century)

**1 :** to prevent disclosure or recognition of
**2 :** to place out of sight
*synonym* see HIDE
— **con·ceal·able** \-'sē-lə-bəl\ *adjective*
— **con·ceal·er** \-'sē-lər\ *noun*
— **con·ceal·ing·ly** \-'sē-liŋ-lē\ *adverb*
— **con·ceal·ment** \-'sē(ə)l-mənt\ *noun*

**con·cede** \kən-'sēd\ *verb* **con·ced·ed; con·ced·ing** [French or Latin; French *concéder*, from Latin *concedere*, from *com-* + *cedere* to yield] (1632)
*transitive verb*
**1 :** to grant as a right or privilege
**2 a :** to accept as true, valid, or accurate ⟨the right of the state to tax is generally *conceded*⟩ **b :** to acknowledge grudgingly or hesitantly
*intransitive verb*
**:** to make concession **:** YIELD
*synonym* see GRANT
— **con·ced·ed·ly** \-'sē-dəd-lē\ *adverb*
— **con·ced·er** *noun*

**¹con·ceit** \kən-'sēt\ *noun* [Middle English, from *conceiven*] (14th century)
**1 a** (1) **:** a result of mental activity **:** THOUGHT (2) **:** individual opinion **b :** favorable opinion; *especially* **:** excessive appreciation of one's own worth or virtue
**2 :** a fancy article
**3 a :** a fanciful idea **b :** an elaborate or strained metaphor **c :** use or presence of such conceits in poetry **d :** an organizing theme or concept ⟨found his *conceit* for the film early —Peter Wilkinson⟩

**²conceit** *transitive verb* (1557)
**1** *obsolete* **:** CONCEIVE, UNDERSTAND
**2** *chiefly dialect* **:** IMAGINE
**3** *dialect British* **:** to take a fancy to

**con·ceit·ed** \-'sē-təd\ *adjective* [¹*conceit*] (1593)
**1 :** ingeniously contrived **:** FANCIFUL
**2 :** having an excessively high opinion of oneself
— **con·ceit·ed·ly** *adverb*
— **con·ceit·ed·ness** *noun*

**con·ceiv·able** \kən-'sē-və-bəl\ *adjective* (15th century)
**:** capable of being conceived **:** IMAGINABLE
— **con·ceiv·abil·i·ty** \kən-ˌsē-və-'bi-lə-tē\ *noun*
— **con·ceiv·able·ness** \-'sē-və-bəl-nəs\ *noun*

**con·ceiv·ably** \-blē\ *adverb* (1625)
**1 :** in a conceivable manner
**2 :** it may be conceived **:** POSSIBLY

**con·ceive** \kən-'sēv\ *verb* **con·ceived; con·ceiv·ing** [Middle English, from Middle French *conceivre*, from Latin *concipere* to take in, conceive, from *com-* + *capere* to take — more at HEAVE] (14th century)
*transitive verb*
**1 a :** to become pregnant with (young) **b :** to cause to begin **:** ORIGINATE
**2 a :** to take into one's mind ⟨*conceive* a prejudice⟩ **b :** to form a conception of **:** IMAGINE
**3 :** to apprehend by reason or imagination **:** UNDERSTAND
**4 :** to be of the opinion
*intransitive verb*
**1 :** to become pregnant
**2 :** to have a conception — usually used with *of* ⟨*conceives* of death as emptiness⟩
*synonym* see THINK
— **con·ceiv·er** *noun*

**con·cel·e·brant** \kən-'se-lə-brənt, kän-\ *noun* (circa 1931)
**:** one that concelebrates a Eucharist or Mass

**con·cel·e·brate** \kən-'se-lə-ˌbrāt, kän-\ *verb* [Medieval Latin *concelebratus*, past participle of *concelebrare*, from Latin, to frequent, celebrate, from *com-* + *celebrare* to celebrate] (1879)
*transitive verb*
**:** to participate in (a Eucharist) as a joint celebrant who recites the canon in unison with other celebrants

*intransitive verb*
**:** to participate as a celebrant in a concelebrated Eucharist
— **con·cel·e·bra·tion** \(ˌ)kän-ˌse-lə-'brā-shən, kən-\ *noun*

**con·cent** \kən-'sent\ *noun* [Latin *concentus*, from *concinere* to sing together, from *com-* + *canere* to sing — more at CHANT] (1585)
*archaic* **:** HARMONY

**con·cen·ter** \kən-'sen-tər, kän-\ *verb* [French *concentrer*, from *com-* + *centre* center] (1598)
*transitive verb*
**:** to draw or direct to a common center **:** CONCENTRATE
*intransitive verb*
**:** to come to a common center

**¹con·cen·trate** \'kän(t)-sən-ˌtrāt, -ˌsen-\ *verb* **-trat·ed; -trat·ing** [*com-* + Latin *centrum* center] (1646)
*transitive verb*
**1 a :** to bring or direct toward a common center or objective **:** FOCUS **b :** to gather into one body, mass, or force ⟨power was *concentrated* in a few able hands⟩ **c :** to accumulate (a toxic substance) in bodily tissues ⟨fish *concentrate* mercury⟩
**2 a :** to make less dilute ⟨*concentrate* syrup⟩ **b :** to express or exhibit in condensed form
*intransitive verb*
**1 :** to draw toward or meet in a common center
**2 :** GATHER, COLLECT
**3 :** to concentrate one's powers, efforts, or attention ⟨*concentrate* on a problem⟩
— **con·cen·trat·ed·ly** \-ˌtrā-təd-lē; ˌkän(t)-sən-'trā-\ *adverb*
— **con·cen·tra·tive** \-ˌtrā-tiv\ *adjective*

**²concentrate** *noun* (1883)
**1 :** something concentrated: as **a :** a mineral-rich product obtained after an initial processing of ore **b :** a food reduced in bulk by elimination of fluid ⟨orange juice *concentrate*⟩
**2 :** a feedstuff (as grains) relatively rich in digestible nutrients — compare FIBER

**con·cen·tra·tion** \ˌkän(t)-sən-'trā-shən, -ˌsen-\ *noun* (1634)
**1 a :** the act or process of concentrating **:** the state of being concentrated; *especially* **:** direction of attention to a single object **b :** MAJOR 4a
**2 :** a concentrated mass or thing
**3 :** the amount of a component in a given area or volume

**concentration camp** *noun* (1901)
**:** a camp where persons (as prisoners of war, political prisoners, or refugees) are detained or confined

**con·cen·tra·tor** \'kän(t)-sən-ˌtrā-tər\ *noun* (1833)
**:** one that concentrates: as **a :** an industrial plant that produces concentrates from ores **b :** a mirror or group of mirrors that focus sunlight for use as an energy source **c :** a device in a computer network that collects data from separate low-volume transmission channels and retransmits it over a single high-volume channel

**con·cen·tric** \kən-'sen-trik, kän-\ *adjective* [Medieval Latin *concentricus*, from Latin *com-* + *centrum* center] (14th century)
**1 :** having a common center ⟨*concentric* circles⟩
**2 :** having a common axis **:** COAXIAL
— **con·cen·tri·cal·ly** \-tri-k(ə-)lē\ *adverb*
— **con·cen·tric·i·ty** \ˌkän-ˌsen-'tri-sə-tē\ *noun*

**con·cept** \'kän-ˌsept\ *noun* [Latin *conceptum*, neuter of *conceptus*, past participle of *concipere* to conceive — more at CONCEIVE] (1556)
**1 :** something conceived in the mind **:** THOUGHT, NOTION
**2 :** an abstract or generic idea generalized from particular instances
*synonym* see IDEA

**con·cep·ta·cle** \kən-'sep-ti-kəl\ *noun* [New Latin *conceptaculum*, from Latin, receptacle,

from *conceptus,* past participle of *concipere* to take in] (1835)
**:** an external cavity containing reproductive cells in algae (as of the genus *Fucus*)

**con·cep·tion** \kən-'sep-shən\ *noun* [Middle English *concepcioun,* from Old French *conception,* from Latin *conception-, conceptio,* from *concipere*] (14th century)
**1 a** (1) **:** the act of becoming pregnant **:** the state of being conceived (2) **:** EMBRYO, FETUS **b** **:** BEGINNING 〈joy had the like *conception* in our eyes —Shakespeare〉
**2 a :** the capacity, function, or process of forming or understanding ideas or abstractions or their symbols **b :** a general idea **:** CONCEPT **c :** a complex product of abstract or reflective thinking **d :** the sum of a person's ideas and beliefs concerning something
**3 :** the originating of something in the mind
*synonym* see IDEA
— **con·cep·tion·al** \-shnəl, -shə-nᵊl\ *adjective*
— **con·cep·tive** \-'sep-tiv\ *adjective*
**con·cep·tu·al** \kən-'sep-chə-wəl, kän-, -chəl, -shwəl\ *adjective* [Medieval Latin *conceptualis* of thought, from Late Latin *conceptus* act of conceiving, thought, from Latin *concipere*] (circa 1834)
**:** of, relating to, or consisting of concepts
— **con·cep·tu·al·i·ty** \-,sep-chə-'wa-lə-tē, -shə-\ *noun*
— **con·cep·tu·al·ly** *adverb*
**conceptual art** *noun* (circa 1969)
**:** an art form in which the artist's intent is to convey a concept rather than to create an art object
— **conceptual artist** *noun*
**con·cep·tu·al·ise** *British variant of* CONCEPTUALIZE
**con·cep·tu·al·ism** \-'sep-chə-wə-,li-zəm, -chə-,li-, -shwə-,li-\ *noun* (circa 1838)
**:** a theory in philosophy intermediate between realism and nominalism that universals exist in the mind as concepts of discourse or as predicates which may be properly affirmed of reality
— **con·cep·tu·al·is·tic** \-,sep-chə-wə-'lis-tik, -chə-'lis-, -shwə-'lis-\ *adjective*
— **con·cep·tu·al·is·ti·cal·ly** \-ti-k(ə-)lē\ *adverb*
**con·cep·tu·al·ist** \-'sep-chə-wə-list, -chə-list, -shwə-list\ *noun* (1785)
**:** an adherent to the tenets of conceptualism or of conceptual art
**con·cep·tu·al·ize** \-'sep-chə-wə-,līz, -chə-,līz, -shwə-,līz\ *transitive verb* **-ized; -iz·ing** (1878)
**:** to form a concept of; *especially* **:** to interpret conceptually
— **con·cep·tu·al·i·za·tion** \-,sep-chə-wə-lə-'zā-shən, -chə-lə-', -shwə-lə-'\ *noun*
— **con·cep·tu·al·iz·er** \-'sep-chə-wə-,lī-zər, chə-,lī-, -shwə-,lī-\ *noun*
**con·cep·tus** \kən-'sep-təs\ *noun* [Latin, one conceived, from past participle of *concipere* to conceive] (circa 1860)
**:** a fertilized egg, embryo, or fetus
**¹con·cern** \kən-'sərn\ *verb* [Middle English, from Middle French & Medieval Latin; Middle French *concerner,* from Medieval Latin *concernere,* from Late Latin, to sift together, mingle, from Latin *com-* + *cernere* to sift — more at CERTAIN] (15th century)
*transitive verb*
**1 a :** to relate to **:** be about 〈the novel *concerns* three soldiers〉 **b :** to bear on
**2 :** to have an influence on **:** INVOLVE; *also* **:** to be the business or affair of 〈the problem *concerns* us all〉
**3 :** to be a care, trouble, or distress to 〈her ill health *concerns* me〉
**4 :** ENGAGE, OCCUPY 〈he *concerns* himself with trivia〉
*intransitive verb*
*obsolete* **:** to be of importance **:** MATTER
**²concern** *noun* (1655)

**1 a :** marked interest or regard usually arising through a personal tie or relationship **b :** an uneasy state of blended interest, uncertainty, and apprehension
**2 :** something that relates or belongs to one **:** AFFAIR
**3 :** matter for consideration
**4 :** an organization or establishment for business or manufacture
**5 :** CONTRIVANCE, GADGET
*synonym* see CARE
**concerned** *adjective* (1656)
**1 a :** ANXIOUS, WORRIED 〈*concerned* for their safety〉 **b :** INTERESTED 〈*concerned* to prove the point〉
**2 a :** interestedly engaged 〈*concerned* with books and music〉 **b :** culpably involved **:** IMPLICATED 〈arrested all *concerned*〉
**concerning** *preposition* (15th century)
**:** relating to **:** REGARDING
**con·cern·ment** \kən-'sərn-mənt\ *noun* (1610)
**1 :** something in which one is concerned
**2 :** IMPORTANCE, CONSEQUENCE
**3** *archaic* **:** INVOLVEMENT, PARTICIPATION
**4 :** SOLICITUDE, ANXIETY
**¹con·cert** \'kän(t)-sərt, 'kän-,sərt\ *noun* [French, from Italian *concerto,* from *concertare*] (1674)
**1** *obsolete* **:** musical harmony **:** CONCORD
**2 a :** agreement in design or plan **:** union formed by mutual communication of opinion and views **b :** a concerted action 〈the sacrifice was hailed with a *concert* of praise〉
**3 :** a public performance (as of music or dancing)
— **concert** *adjective*
— **in concert :** TOGETHER
**²con·cert** \kən-'sərt\ *verb* [Middle French *concerter,* from Old Italian *concertare,* perhaps from *com-* + *certo* certain, decided, from Latin *certus* — more at CERTAIN] (1694)
*transitive verb*
**1 :** to settle or adjust by conferring and reaching an agreement 〈*concerted* their differences〉
**2 :** to make a plan for 〈*concert* measures for aiding the poor〉
*intransitive verb*
**:** to act in harmony or conjunction
**con·cert·ed** \kən-'sər-təd\ *adjective* (1716)
**1 a :** mutually contrived or agreed on 〈a *concerted* effort〉 **b :** performed in unison 〈*concerted* artillery fire〉
**2 :** arranged in parts for several voices or instruments
— **con·cert·ed·ly** *adverb*
— **con·cert·ed·ness** *noun*
**con·cert·go·er** \'kän(t)-sərt-,gō(-ə)r, 'kän-,sərt-\ *noun* (1855)
**:** one who frequently attends concerts
— **con·cert·go·ing** \-,gō-iŋ, -,gȯ(-)iŋ\ *noun or adjective*
**concert grand** *noun* (circa 1891)
**:** a grand piano of the largest size adapted in volume, timbre, and brilliance of tone to concert use
**con·cer·ti·na** \,kän(t)-sər-'tē-nə\ *noun* [probably from ¹*concert* + Italian *-ina,* diminutive suffix] (1837)
**1 :** a musical instrument of the accordion family
**2 :** a coiled barbed wire for use as an obstacle — called also *concertina wire*
**con·cer·ti·no** \,kän-chər-'tē-(,)nō\ *noun,* *plural* **-nos** [Italian, diminutive of *concerto*] (circa 1801)
**1 :** the solo instruments in a concerto grosso
**2 :** a short concerto
**con·cert·ize** \'kän(t)-sər-,tīz\ *intransitive verb* **-ized; -iz·ing** (1883)

**:** to perform professionally in concerts
**con·cert·mas·ter** \'kän(t)-sərt-,mas-tər\ *or* **con·cert·meis·ter** \-,mī-stər\ *noun* [German *Konzertmeister,* from *Konzert* concert + *Meister* master] (circa 1889)
**:** the leader of the first violins of an orchestra and by custom usually the assistant to the conductor
**con·cer·to** \kən-'cher-(,)tō *also* -'chər-\ *noun,* *plural* **-ti** \-(,)tē\ *or* **-tos** [Italian, from *concerto* concert] (1730)
**:** a piece for one or more soloists and orchestra with three contrasting movements
**concerto gros·so** \-'grō-(,)sō, -'grȯ-\ *noun,* *plural* **concerti gros·si** \-(,)sē\ [Italian, literally, big concerto] (1724)
**:** a baroque orchestral composition featuring a small group of solo instruments contrasting with the full orchestra
**concert pitch** *noun* (1767)
**1 :** INTERNATIONAL PITCH
**2 :** a high state of fitness, tension, or readiness
**con·ces·sion** \kən-'se-shən\ *noun* [Middle English, from Middle French or Latin; Middle French, from Latin *concession-, concessio,* from *concedere* to concede] (15th century)
**1 a :** the act or an instance of conceding **b :** the admitting of a point claimed in argument
**2 :** something conceded: **a :** ACKNOWLEDGMENT, ADMISSION **b :** GRANT **c** (1) **:** a grant of land or property especially by a government in return for services or for a particular use (2) **:** a right to undertake and profit by a specified activity (3) **:** a lease of a portion of premises for a particular purpose; *also* **:** the portion leased or the activities carried on
— **con·ces·sion·al** \-'sesh-nəl, -'se-shə-nᵊl\ *adjective*
— **con·ces·sion·ary** \-'se-shə-,ner-ē\ *adjective*
**con·ces·sion·aire** \kən-,se-shə-'nar, -'ner\ *noun* [French *concessionnaire,* from *concession*] (1862)
**:** the owner or operator of a concession; *especially* **:** one that operates a refreshment stand at a recreational center
**con·ces·sion·er** \kən-'se-sh(ə-)nər\ *noun* (circa 1891)
**:** CONCESSIONAIRE
**con·ces·sive** \kən-'se-siv\ *adjective* (1711)
**1 :** denoting concession 〈a *concessive* clause〉
**2 :** making for or being a concession
— **con·ces·sive·ly** *adverb*
**conch** \'käŋk, 'känch, 'kȯŋk\ *noun,* *plural* **conchs** \'käŋks, 'kȯŋks\ *or* **conches** \'kän-chəz\ [Middle English, from Latin *concha* mussel, mussel shell, from Greek *konchē;* akin to Sanskrit *śankha* conch shell] (15th century)
**1 :** any of various large spiral-shelled marine gastropod mollusks (as of the genus *Strombus*); *also* **:** its shell used especially for cameos
**2** *often capitalized* **:** a native or resident of the Florida Keys
**3 :** CONCHA 2
**con·cha** \'kän-kə\ *noun,* *plural* **con·chae** \-,kē, -,kī\ [Italian & Latin; Italian *conca* semidome, apse, from Late Latin *concha,* from Latin, shell] (circa 1639)
**1 a :** the plain semidome of an apse **b :** APSE
**2 :** something shaped like a shell; *especially* **:** the largest and deepest concavity of the external ear
— **con·chal** \-kəl\ *adjective*

conch 1

concertina 1

**con·choi·dal** \kän-'kȯi-dᵊl, kän-\ *adjective* [Greek *konchoeidēs* like a mussel, from *konchē*] (1666)
: having elevations or depressions shaped like the inside surface of a bivalve shell
— **con·choi·dal·ly** \-dᵊl-ē\ *adverb*

**con·chol·o·gy** \kän-'kä-lə-jē\ *noun* [Greek *konchē*] (1776)
**1** : a branch of zoology that deals with shells
**2** : a treatise on shells
— **con·chol·o·gist** \-jist\ *noun*

**con·cierge** \kōⁿ-'syerzh\ *noun, plural* **con·cierges** \-'syerzh, -'syer-zhəz\ [French, from Old French, probably from (assumed) Vulgar Latin *conservius*, alteration of Latin *conservus* fellow slave, from *com-* + *servus* slave] (circa 1697)
**1** : a resident in an apartment building especially in France who serves as doorkeeper, landlord's representative, and janitor
**2** : a usually multilingual hotel staff member who handles luggage and mail, makes reservations, and arranges tours

**con·cil·i·ar** \kən-'si-lē-ər\ *adjective* [Latin *concilium* council] (circa 1677)
: of, relating to, or issued by a council
— **con·cil·i·ar·ly** *adverb*

**con·cil·i·ate** \kən-'si-lē-ˌāt\ *verb* **-at·ed; -at·ing** [Latin *conciliatus*, past participle of *conciliare* to assemble, unite, win over, from *concilium* assembly, council — more at COUNCIL] (1545)
*transitive verb*
**1** : to gain (as goodwill) by pleasing acts
**2** : to make compatible : RECONCILE
**3** : APPEASE
*intransitive verb*
: to become friendly or agreeable
*synonym* SEE PACIFY
— **con·cil·i·a·tion** \-ˌsi-lē-'ā-shən\ *noun*
— **con·cil·i·a·tive** \-'si-lē-ˌā-tiv\ *adjective*
— **con·cil·i·a·tor** \-ˌā-tər\ *noun*
— **con·cil·i·a·to·ry** \-'sil-yə-ˌtȯr-ē, -'si-lē-ə-, -ˌtȯr-\ *adjective*

**con·cin·ni·ty** \kən-'si-nə-tē\ *noun, plural* **-ties** [Latin *concinnitas*, from *concinnus* skillfully put together] (1531)
: harmony or elegance of design especially of literary style in adaptation of parts to a whole or to each other

**con·cise** \kən-'sīs\ *adjective* [Latin *concisus*, from past participle of *concidere* to cut up, from *com-* + *caedere* to cut, strike] (circa 1590)
**1** : marked by brevity of expression or statement : free from all elaboration and superfluous detail
**2** : cut short : BRIEF ☆
— **con·cise·ly** *adverb*
— **con·cise·ness** *noun*

**con·ci·sion** \kən-'si-zhən\ *noun* [Middle English, from Latin *concision-, concisio*, from *concidere*] (14th century)
**1** *archaic* : a cutting up or off
**2** : the quality or state of being concise

**con·clave** \'kän-ˌklāv\ *noun* [Middle English, from Middle French or Medieval Latin; Middle French, from Medieval Latin, from Latin, room that can be locked up, from *com-* + *clavis* key — more at CLAVICLE] (1524)
**1** : a private meeting or secret assembly; especially : a meeting of Roman Catholic cardinals secluded continuously while choosing a pope
**2** : a gathering of a group or association

**con·clude** \kən-'klüd\ *verb* **con·clud·ed; con·clud·ing** [Middle English, from Latin *concludere* to shut up, end, infer, from *com-* + *claudere* to shut — more at CLOSE] (14th century)
*transitive verb*
**1** *obsolete* : to shut up : ENCLOSE
**2** : to bring to an end especially in a particular way or with a particular action 〈*conclude* a meeting with a prayer〉

**3 a** : to reach as a logically necessary end by reasoning : infer on the basis of evidence 〈*concluded* that her argument was sound〉 **b** : to make a decision about : DECIDE 〈*concluded* he would wait a little longer〉 **c** : to come to an agreement on : EFFECT 〈*conclude* a sale〉
**4** : to bring about as a result : COMPLETE
*intransitive verb*
**1** : END
**2 a** : to form a final judgment **b** : to reach a decision or agreement
*synonym* see CLOSE, INFER
— **con·clud·er** *noun*

**con·clu·sion** \kən-'klü-zhən\ *noun* [Middle English, from Middle French, from Latin *conclusion-, conclusio*, from *concludere*] (14th century)
**1 a** : a reasoned judgment : INFERENCE **b** : the necessary consequence of two or more propositions taken as premises; *especially* : the inferred proposition of a syllogism
**2** : the last part of something: as **a** : RESULT, OUTCOME **b** *plural* : trial of strength or skill — used in the phrase *try conclusions* **c** : a final summation **d** : the final decision in a law case **e** : the final part of a pleading in law
**3** : an act or instance of concluding

**con·clu·sion·ary** \kən-'klü-zhə-ˌner-ē\ *adjective* (1948)
: CONCLUSORY

**con·clu·sive** \-'klü-siv, -ziv\ *adjective* (1536)
**1** : of, relating to, or being a conclusion
**2** : putting an end to debate or question especially by reason of irrefutability ☆
— **con·clu·sive·ly** *adverb*
— **con·clu·sive·ness** *noun*

**con·clu·so·ry** \kən-'klüs-rē, -'klü-sə-\ *adjective* (1923)
: consisting of or relating to a conclusion or assertion for which no supporting evidence is offered 〈*conclusory* allegations〉

**con·coct** \kən-'käkt, kän-\ *transitive verb* [Latin *concoctus*, past participle of *concoquere* to cook together, from *com-* + *coquere* to cook — more at COOK] (1675)
**1** : to prepare by combining raw materials
**2** : DEVISE, FABRICATE
— **con·coct·er** *noun*
— **con·coc·tion** \-'käk-shən\ *noun*
— **con·coc·tive** \-'käk-tiv\ *adjective*

**con·com·i·tance** \kən-'kä-mə-tən(t)s, kän-\ *noun* (circa 1535)
: ACCOMPANIMENT; *especially* : a conjunction that is regular and is marked by correlative variation of accompanying elements

**¹con·com·i·tant** \-mə-tənt\ *adjective* [Latin *concomitant-, concomitans*, present participle of *concomitari* to accompany, from *com-* + *comitari* to accompany, from *comit-, comes* companion — more at COUNT] (1607)
: accompanying especially in a subordinate or incidental way
— **con·com·i·tant·ly** *adverb*

**²concomitant** *noun* (1621)
: something that accompanies or is collaterally connected with something else : ACCOMPANIMENT

**con·cord** \'kän-ˌkȯrd, 'käŋ-\ *noun* [Middle English, from Middle French *concorde*, from Latin *concordia*, from *concord-, concors* agreeing, from *com-* + *cord-, cor* heart — more at HEART] (14th century)
**1 a** : a state of agreement : HARMONY **b** : a simultaneous occurrence of two or more musical tones that produces an impression of agreeableness or resolution on a listener — compare DISCORD
**2** : agreement by stipulation, compact, or covenant
**3** : grammatical agreement

**con·cor·dance** \kən-'kȯr-dᵊn(t)s, kän-\ *noun* [Middle English, from Middle French, from Medieval Latin *concordantia*, from Latin *concordant-, concordans*, present participle of

*concordare* to agree, from *concord-, concors*] (14th century)
**1** : an alphabetical index of the principal words in a book or the works of an author with their immediate contexts
**2** : CONCORD, AGREEMENT

**con·cor·dant** \-dᵊnt\ *adjective* [Middle English, from Middle French, from Latin *concordant-, concordans*] (15th century)
: CONSONANT, AGREEING
— **con·cor·dant·ly** *adverb*

**con·cor·dat** \kən-'kȯr-ˌdat\ *noun* [French, from Medieval Latin *concordatum*, from Latin, neuter of *concordatus*, past participle of *concordare*] (1616)
: COMPACT, COVENANT; *specifically* : an agreement between a pope and a sovereign or government for the regulation of ecclesiastical matters

**con·cours d'e·le·gance** \(ˌ)kōⁿ-ˌkür-ˌdā-lā-'gäⁿs\ *noun* [French *concours d'élégance*, literally, competition of elegance] (1950)
: a show or contest of vehicles and accessories in which the entries are judged chiefly on excellence of appearance and turnout

**con·course** \'kän-ˌkȯrs, 'käŋ-, -ˌkȯrs\ *noun* [Middle English, from Middle French & Latin; Middle French *concours*, from Latin *concursus*, from *concurrere* to run together — more at CONCUR] (14th century)
**1** : an act or process of coming together and merging
**2** : a meeting produced by voluntary or spontaneous coming together
**3 a** : an open space where roads or paths meet **b** : an open space or hall (as in a railroad terminal) where crowds gather

**con·cres·cence** \kən-'kre-sᵊn(t)s, kän-\ *noun* [Latin *concrescentia*, from *concrescent-, concrescens*, present participle of *concrescere* to grow together, from *com-* + *crescere* to grow — more at CRESCENT] (1614)
**1** : increase by the addition of particles
**2** : a growing together : COALESCENCE; *especially* : convergence and fusion of the lateral lips of the blastopore to form the primordium of an embryo

---

☆ **SYNONYMS**
**Concise, terse, succinct, laconic, summary, pithy, compendious** mean very brief in statement or expression. CONCISE suggests the removal of all that is superfluous or elaborative 〈a *concise* description〉. TERSE implies pointed conciseness 〈a *terse* reply〉. SUCCINCT implies the greatest possible compression 〈a *succinct* letter of resignation〉. LACONIC implies brevity to the point of seeming rude, indifferent, or mysterious 〈an aloof and *laconic* stranger〉. SUMMARY suggests the statement of main points with no elaboration or explanation 〈a *summary* listing of the year's main events〉. PITHY adds to SUCCINCT or TERSE the implication of richness of meaning or substance 〈a comedy sharpened by *pithy* one-liners〉. COMPENDIOUS applies to what is at once full in scope and brief and concise in treatment 〈a *compendious* dictionary〉.

**Conclusive, decisive, determinative, definitive** mean bringing to an end. CONCLUSIVE applies to reasoning or logical proof that puts an end to debate or questioning 〈*conclusive* evidence〉. DECISIVE may apply to something that ends a controversy, a contest, or any uncertainty 〈a *decisive* battle〉. DETERMINATIVE adds an implication of giving a fixed character or direction 〈the *determinative* factor in the court's decision〉. DEFINITIVE applies to what is put forth as final and permanent 〈the *definitive* biography〉.

— **con·cres·cent** \-s°nt\ *adjective*

¹**con·crete** \(ˌ)kän-'krēt, 'kän-ˌ, kən-\ *adjective* [Middle English, from Latin *concretus*, from past participle of *concrescere*] (14th century)
**1** : naming a real thing or class of things ⟨the word *poem* is concrete, *poetry* is abstract⟩
**2** : formed by coalition of particles into one solid mass
**3 a** : characterized by or belonging to immediate experience of actual things or events **b** : SPECIFIC, PARTICULAR **c** : REAL, TANGIBLE
**4** : relating to or made of concrete
— **con·crete·ly** *adverb*
— **con·crete·ness** *noun*

²**con·crete** \'kän-ˌkrēt, kän-'\ *verb* **con·cret·ed; con·cret·ing** (1590)
*transitive verb*
**1 a** : to form into a solid mass : SOLIDIFY **b** : COMBINE, BLEND
**2** : to make actual or real : cause to take on the qualities of reality
**3** : to cover with, form of, or set in concrete
*intransitive verb*
: to become concreted

³**con·crete** \'kän-ˌkrēt, (ˌ)kän-'\ *noun* (1656)
**1** : a mass formed by concretion or coalescence of separate particles of matter in one body
**2** : a hard strong building material made by mixing a cementing material (as portland cement) and a mineral aggregate (as sand and gravel) with sufficient water to cause the cement to set and bind the entire mass
**3** : a waxy essence of flowers prepared by extraction and evaporation and used in perfumery

**concrete music** *noun* (1953)
: MUSIQUE CONCRÈTE

**concrete poetry** *noun* (1958)
: poetry in which the poet's intent is conveyed by the graphic patterns of letters, words, or symbols rather than by the conventional arrangement of words

**con·cre·tion** \kän-'krē-shən, kən-\ *noun* (1541)
**1** : something concreted: as **a** : a hard usually inorganic mass (as a bezoar or tophus) formed in a living body **b** : a mass of mineral matter found generally in rock of a composition different from its own and produced by deposition from aqueous solution in the rock
**2** : the act or process of concreting : the state of being concreted ⟨*concretion* of ideas in an hypothesis⟩
— **con·cre·tion·ary** \-shə-ˌner-ē\ *adjective*

**con·cre·tism** \kän-'krē-ˌti-zəm, 'kän-ˌ\ *noun* (1865)
: representation of abstract things as concrete; *especially* : the theory or practice of concrete poetry
— **con·cre·tist** \-'krē-tist, -ˌkrē\ *noun*

**con·cret·ize** \-ˌtīz\ *verb* **-ized; -iz·ing** (1884)
*transitive verb*
: to make concrete, specific, or definite ⟨tried to *concretize* his ideas⟩
*intransitive verb*
: to become concrete
— **con·cret·i·za·tion** \(ˌ)kän-ˌkrē-tə-'zā-shən\ *noun*

**con·cu·bi·nage** \kän-'kyü-bə-nij, kən-\ *noun* (14th century)
**1** : cohabitation of persons not legally married
**2** : the state of being a concubine

**con·cu·bine** \'käŋ-kyü-ˌbīn, 'kän-\ *noun* [Middle English, from Middle French, from Latin *concubina*, from *com-* + *cubare* to lie] (14th century)
: a woman with whom a man cohabits without being married: as **a** : one having a recognized social status in a household below that of a wife **b** : MISTRESS 4a

**con·cu·pis·cence** \kän-'kyü-pə-sən(t)s,

kən-\ *noun* [Middle English, from Middle French, from Late Latin *concupiscentia*, from Latin *concupiscent-, concupiscens*, present participle of *concupiscere* to desire ardently, from *com-* + *cupere* to desire] (14th century)
: strong desire; *especially* : sexual desire
— **con·cu·pis·cent** \-sənt\ *adjective*

**con·cu·pis·ci·ble** \-'kyü-pə-sə-bəl\ *adjective* [Middle English, from Middle French or Late Latin; Middle French, from Late Latin *concupiscibilis*, from Latin *concupiscere*] (14th century)
: LUSTFUL, DESIROUS

**con·cur** \kən-'kər, kän-\ *intransitive verb* **con·curred; con·cur·ring** [Middle English *concurren*, from Latin *concurrere*, from *com-* + *currere* to run — more at CAR] (15th century)
**1** : to act together to a common end or single effect
**2 a** : APPROVE ⟨*concur* in a statement⟩ **b** : to express agreement ⟨*concur* with an opinion⟩
**3** *obsolete* : to come together : MEET
**4** : to happen together : COINCIDE
*synonym* see AGREE

**con·cur·rence** \-'kər-ən(t)s, -'kə-rən(t)s\ *noun* (15th century)
**1 a** : the simultaneous occurrence of events or circumstances **b** : the meeting of concurrent lines in a point
**2 a** : agreement or union in action : COOPERATION **b** (1) : agreement in opinion or design (2) : CONSENT
**3** : a coincidence of equal powers in law

**con·cur·ren·cy** \-ən(t)-sē, -rən(t)-sē\ *noun* (1597)
: CONCURRENCE

**con·cur·rent** \-'kər-ənt, -'kə-rənt\ *adjective* [Middle English, from Middle French & Latin; Middle French, from Latin *concurrent-, concurrens*, present participle of *concurrere*] (14th century)
**1** : operating or occurring at the same time
**2 a** : running parallel **b** : CONVERGENT; *specifically* : meeting or intersecting in a point
**3** : acting in conjunction
**4** : exercised over the same matter or area by two different authorities ⟨*concurrent* jurisdiction⟩
— **concurrent** *noun*
— **con·cur·rent·ly** *adverb*

**concurrent resolution** *noun* (1802)
: a resolution passed by both houses of a legislative body that lacks the force of law

**con·cuss** \kən-'kəs\ *transitive verb* [Latin *concussus*, past participle] (1597)
: to affect with or as if with concussion

**con·cus·sion** \kən-'kə-shən\ *noun* [Middle English *concussioun*, from Middle French or Latin; Middle French *concussion*, from Latin *concussion-, concussio*, from *concutere* to shake violently, from *com-* + *quatere* to shake] (14th century)
**1 a** : a stunning, damaging, or shattering effect from a hard blow; *especially* : a jarring injury of the brain resulting in disturbance of cerebral function **b** : a hard blow or collision
**2** : AGITATION, SHAKING
— **con·cus·sive** \-'kə-siv\ *adjective*

**con·demn** \kən-'dem\ *transitive verb* [Middle English, from Middle French *condemner*, from Latin *condemnare*, from *com-* + *damnare* to condemn — more at DAMN] (14th century)
**1** : to declare to be reprehensible, wrong, or evil usually after weighing evidence and without reservation
**2 a** : to pronounce guilty : CONVICT **b** : SENTENCE, DOOM
**3** : to adjudge unfit for use or consumption
**4** : to declare convertible to public use under the right of eminent domain
*synonym* see CRITICIZE
— **con·demn·able** \-'dem-nə-bəl, -'de-mə-\ *adjective*

— **con·dem·na·to·ry** \-'dem-nə-ˌtōr-ē, -'de-mə-, -ˌtòr\ *adjective*
— **con·demn·er** \-'de-mər\ *or* **con·dem·nor** \kən-'de-mər; kən-ˌdem-'nór, ˌkän-\ *noun*

**con·dem·na·tion** \ˌkän-ˌdem-'nā-shən, -dəm-\ *noun* (14th century)
**1** : CENSURE, BLAME
**2** : the act of judicially condemning
**3** : the state of being condemned
**4** : a reason for condemning

**con·den·sate** \'kän-dən-ˌsāt, -ˌden-; kən-'den-\ *noun* (1889)
: a product of condensation; *especially* : a liquid obtained by condensation of a gas or vapor ⟨steam *condensate*⟩

**con·den·sa·tion** \ˌkän-ˌden-'sā-shən, -dən-\ *noun* (1603)
**1** : the act or process of condensing: as **a** : a chemical reaction involving union between molecules often with elimination of a simple molecule (as water) to form a new more complex compound of often greater molecular weight **b** : the conversion of a substance (as water) from the vapor state to a denser liquid or solid state usually initiated by a reduction in temperature of the vapor **c** : compression of a written or spoken work into more concise form
**2** : the quality or state of being condensed
**3** : a product of condensing
— **con·den·sa·tion·al** \-shnəl, -shə-n°l\ *adjective*

**con·dense** \kən-'den(t)s\ *verb* **con·densed; con·dens·ing** [Middle English, from Middle French *condenser*, from Latin *condensare*, from *com-* + *densare* to make dense, from *densus* dense] (15th century)
*transitive verb*
: to make denser or more compact; *especially* : to subject to condensation
*intransitive verb*
: to undergo condensation
*synonym* see CONTRACT
— **con·dens·able** *also* **con·dens·ible** \-'den(t)-sə-bəl\ *adjective*

**condensed** *adjective* (15th century)
: reduced to a more compact or dense form; *also* : having a face narrower than that of a standard typeface

**condensed milk** *noun* (1863)
: evaporated milk with sugar added

**con·dens·er** \kən-'den(t)-sər\ *noun* (1686)
**1** : one that condenses: as **a** : a lens or mirror used to concentrate light on an object **b** : an apparatus in which gas or vapor is condensed
**2** : CAPACITOR

**con·de·scend** \ˌkän-di-'send\ *intransitive verb* [Middle English, from Middle French *condescendre*, from Late Latin *condescendere*, from Latin *com-* + *descendere* to descend] (14th century)
**1 a** : to descend to a less formal or dignified level : UNBEND **b** : to waive the privileges of rank
**2** : to assume an air of superiority

**con·de·scen·dence** \-'sen-dən(t)s\ *noun* (1638)
: CONDESCENSION

**condescending** *adjective* (1707)
: showing or characterized by condescension : PATRONIZING
— **con·de·scend·ing·ly** \-'sen-diŋ-lē\ *adverb*

**con·de·scen·sion** \ˌkän-di-'sen(t)-shən\ *noun* [Late Latin *condescension-, condescensio*, from *condescendere*] (1647)
**1** : voluntary descent from one's rank or dignity in relations with an inferior

\ə\ abut \°\ kitten \ər\ further \a\ ash \ā\ ace
\ä\ mop, mar \aú\ out \ch\ chin \e\ bet \ē\ easy
\g\ go \i\ hit \ī\ ice \j\ job \ŋ\ sing \ō\ go
\ò\ law \òi\ boy \th\ thin \th\ the \ü\ loot \ú\ foot
\y\ yet \zh\ vision *see also* Guide to Pronunciation

**2 :** patronizing attitude or behavior

**con·dign** \kən-'dīn, 'kän-,\ *adjective* [Middle English *condigne,* from Middle French, from Latin *condignus* very worthy, from *com-* + *dignus* worthy — more at DECENT] (15th century)
**:** DESERVED, APPROPRIATE ⟨*condign* punishment⟩
— **con·dign·ly** *adverb*

**con·di·ment** \'kän-də-mənt\ *noun* [Middle English, from Middle French, from Latin *condimentum,* from *condire* to season] (15th century)
**:** something used to enhance the flavor of food; *especially* **:** a pungent seasoning
— **con·di·men·tal** \,kän-də-'men-t°l\ *adjective*

**¹con·di·tion** \kən-'di-shən\ *noun* [Middle English *condicion,* from Middle French, from Latin *condicion-, condicio* terms of agreement, condition, from *condicere* to agree, from *com-* + *dicere* to say, determine — more at DICTION] (14th century)
**1 a :** a premise upon which the fulfillment of an agreement depends **:** STIPULATION **b** *obsolete* **:** COVENANT **c :** a provision making the effect of a legal instrument contingent upon an uncertain event; *also* **:** the event itself
**2 :** something essential to the appearance or occurrence of something else **:** PREREQUISITE: as **a :** an environmental requirement ⟨available oxygen is an essential *condition* for animal life⟩ **b :** the subordinate clause of a conditional sentence
**3 a :** a restricting or modifying factor **:** QUALIFICATION **b :** an unsatisfactory academic grade that may be raised by doing additional work
**4 a :** a state of being **b :** social status **:** RANK **c :** a usually defective state of health ⟨a serious heart *condition*⟩ **d :** a state of physical fitness or readiness for use ⟨the car was in good *condition*⟩ ⟨exercising to get into *condition*⟩ **e** *plural* **:** attendant circumstances
**5 a** *obsolete* **:** temper of mind **b** *obsolete* **:** TRAIT **c** *plural, archaic* **:** MANNERS, WAYS

**²condition** *verb* **con·di·tioned; con·di·tion·ing** \-'di-sh(ə-)niŋ\ (15th century)
*intransitive verb*
*archaic* **:** to make stipulations
*transitive verb*
**1 :** to agree by stipulating
**2 :** to make conditional
**3 a :** to put into a proper state for work or use **b :** AIR-CONDITION
**4 :** to give a grade of condition to
**5 a :** to adapt, modify, or mold so as to conform to an environing culture **b :** to modify so that an act or response previously associated with one stimulus becomes associated with another
— **con·di·tion·able** \-sh(ə-)nə-bəl\ *adjective*
— **con·di·tion·er** \-sh(ə-)nər\ *noun*

**¹con·di·tion·al** \kən-'dish-nəl, -'di-shə-n°l\ *adjective* (14th century)
**1 :** subject to, implying, or dependent upon a condition ⟨a *conditional* promise⟩
**2 :** expressing, containing, or implying a supposition ⟨the *conditional* clause *if he speaks*⟩
**3 a :** true only for certain values of the variables or symbols involved ⟨*conditional* equations⟩ **b :** stating the case when one or more random variables are fixed or one or more events are known ⟨*conditional* frequency distribution⟩
**4 a :** CONDITIONED 2 ⟨*conditional* reflex⟩ ⟨*conditional* response⟩ **b :** established by conditioning as the stimulus eliciting a conditional response
— **con·di·tion·al·i·ty** \-,di-shə-'na-lə-tē\ *noun*
— **con·di·tion·al·ly** \-'dish-nə-lē, -'di-shə-n°l-ē\ *adverb*

**²conditional** *noun* (1828)
**1 :** a conditional word, clause, verb form, or morpheme

**2 :** IMPLICATION 2b

**conditional probability** *noun* (1961)
**:** the probability that a given event will occur if it is certain that another event has taken place or will take place

**conditioned** *adjective* (1537)
**1 :** brought or put into a specified state
**2 :** determined or established by conditioning

**con·do** \'kän-,dō\ *noun* (1964)
**:** CONDOMINIUM 3

**con·dole** \kən-'dōl\ *verb* **con·doled; con·dol·ing** [Late Latin *condolēre,* from Latin *com-* + *dolēre* to feel pain] (1590)
*intransitive verb*
**1** *obsolete* **:** GRIEVE
**2 :** to express sympathetic sorrow
*transitive verb*
*archaic* **:** LAMENT, GRIEVE
— **con·do·la·to·ry** \-'dō-lə-,tōr-ē, -,tôr-\ *adjective*

**con·do·lence** \kən-'dō-lən(t)s *also* 'kän-də-\ *noun* (1603)
**1 :** sympathy with another in sorrow
**2 :** an expression of sympathy
*synonym* see PITY

**con·dom** \'kän-dəm, 'kən-, *dialect* -drəm\ *noun* [origin unknown] (circa 1706)
**:** a sheath commonly of rubber worn over the penis (as to prevent conception or venereal infection during coitus); *also* **:** a similar device inserted into the vagina

**con·do·min·i·um** \,kän-də-'mi-nē-əm\ *noun, plural* **-ums** [New Latin, from Latin *com-* + *dominium* domain] (circa 1714)
**1 a :** joint dominion; *especially* **:** joint sovereignty by two or more nations **b :** a government operating under joint rule
**2 :** a politically dependent territory under condominium
**3 a :** individual ownership of a unit in a multiunit structure (as an apartment building) or on land owned in common (as a town house complex); *also* **:** a unit so owned **b :** a building containing condominiums ◆

**con·do·na·tion** \,kän-də-'nā-shən, -dō-\ *noun* (1625)
**:** implied pardon of an offense by treating the offender as if it had not been committed

**con·done** \kən-'dōn\ *transitive verb* **con·doned; con·don·ing** [Latin *condonare* to absolve, from *com-* + *donare* to give — more at DONATION] (1857)
**:** to pardon or overlook voluntarily; *especially* **:** to treat as if trivial, harmless, or of no importance ⟨*condone* corruption in politics⟩
*synonym* see EXCUSE
— **con·don·able** \-'dō-nə-bəl\ *adjective*
— **con·don·er** *noun*

**con·dor** \'kän-dər, -,dôr\ *noun* [Spanish *cóndor,* from Quechua *kuntur*] (1604)
**1 a :** a very large American vulture (*Vultur gryphus*) of the high Andes having the head and neck bare and the plumage dull black with a downy white neck ruff and white patches on the wings **b :** CALIFORNIA CONDOR
**2** *plural* **condors** *or* **con·do·res** \kən-'dōr-,ās, -'dôr-\ **:** a coin (as the centesimo of Chile) bearing the picture of a condor

**con·dot·tie·re** \,kän-də-'tyer-ē, ,kän-,dä-tē-'er-\ *noun, plural* **-tie·ri** \-ē\ [Italian, from *condotta* troop of mercenaries, from feminine of *condotto,* past participle of *condurre* to conduct, hire, from Latin *conducere*] (1794)
**1 :** a leader of a band of mercenaries common in Europe between the 14th and 16th centuries; *also* **:** a member of such a band
**2 :** a mercenary soldier

**con·duce** \kən-'düs, -'dyüs\ *intransitive verb* **con·duced; con·duc·ing** [Middle English, to conduct, from Latin *conducere* to conduct, conduce, from *com-* + *ducere* to lead — more at TOW] (1586)
**:** to lead or tend to a particular and usually desirable result **:** CONTRIBUTE

**con·du·cive** \-'dü-siv, -'dyü-\ *adjective* (1646)
**:** tending to promote or assist ⟨an atmosphere *conducive* to education⟩
— **con·du·cive·ness** *noun*

**¹con·duct** \'kän-(,)dəkt\ *noun* [Middle English, alteration of *conduit,* from Middle French, act of leading, escort, from Medieval Latin *conductus,* from Latin *conducere*] (15th century)
**1** *obsolete* **:** ESCORT, GUIDE
**2 :** the act, manner, or process of carrying on **:** MANAGEMENT
**3 :** a mode or standard of personal behavior especially as based on moral principles

**²con·duct** \kən-'dəkt *also* 'kän-,dəkt\ (15th century)
*transitive verb*
**1 :** to bring by or as if by leading **:** GUIDE ⟨*conduct* tourists through a museum⟩
**2 a :** to lead from a position of command ⟨*conduct* a siege⟩ ⟨*conduct* a class⟩ **b :** to direct or take part in the operation or management of ⟨*conduct* an experiment⟩ ⟨*conduct* a business⟩ ⟨*conduct* an investigation⟩ **c :** to direct the performance of ⟨*conduct* an orchestra⟩ ⟨*conduct* an opera⟩
**3 a :** to convey in a channel **b :** to act as a medium for conveying or transmitting
**4 :** to cause (oneself) to act or behave in a particular and especially in a controlled manner
*intransitive verb*
**1** *of a road or passage* **:** to show the way **:** LEAD
**2 a :** to act as leader or director **b :** to have the quality of transmitting light, heat, sound, or electricity ☆
— **con·duct·ibil·i·ty** \kən-,dək-tə-'bi-lə-tē\ *noun*
— **con·duct·ible** \-'dək-tə-bəl\ *adjective*

**con·duc·tance** \kən-'dək-tən(t)s\ *noun* (1885)
**1 :** conducting power
**2 :** the readiness with which a conductor transmits an electric current expressed as the reciprocal of electrical resistance

**con·duc·tion** \kən-'dək-shən\ *noun* (1534)
**1 :** the act of conducting or conveying
**2 a :** transmission through or by means of a conductor; *also* **:** the transfer of heat through matter by communication of kinetic energy from particle to particle with no net displacement of the particles — compare CONVECTION, RADIATION **b :** CONDUCTIVITY
**3 :** the transmission of excitation through living tissue and especially nervous tissue

---

◇ **WORD HISTORY**
**condominium** The word *condominium* was coined by European jurists in the 17th century and used in Latin treatises on international law to refer to dual sovereignty exercised by two countries over the same territory; in this sense it was borrowed into English by the early 18th century. Probably the best-known such condominium historically was the joint British and Egyptian rule of the Sudan in Africa, which began in 1899 and ended in 1956 with Sudanese independence. *Condominium* was probably introduced into U.S. real estate terminology in 1961, when the federal government first insured mortgage loans for individually owned units in apartment buildings. Three years earlier condominium mortgages had received U.S. government sanction in Puerto Rico, where the concept of joint ownership of land combined with individual ownership of living space had most likely spread from South America. In the 1960s and 1970s, *condominium* became a common word across the U.S. as state after state passed enabling legislation setting up guidelines for this type of ownership.

**conduction band** *noun* (1953)
: the range of permissible energy values that allow an electron of an atom to dissociate from the atom and become a free charge carrier — compare VALENCE BAND

**con·duc·tive** \kən-'dək-tiv\ *adjective* (1528)
: having conductivity : relating to conduction (as of electricity)

**con·duc·tiv·i·ty** \ˌkän-ˌdək-'ti-və-tē, kən-\ *noun, plural* **-ties** (1837)
: the quality or power of conducting or transmitting : as **a** : the reciprocal of electrical resistivity **b** : the quality of living matter responsible for the transmission of and progressive reaction to stimuli

**con·duc·to·met·ric** *also* **con·duc·ti·met·ric** \kən-ˌdək-tə-'me-trik\ *adjective* (circa 1926)
**1** : of or relating to the measurement of conductivity
**2** : being or relating to titration based on determination of changes in the electrical conductivity of the solution

**con·duc·tor** \kən-'dək-tər\ *noun* (15th century)
: one that conducts: as **a** : GUIDE **b** : a collector of fares in a public conveyance **c** : the leader of a musical ensemble **d** (1) : a material or object that permits an electric current to flow easily — compare INSULATOR, SEMICONDUCTOR (2) : a material capable of transmitting another form of energy (as heat or sound)
— **con·duc·to·ri·al** \ˌkän-ˌdək-'tōr-ē-əl, kən-, -'tȯr-\ *adjective*

**con·duc·tress** \kən-'dək-trəs\ *noun* (1624)
: a woman who is a conductor

**con·duit** \'kän-ˌdü-ət, -ˌdyü- *also* -dwət, -dət\ *noun* [Middle English — more at CONDUCT] (14th century)
**1** : a natural or artificial channel through which something (as a fluid) is conveyed
**2** *archaic* : FOUNTAIN
**3** : a pipe, tube, or tile for protecting electric wires or cables
**4** : a means of transmitting or distributing ⟨a *conduit* for illicit payments⟩ ⟨a *conduit* of information⟩

**con·du·pli·cate** \(ˌ)kän-'dü-pli-kət, -'dyü-\ *adjective* [Latin *conduplicatus,* past participle of *conduplicare* to double, from *com-* + *duplic-, duplex* double — more at DUPLEX] (1777)
: folded lengthwise ⟨*conduplicate* petals in the bud⟩

**con·dy·lar** \'kän-də-lər\ *adjective* (1876)
: of or relating to a condyle

**con·dyle** \'kän-ˌdīl *also* -dᵊl\ *noun* [French & Latin; French, from Latin *condylus* knuckle, from Greek *kondylos*] (1634)
: an articular prominence of a bone; *especially* : one resembling a pair of knuckles
— **con·dy·loid** \-də-ˌlȯid\ *adjective*

**con·dy·lo·ma** \ˌkän-də-'lō-mə\ *noun, plural* **-ma·ta** \-mə-tə\ *also* **-mas** [New Latin, from Greek *kondylōma,* from *kondylos*] (circa 1526)
: a warty growth on the skin or adjoining mucous membrane usually near the anus and genital organs
— **con·dy·lo·ma·tous** \-mə-təs\ *adjective*

**¹cone** \'kōn\ *noun* [Middle French or Latin; Middle French, from Latin *conus,* from Greek *kōnos*] (1545)
**1 a** : a solid generated by rotating a right triangle about one of its legs — called also *right circular cone* **b** : a solid bounded by a circular or other closed plane base and the surface formed by line segments joining every point of the boundary of the base to a common vertex — see VOLUME table **c** : a surface traced by a moving straight line passing through a fixed vertex
**2 a** : a mass of ovule-bearing or pollen-bearing scales or bracts in trees of the pine family or in cycads that are arranged usually

on a somewhat elongated axis **b** : any of several flower or fruit clusters suggesting a cone
**3** : something that resembles a cone in shape: as **a** : any of the conical photosensitive receptor cells of the vertebrate retina that function in color vision — compare ROD 3 **b** : any of a family (Conidae) of tropical marine gastropod mollusks that inject their prey with a potent toxin **c** : the apex of a volcano **d** : a crisp usually cone-shaped wafer for holding ice cream

cone 2a: *1* Sitka spruce, *2* cryptomeria, *3* big tree, *4* white spruce, *5* redwood, *6* lodgepole pine, *7* Douglas fir, *8* bald cypress, *9* jack pine

**²cone** *transitive verb* **coned; con·ing** (circa 1859)
**1** : to make cone-shaped
**2** : to bevel like the slanting surface of a cone ⟨*cone* a tire⟩

**cone·flow·er** \'kōn-ˌflau̇(-ə)r\ *noun* (circa 1818)
: any of several composite plants having cone-shaped flower disks; *especially* : RUDBECKIA

**cone·nose** \'kōn-ˌnōz\ *noun* (circa 1891)
: any of various large bloodsucking bugs and especially some assassin bugs (genus *Triatoma*) including some capable of inflicting painful bites — called also *kissing bug*

**con es·pres·sio·ne** \ˌkän-ˌes-(ˌ)pre-sē-'ō-nē, ˌkōn-, -'ō-(ˌ)nā\ *adverb* [Italian, literally, with expression] (circa 1891)
: with feeling — used as a direction in music

**Con·es·to·ga wagon** \ˌkä-nə-'stō-gə-\ *noun* [*Conestoga,* Pa.] (1717)
: a broad-wheeled covered wagon drawn usually by six horses and used especially for transporting freight across the prairies — called also *Conestoga*

**co·ney** \'kō-nē, *1 also* 'kə-nē\ *noun, plural* **co·neys** [Middle English *conies,* plural, from Old French *conis,* plural of *conil,* from Latin *cuniculus*] (12th century)
**1 a** : rabbit fur **b** (1) : RABBIT; *especially* : the European rabbit (*Oryctolagus cuniculus*) (2) : PIKA **c** : HYRAX
**2** *archaic* : DUPE
**3** : any of several fishes; *especially* : a dusky black-spotted reddish-finned grouper (*Epinephelus fulvus*) of the tropical Atlantic

**con·fab** \kən-'fab, 'kän-\ *intransitive verb* **con·fabbed; con·fab·bing** (1741)
: CONFABULATE
— **con·fab** \'kän-ˌfab, kən-'\ *noun*

**con·fab·u·late** \kən-'fa-byə-ˌlāt\ *intransitive verb* **-lat·ed; -lat·ing** [Latin *confabulatus,* past participle of *confabulari,* from *com-* + *fabulari* to talk, from *fabula* story — more at FABLE] (circa 1604)
**1** : CHAT
**2** : to hold a discussion : CONFER
**3** : to fill in gaps in memory by fabrication
— **con·fab·u·la·tion** \kən-ˌfa-byə-'lā-shən\ *noun*
— **con·fab·u·la·tor** \kən-'fa-byə-ˌlā-tər\ *noun*
— **con·fab·u·la·to·ry** \-lə-ˌtōr-ē, -ˌtȯr-\ *adjective*

**con·fect** \kən-'fekt\ *transitive verb* [Middle English, from Latin *confectus,* past participle of *conficere* to prepare — more at COMFIT] (14th century)
**1** : to put together from varied material

**2 a** : PREPARE **b** : PRESERVE
— **con·fect** \'kän-ˌ\ *noun*

**con·fec·tion** \kən-'fek-shən\ *noun* (15th century)
**1** : the act or process of confecting
**2** : something confected: as **a** : a fancy dish or sweetmeat; *also* : a sweet food **b** : a medicinal preparation usually made with sugar, syrup, or honey **c** : a piece of fine craftsmanship

**con·fec·tion·ary** \-shə-ˌner-ē\ *noun, plural* **-ar·ies** (1605)
**1** *archaic* : CONFECTIONER
**2** : CONFECTIONERY 3
**3** : SWEETS
— **confectionary** *adjective*

**con·fec·tion·er** \-sh(ə-)nər\ *noun* (1591)
: a manufacturer of or dealer in confections

**confectioners' sugar** *noun* (circa 1889)
: a refined finely powdered sugar

**con·fec·tion·ery** \-shə-ˌner-ē\ *noun, plural* **-er·ies** (1769)
**1** : sweet foods (as candy or pastry)
**2** : the confectioner's art or business
**3** : a confectioner's shop

**con·fed·er·a·cy** \kən-'fe-d(ə-)rə-sē\ *noun, plural* **-cies** (14th century)
**1** : a league or compact for mutual support or common action : ALLIANCE
**2** : a combination of persons for unlawful purposes : CONSPIRACY
**3** : the body formed by persons, states, or nations united by a league; *specifically, capitalized* : the 11 southern states seceding from the U.S. in 1860 and 1861

**con·fed·er·al** \-d(ə-)rəl\ *adjective* (1782)
: of or relating to a confederation

**¹con·fed·er·ate** \kən-'fe-d(ə-)rət\ *adjective* [Middle English *confederat,* from Late Latin *confoederatus,* past participle of *confoederare* to unite by a league, from Latin *com-* + *foeder-, foedus* compact — more at FEDERAL] (14th century)
**1** : united in a league : ALLIED
**2** *capitalized* : of or relating to the Confederate States of America

**²confederate** *noun* (15th century)
**1** : ALLY, ACCOMPLICE
**2** *capitalized* : an adherent of the Confederate States of America or their cause

**³con·fed·er·ate** \-'fe-də-ˌrāt\ *verb* **-at·ed; -at·ing** (1531)
*transitive verb*
: to unite in a confederacy
*intransitive verb*
: to band together
— **con·fed·er·a·tive** \-'fe-d(ə-)rə-tiv, -də-ˌrā-\ *adjective*

**Confederate Memorial Day** *noun* (1899)
: any of several days appointed for the commemoration of servicemen of the Confederacy

\ə\ abut \ᵊ\ kitten \ər\ further \a\ ash \ā\ ace \ä\ mop, mar \au̇\ out \ch\ chin \e\ bet \ē\ easy \g\ go \i\ hit \ī\ ice \j\ job \ŋ\ sing \ō\ go \ȯ\ law \ȯi\ boy \th\ thin \t̲h̲\ the \ü\ loot \u̇\ foot \y\ yet \zh\ vision    *see also* Guide to Pronunciation

**con·fed·er·a·tion** \kən-ˌfe-də-'rā-shən\ *noun*
(15th century)
**1** : an act of confederating : a state of being
confederated : ALLIANCE
**2** : LEAGUE
**con·fer** \kən-'fər\ *verb* **con·ferred; con·-
fer·ring** [Latin *conferre* to bring together,
from *com-* + *ferre* to carry — more at BEAR]
(1570)
*transitive verb*
**1** : to bestow from or as if from a position of
superiority ⟨*conferred* an honorary degree on
her⟩ ⟨knowing how to read was a gift *conferred* with manhood —Murray Kempton⟩
**2** : to give (as a property or characteristic) to
someone or something ⟨a reputation for power
will *confer* power —John Spanier⟩
*intransitive verb*
: to compare views or take counsel : CONSULT
**synonym** see GIVE
— **con·fer·ment** \-'fər-mənt\ *noun*
— **con·fer·ra·ble** \-'fər-ə-bəl\ *adjective*
— **con·fer·ral** \-'fər-əl\ *noun*
— **con·fer·rer** \-'fər-ər\ *noun*
**con·fer·ee** \ˌkän-fə-'rē\ *noun* (1771)
: one taking part in a conference
**con·fer·ence** \'kän-f(ə-)rən(t)s, -fərn(t)s, *for*
2 *usually* kən-'fər-ən(t)s\ *noun* (1527)
**1 a** : a meeting of two or more persons for
discussing matters of common concern **b** : a
usually formal interchange of views : CONSUL-
TATION **c** : a meeting of members of the two
branches of a legislature to adjust differences
**d** : CAUCUS
**2** *also* **con·fer·rence** \kən-'fər-ən(t)s\ : BE-
STOWAL, CONFERMENT
**3 a** : a representative assembly or administrative organization of a religious denomination
**b** : a territorial division of a religious denomination
**4** : an association of athletic teams
— **con·fer·en·tial** \ˌkän-fə-'ren(t)-shəl\ *adjective*
**conference call** *noun* (1941)
: a telephone call by which a caller can speak
with several people at the same time
**con·fer·enc·ing** \'kän-f(ə-)rən(t)-siŋ,
-fərn(t)-\ *noun* (1865)
: the holding of conferences especially by
means of an electronic communications system ⟨computer *conferencing*⟩
**con·fess** \kən-'fes\ *verb* [Middle English,
from Middle French *confesser*, from Old
French, from *confes* having confessed, from
Latin *confessus*, past participle of *confitēri* to
confess, from *com-* + *fatēri* to confess; akin to
Latin *fari* to speak — more at BAN] (14th
century)
*transitive verb*
**1** : to tell or make known (as something
wrong or damaging to oneself) : ADMIT
**2 a** : to acknowledge (sin) to God or to a
priest **b** : to receive the confession of (a penitent)
**3** : to declare faith in or adherence to : PROFESS
**4** : to give evidence of
*intransitive verb*
**1 a** : to disclose one's faults; *specifically* : to
unburden one's sins or the state of one's conscience to God or to a priest **b** : to hear a confession
**2** : ADMIT, OWN
**synonym** see ACKNOWLEDGE
— **con·fess·able** \-'fe-sə-bəl\ *adjective*
**con·fessed·ly** \-'fe-səd-lē, -'fest-lē\ *adverb*
(1640)
: by confession
**con·fes·sion** \kən-'fe-shən\ *noun* (14th century)
**1** : an act of confessing; *especially* : a disclosure of one's sins in the sacrament of reconciliation
**2** : a statement of what is confessed: as **a** : a
written acknowledgment of guilt by a party

accused of an offense **b** : a formal statement
of religious beliefs : CREED
**3** : an organized religious body having a common creed
**¹con·fes·sion·al** \-'fesh-nəl, -'fe-shə-n°l\
*noun* (1727)
**1** : a place where a priest hears confessions
**2** : the practice of confessing to a priest
**²confessional** *adjective* (1817)
**1** : of, relating to, or being a confession especially of faith
**2** : of, relating to, or being intimately autobiographical ⟨*confessional* fiction⟩
— **con·fes·sion·al·ism** \-nə-ˌli-zəm\ *noun*
— **con·fes·sion·al·ist** \-list\ *noun*
— **con·fes·sion·al·ly** \-nə-lē, -n°l-ē\ *adverb*
**con·fes·sor** \kən-'fe-sər, 1 & 3 *also* 'kän-ˌfe-
sər, 3 *also* 'kän-fə-ˌsör\ *noun* (12th century)
**1** : one who gives heroic evidence of faith but
does not suffer martyrdom
**2** : one that confesses
**3 a** : a priest who hears confessions **b** : a
priest who is one's regular spiritual guide
**con·fet·ti** \kən-'fe-tē\ *noun* [Italian, plural of
*confetto* sweetmeat, from Medieval Latin *con-
fectum*, from Latin, neuter of *confectus*, past
participle of *conficere* to prepare — more at
COMFIT] (1815)
: small bits or streamers of brightly colored
paper made for throwing (as at weddings)
**con·fi·dant** \'kän-fə-ˌdänt *also* -ˌdant, -dənt\
*noun* [French *confident*, from Italian *confidente*, from *confidente* confident, trustworthy,
from Latin *confident-, confidens*] (1646)
: one to whom secrets are entrusted; *especially*
: INTIMATE
**con·fi·dante** \*same as* CONFIDANT\ *noun*
[French *confidente*, feminine of *confident*]
(1696)
: CONFIDANT; *especially* : one who is a woman
**con·fide** \kən-'fīd\ *verb* **con·fid·ed; con·-
fid·ing** [Middle English, from Middle French
or Latin; Middle French *confider*, from Latin
*confidere*, from *com-* + *fidere* to trust —
more at BIDE] (15th century)
*intransitive verb*
**1** : to have confidence : TRUST
**2** : to show confidence by imparting secrets
*transitive verb*
**1** : to tell confidentially
**2** : to give to the care or protection of another
: ENTRUST
**synonym** see COMMIT
— **con·fid·er** *noun*
**¹con·fi·dence** \'kän-fə-dən(t)s, -ˌden(t)s\
*noun* (14th century)
**1 a** : a feeling or consciousness of one's powers or of reliance on one's circumstances ⟨had
perfect *confidence* in her ability to succeed⟩
⟨met the risk with brash *confidence*⟩ **b** : faith
or belief that one will act in a right, proper, or
effective way ⟨have *confidence* in a leader⟩
**2** : the quality or state of being certain : CERTI-
TUDE ⟨they had every *confidence* of success⟩
**3 a** : a relation of trust or intimacy ⟨took his
friend into his *confidence*⟩ **b** : reliance on another's discretion ⟨their story was told in
strictest *confidence*⟩ **c** : support especially in a
legislative body ⟨vote of *confidence*⟩
**4** : a communication made in confidence : SE-
CRET ☆
**²confidence** *adjective* (1849)
: of, relating to, or adept at swindling by false
promises ⟨a *confidence* game⟩ ⟨a *confidence*
man⟩
**confidence interval** *noun* (1934)
: a group of continuous or discrete adjacent
values that is used to estimate a statistical parameter (as a mean or variance) and that tends
to include the true value of the parameter a
predetermined proportion of the time if the
process of finding the group of values is repeated a number of times
**confidence limits** *noun plural* (1939)
: the end points of a confidence interval

**con·fi·dent** \'kän-fə-dənt, -ˌdent\ *adjective*
[Latin *confident-, confidens*, from present participle of *confidere*] (1576)
**1** : characterized by assurance; *especially*
: SELF-RELIANT
**2** *obsolete* : TRUSTFUL, CONFIDING
**3 a** : full of conviction : CERTAIN **b** : COCKSURE
— **con·fi·dent·ly** *adverb*
**con·fi·den·tial** \ˌkän-fə-'den(t)-shəl\ *adjective*
(1759)
**1** : marked by intimacy or willingness to confide ⟨a *confidential* tone⟩
**2** : PRIVATE, SECRET ⟨*confidential* information⟩
**3** : entrusted with confidences ⟨*confidential*
clerk⟩
**4** : containing information whose unauthorized disclosure could be prejudicial to the national interest — compare SECRET, TOP SECRET
— **con·fi·den·ti·al·i·ty** \-ˌden(t)-shē-'a-lə-
tē\ *noun*
— **con·fi·den·tial·ly** \-'den(t)-sh(ə-)lē\ *adverb*
**con·fid·ing** \kən-'fī-diŋ\ *adjective* (1829)
: tending to confide : TRUSTFUL
— **con·fid·ing·ly** \-diŋ-lē\ *adverb*
— **con·fid·ing·ness** *noun*
**con·fig·u·ra·tion** \kən-ˌfi-gyə-'rā-shən, ˌkän-,
-gə-\ *noun* [Late Latin *configuration-, con-
figuratio* similar formation, from Latin *confi-
gurare* to form from or after, from *com-* + *figurare* to form, from *figura* figure] (1646)
**1 a** : relative arrangement of parts or elements: as (1) : SHAPE (2) : contour of land
⟨*configuration* of the mountains⟩ (3) : functional arrangement ⟨a small business computer
system in its simplest *configuration*⟩ **b** : something (as a figure, contour, pattern, or apparatus) that results from a particular arrangement
of parts or components **c** : the stable structural
makeup of a chemical compound especially
with reference to the space relations of the
constituent atoms
**2** : GESTALT ⟨personality *configuration*⟩
— **con·fig·u·ra·tion·al** \-shnəl, -shə-n°l\
*adjective*
— **con·fig·u·ra·tion·al·ly** *adverb*
— **con·fig·u·ra·tive** \-'fi-gyə-rə-tiv, -'fi-
gə-\ *adjective*
**con·fig·ure** \kən-'fi-gyər, *especially British*
-'fi-gər\ *transitive verb* **-ured; -ur·ing** (1677)
: to set up for operation especially in a particular way ⟨a fighter plane *configured* for the
Malaysian air force⟩
**¹con·fine** \'kän-ˌfīn *also* kən-'\ *noun* [Middle
English, from Middle French or Latin; Middle
French *confines*, plural, from Latin *confine*
border, from neuter of *confinis* adjacent, from
*com-* + *finis* end] (15th century)
**1** *plural* : something (as borders or walls)
that encloses ⟨outside the *confines* of the office or hospital —W. A. Nolen⟩; *also* : something that restrains ⟨escape from the *confines*

---

☆ **SYNONYMS**
**Confidence, assurance, self-pos-
session, aplomb** mean a state of mind or
a manner marked by easy coolness and
freedom from uncertainty, diffidence, or embarrassment. CONFIDENCE stresses faith in
oneself and one's powers without any suggestion of conceit or arrogance ⟨the *confidence* that comes from long experience⟩. AS-
SURANCE carries a stronger implication of
certainty and may suggest arrogance or lack
of objectivity in assessing one's own powers
⟨handled the cross-
examination with complete *assurance*⟩. SELF-
POSSESSION implies an ease or coolness
under stress that reflects perfect self-control
and command of one's powers ⟨answered
the insolent question with complete *self-
possession*⟩. APLOMB implies a manifest self-
possession in trying or challenging situations
⟨handled the reporters with great *aplomb*⟩.

of soot and clutter —E. S. Muskie⟩ **b :** SCOPE 3 ⟨work within the *confines* of a small group —Frank Newman⟩
**2 a** *archaic* **:** RESTRICTION **b** *obsolete* **:** PRISON
²**con·fine** \kən-'fīn\ *verb* **con·fined; con·fin·ing** (1523)
*intransitive verb*
*archaic* **:** BORDER
*transitive verb*
**1 a :** to hold within a location **b :** IMPRISON
**2 :** to keep within limits ⟨will *confine* my remarks to one subject⟩
**synonym** see LIMIT
— **con·fin·er** *noun*
**con·fined** \kən-'fīnd\ *adjective* (1772)
**:** undergoing childbirth
**con·fine·ment** \kən-'fīn-mənt\ *noun* (1646)
**:** an act of confining **:** the state of being confined ⟨solitary *confinement*⟩; *especially* **:** LYING-IN
**con·firm** \kən-'fərm\ *transitive verb* [Middle English, from Old French *confirmer*, from Latin *confirmare*, from *com-* + *firmare* to make firm, from *firmus* firm] (13th century)
**1 :** to give approval to **:** RATIFY
**2 :** to make firm or firmer **:** STRENGTHEN
**3 :** to administer the rite of confirmation to
**4 :** to give new assurance of the validity of **:** remove doubt about by authoritative act or indisputable fact ☆
— **con·firm·abil·i·ty** \-ˌfər-mə-'bi-lə-tē\ *noun*
— **con·firm·able** \-'fər-mə-bəl\ *adjective*
**con·fir·mand** \ˌkän-fər-'mand\ *noun* [Latin *confirmandus*, gerundive of *confirmare*] (1884)
**:** a candidate for religious confirmation
**con·fir·ma·tion** \ˌkän-fər-'mā-shən\ *noun* (14th century)
**1 :** an act or process of confirming: as **a** (1) **:** a Christian rite conferring the gift of the Holy Spirit and among Protestants full church membership (2) **:** a ceremony especially of Reform Judaism confirming youths in their faith **b :** the ratification of an executive act by a legislative body
**2 a :** confirming proof **:** CORROBORATION **b :** the process of supporting a statement by evidence
— **con·fir·ma·tion·al** \-shnəl, -shə-nᵊl\ *adjective*
**con·fir·ma·to·ry** \kən-'fər-mə-ˌtōr-ē, -ˌtor-\ *adjective* (1636)
**:** serving to confirm **:** CORROBORATIVE
**con·firmed** \kən-'fərmd\ *adjective* (14th century)
**1 a :** marked by long continuance and likely to persist ⟨a *confirmed* habit⟩ **b :** fixed in habit and unlikely to change ⟨a *confirmed* do-gooder⟩
**2 :** having received the rite of confirmation
**synonym** see INVETERATE
— **con·firm·ed·ly** \-'fər-məd-lē\ *adverb*
— **con·firmed·ness** \-'fər-məd-nəs, -'fərm(d)-nəs\ *noun*
**con·fis·ca·ble** \kən-'fis-kə-bəl\ *adjective* (circa 1736)
**:** liable to confiscation
**con·fis·cat·able** \'kän-fə-ˌskā-tə-bəl\ *adjective* (1863)
**:** CONFISCABLE
¹**con·fis·cate** \'kän-fə-ˌskāt, kən-'fis-kət\ *adjective* [Latin *confiscatus*, past participle of *confiscare* to confiscate, from *com-* + *fiscus* treasury] (circa 1533)
**1 :** appropriated by the government **:** FORFEITED
**2 :** deprived of property by confiscation
²**con·fis·cate** \'kän-fə-ˌskāt\ *transitive verb* **-cat·ed; -cat·ing** (1552)
**1 :** to seize as forfeited to the public treasury
**2 :** to seize by or as if by authority
— **con·fis·ca·tion** \ˌkän-fə-'skā-shən\ *noun*
— **con·fis·ca·tor** \'kän-fə-ˌskā-tər\ *noun*
— **con·fis·ca·to·ry** \kən-'fis-kə-ˌtōr-ē, -ˌtor-\ *adjective*

**con·fit** \kōn-'fē, kon-, kän-\ *noun* [French, from Old French, preparation, preserves, from past participle of *confire* to prepare — more at COMFIT] (1951)
**:** meat (as goose, duck, or pork) that has been cooked and preserved in its own fat
**con·fi·te·or** \kən-'fē-tē-ˌor, -ər\ *noun* [Middle English, from Latin, literally, I confess, from the opening words — more at CONFESS] (13th century)
**:** a liturgical form in which sinfulness is acknowledged and intercession for God's mercy requested
**con·fi·ture** \'kän-fə-ˌchur, -ˌtyur, -ˌtur\ *noun* [French, from Middle French, from *confit*] (1802)
**:** preserved or candied fruit **:** JAM
**con·fla·grant** \kən-'flā-grənt\ *adjective* [Latin *conflagrant-, conflagrans*, present participle of *conflagrare* to burn, from *com-* + *flagrare* to burn — more at BLACK] (circa 1656)
**:** BURNING, BLAZING
**con·fla·gra·tion** \ˌkän-flə-'grā-shən\ *noun* [Latin *conflagration-, conflagratio*, from *conflagrare*] (circa 1656)
**1 :** FIRE; *especially* **:** a large disastrous fire
**2 :** CONFLICT, WAR
**con·flate** \kən-'flāt\ *transitive verb* **con·flat·ed; con·flat·ing** [Latin *conflatus*, past participle of *conflare* to blow together, fuse, from *com-* + *flare* to blow — more at BLOW] (1610)
**1 a :** to bring together **:** FUSE **b :** CONFUSE
**2 :** to combine (as two readings of a text) into a composite whole
**con·fla·tion** \-'flā-shən\ *noun* (15th century)
**:** BLEND, FUSION; *especially* **:** a composite reading or text
¹**con·flict** \'kän-ˌflikt\ *noun* [Middle English, from Latin *conflictus* act of striking together, from *confligere* to strike together, from *com-* + *fligere* to strike — more at PROFLIGATE] (15th century)
**1 :** FIGHT, BATTLE, WAR
**2 a :** competitive or opposing action of incompatibles **:** antagonistic state or action (as of divergent ideas, interests, or persons) **b :** mental struggle resulting from incompatible or opposing needs, drives, wishes, or external or internal demands
**3 :** the opposition of persons or forces that gives rise to the dramatic action in a drama or fiction
**synonym** see DISCORD
— **con·flict·ful** \'kän-ˌflikt-fəl\ *adjective*
— **con·flic·tu·al** \kän-'flik-chə-wəl, kən-, -chəl, -shwəl\ *adjective*
²**con·flict** \kən-'flikt, 'kän-ˌ\ *intransitive verb* (15th century)
**1** *archaic* **:** to contend in warfare
**2 :** to show antagonism or irreconcilability
— **con·flic·tion** \kən-'flik-shən, kän-\ *noun*
— **con·flic·tive** \kən-'flik-tiv, 'kän-ˌ\ *adjective*
**con·flict·ed** \kən-'flik-təd\ *adjective* (1967)
**:** having or experiencing an emotional conflict ⟨this unhappy and *conflicted* modern woman —John Updike⟩
**conflicting** *adjective* (1607)
**:** being in conflict, collision, or opposition **:** INCOMPATIBLE
— **con·flict·ing·ly** \-'flik-tiŋ-lē, -ˌflik-\ *adverb*
**conflict of interest** (1951)
**:** a conflict between the private interests and the official responsibilities of a person in a position of trust
**con·flu·ence** \'kän-ˌflü-ən(t)s, kən-'\ *noun* (15th century)
**1 :** a coming or flowing together, meeting, or gathering at one point ⟨a happy *confluence* of weather and scenery⟩
**2 a :** the flowing together of two or more streams **b :** the place of meeting of two streams **c :** the combined stream formed by conjunction

¹**con·flu·ent** \-ənt\ *adjective* [Latin *confluent-, confluens*, present participle of *confluere* to flow together, from *com-* + *fluere* to flow — more at FLUID] (15th century)
**1 :** flowing or coming together; *also* **:** run together ⟨*confluent* pustules⟩
**2 :** characterized by confluent lesions ⟨*confluent* smallpox⟩
²**confluent** *noun* (1850)
**:** a confluent stream; *broadly* **:** TRIBUTARY
**con·flux** \'kän-ˌfləks\ *noun* [Medieval Latin *confluxus*, from Latin *confluere*] (1606)
**:** CONFLUENCE
**con·fo·cal** \(ˌ)kän-'fō-kəl\ *adjective* (1867)
**:** having the same foci ⟨*confocal* ellipses⟩ ⟨*confocal* lenses⟩
— **con·fo·cal·ly** \-kə-lē\ *adverb*
**con·form** \kən-'form\ *verb* [Middle English, from Middle French *conformer*, from Latin *conformare*, from *com-* + *formare* to form, from *forma* form] (14th century)
*transitive verb*
**:** to give the same shape, outline, or contour to **:** bring into harmony or accord ⟨*conform* furrows to the slope of the land⟩
*intransitive verb*
**1 :** to be similar or identical; *also* **:** to be in agreement or harmony — used with *to* or *with*
**2 a :** to be obedient or compliant — usually used with *to* **b :** to act in accordance with prevailing standards or customs
**synonym** see ADAPT
— **con·form·er** *noun*
— **con·form·ism** \-'for-ˌmi-zəm\ *noun*
— **con·form·ist** \-mist\ *noun or adjective*
**con·form·able** \kən-'for-mə-bəl\ *adjective* (15th century)
**1 :** corresponding in form or character **:** SIMILAR — usually used with *to*
**2 :** SUBMISSIVE, COMPLIANT
**3 :** following in unbroken sequence — used of geologic strata formed under uniform conditions
— **con·form·ably** \-blē\ *adverb*
**con·for·mal** \kən-'for-məl, (ˌ)kän-\ *adjective* [Late Latin *conformalis* having the same shape, from Latin *com-* + *formalis* formal, from *forma*] (1893)
**1 :** leaving the size of the angle between corresponding curves unchanged ⟨*conformal* transformation⟩
**2** *of a map* **:** representing small areas in their true shape
**con·for·mance** \kən-'for-mən(t)s\ *noun* (1606)

---

☆ **SYNONYMS**
**Confirm, corroborate, substantiate, verify, authenticate, validate** mean to attest to the truth or validity of something. CONFIRM implies the removing of doubts by an authoritative statement or indisputable fact ⟨*confirmed* the reports⟩. CORROBORATE suggests the strengthening of what is already partly established ⟨witnesses *corroborated* his story⟩. SUBSTANTIATE implies the offering of evidence that sustains the contention ⟨the claims have yet to be *substantiated*⟩. VERIFY implies the establishing of correspondence of actual facts or details with those proposed or guessed at ⟨all statements of fact in the article have been *verified*⟩. AUTHENTICATE implies establishing genuineness by adducing legal or official documents or expert opinion ⟨handwriting experts *authenticated* the diaries⟩. VALIDATE implies establishing validity by authoritative affirmation or by factual proof ⟨*validated* the hypothesis by experiments⟩.

---

\ə\ abut \ᵊ\ kitten \ər\ further \a\ ash \ā\ ace
\ä\ mop, mar \au̇\ out \ch\ chin \e\ bet \ē\ easy
\g\ go \i\ hit \ī\ ice \j\ job \ŋ\ sing \ō\ go
\o̊\ law \o̊i\ boy \th\ thin \th̲\ the \ü\ loot \u̇\ foot
\y\ yet \zh\ vision *see also* Guide to Pronunciation

: CONFORMITY

**con·for·ma·tion** \ˌkän-(ˌ)fȯr-'mā-shən, -fər-\ *noun* (1511)
**1** : the act of conforming or producing conformity : ADAPTATION
**2** : formation of something by appropriate arrangement of parts or elements : an assembling into a whole ⟨the gradual *conformation* of the embryo⟩
**3 a** : correspondence especially to a model or plan **b** : STRUCTURE **c** : the shape or proportionate dimensions especially of an animal **d** : any of the spatial arrangements of a molecule that can be obtained by rotation of the atoms about a single bond
— **con·for·ma·tion·al** \-shnəl, -shə-n°l\ *adjective*

**con·for·mi·ty** \kən-'fȯr-mə-tē\ *noun, plural* **-ties** (15th century)
**1** : correspondence in form, manner, or character : AGREEMENT ⟨behaved in *conformity* with her beliefs⟩
**2** : an act or instance of conforming
**3** : action in accordance with some specified standard or authority ⟨*conformity* to social custom⟩

**con·found** \kən-'fau̇nd, kän-\ *transitive verb* [Middle English, from Middle French *confondre*, from Latin *confundere* to pour together, confuse, from *com-* + *fundere* to pour — more at FOUND] (14th century)
**1 a** *archaic* : to bring to ruin : DESTROY **b** : BAFFLE, FRUSTRATE ⟨conferences . . . are not for accomplishment but to *confound* knavish tricks —J. K. Galbraith⟩
**2** *obsolete* : CONSUME, WASTE
**3 a** : to put to shame : DISCOMFIT ⟨a performance that *confounded* the critics⟩ **b** : REFUTE ⟨sought to *confound* his arguments⟩
**4** : DAMN
**5** : to throw (a person) into confusion or perplexity
**6 a** : to fail to discern differences between : mix up **b** : to increase the confusion of
**synonym** see PUZZLE
— **con·found·er** \-'fau̇n-dər\ *noun*
— **con·found·ing·ly** \-diŋ-lē\ *adverb*

**con·found·ed** \kən-'fau̇n-dəd, (ˌ)kän-', 'kän-ˌ\ *adjective* (14th century)
**1** : CONFUSED, PERPLEXED
**2** : DAMNED
— **con·found·ed·ly** *adverb*

**con·fra·ter·ni·ty** \ˌkän-frə-'tər-nə-tē\ *noun* [Middle English *confraternite*, from Middle French *confraternité*, from Medieval Latin *confraternitat-, confraternitas*, from *confrater* fellow, brother, from Latin *com-* + *frater* brother — more at BROTHER] (15th century)
**1** : a society devoted especially to a religious or charitable cause
**2** : fraternal union

**con·frere** *also* **con·frère** \'kän-ˌfrer, kōⁿ-ˌ, kän-', kōⁿ-', kən-\ *noun* [Middle English, from Middle French, translation of Medieval Latin *confrater*] (15th century)
: COLLEAGUE, COMRADE

**con·front** \kən-'frənt\ *transitive verb* [Middle French *confronter* to border on, confront, from Medieval Latin *confrontare* to bound, from Latin *com-* + *front-, frons* forehead, front] (circa 1568)
**1** : to face especially in challenge : OPPOSE
**2 a** : to cause to meet : bring face-to-face ⟨*confront* a reader with statistics⟩ **b** : to meet face-to-face : ENCOUNTER ⟨*confronted* the possibility of failure⟩
— **con·front·al** \-'frən-t°l\ *noun*
— **con·front·er** *noun*

**con·fron·ta·tion** \ˌkän-(ˌ)frən-'tā-shən\ *noun* (1632)
: the act of confronting : the state of being confronted: as **a** : a face-to-face meeting **b** : the clashing of forces or ideas : CONFLICT **c** : COMPARISON ⟨the flashbacks bring into meaningful *confrontation* present and past, near and far —R. J. Clements⟩

— **con·fron·ta·tion·al** \-shnəl, -shə-n°l\ *adjective*
— **con·fron·ta·tion·ist** \-sh(ə-)nist\ *noun or adjective*

**Con·fu·cian** \kən-'fyü-shən\ *adjective* (1837)
: of or relating to the Chinese philosopher Confucius or his teachings or followers
— **Confucian** *noun*
— **Con·fu·cian·ism** \-shə-ˌni-zəm\ *noun*
— **Con·fu·cian·ist** \-nist\ *noun or adjective*

**con·fuse** \kən-'fyüz\ *transitive verb* **con·fused; con·fus·ing** [back-formation from Middle English *confused* perplexed, from Middle French *confus*, from Latin *confusus*, past participle of *confundere*] (14th century)
**1** *archaic* : to bring to ruin
**2 a** : to make embarrassed : ABASH **b** : to disturb in mind or purpose : THROW OFF
**3 a** : to make indistinct : BLUR ⟨stop *confusing* the issue⟩ **b** : to mix indiscriminately : JUMBLE **c** : to fail to differentiate from an often similar or related other ⟨*confuse* money with comfort⟩
— **con·fus·ing·ly** \-'fyü-ziŋ-lē\ *adverb*

**con·fused** \-'fyüzd\ *adjective* (14th century)
**1** : being perplexed or disconcerted ⟨the *confused* students⟩
**2** : INDISTINGUISHABLE ⟨a zigzag, crisscross, *confused* trail —Harry Hervey⟩
**3** : being disordered or mixed up ⟨a contradictory and often *confused* story⟩
— **con·fused·ly** \-'fyü-zəd-lē, -'fyüzd-\ *adverb*
— **con·fused·ness** \-'fyü-zəd-nəs, -'fyüz(d)-\ *noun*

**con·fu·sion** \kən-'fyü-zhən\ *noun* (14th century)
**1** : an act or instance of confusing
**2 a** : the quality or state of being confused **b** : a confused mass or mixture ⟨a *confusion* of voices⟩
— **con·fu·sion·al** \-'fyüzh-nəl, -'fyü-zhə-n°l\ *adjective*

**con·fu·ta·tion** \ˌkän-fyu̇-'tā-shən\ *noun* (15th century)
**1** : the act or process of confuting : REFUTATION
**2** : something (as an argument or statement) that confutes
— **con·fu·ta·tive** \kən-'fyü-tə-tiv\ *adjective*

**con·fute** \kən-'fyüt\ *transitive verb* **con·fut·ed; con·fut·ing** [Latin *confutare* to check, silence] (1529)
**1** : to overwhelm in argument : refute conclusively ⟨Elijah . . . *confuted* the prophets of Baal —G. B. Shaw⟩
**2** *obsolete* : CONFOUND
— **con·fut·er** *noun*

**con·ga** \'käŋ-gə\ *noun* [American Spanish, probably from feminine of *congo* Negro, from *Congo*, region in Africa] (1935)
**1** : a Cuban dance of African origin involving three steps followed by a kick and performed by a group usually in single file
**2** : a tall barrel-shaped or tapering drum of Afro-Cuban origin that is played with the hands

**conga line** *noun* (1947)
: SNAKE DANCE 2

**con·gé** \kōⁿ-'zhā, 'kän-ˌzhā\ *noun* [French, from Latin *commeatus* going back and forth, leave, from *commeare* to go back and forth, from *com-* + *meare* to go — more at PERMEATE] (1702)
**1 a** : a formal permission to depart **b** : DISMISSAL
**2** : a ceremonious bow
**3** : FAREWELL
**4** : an architectural molding of concave profile
— see MOLDING illustration

conga 2

**con·geal** \kən-'jē(ə)l\ *verb* [Middle English *congelen*, from Middle French *congeler*, from Latin *congelare*, from *com-* + *gelare* to freeze — more at COLD] (14th century)
*transitive verb*
**1** : to change from a fluid to a solid state by or as if by cold
**2** : to make viscid or curdled : COAGULATE
**3** : to make rigid, fixed, or immobile
*intransitive verb*
: to become congealed : SOLIDIFY
— **con·geal·ment** \-mənt\ *noun*

**con·gee** \'kän-(ˌ)jē, -(ˌ)zhē\ *noun* (14th century)
: CONGÉ

**con·ge·la·tion** \ˌkän-jə-'lā-shən\ *noun* (15th century)
: the process or result of congealing

**con·ge·ner** \'kän-jə-nər, kən-'jē-\ *noun* [Latin, of the same kind, from *com-* + *gener-, genus* kind — more at KIN] (circa 1736)
**1** : a member of the same taxonomic genus as another plant or animal
**2** : a person or thing resembling another in nature or action ⟨the New England private schools and their *congeners* west of the Alleghenies —Oliver La Farge⟩
— **con·ge·ner·ic** \ˌkän-jə-'ner-ik\ *adjective*
— **con·ge·ner·ous** \kən-'jē-nə-rəs, -'je-nə-, (ˌ)kän-\ *adjective*

**con·ge·nial** \kən-'jē-nē-əl, -'jēn-yəl\ *adjective* [*com-* + *genius*] (circa 1625)
**1** : having the same nature, disposition, or tastes : KINDRED
**2 a** : existing or associated together harmoniously **b** : PLEASANT; *especially* : agreeably suited to one's nature, tastes, or outlook : SOCIABLE, GENIAL
— **con·ge·nial·i·ty** \-ˌjē-nē-'a-lə-tē, -ˌjēn-'ya-\ *noun*
— **con·ge·nial·ly** \-'jē-nē-ə-lē, -'jēn-yə-\ *adverb*

**con·gen·i·tal** \kən-'je-nə-t°l, kän-\ *adjective* [Latin *congenitus*, from *com-* + *genitus*, past participle of *gignere* to bring forth — more at KIN] (1796)
**1 a** : existing at or dating from birth ⟨*congenital* deafness⟩ **b** : constituting an essential characteristic : INHERENT ⟨*congenital* fear of snakes⟩ **c** : acquired during development in the uterus and not through heredity ⟨*congenital* syphilis⟩
**2** : being such by nature ⟨*congenital* liar⟩
**synonym** see INNATE
— **con·gen·i·tal·ly** \-t°l-ē\ *adverb*

**con·ger eel** \'käŋ-gər-\ *noun* [Middle English *congre*, from Old French, from Latin *congr-, conger*, probably from Greek *gongros*] (1602)
: a large strictly marine scaleless eel (*Conger oceanicus*) of the Atlantic; *broadly* : any of various related eels (family Congridae)

**con·ge·ries** \'kän-jə-(ˌ)rēz\ *noun, plural* **con·geries** \*same*\ [Latin, from *congerere*] (circa 1619)
: AGGREGATION, COLLECTION

**con·gest** \kən-'jest\ *verb* [Latin *congestus*, past participle of *congerere* to bring together, from *com-* + *gerere* to bear] (1758)
*transitive verb*
**1** : to cause an excessive fullness of the blood vessels of (as an organ)
**2** : CLOG ⟨traffic *congested* the highways⟩
**3** : to concentrate in a small or narrow space
*intransitive verb*
: to become congested
— **con·ges·tion** \-'jes-chən, -'jesh-\ *noun*
— **con·ges·tive** \-'jes-tiv\ *adjective*

**congestive heart failure** *noun* (1930)
: heart failure in which the heart is unable to maintain an adequate circulation of blood in the bodily tissues or to pump out the venous blood returned to it by the veins

**con·glo·bate** \kän-'glō-ˌbāt, kən-\ *transitive verb* **-bat·ed; -bat·ing** [Latin *conglobatus*, past participle of *conglobare*, from *com-* + *globus* globe] (1635)

: to form into a round compact mass
— **con·glo·bate** \-bət, -ˌbāt\ *adjective*
— **con·glo·ba·tion** \ˌkän-(ˌ)glō-'bā-shən\ *noun*

**con·globe** \kän-'glōb, kən-\ *transitive verb* **con·globed; con·glob·ing** (1535)
: CONGLOBATE

¹**con·glom·er·ate** \kən-'gläm-rət, -'glä-mə-\ *adjective* [Latin *conglomeratus,* past participle of *conglomerare* to roll together, from *com-* + *glomerare* to wind into a ball, from *glomer-, glomus* ball — more at CLAM] (1572)
: made up of parts from various sources or of various kinds

²**con·glom·er·ate** \-'glä-mə-ˌrāt\ *verb* **-at·ed; -at·ing** (1642)
*intransitive verb*
: to gather into a mass or coherent whole ⟨numbers of dull people *conglomerated* round her —Virginia Woolf⟩
*transitive verb*
: ACCUMULATE
— **con·glom·er·a·tive** \-'gläm-rə-tiv, -'glä-mə-; -mə-ˌrā-\ *adjective*
— **con·glom·er·a·tor** \-'glä-mə-ˌrā-tər\ *noun*

³**con·glom·er·ate** \-'gläm-rət, -'glä-mə-\ *noun* (1818)
**1** : a composite mass or mixture; *especially* : rock composed of rounded fragments varying from small pebbles to large boulders in a cement (as of hardened clay)
**2** : a widely diversified corporation
— **con·glom·er·at·ic** \kən-ˌglä-mə-'ra-tik, ˌkän-\ *adjective*

**con·glom·er·a·teur** \kən-ˌglä-mə-rə-'tər, -'tyu̇r, -'tu̇r\ *noun* [³*conglomerate* + *-eur* (as in *entrepreneur*)] (1969)
: a person who forms or heads a conglomerate
: CONGLOMERATOR

**con·glom·er·a·tion** \kən-ˌglä-mə-'rā-shən, ˌkän-\ *noun* (1626)
**1** : the act of conglomerating : the state of being conglomerated
**2** : something conglomerated : a mixed mass or collection

**con·glu·ti·nate** \kən-'glü-tⁿ-ˌāt, kän-\ *verb* **-nat·ed; -nat·ing** [Latin *conglutinatus,* past participle of *conglutinare* to glue together, from *com-* + *glutin-, gluten* glue — more at GLUTEN] (1546)
*transitive verb*
: to unite by or as if by a glutinous substance
*intransitive verb*
: to become conglutinated ⟨blood platelets *conglutinate* in blood clotting⟩
— **con·glu·ti·na·tion** \kən-ˌglü-tⁿ-'ā-shən, kän-\ *noun*

**Congo red** *noun* [*Congo,* territory in Africa] (1885)
: an azo dye $C_{32}H_{22}N_6Na_2O_6S_2$ that is red in alkaline and blue in acid solution and that is used especially as an indicator and as a biological stain

**con·gou** \'käŋ-(ˌ)gō, -(ˌ)gü\ *noun* [probably from Chinese (Xiamen) *kong-hu* pains taken] (1725)
: a black tea from China

**con·grat·u·late** \kən-'gra-chə-ˌlāt, -'gra-jə-\ *transitive verb* **-lat·ed; -lat·ing** [Latin *congratulatus,* past participle of *congratulari* to wish joy, from *com-* + *gratulari* to wish joy, from *gratus* pleasing — more at GRACE] (1539)
**1** *archaic* : to express sympathetic pleasure at (an event)
**2** : to express vicarious pleasure to (a person) on the occasion of success or good fortune; *also* : to feel pleased with ⟨*congratulating* herself for a job well done⟩
**3** *obsolete* : SALUTE, GREET
— **con·grat·u·la·tor** \-ˌlā-tər\ *noun*
— **con·grat·u·la·to·ry** \-lə-ˌtōr-ē, -ˌtȯr-\ *adjective*

**con·grat·u·la·tion** \kən-ˌgra-chə-'lā-shən, -ˌgra-jə-\ *noun* (15th century)

**1** : the act of congratulating
**2** : a congratulatory expression — usually used in plural

**con·gre·gant** \'käŋ-gri-gənt\ *noun* (1886)
: one that congregates; *specifically* : a member of a congregation

¹**con·gre·gate** \-ˌgāt\ *verb* **-gat·ed; -gat·ing** [Middle English, from Latin *congregatus,* past participle of *congregare,* from *com-* + *greg-, grex* flock] (15th century)
*transitive verb*
: to collect into a group or crowd : ASSEMBLE
*intransitive verb*
: to come together into a group, crowd, or assembly
*synonym* see GATHER
— **con·gre·ga·tor** \-ˌgā-tər\ *noun*

²**con·gre·gate** \-gət\ *adjective* (1900)
: providing or being group services or facilities designed especially for elderly persons requiring supportive services ⟨*congregate* housing⟩

**con·gre·ga·tion** \ˌkäŋ-gri-'gā-shən\ *noun* (14th century)
**1 a** : an assembly of persons : GATHERING; *especially* : an assembly of persons met for worship and religious instruction **b** : a religious community: as (1) : an organized body of believers in a particular locality (2) : a Roman Catholic religious institute with only simple vows (3) : a group of monasteries forming an independent subdivision of an order
**2** : the act or an instance of congregating or bringing together : the state of being congregated
**3** : a body of cardinals and officials forming an administrative division of the papal curia

**con·gre·ga·tion·al** \-shnəl, -shə-nᵊl\ *adjective* (1639)
**1** : of or relating to a congregation
**2** *capitalized* : of or relating to a body of Protestant churches deriving from the English Independents of the 17th century and affirming the essential importance and the autonomy of the local congregation
**3** : of or relating to church government placing final authority in the assembly of the local congregation
— **con·gre·ga·tion·al·ism** \-shnə-ˌli-zəm, -shə-nᵊl-ˌi-\ *noun, often capitalized*
— **con·gre·ga·tion·al·ist** \-shnə-list, -shə-nᵊl-ist\ *noun or adjective, often capitalized*

**con·gress** \'käŋ-grəs *also* -rəs, British usually 'käŋ-ˌgres\ *noun* [Latin *congressus,* from *congredi* to come together, from *com-* + *gradi* to go — more at GRADE] (1528)
**1 a** : the act or action of coming together and meeting **b** : COITUS
**2** : a formal meeting of delegates for discussion and usually action on some question
**3** : the supreme legislative body of a nation and especially of a republic
**4** : an association usually made up of delegates from constituent organizations
**5** : a single meeting or session of a group
— **con·gres·sio·nal** \kən-'gresh-nəl, kän-, -'gre-shə-nᵊl\ *adjective*
— **con·gres·sio·nal·ly** *adverb*

**congressional district** *noun* (1812)
: a territorial division of a state from which a member of the U.S. House of Representatives is elected

**Congressional Medal** *noun* (1910)
: MEDAL OF HONOR

**con·gress·man** \'käŋ-(g)rəs-mən\ *noun* (1780)
: a member of a congress; *especially* : a member of the U.S. House of Representatives

**con·gress·peo·ple** \-(g)rəs-ˌpē-pəl\ *noun plural* (1973)
: congressmen or congresswomen

**con·gress·per·son** \-(g)rəs-ˌpər-sən\ *noun* (1972)
: a congressman or congresswoman

**con·gress·wom·an** \-(g)rəs-ˌwu̇-mən\ *noun* (1917)
: a female member of a congress; *especially* : a female member of the U.S. House of Representatives

**con·gru·ence** \kən-'grü-ən(t)s, 'käŋ-grü-ən(t)s\ *noun* (1533)
**1** : the quality or state of agreeing, coinciding, or being congruent
**2** : a statement that two numbers or geometric figures are congruent

**con·gru·en·cy** \-ən(t)-sē\ *noun, plural* **-cies** (15th century)
: CONGRUENCE

**con·gru·ent** \kən-'grü-ənt, 'käŋ-grü-ənt\ *adjective* [Middle English, from Latin *congruent-, congruens,* present participle of *congruere*] (15th century)
**1** : CONGRUOUS
**2** : superposable so as to be coincident throughout
**3** : having the difference divisible by a given modulus ⟨12 is *congruent* to 2 (modulo 5) since $12-2=2\cdot5$⟩
— **con·gru·ent·ly** *adverb*

**con·gru·i·ty** \kən-'grü-ə-tē, kän-\ *noun, plural* **-ties** (14th century)
**1** : the quality or state of being congruent or congruous
**2** : a point of agreement

**con·gru·ous** \'käŋ-grü-əs\ *adjective* [Latin *congruus,* from *congruere* to come together, agree] (1599)
**1 a** : being in agreement, harmony, or correspondence **b** : conforming to the circumstances or requirements of a situation : APPROPRIATE ⟨a *congruous* room to work in —G. B. Shaw⟩
**2** : marked or enhanced by harmonious agreement among constituent elements ⟨a *congruous* theme⟩
— **con·gru·ous·ly** *adverb*
— **con·gru·ous·ness** *noun*

¹**con·ic** \'kä-nik\ *adjective* (1570)
**1** : of or relating to a cone
**2** : CONICAL
— **co·nic·i·ty** \kō-'ni-sə-tē\ *noun*

²**conic** *noun* (1879)
: CONIC SECTION

**con·i·cal** \'kä-ni-kəl\ *adjective* (1570)
: resembling a cone especially in shape
— **con·i·cal·ly** \-k(ə-)lē\ *adverb*

**conic section** *noun* (1664)
**1** : a plane curve, line, pair of intersecting lines, or point that is the intersection of or bounds the intersection of a plane and a cone with two nappes
**2** : a curve generated by a point which always moves so that the ratio of its distance from a fixed point to its distance from a fixed line is constant

**conic section 1:** *1* straight lines, *2* circle, *3* ellipse, *4* parabola, *5* hyperbola

**co·nid·io·phore** \kə-'ni-dē-ə-ˌfōr, -ˌfȯr\ *noun* [New Latin *conidium* + International Scientific Vocabulary *-phore*] (1874)
: a structure that bears conidia; *specifically* : a specialized hyphal branch of some fungi that produces conidia usually by the successive cutting off of parts of the sporophore through the growth of septa

**co·nid·i·um** \kə-'ni-dē-əm\ *noun, plural* **-ia** \-dē-ə\ [New Latin, from Greek *konis* dust — more at INCINERATE] (1856)
: an asexual spore produced on a conidiophore
— **co·nid·i·al** \-dē-əl\ *adjective*

---

\ə\ **abut** \ᵊ\ **kitten** \ər\ **further** \a\ **ash** \ā\ **ace**
\ä\ **mop, mar** \au̇\ **out** \ch\ **chin** \e\ **bet** \ē\ **easy**
\g\ **go** \i\ **hit** \ī\ **ice** \j\ **job** \ŋ\ **sing** \ō\ **go**
\ȯ\ **law** \ȯi\ **boy** \th\ **thin** \th\ **the** \ü\ **loot** \u̇\ **foot**
\y\ **yet** \zh\ **vision** *see also* Guide to Pronunciation

**co·ni·fer** \'kä-nə-fər *also* 'kō-\ *noun* [ultimately from Latin *conifer* cone-bearing, from *conus* cone + *-fer*] (circa 1841)
: any of an order (Coniferales) of mostly evergreen trees and shrubs including forms (as pines) with true cones and others (as yews) with an arillate fruit
— **co·nif·er·ous** \kō-'ni-f(ə-)rəs, kə-\ *adjective*

**co·ni·ine** \'kō-nē-,ēn\ *noun* [German *Koniin*, from Late Latin *conium* hemlock, from Greek *kōneion*] (1831)
: a poisonous alkaloid $C_8H_{17}N$ found in poison hemlock (*Conium maculatum*)

**con·jec·tur·al** \kən-'jek-chə-rəl, -'jek-shrəl\ *adjective* (1553)
**1** : of the nature of or involving or based on conjecture
**2** : given to conjectures
— **con·jec·tur·al·ly** *adverb*

**¹con·jec·ture** \kən-'jek-chər\ *noun* [Middle English, from Middle French or Latin; Middle French, from Latin *conjectura*, from *conjectus*, past participle of *conicere*, literally, to throw together, from *com-* + *jacere* to throw — more at JET] (14th century)
**1** *obsolete* **a** : interpretation of omens **b** : SUPPOSITION
**2 a** : inference from defective or presumptive evidence **b** : a conclusion deduced by surmise or guesswork **c** : a proposition (as in mathematics) before it has been proved or disproved

**²conjecture** *verb* **-tured; -tur·ing** \-'jek-chə-riŋ, -'jek-shriŋ\ (15th century)
*transitive verb*
**1** : to arrive at by conjecture
**2** : to make conjectures as to
*intransitive verb*
: to form conjectures
— **con·jec·tur·er** \-'jek-chər-ər\ *noun*

**con·join** \kən-'join, kän-\ *verb* [Middle English, from Middle French *conjoindre*, from Latin *conjungere*, from *com-* + *jungere* to join — more at YOKE] (14th century)
*transitive verb*
: to join together (as separate entities) for a common purpose
*intransitive verb*
: to join together for a common purpose

**con·joined** \-'joind\ *adjective* (1570)
: being, coming, or brought together so as to meet, touch, or overlap (*conjoined* heads on a coin)

**con·joint** \-'joint\ *adjective* [Middle English, from Middle French, past participle of *conjoindre*] (1725)
**1** : UNITED, CONJOINED
**2** : related to, made up of, or carried on by two or more in combination : JOINT
— **con·joint·ly** *adverb*

**con·ju·gal** \'kän-ji-gəl *also* kən-'jü-\ *adjective* [Middle French or Latin; Middle French, from Latin *conjugalis*, from *conjug-, conjux* husband, wife, from *conjungere* to join, unite in marriage] (1545)
: of or relating to the married state or to married persons and their relations : CONNUBIAL
— **con·ju·gal·i·ty** \,kän-ji-'ga-lə-tē, -jü-\ *noun*
— **con·ju·gal·ly** \'kän-ji-gə-lē *also* kən-'jü-\ *adverb*

**conjugal rights** *noun plural* (circa 1891)
: the sexual rights or privileges implied by and involved in the marriage relationship : the right of sexual intercourse between husband and wife

**con·ju·gant** \'kän-ji-gənt\ *noun* (1910)
: either of a pair of conjugating gametes or organisms

**¹con·ju·gate** \'kän-ji-gət, -jə-,gāt\ *adjective* [Middle English *conjugat*, from Latin *conjugatus*, past participle of *conjugare* to unite, from *com-* + *jugare* to join, from *jugum* yoke — more at YOKE] (15th century)
**1 a** : joined together especially in pairs : COUPLED **b** : acting or operating as if joined

**2 a** : having features in common but opposite or inverse in some particular **b** : relating to or being conjugate complex numbers (complex roots occurring in *conjugate* pairs)
**3** *of an acid or base* : related by the difference of a proton (the acid $NH_4$ and the base $NH_3$ are *conjugate* to each other)
**4** : having the same derivation and therefore usually some likeness in meaning (*conjugate* words)
**5** *of two leaves of a book* : forming a single piece
— **con·ju·gate·ly** *adverb*
— **con·ju·gate·ness** *noun*

**²con·ju·gate** \-jə-,gāt\ *verb* **-gat·ed; -gat·ing** (1530)
*transitive verb*
**1** : to give in prescribed order the various inflectional forms of — used especially of a verb
**2** : to join together
*intransitive verb*
**1** : to become joined together
**2 a** : to pair and fuse in conjugation **b** : to pair in synapsis

**³conjugate** \*same as ¹*\ *noun* (circa 1586)
**1** : something conjugate : a product of conjugating
**2** : CONJUGATE COMPLEX NUMBER
**3** : an element of a mathematical group that is equal to a given element of the group multiplied on the right by another element and on the left by the inverse of the latter element

**conjugate complex number** *noun* (circa 1909)
: one of two complex numbers differing only in the sign of the imaginary part

**con·ju·gat·ed** \-,gā-təd\ *adjective* (1882)
**1** : formed by the union of two compounds or united with another compound (*conjugated* bile acids)
**2** : relating to or containing a system of two double bonds separated by a single bond (*conjugated* fatty acids)

**conjugated protein** *noun* (circa 1909)
: a compound of a protein with a nonprotein (hemoglobin is a *conjugated protein*) — compare SIMPLE PROTEIN

**con·ju·ga·tion** \,kän-jə-'gā-shən\ *noun* (15th century)
**1 a** : a schematic arrangement of the inflectional forms of a verb **b** : verb inflection **c** : a class of verbs having the same type of inflectional forms (the weak *conjugation*) **d** : a set of the simple or derivative inflectional forms of a verb especially in Sanskrit or the Semitic languages (the causative *conjugation*)
**2** : the act of conjugating : the state of being conjugated
**3 a** : fusion of usually similar gametes with ultimate union of their nuclei that among lower thallophytes replaces the typical fertilization of higher forms **b** : temporary cytoplasmic union with exchange of nuclear material that is the usual sexual process in ciliated protozoans **c** : the one-way transfer of DNA between bacteria in cellular contact
— **con·ju·ga·tion·al** \-shnəl, -shə-n°l\ *adjective*
— **con·ju·ga·tion·al·ly** *adverb*

**¹con·junct** \'kän-,jəŋ(k)t, kän-\ *adjective* [Middle English, from Latin *conjunctus*, past participle of *conjungere*] (15th century)
**1** : UNITED, JOINED
**2** : JOINT
**3** : relating to melodic progression by intervals of no more than a major second — compare DISJUNCT

**²con·junct** \,kän-,jəŋ(k)t\ *noun* (1667)
**1** : something joined or associated with another; *specifically* : one of the components of a conjunction
**2** : an adverb or adverbial (as *so, in addition, however, secondly*) that indicates the speaker's or writer's assessment of the connection between linguistic units (as clauses)

**con·junc·tion** \kən-'jəŋ(k)-shən\ *noun* (14th century)
**1** : the act or an instance of conjoining : the state of being conjoined : COMBINATION
**2** : occurrence together in time or space : CONCURRENCE
**3 a** : the apparent meeting or passing of two or more celestial bodies in the same degree of the zodiac **b** : a configuration in which two celestial bodies have their least apparent separation
**4** : an uninflected linguistic form that joins together sentences, clauses, phrases, or words
**5** : a complex sentence in logic true if and only if each of its components is true
— **con·junc·tion·al** \-shnəl, -shə-n°l\ *adjective*
— **con·junc·tion·al·ly** *adverb*

**con·junc·ti·va** \,kän-,jəŋ(k)-'tī-və, kən-\ *noun, plural* **-vas** *or* **-vae** \-(,)vē\ [New Latin, from Late Latin, feminine of *conjunctivus* conjoining, from Latin *conjunctus*] (14th century)
: the mucous membrane that lines the inner surface of the eyelids and is continued over the forepart of the eyeball — see EYE illustration
— **con·junc·ti·val** \-vəl\ *adjective*

**con·junc·tive** \kən-'jəŋ(k)-tiv\ *adjective* (1581)
**1** : CONNECTIVE
**2** : CONJUNCT, CONJOINED
**3** : being or functioning like a conjunction
**4** : COPULATIVE 1a
— **conjunctive** *noun*
— **con·junc·tive·ly** *adverb*

**con·junc·ti·vi·tis** \kən-,jəŋ(k)-ti-'vī-təs\ *noun* (1835)
: inflammation of the conjunctiva

**con·junc·ture** \kən-'jəŋ(k)-chər\ *noun* (1605)
**1** : CONJUNCTION, UNION
**2** : a combination of circumstances or events usually producing a crisis : JUNCTURE

**con·ju·ra·tion** \,kän-jü-'rā-shən, ,kən-\ *noun* (14th century)
**1** : the act or process of conjuring : INCANTATION
**2** : an expression or trick used in conjuring
**3** : a solemn appeal : ADJURATION

**con·jure** \*verb transitive 2 & verb intransitive senses* 'kän-jər *also* 'kən-; *verb transitive 1* kən-'jür\ *verb* **con·jured; con·jur·ing** \'känj-riŋ, 'kän-jə-, 'kənj-, 'kən-jə-; kən-'jür-iŋ\ [Middle English, from Old French *conjurer*, from Latin *conjurare* to swear together, from *com-* + *jurare* to swear — more at JURY] (13th century)
*transitive verb*
**1** : to charge or entreat earnestly or solemnly
**2 a** : to summon by or as if by invocation or incantation **b** (1) : to affect or effect by or as if by magic (2) : IMAGINE, CONTRIVE — often used with *up* (we *conjure* up our own metaphors for our own needs —R. J. Kaufmann) (3) : to bring to mind (words that *conjure* pleasant images)
*intransitive verb*
**1 a** : to summon a devil or spirit by invocation or incantation **b** : to practice magical arts
**2** : to use a conjurer's tricks : JUGGLE

**con·jur·er** *or* **con·ju·ror** \'kän-jər-ər, 'kən-\ *noun* (14th century)
**1** : one that practices magic arts : WIZARD
**2** : one that performs feats of sleight of hand and illusion : MAGICIAN, JUGGLER

**¹conk** \'käŋk, 'kóŋk\ *transitive verb* [English slang *conk* head] (1821)
: to hit especially on the head : KNOCK OUT

**²conk** *noun* [probably alteration of *conch*] (1851)
: the visible fruiting body of a bracket fungus; *also* : decay caused by such a fungus
— **conky** \'käŋ-kē, 'kóŋ-\ *adjective*

**³conk** *intransitive verb* [probably imitative] (1918)

**1 :** BREAK DOWN; *especially* **:** STALL — usually used with *out* 〈the motor suddenly *conked* out〉 **2 a :** FAINT **b :** to go to sleep — usually used with *off* or *out* 〈*conked* out for a while after lunch〉 **c :** DIE 〈I caught pneumonia. I almost *conked* —Truman Capote〉

⁴**conk** *transitive verb* [probably by shortening & alteration from *congolene* preparation used for straightening hair] (1950)
**:** to straighten out (hair) usually by the use of chemicals

⁵**conk** *noun* (1965)
**:** a hairstyle in which the hair is straightened out and flattened down or lightly waved — called also *process*

**conk·er** \'käŋ-kər\ *noun* [*conch* + ²*-er*, from the original use of a snail shell on a string in the game] (circa 1886)
**1 :** a horse chestnut especially when used in conkers
**2** *plural* **:** a game in which each player swings a horse chestnut on a string to try to break one held by the opponent

**con mo·to** \kän-'mō-(ˌ)tō, kōn-\ *adverb* [Italian] (circa 1854)
**:** with movement **:** in a spirited manner — used as a direction in music

¹**conn** \'kän\ *transitive verb* [alteration of Middle English *condien* to conduct, from Middle French *conduire*, from Latin *conducere* — more at CONDUCE] (1626)
**:** to conduct or direct the steering of (as a ship)

²**conn** *noun* (1825)
**:** the control exercised by one who conns a ship

**con·nate** \kä-'nāt, 'kä-ˌ\ *adjective* [Late Latin *connatus*, past participle of *connasci* to be born together, from Latin *com-* + *nasci* to be born — more at NATION] (1641)
**1 :** AKIN, CONGENIAL
**2 :** INNATE, INBORN
**3 :** congenitally or firmly united 〈*connate* leaves〉
**4 :** born or originated together
**5 :** entrapped in sediments at the time of their deposition 〈*connate* water〉
— **con·nate·ly** *adverb*

**con·nat·u·ral** \kä-'nach-rəl, kə-, -'na-chə-\ *adjective* [Medieval Latin *connaturalis*, from Latin *com-* + *naturalis* natural] (1592)
**1 :** connected by nature **:** INBORN
**2 :** of the same nature
— **con·nat·u·ral·i·ty** \-ˌna-chə-'ra-lə-tē\ *noun*
— **con·nat·u·ral·ly** \-'nach-rə-lē, -'na-chə-\ *adverb*

**con·nect** \kə-'nekt\ *verb* [Middle English, from Latin *conectere, connectere*, from *com-* + *nectere* to bind] (15th century)
*intransitive verb*
**1 :** to become joined 〈the two rooms *connect* by a hallway〉 〈ideas that *connect* easily to form a theory〉
**2 :** to make a successful hit, shot, or throw 〈*connected* for a home run〉 〈*connected* on 60 percent of his shots —*N.Y. Times*〉
**3 :** to have or establish a rapport 〈tried to *connect* with the younger generation〉
*transitive verb*
**1 :** to join or fasten together usually by something intervening
**2 :** to place or establish in relationship
**synonym** see JOIN
— **con·nect·able** *also* **con·nect·ible** \-'nek-tə-bəl\ *adjective*
— **con·nec·tor** *also* **con·nect·er** \-'nek-tər\ *noun*

**connected** *adjective* (1712)
**1 :** joined or linked together
**2 :** having the parts or elements logically linked together 〈presented a thoroughly *connected* view of the problem〉
**3 :** related by blood or marriage
**4 :** having social, professional, or commercial relationships 〈a well-*connected* lawyer〉

**5** *of a set* **:** having the property that any two of its points can be joined by a line completely contained in the set; *also* **:** incapable of being separated into two or more closed disjoint subsets
— **con·nect·ed·ly** *adverb*
— **con·nect·ed·ness** *noun*

**connecting rod** *noun* (1839)
**:** a rod that transmits motion from a reciprocating part of a machine (as a piston) to a rotating part or vice versa

**con·nec·tion** \kə-'nek-shən\ *noun* [Latin *connexion-, connexio*, from *conectere*] (14th century)
**1 :** the act of connecting **:** the state of being connected: as **a :** causal or logical relation or sequence 〈the *connection* between two ideas〉 **b** (1) **:** contextual relation or association 〈in this *connection* the word has a different meaning〉 (2) **:** relationship in fact 〈wanted in *connection* with a robbery〉 **c :** a relation of personal intimacy (as of family ties) **d :** COHERENCE, CONTINUITY
**2 a :** something that connects **:** LINK 〈a loose *connection* in the wiring〉 **b :** a means of communication or transport
**3 :** a person connected with another especially by marriage, kinship, or common interest 〈has powerful *connections*〉
**4 :** a political, social, professional, or commercial relationship: as **a :** POSITION, JOB **b :** an arrangement to execute orders or advance interests of another 〈a firm's foreign *connections*〉 **c :** a source of contraband (as illegal drugs)
**5 :** a set of persons associated together: as **a :** DENOMINATION **b :** CLAN
— **con·nec·tion·al** \-shnəl, -shə-nᵊl\ *adjective*

¹**con·nec·tive** \kə-'nek-tiv\ *adjective* (circa 1660)
**:** serving to connect
— **con·nec·tive·ly** *adverb*

²**connective** *noun* (1751)
**:** something that connects: as **a :** a linguistic form that connects words or word groups **b :** the tissue connecting the pollen sacs of an anther **c :** a logical term (as *or, if-then, and, not*) or a symbol for it that relates propositions in such a way that the truth or falsity of the resulting statement is determined by the truth or falsity of the components

**connective tissue** *noun* (1846)
**:** a tissue of mesodermal origin rich in intercellular substance or interlacing processes with little tendency for the cells to come together in sheets or masses; *specifically* **:** connective tissue of stellate or spindle-shaped cells with interlacing processes that pervades, supports, and binds together other tissues and forms ligaments, tendons, and aponeuroses

**con·nec·tiv·i·ty** \(ˌ)kä-ˌnek-'ti-və-tē, kə-\ *noun, plural* **-ties** (1893)
**:** the quality or state of being connective or connected 〈*connectivity* of a surface〉; *especially* **:** the ability to connect to or communicate with another computer or computer system

**Con·ne·ma·ra** \ˌkä-nə-'mär-ə, ˌkò-\ *noun* [*Connemara*, Ireland] (circa 1952)
**:** any of a breed of rugged ponies developed in Ireland

**con·nex·ion** \kə-'nek-shən\ *chiefly British variant of* CONNECTION

**con·ning tower** \'kä-niŋ-\ *noun* (1886)
**:** a raised structure on the deck of a submarine used especially formerly for navigation and attack direction

**con·nip·tion** \kə-'nip-shən\ *noun* [origin unknown] (1833)
**:** a fit of rage, hysteria, or alarm 〈went into *conniptions*〉

**con·niv·ance** \kə-'nī-vən(t)s\ *noun* (1593)
**:** the act of conniving; *especially* **:** knowledge of and active or passive consent to wrongdoing

**con·nive** \kə-'nīv\ *intransitive verb* **con·nived; con·niv·ing**

**conning tower**

[French or Latin; French *conniver*, from Latin *conivēre, connivēre* to close the eyes, connive, from *com-* + *-nivēre* (akin to *nictare* to wink); akin to Old English & Old High German *hnīgan* to bow] (1601)
**1 :** to pretend ignorance of or fail to take action against something one ought to oppose
**2 a :** to be indulgent or in secret sympathy **:** WINK **b :** to cooperate secretly or have a secret understanding
**3 :** CONSPIRE, INTRIGUE
— **con·niv·er** *noun*

**con·ni·vent** \-'nī-vənt\ *adjective* [Latin *conivent-, conivens*, present participle of *conivēre*] (1757)
**:** converging but not fused 〈*connivent* stamens〉

**con·nois·seur** \ˌkä-nə-'sər *also* -'sur\ *noun* [obsolete French (now *connaisseur*), from Old French *connoisseor*, from *connoistre* to know, from Latin *cognoscere* — more at COGNITION] (1714)
**1 :** EXPERT; *especially* **:** one who understands the details, technique, or principles of an art and is competent to act as a critical judge
**2 :** one who enjoys with discrimination and appreciation of subtleties 〈a *connoisseur* of fine wines〉
— **con·nois·seur·ship** \-ˌship\ *noun*

**con·no·ta·tion** \ˌkä-nə-'tā-shən\ *noun* (1532)
**1 a :** the suggesting of a meaning by a word apart from the thing it explicitly names or describes **b :** something suggested by a word or thing **:** IMPLICATION 〈the *connotations* of comfort that surrounded that old chair〉
**2 :** the signification of something 〈that abuse of logic which consists in moving counters about as if they were known entities with a fixed *connotation* —W. R. Inge〉
**3 :** an essential property or group of properties of a thing named by a term in logic — compare DENOTATION
— **con·no·ta·tion·al** \-shnəl, -shə-nᵊl\ *adjective*

**con·no·ta·tive** \'kä-nə-ˌtā-tiv, kə-'nō-tə-tiv\ *adjective* (1614)
**1 :** connoting or tending to connote
**2 :** relating to connotation
— **con·no·ta·tive·ly** *adverb*

**con·note** \kə-'nōt, kä-\ *transitive verb* **con·not·ed; con·not·ing** [Medieval Latin *connotare*, from Latin *com-* + *notare* to note] (1665)
**1 :** to be associated with or inseparable from as a consequence or concomitant 〈the remorse so often *connoted* by guilt〉
**2 a :** to convey in addition to exact explicit meaning 〈all the misery that poverty *connotes*〉 **b :** to imply as a logical connotation

**con·nu·bi·al** \kə-'nü-bē-əl, -'nyü-\ *adjective* [Latin *conubialis*, from *conubium, connubium* marriage, from *com-* + *nubere* to marry — more at NUPTIAL] (circa 1656)
**:** of or relating to the married state **:** CONJUGAL
— **con·nu·bi·al·ism** \-bē-ə-ˌli-zəm\ *noun*
— **con·nu·bi·al·i·ty** \-ˌnü-bē-'a-lə-tē, -ˌnyü-\ *noun*

---

\ə\ abut \ᵊ\ kitten \ər\ further \a\ ash \ā\ ace
\ä\ mop, mar \aú\ out \ch\ chin \e\ bet \ē\ easy
\g\ go \i\ hit \ī\ ice \j\ job \ŋ\ sing \ō\ go
\ò\ law \òi\ boy \th\ thin \t͟h\ the \ü\ loot \ú\ foot
\y\ yet \zh\ vision *see also* Guide to Pronunciation

— **con·nu·bi·al·ly** \-'nü-bē-ə-lē, -'nyü-\ *adverb*

**co·no·dont** \'kō-nə-ˌdänt, 'kä-\ *noun* [International Scientific Vocabulary *con-* (from Greek *kōnos* cone) + *-odont* (1859)]
: a Paleozoic toothlike fossil that is probably the remains of an extinct marine invertebrate

**co·noid** \'kō-ˌnóid\ *or* **co·noi·dal** \kō-'nói-dᵊl\ *adjective* (1668)
: shaped like or nearly like a cone ⟨*conoid* shells⟩ ⟨*conoid* pottery⟩
— **conoid** *noun*

**con·quer** \'kän-kər\ *verb* **con·quered; con·quer·ing** \-k(ə-)riŋ\ [Middle English, to acquire, conquer, from Old French *conquerre*, from (assumed) Vulgar Latin *conquaerere*, alteration of Latin *conquirere* to search for, collect, from *com-* + *quaerere* to ask, search] (14th century)
*transitive verb*
**1** : to gain or acquire by force of arms : SUBJUGATE
**2** : to overcome by force of arms : VANQUISH
**3** : to gain mastery over or win by overcoming obstacles or opposition ⟨*conquered* the mountain⟩
**4** : to overcome by mental or moral power : SURMOUNT ⟨*conquered* her fear⟩
*intransitive verb*
: to be victorious ☆
— **con·quer·or** \-kər-ər\ *noun*

**con·quest** \'kän-ˌkwest, 'kän-; 'käŋ-ˌkwəst\ *noun* [Middle English, from Middle French, from (assumed) Vulgar Latin *conquaesitus*, alteration of Latin *conquisitus*, past participle of *conquirere*] (14th century)
**1** : the act or process of conquering
**2 a** : something conquered; *especially* : territory appropriated in war **b** : a person whose favor or hand has been won

**con·qui·an** \'kän-kē-ən\ *noun* [Mexican Spanish *conquián* — more at COONCAN] (circa 1911)
: a card game for two played with 40 cards from which all games of rummy developed

**con·quis·ta·dor** \kän-'kēs-tə-ˌdór, also -'kwis-, -'kis-\ *noun, plural* **con·quis·ta·do·res** \(ˌ)kän-ˌkēs-tə-'dór-ēz, -'dór-ˌās, kən-; (ˌ)kän-ˌkwis-, -ˌkis-\ *or* **con·quis·ta·dors** [Spanish, ultimately from Latin *conquirere*] (1830)
: one that conquers; *specifically* : a leader in the Spanish conquest of America and especially of Mexico and Peru in the 16th century

**con·san·guine** \kän-'saŋ-gwən, kən-\ *adjective* (1610)
: CONSANGUINEOUS

**con·san·guin·e·ous** \ˌkän-ˌsan-'gwi-nē-əs, -ˌsaŋ-\ *adjective* [Latin *consanguineus*, from *com-* + *sanguin-, sanguis* blood] (1601)
: of the same blood or origin; *specifically* : descended from the same ancestor
— **con·san·guin·e·ous·ly** *adverb*

**con·san·guin·i·ty** \-'gwi-nə-tē\ *noun, plural* **-ties** (14th century)
**1** : the quality or state of being consanguineous
**2** : a close relation or connection

**con·science** \'kän(t)-shən(t)s\ *noun* [Middle English, from Old French, from Latin *conscientia*, from *conscient-, consciens*, present participle of *conscire* to be conscious, be conscious of guilt, from *com-* + *scire* to know — more at SCIENCE] (13th century)
**1 a** : the sense or consciousness of the moral goodness or blameworthiness of one's own conduct, intentions, or character together with a feeling of obligation to do right or be good **b** : a faculty, power, or principle enjoining good acts **c** : the part of the superego in psychoanalysis that transmits commands and admonitions to the ego
**2** *archaic* : CONSCIOUSNESS
**3** : conformity to the dictates of conscience : CONSCIENTIOUSNESS

**4** : sensitive regard for fairness or justice : SCRUPLE
— **con·science·less** \-ləs\ *adjective*
— **in all conscience** *or* **in conscience**
: in all fairness

**conscience money** *noun* (1848)
: money paid usually anonymously to relieve the conscience by restoring what has been wrongfully acquired

**con·sci·en·tious** \ˌkän(t)-shē-'en(t)-shəs\ *adjective* (1611)
**1** : governed by or conforming to the dictates of conscience : SCRUPULOUS ⟨a *conscientious* public servant⟩
**2** : METICULOUS, CAREFUL ⟨a *conscientious* listener⟩
*synonym* see UPRIGHT
— **con·sci·en·tious·ly** *adverb*
— **con·sci·en·tious·ness** *noun*

**conscientious objection** *noun* (1916)
: objection on moral or religious grounds (as to service in the armed forces or to bearing arms)

**conscientious objector** *noun* (1899)
: a person who refuses to serve in the armed forces or bear arms on moral or religious grounds

**con·scio·na·ble** \'kän-sh(ə-)nə-bəl\ *adjective* [irregular from *conscience*] (1549)
: CONSCIENTIOUS

**¹con·scious** \'kän(t)-shəs\ *adjective* [Latin *conscius*, from *com-* + *scire* to know] (1592)
**1** : perceiving, apprehending, or noticing with a degree of controlled thought or observation
**2** *archaic* : sharing another's knowledge or awareness of an inward state or outward fact
**3** : personally felt ⟨*conscious* guilt⟩
**4** : capable of or marked by thought, will, design, or perception
**5** : SELF-CONSCIOUS
**6** : having mental faculties undulled by sleep, faintness, or stupor : AWAKE ⟨became *conscious* after the anesthesia wore off⟩
**7** : done or acting with critical awareness ⟨a *conscious* effort to do better⟩
**8 a** : likely to notice, consider, or appraise ⟨a bargain-*conscious* shopper⟩ **b** : being concerned or interested ⟨a budget-*conscious* businessman⟩ **c** : marked by strong feelings or notions ⟨a race-*conscious* society⟩
*synonym* see AWARE
— **con·scious·ly** *adverb*

**²conscious** *noun* (1919)
: CONSCIOUSNESS 5

**¹con·scious·ness** \-nəs\ *noun* (1632)
**1 a** : the quality or state of being aware especially of something within oneself **b** : the state or fact of being conscious of an external object, state, or fact **c** : AWARENESS; *especially* : concern for some social or political cause
**2** : the state of being characterized by sensation, emotion, volition, and thought : MIND
**3** : the totality of conscious states of an individual
**4** : the normal state of conscious life ⟨regained *consciousness*⟩
**5** : the upper level of mental life of which the person is aware as contrasted with unconscious processes

**consciousness–raising** *noun* (1971)
: an increasing of concerned awareness especially of some social or political issue

**con·scribe** \kən-'skrīb\ *transitive verb* **con·scribed; con·scrib·ing** [Latin *conscribere*] (1613)
**1** : LIMIT, CIRCUMSCRIBE ⟨ill-health . . . *conscribed* the force of his intentions —*Times Literary Supplement*⟩
**2** : to enlist forcibly : CONSCRIPT

**¹con·script** \'kän-ˌskript\ *noun* (1800)
: a conscripted person (as a military recruit)

**²con·script** \kən-'skript\ *transitive verb* (1813)
: to enroll into service by compulsion : DRAFT ⟨was *conscripted* into the army⟩

**³con·script** \'kän-ˌskript\ *adjective* [alteration of French *conscrit*, from Latin *conscriptus*, past participle of *conscribere* to enroll, enlist, from *com-* + *scribere* to write — more at SCRIBE] (1823)
**1** : enrolled into service by compulsion : DRAFTED
**2** : made up of conscripted persons

**con·scrip·tion** \kən-'skrip-shən\ *noun* (1800)
: compulsory enrollment of persons especially for military service : DRAFT

**¹con·se·crate** \'kän(t)-sə-ˌkrāt\ *adjective* (14th century)
: dedicated to a sacred purpose

**²consecrate** *transitive verb* **-crat·ed; -crat·ing** [Middle English, from Latin *consecratus*, past participle of *consecrare*, from *com-* + *sacrare* to consecrate — more at SACRED] (14th century)
**1** : to induct (a person) into a permanent office with a religious rite; *especially* : to ordain to the office of bishop
**2 a** : to make or declare sacred; *especially* : to devote irrevocably to the worship of God by a solemn ceremony **b** : to effect the liturgical transubstantiation of (eucharistic bread and wine) **c** : to devote to a purpose with or as if with deep solemnity or dedication
**3** : to make inviolable or venerable ⟨principles *consecrated* by the weight of history⟩
*synonym* see DEVOTE
— **con·se·cra·tive** \-ˌkrā-tiv\ *adjective*
— **con·se·cra·tor** \-ˌkrā-tər\ *noun*
— **con·se·cra·to·ry** \'kän(t)-si-krə-ˌtōr-ē, -ˌtór-, -ˌkrā-tə-rē\ *adjective*

**con·se·cra·tion** \ˌkän(t)-sə-'krā-shən\ *noun* (14th century)
**1** : the act or ceremony of consecrating
**2** : the state of being consecrated
**3** *capitalized* : the part of a Communion rite in which the bread and wine are consecrated

**con·se·cu·tion** \ˌkän(t)-si-'kyü-shən\ *noun* [Latin *consecution-, consecutio*, from *consequi* to follow along — more at CONSEQUENT] (1651)
: SEQUENCE

**con·sec·u·tive** \kən-'se-kyə-tiv, -kə-tiv\ *adjective* (1611)
: following one after the other in order : SUCCESSIVE
— **con·sec·u·tive·ly** *adverb*
— **con·sec·u·tive·ness** *noun*

**con·sen·su·al** \kən-'sen(t)-sh(ə-)wəl, -shəl\ *adjective* [Latin *consensus* + English *-al*] (1754)
**1 a** : existing or made by mutual consent without an act of writing ⟨a *consensual* contract⟩ **b** : involving or based on mutual consent ⟨*consensual* acts⟩
**2** : relating to or being the constrictive pupillary response of an eye that is covered when the other eye is exposed to light

---

☆ SYNONYMS
**Conquer, vanquish, defeat, subdue, reduce, overcome, overthrow** mean to get the better of by force or strategy. CONQUER implies gaining mastery of ⟨Caesar *conquered* Gaul⟩. VANQUISH implies a complete overpowering ⟨*vanquished* the enemy and ended the war⟩. DEFEAT does not imply the finality or completeness of VANQUISH which it otherwise equals ⟨the Confederates *defeated* the Union forces at Manassas⟩. SUBDUE implies a defeating and suppression ⟨*subdued* the native tribes after years of fighting⟩. REDUCE implies a forcing to capitulate or surrender ⟨the city was *reduced* after a month-long siege⟩. OVERCOME suggests getting the better of with difficulty or after hard struggle ⟨*overcame* a host of bureaucratic roadblocks⟩. OVERTHROW stresses the bringing down or destruction of existing power ⟨violently *overthrew* the old regime⟩.

— **con·sen·su·al·ly** *adverb*
**con·sen·sus** \kən-'sen(t)-səs\ *noun, often attributive* [Latin, from *consentire*] (1858)
**1 a :** general agreement **:** UNANIMITY ⟨the *consensus* of their opinion, based on reports . . . from the border —John Hersey⟩ **b :** the judgment arrived at by most of those concerned ⟨the *consensus* was to go ahead⟩
**2 :** group solidarity in sentiment and belief ▪
¹**con·sent** \kən-'sent\ *intransitive verb* [Middle English, from Latin *consentire*, from *com- + sentire* to feel — more at SENSE] (13th century)
**1 :** to give assent or approval **:** AGREE
**2** *archaic* **:** to be in concord in opinion or sentiment
***synonym*** see ASSENT
— **con·sent·ing·ly** \-'sen-tiŋ-lē\ *adverb*
²**consent** *noun* (14th century)
**1 :** compliance in or approval of what is done or proposed by another **:** ACQUIESCENCE ⟨he shall have power, by and with the advice and *consent* of the Senate, to make treaties —*U.S. Constitution*⟩
**2 :** agreement as to action or opinion; *specifically* **:** voluntary agreement by a people to organize a civil society and give authority to the government
— **con·sent·er** *noun*
**con·sen·ta·ne·ous** \ˌkän(t)-sən-'tā-nē-əs, ˌkän-sen-\ *adjective* [Latin *consentaneus*, from *consentire* to agree] (1625)
**1 :** expressing agreement **:** SUITED
**2 :** done or made by the consent of all
— **con·sen·ta·ne·ous·ly** *adverb*
**consent decree** *noun* (1904)
**:** a judicial decree that sanctions a voluntary agreement between parties in dispute
**con·se·quence** \'kän(t)-sə-ˌkwen(t)s, -si-kwən(t)s\ *noun* (14th century)
**1 :** a conclusion derived through logic **:** INFERENCE
**2 :** something produced by a cause or necessarily following from a set of conditions
**3 a :** importance with respect to power to produce an effect **:** MOMENT **b :** social importance
**4 :** the appearance of importance; *especially* **:** SELF-IMPORTANCE
***synonym*** see IMPORTANCE
— **in consequence :** as a result **:** CONSEQUENTLY
¹**con·se·quent** \-kwənt, -ˌkwent\ *noun* (14th century)
**1 a :** DEDUCTION 2b **b :** the conclusion of a conditional sentence
**2 :** the second term of a ratio
²**consequent** *adjective* [Middle English, from Middle French, from Latin *consequent-, consequens*, present participle of *consequi* to follow along, from *com- + sequi* to follow — more at SUE] (15th century)
**1 :** following as a result or effect ⟨her new job and *consequent* relocation⟩
**2 :** observing logical sequence **:** RATIONAL
**con·se·quen·tial** \ˌkän(t)-sə-'kwen(t)-shəl\ *adjective* (1626)
**1 :** of the nature of a secondary result **:** INDIRECT
**2 :** CONSEQUENT
**3 :** having significant consequences **:** IMPORTANT ⟨a grave and *consequential* event⟩
**4 :** SELF-IMPORTANT
— **con·se·quen·ti·al·i·ty** \-ˌkwen(t)-shē-'a-lə-tē\ *noun*
— **con·se·quen·tial·ly** \-'kwen(t)-sh(ə-)lē\ *adverb*
— **con·se·quen·tial·ness** \-'kwen(t)-shəl-nəs\ *noun*
**con·se·quent·ly** \'kän(t)-sə-ˌkwent-lē, -si-kwənt-\ *adverb* (15th century)
**:** as a result **:** in view of the foregoing **:** ACCORDINGLY
**con·ser·van·cy** \kən-'sər-vən-sē\ *noun, plural* -**cies** [alteration of obsolete *conservacy* conservation, from Anglo-French *conser-*

*vacie*, from Medieval Latin *conservatia*, from Latin *conservare*] (1755)
**1** *British* **:** a board regulating fisheries and navigation in a river or port
**2 a :** CONSERVATION **b :** an organization or area designated to conserve and protect natural resources
**con·ser·va·tion** \ˌkän(t)-sər-'vā-shən\ *noun* [Middle English, from Middle French, from Latin *conservation-, conservatio*, from *conservare*] (14th century)
**1 :** a careful preservation and protection of something; *especially* **:** planned management of a natural resource to prevent exploitation, destruction, or neglect
**2 :** the preservation of a physical quantity during transformations or reactions
— **con·ser·va·tion·al** \-shnəl, -shə-nᵊl\ *adjective*
**con·ser·va·tion·ist** \-sh(ə-)nist\ *noun* (1870)
**:** a person who advocates conservation especially of natural resources
**conservation of charge** (1949)
**:** a principle in physics: the total electric charge of an isolated system remains constant irrespective of whatever internal changes may take place
**conservation of energy** (1853)
**:** a principle in physics: the total energy of an isolated system remains constant irrespective of whatever internal changes may take place with energy disappearing in one form reappearing in another
**conservation of mass** (1884)
**:** a principle in classical physics: the total mass of any material system is neither increased nor diminished by reactions between the parts — called also *conservation of matter*
**con·ser·va·tism** \kən-'sər-və-ˌti-zəm\ *noun* (1835)
**1** *capitalized* **a :** the principles and policies of a Conservative party **b :** the Conservative party
**2 a :** disposition in politics to preserve what is established **b :** a political philosophy based on tradition and social stability, stressing established institutions, and preferring gradual development to abrupt change
**3 :** the tendency to prefer an existing or traditional situation to change
¹**con·ser·va·tive** \kən-'sər-və-tiv\ *adjective* (14th century)
**1 :** PRESERVATIVE
**2 a :** of or relating to a philosophy of conservatism **b** *capitalized* **:** of or constituting a political party professing the principles of conservatism: as (1) **:** of or constituting a party of the United Kingdom advocating support of established institutions (2) **:** PROGRESSIVE CONSERVATIVE
**3 a :** tending or disposed to maintain existing views, conditions, or institutions **:** TRADITIONAL **b :** marked by moderation or caution ⟨a *conservative* estimate⟩ **c :** marked by or relating to traditional norms of taste, elegance, style, or manners ⟨a *conservative* suit⟩
**4 :** of or relating to Conservative Judaism
— **con·ser·va·tive·ly** *adverb*
— **con·ser·va·tive·ness** *noun*
²**conservative** *noun* (1831)
**1 a :** an adherent or advocate of political conservatism **b** *capitalized* **:** a member or supporter of a conservative political party
**2 a :** one who adheres to traditional methods or views **b :** a cautious or discreet person
**Conservative Judaism** *noun* (1946)
**:** Judaism as practiced especially among some U.S. Jews with adherence to the Torah and Talmud but with allowance for some departures in keeping with differing times and circumstances — compare ORTHODOX JUDAISM, REFORM JUDAISM
**con·ser·va·tize** \-ˌtīz\ *verb* -**tized;** -**tiz·ing** (1849)
*intransitive verb*
**:** to grow conservative

*transitive verb*
**:** to make conservative
**con·ser·va·toire** \kən-'sər-və-ˌtwär\ *noun* [French, from Italian *conservatorio*] (1845)
**:** CONSERVATORY 2
**con·ser·va·tor** \kən-'sər-və-tər, -və-ˌtôr; 'kän(t)-sər-ˌvā-tər\ *noun* (15th century)
**1 a :** one that preserves from injury or violation **:** PROTECTOR **b :** one that is responsible for the care, restoration, and repair of archival or museum articles
**2 :** a person, official, or institution designated to take over and protect the interests of an incompetent
**3 :** an official charged with the protection of something affecting public welfare and interests
— **con·ser·va·to·ri·al** \kən-ˌsər-və-'tōr-ē-əl, (ˌ)kän-, -'tôr-\ *adjective*
— **con·ser·va·tor·ship** \kən-'sər-və-tər-ˌship, -və-ˌtôr-; 'kän(t)-sər-ˌvā-tər-\ *noun*
**con·ser·va·to·ry** \kən-'sər-və-ˌtōr-ē, -ˌtôr-\ *noun, plural* -**ries** (1664)
**1 :** a greenhouse for growing or displaying plants
**2** [Italian *conservatorio* home for foundlings, music school, from Latin *conservare*] **:** a school specializing in one of the fine arts ⟨a music *conservatory*⟩
¹**con·serve** \kən-'sərv\ *transitive verb* **con·served; con·serv·ing** [Middle English, from Middle French *conserver*, from Latin *conservare*, from *com- + servare* to keep, guard, observe; akin to Avestan *haurvaiti* he guards] (14th century)
**1 :** to keep in a safe or sound state ⟨he *conserved* his inheritance⟩; *especially* **:** to avoid wasteful or destructive use of ⟨*conserve* natural resources⟩
**2 :** to preserve with sugar
**3 :** to maintain (a quantity) constant during a process of chemical, physical, or evolutionary change
— **con·serv·er** *noun*
²**con·serve** \'kän-ˌsərv\ *noun* (15th century)
**1 :** SWEETMEAT; *especially* **:** a candied fruit
**2 :** PRESERVE; *specifically* **:** one prepared from a mixture of fruits
**con·sid·er** \kən-'si-dər\ *verb* **con·sid·ered; con·sid·er·ing** \-d(ə-)riŋ\ [Middle English, from Middle French *considerer*, from Latin *considerare* to observe, think about, from *com- + sider-, sidus* star] (14th century)
*transitive verb*
**1 :** to think about carefully: as **a :** to think of especially with regard to taking some action ⟨is *considering* you for the job⟩ ⟨*considered* moving to the city⟩ **b :** to take into account ⟨defendant's age must be *considered*⟩
**2 :** to regard or treat in an attentive or kindly way ⟨he *considered* her every wish⟩
**3 :** to gaze on steadily or reflectively
**4 :** to come to judge or classify ⟨*consider* thrift essential⟩
**5 :** REGARD ⟨his works are well *considered* abroad⟩
**6 :** SUPPOSE

☐ **USAGE**
**consensus** The phrase *consensus of opinion*, which is not actually redundant (see sense 1a; the sense that takes the phrase is slightly older), has been so often claimed to be a redundancy that many writers avoid it. You are safe in using *consensus* alone when it is clear you mean consensus of opinion, and most writers in fact do so.

*intransitive verb*
**:** REFLECT, DELIBERATE ⟨paused a moment to *consider*⟩ ☆

**¹con·sid·er·able** \-'si-dər(-ə)-bəl, -'si-drə-bəl\ *adjective* (circa 1619)
**1 :** worth consideration **:** SIGNIFICANT
**2 :** large in extent or degree ⟨a *considerable* number⟩
— **con·sid·er·ably** \-blē\ *adverb*
**²considerable** *noun* (1685)
**:** a considerable amount, degree, or extent
**con·sid·er·ate** \kən-'si-d(ə-)rət\ *adjective* (1572)
**1 :** marked by or given to careful consideration **:** CIRCUMSPECT
**2 :** thoughtful of the rights and feelings of others
— **con·sid·er·ate·ly** *adverb*
— **con·sid·er·ate·ness** *noun*
**con·sid·er·ation** \kən-ˌsi-də-'rā-shən\ *noun* (14th century)
**1 :** continuous and careful thought ⟨after long *consideration* he agreed to their requests⟩
**2 a :** a matter weighed or taken into account when formulating an opinion or plan ⟨economic *considerations* forced her to leave college⟩ **b :** a taking into account
**3 :** thoughtful and sympathetic regard
**4 :** an opinion obtained by reflection
**5 :** ESTEEM, REGARD ⟨the family built themselves a large, ugly villa . . . and became people of *consideration* —V. S. Pritchett⟩
**6 a :** RECOMPENSE, PAYMENT **b :** the inducement to a contract or other legal transaction; *specifically* **:** an act or forbearance or the promise thereof done or given by one party in return for the act or promise of another
— **in consideration of :** as payment or recompense for ⟨a small fee *in consideration of* many kind services⟩
**con·sid·ered** \kən-'si-dərd\ *adjective* (circa 1677)
**1 :** matured by extended deliberative thought ⟨a *considered* opinion⟩
**2 :** viewed with respect or esteem
**¹con·sid·er·ing** \-d(ə-)riŋ\ *preposition* (14th century)
**:** in view of **:** taking into account ⟨he did well *considering* his limitations⟩
**²considering** *conjunction* (15th century)
**:** INASMUCH AS ⟨*considering* he was new at the job, he did quite well⟩
**con·sig·li·e·re** \kōn-(ˌ)sil-'ye-re, -'yer-ē; kän-(ˌ)si-glē-'ye-rä, -rē, -'yer\ *noun, plural* **-ri** \-rē\ [Italian, from *consiglio* advice, counsel, from Latin *consilium* — more at COUNSEL] (1615)
**:** COUNSELOR, ADVISER ⟨*consigliere* of a Mafia family⟩
**con·sign** \kən-'sīn\ *verb* [Middle French *consigner*, from Latin *consignare*, from *com-* + *signum* sign, mark, seal — more at SIGN] (1528)
*transitive verb*
**1 :** to give over to another's care
**2 :** to give, transfer, or deliver into the hands or control of another; *also* **:** to commit especially to a final destination or fate ⟨a writer *consigned* to oblivion⟩
**3 :** to send or address to an agent to be cared for or sold
*intransitive verb*
*obsolete* **:** AGREE, SUBMIT
*synonym* see COMMIT
— **con·sign·able** \-'sī-nə-bəl\ *adjective*
— **con·sig·na·tion** \ˌkän-ˌsī-'nā-shən, ˌkän(t)-sig-\ *noun*
— **con·sign·or** \ˌkän-ˌsī-'nòr, kən-\ *noun*
**con·sign·ee** \ˌkän(t)-sə-'nē, ˌkän-ˌsī-, kən-ˌsī-\ *noun* (1789)
**:** one to whom something is consigned or shipped
**¹con·sign·ment** \kən-'sīn-mənt\ *noun* (circa 1668)
**1 :** the act or process of consigning
**2 :** something consigned especially in a single shipment

— **on consignment :** shipped to a dealer who pays only for what he sells and who may return what is unsold ⟨goods shipped *on consignment*⟩
**²consignment** *adjective* (1913)
**:** of, relating to, or received as goods on consignment ⟨a *consignment* sale⟩
**¹con·sist** \kən-'sist\ *intransitive verb* [Middle French & Latin; Middle French *consister*, from Latin *consistere*, literally, to stop, stand still, from *com-* + *sistere* to take a stand; akin to Latin *stare* to stand — more at STAND] (1526)
**1 :** LIE, RESIDE — usually used with *in* ⟨liberty *consists* in the absence of obstructions —A. E. Housman⟩
**2** *archaic* **a :** EXIST, BE **b :** to be capable of existing
**3 :** to be composed or made up — usually used with *of* ⟨breakfast *consisted* of cereal, milk, and fruit⟩
**4 :** to be consistent ⟨it *consists* with the facts⟩
**²con·sist** \'kän-ˌsist\ *noun* (1898)
**:** makeup or composition (as of coal sizes or a railroad train) by classes, types, or grades and arrangement
**con·sis·tence** \kən-'sis-tən(t)s\ *noun* (1601)
**:** CONSISTENCY
**con·sis·ten·cy** \kən-'sis-tən(t)-sē\ *noun, plural* **-cies** (1594)
**1 a** *archaic* **:** condition of adhering together **:** firmness of material substance **b :** firmness of constitution or character **:** PERSISTENCY
**2 :** degree of firmness, density, viscosity, or resistance to movement or separation of constituent particles ⟨boil the juice to the *consistency* of a thick syrup⟩
**3 a :** agreement or harmony of parts or features to one another or a whole **:** CORRESPONDENCE; *specifically* **:** ability to be asserted together without contradiction **b :** harmony of conduct or practice with profession ⟨followed her own advice with *consistency*⟩
**con·sis·tent** \kən-'sis-tənt\ *adjective* [Latin *consistent-, consistens*, present participle of *consistere*] (1647)
**1** *archaic* **:** possessing firmness or coherence
**2 a :** marked by harmony, regularity, or steady continuity **:** free from variation or contradiction ⟨a *consistent* style in painting⟩ **b :** COMPATIBLE — usually used with *with* **c :** showing steady conformity to character, profession, belief, or custom ⟨a *consistent* patriot⟩
**3 :** tending to be arbitrarily close to the true value of the parameter estimated as the sample becomes large ⟨a *consistent* statistical estimator⟩
— **con·sis·tent·ly** \-lē\ *adverb*
**con·sis·to·ry** \kən-'sis-t(ə-)rē\ *noun, plural* **-ries** [Middle English *consistorie*, from Middle French, from Medieval Latin & Late Latin; Medieval Latin *consistorium* church tribunal, from Late Latin, imperial council, from Latin *consistere*] (14th century)
**1 :** a solemn assembly **:** COUNCIL
**2 :** a church tribunal or governing body: as **a :** a solemn meeting of Roman Catholic cardinals convoked and presided over by the pope **b :** a church session in some Reformed churches
**3 :** the organization that confers the degrees of the Ancient and Accepted Scottish Rite of Freemasonry usually from the 19th to the 32d inclusive; *also* **:** a meeting of such an organization
— **con·sis·to·ri·al** \ˌkän-si-'stòr-ē-əl, -'stòr-\ *adjective*
**con·so·ci·ate** \kən-'sō-sē-ˌāt, -shē-ˌāt\ *verb* **-at·ed; -at·ing** [Latin *consociatus*, past participle of *consociare*, from *com-* + *socius* companion — more at SOCIAL] (1566)
*transitive verb*
**:** to bring into association

*intransitive verb*
**:** to associate especially in fellowship or partnership
**con·so·ci·a·tion** \-ˌsō-sē-'ā-shən, -shē-\ *noun* (1593)
**1 :** association in fellowship or alliance
**2 :** an association of churches or religious societies
**3 :** an ecological community with a single dominant species
— **con·so·ci·a·tion·al** \-shnəl, -shə-nᵊl\ *adjective*
**con·so·la·tion** \ˌkän(t)-sə-'lā-shən\ *noun* (14th century)
**1 :** the act or an instance of consoling **:** the state of being consoled **:** COMFORT
**2 :** something that consoles; *specifically* **:** a contest held for those who have lost early in a tournament ⟨the losers met in a *consolation* game⟩
— **con·so·la·to·ry** \kən-'sō-lə-ˌtòr-ē, -'sä-, -ˌtòr-\ *adjective*
**consolation prize** *noun* (1886)
**:** a prize given to a runner-up or a loser in a contest
**¹con·sole** \'kän-ˌsōl\ *noun* [French] (1664)
**1 :** an architectural member projecting from a wall to form a bracket or from a keystone for ornament
**2 :** CONSOLE TABLE
**3 a :** an upright case which houses the keyboards and controlling mechanisms of an organ and from which the organ is played **b :** a combination of readouts or displays and an input device (as a keyboard or switches) by which an operator can monitor and interact with a system (as a computer or dubber)
**4 a :** a cabinet (as for a radio or television set) designed to rest directly on the floor **b :** a small storage cabinet between bucket seats in an automobile
**²con·sole** \kən-'sōl\ *transitive verb* **con·soled; con·sol·ing** [French *consoler*, from Latin *consolari*, from *com-* + *solari* to console] (1693)
**:** to alleviate the grief, sense of loss, or trouble of **:** COMFORT ⟨*console* a widow⟩
— **con·sol·ing·ly** \-'sō-liŋ-lē\ *adverb*
**console table** *noun* (1813)
**:** a table fixed to a wall with its top supported by consoles or front legs; *broadly* **:** a table designed to fit against a wall
**con·sol·i·date** \kən-'sä-lə-ˌdāt\ *verb* **-dat·ed; -dat·ing** [Latin *consolidatus*, past participle of *consolidare* to make solid, from *com-* + *solidus* solid] (circa 1512)

**console table**

*transitive verb*
**1 :** to join together into one whole **:** UNITE ⟨*consolidate* several small school districts⟩
**2 :** to make firm or secure **:** STRENGTHEN ⟨*consolidate* their hold on first place⟩

---

☆ **SYNONYMS**
**Consider, study, contemplate, weigh** mean to think about in order to arrive at a judgment or decision. CONSIDER may suggest giving thought to in order to reach a suitable conclusion, opinion, or decision ⟨refused even to *consider* my proposal⟩. STUDY implies sustained purposeful concentration and attention to details and minutiae ⟨*study* the plan closely⟩. CONTEMPLATE stresses focusing one's thoughts on something but does not imply coming to a conclusion or decision ⟨*contemplate* the consequences of refusing⟩. WEIGH implies attempting to reach the truth or arrive at a decision by balancing conflicting claims or evidence ⟨*weigh* the pros and cons of the case⟩.

**3 :** to form into a compact mass
*intransitive verb*
**:** to become consolidated; *specifically* **:** MERGE
⟨the two companies *consolidated*⟩
— **con·sol·i·da·tor** \-ˌdā-tər\ *noun*
**consolidated school** *noun* (1911)
**:** a public school formed by merging other
schools
**con·sol·i·da·tion** \kən-ˌsä-lə-'dā-shən\ *noun*
(15th century)
**1 :** the act or process of consolidating **:** the
state of being consolidated
**2 :** the process of uniting **:** the quality or state
of being united; *specifically* **:** the unification
of two or more corporations by dissolution of
existing ones and creation of a single new corporation
**3 :** pathological alteration of lung tissue from
an aerated condition to one of solid consistency
**con·som·mé** \ˌkän(t)-sə-'mā\ *noun* [French,
from past participle of *consommer* to complete, boil down, from Latin *consummare* to
complete — more at CONSUMMATE] (1815)
**:** clear soup made from well-seasoned stock
**con·so·nance** \'kän(t)-s(ə-)nən(t)s\ *noun*
(15th century)
**1 :** harmony or agreement among components
**2 a :** correspondence or recurrence of sounds
especially in words; *specifically* **:** recurrence
or repetition of consonants especially at the
end of stressed syllables without the similar
correspondence of vowels (as in the final
sounds of "stroke" and "luck") **b :** CONCORD 1b
**c :** SYMPATHETIC VIBRATION, RESONANCE
**con·so·nan·cy** \-s(ə-)nən(t)-sē\ *noun, plural*
**-cies** (14th century)
**:** CONSONANCE 1
**¹con·so·nant** \'kän(t)-s(ə-)nənt\ *adjective*
[Middle French, from Latin *consonant-, consonans*, present participle of *consonare* to
sound together, agree, from *com-* + *sonare* to
sound — more at SOUND] (15th century)
**1 :** being in agreement or harmony **:** free from
elements making for discord
**2 :** marked by musical consonances
**3 :** having similar sounds ⟨*consonant* words⟩
**4 :** relating to or exhibiting consonance **:** RESO-
NANT
— **con·so·nant·ly** *adverb*
**²consonant** *noun* [Middle English, from Latin *consonant-, consonans*, from present participle of *consonare*] (14th century)
**:** one of a class of speech sounds (as \p\, \g\,
\n\, \l\, \s\, \r\) characterized by constriction or
closure at one or more points in the breath
channel; *also* **:** a letter representing a consonant — usually used in English of any letter
except *a, e, i, o,* and *u*
**con·so·nan·tal** \ˌkän(t)-sə-'nan-tᵊl\ *adjective*
(1795)
**:** relating to, being, or marked by a consonant
or group of consonants
**consonant shift** *noun* (1888)
**:** a set of regular changes in consonant articulation in the history of a language or dialect: **a**
**:** such a set affecting the Indo-European stops
and distinguishing the Germanic languages
from the other Indo-European languages —
compare GRIMM'S LAW **b :** such a set affecting
the Germanic stops and distinguishing High
German from the other Germanic languages
**¹con·sort** \'kän-ˌsȯrt\ *noun* [Middle English,
from Middle French, from Latin *consort-, consors* partner, sharer, from *com-* + *sort-, sors*
lot, share — more at SERIES] (15th century)
**1 :** ASSOCIATE
**2 :** a ship accompanying another
**3 :** SPOUSE — compare PRINCE CONSORT
**²consort** *noun* [Middle French *consorte*, from
*consort*] (1584)
**1 :** GROUP, ASSEMBLY ⟨a *consort* of specialists⟩
**2 :** CONJUNCTION, ASSOCIATION ⟨he ruled in *consort* with his father⟩

**3 a :** a group of singers or instrumentalists
performing together **b :** a set of musical instruments of the same family
**³con·sort** \kən-'sȯrt, kän-', 'kän-ˌ\ (1588)
*transitive verb*
**1 :** UNITE, ASSOCIATE
**2** *obsolete* **:** ESCORT
*intransitive verb*
**1 :** to keep company ⟨*consorting* with crimi-
nals⟩
**2** *obsolete* **:** to make harmony **:** PLAY
**3 :** ACCORD, HARMONIZE ⟨the illustrations *consort* admirably with the text —*Times Literary
Supplement*⟩
**con·sor·tium** \kən-'sȯr-sh(ē-)əm, -'sȯr-tē-əm\
*noun, plural* **-sor·tia** \-sȯr-sh(ē-)ə, -'sȯr-tē-ə\
*also* **-sortiums** [Latin, fellowship, from
*consort-, consors*] (1829)
**1 :** an agreement, combination, or group (as of
companies) formed to undertake an enterprise
beyond the resources of any one member
**2 :** ASSOCIATION, SOCIETY
**3 :** the legal right of one spouse to the company, affection, and assistance of and to sexual
relations with the other
**con·spe·cif·ic** \ˌkän(t)-spi-'si-fik\ *adjective*
(1859)
**:** of the same species
— **conspecific** *noun*
**con·spec·tus** \kən-'spek-təs\ *noun* [Latin,
from *conspectus*, from *conspicere*] (circa
1837)
**1 :** a usually brief survey or summary (as of
an extensive subject) often providing an overall view
**2 :** OUTLINE, SYNOPSIS
**con·spi·cu·i·ty** \ˌkän(t)-spə-'kyü-ə-tē\ *noun*
(1601)
**:** the quality or state of being conspicuous
**:** CONSPICUOUSNESS
**con·spic·u·ous** \kən-'spi-kyə-wəs\ *adjective*
[Latin *conspicuus*, from *conspicere* to get
sight of, from *com-* + *specere* to look —
more at SPY] (1545)
**1 :** obvious to the eye or mind
**2 :** attracting attention **:** STRIKING
**3 :** marked by a noticeable violation of good
taste
*synonym* see NOTICEABLE
— **con·spic·u·ous·ly** *adverb*
— **con·spic·u·ous·ness** \-nəs\ *noun*
**conspicuous consumption** *noun* (1899)
**:** lavish or wasteful spending thought to enhance social prestige
**con·spir·a·cy** \kən-'spir-ə-sē\ *noun, plural*
**-cies** [Middle English *conspiracie*, from Latin *conspirare*] (14th century)
**1 :** the act of conspiring together
**2 a :** an agreement among conspirators **b :** a
group of conspirators
*synonym* see PLOT
**conspiracy of silence** (1865)
**:** a secret agreement to keep silent about an
occurrence, situation, or subject especially in
order to promote or protect selfish interests
**con·spi·ra·tion** \ˌkän(t)-spə-'rā-shən, ˌkän-
(ˌ)spi-'rā-\ *noun* (14th century)
**1 :** the act or action of plotting or secretly
combining
**2 :** a joint effort toward a particular end
— **con·spi·ra·tion·al** \-shnəl, -shə-nᵊl\ *adjective*
**con·spir·a·tor** \kən-'spir-ə-tər\ *noun* (15th
century)
**:** one that conspires **:** PLOTTER
**con·spir·a·to·ri·al** \kən-ˌspir-ə-'tōr-ē-əl,
-'tȯr-\ *adjective* (1855)
**:** of, relating to, or suggestive of a conspiracy
— **con·spir·a·to·ri·al·ly** \-ē-ə-lē\ *adverb*
**con·spire** \kən-'spīr\ *verb* **con·spired; con-
spir·ing** [Middle English, from Middle
French *conspirer*, from Latin *conspirare* to be
in harmony, conspire, from *com-* + *spirare* to
breathe] (14th century)
*transitive verb*
**:** PLOT, CONTRIVE

*intransitive verb*
**1 a :** to join in a secret agreement to do an unlawful or wrongful act or an act which becomes unlawful as a result of the secret agreement **b :** SCHEME
**2 :** to act in harmony toward a common end
⟨circumstances *conspired* to defeat his efforts⟩
**con spi·ri·to** \kän-'spir-ə-ˌtō, kōn-\ *adverb*
[Italian] (circa 1891)
**:** with spirit or animation — used as a direction in music
**con·sta·ble** \'kän(t)-stə-bəl, 'kən(t)-\ *noun*
[Middle English *conestable*, from Old French,
from Late Latin *comes stabuli*, literally, officer
of the stable] (13th century)
**1 :** a high officer of a medieval royal or noble
household
**2 :** the warden or governor of a royal castle or
a fortified town
**3 a :** a public officer usually of a town or
township responsible for keeping the peace
and for minor judicial duties **b** *British* **:** POLICE
OFFICER; *especially* **:** one ranking below sergeant ◆
**¹con·stab·u·lary** \kən-'sta-byə-ˌler-ē\ *adjective* (1824)
**:** of or relating to a constable or constabulary
**²constabulary** *noun, plural* **-lar·ies** (1837)
**1 :** the organized body of constables of a particular district or country
**2 :** an armed police force organized on military lines but distinct from the regular army
**con·stan·cy** \'kän(t)-stən(t)-sē\ *noun, plural*
**-cies** (15th century)
**1 a :** steadfastness of mind under duress **:** FOR-
TITUDE **b :** FIDELITY, LOYALTY
**2 :** a state of being constant or unchanging
**¹con·stant** \'kän(t)-stənt\ *adjective* [Middle
English, from Middle French, from Latin
*constant-, constans*, from present participle of
*constare* to stand firm, be consistent, from
*com-* + *stare* to stand — more at STAND]
(14th century)
**1 :** marked by firm steadfast resolution or
faithfulness **:** exhibiting constancy of mind and
attachment
**2 :** INVARIABLE, UNIFORM
**3 :** continually occurring or recurring
**:** REGULAR
*synonym* see FAITHFUL, CONTINUAL
— **con·stant·ly** *adverb*
**²constant** *noun* (1832)

◇ WORD HISTORY
**constable** In the late Roman Empire,
*comes stabuli*, literally, "count of the stable,"
became the title of various high-ranking civil
and military officers whose duties extended
far beyond the care of the imperial horses. (A
word whose history shows a similar broadening of meaning is *marshal*.) Shrunk in early
Medieval Latin to *constabulum*, it appears in
Old French as *conestable*, which under the
Capetian rulers of France could denote the
sovereign's chief executive officer, the commander of an army, or the governor of a royal castle or domain. *Conestable* became the
designation for the same functionaries in England after the Norman Conquest. In the
13th century, it was also applied to lower-
ranking officers of the king's peace in English
shires and towns. With the gradual reshaping
of the constabulary in recent centuries into a
police force, *constable* in Britain has now
become virtually synonymous with "police
officer." See in addition MARSHAL.

\ə\ **abut** \ᵊ\ **kitten** \ər\ **further** \a\ **ash** \ā\ **ace**
\ä\ **mop, mar** \au̇\ **out** \ch\ **chin** \e\ **bet** \ē\ **easy**
\g\ **go** \i\ **hit** \ī\ **ice** \j\ **job** \ŋ\ **sing** \ō\ **go**
\ȯ\ **law** \ȯi\ **boy** \th\ **thin** \t̲h̲\ **the** \ü\ **loot** \u̇\ **foot**
\y\ **yet** \zh\ **vision**   *see also* Guide to Pronunciation

: something invariable or unchanging: as **a** : a number that has a fixed value in a given situation or universally or that is characteristic of some substance or instrument **b** : a number that is assumed not to change value in a given mathematical discussion **c** : a term in logic with a fixed designation

**con·stan·tan** \'kän(t)-stən-ˌtan\ *noun* [from the fact that its resistance remains constant under change of temperature] (1903)
: an alloy of copper and nickel used for electrical resistors and in thermocouples

**con·sta·tive** \kən-'stā-tiv, 'kän-stə-tiv\ *adjective* [*constate* to assert positively, from French *constater,* from Latin *constat* it is certain, 3d singular present indicative of *constare*] (1901)
**1** : of, relating to, or being a verbal form that expresses past completed action
**2** : being or relating to an utterance (as an assertion, question, or command) that is capable of being judged true or false
— **constative** *noun*

**con·stel·late** \'kän(t)-stə-ˌlāt\ *verb* **-lat·ed; -lat·ing** (1643)
*transitive verb*
**1** : to unite in a cluster
**2** : to set or adorn with or as if with constellations
*intransitive verb*
: CLUSTER

**con·stel·la·tion** \ˌkän(t)-stə-'lā-shən\ *noun* [Middle English *constellacioun,* from Middle French *constellation,* from Late Latin *constellation-, constellatio,* from Latin *com-* + *stella* star — more at STAR] (14th century)
**1** : the configuration of stars especially at one's birth
**2** : any of 88 arbitrary configurations of stars or an area of the celestial sphere covering one of these configurations
**3** : an assemblage, collection, or gathering of usually related persons, qualities, or things ⟨a *constellation* of . . . relatives, friends, and hangers-on —Brendan Gill⟩
**4** : PATTERN, ARRANGEMENT ⟨taking advantage of the shifting *constellation* of power throughout the known world —H. D. Lasswell⟩
— **con·stel·la·to·ry** \kən-'ste-lə-ˌtōr-ē, -ˌtór\ *adjective*

**con·ster·nate** \'kän(t)-stər-ˌnāt\ *transitive verb* **-nat·ed; -nat·ing** (1651)
: to fill with consternation

**con·ster·na·tion** \ˌkän(t)-stər-'nā-shən\ *noun* [French or Latin; French, from Latin *consternation-, consternatio,* from *consternare* to throw into confusion, from *com-* + *-sternare,* probably from *sternere* to spread, strike down — more at STREW] (circa 1611)
: amazement or dismay that hinders or throws into confusion ⟨the two . . . stared at each other in *consternation,* and neither knew what to do —Pearl Buck⟩

**con·sti·pate** \'kän(t)-stə-ˌpāt\ *transitive verb* **-pat·ed; -pat·ing** [Medieval Latin *constipatus,* past participle of *constipare,* from Latin, to crowd together, from *com-* + *stipare* to pack tight — more at STIFF] (1533)
**1** : to cause constipation in
**2** : to make immobile, inactive, or dull : STULTIFY ⟨so much clutter . . . will tend to *constipate* the novel's working order —*Times Literary Supplement*⟩

**con·sti·pat·ed** \-ˌpā-təd\ *adjective* (1547)
**1** : affected with constipation
**2** : stilted or stodgy in appearance, expression, or action

**con·sti·pa·tion** \ˌkän(t)-stə-'pā-shən\ *noun* (15th century)
**1** : abnormally delayed or infrequent passage of usually dry hardened feces
**2** : STULTIFICATION

**con·stit·u·en·cy** \kən-'stich-wən(t)-sē, -'sti-chə-\ *noun, plural* **-cies** (1831)
**1 a** : a body of citizens entitled to elect a representative (as to a legislative or executive po-

sition) **b** : the residents in an electoral district **c** : an electoral district
**2 a** : a group or body that patronizes, supports, or offers representation ⟨creating . . . a grass-roots *constituency* for continuing the project —Fred Reed⟩ **b** : the people involved in or served by an organization (as a business or institution) ⟨regards its corporate customers as its prime *constituency* —Andrew Hacker⟩

**¹con·stit·u·ent** \-wənt\ *noun* [French *constituant,* from Middle French, from present participle of *constituer* to constitute, from Latin *constituere*] (1622)
**1** : one who authorizes another to act as agent : PRINCIPAL
**2** : a member of a constituency
**3** : an essential part : COMPONENT, ELEMENT
**4** : a structural unit of a definable syntactic, semantic, or phonological category that consists of one or more linguistic elements (as words, morphemes, or features) and that can occur as a component of a larger construction
*synonym* see ELEMENT

**²constituent** *adjective* [Latin *constituent-, constituens,* present participle of *constituere*] (1660)
**1** : serving to form, compose, or make up a unit or whole : COMPONENT
**2** : having the power to create a government or frame or amend a constitution ⟨a *constituent* assembly⟩
— **con·stit·u·ent·ly** *adverb*

**con·sti·tute** \'kän(t)-stə-ˌtüt, -ˌtyüt\ *transitive verb* **-tut·ed; -tut·ing** [Middle English, from Latin *constitutus,* past participle of *constituere* to set up, constitute, from *com-* + *statuere* to set — more at STATUTE] (15th century)
**1** : to appoint to an office, function, or dignity
**2** : SET UP, ESTABLISH: as **a** : ENACT **b** : FOUND **c** (1) : to give due or lawful form to (2) : to legally process
**3** : MAKE UP, FORM, COMPOSE ⟨12 months *constitute* a year⟩ ⟨high school dropouts who *constitute* a major problem in large city slums —J. B. Conant⟩

**con·sti·tu·tion** \ˌkän(t)-stə-'tü-shən, -'tyü-\ *noun* (14th century)
**1** : an established law or custom : ORDINANCE
**2 a** : the physical makeup of the individual comprising inherited qualities modified by environment **b** : the structure, composition, physical makeup, or nature of something
**3** : the act of establishing, making, or setting up
**4** : the mode in which a state or society is organized; *especially* : the manner in which sovereign power is distributed
**5 a** : the basic principles and laws of a nation, state, or social group that determine the powers and duties of the government and guarantee certain rights to the people in it **b** : a written instrument embodying the rules of a political or social organization
— **con·sti·tu·tion·less** \-ləs\ *adjective*

**¹con·sti·tu·tion·al** \-shnəl, -shə-nᵊl\ *adjective* (1682)
**1** : relating to, inherent in, or affecting the constitution of body or mind
**2** : of, relating to, or entering into the fundamental makeup of something : ESSENTIAL
**3** : being in accordance with or authorized by the constitution of a state or society ⟨a *constitutional* government⟩
**4** : regulated by or ruling according to a constitution ⟨a *constitutional* monarchy⟩
**5** : of or relating to a constitution
**6** : loyal to or supporting an established constitution or form of government

**²constitutional** *noun* (1829)
: a walk taken for one's health

**con·sti·tu·tion·al·ism** \-sh(ə)nə-ˌli-zəm\ *noun* (1832)
: adherence to or government according to constitutional principles; *also* : a constitutional system of government
— **con·sti·tu·tion·al·ist** \-list\ *noun*

**con·sti·tu·tion·al·i·ty** \-ˌtü-shə-'na-lə-tē, -ˌtyü-\ *noun* (1787)
: the quality or state of being constitutional; *especially* : accordance with the provisions of a constitution ⟨questioned the *constitutionality* of the law⟩

**con·sti·tu·tion·al·ize** \-'tü-shnə-ˌlīz, -shə-nᵊl-ˌīz\ *transitive verb* **-ized; -iz·ing** (1831)
: to provide with a constitution : organize along constitutional principles
— **con·sti·tu·tion·al·i·za·tion** \-ˌtü-shnə-lə-'zā-shən, -shə-nᵊl-ə-\ *noun*

**con·sti·tu·tion·al·ly** \-'tü-shnə-lē, -'tyü-, -shə-nᵊl-ē\ *adverb* (1742)
**1 a** : in accordance with one's constitution ⟨*constitutionally* unable to grasp subtleties⟩ **b** : in structure, composition, or constitution ⟨despite repeated heatings the material remained *constitutionally* the same⟩
**2** : in accordance with a political constitution ⟨was not *constitutionally* eligible to fill the office⟩

**con·sti·tu·tive** \'kän(t)-stə-ˌtü-tiv, -ˌtyü-; kən-'sti-chə-tiv\ *adjective* (1592)
**1** : having the power to enact or establish : CONSTRUCTIVE
**2** : CONSTITUENT, ESSENTIAL
**3** : relating to or dependent on constitution ⟨a *constitutive* property of all electrolytes⟩
— **con·sti·tu·tive·ly** *adverb*

**con·strain** \kən-'strān\ *transitive verb* [Middle English, from Middle French *constraindre,* from Latin *constringere* to constrict, constrain, from *com-* + *stringere* to draw tight — more at STRAIN] (14th century)
**1 a** : to force by imposed stricture, restriction, or limitation **b** : to restrict the motion of (a mechanical body) to a particular mode
**2** : COMPRESS; *also* : to clasp tightly
**3** : to secure by or as if by bonds : CONFINE; *broadly* : LIMIT
**4** : to force or produce in an unnatural or strained manner ⟨a *constrained* smile⟩
**5** : to hold back by or as if by force ⟨*constraining* my mind not to wander from the task —Charles Dickens⟩
*synonym* see FORCE
— **con·strained·ly** \-'strā-nəd-lē, -'strānd-lē\ *adverb*

**con·straint** \kən-'strānt\ *noun* [Middle English, from Middle French *constrainte,* from *constraindre*] (15th century)
**1 a** : the act of constraining **b** : the state of being checked, restricted, or compelled to avoid or perform some action ⟨the *constraint* and monotony of a monastic life —Matthew Arnold⟩ **c** : a constraining condition, agency, or force : CHECK ⟨put legal *constraints* on the board's activities⟩
**2 a** : repression of one's own feelings, behavior, or actions **b** : a sense of being constrained : EMBARRASSMENT

**con·strict** \kən-'strikt\ *verb* [Latin *constrictus,* past participle of *constringere*] (1732)
*transitive verb*
**1 a** : to make narrow or draw together **b** : COMPRESS, SQUEEZE ⟨*constrict* a nerve⟩
**2** : to stultify, stop, or cause to falter : INHIBIT
*intransitive verb*
: to become constricted
*synonym* see CONTRACT
— **con·stric·tive** \-'strik-tiv\ *adjective*

**con·stric·tion** \-'strik-shən\ *noun* (15th century)
**1** : an act or product of constricting
**2** : the quality or state of being constricted
**3** : something that constricts

**con·stric·tor** \-'strik-tər\ *noun* (1735)
**1** : a muscle that contracts a cavity or orifice or compresses an organ
**2** : a snake (as a boa constrictor) that kills prey by compression in its coils
**3** : one that constricts

**con·stringe** \kən-'strinj\ *transitive verb* **con·stringed; con·string·ing** [Latin *constringere*] (1604)

**1 :** to cause to shrink ⟨cold *constringes* the pores⟩
**2 :** CONSTRICT
— **con·strin·gent** \-'strin-jənt\ *adjective*
**¹con·struct** \kən-'strəkt\ *transitive verb* [Latin *constructus*, past participle of *construere*, from *com-* + *struere* to build — more at STRUCTURE] (1663)
**1 :** to make or form by combining or arranging parts or elements **:** BUILD; *also* **:** CONTRIVE, DEVISE
**2 :** to draw (a geometrical figure) with suitable instruments and under specified conditions
**3 :** to set in logical order
— **con·struct·ible** \-'strək-tə-bəl\ *adjective*
— **con·struc·tor** \-tər\ *noun*
**²con·struct** \'kän-,strəkt\ *noun* (1933)
**1 :** something constructed by the mind: as **a** **:** a theoretical entity ⟨the deductive study of abstract *constructs* —Daniel J. Boorstin⟩ **b :** a working hypothesis or concept ⟨a point of view which made "abroad" singularly containable as a literary *construct* —Jonathan Raban⟩ **c :** a product of mental invention ⟨the novel . . . a verbal *construct* in which invented human characters appear —Anthony Burgess⟩
**2 :** something produced by human effort ⟨the East bloc was always an unnatural *construct* —Walter Isaacson⟩
**con·struc·tion** \kən-'strək-shən\ *noun* (14th century)
**1 :** the act or result of construing, interpreting, or explaining
**2 a :** the process, art, or manner of constructing something; *also* **:** a thing constructed **b :** the construction industry ⟨working in *construction*⟩
**3 :** the arrangement and connection of words or groups of words in a sentence **:** syntactical arrangement
**4 :** a sculpture that is put together out of separate pieces of often disparate materials
— **con·struc·tion·al** \-shnəl, -shə-nᵊl\ *adjective*
— **con·struc·tion·al·ly** *adverb*
**con·struc·tion·ist** \-sh(ə-)nist\ *noun* (1838)
**:** one who construes a legal document (as the U.S. Constitution) in a specific way ⟨a strict *constructionist*⟩
**construction paper** *noun* (circa 1924)
**:** a thick groundwood paper available in many colors and used especially for school artwork
**con·struc·tive** \kən-'strək-tiv\ *adjective* (circa 1680)
**1 :** declared such by judicial construction or interpretation ⟨*constructive* fraud⟩
**2 :** of or relating to construction or creation
**3 :** promoting improvement or development ⟨*constructive* criticism⟩
— **con·struc·tive·ly** *adverb*
— **con·struc·tive·ness** *noun*
**con·struc·tiv·ism** \kən-'strək-ti-,vi-zəm\ *noun, often capitalized* (1925)
**:** a nonobjective art movement originating in Russia and concerned with formal organization of planes and expression of volume in terms of modern industrial materials (as glass and plastic)
— **con·struc·tiv·ist** \-vist\ *adjective or noun, often capitalized*
**¹con·strue** \kən-'strü\ *verb* **con·strued; con·stru·ing** [Middle English, from Late Latin *construere*, from Latin, to construct] (14th century)
*transitive verb*
**1 :** to analyze the arrangement and connection of words in (a sentence or sentence part)
**2 :** to understand or explain the sense or intention of usually in a particular way or with respect to a given set of circumstances ⟨*construed* my actions as hostile⟩
*intransitive verb*
**:** to construe a sentence or sentence part especially in connection with translating
— **con·stru·able** \-'strü-ə-bəl\ *adjective*

**²con·strue** \'kän-,strü\ *noun* (1844)
**:** an act or the result of construing especially by piecemeal translation
**con·sub·stan·tial** \,kän(t)-səb-'stan(t)-shəl\ *adjective* [Late Latin *consubstantialis*, from Latin *com-* + *substantia* substance] (14th century)
**:** of the same substance
**con·sub·stan·ti·a·tion** \,kän(t)-səb-,stan(t)-shē-'ā-shən\ *noun* (1597)
**:** the actual substantial presence and combination of the body and blood of Christ with the eucharistic bread and wine according to a teaching associated with Martin Luther — compare TRANSUBSTANTIATION
**con·sue·tude** \'kän(t)-swi-,tüd, kən-'sü-ə-,tyüd\ *noun* [Middle English, from Latin *consuetudo* — more at CUSTOM] (14th century)
**:** social usage **:** CUSTOM
— **con·sue·tu·di·nary** \,kän(t)-swi-'tü-də-,ner-ē, kən-,sü-ə-, -'tyü-\ *adjective*
**con·sul** \'kän(t)-səl\ *noun* [Middle English, from Latin; perhaps akin to Latin *consulere* to consult] (14th century)
**1 a :** either of two annually elected chief magistrates of the Roman republic **b :** one of three chief magistrates of the French republic from 1799 to 1804
**2 :** an official appointed by a government to reside in a foreign country to represent the commercial interests of citizens of the appointing country
— **con·su·lar** \-s(ə-)lər\ *adjective*
— **con·sul·ship** \-səl-,ship\ *noun*
**con·sul·ate** \-s(ə-)lət\ *noun* (14th century)
**1 :** a government by consuls
**2 :** the office, term of office, or jurisdiction of a consul
**3 :** the residence or official premises of a consul
**consulate general** *noun, plural* **consulates general** (1883)
**:** the residence, office, or jurisdiction of a consul general
**consul general** *noun, plural* **consuls general** (1753)
**:** a consul of the first rank stationed in an important place or having jurisdiction in several places or over several consuls
**¹con·sult** \kən-'səlt\ *verb* [Middle French or Latin; Middle French *consulter*, from Latin *consultare*, frequentative of *consulere* to deliberate, counsel, consult] (1527)
*transitive verb*
**1 :** to have regard to **:** CONSIDER
**2 a :** to ask the advice or opinion of ⟨*consult* a doctor⟩ **b :** to refer to ⟨*consult* a dictionary⟩
*intransitive verb*
**1 :** to consult an individual
**2 :** to deliberate together **:** CONFER
**3 :** to serve as a consultant
— **con·sult·er** *noun*
**²con·sult** \kən-'səlt, 'kän-,\ *noun* (1560)
**:** CONSULTATION
**con·sul·tan·cy** \kən-'səl-tᵊn(t)-sē\ *noun, plural* **-cies** (1955)
**1 :** CONSULTATION
**2 :** an agency that provides consulting services
**3 :** the position of a consultant
**con·sul·tant** \kən-'səl-tᵊnt\ *noun* (1697)
**1 :** one who consults another
**2 :** one who gives professional advice or services **:** EXPERT
— **con·sul·tant·ship** \-,ship\ *noun*
**con·sul·ta·tion** \,kän(t)-səl-'tā-shən\ *noun* (15th century)
**1 :** COUNCIL, CONFERENCE; *specifically* **:** a deliberation between physicians on a case or its treatment
**2 :** the act of consulting or conferring
**con·sul·ta·tive** \kən-'səl-tə-tiv, 'kän(t)-səl-,tā-tiv\ *adjective* (1583)
**:** of, relating to, or intended for consultation **:** ADVISORY ⟨*consultative* committee⟩
**con·sult·ing** \kən-'səl-tiŋ\ *adjective* (1801)

**1 :** providing professional or expert advice ⟨a *consulting* architect⟩
**2 :** of or relating to consultation or a consultant ⟨the *consulting* room of a psychiatrist⟩
**con·sul·tive** \kən-'səl-tiv\ *adjective* (1616)
**:** CONSULTATIVE
**con·sul·tor** \kən-'səl-tər\ *noun* (1611)
**:** one that consults or advises; *especially* **:** an adviser to a Roman Catholic bishop, provincial, or sacred congregation
**¹con·sum·able** \kən-'sü-mə-bəl\ *adjective* (1641)
**:** capable of being consumed
**²consumable** *noun* (1802)
**:** something (as food or fuel) that is consumable — usually used in plural
**con·sume** \kən-'süm\ *verb* **con·sumed; con·sum·ing** [Middle English, from Middle French or Latin; Middle French *consumer*, from Latin *consumere*, from *com-* + *sumere* to take up, take, from *sub-* up + *emere* to take — more at SUB-, REDEEM] (14th century)
*transitive verb*
**1 :** to do away with completely **:** DESTROY ⟨fire *consumed* several buildings⟩
**2 a :** to spend wastefully **:** SQUANDER **b :** USE UP ⟨writing *consumed* much of his time⟩
**3 :** to eat or drink especially in great quantity ⟨*consumed* several kegs of beer⟩
**4 :** to engage fully **:** ENGROSS ⟨*consumed* with curiosity⟩
*intransitive verb*
**1 :** to waste or burn away **:** PERISH
**2 :** to utilize economic goods
**con·sum·ed·ly** \-'sü-məd-lē\ *adverb* (1707)
**:** as if consumed **:** EXCESSIVELY
**con·sum·er** \kən-'sü-mər\ *noun, often attributive* (15th century)
**:** one that consumes: as **a :** one that utilizes economic goods **b :** an organism requiring complex organic compounds for food which it obtains by preying on other organisms or by eating particles of organic matter — compare PRODUCER 4
— **con·sum·er·ship** \-,ship\ *noun*
**consumer credit** *noun* (1927)
**:** credit granted to an individual especially to finance the purchase of consumer goods or to defray personal expenses
**consumer goods** *noun plural* (1890)
**:** goods that directly satisfy human wants
**con·sum·er·ism** \kən-'sü-mə-,ri-zəm\ *noun* (1944)
**1 :** the promotion of the consumer's interests
**2 :** the theory that an increasing consumption of goods is economically desirable; *also* **:** a preoccupation with and an inclination toward the buying of consumer goods
— **con·sum·er·ist** \-rist\ *noun*
— **con·sum·er·is·tic** \kən-,sü-mə-'ris-tik\ *adjective*
**consumer price index** *noun* (1948)
**:** an index measuring the change in the cost of typical wage-earner purchases of goods and services expressed as a percentage of the cost of these same goods and services in some base period — called also *cost-of-living index*
**con·sum·ing** \kən-'sü-miŋ\ *adjective* (1920)
**:** deeply felt **:** ARDENT ⟨a *consuming* interest⟩; *also* **:** ENGROSSING
**¹con·sum·mate** \'kän(t)-sə-mət, kən-'sə-mət\ *adjective* [Middle English *consummat* fulfilled, from Latin *consummatus*, past participle of *consummare* to sum up, finish, from *com-* + *summa* sum] (1527)
**1 :** complete in every detail **:** PERFECT
**2 :** extremely skilled and accomplished ⟨a *consummate* liar⟩
**3 :** of the highest degree ⟨*consummate* skill⟩ ⟨*consummate* cruelty⟩

— **con·sum·mate·ly** adverb

²**con·sum·mate** \ˈkän(t)-sə-ˌmāt\ verb **-mat·ed; -mat·ing** (1530)
transitive verb
**1 a :** FINISH, COMPLETE ⟨consummate a business deal⟩ **b :** to make perfect **c :** ACHIEVE
**2 :** to make (marital union) complete by sexual intercourse ⟨consummate a marriage⟩
intransitive verb
**:** to become perfected
— **con·sum·ma·tive** \ˈkän(t)-sə-ˌmā-tiv, kən-ˈsə-mə-tiv\ adjective
— **con·sum·ma·tor** \ˈkän(t)-sə-ˌmāt-ər\ noun

**con·sum·ma·tion** \ˌkän-sə-ˈmā-shən\ noun (14th century)
**1 :** the act of consummating ⟨the consummation of a contract by mutual signature⟩; specifically **:** the consummating of a marriage
**2 :** the ultimate end **:** FINISH

**con·sum·ma·to·ry** \kən-ˈsə-mə-ˌtōr-ē, -ˌtór-\ adjective (1648)
**1 :** of or relating to consummation **:** CONCLUDING
**2 :** of, relating to, or being a response or act (as eating or copulating) that terminates a period of usually goal-directed behavior

**con·sump·tion** \kən-ˈsəm(p)-shən\ noun [Middle English consumpcioun, from Latin consumption-, consumptio, from consumere] (14th century)
**1 a :** a progressive wasting away of the body especially from pulmonary tuberculosis **b :** TUBERCULOSIS
**2 :** the act or process of consuming
**3 :** the utilization of economic goods in the satisfaction of wants or in the process of production resulting chiefly in their destruction, deterioration, or transformation

¹**con·sump·tive** \-ˈsəm(p)-tiv\ adjective (1664)
**1 :** tending to consume
**2 :** of, relating to, or affected with consumption
— **con·sump·tive·ly** adverb

²**consumptive** noun (1666)
**:** a person affected with consumption

¹**con·tact** \ˈkän-ˌtakt\ noun [French or Latin; French, from Latin contactus, from contingere to have contact with — more at CONTINGENT] (1626)
**1 a :** union or junction of surfaces **b :** the apparent touching or mutual tangency of the limbs of two celestial bodies or of the disk of one body with the shadow of another during an eclipse, transit, or occultation **c** (1) **:** the junction of two electrical conductors through which a current passes (2) **:** a special part made for such a junction
**2 a :** ASSOCIATION, RELATIONSHIP **b :** CONNECTION, COMMUNICATION **c :** an establishing of communication with someone or an observing or receiving of a significant signal from a person or object ⟨radar contact with Mars⟩
**3 :** a person serving as a go-between, messenger, connection, or source of special information ⟨business contacts⟩
**4 :** CONTACT LENS

²**con·tact** \ˈkän-ˌtakt, kən-ˈ\ (1834)
intransitive verb
**:** to make contact
transitive verb
**1 :** to bring into contact
**2 a :** to enter or be in contact with **:** JOIN **b :** to get in communication with ⟨contact your local dealer⟩ ▫

³**con·tact** \ˈkän-ˌtakt\ adjective (1859)
**:** maintaining, involving, or activated or caused by contact ⟨contact poisons⟩ ⟨contact sports⟩

**contact binary** noun (1952)
**:** a binary star system in which the two stars are close enough together for material to pass between them

**contact hitter** noun (1982)
**:** a hitter in baseball who seldom strikes out

**contact inhibition** noun (1965)
**:** cessation of cellular undulating movements upon contact with other cells with accompanying cessation of cell growth and division

**contact language** noun (1950)
**:** PIDGIN

**contact lens** noun (1888)
**:** a thin lens designed to fit over the cornea and usually worn to correct defects in vision

**contact print** noun (1890)
**:** a photographic print made with the negative in contact with the sensitized paper, plate, or film

**con·ta·gion** \kən-ˈtā-jən\ noun [Middle English, from Middle French & Latin; Middle French, from Latin contagion-, contagio, from contingere to have contact with, pollute] (14th century)
**1 a :** a contagious disease **b :** the transmission of a disease by direct or indirect contact **c :** a disease-producing agent (as a virus)
**2 a :** POISON **b :** contagious influence, quality, or nature **c :** corrupting influence or contact
**3 a :** rapid communication of an influence (as a doctrine or emotional state) **b :** an influence that spreads rapidly

**con·ta·gious** \-jəs\ adjective (14th century)
**1 :** communicable by contact **:** CATCHING ⟨contagious diseases⟩
**2 :** bearing contagion
**3 :** used for contagious diseases ⟨a contagious ward⟩
**4 :** exciting similar emotions or conduct in others ⟨contagious enthusiasm⟩
— **con·ta·gious·ly** adverb
— **con·ta·gious·ness** noun

**contagious abortion** noun (1910)
**:** a contagious or infectious disease (as a brucellosis) of domestic animals characterized by abortion

**con·ta·gium** \kən-ˈtā-j(ē-)əm\ noun, plural **-gia** \-j(ē-)ə\ [Latin, contagion, from contingere] (1870)
**:** a virus or living organism capable of causing a communicable disease

**con·tain** \kən-ˈtān\ verb [Middle English conteinen, from Old French contenir, from Latin continēre to hold together, hold in, contain, from com- + tenēre to hold — more at THIN] (14th century)
transitive verb
**1 :** to keep within limits: as **a :** RESTRAIN, CONTROL **b :** CHECK, HALT **c :** to follow successfully a policy of containment toward **d :** to prevent (as an enemy or opponent) from advancing or from making a successful attack
**2 a :** to have within **:** HOLD **b :** COMPRISE, INCLUDE
**3 a :** to be divisible by usually without a remainder **b :** ENCLOSE, BOUND
intransitive verb
**:** to restrain oneself ☆
— **con·tain·able** \-ˈtā-nə-bəl\ adjective

**contained** adjective (1653)
**:** RESTRAINED; also **:** CALM

**con·tain·er** \kən-ˈtā-nər\ noun (15th century)
**:** one that contains; especially **:** a receptacle (as a box or jar) for holding goods
— **con·tain·er·less** \-ləs\ adjective

**con·tain·er·board** \-ˌbōrd, -ˌbórd\ noun (circa 1924)
**:** corrugated or solid paperboard used for making containers

**con·tain·er·i·sa·tion, con·tain·er·ise**
British variant of CONTAINERIZATION, CONTAINERIZE

**con·tain·er·i·za·tion** \kən-ˌtā-nə-rə-ˈzā-shən\ noun (1956)
**:** a shipping method in which a large amount of material (as merchandise) is packaged into large standardized containers

**con·tain·er·ize** \kən-ˈtā-nə-ˌrīz\ transitive verb **-ized; -iz·ing** (1956)
**1 :** to ship by containerization
**2 :** to pack in containers

**con·tain·er·port** \-nər-ˌpōrt, -ˌpórt\ noun (1970)
**:** a shipping port specially equipped to handle containerized cargo

**con·tain·er·ship** \-nər-ˌship\ noun (1966)
**:** a ship specially designed or equipped for carrying containerized cargo

**con·tain·ment** \kən-ˈtān-mənt\ noun (1655)
**1 :** the act, process, or means of containing
**2 :** the policy, process, or result of preventing the expansion of a hostile power or ideology

**con·tam·i·nant** \kən-ˈta-mə-nənt\ noun (1922)
**:** something that contaminates

**con·tam·i·nate** \kən-ˈta-mə-ˌnāt\ transitive verb **-nat·ed; -nat·ing** [Middle English, from Latin contaminatus, past participle of contaminare; akin to Latin contagio contagion] (15th century)
**1 a :** to soil, stain, corrupt, or infect by contact or association ⟨bacteria contaminated the wound⟩ **b :** to make inferior or impure by admixture ⟨iron contaminated with phosphorus⟩
**2 :** to make unfit for use by the introduction of unwholesome or undesirable elements ☆
— **con·tam·i·na·tive** \-ˌnā-tiv\ adjective
— **con·tam·i·na·tor** \-ˌnā-tər\ noun

**con·tam·i·na·tion** \kən-ˌta-mə-ˈnā-shən\ noun (15th century)
**1 :** a process of contaminating **:** a state of being contaminated
**2 :** CONTAMINANT

**conte** \ˈkōⁿt\ noun [French] (1891)
**:** a usually short tale of adventure

**con·temn** \kən-ˈtem\ transitive verb [Middle English contempnen, from Middle French contempner, from Latin contemnere, from com- + temnere to despise] (15th century)
**:** to view or treat with contempt **:** SCORN
**synonym** see DESPISE
— **con·tem·ner** also **con·tem·nor** \-ˈtem-nər, -ˈte-mər\ noun

---

☆ **SYNONYMS**
**Contain, hold, accommodate** mean to have or be capable of having within. CONTAIN implies the actual presence of a specified substance or quantity within something ⟨the can contains a quart of oil⟩. HOLD implies the capacity of containing or the usual or permanent function of containing or keeping ⟨the bookcase will hold all my textbooks⟩. ACCOMMODATE stresses holding without crowding or inconvenience ⟨the hall can accommodate 500 people⟩.

**Contaminate, taint, pollute, defile** mean to make impure or unclean. CONTAMINATE implies intrusion of or contact with dirt or foulness from an outside source ⟨water contaminated by industrial wastes⟩. TAINT stresses the loss of purity or cleanliness that follows contamination ⟨tainted meat⟩ ⟨a politician's tainted reputation⟩. POLLUTE, sometimes interchangeable with contaminate, distinctively may imply that the process which begins with contamination is complete and that what was pure or clean has been made foul, poisoned, or filthy ⟨the polluted waters of the river⟩. DEFILE implies befouling of what could or should have been kept clean and pure or held sacred and commonly suggests violation or desecration ⟨defile a hero's memory with slanderous innuendo⟩.

---

☐ **USAGE**
**contact** The use of contact as a verb, especially in sense 2b, is accepted as standard by almost all commentators except those who write college handbooks.

**con·tem·plate** \'kän-təm-ˌplāt, -ˌtem-\ *verb* **-plat·ed; -plat·ing** [Latin *contemplatus*, past participle of *contemplari*, from *com-* + *templum* space marked out for observation of auguries — more at TEMPLE] (1537) *transitive verb*
**1 :** to view or consider with continued attention **:** meditate on
**2 :** to view as contingent or probable or as an end or intention
*intransitive verb* **:** PONDER, MEDITATE
**synonym** see CONSIDER
— **con·tem·pla·tor** \-ˌplā-tər\ *noun*
**con·tem·pla·tion** \ˌkän-təm-'plā-shən, -ˌtem-\ *noun* (13th century)
**1 a :** concentration on spiritual things as a form of private devotion **b :** a state of mystical awareness of God's being
**2 :** an act of considering with attention **:** STUDY
**3 :** the act of regarding steadily
**4 :** INTENTION, EXPECTATION
**¹con·tem·pla·tive** \kən-'tem-plə-tiv; 'kän-təm-ˌplā-, -ˌtem-\ *adjective* (14th century)
**:** marked by or given to contemplation; *specifically* **:** of or relating to a religious order devoted to prayer and penance
— **con·tem·pla·tive·ly** *adverb*
— **con·tem·pla·tive·ness** *noun*
**²contemplative** *noun* (14th century)
**:** a person who practices contemplation
**con·tem·po·ra·ne·i·ty** \kən-ˌtem-p(ə-)rə-'nē-ə-tē, -'nā-\ *noun* (1772)
**:** the quality or state of being contemporaneous or contemporary
**con·tem·po·ra·ne·ous** \kən-ˌtem-pə-'rā-nē-əs\ *adjective* [Latin *contemporaneus*, from *com-* + *tempor-, tempus* time] (circa 1656)
**:** existing, occurring, or originating during the same time
**synonym** see CONTEMPORARY
— **con·tem·po·ra·ne·ous·ly** *adverb*
— **con·tem·po·ra·ne·ous·ness** *noun*
**¹con·tem·po·rary** \kən-'tem-pə-ˌrer-ē\ *adjective* [*com-* + Latin *tempor-, tempus*] (1631)
**1 :** happening, existing, living, or coming into being during the same period of time
**2 a :** SIMULTANEOUS **b :** marked by characteristics of the present period **:** MODERN, CURRENT ☆
— **con·tem·po·rar·i·ly** \-ˌtem-pə-'rer-ə-lē\ *adverb*
**²contemporary** *noun,* plural **-rar·ies** (1646)
**1 :** one that is contemporary with another
**2 :** one of the same or nearly the same age as another
**con·tem·po·rize** \kən-'tem-pə-ˌrīz\ *transitive verb* **-rized; -riz·ing** (1646)
**:** to make contemporary
**con·tempt** \kən-'tem(p)t\ *noun* [Middle English, from Latin *contemptus,* from *contemnere*] (14th century)
**1 a :** the act of despising **:** the state of mind of one who despises **:** DISDAIN **b :** lack of respect or reverence for something
**2 :** the state of being despised
**3 :** willful disobedience to or open disrespect of a court, judge, or legislative body ⟨*contempt* of court⟩
**con·tempt·ible** \kən-'tem(p)-tə-bəl\ *adjective* (14th century)
**1 :** worthy of contempt
**2** *obsolete* **:** SCORNFUL, CONTEMPTUOUS ☆
— **con·tempt·i·bil·i·ty** \-ˌtem(p)-tə-'bi-lə-tē\ *noun*
— **con·tempt·ible·ness** *noun*
— **con·tempt·ibly** \-'tem(p)-tə-blē\ *adverb*
**con·temp·tu·ous** \kən-'tem(p)-chə-wəs, -chəs, -shwəs\ *adjective* [Latin *contemptus*] (1595)
**:** manifesting, feeling, or expressing contempt
— **con·temp·tu·ous·ly** *adverb*
— **con·temp·tu·ous·ness** *noun*
**con·tend** \kən-'tend\ *verb* [Middle English, from Middle French or Latin; Middle French

*contendre,* from Latin *contendere,* from *com-* + *tendere* to stretch — more at THIN] (15th century)
*intransitive verb*
**1 :** to strive or vie in contest or rivalry or against difficulties **:** STRUGGLE
**2 :** to strive in debate **:** ARGUE
*transitive verb*
**1 :** MAINTAIN, ASSERT ⟨*contended* that he was right⟩
**2 :** to struggle for **:** CONTEST
**con·tend·er** \-'ten-dər\ *noun* (1547)
**:** one that contends; *especially* **:** a competitor for a championship or high honor ⟨a heavyweight title *contender*⟩
**¹con·tent** \kən-'tent\ *adjective* [Middle English, from Middle French, from Latin *contentus,* from past participle of *continēre* to hold in, contain — more at CONTAIN] (15th century)
**:** CONTENTED, SATISFIED
**²content** *transitive verb* (15th century)
**1 :** to appease the desires of
**2 :** to limit (oneself) in requirements, desires, or actions
**³content** *noun* (1579)
**:** CONTENTMENT ⟨ate to his heart's *content*⟩
**⁴con·tent** \'kän-ˌtent\ *noun* [Middle English, from Latin *contentus,* past participle of *continēre* to contain] (15th century)
**1 a :** something contained — usually used in plural ⟨the jar's *contents*⟩ ⟨the drawer's *contents*⟩ **b :** the topics or matter treated in a written work ⟨table of *contents*⟩
**2 a :** SUBSTANCE, GIST **b :** MEANING, SIGNIFICANCE **c :** the events, physical detail, and information in a work of art — compare FORM 10b
**3 a :** the matter dealt with in a field of study **b :** a part, element, or complex of parts
**4 :** the amount of specified material contained **:** PROPORTION
**content analysis** *noun* (1945)
**:** analysis of the manifest and latent content of a body of communicated material (as a book or film) through a classification, tabulation, and evaluation of its key symbols and themes in order to ascertain its meaning and probable effect
**con·tent·ed** \kən-'ten-təd\ *adjective* (1526)
**:** feeling or manifesting satisfaction with one's possessions, status, or situation ⟨a *contented* smile⟩
— **con·tent·ed·ly** *adverb*
— **con·tent·ed·ness** *noun*
**con·ten·tion** \kən-'ten-shən\ *noun* [Middle English *contencioun,* from Middle French, from Latin *contention-, contentio,* from *contendere*] (14th century)
**1 :** an act or instance of contending
**2 :** a point advanced or maintained in a debate or argument
**3 :** RIVALRY, COMPETITION
**synonym** see DISCORD
**con·ten·tious** \kən-'ten(t)-shəs\ *adjective* (15th century)
**1 :** likely to cause contention ⟨a *contentious* argument⟩
**2 :** exhibiting an often perverse and wearisome tendency to quarrels and disputes ⟨a man of a most *contentious* nature⟩
**synonym** see BELLIGERENT
— **con·ten·tious·ly** *adverb*
— **con·ten·tious·ness** *noun*
**con·tent·ment** \kən-'tent-mənt\ *noun* (15th century)
**1 :** the quality or state of being contented
**2 :** something that contents
**content word** \'kän-ˌtent-\ *noun* (1940)
**:** a word that primarily expresses lexical meaning — compare FUNCTION WORD
**con·ter·mi·nous** \kən-'tər-mə-nəs, kän-\ *adjective* [Latin *conterminus,* from *com-* + *terminus* boundary — more at TERM] (1631)
**1 :** having a common boundary
**2 :** COTERMINOUS

**3 :** enclosed within one common boundary ⟨the 48 *conterminous* states⟩
— **con·ter·mi·nous·ly** *adverb*
**¹con·test** \kən-'test, 'kän-ˌ\ *verb* [Middle French *contester,* from Latin *contestari* (*litem*) to bring an action at law, from *contestari* to call to witness, from *com-* + *testis* witness — more at TESTAMENT] (1603)
*intransitive verb* **:** STRIVE, VIE
*transitive verb* **:** to make the subject of dispute, contention, or litigation; *especially* **:** DISPUTE, CHALLENGE
— **con·test·able** \-'tes-tə-bəl\ *adjective*
— **con·test·er** *noun*
**²con·test** \'kän-ˌtest\ *noun* (1647)
**1 :** a struggle for superiority or victory **:** COMPETITION
**2 :** a competition in which each contestant performs without direct contact with or interference from his competitors
**con·tes·tant** \kən-'tes-tənt *also* 'kän-ˌ\ *noun* (1665)
**1 :** one that participates in a contest
**2 :** one that contests an award or decision
**con·tes·ta·tion** \ˌkän-ˌtes-'tā-shən\ *noun* (1580)
**:** CONTROVERSY, DEBATE
**con·text** \'kän-ˌtekst\ *noun* [Middle English, weaving together of words, from Latin *contextus* connection of words, coherence, from *contexere* to weave together, from *com-* + *texere* to weave — more at TECHNICAL] (circa 1568)
**1 :** the parts of a discourse that surround a word or passage and can throw light on its meaning
**2 :** the interrelated conditions in which something exists or occurs **:** ENVIRONMENT, SETTING
— **con·text·less** \-ˌtekst-ləs\ *adjective*

---

☆ **SYNONYMS**
**Contemporary, contemporaneous, coeval, synchronous, simultaneous, coincident** mean existing or occurring at the same time. CONTEMPORARY is likely to apply to people and what relates to them ⟨Abraham Lincoln was *contemporary* with Charles Darwin⟩. CONTEMPORANEOUS applies to events ⟨*contemporaneous* accounts of the kidnapping⟩. COEVAL refers usually to periods, ages, eras, eons ⟨two stars thought to be *coeval*⟩. SYNCHRONOUS implies exact correspondence in time and especially in periodic intervals ⟨*synchronous* timepieces⟩. SIMULTANEOUS implies correspondence in a moment of time ⟨the two shots were *simultaneous*⟩. COINCIDENT is applied to events and may be used in order to avoid implication of causal relationship ⟨the end of World War II was *coincident* with a great vintage year⟩.

**Contemptible, despicable, pitiable, sorry, scurvy** mean arousing or deserving scorn. CONTEMPTIBLE may imply any quality provoking scorn or a low standing in any scale of values ⟨a *contemptible* liar⟩. DESPICABLE may imply utter worthlessness and usually suggests arousing an attitude of moral indignation ⟨a *despicable* crime⟩. PITIABLE applies to what inspires mixed contempt and pity ⟨a *pitiable* attempt at tragedy⟩. SORRY may stress pitiable inadequacy or may suggest wretchedness or sordidness ⟨this rattletrap is a *sorry* excuse for a car⟩. SCURVY adds to DESPICABLE an implication of arousing disgust ⟨a *scurvy* crew of hangers-on⟩.

---

\ə\ abut \ᵊ\ kitten \ər\ further \a\ ash \ā\ ace
\ä\ mop, mar \aů\ out \ch\ chin \e\ bet \ē\ easy
\g\ go \i\ hit \ī\ ice \j\ job \ŋ\ sing \ō\ go
\ȯ\ law \ȯi\ boy \th\ thin \t͟h\ the \ü\ loot \ů\ foot
\y\ yet \zh\ vision *see also* Guide to Pronunciation

— **con·tex·tu·al** \kän-'teks-chə-wəl, kən-, -chəl\ *adjective*

— **con·tex·tu·al·ly** *adverb*

**con·text–free** \'kän-ˌtekst-'frē\ *adjective* (1964)

**:** of, relating to, or being a grammar or language based on rules that describe a change in a string without reference to elements outside of the string; *also* **:** being such a rule

**con·tex·tu·al·ize** \kən-'teks-chə-wə-ˌlīz, -chə-ˌlīz\ *transitive verb* **-ized; -iz·ing** (1934)

**:** to place (as a word or activity) in a context

**con·tex·ture** \kən-'teks-chər, 'kän-ˌ, kän-'\ *noun* [French, from Latin *contextus*, past participle of *contexere*] (1603)

**1 :** the act, process, or manner of weaving parts into a whole; *also* **:** a structure so formed ⟨a *contexture* of lies⟩

**2 :** CONTEXT

**con·ti·gu·i·ty** \ˌkän-tə-'gyü-ə-tē\ *noun, plural* **-ties** (1612)

**:** the quality or state of being contiguous **:** PROXIMITY

**con·tig·u·ous** \kən-'ti-gyə-wəs\ *adjective* [Latin *contiguus*, from *contingere* to have contact with — more at CONTINGENT] (circa 1609)

**1 :** being in actual contact **:** touching along a boundary or at a point

**2** *of angles* **:** ADJACENT 2

**3 :** next or near in time or sequence

**4 :** touching or connected throughout in an unbroken sequence ⟨*contiguous* row houses⟩

*synonym* see ADJACENT

— **con·tig·u·ous·ly** *adverb*

— **con·tig·u·ous·ness** *noun*

**con·ti·nence** \'kän-tᵊn-ən(t)s\ *noun* (14th century)

**1 :** SELF-RESTRAINT; *especially* **:** a refraining from sexual intercourse

**2 :** the ability to retain a bodily discharge voluntarily ⟨fecal *continence*⟩

¹**con·ti·nent** \'kän-tᵊn-ənt\ *adjective* [Middle English, from Middle French, from Latin *continent-, continens*, from present participle of *continēre* to hold in — more at CONTAIN] (14th century)

**1 :** exercising continence

**2** *obsolete* **:** RESTRICTIVE

— **con·ti·nent·ly** *adverb*

²**con·ti·nent** \'kän-tᵊn-ənt, 'känt-nənt\ *noun* [in senses 1 & 2, from Latin *continent-, continens*, present participle of *continēre* to hold together, contain; in senses 3 & 4, from Latin *continent-, continens* continuous mass of land, mainland, from *continent-, continens*, present participle] (1541)

**1** *archaic* **:** CONTAINER, CONFINES

**2** *archaic* **:** EPITOME

**3 :** MAINLAND

**4 a :** one of the six or seven great divisions of land on the globe **b** *capitalized* **:** the continent of Europe — used with *the*

¹**con·ti·nen·tal** \ˌkän-tᵊn-'en-tᵊl\ *adjective* (1760)

**1 a :** of, relating to, or characteristic of a continent ⟨*continental* waters⟩; *specifically, often capitalized* **:** of or relating to the continent of Europe excluding the British Isles **b** *often capitalized* **:** of, relating to, or being a cuisine derived from the classic dishes of Europe and especially France

**2 a** *often capitalized* **:** of or relating to the colonies later forming the U.S. ⟨*Continental* Congress⟩ **b :** being the part of the U.S. on the North American continent; *also* **:** being the part of the U.S. comprising the lower 48 states

— **con·ti·nen·tal·ly** \-tᵊl-ē\ *adverb*

²**continental** *noun* (1777)

**1 a** *often capitalized* **:** an American soldier of the Revolution in the Continental army **b** (1) **:** a piece of Continental paper currency (2) **:** the least bit ⟨not worth a *continental*⟩

**2 :** an inhabitant of a continent and especially the continent of Europe

**continental breakfast** *noun, often C capitalized* (1911)

**:** a light breakfast (as of rolls or toast and coffee)

**continental drift** *noun* (1926)

**:** a hypothetical slow movement of the continents on a deep-seated viscous zone within the earth — compare PLATE TECTONICS

**continental shelf** *noun* (1892)

**:** a shallow submarine plain of varying width forming a border to a continent and typically ending in a steep slope to the oceanic abyss

**continental slope** *noun* (1900)

**:** the usually steep slope from a continental shelf to the ocean floor

**con·tin·gence** \kən-'tin-jən(t)s\ *noun* (circa 1530)

**1 :** CONTINGENCY

**2 :** TANGENCY

**con·tin·gen·cy** \kən-'tin-jən(t)-sē\ *noun, plural* **-cies** (1561)

**1 :** the quality or state of being contingent

**2 :** a contingent event or condition: as **a :** an event (as an emergency) that may but is not certain to occur ⟨trying to provide for every *contingency*⟩ **b :** something liable to happen as an adjunct to or result of something else

*synonym* see JUNCTURE

**contingency fee** *noun* (1945)

**:** a fee for services (as of a lawyer) paid upon successful completion of the services and usually calculated as a percentage of the gain realized for the client — called also *contingent fee*

**contingency table** *noun* (circa 1947)

**:** a table of data in which the row entries tabulate the data according to one variable and the column entries tabulate it according to another variable and which is used especially in the study of the correlation between variables

¹**con·tin·gent** \kən-'tin-jənt\ *adjective* [Middle English, from Middle French, from Latin *contingent-, contingens*, present participle of *contingere* to have contact with, befall, from *com-* + *tangere* to touch — more at TANGENT] (14th century)

**1 :** likely but not certain to happen **:** POSSIBLE

**2 :** not logically necessary; *especially* **:** EMPIRICAL

**3 a :** happening by chance or unforeseen causes **b :** subject to chance or unseen effects **:** UNPREDICTABLE **c :** intended for use in circumstances not completely foreseen

**4 :** dependent on or conditioned by something else

**5 :** not necessitated **:** determined by free choice

*synonym* see ACCIDENTAL

— **con·tin·gent·ly** *adverb*

²**contingent** *noun* (1548)

**1 :** something contingent **:** CONTINGENCY

**2 :** a representative group **:** DELEGATION, DETACHMENT

**con·tin·u·al** \kən-'tin-yü-əl, -yəl\ *adjective* [Middle English, from Middle French, from Latin *continuus* continuous] (14th century)

**1 :** continuing indefinitely in time without interruption ⟨*continual* fear⟩

**2 :** recurring in steady usually rapid succession ⟨a history of *continual* invasions⟩ ☆

— **con·tin·u·al·ly** *adverb*

**con·tin·u·ance** \kən-'tin-yü-ən(t)s\ *noun* (14th century)

**1 :** CONTINUATION

**2 :** the extent of continuing **:** DURATION

**3 :** the quality of enduring **:** PERMANENCE

**4 :** an adjournment of a court case to a future day

**con·tin·u·ant** \-yü-ənt\ *noun* (1861)

**1 :** something that continues or serves as a continuation

**2 :** a speech sound (as a fricative or vowel) that is produced without a complete closure of the breath passage — compare STOP

— **continuant** *adjective*

**con·tin·u·ate** *adjective* (1555)

*obsolete* **:** CONTINUOUS, UNINTERRUPTED

**con·tin·u·a·tion** \kən-ˌtin-yə-'wā-shən\ *noun* (14th century)

**1 :** the act or fact of continuing in or the prolongation of a state or activity

**2 :** resumption after an interruption

**3 :** something that continues, increases, or adds

**con·tin·u·a·tive** \kən-'tin-yə-ˌwā-tiv, -wə-tiv\ *adjective* (1684)

**:** expressing continuity or continuation (as of an idea or action)

**con·tin·u·a·tor** \-ˌwā-tər\ *noun* (1646)

**:** one that continues

**con·tin·ue** \kən-'tin-(ˌ)yü\ *verb* **-tin·ued; -tinu·ing** [Middle English, from Middle French *continuer*, from Latin *continuare*, from *continuus*] (14th century)

*intransitive verb*

**1 :** to maintain without interruption a condition, course, or action

**2 :** to remain in existence **:** ENDURE

**3 :** to remain in a place or condition **:** STAY

**4 :** to resume an activity after interruption

*transitive verb*

**1 a :** KEEP UP, MAINTAIN ⟨*continues* walking⟩ **b :** to keep going or add to **:** PROLONG; *also* **:** to resume after intermission

**2 :** to cause to continue

**3 :** to allow to remain in a place or condition **:** RETAIN

**4 :** to postpone (a legal proceeding) by a continuance ☆

— **con·tinu·er** \-yü-ər\ *noun*

**continued** *adjective* (15th century)

**1 :** lasting or extending without interruption ⟨*continued* success⟩

**2 :** resumed after interruption ⟨a *continued* story⟩

**continued fraction** *noun* (circa 1856)

**:** a fraction whose numerator is an integer and whose denominator is an integer plus a fraction whose numerator is an integer and whose denominator is an integer plus a fraction and so on

**continuing** *adjective* (14th century)

---

☆ **SYNONYMS**

**Continual, continuous, constant, incessant, perpetual, perennial** mean characterized by continued occurrence or recurrence. CONTINUAL often implies a close prolonged succession or recurrence ⟨*continual* showers the whole weekend⟩. CONTINUOUS usually implies an uninterrupted flow or spatial extension ⟨football's oldest *continuous* rivalry⟩. CONSTANT implies uniform or persistent occurrence or recurrence ⟨lived in *constant* pain⟩. INCESSANT implies ceaseless or uninterrupted activity ⟨annoyed by the *incessant* quarreling⟩. PERPETUAL suggests unfailing repetition or lasting duration ⟨a land of *perpetual* snowfall⟩. PERENNIAL implies enduring existence often through constant renewal ⟨a *perennial* source of controversy⟩.

**Continue, last, endure, abide, persist** mean to exist over a period of time or indefinitely. CONTINUE applies to a process going on without ending ⟨the search for peace will *continue*⟩. LAST, especially when unqualified, may stress existing beyond what is normal or expected ⟨buy shoes that will *last*⟩. ENDURE adds an implication of resisting destructive forces or agencies ⟨in spite of everything, her faith *endured*⟩. ABIDE implies stable and constant existing especially as opposed to mutability ⟨a love that *abides* through 40 years of marriage⟩. PERSIST suggests outlasting the normal or appointed time and often connotes obstinacy or doggedness ⟨the sense of guilt *persisted*⟩.

**1 :** CONTINUOUS, CONSTANT 〈*continuing* poverty〉
**2 :** needing no renewal : ENDURING 〈*continuing* fame〉
— **con·tin·u·ing·ly** *adverb*
**continuing education** *noun* (1954)
: formal courses of study for adult part-time students
**con·ti·nu·i·ty** \ˌkän-tᵊn-ˈü-ə-tē, -ˈyü-\ *noun, plural* **-ties** (15th century)
**1 a :** uninterrupted connection, succession, or union **b :** uninterrupted duration or continuation especially without essential change
**2 :** something that has, exhibits, or provides continuity: as **a :** a script or scenario in the performing arts **b :** transitional spoken or musical matter especially for a radio or television program **c :** the story and dialogue of a comic strip
**3 :** the property of being mathematically continuous
**con·tin·uo** \kən-ˈtin-yə-ˌwō, -ˈti-nə-\ *noun, plural* **-u·os** [Italian, from *continuo* continuous, from Latin *continuus*] (1724)
: a bass part (as for a keyboard or stringed instrument) used especially in baroque ensemble music and consisting of a succession of bass notes with figures that indicate the required chords — called also *figured bass, thoroughbass*
**con·tin·u·ous** \kən-ˈtin-yü-əs\ *adjective* [Latin *continuus,* from *continēre* to hold together — more at CONTAIN] (1673)
**1 :** marked by uninterrupted extension in space, time, or sequence
**2** *of a function* : having the property that the absolute value of the numerical difference between the value at a given point and the value at any point in a neighborhood of the given point can be made as close to zero as desired by choosing the neighborhood small enough
*synonym* see CONTINUAL
— **con·tin·u·ous·ly** *adverb*
— **con·tin·u·ous·ness** *noun*
**con·tin·u·um** \kən-ˈtin-yü-əm\ *noun, plural* **-ua** \-yü-ə\ *also* **-u·ums** [Latin, neuter of *continuus*] (1646)
**1 :** a coherent whole characterized as a collection, sequence, or progression of values or elements varying by minute degrees 〈"good" and "bad" . . . stand at opposite ends of a *continuum* —Wayne Shumaker〉
**2 :** the set of real numbers including both the rationals and the irrationals; *broadly* : a compact set which cannot be separated into two sets neither of which contains a limit point of the other
**con·tort** \kən-ˈtȯrt\ *verb* [Middle English, from Latin *contortus,* past participle of *contorquēre,* from *com-* + *torquēre* to twist — more at TORTURE] (15th century)
*transitive verb*
: to twist in a violent manner 〈features *contorted* with fury〉
*intransitive verb*
: to twist into or as if into a strained shape or expression
*synonym* see DEFORM
— **con·tor·tion** \-ˈtȯr-shən\ *noun*
— **con·tor·tive** \-ˈtȯr-tiv\ *adjective*
**con·tor·tion·ist** \kən-ˈtȯr-sh(ə-)nist\ *noun* (1859)
: one who contorts; *specifically* : an acrobat able to twist the body into unusual postures
— **con·tor·tion·is·tic** \-ˌtȯr-shə-ˈnis-tik\ *adjective*
**¹con·tour** \ˈkän-ˌtu̇r\ *noun* [French, from Italian *contorno,* from *contornare* to round off, from Medieval Latin, to turn around, from Latin *com-* + *tornare* to turn on a lathe — more at TURN] (1662)
**1 :** an outline especially of a curving or irregular figure : SHAPE; *also* : the line representing this outline
**2 :** the general form or structure of something **:** CHARACTERISTIC — often used in plural

〈*contours* of a melody〉 〈to delineate the tortured psychological *contours* of the tribal past —B. J. Phillips〉
**3 :** a usually meaningful change in intonation in speech
*synonym* see OUTLINE
**²contour** *adjective* (1844)
**1 :** following contour lines or forming furrows or ridges along them 〈*contour* flooding〉 〈*contour* farming〉
**2 :** made to fit the contour of something 〈a *contour* couch〉 〈*contour* sheets〉
**³contour** *transitive verb* (1871)
**1 a :** to shape the contour of **b :** to shape so as to fit contours
**2 :** to construct (as a road) in conformity to a contour
**contour feather** *noun* (1867)
: one of the medium-sized feathers that form the general covering of a bird and determine the external contour
**contour line** *noun* (1844)
: a line (as on a map) connecting the points on a land surface that have the same elevation
**contour map** *noun* (1862)
: a map having contour lines
**¹con·tra** \ˈkän-trə\ *preposition* [Latin] (15th century)
**1 :** AGAINST — used chiefly in the phrase *pro and contra*
**2 :** in opposition or contrast to — used before a proper name

**contour map**

**²con·tra** \ˈkän-trə, ˈkōn-, -ˌträ\ *noun* [American Spanish, short for *contra-revolucionario* counterrevolutionary] (1981)
: a member of a guerrilla group opposed to the Sandinista government in Nicaragua
**contra-** *prefix* [Middle English, from Latin, from *contra* against, opposite — more at COUNTER]
**1 :** against : contrary : contrasting 〈*contra*distinction〉
**2 :** pitched below normal bass 〈*contra*octave〉
**con·tra·band** \ˈkän-trə-ˌband\ *noun* [Italian *contrabbando,* from Medieval Latin *contrabannum,* from *contra-* + *bannus, bannum* decree, of Germanic origin; akin to Old High German *bannan* to command — more at BAN] (circa 1529)
**1 :** illegal or prohibited traffic in goods **:** SMUGGLING
**2 :** goods or merchandise whose importation, exportation, or possession is forbidden; *also* : smuggled goods
**3 :** a slave who during the Civil War escaped to or was brought within the Union lines
— **contraband** *adjective*
**con·tra·band·ist** \-ˌban-dist\ *noun* (circa 1818)
**:** SMUGGLER
**con·tra·bass** \ˈkän-trə-ˌbās\ *noun* [Italian *contrabbasso,* from *contra-* + *basso* bass] (circa 1611)
**:** DOUBLE BASS
— **con·tra·bass·ist** \-ˌbā-sist\ *noun*
**con·tra·bas·soon** \ˌkän-trə-bə-ˈsün, -ba-\ *noun* (1891)
: a double-reed woodwind instrument having a range an octave lower than that of the bassoon — called also *double bassoon*
**con·tra·cep·tion** \ˌkän-trə-ˈsep-shən\ *noun* [*contra-* + *conception*] (1886)
: deliberate prevention of conception or impregnation
— **con·tra·cep·tive** \-ˈsep-tiv\ *adjective or noun*
**¹con·tract** \ˈkän-ˌtrakt\ *noun* [Middle English, from Latin *contractus,* from *contrahere* to draw together, make a contract, reduce in size, from *com-* + *trahere* to draw] (14th century)
**1 a :** a binding agreement between two or more persons or parties; *especially* : one legal-

ly enforceable **b :** a business arrangement for the supply of goods or services at a fixed price 〈make parts on *contract*〉 **c :** the act of marriage or an agreement to marry
**2 :** a document describing the terms of a contract
**3 :** the final bid to win a specified number of tricks in bridge
**4 :** an order or arrangement for a hired assassin to kill someone
**²con·tract** \*verb transitive* 2a *& verb intransitive* 1 *usually* ˈkän-ˌtrakt, *others usually* kən-ˈ\ *verb* [Middle English, from Middle French or Latin; Middle French *contracter* to agree upon, from Latin *contractus*] (14th century)
*transitive verb*
**1 a :** to bring on oneself especially inadvertently **:** INCUR 〈*contracting* debts〉 **b :** to become affected with 〈*contract* pneumonia〉
**2 a :** to establish or undertake by contract **b :** BETROTH; *also* : to establish (a marriage) formally **c** (1) **:** to hire by contract (2) **:** to purchase (as goods or services) on a contract basis — often used with *out*
**3 a :** LIMIT, RESTRICT **b :** KNIT, WRINKLE 〈frown *contracted* his brow〉 **c :** to draw together **:** CONCENTRATE
**4 :** to reduce to smaller size by or as if by squeezing or forcing together
**5 :** to shorten (as a word) by omitting one or more sounds or letters
*intransitive verb*
**1 :** to make a contract
**2 :** to draw together so as to become diminished in size 〈metal *contracts* on cooling〉; *also* : to become less in compass, duration, or length 〈muscle *contracts* in tetanus〉 ☆
— **con·tract·ibil·i·ty** \kən-ˌtrak-tə-ˈbi-lə-tē, ˌkän-\ *noun*
— **con·tract·ible** \kən-ˈtrak-tə-bəl, ˈkän-ˌ\ *adjective*
**contract bridge** \ˈkän-ˌtrakt-\ *noun* (1924)
: a bridge game distinguished by the fact that overtricks do not count toward game or slam bonuses
**con·trac·tile** \kən-ˈtrak-tᵊl, -ˌtīl\ *adjective* (circa 1706)
: having or concerned with the power or property of contracting 〈*contractile* proteins of muscle fibrils〉
— **con·trac·til·i·ty** \ˌkän-ˌtrak-ˈti-lə-tē\ *noun*
**contractile vacuole** *noun* (1877)

---

☆ **SYNONYMS**
**Contract, shrink, condense, compress, constrict, deflate** mean to decrease in bulk or volume. CONTRACT applies to a drawing together of surfaces or particles or a reduction of area or extent 〈caused her muscles to *contract*〉. SHRINK implies a contracting or a loss of material and stresses a falling short of original dimensions 〈the sweater will *shrink* when washed〉. CONDENSE implies a reducing of something homogeneous to greater compactness without significant loss of content 〈*condense* the essay into a paragraph〉. COMPRESS implies a pressing into a small compass and definite shape usually against resistance 〈*compressed* cotton into bales〉. CONSTRICT implies a tightening that reduces diameter 〈the throat is *constricted* by a tight collar〉. DEFLATE implies a contracting by reducing the internal pressure of contained air or gas 〈*deflate* the balloon〉.

---

\ə\ abut \ᵊ\ kitten \ər\ further \a\ ash \ā\ ace
\ä\ mop, mar \au̇\ out \ch\ chin \e\ bet \ē\ easy
\g\ go \i\ hit \ī\ ice \j\ job \ŋ\ sing \ō\ go
\ȯ\ law \ȯi\ boy \th\ thin \th\ the \ü\ loot \u̇\ foot
\y\ yet \zh\ vision *see also* Guide to Pronunciation

: a vacuole in a unicellular organism that contracts regularly to discharge fluid from the body

**con·trac·tion** \kən-'trak-shən\ *noun* (15th century)
**1 a :** the action or process of contracting **:** the state of being contracted **b :** the shortening and thickening of a functioning muscle or muscle fiber **c :** a reduction in business activity or growth
**2 :** a shortening of a word, syllable, or word group by omission of a sound or letter; *also* **:** a form produced by such shortening
— **con·trac·tion·al** \-shnəl, -shə-n°l\ *adjective*
— **con·trac·tive** \kən-'trak-tiv, 'kän-,\ *adjective*
— **con·trac·tion·ary** \kən-'trak-shə-,ner-ē\ *adjective*

**con·trac·tor** \l *usually* 'kän-,trak-tər, 2 *usually* kən-'\ *noun* (1548)
**1 :** one that contracts or is party to a contract: as **a :** one that contracts to perform work or provide supplies **b :** one that contracts to erect buildings
**2 :** something (as a muscle) that contracts or shortens

**con·trac·tu·al** \kən-'trak-chə-wəl, -chəl, -shwəl\ *adjective* (1861)
**:** of, relating to, or constituting a contract
— **con·trac·tu·al·ly** *adverb*

**con·trac·ture** \kən-'trak-chər\ *noun* (1601)
**:** a permanent shortening (as of muscle, tendon, or scar tissue) producing deformity or distortion

**con·tra·dict** \,kän-trə-'dikt\ *transitive verb* [Latin *contradictus*, past participle of *contradicere*, from *contra-* + *dicere* to say, speak — more at DICTION] (circa 1576)
**1 :** to assert the contrary of **:** take issue with
**2 :** to imply the opposite or a denial of ⟨your actions *contradict* your words⟩
**synonym** see DENY
— **con·tra·dict·able** \-'dik-tə-bəl\ *adjective*
— **con·tra·dic·tor** \-'dik-tər\ *noun*

**con·tra·dic·tion** \,kän-trə-'dik-shən\ *noun* (14th century)
**1 :** act or an instance of contradicting
**2 a :** a proposition, statement, or phrase that asserts or implies both the truth and falsity of something **b :** a statement or phrase whose parts contradict each other ⟨a round square is a *contradiction* in terms⟩
**3 a :** logical incongruity **b :** a situation in which inherent factors, actions, or propositions are inconsistent or contrary to one another

**con·tra·dic·tious** \-shəs\ *adjective* (1604)
**1 :** CONTRADICTORY, OPPOSITE
**2 :** given to or marked by contradiction **:** CONTRARY

**¹con·tra·dic·to·ry** \,kän-trə-'dik-t(ə-)rē\ *noun, plural* **-ries** (14th century)
**:** a proposition so related to another that if either of the two is true the other is false and if either is false the other must be true

**²contradictory** *adjective* (1534)
**:** involving, causing, or constituting a contradiction
**synonym** see OPPOSITE
— **con·tra·dic·to·ri·ly** \-t(ə-)rə-lē\ *adverb*
— **con·tra·dic·to·ri·ness** \-t(ə-)rē-nəs\ *noun*

**con·tra·dis·tinc·tion** \,kän-trə-dis-'tiŋ(k)-shən\ *noun* (1647)
**:** distinction by means of contrast ⟨painting in *contradistinction* to sculpture⟩
— **con·tra·dis·tinc·tive** \-'tiŋ(k)-tiv\ *adjective*
— **con·tra·dis·tinc·tive·ly** *adverb*

**con·tra·dis·tin·guish** \-'tiŋ-gwish\ *transitive verb* (1622)
**:** to distinguish by contrasting qualities

**con·trail** \'kän-,trāl\ *noun* [*condensation trail*] (1943)

: streaks of condensed water vapor created in the air by an airplane or rocket at high altitudes

**con·tra·in·di·cate** \,kän-trə-'in-də-,kāt\ *transitive verb* (1666)
**:** to make (a treatment or procedure) inadvisable

**con·tra·in·di·ca·tion** \-,in-də-'kā-shən\ *noun* (1623)
**:** something (as a symptom or condition) that makes a particular treatment or procedure inadvisable

**con·tra·lat·er·al** \-'la-t(ə-)rəl\ *adjective* [International Scientific Vocabulary] (1882)
**:** occurring on or acting in conjunction with a part on the opposite side of the body

**con·tral·to** \kən-'tral-(,)tō\ *noun, plural* **-tos** [Italian, from *contra-* + *alto*] (1730)
**1 a :** a singing voice having a range between tenor and mezzo-soprano **b :** a person having this voice
**2 :** the part sung by a contralto

**con·tra·oc·tave** \,kän-trə-'äk-tiv, -təv, -,tāv\ *noun* (circa 1891)
**:** the musical octave that begins on the third C below middle C — see PITCH illustration

**con·tra·po·si·tion** \-pə-'zi-shən\ *noun* [Late Latin *contraposition-, contrapositio*, from Latin *contraponere* to place opposite, from *contra-* + *ponere* to place — more at POSITION] (1551)
**:** the relationship between two propositions when the subject and predicate of one are respectively the negation of the predicate and the negation of the subject of the other

**con·tra·pos·i·tive** \-'pä-zə-tiv, -'päz-tiv\ *noun* (1870)
**:** a proposition resulting from an operation of immediate inference in which the terms of a given proposition are permuted and negated ("all not-*P* is not-*S*" is the *contrapositive* of "all *S* is *P*")

**con·trap·tion** \kən-'trap-shən\ *noun* [perhaps blend of *contrivance, trap,* and *invention*] (circa 1825)
**:** DEVICE, GADGET

**con·tra·pun·tal** \,kän-trə-'pən-t°l\ *adjective* [Italian *contrappunto* counterpoint, from Medieval Latin *contrapunctus* — more at COUNTERPOINT] (1845)
**1 :** POLYPHONIC
**2 :** of, relating to, or marked by counterpoint
— **con·tra·pun·tal·ly** \-t°l-ē\ *adverb*

**con·tra·pun·tist** \-'pən-tist\ *noun* (1776)
**:** one who writes counterpoint

**con·trar·i·an** \kən-'trer-ē-ən, kän-\ *noun* (1657)
**:** a person who takes a contrary position or attitude; *specifically* **:** an investor who buys shares of stock when most others are selling and sells when others are buying
— **contrarian** *adjective*

**con·tra·ri·ety** \,kän-trə-'rī-ə-tē\ *noun, plural* **-eties** [Middle English *contrariete*, from Middle French *contrarieté*, from Late Latin *contrarietat-, contrarietas*, from Latin *contrarius* contrary] (14th century)
**1 :** the quality or state of being contrary
**2 :** something contrary

**con·trar·i·ous** \kən-'trer-ē-əs, kän-\ *adjective* (13th century)
**:** PERVERSE, ANTAGONISTIC

**con·trari·wise** \'kän-,trer-ē-,wīz, kən-'\ *adverb* (14th century)
**1 :** on the contrary
**2 :** VICE VERSA
**3 :** in a contrary manner

**¹con·trary** \'kän-,trer-ē\ *noun, plural* **-trar·ies** (13th century)
**1 :** a fact or condition incompatible with another **:** OPPOSITE — usually used with *the*
**2 :** one of a pair of opposites
**3 a :** a proposition so related to another that though both may be false they cannot both be true — compare SUBCONTRARY **b :** either of

two terms (as *good* and *evil*) that cannot both be affirmed of the same subject
— **by contraries** *obsolete* **:** in a manner opposite to what is logical or expected
— **on the contrary :** just the opposite
— **to the contrary 1 :** on the contrary **2** **:** NOTWITHSTANDING

**²con·trary** \'kän-,trer-ē, 4 *often* kən-'trer-ē\ *adjective* [Middle English *contrarie*, from Middle French *contraire*, from Latin *contrarius*, from *contra* opposite] (14th century)
**1 :** being so different as to be at opposite extremes **:** OPPOSITE ⟨come to the *contrary* conclusion⟩ ⟨went off in *contrary* directions⟩; *also* **:** being opposite to or in conflict with each other ⟨*contrary* viewpoints⟩
**2 :** being not in conformity with what is usual or expected ⟨actions *contrary* to company policy⟩ ⟨*contrary* evidence⟩
**3 :** UNFAVORABLE — used of wind or weather
**4 :** temperamentally unwilling to accept control or advice ☆
— **con·trari·ly** \-,trer-ə-lē, -'trer-\ *adverb*
— **con·trari·ness** \-,trer-ē-nəs, -'trer-\ *noun*

**³contrary** \*same as* ²\ *adverb* (15th century)
**:** CONTRARIWISE, CONTRARILY

**contrary to** *preposition* (14th century)
**:** in conflict with **:** DESPITE ⟨*contrary to* orders, he set out alone⟩

**¹con·trast** \kən-'trast, 'kän-,\ *verb* [French *contraster*, from Middle French, to oppose, resist, alteration of *contrester*, from (assumed) Vulgar Latin *contrastare*, from Latin *contra-* + *stare* to stand — more at STAND] (1695)
*transitive verb*
**:** to set off in contrast **:** compare or appraise in respect to differences ⟨*contrast* European and American manners⟩ — often used with *to* or *with* ⟨*contrasting* her with other women —Victoria Sackville-West⟩
*intransitive verb*
**:** to form a contrast
**synonym** see COMPARE
— **con·trast·able** \-'tras-tə-bəl, -,tras-\ *adjective*

**²con·trast** \'kän-,trast\ *noun* (1711)
**1 a :** juxtaposition of dissimilar elements (as color, tone, or emotion) in a work of art **b** **:** degree of difference between the lightest and darkest parts of a picture
**2 a :** the difference or degree of difference between things having similar or comparable natures ⟨the *contrast* between the two forms of government⟩ **b :** comparison of similar objects to set off their dissimilar qualities **:** the state of being so compared ⟨the enforced simplicity in this diary . . . is in *contrast* to the intensity of his former life —*Times Literary Supplement*⟩
**3 :** a person or thing that exhibits differences when compared with another

**con·tras·tive** \kən-'tras-tiv, 'kän-,\ *adjective* (1841)
**:** forming or consisting of a contrast
— **con·tras·tive·ly** *adverb*

**con·trasty** \'kän-,tras-tē\ *adjective* (1891)

---

☆ **SYNONYMS**
**Contrary, perverse, restive, balky, wayward** mean inclined to resist authority or control. CONTRARY implies a temperamental unwillingness to accept orders or advice ⟨a *contrary* child⟩. PERVERSE may imply wrongheaded, determined, or cranky opposition to what is reasonable or normal ⟨a *perverse*, intractable critic⟩. RESTIVE suggests unwillingness or inability to submit to discipline or follow orders ⟨tired soldiers growing *restive*⟩. BALKY suggests a refusing to proceed in a desired direction or course of action ⟨a *balky* witness⟩. WAYWARD suggests strong-willed capriciousness and irregularity in behavior ⟨a school for *wayward* youths⟩. See in addition OPPOSITE.

**:** having or producing in photography great contrast between highlights and shadows

**con·tra·vene** \ˌkän-trə-ˈvēn\ *transitive verb* **-vened; -ven·ing** [Middle French or Late Latin; Middle French *contrevenir*, from Late Latin *contravenire*, from Latin *contra-* + *venire* to come — more at COME] (1567) **1 :** to go or act contrary to **:** VIOLATE ⟨*contravene* a law⟩ **2 :** to oppose in argument **:** CONTRADICT ⟨*contravene* a proposition⟩
*synonym* see DENY
— **con·tra·ven·er** *noun*

**con·tra·ven·tion** \ˌkän-trə-ˈven(t)-shən\ *noun* [Middle French, from Late Latin *contravenire*] (1579)
**:** the act of contravening **:** VIOLATION

**con·tre·danse** \ˈkän-trə-ˌdan(t)s, kōⁿ-trə-däⁿs\ *or* **con·tra dance** \ˈkän-trə-ˌdan(t)s\ *noun* [French *contredanse*, by folk etymology from English *country-dance*] (1803) **1 :** a folk dance in which couples face each other in two lines or in a square **2 :** a piece of music for a contredanse

**con·tre·temps** \ˈkän-trə-ˌtän, kōⁿ-trə-täⁿ\ *noun, plural* **con·tre·temps** \-ˌtäⁿ(z)\ [French, from *contre-* counter- + *temps* time, from Latin *tempus*] (1769)
**:** an inopportune or embarrassing occurrence or situation

**con·trib·ute** \kən-ˈtri-byət, -(ˌ)byüt *also & especially before* -ed *or* -ing -ˈtri-bət; *chiefly British also* ˈkän-trə-ˌbyüt\ *verb* **-ut·ed; -ut·ing** [Latin *contributus*, past participle of *contribuere*, from *com-* + *tribuere* to grant — more at TRIBUTE] (1530)
*transitive verb*
**1 :** to give or supply in common with others
**2 :** to supply (as an article) for a publication
*intransitive verb*
**1 a :** to give a part to a common fund or store **b :** to play a significant part in bringing about an end or result **2 :** to submit articles to a publication
— **con·trib·u·tor** \-byə-tər, -bə-, -ˌbyü-\ *noun*

**con·tri·bu·tion** \ˌkän-trə-ˈbyü-shən\ *noun* (14th century) **1 :** a payment (as a levy or tax) imposed by military, civil, or ecclesiastical authorities usually for a special or extraordinary purpose **2 :** the act of contributing; *also* **:** the thing contributed
— **con·trib·u·tive** \kən-ˈtri-byə-tiv\ *adjective*
— **con·trib·u·tive·ly** *adverb*

**con·trib·u·to·ry** \kən-ˈtri-byə-ˌtōr-ē, -ˌtȯr-\ *adjective* (15th century) **1 a :** subject to a levy of supplies, money, or men **b :** contributing to a common fund or enterprise **2 :** of, relating to, or forming a contribution

**con·trite** \ˈkän-ˌtrīt, kən-ˈ\ *adjective* [Middle English *contrit*, from Middle French, from Medieval Latin *contritus*, from Latin, past participle of *conterere* to grind, bruise, from *com-* + *terere* to rub — more at THROW] (14th century) **1 :** grieving and penitent for sin or shortcoming **2 :** proceeding from contrition ⟨*contrite* sighs⟩
— **con·trite·ly** *adverb*
— **con·trite·ness** *noun*

**con·tri·tion** \kən-ˈtri-shən\ *noun* (14th century)
**:** the state of being contrite **:** REPENTANCE
*synonym* see PENITENCE

**con·triv·ance** \kən-ˈtrī-vən(t)s\ *noun* (circa 1628) **1 a :** a thing contrived; *especially* **:** a mechanical device **b :** an artificial arrangement or development **2 :** the act or faculty of contriving **:** the state of being contrived

**con·trive** \kən-ˈtrīv\ *verb* **con·trived; con·triv·ing** [Middle English *controven, con-*

*treven*, from Middle French *controver*, from Medieval Latin *contropare* to compare, from Latin *com-* + (assumed) Vulgar Latin *tropare* to compose, find — more at TROUBADOR] (14th century)
*transitive verb*
**1 a :** DEVISE, PLAN ⟨*contrive* ways of handling the situation⟩ **b :** to form or create in an artistic or ingenious manner ⟨*contrived* household utensils from stone⟩ **2 :** to bring about by stratagem or with difficulty **:** MANAGE
*intransitive verb*
**:** to make schemes
— **con·triv·er** *noun*

**contrived** *adjective* (15th century)
**:** ARTIFICIAL, LABORED

**¹con·trol** \kən-ˈtrōl\ *transitive verb* **con·trolled; con·trol·ling** [Middle English *controllen*, from Middle French *contreroller*, from *contrerolle* copy of an account, audit, from Medieval Latin *contrarotulus*, from Latin *contra-* + Medieval Latin *rotulus* roll — more at ROLL] (15th century) **1 a** *archaic* **:** to check, test, or verify by evidence or experiments **b :** to incorporate suitable controls in ⟨a *controlled* experiment⟩ **2 a :** to exercise restraining or directing influence over **:** REGULATE **b :** to have power over **:** RULE **c :** to reduce the incidence or severity of especially to innocuous levels ⟨*control* an insect population⟩ ⟨*control* a disease⟩
*synonym* see CONDUCT
— **con·trol·la·bil·i·ty** \-ˌtrō-lə-ˈbi-lə-tē\ *noun*
— **con·trol·la·ble** \-ˈtrō-lə-bəl\ *adjective*
— **con·trol·ment** \-ˈtrōl-mənt\ *noun*

**²control** *noun, often attributive* (1590) **1 a :** an act or instance of controlling; *also* **:** power or authority to guide or manage **b :** skill in the use of a tool, instrument, technique, or artistic medium **c :** the regulation of economic activity especially by government directive — usually used in plural ⟨price *controls*⟩ **2 :** RESTRAINT, RESERVE **3 :** one that controls: as **a** (1) **:** an experiment in which the subjects are treated as in a parallel experiment except for omission of the procedure or agent under test and which is used as a standard of comparison in judging experimental effects — called also *control experiment* (2) **:** one (as an organism, culture, or group) that is part of a control **b :** a device or mechanism used to regulate or guide the operation of a machine, apparatus, or system **c :** an organization that directs a spaceflight ⟨mission *control*⟩ **d :** a personality or spirit believed to actuate the utterances or performances of a spiritualist medium
*synonym* see POWER

**con·trolled** \kən-ˈtrōld\ *adjective* (1586) **1 :** RESTRAINED **2 :** regulated by law with regard to possession and use ⟨*controlled* drugs⟩

**con·trol·ler** \kən-ˈtrō-lər, ˈkän-\ *noun* [Middle English *controllere*, from Middle French *controlleur*, from *controlle*] (15th century) **1 a :** COMPTROLLER 1 **b :** COMPTROLLER 2 **c :** the chief accounting officer of a business enterprise or an institution (as a college) **2 a :** one that controls or has power or authority to control ⟨air traffic *controller*⟩ **b :** CONTROL 3b
— **con·trol·ler·ship** \-ˌship\ *noun*

**controlling interest** *noun* (circa 1924)
**:** sufficient stock ownership in a corporation to exert control over policy

**control surface** *noun* (1917)
**:** a movable airfoil designed to change the attitude of an aircraft

**con·tro·ver·sial** \ˌkän-trə-ˈvər-shəl, -ˈvər-sē-əl\ *adjective* (1583) **1 :** of, relating to, or arousing controversy **:** DISPUTATIOUS **2 :** given to controversy

— **con·tro·ver·sial·ism** \-shə-ˌli-zəm, -sē-ə-ˌ\ *noun*
— **con·tro·ver·sial·ist** \-list\ *noun*
— **con·tro·ver·sial·ly** *adverb*

**con·tro·ver·sy** \ˈkän-trə-ˌvər-sē, *British also* kən-ˈträ-vər-sē\ *noun, plural* **-sies** [Middle English *controversie*, from Latin *controversia*, from *controversus* disputable, literally, turned against, from *contro-* (akin to *contra-*) + *versus*, past participle of *vertere* to turn — more at WORTH] (14th century) **1 :** a discussion marked especially by the expression of opposing views **:** DISPUTE **2 :** QUARREL, STRIFE

**con·tro·vert** \ˈkän-trə-ˌvərt, ˌkän-trə-ˈ\ *verb* [*controversy*] (1609)
*transitive verb*
**:** to dispute or oppose by reasoning ⟨*controvert* a point in a discussion⟩
*intransitive verb*
**:** to engage in controversy
— **con·tro·vert·er** \-ˌvər-tər, -ˈvər-\ *noun*
— **con·tro·vert·ible** \-tə-bəl\ *adjective*

**con·tu·ma·cious** \ˌkän-tü-ˈmā-shəs, -tyü-, -chə-\ *adjective* (circa 1600)
**:** stubbornly disobedient **:** REBELLIOUS
— **con·tu·ma·cious·ly** *adverb*

**con·tu·ma·cy** \kən-ˈtü-mə-sē, -ˈtyü-; ˈkän-tü-, -tyü-, -chə-\ *noun* [Middle English *contumacie*, from Latin *contumacia*, from *contumac-, contumax* rebellious] (13th century)
**:** stubborn resistance to authority; *specifically* **:** willful contempt of court

**con·tu·me·li·ous** \ˌkän-tü-ˈmē-lē-əs, -tyü-, -chə-\ *adjective* (15th century)
**:** insolently abusive and humiliating
— **con·tu·me·li·ous·ly** *adverb*

**con·tume·ly** \ˈkän-ˌtü-mə-lē, kən-, -ˈtyü-; ˈkän-tü-ˌmē-lē, -tyü-, -chə-; *in "Hamlet"* ˈkän-(ˌ)tyüm-lē *or* ˈkän-chəm-\ *noun, plural* **-lies** [Middle English *contumelie*, from Middle French, from Latin *contumelia*] (14th century)
**:** harsh language or treatment arising from haughtiness and contempt; *also* **:** an instance of such language or treatment

**con·tu·sion** \kən-ˈtü-zhən, -ˈtyü-\ *noun* [Middle English *conteschown*, from Middle French *contusion*, from Latin *contusion-, contusio*, from *contundere* to pound, bruise, from *com-* + *tundere* to beat; akin to Gothic *stautan* to strike, Sanskrit *tudati* he pushes] (15th century)
**:** injury to tissue usually without laceration **:** BRUISE 1a
— **con·tuse** \-ˈtüz, -ˈtyüz\ *transitive verb*

**co·nun·drum** \kə-ˈnən-drəm\ *noun* [origin unknown] (1645) **1 :** a riddle whose answer is or involves a pun **2 a :** a question or problem having only a conjectural answer **b :** an intricate and difficult problem

**con·ur·ba·tion** \ˌkä-(ˌ)nər-ˈbā-shən\ *noun* [*com-* + Latin *urb-, urbs* city] (1915)
**:** an aggregation or continuous network of urban communities

**co·nus ar·te·ri·o·sus** \ˈkō-nəs-är-ˌtir-ē-ˈō-səs\ *noun, plural* **co·ni ar·te·ri·o·si** \-ˌnī-är-ˌtir-ē-ˈō-ˌsī\ [New Latin, literally, arterial cone] (circa 1860) **1 :** a conical prolongation of the right ventricle in mammals from which the pulmonary arteries emerge — called also *conus* **2 :** a prolongation of the ventricle of amphibians and some fishes that has a spiral valve separating venous blood going to the respiratory arteries from blood going to the aorta and systemic arteries

**con·va·lesce** \ˌkän-və-ˈles\ *intransitive verb* **-lesced; -lesc·ing** [Latin *convalescere*, from *com-* + *valescere* to grow strong, from

| | | | | |
|---|---|---|---|---|
| \ə\ abut | \ᵊ\ kitten | \ər\ **further** | \a\ ash | \ā\ ace |
| \ä\ mop, mar | \au̇\ out | \ch\ chin | \e\ bet | \ē\ easy |
| \g\ go | \i\ hit | \ī\ ice | \j\ job | \ŋ\ sing | \ō\ go |
| \ȯ\ law | \ȯi\ boy | \th\ thin | \t̷h\ the | \ü\ loot | \u̇\ foot |
| \y\ yet | \zh\ vision | | *see also* Guide to Pronunciation | |

*valēre* to be strong, be well — more at WIELD] (15th century)
**:** to recover health and strength gradually after sickness or weakness
— **con·va·les·cence** \-'le-s°n(t)s\ *noun*
— **con·va·les·cent** \-s°nt\ *adjective or noun*
**con·vect** \kən-'vekt\ *verb* [back-formation from *convection*] (1881)
*intransitive verb*
**:** to transfer heat by convection
*transitive verb*
**:** to circulate (as air) by convection
— **con·vec·tive** \-'vek-tiv\ *adjective*
**con·vec·tion** \kən-'vek-shən\ *noun* [Late Latin *convection-, convectio*, from Latin *convehere* to bring together, from *com-* + *vehere* to carry — more at WAY] (circa 1623)
**1 :** the action or process of conveying
**2 a :** the circulatory motion that occurs in a fluid at a nonuniform temperature owing to the variation of its density and the action of gravity **b :** the transfer of heat by convection — compare CONDUCTION, RADIATION
— **con·vec·tion·al** \-shnəl, -shə-n°l\ *adjective*
**convection oven** *noun* (1973)
**:** an oven having a fan that circulates hot air uniformly and continuously around food
**con·vec·tor** \-'vek-tər\ *noun* (1907)
**:** a heating unit in which air heated by contact with a heating device (as a radiator or a tube with fins) in a casing circulates by convection
**con·vene** \kən-'vēn\ *verb* **con·vened; con·ven·ing** [Middle English, from Middle French *convenir* to come together, from Latin *convenire*] (15th century)
*intransitive verb*
**:** to come together in a body
*transitive verb*
**1 :** to summon before a tribunal
**2 :** to cause to assemble
**synonym** see SUMMON
— **con·ven·er** *or* **con·ve·nor** \-'vē-nər\ *noun*
**¹con·ve·nience** \kən-'vēn-yən(t)s\ *noun* (14th century)
**1 :** fitness or suitability for performing an action or fulfilling a requirement
**2 a :** something (as an appliance, device, or service) conducive to comfort or ease **b** *chiefly British* **:** TOILET 3
**3 :** a suitable or convenient time ⟨at your *convenience*⟩
**4 :** freedom from discomfort **:** EASE
**²convenience** *adjective* (1917)
**:** designed for quick and easy preparation or use ⟨*convenience* foods⟩
**convenience store** *noun* (1965)
**:** a small often franchised market that is open long hours
**con·ve·nien·cy** \-yən(t)-sē\ *noun* (1601)
*archaic* **:** CONVENIENCE
**con·ve·nient** \kən-'vēn-yənt\ *adjective* [Middle English, from Latin *convenient-, conveniens*, from present participle of *convenire* to come together, be suitable, from *com-* + *venire* to come — more at COME] (14th century)
**1** *obsolete* **:** SUITABLE, PROPER
**2 a :** suited to personal comfort or to easy performance **b :** suited to a particular situation **c :** affording accommodation or advantage
**3 :** being near at hand **:** HANDY
— **con·ve·nient·ly** *adverb*
**¹con·vent** \'kän-vənt, -,vent\ *noun* [Middle English *covent*, from Old French, from Medieval Latin *conventus*, from Latin, assembly, from *convenire*] (13th century)
**:** a local community or house of a religious order or congregation; *especially* **:** an establishment of nuns
**²con·vent** \kən-'vent\ *verb* [Latin *conventus*, past participle of *convenire*] (1514)
*obsolete* **:** CONVENE

**con·ven·ti·cle** \kən-'ven-ti-kəl\ *noun* [Middle English, from Latin *conventiculum*, diminutive of *conventus* assembly] (14th century)
**1 :** ASSEMBLY, MEETING
**2 :** an assembly of an irregular or unlawful character
**3 :** an assembly for religious worship; *especially* **:** a secret meeting for worship not sanctioned by law
**4 :** MEETINGHOUSE
— **con·ven·ti·cler** \-k(ə-)lər\ *noun*
**con·ven·tion** \kən-'ven(t)-shən\ *noun* [Middle English, from Middle French or Latin; Middle French, from Latin *convention-, conventio*, from *convenire*] (15th century)
**1 a :** AGREEMENT, CONTRACT **b :** an agreement between states for regulation of matters affecting all of them **c :** a compact between opposing commanders especially concerning prisoner exchange or armistice **d :** a general agreement about basic principles or procedures; *also* **:** a principle or procedure accepted as true or correct by convention
**2 a :** the summoning or convening of an assembly **b :** an assembly of persons met for a common purpose; *especially* **:** a meeting of the delegates of a political party for the purpose of formulating a platform and selecting candidates for office **c :** the usually state or national organization of a religious denomination
**3 a :** usage or custom especially in social matters **b :** a rule of conduct or behavior **c :** a practice in bidding or playing that conveys information between partners in a card game (as bridge) **d :** an established technique, practice, or device (as in literature or the theater)
**con·ven·tion·al** \kən-'vench-nəl, -'ven(t)-shə-n°l\ *adjective* (15th century)
**1 :** formed by agreement or compact
**2 a :** according with, sanctioned by, or based on convention **b :** lacking originality or individuality **:** TRITE **c (1) :** ORDINARY, COMMONPLACE **(2) :** NONNUCLEAR 1 ⟨*conventional* warfare⟩
**3 a :** according with a mode of artistic representation that simplifies or provides symbols or substitutes for natural forms **b :** of traditional design
**4 :** of, resembling, or relating to a convention, assembly, or public meeting
**synonym** see CEREMONIAL
— **con·ven·tion·al·ism** \-nə-,li-zəm, -n°l-,i-zəm\ *noun*
— **con·ven·tion·al·ist** \-list\ *noun or adjective*
— **con·ven·tion·al·i·za·tion** \-,vench-nə-lə-'zā-shən, -,ven(t)-shə-n°l-ə-'zā-\ *noun*
— **con·ven·tion·al·ize** \-'vench-nə-,līz, -'ven(t)-shə-n°l-,īz\ *transitive verb*
— **con·ven·tion·al·ly** *adverb*
**con·ven·tion·al·i·ty** \-,ven(t)-shə-'na-lə-tē\ *noun, plural* **-ties** (circa 1834)
**1 :** a conventional usage, practice, or thing
**2 :** the quality or state of being conventional; *especially* **:** adherence to conventions
**con·ven·tion·eer** \kən-,ven(t)-shə-'nir\ *noun* (1926)
**:** a person attending a convention
**¹con·ven·tu·al** \kən-'ven-chə-wəl, kän-, -'vench-wəl\ *adjective* [Middle English, from Middle French or Medieval Latin; Middle French, from Medieval Latin *conventualis*, from *conventus* convent] (15th century)
**1 :** of, relating to, or befitting a convent or monastic life **:** MONASTIC
**2** *capitalized* **:** of or relating to the Conventuals
— **con·ven·tu·al·ly** *adverb*
**²conventual** *noun* (1533)
**1** *capitalized* **:** a member of the Order of Friars Minor Conventual forming a branch of the first order of Saint Francis of Assisi under a mitigated rule
**2 :** a member of a conventual community
**con·verge** \kən-'vərj\ *verb* **con·verged; con·verg·ing** [Late Latin *convergere*, from

Latin *com-* + *vergere* to bend, incline — more at WRENCH] (1691)
*intransitive verb*
**1 :** to tend or move toward one point or one another **:** come together **:** MEET
**2 :** to come together and unite in a common interest or focus
**3 :** to approach a limit as the number of terms increases without limit
*transitive verb*
**:** to cause to converge
**con·ver·gence** \kən-'vər-jən(t)s\ *noun* (1713)
**1 :** the act of converging and especially moving toward union or uniformity; *especially* **:** coordinated movement of the two eyes so that the image of a single point is formed on corresponding retinal areas
**2 :** the state or property of being convergent
**3 :** independent development of similar characters (as of bodily structure or cultural traits) often associated with similarity of habits or environment
**con·ver·gen·cy** \-jən(t)-sē\ *noun* (1709)
**:** CONVERGENCE
**con·ver·gent** \-jənt\ *adjective* (circa 1751)
**1 :** tending to move toward one point or to approach each other **:** CONVERGING ⟨*convergent* lines⟩
**2 :** exhibiting convergence in form, function, or development ⟨*convergent* evolution⟩
**3 a** *of an improper integral* **:** having a value that is a real number **b :** characterized by having the *n*th term or the sum of the first *n* terms approach a finite limit ⟨a *convergent* sequence⟩ ⟨a *convergent* series⟩
**converging lens** *noun* (1860)
**:** a lens that causes parallel rays (as of light) to come to a focus
**con·vers·able** \kən-'vər-sə-bəl\ *adjective* (circa 1631)
**1** *archaic* **:** relating to or suitable for social interaction
**2 :** pleasant and easy to converse with
**con·ver·sance** \kən-'vər-s°n(t)s *also* 'kän-vər-sən(t)s\ *noun* (1609)
**:** the quality or state of being conversant
**con·ver·san·cy** \-s°n(t)-sē, -sən(t)-\ *noun* (1798)
**:** CONVERSANCE
**con·ver·sant** \kən-'vər-s°nt *also* 'kän-vər-sənt\ *adjective* (14th century)
**1** *archaic* **:** having frequent or familiar association
**2** *archaic* **:** CONCERNED, OCCUPIED
**3 :** having knowledge or experience — used with *with*
**con·ver·sa·tion** \,kän-vər-'sā-shən\ *noun* [Middle English *conversacioun*, from Middle French *conversation*, from Latin *conversation-, conversatio*, from *conversari* to associate with, frequentative of *convertere* to turn around] (14th century)
**1** *obsolete* **:** CONDUCT, BEHAVIOR
**2 a (1) :** oral exchange of sentiments, observations, opinions, or ideas **(2) :** an instance of such exchange **:** TALK **b :** an informal discussion of an issue by representatives of governments, institutions, or groups **c :** an exchange similar to conversation
— **con·ver·sa·tion·al** \-shnəl, -shə-n°l\ *adjective*
— **con·ver·sa·tion·al·ly** *adverb*
**con·ver·sa·tion·al·ist** \-shnə-list, -shə-n°l-ist\ *noun* (1836)
**:** one who converses a great deal or who excels in conversation
**conversation piece** *noun* (1712)
**1 :** a painting of a group of persons in their customary surroundings
**2 :** something (as a novel or unusual object) that stimulates conversation
**con·ver·sa·zi·o·ne** \,kän-vər-,sät-sē-'ō-nē, ,kōn-\ *noun, plural* **-o·nes** *or* **-o·ni** \-'ō-(,)nē\ [Italian, literally, conversation, from Latin *conversation-, conversatio*] (1739)

: a meeting for conversation especially about art, literature, or science

**¹con·verse** \'kän-ˌvərs\ *noun* (15th century)
**1** *obsolete* : social interaction
**2** : CONVERSATION

**²con·verse** \kən-'vərs\ *intransitive verb* **con·versed; con·vers·ing** [Middle English, to live (with), from Middle French *converser,* from Latin *conversari*] (1586)
**1** *archaic* **a** : to become occupied or engaged **b** : to have acquaintance or familiarity
**2 a** : to exchange thoughts and opinions in speech : TALK **b** : to carry on an exchange similar to a conversation (as with a computer)
— **con·vers·er** \-'vər-sər\ *noun*

**³con·verse** \'kän-ˌvərs\ *noun* [Latin *conversus,* past participle of *convertere*] (1570)
: something reversed in order, relation, or action: as **a** : a theorem formed by interchanging the hypothesis and conclusion of a given theorem **b** : a proposition obtained by interchange of the subject and predicate of a given proposition ⟨"no *P* is *S*" is the *converse* of "no *S* is *P*"⟩

**⁴con·verse** \kən-'vərs, 'kän-ˌ\ *adjective* (1794)
**1** : reversed in order, relation, or action
**2** : being a logical or mathematical converse ⟨the *converse* theorem⟩
— **con·verse·ly** *adverb*

**con·ver·sion** \kən-'vər-zhən, -shən\ *noun* [Middle English, from Middle French, from Latin *conversion-, conversio,* from *convertere*] (14th century)
**1** : the act of converting : the process of being converted — compare GENE CONVERSION
**2** : an experience associated with a definite and decisive adoption of religion
**3 a** : the operation of finding a converse in logic or mathematics **b** : reduction of a mathematical expression by clearing of fractions
**4** : a successful try for point or free throw
**5** : something converted from one use to another
— **con·ver·sion·al** \-'vərzh-nəl; -'vər-zhə-, -'vər-shnəl, -shə-nᵊl\ *adjective*

**conversion reaction** *noun* (1945)
: a psychoneurosis in which bodily symptoms (as paralysis of the limbs) appear without physical basis — called also *conversion hysteria*

**¹con·vert** \kən-'vərt\ *verb* [Middle English, from Middle French *convertir,* from Latin *convertere* to turn around, transform, convert, from *com-* + *vertere* to turn — more at WORTH] (14th century)
*transitive verb*
**1 a** : to bring over from one belief, view, or party to another **b** : to bring about a religious conversion in
**2 a** : to alter the physical or chemical nature or properties of especially in manufacturing **b** (1) : to change from one form or function to another (2) : to alter for more effective utilization (3) : to appropriate without right **c** : to exchange for an equivalent
**3** *obsolete* : TURN
**4** : to subject to logical conversion
**5 a** : to make a goal after receiving (a pass) from a teammate **b** : to score on (as a try for point or free throw) **c** : to make (a spare) in bowling
*intransitive verb*
**1** : to undergo conversion
**2** : to make good on a try for point, field goal, or free throw
*synonym* see TRANSFORM

**²con·vert** \'kän-ˌvərt\ *noun* (1561)
: one that is converted

**con·vert·er** \kən-'vər-tər\ *noun* (1533)
: one that converts: as **a** : the furnace used in the Bessemer process **b** *or* **con·ver·tor** \-'vər-tər\ : a device employing mechanical rotation for changing electrical energy from one form to another (as from direct current to alternating current or vice versa); *also* : a radio

device for converting one frequency to another **c** : a device for adapting a television or radio receiver to receive channels or frequencies for which it was not originally designed ⟨a cable *converter*⟩ ⟨FM *converter*⟩ **d** : a device that accepts data in one form and converts it to another ⟨analog-digital *converter*⟩ **e** : CATALYTIC CONVERTER

**¹con·vert·ible** \kən-'vər-tə-bəl\ *adjective* (14th century)
**1** : capable of being converted
**2** : having a top that may be lowered or removed ⟨*convertible* coupe⟩
**3** : capable of being exchanged for a specified equivalent (as another currency or security) ⟨a bond *convertible* to 12 shares of common stock⟩
— **con·vert·ibil·i·ty** \-ˌvər-tə-'bi-lə-tē\ *noun*
— **con·vert·ible·ness** \-'vər-tə-bəl-nəs\ *noun*
— **con·vert·ibly** \-blē\ *adverb*

**²convertible** *noun* (1615)
: something convertible; *especially* : a convertible automobile

**con·verti·plane** *also* **con·verta·plane** \kən-'vər-tə-ˌplān\ *noun* (1949)
: an aircraft that takes off and lands like a helicopter and is convertible to a fixed-wing configuration for forward flight

**con·vex** \kän-'veks; 'kän-ˌ, kən-'\ *adjective* [Middle French or Latin; Middle French *convexe,* from Latin *convexus* vaulted, concave, convex, from *com-* + *-vexus;* perhaps akin to Latin *vehere* to carry — more at WAY] (1571)
**1 a** : curved or rounded like the exterior of a sphere or circle **b** : being a continuous function or part of a continuous function with the property that a line joining any two points on its graph lies on or above the graph
**2 a** *of a set of points* : containing all points in a line joining any two constituent points **b** *of a geometric figure* : comprising a convex set when combined with its interior ⟨a *convex* polygon⟩

**con·vex·i·ty** \kän-'vek-sət-ē, kän-\ *noun, plural* **-ties** (1599)
**1** : the quality or state of being convex
**2** : a convex surface or part

**con·vexo–con·cave** \kən-ˌvek-(ˌ)sō-kän-'kāv, kän-ˌvek-, -'kän-ˌkāv\ *adjective* (1693)
**1** : CONCAVO-CONVEX
**2** : having the convex side of greater curvature than the concave

**con·vey** \kən-'vā\ *transitive verb* **con·veyed; con·vey·ing** [Middle English, from Middle French *conveier* to accompany, escort, from (assumed) Vulgar Latin *conviare,* from Latin *com-* + *via* way — more at WAY] (14th century)
**1** *obsolete* : LEAD, CONDUCT
**2 a** : to bear from one place to another; *especially* : to move in a continuous stream or mass **b** : to impart or communicate by statement, suggestion, gesture, or appearance **c** (1) *archaic* : STEAL (2) *obsolete* : to carry away secretly **d** : to transfer or deliver to another especially by a sealed writing **e** : to cause to pass from one place or person to another

**con·vey·ance** \kən-'vā-ən(t)s\ *noun* (15th century)
**1** : the action of conveying
**2** : a means or way of conveying: as **a** : an instrument by which title to property is conveyed **b** : a means of transport : VEHICLE

**con·vey·anc·er** \-ən(t)-sər\ *noun* (1650)
: one whose business is conveyancing

**con·vey·anc·ing** \-ən(t)-siŋ\ *noun* (1714)
: the act or business of drawing deeds, leases, or other writings for transferring the title to property

**con·vey·or** *also* **con·vey·er** \kən-'vā-ər\ *noun* (circa 1514)
: one that conveys: as **a** : a person who transfers property **b** *usually* **conveyor** : a mechanical apparatus for moving articles or bulk mate-

rial from place to place (as by an endless moving belt or a chain of receptacles)

**con·vey·or·ise** *British variant of* CONVEYORIZE

**con·vey·or·ize** \-ə-ˌrīz\ *transitive verb* **-ized; -iz·ing** (1941)
: to equip with a conveyor
— **con·vey·or·i·za·tion** \-ˌvā-ə-rə-'zā-shən\ *noun*

**¹con·vict** \kən-'vikt\ *adjective* (14th century) *archaic*
: having been convicted

**²con·vict** \kən-'vikt\ *transitive verb* [Middle English, from Latin *convictus,* past participle of *convincere* to refute, convict] (14th century)
**1** : to find or prove to be guilty
**2** : to convince of error or sinfulness

**³con·vict** \'kän-ˌvikt\ *noun* (15th century)
**1** : a person convicted of and under sentence for a crime
**2** : a person serving a usually long prison sentence

**con·vic·tion** \kən-'vik-shən\ *noun* (15th century)
**1** : the act or process of convicting of a crime especially in a court of law
**2 a** : the act of convincing a person of error or of compelling the admission of a truth **b** : the state of being convinced of error or compelled to admit the truth
**3 a** : a strong persuasion or belief **b** : the state of being convinced
*synonym* see CERTAINTY, OPINION

**con·vince** \kən-'vin(t)s\ *transitive verb* **con·vinced; con·vinc·ing** [Latin *convincere* to refute, convict, prove, from *com-* + *vincere* to conquer — more at VICTOR] (1530)
**1** *obsolete* **a** : to overcome by argument **b** : OVERPOWER, OVERCOME
**2** *obsolete* : DEMONSTRATE, PROVE
**3** : to bring (as by argument) to belief, consent, or a course of action : PERSUADE ⟨*convinced* himself that he was all right —William Faulkner⟩ ⟨something I could never *convince* him to read —John Lahr⟩
— **con·vinc·er** *noun*

**con·vinc·ing** \kən-'vin(t)-siŋ\ *adjective* (1624)
**1** : satisfying or assuring by argument or proof ⟨a *convincing* test of a new product⟩
**2** : having power to convince of the truth, rightness, or reality of something : PLAUSIBLE ⟨told a *convincing* story⟩
*synonym* see VALID
— **con·vinc·ing·ly** \-siŋ-lē\ *adverb*
— **con·vinc·ing·ness** *noun*

**con·viv·ial** \kən-'viv-yəl, -'vi-vē-əl\ *adjective* [Late Latin *convivialis,* from Latin *convivium* banquet, from *com-* + *vivere* to live — more at QUICK] (circa 1668)
: relating to, occupied with, or fond of feasting, drinking, and good company
— **con·viv·i·al·i·ty** \-ˌvi-vē-'a-lə-tē\ *noun*
— **con·viv·ial·ly** \-'viv-yə-lē, -'vi-vē-ə-lē\ *adverb*

**con·vo·ca·tion** \ˌkän-və-'kā-shən\ *noun* [Middle English, from Middle French, from Latin *convocation-, convocatio,* from *convocare*] (14th century)
**1 a** : an assembly of persons convoked **b** (1) : an assembly of bishops and representative clergy of the Church of England (2) : a consultative assembly of clergy and lay delegates from one part of an Episcopal diocese; *also* **c** : a territorial division of an Episcopal diocese **c** : a ceremonial assembly of members of a college or university
**2** : the act or process of convoking
— **con·vo·ca·tion·al** \-shnəl, -shə-nᵊl\ *adjective*

---

\ə\ abut \ᵊ\ kitten \ər\ further \a\ ash \ā\ ace \ä\ mop, mar \aů\ out \ch\ chin \e\ bet \ē\ easy \g\ go \i\ hit \ī\ ice \j\ job \ŋ\ sing \ō\ go \ò\ law \òi\ boy \th\ thin \t͟h\ the \ü\ loot \ů\ foot \y\ yet \zh\ vision *see also* Guide to Pronunciation

**con·voke** \kən-'vōk\ *transitive verb* **con·voked; con·vok·ing** [Middle French *convoquer,* from Latin *convocare,* from *com-* + *vocare* to call, from *voc-, vox* voice — more at VOICE] (1598)
: to call together to a meeting
**synonym** see SUMMON

**con·vo·lute** \'kän-və-ˌlüt\ *verb* **-lut·ed; -lut·ing** [Latin *convolutus,* past participle of *convolvere*] (1698)
: TWIST, COIL

**con·vo·lut·ed** \-ˌlü-təd\ *adjective* (1766)
**1** : having convolutions
**2** : INVOLVED, INTRICATE

**convoluted tubule** *noun* (1923)
: all or part of the coiled sections of a nephron: **a** : PROXIMAL CONVOLUTED TUBULE **b** : DISTAL CONVOLUTED TUBULE

**con·vo·lu·tion** \ˌkän-və-'lü-shən\ *noun* (1545)
**1** : a form or shape that is folded in curved or tortuous windings
**2** : one of the irregular ridges on the surface of the brain and especially of the cerebrum of higher mammals
**3** : a complication or intricacy of form, design, or structure

**con·volve** \kən-'välv, -'vȯlv *also* -'väv *or* -'vȯv\ *verb* **con·volved; con·volv·ing** [Latin *convolvere,* from *com-* + *volvere* to roll — more at VOLUBLE] (1650)
*transitive verb*
: to roll together : WRITHE
*intransitive verb*
: to roll together or circulate involvedly

**con·vol·vu·lus** \kən-'väl-vyə-ləs, -'vȯl- *also* -'väv-yə- *or* -'vȯv-yə-\ *noun, plural* **-lus·es** *or* **-li** \-ˌlī, -ˌlē\ [New Latin, from Latin *convolvere*] (1548)
: any of a genus (*Convolvulus*) of erect, trailing, or twining herbs and shrubs of the morning-glory family

**¹con·voy** \'kän-ˌvȯi, kən-'\ *transitive verb* [Middle English, from Middle French *conveier, convoier* — more at CONVEY] (14th century)
: ACCOMPANY; *especially* : to escort for protection

**²con·voy** \'kän-ˌvȯi\ *noun* (1523)
**1** : one that convoys; *especially* : a protective escort (as for ships)
**2** : the act of convoying
**3** : a group convoyed or organized for convenience or protection in moving

**con·vul·sant** \kən-'vəl-sənt\ *adjective* (1875)
: causing convulsions : CONVULSIVE 1a
— **convulsant** *noun*

**con·vulse** \kən-'vəls\ *verb* **con·vulsed; con·vuls·ing** [Latin *convulsus,* past participle of *convellere* to pluck up, convulse, from *com-* + *vellere* to pluck — more at VULNERABLE] (1643)
*transitive verb*
: to shake or agitate violently; *especially* : to shake with or as if with irregular spasms
*intransitive verb*
: to become affected with convulsions
**synonym** see SHAKE

**con·vul·sion** \kən-'vəl-shən\ *noun* (1547)
**1** : an abnormal violent and involuntary contraction or series of contractions of the muscles
**2 a** : a violent disturbance **b** : an uncontrolled fit : PAROXYSM
— **con·vul·sion·ary** \-shə-ˌner-ē\ *adjective*

**con·vul·sive** \kən-'vəl-siv\ *adjective* (1615)
**1 a** : constituting or producing a convulsion **b** : attended or affected with convulsions
**2** : resembling a convulsion in being violent, sudden, frantic, or spasmodic
**synonym** see FITFUL
— **con·vul·sive·ly** *adverb*
— **con·vul·sive·ness** *noun*

**cony** *variant of* CONEY

**coo** \'kü\ *intransitive verb* [imitative] (1670)
**1** : to make the low soft cry of a dove or pigeon or a similar sound

**2** : to talk fondly, amorously, or appreciatively (an album that will be *cooed* over by condescending classical music critics —Ellen Sander)
— **coo** *noun*

**¹cook** \'kùk\ *noun* [Middle English, from Old English *cōc,* from Latin *coquus,* from *coquere* to cook; akin to Old English *āfigen* fried, Greek *pessein* to cook] (before 12th century)
**1** : a person who prepares food for eating
**2** : a technical or industrial process comparable to cooking food; *also* : a substance so processed

**²cook** (14th century)
*intransitive verb*
**1** : to prepare food for eating by means of heat
**2** : to undergo the action of being cooked (the rice is *cooking* now)
**3** : OCCUR, HAPPEN (find out what was *cooking* in the committee)
**4** : to perform, do, or proceed well (the jazz quartet was *cooking* along) (the party *cooked* right through the night)
*transitive verb*
**1** : CONCOCT, FABRICATE — usually used with *up* (*cooked* up a scheme)
**2** : to prepare for eating by a heating process
**3** : FALSIFY, DOCTOR (*cooked* the books with phony spending cuts and accounting gimmickry —Colleen O'Connor)
**4** : to subject to the action of heat or fire
— **cook·able** \'kù-kə-bəl\ *adjective*
— **cook one's goose** : to ruin one irretrievably

**¹cook·book** \-ˌbùk\ *noun* (1809)
: a book of cooking directions and recipes; *broadly* : a book of detailed instructions

**²cookbook** *adjective* (1944)
: involving or using step-by-step procedures whose rationale is usually not explained (a *cookbook* approach)

**cook cheese** *noun* (1941)
: an unripened cheese made from curd that has been cooked to a soft consistency — called also *cooked cheese*

**cook·er** \'kù-kər\ *noun* (1869)
: one that cooks: as **a** : a utensil, device, or apparatus for cooking **b** : a person who tends a cooking process : COOK **c** *British* : STOVE

**cook·ery** \'kù-k(ə-)rē\ *noun, plural* **-er·ies** (14th century)
**1** : the art or practice of cooking
**2** : an establishment for cooking

**cookery book** *noun* (1639)
*chiefly British* : COOKBOOK

**cook·house** \'kùk-ˌhaùs\ *noun* (1795)
: a building for cooking

**cook·ie** *or* **cooky** \'kù-kē\ *noun, plural* **cook·ies** [Dutch *koekje,* diminutive of *koek* cake] (1703)
**1** : a small flat or slightly raised cake
**2 a** : an attractive woman (a buxom French *cookie* who haunts the . . . colony's one night spot —*Newsweek*) **b** : PERSON, GUY (a tough *cookie*)

**cookie–cutter** *adjective* (1963)
: marked by lack of originality or distinction (*cookie-cutter* shopping malls)

**cookie cutter** *noun* (1903)
: a device used to cut rolled cookie dough into shapes before baking

**cookie sheet** *noun* (1926)
: a flat rectangle of metal with at least one rolled edge used especially for the baking of cookies or biscuits

**cooking** *adjective* (circa 1813)
: suitable for or used in cooking (*cooking* apples)

**cook–off** \'kùk-ˌȯf, -ˌäf\ *noun* (1937)
: a cooking competition

**cook off** *intransitive verb* (1945)
*of a cartridge* : to fire as a result of overheating

**cook·out** \'kùk-ˌaùt\ *noun* (1947)
: an outing at which a meal is cooked and served in the open; *also* : the meal cooked

**cook·shack** \-ˌshak\ *noun* (1909)
: a shack used for cooking

**cook·shop** \-ˌshäp\ *noun* (circa 1552)
: a shop supplying or serving cooked food

**Cook's tour** \'kùks-\ *noun* [Thomas *Cook* & Son, English travel agency] (circa 1909)
: a rapid or cursory survey or review

**cook·stove** \'kùk-ˌstōv\ *noun* (1824)
: a stove for cooking

**cook·top** \'kùk-ˌtäp\ *noun* (1948)
**1** : the flat top of a range
**2** : a built-in cabinet-top cooking apparatus containing usually four heating units

**cook·ware** \'kùk-ˌwar, -ˌwer\ *noun* (1953)
: utensils used in cooking

**¹cool** \'kül\ *adjective* [Middle English *col,* from Old English *cōl;* akin to Old High German *kuoli* cool, Old English *ceald* cold — more at COLD] (before 12th century)
**1** : moderately cold : lacking in warmth
**2 a** : marked by steady dispassionate calmness and self-control (a *cool* and calculating administrator —*Current Biography*) **b** : lacking ardor or friendliness (a *cool* impersonal manner) **c** *of jazz* : marked by restrained emotion and the frequent use of counterpoint **d** : free from tensions or violence (meeting with minority groups in an attempt to keep the city *cool*)
**3** — used as an intensive (a *cool* million dollars)
**4** : marked by deliberate effrontery or lack of due respect or discretion (a *cool* reply)
**5** : facilitating or suggesting relief from heat (a *cool* dress)
**6 a** *of a color* : producing an impression of being cool; *specifically* : of a hue in the range violet through blue to green **b** *of a musical tone* : relatively lacking in timbre or resonance
**7** *slang* **a** : very good : EXCELLENT; *also* : ALL RIGHT **b** : FASHIONABLE 1 ☆
— **cool·ish** \'kü-lish\ *adjective*
— **cool·ly** *also* **cooly** \'kü(l)-lē\ *adverb*
— **cool·ness** \'kül-nəs\ *noun*

**²cool** (before 12th century)
*intransitive verb*
**1** : to become cool : lose heat or warmth (placed the pie in the window to *cool*) — sometimes used with *off* or *down*
**2** : to lose ardor or passion (his anger *cooled*)
*transitive verb*
**1** : to make cool : impart a feeling of coolness to (*cooled* the room with a fan) — often used with *off* or *down* (a swim *cooled* us off a little)
**2 a** : to moderate the heat, excitement, or force of : CALM (*cooled* her growing anger)
**b** : to slow or lessen the growth or activity of — usually used with *off* or *down* (wants to *cool* off the economy without freezing it —*Newsweek*)

---

☆ SYNONYMS
**Cool, composed, collected, unruffled, imperturbable, nonchalant** mean free from agitation or excitement. COOL may imply calmness, deliberateness, or dispassionateness (kept a *cool* head). COMPOSED implies freedom from agitation as a result of self-discipline or a sedate disposition (the *composed* pianist gave a flawless concert). COLLECTED implies a concentration of mind that eliminates distractions especially in moments of crisis (the nurse stayed calm and *collected*). UNRUFFLED suggests apparent serenity and poise in the face of setbacks or in the midst of excitement (harried but *unruffled*). IMPERTURBABLE implies coolness or assurance even under severe provocation (the speaker remained *imperturbable* despite the heckling). NONCHALANT stresses an easy coolness of manner or casualness that suggests indifference or unconcern (a *nonchalant* driver).

**— cool it :** to calm down **:** go easy ⟨the word went out to the young to *cool it* —W. M. Young⟩

**— cool one's heels :** to wait or be kept waiting for a long time especially from or as if from disdain or discourtesy

³**cool** *noun* (15th century)
**1 :** a cool time, place, or situation ⟨the *cool* of the evening⟩
**2 a :** absence of excitement or emotional involvement **:** DETACHMENT ⟨must surrender his fine *cool* and enter the closed crazy world of suicide —Wilfrid Sheed⟩ **b :** POISE, COMPOSURE ⟨press questions . . . seemed to rattle him and he lost his *cool* —*New Republic*⟩

⁴**cool** *adverb* (1951)
**:** in a casual and nonchalant manner ⟨play it *cool*⟩

**cool·ant** \'kü-lənt\ *noun* (1926)
**:** a usually fluid cooling agent

**cool·down** \'kül-,daùn\ *noun* (1980)
**:** the act or an instance of allowing physiological activity to return to normal gradually after strenuous exercise by engaging in less strenuous exercise

**cool·er** \'kü-lər\ *noun* (1575)
**1 :** one that cools: as **a :** a container for cooling liquids **b :** REFRIGERATOR
**2 :** LOCKUP, JAIL; *especially* **:** a cell for violent or unmanageable prisoners
**3 :** an iced drink usually with an alcoholic beverage as a base

**Coo·ley's anemia** \'kü-lēz-\ *noun* [Thomas B. *Cooley* (died 1945) American pediatrician] (circa 1935)
**:** a severe thalassemic anemia that is associated with the presence of microcytes, enlargement of the liver and spleen, increase in the erythroid bone marrow, and jaundice and that occurs especially in children of Mediterranean parents

**cool·head·ed** \'kül-,he-dəd\ *adjective* (1777)
**:** not easily excited

**coo·lie** \'kü-lē\ *noun* [Hindi *kulī*] (1638)
**:** an unskilled laborer or porter usually in or from the Far East hired for low or subsistence wages

**coolie hat** *noun* (1924)
**:** a conical-shaped usually straw hat worn especially to protect the head from the heat of the sun

**cool·ing-off** \'kü-liŋ-'òf\ *adjective* (1926)
**:** designed to allow passions to cool or to permit negotiation between parties ⟨a *cooling-off* period⟩

**cooling tower** *noun* (1901)
**:** a structure over which circulated water is trickled to reduce its temperature by partial evaporation

**coombe** *or* **coomb** \'küm\ *variant of* COMBE

**coon** \'kün\ *noun* (1742)
**1 :** RACCOON
**2 :** BLACK 4 — usually taken to be offensive

**coon·can** \'kün-,kan\ *noun* [by folk etymology from Mexican Spanish *conquián* conquian, from Spanish *¿con quién?* with whom?] (1889)
**:** a game of rummy played with two packs including two jokers

**coon cat** *noun* (1901)
**:** MAINE COON

**coon cheese** \'kün-\ *noun* [probably from *coon* (black person); from the color of the coating] (1953)
**:** a sharp cheddar cheese that has been cured at higher than usual temperature and humidity and that is usually coated with black wax

**coon·hound** \'kün-,haùnd\ *noun* (1920)
**:** a sporting dog trained to hunt raccoons; *especially* **:** BLACK-AND-TAN COONHOUND

**coon's age** *noun* (1844)
**:** a long while ⟨best fried chicken I've tasted for a *coon's age* —Sinclair Lewis⟩

**coon·skin** \'kün-,skin\ *noun* (1818)
**1 :** the skin or pelt of the raccoon

**2 :** an article (as a cap or coat) made of coonskin

**coon·tie** \'kün-tē\ *noun* [Creek (Florida dialect) *kuntí*] (1791)
**:** any of several tropical American woody plants (genus *Zamia*) of the cycad family whose roots and stems yield a starchy foodstuff — called also *arrowroot*

¹**coop** \'küp, 'kùp\ *noun* [Middle English *cupe*; akin to Old English *cȳpe* basket] (14th century)
**1 :** a cage or small enclosure (as for poultry); *also* **:** a small building for housing poultry
**2 a :** a confined area **b :** JAIL

²**coop** *transitive verb* (1583)
**1 :** to confine in a restricted and often crowded area — usually used with *up*
**2 :** to place or keep in a coop **:** PEN — often used with *up*

**co–op** \'kō-,äp, kō-'\ *noun* (1869)
**:** COOPERATIVE

¹**coo·per** \'kü-pər, 'kù-\ *noun* [Middle English *couper, cowper*, from Middle Dutch *cūper* (from *cūpe* cask) or Middle Low German *kūper*, from *kūpe* cask; akin to Middle Dutch *cūpe* & Middle Low German *kūpe*, from Latin *cupa*; akin to Greek *kypellon* cup — more at HIVE] (14th century)
**:** one that makes or repairs wooden casks or tubs

²**cooper** *verb* **coo·pered; coo·per·ing** \'kü-p(ə-)riŋ, 'kù-\ (1742)
*transitive verb*
**:** to work as a cooper on
*intransitive verb*
**:** to work at or do coopering

**coo·per·age** \'kü-p(ə-)rij, 'kù-\ *noun* (1705)
**1 :** a cooper's work or products
**2 :** a cooper's place of business

**co·op·er·ate** \kō-'ä-pə-,rāt\ *intransitive verb* [Late Latin *cooperatus*, past participle of *cooperari*, from Latin *co-* + *operari* to work — more at OPERATE] (1582)
**1 :** to act or work with another or others **:** act together
**2 :** to associate with another or others for mutual benefit
**— co·op·er·a·tor** \-,rā-tər\ *noun*

**co·op·er·a·tion** \(,)kō-,ä-pə-'rā-shən\ *noun* (14th century)
**1 :** the action of cooperating **:** common effort
**2 :** association of persons for common benefit
**— co·op·er·a·tion·ist** \-sh(ə-)nist\ *noun*

¹**co·op·er·a·tive** \kō-'ä-p(ə-)rə-tiv, -'ä-pə-,rā-\ *adjective* (1603)
**1 a :** marked by cooperation ⟨*cooperative* efforts⟩ **b :** marked by a willingness and ability to work with others ⟨*cooperative* neighbors⟩
**2 :** of, relating to, or organized as a cooperative
**3 :** relating to or comprising a program of combined liberal arts and technical studies at different schools
**— co·op·er·a·tive·ly** *adverb*
**— co·op·er·a·tive·ness** *noun*

²**cooperative** *noun* (1883)
**:** an enterprise or organization owned by and operated for the benefit of those using its services

**Coo·per's hawk** \'kü-pərz-, 'kù-\ *noun* [William *Cooper* (died 1864) American naturalist] (1828)
**:** an American hawk (*Accipiter cooperii*) that is larger than the similarly colored sharp-shinned hawk and has a more rounded tail

**co–opt** \kō-'äpt\ *transitive verb* [Latin *cooptare*, from *co-* + *optare* to choose] (1651)
**1 a :** to choose or elect as a member **b :** to appoint as a colleague or assistant
**2 a :** to take into a group (as a faction, movement, or culture) **:** ABSORB, ASSIMILATE ⟨the students are *co-opted* by a system they serve even in their struggle against it —A. C. Danto⟩ **b :** TAKE OVER, APPROPRIATE
**— co–op·ta·tion** \,kō-,äp-'tā-shən\ *noun*
**— co–op·ta·tive** \kō-'äp-tə-tiv\ *adjective*

**— co–op·tion** \-'äp-shən\ *noun*
**— co–op·tive** \-'äp-tiv\ *adjective*

¹**co·or·di·nate** \kō-'órd-nət; -'òr-d°n-ət, -də-,nāt\ *adjective* [probably back-formation from *coordination*] (1641)
**1 a :** equal in rank, quality, or significance **b :** being of equal rank in a sentence ⟨*coordinate* clauses⟩
**2 :** relating to or marked by coordination
**3 a :** being a university that awards degrees to men and women taught usually by the same faculty but attending separate classes often on separate campuses **b :** being one of the colleges and especially the women's branch of a coordinate university
**4 :** of, relating to, or being a system of indexing by two or more terms so that documents may be retrieved through the intersection of index terms
**— co·or·di·nate·ly** *adverb*
**— co·or·di·nate·ness** *noun*

²**co·or·di·nate** \kō-'òr-d°n-,āt\ *verb* **-nat·ed; -nat·ing** (1665)
*transitive verb*
**1 :** to put in the same order or rank
**2 :** to bring into a common action, movement, or condition **:** HARMONIZE
**3 :** to attach so as to form a coordination complex
*intransitive verb*
**1 :** to be or become coordinate especially so as to act together in a smooth concerted way
**2 :** to combine by means of a coordinate bond
**— co·or·di·na·tive** \kō-'òrd-nə-tiv; -'òr-d°n-ə-tiv, -də-,nā-\ *adjective*
**— co·or·di·na·tor** \-'òr-də-,nā-tər\ *noun*

³**co·or·di·nate** \*same as* ¹\ *noun* (circa 1823)
**1 a :** any of a set of numbers used in specifying the location of a point on a line, on a surface, or in space **b :** any one of a set of variables used in specifying the state of a substance or the motion of a particle or momentum
**2 :** one who is of equal rank, authority, or importance with another
**3** *plural* **:** articles (as of clothing) designed to be used together and to attain their effect through pleasing contrast (as of color, material, or texture)

**coordinate bond** *noun* (1947)
**:** a covalent bond that consists of a pair of electrons supplied by only one of the two atoms it joins

**co·or·di·nat·ed** \-'òr-də-,nā-təd\ *adjective* (1939)
**:** able to use more than one set of muscle movements to a single end ⟨a well-*coordinated* athlete⟩

**Coordinated Universal Time** *noun* (1969)
**:** the international standard of time that is kept by atomic clocks around the world — abbreviation *UTC*

**coordinate geometry** *noun* (1855)
**:** ANALYTIC GEOMETRY

**coordinating conjunction** *noun* (1916)
**:** a conjunction that joins together words or word groups of equal grammatical rank

**co·or·di·na·tion** \(,)kō-,òr-də-'nā-shən\ *noun* [Late Latin *coordination-, coordinatio*, from Latin *co-* + *ordination-, ordinatio* arrangement, from *ordinare* to arrange — more at ORDAIN] (circa 1643)
**1 :** the act or action of coordinating
**2 :** the harmonious functioning of parts for effective results

**coordination complex** *noun* (1951)
**:** a compound or ion with a central usually metallic atom or ion combined by coordinate bonds with a definite number of surrounding

ions, groups, or molecules — called also *co-ordination compound*

**coordination number** *noun* (1908)
**1** : the number of attachments to the central atom in a coordination complex
**2** : a number used in specifying the spatial arrangement of the constituent groups of crystals

**coot** \'küt\ *noun* [Middle English *coote*; akin to Dutch *koet* coot] (15th century)
**1** : any of various sluggish slow-flying slaty-black birds (genus *Fulica*) of the rail family that somewhat resemble ducks and have lobed toes and the upper mandible prolonged on the forehead as a horny frontal shield
**2** : any of several North American scoters
**3** : a harmless simple person; *broadly* : FELLOW 4c

**coo·ter** \'kü-tər *also* 'ku̇-tə\ *noun* [of African origin; akin to Bambara & Malinke *kuta* turtle] (1832)
*chiefly Southern* : any of several turtles (genus *Pseudemys* and especially *P. concinna*) especially of the southern and eastern U.S.

**coo·tie** \'kü-tē\ *noun* [perhaps modification of Malay *kutu*] (1917)
: BODY LOUSE

**¹cop** \'käp\ *noun* [Middle English, from Old English *copp*] (before 12th century)
**1** *dialect chiefly English* : TOP, CREST
**2** : a cylindrical or conical mass of thread, yarn, or roving wound on a quill or tube; *also* : a quill or tube upon which it is wound

**²cop** *transitive verb* **copped; cop·ping** [perhaps from Dutch *kapen* to steal, from Frisian *kāpia* to take away; akin to Old High German *kouf* trade — more at CHEAP] (1704)
**1** *slang* : to get hold of : CATCH, CAPTURE; *also* : PURCHASE
**2** *slang* : STEAL, SWIPE
— **cop a plea** : to plead guilty to a lesser charge in order to avoid standing trial for a more serious one; *broadly* : to admit fault and plead for mercy

**³cop** *noun* [short for ³*copper*] (1859)
: POLICE OFFICER

**co·pa·cet·ic** *or* **co·pe·set·ic** *also* **co·pa·set·ic** \,kō-pə-'se-tik\ *adjective* [origin unknown] (1919)
: very satisfactory

**co·pai·ba** \kō-'pī-bə, -'pā-\ *noun* [Spanish & Portuguese; Spanish, from Portuguese *copaíba*, from Tupi] (1712)
: a stimulant oleoresin obtained from several pinnate-leaved South American leguminous trees (genus *Copaifera*); *also* : one of these trees

**co·pal** \'kō-pəl, -,pal; kō-'pal\ *noun* [Spanish, from Nahuatl *copalli* resin] (1577)
: a recent or fossil resin from various tropical trees

**co·par·ce·nary** \kō-'pär-s°n-,er-ē\ *noun*, *plural* **-nar·ies** (circa 1504)
**1** : joint heirship
**2** : joint ownership

**co·par·ce·ner** \-'pärs-nər, -'pär-s°n-ər\ *noun* (15th century)
: a joint heir

**co–pay·ment** \'kō-,pā-mənt, ,kō-'\ *noun* (1975)
: a relatively small fixed fee required by a health insurer (as an HMO) to be paid by the patient at the time of each office visit, outpatient service, or filling of a prescription

**¹cope** \'kōp\ *noun* [Middle English, from Old English -*cāp*, from Late Latin *cappa* head covering] (13th century)
**1** : a long enveloping ecclesiastical vestment
**2 a** : something resembling a cope (as by concealing or covering) ⟨the dark sky's starry cope —P. B. Shelley⟩ **b** : COPING

**²cope** *transitive verb* **coped; cop·ing** (14th century)
: to cover or furnish with a cope

**³cope** *verb* **coped; cop·ing** [Middle English *copen, coupen*, from Middle French *couper* to strike, cut, from Old French, from *coup* blow,

from Late Latin *colpus*, alteration of Latin *colaphus*, from Greek *kolaphos* buffet] (14th century)
*intransitive verb*
**1** *obsolete* : STRIKE, FIGHT
**2 a** : to maintain a contest or combat usually on even terms or with success — used with *with* **b** : to deal with and attempt to overcome problems and difficulties — often used with *with*
**3** *archaic* : MEET, ENCOUNTER
*transitive verb*
**1** *obsolete* : to meet in combat
**2** *obsolete* : to come in contact with
**3** *obsolete* : MATCH

**⁴cope** *transitive verb* **coped; cop·ing** [probably from French *couper* to cut] (circa 1901)
**1** : to shape (a structural member) to fit a coping or fit with the shape of another member
**2** : NOTCH

**co·peck** *variant of* KOPECK

**co·pe·pod** \'kō-pə-,päd\ *noun* [ultimately from Greek *kōpē* oar, handle + *pod-, pous* foot; probably akin to Latin *capere* to take — more at HEAVE, FOOT] (1836)
: any of a large subclass (Copepoda) of usually minute freshwater and marine crustaceans
— **copepod** *adjective*

**cop·er** \'kō-pər\ *noun* [English dialect *cope* to trade] (1825)
*British* : a horse dealer; *especially* : a dishonest one

**Co·per·ni·can** \kə-'pər-ni-kən, kō-\ *adjective* [Nicolaus *Copernicus*] (1667)
**1** : of or relating to Copernicus or the belief that the earth rotates daily on its axis and the planets revolve in orbits around the sun
**2** : of radical or major importance or degree ⟨effected a *Copernican* revolution in philosophy —*Times Literary Supplement*⟩
— **Copernican** *noun*
— **Co·per·ni·can·ism** \-kə-,ni-zəm\ *noun*

**cope·stone** \'kōp-,stōn\ *noun* (1567)
**1** : a stone forming a coping
**2** : a finishing touch : CROWN

**copi·er** \'kä-pē-ər\ *noun* (1597)
: one that copies; *specifically* : a machine for making copies of graphic matter (as printing, drawings, or pictures)

**co·pi·lot** \'kō-,pī-lət\ *noun* (1927)
: a qualified pilot who assists or relieves the pilot but is not in command

**cop·ing** \'kō-piŋ\ *noun* (1601)
: the covering course of a wall usually with a sloping top

**cop·ing saw** \'kō-piŋ-\ *noun* [from present participle of ⁴*cope*] (1925)
: a handsaw with a very narrow blade held under tension in a U-shaped frame and used especially for cutting curves in wood

coping saw

**cop·ing·stone** \'kō-piŋ-,stōn\ *noun* (1778)
*chiefly British* : COPESTONE

**co·pi·ous** \'kō-pē-əs\ *adjective* [Middle English, from Latin *copiosus*, from *copia* abundance, from *co-* + *ops* wealth — more at OPULENT] (14th century)
**1 a** : yielding something abundantly ⟨a *copious* harvest⟩ ⟨*copious* springs⟩ **b** : plentiful in number ⟨*copious* references to other writers⟩
**2 a** : full of thought, information, or matter **b** : profuse or exuberant in words, expression, or style ⟨a *copious* talker⟩
**3** : present in large quantity : taking place on a large scale ⟨*copious* weeping⟩ ⟨*copious* food and drink⟩
*synonym* see PLENTIFUL
— **co·pi·ous·ly** *adverb*
— **co·pi·ous·ness** *noun*

**co·pla·nar** \(,)kō-'plā-nər, -,när\ *adjective* (1862)
: lying or acting in the same plane

— **co·pla·nar·i·ty** \,kō-plā-'nar-ə-tē\ *noun*
**co·pol·y·mer** \(,)kō-'pä-lə-mər\ *noun* (1936)
: a product of copolymerization
— **co·pol·y·mer·ic** \,kō-,pä-lə-'mer-ik\ *adjective*
**co·po·ly·mer·i·za·tion** \,kō-pə-,li-mə-rə-'zā-shən, ,kō-,pä-lə-mə-\ *noun* (1936)
: the polymerization of two substances (as different monomers) together
— **co·po·ly·mer·ize** \,kō-pə-'li-mə-,rīz, ,kō-'pä-lə-mə-\ *verb*

**cop–out** \'käp-,au̇t\ *noun* (circa 1942)
**1** : the act or an instance of copping out
**2** : an excuse or means for copping out : PRETEXT
**3** : a person who cops out

**cop out** *intransitive verb* (circa 1961)
**1** : to back out (as of an unwanted responsibility) ⟨*cop out* on jury duty⟩
**2** : to avoid or neglect problems, responsibilities, or commitments ⟨accused the mayor of *copping out* on the issue of homelessness⟩

**¹cop·per** \'kä-pər\ *noun, often attributive* [Middle English *coper*, from Old English, from Late Latin *cuprum* copper, from Latin (*aes*) *Cyprium*, literally, Cyprian metal] (before 12th century)
**1** : a common reddish metallic element that is ductile and malleable and is one of the best conductors of heat and electricity — see ELEMENT table
**2** : a coin or token made of copper or bronze
**3** *chiefly British* : a large boiler (as for cooking)
**4** : any of a subfamily (Lycaeninae of the family Lycaenidae) of small butterflies with usually copper-colored wings

**²copper** *transitive verb* **cop·pered; cop·per·ing** \'kä-p(ə-)riŋ\ (1530)
: to coat or sheathe with or as if with copper

**³copper** *noun* [²*cop*] (1846)
: POLICE OFFICER

**cop·per·as** \'kä-p(ə-)rəs\ *noun* [Middle English *coperas*, from Old French *couperose*, from Medieval Latin *cuprosa*, probably from *aqua cuprosa*, literally, copper water, from Late Latin *cuprum*] (14th century)
: a green hydrated ferrous sulfate $FeSO_4 \cdot 7H_2O$ used especially in making inks and pigments

**cop·per·head** \'kä-pər-,hed\ *noun* (1775)
**1** : a common pit viper (*Agkistrodon contortrix*) of the eastern and central U.S. usually having a copper-colored head and often a reddish brown hourglass pattern on the body

copperhead 1

**2** : a person in the northern states who sympathized with the South during the Civil War

**cop·per·plate** \'kä-pər-,plāt\ *noun* (1663)
**1** : an engraved or etched copper printing plate; *also* : a print made from such a plate
**2** : a neat script handwriting based on engraved models

**copper pyrites** *noun* (1776)
: CHALCOPYRITE

**cop·per·smith** \'kä-pər-,smith\ *noun* (14th century)
: a worker in copper

**copper sulfate** *noun* (circa 1893)
: a sulfate of copper; *especially* : the normal sulfate that is white in the anhydrous form but blue in the crystalline hydrous form $CuSO_4 \cdot 5H_2O$ and that is often used as an algicide and fungicide

**cop·pery** \'kä-p(ə-)rē\ *adjective* (circa 1775)
: resembling or suggesting copper; *especially* : having the reddish to brownish orange color of copper ⟨*coppery* leaves⟩

**¹cop·pice** \'kä-pəs\ *noun* [Middle French *copeiz,* from *couper* to cut — more at COPE] (1534)
**1 :** a thicket, grove, or growth of small trees
**2 :** forest originating mainly from shoots or root suckers rather than seed

**²coppice** *verb* **cop·piced; cop·pic·ing** (1538)
*transitive verb*
**:** to cut back so as to regrow in the form of a coppice
*intransitive verb*
**:** to form a coppice; *specifically, of a tree* **:** to sprout freely from the base

**copr-** *or* **copro-** *combining form* [New Latin, from Greek *kopr-, kopro-,* from *kopros* akin to Sanskrit *śakṛt* dung]
**:** dung **:** feces ⟨*copro*lite⟩

**co·pra** \'kō-prə *also* 'kä-\ *noun* [Portuguese, from Malayalam *koppara*] (1584)
**:** dried coconut meat yielding coconut oil

**co·pro·ces·sor** \(ˌ)kō-'prä-se-sər, -'prō-\ *noun* (1980)
**:** an extra processor in a computer that is designed to perform specialized tasks (as mathematical calculations)

**co·prod·uct** \(ˌ)kō-'prä-(ˌ)dəkt\ *noun* (1942)
**:** BY-PRODUCT 1

**cop·ro·lite** \'kä-prə-ˌlīt\ *noun* (1829)
**:** fossilized excrement
— **cop·ro·lit·ic** \ˌkä-prə-'li-tik\ *adjective*

**co·proph·a·gous** \kə-'prä-fə-gəs\ *adjective* [Greek *koprophagos,* from *kopr-* + *-phagos* -phagous] (1826)
**:** feeding on dung
— **co·proph·a·gy** \-fə-jē\ *noun*

**cop·ro·phil·ia** \ˌkä-prə-'fi-lē-ə\ *noun* [New Latin] (1923)
**:** marked interest in excrement; *especially* **:** the use of feces or filth for sexual excitement
— **cop·ro·phil·i·ac** \-lē-ˌak\ *noun*

**cop·roph·i·lous** \kə-'prä-fə-ləs\ *adjective* (circa 1900)
**:** growing or living on dung ⟨*coprophilous* fungi⟩

**copse** \'käps\ *noun* [by alteration] (1578)
**:** COPPICE 1

**Copt** \'käpt\ *noun* [Arabic *qubṭ* Copts, from Coptic *gyptios* Egyptian, from Greek *Aigyptios*] (1615)
**1 :** a member of the traditional Monophysite Christian church originating and centering in Egypt
**2 :** a member of a people descended from the ancient Egyptians

**cop·ter** \'käp-tər\ *noun* (1943)
**:** HELICOPTER

**¹Cop·tic** \'käp-tik\ *adjective* (1677)
**:** of or relating to the Copts, their liturgical language, or their church

**²Coptic** *noun* (1711)
**:** an Afro-Asiatic language descended from ancient Egyptian and used as the liturgical language of the Coptic church

**cop·u·la** \'kä-pyə-lə\ *noun* [Latin, bond — more at COUPLE] (1619)
**:** something that connects: as **a :** the connecting link between subject and predicate of a proposition **b :** LINKING VERB

**cop·u·late** \'kä-pyə-ˌlāt\ *intransitive verb* **-lat·ed; -lat·ing** [Latin *copulatus,* past participle of *copulare* to join, from *copula*] (1632)
**:** to engage in sexual intercourse
— **cop·u·la·tion** \ˌkä-pyə-'lā-shən\ *noun*
— **cop·u·la·to·ry** \'kä-pyə-lə-ˌtōr-ē, -ˌtor-\ *adjective*

**¹cop·u·la·tive** \'kä-pyə-lə-tiv, -ˌlā-\ *adjective* (14th century)
**1 a :** joining together coordinate words or word groups and expressing addition of their meanings ⟨a *copulative* conjunction⟩ **b :** functioning as a copula
**2 :** relating to or serving for copulation

**²copulative** *noun* (1530)
**:** a copulative word

**¹copy** \'kä-pē\ *noun, plural* **cop·ies** [Middle English *copie,* from Middle French, from Medieval Latin *copia,* from Latin, abundance — more at COPIOUS] (14th century)
**1 :** an imitation, transcript, or reproduction of an original work (as a letter, a painting, a table, or a dress)
**2 :** one of a series of especially mechanical reproductions of an original impression; *also* **:** an individual example of such a reproduction
**3** *archaic* **:** something to be imitated **:** MODEL
**4 a :** matter to be set especially for printing **b :** something considered printable or newsworthy — used without an article ⟨remarks that make good *copy* —Norman Cousins⟩ **c :** text especially of an advertisement
*synonym* see REPRODUCTION

**²copy** *verb* **cop·ied; copy·ing** (14th century)
*transitive verb*
**1 :** to make a copy of
**2 :** to model oneself on
*intransitive verb*
**1 :** to make a copy
**2 :** to undergo copying ⟨the document did not *copy* well⟩ ☆

**copy·book** \'kä-pē-ˌbùk\ *noun* (1588)
**:** a book formerly used in teaching penmanship and containing models for imitation

**copy·boy** \-ˌbòi\ *noun* (1888)
**:** one who carries copy and runs errands

**¹copy·cat** \-ˌkat\ *noun, often attributive* (1896)
**1 :** one who imitates or adopts the behavior or practices of another
**2 :** an imitative act or product ⟨*copycat* board games⟩

**²copycat** *verb* **copy·cat·ted; copy·cat·ting** (1926)
*intransitive verb*
**:** to act as a copycat
*transitive verb*
**:** IMITATE

**copy·desk** \-ˌdesk\ *noun* (1921)
**:** the desk at which newspaper copy is edited

**copy editor** *noun* (1899)
**:** an editor who prepares copy for the printer; *also* **:** one who edits and headlines newspaper copy
— **copy·ed·it** \'kä-pē-ˌe-dət\ *transitive verb*

**copy·hold** \'kä-pē-ˌhōld\ *noun* (15th century)
**1 :** a former tenure of land in England and Ireland by right of being recorded in the court of the manor
**2 :** an estate held by copyhold

**copy·hold·er** \-ˌhōl-dər\ *noun* (1874)
**1 :** a device for holding copy especially for a typesetter
**2 :** one who reads copy for a proofreader

**copy·ist** \'kä-pē-ist\ *noun* (1699)
**1 :** one who makes copies
**2 :** IMITATOR

**copy·read·er** \-ˌrē-dər\ *noun* (1892)
**:** COPY EDITOR
— **copy·read** \-ˌrēd\ *transitive verb*

**¹copy·right** \-ˌrīt\ *noun* (1735)
**:** the exclusive legal right to reproduce, publish, and sell the matter and form (as of a literary, musical, or artistic work)

**²copyright** *transitive verb* (circa 1806)
**:** to secure a copyright
— **copy·right·able** \-ˌrī-tə-bəl\ *adjective*

**³copyright** *adjective* (1870)
**:** secured by copyright

**copy·writ·er** \'kä-pē-ˌrī-tər\ *noun* (1911)
**:** a writer of advertising or publicity copy

**coq au vin** \ˌkōk-ō-'vaⁿ, ˌkäk-ō-\ *noun* [French, cock with wine] (circa 1938)
**:** chicken cooked in usually red wine

**¹co·quet** *noun* [French, diminutive of *coq* cock] (1691)
**1** \kō-'ket, -'kā\ **:** a man who indulges in coquetry
**2** \-'ket\ **:** COQUETTE

**²co·quet** \kō-'ket\ *adjective* (1697)
**:** characteristic of a coquette **:** COQUETTISH

**³co·quet** *or* **co·quette** \-'ket\ *intransitive verb* **co·quet·ted; co·quet·ting** (1701)
**1 :** to play the coquette **:** FLIRT
**2 :** to deal with something playfully rather than seriously
*synonym* see TRIFLE

**co·que·try** \'kō-kə-trē, kō-'ke-trē\ *noun, plural* **-tries** (circa 1656)
**:** a flirtatious act or attitude

**co·quette** \kō-'ket\ *noun* [French, feminine of *coquet*] (circa 1611)
**:** a woman who endeavors without sincere affection to gain the attention and admiration of men
— **co·quett·ish** \-'ke-tish\ *adjective*
— **co·quett·ish·ly** *adverb*
— **co·quett·ish·ness** *noun*

**co·qui·na** \kō-'kē-nə\ *noun* [Spanish, probably diminutive of *coca* head, alteration of *coco* bogeyman, coconut] (1837)
**1 :** a soft whitish limestone formed of broken shells and corals cemented together and used for building
**2 :** a small clam (*Donax variabilis*) used for broth or chowder and occurring in the intertidal zone of sandy Atlantic beaches from Delaware to the Gulf of Mexico

**cor** \'kòr\ *noun* [Middle English, from Late Latin *corus,* from Hebrew *kōr*] (14th century)
**:** an ancient Hebrew and Phoenician unit of measure of capacity

**cor·a·cle** \'kòr-ə-kəl, 'kär-\ *noun* [Welsh *corwgl*] (circa 1547)
**:** a small boat used in Britain from ancient times and made of a frame (as of wicker) covered usually with hide or tarpaulin

**cor·a·coid** \'kòr-ə-ˌkòid, 'kär-\ *adjective* [New Latin *coracoides,* from Greek *korakoeidēs,* literally, like a raven, from *korak-, korax* raven — more at RAVEN] (1741)
**:** of, relating to, or being a process of the scapula in most mammals or a well-developed cartilage bone of many lower vertebrates that extends from the scapula to or toward the sternum
— **coracoid** *noun*

**cor·al** \'kòr-əl, 'kär-\ *noun* [Middle English, from Middle French, from Latin *corallium,* from Greek *korallion*] (14th century)
**1 a :** the calcareous or horny skeletal deposit produced by anthozoan or rarely hydrozoan polyps; *especially* **:** a richly red precious coral secreted by a gorgonian (genus *Corallium*) **b :** a polyp or polyp colony together with its membranes and skeleton
**2 :** a piece of coral and especially of red coral
**3 a :** a bright reddish ovary (as of a lobster or scallop) **b :** a deep pink
— **coral** *adjective*
— **cor·al·loid** \-ə-ˌlòid\ *adjective*

---

☆ **SYNONYMS**
**Copy, imitate, mimic, ape, mock** mean to make something so that it resembles an existing thing. COPY suggests duplicating an original as nearly as possible ⟨*copied* the painting and sold the fake as an original⟩. IMITATE suggests following a model or a pattern but may allow for some variation ⟨*imitate* a poet's style⟩. MIMIC implies a close copying (as of voice or mannerism) often for fun, ridicule, or lifelike imitation ⟨pupils *mimicking* their teacher⟩. APE may suggest presumptuous, slavish, or inept imitating of a superior original ⟨American fashion designers *aped* their European colleagues⟩. MOCK usually implies imitation with derision ⟨*mocking* a vain man's pompous manner⟩.

---

\ə\ abut \ᵊ\ kitten \ər\ further \a\ ash \ā\ ace
\ä\ mop, mar \aù\ out \ch\ chin \e\ bet \ē\ easy
\g\ go \i\ hit \ī\ ice \j\ job \ŋ\ sing \ō\ go
\ò\ law \òi\ boy \th\ thin \th\ the \ü\ loot \ù\ foot
\y\ yet \zh\ vision *see also* Guide to Pronunciation

**cor·al·bells** \'kȯr-əl-ˌbelz, 'kär-\ *noun plural but singular or plural in construction* (circa 1900)
: a perennial alumroot (*Heuchera sanguinea*) widely cultivated for its feathery spikes of tiny bright red campanulate flowers

**cor·al·ber·ry** \-ˌber-ē\ *noun* (circa 1859)
: an American dwarf shrub (*Symphoricarpos orbiculatus*) that bears clusters of small flowers succeeded by red berries

**¹cor·al·line** \'kȯr-ə-ˌlīn, 'kär-\ *noun* (1543)
**1** : a coralline red alga
**2** : a bryozoan or hydroid that resembles a coral

**²coralline** *adjective* [Middle French, from feminine of *corallin* coral-like, from Late Latin *corallinus*, from Latin *corallium*] (circa 1633)
**1** : of, relating to, or resembling coral
**2** : of, relating to, or being any of a family (Corallinaceae) of calcareous red algae

**coral snake** *noun* (circa 1772)
**1** : any of several venomous chiefly tropical New World elapid snakes (genus *Micrurus*) brilliantly banded in red, black, and yellow or white that include two (*M. fulvius* and *M. euryxanthus*) ranging northward into the southern U.S.
**2** : any of several harmless snakes resembling the coral snakes

**co·ran·to** \kə-'ran-(ˌ)tō\ *noun, plural* **-tos** *or* **-toes** [modification of French *courante*] (1564)
: COURANTE

**cor·ban** \'kȯr-ˌban\ *noun* [Hebrew *qorbān* offering] (14th century)
: a sacrifice or offering to God among the ancient Hebrews

**cor·beil** *or* **cor·beille** \'kȯr-bəl, kȯr-'bā\ *noun* [French *corbeille*, literally, basket, from Late Latin *corbicula*] (circa 1734)
: a sculptured basket of flowers or fruit as an architectural decoration

**¹cor·bel** \'kȯr-bəl\ *noun* [Middle English, from Middle French, from diminutive of *corp* raven, from Latin *corvus* — more at RAVEN] (15th century)
: an architectural member that projects from within a wall and supports a weight; *especially* : one that is stepped upward and outward from a vertical surface

**²corbel** *transitive verb* **-beled** *or* **-belled; -bel·ing** *or* **-bel·ling** (1843)
: to furnish with or make into a corbel

**corbeling** *noun* (1548)
**1** : corbel work
**2** : the construction of a corbel

**cor·bic·u·la** \kȯr-'bi-kyə-lə\ *noun, plural* **-lae** \-(ˌ)lē, -ˌlī\ [Late Latin, diminutive of Latin *corbis* basket] (1816)
: POLLEN BASKET

**cor·bie** \'kȯr-bē\ *noun* [Middle English, modification of Middle French *corbin*, from Latin *corvinus* of a raven — more at CORVINE] (15th century)
*chiefly Scottish* : CARRION CROW; *also* : RAVEN

**cor·bi·na** \kȯr-'bē-nə\ *noun* [Mexican Spanish, from Spanish *corvina*, a marine fish (*Argyrosomus regius*), from feminine of *corvino* of a raven, from Latin *corvinus*] (1901)
: a coastal marine croaker (*Menticirrhus undulatus*) favored by surf casters along the California coast

**¹cord** \'kȯrd\ *noun* [Middle English, from Middle French *corde*, from Latin *chorda* string, from Greek *chordē* — more at YARN] (14th century)
**1 a** : a long slender flexible material usually consisting of several strands (as of thread or yarn) woven or twisted together **b** : the hangman's rope
**2** : a moral, spiritual, or emotional bond
**3 a** : an anatomical structure (as a nerve or the umbilical cord) resembling a cord **b** : a small flexible insulated electrical cable having a

plug at one or both ends used to connect a lamp or other appliance with a receptacle
**4** : a unit of wood cut for fuel equal to a stack 4 x 4 x 8 feet or 128 cubic feet
**5 a** : a rib like a cord on a textile **b** (1) : a fabric made with such ribs or a garment made of such a fabric (2) *plural* : trousers made of such a fabric

**²cord** *transitive verb* (15th century)
**1** : to furnish, bind, or connect with a cord
**2** : to pile up (wood) in cords
— **cord·er** *noun*

**cord·age** \'kȯr-dij\ *noun* (1598)
**1** : ropes or cords; *especially* : the ropes in the rigging of a ship
**2** : the number of cords (as of wood) on a given area

**cor·date** \'kȯr-ˌdāt\ *adjective* [New Latin *cordatus*, from Latin *cord-, cor*] (1769)
: shaped like a heart ⟨a *cordate* leaf⟩ — see LEAF illustration
— **cor·date·ly** *adverb*

**cord·ed** \'kȯr-dəd\ *adjective* (14th century)
**1 a** : made of or provided with cords or ridges; *specifically* : muscled in ridges **b** *of a muscle* : TENSE, TAUT
**2** : bound, fastened, or wound about with cords
**3** : striped or ribbed with or as if with cord : TWILLED

**cord·grass** \'kȯrd-ˌgras\ *noun* (1857)
: any of a genus (*Spartina*) of chiefly saltmarsh grasses of coastal regions of Europe, northern Africa, and the New World that have stiff culms and panicled spikelets

**¹cor·dial** \'kȯr-jəl\ *adjective* [Middle English, from Medieval Latin *cordialis*, from Latin *cord-, cor* heart — more at HEART] (14th century)
**1** *obsolete* : of or relating to the heart : VITAL
**2** : tending to revive, cheer, or invigorate
**3 a** : sincerely or deeply felt ⟨a *cordial* dislike for each other⟩ **b** : warmly and genially affable ⟨*cordial* relations⟩
*synonym* see GRACIOUS
— **cor·dial·ly** \'kȯrj-lē, 'kȯr-jə-\ *adverb*
— **cor·dial·ness** \'kȯr-jəl-nəs\ *noun*

**²cordial** *noun* (14th century)
**1** : a stimulating medicine or drink
**2** : LIQUEUR

**cor·dial·i·ty** \ˌkȯr-jē-'a-lə-tē, kȯr-'ja- *also* kȯr-'dya-\ *noun* (1611)
: sincere affection and kindness : cordial regard

**cordia pulmonalia** *plural of* COR PULMONALE

**cor·di·er·ite** \'kȯr-dē-ə-ˌrīt\ *noun* [French, from Pierre L. A. *Cordier* (died 1861) French geologist] (circa 1814)
: a blue mineral of vitreous luster and strong dichroism that consists of a silicate of aluminum, iron, and magnesium

**cor·di·form** \'kȯr-də-ˌfȯrm\ *adjective* [French *cordiforme*, from Latin *cord-, cor* + French *-iforme* -iform] (1828)
: shaped like a heart ⟨a *cordiform* sea-urchin shell⟩

**cor·dil·le·ra** \ˌkȯr-dᵊl-'yer-ə, -də-'ler- *also* kȯr-'di-lə-rə\ *noun* [Spanish] (1704)
: a system of mountain ranges often consisting of a number of more or less parallel chains
— **cor·dil·le·ran** \-'yer-ən, -'ler-, -'di-lə-rən\ *adjective*

**cord·ite** \'kȯr-ˌdīt\ *noun* (1889)
: a smokeless powder composed of nitroglycerin, guncotton, and a petroleum substance usually gelatinized by addition of acetone and pressed into cords resembling brown twine

**cord·less** \'kȯr-dləs\ *adjective* (1906)
: having no cord; *especially* : powered by a battery ⟨*cordless* tools⟩

**cor·do·ba** \'kȯr-də-bə, -və\ *noun* [Spanish *córdoba*, from Francisco Fernández de *Córdoba* (died 1526) Spanish explorer] (1913)
— see MONEY table

**¹cor·don** \'kȯr-dᵊn, -ˌdän\ *noun* [French, diminutive of *corde* cord] (15th century)

**1 a** : an ornamental cord or ribbon **b** : STRINGCOURSE
**2 a** : a line of troops or of military posts enclosing an area to prevent passage **b** : a line of persons or objects around a person or place ⟨a *cordon* of police⟩
**3** : an espalier especially of a fruit tree trained as a single horizontal shoot or two diverging horizontal shoots in a single line

**²cordon** *transitive verb* (1561)
: to form a protective or restrictive cordon around — usually used with *off*

**cor·don sa·ni·taire** \ˌkȯr-ˌdōⁿ-sä-nē-'ter\ *noun* [French, literally, sanitary cordon (quarantine line)] (1920)
: a protective barrier (as of buffer states) against a potentially aggressive nation or a dangerous influence (as an ideology)

**¹cor·do·van** \'kȯr-də-vən\ *adjective* [Old Spanish *cordovano*, from *Córdova* (now *Córdoba*), Spain] (1591)
**1** *capitalized* : of or relating to Córdoba and especially Córdoba, Spain
**2** : made of cordovan leather

**²cordovan** *noun* (circa 1625)
**1** : a soft fine-grained colored leather
**2** : dense nonporous leather tanned from the inner layer of horsehide

**¹cor·du·roy** \'kȯr-də-ˌrȯi\ *noun, plural* **-roys** [origin unknown] (circa 1791)
**1 a** *plural* : trousers of corduroy fabric **b** : a durable usually cotton pile fabric with vertical ribs or wales
**2** : logs laid side by side transversely to make a road surface

**²corduroy** *transitive verb* **-royed; -roy·ing** (1854)
: to build (a road) of logs laid side by side transversely; *also* : to build a corduroy road across

**cord·wain** \'kȯrd-ˌwān\ *noun* [Middle English *cordwane*, from Middle French *cordoan*, from Old Spanish *cordovano, cordován*] (14th century) *archaic*
: cordovan leather

**cord·wain·er** \-ˌwā-nər\ *noun* (14th century)
**1** *archaic* : a worker in cordovan leather
**2** : SHOEMAKER
— **cord·wain·ery** \-ˌwā-nə-rē\ *noun*

**cord·wood** \'kȯrd-ˌwu̇d\ *noun* (circa 1639)
: wood piled or sold in cords

**¹core** \'kȯr, 'kȯr\ *noun, often attributive* [Middle English] (14th century)
**1** : a central and often foundational part usually distinct from the enveloping part by a difference in nature ⟨*core* of the city⟩: as **a** : the usually inedible central part of some fruits (as a pineapple); *especially* : the papery or leathery carpels composing the ripened ovary in a pome fruit **b** : the portion of a foundry mold that shapes the interior of a hollow casting **c** : a vertical space (as for elevator shafts, stairways, or plumbing apparatus) in a multistory building **d** (1) : a mass of iron serving to concentrate and intensify the magnetic field resulting from a current in a surrounding coil (2) : a tiny doughnut-shaped piece of magnetic material (as ferrite) used in computer memories (3) : a computer memory consisting of an array of cores strung on fine wires; *broadly* : the internal memory of a computer **e** : the central part of a celestial body (as the earth or sun) usually having different physical properties from the surrounding parts **f** : a nodule of stone (as flint or obsidian) from which flakes have been struck for making implements **g** : the conducting wire with its insulation in an electric cable **h** : an arrangement of a course of studies that combines under basic topics material from subjects conventionally separated and aims to provide a common background for all students ⟨*core* curriculum⟩ **i** : the place in a nuclear reactor where fission occurs
**2 a** : a basic, essential, or enduring part (as of an individual, a class, or an entity) ⟨the staff had a *core* of experts⟩ ⟨the *core* of her beliefs⟩

**b** : the essential meaning : GIST ⟨the *core* of the argument⟩ **c** : the inmost or most intimate part ⟨honest to the *core*⟩
**3** : a part (as a thin cylinder of material) removed from the interior of a mass especially to determine composition
²**core** *transitive verb* **cored; cor·ing** (15th century)
: to remove a core from
— **cor·er** *noun*
³**core** *noun* [perhaps alteration of Middle English *chore* chorus, company, perhaps from Latin *chorus*] (1622)
*chiefly Scottish* : a group of people
**core city** *noun* (1965)
: INNER CITY
**cored** \'kōrd, 'kȯrd\ *adjective* (1945)
: having a core of a specified kind — usually used in combination
**co·re·li·gion·ist** \,kō-ri-'lij-nist, -'li-jə-\ *noun* (1826)
: a person of the same religion
**co·re·mi·um** \kə-'rē-mē-əm\ *noun*, *plural* **-mia** \-mē-ə\ [New Latin, from Greek *korēma* broom, from *korein* to sweep] (1929)
: a fruiting body characteristic of some fungi (as the one causing Dutch elm disease) that consists of a sterile stalk of parallel or fascicled hyphae and a terminal fertile or spore-bearing head
**co·re·op·sis** \,kōr-ē-'äp-səs, ,kȯr-\ *noun*, *plural* **coreopsis** [New Latin, genus name, from Greek *koris* bedbug + New Latin *-opsis*; akin to Greek *keirein* to cut — more at SHEAR] (circa 1753)
: any of a genus (*Coreopsis*) of widely cultivated composite herbs with showy flower heads and pinnately lobed or dissected leaves
**co·re·pres·sor** \,kō-ri-'pre-sər\ *noun* (1963)
: a substance that activates a particular genetic repressor by combining with it
**co·req·ui·site** \kō-'re-kwə-zət\ *noun* (circa 1948)
: a formal course of study required to be taken simultaneously with another
**co·re·spon·dent** \,kō-ri-'spän-dənt\ *noun* (1857)
: a person named as guilty of adultery with the defendant in a divorce suit
**corf** \'kȯrf\ *noun*, *plural* **corves** \'kȯrvz\ [Middle English, basket, from Middle Dutch *corf* or Middle Low German *korf*, from Latin *corbis* basket] (1653)
*British* : a basket, tub, or truck used in a mine
**cor·gi** \'kȯr-gē\ *noun*, *plural* **corgis** [Welsh, from *cor* dwarf + *ci* dog; akin to Old Irish *cú* dog, Old English *hund* — more at HOUND] (1926)
**1** : CARDIGAN WELSH CORGI
**2** : PEMBROKE WELSH CORGI
**co·ri·a·ceous** \,kōr-ē-'ā-shəs, ,kȯr-\ *adjective* [Late Latin *coriaceus* — more at CUIRASS] (1674)
: resembling leather ⟨*coriaceous* foliage⟩
**co·ri·an·der** \'kōr-ē-,an-dər, ,kōr-ē-', 'kȯr-, ,kȯr-\ *noun* [Middle English *coriandre*, from Old French, from Latin *coriandrum*, from Greek *koriandron, koriannon*] (14th century)
**1** : an Old World herb (*Coriandrum sativum*) of the carrot family with aromatic fruits
**2** : the ripened dried fruit of coriander used as a flavoring — called also *coriander seed*
¹**Co·rin·thi·an** \kə-'rin(t)-thē-ən\ *noun* (1526)
**1** : a native or resident of Corinth, Greece
**2** : a merry profligate man
²**Corinthian** *adjective* (1594)
**1** : of, relating to, or characteristic of Corinth or Corinthians
**2** : of or relating to the lightest and most ornate of the three ancient Greek architectural orders distinguished especially by its large capitals decorated with carved acanthus leaves — see ORDER illustration
**Co·rin·thi·ans** \-thē-ənz\ *noun plural but singular in construction*

: either of two letters written by Saint Paul to the Christians of Corinth and included as books in the New Testament — see BIBLE table
**Co·ri·o·lis effect** \,kōr-ē-'ō-ləs-, ,kȯr-\ *noun* (circa 1946)
: the apparent deflection of a moving object that is the result of the Coriolis force
**Coriolis force** *noun* [Gaspard G. *Coriolis* (died 1843) French civil engineer] (1923)
: an apparent force that as a result of the earth's rotation deflects moving objects (as projectiles or air currents) to the right in the northern hemisphere and to the left in the southern hemisphere
**co·ri·um** \'kōr-ē-əm, 'kȯr-\ *noun*, *plural* **co·ria** \-ē-ə\ [New Latin, from Latin, leather — more at CUIRASS] (1836)
: DERMIS
¹**cork** \'kȯrk\ *noun* [Middle English, cork, bark, probably from Arabic *qurq*, from Latin *cortic-, cortex* bark — more at CUIRASS] (14th century)
**1 a** : the elastic tough outer tissue of the cork oak that is used especially for stoppers and insulation **b** : PHELLEM
**2** : a usually cork stopper for a bottle or jug
**3** : a fishing float
²**cork** *transitive verb* (1535)
**1** : to furnish or fit with cork or a cork
**2** : to stop up with a cork
**3** : to blacken with burnt cork
**cork·age** \'kȯr-kij\ *noun* (1838)
: a charge (as by a restaurant) for opening a bottle of wine bought elsewhere
**cork·board** \'kȯrk-,bōrd, -,bȯrd\ *noun* (circa 1893)
: a heat-insulating material made of compressed granulated cork; *also* : a bulletin board made with this material
**cork cambium** *noun* (1878)
: PHELLOGEN
**corked** \'kȯrkt\ *adjective* (1830)
: CORKY 2
**cork·er** \'kȯr-kər\ *noun* (1881)
**1** : one that corks containers (as bottles)
**2** : one that is excellent or remarkable
**cork·ing** \'kȯr-kiŋ\ *adjective or adverb* (1895)
: extremely fine — often used as an intensive especially before *good* ⟨had a *corking* good time⟩
**cork oak** *noun* (1873)
: an oak (*Quercus suber*) of southern Europe and northern Africa that is the source of the cork of commerce
¹**cork·screw** \'kȯrk-,skrü\ *noun* (1720)
: a device for drawing corks from bottles that has a pointed spiral piece of metal turned by a handle
²**corkscrew** *adjective* (1815)
: resembling a corkscrew : SPIRAL
³**corkscrew** (1837)
*transitive verb*
**1** : WIND
**2** : to draw out with difficulty
**3** : to twist into a spiral
*intransitive verb*
: to move in a winding course
**cork·wood** \'kȯrk-,wu̇d\ *noun* (1756)
: any of several trees having light or corky wood; *especially* : a small or shrubby tree (*Leitneria floridana*) of the southeastern U.S. that has extremely light soft wood
**corky** \'kȯr-kē\ *adjective* **cork·i·er; -est** (1756)
**1** : resembling cork
**2** : having an unpleasant odor and taste (as from a tainted cork) ⟨*corky* wine⟩
— **cork·i·ness** \-kē-nəs\ *noun*
**corm** \'kȯrm\ *noun* [New Latin *cormus*, from Greek *kormos* tree trunk, from *keirein* to cut — more at SHEAR] (1830)
: a rounded thick modified underground stem base bearing membranous or scaly leaves and buds and acting as a vegetative reproductive structure — compare BULB, TUBER

**corm·el** \'kȯr-məl, kȯr-'mel\ *noun* [diminutive of *corm*] (circa 1900)
: a small or secondary corm produced by a larger corm
**cor·mo·rant** \'kȯrm-rənt, 'kȯr-mə-, 'kȯr-mə-,rant\ *noun* [Middle English *cormeraunt*, from Middle French *cormorant*, from Old French *cormareng*, from *corp* raven + *marenc* of the sea, from Latin *marinus* — more at CORBEL, MARINE] (14th century)
**1** : any of a family (Phalacrocoracidae) of dark-colored web-footed water birds that have a long neck, hooked bill, and distensible throat pouch
**2** : a gluttonous, greedy, or rapacious person

**cormorant**

¹**corn** \'kȯrn\ *noun*, *often attributive* [Middle English, from Old English; akin to Old High German & Old Norse *korn* grain, Latin *granum*] (before 12th century)
**1** *chiefly dialect* : a small hard particle : GRAIN
**2** : a small hard seed
**3 a** : the seeds of a cereal grass and especially of the important cereal crop of a particular region (as wheat in Britain, oats in Scotland and Ireland, and Indian corn in the New World and Australia) **b** : the kernels of sweet corn served as a vegetable while still soft and milky
**4** : a plant that produces corn
**5** : CORN WHISKEY
**6 a** : something (as writing, music, or acting) that is corny **b** : the quality or state of being corny : CORNINESS
²**corn** *transitive verb* (1560)
**1** : to form into grains : GRANULATE
**2 a** : to preserve or season with salt in grains **b** : to cure or preserve in brine containing preservatives and often seasonings ⟨*corned* beef⟩
**3** : to feed with corn ⟨*corn* the horses⟩
³**corn** *noun* [Middle English *corne*, from Middle French, horn, corner, from Latin *cornu* horn, point — more at HORN] (15th century)
: a local hardening and thickening of epidermis (as on a toe)
¹**corn·ball** \'kȯrn-,bȯl\ *noun* (circa 1949)
: an unsophisticated person; *also* : something corny
²**cornball** *adjective* (1951)
: CORNY
**corn borer** *noun* (1919)
: any of several insects that bore in maize: as **a** : EUROPEAN CORN BORER **b** : SOUTHWESTERN CORN BORER
**corn bread** *noun* (1750)
: bread made with cornmeal
**corn chip** *noun* (1950)
: a piece of a dry crisp snack food prepared from a seasoned cornmeal batter
**corn·cob** \'kȯrn-,käb\ *noun* (1793)
**1** : the axis on which the kernels of Indian corn are arranged
**2** : an ear of Indian corn
**corncob pipe** *noun* (1832)
: a tobacco pipe with a bowl made of a corncob
**corn cockle** *noun* (1713)
: an annual hairy weed (*Agrostemma githago*) of the pink family with purplish red flowers that is found in grainfields
**corn·crake** \'kȯrn-,krāk\ *noun* (15th century)
: a common Eurasian short-billed rail (*Crex crex*) that frequents grainfields

**corn·crib** \-ˌkrib\ *noun* (1681)
: a crib for storing ears of Indian corn

**corn dodger** *noun* (1834)
*chiefly Southern & Midland* : a cake of corn bread that is fried, baked, or boiled as a dumpling

**corn dog** *noun* (1967)
: a frankfurter dipped in cornmeal batter, fried, and served on a stick

**cor·nea** \ˈkȯr-nē-ə\ *noun* [Middle English, from Medieval Latin, from Latin, feminine of *corneus* horny, from *cornu*] (14th century)
: the transparent part of the coat of the eyeball that covers the iris and pupil and admits light to the interior — see EYE illustration
— **cor·ne·al** \-əl\ *adjective*

**corn ear·worm** \-ˈir-ˌwərm\ *noun* (1802)
: a noctuid moth (*Heliothis zea*) whose large striped yellow-headed larva is especially destructive to Indian corn, tomatoes, tobacco, and cotton bolls

**cor·nel** \ˈkȯr-nᵊl, -ˌnel\ *noun* [ultimately from Latin *cornus* cornel cherry tree; akin to Greek *kranon* cornel cherry tree] (1551)
: any of various shrubs or trees (genus *Cornus*) of the dogwood family with very hard wood and perfect flowers; *specifically* : DOGWOOD

**cor·ne·lian** \kȯr-ˈnēl-yən\ *noun* (15th century)
: CARNELIAN

**cor·ne·ous** \ˈkȯr-nē-əs\ *adjective* [Latin *corneus*] (1646)
: of a horny texture

**¹cor·ner** \ˈkȯr-nər\ *noun* [Middle English, from Old French *cornere*, from *corne* horn, corner] (13th century)
**1 a** : the point where converging lines, edges, or sides meet : ANGLE **b** : the place of intersection of two streets or roads **c** : a piece designed to form, mark, or protect a corner
**2** : the angular part or space between meeting lines, edges, or borders near the vertex of the angle ⟨the southwest *corner* of the state⟩ ⟨the *corners* of the tablecloth⟩: as **a** : the area of a playing field or court near the intersection of the sideline and the goal line or baseline **b** (1) : either of the four angles of a boxing ring; *especially* : the area in which a boxer rests or is worked on by his seconds during periods between rounds (2) : a group of supporters, well-wishers, or adherents associated especially with a contestant **c** : the side of home plate nearest to or farthest from a batter ⟨a fast ball over the outside *corner*⟩ **d** : CORNER KICK **e** (1) : the outside of a football formation (2) : CORNERBACK
**3 a** : a private, secret, or remote place ⟨a quiet *corner* of New England⟩ ⟨to every *corner* of the earth⟩ ⟨dark *corners* of the mind⟩ **b** : a difficult or embarrassing situation : a position from which escape or retreat is difficult or impossible ⟨was backed into a *corner*⟩
**4** : control or ownership of enough of the available supply of a commodity or security especially to permit manipulation of the price
**5** : a point at which significant change occurs — often used in the phrase *turn the corner*
— **cor·nered** \-nərd\ *adjective*
— **around the corner** : at hand : IMMINENT ⟨good times are just *around the corner*⟩

**²corner** *adjective* (13th century)
**1** : situated at a corner ⟨the *corner* drugstore⟩
**2** : used or fitted for use in or on a corner ⟨a *corner* table⟩

**³corner** (1824)
*transitive verb*
**1 a** : to drive into a corner ⟨the animal is dangerous when *cornered*⟩ **b** : to catch and hold the attention of especially to force an interview
**2** : to get a corner on ⟨*corner* the market⟩
*intransitive verb*
**1** : to meet or converge at a corner or angle
**2** : to turn a corner ⟨the car *corners* well⟩

**cor·ner·back** \ˈkȯr-nər-ˌbak\ *noun* (1955)

: a defensive halfback in football who defends the flank

**corner kick** *noun* (1882)
: a free kick from a corner of a soccer field awarded to an attacker when a defender plays the ball out-of-bounds over the end line

**cor·ner·man** \ˈkȯr-nər-ˌman\ *noun* (1957)
**1** : one who plays in or near the corner: as **a** : CORNERBACK **b** : a basketball forward
**2** : a boxer's second

**cor·ner·stone** \-ˌstōn\ *noun* (13th century)
**1** : a stone forming a part of a corner or angle in a wall; *specifically* : such a stone laid at a formal ceremony
**2** : a basic element : FOUNDATION ⟨a *cornerstone* of foreign policy⟩

**cor·ner·ways** \-ˌwāz\ *adverb* (1922)
: DIAGONALLY

**cor·ner·wise** \-ˌwīz\ *adverb* (15th century)
: DIAGONALLY

**cor·net** \kȯr-ˈnet, *British usually* ˈkȯr-nit\ *noun* [Middle English, from Middle French, from diminutive of *corn* horn, from Latin *cornu*] (14th century)
**1** : a valved brass instrument resembling a trumpet in design and range but having a shorter partly conical tube and less brilliant tone
**2** : something shaped like a cone: as **a** : a piece of paper twisted for use as a container **b** : a cone-shaped pastry shell that is often filled with whipped cream **c** *British* : an ice-cream cone
— **cor·net·ist** *or* **cor·net·tist** \kȯr-ˈnet-ist, ˈkȯr-ni-\ *noun*

**corn–fed** \ˈkȯrn-ˌfed\ *adjective* (14th century)
**1** : fed or fattened on grain (as corn) ⟨*corn-fed* hogs⟩
**2** : looking well-fed : PLUMP
**3** : rustically wholesome or corny

**corn·field** \-ˌfēld\ *noun* (14th century)
: a field in which corn is grown

**corn·flakes** \-ˌflāks\ *noun plural* (1907)
: toasted flakes made from the coarse meal of hulled corn for use as a breakfast cereal

**corn flour** *noun* (1791)
*British* : CORNSTARCH

**corn·flow·er** \ˈkȯrn-ˌflau̇(-ə)r\ *noun* (1527)
**1** : CORN COCKLE
**2** : BACHELOR'S BUTTON

**cornflower blue** *noun* (1907)
: a moderate purplish blue

**Corn·husk·er** \ˈkȯrn-ˌhəs-kər\ *noun* (circa 1948)
: a native or resident of Nebraska — used as a nickname

**corn·husk·ing** \-ˌhəs-kiŋ\ *noun* (1692)
: a social gathering especially of farm families to husk corn

**¹cor·nice** \ˈkȯr-nəs, -nish\ *noun* [Middle French, from Italian, frame, cornice, from Latin *cornic-, cornix* crow; akin to Greek *korax* raven — more at RAVEN] (1563)
**1 a** : the molded and projecting horizontal member that crowns an architectural composition **b** : a top course that crowns a wall
**2** : a decorative band of metal or wood used to conceal curtain fixtures
**3** : an overhanging mass of snow, ice, or rock usually on a ridge

*c cornice 1a*

**²cornice** *transitive verb* **cor·niced; cor·nic·ing** (1744)
: to furnish or crown with a cornice

**cor·niche** \kȯr-ˈnēsh\ *noun* [French *cornice, corniche*, literally, cornice, from Italian *cornice*] (1837)
: a road built along a coast and especially along the face of a cliff

**cor·nic·u·late cartilage** \kȯr-ˈni-kyə-lət-\ *noun* [Latin *corniculatus* horned, from *corniculum*, diminutive of *cornu* horn] (circa 1909)

: a small nodule of yellow elastic cartilage articulating with the apex of the arytenoid

**cor·ni·fi·ca·tion** \ˌkȯr-nə-fə-ˈkā-shən\ *noun* [Latin *cornu* horn] (circa 1843)
**1** : conversion into horn or a horny substance or tissue
**2** : the conversion of the vaginal epithelium from the columnar to the squamous type

**¹Cor·nish** \ˈkȯr-nish\ *adjective* [Middle English *Cornysshe*, from *Cornwaile* Cornwall, England] (14th century)
: of, relating to, or characteristic of Cornwall, Cornishmen, or Cornish

**²Cornish** *noun* (1547)
**1** : a Celtic language of Cornwall extinct since the late 18th century
**2** : any of an English breed of domestic fowls much used in crossbreeding for meat production

**Cor·nish·man** \-mən\ *noun* (15th century)
: a native or resident of Cornwall, England

**Corn Law** *noun* (1766)
: one of a series of laws in force in Great Britain before 1846 prohibiting or discouraging the importation of grain

**corn leaf aphid** *noun* (circa 1939)
: a dusky greenish or brownish aphid (*Rhopalosiphum maidis*) that feeds on the flowers and foliage of various commercially important grasses (as Indian corn)

**corn·meal** \ˈkȯrn-ˌmēl\ *noun* (1749)
: meal ground from corn

**corn oil** *noun* (1900)
: a yellow fatty oil obtained from the germ of Indian corn kernels and used chiefly as salad oil, in soft soap, and in margarine

**corn·pone** \ˈkȯrn-ˌpōn\ *adjective* (1972)
: DOWN-HOME, COUNTRIFIED ⟨*cornpone* humor⟩

**corn pone** *noun* (1859)
*Southern & Midland* : corn bread often made without milk or eggs and baked or fried

**corn poppy** *noun* (circa 1859)
: an annual red-flowered Eurasian poppy (*Papaver rhoeas*) common in fields and cultivated in several varieties

**corn rootworm** *noun* (1892)
: any of several chrysomelid beetles (genus *Diabrotica*) whose root-eating larvae are pests especially of corn

**corn·row** \ˈkȯrn-ˌrō\ *noun* (1946)
**1** : a section of hair which is braided usually flat to the scalp
**2** : a hairstyle in which the hair is divided into cornrow sections arranged in rows
— **cornrow** *verb*

*cornrow 2*

**corn salad** *noun* [from its occurrence as a weed in fields of grain] (1597)
: any of several herbs (genus *Valerianella*) of the valerian family; *especially* : a low European herb (*V. locusta* synonym *V. olitoria*) that is widely cultivated as a salad plant and potherb

**corn silk** *noun* (1861)
: the silky styles on an ear of Indian corn

**corn snow** *noun* (1935)
: granular snow formed by alternate thawing and freezing

**corn·stalk** \ˈkȯrn-ˌstȯk\ *noun* (1645)
: a stalk of Indian corn

**corn·starch** \-ˌstärch\ *noun* (1853)
: starch made from corn and used in foods as a thickening agent, in making corn syrup and sugars, and in the manufacture of adhesives and sizes for paper and textiles

**corn sugar** *noun* (1850)
: DEXTROSE

**corn syrup** *noun* (1903)
: a syrup containing dextrins, maltose, and dextrose that is obtained by partial hydrolysis of cornstarch

**cor·nu** \'kȯr-(,)nü, -(,)nyü\ *noun, plural* **cor·nua** \-nü-ə, -nyü-\ [Latin] (1691)
: a horn-shaped anatomical part (as of the uterus)
— **cor·nu·al** \-nü-əl, -nyü-\ *adjective*
**cor·nu·co·pia** \,kȯr-nə-'kō-pē-ə, -nyə-'\ *noun* [Late Latin, from Latin *cornu copiae* horn of plenty] (1508)
**1** : a curved goat's horn overflowing with fruit and ears of grain that is used as a decorative motif emblematic of abundance
**2** : an inexhaustible store : ABUNDANCE

**cornucopia 1**

**3** : a receptacle shaped like a horn or cone
— **cor·nu·co·pi·an** \-pē-ən\ *adjective*
**cor·nu·to** \kȯr-'nü-(,)tō, -'nyü-\ *noun, plural* **-tos** [Italian, from Latin *cornutus* having horns, from *cornu*] (1598)
: CUCKOLD
**corn whiskey** *noun* (1780)
: whiskey distilled from a mash made up of not less than 80 percent corn — compare BOURBON
**¹corny** \'kȯr-nē\ *adjective* **corn·i·er; -est** (14th century)
**1** *archaic* : tasting strongly of malt
**2** : of or relating to corn
**3** : mawkishly old-fashioned : tiresomely simple and sentimental
— **corn·i·ly** \'kȯr-n°l-ē\ *adverb*
— **corn·i·ness** \'kȯr-nē-nəs\ *noun*
**²corny** *adjective* **corn·i·er; -est** (1707)
: relating to or having corns on the feet
**cor·o·dy** \'kȯr-ə-dē, 'kär-\ *noun, plural* **-dies** [Middle English *corrodie*, from Medieval Latin *corrodium*] (15th century)
: an allowance of provisions for maintenance dispensed as a charity
**co·rol·la** \kə-'rä-lə, -'rō-\ *noun* [New Latin, from Latin, diminutive of *corona*] (circa 1753)
: the part of a flower that consists of the separate or fused petals and constitutes the inner whorl of the perianth
— **co·rol·late** \kə-'rä-lət; 'kȯr-ə-,lāt, 'kär-\ *adjective*
**cor·ol·lary** \'kȯr-ə-,ler-ē, 'kär-, *British* kə-'rä-lə-rē\ *noun, plural* **-lar·ies** [Middle English *corolarie*, from Late Latin *corollarium*, from Latin, money paid for a garland, gratuity, from *corolla*] (14th century)
**1** : a proposition inferred immediately from a proved proposition with little or no additional proof
**2 a** : something that naturally follows : RESULT
**b** : something that incidentally or naturally accompanies or parallels
— **corollary** *adjective*
**cor·o·man·del** \,kȯr-ə-'man-d°l, ,kär-\ *noun* [*Coromandel* coast region, India] (1845)
: CALAMANDER
**coromandel screen** *noun, often C capitalized* (1926)
: a Chinese lacquered folding screen
**co·ro·na** \kə-'rō-nə\ *noun* [Latin, garland, crown, cornice — more at CROWN] (1563)
**1** : the projecting part of a classic cornice
**2 a** : a usually colored circle often seen around and close to a luminous body (as the sun or moon) caused by diffraction produced by suspended droplets or occasionally particles of dust **b** : the tenuous outermost part of the atmosphere of a star (as the sun) **c** : a circle of light made by the apparent convergence of the

*a* **corona 2e**

streamers of the aurora borealis **d** : the upper portion of a bodily part (as a tooth or the skull) **e** : an appendage or series of united appendages on the inner side of the corolla in some flowers (as the daffodil, jonquil, or milkweed) **f** : a faint glow adjacent to the surface of an electrical conductor at high voltage
**3** [from *La Corona*, a trademark] : a long cigar having the sides straight to the end to be lit and being roundly blunt at the other end
**Corona Aus·tra·lis** \-ȯ-'strā-ləs, -ä-\ *noun* [New Latin (genitive *Coronae Australis*), literally, southern crown]
: a southern constellation adjoining Sagittarius on the south
**Corona Bo·re·al·is** \-,bȯr-ē-'a-ləs, -,bȯr-\ *noun* [New Latin (genitive *Coronae Borealis*), literally, northern crown]
: a northern constellation between Hercules and Boötes
**cor·o·nach** \'kȯr-ə-nək, 'kär-\ *noun* [Scottish Gaelic *corranach* & Irish *coránach*] (1530)
: a funeral dirge sung or played on the bagpipes in Scotland and Ireland
**co·ro·na·graph** *also* **co·ro·no·graph** \kə-'rō-nə-,graf\ *noun* (1885)
: a telescope for observation of the sun's corona
**¹cor·o·nal** *also* **cor·o·nel** \'kȯr-ə-n°l, 'kär-\ *noun* [Middle English *coronal*, from Anglo-French, from Latin *coronalis* of a crown, from *corona*] (14th century)
: a circlet for the head usually implying rank or dignity
**²co·ro·nal** \'kȯr-ə-n°l, 'kär-; kə-'rō-\ *adjective* (14th century)
**1 a** : lying in the direction of the coronal suture **b** : of or relating to the frontal plane that passes through the long axis of the body
**2** : of or relating to a corona or crown
**coronal suture** *noun* (1615)
: a suture extending across the skull between the parietal and frontal bones
**co·ro·na ra·di·a·ta** \kə-'rō-nə-,rā-dē-'ā-tə, -'ä-tə\ *noun, plural* **co·ro·nae ra·di·a·tae** \-(,)nē-,rā-dē-'ā-(,)tē, -'ä-(,)tē\ [New Latin, literally, crown with rays] (1892)
: the zone of small follicular cells immediately surrounding the ovum in the graafian follicle and accompanying the ovum on its discharge from the follicle
**¹cor·o·nary** \'kȯr-ə-,ner-ē, 'kär-\ *adjective* (1610)
**1** : of, relating to, resembling, or being a crown or coronal
**2** : of, relating to, or being the coronary arteries or veins of the heart; *broadly* : of or relating to the heart
**²coronary** *noun, plural* **-nar·ies** (1893)
**1 a** : CORONARY ARTERY **b** : CORONARY VEIN
**2** : CORONARY THROMBOSIS; *broadly* : HEART ATTACK
**coronary artery** *noun* (1741)
: either of two arteries that arise one from the left and one from the right side of the aorta immediately above the semilunar valves and supply the tissues of the heart itself
**coronary occlusion** *noun* (1946)
: the partial or complete blocking (as by a thrombus, by spasm, or by sclerosis) of a coronary artery
**coronary sinus** *noun* (1831)
: a venous channel that is derived from the sinus venosus, is continuous with the largest of the cardiac veins, receives most of the blood from the walls of the heart, and empties into the right atrium
**coronary thrombosis** *noun* (1926)
: the blocking of a coronary artery of the heart by a thrombus
**coronary vein** *noun* (circa 1828)
: any of several veins that drain the tissues of the heart and empty into the coronary sinus

**co·ro·nate** \'kȯr-ə-,nāt, 'kär-\ *transitive verb* **-nat·ed; -nat·ing** [Latin *coronatus*, past participle of *coronare* to crown, from *corona*] (circa 1623)
: CROWN 1a
**cor·o·na·tion** \,kȯr-ə-'nā-shən, ,kär-\ *noun* [Middle English *coronacion*, from Middle French *coronation*, from *coroner* to crown] (14th century)
: the act or occasion of crowning; *also* : accession to the highest office
**cor·o·ner** \'kȯr-ə-nər, 'kär-\ *noun* [Middle English, an officer of the crown, from Anglo-French, from Old French *corone* crown, from Latin *corona*] (circa 1630)
: a public officer whose principal duty is to inquire by an inquest into the cause of any death which there is reason to suppose is not due to natural causes
**cor·o·net** \,kȯr-ə-'net, ,kär-\ *noun* [Middle French *coronette*, from Old French *coronete*, from *corone*] (15th century)
**1** : a small or lesser crown usually signifying a rank below that of a sovereign
**2** : an ornamental wreath or band for the head usually for wear by women on formal occasions
**3** : the lower part of a horse's pastern where the horn terminates in skin — see HORSE illustration
**co·ro·tate** \(,)kō-'rō-,tāt\ *intransitive verb* (1962)
: to rotate in conjunction with or at the same rate as another rotating body
— **co·ro·ta·tion** \,kō-rō-'tā-shən\ *noun*
**cor·po·ra** *plural of* CORPUS
**¹cor·po·ral** \'kȯr-p(ə-)rəl\ *noun* [Middle English, from Middle French, from Medieval Latin *corporale*, from Latin, neuter of *corporalis*; from the doctrine that the bread of the Eucharist becomes or represents the body of Christ] (14th century)
: a linen cloth on which the eucharistic elements are placed
**²corporal** *adjective* [Middle English, from Middle French, from Latin *corporalis*, from *corpor-, corpus* body — more at MIDRIFF] (14th century)
**1** *obsolete* : CORPOREAL, PHYSICAL
**2** : of, relating to, or affecting the body ⟨*corporal* punishment⟩
— **cor·po·ral·ly** \-p(ə-)rə-lē\ *adverb*
**³corporal** *noun* [Middle French, lowest noncommissioned officer, alteration of *caporal*, from Old Italian *caporale*, from *capo* head, from Latin *caput* — more at HEAD] (1579)
: a noncommissioned officer ranking in the army above a private first class and below a sergeant and in the marine corps above a lance corporal and below a sergeant
**cor·po·ral·i·ty** \,kȯr-pə-'ra-lə-tē\ *noun, plural* **-ties** (14th century)
: the quality or state of being or having a body or a material or physical existence
**corporal's guard** *noun* (1844)
**1** : the small detachment commanded by a corporal
**2** : a small group
**cor·po·rate** \'kȯr-p(ə-)rət\ *adjective* [Latin *corporatus*, past participle of *corporare* to make into a body, from *corpor-, corpus*] (1512)
**1 a** : formed into an association and endowed by law with the rights and liabilities of an individual : INCORPORATED **b** : of or relating to a corporation ⟨a plan to reorganize the *corporate* structure⟩
**2** : of, relating to, or formed into a unified body of individuals ⟨human law arises by the *corporate* action of a people —G. H. Sabine⟩

**3 :** CORPORATIVE 2
— **cor·po·rate·ly** *adverb*
**cor·po·ra·tion** \ˌkȯr-pə-'rā-shən\ *noun* (15th century)
**1 a** *obsolete* **:** a group of merchants or traders united in a trade guild **b :** the municipal authorities of a town or city
**2 :** a body formed and authorized by law to act as a single person although constituted by one or more persons and legally endowed with various rights and duties including the capacity of succession
**3 :** an association of employers and employees in a basic industry or of members of a profession organized as an organ of political representation in a corporative state
**4 :** POTBELLY 1
**cor·po·rat·ism** \'kȯr-p(ə-)rə-ˌti-zəm\ *noun* (1890)
**:** the organization of a society into industrial and professional corporations serving as organs of political representation and exercising some control over persons and activities within their jurisdiction
— **cor·po·rat·ist** \-p(ə-)rə-tist\ *adjective*
**cor·po·ra·tive** \'kȯr-pə-ˌrā-tiv, -p(ə-)rə-\ *adjective* (1833)
**1 :** of or relating to a corporation
**2 :** of or relating to corporatism ⟨a *corporative* state⟩
**cor·po·ra·tiv·ism** \'kȯr-pə-ˌrā-ti-ˌvi-zəm, -p(ə-)rə-\ *noun* (1930)
**:** CORPORATISM
**cor·po·ra·tor** \'kȯr-pə-ˌrā-tər\ *noun* (1784)
**:** a corporation organizer, member, or stockholder
**cor·po·re·al** \kȯr-'pōr-ē-əl, -'pȯr-\ *adjective* [Latin *corporeus* of the body, from *corpor-, corpus*] (15th century)
**1 :** having, consisting of, or relating to a physical material body: as **a :** not spiritual **b :** not immaterial or intangible **:** SUBSTANTIAL
**2** *archaic* **:** CORPORAL
**synonym** see MATERIAL
— **cor·po·re·al·ly** \-ē-ə-lē\ *adverb*
— **cor·po·re·al·ness** *noun*
**cor·po·re·al·i·ty** \(ˌ)kȯr-ˌpōr-ē-'a-lə-tē, -ˌpȯr-\ *noun, plural* **-ties** (1651)
**:** corporeal existence
**cor·po·re·i·ty** \ˌkȯr-pə-'rē-ə-tē, -'rā-\ *noun, plural* **-ties** (1621)
**:** the quality or state of having or being a body **:** MATERIALITY
**cor·po·sant** \'kȯr-pə-ˌsant, -ˌzant\ *noun* [Portuguese *corpo-santo,* literally, holy body] (1655)
**:** SAINT ELMO'S FIRE
**corps** \'kȯr, 'kȯr\ *noun, plural* **corps** \'kȯrz, 'kȯrz\ [French, from Latin *corpus* body] (1711)
**1 a :** an organized subdivision of the military establishment ⟨Marine *Corps*⟩ ⟨Signal *Corps*⟩ **b :** a tactical unit usually consisting of two or more divisions and auxiliary arms and services
**2 :** a group of persons associated together or acting under common direction; *especially* **:** a body of persons having a common activity or occupation ⟨the press *corps*⟩
**3 :** CORPS DE BALLET
**corps de bal·let** \ˌkȯr-də-(ˌ)ba-'lā, ˌkȯr-\ *noun, plural* **corps de ballet** \*same or* ˌkȯrz-də-, ˌkȯrz-\ [French] (1826)
**:** the ensemble of a ballet company
**corps d'elite** \ˌkȯr-dā-'lēt, ˌkȯr-\ *noun, plural* **corps d'elite** \*same or* ˌkȯrz-dā-, ˌkȯrz-\ [French *corps d'élite*] (1884)
**1 :** a body of picked troops
**2 :** a group of the best people in a category
**corpse** \'kȯrps\ *noun* [Middle English *corps,* from Middle French, from Latin *corpus*] (13th century)
**1** *obsolete* **:** a human or animal body whether living or dead
**2 a :** a dead body especially of a human being **b :** the remains of something discarded or defunct ⟨the *corpses* of rusting cars⟩

**corps·man** \'kȯr(z)-mən, 'kȯr(z)-\ *noun* (1901)
**1 :** an enlisted man trained to give first aid and minor medical treatment
**2 :** a member of a government-sponsored service corps
**cor·pu·lence** \'kȯr-pyə-lən(t)s\ *noun* (1581)
**:** the state of being corpulent
**cor·pu·len·cy** \-lən(t)-sē\ *noun, plural* **-cies** (1577)
**:** CORPULENCE
**cor·pu·lent** \-lənt\ *adjective* [Middle English, from Latin *corpulentus,* from *corpus*] (14th century)
**:** having a large bulky body **:** OBESE
— **cor·pu·lent·ly** *adverb*
**cor pul·mo·na·le** \ˌkȯr-ˌpu̇l-mə-'nä-lē, -ˌpȯl-, -'na-\ *noun, plural* **cor·dia pul·mo·na·lia** \'kȯr-dē-ə-ˌpu̇l-mə-'nä-lē-ə, -ˌpȯl-, -'na-\ [New Latin, literally, pulmonary heart] (1857)
**:** disease of the heart characterized by hypertrophy and dilatation of the right ventricle and secondary to disease of the lungs or their blood vessels
**cor·pus** \'kȯr-pəs\ *noun, plural* **cor·po·ra** \-p(ə-)rə\ [Middle English, from Latin] (15th century)
**1 :** the body of a human or animal especially when dead
**2 a :** the main part or body of a bodily structure or organ ⟨the *corpus* of the uterus⟩ **b :** the main body or corporeal substance of a thing; *specifically* **:** the principal of a fund or estate as distinct from income or interest
**3 a :** all the writings or works of a particular kind or on a particular subject; *especially* **:** the complete works of an author **b :** a collection or body of knowledge or evidence; *especially* **:** a collection of recorded utterances used as a basis for the descriptive analysis of a language
**corpus al·la·tum** \-ə-'lā-təm, -'lä-\ *noun, plural* **corpora al·la·ta** \-'lā-tə, -'lä-tə\ [New Latin, literally, applied body] (1947)
**:** one of a pair of separate or fused bodies in many insects that are sometimes closely associated with the corpora cardiaca and that secrete hormones (as juvenile hormone)
**corpus cal·lo·sum** \-kə-'lō-səm\ *noun, plural* **corpora cal·lo·sa** \-sə\ [New Latin, literally, callous body] (1706)
**:** the great band of commissural fibers uniting the cerebral hemispheres of higher mammals including humans — see BRAIN illustration
**corpus car·di·a·cum** \-kär-'dī-ə-kəm\ *noun, plural* **corpora car·di·a·ca** \-ə-kə\ [New Latin, literally, cardiac body] (1960)
**:** one of a pair of separate or fused bodies of nervous tissue in many insects that lie posterior to the brain and dorsal to the esophagus and that function in the storage and secretion of brain hormone
**Cor·pus Chris·ti** \'kȯr-pəs-'kris-tē\ *noun* [Middle English, from Medieval Latin, literally, body of Christ] (14th century)
**:** the Thursday after Trinity observed as a Roman Catholic festival in honor of the Eucharist
**cor·pus·cle** \'kȯr-(ˌ)pə-səl\ *noun* [Latin *corpusculum,* diminutive of *corpus*] (1660)
**1 :** a minute particle
**2 a :** a living cell; *especially* **:** one (as a red or white blood cell or a cell in cartilage or bone) not aggregated into continuous tissues **b :** any of various small circumscribed multicellular bodies
— **cor·pus·cu·lar** \kȯr-'pəs-kyə-lər\ *adjective*
**cor·pus de·lic·ti** \'kȯr-pəs-di-'lik-ˌtī, -(ˌ)tē\ *noun, plural* **corpora delicti** [New Latin, literally, body of the crime] (1832)
**1 :** the substantial and fundamental fact necessary to prove the commission of a crime
**2 :** the material substance (as the body of the victim of a murder) upon which a crime has been committed

**corpus lu·te·um** \-'lü-tē-əm\ *noun, plural* **corpora lu·tea** \-tē-ə\ [New Latin, literally, yellowish body] (1788)
**:** a yellowish mass of progesterone-secreting endocrine tissue that forms immediately after ovulation from the ruptured graafian follicle in the mammalian ovary
**corpus stri·a·tum** \-(ˌ)strī-'ā-təm\ *noun, plural* **corpora stri·a·ta** \-'ā-tə\ [New Latin, literally, striated body] (1851)
**:** either of a pair of masses of nervous tissue within the brain that contain two large nuclei of gray matter separated by sheets of white matter
**cor·rade** \kə-'rād\ *verb* **cor·rad·ed; cor·rad·ing** [Latin *corradere* to scrape together, from *com-* + *radere* to scrape — more at RODENT] (1646)
*transitive verb*
**:** to wear away by abrasion
*intransitive verb*
**:** to crumble away through abrasion
— **cor·ra·sion** \-'rā-zhən\ *noun*
— **cor·ra·sive** \-'rā-siv, -ziv\ *adjective*
**¹cor·ral** \kə-'ral, -'rel\ *noun* [Spanish, from (assumed) Vulgar Latin *currale* enclosure for vehicles, from Latin *currus* cart, from *currere* to run — more at CAR] (1582)
**1 :** a pen or enclosure for confining or capturing livestock
**2 :** an enclosure made with wagons for defense of an encampment
**²corral** *transitive verb* **cor·ralled; cor·ral·ling** (1847)
**1 :** to enclose in a corral
**2 :** to arrange (wagons) so as to form a corral
**3 :** COLLECT, GATHER ⟨*corralling* votes for the upcoming election⟩
**¹cor·rect** \kə-'rekt\ *transitive verb* [Middle English, from Latin *correctus,* past participle of *corrigere,* from *com-* + *regere* to lead straight — more at RIGHT] (14th century)
**1 a :** to make or set right **:** AMEND **b :** COUNTERACT, NEUTRALIZE **c :** to alter or adjust so as to bring to some standard or required condition ⟨*correct* a lens for spherical aberration⟩
**2 a :** to punish (as a child) with a view to reforming or improving **b :** to point out usually for amendment the errors or faults of ⟨spent the day *correcting* tests⟩
— **cor·rect·able** \-'rek-tə-bəl\ *adjective*
— **cor·rec·tor** \-'rek-tər\ *noun*
**²correct** *adjective* [Middle English, corrected, from Latin *correctus,* from past participle of *corrigere*] (1676)
**1 :** conforming to an approved or conventional standard

---

☆ SYNONYMS
**Correct, rectify, emend, remedy, redress, amend, reform, revise** mean to make right what is wrong. CORRECT implies taking action to remove errors, faults, deviations, defects ⟨*correct* your spelling⟩. RECTIFY implies a more essential changing to make something right, just, or properly controlled or directed ⟨*rectify* a misguided policy⟩. EMEND specifically implies correction of a text or manuscript ⟨*emend* a text⟩. REMEDY implies removing or making harmless a cause of trouble, harm, or evil ⟨set out to *remedy* the evils of the world⟩. REDRESS implies making compensation or reparation for an unfairness, injustice, or imbalance ⟨*redress* past social injustices⟩. AMEND, REFORM, REVISE imply an improving by making corrective changes, AMEND usually suggesting slight changes ⟨*amend* a law⟩, REFORM implying drastic change ⟨plans to *reform* the court system⟩, and REVISE suggesting a careful examination of something and the making of necessary changes ⟨*revise* the schedule⟩. See in addition PUNISH.

**2 :** conforming to or agreeing with fact, logic, or known truth **3 :** conforming to a set figure ⟨enclosed the *correct* return postage⟩ ☆ — **cor·rect·ly** \kə-'rek(t)-lē\ *adverb* — **cor·rect·ness** \-'rek(t)-nəs\ *noun*

**corrected time** *noun* (circa 1891)
**:** a boat's elapsed time less its time allowance in yacht racing

**cor·rec·tion** \kə-'rek-shən\ *noun* (14th century)
**1 :** the action or an instance of correcting: as **a :** AMENDMENT, RECTIFICATION **b :** REBUKE, PUNISHMENT **c :** a bringing into conformity with a standard **d :** NEUTRALIZATION, COUNTERACTION ⟨*correction* of acidity⟩ **2 :** a decline in market price or business activity following and counteracting a rise **3 a :** something substituted in place of what is wrong ⟨marking *corrections* on the students' papers⟩ **b :** a quantity applied by way of correcting (as for adjustment of an instrument) **4 :** the treatment and rehabilitation of offenders through a program involving penal custody, parole, and probation; *also* **:** the administration of such treatment as a matter of public policy — usually used in plural — **cor·rec·tion·al** \-shnəl, -shə-nᵊl\ *adjective*

**cor·rec·ti·tude** \kə-'rek-tə-ˌtüd, -ˌtyüd\ *noun* [blend of *correct* and *rectitude*] (1893)
**:** correctness or propriety of conduct

**cor·rec·tive** \kə-'rek-tiv\ *adjective* (1531)
**:** intended to correct ⟨*corrective* lenses⟩ ⟨*corrective* punishment⟩ — **corrective** *noun* — **cor·rec·tive·ly** *adverb*

¹**cor·re·late** \'kȯr-ə-lət, 'kär-, -ˌlāt\ *noun* [back-formation from *correlation*] (1643)
**1 :** either of two things so related that one directly implies or is complementary to the other (as husband and wife) **2 :** a phenomenon (as brain activity) that accompanies another phenomenon (as behavior), is usually parallel to it (as in form, type, development, or distribution), and is related in some way to it — **correlate** *adjective*

²**cor·re·late** \-ˌlāt\ *verb* **-lat·ed; -lat·ing** (circa 1742)
*intransitive verb*
**:** to bear reciprocal or mutual relations **:** CORRESPOND
*transitive verb*
**1 a :** to establish a mutual or reciprocal relation between ⟨*correlate* activities in the lab and the field⟩ **b :** to show correlation or a causal relationship between **2 :** to present or set forth so as to show relationship ⟨he *correlates* the findings of the scientists, the psychologists, and the mystics —Eugene Exman⟩ — **cor·re·lat·able** \-ˌlā-tə-bəl\ *adjective* — **cor·re·lat·or** \-ˌlā-tər\ *noun*

**cor·re·la·tion** \ˌkȯr-ə-'lā-shən, ˌkär-\ *noun* [Medieval Latin *correlation-, correlatio*, from Latin *com-* + *relation-, relatio* relation] (1561)
**1 :** the state or relation of being correlated; *specifically* **:** a relation existing between phenomena or things or between mathematical or statistical variables which tend to vary, be associated, or occur together in a way not expected on the basis of chance alone ⟨the obviously high positive *correlation* between scholastic aptitude and college entrance —J. B. Conant⟩ **2 :** the act of correlating — **cor·re·la·tion·al** \-shnəl, -shə-nᵊl\ *adjective*

**correlation coefficient** *noun* (circa 1909)
**:** a number or function that indicates the degree of correlation between two sets of data or between two random variables and that is equal to their covariance divided by the product of their standard deviations

**cor·rel·a·tive** \kə-'re-lə-tiv\ *adjective* (1530)

**1 :** naturally related **:** CORRESPONDING **2 :** reciprocally related **3 :** regularly used together but typically not adjacent ⟨the *correlative* conjunctions *either . . . or*⟩ — **correlative** *noun* — **cor·rel·a·tive·ly** *adverb*

**cor·re·spond** \ˌkȯr-ə-'spänd, ˌkär-\ *intransitive verb* [Middle French or Medieval Latin; Middle French *correspondre*, from Medieval Latin *correspondēre*, from Latin *com-* + *respondēre* to respond] (1529)
**1 a :** to be in conformity or agreement ⟨the ideal failed . . . to *correspond* with the reality —James Sutherland⟩ **b :** to compare closely **:** MATCH — usually used with *to* or *with* **c :** to be equivalent or parallel **2 :** to communicate with a person by exchange of letters

**cor·re·spon·dence** \-'spän-dən(t)s\ *noun* (15th century)
**1 a :** the agreement of things with one another **b :** a particular similarity **c :** a relation between sets in which each member of one set is associated with one or more members of the other — compare FUNCTION 5a **2 a :** communication by letters; *also* **:** the letters exchanged **b :** the news, information, or opinion contributed by a correspondent to a newspaper or periodical

**correspondence course** *noun* (1902)
**:** a course offered by a correspondence school

**correspondence school** *noun* (1889)
**:** a school that teaches nonresident students by mailing them lessons and exercises which upon completion are returned to the school for grading

**cor·re·spon·den·cy** \ˌkȯr-ə-'spän-dən(t)-sē, ˌkär-\ *noun, plural* **-cies** (1589)
**:** CORRESPONDENCE

¹**cor·re·spon·dent** \ˌkȯr-ə-'spän-dənt, ˌkär-\ *adjective* [Middle English, from Middle French or Medieval Latin; Middle French *correspondent-*, from Medieval Latin *correspondent-, correspondens*, present participle of *correspondēre*] (15th century)
**1 :** CORRESPONDING **2 :** FITTING, CONFORMING — used with *with* or *to* ⟨the outcome was entirely *correspondent* with my wishes⟩

²**correspondent** *noun* (circa 1630)
**1 a :** one who communicates with another by letter **b :** one who has regular commercial relations with another **c :** one who contributes news or commentary to a publication (as a newspaper) or a radio or television network often from a distant place ⟨a war *correspondent*⟩ **2 :** something that corresponds

**corresponding** *adjective* (1579)
**1 a :** having or participating in the same relationship (as kind, degree, position, correspondence, or function) especially with regard to the same or like wholes (as geometric figures or sets) ⟨*corresponding* parts of similar triangles⟩ **b :** RELATED, ACCOMPANYING ⟨all rights carry with them *corresponding* responsibilities —W. P. Paepcke⟩ **2 a :** charged with the duty of writing letters ⟨*corresponding* secretary⟩ **b :** participating or serving at a distance and by mail ⟨a *corresponding* member of the society⟩ — **cor·re·spond·ing·ly** \-'spän-diŋ-lē\ *adverb*

**corresponding angles** *noun plural* (circa 1804)
**:** any pair of angles each of which is on the same side of one of two lines cut by a transversal and on the same side of the transversal

**cor·re·spon·sive** \ˌkȯr-ə-'spän(t)-siv, ˌkär-\ *adjective* (1606)
**:** mutually responsive

**cor·ri·da** \kȯ-'rē-thə\ *noun* [Spanish, literally, act of running] (1898)
**:** BULLFIGHT

**cor·ri·dor** \'kȯr-ə-dər, 'kär-, -ˌdȯr\ *noun* [Middle French, from Old Italian *corridore*, from *correre* to run, from Latin *currere* — more at CAR] (1814)
**1 :** a passageway (as in a hotel) into which compartments or rooms open **2 :** a usually narrow passageway or route: as **a :** a narrow strip of land through foreign-held territory **b :** a restricted lane for air traffic **3 :** a densely populated strip of land including two or more major cities ⟨the Northeast *corridor* stretching from Washington into New England —S. D. Browne⟩

**cor·rie** \'kȯr-ē, 'kär-ē\ *noun* [Scottish Gaelic *coire*, literally, kettle] (1795)
**:** CIRQUE 3

**Cor·rie·dale** \-ˌdāl\ *noun* [*Corriedale*, ranch in New Zealand] (1902)
**:** any of a dual-purpose breed of rather large usually hornless sheep developed in New Zealand

**cor·ri·gen·dum** \ˌkȯr-ə-'jen-dəm, ˌkär-\ *noun, plural* **-da** \-də\ [Latin, neuter of *corrigendus*, gerundive of *corrigere* to correct] (circa 1850)
**:** an error in a printed work discovered after printing and shown with its correction on a separate sheet

**cor·ri·gi·ble** \'kȯr-ə-jə-bəl, 'kär-\ *adjective* [Middle English, from Middle French, from Medieval Latin *corrigibilis*, from Latin *corrigere*] (15th century)
**:** capable of being set right **:** REPARABLE ⟨a *corrigible* defect⟩ — **cor·ri·gi·bil·i·ty** \ˌkȯr-ə-jə-'bi-lə-tē, ˌkär-\ *noun*

**cor·ri·val** \kə-'rī-vəl, kȯ-; kō-\ *noun* [Middle French, from Latin *corrivalis*, from *com-* + *rivalis* rival] (1579)
**:** RIVAL, COMPETITOR — **corrival** *adjective*

**cor·rob·o·rant** \kə-'rä-bə-rənt\ *adjective* (1626) *archaic*
**:** having an invigorating effect — used of a medicine

**cor·rob·o·rate** \kə-'rä-bə-ˌrāt\ *transitive verb* **-rat·ed; -rat·ing** [Latin *corroboratus*, past participle of *corroborare*, from *com-* + *robor-, robur* strength] (1530)
**:** to support with evidence or authority **:** make more certain
**synonym** see CONFIRM — **cor·rob·o·ra·tion** \-ˌrä-bə-'rā-shən\ *noun* — **cor·rob·o·ra·tive** \-'rä-bə-ˌrā-tiv, -'rä-b(ə-)rə-\ *adjective* — **cor·rob·o·ra·tor** \-'rä-bə-ˌrā-tər\ *noun* — **cor·rob·o·ra·to·ry** \-'rä-b(ə-)rə-ˌtōr-ē, -ˌtȯr-\ *adjective*

---

☆ SYNONYMS
**Correct, accurate, exact, precise, nice, right** mean conforming to fact, standard, or truth. CORRECT usually implies freedom from fault or error ⟨*correct* answers⟩ ⟨socially *correct* dress⟩. ACCURATE implies fidelity to fact or truth attained by exercise of care ⟨an *accurate* description⟩. EXACT stresses a very strict agreement with fact, standard, or truth ⟨*exact* measurements⟩. PRECISE adds to EXACT an emphasis on sharpness of definition or delimitation ⟨*precise* calibration⟩. NICE stresses great precision and delicacy of adjustment or discrimination ⟨makes *nice* distinctions⟩. RIGHT is close to CORRECT but has a stronger positive emphasis on conformity to fact or truth rather than mere absence of error or fault ⟨the *right* thing to do⟩.

---

\ə\ **abut** \ᵊ\ **kitten** \ər\ **further** \a\ **ash** \ā\ **ace** \ä\ **mop, mar** \aù\ **out** \ch\ **chin** \e\ **bet** \ē\ **easy** \g\ **go** \i\ **hit** \ī\ **ice** \j\ **job** \ŋ\ **sing** \ō\ **go** \ȯ\ **law** \ȯi\ **boy** \th\ **thin** \t͟h\ **the** \ü\ **loot** \ù\ **foot** \y\ **yet** \zh\ **vision** *see also* Guide to Pronunciation

**cor·rob·o·ree** \kə-'rô-bə-rē, -'rä-\ *noun* [Dharuk (Australian aboriginal language of the Port Jackson area) *garaabara*] (1811)
**1** : a nocturnal festivity with songs and symbolic dances by which the Australian aborigines celebrate events of importance
**2** *Australian* **a** : a noisy festivity **b** : TUMULT
**cor·rode** \kə-'rōd\ *verb* **cor·rod·ed; cor·rod·ing** [Middle English, from Latin *corrodere* to gnaw to pieces, from *com-* + *rodere* to gnaw — more at RODENT] (14th century)
*transitive verb*
**1** : to eat away by degrees as if by gnawing; *especially* : to wear away gradually usually by chemical action ⟨the metal was *corroded* beyond repair⟩
**2** : to weaken or destroy gradually : UNDERMINE ⟨manners and miserliness that *corrode* the human spirit —Bernard DeVoto⟩
*intransitive verb*
: to undergo corrosion
— **cor·rod·ible** \-'rō-də-bəl\ *adjective*
**cor·ro·dy** *variant of* CORODY
**cor·ro·sion** \kə-'rō-zhən\ *noun* [Middle English, from Late Latin *corrosion-, corrosio* act of gnawing, from Latin *corrodere*] (14th century)
**1** : the action, process, or effect of corroding
**2** : a product of corroding
**cor·ro·sive** \-'rō-siv, -ziv\ *adjective* (14th century)
**1** : tending or having the power to corrode ⟨*corrosive* acids⟩ ⟨*corrosive* action⟩ ⟨the *corrosive* effects of alcoholism⟩
**2** : bitingly sarcastic ⟨*corrosive* satire⟩
— **corrosive** *noun*
— **cor·ro·sive·ly** *adverb*
— **cor·ro·sive·ness** *noun*
**corrosive sublimate** *noun* (circa 1751)
: MERCURIC CHLORIDE
**cor·ru·gate** \'kȯr-ə-ˌgāt, 'kär-\ *verb* **-gat·ed; -gat·ing** [Latin *corrugatus*, past participle of *corrugare*, from *com-* + *ruga* wrinkle; probably akin to Lithuanian *raukas* wrinkle — more at ROUGH] (1620)
*transitive verb*
: to form or shape into wrinkles or folds or into alternating ridges and grooves : FURROW
*intransitive verb*
: to become corrugated
**corrugated** *adjective* (1590)
: having corrugations ⟨*corrugated* paper⟩; *also* : made of corrugated material (as paperboard) ⟨*corrugated* boxes⟩
**cor·ru·ga·tion** \ˌkȯr-ə-'gā-shən, ˌkär-\ *noun* (1528)
**1** : the act of corrugating
**2** : a ridge or groove of a surface that has been corrugated
¹**cor·rupt** \kə-'rəpt\ *verb* [Middle English, from Latin *corruptus*, past participle of *corrumpere*, from *com-* + *rumpere* to break — more at REAVE] (14th century)
*transitive verb*
**1 a** : to change from good to bad in morals, manners, or actions; *also* : BRIBE **b** : to degrade with unsound principles or moral values
**2** : ROT, SPOIL
**3** : to subject (a person) to corruption of blood
**4** : to alter from the original or correct form or version
*intransitive verb*
**1 a** : to become tainted or rotten **b** : to become morally debased
**2** : to cause disintegration or ruin
**synonym** see DEBASE
— **cor·rupt·er** *also* **cor·rup·tor** \-'rəp-tər\ *noun*
— **cor·rupt·ibil·i·ty** \-ˌrəp-tə-'bi-lə-tē\ *noun*
— **cor·rupt·ible** \-'rəp-tə-bəl\ *adjective*
— **cor·rupt·ibly** \-blē\ *adverb*
²**corrupt** *adjective* [Middle English, from Middle French or Latin; Middle French, from Latin *corruptus*] (14th century)

**1 a** : morally degenerate and perverted : DEPRAVED **b** : characterized by improper conduct (as bribery or the selling of favors) ⟨*corrupt* judges⟩
**2** : PUTRID, TAINTED
**3** : adulterated or debased by change from an original or correct condition
**synonym** see VICIOUS
— **cor·rupt·ly** \-'rəp(t)-lē\ *adverb*
— **cor·rupt·ness** \-'rəp(t)-nəs\ *noun*
**cor·rup·tion** \kə-'rəp-shən\ *noun* (14th century)
**1 a** : impairment of integrity, virtue, or moral principle : DEPRAVITY **b** : DECAY, DECOMPOSITION **c** : inducement to wrong by improper or unlawful means (as bribery) **d** : a departure from the original or from what is pure or correct
**2** *archaic* : an agency or influence that corrupts
**3** *chiefly dialect* : PUS
**cor·rup·tion·ist** \-sh(ə-)nist\ *noun* (1810)
: one who practices or defends corruption especially in politics
**corruption of blood** (1563)
: the effect of an attainder which bars a person from inheriting, retaining, or transmitting any estate, rank, or title
**cor·rup·tive** \kə-'rəp-tiv\ *adjective* (15th century)
: producing or tending to produce corruption
— **cor·rup·tive·ly** *adverb*
**cor·sage** \kȯr-'säzh, -'säj, 'kȯr-ˌ\ *noun* [French, bust, bodice, from Old French, bust, from *cors* body, from Latin *corpus*] (1843)
**1** : the waist or bodice of a dress
**2** : an arrangement of flowers worn as a fashion accessory
**cor·sair** \'kȯr-ˌsar, -ˌser; kȯr-'\ *noun* [Middle French & Old Italian; Middle French *corsaire* pirate, from Old Provençal *corsari*, from Old Italian *corsaro*, from Medieval Latin *cursarius*, from Latin *cursus* course — more at COURSE] (1549)
: PIRATE; *especially* : a privateer of the Barbary Coast
**corse** \'kȯrs\ *noun* [Middle English *cors*, from Middle French] (13th century)
*archaic* : CORPSE
**corse·let** \*for 1* 'kȯr-slət, *for 2* ˌkȯr-sə-'let\ *noun* (1563)
**1** *or* **cors·let** [Middle French, diminutive of *cors* body, bodice] : a piece of armor covering the trunk
**2** *or* **cor·se·lette** [from *Corselette*, a trademark] : an undergarment combining girdle and brassiere
¹**cor·set** \'kȯr-sət\ *noun* [Middle English, from Old French, diminutive of *cors*] (13th century)
**1** : a usually close-fitting and often laced medieval jacket
**2** : a woman's close-fitting boned supporting undergarment that is often hooked and laced and that extends from above or beneath the bust or from the waist to below the hips and has garters attached
²**corset** *transitive verb* (circa 1847)
**1** : to dress in or fit with a corset
**2** : to restrict closely : control rigidly
**cor·se·tiere** \ˌkȯr-sə-'tir, -'tyer\ *noun* [French *corsetière*, feminine of *corsetier*, from *corset*] (1848)
: one who makes, fits, or sells corsets, girdles, or brassieres
**cor·tege** *also* **cor·tège** \kȯr-'tezh, 'kȯr-ˌ\ *noun* [French *cortège*, from Italian *corteggio*, from *corteggiare* to court, from *corte* court, from Latin *cohort-, cohors* enclosure — more at COURT] (1648)
**1** : a train of attendants : RETINUE
**2** : PROCESSION; *especially* : a funeral procession
**cor·tex** \'kȯr-ˌteks\ *noun, plural* **cor·ti·ces** \'kȯr-tə-ˌsēz\ *or* **cor·tex·es** [Latin *cortic-, cortex* bark — more at CUIRASS] (1677)

**1 a** : the outer or superficial part of an organ or bodily structure (as the kidney, adrenal gland, or a hair); *especially* : the outer layer of gray matter of the cerebrum and cerebellum **b** : the outer part of some organisms (as paramecia)
**2** : a plant bark or rind (as cinchona) used medicinally
**3 a** : the typically parenchymatous layer of tissue external to the vascular tissue and internal to the corky or epidermal tissues of a green plant; *broadly* : all tissues external to the xylem **b** : an outer or investing layer of various algae, lichens, or fungi
**cor·ti·cal** \'kȯr-ti-kəl\ *adjective* (1671)
**1** : of, relating to, or consisting of cortex
**2** : involving or resulting from the action or condition of the cerebral cortex
— **cor·ti·cal·ly** \-k(ə-)lē\ *adverb*
**cortico-** *combining form*
: cortex ⟨*cortico*tropin⟩
**cor·ti·coid** \'kȯr-ti-ˌkȯid\ *noun* (1941)
: CORTICOSTEROID
— **corticoid** *adjective*
**cor·ti·co·ste·roid** \ˌkȯr-ti-kō-'stir-ˌȯid *also* -'ster-\ *noun* (1944)
: any of various adrenal-cortex steroids (as corticosterone, cortisone, and aldosterone) used medically especially as anti-inflammatory agents
**cor·ti·co·ste·rone** \ˌkȯr-tə-'käs-tə-ˌrōn, -ti-kō-stə-'; ˌkȯr-ti-kō-'stir-ˌōn, -'ster-\ *noun* (1937)
: a colorless crystalline corticosteroid $C_{21}H_{30}O_4$ that is important in protein and carbohydrate metabolism
**cor·ti·co·tro·pin** \ˌkȯr-ti-kō-'trō-pən\ *also* **cor·ti·co·tro·phin** \-fən\ *noun* (1946)
: ACTH; *also* : a preparation of ACTH that is used especially in the treatment of rheumatoid arthritis and rheumatic fever
**cor·tin** \'kȯr-tᵊn\ *noun* (1928)
: the active principle of the adrenal cortex
**cor·ti·sol** \'kȯr-tə-ˌsȯl, -ˌzȯl, -ˌsōl, -ˌzōl\ *noun* [*cortis*one + ¹*-ol*] (1951)
: HYDROCORTISONE
**cor·ti·sone** \-ˌsōn, -ˌzōn\ *noun* [alteration of *corticosterone*] (1949)
: a glucocorticoid $C_{21}H_{28}O_5$ of the adrenal cortex used especially in the treatment of rheumatoid arthritis
**co·run·dum** \kə-'rən-dəm\ *noun* [Tamil *kuruntam*; akin to Sanskrit *kuruvinda* ruby] (1804)
: a very hard mineral that consists of aluminum oxide and occurs in massive form and as variously colored crystals (as ruby and sapphire), that can be synthesized, and that is used as an abrasive
**co·rus·cant** \kə-'rəs-kənt\ *adjective* (15th century)
: SHINING, GLITTERING
**cor·us·cate** \'kȯr-ə-ˌskāt, 'kär-\ *intransitive verb* **-cat·ed; -cat·ing** [Latin *coruscatus*, past participle of *coruscare* to flash] (1705)
**1** : to give off or reflect light in bright beams or flashes : SPARKLE
**2** : to be brilliant or showy in technique or style
**cor·us·ca·tion** \ˌkȯr-ə-'skā-shən, ˌkär-\ *noun* (15th century)
**1** : GLITTER, SPARKLE
**2** : a flash of wit
**cor·vée** \'kȯr-ˌvā, kȯr-'\ *noun* [Middle English *corvee*, from Middle French, from Medieval Latin *corrogata*, from Latin, feminine of *corrogatus*, past participle of *corrogare* to collect, requisition, from *com-* + *rogare* to ask — more at RIGHT] (14th century)
**1** : unpaid labor (as toward constructing roads) due from a feudal vassal to his lord
**2** : labor exacted in lieu of taxes by public authorities especially for highway construction or repair
**corves** *plural of* CORF

**cor·vette** \kȯr-'vet\ *noun* [French, from Middle French, probably from Middle Dutch *corf,* a kind of ship, literally, basket — more at CORF] (1636)
**1 :** a warship ranking in the old sailing navies next below a frigate
**2 :** a highly maneuverable armed escort ship that is smaller than a destroyer

**cor·vi·na** \kȯr-'vē-nə\ *variant of* CORBINA

**cor·vine** \'kȯr-ˌvīn\ *adjective* [Latin *corvinus,* from *corvus* raven — more at RAVEN] (circa 1656)
**:** of or relating to the crows **:** resembling a crow

**Cor·vus** \'kȯr-vəs\ *noun* [Latin (genitive *Corvi*), literally, raven]
**:** a small constellation adjoining Virgo on the south

**Cor·y·bant** \'kȯr-ə-ˌbant, 'kär-\ *noun, plural* **Cor·y·bants** \-ˌban(t)s\ *or* **Cor·y·ban·tes** \ˌkȯr-ə-'ban-tēz, ˌkär-\ [Middle French *Corybante,* from Latin *Corybas,* from Greek *Korybas*] (14th century)
**:** one of the attendants or priests of Cybele noted for wildly emotional processions and rites

**cor·y·ban·tic** \ˌkȯr-ē-'ban-tik, ˌkär-\ *adjective* (1642)
**:** like or in the spirit of a Corybant; *especially* **:** WILD, FRENZIED

**co·ryd·a·lis** \kə-'ri-dᵊl-əs\ *noun* [New Latin, genus name, from Greek *korydallis* crested lark (*Galerida cristata*), from *korydos* crested lark] (1818)
**:** any of a large genus (*Corydalis*) of chiefly temperate herbs of the fumitory family with racemose irregular flowers and dissected leaves

**cor·ymb** \'kȯr-ˌim(b), 'kär-, -əm(b)\ *noun, plural* **corymbs** \-ˌimz, -əmz\ [French *corymbe,* from Latin *corymbus* cluster of fruit or flowers, from Greek *korymbos*] (1776)
**:** a flat-topped inflorescence; *specifically* **:** one in which the flower stalks arise at different levels on the main axis and reach about the same height and in which the outer flowers open first and the inflorescence is indeterminate
— **cor·ymbed** \-ˌimd, -əmd\ *adjective*
— **cor·ym·bose** \-əm-ˌbōs\ *adjective*
— **cor·ym·bose·ly** *adverb*

**corymb**

**co·ry·ne·bac·te·ri·um** \ˌkȯr-ə-(ˌ)nē-bak-'tir-ē-əm, kə-ˌri-nə-\ *noun* [New Latin, from Greek *korynē* club] (1909)
**:** any of a large genus (*Corynebacterium*) of usually gram-positive nonmotile bacteria that occur as irregular or branching rods and include numerous important animal and plant parasites
— **co·ry·ne·bac·te·ri·al** \-ē-əl\ *adjective*

**co·ryn·e·form** \kə-'ri-nə-ˌfȯrm\ *adjective* (1952)
**:** being or resembling corynebacteria

**cor·y·phae·us** \ˌkȯr-ə-'fē-əs, ˌkär-\ *noun, plural* **-phaei** \-'fē-ˌī\ [Latin, leader, from Greek *koryphaios,* from *koryphē* summit] (1610)
**1 :** the leader of a party or school of thought
**2 :** the leader of a chorus

**co·ry·phée** \ˌkȯr-i-'fā\ *noun* [French, from Latin *coryphaeus*] (1828)
**:** a ballet dancer who dances in a small group instead of in the corps de ballet or as a soloist

**co·ry·za** \kə-'rī-zə\ *noun* [Late Latin, from Greek *koryza* nasal mucus; akin to Old English *hrot* nasal mucus, Sanskrit *kardama* mud] (1634)
**:** an acute inflammatory contagious disease involving the upper respiratory tract; *especially* **:** COMMON COLD
— **co·ry·zal** \-zəl\ *adjective*

**co·se·cant** \(ˌ)kō-'sē-ˌkant, -kənt\ *noun* [New Latin *cosecant-, cosecans,* from *co-* + *secant-, secans* secant] (circa 1706)
**1 :** a trigonometric function that for an acute angle is the ratio between the hypotenuse of a right triangle of which the angle is considered part and the leg opposite the angle
**2 :** a trigonometric function csc θ that is the reciprocal of the sine for all real numbers θ for which the sine is not zero and that is exactly equal to the cosecant of an angle of measure θ in radians

**co·set** \'kō-ˌset\ *noun* (1910)
**:** a subset of a mathematical group that consists of all the products obtained by multiplying either on the right or the left a fixed element of the group by each of the elements of a given subgroup

**¹cosh** \'käsh\ *noun* [perhaps from Romany *kaš, kašt* stick, piece of wood] (1869)
*chiefly British* **:** a weighted weapon similar to a blackjack

**²cosh** *transitive verb* (1896)
*chiefly British* **:** to strike or assault with or as if with a cosh

**co·sig·na·to·ry** \(ˌ)kō-'sig-nə-ˌtōr-ē, -ˌtȯr-\ *noun* (1865)
**:** a joint signer

**co·sign·er** \'kō-ˌsī-nər\ *noun* (circa 1903)
**:** COSIGNATORY; *especially* **:** a joint signer of a promissory note
— **co·sign** \'kō-ˌsīn\ *verb*

**co·sine** \'kō-ˌsīn\ *noun* [New Latin *cosinus,* from *co-* + Medieval Latin *sinus* sine] (1635)
**1 :** a trigonometric function that for an acute angle is the ratio between the leg adjacent to the angle when it is considered part of a right triangle and the hypotenuse
**2 :** a trigonometric function cos θ that for all real numbers θ is given by the sum of the alternating series

$$\cos \theta = 1 - \frac{\theta^2}{2!} + \frac{\theta^4}{4!} - \frac{\theta^6}{6!} + \frac{\theta^8}{8!} - \cdots$$

and that is exactly equal to the cosine of an angle of measure θ in radians

**cos lettuce** \'käs-, 'kȯs-\ *noun* [Kos, Cos, Greek island] (1699)
**:** ROMAINE

**¹cos·met·ic** \käz-'me-tik\ *adjective* [Greek *kosmētikos* skilled in adornment, from *kosmein* to arrange, adorn, from *kosmos* order] (1650)
**1 :** of, relating to, or making for beauty especially of the complexion **:** BEAUTIFYING ⟨*cosmetic* salves⟩
**2 :** done or made for the sake of appearance: as **a :** correcting defects especially of the face ⟨*cosmetic* surgery⟩ **b :** DECORATIVE, ORNAMENTAL **c :** not substantive **:** SUPERFICIAL ⟨*cosmetic* changes⟩
**3 :** visually appealing
— **cos·met·i·cal·ly** \-ti-k(ə-)lē\ *adverb*

**²cosmetic** *noun* (1650)
**:** something that is cosmetic: as **a :** a cosmetic preparation for external use **b** *plural* **:** superficial features ⟨a poem without rhetorical *cosmetics* —Guy Davenport⟩

**cosmetic case** *noun* (1948)
**:** a small piece of luggage especially for cosmetics

**cos·me·ti·cian** \ˌkäz-mə-'ti-shən\ *noun* (1924)
**:** a person who is professionally trained in the use of cosmetics

**cos·met·i·cize** \käz-'me-tə-ˌsīz\ *transitive verb* **-cized; -ciz·ing** (1824)
**:** to make (something unpleasant or ugly) superficially attractive

**cos·me·tol·o·gist** \ˌkäz-mə-'tä-lə-jist\ *noun* (1926)
**:** a person who gives beauty treatments (as to skin and hair) — called also *beautician*

**cos·me·tol·o·gy** \-jē\ *noun* [French *cosmétologie,* from *cosmétique* cosmetic (from English *cosmetic*) + *-logie* -logy] (1926)
**:** the cosmetic treatment of the skin, hair, and nails

**cos·mic** \'käz-mik\ *also* **cos·mi·cal** \-mi-kəl\ *adjective* [Greek *kosmikos,* from *kosmos* order, universe] (1685)
**1 :** of or relating to the cosmos, the extraterrestrial vastness, or the universe in contrast to the earth alone
**2 :** characterized by greatness especially in extent, intensity, or comprehensiveness ⟨a *cosmic* thinker⟩ ⟨*cosmic* boredom⟩
— **cos·mi·cal·ly** \-mi-k(ə-)lē\ *adverb*

**cosmic background radiation** *noun* (circa 1976)
**:** BACKGROUND RADIATION

**cosmic dust** *noun* (1881)
**:** very fine particles of solid matter found in any part of the universe

**cosmic noise** *noun* (1947)
**:** unidentified celestial radio-frequency radiation; *especially* **:** such radiation originating from outside the Milky Way

**cosmic ray** *noun* (1925)
**:** a stream of atomic nuclei of extremely penetrating character that enter the earth's atmosphere from outer space at speeds approaching that of light

**cosmic string** *noun* (1984)
**:** any of a class of hypothetical supermassive astronomical objects that are extremely thin but are millions of light years long and that are postulated to have formed very early in the history of the universe

**cos·mo·chem·is·try** \ˌkäz-mō-'ke-mə-strē\ *noun* [Greek *kosmos* universe] (1940)
**:** a branch of chemistry that deals with the chemical composition of and changes in the universe
— **cos·mo·chem·i·cal** \-'ke-mi-kəl\ *adjective*
— **cos·mo·chem·ist** \-mist\ *noun*

**cos·mo·gen·ic** \ˌkäz-mə-'je-nik\ *adjective* [*cosmic ray* + *-o-* + *-genic*] (1962)
**:** produced by the action of cosmic rays ⟨*cosmogenic* carbon 14⟩

**cos·mog·o·ny** \käz-'mä-gə-nē\ *noun, plural* **-nies** [New Latin *cosmogonia,* from Greek *kosmogonia,* from *kosmos* + *gonos* offspring; akin to Greek *genos* race — more at KIN] (1766)
**1 :** the creation or origin of the world or universe
**2 :** a theory of the origin of the universe
— **cos·mo·gon·ic** \ˌkäz-mə-'gä-nik\ *or* **cos·mo·gon·i·cal** \-ni-kəl\ *adjective*
— **cos·mog·o·nist** \käz-'mä-gə-nist\ *noun*

**cos·mog·ra·phy** \käz-'mä-grə-fē\ *noun, plural* **-phies** [Middle English *cosmographie,* from Late Latin *cosmographia,* from Greek *kosmographia,* from *kosmos* + *-graphia* -graphy] (14th century)
**1 :** a general description of the world or of the universe
**2 :** the science that deals with the constitution of the whole order of nature
— **cos·mog·ra·pher** \-fər\ *noun*
— **cos·mo·graph·ic** \ˌkäz-mə-'gra-fik\ *or* **cos·mo·graph·i·cal** \-fi-kəl\ *adjective*

**Cos·mo·line** \'käz-mə-ˌlēn\ *trademark*
— used for petroleum jelly

**cos·mol·o·gy** \käz-'mä-lə-jē\ *noun, plural* **-gies** [New Latin *cosmologia,* from Greek *kosmos* + New Latin *-logia* -logy] (circa 1656)
**1 a :** a branch of metaphysics that deals with the nature of the universe **b :** a theory or doctrine describing the natural order of the universe

\ə\ **abut** \ᵊ\ **kitten** \ər\ **further** \a\ **ash** \ā\ **ace**
\ä\ **mop, mar** \au̇\ **out** \ch\ **chin** \e\ **bet** \ē\ **easy**
\g\ **go** \i\ **hit** \ī\ **ice** \j\ **job** \ŋ\ **sing** \ō\ **go**
\ȯ\ **law** \ȯi\ **boy** \th\ **thin** \t͟h\ **the** \ü\ **loot** \u̇\ **foot**
\y\ **yet** \zh\ **vision** *see also* Guide to Pronunciation

**2 :** a branch of astronomy that deals with the origin, structure, and space-time relationships of the universe; *also* **:** a theory dealing with these matters
— **cos·mo·log·i·cal** \,käz-mə-'lä-ji-kəl\ *adjective*
— **cos·mo·log·i·cal·ly** \-ji-k(ə-)lē\ *adverb*
— **cos·mol·o·gist** \käz-'mä-lə-jist\ *noun*
**cos·mo·naut** \'käz-mə-,nȯt, -,nät\ *noun* [Russian *kosmonavt*, from Greek *kosmos* + Russian *-navt* (as in *aeronavt* aeronaut)] (1959)
**:** an astronaut of the Soviet or Russian space program
**cos·mop·o·lis** \käz-'mä-pə-ləs\ *noun* [New Latin, back-formation from *cosmopolites*] (1849)
**:** a cosmopolitan city
**¹cos·mo·pol·i·tan** \,käz-mə-'pä-lə-tᵊn\ *noun* (circa 1645)
**:** COSMOPOLITE
**²cosmopolitan** *adjective* (1844)
**1 :** having worldwide rather than limited or provincial scope or bearing
**2 :** having wide international sophistication **:** WORLDLY
**3 :** composed of persons, constituents, or elements from all or many parts of the world
**4 :** found in most parts of the world and under varied ecological conditions ⟨a *cosmopolitan* herb⟩
— **cos·mo·pol·i·tan·ism** \-tə-,ni-zəm\ *noun*
**cos·mop·o·lite** \käz-'mä-pə-,līt\ *noun* [New Latin *cosmopolites*, from Greek *kosmopolitēs*, from *kosmos* + *politēs* citizen] (circa 1618)
**:** a cosmopolitan person or organism
— **cos·mo·po·li·tism** \käz-'mä-pə-,lī-,ti-zəm, -lə-,ti-; ,käz-mə-'pä-lə-,ti-\ *noun*
**cos·mos** \'käz-məs, *1 & 2 also* -,mōs, -,mäs\ *noun* [Greek *kosmos*] (1650)
**1 a** (1) **:** an orderly harmonious systematic universe — compare CHAOS (2) **:** ORDER, HARMONY **b :** UNIVERSE 1
**2 :** a complex orderly self-inclusive system
**3** *plural* **cosmos** \-məs, -,məz\ *also* **cosmos·es** \-mə-səz\ [New Latin, genus name, from Greek *kosmos*] **:** any of a genus (*Cosmos*) of tropical American composite herbs; *especially* **:** a widely cultivated tall annual (*C. bipinnatus*) with yellow or red disks and showy ray flowers
**cos·sack** \'kä-,sak, -sək\ *noun, often capitalized* [Polish & Ukrainian *kozak*, of Turkic origin; akin to Volga Tatar *kazak* free person] (1589)
**:** a member of a group of frontiersmen of southern Russia organized as cavalry in the czarist army
**¹cos·set** \'kä-sət\ *noun* [origin unknown] (1579)
**:** a pet lamb; *broadly* **:** PET
**²cosset** *transitive verb* (1659)
**:** to treat as a pet **:** PAMPER
**¹cost** \'kȯst\ *noun* (13th century)
**1 a :** the amount or equivalent paid or charged for something **:** PRICE **b :** the outlay or expenditure (as of effort or sacrifice) made to achieve an object
**2 :** loss or penalty incurred especially in gaining something
**3** *plural* **:** expenses incurred in litigation; *especially* **:** those given by the law or the court to the prevailing party against the losing party
— **cost·less** \-ləs\ *adjective*
— **cost·less·ly** *adverb*
**²cost** *verb* **cost; cost·ing** [Middle English, from Middle French *coster*, from Latin *constare* to stand firm, cost — more at CONSTANT] (14th century)
*intransitive verb*
**1 :** to require expenditure or payment ⟨the best goods *cost* more⟩
**2 :** to require effort, suffering, or loss
*transitive verb*
**1 :** to have a price of

**2 :** to cause to pay, suffer, or lose something ⟨frequent absences *cost* him his job⟩
**3** *past* **cost·ed :** to estimate or set the cost of — often used with *out*
**cos·ta** \'käs-tə\ *noun, plural* **cos·tae** \-(,)tē, -,tī\ [Latin — more at COAST] (circa 1864)
**1 :** ¹RIB 1a
**2 :** a part (as the midrib of a leaf or the anterior vein of an insect wing) that resembles a rib
— **cos·tal** \-tᵊl\ *adjective*
**cost accountant** *noun* (1918)
**:** a specialist in cost accounting
**cost accounting** *noun* (1913)
**:** the systematic recording and analysis of the costs of material, labor, and overhead incident to production
**cos·tard** \'käs-tərd\ *noun* [Middle English] (13th century)
**1 :** any of several large English cooking apples
**2** *archaic* **:** NODDLE, PATE
**cost–ben·e·fit** \'kȯs(t)-'be-nə-,fit\ *adjective* (1928)
**:** of, relating to, or being economic analysis that assigns a numerical value to the cost-effectiveness of an operation, procedure, or program
**cost–ef·fec·tive** \'kȯst-ə-'fek-tiv, -,fek-\ *adjective* (1967)
**:** economical in terms of tangible benefits produced by money spent ⟨*cost-effective* measures to combat poverty⟩
— **cost–ef·fec·tive·ness** *noun*
**cost–ef·fi·cient** \-i-'fi-shənt, -,fi-\ *adjective* (1979)
**:** COST-EFFECTIVE
**cos·ter** \'käs-tər\ *noun* (1851)
*British* **:** COSTERMONGER
**cos·ter·mon·ger** \-,mən-gər, -,mäŋ-\ *noun* [*costard* + *monger*] (1514)
*British* **:** a hawker of fruit or vegetables
**cos·tive** \'käs-tiv, 'kȯs-\ *adjective* [Middle English, from Middle French *costivé*, past participle of *costiver* to constipate, from Latin *constipare*] (14th century)
**1 a :** affected with constipation **b :** causing constipation
**2 :** slow in action or expression
**3 :** NIGGARDLY, STINGY
— **cos·tive·ly** *adverb*
— **cos·tive·ness** *noun*
**cost·ly** \'kȯs(t)-lē\ *adjective* **cost·li·er; -est** (14th century)
**1 a :** commanding a high price especially because of intrinsic worth ⟨*costly* gems⟩ **b :** RICH, SPLENDID
**2 :** made or done at heavy expense or sacrifice ⟨a *costly* mistake⟩
— **cost·li·ness** *noun*
**cost·mary** \'kȯst-,mer-ē, 'käst-\ *noun, plural* **-mar·ies** [Middle English *costmarie*, from *coste* costmary (from Old English *cost*, from Latin *costum*, from Greek *kostos*, a fragrant root) + *Marie* the Virgin Mary] (14th century)
**:** an aromatic composite herb (*Chrysanthemum balsamita*) used as a potherb and in flavoring
**cost of living** (1896)
**:** the cost of purchasing those goods and services which are included in an accepted standard level of consumption
**cost–of–living index** *noun* (1913)
**:** CONSUMER PRICE INDEX
**cost–plus** \'kȯs(t)-'pləs\ *adjective* (1918)
**1 :** paid on the basis of a fixed fee or a percentage added to actual cost ⟨a *cost-plus* contract⟩
**2 :** of or relating to a cost-plus contract
**cost–push** \'kȯs(t)-,pùsh\ *noun* (1951)
**:** an increase or upward trend in production costs (as wages) that tends to result in increased consumer prices irrespective of the level of demand — compare DEMAND-PULL
— **cost–push** *adjective*
**cos·trel** \'käs-trəl\ *noun* [Middle English, from Middle French *costerel*, from *costier* at

the side, from *coste* rib, side — more at COAST] (14th century)
**:** a flat usually earthenware container for liquids with loops through which a belt or cord may be passed for easy carrying — called also *pilgrim bottle*
**¹cos·tume** \'käs-,tüm, -,tyüm *also* -təm *or* -,chüm\ *noun* [French, from Italian, custom, dress, from Latin *consuetudin-, consuetudo* custom — more at CUSTOM] (1715)
**1 :** the prevailing fashion in coiffure, jewelry, and apparel of a period, country, or class
**2 :** an outfit worn to create the appearance characteristic of a particular period, person, place, or thing ⟨Halloween *costumes*⟩
**3 :** a person's ensemble of outer garments; *especially* **:** a woman's ensemble of dress with coat or jacket
— **cos·tum·ey** *adjective*
**²cos·tume** \käs-'tüm, -'tyüm *also* -'chüm; *or* 'käs-, *or* -təm\ *transitive verb* **cos·tumed; cos·tum·ing** (1823)
**1 :** to provide with a costume
**2 :** to design costumes for ⟨*costume* a play⟩
**³costume** \*same as* ¹\ *adjective* (1884)
**1 :** characterized by the use of costumes ⟨a *costume* ball⟩ ⟨a *costume* drama⟩
**2 :** suitable for or enhancing the effect of a particular costume ⟨a *costume* handbag⟩
**costume jewelry** *noun* (1933)
**:** jewelry designed for wear with current fashions and usually made of inexpensive materials
**cos·tum·er** \'käs-,tü-mər, -,tyü- *also* -,chü-; käs-'\ *noun* (circa 1859)
**1 :** one that deals in or makes costumes
**2 :** an upright stand with hooks or pegs on which to hang clothes
**cos·tum·ery** \-mə-rē\ *noun* (1838)
**1 :** articles of costume
**2 :** the art of costuming
**cos·tu·mi·er** \käs-'tü-mē-,ā, -'tyü-, -mē-ər\ *noun* [French] (1831)
*chiefly British* **:** COSTUMER 1
**co·sy** \'kō-zē\ *variant of* COZY
**¹cot** \'kät\ *noun* [Middle English, from Old English; akin to Old Norse *kot* small hut] (before 12th century)
**1 :** a small house
**2 :** COVER, SHEATH; *especially* **:** STALL 4
**²cot** *noun* [Hindi *khāṭ* bedstead, from Sanskrit *khaṭvā*, perhaps of Dravidian origin; akin to Tamil *kaṭṭil* bedstead] (1634)
**1 :** a small usually collapsible bed often of fabric stretched on a frame
**2** *British* **:** CRIB 2b
**co·tan·gent** \(,)kō-'tan-jənt, 'kō-,\ *noun* [New Latin *cotangent-, cotangens*, from *co-* + *tangent-, tangens* tangent] (1635)
**1 :** a trigonometric function that for an acute angle is the ratio between the leg adjacent to the angle when it is considered part of a right triangle and the leg opposite
**2 :** a trigonometric function cot θ that is equal to the cosine divided by the sine for all real numbers θ for which the sine is not equal to zero and is exactly equal to the cotangent of an angle of measure θ in radians
**¹cote** \'kōt, 'kät\ *noun* [Middle English, from Old English] (before 12th century)
**1** *dialect English* **:** ¹COT 1
**2 :** a shed or coop for small domestic animals and especially pigeons
**²cote** \'kōt\ *transitive verb* [probably from Middle French *cotoyer*] (1555)
*obsolete* **:** to pass by
**co·te·rie** \'kō-tə-(,)rē, ,kō-tə-'\ *noun* [French, from Middle French, tenants, from Old French *cotier* cotter, of Germanic origin; akin to Old English *cot* hut] (1738)
**:** an intimate and often exclusive group of persons with a unifying common interest or purpose
**co·ter·mi·nous** \(,)kō-'tər-mə-nəs\ *adjective* [alteration of *conterminous*] (1799)

**1 :** having the same or coincident boundaries ⟨*coterminous* states⟩
**2 :** coextensive in scope or duration ⟨an experience of life *coterminous* with the years of his father —Elizabeth Hardwick⟩
— **co·ter·mi·nous·ly** *adverb*
**co·thur·nus** \kō-'thər-nəs\ *noun, plural* **-ni** \-ˌnī, -(ˌ)nē\ [Latin, from Greek *kothornos*] (1606)
**1 :** a high thick-soled laced boot worn by actors in Greek and Roman tragic drama — called also *cothurn* \'kō-ˌthərn, kō-'\
**2 :** the dignified somewhat stilted style of ancient tragedy
**co·tid·al** \(ˌ)kō-'tī-dᵊl\ *adjective* (1833)
**:** indicating equality in the tides or a coincidence in the time of high or low tide
**co·til·lion** \kō-'til-yən, kə-\ *also* **co·til·ion** \kō-'til-yən, kə-, kō-tē-(y)ōⁿ\ *noun* [French *cotillon*, literally, petticoat, from Old French, from *cote* coat] (1766)
**1 :** a ballroom dance for couples that resembles the quadrille
**2 :** an elaborate dance with frequent changing of partners carried out under the leadership of one couple at formal balls
**3 :** a formal ball
**co·to·ne·as·ter** \kə-'tō-nē-ˌas-tər, ˌkä-tᵊn-ē-ˌes-tər\ *noun* [New Latin, genus name; from Latin *cotoneum* quince + New Latin *-aster*] (1796)
**:** any of a genus (*Cotoneaster*) of Old World flowering shrubs of the rose family
**cot·quean** \'kät-ˌkwēn\ *noun* [¹*cot* + *quean*] (1547)
**1** *archaic* **:** a coarse masculine woman
**2** *archaic* **:** a man who busies himself with women's work or affairs
**Cots·wold** \'kät-ˌswōld, -swəld\ *noun* [*Cotswold* Hills, England] (circa 1658)
**:** any of an English breed of large long-wooled sheep
**cot·ta** \'kä-tə\ *noun* [Medieval Latin, of Germanic origin; akin to Old High German *kozza* coarse mantle — more at COAT] (1848)
**:** a waist-length surplice
**cot·tage** \'kä-tij\ *noun* [Middle English *cotage*, from (assumed) Anglo-French, from Middle English *cot* — more at COT] (14th century)
**1 :** the dwelling of a farm laborer or small farmer
**2 :** a usually small frame one-family house
**3 :** a small detached dwelling unit at an institution
**4 :** a usually small house for vacation use
— **cot·tag·ey** \-ti-jē\ *adjective*
**cottage cheese** *noun* (1848)
**:** a bland soft white cheese made from the curds of skim milk — called also *Dutch cheese, pot cheese, smearcase*
**cottage curtains** *noun plural* (1943)
**:** a double set of upper and lower straight-hanging window curtains
**cottage industry** *noun* (1921)
**1 :** an industry whose labor force consists of family units or individuals working at home with their own equipment
**2 :** a small and often informally organized industry
**cottage pie** *noun* (1791)
**:** a shepherd's pie made especially with beef
**cottage pudding** *noun* (circa 1854)
**:** plain cake covered with a hot sweet sauce
**cot·tag·er** \'kä-ti-jər\ *noun* (1550)
**:** a person who lives in a cottage
**cottage tulip** *noun* (1928)
**:** any of various tall late-flowering tulips
**cot·tar** *or* **cot·ter** \'kä-tər\ *noun* [Middle English *cottar*, from Medieval Latin *cotarius*, from Middle English *cot*] (14th century)
**:** a peasant or farm laborer who occupies a cottage and sometimes a small holding of land usually in return for services
**cot·ter** \'kä-tər\ *noun* [origin unknown] (14th century)

**1 :** a wedge-shaped or tapered piece used to fasten together parts of a structure
**2 :** COTTER PIN
— **cot·tered** \-tərd\ *adjective*
— **cot·ter·less** \-tər-ləs\ *adjective*
**cotter pin** *noun* (1881)
**:** a half-round metal strip bent into a pin whose ends can be flared after insertion through a slot or hole
**¹cot·ton** \'kä-tᵊn\ *noun, often attributive* [Middle English *coton*, from Middle French, from Arabic *quṭun*] (14th century)
**1 a :** a soft usually white fibrous substance composed of the hairs surrounding the seeds of various erect freely branching tropical plants (genus *Gossypium*) of the mallow family **b :** a plant producing cotton; *especially* **:** one grown for its cotton
**c :** a crop of cotton
**2 a :** fabric made of cotton **b :** yarn spun from cotton
**3 :** a downy cottony substance produced by various plants (as the cottonwood)

cotton: *1* flowering branch; *2* fruit, unopened; *3* fruit, partly opened

**²cotton** *intransitive verb* **cot·toned; cot·ton·ing** \'kä-tᵊn-iŋ, 'ka-tᵊn-iŋ\ (1605)
**1 :** to take a liking — used with *to* ⟨*cottons* to people easily⟩
**2 :** to come to understand — used with *to* or *on to* ⟨*cottoned* on to the fact that our children work furiously —H. M. McLuhan⟩
**cotton candy** *noun* (1926)
**1 :** a candy made of spun sugar
**2 :** something attractive but insubstantial
**cotton gin** *noun* (1796)
**:** a machine that separates the seeds, hulls, and foreign material from cotton
**cotton grass** *noun* (1597)
**:** any of a genus (*Eriophorum*) of sedges with tufted spikes
**cot·ton·mouth** \'kä-tᵊn-ˌmaùth\ *noun* [from the white interior of its mouth] (1832)
**:** WATER MOCCASIN
**cottonmouth moccasin** *noun* (1879)
**:** WATER MOCCASIN
**cot·ton–pick·ing** \'kä-tᵊn-ˌpi-kiŋ, -ˌpi-kən\ *adjective* (circa 1952)
**1 :** DAMNED — used as a generalized expression of disapproval ⟨a *cotton-picking* hypocrite⟩
**2 :** DAMNED — used as an intensive ⟨out of his *cotton-picking* mind —Irving Kristol⟩
**cot·ton·seed** \'kä-tᵊn-ˌsēd\ *noun* (1774)
**:** the seed of the cotton plant
**cottonseed oil** *noun* (1833)
**:** a pale yellow semidrying fatty oil that is obtained from the cottonseed and is used chiefly in salad and cooking oils and after hydrogenation in shortenings and margarine
**cotton stainer** *noun* (1856)
**:** any of several bugs (genus *Dysdercus*) that damage and stain the lint of developing cotton; *especially* **:** a red and brown bug (*D. suturellus*) that attacks cotton in the southern U.S.
**cot·ton·tail** \'kä-tᵊn-ˌtāl\ *noun* (1869)
**:** any of several rather small North American rabbits (genus *Sylvilagus*) sandy to grayish brown in color with a white-tufted underside of the tail
**cot·ton·weed** \-ˌwēd\ *noun* (1562)
**:** any of various weedy plants (as cudweed) with hoary pubescence or cottony seeds
**cot·ton·wood** \-ˌwùd\ *noun* (1802)
**:** any of several poplars having seeds with cottony hairs; *especially* **:** one (*Populus del-*

*toides*) of the eastern and central U.S. often cultivated for its rapid growth and luxuriant foliage
**cotton wool** *noun* (14th century)
**:** raw cotton; *especially* **:** cotton batting
**cot·tony** \'kät-nē, 'kä-tᵊn-ē\ *adjective* (1578)
**:** resembling cotton in appearance or character: as **a :** covered with hairs or pubescence **b** **:** SOFT
**cot·tony–cush·ion scale** \-'kù-shən-\ *noun* (1886)
**:** a scale insect (*Icerya purchasi*) introduced into the U.S. from Australia that infests citrus and other plants
**-cotyl** *noun combining form* [*cotyledon*]
**:** cotyledon ⟨hypo*cotyl*⟩
**cot·y·le·don** \ˌkä-tə-'lē-dᵊn\ *noun* [New Latin, from Greek *kotylēdōn* cup-shaped hollow, from *kotylē* cup, anything hollow] (1540)
**1 :** a lobule of the mammalian placenta
**2 :** the first leaf or one of the first pair or whorl of leaves developed by the embryo of a seed plant or of some lower plants (as ferns) — see PLUMULE illustration
— **cot·y·le·don·ary** \-'lē-də-ˌner-ē\ *adjective*
**co·ty·lo·saur** \'kä-tᵊl-ō-ˌsòr, kə-'ti-lə-\ *noun* [ultimately from Greek *kotylē* + *sauros* lizard] (circa 1909)
**:** any of an order (Cotylosauria) of extinct primitive reptiles with short legs and massive bodies that were probably the earliest truly terrestrial vertebrate animals
**¹couch** \'kaùch\ *verb* [Middle English, from Middle French *coucher*, from Latin *collocare* to set in place — more at COLLOCATE] (14th century)
*transitive verb*
**1 :** to lay (oneself) down for rest or sleep
**2 :** to embroider (a design) by laying down a thread and fastening it with small stitches at regular intervals
**3 :** to place or hold level and pointed forward ready for use
**4 :** to phrase or express in a specified manner ⟨the comments were *couched* in strong terms⟩
**5 :** to treat (a cataract) by displacing the lens of the eye into the vitreous humor
*intransitive verb*
**1 :** to lie down or recline for sleep or rest
**2 :** to lie in ambush
**²couch** *noun* [Middle English *couche* bed, from Middle French, from *coucher*] (14th century)
**1 a :** an article of furniture for sitting or reclining **b :** a couch on which a patient reclines when undergoing psychoanalysis
**2 :** the den of an animal (as an otter)
— **on the couch :** receiving psychiatric treatment
**couch·ant** \'kaù-chənt\ *adjective* [Middle English, from Middle French, from present participle of *coucher*] (15th century)
**:** lying down especially with the head up ⟨a heraldic lion *couchant*⟩
**couch grass** \'kaùch-, 'küch-\ *noun* [alteration of *quitch*] (1578)
**1 :** QUACK GRASS
**2 :** any of several grasses that resemble quack grass in spreading by creeping rhizomes
**couch potato** *noun* (1982)
**:** a lazy and inactive person; *especially* **:** one who spends a great deal of time watching television
**cou·dé** \kü-'dā\ *adjective* [French *coudé* bent like an elbow, from *coude* elbow, from Latin *cubitum*] (circa 1889)
**:** of, relating to, or being a telescope constructed so that the light is reflected along the polar axis to come to a focus at a point where the

\ə\ **abut** \ᵊ\ **kitten** \ər\ **further** \a\ **ash** \ā\ **ace**
\ä\ **mop, mar** \aù\ **out** \ch\ **chin** \e\ **bet** \ē\ **easy**
\g\ **go** \i\ **hit** \ī\ **ice** \j\ **job** \ŋ\ **sing** \ō\ **go**
\ò\ **law** \òi\ **boy** \th\ **thin** \t̲h̲\ **the** \ü\ **loot** \ù\ **foot**
\y\ **yet** \zh\ **vision** *see also* Guide to Pronunciation

holder for a photographic plate or a spectrograph may be mounted

**cou·gar** \'kü-gər *also* -ˌgär\ *noun, plural* **cougars** *also* **cougar** [French *couguar*, modification of New Latin *cuguacuarana*, from Tupi *siwasuarána*, from *siwasú* deer + *-rana* resembling] (1774)

cougar

: a large powerful tawny brown cat (*Felis concolor*) formerly widespread in the Americas but now reduced in number or extinct in many areas — called also *catamount, mountain lion, panther, puma*

**¹cough** \'kof\ *verb* [Middle English, from (assumed) Old English *cohhian;* akin to Middle High German *kūchen* to breathe heavily] (14th century)
*intransitive verb*
**1 :** to expel air from the lungs suddenly with an explosive noise
**2 :** to make a noise like that of coughing
*transitive verb*
: to expel by coughing — often used with *up* ⟨*cough* up mucus⟩

**²cough** *noun* (14th century)
**1 :** a condition marked by repeated or frequent coughing
**2 :** an act or sound of coughing

**cough drop** *noun* (1831)
: a lozenge or troche used to relieve coughing

**cough syrup** *noun* (1877)
: any of various sweet usually medicated liquids used to relieve coughing

**cough up** *transitive verb* (1894)
: HAND OVER, DELIVER ⟨*cough* up the money⟩

**could** \kəd, 'kůd\ [Middle English *couthe, coude,* from Old English *cūthe;* akin to Old High German *konda* could] *past of* CAN
— used in auxiliary function in the past ⟨we found we *could* go⟩, in the past conditional ⟨we said we would go if we *could*⟩, and as an alternative to *can* suggesting less force or certainty or as a polite form in the present ⟨if you *could* come we would be pleased⟩

**could·est** \'ků-dəst\ *archaic past 2d singular of* CAN

**couldn't** \'ků-d°nt, -d°n, *dialect also* 'kůt-°n(t) *or* 'kůnt\ (1646)
: could not

**couldst** \kədst, 'kůdst, kətst, 'kůtst\ *archaic past 2d singular of* CAN

**cou·lee** \'kü-lē\ *noun* [Canadian French *coulée,* from French, flowing, flow of lava, from *couler* to flow, from Old French, from Latin *colare* to strain, from *colum* sieve] (1807)
**1 a :** a small stream *also* : a dry streambed **c :** a usually small or shallow ravine : GULLY
**2 :** a thick sheet or stream of lava

**cou·lis** \kü-'lē\ *noun* [French, from Old French *coleïs,* from *coleïs, coleïz* flowing] (1978)
: a thick sauce made with pureed vegetable or fruit and often used as a garnish

**cou·lisse** \kü-'lēs, -'lis\ *noun* [French, from Old French *coulice* portcullis, from feminine of *coleïz* flowing, sliding, from *couler*] (1819)
**1 a :** a side scene of a stage; *also* : the space between the side scenes **b :** a backstage area **c :** HALLWAY
**2 :** a piece of timber having a groove in which something glides

**cou·loir** \kül-'wär\ *noun* [French, literally, passage, from *couler*] (1822)
: a steep mountainside gorge

**¹cou·lomb** \'kü-ˌläm, -ˌlōm\ *noun* [Charles A. de *Coulomb*] (1881)
: the practical meter-kilogram-second unit of electric charge equal to the quantity of electricity transferred by a current of one ampere in one second

**²coulomb** *or* **cou·lom·bic** \kü-'läm-bik, -'lōm-, -'lä-mik, -'lō-\ *adjective* (1930)
: of, relating to, or being the electrostatic force of attraction or repulsion between charged particles

**Cou·lomb's law** \'kü-ˌlämz-, -ˌlōmz-\ *noun* (1854)
: a statement in physics: the force of attraction or repulsion acting along a straight line between two electric charges is directly proportional to the product of the charges and inversely to the square of the distance between them

**cou·lo·me·ter** \kü-'lä-mə-tər, 'kü-lə-ˌmē-tər\ *noun* [alteration of *coulombmeter,* from *coulomb* + *-meter*] (circa 1889)
: an instrument of chemical analysis that determines the amount of a substance released in electrolysis by measurement of the quantity of electricity used
— **cou·lo·met·ric** \ˌkü-lə-'me-trik\ *adjective*
— **cou·lo·met·ri·cal·ly** \-tri-k(ə-)lē\ *adverb*
— **cou·lom·e·try** \kü-'lä-mə-trē\ *noun*

**coul·ter** \'kōl-tər\ *noun* [Middle English *colter,* from Old English *culter* & Old French *coltre,* both from Latin *culter* plowshare; akin to Greek *skallein* to hoe — more at SHELL] (before 12th century)
: a cutting tool (as a knife or sharp disc) that is attached to the beam of a plow, makes a vertical cut in the surface, and permits clean separation and effective covering of the soil and materials being turned under

**cou·ma·rin** \'kü-mə-rən\ *noun* [French *coumarine,* from *coumarou* tonka bean tree, from Spanish or Portuguese; Spanish *cumarú,* from Portuguese, from Tupi *kumarú*] (1830)
: a toxic white crystalline lactone $C_9H_6O_2$ with an odor of new-mown hay found in plants or made synthetically and used especially in perfumery; *also* : a derivative of this compound

**¹coun·cil** \'kaůn(t)-səl\ *noun* [Middle English *counceil,* from Old French *concile,* from Latin *concilium,* from *com-* + *calare* to call — more at LOW] (12th century)
**1 :** an assembly or meeting for consultation, advice, or discussion
**2 :** a group elected or appointed as an advisory or legislative body
**3 a :** a usually administrative body **b :** an executive body whose members are equal in power and authority **c :** a governing body of delegates from local units of a federation
**4 :** deliberation in a council
**5 a :** a federation of or a central body uniting a group of organizations **b :** a local chapter of an organization **c :** CLUB, SOCIETY

**²council** *adjective* (14th century)
**1 :** used for councils especially by or with North American Indians ⟨a *council* ground⟩
**2** *British* **:** built, maintained, or operated by a local governing agency ⟨*council* housing⟩ ⟨*council* flats⟩

**coun·cil·lor** *or* **coun·cil·or** \'kaůn(t)-s(ə-)lər\ *noun* (15th century)
: a member of a council
— **coun·cil·lor·ship** \-ˌship\ *noun*

**coun·cil·man** \'kaůn(t)-səl-mən\ *noun* (1659)
: a member of a council (as of a town or city)
— **coun·cil·man·ic** \ˌkaůn(t)-səl-'ma-nik\ *adjective*

**council of ministers** *often C&M capitalized* (circa 1909)
: CABINET 3b

**coun·cil·wom·an** \'kaůn(t)-səl-ˌwů-mən\ *noun* (circa 1928)
: a woman who is a member of a council

**¹coun·sel** \'kaůn(t)-səl\ *noun* [Middle English *conseil,* from Old French, from Latin *consilium,* from *consulere* to consult] (13th century)
**1 a :** advice given especially as a result of consultation **b :** a policy or plan of action or behavior

**2 :** DELIBERATION, CONSULTATION
**3 a** *archaic* **:** PURPOSE **b :** guarded thoughts or intentions
**4 a** *plural* **counsel** (1) **:** a lawyer engaged in the trial or management of a case in court (2) **:** a lawyer appointed to advise and represent in legal matters an individual client or a corporate and especially a public body **b :** CONSULTANT 2

**²counsel** *verb* **-seled** *or* **-selled; -sel·ing** *or* **-sel·ling** \-s(ə-)liŋ\ (14th century)
*transitive verb*
: ADVISE ⟨*counseled* them to avoid rash actions —George Orwell⟩
*intransitive verb*
: CONSULT ⟨*counseled* with her husband⟩

**coun·sel·ee** \ˌkaůn(t)-sə-'lē\ *noun* (1923)
: one who is being counseled

**counseling** *or* **counselling** *noun* (1927)
: professional guidance of the individual by utilizing psychological methods especially in collecting case history data, using various techniques of the personal interview, and testing interests and aptitudes

**coun·sel·or** *or* **coun·sel·lor** \'kaůn(t)-s(ə-)lər\ *noun* (13th century)
**1 :** a person who gives advice or counseling ⟨marriage *counselor*⟩
**2 :** LAWYER; *specifically* **:** one that gives advice in law and manages cases for clients in court
**3 :** one who has supervisory duties at a summer camp
— **coun·sel·or·ship** \-ˌship\ *noun*

**counselor–at–law** *noun, plural* **counselors–at–law** (1617)
: COUNSELOR 2

**¹count** \'kaůnt, *dialect* 'kyaůnt\ *verb* [Middle English, from Middle French *conter, compter,* from Latin *computare,* from *com-* + *putare* to consider] (14th century)
*transitive verb*
**1 a :** to indicate or name by units or groups so as to find the total number of units involved : NUMBER **b :** to name the numbers in order up to and including ⟨*count* ten⟩ **c :** to include in a tallying and reckoning ⟨about 100 present, *counting* children⟩ **d :** to call aloud (beats or time units) ⟨*count* cadence⟩ ⟨*count* eighth notes⟩
**2 a :** CONSIDER, ACCOUNT ⟨*count* oneself lucky⟩ **b :** to record as of an opinion or persuasion ⟨*count* me as uncommitted⟩
**3 :** to include or exclude by or as if by counting ⟨*count* me in⟩
*intransitive verb*
**1 a :** to recite or indicate the numbers in order by units or groups ⟨*count* by fives⟩ **b :** to count the units in a group
**2 :** to rely or depend on someone or something ⟨*counted* on his parents to help with the expenses⟩
**3 :** ADD, TOTAL ⟨it *counts* up to a sizable amount⟩
**4 :** to have value or significance ⟨these are the people who really *count*⟩
— **count heads** *or* **count noses :** to count the number present
— **count on :** to look forward to as certain : ANTICIPATE ⟨*counted* on winning⟩

**²count** *noun* (14th century)
**1 a :** the action or process of counting **b :** a total obtained by counting : TALLY
**2** *archaic* **a :** RECKONING, ACCOUNT **b :** CONSIDERATION, ESTIMATION
**3 a :** ALLEGATION, CHARGE; *specifically* **:** one separately stating the cause of action or prosecution in a legal declaration or indictment ⟨guilty on all *counts*⟩ **b :** a specific point under consideration : ISSUE
**4 :** the total count of individual things in a given unit or sample obtained by counting all or a subsample of them ⟨bacteria *count*⟩
**5 a :** the calling off of the seconds from one to ten when a boxer has been knocked down **b**

: the number of balls and strikes charged to a baseball batter during one turn 〈the *count* stood at 3 and 2〉 **c :** SCORE 〈tied the *count* with a minute to play〉
**6 :** a measurement of the thickness or fineness of yarn by determining the number of hanks or yards per pound it produces

**³count** *noun* [Middle English, from Middle French *comte,* from Late Latin *comit-, comes,* from Latin, companion, one of the imperial court, from *com-* + *ire* to go — more at IS-SUE] (15th century)
: a European nobleman whose rank corresponds to that of a British earl

**count·able** \'kaủn-tə-bəl\ *adjective* (1581)
: capable of being counted; *especially* **:** DENU-MERABLE 〈a *countable* set〉
— **count·abil·i·ty** \ˌkaủn-tə-'bi-lə-tē\ *noun*
— **count·ably** \'kaủn-tə-blē\ *adverb*

**count·down** \'kaủnt-ˌdaủn\ *noun* (circa 1952)
: an audible backward counting in fixed units (as seconds) from an arbitrary starting number to mark the time remaining before an event; *also* **:** preparations carried on during such a count
— **count down** \-'daủn\ *intransitive verb*

**¹coun·te·nance** \'kaủnt-ə°n-ən(t)s, 'kaủnt-nən(t)s\ *noun* [Middle English *contenance,* from Middle French, from Medieval Latin *continentia,* from Latin, restraint, from *continent-, continens,* present participle of *continēre* to hold together — more at CON-TAIN] (13th century)
**1** *obsolete* **:** BEARING, DEMEANOR
**2 a :** calm expression **b :** mental composure **c :** LOOK, EXPRESSION
**3** *archaic* **a :** ASPECT, SEMBLANCE **b :** PRETENSE
**4 :** FACE, VISAGE; *especially* **:** the face as an indication of mood, emotion, or character
**5 :** bearing or expression that offers approval or sanction **:** moral support

**²countenance** *transitive verb* **-nanced; -nanc·ing** (1568)
: to extend approval or toleration to **:** SANCTION
— **coun·te·nanc·er** *noun*

**¹count·er** \'kaủn-tər\ *noun* [Middle English *countour,* from Middle French *comptouer,* from Medieval Latin *computatorium* computing place, from Latin *computare*] (14th century)
**1 :** a piece (as of metal or plastic) used in reckoning or in games
**2 :** something of value in bargaining **:** ASSET
**3 :** a level surface (as a table, shelf or display case) over which transactions are conducted or food is served or on which goods are displayed or work is conducted 〈jewelry *counter*〉 〈a lunch *counter*〉
— **over the counter 1 :** in or through a broker's office rather than through a stock exchange 〈stock bought *over the counter*〉 **2 :** without a prescription 〈drugs available *over the counter*〉
— **under the counter :** by surreptitious means **:** in an illicit and private manner

**²count·er** \'kaủn-tər\ *noun* [Middle English, from Middle French *conteor,* from *compter* to count] (14th century)
: one that counts; *especially* **:** a device for indicating a number or amount

**³coun·ter** *verb* **coun·tered; coun·ter·ing** \'kaủn-t(ə-)riŋ\ [Middle English *countren,* from Middle French *contre* against, opposite, from Latin *contra;* akin to Latin *com-* with, together — more at CO-] (14th century)
*transitive verb*
**1 a :** to act in opposition to **:** OPPOSE **b :** OFF-SET, NULLIFY 〈tried to *counter* the trend toward depersonalization〉
**2 :** to adduce in answer 〈we *countered* that our warnings had been ignored〉
*intransitive verb*
: to meet attacks or arguments with defensive or retaliatory steps

**⁴coun·ter** *adverb* [Middle English *contre,* from Middle French] (15th century)

**1 :** in an opposite or wrong direction
**2 :** to or toward a different or opposite direction, result, or effect 〈values that run *counter* to those of society〉

**⁵coun·ter** *noun* (15th century)
**1 :** CONTRARY, OPPOSITE
**2 :** the after portion of a boat from the waterline to the extreme outward swell or stern overhang
**3 a :** the act of making an attack while parrying one (as in boxing or fencing); *also* **:** a blow thus given in boxing **b :** an agency or force that offsets **:** CHECK
**4 :** a stiffener to give permanent form to a boot or shoe upper around the heel
**5 :** an area within the face of a letter wholly or partly enclosed by strokes
**6 :** a football play in which the ballcarrier goes in a direction opposite to the movement of the play

**⁶coun·ter** *adjective* (1596)
**1 :** marked by or tending toward or in an opposite direction or effect
**2 :** given to or marked by opposition, hostility, or antipathy
**3 :** situated or lying opposite 〈the *counter* side〉
**4 :** recalling or ordering back by a superseding contrary order **:** COUNTERMANDING 〈*counter* orders from the colonel〉

**counter-** *prefix* [Middle English *contre-,* from Middle French, from *contre*]
**1 a :** contrary **:** opposite 〈*counter*clockwise〉 〈*counter*march〉 **b :** opposing **:** retaliatory 〈*counter*force〉 〈*counter*offensive〉
**2 :** complementary **:** corresponding 〈*counter*weight〉 〈*counter*part〉
**3 :** duplicate **:** substitute 〈*counter*foil〉

coun·ter·ac·cu·sa·tion
coun·ter·ad·ap·ta·tion
coun·ter·ad·ver·tis·ing
coun·ter·agent
coun·ter·ag·gres·sion
coun·ter·ar·gue
coun·ter·ar·gu·ment
coun·ter·as·sault
coun·ter·at·tack
coun·ter·at·tack·er
coun·ter·bid
coun·ter·blast
coun·ter·block·ade
coun·ter·blow
coun·ter·cam·paign
coun·ter·charge
coun·ter·com·mer·cial
coun·ter·com·plaint
coun·ter·con·spir·a·cy
coun·ter·con·ven·tion
coun·ter·coun·ter·mea·sure
coun·ter·coup
coun·ter·crit·i·cism
coun·ter·cry
coun·ter·de·mand
coun·ter·dem·on·strate
coun·ter·dem·on·stra·tion
coun·ter·dem·on·stra·tor
coun·ter·de·ploy·ment
coun·ter·ed·u·ca·tion·al
coun·ter·ef·fort
coun·ter·ev·i·dence
coun·ter·fire
coun·ter·force

coun·ter·gov·ern·ment
coun·ter·hy·poth·e·sis
coun·ter·im·age
coun·ter·in·cen·tive
coun·ter·in·fla·tion
coun·ter·in·fla·tion·ary
coun·ter·in·flu·ence
coun·ter·in·stance
coun·ter·in·sti·tu·tion
coun·ter·in·ter·pre·ta·tion
coun·ter·memo
coun·ter·mo·bi·li·za·tion
coun·ter·move
coun·ter·move·ment
coun·ter·myth
coun·ter·or·der
coun·ter·pe·ti·tion
coun·ter·pick·et
coun·ter·play
coun·ter·play·er
coun·ter·ploy
coun·ter·pow·er
coun·ter·pres·sure
coun·ter·pro·ject
coun·ter·pro·pa·gan·da
coun·ter·pro·test
coun·ter·ques·tion
coun·ter·raid
coun·ter·ral·ly
coun·ter·re·ac·tion
coun·ter·re·form
coun·ter·re·form·er
coun·ter·re·sponse
coun·ter·re·tal·i·a·tion
coun·ter·sci·en·tif·ic
coun·ter·shot
coun·ter·snip·er
coun·ter·spell

coun·ter·state
coun·ter·state·ment
coun·ter·step
coun·ter·strat·e·gist
coun·ter·strat·e·gy
coun·ter·stream
coun·ter·strike
coun·ter·stroke
coun·ter·style
coun·ter·sue
coun·ter·sug·ges·tion
coun·ter·suit

coun·ter·sur·veil·lance
coun·ter·tac·tics
coun·ter·ten·den·cy
coun·ter·ter·ror
coun·ter·ter·ror·ism
coun·ter·ter·ror·ist
coun·ter·threat
coun·ter·thrust
coun·ter·tra·di·tion
coun·ter·trend
coun·ter·vi·o·lence
coun·ter·world

**coun·ter·act** \ˌkaủn-tə-'rakt\ *transitive verb* (1678)
: to make ineffective or restrain or neutralize the usually ill effects of by an opposite force
— **coun·ter·ac·tion** \-'rak-shən\ *noun*
— **coun·ter·ac·tive** \-'rak-tiv\ *adjective*

**¹coun·ter·bal·ance** \'kaủn-tər-ˌba-lən(t)s, ˌkaủn-tər-'\ *noun* (1611)
**1 :** a weight that balances another
**2 :** a force or influence that offsets or checks an opposing force

**²counterbalance** \ˌkaủn-tər-', 'kaủn-tər-ˌ\ *transitive verb* (1611)
**1 :** to oppose or balance with an equal weight or force
**2 :** to equip with counterbalances

**coun·ter·change** \'kaủn-tər-ˌchānj\ *transitive verb* (circa 1604)
**1 :** INTERCHANGE, TRANSPOSE
**2 :** CHECKER 1a

**¹coun·ter·check** \-ˌchek\ *noun* (1559)
: a check or restraint often operating against something that is itself a check

**²countercheck** *transitive verb* (1587)
**1 :** CHECK, COUNTERACT
**2 :** to check a second time for verification

**counter check** *noun* (1856)
: a check obtainable at a bank usually to be cashed only at the bank by the drawer

**¹coun·ter·claim** \'kaủn-tər-ˌklām\ *noun* (1784)
: an opposing claim; *especially* **:** a claim brought by a defendant against a plaintiff in a legal action

**²counterclaim** (1881)
*intransitive verb*
: to enter or plead a counterclaim
*transitive verb*
: to ask in a counterclaim

**coun·ter·clock·wise** \ˌkaủn-tər-'kläk-ˌwīz\ *adverb* (1888)
: in a direction opposite to that in which the hands of a clock rotate as viewed from in front
— **counterclockwise** *adjective*

**coun·ter·con·di·tion·ing** \-kən-'di-sh(ə-)niŋ\ *noun* (1962)
: conditioning in order to replace an undesirable response (as fear) to a stimulus (as an engagement in public speaking) by a favorable one

**coun·ter·cul·ture** \'kaủn-tər-ˌkəl-chər\ *noun* (1968)
: a culture with values and mores that run counter to those of established society
— **coun·ter·cul·tur·al** \ˌkaủn-tər-'kəlch-rəl, -'kəl-chə-\ *adjective*
— **coun·ter·cul·tur·al·ism** \-rə-ˌli-zəm\ *noun*
— **coun·ter·cul·tur·ist** \-rist\ *noun*

**¹coun·ter·cur·rent** \'kaủn-tər-ˌkər-ənt, -ˌkə-rənt\ *noun* (1684)
: a current flowing in a direction opposite that of another current

**²countercurrent** \ˌkaủn-tər-'\ *adjective* (1799)
**1 :** flowing in an opposite direction

**2 :** involving flow of materials in opposite directions ⟨*countercurrent* dialysis⟩
— **coun·ter·cur·rent·ly** *adverb*

**coun·ter·cy·cli·cal** \-'sī-kli-kəl, -'si-\ *adjective* (1944)
**:** calculated to check excessive developments in a business cycle **:** COMPENSATORY ⟨*countercyclical* budget policies⟩
— **coun·ter·cy·cli·cal·ly** \-k(ə-)lē\ *adverb*

**coun·ter·es·pi·o·nage** \,kaùn-tər-'es-pē-ə-,näzh, -,näj, -nij, *Canadian also* -,nazh; -,es-pē-ə-'näzh; -ə-'spē-ə-nij\ *noun* (1899)
**:** the activity concerned with detecting and thwarting enemy espionage

**coun·ter·ex·am·ple** \'kaùn-tər-ig-,zam-pəl\ *noun* (1957)
**:** an example that disproves a proposition or theory

**coun·ter·fac·tu·al** \,kaùn-tər-'fak-chə-wəl, -chəl, -shwəl\ *adjective* (1946)
**:** contrary to fact ⟨*counterfactual* assumptions⟩

**¹coun·ter·feit** \'kaùnt-ər-,fit\ *adjective* [Middle English *countrefet,* from Middle French *contrefait,* from past participle of *contrefaire* to imitate, from *contre-* + *faire* to make, from Latin *facere* — more at DO] (14th century)
**1 :** made in imitation of something else with intent to deceive **:** FORGED ⟨*counterfeit* money⟩
**2 a :** INSINCERE, FEIGNED ⟨*counterfeit* sympathy⟩ **b :** IMITATION ⟨*counterfeit* Georgian houses⟩

**²counterfeit** (14th century)
*transitive verb*
**:** to imitate or feign especially with intent to deceive; *also* **:** to make a fraudulent replica of ⟨*counterfeiting* $20 bills⟩
*intransitive verb*
**1 :** to try to deceive by pretense or dissembling
**2 :** to engage in counterfeiting something of value
*synonym* see ASSUME
— **coun·ter·feit·er** *noun*

**³counterfeit** *noun* (15th century)
**1 :** something counterfeit **:** FORGERY
**2 :** something likely to be mistaken for something of higher value ⟨pity was a *counterfeit* of love —Harry Hervey⟩
*synonym* see IMPOSTURE

**coun·ter·flow** \'kaùn-tər-,flō\ *noun* (1870)
**:** the flow of a fluid in opposite directions (as in an apparatus)

**coun·ter·foil** \-,fòil\ *noun* (1706)
**:** a detachable stub (as on a check or ticket) usually serving as a record or receipt

**coun·ter·guer·ril·la** *also* **coun·ter·gue·ril·la** \,kaùn-tər-gə-'ri-lə, -gi-, -gyi-, -ge-\ *noun* (1901)
**:** a guerrilla who is trained to thwart enemy guerrilla operations

**coun·ter·in·sur·gen·cy** \,kaùn-tər-in-'sər-jən(t)-sē\ *noun* (1962)
**:** organized military activity designed to combat insurgency
— **coun·ter·in·sur·gent** \-jənt\ *noun*

**coun·ter·in·tel·li·gence** \,kaùn-tər-in-'te-lə-jən(t)s\ *noun* (1940)
**:** organized activity of an intelligence service designed to block an enemy's sources of information, to deceive the enemy, to prevent sabotage, and to gather political and military information

**coun·ter·in·tu·i·tive** \-in-'tü-ə-tiv, -'tyü-\ *adjective* (1955)
**:** contrary to what one would intuitively expect
— **coun·ter·in·tu·i·tive·ly** \-lē\ *adverb*

**coun·ter·ion** \'kaùn-tər-,ī-ən, -,än\ *noun* (1940)
**:** an ion having a charge opposite to that of the substance with which it is associated

**coun·ter·ir·ri·tant** \,kaùn-tər-'ir-ə-tənt\ *noun* (1854)

**1 :** an agent applied locally to produce superficial inflammation with the object of reducing inflammation in deeper adjacent structures
**2 :** an irritation or discomfort that diverts attention from another
— **counterirritant** *adjective*

**count·er·man** \'kaùn-tər-,man, -mən\ *noun* (1853)
**:** one who tends a counter

**¹coun·ter·mand** \'kaùn-tər-,mand, ,kaùn-tər-'\ *transitive verb* [Middle English *countermaunden,* from Middle French *contremander,* from *contre-* counter- + *mander* to command, from Latin *mandare* — more at MANDATE] (15th century)
**1 :** to revoke (a command) by a contrary order
**2 :** to recall or order back by a superseding contrary order ⟨*countermand* reinforcements⟩

**²coun·ter·mand** \'kaùn-tər-,mand\ *noun* (1548)
**1 :** a contrary order
**2 :** the revocation of an order or command

**coun·ter·march** \'kaùn-tər-,märch\ *noun* (1598)
**1 :** a marching back; *specifically* **:** a movement in marching by which a unit of troops reverses direction while marching but keeps the same order
**2 :** a march (as of political demonstrators) designed to counter the effect of another march
— **countermarch** *intransitive verb*

**coun·ter·mea·sure** \-,me-zhər, -,mā-\ *noun* (1923)
**:** an action or device designed to negate or offset another; *especially* **:** a military system or device intended to thwart a sensing mechanism (as radar) ⟨electronic *countermeasures*⟩

**coun·ter·mel·o·dy** \-,me-lə-dē\ *noun* (1926)
**:** a secondary melody that is sounded simultaneously with the principal one

**coun·ter·mine** \-,mīn\ *noun* (1548)
**:** a tunnel for intercepting an enemy mine

**coun·ter·of·fen·sive** \'kaùn-tər-ə-,fen(t)-siv\ *noun* (1909)
**:** a large-scale military offensive undertaken by a force previously on the defensive

**coun·ter·of·fer** \-,ò-fər, -,ä-fər\ *noun* (1788)
**:** a return offer made by one who has rejected an offer

**coun·ter·pane** \'kaùn-tər-,pān\ *noun* [alteration of Middle English *countrepointe,* modification of Middle French *coute pointe,* literally, embroidered quilt] (15th century)
**:** BEDSPREAD

**coun·ter·part** \-,pärt\ *noun* (15th century)
**1 :** one of two corresponding copies of a legal instrument **:** DUPLICATE
**2 a :** a thing that fits another perfectly **b :** something that completes **:** COMPLEMENT
**3 a :** one remarkably similar to another **b :** one having the same function or characteristics as another ⟨college presidents and their *counterparts* in business⟩

**coun·ter·plan** \'kaùn-tər-,plan\ *noun* (1788)
**1 :** a plan designed to counter another plan
**2 :** an alternate or substitute plan

**coun·ter·plea** \-,plē\ *noun* (1523)
**:** a replication to a legal plea

**¹coun·ter·plot** \-,plät\ *noun* (circa 1611)
**:** a plot designed to thwart an opponent's plot

**²counterplot** *transitive verb* (1662)
**:** to intrigue against **:** foil with a plot

**¹coun·ter·point** \'kaùn-tər-,pòint\ *noun* [Middle French *contrepoint,* from Medieval Latin *contrapunctus,* from Latin *contra-* counter- + Medieval Latin *punctus* musical note, melody, from Latin, act of pricking, from *pungere* to prick — more at PUNGENT] (15th century)
**1 a :** one or more independent melodies added above or below a given melody **b :** the combination of two or more independent melodies into a single harmonic texture in which each retains its linear character **:** POLYPHONY

**2 a :** a complementing or contrasting item **:** OPPOSITE **b :** use of contrast or interplay of elements in a work of art (as a drama)

**²counterpoint** *transitive verb* (1875)
**1 :** to compose or arrange in counterpoint
**2 :** to set off or emphasize by juxtaposition **:** set in contrast ⟨*counterpoints* the public and the private man —Tom Bishop⟩

**¹coun·ter·poise** \-,pòiz\ *transitive verb* [Middle English *countrepesen,* from Middle French *contrepeser,* from *contre-* + *peser* to weigh — more at POISE] (14th century)
**:** COUNTERBALANCE

**²counterpoise** *noun* (15th century)
**1 :** COUNTERBALANCE
**2 :** an equivalent power or force acting in opposition
**3 :** a state of balance

**coun·ter·pose** \,kaùn-tər-'pōz\ *transitive verb* [*counter-* + *-pose* (as in *compose*)] (1594)
**:** to place in opposition, contrast, or equilibrium ⟨*counterpose* a positive view to the negative assessment⟩

**coun·ter·pro·duc·tive** \-prə-'dək-tiv\ *adjective* (1959)
**:** tending to hinder the attainment of a desired goal ⟨violence as a means to achieve an end is *counterproductive* —W. E. Brock (born 1930)⟩

**coun·ter·pro·gram·ming** \,kaùn-tər-'prō-,gra-miŋ, -grə-\ *noun* (circa 1966)
**:** the scheduling of programs by television networks so as to attract audiences away from simultaneously telecast programs of competitors

**coun·ter·pro·pos·al** \'kaùn-tər-prə-,pō-zəl\ *noun* (1885)
**:** a return proposal made by one who has rejected a proposal

**coun·ter·punch** \'kaùn-tər-,pənch\ *noun* (1942)
**:** a counter in boxing; *also* **:** a countering blow or attack
— **counterpunch** *intransitive verb*
— **coun·ter·punch·er** \-,pən-chər\ *noun*

**coun·ter·ref·or·ma·tion** \,kaùn-tə(r),re-fər-'mā-shən\ *noun* (1840)
**1** *usually* **Counter-Reformation :** the reform movement in the Roman Catholic Church following the Reformation
**2 :** a reformation designed to counter the effects of a previous reformation

**coun·ter·rev·o·lu·tion** \-,re-və-'lü-shən\ *noun* (1793)
**1 :** a revolution directed toward overthrowing a government or social system established by a previous revolution
**2 :** a movement to counteract revolutionary trends
— **coun·ter·rev·o·lu·tion·ary** \-shə-,ner-ē\ *adjective or noun*

**coun·ter·shad·ing** \'kaùn-tər-,shā-diŋ\ *noun* (1896)
**:** cryptic coloration of an animal with parts normally in shadow being light and parts normally illuminated being dark thereby reducing shadows and contours

**coun·ter·sign** \-,sīn\ *noun* (1591)
**1 :** a signature attesting the authenticity of a document already signed by another
**2 :** a sign given in reply to another; *specifically* **:** a military secret signal that must be given by one wishing to pass a guard
— **countersign** *transitive verb*
— **coun·ter·sig·na·ture** \,kaùn-tər-'sig-nə-,chúr, -chər, -,tyùr, -,túr\ *noun*

**¹coun·ter·sink** \'kaùn-tər-,siŋk\ *transitive verb* **-sunk** \-,səŋk\; **-sink·ing** (1816)
**1 :** to make a countersink on
**2 :** to set the head of (as a screw) at or below the surface

**²countersink** *noun* (1816)
**1 :** a bit or drill for making a funnel-shaped enlargement at the outer end of a drilled hole
**2 :** the enlargement made by a countersink

**coun·ter·spy** \'kaùn-tər-,spī\ *noun* (1939)
**:** a spy engaged in counterespionage

**coun·ter·stain** \-ˌstān\
*transitive verb* (1895)
**:** to stain (as a microscopy specimen) so as to color parts (as the cytoplasm of cells) not colored by another stain (as a nuclear stain)
— **counterstain** *noun*

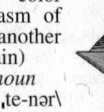

**countersink**

**coun·ter·ten·or** \-ˌte-nər\ *noun* [Middle English *countretenour*, from Middle French *contreteneur*, from *contre-* + *teneur* tenor] (15th century)
**:** a tenor with an unusually high range (as an alto range)

**coun·ter·top** \-ˌtäp\ *noun* [¹*counter* + ¹*top*] (1897)
**:** the flat working surface on top of waist-level kitchen cabinets

**coun·ter·trade** \-ˌtrād\ *noun* (1978)
**:** a form of international trade in which purchases made by an importing nation are linked to offsetting purchases made by the exporting nation

**coun·ter·trans·fer·ence** \ˌkaún-tər-(ˌ)tran(t)s-ˈfər-ən(t)s, -ˈtran(t)s-(ˌ)\ *noun* (1920)
**1 :** psychological transference especially by a psychotherapist during the course of treatment; *especially* **:** the psychotherapist's reactions to the patient's transference
**2 :** the complex of feelings of a psychotherapist toward the patient

**coun·ter·vail** \ˌkaún-tər-ˈvā(ə)l\ *verb* [Middle English *countrevailen*, from Middle French *contrevaloir*, from *contre-* counter- + *valoir* to be worth, from Latin *valēre* — more at WIELD] (14th century)
*transitive verb*
**1 :** to compensate for
**2** *archaic* **:** EQUAL, MATCH
**3 :** to exert force against **:** COUNTERACT
*intransitive verb*
**:** to exert force against an opposing and often bad or harmful force or influence

**coun·ter·view** \ˈkaún-tər-ˌvyü\ *noun* (1590)
**1** *archaic* **:** CONFRONTATION
**2 :** an opposite point of view

**coun·ter·weight** \-ˌwāt\ *noun* (1693)
**:** an equivalent weight or force **:** COUNTERBALANCE
— **counterweight** *transitive verb*

**count·ess** \ˈkaún-təs\ *noun* (12th century)
**1 :** the wife or widow of an earl or count
**2 :** a woman who holds in her own right the rank of earl or count

**coun·ti·an** \ˈkaún-tē-ən\ *noun* (15th century)
**:** a native or resident of a usually specified county

**count·ing·house** \ˈkaún-tiŋ-ˌhaús\ *noun* (15th century)
**:** a building, room, or office used for keeping books and transacting business

**counting number** *noun* (circa 1965)
**:** NATURAL NUMBER

**counting room** *noun* (1712)
**:** COUNTINGHOUSE

**count·less** \ˈkaúnt-ləs\ *adjective* (1588)
**:** too numerous to be counted **:** MYRIAD, MANY
— **count·less·ly** *adverb*

**count noun** *noun* (1952)
**:** a noun (as *bean* or *sheet*) that forms a plural and is used with a numeral, with words such as *many* or *few*, or with the indefinite article *a* or *an* — compare MASS NOUN

**count palatine** *noun* (1539)
**1 a :** a count of the Holy Roman Empire having imperial powers in his own domain **b :** a high judicial official in the Holy Roman Empire
**2 :** the proprietor of a county palatine in England or Ireland

**coun·tri·fied** *also* **coun·try·fied** \ˈkən-tri-ˌfīd\ *adjective* [*country* + *-fied* (as in *glorified*)] (1653)
**1 :** RURAL, RUSTIC
**2 :** UNSOPHISTICATED

**3 :** played or sung in the manner of country music ⟨*countrified* rock⟩

**¹coun·try** \ˈkən-trē\ *noun, plural* **countries** [Middle English *contree*, from Old French *contrée*, from Medieval Latin *contrata*, from Latin *contra* against, on the opposite side] (13th century)
**1 :** an indefinite usually extended expanse of land **:** REGION
**2 a :** the land of a person's birth, residence, or citizenship **b :** a political state or nation or its territory
**3 a :** the people of a state or district **:** POPULACE **b :** JURY **c :** ELECTORATE 2
**4 :** rural as distinguished from urban areas
**5 :** COUNTRY MUSIC ◆
— **coun·try·ish** \-trē-ish\ *adjective*

**²country** *adjective* (14th century)
**1 :** of, relating to, or characteristic of the country
**2 a :** of or relating to a decorative style associated with life in the country ⟨an English *country* look⟩; *also* **:** possessing a style of rustic simplicity ⟨*country* furniture⟩ **b :** prepared or processed with farm supplies and procedures ⟨*country* ham⟩
**3 :** of, relating to, suitable for, or featuring country music ⟨*country* singers⟩

**country and western** *noun* (1960)
**:** COUNTRY MUSIC — usually hyphenated in attributive use

**country club** *noun* (1867)
**:** a suburban club for social life and recreation; *especially* **:** one having a golf course — usually hyphenated in attributive use

**coun·try–dance** \ˈkən-trē-ˌdan(t)s\ *noun* (1579)
**:** any of various native English dances in which partners face each other especially in rows

**country gentleman** *noun* (1632)
**1 :** a well-to-do country resident **:** an owner of a country estate
**2 :** one of the English landed gentry

**country house** *noun* (14th century)
**:** a house and especially a mansion in the country

**coun·try·man** \ˈkən-trē-mən, *3 often* -ˌman\ *noun* (14th century)
**1 :** an inhabitant or native of a specified country
**2 :** COMPATRIOT
**3 :** one living in the country or marked by country ways **:** RUSTIC

**country mile** *noun* (1950)
**:** a long distance

**country music** *noun* (1952)
**:** music derived from or imitating the folk style of the Southern U.S. or of the Western cowboy

**country rock** *noun* (1968)
**:** ROCKABILLY

**coun·try·seat** \ˌkən-trē-ˈsēt\ *noun* (1583)
**:** a house or estate in the country

**coun·try·side** \ˈkən-trē-ˌsīd\ *noun* (1727)
**1 :** a rural area
**2 :** the inhabitants of a countryside

**coun·try·wide** \ˈkən-trē-ˈwīd\ *adjective* (1915)
**:** extending throughout a country

**coun·try·wom·an** \ˈkən-trē-ˌwú-mən\ *noun* (15th century)
**1 :** a woman compatriot
**2 :** a woman resident of the country

**¹coun·ty** \ˈkaún-tē\ *noun, plural* **counties** [Middle English *counte*, from Middle French *conté*, from Medieval Latin *comitatus*, from Late Latin, office of a count, from *comit-, comes* count — more at COUNT] (14th century)
**1 :** the domain of a count
**2 a :** one of the territorial divisions of England and Wales and formerly also of Scotland and Northern Ireland constituting the chief units for administrative, judicial, and political pur-

poses **b** (1) **:** the people of a county (2) *British* **:** the gentry of a county
**3 :** the largest territorial division for local government within a state of the U.S.
**4 :** the largest local administrative unit in various countries
— **county** *adjective*

**²county** *noun, plural* **counties** [modification of Middle French *comte*] (1550)
*archaic* **:** ³COUNT

**county agent** *noun* (1705)
**:** a consultant employed jointly by federal and state governments to provide information about agriculture and home economics

**county court** *noun* (1639)
**:** a court in some states that has a designated jurisdiction usually both civil and criminal within the limits of a county

**county fair** *noun* (1856)
**:** a fair usually held annually at a set location in a county especially to exhibit local agricultural products and livestock

**county palatine** *noun* (15th century)
**:** the territory of a count palatine

**county seat** *noun* (1803)
**:** a town that is the seat of county administration

**county town** *noun* (1670)
*chiefly British* **:** COUNTY SEAT

**¹coup** \ˈkōp\ *verb* [Middle English, to strike, from Middle French *couper* — more at COPE] (circa 1572)
*chiefly Scottish* **:** OVERTURN, UPSET

**²coup** \ˈkü\ *noun, plural* **coups** \ˈküz\ [French, blow, stroke — more at COPE] (1791)
**1 :** a brilliant, sudden, and usually highly successful stroke or act
**2 :** COUP D'ÉTAT

**coup de grâce** *or* **coup de grace** \ˌkü-də-ˈgräs\ *noun, plural* **coups de grâce** *or* **coups de grace** \ˌkü-də-\ [French *coup de grâce*, literally, stroke of mercy] (1699)
**1 :** a death blow or shot administered to end the suffering of one mortally wounded
**2 :** a decisive finishing blow, act, or event

**coup de main** \-ˈmaⁿ\ *noun, plural* **coups de main** \ˌkü-də-\ [French, literally, hand stroke] (1758)
**:** a sudden attack in force

**coup d'état** *or* **coup d'etat** \ˌkü-(ˌ)dā-ˈtä, ˈkü-(ˌ)dā-ˌ, -də-\ *noun, plural* **coups d'état** *or* **coups d'etat** \-ˈtä(z), -ˌtä(z)\ [French, literally, stroke of state] (1646)
**:** a sudden decisive exercise of force in politics; *especially* **:** the violent overthrow or alteration of an existing government by a small group

**coup de thé·âtre** *or* **coup de the·atre** \ˌkü-də-tā-ˈätrᵊ\ *noun, plural* **coups de thé·âtre** *or* **coups de theatre** \ˌkü-də-\

---

◇ WORD HISTORY
**country** In Latin the adverb and preposition *contra* means "against" or "on the opposite side." The spoken Latin from which the Romance languages descend formed the derivative *contrata*, which literally meant "that which is situated on the opposite side." But in the Romance words, such as Old Italian *contrata* and Old French *contree*, the attested sense is invariably "environs," "area of land," or "region." Borrowed from French as *contree* in the 13th century, English *country* has had a rich development in its adopted home, acquiring significant new senses, such as "populace" and "rural as opposed to urban areas," that are not shared by Modern French *contrée*.

---

\ə\ abut \ᵊ\ kitten \ər\ further \a\ ash \ā\ ace
\ä\ mop, mar \aú\ out \ch\ chin \e\ bet \ē\ easy
\g\ go \i\ hit \ī\ ice \j\ job \ŋ\ sing \ō\ go
\ò\ law \òi\ boy \th\ thin \th\ the \ü\ loot \ú\ foot
\y\ yet \zh\ vision *see also* Guide to Pronunciation

[French *coup de théâtre*, literally, stroke of theater] (1747)
**1 :** a sudden sensational turn in a play; *also* **:** a sudden dramatic effect or turn of events
**2 :** a theatrical success

**coup d'oeil** \kü-'də(r), -'dȯi\ *noun, plural* **coups d'oeil** \*same*\ [French, literally, stroke of the eye] (1739)
**:** a brief survey **:** GLANCE

**cou·pé** *or* **coupe** \kü-'pā, *2 often* 'küp\ *noun* [French *coupé,* from past participle of *couper* to cut, strike] (1834)
**1 :** a four-wheeled closed horse-drawn carriage for two persons inside with an outside seat for the driver in front
**2** *usually* **coupe :** a 2-door automobile often seating only two persons; *also* **:** one with a tight-spaced rear seat — compare SEDAN

**¹cou·ple** \'kə-pəl; "*couple of*" *is often* ‚kə-plə(v)\ *noun* [Middle English, pair, bond, from Old French *cople,* from Latin *copula* bond, from *co-* + *apere* to fasten — more at APT] (13th century)
**1 a :** a man and a woman married, engaged, or otherwise paired **b :** two persons paired together
**2 :** PAIR, BRACE
**3 :** something that joins or links two things together: as **a :** two equal and opposite forces that act along parallel lines **b :** a pair of substances that in contact with an electrolyte participate in a transfer of electrons which causes an electric current to flow
**4 :** an indefinite small number **:** FEW ⟨a *couple* of days ago⟩ ☐

**²cou·ple** \'kə-pəl\ *verb* **cou·pled; cou·pling** \-p(ə-)liŋ\ (13th century)
*transitive verb*
**1 a :** to connect for consideration together **b :** to join for combined effect
**2 a :** to fasten together **:** LINK **b :** to bring (two electric circuits) into such close proximity as to permit mutual influence
**3 :** to join in marriage or sexual union
*intransitive verb*
**1 :** to unite in sexual union
**2 :** JOIN
**3 :** to unite chemically

**³couple** *adjective* (1924)
**:** TWO; *also* **:** FEW — used with *a* ⟨a *couple* drinks⟩ ☐

**cou·ple·ment** \'kə-pəl-mənt\ *noun* [Middle French, from *coupler* to join, from Latin *copulare,* from *copula*] (1548)
*archaic* **:** the act or result of coupling

**cou·pler** \'kə-p(ə-)lər\ *noun* (1552)
**1 :** one that couples
**2 :** a contrivance on a keyboard instrument by which keyboards or keys are connected to play together

**cou·plet** \'kə-plət\ *noun* [Middle French, diminutive of *cople*] (1580)
**1 :** two successive lines of verse forming a unit marked usually by rhythmic correspondence, rhyme, or the inclusion of a self-contained utterance **:** DISTICH
**2 :** COUPLE
**3 :** one of the musical episodes alternating with the main theme (as in a rondo)

**cou·pling** \'kə-pliŋ (*usual for 2*), -pə-liŋ\ *noun* (14th century)
**1 :** the act of bringing or coming together **:** PAIRING; *specifically* **:** sexual union
**2 :** a device that serves to connect the ends of adjacent parts or objects
**3 :** the joining of or the part of the body that joins the hindquarters to the forequarters of a quadruped
**4 :** a means of electric connection of two electric circuits by having a part common to both

**cou·pon** \'kü-‚pän, 'kyü-\ *noun* [French, from Old French, piece, from *couper* to cut — more at COPE] (1822)
**1 :** a statement of due interest to be cut from a bearer bond when payable and presented for payment; *also* **:** the interest rate of a coupon

**2 :** a form surrendered in order to obtain an article, service, or accommodation: as **a :** one of a series of attached tickets or certificates often to be detached and presented as needed **b :** a ticket or form authorizing purchases of rationed commodities **c :** a certificate or similar evidence of a purchase redeemable in premiums **d :** a part of a printed advertisement to be cut off to use as an order blank or inquiry form or to obtain a discount on merchandise ☐

**cou·pon·ing** \'kü-‚pä-niŋ, 'kyü-\ *noun* (1954)
**:** the distribution or redemption of coupons

**cour·age** \'kər-ij, 'kə-rij\ *noun* [Middle English *corage,* from Old French, from *cuer* heart, from Latin *cor* — more at HEART] (14th century)
**:** mental or moral strength to venture, persevere, and withstand danger, fear, or difficulty ☆

**cou·ra·geous** \kə-'rā-jəs\ *adjective* (14th century)
**:** having or characterized by courage **:** BRAVE
**— cou·ra·geous·ly** *adverb*
**— cou·ra·geous·ness** *noun*

**cou·rante** \kü-'ränt, -'rant\ *noun* [Middle French, from *courir* to run, from Latin *currere*] (1586)
**1 :** a dance of Italian origin marked by quick running steps
**2 :** music in quick triple time or in a mixture of ³/₂ and ⁶/₄ time

**cou·reur de bois** \kü-‚rər-də-'bwä\ *noun, plural* **coureurs de bois** \*same*\ [Canadian French, literally, woods runner] (1700)
**:** a French or métis trapper of North America and especially of Canada

**cour·gette** \kùr-'zhet\ *noun* [French, diminutive of *courge* gourd, from Latin *cucurbita*] (1931)
*chiefly British* **:** ZUCCHINI

**cou·ri·er** \'kùr-ē-ər, 'kər-ē-, 'kə-rē-\ *noun* [Middle French *courrier,* from Old Italian *corriere,* from *correre* to run, from Latin *currere*] (1579)
**1 :** MESSENGER: as **a :** a member of a diplomatic service entrusted with bearing messages **b** (1) **:** an espionage agent transferring secret information (2) **:** a runner of contraband **c :** a member of the armed services whose duties include carrying mail, information, or supplies
**2 :** a traveler's paid attendant; *especially* **:** a tourists' guide employed by a travel agency

**¹course** \'kōrs, 'kȯrs\ *noun* [Middle English, from Old French, from Latin *cursus,* from *currere* to run — more at CAR] (14th century)
**1 :** the act or action of moving in a path from point to point
**2 :** the path over which something moves or extends: as **a :** RACECOURSE **b** (1) **:** the direction of travel of a vehicle (as a ship or airplane) usually measured as a clockwise angle from north; *also* **:** the projected path of travel (2) **:** a point of the compass **c :** WATERCOURSE **d :** GOLF COURSE
**3 a :** accustomed procedure or normal action ⟨the law taking its *course*⟩ **b :** a chosen manner of conducting oneself **:** way of acting ⟨our wisest *course* is to retreat⟩ **c** (1) **:** progression through a development or period or a series of acts or events (2) **:** LIFE HISTORY, CAREER
**4 :** an ordered process or succession: as **a :** a number of lectures or other matter dealing with a subject; *also* **:** a series of such courses constituting a curriculum ⟨a premed *course*⟩ **b :** a series of doses or medications administered over a designated period
**5 a :** a part of a meal served at one time **b :** LAYER; *especially* **:** a continuous level range of brick or masonry throughout a wall **c :** the lowest sail on a square-rigged mast
**— in due course :** after a normal passage of time **:** in the expected or allotted time
**— of course 1 :** following the ordinary way or procedure **2 :** as might be expected

**²course** *verb* **coursed; cours·ing** (15th century)

*transitive verb*
**1 :** to follow close upon **:** PURSUE

**2 a :** to hunt or pursue (game) with hounds **b :** to cause (dogs) to run (as after game) **3 :** to run or move swiftly through or over **:** TRAVERSE ⟨jets *coursed* the area daily⟩ *intransitive verb* **:** to run or pass rapidly along or as if along an indicated path ⟨blood *coursing* through the veins⟩

**course of study** (1781) **1 :** CURRICULUM **2 :** COURSE 4a

¹**cours·er** \'kōr-sər, 'kȯr-\ *noun* [Middle English, from Middle French *coursier*, from Old French *course* course, run] (14th century) **:** a swift or spirited horse **:** CHARGER

²**courser** *noun* (1600) **1 :** a dog for coursing **2 :** one that courses **:** HUNTSMAN **3 :** any of various Old World birds (subfamily Cursoriinae of the family Glareolidae) noted for their speed in running

**course·ware** \'kōrs-,war, 'kȯrs-, -,wer\ *noun* (1972) **:** educational software

**coursing** *noun* (1538) **1 :** the pursuit of running game with dogs that follow by sight instead of by scent **2 :** the act of one that courses

¹**court** \'kōrt, 'kȯrt\ *noun, often attributive* [Middle English, from Old French, from Latin *cohort-, cohors* enclosure, group, retinue, cohort, from *co-* + *-hort-, -hors* (akin to *hortus* garden) — more at YARD] (12th century) **1 a :** the residence or establishment of a sovereign or similar dignitary **b :** a sovereign's formal assembly of councillors and officers **c :** the sovereign and officers and advisers who are the governing power **d :** the family and retinue of a sovereign **e :** a reception held by a sovereign **2 a** (1) **:** a manor house or large building surrounded by usually enclosed grounds (2) **:** MOTEL **b :** an open space enclosed wholly or partly by buildings or circumscribed by a single building **c :** a quadrangular space walled or marked off for playing one of various games with a ball (as lawn tennis, handball, or basketball); *also* **:** a division of such a court **d :** a wide alley with only one opening onto a street **3 a :** an official assembly for the transaction of judicial business **b :** a session of such a court ⟨*court* is now adjourned⟩ **c :** a place (as a chamber) for the administration of justice **d :** a judge or judges in session; *also* **:** a faculty or agency of judgment or evaluation ⟨rest our case in the *court* of world opinion —L. H. Marks⟩ **4 a :** an assembly or board with legislative or administrative powers **b :** PARLIAMENT, LEGISLATURE **5 :** conduct or attention intended to win favor or dispel hostility **:** HOMAGE ⟨pay *court* to the king⟩

²**court** (1571) *transitive verb* **1 a :** to seek to gain or achieve **b** (1) **:** ALLURE, TEMPT (2) **:** to act so as to invite or provoke ⟨*courts* disaster⟩ **2 a :** to seek the affections of; *especially* **:** to seek to win a pledge of marriage from **b** *of an animal* **:** to perform actions in order to attract for mating **3 a :** to seek to attract (as by solicitous attention or offers of advantages) ⟨college teams *courting* high school basketball stars⟩ **b :** to seek an alliance with *intransitive verb* **1 :** to engage in social activities leading to engagement and marriage **2** *of an animal* **:** to engage in activity leading to mating

**court bouil·lon** \'kur-(,)bü-'yȯⁿ, -(,)bwē-, 'kōr-, 'kȯr-\ *noun* [French *court-bouillon*, literally, short bouillon] (1723)

**:** a liquid made usually with water, white wine, vegetables, and seasonings and used to poach fish

**cour·te·ous** \'kər-tē-əs, *British also* 'kȯr-\ *adjective* [Middle English, from Old French, from *court*] (13th century) **1 :** marked by polished manners, gallantry, or ceremonial usage of a court **2 :** marked by respect for and consideration of others
*synonym* see CIVIL
— **cour·te·ous·ly** *adverb*
— **cour·te·ous·ness** *noun*

**cour·te·san** \'kȯr-tə-zən, 'kȯr-, -,zan *also* 'kər-, -,zän; *especially British* ,kȯr-tə-'zan\ *noun* [Middle French *courtisane*, from northern Italian dialect form of Italian *cortigiana* woman courtier, feminine of *cortigiano* courtier, from *corte* court, from Latin *cohort-, cohors*] (1533) **:** a prostitute with a courtly, wealthy, or upper-class clientele

¹**cour·te·sy** \'kər-tə-sē, *British also* 'kȯr-\ *noun, plural* **-sies** [Middle English *corteisie*, from Old French, from *corteis*] (13th century) **1 a :** courteous behavior **b :** a courteous act or expression **2 a :** general allowance despite facts **:** INDULGENCE ⟨hills called mountains by *courtesy* only⟩ **b :** consideration, cooperation, and generosity in providing (as a gift or privilege); *also* **:** AGENCY, MEANS — used chiefly in the phrases *through the courtesy of* or *by courtesy of* or sometimes simply *courtesy of*

²**courtesy** *adjective* (1613) **:** granted, provided, or performed as a courtesy or by way of courtesy ⟨made a *courtesy* call on the ambassador⟩

**courtesy card** *noun* (1934) **:** a card entitling its holder to some special privilege

**courtesy title** *noun* (1865) **1 :** a title (as "Lord" added to the Christian name of a peer's younger son) used in addressing certain lineal relatives of British peers **2 :** a title (as "Professor" for any teacher) taken by the user and commonly accepted without consideration of official right

**court·house** \'kōrt-,haus, 'kȯrt-\ *noun* (15th century) **1 a :** a building in which courts of law are regularly held **b :** the principal building in which county offices are housed **2 :** COUNTY SEAT

**cour·tier** \'kōrt-tē-ər, 'kȯr-; 'kōrt-yər, 'kȯrt-; 'kōr-chər, 'kȯr-\ *noun* (14th century) **1 :** one in attendance at a royal court **2 :** one who practices flattery

¹**court·ly** \'kōrt-lē, 'kȯrt-\ *adjective* **court·li·er; -est** (15th century) **1 a :** of a quality befitting the court **:** ELEGANT **b :** insincerely flattering **2 :** favoring the policy or party of the court
— **court·li·ness** *noun*

²**courtly** *adverb* (circa 1592) **:** in a courtly manner **:** POLITELY

**courtly love** *noun* (1896) **:** a late medieval conventionalized code prescribing conduct and emotions of ladies and their lovers

¹**court-mar·tial** \'kōrt-,mär-shəl, 'kȯrt-, -'mär-\ *noun, plural* **courts-martial** *also* **court-martials** (1651) **1 :** a court consisting of commissioned officers and in some instances enlisted personnel for the trial of members of the armed forces or others within its jurisdiction **2 :** a trial by court-martial

²**court-martial** *transitive verb* **–mar·tialed** *also* **–mar·tialled; –mar·tial·ing** *also* **–mar·tial·ling** \-,mär-sh(ə-)liŋ, -'mär-\ (1859) **:** to subject to trial by court-martial

**court of appeals** *often C&A capitalized* (1777)

**:** a court hearing appeals from the decisions of lower courts — called also *court of appeal*

**court of claims** (1691) **:** a court that has jurisdiction over claims (as against a government)

**court of common pleas** (1687) **1 :** a former English superior court having civil jurisdiction **2 :** an intermediate court in some American states that usually has civil and criminal jurisdiction

**court of domestic relations** (1926) **:** a court that has jurisdiction and often special advisory powers over family disputes involving the rights and duties of husband, wife, parent, or child especially in matters affecting the support, custody, and welfare of children

**court of honor** (1687) **:** a tribunal (as a military court) for investigating questions of personal honor

**court of inquiry** (1757) **:** a military court that inquires into and reports on some military matter (as an officer's questionable conduct)

**court of law** (14th century) **:** a court that hears cases and decides them on the basis of statutes or the common law

**court of record** (15th century) **:** a court whose acts and proceedings are kept on permanent record

**Court of St· James's** \-sənt-'jāmz, -'jām-zəz, -,sänt-\ [from *Saint James's* Palace, London, former seat of the British court] (1848) **:** the British court

**court of sessions** (circa 1889) **:** any of various state criminal courts of record

**court order** *noun* (1650) **:** an order issuing from a competent court that requires a party to do or abstain from doing a specified act

**court plaster** *noun* [from its use for beauty spots by ladies at royal courts] (1772) **:** an adhesive plaster especially of silk coated with isinglass and glycerin

**court reporter** *noun* (1894) **:** a stenographer who records and transcribes a verbatim report of all proceedings in a court of law

**court·room** \'kōrt-,rüm, 'kȯrt-, -,rum\ *noun* (1677) **:** a room in which a court of law is held

**court·ship** \-,ship\ *noun* (1596) **:** the act, process, or period of courting

**court·side** \-,sīd\ *noun* (1969) **:** the area at the edge of a court (as for tennis or basketball)

**court tennis** *noun* (circa 1890) **:** a game played with a ball and racket in an enclosed court divided by a net

**court·yard** \'kōrt-,yärd, 'kȯrt-\ *noun* (1552) **:** a court or enclosure adjacent to a building (as a house or palace)

**cous·cous** \'küs-,küs\ *noun* [French *couscous, couscoussou*, from Arabic *kuskus, kuskusū*] (1759) **:** a North African dish of steamed semolina usually served with meat or vegetables; *also* **:** the semolina itself

**cous·in** \'kə-zən\ *noun* [Middle English *cosin*, from Old French, from Latin *consobrinus*, from *com-* + *sobrinus* second cousin, from *soror* sister — more at SISTER] (13th century) **1 a :** a child of one's uncle or aunt **b :** a relative descended from one's grandparent or more remote ancestor by two or more steps and in a different line **c :** KINSMAN, RELATIVE ⟨a distant *cousin*⟩ **2 :** one associated with or related to another **:** COUNTERPART

\ə\ abut \ᵊ\ kitten \ər\ further \a\ ash \ā\ ace \ä\ mop, mar \au\ out \ch\ chin \e\ bet \ē\ easy \g\ go \i\ hit \ī\ ice \j\ job \ŋ\ sing \ō\ go \ȯ\ law \ȯi\ boy \th\ thin \th\ the \ü\ loot \u̇\ foot \y\ yet \zh\ vision *see also* Guide to Pronunciation

**3** — used as a title by a sovereign in addressing a nobleman
**4 :** a person of a race or people ethnically or culturally related ⟨our English *cousins*⟩
— **cous·in·hood** \-ˌhu̇d\ *noun*
— **cous·in·ly** *adjective*
— **cous·in·ship** \-ˌship\ *noun*

**cous·in·age** \'kə-zə-nij\ *noun* (14th century)
**1 :** relationship of cousins : KINSHIP
**2 :** a collection of cousins : KINFOLK

**cous·in–ger·man** \ˌkə-zən-'jər-mən\ *noun, plural* **cous·ins–ger·man** \-zənz-\ [Middle English *cosin germain*, from Middle French, from Old French, from *cosin* + *germain* german] (14th century)
**:** COUSIN 1a

**Cousin Jack** \ˌkə-zən-'jak\ *noun* (1890)
**:** CORNISHMAN; *especially* **:** a Cornish miner

**¹couth** \'küth\ *adjective* [back-formation from *uncouth*] (1896)
**:** SOPHISTICATED, POLISHED

**²couth** *noun* (1956)
**:** POLISH, REFINEMENT ⟨I expected kindness and gentility . . . but there is such a thing as too much *couth* —S. J. Perelman⟩

**couth·ie** \'kü-thē\ *adjective* [Middle English *couth* familiar, from Old English *cūth* — more at UNCOUTH] (1719)
*chiefly Scottish* **:** PLEASANT, KINDLY

**cou·ture** \kü-'tu̇r, -'tu̇er\ *noun* [French, from Old French *cousture* sewing, from (assumed) Vulgar Latin *consutura*, from Latin *consutus*, past participle of *consuere* to sew together, from *com-* + *suere* to sew — more at SEW] (1908)
**1 :** the business of designing, making, and selling fashionable custom-made women's clothing
**2 :** the designers and establishments engaged in couture
**3 :** the clothes created by couture

**cou·tu·ri·er** \kü-'tu̇r-ē-ər, -ē-ˌā\ *noun* [French, dressmaker, from Old French *cousturier* tailor's assistant, from *cousture*] (1899)
**:** an establishment engaged in couture; *also*
**:** the proprietor of or designer for such an establishment

**cou·tu·ri·ere** \kü-'tu̇r-ē-ər, -ē-ˌer\ *noun* [French *couturière*, from Old French *cousturiere*, feminine of *cousturier*] (1818)
**:** a woman who is a couturier

**cou·vade** \kü-'väd\ *noun* [French, from Middle French, cowardly inactivity, from *cover* to sit on, brood over — more at COVEY] (1865)
**:** a custom in some cultures in which when a child is born the father takes to bed as if bearing the child and submits himself to fasting, purification, or taboos

**co·va·lence** \ˌkō-'vā-lən(t)s, 'kō-ˌ\ *noun* (1919)
**:** valence characterized by the sharing of electrons

**co·va·len·cy** \-lən(t)-sē\ *noun* (1919)
**:** COVALENCE

**co·va·lent** \ˌkō-'vā-lənt, 'kō-ˌ\ *adjective* (circa 1926)
**:** of, relating to, or characterized by covalent bonds
— **co·va·lent·ly** \-lē\ *adverb*

**covalent bond** *noun* (1939)
**:** a chemical bond formed between atoms by the sharing of electrons

**co·vari·ance** \ˌkō-'ver-ē-ən(t)s, -'var-; 'kō-ˌ\ *noun* (1931)
**1 :** the expected value of the product of the deviations of two random variables from their respective means
**2 :** the arithmetic mean of the products of the deviations of corresponding values of two quantitative variables from their respective means

**co·vari·ant** \-ənt\ *adjective* [International Scientific Vocabulary] (1893)
**:** varying with something else so as to preserve certain mathematical interrelations

**co·vari·a·tion** \ˌkō-ˌver-ē-'ā-shən, -ˌvar-\ *noun* (1906)
**:** correlated variation of two or more variables

**¹cove** \'kōv\ *noun* [Middle English, den, from Old English *cofa;* akin to Old High German *chubisi* hut] (before 12th century)
**1 :** a recessed place : CONCAVITY: as **a :** an architectural member with a concave cross section **b :** a trough for concealed lighting at the upper part of a wall
**2 :** a small sheltered inlet or bay
**3 a :** a deep recess or small valley in the side of a mountain **b :** a level area sheltered by hills or mountains

**²cove** *transitive verb* **coved; cov·ing** (1756)
**:** to make in a hollow concave form

**³cove** *noun* [Romany *kova* thing, person] (1567)
*British* **:** MAN, FELLOW

**co·vel·lite** \kō-'ve-ˌlīt, 'kō-və-\ *also* **co·vel·line** \-ˌlēn\ *noun* [French *covelline*, from Niccolò *Covelli* (died 1829) Italian chemist] (1850)
**:** a native copper sulfide

**co·ven** \'kə-vən *also* 'kō-\ *noun* [Middle English *covin* band, from Middle French, from Medieval Latin *convenium* agreement, from Latin *convenire* to agree — more at CONVENIENT] (circa 1520)
**1 :** a collection of individuals with similar interests or activities ⟨a *coven* of intellectuals⟩
**2 :** an assembly or band of usually 13 witches

**¹cov·e·nant** \'kəv-nənt, 'kə-və-\ *noun* [Middle English, from Middle French, from present participle of *covenir* to agree, from Latin *convenire*] (14th century)
**1 :** a usually formal, solemn, and binding agreement : COMPACT
**2 a :** a written agreement or promise usually under seal between two or more parties especially for the performance of some action **b :** the common-law action to recover damages for breach of such a contract
— **cov·e·nan·tal** \ˌkə-və-'nan-t°l\ *adjective*

**²cov·e·nant** \-nənt, -ˌnant\ (14th century)
*transitive verb*
**:** to promise by a covenant : PLEDGE
*intransitive verb*
**:** to enter into a covenant : CONTRACT

**cov·e·nan·tee** \ˌkə-və-ˌnan-'tē, -nən-\ *noun* (1649)
**:** the person to whom a promise in the form of a covenant is made

**cov·e·nant·er** \'kə-və-ˌnan-tər, *1 also* ˌkə-və-'\ *noun* (1638)
**1** *capitalized* **:** a signer or adherent of the Scottish National Covenant of 1638
**2 :** one that makes a covenant

**cov·e·nan·tor** \'kə-və-ˌnan-tər; ˌkə-və-ˌnan-'tȯr, -nən-\ *noun* (1649)
**:** a party bound by a covenant

**Cov·en·try** \'kə-vən-trē *also* 'kä-\ *noun* [*Coventry*, England] (1765)
**:** a state of ostracism or exclusion ⟨sent to *Coventry*⟩

**¹cov·er** \'kə-vər\ *verb* **cov·ered; cov·er·ing** \'kəv-riŋ, 'kə-və-\ [Middle English, from Old French *covrir*, from Latin *cooperire*, from *co-* + *operire* to close, cover] (13th century)
*transitive verb*
**1 a :** to guard from attack **b** (1) **:** to have within the range of one's guns : COMMAND (2) **:** to hold within range of an aimed firearm **c** (1) **:** to afford protection or security to : INSURE (2) **:** to afford protection against or compensation for **d** (1) **:** to guard (an opponent) in order to obstruct a play (2) **:** to be in position to receive a throw to (a base in baseball) **e** (1) **:** to make provision for (a demand or charge) by means of a reserve or deposit ⟨your balance is insufficient to *cover* the check⟩ (2) **:** to maintain a check on especially by patrolling (3) **:** to protect by contrivance or expedient
**2 a :** to hide from sight or knowledge : CONCEAL ⟨*cover* up a scandal⟩ **b :** to lie over : ENVELOP
**3 :** to lay or spread something over : OVERLAY

**4 a :** to spread over **b :** to appear here and there on the surface of
**5 :** to place or set a cover or covering over
**6 a :** to copulate with (a female animal) ⟨a horse *covers* a mare⟩ **b :** to sit on and incubate (eggs)
**7 :** to invest with a large or excessive amount of something ⟨*covered* herself with glory⟩
**8 :** to play a higher-ranking card on (a previously played card)
**9 :** to have sufficient scope to include or take into account : COMPRISE
**10 :** to deal with : TREAT
**11 a :** to have as one's territory or field of activity ⟨one sales rep *covers* the whole state⟩ **b :** to report news about
**12 :** to pass over : TRAVERSE
**13 :** to place one's stake in equal jeopardy with in a bet
**14 :** to buy securities or commodities for delivery against (an earlier short sale)
**15 :** to record a cover of (a song)
*intransitive verb*
**1 :** to conceal something illicit, blameworthy, or embarrassing from notice — usually used with *up*
**2 :** to act as a substitute or replacement during an absence
— **cov·er·able** \'kə-və-rə-bəl, 'kə-və-\ *adjective*
— **cov·er·er** \'kə-və-rər\ *noun*
— **cover one's tracks :** to conceal traces in order to elude pursuers
— **cover the ground** *or* **cover ground :** to deal with a subject or assignment in a particular manner ⟨the new book *covers* a lot of ground⟩

**²cover** *noun, often attributive* (14th century)
**1 :** something that protects, shelters, or guards: as **a :** natural shelter for an animal; *also* **:** the factors that provide such shelter **b** (1) **:** a position or situation affording protection from enemy fire (2) **:** the protection offered by airplanes in tactical support of a military operation **c** *British* **:** COVERAGE 1a, b, 2a
**2 :** something that is placed over or about another thing: **a :** LID, TOP **b :** a binding or case for a book or the analogous part of a magazine; *also* **:** the front or back of such a binding **c :** an overlay or outer layer especially for protection ⟨a mattress *cover*⟩ **d :** a tablecloth and the other table accessories **e :** COVER CHARGE **f :** ROOF **g :** a cloth used on a bed **h :** something (as vegetation or snow) that covers the ground **i :** the extent to which clouds obscure the sky
**3 a :** something that conceals or obscures ⟨under *cover* of darkness⟩ **b :** a masking device **:** PRETEXT ⟨the project was a *cover* for intelligence operations⟩
**4 :** an envelope or wrapper for mail
**5 :** one who substitutes for another during an absence
**6 :** a recording of a song previously recorded usually by another performer
— **cov·er·less** \'kə-vər-ləs\ *adjective*
— **under cover 1 :** in an envelope or wrapper **2 :** under concealment : in secret

**cov·er·age** \'kəv-rij, 'kə-və-\ *noun* (1912)
**1 :** something that covers: as **a :** inclusion within the scope of an insurance policy or protective plan : INSURANCE **b :** the amount available to meet liabilities **c :** inclusion within the scope of discussion or reporting ⟨the news *coverage* of the trial⟩
**2 :** the total group covered : SCOPE: as **a :** all the risks covered by the terms of an insurance contract **b :** the number or percentage of persons reached by a communications medium
**3 :** the act or fact of covering

**cov·er·all** \'kə-və-ˌrȯl\ *noun* (1824)
**:** a one-piece outer garment worn to protect other garments — usually used in plural
— **cov·er·alled** \-ˌrȯld\ *adjective*

**cov·er–all** \'kə-və-ˌrȯl\ *adjective* (1895)
**:** COMPREHENSIVE ⟨*cover-all* provisions⟩

**cover charge** *noun* (1921)
: a charge made by a restaurant or nightclub in addition to the charge for food and drink

**cover crop** *noun* (1899)
: a crop planted to prevent soil erosion and to provide humus

**covered bridge** *noun* (1809)
: a bridge that has its roadway protected by a roof and enclosing sides

**covered smut** *noun* (1900)
: a smut disease of grains in which the spore masses are held together by the persistent grain membrane and glumes

**covered wagon** *noun* (1745)
: a wagon with a canvas top supported by bowed strips of wood or metal

**cover girl** *noun* (1915)
: an attractive young woman whose picture appears on a magazine cover

**cover glass** *noun* (1881)
: a piece of very thin glass used to cover material on a glass microscope slide

**¹cov·er·ing** \'kəv-riŋ, 'kə-və-\ *noun* (14th century)
: something that covers or conceals

**²covering** *adjective* (1887)
: containing explanation of or additional information about an accompanying communication ⟨a *covering* letter⟩

**cov·er·let** \'kə-vər-lət, -(,)lid\ *noun* [Middle English, alteration of *coverlite*, from Anglo-French *coverelyth*, from Old French *covrir* + literally bed, from Latin *lectus* — more at LIE] (14th century)
: BEDSPREAD

**word history** see CURFEW

**cov·er·slip** \'kə-vər-,slip\ *noun* (1875)
: COVER GLASS

**cover story** *noun* (1948)
: a story accompanying a magazine-cover illustration

**¹co·vert** \'kō-(,)vərt, kō-'; 'kə-vərt\ *adjective* [Middle English, from Middle French, past participle of *covrir* to cover] (14th century)
**1** : not openly shown, engaged in, or avowed : VEILED ⟨a *covert* alliance⟩
**2** : covered over : SHELTERED

*synonym* see SECRET
— **co·vert·ly** *adverb*
— **co·vert·ness** *noun*

**²co·vert** \'kə-vərt, 'kō-vərt *also* 'kə-vər\ *noun* (14th century)
**1 a** : hiding place : SHELTER **b** : a thicket affording cover for game **c** : a masking or concealing device
**2** : a feather covering the bases of the quills of the wings and tail of a bird — see BIRD illustration
**3** : a firm durable twilled sometimes waterproofed cloth usually of mixed-color yarns

**cov·er·ture** \'kə-vər-,chûr, -chər, -,tyùr, -,tùr\ *noun* (13th century)
**1 a** : COVERING **b** : SHELTER
**2** : the status a woman acquires upon marriage under common law

**cov·er·up** \'kə-və-,rəp\ *noun* (1927)
**1** : a device or stratagem for masking or concealing ⟨his garrulousness is a *cover-up* for insecurity⟩; *also* : a usually concerted effort to keep an illegal or unethical act or situation from being made public
**2** : a loose outer garment

**cov·et** \'kə-vət\ *verb* [Middle English *coveiten*, from Old French *coveitier*, from *coveitié* desire, modification of Latin *cupiditat-*, *cupiditas*, from *cupidus* desirous, from *cupere* to desire] (14th century)
*transitive verb*
**1** : to wish for enviously
**2** : to desire (what belongs to another) inordinately or culpably
*intransitive verb*
: to feel inordinate desire for what belongs to another

*synonym* see DESIRE
— **cov·et·able** \-və-tə-bəl\ *adjective*

**cov·et·er** \-tər\ *noun*
— **cov·et·ing·ly** \-tiŋ-lē\ *adverb*

**cov·et·ous** \'kə-və-təs\ *adjective* (13th century)
**1** : marked by inordinate desire for wealth or possessions or for another's possessions
**2** : having a craving for possession ⟨*covetous* of power⟩ ☆
— **cov·et·ous·ly** *adverb*
— **cov·et·ous·ness** *noun*

**cov·ey** \'kə-vē\ *noun, plural* **coveys** [Middle English, from Middle French *covee*, from Old French, from *cover* to sit on, brood over, from Latin *cubare* to lie] (14th century)
**1** : a mature bird or pair of birds with a brood of young; *also* : a small flock
**2** : COMPANY, GROUP

**¹cow** \'kaù\ *noun* [Middle English *cou*, from Old English *cū*; akin to Old High German *kuo* cow, Latin *bos* head of cattle, Greek *bous*, Sanskrit *go*] (before 12th century)
**1 a** : the mature female of cattle (genus *Bos*) **b** : the mature female of various usually large animals (as an elephant, whale, or moose)
**2** : a domestic bovine animal regardless of sex or age
— **cowy** \-ē\ *adjective*

cow 1: *1* hoof, *2* pastern, *3* dewclaw, *4* switch, *5* hock, *6* rear udder, *7* flank, *8* thigh, *9* tail, *10* pinbone, *11* tail head, *12* thurl, *13* hip, *14* barrel, *15* ribs, *16* crops, *17* withers, *18* heart girth, *19* neck, *20* horn, *21* poll, *22* forehead, *23* bridge of nose, *24* muzzle, *25* jaw, *26* throat, *27* point of shoulder, *28* dewlap, *29* point of elbow, *30* brisket, *31* chest floor, *32* knee, *33* milk well, *34* milk vein, *35* fore udder, *36* teats, *37* rump, *38* loin

**²cow** *transitive verb* [probably of Scandinavian origin; akin to Danish *kue* to subdue] (1605)
: to destroy the resolve or courage of ⟨the party that Stalin had *cowed* —*World Press Review*⟩; *also* : to bring to a state or an action by intimidation — used with *into* ⟨like too many Asian armies, adept at *cowing* a population into feeding them —Edward Lansdale⟩

*synonym* see INTIMIDATE
— **cowed·ly** \'kaù(-ə)d-lē\ *adverb*

**cow·ard** \'kaù(-ə)rd\ *noun* [Middle English, from Old French *coart*, from *coe* tail, from Latin *cauda*] (13th century)
: one who shows disgraceful fear or timidity
◆
— **coward** *adjective*

**cow·ard·ice** \'kaù(-ə)r-dəs, *dialect* -(,)dīs\ *noun* [Middle English *cowardise*, from Middle French *coardise*, from *coart*] (14th century)
: lack of courage or resolution

**¹cow·ard·ly** \-lē\ *adverb* (14th century)
: in a cowardly manner

**²cowardly** *adjective* (1551)
: being, resembling, or befitting a coward ⟨a *cowardly* retreat⟩ ☆
— **cow·ard·li·ness** *noun*

**cow·bane** \'kaù-,bān\ *noun* (1776)
: any of several poisonous plants (as a water hemlock) of the carrot family

**cow·bell** \-,bel\ *noun* (1652)
: a bell hung around the neck of a cow to make a sound by which the cow can be located

**cow·ber·ry** \-,ber-ē\ *noun* (1800)
: MOUNTAIN CRANBERRY; *also* : its fruit

**cow·bird** \-,bərd\ *noun* (1810)
: a small North American blackbird (*Molothrus ater*) that lays its eggs in the nests of other birds

**cow·boy** \-,bòi\ *noun* (1623)
**1** : one who tends cattle or horses; *especially* : a usually mounted cattle-ranch hand
**2** : a rodeo performer

**cowboy boot** *noun* (1895)
: a boot made with a high arch, a high Cuban heel, and usually fancy stitching

**cowboy hat** *noun* (1895)
: a wide-brimmed hat with a large soft crown — called also *ten-gallon hat*

**cow·catch·er** \'kaù-,ka-chər, -,ke-\ *noun* (1838)
: an inclined frame on the front of a railroad locomotive for throwing obstacles off the track

**cow college** *noun* (circa 1915)
**1** : a college that specializes in agriculture

☆ SYNONYMS
**Covetous, greedy, acquisitive, grasping, avaricious** mean having or showing a strong desire for especially material possessions. COVETOUS implies inordinate desire often for another's possessions ⟨*covetous* of his brother's country estate⟩. GREEDY stresses lack of restraint and often of discrimination in desire ⟨*greedy* for status symbols⟩. ACQUISITIVE implies both eagerness to possess and ability to acquire and keep ⟨an eagerly *acquisitive* mind⟩. GRASPING adds to COVETOUS and GREEDY an implication of selfishness and often suggests unfair or ruthless means ⟨a hard *grasping* trader who cheated the natives⟩. AVARICIOUS implies obsessive acquisitiveness especially of money and strongly suggests stinginess ⟨an *avaricious* miser⟩.

**Cowardly, pusillanimous, craven, dastardly** mean having or showing a lack of courage. COWARDLY implies a weak or ignoble lack of courage ⟨a *cowardly* failure to stand up for principle⟩. PUSILLANIMOUS suggests a contemptible lack of courage ⟨the *pusillanimous* fear of a future full of possibility⟩. CRAVEN suggests extreme defeatism and complete lack of resistance ⟨secretly despised her own *craven* yes-men⟩. DASTARDLY often implies behavior that is both cowardly and treacherous or skulking or outrageous ⟨a *dastardly* attack on unarmed civilians⟩.

◇ WORD HISTORY
**coward** A frightened animal may draw its tail between its hind legs—or it may simply turn tail and run. If the fleeing animal has a white tail, as does the hare, the flash of white can leave a keen impression. But fear can be found in humans as well as animals, and armies have their tail ends also. A traditional belief holds that it is in the tail end of an advancing army that one is most likely to find the cowards lurking. Although it is not known whether the original reference was to the tail of an army or an animal, it is certain that the Old French word *cuart* or *coart*, the source of our word *coward*, comes from *coe* or *coue*, meaning "tail."

**2 :** a provincial college or university that lacks culture, sophistication, and tradition

**cow·er** \'kau̇(-ə)r\ *intransitive verb* [Middle English *couren*, of Scandinavian origin; akin to Old Norse *kura* to cower] (14th century)
**:** to shrink away or crouch especially for shelter from something that menaces, domineers, or dismays
***synonym*** see FAWN

**cow·fish** \'kau̇-ˌfish\ *noun* (1870)
**:** any of various small bright-colored fishes (family Ostraciidae) with hornlike projections over the eyes

**cow·girl** \-ˌgər(-ə)l\ *noun* (1884)
**1 :** a girl or woman who tends cattle or horses
**2 :** a girl or woman who is a rodeo performer

**cow·hage** *also* **cow·age** \'kau̇-ij\ *noun* [Hindi *kavā̃c*] (1640)
**:** a tropical leguminous woody vine (*Mucuna pruriens*) with crooked pods covered with barbed hairs that cause severe itching; *also*
**:** these hairs formerly used as a vermifuge

**cow·hand** \'kau̇-ˌhand\ *noun* (1852)
**:** COWBOY 1

**cow·herd** \-ˌhərd\ *noun* (before 12th century)
**:** one who tends cows

**¹cow·hide** \-ˌhīd\ *noun* (14th century)
**1 :** the hide of a cow; *also* **:** leather made from this hide
**2 :** a coarse whip of rawhide or braided leather

**²cowhide** *transitive verb* **cow·hid·ed; cow·hid·ing** (1794)
**:** to flog with a cowhide whip

**cow horse** *noun* (1853)
**:** COW PONY

**¹cowl** \'kau̇(ə)l\ *noun* [Middle English *cowle*, from Old English *cugele*, from Late Latin *cuculla* monk's hood, from Latin *cucullus* hood] (before 12th century)
**1 a :** a hood or long hooded cloak especially of a monk **b :** a draped neckline on a woman's garment
**2 a :** a chimney covering designed to improve the draft **b :** the top portion of the front part of an automobile body forward of the two front doors to which are attached the windshield and instrument board **c :** COWLING

**²cowl** *transitive verb* (1536)
**:** to cover with or as if with a cowl

**cow·lick** \'kau̇-ˌlik\ *noun* (1598)
**:** a lock or tuft of hair growing in a different direction from the rest of the hair

**cowl·ing** \'kau̇-liŋ\ *noun* (1917)
**:** a removable metal covering that houses the engine and sometimes a part of the fuselage or nacelle of an airplane; *also* **:** a metal cover for an engine

**cowl·staff** \'kōl-ˌstaf, 'kau̇(ə)l-, 'kül-\ *noun* [Middle English *cuvelstaff*, from *cuvel* vessel (from Old English *cȳfel*, from Old North French *cuvele* small vat) + ¹*staff*] (13th century)
*archaic* **:** a staff from which a vessel is suspended and carried between two persons

**cow·man** \'kau̇-mən, -ˌman\ *noun* (1677)
**1 :** COWHERD, COWBOY
**2 :** a cattle owner or rancher

**cow parsnip** *noun* (1548)
**:** a tall perennial North American plant (*Heracleum lanatum*) of the carrot family with large compound leaves and broad umbels of white or purplish flowers; *also* **:** a related Eurasian plant (*H. sphondylium*) naturalized in the U.S.

**cow·pat** \'kau̇-ˌpat\ *noun* (1937)
**:** a dropping of cow dung

**cow·pea** \'kau̇-ˌpē\ *noun* (1776)
**:** a sprawling leguminous herb (*Vigna unguiculata* synonym *V. sinensis*) related to the bean and widely cultivated in the southern U.S. especially for forage and green manure; *also* **:** its edible seed — called also *black-eyed pea*

**Cow·per's gland** \'kau̇-pərz-, 'kü-, 'ku̇-\ *noun* [William *Cowper* (died 1709) English surgeon] (1738)
**:** either of two small glands lying on either side of the male urethra below the prostate gland and discharging a secretion into the semen — called also *bulbourethral gland*; compare BARTHOLIN'S GLAND

**cow·poke** \'kau̇-ˌpōk\ *noun* (circa 1881)
**:** COWBOY 1

**cow pony** *noun* (1874)
**:** a strong and agile saddle horse trained for herding cattle

**cow·pox** \'kau̇-ˌpäks\ *noun* (1798)
**:** a mild eruptive disease of the cow that when communicated to humans protects against smallpox

**cow·punch·er** \-ˌpən-chər\ *noun* (1878)
**:** COWBOY 1

**cow·rie** *or* **cow·ry** \'kau̇-rē\ *noun, plural* **cowries** [Hindi *kaurī*] (1662)
**:** any of various marine gastropods (family Cypraeidae) that are widely distributed in warm seas and have glossy and often brightly colored shells; *also* **:** the shell of a cowrie

**cow·shed** \'kau̇-ˌshed\ *noun* (1835)
**:** a shed for the housing of cows

**cow·slip** \'kau̇-ˌslip\ *noun* [Middle English *cowslyppe*, from Old English *cūslyppe*, literally, cow dung, from *cū* cow + *slypa, slyppe* paste] (before 12th century)
**1 :** a common European primrose (*Primula veris*) with fragrant yellow flowers
**2 :** MARSH MARIGOLD

**cow town** *noun* (1885)
**1 :** a town or city that serves as a market center or shipping point for cattle
**2 :** a small unsophisticated town within a cattle-raising area

**¹cox** \'käks\ *noun* (1869)
**:** COXSWAIN

**²cox** *verb* (1881)
**:** COXSWAIN

**coxa** \'käk-sə\ *noun, plural* **cox·ae** \-ˌsē, -ˌsī\ [Latin, hip; akin to Old High German *hāhsina* hock, Sanskrit *kakṣa* armpit] (1826)
**:** the basal segment of a limb of various arthropods (as an insect)
— **cox·al** \-səl\ *adjective*

**cox·comb** \'käk-ˌskōm\ *noun* [Middle English *cokkes comb*, literally, cock's comb] (1573)
**1 a** *obsolete* **:** a jester's cap adorned with a strip of red **b** *archaic* **:** PATE, HEAD
**2 a** *obsolete* **:** FOOL **b :** a conceited foolish person **:** FOP
— **cox·comb·i·cal** \käk-'skō-mi-kəl, -'skä-\ *adjective*

**cox·comb·ry** \'käk-skəm-rē, -ˌskōm-\ *noun, plural* **-ries** (1608)
**:** behavior that is characteristic of a coxcomb **:** FOPPERY

**Cox·sack·ie virus** \(ˌ)käk-'sa-kē-\ *noun* [*Coxsackie*, N.Y.] (1949)
**:** any of several enteroviruses associated with human diseases (as meningitis)

**¹cox·swain** \'käk-sən, -ˌswān\ *noun* [Middle English *cokswayne*, from *cok* cockboat + *swain* servant] (15th century)
**1 :** a sailor who has charge of a ship's boat and its crew and who usually steers
**2 :** a steersman of a racing shell who usually directs the rowers

**²coxswain** (1928)
*transitive verb*
**:** to direct as coxswain
*intransitive verb*
**:** to act as coxswain

**¹coy** \'kȯi\ *adjective* [Middle English, quiet, shy, from Middle French *coi* calm, from Latin *quietus* quiet] (14th century)
**1 a :** shrinking from contact or familiarity **b :** marked by cute, coquettish, or artful playfulness
**2 :** showing reluctance to make a definite commitment
***synonym*** see SHY
— **coy·ly** *adverb*
— **coy·ness** *noun*

**²coy** (1583)
*transitive verb*
*obsolete* **:** CARESS
*intransitive verb*
*archaic* **:** to act coyly

**coy·dog** \'kȯi-ˌdȯg\ *noun* [*coyote* + *dog*] (1950)
**:** a hybrid between a coyote and a feral dog

**coy·ote** \'kī-ˌōt, kī-'ō-tē\ *noun, plural* **coy·otes** *or* **coyote** [Mexican Spanish, from Nahuatl *coyōtl*] (1759)
**1 :** a buff-gray to reddish gray North American canid (*Canis latrans*) closely related to but smaller than the wolf
**2 :** one who smuggles immigrants into the U.S.

*coyote 1*

**coy·o·til·lo** \ˌkī-ə-'ti-(ˌ)lō, ˌkȯi-ə-, -'tē-(ˌ)yōl\ *noun* [Mexican Spanish, diminutive of *coyote*] (circa 1892)
**:** a shrub (*Karwinskia humboldtiana*) of the buckthorn family of the southwestern U.S. and Mexico having poisonous berries

**coy·pu** \'kȯi-(ˌ)pü, kȯi-'\ *noun* [American Spanish *coipú*, from Araucanian *coipu*] (1793)
**:** NUTRIA

**coz** \'kəz\ *noun* [by shortening & alteration] (1559)
**:** COUSIN

**coz·en** \'kə-zən\ *transitive verb* **coz·ened; coz·en·ing** \'kəz-niŋ, 'kə-zə-\ [perhaps from obsolete Italian *cozzonare*, from Italian *cozzone* horse trader, from Latin *cocion-, cocio* trader] (1573)
**1 :** to deceive, win over, or induce to do something by artful coaxing and wheedling or shrewd trickery
**2 :** to gain by cozening someone ⟨*cozened* his supper out of the old couple⟩
***synonym*** see CHEAT
— **coz·en·er** \'kəz-nər, 'kə-zə-\ *noun*

**coz·en·age** \'kəz-nij, 'kə-zə-\ *noun* (1583)
**1 :** the art or practice of cozening **:** FRAUD
**2 :** an act or an instance of cozening

**¹co·zy** \'kō-zē\ *adjective* **co·zi·er; -est** [probably of Scandinavian origin; akin to Norwegian *koselig* cozy] (1709)
**1 :** enjoying or affording warmth and ease **:** SNUG
**2 a :** marked by the intimacy of the family or a close group **b :** marked by or suggesting close association or connivance ⟨a *cozy* agreement⟩
**3 :** marked by a discreet and cautious attitude or procedure
***synonym*** see COMFORTABLE
— **co·zi·ly** \-zə-lē\ *adverb*
— **co·zi·ness** \-zē-nəs\ *noun*

**²cozy** *noun, plural* **co·zies** (1863)
**:** a padded covering especially for a teapot to keep the contents hot

**³cozy** *adverb* (1946)
**:** in a cautious manner ⟨play it *cozy* and wait for the other team to make a mistake —Bobby Dodd⟩

**cozy up** *intransitive verb* (1937)
**:** to attain or try to attain familiarity, friendship, or intimacy **:** ingratiate oneself ⟨*cozying* up to the boss⟩

**¹crab** \'krab\ *noun, often attributive* [Middle English *crabbe*, from Old English *crabba*; akin to Old High German *krebiz* crab, Old English *ceorfan* to carve — more at CARVE] (before 12th century)
**1 :** any of numerous chiefly marine broadly built decapod crustaceans: **a :** any of a group (Brachyura) with a short broad usually flattened carapace, a small abdomen that curls forward beneath the body, short antennae, and the anterior pair of limbs modified as grasping pincers **b :** any of various crustaceans of a

group (Anomura) resembling true crabs in the more or less reduced condition of the abdomen

**2** *capitalized* : CANCER 1
**3** *plural* : infestation with crab lice
**4** : the angular difference between an aircraft's course and the heading necessary to make that course in the presence of a crosswind

²**crab** *verb* **crabbed; crab·bing** (1918)
*transitive verb*
**1** : to cause to move sideways or in an indirect or diagonal manner; *specifically* : to head (an airplane) into a crosswind to counteract drift
**2** : to subject to crabbing
*intransitive verb*
**1 a** (1) : to move sideways indirectly or diagonally (2) : to crab an airplane **b** : to scuttle or scurry sideways
**2** : to fish for crabs
— **crab·ber** *noun*

³**crab** *noun* [Middle English *crabbe*, perhaps from *crabbe* ¹crab] (14th century)
: CRAB APPLE

⁴**crab** *noun* (1580)
: an ill-tempered person : CROSSPATCH

⁵**crab** *verb* **crabbed; crab·bing** [Middle English *crabben*, probably back-formation from *crabbed*] (1662)
*transitive verb*
**1** : to make sullen : SOUR (old age has *crabbed* his nature)
**2** : to complain about peevishly
**3** : SPOIL, RUIN
*intransitive verb*
: CARP, GROUSE (always *crabs* about the weather)
— **crab·ber** *noun*

**crab apple** *noun* [³crab] (1712)
: any of various wild or cultivated trees (genus *Malus*) that are cultivars or relatives of the cultivated apple and that produce small sour fruit; *also* : the fruit

**crab·bed** \'kra-bəd\ *adjective* [Middle English, partly from *crabbe* ¹crab, partly from *crabbe* crab apple] (14th century)
**1** : marked by a forbidding moroseness
**2** : difficult to read or understand (*crabbed* handwriting)
*synonym* see SULLEN
— **crab·bed·ness** *noun*

**crab·by** \'kra-bē\ *adjective* **crab·bi·er; -est** [⁴crab] (1776)
: CROSS, ILL-NATURED

**crab cactus** *noun* (1900)
: CHRISTMAS CACTUS

**crab·grass** \'krab-,gras\ *noun* (1743)
: a grass (especially *Digitaria sanguinalis*) that has creeping or decumbent stems which root freely at the nodes and that is often a pest in turf or cultivated lands

**crab louse** *noun* (1547)
: a sucking louse (*Phthirus pubis*) infesting the pubic region of the human body

**crab·meat** \'krab-,mēt\ *noun* (1876)
: the edible part of a crab

**crab·stick** \-,stik\ *noun* (1703)
**1** : a stick, cane, or cudgel of crab apple tree wood
**2** : a crabbed ill-natured person

**crab·wise** \-,wīz\ *adverb* (1898)
**1** : SIDEWAYS
**2** : in a sidling or cautiously indirect manner

¹**crack** \'krak\ *verb* [Middle English *crakken*, from Old English *cracian;* akin to Old High German *chrahhōn* to resound] (before 12th century)
*intransitive verb*
**1** : to make a very sharp explosive sound (the whip *cracks* through the air)
**2** : to break, split, or snap apart
**3** : FAIL: as **a** : to lose control or effectiveness under pressure — often used with *up* **b** : to fail in tone (his voice *cracked*)
**4** : to go or travel at good speed — usually used with *on* (the steamboat *cracked* on)
*transitive verb*

**1 a** : to break so that fissures appear on the surface (*crack* a mirror) **b** : to break with a sudden sharp sound (*crack* nuts)
**2** : to tell especially suddenly or strikingly (*crack* a joke)
**3** : to strike with a sharp noise : RAP (then *cracks* him over the head) (*cracked* a two-run homer in the fifth —*N.Y. Times*)
**4 a** (1) : to open (as a bottle) for drinking (2) : to open (a book) for studying **b** : to puzzle out and expose, solve, or reveal the mystery of (*crack* a code) **c** : to break into (*crack* a safe) **d** : to open slightly (*crack* the throttle) **e** : to break through (as a barrier) so as to gain acceptance or recognition
**5 a** : to impair seriously or irreparably : WRECK (*crack* a car up) **b** : to destroy the tone of (a voice) **c** : DISORDER, CRAZE **d** : to interrupt sharply or abruptly (the criticism *cracked* our complacency)
**6** : to cause to make a sharp noise (*cracks* his knuckles)
**7 a** (1) : to subject (hydrocarbons) to cracking (2) : to produce by cracking (*cracked* gasoline) **b** : to break up (chemical compounds) into simpler compounds by means of heat

²**crack** *noun* (14th century)
**1 a** : a loud roll or peal (a *crack* of thunder) **b** : a sudden sharp noise (the *crack* of rifle fire)
**2** : a sharp witty remark : QUIP
**3 a** : a narrow break : FISSURE (a *crack* in the ice) **b** : a narrow opening (leave the door open a *crack*)
**4 a** : a weakness or flaw caused by decay, age, or deficiency : UNSOUNDNESS **b** : a broken tone of the voice **c** : CRACKPOT
**5** : MOMENT, INSTANT (the *crack* of dawn)
**6** : HOUSEBREAKING, BURGLARY
**7** : a sharp resounding blow (gave him a *crack* on the head)
**8** : ATTEMPT, TRY (her first *crack* at writing a novel)
**9** : highly purified cocaine in small chips used illicitly usually for smoking

³**crack** *adjective* (1793)
: of superior excellence or ability (a *crack* marksman)

**crack·back** \'krak-,bak\ *noun* (1967)
: a blind-side block on a defensive back in football by a pass receiver who starts downfield and then cuts back to the middle of the line

**crack·brain** \-,brān\ *noun* (circa 1570)
: an erratic person : CRACKPOT
— **crack·brained** \-'brānd\ *adjective*

**crack·down** \-,daun\ *noun* (1935)
: an act or instance of cracking down

**crack down** *intransitive verb* (1939)
: to take positive regulatory or disciplinary action

**cracked** \'krakt\ *adjective* (1503)
**1 a** : broken (as by a sharp blow) so that the surface is fissured (*cracked* china) **b** : broken into coarse particles (*cracked* wheat) **c** : marked by harshness, dissonance, or failure to sustain a tone (a *cracked* voice)
**2** : mentally disturbed : CRAZY

**crack·er** \'kra-kər\ *noun* (15th century)
**1** *chiefly dialect* : a bragging liar : BOASTER
**2** : something that makes a cracking or snapping noise: as **a** : FIRECRACKER **b** : the snapping end of a whiplash : SNAPPER **c** : a paper holder for a party favor that pops when the ends are pulled sharply
**3** *plural* : NUTCRACKER
**4** : a dry thin crispy baked bread product that may be leavened or unleavened
**5 a** : a poor usually Southern white — usually used disparagingly **b** *capitalized* : a native or resident of Florida or Georgia — used as a nickname
**6** : the equipment in which cracking (as of petroleum) is carried out

**crack·er-bar·rel** \-,bar-əl\ *adjective* [from the cracker barrel in country stores around

which customers lounged for informal conversation] (1916)
: suggestive of the friendly homespun character of a country store (a *cracker-barrel* philosopher)

**crack·er·jack** \'kra-kər-,jak\ *also* **crack·a·jack** \-kə-,jak\ *noun* [probably alteration of ³*crack + jack* (man)] (1895)
: a person or thing of marked excellence
— **crackerjack** *adjective*

**Cracker Jack** *trademark*
— used for a candied popcorn confection

**crack·ers** \'kra-kərz\ *adjective* [probably *cracked + -ers* (as in *starkers*)] (1928)
: CRAZY

*word history* see NUTS

¹**crack·ing** \'kra-kiŋ\ *adjective* (1830)
: very impressive or effective : GREAT

²**cracking** *adverb* (1903)
: VERY, EXTREMELY (a *cracking* good book)

³**cracking** *noun* (1868)
: a process in which relatively heavy hydrocarbons are broken up by heat into lighter products (as gasoline)

¹**crack·le** \'kra-kəl\ *verb* **crack·led; crack·ling** \-k(ə-)liŋ\ [frequentative of ¹*crack*] (circa 1560)
*intransitive verb*
**1 a** : to make small sharp sudden repeated noises (the fire *crackles* on the hearth) **b** : to show animation : SPARKLE (the essays *crackle* with wit)
**2** : CRAZE 3
*transitive verb*
: to crush or crack with snapping noises

²**crackle** *noun* (1833)
**1 a** : the noise of repeated small cracks or reports **b** : SPARKLE, EFFERVESCENCE
**2** : a network of fine cracks on an otherwise smooth surface

**crack·le·ware** \'kra-kəl-,war, -,wer\ *noun* (1881)
: ceramic ware with a decorative crazed glaze

**crack·ling** *noun* (1599)
**1** \'kra-k(ə-)liŋ\ : a series of small sharp noises (the *crackling* of frozen snow as we walk)
**2** \'kra-klən, -kliŋ\ : the crisp residue left after the rendering of lard from fat or the frying or roasting of the skin (as of pork) — usually used in plural

**crack·ly** \'kra-k(ə-)lē\ *adjective* (1859)
: inclined to crackle : CRISP

**crack·nel** \'krak-nᵊl\ *noun* [Middle English *krakenelle*] (14th century)
**1** : a hard brittle biscuit
**2** : CRACKLING 2 — usually used in plural

**crack·pot** \'krak-,pät\ *noun* (1883)
: one given to eccentric or lunatic notions
— **crackpot** *adjective*

**cracks·man** \'krak-smən\ *noun* (circa 1812)
: BURGLAR; *also* : SAFECRACKER

**crack·up** \'krak-,əp\ *noun* (circa 1926)
**1** : CRASH, WRECK (an automobile *crack-up*)
**2 a** : a mental collapse : NERVOUS BREAKDOWN (his wife's death brought on his *crack-up*) **b** : COLLAPSE, BREAKDOWN

**crack up** (1829)
*transitive verb*
**1** : PRAISE, TOUT 4 (wasn't all that it was *cracked up* to be)
**2** : to cause to laugh out loud (that joke really *cracks* him *up*)
*intransitive verb*
**1** : to smash up a vehicle (as by losing control) (*cracked up* on a curve)
**2** : to laugh out loud

**-cracy** *noun combining form* [Middle French & Late Latin; Middle French *-cratie*, from Late Latin *-cratia*, from Greek *-kratia*, from *kratos* strength, power — more at HARD]

\ə\ abut \ᵊ\ kitten \ər\ further \a\ ash \ā\ ace
\ä\ mop, mar \au\ out \ch\ chin \e\ bet \ē\ easy
\g\ go \i\ hit \ī\ ice \j\ job \ŋ\ sing \ō\ go
\o\ law \oi\ boy \th\ thin \th\ the \ü\ loot \u\ foot
\y\ yet \zh\ vision *see also* Guide to Pronunciation

**1 :** form of government; *also* **:** state having such a form ⟨mono*cracy*⟩
**2 :** social or political class (as of powerful persons) ⟨mobo*cracy*⟩
**3 :** theory of social organization ⟨techno*cracy*⟩

**¹cra·dle** \'krā-d°l\ *noun* [Middle English *cradel*, from Old English *cradol*; perhaps akin to Old High German *kratto* basket, Sanskrit *grantha* knot] (before 12th century)
**1 a :** a bed or cot for a baby usually on rockers or pivots **b :** a framework or support suggestive of a baby's cradle: as (1) **:** a framework of bars and rods (2) **:** the support for a telephone receiver or handset **c :** an implement with rods like fingers attached to a scythe and used formerly for harvesting grain **d :** a frame to keep the bedclothes from contact with an injured part of the body
**2 a :** the earliest period of life **:** INFANCY ⟨from the *cradle* to the grave⟩ **b :** a place of origin ⟨the *cradle* of civilization⟩
**3 :** a rocking device used in panning for gold

**²cradle** *verb* **cra·dled; cra·dling** \'krād-liŋ, 'krā-d°l-iŋ\ (15th century)
*transitive verb*
**1 a :** to place or keep in or as if in a cradle **b :** SHELTER, REAR **c :** to support protectively or intimately ⟨*cradling* the injured man's head in her arms⟩
**2 :** to cut (grain) with a cradle scythe
**3 :** to place, raise, support, or transport on a cradle
*intransitive verb*
*obsolete* **:** to rest in or as if in a cradle

**cradle cap** *noun* (circa 1890)
**:** a seborrheic condition in infants that usually affects the scalp and is characterized by greasy gray or dark brown adherent scaly crusts

**cra·dle·song** \'krā-d°l-,soŋ\ *noun* (14th century)
**:** LULLABY

**¹craft** \'kraft\ *noun* [Middle English, strength, skill, from Old English *cræft*; akin to Old High German *kraft* strength] (before 12th century)
**1 :** skill in planning, making, or executing **:** DEXTERITY
**2 :** an occupation or trade requiring manual dexterity or artistic skill ⟨the carpenter's *craft*⟩ ⟨the *craft* of writing plays⟩ ⟨*crafts* such as pottery, carpentry, and sewing⟩
**3 :** skill in deceiving to gain an end ⟨used *craft* and guile to close the deal⟩
**4 :** the members of a trade or trade association
**5** *plural usually* **craft a :** a boat especially of small size **b :** AIRCRAFT **c :** SPACECRAFT
**synonym** see ART

**²craft** *transitive verb* (15th century)
**:** to make or produce with care, skill, or ingenuity ⟨is *crafting* a new sculpture⟩ ⟨a carefully *crafted* story⟩

**crafts·man** \'kraf(t)s-mən\ *noun* (13th century)
**1 :** a worker who practices a trade or handicraft
**2 :** one who creates or performs with skill or dexterity especially in the manual arts ⟨jewelry made by European *craftsmen*⟩
— **crafts·man·like** \-,līk\ *adjective*
— **crafts·man·ly** \-lē\ *adjective*
— **crafts·man·ship** \-,ship\ *noun*

**crafts·peo·ple** \-,pē-pəl\ *noun plural* (1953)
**:** workers who practice a trade or craft

**crafts·per·son** \-,pər-s°n\ *noun* (1920)
**:** a craftsman or craftswoman

**crafts·wom·an** \'kraf(t)s-,wu̇-mən\ *noun* (1886)
**1 :** a woman artisan
**2 :** a woman who is skilled in a craft

**craft union** *noun* (1922)
**:** a labor union with membership limited to workers of the same craft — compare INDUSTRIAL UNION

**crafty** \'kraf-tē\ *adjective* **craft·i·er; -est** (before 12th century)
**1** *dialect chiefly British* **:** SKILLFUL, CLEVER

**2 a :** adept in the use of subtlety and cunning
**b :** marked by subtlety and guile ⟨a *crafty* scheme⟩
**synonym** see SLY
— **craft·i·ly** \'kraf-tə-lē\ *adverb*
— **craft·i·ness** \-tē-nəs\ *noun*

**¹crag** \'krag\ *noun* [Middle English, of Celtic origin; akin to Welsh *craig* rock] (14th century)
**1 :** a steep rugged rock or cliff
**2** *archaic* **:** a sharp detached fragment of rock
— **crag·ged** \'kra-gəd\ *adjective*

**²crag** *noun* [Middle English, from Middle Dutch *crāghe*; akin to Old English *cræga* throat — more at CRAW] (14th century)
*chiefly Scottish* **:** NECK, THROAT

**crag·gy** \'kra-gē\ *adjective* **crag·gi·er; -est** (15th century)
**1 :** full of crags ⟨*craggy* slopes⟩
**2 :** ROUGH, RUGGED ⟨a *craggy* face⟩
— **crag·gi·ly** \'kra-gə-lē\ *adverb*
— **crag·gi·ness** \'kra-gē-nəs\ *noun*

**crags·man** \'kragz-mən\ *noun* (1816)
**:** one that is expert in climbing crags or cliffs

**crake** \'krāk\ *noun* [Middle English, probably from Old Norse *krāka* crow or *krākr* raven; akin to Old English *crāwan* to crow] (14th century)
**1 :** any of various rails; *especially* **:** a short-billed rail (as the corncrake)
**2 :** the corncrake's cry

**¹cram** \'kram\ *verb* **crammed; cram·ming** [Middle English *crammen*, from Old English *crammian*; akin to Old Norse *kremja* to squeeze] (before 12th century)
*transitive verb*
**1 :** to pack tight **:** JAM ⟨*cram* a suitcase with clothes⟩
**2 a :** to fill with food to satiety **:** STUFF **b :** to eat voraciously **:** BOLT ⟨the child *crams* her food⟩
**3 :** to thrust in or as if in a rough or forceful manner ⟨*crammed* the letters into his pocket⟩
**4 :** to prepare hastily for an examination ⟨*cram* the students for the test⟩
*intransitive verb*
**1 :** to eat greedily or to satiety **:** STUFF
**2 :** to study hastily for an imminent examination
— **cram·mer** *noun*

**²cram** *noun* (1810)
**1 :** a compressed multitude or crowd **:** CRUSH
**2 :** last-minute study for an examination

**cram·bo** \'kram-(,)bō\ *noun, plural* **cram·boes** [alteration of earlier *crambe*, from Latin, cabbage, from Greek *krambē*] (1660)
**:** a game in which one player gives a word or line of verse to be matched in rhyme by other players

**cram·oi·sie** *or* **cram·oi·sy** \'kra-,mȯi-zē, 'kra-mə-zē\ *noun, plural* **-sies** [Middle English *crammassy*, from Middle French *cramoisi*, from *cramoisi* crimson] (15th century)
**:** crimson cloth

**¹cramp** \'kramp\ *noun* [Middle English *crampe*, from Middle French, of Germanic origin; akin to Middle Dutch *crampe*; akin to Old High German *krampf* bent] (14th century)
**1 :** a painful involuntary spasmodic contraction of a muscle
**2 :** a temporary paralysis of muscles from overuse — compare WRITER'S CRAMP
**3 a :** sharp abdominal pain — usually used in plural **b :** persistent and often intense though dull lower abdominal pain associated with dysmenorrhea — usually used in plural

**²cramp** *noun* [Middle English *crampe*, from Middle Dutch] (15th century)
**1 a :** a usually iron device bent at the ends and used to hold timbers or blocks of stone together **b :** CLAMP
**2 a :** something that confines **:** SHACKLE **b :** the state of being confined

**³cramp** (15th century)
*transitive verb*

**1 :** to affect with or as if with a cramp or cramps
**2 a :** CONFINE, RESTRAIN ⟨was *cramped* in the tiny apartment⟩ **b :** to restrain from free expression — used especially in the phrase *cramp one's style*
**3 :** to turn (the front wheels of a vehicle) to right or left
**4 :** to fasten or hold with a cramp
*intransitive verb*
**:** to suffer from cramps

**⁴cramp** *adjective* (1674)
**1 :** hard to understand or figure out ⟨*cramp* law terms⟩ ⟨*cramp* handwriting⟩
**2 :** being cramped ⟨a *cramp* corner⟩

**cram·pon** \'kram-,pän\ *noun* [Middle English, from Middle French *crampon*, of Germanic origin; akin to Middle Dutch *crampe*] (15th century)
**1 :** a hooked clutch or dog for raising heavy objects — usually used in plural
**2 :** a climbing iron used especially on ice and snow in mountaineering — usually used in plural

**crampon 2**

**cran·ber·ry** \'kran-,ber-ē, -b(ə-)rē\ *noun* [part translation of Low German *kraanbere*, from *kraan* crane + *bere* berry] (1647)
**1 :** the red acid berry produced by some plants (as *Vaccinium oxycoccos* and *V. macrocarpon*) of the heath family; *also* **:** a plant producing these
**2 :** any of various plants with a fruit that resembles a cranberry

**cranberry bush** *noun* (1778)
**:** a shrubby or arborescent viburnum (*Viburnum opulus*) of North America and Europe with prominently 3-lobed leaves and red fruit

**cranch** \'kränch\ *variant of* CRAUNCH

**¹crane** \'krān\ *noun* [Middle English *cran*, from Old English; akin to Old High German *krano* crane, Greek *geranos*, Latin *grus*] (before 12th century)
**1 :** any of a family (Gruidae of the order Gruiformes) of tall wading birds superficially resembling the herons but structurally more nearly related to the rails
**2 :** any of several herons
**3 :** an often horizontal projection swinging about a vertical axis: as **a :** a machine for raising, shifting, and lowering heavy weights by means of a projecting swinging arm or with the hoisting apparatus supported on an overhead track **b :** an iron arm in a fireplace for supporting kettles **c :** a boom for holding a motion-picture or television camera

**crane 1**

**²crane** *verb* **craned; cran·ing** (1570)
*transitive verb*
**1 :** to raise or lift by or as if by a crane
**2 :** to stretch (as the neck) toward an object of attention ⟨*craning* her neck to get a better view⟩
*intransitive verb*
**1 :** to stretch one's neck toward an object of attention ⟨I *craned* out of the window of my compartment —Webb Waldron⟩
**2 :** HESITATE

**crane fly** *noun* (1658)
: any of a family (Tipulidae) of long-legged slender dipteran flies that resemble large mosquitoes but do not bite

**cranes·bill** \'krānz-ˌbil\ *noun* (1548)
: GERANIUM 1

**crani-** *or* **cranio-** *combining form* [Medieval Latin *cranium*]
: cranium ⟨*crani*ate⟩ : cranial and ⟨*cranio*sacral⟩

**cra·ni·al** \'krā-nē-əl\ *adjective* (1800)
**1** : of or relating to the skull or cranium
**2** : CEPHALIC
— **cra·ni·al·ly** \-ə-lē\ *adverb*

**cranial index** *noun* (1868)
: the ratio multiplied by 100 of the maximum breadth of the bare skull to its maximum length from front to back

**cranial nerve** *noun* (1840)
: any of the nerves that arise in pairs from the lower surface of the brain one on each side and pass through openings in the skull to the periphery of the body and that comprise 12 pairs in reptiles, birds, and mammals and usually 10 in fishes and amphibians

**cra·ni·ate** \'krā-nē-ət, -ˌāt\ *adjective* (1879)
: having a cranium
— **craniate** *noun*

**cra·nio·ce·re·bral** \ˌkrā-nē-ō-sə-'rē-brəl, -'ser-ə-\ *adjective* (circa 1903)
: involving both cranium and brain ⟨*craniocerebral* injury⟩

**cra·nio·fa·cial** \-'fā-shəl\ *adjective* (circa 1859)
: of, relating to, or involving both the cranium and the face

**cra·ni·ol·o·gy** \ˌkrā-nē-'ä-lə-jē\ *noun* [probably from German *Kraniologie*, from *kranio-* crani- + *-logie* -logy] (1851)
: a science dealing with variations in size, shape, and proportions of skulls among human races

**cra·ni·om·e·try** \-'ä-mə-trē\ *noun* [International Scientific Vocabulary] (circa 1828)
: a science dealing with cranial measurement — compare CEPHALOMETRY

**cra·nio·sa·cral** \ˌkrā-nē-ō-'sa-krəl, -'sā-\ *adjective* (circa 1923)
: PARASYMPATHETIC

**cra·ni·ot·o·my** \ˌkrā-nē-'ä-tə-mē\ *noun* [International Scientific Vocabulary] (1855)
: surgical opening of the skull

**cra·ni·um** \'krā-nē-əm\ *noun, plural* **-ni·ums** *or* **-nia** \-nē-ə\ [Medieval Latin, from Greek *kranion;* akin to Greek *kara* head — more at CEREBRAL] (15th century)
: SKULL; *specifically* : the part that encloses the brain : BRAINCASE

**¹crank** \'kraŋk\ *noun* [Middle English *cranke,* from Old English *cranc-* (as in *crancstæf,* a weaving instrument); probably akin to Middle High German *krank* weak, sick — more at CRINGE] (13th century)
**1** : a bent part of an axle or shaft or an arm keyed at right angles to the end of a shaft by which circular motion is imparted to or received from the shaft or by which reciprocating motion is changed into circular motion or vice versa
**2 a** *archaic* : BEND **b** : a twist or turn of speech : CONCEIT — used especially in the phrase *quips and cranks* **c** : CAPRICE, CROTCHET (2) : an annoyingly eccentric person; *also* : one that is overly enthusiastic about a particular subject or activity **d** : a bad-tempered person : GROUCH
**3** : CRYSTAL 7
— **crank·ish** \'kraŋ-kish\ *adjective*

**²crank** (1592)
*intransitive verb*
**1** : to move with a winding course : ZIGZAG
**2 a** : to turn a crank **b** : to get started by or as if by the turning of a crank **c** : to gain speed, momentum, or intensity — usually used with *up* ⟨the campaign is *cranking* up⟩
*transitive verb*

**1** : to move or operate by or as if by a crank ⟨*crank* the window down⟩
**2 a** : to cause to start (as an automobile) **b** : to rotate the shaft (as a crankshaft) of especially with a starter ⟨*crank* over an engine⟩ **c** : to use in trying to start an engine ⟨*crank* the starter⟩
**3 a** : to start as if by use of a crank — usually used with *up* ⟨*crank* up an atom smasher⟩ **b** : TURN UP 2 — usually used with *up* ⟨*crank* up the volume⟩

**³crank** *adjective* (1924)
: of, relating to, or being a cranky or eccentric person; *also* : made or sent by such a person ⟨*crank* calls⟩ ⟨a *crank* letter⟩

**⁴crank** *adjective* [Middle English *cranke,* of unknown origin] (15th century)
**1** *chiefly dialect* : MERRY, HIGH-SPIRITED
**2** *chiefly dialect* : COCKY, CONFIDENT

**⁵crank** *adjective* [short for *crank-sided* (easily tipped)] (circa 1649)
*of a boat* : easily tipped by an external force

**crank·case** \'kraŋk-ˌkās\ *noun* (circa 1878)
: the housing of a crankshaft

**crank out** *transitive verb* (1956)
: to produce especially in a mechanical manner

**crank·pin** \'kraŋk-ˌpin\ *noun* (1839)
: the cylindrical piece which forms the handle of a crank or to which a connecting rod is attached

**crank·shaft** \'kraŋk-ˌshaft\ *noun* (1854)
**1** : a shaft driven by or driving a crank
**2** : a shaft consisting of a series of cranks and crankpins to which the connecting rods of an engine are attached

**¹cranky** \'kraŋ-kē\ *adjective* **crank·i·er; -est** [¹*crank*] (1821)
**1 a** : given to fretful fussiness : readily angered when opposed : CROTCHETY **b** : marked by eccentricity
**2** : full of twists and turns : TORTUOUS ⟨a *cranky* road⟩
**3** : working erratically : UNPREDICTABLE ⟨a *cranky* old tractor⟩
**4** *dialect* : CRAZY, IMBECILE
— **crank·i·ly** \-kə-lē\ *adverb*
— **crank·i·ness** \-kē-nəs\ *noun*

**²cranky** *adjective* (1841) *of a boat*
: ⁵CRANK

**cran·nog** \'kra-ˌnóg, kra-'nóg\ *noun* [Scottish Gaelic *crannag* & Irish *crannóg*] (1608)
: an artificial fortified island constructed in a lake or marsh originally in prehistoric Ireland and Scotland

**cran·ny** \'kra-nē\ *noun, plural* **crannies** [Middle English *crany,* from Middle French *cren, cran* notch] (15th century)
**1** : a small break or slit : CREVICE
**2** : an obscure nook or corner
— **cran·nied** \-nēd\ *adjective*

**cran·reuch** \'kran-ˌrúk\ *noun* [probably modification of Scottish Gaelic *crannreotha*] (1682)
*Scottish* : HOARFROST, RIME

**¹crap** \'krap\ *intransitive verb* **crapped; crap·ping** (1846)
: DEFECATE — usually considered vulgar

**²crap** *noun* [Middle English *crappe* chaff, residue from rendered fat, perhaps from Old French *crappe* chaff, residue, from Medieval Latin *crappa*] (circa 1897)
**1 a** : EXCREMENT — usually considered vulgar **b** : the act of defecating — usually considered vulgar
**2** : NONSENSE, RUBBISH; *also* : STUFF 4b — sometimes considered vulgar

**³crap** *noun* [singular of *craps*] (1885)
**1** — used as an attributive form of *craps* ⟨*crap* game⟩ ⟨*crap* table⟩
**2** : a throw of 2, 3, or 12 in the game of craps losing the shooter his bet unless he has a point — called also *craps;* compare NATURAL

**⁴crap** *intransitive verb* **crapped; crap·ping** (circa 1930)
**1** : to throw a crap

**2** : to throw a seven while trying to make a point — usually used with *out*

**¹crape** \'krāp\ *noun* [alteration of French *crêpe,* from Middle French *crespe,* from *crespe* curly, from Latin *crispus* — more at CRISP] (1633)
**1** : CREPE
**2** : a band of crepe worn on a hat or sleeve as a sign of mourning

**²crape** *transitive verb* **craped; crap·ing** (1815)
: to cover or shroud with or as if with crape

**³crape** *transitive verb* **craped; crap·ing** [French *crêper,* from Latin *crispare,* from *crispus*] (1774)
: to make (the hair) curly

**crape myrtle** *noun* (1850)
: an Asian shrub (*Lagerstroemia indica*) of the loosestrife family widely grown in warm regions for its flowers

**crap·per** \'kra-pər\ *noun* [¹*crap*] (circa 1932)
: TOILET — usually considered vulgar

**crap·pie** \'krä-pē\ *noun* [Canadian French *crapet*] (circa 1827)
**1** : BLACK CRAPPIE
**2** : WHITE CRAPPIE

**crap·py** \'kra-pē\ *adjective* **crap·pi·er; -est** (1846)
*slang* : markedly inferior in quality : LOUSY

**craps** \'kraps\ *noun plural but singular or plural in construction* [Louisiana French, from French *crabs, craps,* from English *crabs* lowest throw at hazard, from plural of ¹*crab*] (1843)
**1** : a gambling game played with two dice
**2** : ³CRAP 2

**crap·shoot** \'krap-ˌshüt\ *noun* (1971)
: something (as a business venture) that has an unpredictable outcome

**crap·shoot·er** \'krap-ˌshü-tər\ *noun* (1895)
: one who plays craps

**crap·u·lous** \'kra-pyə-ləs\ *adjective* [Late Latin *crapulosus,* from Latin *crapula* intoxication, from Greek *kraipalē*] (1536)
**1** : marked by intemperance especially in eating or drinking
**2** : sick from excessive indulgence in liquor

**¹crash** \'krash\ *verb* [Middle English *crasschen*] (15th century)
*transitive verb*
**1 a** : to break violently and noisily : SMASH **b** : to damage (an airplane) in landing
**2 a** : to cause to make a loud noise ⟨*crash* the cymbals together⟩ **b** : to force (as one's way) through with loud crashing noises
**3** : to enter or attend without invitation or without paying ⟨*crash* the party⟩
*intransitive verb*
**1 a** : to break or go to pieces with or as if with violence and noise **b** : to fall, land, or hit with destructive force **c** : to decline suddenly and steeply **d** *of a computer system or program* : to suffer a sudden major failure usually with attendant loss of data
**2** : to make a smashing noise ⟨thunder *crashing* overhead⟩
**3** : to move or force one's way with or as if with a crash ⟨*crashes* into the room⟩
**4** *slang* : to experience the aftereffects (as dysphoria or depression) of drug intoxication
**5** *slang* : to go to bed or fall asleep; *also* : to reside temporarily : STAY ⟨*crashing* with friends for a few days⟩
— **crash·er** *noun*

**²crash** *noun* (circa 1580)
**1** : a loud sound (as of things smashing) ⟨a *crash* of thunder⟩
**2 a** : a breaking to pieces by or as if by collision **b** : an instance of crashing ⟨a plane *crash*⟩ ⟨a system *crash*⟩

\ə\ abut \ᵊ\ kitten \ər\ further \a\ ash \ā\ ace
\ä\ mop, mar \aú\ out \ch\ chin \e\ bet \ē\ easy
\g\ go \i\ hit \ī\ ice \j\ job \ŋ\ sing \ō\ go
\ó\ law \ói\ boy \th\ thin \t͟h\ the \ü\ loot \ú\ foot
\y\ yet \zh\ vision *see also* Guide to Pronunciation

**3** : a sudden decline (as of a population) or failure (as of a business) ⟨a stockmarket *crash*⟩
**4** *slang* : the process of crashing after drug intoxication

³**crash** *adjective* (1945)
: marked by a concerted effort and effected in the shortest possible time ⟨a *crash* program⟩

⁴**crash** *noun* [probably from Russian *krashenina* colored linen] (1812)
: a coarse fabric used for draperies, toweling, and clothing and for strengthening joints of cased-in books

**crash dive** *noun* (1918)
: a dive made by a submarine in the least possible time
— **crash–dive** *intransitive verb*

**crash helmet** *noun* (circa 1918)
: a helmet that is worn (as by motorcyclists) as protection for the head in the event of an accident

**crash·ing** \'kra-shiŋ\ *adjective* (1924)
**1** : UTTER, ABSOLUTE ⟨a *crashing* bore⟩
**2** : SUPERLATIVE ⟨a *crashing* effect⟩
— **crash·ing·ly** \-lē\ *adverb*

**crash–land** \'krash-'land\ (1941)
*transitive verb*
: to land (an airplane or spacecraft) under emergency conditions usually with damage to the craft
*intransitive verb*
: to crash-land an airplane or spacecraft
— **crash landing** *noun*

**crash pad** *noun* (1939)
**1** : protective padding (as on the inside of an automobile or a tank)
**2** : a place to stay temporarily

**crash·wor·thy** \'krash-,wər-thē\ *adjective* (1966)
: resistant to the effects of collision ⟨*crashworthy* cars⟩
— **crash·wor·thi·ness** *noun*

**crass** \'kras\ *adjective* [Latin *crassus* thick, gross] (1653)
**1 a** : GROSS 6a; *especially* : having or indicating such grossness of mind as precludes delicacy and discrimination **b** : being beneath one's dignity ⟨*crass* concerns of daily life⟩ **c** — used as a pejorative intensifier ⟨*crass* flattery⟩ ⟨*crass* propaganda⟩
**2** : guided by or indicative of base or materialistic values ⟨*crass* commercialism⟩ ⟨*crass* measures of success⟩
**synonym** see STUPID
— **crass·ly** *adverb*
— **crass·ness** *noun*

**cras·si·tude** \'kra-sə-,tüd, -,tyüd\ *noun* (1679)
: the quality or state of being crass : GROSSNESS; *also* : an instance of grossness

-**crat** *noun combining form* [French *-crate*, back-formation from *-cratie* -cracy]
**1** : advocate or partisan of a (specified) theory of government ⟨theo*crat*⟩
**2** : member of a (specified) dominant class ⟨pluto*crat*⟩
— -**cratic** *adjective combining form*

**cratch** \'krach\ *noun* [Middle English *cracche*, from Old French *creche* manger — more at CRÈCHE] (13th century)
**1** *archaic* : MANGER
**2** : a crib or rack especially for fodder; *also* : FRAME

¹**crate** \'krāt\ *noun* [Middle English, from Latin *cratis*] (15th century)
**1** : an open box of wooden slats or a usually wooden protective case or framework for shipping
**2** : JALOPY

²**crate** *transitive verb* **crat·ed; crat·ing** (1871)
: to pack in a crate

¹**cra·ter** \'krā-tər\ *noun* [Latin, mixing bowl, crater, from Greek *kratēr*, from *kerannynai* to mix; akin to Sanskrit *śṛṇāti* he mixes] (1613)

**1** \'krā-tər\ **a** : the bowl-shaped depression around the orifice of a volcano **b** : a depression formed by the impact of a meteorite **c** : a hole in the ground made by the explosion of a bomb or shell **d** : an eroded lesion **e** : a dimple in a painted surface
**2** \'krā-tər, krä-'ter\ : KRATER
— **cra·ter·like** \'krā-tər-,līk\ *adjective*

²**crater** (1884)
*intransitive verb*
: to exhibit or form craters
*transitive verb*
: to form craters in

**cra·ter·let** \'krā-tər-lət\ *noun* (1881)
: a small crater

**C ration** *noun* (1942)
: a canned field ration of the U.S. Army

**cra·ton** \'krā-,tän, 'kra-\ *noun* [German *Kraton*, modification of Greek *kratos* strength — more at HARD] (1944)
: a stable relatively immobile area of the earth's crust that forms the nuclear mass of a continent or the central basin of an ocean
— **cra·ton·ic** \krə-'tä-nik, krā-, kra-\ *adjective*

**craunch** \'krȯnch, 'kränch\ *verb* [probably imitative] (1631)
: CRUNCH
— **craunch** *noun*

**cra·vat** \krə-'vat\ *noun* [French *cravate*, from *Crabate, Cravate* Croatian] (circa 1656)
**1** : a band or scarf worn around the neck
**2** : NECKTIE

**crave** \'krāv\ *verb* **craved; crav·ing** [Middle English, from Old English *crafian*; akin to Old Norse *krefja* to crave, demand] (before 12th century)
*transitive verb*
**1** : to ask for earnestly : BEG, DEMAND ⟨*crave* a pardon for neglect⟩
**2 a** : to want greatly : NEED ⟨*craves* drugs⟩ **b** : to yearn for ⟨*crave* a vanished youth⟩
*intransitive verb*
: to have a strong or inward desire ⟨*craves* after affection⟩
**synonym** see DESIRE
— **crav·er** *noun*

**cra·ven** \'krā-vən\ *adjective* [Middle English *cravant*] (13th century)
**1** *archaic* : DEFEATED, VANQUISHED
**2** : lacking the least bit of courage : contemptibly fainthearted
**synonym** see COWARDLY
— **craven** *noun*
— **cra·ven·ly** *adverb*
— **cra·ven·ness** \-vən-nəs\ *noun*

**crav·ing** \'krā-viŋ\ *noun* (1633)
: an intense, urgent, or abnormal desire or longing

**craw** \'krȯ\ *noun* [Middle English *crawe*, from (assumed) Old English *cræga*; perhaps akin to Latin *vorare* to devour — more at VORACIOUS] (14th century)
**1** : the crop of a bird or insect
**2** : the stomach especially of a lower animal

**craw·dad** \'krȯ-,dad\ *noun* [alteration of *crawfish*] (circa 1905)
: CRAYFISH 1 — used chiefly west of the Appalachians

¹**craw·fish** \'krȯ-,fish\ *noun* [by folk etymology from Middle English *crevis, kraveys*] (1624)
**1** : CRAYFISH 1
**2** : SPINY LOBSTER

²**crawfish** *intransitive verb* (1842)
: to retreat from a position : back out

¹**crawl** \'krȯl\ *verb* [Middle English, from Old Norse *krafla*] (14th century)
*intransitive verb*
**1** : to move slowly in a prone position without or as if without the use of limbs ⟨the snake *crawled* into its hole⟩
**2** : to move or progress slowly or laboriously ⟨traffic *crawls* along at 10 miles an hour⟩
**3** : to advance by guile or servility ⟨*crawling* into favor by toadying to his boss⟩

**4** : to spread by extending stems or tendrils
**5 a** : to be alive or swarming with or as if with creeping things ⟨a kitchen *crawling* with ants⟩ **b** : to have the sensation of insects creeping over one ⟨the story made her flesh *crawl*⟩
**6** : to fail to stay evenly spread — used of paint, varnish, or glaze
*transitive verb*
**1** : to move upon in or as if in a creeping manner
**2** : to reprove harshly ⟨they got no good right to *crawl* me for what I wrote —Marjorie K. Rawlings⟩

²**crawl** *noun* (1818)
**1 a** : the act or action of crawling **b** : slow or laborious progress **c** *chiefly British* : a going from one pub to another
**2** : a prone speed swimming stroke consisting of alternating overarm strokes and a flutter kick
**3** : lettering that moves vertically or horizontally across a television or motion-picture screen to give information (as performer credits or news bulletins)

**crawl·er** \'krȯ-lər\ *noun* (circa 1629)
**1** : one that crawls
**2** : a vehicle (as a crane) that travels on endless chain belts

**crawl space** *noun* (1946)
: a shallow unfinished space beneath the first floor or under the roof of a building especially for access to plumbing or wiring

**crawl·way** \'krȯl-,wā\ *noun* (1909)
: a low passageway (as in a cave) that can be traversed only by crawling

**crawly** \'krȯ-lē\ *adjective* (1857)
**1** : CREEPY 1
**2** : marked by crawling or slow motion ⟨*crawly* creatures⟩

**cray·fish** \'krā-,fish\ *noun* [by folk etymology from Middle English *crevis*, from Middle French *crevice*, of Germanic origin; akin to Old High German *krebiz* crab — more at CRAB] (14th century)
**1** : any of numerous freshwater decapod crustaceans (superfamily Astacoidea) resembling the lobster but usually much smaller
**2** : SPINY LOBSTER

crayfish 1

¹**cray·on** \'krā-,än, -ən *also* 'kran\ *noun* [French, crayon, pencil, from diminutive of *craie* chalk, from Latin *creta*] (1644)
**1** : a stick of white or colored chalk or of colored wax used for writing or drawing
**2** : a crayon drawing

²**crayon** *transitive verb* (1662)
: to draw with a crayon
— **cray·on·ist** \'krā-ə-nist\ *noun*

¹**craze** \'krāz\ *verb* **crazed; craz·ing** [Middle English *crasen* to crush, craze, of Scandinavian origin; akin to Old Swedish *krasa* to crush] (14th century)
*transitive verb*
**1** *obsolete* : BREAK, SHATTER
**2** : to produce minute cracks on the surface or glaze of
**3** : to make insane or as if insane ⟨*crazed* by pain and fear⟩
*intransitive verb*
**1** *archaic* : SHATTER, BREAK
**2** : to become insane
**3** : to develop a mesh of fine cracks

²**craze** *noun* (1813)
**1** : an exaggerated and often transient enthusiasm : MANIA
**2** : a crack in a surface or coating (as of glaze or enamel)
**synonym** see FASHION

¹**cra·zy** \'krā-zē\ *adjective* **cra·zi·er; -est** (1583)

**1 a :** full of cracks or flaws **:** UNSOUND **b :** CROOKED, ASKEW
**2 a :** MAD, INSANE **b** (1) **:** IMPRACTICAL (2) **:** ERRATIC **c :** being out of the ordinary **:** UNUSUAL ⟨a taste for *crazy* hats⟩
**3 a :** distracted with desire or excitement ⟨a thrill-*crazy* mob⟩ **b :** absurdly fond **:** INFATUATED ⟨he's *crazy* about the girl⟩ **c :** passionately preoccupied **:** OBSESSED ⟨*crazy* about boats⟩
— **cra·zi·ly** \-zə-lē\ *adverb*
— **cra·zi·ness** \-zē-nəs\ *noun*
— **like crazy :** to an extreme degree ⟨everyone dancing *like crazy*⟩
**²crazy** *noun, plural* **cra·zies** (1867)
**:** one who is or acts crazy; *especially* **:** such a one associated with a radical or extremist political cause
**crazy bone** *noun* (1876)
**:** FUNNY BONE
**crazy quilt** *noun* (1886)
**1 :** a patchwork quilt without a design
**2 :** JUMBLE, HODGEPODGE ⟨a *crazy quilt* of regulations⟩
**cra·zy·weed** \'krā-zē-ˌwēd\ *noun* (circa 1889)
**:** LOCOWEED
**C–re·ac·tive protein** \'sē-rē-'ak-tiv-\ *noun* [*C-polysaccharide,* a polysaccharide found in the cell wall of pneumococci and precipitated by this protein, from *carbohydrate*] (1955)
**:** a protein present in blood serum in various abnormal states (as inflammation or neoplasia)
**¹creak** \'krēk\ *intransitive verb* [Middle English *creken* to croak, of imitative origin] (1583)
**:** to make a prolonged grating or squeaking sound often as a result of being worn-out; *also* **:** to proceed slowly with or as if with creaking wheels ⟨the story *creaks* along to a dull conclusion⟩
**²creak** *noun* (1605)
**:** a rasping or grating noise
**creaky** \'krē-kē\ *adjective* **creak·i·er; -est** (1834)
**1 :** marked by creaking **:** SQUEAKY ⟨*creaky* shoes⟩
**2 :** showing signs of deterioration or decrepitude ⟨a *creaky* old house⟩ ⟨a *creaky* economy⟩
— **creak·i·ly** \-kə-lē\ *adverb*
— **creak·i·ness** \-nəs\ *noun*
**¹cream** \'krēm\ *noun, often attributive* [Middle English *creime, creme,* from Middle French *craime, cresme,* from Late Latin *cramum,* of Celtic origin; akin to Welsh *cramen* scab, crust] (14th century)
**1 :** the yellowish part of milk containing from 18 to about 40 percent butterfat
**2 a :** a food prepared with cream **b :** something having the consistency of cream; *especially* **:** a usually emulsified medicinal or cosmetic preparation
**3 :** the choicest part **:** BEST ⟨the *cream* of the crop⟩
**4 :** CREAMER 1
**5 a :** a pale yellow **b :** a cream-colored animal
— **cream·i·ly** \'krē-mə-lē\ *adverb*
— **cream·i·ness** \-mē-nəs\ *noun*
— **creamy** \-mē\ *adjective*
**²cream** (1596)
*intransitive verb*
**1 :** to form cream or a surface layer like the cream on standing milk
**2 :** to break into or cause something to break into a creamy froth; *also* **:** to move like froth
*transitive verb*
**1 a :** SKIM 1c **b :** to remove (something choice) from an aggregate ⟨she has *creamed* off her favorite stories from her earlier books —*Times Literary Supplement*⟩
**2 :** to furnish, prepare, or treat with cream; *also* **:** to dress with a cream sauce
**3 a :** to beat into a creamy froth **b :** to work or blend to the consistency of cream ⟨*cream* butter and sugar together⟩ **c :** to cause to form a surface layer of or like cream

**4 a :** to defeat decisively ⟨was *creamed* in the first round⟩ **b :** WRECK ⟨*creamed* the car on the turnpike⟩
**cream cheese** *noun* (1583)
**:** a mild soft unripened cheese made from whole sweet milk enriched with cream
**cream·cups** \'krēm-ˌkəps\ *noun plural but singular or plural in construction* (1888)
**:** a California annual (*Platystemon californicus*) of the poppy family
**cream·er** \'krē-mər\ *noun* (1858)
**1 :** a small vessel for serving cream
**2 :** a nondairy product used as a substitute for cream (as in coffee)
**cream·ery** \'krēm-rē, 'krē-mə-\ *noun, plural* **-er·ies** (1872)
**:** an establishment where butter and cheese are made or where milk and cream are prepared or sold
**cream of tartar** (1662)
**:** a white crystalline salt $C_4H_5KO_6$ used especially in baking powder and in certain treatments of metals
**cream puff** *noun* (1880)
**1 :** a round shell of light pastry filled with whipped cream or a cream filling
**2 :** an ineffectual person
**3 :** something trifling, inconsiderable, or easily dealt with
**4 :** a usually used motor vehicle that is in especially good condition
**cream soda** *noun* (1854)
**:** a carbonated soft drink flavored with vanilla
**cream·ware** \'krēm-ˌwar, -ˌwer\ *noun* (1780)
**:** earthenware having a cream-colored glaze
**¹crease** \'krēs\ *noun* [probably alteration of earlier *creaste,* from Middle English *creste* crest] (1578)
**1 :** a line, mark, or ridge made by or as if by folding a pliable substance
**2 :** a specially marked area in various sports; *especially* **:** an area surrounding or in front of a goal (as in lacrosse or hockey)
— **crease·less** \-ləs\ *adjective*
**²crease** *verb* **creased; creas·ing** (1588)
*transitive verb*
**1 :** to make a crease in or on **:** WRINKLE ⟨a smile *creased* her face⟩
**2 :** to wound slightly especially by grazing
*intransitive verb*
**:** to become creased
— **creas·er** *noun*
**¹cre·ate** \krē-'āt, 'krē-\ *verb* **cre·at·ed; cre·at·ing** [Middle English, from Latin *creatus,* past participle of *creare;* akin to Latin *crescere* to grow — more at CRESCENT] (14th century)
*transitive verb*
**1 :** to bring into existence ⟨God *created* the heaven and the earth —Genesis 1:1 (Authorized Version)⟩
**2 a :** to invest with a new form, office, or rank ⟨was *created* a lieutenant⟩ **b :** to produce or bring about by a course of action or behavior ⟨her arrival *created* a terrible fuss⟩ ⟨*create* new jobs⟩
**3 :** CAUSE, OCCASION ⟨famine *creates* high food prices⟩
**4 a :** to produce through imaginative skill ⟨*create* a painting⟩ **b :** DESIGN ⟨*creates* dresses⟩
*intransitive verb*
**:** to make or bring into existence something new
**²create** *adjective* (15th century)
*archaic* **:** CREATED
**cre·a·tine** \'krē-ə-ˌtēn, -t°n\ *noun* [French *créatine,* from Greek *kreat-, kreas* flesh — more at RAW] (1840)
**:** a white crystalline nitrogenous substance $C_4H_9N_3O_2$ found especially in the muscles of vertebrates either free or as phosphocreatine
**creatine phosphate** *noun* (1945)
**:** PHOSPHOCREATINE
**cre·at·i·nine** \krē-'a-t°n-ˌēn, -ən\ *noun* [German *Kreatinin,* from *Kreatin* creatine] (1851)

**:** a white crystalline strongly basic compound $C_4H_7N_3O$ formed from creatine and found especially in muscle, blood, and urine
**cre·a·tion** \krē-'ā-shən\ *noun* (14th century)
**1 :** the act of creating; *especially* **:** the act of bringing the world into ordered existence
**2 :** the act of making, inventing, or producing: as **a :** the act of investing with a new rank or office **b :** the first representation of a dramatic role
**3 :** something that is created: as **a :** WORLD **b :** creatures singly or in aggregate **c :** an original work of art **d :** a new usually striking article of clothing
**cre·a·tion·ism** \-shə-ˌni-zəm\ *noun* (1880)
**:** a doctrine or theory holding that matter, the various forms of life, and the world were created by God out of nothing and usually in the way described in Genesis — compare EVOLUTION 4b
— **cre·a·tion·ist** \-shə-nist\ *noun or adjective*
**creation science** *noun* (1979)
**:** CREATIONISM; *also* **:** scientific evidence or arguments put forth in support of creationism
**cre·a·tive** \krē-'ā-tiv, 'krē-\ *adjective* (1678)
**1 :** marked by the ability or power to create **:** given to creating ⟨the *creative* impulse⟩
**2 :** having the quality of something created rather than imitated **:** IMAGINATIVE ⟨the *creative* arts⟩
**3 :** managed so as to get around legal or conventional limits ⟨*creative* financing⟩; *also* **:** deceptively arranged so as to conceal or defraud ⟨*creative* accounting⟩
— **cre·a·tive·ly** *adverb*
— **cre·a·tive·ness** *noun*
**creative evolution** *noun* (1909)
**:** evolution that is a creative product of a vital force rather than a spontaneous process explicable in terms of scientific laws — compare EMERGENT EVOLUTION
**cre·a·tiv·i·ty** \krē-(ˌ)ā-'ti-və-tē, ˌkrē-ə-\ *noun* (1875)
**1 :** the quality of being creative
**2 :** the ability to create
**cre·a·tor** \krē-'ā-tər\ *noun* (13th century)
**:** one that creates usually by bringing something new or original into being; *especially,* *capitalized* **:** GOD 1
**crea·ture** \'krē-chər\ *noun* [Middle English, from Old French, from Late Latin *creatura,* from Latin *creatus,* past participle of *creare*] (14th century)
**1 :** something created either animate or inanimate: as **a :** a lower animal; *especially* **:** a farm animal **b :** a human being **c :** a being of anomalous or uncertain aspect or nature ⟨*creatures* of fantasy⟩
**2 :** one that is the servile dependent or tool of another **:** INSTRUMENT
— **crea·tur·al** \'krē-chə-rəl\ *adjective*
— **crea·ture·hood** \'krē-chər-ˌhud\ *noun*
— **crea·ture·li·ness** \-lē-nəs\ *noun*
— **crea·ture·ly** \-lē\ *adjective*
**creature comfort** *noun* (1659)
**:** something (as food, warmth, or special accommodations) that gives bodily comfort
**crèche** \'kresh, 'krāsh\ *noun* [French, from Old French *creche* manger, crib, of Germanic origin; akin to Old High German *krippa* manger — more at CRIB] (1792)
**1 :** a representation of the Nativity scene
**2 :** DAY NURSERY
**3 :** a foundling hospital
**cre·dence** \'krē-d°n(t)s\ *noun* [Middle English, from Middle French or Medieval Latin;

\ə\ abut \ᵊ\ kitten \ər\ further \a\ ash \ā\ ace
\ä\ mop, mar \aú\ out \ch\ chin \e\ bet \ē\ easy
\g\ go \i\ hit \ī\ ice \j\ job \ŋ\ sing \ō\ go
\ò\ law \òi\ boy \th\ thin \t͟h\ the \ü\ loot \ú\ foot
\y\ yet \zh\ vision *see also* Guide to Pronunciation

Middle French, from Medieval Latin *credentia*, from Latin *credent-, credens,* present participle of *credere* to believe, trust — more at CREED] (14th century) **1 a :** mental acceptance as true or real ⟨give *credence* to gossip⟩ **b :** CREDIBILITY 1 ⟨lends *credence* to the theory⟩ **2 :** CREDENTIALS — used in the phrase *letters of credence* **3** [Middle French, from Old Italian *credenza*] **:** a Renaissance sideboard used chiefly for valuable plate **4 :** a small table where the bread and wine rest before consecration

**synonym** see BELIEF

**cre·dent** \'krē-d°nt\ *adjective* [Latin *credent-, credens,* present participle] (1602) **1 :** giving credence **:** CONFIDING **2** *obsolete* **:** CREDIBLE

**¹cre·den·tial** \kri-'den(t)-shəl\ *adjective* (15th century) **:** warranting credit or confidence — used chiefly in the phrase *credential letters*

**²credential** *noun* (circa 1674) **1 :** something that gives a title to credit or confidence **2** *plural* **:** testimonials showing that a person is entitled to credit or has a right to exercise official power **3 :** CERTIFICATE, DIPLOMA

**³credential** *transitive verb* **-tialed** *also* **-tialled; -tial·ing** *also* **-tial·ling** (1888) **:** to furnish with credentials ⟨to *credential* adequate academic performance —K. Patricia Cross⟩

**cre·den·tial·ism** \-chə,li-zəm\ *noun* (1967) **:** undue emphasis on credentials (as college degrees) as prerequisites to employment

**cre·den·za** \kri-'den-zə\ *noun* [Italian, literally, belief, confidence, from Medieval Latin *credentia*] (1880) **1 :** CREDENCE 3 **2 :** a sideboard, buffet, or bookcase patterned after a Renaissance credence; *especially* **:** one without legs ◆

**cred·i·bil·i·ty** \,kre-də-'bi-lə-tē\ *noun* (1594) **1 :** the quality or power of inspiring belief ⟨an account lacking in *credibility*⟩ **2 :** capacity for belief ⟨strains her reader's *credibility* —*Times Literary Supplement*⟩

**credibility gap** *noun* (1966) **1 a :** lack of trust ⟨a *credibility gap* between generations⟩ **b :** lack of believability ⟨a *credibility gap* created by contradictory official statements —Samuel Ellenport⟩ **2 :** DISCREPANCY ⟨the *credibility gap* between the professed ideals . . . and their actual practices —Jeanne L. Noble⟩

**cred·i·ble** \'kre-də-bəl\ *adjective* [Middle English, from Latin *credibilis,* from *credere*] (14th century) **1 :** offering reasonable grounds for being believed ⟨a *credible* account of an accident⟩ ⟨*credible* witnesses⟩ **2 :** of sufficient capability to be militarily effective ⟨a *credible* deterrent⟩ ⟨*credible* forces⟩ — **cred·i·bly** \'kre-də-blē\ *adverb*

**¹cred·it** \'kre-dit\ *noun* [Middle French, from Old Italian *credito,* from Latin *creditum* something entrusted, loan, from neuter of *creditus,* past participle of *credere* to believe, entrust — more at CREED] (1537) **1 :** reliance on the truth or reality of something ⟨gave *credit* to everything he said⟩ **2 a :** the balance in a person's favor in an account **b :** an amount or sum placed at a person's disposal by a bank **c :** time given for payment for goods or services sold on trust ⟨long-term *credit*⟩ **d** (1) **:** an entry on the right-hand side of an account constituting an addition to a revenue, net worth, or liability account (2) **:** a deduction from an expense or asset account **e :** any one of or the sum of the items entered on the right-hand side of an account **f :** a deduction from an amount otherwise due

**3 a :** influence or power derived from enjoying the confidence of another or others **b :** good name **:** ESTEEM; *also* **:** financial or commercial trustworthiness **4** *archaic* **:** CREDIBILITY **5 :** a source of honor ⟨a *credit* to the school⟩ **6 a :** something that gains or adds to reputation or esteem **:** HONOR ⟨took no *credit* for his kindly act⟩ **b :** RECOGNITION, ACKNOWLEDGMENT ⟨quite willing to accept undeserved *credit*⟩ **7 :** recognition by name of a person contributing to a performance (as a film or telecast) ⟨the opening *credits*⟩ **8 a :** recognition by a school or college that a student has fulfilled a requirement leading to a degree **b :** CREDIT HOUR

**synonym** see BELIEF, INFLUENCE

**²credit** *transitive verb* [partly from ¹*credit*; partly from Latin *creditus,* past participle] (1541) **1 :** to supply goods on credit **2 :** to trust in the truth of **:** BELIEVE **3** *archaic* **:** to bring credit or honor upon **4 a :** to enter upon the credit side of an account **b :** to place an amount to the credit of ⟨*credit* his account with ten dollars⟩ **5 a :** to consider usually favorably as the source, agent, or performer of an action or the possessor of a trait ⟨*credits* him with an excellent sense of humor⟩ **b :** to attribute to some person ⟨they *credit* the invention to him⟩

**synonym** see ASCRIBE

**cred·it·able** \'kre-di-tə-bəl\ *adjective* (1526) **1 :** worthy of belief **2 :** sufficiently good to bring esteem or praise **3 :** worthy of commercial credit **4 :** capable of being assigned — **cred·it·abil·i·ty** \,kre-di-tə-'bi-lə-tē\ *noun* — **cred·it·able·ness** \'kre-di-tə-bəl-nəs\ *noun* — **cred·it·ably** \-blē\ *adverb*

**credit card** *noun* (1888) **:** a card authorizing purchases on credit

**credit hour** *noun* (circa 1927) **:** the unit of measuring educational credit usually based on the number of classroom hours per week throughout a term

**credit line** *noun* (1914) **1 :** a line, note, or name that acknowledges the source of an item (as a news dispatch or television program) **2 :** LINE OF CREDIT

**cred·i·tor** \'kre-di-tər, -,tor\ *noun* (15th century) **:** one to whom a debt is owed; *especially* **:** a person to whom money or goods are due

**credit union** *noun* (1881) **:** a cooperative association that makes small loans to its members at low interest rates

**cred·it·wor·thy** \'kre-dit-,wər-thē\ *adjective* (1924) **:** financially sound enough to justify the extension of credit — **cred·it·wor·thi·ness** *noun*

**cre·do** \'krē-(,)dō, 'krā-\ *noun, plural* **credos** [Middle English, from Latin, I believe] (12th century) **:** CREED

**cre·du·li·ty** \kri-'dü-lə-tē, -'dyü-\ *noun* (15th century) **:** readiness or willingness to believe especially on slight or uncertain evidence

**cred·u·lous** \'kre-jə-ləs\ *adjective* [Latin *credulus,* from *credere*] (1576) **1 :** ready to believe especially on slight or uncertain evidence **2 :** proceeding from credulity — **cred·u·lous·ly** *adverb* — **cred·u·lous·ness** *noun*

**Cree** \'krē\ *noun, plural* **Cree** *or* **Crees** [Canadian French *Cris,* plural, short for *Cristinaux,* from Ojibwa dialect *kiristino·,* singular, member of a band living south of James Bay] (1744)

**1 :** a member of an American Indian people of Quebec, Ontario, Manitoba, and Saskatchewan **2 :** the Algonquian language of the Cree people

**creed** \'krēd\ *noun* [Middle English *crede,* from Old English *crēda,* from Latin *credo* (first word of the Apostles' and Nicene Creeds), from *credere* to believe, trust, entrust; akin to Old Irish *cretid* he believes, Sanskrit *śrad-dadhāti*] (before 12th century) **1 :** a brief authoritative formula of religious belief **2 :** a set of fundamental beliefs; *also* **:** a guiding principle — **creed·al** *or* **cre·dal** \'krē-d°l\ *adjective*

**creek** \'krēk, 'krik\ *noun* [Middle English *crike, creke,* from Old Norse *-kriki* bend] (13th century) **1** *chiefly British* **:** a small inlet or bay narrower and extending farther inland than a cove **2 :** a natural stream of water normally smaller than and often tributary to a river **3** *archaic* **:** a narrow or winding passage — **up the creek :** in a difficult or perplexing situation

**Creek** \'krēk\ *noun* (1725) **1 :** an American Indian confederacy of peoples chiefly of Muskogean stock of Alabama, Georgia, and Florida **2 :** a member of any of the Creek peoples **3 :** the Muskogean language of the Creek Indians

**¹creel** \'krē(ə)l\ *noun* [Middle English *creille, crele*] (14th century) **1 :** a wicker basket (as for carrying newly caught fish) **2 :** a bar with skewers for holding bobbins in a spinning machine

**²creel** *transitive verb* (1844) **:** to put (caught fish) in a creel

**¹creep** \'krēp\ *intransitive verb* **crept** \'krept\; **creep·ing** [Middle English *crepen,* from Old English *crēopan;* akin to Old Norse *krjūpa* to creep] (before 12th century) **1 a :** to move along with the body prone and close to the ground **b :** to move slowly on hands and knees **2 a :** to go very slowly ⟨the hours *crept* by⟩ **b :** to go timidly or cautiously so as to escape notice ⟨she *crept* away from the festive scene⟩ **c :** to enter or advance gradually so as to be almost unnoticed ⟨age *creeps* up on us⟩ ⟨a note of irritation *crept* into her voice⟩ **3 :** to have the sensation of being covered with creeping things ⟨the thought made his flesh *creep*⟩ **4** *of a plant* **:** to spread or grow over a surface rooting at intervals or clinging with tendrils, stems, or aerial roots **5 a :** to slip or gradually shift position **b :** to change shape permanently from prolonged stress or exposure to high temperatures

**²creep** *noun* (1818)

---

◇ **WORD HISTORY**

**credenza** In Italian *credenza* literally means "belief" or "confidence," the latter being just what a member of a royal or noble household needed to have in his food and drink during the Middle Ages and Renaissance. Being poisoned by one's enemies, employees, or even one's own family was an ever-present danger during those times. As a result, it became customary for royalty and noblemen to have a servant taste their food and drink after it had left the kitchen and just before it was served. The tasting was accomplished at a dining room sideboard reserved for the purpose. If the servant survived the tasting, the master had every reason to believe that he would also. The name for the sideboard became *credenza* in Italian. Sideboards and buffets of Italian Renaissance style are still called credenzas.

**1 :** a movement of or like creeping ⟨traffic moving at a *creep*⟩
**2 :** a distressing sensation like that caused by the creeping of insects over one's flesh; *especially* **:** a feeling of apprehension or horror — usually used in plural with *the* ⟨that gives me the *creeps*⟩
**3 :** a feed trough or enclosure that young animals can enter while adults are excluded
**4 :** the slow change of dimensions of an object from prolonged exposure to high temperature or stress
**5 :** an unpleasant or obnoxious person
**creep·age** \'krē-pij\ *noun* (1903)
**:** gradual movement **:** CREEP
**creep·er** \'krē-pər\ *noun* (before 12th century)
**1 :** one that creeps: as **a :** a creeping plant **b :** a bird (as of the family Certhiidae) that creeps about on trees or bushes searching for insects **c :** a creeping insect or reptile
**2 :** any of various devices used for creeping: as **a :** a fixture with iron points worn on the shoe to prevent slipping **b :** a low wheeled platform for supporting the body when working under an automobile
**3 :** a usually one-piece garment for a child at the crawling age
**creep·ing** \'krē-piŋ\ *adjective* (14th century)
**:** developing or advancing by slow imperceptible degrees ⟨a period of *creeping* inflation⟩
**creeping eruption** *noun* (1926)
**:** a skin disorder marked by a spreading red line of eruption and caused especially by larvae (as of hookworms not normally parasitic in humans) burrowing beneath the human skin
**creepy** \'krē-pē\ *adjective* **creep·i·er; -est** (1883)
**1 :** producing a nervous shivery apprehension ⟨*creepy* things were crawling over us⟩ ⟨a *creepy* horror story⟩
**2 :** of, relating to, or being a creep **:** annoyingly unpleasant
— **creep·i·ly** \-pə-lē\ *adverb*
— **creep·i·ness** \-pē-nəs\ *noun*
**creese** *variant of* KRIS
**cre·mains** \kri-'mānz\ *noun plural* [blend of *cremated* and *remains*] (1947)
**:** the ashes of a cremated human body
**cre·mate** \'krē-,māt, kri-'\ *transitive verb* **cre·mat·ed; cre·mat·ing** [Latin *crematus*, past participle of *cremare* to burn up, cremate] (1874)
**:** to reduce (as a dead body) to ashes by burning
— **cre·ma·tion** \kri-'mā-shən\ *noun*
**cre·ma·to·ri·um** \,krē-mə-'tōr-ē-əm, ,kre-, -'tȯr-\ *noun, plural* **-ri·ums** *or* **-ria** \-ē-ə\ (1880)
**:** CREMATORY
**cre·ma·to·ry** \'krē-mə-,tōr-ē, 'kre-, -,tȯr-\ *noun, plural* **-ries** (1876)
**:** a furnace for cremating; *also* **:** an establishment containing such a furnace
— **crematory** *adjective*
**crème** *or* **creme** \'krem *also* 'krēm *or* 'krām\ *noun, plural* **crèmes** *or* **cremes** \'krem(z), 'krēmz\ [French, from Old French *cresme* — more at CREAM] (circa 1821)
**1 :** a sweet liqueur
**2 :** cream or a preparation made with or resembling cream used in cooking
**3 :** CREAM 2b
**crème an·glaise** \,äⁿ-'glāz, -aⁿ-, -äⁿ-'glez\ *noun* [French, literally, English cream] (1975)
**:** a vanilla-flavored custard sauce usually served with desserts
**crème brû·lée** \-brᴜᴇ-'lā, -brü-\ *noun* [French, literally, scorched cream] (1886)
**:** a rich custard topped with caramelized sugar
**crème car·a·mel** \-kár-à-'mel, *or see* CARA-MEL\ *noun* [French, literally, caramel cream] (1906)
**:** a custard that has been baked with caramel sauce

**crème de ca·cao** \'krem-də-'kō-(,)kō; ,krem-də-kə-'kaᴜ, -kə-'kā-(,)ō\ *noun* [French, literally, cream of cacao] (1904)
**:** a sweet brown or colorless liqueur flavored with cacao beans and vanilla
**crème de la crème** \'krem-də-lä-'krem, -lə-\ *noun* [French, literally, cream of the cream] (1848)
**:** the very best
**crème de menthe** \'krem-də-'men(t)th, 'krēm-, -'mint, 'krem-də-'mänt\ *noun* [French, literally, cream of mint] (1901)
**:** a sweet green or colorless mint-flavored liqueur
**crème fraîche** *or* **crème fraiche** \'krem-'fresh *also* 'krēm- *or* 'krām-\ *noun* [French, literally, fresh cream] (1950)
**:** heavy cream thickened and slightly soured with buttermilk and often served on fruit
**cre·nate** \'krē-,nāt\ *or* **cre·nat·ed** \-,nā-təd\ *adjective* [New Latin *crenatus*, from Medieval Latin *crena* notch] (1794)
**:** having the margin or surface cut into rounded scallops ⟨a *crenate* leaf⟩
**cre·na·tion** \kri-'nā-shən\ *noun* (1846)
**1 a :** a crenate formation; *especially* **:** one of the rounded projections on an edge (as of a coin) **b :** the quality or state of being crenate
**2 :** shrinkage of red blood cells resulting in crenate margins
**cren·el·lat·ed** *or* **cren·el·at·ed** \'kre-nᵊl-,ā-təd\ *adjective* [French *créneler* to furnish with embrasures, from Old French *querneler*, from *kernel, crenel* embrasure, diminutive of *cren* notch, from *crener* to notch; akin to Medieval Latin *crena*] (circa 1823)
**:** having crenellations
**cren·el·la·tion** *also* **cren·el·a·tion** \,kre-nᵊl-'ā-shən\ *noun* (1849)
**1 :** BATTLEMENT
**2 :** any of the embrasures alternating with merlons in a battlement — see BATTLEMENT illustration
**cren·u·lat·ed** \'kren-yə-,lā-təd\ *or* **cren·u·late** \-lət, -,lāt\ *adjective* [New Latin *crenulatus*, from *crenula*, diminutive of Medieval Latin *crena*] (1794)
**:** having an irregularly wavy or serrate outline ⟨a *crenulated* shoreline⟩
— **cren·u·la·tion** \,kren-yə-'lā-shən\ *noun*
**cre·ole** \'krē-,ōl\ *adjective* (1748)
**1** *often capitalized* **:** of or relating to Creoles or their language
**2** *often capitalized* **:** relating to or being highly seasoned food typically prepared with rice, okra, tomatoes, and peppers ⟨shrimp *creole*⟩
**Cre·ole** \'krē-,ōl\ *noun* [French *créole*, from Spanish *criollo*, from Portuguese *crioulo* white person born in the colonies] (1737)
**1 :** a person of European descent born especially in the West Indies or Spanish America
**2 :** a white person descended from early French or Spanish settlers of the U.S. Gulf states and preserving their speech and culture
**3 :** a person of mixed French or Spanish and black descent speaking a dialect of French or Spanish
**4 a :** a language evolved from pidginized French that is spoken by blacks in southern Louisiana **b :** HAITIAN **c** *not capitalized* **:** a language that has evolved from a pidgin but serves as the native language of a speech community
**cre·ol·ise** *British variant of* CREOLIZE
**cre·ol·ize** \'krē-ə-,līz, 'krē-,ō-\ *transitive verb* **-ized; -iz·ing** (circa 1932)
**:** to cause (a pidginized language) to become a creole in a speech community
— **cre·ol·i·za·tion** \,krē-ə-lə-'zā-shən, ,krē-(,)ō-\ *noun*
**cre·o·sote** \'krē-ə-,sōt\ *noun* [German *Kreosot*, from Greek *kreas* flesh + *sōtēr* preserver, from *sōzein* to preserve, from *sōs* safe (probably akin to Sanskrit *tavīti* he is strong); from its antiseptic properties — more at RAW] (1835)

**1 :** a clear or yellowish flammable oily liquid mixture of phenolic compounds obtained by the distillation of wood tar especially from beech wood
**2 :** a brownish oily liquid consisting chiefly of aromatic hydrocarbons obtained by distillation of coal tar and used especially as a wood preservative
**3 :** a dark brown or black flammable tar deposited from especially wood smoke on the walls of a chimney
**²creosote** *transitive verb* **-sot·ed; -sot·ing** (1846)
**:** to treat with creosote
**creosote bush** *noun* (1846)
**:** a resinous desert shrub (*Larrea tridentata*) of the caltrop family found in the southwestern U.S. and Mexico
**crepe** *or* **crêpe** \'krāp\ *noun* [French *crêpe* — more at CRAPE] (1797)
**1 :** a light crinkled fabric woven of any of various fibers
**2 :** CRAPE 2
**3 :** crude rubber in the form of nearly white to brown crinkled sheets used especially for shoe soles ⟨*crepe*-soled shoes⟩
**4 :** a small very thin pancake
— **crepe** *adjective*
— **crep·ey** *or* **crepy** \'krā-pē\ *adjective*
**crepe de chine** *or* **crêpe de chine** \,krāp-də-'shēn\ *noun, often 2d C capitalized* [French *crêpe de Chine*, literally, China crepe] (1872)
**:** a soft fine or sheer clothing crepe especially of silk
**crepe myrtle** *or* **crêpe myrtle** *noun* (1916)
**:** CRAPE MYRTLE
**crepe paper** *noun* (1897)
**:** paper with a crinkled or puckered texture
**crêpe su·zette** \,krāp-sᴜ-'zet\ *noun, plural* **crêpes suzette** \,krāp(s)-sᴜ-'zet\ *or* **crêpe suzettes** \,krāp-sᴜ-'zets\ *often S capitalized* [French *crêpe Suzette*, probably from *Suzette*, nickname of Suzanne Reichenberg (died 1924) French actress] (1922)
**:** a thin folded or rolled pancake in a hot orange-butter sauce that is sprinkled with a liqueur (as cognac or curaçao) and set ablaze for serving
**crep·i·tant** \'kre-pə-tənt\ *adjective* (1855)
**:** having or making a crackling sound ⟨*crepitant* sounds in breathing⟩
**crep·i·tate** \'kre-pə-,tāt\ *intransitive verb* **-tat·ed; -tat·ing** [Latin *crepitatus*, past participle of *crepitare* to crackle, frequentative of *crepare* to rattle, crack] (circa 1828)
**:** to make a crackling sound **:** CRACKLE
— **crep·i·ta·tion** \,kre-pə-'tā-shən\ *noun*
**cre·pon** \'krā-,pän\ *noun* [French, from *crêpe*] (circa 1864)
**:** a heavy crepe fabric with lengthwise crinkles
**crept** *past and past participle of* CREEP
**cre·pus·cu·lar** \kri-'pəs-kyə-lər\ *adjective* (1668)
**1 :** of, relating to, or resembling twilight **:** DIM
**2 :** active in the twilight ⟨*crepuscular* insects⟩
**cre·pus·cule** \kri-'pəs-(,)kyü(ə)l\ *or* **cre·pus·cle** \-'pə-səl\ *noun* [Latin *crepusculum*, from *creper* dusky] (14th century)
**:** TWILIGHT
**¹cre·scen·do** \krə-'shen-(,)dō\ *noun, plural* **-dos** *or* **-does** *also* **-di** \-dē\ [Italian, from *crescendo*, adjective, increasing, gerund of *crescere* to grow, increase, from Latin] (1776)
**1 a :** a gradual increase; *specifically* **:** a gradual increase in volume of a musical passage **b :** the peak of a gradual increase **:** CLIMAX ⟨complaints about stifling smog conditions reach a *crescendo* —*Down Beat*⟩

---

\ə\ abut \ᵊ\ kitten \ər\ further \a\ ash \ā\ ace
\ä\ mop, mar \aᴜ\ out \ch\ chin \e\ bet \ē\ easy
\g\ go \i\ hit \ī\ ice \j\ job \ŋ\ sing \ō\ go
\ȯ\ law \ȯi\ boy \th\ thin \ṯẖ\ the \ü\ loot \ᴜ\ foot
\y\ yet \zh\ vision     *see also* Guide to Pronunciation

**2** : a crescendo musical passage ◻
— **crescendo** *intransitive verb*

**mark indicating crescendo 2**

²**crescendo** *adverb or adjective* (1859)
: with an increase in volume — used as a direction in music

¹**cres·cent** \'kre-s°nt\ *noun* [Middle English *cressant,* from Middle French *creissant,* from present participle of *creistre* to grow, increase, from Latin *crescere;* akin to Old High German *hirsi* millet, Lithuanian *šerti* to feed, Greek *koros* boy] (15th century)
**1 a** : the moon at any stage between new moon and first quarter and between last quarter and the succeeding new moon when less than half of the illuminated hemisphere is visible **b** : the figure of the moon at such a stage defined by a convex and a concave edge
**2** : something shaped like a crescent
— **cres·cen·tic** \kre-'sen-tik, krə-\ *adjective*

²**crescent** *adjective* [Latin *crescent-, crescens,* present participle of *crescere*] (1574)
: marked by an increase

**Cres·cent** \'kre-s°nt\ *trademark*
— used for an adjustable open-end wrench

**cres·cive** \'kre-siv\ *adjective* [Latin *crescere* to grow] (1566)
: marked by gradual spontaneous development
— **cres·cive·ly** *adverb*

**cre·sol** \'krē-,sȯl, -,sōl\ *noun* [International Scientific Vocabulary, irregular from *creosote*] (circa 1869)
: any of three poisonous colorless crystalline or liquid isomeric phenols $C_7H_8O$

**cress** \'kres\ *noun* [Middle English *cresse,* from Old English *cærse, cressa;* akin to Old High German *kressa* cress] (before 12th century)
: any of numerous crucifers (especially genera *Lepidium* and *Nasturtium*) with moderately pungent leaves used especially in salads

**cres·set** \'kre-sət\ *noun* [Middle English, from Middle French, from Old French *craisset,* from *craisse* grease — more at GREASE] (14th century)
: an iron vessel or basket used for holding an illuminant (as oil) and mounted as a torch or suspended as a lantern

**Cres·si·da** \'kre-sə-də\ *noun*
: a Trojan woman of medieval legend who pledges herself to Troilus but while a captive of the Greeks gives herself to Diomedes

¹**crest** \'krest\ *noun* [Middle English *creste,* from Middle French, from Latin *crista;* probably akin to Latin *crinis* hair] (14th century)
**1 a** : a showy tuft or process on the head of an animal and especially a bird — see BIRD illustration **b** : the plume or identifying emblem worn on a knight's helmet; *also* : the top of a helmet **c** (1) : a heraldic representation of the crest (2) : a heraldic device depicted above the escutcheon but not upon a helmet (3) : COAT OF ARMS 2a **d** : a ridge or prominence on a part of an animal body
**2** : something suggesting a crest especially in being an upper prominence, edge, or limit: as **a** : PEAK; *especially* : the top line of a mountain or hill **b** : the ridge of a roof **c** : the top of a wave
**3 a** : a high point of an action or process and especially of one that is rhythmic **b** : CLIMAX, CULMINATION ⟨at the *crest* of his fame⟩
— **crest·al** \'kres-t°l\ *adjective*
— **crest·less** \-ləs\ *adjective*

²**crest** (15th century)
*transitive verb*
**1** : to furnish with a crest; *also* : CROWN
**2** : to reach the crest of ⟨*crested* the hill and looked around⟩
*intransitive verb*
: to rise to a crest ⟨waves *cresting* in the storm⟩

**crest·ed** \'kres-təd\ *adjective* (14th century)
: having a crest ⟨a *crested* bird⟩

**crested wheatgrass** *noun* (1923)
: either of two Eurasian grasses (*Agropyron cristatum* or *A. sibericum* synonym *A. desertorum*) that are grown in the U.S. for forage and for erosion control

**crest·fall·en** \'krest-,fȯ-lən\ *adjective* (1589)
**1** : having a drooping crest or hanging head
**2** : feeling shame or humiliation : DEJECTED
— **crest·fall·en·ly** *adverb*
— **crest·fall·en·ness** \-lən-nəs\ *noun*

**crest·ing** \'kres-tiŋ\ *noun* (1908)
: a decorative edging or railing (as on pottery or furniture)

**cre·syl** \'kre-səl, 'krē-,sil\ *noun* [International Scientific Vocabulary *cresol* + *-yl*] (circa 1872)
: TOLYL

**Cre·ta·ceous** \kri-'tā-shəs\ *adjective* [Latin *cretaceus* resembling chalk, from *creta* chalk] (1832)
: of, relating to, or being the last period of the Mesozoic era characterized by continued dominance of reptiles, emergent dominance of angiosperms, diversification of mammals, and the extinction of many types of organisms at the close of the period; *also* : of, relating to, or being the corresponding system of rocks — see GEOLOGIC TIME table
— **Cretaceous** *noun*

**cre·tin** \'krē-t°n\ *noun* [French *crétin,* from French dialect *cretin,* literally, wretch, innocent victim, from Latin *christianus* Christian] (1779)
**1** : one afflicted with cretinism
**2** : a stupid, vulgar, or insensitive person : CLOD, LOUT ◆
— **cre·tin·ous** \-t°n-əs\ *adjective*

**cre·tin·ism** \-t°n-,i-zəm\ *noun* (1801)
: a usually congenital abnormal condition marked by physical stunting and mental retardation and caused by severe hypothyroidism

**cre·tonne** \'krē-,tän, kri-\ *noun* [French, from *Creton,* Normandy] (1870)
: a strong cotton or linen cloth used especially for curtains and upholstery

**Creutz·feldt–Ja·kob disease** *also* **Creutz·feld–Ja·cob disease** \'krȯits-,felt-'yä-(,)kōb-\ *noun* [Hans G. *Creutzfeldt* (died 1964) German psychiatrist and Alfons M. *Jakob* (died 1931) German psychiatrist] (1963)
: a rare progressive fatal encephalopathy caused by a slow virus and marked by development of porous brain tissue, premature dementia in middle age, and gradual loss of muscular coordination

**cre·val·le** \kri-'va-lē\ *noun* [by alteration] (1879)
: CAVALLA 1; *especially* : JACK CREVALLE

**cre·vasse** \kri-'vas\ *noun* [French, from Old French *crevace*] (1813)
**1** : a breach in a levee
**2** : a deep crevice or fissure (as in a glacier or the earth)

**crev·ice** \'kre-vəs\ *noun* [Middle English, from Middle French *crevace,* from Old French, from *crever* to break, from Latin *crepare* to crack] (14th century)
: a narrow opening resulting from a split or crack (as in a cliff) : FISSURE

¹**crew** \'krü\ *chiefly British past of* CROW

²**crew** \'krü\ *noun* [Middle English *crue,* literally, reinforcement, from Middle French *creue* increase, from *creistre* to grow — more at CRESCENT] (15th century)
**1** *archaic* : a band or force of armed men
**2** : a group of people associated together in a common activity or by common traits or interests
**3 a** : a company of people working on one job or under one foreman or operating a machine **b** : the whole company belonging to a ship sometimes including the officers and master; *also* : one who assists the skipper of a sailboat

**c** : the persons who have duties on an aircraft in flight **d** : the rowers and coxswain of a racing shell; *also* : ROWING
— **crew·less** \-ləs\ *adjective*

³**crew** (1935)
*intransitive verb*
: to act as a member of a crew
*transitive verb*
: to serve as a crew member on (as a ship or aircraft)

**crew cut** *noun* (1942)
: a very short haircut usually for men or boys in which the hair resembles the bristle surface of a brush

**crew·el** \'krü-əl\ *noun* [Middle English *crule*] (15th century)
**1** : slackly twisted worsted yarn used for embroidery
**2** : CREWELWORK

**crew·el·work** \-,wərk\ *noun* (1863)
: embroidery work with crewel

**crew·man** \'krü-mən\ *noun* (circa 1927)
: a member of a crew

**crew·mate** \-,māt\ *noun* (1938)
: a fellow crewman

**crew neck** *noun* [from the sweaters with this neckline worn by oarsmen] (1940)
**1** : a round collarless neckline
**2** *usually* **crew·neck** \'krü-,nek\ : a sweater with a crew neck

**crew sock** *noun* (1948)
: a short bulky usually ribbed sock

¹**crib** \'krib\ *noun* [Middle English, from Old English *cribb;* akin to Old High German *krippa* manger, and perhaps to Greek *griphos* reed basket] (before 12th century)
**1** : a manger for feeding animals
**2** : an enclosure especially of framework: as **a** : a stall for a stabled animal **b** : a small child's bedstead with high enclosing usually slatted sides **c** : any of various devices resembling a crate or framework in structure **d** : a building for storage : BIN

**3 a :** a small narrow room or dwelling **:** HUT, SHACK **b :** a room or shack used for prostitution
**4 :** the cards discarded in cribbage for the dealer to use in scoring
**5 a :** a small theft **b :** PLAGIARISM **c :** a literal translation; *especially* **:** PONY 3 **d :** a summary and key to understanding a literary work **e :** something used for cheating in an examination
**6 :** CRÈCHE 1
**²crib** *verb* **cribbed; crib·bing** (1605)
*transitive verb*
**1 :** CONFINE, CRAMP
**2 :** to provide with or put into a crib; *especially* **:** to line or support with a framework of timber
**3 :** PILFER, STEAL; *especially* **:** PLAGIARIZE
*intransitive verb*
**1 a :** STEAL, PLAGIARIZE **b :** to use a crib **:** CHEAT
**2 :** to have the vice of cribbing
— **crib·ber** *noun*
**crib·bage** \'kri-bij\ *noun* [¹*crib*] (1630)
**:** a card game for two players in which each player tries to form various counting combinations of cards
**crib·bing** \'kri-biŋ\ *noun* (1841)
**1 :** material for use in making a crib
**2 :** a vice of horses in which they gnaw (as at the manger) while slobbering and salivating
**crib biting** *noun* (1831)
**:** CRIBBING 2
**crib death** *noun* (1965)
**:** SUDDEN INFANT DEATH SYNDROME
**crib·ri·form** \'kri-brə-ˌfórm\ *adjective* [Latin *cribrum* sieve; akin to Latin *cernere* to sift — more at CERTAIN] (1741)
**:** pierced with small holes
**cri·ce·tid** \krī-'sē-təd, -'se-\ *noun* [ultimately from New Latin *Cricetus,* genus name, of Slavic origin; akin to Czech *křeček* hamster] (1960)
**:** any of a family (Cricetidae) of small rodents including the hamsters
— **cricetid** *adjective*
**¹crick** \'krik\ *noun* [Middle English *cryk*] (15th century)
**:** a painful spasmodic condition of muscles (as of the neck or back)
**²crick** *transitive verb* (1884)
**1 :** to cause a crick in (as the neck)
**2 :** to turn or twist (as the head) especially into a strained position
**¹crick·et** \'kri-kət\ *noun* [Middle English *criket,* from Middle French *criquet,* of imitative origin] (14th century)
**1 :** any of a family (Gryllidae) of leaping orthopteran insects noted for the

cricket 1

chirping notes produced by the male by rubbing together specially modified parts of the forewings
**2 :** a low wooden footstool
**3 :** a small metal toy or signaling device that makes a sharp click or snap when pressed
**²cricket** *noun* [Middle French *criquet* goal stake in a bowling game] (1598)
**1 :** a game played with a ball and bat by two sides of usually 11 players each on a large field centering upon two wickets each defended by a batsman
**2 :** fair and honorable behavior ⟨it wasn't *cricket* for her to break her contract —Gerry Nadel⟩
**³cricket** *intransitive verb* (circa 1809)
**:** to play the game of cricket
— **crick·et·er** *noun*
**cri·coid** \'krī-ˌkòid\ *adjective* [New Latin *cricoides,* from Greek *krikoeidēs* ring-shaped, from *krikos* ring — more at CIRCLE] (1746)

**:** of, relating to, or being a cartilage of the larynx with which arytenoid cartilages articulate
**cri de coeur** \krē-də-'kər\ *noun, plural* **cris de coeur** \*same*\ [French, literally, cry from the heart] (1904)
**:** a passionate outcry (as of appeal or protest)
**cri·er** \'krī-(-ə)r\ *noun* (14th century)
**:** one that cries: **a :** an officer who proclaims the orders of a court **b :** TOWN CRIER
**cri·key** \'krī-kē\ *or* **crick·ey** \'kri-kē\ *interjection* [euphemism for *Christ*] (1838)
— used as a mild oath
**crime** \'krīm\ *noun* [Middle English, from Middle French, from Latin *crimen* accusation, reproach, crime; probably akin to Latin *cernere* to sift, determine] (14th century)
**1 :** an act or the commission of an act that is forbidden or the omission of a duty that is commanded by a public law and that makes the offender liable to punishment by that law; *especially* **:** a gross violation of law
**2 :** a grave offense especially against morality
**3 :** criminal activity ⟨efforts to fight *crime*⟩
**4 :** something reprehensible, foolish, or disgraceful ⟨it's a *crime* to waste good food⟩
**synonym** see OFFENSE
— **crime·less** \-ləs\ *adjective*
**crime against humanity** (1945)
**:** atrocity (as extermination or enslavement) that is directed especially against an entire population or part of a population on specious grounds and without regard to individual guilt or responsibility even on such grounds
**crime against nature** (1828)
**:** SODOMY
**¹crim·i·nal** \'kri-mə-nᵊl, 'krim-nəl\ *adjective* [Middle English, from Middle French or Late Latin; Middle French *criminel,* from Late Latin *criminalis,* from Latin *crimin- crimen* crime] (15th century)
**1 :** relating to, involving, or being a crime ⟨*criminal* neglect⟩
**2 :** relating to crime or to the prosecution of suspects in a crime ⟨*criminal* statistics⟩ ⟨brought *criminal* action⟩
**3 :** guilty of crime; *also* **:** of or befitting a criminal ⟨a *criminal* mind⟩
**4 :** DISGRACEFUL
— **crim·i·nal·ly** *adverb*
**²criminal** *noun* (circa 1626)
**1 :** one who has committed a crime
**2 :** a person who has been convicted of a crime
**criminal conversation** *noun* (1768)
**:** adultery considered as a tort
**criminal court** *noun* (1678)
**:** a court that has jurisdiction to try and punish offenders against criminal law
**crim·i·nal·is·tics** \ˌkri-mə-nᵊl-'is-tiks, ˌkrim-nə-'lis-\ *noun plural but singular in construction* (1943)
**:** application of scientific techniques in collecting and analyzing physical evidence in criminal cases
**crim·i·nal·i·ty** \ˌkri-mə-'na-lə-tē\ *noun* (1611)
**1 :** the quality or state of being criminal
**2 :** criminal activity ⟨urban *criminality*⟩
**crim·i·nal·ize** \'kri-mə-nᵊl-ˌīz, 'krim-nə-ˌlīz\ *transitive verb* **-ized; -iz·ing** (circa 1956)
**:** to make illegal **:** OUTLAW; *also* **:** to turn into or treat as a criminal
— **crim·i·nal·i·za·tion** \ˌkri-mə-nᵊl-ə-'zā-shən, ˌkrim-nə-lə-'zā-\ *noun*
**criminal law** *noun* (1864)
**:** the law of crimes and their punishments
**criminal lawyer** *noun* (1869)
**:** a lawyer who specializes in criminal law; *especially* **:** a lawyer who represents defendants in criminal cases
**crim·i·nate** \'kri-mə-ˌnāt\ *transitive verb* **-nat·ed; -nat·ing** [Latin *criminatus,* past participle of *criminari,* from *crimin-, crimen* accusation] (1645)
**:** INCRIMINATE
— **crim·i·na·tion** \ˌkri-mə-'nā-shən\ *noun*

**crim·i·nol·o·gy** \ˌkri-mə-'nä-lə-jē\ *noun* [Italian *criminologia,* from Latin *crimin-, crimen* + Italian *-o- + -logia* -logy] (1890)
**:** the scientific study of crime as a social phenomenon, of criminals, and of penal treatment
— **crim·i·no·log·i·cal** \-mə-nᵊl-'ä-ji-kəl\ *adjective*
— **crim·i·no·log·i·cal·ly** \-k(ə-)lē\ *adverb*
— **crim·i·nol·o·gist** \ˌkri-mə-'nä-lə-jist\ *noun*
**crim·i·nous** \'kri-mə-nəs\ *adjective* (15th century)
**:** CRIMINAL
**¹crimp** \'krimp\ *transitive verb* [Dutch or Low German *krimpen* to shrivel; akin to Middle Dutch *crampe* hook, cramp] (1712)
**1 :** to cause to become wavy, bent, or pinched: as **a :** to form (leather) into a desired shape **b :** to give (synthetic fibers) a curl or wave like that of natural fibers **c :** to pinch or press together (as the margins of a pie crust) in order to seal
**2 :** to be an inhibiting or restraining influence on **:** CRAMP ⟨sales had been *crimped* by credit controls —*Time*⟩
— **crimp·er** \'krim-pər\ *noun*
**²crimp** *noun* (1863)
**1 :** something produced by or as if by crimping: as **a :** a section of hair artificially waved or curled **b :** a succession of waves (as in wool fiber) **c :** a bend or crease formed in something
**2 :** something that cramps or inhibits **:** RESTRAINT, CURB
**³crimp** *noun* [perhaps from ¹*crimp*] (1758)
**:** a person who entraps or forces men into shipping or into enlisting in an army or navy
**⁴crimp** *transitive verb* (1812)
**:** to trap into military or sea service **:** IMPRESS
**crimpy** \'krim-pē\ *adjective* **crimp·i·er; -est** (1888)
**:** FRIZZY
**¹crim·son** \'krim-zən\ *noun* [Middle English *crimsin,* from Old Spanish *cremesín,* from Arabic *qirmizī,* from *qirmiz* kermes] (15th century)
**:** any of several deep purplish reds
**²crimson** *adjective* (15th century)
**:** of the color crimson
**³crimson** (1601)
*transitive verb*
**:** to make crimson
*intransitive verb*
**:** to become crimson; *especially* **:** BLUSH
**¹cringe** \'krinj\ *intransitive verb* **cringed; cring·ing** [Middle English *crengen;* akin to Old English *cringan* to yield, Middle High German *krank* weak] (13th century)
**1 :** to draw in or contract one's muscles involuntarily (as from cold or pain)
**2 :** to shrink in fear or servility
**3 :** to behave in an excessively humble or servile way
**synonym** see FAWN
— **cring·er** *noun*
**²cringe** *noun* (1597)
**:** a cringing act; *specifically* **:** a servile bow
**crin·gle** \'kriŋ-gəl\ *noun* [Low German *kringel,* diminutive of *kring* ring] (1627)
**:** a loop or grommet at the corner of a sail to which a line is attached
**¹crin·kle** \'kriŋ-kəl\ *verb* **crin·kled; crin·kling** \-k(ə-)liŋ\ [Middle English *crynkelen;* akin to Old English *cringan* to yield] (14th century)
*intransitive verb*
**1 a :** to form many short bends or ripples **b :** WRINKLE

**2 :** to give forth a thin crackling sound **:** RUSTLE ⟨*crinkling* silks⟩
*transitive verb*
**:** to cause to crinkle **:** make crinkles in
**²crinkle** *noun* (1596)
**1 :** WRINKLE, CORRUGATION, PUCKER
**2 :** any of several plant diseases marked by crinkling of leaves
— **crin·kly** \-k(ə-)lē\ *adjective*
**cri·noid** \'krī-,nȯid\ *noun* [ultimately from Greek *krinon* lily] (1847)
**:** any of a large class (Crinoidea) of echinoderms usually having a somewhat cup-shaped body with five or more feathery arms
— **crinoid** *adjective*
**crin·o·line** \'kri-n°l-ən\ *noun* [French, from Italian *crinolino*, from *crino* horsehair (from Latin *crinis* hair) + *lino* flax, linen, from Latin *linum* — more at CREST] (1830)
**1 :** an open-weave fabric of horsehair or cotton that is usually stiffened and used especially for interlinings and millinery
**2 :** a full stiff skirt or underskirt made of crinoline; *also* **:** HOOPSKIRT
— **crinoline** *or* **crin·o·lined** \-ənd\ *adjective*
**cri·o·llo** \krē-'ōl-(,)yō, -'ō-(,)yō\ *noun, plural* **-llos** [Spanish — more at CREOLE] (1604)
**1 a :** a person of pure Spanish descent born in Spanish America **b :** a person born and usually raised in a Spanish-American country
**2 :** a domestic animal of a breed or strain developed in Latin America; *especially, often capitalized* **:** a hardy muscular pony of a breed originally developed in Argentina
— **criollo** *adjective*
**cripes** \'krīps\ *interjection* [euphemism for *Christ*] (1910)
**—** used as a mild oath
**¹crip·ple** \'kri-pəl\ *noun* [Middle English *cripel*, from Old English *crypel*; akin to Old English *crēopan* to creep — more at CREEP] (before 12th century)
**1 a :** a lame or partly disabled person or animal — sometimes taken to be offensive **b :** one that is disabled or deficient in a specified manner ⟨a social *cripple*⟩
**2 :** something flawed or imperfect
**²cripple** *adjective* (13th century)
**:** being a cripple **:** LAME
**³cripple** *transitive verb* **crip·pled; crip·pling** \-p(ə-)liŋ\ (14th century)
**1 :** to deprive of the use of a limb and especially a leg
**2 :** to deprive of capability for service or of strength, efficiency, or wholeness
*synonym* see MAIM, WEAKEN
— **crip·pler** \-p(ə-)lər\ *noun*
— **crip·pling·ly** \-p(ə-)liŋ-lē\ *adverb*
**cri·sis** \'krī-səs\ *noun, plural* **cri·ses** \'krī-,sēz\ [Middle English, from Latin, from Greek *krisis*, literally, decision, from *krinein* to decide — more at CERTAIN] (15th century)
**1 a :** the turning point for better or worse in an acute disease or fever **b :** a paroxysmal attack of pain, distress, or disordered function **c :** an emotionally significant event or radical change of status in a person's life ⟨a midlife *crisis*⟩
**2 :** the decisive moment (as in a literary plot)
**3 a :** an unstable or crucial time or state of affairs in which a decisive change is impending; *especially* **:** one with the distinct possibility of a highly undesirable outcome ⟨a financial *crisis*⟩ **b :** a situation that has reached a critical phase ⟨the environmental *crisis*⟩
*synonym* see JUNCTURE
**¹crisp** \'krisp\ *adjective* [Middle English, from Old English, from Latin *crispus*; akin to Welsh *crych* curly] (before 12th century)
**1 :** CURLY, WAVY; *also* **:** having close stiff or wiry curls or waves
**2 a :** easily crumbled **:** BRITTLE **b :** being desirably firm and fresh ⟨*crisp* lettuce⟩
**3 a :** being sharp, clean-cut, and clear ⟨a *crisp* illustration⟩; *also* **:** concise and to the point ⟨a

*crisp* reply⟩ **b :** noticeably neat ⟨*crisp* new clothes⟩ **c :** BRISK, LIVELY ⟨a *crisp* tale of intrigue⟩ ⟨*crisp* musical tempi⟩ **d :** FROSTY, SNAPPY ⟨*crisp* winter weather⟩; *also* **:** FRESH, INVIGORATING ⟨*crisp* autumn air⟩ ⟨a *crisp* white wine⟩
*synonym* see FRAGILE
— **crisp·ly** *adverb*
— **crisp·ness** *noun*
**²crisp** (14th century)
*transitive verb*
**1 :** CURL, CRIMP
**2 :** to cause to ripple **:** WRINKLE
**3 :** to make or keep crisp
*intransitive verb*
**1 :** CURL
**2 :** RIPPLE
**3 :** to become crisp
**³crisp** *noun* (14th century)
**1 a :** something crisp or brittle ⟨burned to a *crisp*⟩ **b** *chiefly British* **:** POTATO CHIP — usually used in plural
**2 :** a baked dessert of fruit with crumb topping ⟨apple *crisp*⟩
**crisp·bread** \'krisp-,bred\ *noun* (circa 1927)
**:** a plain dry unsweetened cracker made from crushed grain (as wheat or rye)
**crisp·en** \'kris-pən\ (1943)
*transitive verb*
**:** to make crisp
*intransitive verb*
**:** to become crisp
**crisp·er** \'kris-pər\ *noun* (1835)
**:** one that crisps; *specifically* **:** a closed container in a refrigerator intended to prevent loss of moisture from fresh produce
**crispy** \'kris-pē\ *adjective* **crisp·i·er; -est** (14th century)
**:** CRISP
— **crisp·i·ness** *noun*
**¹criss·cross** \'kris-,krȯs\ *verb* [obsolete *christcross, crisscross* mark of a cross] (1818)
*transitive verb*
**1 :** to mark with intersecting lines
**2 :** to pass back and forth through or over
*intransitive verb*
**:** to go or pass back and forth
**²crisscross** *adjective* (1846)
**:** marked or characterized by crisscrossing
— **crisscross** *adverb*
**³crisscross** *noun* (1876)
**1 :** a crisscross pattern **:** NETWORK
**2 :** the state of being at cross-purposes; *also* **:** a confused state
**cris·ta** \'kris-tə\ *noun, plural* **cris·tae** \-,tē, -,tī\ [New Latin, from Latin, crest — more at CREST] (1959)
**:** any of the inwardly projecting folds of the inner membrane of a mitochondrion
**cri·te·ri·on** \krī-'tir-ē-ən *also* krə-\ *noun, plural* **-ria** \-ē-ə\ *also* **-ri·ons** [Greek *kritērion*, from *krinein* to judge, decide — more at CERTAIN] (1622)
**1 :** a standard on which a judgment or decision may be based
**2 :** a characterizing mark or trait
*synonym* see STANDARD ◾
**cri·te·ri·um** \krī-'tir-ē-əm, krē-ter-'yȯm\ *noun* [French *critérium* competition, literally, criterion, from Late Latin *criterium*, from Greek *kritērion*] (1970)
**:** a bicycle race of a specified number of laps on a closed course over public roads closed to normal traffic
**¹crit·ic** \'kri-tik\ *noun* [Latin *criticus*, from Greek *kritikos*, from *kritikos* able to discern or judge, from *krinein*] (1588)
**1 a :** one who expresses a reasoned opinion on any matter especially involving a judgment of its value, truth, righteousness, beauty, or technique **b :** one who engages often professionally in the analysis, evaluation, or appreciation of works of art or artistic performances
**2 :** one given to harsh or captious judgment
**²critic** *noun* [Greek *kritikē* art of the critic, from feminine of *kritikos*] (1656)
**1** *archaic* **:** CRITICISM

**2** *archaic* **:** CRITIQUE
**crit·i·cal** \'kri-ti-kəl\ *adjective* (1547)
**1 a :** of, relating to, or being a turning point or specially important juncture ⟨*critical* phase⟩: as (1) **:** relating to or being the stage of a disease at which an abrupt change for better or worse may be expected; *also* **:** being or relating to an illness or condition involving danger of death ⟨*critical* care⟩ (2) **:** relating to or being a state in which or a measurement or point at which some quality, property, or phenomenon suffers a definite change ⟨*critical* temperature⟩ **b :** CRUCIAL, DECISIVE ⟨*critical* test⟩ **c :** INDISPENSABLE, VITAL ⟨a *critical* waterfowl habitat⟩ ⟨a component *critical* to the operation of a machine⟩ **d :** being in or approaching a state of crisis ⟨a *critical* shortage⟩ ⟨a *critical* situation⟩
**2 a :** inclined to criticize severely and unfavorably **b :** consisting of or involving criticism ⟨*critical* writings⟩; *also* **:** of or relating to the judgment of critics ⟨the play was a *critical* success⟩ **c :** exercising or involving careful judgment or judicious evaluation **d :** including variant readings and scholarly emendations ⟨a *critical* edition⟩
**3 :** characterized by risk or uncertainty
**4 a :** of sufficient size to sustain a chain reaction — used of a mass of fissionable material **b :** sustaining a chain reaction — used of a nuclear reactor ☆
— **crit·i·cal·i·ty** \,kri-tə-'ka-lə-tē\ *noun*
— **crit·i·cal·ly** \'kri-ti-k(ə-)lē\ *adverb*
— **crit·i·cal·ness** \-kəl-nəs\ *noun*
**critical angle** *noun* (1873)
**:** the least angle of incidence at which total reflection takes place
**critical mass** *noun* (1964)
**:** a size, number, or amount large enough to produce a particular result ⟨the *critical mass* of activity needed for a retail store⟩

critical angle: *AOB, AO'B', AO"B"* angles of incidence; *AOC* refracted ray; *AO"C"* totally reflected ray; *AO'B'* critical angle

☆ SYNONYMS
**Critical, hypercritical, faultfinding, captious, carping, censorious** mean inclined to look for and point out faults and defects. CRITICAL may also imply an effort to see a thing clearly and truly in order to judge it fairly ⟨a *critical* essay⟩. HYPERCRITICAL suggests a tendency to judge by unreasonably strict standards ⟨*hypercritical* disparagement of other people's work⟩. FAULTFINDING implies a querulous or exacting temperament ⟨a *faultfinding* reviewer⟩. CAPTIOUS suggests a readiness to detect trivial faults or raise objections on trivial grounds ⟨a *captious* critic⟩. CARPING implies an ill-natured or perverse picking of flaws ⟨a *carping* editorial⟩. CENSORIOUS implies a disposition to be severely critical and condemnatory ⟨the *censorious* tone of the review⟩. See in addition ACUTE.

◻ USAGE
**criterion** The plural *criteria* has been used as a singular for nearly half a century ⟨let me now return to the third *criteria* —R. M. Nixon⟩ ⟨that really is the *criteria* —Burt Lance⟩. Many of our examples, like the two foregoing, are taken from speech. But singular *criteria* is not uncommon in edited prose, and its use both in speech and writing seems to be increasing. Only time will tell whether it will reach the unquestioned acceptability of *agenda*.

**critical point** *noun* (circa 1889)
: a point on the graph of a function where the derivative is zero or infinite

**critical region** *noun* (1951)
: the set of outcomes of a statistical test for which the null hypothesis is to be rejected

**critical value** *noun* (circa 1909)
: the value of an independent variable corresponding to a critical point of a function

**crit·ic·as·ter** \'kri-ti-ˌkas-tər\ *noun* (1684)
: an inferior or petty critic

**crit·i·cise** *British variant of* CRITICIZE

**crit·i·cism** \'kri-tə-ˌsi-zəm\ *noun* (1607)
**1 a :** the act of criticizing usually unfavorably **b :** a critical observation or remark **c :** CRITIQUE
**2 :** the art of evaluating or analyzing works of art or literature
**3 :** the scientific investigation of literary documents (as the Bible) in regard to such matters as origin, text, composition, or history

**crit·i·cize** \'kri-tə-ˌsīz\ *verb* **-cized; -ciz·ing** (1649)
*intransitive verb*
: to act as a critic
*transitive verb*
**1 :** to consider the merits and demerits of and judge accordingly : EVALUATE
**2 :** to find fault with : point out the faults of ☆
**— crit·i·ciz·able** \-ˌsī-zə-bəl\ *adjective*
**— crit·i·ciz·er** *noun*

**¹cri·tique** \krə-'tēk, kri-\ *noun* [alteration of ²*critic*] (1702)
: an act of criticizing; *especially* : a critical estimate or discussion

**²critique** *transitive verb* **cri·tiqued; cri·tiqu·ing** (1751)
: REVIEW, CRITICIZE

**crit·ter** \'kri-tər\ *noun* [by alteration] (1815)
: CREATURE

**¹croak** \'krōk\ *verb* [Middle English *croken*, of imitative origin] (15th century)
*intransitive verb*
**1 a :** to make a deep harsh sound **b :** to speak in a hoarse throaty voice
**2 :** GRUMBLE 1
**3** *slang* : DIE
*transitive verb*
**1 :** to utter in a hoarse raucous voice
**2** *slang* : KILL

**²croak** *noun* (1561)
: a hoarse harsh cry or sound
**— croaky** \'krō-kē\ *adjective*

**croak·er** \'krō-kər\ *noun* (1651)
**1 :** an animal that croaks
**2 :** any of various fishes (especially family Sciaenidae) that produce croaking or grunting noises
**3** *slang* : DOCTOR

**Croat** \'krō-ˌat *also* 'krō(-ə)t\ *noun* [New Latin *Croata*, from Serbo-Croatian *Hrvat*] (circa 1702)
: CROATIAN

**Cro·atian** \krō-'ā-shən\ *noun* (1555)
**1 :** a native or inhabitant of Croatia
**2 :** a south Slavic language spoken by the Croatian people and distinct from Serbian chiefly in its use of the Latin alphabet
**— Croatian** *adjective*

**croc** \'kräk\ *noun* (1884)
: CROCODILE

**¹cro·chet** \krō-'shā\ *noun* [French, hook, crochet, from Middle French, diminutive of *croche* hook, of Scandinavian origin; akin to Old Norse *krōkr* hook] (1846)
: needlework consisting of the interlocking of looped stitches formed with a single thread and a hooked needle

**²crochet** (1858)
*transitive verb*
: to make of crochet ⟨*crocheted* a doily⟩
*intransitive verb*
: to work with crochet
**— cro·chet·er** \-'shā-ər\ *noun*

**cro·cid·o·lite** \krō-'si-də-ˌlīt\ *noun* [German *Krokydolith*, from Greek *krokyd-, krokys* nap

on cloth (akin to Greek *krekein* to weave) + German *-lith* -lite — more at REEL] (1835)
: a lavender-blue or light green mineral of the amphibole group that occurs in silky fibers and in massive form and is a type of asbestos
— compare TIGEREYE

**¹crock** \'kräk\ *noun* [Middle English, from Old English *crocc;* akin to Middle High German *krūche* crock] (before 12th century)
**1 :** a thick earthenware pot or jar
**2** [from its formation on cooking pots] *dialect* : SOOT, SMUT
**3 :** coloring matter that rubs off from cloth or dyed leather
**4 :** BUNKUM — usually used with *a*

**²crock** (1594)
*transitive verb*
**1 :** to put or preserve in a crock
**2** *dialect* : to soil with crock : SMUDGE
*intransitive verb*
: to transfer color (as when rubbed or washed) ⟨a suede that will not *crock*⟩

**³crock** *noun* [Middle English *crok*, probably of Scandinavian origin; akin to Norwegian dialect *krokje* crock] (1528)
**1 :** one that is broken-down, disabled, or impaired
**2 :** a complaining medical patient whose illness is largely imaginary or psychosomatic

**⁴crock** (1896)
*transitive verb*
: to cause to become disabled
*intransitive verb*
: BREAK DOWN

**crocked** \'kräkt\ *adjective* (circa 1927)
: DRUNK

**crock·ery** \'krä-k(ə-)rē\ *noun* (circa 1755)
: EARTHENWARE

**crock·et** \'krä-kət\ *noun* [Middle English *croket*, from Old North French *croquet* crook, diminutive of *croc* hook, of Scandinavian origin; akin to Old Norse *krōkr* hook] (1673)
: an ornament usually in the form of curved and bent foliage used on the edge of a gable or spire
**— crock·et·ed** \-kə-təd\ *adjective*

**Crock–Pot** \'kräk-ˌpät\ *trademark*
— used for an electric cooking pot

**croc·o·dile** \'krä-kə-ˌdīl\ *noun* [Middle English & Latin; Middle English *cocodrille*, from Middle French, from Medieval Latin *cocodrillus*, alteration of Latin *crocodilus*, from Greek *krokodilos* lizard, crocodile, from *krokē* shingle, pebble + *drilos* worm; akin to Sanskrit *śarkara* pebble] (1684)
**1 a :** any of several large carnivorous thick-skinned long-bodied aquatic reptiles (family Crocodilidae) of tropical and subtropical waters; *broadly* : CROCODILIAN **b :** the skin or hide of a crocodile

crocodile 1a

**2** *chiefly British* : a line of people (as schoolchildren) usually walking in pairs

**crocodile bird** *noun* (1868)
: an African bird (*Pluvianus aegyptius*) that is related to the pratincoles and lights on the crocodile and eats its insect parasites

**crocodile tears** *noun plural* (1563)
: false or affected tears; *also* : hypocritical sorrow

**croc·o·dil·ian** \ˌkrä-kə-'di-lē-ən, -'dil-yən\ *noun* (1837)
: any of an order (Crocodylia) of reptiles including the crocodiles, alligators, caimans, gavials, and related extinct forms
**— crocodilian** *adjective*

**cro·cus** \'krō-kəs\ *noun, plural* **cro·cus·es** [Middle English, the saffron plant, from Latin, from Greek *krokos,* of Semitic origin; akin to Akkadian *kurkānū* saffron] (14th century)
**1 a** *plural also* **crocus** *or* **cro·ci** \-ˌkē, -ˌkī, -ˌsī\ : any of a large genus (*Crocus*) of herbs

of the iris family developing from corms and having solitary long-tubed flowers and slender linear leaves **b :** SAFFRON 1a
**2 :** a dark red ferric oxide used for polishing metals

**Croe·sus** \'krē-səs\ *noun* [*Croesus,* king of Lydia, famed for his wealth] (1650)
: a very rich man

**croft** \'kròft\ *noun* [Middle English, from Old English; akin to Middle Dutch *krocht* hill] (before 12th century)
**1** *chiefly British* : a small enclosed field usually adjoining a house
**2** *chiefly British* : a small farm worked by a tenant
**— croft·er** \'kròf-tər\ *noun, chiefly British*

**crois·sant** \krò-'sänt, krə-; krwä-'sä[n]\ *noun, plural* **croissants** \-'sänt(s), -'sä[n](z)\ [French, literally, crescent, from Middle French *creissant*] (1899)
: a flaky rich crescent-shaped roll

**Croix de Guerre** \ˌkrwä-di-'ger\ *noun* [French, literally, war cross] (1915)
: a French military decoration awarded for gallant action in war

**cro·ker sack** \'krō-kər-\ *noun* [alteration of *crocus sack, crocus bag,* of unknown origin] (1895)
*chiefly Southern* : a sack of a coarse material (as burlap)

**Cro–Ma·gnon** \krō-'mag-nən, -'man-yən\ *noun* [*Cro-Magnon,* a cave near Les Eyzies, France] (1869)
: a tall erect race of hominids of the Upper Paleolithic known from skeletal remains found chiefly in southern France and classified as the same species (*Homo sapiens*) as present day humans

**crom·lech** \'kräm-ˌlek\ *noun* [Welsh, literally, bent stone] (1695)
**1 :** DOLMEN
**2 :** a circle of monoliths usually enclosing a dolmen or mound

**crone** \'krōn\ *noun* [Middle English, from Old North French *carogne,* literally, carrion, from (assumed) Vulgar Latin *caronia* — more at CARRION] (14th century)
: a withered old woman

**Cro·nus** \'krō-nəs, 'krä-\ *noun* [Latin, from Greek *Kronos*]
: a Titan dethroned by his son Zeus

**cro·ny** \'krō-nē\ *noun, plural* **cronies** [perhaps from Greek *chronios* long-lasting, from *chronos* time] (1663)
: a close friend especially of long standing
: PAL

**cro·ny·ism** \-nē-ˌi-zəm\ *noun* (1840)

---

☆ **SYNONYMS**
**Criticize, reprehend, censure, reprobate, condemn, denounce** mean to find fault with openly. CRITICIZE implies finding fault especially with methods or policies or intentions ⟨*criticized* the police for using violence⟩. REPREHEND implies both criticism and severe rebuking ⟨*reprehends* the self-centeredness of today's students⟩. CENSURE carries a strong suggestion of authority and of reprimanding ⟨a Senator formally *censured* by his peers⟩. REPROBATE implies strong disapproval or firm refusal to sanction ⟨*reprobated* his son's unconventional lifestyle⟩. CONDEMN usually suggests an unqualified and final unfavorable judgment ⟨*condemned* the government's racial policies⟩. DENOUNCE adds to CONDEMN the implication of a public declaration ⟨a pastoral letter *denouncing* abortion⟩.

---

\ə\ abut \ə\ kitten \ər\ further \a\ ash \ā\ ace \ä\ mop, mar \au̇\ out \ch\ chin \e\ bet \ē\ easy \g\ go \i\ hit \ī\ ice \j\ job \ŋ\ sing \ō\ go \ȯ\ law \ȯi\ boy \th\ thin \th\ the \ü\ loot \u̇\ foot \y\ yet \zh\ vision    *see also* Guide to Pronunciation

: partiality to cronies especially as evidenced in the appointment of political hangers-on to office without regard to their qualifications

¹**crook** \'krùk\ (12th century)
*transitive verb*
: BEND
*intransitive verb*
: CURVE, WIND

²**crook** *noun* [Middle English *crok,* from Old Norse *krōkr* hook] (13th century)
**1** : an implement having a bent or hooked form: as **a** : POTHOOK **b** (1) : a shepherd's staff (2) : CROSIER 1
**2** : a part of something that is hook-shaped, curved, or bent ⟨the *crook* of an umbrella handle⟩
**3** : BEND, CURVE
**4** : a person who engages in fraudulent or criminal practices

³**crook** *adjective* [probably short for *crooked*] (1898)
*Australian & New Zealand* : not right: **a** : UNSATISFACTORY **b** : DISHONEST, CROOKED **c** : IRRITABLE, ANGRY — used especially in the phrase *go crook* **d** : ILL, UNWELL

**crook·back** \'krùk-ˌbak\ *noun* (1508)
**1** *obsolete* : a crooked back
**2** *obsolete* : HUNCHBACK
— **crook·backed** \-ˌbakt\ *adjective*

**crook·ed** \'krù-kəd\ *adjective* (13th century)
**1** : not straight ⟨a *crooked* road⟩ ⟨your tie is *crooked*⟩
**2** : DISHONEST ⟨a *crooked* election⟩ ⟨*crooked* politicians⟩
— **crook·ed·ly** *adverb*
— **crook·ed·ness** *noun*

**crook·ery** \'krù-kə-rē\ *noun* (1927)
: crooked dealings or practices

**crook·neck** \'krùk-ˌnek\ *noun* (1784)
: a squash with a long recurved neck

**croon** \'krün\ *verb* [Middle English *croynen,* from Middle Dutch *cronen;* akin to Old High German *crōnen* to chatter] (15th century)
*intransitive verb*
**1** *chiefly Scottish* : BELLOW, BOOM
**2** : to sing or speak in a gentle murmuring manner; *especially* : to sing in a soft intimate manner adapted to amplifying systems
*transitive verb*
: to sing (as a popular song or a lullaby) in a crooning manner
— **croon** *noun*

**croon·er** \'krü-nər\ *noun* (1930)
: one that croons; *especially* : a singer of popular songs

¹**crop** \'kräp\ *noun* [Middle English, craw, head of a plant, yield of a field, from Old English *cropp* craw, head of a plant; akin to Old High German *kropf* goiter, craw] (before 12th century)
**1** : a pouched enlargement of the gullet of many birds that serves as a receptacle for food and for its preliminary maceration; *also* : an enlargement of the gullet of another animal (as an insect)
**2 a** (1) : a plant or animal or plant or animal product that can be grown and harvested extensively for profit or subsistence ⟨an apple *crop*⟩ ⟨a *crop* of wool⟩ (2) : the total yearly production from a specified area **b** : the product or yield of something formed together ⟨the ice *crop*⟩ **c** : a batch or lot of something produced during a particular cycle ⟨the current *crop* of films⟩ **d** : COLLECTION ⟨a *crop* of lies⟩
**3** : the stock or handle of a whip; *also* : a riding whip with a short straight stock and a loop
**4** [²*crop*] **a** : the part of the chine of a quadruped (as a domestic cow) lying immediately behind the withers — usually used in plural; see COW illustration **b** : an earmark on an animal; *especially* : one made by a straight cut squarely removing the upper part of the ear **c** : a close cut of the hair

²**crop** *verb* **cropped; crop·ping** (13th century)

*transitive verb*
**1 a** : to remove the upper or outer parts of ⟨*crop* a hedge⟩ ⟨*crop* a dog's ears⟩ **b** : HARVEST ⟨*crop* trout⟩ **c** : to cut off short : TRIM ⟨*crop* a photograph⟩
**2** : to cause (land) to bear a crop ⟨will *crop* another 40 acres⟩; *also* : to grow as a crop
*intransitive verb*
**1** : to feed by cropping something
**2** : to yield or make a crop
**3** : to appear unexpectedly or casually ⟨problems *crop* up daily⟩

**crop duster** *noun* (1939)
: a person who sprays crops with fungicidal or insecticidal dusts from an airplane; *also* : the airplane used for such spraying

**crop-eared** \'kräp-ˌird\ *adjective* (1530)
: having the ears cropped

**crop·land** \-ˌland\ *noun* (1846)
: land that is suited to or used for crops

¹**crop·per** \'krä-pər\ *noun* (15th century)
**1** : one that crops
**2** : one that raises crops; *specifically* : SHARECROPPER

²**cropper** *noun* [probably from English dialect *crop* neck, from ¹*crop*] (1858)
**1** : a severe fall
**2** : a sudden or violent failure or collapse

**crop rotation** *noun* (1909)
: the practice of growing different crops in succession on the same land chiefly to preserve the productive capacity of the soil

**cro·quet** \krō-'kā\ *noun* [French dialect, hockey stick, from Old North French, crook — more at CROCKET] (1858)
**1** : a game in which players using mallets drive wooden balls through a series of wickets set out on a lawn
**2** : the act of driving away an opponent's croquet ball by striking one's own ball placed against it
— **croquet** *transitive verb*

**cro·quette** \krō-'ket\ *noun* [French, from *croquer* to crunch, of imitative origin] (1706)
: a small often rounded mass consisting usually of minced meat, fish, or vegetable coated with egg and bread crumbs and deep-fried

**cro·qui·gnole** \'krō-kə-ˌnōl *also* -kən-ˌyōl\ *noun* [French, light blow, fillip] (1932)
: a method used in waving the hair by winding it on curlers from the ends of the hair toward the scalp

**cro·quis** \krō-'kē\ *noun, plural* **cro·quis** \-'kē(z)\ [French, from *croquer* to sketch, rough out, literally, to crunch] (1805)
: a rough draft : SKETCH

**crore** \'krōr, 'krȯr\ *noun, plural* **crores** *also* **crore** [Hindi *karoṛ*] (1609)
: a unit of value equal to ten million rupees or 100 lakhs

**cro·sier** \'krō-zhər\ *noun* [Middle English *crocer* crosier bearer, from Middle French *crossier,* from *crosse* crosier, of Germanic origin; akin to Old English *crycc* crutch — more at CRUTCH] (1500)
**1** : a staff resembling a shepherd's crook carried by bishops and abbots as a symbol of office
**2** : a plant structure with a coiled end

¹**cross** \'krȯs\ *noun* [Middle English, from Old English, from Old Norse or Old Irish; Old Norse *kross,* from Old Irish *cros,* from Latin *cruc-, crux*] (before 12th century)
**1 a** : a structure consisting of an upright with a transverse beam used especially by the ancient Romans for execution **b** *often capitalized* : the cross on which Jesus was crucified
**2 a** : CRUCIFIXION **b** : an affliction that tries one's virtue, steadfastness, or patience
**3** : a cruciform sign made to invoke the blessing of Christ especially by touching the forehead, breast, and shoulders
**4 a** : a device composed of an upright bar traversed by a horizontal one; *specifically* : one used as a Christian symbol **b** *capitalized* : the Christian religion

**5** : a structure (as a monument) shaped like or surmounted by a cross
**6** : a figure or mark formed by two intersecting lines crossing at their midpoints; *specifically* : such a mark used as a signature
**7** : a cruciform badge, emblem, or decoration
**8** : the intersection of two ways or lines : CROSSING
**9** : ANNOYANCE, THWARTING ⟨a *cross* in love⟩
**10 a** : an act of crossing dissimilar individuals **b** : a crossbred individual or kind **c** : one that combines characteristics of two different types or individuals
**11 a** : a fraudulent or dishonest contest **b** : dishonest or illegal practices — used especially in the phrase *on the cross*
**12** : a movement from one part of a theater stage to another
**13** : a hook thrown over the opponent's lead in boxing
**14** : a security transaction in which a broker acts for both buyer and seller (as in the placing of a large lot of common stock) — called also *cross-trade*

cross 4a: *1* Latin, *2* Calvary, *3* patriarchal, *4* papal, *5* Lorraine, *6* Greek, *7* Celtic, *8* Maltese, *9* Saint Andrew's, *10* tau, *11* pommée, *12* botonée, *13* fleury, *14* avellan, *15* moline, *16* formée, *17* fourchée, *18* crosslet, *19* quadrate, *20* potent

²**cross** (14th century)
*transitive verb*
**1 a** : to lie or be situated across **b** : INTERSECT
**2** : to make the sign of the cross upon or over
**3** : to cancel by marking a cross on or drawing a line through : strike out ⟨*cross* names off a list⟩
**4** : to place or fold crosswise one over the other ⟨*cross* the arms⟩
**5 a** (1) : to run counter to : OPPOSE (2) : to deny the validity of : CONTRADICT **b** : to confront in a troublesome manner : OBSTRUCT **c** (1) : to spoil completely : DISRUPT — used with *up* ⟨his failure to appear *crossed* up the whole program⟩ (2) : to turn against : BETRAY ⟨*crossed* me up on the deal⟩
**6 a** : to extend across or over : TRAVERSE ⟨a highway *crossing* the entire state⟩ **b** : REACH, ATTAIN ⟨only two *crossed* the finish line⟩ **c** : to go from one side of to the other ⟨*cross* a street⟩ ⟨*crosses* racial barriers⟩
**7 a** : to draw a line across **b** : to mark or figure with lines : STREAK
**8** : to cause (an animal or plant) to interbreed with one of a different kind : HYBRIDIZE
**9** : to meet and pass on the way ⟨our letters must have *crossed* each other⟩
**10** : to occur to ⟨it never *crossed* my mind⟩
**11** : to carry or take across something ⟨*crossed* the children at the intersection⟩
*intransitive verb*

**1 a :** to move, pass, or extend across something ⟨*crossed* through France⟩ ⟨*crossed* over to the other side of the river⟩ **b :** to move or pass from one character, condition, or allegiance to another — used with *over* **2 :** to lie or be athwart each other **3 :** to meet in passing especially from opposite directions **4 :** INTERBREED, HYBRIDIZE — **cross·er** *noun* — **cross swords :** to engage in a dispute

³**cross** *adjective* (14th century) **1 a :** lying across or athwart **b :** moving across ⟨*cross* traffic⟩ **2 a :** running counter : OPPOSITE **b :** mutually opposed ⟨*cross* purposes⟩ **3 :** involving mutual interchange : RECIPROCAL **4 :** marked by typically transitory bad temper **5 :** extending over or treating several groups or classes ⟨a *cross* sample from 25 colleges⟩ **6 :** CROSSBRED, HYBRID — **cross·ly** *adverb* — **cross·ness** *noun*

⁴**cross** *preposition* (1551) **:** ACROSS

⁵**cross** *adverb* (1577) **:** not parallel : CRISSCROSS, CROSSWISE

**cross·abil·i·ty** \ˌkrȯ-sə-ˈbi-lə-tē\ *noun* (1916) **:** the ability of different species or varieties to cross with each other

**cross·able** \ˈkrȯ-sə-bəl\ *adjective* (1865) **:** capable of being crossed

**cross action** *noun* (circa 1859) **:** a legal action in which the defendant in an existing action files a suit against the plaintiff on the same subject matter : COUNTERSUIT

**cross·band·ing** \ˈkrȯs-ˌban-diŋ\ *noun* (1904) **:** a veneer border (as on furniture) with its grain at right angles to the grain of the adjacent wood — **cross·band·ed** \-ˌban-dəd\ *adjective*

**cross·bar** \ˈkrȯs-ˌbär\ *noun* (1562) **:** a transverse bar or stripe

**cross·bear·er** \ˈkrȯs-ˌbar-ər, -ˌber-\ *noun* (1568) **:** CRUCIFER 1

**cross·bill** \-ˌbil\ *noun* (circa 1672) **:** any of a small genus (*Loxia*) of finches with strongly curved mandibles that cross each other

**cross·bones** \-ˌbōnz\ *noun plural* (1798) **:** two leg or arm bones placed or depicted crosswise — compare SKULL AND CROSSBONES

**cross·bow** \-ˌbō\ *noun* (15th century) **:** a weapon for discharging quarrels and stones that consists chiefly of a short bow mounted crosswise near the end of a stock

crossbow

**cross·bow·man** \-mən\ *noun* (circa 1500) **:** a person (as a soldier or a hunter) whose weapon is a crossbow

**cross·bred** \ˈkrȯs-ˈbred\ *adjective* (1856) **:** produced by crossbreeding : HYBRID — **cross·bred** \-ˌbred\ *noun*

¹**cross·breed** \ˈkrȯs-ˌbrēd, -ˈbrēd\ *verb* **-bred** \-ˌbred, -ˈbred\; **-breed·ing** (1675) *transitive verb* **:** HYBRIDIZE, CROSS; *especially* **:** to cross (two varieties or breeds) within the same species *intransitive verb* **:** to engage in or undergo hybridization

²**cross·breed** \-ˌbrēd\ *noun* (1774) **:** HYBRID

¹**cross–check** \-ˌchek\ *transitive verb* (circa 1930) **1 :** to obstruct in ice hockey or lacrosse by thrusting one's stick held in both hands across an opponent's face or body

**2 :** to check (as data or reports) from various angles or sources to determine validity or accuracy

²**cross–check** *noun* (1937) **:** an act or instance of cross-checking

**cross–claim** \-ˌklām\ *noun* (1952) **:** a claim against a party on the same side of a legal action

¹**cross–coun·try** \ˈkrȯs-ˈkən-trē, -ˌkən-\ *adjective* (1767) **1 :** extending or moving across a country ⟨a *cross-country* concert tour⟩ **2 :** proceeding over countryside (as across fields and through woods) and not by roads **3 :** of or relating to racing or skiing over the countryside instead of over a track or run — **cross–country** *adverb*

²**cross–country** *noun* (1925) **:** cross-country racing or skiing

**cross–court** \ˈkrȯs-ˈkōrt, -ˈkȯrt\ *adverb or adjective* (1915) **:** to or toward the opposite side of a court (as in tennis or basketball)

**cross–cul·tur·al** \ˈkrȯs-ˈkəlch-rəl, -ˈkəl-chə-\ *adjective* (circa 1942) **:** dealing with or offering comparison between two or more different cultures or cultural areas — **cross–cul·tur·al·ly** \-rə-lē\ *adverb*

**cross–cur·rent** \ˈkrȯs-ˌkər-ənt, -ˌkə-rənt\ *noun* (1598) **1 :** a current running counter to the general forward direction **2 :** a conflicting tendency — usually used in plural ⟨political *crosscurrents*⟩

¹**cross·cut** \ˈkrȯs-ˌkət, -ˈkət\ *transitive verb* (1590) **1 :** to cut, go, or move across or through **2 :** to cut with a crosscut saw **3 :** to subject (as movie scenes) to crosscutting

²**crosscut** *adjective* (1645) **1 :** made or used for cutting transversely ⟨a saw with *crosscut* teeth⟩ **2 :** cut across or transversely ⟨a *crosscut* incision⟩

³**cross·cut** \ˈkrȯs-ˌkət\ *noun* (1789) **1 :** something that cuts across or through; *specifically* **:** a mine working driven horizontally and at right angles to an adit, drift, or level **2 :** CROSS SECTION **3 :** CROSSCUT SAW **4 :** an instance of crosscutting (as in a movie)

**crosscut saw** *noun* (1645) **:** a saw designed chiefly to cut across the grain of wood — compare RIPSAW

**cross·cut·ting** \ˈkrȯs-ˌkə-tiŋ\ *noun* (1930) **:** a technique especially in filmmaking of interweaving bits of two or more separate scenes

**cross–dress·ing** \ˈkrȯs-ˌdre-siŋ\ *noun* (1911) **:** the wearing of clothes designed for the opposite sex — **cross–dress** *intransitive verb* — **cross–dress·er** *noun*

**crosse** \ˈkrȯs\ *noun* [French, literally, crosier — more at CROSIER] (1867) **:** a stick with a small net at one end that is used in lacrosse

**cross–ex·am·i·na·tion** \ˈkrȯs-ig-ˌza-mə-ˈnā-shən\ *noun* (1824) **:** the examination of a witness who has already testified in order to check or discredit the witness's testimony, knowledge, or credibility — compare DIRECT EXAMINATION — **cross–ex·am·ine** \-ig-ˈza-mən\ *transitive verb* — **cross–ex·am·in·er** \-ˈzam-nər, -ˈza-mə-\ *noun*

**cross–eye** \ˈkrȯ-ˌsī\ *noun* (1826) **1 :** strabismus in which the eye turns inward toward the nose **2** *plural* **:** eyes affected with cross-eye — **cross–eyed** \-ˌsīd\ *adjective*

**cross–fer·tile** \ˈkrȯs-ˈfər-tᵊl, -ˌfər-\ *adjective* (1929) **:** fertile in a cross or capable of cross-fertilization

**cross–fer·til·i·za·tion** \-ˌfər-tᵊl-ə-ˈzā-shən\ *noun* (1876) **1 a :** fertilization in which the gametes are produced by separate individuals or sometimes by individuals of different kinds **b :** CROSS-POLLINATION **2 :** interchange or interaction (as between different ideas, cultures, or categories) especially of a broadening or productive nature

**cross–fer·til·ize** \-ˈfər-tᵊl-ˌīz\ (1876) *transitive verb* **:** to accomplish cross-fertilization of *intransitive verb* **:** to undergo cross-fertilization

**cross–file** \-ˈfī(ə)l\ (1949) *intransitive verb* **:** to register as a candidate in the primary elections of more than one political party *transitive verb* **:** to register (a person) as a candidate for more than one party

**cross fire** *noun* (circa 1859) **1 a :** firing (as in combat) from two or more points so that the lines of fire cross **b :** a situation wherein the forces of opposing factions meet, cross, or clash ⟨caught in a political *cross fire*⟩ **2 :** rapid or heated exchange of words

**cross–grained** \ˈkrȯs-ˌgrānd\ *adjective* (1647) **1 :** difficult to deal with **2 :** having the grain or fibers running diagonally, transversely, or irregularly

**cross·hair** \-ˌhar, -ˌher\ *noun* (circa 1884) **:** a fine wire or thread in the focus of the eyepiece of an optical instrument used as a reference line in the field or for marking the instrumental axis

**cross·hatch** \ˈkrȯs-ˌhach\ *transitive verb* (1822) **:** to mark with two series of parallel lines that intersect — **crosshatch** *noun* — **cross–hatch·ing** *noun*

**cross·head** \-ˌhed\ *noun* (1827) **1 :** a metal block to which one end of a piston rod is secured **2 :** a heading centered usually between portions of text

**cross–in·dex** \ˈkrȯs-ˈin-ˌdeks\ *transitive verb* (1892) **1 :** to index (an item) under a second or under more than one heading **2 :** to supply (as a book) with a cross-referenced index — **cross–index** *noun*

**cross·ing** \ˈkrȯ-siŋ\ *noun* (1575) **1 :** the act or action of crossing: as **a :** a traversing or traveling across **b :** an opposing, blocking, or thwarting especially in an unfair or dishonest manner **2 a :** a place or structure (as on a street or over a river) where pedestrians or vehicles cross; *especially* **:** CROSSWALK **b :** the place in a cruciform church where the transept crosses the nave **c :** a place where a railroad track crosses a street

**cross·ing–over** \ˌkrȯ-siŋ-ˈō-vər\ *noun* (1912) **:** an interchange of genes or segments between homologous chromosomes

**cross·legged** \ˈkrȯs-ˈle-gəd, -ˈlā-; -ˌlegd, -ˌlāgd\ *adverb or adjective* (circa 1530) **1 :** with legs crossed and knees spread wide apart **2 :** with one leg placed over and across the other

**cross·let** \ˈkrȯs-lət\ *noun* (15th century) **:** a small cross usually with crossed arms; *especially* **:** one used as a heraldic bearing — see CROSS illustration

---

\ə\ abut \ᵊ\ kitten \ər\ further \a\ ash \ā\ ace \ä\ mop, mar \au̇\ out \ch\ chin \e\ bet \ē\ easy \g\ go \i\ hit \ī\ ice \j\ job \ŋ\ sing \ō\ go \ȯ\ law \ȯi\ boy \th\ thin \t͟h\ the \ü\ loot \u̇\ foot \y\ yet \zh\ vision    *see also* Guide to Pronunciation

**cross·lin·guis·tic** \-liŋ-'gwis-tik\ *adjective* (1954)
**:** of or relating to languages of different families and types; *especially* **:** relating to the comparison of different languages
— **cross·lin·guis·ti·cal·ly** \-ti-k(ə-)lē\ *adverb*

**cross–link** \'kròs-,liŋk\ *noun* (1936)
**:** a crosswise connecting part (as an atom or group) that connects parallel chains in a complex chemical molecule (as a polymer)
— **cross–link** *verb*

**cross–link·age** \'kròs-'liŋ-kij\ *noun* (1937)
**:** the process of forming cross-links; *also* **:** CROSS-LINK

**cross multiply** *intransitive verb* (1951)
**:** to find the two products obtained by multiplying the numerator of each of two fractions by the denominator of the other
— **cross multiplication** *noun*

**cross–na·tion·al** \'kròs-'nash-nəl, -'na-shə-n²l\ *adjective* (1965)
**:** of or relating to two or more nations

**cross of Lor·raine** \-lə-'rān, -lò-\ [*Lorraine*, France] (circa 1889)
**:** a cross with two crossbars the lower one of which is longer than the upper one — see CROSS illustration

**cros·sop·ter·yg·ian** \,krò-,säp-tə-'ri-j(ē-)ən\ *noun* [New Latin *Crossopterygii*, subclass name, from Greek *krossoi* fringe + *pterygion*, diminutive of *pteryg-, pteryx* wing, fin; akin to Greek *pteron* wing — more at FEATHER] (1861)
**:** any of a subclass (Crossopterygii) of fishes (as a coelacanth) that have paired fins suggesting limbs, that may be ancestral to the terrestrial vertebrates, and that are mostly extinct — called also *lobe-fin*
— **crossopterygian** *adjective*

**¹cross·over** \'kròs-,ō-vər\ *noun* (1884)
**1 :** CROSSING 2a
**2 :** an instance or product of genetic crossing-over
**3 :** a voter registered as a member of one political party who votes in the primary of the other party
**4 :** a broadening of the popular appeal of an artist (as a musician) or an artist's work that is often the result of a change of the artist's medium or style; *also* **:** an artist or artistic work that has achieved a crossover
**5 :** an instance of breaking into another category ⟨trying to make the *crossover* to serious acting —Michael Neill⟩

**²crossover** *adjective* (1893)
**1 :** having two pieces that cross especially one over the other ⟨a *crossover* vest⟩
**2 :** CRITICAL 1 ⟨the *crossover* point⟩

**cross–own·er·ship** \-'ō-nər-,ship\ *noun* (1969)
**:** single ownership of two or more related businesses (as a newspaper and a television station) that allows the owner to control competition

**cross–patch** \'kròs-,pach\ *noun* [³*cross* + ³*patch*] (circa 1700)
**:** GROUCH 2

**cross·piece** \'kròs-,pēs\ *noun* (1607)
**:** a horizontal member (as of a structure)

**cross–pol·li·nate** \'kròs-'pä-lə-,nāt\ *transitive verb* (circa 1900)
**:** to subject to cross-pollination

**cross–pol·li·na·tion** \,kròs-,pä-lə-'nā-shən\ *noun* (1882)
**1 :** the transfer of pollen from one flower to the stigma of another
**2 :** CROSS-FERTILIZATION 2

**cross product** *noun* (1929)
**1 :** VECTOR PRODUCT
**2 :** either of the two products obtained by multiplying the two means or the two extremes of a proportion

**cross–pur·pose** \'kròs-'pər-pəs\ *noun* (1681)
**:** a purpose usually unintentionally contrary to another purpose of oneself or of someone or

something else — usually used in plural ⟨the two were always working at *cross-purposes*⟩

**cross–ques·tion** \'kròs-'kwes-chən, -'kwesh-\ *noun* (circa 1694)
**:** a question asked in cross-examination
— **cross–question** *transitive verb*

**cross–re·ac·tion** \,kròs-rē-'ak-shən\ *noun* (1946)
**:** reaction of one antigen with antibodies developed against another antigen
— **cross–re·act** \-rē-'akt\ *intransitive verb*
— **cross–re·ac·tive** \-'ak-tiv\ *adjective*
— **cross–re·ac·tiv·i·ty** \-(,)rē-,ak-'ti-və-tē\ *noun*

**cross–re·fer** \,kròs-ri-'fər\ (1879)
*transitive verb*
**:** to refer (a reader) by a notation or direction from one place to another (as in a book, list, or catalog)
*intransitive verb*
**:** to make a cross-reference

**¹cross–ref·er·ence** \'kròs-'re-fərn(t)s, -'re-f(ə-)rən(t)s\ *noun* (1834)
**:** a notation or direction at one place (as in a book or filing system) to pertinent information at another place

**²cross–reference** *transitive verb* (1902)
**:** to supply with cross-references

**cross–re·sis·tance** \,kròs-ri-'zis-tən(t)s\ *noun* (1946)
**:** tolerance (as of an insect population) to a normally toxic substance (as an insecticide) that is acquired not as a result of direct exposure but by exposure to a related substance

**cross·road** \'kròs-,rōd *also* -'rōd\ *noun* (1719)
**1 :** a road that crosses a main road or runs cross-country between main roads
**2** *usually plural but singular or plural in construction* **a :** the place of intersection of two or more roads **b** (1) **:** a small community located at such a crossroads (2) **:** a central meeting place **c :** a crucial point especially where a decision must be made

**cross–ruff** \'kròs-,rəf, -'rəf\ *noun* (1862)
**:** a series of plays in a card game (as bridge) in which partners alternately trump different suits and lead to each other for that purpose
— **crossruff** *verb*

**cross section** *noun* (1835)
**1 a :** a cutting or piece of something cut off at right angles to an axis; *also* **:** a representation of such a cutting **b :** SECTION 3b
**2 :** a measure of the probability of an encounter between particles such as will result in a specified effect (as scattering or capture)
**3 :** a composite representation typifying the constituents of a thing in their relations
— **cross–section** *transitive verb*
— **cross–sec·tion·al** \'kròs-'sek-shnəl, -shə-n²l\ *adjective*

**cross–stitch** \'krò(s)-,stich\ *noun* (circa 1710)
**1 :** a needlework stitch that forms an X
**2 :** work having cross-stitch
— **cross–stitch** *verb*

**cross talk** *noun* (1887)
**:** unwanted signals in a communication channel (as in a telephone, radio, or computer) caused by transference of energy from another circuit (as by leakage or coupling)

**cross–tol·er·ance** \'kròs-'täl-rən(t)s, -'tä-lə-\ *noun* (circa 1923)
**:** tolerance or resistance to a drug that develops through continued use of another drug with similar pharmacological action

**cross–town** \'kròs-'taùn\ *adjective* (1886)
**1 :** situated at opposite points of a town
**2 :** extending or running across a town ⟨a *crosstown* street⟩ ⟨a *crosstown* bus⟩

**cross–trade** \'kròs-,trād\ *noun* (circa 1923)
**:** CROSS 14

**cross·trees** \-(,)trēz\ *noun plural* (1626)
**:** two horizontal crosspieces of timber or metal supported by trestletrees at a masthead that spread the upper shrouds in order to support the mast

**cross vault** *noun* (1850)
**:** a vault formed by the intersection of two or more simple vaults — called also *cross vaulting*

**cross·walk** \'kròs-,wòk\ *noun* (1744)
**:** a specially paved or marked path for pedestrians crossing a street or road

**cross·way** \-,wā\ *noun* (14th century)
**:** CROSSROAD — often used in plural

**cross·ways** \-,wāz\ *adverb* (1564)
**:** CROSSWISE, DIAGONALLY

**cross·wind** \-,wind\ *noun* (1677)
**:** a wind blowing in a direction not parallel to a course (as of an airplane)

**¹cross·wise** \-,wīz\ *adverb* (14th century)
**1** *archaic* **:** in the form of a cross
**2 :** so as to cross something **:** ACROSS ⟨logs laid *crosswise*⟩

**²crosswise** *adjective* (1903)
**:** TRANSVERSE, CROSSING

**cross·word** \'kròs-,wərd\ *noun* (1914)
**:** a puzzle in which words are filled into a pattern of numbered squares in answer to correspondingly numbered clues and in such a way that the words read across and down

**crotch** \'kräch\ *noun* [probably alteration of ¹*crutch*] (1573)
**1 :** a pole with a forked end used especially as a prop
**2 :** an angle formed by the parting of two legs, branches, or members
— **crotched** \'krächt\ *adjective*

**crotch·et** \'krä-chət\ *noun* [Middle English *crochet*, from Middle French — more at CROCHET] (14th century)
**1** *obsolete* **a :** a small hook or hooked instrument **b :** BROOCH
**2 a :** a highly individual and usually eccentric opinion or preference **b :** a peculiar trick or device
**3 :** QUARTER NOTE
**synonym** see CAPRICE

**crotch·ety** \'krä-chə-tē\ *adjective* (1825)
**1 :** given to crotchets **:** subject to whims, crankiness, or ill temper ⟨a *crotchety* old man⟩
**2 :** full of or arising from crotchets
— **crotch·et·i·ness** \-tē-nəs\ *noun*

**cro·ton** \'krō-t²n\ *noun* [New Latin, genus name, from Greek *krotōn* castor-oil plant] (1751)
**1 :** any of a genus (Croton) of herbs, shrubs, and trees of the spurge family: as **a :** one (C. *eluteria*) of the Bahamas yielding cascarilla bark **b :** an Asian plant (C. *tiglium*) yielding croton oil
**2 :** any of a genus (Codiaeum) of shrubs and trees related to the crotons

**Cro·ton bug** \'krō-t²n-\ *noun* [*Croton* River, N.Y., used as a water supply for New York City] (1877)
**:** GERMAN COCKROACH

**croton oil** *noun* (circa 1831)
**:** a viscid acrid fixed oil from an Asian croton (*Croton tiglium*) formerly used as a drastic cathartic but now used especially in pharmacological experiments as an irritant

**crouch** \'kraùch\ *verb* [Middle English] (14th century)
*intransitive verb*
**1 a :** to lower the body stance especially by bending the legs ⟨a sprinter *crouched* ready to go⟩ **b :** to lie close to the ground with the legs bent ⟨a pair of cats, *crouching* on the brink of a fight —Aldous Huxley⟩
**2 :** to bend or bow servilely **:** CRINGE
*transitive verb*
**:** to bow especially in humility or fear **:** BEND
— **crouch** *noun*

**¹croup** \'krüp\ *noun* [Middle English *croupe*, from Old French, of Germanic origin; akin to Old High German *kropf* craw — more at CROP] (14th century)
**:** the rump of a quadruped

**²croup** *noun* [English dialect *croup* to cry hoarsely, cough, probably of imitative origin] (1765)

: a spasmodic laryngitis especially of infants marked by episodes of difficult breathing and hoarse metallic cough
— **croup·ous** \'krü-pəs\ *adjective*
— **croupy** \-pē\ *adjective*
**crou·pi·er** \'krü-pē-ər, -pē-ˌā\ *noun* [French, literally, rider on the croup of a horse, from *croupe* croup] (1709)
: an employee of a gambling casino who collects and pays bets and assists at the gaming tables
**crouse** \'krüs\ *adjective* [Middle English] (15th century)
*chiefly Scottish* : BRISK, LIVELY
**crous·tade** \krü-'städ\ *noun* [French, probably from Italian *crostata* tart, from *crosta* pastry shell, crust, from Latin *crusta* — more at CRUST] (circa 1845)
: a crisp shell (as of toast or puff pastry) in which to serve food
**crou·ton** \'krü-ˌtän, krü-'\ *noun* [French *croûton*, diminutive of *croûte* crust, from Middle French *crouste*, from Old French, from Latin *crusta*] (1806)
: a small cube of toasted or crisply fried bread
¹**crow** \'krō\ *noun* [Middle English *crowe*, from Old English *crāwe*; akin to Old High German *krāwa* crow, Old English *crāwan* to crow] (before 12th century)
**1** : any of various large usually entirely glossy black passerine birds (family Corvidae and especially genus *Corvus*)
**2** *capitalized* **a** : a member of an American Indian people of the region between the Platte and Yellowstone rivers **b** : the language of the Crow people
**3** *capitalized* : CORVUS
— **as the crow flies** : in a straight line
²**crow** *verb* **crowed** \'krōd\ *also in sense 1 chiefly British* **crew** \'krü\; **crow·ing** [Middle English, from Old English *crāwan*] (before 12th century)
*intransitive verb*
**1** : to make the loud shrill sound characteristic of a cock
**2** : to utter a sound expressive of pleasure
**3 a** : to exult gloatingly especially over the distress of another **b** : to brag exultantly or blatantly
*transitive verb*
: to say with self-satisfaction
**synonym** see BOAST
³**crow** *noun* (13th century)
**1** : the cry of the cock
**2** : a triumphant cry
**crow·bar** \'krō-ˌbär\ *noun* (1748)
: an iron or steel bar that is usually wedge-shaped at the working end for use as a pry or lever
— **crowbar** *transitive verb*
**crow·ber·ry** \'krō-ˌber-ē\ *noun* (1597)
**1** : an evergreen subshrub (*Empetrum nigrum* of the family Empetraceae) of arctic and alpine regions with an insipid black berry
**2** : the fruit of a crowberry
¹**crowd** \'kraüd\ *verb* [Middle English *crouden*, from Old English *crūdan*; akin to Middle High German *kroten* to crowd, Old English *crod* multitude, Middle Irish *gruth* curds] (before 12th century)
*intransitive verb*
**1 a** : to press on : HURRY **b** : to press close
**2** : to collect in numbers
*transitive verb*
**1 a** : to fill by pressing or thronging together **b** : to press, force, or thrust into a small space
**2** : PUSH, FORCE — often used with *off* or *out*
**3 a** : to urge on **b** : to put on (sail) in excess of the usual for greater speed
**4** : to put pressure on ⟨don't *crowd* me, I'll pay⟩
**5** : THRONG, JOSTLE
**6** : to press or stand close to
²**crowd** *noun* (1567)
**1** : a large number of persons especially when collected together : THRONG

**2 a** : the great body of the people : POPULACE
**b** : most of one's peers ⟨follow the *crowd*⟩
**3** : a large number of things close together
**4** : a group of people having something (as a habit, interest, or occupation) in common ⟨in with the wrong *crowd*⟩ ☆
³**crowd** \'kraüd, 'krüd\ *noun* [Middle English *crowde*, from Middle Welsh *crwth*] (14th century)
**1** : an ancient Celtic stringed instrument that is plucked or bowed — called also *crwth*
**2** *dialect English* : VIOLIN

**crowd 1**

**crowd·ed·ness** \'kraü-dəd-nəs\ *noun* (1823)
: the quality or state of being crowded
**crow·die** \'kraü-dē\ *noun* [alteration of *crud* curd] (1820)
: a Scottish cottage cheese that is partially cooked
**crow·foot** \'krō-ˌfüt\ *noun, plural* **crow·feet** \-ˌfēt\ (14th century)
**1** *plural usually* **crow·foots** : any of numerous plants having leaves with cleft lobes; especially : BUTTERCUP
**2** : CROW'S-FOOT 1 — usually used in plural
**crow·keep·er** \'krō-ˌkē-pər\ *noun* (1562)
*dialect English* : a person employed to scare off crows
¹**crown** \'kraün\ *noun, often attributive* [Middle English *coroune, crowne*, from Old French *corone*, from Latin *corona* wreath, crown, from Greek *korōnē* culmination, something curved like a crow's beak, literally, crow; akin to Latin *cornix* crow, Greek *korax* raven — more at RAVEN] (12th century)
**1** : a reward of victory or mark of honor; *especially* : the title representing the championship in a sport
**2** : a royal or imperial headdress or cap of sovereignty : DIADEM
**3** : the highest part: as **a** : the topmost part of the skull or head **b** : the summit of a mountain **c** : the head of foliage of a tree or shrub **d** : the part of a hat or other headgear covering the crown of the head **e** : the part of a tooth external to the gum or an artificial substitute for this — see TOOTH illustration
**4** : a wreath, band, or circular ornament for the head
**5 a** : something resembling a wreath or crown **b** : the knurled cap on top of a watch stem
**6** *often capitalized* **a** (1) : imperial or regal power : SOVEREIGNTY (2) : the government under a constitutional monarchy **b** : MONARCH
**7** : something that imparts splendor, honor, or finish : CULMINATION
**8 a** : any of several old gold coins with a crown as part of the device **b** : an old usually silver British coin worth five shillings
**9 a** : KORUNA **b** : KRONA **c** : KRONE
**10 a** : the region of a seed plant at which stem and root merge **b** : the thick arching end of the shank of an anchor where the arms join it — see ANCHOR illustration
— **crowned** \'kraünd\ *adjective*
— **crown·less** \-ləs\ *adjective*
²**crown** *verb* [Middle English *corounen*, from Old French *coroner*, from Latin *coronare*, from *corona*] (12th century)
*transitive verb*
**1 a** : to place a crown or wreath on the head of; *specifically* : to invest with regal dignity and power **b** : to recognize officially as ⟨they *crowned* her athlete of the year⟩
**2** : to bestow something on as a mark of honor or recompense : ADORN
**3** : SURMOUNT, TOP; *especially* : to top (a checker) with a checker to make a king
**4** : to bring to a successful conclusion : CLIMAX

**5** : to provide with something like a crown: as **a** : to fill so that the surface forms a crown **b** : to put an artificial crown on (a tooth)
**6** : to hit on the head
*intransitive verb*
*of a forest fire* : to burn rapidly through the tops of trees
**crown colony** *noun, often both Cs capitalized* (1845)
: a colony of the Commonwealth over which the Crown retains some control
**crown court** *noun* (1827)
: a court in England and Wales that exercises jurisdiction over matters formerly heard by the quarter sessions and criminal matters formerly heard by the courts of assize
**crow·ner** \'krü-nər, 'kraü-\ *noun* [Middle English, alteration of *coroner*] (14th century)
*dialect chiefly English* : CORONER
**crown·et** \'kraü-nət\ *noun* (15th century)
*archaic* : CORONET
**crown gall** *noun* (1900)
: a disease that affects many species of plants and is caused by a bacterium (*Agrobacterium tumefaciens*) which forms tumorous enlargements just below the ground on the stem
**crown glass** *noun* (1706)
**1** : a glass blown and whirled into the form of a disk with a center lump left by the worker's rod
**2** : alkali-lime silicate optical glass having relatively low index of refraction and low dispersion value
**crown jewel** *noun* (1649)
**1** *plural* : the jewels (as crown and scepter) belonging to a sovereign's regalia
**2** : the most attractive or valuable one of a collection or group
**crown land** *noun* (circa 1625)
**1** : land belonging to the crown and yielding revenues that the reigning sovereign is entitled to
**2** : public land in some British dominions or colonies
**crown of thorns** (1964)
: a starfish (*Acanthaster planci*) of the Pacific region that is covered with long spines and is destructive to the coral of coral reefs — called also *crown-of-thorns starfish*
**crown prince** *noun* (1791)
: a male heir apparent to a crown or throne
**crown princess** *noun* (1863)
**1** : the wife of a crown prince
**2** : a female heir apparent or heir presumptive to a crown or throne
**crown roast** *noun* (circa 1909)
: a fancy roast of lamb, veal, or pork made from the rib portions of two loins skewered together at the ends to form a circle
**crown rust** *noun* (circa 1899)

---

☆ **SYNONYMS**
**Crowd, throng, crush, mob, horde** mean an assembled multitude usually of people. CROWD implies a close gathering and pressing together ⟨a small *crowd* gathered⟩. THRONG strongly suggests movement and pushing ⟨a *throng* of reporters⟩. CRUSH emphasizes the compactness of the group, the difficulty of individual movement, and the attendant discomfort ⟨a *crush* of fans⟩. MOB implies a disorderly crowd with the potential for violence ⟨an angry *mob* outside the jail⟩. HORDE suggests a rushing or tumultuous crowd ⟨a *horde* of shoppers⟩.

---

\ə\ **abut** \ᵊ\ **kitten** \ər\ **further** \a\ **ash** \ā\ **ace** \ä\ **mop, mar** \au̇\ **out** \ch\ **chin** \e\ **bet** \ē\ **easy** \g\ **go** \i\ **hit** \ī\ **ice** \j\ **job** \ŋ\ **sing** \ō\ **go** \ȯ\ **law** \ȯi\ **boy** \th\ **thin** \t̲h̲\ **the** \ü\ **loot** \u̇\ **foot** \y\ **yet** \zh\ **vision** · *see also* Guide to Pronunciation

: a leaf rust of oats and other grasses that is caused by a fungus (*Puccinia coronata*) and is characterized by rounded light-orange uredinia and buried telia

**crown vetch** *noun* (circa 1900)
: a European leguminous herb (*Coronilla varia*) that is naturalized in the eastern U.S. and has umbels of pink-and-white flowers and sharp-angled pods

**crow's–foot** \'krōz-ˌfůt\ *noun*, *plural* **crow's–feet** \-ˌfēt\ (14th century)
**1** : a wrinkle extending from the outer corner of the eye — usually used in plural
**2** : CROWFOOT 1

**crow's nest** *noun* (1818)
: a partly enclosed platform high on a ship's mast for use as a lookout; *also* : a similar lookout (as for traffic control)

**crow·step** \'krō-ˌstep\ *noun* (1822)
: any of a series of steps at the top of a gable wall
— **crow·stepped** \-ˌstept\ *adjective*

**cro·zier** *variant of* CROSIER

**CRT** \ˌsē-(ˌ)är-'tē\ *noun*, *plural* **CRTs** *or* **CRT's** (circa 1945)
: CATHODE-RAY TUBE; *also* : a display device incorporating a cathode-ray tube

**cruces** *plural of* CRUX

**cru·cial** \'krü-shəl\ *adjective* [French, from Latin *cruc-*, *crux* cross] (1706)
**1** *archaic* : CRUCIFORM
**2 a** : important or essential as resolving a crisis : DECISIVE ⟨a *crucial* step⟩ **b** : marked by final determination of a doubtful issue ⟨the *crucial* game of a series⟩ **c** : IMPORTANT, SIGNIFICANT ⟨what use we make of them will be the *crucial* question —Stanley Kubrick⟩
*synonym* see ACUTE

**cru·cial·ly** \'krü-sh(ə-)lē\ *adverb* (1879)
**1** : in a crucial manner
**2** : very importantly

**cru·cian carp** \'krü-shən-\ *noun* [modification of Low German *karuse*, from Middle Low German *karusse*, perhaps of Baltic origin; akin to Lithuanian *karušis* carp] (1836)
: a European carp (*Carassius carassius*) — called also *crucian*

**cru·ci·ate** \'krü-shē-ˌāt\ *adjective* [New Latin *cruciatus*, from Latin *cruc-*, *crux*] (1826)
: cross-shaped : CRUCIFORM

**cru·ci·ble** \'krü-sə-bəl\ *noun* [Middle English *corusible*, from Medieval Latin *crucibulum* earthen pot for melting metals] (15th century)
**1** : a vessel of a very refractory material (as porcelain) used for melting and calcining a substance that requires a high degree of heat
**2** : a severe test
**3** : a place or situation in which concentrated forces interact to cause or influence change or development ⟨conditioned by having grown up within the *crucible* of Chinatown —Tom Wolfe⟩

**crucible steel** *noun* (circa 1879)
: hard cast steel made in pots that are lifted from the furnace before the metal is poured into molds

**cru·ci·fer** \'krü-sə-fər\ *noun* [Late Latin, from Latin *cruc-*, *crux* + *-fer*] (1574)
**1** : one who carries a cross especially at the head of an ecclesiastical procession
**2** : any of a family (Cruciferae) of plants including the cabbage, turnip, and mustard
— **cru·cif·er·ous** \krü-'si-f(ə-)rəs\ *adjective*

**cru·ci·fix** \'krü-sə-ˌfiks\ *noun* [Middle English, from Late Latin *crucifixus* the crucified Christ, from *crucifixus*, past participle of *crucifigere* to crucify, from Latin *cruc-*, *crux* + *figere* to fasten — more at FIX] (13th century)
: a representation of Christ on the cross

**cru·ci·fix·ion** \ˌkrü-sə-'fik-shən\ *noun* (15th century)
**1 a** *capitalized* : the crucifying of Christ **b** : the act of crucifying
**2** : extreme and painful punishment, affliction, or suffering

**cru·ci·form** \'krü-sə-ˌfȯrm\ *adjective* [Latin *cruc-*, *crux* + English *-form*] (1661)
: forming or arranged in a cross
— **cruciform** *noun*

**cru·ci·fy** \'krü-sə-ˌfī\ *transitive verb* **-fied**; **-fy·ing** [Middle English *crucifien*, from Old French *crucifier*, from Late Latin *crucifigere*] (14th century)
**1** : to put to death by nailing or binding the wrists or hands and feet to a cross
**2** : to destroy the power of : MORTIFY ⟨*crucify* the flesh⟩
**3 a** : to treat cruelly : TORMENT **b** : PILLORY 2

**cruck** \'krək\ *noun* [probably from dialect form of ²*crook* (curved timber)] (1888)
: one of a pair of curved timbers forming a principal support of a roof in primitive English house construction

**¹crud** \'krəd\ *noun* [Middle English *curd*, *crudd*] (14th century)
**1** *dialect* : CURD
**2 a** : a deposit or incrustation of filth, grease, or refuse **b** : something disagreeable or disgusting : RUBBISH **c** *slang* : a despicable or contemptible person
**3** : a usually ill-defined or imperfectly identified bodily disorder
— **crud·dy** \'krə-dē\ *adjective*

**²crud** *verb* **crud·ded**; **crud·ding** (14th century)
*dialect* : ²CURD

**¹crude** \'krüd\ *adjective* **crud·er**; **crud·est** [Middle English, from Latin *crudus* raw, crude, undigested — more at RAW] (14th century)
**1** : existing in a natural state and unaltered by cooking or processing ⟨*crude* oil⟩
**2** *archaic* : UNRIPE, IMMATURE
**3** : marked by the primitive, gross, or elemental or by uncultivated simplicity or vulgarity ⟨a *crude* stereotype⟩
**4** : rough or inexpert in plan or execution ⟨a *crude* shelter⟩
**5** : lacking a covering, glossing, or concealing element : OBVIOUS ⟨*crude* facts⟩
**6** : tabulated without being broken down into classes ⟨the *crude* death rate⟩
*synonym* see RUDE
— **crude·ly** *adverb*
— **crude·ness** *noun*

**²crude** *noun* (1904)
: a substance in its natural unprocessed state; *especially* : unrefined petroleum

**cru·di·tés** \krə-dē-tā, ˌkrü-di-'tā\ *noun plural* [French, from plural of *crudité* rawness, from Latin *cruditas* indigestion, from *crudus*] (1960)
: pieces of raw vegetables (as celery or carrot sticks) served as an hors d'oeuvre often with a dip

**cru·di·ty** \'krü-də-tē\ *noun*, *plural* **-ties** (1547)
**1** : the quality or state of being crude
**2** : something that is crude

**cru·el** \'krü(-ə)l\ *adjective* **cru·el·er** *or* **cru·el·ler**; **cru·el·est** *or* **cru·el·lest** [Middle English, from Old French, from Latin *crudelis*, from *crudus*] (14th century)
**1** : disposed to inflict pain or suffering : devoid of humane feelings
**2 a** : causing or conducive to injury, grief, or pain ⟨a *cruel* joke⟩ **b** : unrelieved by leniency
*synonym* see FIERCE
— **cru·el·ly** \'krü-(ə-)lē\ *adverb*
— **cru·el·ness** *noun*

**cru·el·ty** \'krü(-ə)l-tē\ *noun*, *plural* **-ties** [Middle English *cruelte*, from Old French *cruelté*, from Latin *crudelitat-*, *crudelitas*, from *crudelis*] (13th century)
**1** : the quality or state of being cruel
**2 a** : a cruel action **b** : inhuman treatment
**3** : marital conduct held (as in a divorce action) to endanger life or health or to cause mental suffering or fear

**cru·et** \'krü-ət\ *noun* [Middle English, from Anglo-French, diminutive of Old French *crue*,

of Germanic origin; akin to Old English *crūce*] (14th century)
**1** : a vessel to hold wine or water for the Eucharist
**2** : a usually glass bottle used to hold a condiment (as oil or vinegar) for use at the table

**¹cruise** \'krüz\ *verb* **cruised**; **cruis·ing** [Dutch *kruisen* to make a cross, cruise, from Middle Dutch *crucen*, from *crūce* cross, from Latin *cruc-*, *crux*] (1651)
*intransitive verb*
**1** : to sail about touching at a series of ports
**2** : to move or proceed speedily, smoothly, or effortlessly ⟨I'll *cruise* over to her house to see if she's home⟩
**3** : to travel without destination or purpose
**4 a** : to go about the streets at random but on the lookout for possible developments ⟨the cabdriver *cruised* for an hour before being hailed⟩ **b** : to search (as in public places) for a sexual partner
**5 a** *of an airplane* : to fly at the most efficient operating speed **b** *of an automobile* : to travel at a speed suitable for being maintained for a long distance
*transitive verb*
**1** : to cruise over or about
**2** : to inspect (as land) with reference to possible lumber yield
**3 a** : to search in (a public place) for a sexual partner **b** : to approach and suggest sexual relations to

**²cruise** *noun* (circa 1706)
: an act or an instance of cruising; *especially* : a tour by ship

**cruise control** *noun* (1968)
**1** : an electronic device in an automobile that controls the throttle so as to maintain a constant speed
**2** : a relaxed and seemingly automatic pace that is easily maintained

**cruise missile** *noun* (1959)
: a guided missile that has a terrain-following radar system and that flies at moderate speed and low altitude

**cruis·er** \'krü-zər\ *noun* (1695)
**1** : a vehicle that cruises: as **a** : SQUAD CAR **b** : a powerboat with facilities (as a cabin and plumbing) necessary for living aboard — called also *cabin cruiser*
**2** : a large fast moderately armored and gunned warship usually of 6000 to 15,000 tons displacement
**3** : a person who cruises

**crul·ler** \'krə-lər\ *noun* [Dutch *krulle*, a twisted cake, from *krul* curly, from Middle Dutch *crul* — more at CURL] (1818)
**1** : a small sweet cake in the form of a twisted strip fried in deep fat
**2** *Northern & Midland* : an unraised doughnut

**¹crumb** \'krəm\ *noun* [Middle English *crumme*, from Old English *cruma*; akin to Middle High German *krume* crumb] (before 12th century)
**1 a** : a small fragment especially of something baked (as bread) **b** : a porous aggregate of soil particles
**2** : BIT ⟨a *crumb* of good news⟩
**3** : the soft part of bread
**4** *slang* : a worthless person

**²crumb** *transitive verb* (14th century)
**1** : to break into crumbs
**2** : to cover or thicken with crumbs
**3** : to remove crumbs from ⟨*crumb* a table⟩

**¹crum·ble** \'krəm-bəl\ *verb* **crum·bled**; **crum·bling** \-b(ə-)liŋ\ [alteration of Middle English *kremelen*, frequentative of Old English *gecrymian* to crumble, from *cruma*] (1570)
*transitive verb*
: to break into small pieces
*intransitive verb*
**1** : to fall into small pieces : DISINTEGRATE
**2** : to break down completely : COLLAPSE ⟨marriages *crumble*⟩

**²crumble** *noun* (1820)

**1** : something crumbled : fine debris
**2** : CRISP 2
**crum·blings** \'krəm-b(ə-)liŋz\ *noun plural* (1660)
: crumbled particles : CRUMBS
**crum·bly** \-b(ə-)lē\ *adjective* **crum·bli·er;
-est** (1523)
: easily crumbled : FRIABLE ⟨*crumbly* soil⟩
— **crum·bli·ness** *noun*
**crumb structure** *noun* (circa 1906)
: a soil condition suitable for farming in which
the soil particles are aggregated into crumbs
**crumhorn** *variant of* KRUMMHORN
**crum·mie** *or* **crum·my** \'krə-mē\ *noun, plural* **crummies** [Scots *crumb* crooked, from
Middle English, from Old English] (1724)
*chiefly Scottish* : COW; *especially* : one with
crumpled horns
**crum·my** *also* **crumby** \'krə-mē\ *adjective*
**crum·mi·er** *also* **crumb·i·er; -est** [Middle
English *crumme*] (1567)
**1** *obsolete* : CRUMBLY
**2 a** : MISERABLE, FILTHY **b** : CHEAP, WORTHLESS
— **crum·mi·ness** *noun*
**¹crump** \'krəmp\ *intransitive verb* [imitative]
(1646)
**1** : CRUNCH
**2** : to explode heavily
**²crump** *noun* (1914)
**1** : a crunching sound
**2** : SHELL, BOMB
**³crump** *adjective* [perhaps alteration of *crimp*]
friable (1787)
*chiefly Scottish* : BRITTLE
**crum·pet** \'krəm-pət\ *noun* [perhaps from
Middle English *crompid* (*cake*) wafer, literally,
curled-up cake, from *crumped*, past participle
of *crumpen* to curl up, from *crump, crumb*
crooked, from Old English *crumb*; akin to Old
High German *krump* crooked] (1769)
: a small round unsweetened bread cooked on
a griddle and usually split and toasted before
serving
**¹crum·ple** \'krəm-pəl\ *verb* **crum·pled;
crum·pling** \-p(ə-)liŋ\ [Middle English
*crumplen*, frequentative of Middle English
*crumpen*] (14th century)
*transitive verb*
**1** : to press, bend, or crush out of shape : RUM-
PLE
**2** : to cause to collapse
*intransitive verb*
**1** : to become crumpled
**2** : COLLAPSE
**²crumple** *noun* (15th century)
: a wrinkle or crease made by crumpling
— **crum·ply** \'krəm-p(ə-)lē\ *adjective*
**¹crunch** \'krənch\ *verb* [alteration of *craunch*]
(1814)
*intransitive verb*
**1** : to chew or press with a crushing noise
**2** : to make one's way with a crushing noise
*transitive verb*
**1** : to chew, press, or grind with a crunching
sound
**2** : PROCESS; *especially* : to perform mathematical computations on ⟨*crunch* numbers⟩
— **crunch·able** \'krən-chə-bəl\ *adjective*
**²crunch** *noun* (1836)
**1** : an act of crunching
**2** : a sound made by crunching
**3** : a tight or critical situation: as **a** : a critical
point in the buildup of pressure between opposing elements : SHOWDOWN **b** : a severe economic squeeze (as on credit) **c** : SHORTAGE ⟨an
energy *crunch*⟩
**crunch·er** \'krən-chər\ *noun* (1946)
**1** : one that crunches
**2** : a finishing blow
**crunchy** \'krən-chē\ *adjective* **crunch·i·er;
-est** (1913)
: making a crunching sound when chewed or
pressed
— **crunch·i·ly** \-chə-lē\ *adverb*
— **crunch·i·ness** \-chē-nəs\ *noun*

**crup·per** \'krə-pər, 'krù-\ *noun* [Middle English *cruper*, from Old French *crupiere*, from
*croupe* hindquarters — more at CROUP] (14th
century)
**1** : a leather loop passing under a horse's tail
and buckled to the saddle
**2** : ¹CROUP; *broadly* : BUTTOCKS
**cru·ral** \'krùr-əl\ *adjective* [Latin *crur-, crus*
leg] (1599)
: of or relating to the thigh or leg; *specifically*
: FEMORAL ⟨*crural* artery⟩
**crus** \'krüs, 'krəs\ *noun, plural* **cru·ra** \'krùr-ə\
[Latin *crur-, crus*] (circa 1751)
: any of various anatomical parts that resemble
a leg or a pair of legs
**¹cru·sade** \krü-'sād\ *noun* [blend of Middle
French *croisade* & Spanish *cruzada*; both ultimately from Latin *cruc-, crux* cross] (circa
1708)
**1** *capitalized* : any of the military expeditions
undertaken by Christian powers in the 11th,
12th, and 13th centuries to win the Holy Land
from the Muslims
**2** : a remedial enterprise undertaken with zeal
and enthusiasm ◆
**²crusade** *intransitive verb* **cru·sad·ed;
cru·sad·ing** (1732)
: to engage in a crusade
— **cru·sad·er** *noun*
**cru·sa·do** \krü-'sā-(ˌ)dō\ *also* **cru·za·do**
\-'zä-(ˌ)dō, -(ˌ)dü\ *noun, plural* **-does** *or* **-dos**
[Portuguese *cruzado*, literally, marked with a
cross] (1544)
: an old gold or silver coin of Portugal having
a cross on the reverse
**cruse** \'krüz, 'krüs\ *noun* [Middle English;
akin to Old English *crūse* pitcher] (13th century)
: a small vessel (as a jar or pot) for holding a
liquid (as water or oil)
**¹crush** \'krəsh\ *verb* [Middle English *crusshen*,
from Middle French *cruisir*, of Germanic origin; akin to Middle Low German *krossen* to
crush] (15th century)
*transitive verb*
**1 a** : to squeeze or force by pressure so as to
alter or destroy structure **b** : to squeeze together into a mass
**2** : HUG, EMBRACE
**3** : to reduce to particles by pounding or
grinding
**4 a** : to suppress or overwhelm as if by pressure or weight **b** : to oppress or burden grievously **c** : to subdue completely
**5** : CROWD, PUSH
**6** *archaic* : DRINK
*intransitive verb*
**1** *obsolete* : CRASH
**2** : to become crushed
**3** : to advance with or as if with crushing
— **crush·able** \'krə-shə-bəl\ *adjective*
— **crush·er** *noun*
— **crush·ing·ly** *adverb*
**²crush** *noun* (1599)
**1** : an act of crushing
**2** : the quantity of material crushed
**3 a** : a crowding together (as of people) **b**
: CROWD, MOB; *especially* : a crowd of people
pressing against one another
**4** : an intense and usually passing infatuation
⟨have a *crush* on someone⟩; *also* : the object
of infatuation
**synonym** *see* CROWD
— **crush-proof** \-ˌprüf\ *adjective*
**crust** \'krəst\ *noun* [Middle English, from Latin *crusta*; akin to Old English *hrūse* earth,
Greek *kryos* icy cold, *krystallos* ice, crystal]
(14th century)
**1 a** : the hardened exterior or surface part of
bread **b** : a piece of this or of bread grown dry
or hard
**2** : the pastry cover of a pie

**3** : a hard or brittle external coat or covering:
as **a** : a hard surface layer (as of soil or snow)
**b** : the outer part of a planet, moon, or asteroid
composed essentially of crystalline rocks **c** : a
deposit built up on the interior surface of a
wine bottle during long aging **d** : an encrusting deposit of dried secretions or exudate; *especially* : SCAB
**4** : GALL, NERVE
— **crust** *verb*
— **crust·al** \'krəs-t°l\ *adjective*
— **crust·less** \'krəs(t)-ləs\ *adjective*
**crus·ta·cea** \ˌkrəs-'tā-sh(ē-)ə\ *noun plural*
[New Latin, group name, from neuter plural of
*crustaceus*] (1814)
: arthropods that are crustaceans
**crus·ta·cean** \ˌkrəs-'tā-shən\ *noun* (1835)
: any of a large class (Crustacea) of mostly
aquatic mandibulate arthropods that have a
chitinous or calcareous and chitinous exoskeleton, a pair of often much modified appendages on each segment, and two pairs of antennae
and that include the lobsters, shrimps, crabs,
wood lice, water fleas, and barnacles
— **crustacean** *adjective*
**crus·ta·ceous** \-shəs\ *adjective* [New Latin
*crustaceus*, from Latin *crusta* crust, shell] (circa 1656)
: of, relating to, having, or forming a crust or
shell; *especially* : CRUSTOSE
**crus·tose** \'krəs-ˌtōs\ *adjective* [Latin *crusto-
sus* crusted, from *crusta*] (circa 1879)
: having a thin thallus adhering closely to a
substrate (as of rock, bark, or soil) ⟨*crustose*
lichens⟩ — compare FOLIOSE, FRUTICOSE
**crusty** \'krəs-tē\ *adjective* **crust·i·er; -est**
(14th century)
**1** : having or being a crust
**2** : giving an effect of surly incivility in address or disposition
**synonym** *see* BLUFF
— **crust·i·ly** \-tə-lē\ *adverb*
— **crust·i·ness** \-tē-nəs\ *noun*
**¹crutch** \'krəch\ *noun* [Middle English
*crucche*, from Old English *crycc*; akin to Old
High German *krucka* crutch] (before 12th century)
**1 a** : a support typically fitting under the armpit for use by the disabled in walking **b** : PROP,
STAY
**2** : a forked leg rest constituting the pommel
of a sidesaddle
**3** : the crotch of a human being or an animal

---

◇ **WORD HISTORY**
**crusade**   In 1095 when Palestinian lands
sacred to Christians were held by Muslims,
Pope Urban II convoked a council at
Clermont-Ferrand in France and exhorted
the assembly to go forth and reclaim the
Holy Sepulcher and other venerated sites
from the infidels. Those who responded to
the call wore on their breasts crosses of
cloth to identify themselves as soldiers in
Christ's army. These crosses would provide
the name for their enterprise and succeeding
invasions of the Holy Land in following centuries. Medieval French words for such a holy
war against infidels were *croisement, croi-
serie, croisée*, and *croisade*, all derivatives of
*crois* "cross." The last word, *croisade*, was
formed under the influence of Old Provençal
*crozata* and Spanish *cruzada*, likewise
formed from words meaning "cross." English
borrowed both French *croisade* and Spanish
*cruzada*, blending the two to produce *crusade* in the 18th century, long after the crusades themselves had ceased.

---

\ə\ abut \ᵊ\ kitten \ər\ further \a\ ash \ā\ ace
\ä\ mop, mar \aù\ out \ch\ chin \e\ bet \ē\ easy
\g\ go \i\ hit \ī\ ice \j\ job \ŋ\ sing \ō\ go
\ò\ law \òi\ boy \th\ thin \t͟h\ the \ü\ loot \ù\ foot
\y\ yet \zh\ vision   *see also* Guide to Pronunciation

**4 :** a forked support
**²crutch** *transitive verb* (1681)
**:** to support on crutches **:** prop up
**crux** \'krəks, 'krŭks\ *noun, plural* **crux·es** *also* **cru·ces** \'krü-,sēz\ [Latin *cruc-, crux* cross, torture] (1718)
**1 :** a puzzling or difficult problem **:** an unsolved question
**2 :** an essential point requiring resolution or resolving an outcome ⟨the *crux* of the problem⟩
**3 :** a main or central feature (as of an argument)
**cru·za·do** \krü-'zä-(,)dō, -(,)dü\ *noun, plural* **-dos** [Portuguese] (1986)
**:** the basic monetary unit of Brazil 1986–90
**Cru·zan** \krü-'zan\ *noun* [(assumed) American Spanish *cruzano,* from *Santa Cruz* Saint Croix] (1958)
**:** a native or inhabitant of Saint Croix
**— Cruzan** *adjective*
**cru·zei·ro** \krü-'zer-(,)ō, -(,)ü\ *noun, plural* **-ros** [Portuguese] (1927)
**:** the basic monetary unit of Brazil 1942–85 and 1991–93
**crwth** \'krüth\ *noun* [Welsh] (circa 1837)
**:** ³CROWD 1
**¹cry** \'krī\ *verb* **cried; cry·ing** [Middle English *crien,* from Old French *crier,* from Latin *quiritare* to make a public outcry, perhaps from *Quirit-, Quiris,* name for the Roman citizen] (13th century)
*transitive verb*
**1 :** to utter loudly **:** SHOUT
**2** *archaic* **:** BEG, BESEECH
**3 :** to proclaim publicly **:** ADVERTISE ⟨*cry* their wares⟩
*intransitive verb*
**1 :** to call loudly **:** SHOUT
**2 :** to shed tears often noisily **:** WEEP, SOB
**3 :** to utter a characteristic sound or call
**4 :** to require or suggest strongly a remedy or disposition ⟨a hundred things which *cry* out for planning —Roger Burlingame⟩
**— cry havoc :** to sound an alarm
**— cry over spilled milk :** to express vain regrets for what cannot be recovered or undone
**— cry wolf :** to give alarm unnecessarily
**²cry** *noun, plural* **cries** (13th century)
**1 :** an instance of crying: as **a :** an inarticulate utterance of distress, rage, or pain **b** *obsolete* **:** OUTCRY, CLAMOR
**2 a** *obsolete* **:** PROCLAMATION **b** *plural, Scottish* **:** BANNS
**3 :** ENTREATY, APPEAL
**4 :** a loud shout
**5 :** WATCHWORD, SLOGAN
**6 a :** common report **b :** a general opinion
**7 :** the public voice raised in protest or approval
**8 :** a fit of weeping
**9 :** the characteristic sound or call of an animal
**10 a :** a pack of hounds **b :** PURSUIT — used in the phrase *in full cry*
**11 :** DISTANCE — usually used in the phrase *a far cry*
**cry- or cryo-** *combining form* [German *kryo-,* from Greek, from *kryos* — more at CRUST]
**:** cold **:** freezing ⟨*cryonics*⟩ ⟨*cryogen*⟩
**cry·ba·by** \'krī-,bā-bē\ *noun* (1851)
**:** one who cries or complains easily or often
**cry down** *transitive verb* (1598)
**:** DISPARAGE, DEPRECIATE
**cry·ing** \'krī-iŋ\ *adjective* (1607)
**1 :** calling for notice ⟨a *crying* need⟩
**2 :** NOTORIOUS, HEINOUS ⟨a *crying* shame⟩
**cryo·bi·ol·o·gy** \,krī-ō-bī-'ä-lə-jē\ *noun* (1960)
**:** the study of the effects of extremely low temperature on biological systems
**— cryo·bi·o·log·i·cal** \-,bī-ə-'lä-ji-kəl\ *adjective*
**— cryo·bi·ol·o·gist** \-bī-'ä-lə-jist\ *noun*
**cry off** (1928)

*transitive verb*
**:** to call off (as a bargain)
*intransitive verb*
*chiefly British* **:** to beg off
**cryo·gen** \'krī-ə-jən\ *noun* (1875)
**:** a substance for obtaining low temperatures **:** REFRIGERANT — called also *cryogenic*
**cryo·gen·ic** \,krī-ə-'je-nik\ *adjective* (1896)
**1 a :** of or relating to the production of very low temperatures **b :** being or relating to very low temperatures
**2 a :** requiring or involving the use of a cryogenic temperature **b :** requiring cryogenic storage **c :** suitable for storage of a cryogenic substance
**— cryo·gen·i·cal·ly** \-ni-k(ə-)lē\ *adverb*
**cryo·gen·ics** \-niks\ *noun plural but singular in construction* (circa 1934)
**:** a branch of physics that deals with the production and effects of very low temperatures
**cryo·lite** \'krī-ə-,līt\ *noun* (1801)
**:** a mineral consisting of a fluoride of sodium and aluminum found in Greenland usually in white cleavable masses and used as a source of aluminum
**cry·on·ics** \krī-'ä-niks\ *noun plural but usually singular in construction* [*cry-* + *-onics* (as in *electronics*)] (1967)
**:** the practice of freezing a dead diseased human in hopes of restoring life at some future time when a cure for the disease has been developed
**— cry·on·ic** \-nik\ *adjective*
**cryo·phil·ic** \,krī-ə-'fi-lik\ *adjective* (1942)
**:** thriving at low temperatures
**cryo·pres·er·va·tion** \,krī-ō-,pre-zər-'vā-shən\ *noun* (1968)
**:** preservation (as of cells) by subjection to extremely low temperatures
**— cryo·pre·serve** \,krī-ō-pri-'zərv, 'krī-ō-pri-,\ *transitive verb*
**cryo·probe** \'krī-ə-,prōb\ *noun* (1965)
**:** a blunt chilled instrument used to freeze tissues in cryosurgery
**cryo·pro·tec·tive** \,krī-ō-prə-'tek-tiv\ *adjective* (1967)
**:** serving to protect from freezing ⟨an extracellular *cryoprotective* agent⟩
**— cryo·pro·tec·tant** \-'tek-tənt\ *noun or adjective*
**cryo·scope** \'krī-ə-,skōp\ *noun* (1920)
**:** an instrument for determining freezing points
**cry·os·co·py** \krī-'äs-kə-pē\ *noun* [International Scientific Vocabulary] (circa 1900)
**:** the determination of the lowered freezing points produced in liquid by dissolved substances in order to determine molecular weights of solutes and various properties of solutions
**— cryo·scop·ic** \,krī-ə-'skä-pik\ *adjective*
**cryo·stat** \'krī-ə-,stat\ *noun* [International Scientific Vocabulary] (1913)
**:** an apparatus for maintaining a constant low temperature especially below 0°C
**— cryo·stat·ic** \,krī-ə-'sta-tik\ *adjective*
**cryo·sur·gery** \,krī-ō-'sərj-rē, -'sər-jə-\ *noun* (1962)
**:** surgery in which the tissue to be treated or operated on is frozen (as by liquid nitrogen)
**— cryo·sur·geon** \-'sər-jən\ *noun*
**— cryo·sur·gi·cal** \-ji-kəl\ *adjective*
**cryo·ther·a·py** \-'ther-ə-pē\ *noun* (1926)
**:** the therapeutic use of cold
**crypt** \'kript\ *noun* [Latin *crypta,* from Greek *kryptē,* from feminine of *kryptos* hidden, from *kryptein* to hide; perhaps akin to Lithuanian *krauti* to pile up] (1789)
**1 a :** a chamber (as a vault) wholly or partly underground; *especially* **:** a vault under the main floor of a church **b :** a chamber in a mausoleum
**2 a :** an anatomical pit or depression **b :** a simple tubular gland
**crypt- or crypto-** *combining form* [New Latin, from Greek *kryptos*]
**1 :** hidden **:** covered ⟨*crypto*genic⟩

**2 :** CRYPTOGRAPHIC ⟨*crypt*analysis⟩
**crypt·anal·y·sis** \,krip-tə-'na-lə-səs\ *noun* (1923)
**1 :** the solving of cryptograms or cryptographic systems
**2 :** the theory of solving cryptograms or cryptographic systems **:** the art of devising methods for this
**— crypt·an·a·lyt·ic** \,krip-,ta-nᵊl-'i-tik\ *also* **crypt·an·a·lyt·i·cal** \-ti-kəl\ *adjective*
**crypt·an·a·lyst** \krip-'ta-nᵊl-ist\ *noun* (1921)
**:** a specialist in cryptanalysis
**cryp·ta·rithm** \'krip-tə-,ri-thəm\ *noun* [*crypt-* + *-arithm* (as in *logarithm*)] (1943)
**:** an arithmetic problem in which letters have been substituted for numbers and which is solved by finding all possible pairings of digits with letters that produce a numerically correct answer
**cryp·tic** \'krip-tik\ *adjective* [Late Latin *crypticus,* from Greek *kryptikos,* from *kryptos*] (circa 1638)
**1 :** SECRET, OCCULT
**2 a :** having or seeming to have a hidden or ambiguous meaning **:** MYSTERIOUS ⟨*cryptic* messages⟩ **b :** marked by an often perplexing brevity ⟨*cryptic* marginal notes⟩
**3 :** serving to conceal ⟨*cryptic* coloration in animals⟩; *also* **:** exhibiting cryptic coloration ⟨*cryptic* animals⟩
**4 :** UNRECOGNIZED ⟨a *cryptic* infection⟩
**5 :** employing cipher or code
*synonym* SEE OBSCURE
**— cryp·ti·cal·ly** \-ti-k(ə-)lē\ *adverb*
**¹cryp·to** \'krip-(,)tō\ *noun, plural* **cryptos** [*crypt-*] (1946)
**:** a person who adheres or belongs secretly to a party, sect, or other group
**²crypto** *adjective* (1952)
**1 :** CRYPTOGRAPHIC
**2 :** not openly avowed or declared — often used in combination ⟨*crypto*-fascist⟩
**cryp·to·coc·co·sis** \,krip-tə-(,)kä-'kō-səs\ *noun, plural* **-co·ses** \-(,)sēz\ [New Latin] (1938)
**:** an infectious disease that is caused by a fungus (*Cryptococcus neoformans*) and is characterized by the production of nodular lesions or abscesses in the lungs, subcutaneous tissues, joints, and especially the brain and meninges
**cryp·to·coc·cus** \-'kä-kəs\ *noun, plural* **-coc·ci** \-'käk-,sī, -,sē, -'kä-,kī, -,kē\ [New Latin] (circa 1902)
**:** any of a genus (*Cryptococcus*) of budding imperfect fungi that resemble yeasts and include a number of saprophytes and a few serious pathogens
**— cryp·to·coc·cal** \-'kä-kəl\ *adjective*
**cryp·to·crys·tal·line** \,krip-tō-'kris-tə-lən\ *adjective* [International Scientific Vocabulary] (1862)
**:** having a crystalline structure so fine that no distinct particles are recognizable under the microscope ⟨*cryptocrystalline* quartz⟩
**cryp·to·gam** \'krip-tə-,gam\ *noun* [ultimately from Greek *kryptos* + *-gamia* -gamy] (1847)
**:** a plant (as a fern, moss, alga, or fungus) reproducing by spores and not producing flowers or seed
**— cryp·to·gam·ic** \,krip-tə-'ga-mik\ *or* **cryp·tog·a·mous** \krip-'tä-gə-məs\ *adjective*
**cryp·to·gen·ic** \,krip-tə-'je-nik\ *adjective* (1908)
**:** of obscure or unknown origin ⟨a *cryptogenic* disease⟩
**cryp·to·gram** \'krip-tə-,gram\ *noun* [French *cryptogramme,* from *crypt-* + *-gramme* -gram] (1880)
**1 :** a communication in cipher or code
**2 :** a figure or representation having a hidden significance
**cryp·to·graph** \'krip-tə-,graf\ *noun* (1849)
**:** CRYPTOGRAM
**cryp·tog·ra·pher** \krip-'tä-grə-fər\ *noun* (1641)

: a specialist in cryptography: as **a** : a clerk who enciphers and deciphers messages **b** : one who devises cryptographic methods or systems **c** : CRYPTANALYST

**cryp·to·graph·ic** \,krip-tə-'gra-fik\ *adjective* (1824)
: of, relating to, or using cryptography
— **cryp·to·graph·i·cal·ly** \-fi-k(ə-)lē\ *adverb*

**cryp·tog·ra·phy** \krip-'tä-grə-fē\ *noun* [New Latin *cryptographia*, from *crypt-* + *-graphia* -graphy] (1658)
**1** : secret writing
**2** : the enciphering and deciphering of messages in secret code or cipher
**3** : CRYPTANALYSIS

**cryp·tol·o·gy** \krip-'tä-lə-jē\ *noun* (1935)
: the scientific study of cryptography and cryptanalysis
— **cryp·to·log·i·cal** \,krip-tə-'lä-ji-kəl\ *or* **cryp·to·log·ic** \-jik\ *adjective*
— **cryp·tol·o·gist** \krip-'tä-lə-jist\ *noun*

**cryp·to·me·ria** \,krip-tə-'mir-ē-ə\ *noun* [New Latin, genus name, from *crypt-* + Greek *meros* part — more at MERIT] (1841)
: an evergreen tree (*Cryptomeria japonica*) of the pine family that is a valuable timber tree of Japan

**cryp·to·nym** \'krip-tə-,nim\ *noun* (1876)
: a secret name

**crypt·or·chid** \krip-'tȯr-kəd\ *noun* [New Latin *cryptorchid-, cryptorchis*, from *crypt-* + *orchid-, orchis* testicle, from Greek *orchis* — more at ORCHIS] (1874)
: one affected with cryptorchidism
— **cryptorchid** *adjective*

**crypt·or·chi·dism** \-kə-,di-zəm\ *or* **crypt·or·chism** \-,ki-zəm\ *noun* (circa 1882)
: a condition in which one or both testes fail to descend normally

**cryp·to·zo·ol·o·gy** \,krip-tə-zō-'ä-lə-jē, -zə-'wä-\ *noun* (1969)
: the study of the lore concerning legendary animals (as Sasquatch) especially in order to evaluate the possibility of their existence
— **cryp·to·zo·ol·o·gist** \-'ä-lə-jist, -'wä-\ *noun*

**¹crys·tal** \'kris-t°l\ *noun* [Middle English *cristal*, from Old French, from Latin *crystallum*, from Greek *krystallos* — more at CRUST] (13th century)
**1** : quartz that is transparent or nearly so and that is either colorless or only slightly tinged
**2** : something resembling crystal in transparency and colorlessness
**3** : a body that is formed by the solidification of a chemical element, a compound, or a mixture and has a regularly repeating internal arrangement of its atoms and often external plane faces
**4** : a clear colorless glass of superior quality; *also* : objects or ware of such glass
**5** : the glass or transparent plastic cover over a watch or clock dial
**6** : a crystalline material used in electronics as a frequency-determining element or for rectification
**7** : powdered methamphetamine

**²crystal** *adjective* (14th century)
**1** : consisting of or resembling crystal : CLEAR, LUCID
**2** : relating to or using a crystal ⟨a *crystal* radio receiver⟩

**crystal ball** *noun* (1855)
**1** : a sphere especially of quartz crystal traditionally used by fortune-tellers
**2** : a means or method of predicting future events

**crystal gazing** *noun* (1889)
**1** : the art or practice of concentrating on a glass or crystal globe with the aim of inducing a psychic state in which divination can be performed
**2** : the attempt to predict future events or make difficult judgments especially without adequate data

— **crystal gazer** *noun*

**crystall-** *or* **crystallo-** *combining form* [Greek *krystallos*]
: crystal ⟨*crystall*ography⟩

**crys·tal·line** \'kris-tə-lən *also* -,līn, -,lēn\ *adjective* [Middle English *cristallin*, from Middle French & Latin; Middle French, from Latin *crystallinus*, from Greek *krystallinos*, from *krystallos*] (15th century)
**1** : resembling crystal: as **a** : strikingly clear or sparkling ⟨*crystalline* air⟩ ⟨a *crystalline* lake⟩ **b** : CLEAR-CUT
**2** : made of crystal : composed of crystals
**3** : constituting or relating to a crystal
— **crys·tal·lin·i·ty** \,kris-tə-'li-nə-tē\ *noun*

**crystalline lens** *noun* (1794)
: the lens of the eye in vertebrates

**crys·tal·lise** *British variant of* CRYSTALLIZE

**crys·tal·lite** \'kris-tə-,līt\ *noun* [German *Kristallit*, from Greek *krystallos*] (1805)
**1 a** : a minute mineral form (as in glassy volcanic rocks) that marks the beginning of crystallization **b** : a single grain in a polycrystalline substance
**2** : MICELLE

**crys·tal·lize** *also* **crys·tal·ize** \'kris-tə-,līz\ *verb* **-lized; -liz·ing** (1598)
*transitive verb*
**1** : to cause to form crystals or assume crystalline form
**2** : to cause to take a definite form ⟨tried to *crystallize* his thoughts⟩
**3** : to coat with crystals especially of sugar ⟨*crystallize* grapes⟩
*intransitive verb*
: to become crystallized
— **crys·tal·liz·able** \-,lī-zə-bəl, ,kris-tə-'\ *adjective*
— **crys·tal·li·za·tion** \,kris-tə-li-'zā-shən\ *noun*
— **crys·tal·liz·er** *noun*

**crys·tal·lo·graph·ic** \,kris-tə-lə-'gra-fik\ *adjective* (1804)
: of or relating to crystals or crystallography
— **crys·tal·lo·graph·i·cal·ly** \-fi-k(ə-)lē\ *adverb*

**crys·tal·log·ra·phy** \,kris-tə-'lä-grə-fē\ *noun* (1802)
: a science that deals with the forms and structures of crystals
— **crys·tal·log·ra·pher** \-fər\ *noun*

**crys·tal·loid** \'kris-tə-,lȯid\ *noun* (1861)
: a substance that forms a true solution and is capable of being crystallized
— **crystalloid** *or* **crys·tal·loi·dal** \,kris-tə-'lȯi-d°l\ *adjective*

**crystal pleat** *noun* (1976)
: any of a series of narrow sharply pressed pleats all turned in one direction
— **crystal pleated** *adjective*

**crystal violet** *noun* (circa 1893)
: a triphenylmethane dye found in gentian violet

**cry up** *transitive verb* (1593)
: to praise publicly in order to enhance in value or repute

**CS** \,sē-'es\ *noun* [Ben B. *Corson* (born 1896) and Roger W. *Staughton* (died 1957) American chemists] (1960)
: a potent tear gas used especially for riot control

**C–sec·tion** \'sē-,sek-shən\ *noun* (1973)
: CESAREAN SECTION

**cte·noid** \'te-,nȯid, 'tē-\ *adjective* [International Scientific Vocabulary, from Greek *ktenoeidēs*, from *kten-, kteis* comb — more at PECTINATE] (1872)
: having the margin toothed ⟨*ctenoid* scale⟩; *also* : having or consisting of ctenoid scales ⟨*ctenoid* fishes⟩

**cteno·phore** \'te-nə-,fȯr, -,fȯr\ *noun* [ultimately from Greek *kten-, kteis* + *pherein* to carry — more at BEAR] (circa 1882)
: any of a phylum (Ctenophora) of marine animals superficially resembling jellyfishes but having biradial symmetry and swimming by

means of eight meridional bands of transverse ciliated plates — called also *comb jelly*
— **cte·noph·o·ran** \tə-'nä-fə-rən\ *noun or adjective*

**CT scan** \,sē-'tē-\ *noun* [computerized tomography] (1974)
: CAT SCAN
— **CT scanner** *noun*

**C–type** \'sē-,tīp\ *adjective* (1967)
: relating to or being any of the oncornaviruses in which the structure containing the nucleic acid is spherical and centrally located ⟨*C-type* virus particles⟩

**cua·dri·lla** \kwä-'drē-yə, -'drēl-\ *noun* [Spanish, diminutive of *cuadra* square, from Latin *quadra*] (1893)
: the team assisting the matador in the bullring

**cub** \'kəb\ *noun* [origin unknown] (1530)
**1 a** : a young carnivorous mammal (as a bear, fox, or lion) **b** : a young shark
**2** : a young person
**3** : APPRENTICE; *especially* : an inexperienced newspaper reporter

**cub·age** \'kyü-bij\ *noun* (1840)
: cubic content, volume, or displacement

**Cu·ban heel** \'kyü-bən-\ *noun* [*Cuba*, West Indies] (1908)
: a broad medium-high heel with a moderately curved back

**cu·ba·ture** \'kyü-bə-,chu̇r, -,chər, -,tyu̇r, -,tu̇r\ *noun* [*cube* + *-ature* (as in *quadrature*)] (1679)
: the process of determining the volume of a solid

**cub·by** \'kə-bē\ *noun, plural* **cubbies** [obsolete English *cub* pen, from Dutch *kub* fish basket; akin to Old English *cofa* den] (circa 1859)
: CUBBYHOLE

**cub·by·hole** \'kə-bē-,hōl\ *noun* (circa 1842)
: a small snug place (as for hiding or storage); *also* : a cramped space

**¹cube** \'kyüb\ *noun* [Latin *cubus*, from Greek *kybos* die, cube] (1551)
**1 a** : the regular solid of six equal square sides — see VOLUME table **b** : something shaped like a cube ⟨ice *cube*⟩
**2** : the product got by taking a number three times as a factor

**²cube** *adjective* (1570)
: raised to the third power

**³cube** *transitive verb* **cubed; cub·ing** (1588)
**1** : to raise to the third power
**2** : to form into a cube
**3** : to cut partly through (a steak) in a checkered pattern to increase tenderness by breaking the fibers
— **cub·er** *noun*

**⁴cu·be** *or* **cu·bé** \'kyü-,bā, kyü-'\ *noun* [American Spanish *cubé*] (1924)
: any of several tropical American plants (genus *Lonchocarpus*) furnishing rotenone

**cu·beb** \'kyü-,beb\ *noun* [Middle French *cubebe*, from Old French, from Medieval Latin *cubeba*, from Arabic *kubābah*] (14th century)
: the dried unripe berry of a tropical shrub (*Piper cubeba*) of the pepper family that is crushed and smoked in cigarettes for catarrh

**cube root** *noun* (circa 1696)
: a number whose cube is a given number

**cube steak** *noun* (1930)
: a thin slice of beef that has been cubed

**¹cu·bic** \'kyü-bik\ *adjective* (15th century)
**1** : having the form of a cube : CUBICAL
**2 a** : relating to the cube considered as a crystal form **b** : ISOMETRIC 1
**3 a** : THREE-DIMENSIONAL **b** : being the volume of a cube whose edge is a specified unit ⟨*cubic* inch⟩

\ə\ abut \°\ kitten \ər\ further \a\ ash \ā\ ace
\ä\ mop, mar \au̇\ out \ch\ chin \e\ bet \ē\ easy
\g\ go \i\ hit \ī\ ice \j\ job \ŋ\ sing \ō\ go
\ȯ\ law \ȯi\ boy \th\ thin \t̲h̲\ the \ü\ loot \u̇\ foot
\y\ yet \zh\ vision *see also* Guide to Pronunciation

**4 :** of third degree, order, or power ⟨a *cubic* polynomial⟩
**²cubic** *noun* (1799)
**:** a cubic curve, equation, or polynomial
**cu·bi·cal** \'kyü-bi-kəl\ *adjective* (15th century)
**1 :** CUBIC; *especially* **:** shaped like a cube
**2 :** relating to volume
— **cu·bi·cal·ly** \-k(ə-)lē\ *adverb*
**cubic equation** *noun* (circa 1751)
**:** a polynomial equation in which the highest sum of exponents of variables in any term is three
**cu·bi·cle** \'kyü-bi-kəl\ *noun* [Latin *cubiculum*, from *cubare* to lie, recline] (15th century)
**1 :** a sleeping compartment partitioned off from a large room
**2 :** a small partitioned space; *especially* **:** CARREL
**cubic measure** *noun* (1660)
**:** a unit (as cubic inch or cubic centimeter) for measuring volume — see METRIC SYSTEM table, WEIGHT table
**cub·ism** \'kyü-bi-zəm\ *noun, often capitalized* (1911)
**:** a style of art that stresses abstract structure at the expense of other pictorial elements especially by displaying several aspects of the same object simultaneously and by fragmenting the form of depicted objects
— **cub·ist** \-bist\ *noun or adjective, often capitalized*
— **cu·bis·tic** \kyü-'bis-tik\ *adjective*
**cu·bit** \'kyü-bət\ *noun* [Middle English, from Latin *cubitum* elbow, cubit] (14th century)
**:** any of various ancient units of length based on the length of the forearm from the elbow to the tip of the middle finger and usually equal to about 18 inches (45.7 centimeters)
**¹cu·boid** \'kyü-ˌbȯid\ *adjective* (circa 1828)
**1 :** approximately cubical in shape
**2 :** relating to or being the cuboid
**²cuboid** *noun* (1839)
**:** the outermost bone in the distal row of tarsal bones of many higher vertebrates
**cu·boi·dal** \kyü-'bȯi-d°l\ *adjective* (1803)
**1 :** somewhat cubical
**2 :** composed of nearly cubical elements ⟨*cuboidal* epithelium⟩
**Cub Scout** *noun* (circa 1935)
**:** a member of the scouting program of the Boy Scouts for boys in the first through fifth grades in school
**cuck·ing stool** \'kə-kiŋ-\ *noun* [Middle English *cucking stol*, literally, defecating chair] (12th century)
**:** a chair formerly used for punishing offenders (as dishonest tradesmen) by public exposure or ducking in water
**cuck·old** \'kə-kəld, -(ˌ)kōld\ *noun* [Middle English *cokewold*] (13th century)
**:** a man whose wife is unfaithful
— **cuckold** *transitive verb*
**cuck·old·ry** \-kəl-drē\ *noun* (1529)
**1 :** the practice of making cuckolds
**2 :** the state of being a cuckold
**¹cuck·oo** \'kü-(ˌ)kü, 'kù-\ *noun, plural* **cuck·oos** [Middle English *cuccu*, of imitative origin] (13th century)
**1 :** a largely grayish brown European bird (*Cuculus canorus*) that is a parasite given to laying its eggs in the nests of other birds which hatch them and rear the offspring; *broadly* **:** any of a large family (Cuculidae of the order Cuculiformes) to which this bird belongs
**2 :** the call of the cuckoo
**3 :** a silly or slightly crackbrained person

cuckoo 1

**²cuckoo** *transitive verb* (1648)
**:** to repeat monotonously as a cuckoo does its call

**³cuckoo** *adjective* (1627)
**1 :** of, relating to, or resembling the cuckoo
**2 :** deficient in sense or intelligence **:** SILLY
**cuckoo clock** *noun* (1789)
**:** a wall or shelf clock that announces the hours by sounds resembling a cuckoo's call
**cuck·oo·flow·er** \'kü-(ˌ)kü-ˌflaú(-ə)r, 'kù-\ *noun* (1578)
**1 :** a bitter cress (*Cardamine pratensis*) of Eurasia and North America
**2 :** RAGGED ROBIN
**cuck·oo·pint** \-ˌpint\ *noun* [Middle English *cuccupintel*, from *cuccu* + *pintel* pintle] (1551)
**:** a European arum (*Arum maculatum*) with erect spathe and short purple spadix
**cuckoo spit** *noun* (1592)
**1 :** a frothy secretion exuded on plants by the nymphs of spittle insects
**2 :** SPITTLEBUG
**cu·cul·late** \'kyü-kə-ˌlāt, kyü-'kə-lət\ *adjective* [Medieval Latin *cucullatus*, from Latin *cucullus* hood] (1794)
**:** having the shape of a hood ⟨a *cucullate* leaf⟩
**cu·cum·ber** \'kyü-(ˌ)kəm-bər\ *noun* [Middle English, from Middle French *cocombre*, from Latin *cucumer-, cucumis*] (14th century)
**:** the fruit of a vine (*Cucumis sativus*) of the gourd family cultivated as a garden vegetable; *also* **:** this vine
**cucumber mosaic** *noun* (1916)
**:** a virus disease especially of cucumbers that is transmitted chiefly by an aphid and produces mottled foliage and often pale warty fruits
**cucumber tree** *noun* (circa 1782)
**:** a magnolia (*Magnolia acuminata*) of the eastern U.S. having fruit resembling a small cucumber
**cu·cur·bit** \kyü-'kər-bət\ *noun* [Middle English *cucurbite*, from Middle French, from Latin *cucurbita* gourd] (14th century)
**1 :** a vessel or flask for distillation used with or forming part of an alembic
**2 :** a plant of the gourd family
**cud** \'kəd, *chiefly Southern* 'kùd *or* 'küd\ *noun* [Middle English *cudde*, from Old English *cwudu*; akin to Old High German *kuti* glue, Sanskrit *jatu* gum] (before 12th century)
**1 :** food brought up into the mouth by a ruminating animal from its first stomach to be chewed again
**2 :** ²QUID
**cud·bear** \'kəd-ˌbar, -ˌber\ *noun* [irregular from Dr. *Cuthbert* Gordon, 18th century Scottish chemist] (1764)
**:** a reddish coloring matter from lichens
**¹cud·dle** \'kə-d°l\ *verb* **cud·dled; cud·dling** \'kəd-liŋ, 'kə-d°l-iŋ\ [origin unknown] (1520)
*transitive verb*
**:** to hold close for warmth or comfort or in affection
*intransitive verb*
**:** to lie close or snug **:** NESTLE, SNUGGLE
— **cud·dler** \'kəd-lər, 'kə-d°l-ər\ *noun*
**²cuddle** *noun* (1825)
**:** a close embrace
**cud·dle·some** \'kə-d°l-səm\ *adjective* (1876)
**:** CUDDLY
**cud·dly** \'kəd-lē, 'kə-d°l-ē\ *adjective* **cud·dli·er; -est** (1863)
**:** fit for or inviting cuddling
**¹cud·dy** \'kə-dē\ *noun, plural* **cuddies** [origin unknown] (1660)
**1 :** a usually small cabin or shelter (as on a sailboat)
**2 :** a small room or cupboard
**²cud·dy** *or* **cud·die** \'kù-dē, 'kə-\ *noun, plural* **cuddies** [perhaps from *Cuddy*, nickname for *Cuthbert*] (circa 1715)
**1** *dialect British* **:** DONKEY
**2** *dialect British* **:** BLOCKHEAD
**¹cud·gel** \'kə-jəl\ *noun* [Middle English *kuggel*, from Old English *cycgel*; perhaps akin to Middle High German *kugele* ball] (before 12th century)

**:** a short heavy club
**²cudgel** *transitive verb* **-geled** *or* **-gelled; -gel·ing** *or* **-gel·ling** \'kəj-liŋ, 'kə-jə-\ (1596)
**:** to beat with or as if with a cudgel
— **cudgel one's brains :** to think hard (as for a solution to a problem)
**cud·weed** \'kəd-ˌwēd, *chiefly Southern* 'kùd-*or* 'küd-\ *noun* (1548)
**:** any of several composite plants (as of the genus *Gnaphalium*) with silky or woolly foliage
**¹cue** \'kyü\ *noun* [Middle English *cu* half a farthing (spelled form of *q*, abbreviation for Latin *quadrans* quarter of an as)] (circa 1755)
**:** the letter *q*
**²cue** *noun* [probably from *qu*, abbreviation (used as a direction in actors' copies of plays) of Latin *quando* when] (1553)
**1 a :** a signal (as a word, phrase, or bit of stage business) to a performer to begin a specific speech or action **b :** something serving a comparable purpose **:** HINT
**2 :** a feature indicating the nature of something perceived
**3** *archaic* **:** the part one has to perform in or as if in a play
**4** *archaic* **:** MOOD, HUMOR
**³cue** *transitive verb* **cued; cu·ing** *or* **cue·ing** (1922)
**1 :** to give a cue to **:** PROMPT
**2 :** to insert into a continuous performance ⟨*cue* in sound effects⟩
**⁴cue** *noun* [French *queue*, literally, tail, from Latin *cauda*] (circa 1749)
**1 a :** a leather-tipped tapering rod for striking the cue ball (as in billiards and pool) **b :** a long-handled instrument with a concave head for shoving disks in shuffleboard
**2 :** QUEUE 2
**⁵cue** *verb* **cued; cu·ing** *or* **cue·ing** (circa 1784)
*transitive verb*
**1 :** QUEUE
**2 :** to strike with a cue
*intransitive verb*
**1 :** QUEUE
**2 :** to use a cue
**cue ball** *noun* (1881)
**:** the ball a player strikes with the cue in billiards and pool
**cues·ta** \'kwes-tə\ *noun* [Spanish, from Latin *costa* side, rib — more at COAST] (1818)
**:** a hill or ridge with a steep face on one side and a gentle slope on the other
**¹cuff** \'kəf\ *noun* [Middle English *coffe, cuffe* mitten] (1522)
**1 :** something (as a part of a sleeve or glove) encircling the wrist
**2 :** the turned-back hem of a trouser leg
**3 a :** HANDCUFF — usually used in plural **b :** a usually wide metal band worn as a bracelet
**4 :** an inflatable band that is wrapped around an extremity to control the flow of blood through the part when recording blood pressure with a sphygmomanometer
— **cuff·less** \'kə-fləs\ *adjective*
— **off the cuff :** without preparation **:** AD LIB
— **on the cuff :** on credit
**²cuff** *transitive verb* (1693)
**1 :** to furnish with a cuff
**2 :** HANDCUFF
**³cuff** *verb* [perhaps from obsolete English, glove, from Middle English] (1530)
*transitive verb*
**:** to strike especially with or as if with the palm of the hand **:** BUFFET
*intransitive verb*
**:** FIGHT, SCUFFLE
**⁴cuff** *noun* (1570)
**:** a blow with the hand especially when open **:** SLAP
**cuff link** *noun* (1897)
**:** a usually ornamental device consisting of two parts joined by a shank, chain, or bar for

passing through buttonholes to fasten shirt cuffs — usually used in plural

**cui bo·no** \'kwē-'bō-(,)nō\ *noun* [Latin, to whose advantage?] (1604)
**1** : a principle that probable responsibility for an act or event lies with one having something to gain
**2** : usefulness or utility as a principle in estimating the value of an act or policy

**cui·rass** \kwi-'ras, kyù-\ *noun* [Middle English *curas*, from Middle French *curasse*, from Late Latin *coreacea*, feminine of *coreaceus* leathern; from Latin *corium* skin, leather; akin to Old English *heortha* deerskin, Latin *cortex* bark, Greek *keirein* to cut — more at SHEAR] (15th century)
**1** : a piece of armor covering the body from neck to waist; *also* : the breastplate of such a piece
**2** : something (as bony plates covering an animal) resembling a cuirass
— **cui·rassed** *adjective*

**cui·ras·sier** \,kwir-ə-'sir, kyùr-\ *noun* (1625)
: a mounted soldier wearing a cuirass

**Cui·se·naire rod** \,kwē-zə-'nar-, -'ner-\ *noun* [from *Cuisenaire*, a trademark] (1954)
: any of a set of colored rods usually of 1 centimeter cross section and of 10 lengths from 1 to 10 centimeters that are used for teaching number concepts and the basic operations of arithmetic

**cui·sine** \kwi-'zēn, kwē-\ *noun* [French, literally, kitchen, from Late Latin *coquina* — more at KITCHEN] (1786)
: manner of preparing food : style of cooking; *also* : the food prepared

**cuisse** \'kwis\ *also* **cuish** \'kwish\ *noun* [Middle English *cusseis*, plural, from Middle French *cuissaux*, plural of *cuissel*, from *cuisse* thigh, from Latin *coxa* hip — more at COXA] (15th century)
: a piece of plate armor for the front of the thigh — see ARMOR illustration

**cuke** \'kyük\ *noun* (1903)
: CUCUMBER

**cul-de-sac** \'kəl-di-,sak, 'kùl-; ,kəl-di-', ,kùl-\ *noun, plural* **culs-de-sac** \'kəl(z)-, 'kùl(z)-, ,kəl(z)-, ,kùl(z)-\ *also* **cul-de-sacs** \-,saks, -'saks\ [French, literally, bottom of the bag] (1738)
**1** : a blind diverticulum or pouch
**2** : a street or passage closed at one end
**3** : BLIND ALLEY

**cu·let** \'kyü-lət, 'kə-lət\ *noun* [French, from diminutive of *cul* backside, from Latin *culus*; akin to Old Irish *cúl* back] (1678)
**1** : the small flat facet at the bottom of a brilliant parallel to the table
**2** : plate armor covering the buttocks

**cu·lex** \'kyü-,leks\ *noun* [New Latin, from Latin, gnat; akin to Old Irish *cuil* fly] (15th century)
: any of a large cosmopolitan genus (*Culex*) of mosquitoes that includes the common house mosquito (*C. pipiens*) of Europe and North America
— **cu·li·cine** \'kyü-lə-,sīn\ *adjective or noun*

**cu·li·nar·i·an** \,kə-lə-'ner-ē-ən, ,kyü-\ *noun* (1949)
: COOK, CHEF

**cu·li·nary** \'kə-lə-,ner-ē, 'kyü-\ *adjective* [Latin *culinarius*, from *culina* kitchen — more at KILN] (1638)
: of or relating to the kitchen or cookery
— **cu·li·nar·i·ly** \,kə-lə-'ner-ə-lē, ,kyü-\ *adverb*

**¹cull** \'kəl\ *transitive verb* [Middle English, from Middle French *cuillir*, from Latin *colligere* to bind together — more at COLLECT] (13th century)
**1** : to select from a group : CHOOSE ⟨*culled* the best passages from the poet's work⟩
**2** : to identify and remove the culls from
— **cull·er** *noun*

**²cull** *noun* (1809)
: something rejected especially as being inferior or worthless ⟨how to separate good-looking pecans from *culls* —*Washington Post*⟩

**cul·len·der** \'kə-lən-dər\ *variant of* COLANDER

**cul·let** \'kə-lət\ *noun* [perhaps from French *cueillette* act of gathering, from Latin *collecta*, from feminine of *collectus*, past participle of *colligere*] (1817)
: broken or refuse glass usually added to new material to facilitate melting in making glass

**cul·lion** \'kəl-yən\ *noun* [Middle English *coillon* testicle, from Middle French, from (assumed) Vulgar Latin *coleon-, coleo*, from Latin *coleus* scrotum] (1575) *archaic*
: a mean or base fellow

**¹cul·ly** \'kə-lē\ *noun, plural* **cullies** [perhaps alteration of *cullion*] (1664)
: one easily tricked or imposed on : DUPE

**²cully** *transitive verb* **cul·lied; cul·ly·ing** (1676)
*archaic* : CHEAT, DECEIVE

**¹culm** \'kəlm\ *noun* [Middle English] (14th century)
: refuse coal screenings : SLACK

**²culm** *noun* [Latin *culmus* stalk — more at HAULM] (circa 1657)
: a monocotyledonous stem (as of a grass or sedge)

**cul·mi·nant** \'kəl-mə-nənt\ *adjective* (1605)
**1** : being at greatest altitude or on the meridian
**2** : fully developed

**cul·mi·nate** \'kəl-mə-,nāt\ *verb* **-nat·ed; -nat·ing** [Medieval Latin *culminatus*, past participle of *culminare*, from Late Latin, to crown, from Latin *culmin-, culmen* top — more at HILL] (1647)
*intransitive verb*
**1** *of a celestial body* : to reach its highest altitude; *also* : to be directly overhead
**2 a** : to rise to or form a summit **b** : to reach the highest or a climactic or decisive point
*transitive verb*
: to bring to a head or to the highest point

**cul·mi·na·tion** \,kəl-mə-'nā-shən\ *noun* (1633)
**1** : the action of culminating
**2** : culminating position : CLIMAX
*synonym* see SUMMIT

**cu·lotte** \'kü-,lät, 'kyü-; kü-'lät, kyü-'\ *noun* [French, breeches, from diminutive of *cul* backside — more at CULET] (1911)
: a divided skirt; *also* : a garment having a divided skirt — often used in plural

**cul·pa·ble** \'kəl-pə-bəl\ *adjective* [Middle English *coupable*, from Middle French, from Latin *culpabilis*, from *culpare* to blame, from *culpa* guilt] (14th century)
**1** *archaic* : GUILTY, CRIMINAL
**2** : meriting condemnation or blame especially as wrong or harmful ⟨*culpable* negligence⟩
*synonym* see BLAMEWORTHY
— **cul·pa·bil·i·ty** \,kəl-pə-'bi-lə-tē\ *noun*
— **cul·pa·ble·ness** \'kəl-pə-bəl-nəs\ *noun*
— **cul·pa·bly** \-blē\ *adverb*

**cul·prit** \'kəl-prət, -,prit\ *noun* [Anglo-French *cul.* (abbreviation of *culpable* guilty) + *prest, prit* ready (i.e., to prove it), from Latin *praestus* — more at PRESTO] (1678)
**1** : one accused of or charged with a crime
**2** : one guilty of a crime or a fault
**3** : the source or cause of a problem

**cult** \'kəlt\ *noun, often attributive* [French & Latin; French *culte*, from Latin *cultus* care, adoration, from *colere* to cultivate — more at WHEEL] (1617)
**1** : formal religious veneration : WORSHIP
**2** : a system of religious beliefs and ritual; *also* : its body of adherents
**3** : a religion regarded as unorthodox or spurious; *also* : its body of adherents
**4** : a system for the cure of disease based on dogma set forth by its promulgator ⟨health *cults*⟩

**5 a** : great devotion to a person, idea, object, movement, or work (as a film or book); *especially* : such devotion regarded as a literary or intellectual fad **b** : a usually small group of people characterized by such devotion
— **cul·tic** \'kəl-tik\ *adjective*
— **cult·ish** \-tish\ *adjective*
— **cult·ish·ly** \-lē\ *adverb*
— **cult·ish·ness** \-nəs\ *noun*
— **cult·ism** \'kəl-,ti-zəm\ *noun*
— **cult·ist** \'kəl-tist\ *noun*
— **cult·like** \-,līk\ *adjective*

**cultch** *also* **culch** \'kəlch\ *noun* [perhaps from a French dialect form of French *couche* couch] (1667)
**1** : material (as oyster shells) laid down on oyster grounds to furnish points of attachment for the spat
**2** *chiefly New England* : CLUTTER, TRASH

**cul·ti·gen** \'kəl-tə-jən\ *noun* [*culti*vated + -*gen*] (1924)
**1** : a cultivated or domestic organism of a variety or species for which a wild ancestor is unknown
**2** : CULTIVAR

**cul·ti·va·ble** \'kəl-tə-və-bəl\ *adjective* (1682)
: capable of being cultivated
— **cul·ti·va·bil·i·ty** \,kəl-tə-və-'bi-lə-tē\ *noun*

**cul·ti·var** \'kəl-tə-,vär, -,ver, -,var\ *noun* [*culti*vated + *variety*] (1923)
: an organism of a kind originating and persistent under cultivation

**cul·ti·vate** \'kəl-tə-,vāt\ *transitive verb* **-vat·ed; -vat·ing** [Medieval Latin *cultivatus*, past participle of *cultivare*, from *cultivus* cultivable, from Latin *cultus*, past participle of *colere*] (circa 1655)
**1** : to prepare or prepare and use for the raising of crops; *also* : to loosen or break up the soil about ⟨growing plants⟩
**2 a** : to foster the growth of ⟨*cultivate* vegetables⟩ **b** : CULTURE 2a **c** : to improve by labor, care, or study : REFINE ⟨*cultivate* the mind⟩
**3** : FURTHER, ENCOURAGE ⟨*cultivate* the arts⟩
**4** : to seek the society of : make friends with
— **cul·ti·vat·able** \-,vā-tə-bəl\ *adjective*

**cultivated** *adjective* (1665)
: REFINED, EDUCATED ⟨*cultivated* speech⟩ ⟨*cultivated* tastes⟩

**cul·ti·va·tion** \,kəl-tə-'vā-shən\ *noun* (circa 1716)
**1** : CULTURE, REFINEMENT
**2** : the act or art of cultivating or tilling

**cul·ti·va·tor** \'kəl-tə-,vā-tər\ *noun* (1665)
: one that cultivates; *especially* : an implement for loosening the soil while crops are growing

**cul·tur·al** \'kəlch-rəl, 'kəl-chə-\ *adjective* (circa 1864)
**1** : of or relating to culture or culturing
**2** : concerned with the fostering of plant or animal growth
— **cul·tur·al·ly** \-rə-lē\ *adverb*

**cultural anthropology** *noun* (1933)
: anthropology that deals with human culture especially with respect to social structure, language, law, politics, religion, magic, art, and technology — compare PHYSICAL ANTHROPOLOGY
— **cultural anthropologist** *noun*

**cul·tur·a·ti** \,kəl-chə-'rä-(,)tē\ *noun plural* [¹*culture* + -*ati* (as in *literati*)] (1964)
: people intensely interested in cultural affairs

**¹cul·ture** \'kəl-chər\ *noun* [Middle English, from Middle French, from Latin *cultura*, from *cultus*, past participle] (15th century)
**1** : CULTIVATION, TILLAGE
**2** : the act of developing the intellectual and moral faculties especially by education
**3** : expert care and training ⟨beauty *culture*⟩

**4 a :** enlightenment and excellence of taste acquired by intellectual and aesthetic training **b :** acquaintance with and taste in fine arts, humanities, and broad aspects of science as distinguished from vocational and technical skills **5 a :** the integrated pattern of human knowledge, belief, and behavior that depends upon man's capacity for learning and transmitting knowledge to succeeding generations **b :** the customary beliefs, social forms, and material traits of a racial, religious, or social group **c :** the set of shared attitudes, values, goals, and practices that characterizes a company or corporation **6 :** cultivation of living material in prepared nutrient media; *also* **:** a product of such cultivation

²**culture** *transitive verb* **cul·tured; cul·tur·ing** \'kəlch-riŋ, 'kəl-chə-\ (1510) **1 :** CULTIVATE **2 a :** to grow in a prepared medium **b :** to start a culture from

**cultured** *adjective* (circa 1746) **1 :** CULTIVATED **2 :** produced under artificial conditions ⟨*cultured* viruses⟩ ⟨*cultured* pearls⟩

**culture shock** *noun* (circa 1940) **:** a sense of confusion and uncertainty sometimes with feelings of anxiety that may affect people exposed to an alien culture or environment without adequate preparation

**cul·tus** \'kəl-təs\ *noun* [Latin, adoration] (1640) **:** CULT

**cul·ver** \'kəl-vər, 'kúl-\ *noun* [Middle English, from Old English *culfer*, from (assumed) Vulgar Latin *columbra*, from Latin *columbula*, diminutive of Latin *columba* dove — more at COLUMBINE] (before 12th century) **:** PIGEON

**cul·ver·in** \'kəl-və-rən\ *noun* [Middle English, from Middle French *couleuvrine*, from *couleuvre* snake, from Latin *colubra*] (15th century) **:** an early firearm: **a :** a rude musket **b :** a long cannon (as an 18-pounder) of the 16th and 17th centuries

**cul·vert** \'kəl-vərt\ *noun* [origin unknown] (1773) **1 :** a transverse drain **2 :** a conduit for a culvert **3 :** a bridge over a culvert

**cum** \'kùm, 'kəm\ *conjunction* [Latin, with; akin to Latin *com-* — more at CO-] (circa 1873) **:** along with being **:** AND — used to form usually hyphenated phrases ⟨a credible mining camp elder-*cum*-publican —G. B. Shaw⟩ ⟨Christian and Christian-*cum*-voodoo churches —David Binder⟩

¹**cum·ber** \'kəm-bər\ *transitive verb* **cum·bered; cum·ber·ing** \-b(ə-)riŋ\ [Middle English *combren*, perhaps from Old French *combrer* to prevent, from (assumed) Old French *combre* abatis] (14th century) **1** *archaic* **:** TROUBLE, HARASS **2 a :** to hinder or encumber by being in the way ⟨*cumbered* with heavy clothing⟩ **b :** to clutter up ⟨rocks *cumbering* the yard⟩

²**cumber** *noun* (14th century) **:** something that cumbers; *especially* **:** HINDRANCE

**cum·ber·some** \'kəm-bər-səm\ *adjective* (1535) **1** *dialect* **:** BURDENSOME, TROUBLESOME **2 :** unwieldy because of heaviness and bulk **3 :** slow-moving **:** PONDEROUS **synonym** see HEAVY — **cum·ber·some·ly** *adverb* — **cum·ber·some·ness** *noun*

**cum·brous** \'kəm-b(ə-)rəs\ *adjective* (15th century) **:** CUMBERSOME **synonym** see HEAVY — **cum·brous·ly** *adverb* — **cum·brous·ness** *noun*

**cum·in** \'kə-mən, 'kyü-\ *noun* [Middle English, from Old English *cymen*, from Latin *cuminum*, from Greek *kyminon*, of Semitic origin; akin to Akkadian *kamūnu* cumin] (before 12th century) **:** a low plant (*Cuminum cyminum*) of the carrot family long cultivated for its aromatic seeds; *also* **:** the fruit or seed of cumin used as a spice

**cum lau·de** \kúm-'laú-də, -dē; ˌkəm-'lô-dē\ *adverb or adjective* [New Latin, with praise] (1893) **:** with distinction ⟨graduated *cum laude*⟩ — compare MAGNA CUM LAUDE, SUMMA CUM LAUDE

**cum·mer·bund** \'kə-mər-ˌbənd, 'kəm-bər-\ *also* **cum·ber·bund** \'kəm-bər-\ *noun* [Hindi *kamarband*, from Persian, from *kamar* waist + *band* band] (1616) **:** a broad waistband usually worn in place of a vest with men's dress clothes and adapted in various styles of women's clothes

**cum·shaw** \'kəm-ˌshô\ *noun* [Chinese (Xiamen) *kam siā* grateful thanks] (1839) **:** PRESENT, GRATUITY

**cumul-** *or* **cumuli-** *or* **cumulo-** *combining form* [New Latin, from Latin *cumulus*] **:** cumulus and ⟨*cumulo*nimbus⟩

**cu·mu·late** \'kyü-myə-ˌlāt\ *verb* **-lat·ed; -lat·ing** [Latin *cumulatus*, past participle of *cumulare*, from *cumulus* mass] (1534) *transitive verb* **1 :** to gather or pile in a heap **2 :** to combine into one **3 :** to build up by addition of new material *intransitive verb* **:** to become massed — **cu·mu·late** \-lət, -ˌlāt\ *adjective* — **cu·mu·la·tion** \ˌkyü-myə-'lā-shən\ *noun*

**cu·mu·la·tive** \'kyü-myə-lə-tiv, -ˌtā-\ *adjective* (1605) **1 a :** made up of accumulated parts **b :** increasing by successive additions **2 a :** tending to prove the same point ⟨*cumulative* evidence⟩ **b :** additional rather than repeated ⟨*cumulative* legacy⟩ **3 a :** taking effect upon completion of another penal sentence ⟨*cumulative* sentence⟩ **b :** increasing in severity with repetition of the offense ⟨*cumulative* penalty⟩ **4 :** formed by the addition of new material of the same kind ⟨*cumulative* book index⟩ **5 :** summing or integrating overall data or values of a random variable less than or less than or equal to a specified value ⟨*cumulative* normal distribution⟩ ⟨*cumulative* frequency distribution⟩ — **cu·mu·la·tive·ly** *adverb* — **cu·mu·la·tive·ness** *noun*

**cumulative distribution function** *noun* (circa 1965) **:** DISTRIBUTION FUNCTION

**cu·mu·li·form** \'kyü-myə-lə-ˌfôrm\ *adjective* (1885) **:** of the form of a cumulus

**cu·mu·lo·nim·bus** \-'nim-bəs\ *noun* [New Latin] (1887) **:** cumulus cloud often spread out in the shape of an anvil extending to great heights — see CLOUD illustration

**cu·mu·lous** \'kyü-myə-ləs\ *adjective* (1815) **:** resembling cumulus

**cu·mu·lus** \-ləs\ *noun, plural* **-li** \-ˌlī, -ˌlē\ [Latin] (1659) **1 :** HEAP, ACCUMULATION **2** [New Latin, from Latin] **:** a massy cloud form having a flat base and rounded outlines often piled up like a mountain — see CLOUD illustration

**cunc·ta·tion** \ˌkəŋ(k)-'tā-shən\ *noun* [Latin *cunctation-, cunctatio*, from *cunctari* to hesitate; akin to Sanskrit *śaṅkate* he wavers, Old English *hangian* to hang] (1585) **:** DELAY — **cunc·ta·tive** \'kəŋ(k)-ˌtā-tiv, -tə-tiv\ *adjective*

**cu·ne·ate** \'kyü-nē-ˌāt, -ət\ *adjective* [Latin *cuneatus*, from *cuneus* wedge] (1810) **:** narrowly triangular with the acute angle toward the base — see LEAF illustration

¹**cu·ne·i·form** \kyú-'nē-ə-ˌfôrm, 'kyü-n(ē-)ə-\ *adjective* [probably from French *cunéiforme*, from Middle French, from Latin *cuneus* + Middle French *-iforme* -iform] (1677) **1 :** having the shape of a wedge **2 :** composed of or written in wedge-shaped characters ⟨*cuneiform* syllabary⟩

²**cuneiform** *noun* (1808) **1 :** a cuneiform part; *specifically* **:** a cuneiform bone or cartilage **2 :** cuneiform writing

**cun·ner** \'kə-nər\ *noun* [origin unknown] (1602) **:** either of two wrasses: **a :** a European wrasse (*Crenilabrus melops*) **b :** a wrasse (*Tautogolabrus adspersus*) common along the northeastern U.S. and adjacent Canadian coast

cuneiform 2

**cun·ni·lin·gus** \ˌkə-ni-'liŋ-gəs\ *also* **cun·ni·linc·tus** \-'liŋ(k)-təs\ *noun* [*cunnilingus*, New Latin, from Latin, one who licks the vulva, from *cunnus* vulva + *lingere* to lick; *cunnilinctus*, New Latin, from Latin *cunnus* + *linctus*, act of licking, from *lingere* — more at LICK] (1887) **:** oral stimulation of the vulva or clitoris

¹**cun·ning** \'kə-niŋ\ *adjective* [Middle English, from present participle of *can* know] (14th century) **1 :** dexterous or crafty in the use of special resources (as skill or knowledge) or in attaining an end ⟨a *cunning* plotter⟩ **2 :** displaying keen insight ⟨a *cunning* observation⟩ **3 :** characterized by wiliness and trickery ⟨*cunning* schemes⟩ **4 :** prettily appealing **:** CUTE **synonym** see CLEVER, SLY — **cun·ning·ly** \-niŋ-lē\ *adverb* — **cun·ning·ness** *noun*

²**cunning** *noun* (14th century) **1** *obsolete* **a :** KNOWLEDGE, LEARNING **b :** magic art **2 :** dexterous skill and subtlety (as in inventing, devising, or executing) ⟨high-ribbed vault . . . with perfect *cunning* framed —William Wordsworth⟩ **3 :** CRAFT, SLYNESS **synonym** see ART

**cunt** \'kənt\ *noun* [Middle English *cunte*; akin to Middle Low German *kunte* female pudenda] (14th century) **1 :** the female pudenda; *also* **:** coitus with a woman — usually considered obscene **2 :** WOMAN 1a — usually used disparagingly; usually considered obscene

¹**cup** \'kəp\ *noun* [Middle English *cuppe*, from Old English, from Late Latin *cuppa* cup, alteration of Latin *cupa* tub — more at HIVE] (before 12th century) **1 :** an open usually bowl-shaped drinking vessel **2 a :** a drinking vessel and its contents **b :** the consecrated wine of the Communion **3 :** something that falls to one's lot **4 :** an ornamental cup offered as a prize (as in a championship) **5 a :** something resembling a cup **b :** a cup-shaped plant organ **c :** an athletic supporter reinforced usually with plastic to provide extra protection to the wearer **d :** either of two parts of a brassiere that are shaped like and fit over the breasts **e :** the metal case inside a hole in golf; *also* **:** the hole itself **6 :** a usually iced beverage resembling punch but served from a pitcher rather than a bowl **7 :** a half pint **:** eight fluid ounces **8 :** a food served in a cup-shaped usually footed vessel ⟨fruit *cup*⟩

**9 :** the symbol ∪ indicating the union of two sets — compare CAP 7
— **cup·like** \-ˌlīk\ *adjective*
— **in one's cups :** DRUNK

²**cup** *transitive verb* **cupped; cup·ping** (14th century)
**1 :** to treat by cupping
**2 a :** to curve into the shape of a cup ⟨*cupped* his hands around his mouth⟩ **b :** to place in or as if in a cup

**cup·bear·er** \'kəp-ˌbar-ər, -ˌber-\ *noun* (15th century)
**:** one who has the duty of filling and handing around the cups in which wine is served

**cup·board** \'kə-bərd\ *noun* (1530)
**:** a closet with shelves where dishes, utensils, or food is kept; *also* **:** a small closet

**cup·cake** \'kəp-ˌkāk\ *noun* (1828)
**:** a small cake baked in a cuplike mold

¹**cu·pel** \kyü-'pel, 'kyü-pəl\ *noun* [French *coupelle*, diminutive of *coupe* cup, from Late Latin *cuppa*] (1605)
**:** a small shallow porous cup especially of bone ash used in assaying to separate precious metals from lead

²**cupel** *transitive verb* **-pelled** *or* **-peled; -pel·ling** *or* **-pel·ing** (1644)
**:** to refine by means of a cupel
— **cu·pel·ler** *noun*

**cu·pel·la·tion** \ˌkyü-pə-'lā-shən, -ˌpe-\ *noun* (circa 1691)
**:** refinement (as of gold or silver) in a cupel by exposure to high temperature in a blast of air by which the lead, copper, tin, and other unwanted metals are oxidized and partly sink into the porous cupel

**cup·ful** \'kəp-ˌfül\ *noun, plural* **cup·fuls** \-ˌfülz\ *also* **cups·ful** \'kəps-ˌfül\ (12th century)
**1 :** as much as a cup will hold
**2 :** CUP 7
*usage* see ²-FUL

**cup fungus** *noun* (circa 1905)
**:** any of an order (Pezizales) of mostly saprophytic fungi with a fleshy or horny apothecium that is often colored and is typically shaped like a cup, saucer, or disk

**Cu·pid** \'kyü-pəd\ *noun* [Latin *Cupido*]
**1 :** the Roman god of erotic love — compare EROS
**2** *not capitalized* **:** a figure that represents Cupid as a naked usually winged boy often holding a bow and arrow
*word history* see EROTIC

**cu·pid·i·ty** \kyü-'pi-də-tē\ *noun, plural* **-ties** [Middle English *cupidite*, from Middle French *cupidité*, from Latin *cupiditat-, cupiditas* — more at COVET] (15th century)
**1 :** inordinate desire for wealth **:** AVARICE, GREED
**2 :** strong desire **:** LUST

**Cupid's bow** *noun* (1858)
**:** a bow that consists of two convex curves usually with recurved ends

**cup of tea** (1932)
**1 :** something one likes or excels in ⟨I see already that storytelling isn't my *cup of tea* —John Barth⟩; *also* **:** a person suited to one's taste
**2 :** a thing to be reckoned with **:** MATTER ⟨poltergeists are a different *cup of tea* —D. B. W. Lewis⟩

**cu·po·la** \'kyü-pə-lə, ÷-ˌlō\ *noun* [Italian, from Latin *cupula*, diminutive of *cupa* tub] (1549)
**1 a :** a rounded vault resting on a usually circular base and forming a roof or a ceiling **b :** a small structure built on top of a roof
**2 :** a vertical cylindrical furnace for melting iron in the foundry that has tuyeres and tapping spouts near the bottom
**3 :** a raised observation post in the roof of a railroad caboose
— **cu·po·laed** \-ləd, ÷-ˌlōd\ *adjective*

**cup·pa** \'kə-pə\ *noun* [short for *cuppa tea*, pronunciation spelling of *cup of tea*] (1934)
*chiefly British* **:** a cup of tea

**cup·ping** *noun* (14th century)
**:** an operation of drawing blood to the surface of the body by use of a glass vessel evacuated by heat

**cup·py** \'kə-pē\ *adjective* **cup·pi·er; -est** (1882)
**1 :** resembling a cup
**2 :** full of small depressions ⟨a *cuppy* racetrack⟩

**cupr-** *or* **cupri-** *or* **cupro-** *combining form* [Late Latin *cuprum* — more at COPPER]
**1 :** copper ⟨*cupriferous*⟩
**2 :** copper and ⟨*cupronickel*⟩

**cu·pric** \'kyü-prik, 'kü-\ *adjective* (1799)
**:** of, relating to, or containing copper with a valence of two

**cu·prif·er·ous** \kyü-'pri-f(ə-)rəs, kü-\ *adjective* (1784)
**:** containing copper

**cu·prite** \'kyü-ˌprīt, 'kü-\ *noun* [German *Kuprit*, from Late Latin *cuprum*] (circa 1850)
**:** a mineral consisting of copper oxide and constituting an ore of copper

**cu·pro·nick·el** \ˌkyü-prō-'ni-kəl, ˌkü-\ *noun* (1900)
**:** an alloy of copper and nickel; *especially* **:** one containing about 70 percent copper and 30 percent nickel

**cu·prous** \'kyü-prəs, 'kü-\ *adjective* (1669)
**:** of, relating to, or containing copper with a valence of one

**cu·pu·late** \'kyü-pyə-ˌlāt, -lət\ *adjective* (1835)
**:** shaped like, having, or bearing a cupule

**cu·pule** \'kyü-(ˌ)pyü(ə)l\ *noun* [New Latin *cupula*, from Late Latin, diminutive of Latin *cupa* tub — more at HIVE] (1826)
**:** a cup-shaped anatomical structure: as **a :** an involucre characteristic of the oak in which the bracts are indurated and coherent **b :** an outer integument partially enclosing the seed of some seed ferns

**cur** \'kər\ *noun* [Middle English, short for *curdogge*, from (assumed) Middle English *curren* to growl (perhaps from Old Norse *kurra* to grumble) + Middle English *dogge* dog] (13th century)
**1 :** a mongrel or inferior dog
**2 :** a surly or cowardly fellow

**cur·able** \'kyür-ə-bəl\ *adjective* (14th century)
**:** capable of being cured
— **cur·abil·i·ty** \ˌkyür-ə-'bi-lə-tē\ *noun*
— **cur·able·ness** \'kyür-ə-bəl-nəs\ *noun*
— **cur·ably** \-blē\ *adverb*

**cu·ra·çao** \'kyür-ə-ˌsō, -ˌsaú, 'kúr-; ˌk(y)úr-ə-'-\ *also* **cu·ra·çoa** \*same, or* ˌkyür-ə-'sō-ə\ *noun* [Dutch *curaçao*, from *Curaçao*, Netherlands Antilles] (1813)
**:** a liqueur flavored with the dried peel of the sour orange

**cu·ra·cy** \'kyür-ə-sē\ *noun, plural* **-cies** (1682)
**:** the office or term of office of a curate

**cu·ra·re** *also* **cu·ra·ri** \kyú-'rär-ē, kú-\ *noun* [Portuguese & Spanish *curare*, from Carib *kurari*] (1777)
**:** a dried aqueous extract especially of a vine (as *Strychnos toxifera* of the family Loganiaceae or *Chondodendron tomentosum* of the family Menispermaceae) used by South American Indians to poison arrow tips and in medicine to produce muscular relaxation

**cu·ra·rine** \-'rär-ən, -ˌēn\ *noun* (circa 1872)
**:** any of several alkaloids from curare

**cu·ra·rize** \-'rär-ˌīz\ *transitive verb* **-rized; -riz·ing** (1875)
**:** to treat with curare
— **cu·ra·ri·za·tion** \-ˌrär-ə-'zā-shən\ *noun*

**cu·ras·sow** \'kyür-ə-ˌsō, 'kúr-\ *noun* [alteration of *Curaçao*] (1685)
**:** any of several large arboreal game birds (family Cracidae, especially genus *Crax*) of South and Central America related to the domestic fowls

¹**cu·rate** \'kyúr-ət *also* 'kyúr-ˌāt\ *noun* [Middle English, from Medieval Latin *curatus*, from *cura* cure of souls, from Latin, care] (14th century)
**1 :** a clergyman in charge of a parish
**2 :** a clergyman serving as assistant (as to a rector) in a parish

²**cu·rate** \-ˌāt, kyú-'rāt\ *transitive verb* **cu·rat·ed; cu·rat·ing** (1909)
**:** to act as curator of

**curate's egg** *noun* [from the story of a curate who was given a stale egg by his bishop and declared that parts of it were excellent] (1905) *British* **:** something with both good and bad parts or qualities

**cu·ra·tive** \'kyúr-ə-tiv\ *adjective* (15th century)
**:** relating to or used in the cure of diseases **:** tending to cure
— **curative** *noun*
— **cu·ra·tive·ly** *adverb*

**cu·ra·tor** \'kyúr-ˌā-tər, kyú-'rā-, 'kyúr-ə-\ *noun* [Latin, from *curatus*, past participle of *curare* to care, from *cura* care] (1632)
**:** one that has the care and superintendence of something; *especially* **:** one in charge of a museum, zoo, or other place of exhibit
— **cu·ra·to·ri·al** \ˌkyúr-ə-'tōr-ē-əl, -'tòr-\ *adjective*
— **cu·ra·tor·ship** \'kyúr-ˌā-tər-ˌship, kyú-'rā-, 'kyúr-ə-\ *noun*

¹**curb** \'kərb\ *noun* [Middle French *courbe* curve, curved piece of wood or iron, from *courbe* curved, from Latin *curvus*] (15th century)
**1 :** a bit that exerts severe pressure on a horse's jaws; *also* **:** the chain or strap attached to it
**2 :** an enclosing frame, border, or edging
**3 :** CHECK, RESTRAINT ⟨a price *curb*⟩
**4 :** a raised edge or margin to strengthen or confine
**5 :** an edging (as of concrete) built along a street to form part of a gutter
**6** [from the fact that it originally transacted its business on the street] **:** a market for trading in securities not listed on a stock exchange

²**curb** *transitive verb* (1530)
**1 :** to furnish with a curb
**2 :** to check or control with or as if with a curb ⟨trying to *curb* her curiosity⟩
**3 :** to lead (a dog) to a suitable place (as a gutter) for defecation
*synonym* see RESTRAIN

**curb·ing** \'kər-biŋ\ *noun* (1838)
**1 :** the material for a curb
**2 :** CURB

**curb service** *noun* (1931)
**:** service extended (as by a restaurant) to persons sitting in parked automobiles

**curb·side** \'kərb-ˌsīd\ *noun* (1946)
**1 :** the side of a pavement bordered by a curb
**2 :** SIDEWALK

¹**curb·stone** \-ˌstōn\ *noun* (1791)
**:** a stone or edging of concrete forming a curb

²**curbstone** *adjective* (1848)
**1 :** operating on the street without maintaining an office ⟨a *curbstone* broker⟩
**2 :** not having the benefit of training or experience ⟨a *curbstone* critic⟩

**curb weight** *noun* (1949)
**:** the weight of an automobile with standard equipment and fuel, oil, and coolant

**curch** \'kərch\ *noun* [Middle English] (14th century)
*Scottish* **:** KERCHIEF 1

**cur·cu·lio** \(ˌ)kər-'kyü-lē-ˌō\ *noun, plural* **-lios** [Latin, grain weevil] (1756)

: any of various weevils; *especially* : one that injures fruit

**¹curd** \'kərd\ *noun* [Middle English *crud;* probably akin to Old English *crūdan* to press — more at CROWD] (15th century)
**1** : the thick casein-rich part of coagulated milk
**2** : something suggesting the curd of milk
— **curdy** \'kər-dē\ *adjective*

**²curd** *verb* (15th century)
: COAGULATE, CURDLE

**cur·dle** \'kər-d°l\ *verb* **cur·dled; cur·dling** \'kərd-liŋ, 'kər-d°l-iŋ\ [frequentative of ²*curd*] (1590)
*intransitive verb*
**1** : to form curds; *also* : to congeal as if by forming curds 〈a scream *curdled* in her throat〉
**2** : to go bad or wrong : SPOIL
*transitive verb*
**1** : to cause curds to form in
**2** : SPOIL, SOUR

**¹cure** \'kyùr\ *noun* [Middle English, from Old French, from Medieval Latin & Latin; Medieval Latin *cura,* cure of souls, from Latin, care] (14th century)
**1 a** : spiritual charge : CARE **b** : pastoral charge of a parish
**2 a** : recovery or relief from a disease **b** : something (as a drug or treatment) that cures a disease **c** : a course or period of treatment 〈take the *cure* for alcoholism〉 **d** : SPA
**3** : a complete or permanent solution or remedy 〈seeking a *cure* for unemployment〉
**4** : a process or method of curing
— **cure·less** \-ləs\ *adjective*

**²cure** *verb* **cured; cur·ing** (14th century)
*transitive verb*
**1 a** : to restore to health, soundness, or normality **b** : to bring about recovery from
**2 a** : to deal with in a way that eliminates or rectifies 〈his small size, which time would *cure* for him —William Faulkner〉 **b** : to free from something objectionable or harmful
**3** : to prepare or alter especially by chemical or physical processing for keeping or use
*intransitive verb*
**1 a** : to undergo a curing process **b** : SET 11
**2** : to effect a cure
— **cur·er** *noun*

**cu·ré** \kyù-'rā, 'kyùr-ˌā\ *noun* [French, from Old French, from Medieval Latin *curatus* — more at CURATE] (1655)
: a parish priest

**cure–all** \'kyùr-ˌol\ *noun* (1821)
: a remedy for all ills : PANACEA

**cu·ret·tage** \ˌkyùr-ə-'täzh\ *noun* (1897)
: a surgical scraping or cleaning by means of a curette

**¹cu·rette** *also* **cu·ret** \kyù-'ret\ *noun* [French *curette,* from *curer* to cure, from Latin *curare,* from *cura*] (1753)
: a surgical instrument that has a scoop, ring, or loop at the tip and is used in performing curettage

**²curette** *also* **curet** *transitive verb* **cu·rett·ed; cu·rett·ing** (1888)
: to perform curettage on
— **cu·rette·ment** \kyù-'ret-mənt\ *noun*

**cur·few** \'kər-ˌfyü\ *noun* [Middle English, from Middle French *covrefeu,* signal given to bank the hearth fire, curfew, from *covrir* to cover + *feu* fire, from Latin *focus* hearth] (14th century)
**1** : the sounding of a bell at evening 〈the *Curfew* tolls the knell of parting day —Thomas Gray〉
**2 a** : a regulation enjoining the withdrawal of usually specified persons (as juveniles or military personnel) from the streets or the closing of business establishments or places of assembly at a stated hour **b** : a signal to announce the beginning of a curfew **c** : the hour at which a curfew becomes effective **d** : the period during which a curfew is in effect ◆

**cu·ria** \'kyùr-ē-ə, 'kùr-\ *noun, plural* **cu·ri·ae** \'kyùr-ē-ˌē, 'kùr-ē-ˌī\ [Latin, perhaps from *co- + vir* man — more at VIRILE] (1600)
**1 a** : a division of the ancient Roman people comprising several gentes of a tribe **b** : the place of assembly of one of these divisions
**2 a** : the court of a medieval king **b** : a court of justice
**3** *often capitalized* : the body of congregations, tribunals, and offices through which the pope governs the Roman Catholic Church
— **cu·ri·al** \'kyùr-ē-əl, 'kùr-\ *adjective*

**cu·rie** \'kyùr-(ˌ)ē, kyù-'rē\ *noun* [Marie & Pierre *Curie*] (1910)
**1** : a unit quantity of any radioactive nuclide in which $3.7 \times 10^{10}$ disintegrations occur per second
**2** : a unit of radioactivity equal to $3.7 \times 10^{10}$ disintegrations per second ◆

**Curie point** *noun* (1911)
**1** : the temperature at which there is a transition between the ferromagnetic and paramagnetic phases
**2** : a temperature at which the anomalies that characterize a ferroelectric substance disappear — called also *Curie temperature*

**cu·rio** \'kyùr-ē-ˌō\ *noun, plural* **cu·ri·os** [short for *curiosity*] (1851)
: something (as a decorative object) considered novel, rare, or bizarre : CURIOSITY; *also* : an unusual or bizarre person

**cu·ri·o·sa** \ˌkyùr-ē-'ō-sə, -'ō-zə\ *noun plural* [New Latin, from Latin, neuter plural of *curiosus*] (1883)
: CURIOSITIES, RARITIES; *especially* : unusual or erotic books

**cu·ri·os·i·ty** \ˌkyùr-ē-'ä-s(ə-)tē\ *noun, plural* **-ties** (14th century)
**1** : desire to know: **a** : inquisitive interest in others' concerns : NOSINESS **b** : interest leading to inquiry 〈intellectual *curiosity*〉
**2** *archaic* : undue nicety or fastidiousness
**3 a** : one that arouses interest especially for uncommon or exotic characteristics **b** : an unusual knickknack : CURIO **c** : a curious trait or aspect

**cu·ri·ous** \'kyùr-ē-əs\ *adjective* [Middle English, from Middle French *curios,* from Latin *curiosus* careful, inquisitive, from *cura* cure] (14th century)
**1 a** *archaic* : made carefully **b** *obsolete* : ABSTRUSE **c** *archaic* : precisely accurate
**2 a** : marked by desire to investigate and learn **b** : marked by inquisitive interest in others' concerns : NOSY
**3** : exciting attention as strange, novel, or unexpected : ODD ☆
— **cu·ri·ous·ness** *noun*

**cu·ri·ous·ly** \-lē\ *adverb* (1665)
**1** : in a curious manner 〈seemed *curiously* calm〉
**2** : as is curious 〈*curiously,* he continues to win reelection〉

**cu·ri·um** \'kyùr-ē-əm\ *noun* [New Latin, from Marie & Pierre *Curie*] (1946)
: a metallic radioactive element produced artificially — see ELEMENT table

**¹curl** \'kər(-ə)l\ *verb* [Middle English, from *crul* curly, probably from Middle Dutch; akin to Old High German *krol* curly] (14th century)
*transitive verb*
**1** : to form (as the hair) into coils or ringlets
**2** : to form into a curved shape : TWIST 〈*curled* his lip in a sneer〉
**3** : to furnish with curls
*intransitive verb*
**1 a** : to grow in coils or spirals **b** : to form ripples or crinkles 〈bacon *curling* in a pan〉
**2** : to move or progress in curves or spirals : WIND 〈the path *curled* along the mountainside〉
**3** : TWIST, CONTORT
**4** : to play the game of curling

**²curl** *noun* (1602)
**1** : a lock of hair that coils : RINGLET

**2** : something having a spiral or winding form : COIL
**3** : the action of curling : the state of being curled
**4** : a curved or spiral marking in the grain of wood
**5** : a hollow arch of water formed when the crest of a breaking wave spills forward

**curl·er** \'kər-lər\ *noun* (1638)
**1** : a player of curling
**2** : one that curls; *especially* : a device on which hair is wound for curling

**cur·lew** \'kər-(ˌ)lü, 'kərl-(ˌ)yü\ *noun, plural* **curlews** *or* **curlew** [Middle English, from Middle French *corlieu,* of imitative origin] (14th century)
: any of various largely brownish chiefly migratory birds (especially genus *Numenius*) having long legs and a long slender downcurved bill and related to the sandpipers and snipes

**¹cur·li·cue** *also* **cur·ly·cue** \'kər-lē-ˌkyü, -li-\ *noun* [*curly* + *cue* a braid of hair] (1843)
: a fancifully curved or spiral figure : FLOURISH

**²curlicue** *verb* **-cued; -cu·ing** (1844)
*intransitive verb*
: to form curlicues

---

☆ **SYNONYMS**
**Curious, inquisitive, prying** mean interested in what is not one's personal or proper concern. CURIOUS, a neutral term, basically connotes an active desire to learn or to know 〈children are *curious* about everything〉. INQUISITIVE suggests impertinent and habitual curiosity and persistent quizzing 〈dreaded the visits of their *inquisitive* relatives〉. PRYING implies busy meddling and officiousness 〈*prying* neighbors who refuse to mind their own business〉.

---

◇ **WORD HISTORY**
**curfew** In Europe in the Middle Ages people were required to put out or cover their hearth fires by a certain time in the evening. Given the fact that houses were usually of wood and closely adjoining, a hearth fire left unattended overnight might spread and destroy neighboring houses or even the entire town. A bell was rung to let people know that the time had come for covering their fires. In Middle French this signal was called *covrefeu,* a compound of *covrir* "to cover," and *feu* "fire." The meaning of *covrefeu* was extended to any public signal calling on people to retire in the evening, and also to the time of evening when the signal was given. It was in these senses that English borrowed the word as *corfu* or *curfew* in the 14th century. Another English word based on French *covre* and a following noun object is *coverlet.*

**curie** The unit of measurement called the *curie* is named after Pierre (1859–1906) and Marie (1867–1934) Curie, the French chemists and physicists. The Curies were two of the most important and influential figures in modern physics. Their major joint contributions include the discovery (with Henri Becquerel) of radioactivity and the discovery and isolation of radium and polonium in 1898. In 1910 the first International Congress of Radiology honored the husband and wife team by establishing *curie* as a standard unit of measurement for radioactive material. Later it was used as a unit of radioactivity itself. The Curies were awarded the Nobel Prize for Physics in 1903, and Marie Curie was awarded the Nobel Prize for Chemistry in 1911.

*transitive verb*
: to embellish with curlicues
**curl·ing** \'kər-liŋ\ *noun* (1620)
: a game in which two teams of four players each slide curling stones over a stretch of ice toward a target circle
**curling iron** *noun* (1616)
: a rod-shaped usually metal instrument which is heated and around which a lock of hair to be curled or waved is wound
**curling stone** *noun* (1620)
: an ellipsoid stone or occasionally piece of iron with a gooseneck handle used in the game of curling
**curl·pa·per** \'kər(-ə)l-ˌpā-pər\ *noun* (circa 1817)
: a strip or piece of paper around which a lock of hair is wound for curling
**curl up** *intransitive verb* (1861)
: to arrange oneself in or as if in a ball or curl ⟨*curl up* by the fire⟩ ⟨*curl up* with a good book⟩
**curly** \'kər-lē\ *adjective* **curl·i·er; -est** (circa 1784)
**1** : tending to curl; *also* : having curls
**2** : having the grain composed of fibers that undulate without crossing and that often form alternating light and dark lines ⟨*curly* maple⟩
— **curl·i·ness** *noun*
**curly–coat·ed retriever** \'kər-lē-'kō-təd-\ *noun* (1885)
: any of a breed of sporting dogs with a short curly black or liver-colored coat
**curly top** *noun* (1901)
: a destructive virus disease especially of beets that kills young plants and causes curling and puckering of the leaves in older plants
**cur·mud·geon** \(ˌ)kər-'mə-jən\ *noun* [origin unknown] (1577)
**1** *archaic* : MISER
**2** : a crusty, ill-tempered, and usually old man
— **cur·mud·geon·li·ness** \-lē-nəs\ *noun*
— **cur·mud·geon·ly** \-lē\ *adjective*
**curn** \'kərn\ *or* **cur·ran** \'kə-rən\ *noun* [Middle English *curn;* akin to Middle English *corn*] (14th century)
**1** *Scottish* : GRAIN
**2** *Scottish* : a small number : FEW
**curr** \'kər\ *intransitive verb* [imitative] (1677)
: to make a murmuring sound (as of doves)
**cur·ragh** *or* **cur·rach** \'kə-rə, -ˌrək\ *noun* [Middle English *currok,* from Irish *currach, curach*] (15th century)
: a usually large coracle used especially on the west coast of Ireland
**cur·rant** \'kər-ənt, 'kə-rənt\ *noun* [Middle English *raison of Coraunte,* literally, raisin of Corinth] (14th century)
**1** : a small seedless raisin grown chiefly in the Levant
**2** : the acid edible fruit of several shrubs (genus *Ribes*) of the saxifrage family; *also* : a plant bearing currants
**cur·ren·cy** \'kər-ən(t)-sē, 'kə-rən(t)-\ *noun, plural* **-cies** (1699)
**1 a** : circulation as a medium of exchange **b** : general use, acceptance, or prevalence **c** : the quality or state of being current : CURRENTNESS
**2 a** : something (as coins, treasury notes, and banknotes) that is in circulation as a medium of exchange **b** : paper money in circulation **c** : a common article for bartering **d** : a medium of verbal or intellectual expression
**¹cur·rent** \'kər-ənt, 'kə-rənt\ *adjective* [Middle English *curraunt,* from Old French *curant,* present participle of *courre* to run, from Latin *currere* — more at CAR] (14th century)
**1 a** *archaic* : RUNNING, FLOWING **b** (1) : presently elapsing (2) : occurring in or existing at the present time (3) : most recent ⟨the *current* issue⟩
**2** : used as a medium of exchange
**3** : generally accepted, used, practiced, or prevalent at the moment
— **cur·rent·ly** *adverb*
— **cur·rent·ness** *noun*

**²current** *noun* (14th century)
**1 a** : the part of a fluid body (as air or water) moving continuously in a certain direction **b** : the swiftest part of a stream **c** : a tidal or nontidal movement of lake or ocean water **d** : flow marked by force or strength
**2 a** : a tendency or course of events that is usually the result of an interplay of forces ⟨*currents* of public opinion⟩ **b** : a prevailing mood : STRAIN
**3** : a flow of electric charge; *also* : the rate of such flow
**synonym** see TENDENCY
**current assets** *noun plural* (circa 1909)
: assets of a short-term nature that are readily convertible to cash
**cur·ri·cle** \'kər-i-kəl, 'kə-ri-\ *noun* [Latin *curriculum* running, chariot, from *currere*] (1752)
: a 2-wheeled chaise usually drawn by two horses
**cur·ric·u·lar** \kə-'ri-kyə-lər\ *adjective* (circa 1909)
: of or relating to a curriculum
**cur·ric·u·lum** \-ləm\ *noun, plural* **-la** \-lə\ *also* **-lums** [New Latin, from Latin, running, course] (1633)
**1** : the courses offered by an educational institution
**2** : a set of courses constituting an area of specialization
**cur·ric·u·lum vi·tae** \kə-'ri-kyə-ləm-'vē-ˌtī, -kə-ləm-, -'wē-ˌtī, -'vī-ˌtē\ *noun, plural* **cur·ric·u·la vitae** \-lə-\ [Latin, course of (one's) life] (1902)
: a short account of one's career and qualifications prepared typically by an applicant for a position
**cur·ri·ery** \'kər-ē-ə-rē, 'kə-rē-\ *noun, plural* **-er·ies** (circa 1889)
**1** : the trade of a currier of leather
**2** : a place where currying is done
**cur·rish** \'kər-ish\ *adjective* (15th century)
**1** : IGNOBLE
**2** : resembling a cur : MONGREL
— **cur·rish·ly** *adverb*
**¹cur·ry** \'kər-ē, 'kə-rē\ *transitive verb* **cur·ried; cur·ry·ing** [Middle English *currayen,* from Old French *correer* to prepare, curry, from (assumed) Vulgar Latin *conredare,* from Latin *com-* + a base of Germanic origin; akin to Gothic *garaiths* arrayed — more at READY] (13th century)
**1** : to clean the coat of (as a horse) with a currycomb
**2** : to treat (tanned leather) especially by incorporating oil or grease
**3** : BEAT, THRASH
— **cur·ri·er** *noun*
— **curry favor** [Middle English *currayen favel* to curry a chestnut horse] : to seek to gain favor by flattery or attention
**²cur·ry** *also* **cur·rie** \'kər-ē, 'kə-rē\ *noun, plural* **curries** [Tamil *kari*] (1681)
**1** : a food, dish, or sauce in Indian cuisine seasoned with a mixture of pungent spices; *also* : a food or dish seasoned with curry powder
**2** : CURRY POWDER
**³curry** *transitive verb* **cur·ried; cur·ry·ing** (1839)
: to flavor or cook with curry powder or a curry sauce
**cur·ry·comb** \-ˌkōm\ *noun* (1573)
: a comb made of rows of metallic teeth or serrated ridges and used especially to curry horses
— **currycomb** *transitive verb*
**curry powder** *noun* (1810)
: a condiment consisting of several pungent ground spices (as cayenne pepper, fenugreek, and turmeric)
**¹curse** \'kərs\ *noun* [Middle English *curs,* from Old English] (before 12th century)
**1** : a prayer or invocation for harm or injury to come upon one : IMPRECATION
**2** : something that is cursed or accursed

**3** : evil or misfortune that comes as if in response to imprecation or as retribution
**4** : a cause of great harm or misfortune : TORMENT
**5** : MENSTRUATION — used with *the*
**²curse** *verb* **cursed; curs·ing** (before 12th century)
*transitive verb*
**1** : to use profanely insolent language against : BLASPHEME
**2 a** : to call upon divine or supernatural power to send injury upon **b** : to execrate in fervent and often profane terms
**3** : to bring great evil upon : AFFLICT
*intransitive verb*
: to utter imprecations : SWEAR
**synonym** see EXECRATE
**cursed** \'kər-səd, 'kərst\ *also* **curst** \'kərst\ *adjective* (13th century)
: being under or deserving a curse
— **cursed·ly** *adverb*
— **cursed·ness** *noun*
**¹cur·sive** \'kər-siv\ *adjective* [French or Medieval Latin; French *cursif,* from Medieval Latin *cursivus,* literally, running, from Latin *cursus,* past participle of *currere* to run] (1784)
: RUNNING, COURSING: as **a** *of writing* : flowing often with the strokes of successive characters joined and the angles rounded **b** : having a flowing, easy, impromptu character
— **cur·sive·ly** *adverb*
— **cur·sive·ness** *noun*
**²cursive** *noun* (1861)
**1** : a manuscript written in cursive writing; *also* : cursive writing
**2** : a style of printed letter resembling handwriting
**cur·sor** \'kər-sər, -ˌsȯr\ *noun* [Latin, runner, from *currere*] (1594)
: a movable item used to mark a position: as **a** : a transparent slide with a line attached to a slide rule **b** : a visual cue (as a flashing rectangle) on a video display that indicates position (as for data entry)
**cur·so·ri·al** \ˌkər-'sȯr-ē-əl, -'sȯr-\ *adjective* (1836)
: adapted to or involving running
**cur·so·ry** \'kərs-rē, 'kər-sə-\ *adjective* [Late Latin *cursorius* of running, from Latin *currere*] (1601)
: rapidly and often superficially performed or produced : HASTY ⟨a *cursory* glance⟩
**synonym** see SUPERFICIAL
— **cur·so·ri·ly** \-rə-lē\ *adverb*
— **cur·so·ri·ness** \-rē-nəs\ *noun*
**curt** \'kərt\ *adjective* [Latin *curtus* shortened — more at SHEAR] (1630)
**1 a** : sparing of words : TERSE **b** : marked by rude or peremptory shortness : BRUSQUE
**2** : shortened in linear dimension
**synonym** see BLUFF
— **curt·ly** *adverb*
— **curt·ness** *noun*
**cur·tail** \(ˌ)kər-'tā(ə)l\ *transitive verb* [by folk etymology from earlier *curtal* to dock an animal's tail, from *curtal,* noun, animal with a docked tail, from Middle French *courtault* — more at CURTAL] (1580)
: to make less by or as if by cutting off or away some part ⟨*curtail* the power of the executive branch⟩ ⟨*curtail* inflation⟩
**synonym** see SHORTEN
— **cur·tail·er** \-'tā-lər\ *noun*
**cur·tail·ment** \-'tā(ə)l-mənt\ *noun* (1794)
: the act of curtailing : the state of being curtailed
**¹cur·tain** \'kər-t³n\ *noun* [Middle English *curtine,* from Old French, from Late Latin *cortina* (translation of Greek *aulaia,* from *aulē* court),

from Latin *cohort-, cohors* enclosure, court — more at COURT] (14th century)
**1 :** a hanging screen usually capable of being drawn back or up; *especially* **:** window drapery
**2 :** a device or agency that conceals or acts as a barrier — compare IRON CURTAIN
**3 a :** the part of a bastioned front that connects two neighboring bastions **b** (1) **:** a similar stretch of plain wall (2) **:** a nonbearing exterior wall
**4 a :** the movable screen separating the stage from the auditorium of a theater **b :** the ascent or opening (as at the beginning of a play) of a stage curtain; *also* **:** its descent or closing (as at the end of an act) **c :** the final situation, line, or scene of an act or play **d :** the time at which a theatrical performance begins **e** *plural* **:** END; *especially* **:** DEATH ⟨it will be *curtains* for us if we're caught⟩
— **cur·tain·less** \-ləs\ *adjective*

**²curtain** *transitive verb* **cur·tained; cur·tain·ing** \'kərt-niŋ, -'kər-t³n-iŋ\ (14th century)
**1 :** to furnish with or as if with curtains
**2 :** to veil or shut off with or as if with a curtain

**curtain call** *noun* (1884)
**:** an appearance by a performer (as after the final curtain of a play) in response to the applause of the audience

**curtain lecture** *noun* [from its originally being given behind the curtains of a bed] (1633)
**:** a private lecture by a wife to her husband

**cur·tain–rais·er** \'kər-t³n-ˌrā-zər\ *noun* (1886)
**1 :** a short play usually of one scene that is presented before the main full-length drama
**2 :** a usually short preliminary to a main event

**curtain wall** *noun* (1853)
**:** a nonbearing exterior wall between columns or piers

**cur·tal** \'kərt-³l\ *adjective* [Middle French *courtault,* from *court* short, from Latin *curtus*] (1576)
**1** *obsolete* **:** having a docked tail
**2** *obsolete* **:** BRIEF, CURTAILED
**3** *archaic* **:** wearing a short frock

**cur·tal ax** *or* **cur·tle ax** \'kərt-³l-\ *noun* [modification of Middle French *coutelas*] (circa 1580)
*archaic* **:** CUTLASS

**cur·te·sy** \'kərt-ə-sē\ *noun, plural* **-sies** [Middle English *corteisie* courtesy] (1523)
**:** a husband's interest upon the death of his wife in the real property of an estate that she either solely owned or inherited provided they bore a child capable of inheriting the estate — compare DOWER

**cur·ti·lage** \'kərt-³l-ij\ *noun* [Middle English, from Middle French *cortillage,* from *cortil* courtyard, from *cort* court] (14th century)
**:** a piece of ground (as a yard or courtyard) within the fence surrounding a house

**¹curt·sy** *also* **curt·sey** \'kərt-sē\ *intransitive verb* **curt·sied** *also* **curt·seyed; curt·sy·ing** *also* **curt·sey·ing** [alteration of *courtesy*] (circa 1553)
**:** to make a curtsy

**²curtsy** *also* **curtsey** *noun, plural* **curtsies** *also* **curtseys** (1575)
**:** an act of civility, respect, or reverence made mainly by women and consisting of a slight lowering of the body with bending of the knees

**cu·rule** \'kyùr-ˌül\ *adjective* [Latin *curulis,* perhaps alteration of *currulis* of a chariot, from *currus* chariot, from *currere* to run] (1600)
**:** privileged to sit in a seat reserved in ancient Rome for the use of the highest dignitaries; *also* **:** of or relating to a curule chair

**cur·va·ceous** *also* **cur·va·cious** \ˌkər-'vā-shəs\ *adjective* (circa 1935)
**:** having curves suggestive of a well-proportioned feminine figure

**cur·va·ture** \'kər-və-ˌchùr, -chər, -ˌtyùr, -ˌtùr\ *noun* (1603)
**1 :** the act of curving **:** the state of being curved
**2 :** a measure or amount of curving; *specifically* **:** the rate of change of the angle through which the tangent to a curve turns in moving along the curve and which for a circle is equal to the reciprocal of the radius
**3 a :** an abnormal curving (as of the spine) **b :** a curved surface of an organ

**¹curve** \'kərv\ *adjective* [Middle English, from Latin *curvus;* akin to Greek *kyrtos* convex, Middle Irish *cruinn* round] (15th century)
*archaic* **:** bent or formed into a curve

**²curve** *verb* **curved; curv·ing** [Latin *curvare,* from *curvus*] (1594)
*intransitive verb*
**:** to have or take a turn, change, or deviation from a straight line or plane surface without sharp breaks or angularity
*transitive verb*
**1 :** to cause to curve
**2 :** to throw a curveball to (a batter)
**3 :** to grade (as an examination) on a curve

**³curve** *noun* (1696)
**1 a :** a line especially when curved: as (1) **:** the path of a moving point (2) **:** a line defined by an equation so that the coordinates of its points are functions of a single independent variable or parameter **b :** the graph of a variable
**2 :** something curved: as **a :** a curving line of the human body **b** *plural* **:** PARENTHESIS
**3 a :** CURVEBALL **b :** TRICK, DECEPTION
**4 :** a distribution indicating the relative performance of individuals measured against each other that is used especially in assigning good, medium, or poor grades to usually predetermined proportions of students rather than in assigning grades based on predetermined standards of achievement
— **curvy** \'kər-vē\ *adjective*

**curve·ball** \'kərv-ˌbòl\ *noun* (1936)
**:** a slow or moderately fast baseball pitch thrown with spin to make it swerve downward and usually to the left when thrown from the right hand or to the right when thrown from the left hand
— **curveball** *verb*

**curve fitting** *noun* (circa 1924)
**:** the empirical determination of a curve or function that approximates a set of data

**¹cur·vet** \(ˌ)kər-'vet\ *noun* [Italian *corvetta,* from Middle French *courbette,* from *courber* to curve, from Latin *curvare*] (1575)
**:** a prancing leap of a horse in which the hind legs are raised just before the forelegs touch the ground

**²curvet** *intransitive verb* **-vet·ted** *or* **-vet·ed; -vet·ting** *or* **-vet·ing** (1592)
**:** to make a curvet; *also* **:** PRANCE, CAPER

**cur·vi·lin·ear** \ˌkər-və-'li-nē-ər\ *adjective* [Latin *curvus* + *linea* line] (1710)
**1 :** consisting of or bounded by curved lines **:** represented by a curved line
**2 :** marked by flowing tracery ⟨*curvilinear* Gothic⟩
— **cur·vi·lin·ear·i·ty** \-ˌli-nē-'ar-ə-tē\ *noun*

**cu·sec** \'kyü-ˌsek\ *noun* [*cubic foot per second*] (circa 1903)
**:** a volumetric unit of flow equal to a cubic foot per second

**cush·at** \'kə-shət\ *noun* [Middle English *cowschote,* from Old English *cūscote*] (before 12th century)
*chiefly Scottish* **:** RINGDOVE 1

**cu·shaw** \kù-'shò, 'kü-ˌ\ *noun* [origin unknown] (1698)
**:** a squash of any of several cultivars of a winter squash (*Cucurbita mixta*)

**Cush·ing's disease** \'kù-shiŋz-\ *noun* [Harvey *Cushing*] (circa 1935)

**:** Cushing's syndrome especially when caused by excessive production of ACTH by the pituitary gland

**Cushing's syndrome** *noun* (1937)
**:** an abnormal bodily condition characterized by obesity and muscular weakness due to excess corticosteroids and especially hydrocortisone from adrenal or pituitary hyperfunction

**¹cush·ion** \'kù-shən\ *noun* [Middle English *cusshin,* from Middle French *coissin,* from (assumed) Vulgar Latin *coxinus,* from Latin *coxa* hip — more at COXA] (14th century)
**1 :** a soft pillow or pad usually used for sitting, reclining, or kneeling
**2 :** a bodily part resembling a pad
**3 :** something resembling a cushion: as **a :** PILLOW 2 **b :** RAT 3 **c :** a pad of springy rubber along the inside of the rim of a billiard table **d :** a padded insert in a shoe **e :** an elastic body for reducing shock **f :** a mat laid under a large rug to ease the effect of wear
**4 a :** something (as an economic factor or a medical procedure) serving to mitigate the effects of disturbances or disorders **b :** a reserve supply (as of money) **c :** a comfortable lead ⟨a 4–0 *cushion* in the ninth inning⟩
— **cush·ion·less** \-ləs\ *adjective*
— **cush·iony** \-shə-nē\ *adjective*

**²cushion** *transitive verb* **cush·ioned; cush·ion·ing** \'kù-sh(ə-)niŋ\ (circa 1738)
**1 :** to seat or place on a cushion
**2 :** to suppress by ignoring
**3 :** to furnish with a cushion
**4 a :** to mitigate the effects of **b :** to protect against force or shock
**5 :** to check gradually so as to minimize shock of moving parts

**Cush·it·ic** \kə-'shi-tik, kù-\ *noun* [*Cush* (Kush), Africa] (circa 1903)
**:** a subfamily of the Afro-Asiatic language family comprising various languages spoken in eastern Africa and especially in Ethiopia, Djibouti, and Somalia
— **Cushitic** *adjective*

**cushy** \'kù-shē\ *adjective* **cush·i·er; cush·i·est** [Hindi *khush* pleasant, from Persian *khūsh*] (1915)
**:** entailing little hardship or difficulty ⟨a *cushy* job with a high salary⟩
— **cush·i·ly** \'kù-shə-lē\ *adverb*

**cusk** \'kəsk\ *noun, plural* **cusk** *or* **cusks** [probably alteration of *tusk,* a kind of codfish] (1616)
**1 :** a large edible North Atlantic fish (*Brosme brosme*) of the cod family
**2 :** BURBOT

**cusp** \'kəsp\ *noun* [Latin *cuspis* point] (1585)
**:** POINT, APEX: as **a :** either horn of a crescent moon **b :** a fixed point on a mathematical curve at which a point tracing the curve would exactly reverse its direction of motion **c :** an ornamental pointed projection formed by or arising from the intersection of two arcs or foils **d** (1) **:** a point on the grinding surface of a tooth (2) **:** a fold or flap of a cardiac valve **e :** a point of transition (as from one astrological sign to another or one historical period to the next) **:** TURNING POINT; *also* **:** EDGE, VERGE ⟨on the *cusp* of stardom⟩

*1 cusp c*

— **cus·pate** \'kəs-ˌpāt, -pət\ *adjective*
— **cusped** \'kəspt\ *adjective*

**cus·pid** \'kəs-pəd\ *noun* [*bicuspid*] (1878)
**:** CANINE 1

**cus·pi·date** \'kəs-pə-ˌdāt\ *adjective* [Latin *cuspidatus,* past participle of *cuspidare* to make pointed, from *cuspid-, cuspis* point] (1692)
**:** having a cusp **:** terminating in a point ⟨a *cuspidate* leaf⟩ ⟨*cuspidate* molars⟩

**cus·pi·da·tion** \ˌkəs-pə-'dā-shən\ *noun* (1848)
**:** decoration with cusps

**cus·pi·dor** \'kəs-pə-ˌdòr, -ˌdōr\ *noun* [Portuguese *cuspidouro* place for spitting, from *cuspir* to spit, from Latin *conspuere*, from *com-* + *spuere* to spit — more at SPEW] (1735)
: SPITTOON

**¹cuss** \'kəs\ *noun* [alteration of *curse*] (1775)
**1** : FELLOW 4c
**2** : CURSE 1, 2

**²cuss** *verb* (1815)
: CURSE
— **cuss·er** *noun*

**cuss·ed** \'kə-səd\ *adjective* (1840)
**1** : CURSED
**2** : OBSTINATE, CANTANKEROUS
— **cuss·ed·ly** *adverb*
— **cuss·ed·ness** \-nəs\ *noun*

**cuss·word** \'kəs-ˌwərd\ *noun* (1872)
**1** : SWEARWORD
**2** : a term of abuse : a derogatory term

**cus·tard** \'kəs-tərd\ *noun* [Middle English, a kind of pie, alteration of *crustarde, crustade*, probably from (assumed) Anglo-French *crustade*, from Old French *crouste* crust, from Latin *crusta* — more at CRUST] (1740)
: a pudding-like usually sweetened mixture made with eggs and milk
— **cus·tardy** \-tər-dē\ *adjective*

**custard apple** *noun* (1657)
**1 a** : any of several chiefly tropical American soft-fleshed edible fruits **b** : any of a genus (*Annona* of the family Annonaceae, the custard-apple family) of trees or shrubs bearing this fruit; *especially* : a small West Indian tree (*A. reticulata*)
**2** : PAPAW 2

**cus·to·di·al** \ˌkəs-'tō-dē-əl\ *adjective* (1772)
: relating to guardianship; *specifically* : marked by or given to watching and protecting rather than seeking to cure ⟨*custodial* care⟩

**cus·to·di·an** \ˌkəs-'tō-dē-ən\ *noun* (1781)
: one that guards and protects or maintains; *especially* : one entrusted with guarding and keeping property or records or with custody or guardianship of prisoners or inmates
— **cus·to·di·an·ship** \-ˌship\ *noun*

**cus·to·dy** \'kəs-tə-dē\ *noun, plural* **-dies** [Middle English *custodie*, from Latin *custodia* guarding, from *custod-, custos* guardian] (15th century)
: immediate charge and control (as over a ward or a suspect) exercised by a person or an authority; *also* : SAFEKEEPING

**¹cus·tom** \'kəs-təm\ *noun* [Middle English *custume*, from Old French, from Latin *consuetudin-, consuetudo*, from *consuescere* to accustom, from *com-* + *suescere* to accustom; akin to *suus* one's own — more at SUICIDE] (13th century)
**1 a** : a usage or practice common to many or to a particular place or class or habitual with an individual **b** : long-established practice considered as unwritten law **c** : repeated practice **d** : the whole body of usages, practices, or conventions that regulate social life
**2** *plural* **a** : duties, tolls, or imposts imposed by the sovereign law of a country on imports or exports **b** *usually singular in construction* : the agency, establishment, or procedure for collecting such customs
**3 a** : business patronage **b** : usually habitual patrons : CUSTOMERS
**synonym** see HABIT

**²custom** *adjective* (1830)
**1** : made or performed according to personal order
**2** : specializing in custom work or operation ⟨a *custom* tailor⟩

**cus·tom·ary** \'kəs-tə-ˌmer-ē\ *adjective* (1535)
**1** : based on or established by custom
**2** : commonly practiced, used, or observed
**synonym** see USUAL
— **cus·tom·ar·i·ly** \ˌkəs-tə-'mer-ə-lē\ *adverb*
— **cus·tom·ar·i·ness** \'kəs-tə-ˌmer-ē-nəs\ *noun*

**cus·tom–built** \'kəs-təm-'bilt\ *adjective* (1925)
: built to individual specifications

**cus·tom·er** \'kəs-tə-mər\ *noun* [Middle English *custumer*, from *custume*] (15th century)
**1** : one that purchases a commodity or service
**2** : an individual usually having some specified distinctive trait ⟨a real tough *customer*⟩

**cus·tom·house** \'kəs-təm-ˌhaus\ *also* **cus·toms·house** \-təmz-\ *noun* (15th century)
: a building where customs and duties are paid or collected and where vessels are entered and cleared

**cus·tom·ise** *British variant of* CUSTOMIZE

**cus·tom·ize** \'kəs-tə-ˌmīz\ *transitive verb* **-ized; -iz·ing** (1926)
: to build, fit, or alter according to individual specifications
— **cus·tom·iz·er** *noun*

**cus·tom–made** \ˌkəs-tə(m)-'mād\ *adjective* (1855)
: made to individual specifications

**cus·tom–tai·lor** \-'tā-lər\ *transitive verb* (1895)
: to alter, plan, or build according to individual specifications or needs

**¹cut** \'kət\ *verb* **cut; cut·ting** [Middle English *cutten*] (13th century)
*transitive verb*
**1 a** : to penetrate with or as if with an edged instrument **b** : to hurt the feelings of **c** : to strike sharply with a cutting effect **d** : to strike (a ball) with a glancing blow that imparts a reverse spin **e** : to experience the growth of (a tooth) through the gum
**2 a** : TRIM, PARE ⟨*cut* one's nails⟩ **b** : to shorten by omissions **c** : DISSOLVE, DILUTE, ADULTERATE **d** : to reduce in amount ⟨*cut* costs⟩
**3 a** : MOW, REAP **b** (1) : to divide into parts with an edged tool ⟨*cut* bread⟩ (2) : FELL, HEW **c** (1) : to separate or discharge from an organization : DETACH (2) : to single out and isolate ⟨*cut* a calf out from the herd⟩ **d** : to change the direction of sharply **e** : to go or pass around or about
**4 a** : to divide into segments **b** : INTERSECT, CROSS **c** : BREAK, INTERRUPT ⟨*cut* our supply lines⟩ **d** (1) : to divide (a deck of cards) into two portions (2) : to draw (a card) from the deck **e** : to divide into shares : SPLIT
**5 a** : to make by or as if by cutting: as (1) : CARVE ⟨*cut* stone⟩ (2) : to shape by grinding ⟨*cut* a diamond⟩ (3) : ENGRAVE (4) : to shear or hollow out **b** : to record sounds (as speech or music) on ⟨*cut* a record⟩ **c** : to type on a stencil
**6 a** : STOP, CEASE ⟨*cut* the nonsense⟩ **b** : to refuse to recognize (an acquaintance) : OSTRACIZE **c** : to absent oneself from (as a class) **d** : to stop (a motor) by opening a switch **e** : to stop the filming of (a motion-picture scene)
**7 a** : to engage in (a frolicsome or mischievous action) ⟨on summer nights strange capers are *cut* under the thin guise of a Christian festival —D. C. Peattie⟩ **b** : to give the appearance or impression of ⟨*cut* a fine figure⟩
**8** : to be able to manage or handle — usually used in negative constructions ⟨can't *cut* that kind of work anymore⟩
*intransitive verb*
**1 a** : to function as or as if as an edged tool **b** : to undergo incision or severance ⟨cheese *cuts* easily⟩ **c** : to perform the operation of dividing, severing, incising, or intersecting **d** : to make a stroke with a whip, sword, or other weapon **e** : to wound feelings or sensibilities **f** : to cause constriction or chafing **g** : to be of effect, influence, or significance ⟨an analysis that *cuts* deep⟩
**2 a** (1) : to divide a pack of cards especially in order to decide the deal or settle a bet (2) : to draw a card from the pack **b** : to divide spoils : SPLIT

**3 a** : to proceed obliquely from a straight course ⟨*cut* across the yard⟩ **b** : to move swiftly ⟨a yacht *cutting* through the water⟩ **c** : to describe an oblique or diagonal line **d** : to change sharply in direction : SWERVE **e** : to make an abrupt transition from one sound or image to another in motion pictures, radio, or television
**4** : to stop photographing motion pictures
— **cut a deal** : to negotiate an agreement
— **cut both ways** : to have both favorable and unfavorable results or implications
— **cut corners** : to perform some action in the quickest, easiest, or cheapest way
— **cut ice** : to be of importance — usually used in negative constructions
— **cut it** : to cut the mustard
— **cut the mustard** : to achieve the standard of performance necessary for success

**²cut** *noun* (1548)
**1** : a product of cutting: as **a** : a creek, channel, or inlet made by excavation or worn by natural action **b** (1) : an opening made with an edged instrument (2) : a wound made by something sharp : GASH **c** : a surface or outline left by cutting **d** : a passage cut as a roadway **e** : a grade or step especially in a social scale ⟨a *cut* above the ordinary⟩ **f** : a subset of a set such that when it is subtracted from the set the remainder is not connected **g** : a pictorial illustration **h** : TRACK 1e(2)
**2** : the act or an instance of cutting: as **a** : a gesture or expression that hurts the feelings ⟨made an unkind *cut*⟩ **b** : a straight passage or course **c** : a stroke or blow with the edge of a knife or other edged tool **d** : a lash with or as if with a whip **e** : the act of reducing or removing a part ⟨a *cut* in pay⟩ **f** : an act or turn of cutting cards; *also* : the result of cutting **g** : the elimination of part of a large field from further competition (as in a golf tournament) — often used with *miss* or *make* to denote respectively being or not being among those eliminated ⟨played poorly and missed the *cut*⟩
**3** : something that is cut or cut off: as **a** : a length of cloth varying from 40 to 100 yards (36.6 to 91.4 meters) **b** : the yield of products cut especially during one harvest **c** : a segment or section of a meat carcass or a part of one **d** : a group of animals selected from a herd **e** : SHARE ⟨took his *cut* of the profits⟩
**4** : a voluntary absence from a class
**5 a** : a stroke that cuts a ball; *also* : the spin imparted by such a stroke **b** : a swing by a batter at a pitched baseball **c** : an exchange of captures in checkers
**6** : an abrupt transition from one sound or image to another in motion pictures, radio, or television
**7 a** : the shape and style in which a thing is cut, formed, or made ⟨clothes of the latest *cut*⟩ **b** : PATTERN, TYPE **c** : HAIRCUT
— **cut of one's jib** : APPEARANCE, STYLE

**cut·abil·i·ty** \ˌkə-tə-'bi-lə-tē\ *noun* (1965)
: the proportion of lean salable meat yielded by a carcass

**cut–and–dried** \ˌkət-ᵊn-'drīd\ *also* **cut–and–dry** \-'drī\ *adjective* (1710)
: being or done according to a plan, set procedure, or formula : ROUTINE

**cut–and–paste** \-'pāst\ *adjective* (1953)
: pieced together by excerpting and combining passages from many sources ⟨the book was a *cut-and-paste* job⟩

**cut–and–try** \-'trī\ *adjective* (1903)
: marked by experimental procedure : EMPIRICAL

**cu·ta·ne·ous** \kyù-'tā-nē-əs\ *adjective* [New Latin *cutaneus*, from Latin *cutis* skin — more at HIDE] (1578)

\ə\ abut \ᵊ\ kitten \ər\ further \a\ ash \ā\ ace \ä\ mop, mar \aù\ out \ch\ chin \e\ bet \ē\ easy \g\ go \i\ hit \ī\ ice \j\ job \ŋ\ sing \ō\ go \ò\ law \òi\ boy \th\ thin \th\ the \ü\ loot \ù\ foot \y\ yet \zh\ vision *see also* Guide to Pronunciation

: of, relating to, or affecting the skin
— **cu·ta·ne·ous·ly** *adverb*
**¹cut·away** \'kə-tə-ˌwā\ *adjective* (1841)
: having or showing parts cut away
**²cutaway** *noun* (1849)
**1** : a coat with skirts tapering from the front waistline to form tails at the back
**2 a** : a cutaway picture or representation **b** : a shot that interrupts the main action of a film or television program to take up a related subject or to depict action supposed to be going on at the same time as the main action
**3** : a back dive in which the head is lowered toward the board after the takeoff
**cut·back** \'kət-ˌbak\ *noun* (1897)
**1** : something cut back
**2** : REDUCTION
**cut back** (1871)
*transitive verb*
: to shorten by cutting : PRUNE
*intransitive verb*
**1** : to interrupt the sequence of a plot (as of a movie) by introducing events prior to those last presented
**2** : CUT DOWN ⟨*cut back* on sugar⟩
**cutch** \'kəch\ *noun* [modification of Malay *kachu*] (1759)
: CATECHU a
**cut down** (1821)
*transitive verb*
**1 a** : to strike down and kill or incapacitate **b** : KNOCK DOWN
**2 a** : to remodel by removing extras or unwanted furnishings and fittings **b** : to remake in a smaller size
*intransitive verb*
: to reduce or curtail volume or activity ⟨*cut down* on smoking⟩
— **cut down to size** : to reduce from an inflated or exaggerated importance to true or suitable stature
**cute** \'kyüt\ *adjective* **cut·er; cut·est** [short for *acute*] (circa 1731)
**1 a** : clever or shrewd often in an underhanded manner **b** : IMPERTINENT, SMART-ALECKY ⟨don't get *cute* with me⟩
**2** : attractive or pretty especially in a dainty or delicate way
**3** : obviously straining for effect
— **cute·ly** *adverb*
— **cute·ness** *noun*
**cute·sy** \'kyüt-sē\ *adjective* **cute·si·er; -est** [*cute* + *-sy* (as in *folksy*)] (1914)
: self-consciously or excessively cute
**cut glass** *noun* (1800)
: glass ornamented with patterns cut into its surface by an abrasive wheel and polished
**cut–grass** \'kət-ˌgras\ *noun* (circa 1818)
: a grass (especially genus *Leersia*) with minute hooked bristles along the edges of the leaf blade
**cu·ti·cle** \'kyü-ti-kəl\ *noun* [Latin *cuticula*, diminutive of *cutis* skin — more at HIDE] (1615)
**1** : SKIN, PELLICLE: as **a** : an external investment (as of an insect) secreted usually by epidermal cells **b** : the outermost layer of animal integument (as in humans) when composed of epidermis **c** : a thin continuous fatty or waxy film on the external surface of many higher plants that consists chiefly of cutin
**2** : dead or horny epidermis
— **cu·tic·u·lar** \kyü-'ti-kyə-lər\ *adjective*
**cut·ie** *or* **cut·ey** \'kyü-tē\ *noun, plural* **cuties** *or* **cuteys** [*cute* + *-ie*] (1908)
: an attractive person; *especially* : a pretty girl
**cu·tin** \'kyü-t°n\ *noun* [International Scientific Vocabulary, from Latin *cutis*] (circa 1872)
: an insoluble mixture containing waxes, fatty acids, soaps, and resinous material that forms a continuous layer on the outer epidermal wall of a plant
**cut–in** \'kət-ˌin\ *noun* (1883)
: something cut in
— **cut–in** *adjective*
**cut in** (1612)
*intransitive verb*

**1** : to thrust oneself into a position between others or belonging to another
**2** : to join in something suddenly ⟨*cut in* on the conversation⟩
**3** : to interrupt a dancing couple and take one as one's partner
**4** : to become automatically connected or started in operation
*transitive verb*
**1** : to mix with cutting motions ⟨after sifting the flour into a mixing bowl, *cut* the lard *in*⟩
**2** : to introduce into a number, group, or sequence
**3** : to connect into an electrical circuit to a mechanical apparatus so as to permit operation
**4** : to include especially among those benefiting or favored ⟨*cut* them *in* on the profits⟩
**cu·tin·ized** \'kyü-t°n-ˌīzd\ *adjective* (1901)
: infiltrated with cutin ⟨*cutinized* epidermal cells⟩
**cu·tis** \'kyü-təs\ *noun, plural* **cu·tes** \'kyü-ˌtēz\ *or* **cu·tis·es** [Latin] (1603)
: DERMIS
**cut·lass** \'kət-ləs\ *noun* [Middle French *coutelas*, augmentative of *coutel* knife, from Latin *cultellus*, diminutive of *culter* knife, plowshare] (1594)
**1** : a short curving sword formerly used by sailors on warships
**2** : MACHETE
**cut·ler** \'kət-lər\ *noun* [Middle English, from Middle French *coutelier*, from Late Latin *cultellarius*, from Latin *cultellus*] (14th century)
: one who makes, deals in, or repairs cutlery
**cut·lery** \'kət-lə-rē\ *noun* (15th century)
**1** : the business of a cutler
**2** : edged or cutting tools; *specifically* : implements for cutting and eating food
**cut·let** \'kət-lət\ *noun* [French *côtelette*, from Old French *costelette*, diminutive of *coste* rib, side, from Latin *costa* — more at COAST] (circa 1706)
**1** : a small slice of meat ⟨a veal *cutlet*⟩
**2** : a flat croquette of chopped meat or fish
**cut·line** \'kət-ˌlīn\ *noun* (1943)
: CAPTION, LEGEND
**cut·off** \'kət-ˌof\ *noun* (1741)
**1** : the act or action of cutting off
**2 a** : the new and relatively short channel formed when a stream cuts through the neck of an oxbow **b** : SHORTCUT 1 **c** : a channel made to straighten a stream
**3** : a device for cutting off
**4 a** : something cut off **b** *plural* : shorts originally made from jeans with the legs cut off at the knees or higher
**5** : the point, date, or period for a cutoff
— **cutoff** *adjective*
**cut off** (14th century)
*transitive verb*
**1** : to bring to an untimely end
**2** : to stop the passage of
**3** : SHUT OFF, BAR
**4** : DISCONTINUE, TERMINATE
**5** : SEPARATE, ISOLATE
**6** : DISINHERIT
**7 a** : to stop the operation of : TURN OFF **b** : to stop or interrupt while in communication ⟨the operator *cut* me *off*⟩
*intransitive verb*
: to cease operating
**cutoff man** *noun* (1967)
: a player in baseball who relays a ball from an outfielder to the infield
**cut·out** \'kət-ˌaut\ *noun* (1851)
**1** : something cut out or off from something else; *also* : the space or hole left after cutting
**2** : one that cuts out
**3** : one serving as an intermediary for clandestine operations
— **cutout** *adjective*
**¹cut out** (15th century)
*transitive verb*
**1** : to form by erosion
**2** : to determine or assign through necessity ⟨you've got your work *cut out* for you⟩

**3** : to take the place of : SUPPLANT
**4** : to put an end to : desist from
**5** : DEPRIVE, DEFRAUD
**6 a** : to remove from a series or circuit : DISCONNECT **b** : to make inoperative
*intransitive verb*
**1** : to depart in haste
**2** : to cease operating
**3** : to swerve out of a traffic line
**²cut out** *adjective* (1645)
: naturally fitted or suited ⟨not *cut out* to be a vet⟩
**cut·over** \'kət-ˌō-vər\ *adjective* (1899)
: having most of the salable timber cut down
**cut–price** \-'prīs\ *adjective* (1897)
*chiefly British* : CUT-RATE
**cut·purse** \'kət-ˌpərs\ *noun* (14th century)
: PICKPOCKET
**cut–rate** \'kət-ˌrāt\ *adjective* (1881)
**1** : marked by, offering, or making use of a reduced rate or price ⟨*cut-rate* stores⟩
**2** : SECOND-RATE, CHEAP
**cut·ta·ble** \'kə-tə-bəl\ *adjective* (15th century)
: capable of being cut : ready for cutting
**cut·ter** \'kət-ər\ *noun* (15th century)
**1** : one that cuts: **a** : one whose work is cutting or involves cutting **b** (1) : an instrument, machine, machine part, or tool that cuts (2) : a device for vibrating a cutting stylus in disc recording; *also* : the stylus or its point
**2 a** : a ship's boat for carrying stores or passengers **b** : a single-masted fore-and-aft rigged sailing vessel **c** : a small armed vessel in government service
**3** : a light sleigh
**¹cut·throat** \'kət-ˌthrōt\ *noun* (1535)
**1** : KILLER, MURDERER
**2** : a cruel unprincipled person
**²cutthroat** *adjective* (1567)
**1** : MURDEROUS, CRUEL
**2** : marked by unprincipled practices : RUTHLESS ⟨*cutthroat* competition⟩
**3** : characterized by each player playing independently rather than having a permanent partner — used especially of partnership games adapted for three players ⟨*cutthroat* bridge⟩
**cutthroat contract** *noun* (circa 1944)
: contract bridge in which partnerships are determined by the bidding
**cutthroat trout** *noun* (circa 1891)
: a large spotted trout (*Oncorhynchus clarki* synonym *Salmo clarki*) chiefly of northwestern North America that has reddish streaks on the integument of the lower jaw — called also *cutthroat*

**cutthroat trout**

**cut time** *noun* (1951)
: duple or quadruple time with the beat represented by a half note
**¹cut·ting** \'kə-tiŋ\ *noun* (14th century)
**1** : something cut or cut off or out: as **a** : a plant section originating from stem, leaf, or root and capable of developing into a new plant **b** : HARVEST
**2** : something made by cutting; *especially* : RECORD 4
**²cutting** *adjective* (15th century)
**1** : given to or designed for cutting; *especially* : SHARP, EDGED
**2** : marked by sharp piercing cold
**3** : inclined or likely to wound the feelings of others especially because of a ruthless incisiveness ⟨a *cutting* remark⟩
**4** : INTENSE, PIERCING ⟨a *cutting* pain⟩
— **cut·ting·ly** \-tiŋ-lē\ *adverb*
**cutting board** *noun* (1825)
: a board on which something (as food or cloth) is placed for cutting
**cutting edge** *noun* (1951)
**1** : the foremost part or place : VANGUARD

**2 :** a sharp effect or quality
**cutting horse** *noun* (1881)
: an agile saddle horse trained to separate individual animals from a cattle herd
**cut·tle·bone** \'kə-t'l-ˌbōn\ *noun* [Middle English *cotul* cuttlefish (from Old English *cudele*) + English *bone*] (1547)
: the shell of cuttlefishes that is sometimes used for polishing powder or for supplying cage birds with lime and salts
**cut·tle·fish** \-ˌfish\ *noun* [Middle English *cotul* + English *fish*] (circa 1828)
: any of various 10-armed marine cephalopod mollusks (order Sepioidea, especially genus *Sepia*) differing from the related squid in having a calcified internal shell
**cut·ty sark** \'kə-tē-'särk\ *noun* [English dialect *cutty* short + *sark*] (1779)
*chiefly Scottish* : a short garment; *especially*
: a woman's short undergarment
**cutty stool** *noun* (1820)
**1** *chiefly Scottish* : a low stool
**2 :** a seat in a Scottish church where offenders formerly sat for public rebuke
**cut·up** \'kət-ˌəp\ *noun* (1843)
: a person who clowns or acts boisterously
**cut up** (1580)
*transitive verb*
**1 a :** to cut into parts or pieces **b :** to injure or damage by or as if by cutting **:** GASH, SLASH
**2 :** to subject to hostile criticism **:** CENSURE
*intransitive verb*
**1 :** to undergo being cut up
**2 :** to behave in a comic, boisterous, or unruly manner **:** CLOWN
**cut·wa·ter** \'kət-ˌwȯ-tər, -ˌwä-\ *noun* (1644)
: the forepart of a ship's stem
**cut·work** \-ˌwərk\ *noun* (15th century)
: embroidery usually on linen in which a design is outlined in buttonhole stitch and the enclosed material cut away
**cut·worm** \-ˌwərm\ *noun* (1816)
: any of various smooth-bodied chiefly nocturnal noctuid moth caterpillars which often feed on young plant stems near ground level
**cu·vette** \kyü-'vet\ *noun* [French, diminutive of *cuve* tub, from Latin *cupa* — more at HIVE] (circa 1909)
: a small often transparent laboratory vessel (as a tube)
**cwm** \'küm\ *noun* [Welsh, valley] (1853)
*chiefly British* **:** CIRQUE 3
**-cy** *noun suffix* [Middle English *-cie*, from Old French, from Latin *-tia*, partly from *-t-* (final stem consonant) + *-ia* -y, partly from Greek *-tia*, *-teia*, from *-t-* (final stem consonant) + *-ia*, *-eia* -y]
**1 :** action **:** practice ⟨mendican*cy*⟩
**2 :** rank **:** office ⟨baronet*cy*⟩ ⟨chaplain*cy*⟩
**3 :** body **:** class ⟨magistra*cy*⟩
**4 :** state **:** quality ⟨accura*cy*⟩ — often replacing a final *-t* or *-te* of the base word
**cy·an** \'sī-ˌan, -ən\ *noun* [Greek *kyanos*] (circa 1889)
: a greenish blue color — used in photography and color printing of one of the primary colors
**cyan-** *or* **cyano-** *combining form* [German, from Greek *kyan-, kyano-,* from *kyanos* dark blue enamel]
**1 :** dark blue **:** blue ⟨*cyano*bacterium⟩
**2 :** cyanogen ⟨*cyan*ide⟩
**3 :** cyanide ⟨*cyan*ogenetic⟩
**cy·an·a·mide** \sī-'a-nə-məd\ *noun* [International Scientific Vocabulary] (1838)
**1 :** a caustic acidic compound $CH_2N_2$
**2 :** CALCIUM CYANAMIDE
**cy·a·nate** \'sī-ə-ˌnāt, -nət\ *noun* [International Scientific Vocabulary] (circa 1846)
: a salt (as ammonium cyanate) or ester of cyanic acid
**cy·an·ic acid** \sī-'a-nik\ *noun* (1832)
: a strong acid HOCN used to prepare cyanates

**cy·a·nide** \'sī-ə-ˌnīd, -nəd\ *noun* [International Scientific Vocabulary] (1826)
**1 :** a compound of cyanogen with a more electropositive element or group: as **a :** POTASSIUM CYANIDE **b :** SODIUM CYANIDE
**2 :** CYANOGEN 1
**cy·a·nine** \'sī-ə-ˌnēn, -nən\ *noun* [International Scientific Vocabulary] (circa 1872)
: any of various dyes that sensitize photographic film to light from the green, yellow, red, and infrared regions of the spectrum
**cy·a·no** \'sī-ə-(ˌ)nō, sī-'a-(ˌ)nō\ *adjective* [*cyan-*] (1929)
: relating to or containing the cyanogen group — often used in combination
**cy·a·no·ac·ry·late** \ˌsī-ə-nō-'a-krə-ˌlāt, sī-ˌa-nō-\ *noun* (1963)
: any of several liquid acrylate monomers that readily polymerize as anions and are used as adhesives in industry and in closing wounds in surgery
**cy·a·no·bac·te·ri·um** \-bak-'tir-ē-əm\ *noun* [New Latin] (1974)
**:** BLUE-GREEN ALGA
**cy·a·no·co·bal·a·min** \-kō-'ba-lə-mən\ *also* **cy·a·no·co·bal·a·mine** \-ˌmēn\ *noun* [*cyan-* + *cobalt* + *vitamin*] (1950)
**:** VITAMIN B₁₂ 1
**cy·a·no·eth·yl·ate** \-'e-thə-ˌlāt\ *transitive verb* (1942)
: to introduce a cyano-ethyl group $CNC_2H_4$ into (a compound) usually by means of acrylonitrile ⟨*cyanoethylate* cotton⟩
— **cy·a·no·eth·yl·ation** \-ˌe-thə-'lā-shən\ *noun*
**cy·an·o·gen** \sī-'a-nə-jən\ *noun* [French *cyanogène,* from *cyan-* + *gène* -gen] (1826)
**1 :** a univalent group —CN present in cyanides
**2 :** a colorless flammable poisonous gas $(CN)_2$
**cy·a·no·ge·net·ic** \ˌsī-ə-nō-jə-'ne-tik, sī-ˌa-nō-\ *or* **cy·a·no·gen·ic** \-'je-nik\ *adjective* (1902)
: capable of producing cyanide (as hydrogen cyanide) ⟨a *cyanogenetic* plant⟩ ⟨a *cyanogenetic* glucoside⟩
— **cy·a·no·gen·e·sis** \-'je-nə-səs\ *noun*
**cy·a·no·hy·drin** \-'hī-drən\ *noun* [International Scientific Vocabulary, from *cyan-* + *hydr-* + ¹*-in*] (1925)
: any of various compounds containing both cyano and hydroxyl groups
**cy·a·no·sis** \ˌsī-ə-'nō-səs\ *noun* [New Latin, from Greek *kyanōsis* dark blue color, from *kyanos*] (1834)
: a bluish or purplish discoloration (as of skin) due to deficient oxygenation of the blood
— **cy·a·not·ic** \-'nä-tik\ *adjective*
**cy·an·uric acid** \ˌsī-ə-'nùr-ik-, -'nyùr-\ *noun* [*cyan-* + *urea*] (1838)
: a crystalline weak acid $C_3N_3(OH)_3$ that yields cyanic acid when heated
**Cyb·e·le** \'si-bə-(ˌ)lē\ *noun* [Latin, from Greek *Kybelē*]
: a nature goddess of the ancient peoples of Asia Minor
**cy·ber·na·tion** \ˌsī-bər-'nā-shən\ *noun* [*cybernetics* + *-ation*] (1962)
: the automatic control of a process or operation (as in manufacturing) by means of computers
— **cy·ber·nat·ed** \'sī-bər-ˌnā-təd\ *adjective*
**cy·ber·ne·ti·cian** \ˌsī-(ˌ)bər-nə-'ti-shən\ *noun* (1951)
: a specialist in cybernetics
**cy·ber·net·i·cist** \ˌsī-bər-'ne-tə-sist\ *noun* (1948)
**:** CYBERNETICIAN
**cy·ber·net·ics** \ˌsī-bər-'ne-tiks\ *noun plural but singular in construction* [Greek *kybernētēs* pilot, governor (from *kybernan* to steer, govern) + English *-ics*] (1948)
: the science of communication and control theory that is concerned especially with the comparative study of automatic control systems (as the nervous system and brain and mechanical-electrical communication systems)

— **cy·ber·net·ic** \-tik\ *also* **cy·ber·net·i·cal** \-ti-kəl\ *adjective*
— **cy·ber·net·i·cal·ly** \-ti-k(ə-)lē\ *adverb*
**cy·ber·punk** \'sī-bər-ˌpəŋk\ *noun* [*cyber*netic + ¹*punk*] (1984)
**1 :** science fiction dealing with future urban societies dominated by computer technology
**2 :** an opportunistic computer hacker
**cy·ber·space** \-ˌspās\ *noun* [*cyber*netic + *space*] (1986)
: the on-line world of computer networks
**cy·borg** \'sī-ˌbȯrg\ *noun* [*cyb*ernetic + *org*anism] (1960)
: a bionic human
**cy·cad** \'sī-kəd\ *noun* [New Latin *Cycad-, Cycas,* genus name, from Greek *kykas,* manuscript variant of *koïkas,* accusative plural of *koïx,* a kind of palm] (1845)
: any of an order (Cycadales) of dioecious cycadophytes that are represented by a single surviving family (Cycadaceae) of palmlike tropical plants that reproduce by means of spermatozoids
**cy·cad·e·oid** \sī-'ka-dē-ˌȯid\ *noun* [New Latin *Cycadeoidales,* group name, ultimately from *Cycad-, Cycas*] (1928)
: any of an extinct order (Cycadeoidales or Bennettitales) of Mesozoic cycadophytes that differ from the cycads chiefly in having the reproductive organs on the trunk embedded in a thick external covering of persistent leaf bases
**cy·cad·o·phyte** \sī-'ka-də-ˌfīt\ *noun* [ultimately from New Latin *Cycad-, Cycas* + Greek *phyton* plant — more at -PHYTE] (1911)
: any of a subclass (Cycadophytae) of usually unbranched gymnosperms with pinnate leaves, large pith, little xylem, and a thick cortex that includes the cycads, cycadeoids, and seed ferns
**cy·ca·sin** \'sī-kə-sən\ *noun* [New Latin *Cycas* cycad + International Scientific Vocabulary ¹*-in*] (circa 1965)
: a glucoside $C_8H_{16}N_2O_7$ that occurs in cycads and results in toxic and carcinogenic effects when introduced into mammals
**cycl-** *or* **cyclo-** *combining form* [New Latin, from Greek *kykl-, kyklo-,* from *kyklos*]
**1 :** circle ⟨*cyclo*meter⟩
**2 :** cyclic ⟨*cyclo*hexane⟩
**cy·cla·mate** \'sī-klə-ˌmāt, -mət\ *noun* [*cyclo*hexyl-sulf*amate*] (1954)
: an artificially prepared salt of sodium or calcium used especially formerly as a sweetener
**cy·cla·men** \'sī-klə-mən, 'si-\ *noun* [New Latin, genus name, from Greek *kyklaminos*] (circa 1550)
: any of a genus (*Cyclamen*) of plants of the primrose family having showy nodding flowers
**cy·clase** \'sī-ˌklās, -ˌklāz\ *noun* [*cycl-* + *-ase*] (1946)
: an enzyme (as adenylate cyclase) that catalyzes cyclization of a compound
**cy·claz·o·cine** \sī-'kla-zə-ˌsēn, -sən\ *noun* [*cycl-* + *azocine* ($C_7H_7N$), probably from *az-* + *octa-* + ²*-ine*] (1966)
: an analgesic drug $C_{18}H_{25}NO$ that inhibits the effect of morphine and related addictive drugs and is used in the treatment of drug addiction
**¹cy·cle** \'sī-kəl\ *noun* [Middle English *cicle,* from Late Latin *cyclus,* from Greek *kyklos* circle, wheel, cycle — more at WHEEL] (14th century)
**1 :** an interval of time during which a sequence of a recurring succession of events or phenomena is completed
**2 a :** a course or series of events or operations that recur regularly and usually lead back to

the starting point **b** : one complete performance of a vibration, electric oscillation, current alternation, or other periodic process **c** : a permutation of a set of ordered elements in which each element takes the place of the next and the last becomes first
**3** : a circular or spiral arrangement: as **a** : an imaginary circle or orbit in the heavens **b** : WHORL **c** : RING 10
**4** : a long period of time : AGE
**5 a** : a group of poems, plays, novels, or songs treating the same theme **b** : a series of narratives dealing typically with the exploits of a legendary hero
**6 a** : BICYCLE **b** : TRICYCLE **c** : MOTORCYCLE
**7** : the series of a single, double, triple, and home run hit in any order by one player during one baseball game
**²cycle** *verb* **cy·cled; cy·cling** \'sī-k(ə-)liŋ\ (1842)
*intransitive verb*
**1 a** : to pass through a cycle **b** : to recur in cycles
**2** : to ride a cycle; *specifically* : BICYCLE
*transitive verb*
: to cause to go through a cycle
— **cy·cler** \'sī-k(ə-)lər\ *noun*
**cy·clic** \'sī-klik *also* 'si-\ *or* **cy·cli·cal** \'sī-kli-kəl, 'si-\ *adjective* (1794)
**1 a** : of, relating to, or being a cycle **b** : moving in cycles ⟨*cyclic* time⟩ **c** : of, relating to, or being a chemical compound containing a ring of atoms
**2** *cyclic* : being a mathematical group that has an element such that every element of the group can be expressed as one of its powers
— **cy·cli·cal·ly** \-k(ə-)lē\ *also* **cy·clic·ly** \'sī-kli-klē, 'si-\ *adverb*
**cyclic AMP** *noun* (1966)
: a cyclic mononucleotide of adenosine that is formed from ATP and is responsible for the intracellular mediation of hormonal effects on various cellular processes — called also *adenosine 3',5'-monophosphate*
**cyclic GMP** \-,jē-(,)em-'pē\ *noun* [guanosine + *mon-* + *p*hosphate] (1969)
: a cyclic mononucleotide of guanosine that acts similarly to cyclic AMP as a secondary messenger in response to hormones
**cy·clic·i·ty** \sī-'kli-sə-tē, si-\ *noun* (1944)
: the quality or state of being cyclic ⟨estrous *cyclicity*⟩ — called also *cy·cli·cal·i·ty* \,sī-klə-'ka-lə-tē, ,si-\
**cy·clist** \'sī-k(ə-)ləst\ *noun* (1882)
: one who rides a cycle
**cy·cli·tol** \'sī-klə-,tol, 'si-, -,tōl\ *noun* [*cycl-* + *-itol* (as in *inositol*)] (1943)
: an alicyclic polyhydroxy compound (as inositol)
**cy·cli·za·tion** \,sī-k(ə-)lə-'zā-shən, ,si-\ *noun* (1909)
: formation of one or more rings in a chemical compound
— **cy·clize** \'sī-kə-,līz, 'si-, -,klīz\ *verb*
**cy·clo** \'sē-(,)klō, 'si-\ *noun, plural* **cyclos** [French, bicycle, moped, from *cyclo-* (as in *cyclomoteur* moped), from *cycle* two- or three-wheeled vehicle] (1964)
: a 3-wheeled often motor-driven taxi
**cy·clo·ad·di·tion** \,sī-(,)klō-ə-'di-shən\ *noun* (1963)
: a chemical reaction leading to ring formation in a compound
**cy·clo·al·i·phat·ic** \,sī-klō-,a-lə-'fa-tik\ *adjective* (1936)
: ALICYCLIC
**cy·clo·dex·trin** \-'dek-strən\ *noun* (1960)
: any of a class of complex cyclic sugars that are products of the enzymatic decomposition of starch and that can catalyze reactions between simpler molecules which come together within the cylindrical body of the sugar
**cy·clo·di·ene** \-'dī-,ēn, -dī-'\ *noun* (1942)

: an organic insecticide (as dieldrin or chlordane) with a chlorinated methylene group forming a bridge across a 6-membered carbon ring
**cy·clo·gen·e·sis** \-'je-nə-səs\ *noun* [*cyclone* + *genesis*] (circa 1938)
: the development or intensification of a cyclone
**cy·clo·hex·ane** \,sī-klō-'hek-,sān\ *noun* [International Scientific Vocabulary] (circa 1909)
: a pungent saturated cyclic hydrocarbon $C_6H_{12}$ found in petroleum or made synthetically and used chiefly as a solvent and in organic synthesis
**cy·clo·hex·a·none** \-'hek-sə-,nōn\ *noun* (circa 1909)
: a liquid ketone $C_6H_{10}O$ used especially as a solvent and in organic synthesis
**cy·clo·hex·i·mide** \-'hek-sə-,mīd, -məd\ *noun* [*cyclohex*ane + *imide*] (1950)
: an agricultural fungicide $C_{15}H_{23}NO_4$ that inhibits protein synthesis and is obtained from a soil bacterium (*Streptomyces griseus*)
**cy·clo·hex·yl·amine** \-hek-'si-lə-,mēn\ *noun* [*cyclohex*ane + *-yl* + *amine*] (1943)
: a colorless liquid amine $C_6H_{11}NH_2$ that is used in organic synthesis and to prevent corrosion in boilers and that is believed to be harmful as a metabolic breakdown product of cyclamate
**¹cy·cloid** \'sī-,klȯid\ *noun* [French *cycloïde*, from Greek *kykloeidēs* circular, from *kyklos*] (1661)
: a curve that is generated by a point on the circumference of a circle as it rolls along a straight line

**cycloid**

— **cy·cloi·dal** \sī-'klȯi-d°l\ *adjective*
**²cycloid** *adjective* (1847)
**1** : smooth with concentric lines of growth ⟨*cycloid* scales⟩; *also* : having or consisting of cycloid scales
**2** : relating to or being a personality characterized by alternating high and low moods — compare CYCLOTHYMIC
**cy·clom·e·ter** \sī-'klä-mə-tər\ *noun* (1880)
: a device made for recording the revolutions of a wheel and often used for registering distance traversed by a wheeled vehicle
**cy·clone** \'sī-,klōn\ *noun* [modification of Greek *kyklōma* wheel, coil, from *kykloun* to go around, from *kyklos* circle] (1848)
**1 a** : a storm or system of winds that rotates about a center of low atmospheric pressure, advances at a speed of 20 to 30 miles (about 30 to 50 kilometers) an hour, and often brings heavy rain **b** : TORNADO **c** : LOW 1b
**2** : any of various centrifugal devices for separating materials (as solid particles from gases)
— **cy·clon·ic** \sī-'klä-nik\ *adjective*
— **cy·clon·i·cal·ly** \-ni-k(ə-)lē\ *adverb*
**Cy·clone** \'sī-,klōn\ *trademark*
— used for a chain-link fence
**cyclone cellar** *noun* (1887)
: STORM CELLAR
**cy·clo·ole·fin** \,sī-klō-'ō-lə-fən\ *noun* [International Scientific Vocabulary] (circa 1929)
: a hydrocarbon containing a ring having one or more double bonds
— **cy·clo·ole·fin·ic** \-,ō-lə-'fi-nik\ *adjective*
**cy·clo·par·af·fin** \-'par-ə-fən\ *noun* (1900)
: a saturated cyclic hydrocarbon of the formula $C_nH_{2n}$
**cy·clo·pe·an** \,sī-klə-'pē-ən, sī-'klō-pē-\ *adjective* (1626)
**1** *often capitalized* : of, relating to, or characteristic of a Cyclops
**2** : HUGE, MASSIVE
**3** : of or relating to a style of stone construction marked typically by the use of large irregular blocks without mortar

**cy·clo·pe·dia** *also* **cy·clo·pae·dia** \,sī-klə-'pē-dē-ə\ *noun* (1728)
: ENCYCLOPEDIA
— **cy·clo·pe·dic** \-'pē-dik\ *adjective*
**cy·clo·phos·pha·mide** \,sī-klō-'fäs-fə-,mīd\ *noun* (1960)
: an immunosuppressive and antineoplastic agent $C_7H_{15}Cl_2N_2O_2P$ used especially in the treatment of lymphomas and some leukemias
**cy·clo·pro·pane** \,sī-klə-'prō-,pān\ *noun* [International Scientific Vocabulary] (1894)
: a flammable gaseous saturated cyclic hydrocarbon $C_3H_6$ sometimes used as a general anesthetic
**cy·clops** \'sī-,kläps\ *noun* [Latin, from Greek *Kyklōps*, from *kykl-* cycl- + *ōps* eye] (1513)
**1** *plural* **cy·clo·pes** \sī-'klō-(,)pēz\ *capitalized* : any of a race of giants in Greek mythology with a single eye in the middle of the forehead
**2** *plural* **cyclops** [New Latin, genus name, from Latin] : any of a genus (*Cyclops*) of freshwater predatory copepods having a median eye
**cy·clo·ra·ma** \,sī-klə-'ra-mə, -'rä-\ *noun* [*cycl-* + *-orama* (as in *panorama*)] (1840)
**1** : a large pictorial representation encircling the spectator and often having real objects as a foreground
**2** : a curved curtain or wall used as a background of a stage set to suggest unlimited space
— **cy·clo·ram·ic** \-'ra-mik\ *adjective*
**cy·clo·ser·ine** \,sī-klō-'ser-,ēn\ *noun* (1952)
: an amino antibiotic $C_3H_6N_2O_2$ produced by an actinomycete (*Streptomyces orchidaceus*) and used especially in the treatment of tuberculosis
**cy·clo·sis** \sī-'klō-səs\ *noun* [New Latin, from Greek *kyklōsis* encirclement, from *kykloun* to go around] (1835)
: the streaming of protoplasm within a cell
**cy·clo·spor·ine** \,sī-klə-'spȯr-°n, -,ēn\ *noun* [International Scientific Vocabulary *cycl-* + *spor-* + *²-ine*] (1976)
: an immunosuppressive polypeptide drug $C_{62}H_{111}N_{11}O_{12}$ obtained from various imperfect fungi and used especially to prevent rejection of organ transplants
**cy·clo·stome** \'sī-klə-,stōm\ *noun* [ultimately from Greek *kykl-* + *stoma* mouth — more at STOMACH] (1835)
: any of a class (Cyclostomata) of jawless fishes having a large sucking mouth and comprising the hagfishes and lampreys
**cy·clo·style** \-,stīl\ *noun* [from *Cyclostyle*, a trademark] (1883)
: a machine for making multiple copies that utilizes a stencil cut by a graver whose tip is a small rowel
— **cyclostyle** *transitive verb*
**cy·clo·thy·mic** \,sī-klə-'thī-mik\ *adjective* [New Latin *cyclothymia* (from German *Zyklothymie*, from *zykl-* cycl- + *-thymie* -thymia) + English *-ic*] (1923)
: relating to or being an affective disorder characterized by the alternation of depressed moods with elevated, expansive, or irritable moods without psychotic features — compare CYCLOID 2
— **cy·clo·thy·mia** \-'thī-mē-ə\ *noun*
**cy·clo·tom·ic** \-'tä-mik\ *adjective* [*cyclotomy* mathematical theory of the division of the circle into equal parts, from *cycl-* + *-tomy*] (1879)
: relating to, being, or containing a polynomial of the form $x^p - 1 + x^p - 2 + . . . + x + 1$ where $p$ is a prime number
**cy·clo·tron** \'sī-klə-,trän\ *noun* [*cycl-* + *-tron*; from the circular movement of the particles] (1935)
: an accelerator in which charged particles (as protons, deuterons, or ions) are propelled by an alternating electric field in a constant magnetic field
**cy·der** *British variant of* CIDER

**cyg·net** \'sig-nət\ *noun* [Middle English *sygnett*, from Middle French *cygne* swan, from Latin *cycnus, cygnus,* from Greek *kyknos*] (15th century)
**:** a young swan

**Cyg·nus** \'sig-nəs\ *noun* [Latin (genitive *Cygni*), literally, swan]
**:** a northern constellation between Lyra and Pegasus in the Milky Way

**cyl·in·der** \'si-lən-dər\ *noun* [Middle French or Latin; Middle French *cylindre,* from Latin *cylindrus,* from Greek *kylindros,* from *kylindein* to roll; perhaps akin to Greek *kyklos* wheel — more at WHEEL] (1570)
**1 a :** the surface traced by a straight line moving parallel to a fixed straight line and intersecting a fixed planar closed curve **b :** the space bounded by a cylinder and two parallel planes cutting all its elements — see VOLUME table
**2 :** a cylindrical body or space: as **a :** the turning chambered breech of a revolver **b** (1) **:** the piston chamber in an engine (2) **:** a chamber in a pump from which the piston expels the fluid **c :** any of various rotating members in a press (as a printing press); *especially* **:** one that impresses paper on an inked form **d :** a cylindrical clay object inscribed with cuneiform inscriptions
— **cyl·in·dered** \-dərd\ *adjective*

**cylinder head** *noun* (1884)
**:** the closed end of an engine or pump cylinder

**cylinder seal** *noun* (1887)
**:** a cylinder (as of stone) engraved in intaglio and used especially in ancient Mesopotamia to roll an impression on wet clay

**cy·lin·dri·cal** \sə-'lin-dri-kəl\ *also* **cy·lin·dric** \-drik\ *adjective* (1646)
**:** relating to or having the form or properties of a cylinder
— **cy·lin·dri·cal·ly** \-dri-k(ə-)lē\ *adverb*

**cylindrical coordinate** *noun* (circa 1934)
**:** any of the coordinates in space obtained by constructing in a plane a polar coordinate system and on a line perpendicular to the plane a linear coordinate system

**cy·ma** \'sī-mə\ *noun* [Greek *kyma,* literally, wave] (1563)
**1 :** a projecting molding whose profile is an S-shaped curve
**2 :** an S-shaped curve formed by the union of a concave line and a convex line

**cy·ma·tium** \sī-'mā-sh(ē-)əm\ *noun, plural* **-tia** \-sh(ē-)ə\ [Latin, from Greek *kymation,* diminutive of *kymat-, kyma*] (1563)
**:** a crowning molding in classic architecture; *especially* **:** CYMA

**cym·bal** \'sim-bəl\ *noun* [Middle English, from Old English *cymbal* & Middle French *cymbale,* from Latin *cymbalum,* from Greek *kymbalon,* from *kymbē* bowl, boat] (before 12th century)
**:** a concave brass plate that produces a brilliant clashing tone and that is struck with a drumstick or is used in pairs struck glancingly together
— **cym·bal·ist** \-bə-list\ *noun*

**cym·bid·i·um** \sim-'bi-dē-əm\ *noun* [New Latin, genus name, from Latin *cymba* boat, from Greek *kymbē*] (1815)
**:** any of a genus (*Cymbidium*) of tropical Old World epiphytic orchids with showy flowers

**cyme** \'sīm\ *noun* [New Latin *cyma,* from Latin, cabbage sprout, from Greek *kyma* swell, wave, cabbage sprout, from *kyein* to be pregnant; akin to Sanskrit *śvayati* it swells, grows] (1794)
**:** an inflorescence in which each floral axis terminates in a single flower; *especially* **:** a determinate inflorescence of this type containing several flowers with the first-opening central flower terminating the main axis and subsequent flowers developing from lateral buds — see INFLORESCENCE illustration

**cym·ling** \'sim-lən, -liŋ\ *noun* [probably alteration of *simnel*] (1779)

**:** PATTYPAN

**cy·mo·phane** \'sī-mə-ˌfān\ *noun* [French, from Greek *kyma* wave + French *-phane* -phane] (circa 1804)
**:** CHRYSOBERYL; *especially* **:** an opalescent chrysoberyl

**cy·mose** \'sī-ˌmōs\ *adjective* (1807)
**:** of, relating to, being, or bearing a cyme

**¹Cym·ric** \'kəm-rik, 'kim-\ *adjective* (1839)
**:** of, relating to, or characteristic of the non-Gaelic Celtic people of Britain or their language; *specifically* **:** WELSH

**²Cymric** *noun* (circa 1889)
**:** BRYTHONIC; *specifically* **:** the Welsh language

**Cym·ry** \-rē\ *noun* [Welsh] (1833)
**:** WELSH 2

**cyn·ic** \'si-nik\ *noun* [Middle French or Latin, Middle French *cynique,* from Latin *cynicus,* from Greek *kynikos,* literally, like a dog, from *kyn-, kyōn* dog — more at HOUND] (circa 1564)
**1** *capitalized* **:** an adherent of an ancient Greek school of philosophers who held the view that virtue is the only good and that its essence lies in self-control and independence
**2 :** a faultfinding captious critic; *especially* **:** one who believes that human conduct is motivated wholly by self-interest ◆
— **cynic** *adjective*

**cyn·i·cal** \'si-ni-kəl\ *adjective* (1584)
**1 :** CAPTIOUS, PEEVISH
**2 :** having or showing the attitude or temper of a cynic; *especially* **:** contemptuously distrustful of human nature and motives ⟨those *cynical* men who say that democracy cannot be honest and efficient — F. D. Roosevelt⟩ ☆
— **cyn·i·cal·ly** \-k(ə-)lē\ *adverb*

**cyn·i·cism** \'si-nə-ˌsi-zəm\ *noun* (1672)
**1** *capitalized* **:** the doctrine of the Cynics
**2 :** cynical character, attitude, or quality; *also* **:** an expression of such quality

**cy·no·mol·gus monkey** \ˌsī-nə-'mäl-gəs-\ *noun* [New Latin, alteration of *cynamolgus,* from Latin, member of an ancient tribe in Africa, from Greek *Kynamolgoi,* literally, dog milkers] (1936)
**:** a macaque (*Macaca fascicularis* synonym *M. cynomolgus*) of southeastern Asia, Borneo, and the Philippines that sometimes feeds on marine crustaceans and shellfish and is often used in medical research

**cy·no·sure** \'sī-nə-ˌshu̇r, 'si-\ *noun* [Middle French & Latin; Middle French, Ursa Minor, guide, from Latin *cynosura* Ursa Minor, from Greek *kynosoura,* from *kynos oura,* literally, dog's tail]
**1** *capitalized* **:** the northern constellation Ursa Minor; *also* **:** NORTH STAR
**2 :** one that serves to direct or guide
**3 :** a center of attraction or attention

**Cyn·thia** \'sin(t)-thē-ə\ *noun* [Latin, from feminine of *Cynthius* of Cynthus, from *Cynthus,* mountain on Delos where she was born, from Greek *Kynthos*]
**1 :** ARTEMIS
**2 :** MOON 1a

**cy·pher** *chiefly British variant of* CIPHER

**¹cy pres** \ˌsī-'prā, ˌsē-\ *noun* [Anglo-French, so near, as near (as may be)] (1802)
**:** a rule providing for the interpretation of instruments in equity as nearly as possible in conformity to the intention of the testator when literal construction is illegal, impracticable, or impossible — called also *cy pres doctrine*

**²cy pres** *adverb* (1885)
**:** in accordance with the rule of cy pres

**¹cy·press** \'sī-prəs\ *noun* [Middle English, from Middle French *ciprès,* from Latin *cyparissus,* from Greek *kyparissos*] (14th century)
**1 a** (1) **:** any of a genus (*Cupressus* of the family Cupressaceae, the cypress family) of evergreen trees and shrubs with small overlapping leaves resembling scales (2) **:** any of several coniferous trees of the cypress family or the

bald cypress family; *especially* **:** BALD CYPRESS
**1 b :** the wood of a cypress tree
**2 :** branches of cypress used as a symbol of mourning

**²cypress** *noun* [Middle English *ciprus, cipres,* from *Cyprus,* Mediterranean island] (15th century)
**:** a silk or cotton usually black gauze formerly used for mourning

**cypress vine** *noun* (1819)
**:** a tropical American vine (*Ipomoea quamoclit* synonym *Quamoclit pennata*) of the morning-glory family with usually red or white tubular flowers and finely dissected leaves

**cyp·ri·an** \'si-prē-ən\ *noun, often capitalized* [Latin *cyprius* of Cyprus, from Greek *kyprios,* from *Kypros* Cyprus, birthplace of Aphrodite] (1819)
**:** PROSTITUTE

**cyp·ri·nid** \'si-prə-nəd\ *noun* [ultimately from Latin *cyprinus* carp, from Greek *kyprinos*] (circa 1889)
**:** any of a family (Cyprinidae) of soft-finned freshwater fishes including the carps and minnows
— **cyprinid** *adjective*

**cyp·ri·pe·di·um** \ˌsi-prə-'pē-dē-əm\ *noun* [New Latin, genus name, from Late Latin *Cypris,* a name for Venus + Greek *pedilon* sandal] (1813)
**1 :** any of a genus (*Cypripedium*) of Eurasian and North American terrestrial orchids having large usually showy drooping flowers with the lip inflated or pouched — compare LADY'S SLIPPER
**2 :** any of a genus (*Paphiopedalum*) of widely cultivated Asian orchids

**cy·pro·hep·ta·dine** \ˌsī-prō-'hep-tə-ˌdēn\ *noun* [*cyclic* + *pro*pyl + *hepta-* + piperi*dine*] (1971)

---

☆ SYNONYMS
**Cynical, misanthropic, pessimistic** mean deeply distrustful. CYNICAL implies having a sneering disbelief in sincerity or integrity ⟨*cynical* about politicians' motives⟩. MISANTHROPIC suggests a rooted distrust and dislike of human beings and their society ⟨a solitary and *misanthropic* artist⟩. PESSIMISTIC implies having a gloomy, distrustful view of life ⟨*pessimistic* about the future⟩.

---

◇ WORD HISTORY
**cynic** The ancient school of philosophers known collectively as the Cynics was founded by Antisthenes (c. 445–c. 360 B.C.), a contemporary of Plato. Antisthenes is said to have taught at a gymnasium outside Athens called the Kynosarges, from which the Greek name of the school *kynikoi,* literally, "doglike ones," may be derived. On the other hand, Antisthenes' most famous follower, Diogenes of Sinope (c. 400–c. 325 B.C. ), is most closely associated with the appellation. Diogenes rejected social conventions as impeding the most convenient satisfaction of one's needs; whatever was natural and easy could not be indecent, and therefore can and should be done in public. This shamelessness earned him the label *ho kyōn* "the dog," *kyōn* being an epithet applied to shameless or audacious people as far back as Homer. What English *cynic* and *cynical* now reflect, however, is not the Cynics' shamelessness, but their biting criticism of conventional mores.

---

\ə\ **abut** \ᵊ\ **kitten** \ər\ **further** \a\ **ash** \ā\ **ace** \ä\ **mop, mar** \au̇\ **out** \ch\ **chin** \e\ **bet** \ē\ **easy** \g\ **go** \i\ **hit** \ī\ **ice** \j\ **job** \ŋ\ **sing** \ō\ **go** \ȯ\ **law** \ȯi\ **boy** \th\ **thin** \t͟h\ **the** \ü\ **loot** \u̇\ **foot** \y\ **yet** \zh\ **vision** *see also* Guide to Pronunciation

: a drug $C_{21}H_{21}N$ that acts antagonistically to histamine and serotonin and is used especially in the treatment of asthma

**cy·prot·er·one** \sī-'prä-tə-ˌrōn\ *noun* [probably from *cycl-* + *progesterone*] (1966)
: a synthetic steroid $C_{22}H_{27}ClO_3$ that inhibits androgenic secretions (as testosterone)

**Cy·re·na·ic** \ˌsir-ə-'nā-ik, ˌsī-rə-\ *noun* [Latin *cyrenaicus,* from Greek *kyrēnaikos,* from *Kyrēnē* Cyrene, Africa, home of Aristippus, author of the doctrine] (1586)
: an adherent of the doctrine that pleasure is the chief end of life
— **Cyrenaic** *adjective*
— **Cy·re·na·icism** \-'nā-ə-ˌsi-zəm\ *noun*

**Cy·ril·lic** \sə-'ri-lik\ *adjective* [Saint *Cyril,* reputed inventor of the Cyrillic alphabet] (1842)
: of, relating to, or constituting an alphabet used for writing Old Church Slavonic and for Russian and a number of other languages of eastern Europe and Asia

**cyst** \'sist\ *noun* [New Latin *cystis,* from Greek *kystis* bladder, pouch; akin to Sanskrit *śvasiti* he blows, snorts — more at WHEEZE] (circa 1720)
**1** : a closed sac having a distinct membrane and developing abnormally in a cavity or structure of the body
**2** : a body resembling a cyst: as **a** : a resting spore of many algae **b** : a gas-filled vesicle (as of a rockweed or bladderwort) **c** : a capsule formed about a minute organism going into a resting or spore stage; *also* : this capsule with its contents **d** : a resistant cover about a parasite produced by the parasite or the host

**cyst-** *or* **cysti-** *or* **cysto-** *combining form* [French, from Greek *kyst-, kysto-,* from *kystis*]
: bladder ⟨*cystitis*⟩ : sac ⟨*cystocarp*⟩

**-cyst** *noun combining form* [New Latin *-cystis,* from Greek *kystis*]
: bladder : sac ⟨blasto*cyst*⟩

**cys·te·amine** \sis-'tē-ə-mən\ *noun* [*cysteine* + *amine*] (1943)
: a cysteine derivative $C_2H_7NS$ that has been used experimentally in the prevention of radiation sickness (as of cancer patients)

**cys·te·ine** \'sis-tə-ˌēn\ *noun* [International Scientific Vocabulary, from *cystine* + *-ein*] (1884)
: a crystalline sulfur-containing amino acid $C_3H_7NO_2S$ readily oxidizable to cystine

**cys·tic** \'sis-tik\ *adjective* (1713)
**1** : relating to, composed of, or containing cysts
**2** : of or relating to the urinary bladder or the gallbladder
**3** : enclosed in a cyst

**cys·ti·cer·coid** \ˌsis-tə-'sər-ˌkȯid\ *noun* (1858)
: a tapeworm larva having an invaginated scolex and solid tailpiece

**cys·ti·cer·co·sis** \ˌsis-tə-(ˌ)sər-'kō-səs\ *noun, plural* **-co·ses** \-'kō-ˌsēz\ [New Latin] (1905)
: infestation with or disease caused by cysticerci

**cys·ti·cer·cus** \-'sər-kəs\ *noun, plural* **-cer·ci** \-'sər-ˌsī, -ˌkī\ [New Latin, from *cyst-* + Greek *kerkos* tail] (circa 1871)
: a tapeworm larva that consists of a fluid-filled sac containing an invaginated scolex and is situated in the tissues of an intermediate host

**cystic fibrosis** *noun* (1938)
: a common hereditary disease especially among whites that appears usually in early childhood, involves functional disorder of the exocrine glands, and is marked especially by faulty digestion due to a deficiency of pancreatic enzymes, by difficulty in breathing due to mucus accumulation in airways, and by excessive loss of salt in the sweat

**cys·tine** \'sis-ˌtēn\ *noun* [from its discovery in bladder stones] (1843)
: a crystalline amino acid $C_6H_{12}N_2O_4S_2$ that is widespread in proteins (as keratins) and is a major metabolic sulfur source

**cys·tin·uria** \ˌsis-tə-'nu̇r-ē-ə, -'nyu̇r-\ *noun* [New Latin] (1853)
: a metabolic defect characterized by excretion of excessive amounts of cystine in the urine and inherited as an autosomal recessive trait

**cys·ti·tis** \sis-'tī-təs\ *noun* [New Latin] (circa 1783)
: inflammation of the urinary bladder

**cys·to·carp** \'sis-tə-ˌkärp\ *noun* [International Scientific Vocabulary] (1875)
: the fruiting structure produced in the red algae after fertilization

**cys·to·lith** \'sis-tə-ˌlith\ *noun* [German *Zystolith,* from *zyst-* cyst- + *-lith*] (1857)
: a calcium carbonate concretion arising from the cellulose wall of cells of higher plants

**cys·to·scope** \'sis-tə-ˌskōp\ *noun* [International Scientific Vocabulary] (1889)
: a medical instrument for the visual examination of the bladder and for the passage of instruments under visual control
— **cys·to·scop·ic** \ˌsis-tə-'skä-pik\ *adjective*
— **cys·tos·co·py** \si-'stäs-kə-pē\ *noun*

**cyt-** *or* **cyto-** *combining form* [German *zyt-, zyto-,* from Greek *kytos* hollow vessel — more at HIDE]
**1** : cell ⟨*cytology*⟩
**2** : cytoplasm ⟨*cytokinesis*⟩

**-cyte** *noun combining form* [New Latin *-cyta,* from Greek *kytos* hollow vessel]
: cell ⟨leuko*cyte*⟩

**Cyth·er·ea** \ˌsi-thə-'rē-ə\ *noun* [Latin, from Greek *Kythereia,* from *Kythēra* Cythera, island associated with Aphrodite]
: APHRODITE

**Cyth·er·e·an** \-'rē-ən\ *adjective* (1885)
: of or relating to the planet Venus

**cy·ti·dine** \'si-tə-ˌdēn, 'sī-\ *noun* [*cytosine* + *-idine*] (1911)
: a nucleoside containing cytosine

**cy·ti·dyl·ic acid** \ˌsi-tə-'di-lik-, ˌsī-\ *noun* [*cytidi*ne + *-yl* + $^1$*-ic*] (1936)
: a nucleotide containing cytosine

**cy·to·cha·la·sin** \ˌsī-tō-kə-'lā-sən\ *noun* [*cyt-* + Greek *chalasis* slackening + English $^1$*-in*] (1967)
: any of a group of metabolites isolated from fungi (especially *Helminthosporium dematioideum*) that inhibit various cell processes

**cy·to·chem·is·try** \-'ke-mə-strē\ *noun* (circa 1905)
**1** : microscopical biochemistry
**2** : the chemistry of cells
— **cy·to·chem·i·cal** \-'ke-mi-kəl\ *adjective*

**cy·to·chrome** \'sī-tə-ˌkrōm\ *noun* (1925)
: any of several intracellular hemoprotein respiratory pigments that are enzymes functioning in electron transport as carriers of electrons

**cytochrome c** *noun, often 2d c italic* (1940)
: the most abundant and stable of the cytochromes

**cytochrome oxidase** *noun* (1942)
: an iron-porphyrin enzyme important in cell respiration because of its ability to catalyze the oxidation of reduced cytochrome c in the presence of oxygen

**cy·to·dif·fer·en·ti·a·tion** \'sī-tō-ˌdi-fə-ˌren(t)-shē-'ā-shən\ *noun* (1959)
: the development of specialized cells (as muscle, blood, or nerve cells) from undifferentiated precursors

**cy·to·ge·net·ics** \ˌsī-tō-jə-'ne-tiks\ *noun plural but singular or plural in construction* [International Scientific Vocabulary] (1942)
: a branch of biology that deals with the study of heredity and variation by the methods of both cytology and genetics
— **cy·to·ge·net·ic** \-jə-'ne-tik\ *or* **cy·to·ge·net·i·cal** \-ti-kəl\ *adjective*
— **cy·to·ge·net·i·cal·ly** \-ti-k(ə-)lē\ *adverb*
— **cy·to·ge·net·i·cist** \-'ne-tə-sist\ *noun*

**cy·to·kine** \'sī-tə-ˌkīn\ *noun* [*cyt-* + *-kine* (as in *lymphokine*)] (1979)
: any of a class of immunoregulatory substances (as lymphokines) that are secreted by cells of the immune system

**cy·to·ki·ne·sis** \ˌsī-tō-kə-'nē-səs, -kī-\ *noun* [New Latin] (1919)
**1** : the cytoplasmic changes accompanying mitosis
**2** : cleavage of the cytoplasm into daughter cells following nuclear division
— **cy·to·ki·net·ic** \-'ne-tik\ *adjective*

**cy·to·ki·nin** \ˌsī-tə-'kī-nən\ *noun* [*cyt-* + ki*nin*] (1965)
: any of various plant growth substances (as kinetin) that are usually derivatives of adenine

**cy·tol·o·gy** \sī-'tä-lə-jē\ *noun* [International Scientific Vocabulary] (1889)
**1** : a branch of biology dealing with the structure, function, multiplication, pathology, and life history of cells
**2** : the cytological aspects of a process or structure
— **cy·to·log·i·cal** \ˌsī-tᵊl-'ä-ji-kəl\ *or* **cy·to·log·ic** \-'ä-jik\ *adjective*
— **cy·to·log·i·cal·ly** \-ji-k(ə-)lē\ *adverb*
— **cy·tol·o·gist** \sī-'tä-lə-jist\ *noun*

**cy·to·ly·sin** \ˌsī-tᵊl-'ī-sᵊn\ *noun* [International Scientific Vocabulary] (circa 1903)
: a substance (as an antibody that lyses bacteria) producing cytolysis

**cy·tol·y·sis** \sī-'tä-lə-səs\ *noun* [New Latin] (1907)
: the usually pathologic dissolution or disintegration of cells
— **cy·to·lyt·ic** \ˌsī-tᵊl-'i-tik\ *adjective*

**cy·to·meg·al·ic** \ˌsī-tō-mi-'ga-lik\ *adjective* [New Latin *cytomegalia* condition of having enlarged cells, from *cyt-* + *megal-* + *-ia*] (1952)
: characterized by or causing the formation of enlarged cells

**cy·to·meg·a·lo·vi·rus** \ˌsī-tə-ˌme-gə-lō-'vī-rəs\ *noun* [New Latin, from *cytomegalia* + *-o-* + *virus*] (1963)
: any of several viruses that cause cellular enlargement and formation of eosinophilic inclusion bodies especially in the nucleus and include some acting as opportunistic infectious agents in immunosuppressed conditions (as AIDS)

**cy·to·mem·brane** \ˌsī-tō-'mem-ˌbrān\ *noun* (1962)
: one of the cellular membranes including those of the plasmalemma, endoplasmic reticulum, nuclear envelope, and Golgi apparatus; *specifically* : UNIT MEMBRANE

**cy·to·path·ic** \ˌsī-tə-'pa-thik\ *adjective* (1952)
: of, relating to, characterized by, or producing pathological changes in cells

**cy·to·path·o·gen·ic** \-ˌpa-thə-'je-nik\ *adjective* (1952)
: pathologic for or destructive to cells
— **cy·to·path·o·ge·nic·i·ty** \-jə-'ni-sə-tē\ *noun*

**cy·to·phil·ic** \ˌsī-tə-'fi-lik\ *adjective* (circa 1909)
: having an affinity for cells ⟨*cytophilic* antibodies⟩

**cy·to·pho·tom·e·try** \-fō-'tä-mə-trē\ *noun* (1955)
: photometry applied to the study of the cell or its constituents
— **cy·to·pho·to·met·ric** \-ˌfō-tə-'me-trik\ *adjective*

**cy·to·plasm** \'sī-tə-ˌpla-zəm\ *noun* [International Scientific Vocabulary] (1874)
: the organized complex of inorganic and organic substances external to the nuclear membrane of a cell and including the cytosol and membrane-bound organelles (as mitochondria or chloroplasts) — see CELL illustration
— **cy·to·plas·mic** \ˌsī-tə-'plaz-mik\ *adjective*
— **cy·to·plas·mi·cal·ly** \-mi-k(ə-)lē\ *adverb*

**cy·to·sine** \'sī-tə-,sēn\ *noun* [International Scientific Vocabulary *cyt-* + *-ose* + ²*-ine*] (1894)
**:** a pyrimidine base C₄H₅N₃O that codes genetic information in the polynucleotide chain of DNA or RNA — compare ADENINE, GUANINE, THYMINE, URACIL

**cy·to·skel·e·ton** \,sī-tə-'ske-lə-t°n\ *noun* (1940)
**:** the network of protein filaments and microtubules in the cytoplasm that controls cell shape, maintains intracellular organization, and is involved in cell movement
— **cy·to·skel·e·tal** \-t°l\ *adjective*

**cy·to·sol** \'sī-tə-,säl, -,sòl\ *noun* (1970)
**:** the fluid portion of the cytoplasm exclusive of organelles and membranes — called also *hyaloplasm, ground substance*
— **cy·to·sol·ic** \,sī-tə-'sä-lik, -'sò-\ *adjective*

**cy·to·stat·ic** \,sī-tə-'sta-tik\ *adjective* (1949)
**:** tending to retard cellular activity and multiplication ⟨*cytostatic* treatment of tumor cells⟩
— **cytostatic** *noun*
— **cy·to·stat·i·cal·ly** \-ti-k(ə-)lē\ *adverb*

**cy·to·tax·on·o·my** \,sī-tō-(,)tak-'sä-nə-mē\ *noun* (1930)
**1 :** study of the relationships and classification of organisms using both classical systematic techniques and comparative studies of chromosomes
**2 :** the nuclear cytologic makeup of a kind of organism
— **cy·to·tax·o·nom·ic** \-,tak-sə-'nä-mik\ *adjective*
— **cy·to·tax·o·nom·i·cal·ly** \-mi-k(ə-)lē\ *adverb*

**cy·to·tech·nol·o·gist** \,sī-tə-tek-'nä-lə-jist\ *noun* (1961)
**:** a medical technician trained in the identification of cells and cellular abnormalities (as in cancer)
— **cy·to·tech·nol·o·gy** \-lə-jē\ *noun*

**cy·to·tox·ic** \,sī-tə-'täk-sik\ *adjective* (1904)
**1 :** of or relating to a cytotoxin
**2 :** toxic to cells ⟨*cytotoxic* properties of platinum⟩
— **cy·to·tox·ic·i·ty** \-(,)täk-'si-sə-tē\ *noun*

**cy·to·tox·in** \-'täk-sən\ *noun* (1902)
**:** a substance (as a toxin or antibody) having a toxic effect on cells

**czar** \'zär, '(t)sär\ *noun* [New Latin *czar,* from Russian *tsar',* from Old Russian *tsĭsarĭ,* from Gothic *kaisar,* from Greek or Latin; Greek, from Latin *Caesar* — more at CAESAR] (1555)
**1 :** EMPEROR; *specifically* **:** the ruler of Russia until the 1917 revolution
**2 :** one having great power or authority ⟨a banking *czar*⟩ ◆
— **czar·dom** \'zär-dəm, '(t)sär-\ *noun*

**czar·das** \'chär-,dash, -,däsh\ *noun, plural* **czardas** [Hungarian *csárdás*] (1860)
**:** a Hungarian dance to music in duple time in which the dancers start slowly and finish with a rapid whirl

**czar·e·vitch** \'zär-ə-,vich, '(t)sär-\ *noun* [Russian *tsarevich,* from *tsar'* + *-evich,* patronymic suffix] (1710)
**:** an heir apparent of a Russian czar

**cza·ri·na** \zä-'rē-nə, (t)sä-\ *noun* [probably modification of German *Zarin,* from *Zar* czar, from Russian *tsar'*] (1717)
**:** the wife of a czar

**czar·ism** \'zär-,i-zəm, '(t)sär-\ *noun* (1855)
**1 :** the government of Russia under the czars
**2 :** autocratic rule
— **czar·ist** \'zär-ist, '(t)sär-\ *noun or adjective*

**Czech** \'chek\ *noun* [Czech *Čech*] (1841)
**1 :** a native or inhabitant of western Czechoslovakia including Bohemia and Moravia
**2 :** the Slavic language of the Czechs
**3 :** a native or inhabitant of Czechoslovakia or the Czech Republic
— **Czech** *adjective*
— **Czech·ish** \'che-kish\ *adjective*

---

◇ WORD HISTORY

**czar** *Czar* or *tsar* is the English word for a pre-Soviet Russian emperor. *Tsar* is a straightforward transliteration of the Russian word and is now the usual form in Slavic studies; but *czar,* now usually used figuratively (as in "drug czar") has an older and more involved origin. We owe this spelling to the Austrian diplomat Seigmund, Freiherr (Baron) von Herberstein (1486–1566), who was an ambassador to the court at Moscow during the reigns of the Holy Roman Emperors Maximilian I and Charles V. In 1549 he published *Rerum moscovitarum commentarii* ("Commentaries on Muscovite Matters"), one of the first Western books concerning things Russian and long a major source of information about Russia in Western Europe. Herberstein wrote in Latin, but his use of *cz* to represent the sound \ts\ reflected a largely obsolete spelling convention in Hungarian. In English words such as *czardas* and *Czech,* *cz* represents, in contrast, \ch\, which is a convention continued in modern Polish.

---

\ə\ **abut** \°\ **kitten** \ər\ **further** \a\ **ash** \ā\ **ace**
\ä\ **mop, mar** \aú\ **out** \ch\ **chin** \e\ **bet** \ē\ **easy**
\g\ **go** \i\ **hit** \ī\ **ice** \j\ **job** \ŋ\ **sing** \ō\ **go**
\ò\ **law** \òi\ **boy** \th\ **thin** \t̲h̲\ **the** \ü\ **loot** \ú\ **foot**
\y\ **yet** \zh\ **vision** *see also* Guide to Pronunciation

**D** *is the fourth letter of the English alphabet and of most alphabets that are closely related to that of English. It came to Latin through Etruscan from a western Greek alphabet. The Greeks took it from the Phoenician alphabet, naming the letter* delta *after Phoenician* dāleth. *In modern English* d *usually represents the voiced alveolar stop, a consonant sound made with the tip of the tongue touching the inner surface of the gums above the upper front teeth (as the* d *sound in English* dog*). Small* d *evolved from a Roman variant of captial* D *in which the top of the curved line swept beyond the straight upright line of the letter (*Ɒ*). The straight line was later rounded on the left to form a lobe, and the original curved line ascended above the lobe from its right side (*∂*). Eventually, this ascender was straightened to produce the modern form of the letter.*

**d** \'dē\ *noun, plural* **d's** *or* **ds** \'dēz\ *often capitalized, often attributive* (before 12th century)
**1 a :** the 4th letter of the English alphabet **b :** a graphic representation of this letter **c :** a speech counterpart of orthographic *d*
**2 :** 500 — see NUMBER table
**3 :** the 2d tone of a C-major scale
**4 :** a graphic device for reproducing the letter *d*
**5 :** one designated *d* especially as the 4th in order or class
**6 a :** a grade rating a student's work as poor in quality **b :** one graded or rated with a D
**7 :** something shaped like the letter D; *specifically :* a semicircle on a pool table about 23 inches in diameter for use especially in snooker
**8 :** DEFENSE 2b, 4b ⟨play tough *D*⟩

**d-** \ˌdē, 'dē\ *prefix* [International Scientific Vocabulary, from *dextr-*]
**1 :** dextrorotatory ⟨*d*-tartaric acid⟩
**2 :** having a similar configuration at a selected carbon atom to the configuration of dextrorotatory glyceraldehyde — usually printed as a small capital ⟨D-fructose⟩

**-d** *symbol*
— used after the figure 2 or 3 to indicate the ordinal number second or third ⟨2*d*⟩ ⟨53*d*⟩

**'d** \d, əd, id\ *verb*
**1 :** HAD
**2 :** WOULD
**3 :** DID

**DA** \ˌdē-'ā\ *noun* [*duck's ass*; from its resemblance to the tail of a duck] (1951)
**:** DUCKTAIL

**¹dab** \'dab\ *noun* [Middle English *dabbe*] (14th century)
**1 :** a sudden blow or thrust : POKE
**2 :** a small amount
**3 :** a gentle touch or stroke : PAT
**4 :** DAUB

**²dab** *verb* **dabbed; dab·bing** (1562)
*transitive verb*
**1 :** to strike or touch lightly : PAT
**2 :** to apply lightly or irregularly : DAUB
*intransitive verb*
**:** to make a dab
— **dab·ber** *noun*

**³dab** *noun* [Anglo-French *dabbe*] (15th century)
**:** FLATFISH; *especially :* any of several flounders (genus *Limanda*)

**⁴dab** *noun* [origin unknown] (1691)
*chiefly British :* a skillful person

**dab·ble** \'da-bəl\ *verb* **dab·bled; dab·bling** \-b(ə-)liŋ\ [perhaps frequentative of ²*dab*] (1557)
*transitive verb*
**:** to wet by splashing or by little dips or strokes : SPATTER
*intransitive verb*

**1 a :** to paddle, splash, or play in or as if in water **b :** to reach with the bill to the bottom of shallow water in order to obtain food
**2 :** to work or involve oneself superficially or intermittently especially in a secondary activity or interest ⟨*dabbles* in art⟩

**dab·bler** \-b(ə-)lər\ *noun* (1611)
**:** one that dabbles: as **a :** one not deeply engaged in or concerned with something **b :** a duck (as a mallard or shoveler) that feeds by dabbling — called also *dabbling duck, puddle duck*
**synonym** see AMATEUR

**dab·bling** \-b(ə-)liŋ\ *noun* (circa 1847)
**:** a superficial or intermittent interest, investigation, or experiment ⟨his *dabblings* in philosophy and art⟩

**dab·chick** \'dab-ˌchik\ *noun* [probably irregular from obsolete English *dop* (to dive) + English *chick*] (circa 1550)
**:** any of several small grebes

**dab hand** *noun* [⁴*dab*] (circa 1828)
*chiefly British :* EXPERT

**da ca·po** \dä-'kä-(ˌ)pō, də-\ *adverb or adjective* [Italian] (circa 1724)
**:** from the beginning — used as a direction in music to repeat

**dace** \'dās\ *noun, plural* **dace** [Middle English *dace, darce*, from Middle French *dars*, from Medieval Latin *darsus*] (15th century)
**1 :** a small freshwater European cyprinid fish (*Leuciscus leuciscus*)
**2 :** any of various small North American freshwater cyprinid fishes

**da·cha** \'dä-chə *also* 'da-\ *noun* [Russian, from Old Russian, land allotted by a prince; akin to Latin *dos* dowry — more at DATE] (1896)
**:** a Russian country cottage used especially in the summer

**dachs·hund** \'däks-ˌhunt, -ˌhund; 'däk-sənt; *especially British* 'dak-sənd\ *noun* [German, from *Dachs* badger + *Hund* dog] (1882)
**:** any of a breed of long-bodied, short-legged dogs of German origin that occur in short-haired, long-haired, and wirehaired varieties

dachshund

**Da·cron** \'dā-ˌkrän, 'da-\ *trademark*
— used for a synthetic polyester textile fiber

**dac·tyl** \'dak-tᵊl, -ˌtil\ *noun* [Middle English *dactile*, from Latin *dactylus*, from Greek *daktylos*, literally, finger; from the fact that the first of three syllables is the longest, like the joints of the finger] (14th century)
**:** a metrical foot consisting of one long and two short syllables or of one stressed and two unstressed syllables (as in *tenderly*)
— **dac·tyl·ic** \dak-'ti-lik\ *adjective or noun*

**dactyl-** *or* **dactylo-** *combining form* [Greek *daktyl-, daktylo-*, from *daktylos*]

**:** finger : toe : digit ⟨*dactylology*⟩

**dac·ty·lol·o·gy** \ˌdak-tə-'lä-lə-jē\ *noun* (circa 1656)
**:** FINGER SPELLING

**dad** \'dad\ *noun* [probably baby talk] (15th century)
**:** FATHER 1a

**Da·da** \'dä-(ˌ)dä\ *noun* [French] (1919)
**:** a movement in art and literature based on deliberate irrationality and negation of traditional artistic values; *also :* the art and literature produced by this movement ◆

**da·da·ism** \-ˌi-zəm\ *noun, often capitalized* [French *dadaïsme*] (1919)
**:** DADA
— **da·da·ist** \-ˌist\ *noun or adjective, often capitalized*
— **da·da·is·tic** \ˌdä-dä-'is-tik\ *adjective, often capitalized*

**dad·dy** \'da-dē\ *noun, plural* **daddies** (15th century)
**1 :** FATHER 1a
**2 :** GRANDDADDY 2

**dad·dy long·legs** \ˌda-dē-'lóŋ-ˌlegz, -ˌlägz\ *noun, plural* **daddy longlegs** (circa 1814)
**1 :** CRANE FLY
**2 :** HARVESTMAN

**¹da·do** \'dä-(ˌ)dō\ *noun, plural* **da·does** [Italian, die, plinth] (1664)
**1 a :** the part of a pedestal of a column between the base and the surbase **b :** the lower part of an interior wall when specially decorated or faced; *also :* the decoration adorning this part of a wall
**2 :** a rectangular groove cut to make a joint in woodworking; *specifically :* one cut across the grain

dado 1a: *1* surbase, *2* dado, *3* base

**²dado** *transitive verb* **da·doed; da·do·ing** (1881)
**1 :** to provide with a dado
**2 a :** to set into a groove **b :** to cut a dado in (as a plank)

**dae·dal** \'dē-dᵊl\ *adjective* [Latin *daedalus*, from Greek *daidalos*] (1590)
**1 a :** SKILLFUL, ARTISTIC **b :** INTRICATE ⟨the computer's *daedal* circuitry⟩
**2 :** adorned with many things ⟨visions of cloud and light and *daedal* earth are the airman's daily scene —Laurence Binyon⟩

**Dae·da·lus** \'de-dᵊl-əs, 'dē-\ *noun* [Latin, from Greek *Daidalos*]
**:** the legendary builder of the Cretan labyrinth who makes wings to enable himself and his son Icarus to escape imprisonment

◇ WORD HISTORY
**Dada** In February 1916, while Europe was engulfed in World War I, a group of aesthetes and war resisters, including the artists Marcel Duchamp and Jean Arp and the poet Tristan Tzara, sought refuge in tranquil, neutral Switzerland. They decided to respond to the madness about them by creating an artistic movement based on irrationality, one that would repudiate traditional values and conventions and would shock bourgeois sensibilities. At a café in Zurich one evening, they hit upon a name for the new movement. Recollections of the movement's founding members differ regarding the arbitrariness of the naming process, but in any case the word chosen was *dada*, in French a child's word for a hobbyhorse; its very childishness was a way the group could mock the world around them. Though the Zurich group soon broke up and Dadaism as a movement lost its steam in the 1920s, it had far-reaching effects on the art of the 20th century, for trends as diverse as surrealism and conceptual art have their roots in Dada.

— **Dae·da·lian** or **Dae·da·lean** \di-'dāl-yən\ adjective

**dae·mon** variant of DEMON

**daff** \'daf\ transitive verb [alteration of doff] (1596)
**1** archaic **:** to thrust aside
**2** obsolete **:** to put off (as with an excuse)

**daf·fo·dil** \'da-fə-ˌdil\ noun [perhaps from Dutch de affodil the asphodel, from de the (from Middle Dutch) + affodil asphodel, from Middle French afrodille, from Latin asphodelus; akin to Old High German thaz the — more at THAT, ASPHODEL] (1548)
**:** any of various bulbous herbs (genus Narcissus); especially **:** a plant whose flowers have a large corona elongated into a trumpet — compare JONQUIL

**daf·fy** \'da-fē\ adjective **daf·fi·er; -est** [obsolete English daff, noun (fool)] (circa 1884)
**:** CRAZY, FOOLISH
— **daf·fi·ly** \'da-fə-lē\ adverb

**daft** \'daft also 'däft\ adjective [Middle English dafte gentle, stupid; akin to Old English gedæfte mild, gentle, Middle English defte deft, Old Church Slavonic podobati to be fitting] (14th century)
**1 a :** SILLY, FOOLISH **b :** MAD, INSANE
**2** Scottish **:** frivolously gay
— **daft·ly** adverb
— **daft·ness** \'daf(t)-nəs\ noun

**dag** \'dag\ noun [Middle English dagge] (14th century)
**1 :** a hanging end or shred
**2 :** matted or manure-coated wool

**dag·ger** \'da-gər\ noun [Middle English] (14th century)
**1 :** a sharp pointed knife for stabbing
**2 a :** something that resembles a dagger **b :** a character † used as a reference mark or to indicate a death date
— **dag·ger·like** \-ˌlīk\ adjective
— **at daggers drawn :** in a state of open hostility or conflict

**da·go** \'dā-(ˌ)gō\ noun, plural **dagos** or **dagoes** [alteration of earlier diego, from Diego, a common Spanish given name] (1832)
**:** a person of Italian or Spanish birth or descent — usually used disparagingly

**da·guerre·o·type** \də-'ge-rō-ˌtīp, -rə- also də-'ge-rē-ō-ˌtīp\ noun [French daguerréotype, from L. J. M. Daguerre + French -o- + type] (1839)
**:** an early photograph produced on a silver or a silver-covered copper plate; also **:** the process of producing such photographs
— **daguerreotype** transitive verb
— **da·guerre·o·typ·ist** \-ˌtī-pist\ noun
— **da·guerre·o·typy** \-ˌtī-pē\ noun

**dah** \'dä\ noun [imitative] (1940)
**:** DASH 7

**dahl·ia** \'dal-yə, 'däl-, U.S. also & British usually 'dāl-\ noun [New Latin, genus name, from Anders Dahl (died 1789) Swedish botanist] (1840)
**:** any of a genus (Dahlia) of American tuberous-rooted composite herbs having opposite pinnate leaves and rayed flower heads and including many that are cultivated as ornamentals

**dai·kon** \'dī-kən\ noun [Japanese, from dai big + kon root] (1876)
**:** a large long hard white radish used especially in Oriental cuisine; also **:** a plant (Raphanus sativus longipinnatus) whose root is a daikon

**dai·li·ness** \'dā-lē-nəs, -li-\ noun (1596)
**:** daily or routine quality **:** ORDINARINESS (the dailiness of family life)

**¹dai·ly** \'dā-lē\ adjective (15th century)
**1 a :** occurring, made, or acted upon every day **b :** issued every day or every weekday **c :** of or providing for every day
**2 a :** reckoned by the day (average daily wage) **b :** covering the period of or based on a day (daily statistics)

**²daily** adverb (15th century)
**1 :** every day
**2 :** every weekday

**³daily** noun, plural **dai·lies** (1832)
**1 :** a newspaper published every weekday
**2** British **:** a servant who works on a daily basis
**3** plural **:** RUSH 6

**daily double** noun (1942)
**:** a system of betting (as on horse races) in which the bettor must pick the winners of two stipulated races in order to win

**daily dozen** noun (1919)
**1 :** a series of physical exercises to be performed daily **:** WORKOUT
**2 :** a set of routine duties or tasks

**dai·mon** \'dī-ˌmōn\ noun, plural **dai·mo·nes** \'dī-mə-ˌnēz\ or **daimons** [Greek daimōn] (1852)
**:** DEMON 2, 3
— **dai·mon·ic** \dī-'mä-nik\ adjective

**dai·myo** also **dai·mio** \'dī-mē-ˌō, -(ˌ)myō\ noun, plural **-myo** or **-myos** also **-mio** or **-mios** [Japanese daimyō] (1727)
**:** a Japanese feudal baron

**¹dain·ty** \'dān-tē\ noun, plural **dain·ties** [Middle English deinte, from Old French deintié, from Latin dignitat-, dignitas dignity, worth] (14th century)
**1 a :** something delicious to the taste **b :** something choice or pleasing
**2** obsolete **:** FASTIDIOUSNESS

**²dainty** adjective **dain·ti·er; -est** (14th century)
**1 a :** tasting good **:** TASTY **b :** attractively prepared and served
**2 :** marked by delicate or diminutive beauty, form, or grace
**3** obsolete **:** CHARY, RELUCTANT
**4 a :** marked by fastidious discrimination or finical taste **b :** showing avoidance of anything rough
**synonym** see CHOICE
— **dain·ti·ly** \'dān-tə-lē\ adverb
— **dain·ti·ness** \'dān-tē-nəs\ noun

**dai·qui·ri** \'da-kə-rē, 'dī-\ noun [Daiquirí, Cuba] (1920)
**:** a cocktail made of rum, lime juice, and sugar

**dairy** \'der-ē, 'dar-\ noun, plural **dair·ies** often attributive [Middle English deyerie, from deye dairymaid, from Old English dæge kneader of bread; akin to Old English dāg dough — more at DOUGH] (14th century)
**1 :** a room, building, or establishment where milk is kept and butter or cheese is made
**2 a :** the department of farming or of a farm that is concerned with the production of milk, butter, and cheese **b :** a farm devoted to such production
**3 :** an establishment for the sale or distribution chiefly of milk and milk products

**dairy cattle** noun plural (1895)
**:** cattle kept for milk production

**dairy·ing** \'der-ē-iŋ\ noun (1649)
**:** the business of operating a dairy

**dairy·maid** \-ˌmād\ noun (1599)
**:** a woman employed in a dairy

**dairy·man** \-mən, -ˌman\ noun (circa 1617)
**:** one who operates a dairy farm or works in a dairy

**da·is** \'dā-əs, ÷'dīs-\ noun [Middle English deis, from Old French, from Late Latin discus high table, from Latin, dish, quoit — more at DISH] (13th century)
**:** a raised platform (as in a hall or large room)

**dai·shi·ki** \dī-'shē-kē\ variant of DASHIKI

**dai·sy** \'dā-zē\ noun, plural **daisies** [Middle English dayeseye, from Old English dægesēage, from dæg day + ēage eye] (before 12th century)
**1 :** a composite plant (as of the genera Bellis or Chrysanthemum) having a flower head with well-developed ray flowers usually arranged in one or a few whorls: as **a :** a low European herb (Bellis perennis) with white or pink ray flowers — called also English daisy **b :** a leafy-stemmed perennial herb (Chrysanthemum leucanthemum) with long white ray flowers and a yellow disk that was introduced into the U.S. from Europe — called also ox-eye daisy
**2 :** the flower head of a daisy
**3 :** a first-rate person or thing
**4** capitalized **:** a member of a program of the Girl Scouts for girls in kindergarten and first grade in school

**daisy chain** noun (1841)
**1 :** a string of daisies with stems linked to form a chain
**2 :** an interlinked series

**daisy ham** noun (circa 1938)
**:** a boned and smoked piece of pork from the shoulder

**daisy wheel** noun [from its resemblance to the flower] (circa 1977)
**:** a disk with spokes bearing type that serves as the printing element of an electric typewriter or printer; also **:** a printer that uses such a disk

**Da·ko·ta** \də-'kō-tə\ noun, plural **Dakotas** also **Dakota** (1804)
**1 :** a member of an American Indian people of the northern Mississippi valley
**2 :** the language of the Dakota people

**dal** also **dahl** \'däl\ noun [Hindi dāl] (1673)
**:** a dried legume (as lentils, beans, or peas); also **:** an Indian dish made of simmered and usually pureed and spiced legumes

**Da·lai La·ma** \dä-lī-'lä-mə, ˌdä-lā-, ˌda-\ noun [Mongolian dalai ocean] (1698)
**:** the spiritual head of Lamaism

**da·la·si** \dä-'lä-sē\ noun, plural **dalasi** or **dalasis** [Wolof] (1966)
— see MONEY table

**dale** \'dā(ə)l\ noun [Middle English, from Old English dæl; akin to Old High German tal valley, Welsh dôl] (before 12th century)
**:** VALLEY, VALE (went riding over hill and dale)

**dales·man** \'dā(ə)lz-mən\ noun (1769)
British **:** one living or born in a dale

**da·leth** \'dä-ˌleth, -ˌlet also -ləd\ noun [Hebrew dāleth, from deleth door] (1823)
**:** the 4th letter of the Hebrew alphabet — see ALPHABET table

**dal·li·ance** \'da-lē-ən(t)s\ noun (14th century)
**:** an act of dallying: as **a :** PLAY; especially **:** amorous play **b :** frivolous action **:** TRIFLING

**Dal·lis grass** \'da-ləs-\ noun [A. T. Dallis, 19th century American farmer] (1907)
**:** a tall tufted tropical perennial grass (Paspalum dilatatum) introduced as a pasture and forage grass in the southern U.S.

**Dall por·poise** \'dȯl-\ noun [William H. Dall (died 1927) American naturalist] (1951)
**:** a black-and-white porpoise (Phocoenoides dalli) of temperate and arctic waters of the rim of the North Pacific Ocean — called also Dall's porpoise \'dȯlz-\

**Dall sheep** noun [W. H. Dall] (1887)
**:** a large white wild sheep (Ovis dalli) of Alaska and northern British Columbia — called also Dall's sheep

**dal·ly** \'da-lē\ intransitive verb **dal·lied; dal·ly·ing** [Middle English dalyen, from Anglo-French dalier] (15th century)
**1 a :** to act playfully; especially **:** to play amorously **b :** to deal lightly **:** TOY (accused him of dallying with a serious problem)
**2 a :** to waste time **b :** LINGER, DAWDLE
**synonym** see TRIFLE, DELAY
— **dal·li·er** noun

**dal·ma·tian** \dal-'mā-shən\ noun, often capitalized [from the supposed origin of the breed in Dalmatia] (1824)
**:** any of a breed of medium-sized dogs having a

---

\ə\ abut \ˀ\ kitten \ər\ further \a\ ash \ā\ ace
\ä\ mop, mar \au̇\ out \ch\ chin \e\ bet \ē\ easy
\g\ go \i\ hit \ī\ ice \j\ job \ŋ\ sing \ō\ go
\ȯ\ law \ȯi\ boy \th\ thin \t͟h\ the \ü\ loot \u̇\ foot
\y\ yet \zh\ vision _see also_ Guide to Pronunciation

white short-haired coat with black or brown spots
**dal·mat·ic** \dal-'ma-tik\ *noun* [Middle English *dalmatyk,* from Old English *dalmatice,* from Late Latin *dalmatica,* from Latin, feminine of *dalmaticus* Dalmatian, from *Dalmatia*] (before 12th century)

**dalmatian**

**1 :** a wide-sleeved overgarment with slit sides worn by a deacon or prelate
**2 :** a robe worn by a British sovereign at his or her coronation
**dal se·gno** \däl-'sā-(,)nyō\ *adverb* [Italian, from the sign] (circa 1854)
— used as a direction in music to return to the sign that marks the beginning of a repeat
**dal·ton** \'dol-t°n\ *noun* [John *Dalton* (died 1844) English chemist] (circa 1928)
**:** ATOMIC MASS UNIT — used chiefly in biochemistry
**¹dam** \'dam\ *noun* [Middle English *dam, dame* lady, dam — more at DAME] (13th century)
**:** a female parent — used especially of a domestic animal
**²dam** *noun* [Middle English, probably from Middle Dutch; akin to Old English for*demman* to stop up] (14th century)
**1 :** a body of water confined by a barrier
**2 a :** a barrier preventing the flow of water or of loose solid materials (as soil or snow); *especially* **:** a barrier built across a watercourse for impounding water **b :** a barrier to check the flow of liquid, gas, or air
**³dam** *transitive verb* **dammed; dam·ming** (15th century)
**1 :** to provide or restrain with a dam
**2 :** to stop up **:** BLOCK
**¹dam·age** \'da-mij\ *noun* [Middle English, from Middle French, from *dam* damage, from Latin *damnum*] (14th century)
**1 :** loss or harm resulting from injury to person, property, or reputation
**2** *plural* **:** compensation in money imposed by law for loss or injury
**3 :** EXPENSE, COST ("What's the *damage*?" he asked the waiter)
**²damage** *transitive verb* **dam·aged; dam·ag·ing** (14th century)
**:** to cause damage to
**synonym** see INJURE
— **dam·age·abil·i·ty** \,da-mi-jə-'bi-lə-tē\ *noun*
— **dam·ag·er** *noun*
**dam·ag·ing** *adjective* (circa 1828)
**:** causing or able to cause damage **:** INJURIOUS (has a *damaging* effect on wildlife)
— **dam·ag·ing·ly** \'da-mi-jiŋ-lē\ *adverb*
**dam·ar** *or* **dam·mar** \'da-mər\ *noun* [Malay] (1698)
**:** any of various resins used in varnishes and inks and obtained chiefly in Malaya and Indonesia from several timber trees (families Dipterocarpaceae and Burseraceae)
**¹dam·a·scene** \'da-mə-,sēn, ,da-mə-'-\ *noun* (14th century)
**1** *capitalized* **:** a native or inhabitant of Damascus
**2 :** the characteristic markings of Damascus steel
**²damascene** *adjective* (14th century)
**1** *capitalized* **:** of, relating to, or characteristic of Damascus or the Damascenes
**2 :** of or relating to damask or the art of damascening
**³damascene** *transitive verb* **-scened; -scen·ing** [Middle French *damasquiner,* from *damasquin* of Damascus] (1585)
**:** to ornament (as iron or steel) with wavy patterns like those of watered silk or with inlaid work of precious metals

**Da·mas·cus steel** \də-'mas-kəs-\ *noun* (circa 1727)
**:** hard elastic steel ornamented with wavy patterns and used especially for sword blades
**¹dam·ask** \'da-məsk\ *noun* [Middle English *damaske,* from Medieval Latin *damascus,* from *Damascus*] (14th century)
**1 :** a firm lustrous fabric (as of linen, cotton, silk, or rayon) made with flat patterns in a satin weave on a plain-woven ground on jacquard looms
**2 :** DAMASCUS STEEL; *also* **:** the characteristic markings of this steel
**3 :** a grayish red
**²damask** *adjective* (15th century)
**1 :** made of or resembling damask
**2 :** of the color damask
**damask rose** *noun* [obsolete *Damask* of Damascus, from obsolete *Damask* Damascus] (1540)
**:** a large hardy fragrant pink rose (*Rosa damascena*) widely introduced from Asia Minor and the major source of attar of roses
**dame** \'dām\ *noun* [Middle English, from Old French *dame,* from Latin *domina,* feminine of *dominus* master; akin to Latin *domus* house — more at DOME] (13th century)
**1 :** a woman of rank, station, or authority: as **a** *archaic* **:** the mistress of a household **b :** the wife or daughter of a lord **c :** a female member of an order of knighthood — used as a title prefixed to the given name
**2 a :** an elderly woman **b :** WOMAN
**dame school** *noun* (1817)
**:** a school in which the rudiments of reading and writing were taught by a woman in her own home
**dame's rocket** *noun* (circa 1900)
**:** a Eurasian perennial plant (*Hesperis matronalis*) of the mustard family cultivated for its spikes of showy fragrant white or purple flowers — called also *dame's violet, rocket*
**¹damn** \'dam\ *verb* **damned; damn·ing** \'da-miŋ\ [Middle English *dampnen,* from Old French *dampner,* from Latin *damnare,* from *damnum* damage, loss, fine] (13th century)
*transitive verb*
**1 :** to condemn to a punishment or fate; *especially* **:** to condemn to hell
**2 a :** to condemn vigorously and often irascibly for some real or fancied fault or defect (*damned* the storm for their delay) **b :** to condemn as a failure by public criticism
**3 :** to bring ruin on
**4 :** to swear at **:** CURSE — often used to express annoyance, disgust, or surprise
*intransitive verb*
**:** CURSE, SWEAR
**synonym** see EXECRATE
**²damn** *noun* (1619)
**1 :** the utterance of the word *damn* as a curse
**2 :** a minimum amount or degree (as of care or consideration) **:** the least bit (don't give a *damn*)
**³damn** *adjective or adverb* (1775)
**:** DAMNED (a *damn* nuisance) (ran *damn* fast)
— **damn well :** beyond doubt or question **:** CERTAINLY (knew *damn well* what would happen)
**dam·na·ble** \'dam-nə-bəl\ *adjective* (14th century)
**1 :** liable to or deserving condemnation
**2 :** very bad **:** DETESTABLE (*damnable* weather)
— **dam·na·ble·ness** *noun*
— **dam·na·bly** \-blē\ *adverb*
**dam·na·tion** \dam-'nā-shən\ *noun* (14th century)
**:** the act of damning **:** the state of being damned
**dam·na·to·ry** \'dam-nə-,tōr-ē, -,tor-\ *adjective* (1682)
**:** expressing, imposing, or causing condemnation **:** CONDEMNATORY
**¹damned** \'dam(d)\ *adjective* **damned·er** \'dam-dər\; **damned·est** *or* **damnd·est** \-dəst\ (1563)

**1 :** DAMNABLE (this *damned* smog)
**2 :** COMPLETE, UTTER — often used as an intensive
**3 :** EXTRAORDINARY — used in the superlative (the *damnedest* contraption you ever saw)
**²damned** \'dam(d)\ *adverb* (1757)
**:** EXTREMELY, VERY (a *damned* good job)
**damned·est** *or* **damnd·est** \'dam-dəst\ *noun* (1830)
**:** UTMOST, BEST — used chiefly in the phrase *do one's damnedest* (doing my *damnedest* to win)
**dam·ni·fy** \'dam-nə-,fī\ *transitive verb* **-fied; -fy·ing** [Middle French *damnifier,* from Old French, from Late Latin *damnificare,* from Latin *damnificus* injurious, from *damnum* damage] (1512)
**:** to cause loss or damage to
**damn·ing** \'da-miŋ\ *adjective* (1599)
**1 :** bringing damnation (a *damning* sin)
**2 :** causing or leading to condemnation or ruin (presented some *damning* testimony)
— **damn·ing·ly** \-miŋ-lē\ *adverb*
**Dam·o·cles** \'da-mə-,klēz\ *noun* [Latin, from Greek *Damoklēs*]
**:** a courtier of ancient Syracuse held to have been seated at a banquet beneath a sword hung by a single hair
— **Dam·o·cle·an** \,da-mə-'klē-ən\ *adjective*
**Da·mon** \'dā-mən\ *noun* [Latin, from Greek *Damōn*]
**:** a legendary Sicilian who pledges his life for his condemned friend Pythias
**¹damp** \'damp\ *noun* [Middle Dutch or Middle Low German, vapor; akin to Old High German *damph* vapor] (14th century)
**1 :** a noxious gas — compare BLACK DAMP, FIREDAMP
**2 :** MOISTURE: **a :** HUMIDITY, DAMPNESS **b** *archaic* **:** FOG, MIST
**3 a :** DISCOURAGEMENT, CHECK **b** *archaic* **:** DEPRESSION, DEJECTION
**²damp** (14th century)
*transitive verb*
**1 a :** to affect with or as if with a noxious gas **:** CHOKE **b :** to diminish the activity or intensity of (*damping* down the causes of inflation) (liquid *damps* out compass oscillations) **c :** to check the vibration or oscillation of (as a string or voltage)
**2 :** DAMPEN
*intransitive verb*
**:** to diminish progressively in vibration or oscillation
**³damp** *adjective* (1590)
**1 a** *archaic* **:** being confused, bewildered, or shocked **:** STUPEFIED **b :** DEPRESSED, DULL
**2 :** slightly or moderately wet **:** MOIST; *also* **:** HUMID
**synonym** see WET
— **damp·ish** \'dam-pish\ *adjective*
— **damp·ly** *adverb*
— **damp·ness** *noun*
**damp·en** \'dam-pən\ *verb* **damp·ened; damp·en·ing** \'damp-niŋ, 'dam-pə-\ (1547)
*transitive verb*
**1 :** to check or diminish the activity or vigor of **:** DEADEN (the heat *dampened* our spirits)
**2 :** to make damp (the shower barely *dampened* the ground)
**3 :** DAMP 1c
*intransitive verb*
**1 :** to become damp
**2 :** to become deadened or depressed
— **damp·en·er** \-nər\ *noun*
**damp·er** \'dam-pər\ *noun* (1748)
**1 :** a dulling or deadening influence (put a *damper* on the celebration)
**2 :** a device that damps: as **a :** a valve or plate (as in the flue of a furnace) for regulating the draft **b :** a small felted block to stop the vibration of a piano string **c** *chiefly British* **:** SHOCK ABSORBER
**damp·ing–off** \,dam-piŋ-'of\ *noun* (1890)

: a diseased condition of seedlings or cuttings caused by fungi and marked by wilting or rotting

**dam·sel** \'dam-zəl\ *also* **dam·o·sel** *or* **dam·o·zel** \'da-mə-,zel\ *noun* [Middle English *dameisel*, from Old French *dameisele*, from (assumed) Vulgar Latin *domnicella* young noblewoman, diminutive of Latin *domina* lady] (13th century)
: a young woman: **a** *archaic* : a young unmarried woman of noble birth **b** : GIRL

**dam·sel·fish** \'dam-zəl-,fish\ *noun* (1904)
: any of numerous often brilliantly colored marine fishes (family Pomacentridae) living especially along coral reefs — called also *demoiselle*

**dam·sel·fly** \-,flī\ *noun* (1815)
: any of numerous odonate insects (suborder Zygoptera) distinguished from dragonflies by laterally projecting eyes and petiolate wings folded above the body when at rest

**dam·son** \'dam-zən\ *noun* [Middle English, from Latin (*prunum*) *damascenum*, literally, plum of Damascus] (14th century)
: the small tart fruit of a widely cultivated Asian plum tree (*Prunus insititia*); *also* : this tree

**¹Dan** \'dan\ *noun* [Hebrew *Dān*]
: a son of Jacob and the traditional eponymous ancestor of one of the tribes of Israel

**²Dan** \'dan\ *noun* [Middle English, title of members of religious orders, from Middle French, from Latin *dominus* master] (13th century)
*archaic* : MASTER, SIR

**Dan·aë** \'da-nə-,ē\ *noun* [Latin, from Greek *Danaē*]
: a princess of Argos visited by Zeus in the form of a shower of gold and by him the mother of Perseus

**¹dance** \'dan(t)s, 'dàn(t)s\ *verb* **danced; danc·ing** [Middle English *dauncen*, from Old French *dancier*] (14th century)
*intransitive verb*
**1** : to engage in or perform a dance
**2** : to move or seem to move up and down or about in a quick or lively manner
*transitive verb*
**1** : to perform or take part in as a dancer
**2** : to cause to dance
**3** : to bring into a specified condition by dancing
— **dance·able** \'dan(t)-sə-bəl\ *adjective*
— **danc·er** *noun*

**²dance** *noun, often attributive* (14th century)
**1** : an act or instance of dancing
**2** : a series of rhythmic and patterned bodily movements usually performed to music
**3** : a social gathering for dancing
**4** : a piece of music by which dancing may be guided
**5** : the art of dancing

**dan·de·li·on** \'dan-də-,lī-ən, -dē-\ *noun* [Middle French *dent de lion*, literally, lion's tooth] (14th century)
: any of a genus (*Taraxacum*) of yellow-flowered composite plants; *especially* : an herb (*T. officinale*) sometimes grown as a potherb and nearly cosmopolitan as a weed

**dan·der** \'dan-dər\ *noun* [alteration of *dandruff*] (1786)
**1** : DANDRUFF; *specifically* : minute scales from hair, feathers, or skin that may be allergenic
**2** : ANGER, TEMPER ⟨don't get your *dander* up⟩

**dan·di·a·cal** \dan-'dī-ə-kəl\ *adjective* [¹*dandy* + *-acal* (as in *demoniacal*)] (1831)
: of, relating to, or suggestive of a dandy

**Dan·die Din·mont terrier** \'dan-dē-'din-,mänt-\ *noun* [*Dandie Dinmont*, character owning six such dogs in the novel *Guy Mannering* by Sir Walter Scott] (1875)
: any of a breed of terriers characterized by short legs, a long body, pendulous ears, a rough coat, and a full silky topknot

**dan·di·fy** \'dan-di-,fī\ *transitive verb* **-fied; -fy·ing** (1823)

: to cause to resemble a dandy
— **dan·di·fi·ca·tion** \,dan-di-fə-'kā-shən\ *noun*

**dan·dle** \'dan-d°l\ *transitive verb* **dan·dled; dan·dling** \-(d)liŋ, -d°l-iŋ\ [origin unknown] (1530)
**1** : to move (as a baby) up and down in one's arms or on one's knee in affectionate play
**2** : PAMPER, PET

**Dandie Dinmont terrier**

**dan·druff** \'dan-drəf\ *noun* [probably from *dand-* (origin unknown) + *-ruff*, from Middle English *rove* scabby condition, from Old Norse *hrūfa* scab; akin to Old High German *hruf* scurf, Lithuanian *kraupus* rough] (1545)
: a scurf that forms on skin especially of the scalp and comes off in small white or grayish scales
— **dan·druffy** \-drə-fē\ *adjective*

**¹dan·dy** \'dan-dē\ *noun, plural* **dandies** [probably short for *jack-a-dandy*, from ¹*jack* + *a* (of) + *dandy* (origin unknown)] (circa 1780)
**1** : a man who gives exaggerated attention to personal appearance
**2** : something excellent in its class
— **dan·dy·ish** \-dē-ish\ *adjective*
— **dan·dy·ish·ly** *adverb*

**²dandy** *adjective* **dan·di·er; -est** (1792)
**1** : of, relating to, or suggestive of a dandy : FOPPISH
**2** : very good : FIRST-RATE ⟨a *dandy* place to stay⟩

**dan·dy·ism** \'dan-dē-,i-zəm\ *noun* (1819)
**1** : the style or conduct of a dandy
**2** : a literary and artistic style of the latter part of the 19th century marked by artificiality and excessive refinement

**Dane** \'dān\ *noun* [Middle English *Dan*, from Old Norse *Danr*] (14th century)
**1** : a native or inhabitant of Denmark
**2** : a person of Danish descent
**3** : GREAT DANE

**dane·geld** \'dān-,geld\ *noun, often capitalized* (before 12th century)
: an annual tax believed to have been imposed originally to buy off Danish invaders in England or to maintain forces to oppose them but continued as a land tax

**Dane·law** \'dān-,lȯ\ *noun* (before 12th century)
**1** : the law in force in the part of England held by the Danes before the Norman Conquest
**2** : the part of England under the Danelaw

**¹dang** \'daŋ\ *transitive verb* [euphemism] (1797)
: DAMN 4

**²dang** *adjective or adverb* (1914)
: DAMNED

**¹dan·ger** \'dān-jər\ *noun* [Middle English *daunger*, from Old French *dangier*, alteration of *dongier*, from (assumed) Vulgar Latin *dominiarium*, from Latin *dominium* ownership] (13th century)
**1 a** *archaic* : JURISDICTION **b** *obsolete* : REACH, RANGE
**2** *obsolete* : HARM, DAMAGE
**3** : exposure or liability to injury, pain, harm, or loss ⟨could play there without *danger*⟩
**4** : a case or cause of danger ⟨the *dangers* of mining⟩

**²danger** *transitive verb* (14th century)
*archaic* : ENDANGER

**dan·ger·ous** \'dān-jə-rəs; 'dān-jərs, -zhrəs\ *adjective* (15th century)
**1** : exposing to or involving danger
**2** : able or likely to inflict injury or harm ☆
— **dan·ger·ous·ly** *adverb*
— **dan·ger·ous·ness** *noun*

**¹dan·gle** \'daŋ-gəl\ *verb* **dan·gled; dan·gling** \-g(ə-)liŋ\ [probably of Scandinavian origin; akin to Danish *dangle* to dangle] (circa 1590)

*intransitive verb*
**1** : to hang loosely and usually so as to be able to swing freely
**2** : to be a hanger-on or a dependent
**3** : to occur in a sentence without having a normally expected syntactic relation to the rest of the sentence ⟨the word *climbing* in "Climbing the mountain the cabin came into view" is *dangling*⟩
*transitive verb*
**1** : to cause to dangle : SWING
**2 a** : to keep hanging uncertainly **b** : to hold out as an inducement
— **dan·gler** \-g(ə-)lər\ *noun*

**²dangle** *noun* (1756)
**1** : the action of dangling
**2** : something that dangles

**Dan·iel** \'da-nyəl *also* 'da-n°l\ *noun* [Hebrew *Dānī'ēl*]
**1** : the Jewish hero of the Book of Daniel who as an exile in Babylon interprets dreams, gives accounts of apocalyptic visions, and is divinely delivered from a den of lions
**2** : a book of narratives, visions, and prophecies in canonical Jewish and Christian Scripture — see BIBLE table

**da·nio** \'dā-nē-,ō\ *noun, plural* **da·ni·os** [New Latin, genus name] (circa 1889)
: any of several small brightly colored Asian cyprinid fishes

**¹Dan·ish** \'dā-nish\ *adjective* (14th century)
: of, relating to, or characteristic of Denmark, the Danes, or the Danish language

**²Danish** *noun* (15th century)
**1** : the Germanic language of the Danes
**2** *plural* **Danish** : a piece of Danish pastry

**Danish pastry** *noun* (circa 1928)
: a pastry made of a rich raised dough

**dank** \'daŋk\ *adjective* [Middle English *danke*] (1573)
: unpleasantly moist or wet
**synonym** see WET
— **dank·ly** *adverb*
— **dank·ness** *noun*

**dan·seur** \dä�207-'sər, dän-\ *noun* [French, from *danser* to dance] (1828)
: a male ballet dancer

**dan·seuse** \dä�207-'sœz; dä�207-'sə(r)z, dän-'süz\ *noun* [French, feminine of *danseur*] (1828)
: a female ballet dancer

**Dan·te·an** \'dan-tē-ən, 'dän-\ *noun* (circa 1850)
: a student or admirer of Dante

**Dao·ism, Dao·ist, Dao·is·tic** *variant of* TAOISM, TAOIST, TAOISTIC

**daph·ne** \'daf-nē\ *noun* [New Latin, genus name, from Latin, laurel, from Greek *daphnē*] (1862)
: any of a genus (*Daphne*) of Eurasian shrubs of the mezereon family with apetalous flowers whose colored calyx resembles a corolla

---

☆ **SYNONYMS**
**Dangerous, hazardous, precarious, perilous, risky** mean bringing or involving the chance of loss or injury. DANGEROUS applies to something that may cause harm or loss unless dealt with carefully ⟨soldiers on a *dangerous* mission⟩. HAZARDOUS implies great and continuous risk of harm or failure ⟨claims that smoking is *hazardous* to your health⟩. PRECARIOUS suggests both insecurity and uncertainty ⟨earned a *precarious* living by gambling⟩. PERILOUS strongly implies the immediacy of danger ⟨*perilous* mountain roads⟩. RISKY often applies to a known and accepted danger ⟨made *risky* decisions⟩.

---

\ə\ abut \°\ kitten \ər\ further \a\ ash \ā\ ace
\ä\ mop, mar \au̇\ out \ch\ chin \e\ bet \ē\ easy
\g\ go \i\ hit \ī\ ice \j\ job \ŋ\ sing \ō\ go
\ȯ\ law \ȯi\ boy \th\ thin \t͟h\ this \ü\ loot \u̇\ foot
\y\ yet \zh\ vision *see also* Guide to Pronunciation

**Daph·ne** \'daf-nē\ *noun* [Latin, from Greek *Daphnē*]
: a nymph who is transformed into a laurel tree to escape the pursuing Apollo

**daph·nia** \'daf-nē-ə\ *noun* [New Latin, genus name] (1847)
: any of a genus (*Daphnia*) of minute freshwater branchiopod crustaceans with biramous antennae used as locomotor organs — compare WATER FLEA

**Daph·nis** \'daf-nəs\ *noun* [Latin, from Greek]
: a Sicilian shepherd renowned in Greek mythology as the inventor of pastoral poetry

**dap·per** \'da-pər\ *adjective* [Middle English *dapyr*, from Middle Dutch *dapper* quick, strong; akin to Old High German *tapfar* heavy, Old Church Slavonic *debelŭ* thick] (15th century)
**1 a** : neat and trim in appearance **b** : excessively spruce and stylish
**2** : alert and lively in movement and manners
— **dap·per·ly** *adverb*
— **dap·per·ness** *noun*

**¹dap·ple** \'da-pəl\ *noun* [Middle English *dappel-gray*, adjective, gray marked with spots of another color] (1580)
**1** : any of numerous usually cloudy and rounded spots or patches of a color or shade different from their background
**2** : the quality or state of being dappled
**3** : a dappled animal

**²dapple** *verb* **dap·pled; dap·pling** \-p(ə-)liŋ\ (1599)
*transitive verb*
: to mark with dapples
*intransitive verb*
: to produce a dappled pattern ⟨sun *dappling* through trees⟩

**dap·pled** *also* **dap·ple** *adjective* (15th century)
: marked with small spots or patches contrasting with the background ⟨a *dappled* fawn⟩

**dap·sone** \'dap-,sōn\ *noun* [*di*amine + *p*henyl + *sulfone*] (1952)
: an antimicrobial agent $C_{12}H_{12}N_2O_2S$ used especially against leprosy

**Dar·by and Joan** \,där-bē-ən-'jōn\ *noun* [probably from *Darby & Joan*, couple in an 18th century song] (1857)
: a happily married usually elderly couple

**Dard** \'därd\ *noun* (circa 1885)
: DARDIC

**Dar·dan** \'där-d°n\ *adjective or noun* [Latin *Dardanus*, from Greek *Dardanos*] (1606)
*archaic* : TROJAN

**Dar·da·ni·an** \där-'dā-nē-ən\ *adjective* (1596)
: TROJAN

**Dar·dic** \'där-dik\ *noun* (1910)
: a complex of Indic languages spoken in the upper valley of the Indus

**¹dare** \'dar, 'der\ *verb* **dared; dar·ing; dares** *or (auxiliary)* **dare** [Middle English *dar* (1st & 3d singular present indicative), from Old English *dear*; akin to Old High German *gitar* (1st & 3d singular present indicative) *dare*, Greek *tharsos* courage] (before 12th century)
*verbal auxiliary*
: to be sufficiently courageous to ⟨no one *dared* say a word⟩ ⟨she *dare* not let herself love —G. B. Shaw⟩
*intransitive verb*
: to have sufficient courage ⟨try it if you *dare*⟩
*transitive verb*
**1 a** : to challenge to perform an action especially as a proof of courage ⟨*dared* him to jump⟩ **b** : to confront boldly : ⟨*dared* the mob⟩
**2** : to have the courage to contend against, venture, or try ⟨the actress *dared* a new interpretation of this classic role⟩
— **dar·er** \'dar-ər, 'der-\ *noun*

**²dare** *noun* (1594)
**1** : an act or instance of daring : CHALLENGE ⟨foolishly took a *dare*⟩
**2** : imaginative or vivacious boldness : DARING

**¹dare·dev·il** \'dar-,de-v°l, 'der-\ *noun* (1794)

: a recklessly bold person
— **dare·dev·il·ry** \-v°l-rē\ *noun*
— **dare·dev·il·try** \-v°l-trē\ *noun*

**²daredevil** *adjective* (1832)
: recklessly and often ostentatiously daring
*synonym* see ADVENTUROUS

**dare·ful** *adjective* (1605)
*obsolete* : DARING

**daren't** \'dar-ənt, 'der-\
: dare not : dared not

**dare·say** \,dar-'sā, ,der-\ (13th century)
*transitive verb*
: venture to say : think probable — used in present 1st singular
*intransitive verb*
: AGREE, SUPPOSE — used in present 1st singular

**¹dar·ing** *adjective* (1582)
: venturesomely bold in action or thought
*synonym* see ADVENTUROUS
— **dar·ing·ly** \-iŋ-lē\ *adverb*
— **dar·ing·ness** *noun*

**²daring** *noun* (1651)
: venturesome boldness

**Dar·jee·ling** \där-'jē-liŋ\ *noun* [*Darjeeling*, India] (1907)
: a tea of high quality grown especially in the mountainous districts of northern India

**¹dark** \'därk\ *adjective* [Middle English *derk*, from Old English *deorc*; akin to Old High German *tarchannen* to hide] (before 12th century)
**1 a** : devoid or partially devoid of light : not receiving, reflecting, transmitting, or radiating light **b** : transmitting only a portion of light
**2 a** : wholly or partially black **b** *of a color* : of low or very low lightness
**3 a** : arising from or showing evil traits or desires : EVIL ⟨the *dark* powers that lead to war⟩ **b** : DISMAL, GLOOMY ⟨had a *dark* view of the future⟩ **c** : lacking knowledge or culture
**4** : not clear to the understanding
**5** : not fair in complexion : SWARTHY
**6** : SECRET ⟨kept his plans *dark*⟩
**7** : possessing depth and richness ⟨a *dark* voice⟩
**8** : closed to the public ⟨the theater is *dark* in the summer⟩
*synonym* see OBSCURE
— **dark·ish** \'där-kish\ *adjective*
— **dark·ly** *adverb*
— **dark·ness** *noun*

**²dark** *noun* (13th century)
**1 a** : a place or time of little or no light : NIGHT, NIGHTFALL **b** : absence of light : DARKNESS
**2** : a dark or deep color
— **in the dark 1** : in secrecy ⟨most of his dealings were done *in the dark*⟩ **2** : in ignorance ⟨kept the public *in the dark* about the agreement⟩

**³dark** (14th century)
*intransitive verb*
*obsolete* : to grow dark
*transitive verb*
: to make dark

**dark adaptation** *noun* (1909)
: the phenomena usually including dilation of the pupil, increase in retinal sensitivity, shift of the region of maximum luminosity toward the blue, and regeneration of visual purple by which the eye adapts to conditions of reduced illumination
— **dark–adapt·ed** \,därk-ə-'dap-təd\ *adjective*

**dark age** *noun* (1730)
**1** : a time during which a civilization undergoes a decline: as **a** *plural, D&A capitalized* : the European historical period from about A.D. 476 to about 1000; *broadly* : MIDDLE AGES **b** *often plural, often D&A capitalized* : the Greek historical period of three to four centuries from about 1100 B.C.
**2 a** *often plural, often D&A capitalized* : the primitive period in the development of something ⟨in the 1890s, way back in baseball's

*Dark Ages* —R. W. Creamer⟩ **b** *often plural, often D&A capitalized* : a state of stagnation or decline

**dark·en** \'där-kən\ *verb* **dark·ened; dark·en·ing** \'där-kə-niŋ\ (14th century)
*intransitive verb*
**1** : to grow dark : become obscured
**2** : to become gloomy
*transitive verb*
**1** : to make dark
**2** : to make less clear : OBSCURE ⟨the financial crisis *darkened* the future of the company⟩
**3** : TAINT, TARNISH
**4** : to cast a gloom over
**5** : to make of darker color
— **dark·en·er** \-kə-nər\ *noun*

**dark field** *noun* (1865)
: the dark area that serves as the background for objects viewed in an ultramicroscope

**dark–field microscope** *noun* (1926)
: ULTRAMICROSCOPE

**dark horse** *noun* (1831)
**1 a** : a usually little known contender (as a racehorse) that makes an unexpectedly good showing **b** : an entrant in a contest that is judged unlikely to succeed
**2** : a political candidate unexpectedly nominated usually as a compromise between factions ◆

**dark lantern** *noun* (1650)
: a lantern that can be closed to conceal the light

**dar·kle** \'där-kəl\ *intransitive verb* **dar·kled; dar·kling** \-k(ə-)liŋ\ [back-formation from *darkling*] (1800)
**1 a** : to become clouded or gloomy **b** : to grow dark
**2** : to become concealed in the dark

**¹dark·ling** \'där-kliŋ\ *adverb* [Middle English *derkelyng*, from *derk* dark + *-lyng* -ling] (15th century)
: in the dark

**²dark·ling** *adjective* (1739)
**1** : DARK
**2** : done or taking place in the dark

**darkling beetle** *noun* (1816)
: TENEBRIONID

**dark matter** *noun* (1982)
: nonluminous matter not yet directly detected by astronomers that is hypothesized to exist because the visible matter in the universe is insufficient to account for various observed gravitational effects

**dark reaction** *noun* (1927)
: any of a series of chemical reactions in photosynthesis not requiring the presence of light and involving the reduction of carbon dioxide to form carbohydrate; *also* : CALVIN CYCLE

**dark·room** \'därk-,rüm, -,rům\ *noun* (1841)
: a room with no light or with a safelight for handling and processing light-sensitive photographic materials

**dark·some** \'därk-səm\ *adjective* (circa 1530)
: gloomily somber : DARK

**darky** *or* **dark·ie** \'där-kē\ *noun, plural* **dark·ies** (1775)
: a black person — usually taken to be offensive

**¹dar·ling** \'där-liŋ\ *noun* [Middle English *der-*

ling, from Old English *dēorling,* from *dēore*
dear] (before 12th century)
**1 :** a dearly loved person
**2 :** FAVORITE
**²darling** *adjective* (1509)
**1 :** dearly loved **:** FAVORITE
**2 :** very pleasing **:** CHARMING
— **dar·ling·ly** \-liŋ-lē\ *adverb*
— **dar·ling·ness** *noun*
**¹darn** \'därn\ *verb* [perhaps from French dialect *darner*] (circa 1600)
*transitive verb*
**1 :** to mend with interlacing stitches
**2 :** to embroider by filling in with long running or interlacing stitches
*intransitive verb*
**:** to do darning
— **darn·er** *noun*
**²darn** *noun* (1720)
**:** a place that has been darned ⟨a sweater full of *darns*⟩
**³darn** *adjective or adverb* [euphemism] (1781)
**:** DAMNED
**⁴darn** *verb* (1781)
**:** DAMN
— **darned** \'därn(d)\ *adjective or adverb*
**⁵darn** *noun* (1840)
**:** DAMN
**dar·nel** \'där-n°l\ *noun* [Middle English] (14th century)
**:** any of several usually weedy grasses (genus *Lolium*)
**darning needle** *noun* (1761)
**1 :** a long needle with a large eye for use in darning
**2 :** DRAGONFLY, DAMSELFLY
**¹dart** \'därt\ *noun* [Middle English, from Middle French, of Germanic origin; akin to Old High German *tart* dart, Old English *daroth*] (14th century)
**1 a** *archaic* **:** a light spear **b** (1) **:** a small missile usually with a pointed shaft at one end and feathers at the other (2) *plural but singular in construction* **:** a game in which darts are thrown at a target
**2 a :** something projected with sudden speed; *especially* **:** a sharp glance **b :** something causing sudden pain or distress ⟨*darts* of sarcasm⟩
**3 :** something with a slender pointed shaft or outline; *specifically* **:** a stitched tapering fold in a garment
**4 :** a quick movement ⟨made a *dart* for the door⟩
**²dart** (1580)
*transitive verb*
**1 :** to throw with a sudden movement
**2 :** to thrust or move with sudden speed
**3 :** to shoot with a dart containing a usually tranquilizing drug
*intransitive verb*
**:** to move suddenly or rapidly ⟨*darted* across the street⟩
**dart·board** \'därt-,bōrd, -,bȯrd\ *noun* (1901)
**:** a usually circular board (as of compressed bristles) used as a target in the game of darts
**dart·er** \'där-tər\ *noun* (1813)
**1 :** ANHINGA
**2 :** any of numerous small American freshwater bony fishes (especially genera *Ammocrypta, Etheostoma,* and *Percina* of the family Percidae)
**Dar·win·i·an** \där-'wi-nē-ən\ *adjective* (1860)
**:** of or relating to Charles Darwin, his theories especially of evolution, or his followers
— **Darwinian** *noun*
**Dar·win·ism** \'där-wə-,ni-zəm\ *noun* (1864)
**:** a theory of the origin and perpetuation of new species of animals and plants that offspring of a given organism vary, that natural selection favors the survival of some of these variations over others, that new species have arisen and may continue to arise by these processes, and that widely divergent groups of plants and animals have arisen from the same ancestors; *broadly* **:** biological evolutionism ◆

— **Dar·win·ist** \-wə-nist\ *noun or adjective*
**Dar·win's finches** \,där-wənz-\ *noun plural* [Charles *Darwin*] (1947)
**:** finches of a subfamily (Geospizinae) having great variation in bill shape and confined mostly to the Galapagos islands
**Dar·win tulip** \,där-wən-\ *noun* (1889)
**:** a tall late-flowering tulip with the flowers single and of one color
**¹dash** \'dash\ *verb* [Middle English *dasshen*] (13th century)
*transitive verb*
**1 :** to break by striking or knocking
**2 :** to knock, hurl, or thrust violently
**3 :** SPLASH, SPATTER
**4 a :** RUIN, DESTROY ⟨the news *dashed* his hopes⟩ **b :** DEPRESS, SADDEN **c :** to make ashamed
**5 :** to affect by mixing in something different ⟨his delight was *dashed* with bitterness over the delay⟩
**6 :** to complete, execute, or finish off hastily — used with *down* or *off* ⟨*dashed* down a drink⟩ ⟨*dash* off a letter⟩
**7** [euphemism] **:** ¹DAMN 4
*intransitive verb*
**1 :** to move with sudden speed ⟨*dashed* through the rain⟩
**2 :** SMASH
**²dash** *noun* (14th century)
**1 a** *archaic* **:** BLOW **b** (1) **:** a sudden burst or splash (2) **:** the sound produced by such a burst
**2 a :** a stroke of a pen **b :** a punctuation mark — that is used especially to indicate a break in the thought or structure of a sentence
**3 :** a small usually distinctive addition ⟨a *dash* of salt⟩ ⟨a *dash* of humor⟩
**4 :** flashy display
**5 :** animation in style and action
**6 a :** a sudden onset, rush, or attempt **b :** a short fast race
**7 :** a long click or buzz forming a letter or part of a letter (as in Morse code)
**8 :** DASHBOARD 2
**dash·board** \'dash-,bōrd, -,bȯrd\ *noun* (1846)
**1 :** a screen on the front of a usually horse-drawn vehicle to intercept water, mud, or snow
**2 :** a panel extending across the interior of a vehicle (as an automobile) below the windshield and usually containing dials and controls
**dashed** \'dasht\ *adjective* (circa 1889)
**:** made up of a series of dashes
**da·sheen** \da-'shēn, də-\ *noun* [origin unknown] (circa 1899)
**:** TARO
**dash·er** \'da-shər\ *noun* (1790)
**1 :** a dashing person
**2 :** one that dashes; *specifically* **:** a device having blades for agitating a liquid or semisolid
**dashi** \'dä-(,)shē\ *noun* [Japanese, broth] (circa 1961)
**:** a fish broth made from dried bonito
**da·shi·ki** \də-'shē-kē, dä-, da-\ *noun* [modification of Yoruba *dànṣíkí*] (circa 1968)
**:** a usually brightly colored loose-fitting pullover garment
**dash·ing** *adjective* (1796)
**1 :** marked by vigorous action **:** SPIRITED ⟨a *dashing* young horse⟩
**2 :** marked by smartness especially in dress and manners
— **dash·ing·ly** \-iŋ-lē\ *adverb*
**dash·pot** \'dash-,pät\ *noun* (1861)
**:** a device for cushioning or damping a movement (as of a mechanical part) to avoid shock
**das·sie** \'da-sē\ *noun* [Afrikaans] (1786)
**:** HYRAX
**das·tard** \'das-tərd\ *noun* [Middle English] (15th century)
**1 :** COWARD
**2 :** a person who acts treacherously or underhandedly
**das·tard·ly** \-lē\ *adjective* (1576)

**1 :** COWARDLY
**2 :** characterized by underhandedness or treachery ⟨a *dastardly* attack⟩ ⟨a *dastardly* villain⟩
*synonym* see COWARDLY
— **das·tard·li·ness** *noun*
**da·ta** \'dā-tə, 'da- *also* 'dä-\ *noun plural but singular or plural in construction, often attributive* [Latin, plural of *datum*] (1646)
**1 :** factual information (as measurements or statistics) used as a basis for reasoning, discussion, or calculation ⟨the *data* is plentiful and easily available —H. A. Gleason, Jr.⟩ ⟨comprehensive *data* on economic growth have been published —N. H. Jacoby⟩
**2 :** information output by a sensing device or organ that includes both useful and irrelevant or redundant information and must be processed to be meaningful
**3 :** information in numerical form that can be digitally transmitted or processed ■
**data bank** *noun* (1966)
**:** DATABASE
**da·ta·base** \'dā-tə-,bās, 'da- *also* 'dä-\ *noun* (circa 1962)
**:** a usually large collection of data organized especially for rapid search and retrieval (as by a computer)
**data processing** *noun* (1954)
**:** the converting of raw data to machine-readable form and its subsequent processing (as storing, updating, combining, rearranging, or printing out) by a computer
— **data processor** *noun*
**data structure** *noun* (1963)
**:** any of various methods of organizing data items (as records) in a computer

□ **USAGE**
**data** *Data* leads a life of its own quite independent of *datum,* of which it was originally the plural. It occurs in two constructions: as a plural noun (like *earnings*), taking a plural verb and plural modifiers (as *these, many, a few*) but not cardinal numbers, and serving as a referent for plural pronouns (as *they, them*); and as an abstract mass noun (like *information*), taking a singular verb and singular modifiers (as *this, much, little*), and being referred to by a singular pronoun (*it*). Both constructions are standard. The plural construction is more common in print, evidently because the house style of several publishers mandates it.

◇ **WORD HISTORY**
**Darwinism** *Darwinism* is the theory initiated by the British naturalist Charles Robert Darwin (1809–1882). Although he was not the first to question the immutability of species in nature or to conceive the notion of evolution, Darwin is credited with providing voluminous evidence for evolution and with developing the principle of natural selection. In 1831 he embarked on a five-year voyage around the world, making stopovers in South America and the Galápagos Islands, where he gained critical insight into the variation between populations of animals. His landmark *On the Origin of Species by Means of Natural Selection* (1859) brought about a revolution in biological thinking and firmly established the study of evolution as part of the science of biology. *The Descent of Man* (1871) was a follow-up work that presented his related theory of sexual selection.

**¹date** \ˈdāt\ *noun* [Middle English, from Old French, ultimately from Latin *dactylus* — more at DACTYL] (14th century)
**1 :** the oblong edible fruit of a palm (*Phoenix dactylifera*)
**2 :** the tall palm with pinnate leaves that yields the date ◆

**²date** *noun* [Middle English, from Middle French, from Late Latin *data,* from *data* (as in *data Romae* given at Rome), feminine of Latin *datus,* past participle of *dare* to give; akin to Latin *dos* gift, dowry, Greek *didonai* to give] (14th century)
**1 a :** the time at which an event occurs ⟨the *date* of his birth⟩ **b :** a statement of the time of execution or making ⟨the *date* on the letter⟩
**2 :** DURATION
**3 :** the period of time to which something belongs
**4 a :** an appointment to meet at a specified time; *especially* **:** a social engagement between two persons that often has a romantic character **b :** a person with whom one has a usually romantic date
**5 :** an engagement for a professional performance (as of a dance band)
**— to date :** up to the present moment

**³date** *verb* **dat·ed; dat·ing** (15th century)
*transitive verb*
**1 :** to determine the date of ⟨*date* an antique⟩
**2 :** to record the date of **:** mark with the date
**3 a :** to mark with characteristics typical of a particular period **b :** to show up plainly the age of
**4 :** to make or have a date with
*intransitive verb*
**1 :** to reckon chronologically
**2 :** ORIGINATE ⟨a friendship *dating* from college days⟩
**3 :** to become dated
**— dat·able** *also* **date·able** \ˈdā-tə-bəl\ *adjective*
**— dat·er** \ˈdā-tər\ *noun*

**dat·ed** *adjective* (1731)
**1 :** provided with a date ⟨a *dated* document⟩
**2 :** OUTMODED, OLD-FASHIONED ⟨*dated* formalities⟩
**— dat·ed·ly** *adverb*
**— dat·ed·ness** *noun*

**date·less** \ˈdāt-ləs\ *adjective* (1593)
**1 :** ENDLESS
**2 :** having no date
**3 :** too ancient to be dated
**4 :** TIMELESS ⟨the play's *dateless* theme⟩

**date·line** \ˈdāt-ˌlīn\ *noun* (1888)
**1 :** a line in a written document or a printed publication giving the date and place of composition or issue
**2** *usually* **date line :** INTERNATIONAL DATE LINE
**— dateline** *transitive verb*

**date rape** *noun* (circa 1983)
**:** rape committed by someone known to the victim

**¹da·tive** \ˈdā-tiv\ *adjective* [Middle English *datif,* from Latin *dativus,* from *datus*] (15th century)
**:** of, relating to, or being the grammatical case that marks typically the indirect object of a verb, the object of some prepositions, or a possessor

**²dative** *noun* (15th century)
**:** a dative case or form

**dative bond** *noun* [from the donation of electrons by one of the atoms] (circa 1929)
**:** COORDINATE BOND

**da·tum** \ˈdā-təm, ˈda-, ˈdä-\ *noun* [Latin, from neuter of *datus*] (1646)
**1** *plural* **da·ta** \-ə\ **:** something given or admitted especially as a basis for reasoning or inference
**2** *plural* **datums :** something used as a basis for calculating or measuring
*usage* see DATA

**da·tu·ra** \də-ˈt(y)ur-ə\ *noun* [New Latin, genus name, from Hindi *dhatūrā* jimsonweed] (1598)
**:** any of a genus (*Datura*) of widely distributed strong-scented herbs, shrubs, or trees of the nightshade family including some used as sources of medicinal alkaloids (as stramonium) or in folk rites or illicitly for their poisonous, narcotic, or hallucinogenic properties — compare JIMSONWEED

**¹daub** \ˈdȯb, ˈdäb\ *verb* [Middle English, from Middle French *dauber*] (14th century)
*transitive verb*
**1 :** to cover or coat with soft adhesive matter **:** PLASTER
**2 :** to coat with a dirty substance
**3 a :** to apply coloring material crudely to **b :** to apply (as paint) crudely
*intransitive verb*
**1** *archaic* **:** to put on a false exterior
**2 :** to apply colors crudely
**— daub·er** *noun*

**²daub** *noun* (15th century)
**1 :** material used to daub walls
**2 :** an act or instance of daubing
**3 :** something daubed on **:** SMEAR
**4 :** a crude picture

**daube** \ˈdōb\ *noun* [French] (1723)
**:** a stew of braised meat, vegetables, herbs, and spices

**¹daugh·ter** \ˈdȯ-tər, ˈdä-\ *noun* [Middle English, *doughter,* from Old English *dohtor;* akin to Old High German *tohter* daughter, Greek *thygatēr*] (before 12th century)
**1 a** (1) **:** a human female having the relation of child to parent (2) **:** a female offspring of a lower animal **b :** a human female having a specified ancestor or belonging to a group of common ancestry
**2 :** something considered as a daughter ⟨the United States is a *daughter* of Great Britain⟩
**3 :** an atomic species that is the product of the radioactive decay of a given element
**— daugh·ter·less** \-ləs\ *adjective*

**²daughter** *adjective* (1614)
**1 :** having the characteristics or relationship of a daughter
**2 :** belonging to the first generation of offspring, organelles, or molecules produced by reproduction, division, or replication ⟨*daughter* cell⟩ ⟨*daughter* DNA molecules⟩

**daugh·ter–in–law** \ˈdȯ-tər-in-ˌlȯ, ˈdȯ-tərn-\ *noun, plural* **daugh·ters–in–law** \-tər-zin-\ (14th century)
**:** the wife of one's son

**dau·no·my·cin** \ˌdȯ-nə-ˈmī-sᵊn, ˌdaù-\ *noun* [International Scientific Vocabulary *dauno-* (from Latin *Daunus* Apulian) + *-mycin*] (1964)
**:** DAUNORUBICIN

**dau·no·ru·bi·cin** \-ˈrü-bə-sᵊn\ *noun* [*dauno-* (as in *daunomycin*) + *rubi*domycin, a substance found to be identical with daunomycin (from International Scientific Vocabulary *rubido-* — from Latin *rubidus* red — + *-mycin*)] (circa 1968)
**:** an antibiotic $C_{27}H_{29}NO_{10}$ that is a nitrogenous glycoside and is used especially in the treatment of leukemia

**daunt** \ˈdȯnt, ˈdänt\ *transitive verb* [Middle English, from Middle French *danter,* alteration of *donter,* from Latin *domitare* to tame, frequentative of *domare* — more at TAME] (14th century)
**:** to lessen the courage of **:** COW, SUBDUE
*synonym* see DISMAY
**— daunt·ing·ly** \-iŋ-lē\ *adverb*

**daunt·less** \-ləs\ *adjective* (1593)
**:** FEARLESS, UNDAUNTED ⟨a *dauntless* hero⟩
**— daunt·less·ly** *adverb*
**— daunt·less·ness** *noun*

**dau·phin** \ˈdȯ-fən, ˈdȯ-; ˌdō-ˈfaⁿ\ *noun, often capitalized* [Middle English *dolphin,* from Middle French *dalfin,* from Old French, title of lords of the Dauphiné, from *Dalfin,* a surname] (15th century)

**:** the eldest son of a king of France

**dau·phine** \dȯ-ˈfēn, dō-\ *noun, often capitalized* [French] (circa 1864)
**:** the wife of the dauphin

**da·ven** \ˈdä-vən\ *intransitive verb* [Yiddish *davnen*] (circa 1930)
**:** to recite the prescribed prayers in a Jewish liturgy

**dav·en·port** \ˈda-vᵊn-ˌpȯrt, ˈda-vᵊm-, -ˌpȯrt\ *noun* [probably from the name *Davenport*] (1853)
**1 :** a small compact writing desk
**2 :** a large upholstered sofa often convertible into a bed

**Da·vid** \ˈdā-vəd\ *noun* [Hebrew *Dāwīdh*]
**1 :** a Hebrew shepherd who became the second king of Israel in succession to Saul according to biblical accounts
**2 :** UNDERDOG 1
**— Da·vid·ic** \də-ˈvi-dik, dā-\ *adjective*

**da·vit** \ˈdā-vət, ˈda-\ *noun* [probably from the name *David*] (15th century)
**:** a crane that projects over the side of a ship or a hatchway and is used especially for boats, anchors, or cargo

**Da·vy Jones** \ˌdā-vē-ˈjōnz\ *noun* (1751)
**:** the bottom of the sea personified

**Da·vy Jones's lock·er** \ˌdā-vē-ˌjōnz(-əz)-\ *noun* (circa 1777)
**:** the bottom of the ocean

davit

**¹daw** \ˈdȯ, ˈdä\ *intransitive verb* [Middle English, from Old English *dagian;* akin to Old High German *tagēn* to dawn, Old English *dæg* day] (13th century)
*chiefly Scottish* **:** DAWN

**²daw** \ˈdȯ\ *noun* [Middle English *dawe;* akin to Old High German *taha* jackdaw] (15th century)
**:** JACKDAW

**daw·dle** \ˈdȯ-dᵊl\ *verb* **daw·dled; daw·dling** \ˈdȯ-dliŋ, -dᵊl-iŋ\ [origin unknown] (circa 1656)
*intransitive verb*
**1 :** to spend time idly
**2 :** to move lackadaisically ⟨*dawdled* up the hill⟩
*transitive verb*
**:** to spend fruitlessly or lackadaisically ⟨*dawdled* the day away⟩
*synonym* see DELAY
**— daw·dler** \ˈdȯ-dlər, -dᵊl-ər\ *noun*

◇ WORD HISTORY
**date** The English word *date* in its temporal sense has nothing to do etymologically with *day,* but rather is descended from the Latin verb *dare* "to give." In ancient Rome, the date of a letter was written in the following manner: *Dabam Romae Kal. Aprilis* ("I gave [this letter] at Rome on the calends of April [April 1]."") A later formula used *data Romae* "given at Rome," instead of *dabam Romae. Data,* past participle of *dare* "to give," had the feminine case ending because it was understood to refer to the unexpressed feminine noun *epistula* "letter." By the 6th century of the modern era, *data* itself had become a noun, used for the formula indicating the date on a letter. Borrowed into French as *date,* it was used not only for the formula on a letter, but also for the time that such a formula indicated, or indeed for any point in time. The English word *date,* borrowed from French in the late Middle Ages, did not come to mean an appointment or engagement until the late 19th century.

**¹dawn** \'dȯn, 'dän\ *intransitive verb* [Middle English, probably back-formation from *dawning* daybreak, alteration of *dawing*, from Old English *dagung*, from *dagian*] (15th century)
**1 :** to begin to grow light as the sun rises
**2 :** to begin to appear or develop
**3 :** to begin to be perceived or understood ⟨the truth finally *dawned* on us⟩
**²dawn** *noun* (1599)
**1 :** the first appearance of light in the morning followed by sunrise
**2 :** BEGINNING ⟨the *dawn* of the space age⟩
**dawn horse** *noun* (1930)
**:** EOHIPPUS
**dawn redwood** *noun* (1948)
**:** a metasequoia (*Metasequoia glyptostroboides*) of China resembling the coast redwood but having deciduous foliage
**daw·son·ite** \'dȯ-sə-ˌnīt\ *noun* [Sir John W. *Dawson*] (1874)
**:** a mineral consisting of a basic sodium aluminum carbonate
**day** \'dā\ *noun* [Middle English, from Old English *dæg*; akin to Old High German *tag* day] (before 12th century)
**1 a :** the time of light between one night and the next **b :** DAYLIGHT 1, 2
**2 :** the period of rotation of a planet (as earth) or a moon on its axis
**3 :** the mean solar day of 24 hours beginning at mean midnight
**4 :** a specified day or date
**5 :** a specified time or period **:** AGE ⟨in grandfather's *day*⟩
**6 :** the conflict or contention of the day ⟨played hard and won the *day*⟩
**7 :** the time established by usage or law for work, school, or business
**8 :** a period of existence or prominence of a person or thing
**— day after day :** for an indefinite or seemingly endless number of days
**— day in, day out :** for an indefinite number of successive days
**Day·ak** \'dī-ˌak\ *noun* [Malay, literally, up-country] (1836)
**:** a member of any of several Indonesian peoples of the interior of Borneo
**day·bed** \'dā-ˌbed\ *noun* (1818)
**1 :** a chaise longue of a type made 1680–1780
**2 :** a couch that can be converted into a bed
**day·book** \-ˌbůk\ *noun* (1580)
**:** DIARY, JOURNAL
**day·break** \-ˌbrāk\ *noun* (1530)
**:** DAWN
**day care** *noun* (1947)
**1 :** supervision of and care for children or disabled adults that is provided during the day by a person or organization
**2 :** a program, facility, or organization offering day care
**¹day·dream** \'dā-ˌdrēm\ *noun* (1685)
**:** a pleasant visionary usually wishful creation of the imagination
**— day·dream·like** \-ˌlīk\ *adjective*
**²daydream** *intransitive verb* (1820)
**:** to have a daydream
**— day·dream·er** *noun*
**day·flow·er** \'dā-ˌflaů(-ə)r\ *noun* (circa 1688)
**:** any of a genus (*Commelina*) of herbs of the spiderwort family having one petal smaller than the other two; *especially* **:** a blue-flowered weed (*C. communis*) with the smaller petal white
**Day–Glo** \'dā-ˌglō\ *trademark*
**—** used for fluorescent materials or colors
**day·glow** \'dā-ˌglō\ *noun* (circa 1960)
**:** airglow seen during the day
**day laborer** *noun* (1548)
**:** one who works for daily wages especially as an unskilled laborer
**day letter** *noun* (circa 1913)
**:** a telegram sent during the day that has a lower priority than a regular telegram
**day·light** \'dā-ˌlīt\ *noun* (13th century)
**1 :** the light of day

**2 :** DAYTIME
**3 :** DAWN
**4 a :** knowledge or understanding of something that has been obscure ⟨began to see *daylight* on the problem⟩ **b :** the quality or state of being open **:** OPENNESS
**5** *plural* **a :** CONSCIOUSNESS **b :** mental soundness or stability **:** WITS ⟨scared the *daylights* out of him⟩
**6 :** an opening or opportunity especially for action
**day·light·ing** \'dā-ˌlī-tiŋ\ *noun* (1929)
**:** illumination of indoor spaces by natural light
**daylight saving time** *noun* (1919)
**:** time usually one hour ahead of standard time
— called also *daylight saving, daylight time*
**day·lily** \'dā-ˌli-lē\ *noun* (1597)
**:** any of various Eurasian plants (genus *Hemerocallis*) of the lily family that have short-lived flowers resembling lilies and are widespread in cultivation and as escapes
**day·long** \'dā-ˌlȯŋ\ *adjective* (1855)
**:** lasting all day ⟨a *daylong* tour⟩
**day·mare** \'dā-ˌmar, -ˌmer\ *noun* [ *day* + *-mare* (as in *nightmare*)] (1737)
**:** a nightmarish fantasy experienced while awake
**day–neutral** *adjective* (1941)
**:** developing and maturing regardless of relative length of alternating exposures to light and dark periods — used especially of a plant; compare LONG-DAY, SHORT-DAY
**day nursery** *noun* (1844)
**:** a public center for the care and training of young children; *specifically* **:** NURSERY SCHOOL
**Day of Atonement** (1611)
**:** YOM KIPPUR
**day one** *noun, often D&O capitalized* (1971)
**:** the first day or very beginning of something
**day·room** \'dā-ˌrüm, -ˌrům\ *noun* (1823)
**:** a room (as in a hospital) equipped for reading, writing, and recreation
**days** \'dāz\ *adverb* (before 12th century)
**:** in the daytime repeatedly **:** on any day
**day school** *noun* (1838)
**:** an elementary or secondary school held on weekdays; *specifically* **:** a private school without boarding facilities
**day·side** \'dā-ˌsīd\ *noun* (1963)
**:** the side of a planet in sunlight
**days of grace** (1726)
**:** the days allowed for payment of a note or an insurance premium after it becomes due
**day·star** \'dā-ˌstär\ *noun* (before 12th century)
**1 :** MORNING STAR
**2 :** SUN 1a
**day student** *noun* (1883)
**:** a student who attends regular classes at a college or preparatory school but does not live at the institution
**day·time** \'dā-ˌtīm\ *noun, often attributive* (1535)
**:** the time during which there is daylight
**day·times** \'dā-ˌtīmz\ *adverb* (1854)
**:** during the day or during the workday repeatedly **:** DAYS ⟨has a housekeeper *daytimes*⟩
**day–to–day** \ˌdā-tə-ˈdā\ *adjective* (1883)
**1 :** taking place, made, or done in the course of successive days ⟨*day-to-day* problems⟩
**2 :** providing for a day at a time with little thought for the future ⟨lived an aimless *day-to-day* existence⟩
**day–trip·per** \'dā-ˌtri-pər\ *noun* (1897)
**:** one who takes a trip that does not last overnight
**daze** \'dāz\ *transitive verb* **dazed; daz·ing** [Middle English *dasen*, from (assumed) Old Norse *dasa*; akin to Old Norse *dasask* to become exhausted] (14th century)
**1 :** to stupefy especially by a blow **:** STUN
**2 :** to dazzle with light
**— daze** *noun*
**— dazed·ly** \'dā-zəd-lē\ *adverb*
**— dazed·ness** \'dā-zəd-nəs, 'dāzd-\ *noun*

**daz·zle** \'da-zəl\ *verb* **daz·zled; daz·zling** \-z(ə-)liŋ\ [frequentative of *daze*] (15th century)
*intransitive verb*
**1 :** to lose clear vision especially from looking at bright light
**2 a :** to shine brilliantly **b :** to arouse admiration by an impressive display
*transitive verb*
**1 :** to overpower with light
**2 :** to impress deeply, overpower, or confound with brilliance ⟨*dazzled* us with her wit⟩
**— dazzle** *noun*
**— daz·zler** \-z(ə-)lər\ *noun*
**— daz·zling·ly** \-z(ə-)liŋ-lē\ *adverb*
**DBCP** \ˌdē-(ˌ)bē-(ˌ)sē-ˈpē\ *noun* [*di*- + *brom*- + *chlor*- + *propane*] (1967)
**:** a halocarbon compound $C_3H_5Br_2Cl$ used as an agricultural pesticide that is a suspected carcinogen and cause of sterility in human males
**D day** *noun* [*D*, abbreviation for *day*] (1918)
**:** a day set for launching an operation; *specifically* **:** June 6, 1944, on which Allied forces began the invasion of France in World War II
**DDC** \ˌdē-(ˌ)dē-ˈsē\ *noun* [*di*- + *deoxy* + *cytidine*] (1987)
**:** an antiviral drug $C_{10}H_{13}N_3O_3$ used to reduce virus growth and reproduction in AIDS and HIV infection
**DDD** \ˌdē-(ˌ)dē-ˈdē\ *noun* [*dichlor*- + *diphenyl* + *dichlor*-] (1946)
**:** an insecticide $(ClC_6H_4)_2CHCHCl_2$ closely related chemically and similar in properties to DDT
**DDE** \ˌdē-(ˌ)dē-ˈē\ *noun* [*dichlor*- + *diphenyl* + *ethylene*] (1949)
**:** a persistent organochlorine $C_{15}H_8Cl_4$ that is produced by the metabolic breakdown of DDT
**DDI** \ˌdē-(ˌ)dē-ˈī\ *noun* [*di*- + *deoxy* + *inosine*, a nucleoside] (1988)
**:** an antiviral drug $C_{10}H_{12}N_4O_3$ used to reduce virus growth and reproduction in AIDS and HIV infection
**DDT** \ˌdē-(ˌ)dē-ˈtē\ *noun* [*dichlor*- + *diphenyl* + *trichlor*- (from *tri*- +*chlor*-)] (1943)
**:** a colorless odorless water-insoluble crystalline insecticide $C_{14}H_9Cl_5$ that tends to accumulate in ecosystems and has toxic effects on many vertebrates
**DDVP** \ˌdē-(ˌ)dē-ˌvē-ˈpē\ *noun* [*dimethyl* + *dichlor*- + *vinyl* + *phosphate*] (1954)
**:** DICHLORVOS
**de-** *prefix* [Middle English, from Old French *de-, des-*, partly from Latin *de-* from, down, away (from *de*, preposition) and partly from Latin *dis-*; Latin *de* akin to Old Irish *di* from, Old English *tō* to — more at TO, DIS-]
**1 a :** do the opposite of ⟨*deactivate*⟩ **b :** reverse of ⟨*de-emphasis*⟩
**2 a :** remove (a specified thing) from ⟨*delouse*⟩ **b :** remove from (a specified thing) ⟨*dethrone*⟩
**3 :** reduce ⟨*devalue*⟩
**4 :** something derived from (a specified thing) ⟨*decompound*⟩ **:** derived from something (of a specified nature) ⟨*denominative*⟩
**5 :** get off of (a specified thing) ⟨*detrain*⟩
**6 :** having a molecule characterized by the removal of one or more atoms (of a specified element) ⟨*deoxy*-⟩
**de·acid·i·fy** \ˌdē-ə-ˈsi-də-ˌfī\ *transitive verb* (1786)
**:** to remove acid from **:** reduce the acidity of (as by neutralization)
**— de·acid·i·fi·ca·tion** \-ˌsi-də-fə-ˈkā-shən\ *noun*
**dea·con** \'dē-kən\ *noun* [Middle English *dekene*, from Old English *dēacon*, from Late Latin *diaconus*, from Greek *diakonos*, literally,

servant, from *dia-* + *-konos* (akin to en*konein* to be active); perhaps akin to Latin *conari* to attempt] (before 12th century)
**:** a subordinate officer in a Christian church: as **a :** a Roman Catholic, Anglican, or Eastern Orthodox cleric ranking next below a priest **b :** one of the laymen elected by a church with congregational polity to serve in worship, in pastoral care, and on administrative committees **c :** a Mormon in the lowest grade of the Aaronic priesthood

**dea·con·ess** \'dē-kə-nəs\ *noun* (15th century)
**:** a woman chosen to assist in the church ministry; *specifically* **:** one in a Protestant order

**deacon's bench** *noun* (1922)
**:** a bench with usually spindled arms and back

deacon's bench

**de·ac·ti·vate** \(ˌ)dē-'ak-tə-ˌvāt\ *transitive verb* (1926)
**:** to make inactive or ineffective
— **de·ac·ti·va·tion** \(ˌ)dē-ˌak-tə-'vā-shən\ *noun*
— **de·ac·ti·va·tor** \(ˌ)dē-'ak-tə-ˌvā-tər\ *noun*

**¹dead** \'ded\ *adjective* [Middle English *deed*, from Old English *dēad;* akin to Old Norse *dauthr* dead, *deyja* to die, Old High German *tōt* dead — more at DIE] (before 12th century)
**1 :** deprived of life **:** having died
**2 a** (1) **:** having the appearance of death **:** DEATHLY ⟨in a *dead* faint⟩ (2) **:** lacking power to move, feel, or respond **:** NUMB **b :** very tired **c** (1) **:** incapable of being stirred emotionally or intellectually **:** UNRESPONSIVE ⟨*dead* to pity⟩ **2 :** grown cold **:** EXTINGUISHED ⟨*dead* coals⟩ **3 a :** INANIMATE, INERT ⟨*dead* matter⟩ **b :** BARREN, INFERTILE ⟨*dead* soil⟩ **c :** no longer producing or functioning **:** EXHAUSTED ⟨a *dead* battery⟩
**4 a** (1) **:** lacking power or effect ⟨a *dead* law⟩ (2) **:** no longer having interest, relevance, or significance ⟨a *dead* issue⟩ **b :** no longer in use **:** OBSOLETE ⟨a *dead* language⟩ **c :** no longer active **:** EXTINCT ⟨a *dead* volcano⟩ **d :** lacking in gaiety or animation ⟨a *dead* party⟩ **e** (1) **:** lacking in commercial activity **:** QUIET (2) **:** commercially idle or unproductive ⟨*dead* capital⟩ **f :** lacking elasticity ⟨a *dead* tennis ball⟩ **g :** being out of action or out of use; *specifically* **:** free from any connection to a source of voltage and free from electric charges **h** (1) **:** being out of play ⟨a *dead* ball⟩ (2) **:** temporarily forbidden to play or to make a certain play in croquet
**5 a :** not running or circulating **:** STAGNANT ⟨*dead* water⟩ **b :** not turning ⟨a *dead* lathe center⟩ **c :** not imparting motion or power although otherwise functioning ⟨a *dead* rear axle⟩ **d :** lacking warmth, vigor, or taste
**6 a :** absolutely uniform ⟨a *dead* level⟩ **b** (1) **:** UNERRING (2) **:** EXACT ⟨*dead* center of the target⟩ (3) **:** certain to be doomed ⟨he's *dead* if he's late for curfew⟩ (4) **:** IRREVOCABLE ⟨a *dead* loss⟩ **c :** ABRUPT ⟨brought to a *dead* stop⟩ **d** (1) **:** COMPLETE, ABSOLUTE ⟨a *dead* silence⟩ (2) **:** ALL-OUT ⟨caught it on the *dead* run⟩
**7 :** devoid of former occupants ⟨*dead* villages⟩ ☆
— **dead·ness** *noun*
— **dead in the water 1 :** incapable of being effective **:** STALLED **2 :** ¹DEAD 6b(3)

**²dead** *noun, plural* **dead** (before 12th century)
**1 :** one that is dead — usually used collectively
**2 :** the state of being dead ⟨raised him from the *dead* —Colossians 2:12(Revised Standard Version)⟩
**3 :** the time of greatest quiet ⟨the *dead* of night⟩

**³dead** *adverb* (14th century)

**1 :** ABSOLUTELY, UTTERLY ⟨*dead* certain⟩
**2 :** suddenly and completely ⟨stopped *dead*⟩
**3 :** DIRECTLY ⟨*dead* ahead⟩

**dead air** *noun* (circa 1943)
**:** a period of silence especially during a broadcast

**dead–air space** \'ded-'ar-, -'er-\ *noun* (1902)
**:** an unventilated air space

**¹dead·beat** \'ded-ˌbēt\ *noun* (1863)
**1 :** LOAFER
**2 :** one who persistently fails to pay personal debts or expenses

**²deadbeat** *adjective* (circa 1864)
**:** having a pointer that gives a reading with little or no oscillation

**dead bolt** *noun* (circa 1902)
**:** a lock bolt that is moved by turning the knob or key without action of a spring

**dead duck** *noun* (1943)
**:** one that is doomed

**dead·en** \'de-dᵊn\ *verb* **dead·ened; dead·en·ing** \'ded-niŋ, 'de-dᵊn-iŋ\ (1665)
*transitive verb*
**1 :** to impair in vigor or sensation **:** BLUNT ⟨*deadened* his enthusiasm⟩
**2 a :** to deprive of brilliance **b :** to make vapid or spiritless **c :** to make (as a wall) impervious to sound
**3 :** to deprive of life **:** KILL
*intransitive verb*
**:** to become dead **:** lose life or vigor
— **dead·en·er** \'ded-nər, -dᵊn-ər\ *noun*
— **dead·en·ing·ly** \-niŋ-lē, -dᵊn-iŋ-\ *adverb*

**¹dead–end** \'ded-ˌend\ *adjective* (1919)
**1 a :** lacking opportunities especially for advancement ⟨a *dead-end* job⟩ **b :** lacking an exit ⟨a *dead-end* street⟩
**2 :** UNRULY ⟨*dead-end* kids⟩
— **dead–end·ed·ness** \ˌded-'en-dəd-nəs\ *noun*

**²dead–end** \'ded-'end\ *intransitive verb* (1944)
**:** to come to a dead end **:** TERMINATE

**dead end** \'ded-'end\ *noun* (1886)
**1 :** an end (as of a street) without an exit
**2 :** a position, situation, or course of action that leads to nothing further

**dead·en·ing** *noun* (circa 1874)
**:** material used to soundproof walls or floors

**dead·eye** \'ded-ˌī\ *noun* (1748)
**1 :** a rounded wood block encircled by a rope or an iron band and having holes to receive the lanyard that is used especially to set up shrouds and stays
**2 :** an unerring marksman

**dead·fall** \-ˌfȯl\ *noun* (1611)
**1 :** a trap so constructed that a weight (as a heavy log) falls on an animal and kills or disables it
**2 :** a tangled mass of fallen trees and branches

**dead hand** *noun* (14th century)
**1 :** MORTMAIN 1
**2 :** the oppressive influence of the past

**¹dead·head** \'ded-ˌhed\ *noun* (1841)
**1 :** one who has not paid for a ticket
**2 :** a dull or stupid person

**²deadhead** (1911)
*intransitive verb*
**:** to make a return trip without a load
*transitive verb*
**:** to remove the faded flowers of (a plant) especially to keep a neat appearance and to promote reblooming by preventing seed production

**dead heat** *noun* (1796)
**:** a tie with no single winner of a race

**dead horse** *noun* (1830)
**:** an exhausted or profitless topic or issue — usually used in the phrases *beat a dead horse* and *flog a dead horse*

**dead letter** *noun* (1663)
**1 :** something that has lost its force or authority without being formally abolished
**2 :** a letter that is undeliverable and unreturnable by the post office

**dead lift** *noun* (1963)

**:** a lift in weight lifting in which the weight is lifted from the floor to hip level
— **dead·lift** \'ded-ˌlift\ *transitive verb*

**dead·light** \'ded-ˌlīt\ *noun* (1726)
**:** a metal cover or shutter fitted to a port to keep out light and water

**dead·line** \-ˌlīn\ *noun* (1864)
**1 :** a line drawn within or around a prison that a prisoner passes at the risk of being shot
**2 a :** a date or time before which something must be done **b :** the time after which copy is not accepted for a particular issue of a publication

**dead load** *noun* (circa 1888)
**:** a constant load in a structure (as a bridge, building, or machine) that is due to the weight of the members, the supported structure, and permanent attachments or accessories

**dead·lock** \'ded-ˌläk\ *noun* (1779)
**1 :** a state of inaction or neutralization resulting from the opposition of equally powerful uncompromising persons or factions **:** STANDSTILL
**2 :** a tie score
— **deadlock** *verb*

**¹dead·ly** \'ded-lē\ *adjective* **dead·li·er; -est** (before 12th century)
**1 :** likely to cause or capable of producing death
**2 a :** aiming to kill or destroy **:** IMPLACABLE ⟨a *deadly* enemy⟩ **b :** highly effective ⟨a *deadly* exposé⟩ **c :** UNERRING ⟨a *deadly* marksman⟩ **d :** marked by determination or extreme seriousness
**3 a :** tending to deprive of force or vitality ⟨a *deadly* habit⟩ **b :** suggestive of death especially in dullness or lack of animation ⟨*deadly* bores⟩ ⟨a *deadly* conversation⟩
**4 :** very great **:** EXTREME ☆
— **dead·li·ness** *noun*

**²deadly** *adverb* (before 12th century)
**1** *archaic* **:** in a manner to cause death **:** MORTALLY
**2 :** suggesting death
**3 :** EXTREMELY ⟨*deadly* serious⟩

**deadly nightshade** *noun* (1578)
**:** BELLADONNA 1

**deadly sin** *noun* (13th century)
**:** one of seven sins of pride, covetousness, lust, anger, gluttony, envy, and sloth held to be fatal to spiritual progress

**dead man's float** *noun* (circa 1946)

: a prone floating position with the arms extended forward

**dead march** *noun* (1603)
: a solemn march for a funeral

**dead metaphor** *noun* (1922)
: a word or phrase (as *time is running out*) that has lost its metaphoric force through common usage

**dead-on** \'ded-'òn, -'än\ *adjective* (circa 1889)
: exactly correct or accurate

**¹dead·pan** \'ded-,pan\ *adjective* (circa 1928)
: marked by an impassive matter-of-fact manner, style, or expression (a *deadpan* comedy)
— **deadpan** *adverb*

**²deadpan** *noun* (circa 1930)
**1** : a completely expressionless face
**2** : a deadpan manner of behavior or presentation

**³deadpan** *transitive verb* (circa 1942)
: to express in a deadpan manner
— **dead·pan·ner** *noun*

**dead reckoning** *noun* (1613)
**1** : the determination without the aid of celestial observations of the position of a ship or aircraft from the record of the courses sailed or flown, the distance made, and the known or estimated drift
**2** : GUESSWORK
— **dead reckon** *verb*

**dead space** *noun* (circa 1923)
: the portion of the respiratory system which is external to the bronchioles and through which air must pass to reach the bronchioles and alveoli

**dead–stick landing** \'ded-,stik-\ *noun* (circa 1917)
: a landing of an airplane or spacecraft made without power

**dead·weight** \'ded-'wāt\ *noun* (1660)
**1** : the unrelieved weight of an inert mass
**2** : DEAD LOAD
**3** : a ship's load including the total weight of cargo, fuel, stores, crew, and passengers

**deadweight ton** *noun* (circa 1917)
: a long ton used in indicating a ship's gross capacity — abbreviation *dwt*

**dead·wood** \-,wùd\ *noun* (15th century)
**1** : wood dead on the tree
**2** : useless personnel or material
**3** : solid timbers built in at the extreme bow and stern of a ship when too narrow to permit framing
**4** : bowling pins that have been knocked down but remain on the alley

**de·aer·ate** \,dē-'ar-,āt, -'er-\ *transitive verb* (1791)
: to remove air or gas from
— **de·aer·a·tion** \,dē-,ar-'ā-shən, -,er-\ *noun*
— **de·aer·a·tor** \-'ar-,ā-tər, -'er-\ *noun*

**deaf** \'def, *dialect* 'dēf\ *adjective* [Middle English *deef*, from Old English *dēaf*; akin to Greek *typhlos* blind, *typhein* to smoke, Latin *fumus* smoke — more at FUME] (before 12th century)
**1** : lacking or deficient in the sense of hearing
**2** : unwilling to hear or listen : not to be persuaded (was overwrought and *deaf* to reason)
— **deaf·ish** \'de-fish\ *adjective*
— **deaf·ly** *adverb*
— **deaf·ness** *noun*

**deaf·en** \'de-fən\ *transitive verb* **deaf·ened; deaf·en·ing** \-fə-niŋ, 'def-niŋ\ (1597)
: to make deaf

**deaf·en·ing** *adjective* (1597)
**1** : that deafens
**2** : very loud : EARSPLITTING (fell with a *deafening* clap)
— **deaf·en·ing·ly** *adverb*

**deaf–mute** \'def-'myüt\ *noun* (circa 1837)
: a deaf person who cannot speak
— **deaf–mute** *adjective*

**¹deal** \'dē(ə)l\ *noun* [Middle English *deel*, from Old English *dǣl*; akin to Old English *dāl* division, portion, Old High German *teil* part] (before 12th century)

**1** *obsolete* : PART, PORTION
**2** : a usually large or indefinite quantity or degree (a great *deal* of support) (a good *deal* faster)
**3 a** : the act or right of distributing cards to players in a card game **b** : HAND 9b

**²deal** *verb* **dealt** \'delt\; **deal·ing** \'dē-liŋ\ (before 12th century)
*transitive verb*
**1 a** : to give as one's portion : APPORTION (tried to *deal* justice to all) (*dealt* out three sandwiches apiece) **b** : to distribute (playing cards) to players in a game
**2** : ADMINISTER, DELIVER (*dealt* him a blow)
**3** : SELL (*deals* marijuana)
*intransitive verb*
**1** : to distribute the cards in a card game
**2** : to concern oneself or itself (the book *deals* with education)
**3 a** : to engage in bargaining : TRADE **b** : to sell or distribute something as a business (*deal* in insurance)
**4 a** : to take action with regard to someone or something (*deal* with an offender) **b** : to reach or try to reach a state of acceptance or reconcilement (trying to *deal* with her son's death)
**synonym** see DISTRIBUTE
— **deal·er** \'dē-lər\ *noun*

**³deal** *noun* (15th century)
**1 a** : an act of dealing : TRANSACTION **b** : BARGAIN
**2** : PACKAGE DEAL
**3** : treatment received (a dirty *deal*)
**4** : an arrangement for mutual advantage
**5** : AFFAIR 2 (dinner was an informal *deal*)

**⁴deal** *noun* [Middle English *dele*, from Middle Dutch or Middle Low German, plank; akin to Old High German *dili* plank — more at THILL] (14th century)
**1 a** *British* : a board of fir or pine **b** : sawed yellow-pine lumber nine inches (22.5 centimeters) or wider and three, four, or five inches (7.6 to 12.4 centimeters) thick
**2** : pine or fir wood
— **deal** *adjective*

**de·alat·ed** \(,)dē-'ā-,lā-təd\ *adjective* (1904)
: divested of the wings — used of postnuptial adults of insects (as ants) that drop their wings after a nuptial flight
— **de·ala·tion** \,dē-(,)ā-'lā-shən\ *noun*

**deal·er·ship** \'dē-lər-,ship\ *noun* (1916)
: an authorized sales agency (an automobile *dealership*)

**deal·fish** \'dē(ə)l-,fish\ *noun* [⁴*deal*] (1845)
: any of several long thin fishes (genus *Trachipterus* especially *T. arcticus* of the family Trachipteridae) inhabiting the deep sea

**deal·ing** *noun* (15th century)
**1** : method of business : manner of conduct
**2** *plural* : friendly or business interactions

**dealing box** *noun* (1897)
: a case that holds a deck of playing cards so that they may be dealt one by one

**de·am·i·nase** \(,)dē-'a-mi-,nās, -,nāz\ *noun* [*de-* + *amino* + *-ase*] (1920)
: an enzyme that hydrolyzes amino compounds (as amino acids) with removal of the amino group

**de·am·i·nate** \-,nāt\ *transitive verb* **-nat·ed; -nat·ing** (1926)
: to remove the amino group from (a compound)
— **de·am·i·na·tion** \(,)dē-,a-mi-'nā-shən\ *noun*

**dean** \'dēn\ *noun* [Middle English *deen*, from Old French *deien*, from Late Latin *decanus* chief of ten, from Greek *dekanos*, from *deka* ten — more at TEN] (13th century)
**1 a** : the head of the chapter of a collegiate or cathedral church **b** : a Roman Catholic priest who supervises one district of a diocese
**2 a** : the head of a division, faculty, college, or school of a university **b** : a college or secondary school administrator in charge of counseling and disciplining students
**3** : DOYEN 1

— **dean** *intransitive verb*
— **dean·ship** \-,ship\ *noun*

**dean·ery** \'dēn-rē, 'dē-nə-rē\ *noun, plural* **-er·ies** (15th century)
: the office, jurisdiction, or official residence of a clerical dean

**dean's list** *noun* (circa 1926)
: a list of students receiving special recognition from the dean of a college because of superior scholarship

**¹dear** \'dir\ *adjective* [Middle English *dere*, from Old English *dēor*] (before 12th century)
: SEVERE, SORE (in our *dear* peril —Shakespeare)

**²dear** *adjective* [Middle English *dere*, from Old English *dēore*; akin to Old High German *tiuri* distinguished, costly] (before 12th century)
**1** *obsolete* : NOBLE
**2** : highly valued : PRECIOUS (a *dear* friend) — often used in a salutation (*dear* Sir)
**3** : AFFECTIONATE, FOND
**4** : high or exorbitant in price : EXPENSIVE (eggs are very *dear* just now)
**5** : HEARTFELT
— **dear** *adverb*
— **dear·ly** *adverb*
— **dear·ness** *noun*

**³dear** *noun* (13th century)
**1** : a loved one : SWEETHEART
**2** : a lovable person

**⁴dear** *interjection* (1694)
— used especially to express annoyance or dismay

**Dear John** \-'jän\ *noun* (1945)
: a letter (as to a soldier) in which a wife asks for a divorce or a girlfriend breaks off an engagement or a friendship

**dearth** \'dərth\ *noun* [Middle English *derthe*, from (assumed) Old English *dierth*, from *dēore* dear] (13th century)
**1** : scarcity that makes dear; *specifically* : FAMINE
**2** : an inadequate supply : LACK

**dea·sil** \'dē-zəl\ *adverb* [Scottish Gaelic *deiseil*; akin to Latin *dexter* right hand] (1771)
: CLOCKWISE — compare WIDDERSHINS

**death** \'deth\ *noun* [Middle English *deeth*, from Old English *dēath*; akin to Old Norse *dauthi* death, *deyja* to die — more at DIE] (before 12th century)
**1** : a permanent cessation of all vital functions : the end of life — compare BRAIN DEATH
**2** : the cause or occasion of loss of life (drinking was the *death* of him)
**3** *capitalized* : the destroyer of life represented usually as a skeleton with a scythe
**4** : the state of being dead
**5 a** : the passing or destruction of something inanimate (the *death* of vaudeville) **b** : EXTINCTION
**6** : CIVIL DEATH
**7** : SLAUGHTER
**8** *Christian Science* : the lie of life in matter : that which is unreal and untrue : ILLUSION
— **at death's door** : close to death : critically ill
— **to death** : beyond endurance : EXCESSIVELY (bored *to death*)

**death·bed** \'deth-,bed\ *noun* (before 12th century)
**1** : the bed in which a person dies
**2** : the last hours of life
— **on one's deathbed** : near the point of death

**death benefit** *noun* (1921)
: money payable to the beneficiary of a deceased

**death·blow** \'deth-,blō\ *noun* (1795)
: a destructive or killing stroke or event

\ə\ abut \ᵊ\ kitten \ər\ further \a\ ash \ā\ ace
\ä\ mop, mar \aù\ out \ch\ chin \e\ bet \ē\ easy
\g\ go \i\ hit \ī\ ice \j\ job \ŋ\ sing \ō\ go
\ò\ law \òi\ boy \th\ thin \th\ the \ü\ loot \ù\ foot
\y\ yet \zh\ vision   *see also* Guide to Pronunciation

**death camas** *noun* (circa 1889)
: any of several plants (genus *Zigadenus*) of the lily family that cause poisoning of livestock in the western U.S.

**death camp** *noun* (1944)
: a concentration camp in which large numbers of prisoners are systematically killed

**death cap** *noun* (1925)
: a very poisonous mushroom (*Amanita phalloides*) of deciduous woods of North America and Europe that varies in color from pure white to olive or yellow and has a prominent volva at the base — called also *death cup*

**death duty** *noun* (1881)
*chiefly British* : DEATH TAX

**death instinct** *noun* (1922)
: an innate and unconscious tendency toward self-destruction postulated in psychoanalytic theory to explain aggressive and destructive behavior not satisfactorily explained by the pleasure principle — called also *Thanatos*; compare EROS 2

**death·less** \'deth-ləs\ *adjective* (1589)
: IMMORTAL, IMPERISHABLE ⟨*deathless* fame⟩
— **death·less·ly** *adverb*
— **death·less·ness** *noun*

**death·ly** \'deth-lē\ *adjective* (before 12th century)
**1** : FATAL
**2** : of, relating to, or suggestive of death ⟨a *deathly* pallor⟩
— **deathly** *adverb*

**death mask** *noun* (1877)
: a cast taken from the face of a dead person

**death rattle** *noun* (1822)
: a rattling or gurgling sound produced by air passing through mucus in the lungs and air passages of a dying person

**death ray** *noun* (1919)
: a weapon that generates an intense beam of particles or radiation by which it destroys its target

**death row** *noun* (1950)
: a prison area housing inmates sentenced to death

**death's–head** \'deths-,hed\ *noun* (1596)
: a human skull or a depiction of a human skull symbolizing death

**death's–head hawkmoth** *noun* (1879)
: a large dark hawkmoth (*Acherontia atropos*) with markings resembling a human skull on the back of the thorax — called also *death's-head moth*

**deaths·man** \'deths-mən\ *noun* (1589)
*archaic* : EXECUTIONER

**death squad** *noun* (1969)
: any of various right-wing vigilante groups in Latin America whose members kill suspected political adversaries and criminals

**death tax** *noun* (1937)
: a tax arising on the transmission of property after the owner's death; *especially* : ESTATE TAX

**death trap** *noun* (1835)
: a structure or situation that is potentially very dangerous to life

**death warrant** *noun* (1692)
**1** : a warrant for the execution of a death sentence
**2** : DEATHBLOW

¹**death·watch** \'deth-,wäch\ *noun* [*death* + *watch* (timepiece); from the superstition that its ticking presages death] (1646)
: a small insect that makes a ticking sound; *especially* : DEATHWATCH BEETLE

²**deathwatch** *noun* [*death* + *watch* (vigil)] (circa 1890)
**1** : a vigil kept over the dead or dying
**2** : the guard set over a criminal to be executed

**deathwatch beetle** *noun* (1877)
: any of various small beetles (family Anobiidae) that are common in old houses where they bore in woodwork and furniture and make a tapping noise as a mating call

**death wish** *noun* (1913)
: the conscious or unconscious desire for the death of oneself or of another

**deb** \'deb\ *noun* (1920)
: DEBUTANTE

**de·ba·cle** \dē-'bä-kəl, -'ba-; ÷'de-bə-kəl\ *also* **dé·bâ·cle** \*also* dā-'bäk(l°)\ *noun* [French *débâcle*, from *débâcler* to clear, from Middle French *desbacler*, from *des-* de- + *bacler* to block, perhaps from (assumed) Vulgar Latin *bacculare*, from Latin *baculum* staff] (1802)
**1** : a tumultuous breakup of ice in a river
**2** : a violent disruption (as of an army) : ROUT
**3 a** : a great disaster **b** : a complete failure : FIASCO

**de·bar** \di-'bär, dē-\ *transitive verb* [Middle English *debarren*, from Middle French *desbarrer* to unbar, from *des-* de- + *barrer* to bar] (15th century)
: to bar from having or doing something : PRECLUDE
— **de·bar·ment** \-mənt\ *noun*

¹**de·bark** \di-'bärk, dē-\ *verb* [French *debarquer*, from *de-* + *barque* bark (ship)] (1654)
: DISEMBARK
— **de·bar·ka·tion** \,dē-,bär-'kā-shən\ *noun*

²**de·bark** \(,)dē-'bärk\ *transitive verb* (1742)
: to remove bark from

**de·base** \di-'bās, dē-\ *transitive verb* (1565)
**1** : to lower in status, esteem, quality, or character
**2 a** : to reduce the intrinsic value of (a coin) by increasing the base-metal content **b** : to reduce the exchange value of (a monetary unit) ☆
— **de·base·ment** \-'bās-mənt\ *noun*
— **de·bas·er** \-'bā-sər\ *noun*

**de·bat·able** \di-'bā-tə-bəl, dē-\ *adjective* (1536)
**1** : claimed by more than one country ⟨*debatable* border territory⟩
**2 a** : open to dispute : QUESTIONABLE **b** : open to debate
**3** : capable of being debated

¹**de·bate** \di-'bāt, dē-\ *noun* (13th century)
: a contention by words or arguments: as **a** : the formal discussion of a motion before a deliberative body according to the rules of parliamentary procedure **b** : a regulated discussion of a proposition between two matched sides

²**debate** *verb* **de·bat·ed; de·bat·ing** [Middle English, from Middle French *debatre*, from Old French, from *de-* + *batre* to beat, from Latin *battuere*] (14th century)
*intransitive verb*
**1** *obsolete* : FIGHT, CONTEND
**2 a** : to contend in words **b** : to discuss a question by considering opposed arguments
**3** : to participate in a debate
*transitive verb*
**1 a** : to argue about **b** : to engage (an opponent) in debate
**2** : to turn over in one's mind
*synonym* see DISCUSS
— **de·bate·ment** \-'bāt-mənt\ *noun*
— **de·bat·er** *noun*

¹**de·bauch** \di-'bóch, -'bäch, dē-\ *transitive verb* [Middle French *debaucher*, from Old French *desbauchier* to scatter, disperse, from *des-* de- + *bauch* beam, of Germanic origin; akin to Old High German *balko* beam — more at BALK] (1595)
**1 a** *archaic* : to make disloyal **b** : to seduce from chastity
**2 a** : to lead away from virtue or excellence **b** : to corrupt by intemperance or sensuality
*synonym* see DEBASE
— **de·bauch·er** *noun*

²**debauch** *noun* (1603)
**1** : an act or occasion of debauchery
**2** : ORGY

**de·bauch·ee** \di-'bó-'chē, -,bä-; ,de-bə-'shē, -'shā\ *noun* [French *débauché*, from past participle of *débaucher*] (1661)
: one given to debauchery

**de·bauch·ery** \di-'bó-chə-rē, -chrē, -'bä-\ *noun, plural* **-er·ies** (1642)

**1 a** : extreme indulgence in sensuality **b** *plural* : ORGIES
**2** *archaic* : seduction from virtue or duty

**de·beak** \(,)dē-'bēk\ *transitive verb* (1937)
: to remove the tip of the upper mandible of (as a chicken) to prevent cannibalism and fighting

**de·ben·ture** \di-'ben-chər\ *noun* [Middle English *debentur*, from Latin, they are due, 3d plural present passive of *debēre* to owe — more at DEBT] (15th century)
**1** *British* : a corporate security other than an equity security : BOND
**2** : a bond backed by the general credit of the issuer rather than a specific lien on particular assets

**de·bil·i·tate** \di-'bi-lə-,tāt, dē-\ *transitive verb* **-tat·ed; -tat·ing** [Latin *debilitatus*, past participle of *debilitare* to weaken, from *debilis* weak] (1533)
: to impair the strength of : ENFEEBLE
*synonym* see WEAKEN
— **de·bil·i·ta·tion** \-,bi-lə-'tā-shən\ *noun*

**de·bil·i·ty** \di-'bi-lə-tē, dē-\ *noun, plural* **-ties** [Middle French *debilité*, from Latin *debilitat-, debilitas*, from *debilis*, from *de-* de- + *-bilis*; akin to Sanskrit *bala* strength] (15th century)
: WEAKNESS, INFIRMITY

¹**deb·it** \'de-bət\ *transitive verb* (1682)
: to enter upon the debit side of an account : charge with a debit

²**debit** *noun* [Latin *debitum* debt] (1776)
**1 a** : a record of an indebtedness; *specifically* : an entry on the left-hand side of an account constituting an addition to an expense or asset account or a deduction from a revenue, net worth, or liability account **b** : the sum of the items charged as debits
**2** : a charge against a bank deposit account
**3** : DRAWBACK, SHORTCOMING

**debit card** *noun* (1977)
: a card like a credit card by which money may be withdrawn or the cost of purchases paid directly from the holder's bank account without the payment of interest

**deb·o·nair** \,de-bə-'nar, -'ner\ *adjective* [Middle English *debonere*, from Old French *debonaire*, from *de bon aire* of good family or nature] (13th century)
**1** *archaic* : GENTLE, COURTEOUS
**2 a** : SUAVE, URBANE **b** : LIGHTHEARTED, NONCHALANT
— **deb·o·nair·ly** *adverb*
— **deb·o·nair·ness** *noun*

**de·bone** \(,)dē-'bōn\ *transitive verb* (1944)
: BONE ⟨*debone* a roast⟩
— **de·bon·er** *noun*

**Deb·o·rah** \'de-b(ə-)rə\ *noun* [Hebrew *Dĕbhōrāh*]
: a Hebrew prophetess who rallied the Israelites in their struggles against the Canaanites

---

☆ SYNONYMS
**Debase, vitiate, deprave, corrupt, debauch, pervert** mean to cause deterioration or lowering in quality or character. DEBASE implies a loss of position, worth, value, or dignity ⟨commercialism has *debased* the holiday⟩. VITIATE implies a destruction of purity, validity, or effectiveness by allowing entrance of a fault or defect ⟨a foreign policy *vitiated* by partisanship⟩. DEPRAVE implies moral deterioration by evil thoughts or influences ⟨the claim that society is *depraved* by pornography⟩. CORRUPT implies loss of soundness, purity, or integrity ⟨the belief that bureaucratese *corrupts* the language⟩. DEBAUCH implies a debasing through sensual indulgence ⟨the long stay on a tropical isle had *debauched* the ship's crew⟩. PERVERT implies a twisting or distorting from what is natural or normal ⟨*perverted* the original goals of the institute⟩.

**de·bouch** \di-'baùch, -'büsh, dē-\ *verb* [French *déboucher,* from *dé-* de- + *bouche* mouth, from Latin *bucca* cheek] (1745)
*transitive verb*
**:** to cause to emerge **:** DISCHARGE
*intransitive verb*
**1 :** to march out into open ground
**2 :** EMERGE, ISSUE
— **de·bouch·ment** \-mənt\ *noun*
**de·bride·ment** \di-'brēd-mənt, dā-, -,mänt, dā-brēd-'mäⁿ\ *noun* [French *débridement,* from *débrider* to remove adhesions, literally, to unbridle, from Middle French *desbrider,* from *des-* de- + *bride* bridle, from Middle High German *brīdel* — more at BRIDLE] (circa 1842)
**:** the surgical removal of lacerated, devitalized, or contaminated tissue
— **de·bride** \di-'brēd, dā-\ *transitive verb*
**de·brief** \(,)dē-'brēf\ *transitive verb* (1945)
**:** to interrogate (as a pilot) usually upon return (as from a mission) in order to obtain useful information
**de·bris** \də-'brē, dā-, 'dā-,, *British usually* 'de-(,)brē\ *noun, plural* **de·bris** \-'brēz, -,brēz\ [French *débris,* from Middle French, from *debriser* to break to pieces, from Old French *debrisier,* from *de-* + *brisier* to break — more at BRISANCE] (1708)
**1 :** the remains of something broken down or destroyed
**2 :** an accumulation of fragments of rock
**3 :** something discarded **:** RUBBISH
**debt** \'det\ *noun* [Middle English *dette, debte,* from Old French *dette* something owed, from (assumed) Vulgar Latin *debita,* from Latin, plural of *debitum* debt, from neuter of *debitus,* past participle of *debēre* to owe, from *de-* + *habēre* to have — more at GIVE] (13th century)
**1 :** SIN, TRESPASS
**2 :** something owed **:** OBLIGATION
**3 :** a state of owing
**4 :** the common-law action for the recovery of money held to be due
— **debt·less** \-ləs\ *adjective*
**debt·or** \'de-tər\ *noun* (13th century)
**1 :** one guilty of neglect or violation of duty
**2 :** one who owes a debt
**debt service** *noun* (1929)
**:** the amount of interest and sinking fund payments due annually on long-term debt
**de·bug** \(,)dē-'bəg\ *transitive verb* (1944)
**1 :** to remove insects from
**2 :** to eliminate errors in or malfunctions of
**3 :** to remove a concealed microphone or wiretapping device from
— **de·bug·ger** *noun*
**de·bunk** \(,)dē-'bəŋk\ *transitive verb* (1923)
**:** to expose the sham or falseness of ⟨debunk a legend⟩
— **de·bunk·er** *noun*
**¹de·but** *also* **dé·but** \'dā-,byü, dā-'\ *noun* [French *début,* from *débuter* to begin, from Middle French *desbuter* to play first, from *des-* de- + *but* starting point, goal — more at BUTT] (1751)
**1 :** a first appearance ⟨made her singing *debut*⟩
**2 :** a formal entrance into society
**²debut** (1830)
*intransitive verb*
**:** to make a debut
*transitive verb*
**:** to present to the public for the first time **:** INTRODUCE
**deb·u·tant** \'de-byu-,tänt\ *noun* [French *débutant,* from present participle of *débuter*] (1821)
**:** one making a debut
**deb·u·tante** \'de-byu-,tänt\ *noun* [French *débutante,* feminine of *débutant*] (1801)
**:** DEBUTANT; *especially* **:** a young woman making her formal entrance into society
**deca-** *or* **dec-** *or* **deka-** *or* **dek-** *combining form* [Middle English, from Latin, from Greek *deka-, dek-,* from *deka* — more at TEN]
**:** ten ⟨*deca*syllabic⟩ ⟨*deka*meter⟩

**de·cade** \'de-,kād, de-'kād; *especially sense 1b* 'de-kəd\ *noun* [Middle English, from Middle French *décade,* from Late Latin *decad-, decas,* from Greek *dekad-, dekas,* from *deka*] (15th century)
**1 :** a group or set of 10: as **a :** a period of 10 years **b :** a division of the rosary that consists primarily of 10 Hail Marys
**2 :** a ratio of 10 to 1 **:** ORDER OF MAGNITUDE
— **de·cad·al** \'de-kə-dᵊl\ *adjective*
**dec·a·dence** \'de-kə-dən(t)s *also* di-'kā-\ *noun* [Middle French, from Medieval Latin *decadentia,* from Late Latin *decadent-, decadens,* present participle of *decadere* to fall, sink — more at DECAY] (1549)
**1 :** the process of becoming decadent **:** the quality or state of being decadent
**2 :** a period of decline
*synonym* see DETERIORATION
**dec·a·den·cy** \-dᵊn-sē\ *noun* (1632)
**:** DECADENCE 1
**¹dec·a·dent** \'de-kə-dənt *also* di-'kā-\ *adjective* [back-formation from *decadence*] (1837)
**1 :** marked by decay or decline
**2 :** of, relating to, or having the characteristics of the decadents
**3 :** characterized by or appealing to self-indulgence
— **dec·a·dent·ly** *adverb*
**²decadent** *noun* (1886)
**1 :** one of a group of late 19th century French and English writers tending toward artificial and unconventional subjects and subtilized style
**2 :** one that is decadent
**de·caf** \'dē-,kaf\ *noun* [short for *decaffeinated*] (1984)
**:** decaffeinated coffee
**de·caf·fein·at·ed** \(,)dē-'ka-fə-nā-təd, -fē-ə-\ *adjective* (1921)
**:** having the caffeine removed ⟨*decaffeinated* coffee⟩ ⟨*decaffeinated* tea⟩
**deca·gon** \'de-kə-,gän\ *noun* [New Latin *decagonum,* from Greek *dekagōnon,* from *deka-* deca- + *-gōnon* -gon] (1571)
**:** a plane polygon of 10 angles and 10 sides
**deca·gram** \-,gram\ *noun* [French *décagramme,* from *déca-* deca- + *gramme* gram] (1810)
**:** DEKAGRAM
**deca·he·dron** \,de-kə-'hē-drən\ *noun* [International Scientific Vocabulary] (circa 1828)
**:** a polyhedron of 10 faces
**de·cal** \'dē-,kal, di-'kal; *Canadian usually* 'de-kəl\ *noun* [short for *decalcomania*] (1937)
**:** a picture, design, or label made to be transferred (as to glass) from specially prepared paper
**de·cal·ci·fi·ca·tion** \(,)dē-,kal-sə-fə-'kā-shən\ *noun* (1859)
**:** the removal or loss of calcium or calcium compounds (as from bones or soil)
— **de·cal·ci·fy** \(,)dē-'kal-sə-fī\ *transitive verb*
**de·cal·co·ma·nia** \di-,kal-kə-'mā-nē-ə\ *noun* [French *décalcomanie,* from *décalquer* to copy by tracing (from *dé-* de- + *calquer* to trace, from Italian *calcare,* literally, to tread, from Latin) + *manie* mania, from Late Latin *mania* — more at CAULK] (1864)
**1 :** the art or process of transferring pictures and designs from specially prepared paper (as to glass)
**2 :** DECAL
**deca·li·ter** \'de-kə-,lē-tər\ *noun* [French *décalitre,* from *déca-* + *litre* liter] (1810)
**:** DEKALITER
**deca·logue** \'de-kə-,lòg, -,läg\ *noun* [Middle English *decaloge,* from Late Latin *decalogus,* from Greek *dekalogos,* from *deka-* + *logos* word — more at LEGEND] (14th century)
**1** *capitalized* **:** TEN COMMANDMENTS

**2 :** a basic set of rules carrying binding authority
**¹deca·me·ter** \'de-kə-,mē-tər\ *noun* [French *décamètre,* from *déca-* + *mètre* meter] (1810)
**:** DEKAMETER
**²de·cam·e·ter** \de-'ka-mə-tər, də-\ *noun* [Greek *dekametron,* from *deka-* + *metron* measure, meter] (1821)
**:** a line of verse consisting of 10 metrical feet
**deca·me·tho·ni·um** \,de-kə-mə-'thō-nē-əm\ *noun* [*deca-* + *methylene* + *-onium*] (circa 1949)
**:** a synthetic ion used in the form of either its bromide or iodide salts ($C_{16}H_{38}Br_2N_2$ or $C_{16}H_{38}I_2N_2$) as a skeletal muscle relaxant; *also* **:** either of these salts
**deca·met·ric** \,de-kə-'me-trik\ *adjective* [*decameter* + *-ic*; from the wavelength range being between 1 and 10 dekameters] (1950)
**:** of, relating to, or being a radio wave of high frequency
**de·camp** \di-'kamp, dē-\ *intransitive verb* [French *décamper,* from Middle French *descamper,* from *des-* de- + *camper* to camp] (1676)
**1 :** to break up a camp
**2 :** to depart suddenly **:** ABSCOND
— **de·camp·ment** \-mənt\ *noun*
**dec·ane** \'de-,kān\ *noun* [International Scientific Vocabulary *deca-*] (circa 1875)
**:** any of several isomeric liquid alkanes $C_{10}H_{22}$
**de·cant** \di-'kant, dē-\ *transitive verb* [New Latin *decantare,* from Latin *de-* + Medieval Latin *cantus* edge, from Latin, iron ring round a wheel — more at CANT] (1633)
**1 :** to draw off (a liquid) without disturbing the sediment or the lower liquid layers
**2 :** to pour from one vessel into another
**3 :** to pour out, transfer, or unload as if by pouring
— **de·can·ta·tion** \,dē-,kan-'tā-shən\ *noun*
**de·cant·er** \di-'kan-tər, dē-\ *noun* (1712)
**:** a vessel used to decant or to receive decanted liquids; *especially* **:** an ornamental glass bottle used for serving wine
**de·cap·i·tate** \di-'ka-pə-,tāt, dē-\ *transitive verb* **-tat·ed; -tat·ing** [Late Latin *decapitatus,* past participle of *decapitare,* from Latin *de-* + *capit-, caput* head — more at HEAD] (circa 1611)
**1 :** to cut off the head of **:** BEHEAD
**2 :** to make ineffective **:** DESTROY
— **de·cap·i·ta·tion** \-,ka-pə-'tā-shən\ *noun*
— **de·cap·i·ta·tor** \-'ka-pə-,tā-tər\ *noun*

decanter

**deca·pod** \'de-kə-,päd\ *noun* [New Latin *Decapoda,* order name] (1836)
**1 :** any of an order (Decapoda) of crustaceans (as shrimps, lobsters, and crabs) with five pairs of thoracic appendages one or more of which are modified into pincers, with stalked eyes, and with the head and thorax fused into a cephalothorax and covered by a carapace
**2 :** any of the cephalopod mollusks (orders Sepioidea and Teuthoidea) with 10 arms including cuttlefishes, squids, and related forms
— **decapod** *adjective*
— **de·cap·o·dan** \di-'ka-pə-dən\ *adjective or noun*
— **de·cap·o·dous** \-ə-dəs\ *adjective*
**de·car·bon·ate** \(,)dē-'kär-bə-,nāt\ *transitive verb* (1831)
**:** to remove carbon dioxide or carbonic acid from
— **de·car·bon·ation** \-,kär-bə-'nā-shən\ *noun*

\ə\ abut \ᵊ\ kitten \ər\ further \a\ ash \ā\ ace \ä\ mop, mar \aù\ out \ch\ chin \e\ bet \ē\ easy \g\ go \i\ hit \ī\ ice \j\ job \ŋ\ sing \ō\ go \ò\ law \òi\ boy \th\ thin \t͟h\ the \ü\ loot \ù\ foot \y\ yet \zh\ vision *see also* Guide to Pronunciation

**de·car·bon·ize** \(,)dē-'kär-bə-,nīz\ *transitive verb* [International Scientific Vocabulary] (1825)
: to remove carbon from
— **de·car·bon·iz·er** *noun*

**de·car·box·yl·ase** \,dē-kär-'bäk-sə-,lās, -,lāz\ *noun* (1940)
: any of a group of enzymes that accelerate decarboxylation especially of amino acids

**de·car·box·yl·ation** \-,bäk-sə-'lā-shən\ *noun* (1922)
: the removal or elimination of carboxyl from a molecule
— **de·car·box·yl·ate** \-'bäk-sə-,lāt\ *transitive verb*

**de·car·bu·rize** \(,)dē-'kär-b(y)ə-,rīz\ *transitive verb* (1856)
: DECARBONIZE
— **de·car·bu·ri·za·tion** \-,kär-b(y)ə-rə-'zā-shən\ *noun*

**dec·are** \'de-,kar, -,ker, -,kär\ *noun* [French *décare*, from *déca-* deca- + *are*] (1810)
: a metric unit of area equal to 10 ares or 0.2471 acre

**de·ca·su·al·iza·tion** \(,)dē-,ka-zh(ə-)wə-lə-'zā-shən, -,ka-zhə-lə-\ *noun* (1892)
: the process of eliminating the employment of casual workers to stabilize the work force

**deca·syl·lab·ic** \,de-kə-sə-'la-bik\ *adjective* [probably from French *décasyllabique*, from Greek *dekasyllabos*, from *deka-* deca- + *syllabē* syllable] (1771)
: consisting of 10 syllables or composed of verses of 10 syllables
— **decasyllabic** *noun*
— **deca·syl·la·ble** \'de-kə-,si-lə-bəl, ,de-kə-'\ *noun*

**de·cath·lete** \di-'kath-,lēt\ *noun* [blend of *decathlon* and *athlete*] (1968)
: an athlete who competes in the decathlon

**de·cath·lon** \di-'kath-lən, -,län\ *noun* [French *décathlon*, from *déca-* deca- + *-athlon* (as in *pentathlon*)] (1912)
: a 10-event athletic contest; *specifically* : a composite contest that consists of the 100-meter, 400-meter, and 1500-meter runs, the 110-meter high hurdles, the javelin and discus throws, shot put, pole vault, high jump, and long jump

¹**de·cay** \di-'kā\ *verb* [Middle English, from Old North French *decaïr*, from Late Latin *decadere* to fall, sink, from Latin *de-* + *cadere* to fall — more at CHANCE] (15th century)
*intransitive verb*
**1** : to decline from a sound or prosperous condition
**2** : to decrease gradually in quantity, activity, or force
**3** : to fall into ruin
**4** : to decline in health, strength, or vigor
**5** : to undergo decomposition
*transitive verb*
**1** *obsolete* : to cause to decay : IMPAIR ⟨infirmity that *decays* the wise —Shakespeare⟩
**2** : to destroy by decomposition ☆
— **de·cay·er** *noun*

²**decay** *noun* (15th century)
**1** : gradual decline in strength, soundness, or prosperity or in degree of excellence or perfection
**2** : a wasting or wearing away : RUIN
**3** *obsolete* : DESTRUCTION, DEATH
**4 a** : ROT; *specifically* : aerobic decomposition of proteins chiefly by bacteria **b** : the product of decay
**5** : a decline in health or vigor
**6** : decrease in quantity, activity, or force: as **a** : spontaneous decrease in the number of radioactive atoms in radioactive material **b** : spontaneous disintegration (as of an atom or a particle)

**Dec·ca** \'de-kə\ *noun* [*Decca* Co., British firm which developed it] (1946)
: a system of long-range navigation used chiefly in Europe that utilizes the phase differences of continuous-wave signals from synchronized ground transmitters to establish position

**de·cease** \di-'sēs\ *noun* [Middle English *deces*, from Middle French, from Latin *decessus* departure, death, from *decedere* to depart, die, from *de-* + *cedere* to go] (14th century)
: departure from life : DEATH
— **decease** *intransitive verb*

¹**de·ceased** \-'sēst\ *adjective* (15th century)
: no longer living; *especially* : recently dead — used of persons
*synonym* see DEAD

²**deceased** *noun, plural* **deceased** (1625)
: a dead person ⟨the will of the *deceased*⟩

**de·ce·dent** \di-'sē-dᵊnt\ *noun* [Latin *decedent-, decedens,* present participle of *decedere*] (1599)
: a deceased person — used chiefly in law

**de·ceit** \di-'sēt\ *noun* [Middle English *deceite*, from Middle French, from Latin *decepta*, feminine of *deceptus*, past participle of *decipere*] (14th century)
**1** : the act or practice of deceiving : DECEPTION
**2** : an attempt or device to deceive : TRICK
**3** : the quality of being deceitful : DECEITFULNESS

**de·ceit·ful** \-fəl\ *adjective* (15th century)
: having a tendency or disposition to deceive: **a** : not honest ⟨a *deceitful* child⟩ **b** : DECEPTIVE, MISLEADING
*synonym* see DISHONEST
— **de·ceit·ful·ly** \-fə-lē\ *adverb*
— **de·ceit·ful·ness** *noun*

**de·ceiv·able** \di-'sē-və-bəl\ *adjective* (14th century)
**1** *archaic* : DECEITFUL, DECEPTIVE
**2** *archaic* : capable of being deceived

**de·ceive** \di-'sēv\ *verb* **de·ceived; de·ceiv·ing** [Middle English, from Middle French *deceivre*, from Latin *decipere*, from *de-* + *capere* to take — more at HEAVE] (13th century)
*transitive verb*
**1** *archaic* : ENSNARE
**2 a** *obsolete* : to be false to **b** *archaic* : to fail to fulfill
**3** *obsolete* : CHEAT
**4** : to cause to accept as true or valid what is false or invalid
**5** *archaic* : to while away
*intransitive verb*
: to practice deceit; *also* : to give a false impression ⟨appearances can *deceive*⟩ ☆
— **de·ceiv·er** *noun*
— **de·ceiv·ing·ly** \-'sē-viŋ-lē\ *adverb*

**de·cel·er·ate** \(,)dē-'se-lə-,rāt\ *verb* **-at·ed; -at·ing** [*de-* + *accelerate*] (1899)
*transitive verb*
**1** : to reduce the speed of : slow down
**2** : to decrease the rate of progress of
*intransitive verb*
: to move at decreasing speed
— **de·cel·er·a·tion** \(,)dē-,se-lə-'rā-shən\ *noun*
— **de·cel·er·a·tor** \(,)dē-'se-lə-,rā-tər\ *noun*

**De·cem·ber** \di-'sem-bər, dē-\ *noun* [Middle English *Decembre*, from Old English or Old French, both from Latin *December* (tenth month), from *decem* ten — more at TEN] (before 12th century)
: the 12th month of the Gregorian calendar
**word history** see SEPTEMBER

**De·cem·brist** \-brist\ *noun* (1877)
: one taking part in the unsuccessful uprising against the Russian emperor Nicholas I in December 1825

**de·cem·vir** \di-'sem-vər\ *noun* [Middle English, from Latin, back-formation from *decemviri*, plural, from *decem* + *viri*, plural of *vir* man — more at VIRILE] (1579)
: one of a ruling body of 10; *specifically* : one of a body of 10 magistrates in ancient Rome
— **de·cem·vi·ral** \-vər-əl\ *adjective*
— **de·cem·vi·rate** \-vər-ət\ *noun*

**de·cen·cy** \'dē-sᵊn-sē\ *noun, plural* **-cies** (1567)
**1** *archaic* **a** : FITNESS **b** : ORDERLINESS
**2 a** : the quality or state of being decent : PROPRIETY **b** : conformity to standards of taste, propriety, or quality
**3** : standard of propriety — usually used in plural
**4** *plural* : conditions or services considered essential for a proper standard of living
**5** : literary decorum

**de·cen·ni·al** \di-'se-nē-əl\ *adjective* (circa 1656)
**1** : consisting of or lasting for 10 years
**2** : occurring or being done every 10 years ⟨the *decennial* census⟩
— **decennial** *noun*
— **de·cen·ni·al·ly** \-nē-ə-lē\ *adverb*

**de·cen·ni·um** \-nē-əm\ *noun, plural* **-ni·ums** *or* **-nia** \-nē-ə\ [Latin, from *decem* + *annus* year — more at ANNUAL] (1685)
: a period of 10 years : DECADE

**de·cent** \'dē-sᵊnt\ *adjective* [Middle French or Latin; Middle French, from Latin *decent-, decens,* present participle of *decēre* to be fitting; akin to Latin *decus* honor, *dignus* worthy, Greek *dokein* to seem, seem good] (1539)
**1** *archaic* **a** : APPROPRIATE **b** : well-formed : HANDSOME
**2 a** : conforming to standards of propriety, good taste, or morality **b** : modestly clothed
**3** : free from immodesty or obscenity
**4** : fairly good but not excellent : ADEQUATE, SATISFACTORY ⟨*decent* wages⟩
**5** : marked by moral integrity, kindness, and goodwill ⟨hard-working and *decent* folks⟩
*synonym* see CHASTE
— **de·cent·ly** *adverb*

**de·cen·tral·iza·tion** \(,)dē-,sen-trə-lə-'zā-shən\ *noun* (1846)
**1** : the dispersion or distribution of functions and powers; *specifically* : the delegation of power from a central authority to regional and local authorities
**2** : the redistribution of population and industry from urban centers to outlying areas
— **de·cen·tral·ize** \(,)dē-'sen-trə-,līz\ *verb*

**de·cep·tion** \di-'sep-shən\ *noun* [Middle English *decepcioun*, from Middle French *deception*, from Late Latin *deception-, deceptio,* from Latin *decipere* to deceive] (15th century)
**1 a** : the act of deceiving **b** : the fact or condition of being deceived

---

☆ **SYNONYMS**
**Decay, decompose, rot, putrefy, spoil** mean to undergo destructive dissolution. DECAY implies a slow change from a state of soundness or perfection ⟨a *decaying* mansion⟩. DECOMPOSE stresses a breaking down by chemical change and when applied to organic matter a corruption ⟨the strong odor of *decomposing* vegetation⟩. ROT is a close synonym of DECOMPOSE and often connotes foulness ⟨fruit was left to *rot* in warehouses⟩. PUTREFY implies the rotting of animal matter and offensiveness to sight and smell ⟨corpses *putrefying* on the battlefield⟩. SPOIL applies chiefly to the decomposition of foods ⟨keep the ham from *spoiling*⟩.

**Deceive, mislead, delude, beguile** mean to lead astray or frustrate usually by underhandedness. DECEIVE implies imposing a false idea or belief that causes ignorance, bewilderment, or helplessness ⟨tried to *deceive* me about the cost⟩. MISLEAD implies a leading astray that may or may not be intentional ⟨I was *misled* by the confusing sign⟩. DELUDE implies deceiving so thoroughly as to obscure the truth ⟨we were *deluded* into thinking we were safe⟩. BEGUILE stresses the use of charm and persuasion in deceiving ⟨was *beguiled* by false promises⟩.

**2 :** something that deceives **:** TRICK ☆
— **de·cep·tion·al** \-shə-nəl\ *adjective*
**de·cep·tive** \di-'sep-tiv\ *adjective* (circa 1611)
**:** tending or having power to deceive **:** MISLEADING
— **de·cep·tive·ly** *adverb*
— **de·cep·tive·ness** *noun*
**¹de·cer·e·brate** \(ˌ)dē-'ser-ə-brət, -ˌbrāt\ *adjective* (1897)
**1 :** characteristic of decerebration ⟨*decerebrate* rigidity⟩
**2 :** having the cerebrum removed or made inactive
**²de·cer·e·brate** \(ˌ)dē-'ser-ə-ˌbrāt\ *transitive verb* (circa 1900)
**:** to remove the cerebrum from; *also* **:** to make incapable of cerebral activity
— **de·cer·e·bra·tion** \(ˌ)dē-ˌser-ə-'brā-shən\ *noun*
**de·cer·ti·fy** \(ˌ)dē-'sər-tə-ˌfī\ *transitive verb* (1918)
**:** to withdraw or revoke the certification of
— **de·cer·ti·fi·ca·tion** \(ˌ)dē-ˌsər-tə-fə-'kā-shən\ *noun*
**de·chlo·ri·nate** \(ˌ)dē-'klōr-ə-ˌnāt, -'klȯr-\ *transitive verb* (1941)
**:** to remove chlorine from ⟨*dechlorinate* water⟩
— **de·chlo·ri·na·tion** \(ˌ)dē-ˌklōr-ə-'nā-shən, -ˌklȯr-\ *noun*
**deci-** *combining form* [French *déci-*, from Latin *decimus* tenth, from *decem* ten — more at TEN]
**:** tenth part ⟨*decimeter*⟩
**deci·bel** \'de-sə-ˌbel, -bəl\ *noun* [International Scientific Vocabulary *deci- + bel*] (1928)
**1 a :** a unit for expressing the ratio of two amounts of electric or acoustic signal power equal to 10 times the common logarithm of this ratio **b :** a unit for expressing the ratio of the magnitudes of two electric voltages or currents or analogous acoustic quantities equal to 20 times the common logarithm of the voltage or current ratio
**2 :** a unit for expressing the relative intensity of sounds on a scale from zero for the average least perceptible sound to about 130 for the average pain level
**3 :** degree of loudness; *also* **:** extremely loud sound — usually used in plural
**de·cide** \di-'sīd, dē-\ *verb* **de·cid·ed; de·cid·ing** [Middle English, from Middle French *decider*, from Latin *decidere*, literally, to cut off, from *de- + caedere* to cut] (14th century)
*transitive verb*
**1 a :** to arrive at a solution that ends uncertainty or dispute about ⟨*decide* what to do⟩ **b :** to select as a course of action — used with an infinitive ⟨*decided* to go⟩
**2 :** to bring to a definitive end ⟨one blow *decided* the fight⟩
**3 :** to induce to come to a choice ⟨her pleas *decided* him to help⟩
*intransitive verb*
**:** to make a choice or judgment ☆
— **de·cid·abil·i·ty** \di-ˌsī-də-'bi-lə-tē\ *noun*
— **de·cid·able** \di-'sī-də-bəl\ *adjective*
— **de·cid·er** *noun*
**de·cid·ed** *adjective* (1790)
**1 :** UNQUESTIONABLE ⟨a *decided* advantage⟩
**2 :** free from doubt or wavering
— **de·cid·ed·ly** *adverb*
— **de·cid·ed·ness** *noun*
**de·cid·ing** *adjective* (1658)
**:** that decides **:** DECISIVE ⟨drove in the *deciding* run⟩
**de·cid·ua** \di-'si-jə-wə\ *noun, plural* **-u·ae** \-jə-ˌwē\ [New Latin, from Latin, feminine of *deciduus*] (1785)
**1 :** the part of the mucous membrane lining the uterus that in higher placental mammals undergoes special modifications in preparation for and during pregnancy and is cast off at parturition

**2 :** the part of the mucous membrane of the uterus cast off in the process of menstruation
— **de·cid·u·al** \-wəl\ *adjective*
**de·cid·u·ate** \-wət\ *adjective* (1868)
**:** having the fetal and maternal tissues firmly interlocked so that a layer of maternal tissue is torn away at parturition and forms part of the afterbirth
**de·cid·u·ous** \di-'si-jə-wəs\ *adjective* [Latin *deciduus*, from *decidere* to fall off, from *de- + cadere* to fall — more at CHANCE] (1688)
**1 :** falling off or shed seasonally or at a certain stage of development in the life cycle ⟨*deciduous* leaves⟩ ⟨*deciduous* teeth⟩
**2 a :** having deciduous parts ⟨*deciduous* trees⟩ **b :** having the dominant plants deciduous ⟨a *deciduous* forest⟩
**3 :** EPHEMERAL
— **de·cid·u·ous·ness** *noun*
**deci·gram** \'de-sə-ˌgram\ *noun* [French *décigramme*, from *déci- + gramme* gram] (1810)
— see METRIC SYSTEM table
**dec·ile** \'de-ˌsīl, -səl\ *noun* [Latin *decem* ten — more at TEN] (1882)
**:** any one of nine numbers that divide a frequency distribution into 10 classes such that each contains the same number of individuals; *also* **:** any one of these 10 classes
— **decile** *adjective*
**deci·li·ter** \'de-sə-ˌlē-tər\ *noun* [French *décilitre*, from *déci- + litre* liter] (1801)
— see METRIC SYSTEM table
**de·cil·lion** \di-'sil-yən\ *noun, often attributive* [Latin *decem* + English *-illion* (as in *million*)] (1847)
— see NUMBER table
**¹dec·i·mal** \'de-sə-məl, 'des-məl\ *adjective* [French *décimal*, from Medieval Latin *decimalis* of a tithe, from Latin *decima* tithe — more at DIME] (1608)
**:** numbered or proceeding by tens: **a :** based on the number 10; *especially* **:** expressed in or utilizing a decimal system especially with a decimal point **b :** subdivided into 10th or 100th units ⟨*decimal* coinage⟩
— **dec·i·mal·ly** \-mə-lē\ *adverb*
**²decimal** *noun* (1651)
**:** any real number expressed in base 10; *especially* **:** DECIMAL FRACTION
**decimal fraction** *noun* (1660)
**:** a fraction (as $.25 = {}^{25}/_{100}$ or $.025 = {}^{25}/_{1000}$) or mixed number (as $3.025 = 3{}^{25}/_{1000}$) in which the denominator is a power of 10 usually expressed by use of the decimal point
**dec·i·mal·i·za·tion** \ˌde-sə-mə-lə-'zā-shən\ *noun* (1855)
**:** conversion (as of a currency) to a decimal system
— **dec·i·mal·ize** \'de-sə-mə-ˌlīz\ *transitive verb*
**decimal point** *noun* (circa 1864)
**:** a period, centered dot, or in some countries a comma at the left of a proper decimal fraction (as .678) or between the parts of a mixed number (as 3.678) expressed by a whole number and a decimal fraction
**decimal system** *noun* (1864)
**1 :** a number system that uses a notation in which each number is expressed in base 10 by using one of the first nine integers or 0 in each place and letting each place value be a power of 10
**2 :** a system of measurement or currency in which the basic units increase by powers of 10
**dec·i·mate** \'de-sə-ˌmāt\ *transitive verb* **-mat·ed; -mat·ing** [Latin *decimatus*, past participle of *decimare*, from *decimus* tenth, from *decem* ten] (1660)
**1 :** to select by lot and kill every tenth man of
**2 :** to exact a tax of 10 percent from ⟨poor as a *decimated* Cavalier —John Dryden⟩
**3 a :** to reduce drastically especially in number ⟨cholera *decimated* the population⟩ **b :** to destroy a large part of ⟨firebombs *decimated* large sections of the city⟩ ∎

☐ **USAGE**
**decimate** The first sense of *decimate* was born in the Roman practice of disciplining refractory military units by selecting one tenth of the men by lot and executing them. A bit harsh, from a modern standpoint, but presumably the Romans thought it effective. Sense 1 is used only in historical contexts. Sense 2 is also historical; it refers in the main to a tax levied by Oliver Cromwell on the defeated Royalists. Sense 3 is the live sense. It remembers not the arithmetic of the Romans, but the ferocity of their methods, and it has been in continuous use since the second half of the 17th century. Beginning around 1870 and continuing for more than a century, a school of critics—many of them newspaper editors—has emphasized the etymology and disapproved of the use that is regularly met in current writing. All the same, uses like those that follow are standard ⟨though the buffalo herds have been *decimated* . . . this is still the frontier —John Updike⟩ ⟨the curse of scurvy, which *decimated* the crew —Daniel J. Boorstin⟩ ⟨injuries *decimated* the Yankees in the first half of the season —Murray Chass⟩ ⟨tanks and enough weaponry to *decimate* the continent —William Safire⟩ ⟨logrolling that ultimately brought a new tariff compromise bill, the price of which was to *decimate* the distribution act —James MacGregor Burns⟩. This sense is even used occasionally for humorous overstatement ⟨is there a homicidal maniac on the loose, who intends to *decimate* the Detroit priesthood? —Newgate Callendar⟩.

— **dec·i·ma·tion** \,de-sə-'mā-shən\ *noun*

**deci·me·ter** \'de-sə-,mē-tər\ *noun* [French *décimètre*, from *déci-* deci- + *mètre* meter] (1809)
— see METRIC SYSTEM table

**de·ci·pher** \dē-'sī-fər\ *transitive verb* (1545)
**1** : DECODE 1a
**2** *obsolete* : DEPICT
**3 a** : to make out the meaning of despite indistinctness or obscurity **b** : to interpret the meaning of
— **de·ci·pher·able** \-f(ə-)rə-bəl\ *adjective*
— **de·ci·pher·er** \-fər-ər\ *noun*
— **de·ci·pher·ment** \-fər-mənt\ *noun*

**¹de·ci·sion** \di-'si-zhən\ *noun* [Middle French, from Latin *decision-, decisio,* from *decidere* to decide] (15th century)
**1 a** : the act or process of deciding **b** : a determination arrived at after consideration : CONCLUSION
**2** : a report of a conclusion
**3** : promptness and firmness in deciding : DETERMINATION
**4 a** : WIN; *specifically* : a victory in boxing decided on points **b** : a win or loss officially credited to a pitcher in baseball
— **de·ci·sion·al** \-'si-zhnəl, -'si-zhə-n°l\ *adjective*

**²decision** *transitive verb* (1943)
: to win a decision over (a boxing opponent)

**decision theory** *noun* (1961)
: a branch of statistical theory concerned with quantifying the process of making choices between alternatives

**decision tree** *noun* (1964)
: a tree diagram which is used for making decisions in business or computer programming and in which the branches represent choices with associated risks, costs, results, or probabilities

**de·ci·sive** \di-'sī-siv\ *adjective* (1611)
**1** : having the power or quality of deciding
**2** : RESOLUTE, DETERMINED
**3** : UNMISTAKABLE, UNQUESTIONABLE ⟨a *decisive* superiority⟩
**synonym** see CONCLUSIVE
— **de·ci·sive·ly** *adverb*
— **de·ci·sive·ness** *noun*

**¹deck** \'dek\ *noun* [Middle English *dekke* covering of a ship, from (assumed) Middle Dutch *dec* covering, probably from Middle Low German *vordeck,* from *vordecken* to cover, from *vor-* for- + *decken* to cover; akin to Old High German *decchen* to cover — more at THATCH] (1509)
**1** : a platform in a ship serving usually as a structural element and forming the floor for its compartments
**2** : something resembling the deck of a ship: as **a** : a story or tier of a building **b** : the roadway of a bridge **c** : a flat floored roofless area adjoining a house **d** : the lid of the compartment at the rear of the body of an automobile; *also* : the compartment **e** : a layer of clouds
**3 a** : a pack of playing cards **b** : a packet of narcotics
**4** : TAPE DECK
— **on deck 1** : ready for duty **2** : next in line : next in turn

**²deck** *transitive verb* [Dutch *dekken* to cover; akin to Old High German *decchen*] (1513)
**1** *obsolete* : COVER
**2 a** : to clothe elegantly : ARRAY ⟨*decked* out in furs⟩ **b** : DECORATE ⟨*deck* the halls with boughs of holly —*English carol*⟩ **c** : to portray or present with embellishments
**3** [¹*deck*] : to furnish with or as if with a deck
**4** [¹*deck*] : to knock down forcibly : FLOOR ⟨*decked* him with one punch⟩
**synonym** see ADORN

**deck chair** *noun* (1884)
: a folding chair often having an adjustable leg rest

**deck·er** \'de-kər\ *noun* (1790)
: something having a specified number of decks, levels, floors, or layers — used in combination ⟨many of the city's buses are double-*deckers*⟩

**deck·hand** \'dek-,hand\ *noun* (1844)
: a seaman who performs manual duties

**deck·house** \-,haús\ *noun* (1856)
: a superstructure on a ship's upper deck

**deck·ing** \'de-kiŋ\ *noun* (1580)
: DECK; *also* : material for a deck

**deck chair**

**deck·le** \'de-kəl\ *noun* [German *Deckel,* literally, cover, from *decken* to cover, from Old High German *decchen*] (1816)
: a frame around the edges of a mold used in making paper by hand; *also* : either of the bands around the edge of the wire of a papermaking machine that determine the width of the web

**deckle edge** *noun* (circa 1874)
: the rough untrimmed edge of paper left by a deckle or produced artificially
— **deck·le-edged** \-'ejd\ *adjective*

**deck tennis** *noun* [from its being played on the decks of ocean liners] (1927)
: a game in which players toss a ring or quoit back and forth over a net stretched across a small court

**de·claim** \di-'klām, dē-\ *verb* [Middle English *declamen,* from Latin *declamare,* from *de-* + *clamare* to cry out; akin to Latin *calare* to call — more at LOW] (14th century)
*intransitive verb*
**1** : to speak rhetorically; *specifically* : to recite something as an exercise in elocution
**2** : to speak pompously or bombastically : HARANGUE
*transitive verb*
: to deliver rhetorically; *specifically* : to recite in elocution
— **de·claim·er** *noun*
— **dec·la·ma·tion** \,de-klə-'mā-shən\ *noun*

**de·clam·a·to·ry** \di-'kla-mə-,tōr-ē, -,tór-\ *adjective* (1581)
: of, relating to, or marked by declamation or rhetorical display

**de·clar·ant** \di-'klar-ənt, -'kler-\ *noun* (1681)
: a person who makes a statement or declaration especially in connection with a legal proceeding

**dec·la·ra·tion** \,de-klə-'rā-shən\ *noun* (15th century)
**1** : the act of declaring : ANNOUNCEMENT
**2 a** : the first pleading in a common-law action **b** : a statement made by a party to a legal transaction usually not under oath
**3 a** : something that is declared **b** : the document containing such a declaration

**de·clar·a·tive** \di-'klar-ə-tiv, -'kler-\ *adjective* (1628)
: making a declaration : DECLARATORY ⟨a *declarative* sentence⟩
— **de·clar·a·tive·ly** *adverb*

**de·clar·a·to·ry** \-ə-,tōr-ē, -,tór-\ *adjective* (15th century)
**1** : serving to declare, set forth, or explain
**2 a** : declaring what is the existing law ⟨*declaratory* statute⟩ **b** : declaring a legal right or interpretation ⟨a *declaratory* judgment⟩

**de·clare** \di-'klar, -'kler\ *verb* **de·clared; de·clar·ing** [Middle English, from Middle French & Latin; Middle French *declarer,* from Latin *declarare,* from *de-* + *clarare* to make visible, from *clarus* clear — more at CLEAR] (14th century)
*transitive verb*
**1** : to make known formally, officially, or explicitly
**2** *obsolete* : to make clear
**3** : to make evident : SHOW
**4** : to state emphatically : AFFIRM ⟨*declares* his innocence⟩

**5** : to make a full statement of (one's taxable or dutiable property)
**6 a** : to announce (as a trump suit) in a card game **b** : MELD
**7** : to make payable ⟨*declare* a dividend⟩
*intransitive verb*
**1** : to make a declaration
**2** : to avow one's opinion or support ☆
— **de·clar·able** \-'klar-ə-bəl, -'kler-\ *adjective*

**de·clar·er** \di-'klar-ər, -'kler-\ *noun* (14th century)
: one that declares; *specifically* : the bridge player who names the trump and plays both his own hand and that of the dummy

**de·class** \(,)dē-'klas\ *transitive verb* (1888)
: to remove from a class; *especially* : to assign to a lower social status

**dé·clas·sé** \,dā-,kla-'sā, -,klä-\ *adjective* [French, from past participle of *déclasser* to declass] (1887)
**1** : fallen or lowered in class, rank, or social position
**2** : of inferior status

**de·clas·si·fy** \(,)dē-'kla-sə-,fī\ *transitive verb* (1945)
: to remove or reduce the security classification of ⟨*declassify* a secret document⟩
— **de·clas·si·fi·ca·tion** \(,)dē-,kla-sə-fə-'kā-shən\ *noun*

**de·claw** \-'kló\ *transitive verb* (1953)
: to remove the claws of (as a cat) surgically

**de·clen·sion** \di-'klen(t)-shən\ *noun* [Middle English *declenson,* modification of Middle French *declinaison,* from Latin *declination-, declinatio* grammatical inflection, turning aside, from *declinare* to inflect, turn aside] (15th century)
**1 a** : noun, adjective, or pronoun inflection especially in some prescribed order of the forms **b** : a class of nouns or adjectives having the same type of inflectional forms
**2** : a falling off or away : DETERIORATION
**3** : DESCENT, SLOPE
— **de·clen·sion·al** \-'klen(t)-shə-n°l\ *adjective*

**dec·li·na·tion** \,de-klə-'nā-shən\ *noun* [Middle English *declinacioun,* from Middle French *declination,* from Latin *declination-, declinatio* angle of the heavens, turning aside] (14th century)
**1** : angular distance north or south from the celestial equator measured along a great circle passing through the celestial poles
**2** : a turning aside or swerving
**3** : DETERIORATION ⟨moral *declination*⟩
**4** : a bending downward : INCLINATION
**5** : a formal refusal
**6** : the angle formed between a magnetic needle and the geographical meridian
— **dec·li·na·tion·al** \-shnəl, -shə-n°l\ *adjective*

**¹de·cline** \di-'klīn, dē-\ *verb* **de·clined; de·clin·ing** [Middle English, from Middle French *decliner,* from Latin *declinare* to turn aside, inflect, from *de-* + *clinare* to incline — more at LEAN] (14th century)
*intransitive verb*

☆ **SYNONYMS**
**Declare, announce, proclaim, promulgate** mean to make known publicly. DECLARE implies explicitness and usually formality in making known ⟨the referee *declared* the contest a draw⟩. ANNOUNCE implies the declaration of something for the first time ⟨*announced* their engagement at a party⟩. PROCLAIM implies declaring clearly, forcefully, and authoritatively ⟨the president *proclaimed* a national day of mourning⟩. PROMULGATE implies the proclaiming of a dogma, doctrine, or law ⟨*promulgated* an edict of religious toleration⟩. See in addition ASSERT.

**1** *archaic* **:** to turn from a straight course **:** STRAY
**2 a :** to slope downward **:** DESCEND **b :** to bend down **:** DROOP **c :** to stoop to what is unworthy
**3 a** *of a celestial body* **:** to sink toward setting **b :** to draw toward a close **:** WANE ⟨the day *declined*⟩
**4 :** to tend toward an inferior state or weaker condition ⟨his health *declined*⟩
**5 :** to withhold consent
**6 :** to become less in amount ⟨prices *declined*⟩ *transitive verb*
**1 :** to give in prescribed order the grammatical forms of (a noun, pronoun, or adjective)
**2** *obsolete* **a :** AVERT **b :** AVOID
**3 :** to cause to bend or bow downward
**4 a :** to refuse to undertake, undergo, engage in, or comply with **b :** to refuse especially courteously ⟨*decline* an invitation⟩ ☆
— **de·clin·able** \-'klī-nə-bəl\ *adjective*
— **de·clin·er** \-'klī-nər\ *noun*
²**decline** \*also* 'dē-,klīn\ *noun* (14th century)
**1 :** the process of declining: **a :** a gradual physical or mental sinking and wasting away **b :** a change to a lower state or level
**2 :** the period during which something is deteriorating or approaching its end
**3 :** a downward slope
**4 :** a wasting disease; *especially* **:** pulmonary tuberculosis
***synonym*** see DETERIORATION
**de·clin·ing** \-niŋ\ *adjective* (1593)
**:** of or relating to the period during which something is deteriorating or nearing its end ⟨her *declining* years⟩
**de·cliv·i·tous** \di-'kliv-ət-əs\ *adjective* (1799)
**:** moderately steep
**de·cliv·i·ty** \-ət-ē\ *noun, plural* **-ties** [Latin *declivitat-, declivitas,* from *declivis* sloping down, from *de-* + *clivus* slope, hill; akin to Latin *clinare*] (1612)
**1 :** downward inclination
**2 :** a descending slope
**de·co** \'de-(,)kō, dā-'kō, 'dā-\ *noun, often capitalized* (1969)
**:** ART DECO
**de·coct** \di-'käkt\ *transitive verb* [Latin *decoctus,* past participle of *decoquere,* from *de-* + *coquere* to cook — more at COOK] (15th century)
**1 :** to extract the flavor of by boiling
**2 :** BOIL DOWN, CONCENTRATE
**de·coc·tion** \di-'käk-shən\ *noun* (15th century)
**1 :** an extract obtained by decocting
**2 :** the act or process of decocting
**de·code** \(,)dē-'kōd\ *transitive verb* (1896)
**1 a :** to convert (as a coded message) into intelligible form **b :** to recognize and interpret (an electronic signal)
**2 a :** DECIPHER 3a **b :** to discover the underlying meaning of ⟨*decode* the play's imagery⟩
**de·cod·er** \-'kō-dər\ *noun* (1920)
**:** one that decodes; *especially* **:** an electronic device for unscrambling a television transmission
**de·col·late** \dē-'kä-,lāt\ *transitive verb* **-lat·ed; -lat·ing** [Latin *decollatus,* past participle of *decollare,* from *de-* + *collum* neck — more at COLLAR] (1599)
**:** BEHEAD
— **de·col·la·tion** \,dē-kä-'lā-shən\ *noun*
**dé·col·le·tage** \(,)dā-,kä-lə-'täzh, (,)dā-,kȯl-'täzh, ,de-klə-\ *noun* [French, action of cutting or wearing a low neckline, from *décolleter*] (1894)
**1 :** the low-cut neckline of a dress
**2 :** a décolleté dress
**3 :** ¹BUST 2
¹**dé·col·le·té** \(,)dā-,käl-'tā, -,kȯl-, -lə-'tā; *also* dā-'kȯl-tā\ *adjective* [French, from past participle of *décolleter* to give a low neckline to, from *dé-* de- + *collet* collar, from Old French *colet,* from *col* collar, neck, from Latin *collum* neck] (1831)
**1 :** wearing a strapless or low-necked dress

**2 :** having a low-cut neckline
²**dé·col·le·té** *also* **de·col·le·te** *noun* (1900)
**:** DÉCOLLETAGE
**de·col·o·nize** \(,)dē-'kä-lə-,nīz\ *transitive verb* (1963)
**:** to free from colonial status
— **de·col·o·ni·za·tion** \(,)dē-,kä-lə-nə-'zā-shən\ *noun*
**de·col·or·ize** \(,)dē-'kə-lə-,rīz\ *transitive verb* **-ized; -iz·ing** (1839)
**:** to remove color from ⟨*decolorize* vinegar by adsorption of impurities on activated charcoal⟩
— **de·col·or·iza·tion** \(,)dē-,kə-lə-rə-'zā-shən\ *noun*
— **de·col·or·iz·er** \(')dē-'kə-lə-,rī-zər\ *noun*
**de·com·mis·sion** \,dē-kə-'mi-shən\ *transitive verb* (1922)
**:** to remove (as a ship or nuclear power plant) from service
**de·com·pen·sa·tion** \(,)dē-,käm-pən-'sā-shən, -,pen-\ *noun* [International Scientific Vocabulary] (circa 1903)
**:** loss of physiological compensation or psychological balance; *especially* **:** inability of the heart to maintain adequate circulation
— **de·com·pen·sate** \(,)dē-'käm-pən-,sāt, -,pen-\ *verb*
**de·com·pose** \,dē-kəm-'pōz\ *verb* [French *décomposer,* from *dé-* de- + *composer* to compose] (circa 1751)
*transitive verb*
**1 :** to separate into constituent parts or elements or into simpler compounds ⟨*decompose* water by electrolysis⟩ ⟨*decompose* a word into its base and affixes⟩
**2 :** ROT
*intransitive verb*
**:** to break up into constituent parts by or as if by a chemical process **:** DECAY, ROT ⟨fruit *decomposes*⟩
***synonym*** see DECAY
— **de·com·pos·abil·i·ty** \-,pō-zə-'bi-lə-tē\ *noun*
— **de·com·pos·able** \-'pō-zə-bəl\ *adjective*
— **de·com·po·si·tion** \(,)dē-,käm-pə-'zi-shən\ *noun*
**de·com·pos·er** \,dē-kəm-'pō-zər\ *noun* (1959)
**:** any of various organisms (as many bacteria and fungi) that return constituents of organic substances to ecological cycles by feeding on and breaking down dead protoplasm
**de·com·pound** \,dē-'käm-,paůnd, ,dē-kəm-'\ *adjective* (circa 1793)
*of a leaf* **:** having divisions that are themselves compound
**de·com·press** \,dē-kəm-'pres\ (1905)
*transitive verb*
**:** to release from pressure or compression
*intransitive verb*
**:** to undergo release from pressure; *especially* **:** RELAX ⟨need a week off to *decompress*⟩
— **de·com·pres·sion** \-'pre-shən\ *noun*
**decompression sickness** *noun* (circa 1941)
**:** ²BEND 3, AEROEMBOLISM
**de·con·cen·trate** \(,)dē-'kän(t)-sən-,trāt\ *transitive verb* (circa 1889)
**:** to reduce or abolish the concentration of **:** DECENTRALIZE
— **de·con·cen·tra·tion** \(,)dē-,kän(t)-sən-'trā-shən\ *noun*
**de·con·di·tion** \,dē-kən-'di-shən\ *transitive verb* (1941)
**1 :** to cause extinction of (a conditioned response)
**2 :** to cause to lose physical fitness
**de·con·ges·tant** \,dē-kən-'jes-tənt\ *noun* (1947)
**:** an agent that relieves congestion (as of mucous membranes)
— **decongestant** *adjective*
**de·con·ges·tion** \,dē-kən-'jes(h)-chən\ *noun* (1908)
**:** the process of relieving congestion

— **de·con·gest** \-'jest\ *transitive verb*
— **de·con·ges·tive** \-'jes-tiv\ *adjective*
**de·con·se·crate** \(,)dē-'kän(t)-sə-,krāt\ *transitive verb* (1876)
**:** to remove the sacred character of ⟨*deconsecrate* a church⟩
— **de·con·se·cra·tion** \(,)dē-,kän(t)-sə-'krā-shən\ *noun*
**de·con·struct** \,dē-kən-'strəkt\ *transitive verb* (1973)
**:** to discuss (as a work of literature) using the methods of deconstruction
— **de·con·struc·tive** \-tiv\ *adjective*
— **de·con·struc·tor** \-tər\ *noun*
**de·con·struc·tion** \,dē-kən-'strək-shən\ *noun* [French *déconstruction,* from *dé-* de- + *construction*] (1973)
**:** a method of literary criticism that assumes language refers only to itself rather than to an extratextual reality, that asserts multiple conflicting interpretations of a text, and that bases such implications on the philosophical, political, or social implications of the use of language in the text rather than on the author's intention
— **de·con·struc·tion·ist** \-shə-nist\ *noun*
**de·con·tam·i·nate** \,dē-kən-'ta-mə-,nāt\ *transitive verb* (1936)
**:** to rid of contamination (as radioactive material)
— **de·con·tam·i·na·tion** \-,ta-mə-'nā-shən\ *noun*
— **de·con·tam·i·na·tor** \-'ta-mə-,nā-tər\ *noun*
**de·con·trol** \,dē-kən-'trōl\ *transitive verb* (1919)
**:** to end control of
— **decontrol** *noun*
**de·cor** *or* **dé·cor** \dā-'kȯr, di-'; 'de-,kȯr, 'dā-\ *noun* [French *décor,* from *décorer* to decorate, from Latin *decorare*] (1897)
**1 :** a stage setting
**2 a :** DECORATION **2 b :** the style and layout of interior furnishings
**dec·o·rate** \'de-kə-,rāt\ *transitive verb* **-rat·ed; -rat·ing** [Latin *decoratus,* past participle of *decorare,* from *decor-, decus* ornament, honor — more at DECENT] (1530)
**1 :** to add honor to
**2 :** to furnish with something ornamental ⟨*decorate* a room⟩
**3 :** to award a mark of honor to
***synonym*** see ADORN
**dec·o·ra·tion** \,de-kə-'rā-shən\ *noun* (1530)
**1 :** the act or process of decorating
**2 :** something that adorns, enriches, or beautifies **:** ORNAMENT
**3 :** a badge of honor (as a U.S. military award)

---

☆ **SYNONYMS**
**Decline, refuse, reject, repudiate, spurn** mean to turn away by not accepting, receiving, or considering. DECLINE often implies courteous refusal especially of offers or invitations ⟨*declined* his party's nomination⟩. REFUSE suggests more positiveness or ungraciousness and often implies the denial of something asked for ⟨*refused* to lend them the money⟩. REJECT implies a peremptory refusal by sending away or discarding ⟨*rejected* the manuscript as unpublishable⟩. REPUDIATE implies a casting off or disowning as untrue, unauthorized, or unworthy of acceptance ⟨teenagers who *repudiate* the values of their parents⟩. SPURN stresses contempt or disdain in rejection or repudiation ⟨*spurned* his overtures of friendship⟩.

---

\ə\ **abut** \ˈə\ **kitten** \ər\ **further** \a\ **ash** \ā\ **ace**
\ä\ **mop, mar** \aů\ **out** \ch\ **chin** \e\ **bet** \ē\ **easy**
\g\ **go** \i\ **hit** \ī\ **ice** \j\ **job** \ŋ\ **sing** \ō\ **go**
\ȯ\ **law** \ȯi\ **boy** \th\ **thin** \t̶h\ **the** \ü\ **loot** \ů\ **foot**
\y\ **yet** \zh\ **vision** *see also* Guide to Pronunciation

**Decoration Day** *noun* [from the custom of decorating graves on this day] (1871)
**:** MEMORIAL DAY

**dec·o·ra·tive** \'de-k(ə-)rə-tiv, 'de-kə-,rā-\ *adjective* (1791)
**:** serving to decorate; *especially* **:** purely ornamental
— **dec·o·ra·tive·ly** *adverb*
— **dec·o·ra·tive·ness** *noun*

**decorative art** *noun* (1967)
**1 :** an art concerned primarily with the creation of useful items (as furniture, ceramics, and textiles) — usually used in plural
**2 :** objects of decorative art

¹**dec·o·ra·tor** \'de-kə-,rā-tər\ *noun* (circa 1755)
**:** one that decorates; *especially* **:** one that designs or executes interiors and their furnishings

²**decorator** *adjective* (1950)
**:** suitable for interior decoration ⟨*decorator* fabrics⟩

**dec·o·rous** \'de-kər-əs *also* di-'kōr-əs *or* -'kȯr-\ *adjective* [Latin *decorus,* from *decor* beauty, grace; akin to Latin *decēre* to be fitting — more at DECENT] (1673)
**:** marked by propriety and good taste **:** CORRECT ⟨*decorous* conduct⟩
— **dec·o·rous·ly** *adverb*
— **dec·o·rous·ness** *noun*

**de·cor·ti·ca·tion** \(,)dē-,kȯr-tə-'kā-shən\ *noun* [Latin *decortication-, decorticatio,* from *decorticare* to remove the bark, from *de-* + *cortic-, cortex* bark — more at CUIRASS] (circa 1623)
**1 :** the act or process of removing the outer coverings (as bark or husks) from something (as fiber or seed)
**2 :** the surgical removal of the cortex of an organ (as the brain), an enveloping membrane, or a constrictive fibrinous covering
— **de·cor·ti·cate** \(,)dē-'kȯr-tə-,kāt\ *transitive verb*
— **de·cor·ti·cat·or** \-,kā-tər\ *noun*

**de·co·rum** \di-'kȯr-əm, -'kȯr-\ *noun* [Latin, from neuter of *decorus*] (1576)
**1 :** literary and dramatic propriety **:** FITNESS
**2 :** propriety and good taste in conduct or appearance
**3 :** ORDERLINESS
**4** *plural* **:** the conventions of polite behavior

**de·cou·page** *or* **dé·cou·page** \,dā-(,)kü-'päzh\ *noun* [French *découpage,* literally, act of cutting out, from Middle French, from *decouper* to cut out, from *de-* + *couper* to cut — more at COPE] (1946)
**1 :** the art of decorating surfaces by applying cutouts (as of paper) and then coating with usually several layers of finish (as lacquer or varnish)
**2 :** work produced by decoupage
— **decoupage** *or* **découpage** *transitive verb*

**de·cou·ple** \(,)dē-'kə-pəl\ *transitive verb* (1953)
**:** to eliminate the interrelationship of **:** SEPARATE

¹**de·coy** \'dē-,kȯi, di-'\ *noun* [probably from Dutch *de kooi,* literally, the cage, from *de,* masculine definite article (akin to Old English *thæt,* neuter definite article) + *kooi* cage, from Latin *cavea* — more at THAT, CAGE] (1641)
**1 :** a pond into which wildfowl are lured for capture
**2 :** someone or something used to lure or lead another into a trap; *especially* **:** an artificial bird used to attract live birds within shot
**3 :** someone or something used to draw attention away from another

²**de·coy** \di-'kȯi, 'dē-,\ *transitive verb* (circa 1674)
**:** to lure by or as if by a decoy **:** ENTICE
**synonym** SEE LURE

¹**de·crease** \di-'krēs, 'dē-,\ *verb* **de·creased; de·creas·ing** [Middle English *decreessen,* from (assumed) Anglo-French *de-*

*creistre,* from Latin *decrescere,* from *de-* + *crescere* to grow — more at CRESCENT] (14th century)
*intransitive verb*
**:** to grow progressively less (as in size, amount, number, or intensity)
*transitive verb*
**:** to cause to decrease ☆
— **de·creas·ing·ly** \di-'krē-siŋ-lē, dē-\ *adverb*

²**de·crease** \'dē-,krēs, di-'\ *noun* (14th century)
**1 :** the process of decreasing
**2 :** an amount of diminution **:** REDUCTION

¹**de·cree** \di-'krē\ *noun* [Middle English, from Middle French *decré,* from Latin *decretum,* from neuter of *decretus,* past participle of *decernere* to decide, from *de-* + *cernere* to sift, decide — more at CERTAIN] (14th century)
**1 :** an order usually having the force of law
**2 a :** a religious ordinance enacted by council or titular head **b :** a foreordaining will
**3 a :** a judicial decision of the Roman emperor **b :** a judicial decision especially in an equity or probate court

²**decree** *verb* **de·creed; de·cree·ing** (14th century)
*transitive verb*
**1 :** to command or enjoin by or as if by decree ⟨*decree* an amnesty⟩
**2 :** to determine or order judicially ⟨*decree* a punishment⟩
*intransitive verb*
**:** ORDAIN
— **de·cre·er** \-'krē-ər\ *noun*

**de·cree-law** \di-'krē-,lȯ\ *noun* (1926)
**:** a decree of a ruler or ministry having the force of a law enacted by the legislature

**dec·re·ment** \'de-krə-mənt\ *noun* [Latin *decrementum,* from *decrescere*] (1610)
**1 :** a gradual decrease in quality or quantity
**2 a :** the quantity lost by diminution or waste **b :** the amount of decrease (as of a variable)
— **dec·re·men·tal** \,de-krə-'men-t°l\ *adjective*

**de·crep·it** \di-'kre-pət\ *adjective* [Middle English, from Middle French, from Latin *decrepitus*] (15th century)
**1 :** wasted and weakened by or as if by the infirmities of old age
**2 a :** impaired by use or wear **:** WORN-OUT **b :** fallen into ruin or disrepair
**3 :** DILAPIDATED, RUN-DOWN
**synonym** SEE WEAK
— **de·crep·it·ly** *adverb*

**de·crep·i·tate** \di-'kre-pə-,tāt\ *verb* [probably from (assumed) New Latin *decrepitatus,* past participle of *decrepitare,* from Latin *de-* + *crepitare* to crackle — more at CREPITATE] (1646)
*transitive verb*
**:** to roast or calcine (as salt) so as to cause crackling or until crackling stops
*intransitive verb*
**:** to become decrepitated
— **de·crep·i·ta·tion** \-,kre-pə-'tā-shən\ *noun*

**de·crep·i·tude** \di-'kre-pə-,tüd, -,tyüd\ *noun* (1603)
**:** the quality or state of being decrepit

¹**de·cre·scen·do** \,dā-krə-'shen-(,)dō\ *noun, plural* **-dos** [Italian, literally, decreasing, from Latin *decrescendum,* gerund of *decrescere*] (circa 1880)
**1 :** a gradual decrease in volume of a musical passage
**2 :** a decrescendo musical passage

²**decrescendo** *adverb or adjective* (circa 1890)
**:** with a decrease in volume — used as a direction in music

**mark indicating decrescendo 2**

**de·cres·cent** \di-'kre-s°nt\ *adjective* [alteration of earlier *decrescant,* probably from Anglo-French, present participle of (assumed) Anglo-French *decreistre* to decrease] (1610)
**:** becoming less by gradual diminution **:** DECREASING, WANING

**de·cre·tal** \di-'krē-t°l, 'de-kri-t°l\ *noun* [Middle English, from Middle French, from Late Latin *decretalis* of a decree, from Latin *decretum* decree] (14th century)
**:** DECREE; *especially* **:** a papal letter giving an authoritative decision on a point of canon law

**de·cre·tive** \-'krē-tiv\ *adjective* (1609)
**:** having the force of a decree **:** DECRETORY

**de·cre·to·ry** \'de-krə-,tōr-ē, -,tȯr-; di-'krē-tər-ē\ *adjective* (circa 1631)
**:** relating to or fixed by a decree or decision

**de·crim·i·nal·ize** \(,)dē-'kri-mə-nə-,līz, -'krim-nəl-\ *transitive verb* (1969)
**:** to remove or reduce the criminal classification or status of; *especially* **:** to repeal a strict ban on while keeping under some form of regulation ⟨*decriminalize* the possession of marijuana⟩
— **de·crim·i·nal·iza·tion** \(,)dē-,kri-mə-nə-lə-'zā-shən, -,krim-nəl-\ *noun*

**de·cry** \di-'krī, dē-\ *transitive verb* [French *décrier,* from Old French *descrier,* from *des-* + *crier* to cry] (1614)
**1 :** to depreciate (as a coin) officially or publicly
**2 :** to express strong disapproval of ⟨*decry* the emphasis on sex⟩ ☆
— **de·cri·er** \-'krī(-ə)r\ *noun*

**de·crypt** \(,)dē-'kript\ *transitive verb* [International Scientific Vocabulary *de-* + *crypt*ogram, *crypt*ograph] (1935)
**:** DECODE 1a
— **de·cryp·tion** \-'krip-shən\ *noun*

**de·cum·bent** \di-'kəm-bənt, dē-\ *adjective* [Latin *decumbent-, decumbens,* present participle of *decumbere* to lie down, from *de-* + *-cumbere* to lie down; akin to Latin *cubare* to lie] (1656)
**1 :** lying down
**2** *of a plant* **:** reclining on the ground but with ascending apex or extremity

**dec·u·ple** \'de-kyə-pəl\ *adjective* [French *décuple,* from Middle French, from Late Latin *decuplus,* from Latin *decem* ten + *-uplus* (as in *quadruplus* quadruple)] (1613)
**1 :** TENFOLD
**2 :** taken in groups of 10

**de·cu·ri·on** \di-'kyur-ē-ən\ *noun* [Middle English *decurioun,* from Latin *decurion-, decurio,* from *decuria* division of ten, from *decem*] (14th century)
**1 :** a Roman cavalry officer in command of 10 men
**2 :** a member of a Roman senate

**de·cur·rent** \di-'kər-ənt, -'kə-rənt\ *adjective* [Latin *decurrent-, decurrens,* present participle of *decurrere* to run down, from *de-* + *currere* to run — more at CAR] (circa 1753)

---

☆ **SYNONYMS**
**Decrease, lessen, diminish, reduce, abate, dwindle** mean to grow or make less. DECREASE suggests a progressive decline in size, amount, numbers, or intensity ⟨slowly *decreased* the amount of pressure⟩. LESSEN suggests a decline in amount rather than in number ⟨has been unable to *lessen* her debt⟩. DIMINISH emphasizes a perceptible loss and implies its subtraction from a total ⟨his visual acuity has *diminished*⟩. REDUCE implies a bringing down or lowering ⟨you must *reduce* your caloric intake⟩. ABATE implies a reducing of something excessive or oppressive in force or amount ⟨the storm *abated*⟩. DWINDLE implies progressive lessening and is applied to things growing visibly smaller ⟨their provisions *dwindled* slowly⟩.

: running or extending downward along the stem ⟨*decurrent* leaves⟩

**de·curved** \(ˌ)dē-'kərvd\ *adjective* [part translation of Late Latin *decurvatus,* from Latin *de-* + *curvatus* curved] (1835)
: curved downward : bent down

¹**de·cus·sate** \'de-kə-ˌsāt, di-'kə-ˌsāt\ *verb* **-sat·ed; -sat·ing** [Latin *decussatus,* past participle of *decussare* to arrange crosswise, from *decussis* the number ten, numeral X, intersection, from *decem* + *ass-,* as unit — more at ACE] (1658)
: INTERSECT, CROSS

²**de·cus·sate** \'de-kə-ˌsāt, di-'kə-sət\ *adjective* (circa 1823)
: arranged in pairs each at right angles to the next pair above or below ⟨*decussate* leaves⟩

**de·cus·sa·tion** \ˌde-kə-'sā-shən, ˌdē-kə-\ *noun* (circa 1656)
**1** : the action of crossing (as of nerve fibers) especially in the form of an X
**2** : a crossed tract of nerve fibers passing between centers on opposite sides of the nervous system

¹**ded·i·cate** \'de-di-kət\ *adjective* [Middle English, from Latin *dedicatus,* past participle of *dedicare* to dedicate, from *de-* + *dicare* to proclaim, dedicate — more at DICTION] (14th century)
: DEDICATED

²**ded·i·cate** \'de-di-ˌkāt also 'de-ˌdē-\ *transitive verb* **-cat·ed; -cat·ing** (15th century)
**1** : to devote to the worship of a divine being; *specifically* : to set apart (a church) to sacred uses with solemn rites
**2 a** : to set apart to a definite use ⟨money *dedicated* to their vacation fund⟩ **b** : to commit to a goal or way of life ⟨ready to *dedicate* his life to public service⟩
**3** : to inscribe or address by way of compliment ⟨*dedicate* a book to a friend⟩
**4** : to open to public use
*synonym* see DEVOTE
— **ded·i·ca·tor** \-ˌkā-tər\ *noun*

**ded·i·cat·ed** *adjective* (circa 1600)
**1** : devoted to a cause, ideal, or purpose : ZEALOUS ⟨a *dedicated* scholar⟩
**2** : given over to a particular purpose ⟨a *dedicated* process control computer⟩
— **ded·i·cat·ed·ly** *adverb*

**ded·i·ca·tee** \ˌde-di-kə-'tē\ *noun* (1760)
: one to whom a thing is dedicated

**ded·i·ca·tion** \ˌde-di-'kā-shən\ *noun* (14th century)
**1** : an act or rite of dedicating to a divine being or to a sacred use
**2** : a devoting or setting aside for a particular purpose
**3** : a name and often a message prefixed to a literary, musical, or artistic production in tribute to a person or cause
**4** : self-sacrificing devotion
— **ded·i·ca·to·ry** \'de-di-kə-ˌtōr-ē, -ˌtor-\ *adjective*

**de·dif·fer·en·ti·a·tion** \(ˌ)dē-ˌdi-fə-ˌren-chē-'ā-shən\ *noun* (1915)
: reversion of specialized structures (as cells) to a more generalized or primitive condition often as a preliminary to major physiological or structural change
— **de·dif·fer·en·ti·ate** \-'ren-chē-ˌāt\ *intransitive verb*

**de·duce** \di-'düs, dē-; *chiefly British* -'dyüs\ *transitive verb* **de·duced; de·duc·ing** [Middle English, from Latin *deducere,* literally, to lead away, from *de-* + *ducere* to lead — more at TOW] (15th century)
**1** : to determine by deduction; *specifically* : to infer from a general principle
**2** : to trace the course of
*synonym* see INFER
— **de·duc·ible** \-'d(y)ü-sə-bəl\ *adjective*

**de·duct** \di-'dəkt, dē-\ *transitive verb* [Latin *deductus,* past participle of *deducere*] (15th century)

**1** : to take away (an amount) from a total : SUBTRACT
**2** : DEDUCE, INFER

¹**de·duct·ible** \di-'dək-tə-bəl, dē-\ *adjective* (1856)
: allowable as a deduction
— **de·duct·ibil·i·ty** \-ˌdək-tə-'bi-lə-tē\ *noun*

²**deductible** *noun* (1929)
: a clause in an insurance policy that relieves the insurer of responsibility for an initial specified loss of the kind insured against; *also* : the amount of the loss specified in such a clause

**de·duc·tion** \di-'dək-shən, dē-\ *noun* (15th century)
**1 a** : an act of taking away ⟨*deduction* of legitimate business expenses⟩ **b** : something that is or may be subtracted ⟨*deductions* from his taxable income⟩
**2 a** : the deriving of a conclusion by reasoning; *specifically* : inference in which the conclusion about particulars follows necessarily from general or universal premises — compare INDUCTION **b** : a conclusion reached by logical deduction

**de·duc·tive** \di-'dək-tiv, dē-\ *adjective* (1665)
**1** : of, relating to, or provable by deduction
**2** : employing deduction in reasoning
— **de·duc·tive·ly** *adverb*

**dee** \'dē\ *noun* (13th century)
**1** : the letter *d*
**2** : something shaped like the letter D

¹**deed** \'dēd\ *noun* [Middle English *dede,* from Old English *dǣd;* akin to Old English *dōn* to do] (before 12th century)
**1** : something that is done ⟨evil *deeds*⟩
**2** : a usually illustrious act or action : FEAT, EXPLOIT
**3** : the act of performing : ACTION ⟨righteous in word and in *deed*⟩
**4** : a signed and usually sealed instrument containing some legal transfer, bargain, or contract
— **deed·less** \-ləs\ *adjective*

²**deed** *transitive verb* (1806)
: to convey or transfer by deed

**deed poll** \-'pōl\ *noun, plural* **deeds poll** [¹*deed* + *poll,* adjective (having the edges cut even rather than indented), from ²*poll*] (1588)
*British* : a deed (as to change one's name) made and executed by only one party

**deedy** \'dē-dē\ *adjective* **deed·i·er; -est** (1615)
*dialect chiefly English* : INDUSTRIOUS

**dee·jay** \'dē-ˌjā\ *noun* [*disc jockey*] (circa 1949)
: DISC JOCKEY

**deem** \'dēm\ *verb* [Middle English *demen,* from Old English *dēman;* akin to Old High German *tuomen* to judge, Old English *dōm* doom] (before 12th century)
*transitive verb*
: to come to think or judge : CONSIDER ⟨*deemed* it wise to go slow⟩
*intransitive verb*
: to have an opinion : BELIEVE

**de-em·pha·size** \(ˌ)dē-'em(p)-fə-ˌsīz\ *transitive verb* (1938)
: to reduce in relative importance; *also* : PLAY DOWN
— **de-em·pha·sis** \-fə-səs\ *noun*

**de-en·er·gize** \ˌdē-'e-nər-ˌjīz\ *transitive verb* (1925)
: to disconnect from a source of electricity : shut off the power to

¹**deep** \'dēp\ *adjective* [Middle English *dep,* from Old English *dēop;* akin to Old High German *tiof* deep, Old English *dyppan* to dip — more at DIP] (before 12th century)
**1** : extending far from some surface or area: as **a** : extending far downward ⟨a *deep* well⟩ **b** (1) : extending well inward from an outer surface ⟨a *deep* gash⟩ ⟨a *deep*-chested animal⟩ (2) : not located superficially within the body ⟨*deep* pressure receptors in muscles⟩ **c** : extending well back from a surface accepted as

front ⟨a *deep* closet⟩ **d** : extending far laterally from the center ⟨*deep* borders of lace⟩ **e** : occurring or located near the outer limits of the playing area ⟨hit to *deep* right field⟩ **f** : thrown deep ⟨a *deep* pass⟩
**2** : having a specified extension in an implied direction usually downward or backward ⟨a shelf 20 inches *deep*⟩ ⟨cars parked three-*deep*⟩
**3 a** : difficult to penetrate or comprehend : RECONDITE ⟨*deep* mathematical problems⟩ **b** : MYSTERIOUS, OBSCURE ⟨a *deep* dark secret⟩ **c** : grave in nature or effect ⟨in *deepest* disgrace⟩ **d** : of penetrating intellect : WISE ⟨*deep* thinker⟩ **e** : INVOLVED, ENGROSSED ⟨*deep* in debt⟩ **f** : characterized by profundity of feeling or quality ⟨a *deep* sleep⟩; *also* : DEEP-SEATED ⟨*deep* religious beliefs⟩
**4 a** *of color* : high in saturation and low in lightness **b** : having a low musical pitch or pitch range ⟨a *deep* voice⟩
**5 a** : situated well within the boundaries ⟨a house *deep* in the woods⟩ **b** : remote in time or space **c** : being below the level of the conscious ⟨*deep* neuroses⟩ **d** : covered, enclosed, or filled to a specified degree — usually used in combination ⟨ankle-*deep* in mud⟩
**6** : LARGE ⟨*deep* discounts⟩
**7** : having many good players ⟨a *deep* bull pen⟩
*synonym* see BROAD
— **deep·ly** *adverb*
— **deep·ness** *noun*
— **in deep water** : in difficulty or distress

²**deep** *adverb* (before 12th century)
**1** : to a great depth : DEEPLY ⟨still waters run *deep*⟩
**2** : far on : LATE ⟨danced *deep* into the night⟩
**3 a** : near the outer limits of the playing area ⟨the shortstop was playing *deep*⟩ **b** : LONG 6

³**deep** *noun* (before 12th century)
**1 a** : a vast or immeasurable extent : ABYSS **b** (1) : the extent of surrounding space or time (2) : OCEAN
**2** : any of the deep portions of a body of water; *specifically* : a generally long and narrow area in the ocean where the depth exceeds 3000 fathoms (5500 meters)
**3** : the middle or most intense part ⟨the *deep* of winter⟩
**4** : any of the fathom points on a sounding line other than the marks

**deep–dish pie** *noun* (1918)
: a pie usually with a fruit filling and no bottom crust that is baked in a deep dish

**deep·en** \'dē-pən\ *verb* **deep·ened; deep·en·ing** \'dē-pə-niŋ, 'dēp-niŋ\ (1598)
*transitive verb*
: to make deep or deeper
*intransitive verb*
: to become deeper or more profound

**deep fat** *noun* (1921)
: hot fat or oil deep enough in a cooking utensil to cover the food to be fried

---

☆ **SYNONYMS**
**Decry, depreciate, disparage, belittle** mean to express a low opinion of. DECRY implies open condemnation with intent to discredit ⟨*decried* their defeatist attitude⟩. DEPRECIATE implies a representing as being of less value than commonly believed ⟨critics *depreciate* his plays for being unabashedly sentimental⟩. DISPARAGE implies depreciation by indirect means such as slighting or invidious comparison ⟨*disparaged* polo as a game for the rich⟩. BELITTLE usually suggests a contemptuous or envious attitude ⟨*belittled* the achievements of others⟩.

---

\ə\ abut \ᵊ\ kitten \ər\ further \a\ ash \ā\ ace \ä\ mop, mar \au̇\ out \ch\ chin \e\ bet \ē\ easy \g\ go \i\ hit \ī\ ice \j\ job \ŋ\ sing \ō\ go \ȯ\ law \ȯi\ boy \th\ thin \th\ the \ü\ loot \u̇\ foot \y\ yet \zh\ vision *see also* Guide to Pronunciation

**Deep·freeze** \'dēp-ˌfrēz\ *trademark*
— used for a freezer for food storage
**deep–freeze** \'dēp-'frēz\ *transitive verb*
**-froze** \-'frōz\; **-fro·zen** \-'frō-zᵊn\ (1943)
**1 :** QUICK-FREEZE
**2 :** to store in a frozen state
**deep freeze** \'dēp-ˌfrēz\ *noun* (1948)
**1 :** COLD STORAGE 2 ⟨a bill presently in *deep freeze* awaiting a new congress —*Newsweek*⟩
**2 :** intense cold
**deep–fry** \'dēp-'frī\ *transitive verb* (1922)
**:** to cook in deep fat
**deep fryer** *noun* (1950)
**:** a utensil suitable for deep-fat frying
**deep pocket** *noun* (1976)
**1 :** a person or an organization having substantial financial resources
**2** *plural* **:** substantial financial resources
**deep–root·ed** \'dēp-'rü-təd, -'ru̇-\ *adjective* (15th century)
**:** deeply implanted or established ⟨a *deep-rooted* loyalty⟩
**synonym** see INVETERATE
**deep–sea** \'dēp-'sē\ *adjective* (1626)
**:** of, relating to, or occurring in the deeper parts of the sea ⟨*deep-sea* fishing⟩
**deep–seat·ed** \'dēp-'sē-təd\ *adjective* (1741)
**1 :** situated far below the surface ⟨a *deep-seated* inflammation⟩
**2 :** firmly established ⟨a *deep-seated* tradition⟩
**synonym** see INVETERATE
**deep–six** \'dēp-'siks\ *transitive verb* (1952)
**1** *slang* **:** to throw away : DISCARD
**2** *slang* **:** to throw overboard
**deep six** *noun* [from the leadsman's call *by the deep six* for a depth corresponding to the sixth deep on a sounding line] (1944)
*slang* **:** a place of disposal or abandonment — used especially in the phrase *give it the deep six*
**deep–sky** \'dēp-ˌskī\ *adjective* (1968)
**:** relating to or existing in space outside the solar system ⟨*deep-sky* objects⟩
**deep space** *noun* (circa 1952)
**:** space well outside the earth's atmosphere and especially that part lying beyond the earth-moon system
**deep structure** *noun* (1964)
**:** a formal representation of the underlying semantic content of a sentence; *also* **:** the structure which such a representation specifies
**deep throat** *noun, often D&T capitalized* [from the nickname given to such an informant in the Watergate scandal by Bob Woodward (born 1943) U.S. journalist, from the title of a pornographic film (1972)] (1973)
**:** an informant who divulges damaging information under cover of anonymity
**deep·wa·ter** \'dēp-ˌwȯ-tər, -ˌwä-\ *adjective* (1795)
**:** of, relating to, or characterized by water of considerable depth; *especially* **:** able to accommodate oceangoing vessels ⟨*deepwater* ports⟩
**deer** \'dir\ *noun, plural* **deer** *also* **deers** [Middle English, deer, animal, from Old English *dēor* beast; akin to Old High German *tior* wild animal, Lithuanian *dvasia* breath, spirit] (before 12th century)
**1** *archaic* **:** ANIMAL; *especially* **:** a small mammal
**2 :** any of numerous ruminant mammals (family Cervidae, the deer family) having two large and two small hooves on each foot and antlers borne by the males of nearly all and by the females of a few forms ◆
— **deer·like** \-ˌlīk\ *adjective*
**deer·ber·ry** \-ˌber-ē\ *noun* (1814)
**1 :** either of two shrubs (*Vaccinium stamineum* or *V. caesium*) of dry woods and scrub of the eastern U.S.
**2 :** the edible fruit of a deerberry
**deer·fly** \'dir-ˌflī\ *noun* (1853)
**:** any of numerous small horseflies (as of the genus *Chrysops*) that include important vectors of tularemia
**deer·hound** \-ˌhau̇nd\ *noun* (1818)

**:** SCOTTISH DEERHOUND
**deer mouse** *noun* [from its agility] (1833)
**:** WHITE-FOOTED MOUSE; *especially* **:** a mouse (*Peromyscus maniculatus*) widely distributed in forests and grasslands of North America and Mexico
**deer·skin** \'dir-ˌskin\ *noun* (14th century)
**:** leather made from the skin of a deer; *also* **:** a garment of this leather
**deer·stalk·er** \-ˌstȯ-kər\ *noun* (1870)
**:** a close-fitting hat with a visor at the front and the back and with earflaps that may be worn up or down — called also *deerstalker cap, deerstalker hat*
**deer tick** *noun* (1982)
**:** an ixodid tick (*Ixodes dammini*) that transmits the bacterium causing Lyme disease
**deer·yard** \'dir-ˌyärd\ *noun* (1849)
**:** a place where deer herd in winter

deerstalker

**de–es·ca·late** \(ˌ)dē-'es-kə-ˌlāt, ÷-kyə-\ (1964)
*transitive verb*
**:** LIMIT 2b
*intransitive verb*
**:** to decrease in extent, volume, or scope
— **de·es·ca·la·tion** \(ˌ)dē-ˌes-kə-'lā-shən, ÷-kyə-\ *noun*
— **de·es·ca·la·to·ry** \(ˌ)dē-'es-kə-lə-ˌtȯr-ē, -ˌtȯr-, ÷-kyə-\ *adjective*
**deet** \'dēt\ *noun, often all capitalized* [probably from *d. e. t.*, from *di-* + *ethyl* + *toluamide* (C₈H₉NO)] (1962)
**:** a colorless oily liquid insect repellent $C_{12}H_{17}NO$
**de·face** \di-'fās, dē-\ *transitive verb* [Middle English, from Middle French *desfacier*, from Old French, from *des-* de- + *face* front, face] (14th century)
**1 :** to mar the external appearance of : injure by effacing significant details ⟨*deface* an inscription⟩
**2 :** IMPAIR
**3** *obsolete* **:** DESTROY
— **de·face·ment** \-'fās-mənt\ *noun*
— **de·fac·er** *noun*
**¹de fac·to** \di-'fak-(ˌ)tō, dā-, dē-\ *adverb* [Medieval Latin, literally, from the fact] (1601)
**:** in reality **:** ACTUALLY
**²de facto** *adjective* (1696)
**1 :** ACTUAL; *especially* **:** being such in effect though not formally recognized ⟨a *de facto* state of war⟩
**2 :** exercising power as if legally constituted ⟨a *de facto* government⟩
**de·fal·cate** \di-'fal-ˌkāt, -'fȯl-, dē-; 'de-fəl-\ *verb* **-cat·ed; -cat·ing** [Medieval Latin *defalcatus*, past participle of *defalcare*, from Latin *de-* + *falc-, falx* sickle] (1540)
*transitive verb*
*archaic* **:** DEDUCT, CURTAIL
*intransitive verb*
**:** to engage in embezzlement
— **de·fal·ca·tor** \-ˌkā-tər\ *noun*
**de·fal·ca·tion** \ˌdē-fal-'kā-shən, ˌdē-ˌfȯl-, di-; ˌde-fəl-\ *noun* (15th century)
**1** *archaic* **:** DEDUCTION
**2 :** the act or an instance of embezzling
**3 :** a failure to meet a promise or an expectation
**def·a·ma·tion** \ˌde-fə-'mā-shən\ *noun* (14th century)
**:** the act of defaming another **:** CALUMNY
— **de·fam·a·to·ry** \di-'fa-mə-ˌtȯr-ē, dē-, -ˌtȯr-\ *adjective*
**de·fame** \di-'fām, dē-\ *transitive verb* **de·famed; de·fam·ing** [Middle English, from Middle French & Medieval Latin; Middle French *defamer*, from Medieval Latin *defamare*, alteration of Latin *diffamare*, from *dis-* + *fama* reputation, fame] (14th century)
**1** *archaic* **:** DISGRACE

**2 :** to harm the reputation of by libel or slander
**3** *archaic* **:** ACCUSE
**synonym** see MALIGN
— **de·fam·er** *noun*
**de·fang** \(ˌ)dē-'faŋ\ *transitive verb* (1953)
**:** to make harmless or less powerful
**de·fat** \(ˌ)dē-'fat\ *transitive verb* (1919)
**:** to remove fat from
**¹de·fault** \di-'fȯlt, dē-; 'dē-ˌfȯlt\ *noun* [Middle English *defaute, defaulte*, from Old French *defaute, defaulte*, from *defaillir* to be lacking, fail, from *de-* + *faillir* to fail] (13th century)
**1 :** failure to do something required by duty or law **:** NEGLECT
**2** *archaic* **:** FAULT
**3 :** a failure to pay financial debts
**4 a :** failure to appear at the required time in a legal proceeding **b :** failure to compete in or to finish an appointed contest
**5 :** a selection automatically used by a computer program in the absence of a choice made by the user
— **in default of :** in the absence of
**²default** (15th century)
*intransitive verb*
**:** to fail to fulfill a contract, agreement, or duty: as **a :** to fail to meet a financial obligation **b :** to fail to appear in court **c :** to fail to compete in or to finish an appointed contest; *also* **:** to forfeit a contest by such failure
*transitive verb*
**1 :** to fail to perform, pay, or make good
**2 a :** FORFEIT **b :** to exclude (a player or a team) from a contest by default
— **de·fault·er** *noun*
**de·fea·sance** \di-'fē-zən(t)s\ *noun* [Middle English *defesance*, from Anglo-French, from Old French *deffesant*, present participle of *deffaire*] (15th century)
**1 a** (1) **:** the termination of a property interest in accordance with stipulated conditions (as in a deed) (2) **:** an instrument stating such conditions of limitation **b :** a rendering null or void
**2 :** DEFEAT, OVERTHROW
**de·fea·si·ble** \di-'fē-zə-bəl\ *adjective* (15th century)
**:** capable of being annulled or made void ⟨a *defeasible* claim⟩
— **de·fea·si·bil·i·ty** \-ˌfē-zə-'bi-lə-tē\ *noun*
**¹de·feat** \di-'fēt, dē-\ *transitive verb* [Middle English *deffeten*, from Middle French *deffait*, past participle of *deffaire* to destroy, from Old French *desfaire*, from Medieval Latin *disfacere*, from Latin *dis-* + *facere* to do — more at DO] (14th century)
**1** *obsolete* **:** DESTROY
**2 a :** NULLIFY ⟨*defeat* an estate⟩ **b :** FRUSTRATE 2a(1) ⟨*defeat* a hope⟩
**3 :** to win victory over **:** BEAT ⟨*defeat* the opposing team⟩
**synonym** see CONQUER

◇ WORD HISTORY
**deer** In English the development of a word's meaning is sometimes from the general to the specific. For instance, *deer* is used in modern English to refer to several animals, including the white-tailed deer, reindeer, elk, and moose, that belong to the same zoological family. In Old English, however, *dēor* could refer to any animal, tame or wild, or to wild animals collectively. In time, *deer* came to be used only for wild animals that were hunted and then quite specifically for the red deer, which was once the primary object of the hunt in England. From that rather narrow usage, *deer* has expanded to the other members of its family mentioned above, thereby becoming somewhat more general again, though not as general as it once was.

**²defeat** *noun* (1590)
**1 :** frustration by nullification or by prevention of success ⟨the bill suffered *defeat* in the Senate⟩
**2** *obsolete* **:** DESTRUCTION
**3 a :** an overthrow especially of an army in battle **b :** the loss of a contest
**de·feat·ism** \di-'fē-‚ti-zəm, dē-\ *noun* (1918)
**:** acceptance or expectation of or resignation to defeat
— **de·feat·ist** \-tist\ *noun or adjective*
**de·fea·ture** \di-'fē-chər, dē-\ *noun* [probably from *de-* + *feature*] (1590)
**1** *archaic* **:** DISFIGUREMENT
**2** *archaic* **:** DEFEAT
**def·e·cate** \'de-fi-‚kāt\ *verb* **-cat·ed; -cat·ing** [Latin *defaecatus,* past participle of *defaecare,* from *de-* + *faec-, faex* dregs, lees] (1575)
*transitive verb*
**1 :** to free from impurity or corruption
**2 :** to discharge from the anus
*intransitive verb*
**:** to discharge feces from the bowels
— **def·e·ca·tion** \‚de-fi-'kā-shən\ *noun*
**¹de·fect** \'dē-‚fekt, di-'\ *noun* [Middle English, from Middle French, from Latin *defectus* lack, from *deficere* to desert, fail, from *de-* + *facere* to do — more at DO] (15th century)
**1 a :** an imperfection that impairs worth or utility **:** SHORTCOMING ⟨the grave *defects* in our foreign policy⟩ **b :** an imperfection (as a vacancy or a foreign atom) in a crystal lattice
**2** [Latin *defectus*] **:** a lack of something necessary for completeness, adequacy, or perfection **:** DEFICIENCY ⟨a hearing *defect*⟩
**²de·fect** \di-'fekt\ *intransitive verb* [Latin *defectuš,* past participle of *deficere*] (1596)
**1 :** to forsake one cause, party, or nation for another often because of a change in ideology
**2 :** to leave one situation (as a job) often to go over to a rival ⟨the reporter *defected* to another network⟩
— **de·fec·tor** \-'fek-tər\ *noun*
**de·fec·tion** \di-'fek-shən\ *noun* (1552)
**:** conscious abandonment of allegiance or duty (as to a person, cause, or doctrine) **:** DESERTION
**¹de·fec·tive** \di-'fek-tiv\ *adjective* (14th century)
**1 a :** imperfect in form or function **:** FAULTY ⟨a *defective* pane of glass⟩ **b :** falling below the norm in structure or in mental or physical function ⟨*defective* eyesight⟩
**2 :** lacking one or more of the usual forms of grammatical inflection ⟨*must* is a *defective* verb⟩
— **de·fec·tive·ly** *adverb*
— **de·fec·tive·ness** *noun*
**²defective** *noun* (1881)
**:** a person who is subnormal physically or mentally
**de·fem·i·nize** \(‚)dē-'fe-mə-‚nīz\ *transitive verb* (1907)
**:** to divest of feminine qualities or characteristics **:** MASCULINIZE
— **de·fem·i·ni·za·tion** \(‚)dē-‚fe-mə-nə-'zā-shən\ *noun*
**de·fence, de·fence·man** *chiefly British variant of* DEFENSE, DEFENSEMAN
**de·fend** \di-'fend\ *verb* [Middle English, from Old French *defendre,* from Latin *defendere,* from *de-* + *-fendere* to strike; akin to Old English *gūth* battle, war, Greek *theinein* to strike] (14th century)
*transitive verb*
**1 a :** to drive danger or attack away from **b** (1) **:** to maintain or support in the face of argument or hostile criticism (2) **:** to prove (as a doctoral thesis) valid by answering questions in an oral exam **c :** to attempt to prevent an opponent from scoring at ⟨elects to *defend* the south goal⟩
**2** *archaic* **:** PREVENT, FORBID
**3 :** to act as attorney for

**4 :** to deny or oppose the right of a plaintiff in regard to (a suit or a wrong charged) **:** CONTEST
**5 :** to seek to retain (as a title or position) against a challenge in a contest
*intransitive verb*
**1 :** to take action against attack or challenge ⟨couldn't fight back, could only *defend*⟩
**2 :** to play or be on defense ⟨playing deep to *defend* against a pass⟩
**3 :** to play against the high bidder in a card game ☆
— **de·fend·able** \'fen-də-bəl\ *adjective*
**¹de·fen·dant** \di-'fen-dənt, *in legal circles often* -‚dant\ *noun* (14th century)
**:** a person required to make answer in a legal action or suit — compare PLAINTIFF
**²defendant** *adjective* (15th century)
**:** being on the defensive **:** DEFENDING
**de·fend·er** \di-'fen-dər\ *noun* (14th century)
**1 :** one that defends
**2 :** a player in a sport (as football) assigned to a defensive position
**de·fen·es·tra·tion** \(‚)dē-‚fe-nə-'strā-shən\ *noun* [*de-* + Latin *fenestra* window] (1620)
**:** a throwing of a person or thing out of a window
— **de·fen·es·trate** \(‚)dē-'fe-nə-‚strāt\ *transitive verb*
**¹de·fense** \di-'fen(t)s; *as antonym of* "offense," *often* 'dē-\ *noun* [Middle English, from Middle French, from Late Latin *defensa* vengeance, from Latin, feminine of *defensus,* past participle of *defendere*] (14th century)
**1 a :** the act or action of defending ⟨the *defense* of our country⟩ ⟨speak out in *defense* of justice⟩ **b :** a defendant's denial, answer, or plea
**2 a :** capability of resisting attack **b :** defensive play or ability ⟨a player known for good *defense*⟩
**3 a :** means or method of defending or protecting oneself, one's team, or another; *also* **:** a defensive structure **b :** an argument in support or justification **c :** the collected facts and method adopted by a defendant to protect himself against a plaintiff's action **d :** a sequence of moves available in chess to the second player in the opening
**4 a :** a defending party or group (as in a court of law) ⟨the *defense* rests⟩ **b :** a defensive team
**5 :** the military and industrial aggregate that authorizes and supervises arms production ⟨appropriations for *defense*⟩ ⟨*defense* contract⟩
— **de·fense·less** \-ləs\ *adjective*
— **de·fense·less·ly** *adverb*
— **de·fense·less·ness** *noun*
**²defense** *transitive verb* **de·fensed; de·fens·ing** (1950)
**:** to take specific defensive action against (an opposing team or player or an offensive play)
**de·fense·man** \-mən, -‚man\ *noun* (1895)
**:** a player in a sport (as hockey) who is assigned to a defensive zone or position
**defense mechanism** *noun* (1913)
**1 :** an often unconscious mental process (as repression) that makes possible compromise solutions to personal problems
**2 :** a defensive reaction by an organism
**de·fen·si·ble** \di-'fen(t)-sə-bəl\ *adjective* (14th century)
**:** capable of being defended
— **de·fen·si·bil·i·ty** \di-‚fen(t)-sə-'bi-lə-tē, ‚dē-\ *noun*
— **de·fen·si·bly** \-blē\ *adverb*
**¹de·fen·sive** \di-'fen(t)-siv, 'dē-‚\ *adjective* (14th century)
**1 :** serving to defend or protect
**2 a :** devoted to resisting or preventing aggression or attack **b :** of or relating to the attempt to keep an opponent from scoring in a game or contest
**3 a :** valuable in defensive play ⟨a *defensive* card in bridge⟩ **b :** designed to keep an opponent from being the highest bidder ⟨a *defensive* bid⟩

— **de·fen·sive·ly** *adverb*
— **de·fen·sive·ness** *noun*
**²defensive** *noun* (1601)
**:** a defensive position
— **on the defensive :** in the state or condition of being prepared for an expected aggression or attack
**¹de·fer** \di-'fər\ *transitive verb* **de·ferred; de·fer·ring** [Middle English *deferren, differren,* from Middle French *differer,* from Latin *differre* to postpone, be different — more at DIFFER] (14th century)
**1 :** PUT OFF, DELAY
**2 :** to postpone induction of (a person) into military service ☆
— **de·fer·rer** *noun*
**²defer** *verb* **deferred; deferring** [Middle English *deferren, differren,* from Middle French *deferer, defferer,* from Late Latin *deferre,* from Latin, to bring down, bring, from *de-* + *ferre* to carry — more at BEAR] (15th century)
*transitive verb*
**:** to delegate to another ⟨he could *defer* his job to no one —J. A. Michener⟩
*intransitive verb*
**:** to submit to another's wishes, opinion, or governance usually through deference or respect ⟨*deferred* to her father's wishes⟩
**synonym** see YIELD
**def·er·ence** \'de-fə-rən(t)s, 'def-rən(t)s\ *noun* (1660)
**:** respect and esteem due a superior or an elder; *also* **:** affected or ingratiating regard for another's wishes
**synonym** see HONOR
— **in deference to :** in consideration of
**def·er·ent** \'de-fə-rənt, 'def-rənt\ *adjective* [back-formation from *deference*] (1822)
**:** DEFERENTIAL
**def·er·en·tial** \‚de-fə-'ren-chəl\ *adjective* (1822)
**:** showing or expressing deference ⟨*deferential* attention⟩

---

☆ **SYNONYMS**
**Defend, protect, shield, guard, safeguard** mean to keep secure from danger or against attack. DEFEND denotes warding off actual or threatened attack ⟨*defend* the country⟩. PROTECT implies the use of something (as a covering) as a bar to the admission or impact of what may attack or injure ⟨a hard hat to *protect* your head⟩. SHIELD suggests protective intervention in imminent danger or actual attack ⟨*shielded* her eyes from the sun with her hand⟩. GUARD implies protecting with vigilance and force against expected danger ⟨White House entrances are well *guarded*⟩. SAFEGUARD implies taking precautionary protective measures against merely possible danger ⟨our civil liberties must be *safeguarded*⟩. See in addition MAINTAIN.

**Defer, postpone, suspend, stay** mean to delay an action or proceeding. DEFER implies a deliberate putting off to a later time ⟨*deferred* buying a car until spring⟩. POSTPONE implies an intentional deferring usually to a definite time ⟨the game is *postponed* until Saturday⟩. SUSPEND implies temporary stoppage with an added suggestion of waiting until some condition is satisfied ⟨business will be *suspended* while repairs are under way⟩. STAY often suggests the stopping or checking by an intervening agency or authority ⟨the governor *stayed* the execution⟩.

---

\ə\ abut \ᵊ\ kitten \ər\ **further** \a\ ash \ā\ ace
\ä\ mop, mar \au̇\ out \ch\ chin \e\ bet \ē\ easy
\g\ go \i\ hit \ī\ ice \j\ job \ŋ\ sing \ō\ go
\ȯ\ law \ȯi\ boy \th\ thin \t͟h\ the \ü\ loot \u̇\ foot
\y\ yet \zh\ vision *see also* Guide to Pronunciation

— **def·er·en·tial·ly** \-'ren-chə-lē\ *adverb*
**de·fer·ment** \di-'fər-mənt\ *noun* (1612)
: the act of delaying or postponing; *specifically* : official postponement of military service
**de·fer·ra·ble** \di-'fər-ə-bəl\ *adjective* (1943)
: capable of or suitable or eligible for being deferred
— **deferrable** *noun*
**de·fer·ral** \di-'fər-əl\ *noun* (1895)
: the act of delaying : POSTPONEMENT
**de·ferred** *adjective* (1651)
**1** : withheld for or until a stated time ⟨a *deferred* payment⟩
**2** : charged in cases of delayed handling ⟨a *deferred* rate⟩
**de·fer·ves·cence** \dē-(,)fər-'ve-sᵊn(t)s, ,de-fər-\ *noun* [German *Deferveszenz,* from Latin *defervescent-, defervescens,* present participle of *defervescere* to stop boiling, from *de-* + *fervescere* to begin to boil — more at EFFERVESCE] (1866)
: the subsidence of a fever
**de·fi·ance** \di-'fī-ən(t)s, dē-\ *noun* (15th century)
**1** : the act or an instance of defying : CHALLENGE
**2** : disposition to resist : willingness to contend or fight
— **in defiance of** : contrary to : DESPITE
**de·fi·ant** \-ənt\ *adjective* [French *défiant,* from Old French, present participle of *defier* to defy] (circa 1837)
: full of defiance : BOLD
— **de·fi·ant·ly** *adverb*
**de·fi·bril·la·tor** \(,)dē-'fi-brə-,lā-tər\ *noun* (1952)
: an electronic device that applies an electric shock to restore the rhythm of a fibrillating heart
— **de·fi·bril·late** \-,lāt\ *transitive verb*
— **de·fi·bril·la·tion** \-,fi-brə-'lā-shən\ *noun*
**de·fi·brin·ate** \(,)dē-'fi-brə-,nāt, -'fī-\ *transitive verb* **-at·ed; -at·ing** (1845)
: to remove fibrin from ⟨blood⟩
— **de·fi·brin·ation** \(,)dē-,fi-brə-'nā-shən, -,fī-\ *noun*
**de·fi·cien·cy** \di-'fi-shən-sē\ *noun, plural* **-cies** (1634)
**1** : the quality or state of being deficient : INADEQUACY
**2** : an amount that is lacking or inadequate : SHORTAGE: as **a** : a shortage of substances necessary to health **b** : DELETION 2b(1)
**deficiency disease** *noun* (1912)
: a disease (as scurvy) caused by a lack of essential dietary elements and especially a vitamin or mineral
**¹de·fi·cient** \di-'fi-shənt\ *adjective* [Latin *deficient-, deficiens,* present participle of *deficere* to be wanting — more at DEFECT] (1581)
**1** : lacking in some necessary quality or element ⟨*deficient* in judgment⟩
**2** : not up to a normal standard or complement : DEFECTIVE ⟨*deficient* strength⟩
— **de·fi·cient·ly** *adverb*
**²deficient** *noun* (1906)
: one that is deficient ⟨a mental *deficient*⟩
**def·i·cit** \'de-fə-sət, *British also* di-'fis-ət *or* 'dē-fə-sət\ *noun* [French *déficit,* from Latin *deficit* it is wanting, 3d singular present indicative of *deficere*] (1782)
**1 a** (1) : deficiency in amount or quality ⟨a *deficit* in rainfall⟩ (2) : a lack or impairment in a functional capacity ⟨cognitive *deficits*⟩ ⟨a hearing *deficit*⟩ **b** : DISADVANTAGE ⟨scored two runs to overcome a 2–1 *deficit*⟩
**2 a** : an excess of expenditure over revenue **b** : a loss in business operations
**deficit spending** *noun* (1938)
: the spending of public funds raised by borrowing rather than by taxation
**de·fi·er** \di-'fī(-ə)r\ *noun* (1585)
: one that defies
**def·i·lade** \'de-fə-,lād, -,läd\ *transitive verb* **-lad·ed; -lad·ing** [probably from *de-* + *-filade* (as in *enfilade*)] (1828)

: to arrange (fortifications) so as to protect the lines from frontal or enfilading fire and the interior from fire from above or behind
— **defilade** *noun*
**¹de·file** \di-'fī(ə)l, dē-\ *transitive verb* **de·filed; de·fil·ing** [Middle English, alteration (influenced by Old English *fȳlan* to defile) of *defoulen* to trample, defile, from Old French *defouler* to trample, from *de-* + *fouler* to trample, literally, to full — more at FULL] (14th century)
: to make unclean or impure: as **a** : to corrupt the purity or perfection of : DEBASE ⟨the countryside *defiled* by billboards⟩ **b** : to violate the chastity of : DEFLOWER **c** : to make physically unclean especially with something unpleasant or contaminating ⟨boots *defiled* with blood⟩ **d** : to violate the sanctity of : DESECRATE ⟨*defile* a sanctuary⟩ **e** : SULLY, DISHONOR
**synonym** see CONTAMINATE
— **de·file·ment** \-'fī(ə)l-mənt\ *noun*
— **de·fil·er** \-'fī-lər\ *noun*
**²de·file** \di-'fī(ə)l, 'dē-,fīl\ *noun* [French *défilé,* from past participle of *défiler*] (1685)
: a narrow passage or gorge
**³de·file** \di-'fī(ə)l, 'dē-,fīl\ *intransitive verb* **de·filed; de·fil·ing** [French *défiler,* from *dé-* + *filer* to move in a column — more at FILE] (1705)
: to march off in a line
**de·fin·able** \di-'fī-nə-bəl\ *adjective* (circa 1660)
**1** : able to be defined
**2** : able to be specified to have a particular function or operation ⟨*definable* keys⟩
— **de·fin·ably** \-'fī-nə-blē\ *adverb*
**de·fine** \di-'fīn\ *verb* **de·fined; de·fin·ing** [Middle English, from Middle French & Latin; Middle French *definer,* from Latin *definire,* from *de-* + *finire* to limit, end, from *finis* boundary, end] (14th century)
*transitive verb*
**1 a** : to determine or identify the essential qualities or meaning of ⟨whatever *defines* us as human⟩ **b** : to discover and set forth the meaning of (as a word) **c** : to create on a computer ⟨*define* a window⟩ ⟨*define* a procedure⟩
**2 a** : to fix or mark the limits of : DEMARCATE ⟨rigidly *defined* property lines⟩ **b** : to make distinct, clear, or detailed especially in outline ⟨the issues aren't too well *defined*⟩
**3** : CHARACTERIZE, DISTINGUISH ⟨you *define* yourself by the choices you make —*Denison University Bulletin*⟩
*intransitive verb*
: to make a definition
— **de·fine·ment** \-'fīn-mənt\ *noun*
— **de·fin·er** \-'fī-nər\ *noun*
**de·fin·i·en·dum** \di-,fi-nē-'en-dəm\ *noun, plural* **-da** \-də\ [Latin, something to be defined, neuter of *definiendus,* gerundive of *definire*] (1871)
: an expression that is being defined
**de·fin·i·ens** \di-'fi-nē-,enz\ *noun, plural* **de·fin·i·en·tia** \di-,fi-nē-'en(t)-shē-ə\ [Latin, present participle of *definire*] (1871)
: an expression that defines : DEFINITION
**def·i·nite** \'de-fə-nit, 'def-nət\ *adjective* [Latin *definitus,* past participle of *definire*] (1553)
**1** : having distinct or certain limits ⟨set *definite* standards for pupils to meet⟩
**2 a** : free of all ambiguity, uncertainty, or obscurity ⟨demanded a *definite* answer⟩ **b** : UNQUESTIONABLE, DECIDED ⟨the quarterback was a *definite* hero today⟩
**3** : typically designating an identified or immediately identifiable person or thing ⟨the *definite* article *the*⟩
**4 a** : being constant in number, usually less than 20, and occurring in multiples of the petal number ⟨stamens *definite*⟩ **b** : CYMOSE ⟨a *definite* inflorescence⟩
**synonym** see EXPLICIT
— **def·i·nite·ly** *adverb*
— **def·i·nite·ness** *noun*

**definite integral** *noun* (1860)
: the difference between the values of the integral of a given function *f*(*x*) for an upper value *b* and a lower value *a* of the independent variable *x*
**def·i·ni·tion** \,de-fə-'ni-shən\ *noun* [Middle English *diffinicioun,* from Middle French *definition,* from Latin *definition-, definitio,* from *definire*] (14th century)
**1** : an act of determining; *specifically* : the formal proclamation of a Roman Catholic dogma
**2 a** : a statement expressing the essential nature of something **b** : a statement of the meaning of a word or word group or a sign or symbol ⟨dictionary *definitions*⟩ **c** : a product of defining
**3** : the action or process of defining
**4 a** : the action or the power of describing, explaining, or making definite and clear ⟨the *definition* of a telescope⟩ ⟨her comic genius is beyond *definition*⟩ **b** (1) : clarity of visual presentation : distinctness of outline or detail ⟨high-*definition* television⟩ (2) : clarity especially of musical sound in reproduction **c** : sharp demarcation of outlines or limits ⟨a jacket with distinct waist *definition*⟩
— **def·i·ni·tion·al** \-'ni-shə-nᵊl\ *adjective*
**¹de·fin·i·tive** \di-'fi-nə-tiv\ *adjective* [Middle English *diffinityf,* from Middle French *definitif,* from Latin *definitivus,* from *definitus*] (14th century)
**1** : serving to provide a final solution or to end a situation ⟨a *definitive* victory⟩
**2** : authoritative and apparently exhaustive ⟨a *definitive* edition⟩
**3 a** : serving to define or specify precisely ⟨*definitive* laws⟩ **b** : serving as a perfect example : QUINTESSENTIAL ⟨a *definitive* bourgeois⟩
**4** : fully differentiated or developed ⟨a *definitive* organ⟩
**5** *of a postage stamp* : issued as a regular stamp for the country or territory in which it is to be used
**synonym** see CONCLUSIVE
— **de·fin·i·tive·ly** *adverb*
— **de·fin·i·tive·ness** *noun*
**²definitive** *noun* (1951)
: a definitive postage stamp — compare PROVISIONAL
**definitive host** *noun* (1901)
: the host in which the sexual reproduction of a parasite takes place — compare INTERMEDIATE HOST 1
**de·fi·ni·tize** \'de-fə-nə-,tīz, di-'fi-\ *transitive verb* **-tized; -tiz·ing** (1876)
: to make definite
**de·fi·ni·tude** \di-'fi-nə-,tüd, -,tyüd\ *noun* [irregular from *definite*] (1836)
: PRECISION, DEFINITENESS
**def·la·grate** \'def-lə-,grāt\ *verb* **-grat·ed; -grat·ing** [Latin *deflagratus,* past participle of *deflagrare* to burn down, from *de-* + *flagrare* to burn — more at BLACK] (circa 1727)
*transitive verb*
: to cause to deflagrate — compare DETONATE 1
*intransitive verb*
: to burn rapidly with intense heat and sparks being given off
— **def·la·gra·tion** \,def-lə-'grā-shən\ *noun*
**de·flate** \di-'flāt, dē-\ *verb* **de·flat·ed; de·flat·ing** [*de-* + *-flate* (as in *inflate*)] (1891)
*transitive verb*
**1** : to release air or gas from
**2** : to reduce in size, importance, or effectiveness ⟨*deflate* his ego with cutting remarks⟩
**3** : to reduce (a price level) or cause (a volume of credit) to contract
*intransitive verb*
: to lose firmness through or as if through the escape of contained gas
**synonym** see CONTRACT
— **de·fla·tor** *also* **de·fla·ter** \-'flā-tər\ *noun*

**de·fla·tion** \di-'flā-shən, ,dē-\ *noun* (1891)
**1** : an act or instance of deflating : the state of being deflated
**2** : a contraction in the volume of available money or credit that results in a general decline in prices
**3** : the erosion of soil by the wind
— **de·fla·tion·ary** \-shə-,ner-ē\ *adjective*

**de·flect** \di-'flekt, dē-\ *verb* [Latin *deflectere* to bend down, turn aside, from *de-* + *flectere* to bend] (circa 1555)
*transitive verb*
: to turn aside especially from a straight course or fixed direction
*intransitive verb*
: to turn aside : DEVIATE
— **de·flect·able** \-'flek-tə-bəl\ *adjective*
— **de·flec·tive** \-tiv\ *adjective*
— **de·flec·tor** \-tər\ *noun*

**de·flec·tion** \di-'flek-shən, dē-\ *noun* (1605)
**1** : a turning aside or off course : DEVIATION
**2** : the departure of an indicator or pointer from the zero reading on the scale of an instrument

**de·flexed** \'dē-,flekst, di-'\ *adjective* [Latin *deflexus*, past participle of *deflectere*] (1826)
: turned abruptly downward ⟨a *deflexed* leaf⟩

**de·flo·ra·tion** \,def-lə-'rā-shən, ,dē-flō-\ *noun* [Middle English *defloracioun*, from Middle French & Late Latin; Middle French *defloracion*, from Late Latin *defloration-, defloratio*, from *deflorare*] (15th century)
: rupture of the hymen

**de·flow·er** \(,)dē-'flaů(-ə)r\ *transitive verb* [Middle English *deflouren*, from Middle French or Late Latin; Old French *desflorer*, from Late Latin *deflorare*, from Latin *de-* + *flor-, flos* flower — more at BLOW] (14th century)
**1** : to deprive of virginity
**2** : to take away the prime beauty of
— **de·flow·er·er** *noun*

**de·fog** \(,)dē-'fóg, -'fäg\ *transitive verb* (1904)
: to remove fog or condensed moisture from
— **de·fog·ger** *noun*

**de·fo·li·ant** \(,)dē-'fō-lē-ənt\ *noun* (1943)
: a chemical spray or dust applied to plants in order to cause the leaves to drop off prematurely

**de·fo·li·ate** \-lē-,āt\ *transitive verb* [Late Latin *defoliatus*, past participle of *defoliare*, from Latin *de-* + *folium* leaf — more at BLADE] (1791)
: to deprive of leaves especially prematurely
— **de·fo·li·a·tion** \(,)dē-,fō-lē-'ā-shən\ *noun*
— **de·fo·li·a·tor** \(,)dē-'fō-lē-,ā-tər\ *noun*

**de·force** \(,)dē-'fōrs, -'fòrs\ *transitive verb* [Middle English, from Middle French *deforcier*, from *de-* + *forcier* to force] (15th century)
**1** : to keep (as lands) by force from the rightful owner
**2** : to eject (a person) from possession by force
— **de·force·ment** \-'fōr-smənt, -'fòr-\ *noun*

**de·for·es·ta·tion** \(,)dē-,fòr-ə-'stā-shən, -,fär-\ *noun* (1874)
: the action or process of clearing of forests; *also* : the state of having been cleared of forests
— **de·for·est** \(')dē-'fòr-əst, -'fär-\ *transitive verb*

**de·form** \di-'fòrm, dē-\ *verb* [Middle English, from Old French or Latin; Old French *deformer*, from Latin *deformare*, from *de-* + *formare* to form, from *forma* form] (15th century)
*transitive verb*
**1** : to spoil the form of
**2 a** : to spoil the looks of : DISFIGURE ⟨a face *deformed* by bitterness⟩ **b** : to mar the character of ⟨a marriage *deformed* by jealousy⟩
**3** : to alter the shape of by stress
*intransitive verb*
: to become misshapen or changed in shape ☆

— **de·form·able** \-mə-bəl\ *adjective*

**de·for·mal·ize** \(,)dē-'fòr-mə-,līz\ *transitive verb* (1880)
: to make less formal

**de·for·ma·tion** \,dē-,fòr-'mā-shən, ,de-fər-\ *noun* (15th century)
**1** : alteration of form or shape; *also* : the product of such alteration
**2** : the action of deforming : the state of being deformed
**3** : change for the worse
— **de·for·ma·tion·al** \-shə-nᵊl\ *adjective*

**de·for·ma·tive** \di-'fòr-mə-tiv, dē-\ *adjective* (1641)
: tending to deform

**de·formed** *adjective* (15th century)
: distorted or unshapely in form : MISSHAPEN

**de·for·mi·ty** \di-'fòr-mə-tē, dē-\ *noun, plural* **-ties** [Middle English *deformite*, from Middle French *defformeteit*, from Latin *deformitat-, deformitas*, from *deformis* deformed, from *de-* + *forma*] (15th century)
**1** : the state of being deformed
**2** : IMPERFECTION, BLEMISH: as **a** : a physical blemish or distortion : DISFIGUREMENT **b** : a moral or aesthetic flaw or defect

**de·fraud** \di-'fród, dē-\ *transitive verb* [Middle English, from Middle French *defrauder*, from Latin *defraudare*, from *de-* + *fraudare* to cheat, from *fraud-, fraus* fraud] (14th century)
: to deprive of something by deception or fraud
*synonym* see CHEAT
— **de·fraud·er** \di-'fró-dər\ *noun*

**de·fray** \di-'frā, dē-\ *transitive verb* [Middle French *deffrayer*, from *des-* de- + *frayer* to expend, from Old French, from (assumed) Old French *frai* expenditure, literally, damage by breaking, from Latin *fractum*, neuter of *fractus*, past participle of *frangere* to break — more at BREAK] (1536)
**1** : to provide for the payment of : PAY
**2** *archaic* : to bear the expenses of
— **de·fray·able** \-ə-bəl\ *adjective*
— **de·fray·al** \-'frā(-ə)l\ *noun*

**de·frock** \(,)dē-'fräk\ *transitive verb* (1581)
**1** : to deprive (as a priest) of the right to exercise the functions of office
**2** : to remove from a position of honor or privilege

**de·frost** \di-'fròst, 'dē-,\ (1895)
*transitive verb*
**1** : to release from a frozen state ⟨*defrost* meat⟩
**2** : to free from ice ⟨*defrost* the refrigerator⟩
*intransitive verb*
: to thaw out especially from a deep-frozen state
— **de·frost·er** *noun*

**deft** \'deft\ *adjective* [Middle English *defte* gentle — more at DAFT] (15th century)
: characterized by facility and skill
*synonym* see DEXTEROUS
— **deft·ly** *adverb*
— **deft·ness** \'def(t)-nəs\ *noun*

**de·funct** \di-'fəŋkt, dē-\ *adjective* [Latin *defunctus*, from past participle of *defungi* to finish, die, from *de-* + *fungi* to perform — more at FUNCTION] (1599)
: no longer living, existing, or functioning ⟨the committee is now *defunct*⟩
*synonym* see DEAD

**de·fund** \(,)dē-'fənd\ *transitive verb* (1948)
: to withdraw funding from

**de·fuse** \(,)dē-'fyüz\ *transitive verb* (1943)
**1** : to remove the fuse from (as a mine or bomb)
**2** : to make less harmful, potent, or tense ⟨*defuse* the crisis⟩

**¹de·fy** \di-'fī, dē-\ *transitive verb* **de·fied; de·fy·ing** [Middle English, to renounce faith in, challenge, from Middle French *defier*, from *de-* + *fier* to entrust, from (assumed) Vulgar Latin *fidare*, alteration of Latin *fidere* to trust — more at BIDE] (14th century)
**1** *archaic* : to challenge to combat

**2** : to challenge to do something considered impossible : DARE
**3** : to confront with assured power of resistance : DISREGARD ⟨*defy* public opinion⟩
**4** : to resist attempts at : WITHSTAND ⟨the paintings *defy* classification⟩

**²de·fy** \di-'fī, 'dē-,\ *noun, plural* **defies** (1580)
: CHALLENGE, DEFIANCE

**dé·ga·gé** \,dā-,gä-'zhā\ *adjective* [French, from past participle of *dégager* to put at ease, from Old French *desgagier* to redeem a pledge, free, from *des-* de- + *gage* pledge — more at GAGE] (1696)
**1** : free of constraint : NONCHALANT
**2** : being free and easy ⟨clothes with a *dégagé* look⟩
**3** : extended with toe pointed in preparation for a ballet step

**de·gas** \(,)dē-'gas\ *transitive verb* (1928)
: to remove gas from ⟨*degas* an electron tube⟩

**de Gaull·ism** \di-'gō-,li-zəm, -'gó-\ *noun* (1943)
: GAULLISM
— **de Gaull·ist** \-ləst\ *noun*

**de·gauss** \(,)dē-'gaůs\ *transitive verb* [*de-* + *gauss*, after Karl F. *Gauss*] (circa 1940)
: to remove or neutralize the magnetic field of ⟨*degauss* a ship⟩ ⟨*degauss* a magnetic tape⟩
— **de·gauss·er** *noun*

**de·gen·er·a·cy** \di-'jen-rə-sē, -'je-nə-, dē-\ *noun, plural* **-cies** (1664)
**1** : the state of being degenerate
**2** : the process of becoming degenerate
**3** : sexual perversion
**4** : the coding of an amino acid by more than one codon

**¹de·gen·er·ate** \di-'jen-rət, -'je-nə-, dē-\ *adjective* [Middle English *degenerat*, from Latin *degeneratus*, past participle of *degenerare* to degenerate, from *de-* + *gener-, genus* race, kind — more at KIN] (15th century)
**1 a** : having declined (as in nature, character, structure, or function) from an ancestral or former state **b** : having sunk to a condition below that which is normal to a type; *especially* : having sunk to a lower and usually corrupt and vicious state **c** : DEGRADED 2
**2** : being mathematically simpler (as by having a factor or constant equal to zero) than the typical case ⟨a *degenerate* hyperbola⟩
**3** : characterized by atoms stripped of their electrons and by very great density ⟨*degenerate* matter⟩; *also* : consisting of degenerate matter ⟨a *degenerate* star⟩
**4** : having two or more states or subdivisions ⟨*degenerate* energy level⟩
**5** : having more than one codon representing an amino acid; *also* : being such a codon
*synonym* see VICIOUS
— **de·gen·er·ate·ly** *adverb*
— **de·gen·er·ate·ness** *noun*

---

☆ SYNONYMS
**Deform, distort, contort, warp** means to mar or spoil by or as if by twisting. DEFORM may imply a change of shape through stress, injury, or some accident of growth ⟨his face was *deformed* by hatred⟩. DISTORT and CONTORT both imply a wrenching from the natural, normal, or justly proportioned, but CONTORT suggests a more involved twisting and a more grotesque and painful result ⟨the odd camera angle *distorts* the figure in the photograph⟩ ⟨disease had painfully *contorted* her body⟩. WARP indicates physically an uneven shrinking that bends or twists out of a flat plane ⟨*warped* floorboards⟩.

---

\ə\ **abut** \ᵊ\ **kitten** \ər\ **further** \a\ **ash** \ā\ **ace**
\ä\ **mop, mar** \aů\ **out** \ch\ **chin** \e\ **bet** \ē\ **easy**
\g\ **go** \i\ **hit** \ī\ **ice** \j\ **job** \ŋ\ **sing** \ō\ **go**
\ò\ **law** \òi\ **boy** \th\ **thin** \th\ **the** \ü\ **loot** \ů\ **foot**
\y\ **yet** \zh\ **vision** *see also* Guide to Pronunciation

**²de·gen·er·ate** \di-'je-nə-ˌrāt, dē-\ (1545)
*intransitive verb*
**1 :** to pass from a higher to a lower type or condition : DETERIORATE
**2 :** to sink into a low intellectual or moral state
**3 :** to decline in quality ⟨the poetry gradually *degenerates* into jingles⟩
**4 :** to decline from a condition or from the standards of a species, race, or breed
**5 :** to evolve or develop into a less autonomous or less functionally active form ⟨*degenerated* into dependent parasites⟩
*transitive verb*
**:** to cause to degenerate

**³de·gen·er·ate** \di-'jen-rət, -'je-nə-, dē-\ *noun* (1555)
**:** one that is degenerate: as **a :** one degraded from the normal moral standard **b :** a sexual pervert **c :** one showing signs of reversion to an earlier culture stage

**de·gen·er·a·tion** \di-ˌje-nə-'rā-shən, ˌdē-\ *noun* (15th century)
**1 :** degenerate condition
**2 :** a lowering of effective power, vitality, or essential quality to an enfeebled and worsened kind or state
**3 :** intellectual, moral, or artistic decline
**4 a :** progressive deterioration of physical characters from a level representing the norm of earlier generations or forms **b :** deterioration of a tissue or an organ in which its function is diminished or its structure is impaired
*synonym* see DETERIORATION

**de·gen·er·a·tive** \di-'je-nə-ˌrā-tiv, -'jen-rə-; -'je-nə-ˌrā-; dē-\ *adjective* (circa 1846)
**:** of, relating to, involving, or causing degeneration ⟨a *degenerative* disease⟩

**de·gla·ci·a·tion** \(ˌ)dē-ˌglā-s(h)ē-'ā-shən\ *noun* (1895)
**:** the melting of ice; *specifically* **:** the retreat of a glacier or ice sheet
— **de·gla·ci·at·ed** \-'glā-s(h)ē-ˌā-təd\ *adjective*

**de·glam·or·ize** \(ˌ)dē-'gla-mə-ˌrīz\ *transitive verb* (1938)
**:** to remove the glamor from
— **de·glam·or·iza·tion** \(ˌ)dē-ˌgla-mə-rə-'zā-shən\ *noun*

**¹de·glaze** \(ˌ)dē-'glāz\ *transitive verb* (circa 1889)
**:** to remove the glaze from

**²deglaze** *transitive verb* [modification of French *déglacer*, literally, to melt the ice from, from *dé-* + *glacer* to freeze — more at GLACÉ] (1968)
**:** to dissolve the small particles of sautéed meat remaining in (a pan) by adding a liquid and heating

**de·glu·ti·tion** \ˌdē-glü-'ti-shən, ˌdē-glü-\ *noun* [French *déglutition*, from Latin *deglutire* to swallow down, from *de-* + *glutire, gluttire* to swallow — more at GLUTTON] (1650)
**:** the act or process of swallowing

**de·grad·able** \di-'grā-də-bəl, dē-\ *adjective* (circa 1962)
**:** capable of being chemically degraded ⟨*degradable* detergents⟩ — compare BIODEGRADABLE

**deg·ra·da·tion** \ˌde-grə-'dā-shən\ *noun* (circa 1535)
**1 :** the act or process of degrading
**2 a :** decline to a low, destitute, or demoralized state **b :** moral or intellectual decadence **:** DEGENERATION
— **deg·ra·da·tive** \'de-grə-ˌdā-tiv\ *adjective*

**de·grade** \di-'grād, dē-\ *verb* [Middle English, from Old French *degrader*, from Late Latin *degradare*, from Latin *de-* + *gradus* step, grade — more at GRADE] (14th century)
*transitive verb*
**1 a :** to lower in grade, rank, or status : DEMOTE **b :** to strip of rank or honors **c :** to lower to an inferior or less effective level **d :** to scale down in desirability or salability

**2 a :** to bring to low esteem or into disrepute **b :** to drag down in moral or intellectual character : CORRUPT
**3 :** to impair in respect to some physical property
**4 :** to wear down by erosion
**5 :** to reduce the complexity of (a chemical compound) **:** DECOMPOSE
*intransitive verb*
**1 :** to pass from a higher grade or class to a lower
**2** *of a chemical compound* **:** to become reduced in complexity
— **de·grad·er** *noun*
— **de·grad·ing·ly** \-'grā-diŋ-lē\ *adverb*

**de·grad·ed** *adjective* (1643)
**1 :** reduced far below ordinary standards of civilized life and conduct
**2 :** characterized by degeneration of structure or function
— **de·grad·ed·ly** *adverb*

**de·gran·u·la·tion** \(ˌ)dē-ˌgra-nyə-'lā-shən\ *noun* (circa 1941)
**:** the process of losing granules ⟨*degranulation* of leukocytes⟩

**de·grease** \(ˌ)dē-'grēs, -'grēz\ *transitive verb* (circa 1889)
**:** to remove grease from
— **de·greas·er** \-'grē-sər, -zər\ *noun*

**de·gree** \di-'grē\ *noun* [Middle English, from Old French *degré*, from (assumed) Vulgar Latin *degradus*, from Latin *de-* + *gradus*] (13th century)
**1 :** a step or stage in a process, course, or order of classification ⟨advanced by *degrees*⟩
**2 a :** a rank or grade of official, ecclesiastical, or social position ⟨people of low *degree*⟩ **b** *archaic* **:** a particular standing especially as to dignity or worth **c :** the civil condition or status of a person
**3 :** a step in a direct line of descent or in the line of ascent to a common ancestor
**4 a** *obsolete* **:** STEP, STAIR **b** *archaic* **:** a member of a series arranged in steps
**5 :** a measure of damage to tissue caused by injury or disease — compare FIRST-DEGREE BURN, SECOND-DEGREE BURN, THIRD-DEGREE BURN
**6 a :** the extent, measure, or scope of an action, condition, or relation ⟨different in *degree* but not in kind⟩ **b :** relative intensity ⟨a high *degree* of stress⟩ **c :** the forms or sets of forms used in the comparison of an adjective or adverb **d :** a legal measure of guilt or negligence ⟨found guilty of robbery in the first *degree*⟩
**7 a :** a title conferred on students by a college, university, or professional school on completion of a program of study **b :** a grade of membership attained in a ritualistic order or society **c :** an academic title conferred to honor distinguished achievement or service **d :** the formal ceremonies observed in the conferral of such a distinction
**8 :** a unit of measure for angles equal to an angle with its vertex at the center of a circle and its sides cutting off $\frac{1}{360}$ of the circumference; *also* **:** a unit of measure for arcs of a circle equal to the amount of arc that subtends a central angle of one degree
**9** *archaic* **:** a position or space on the earth or in the heavens as measured by degrees of latitude
**10 a :** a step, note, or tone of a musical scale **b :** a line or space of the musical staff
**11 :** one of the divisions or intervals marked on a scale of a measuring instrument; *specifically* **:** any of various units for measuring temperature
**12 a :** the sum of the exponents of the variables in the term of highest degree in a polynomial, polynomial function, or polynomial equation **b :** the sum of the exponents of the variable factors of a monomial **c :** the greatest power of the derivative of highest order in a differential equation after the equation has

been rationalized and cleared of fractions with respect to the derivative
— **de·greed** \-'grēd\ *adjective*
— **to a degree 1 :** to a remarkable extent **2 :** in a small way

**de·gree–day** \di-'grē-ˌdā\ *noun* (1832)
**:** a unit that represents one degree of difference from a given point (as 65°) in the mean daily outdoor temperature and that is used especially to measure heat requirements

**degree of freedom** (1867)
**1 :** any of a limited number of ways in which a body may move or in which a dynamic system may change
**2 :** one of the capabilities of a statistic for variation of which there are as many as the number of unrestricted and independent variables determining its value

**de·gres·sive** \di-'gre-siv, 'dē-\ *adjective* [*de-* + *-gressive* (as in *progressive*)] (1886)
**:** tending to descend or decrease
— **de·gres·sive·ly** *adverb*

**dé·grin·go·lade** \ˌdā-ˌgraⁿ(ŋ)-gə-'läd\ *noun* [French, from *dégringoler* to tumble down, from Middle French *desgringueler*, from *desde-* + *gringueler* to tumble, from Middle Dutch *crinkelen* to make curl, from *crinc, cring* ring, circle] (1883)
**:** a rapid decline or deterioration (as in strength, position, or condition) **:** DOWNFALL

**de·gum** \(ˌ)dē-'gəm\ *transitive verb* (1887)
**:** to free from gum, a gummy substance, or sericin

**de·gus·ta·tion** \ˌdē-ˌgəs-'tā-shən, de-\ *noun* [French *dégustation*, from Latin *degustation-, degustatio*, from *degustare* to taste, from *de-* + *gustare* to taste — more at CHOOSE] (circa 1656)
**:** the action or an instance of tasting especially in a series of small portions
— **de·gust** \di-'gəst, dē-\ *transitive verb*

**de haut en bas** \də-ō-täⁿ-bä\ *adjective or adverb* [French, literally, from top to bottom] (1696)
**:** of superiority **:** of or with condescension

**de·hisce** \di-'his\ *intransitive verb* **de·hisced; de·hisc·ing** [Latin *dehiscere* to split open, from *de-* + *hiscere* to gape; akin to Latin *hiare* to yawn — more at YAWN] (1657)
**:** to split along a natural line; *also* **:** to discharge contents by so splitting ⟨seedpods *dehiscing* at maturity⟩

**de·his·cence** \di-'hi-sᵊn(t)s\ *noun* [New Latin *dehiscentia*, from Latin *dehiscent-, dehiscens*, present participle of *dehiscere*] (circa 1828)
**:** an act or instance of dehiscing ⟨pollen freed by *dehiscence* of the anther⟩
— **de·his·cent** \-sᵊnt\ *adjective*

**de·horn** \(ˌ)dē-'hórn\ *transitive verb* (1888)
**1 :** to deprive of horns
**2 :** to prevent the growth of the horns of
— **de·horn·er** *noun*

**de·hu·man·ize** \(ˌ)dē-'hyü-mə-ˌnīz, (ˌ)dē-'yü-\ *transitive verb* (1818)
**:** to deprive of human qualities, personality, or spirit
— **de·hu·man·iza·tion** \(ˌ)dē-ˌhyü-mə-nə-'zā-shən, (ˌ)dē-ˌyü-\ *noun*

**de·hu·mid·i·fy** \ˌdē-hyü-'mi-də-ˌfī, ˌdē-yü-\ *transitive verb* (1927)
**:** to remove moisture from (as air)
— **de·hu·mid·i·fi·ca·tion** \-ˌmi-də-fə-'kā-shən\ *noun*
— **de·hu·mid·i·fi·er** \-'mi-də-ˌfī(-ə)r\ *noun*

**de·hy·drate** \(ˌ)dē-'hī-ˌdrāt\ (1876)
*transitive verb*
**1 a :** to remove bound water or hydrogen and oxygen from (a chemical compound) in the proportion in which they form water **b :** to remove water from (as foods)
**2 :** to deprive of vitality or savor
*intransitive verb*
**:** to lose water or body fluids
— **de·hy·dra·tor** \-ˌdrā-tər\ *noun*

**de·hy·dra·tion** \dē-,hī-'drā-shən\ *noun* (1854)
: the process of dehydrating; *especially* : an abnormal depletion of body fluids

**de·hy·dro·chlo·ri·nase** \(,)dē-,hī-drə-'klōr-ə-,nās, -'klȯr-, -,nāz\ *noun* (1956)
: an enzyme that dehydrochlorinates a chlorinated hydrocarbon (as DDT) and is found especially in some DDT resistant insects

**de·hy·dro·chlo·ri·na·tion** \-,klōr-ə-'nā-shən, -,klȯr-\ *noun* (1936)
: the process of removing hydrogen and chlorine or hydrogen chloride from a compound
— **de·hy·dro·chlo·ri·nate** \-'klōr-ə-,nāt, -'klȯr-\ *transitive verb*

**de·hy·dro·ge·nase** \dē-(,)hī-'drä-jə-,nās, (,)dē-'hī-drə-jə-, -,nāz\ *noun* [International Scientific Vocabulary] (1923)
: an enzyme that accelerates the removal of hydrogen from metabolites and its transfer to other substances ⟨succinic *dehydrogenase*⟩

**de·hy·dro·ge·na·tion** \dē-(,)hī-,drä-jə-'nā-shən, (,)dē-,hī-drə-jə-\ *noun* (1866)
: the removal of hydrogen from a chemical compound
— **de·hy·dro·ge·nate** \dē-(,)hī-'drä-jə-,nāt, (,)dē-'hī-drə-jə-\ *transitive verb*

**de·ice** \(,)dē-'īs\ *transitive verb* (1934)
: to rid or keep free of ice
— **de·ic·er** *noun*

**de·i·cide** \'dē-ə-,sīd, 'dā-ə-\ *noun* [ultimately from Latin *deus* god + *-cidium, -cida* -cide — more at DEITY] (1611)
**1** : the act of killing a divine being or a symbolic substitute of such a being
**2** : the killer or destroyer of a god

**deic·tic** \'dīk-tik *also* 'dāk-\ *adjective* [Greek *deiktikos* able to show, from *deiktos,* verbal of *deiknynai* to show — more at DICTION] (1876)
: showing or pointing out directly ⟨the words *this, that,* and *those* have a *deictic* function⟩

**de·i·fi·ca·tion** \,dē-ə-fə-'kā-shən, ,dā-\ *noun* (14th century)
: the act or an instance of deifying

**de·i·fy** \'dē-ə-,fī, 'dā-\ *transitive verb* **-fied; -fy·ing** [Middle English, from Middle French *deifier,* from Late Latin *deificare,* from Latin *deus* god + *-ficare* -fy] (14th century)
**1 a** : to make a god of **b** : to take as an object of worship
**2** : to glorify as of supreme worth

**deign** \'dān\ *verb* [Middle English, from Old French *deignier,* from Latin *dignare, dignari,* from *dignus* worthy — more at DECENT] (14th century)
*intransitive verb*
: to condescend reluctantly and with a strong sense of the affront to one's superiority that is involved
*transitive verb*
: to condescend to give or offer

**deil** \'dē(ə)l\ *noun* [Middle English *devel, del*] (15th century)
*Scottish* : DEVIL

**de·in·dus·tri·al·iza·tion** \(,)dē-in-,dəs-trē-ə-lə-'zā-shən\ *noun* (1940)
: the reduction or destruction of a nation's industrial capacity
— **de·in·dus·tri·al·ize** \(,)dē-in-'dəs-trē-ə-,līz\ *verb*

**dei·non·y·chus** \(,)dī-'nä-ni-kəs\ *noun* [New Latin, from Greek *deinos* terrifying + *-onychos* -clawed (from *onych-, onyx* claw, nail] — more at DIRE, NAIL] (1969)
: any of a genus (*Deinonychus*) of small bipedal carnivorous dinosaurs from the Cretaceous

**de·in·sti·tu·tion·al·iza·tion** \(,)dē-,in(t)-stə-,tü-shə-nə-lə-'zā-shən, -,tyü-\ *noun* (1955)
**1** : the release of institutionalized individuals (as mental patients) from institutional care to care in the community
**2** : the reform or modification of an institution to remove or disguise its institutional character
— **de·in·sti·tu·tion·al·ize** \-'tü-shə-nə-,līz, -'tyü-\ *transitive verb*

**de·ion·ize** \(,)dē-'ī-ə-,nīz\ *transitive verb* (1906)
: to remove ions from ⟨*deionize* water by ion exchange⟩
— **de·ion·iza·tion** \(,)dē-,ī-ə-nə-'zā-shən\ *noun*
— **de·ion·iz·er** \-,nī-zər\ *noun*

**de·ism** \'dē-,i-zəm, 'dā-\ *noun, often capitalized* (1682)
: a movement or system of thought advocating natural religion, emphasizing morality, and in the 18th century denying the interference of the Creator with the laws of the universe
— **de·ist** \'dē-ist, 'dā-\ *noun, often capitalized*
— **de·is·tic** \dē-'is-tik, dā-\ *adjective*
— **de·is·ti·cal** \-ti-kəl\ *adjective*
— **de·is·ti·cal·ly** \-ti-k(ə-)lē\ *adverb*

**de·i·ty** \'dē-ə-tē, 'dā-\ *noun, plural* **-ties** [Middle English *deitee,* from Old French *deité,* from Late Latin *deitat-, deitas,* from Latin *deus* god; akin to Old English *Tīw,* god of war, Latin *divus* god, *dies* day, Greek *dios* heavenly, Sanskrit *deva* heavenly, god] (14th century)
**1 a** : the rank or essential nature of a god : DIVINITY **b** *capitalized* : GOD 1, SUPREME BEING
**2** : a god or goddess ⟨the *deities* of ancient Greece⟩
**3** : one exalted or revered as supremely good or powerful

**deix·is** \'dīk-sis *also* 'dāk-\ *noun* [Greek, literally, display, from *deiknynai* to show — more at DICTION] (1949)
: the pointing or specifying function of some words (as definite articles and demonstrative pronouns) whose denotation changes from one discourse to another

**dé·jà vu** \,dā-,zhä-'vü, dā-zhà-vu̇\ *noun* [French, adjective, literally, already seen] (1903)
**1 a** : the illusion of remembering scenes and events when experienced for the first time **b** : a feeling that one has seen or heard something before
**2** : something overly or unpleasantly familiar

**¹de·ject** \di-'jekt, dē-\ *adjective* (15th century)
*archaic* : DEJECTED

**²deject** *transitive verb* [Middle English, to throw down, from Latin *dejectus,* past participle of *deicere,* from *de-* + *jacere* to throw — more at JET] (1581)
: to make gloomy

**de·jec·ta** \di-'jek-tə, dē-\ *noun plural* [New Latin, from Latin, neuter plural of *dejectus*] (1887)
: FECES, EXCREMENT

**de·ject·ed** \di-'jek-təd, dē-\ *adjective* (1581)
**1** : cast down in spirits : DEPRESSED
**2 a** *obsolete, of the eyes* : DOWNCAST **b** *archaic* : thrown down
**3** *obsolete* : lowered in rank or condition
— **de·ject·ed·ly** *adverb*
— **de·ject·ed·ness** *noun*

**de·jec·tion** \di-'jek-shən, dē-\ *noun* (15th century)
: lowness of spirits

**de ju·re** \(,)dē-'juṙ-ē, (,)dā-'yuṙ-\ *adverb or adjective* [Medieval Latin] (1611)
: by right : of right

**deka-** *or* **dek-** — see DECA-

**deka·gram** \'de-kə-,gram\ *noun* (circa 1879)
— see METRIC SYSTEM table

**deka·li·ter** \-,lē-tər\ *noun* (circa 1879)
— see METRIC SYSTEM table

**deka·me·ter** \-,mē-tər\ *noun* (circa 1879)
— see METRIC SYSTEM table

**deka·met·ric** \,de-kə-'me-trik\ *adjective* (1968)
: DECAMETRIC

**de·lam·i·na·tion** \(,)dē-,la-mə-'nā-shən\ *noun* (1877)
**1** : gastrula formation in which the endoderm is split off as a layer from the inner surface of the blastoderm and the archenteron is represented by the space between this endoderm and the yolk mass

**2** : separation into constituent layers
— **de·lam·i·nate** \(,)dē-'la-mə-,nāt\ *intransitive verb*

**de·late** \di-'lāt, dē-\ *transitive verb* **de·lat·ed; de·lat·ing** [Latin *delatus* (past participle of *deferre* to bring down, report, accuse), from *de-* + *latus,* past participle of *ferre* to bear — more at TOLERATE] (15th century)
**1** : ACCUSE, DENOUNCE
**2** : REPORT, RELATE
— **de·la·tion** \-'lā-shən\ *noun*
— **de·la·tor** \-'lā-tər\ *noun*

**Del·a·ware** \'de-lə-,war, -,wer, -wər\ *noun, plural* **Delaware** *or* **Delawares** [*Delaware* River] (1721)
**1** : a member of an American Indian people originally of the Delaware valley
**2** : the Algonquian language of the Delaware

**¹de·lay** \di-'lā, dē-\ *noun* (13th century)
**1 a** : the act of delaying : the state of being delayed **b** : an instance of being delayed
**2** : the time during which something is delayed

**²delay** *verb* [Middle English, from Old French *delaier,* from *de-* + *laier* to leave, perhaps alteration of *laissier,* from Latin *laxare* to slacken, from *laxus* loose — more at SLACK] (14th century)
*transitive verb*
**1** : PUT OFF, POSTPONE
**2** : to stop, detain, or hinder for a time
*intransitive verb*
: to move or act slowly; *also* : to cause delay
☆ ☆
— **de·lay·er** *noun*

**¹de·le** \'dē-(,)lē\ *transitive verb* **de·led; de·le·ing** [Latin, imperative singular of *delēre*] (1705)
: to delete especially from typeset matter

---

\ə\ abut \ᵊ\ kitten \ər\ further \a\ ash \ā\ ace
\ä\ mop, mar \au̇\ out \ch\ chin \e\ bet \ē\ easy
\g\ go \i\ hit \ī\ ice \j\ job \ŋ\ sing \ō\ go
\ȯ\ law \ȯi\ boy \th\ thin \t͟h\ the \ü\ loot \u̇\ foot
\y\ yet \zh\ vision *see also* Guide to Pronunciation

²**dele** *noun* (circa 1751)
: a mark indicating that something is to be deled

¹**de·lec·ta·ble** \di-'lek-tə-bəl\ *adjective* [Middle English, from Old French, from Latin *delectabilis,* from *delectare* to delight — more at DELIGHT] (15th century)
**1** : highly pleasing : DELIGHTFUL
**2** : DELICIOUS
— **de·lec·ta·bil·i·ty** \-,lek-tə-'bi-lə-tē\ *noun*
— **de·lec·ta·bly** \-blē\ *adverb*
²**delectable** *noun* (1921)
: something that is delectable

**de·lec·ta·tion** \,dē-,lek-'tā-shən, di-; ,de-lək-\ *noun* (14th century)
: DELIGHT, ENJOYMENT

**del·e·ga·ble** \'de-li-gə-bəl\ *adjective* (1660)
: capable of being delegated

**del·e·ga·cy** \-gə-sē\ *noun, plural* **-cies** (15th century)
**1** : a body of delegates : BOARD
**2 a** : the act of delegating **b** : appointment as delegate

¹**del·e·gate** \'de-li-gət, -,gāt\ *noun* [Middle English *delegat,* from Medieval Latin *delegatus,* from Latin, past participle of *delegare* to delegate, from *de-* + *legare* to send — more at LEGATE] (15th century)
: a person acting for another: as **a** : a representative to a convention or conference **b** : a representative of a U.S. territory in the House of Representatives **c** : a member of the lower house of the legislature of Maryland, Virginia, or West Virginia

²**del·e·gate** \-,gāt\ *verb* **-gat·ed; -gat·ing** (1530)
*transitive verb*
**1** : to entrust to another ⟨*delegate* authority⟩
**2** : to appoint as one's representative
*intransitive verb*
: to assign responsibility or authority
— **del·e·ga·tee** \,de-li-gə-'tē\ *noun*
— **del·e·ga·tor** \'de-li-gā-tər\ *noun*

**del·e·ga·tion** \,de-li-'gā-shən\ *noun* (1612)
**1** : the act of empowering to act for another
**2** : a group of persons chosen to represent others

**de·le·git·i·ma·tion** \,dē-lə-,ji-tə-'mā-shən\ *noun* (1968)
: a decline in or loss of prestige or authority

**de·lete** \di-'lēt, dē-\ *transitive verb* **de·let·ed; de·let·ing** [Latin *deletus,* past participle of *delēre* to wipe out, destroy] (circa 1605)
: to eliminate especially by blotting out, cutting out, or erasing

**del·e·te·ri·ous** \,de-lə-'ti-rē-əs\ *adjective* [Greek *dēlētērios,* from *dēleisthai* to hurt] (1643)
: harmful often in a subtle or unexpected way ⟨*deleterious* effects⟩ ⟨*deleterious* to health⟩
*synonym* see PERNICIOUS
— **del·e·te·ri·ous·ly** *adverb*
— **del·e·te·ri·ous·ness** *noun*

**de·le·tion** \di-'lē-shən, dē-\ *noun* [Latin *deletion-, deletio* destruction, from *delēre*] (1590)
**1** : the act of deleting
**2 a** : something deleted **b** (1) : the absence of a section of genetic material from a chromosome (2) : the mutational process that results in a deletion

**delft** \'delft\ *noun* [*Delft,* Netherlands] (1723)
**1** : tin-glazed Dutch earthenware with blue and white or polychrome decoration
**2** : a ceramic ware resembling or imitative of Dutch delft

**delft·ware** \'delft-,war, -,wer\ *noun* (1714)
: DELFT

**deli** \'de-lē\ *noun, plural* **del·is** (circa 1954)
: DELICATESSEN

¹**de·lib·er·ate** \di-'li-bə-,rāt\ *verb* **-at·ed; -at·ing** (14th century)
*intransitive verb*

: to think about or discuss issues and decisions carefully
*transitive verb*
: to think about deliberately and often with formal discussion before reaching a decision
*synonym* see THINK

²**de·lib·er·ate** \di-'li-bə-rət, -'lib-rət\ *adjective* [Latin *deliberatus,* past participle of *deliberare* to consider carefully, perhaps alteration of (assumed) *delibrare,* from *de-* + *libra* scale, pound] (15th century)
**1** : characterized by or resulting from careful and thorough consideration ⟨a *deliberate* decision⟩
**2** : characterized by awareness of the consequences ⟨*deliberate* falsehood⟩
**3** : slow, unhurried, and steady as though allowing time for decision on each individual action involved ⟨a *deliberate* pace⟩
*synonym* see VOLUNTARY
— **de·lib·er·ate·ly** *adverb*
— **de·lib·er·ate·ness** *noun*

**de·lib·er·a·tion** \di-,li-bə-'rā-shən\ *noun* (14th century)
**1 a** : the act of deliberating **b** : a discussion and consideration by a group of persons of the reasons for and against a measure
**2** : the quality or state of being deliberate
— **de·lib·er·a·tive** \-'li-bə-,rāt-iv, -'li-b(ə-)rət-\ *adjective*
— **de·lib·er·a·tive·ly** *adverb*
— **de·lib·er·a·tive·ness** *noun*

**del·i·ca·cy** \'de-li-kə-sē\ *noun, plural* **-cies** (14th century)
**1** *obsolete* **a** : the quality or state of being luxurious **b** : INDULGENCE
**2** : something pleasing to eat that is considered rare or luxurious ⟨considered caviar a *delicacy*⟩
**3 a** : the quality or state of being dainty : FINENESS ⟨lace of great *delicacy*⟩ **b** : FRAILTY 1
**4** : fineness or subtle expressiveness of touch (as in painting or music)
**5 a** : precise and refined perception and discrimination **b** : extreme sensitivity : PRECISION ⟨an electronic instrument of great *delicacy*⟩
**6 a** : refined sensibility in feeling or conduct **b** : the quality or state of being squeamish
**7** : the quality or state of requiring delicate handling

¹**del·i·cate** \'de-li-kət\ *adjective* [Middle English *delicat,* from Latin *delicatus* delicate, addicted to pleasure; akin to Latin *delicere* to allure] (14th century)
**1** : pleasing to the senses: **a** : generally pleasant ⟨the climate's *delicate,* the air most sweet —Shakespeare⟩ **b** : pleasing to the sense of taste or smell especially in a mild or subtle way ⟨a *delicate* aroma⟩ ⟨a robust wine will dominate *delicate* dishes⟩ **c** : marked by daintiness or charm of color, lines, or proportions ⟨a *delicate* floral print⟩ ⟨an ample tear trilled down her *delicate* cheek —Shakespeare⟩ **d** : marked by fineness of structure, workmanship, or texture ⟨a *delicate* tracery⟩ ⟨a *delicate* lace⟩
**2 a** : marked by keen sensitivity or fine discrimination ⟨*delicate* insights⟩ ⟨a more *delicate* syntactic analysis —R. H. Robins⟩ **b** : FASTIDIOUS, SQUEAMISH ⟨a person of *delicate* tastes⟩
**3 a** : not robust in health or constitution : WEAK, SICKLY ⟨had been considered a *delicate* child⟩ **b** : easily torn or damaged : FRAGILE ⟨the *delicate* chain of life⟩
**4 a** : requiring careful handling: (1) : easily unsettled or upset ⟨a *delicate* balance⟩ ⟨the *delicate* relationships defined by the Constitution —*New Yorker*⟩ (2) : requiring skill or tact ⟨in a *delicate* position⟩ ⟨*delicate* negotiations⟩ ⟨a *delicate* operation⟩ (3) : involving matters of a deeply personal nature : SENSITIVE ⟨this is a

*delicate* matter. Could I possibly speak to you alone —Daphne Du Maurier⟩ **b** : marked by care, skill, or tact ⟨*delicate* handling of a difficult situation⟩
**5** : marked by great precision or sensitivity ⟨a *delicate* instrument⟩
*synonym* see CHOICE
— **del·i·cate·ly** *adverb*
²**delicate** *noun* (15th century)
: something delicate

**del·i·ca·tes·sen** \,de-li-kə-'te-s²n\ *noun plural* [obsolete German (now *Delikatessen*), plural of *Delicatesse* delicacy, from French *délicatesse,* probably from Old Italian *delicatezza,* from *delicato* delicate, from Latin *delicatus*] (1889)
**1** : ready-to-eat food products (as cooked meats and prepared salads)
**2** *singular, plural* **delicatessens** [*delicatessen (store)*] : a store where delicatessen are sold ◆

**de·li·cious** \di-'li-shəs\ *adjective* [Middle English, from Middle French, from Late Latin *deliciosus,* from Latin *deliciae* delights, from *delicere* to allure] (14th century)
**1** : affording great pleasure : DELIGHTFUL ⟨*delicious* anecdotes⟩
**2** : appealing to one of the bodily senses especially of taste or smell
— **de·li·cious·ly** *adverb*
— **de·li·cious·ness** *noun*

**Delicious** *noun, plural* **De·li·cious·es** *or* **Delicious** (circa 1903)
: an important red or yellow market apple of American origin that has a crown of five rounded prominences on the end opposite the stem

**de·lict** \di-'likt, dē-\ *noun* [Latin *delictum* fault, from neuter of *delictus,* past participle of *delinquere*] (1523)
: an offense against the law

¹**de·light** \di-'līt, dē-\ *noun* (13th century)
**1** : a high degree of gratification : JOY; *also* : extreme satisfaction
**2** : something that gives great pleasure
**3** *archaic* : the power of affording pleasure

²**delight** *verb* [Middle English *deliten,* from Old French *delitier,* from Latin *delectare,* frequentative of *delicere* to allure, from *de-* + *lacere* to allure] (13th century)
*intransitive verb*
**1** : to take great pleasure ⟨*delighted* in playing the guitar⟩
**2** : to give keen enjoyment ⟨a book certain to *delight*⟩
*transitive verb*
: to give joy or satisfaction to

---

◇ **WORD HISTORY**
**delicatessen** The word *delicatessen,* borrowed from a German plural noun meaning "delicacies," began to appear in U.S. publications toward the end of the 19th century, usually in combination with *store* or *shop.* These collocations are partial translations of German compound words such as *Delikatessenhandlung* or *Delikatessengeschäft.* By the 1920s the noun *store* or *shop* was dropped and the word *delicatessen* was used alone for the store. The delicatessen has become an American institution, especially in large urban centers such as New York City, where the *deli* (a clipping that first appeared in the 1950s) is typically a sparely furnished restaurant that serves traditional American Jewish fare such as pastrami and corned beef sandwiches, knishes, and matzo ball soup. More generally in the U.S., *deli* evokes a store or now more commonly a supermarket department that sells cold cuts and prepared foods. It is worth noting that, contrary to some popular notions, *delicatessen* has no etymological connection with the German verb *essen* "to eat."

— **de·light·er** *noun*
**de·light·ed** *adjective* (1603)
**1** *obsolete* : DELIGHTFUL
**2** : highly pleased
— **de·light·ed·ly** *adverb*
— **de·light·ed·ness** *noun*
**de·light·ful** \di-'līt-fəl, dē-\ *adjective* (circa 1530)
: highly pleasing
— **de·light·ful·ly** \-fə-lē\ *adverb*
— **de·light·ful·ness** *noun*
**de·light·some** \-'līt-səm\ *adjective* (1520)
: very pleasing : DELIGHTFUL
**De·li·lah** \di-'lī-lə\ *noun* [Hebrew *Dĕlīlāh*]
: the mistress and betrayer of Samson in the book of Judges
**de·lim·it** \di-'li-mət\ *transitive verb* [French *délimiter*, from Latin *delimitare*, from *de-* + *limitare* to limit, from *limit-, limes* boundary, limit] (1852)
: to fix or define the limits of
— **de·lim·i·ta·tion** \di-,li-mə-'tā-shən, ,dē-\ *noun*
**de·lim·it·er** \di-'li-mə-tər\ *noun* (1960)
: a character that marks the beginning or end of a unit of data
**de·lin·eate** \di-'li-nē-,āt\ *transitive verb* **-eat·ed; -eat·ing** [Latin *delineatus*, past participle of *delineare*, from *de-* + *linea* line] (1559)
**1 a** : to indicate or represent by drawn or painted lines **b** : to mark the outline of ⟨lights *delineating* the narrow streets⟩
**2** : to describe, portray, or set forth with accuracy or in detail ⟨*delineate* a character in the story⟩ ⟨*delineate* the steps to be taken by the government⟩
— **de·lin·ea·tor** \-ē-,ā-tər\ *noun*
**de·lin·ea·tion** \di-,li-nē-'ā-shən\ *noun* (1570)
**1** : the act of delineating
**2** : something made by delineating
— **de·lin·ea·tive** \-'li-nē-,ā-tiv\ *adjective*
**de·lin·quen·cy** \di-'liŋ-kwən-sē, -'lin-\ *noun, plural* **-cies** (1636)
**1 a** : a delinquent act **b** : conduct that is out of accord with accepted behavior or the law; *especially* : JUVENILE DELINQUENCY
**2** : a debt on which payment is overdue
¹**de·lin·quent** \-kwənt\ *noun* (15th century)
: a delinquent person
²**delinquent** *adjective* [Latin *delinquent-, delinquens*, present participle of *delinquere* to fail, offend, from *de-* + *linquere* to leave — more at LOAN] (1603)
**1** : offending by neglect or violation of duty or of law
**2** : being overdue in payment ⟨a *delinquent* charge account⟩
**3** : of, relating to, or characteristic of delinquents : marked by delinquency
— **de·lin·quent·ly** *adverb*
**del·i·quesce** \,de-li-'kwes\ *intransitive verb* **-quesced; -quesc·ing** [Latin *deliquescere*, from *de-* + *liquescere*, inchoative of *liquēre* to be fluid — more at LIQUID] (1756)
**1** : to dissolve or melt away
**2** : to become soft or liquid with age — used of plant structures (as mushrooms)
**del·i·ques·cent** \-'kwe-s°nt\ *adjective* [Latin *deliquescent-, deliquescens*, present participle of *deliquescere*] (1791)
**1** : tending to melt or dissolve; *especially* : tending to undergo gradual dissolution and liquefaction by the attraction and absorption of moisture from the air
**2** : having repeated division into branches ⟨elms are *deliquescent* trees⟩ — compare EXCURRENT 2a
— **del·i·ques·cence** \-s°n(t)s\ *noun*
**de·lir·i·ous** \di-'lir-ē-əs\ *adjective* (1599)
**1** : of, relating to, or characteristic of delirium
**2** : affected with or marked by delirium
— **de·lir·i·ous·ly** *adverb*
— **de·lir·i·ous·ness** *noun*

**de·lir·i·um** \di-'lir-ē-əm\ *noun* [Latin, from *delirare* to be crazy, literally, to leave the furrow (in plowing), from *de-* + *lira* furrow — more at LEARN] (circa 1563)
**1** : a mental disturbance characterized by confusion, disordered speech, and hallucinations
**2** : frenzied excitement ⟨he would stride about his room in a *delirium* of joy —Thomas Wolfe⟩
**delirium tre·mens** \-'trē-mənz, -'tre-\ *noun* [New Latin, literally, trembling delirium] (1865)
: a violent delirium with tremors that is induced by excessive and prolonged use of alcoholic liquors — called also *d.t.'s*
**de·list** \(,)dē-'list\ *transitive verb* (1933)
: to remove from a list; *especially* : to remove (a security) from the list of securities that may be dealt in on a particular exchange
**de·liv·er** \di-'li-vər, dē-\ *verb* **de·liv·ered; de·liv·er·ing** \-v(ə-)riŋ\ [Middle English, from Old French *delivrer*, from Late Latin *deliberare*, from Latin *de-* + *liberare* to liberate] (13th century)
*transitive verb*
**1** : to set free ⟨and lead us not into temptation, but *deliver* us from evil —Matthew 6:13 (Authorized Version)⟩
**2 a** : to take and hand over to or leave for another : CONVEY ⟨*deliver* a package⟩ **b** : HAND OVER, SURRENDER ⟨*delivered* the prisoners to the sheriff⟩ ⟨*delivered* themselves over to God⟩
**3 a** : to assist in giving birth (2) : to aid in the birth of **b** : to give birth to **c** : to cause (oneself) to produce as if by giving birth ⟨has *delivered* himself of half an autobiography —H. C. Schonberg⟩
**4** : SPEAK, SING, UTTER ⟨*delivered* their lines with style⟩ ⟨*deliver* a song⟩ ⟨*deliver* a speech⟩
**5** : to send (something aimed or guided) to an intended target or destination ⟨ability to *deliver* nuclear warheads⟩ ⟨*delivered* a fastball⟩
**6 a** : to bring (as votes) to the support of a candidate or cause **b** : to come through with : PRODUCE ⟨can *deliver* the goods⟩ ⟨new car *delivers* high gas mileage⟩
*intransitive verb*
: to produce the promised, desired, or expected results : COME THROUGH ⟨can't *deliver* on all these promises⟩
**synonym** see RESCUE
— **de·liv·er·abil·i·ty** \-,li-v(ə-)rə-'bi-lə-tē\ *noun*
— **de·liv·er·able** \-'li-v(ə-)rə-bəl\ *adjective*
— **de·liv·er·er** \-'li-vər-ər\ *noun*
— **deliver the goods** : to give results that are promised, expected, or desired
**de·liv·er·ance** \di-'li-v(ə-)rən(t)s, dē-\ *noun* (14th century)
**1** : the act of delivering someone or something : the state of being delivered; *especially* : LIBERATION, RESCUE
**2** : something delivered; *especially* : an opinion or decision (as the verdict of a jury) expressed publicly
**de·liv·ery** \di-'li-v(ə-)rē, dē-\ *noun, plural* **-eries** (15th century)
: the act of delivering something; *also* : something delivered
**delivery boy** *noun* (1920)
: a person employed by a retail store to deliver small orders to customers on call
**de·liv·ery·man** \-v(ə-)rē-mən, -,man\ *noun* (1920)
: a person who delivers wholesale or retail goods to customers usually over a regular local route
**dell** \'del\ *noun* [Middle English *delle*; akin to Middle High German *telle* ravine, Old English *dæl* valley — more at DALE] (13th century)
: a secluded hollow or small valley usually covered with trees or turf
**delly** *variant of* DELI

**Del·mon·i·co steak** \del-'mä-ni-(,)kō-\ *noun* [from the *Delmonico* restaurants, New York City, after Lorenzo Delmonico (died 1881) American restaurateur] (1925)
: CLUB STEAK — called also *Delmonico*
**de·lo·cal·ize** \(,)dē-'lō-kə-,līz\ *transitive verb* (1855)
: to free from the limitations of locality; *specifically* : to remove (a charge or charge carrier) from a particular position
— **de·lo·cal·iza·tion** \(,)dē-,lō-kə-lə-'zā-shən\ *noun*
**de·louse** \(,)dē-'laůs, -'laůz\ *transitive verb* (circa 1919)
: to remove lice from
**Del·phi·an** \'del-fē-ən\ *adjective* (1625)
: DELPHIC
**Del·phic** \'del-fik\ *adjective* (circa 1599)
**1** : of or relating to ancient Delphi or its oracle
**2** *often not capitalized* : AMBIGUOUS, OBSCURE ⟨*Delphic* utterances⟩ ◆
— **del·phi·cal·ly** \-fi-k(ə-)lē\ *adverb*

delphinium

**del·phin·i·um** \del-'fi-nē-əm\ *noun* [New Latin, genus name, from Greek *delphinion* larkspur, diminutive of *delphin-, delphis* dolphin; probably from the shape of the nectary] (1664)
: any of a large genus (*Delphinium*) of the buttercup family that comprises chiefly perennial erect branching herbs with palmately divided leaves and irregular flowers in showy spikes and includes several that are poisonous — compare LARKSPUR
**Del·phi·nus** \del-'fī-nəs, -'fē-\ *noun* [Latin (genitive *Delphini*), literally, dolphin, from Greek *delphin-, delphis*]
: a northern constellation nearly west of Pegasus
¹**del·ta** \'del-tə\ *noun* [Middle English *deltha*, from Greek *delta*, of Semitic origin; akin to Hebrew *dāleth* daleth] (13th century)
**1** : the 4th letter of the Greek alphabet — see ALPHABET table
**2** : something shaped like a capital Greek delta; *especially* : the alluvial deposit at the mouth of a river
**3** : an increment of a variable — symbol $\Delta$
— **del·ta·ic** \del-'tā-ik\ *adjective*

---

◇ **WORD HISTORY**

**Delphic** *Delphic* alludes to the ancient Greek town of Delphoi (better known now in its Latin form *Delphi*). Situated on the southern slopes of Mount Parnassus, Delphi was the site of classical Greece's most important oracle. The oracular medium or priestess, known as a Pythia, would chew the leaves of the laurel, the tree sacred to Apollo, as vapors from the earth below engulfed her. While in her divine ecstasy, she would utter incoherent responses to questions posed in advance by those wishing to know what the future might hold or how the gods might be propitiated or evil averted. The Pythia's responses were interpreted by attending priests who recast them into verses that were often highly ambiguous or obscure—so much so that they allowed for just about any interpretation. This ambiguity is the source of a common modern meaning of English *Delphic*.

---

\ə\ abut \°\ kitten \ər\ further \a\ ash \ā\ ace
\ä\ mop, mar \aů\ out \ch\ chin \e\ bet \ē\ easy
\g\ go \i\ hit \ī\ ice \j\ job \ŋ\ sing \ō\ go
\ȯ\ law \ȯi\ boy \th\ thin \ṯẖ\ the \ü\ loot \ů\ foot
\y\ yet \zh\ vision *see also* Guide to Pronunciation

²**delta** *adjective* (circa 1929)
: fourth in position in the structure of an organic molecule from a particular group or atom — symbol δ

**Delta** (1952)
— a communications code word for the letter *d*

**delta ray** *noun* (1908)
: an electron ejected by an ionizing particle in its passage through matter

**delta wave** *noun* (1936)
: a high amplitude electrical rhythm of the brain with a frequency of less than 6 cycles per second that occurs especially in deep sleep, in infancy, and in many diseased conditions of the brain — called also *delta, delta rhythm*

**delta wing** *noun* [¹*delta;* from its shape] (1946)
: a triangular swept-back airplane wing with a usually straight trailing edge

¹**del·toid** \'del-,tȯid\ *noun* [New Latin *deltoides,* from Greek *deltoeidēs* shaped like a delta, from *delta*] (circa 1681)
: a large triangular muscle that covers the shoulder joint and serves to raise the arm laterally

²**deltoid** *adjective* (circa 1753)
**1** : having a triangular shape ⟨a *deltoid* leaf⟩
— see LEAF illustration
**2** : relating to, associated with, or supplying the deltoid

**del·toi·de·us** \del-'tȯi-dē-əs\ *noun, plural* **del·toi·dei** \-ē-,ī\ [New Latin, alteration of *deltoides*] (circa 1860)
: DELTOID

**de·lude** \di-'lüd, dē-\ *transitive verb* **de·lud·ed; de·lud·ing** [Middle English, from Latin *deludere,* from *de-* + *ludere* to play — more at LUDICROUS] (15th century)
**1** : to mislead the mind or judgment of : DECEIVE, TRICK
**2** *obsolete* **a** : FRUSTRATE, DISAPPOINT **b** : EVADE, ELUDE
**synonym** see DECEIVE
— **de·lud·er** *noun*

¹**del·uge** \'del-,yüj, -,yüzh; ÷də-'lüj, 'dā-,lüj\ *noun* [Middle English, from Old French, from Latin *diluvium,* from *diluere* to wash away, from *dis-* + *lavere* to wash — more at LYE] (14th century)
**1 a** : an overflowing of the land by water **b** : a drenching rain
**2** : an overwhelming amount or number

²**deluge** *transitive verb* **del·uged; del·ug·ing** (1593)
**1** : to overflow with water : INUNDATE
**2** : OVERWHELM, SWAMP

**de·lu·sion** \di-'lü-zhən, dē-\ *noun* [Middle English, from Late Latin *delusion-, delusio,* from *deludere*] (15th century)
**1 a** : the act of deluding : the state of being deluded **b** : an abnormal mental state characterized by the occurrence of psychotic delusions
**2 a** : something that is falsely or delusively believed or propagated **b** : a persistent false psychotic belief regarding the self or persons or objects outside the self
— **de·lu·sion·al** \-'lüzh-nəl, -'lü-zhə-n°l\ *adjective*
— **de·lu·sion·ary** \-zhə-,ner-ē\ *adjective*

**de·lu·sive** \-'lü-siv, -'lü-ziv\ *adjective* (1605)
**1** : likely to delude
**2** : constituting a delusion
— **de·lu·sive·ly** *adverb*
— **de·lu·sive·ness** *noun*

**de·lu·so·ry** \-sə-rē, -zə-\ *adjective* (15th century)
: DECEPTIVE, DELUSIVE

**de·lus·ter** \(,)dē-'ləs-tər\ *transitive verb* (1926)
: to reduce the sheen of (as yarn or fabric)

**de·luxe** \di-'ləks, dē- *also* -'lu̇ks, -'lüks\ *adjective* [French *de luxe,* literally, of luxury] (1819)
: notably luxurious, elegant, or expensive ⟨a *deluxe* edition⟩ ⟨*deluxe* hotels⟩

¹**delve** \'delv\ *verb* **delved; delv·ing** [Middle English, from Old English *delfan;* akin to Old High German *telban* to dig] (before 12th century)
*transitive verb*
*archaic* : EXCAVATE
*intransitive verb*
**1** : to dig or labor with or as if with a spade
**2** : to make a careful or detailed search for information ⟨*delved* into the past⟩
— **delv·er** *noun*

²**delve** *noun* (14th century)
*archaic* : CAVE, HOLLOW

**de·mag·ne·tize** \(,)dē-'mag-nə-,tīz\ *transitive verb* (1839)
: to deprive of magnetic properties
— **de·mag·ne·ti·za·tion** \(,)dē-,mag-nə-tə-'zā-shən\ *noun*
— **de·mag·ne·tiz·er** \(,)dē-'mag-nə-,tī-zər\ *noun*

**dem·a·gog·ic** \,de-mə-'gä-gik *also* -'gä-jik *or* -'gō-jik\ *adjective* (1831)
: of, relating to, or characteristic of a demagogue : employing demagoguery
— **dem·a·gog·i·cal·ly** \-gi-k(ə-)lē, -ji-\ *adverb*

¹**dem·a·gogue** *or* **dem·a·gog** \'de-mə-,gäg\ *noun* [Greek *dēmagōgos,* from *dēmos* people (perhaps akin to Greek *daiesthai* to divide) + *agōgos* leading, from *agein* to lead — more at TIDE, AGENT] (1648)
**1** : a leader who makes use of popular prejudices and false claims and promises in order to gain power
**2** : a leader championing the cause of the common people in ancient times
— **dem·a·gogu·ery** \-,gä-g(ə-)rē\ *noun*
— **dem·a·gogy** \-,gä-gē, -,gä-jē, -,gō-jē\ *noun*

²**demagogue** *or* **demagog** *verb* **-gogued** *or* **-goged; -gogu·ing** *or* **-gog·ing** (1656)
*intransitive verb*
: to behave like a demagogue
*transitive verb*
: to treat (as an issue) in a demogic manner

¹**de·mand** \di-'mand, -'mand, dē-\ *noun* (13th century)
**1 a** : an act of demanding or asking especially with authority **b** : something claimed as due
**2** *archaic* : QUESTION
**3 a** : willingness and ability to purchase a commodity or service **b** : the quantity of a commodity or service wanted at a specified price and time
**4 a** : a seeking or state of being sought after ⟨in great *demand* as an entertainer⟩ **b** : urgent need
**5** : the requirement of work or of the expenditure of a resource ⟨equal to the *demands* of the office⟩ ⟨oxygen *demand* for waste oxidation⟩
— **on demand** : upon presentation and request for payment; *also* : when requested or needed

²**demand** *verb* [Middle English *demaunden,* from Old French *demander,* from Medieval Latin *demandare,* from Latin, to entrust, charge, from *de-* + *mandare* to enjoin — more at MANDATE] (14th century)
*intransitive verb*
: to make a demand : ASK
*transitive verb*
**1** : to ask or call for with authority : claim as due or just ⟨*demanded* to see a lawyer⟩
**2** : to call for urgently, peremptorily, or insistently ⟨*demanded* that the rioters disperse⟩
**3 a** : to ask authoritatively or earnestly to be informed of **b** : to require to come : SUMMON
**4** : to call for as useful or necessary ☆

— **de·mand·able** \-'man-də-bəl\ *adjective*
— **de·mand·er** *noun*

**de·man·dant** \di-'man-dənt\ *noun* (15th century)
**1** *archaic* : the plaintiff in a real action
**2** *archaic* : one who makes a demand or claim

**demand deposit** *noun* (1923)
: a bank deposit that can be withdrawn without advance notice

**de·mand·ing** *adjective* (1926)
: requiring much time, effort, or attention : EXACTING
— **de·mand·ing·ly** \-'man-diŋ-lē\ *adverb*
— **de·mand·ing·ness** *noun*

**demand loan** *noun* (1913)
: CALL LOAN

**demand note** *noun* (1862)
: a note payable on demand

**de·mand–pull** \di-'man(d)-,pu̇l\ *noun* (1952)
: an increase or upward trend in spendable money that tends to result in increased competition for available goods and services and a corresponding increase in consumer prices — compare COST-PUSH
— **demand–pull** *adjective*

**de·mand–side** \di-'mand-,sīd\ *adjective* (1980)
: of, relating to, or being an economic theory that advocates use of government spending and growth in the money supply to stimulate the demand for goods and services and therefore expand economic activity — compare SUPPLY-SIDE

**de·man·toid** \'de-mən-,tȯid\ *noun* [German, from obsolete German *Demant* diamond, from Middle High German *diemant,* from Old French *diamant* — more at DIAMOND] (circa 1890)
: a green garnet used as a gem

**de·mar·cate** \di-'mär-,kāt, 'dē-,\ *transitive verb* **-cat·ed; -cat·ing** [back-formation from *demarcation,* from Spanish *demarcación,* from *demarcar* to delimit, from *de-* + *marcar* to mark, probably from Italian *marcare,* of Germanic origin; akin to Old High German *marha* boundary — more at MARK] (1816)
**1** : DELIMIT
**2** : to set apart : SEPARATE
— **de·mar·ca·tion** \,dē-,mär-'kā-shən\ *noun*

**dé·marche** *or* **de·marche** \dā-'märsh, di-', 'dā-,\ *noun* [French *démarche,* literally, gait, from Middle French, from *demarcher* to march, from Old French *demarchier,* from *de-* + *marchier* to march] (1658)
**1 a** : a course of action : MANEUVER **b** : a diplomatic or political initiative or maneuver
**2** : a petition or protest presented through diplomatic channels

**de·mark** \di-'märk\ *transitive verb* (1834)
: DEMARCATE

**de·ma·te·ri·al·ize** \,dē-mə-'tir-ē-ə-,līz\ (circa 1864)
*transitive verb*

---

☆ SYNONYMS
**Demand, claim, require, exact** mean to ask or call for something as due or as necessary. DEMAND implies peremptoriness and insistence and often the right to make requests that are to be regarded as commands ⟨*demanded* payment of the debt⟩. CLAIM implies a demand for the delivery or concession of something due as one's own or one's right ⟨*claimed* the right to manage his own affairs⟩. REQUIRE suggests the imperativeness that arises from inner necessity, compulsion of law or regulation, or the exigencies of the situation ⟨the patient *requires* constant attention⟩. EXACT implies not only demanding but getting what one demands ⟨*exacts* absolute loyalty⟩.

: to cause to become or appear immaterial
*intransitive verb*
: to lose or appear to lose materiality
— **de·ma·te·ri·al·iza·tion** \-ˌtir-ē-ə-lə-ˈzā-shən\ *noun*

**deme** \ˈdēm\ *noun* [Greek *dēmos* people, deme] (1833)
**1** : a unit of local government in ancient Attica
**2** : a local population of closely related interbreeding organisms

¹**de·mean** \di-ˈmēn\ *transitive verb* **de·meaned; de·mean·ing** [Middle English *demenen*, from Middle French *demener* to conduct, from *de-* + *mener* to lead, from Latin *minare* to drive, from *minari* to threaten — more at MOUNT] (14th century)
: to conduct or behave (oneself) usually in a proper manner

²**demean** *transitive verb* **de·meaned; de·mean·ing** [*de-* + ¹*mean*] (1601)
: to lower in character, status, or reputation

**de·mean·or** \di-ˈmē-nər\ *noun* [¹*demean*] (circa 1485)
: behavior toward others : outward manner
**synonym** see BEARING

**demeanour** *British variant of* DEMEANOR

**de·ment·ed** \di-ˈmen-təd\ *adjective* (1644)
: MAD, INSANE
— **de·ment·ed·ly** *adverb*
— **de·ment·ed·ness** *noun*

**de·men·tia** \di-ˈmen(t)-shə, -shē-ə\ *noun* [Latin, from *dement-, demens* mad, from *de-* + *ment-, mens* mind — more at MIND] (1806)
**1** : a condition of deteriorated mentality often with emotional apathy
**2** : MADNESS, INSANITY ⟨a fanaticism bordering on *dementia*⟩
— **de·men·tial** \-shəl\ *adjective*

**dementia prae·cox** \-ˈprē-ˌkäks\ *noun* [New Latin, literally, premature dementia] (1899)
: SCHIZOPHRENIA

**de·mer·it** \di-ˈmer-ət, dē-\ *noun* [Middle English, from Middle French & Medieval Latin; Middle French *demerite*, from Medieval Latin *demeritum*, from neuter of *demeritus*, past participle of *demerēre* to be undeserving of, from Latin, to earn, from *de-* + *merēre* to merit] (15th century)
**1** *obsolete* : OFFENSE
**2 a** : a quality that deserves blame or lacks merit : FAULT, DEFECT **b** : lack of merit
**3** : a mark usually entailing a loss of privilege given to an offender

**De·mer·ol** \ˈde-mə-ˌról, -ˌrōl\ *trademark*
— used for meperidine

**de·mer·sal** \di-ˈmər-səl\ *adjective* [Latin *demersus* (past participle of *demergere* to sink, from *de-* + *mergere* to dip, sink) + English ¹*-al* — more at MERGE] (1889)
: living near, deposited on, or sinking to the bottom of the sea ⟨*demersal* fish eggs⟩

**de·mesne** \di-ˈmān, -ˈmēn\ *noun* [Middle English, from Anglo-French, modification of Old French *demaine* — more at DOMAIN] (14th century)
**1** : legal possession of land as one's own
**2** : REALM 4b, DOMAIN
**3** : manorial land actually possessed by the lord and not held by tenants
**4 a** : the land attached to a mansion **b** : landed property : ESTATE **c** : REGION 2, TERRITORY

**De·me·ter** \di-ˈmē-tər\ *noun* [Latin, from Greek *Dēmētēr*]
: the Greek goddess of agriculture — compare CERES

**demi-** *prefix* [Middle English, from *demi*, from Middle French, from (assumed) Vulgar Latin *dimedius*, modification of Latin *dimidius*, from *dis-* + *medius* mid — more at MID]
**1** : half ⟨*demi*semiquaver⟩
**2** : one that partly belongs to (a specified type or class) ⟨*demi*god⟩

**demi·god** \ˈde-mē-ˌgäd\ *noun* (1530)

**1** : a mythological being with more power than a mortal but less than a god
**2** : a person so outstanding as to seem to approach the divine

**demi·god·dess** \ˈde-mē-ˌgä-dəs\ *noun* (1603)
: a female demigod

**demi·john** \ˈde-mē-ˌjän\ *noun* [by folk etymology from French *dame-jeanne*, literally, Lady Jane] (1806)
: a large narrow-necked bottle usually enclosed in wickerwork

**demijohn**

**de·mil·i·ta·rize** \ˌ(ˌ)dē-ˈmi-lə-tə-ˌrīz, di-\ *transitive verb* (1883)
**1 a** : to do away with the military organization or potential of **b** : to prohibit (as a zone or frontier area) from being used for military purposes
**2** : to rid of military characteristics or uses
— **de·mil·i·tar·iza·tion** \ˌ(ˌ)dē-ˌmi-lə-t(ə-)rə-ˈzā-shən, di-\ *noun*

**demi·mon·daine** \ˌde-mi-ˌmän-ˈdān, -ˈmän-ˌ, -mē-\ *noun* [French *demi-mondaine*, from feminine of *demi-mondain*, from *demi-monde*] (1894)
: a woman of the demimonde

**demi·monde** \ˈde-mi-ˌmänd, -mē-\ *noun* [French *demi-monde*, from *demi-* + *monde* world, from Latin *mundus*] (1855)
**1 a** : a class of women on the fringes of respectable society supported by wealthy lovers **b** : PROSTITUTES
**2** : DEMIMONDAINE
**3** : a distinctive class, group, or activity that is often an isolated part of a larger class, group, or activity ⟨the pop music *demimonde*⟩ ⟨the literary *demimonde*⟩; *especially* : one having little reputation or prestige

**de·min·er·al·iza·tion** \ˌ(ˌ)dē-ˌmi-nə-rə-lə-ˈzā-shən, di-\ *noun* (1903)
**1** : loss of bodily minerals (as calcium salts) especially in disease
**2** : the process of removing mineral matter or salts (as from water)
— **de·min·er·al·ize** \ˌ(ˌ)dē-ˈmi-nə-rə-ˌlīz\ *transitive verb*
— **de·min·er·al·iz·er** \-ˌlī-zər\ *noun*

**demi·rep** \ˈde-mi-ˌrep, -mē-\ *noun* [*demi-* + *rep* (reprobate)] (1749)
: DEMIMONDAINE

¹**de·mise** \di-ˈmīz\ *verb* **de·mised; de·mis·ing** (15th century)
*transitive verb*
**1** : to convey (as an estate) by will or lease
**2** *obsolete* : CONVEY, GIVE
**3** : to transmit by succession or inheritance
*intransitive verb*
**1** : DIE, DECEASE
**2** : to pass by descent or bequest ⟨the property has *demised* to the king⟩

²**demise** *noun* [Middle French, feminine of *demis*, past participle of *demettre* to dismiss, from Latin *demittere* to send down, from *de-* + *mittere* to send] (15th century)
**1** : the conveyance of an estate
**2** : transfer of the sovereignty to a successor
**3 a** : DEATH **b** : a cessation of existence or activity **c** : a loss of position or status

**demi·sec** \ˌde-mi-ˈsek, -mē-\ *adjective* [French] (1926)
*of champagne* : moderately sweet

**demi·semi·qua·ver** \ˌde-mē-ˈse-mē-ˌkwā-vər\ *noun* (circa 1706)
: THIRTY-SECOND NOTE

**de·mis·sion** \di-ˈmi-shən\ *noun* [Middle French, from Latin *demission-, demissio* lowering, from *demittere*] (15th century)
: RESIGNATION, ABDICATION

**de·mit** \di-ˈmit\ *verb* **de·mit·ted; de·mit·ting** [Middle French *demettre*] (15th century)

*transitive verb*
**1** *archaic* : DISMISS
**2** : RESIGN
*intransitive verb*
: to withdraw from office or membership

**demi·tasse** \ˈde-mi-ˌtas, -ˌtäs, -mē\ *noun* [French *demi-tasse*, from *demi-* + *tasse* cup, from Middle French, from Arabic *ṭass*, from Persian *tast*] (1842)
: a small cup of black coffee; *also* : the cup used to serve it

**demi·urge** \ˈde-mē-ˌərj\ *noun* [Late Latin *demiurgus*, from Greek *dēmiourgos*, literally, artisan, one with special skill, from *dēmios* of the people (from *dēmos* people) + *-ourgos* worker (from *ergon* work) — more at DEMAGOGUE, WORK] (1678)
**1** *capitalized* **a** : a Platonic subordinate deity who fashions the sensible world in the light of eternal ideas **b** : a Gnostic subordinate deity who is the creator of the material world
**2** : one that is an autonomous creative force or decisive power
— **demi·ur·gic** \-ˈjik\ *also* **demi·ur·gi·cal** \-ji-kəl\ *adjective*

**demi·world** \ˈde-mē-ˌwərld\ *noun* (1862)
: DEMIMONDE 3

**demo** \ˈde-(ˌ)mō\ *noun, plural* **dem·os** (1793)
**1** *capitalized* : DEMOCRAT 2
**2 a** : DEMONSTRATION 1b **b** *British* : DEMONSTRATION 4
**3 a** : DEMONSTRATOR a **b** : a recording intended to show off a song or performer to a record producer

¹**de·mob** \ˌ(ˌ)dē-ˈmäb, di-\ *transitive verb* (1919)
*chiefly British* : DEMOBILIZE

²**demob** *noun* (1945)
*chiefly British* : the act or process of demobilizing

**de·mo·bi·lize** \di-ˈmō-bə-ˌlīz, ˌdē-\ *transitive verb* (1882)
**1** : DISBAND
**2** : to discharge from military service
— **de·mo·bi·li·za·tion** \di-ˌmō-bə-lə-ˈzā-shən, ˌdē-\ *noun*

**de·moc·ra·cy** \di-ˈmä-krə-sē\ *noun, plural* **-cies** [Middle French *democratie*, from Late Latin *democratia*, from Greek *dēmokratia*, from *dēmos* + *-kratia* -cracy] (1576)
**1 a** : government by the people; *especially* : rule of the majority **b** : a government in which the supreme power is vested in the people and exercised by them directly or indirectly through a system of representation usually involving periodically held free elections
**2** : a political unit that has a democratic government
**3** *capitalized* : the principles and policies of the Democratic party in the U.S.
**4** : the common people especially when constituting the source of political authority
**5** : the absence of hereditary or arbitrary class distinctions or privileges

**dem·o·crat** \ˈde-mə-ˌkrat\ *noun* (1740)
**1 a** : an adherent of democracy **b** : one who practices social equality
**2** *capitalized* : a member of the Democratic party of the U.S.

**dem·o·crat·ic** \ˌde-mə-ˈkra-tik\ *adjective* (1602)
**1** : of, relating to, or favoring democracy
**2** *often capitalized* : of or relating to one of the two major political parties in the U.S. evolving in the early 19th century from the antifederalists and the Democratic-Republican party and associated in modern times with policies of broad social reform and internationalism

**3 :** relating to, appealing to, or available to the broad masses of the people ⟨*democratic* art⟩
**4 :** favoring social equality **:** not snobbish
— **dem·o·crat·i·cal·ly** \-ti-k(ə-)lē\ *adverb*
**democratic centralism** *noun* (1926)
**:** a principle of Communist party organization by which members take part in policy discussions and elections at all levels but must follow decisions made at higher levels
**Democratic–Republican** *adjective* (1818)
**:** of or relating to a major American political party of the early 19th century favoring a strict interpretation of the constitution to restrict the powers of the federal government and emphasizing states' rights
**de·moc·ra·tize** \di-'mä-krə-,tīz\ *transitive verb* **-tized; -tiz·ing** (1798)
**:** to make democratic
— **de·moc·ra·ti·za·tion** \-,mä-krə-tə-'zā-shən\ *noun*
— **de·moc·ra·tiz·er** \-'mä-krə-,tī-zər\ *noun*
**dé·mo·dé** \,dā-mō-'dā\ *adjective* [French, from *dé-* de- + *mode*] (1873)
**:** no longer fashionable **:** OUT-OF-DATE
**de·mod·ed** \(,)dē-'mō-dəd\ *adjective* (1887)
**:** DÉMODÉ
**de·mod·u·late** \(,)dē-'mä-jə-,lāt\ *transitive verb* (1927)
**:** to extract the intelligence from (a modulated signal)
— **de·mod·u·la·tion** \(,)dē-,mä-jə-'lā-shən\ *noun*
— **de·mod·u·la·tor** \(')dē-'mä-jə-,lā-tər\ *noun*
**De·mo·gor·gon** \dē-mə-'gȯr-gən, 'dē-mə-,\ *noun* [Late Latin]
**:** a mysterious spirit or deity often explained as a primeval creator god who antedates the gods of Greek mythology
**de·mo·graph·ic** \,de-mə-'gra-fik, ,dē-mə-\ *also* **de·mo·graph·i·cal** \-fi-kəl\ *adjective* (1882)
**1 :** of or relating to demography or demographics
**2 :** relating to the dynamic balance of a population especially with regard to density and capacity for expansion or decline
— **de·mo·graph·i·cal·ly** \-fi-k(ə-)lē\ *adverb*
**de·mo·graph·ics** \-fiks\ *noun plural* (circa 1966)
**1 :** the statistical characteristics of human populations (as age or income) used especially to identify markets
**2 :** the demographic profile of a market (as the viewers of a TV show)
**de·mog·ra·phy** \di-'mä-grə-fē\ *noun* [French *démographie*, from Greek *dēmos* people + French *-graphie* -graphy] (1880)
**:** the statistical study of human populations especially with reference to size and density, distribution, and vital statistics
— **de·mog·ra·pher** \-fər\ *noun*
**dem·oi·selle** \,dem-wə-'zel\ *noun* [French, from Old French *dameisele* — more at DAMSEL] (1520)
**1 :** a young lady
**2 :** DAMSELFLY
**3 :** DAMSELFISH
**De·Moi·vre's theorem** \di-'mȯi-vərz-, -'mwäv(-rə)z-\ *noun* [Abraham *De Moivre* (died 1754) French mathematician] (circa 1891)
**:** a theorem of complex numbers: the *n*th power of a complex number has for its absolute value and its argument respectively the *n*th power of the absolute value and *n* times the argument of the complex number
**de·mol·ish** \di-'mä-lish\ *transitive verb* [Middle French *demoliss-*, stem of *demolir*, from Latin *demoliri*, from *de-* + *moliri* to construct, from *moles* mass — more at MOLE] (1570)
**1 a :** TEAR DOWN, RAZE **b :** to break to pieces **:** SMASH
**2 a :** to do away with **:** DESTROY **b :** to strip of any pretense of merit or credence

— **de·mol·ish·er** *noun*
— **de·mol·ish·ment** \-lish-mənt\ *noun*
**de·mo·li·tion** \,de-mə-'li-shən, ,dē-mə-\ *noun* (1549)
**1 :** the act of demolishing; *especially* **:** destruction in war by means of explosives
**2 *plural* :** explosives for destruction in war
— **de·mo·li·tion·ist** \-'li-sh(ə-)nəst\ *noun*
**demolition derby** *noun* (circa 1953)
**:** a contest in which skilled drivers ram old cars into one another until only one car remains running
**de·mon** *or* **dae·mon** \'dē-mən\ *noun* [Middle English *demon*, from Late Latin & Latin; Late Latin *daemon* evil spirit, from Latin, divinity, spirit, from Greek *daimōn*, probably from *daiesthai* to distribute — more at TIDE] (13th century)
**1 a :** an evil spirit **b :** a source or agent of evil, harm, distress, or ruin
**2** *usually* **daemon :** an attendant power or spirit **:** GENIUS
**3** *usually* **daemon :** a supernatural being of Greek mythology intermediate between gods and men
**4 :** one that has exceptional enthusiasm, drive, or effectiveness ⟨a *demon* for work⟩
— **de·mo·ni·an** \di-'mō-nē-ən\ *adjective*
— **de·mon·iza·tion** \,dē-mə-nə-'zā-shən\ *noun*
— **de·mon·ize** \'dē-mə-,nīz\ *transitive verb*
**de·mon·e·tize** \(,)dē-'mä-nə-,tīz, -'mä-\ *transitive verb* [French *démonétiser*, from *dé-* de- + Latin *moneta* coin — more at MINT] (1852)
**1 :** to stop using (a metal) as a monetary standard
**2 :** to deprive of value for official payment
— **de·mon·e·ti·za·tion** \(,)dē-,mä-nə-tə-'zā-shən, -,mə-\ *noun*
**¹de·mo·ni·ac** \di-'mō-nē-,ak\ *also* **de·mo·ni·a·cal** \,dē-mə-'nī-ə-kəl\ *adjective* [Middle English *demoniak*, from Late Latin *daemoniacus*, from Greek *daimoniakos*, from *daimon-, daimōn*] (14th century)
**1 :** possessed or influenced by a demon
**2 :** of, relating to, or suggestive of a demon **:** FIENDISH ⟨*demoniac* cruelty⟩
— **de·mo·ni·a·cal·ly** \,dē-mə-'nī-ə-k(ə-)lē\ *adverb*
**²demoniac** *noun* (14th century)
**:** one possessed by a demon
**de·mon·ic** \di-'mä-nik, dē-\ *also* **de·mon·i·cal** \-ni-kəl\ *adjective* (1662)
**:** DEMONIAC 2
— **de·mon·i·cal·ly** \-ni-k(ə-)lē\ *adverb*
**de·mon·ol·o·gy** \,dē-mə-'nä-lə-jē\ *noun* (1597)
**1 :** the study of demons or evil spirits
**2 :** belief in demons **:** a doctrine of evil spirits
**3 :** a catalog of enemies ⟨the liberal creed at that time put Big Business in a central place in its *demonology* —Carl Kaysen⟩
— **de·mon·o·log·i·cal** \,dē-mə-nə-'lä-ji-kəl\ *adjective*
— **de·mon·ol·o·gist** \-'nä-lə-jist\ *noun*
**de·mon·stra·ble** \di-'män(t)-strə-bəl\ *adjective* (15th century)
**1 :** capable of being demonstrated
**2 :** APPARENT, EVIDENT
— **de·mon·stra·bil·i·ty** \-,män(t)-strə-'bi-lə-tē\ *noun*
— **de·mon·stra·bly** \-blē\ *adverb*
**dem·on·strate** \'de-mən-,strāt\ *verb* **-strat·ed; -strat·ing** [Latin *demonstratus*, past participle of *demonstrare*, from *de-* + *monstrare* to show — more at MUSTER] (1552)
*transitive verb*
**1 :** to show clearly
**2 a :** to prove or make clear by reasoning or evidence **b :** to illustrate and explain especially with many examples
**3 :** to show or prove the value or efficiency of to a prospective buyer

*intransitive verb*
**:** to make a demonstration
**synonym** see SHOW
**dem·on·stra·tion** \,de-mən-'strā-shən\ *noun* (14th century)
**1 :** an act, process, or means of demonstrating to the intelligence: as **a** (1) **:** conclusive evidence **:** PROOF (2) **:** DERIVATION 5 **b :** a showing of the merits of a product or service to a prospective consumer
**2 :** an outward expression or display
**3 :** a show of armed force
**4 :** a public display of group feelings toward a person or cause
— **dem·on·stra·tion·al** \-shnəl, -shə-n°l\ *adjective*
**¹de·mon·stra·tive** \di-'män(t)-strə-tiv\ *adjective* (14th century)
**1 a :** demonstrating as real or true **b :** characterized or established by demonstration
**2 :** pointing out the one referred to and distinguishing it from others of the same class ⟨*demonstrative* pronouns⟩
**3 a :** marked by display of feeling **b :** inclined to display feelings openly
— **de·mon·stra·tive·ly** *adverb*
— **de·mon·stra·tive·ness** *noun*
**²demonstrative** *noun* (15th century)
**:** a demonstrative word or morpheme
**dem·on·stra·tor** \'de-mən-,strā-tər\ *noun* (1611)
**:** one that demonstrates: **a :** a product (as an automobile) used to demonstrate performance or merits to prospective buyers **b :** someone who engages in a public demonstration
**de·mor·al·ize** \di-'mȯr-ə-,līz, dē-, -'mär-\ *transitive verb* (circa 1793)
**1 :** to corrupt the morals of
**2 a :** to weaken the morale of **:** DISCOURAGE, DISPIRIT **b :** to upset or destroy the normal functioning of **c :** to throw into disorder
— **de·mor·al·iza·tion** \di-,mȯr-ə-lə-'zā-shən, ,dē-, -,mär-\ *noun*
— **de·mor·al·iz·er** \di-'mȯr-ə-,lī-zər, ,dē-, -'mär-\ *noun*
— **de·mor·al·iz·ing·ly** \-ziŋ-lē\ *adverb*
**de·mos** \'dē-,mäs\ *noun* [Greek *dēmos* — more at DEMAGOGUE] (1831)
**1 :** POPULACE
**2 :** the common people of an ancient Greek state
**de·mote** \di-'mōt, ,dē-\ *transitive verb* **de·mot·ed; de·mot·ing** [*de-* + *-mote* (as in *promote*)] (circa 1891)
**1 :** to reduce to a lower grade or rank
**2 :** to relegate to a less important position
— **de·mo·tion** \-'mō-shən\ *noun*
**de·mot·ic** \di-'mä-tik\ *adjective* [Greek *dēmotikos*, from *dēmotēs* commoner, from *dēmos*] (1822)
**1 :** of, relating to, or written in a simplified form of the ancient Egyptian hieratic writing
**2 :** POPULAR, COMMON ⟨*demotic* idiom⟩
**3 :** of or relating to the form of Modern Greek that is based on everyday speech
**de·mount** \(,)dē-'mau̇nt\ *transitive verb* (circa 1930)
**1 :** to remove from a mounted position
**2 :** DISASSEMBLE
— **de·mount·able** \-tə-bəl\ *adjective*
**¹de·mul·cent** \di-'məl-sənt\ *adjective* [Latin *demulcent-, demulcens*, present participle of *demulcēre* to soothe, from *de-* + *mulcēre* to soothe] (1732)
**:** SOOTHING
**²demulcent** *noun* (1732)
**:** a usually mucilaginous or oily substance (as tragacanth) that can soothe or protect an abraded mucous membrane
**de·mul·ti·plex·er** \(,)dē-'məl-tə-,plek-sər\ *noun* (1963)
**:** an electronic device that separates a multiplex signal into its component parts

¹**de·mur** \di-'mər\ *intransitive verb* **de·murred; de·mur·ring** [Middle English *demeoren* to linger, from Old French *demorer,* from Latin *demorari,* from *de-* + *morari* to linger, from *mora* delay — more at MORA] (13th century)
**1** *archaic* **:** DELAY, HESITATE
**2 :** to file a demurrer
**3 :** to take exception **:** OBJECT — often used with *to* or *at*

²**demur** *noun* (13th century)
**1 :** hesitation (as in doing or accepting) usually based on doubt of the acceptability of something offered or proposed
**2 :** the act or an instance of objecting **:** PROTEST
*synonym* see QUALM

**de·mure** \di-'myu̇r\ *adjective* [Middle English] (14th century)
**1 :** RESERVED, MODEST
**2 :** affectedly modest, reserved, or serious **:** COY
— **de·mure·ly** *adverb*
— **de·mure·ness** *noun*

**de·mur·rage** \di-'mər-ij, -'mə-rij\ *noun* (1641)
**1 :** the detention of a ship by the freighter beyond the time allowed for loading, unloading, or sailing
**2 :** a charge for detaining a ship, freight car, or truck

**de·mur·ral** \di-'mər-əl, -'mə-rəl\ *noun* (1810)
**:** the act or an instance of demurring

¹**de·mur·rer** \di-'mər-ər, -'mə-rər\ *noun* [Middle French *demorer,* verb] (circa 1521)
**1 :** a response in a court proceeding in which the defendant does not dispute the truth of the allegation but claims it is not sufficient grounds to justify legal action
**2 :** OBJECTION

²**de·mur·rer** \-'mər-ər\ *noun* [¹*demur*] (1711)
**:** one that demurs

**de·my·e·lin·at·ing** \(,)dē-'mī-ə-lə-,nā-tiŋ\ *adjective* (1939)
**:** causing or characterized by the loss or destruction of myelin ⟨*demyelinating* diseases⟩ ⟨a *demyelinating* agent⟩
— **de·my·e·lin·ation** \(,)dē-,mī-ə-lə-'nā-shən\ *noun*

**de·mys·ti·fy** \(,)dē-'mis-tə-,fī\ *transitive verb* (1963)
**:** to eliminate the mystifying features of
— **de·mys·ti·fi·ca·tion** \(,)dē-,mis-tə-fə-'kā-shən\ *noun*

**de·my·thol·o·gize** \,dē-mi-'thä-lə-,jīz\ *transitive verb* (1950)
**1 :** to divest of mythological forms in order to uncover the meaning underlying them ⟨*demythologize* the Gospels⟩
**2 :** to divest of mythical elements or associations
— **de·my·thol·o·gi·za·tion** \-,thä-lə-jə-'zā-shən\ *noun*
— **de·my·thol·o·giz·er** \-'thä-lə-,jī-zər\ *noun*

¹**den** \'den\ *noun* [Middle English, from Old English *denn;* akin to Old English *denu* valley, Old High German *tenni* threshing floor] (before 12th century)
**1 :** the lair of a wild usually predatory animal
**2 a** (1) **:** a hollow or cavern used especially as a hideout (2) **:** a center of secret activity **b :** a small usually squalid dwelling
**3 :** a comfortable usually secluded room
**4 :** a subdivision of a Cub Scout pack made up of two or more boys

²**den** *verb* **denned; den·ning** (13th century)
*intransitive verb*
**:** to live in or retire to a den
*transitive verb*
**:** to drive into a den

**de·nar·i·us** \di-'nar-ē-əs, -'ner-\ *noun, plural* **de·nar·ii** \-ē-,ī, -ē-,ē\ [Middle English, from Latin — more at DENIER] (14th century)
**1 :** a small silver coin of ancient Rome
**2 :** a gold coin of the Roman Empire equivalent to 25 denarii

**de·na·tion·al·ize** \(')dē-'nash-nə-,līz, -'na-shə-nᵊl-,īz\ *transitive verb* (1807)
**1 :** to divest of national character or rights
**2 :** to remove from ownership or control by the national government
— **de·na·tion·al·iza·tion** \(,)dē-,nash-nə-lə-'zā-shən, -,na-shə-nᵊl-ə-'zā-\ *noun*

**de·nat·u·ral·ize** \(,)dē-'na-ch(ə-)rə-,līz\ *transitive verb* (1800)
**1 :** to make unnatural
**2 :** to deprive of the rights and duties of a citizen
— **de·nat·u·ral·iza·tion** \(,)dē-,na-ch(ə-)rə-lə-'zā-shən\ *noun*

**de·na·ture** \(,)dē-'nā-chər\ *verb* **de·na·tured; de·na·tur·ing** \-'nā-ch(ə-)riŋ\ (1685)
*transitive verb*
**1 :** DEHUMANIZE
**2 :** to deprive of natural qualities **:** change the nature of: as **a :** to make (alcohol) unfit for drinking (as by adding an obnoxious substance) without impairing usefulness for other purposes **b :** to modify the molecular structure of (as a protein or DNA) especially by heat, acid, alkali, or ultraviolet radiation so as to destroy or diminish some of the original properties and especially the specific biological activity
*intransitive verb*
**:** to become denatured
— **de·na·tur·ant** \(,)dē-'nā-chər-ənt\ *noun*
— **de·na·tur·ation** \(,)dē-,nā-chə-'rā-shən\ *noun*

**de·na·zi·fy** \(,)dē-'nät-si-,fī, -'nat-\ *transitive verb* **-fied; -fy·ing** (1940)
**:** to rid of Nazism and its influence
— **de·na·zi·fi·ca·tion** \(,)dē-,nät-si-fə-'kā-shən, -,nat-\ *noun*

**dendr-** *or* **dendro-** *combining form* [Greek, from *dendron;* akin to Greek *drys* tree — more at TREE]
**:** tree ⟨*dendro*logy⟩ **:** resembling a tree ⟨*dend*rite⟩

**den·dri·form** \'den-drə-,fȯrm\ *adjective* (circa 1847)
**:** resembling a tree in structure

**den·drite** \'den-,drīt\ *noun* (1751)
**1 :** a branching treelike figure produced on or in a mineral by a foreign mineral; *also* **:** the mineral so marked
**2 :** a crystallized arborescent form
**3 :** any of the usually branching protoplasmic processes that conduct impulses toward the body of a nerve cell
**den·drit·ic** \(,)den-'dri-tik\ *adjective* (1816)
**:** resembling or having dendrites **:** branching like a tree ⟨a *dendritic* drainage system⟩ ⟨*dendritic* cells⟩

**den·dro·chro·nol·o·gy** \,den-(,)drō-krə-'nä-lə-jē\ *noun* (circa 1928)
**:** the science of dating events and variations in environment in former periods by comparative study of growth rings in trees and aged wood
— **den·dro·chro·no·log·i·cal** \-,krä-nə-'lä-ji-kəl, -,krō-\ *adjective*
— **den·dro·chro·no·log·i·cal·ly** \-ji-k(ə-)lē\ *adverb*
— **den·dro·chro·nol·o·gist** \-krə-'nä-lə-jist\ *noun*

**den·dro·gram** \'den-drə-,gram\ *noun* (circa 1953)
**:** a branching diagram representing a hierarchy of categories based on degree of similarity or number of shared characteristics especially in biological taxonomy — compare CLADOGRAM

**den·droid** \'den-,drȯid\ *adjective* [Greek *dendroeidēs,* from *dendron*] (circa 1828)
**:** resembling a tree in form **:** ARBORESCENT

denarius of Julius Caesar, 44 B.C.

**den·drol·o·gy** \den-'drä-lə-jē\ *noun* (circa 1708)
**:** the study of trees
— **den·dro·log·ic** \,den-drə-'lä-jik\ *or* **den·dro·log·i·cal** \-ji-kəl\ *adjective*
— **den·drol·o·gist** \den-'drä-lə-jist\ *noun*

**dene** \'dēn\ *noun* [Middle English, from Old English *denu*] (before 12th century)
*British* **:** VALLEY

**Dé·né** \de-'nā, dā-\ *noun, plural* **Dé·né** *or* **Dé·nés** \-āz\ [Canadian French, from Athabascan; akin to Chipewyan *dene* person] (1891)
**:** a member of any of the Athabascan-speaking peoples of the interior of Alaska and northwestern Canada; *also* **:** the languages of these peoples

**Den·eb** \'de-,neb, -nəb\ *noun* [Arabic *dhanab al-dajāja,* literally, the tail of the hen]
**:** a star of the first magnitude in Cygnus

**den·e·ga·tion** \,de-ni-'gā-shən\ *noun* [Middle English *denegacioun,* from Middle French or Latin; Middle French *denegation,* from Latin *denegation-, denegatio,* from *denegare* to deny — more at DENY] (15th century)
**:** DENIAL

**de·ner·vate** \'dē-(,)nər-,vāt\ *transitive verb* **-vat·ed; -vat·ing** (1905)
**:** to deprive of a nerve supply (as by cutting a nerve)
— **de·ner·va·tion** \dē-(,)nər-'vā-shən\ *noun*

**den·gue** \'deŋ-gē, -,gā\ *noun* [American Spanish] (1828)
**:** an acute infectious disease caused by an arbovirus, transmitted by aedes mosquitoes, and characterized by headache, severe joint pain, and a rash — called also *breakbone fever, dengue fever*

**de·ni·abil·i·ty** \di-,nī-ə-'bi-lə-tē\ *noun* (1973)
**:** the ability to deny something especially on the basis of being officially uninformed

**de·ni·able** \di-'nī-ə-bəl, dē-\ *adjective* (1548)
**:** capable of being denied

**de·ni·al** \di-'nī(-ə)l, dē-\ *noun* (1528)
**1 :** refusal to satisfy a request or desire
**2 a** (1) **:** refusal to admit the truth or reality (as of a statement or charge) (2) **:** assertion that an allegation is false **b :** refusal to acknowledge a person or a thing **:** DISAVOWAL
**3 :** the opposing by the defendant of an allegation of the opposite party in a lawsuit
**4 :** SELF-DENIAL
**5 :** negation in logic
**6 :** a psychological defense mechanism in which confrontation with a personal problem or with reality is avoided by denying the existence of the problem or reality

¹**de·ni·er** \di-'nī(-ə)r, dē-\ *noun* (15th century)
**:** one that denies

²**de·nier** *noun* [Middle English *denere,* from Middle French *denier,* from Latin *denarius,* coin worth ten asses, from *denarius* containing ten, from *deni* ten each, from *decem* ten — more at TEN] (15th century)
**1** \də-'ni(ə)r, də-'nyā\ **:** a small originally silver coin formerly used in western Europe
**2** \'de-nyər\ **:** a unit of fineness for yarn equal to the fineness of a yarn weighing one gram for each 9000 meters ⟨100-*denier* yarn is finer than 150-*denier* yarn⟩

**den·i·grate** \'de-ni-,grāt\ *transitive verb* **-grat·ed; -grat·ing** [Latin *denigratus,* past participle of *denigrare,* from *de-* + *nigrare* to blacken, from *nigr-, niger* black] (1526)
**1 :** to cast aspersions on **:** DEFAME
**2 :** to deny the importance or validity of **:** BELITTLE
— **den·i·gra·tion** \,de-ni-'grā-shən\ *noun*
— **den·i·gra·tive** \'de-ni-,grā-tiv\ *adjective*
— **den·i·gra·tor** \-,grā-tər\ *noun*

**— den·i·gra·to·ry** \'de-ni-grə-ˌtōr-ē, -ˌtȯr-\ *adjective*

**den·im** \'de-nəm\ *noun* [French (*serge*) *de Nîmes* serge of Nîmes, France] (1695)
**1 a :** a firm durable twilled usually cotton fabric woven with colored warp and white filling threads **b :** a similar fabric woven in colored stripes
**2** *plural* **:** overalls or trousers usually of blue denim ◆

**de·ni·tri·fi·ca·tion** \(ˌ)dē-ˌnī-trə-fə-'kā-shən\ *noun* (1883)
**:** the loss or removal of nitrogen or nitrogen compounds; *specifically* **:** reduction of nitrates or nitrites commonly by bacteria (as in soil) that usually results in the escape of nitrogen into the air
**— de·ni·tri·fi·er** \-'nī-trə-ˌfī-ər\ *noun*
**— de·ni·tri·fy** \-'nī-trə-ˌfī\ *transitive verb*

**den·i·zen** \'de-nə-zən\ *noun* [Middle English *denizeine*, from Anglo-French *denzein* inhabitant, inner part, inner, from Old French *denz* within, from Late Latin *deintus*, from Latin *de-* + *intus* within — more at ENT-] (15th century)
**1 :** INHABITANT
**2 :** one admitted to residence in a foreign country; *especially* **:** an alien admitted to rights of citizenship
**3 :** one that frequents a place

**den mother** *noun* (1946)
**:** a female adult leader of a Cub Scout den; *also* **:** a person seen in the role of leader or protector of a group

**de·nom·i·nal** \dē-'nä-mə-n°l\ *adjective* (1951)
**:** derived from a noun

**de·nom·i·nate** \di-'nä-mə-ˌnāt, dē-\ *transitive verb* [Latin *denominatus*, past participle of *denominare*, from *de-* + *nominare* to name — more at NOMINATE] (circa 1552)
**1 :** to give a name to **:** DESIGNATE
**2 :** to express or designate in some denomination ⟨will *denominate* prices in U.S. dollars⟩

**de·nom·i·nate number** \di-ˌnä-mə-nət-\ *noun* [Latin *denominatus*] (1579)
**:** a number (as *7* in *7 feet*) that specifies a quantity in terms of a unit of measurement

**de·nom·i·na·tion** \di-ˌnä-mə-'nā-shən\ *noun* (15th century)
**1 :** an act of denominating
**2 :** a value or size of a series of values or sizes (as of money)
**3 :** NAME, DESIGNATION; *especially* **:** a general name for a category
**4 :** a religious organization uniting local congregations in a single legal and administrative body
**— de·nom·i·na·tion·al** \-shnəl, -shə-n°l\ *adjective*

**de·nom·i·na·tion·al·ism** \-shə-nə-ˌli-zəm\ *noun* (circa 1855)
**1 :** devotion to denominational principles or interests
**2 :** the emphasizing of denominational differences to the point of being narrowly exclusive **:** SECTARIANISM

**de·nom·i·na·tive** \di-'nä-mə-nə-tiv\ *adjective* [Latin *de* from + *nomin-, nomen* name] (circa 1783)
**:** derived from a noun or adjective
**— denominative** *noun*

**de·nom·i·na·tor** \di-'nä-mə-ˌnā-tər\ *noun* (circa 1542)
**1 :** the part of a fraction below the line signifying division that functions as the divisor of the numerator and in fractions with 1 as the numerator indicates into how many parts the unit is divided
**2 a :** a common trait **b :** the average level (as of taste or opinion) **:** STANDARD

**de·no·ta·tion** \ˌdē-nō-'tā-shən\ *noun* (circa 1532)
**1 :** an act or process of denoting
**2 :** MEANING; *especially* **:** a direct specific meaning as distinct from an implied or associated idea

**3 a :** a denoting term **:** NAME **b :** SIGN, INDICATION ⟨visible *denotations* of divine wrath⟩
**4 :** the totality of things to which a term is applicable especially in logic — compare CONNOTATION

**de·no·ta·tive** \'dē-nō-ˌtā-tiv, di-'nō-tə-tiv\ *adjective* (circa 1611)
**1 :** denoting or tending to denote
**2 :** relating to denotation

**de·note** \di-'nōt, dē-\ *transitive verb* [Middle French *denoter*, from Latin *denotare*, from *de-* + *notare* to note] (1592)
**1 :** to serve as an indication of **:** BETOKEN ⟨the swollen bellies that *denote* starvation⟩
**2 :** to serve as an arbitrary mark for ⟨red flares *denoting* danger⟩
**3 :** to make known **:** ANNOUNCE ⟨his crestfallen look *denoted* his distress⟩
**4 a :** to serve as a linguistic expression of the notion of **:** MEAN **b :** to stand for **:** DESIGNATE
**— de·note·ment** \-'nōt-mənt\ *noun*

**de·noue·ment** *also* **dé·noue·ment** \ˌdā-ˌnü-'mäⁿ, dā-'nü-\ *noun* [French *dénouement*, literally, untying, from Middle French *desnouement*, from *desnouer* to untie, from Old French *desnoer*, from *des-* de- + *noer* to tie, from Latin *nodare*, from *nodus* knot — more at NODE] (1752)
**1 :** the final outcome of the main dramatic complication in a literary work
**2 :** the outcome of a complex sequence of events

**de·nounce** \di-'naun(t)s, dē-\ *transitive verb* **de·nounced; de·nounc·ing** [Middle English, from Old French *denoncier* to proclaim, from Latin *denuntiare*, from *de-* + *nuntiare* to report — more at ANNOUNCE] (13th century)
**1 :** to pronounce especially publicly to be blameworthy or evil
**2** *archaic* **a :** PROCLAIM **b :** to announce threateningly
**3 :** to inform against **:** ACCUSE
**4** *obsolete* **:** PORTEND
**5 :** to announce formally the termination of (as a treaty)
**synonym** see CRITICIZE
**— de·nounce·ment** \-'naun(t)-smənt\ *noun*
**— de·nounc·er** *noun*

**de no·vo** \di-'nō-(ˌ)vō, dā-, dē-\ *adverb or adjective* [Latin] (1536)
**:** over again **:** ANEW

**dense** \'den(t)s\ *adjective* **dens·er; dens·est** [Latin *densus*; akin to Greek *dasys* thick with hair or leaves] (15th century)
**1 a :** marked by compactness or crowding together of parts **b :** having a high mass per unit volume ⟨carbon dioxide is a *dense* gas⟩
**2 a :** marked by a stupid imperviousness to ideas or impressions **:** THICKHEADED **b :** EXTREME ⟨*dense* ignorance⟩
**3 :** having between any two elements at least one element ⟨the set of rational numbers is *dense*⟩
**4 :** demanding concentration to follow or comprehend ⟨*dense* prose⟩
**5 :** having high or relatively high opacity ⟨a *dense* fog⟩ ⟨a *dense* photographic negative⟩
**synonym** see STUPID
**— dense·ly** *adverb*
**— dense·ness** \'den(t)-snəs\ *noun*

**den·si·fy** \'den(t)-sə-ˌfī\ *transitive verb* **-fied; -fy·ing** (1820)
**:** to make denser **:** COMPRESS
**— den·si·fi·ca·tion** \ˌden(t)-sə-fə-'kā-shən\ *noun*

**den·si·tom·e·ter** \ˌden(t)-sə-'tä-mə-tər\ *noun* (1901)
**:** an instrument for determining optical or photographic density
**— den·si·to·met·ric** \ˌden(t)-sə-tə-'me-trik\ *adjective*
**— den·si·tom·e·try** \ˌden(t)-sə-'tä-mə-trē\ *noun*

**den·si·ty** \'den(t)-sə-tē\ *noun, plural* **-ties** (1603)

**1 :** the quality or state of being dense
**2 :** the quantity per unit volume, unit area, or unit length: as **a :** the mass of a substance per unit volume **b :** the distribution of a quantity (as mass, electricity, or energy) per unit usually of space (as length, area, or volume) **c :** the average number of individuals or units per space unit ⟨a population *density* of 500 per square mile⟩ ⟨a housing *density* of 10 houses per acre⟩
**3 a :** the degree of opacity of a translucent medium **b :** the common logarithm of the opacity

**density function** *noun* (circa 1962)
**:** PROBABILITY DENSITY FUNCTION

**¹dent** \'dent\ *verb* [Middle English, short for *indenten* to make dents in, indent] (14th century)
*transitive verb*
**1 :** to make a dent in
**2 :** to have a weakening effect on
*intransitive verb*
**:** to form a dent by sinking inward **:** become dented

**²dent** *noun* (1565)
**1 :** a depression or hollow made by a blow or by pressure
**2 a :** an impression or effect often made against resistance and usually having a weakening effect **b :** initial progress **:** HEADWAY

**³dent** *noun* [French, literally, tooth, from Latin *dent-, dens*] (1703)
**:** TOOTH 3a

**dent-** *or* **denti-** *or* **dento-** *combining form* [Middle English *denti-*, from Latin, from *dent-, dens* tooth — more at TOOTH]
**:** tooth **:** teeth ⟨*dentiform*⟩

**¹den·tal** \'den-t°l\ *adjective* [Latin *dentalis*, from *dent-, dens*] (1594)
**1 :** articulated with the tip or blade of the tongue against or near the upper front teeth
**2 :** of or relating to the teeth or dentistry
**— den·tal·ly** \-ē\ *adverb*

**²dental** *noun* (circa 1727)
**:** a dental consonant

**dental floss** *noun* (1910)
**:** a thread used to clean between the teeth

**dental hygienist** *noun* (circa 1922)
**:** a licensed dental professional who cleans and examines teeth

**den·ta·li·um** \den-'tä-lē-əm\ *noun, plural* **-lia** \-lē-ə\ [New Latin, genus name, from Latin *dentalis*] (1864)
**:** any of a genus (*Dentalium*) of widely distributed tooth shells; *broadly* **:** TOOTH SHELL

**dental technician** *noun* (1946)
**:** one who makes dental appliances

**den·tate** \'den-ˌtāt\ *adjective* [Latin *dentatus*, from *dent-, dens*] (1810)
**:** having teeth or pointed conical projections ⟨a *dentate* margin of a leaf⟩

**dent corn** *noun* (1873)
**:** an Indian corn having kernels that contain both hard and soft starch and that become indented at maturity

**den·ti·cle** \'den-ti-kəl\ *noun* [Middle English, from Latin *denticulus*, diminutive of *dent-, dens*] (14th century)
**:** a conical pointed projection (as a small tooth)

**den·tic·u·late** \den-'ti-kyə-lət\ *or* **den·tic·u·lat·ed** \-,lā-təd\ *adjective* (1661)
**1** : finely dentate or serrate ⟨a *denticulate* shell⟩ ⟨a *denticulate* margin of a leaf⟩
**2** : cut into dentils
— **den·tic·u·la·tion** \(,)den-,ti-kyə-'lā-shən\ *noun*

**den·ti·form** \'den-tə-,form\ *adjective* (1708)
: shaped like a tooth

**den·ti·frice** \'den-tə-frəs\ *noun* [Middle French, from Latin *dentifricium*, from *denti-* + *fricare* to rub — more at FRICTION] (15th century)
: a powder, paste, or liquid for cleaning the teeth

**den·til** \'den-t°l, -,til\ *noun* [obsolete French *dentille*, from Middle French, diminutive of *dent*] (1663)
: one of a series of small projecting rectangular blocks forming a molding especially under a cornice
— **den·tiled** \-t°ld, -,tild\ *adjective*

**den·tin** \'den-t°n\ *or* **den·tine** \'den-,tēn, den-'\ *noun* (1845)
: a calcareous material similar to but harder and denser than bone that composes the principal mass of a tooth — see TOOTH illustration
— **den·tin·al** \den-'tē-n°l, 'den-t°n-əl\ *adjective*

**den·tist** \'den-təst\ *noun* [French *dentiste*, from *dent*] (1752)
: one who is skilled in and licensed to practice the prevention, diagnosis, and treatment of diseases, injuries, and malformations of the teeth, jaws, and mouth and who makes and inserts false teeth

**den·tist·ry** \'den-tə-strē\ *noun* (1838)
: the art or profession of a dentist

**den·ti·tion** \den-'ti-shən\ *noun* [Latin *dentition-, dentitio*, from *dentire* to cut teeth, from *dent-, dens*] (1615)
**1** : the development and cutting of teeth
**2** : the character of a set of teeth especially with regard to their number, kind, and arrangement — see TOOTH illustration
**3** : TEETH

**den·tu·lous** \'den-chə-ləs\ *adjective* [back-formation from *edentulous*] (1926)
: having teeth

**den·ture** \'den-chər\ *noun* [French, from Middle French, from *dent*] (1874)
**1** : a set of teeth
**2** : an artificial replacement for one or more teeth; *especially* : a set of false teeth

**den·tur·ist** \'den-chə-rist\ *noun* (1965)
: a dental technician who makes, fits, and repairs dentures directly for the public

**de·nu·cle·ar·ize** \(')dē-'n(y)ü-klē-ə-,rīz, ÷-kyə-lə-,rīz\ *transitive verb* **-ized; -iz·ing** (1958)
: to remove nuclear arms from : prohibit the use of nuclear arms in
— **de·nu·cle·ar·iza·tion** \(,)dē-,n(y)ü-klē-ə-rə-'zā-shən, ÷-kyə-lə-rə-\ *noun*

**de·nude** \di-'n(y)üd, dē-\ *transitive verb* **de·nud·ed; de·nud·ing** [Latin *denudare*, from *de-* + *nudus* bare — more at NAKED] (15th century)
**1** : to deprive of something important
**2 a** : to strip of all covering or surface layers **b** : to lay bare by erosion **c** : to strip (land) of forests
— **de·nu·da·tion** \,dē-(,)n(y)ü-'dā-shən, ,den-yü-\ *noun*
— **de·nude·ment** \di-'n(y)üd-mənt\ *noun*

**de·nu·mer·a·ble** \di-'n(y)ü-mə-rə-bəl\ *adjective* (1902)
: capable of being put into one-to-one correspondence with the positive integers
— **de·nu·mer·a·bil·i·ty** \-,n(y)ü-mə-rə-'bi-lə-tē\ *noun*
— **de·nu·mer·a·bly** \-'n(y)ü-mə-rə-blē\ *adverb*

**de·nun·ci·a·tion** \di-,nən(t)-sē-'ā-shən\ *noun* (1842)

: an act of denouncing; *especially* : a public condemnation
— **de·nun·ci·a·tive** \-'nən(t)-sē-,ā-tiv\ *adjective*
— **de·nun·ci·a·to·ry** \-sē-ə-,tōr-ē, -,tòr-\ *adjective*

**Den·ver boot** \'den-vər-\ *noun* [*Denver, Colo.*] (1968)
: a metal clamp that is locked onto one of the wheels of an automobile to immobilize it especially until its owner pays accumulated parking fines

**Denver omelet** *noun* (1954)
: WESTERN OMELET

**Denver sandwich** *noun* (1950)
: WESTERN SANDWICH

**de·ny** \di-'nī, dē-\ *transitive verb* **de·nied; de·ny·ing** [Middle English, from Middle French *denier*, from Latin *denegare*, from *de-* + *negare* to deny — more at NEGATE] (14th century)
**1** : to declare untrue
**2** : to disclaim connection with or responsibility for : DISAVOW
**3 a** : to give a negative answer to **b** : to refuse to grant **c** : to restrain (oneself) from gratification of desires
**4** *archaic* : DECLINE
**5** : to refuse to accept the existence, truth, or validity of ☆
— **de·ny·ing·ly** \-'nī-iŋ-lē\ *adverb*

**deoch an dor·is** \,d(y)ók-°n-'dōr-əs\ *Scottish & Irish variant of* DOCH-AN-DORRIS

**de·o·dar** \'dē-ə-,där\ *also* **de·o·da·ra** \,dē-ə-'där-ə\ *noun* [Hindi *deodār*, from Sanskrit *devadāru*, literally, timber of the gods, from *deva* god + *dāru* wood — more at DEITY, TREE] (1842)
: an East Indian cedar (*Cedrus deodara*)

**de·odor·ant** \dē-'ō-də-rənt\ *noun* (1869)
: a preparation that destroys or masks unpleasant odors
— **deodorant** *adjective*

**de·odor·ize** \dē-'ō-də-,rīz\ *transitive verb* (1856)
**1** : to eliminate or prevent the offensive odor of
**2** : to make (something unpleasant or reprehensible) more acceptable ⟨the movie *deodorizes* his scandalous career⟩
— **de·odor·iza·tion** \-,ō-də-rə-'zā-shən\ *noun*
— **de·odor·iz·er** *noun*

**de·on·tic** \(,)dē-'än-tik\ *adjective* [Greek *deont-, deon* that which is obligatory, from neuter of present participle of *dein* to lack, be needful — more at DEUTER-] (circa 1866)
: of or relating to moral obligation : DEONTOLOGICAL

**de·on·tol·o·gy** \,dē-,än-'tä-lə-jē\ *noun* (1826)
: the theory or study of moral obligation
— **de·on·to·log·i·cal** \,dē-,än-tə-'lä-ji-kəl\ *adjective*
— **de·on·tol·o·gist** \dē-,än-'tä-lə-jist\ *noun*

**Deo vo·len·te** \,dā-(,)ō-vō-'len-tē, ,dē-\ [Latin] (1767)
: God being willing

**de·ox·i·dize** \(,)dē-'äk-sə-,dīz\ *transitive verb* (1794)
: to remove oxygen from
— **de·ox·i·da·tion** \(,)dē-,äk-sə-'dā-shən\ *noun*
— **de·ox·i·diz·er** \(,)dē-'äk-sə-,dī-zər\ *noun*

**de·oxy** \(,)dē-'äk-sē\ *also* **des·oxy** \(,)dē-'zäk-sē, -'säk-\ *adjective* [International Scientific Vocabulary]
: containing less oxygen in the molecule than the compound from which it is derived ⟨*deoxy* sugars⟩ — usually used in combination ⟨*de*oxyribonucleic acid⟩

**de·ox·y·gen·ate** \(,)dē-'äk-si-jə-,nāt, ,dē-,äk-'si-jə-\ *transitive verb* (1799)
: to remove oxygen from
— **de·ox·y·gen·ation** \(,)dē-,äk-si-jə-'nā-shən, ,dē-,äk-,si-jə-\ *noun*

**de·ox·y·gen·at·ed** *adjective* (1799)
: having the hemoglobin in the reduced state

**de·oxy·ri·bo·nu·cle·ase** \(,)dē-,äk-si-,rī-bō-'n(y)ü-klē-,ās, -,āz\ *noun* (1946)
: an enzyme that hydrolyzes DNA to nucleotides — called also *DNase*

**de·oxy·ri·bo·nu·cle·ic acid** \(,)dē-,äk-si-,rī-bō-n(y)ü-,klē-ik-, -,klā-\ *noun* [*deoxyribose* + *nucleic acid*] (1938)
: DNA

**de·oxy·ri·bo·nu·cle·o·tide** \-'n(y)ü-klē-ə-,tīd\ *noun* (1972)
: a nucleotide that contains deoxyribose and is a constituent of DNA

**de·oxy·ri·bose** \(,)dē-,äk-si-'rī-,bōs, -,bōz\ *noun* [International Scientific Vocabulary] (1957)
: a pentose sugar $C_5H_{10}O_4$ that is a structural element of DNA

**de·part** \di-'pärt\ *verb* [Middle English, to divide, part company, from Old French *departir*, from *de-* + *partir* to divide, from Latin *partire*, from *part-, pars* part] (13th century)
*intransitive verb*
**1 a** : to go away : LEAVE **b** : DIE
**2** : to turn aside : DEVIATE
*transitive verb*
: to go away from : LEAVE
*synonym* see SWERVE

**de·part·ed** *adjective* (14th century)
**1** : BYGONE
**2** : having died especially recently ⟨mourning our *departed* friend⟩
*synonym* see DEAD

**de·part·ment** \di-'pärt-mənt\ *noun* [French *département*, from Old French, act of dividing, from *departir*] (1735)
**1 a** : a distinct sphere : PROVINCE ⟨that's not my *department*⟩ **b** : a category consisting especially of a measurable activity or attribute ⟨lacking in the trustworthiness *department* —Garrison Keillor⟩
**2** : a functional or territorial division: as **a** : a major administrative division of a government **b** : a major territorial administrative subdivision **c** : a division of a college or school giving instruction in a particular subject **d** : a major division of a business **e** : a section of a department store handling a particular kind of merchandise **f** : a territorial subdivision made for the administration and training of military units
— **de·part·men·tal** \di-,pärt-'men-t°l, ,dē-\ *adjective*
— **de·part·men·tal·ly** \-t°l-ē\ *adverb*

**de·part·men·tal·ize** \di-,pärt-'men-t°l-,īz, ,dē-\ *transitive verb* **-ized; -iz·ing** (circa 1895)
: to divide into departments
— **de·part·men·tal·iza·tion** \-,men-t°l-ə-'zā-shən\ *noun*

**department store** *noun* (1887)
: a store selling a wide variety of goods and arranged in several departments

---

☆ SYNONYMS
**Deny, gainsay, contradict, contravene** mean to refuse to accept as true or valid. DENY implies a firm refusal to accept as true, to grant or concede, or to acknowledge the existence or claims of ⟨*denied* the charges⟩. GAINSAY implies disputing the truth of what another has said ⟨no one can *gainsay* her claims⟩. CONTRADICT implies an open or flat denial ⟨her account *contradicts* his⟩. CONTRAVENE implies not so much an intentional opposition as some inherent incompatibility ⟨laws that *contravene* tradition⟩.

---

**de·par·ture** \di-'pär-chər\ *noun* (15th century) **1 a** (1) **:** the act or an instance of departing (2) *archaic* **:** DEATH **b :** a setting out (as on a new course) **2 :** DIVERGENCE 2

**de·pau·per·ate** \di-'pö-pə-rət\ *adjective* [Middle English *depauperat*, from Medieval Latin *depauperatus*, past participle of *depauperare* to impoverish, from Latin *de-* + *pauperare* to impoverish, from *pauper* poor — more at POOR] (1670) **1 :** falling short of natural development or size **2 :** IMPOVERISHED ⟨a *depauperate* fauna⟩

**de·pend** \di-'pend\ *intransitive verb* [Middle English, from Middle French *dependre*, modification of Latin *dependēre*, from *de-* + *pendēre* to hang — more at PENDANT] (15th century) **1 :** to be determined, based, or contingent ⟨life *depends* on food⟩ ⟨the value of *Y depends* on *X*⟩ **2 :** to be pending or undecided **3 a :** to place reliance or trust ⟨you can *depend* on me⟩ **b :** to be dependent especially for financial support **4 :** to hang down

**de·pend·able** \di-'pen-də-bəl\ *adjective* (1735) **:** capable of being depended on **:** RELIABLE — **de·pend·abil·i·ty** \-,pen-də-'bi-lə-tē\ *noun* — **de·pend·able·ness** *noun* — **de·pend·ably** \-blē\ *adverb*

**de·pen·dence** *also* **de·pen·dance** \di-'pen-dən(t)s\ *noun* (15th century) **1 :** the quality or state of being dependent; *especially* **:** the quality or state of being influenced or determined by or subject to another **2 :** RELIANCE, TRUST **3 :** one that is relied on **4 a :** drug addiction **b :** HABITUATION 2b

**de·pen·den·cy** \-dən(t)-sē\ *noun, plural* **-cies** (1594) **1 :** DEPENDENCE 1 **2 :** something that is dependent on something else; *especially* **:** a territorial unit under the jurisdiction of a nation but not formally annexed by it **3 :** a building (as a stable) that is an adjunct to a main dwelling

**¹de·pen·dent** \di-'pen-dənt\ *adjective* [Middle English *dependant*, from Middle French, present participle of *dependre*] (14th century) **1 :** hanging down **2 a :** determined or conditioned by another **:** CONTINGENT **b** (1) **:** relying on another for support (2) **:** affected with a drug dependence **c :** subject to another's jurisdiction **d :** SUBORDINATE 3a **3 a :** not mathematically or statistically independent ⟨a *dependent* set of vectors⟩ ⟨*dependent* events⟩ **b :** EQUIVALENT 6a ⟨*dependent* equations⟩ — **de·pen·dent·ly** *adverb*

**²dependent** *also* **de·pen·dant** \-dənt\ *noun* (1523) **1** *archaic* **:** DEPENDENCY **2 :** one that is dependent; *especially* **:** a person who relies on another for support

**dependent variable** *noun* (circa 1852) **:** a mathematical variable whose value is determined by that of one or more other variables in a function

**de·per·son·al·iza·tion** \(,)dē-,pər-snə-lə-'zā-shən, -,pər-s°n-ə-lə-\ *noun* (1906) **1 a :** an act or process of depersonalizing **b :** the quality or state of being depersonalized **2 :** a psychopathological syndrome characterized by loss of identity and feelings of unreality and strangeness about one's own behavior

**de·per·son·al·ize** \(')dē-'pər-snə-,līz, -'pər-s°n-ə-\ *transitive verb* (1866) **1 :** to deprive of the sense of personal identity ⟨schools that *depersonalize* students⟩ **2 :** to make impersonal

**de·phos·phor·y·la·tion** \(,)dē-,fäs-fȯr-ə-'lā-shən\ *noun* (1931) **:** the process of removing phosphate groups from an organic compound (as ATP) by hydrolysis; *also* **:** the resulting state — **de·phos·phor·y·late** \(,)dē-fäs-'fȯr-ə-,lāt\ *transitive verb*

**de·pict** \di-'pikt, dē-\ *transitive verb* [Latin *depictus*, past participle of *depingere*, from *de-* + *pingere* to paint — more at PAINT] (15th century) **1 :** to represent by or as if by a picture **2 :** DESCRIBE 1 — **de·pic·ter** \-'pik-tər\ *noun* — **de·pic·tion** \-'pik-shən\ *noun*

**de·pig·men·ta·tion** \(,)dē-,pig-mən-'tā-shən, -,men-\ *noun* (1889) **:** loss of normal pigmentation

**dep·i·la·tion** \,de-pə-'lā-shən\ *noun* [Middle French or Medieval Latin; Middle French, from Medieval Latin *depilation-, depilatio*, from Latin *depilare*, from *de-* + *pilus* hair — more at PILE] (1547) **:** the removal of hair, wool, or bristles by chemical or mechanical methods — **dep·i·late** \'de-pə-,lāt\ *transitive verb*

**de·pil·a·to·ry** \di-'pi-lə-,tōr-ē, -,tȯr-\ *noun, plural* **-ries** (1606) **:** an agent for removing hair, wool, or bristles — **depilatory** *adjective*

**de·plane** \(,)dē-'plān\ *intransitive verb* (1923) **:** to disembark from an airplane

**de·plete** \di-'plēt\ *transitive verb* **de·plet·ed; de·plet·ing** [Latin *depletus*, past participle of *deplēre*, from *de-* + *plēre* to fill — more at FULL] (1807) **1 :** to empty of a principal substance **2 :** to lessen markedly in quantity, content, power, or value ☆ — **de·plet·able** \-'plē-tə-bəl\ *adjective* — **de·ple·tion** \-'plē-shən\ *noun* — **de·ple·tive** \-'plē-tiv\ *adjective*

**de·plor·able** \di-'plȯr-ə-bəl, -'plȯr-\ *adjective* (1612) **1 :** LAMENTABLE **2 :** deserving censure or contempt **:** WRETCHED — **de·plor·able·ness** *noun* — **de·plor·ably** \-blē\ *adverb*

**de·plore** \di-'plȯr, -'plȯr\ *transitive verb* **de·plored; de·plor·ing** [Middle French or Latin; Middle French *deplorer*, from Latin *deplorare*, from *de-* + *plorare* to wail] (1567) **1 a :** to feel or express grief for **b :** to regret strongly **2 :** to consider unfortunate or deserving of deprecation ☆ — **de·plor·er** \-'plȯr-ər\ *noun* — **de·plor·ing·ly** \-iŋ-lē\ *adverb*

**de·ploy** \di-'plȯi\ *verb* [French *déployer*, literally, to unfold, from Old French *desploier*, from *des-* dis- + *ploier, plier* to fold — more at PLY] (1786) *transitive verb* **1 a :** to extend (a military unit) especially in width **b :** to place in battle formation or appropriate positions **2 :** to spread out, utilize, or arrange especially strategically *intransitive verb* **:** to move in being deployed — **de·ploy·able** \-ə-bəl\ *adjective* — **de·ploy·ment** \-mənt\ *noun*

**de·po·lar·ize** \(,)dē-'pō-lə-,rīz\ *transitive verb* (1818) **1 :** to cause to become partially or wholly unpolarized **2 :** to prevent or remove polarization of (as a dry cell or cell membrane) — **de·po·lar·iza·tion** \(,)dē-,pō-lə-rə-'zā-shən\ *noun* — **de·po·lar·iz·er** \(,)dē-'pō-lə-,rī-zər\ *noun*

**de·po·lit·i·cize** \,dē-pə-'li-tə-,sīz\ *transitive verb* (1937)

**:** to remove the political character of **:** take out of the realm of politics ⟨*depoliticize* foreign aid⟩ — **de·po·lit·i·ci·za·tion** \,dē-pə-,li-tə-sə-'zā-shən\ *noun*

**de·po·ly·mer·ize** \(,)dē-pə-'li-mə-,rīz, -'pä-lə-mə-\ (circa 1909) *transitive verb* **:** to decompose (macromolecules) into simpler compounds (as monomers) *intransitive verb* **:** to undergo decomposition into simpler compounds — **de·po·ly·mer·iza·tion** \,dē-pə-,li-mə-rə-'zā-shən, (,)dē-,pä-lə-mə-rə-\ *noun*

**de·pone** \di-'pōn\ *verb* **de·poned; de·pon·ing** [Medieval Latin *deponere*, from Latin, to put down, from *de-* + *ponere* to put — more at POSITION] (15th century) **:** TESTIFY

**¹de·po·nent** \di-'pō-nənt\ *adjective* [Late Latin *deponent-, deponens*, from Latin, present participle of *deponere*] (15th century) **:** occurring with passive or middle voice forms but with active voice meaning ⟨the *deponent* verbs in Latin and Greek⟩

**²deponent** *noun* (1530) **1 :** a deponent verb **2 :** one who gives evidence

**de·pop·u·late** \(,)dē-'pä-pyə-,lāt\ *transitive verb* [Latin *depopulatus*, past participle of *depopulari*, from *de-* + *populari* to ravage] (1548) **1** *obsolete* **:** RAVAGE **2 :** to reduce greatly the population of — **de·pop·u·la·tion** \(,)dē-,pä-pyə-'lā-shən\ *noun*

**de·port** \di-'pōrt, -'pȯrt, dē-\ *transitive verb* [Middle French *deporter*, from Latin *deportare* to carry away, from *de-* + *portare* to carry — more at FARE] (1598) **1 :** to behave or comport (oneself) especially in accord with a code **2** [Latin *deportare*] **a :** to carry away **b :** to send out of the country by legal deportation **synonym** see BANISH, BEHAVE

**de·port·able** \di-'pōr-tə-bəl, -'pȯr-, dē-\ *adjective* (1891) **1 :** punishable by deportation ⟨*deportable* offenses⟩

---

☆ **SYNONYMS**

**Deplete, drain, exhaust, impoverish, bankrupt** mean to deprive of something essential to existence or potency. DEPLETE implies a reduction in number or quantity so as to endanger the ability to function ⟨*depleting* our natural resources⟩. DRAIN implies a gradual withdrawal and ultimate deprivation of what is necessary to an existence ⟨personal tragedy had *drained* him of all spirit⟩. EXHAUST stresses a complete emptying ⟨her lecture *exhausted* the subject⟩. IMPOVERISH suggests a deprivation of something essential to richness or productiveness ⟨*impoverished* soil⟩. BANKRUPT suggests impoverishment to the point of imminent collapse ⟨war had *bankrupted* the nation of resources⟩.

**Deplore, lament, bewail, bemoan** mean to express grief or sorrow for something. DEPLORE implies regret for the loss or impairment of something of value ⟨*deplores* the breakdown in family values⟩. LAMENT implies a profound or demonstrative expression of sorrow ⟨*lamenting* the loss of their only child⟩. BEWAIL and BEMOAN imply sorrow, disappointment, or protest finding outlet in words or cries, BEWAIL commonly suggesting loudness, and BEMOAN lugubriousness ⟨fans *bewailed* the defeat⟩ ⟨purists *bemoaning* the corruption of the language⟩.

**2 :** subject to deportation ⟨*deportable* aliens⟩

**de·por·ta·tion** \dē-ˌpȯr-'tā-shən, -ˌpȯr-, -pər-\ *noun* (1595)
**1 :** an act or instance of deporting
**2 :** the removal from a country of an alien whose presence is unlawful or prejudicial

**de·por·tee** \ˌdē-pȯr-'tē, di-, -ˌpȯr-\ *noun* (1865)
**:** one who has been deported or is under sentence of deportation

**de·port·ment** \di-'pōrt-mənt, -'pȯrt-, dē-\ *noun* (1601)
**:** the manner in which one conducts oneself **:** BEHAVIOR
**synonym** see BEARING

**de·pos·al** \di-'pō-zəl, dē-\ *noun* (14th century)
**:** an act of deposing from office

**de·pose** \di-'pōz, dē-\ *verb* **de·posed; de·pos·ing** [Middle English, from Middle French *deposer*, from Late Latin *deponere* (perfect indicative *deposui*), from Latin, to put down] (14th century)
*transitive verb*
**1 :** to remove from a throne or other high position
**2 :** to put down **:** DEPOSIT
**3 a** [Middle English, from Medieval Latin *deponere*, from Late Latin] **:** to testify to under oath or by affidavit **b :** AFFIRM, ASSERT
*intransitive verb*
**:** to bear witness

¹**de·pos·it** \di-'pä-zət\ *verb* **de·pos·it·ed** \-'pä-zə-təd, -'päz-təd\; **de·pos·it·ing** \-'pä-zə-tiŋ, -'päz-tiŋ\ [Latin *depositus*, past participle of *deponere*] (1624)
*transitive verb*
**1 :** to place especially for safekeeping or as a pledge; *especially* **:** to put in a bank
**2 a :** to lay down **:** PLACE **b :** to let fall (as sediment)
*intransitive verb*
**:** to become deposited
— **de·pos·i·tor** \-'pä-zə-tər, -'päz-tər\ *noun*

²**deposit** *noun* (1624)
**1 :** the state of being deposited
**2 :** something placed for safekeeping: as **a :** money deposited in a bank **b :** money given as a pledge or down payment
**3 :** a place of deposit **:** DEPOSITORY
**4 :** an act of depositing
**5 a :** something laid down; *especially* **:** matter deposited by a natural process **b :** a natural accumulation (as of iron ore, coal, or gas)

**de·pos·i·tary** \di-'pä-zə-ˌter-ē\ *noun, plural* **-tar·ies** (1605)
**1 :** a person to whom something is entrusted
**2 :** DEPOSITORY 2

**de·po·si·tion** \ˌde-pə-'zi-shən, ˌdē-pə-\ *noun* (14th century)
**1 :** an act of removing from a position of authority
**2 a :** a testifying especially before a court **b :** DECLARATION; *specifically* **:** testimony taken down in writing under oath
**3 :** an act or process of depositing
**4 :** something deposited **:** DEPOSIT
— **de·po·si·tion·al** \-'zish-nəl, -shə-nᵊl\ *adjective*

**de·pos·i·to·ry** \di-'pä-zə-ˌtōr-ē, -ˌtȯr-\ *noun, plural* **-ries** (1656)
**1 :** DEPOSITARY 1
**2 :** a place where something is deposited especially for safekeeping

**depository library** *noun* (circa 1930)
**:** a library designated to receive U.S. government publications

**de·pot** \*1 & 2 are* 'de-(ˌ)pō *also* 'dē-, *3 is* 'dē- *sometimes* 'de-\ *noun* [French *dépôt*, from Middle French *depost*, Medieval Latin *depositum*, from Latin, neuter of *depositus*] (1795)
**1 a :** a place for storing goods or motor vehicles **b :** STORE, CACHE
**2 a :** a place for the storage of military supplies **b :** a place for the reception and forwarding of military replacements

**3 :** a building for railroad or bus passengers or freight

**de·prave** \di-'prāv\ *transitive verb* **de·praved; de·prav·ing** [Middle English, from Middle French *depraver*, from Latin *depravare* to pervert, from *de-* + *pravus* crooked, bad] (14th century)
**1** *archaic* **:** to speak ill of **:** MALIGN
**2 :** to make bad **:** CORRUPT; *especially* **:** to corrupt morally
**synonym** see DEBASE
— **de·pra·va·tion** \ˌde-prə-'vā-shən, ˌdē-ˌprā-\ *noun*
— **de·prave·ment** \di-'prāv-mənt\ *noun*
— **de·prav·er** \di-'prā-vər\ *noun*

**de·praved** \di-'prāvd\ *adjective* (14th century)
**:** marked by corruption or evil; *especially* **:** PERVERTED
— **de·praved·ly** \-'prā-vəd-lē, -'prāvd-lē\ *adverb*
— **de·praved·ness** \-'prā-vəd-nəs, -'prāvd-nəs\ *noun*

**de·prav·i·ty** \di-'pra-və-tē *also* -'prā-\ *noun, plural* **-ties** (1641)
**1 :** the quality or state of being depraved
**2 :** a corrupt act or practice

**dep·re·cate** \'de-pri-ˌkāt\ *transitive verb* **-cat·ed; -cat·ing** [Latin *deprecatus,* past participle of *deprecari* to avert by prayer, from *de-* + *precari* to pray — more at PRAY] (1628)
**1 a** *archaic* **:** to pray against (as an evil) **b :** to seek to avert ⟨*deprecate* the wrath . . . of the Roman people —Tobias Smollett⟩
**2 :** to express disapproval of
**3 a :** PLAY DOWN **:** make little of ⟨speaks five languages . . . but *deprecates* this facility —*Time*⟩ **b :** BELITTLE, DISPARAGE ⟨the most reluctantly admired and least easily *deprecated* of . . . novelists —*New Yorker*⟩
— **dep·re·cat·ing·ly** \-ˌkā-tiŋ-lē\ *adverb*
— **dep·re·ca·tion** \ˌde-pri-'kā-shən\ *noun*

**dep·re·ca·to·ry** \'de-pri-kə-ˌtōr-ē, -ˌtȯr-, 'de-prə-ˌkā-tə-rē\ *adjective* (1586)
**1 :** seeking to avert disapproval **:** APOLOGETIC
**2 :** serving to deprecate **:** DISAPPROVING
— **dep·re·ca·to·ri·ly** \ˌde-pri-kə-'tōr-ə-lē, -'tȯr-\ *adverb*

**de·pre·ci·ate** \di-'prē-shē-ˌāt\ *verb* **-at·ed; -at·ing** [Late Latin *depretiatus,* past participle of *depretiare*, from Latin *de-* + *pretium* price — more at PRICE] (15th century)
*transitive verb*
**1 :** to lower in estimation or esteem
**2 :** to lower the price or estimated value of
*intransitive verb*
**:** to fall in value
**synonym** see DECRY
— **de·pre·cia·ble** \-shə-bəl\ *adjective*
— **de·pre·ci·at·ing·ly** \-shē-ˌā-tiŋ-lē\ *adverb*
— **de·pre·ci·a·tion** \-ˌprē-shē-'ā-shən\ *noun*
— **de·pre·ci·a·tive** \-'prē-shə-tiv, -shē-ˌā-tiv\ *adjective*
— **de·pre·ci·a·tor** \-shē-ˌā-tər\ *noun*
— **de·pre·cia·to·ry** \-shə-ˌtōr-ē, -ˌtȯr-\ *adjective*

**dep·re·date** \'de-prə-ˌdāt\ *verb* **-dat·ed; -dat·ing** [Late Latin *depraedatus,* past participle of *depraedari,* from Latin *de-* + *praedari* to plunder — more at PREY] (1626)
*transitive verb*
**:** to lay waste **:** PLUNDER, RAVAGE
*intransitive verb*
**:** to engage in plunder
— **dep·re·da·tion** \ˌde-prə-'dā-shən\ *noun*
— **dep·re·da·tor** \'de-prə-ˌdā-tər, di-'pre-də-\ *noun*
— **dep·re·da·to·ry** \di-'pre-də-ˌtōr-ē, 'de-pri-də-, -ˌtȯr-\ *adjective*

**de·press** \di-'pres, dē-\ *transitive verb* [Middle English, from Middle French *depresser,* from Latin *depressus,* past participle of *deprimere* to press down, from *de-* + *premere* to press — more at PRESS] (14th century)
**1** *obsolete* **:** REPRESS, SUBJUGATE

**2 a :** to press down ⟨*depress* a typewriter key⟩
**b :** to cause to sink to a lower position
**3 :** to lessen the activity or strength of
**4 :** SADDEN, DISCOURAGE
**5 :** to decrease the market value or marketability of
— **de·press·ible** \-'pre-sə-bəl\ *adjective*

**de·pres·sant** \di-'pre-sᵊnt, dē-\ *noun* (1876)
**:** one that depresses; *specifically* **:** an agent that reduces a bodily functional activity or an instinctive desire (as appetite)
— **depressant** *adjective*

**de·pressed** *adjective* (1621)
**1 :** low in spirits **:** SAD; *especially* **:** affected by psychological depression
**2 a :** vertically flattened ⟨a *depressed* cactus⟩ **b :** having the central part lower than the margin **c :** lying flat or prostrate **d :** dorsoventrally flattened
**3 :** suffering from economic depression; *especially* **:** UNDERPRIVILEGED
**4 :** being below the standard

**de·press·ing** *adjective* (1789)
**:** that depresses; *especially* **:** causing emotional depression ⟨a *depressing* story⟩
— **de·press·ing·ly** \-siŋ-lē\ *adverb*

**de·pres·sion** \di-'pre-shən, dē-\ *noun* (14th century)
**1 a :** the angular distance of a celestial object below the horizon **b :** the size of an angle of depression
**2 :** an act of depressing or a state of being depressed: as **a :** a pressing down **:** LOWERING **b** (1) **:** a state of feeling sad **:** DEJECTION (2) **:** a psychoneurotic or psychotic disorder marked especially by sadness, inactivity, difficulty in thinking and concentration, a significant increase or decrease in appetite and time spent sleeping, feelings of dejection and hopelessness, and sometimes suicidal tendencies **c** (1) **:** a reduction in activity, amount, quality, or force (2) **:** a lowering of vitality or functional activity
**3 :** a depressed place or part **:** HOLLOW
**4 :** LOW 1b
**5 :** a period of low general economic activity marked especially by rising levels of unemployment

**Depression glass** *noun* [Great *Depression* of 1929 to circa 1939] (1971)
**:** tinted glassware machine-produced during the 1930s

¹**de·pres·sive** \di-'pre-siv, dē-\ *adjective* (1620)
**1 :** tending to depress
**2 :** of, relating to, marked by, or affected by psychological depression
— **de·pres·sive·ly** *adverb*

²**depressive** *noun* (1937)
**:** one who is affected with or prone to psychological depression

**de·pres·sor** \di-'pre-sər, dē-\ *noun* [Late Latin, from Latin *deprimere*] (1611)
**:** one that depresses: as **a :** a muscle that draws down a part — compare LEVATOR **b :** a device for pressing down or aside **c :** a nerve or nerve fiber that decreases the activity or the tone of the organ or part it innervates

**de·pres·sur·ize** \(ˌ)dē-'pre-shə-ˌrīz\ *transitive verb* (1944)
**:** to release pressure from
— **de·pres·sur·iza·tion** \(ˌ)dē-ˌpre-shə-rə-'zā-shən\ *noun*

**dep·ri·va·tion** \ˌde-prə-'vā-shən *also* ˌdē-ˌprī-\ *noun* (15th century)
**1 :** the state of being deprived **:** PRIVATION; *especially* **:** removal from an office, dignity, or benefice
**2 :** an act or instance of depriving **:** LOSS

**de·prive** \di-'prīv\ *transitive verb* **de·prived; de·priv·ing** [Middle English *depriven*, from Medieval Latin *deprivare*, from Latin *de-* + *privare* to deprive — more at PRIVATE] (14th century)
**1** *obsolete* : REMOVE
**2** : to take something away from ⟨*deprived* him of his professorship —J. M. Phalen⟩
**3** : to remove from office
**4** : to withhold something from ⟨*deprived* a citizen of her rights⟩

**de·prived** *adjective* (circa 1522)
: marked by deprivation especially of the necessities of life or of healthful environmental influences ⟨culturally *deprived* children⟩

**de·pro·gram** \(,)dē-'prō-,gram, -grəm\ *transitive verb* (1973)
: to dissuade from convictions usually of a religious nature often by coercive means
— **de·pro·gram·mer** \-mər\ *noun*

**depth** \'depth\ *noun, plural* **depths** \'depths, 'dep(t)s\ [Middle English, probably from *dep* deep] (14th century)
**1 a** (1) : a deep place in a body of water (2) : a part that is far from the outside or surface ⟨the *depths* of the woods⟩ (3) : ABYSS **2 b** (1) : a profound or intense state (as of thought or feeling) ⟨the *depths* of misery⟩; *also* : a reprehensibly low condition ⟨hadn't realized that standards had fallen to such *depths*⟩ (2) : the middle of a time (as winter) (3) : the worst part
**2 a** : the perpendicular measurement downward from a surface **b** : the direct linear measurement from front to back
**3** : the quality of being deep
**4** : the degree of intensity ⟨*depth* of a color⟩; *also* : the quality of being profound (as in insight) or full (as of knowledge)
**5** : the quality or state of being complete or thorough ⟨a study will be made in *depth*⟩
— **depth·less** \'depth-ləs\ *adjective*

**depth charge** *noun* (1917)
: an antisubmarine weapon that consists essentially of a drum filled with explosives which is dropped near a target and descends to a predetermined depth where it explodes — called also *depth bomb*

**depth of field** (1911)
: the range of distances of the object in front of an image-forming device (as a camera lens) measured along the axis of the device throughout which the image has acceptable sharpness

**depth perception** *noun* (circa 1911)
: the ability to judge the distance of objects and the spatial relationship of objects at different distances

**depth psychology** *noun* (1924)
: PSYCHOANALYSIS; *also* : psychology concerned especially with the unconscious mind

**dep·u·ta·tion** \,de-pyə-'tā-shən\ *noun* (14th century)
**1** : the act of appointing a deputy
**2** : a group of people appointed to represent others

**de·pute** \di-'pyüt\ *transitive verb* **de·put·ed; de·put·ing** [Middle English, to appoint, from Middle French *deputer*, from Late Latin *deputare* to assign, from Latin, to consider (as), from *de-* + *putare* to consider — more at PAVE] (14th century)
: DELEGATE

**dep·u·tize** \'de-pyə-,tīz\ *verb* **-tized; -tiz·ing** (circa 1736)
*transitive verb*
: to appoint as deputy
*intransitive verb*
: to act as deputy
— **dep·u·ti·za·tion** \,de-pyə-tə-'zā-shən\ *noun*

**dep·u·ty** \'de-pyə-tē\ *noun, plural* **-ties** [Middle English, from Middle French *deputé*, past participle of *deputer*] (15th century)

**1 a** : a person appointed as a substitute with power to act **b** : a second in command or assistant who usually takes charge when his or her superior is absent
**2** : a member of the lower house of some legislative assemblies

**de·rac·i·nate** \(,)dē-'ra-s°n-,āt\ *transitive verb* **-nat·ed; -nat·ing** [Middle French *desraciner*, from *des-* de- + *racine* root, from Late Latin *radicina*, from Latin *radic-, radix* — more at ROOT] (1599)
: UPROOT
— **de·rac·i·na·tion** \(,)dē-,ra-s°n-'ā-shən\ *noun*

**de·rail** \di-'rā(ə)l, dē-\ *verb* [French *dérailler* to throw off the track, from *dé-* de- + *rail*, from English] (1850)
*transitive verb*
**1** : to cause to run off the rails
**2** : to obstruct the progress of : FRUSTRATE
*intransitive verb*
: to leave the rails
— **de·rail·ment** \-mənt\ *noun*

**de·rail·leur** \di-'rā-lər\ *noun* [French *dérailleur*, from *dérailler*] (1930)
: a mechanism for shifting gears on a bicycle that operates by moving the chain from one set of exposed gears to another

**de·range** \di-'rānj\ *transitive verb* **de·ranged; de·rang·ing** [French *déranger*, from Old French *desrengier*, from *des-* de- + *reng* line, row — more at RANK] (1776)
**1** : to disturb the operation or functions of
**2** : DISARRANGE ⟨hatless, with tie *deranged* —G. W. Stonier⟩
**3** : to make insane
— **de·range·ment** \-mənt\ *noun*

**de·rate** \(,)dē-'rāt\ *transitive verb* (1947)
: to lower the rated capability of (as electrical or mechanical apparatus) because of deterioration or inadequacy

**der·by** \'dər-bē, *especially British* 'där-\ *noun, plural* **derbies** [Edward Stanley (died 1834), 12th earl of *Derby*] (1844)
**1** : any of several horse races held annually and usually restricted to three-year-olds
**2** : a race or contest open to all comers or to a specified category of contestants ⟨bicycle *derby*⟩
**3** : a man's stiff felt hat with dome-shaped crown and narrow brim ◆

*derby 3*

**de·re·al·iza·tion** \(,)dē-,rē-ə-lə-'zā-shən, -,ri-ə-\ *noun* (1942)
: a feeling of altered reality that occurs often in schizophrenia and in some drug reactions

**de·reg·u·la·tion** \(,)dē-,re-gyə-'lā-shən\ *noun* (1963)
: the act or process of removing restrictions and regulations
— **de·reg·u·late** \('dē-'re-gyə-,lāt\ *transitive verb*

**¹der·e·lict** \'der-ə-,likt\ *adjective* [Latin *derelictus*, past participle of *derelinquere* to abandon, from *de-* + *relinquere* to leave — more at RELINQUISH] (1649)
**1** : abandoned especially by the owner or occupant : RUN-DOWN
**2** : lacking a sense of duty : NEGLIGENT

**²derelict** *noun* (1670)
**1 a** : something voluntarily abandoned; *specifically* : a ship abandoned on the high seas **b** : a tract of land left dry by receding water
**2** : a destitute homeless social misfit : VAGRANT, BUM

**der·e·lic·tion** \,der-ə-'lik-shən\ *noun* (1597)
**1 a** : an intentional abandonment **b** : the state of being abandoned
**2** : a recession of water leaving permanently dry land

**3 a** : intentional or conscious neglect : DELINQUENCY ⟨*dereliction* of duty⟩ **b** : FAULT, SHORTCOMING

**de·re·press** \,dē-ri-'pres\ *transitive verb* (1962)
: to activate (a gene or enzyme) by releasing from a blocked state
— **de·re·pres·sion** \-'pre-shən\ *noun*

**de·ride** \di-'rīd, dē-\ *transitive verb* **de·rid·ed; de·rid·ing** [Latin *deridēre*, from *de-* + *ridēre* to laugh] (1530)
**1** : to laugh at contemptuously
**2** : to subject to usually bitter or contemptuous ridicule
*synonym* see RIDICULE
— **de·rid·er** *noun*
— **de·rid·ing·ly** \-'rī-diŋ-lē\ *adverb*

**de ri·gueur** \də-(,)rē-'gər\ *adjective* [French] (1833)
: prescribed or required by fashion, etiquette, or custom : PROPER

**de·ri·sion** \di-'ri-zhən\ *noun* [Middle English, from Middle French, from Late Latin *derision-, derisio*, from Latin *deridēre*] (14th century)
**1 a** : the use of ridicule or scorn to show contempt **b** : a state of being derided
**2** : an object of ridicule or scorn

**de·ri·sive** \di-'rī-siv, -ziv; 'ri-ziv, -'ri-siv\ *adjective* (circa 1662)
: expressing or causing derision
— **de·ri·sive·ly** *adverb*
— **de·ri·sive·ness** *noun*

**de·ri·so·ry** \di-'rī-sə-rē, -zə-\ *adjective* (1618)
**1** : expressing derision : DERISIVE
**2** : worthy of derision; *especially* : laughably small ⟨a *derisory* sum⟩

**de·riv·able** \di-'rī-və-bəl\ *adjective* (1653)
: capable of being derived

**der·i·vate** \'der-ə-,vāt\ *noun* (1660)
: DERIVATIVE

**der·i·va·tion** \,der-ə-'vā-shən\ *noun* (15th century)
**1 a** (1) : the formation of a word from another word or base (as by the addition of a usually noninflectional affix) (2) : an act of ascertaining or stating the derivation of a word (3) : ETYMOLOGY 1 **b** : the relation of a word to its base
**2 a** : SOURCE, ORIGIN **b** : DESCENT, ORIGINATION
**3** : something derived : DERIVATIVE
**4** : an act or process of deriving
**5** : a sequence of statements (as in logic or mathematics) showing that a result is a necessary consequence of previously accepted statements
— **der·i·va·tion·al** \-shnəl, -shə-n°l\ *adjective*

**¹de·riv·a·tive** \di-'ri-və-tiv\ *noun* (15th century)
**1** : a word formed by derivation
**2** : something derived
**3** : the limit of the ratio of the change in a function to the corresponding change in its independent variable as the latter change approaches zero

**4 a :** a chemical substance related structurally to another substance and theoretically derivable from it **b :** a substance that can be made from another substance

**²derivative** *adjective* (circa 1530)
**1 :** formed by derivation
**2 :** made up of or marked by derived elements
**3 :** lacking originality : BANAL
— **de·riv·a·tive·ly** *adverb*
— **de·riv·a·tive·ness** *noun*

**de·riv·a·ti·za·tion** \də-ˌri-və-tə-ˈzā-shən\ *noun* (1967)
: the conversion of a chemical compound into a derivative (as for identification)
— **de·riv·a·tize** \də-ˈri-və-ˌtīz\ *transitive verb*

**de·rive** \di-ˈrīv, dē-\ *verb* **de·rived; de·riv·ing** [Middle English, from Middle French *deriver*, from Latin *derivare*, literally, to draw off (water), from *de-* + *rivus* stream — more at RUN] (14th century)
*transitive verb*
**1 a :** to take, receive, or obtain especially from a specified source **b :** to obtain (a chemical substance) actually or theoretically from a parent substance
**2 :** INFER, DEDUCE
**3** *archaic* **:** BRING
**4 :** to trace the derivation of
*intransitive verb*
: to have or take origin : come as a derivative
**synonym** see SPRING
— **de·riv·er** *noun*

**derm-** *or* **derma-** *or* **dermo-** *combining form* [New Latin, from Greek *derm-, dermo-,* from *derma,* from *derein* to skin — more at TEAR] : skin 〈*dermal*〉

**-derm** \ˌdərm\ *noun combining form* [probably from French *-derme,* from Greek *derma*] : skin : covering 〈ecto*derm*〉

**-der·ma** \ˈdər-mə\ *noun combining form, plural* **-dermas** *or* **-der·ma·ta** \-mə-tə\ [New Latin, from Greek *dermat-, derma* skin] : skin or skin ailment of a (specified) type 〈sclero*derma*〉

**derm·abra·sion** \ˌdər-mə-ˈbrā-zhən\ *noun* (circa 1954)
: surgical removal of skin blemishes or imperfections (as scars or tattoos) by abrasion (as with sandpaper or wire brushes)

**der·mal** \ˈdər-məl\ *adjective* (circa 1803)
**1 :** of or relating to skin and especially to the dermis : CUTANEOUS
**2 :** EPIDERMAL

**dermat-** *or* **dermato-** *combining form* [Greek, from *dermat-, derma*] : skin 〈*dermat*itis〉 〈*dermato*logy〉

**der·ma·ti·tis** \ˌdər-mə-ˈtī-təs\ *noun* (1876)
: inflammation of the skin

**der·mat·o·gen** \ˌdər-ˈma-tə-jən\ *noun* [International Scientific Vocabulary] (1882)
: PROTODERM

**der·ma·to·glyph·ics** \ˌdər-mə-tə-ˈgli-fiks\ *noun plural but singular or plural in construction* [*dermat-* + Greek *glyphein* to carve + English *-ics* — more at CLEAVE] (1926)
**1 :** skin patterns; *especially* **:** patterns of the specialized skin of the inferior surfaces of the hands and feet
**2 :** the science of the study of skin patterns
— **der·ma·to·glyph·ic** \-fik\ *adjective*

**der·ma·tol·o·gy** \ˌdər-mə-ˈtä-lə-jē\ *noun* (1819)
: a branch of science dealing with the skin, its structure, functions, and diseases
— **der·ma·to·log·ic** \-mə-tᵊl-ˈä-jik\ *or* **der·ma·to·log·i·cal** \-ji-kəl\ *adjective*
— **der·ma·tol·o·gist** \-mə-ˈtä-lə-jist\ *noun*

**der·ma·tome** \ˈdər-mə-ˌtōm\ *noun* [International Scientific Vocabulary *dermat-* + *-ome*] (1910)
: the lateral wall of a somite from which the dermis is produced
— **der·ma·to·mal** \ˌdər-mə-ˈtō-məl\ *adjective*

**der·ma·to·phyte** \ˌdər-ˈma-tə-ˌfīt, ˈdər-mə-\ *noun* [International Scientific Vocabulary] (1882)
: a fungus parasitic on the skin or skin derivatives (as hair or nails)

**der·ma·to·sis** \ˌdər-mə-ˈtō-səs\ *noun, plural* **-to·ses** \-ˌsēz\ (1866)
: a disease of the skin

**-der·ma·tous** \ˈdər-mə-təs\ *adjective combining form* [Greek *dermat-, derma* skin] : having a (specified) type of skin 〈pachy*dermatous*〉

**der·mes·tid** \ˌdər-ˈmes-təd\ *noun* [ultimately from Greek *dermēstēs,* a leather-eating worm, literally, skin eater, from *derm-* + *edmenai* to eat — more at EAT] (circa 1888)
: any of a family (Dermestidae) of beetles with clubbed antennae that are very destructive to organic material of animal origin (as dried meat, wool, or museum specimens)
— **dermestid** *adjective*

**der·mis** \ˈdər-məs\ *noun* [New Latin, from Late Latin *-dermis*] (circa 1830)
: the sensitive vascular inner mesodermic layer of the skin — called also *corium, cutis*

**-der·mis** \ˈdər-məs\ *noun combining form* [Late Latin, from Greek, from *derma*] : layer of skin or tissue 〈endo*dermis*〉

**der·moid cyst** \ˈdər-ˌmȯid-\ *noun* (1872)
: a cystic tumor often of the ovary that contains skin and skin derivatives (as hair or teeth) — called also *dermoid*

**der·nier cri** \ˌdern-ˌyā-ˈkrē\ *noun* [French, literally, last cry] (1896)
: the newest fashion

**der·o·gate** \ˈder-ə-ˌgāt\ *verb* **-gat·ed; -gat·ing** [Middle English, from Late Latin *derogatus,* past participle of *derogare,* from Latin, to annul (a law), detract, from *de-* + *rogare* to ask, propose (a law) — more at RIGHT] (15th century)
*transitive verb*
: to cause to seem inferior : DISPARAGE
*intransitive verb*
**1 :** to take away a part so as to impair : DETRACT
**2 :** to act beneath one's position or character
— **der·o·ga·tion** \ˌder-ə-ˈgā-shən\ *noun*
— **de·rog·a·tive** \di-ˈrä-gə-tiv\ *adjective*

**de·rog·a·to·ry** \di-ˈrä-gə-ˌtōr-ē, -ˌtȯr-\ *adjective* (1503)
**1 :** detracting from the character or standing of something — often used with *to, of,* or *from*
**2 :** expressive of a low opinion : DISPARAGING 〈*derogatory* remarks〉
— **de·rog·a·to·ri·ly** \-ˌrä-gə-ˈtōr-ə-lē, -ˈtȯr-\ *adverb*

**der·rick** \ˈder-ik\ *noun* [obsolete *derrick* hangman, gallows, from *Derick,* name of 17th century English hangman] (circa 1752)
**1 :** a hoisting apparatus employing a tackle rigged at the end of a beam
**2 :** a framework or tower over a deep drill hole (as of an oil well) for supporting boring tackle or for hoisting and lowering ◇

**der·ri·ere** *or* **der·ri·ère** \ˌder-ē-ˈer\ *noun* [French *derrière,* from Old French *derière* back part, rear, from *derier,* adverb, behind, from Late Latin *deretro,* from Latin *de* from + *retro* back] (1774)
: BUTTOCKS

**der·ring-do** \ˌder-iŋ-ˈdü\ *noun* [Middle English *dorring don* daring to do, from *dorring* (gerund of *dorren* to dare) + *don* to do] (1579)
: daring action : DARING 〈deeds of *derring-do*〉

**der·rin·ger** \ˈder-ən-jər\ *noun* [Henry Deringer (died 1869) American inventor] (1853)
: a short-barreled pocket pistol

derrick 2

**der·ris** \ˈder-əs\ *noun* [New Latin, genus name, from Greek, skin, from *derein* to skin — more at TEAR] (1919)
**1 :** a preparation of derris roots and stems used as an insecticide
**2 :** any of a large genus (*Derris*) of leguminous tropical Old World shrubs and woody vines including sources of poisons and especially commercial sources of rotenone

**der·vish** \ˈdər-vish\ *noun* [Turkish *derviş,* literally, beggar, from Persian *darvīsh*] (1585)
**1 :** a member of a Muslim religious order noted for devotional exercises (as bodily movements leading to a trance)
**2 :** one that whirls or dances with or as if with the abandonment of a dervish

**des-** *prefix* [French *dés-,* from Old French *des-* — more at DE-]
: DE- 6 — especially before vowels 〈*des*oxy〉

**DES** \ˌdē-ˌē-ˈes\ *noun* (1971)
: DIETHYLSTILBESTROL

**de·sa·cral·ize** \ˌdē-ˈsā-krə-ˌlīz, -ˈsa-\ *transitive verb* **-ized; -iz·ing** (1911)
: to divest of sacred qualities
— **de·sa·cral·iza·tion** \ˌdē-ˌsā-krə-lī-ˈzā-shən, -ˌsa-\ *noun*

**de·sa·li·nate** \ˌdē-ˈsa-lə-ˌnāt *also* -ˈsā-\ *transitive verb* **-nat·ed; -nat·ing** (1949)
: DESALT
— **de·sa·li·na·tion** \ˌdē-ˌsa-lə-ˈnā-shən *also* -ˌsā-\ *noun*
— **de·sa·li·na·tor** \ˌdē-ˈsa-lə-ˌnā-tər *also* -ˈsā-\ *noun*

**de·sa·li·nize** \ˌdē-ˈsa-lə-ˌnīz *also* -ˈsā-\ *transitive verb* **-nized; -niz·ing** (1963)
: DESALT
— **de·sa·li·ni·za·tion** \ˌdē-ˌsa-lə-nə-ˈzā-shən *also* -ˌsā-\ *noun*

**de·salt** \ˌdē-ˈsȯlt\ *transitive verb* (circa 1904)
: to remove salt from
— **de·salt·er** *noun*

**¹des·cant** \ˈdes-ˌkant\ *noun* [Middle English *dyscant,* from Old North French & Medieval Latin; Old North French *descant,* from Medieval Latin *discantus,* from Latin *dis-* + *cantus* song — more at CHANT] (14th century)
**1 a :** a melody or counterpoint sung above the plainsong of the tenor **b :** the art of composing or improvising contrapuntal part music; *also* **:** the music so composed or improvised **c :** SOPRANO, TREBLE **d :** a superimposed counterpoint to a simple melody sung typically by some or all of the sopranos
**2 :** discourse or comment on a theme

◇ WORD HISTORY

**derrick** *Derick* or *Derrick* was apparently the surname of a well-known public executioner active about 1600 at Tyburn, an execution site in what is now central London. Our sole evidence for his existence, however, consists of a few references in plays and popular ballads that circulated in the first decade of the 17th century. According to Thomas Blount's *Glossographia,* an English dictionary published in 1656, *Deric* had become an abusive byword for a hangman. Nothing more is heard of this word for a time, but then *derrick* turns up in the 18th century applied to a kind of block and tackle used aboard ships, and the habitual, if tenuous, assumption is that the famous hangman's name was transferred to a gallows, and the name for a gallows applied to other hoisting apparatuses. In the United States, *derrick* is probably most frequently used for the tower-like structure suspended over an oil well.

²**des·cant** \'des-ˌkant, des-', dis-'\ *intransitive verb* (15th century)
**1 :** to sing or play a descant; *broadly* **:** SING
**2 :** COMMENT, DISCOURSE

**de·scend** \di-'send, dē-\ *verb* [Middle English, from Old French *descendre*, from Latin *descendere*, from *de-* + *scandere* to climb — more at SCAN] (13th century)
*intransitive verb*
**1 :** to pass from a higher place or level to a lower one ⟨*descended* from the platform⟩
**2 :** to pass in discussion from what is logically prior or more comprehensive
**3 a :** to come down from a stock or source **:** DERIVE ⟨*descends* from an old merchant family⟩ **b :** to pass by inheritance ⟨a desk that has *descended* in the family⟩ **c :** to pass by transmission ⟨songs *descended* from old ballads⟩
**4 :** to incline, lead, or extend downward ⟨the road *descends* to the river⟩
**5 a :** to swoop or pounce down (as in a sudden attack) **b :** to appear suddenly and often disconcertingly as if from above ⟨reporters *descended* on the candidate⟩
**6 :** to proceed in a sequence or gradation from higher to lower or from more remote to nearer or more recent
**7 a :** to lower oneself in status or dignity **:** STOOP **b :** to worsen and sink in condition or estimation
*transitive verb*
**1 :** to pass, move, or climb down or down along
**2 :** to extend down along
— **de·scend·ible** \-'sen-də-bəl\ *adjective*

¹**de·scen·dant** *or* **de·scen·dent** \di-'sendənt\ *adjective* [Middle French & Latin; Middle French *descendant*, from Latin *descendent-, descendens*, present participle of *descendere*] (1572)
**1 :** moving or directed downward
**2 :** proceeding from an ancestor or source

²**descendant** *or* **descendent** *noun* [French & Latin; French *descendant*, from Late Latin *descendent-, descendens*, from Latin] (1600)
**1 :** one descended from another or from a common stock
**2 :** one deriving directly from a precursor or prototype

**de·scend·er** \di-'sen-dər, 'dē-,\ *noun* (1802)
**:** the part of a lowercase letter (as p) that descends below the main body of the letter; *also* **:** a letter that has such a part

**de·scen·sion** \di-'sen-chən\ *noun* (15th century)
*archaic* **:** DESCENT 2

**de·scent** \di-'sent\ *noun* [Middle English, from Middle French *descente*, from Old French *descendre*] (14th century)
**1 a :** derivation from an ancestor **:** BIRTH, LINEAGE ⟨of French *descent*⟩ **b :** transmission or devolution of an estate by inheritance usually in the descending line **c :** the fact or process of originating from an ancestral stock **d :** the shaping or development in nature and character by transmission from a source **:** DERIVATION
**2 :** the act or process of descending
**3 :** a step downward in a scale of gradation; *specifically* **:** one generation in an ancestral line or genealogical scale
**4 a :** an inclination downward **:** SLOPE **b :** a descending way (as a downgrade or stairway) **c** *obsolete* **:** the lowest part
**5 a :** ATTACK, INVASION **b :** a sudden disconcerting appearance (as for a visit)
**6 :** a downward step (as in station or value) **:** DECLINE ⟨*descent* of the family to actual poverty⟩

**de·scribe** \di-'skrīb\ *transitive verb* **de·scribed; de·scrib·ing** [Middle English, from Latin *describere*, from *de-* + *scribere* to write — more at SCRIBE] (15th century)
**1 :** to represent or give an account of in words ⟨*describe* a picture⟩
**2 :** to represent by a figure, model, or picture **:** DELINEATE

**3** *obsolete* **:** DISTRIBUTE
**4 :** to trace or traverse the outline of ⟨*describe* a circle⟩
**5** *archaic* **:** OBSERVE, PERCEIVE
— **de·scrib·able** \-'skrī-bə-bəl\ *adjective*
— **de·scrib·er** *noun*

**de·scrip·tion** \di-'skrip-shən\ *noun* [Middle English *descripcioun*, from Middle French & Latin; Middle French *description*, from Latin *description-, descriptio*, from *describere*] (14th century)
**1 a :** an act of describing; *specifically* **:** discourse intended to give a mental image of something experienced **b :** a descriptive statement or account
**2 :** kind or character especially as determined by salient features ⟨opposed to any tax of so radical a *description*⟩
*synonym* see TYPE

**de·scrip·tive** \di-'skrip-tiv\ *adjective* (1751)
**1 :** serving to describe ⟨a *descriptive* account⟩
**2 a :** referring to, constituting, or grounded in matters of observation or experience ⟨the *descriptive* basis of science⟩ **b :** factually grounded or informative rather than normative, prescriptive, or emotive ⟨*descriptive* cultural studies⟩
**3** *of a modifier* **a :** expressing the quality, kind, or condition of what is denoted by the modified term ⟨hot in "hot water" is a *descriptive* adjective⟩ **b :** NONRESTRICTIVE
**4 :** of, relating to, or dealing with the structure of a language at a particular time usually with exclusion of historical and comparative data ⟨*descriptive* linguistics⟩
— **de·scrip·tive·ly** *adverb*
— **de·scrip·tive·ness** *noun*

**de·scrip·tor** \di-'skrip-tər\ *noun* (1933)
**:** something (as a word or characteristic feature) that serves to describe or identify; *especially* **:** a word or phrase (as an index term) used to identify an item (as a subject or document) in an information retrieval system

¹**de·scry** \di-'skrī\ *transitive verb* **de·scried; de·scry·ing** [Middle English *descrien*, from Middle French *descrier* to proclaim, decry] (14th century)
**1 a :** to catch sight of **b :** FIND OUT, DISCOVER
**2** *obsolete* **:** to make known **:** REVEAL

²**descry** *noun* (1605)
*obsolete* **:** discovery or view from afar

**Des·de·mo·na** \ˌdez-də-'mō-nə\ *noun*
**:** the wife of Othello in Shakespeare's *Othello*

**des·e·crate** \'de-si-ˌkrāt\ *transitive verb* **-crat·ed; -crat·ing** [*de-* + *-secrate* (as in *consecrate*)] (1677)
**1 :** to violate the sanctity of **:** PROFANE
**2 :** to treat disrespectfully, irreverently, or outrageously ⟨the kind of shore development . . . that has *desecrated* so many waterfronts —John Fischer⟩
— **des·e·crat·er** *or* **des·e·cra·tor** \-ˌkrātər\ *noun*

**des·e·cra·tion** \ˌde-si-'krā-shən\ *noun* (circa 1717)
**:** an act or instance of desecrating **:** the state of being desecrated

**de·seg·re·gate** \(ˌ)dē-'se-gri-ˌgāt\ (1944)
*transitive verb*
**:** to eliminate segregation in; *specifically* **:** to free of any law, provision, or practice requiring isolation of the members of a particular race in separate units
*intransitive verb*
**:** to become desegregated

**de·seg·re·ga·tion** \(ˌ)dē-ˌse-gri-'gā-shən\ *noun* (1951)
**1 :** the action or an instance of desegregating
**2 :** the state of being desegregated

**de·se·lect** \ˌdē-sə-'lekt\ *transitive verb* (1965)
**:** DISMISS, REJECT

**de·sen·si·tize** \(ˌ)dē-'sen(t)-sə-ˌtīz\ *transitive verb* (1898)
**1 :** to make (a sensitized or hypersensitive individual) insensitive or nonreactive to a sensitizing agent

**2 :** to make emotionally insensitive or callous; *specifically* **:** to extinguish an emotional response (as of fear, anxiety, or guilt) to stimuli that formerly induced it
— **de·sen·si·ti·za·tion** \(ˌ)dē-ˌsen(t)-sə-tə-'zā-shən\ *noun*
— **de·sen·si·tiz·er** \(ˌ)dē-'sen-sə-ˌtī-zər\ *noun*

¹**des·ert** \'de-zərt\ *noun* [Middle English, from Old French, from Late Latin *desertum*, from Latin, neuter of *desertus*, past participle of *deserere* to desert, from *de-* + *serere* to join together — more at SERIES] (13th century)
**1 a :** arid barren land; *especially* **:** a tract incapable of supporting any considerable population without an artificial water supply **b :** an area of water apparently devoid of life
**2** *archaic* **:** a wild uninhabited and uncultivated tract
**3 :** a desolate or forbidding area ⟨lost in a *desert* of doubt⟩
— **de·ser·tic** \de-'zər-tik\ *adjective*

²**des·ert** \'de-zərt\ *adjective* (13th century)
**1 :** desolate and sparsely occupied or unoccupied ⟨a *desert* island⟩
**2 :** of or relating to a desert
**3** *archaic* **:** FORSAKEN

³**de·sert** \di-'zərt\ *noun* [Middle English *deserte*, from Old French, from feminine of *desert*, past participle of *deservir* to deserve] (13th century)
**1 :** the quality or fact of deserving reward or punishment
**2 :** deserved reward or punishment — usually used in plural ⟨got their just *deserts*⟩
**3 :** EXCELLENCE, WORTH

⁴**de·sert** \di-'zərt\ *verb* [French *déserter*, from Late Latin *desertare*, frequentative of Latin *deserere*] (1603)
*transitive verb*
**1 :** to withdraw from or leave usually without intent to return
**2 a :** to leave in the lurch ⟨*desert* a friend in trouble⟩ **b :** to abandon (military service) without leave
*intransitive verb*
**:** to quit one's post, allegiance, or service without leave or justification; *especially* **:** to abandon military duty without leave and without intent to return
*synonym* see ABANDON
— **de·sert·er** *noun*

**de·sert·i·fi·ca·tion** \di-ˌzər-tə-fə-'kā-shən\ *noun* (1974)
**:** the process of becoming desert (as from land mismanagement or climate change)

**de·ser·tion** \di-'zər-shən\ *noun* (1591)
**1 :** an act of deserting; *especially* **:** the abandonment without consent or legal justification of a person, post, or relationship and the associated duties and obligations ⟨sued for divorce on grounds of *desertion*⟩
**2 :** a state of being deserted or forsaken

**desert locust** *noun* (1944)
**:** a destructive migratory locust (*Schistocerca gregaria*) of southwestern Asia and parts of northern Africa

**desert soil** *noun* (circa 1938)
**:** a soil that develops under sparse shrub vegetation in warm to cool arid climates with a light-colored surface soil usually underlain by calcareous material and a hardpan layer

**desert varnish** *noun* (circa 1898)
**:** a dark coating which is found on rocks after long exposure in desert regions and whose color is due to iron and manganese oxides

**de·serve** \di-'zərv\ *verb* **de·served; de·serv·ing** [Middle English, from Old French *deservir*, from Latin *deservire* to devote oneself to, from *de-* + *servire* to serve] (13th century)
*transitive verb*
**:** to be worthy of **:** MERIT ⟨*deserves* another chance⟩
*intransitive verb*
**:** to be worthy, fit, or suitable for some reward

or requital ⟨have become recognized as they *deserve* —T. S. Eliot⟩
— **de·serv·er** *noun*
**de·served** \-'zərvd\ *adjective* (circa 1552)
: of, relating to, or being that which one deserves ⟨a *deserved* reputation⟩
— **de·served·ly** \-'zər-vəd-lē, -'zərvd-lē\ *adverb*
— **de·served·ness** \-'zər-vəd-nəs, -'zərvd-nəs\ *noun*
¹**de·serv·ing** \-'zər-viŋ\ *noun* (14th century)
: DESERT, MERIT ⟨reward the proud according to their *deservings* —Charles Kingsley⟩
²**deserving** *adjective* (1576)
: MERITORIOUS, WORTHY; *especially* : meriting financial aid ⟨scholarships for *deserving* students⟩
**de·sex** \(,)dē-'seks\ *transitive verb* (1911)
**1** : CASTRATE, SPAY
**2** : to eliminate perceived sexism from ⟨*desex* the language of church Bible study programs —R. M. Harley⟩
**de·sex·u·al·ize** \(,)dē-'sek-sh(ə-)wə-,līz, -'sek-shə-,līz\ *transitive verb* (1894)
**1** : to deprive of sexual characters or power
**2** : to divest of sexual quality
— **de·sex·u·al·iza·tion** \(,)dē-,sek-sh(ə-)wə-lə-'zā-shən, -'sek-shə-lə-\ *noun*
**des·ha·bille** \,de-sə-'bē(ə)l, -'bil, -'bē\ *variant of* DISHABILLE
**des·ic·cant** \'de-si-kənt\ *noun* (1676)
: a drying agent (as calcium chloride)
**des·ic·cate** \'de-si-,kāt\ *verb* **-cat·ed; -cat·ing** [Latin *desiccatus*, past participle of *desiccare* to dry up, from *de-* + *siccare* to dry, from *siccus* dry — more at SACK] (1575)
*transitive verb*
**1** : to dry up
**2** : to preserve (a food) by drying : DEHYDRATE
**3** : to drain of emotional or intellectual vitality
*intransitive verb*
: to become dried up
— **des·ic·ca·tion** \,de-si-'kā-shən\ *noun*
— **de·sic·ca·tive** \'de-si-,kā-tiv\ *adjective*
— **des·ic·ca·tor** \'de-si-,kā-tər\ *noun*
**de·sid·er·ate** \di-'si-də-,rāt, -'zi-\ *transitive verb* **-at·ed; -at·ing** [Latin *desideratus*, past participle of *desiderare* to desire] (1645)
: to entertain or express a wish to have or attain
— **de·sid·er·a·tion** \-,si-də-'rā-shən, -,zi-\ *noun*
— **de·sid·er·a·tive** \-'si-də-,rā-tiv, -'si-d(ə-)rət-, -'zi-\ *adjective*
**de·sid·er·a·tum** \di-,si-də-'rä-təm, -,zi-, -'rā-\ *noun, plural* **-ta** \-tə\ [Latin, neuter of *desideratus*] (1652)
: something desired as essential
¹**de·sign** \di-'zīn\ *verb* [Middle English, to outline, indicate, mean, from Middle French & Medieval Latin; Middle French *designer* to designate, from Medieval Latin *designare*, from Latin, to mark out, from *de-* + *signare* to mark — more at SIGN] (14th century)
*transitive verb*
**1** : to create, fashion, execute, or construct according to plan : DEVISE, CONTRIVE
**2 a** : to conceive and plan out in the mind ⟨he *designed* the perfect crime⟩ **b** : to have as a purpose : INTEND ⟨she *designed* to excel in her studies⟩ **c** : to devise for a specific function or end ⟨a book *designed* primarily as a college textbook⟩
**3** *archaic* : to indicate with a distinctive mark, sign, or name
**4 a** : to make a drawing, pattern, or sketch of **b** : to draw the plans for
*intransitive verb*
**1** : to conceive or execute a plan
**2** : to draw, lay out, or prepare a design
— **de·sign·ed·ly** \-'zī-nəd-lē\ *adverb*
²**design** *noun* (1588)
**1 a** : a particular purpose held in view by an individual or group ⟨he has ambitious *designs* for his son⟩ **b** : deliberate purposive planning ⟨more by accident than *design*⟩

**2** : a mental project or scheme in which means to an end are laid down
**3 a** : a deliberate undercover project or scheme : PLOT **b** *plural* : aggressive or evil intent — used with *on* or *against* ⟨he has *designs* on the money⟩
**4** : a preliminary sketch or outline showing the main features of something to be executed : DELINEATION
**5 a** : an underlying scheme that governs functioning, developing, or unfolding : PATTERN, MOTIF ⟨the general *design* of the epic⟩ **b** : a plan or protocol for carrying out or accomplishing something (as a scientific experiment); *also* : the process of preparing this
**6** : the arrangement of elements or details in a product or work of art
**7** : a decorative pattern
**8** : the creative art of executing aesthetic or functional designs
**synonym** *see* INTENTION, PLAN
¹**des·ig·nate** \'de-zig-,nāt, -nət\ *adjective* [Latin *designatus*, past participle of *designare*] (1646)
: chosen but not yet installed ⟨ambassador *designate*⟩
²**des·ig·nate** \-,nāt\ *transitive verb* **-nat·ed; -nat·ing** (1791)
**1** : to indicate and set apart for a specific purpose, office, or duty ⟨*designate* a group to prepare a plan⟩
**2 a** : to point out the location of ⟨a marker *designating* the battle⟩ **b** : to distinguish as to class ⟨the area we *designate* as that of spiritual values —J. B. Conant⟩ **c** : SPECIFY, STIPULATE ⟨to be sent by a *designated* shipper⟩
**3** : DENOTE ⟨associate names with the people they *designate*⟩
**4** : to call by a distinctive title, term, or expression ⟨a particle *designated* the neutron⟩
— **des·ig·na·tive** \-,nā-tiv\ *adjective*
— **des·ig·na·tor** \-,nā-tər\ *noun*
— **des·ig·na·to·ry** \-nə-,tōr-ē, -,tor-\ *adjective*
**designated hitter** *noun* (1973)
: a baseball player designated at the start of the game to bat in place of the pitcher without causing the pitcher to be removed from the game
**des·ig·na·tion** \,de-zig-'nā-shən\ *noun* (14th century)
**1** : the act of indicating or identifying
**2** : appointment to or selection for an office, post, or service
**3** : a distinguishing name, sign, or title
**4** : the relation between a sign and the thing signified
**des·ig·nee** \,de-zig-'nē\ *noun* (1925)
: one who is designated
¹**de·sign·er** \di-'zī-nər\ *noun* (1662)
: one that designs: as **a** : one who creates and often executes plans for a project or structure ⟨urban *designers*⟩ ⟨a theater set *designer*⟩ **b** : one that creates and manufactures a new product style or design; *especially* : one who designs and manufactures high-fashion clothing ⟨the *designer's* new fall line⟩
²**designer** *adjective* (1966)
**1** : of, relating to, or produced by a designer ⟨*designer* wallpaper⟩ ⟨wearing a *designer* original⟩; *also* : displaying the name, signature, or logo of a designer or manufacturer ⟨*designer* jeans⟩
**2** : intended to reflect the latest in sophisticated taste or fashion ⟨*designer* ice cream⟩ ⟨a *designer* haircut⟩
**designer drug** *noun* (1983)
: a synthetic version of a controlled substance (as heroin) that is produced with a slightly altered molecular structure to avoid having it classified as an illicit drug
**de·sign·ing** \di-'zī-niŋ\ *adjective* (1653)
**1** : practicing forethought
**2** : CRAFTY, SCHEMING
**de·sign·ment** \di-'zīn-mənt\ *noun* (1583)
*obsolete* : PLAN, PURPOSE

**de·si·pra·mine** \də-'zi-prə-,mēn\ *noun* [*desmethyl* (from *des-* + *methyl*) + *imipramine*] (1965)
: a tricyclic antidepressant $C_{18}H_{22}N_2$
**de·sir·abil·i·ty** \di-,zī-rə-'bi-lə-tē\ *noun, plural* **-ties** (1824)
**1** *plural* : desirable conditions ⟨had understood and studied certain *desirabilities* —D. D. Eisenhower⟩
**2** : the quality, fact, or degree of being desirable
¹**de·sir·able** \di-'zī-rə-bəl\ *adjective* (14th century)
**1** : having pleasing qualities or properties : ATTRACTIVE ⟨a *desirable* woman⟩
**2** : worth seeking or doing as advantageous, beneficial, or wise : ADVISABLE ⟨*desirable* legislation⟩
— **de·sir·able·ness** *noun*
— **de·sir·ably** \-blē\ *adverb*
²**desirable** *noun* (1645)
: one that is desirable
¹**de·sire** \di-'zīr, dē-\ *verb* **de·sired; de·sir·ing** [Middle English, from Old French *desirer*, from Latin *desiderare*, from *de-* + *sider-, sidus* heavenly body] (13th century)
*transitive verb*
**1** : to long or hope for : exhibit or feel desire for
**2 a** : to express a wish for : REQUEST **b** *archaic* : to express a wish to : ASK
**3** *obsolete* : INVITE
**4** *archaic* : to feel the loss of
*intransitive verb*
: to have or feel desire ☆
²**desire** *noun* (14th century)
**1** : conscious impulse toward something that promises enjoyment or satisfaction in its attainment
**2 a** : LONGING, CRAVING **b** : sexual urge or appetite
**3** : a usually formal request or petition for some action
**4** : something desired
**de·sir·ous** \di-'zīr-əs\ *adjective* (14th century)
: impelled or governed by desire ⟨*desirous* of fame⟩
— **de·sir·ous·ly** *adverb*
— **de·sir·ous·ness** *noun*
**de·sist** \di-'zist, -'sist, dē-\ *intransitive verb* [Middle English, from Middle French *desister*, from Latin *desistere*, from *de-* + *sistere* to stand, stop; akin to Latin *stare* to stand — more at STAND] (15th century)
: to cease to proceed or act
**synonym** *see* STOP
— **de·sis·tance** \-'zis-tən(t)s, -'sis-\ *noun*
**desk** \'desk\ *noun* [Middle English *deske*, from Medieval Latin *desca*, modification of Old Italian *desco* table, from Latin *discus* dish, disc — more at DISH] (14th century)
**1 a** : a table, frame, or case with a sloping or horizontal surface especially for writing and

\ə\ abut \ᵊ\ kitten \ər\ further \a\ ash \ā\ ace \ä\ mop, mar \aú\ out \ch\ chin \e\ bet \ē\ easy \g\ go \i\ hit \ī\ ice \j\ job \ŋ\ sing \ō\ go \ò\ law \oi\ boy \th\ thin \t̲h̲\ the \ü\ loot \ú\ foot \y\ yet \zh\ vision *see also* Guide to Pronunciation

reading and often with drawers, compartments, and pigeonholes **b** : a reading table or lectern from which a liturgical service is read **c** : a table, counter, stand, or booth at which a person works
**2 a** : a division of an organization specializing in a particular phase of activity ⟨the Russian *desk* in the Department of State⟩ **b** : a seating position according to rank in an orchestra ⟨a first-*desk* violinist⟩
**desk·bound** \'desk-,baund\ *adjective* (1944)
: restricted to work at a desk
**de–skill** \,dē-'skil\ *transitive verb* (1941)
**1** : to reduce the level of skill needed for (a job)
**2** : to reduce the level of skill needed for a job by (a worker)
**desk·man** \'desk-,man, -mən\ *noun* (1913)
: one that works at a desk; *specifically* : a newspaperman who processes news and prepares copy
**1desk·top** \'desk-,täp\ *noun* (1929)
**1** : the top of a desk; *also* : an office desktop simulated by a computer program
**2** : a desktop computer
**2desktop** *adjective* (1958)
: of a size that can be conveniently used on a desk or table ⟨*desktop* computers⟩ — compare LAPTOP
**desktop publishing** *noun* (1984)
: the production of printed matter by means of a desktop computer having a layout program that integrates text and graphics
**desm-** *or* **desmo-** *combining form* [New Latin, from Greek, from *desmos*, from *dein* to bind — more at DIADEM]
: bond : ligament ⟨*desmosome*⟩
**des·mid** \'dez-məd\ *noun* [ultimately from Greek *desmos*] (1862)
: any of numerous unicellular or colonial green algae (order Zygnematales)
**des·mo·some**
\'dez-mə-,sōm\
*noun* (circa 1932)
: a specialized local thickening of the cell membrane of an epithelial cell that serves to anchor contiguous cells together

desmid

— **des·mo·som·al** \-,sō-məl\ *adjective*
**1des·o·late** \'de-sə-lət, 'de-zə-\ *adjective* [Middle English *desolat*, from Latin *desolatus*, past participle of *desolare* to abandon, from *de-* + *solus* alone] (14th century)
**1** : devoid of inhabitants and visitors : DESERTED
**2** : joyless, disconsolate, and sorrowful through or as if through separation from a loved one
**3 a** : showing the effects of abandonment and neglect : DILAPIDATED **b** : BARREN, LIFELESS ⟨a *desolate* landscape⟩ **c** : devoid of warmth, comfort, or hope : GLOOMY ⟨*desolate* memories⟩
*synonym* see ALONE
— **des·o·late·ly** *adverb*
— **des·o·late·ness** *noun*
**2des·o·late** \-,lāt\ *transitive verb* **-lat·ed;** **-lat·ing** (14th century)
: to make desolate: **a** : to deprive of inhabitants **b** : to lay waste **c** : FORSAKE **d** : to make wretched
— **des·o·lat·er** *or* **des·o·la·tor** \-,lā-tər\ *noun*
— **des·o·lat·ing·ly** \-,lā-tiŋ-lē\ *adverb*
**des·o·la·tion** \,de-sə-'lā-shən, ,de-zə-\ *noun* (14th century)
**1** : the action of desolating
**2 a** : GRIEF, SADNESS **b** : LONELINESS
**3** : DEVASTATION, RUIN
**4** : barren wasteland

**de·sorb** \(,)dē-'sorb, -'zorb\ *transitive verb* (1924)
: to remove (a sorbed substance) by the reverse of adsorption or absorption
**de·sorp·tion** \-'sorp-shən, -'zorp-\ *noun* (1924)
: the process of desorbing
**desoxy-** — see DEOXY-
**des·oxy·ri·bo·nu·cle·ic acid** \de-,zäk-sē-'rī-bō-n(y)ù-,klē-ik-, -,klä-\ *noun* (1931)
: DNA
**1de·spair** \di-'spar, -'sper\ *verb* [Middle English *despeiren*, from Middle French *desperer*, from Latin *desperare*, from *de-* + *sperare* to hope; akin to Latin *spes* hope — more at SPEED] (14th century)
*intransitive verb*
: to lose all hope or confidence ⟨*despair* of winning⟩
*transitive verb*
*obsolete* : to lose hope for
— **de·spair·er** *noun*
**2despair** *noun* (14th century)
**1** : utter loss of hope
**2** : a cause of hopelessness ⟨an incorrigible child is the *despair* of his parents⟩
**de·spair·ing** *adjective* (1589)
: given to, arising from, or marked by despair : devoid of hope
*synonym* see DESPONDENT
— **de·spair·ing·ly** \-iŋ-lē\ *adverb*
**des·patch** \dis-'pach\ *variant of* DISPATCH
**des·per·a·do** \,des-pə-'rä-(,)dō, -'rä-\ *noun, plural* **-does** *or* **-dos** [probably alteration of obsolete *desperate* desperado, from *desperate, adjective*] (1647)
: a bold or violent criminal; *especially* : a bandit of the western U.S. in the 19th century
**des·per·ate** \'des-p(ə-)rət, -pərt\ *adjective* [Latin *desperatus*, past participle of *desperare*] (15th century)
**1 a** : having lost hope ⟨a *desperate* spirit crying for relief⟩ **b** : giving no ground for hope ⟨the outlook was *desperate*⟩
**2 a** : moved by despair ⟨victims made *desperate* by abuse⟩ **b** : involving or employing extreme measures in an attempt to escape defeat or frustration ⟨made a *desperate* leap for the rope⟩
**3** : suffering extreme need or anxiety ⟨*desperate* for money⟩
**4** : involving extreme danger or possible disaster ⟨a *desperate* situation⟩
**5** : of extreme intensity
**6** : SHOCKING, OUTRAGEOUS
*synonym* see DESPONDENT
— **des·per·ate·ly** *adverb*
— **des·per·ate·ness** *noun*
**des·per·a·tion** \,des-pə-'rā-shən\ *noun* (14th century)
**1** : loss of hope and surrender to despair
**2** : a state of hopelessness leading to rashness
**de·spi·ca·ble** \di-'spi-kə-bəl, 'des-(,)pi-\ *adjective* [Late Latin *despicabilis*, from Latin *despicari* to despise] (1553)
: deserving to be despised : so worthless or obnoxious as to rouse moral indignation ⟨*despicable* behavior⟩
*synonym* see CONTEMPTIBLE
— **de·spi·ca·ble·ness** *noun*
— **de·spi·ca·bly** \-blē\ *adverb*
**de·spir·i·tu·al·ize** \(,)dē-'spi-ri-ch(ə-)wə-,līz, -chə-,līz\ *transitive verb* (1868)
: to deprive of spiritual character or influence
**de·spise** \di-'spīz\ *transitive verb* **de·spised; de·spis·ing** [Middle English, from Old French *despis-*, stem of *despire*, from Latin *despicere*, from *de-* + *specere* to look — more at SPY] (14th century)
**1** : to look down on with contempt or aversion ⟨*despised* the weak⟩
**2** : to regard as negligible, worthless, or distasteful ☆
— **de·spise·ment** \-'spīz-mənt\ *noun*
— **de·spis·er** \-'spī-zər\ *noun*

**1de·spite** \di-'spīt\ *noun* [Middle English, from Old French *despit*, from Latin *despectus*, from *despicere*] (13th century)
**1** : the feeling or attitude of despising : CONTEMPT
**2** : MALICE, SPITE
**3 a** : an act showing contempt or defiance **b** : DETRIMENT, DISADVANTAGE ⟨I know of no government which stands to its obligations, even in its own *despite*, more solidly —Sir Winston Churchill⟩
— **in despite of** : in spite of
**2despite** *transitive verb* **de·spit·ed; de·spit·ing** (14th century)
**1** *archaic* : to treat with contempt
**2** *obsolete* : to provoke to anger : VEX
**3despite** *preposition* (15th century)
: in spite of ⟨played *despite* an injury⟩
**de·spite·ful** \di-'spīt-fəl\ *adjective* (15th century)
: expressing malice or hate
— **de·spite·ful·ly** \-fə-lē\ *adverb*
— **de·spite·ful·ness** *noun*
**de·spit·eous** \dis-'pi-tē-əs\ *adjective* (14th century)
*archaic* : feeling or showing despite : MALICIOUS
— **de·spit·eous·ly** *adverb, archaic*
**de·spoil** \di-'spoi(ə)l\ *transitive verb* [Middle English *despoylen*, from Middle French *despoillier*, from Latin *despoliare*, from *de-* + *spoliare* to strip, rob — more at SPOIL] (14th century)
: to strip of belongings, possessions, or value : PILLAGE
*synonym* see RAVAGE
— **de·spoil·er** *noun*
— **de·spoil·ment** \-mənt\ *noun*
**de·spo·li·a·tion** \di-,spō-lē-'ā-shən\ *noun* [Late Latin *despoliation-, despoliatio,* from *despoliare*] (circa 1657)
: the condition of being despoiled : SPOLIATION
**1de·spond** \di-'spänd\ *intransitive verb* [Latin *despondēre*, from *de-* + *spondēre* to promise solemnly — more at SPOUSE] (1655)
: to become despondent
**2despond** *noun* (1678)
: DESPONDENCY
**de·spon·dence** \di-'spän-dən(t)s\ *noun* (1676)
: DESPONDENCY
**de·spon·den·cy** \-dən-sē\ *noun* (1653)
: the state of being despondent : DEJECTION, HOPELESSNESS
**de·spon·dent** \-dənt\ *adjective* [Latin *despondent-, despondens,* present participle of *despondēre*] (circa 1699)
: feeling or showing extreme discouragement, dejection, or depression ⟨*despondent* about his health⟩ ☆
— **de·spon·dent·ly** *adverb*
**des·pot** \'des-pət, -,pät\ *noun* [Middle French *despote*, from Greek *despotēs* master, lord, autocrat, from *des-* (akin to *domos* house) + *-potēs* (akin to *posis* husband); akin to Sanskrit *dampati* lord of the house — more at DOME, POTENT] (1585)

---

☆ SYNONYMS
**Despise, contemn, scorn, disdain**
mean to regard as unworthy of one's notice or consideration. DESPISE may suggest an emotional response ranging from strong dislike to loathing ⟨*despises* cowards⟩. CONTEMN implies a vehement condemnation of a person or thing as low, vile, feeble, or ignominious ⟨*contemns* the image of women promoted by advertisers⟩. SCORN implies a ready or indignant contempt ⟨*scorns* the very thought of retirement⟩. DISDAIN implies an arrogant or supercilious aversion to what is regarded as unworthy ⟨*disdained* popular music⟩.

**1 a :** a Byzantine emperor or prince **b :** a bishop or patriarch of the Eastern Orthodox Church **c :** an Italian hereditary prince or military leader during the Renaissance
**2 a :** a ruler with absolute power and authority **b :** a person exercising power tyrannically
**des·pot·ic** \des-'pä-tik, dis-\ *adjective* (1650)
: of, relating to, or characteristic of a despot
— **des·pot·i·cal·ly** \-ti-k(ə-)lē\ *adverb*
**des·po·tism** \'des-pə-ˌti-zəm\ *noun* (circa 1727)
**1 a :** rule by a despot **b :** despotic exercise of power
**2 a :** a system of government in which the ruler has unlimited power : ABSOLUTISM **b :** a despotic state
**des·qua·mate** \'des-kwə-ˌmāt\ *intransitive verb* **-mat·ed; -mat·ing** [Latin *desquamatus*, past participle of *desquamare* to scale, from *de-* + *squama* scale] (1828)
: to peel off in scales
— **des·qua·ma·tion** \ˌdes-kwə-'mā-shən\ *noun*
**des·sert** \di-'zərt\ *noun* [Middle French, from *desservir* to clear the table, from *des-* de- + *servir* to serve, from Latin *servire*] (1600)
**1 :** a usually sweet course or dish (as of pastry or ice cream) served at the end of a meal
**2** *British* **:** a fresh fruit served after a sweet course
**des·sert·spoon** \-ˌspün\ *noun* (1754)
**1 :** a spoon intermediate in size between a teaspoon and a tablespoon for use in eating dessert
**2 :** DESSERTSPOONFUL
**des·sert·spoon·ful** \di-'zərt-ˌspün-ˌful\ *noun* (1875)
**1 :** as much as a dessertspoon will hold
**2** *chiefly British* **:** a unit of measure equal to about 2½ fluidrams
**dessert wine** *noun* (1773)
: a usually sweet wine typically served with dessert or afterward
**de·sta·bi·lize** \(ˌ)dē-'stā-bə-ˌlīz\ *transitive verb* (1924)
**1 :** to make unstable
**2 :** to cause (as a government) to be incapable of functioning or surviving
— **de·sta·bi·li·za·tion** \(ˌ)dē-ˌstā-bə-lə-'zā-shən\ *noun*
**de·stain** \(ˌ)dē-'stān\ *transitive verb* (1927)
: to selectively remove stain from (a specimen for microscopic study)
**de–Sta·lin·iza·tion** \(ˌ)dē-ˌstä-lə-nə-'zā-shən, -ˌsta-\ *noun* (1951)
: the discrediting of Stalin and his policies
**de Stijl** \də-'stī(ə)l, -'stā(ə)l\ *noun* [Dutch *De Stijl*, literally, the style, magazine published by members of the school] (1934)
: a school of art founded in Holland in 1917 typically using rectangular forms and the primary colors plus black and white and asymmetric balance
**des·ti·na·tion** \ˌdes-tə-'nā-shən\ *noun* (14th century)
**1 :** the purpose for which something is destined
**2 :** an act of appointing, setting aside for a purpose, or predetermining
**3 :** a place to which one is journeying or to which something is sent (kept their *destination* secret)
**des·tine** \'des-tən\ *transitive verb* **des·tined; des·tin·ing** [Middle English, from Middle French *destiner*, from Latin *destinare*, from *de-* + *-stinare* (akin to Latin *stare* to stand) — more at STAND] (14th century)
**1 :** to decree beforehand : PREDETERMINE
**2 a :** to designate, assign, or dedicate in advance (the younger son was *destined* for the priesthood) **b :** to direct, devise, or set apart for a specific purpose or place (freight *destined* for European ports)
**des·ti·ny** \'des-tə-nē\ *noun, plural* **-nies** [Middle English *destinee*, from Middle

French, from feminine of *destiné*, past participle of *destiner*] (14th century)
**1 :** something to which a person or thing is destined : FORTUNE
**2 :** a predetermined course of events often held to be an irresistible power or agency
*synonym* see FATE
**des·ti·tute** \'des-tə-ˌtüt, -ˌt(y)üt\ *adjective* [Middle English, from Latin *destitutus*, past participle of *destituere* to abandon, deprive, from *de-* + *statuere* to set up — more at STATUTE] (14th century)
**1 :** lacking something needed or desirable (a lake *destitute* of fish)
**2 :** lacking possessions and resources; *especially* **:** suffering extreme poverty (a *destitute* old man)
— **des·ti·tute·ness** *noun*
**des·ti·tu·tion** \ˌdes-tə-'tü-shən, -'tyü-\ *noun* (15th century)
: the state of being destitute; *especially* **:** such extreme want as threatens life unless relieved
*synonym* see POVERTY
**des·trier** \'des-trē-ər, də-'stri(ə)r\ *noun* [Middle English, from Middle French, from *destre* right hand, from Latin *dextra*, from feminine of *dexter*] (14th century)
*archaic* **:** WAR-HORSE; *also* **:** a charger used especially in medieval tournaments
**de·stroy** \di-'stroi, dē-\ *verb* [Middle English, from Old French *destruire*, from (assumed) Vulgar Latin *destruere*, alteration of Latin *destruere*, from *de-* + *struere* to build — more at STRUCTURE] (13th century)
*transitive verb*
**1 :** to ruin the structure, organic existence, or condition of (*destroyed* the files); *also* **:** to ruin as if by tearing to shreds (their reputation was *destroyed*)
**2 a :** to put out of existence : KILL **b :** NEUTRALIZE (the moon *destroys* the light of the stars) **c :** ANNIHILATE, VANQUISH (armies had been crippled but not *destroyed* —W. L. Shirer)
*intransitive verb*
: to cause destruction
**de·stroy·er** \di-'stroi(-ə)r, dē-\ *noun* (14th century)
**1 :** one that destroys
**2 :** a small fast warship used especially to support larger vessels and usually armed with 5-inch guns, depth charges, torpedoes, and often guided missiles
**destroyer escort** *noun* (1924)
: a warship similar to but smaller than a destroyer
**destroying angel** *noun* (circa 1900)
: DEATH CAP; *also* **:** a related poisonous mushroom (*Amanita verna*)
**de·struc·ti·ble** \di-'strək-tə-bəl\ *adjective* (circa 1755)
: capable of being destroyed
— **de·struc·ti·bil·i·ty** \di-ˌstrək-tə-'bi-lə-tē\ *noun*
**de·struc·tion** \di-'strək-shən\ *noun* [Middle English *destruccioun*, from Middle French *destruction*, from Latin *destruction-, destructio*, from *destruere*] (14th century)
**1 :** the state or fact of being destroyed : RUIN
**2 :** the action or process of destroying something
**3 :** a destroying agency
**de·struc·tion·ist** \-sh(ə-)nəst\ *noun* (1833)
: one who delights in or advocates destruction
**de·struc·tive** \di-'strək-tiv\ *adjective* (15th century)
**1 :** causing destruction : RUINOUS (*destructive* storm)
**2 :** designed or tending to destroy (*destructive* criticism)
— **de·struc·tive·ly** *adverb*
— **de·struc·tive·ness** *noun*
**destructive distillation** *noun* (circa 1831)

: decomposition of a substance (as wood, coal, or oil) by heat in a closed container and collection of the volatile products produced
**de·struc·tiv·i·ty** \di-ˌstrək-'ti-və-tē, ˌdē-\ *noun* (1902)
: capacity for destruction
**de·sue·tude** \'de-swi-ˌtüd, -ˌtyüd, di-'sü-ə-, -'syü-\ *noun* [Middle English *dissuetude*, from Latin *desuetudo*, from *desuescere* to become unaccustomed, from *de-* + *suescere* to become accustomed; akin to Latin *sodalis* comrade — more at SIB] (15th century)
: discontinuance from use or exercise : DISUSE
**de·sul·fur·iza·tion** \(ˌ)dē-ˌsəl-fər-ə-'zā-shən\ *noun* (1854)
: the removal of sulfur or sulfur compounds (as from coal or flue gas)
— **de·sul·fur·ize** \(ˌ)dē-'səl-fər-ˌīz\ *transitive verb*
**des·ul·to·ry** \'de-səl-ˌtōr-ē, -ˌtȯr- *also* -zəl-\ *adjective* [Latin *desultorius*, literally, of a circus rider who leaps from horse to horse, from *desilire* to leap down, from *de-* + *salire* to leap — more at SALLY] (1581)
**1 :** marked by lack of definite plan, regularity, or purpose (a dragged-out ordeal of . . . *desultory* shopping —Herman Wouk)
**2 :** not connected with the main subject
**3 :** disappointing in progress or performance : SLUGGISH
— **des·ul·to·ri·ly** \ˌde-səl-'tōr-ə-lē, -'tȯr-\ *adverb*
— **des·ul·to·ri·ness** \'de-səl-ˌtōr-ē-nəs, -ˌtȯr-\ *noun*
**de·tach** \di-'tach, dē-\ *transitive verb* [French *détacher*, from Old French *destachier*, from *des-* de- + *-tachier* (as in *atachier* to attach)] (1686)
**1 :** to separate especially from a larger mass and usually without violence or damage
**2 :** DISENGAGE, WITHDRAW
— **de·tach·abil·i·ty** \-ˌta-chə-'bi-lə-tē\ *noun*
— **de·tach·able** \-'ta-chə-bəl\ *adjective*
— **de·tach·ably** \-blē\ *adverb*
**de·tached** \di-'tacht, dē-\ *adjective* (circa 1706)
**1 :** standing by itself : SEPARATE, UNCONNECTED; *especially* **:** not sharing any wall with another building (a *detached* house)
**2 :** exhibiting an aloof objectivity usually free from prejudice or self-interest (a *detached* observer)
*synonym* see INDIFFERENT
— **de·tached·ly** \-'ta-chəd-lē, -'tacht-lē\ *adverb*
— **de·tached·ness** \-'ta-chəd-nəs, -'tacht-nəs\ *noun*
**detached service** *noun* (circa 1889)

---

☆ SYNONYMS
**Despondent, despairing, desperate, hopeless** mean having lost all or nearly all hope. DESPONDENT implies a deep dejection arising from a conviction of the uselessness of further effort (*despondent* about yet another rejection). DESPAIRING suggests the slipping away of all hope and often despondency (*despairing* appeals for the return of the kidnapped child). DESPERATE implies despair that prompts reckless action or violence in the face of defeat or frustration (one last *desperate* attempt to turn the tide of battle). HOPELESS suggests despair and the cessation of effort or resistance and often implies acceptance or resignation (the situation of the trapped miners is *hopeless*).

---

\ə\ abut \ᵊ\ kitten \ər\ further \a\ ash \ā\ ace
\ä\ mop, mar \aù\ out \ch\ chin \e\ bet \ē\ easy
\g\ go \i\ hit \ī\ ice \j\ job \ŋ\ sing \ō\ go
\ò\ law \òi\ boy \th\ thin \th\ the \ü\ loot \ù\ foot
\y\ yet \zh\ vision *see also* Guide to Pronunciation

: military service away from one's assigned organization

**de·tach·ment** \di-'tach-mənt, dē-\ noun (1669)
**1 :** the action or process of detaching : SEPARATION
**2 a :** the dispatch of a body of troops or part of a fleet from the main body for a special mission or service **b :** the part so dispatched **c :** a permanently organized separate unit usually smaller than a platoon and of special composition
**3 a :** indifference to worldly concerns : ALOOFNESS **b :** freedom from bias or prejudice

¹**de·tail** \di-'tā(ə)l, 'dē-,tāl\ noun [French détail, from Old French detail slice, piece, from detaillier to cut in pieces, from de- + taillier to cut — more at TAILOR] (1603)
**1 :** extended treatment of or attention to particular items
**2 :** a part of a whole: as **a :** a small and subordinate part : PARTICULAR; also : a reproduction of such a part of a work of art **b :** a part considered or requiring to be considered separately from the whole **c :** the small elements that collectively constitute a work of art **d :** the small elements of a photographic image corresponding to those of the subject
**3 a :** selection of a person or group for a particular task (as in military service) **b** (1) : the person or group selected (2) : the task to be performed
**synonym** see ITEM
**— in detail :** with all the particulars

²**detail** (1650)
transitive verb
**1 :** to report minutely and distinctly : SPECIFY ⟨detailed their grievances⟩
**2 :** to assign to a particular task
**3 :** to furnish with the smaller elements of design and finish ⟨trimmings that detail slips and petticoats⟩
intransitive verb
**:** to make detail drawings
**— de·tail·er** noun

**de·tailed** \di-'tā(ə)ld, 'dē-,tāld\ adjective (1740)
**:** marked by abundant detail or by thoroughness in treating small items or parts ⟨the detailed study of history⟩
**synonym** see CIRCUMSTANTIAL
**— de·tailed·ly** \di-'tāld-lē, -'tā-ləd-, 'dē-\ adverb
**— de·tailed·ness** \di-'tā-ləd-nəs, -'tāld-, 'dē-\ noun

**detail man** noun (1928)
**:** a representative of a drug manufacturer who introduces new drugs especially to physicians and pharmacists

**de·tain** \di-'tān, dē-\ transitive verb [Middle English deteynen, from Middle French detenir, modification of Latin detinēre, from de- + tenēre to hold — more at THIN] (15th century)
**1 :** to hold or keep in or as if in custody
**2** obsolete **:** to keep back (as something due) : WITHHOLD
**3 :** to restrain especially from proceeding : STOP
**synonym** see KEEP, DELAY
**— de·tain·ment** \-mənt\ noun

**de·tain·ee** \di-,tā-'nē, ,dē-\ noun (circa 1928)
**:** a person held in custody especially for political reasons

**de·tain·er** \di-'tā-nər\ noun [Anglo-French detener, from detener to detain, from Latin detinēre] (1619)
**1 :** the act of keeping something in one's possession; specifically : the withholding from the rightful owner of something that has lawfully come into the possession of the holder
**2 :** detention in custody
**3 :** a writ authorizing the keeper of a prison to continue to hold a person in custody

**de·tect** \di-'tekt, dē-\ verb [Middle English, from Latin detectus, past participle of detegere

to uncover, detect, from de- + tegere to cover — more at THATCH] (1581)
transitive verb
**1 :** to discover the true character of
**2 :** to discover or determine the existence, presence, or fact of ⟨detect alcohol in the blood⟩
**3 :** DEMODULATE
intransitive verb
**:** to work as a detective
**— de·tect·abil·i·ty** \-,tek-tə-'bi-lə-tē\ noun
**— de·tect·able** \-'tek-tə-bəl\ adjective

**de·tec·tion** \di-'tek-shən\ noun (15th century)
**1 :** the act of detecting : the state or fact of being detected
**2 :** the process of demodulating

¹**de·tec·tive** \di-'tek-tiv\ adjective (1843)
**1 :** fitted for or used in detecting something ⟨had perfected his detective sensibilities⟩
**2 :** of or relating to detectives or their work ⟨a detective novel⟩
**— de·tec·tive·like** \-,līk\ adjective

²**detective** noun (1850)
**:** one employed or engaged in detecting lawbreakers or in getting information that is not readily or publicly accessible

**de·tec·tor** \di-'tek-tər\ noun (1541)
**:** one that detects: as **a :** a device for detecting the presence of electromagnetic waves or of radioactivity **b :** a rectifier of high-frequency current used especially for extracting the intelligence from a radio signal

**de·tent** \'dē-,tent, di-\ noun [French détente, from Middle French destente, from destendre to slacken, from Old French, from des- de- + tendre to stretch, from Latin tendere — more at THIN] (1688)
**:** a device (as a catch, dog, or spring-operated ball) for positioning and holding one mechanical part in relation to another so that the device can be released by force applied to one of the parts

**dé·tente** or **detente** \dā-'tänt\ noun [French] (1908)
**1 :** the relaxation of strained relations or tensions (as between nations); also : a policy promoting this
**2 :** a period of détente

**de·ten·tion** \di-'ten-chən\ noun [Middle English detencion, from Middle French or Latin; Middle French, from Latin detention-, detentio, from detinēre to detain] (15th century)
**1 :** the act or fact of detaining or holding back; especially : a holding in custody
**2 :** the state of being detained; especially : a period of temporary custody prior to disposition by a court

**detention home** noun (circa 1930)
**:** a house of detention for juvenile delinquents usually under the supervision of a juvenile court

**de·ter** \di-'tər, dē-\ transitive verb **de·terred; de·ter·ring** [Latin deterrēre, from de- + terrēre to frighten — more at TERROR] (1579)
**1 :** to turn aside, discourage, or prevent from acting
**2 :** INHIBIT
**— de·ter·ment** \-'tər-mənt\ noun
**— de·ter·ra·bil·i·ty** \-,tər-ə-'bi-lə-tē\ noun
**— de·ter·ra·ble** \-'tər-ə-bəl\ adjective

**de·terge** \di-'tərj\ transitive verb **de·terged; de·terg·ing** [French or Latin; French déterger, from Latin detergēre, from de- + tergēre to wipe] (circa 1623)
**:** to wash off : CLEANSE
**— de·terg·er** noun

**de·ter·gen·cy** \di-'tər-jən(t)-sē\ noun (1710)
**:** cleansing quality or power

¹**de·ter·gent** \-jənt\ adjective (1616)
**:** that cleanses : CLEANSING

²**detergent** noun (1676)
**:** a cleansing agent: as **a :** SOAP **b :** any of numerous synthetic water-soluble or liquid organic preparations that are chemically different from soaps but are able to emulsify oils, hold dirt in suspension, and act as wetting

agents **c :** an oil-soluble substance that holds insoluble foreign matter in suspension and is used in lubricating oils and dry-cleaning solvents

**de·te·ri·o·rate** \di-'tir-ē-ə-,rāt, dē-\ verb **-rat·ed; -rat·ing** [Late Latin deterioratus, past participle of deteriorare, from Latin deterior worse, from de- + -ter (suffix as in Latin uter which of two) + -ior (comparative suffix) — more at WHETHER, -ER] (1572)
transitive verb
**1 :** to make inferior in quality or value : IMPAIR
**2 :** DISINTEGRATE
intransitive verb
**:** to become impaired in quality, functioning, or condition : DEGENERATE ⟨allowed a tradition of academic excellence to deteriorate⟩ ⟨his health deteriorated⟩
**— de·te·ri·o·ra·tive** \-,rā-tiv\ adjective

**de·te·ri·o·ra·tion** \di-,tir-ē-ə-'rā-shən, dē-\ noun (circa 1658)
**:** the action or process of deteriorating : the state of having deteriorated ☆

**de·ter·min·able** \-'tər-mə-nə-bəl\ adjective (15th century)
**1 :** capable of being determined, definitely ascertained, or decided upon
**2 :** liable to be terminated : TERMINABLE
**— de·ter·min·able·ness** noun
**— de·ter·min·ably** \-blē\ adverb

**de·ter·mi·na·cy** \di-'tər-mə-nə-sē\ noun, plural **-cies** (1873)
**1 :** the quality or state of being determinate
**2 a :** the state of being definitely and unequivocally characterized : EXACTNESS **b :** the state of being determined or necessitated

**de·ter·mi·nant** \di-'tər-mə-nənt\ noun (1686)
**1 :** an element that identifies or determines the nature of something or that fixes or conditions an outcome
**2 :** a square array of numbers bordered on the left and right by a vertical line and having a value equal to the algebraic sum of all possible products where the number of factors in each product is the same as the number of rows or columns, each factor in a given product is taken from a different row and column, and the sign of a product is positive or negative depending upon whether the number of permutations necessary to place the indices representing each factor's position in its row or column in the order of the natural numbers is odd or even
**3 :** GENE
**4 :** EPITOPE
**— de·ter·mi·nan·tal** \-,tər-mə-'nan-t°l\ adjective

**de·ter·mi·nate** \di-'tər-mə-nət\ adjective [Middle English, from Latin determinatus, past participle of determinare] (14th century)
**1 :** having defined limits
**2 :** definitely settled

☆ SYNONYMS
**Deterioration, degeneration, decadence, decline** mean the falling from a higher to a lower level in quality, character, or vitality. DETERIORATION implies generally the impairment of value or usefulness ⟨the deterioration of the house through neglect⟩. DEGENERATION stresses physical, intellectual, or especially moral retrogression ⟨the degeneration of their youthful idealism into cynicism⟩. DECADENCE presupposes a reaching and passing the peak of development and implies a turn downward with a consequent loss in vitality or energy ⟨cited love of luxury as a sign of cultural decadence⟩. DECLINE differs from DECADENCE in suggesting a more markedly downward direction and greater momentum as well as more obvious evidence of deterioration ⟨the meteoric decline of his career after the scandal⟩.

**3 :** conclusively determined **:** DEFINITIVE
**4 :** characterized by sequential flowering from the central or uppermost bud to the lateral or basal buds; *also* **:** characterized by growth in which the main stem ends in an inflorescence and stops growing with only branches from the main stem having further and similarly restricted growth ⟨*determinate* tomato plants⟩ — compare INDETERMINATE 4
**5 :** relating to, being, or undergoing egg cleavage in which each division irreversibly separates portions of the zygote with specific potencies for further development
— **de·ter·mi·nate·ly** *adverb*
— **de·ter·mi·nate·ness** *noun*
**de·ter·mi·na·tion** \di-ˌtər-mə-ˈnā-shən\ *noun* (14th century)
**1 a :** a judicial decision settling and ending a controversy **b :** the resolving of a question by argument or reasoning
**2** *archaic* **:** TERMINATION
**3 a :** the act of deciding definitely and firmly; *also* **:** the result of such an act of decision **b :** the power or habit of deciding definitely and firmly
**4 :** a fixing or finding of the position, magnitude, value, or character of something: as **a :** the act, process, or result of an accurate measurement **b :** an identification of the taxonomic position of a plant or animal
**5 a :** the definition of a concept in logic by its essential constituents **b :** the addition of a differentia to a concept to limit its denotation
**6 :** direction or tendency to a certain end **:** IMPULSION
**7 :** the fixation of the destiny of undifferentiated embryonic tissue
**de·ter·mi·na·tive** \-ˈtər-mə-ˌnā-tiv, -ˈtər-mə-nə-\ *adjective* (1655)
**:** having power or tendency to determine **:** tending to fix, settle, or define something ⟨regard experiments as *determinative* of the principles from which deductions could be made —S. F. Mason⟩
**synonym** see CONCLUSIVE
— **determinative** *noun*
**de·ter·mi·na·tor** \di-ˈtər-mə-ˌnā-tər\ *noun* (1556)
**:** DETERMINER
**de·ter·mine** \di-ˈtər-mən, dē-\ *verb* **de·ter·mined; de·ter·min·ing** [Middle English, from Middle French *determiner*, from Latin *determinare*, from *de-* + *terminare* to limit, from *terminus* boundary, limit — more at TERM] (14th century)
*transitive verb*
**1 a :** to fix conclusively or authoritatively **b :** to decide by judicial sentence **c :** to settle or decide by choice of alternatives or possibilities **d :** RESOLVE
**2 a :** to fix the form, position, or character of beforehand **:** ORDAIN ⟨two points *determine* a straight line⟩ **b :** to bring about as a result **:** REGULATE ⟨demand *determines* the price⟩
**3 a :** to fix the boundaries of **b :** to limit in extent or scope **c :** to put or set an end to **:** TERMINATE ⟨*determine* an estate⟩
**4 :** to find out or come to a decision about by investigation, reasoning, or calculation ⟨*determine* the answer to the problem⟩ ⟨*determine* a position at sea⟩
**5 :** to bring about the determination of ⟨*determine* the fate of a cell⟩
*intransitive verb*
**1 :** to come to a decision
**2 :** to come to an end or become void
**synonym** see DECIDE, DISCOVER
**de·ter·mined** \-ˈtər-mənd\ *adjective* (1513)
**1 :** having reached a decision **:** firmly resolved ⟨*determined* to be a pilot⟩
**2 a :** showing determination ⟨a *determined* effort⟩ **b :** characterized by determination ⟨will deter all but the most *determined* thief —*Security World*⟩
— **de·ter·mined·ly** \-mənd-lē, -mə-nəd-lē\ *adverb*

— **de·ter·mined·ness** \-mənd-nəs\ *noun*
**de·ter·min·er** \-ˈtər-mə-nər\ *noun* (circa 1530)
**:** one that determines: as **a :** GENE **b :** a word (as an article, possessive, demonstrative, or quantifier) that makes specific the denotation of a noun phrase
**de·ter·min·ism** \di-ˈtər-mə-ˌni-zəm, dē-\ *noun* (1846)
**1 a :** a theory or doctrine that acts of the will, occurrences in nature, or social or psychological phenomena are causally determined by preceding events or natural laws **b :** a belief in predestination
**2 :** the quality or state of being determined
— **de·ter·min·ist** \-nəst\ *noun or adjective*
— **de·ter·min·is·tic** \-ˌtər-mə-ˈnis-tik\ *adjective*
— **de·ter·min·is·ti·cal·ly** \-ti-k(ə-)lē\ *adverb*
**de·ter·rence** \di-ˈtər-ən(t)s, -ˈter-; -ˈtə-rən(t)s, dē-\ *noun* (1861)
**:** the inhibition of criminal behavior by fear especially of punishment; *also* **:** the maintenance of military power for the purpose of discouraging attack
**de·ter·rent** \-ənt, -ˌrənt\ *adjective* [Latin *deterrent-, deterrens*, present participle of *deterrēre* to deter] (1829)
**1 :** serving to deter
**2 :** relating to deterrence
— **deterrent** *noun*
— **de·ter·rent·ly** *adverb*
**de·ter·sive** \di-ˈtər-siv, -ziv\ *adjective* [Middle French *detersif*, from Latin *detersus*, past participle of *detergēre* to deterge] (1586)
**:** DETERGENT
— **detersive** *noun*
**de·test** \di-ˈtest, dē-\ *transitive verb* [Middle French *detester* or Latin *detestari*; Middle French *detester*, from Latin *detestari*, literally, to curse while calling a deity to witness, from *de-* + *testari* to call to witness — more at TESTAMENT] (circa 1535)
**1 :** to feel intense and often violent antipathy toward **:** LOATHE
**2** *obsolete* **:** CURSE, DENOUNCE
**synonym** see HATE
— **de·test·er** *noun*
**de·test·able** \di-ˈtes-tə-bəl, dē-\ *adjective* (15th century)
**:** arousing or meriting intense dislike **:** ABOMINABLE
— **de·test·able·ness** *noun*
— **de·test·ably** \-blē\ *adverb*
**de·tes·ta·tion** \ˌdē-ˌtes-ˈtā-shən, di-\ *noun* (15th century)
**1 :** extreme hatred or dislike **:** ABHORRENCE, LOATHING
**2 :** an object of hatred or contempt
**de·throne** \di-ˈthrōn, dē-\ *transitive verb* (1609)
**:** to remove from a throne or place of power or prominence **:** DEPOSE
— **de·throne·ment** \-mənt\ *noun*
— **de·thron·er** *noun*
**de·tick** \(ˌ)dē-ˈtik\ *transitive verb* (1925)
**:** to remove ticks from
— **de·tick·er** *noun*
**det·i·nue** \ˈde-tᵊn-ˌ(y)ü\ *noun* [Middle English *detenewe*, from Middle French *detenue* detention, from feminine of *detenu*, past participle of *detenir* to detain] (15th century)
**1 :** a common-law action for the recovery of a personal chattel wrongfully detained or of its value
**2 :** detention of something due; *especially* **:** the unlawful detention of a personal chattel from another
**det·o·na·ble** \ˈde-tᵊn-ə-bəl, -tə-nə-\ *adjective* (1884)
**:** capable of being detonated
— **det·o·na·bil·i·ty** \ˌdet-ᵊn-ə-ˈbil-ət-ē, ˌdet-ə-nə-\ *noun*
**det·o·nate** \ˈde-tᵊn-ˌāt, ˈde-tə-ˌnāt\ *verb* **-nat·ed; -nat·ing** [French *détoner* to explode,

from Latin *detonare* to expend thunder, from *de-* + *tonare* to thunder — more at THUNDER] (1729)
*intransitive verb*
**:** to explode with sudden violence
*transitive verb*
**1 :** to cause to detonate ⟨*detonate* a bomb⟩ — compare DEFLAGRATE
**2 :** to set off in a burst of activity **:** SPARK ⟨programs that *detonated* controversies⟩
— **det·o·nat·able** \-ˌā-tə-bəl, -ˌnā-\ *adjective*
— **det·o·na·tive** \ˈde-tᵊn-ˌā-tiv, ˈde-tə-ˌnā-\ *adjective*
**det·o·na·tion** \ˌde-tᵊn-ˈā-shən, ˌde-tə-ˈnā-\ *noun* (1686)
**1 :** the action or process of detonating
**2 :** rapid combustion in an internal combustion engine that results in knocking
**det·o·na·tor** \ˈde-tᵊn-ˌā-tər, -tə-ˌnā-\ *noun* (1822)
**:** a device or small quantity of explosive used for detonating a high explosive
**¹de·tour** \ˈdē-ˌtu̇r *also* di-ˈtu̇ər\ *noun* [French *détour*, from Old French *destor*, from *destorner* to divert, from *des-* de- + *torner* to turn — more at TURN] (1738)
**:** a deviation from a direct course or the usual procedure; *especially* **:** a roundabout way temporarily replacing part of a route
**²detour** (1836)
*intransitive verb*
**:** to proceed by a detour ⟨*detour* around road construction⟩
*transitive verb*
**1 :** to send by a circuitous route
**2 :** to avoid by going around **:** BYPASS
**de·tox** \ˈdē-ˌtäks, di-ˈtäks\ *noun, often attributive* (1973)
**:** detoxification from an intoxicating or an addictive substance
— **detox** *verb*
**de·tox·i·cate** \(ˌ)dē-ˈtäk-sə-ˌkāt\ *transitive verb* **-cat·ed; -cat·ing** [*de-* + *²intoxicate*] (1867)
**:** DETOXIFY 1, 2
— **de·tox·i·cant** \-si-kənt\ *noun*
— **de·tox·i·ca·tion** \(ˌ)dē-ˌtäk-sə-ˈkā-shən\ *noun*
**de·tox·i·fy** \(ˌ)dē-ˈtäk-sə-ˌfī\ *transitive verb* **-fied; -fy·ing** (circa 1905)
**1 a :** to remove a poison or toxin or the effect of such from **b :** to render (a harmful substance) harmless
**2 :** to free (as a drug user or an alcoholic) from an intoxicating or an addictive substance in the body or from dependence on or addiction to such a substance
**3 :** NEUTRALIZE 2
— **de·tox·i·fi·ca·tion** \(ˌ)dē-ˌtäk-sə-fə-ˈkā-shən\ *noun*
**de·tract** \di-ˈtrakt, dē-\ *verb* [Middle English, from Latin *detractus*, past participle of *detrahere* to pull down, disparage, from *de-* + *trahere* to draw] (15th century)
*transitive verb*
**1** *archaic* **:** to speak ill of
**2** *archaic* **:** to take away
**3 :** DIVERT ⟨*detract* attention⟩
*intransitive verb*
**:** to diminish the importance, value, or effectiveness of something — often used with *from*
— **de·trac·tor** \-ˈtrak-tər\ *noun*
**de·trac·tion** \di-ˈtrak-shən, dē-\ *noun* (14th century)
**1 :** a lessening of reputation or esteem especially by envious, malicious, or petty criticism **:** BELITTLING, DISPARAGEMENT
**2 :** a taking away ⟨it is no *detraction* from its dignity or prestige —J. F. Golay⟩

\ə\ abut \ᵊ\ kitten \ər\ **further** \a\ ash \ā\ ace
\ä\ mop, mar \au̇\ out \ch\ chin \e\ bet \ē\ **easy**
\g\ go \i\ hit \ī\ ice \j\ job \ŋ\ sing \ō\ go
\ȯ\ law \ȯi\ boy \th\ thin \t̲h̲\ the \ü\ loot \u̇\ foot
\y\ yet \zh\ vision *see also* Guide to Pronunciation

— **de·trac·tive** \-'trak-tiv\ *adjective*
— **de·trac·tive·ly** *adverb*
**de·train** \(,)dē-'trān\ (1881)
*intransitive verb*
: to get off a railroad train
*transitive verb*
: to remove from a railroad train
— **de·train·ment** \-mənt\ *noun*
**de·trib·al·ize** \(,)dē-'trī-bə-,līz\ *transitive verb* **-ized; -iz·ing** (1920)
: to cause to lose tribal identity : ACCULTURATE
— **de·trib·al·iza·tion** \(,)dē-,trī-bə-lə-'zā-shən\ *noun*
**det·ri·ment** \'de-trə-mənt\ *noun* [Middle English, from Middle French or Latin; Middle French, from Latin *detrimentum*, from *deterere* to wear away, impair, from *de-* + *terere* to rub — more at THROW] (15th century)
**1** : INJURY, DAMAGE ⟨did hard work without *detriment* to his health⟩
**2** : a cause of injury or damage ⟨a *detriment* to progress⟩
**¹det·ri·men·tal** \,de-trə-'men-t°l\ *adjective* (1590)
: obviously harmful : DAMAGING ⟨the *detrimental* effects of pollution⟩
**synonym** see PERNICIOUS
— **det·ri·men·tal·ly** \-t°l-ē\ *adverb*
**²detrimental** *noun* (1831)
: an undesirable or harmful person or thing
**de·tri·tion** \di-'tri-shən\ *noun* (1674)
: a wearing off or away
**de·tri·tus** \di-'trī-təs\ *noun, plural* **de·tri·tus** \-'trī-təs, -'trī-,tüs\ [French *détritus*, from Latin *detritus*, past participle of *deterere*] (1802)
**1** : loose material (as rock fragments or organic particles) that results directly from disintegration
**2** : a product of disintegration, destruction, or wearing away : DEBRIS
— **de·tri·tal** \-'trī-t°l\ *adjective*
**de trop** \də-'trō\ *adjective* [French] (1752)
: too much or too many : SUPERFLUOUS
**de·tu·mes·cence** \,dē-t(y)ü-'me-s°n(t)s\ *noun* [Latin *detumescere* to become less swollen, from *de-* + *tumescere* to swell — more at TUMESCENT] (1678)
: subsidence or diminution of swelling or erection
— **de·tu·mes·cent** \-s°nt\ *adjective*
**Deu·ca·lion** \d(y)ü-'kāl-yən\ *noun* [Latin, from Greek *Deukaliōn*]
: a survivor with his wife Pyrrha of a great flood by which Zeus destroys the rest of the human race
**¹deuce** \'düs *also* 'dyüs\ *noun* [Middle French *deus* two, from Latin *duos*, accusative masculine of *duo* two — more at TWO] (15th century)
**1 a** (1) : the face of a die that bears two spots (2) : a playing card bearing an index number two **b** : a throw of the dice yielding two points
**2** : a tie in tennis after each side has scored 40 requiring two consecutive points by one side to win
**3** [obsolete English *deuce* bad luck] **a** : DEVIL, DICKENS — used chiefly as a mild oath ⟨what the *deuce* is he up to now⟩ **b** : something notable of its kind ⟨a *deuce* of a mess⟩
**²deuce** *transitive verb* **deuced; deuc·ing** (1919)
: to bring the score of (a tennis game or set) to deuce
**deuc·ed** \'dü-səd *also* 'dyü-\ *adjective* (1782)
: DAMNED, CONFOUNDED ⟨in a *deuced* fix⟩
— **deuc·ed** *or* **deuc·ed·ly** *adverb*
**deuces wild** *noun* (1927)
: a card game (as poker) in which each deuce may represent any card designated by its holder
**de·us ex ma·chi·na** \'dā-əs-,eks-'mä-ki-nə, -'ma-, -,nä; -mə-'shē-nə\ *noun* [New Latin, a god from a machine, translation of Greek *theos ek mēchanēs*] (1697)

**1** : a god introduced by means of a crane in ancient Greek and Roman drama to decide the final outcome
**2** : a person or thing (as in fiction or drama) that appears or is introduced suddenly and unexpectedly and provides a contrived solution to an apparently insoluble difficulty ◆
**deuter-** *or* **deutero-** *combining form* [alteration of Middle English *deutro-*, modification of Late Latin *deutero-*, from Greek *deuter-*, *deutero-*, from *deuteros*; probably akin to Greek *dein* to lack, Sanskrit *doṣa* fault, lack]
**1** : second : secondary ⟨*deuteranopia*⟩
**2** : second : secondary
**deu·ter·ag·o·nist** \,dü-tə-'ra-gə-nist *also* ,dyü-\ *noun* [Greek *deuteragōnistēs*, from *deuter-* + *agōnistēs* combatant, actor — more at PROTAGONIST] (1855)
**1** : the actor taking the part of second importance in a classical Greek drama
**2** : a person who serves as a foil to another
**deu·ter·anom·a·lous** \,dü-tə-rə-'nä-mə-ləs *also* ,dyü-\ *adjective* [New Latin *deuteranomali*a (from *deuter-* + Latin *anomalia* anomaly) abnormal trichromatism + English *-ous*] (circa 1931)
: exhibiting partial loss of green color vision so that an increased intensity of this color is required in a mixture of red and green to match a given yellow
— **deu·ter·anom·a·ly** \-'nä-mə-lē\ *noun*
**deu·ter·an·ope** \'dü-tə-rə-,nōp *also* 'dyü-\ *noun* (1902)
: an individual affected with deuteranopia
**deu·ter·an·opia** \,dü-tə-rə-'nō-pē-ə *also* ,dyü-\ *noun* [New Latin, from *deuter-* + ²*a-* + *-opia*; from the blindness to green, regarded as the second primary color] (circa 1901)
: color blindness marked by confusion of purplish red and green
— **deu·ter·an·opic** \-'nō-pik, -'nä-pik\ *adjective*
**deu·ter·ate** \'dü-tə-,rāt *also* 'dyü-\ *transitive verb* **-at·ed; -at·ing** (1947)
: to introduce deuterium into (a compound)
— **deu·ter·a·tion** \,dü-tə-'rā-shən\ *noun*
**deu·te·ri·um** \dü-'tir-ē-əm *also* dyü-\ *noun* [New Latin, from Greek *deuteros* second] (1933)
: an isotope of hydrogen that has one proton and one neutron in its nucleus and that has twice the mass of ordinary hydrogen — symbol *D*; called also *heavy hydrogen*
**deuterium oxide** *noun* (1934)
: HEAVY WATER 1
**deu·tero·ca·non·i·cal** \,dü-tə-rō-kə-'nä-ni-kəl *also* ,dyü-\ *adjective* [New Latin *deuterocanonicus*, from *deuter-* + Late Latin *canonicus* canonical] (1684)
: of, relating to, or constituting the books of Scripture contained in the Septuagint but not in the Hebrew canon
**deu·ter·on** \'dü-tə-,rän *also* 'dyü-\ *noun* (1933)
: a deuterium nucleus
**Deu·ter·o·nom·ic** \,dü-tə-rə-'nä-mik *also* ,dyü-\ *adjective* (1857)
: of or relating to the book of Deuteronomy, its style, or its contents
**Deu·ter·on·o·mist** \,dü-tə-'rä-nə-mist *also* ,dyü-\ *noun* (1862)
: any of the writers or editors of a Deuteronomic body of source material often distinguished in the earlier books of the Old Testament
— **Deu·ter·on·o·mis·tic** \-,rä-nə-'mis-tik\ *adjective*
**Deu·ter·on·o·my** \,dü-tə-'rä-nə-mē *also* ,dyü-\ *noun* [Middle English *Deutronomie*, from Late Latin *Deuteronomium*, from Greek *Deuteronomion*, from *deuter-* + *nomos* law — more at NIMBLE]
: the fifth book of canonical Jewish and Christian Scripture containing narrative and Mosaic laws — see BIBLE table
**deu·tero·stome** \'dü-tə-rō-,stōm *also* 'dyü-\ *noun* [New Latin *Deuterostomia*, group name,

from *deuter-* + Greek *stoma* mouth — more at STOMACH] (1950)
: any of a major division (Deuterostomia) of the animal kingdom that includes the bilaterally symmetrical animals (as the chordates) with indeterminate cleavage and a mouth that does not arise from the blastopore
**deu·to·plasm** \'dü-tō-,pla-zəm *also* 'dyü-\ *noun* [International Scientific Vocabulary *deuter-* + *-plasm*] (1884)
: the nutritive inclusions of protoplasm; *especially* : the yolk reserves of an egg
**deut·sche mark** \'dóich-,märk, 'doi-chə-\ *noun* [German, German mark] (1948)
— see MONEY table
**deut·zia** \'düt-sē-ə *also* 'dyüt-\ *noun* [New Latin, from Jean *Deutz* (died 1784?) Dutch patron of botanical research] (1837)
: any of a genus (*Deutzia*) of the saxifrage family of ornamental shrubs with white or pink flowers
**de·val·u·ate** \(,)dē-'val-yə-,wāt\ *verb* (1898)
: DEVALUE
**de·val·u·a·tion** \(,)dē-,val-yə-'wā-shən\ *noun* (1914)
**1** : an official reduction in the exchange value of a currency by a lowering of its gold equivalency or its value relative to another currency
**2** : a lessening especially of status or stature : DECLINE
**de·val·ue** \(,)dē-'val-(,)yü, -yə(-w)\ (1918)
*transitive verb*
**1** : to institute the devaluation of (money)
**2** : to lessen the value of
*intransitive verb*
: to institute devaluation
**De·va·na·ga·ri** \,dā-və-'nä-gə-rē\ *noun* [Sanskrit *devanāgarī*, from *deva* divine + *nāgarī* script of the city — more at DEITY] (1781)
: an alphabet usually employed for Sanskrit and also used as a literary hand for various modern languages of India — see ALPHABET table
**dev·as·tate** \'de-və-,stāt\ *transitive verb* **-tat·ed; -tat·ing** [Latin *devastatus*, past participle of *devastare*, from *de-* + *vastare* to lay waste — more at WASTE] (1638)
**1** : to bring to ruin or desolation by violent action
**2** : to reduce to chaos, disorder, or helplessness : OVERWHELM ⟨*devastated* by grief⟩ ⟨her wisecrack *devastated* the class⟩
**synonym** see RAVAGE
— **dev·as·tat·ing·ly** \-,stā-tiŋ-lē\ *adverb*
— **dev·as·ta·tion** \,de-və-'stā-shən\ *noun*
— **dev·as·tat·ive** \'de-və-,stā-tiv\ *adjective*
— **dev·as·ta·tor** \-,stā-tər\ *noun*

◇ WORD HISTORY
**deus ex machina** Since the birth of the drama, playwrights have wrestled with the problem of how to resolve the conflicts that they develop in their dramatic works. In antiquity, even the greatest playwrights often resorted to divine intervention to resolve seemingly irresolvable dramatic situations. In Greek drama of the 4th century B.C., divine intervention took the form of the sudden appearance of a god in the sky. The use of a machine like a crane to achieve this primitive stage effect gave birth to the term *theos ek mēchanēs*, which literally means "a god from a machine." The resolving of a tangled plot by the timely intervention of a god hoisted on a crane became a standard convention in the Greek and Roman theater. The extended application of the term for this stage effect to any unlikely but providential savior, whether person or event, also became established during classical times. It was in this extended sense that *deus ex machina*, the New Latin translation of the Greek phrase, first appeared in English contexts in the 17th century.

**de·vein** \(ˌ)dē-'vān\ *transitive verb* (1953)
: to remove the dark dorsal vein from (shrimp)
**de·vel·op** \di-'vel-əp, dē-\ *verb* [French *développer*, from Old French *desveloper, desvoluper* to unwrap, expose, from *des-* de- + *enveloper* to enclose — more at ENVELOP] (1750)
*transitive verb*
**1 a :** to set forth or make clear by degrees or in detail : EXPOUND **b :** to make visible or manifest **c :** to treat (as in dyeing) with an agent to cause the appearance of color **d :** to subject (exposed photograph material) especially to chemicals in order to produce a visible image; *also* : to make visible by such a method **e :** to elaborate (a musical idea) by the working out of rhythmic and harmonic changes in the theme
**2 :** to work out the possibilities of
**3 a :** to make active or promote the growth of ⟨*developed* his muscles⟩ **b** (1) : to make available or usable ⟨*develop* natural resources⟩ (2) : to make suitable for commercial or residential purposes **c :** to move (as a chess piece) from the original position to one providing more opportunity for effective use
**4 a :** to cause to unfold gradually ⟨*developed* his argument⟩ **b :** to expand by a process of growth ⟨*developed* a strong organization⟩ **c :** to cause to grow and differentiate along lines natural to its kind ⟨rain and sun *develop* the grain⟩ **d :** to have unfold or differentiate within one ⟨*developed* pneumonia⟩
**5 :** to acquire gradually ⟨*develop* an appreciation for ballet⟩
*intransitive verb*
**1 a :** to go through a process of natural growth, differentiation, or evolution by successive changes ⟨a blossom *develops* from a bud⟩ **b :** to acquire secondary sex characters
**2 :** to become gradually manifest
**3 :** to come into being gradually ⟨the situation *developing* in eastern Europe⟩; *also* : TURN OUT ⟨*intransitive verb* 2a ⟨it *developed* that no one had paid the bill⟩
**— de·vel·op·able** \-'ve-lə-pə-bəl\ *adjective*

**de·vel·oped** \di-'ve-ləpt\ *adjective* (1945)
: having a relatively high level of industrialization and standard of living ⟨a *developed* country⟩
**de·vel·op·er** \-lə-pər\ *noun* (1883)
: one that develops: as **a :** a chemical used to develop exposed photographic materials **b :** a person who develops real estate
**de·vel·op·ing** \-lə-piŋ\ *adjective* (1964)
: UNDERDEVELOPED 2 ⟨*developing* nations⟩
**de·vel·op·ment** \di-'ve-ləp-mənt, dē-\ *noun* (1756)
**1 :** the act, process, or result of developing
**2 :** the state of being developed
**3 :** a developed tract of land; *especially* : one with houses built on it
**de·vel·op·men·tal** \dē-ˌve-ləp-'men-tᵊl\ *adjective* (1849)
**1 a :** of, relating to, or being development ⟨*developmental* processes⟩; *broadly* : EXPERIMENTAL 2 ⟨*developmental* aircraft⟩ **b :** serving economic development ⟨*developmental* highways⟩
**2 :** designed to assist growth or bring about improvement (as of a skill) ⟨*developmental* toys⟩
**— de·vel·op·men·tal·ly** \-tᵊl-ē\ *adverb*
**developmentally disabled** *adjective* (1975)
: having a physical or mental handicap that impedes or prevents normal development
**de·verb·al** \(ˌ)dē-'vər-bəl\ *adjective* (1943)
: DEVERBATIVE
**de·verb·a·tive** \(ˌ)dē-'vər-bə-tiv\ *adjective* (1930)
**1 :** derived from a verb ⟨the *deverbative* noun *developer* is derived from *develop*⟩
**2 :** used in derivation from a verb ⟨the *deverbative* suffix *-er* in *developer*⟩
**— deverbative** *noun*

**de·vest** \di-'vest\ *transitive verb* [Middle French *desvestir,* from Medieval Latin *disvestire,* from Latin *dis-* + *vestire* to clothe — more at VEST] (1563)
: DIVEST
**de·vi·ance** \'dē-vē-ən(t)s\ *noun* (1944)
: deviant quality, state, or behavior
**de·vi·an·cy** \-ən-sē\ *noun, plural* **-cies** (1947)
: DEVIANCE
**de·vi·ant** \-ənt\ *adjective* (15th century)
: deviating especially from an accepted norm ⟨*deviant* behavior⟩
**— deviant** *noun*
**¹de·vi·ate** \'dē-vē-ˌāt\ *verb* **-at·ed; -at·ing** [Late Latin *deviatus,* past participle of *deviare,* from Latin *de-* + *via* way — more at WAY] (circa 1633)
*intransitive verb*
**1 :** to stray especially from a standard, principle, or topic
**2 :** to depart from an established course or norm
*transitive verb*
: to cause to turn out of a previous course
**synonym** see SWERVE
**— de·vi·a·tor** \-ˌā-tər\ *noun*
**— de·vi·a·to·ry** \-ə-ˌtōr-ē, -ˌtòr-\ *adjective*
**²de·vi·ate** \-vē-ət, -vē-ˌāt\ *noun* (1912)
**1 :** one that deviates from a norm; *especially* : a person who differs markedly from a group norm
**2 :** a statistical variable that gives the deviation of another variable from a fixed value (as the mean)
**³de·vi·ate** \-vē-ət, -vē-ˌāt\ *adjective* (1929)
: departing significantly from the behavioral norms of a particular society
**de·vi·a·tion** \ˌdē-vē-'ā-shən\ *noun* (15th century)
: an act or instance of deviating: as **a :** deflection of the needle of a compass caused by local magnetic influences (as in a ship) **b :** the difference between a value in a frequency distribution and a fixed number (as the mean) **c :** departure from an established ideology or party line **d :** noticeable or marked departure from accepted norms of behavior
**— de·vi·a·tion·ism** \-shə-ˌni-zəm\ *noun*
**— de·vi·a·tion·ist** \-sh(ə-)nist\ *noun or adjective*
**de·vice** \di-'vīs\ *noun* [Middle English *devis,* *devise,* from Middle French, division, intention, from Old French *deviser* to divide, regulate, tell — more at DEVISE] (14th century)
**1 :** something devised or contrived: as **a** (1) : PLAN, PROCEDURE, TECHNIQUE (2) : a scheme to deceive : STRATAGEM, TRICK **b :** something fanciful, elaborate, or intricate in design **c :** something (as a figure of speech) in a literary work designed to achieve a particular artistic effect **d** *archaic* : MASQUE, SPECTACLE **e :** a conventional stage practice or means (as a stage whisper) used to achieve a particular dramatic effect **f :** a piece of equipment or a mechanism designed to serve a special purpose or perform a special function
**2 :** DESIRE, INCLINATION ⟨left to my own *devices*⟩
**3 :** an emblematic design used especially as a heraldic bearing
**¹dev·il** \'de-vᵊl, dialect 'di-\ *noun* [Middle English *devel,* from Old English *dēofol,* from Late Latin *diabolus,* from Greek *diabolos,* literally, slanderer, from *diaballein* to throw across, slander, from *dia-* + *ballein* to throw; probably akin to Sanskrit *gurate* he lifts up] (before 12th century)
**1** *often capitalized* : the personal supreme spirit of evil often represented in Jewish and Christian belief as the tempter of mankind, the leader of all apostate angels, and the ruler of hell — usually used with *the*; often used as an interjection, an intensive, or a generalized term of abuse ⟨what the *devil* is this?⟩ ⟨the *devil* you say!⟩

**2 :** an evil spirit : DEMON
**3 a :** an extremely wicked person : FIEND **b** *archaic* : a great evil
**4 :** a person of notable energy, recklessness, and dashing spirit; *also* : one who is mischievous ⟨those kids are little *devils* today⟩
**5 :** FELLOW — usually used in the phrases *poor devil, lucky devil*
**6 a :** something very trying or provoking ⟨having a *devil* of a time with this problem⟩ **b :** severe criticism or rebuke : HELL — used with *the* ⟨I'll probably catch the *devil* for this⟩
**7 :** DUST DEVIL
**8** *Christian Science* : the opposite of Truth : a belief in sin, sickness, and death : EVIL, ERROR
**— between the devil and the deep blue sea :** faced with two equally objectionable alternatives
**— devil to pay :** severe consequences — used with *the*
**²devil** *transitive verb* **-iled** *or* **-illed; -il·ing** *or* **-il·ling** \'de-vᵊl-iŋ, 'dev-liŋ\ (1800)
**1 :** to season highly ⟨*deviled* eggs⟩
**2 :** TEASE, ANNOY
**dev·il·fish** \'de-vᵊl-ˌfish\ *noun* (1709)
**1 :** any of several extremely large rays (genera *Manta* and *Mobula*) widely distributed in warm seas
**2 :** OCTOPUS; *broadly* : any large cephalopod

devilfish 1

**dev·il·ish** \'de-vᵊl-ish, 'dev-lish\ *adjective* (15th century)
**1 :** resembling or befitting a devil: as **a :** EVIL, SINISTER **b :** MISCHIEVOUS, ROGUISH
**2 :** EXTREME ⟨in a *devilish* hurry⟩
**— devilish** *adverb*
**— dev·il·ish·ly** *adverb*
**— dev·il·ish·ness** *noun*
**dev·il—may—care** \ˌde-vᵊl-(ˌ)mā-'ker, -'kar\ *adjective* (1837)
: EASYGOING, CAREFREE
**dev·il·ment** \'de-vᵊl-mənt, -ˌment\ *noun* (1771)
: MISCHIEF
**dev·il·ry** \'de-vᵊl-rē\ *or* **dev·il·try** \-vᵊl-trē\ *noun, plural* **-ries** *or* **-tries** (14th century)
**1 a :** action performed with the help of the devil : WITCHCRAFT **b :** WICKEDNESS **c :** MISCHIEF
**2 :** an act of devilry
**devil's advocate** *noun* [translation of New Latin *advocatus diaboli*] (1760)
**1 :** a Roman Catholic official whose duty is to examine critically the evidence on which a demand for beatification or canonization rests
**2 :** a person who champions the less accepted cause for the sake of argument
**devil's claw** *noun* (circa 1900)
: any of several herbs (genus *Proboscidea* synonym *Martynia* of the family Martyniaceae) of the southwestern U.S. and Mexico that have edible pods yielding a black sewing material used in basket making
**devil's darning needle** *noun* (1809)
**1 :** DRAGONFLY
**2 :** DAMSELFLY
**devil's food cake** *noun* (1905)
: a rich chocolate cake
**devil's paintbrush** *noun* (1900)
: ORANGE HAWKWEED; *broadly* : any of various hawkweeds that are naturalized weeds in the eastern U.S.
**devil theory** *noun* (1937)

\ə\ abut \ᵊ\ kitten \ər\ further \a\ ash \ā\ ace \ä\ mop, mar \aù\ out \ch\ chin \e\ bet \ē\ easy \g\ go \i\ hit \ī\ ice \j\ job \ŋ\ sing \ō\ go \ò\ law \òi\ boy \th\ thin \th̲\ the \ü\ loot \ù\ foot \y\ yet \zh\ vision    *see also* Guide to Pronunciation

: a theory of history: political and social crises arise from the deliberate actions of evil or misguided leaders rather than as a natural result of conditions

**dev·il·wood** \'de-v°l-,wùd\ *noun* (1818)
: a small tree (*Osmanthus americanus*) of the southern U.S. that is related to the olive

**de·vi·ous** \'dē-vē-əs, -vyəs\ *adjective* [Latin *devius*, from *de* from + *via* way — more at DE-, WAY] (1599)
**1 :** OUT-OF-THE-WAY, REMOTE
**2 a :** WANDERING, ROUNDABOUT ⟨a *devious* path⟩ **b :** moving without a fixed course : ERRANT ⟨*devious* breezes⟩
**3 a :** deviating from a right, accepted, or common course **b :** not straightforward : CUNNING; *also* : DECEPTIVE
— **de·vi·ous·ly** *adverb*
— **de·vi·ous·ness** *noun*

**¹de·vise** \di-'vīz\ *transitive verb* **de·vised; de·vis·ing** [Middle English, from Old French *deviser* to divide, regulate, tell, modification of (assumed) Vulgar Latin *divisare*, frequentative of Latin *dividere* to divide] (13th century)
**1 a :** to form in the mind by new combinations or applications of ideas or principles : INVENT **b** *archaic* : CONCEIVE, IMAGINE **c :** to plan to obtain or bring about : PLOT
**2 :** to give (real estate) by will — compare BEQUEATH
— **de·vis·able** \-'vī-zə-bəl\ *adjective*
— **de·vis·er** *noun*

**²devise** *noun* (15th century)
**1 :** the act of giving or disposing of real property by will
**2 :** a will or clause of a will disposing of real property
**3 :** property devised by will

**de·vi·see** \,de-və-'zē, di-,vī-'zē\ *noun* (1543)
: one to whom a devise of property is made

**de·vi·sor** \,de-və-'zór; di-'vī-zər, -,vī-'zór\ *noun* (1543)
: one who devises property in a will

**de·vi·tal·ize** \(,)dē-'vī-t°l-,īz\ *transitive verb* (1849)
: to deprive of life, vigor, or effectiveness

**de·vit·ri·fy** \(,)dē-'vi-trə-,fī\ *transitive verb* [French *dévitrifier*, from *dé-* de- + *vitrifier* to vitrify] (1832)
: to deprive of glassy luster and transparency; *especially* : to change (as a glass) from a vitreous to a crystalline condition
— **de·vit·ri·fi·ca·tion** \(,)dē-,vi-trə-fə-'kā-shən\ *noun*

**de·vo·cal·ize** \(,)dē-'vō-kə-,līz\ *transitive verb* (1877)
: DEVOICE

**de·voice** \(,)dē-'vòis\ *transitive verb* (1932)
: to pronounce (as a sometimes or formerly voiced sound) without vibration of the vocal cords

**de·void** \di-'vòid\ *adjective* [Middle English, past participle of *devoiden* to dispel, from Middle French *desvuidier* to empty, from Old French, from *des-* dis- + *vuidier* to empty — more at VOID] (15th century)
: being without a usual, typical, or expected attribute or accompaniment ⟨an argument *devoid* of sense⟩

**de·voir** \də-'vwär, 'de-,\ *noun* [Middle English, alteration of *dever*, from Anglo-French *deveir*, from Old French *devoir, deveir* to owe, be obliged, from Latin *debēre* — more at DEBT] (14th century)
**1 :** DUTY, RESPONSIBILITY
**2 :** a usually formal act of civility or respect

**de·vo·lu·tion** \,de-və-'lü-shən *also* ,dē-və-\ *noun* [Medieval Latin *devolution-, devolutio*, from Latin *devolvere*] (1545)
**1 :** transference (as of rights, powers, property, or responsibility) to another; *especially* : the surrender of powers to local authorities by a central government
**2 :** retrograde evolution : DEGENERATION
— **de·vo·lu·tion·ary** \-shə-,ner-ē\ *adjective*

— **de·vo·lu·tion·ist** \-sh(ə-)nist\ *noun*

**de·volve** \di-'välv, -'vòlv, dē-\ *verb* **de·volved; de·volv·ing** [Middle English, from Latin *devolvere*, from *de- + volvere* to roll — more at VOLUBLE] (15th century)
*transitive verb*
: to pass on (as responsibility, rights, or powers) from one person or entity to another ⟨*devolving* to western Europe full responsibility for its own defense —Christopher Lane⟩
*intransitive verb*
**1 a :** to pass by transmission or succession ⟨the estate *devolved* on a distant cousin⟩ **b :** to fall or be passed usually as a responsibility or obligation ⟨the responsibility for breadwinning has *devolved* increasingly upon women —Barbara Ehrenreich⟩
**2 :** to come by or as if by flowing down ⟨his allegedly subversive campaigns . . . *devolve* from his belief in basic American rights —Frank Deford⟩
**3 :** to degenerate through a gradual change or evolution ⟨where order *devolves* into chaos —*Johns Hopkins Magazine*⟩

**dev·on** \'de-vən\ *noun, often capitalized* [*Devon*, England] (1834)
: any of a breed of vigorous red dual-purpose cattle of English origin

**De·vo·ni·an** \di-'vō-nē-ən\ *adjective* [*Devon*, England] (1612)
**1 :** of or relating to Devonshire, England
**2 :** of, relating to, or being the period of the Paleozoic era between the Silurian and the Mississippian or the corresponding system of rocks — see GEOLOGIC TIME table
— **Devonian** *noun*

**Dev·on·shire cream** \,de-vən-,shir-, -shər-\ *noun* (1825)
: CLOTTED CREAM

**de·vote** \di-'vōt, dē-\ *transitive verb* **de·vot·ed; de·vot·ing** [Latin *devotus*, past participle of *devovēre*, from *de- + vovēre* to vow] (1586)
**1 :** to commit by a solemn act ⟨*devoted* herself to serving God⟩
**2 :** to give over or direct (as time, money, or effort) to a cause, enterprise, or activity ☆
— **de·vote·ment** \-'vōt-mənt\ *noun*

**de·vot·ed** *adjective* (1593)
: characterized by loyalty and devotion
— **de·vot·ed·ly** *adverb*
— **de·vot·ed·ness** *noun*

**dev·o·tee** \,de-və-'tē, -'tā; dē-,vō-'tē\ *noun* (1645)
: an ardent follower, supporter, or enthusiast (as of a religion, art form, or sport)

**de·vo·tion** \di-'vō-shən, dē-\ *noun* (13th century)
**1 a :** religious fervor : PIETY **b :** an act of prayer or private worship — usually used in plural **c :** a religious exercise or practice other than the regular corporate worship of a congregation
**2 a :** the act of devoting **b :** the fact or state of being ardently dedicated and loyal (as to an idea or person)
**3** *obsolete* : the object of one's devotion
*synonym* see FIDELITY

**¹de·vo·tion·al** \-shnəl, -shə-n°l\ *adjective* (1648)
: of, relating to, or characterized by devotion
— **de·vo·tion·al·ly** \-ē\ *adverb*

**²devotional** *noun* (1659)
: a short worship service

**de·vour** \di-'vaù(ə)r, dē-\ *transitive verb* [Middle English, from Middle French *devourer*, from Latin *devorare*, from *de- + vorare* to devour — more at VORACIOUS] (14th century)
**1 :** to eat up greedily or ravenously
**2 :** to use up or destroy as if by eating ⟨we are *devouring* the world's resources⟩
**3 :** to prey upon ⟨*devoured* by guilt⟩
**4 :** to enjoy avidly ⟨*devours* books⟩
— **de·vour·er** *noun*

**de·vout** \di-'vaùt\ *adjective* [Middle English *devot*, from Old French, from Late Latin *devo-*

*tus*, from Latin, past participle of *devovēre*] (13th century)
**1 :** devoted to religion or to religious duties or exercises
**2 :** expressing devotion or piety ⟨a *devout* attitude⟩
**3 :** devoted to a pursuit, belief, or mode of behavior : SERIOUS, EARNEST ⟨a *devout* baseball fan⟩ ⟨born a *devout* coward —G. B. Shaw⟩
— **de·vout·ly** *adverb*
— **de·vout·ness** *noun*

**dew** \'dü *also* 'dyü\ *noun* [Middle English, from Old English *dēaw;* akin to Old High German *tou* dew, Greek *thein* to run] (before 12th century)
**1 :** moisture condensed upon the surfaces of cool bodies especially at night
**2 :** something resembling dew in purity, freshness, or power to refresh
**3 :** moisture especially when appearing in minute droplets: as **a :** TEARS **b :** SWEAT **c** : droplets of water produced by a plant in transpiration
— **dew** *transitive verb*
— **dew·less** \-ləs\ *adjective*

**dew·ar** \'dü-ər *also* 'dyü-\ *noun, often capitalized* [Sir James *Dewar*] (circa 1909)
: a glass or metal container made like a vacuum bottle that is used especially for storing liquefied gases — called also *Dewar flask*

**de·wa·ter** \(,)dē-'wòt-ər, -'wät-\ *transitive verb* (circa 1909)
: to remove water from
— **de·wa·ter·er** *noun*

**dew·ber·ry** \'dü-,ber-ē *also* 'dyü-\ *noun* (circa 1578)
**1 :** any of several sweet edible berries related to and resembling blackberries
**2 :** a trailing or decumbent bramble (genus *Rubus*) that bears dewberries

**dew·claw** \'dü-,klò *also* 'dyü-\ *noun* (1576)
: a vestigial digit not reaching to the ground on the foot of a mammal; *also* : a claw or hoof terminating such a digit — see COW illustration

**dew·drop** \'dü-,dräp *also* 'dyü-\ *noun* (13th century)
: a drop of dew

**Dew·ey decimal classification** \'dü-ē-*also* 'dyü-\ *noun* [Melvil *Dewey*] (1924)
: a system of classifying books and other publications whereby main classes are designated by a three-digit number and subdivisions are shown by numbers after a decimal point — called also *Dewey decimal system*

**dew·fall** \'dü-,fòl *also* 'dyü-\ *noun* (1622)
: formation of dew; *also* : the time when dew begins to deposit

**dew·lap** \'dü-,lap *also* 'dyü-\ *noun* (14th century)
**1 :** loose skin hanging under the neck of an animal — see COW illustration
**2 :** loose flesh on the human throat
— **dew·lapped** \-,lapt\ *adjective*

**de·worm** \(,)dē-'wərm\ *transitive verb* (1926)
: to rid (as a dog) of worms : WORM 4
— **de·worm·er** \(,)dē-'wər-mər\ *noun*

---

☆ SYNONYMS
**Devote, dedicate, consecrate, hallow** mean to set apart for a special and often higher end. DEVOTE is likely to imply compelling motives and often attachment to an objective ⟨*devoted* his evenings to study⟩. DEDICATE implies solemn and exclusive devotion to a sacred or serious use or purpose ⟨*dedicated* her life to medical research⟩. CONSECRATE stresses investment with a solemn or sacred quality ⟨*consecrate* a church to the worship of God⟩. HALLOW, often differing little from *dedicate* or *consecrate,* may distinctively imply an attribution of intrinsic sanctity ⟨battlegrounds *hallowed* by the blood of patriots⟩.

**dew point** *noun* (circa 1833)
: the temperature at which a vapor begins to condense

**dew worm** *noun* (1599)
: NIGHT CRAWLER

**dewy** \'dü-ē *also* 'dyü-\ *adjective* **dew·i·er; -est** (before 12th century)
**1** : moist with, affected by, or suggestive of dew
**2** : INNOCENT, UNSOPHISTICATED ⟨from a *dewy* bride to an ill-mannered, murderous courtesan —Melvin Gussow⟩
— **dew·i·ly** \'dü-ə-lē, 'dyü-\ *adverb*
— **dew·i·ness** \'dü-ē-nəs, 'dyü-\ *noun*

**dewy–eyed** \'dü-ē-ˌīd *also* 'dyü-\ *adjective* (1938)
: naively credulous

**dex** \'deks\ *noun* (circa 1961)
: the sulfate of dextroamphetamine

**dexa·meth·a·sone** \ˌdek-sə-'me-thə-ˌsōn, -ˌzōn\ *noun* [*dexa*- (blend of *deca*- and *hexa*-) + *methyl* + *-a*- (perhaps from *pregnane*, a parent compound of corticoid hormones) + *-sone* (as in *cortisone*)] (1958)
: a synthetic glucocorticoid $C_{22}H_{29}FO_5$ used especially as an anti-inflammatory agent

**Dex·e·drine** \'dek-sə-ˌdrēn, -drən\ *trademark*
— used for a preparation of the sulfate of dextroamphetamine

**dex·ies** \'dek-sēz\ *noun plural* [*Dexedrine* + *-ie* + [1]*-s*] (1956)
: tablets or capsules of the sulfate of dextro-amphetamine

**dex·ter** \'dek-stər\ *adjective* [Latin; akin to Old High German *zeso* situated on the right, Greek *dexios*] (1562)
**1** : relating to or situated on the right
**2** : being or relating to the side of a heraldic shield at the right of the person bearing it
— **dexter** *adverb*

**dex·ter·i·ty** \dek-'ster-ə-tē\ *noun, plural* **-ties** [Middle French or Latin; Middle French *dexterité*, from Latin *dexteritat-, dexteritas*, from *dexter*] (1527)
**1** : mental skill or quickness : ADROITNESS
**2** : readiness and grace in physical activity; *especially* : skill and ease in using the hands

**dex·ter·ous** *also* **dex·trous** \'dek-st(ə-)rəs\ *adjective* [Latin *dextr-, dexter* on the right side, skillful] (1622)
**1** : mentally adroit and skillful : CLEVER
**2** : done with dexterity : ARTFUL
**3** : skillful and competent with the hands ☆
— **dex·ter·ous·ly** *adverb*
— **dex·ter·ous·ness** *noun*

**dextr-** *or* **dextro-** *combining form* [Latin *dextr-, dexter*]
**1** : right : on or toward the right ⟨*dextro*rotatory⟩
**2** *usually* **dextro-** : dextrorotatory ⟨*dextro*amphetamine⟩

**dex·tral** \'dek-strəl\ *adjective* (1646)
: of or relating to the right : inclined to the right: as **a** : RIGHT-HANDED **3 b** *of a gastropod shell* : having the whorls coiling clockwise down the spire when viewed with the apex toward the observer and having the aperture situated on the right of the axis when held with the spire uppermost and with the aperture opening toward the observer — compare SINISTRAL

**dex·tran** \'dek-stran, -ˌstran\ *noun* [International Scientific Vocabulary] (1879)
: any of numerous glucose biopolymers of variable molecular weight produced especially by bacteria (as genus *Leuconostoc*), occurring in dental plaque, and used after chemical modification as blood plasma substitutes, as packing materials in chromatography, and as pharmaceutical agents

**dex·tran·ase** \-strə-ˌnās, -ˌnāz\ *noun* (circa 1949)
: a hydrolase that prevents tooth decay by breaking down dextran and eliminating dental plaque

**dex·trin** \'dek-strən\ *also* **dex·trine** \-ˌstren, -strən\ *noun* [French *dextrine*, from *dextr-*] (1838)
: any of various water-soluble gummy polysaccharides $(C_6H_{10}O_5)n$ obtained from starch by the action of heat, acids, or enzymes and used as adhesives, as sizes for paper and textiles, as thickening agents (as in syrups), and in beer

**dex·tro** \'dek-(ˌ)strō\ *adjective* [*dextr-*] (circa 1929)
: DEXTROROTATORY

**dex·tro·am·phet·amine** \ˌdek-(ˌ)strō-am-'fe-tə-ˌmēn, -mən\ *noun* (1943)
: dextrorotatory amphetamine sulfate

**dex·tro·ro·ta·to·ry** \-'rō-tə-ˌtōr-ē, -ˌtȯr-\ *also* **dex·tro·ro·ta·ry** \-'rō-tə-rē\ *adjective* (1878)
: turning clockwise or toward the right; *especially* : rotating the plane of polarization of light toward the right ⟨*dextrorotatory* crystals⟩ — compare LEVOROTATORY

**dex·trose** \'dek-ˌstrōs, -ˌstrōz\ *noun* (circa 1869)
: dextrorotatory glucose

**dey** \'dā\ *noun* [French, from Turkish *dayı*, literally, maternal uncle] (1659)
: a ruling official of the Ottoman Empire in northern Africa

[1]**DH** \ˌdē-'āch\ *noun* (1973)
: DESIGNATED HITTER

[2]**DH** \ˌdē-'āch, 'dē-ˌāch\ *intransitive verb* **DH–d; DH–ing** (1975)
: to play the position of designated hitter

**dhar·ma** \'där-mə, 'där-\ *noun* [Sanskrit; akin to Latin *firmus* firm] (1796)
**1** *Hinduism* : an individual's duty fulfilled by observance of custom or law
**2** *Hinduism & Buddhism* **a** : the basic principles of cosmic or individual existence : divine law **b** : conformity to one's duty and nature
— **dhar·mic** \-mik\ *adjective*

**dhar·na** \'dər-nə, 'där-\ *noun* [Hindi *dharnā*, from Sanskrit *dharaṇa* support, prop; akin to Latin *firmus* firm] (1747)
: a fast held at the door of an offender in India as an appeal for justice

**dhole** \'dōl\ *noun* [perhaps from Kannada *tōḷa* wolf] (circa 1827)
: a wild dog (*Cuon alpinus*) occurring from India to southern Siberia

**dho·ti** \'dō-tē\ *noun, plural* **dhotis** [Hindi *dhotī*] (1614)
: a loincloth worn by men in some parts of India

**dhow** \'daù\ *noun* [Arabic *dāwa*] (1785)
: an Arab lateen-rigged boat usually having a long overhang forward, a high poop, and a low waist

**Dhu'l–Hij·ja** \ˌdül-'hi-(ˌ)jä, ˌthül-\ *noun* [Arabic *Dhū-l-ḥijjah*, literally, the one of the pilgrimage] (circa 1771)
: the 12th month of the Islamic year — see MONTH table

**dhow**

**Dhu'l–Qa'·dah** \-'kä-(ˌ)dä\ *noun* [Arabic *Dhū-l-qa'dah*, literally, the one of the sitting] (circa 1771)
: the 11th month of the Islamic year — see MONTH table

**dhur·rie** \'də-rē, 'dər-ē\ *noun* [Hindi *darī*] (1880)
: a thick flat-woven cotton or wool cloth or rug made in India

**di-** *combining form* [Middle English, from Middle French, from Latin, from Greek; akin to Old English *twi-*]
**1** : twice : twofold : double ⟨*di*chromatic⟩
**2** : containing two atoms, radicals, or groups ⟨*di*oxide⟩

**dia-** *also* **di-** *prefix* [Middle English, from Old French, from Latin, from Greek, through, apart, from *dia*; akin to Latin *dis-*]
: through ⟨*dia*positive⟩ : across ⟨*dia*dromous⟩

**di·a·base** \'dī-ə-ˌbās\ *noun* [French, probably from Greek *diabasis* act of crossing over, from *diabainein* to cross over, from *dia-* + *bainein* to go — more at COME] (circa 1816)
**1** *archaic* : DIORITE
**2** *chiefly British* : an altered basalt
**3** : a fine-grained rock of the composition of gabbro but with an ophitic texture
— **di·a·ba·sic** \ˌdī-ə-'bā-sik\ *adjective*

**di·a·be·tes** \ˌdī-ə-'bē-tēz, -'bē-təs\ *noun* [Latin, from Greek *diabētēs* diabetes insipidus, from *diabainein* to walk with the legs apart, cross over] (15th century)
: any of various abnormal conditions characterized by the secretion and excretion of excessive amounts of urine; *especially* : DIABETES MELLITUS ▪

**diabetes in·sip·i·dus** \-in-'si-pə-dəs\ *noun* [New Latin, literally, bland diabetes] (circa 1860)
: a disorder of the pituitary gland characterized by intense thirst and by the excretion of large amounts of urine

**diabetes mel·li·tus** \-'me-lə-təs\ *noun* [New Latin, literally, honey-sweet diabetes] (circa 1860)
: a variable disorder of carbohydrate metabolism caused by a combination of hereditary and environmental factors and usually characterized by inadequate secretion or utilization of insulin, by excessive urine production, by excessive amounts of sugar in the blood and urine, and by thirst, hunger, and loss of weight

[1]**di·a·bet·ic** \ˌdī-ə-'be-tik\ *adjective* (1799)
**1** : of or relating to diabetes or diabetics
**2** : affected with diabetes
**3** : occurring in or caused by diabetes ⟨*diabetic* coma⟩
**4** : suitable for diabetics ⟨*diabetic* food⟩

[2]**diabetic** *noun* (1840)

---

☆ **SYNONYMS**
**Dexterous, adroit, deft** mean ready and skilled in physical movement. DEXTEROUS implies expertness with consequent facility and quickness in manipulation ⟨unrolled the sleeping bag with a *dexterous* toss⟩. ADROIT implies dexterity but usually also stresses resourcefulness or artfulness or inventiveness ⟨the magician's *adroit* response to the failure of her prop won applause⟩. DEFT emphasizes lightness, neatness, and sureness of touch or handling ⟨a surgeon's *deft* manipulation of the scalpel⟩.

---

□ **USAGE**
**diabetes** One of the forces in linguistic change is *analogy*, the alteration of one word to make it similar to other words which are perceived to be related. Analogy has probably been the source of the variant pronunciation of *diabetes* in which the last syllable has a reduced form \-təs\, and not the older, fuller \-tēz\. The \-təs\ ending is more like the final syllable of the names of other diseases and conditions: *phlebitis, arthritis, conjunctivitis*. Although *diabetes* shares no word elements with these names, the last syllable has come to be pronounced as if it were parallel in form to these words. The newer pronunciation has been labelled "colloquial" by some, but it is common in all circles today.

---

\ə\ abut  \ᵊ\ kitten  \ər\ further  \a\ ash  \ā\ ace
\ä\ mop, mar  \aù\ out  \ch\ chin  \e\ bet  \ē\ easy
\g\ go  \i\ hit  \ī\ ice  \j\ job  \ŋ\ sing  \ō\ go
\ȯ\ law  \ȯi\ boy  \th\ thin  \t͟h\ the  \ü\ loot  \ů\ foot
\y\ yet  \zh\ vision      *see also* Guide to Pronunciation

: a person affected with diabetes

**di·a·be·to·gen·ic** \ˌdī-ə-ˌbe-tə-'je-nik, -ˌbē-\ *adjective* (circa 1903)
: producing diabetes

**di·a·be·tol·og·ist** \ˌdī-ə-(ˌ)be-'tä-lə-jist, -ˌbē-\ *noun* (1970)
: a specialist in diabetes

**di·a·ble·rie** \dē-'ä-blə-(ˌ)rē, -'ä-blə-\ *noun* [French, from Old French, from *dïable* devil, from Late Latin *diabolus* — more at DEVIL] (1751)
1 : black magic : SORCERY
2 a : a representation in words or pictures of black magic or of dealings with the devil **b** : demon lore
3 : mischievous conduct or manner

**di·a·bol·i·cal** \ˌdī-ə-'bä-li-kəl\ *or* **di·a·bol·ic** \-'bä-lik\ *adjective* [Middle English *deabolik*, from Middle French *diabolique*, from Late Latin *diabolicus*, from *diabolus*] (14th century)
: of, relating to, or characteristic of the devil : DEVILISH
— **di·a·bol·i·cal·ly** \-li-k(ə-)lē\ *adverb*
— **di·a·bol·i·cal·ness** \-li-kəl-nəs\ *noun*

**di·ab·o·lism** \dī-'a-bə-ˌli-zəm\ *noun* (1614)
1 : dealings with or possession by the devil
2 : belief in or worship of devils
3 : evil character or conduct
— **di·ab·o·list** \-list\ *noun*

**di·ab·o·lize** \-ˌlīz\ *transitive verb* **-lized; -liz·ing** (1702)
: to represent as or make diabolic

**dia·chron·ic** \ˌdī-ə-'krä-nik\ *adjective* (1927)
: of, relating to, or dealing with phenomena (as of language or culture) as they occur or change over a period of time
— **dia·chron·i·cal·ly** \-'krä-ni-k(ə-)lē\ *adverb*

**di·ach·ro·ny** \dī-'a-krə-nē\ *noun* [International Scientific Vocabulary *dia-* + *-chrony* (as in *synchrony*)] (circa 1939)
1 : diachronic analysis
2 : change extending through time

¹**di·ac·id** \(ˌ)dī-'a-səd\ *or* **di·acid·ic** \ˌdī-ə-'si-dik\ *adjective* (1866)
: able to react with two molecules of a monobasic acid or one of a dibasic acid to form a salt or ester — used especially of bases

²**diacid** *noun* [International Scientific Vocabulary] (circa 1929)
: an acid with two acid hydrogen atoms

**di·ac·o·nal** \dī-'a-kə-n°l, dē-\ *adjective* [Late Latin *diaconalis*, from *diaconus* deacon — more at DEACON] (circa 1611)
: of or relating to a deacon or deaconess

**di·ac·o·nate** \-'a-kə-nət, -ˌnāt\ *noun* (circa 1751)
1 : the office or period of office of a deacon or deaconess
2 : an official body of deacons

**di·a·crit·ic** \ˌdī-ə-'kri-tik\ *noun* (1866)
: an accent near or through an orthographic or phonetic character or combination of characters indicating a phonetic value different from that given the unmarked or otherwise marked element

**di·a·crit·i·cal** \ˌdī-ə-'kri-ti-kəl\ *also* **di·a·crit·ic** \-'kri-tik\ *adjective* [Greek *diakritikos* separative, from *diakrinein* to distinguish, from *dia-* + *krinein* to separate — more at CERTAIN] (1749)
1 : serving as a diacritic
2 a : DISTINCTIVE (the *diacritical* elements in culture —S. F. Nadel) **b** : capable of distinguishing (students of superior *diacritical* powers)

**di·adel·phous** \ˌdī-ə-'del-fəs\ *adjective* [*di-* + *-adelphous*] (1807)
: united by filaments into two fascicles — used of stamens

**di·a·dem** \'dī-ə-ˌdem, -dəm\ *noun* [Middle English *diademe*, from Old French, from Latin *diadema*, from Greek *diadēma*, from *diadein* to bind around, from *dia-* + *dein* to bind; akin to Sanskrit *dāman* rope] (13th century)

---

# DIACRITICS

| | | |
|---|---|---|
| ´ | (é) | acute accent |
| ` | (è) | grave accent |
| ^ *or* ˆ *or* ~ | (ô) | circumflex |
| ~ | (ñ) | tilde |
| ˉ | (ō) | macron |
| ˘ | (ŭ) | breve |
| ˇ | (č) | haček |
| ·· | (oö) | diaeresis |
| ¸ | (ç) | cedilla |

1 a : CROWN 1; *specifically* : a royal headband **b** : CROWN 6a(1)
2 : something that adorns like a crown

**di·ad·ro·mous** \dī-'a-drə-məs\ *adjective* (circa 1949)
*of a fish* : migratory between salt and fresh waters

**di·aer·e·sis** \dī-'er-ə-səs, *British also* -'ir-\ *noun, plural* **-e·ses** \-ˌsēz\ [Late Latin *diaeresis*, from Greek *diairesis*, literally, division, from *diairein* to divide, from *dia-* + *hairein* to take] (circa 1611)
1 : a mark ¨ placed over a vowel to indicate that the vowel is pronounced in a separate syllable (as in *naïve* or *Brontë*)
2 : the break in a verse caused by the coincidence of the end of a foot with the end of a word
— **di·ae·ret·ic** \ˌdī-ə-'re-tik\ *adjective*

**dia·gen·e·sis** \ˌdī-ə-'je-nə-səs\ *noun* [New Latin] (circa 1886)
1 : recombination or rearrangement of constituents (as of a chemical or mineral) resulting in a new product
2 : the conversion (as by compaction or chemical reaction) of sediment into rock
— **dia·ge·net·ic** \ˌdī-ə-jə-'ne-tik\ *adjective*
— **dia·ge·net·i·cal·ly** \-'ne-ti-k(ə-)lē\ *adverb*

**dia·geo·tro·pic** \ˌdī-ə-ˌjē-ə-'trō-pik, -'trä-pik\ *adjective* (1880)
: tending to grow at right angles to the line of gravity (*diageotropic* branches and roots)

**di·ag·nose** \'dī-ig-ˌnōs, -ˌnōz, ˌdī-ig-', -əg-\ *verb* **-nosed; -nos·ing** [back-formation from *diagnosis*] (circa 1859)
*transitive verb*
1 a : to recognize (as a disease) by signs and symptoms **b** : to diagnose a disease or condition in (*diagnosed* the patient)
2 : to analyze the cause or nature of (*diagnose* the problem)
*intransitive verb*
: to make a diagnosis
— **di·ag·nos·able** *or* **di·ag·nose·able** \ˌdī-ig-'nō-sə-bəl, -əg-, -zə-\ *adjective*

**di·ag·no·sis** \ˌdī-ig-'nō-səs, -əg-\ *noun, plural* **-no·ses** \-ˌsēz\ [New Latin, from Greek *diagnōsis*, from *diagignōskein* to distinguish, from *dia-* + *gignōskein* to know — more at KNOW] (circa 1681)
1 a : the art or act of identifying a disease from its signs and symptoms **b** : the decision reached by diagnosis
2 : a concise technical description of a taxon
3 a : investigation or analysis of the cause or nature of a condition, situation, or problem (*diagnosis* of engine trouble) **b** : a statement or conclusion from such an analysis

¹**di·ag·nos·tic** \-'näs-tik\ *also* **di·ag·nos·ti·cal** \-ti-kəl\ *adjective* (1625)
1 a : of, relating to, or used in diagnosis **b** : using the methods of or yielding a diagnosis
2 : serving to distinguish or identify
— **di·ag·nos·ti·cal·ly** \-ti-k(ə-)lē\ *adverb*

²**diagnostic** *noun* (1625)
1 : the art or practice of diagnosis — often used in plural
2 : a distinguishing mark
— **di·ag·nos·ti·cian** \-(ˌ)näs-'ti-shən\ *noun*

¹**di·ag·o·nal** \dī-'a-gə-n°l, -'ag-nəl\ *adjective* [Latin *diagonalis,* from Greek *diagōnios* from angle to angle, from *dia-* + *gōnia* angle; akin to Greek *gony* knee — more at KNEE] (1563)
1 a : joining two vertices of a rectilinear figure that are nonadjacent or two vertices of a polyhedral figure that are not in the same face **b** : passing through two nonadjacent edges of a polyhedron (a *diagonal* plane)
2 a : inclined obliquely from a reference line (as the vertical) (wood with a *diagonal* grain) **b** : having diagonal markings or parts (a *diagonal* weave)

²**diagonal** *noun* (1571)
1 : a diagonal straight line or plane
2 a (1) : a diagonal direction (2) : a diagonal row, arrangement, or pattern **b** : something oriented in diagonal position
3 : a mark / used typically to denote "or" (as in *and/or*), "and or" (as in *straggler/deserter*), or "per" (as in *feet/second*) — called also *solidus, virgule*
— **on the diagonal** : in an oblique direction : DIAGONALLY

**di·ag·o·nal·ize** \-nə-ˌlīz\ *transitive verb* **-ized; -iz·ing** (1942)
: to put (a matrix) in a form with all the nonzero elements along the diagonal from upper left to lower right
— **di·ag·o·nal·iz·able** \-ˌlī-zə-bəl\ *adjective*
— **di·ag·o·nal·iza·tion** \-ˌa-gə-n°l-ə-'zā-shən, -ˌag-nə-lə-'zā-\ *noun*

**di·ag·o·nal·ly** \dī-'a-gə-n°l-ē, -'ag-nə-lē\ *adverb* (1541)
: in a diagonal manner

**diagonal matrix** *noun* (circa 1928)
: a diagonalized matrix

¹**di·a·gram** \'dī-ə-ˌgram\ *noun* [Greek *diagramma,* from *diagraphein* to mark out by lines, from *dia-* + *graphein* to write — more at CARVE] (1619)
1 : a graphic design that explains rather than represents; *especially* : a drawing that shows arrangement and relations (as of parts)
2 : a line drawing made for mathematical or scientific purposes
— **di·a·gram·ma·ble** \-ˌgra-mə-bəl\ *adjective*
— **di·a·gram·mat·ic** \ˌdī-ə-grə-'ma-tik\ *also* **di·a·gram·mat·i·cal** \-'ma-ti-kəl\ *adjective*
— **di·a·gram·mat·i·cal·ly** \-ti-k(ə-)lē\ *adverb*

²**diagram** *transitive verb* **-grammed** *or* **-gramed** \-ˌgramd\; **-gram·ming** *or* **-gram·ing** \-ˌgra-min\ (1840)
: to represent by or put into the form of a diagram

**dia·ki·ne·sis** \ˌdī-ə-kə-'nē-səs, -(ˌ)kī-\ *noun, plural* **-ne·ses** \-ˌsēz\ [New Latin] (circa 1902)
: the final stage of the meiotic prophase marked by contraction of the bivalents

¹**di·al** \'dī(-ə)l\ *noun* [Middle English *dyal,* from Medieval Latin *dialis* clock wheel revolving daily, from Latin *dies* day — more at DEITY] (15th century)
1 : the face of a sundial
2 *obsolete* : TIMEPIECE
3 : the graduated face of a timepiece
4 a : a face upon which some measurement is registered usually by means of graduations and a pointer (the thermometer *dial* reads 70°F) **b** : a device that may be operated to make electrical connections or to regulate the operation of a machine (a radio *dial*) (a telephone *dial*)

²**dial** *verb* **di·aled** *or* **di·alled; di·al·ing** *or* **di·al·ling** (1821)
*transitive verb*

**1 :** to measure with a dial
**2 a :** to manipulate a device (as a dial) so as to operate, regulate, or select ⟨*dial* your favorite program⟩ ⟨*dialed* the wrong number⟩ **b :** CALL 1m(1) ⟨*dialed* the office⟩
*intransitive verb*
**1 :** to manipulate a dial
**2 :** to make a telephone call or connection
— **di·al·er** *noun*
**di·a·lect** \'dī-ə-ˌlekt\ *noun, often attributive* [Middle French *dialecte,* from Latin *dialectus,* from Greek *dialektos* conversation, dialect, from *dialegesthai* to converse — more at DIA-LOGUE] (1577)
**1 a :** a regional variety of language distinguished by features of vocabulary, grammar, and pronunciation from other regional varieties and constituting together with them a single language ⟨the Doric *dialect* of ancient Greek⟩ **b :** one of two or more cognate languages ⟨French and Italian are Romance *dialects*⟩ **c :** a variety of a language used by the members of a group ⟨such *dialects* as politics and advertising —Philip Howard⟩ **d :** a variety of language whose identity is fixed by a factor other than geography (as social class) ⟨spoke a rough peasant *dialect*⟩ **e :** REGISTER 4c **f :** a version of a computer programming language
**2 :** manner or means of expressing oneself **:** PHRASEOLOGY
— **di·a·lec·tal** \ˌdī-ə-'lek-t²l\ *adjective*
— **di·a·lec·tal·ly** \-t²l-ē\ *adverb*
**dialect atlas** *noun* (1932)
**:** LINGUISTIC ATLAS
**dialect geography** *noun* (1929)
**:** LINGUISTIC GEOGRAPHY
**di·a·lec·tic** \ˌdī-ə-'lek-tik\ *noun* [Middle English *dialetik,* from Middle French *dialetique,* from Latin *dialectica,* from Greek *dialektikē,* from feminine of *dialektikos* of conversation, from *dialektos*] (14th century)
**1 :** LOGIC 1a(1)
**2 a :** discussion and reasoning by dialogue as a method of intellectual investigation; *specifically* **:** the Socratic techniques of exposing false beliefs and eliciting truth **b :** the Platonic investigation of the eternal ideas
**3 :** the logic of fallacy
**4 a :** the Hegelian process of change in which a concept or its realization passes over into and is preserved and fulfilled by its opposite; *also* **:** the critical investigation of this process **b** (1) *usually plural but singular or plural in construction* **:** development through the stages of thesis, antithesis, and synthesis in accordance with the laws of dialectical materialism (2) **:** the investigation of this process (3) **:** the theoretical application of this process especially in the social sciences
**5** *usually plural but singular or plural in construction* **a :** any systematic reasoning, exposition, or argument that juxtaposes opposed or contradictory ideas and usually seeks to resolve their conflict **b :** an intellectual exchange of ideas
**6 :** the dialectical tension or opposition between two interacting forces or elements
**di·a·lec·ti·cal** \ˌdī-ə-'lek-ti-kəl\ *also* **di·a·lec·tic** \-tik\ *adjective* (1548)
**1 a :** of, relating to, or in accordance with dialectic ⟨*dialectical* method⟩ **b :** practicing, devoted to, or employing dialectic ⟨a *dialectical* philosopher⟩
**2 :** of, relating to, or characteristic of a dialect
— **di·a·lec·ti·cal·ly** \-ti-k(ə-)lē\ *adverb*
**dialectical materialism** *noun* (1927)
**:** the Marxist theory that maintains the material basis of a reality constantly changing in a dialectical process and the priority of matter over mind — compare HISTORICAL MATERIALISM
**di·a·lec·ti·cian** \ˌdī-ə-ˌlek-'ti-shən\ *noun* (circa 1693)
**1 :** one who is skilled in or practices dialectic
**2 :** a student of dialects
**di·a·lec·tol·o·gist** \-'tä-lə-jist\ *noun* (1883)

**:** a specialist in dialectology
**di·a·lec·tol·o·gy** \-jē\ *noun* [International Scientific Vocabulary] (circa 1864)
**1 :** the systematic study of dialect
**2 :** the body of data available for study of a dialect
— **di·a·lec·to·log·i·cal** \-ˌlek-tə-'lä-ji-kəl\ *adjective*
— **di·a·lec·to·log·i·cal·ly** \-k(ə-)lē\ *adverb*
**di·al·lel** \'dī-ə-ˌlel\ *adjective* [Greek *diallēlos* reciprocating, from *dia* through + *allēlōn* one another — more at ALLELO-] (1920)
**:** relating to or being the crossing of each of several individuals with two or more others in order to determine the relative genetic contribution of each parent to specific characters in the offspring
**di·a·log·ic** \ˌdī-ə-'lä-jik\ *or* **di·a·log·i·cal** \-ji-kəl\ *adjective* (1833)
**:** of, relating to, or characterized by dialogue ⟨*dialogic* writing⟩
— **di·a·log·i·cal·ly** \-ji-k(ə-)lē\ *adverb*
**di·a·lo·gist** \dī-'a-lə-jist; 'dī-ə-ˌlo-gist, -ˌlä-\ *noun* (circa 1660)
**1 :** a writer of dialogues
**2 :** one who participates in a dialogue
— **di·a·lo·gis·tic** \(ˌ)dī-ˌa-lə-'jis-tik; ˌdī-ə-ˌlo-'gis-, -ˌlä-'gis-\ *adjective*
¹**di·a·logue** *also* **di·a·log** \'dī-ə-ˌlog, -ˌläg\ *noun* [Middle English *dialoge,* from Old French *dialogue,* from Latin *dialogus,* from Greek *dialogos,* from *dialegesthai* to converse, from *dia-* + *legein* to speak — more at LEGEND] (13th century)
**1 :** a written composition in which two or more characters are represented as conversing
**2 a :** a conversation between two or more persons; *also* **:** a similar exchange between a person and something else (as a computer) **b :** an exchange of ideas and opinions **c :** a discussion between representatives of parties to a conflict that is aimed at resolution
**3 :** the conversational element of literary or dramatic composition
**4 :** a musical composition for two or more parts suggestive of a conversation
²**dialogue** *verb* **-logued; -logu·ing** (1597)
*transitive verb*
**:** to express in dialogue
*intransitive verb*
**:** to take part in a dialogue
**dial tone** *noun* (1923)
**:** a tone emitted by a telephone as a signal that the system is ready for dialing
**dial–up** \'dī-(ə)l-ˌəp\ *adjective* (1972)
**:** relating to or being a standard telephone line used for computer communications; *also* **:** accessible via a standard telephone line ⟨a *dial–up* information service⟩
**di·al·y·sate** \dī-'a-lə-ˌzāt, -ˌsāt\ *also* **di·al·y·zate** \-ˌzāt\ *noun* (circa 1867)
**:** the material that passes through the membrane in dialysis; *also* **:** the liquid into which this material passes
**di·al·y·sis** \dī-'a-lə-səs\ *noun, plural* **-y·ses** \-ˌsēz\ [New Latin, from Greek, separation, from *dialyein* to dissolve, from *dia-* + *lyein* to loosen — more at LOSE] (1861)
**1 :** the separation of substances in solution by means of their unequal diffusion through semipermeable membranes; *especially* **:** such a separation of colloids from soluble substances
**2 :** HEMODIALYSIS
— **di·a·lyt·ic** \ˌdī-ə-'li-tik\ *adjective*
**di·a·lyze** \'dī-ə-ˌlīz\ *verb* **-lyzed; -lyz·ing** (1861)
*transitive verb*
**:** to subject to dialysis
*intransitive verb*
**:** to undergo dialysis
— **di·a·lyz·able** \-ˌlī-zə-bəl\ *adjective*
— **di·a·lyz·er** \-ˌlī-zər\ *noun*
**dia·mag·net·ic** \ˌdī-ə-mag-'ne-tik\ *adjective* (1846)

**:** having a magnetic permeability less than that of a vacuum **:** slightly repelled by a magnet
— **dia·mag·ne·tism** \-'mag-nə-ˌti-zəm\ *noun*
**di·a·man·té** \ˌdē-ə-ˌmän-'tā\ *noun* [French, adjective, like a diamond, from *diamant* diamond, from Middle French] (1904)
**:** a sparkling decoration (as of sequins) or material decorated with this ⟨a gown trimmed with *diamanté*⟩
**di·am·e·ter** \dī-'a-mə-tər\ *noun* [Middle English *diametre,* from Middle French, from Latin *diametros,* from Greek, from *dia-* + *metron* measure — more at MEASURE] (14th century)
**1 :** a chord passing through the center of a figure or body
**2 :** the length of a straight line through the center of an object
**3 :** a unit of magnification for an optical instrument equal to the number of times the linear dimensions of an object are apparently increased ⟨a microscope magnifying 60 *diameters*⟩
— **di·am·e·tral** \-'a-mə-trəl\ *adjective*
**di·a·met·ric** \ˌdī-ə-'me-trik\ *or* **di·a·met·ri·cal** \-tri-kəl\ *adjective* (1553)
**1 :** of, relating to, or constituting a diameter **:** located at the diameter
**2 :** completely opposed **:** being at opposite extremes ⟨in *diametric* contradiction to his claims⟩
— **di·a·met·ri·cal·ly** \-tri-k(ə-)lē\ *adverb*
**di·amide** \'dī-ə-ˌmīd, dī-'a-məd\ *noun* (1866)
**:** a compound containing two amido groups
**di·amine** \'dī-ə-ˌmēn, dī-'a-mən\ *noun* [International Scientific Vocabulary] (1866)
**:** a compound containing two amino groups
**di·am·mo·ni·um phosphate** \ˌdī-ə-'mō-nē-əm-\ *noun* (circa 1929)
**:** a white crystalline compound $(NH_4)_2HPO_4$ used especially as a fertilizer and as a fire retardant
¹**di·a·mond** \'dī-(ə-)mənd\ *noun, often attributive* [Middle English *diamaunde,* from Middle French *diamant,* from Old French, from Late Latin *diamant-, diamas,* alteration of Latin *adamant-, adamas* hardest metal, diamond, from Greek] (14th century)
**1 a :** native crystalline carbon that is usually nearly colorless, that when transparent and free from flaws is highly valued as a precious stone, and that is used industrially as an abrasive powder and in rock drills because of its great hardness; *also* **:** a piece of this substance **b :** crystallized carbon produced artificially
**2 :** something that resembles a diamond (as in brilliance, value, or fine quality)
**3 :** a square or rhombus-shaped figure usually oriented with the long diagonal vertical
**4 a :** a playing card marked with a stylized figure of a red diamond **b** *plural but singular or plural in construction* **:** the suit comprising cards marked with diamonds
**5 :** a baseball infield; *also* **:** the entire playing field
²**diamond** *transitive verb* (1751)
**:** to adorn with or as if with diamonds
³**diamond** *adjective* (1872)
**:** of, relating to, or being a 60th or 75th anniversary or its celebration ⟨*diamond* jubilee⟩
**di·a·mond·back** \'dī-(ə-)mən(d)-ˌbak\ *adjective* (1887)
**:** having marks like diamonds or lozenges on the back
**diamondback moth** *noun* (1891)
**:** a nearly cosmopolitan moth (*Plutella xylostella* of the family Plutellidae) whose larva is a pest on cruciferous plants
**diamondback rattlesnake** *noun* (1894)

\ə\ abut  \ᵊ\ kitten  \ər\ further  \a\ ash  \ā\ ace
\ä\ mop, mar  \aú\ out  \ch\ chin  \e\ bet  \ē\ easy
\g\ go  \i\ hit  \ī\ ice  \j\ job  \ŋ\ sing  \ō\ go
\ó\ law  \ói\ boy  \th\ thin  \th\ the  \ü\ loot  \ù\ foot
\y\ yet  \zh\ vision  *see also* Guide to Pronunciation

: either of two large and deadly rattlesnakes (*Crotalus adamanteus* of the southeastern U.S. and *C. atrox* of the south central and southwestern U.S. and Mexico) — called also *diamondback, diamondback rattler*

**diamondback terrapin** *noun* (1887)
: any of several terrapins (genus *Malaclemys*) formerly widely distributed in salt marshes along the Atlantic and Gulf coasts but now much restricted

**di·a·mond·if·er·ous** \ˌdī-(ə-)mən-'di-fə-rəs\ *adjective* (1870)
: containing diamonds ⟨*diamondiferous* earth⟩

**diamond in the rough** (circa 1947)
: a person of exceptional qualities or potential but lacking refinement or polish

**Di·ana** \dī-'a-nə\ *noun* [Latin]
: an ancient Italian goddess of the forest and of childbirth who was identified with Artemis by the Romans

**di·an·thus** \dī-'an(t)-thəs\ *noun* [New Latin, genus name, from Greek *dios* heavenly + *anthos* flower — more at DEITY, ANTHOLOGY] (1849)
: [2]PINK 1

**di·a·pa·son** \ˌdī-ə-'pā-z°n, -s°n\ *noun* [Middle English, from Latin, from Greek *(hē) dia pasōn (chordōn symphōnia)*, literally, the concord through all the notes, from *dia* through + *pasōn*, genitive feminine plural of *pas* all — more at DIA-, PAN-] (circa 1501)
**1 a :** a burst of sound ⟨*diapasons* of laughter⟩ **b :** the principal foundation stop in the organ extending through the complete range of the instrument **c** (1) **:** the entire compass of musical tones (2) **:** RANGE, SCOPE
**2 a :** TUNING FORK **b :** a standard of pitch

**dia·pause** \'dī-ə-ˌpòz\ *noun* [Greek *diapausis* pause, from *diapauein* to pause, from *dia-* + *pauein* to stop] (1893)
: a period of physiologically enforced dormancy between periods of activity

**dia·paus·ing** \-ˌpò-ziŋ\ *adjective* (1944)
: undergoing diapause

**di·a·pe·de·sis** \ˌdī-ə-pə-'dē-səs\ *noun, plural* **-de·ses** \-ˌsēz\ [New Latin, from Greek *diapēdēsis*, literally, act of leaping through, from *diapēdan* to leap through, from *dia-* + *pēdan* to leap] (1625)
: the passage of blood cells through capillary walls into the tissues

**[1]di·a·per** \'dī-pər *also* 'dī-ə-\ *noun* [Middle English *diapre*, from Middle French, from Medieval Latin *diasprum*] (14th century)
**1 :** a fabric with a distinctive pattern: **a :** a rich silk fabric **b :** a soft usually white linen or cotton fabric used for tablecloths or towels
**2 :** an allover pattern consisting of one or more small repeated units of design (as geometric figures) connecting with one another or growing out of one another with continuously flowing or straight lines
**3 :** a basic garment for infants consisting of a folded cloth or other absorbent material drawn up between the legs and fastened about the waist

diaper 2

**[2]diaper** *transitive verb* **di·a·pered; di·a·per·ing** \-p(ə-)riŋ\ (14th century)
**1 :** to ornament with diaper designs
**2 :** to put on or change the diaper of (an infant)

**diaper rash** *noun*
: skin irritation of the diaper-covered area of an infant especially from excessive urinary ammonia

**di·a·pha·ne·ity** \ˌ(ˌ)dī-ˌa-fə-'nē-ə-tē, ˌdī-ə-fə-, -'nā-\ *noun* (15th century)
: the quality or state of being diaphanous

**di·aph·a·nous** \dī-'a-fə-nəs\ *adjective* [Medieval Latin *diaphanus*, from Greek *diaphanēs*,

from *diaphainein* to show through, from *dia-* + *phainein* to show — more at FANCY] (1614)
**1 :** characterized by such fineness of texture as to permit seeing through
**2 :** characterized by extreme delicacy of form **:** ETHEREAL ⟨painted *diaphanous* landscapes⟩
**3 :** INSUBSTANTIAL, VAGUE ⟨had only a *diaphanous* hope of success⟩
**— di·aph·a·nous·ly** *adverb*
**— di·aph·a·nous·ness** *noun*

**dia·phone** \'dī-ə-ˌfōn\ *noun* (1906)
: a fog signal similar to a siren but producing a blast of two tones

**di·aph·o·rase** \dī-'a-fə-ˌrās, -ˌrāz\ *noun* [International Scientific Vocabulary *diaphor-* (from Greek *diaphoros* different, from *diapherein* to differ, from *dia-* + *pherein* to carry) + *-ase* — more at BEAR] (1938)
: a flavoprotein enzyme capable of oxidizing the reduced form of NAD

**di·a·pho·re·sis** \ˌdī-ə-fə-'rē-səs, ˌ(ˌ)dī-ˌa-fə-\ *noun, plural* **-re·ses** \-ˌsēz\ [Late Latin, from Greek *diaphorēsis*, from *diaphorein* to dissipate by perspiration, from *dia-* + *phorein*, frequentative of *pherein* to carry] (circa 1681)
: PERSPIRATION; *especially* : profuse perspiration artificially induced

**di·a·pho·ret·ic** \-'re-tik\ *adjective* (15th century)
: having the power to increase perspiration
**— diaphoretic** *noun*

**di·a·phragm** \'dī-ə-ˌfram\ *noun* [Middle English *diafragma*, from Late Latin *diaphragma*, from Greek, from *diaphrassein* to barricade, from *dia-* + *phrassein* to enclose] (14th century)
**1 :** a body partition of muscle and connective tissue; *specifically* **:** the partition separating the chest and abdominal cavities in mammals
**2 :** a dividing membrane or thin partition especially in a tube
**3 a :** a more or less rigid partition in the body or shell of an invertebrate **b :** a transverse septum in a plant stem
**4 :** a device that limits the aperture of a lens or optical system — compare IRIS DIAPHRAGM
**5 :** a thin flexible disk (as in a microphone or loudspeaker) that vibrates when struck by sound waves or that vibrates to generate sound waves
**6 :** a molded cap usually of thin rubber fitted over the uterine cervix to act as a mechanical contraceptive barrier
**— di·a·phrag·mat·ic** \ˌdī-ə-frə(g)-'ma-tik, -ˌfrag-\ *adjective*
**— di·a·phrag·mat·i·cal·ly** \-'ma-ti-k(ə-)lē\ *adverb*

**di·aph·y·sis** \dī-'a-fə-səs\ *noun, plural* **-y·ses** \-ˌsēz\ [New Latin, from Greek, spinous process of the tibia, from *diaphyesthai* to grow between, from *dia-* + *phyein* to bring forth — more at BE] (1831)
: the shaft of a long bone
**— di·aph·y·se·al** \ˌ(ˌ)dī-ˌa-fə-'sē-əl\ *or* **di·a·phys·i·al** \ˌdī-ə-'fi-zē-əl\ *adjective*

**di·a·pir** \'dī-ə-ˌpir\ *noun* [French, probably from Greek *diapeirein* to drive through, from *dia-* + *peirein* to pierce; akin to Greek *poros* passage — more at FARE] (1918)
: an anticlinal fold in which a mobile core has broken through brittle overlying rocks
**— di·a·pir·ic** \ˌdī-ə-'pir·ik\ *adjective*

**dia·pos·i·tive** \ˌdī-ə-'pä-zə-tiv, -'päz-tiv\ *noun* (1893)
: a positive photographic image on transparent material (as glass or film)

**di·ap·sid** \dī-'ap-səd\ *adjective* [ultimately from Greek *di-* + *hapsid-, hapsis* loop, arch — more at APSIS] (circa 1909)
: of, relating to, or including reptiles (as the crocodiles) with two pairs of temporal openings in the skull

**di·ar·chy** *variant of* DYARCHY

**di·a·rist** \'dī-ə-rəst\ *noun* (circa 1818)
: one who keeps a diary

**di·ar·rhea** \ˌdī-ə-'rē-ə\ *noun* [Middle English *diaria*, from Late Latin *diarrhoea*, from Greek *diarrhoia*, from *diarrhein* to flow through, from *dia-* + *rhein* to flow — more at STREAM] (14th century)
**1 :** abnormally frequent intestinal evacuations with more or less fluid stools
**2 :** excessive flow ⟨verbal *diarrhea*⟩
**— di·ar·rhe·ic** \-'rē-ik\ *adjective*
**— di·ar·rhe·al** \-'rē-əl\ *adjective*
**— di·ar·rhet·ic** \-'re-tik\ *adjective*

**di·ar·rhoea** *chiefly British variant of* DIARRHEA

**di·ar·thro·sis** \ˌdī-är-'thrō-səs\ *noun, plural* **-thro·ses** \-ˌsēz\ [New Latin, from Greek *diarthrōsis*, from *diarthroun* to joint, from *dia-* + *arthroun* to fasten by a joint, from *arthron* joint — more at ARTHR-] (1578)
**1 :** articulation that permits free movement
**2 :** a freely movable joint

**di·a·ry** \'dī-(ə-)rē\ *noun, plural* **-ries** [Latin *diarium*, from *dies* day — more at DEITY] (1581)
**1 :** a record of events, transactions, or observations kept daily or at frequent intervals **:** JOURNAL; *especially* **:** a daily record of personal activities, reflections, or feelings
**2 :** a book intended or used for a diary

**di·as·po·ra** \dī-'as-p(ə-)rə, dē-\ *noun* [Greek, dispersion, from *diaspeirein* to scatter, from *dia-* + *speirein* to sow] (1881)
**1** *capitalized* **a :** the settling of scattered colonies of Jews outside Palestine after the Babylonian exile **b :** the area outside Palestine settled by Jews **c :** the Jews living outside Palestine or modern Israel
**2 a :** the breaking up and scattering of a people **:** MIGRATION ⟨the black *diaspora* to northern cities⟩ **b :** people settled far from their ancestral homelands ⟨African *diaspora*⟩ **c :** the place where these people live

**di·a·spore** \'dī-ə-ˌspōr, -ˌspòr\ *noun* [French, from Greek *diaspora*] (1805)
: a mineral consisting of aluminum hydrogen oxide

**di·a·stase** \'dī-ə-ˌstās, -ˌstāz\ *noun* [French, from Greek *diastasis* separation, interval, from *diistanai* to separate, from *dia-* + *histanai* to cause to stand — more at STAND] (1838)
**1 :** AMYLASE; *especially* : a mixture of amylases from malt
**2 :** ENZYME

**di·a·stat·ic** \ˌdī-ə-'sta-tik\ *adjective* (1881)
: relating to or having the properties of diastase; *especially* : converting starch into sugar

**di·a·ste·ma** \ˌdī-ə-'stē-mə\ *noun, plural* **-ma·ta** \-mə-tə\ [New Latin, from Late Latin, interval, from Greek *diastēma*, from *diistanai*] (1854)
: a space between teeth in a jaw

**di·a·ste·reo·mer** \ˌdī-ə-'ster-ē-ō-(ˌ)mər, -'stir-\ *or* **di·a·ste·reo·iso·mer** \-ˌster-ē-ō-'ī-sə-mər, -ˌstir-\ *noun* (1936)
: a stereoisomer of a compound having two or more chiral centers that is not a mirror image of another stereoisomer of the same compound — compare ENANTIOMORPH
**— di·a·ste·reo·mer·ic** \-ˌster-ē-ō-'mer-ik, -ˌstir-\ *or* **di·a·ste·reo·iso·mer·ic** \-ˌī-sə-'mer-ik\ *adjective*
**— di·a·ste·reo·isom·er·ism** \-ˌī-'sä-mə-ˌri-zəm\ *noun*

**di·as·to·le** \dī-'as-tə-(ˌ)lē\ *noun* [Greek *diastolē* dilatation, from *diastellein* to expand, from *dia-* + *stellein* to prepare, send] (circa 1578)
: a rhythmically recurrent expansion; *especially* : the dilatation of the cavities of the heart during which they fill with blood
**— di·a·stol·ic** \ˌdī-ə-'stä-lik\ *adjective*

**di·a·stro·phism** \dī-'as-trə-ˌfi-zəm\ *noun* [Greek *diastrophē* twisting, from *diastrephein* to distort, from *dia-* + *strephein* to twist] (1890)

: the process of deformation that produces in the earth's crust its continents and ocean basins, plateaus and mountains, folds of strata, and faults
— **di·a·stroph·ic** \ˌdī-ə-'strä-fik\ *adjective*
— **di·a·stroph·i·cal·ly** \-fi-k(ə-)lē\ *adverb*
**di·a·tes·sa·ron** \ˌdī-ə-'te-sə-rən\ *noun* [Greek (*Euangelion*) *dia tessarōn*, literally, Gospel out of four, from *dia* through, out of + *tessarōn*, genitive of *tessares* four — more at DIA-, FOUR] (1803)
: a harmony of the four Gospels edited and arranged into a single connected narrative
**dia·ther·ma·nous** \ˌdī-ə-'thər-mə-nəs\ *adjective* [French *diathermane*, modification of Greek *diathermainein* to heat through, from *dia-* + *thermainein* to heat, from *thermos* hot — more at THERM] (1834)
: DIATHERMIC 1
**dia·ther·mic** \ˌdī-ə-'thər-mik\ *adjective* (1840)
**1** : transmitting infrared radiation
**2** : of or relating to diathermy ⟨*diathermic* treatment⟩
**dia·ther·my** \'dī-ə-ˌthər-mē\ *noun* [International Scientific Vocabulary] (1909)
: the generation of heat in tissue by electric currents for medical or surgical purposes
**di·ath·e·sis** \dī-'a-thə-səs\ *noun, plural* **-e·ses** \-ˌsēz\ [New Latin, from Greek, literally, arrangement, from *diatithenai* to arrange, from *dia-* + *tithenai* to set — more at DO] (1651)
: a constitutional predisposition toward a particular state or condition and especially one that is abnormal or diseased
— **di·a·thet·ic** \ˌdī-ə-'the-tik\ *adjective*
**di·a·tom** \'dī-ə-ˌtäm\ *noun* [ultimately from Greek *diatomos* cut in half, from *diatemnein* to cut through, from *dia-* + *temnein* to cut — more at TOME] (1845)
: any of a class (Bacillariophyceae) of minute planktonic unicellular or colonial algae with silicified skeletons that form diatomite
**di·a·to·ma·ceous** \ˌdī-ə-tə-'mā-shəs, ˌ)dī-ˌa-tə-\ *adjective* (1847)
: consisting of or abounding in diatoms or their siliceous remains ⟨*diatomaceous* silica⟩
**diatomaceous earth** *noun* (1883)
: DIATOMITE
**di·atom·ic** \ˌdī-ə-'tä-mik\ *adjective* [International Scientific Vocabulary] (circa 1859)
: consisting of two atoms : having two atoms in the molecule
**di·at·o·mite** \dī-'a-tə-ˌmīt\ *noun* (1887)
: a light friable siliceous material derived chiefly from diatom remains and used especially as a filter
**dia·ton·ic** \ˌdī-ə-'tä-nik\ *adjective* [Late Latin *diatonicus*, from Greek *diatonikos*, from *diatonos* stretching, from *diateinein* to stretch out, from *dia-* + *teinein* to stretch — more at THIN] (1694)
: of or relating to a major or minor musical scale comprising intervals of five whole steps and two half steps
— **dia·ton·i·cal·ly** \-'tä-ni-k(ə-)lē\ *adverb*
**di·a·tribe** \'dī-ə-ˌtrīb\ *noun* [Latin *diatriba*, from Greek *diatribē* pastime, discourse, from *diatribein* to spend (time), wear away, from *dia-* + *tribein* to rub — more at THROW] (1581)
**1** *archaic* : a prolonged discourse
**2** : a bitter and abusive speech or writing
**3** : ironical or satirical criticism
**di·az·e·pam** \dī-'a-zə-ˌpam\ *noun* [benzo*diaz*epine + -*am* (of unknown origin)] (circa 1961)
: a tranquilizer $C_{16}H_{13}ClN_2O$ used especially to relieve anxiety and tension and as a muscle relaxant — compare VALIUM
**Di·az·i·non** \dī-'a-zi-ˌnän\ *trademark*
— used for a cholinesterase-inhibiting organophosphate insecticide
**di·azo** \dī-'a-(ˌ)zō, -'ā-\ *adjective* [International Scientific Vocabulary *diaz-, diazo-,* from *di-* + *az-*] (1878)

**1 a** : relating to or containing the group $N_2$ composed of two nitrogen atoms united to a single carbon atom of an organic radical — often used in combination **b** : relating to or containing diazonium — often used in combination
**2** : of or relating to a photograph or photocopy whose production involves the use of a coating of a diazo compound that is decomposed by exposure to light
**di·a·zo·ni·um** \ˌdī-ə-'zō-nē-əm\ *noun* [International Scientific Vocabulary *di-* + *az-* + -*onium*] (1895)
: the univalent cation $N_2^+$ that is composed of two nitrogen atoms united to carbon in an organic radical and that usually exists in salts used in the manufacture of azo dyes
**di·az·o·tize** \dī-'a-zə-ˌtīz\ *transitive verb* **-tized; -tiz·ing** [International Scientific Vocabulary *di-* + *azote* nitrogen + -*ize* — more at AZ-] (circa 1889)
: to convert (a compound) into a diazo compound (as a diazonium salt)
— **di·az·o·ti·za·tion** \-ˌa-zə-tə-'zā-shən\ *noun*
**di·ba·sic** \(ˌ)dī-'bā-sik\ *adjective* (1868)
: having two replaceable hydrogen atoms — used of acids
**dib·ber** \'di-bər\ *noun* (circa 1736)
: DIBBLE
**¹dib·ble** \'di-bəl\ *noun* [Middle English *debylle*] (15th century)
: a small hand implement used to make holes in the ground for plants, seeds, or bulbs
**²dibble** *transitive verb* **dib·bled; dib·bling** \'di-b(ə-)liŋ\ (1583)
**1** : to plant with a dibble
**2** : to make holes in (soil) with or as if with a dibble
**di·ben·zo·fu·ran** \ˌdī-ˌben-zō-'fyu̇-ˌran, -fyə-'ran\ *noun* (1940)
: a highly toxic chemical compound $C_{12}H_8O$ that is used in chemical synthesis and as an insecticide and is a hazardous pollutant in its chlorinated form
**dibs** \'dibz\ *noun plural* [short for *dibstones* (jacks), from obsolete *dib* (to dab)] (1812)
**1** *slang* : money especially in small amounts
**2** : CLAIM, RIGHTS ⟨I have *dibs* on that piece of cake⟩
**di·bu·tyl phthal·ate** \ˌdī-ˌbyü-t²l-'tha-ˌlāt\ *noun* [*phthal*ic acid + ¹-*ate*] (1925)
: a colorless oily ester $C_{16}H_{22}O_4$ used chiefly as a solvent, plasticizer, pesticide, and repellent (as for chiggers and mites)
**di·cal·ci·um silicate** \(ˌ)dī-'kal-sē-əm-\ *noun* (1925)
: a calcium silicate $2CaO \cdot SiO_2$ that is an essential ingredient of portland cement
**di·car·box·yl·ic** \ˌdī-ˌkär-ˌbäk-'si-lik\ *adjective* (circa 1890)
: containing two carboxyl groups in the molecule ⟨*dicarboxylic* acids⟩
**di·cast** \'dī-ˌkast, 'di-\ *noun* [Greek *dikastēs*, from *dikazein* to judge, from *dikē* judgment — more at DICTION] (1822)
: an ancient Athenian performing the functions of both judge and juror at a trial
**¹dice** \'dīs\ *noun, plural* **dice** [Middle English *dyce,* from *dees, dyce,* plural of *dee* die — more at DIE] (14th century)
**1 a** : DIE 1 **b** : a gambling game played with dice
**2** *plural also* **dic·es** : a small cubical piece (as of food)
**3** : a close contest between two racing-car drivers for position during a race
— **no dice 1** : of no avail : no use : FUTILE **2** : ¹NO 3 ⟨said *no dice* to my request⟩
**²dice** *verb* **diced; dic·ing** [Middle English *dycen,* from *dyce*] (14th century)
*transitive verb*
**1 a** : to cut into small cubes **b** : to ornament with square markings ⟨*diced* leather⟩

**2 a** : to bring by playing dice ⟨*dice* himself into debt⟩ **b** : to lose by dicing ⟨*dice* her money away⟩
*intransitive verb*
**1** : to play games with dice ⟨*dice* for drinks in the bar —Malcolm Lowry⟩
**2** : to take a chance ⟨the temptation to *dice* with death —*Newsweek*⟩
— **dic·er** *noun*
**di·cen·tric** \(ˌ)dī-'sen-trik\ *adjective* (1937)
: having two centromeres ⟨a *dicentric* chromosome⟩
— **dicentric** *noun*
**dic·ey** \'dī-sē\ *adjective* **dic·i·er; -est** [¹*dice* + -*y*] (1950)
: RISKY, UNPREDICTABLE ⟨a *dicey* proposition⟩ ⟨*dicey* weather⟩
**dich-** *or* **dicho-** *combining form* [Late Latin, from Greek, from *dicha;* akin to Greek *di-*]
: in two : apart ⟨*dicho*gamous⟩
**di·cha·si·um** \dī-'kā-z(h)ē-əm, -zhəm\ *noun, plural* **-sia** \-z(h)ē-ə, -zhə\ [New Latin, from Greek *dichasis* halving, from *dichazein* to halve, from *dicha*] (1875)
: a cymose inflorescence that produces two main axes
**dichlor-** *or* **dichloro-** *combining form*
: containing two atoms of chlorine ⟨*dichloro*ethane⟩
**di·chlo·ro·ben·zene** \(ˌ)dī-ˌklōr-ə-'ben-ˌzēn, -ˌklȯr-, -(ˌ)ben-'\ *noun* (1873)
: any of three isomeric compounds $C_6H_4Cl_2$; *especially* : PARADICHLOROBENZENE
**di·chlo·ro·di·flu·o·ro·meth·ane** \-ˌdī-ˌflu̇r-ə-'me-ˌthän\ *noun* (1936)
: a chlorofluoromethane $CCl_2F_2$
**di·chlo·ro·eth·ane** \(ˌ)dī-ˌklō-rō-'e-ˌthän\ *noun* (1936)
: a colorless toxic liquid compound $C_2H_4Cl_2$ that is used chiefly as a solvent
**di·chlor·vos** \(')dī-'klȯr-ˌväs, -'klȯr-, -vəs\ *noun* [*dichlor-* + *vinyl* + *phosphate*] (1957)
: an organophosphorus insecticide and anthelmintic $C_4H_7Cl_2O_4P$ used especially in veterinary medicine — called also *DDVP*
**di·chog·a·my** \dī-'kä-gə-mē\ *noun, plural* **-mies** [German *Dichogamie,* from *dich-* + -*gamie* -gamy] (1862)
: the production of male and female reproductive elements at different times by a hermaphroditic organism in order to ensure cross-fertilization
— **di·chog·a·mous** \-gə-məs\ *adjective*
**di·chon·dra** \dī-'kän-drə\ *noun* [New Latin, genus name, from *di-* + Greek *chondros* grain — more at GRIND] (1947)
: any of a genus (*Dichondra*) of chiefly tropical perennial herbs of the morning glory family that includes some (especially *D. repens* and its varieties) used as a ground cover and a substitute for lawn grasses in warmer parts of the U.S.
**di·chot·ic** \(ˌ)dī-'kō-tik\ *adjective* [*dich-* + ²-*otic*] (circa 1911)
: affecting or relating to the two ears differently in regard to a conscious aspect (as pitch or loudness) or a physical aspect (as frequency or energy) of sound
— **di·chot·i·cal·ly** \-ti-k(ə-)lē\ *adverb*
**di·chot·o·mist** \dī-'kä-tə-məst *also* də-\ *noun* (circa 1592)
: one that dichotomizes
**di·chot·o·mize** \-ˌmīz\ *verb* **-mized; -miz·ing** [Late Latin *dichotomos*] (1606)
*transitive verb*
: to divide into two parts, classes, or groups
*intransitive verb*
: to exhibit dichotomy
— **di·chot·o·mi·za·tion** \-ˌkä-tə-mə-'zā-shən\ *noun*

---

\ə\ abut \ᵊ\ kitten \ər\ further \a\ ash \ā\ ace
\ä\ mop, mar \au̇\ out \ch\ chin \e\ bet \ē\ easy
\g\ go \i\ hit \ī\ ice \j\ job \ŋ\ sing \ō\ go
\ȯ\ law \ȯi\ boy \th\ thin \th\ the \ü\ loot \u̇\ foot
\y\ yet \zh\ vision *see also* Guide to Pronunciation

**di·chot·o·mous** \dī-'kä-tə-məs *also* də-\ *adjective* [Late Latin *dichotomos,* from Greek, from *dich-* + *temnein* to cut — more at TOME] (1752)
**1** : dividing into two parts
**2** : relating to, involving, or proceeding from dichotomy
— **di·chot·o·mous·ly** *adverb*
— **di·chot·o·mous·ness** *noun*
**dichotomous key** *noun* (circa 1889)
: a key for the identification of organisms based on a series of choices between alternative characters
**di·chot·o·my** \dī-'kä-tə-mē *also* də-\ *noun,* plural **-mies** [Greek *dichotomia,* from *dichotomos*] (1610)
**1** : a division or the process of dividing into two especially mutually exclusive or contradictory groups or entities
**2** : the phase of the moon or an inferior planet in which half its disk appears illuminated
**3 a** : BIFURCATION; *especially* : repeated bifurcation (as of a plant's stem) **b** : a system of branching in which the main axis forks repeatedly into two branches **c** : branching of an ancestral line into two equal diverging branches
**4** : something with seemingly contradictory qualities
**di·chro·ic** \dī-'krō-ik\ *adjective* [Greek *dichroos* two-colored, from *di-* + *chrōs* color, literally, skin] (circa 1859)
**1** : having the property of dichroism (a *dichroic* crystal) (a *dichroic* mirror)
**2** : DICHROMATIC
**di·chro·ism** \'dī-(ˌ)krō-i-zəm\ *noun* (1819)
: the property of some crystals and solutions of absorbing one of two plane-polarized components of transmitted light more strongly than the other; *also* : the property of exhibiting different colors by reflected or transmitted light — compare CIRCULAR DICHROISM
**di·chro·mat** \'dī-krō-ˌmat, (ˌ)dī-'\ *noun* [back-formation from *dichromatic*] (circa 1909)
: one affected with dichromatism
**di·chro·mate** \(ˌ)dī-'krō-ˌmāt, 'dī-krō-\ *noun* [International Scientific Vocabulary] (circa 1864)
: a usually orange to red chromium salt containing the anion $Cr_2O_7{}^{2-}$ (*dichromate* of potassium) — called also *bichromate*
**di·chro·mat·ic** \ˌdī-krō-'ma-tik\ *adjective* (circa 1847)
**1** : having or exhibiting two colors
**2** : of, relating to, or exhibiting dichromatism
**di·chro·ma·tism** \dī-'krō-mə-ˌti-zəm\ *noun* (circa 1901)
: partial color blindness in which only two colors are perceptible
**di·chro·scope** \'dī-krə-ˌskōp\ *noun* (1857)
: an instrument for examining crystals for dichroism
**dick** \'dik\ *noun* [*Dick,* nickname for *Richard*] (1553)
**1** *chiefly British* : FELLOW, CHAP
**2** : PENIS — usually considered vulgar
**3** [by shortening & alteration] : DETECTIVE
**dick·cis·sel** \dik-'si-səl, 'dik-ˌ\ *noun* [imitative] (1886)
: a common migratory black-throated finch (*Spiza americana*) of the central U.S.
**dick·ens** \'di-kənz\ *noun* [euphemism] (1598)
: DEVIL, DEUCE
**¹dick·er** \'di-kər\ *noun* [Middle English *dyker,* from Latin *decuria* quantity of ten, from *decem* ten — more at TEN] (14th century)
: the number or quantity of 10 especially of hides or skins

dickcissel

**²dicker** *intransitive verb* **dick·ered; dick·er·ing** \'di-k(ə-)riŋ\ [origin unknown] (circa 1802)
: BARGAIN (*dickered* over the price)
**³dicker** *noun* (1823)
**1** : BARTER
**2** : an act or session of bargaining
**dick·ey** *or* **dicky** *also* **dick·ie** \'di-kē\ *noun,* plural **dickeys** *or* **dick·ies** [*Dicky,* nickname for *Richard*] (1753)
**1** : any of various articles of clothing: as **a** : a man's separate or detachable shirtfront **b** : a small fabric insert worn to fill in the neckline
**2** *chiefly British* **a** : the driver's seat in a carriage **b** : a seat at the back of a carriage or automobile
**3** : a small bird
**Dick test** \'dik-\ *noun* [George French *Dick* and Gladys H. *Dick*] (1925)
: a test to determine susceptibility or immunity to scarlet fever by an injection of scarlet fever toxin
**di·cli·nous** \(ˌ)dī-'klī-nəs\ *adjective* (1830)
: having the stamens and pistils in separate flowers
**di·cot** \'dī-ˌkät\ *noun* (1877)
: DICOTYLEDON
**di·cot·y·le·don** \ˌdī-ˌkä-tᵊl-'ē-dᵊn\ *noun* [New Latin] (circa 1727)
: any of a class or subclass (Magnoliopsida or Dicotyledoneae) of angiospermous plants that produce an embryo with two cotyledons and usually have floral organs arranged in cycles of four or five and leaves with reticulate venation — compare MONOCOTYLEDON
— **di·cot·y·le·don·ous** \-dᵊn-əs\ *adjective*
**di·cou·ma·rin** \(ˌ)dī-'kü-mə-rən\ *noun* (1886)
: DICUMAROL
**di·crot·ic** \dī-'krä-tik\ *adjective* [Greek *dikrotos,* from *di-* + *krotos* rattling noise, beat] (circa 1811)
**1** *of the pulse* : having a double beat
**2** : being or relating to the second part of the arterial pulse occurring during diastole of the heart or of an arterial pressure recording made during the same period
— **di·cro·tism** \'dī-krə-ˌti-zəm\ *noun*
**Dic·ta·phone** \'dik-tə-ˌfōn\ *trademark*
— used for a dictating machine
**¹dic·tate** \'dik-ˌtāt, dik-'\ *verb* **dic·tat·ed; dic·tat·ing** [Latin *dictatus,* past participle of *dictare* to assert, dictate, frequentative of *dicere* to say — more at DICTION] (1592)
*intransitive verb*
**1** : to give dictation
**2** : to speak or act domineeringly : PRESCRIBE
*transitive verb*
**1** : to speak or read for a person to transcribe or for a machine to record
**2 a** : to issue as an order **b** : to impose, pronounce, or specify authoritatively **c** : to require or determine necessarily (injuries *dictated* the choice of players)
**²dictate** \'dik-ˌtāt\ *noun* (1594)
**1 a** : an authoritative rule, prescription, or injunction **b** : a ruling principle (according to the *dictates* of your conscience)
**2** : a command by one in authority
**dictating machine** *noun* (1907)
: a machine used especially for the recording of human speech for transcription
**dic·ta·tion** \dik-'tā-shən\ *noun* (circa 1656)
**1 a** : PRESCRIPTION **b** : arbitrary command
**2 a** (1) : the act or manner of uttering words to be transcribed (2) : material that is dictated or transcribed **b** (1) : the performing of music to be reproduced by a student (2) : music so reproduced
**dic·ta·tor** \'dik-ˌtā-tər, dik-'\ *noun* [Latin, from *dictare*] (14th century)
**1 a** : a person granted absolute emergency power; *especially* : one appointed by the senate of ancient Rome **b** : one holding complete autocratic control **c** : one ruling absolutely and often oppressively
**2** : one that dictates

**dic·ta·to·ri·al** \ˌdik-tə-'tōr-ē-əl, -'tor-\ *adjective* (1701)
**1 a** : of, relating to, or befitting a dictator (*dictatorial* power) **b** : ruled by a dictator
**2** : oppressive to or arrogantly overbearing toward others ☆
— **dic·ta·to·ri·al·ly** \-ē-ə-lē\ *adverb*
— **dic·ta·to·ri·al·ness** *noun*
**dic·ta·tor·ship** \dik-'tā-tər-ˌship, 'dik-\ *noun* (1542)
**1** : the office of dictator
**2** : autocratic rule, control, or leadership
**3 a** : a form of government in which absolute power is concentrated in a dictator or a small clique **b** : a government organization or group in which absolute power is so concentrated **c** : a despotic state
**dic·tion** \'dik-shən\ *noun* [Latin *diction-, dictio* speaking, style, from *dicere* to say; akin to Old English *tēon* to accuse, Latin *dicare* to proclaim, dedicate, Greek *deiknynai* to show, *dikē* judgment, right] (1581)
**1** *obsolete* : verbal description
**2** : choice of words especially with regard to correctness, clearness, or effectiveness
**3 a** : vocal expression : ENUNCIATION **b** : pronunciation and enunciation of words in singing
— **dic·tion·al** \-shnəl, -shə-nᵊl\ *adjective*
— **dic·tion·al·ly** \-ē\ *adverb*
**dic·tio·nary** \'dik-shə-ˌner-ē\ *noun,* plural **-nar·ies** [Medieval Latin *dictionarium,* from Late Latin *diction-, dictio* word, from Latin, speaking] (1526)
**1** : a reference book containing words usually alphabetically arranged along with information about their forms, pronunciations, functions, etymologies, meanings, and syntactical and idiomatic uses
**2** : a reference book listing alphabetically terms or names important to a particular subject or activity along with discussion of their meanings and applications
**3** : a reference book giving for words of one language equivalents in another
**4** : a list (as of items of data or words) stored in a computer for reference (as for information retrieval or word processing)
**dic·tum** \'dik-təm\ *noun, plural* **dic·ta** \-tə\ *also* **dictums** [Latin, from neuter of *dictus,* past participle of *dicere*] (1599)
**1** : a noteworthy statement: as **a** : a formal pronouncement of a principle, proposition, or opinion **b** : an observation intended or regarded as authoritative
**2** : a judicial opinion on a point other than the precise issue involved in determining a case
**dicty-** *or* **dictyo-** *combining form* [New Latin, from Greek *dikty-, diktyo-,* from *diktyon,* from *dikein* to throw]
: net (*dicty*ostele) (*dictyo*some)

☆ **SYNONYMS**
**Dictatorial, magisterial, dogmatic, doctrinaire, oracular** mean imposing one's will or opinions on others. DICTATORIAL stresses autocratic, high-handed methods and a domineering manner (exercised *dictatorial* control over the office). MAGISTERIAL stresses assumption or use of prerogatives appropriate to a magistrate or schoolmaster in forcing acceptance of one's opinions (the *magisterial* tone of his pronouncements). DOGMATIC implies being unduly and offensively positive in laying down principles and expressing opinions (*dogmatic* about what is art and what is not). DOCTRINAIRE implies a disposition to follow abstract theories in framing laws or policies affecting people (a *doctrinaire* approach to improving the economy). ORACULAR implies the manner of one who delivers opinions in cryptic phrases or with pompous dogmatism (a designer who is the *oracular* voice of fashion).

**dic·tyo·some** \'dik-tē-ə-ˌsōm\ *noun* (circa 1930)
: any of the membranous or vesicular structures making up the Golgi apparatus

**dic·tyo·stele** \'dik-tē-ə-ˌstēl, ˌdik-tē-ə-'stē-lē\ *noun* (circa 1902)
: a stele in which the vascular cylinder is broken up into a longitudinal series or network of vascular strands around a central pith (as in many ferns)

**di·cu·ma·rol** *also* **di·cou·ma·rol** \dī-'k(y)ü-mə-ˌról, -ˌról\ *noun* [*di-* + *coumar*in + ¹*-ol*] (1943)
: a crystalline compound $C_{19}H_{12}O_6$ originally obtained from spoiled sweet clover hay and used to delay clotting of blood especially in preventing and treating thromboembolic disease

**di·cyn·o·dont** \(ˌ)dī-'si-nō-ˌdänt, -'sī-\ *noun* [ultimately from Greek *di-* + *kyn-*, *kyōn* dog + *odont-*, *odous* tooth — more at HOUND, TOOTH] (1854)
: any of a suborder (Dicynodontia) of small herbivorous therapsid reptiles with reduced dentition
— **dicynodont** *adjective*

**did** *past of* DO

**di·dact** \'dī-ˌdakt\ *noun* [back-formation from *didactic*] (1954)
: a didactic person

**di·dac·tic** \dī-'dak-tik, də-\ *adjective* [Greek *didaktikos*, from *didaskein* to teach] (1658)
**1 a :** designed or intended to teach **b :** intended to convey instruction and information as well as pleasure and entertainment
**2 :** making moral observations
— **di·dac·ti·cal** \-ti-kəl\ *adjective*
— **di·dac·ti·cal·ly** \-ti-k(ə-)lē\ *adverb*
— **di·dac·ti·cism** \-tə-ˌsi-zəm\ *noun*

**di·dac·tics** \-tiks\ *noun plural but singular or plural in construction* (1644)
: systematic instruction : PEDAGOGY

**did·dle** \'di-dᵊl\ *verb* **did·dled; did·dling** \'did-liŋ, -dᵊl-iŋ\ [origin unknown] (1786)
*transitive verb*
**1** *chiefly dialect* : to move with short rapid motions
**2 :** to waste (as time) in trifling
**3 :** HOAX, SWINDLE
**4 :** to copulate with — often considered vulgar
*intransitive verb*
**1 :** DAWDLE, FOOL
**2 :** FIDDLE, TOY — usually used with *with* ⟨*diddled* with the machine until it broke⟩
— **did·dler** \'did-lər, -dᵊl-ər\ *noun*

**did·dly** \'di-dᵊl-ē, 'did-lē\ *noun* (1964)
*slang* : DIDDLY-SQUAT

**did·dly–squat** \-ˌskwät\ *noun* [probably alteration of *doodly-squat*] (1974)
*slang* : the least amount : anything at all ⟨didn't know *diddly-squat* about sports —Sam Toperoff⟩

**did·ger·i·doo** *also* **did·jer·i·doo** \'di-jə-rē-ˌdü, ˌdi-jə-rē-'\ *noun* [Yolngu (Australian aboriginal language group of Arnhem Land) *didjeridu*] (1919)
: a large bamboo or wooden trumpet of the Australian Aborigines

**didn't** \'di-dᵊnt, -dᵊn, *dialect also* 'dit-ᵊn(t) *or* 'dint\ (1705)
: did not

**di·do** \'dī-(ˌ)dō\ *noun, plural* **didoes** *or* **didos** [origin unknown] (1807)
**1 :** a mischievous or capricious act : PRANK, ANTIC — often used in the phrase *cut didoes*
**2 :** something that is frivolous or showy

**Di·do** \'dī-(ˌ)dō\ *noun* [Latin, from Greek *Didō*]
: a legendary queen of Carthage in Virgil's *Aeneid* who kills herself when Aeneas leaves her

**didst** \'didst, 'ditst\ *archaic past 2d singular of* DO

**di·dym·i·um** \dī-'di-mē-əm\ *noun* [New Latin, from Greek *didymos* twin, from *dyo* two — more at TWO] (1842)
: a mixture of rare-earth elements made up chiefly of neodymium and praseodymium and used especially for coloring glass for optical filters

**¹die** \'dī\ *intransitive verb* **died; dy·ing** \'dī-iŋ\ [Middle English *dien*, from or akin to Old Norse *deyja* to die; akin to Old High German *touwen* to die] (12th century)
**1 :** to pass from physical life : EXPIRE
**2 a :** to pass out of existence : CEASE ⟨their anger *died* at these words⟩ **b :** to disappear or subside gradually — often used with *away*, *down*, or *out* ⟨the storm *died* down⟩
**3 a :** SINK, LANGUISH ⟨*dying* from fatigue⟩ **b :** to long keenly or desperately ⟨*dying* to go⟩ **c :** to be overwhelmed by emotion ⟨*die* of embarrassment⟩
**4 a :** to cease functioning : STOP ⟨the motor *died*⟩ **b :** to end in failure ⟨the bill *died* in committee⟩
**5 :** to become indifferent ⟨*die* to worldly things⟩
— **die hard 1 :** to be long in dying ⟨such rumors *die hard*⟩ **2 :** to continue resistance against hopeless odds ⟨hard-shell conservatism *dies hard*⟩
— **die on the vine :** to fail especially at an early stage through lack of support or enthusiasm ⟨let the proposal *die on the vine*⟩

**²die** \'dī\ *noun, plural* **dice** \'dīs\ *or* **dies** \'dīz\ [Middle English *dee*, from Middle French *dé*] (14th century)
**1** *plural* **dice :** a small cube marked on each face with from one to six spots and used usually in pairs in various games and in gambling by being shaken and thrown to come to rest at random on a flat surface — often used figuratively in expressions concerning chance or the irrevocability of a course of action ⟨the *die* was cast⟩
**2** *plural* **dies :** DADO 1a
**3** *plural* **dies :** any of various tools or devices for imparting a desired shape, form, or finish to a material or for impressing an object or material: as **a** (1) : the larger of a pair of cutting or shaping tools that when moved toward each other produce a desired form in or impress a desired device on an object by pressure or by a blow (2) : a device composed of a pair of such tools **b :** a hollow internally threaded screw-cutting tool used for forming screw threads **c :** a mold into which molten metal or other material is forced **d :** a perforated block through which metal or plastic is drawn or extruded for shaping

**die·back** \'dī-ˌbak\ *noun* (circa 1886)
: a condition in woody plants in which peripheral parts are killed especially by parasites

**di·e·cious** *variant of* DIOECIOUS

**dief·fen·bach·ia** \ˌdē-fən-'ba-kē-ə, ˌdi-, -'bä-\ *noun* [New Latin, from Ernst *Dieffenbach* (died 1855) German naturalist] (circa 1900)
: any of a genus (*Dieffenbachia* of the family Araceae) of erect poisonous tropical American plants that have oblong usually variegated leaves and are often used as houseplants

**die–hard** \'dī-ˌhärd\ *adjective* (1922)
: strongly or fanatically determined or devoted ⟨*die-hard* fans⟩; *especially* : strongly resisting change ⟨a *die-hard* conservative⟩
— **die·hard** *noun*
— **die–hard·ism** \-ˌiz-əm\ *noun*

**di·el** \'dī-əl, -ˌel\ *adjective* [irregular from Latin *dies* day + English *-al*] (circa 1935)
: involving a 24-hour period that usually includes a day and the adjoining night ⟨*diel* fluctuations in temperature⟩

**diel·drin** \'dē(ə)l-drən\ *noun* [*Diel*s-A*l*der reaction (an addition reaction forming a 6-membered ring), after Otto *Diels* & Kurt *Alder*] (circa 1949)
: a white crystalline persistent chlorinated hydrocarbon insecticide $C_{12}H_8Cl_6O$ that accumulates in and becomes toxic to vertebrates

**di·elec·tric** \ˌdī-ə-'lek-trik\ *noun* [*dia-* + *electric*] (1837)
: a nonconductor of direct electric current
— **dielectric** *adjective*

**dielectric constant** *noun* (1875)
: PERMITTIVITY

**dielectric heating** *noun* (1944)
: the rapid and uniform heating throughout a nonconducting material by means of a high-frequency electromagnetic field

**di·en·ceph·a·lon** \ˌdī-ən-'se-fə-ˌlän, ˌdī-(ˌ)en-, -lən\ *noun* [New Latin, from *dia-* + *encephalon*] (circa 1883)
: the posterior subdivision of the forebrain — called also *betweenbrain*
— **di·en·ce·phal·ic** \-sə-'fa-lik\ *adjective*

**di·ene** \'dī-ˌēn\ *noun* [*di-* + *-ene*] (1917)
: a compound containing two double bonds between carbon atoms

**die–off** \'dī-ˌóf\ *noun* (1936)
: a sudden sharp decline of a population (as of rabbits) that is not caused directly by human activity (as hunting)

**die off** \'dī-'óf\ *intransitive verb* (1697)
: to die sequentially either singly or in numbers so that the total number is greatly diminished

**die out** *intransitive verb* (1853)
: to become extinct

**di·er·e·sis** *variant of* DIAERESIS

**die·sel** \'dē-zəl, -səl\ *noun* [Rudolf *Diesel*] (1894)
**1 :** DIESEL ENGINE
**2 :** a vehicle driven by a diesel engine

**diesel–electric** *adjective* (1914)
: of, relating to, or employing the combination of a diesel engine driving an electric generator ⟨a *diesel-electric* locomotive⟩

**diesel engine** *noun* (1894)
: an internal combustion engine in which air is compressed to a temperature sufficiently high to ignite fuel injected into the cylinder where the combustion and expansion actuate a piston

**die·sel·ing** \'dē-zə-liŋ, -sə-\ *noun* (circa 1955)
: the continued operation of an internal combustion engine after the ignition is turned off

**die·sel·ize** \'dē-zə-ˌlīz, -sə-\ *transitive verb* **-ized; -iz·ing** (1925)
: to equip with a diesel engine or with electric locomotives having generators powered by diesel engines
— **die·sel·iza·tion** \ˌdē-zə-lə-'zā-shən, -sə-\ *noun*

**Di·es Irae** \ˌdē-(ˌ)ās-'ē-ˌrā\ *noun* [Medieval Latin, day of wrath; from the first words of the hymn] (1860)
: a medieval Latin hymn on the Day of Judgment sung in requiem masses

**di·esis** \'dī-ə-səs\ *noun, plural* **di·eses** \-ˌsēz\ [probably from Italian, sharp (in music), symbol for a sharp, from Medieval Latin, quarter tone, from Latin, from Greek *diiēnai* to send through, from *dia-* + *hienai* to send — more at JET] (circa 1706)
: DOUBLE DAGGER

**di·es·ter** \'dī-ˌes-tər\ *noun* (1935)
: a compound containing two ester groups

**die·stock** \'dī-ˌstäk\ *noun* (circa 1859)
: a stock to hold dies used for cutting threads

**di·es·trus** \(ˌ)dī-'es-trəs\ *noun* [New Latin, from *dia-* + *estrus*] (1942)
: a period of sexual quiescence that intervenes between two periods of estrus
— **di·es·trous** \-trəs\ *adjective*

**¹di·et** \'dī-ət\ *noun* [Middle English *diete*, from Old French, from Latin *diaeta*, from Greek *diaita*, literally, manner of living, from *diaitasthai* to lead one's life] (13th century)
**1 a :** food and drink regularly provided or consumed **b :** habitual nourishment **c :** the kind and amount of food prescribed for a person or animal for a special reason

**2 :** something provided especially habitually ⟨a *diet* of Broadway shows and nightclubs —Frederick Wyatt⟩

²**diet** (14th century)
*transitive verb*
**1 :** to cause to take food : FEED
**2 :** to cause to eat and drink sparingly or according to prescribed rules
*intransitive verb*
**:** to eat sparingly or according to prescribed rules
— **di·et·er** *noun*

³**diet** *adjective* (1969)
**:** reduced in calories ⟨a *diet* soft drink⟩

⁴**diet** *noun* [Middle English *diete* day's journey, day set for a meeting, from Medieval Latin *dieta*, literally, daily regimen, diet (taken as a derivative of Latin *dies* day), from Latin *diaeta*] (1565)
**1 :** a formal deliberative assembly of princes or estates
**2 :** any of various national or provincial legislatures

¹**di·e·tary** \'dī-ə-,ter-ē\ *noun, plural* **di·e·tar·ies** (1838)
**:** the kinds and amounts of food available to or eaten by an individual, group, or population

²**dietary** *adjective* (1614)
**:** of or relating to a diet or to the rules of a diet
— **di·e·tar·i·ly** \,dī-ə-'ter-ə-lē\ *adverb*

**dietary law** *noun* (circa 1930)
**:** any of the laws observed by Orthodox Jews that permit or prohibit certain foods

**di·e·tet·ic** \,dī-ə-'te-tik\ *adjective* (1579)
**1 :** of or relating to diet
**2 :** adapted for use in special diets
— **di·e·tet·i·cal·ly** \-ti-k(ə-)lē\ *adverb*

**di·e·tet·ics** \-'te-tiks\ *noun plural but singular or plural in construction* (1799)
**:** the science or art of applying the principles of nutrition to the diet

**di·ether** \(,)dī-'ē-thər\ *noun* (1950)
**:** a compound containing two atoms of oxygen with ether linkages

**di·eth·yl·car·bam·a·zine** \,dī-,e-thəl-kär-'ba-mə-,zēn, -zən\ *noun* [*di-* + *ethyl* + *carboxy-* + *amide* + *azine*] (1948)
**:** an anthelmintic administered in the form of its crystalline citrate $C_{10}H_{21}N_3O \cdot C_6H_8O_7$ especially to control human filariasis and large roundworms in dogs and cats

**di·eth·yl ether** \(,)dī-,e-thəl-\ *noun* (circa 1930)
**:** ETHER 3a

**di·eth·yl·stil·bes·trol** \-stil-'bes-,trol, -,trōl\ *noun* [International Scientific Vocabulary] (1938)
**:** a colorless crystalline synthetic compound $C_{18}H_{20}O_2$ used as a potent estrogen but contraindicated in pregnancy for its tendency to cause cancer or birth defects in offspring — called also *stilbestrol*

**di·eth·yl zinc** *noun* (1952)
**:** a volatile pyrophoric liquid organometallic compound $C_4H_{10}Zn$ used especially to catalyze polymerization reactions and to deacidify paper

**di·e·ti·tian** *or* **di·e·ti·cian** \,dī-ə-'ti-shən\ *noun* [*dietitian* irregular from ¹*diet* + *-ician*] (circa 1846)
**:** a specialist in dietetics

**dif·fer** \'di-fər\ *intransitive verb* **dif·fered; dif·fer·ing** \-f(ə-)riŋ\ [Middle English, from Middle French or Latin; Middle French *differer* to postpone, be different, from Latin *differre*, from *dis-* + *ferre* to carry — more at BEAR] (14th century)
**1 a :** to be unlike or distinct in nature, form, or characteristics ⟨the law of one state *differs* from that of another⟩ **b :** to change from time to time or from one instance to another : VARY ⟨the number of cookies in a box may *differ*⟩
**2 :** to be of unlike or opposite opinion : DISAGREE ⟨they *differ* on religious matters⟩

¹**dif·fer·ence** \'di-fərn(t)s, 'di-f(ə-)rən(t)s\ *noun* (14th century)

**1 a :** the quality or state of being different **b :** an instance of differing in nature, form, or quality **c** *archaic* **:** a characteristic that distinguishes one from another or from the average **d :** the element or factor that separates or distinguishes contrasting situations
**2 :** distinction or discrimination in preference
**3 a :** disagreement in opinion : DISSENSION **b :** an instance or cause of disagreement
**4 :** the degree or amount by which things differ in quantity or measure; *specifically* : REMAINDER 2b(1)
**5 :** a significant change in or effect on a situation

²**difference** *transitive verb* **-enced; -enc·ing** (1576)
**:** DIFFERENTIATE, DISTINGUISH

¹**dif·fer·ent** \'di-fərnt, 'di-f(ə-)rənt\ *adjective* [Middle French, from Latin *different-, differens*, present participle of *differre*] (14th century)
**1 :** partly or totally unlike in nature, form, or quality : DISSIMILAR ⟨could hardly be more *different*⟩ — often followed by *from, than,* or chiefly British *to* ⟨small, neat hand, very *different* from the captain's tottery characters —R. L. Stevenson⟩ ⟨vastly *different* in size than it was twenty-five years ago —N. M. Pusey⟩ ⟨a very *different* situation to the . . . one under which we live —Sir Winston Churchill⟩
**2 :** not the same: as **a :** DISTINCT ⟨*different* age groups⟩ **b :** VARIOUS ⟨*different* members of the class⟩ **c :** ANOTHER ⟨switched to a *different* TV program⟩
**3 :** UNUSUAL, SPECIAL ⟨she was *different* and superior⟩ ☆ ■
— **dif·fer·ent·ness** *noun*

²**different** *adverb* (1744)
**:** DIFFERENTLY

**dif·fer·en·tia** \,di-fə-'ren(t)-sh(ē-)ə\ *noun, plural* **-ti·ae** \-shē-,ē, -shē-,ī\ [Latin, difference, from *different-, differens*] (1690)
**:** an element, feature, or factor that distinguishes one entity, state, or class from another; *especially* : a characteristic trait distinguishing a species from other species of the same genus

¹**dif·fer·en·tial** \,di-fə-'ren(t)-shəl\ *adjective* (1647)
**1 a :** of, relating to, or constituting a difference : DISTINGUISHING **b :** making a distinction between individuals or classes **c :** based on or resulting from a differential **d :** functioning or proceeding differently or at a different rate
**2 :** being, relating to, or involving a differential or differentiation
**3 a :** relating to quantitative differences **b :** producing effects by reason of quantitative differences
— **dif·fer·en·tial·ly** \-'ren(t)-shə-lē\ *adverb*

²**differential** *noun* (1704)
**1 a :** the product of the derivative of a function of one variable by the increment of the independent variable **b :** a sum of products in which each product consists of a partial derivative of a given function of several variables multiplied by the corresponding increment and which contains as many products as there are independent variables in the function
**2 :** a difference between comparable individuals or classes ⟨a price *differential*⟩; *also* : the amount of such a difference
**3 a :** DIFFERENTIAL GEAR **b :** a case covering a differential gear

**differential calculus** *noun* (1702)
**:** a branch of mathematics concerned chiefly with the study of the rate of change of functions with respect to their variables especially through the use of derivatives and differentials

**differential equation** *noun* (1763)
**:** an equation containing differentials or derivatives of functions — compare PARTIAL DIFFERENTIAL EQUATION

**differential gear** *noun* (circa 1859)
**:** an arrangement of gears forming an epicyclic train for connecting two shafts or axles in the same line, dividing the driving force equally

between them, and permitting one shaft to revolve faster than the other — called also *differential gearing*

**differential geometry** *noun* (circa 1909)
**:** a branch of mathematics using calculus to study the geometric properties of curves and surfaces

**dif·fer·en·ti·ate** \,dif-ə-'ren(t)-shē-,āt\ *verb* **-at·ed; -at·ing** (1816)
*transitive verb*
**1 :** to obtain the mathematical derivative of
**2 :** to mark or show a difference in : constitute a difference that distinguishes
**3 :** to develop differential characteristics in
**4 :** to cause differentiation of in the course of development
**5 :** to express the specific distinguishing quality of : DISCRIMINATE
*intransitive verb*
**1 :** to recognize or give expression to a difference
**2 :** to become distinct or different in character
**3 :** to undergo differentiation
— **dif·fer·en·tia·bil·i·ty** \-,ren(t)-sh(ē-)ə-'bi-lə-tē\ *noun*
— **dif·fer·en·tia·ble** \-'ren(t)-sh(ē-)ə-bəl\ *adjective*

**dif·fer·en·ti·a·tion** \-,ren(t)-shē-'ā-shən\ *noun* (1802)
**1 :** the act or process of differentiating
**2 :** development from the one to the many, the simple to the complex, or the homogeneous to the heterogeneous
**3 a :** modification of body parts for performance of particular functions **b :** the sum of the processes whereby apparently indifferent cells, tissues, and structures attain their adult form and function
**4 :** the processes by which various rock types are produced from a common magma

**dif·fer·ent·ly** \'di-fərnt-lē, 'di-f(ə-)rənt-\ *adverb* (14th century)
**1 :** in a different manner
**2 :** OTHERWISE

**dif·fi·cile** \dē-fi-'sē(ə)l\ *adjective* [French, literally, difficult] (1536)
**:** STUBBORN, UNREASONABLE

**dif·fi·cult** \'di-fi-(,)kəlt\ *adjective* [Middle English, back-formation from *difficulty*] (14th century)
**1 :** hard to do, make, or carry out : ARDUOUS ⟨a *difficult* climb⟩

---

☆ **SYNONYMS**
**Different, diverse, divergent, disparate, various** mean unlike in kind or character. DIFFERENT may imply little more than separateness but it may also imply contrast or contrariness ⟨*different* foods⟩. DIVERSE implies both distinctness and marked contrast ⟨such *diverse* interests as dancing and football⟩. DIVERGENT implies movement away from each other and unlikelihood of ultimate meeting or reconciliation ⟨went on to pursue *divergent* careers⟩. DISPARATE emphasizes incongruity or incompatibility ⟨*disparate* notions of freedom⟩. VARIOUS stresses the number of sorts or kinds ⟨tried *various* methods⟩.

---

▢ **USAGE**
**different** Numerous commentators have condemned *different than* in spite of its use since the 17th century by many of the best-known names in English literature. It is nevertheless standard and is even recommended in many handbooks when followed by a clause. *Different from*, the generally safe choice, is more common and is even used in constructions where *than* would work more smoothly.

**2 a :** hard to deal with, manage, or overcome ⟨a *difficult* child⟩ **b :** hard to understand **:** PUZZLING ⟨*difficult* reading⟩
**synonym** see HARD
— **dif·fi·cult·ly** *adverb*
**dif·fi·cul·ty** \-(,)kəl-tē\ *noun, plural* **-ties** [Middle English *difficulte*, from Latin *difficultas*, from *difficilis* not easy, from *dis-* + *facilis* easy — more at FACILE] (14th century)
**1 :** the quality or state of being difficult
**2 :** CONTROVERSY, DISAGREEMENT
**3 :** OBJECTION
**4 :** something difficult **:** IMPEDIMENT
**5 :** EMBARRASSMENT, TROUBLE — usually used in plural
**dif·fi·dence** \'di-fə-dən(t)s, -fə-,den(t)s\ *noun* (14th century)
**:** the quality or state of being diffident
**dif·fi·dent** \-dənt, -,dent\ *adjective* [Middle English, from Latin *diffident-, diffidens*, present participle of *diffidere* to distrust, from *dis-* + *fidere* to trust — more at BIDE] (15th century)
**1 :** hesitant in acting or speaking through lack of self-confidence
**2** *archaic* **:** DISTRUSTFUL
**3 :** RESERVED, UNASSERTIVE
**synonym** see SHY
— **dif·fi·dent·ly** *adverb*
**dif·fract** \di-'frakt\ *transitive verb* [back-formation from *diffraction*] (1803)
**:** to cause to undergo diffraction
**dif·frac·tion** \di-'frak-shən\ *noun* [New Latin *diffraction-, diffractio*, from Latin *diffringere* to break apart, from *dis-* + *frangere* to break — more at BREAK] (1671)
**:** a modification which light undergoes in passing by the edges of opaque bodies or through narrow slits or in being reflected from ruled surfaces and in which the rays appear to be deflected and to produce fringes of parallel light and dark or colored bands; *also* **:** a similar modification of other waves (as sound waves)
**diffraction grating** *noun* (1867)
**:** GRATING 3
**dif·frac·tom·e·ter** \di-,frak-'tä-mə-tər\ *noun* (circa 1909)
**:** an instrument for analyzing the structure of a usually crystalline substance from the scattering pattern produced when a beam of radiation or particles (as X rays or neutrons) strikes it
— **dif·frac·to·met·ric** \di-,frak-tə-'me-trik\ *adjective*
— **dif·frac·tom·e·try** \di-,frak-'tä-mə-trē\ *noun*
**¹dif·fuse** \di-'fyüs\ *adjective* [Middle English, from Latin *diffusus*, past participle of *diffundere* to spread out, from *dis-* + *fundere* to pour — more at FOUND] (15th century)
**1 :** being at once verbose and ill-organized
**2 :** not concentrated or localized ⟨*diffuse* sclerosis⟩
**synonym** see WORDY
— **dif·fuse·ly** *adverb*
— **dif·fuse·ness** *noun*
**²dif·fuse** \di-'fyüz\ *verb* **dif·fused; dif·fus·ing** [Middle English *diffused*, past participle, from Latin *diffusus*, past participle] (14th century)
*transitive verb*
**1 a :** to pour out and permit or cause to spread freely **b :** EXTEND, SCATTER **c :** to spread thinly or wastefully
**2 :** to subject to diffusion; *especially* **:** to break up and distribute (incident light) by reflection
*intransitive verb*
**1 :** to spread out or become transmitted especially by contact
**2 :** to undergo diffusion
— **dif·fus·ible** \di-'fyü-zə-bəl\ *adjective*
**dif·fuse–po·rous** \di-,fyüs-'pōr-əs, -'pòr-əs\ *adjective* [¹*diffuse*] (circa 1902)
**:** having vessels more or less evenly distributed throughout an annual ring and not varying greatly in size — compare RING-POROUS

**dif·fus·er** \di-'fyü-zər\ *noun* (circa 1679)
**1 :** one that diffuses: as **a :** a device (as a reflector) for distributing the light of a lamp evenly **b :** a screen (as of cloth or frosted glass) for softening lighting (as in photography) **c :** a device (as slats at different angles) for deflecting air from an outlet in various directions
**2 :** a device for reducing the velocity and increasing the static pressure of a fluid passing through a system
**dif·fu·sion** \di-'fyü-zhən\ *noun* (14th century)
**1 :** the action of diffusing **:** the state of being diffused
**2 :** PROLIXITY, DIFFUSENESS
**3 a :** the process whereby particles of liquids, gases, or solids intermingle as the result of their spontaneous movement caused by thermal agitation and in dissolved substances move from a region of higher to one of lower concentration **b** (1) **:** reflection of light by a rough reflecting surface (2) **:** transmission of light through a translucent material **:** SCATTERING
**4 :** the spread of cultural elements from one area or group of people to others by contact
**5 :** the softening of sharp outlines in a photographic image
— **dif·fu·sion·al** \-'fyü-zhə-n°l\ *adjective*
**dif·fu·sion·ist** \-'fyü-zhə-nəst\ *noun* (1938)
**:** an anthropologist who emphasizes the role of diffusion in the history of culture rather than independent invention or discovery
— **dif·fu·sion·ism** \-'fyü-zhə-,ni-zəm\ *noun*
— **diffusionist** *adjective*
**dif·fu·sive** \di-'fyü-siv, -ziv\ *adjective* (1614)
**:** tending to diffuse **:** characterized by diffusion ⟨*diffusive* motion of atoms⟩
— **dif·fu·sive·ly** *adverb*
— **dif·fu·sive·ness** *noun*
— **dif·fu·siv·i·ty** \di-,fyü-'si-və-tē, -'zi-\ *noun*
**di·func·tion·al** \(,)dī-'fəŋ(k)-shnəl, -shə-n°l\ *adjective* (1943)
**:** of, relating to, or being a compound with two highly reactive sites in each molecule
**¹dig** \'dig\ *verb* **dug** \'dəg\; **dig·ging** [Middle English *diggen*] (13th century)
*transitive verb*
**1 a :** to break up, turn, or loosen (earth) with an implement **b :** to prepare the soil of ⟨*dig* a garden⟩
**2 a :** to bring to the surface by digging **:** UNEARTH **b :** to bring to light or out of hiding ⟨*dig* up facts⟩
**3 :** to hollow out or form by removing earth **:** EXCAVATE
**4 :** to drive down so as to penetrate **:** THRUST
**5 :** POKE, PROD
**6 a :** to pay attention to **:** NOTICE ⟨*dig* that fancy hat⟩ **b :** UNDERSTAND, APPRECIATE ⟨if you . . . do something subtle . . . only one tenth of the audience will *dig* it —Nat Hentoff⟩ **c :** LIKE, ADMIRE ⟨high school students *dig* short poetry —David Burmester⟩
*intransitive verb*
**1 :** to turn up, loosen, or remove earth **:** DELVE
**2 :** to work hard or laboriously
**3 :** to advance by or as if by removing or pushing aside material
**²dig** *noun* (1819)
**1 a :** THRUST, POKE **b :** a cutting remark
**2** *plural* **a :** living accommodations **b** *chiefly British* **:** LODGING, HOTEL
**3 :** an archaeological excavation site; *also* **:** the excavation itself
**dig·a·my** \'di-gə-mē\ *noun, plural* **-mies** [Late Latin *digamia*, from Late Greek, from Greek *digamos* married to two people, from *di-* + *-gamos* -gamous] (1635)
**:** a second marriage after the termination of the first
**di·gas·tric** \(,)dī-'gas-trik\ *adjective* [New Latin *digastricus*, from *di-* + *gastricus* gastric] (circa 1721)

**:** of, relating to, or being a muscle with two bellies separated by a median tendon
**di·ge·net·ic** \,dī-jə-'ne-tik\ *adjective* [New Latin *Digenetica*, subclass name (synonym of *Digenea*), from *di-* + *genetica*, neuter plural of *geneticus* genetic] (circa 1883)
**:** of or relating to a subclass (Digenea) of trematode worms in which sexual reproduction as an internal parasite of a vertebrate alternates with asexual reproduction in a mollusk
**¹di·gest** \'dī-,jest\ *noun* [Middle English, systematic arrangement of laws, from Latin *digesta*, from neuter plural of *digestus*, past participle of *digerere* to arrange, distribute, digest, from *dis-* + *gerere* to carry] (14th century)
**1 :** a summation or condensation of a body of information: as **a :** a systematic compilation of legal rules, statutes, or decisions **b :** a periodical devoted to condensed versions of previously published articles
**2 :** a product of digestion
**²di·gest** \dī-'jest, də-\ *verb* [Middle English, from Latin *digestus*] (14th century)
*transitive verb*
**1 :** to distribute or arrange systematically **:** CLASSIFY
**2 :** to convert (food) into absorbable form
**3 :** to take into the mind or memory; *especially* **:** to assimilate mentally
**4 a :** to soften, decompose, or break down by heat and moisture or chemicals **b :** to extract soluble ingredients from by warming with a liquid
**5 :** to compress into a short summary
**6 :** ABSORB 1 ⟨the capacity of the U.S. to *digest* immigrants⟩
*intransitive verb*
**1 :** to digest food
**2 :** to become digested
**di·gest·er** \-'jes-tər\ *noun* (1614)
**1 :** one that digests or makes a digest
**2 :** a vessel for digesting especially plant or animal materials
**di·gest·ibil·i·ty** \-,jes-tə-'bi-lə-tē\ *noun, plural* **-ties** (1740)
**1 :** the fitness of something for digestion
**2 :** the percentage of a foodstuff taken into the digestive tract that is absorbed into the body
**di·gest·ible** \-'jes-tə-bəl\ *adjective* (14th century)
**:** capable of being digested
**di·ges·tion** \dī-'jes-chən, də-, -'jesh-\ *noun* (14th century)
**:** the action, process, or power of digesting: as **a :** the process of making food absorbable by dissolving it and breaking it down into simpler chemical compounds that occurs in the living body chiefly through the action of enzymes secreted into the alimentary canal **b :** the process in sewage treatment by which organic matter in sludge is decomposed by anaerobic bacteria with the release of a burnable mixture of gases
**¹di·ges·tive** \-'jes-tiv\ *noun* (14th century)
**:** an aid to digestion especially of food
**²digestive** *adjective* (15th century)
**1 :** relating to or functioning in digestion ⟨the *digestive* system⟩
**2 :** having the power to cause or promote digestion ⟨*digestive* enzymes⟩
— **di·ges·tive·ly** *adverb*
**digestive gland** *noun* (1940)
**:** a gland secreting digestive enzymes
**dig·ger** \'di-gər\ *noun* (15th century)
**1 a :** one that digs **b :** a tool or machine for digging

**2** *capitalized* **:** a North American Indian (as a Paiute) who dug roots for food — usually used disparagingly especially formerly
**3** *often capitalized, chiefly Australian & New Zealand* **:** an Australian or New Zealand soldier

**digger wasp** *noun* (1880)
**:** a burrowing wasp; *especially* **:** a usually solitary wasp (superfamily Sphecoidea) that digs nest burrows in the soil and provisions them with insects or spiders paralyzed by stinging

**dig·gings** *noun plural* (1538)
**1 :** a place of excavating especially for ore, metals, or precious stones
**2 :** material dug out
**3 a :** QUARTERS, PREMISES **b** *chiefly British* **:** lodgings for a student

**dight** \'dīt\ *transitive verb* **dight·ed** *or* **dight; dight·ing** [Middle English, from Old English *dihtan* to arrange, compose, from Latin *dictare* to dictate, compose] (13th century)
*archaic* **:** DRESS, ADORN

**dig in** (1839)
*transitive verb*
**1 :** to cover or incorporate by burying ⟨*dig in* compost⟩
**2 :** to establish in a dug defensive position ⟨the platoon was well *dug in*⟩
*intransitive verb*
**1 :** to establish a defensive position especially by digging trenches
**2 a :** to go resolutely to work **b :** to begin eating
**3 :** to hold stubbornly to a position
**4 :** to scuff the ground for better footing while batting (as in baseball)
**— dig in one's heels :** to take or persist in an uncompromising position or attitude despite opposition

**dig·it** \'di-jət\ *noun* [Middle English, from Latin *digitus* finger, toe; perhaps akin to Greek *deiknynai* to show — more at DICTION] (14th century)
**1 a :** any of the Arabic numerals 1 to 9 and usually the symbol 0 **b :** one of the elements that combine to form numbers in a system other than the decimal system
**2 :** a unit of length based on the breadth of a finger and equal in English measure to ¾ inch
**3 :** any of the divisions in which the limbs of amphibians and all higher vertebrates terminate, which are typically five in number but may be reduced (as in the horse), and which typically have a series of phalanges bearing a nail, claw, or hoof at the tip — compare FINGER 1, TOE 1a

**dig·i·tal** \'di-jə-t°l\ *adjective* [Latin *digitalis*] (circa 1656)
**1 :** of or relating to the fingers or toes **:** DIGITATE
**2 :** done with a finger
**3 :** of, relating to, or using calculation by numerical methods or by discrete units
**4 :** of or relating to data in the form of numerical digits
**5 :** providing a readout in numerical digits ⟨a *digital* voltmeter⟩
**6 :** relating to an audio recording method in which sound waves are represented digitally (as on magnetic tape) so that in the recording wow and flutter are eliminated and background noise is reduced
**— dig·i·tal·ly** \-t°l-ē\ *adverb*

**digital computer** *noun* (1947)
**:** a computer that operates with numbers expressed directly as digits — compare ANALOG COMPUTER, HYBRID COMPUTER

**dig·i·tal·in** \,di-jə-'ta-lən *also* -'tā-\ *noun* [New Latin *Digitalis*] (1837)
**1 :** a white crystalline steroid glycoside $C_{36}H_{56}O_{14}$ obtained from seeds especially of the common foxglove
**2 :** a mixture of the glycosides of digitalis leaves or seeds

**dig·i·tal·is** \-'ta-ləs *also* -'tā-\ *noun* [New Latin, genus name, from Latin, of a finger, from *digitus;* from its finger-shaped corolla] (1664)
**1 :** FOXGLOVE
**2 :** the dried powdered leaf of the common foxglove containing important glycosides and serving as a powerful cardiac stimulant and a diuretic

**dig·i·ta·li·za·tion** \,di-jə-t°l-ə-'zā-shən\ *noun* [*digitalis*] (1882)
**:** the administration of digitalis until the desired physiological adjustment is attained; *also* **:** the bodily state so produced

¹**dig·i·ta·lize** \'di-jə-t°l-,īz\ *transitive verb* **-lized; -liz·ing** [*digitalis*] (1927)
**:** to subject to digitalization

²**dig·i·tal·ize** \'di-jə-t°l-,īz\ *transitive verb* **-ized; -iz·ing** [*digital*] (1962)
**:** DIGITIZE

**dig·i·tate** \'di-jə-,tāt\ *adjective* (1661)
**:** having divisions arranged like those of a bird's foot ⟨*digitate* leaves⟩
**— dig·i·tate·ly** *adverb*

**digiti-** *combining form* [French, from Latin *digitus*]
**:** digit **:** finger ⟨*digiti*grade⟩

**dig·i·ti·grade** \'di-jə-tə-,grād\ *adjective* [French, from *digiti-* + *-grade*] (circa 1833)
**:** walking on the digits with the posterior of the foot more or less raised

**dig·i·tize** \'di-jə-,tīz\ *transitive verb* **-tized; -tiz·ing** (1953)
**:** to convert (as data or an image) to digital form
**— dig·i·ti·za·tion** \,di-jə-tə-'zā-shən\ *noun*
**— dig·i·tiz·er** \'di-jə-,tī-zər\ *noun*

**dig·i·to·nin** \,di-jə-'tō-nən\ *noun* [International Scientific Vocabulary *digit-* (from New Latin *Digitalis*) + *saponin*] (1875)
**:** a steroid saponin $C_{56}H_{92}O_{29}$ occurring in the leaves and seeds of foxglove

**digi·toxi·gen·in** \,di-jə-,täk-sə-'je-nən\ *noun* [International Scientific Vocabulary, blend of *digitoxin* and *-gen*] (circa 1909)
**:** a steroid lactone $C_{23}H_{34}O_4$ obtained especially by hydrolysis of digitoxin

**digi·tox·in** \,di-jə-'täk-sən\ *noun* [International Scientific Vocabulary, blend of New Latin *Digitalis* and International Scientific Vocabulary *toxin*] (circa 1883)
**:** a poisonous glycoside $C_{41}H_{64}O_{13}$ that is the most active constituent of digitalis; *also* **:** a mixture of digitalis glycosides consisting chiefly of digitoxin

**di·glyc·er·ide** \dī-'gli-sə-,rīd\ *noun* (1918)
**:** an ester formed from glycerol by reacting two of its alcohol hydroxy groups with fatty acids

**dig·ni·fied** \'dig-nə-,fīd\ *adjective* (1763)
**:** showing or expressing dignity

**dig·ni·fy** \'dig-nə-,fī\ *transitive verb* **-fied; -fy·ing** [Middle French *dignifier*, from Late Latin *dignificare*, from Latin *dignus* worthy — more at DECENT] (15th century)
**1 :** to give distinction to **:** ENNOBLE
**2 :** to confer dignity upon; *also* **:** to give undue attention or status to ⟨won't *dignify* that remark with a reply⟩

**dig·ni·tary** \'dig-nə-,ter-ē\ *noun, plural* **-tar·ies** (1673)
**:** one who possesses exalted rank or holds a position of dignity or honor
**— dignitary** *adjective*

**dig·ni·ty** \'dig-nə-tē\ *noun, plural* **-ties** [Middle English *dignete*, from Old French *digneté*, from Latin *dignitat-, dignitas*, from *dignus*] (13th century)
**1 :** the quality or state of being worthy, honored, or esteemed
**2 a :** high rank, office, or position **b :** a legal title of nobility or honor
**3** *archaic* **:** DIGNITARY
**4 :** formal reserve or seriousness of manner, appearance, or language

**dig out** (14th century)
*transitive verb*
**1 :** FIND, UNEARTH
**2 :** to make hollow by digging
*intransitive verb*
**:** TAKE OFF 2a

**di·gox·in** \di-'jäk-sən, -'gäk-\ *noun* [International Scientific Vocabulary *dig-* (from New Latin *Digitalis*) + *toxin*] (circa 1930)
**:** a poisonous cardiotonic steroid $C_{41}H_{64}O_{14}$ obtained from a foxglove (*Digitalis lanata*) and used similarly to digitalis

**di·graph** \'dī-,graf\ *noun* (1780)
**1 :** a group of two successive letters whose phonetic value is a single sound (as *ea* in *bread* or *ng* in *sing*) or whose value is not the sum of a value borne by each in other occurrences (as *ch* in *chin* where the value is \t\ + \sh\)
**2 :** a group of two successive letters
**3 :** LIGATURE 4
**— di·graph·ic** \dī-'gra-fik\ *adjective*
**— di·graph·i·cal·ly** \-fi-k(ə-)lē\ *adverb*

**di·gress** \dī-'gres, də-\ *intransitive verb* [Latin *digressus*, past participle of *digredi*, from *dis- + gradi* to step — more at GRADE] (1530)
**:** to turn aside especially from the main subject of attention or course of argument
*synonym* see SWERVE

**di·gres·sion** \-'gre-shən\ *noun* (14th century)
**1 :** the act or an instance of digressing in a discourse or other usually organized literary work
**2** *archaic* **:** a going aside
**— di·gres·sion·al** \-'gresh-nəl, -ən-°l\ *adjective*
**— di·gres·sion·ary** \-'gre-shə-,ner-ē\ *adjective*

**di·gres·sive** \-'gre-siv\ *adjective* (circa 1611)
**:** characterized by digressions ⟨a *digressive* talk⟩
**— di·gres·sive·ly** *adverb*
**— di·gres·sive·ness** *noun*

**dig up** *transitive verb* (14th century)
**:** FIND, UNEARTH

**di·he·dral** \(,)dī-'hē-drəl\ *noun* (circa 1911)
**1 :** DIHEDRAL ANGLE
**2 :** the angle between an aircraft supporting surface (as a wing) and a horizontal transverse line

**dihedral angle** *noun* [*di-* + *-hedral*] (1826)
**:** a figure formed by two intersecting planes

**di·hy·brid** \(,)dī-'hī-brəd\ *adjective* [International Scientific Vocabulary] (1907)
**:** of, relating to, involving, or being an individual or strain that is heterozygous at two genetic loci
**— dihybrid** *noun*

**dihydr-** *or* **dihydro-** *combining form*
**:** combined with two atoms of hydrogen ⟨*dihydro*ergotamine⟩

**di·hy·dro·er·got·a·mine** \(,)dī-,hī-drō-,ər-'gä-tə-,mēn\ *noun* (1945)
**:** a hydrogenated derivative $C_{33}H_{37}N_5O_5$ of ergotamine that is used in the treatment of migraine

**dihydroxy-** *combining form*
**:** containing two hydroxyl groups ⟨*dihydroxy*acetone⟩

**di·hy·droxy·ac·e·tone** \dī-hī-,dräk-sē-'a-sə-,tōn\ *noun* (1895)
**:** a glyceraldehyde isomer $C_3H_6O_3$ used especially to stain the skin to resemble a tan

**dik-dik** \'dik-,dik\ *noun, plural* **dik-diks** *or* **dik-dik** [origin unknown] (1883)
**:** any of a genus (*Madoqua*) of small eastern African antelopes

¹**dike** \'dīk\ *noun* [Middle English, probably from Old Norse *dīk* ditch and Middle Low German *dīk* dam; akin to Old

**dik-dik**

English *dīc* ditch — more at DITCH] (13th century)
**1 :** an artificial watercourse **:** DITCH
**2 a :** a bank usually of earth constructed to control or confine water **:** LEVEE **b :** a barrier preventing passage especially of something undesirable
**3 a :** a raised causeway **b :** a tabular body of igneous rock that has been injected while molten into a fissure
²**dike** *transitive verb* **diked; dik·ing** (14th century)
**1 :** to surround or protect with a dike
**2 :** to drain by a dike
— **dik·er** *noun*
³**dike** *variant of* ²DYKE
**dik·tat** \dik-'tät\ *noun* [German, literally, something dictated, from New Latin *dictatum,* from Latin, neuter of *dictatus,* past participle of *dictare* to dictate] (1933)
**1 :** a harsh settlement unilaterally imposed (as on a defeated nation)
**2 :** DECREE, ORDER
**Di·lan·tin** \dī-'lan-t°n, də-\ *trademark*
— used for phenytoin
**di·lap·i·date** \də-'la-pə-ˌdāt\ *verb* **-dat·ed; -dat·ing** [Latin *dilapidatus,* past participle of *dilapidare* to squander, destroy, from *dis-* + *lapidare* to pelt with stones, from *lapid-, lapis* stone] (circa 1570)
*transitive verb*
**1 :** to bring into a condition of decay or partial ruin ⟨furniture is *dilapidated* by use —Janet Flanner⟩
**2** *archaic* **:** SQUANDER
*intransitive verb*
**:** to become dilapidated
— **di·lap·i·da·tion** \-ˌla-pə-'dā-shən\ *noun*
**di·lap·i·dat·ed** *adjective* (circa 1806)
**:** decayed, deteriorated, or fallen into partial ruin especially through neglect or misuse ⟨a *dilapidated* old house⟩
**di·lat·an·cy** \dī-'lā-t°n(t)-sē\ *noun* (1885)
**:** the property of being dilatant
**di·lat·ant** \-t°nt\ *adjective* (1885)
**:** increasing in viscosity and setting to a solid as a result of deformation by expansion, pressure, or agitation
**di·la·ta·tion** \ˌdi-lə-'tā-shən, ˌdī-\ *noun* (14th century)
**1 :** amplification in writing or speech
**2 a :** the condition of being stretched beyond normal dimensions especially as a result of overwork, disease, or abnormal relaxation ⟨*dilatation* of the heart⟩ ⟨*dilatation* of the stomach⟩ **b :** DILATION 2
**3 :** the action of expanding **:** the state of being expanded
**4 :** a dilated part or formation
— **di·la·ta·tion·al** \-shnəl, -shə-n°l\ *adjective*
**di·late** \'dī-ˌlāt, dī-'\ *verb* **di·lat·ed; di·lat·ing** [Middle English, from Middle French *dilater,* from Latin *dilatare,* literally, to spread wide, from *dis-* + *latus* wide — more at LATITUDE] (14th century)
*transitive verb*
**1** *archaic* **:** to describe or set forth at length or in detail
**2 :** to enlarge or expand in bulk or extent **:** DISTEND, WIDEN
*intransitive verb*
**1 :** to comment at length **:** DISCOURSE — usually used with *on* or *upon*
**2 :** to become wide **:** SWELL
**synonym** see EXPAND
— **di·lat·abil·i·ty** \(ˌ)dī-ˌlā-tə-'bi-lə-tē\ *noun*
— **di·lat·able** \dī-'lā-tə-bəl, 'dī-\ *adjective*
— **di·la·tor** \dī-'lā-tər, 'dī-\ *noun*
**di·lat·ed** *adjective* (15th century)
**1 :** expanded laterally; *especially* **:** being flat and widened ⟨*dilated* leaves⟩
**2 :** expanded normally or abnormally in all dimensions
**di·la·tion** \dī-'lā-shən\ *noun* (15th century)

**1 :** the act or action of dilating **:** the state of being dilated **:** EXPANSION, DILATATION
**2 :** the action of stretching or enlarging an organ or part of the body
**di·la·tive** \dī-'lā-tiv, 'dī-\ *adjective* (1634)
**:** causing dilation **:** tending to dilate
**di·la·tom·e·ter** \ˌdi-lə-'tä-mə-tər, ˌdī-\ *noun* [International Scientific Vocabulary] (circa 1883)
**:** an instrument for measuring expansion
— **di·la·to·met·ric** \-tō-'me-trik\ *adjective*
— **di·la·tom·e·try** \-'tä-mə-trē\ *noun*
**dil·a·to·ry** \'di-lə-ˌtōr-ē, -ˌtȯr-\ *adjective* [Middle English, from Late Latin *dilatorius,* from Latin *differre* (past participle *dilatus*) to postpone, differ — more at DIFFER, TOLERATE] (15th century)
**1 :** tending or intended to cause delay ⟨*dilatory* tactics⟩
**2 :** characterized by procrastination **:** TARDY ⟨*dilatory* in answering letters⟩
— **dil·a·to·ri·ly** \ˌdi-lə-'tȯr-ə-lē, -'tōr-\ *adverb*
— **dil·a·to·ri·ness** \'di-lə-ˌtōr-ē-nəs, -ˌtȯr-\ *noun*
**dil·do** \'dil-(ˌ)dō\ *noun, plural* **dildos** *also* **dil·does** [origin unknown] (circa 1593)
**:** an object serving as a penis substitute for vaginal insertion
**di·lem·ma** \də-'le-mə *also* dī-\ *noun* [Late Latin, from Late Greek *dilēmmat-, dilēmma,* probably back-formation from Greek *dilēmmatos* involving two assumptions, from *di-* + *lēmmat-, lēmma* assumption — more at LEMMA] (1523)
**1 :** an argument presenting two or more equally conclusive alternatives against an opponent
**2 a :** a usually undesirable or unpleasant choice ⟨faces this *dilemma*: raise interest rates and slow the economy or lower them and risk serious inflation⟩ **b :** a situation involving such a choice ⟨here am I brought to a very pretty *dilemma*; I must commit murder or commit matrimony —George Farquhar⟩; *broadly* **:** PREDICAMENT ⟨lords and bailiffs were in a terrible *dilemma* —G. M. Trevelyan⟩
**3 a :** a problem involving a difficult choice ⟨the *dilemma* of "liberty versus order" —J. M. Burns⟩ **b :** a difficult or persistent problem ⟨unemployment . . . the great central *dilemma* of our advancing technology —August Heckscher⟩ ■
— **di·lem·mat·ic** \ˌdi-lə-'ma-tik *also* ˌdī-\ *adjective*
**dil·et·tante** \'di-lə-ˌtänt, -ˌtant; ˌdi-lə-'\ *noun, plural* **-tantes** *or* **-tan·ti** \-'tän-tē, -'tan-tē\ [Italian, from present participle of *dilettare* to delight, from Latin *dilectare* — more at DELIGHT] (1748)
**1 :** an admirer or lover of the arts
**2 :** a person having a superficial interest in an art or a branch of knowledge **:** DABBLER
**synonym** see AMATEUR
— **dilettante** *adjective*
— **dil·et·tant·ish** \-ˌtän-tish, -ˌtan-, ˌdi-lə-'\ *adjective*
— **dil·et·tan·tism** \-ˌtän-ˌti-zəm, -ˌtan-, ˌdi-lə-'\ *noun*
¹**dil·i·gence** \'di-lə-jən(t)s\ *noun* [Middle English, from Middle French, from Latin *diligentia,* from *diligent-, diligens*] (14th century)
**1 a :** persevering application **:** ASSIDUITY **b** *obsolete* **:** SPEED, HASTE
**2 :** the attention and care legally expected or required of a person (as a party to a contract)
²**di·li·gence** \'di-lə-ˌzhäⁿs, 'di-lə-jən(t)s\ *noun* [French, literally, haste, from Middle French, persevering application] (1742)
**:** STAGECOACH
**dil·i·gent** \'di-lə-jənt\ *adjective* [Middle English, from Middle French, from Latin *diligent-, diligens,* from present participle of *diligere* to esteem, love, from *di-* (from *dis-* apart) + *legere* to select — more at LEGEND] (14th century)

**:** characterized by steady, earnest, and energetic effort **:** PAINSTAKING
**synonym** see BUSY
— **dil·i·gent·ly** *adverb*
**dill** \'dil\ *noun* [Middle English *dile,* from Old English; akin to Old High German *tilli* dill] (before 12th century)
**1 :** any of several plants of the carrot family; *especially* **:** a European herb (*Anethum graveolens*) with aromatic foliage and seeds both of which are used in flavoring foods and especially pickles
**2 :** DILL PICKLE
— **dilled** *adjective*
**dill pickle** *noun* (1904)
**:** a pickle seasoned with fresh dill or dill juice
**dil·ly** \'di-lē\ *noun, plural* **dillies** [obsolete *dilly,* adjective (delightful), perhaps by shortening & alteration from *delightful*] (1935)
**:** one that is remarkable or outstanding ⟨had a *dilly* of a storm⟩ ⟨for a practical joke, that was a *dilly*⟩
**dil·ly bag** \'di-lē-\ *noun* [Jagara (Australian aboriginal language of Queensland) *dili* coarse grass, fiber bag] (1867)
**:** an Australian mesh bag made of native fibers
**dil·ly-dal·ly** \'di-lē-ˌda-lē\ *intransitive verb* [reduplication of *dally*] (1741)
**:** to waste time by loitering or delaying **:** DAWDLE
**dil·u·ent** \'dil-yə-wənt\ *noun* [Latin *diluent-, diluens,* present participle of *diluere*] (circa 1721)
**:** a diluting agent (as the vehicle in a medicinal preparation)
¹**di·lute** \dī-'lüt, də-\ *transitive verb* **di·lut·ed; di·lut·ing** [Latin *dilutus,* past participle of *diluere* to wash away, dilute, from *di-* + *lavere* to wash — more at LYE] (circa 1555)
**1 :** ATTENUATE
**2 :** to make thinner or more liquid by admixture
**3 :** to diminish the strength, flavor, or brilliance of by admixture
**4 :** to decrease the per share value of (common stock) by increasing the total number of shares
— **di·lut·er** *or* **di·lu·tor** \-'lü-tər\ *noun*
— **di·lu·tive** \-'lü-tiv\ *adjective*
²**dilute** *adjective* (1605)
**:** WEAK, DILUTED
— **di·lute·ness** *noun*
**di·lu·tion** \dī-'lü-shən, də-\ *noun* (1646)
**1 :** the action of diluting **:** the state of being diluted
**2 :** something (as a solution) that is diluted
**3 :** a lessening of real value (as of equity) by a decrease in relative worth; *specifically* **:** a decrease of per share value of common stock by an increase in the total number of shares

\ə\ abut \°\ kitten \ər\ further \a\ ash \ā\ ace
\ä\ mop, mar \aú\ out \ch\ chin \e\ bet \ē\ easy
\g\ go \i\ hit \ī\ ice \j\ job \ŋ\ sing \ō\ go
\ȯ\ law \ȯi\ boy \th\ thin \t͟h\ the \ü\ loot \ú\ foot
\y\ yet \zh\ vision *see also* Guide to Pronunciation

**di·lu·vi·al** \də-'lü-vē-əl, dī-\ *or* **di·lu·vi·an** \-vē-ən\ *adjective* [Late Latin *diluvialis,* from Latin *diluvium* deluge — more at DELUGE] (circa 1656)
**:** of, relating to, or brought about by a flood

**¹dim** \'dim\ *adjective* **dim·mer; dim·mest** [Middle English, from Old English *dimm;* akin to Old High German *timber* dark] (before 12th century)
**1 a :** emitting a limited or insufficient amount of light **b :** DULL, LUSTERLESS **c :** lacking pronounced, clear-cut, or vigorous quality or character
**2 a :** seen indistinctly or without clear outlines or details **b :** perceived by the senses or mind indistinctly or weakly **:** FAINT ⟨had only a *dim* notion of what was going on⟩ **c :** having little prospect of favorable result or outcome ⟨a *dim* future⟩ **d :** characterized by an unfavorable, skeptical, or pessimistic attitude — usually used in the phrase *take a dim view of*
**3 :** not perceiving clearly and distinctly ⟨*dim* eyes⟩
**4 :** DIM-WITTED
— **dim·ly** *adverb*
— **dim·ma·ble** \'di-mə-bəl\ *adjective*
— **dim·ness** *noun*

**²dim** *verb* **dimmed; dim·ming** (before 12th century)
*transitive verb*
**1 :** to make dim or lusterless
**2 :** to reduce the light from
*intransitive verb*
**:** to become dim

**³dim** *noun* (14th century)
**1** *archaic* **:** DUSK, DIMNESS
**2 :** LOW BEAM

**dim bulb** *noun* (1927)
*slang* **:** DIMWIT

**dime** \'dīm\ *noun* [Middle English, tenth part, tithe, from Middle French, from Latin *decima,* from feminine of *decimus* tenth, from *decem* ten — more at TEN] (1786)
**1 a :** a coin of the U.S. worth ¹/₁₀ dollar **b :** a petty sum of money
**2 :** a Canadian 10-cent piece
— **a dime a dozen :** so plentiful or commonplace as to be of little esteem or slight value
— **on a dime 1 :** in a very small area ⟨these cars can turn *on a dime*⟩ **2 :** INSTANTLY

**dim·en·hy·dri·nate** \,dī-,men-'hī-drə-,nāt\ *noun* [*dim*ethyl + *a*mi*ne* + *hydr-* + *a*mi*ne* + *¹-ate*] (circa 1950)
**:** a crystalline antihistaminic compound $C_{24}H_{28}ClN_5O_3$ used especially to prevent nausea

**dime novel** *noun* (1864)
**:** a usually paperback melodramatic novel; *especially* **:** one popular in the U.S. from about the mid-19th century to the early 20th often featuring a Western theme

**¹di·men·sion** \də-'men(t)-shən *also* dī-\ *noun* [Middle English, from Middle French, from Latin *dimension-, dimensio,* from *dimetiri* to measure out, from *dis-* + *metiri* to measure — more at MEASURE] (14th century)
**1 a** (1) **:** measure in one direction; *specifically* **:** one of three coordinates determining a position in space or four coordinates determining a position in space and time (2) **:** one of a group of properties whose number is necessary and sufficient to determine uniquely each element of a system of usually mathematical entities (as an aggregate of points in real or abstract space) ⟨the surface of a sphere has two *dimensions*⟩; *also* **:** a parameter or coordinate variable assigned to such a property ⟨the three *dimensions* of momentum⟩ (3) **:** the number of elements in a basis of a vector space **b :** the quality of spatial extension **:** MAGNITUDE, SIZE **c :** a lifelike or realistic quality **d :** the range over which or the degree to which something extends **:** SCOPE — usually used in plural **e :** one of the elements or factors making up a complete personality or entity **:** ASPECT

**2** *obsolete* **:** bodily form or proportions
**3 :** any of the fundamental units (as of mass, length, or time) on which a derived unit is based; *also* **:** the power of such a unit
**4 :** wood or stone cut to pieces of specified size
**5 :** a level of existence or consciousness
— **di·men·sion·al** \-'mench-nəl, -'men(t)-shə-n°l\ *adjective*
— **di·men·sion·al·i·ty** \-,men(t)-shə-'na-lə-tē\ *noun*
— **di·men·sion·al·ly** \-'mench-nə-lē, -'men(t)-shə-n°l-ē\ *adverb*
— **di·men·sion·less** \-'men(t)-shən-ləs\ *adjective*

**²dimension** *transitive verb* **di·men·sioned; di·men·sion·ing** \-'men(t)-shə-niŋ\ (1754)
**1 :** to form to the required dimensions
**2 :** to indicate the dimensions of (as on a drawing)

**di·mer** \'dī-mər\ *noun* [International Scientific Vocabulary] (circa 1926)
**:** a compound formed by the union of two radicals or two molecules of a simpler compound; *specifically* **:** a polymer formed from two molecules of a monomer
— **di·mer·ic** \(,)dī-'mer-ik\ *adjective*
— **di·mer·iza·tion** \,dī-mə-rə-'zā-shən\ *noun*
— **di·mer·ize** \'dī-mə-,rīz\ *transitive verb*

**di·mer·cap·rol** \,dī-mər-'ka-,prȯl, -,prōl\ *noun* [*di-* + *mercap*tan + *propane* + *¹-ol*] (1947)
**:** a compound $C_3H_8OS_2$ developed as an antidote against lewisite and used against arsenic, mercury, and gold poisoning — called also *BAL*

**dime-store** \'dīm-,stōr, -,stȯr\ *adjective* (1938)
**1 :** INEXPENSIVE ⟨*dime-store* perfume⟩
**2 :** TAWDRY, SECOND-RATE ⟨*dime-store* philosophy⟩

**dime store** *noun* (circa 1928)
**:** FIVE-AND-TEN

**dim·e·ter** \'di-mə-tər\ *noun* [Late Latin, from Greek *dimetros,* adjective, being a dimeter, from *di-* + *metron* measure — more at MEASURE] (1589)
**:** a line of verse consisting of two metrical feet or of two dipodies

**di·meth·o·ate** \dī-'me-thə-,wāt\ *noun* [*di*methyl + *thio* acid + *¹-ate*] (1960)
**:** an insecticide $C_5H_{12}NO_3PS_2$ used in agriculture and animal husbandry

**di·meth·yl** \dī-'me-thəl\ *adjective*
**:** containing two methyl groups in the molecule — often used in combination

**di·meth·yl·hy·dra·zine** \,dī-,me-thəl-'hī-drə-,zēn\ *noun* (1961)
**:** either of two flammable corrosive isomeric liquids $C_2H_8N_2$ which are methylated derivatives of hydrazine and of which one is used as a rocket fuel

**di·meth·yl·ni·tro·sa·mine** \-nī-'trō-sə-,mēn\ *noun* (1965)
**:** a carcinogenic nitrosamine $C_2H_6N_2O$ that occurs especially in tobacco smoke

**dimethyl sulfoxide** *noun* (1964)
**:** a compound $(CH_3)_2SO$ obtained as a by-product in wood-pulp manufacture and used as a solvent and in veterinary medicine as an anti-inflammatory — called also *DMSO*

**di·meth·yl·tryp·ta·mine** \-'trip-tə-,mēn\ *noun* (1966)
**:** a naturally occurring or easily synthesized hallucinogenic drug $C_{12}H_{16}N_2$ that is chemically similar to but shorter acting than psilocybin — called also *DMT*

**di·min·ish** \də-'mi-nish\ *verb* [Middle English *deminishen,* alteration of *diminuen,* from Middle French *diminuer,* from Late Latin *diminuere,* alteration of Latin *deminuere,* from *de-* + *minuere* to lessen — more at MINOR] (15th century)
*transitive verb*
**1 :** to make less or cause to appear less

**2 :** to lessen the authority, dignity, or reputation of **:** BELITTLE
**3 :** to cause to taper
*intransitive verb*
**1 :** to become gradually less (as in size or importance) **:** DWINDLE
**2 :** TAPER
*synonym* see DECREASE
— **di·min·ish·able** \-ni-shə-bəl\ *adjective*
— **di·min·ish·ment** \-mənt\ *noun*

**di·min·ished** *adjective* (circa 1751)
*of a musical interval* **:** made one half step less than perfect or minor ⟨a *diminished* fifth⟩

**diminishing returns** *noun plural* (1815)
**:** a rate of yield that beyond a certain point fails to increase in proportion to additional investments of labor or capital

**di·min·u·en·do** \də-,min-yə-'wen-(,)dō *also* -,mi-nə-\ *adverb or adjective* [Italian, literally, diminishing, from Late Latin *diminuendum,* gerund of *diminuere*] (1775)
**:** DECRESCENDO
— **diminuendo** *noun*

**dim·i·nu·tion** \,di-mə-'nü-shən *also* -'nyü-\ *noun* [Middle English *diminucioun,* from Middle French *diminution,* from Medieval Latin *diminution-, diminutio,* alteration of Latin *deminution-, deminutio,* from *deminuere*] (14th century)
**:** the act, process, or an instance of diminishing **:** DECREASE

**¹di·min·u·tive** \də-'mi-nyə-tiv\ *noun* [Middle English *diminutif,* from Medieval Latin *diminutivum,* alteration of Late Latin *deminutivum,* from neuter of *deminutivus,* adjective, from *deminutus,* past participle of *deminuere*] (14th century)
**1 :** a diminutive word, affix, or name
**2 :** a diminutive individual

**²diminutive** *adjective* (14th century)
**1 :** indicating small size and sometimes the state or quality of being familiarly known, lovable, pitiable, or contemptible — used of affixes (as *-ette, -kin, -ling*) and of words formed with them (as *kitchenette, manikin, duckling*), of clipped forms (as *Jim*), and of altered forms (as *Peggy*); compare AUGMENTATIVE
**2 :** exceptionally or notably small **:** TINY
*synonym* see SMALL
— **di·min·u·tive·ly** *adverb*
— **di·min·u·tive·ness** *noun*

**dim·i·ty** \'di-mə-tē\ *noun, plural* **-ties** [alteration of Middle English *demyt,* from Medieval Latin *dimitum,* from Middle Greek *dimitos* of double thread, from Greek *di-* + *mitos* warp thread] (1570)
**:** a sheer usually corded cotton fabric of plain weave in checks or stripes

**dim·mer** \'di-mər\ *noun* (circa 1896)
**1 :** a device for regulating the intensity of an electric lighting unit
**2 :** LOW BEAM

**di·mor·phic** \(,)dī-'mȯr-fik\ *adjective* (1859)
**1 a :** DIMORPHOUS 1 **b :** occurring in two distinct forms ⟨*dimorphic* leaves of emergent plants⟩ ⟨sexually *dimorphic* coloration in birds⟩
**2 :** combining qualities of two kinds of individuals in one

**di·mor·phism** \-,fi-zəm\ *noun* (1832)
**:** the condition or property of being dimorphic or dimorphous: as **a :** the existence of two different forms (as of color or size) of a species especially in the same population ⟨sexual *dimorphism*⟩ **b :** the existence of an organ (as the leaves of a plant) in two different forms

**di·mor·phous** \(,)dī-'mȯr-fəs\ *adjective* [Greek *dimorphos* having two forms, from *di-* + *-morphos* -morphous] (1832)
**1 :** crystallizing in two different forms
**2 :** DIMORPHIC 1b

**dim·out** \'dim-,aút\ *noun* (1942)
**:** a restriction limiting the use or showing of lights at night especially during the threat of

an air raid; *also* **:** a condition of partial darkness produced by this restriction

**¹dim·ple** \'dim-pəl\ *noun* [Middle English *dympull;* akin to Old High German *tumphilo* whirlpool, Old English *dyppan* to dip — more at DIP] (15th century)
**1 :** a slight natural indentation in the surface of some part of the human body
**2 :** a depression or indentation on a surface (as of a golf ball)
— **dim·ply** \-p(ə-)lē\ *adjective*
**²dimple** *verb* **dim·pled; dim·pling** \-p(ə-)liŋ\ (1602)
*transitive verb*
**:** to mark with dimples
*intransitive verb*
**:** to exhibit or form dimples

**dim sum** \'dim-'səm\ *noun* [Chinese (Guangdong) *dímsām,* from *dím* dot, speck + *sām* heart] (1948)
**:** traditional Chinese food consisting of a variety of items (as steamed or fried dumplings, pieces of cooked chicken, and rice balls) served in small portions

**dim-wit** \'dim-,wit\ *noun* (circa 1922)
**:** a stupid or mentally slow person

**dim—wit·ted** \-'wi-təd\ *adjective* (1934)
**:** not mentally bright **:** STUPID
— **dim—wit·ted·ly** *adverb*
— **dim—wit·ted·ness** *noun*

**¹din** \'din\ *noun* [Middle English, from Old English *dyne;* akin to Old Norse *dynr* din, Sanskrit *dhvanati* it roars] (before 12th century)
**1 :** a loud continued noise; *especially* **:** a welter of discordant sounds
**2 :** a situation or condition resembling a din

**²din** *verb* **dinned; din·ning** (before 12th century)
*intransitive verb*
**:** to make a loud noise
*transitive verb*
**1 :** to assail with loud continued noise
**2 :** to impress by insistent repetition — often used with *into*

**di·nar** \di-'när, 'dē-,\ *noun* [Arabic *dīnār,* from Late Greek *dēnarion* denarius, from Latin *denarius* — more at DENIER] (1634)
**1 :** a gold coin formerly used in countries of southwest Asia and north Africa
**2 a** — see MONEY table **b** — see *rial* at MONEY table

**¹dine** \'dīn\ *verb* **dined; din·ing** [Middle English, from Old French *diner,* from (assumed) Vulgar Latin *disjejunare* to break one's fast, from Latin *dis-* + Late Latin *jejunare* to fast, from Latin *jejunus* fasting] (13th century)
*intransitive verb*
**:** to take dinner
*transitive verb*
**:** to give a dinner to

**²dine** *noun* (15th century)
*Scottish* **:** DINNER

**dine out** *intransitive verb* (1816)
**:** to eat a meal away from home
— **dine out on :** to use as a subject for dining table conversation

**din·er** \'dī-nər\ *noun* (1815)
**1 :** one that dines
**2 a :** DINING CAR **b :** a restaurant usually resembling a dining car in shape

**din·er—out** \,dī-nə-'raút\ *noun, plural* **diners—out** \-nər-'zaút\ (1808)
**:** one who dines out

**di·nette** \dī-'net\ *noun* (1925)
**:** a small space usually off a kitchen used for informal dining; *also* **:** furniture for such a space

**¹ding** \'diŋ\ *verb* [probably imitative] (1582)
*transitive verb*
**:** to dwell on with tiresome repetition ⟨keeps *dinging* it into him that the less he smokes the better —Samuel Butler (died 1902)⟩
*intransitive verb*
**1 :** to make a ringing sound **:** CLANG
**2 :** to speak with tiresome reiteration

**²ding** *noun* [*ding* (to strike), from Middle English *dingen*] (circa 1945)
**:** an instance of minor surface damage (as a dent)

**ding—a—ling** \'diŋ-ə-,liŋ\ *noun* [reduplication of ¹*ding*] (circa 1935)
**:** NITWIT, KOOK

**ding·bat** \'diŋ-,bat\ *noun* [origin unknown] (1904)
**1 :** a typographical symbol or ornament (as *, ¶, or ☞)
**2 :** NITWIT, KOOK

**¹ding—dong** \'diŋ-,dòŋ, -,däŋ\ *noun* [imitative] (1611)
**:** the ringing sound produced by repeated strokes especially on a bell

**²dingdong** *intransitive verb* (1659)
**1 :** to make a dingdong sound
**2 :** to repeat a sound or action tediously or insistently

**³dingdong** *adjective* (1792)
**1 :** of, relating to, or resembling the ringing sound made by a bell
**2 :** marked by a rapid exchange or alternation

**dinge** \'dinj\ *noun* [back-formation from *dingy*] (1846)
**:** the condition of being dingy

**ding·er** \'diŋ-ər\ *noun* [perhaps from *ding* (to strike) + ²*-er*] (1974)
**:** HOME RUN

**din·ghy** \'diŋ-ē, -gē\ *noun, plural* **dinghies** [Bengali *ḍiṅgi* & Hindi *ḍiṅgī*] (1810)
**1 :** an East Indian rowboat or sailboat
**2 a :** a small boat carried on or towed behind a larger boat as a tender or a lifeboat **b :** a small sailboat
**3 :** a rubber life raft

**din·gle** \'diŋ-gəl\ *noun* [Middle English, deep hollow] (13th century)
**:** a small wooded valley **:** DELL

**din·gle·ber·ry** \'diŋ-gəl-,ber-ē\ *noun* [origin unknown] (1955)
**:** a piece of dried fecal matter clinging to the hair around the anus

**din·go** \'diŋ-(,)gō\ *noun, plural* **dingoes** [Dharuk (Australian aboriginal language of the Port Jackson area) *ḍiṅgu*] (1789)
**:** a reddish brown wild dog (*Canis dingo*) of Australia

dingo

**din·gus** \'diŋ-(g)əs\ *noun* [Dutch or German; Dutch *dinges,* probably from German *Dings,* from genitive of *Ding* thing, from Old High German — more at THING] (1876)
**:** DOODAD 2

**din·gy** \'din-jē\ *adjective* **din·gi·er; -est** [origin unknown] (circa 1736)
**1 :** DIRTY, DISCOLORED
**2 :** SHABBY, SQUALID
— **din·gi·ly** \-jə-lē\ *adverb*
— **din·gi·ness** \-jē-nəs\ *noun*

**dining car** *noun* (1838)
**:** a railroad car in which meals are served

**dining room** *noun* (1601)
**:** a room used for eating meals

**di·ni·tro** \(,)dī-'nī-trō\ *adjective*
**:** containing two nitro groups — often used in combination

**di·ni·tro·ben·zene** \(,)dī-,nī-trō-'ben-,zēn, -(,)ben-'\ *noun* [International Scientific Vocabulary] (1873)
**:** any of three isomeric toxic compounds $C_6H_4(NO_2)_2$

**di·ni·tro·phe·nol** \-'fē-,nól, -fi-'\ *noun* (circa 1897)
**:** any of six isomeric crystalline compounds $C_6H_4N_2O_5$ some of whose derivatives are pesticides

**¹dink** \'diŋk\ *noun* [by shortening & alteration] (1903)
**:** DINGHY

**²dink** *noun* [*dink* (to hit with a drop shot), probably of imitative origin] (1939)
**:** DROP SHOT

**³dink** *noun* [perhaps from *dink,* disparaging name for a Vietnamese] (1974)
*slang* **:** NITWIT, JERK, NERD

**Din·ka** \'diŋ-kə\ *noun, plural* **Dinkas** *also* **Dinka** (1861)
**1 :** a member of a pastoral people of the Nile Valley in south central Sudan
**2 :** the Nilotic language of the Dinkas

**din·key** *or* **din·ky** \'diŋ-kē\ *noun, plural* **dinkeys** *or* **dinkies** [probably from *dinky*] (1874)
**:** a small locomotive

**¹din·kum** \'diŋ-kəm\ *adjective* [English dialect *dinkum,* noun, work, share of work] (1905)
*Australian & New Zealand* **:** AUTHENTIC, GENUINE — often used with *fair*

**²dinkum** *adverb* (1915)
*Australian & New Zealand* **:** TRULY, HONESTLY — often used with *fair;* often used interjectionally

**din·ky** \'diŋ-kē\ *adjective* **din·ki·er; -est** [Scots *dink* neat] (1880)
**:** SMALL 1a; *also* **:** INSIGNIFICANT

**din·ner** \'di-nər\ *noun, often attributive* [Middle English *diner,* from Old French, from *diner* to dine] (13th century)
**1 a :** the principal meal of the day **b :** a formal feast or banquet
**2 :** TABLE D'HÔTE 2
**3 :** the food prepared for a dinner ⟨eat your *dinner*⟩
**4 :** a packaged meal usually for quick preparation ⟨warmed up a frozen *dinner*⟩
— **din·ner·less** \-ləs\ *adjective*

**dinner jacket** *noun* (1891)
**:** a jacket for formal evening wear

**dinner theater** *noun* (1960)
**:** a restaurant in which a play is presented after the meal is over

**din·ner·time** \'di-nər-,tīm\ *noun* (14th century)
**:** the customary time for dinner

**din·ner·ware** \-,war, -,wer\ *noun* (1895)
**:** tableware other than flatware

**di·no·fla·gel·late** \,dī-nō-'fla-jə-lət, -,lāt; -flə-'je-lət\ *noun* [ultimately from Greek *dinos* rotation, eddy + New Latin *flagellum*] (1889)
**:** any of an order (Dinoflagellata) of chiefly marine planktonic usually solitary unicellular phytoflagellates that include luminescent forms, forms important in marine food chains, and forms causing red tide

**di·no·saur** \'dī-nə-,sór\ *noun* [New Latin *Dinosaurus,* genus name, from Greek *deinos* terrifying + *sauros* lizard — more at DIRE] (1841)
**1 :** any of a group (Dinosauria) of extinct chiefly terrestrial carnivorous or herbivorous reptiles of the Mesozoic era
**2 :** any of various large extinct reptiles other than the true dinosaurs
**3 :** one that is impractically large, out-of-date, or obsolete
— **di·no·sau·ri·an** \,dī-nə-'sór-ē-ən\ *adjective*

**¹dint** \'dint\ *noun* [Middle English, from Old English *dynt;* akin to Old Norse *dyntr* noise] (before 12th century)
**1** *archaic* **:** BLOW, STROKE
**2 :** FORCE, POWER
**3 :** ²DENT
— **by dint of :** by force of **:** BECAUSE OF

**²dint** *transitive verb* (1597)
**1 :** to make a dent in
**2 :** to impress or drive in with force

---

\ə\ abut \ᵊ\ kitten \ər\ further \a\ ash \ā\ ace
\ä\ mop, mar \aú\ out \ch\ chin \e\ bet \ē\ easy
\g\ go \i\ hit \ī\ ice \j\ job \ŋ\ sing \ō\ go
\ó\ law \ói\ boy \th\ thin \t͟h\ the \ü\ loot \ú\ foot
\y\ yet \zh\ vision   *see also* Guide to Pronunciation

**di·nu·cle·o·tide** \(ˌ)dī-'n(y)ü-klē-ə-ˌtīd\ *noun* (circa 1927)
: a nucleotide consisting of two units each composed of a phosphate, a pentose, and a nitrogen base

**di·oc·e·san** \dī-'ä-sə-sən *also* 'dī-ə-ˌsē-sᵊn\ *noun* (15th century)
: a bishop having jurisdiction over a diocese

**di·o·cese** \'dī-ə-səs, -ˌsēs, -ˌsēz\ *noun, plural* **-ces·es** \'dī-ə-sə-səz, -ˌsē-zəz, ÷'dī-ə-ˌsēz\ [Middle English *diocise*, from Middle French, from Late Latin *diocesis*, alteration of *dioecesis*, from Latin, administrative division, from Greek *dioikēsis* administration, administrative division, from *dioikein* to keep house, govern, from *dia-* + *oikein* to dwell, manage, from *oikos* house — more at VICINITY] (14th century)
: the territorial jurisdiction of a bishop
— **di·oc·e·san** \dī-'ä-sə-sən *also* 'dī-ə-ˌsē-sᵊn\ *adjective*

**di·ode** \'dī-ˌōd\ *noun* [International Scientific Vocabulary] (1919)
: an electronic device that has two electrodes or terminals and is used especially as a rectifier

**di·oe·cious** \(ˌ)dī-'ē-shəs\ *adjective* [ultimately from Greek *di-* + *oikos*] (1752)
**1** : having male reproductive organs in one individual and female in another
**2** : having staminate and pistillate flowers borne on different individuals
— **di·oe·cism** \-'ē-ˌsi-zəm\ *noun*
— **di·oe·cy** \'dī-ˌē-sē\ *noun*

**di·ol** \'dī-ˌōl, -ˌól\ *noun* [International Scientific Vocabulary] (1923)
: a compound containing two hydroxyl groups

**di·ole·fin** \dī-'ō-lə-fən\ *noun* [International Scientific Vocabulary] (circa 1909)
: DIENE

**Di·o·me·des** \ˌdī-ə-'mē-dēz\ *noun* [Latin, from Greek *Diomēdēs*]
: one of the Greek heroes of the Trojan War

**Di·o·ny·sia** \ˌdī-ə-'ni-zhē-ə, -'nē-, -shē-, -zē-, -sē-\ *noun plural* [Latin, from Greek, from neuter plural of *dionysios* of Dionysus, from *Dionysos*] (circa 1895)
: ancient Greek festival observances held in seasonal cycles in honor of Dionysus; *especially* : such observances marked by dramatic performances

**Di·o·ny·si·ac** \-'ni-zhē-ˌak, -'nē-, -shē-, -zē-, -sē-\ *adjective* [Latin *dionysiacus*, from Greek *dionysiakos*, from *Dionysos*] (1844)
: DIONYSIAN 2
— **Dionysiac** *noun*

**Di·o·ny·sian** \-'ni-zhē-ən, -'nē-, -shē-, -zē-, -sē-; -zhən, -shən\ *adjective* (1607)
**1 a** : of or relating to Dionysius **b** : of or related to the theological writings once mistakenly attributed to Dionysius the Areopagite
**2 a** : devoted to the worship of Dionysus **b** : characteristic of Dionysus or the cult of worship of Dionysus; *especially* : being of a frenzied or orgiastic character — compare APOLLONIAN

**Di·o·ny·sus** \ˌdī-ə-'nī-səs, -'nē-\ *noun* [Latin, from Greek *Dionysos*]
: BACCHUS

**Di·o·phan·tine equation** \ˌdī-ə-'fan-ˌtīn-, -'fan-tᵊn-\ *noun* [*Diophantus*, 3d century A.D. Greek mathematician] (circa 1928)
: an indeterminate polynomial equation with integral coefficients for which it is required to find all integral solutions

**di·op·side** \dī-'äp-ˌsīd\ *noun* [French, from *di-* + Greek *opsis* appearance — more at OPTIC] (circa 1808)
: a green to white mineral that consists of pyroxene containing little or no aluminum
— **di·op·sid·ic** \ˌdī-ˌäp-'si-dik\ *adjective*

**di·op·ter** \dī-'äp-tər, 'dī-ˌäp-\ *noun* [*diopter* (an optical instrument), from Middle French *dioptre*, from Latin *dioptra*, from Greek, from *dia-* + *opsesthai* to be going to see — more at OPTIC] (circa 1864)
: a unit of measurement of the refractive power of lenses equal to the reciprocal of the focal length in meters

**di·op·tric** \dī-'äp-trik\ *adjective* [Greek *dioptrikos* of a diopter (instrument), from *dioptra*] (1653)
: REFRACTIVE; *specifically* : assisting vision by refracting and focusing light

**di·o·ra·ma** \ˌdī-ə-'ra-mə, -'rä-\ *noun* [French, from *dia-* + *-orama* (as in *panorama*, from English)] (1823)
**1** : a scenic representation in which a partly translucent painting is seen from a distance through an opening
**2 a** : a scenic representation in which sculptured figures and lifelike details are displayed usually in miniature so as to blend indistinguishably with a realistic painted background **b** : a life-size exhibit (as of a wildlife specimen or scene) with realistic natural surroundings and a painted background
— **di·o·ram·ic** \-'ra-mik\ *adjective*

**di·o·rite** \'dī-ə-ˌrīt\ *noun* [French, irregular from Greek *diorizein* to distinguish, from *dia-* + *horizein* to define — more at HORIZON] (1826)
: a granular crystalline igneous rock commonly of acid plagioclase and hornblende, pyroxene, or biotite
— **di·o·rit·ic** \ˌdī-ə-'ri-tik\ *adjective*

**Di·os·cu·ri** \ˌdī-əs-'kyủ(ə)r-ˌī, dī-'äs-kyə-ˌrī\ *noun plural* [New Latin, from Greek *Dioskouroi*, literally, sons of Zeus, from *Dios* (genitive of *Zeus;* akin to Latin *divus* divine) + *kouroi*, plural of *kouros, koros* boy — more at DEITY, CRESCENT]
: the twins Castor and Pollux reunited as stars in the sky by Zeus after Castor's death and regarded as patrons of athletes and sailors

**di·ox·ane** \dī-'äk-ˌsān\ *also* **di·ox·an** \-ˌsan, -sən\ *noun* [International Scientific Vocabulary] (1912)
: a flammable toxic liquid diether $C_4H_8O_2$ used especially as a solvent

**di·ox·ide** \(ˌ)dī-'äk-ˌsīd\ *noun* [International Scientific Vocabulary] (circa 1847)
: an oxide (as carbon dioxide) containing two atoms of oxygen in the molecule

**di·ox·in** \(ˌ)dī-'äk-sən\ *noun* (circa 1919)
: any of several heterocyclic hydrocarbons that occur especially as persistent toxic impurities in herbicides; *especially* : TCDD

**¹dip** \'dip\ *verb* **dipped; dip·ping** [Middle English *dippen*, from Old English *dyppan;* akin to Old High German *tupfen* to wash, Lithuanian *dubus* deep] (before 12th century)
*transitive verb*
**1 a** : to plunge or immerse momentarily or partially under the surface (as of a liquid) so as to moisten, cool, or coat ⟨*dip* candles⟩ **b** : to thrust in a way to suggest immersion **c** : to immerse (as a sheep or dog) in an antiseptic or parasiticidal solution
**2 a** : to lift a portion of by reaching below the surface with something shaped to hold liquid : LADLE **b** : to take a portion of (snuff)
**3 a** *archaic* : INVOLVE **b** : MORTGAGE
**4 a** : to lower and then raise again ⟨*dip* a flag in salute⟩ **b** *chiefly British* : DIM 2
*intransitive verb*
**1 a** : to plunge into a liquid and quickly emerge **b** : to immerse something into a processing liquid or finishing material
**2 a** : to suddenly drop down or out of sight **b** *of an airplane* : to drop suddenly before climbing **c** : to decline or decrease moderately and usually temporarily ⟨prices *dipped*⟩ **d** : to lower the body momentarily especially as part of an athletic or dancing motion
**3 a** : to reach down inside or below or as if inside or below a surface especially to withdraw a part of the contents — used with *into* ⟨*dipped* into the family's savings⟩
**4** : to examine or read something casually or superficially — used with *into*

**5** : to incline downward from the plane of the horizon
— **dip·pa·ble** \'di-pə-bəl\ *adjective*

**²dip** *noun* (1599)
**1** : an act of dipping; *especially* : a brief plunge into the water for sport or exercise
**2** : inclination downward: **a** : PITCH **b** : a sharp downward course : DROP **c** : the angle that a stratum or similar geological feature makes with a horizontal plane
**3** : the angle formed with the horizon by a magnetic needle free to rotate in the vertical plane
**4** : HOLLOW, DEPRESSION
**5** : something obtained by or used in dipping
**6 a** : a sauce or soft mixture into which food may be dipped **b** : a liquid preparation for the dipping of something; *especially* : an insecticide or parasiticide for the dipping of animals — compare SHEEP-DIP
**7** *slang* : PICKPOCKET
**8** : a stupid or unsophisticated person

**di·pep·ti·dase** \dī-'pep-tə-ˌdās, -ˌdāz\ *noun* (1927)
: any of various enzymes that hydrolyze dipeptides but not polypeptides

**di·pep·tide** \(ˌ)dī-'pep-ˌtīd\ *noun* (1903)
: a peptide that yields two molecules of amino acid on hydrolysis

**di·pha·sic** \(ˌ)dī-'fā-zik\ *adjective* (1881)
: having two phases

**di·phen·hy·dra·mine** \ˌdī-ˌfen-'hī-drə-ˌmēn\ *noun* (1948)
: an antihistamine $C_{17}H_{21}NO$ used especially in the form of its hydrochloride to treat allergy symptoms and motion sickness

**di·phe·nyl·amine** \(ˌ)dī-ˌfe-nᵊl-ə-'mēn, -ˌfē-, -nᵊl-'a-mən\ *noun* [International Scientific Vocabulary] (1872)
: a crystalline pleasant-smelling compound $(C_6H_5)_2NH$ used chiefly in the manufacture of dyes and as an indicator

**di·phe·nyl·hy·dan·to·in** \-hī-'dan-tə-wən\ *noun* [*di-* + *phenyl* + *hyd*rogen + all*antoin*] (1937)
: PHENYTOIN

**di·phos·gene** \(ˌ)dī-'fäz-ˌjēn\ *noun* [International Scientific Vocabulary] (circa 1922)
: a liquid compound $C_2Cl_4O_2$ used as a poison gas in World War I

**di·phos·phate** \(ˌ)dī-'fäs-ˌfāt\ *noun* (1826)
: a phosphate containing two phosphate groups

**di·phos·pho·glyc·er·ic acid** \(ˌ)dī-'fäs-fō-gli-ˌser-ik-\ *noun* (1959)
: a diphosphate of glyceric acid that is an important intermediate in photosynthesis and in glycolysis and fermentation

**di·phos·pho·pyr·i·dine nucleotide** \-ˌpir-ə-ˌdēn-\ *noun* (1938)
: NAD

**diph·the·ria** \dif-'thir-ē-ə, ÷dip-\ *noun* [New Latin, from French *diphthérie*, from Greek *diphthera* leather; from the toughness of the false membrane] (circa 1851)
: an acute febrile contagious disease marked by the formation of a false membrane especially in the throat and caused by a bacterium (*Corynebacterium diphtheriae*) that produces a toxin causing inflammation of the heart and nervous system
— **diph·the·ri·al** \-ē-əl\ *adjective*
— **diph·the·rit·ic** \ˌdif-thə-'ri-tik, ÷ˌdip-\ *adjective*

**¹diph·the·roid** \'dif-thə-ˌróid\ *adjective* (1861)
: resembling diphtheria

**²diphtheroid** *noun* (1908)
: a bacterium (especially genus *Corynebacterium*) that resembles the bacterium of diphtheria but does not produce diphtheria toxin

**diph·thong** \'dif-ˌthón, 'dip-\ *noun* [Middle English *diptonge*, from Middle French *diptongue*, from Late Latin *dipthongus*, from Greek *diphthongos*, from *di-* + *phthongos* voice, sound] (15th century)

**1 :** a gliding monosyllabic speech sound (as the vowel combination at the end of *toy*) that starts at or near the articulatory position for one vowel and moves to or toward the position of another
**2 :** DIGRAPH
**3 :** the ligature æ or œ
— **diph·thon·gal** \dif-'thŏŋ-(g)əl, dip-\ *adjective*

**diph·thong·i·za·tion** \(͵)dif-͵thŏŋ-ə-'zā-shən, (͵)dip-\ *noun* (1874)
**:** the act of diphthongizing **:** the state of being diphthongized

**diph·thong·ize** \'dif-͵thŏŋ-͵īz, 'dip-\ *verb* **-ized; -iz·ing** (1867)
*intransitive verb*
*of a simple vowel* **:** to change into a diphthong
*transitive verb*
**:** to pronounce as a diphthong

**diphy-** *or* **diphyo-** *combining form* [New Latin, from Greek *diphy-*, from *diphyēs*, from *di-* + *phyein* to bring forth — more at BE]
**:** double **:** bipartite ⟨*diphy*odont⟩

**di·phy·let·ic** \͵dī-fī-'le-tik\ *adjective* (1902)
**:** derived from two lines of evolutionary descent ⟨*diphyletic* dinosaurs⟩

**di·phy·odont** \(͵)dī-'fī-ə-͵dänt\ *adjective* [International Scientific Vocabulary] (1854)
**:** marked by the successive development of deciduous and permanent sets of teeth

**dipl-** *or* **diplo-** *combining form* [Greek, from *diploos* — more at DOUBLE]
**1 :** double **:** twofold ⟨*diplo*pia⟩
**2 :** diploid ⟨*diplo*phase⟩

**di·ple·gia** \dī-'plē-j(ē-)ə\ *noun* [New Latin] (circa 1881)
**:** paralysis of corresponding parts on both sides of the body

**dip·lo·blas·tic** \͵dip-lō-'blas-tik\ *adjective* (circa 1885)
**:** having two germ layers — used of an embryo or lower invertebrate that lacks a true mesoderm

**dip·lo·coc·cus** \-'kä-kəs\ *noun* [New Latin, genus name] (circa 1881)
**:** any of various encapsulated bacteria (as *Streptococcus pneumoniae,* a common cause of pneumonia) that usually occur in pairs and that were formerly grouped in a single taxon (genus *Diplococcus*) but are now all assigned to other genera

**di·plod·o·cus** \də-'plä-də-kəs, dī-\ *noun* [New Latin, genus name, from *dipl-* + Greek *dokos* beam, from *dekesthai, dechesthai* to receive; akin to Latin *decēre* to be fitting — more at DECENT] (1928)
**:** any of a genus (*Diplodocus*) of large herbivorous sauropod dinosaurs of the late Jurassic period in Colorado and Wyoming

**dip·loe** \'di-plə-͵wē\ *noun* [New Latin, from Greek *diploē,* from *diploos* double] (circa 1696)
**:** cancellous bony tissue between the external and internal layers of the skull
— **di·plo·ic** \di-'plō-ik, -'plō-\ *adjective*

**¹dip·loid** \'di-͵plŏid\ *adjective* [International Scientific Vocabulary] (1908)
**:** having the basic chromosome number doubled
— **dip·loi·dy** \-͵plŏi-dē\ *noun*

**²diploid** *noun* (1908)
**:** a single cell, individual, or generation characterized by the diploid chromosome number

**di·plo·ma** \də-'plō-mə\ *noun, plural* **diplomas** [Latin, passport, diploma, from Greek *diplōma* folded paper, passport, from *diploun* to double, from *diploos*] (1622)
**1** *plural also* **di·plo·ma·ta** \-mə-tə\ **:** an official or state document **:** CHARTER
**2 :** a writing usually under seal conferring some honor or privilege
**3 :** a document bearing record of graduation from or of a degree conferred by an educational institution

**di·plo·ma·cy** \də-'plō-mə-sē\ *noun* (1796)

**1 :** the art and practice of conducting negotiations between nations
**2 :** skill in handling affairs without arousing hostility **:** TACT

**diploma mill** *noun* (1914)
**:** a usually unregulated institution of higher education granting degrees with few or no academic requirements

**dip·lo·mat** \'di-plə-͵mat\ *noun* [French *diplomate,* back-formation from *diplomatique*] (1813)
**:** one employed or skilled in diplomacy

**dip·lo·mate** \'di-plə-͵māt\ *noun* (1879)
**:** one who holds a diploma; *especially* **:** a physician qualified to practice in a medical specialty by advanced training and experience in the specialty followed by passing an intensive examination by a national board of senior specialists

**dip·lo·mat·ic** \͵di-plə-'ma-tik\ *adjective* [in sense 1, from New Latin *diplomaticus,* from Latin *diplomat-, diploma;* in other senses, from French *diplomatique* connected with documents regulating international relations, from New Latin *diplomaticus*] (1711)
**1 a :** PALEOGRAPHIC **b :** exactly reproducing the original ⟨a *diplomatic* edition⟩
**2 :** of, relating to, or concerned with diplomacy or diplomats ⟨*diplomatic* relations⟩
**3 :** employing tact and conciliation especially in situations of stress
**synonym** see SUAVE
— **dip·lo·mat·i·cal·ly** \-ti-k(ə-)lē\ *adverb*

**di·plo·ma·tist** \də-'plō-mə-tist\ *noun* (1815)
**:** DIPLOMAT

**dip·lont** \'di-͵plänt\ *noun* [International Scientific Vocabulary] (1925)
**:** an organism with somatic cells having the diploid chromosome number — compare HAPLONT
— **dip·lon·tic** \di-'plän-tik\ *adjective*

**dip·lo·phase** \'di-plə-͵fāz\ *noun* (circa 1925)
**:** a diploid phase in a life cycle

**dip·lo·pia** \di-'plō-pē-ə\ *noun* [New Latin] (circa 1811)
**:** a disorder of vision in which two images of a single object are seen because of unequal action of the eye muscles — called also *double vision*
— **dip·lo·pic** \-'plō-pik, -'plä-pik\ *adjective*

**dip·lo·pod** \'di-plə-͵päd\ *noun* [ultimately from Greek *dipl-* + *pod-, pous* foot — more at FOOT] (circa 1864)
**:** MILLIPEDE

**dip·lo·tene** \'di-plə-͵tēn\ *noun* [International Scientific Vocabulary] (1925)
**:** a stage of meiotic prophase which follows the pachytene and during which the paired homologous chromosomes begin to separate and chiasmata become visible
— **diplotene** *adjective*

**dip net** *noun* (1820)
**:** a bag net with a handle that is used especially to scoop fish from the water
— **dip·net** \'dip-͵net\ *transitive verb*

**dip·no·an** \'dip-nə-wən\ *adjective* [ultimately from Greek *dipnoos* having two breathing apertures, from *di-* + *pnoē* breath, from *pnein* to breathe — more at SNEEZE] (1883)
**:** of or relating to a group (Dipnoi) of fishes with pulmonary circulation, gills, and lungs
— **dipnoan** *noun*

**dip·o·dy** \'di-pə-dē\ *noun, plural* **-dies** [Late Latin *dipodia,* from Greek, from *dipod-, dipous* having two feet, from *di-* + *pod-, pous*] (circa 1844)
**:** a prosodic unit or measure of two feet
— **di·pod·ic** \dī-'pä-dik\ *adjective*

**di·pole** \'dī-͵pōl\ *noun* [International Scientific Vocabulary] (1912)
**1 a :** a pair of equal and opposite electric charges or magnetic poles of opposite sign separated especially by a small distance **b :** a body or system (as a molecule) having such charges

**2 :** a radio antenna consisting of two horizontal rods in line with each other with their ends slightly separated
— **di·po·lar** \'dī-͵pō-lər, ͵dī-'pō-\ *adjective*

**dipole moment** *noun* (1926)
**:** the product of the distance between the two poles (as magnetic or electric) of a dipole and the magnitude of either pole

**dip·per** \'di-pər\ *noun* (1611)
**1 :** one that dips: as **a :** a worker who dips articles **b :** something (as a long-handled cup) used for dipping **c** *slang* **:** PICKPOCKET
**2 :** any of a genus (*Cinclus* and especially *C. cinclus* of the Old World and *C. mexicanus* of North America) of birds that comprise an oscine family (Cinclidae) related to the thrushes and including individuals that are not web-footed but dive into swift mountain streams and walk on the bottom in search of food — called also *water ouzel*
**3** *capitalized* **:** a group of stars that resembles a dipper: as **a :** BIG DIPPER **b :** LITTLE DIPPER
— **dip·per·ful** \-͵fůl\ *noun*

**dip·py** \'di-pē\ *adjective* **dip·pi·er; -est** [origin unknown] (1911)
**:** FOOLISH

**dip·so** \'dip-(͵)sō\ *noun, plural* **dipsos** [by shortening] (1880)
**:** one affected with dipsomania

**dip·so·ma·nia** \͵dip-sə-'mā-nē-ə, -nyə\ *noun* [New Latin, from Greek *dipsa* thirst + Late Latin *mania*] (circa 1844)
**:** an uncontrollable craving for alcoholic liquors
— **dip·so·ma·ni·ac** \-nē-͵ak\ *noun*
— **dip·so·ma·ni·a·cal** \͵dip-sō-mə-'nī-ə-kəl\ *adjective*

**dip·stick** \'dip-͵stik\ *noun* (1927)
**:** a graduated rod for indicating depth (as of oil in a crankcase)

**dip·ter·an** \'dip-tə-rən\ *adjective* [ultimately from Greek *dipteros* two-winged, from *di-* + *pteron* wing — more at FEATHER] (circa 1842)
**:** of, relating to, or being a fly (sense 2a)
— **dipteran** *noun*
— **dip·ter·ous** \'dip-t(ə-)rəs\ *adjective*

**dip·tero·carp** \'dip-tə-rō-͵kärp\ *noun* [ultimately from Greek *dipteros* + *-karpos* -carpous] (circa 1876)
**:** any of a family (Dipterocarpaceae) of tall hardwood trees of tropical Asia, Indonesia, and the Philippines that have a 2-winged fruit and are the source of valuable timber, aromatic oils, and resins; *especially* **:** a member of the type genus (*Dipterocarpus*)

**dip·ter·on** \'dip-tə-͵rän\ *noun, plural* **-tera** \-rə\ [Greek, neuter of *dipteros*] (circa 1891)
**:** ⁴FLY 2a

**dip·tych** \'dip-(͵)tik\ *noun* [Late Latin *diptycha,* plural, from Greek, from neuter plural of *diptychos* folded in two, from *di-* + *ptychē* fold] (1622)
**1 :** a 2-leaved hinged tablet folding together to protect writing on its waxed surfaces
**2 :** a picture or series of pictures (as an altarpiece) painted or carved on two hinged tablets
**3 :** a work made up of two matching parts

**di·quat** \'dī-͵kwät\ *noun* [*di-* + *quat*ernary] (1960)
**:** a powerful nonpersistent herbicide $C_{12}H_{12}Br_2N_2$ that has been used to control water weeds (as the water hyacinth)

**diptych 2**

**dir·dum** \'dir-dəm, 'dər-\ *noun* [Middle English (northern dialect) *durdan, durdum* uproar, from Celtic; akin to Welsh *dwrdd* noise, clamor, Middle Irish *dordán* humming, droning] (circa 1693)
*Scottish* : BLAME

**dire** \'dīr\ *adjective* **dir·er; dir·est** [Latin *dirus;* akin to Greek *deinos* terrifying, Sanskrit *dveṣṭi* he hates] (1567)
**1 a** : exciting horror ⟨*dire* suffering⟩ **b** : DISMAL, OPPRESSIVE ⟨*dire* days⟩
**2** : warning of disaster ⟨a *dire* forecast⟩
**3 a** : desperately urgent ⟨*dire* need⟩ **b** : EXTREME ⟨*dire* poverty⟩
— **dire·ly** *adverb*
— **dire·ness** *noun*

**¹di·rect** \də-'rekt, dī-\ *verb* [Middle English, from Latin *directus* straight, from past participle of *dirigere* to direct — more at DRESS] (14th century)
*transitive verb*
**1 a** *obsolete* : to write (a letter) to a person **b** : to mark with the name and address of the intended recipient **c** : to impart orally **d** : to adapt in expression so as to have particular applicability ⟨a lawyer who *directs* his appeals to intelligence⟩
**2 a** : to regulate the activities or course of **b** : to carry out the organizing, energizing, and supervising of **c** : to dominate and determine the course of **d** : to train and lead performances of
**3** : to cause to turn, move, or point undeviatingly or to follow a straight course ⟨X rays are *directed* through the body⟩
**4** : to point, extend, or project in a specified line or course
**5** : to request or enjoin with authority
**6** : to show or point out the way for
*intransitive verb*
**1** : to point out, prescribe, or determine a course or procedure
**2** : to act as director
**synonym** see COMMAND, CONDUCT

**²direct** *adjective* [Middle English, from Latin *directus*] (15th century)
**1** *of a celestial body* : moving in the general planetary direction from west to east : not retrograde
**2 a** : stemming immediately from a source ⟨*direct* result⟩ **b** : being or passing in a straight line of descent from parent to offspring : LINEAL ⟨*direct* ancestor⟩ **c** : having no compromising or impairing element ⟨*direct* insult⟩
**3 a** : proceeding from one point to another in time or space without deviation or interruption : STRAIGHT **b** : proceeding by the shortest way ⟨the *direct* route⟩
**4** : NATURAL, STRAIGHTFORWARD ⟨*direct* manner⟩
**5 a** : marked by absence of an intervening agency, instrumentality, or influence **b** : effected by the action of the people or the electorate and not by representatives ⟨*direct* democracy⟩ **c** : consisting of or reproducing the exact words of a speaker or writer
**6** : characterized by close logical, causal, or consequential relationship ⟨*direct* evidence⟩
**7** : capable of dyeing without the aid of a mordant

**³direct** *adverb* (14th century)
: in a direct way: as **a** : from point to point without deviation : by the shortest way ⟨flew *direct* to Miami⟩ **b** : from the source without interruption or diversion ⟨the writer must take his material *direct* from life —Douglas Stewart⟩ **c** : without an intervening agency or step ⟨buy *direct* from the manufacturer⟩

**direct action** *noun* (1912)
: action that seeks to achieve an end directly and by the most immediately effective means (as boycott or strike)

**direct current** *noun* (circa 1889)
: an electric current flowing in one direction only and substantially constant in value — abbreviation *DC*

**di·rect·ed** *adjective* (1891)
**1** : subject to supervision or regulation ⟨a *directed* reading program for students⟩
**2** : having a positive or negative sense ⟨*directed* line segment⟩
— **di·rect·ed·ness** *noun*

**direct examination** *noun* (circa 1859)
: the first examination of a witness by the party calling the witness — compare CROSS-EXAMINATION

**di·rec·tion** \də-'rek-shən, dī-\ *noun* (15th century)
**1** : guidance or supervision of action or conduct : MANAGEMENT
**2** *archaic* : SUPERSCRIPTION
**3 a** : an explicit instruction : ORDER **b** : assistance in pointing out the proper route — usually used in plural ⟨asked for *directions* to the beach⟩
**4** : the line or course on which something is moving or is aimed to move or along which something is pointing or facing
**5** *archaic* : DIRECTORATE 1
**6 a** : a channel or direct course of thought or action **b** : TENDENCY, TREND **c** : a guiding, governing, or motivating purpose
**7 a** : the art and technique of directing an orchestra, band, or a show (as for stage or screen) **b** : a word, phrase, or sign indicating the appropriate tempo, mood, or intensity of a passage or movement in music
— **di·rec·tion·less** \-ləs\ *adjective*
— **di·rec·tion·less·ness** \-nəs\ *noun*

**di·rec·tion·al** \-shnəl, -shə-n⁰l\ *adjective* (1881)
**1** : of, relating to, or indicating direction in space: **a** : suitable for detecting the direction from which radio signals come or for sending out radio signals in one direction only **b** : operating most effectively in a particular direction
**2** : relating to direction or guidance especially of thought or effort
— **di·rec·tion·al·i·ty** \-,rek-shə-'na-lə-tē\ *noun*

**direction angle** *noun* (circa 1909)
: an angle made by a given line with an axis of reference; *specifically* : such an angle made by a straight line with the three axes of a rectangular Cartesian coordinate system — usually used in plural

**direction cosine** *noun* (circa 1889)
: any of the cosines of the three angles between a directed line in space and the positive direction of the axes of a rectangular Cartesian coordinate system — usually used in plural

**direction finder** *noun* (1913)
: a radio receiving device for determining the direction of incoming radio waves that typically consists of a coil antenna rotating freely on a vertical axis

**¹di·rec·tive** \də-'rek-tiv, dī-\ *adjective* (15th century)
**1** : serving or intended to guide, govern, or influence
**2** : serving to point direction; *specifically* : DIRECTIONAL 1b
**3** : of or relating to psychotherapy or counseling in which the counselor introduces information, content, or attitudes not previously expressed by the client

**²directive** *noun* (1902)
: something that serves to direct, guide, and usually impel toward an action or goal; *especially* : an authoritative instrument issued by a high-level body or official

**di·rec·tiv·i·ty** \də-,rek-'ti-və-tē, (,)dī-\ *noun* (1928)
: the property of being directional

**direct lighting** *noun* (1928)
: lighting in which the greater part of the light goes directly from the source to the area lit

**¹di·rect·ly** \də-'rek(t)-lē, dī-, *in sense 2 especially* də-'rek-lē *or* 'drek-lē\ *adverb* (15th century)

**1 a** : in a direct manner ⟨*directly* relevant⟩ ⟨the road runs *directly* east and west⟩ **b** : in immediate physical contact **c** : in the manner of direct variation
**2 a** : without delay : IMMEDIATELY **b** : in a little while : SHORTLY

**²di·rect·ly** \də-'rek(t)-lē, dī-; 'drek-lē\ *conjunction* (1795)
*chiefly British* : immediately after : AS SOON AS ⟨*directly* I received it I rang up the shipping company —F. W. Crofts⟩

**directly proportional** *noun* (1796)
: related by direct variation — compare INVERSELY PROPORTIONAL

**direct mail** *noun* (circa 1923)
: printed matter (as circulars) prepared for soliciting business or contributions and mailed directly to individuals

**di·rect·ness** \də-'rek(t)-nəs, dī-\ *noun* (1598)
**1** : the character of being accurate in course or aim
**2** : strict pertinence : STRAIGHTFORWARDNESS ⟨her *directness* was disarming —Robin Cook⟩

**direct object** *noun* (1879)
: a word or phrase denoting the goal or the result of the action of a verb

**Di·rec·toire** \dē-(,)rek-'twä(r), -'rek-,\ *adjective* [French, from *Directoire,* the group of five officials who governed France from 1795–99, from *directeur* director] (1878)
: of, relating to, or imitative of the style of clothing, furniture, or decoration prevalent in France during the period of the Directory

**di·rec·tor** \də-'rek-tər, dī-\ *noun* (15th century)
: one that directs: as **a** : the head of an organized group or administrative unit (as a bureau or school) **b** : one of a group of persons entrusted with the overall direction of a corporate enterprise **c** : one that supervises the production of a show (as for stage or screen) usually with responsibility for action, lighting, music, and rehearsals **d** : CONDUCTOR c
— **di·rec·tor·ship** \-,ship\ *noun*

**di·rec·tor·ate** \də-'rek-t(ə-)rət, dī-\ *noun* (1837)
**1** : the office of director
**2 a** : a board of directors (as of a corporation) **b** : membership on a board of directors
**3** : an executive staff (as of a department)

**di·rec·to·ri·al** \də-,rek-'tōr-ē-əl, (,)dī-, -'tor-\ *adjective* (1770)
**1** : serving to direct
**2** : of or relating to a director or to theatrical or motion-picture direction
**3** : of, relating to, or administered by a directory

**director's chair** *noun* [from its use by motion-picture directors on the set] (1953)
: a lightweight folding armchair with a back and seat usually of cotton duck

**¹di·rec·to·ry** \də-'rek-t(ə-)rē, dī-\ *adjective* (15th century)
: serving to direct; *specifically* : providing advisory but not compulsory guidance

**²directory** *noun, plural* **-ries** [Middle English *directorie* guide, from Medieval Latin

**director's chair**

*directorium,* from neuter of Late Latin *directorius* directorial, from Latin *dirigere*] (1543)
**1 a** : a book or collection of directions, rules, or ordinances **b** : an alphabetical or classified list (as of names and addresses)
**2** : a body of directors

**direct primary** *noun* (1900)
: a primary in which nominations of candidates for office are made by direct vote

**direct product** *noun* (circa 1925)
: CARTESIAN PRODUCT; *especially* : a group that is the Cartesian product of two other groups

**di·rec·tress** \də-'rek-trəs, dī-\ *noun* (1580)
: a woman who is a director

**di·rec·trice** \də-,rek-'trēs\ *noun* [French, from Medieval Latin *directric-, directrix*] (1631)
: DIRECTRESS

**di·rec·trix** \-'rek-triks\ *noun, plural* **-trix·es** \-trik-səz\ *also* **-tri·ces** \-trə-,sēz\ [Medieval Latin, feminine of Late Latin *director,* from Latin *dirigere*] (1622)
**1** *archaic* : DIRECTRESS
**2** : a fixed curve with which a generatrix maintains a given relationship in generating a geometric figure; *specifically* : a straight line the distance to which from any point of a conic section is in fixed ratio to the distance from the same point to a focus

**direct sum** *noun* (circa 1928)
: CARTESIAN PRODUCT — compare DIRECT PRODUCT

**direct tax** *noun* (1801)
: a tax exacted directly from the taxpayer

**direct variation** *noun* (1949)
**1** : mathematical relationship between two variables that can be expressed by an equation in which one variable is equal to a constant times the other
**2** : an equation or function expressing direct variation — compare INVERSE VARIATION

**dire·ful** \'dīr-fəl\ *adjective* (1583)
**1** : DREADFUL
**2** : OMINOUS
— **dire·ful·ly** \-fə-lē\ *adverb*

**dire wolf** *noun* (1925)
: a large extinct lupine mammal (*Canis dirus*) known from Pleistocene deposits of North America

**dirge** \'dərj\ *noun* [Middle English *dirige,* the Office of the Dead, from the first word of a Late Latin antiphon, from Latin, imperative of *dirigere* to direct — more at DRESS] (13th century)
**1** : a song or hymn of grief or lamentation; *especially* : one intended to accompany funeral or memorial rites
**2** : a slow, solemn, and mournful piece of music
**3** : something (as a poem) that has the qualities of a dirge ◆
— **dirge·like** \-,līk\ *adjective*

**dir·ham** \'dir-həm\ *noun* [Arabic, from Latin *drachma* drachma] (1788)
**1** — see MONEY table
**2** — see *dinar, riyal* at MONEY table

**¹di·ri·gi·ble** \'dir-ə-jə-bəl, də-'ri-jə-\ *adjective* [Latin *dirigere*] (1581)
: capable of being steered

**²dirigible** *noun* [*dirigible (balloon)*] (1885)
: AIRSHIP

**di·ri·gisme** \di-ri-'zhi-z⁵m, dē-rē-zhēs-m⁵\ *noun* [French, from *dirig*er to direct (from Latin *dirigere*) + *-isme* -ism] (1947)
: economic planning and control by the state
— **di·ri·giste** \di-ri-'zhēst, dē-rē-\ *adjective*

**¹dirk** \'dərk\ *noun* [Scots *durk*] (1557)
: a long straight-bladed dagger

**²dirk** *transitive verb* (1599)
: to stab with a dirk

**dirl** \'dir(-ə)l, 'dərl\ *intransitive verb* [perhaps alteration of *thirl*] (1715)
*Scottish* : TREMBLE, QUIVER

**dirndl** \'dərn-d⁵l\ *noun* [short for German *Dirndlkleid,* from German dialect *Dirndl* girl + German *Kleid* dress] (1937)
**1** : a dress style with tight bodice, short sleeves, low neck, and gathered skirt
**2** : a full skirt with a tight waistband

**dirt** \'dərt\ *noun* [Middle English *drit,* from Old Norse; akin to Old English *drītan* to defecate] (13th century)
**1 a** : EXCREMENT **b** : a filthy or soiling substance (as mud, dust, or grime) **c** *archaic* : something worthless **d** : a contemptible person
**2** : loose or packed soil or sand : EARTH

**3 a** : an abject or filthy state : SQUALOR **b** : CORRUPTION, CHICANERY **c** : licentiousness of language or theme **d** : scandalous or malicious gossip **e** : embarrassing or incriminating information

**dirt·bag** \'dərt-,bag\ *noun* (circa 1967)
*slang* : a dirty, unkempt, or contemptible person

**dirt bike** *noun* (1970)
: a usually lightweight motorcycle designed for operation on unpaved surfaces

**dirt cheap** *adjective or adverb* (1821)
: exceedingly cheap

**dirt farmer** *noun* (1920)
: a farmer who earns his living by farming his own land especially without the help of hired hands or tenants

**dirt–poor** \'dərt-'pùr\ *adjective* (1937)
: suffering extreme poverty

**¹dirty** \'dər-tē\ *adjective* **dirt·i·er; -est** (14th century)
**1 a** : not clean or pure ⟨*dirty* clothes⟩ **b** : likely to befoul or defile with dirt ⟨*dirty* jobs⟩ **c** : tedious, disagreeable, and unrecognized or thankless ⟨had to do the *dirty* work⟩ **d** : contaminated with infecting organisms ⟨*dirty* wounds⟩ **e** : containing impurities ⟨*dirty* coal⟩
**2 a** : morally unclean or corrupt: as (1) : INDECENT, VULGAR ⟨*dirty* jokes⟩ ⟨a *dirty* movie⟩ (2) : DISHONORABLE, BASE ⟨*dirty* tricks⟩ (3) : UNSPORTSMANLIKE ⟨*dirty* players⟩ **b** : acquired by disreputable or illegal means : ILL-GOTTEN ⟨*dirty* money⟩
**3 a** : ABOMINABLE, HATEFUL ⟨war is a *dirty* business⟩ **b** : highly regrettable ⟨a *dirty* shame⟩
**4** : FOGGY, STORMY ⟨*dirty* weather⟩
**5 a** *of color* : not clear and bright : DULLISH ⟨*dirty* blond⟩ **b** : characterized by a husky, rasping, or raw tonal quality ⟨*dirty* trumpet tones⟩
**6** : conveying ill-natured resentment ⟨gave him a *dirty* look⟩
**7** : having considerable fallout ⟨*dirty* bombs⟩ ☆
— **dirt·i·ly** \'dər-t⁵l-ē\ *adverb*
— **dirt·i·ness** \'dər-tē-nəs\ *noun*

**²dirty** *adverb* **dirt·i·er; -est** (circa 1934)
: in a dirty manner: as **a** : DECEPTIVELY, UNDERHANDEDLY ⟨fight *dirty*⟩ **b** : INDECENTLY ⟨talk *dirty*⟩

**³dirty** *verb* **dirt·ied; dirty·ing** (1591)
*transitive verb*
**1** : to make dirty
**2 a** : to stain with dishonor : SULLY **b** : to debase by distorting the real nature of
*intransitive verb*
: to become soiled

**dirty linen** *noun* (1946)
: private matters whose public exposure brings distress and embarrassment — called also *dirty laundry*

**dirty old man** *noun* (1932)
: a lecherous older man

**dirty pool** *noun* (1940)
: underhanded or unsportsmanlike conduct

**dirty rice** *noun* (circa 1967)
: a Cajun dish of white rice cooked with chopped or ground giblets

**dirty word** *noun* (1842)
: a word, expression, or idea that is disagreeable or unpopular in a particular frame of reference

**dis** \'dis\ *transitive verb* **dissed; dis·sing** [perhaps short for *disrespect*] (1986)
**1** *slang* : to treat with disrespect or contempt : INSULT
**2** *slang* : to find fault with : CRITICIZE

**Dis** \'dis\ *noun* [Latin]
: the Roman god of the underworld — compare PLUTO

**dis-** *prefix* [Middle English *dis-, des-,* from Old French & Latin; Old French *des-, dis-,* from Latin *dis-,* literally, apart; akin to Old English *te-* apart, Latin *duo* two — more at TWO]
**1 a** : do the opposite of ⟨*dis*establish⟩ **b** : deprive of (a specified quality, rank, or object)

⟨*dis*franchise⟩ **c** : exclude or expel from ⟨*dis*bar⟩
**2** : opposite or absence of ⟨*dis*union⟩ ⟨*dis*affection⟩
**3** : not ⟨*dis*agreeable⟩
**4** : completely ⟨*dis*annul⟩
**5** [by folk etymology] : DYS- ⟨*dis*function⟩

**dis·abil·i·ty** \,di-sə-'bi-lə-tē\ *noun* (1580)
**1 a** : the condition of being disabled **b** : inability to pursue an occupation because of physical or mental impairment
**2** : lack of legal qualification to do something
**3** : a disqualification, restriction, or disadvantage

**dis·able** \di-'sā-bəl, di-'zā-\ *transitive verb* **dis·abled; dis·abling** \-b(ə-)liŋ\ (15th century)
**1** : to deprive of legal right, qualification, or capacity
**2** : to make incapable or ineffective; *especially* : to deprive of physical, moral, or intellectual strength
*synonym* see WEAKEN
— **dis·able·ment** \-bəl-mənt\ *noun*

**dis·abled** *adjective* (1633)

---

☆ **SYNONYMS**
**Dirty, filthy, foul, nasty, squalid** mean conspicuously unclean or impure. DIRTY emphasizes the presence of dirt more than an emotional reaction to it ⟨a *dirty* littered street⟩. FILTHY carries a strong suggestion of offensiveness and typically of gradually accumulated dirt that begrimes and besmears ⟨a stained greasy floor, utterly *filthy*⟩. FOUL implies extreme offensiveness and an accumulation of what is rotten or stinking ⟨a *foul*-smelling open sewer⟩. NASTY applies to what is actually foul or is repugnant to one expecting freshness, cleanliness, or sweetness ⟨it's a *nasty* job to clean up after a sick cat⟩. In practice, *nasty* is often weakened to the point of being no more than a synonym of *unpleasant* or *disagreeable* ⟨had a *nasty* fall⟩ ⟨his answer gave her a *nasty* shock⟩. SQUALID adds to the idea of dirtiness and filth that of slovenly neglect ⟨*squalid* slums⟩. All these terms are also applicable to moral uncleanness or baseness or obscenity. DIRTY then stresses meanness or despicableness ⟨don't ask me to do your *dirty* work⟩, while FILTHY and FOUL describe disgusting obscenity or loathsome behavior ⟨*filthy* street language⟩ ⟨a *foul* story of lust and greed⟩, and NASTY implies a peculiarly offensive unpleasantness ⟨a stand-up comedian known for *nasty* humor⟩. Distinctively, SQUALID implies sordidness as well as baseness and dirtiness ⟨engaged in a series of *squalid* affairs⟩.

---

◇ **WORD HISTORY**
**dirge** *Dirge* is a borrowed word whose English meaning is derived from its use, as distinct from its meaning, in its original language. *Dirge* and its earlier form *dirige,* meaning "a song or hymn of mourning," come from the first word of a Latin chant used in the church service for the dead: "Dirige, Domine deus meus, in conspectu tuo viam meam." ("Direct, O Lord my God, my way in thy sight.") Because hymns and chants were often referred to by their first words, *dirge* became the common word for this chant. Later it was used for any slow, solemn piece of music.

---

\ə\ abut \⁵\ kitten \ər\ further \a\ ash \ā\ ace \ä\ mop, mar \aù\ out \ch\ chin \e\ bet \ē\ easy \g\ go \i\ hit \ī\ ice \j\ job \ŋ\ sing \ō\ go \ò\ law \òi\ boy \th\ thin \t̲h\ the \ü\ loot \ù\ foot \y\ yet \zh\ vision *see also* Guide to Pronunciation

: incapacitated by illness, injury, or wounds;
*broadly* : physically or mentally impaired

**dis·abuse** \,di-sə-'byüz\ *transitive verb*
[French *désabuser*, from *dés-* dis- + *abuser* to
abuse] (1611)
: to free from error, fallacy, or misconception

**di·sac·cha·ri·dase** \(,)dī-'sa-kə-rə-,dās,
-,dāz\ *noun* (1961)
: an enzyme (as maltase or lactase) that hydrolyzes disaccharides

**di·sac·cha·ride** \(,)dī-'sa-kə-,rīd\ *noun*
(1892)
: any of a class of sugars (as sucrose) that
yields on hydrolysis two monosaccharide molecules

**dis·ac·cord** \,di-sə-'kórd\ *intransitive verb*
[Middle English *disacorden*, from Middle
French *desacorder*, from *desacort* disagreement, from *des-* dis- + *acort* accord] (15th
century)
: CLASH, DISAGREE
— **disaccord** *noun*

**dis·ac·cus·tom** \,di-sə-'kəs-təm\ *transitive
verb* [Middle French *desaccoustumer*, from
Old French *desacostumer*, from *des-* dis- +
*acostumer* to accustom] (1530)
: to free from a habit

**¹dis·ad·van·tage** \,di-səd-'van-tij\ *noun*
[Middle English *disavauntage*, from Middle
French *desavantage*, from Old French, from
*des-* dis- + *avantage* advantage] (14th century)
**1** : loss or damage especially to reputation,
credit, or finances :DETRIMENT
**2 a** : an unfavorable, inferior, or prejudicial
condition ⟨we were at a *disadvantage*⟩ **b**
: HANDICAP ⟨it put us under a serious *disadvantage*⟩

**²disadvantage** *transitive verb* (circa 1534)
: to place at a disadvantage : HARM

**dis·ad·van·taged** \-tijd\ *adjective* (1648)
: lacking in the basic resources or conditions
(as standard housing, medical and educational
facilities, and civil rights) believed to be necessary for an equal position in society
— **dis·ad·van·taged·ness** \-tijd-nəs\
*noun*

**dis·ad·van·ta·geous** \(,)dis-,ad-,van-'tā-jəs,
-vən-\ *adjective* (1603)
**1** : constituting a disadvantage
**2** : DEROGATORY, DISPARAGING
— **dis·ad·van·ta·geous·ly** *adverb*
— **dis·ad·van·ta·geous·ness** *noun*

**dis·af·fect** \,di-sə-'fekt\ *transitive verb* (1641)
: to alienate the affection or loyalty of
**synonym** see ESTRANGE
— **dis·af·fec·tion** \-'fek-shən\ *noun*

**dis·af·fect·ed** *adjective* (1632)
: discontented and resentful especially against
authority : REBELLIOUS

**dis·af·fil·i·ate** \,di-sə-'fi-lē-,āt\ (1870)
*transitive verb*
: DISASSOCIATE
*intransitive verb*
: to terminate an affiliation
— **dis·af·fil·i·a·tion** \-,fil-ē-'ā-shən\ *noun*

**dis·af·firm** \,di-sə-'fərm\ *transitive verb*
(1531)
**1** : to refuse to confirm : ANNUL, REPUDIATE
**2** : CONTRADICT
— **dis·af·fir·mance** \-'fər-mən(t)s\ *noun*

**dis·ag·gre·gate** \(,)dis-'a-gri-,gāt\ (circa
1828)
*transitive verb*
: to separate into component parts ⟨*disaggregate* sandstone⟩ ⟨*disaggregate* demographic
data⟩
*intransitive verb*
: to break up or apart ⟨the molecules of a gel
*disaggregate* to form a sol⟩
— **dis·ag·gre·ga·tion** \(,)dis-,a-gri-'gā-
shən\ *noun*
— **dis·ag·gre·ga·tive** \(,)dis-'a-gri-,gā-tiv\
*adjective*

**dis·agree** \,di-sə-'grē\ *intransitive verb* [Mid-
dle English, from Middle French *desagreer*,
from *des-* dis- + *agreer* to agree] (15th century)
**1** : to fail to agree ⟨the two accounts *disagree*⟩
**2** : to differ in opinion ⟨he *disagreed* with me
on every topic⟩
**3** : to cause discomfort or distress ⟨fried foods
*disagree* with me⟩

**dis·agree·able** \-ə-bəl\ *adjective* (15th century)
**1** : causing discomfort : UNPLEASANT, OFFEN-
SIVE
**2** : marked by ill temper : PEEVISH
— **dis·agree·able·ness** *noun*
— **dis·agree·ably** \-blē\ *adverb*

**dis·agree·ment** \,di-sə-'grē-mənt\ *noun* (15th
century)
**1** : the act of disagreeing
**2 a** : the state of being at variance : DISPARITY
**b** : QUARREL

**dis·al·low** \,di-sə-'laú\ *transitive verb* (14th
century)
**1** : to deny the force, truth, or validity of
**2** : to refuse to allow
— **dis·al·low·ance** \-ən(t)s\ *noun*

**dis·am·big·u·ate** \,di-sam-'bi-gyə-,wāt\ *transitive verb* **-at·ed; -at·ing** (1963)
: to establish a single semantic or grammatical
interpretation for
— **dis·am·big·u·a·tion** \-,bi-gyə-'wā-
shən\ *noun*

**dis·an·nul** \,di-sə-'nəl\ *transitive verb* (15th
century)
: ANNUL, CANCEL

**dis·ap·pear** \,di-sə-'pir\ (15th century)
*intransitive verb*
**1** : to pass from view
**2** : to cease to be : pass out of existence or notice
*transitive verb*
: to cause the disappearance of
— **dis·ap·pear·ance** \-'pir-ən(t)s\ *noun*

**dis·ap·point** \,di-sə-'póint\ *verb* [Middle English *disapoynten*, from Middle French *desa-
pointier*, from *des-* dis- + *apointier* to arrange
— more at APPOINT] (15th century)
*transitive verb*
: to fail to meet the expectation or hope of
: FRUSTRATE
*intransitive verb*
: to cause disappointment ⟨where the show
*disappoints* most is in the work of the younger
generation —John Ashbery⟩

**dis·ap·point·ed** *adjective* (1537)
**1** : defeated in expectation or hope
**2** *obsolete* : not adequately equipped
— **dis·ap·point·ed·ly** *adverb*

**dis·ap·point·ing** *adjective* (1530)
: failing to meet expectations
— **dis·ap·point·ing·ly** \-'póin-tiŋ-lē\ *adverb*

**dis·ap·point·ment** \,di-sə-'póint-mənt\ *noun*
(1614)
**1** : the act or an instance of disappointing : the
state or emotion of being disappointed
**2** : one that disappoints

**dis·ap·pro·ba·tion** \(,)di-,sa-prə-'bā-shən\
*noun* (1647)
: the act or state of disapproving : the state of
being disapproved : CONDEMNATION

**dis·ap·prov·al** \,di-sə-'prü-vəl\ *noun* (1662)
: DISAPPROVAL, CENSURE

**dis·ap·prove** \-'prüv\ (1647)
*transitive verb*
**1** : to pass unfavorable judgment on
**2** : to refuse approval to : REJECT
*intransitive verb*
: to feel or express disapproval
— **dis·ap·prov·er** *noun*
— **dis·ap·prov·ing·ly** \-'prü-viŋ-lē\ *adverb*

**dis·arm** \di-'särm, -'zärm, 'di-,särm\ *verb*
[Middle English *desarmen*, literally, to divest
of arms, from Middle French *desarmer*, from
Old French, from *des-* dis- + *armer* to arm]
(14th century)

*transitive verb*
**1 a** : to deprive of means, reason, or disposition to be hostile **b** : to win over
**2 a** : to divest of arms **b** : to deprive of a
means of attack or defense **c** : to make harmless
*intransitive verb*
**1** : to lay aside arms
**2** : to give up or reduce armed forces
— **dis·ar·ma·ment** \-'sär-mə-mənt, -'zär-\
*noun*
— **dis·arm·er** *noun*

**dis·arm·ing** *adjective* (1839)
: allaying criticism or hostility : INGRATIATING
— **dis·arm·ing·ly** \-'sär-miŋ-lē, -'zär-\ *adverb*

**dis·ar·range** \,di-sə-'rānj\ *transitive verb*
(1744)
: to disturb the arrangement or order of
— **dis·ar·range·ment** \-mənt\ *noun*

**¹dis·ar·ray** \,di-sə-'rā\ *noun* (15th century)
**1** : a lack of order or sequence : CONFUSION,
DISORDER
**2** : disorderly dress : DISHABILLE

**²disarray** *transitive verb* [Middle English
*disarayen*, from Middle French *desarroyer*,
from Old French *desareer*, from *des-* dis- +
*areer* to array] (14th century)
**1** : to throw into disorder
**2** : UNDRESS

**dis·ar·tic·u·late** \,di-sär-'ti-kyə-,lāt\ (1830)
*intransitive verb*
: to become disjointed
*transitive verb*
: DISJOINT
— **dis·ar·tic·u·la·tion** \-,ti-kyə-'lā-shən\
*noun*

**dis·as·sem·ble** \,di-sə-'sem-bəl\ (1903)
*transitive verb*
: to take apart ⟨*disassemble* a watch⟩
*intransitive verb*
**1** : to come apart ⟨the frame *disassembles* into
sections⟩
**2** : DISPERSE, SCATTER ⟨the crowd began to *disassemble*⟩
— **dis·as·sem·bly** \-blē\ *noun*

**dis·as·so·ci·ate** \,di-sə-'sō-sē-,āt, -shē-\ *transitive verb* (1603)
: to detach from association : DISSOCIATE
— **dis·as·so·ci·a·tion** \-,sō-sē-'ā-shən,
-shē-\ *noun*

**di·sas·ter** \di-'zas-tər, -'sas-\ *noun* [Middle
French & Old Italian; Middle French *desastre*,
from Old Italian *disastro*, from *dis-* (from Latin) + *astro* star, from Latin *astrum* — more at
ASTRAL] (1591)
**1** : a sudden calamitous event bringing great
damage, loss, or destruction; *broadly* : a sudden or great misfortune or failure
**2** *obsolete* : an unfavorable aspect of a planet
or star ◆

**disaster area** *noun* (1953)

◇ **WORD HISTORY**
**disaster** People who are beset by bad
luck are regularly described as "star-
crossed." This expression comes from the
traditional belief that the position of the stars
and planets can have a direct influence on
earthly events. The origins of the word *disaster* can likewise be traced to this belief. *Disaster* is ultimately borrowed from *disastro*,
an Italian word formed by compounding the
negative prefix *dis-* and the noun *astro*,
meaning "star." *Disastro* originally referred to
an unfortunate event, such as a military defeat, that took place under an unlucky conjunction of heavenly bodies. Eventually the
astrological connection became superfluous,
and *disastro*, like English *disaster*, was used
for any calamity.

: an area officially declared to be the scene of an emergency created by a disaster and therefore qualified to receive certain types of governmental aid (as emergency loans and relief supplies)

**di·sas·trous** \di-'zas-trəs *also* -'sas-\ *adjective* (1603)
**1** : attended by or causing suffering or disaster : CALAMITOUS
**2** : TERRIBLE, HORRENDOUS ⟨a *disastrous* score⟩
— **di·sas·trous·ly** *adverb*

**dis·avow** \ˌdi-sə-'vaů\ *transitive verb* [Middle English *desavowen*, from Middle French *desavouer*, from Old French, from *des-* dis- + *avouer* to avow] (14th century)
**1** : to deny responsibility for : REPUDIATE
**2** : to refuse to acknowledge : DISCLAIM
— **dis·avow·able** \-ə-bəl\ *adjective*
— **dis·avow·al** \-'vaů(-ə)l\ *noun*

**dis·band** \dis-'band\ *verb* [Middle French *desbander*, from *des-* dis- + *bande* band] (1591)
*transitive verb*
: to break up the organization of : DISSOLVE
*intransitive verb*
: to break up as an organization : DISPERSE
— **dis·band·ment** \-'ban(d)-mənt\ *noun*

**dis·bar** \dis-'bär\ *transitive verb* (1633)
: to expel from the bar or the legal profession : deprive (an attorney) of legal status and privileges
— **dis·bar·ment** \-mənt\ *noun*

**dis·be·lief** \ˌdis-bə-'lēf\ *noun* (1672)
: the act of disbelieving : mental rejection of something as untrue

**dis·be·lieve** \-'lēv\ (circa 1644)
*transitive verb*
: to hold not worthy of belief : not believe
*intransitive verb*
: to withhold or reject belief
— **dis·be·liev·er** *noun*

**dis·ben·e·fit** \ˌ(ˌ)dis-'be-nə-fit\ *noun* (1968)
: something disadvantageous or objectionable : DRAWBACK

**dis·bud** \ˌ(ˌ)dis-'bəd\ *transitive verb* (1727)
**1** : to thin out flower buds in order to improve the quality of bloom of
**2** : to dehorn (cattle) by destroying the undeveloped horn bud

**dis·bur·den** \ˌ(ˌ)dis-'bər-d°n\ (1532)
*transitive verb*
**1 a** : to rid of a burden ⟨*disburden* a pack animal⟩ **b** : UNBURDEN ⟨*disburden* your conscience⟩
**2** : UNLOAD ⟨*disburdened* their merchandise in the town square⟩
*intransitive verb*
: DISCHARGE ⟨the vessels *disburdened* at the dock⟩
— **dis·bur·den·ment** \-mənt\ *noun*

**dis·burse** \dis-'bərs\ *transitive verb* **disbursed; dis·burs·ing** [Middle French *desbourser*, from Old French *desborser*, from *des-* dis- + *borser* to get money, from *borse* burse] (1530)
**1 a** : to pay out : expend especially from a fund **b** : to make a payment in settlement of
**2** : DISTRIBUTE
— **dis·burs·er** *noun*

**dis·burse·ment** \-'bər-smənt\ *noun* (1596)
: the act of disbursing; *also* : funds paid out

**disc** *variant of* DISK

**disc-** *or* **disci-** *or* **disco-** *combining form* [Latin, from Greek *disk-*, *disko-*, from *diskos*]
**1** : disk ⟨*discoid*⟩
**2** : phonograph record ⟨*discophile*⟩

**dis·calced** \ˌ(ˌ)dis-'kalst\ *adjective* [part translation of Latin *discalceatus*, from *dis-* + *calceatus*, past participle of *calceare* to put on shoes, from *calceus* shoe, from *calc-*, *calx* heel] (1631)
: UNSHOD, BAREFOOT ⟨*discalced* friars⟩

**dis·cant** \'dis-ˌkant\ *variant of* DESCANT

**¹dis·card** \dis-'kärd, 'dis-ˌ\ (circa 1586)
*transitive verb*
**1** : to get rid of especially as useless or unpleasant

**2 a** : to remove (a playing card) from one's hand **b** : to play (any card except a trump) from a suit different from the one led
*intransitive verb*
: to discard a playing card ☆
— **dis·card·able** \-ə-bəl\ *adjective*
— **dis·card·er** *noun*

**²dis·card** \'dis-ˌkärd\ *noun* (1744)
**1 a** : the act of discarding in a card game **b** : a card discarded
**2** : one that is cast off or rejected

**dis·car·nate** \dis-'kär-nət, -ˌnāt\ *adjective* [*dis-* + *-carnate* (as in *incarnate*)] (1895)
: having no physical body : INCORPOREAL

**disc brake** *noun* (1904)
: a brake that operates by the friction of a caliper pressing against the sides of a rotating disc

disc brake: *1* caliper, *2* disc

**dis·cern** \di-'sərn, -'zərn\ *verb* [Middle English, from Middle French *discerner*, from Latin *discernere* to separate, distinguish between, from *dis-* apart + *cernere* to sift — more at DIS-, CERTAIN] (14th century)
*transitive verb*
**1 a** : to detect with the eyes **b** : to detect with senses other than vision
**2** : to recognize or identify as separate and distinct : DISCRIMINATE
**3** : to come to know or recognize mentally
*intransitive verb*
: to see or understand the difference
— **dis·cern·er** *noun*
— **dis·cern·ible** *also* **dis·cern·able** \-'sər-nə-bəl, -'zər-\ *adjective*
— **dis·cern·ibly** \-blē\ *adverb*

**dis·cern·ing** *adjective* (1589)
: showing insight and understanding : DISCRIMINATING ⟨a *discerning* critic⟩
— **dis·cern·ing·ly** \-'sər-niŋ-lē, -'zər-\ *adverb*

**dis·cern·ment** \di-'sərn-mənt, -'zərn-\ *noun* (1586)
**1** : the quality of being able to grasp and comprehend what is obscure : skill in discerning
**2** : an act of discerning ☆

**¹dis·charge** \dis-'chärj, 'dis-ˌ\ *verb* [Middle English, from Middle French *descharger*, from Late Latin *discarricare*, from Latin *dis-* + Late Latin *carricare* to load — more at CHARGE] (14th century)
*transitive verb*
**1** : to relieve of a charge, load, or burden: **a** : UNLOAD **b** : to release from an obligation **c** : to release electrical energy from (as a battery or capacitor) by a discharge
**2 a** : to let go or put off ⟨*discharge* passengers⟩ ⟨*discharge* cargo⟩ **b** : SHOOT ⟨*discharge* an arrow⟩ **c** : to release from confinement, custody, or care ⟨*discharge* a prisoner⟩ **d** : to give outlet or vent to : EMIT
**3 a** (1) : to dismiss from employment (2) : to release from service or duty ⟨*discharge* a soldier⟩ **b** : to get rid of (as a debt or obligation) by performing an appropriate action (as payment) **c** : to set aside : ANNUL **d** : to order (a legislative committee) to end consideration of a bill in order to bring it before the house for action
**4** : to bear and distribute (as the weight of a wall above an opening)
**5** : to bleach out or remove (color or dye) in dyeing and printing textiles
**6** : to cancel the record of the loan of (a library book) upon return
*intransitive verb*
**1 a** : to throw off or deliver a load, charge, or burden **b** : to release electrical energy by a discharge

**2 a** : GO OFF, FIRE — used of a gun **b** : SPREAD, RUN ⟨some dyes *discharge*⟩ **c** : to pour forth fluid or other contents
**synonym** *see* PERFORM
— **dis·charge·able** \-jə-bəl\ *adjective*
— **dis·charg·ee** \ˌ(ˌ)dis-ˌchär-'jē\ *noun*
— **dis·charg·er** \dis-'chär-jər, 'dis-ˌ\ *noun*

**²dis·charge** \'dis-ˌchärj, dis-'\ *noun* (14th century)
**1 a** : the act of relieving of something that oppresses : RELEASE **b** : something that discharges or releases; *especially* : a certification of release or payment
**2** : the state of being discharged or relieved
**3** : the act of discharging or unloading
**4** : legal release from confinement
**5** : a firing off
**6 a** : a flowing or issuing out ⟨a *discharge* of spores⟩; *also* : a rate of flow **b** : something that is emitted ⟨a purulent *discharge*⟩
**7** : the act of removing an obligation or liability
**8 a** : release or dismissal especially from an office or employment **b** : complete separation from military service
**9 a** : the equalization of a difference of electric potential between two points **b** : the conversion of the chemical energy of a battery into electrical energy

**discharge lamp** *noun* (1936)
: an electric lamp in which an enclosed gas or vapor glows or causes a phosphor coating on the lamp's inner surface to glow

**discharge tube** *noun* (1898)

---

☆ **SYNONYMS**

**Discard, cast, shed, slough, scrap, junk** mean to get rid of. DISCARD implies the letting go or throwing away of something that has become useless or superfluous though often not intrinsically valueless ⟨*discard* old clothes⟩. CAST, especially when used with *off*, *away*, or *out*, implies a forceful rejection or repudiation ⟨*cast* off her friends⟩. SHED and SLOUGH imply a throwing off of something both useless and encumbering and often suggest a consequent renewal of vitality or luster ⟨*shed* a bad habit⟩ ⟨finally *sloughed* off the depression⟩. SCRAP and JUNK imply throwing away or breaking up as worthless in existent form ⟨*scrap* all the old ways⟩ ⟨would *junk* our educational system⟩.

**Discernment, discrimination, perception, penetration, insight, acumen** mean a power to see what is not evident to the average mind. DISCERNMENT stresses accuracy (as in reading character or motives or appreciating art) ⟨the *discernment* to know true friends⟩. DISCRIMINATION stresses the power to distinguish and select what is true or appropriate or excellent ⟨the *discrimination* that develops through listening to a lot of great music⟩. PERCEPTION implies quick and often sympathetic discernment (as of shades of feeling) ⟨a novelist of keen *perception* into human motives⟩. PENETRATION implies a searching mind that goes beyond what is obvious or superficial ⟨lacks the *penetration* to see the scorn beneath their friendly smiles⟩. INSIGHT suggests depth of discernment coupled with understanding sympathy ⟨a documentary providing *insight* into the plight of the homeless⟩. ACUMEN implies characteristic penetration combined with keen practical judgment ⟨a director of reliable box-office *acumen*⟩.

---

: an electron tube which contains gas or vapor at low pressure and through which conduction takes place when a high voltage is applied

**disci-** — see DISC-

**dis·ci·form** \'di-sə-ˌform\ *adjective* (1830)
: round or oval in shape

**dis·ci·ple** \di-'sī-pəl\ *noun* [Middle English, from Old English *discipul* & Old French *desciple*, from Late Latin and Latin; Late Latin *discipulus* follower of Jesus Christ in his lifetime, from Latin, pupil] (before 12th century)
**1** : one who accepts and assists in spreading the doctrines of another: as **a** : one of the twelve in the inner circle of Christ's followers according to the Gospel accounts **b** : a convinced adherent of a school or individual
**2** *capitalized* : a member of the Disciples of Christ founded in the U.S. in 1809 that holds the Bible alone to be the rule of faith and practice, usually baptizes by immersion, and has a congregational polity
**synonym** see FOLLOWER
— **dis·ci·ple·ship** \-ˌship\ *noun*

**dis·ci·plin·able** \'di-sə-'pli-nə-bəl; 'di-sə-pli-\ *adjective* (15th century)
**1** : DOCILE, TEACHABLE
**2** : subject to or deserving discipline ⟨a *disciplinable* offense⟩

**dis·ci·pli·nar·i·an** \ˌdi-sə-plə-'ner-ē-ən\ *noun* (1639)
: one who disciplines or enforces order
— **disciplinarian** *adjective*

**dis·ci·plin·ary** \'di-sə-plə-ˌner-ē, *especially British* ˌdi-sə-'pli-nə-rē\ *adjective* (1598)
**1 a** : of or relating to discipline **b** : designed to correct or punish breaches of discipline ⟨took *disciplinary* action⟩
**2** : of or relating to a particular field of study
— **dis·ci·plin·ar·i·ly** \ˌdi-sə-plə-'ner-ə-lē\ *adverb*
— **dis·ci·plin·ar·i·ty** \-'nar-ə-tē\ *noun*

**¹dis·ci·pline** \'di-sə-plən\ *noun* [Middle English, from Old French & Latin; Old French, from Latin *disciplina* teaching, learning, from *discipulus* pupil] (13th century)
**1** : PUNISHMENT
**2** *obsolete* : INSTRUCTION
**3** : a field of study
**4** : training that corrects, molds, or perfects the mental faculties or moral character
**5 a** : control gained by enforcing obedience or order **b** : orderly or prescribed conduct or pattern of behavior **c** : SELF-CONTROL
**6** : a rule or system of rules governing conduct or activity
— **dis·ci·plin·al** \-plə-nᵊl\ *adjective*

**²discipline** *transitive verb* **-plined; -plin·ing** (14th century)
**1** : to punish or penalize for the sake of discipline
**2** : to train or develop by instruction and exercise especially in self-control
**3 a** : to bring (a group) under control ⟨*discipline* troops⟩ **b** : to impose order upon ⟨serious writers *discipline* and refine their writing styles⟩
**synonym** see PUNISH, TEACH
— **dis·ci·plin·er** *noun*

**dis·ci·plined** *adjective* (14th century)
: marked by or possessing discipline ⟨a *disciplined* mind⟩

**disc jockey** *noun* (1941)
: an announcer of a radio show of popular recorded music; *also* : one who plays recorded music for dancing at a nightclub or party

**dis·claim** \dis-'klām\ *verb* [Middle English, from Anglo-French *disclaimer*, from *dis-* + *claimer* to claim, from Old French *clamer*] (15th century)
*intransitive verb*
**1** : to make a disclaimer
**2 a** *obsolete* : to disavow all part or share **b** : to utter denial
*transitive verb*
**1** : to renounce a legal claim to

**2** : DENY, DISAVOW ⟨*disclaimed* any knowledge of the contents of the letter⟩

**dis·claim·er** \-'klā-mər\ *noun* (15th century)
**1 a** : a denial or disavowal of legal claim : relinquishment of or formal refusal to accept an interest or estate **b** : a writing that embodies a legal disclaimer
**2 a** : DENIAL, DISAVOWAL **b** : REPUDIATION

**dis·cla·ma·tion** \ˌdis-klə-'mā-shən\ *noun* (1592)
: RENUNCIATION, DISAVOWAL

**dis·cli·max** \(ˌ)dis-'klī-ˌmaks\ *noun* (1935)
: a relatively stable ecological community often including kinds of organisms foreign to the region and displacing the climax because of disturbance especially by man

**¹dis·close** \dis-'klōz\ *transitive verb* [Middle English, from Middle French *desclos-*, stem of *desclore* to disclose, from Medieval Latin *dis-claudere* to open, from Latin *dis-* + *claudere* to close — more at CLOSE] (14th century)
**1** *obsolete* : to open up
**2 a** : to expose to view **b** *archaic* : HATCH **c** : to make known or public ⟨demands that politicians *disclose* the sources of their income⟩
**synonym** see REVEAL
— **dis·clos·er** *noun*

**²disclose** *noun* (1548)
*obsolete* : DISCLOSURE

**dis·clos·ing** \-'klō-ziŋ\ *adjective* (1965)
: being or using an agent (as a tablet or liquid) that contains a usually red dye that stains dental plaque

**dis·clo·sure** \dis-'klō-zhər\ *noun* (circa 1598)
**1** : the act or an instance of disclosing : EXPOSURE
**2** : something disclosed : REVELATION

**¹dis·co** \'dis-(ˌ)kō\ *noun, plural* **discos** [short for *discotheque*] (1964)
**1** : a nightclub for dancing to live and recorded music
**2** : popular dance music characterized by hypnotic rhythm, repetitive lyrics, and electronically produced sounds

**²disco** *intransitive verb* (1979)
: to dance to disco music

**disco-** — see DISC-

**dis·cog·ra·pher** \dis-'kä-grə-fər\ *noun* (1941)
: a person who compiles discographies

**dis·cog·ra·phy** \-fē\ *noun, plural* **-phies** [French *discographie*, from *disc-* + *-graphie* -graphy] (1933)
**1** : a descriptive list of phonograph records by category, composer, performer, or date of release
**2** : the history of recorded music
— **dis·co·graph·i·cal** \ˌdis-kə-'gra-fi-kəl\ *also* **dis·co·graph·ic** \-fik\ *adjective*

**dis·coid** \'dis-ˌkȯid\ *adjective* [Late Latin *discoides* quoit-shaped, from Greek *diskoeidēs*, from *diskos* disk] (1794)
**1** : relating to or having a disk: as **a** *of a composite floret* : situated in the floral disk **b** *of a composite flower head* : having only tubular florets
**2** : flat and circular like a disc

**dis·coi·dal** \dis-'kȯi-dᵊl\ *adjective* (circa 1706)
: of, resembling, or producing a disk

**discoidal cleavage** *noun* (circa 1909)
: meroblastic cleavage in which a disk of cells is produced at the animal pole of the zygote (as in bird eggs)

**dis·col·or** \(ˌ)dis-'kə-lər\ *verb* [Middle English *discolouren*, from Middle French *descolourer*, from Late Latin *discolorari*, from Latin *discolor* of another color, from *dis-* + *color* color] (14th century)
*transitive verb*
: to alter or change the hue or color of
*intransitive verb*
: to change color especially for the worse

**dis·col·or·ation** \(ˌ)dis-ˌkə-lə-'rā-shən\ *noun* (1642)
**1** : the act of discoloring : the state of being discolored

**2** : a discolored spot or formation : STAIN

**dis·com·bob·u·late** \ˌdis-kəm-'bä-b(y)ə-ˌlāt\ *transitive verb* **-lat·ed; -lat·ing** [probably alteration of *discompose*] (circa 1916)
: UPSET, CONFUSE ⟨the offensive had *discombobulated* all the German defensive arrangements —A. J. Liebling⟩
— **dis·com·bob·u·la·tion** \-ˌbä-b(y)ə-'lā-shən\ *noun*

**¹dis·com·fit** \dis-'kəm(p)-fət, *especially Southern* ˌdis-kəm-'fit\ *transitive verb* [Middle English, from Old French *desconfit*, past participle of *desconfire*, from *des-* dis- + *confire* to prepare — more at COMFIT] (13th century)
**1 a** *archaic* : to defeat in battle **b** : to frustrate the plans of : THWART
**2** : to put into a state of perplexity and embarrassment : DISCONCERT
**synonym** see EMBARRASS

**²discomfit** *noun* (15th century)
: DISCOMFITURE

**dis·com·fi·ture** \dis-'kəm(p)-fə-ˌchùr, -chər, *especially Southern* -ˌt(y)ùr\ *noun* (14th century)
: the act of discomfiting : the state of being discomfited

**¹dis·com·fort** \dis-'kəm(p)-fərt\ *transitive verb* [Middle English, from Middle French *desconforter*, from Old French, from *des-* dis- + *conforter* to comfort] (14th century)
**1** *archaic* : DISMAY
**2** : to make uncomfortable or uneasy
— **dis·com·fort·able** \-'kəm(p)-fər-tə-bəl, -'kəm(p)f-tər-bəl\ *adjective*

**²discomfort** *noun* (14th century)
**1** *archaic* : DISTRESS, GRIEF
**2** : mental or physical uneasiness : ANNOYANCE

**dis·com·mend** \ˌdis-kə-'mend\ *transitive verb* [Middle English *dyscommenden*] (15th century)
**1** : DISAPPROVE, DISPARAGE
**2** : to cause to be viewed unfavorably

**dis·com·mode** \ˌdis-kə-'mōd\ *transitive verb* **-mod·ed; -mod·ing** [Middle French *discommoder*, from *dis-* + *commode* convenient — more at COMMODE] (circa 1721)
: to cause inconvenience to : TROUBLE

**dis·com·pose** \ˌdis-kəm-'pōz\ *transitive verb* [Middle English] (15th century)
**1** : to destroy the composure of
**2** : to disturb the order of ☆
— **dis·com·po·sure** \-'pō-zhər\ *noun*

**dis·con·cert** \ˌdis-kən-'sərt\ *transitive verb* [obsolete French *disconcerter*, alteration of Middle French *desconcerter*, from *des-* dis- + *concerter* to concert] (1687)
**1** : to throw into confusion

---

☆ **SYNONYMS**
**Discompose, disquiet, disturb, perturb, agitate, upset, fluster** mean to destroy capacity for collected thought or decisive action. DISCOMPOSE implies some degree of loss of self-control or self-confidence especially through emotional stress ⟨*discomposed* by the loss of his beloved wife⟩. DISQUIET suggests loss of sense of security or peace of mind ⟨the *disquieting* news of factories closing⟩. DISTURB implies interference with one's mental processes caused by worry, perplexity, or interruption ⟨the discrepancy in accounts *disturbed* me⟩. PERTURB implies deep disturbance of mind and emotions ⟨*perturbed* by her husband's strange behavior⟩. AGITATE suggests obvious external signs of nervous or emotional excitement ⟨in his *agitated* state we could see he was unable to work⟩. UPSET implies the disturbance of normal or habitual functioning by disappointment, distress, or grief ⟨the family's constant bickering *upsets* the youngest child⟩. FLUSTER suggests bewildered agitation ⟨his declaration of love completely *flustered* her⟩.

**2 :** to disturb the composure of
**synonym** see EMBARRASS
— **dis·con·cert·ing** *adjective*
— **dis·con·cert·ing·ly** \-tiŋ-lē\ *adverb*
— **dis·con·cert·ment** \-mənt\ *noun*
**dis·con·firm** \ˌdis-kən-ˈfərm\ *transitive verb* (1936)
**:** to deny the validity of
**dis·con·for·mi·ty** \ˌdis-kən-ˈfòr-mə-tē\ *noun* (1587)
**1 :** NONCONFORMITY
**2 :** a break in a sequence of sedimentary rocks all of which have approximately the same dip
**dis·con·nect** \ˌdis-kə-ˈnekt\ (1770)
*transitive verb*
**:** to sever the connection of or between
*intransitive verb*
**1 :** to terminate a connection
**2 :** to become detached or withdrawn ⟨*disconnects* into dark moods⟩
— **dis·con·nec·tion** \-ˈnek-shən\ *noun*
**dis·con·nect·ed** *adjective* (1783)
**:** not connected **:** SEPARATE; *also* **:** INCOHERENT
— **dis·con·nect·ed·ly** *adverb*
— **dis·con·nect·ed·ness** *noun*
**dis·con·so·late** \dis-ˈkän(t)-sə-lət\ *adjective* [Middle English, from Medieval Latin *disconsolatus*, from Latin *dis-* + *consolatus*, past participle of *consolari* to console] (14th century)
**1 :** CHEERLESS ⟨a clutch of *disconsolate* houses —D. H. Lawrence⟩
**2 :** DEJECTED, DOWNCAST ⟨the team returned *disconsolate* from three losses⟩
— **dis·con·so·late·ly** *adverb*
— **dis·con·so·late·ness** *noun*
— **dis·con·so·la·tion** \ˌ(ˌ)dis-ˌkän(t)-sə-ˈlā-shən\ *noun*
**¹dis·con·tent** \ˌdis-kən-ˈtent\ *adjective* (15th century)
**:** DISCONTENTED
**²discontent** *transitive verb* (1549)
**:** to make discontented
— **dis·con·tent·ment** \-mənt\ *noun*
**³discontent** *noun* (1591)
**:** lack of contentment: **a :** a sense of grievance **:** DISSATISFACTION ⟨the winter of our *discontent* —Shakespeare⟩ **b :** restless aspiration for improvement
**⁴discontent** *noun* (1596)
**:** one who is discontented **:** MALCONTENT
**dis·con·tent·ed** *adjective* (1525)
**:** DISSATISFIED, MALCONTENT
— **dis·con·tent·ed·ly** *adverb*
— **dis·con·tent·ed·ness** *noun*
**dis·con·tin·u·ance** \ˌdis-kən-ˈtin-yə-wən(t)s\ *noun* (14th century)
**1 :** the act or an instance of discontinuing
**2 :** the interruption or termination of a legal action by the plaintiff's not continuing it
**dis·con·tin·ue** \ˌdis-kən-ˈtin-(ˌ)yü, -yə(-w)\ *verb* [Middle English, from Middle French *discontinuer*, from Medieval Latin *discontinuare*, from Latin *dis-* + *continuare* to continue] (14th century)
*transitive verb*
**1 :** to break the continuity of **:** cease to operate, administer, use, produce, or take
**2 :** to abandon or terminate by a legal discontinuance
*intransitive verb*
**:** to come to an end
**synonym** see STOP
— **dis·con·tin·u·a·tion** \-kən-ˌtin-yə-ˈwā-shən\ *noun*
**dis·con·ti·nu·ity** \ˌ(ˌ)dis-ˌkän-tə-ˈnü-ə-tē, -ˈnyü-\ *noun* (1570)
**1 :** lack of continuity or cohesion
**2 :** GAP 5
**3 a :** the property of being not mathematically continuous ⟨a point of *discontinuity*⟩ **b :** an instance of being not mathematically continuous; *especially* **:** a value of an independent variable at which a function is not continuous

**dis·con·tin·u·ous** \ˌdis-kən-ˈtin-yə-wəs\ *adjective* (1718)
**1 a** (1) **:** not continuous ⟨a *discontinuous* series of events⟩ (2) **:** not continued **:** DISCRETE ⟨*discontinuous* features of terrain⟩ **b :** lacking sequence or coherence
**2 :** having one or more mathematical discontinuities — used of a variable or a function
— **dis·con·tin·u·ous·ly** *adverb*
**dis·co·phile** \ˈdis-kə-ˌfīl\ *noun* (1940)
**:** one who studies and collects phonograph records
**¹dis·cord** \ˈdis-ˌkòrd\ *noun* (13th century)
**1 a :** lack of agreement or harmony (as between persons, things, or ideas) **b :** active quarreling or conflict resulting from discord among persons or factions **:** STRIFE
**2 a** (1) **:** a combination of musical sounds that strikes the ear harshly (2) **:** DISSONANCE **b :** a harsh or unpleasant sound ☆
**²dis·cord** \ˈdis-ˌkòrd, dis-ˈ\ *intransitive verb* [Middle English, from Old French *discorder*, from Latin *discordare*, from *discord-*, *discors* discordant, from *dis-* + *cord-*, *cor* heart — more at HEART] (14th century)
**:** DISAGREE, CLASH
**dis·cor·dance** \dis-ˈkòr-dᵊn(t)s\ *noun* (14th century)
**1 :** the state or an instance of being discordant
**2 :** DISSONANCE
**dis·cor·dan·cy** \-dᵊn-sē\ *noun, plural* **-cies** (1607)
**:** DISCORDANCE
**dis·cor·dant** \-dᵊnt\ *adjective* (14th century)
**1 a :** being at variance **:** DISAGREEING **b :** QUARRELSOME
**2 :** relating to a discord
— **dis·cor·dant·ly** *adverb*
**dis·co·theque** *or* **discothèque** \ˈdis-kə-ˌtek, ˌdis-kə-ˈ\ *noun* [French *discothèque*, from *disque* disk, record + *-o-* + *-thèque* (as in *bibliothèque* library)] (1954)
**:** DISCO 1
**¹dis·count** \ˈdis-ˌkaùnt\ *noun* (1622)
**1 :** a reduction made from the gross amount or value of something: as **a** (1) **:** a reduction made from a regular or list price (2) **:** a proportionate deduction from a debt account usually made for cash or prompt payment **b :** a deduction made for interest in advancing money upon or purchasing a bill or note not due
**2 :** the act or practice of discounting
**3 :** a deduction taken or allowance made
**²dis·count** \ˈdis-ˌkaùnt, dis-ˈ\ *verb* [modification of French *décompter*, from Old French *desconter*, from Medieval Latin *discomputare*, from Latin *dis-* + *computare* to count — more at COUNT] (1629)
*transitive verb*
**1 a :** to make a deduction from usually for cash or prompt payment **b :** to sell or offer for sale at a discount
**2 :** to lend money on after deducting the discount
**3 a :** to leave out of account **:** DISREGARD **b :** to minimize the importance of **c** (1) **:** to make allowance for bias or exaggeration in (2) **:** to view with doubt **d :** to take into account (as a future event) in present calculations
*intransitive verb*
**:** to give or make discounts
— **dis·count·er** \-ˌkaùn-tər, -ˈkaùn-\ *noun*
**³dis·count** \ˈdis-ˌkaùnt\ *adjective* (1889)
**1 a :** selling goods or services at a discount ⟨*discount* stores⟩ ⟨a *discount* broker⟩ ⟨*discount* airlines⟩ **b :** offered or sold at a discount
**2 :** reflecting a discount ⟨*discount* prices⟩
**dis·count·able** \dis-ˈkaùn-tə-bəl, ˈdis-ˌ\ *adjective* (1800)
**1 :** set apart for discounting ⟨within the *discountable* period⟩
**2 :** subject to being discounted ⟨a *discountable* note⟩

**¹dis·coun·te·nance** \dis-ˈkaùn-tᵊn-ən(t)s, -ˈkaùnt-nən(t)s\ *transitive verb* (1580)
**1 :** ABASH, DISCONCERT
**2 :** to look with disfavor on **:** discourage by evidence of disapproval
**²discountenance** *noun* (1580)
**:** DISAPPROBATION, DISFAVOR
**discount rate** *noun* (circa 1927)
**1 :** the interest on an annual basis deducted in advance on a loan
**2 :** the charge levied by a central bank for advances and rediscounts
**dis·cour·age** \dis-ˈkər-ij, -ˈkə-rij\ *transitive verb* **-aged; -ag·ing** [Middle English *discoragen*, from Middle French *descoragier*, from Old French *descoragier*, from *des-* dis- + *corage* courage] (15th century)
**1 :** to deprive of courage or confidence **:** DISHEARTEN
**2 a :** to hinder by disfavoring **b :** to attempt to dissuade
— **dis·cour·age·able** \-jə-bəl\ *adjective*
— **dis·cour·ag·er** *noun*
— **dis·cour·ag·ing·ly** \-jiŋ-lē\ *adverb*
**dis·cour·age·ment** \-mənt\ *noun* (1561)
**1 :** the act of discouraging **:** the state of being discouraged
**2 :** something that discourages
**¹dis·course** \ˈdis-ˌkōrs, -ˌkòrs, dis-ˈ\ *noun* [Middle English *discours*, from Medieval Latin & Late Latin *discursus*; Medieval Latin, argument, from Late Latin, conversation, from Latin, act of running about, from *discurrere* to run about, from *dis-* + *currere* to run — more at CAR] (14th century)
**1** *archaic* **:** the capacity of orderly thought or procedure **:** RATIONALITY
**2 :** verbal interchange of ideas; *especially* **:** CONVERSATION
**3 a :** formal and orderly and usually extended expression of thought on a subject **b :** connected speech or writing **c :** a linguistic unit (as a conversation or a story) larger than a sentence
**4** *obsolete* **:** social familiarity
**²dis·course** \dis-ˈkōrs, -ˈkòrs, ˈdis-ˌ\ *verb* **dis·coursed; dis·cours·ing** (1559)
*intransitive verb*
**1 :** to express oneself especially in oral discourse

---

☆ SYNONYMS
**Discord, strife, conflict, contention, dissension, variance** mean a state or condition marked by a lack of agreement or harmony. DISCORD implies an intrinsic or essential lack of harmony producing quarreling, factiousness, or antagonism ⟨a political party long racked by *discord*⟩. STRIFE emphasizes a struggle for superiority rather than the incongruity or incompatibility of the persons or things involved ⟨during his brief reign the empire was never free of civil *strife*⟩. CONFLICT usually stresses the action of forces in opposition but in static applications implies an irreconcilability as of duties or desires ⟨the *conflict* of freedom and responsibility⟩. CONTENTION applies to strife or competition that shows itself in quarreling, disputing, or controversy ⟨several points of *contention* about the new zoning law⟩. DISSENSION implies strife or discord and stresses a division into factions ⟨religious *dissension* threatened to split the colony⟩. VARIANCE implies a clash between persons or things owing to a difference in nature, opinion, or interest ⟨cultural *variances* that work against a national identity⟩.

---

**2 :** TALK, CONVERSE
*transitive verb*
*archaic* **:** to give forth **:** UTTER
— **dis·cours·er** *noun*
**discourse analysis** *noun* (1952)
**:** the study of linguistic relations and structures in discourse
**dis·cour·te·ous** \(ˌ)dis-ˈkər-tē-əs\ *adjective* (1578)
**:** lacking courtesy **:** RUDE
— **dis·cour·te·ous·ly** *adverb*
— **dis·cour·te·ous·ness** *noun*
**dis·cour·te·sy** \-ˈkər-tə-sē\ *noun* (1555)
**1 :** RUDENESS
**2 :** a rude act
**dis·cov·er** \dis-ˈkə-vər\ *verb* **dis·cov·ered; dis·cov·er·ing** \-ˈkə-v(ə-)riŋ\ [Middle English, from Middle French *descovrir*, from Late Latin *discooperire*, from Latin *dis-* + *cooperire* to cover — more at COVER] (14th century)
*transitive verb*
**1 a :** to make known or visible **:** EXPOSE **b** *archaic* **:** DISPLAY
**2 a :** to obtain sight or knowledge of for the first time **:** FIND ⟨*discover* the solution⟩ **b :** FIND OUT ⟨*discovered* he was out of gas⟩
*intransitive verb*
**:** to make a discovery ☆
— **dis·cov·er·able** \-ˈkə-v(ə-)rə-bəl\ *adjective*
— **dis·cov·er·er** \-ər-ər\ *noun*
**dis·cov·ery** \dis-ˈkə-v(ə-)rē\ *noun, plural* **-er·ies** (1539)
**1 a :** the act or process of discovering **b** (1) *archaic* **:** DISCLOSURE (2) *obsolete* **:** DISPLAY **c** *obsolete* **:** EXPLORATION
**2 :** something discovered
**3 :** the usually pretrial disclosure of pertinent facts or documents by one or both parties to a legal action or proceeding
**Discovery Day** *noun* (circa 1913)
**:** COLUMBUS DAY
**¹dis·cred·it** \(ˌ)dis-ˈkre-dət\ *transitive verb* (1559)
**1 :** to refuse to accept as true or accurate **:** DISBELIEVE
**2 :** to cause disbelief in the accuracy or authority of
**3 :** to deprive of good repute **:** DISGRACE
**²discredit** *noun* (1565)
**1 :** loss of credit or reputation ⟨I knew stories to the *discredit* of England —W. B. Yeats⟩
**2 :** lack or loss of belief or confidence **:** DOUBT ⟨contradictions cast *discredit* on his testimony⟩
**dis·cred·it·able** \-tə-bəl\ *adjective* (1640)
**:** injurious to reputation **:** DISGRACEFUL
— **dis·cred·it·ably** \-blē\ *adverb*
**dis·creet** \di-ˈskrēt\ *adjective* [Middle English, from Middle French *discret*, from Medieval Latin *discretus*, from Latin, past participle of *discernere* to separate, distinguish between — more at DISCERN] (14th century)
**1 :** having or showing discernment or good judgment in conduct and especially in speech **:** PRUDENT; *especially* **:** capable of preserving prudent silence
**2 :** UNPRETENTIOUS, MODEST ⟨the warmth and *discreet* elegance of a civilized home —Joseph Wechsberg⟩
**3 :** UNOBTRUSIVE, UNNOTICEABLE ⟨followed at a *discreet* distance⟩
— **dis·creet·ly** *adverb*
— **dis·creet·ness** *noun*
**dis·crep·an·cy** \dis-ˈkre-pən-sē\ *noun, plural* **-cies** (circa 1623)
**1 :** the quality or state of being discrepant
**2 :** an instance of being discrepant
**dis·crep·ant** \-pənt\ *adjective* [Middle English *discrepaunt*, from Latin *discrepant-*, *discrepans*, present participle of *discrepare* to sound discordantly, from *dis-* + *crepare* to rattle, creak — more at RAVEN] (15th century)

**:** being at variance **:** DISAGREEING ⟨widely *discrepant* conclusions⟩
— **dis·crep·ant·ly** *adverb*
**dis·crete** \dis-ˈkrēt, ˈdis-ˌ\ *adjective* [Middle English, from Latin *discretus*] (14th century)
**1 :** constituting a separate entity **:** individually distinct
**2 a :** consisting of distinct or unconnected elements **:** NONCONTINUOUS **b :** taking on or having a finite or countably infinite number of values ⟨*discrete* probabilities⟩ ⟨a *discrete* random variable⟩
*synonym* see DISTINCT
— **dis·crete·ly** *adverb*
— **dis·crete·ness** *noun*
**dis·cre·tion** \dis-ˈkre-shən\ *noun* (14th century)
**1 :** the quality of being discreet **:** CIRCUMSPECTION; *especially* **:** cautious reserve in speech
**2 :** ability to make responsible decisions
**3 a :** individual choice or judgment ⟨left the decision to his *discretion*⟩ **b :** power of free decision or latitude of choice within certain legal bounds ⟨reached the age of *discretion*⟩
**4 :** the result of separating or distinguishing
**dis·cre·tion·ary** \-ˈkre-shə-ˌner-ē\ *adjective* (1698)
**1 :** left to discretion **:** exercised at one's own discretion
**2 :** available for discretionary use ⟨*discretionary* purchasing power⟩
**discretionary account** *noun* (circa 1920)
**:** a security or commodity market account in which an agent (as a broker) is given power of attorney so as to be able to make independent decisions and buy and sell for the principal's account
**dis·crim·i·na·bil·i·ty** \-ˌkri-mə-nə-ˈbi-lə-tē\ *noun, plural* **-ties** (circa 1901)
**1 :** the quality of being discriminable
**2 :** the ability to discriminate
**dis·crim·i·na·ble** \dis-ˈkri-mə-nə-bəl\ *adjective* (1736)
**:** capable of being discriminated
— **dis·crim·i·na·bly** \-blē\ *adverb*
**dis·crim·i·nant** \-ˈkri-mə-nənt\ *noun* (circa 1948)
**:** a mathematical expression providing a criterion for the behavior of another more complicated expression, relation, or set of relations
**discriminant function** *noun* (circa 1936)
**:** a function of a set of variables (as measurements of taxonomic specimens) that is evaluated for samples of events or objects and used as an aid in discriminating between or classifying them
**dis·crim·i·nate** \dis-ˈkri-mə-ˌnāt\ *verb* **-nat·ed; -nat·ing** [Latin *discriminatus*, past participle of *discriminare*, from *discrimin-*, *discrimen* distinction, from *discernere* to distinguish between — more at DISCERN] (1628)
*transitive verb*
**1 a :** to mark or perceive the distinguishing or peculiar features of **b :** DISTINGUISH, DIFFERENTIATE ⟨*discriminate* hundreds of colors⟩
**2 :** to distinguish by discerning or exposing differences; *especially* **:** to distinguish from another like object
*intransitive verb*
**1 a :** to make a distinction ⟨*discriminate* among historical sources⟩ **b :** to use good judgment
**2 :** to make a difference in treatment or favor on a basis other than individual merit ⟨*discriminate* in favor of your friends⟩ ⟨*discriminate* against a certain nationality⟩
**dis·crim·i·nat·ing** *adjective* (1647)
**1 :** making a distinction **:** DISTINGUISHING
**2 :** marked by discrimination: **a :** DISCERNING, JUDICIOUS **b :** DISCRIMINATORY
— **dis·crim·i·nat·ing·ly** \-ˌnā-tiŋ-lē\ *adverb*
**dis·crim·i·na·tion** \dis-ˌkri-mə-ˈnā-shən\ *noun* (1648)

**1 a :** the act of discriminating **b :** the process by which two stimuli differing in some aspect are responded to differently
**2 :** the quality or power of finely distinguishing
**3 a :** the act, practice, or an instance of discriminating categorically rather than individually **b :** prejudiced or prejudicial outlook, action, or treatment ⟨racial *discrimination*⟩
*synonym* see DISCERNMENT
— **dis·crim·i·na·tion·al** \-shnəl, -shə-nᵊl\ *adjective*
**dis·crim·i·na·tive** \dis-ˈkri-mə-ˌnā-tiv, -ˈkri-mə-nət-\ *adjective* (1677)
**1 :** making distinctions
**2 :** DISCRIMINATORY 2
**dis·crim·i·na·tor** \dis-ˈkri-mə-ˌnā-tər\ *noun* (1828)
**:** one that discriminates; *especially* **:** a circuit that can be adjusted to accept or reject signals of different characteristics (as amplitude or frequency)
**dis·crim·i·na·to·ry** \dis-ˈkri-mə-nə-ˌtōr-ē, -ˌtòr-, -ˈkrim-nə-\ *adjective* (1828)
**1 :** DISCRIMINATIVE 1
**2 :** applying or favoring discrimination in treatment
— **dis·crim·i·na·to·ri·ly** \-ˌkri-mə-nə-ˈtōr-ə-lē, -ˈtòr-, -ˌkrim-nə-\ *adverb*
**dis·cur·sive** \dis-ˈkər-siv\ *adjective* [Medieval Latin *discursivus*, from Latin *discursus*, past participle of *discurrere* to run about — more at DISCOURSE] (1598)
**1 a :** moving from topic to topic without order **:** RAMBLING **b :** proceeding coherently from topic to topic
**2 :** marked by analytical reasoning
— **dis·cur·sive·ly** *adverb*
— **dis·cur·sive·ness** *noun*
**dis·cus** \ˈdis-kəs\ *noun, plural* **dis·cus·es** [Latin — more at DISH] (1656)
**:** a disk (as of wood or plastic) that is thicker in the center than at the perimeter and that is hurled for distance as a track-and-field event; *also* **:** the event
**dis·cuss** \di-ˈskəs\ *transitive verb* [Middle English, from Latin *discussus*, past participle of *discutere* to disperse, from *dis-* apart + *quatere* to shake — more at DIS-, QUASH] (14th century)

discus

**1** *obsolete* **:** DISPEL
**2 a :** to investigate by reasoning or argument **b :** to present in detail for examination or consideration ⟨*discussed* plans for the party⟩ **c :** to talk about

☆ SYNONYMS
**Discover, ascertain, determine, unearth, learn** mean to find out what one did not previously know. DISCOVER may apply to something requiring exploration or investigation or to a chance encounter ⟨*discovered* the source of the river⟩. ASCERTAIN implies effort to find the facts or the truth proceeding from awareness of ignorance or uncertainty ⟨attempts to *ascertain* the population of the region⟩. DETERMINE emphasizes the intent to establish the facts definitely or precisely ⟨unable to *determine* the origin of the word⟩. UNEARTH implies bringing to light something forgotten or hidden ⟨*unearth* old records⟩. LEARN may imply acquiring knowledge with little effort or conscious intention (as by simply being told) or it may imply study and practice ⟨I *learned* her name only today⟩ ⟨*learning* Greek⟩.

**3** *obsolete* : DECLARE ☆
— **dis·cuss·able** *or* **dis·cuss·ible**
\-'skə-sə-bəl\ *adjective*
— **dis·cuss·er** *noun*
**dis·cus·sant** \di-'skə-s°nt\ *noun* (1926)
: one who takes part in a formal discussion or symposium
**dis·cus·sion** \di-'skə-shən\ *noun* (14th century)
**1** : consideration of a question in open and usually informal debate
**2** : a formal treatment of a topic in speech or writing
**¹dis·dain** \dis-'dān\ *noun* [Middle English *desdeyne*, from Old French *desdeign*, from *desdeignier*] (14th century)
: a feeling of contempt for what is beneath one : SCORN
**²disdain** *transitive verb* [Middle English *desdeynen*, from Middle French *desdeignier*, from Old French, from (assumed) Vulgar Latin *disdignare*, from Latin *dis-* + *dignare* to deign — more at DEIGN] (14th century)
**1** : to look on with scorn
**2** : to refuse or abstain from because of disdain
**3** : to treat as beneath one's notice or dignity
*synonym* see DESPISE
**dis·dain·ful** \-fəl\ *adjective* (circa 1542)
: full of or expressing disdain
*synonym* see PROUD
— **dis·dain·ful·ly** \-fə-lē\ *adverb*
— **dis·dain·ful·ness** *noun*
**dis·ease** \di-'zēz\ *noun* [Middle English *disese*, from Middle French *desaise*, from *des-* + *aise* ease] (14th century)
**1** *obsolete* : TROUBLE
**2** : a condition of the living animal or plant body or of one of its parts that impairs normal functioning : SICKNESS, MALADY
**3** : a harmful development (as in a social institution)
— **dis·eased** \-'zēzd\ *adjective*
**dis·econ·o·my** \di-si-'kä-nə-mē\ *noun* (1937)
**1** : a lack of economy
**2** : a factor responsible for an increase in cost
**dis·em·bark** \di-səm-'bärk\ *verb* [Middle French *desembarquer*, from *des-* dis- + *embarquer* to embark] (1582)
*transitive verb*
: to remove to shore from a ship
*intransitive verb*
**1** : to go ashore out of a ship
**2** : to get out of a vehicle or craft
— **dis·em·bar·ka·tion** \(,)di-,sem-,bär-'kā-shən, -bər-\ *noun*
**dis·em·bar·rass** \di-səm-'bar-əs\ *transitive verb* (1726)
: to free (as oneself) from something troublesome or superfluous
*synonym* see EXTRICATE
**dis·em·body** \di-səm-'bä-dē\ *transitive verb* (1714)
: to divest of a body, of corporeal existence, or of reality
**dis·em·bogue** \di-sim-'bōg\ *verb* -bogued; -bogu·ing [modification of Spanish *desembocar*, from *des-* dis- (from Latin *dis-*) + *embocar* to put into the mouth, from *en* in (from Latin *in*) + *boca* mouth, from Latin *bucca*] (1595)
*intransitive verb*
: to flow or come forth from or as if from a channel
*transitive verb*
*archaic* : to pour out from or as if from a container
**dis·em·bow·el** \di-səm-'baú(-ə)l\ *transitive verb* (1618)
**1** : to take out the bowels of : EVISCERATE
**2** : to remove the substance of
— **dis·em·bow·el·ment** \-mənt\ *noun*
**dis·en·chant** \di-s°n-'chant\ *transitive verb* [Middle French *desenchanter*, from *des-* dis- + *enchanter* to enchant] (circa 1586)

: to free from illusion
— **dis·en·chant·er** *noun*
— **dis·en·chant·ing** *adjective*
— **dis·en·chant·ing·ly** \-'chan-tiŋ-lē\ *adverb*
— **dis·en·chant·ment** \-mənt\ *noun*
**dis·en·chant·ed** \-'chan-təd\ *adjective* (1838)
: DISAPPOINTED, DISSATISFIED
**dis·en·cum·ber** \di-s°n-'kəm-bər\ *transitive verb* [Middle French *desencombrer*, from *des-* dis- + *encombrer* to encumber] (1598)
: to free from encumbrance : DISBURDEN
*synonym* see EXTRICATE
**dis·en·dow** \di-s°n-'daú\ *transitive verb* (1861)
: to strip of endowment
— **dis·en·dow·er** \-'daú(-ə)r\ *noun*
— **dis·en·dow·ment** \-'daú-mənt\ *noun*
**dis·en·fran·chise** \di-s°n-'fran-,chīz\ *transitive verb* (1664)
: DISFRANCHISE
— **dis·en·fran·chise·ment** \-,chīz-mənt, -chəz-\ *noun*
**dis·en·gage** \di-s°n-'gāj\ *verb* [French *désengager*, from Middle French, from *des-* dis- + *engager* to engage] (1611)
*transitive verb*
: to release from something that engages or involves
*intransitive verb*
: to release or detach oneself : WITHDRAW
— **dis·en·gage·ment** \-mənt\ *noun*
**dis·en·tail** \di-s°n-'tā(ə)l\ *transitive verb* (1641)
: to free from entail
**dis·en·tan·gle** \di-s°n-'taŋ-gəl\ *transitive verb* (1598)
*transitive verb*
: to free from entanglement : UNRAVEL
*intransitive verb*
: to become disentangled
*synonym* see EXTRICATE
— **dis·en·tan·gle·ment** \-mənt\ *noun*
**dis·en·thrall** *also* **dis·en·thral** \di-s°n-'thrȯl\ *transitive verb* (1643)
: to free from bondage : LIBERATE
**dis·en·tit·le** \di-s°n-'tī-t°l\ *transitive verb* (1654)
: to deprive of title, claim, or right
**dis·equil·i·brate** \di-si-'kwi-lə-,brāt\ *transitive verb* (1891)
: to put out of balance
— **dis·equil·i·bra·tion** \-,kwi-lə-'brā-shən\ *noun*
**dis·equi·lib·ri·um** \(,)di-,sē-kwə-'li-brē-əm, -,se-kwə-\ *noun* (1840)
: loss or lack of equilibrium
**dis·es·tab·lish** \di-sə-'stab-lish\ *transitive verb* (1598)
: to deprive of an established status; *especially* : to deprive of the status and privileges of an established church
— **dis·es·tab·lish·ment** \-mənt\ *noun*
**dis·es·tab·lish·men·tar·i·an** \-,stab-lish-,men-'ter-ē-ən, -mən-\ *noun, often capitalized* [*disestablishment*] (1885)
: one who opposes an established order
— **disestablishmentarian** *adjective, often capitalized*
**¹dis·es·teem** \di-sə-'stēm\ *transitive verb* (1594)
: to regard with disfavor
**²disesteem** *noun* (1603)
: DISFAVOR, DISREPUTE
**di·seuse** \dē-'züz, -'zœz\ *noun, plural* **di·seuses** \*same*\ [French, feminine of *diseur*, from Old French, from *dire* to say, from Latin *dicere* — more at DICTION] (1896)
: a skilled and usually professional woman reciter
**¹dis·fa·vor** \(,)dis-'fā-vər\ *noun* [probably from Middle French *desfaveur*, from *des-* dis- + *faveur* favor, from Old French *favor*] (circa 1533)

**1** : DISAPPROVAL, DISLIKE ⟨practices looked upon with *disfavor*⟩
**2** : the state or fact of being no longer favored ⟨fell into *disfavor*⟩
**3** : DISADVANTAGE
**²disfavor** *transitive verb* (1570)
: to withhold or withdraw favor from
**dis·fig·ure** \dis-'fi-gyər, *especially British* -'fi-gər\ *transitive verb* [Middle English, from Middle French *desfigurer*, from *des-* dis- + *figure* figure] (14th century)
**1** : to impair (as in beauty) by deep and persistent injuries ⟨a face *disfigured* by smallpox⟩
**2** *obsolete* : DISGUISE
— **dis·fig·ure·ment** \-mənt\ *noun*
**dis·fran·chise** \(,)dis-'fran-,chīz\ *transitive verb* (15th century)
: to deprive of a franchise, of a legal right, or of some privilege or immunity; *especially* : to deprive of the right to vote
— **dis·fran·chise·ment** \-,chīz-mənt, -chəz-\ *noun*
**dis·frock** \(,)dis-'fräk\ *transitive verb* (1837)
: DEFROCK
**dis·func·tion** *variant of* DYSFUNCTION
**dis·fur·nish** \(,)dis-'fər-nish\ *transitive verb* [Middle French *desfourniss-*, stem of *desfournir*, from *des-* dis- + *fournir* to furnish] (1531)
: to make destitute of possessions : DIVEST
— **dis·fur·nish·ment** \-mənt\ *noun*
**dis·gorge** \(,)dis-'gȯrj\ *verb* [Middle English, from Middle French *desgorger*, from *des-* dis- + *gorge* gorge] (15th century)
*transitive verb*
**1 a** : to discharge by the throat and mouth : VOMIT **b** : to discharge or let go of in a manner suggesting vomiting ⟨the train *disgorged* its passengers⟩ **c** : to give up on request or under pressure ⟨refused to *disgorge* his ill-gotten gains⟩
**2** : to discharge the contents of (as the stomach)
*intransitive verb*
: to discharge contents ⟨where the river *disgorges* into the sea⟩
**¹dis·grace** \di-'skrās, dis-'grās\ *transitive verb* (1580)
**1** *archaic* : to humiliate by a superior showing
**2** : to be a source of shame to ⟨your actions *disgraced* the family⟩
**3** : to cause to lose favor or standing ⟨was *disgraced* by the hint of scandal⟩
— **dis·grac·er** *noun*
**²disgrace** *noun* [Middle French, from Old Italian *disgrazia*, from *dis-* (from Latin) + *grazia* grace, from Latin *gratia* — more at GRACE] (1586)
**1 a** : the condition of one fallen from grace or honor **b** : loss of grace, favor, or honor

---

☆ **SYNONYMS**
**Discuss, argue, debate** mean to discourse about in order to reach conclusions or to convince. DISCUSS implies a sifting of possibilities especially by presenting considerations pro and con ⟨*discussed* the need for a new highway⟩. ARGUE implies the offering of reasons or evidence in support of convictions already held ⟨*argued* that the project would be too costly⟩. DEBATE suggests formal or public argument between opposing parties ⟨*debated* the merits of the amendment⟩; it may also apply to deliberation with oneself ⟨I'm *debating* whether I should go⟩.

---

\ə\ abut \°\ kitten \ər\ further \a\ ash \ā\ ace
\ä\ mop, mar \aú\ out \ch\ chin \e\ bet \ē\ easy
\g\ go \i\ hit \ī\ ice \j\ job \ŋ\ sing \ō\ go
\ȯ\ law \ȯi\ boy \th\ thin \th\ the \ü\ loot \ú\ foot
\y\ yet \zh\ vision *see also* Guide to Pronunciation

**2 :** something that disgraces ⟨your manners are a *disgrace*⟩ ☆
**dis·grace·ful** \-fəl\ *adjective* (1597)
**:** bringing or involving disgrace
— **dis·grace·ful·ly** \-fə-lē\ *adverb*
— **dis·grace·ful·ness** *noun*
**dis·grun·tle** \dis-'grən-t°l\ *transitive verb* **dis·grun·tled; dis·grun·tling** \-'grənt-liŋ, -'grən-t°l-iŋ\ [*dis-* + *gruntle* (to grumble), from Middle English *gruntlen,* frequentative of *grunten* to grunt] (1682)
**:** to make ill-humored or discontented — usually used as a participial adjective ⟨they were a very *disgruntled* crew —Flannery O'Connor⟩
— **dis·grun·tle·ment** \-t°l-mənt\ *noun*
¹**dis·guise** \də-'skīz, dis-'gīz *also* diz-\ *transitive verb* **dis·guised; dis·guis·ing** [Middle English *disgisen,* from Middle French *desguiser,* from Old French, from *des-* dis- + *guise* guise] (14th century)
**1 a :** to change the customary dress or appearance of **b :** to furnish with a false appearance or an assumed identity
**2** *obsolete* **:** DISFIGURE
**3 :** to obscure the existence or true state or character of **:** CONCEAL ☆
— **dis·guis·ed·ly** \-'gīz(-ə)d-lē, -'kīz(-ə)d-\ *adverb*
— **dis·guise·ment** \-'gīz-mənt, -'kīz-\ *noun*
— **dis·guis·er** *noun*
²**disguise** *noun* (14th century)
**1 :** apparel assumed to conceal one's identity or counterfeit another's
**2 :** the act of disguising
**3 a :** form misrepresenting the true nature of something ⟨blessings in *disguise*⟩ **b :** an artificial manner **:** PRETENSE ⟨threw off all *disguise*⟩
¹**dis·gust** \di-'skəst, dis-'gəst *also* diz-\ *noun* (1598)
**:** marked aversion aroused by something highly distasteful **:** REPUGNANCE
²**disgust** *verb* [Middle French *desgouster,* from *des-* dis- + *goust* taste, from Latin *gustus;* akin to Latin *gustare* to taste — more at CHOOSE] (1616)
*transitive verb*
**1 :** to provoke to loathing, repugnance, or aversion **:** be offensive to
**2 :** to cause (one) to lose an interest or intention
*intransitive verb*
**:** to cause disgust
— **dis·gust·ed** *adjective*
— **dis·gust·ed·ly** *adverb*
**dis·gust·ful** \-fəl\ *adjective* (circa 1616)
**1 :** provoking disgust
**2 :** full of or accompanied by disgust
— **dis·gust·ful·ly** \-fə-lē\ *adverb*
**dis·gust·ing** *adjective* (1754)
**:** causing disgust
— **dis·gust·ing·ly** \di-'skəs-tiŋ-lē, dis-'gəs- *also* diz-\ *adverb*
¹**dish** \'dish\ *noun* [Middle English, from Old English *disc* plate, from Latin *discus* quoit, disk, dish, from Greek *diskos,* from *dikein* to throw] (before 12th century)
**1 a :** a more or less concave vessel from which food is served **b :** the contents of a dish ⟨a *dish* of strawberries⟩
**2 a :** food prepared in a particular way **b :** something one particularly enjoys **:** CUP OF TEA
**3 a** (1) **:** any of various shallow concave vessels; *broadly* **:** anything shallowly concave (2) **:** a directional receiver having a concave usually parabolic reflector; *especially* **:** one used as a microwave antenna **b :** the state of being concave or the degree of concavity
**4 a :** something that is favored ⟨entertainment that is just his *dish*⟩ **b :** an attractive or sexy person
²**dish** (14th century)
*transitive verb*

**1 :** to put (as food for serving) into a dish — often used with *up*
**2 :** PRESENT — usually used with *up*
**3 :** to make concave like a dish
*intransitive verb*
**:** to pass to a teammate (as in basketball) — usually used with *off*
**dis·ha·bille** \ˌdis-ə-'bē(ə)l, -'bil\ *noun* [French *déshabillé,* from past participle of *déshabiller* to undress, from *dés-* dis- + *habiller* to dress — more at HABILIMENT] (1673)
**1 a** *archaic* **:** NEGLIGEE **b :** the state of being dressed in a casual or careless style
**2 :** a deliberately careless or casual manner
**dis·har·mo·ni·ous** \ˌdis-(ˌ)här-'mō-nē-əs\ *adjective* (1659)
**:** lacking in harmony
**dis·har·mo·nize** \(ˌ)dis-'här-mə-ˌnīz\ *transitive verb* (1801)
**:** to make disharmonious
**dis·har·mo·ny** \-nē\ *noun* (circa 1602)
**:** lack of harmony **:** DISCORD
**dish·cloth** \'dish-ˌklȯth\ *noun* (circa 1828)
**:** a cloth for washing dishes
**dish·clout** \'dish-ˌklaȯt\ *noun* (circa 1530)
*British* **:** DISHCLOTH
**dis·heart·en** \(ˌ)dis-'härt-°n\ *transitive verb* (1590)
**:** to cause to lose spirit or morale
— **dis·heart·en·ing·ly** \-'härt-niŋ-lē, -'härt-°n-iŋ-\ *adverb*
— **dis·heart·en·ment** \-'härt-°n-mənt\ *noun*
**dished** \'disht\ *adjective* (1737)
**:** CONCAVE
**di·shev·el** \di-'shev-əl\ *transitive verb* **di·shev·eled** *or* **di·shev·elled; di·shev·el·ing** *or* **di·shev·el·ling** \-'shev-(ə-)liŋ\ [back-formation from *disheveled*] (1598)
**:** to throw into disorder or disarray
**di·shev·eled** *or* **di·shev·elled** *adjective* [Middle English *discheveled* with disordered hair, part translation of Middle French *deschevelé,* from past participle of *descheveler* to disarrange the hair, from *des-* dis- + *chevel* hair, from Latin *capillus*] (1583)
**:** marked by disorder or disarray
**dis·hon·est** \(ˌ)di-'sä-nəst *also* -'zä-\ *adjective* [Middle English, from Middle French *deshoneste,* from *des-* dis- + *honeste* honest] (14th century)
**1** *obsolete* **:** SHAMEFUL, UNCHASTE
**2 :** characterized by lack of truth, honesty, or trustworthiness **:** UNFAIR, DECEPTIVE ☆
— **dis·hon·est·ly** *adverb*
**dis·hon·es·ty** \-nə-stē\ *noun* (1599)
**1 :** lack of honesty or integrity **:** disposition to defraud or deceive
**2 :** a dishonest act **:** FRAUD
¹**dis·hon·or** \(ˌ)di-'sä-nər *also* -'zä-\ *noun* [Middle English *dishonour,* from Middle French *deshonor,* from *des-* dis- + *honor* honor] (13th century)
**1 :** lack or loss of honor or reputation
**2 :** the state of one who has lost honor or prestige **:** SHAME
**3 :** a cause of disgrace
**4 :** the nonpayment or nonacceptance of commercial paper by the party on whom it is drawn
*synonym* see DISGRACE
— **dis·hon·or·er** \-'sän-ər-ər *also* -'zä-\ *noun*
²**dishonor** *transitive verb* (13th century)
**1 a :** to treat in a degrading manner **b :** to bring shame on
**2 :** to refuse to accept or pay (as a bill or check)
**dis·hon·or·able** \(ˌ)di-'sä-nə-rə-bəl, -'sä-nər-bəl\ *adjective* (1534)
**1 :** lacking honor **:** SHAMEFUL ⟨*dishonorable* conduct⟩
**2** *archaic* **:** not honored
— **dis·hon·or·able·ness** *noun*
— **dis·hon·or·ably** \-blē\ *adverb*

**dish out** *transitive verb* (1641)
**:** to give or dispense freely ⟨*dish out* gifts⟩ ⟨*dish out* advice⟩ ⟨*dish out* punishment⟩
**dish·pan** \'dish-ˌpan\ *noun* (1872)
**:** a large flat-bottomed pan used for washing dishes
**dishpan hands** *noun plural but singular or plural in construction* (1944)
**:** a condition of dryness, redness, and scaling of the hands that results typically from repeated exposure to, sensitivity to, or overuse of cleaning materials (as detergents) used in housework
**dish·rag** \'dish-ˌrag\ *noun* (1839)
**:** DISHCLOTH
**dish·ware** \'dish-ˌwar, -ˌwer\ *noun* (1946)
**:** tableware (as of china) used in serving food
**dish·wash·er** \-ˌwȯ-shər, -ˌwä-\ *noun* (15th century)
**1 :** a worker employed to wash dishes
**2 :** a machine for washing dishes
**dish·wa·ter** \-ˌwȯ-tər, -ˌwä-\ *noun* (15th century)
**:** water in which dishes have been or are to be washed
**dishy** \'di-shē\ *adjective* **dish·i·er; -est** (1961)
**:** ATTRACTIVE 2
¹**dis·il·lu·sion** \ˌdi-sə-'lü-zhən\ *noun* (1851)
**:** the condition of being disenchanted
²**disillusion** *transitive verb* **dis·il·lu·sioned; dis·il·lu·sion·ing** \-'lü-zhə-niŋ\ (1855)
**:** to leave without illusion or naive faith and trust
— **dis·il·lu·sion·ment** \-'lü-zhən-mənt\ *noun*

---

**disillusioned** *adjective* (1871)
: DISAPPOINTED, DISSATISFIED

**dis·in·cen·tive** \ˌdi-s°n-'sen-tiv\ *noun* (1946)
: DETERRENT

**dis·in·cli·na·tion** \ˌ(ˌ)di-ˌsin-klə-'nā-shən, -ˌsiŋ-\ *noun* (1647)
: a preference for avoiding something : slight aversion

**dis·in·cline** \ˌdi-s°n-'klīn\ *transitive verb* (1647)
: to make unwilling

**dis·in·clined** *adjective* (1647)
: unwilling because of mild dislike or disapproval ☆

**dis·in·fect** \ˌdi-s°n-'fekt\ *transitive verb* [Middle French *desinfecter,* from *des-* dis- + *infecter* to infect] (1598)
: to free from infection especially by destroying harmful microorganisms; *broadly* : CLEANSE
— **dis·in·fec·tion** \-'fek-shən\ *noun*

**dis·in·fec·tant** \-'fek-tənt\ *noun* (1837)
: an agent that frees from infection; *especially* : a chemical that destroys vegetative forms of harmful microorganisms especially on inanimate objects but that may be less effective in destroying bacterial spores

**dis·in·fest** \ˌdi-s°n-'fest\ *transitive verb* (circa 1920)
: to rid of small animal pests (as insects or rodents)
— **dis·in·fes·ta·tion** \ˌ(ˌ)di-ˌsin-ˌfes-'tā-shən\ *noun*

**dis·in·fes·tant** \ˌdi-s°n-'fes-tənt\ *noun* (1943)
: a disinfesting agent

**dis·in·fla·tion** \ˌdi-s°n-'flā-shən\ *noun* (1880)
: a reversal of inflationary pressures
— **dis·in·fla·tion·ary** \-shə-ˌner-ē\ *adjective*

**dis·in·for·ma·tion** \ˌ(ˌ)di-ˌsin-fər-'mā-shən\ *noun* (1939)
: false information deliberately and often covertly spread (as by the planting of rumors) in order to influence public opinion or obscure the truth ◆

**dis·in·gen·u·ous** \ˌdi-s°n-'jen-yə-wəs\ *adjective* (1655)
: lacking in candor; *also* : giving a false appearance of simple frankness : CALCULATING
— **dis·in·gen·u·ous·ly** *adverb*
— **dis·in·gen·u·ous·ness** *noun*

**dis·in·her·it** \ˌdi-s°n-'her-ət\ *transitive verb* [Middle English] (15th century)
**1** : to prevent deliberately from inheriting something (as by making a will)
**2** : to deprive of natural or human rights or of previously held special privileges
— **dis·in·her·i·tance** \-'her-ə-tən(t)s\ *noun*

**dis·in·hi·bi·tion** \ˌ(ˌ)di-ˌsin-(h)ə-'bi-shən\ *noun* (circa 1927)
: loss or reduction of an inhibition (as by the action of interfering stimuli or events) ⟨*disinhibition* of a reflex⟩ ⟨*disinhibition* of violent tendencies⟩
— **dis·in·hib·it** \ˌ(ˌ)di-s°n-'hi-bət\ *transitive verb*

**dis·in·te·grate** \ˌ(ˌ)di-'sin-tə-ˌgrāt\ (1796) *transitive verb*
**1** : to break or decompose into constituent elements, parts, or small particles
**2** : to destroy the unity or integrity of
*intransitive verb*
**1** : to break or separate into constituent elements or parts
**2** : to lose unity or integrity by or as if by breaking into parts
**3** : to undergo a change in composition ⟨an atomic nucleus that *disintegrates* because of radioactivity⟩
— **dis·in·te·gra·tion** \ˌ(ˌ)di-ˌsin-tə-'grā-shən\ *noun*
— **dis·in·te·gra·tive** \ˌ(ˌ)di-'sin-tə-ˌgrā-tiv\ *adjective*
— **dis·in·te·gra·tor** \-ˌgrā-tər\ *noun*

**dis·in·ter** \ˌdi-s°n-'tər\ *transitive verb* (1611)
**1** : to take out of the grave or tomb

**2** : to bring back into awareness or prominence; *also* : to bring to light : UNEARTH
— **dis·in·ter·ment** \-'mənt\ *noun*

**¹dis·in·ter·est** \ˌ(ˌ)dis-'in-trəst; -'in-tə-ˌrest, -tə-rəst, -tərst; -'in-ˌtrest\ *transitive verb* (1612)
: to cause to regard something with no interest or concern

**²disinterest** *noun* (1658)
**1** : DISINTERESTEDNESS
**2** : lack of interest : INDIFFERENCE

**dis·in·ter·est·ed** \-təd\ *adjective* (circa 1612)
**1 a** : not having the mind or feelings engaged : not interested ⟨telling them in a *disinterested* voice —Tom Wicker⟩ ⟨Introverted. Unsocial . . . Disinterested in women —J. A. Brussel⟩ **b** : no longer interested ⟨husband and wife become *disinterested* in each other —T. I. Rubin⟩
**2** : free from selfish motive or interest : UNBIASED ⟨a *disinterested* decision⟩ ⟨*disinterested* intellectual curiosity is the lifeblood of real civilization —G. M. Trevelyan⟩ ▪
*synonym* see INDIFFERENT
— **dis·in·ter·est·ed·ly** *adverb*

**dis·in·ter·est·ed·ness** \-təd-nəs\ *noun* (circa 1682)
: the quality of being objective or impartial

**dis·in·ter·me·di·a·tion** \ˌdi-ˌsin-tər-ˌmē-dē-'ā-shən\ *noun* (1967)
: the diversion of savings from accounts with low fixed interest rates to direct investment in high-yielding instruments

**dis·in·tox·i·cate** \ˌdi-s°n-'täk-sə-ˌkāt\ *transitive verb* (1685)
: DETOXIFY 2
— **dis·in·tox·i·ca·tion** \-ˌtäk-sə-'kā-shən\ *noun*

**dis·in·vest** \ˌ(ˌ)di-s°n-'vest\ *intransitive verb* (1945)
: to reduce or eliminate capital investment (as in an industry or area)

**dis·in·vest·ment** \ˌdi-s°n-'ves(t)-mənt\ *noun* (1936)
: consumption of capital; *also* : the withdrawing of investment

**dis·in·vite** \ˌ(ˌ)di-s°n-'vīt\ *transitive verb* (1580)
: to withdraw an invitation to

**dis·join** \ˌ(ˌ)dis-'jȯin\ *verb* [Middle English *disjoynen,* from Middle French *desjoindre,* from Latin *disjungere,* from *dis-* + *jungere* to join — more at YOKE] (15th century)
*transitive verb*
: to end the joining of
*intransitive verb*
: to become detached

**¹dis·joint** \-'jȯint\ *adjective* [Middle English *disjoynt,* from Middle French *desjoint,* past participle of *desjoindre*] (15th century)
**1** *obsolete* : DISJOINTED 1a
**2** : having no elements in common ⟨*disjoint* mathematical sets⟩

**²disjoint** (15th century)
*transitive verb*
**1** : to disturb the orderly structure or arrangement of
**2** : to take apart at the joints
*intransitive verb*
: to come apart at the joints

**dis·joint·ed** *adjective* (circa 1586)
**1 a** : being thrown out of orderly function ⟨a *disjointed* society⟩ **b** : lacking coherence or orderly sequence ⟨an incomplete and *disjointed* history⟩
**2** : separated at or as if at the joint
— **dis·joint·ed·ly** *adverb*
— **dis·joint·ed·ness** *noun*

**¹dis·junct** \dis-'jəŋ(k)t\ *adjective* [Middle English, from Latin *disjunctus,* past participle of *disjungere* to disjoin] (15th century)
: marked by separation of or from usually contiguous parts or individuals: as **a** : DISCONTINUOUS **b** : relating to melodic progression by intervals larger than a major second — compare CONJUNCT

☐ USAGE

**disinterested**   *Disinterested* and *uninterested* have a tangled history. *Uninterested* originally meant impartial, but this sense fell into disuse during the 18th century. About the same time the original sense of *disinterested* also disappeared, with *uninterested* developing a new sense—the present meaning—to take its place. The original sense of *uninterested* is still out of use, but the original sense of *disinterested* revived in the early 20th century. The revival has since been under frequent attack as an illiteracy and a blurring or loss of a useful distinction. Actual usage shows otherwise. Sense 2 of *disinterested* is still its most frequent sense, especially in edited prose; it shows no sign of vanishing. A careful writer may choose sense 1a of *disinterested* in preference to *uninterested* for emphasis ⟨teaching the letters of the alphabet to her wiggling and supremely *disinterested* little daughter —C. L. Sulzberger⟩ Further, *disinterested* has developed a sense (1b), perhaps influenced by sense 1 of the prefix *dis-,* that contrasts with *uninterested* ⟨when I grow tired or *disinterested* in anything, I experience a disgust —Jack London (letter, 1914)⟩ Still, use of senses 1a and 1b will incur the disapproval of some who may not fully appreciate the history of this word or the subtleties of its present use.

◇ WORD HISTORY

**disinformation**   Though its roots are several decades older, *disinformation* became a common word in the 1970s and '80s. Many uses of the word during this period associate *disinformation* with the KGB, the Soviet secret police; and claims have been made that the KGB established a branch in the 1950s called, presumably unofficially, the "Department of Disinformation." It has been said that the word first appeared in English in the *Times* of London in 1955, but actually the U.S. magazine *Time* used it a year earlier to refer to Communist propaganda. The earliest known attestation of *disinformation,* however, is in the 1939 book *In Stalin's Secret Police,* a pioneering exposé of Stalin's purges, written by Walter Krivitsky, a Soviet intelligence officer who defected in the fall of 1937 and—meeting a fate common among Stalin's enemies in those days—was found shot in his hotel room in February 1941. In all likelihood, *disinformation* in Krivitsky's book as well as later uses are translations of Russian *dezinformatsiya,* which began to appear in Russian dictionaries in 1949.

\ə\ **abut** \ə\ **kitten** \ər\ **further** \a\ **ash** \ā\ **ace**
\ä\ **mop, mar** \aù\ **out** \ch\ **chin** \e\ **bet** \ē\ **easy**
\g\ **go** \i\ **hit** \ī\ **ice** \j\ **job** \ŋ\ **sing** \ō\ **go**
\ȯ\ **law** \ȯi\ **boy** \th\ **thin** \th\ **the** \ü\ **loot** \ù\ **foot**
\y\ **yet** \zh\ **vision**    *see also* Guide to Pronunciation

**²dis·junct** \'dis-ˌjəŋ(k)t, dis-'\ *noun* (1921)
**1 :** any of the alternatives that make up a logical disjunction
**2 :** an adverb or adverbial (as *luckily* in "Luckily we had an extra set" or *in short* in "In short, there is nothing we can do") that is loosely connected to a sentence and conveys the speaker's or writer's comment on its content, truth, or manner — compare ADJUNCT 2b
**dis·junc·tion** \dis-'jəŋ(k)-shən\ *noun* (14th century)
**1 :** a sharp cleavage : DISUNION, SEPARATION ⟨the *disjunction* between theory and practice⟩
**2 :** a compound sentence in logic formed by joining two simple statements by *or:* **a :** INCLUSIVE DISJUNCTION **b :** EXCLUSIVE DISJUNCTION
**¹dis·junc·tive** \-'jəŋ(k)-tiv\ *adjective* (15th century)
**1 a :** relating to, being, or forming a logical disjunction **b :** expressing an alternative or opposition between the meanings of the words connected ⟨the *disjunctive* conjunction *or*⟩ **c :** expressed by mutually exclusive alternatives joined by *or* ⟨*disjunctive* pleading⟩
**2 :** marked by breaks or disunity ⟨a *disjunctive* narrative sequence⟩
**3** *of a pronoun form* **:** stressed and not attached to the verb as an enclitic or proclitic
— **dis·junc·tive·ly** *adverb*
**²disjunctive** *noun* (1530)
**:** a disjunctive conjunction
**dis·junc·ture** \-'jəŋ(k)-chər\ *noun* [Middle English, modification (influenced by Latin *disjunctus*) of Middle French *desjointure,* from *desjoint* disjoint] (14th century)
**:** DISJUNCTION 1
**¹disk** *or* **disc** \'disk\ *noun, often attributive* [Latin *discus* — more at DISH] (1664)
**1 a :** the seemingly flat figure of a celestial body ⟨the solar *disk*⟩ **b** *archaic* **:** DISCUS
**2 :** any of various rounded and flattened animal anatomical structures (as an intervertebral disk) — compare SLIPPED DISK
**3 :** the central part of the flower head of a typical composite made up of closely packed tubular flowers
**4 a :** a thin circular object **b** *usually* **disc :** a phonograph record **c :** a round flat plate coated with a magnetic substance on which data for a computer is stored **d** *usually* **disc :** OPTICAL DISK: as (1) : VIDEODISC (2) : COMPACT DISC
**5** *usually* **disc :** one of the concave circular steel tools with sharpened edge making up the working part of a disc harrow or plow; *also* **:** an implement employing such tools
— **disk·like** \-ˌlīk\ *adjective*
**²disk** *or* **disc** *transitive verb* (circa 1884)
**:** to cultivate with an implement (as a harrow or plow) that turns and loosens the soil with a series of disks
**dis·kette** \ˌdis-'ket\ *noun* (1973)
**:** FLOPPY DISK
**disk flower** *noun* (1870)
**:** one of the tubular flowers in the disk of a composite plant — called also *disk floret*
**dis·lik·able** *also* **dis·like·able** \(ˌ)dis-'lī-kə-bəl\ *adjective* (1843)
**:** easy to dislike
**¹dis·like** \(ˌ)dis-'līk, 'dis-\ *noun* (1577)
**1 :** a feeling of aversion or disapproval
**2** *obsolete* **:** DISCORD
**²dislike** *transitive verb* (1579)
**1** *archaic* **:** DISPLEASE
**2 :** to regard with dislike : DISAPPROVE
**3** *obsolete* **:** to show aversion to
— **dis·lik·er** *noun*
**dis·limn** \(ˌ)dis-'lim\ *verb* (1606)
**:** DIM
**dis·lo·cate** \'dis-lō-ˌkāt, -lə-; (ˌ)dis-'lō-\ *transitive verb* [Medieval Latin *dislocatus,* past participle of *dislocare,* from Latin *dis-* + *locare* to locate] (1605)
**1 :** to put out of place; *specifically* **:** to displace (a bone) from normal connections with another bone

**2 :** to force a change in the usual status, relationship, or order of : DISRUPT
**dis·lo·ca·tion** \ˌdis-(ˌ)lō-'kā-shən, -lə-\ *noun* (14th century)
**:** the act of dislocating : the state of being dislocated: as **a :** displacement of one or more bones at a joint : LUXATION **b :** a discontinuity in the otherwise normal lattice structure of a crystal **c :** disruption of an established order
**dis·lodge** \(ˌ)dis-'läj\ *verb* [Middle English *disloggen,* from Middle French *desloger,* from *des-* dis- + *loger* to lodge, from Old French *loge* lodge] (15th century)
*transitive verb*
**1 :** to drive from a position of hiding, defense, or advantage
**2 :** to force out of a secure or settled position ⟨*dislodged* the rock with a shovel⟩
*intransitive verb*
**:** to leave a lodging place
— **dis·lodg·ment** *or* **dis·lodge·ment** *noun*
**dis·loy·al** \(ˌ)dis-'lȯi(-ə)l\ *adjective* [Middle English, from Middle French *desloial,* from Old French, from *des-* dis- + *loial* loyal] (15th century)
**:** lacking in loyalty; *also* **:** showing an absence of allegiance, devotion, obligation, faith, or support ⟨his *disloyal* refusal to help his friend⟩
*synonym* see FAITHLESS
— **dis·loy·al·ly** \-'lȯi-ə-lē\ *adverb*
**dis·loy·al·ty** \-'lȯi(-ə)l-tē\ *noun* (15th century)
**:** lack of loyalty
**dis·mal** \'diz-məl\ *adjective* [Middle English, from *dismal,* noun, days marked as unlucky in medieval calendars, from Anglo-French, from Medieval Latin *dies mali,* literally, evil days] (15th century)
**1** *obsolete* **:** DISASTROUS, DREADFUL
**2 :** showing or causing gloom or depression
**3 :** lacking merit : particularly bad ◆
— **dis·mal·ly** \-mə-lē\ *adverb*
— **dis·mal·ness** *noun*
**dis·man·tle** \(ˌ)dis-'man-tᵊl\ *transitive verb* **dis·man·tled; dis·man·tling** \-'mant-liŋ, -'man-tᵊl-\ [Middle French *desmanteler,* from *des-* dis- + *mantel* mantle] (1602)
**1 :** to take to pieces; *also* **:** to destroy the integrity or functioning of
**2 :** to strip of dress or covering : DIVEST
**3 :** to strip of furniture and equipment
— **dis·man·tle·ment** \-'man-tᵊl-mənt\ *noun*
**dis·mast** \(ˌ)dis-'mast\ *transitive verb* (1747)
**:** to remove or break off the mast of
**¹dis·may** \dis-'mā, diz-\ *transitive verb* **dis·mayed; dis·may·ing** [Middle English, from (assumed) Old French *desmaiier,* from Old French *des-* dis- + *-maiier* (as in *esmaiier* to dismay), from (assumed) Vulgar Latin *-magare,* of Germanic origin; akin to Old High German *magan* to be able — more at MAY] (13th century)
**:** to deprive of courage, resolution, and initiative through the pressure of sudden fear or anxiety or great perplexity ☆
— **dis·may·ing·ly** \-iŋ-lē\ *adverb*
**²dismay** *noun* (14th century)
**1 :** sudden loss of courage or resolution from alarm or fear
**2 a :** sudden disappointment **b :** PERTURBATION 1
**disme** \'dīm\ *noun* [obsolete English, tenth, from obsolete French, from Middle French *disme, dime* — more at DIME] (1792)
**:** a U.S. 10-cent coin struck in 1792
**dis·mem·ber** \(ˌ)dis-'mem-bər\ *transitive verb* **-bered; -ber·ing** \-b(ə-)riŋ\ [Middle English *dismembren,* from Old French *desmembrer,* from *des-* dis- + *membre* member] (14th century)
**1 :** to cut off or disjoin the limbs, members, or parts of
**2 :** to break up or tear into pieces
— **dis·mem·ber·ment** \-bər-mənt\ *noun*

**dis·miss** \dis-'mis\ *transitive verb* [Middle English, modification of Latin *dimissus,* past participle of *dimittere,* from *dis-* + *mittere* to send — more at DIS-, SMITE] (15th century)
**1 :** to permit or cause to leave ⟨*dismissed* the visitors⟩
**2 :** to remove from position or service : DISCHARGE
**3 a :** to reject serious consideration of ⟨*dismissed* the thought⟩ **b :** to put out of judicial consideration ⟨*dismissed* all charges⟩
— **dis·mis·sion** \-'mi-shən\ *noun*
— **dis·mis·sive** \-'mi-siv\ *adjective*
— **dis·mis·sive·ly** *adverb*
**dis·miss·al** \-'mi-səl\ *noun* (1816)
**:** the act of dismissing : the fact or state of being dismissed
**¹dis·mount** \(ˌ)dis-'maünt\ *verb* [probably modification of Middle French *desmonter,* from *des-* dis- + *monter* to mount] (1579)
*intransitive verb*
**1** *obsolete* **:** DESCEND
**2 :** to alight from an elevated position (as on a horse); *also* **:** to get out of an enclosed craft or vehicle
*transitive verb*
**1 :** to throw down or remove from a mount or an elevated position; *especially* **:** UNHORSE
**2 :** DISASSEMBLE
**²dismount** *noun* (1654)
**:** the act of dismounting
**dis·obe·di·ence** \ˌdi-sə-'bē-dē-ən(t)s\ *noun* (15th century)
**:** refusal or neglect to obey
**dis·obe·di·ent** \-ənt\ *adjective* [Middle English, from Middle French *desobedient,* from Old French, from *des-* dis- + *obedient* obedient] (15th century)
**:** refusing or neglecting to obey
— **dis·obe·di·ent·ly** *adverb*

---

☆ **SYNONYMS**
**Dismay, appall, horrify, daunt** mean to unnerve or deter by arousing fear, apprehension, or aversion. DISMAY implies that one is disconcerted and at a loss as to how to deal with something ⟨*dismayed* at the size of the job⟩. APPALL implies that one is faced with that which perturbs, confounds, or shocks ⟨I am *appalled* by your behavior⟩. HORRIFY stresses a reaction of horror or revulsion ⟨was *horrified* by such wanton cruelty⟩. DAUNT suggests a cowing, disheartening, or frightening in a venture requiring courage ⟨a cliff that would *daunt* the most intrepid climber⟩.

---

◇ **WORD HISTORY**
**dismal** In late antiquity, certain days of each month, called in Latin *dies Aegyptiaci* "Egyptian days," were regarded as unlucky times, when new enterprises of any sort were not to be undertaken. These days of ill omen were probably a relic of ancient Egyptian astrological practices, but their source had been forgotten by the Middle Ages. People then took them to be anniversaries of the plagues visited on Egypt in Moses' time—despite the fact that there were 24 Egyptian days in the year and only ten Biblical plagues. In a 13th century Anglo-French calendar, the Egyptian days were called collectively *dismal* (from Latin *dies mali* "evil days"), and this word was borrowed into Middle English. Any day of the 24 was a *dismal day,* but the original sense "evil days" was forgotten, and *dismal* in the phrase was simply taken as an adjective meaning "disastrous." In Modern English this sense has been weakened to "causing gloom," perhaps by association with *dismay.*

**dis·obey** \,di-sə-'bā\ *verb* [Middle English, from Middle French *desobeir*, from Old French, from *des-* dis- + *obeir* to obey] (14th century)
*intransitive verb*
: to be disobedient
*transitive verb*
: to fail to obey
— **dis·obey·er** *noun*

**dis·oblige** \,di-sə-'blīj\ *transitive verb* [French *désobliger*, from Middle French, from *des-* dis- + *obliger* to oblige] (1632)
**1** : to go counter to the wishes of
**2** : INCONVENIENCE

**di·so·di·um phosphate** \,(,)dī-'sō-dē-əm-\ *noun* (circa 1928)
: a sodium phosphate $Na_2HPO_4$

**di·so·mic** \,(,)dī-'sō-mik\ *adjective* [*di-* + *-somic*] (1924)
: having one or more chromosomes present in twice the normal number but not having the entire genome doubled

**¹dis·or·der** \,(,)di-'sòr-dər, -'zòr-\ *transitive verb* (15th century)
**1** : to disturb the order of
**2** : to disturb the regular or normal functions of

**²disorder** *noun* (1530)
**1** : lack of order ⟨clothes in *disorder*⟩
**2** : breach of the peace or public order ⟨troubled times marked by social *disorders*⟩
**3** : an abnormal physical or mental condition : AILMENT ⟨a nervous *disorder*⟩

**dis·or·dered** *adjective* (1548)
**1** *obsolete* **a** : morally reprehensible **b** : UNRULY
**2 a** : marked by disorder **b** : not functioning in a normal orderly healthy way
— **dis·or·dered·ly** *adverb*
— **dis·or·dered·ness** *noun*

**¹dis·or·der·ly** \-'sòrd-ər-lē\ *adverb* (1564)
*archaic* : in a disorderly manner

**²disorderly** *adjective* (1585)
**1** : engaged in conduct offensive to public order ⟨charged with being drunk and *disorderly*⟩
**2** : characterized by disorder ⟨a *disorderly* pile of clothes⟩
— **dis·or·der·li·ness** *noun*

**disorderly conduct** *noun* (circa 1845)
: a petty offense chiefly against public order and decency that falls short of an indictable misdemeanor

**disorderly house** *noun* [euphemism] (circa 1809)
: BORDELLO

**dis·or·ga·nize** \,(,)di-'sòr-gə-,nīz\ *transitive verb* [French *désorganiser*, from *dés-* dis- + *organiser* to organize] (1793)
: to destroy or interrupt the orderly structure or function of
— **dis·or·ga·ni·za·tion** \,(,)di-,sòr-gə-nə-'zā-shən\ *noun*

**dis·or·ga·nized** *adjective* (1812)
: lacking coherence, system, or central guiding agency ⟨*disorganized* work habits⟩

**dis·ori·ent** \,(,)di-'sòr-ē-,ent, -'sòr-\ *transitive verb* [French *désorienter*, from *dés-* dis- + *orienter* to orient] (1655)
**1 a** : to cause to lose bearings : displace from normal position or relationship **b** : to cause to lose the sense of time, place, or identity
**2** : CONFUSE

**dis·ori·en·tate** \-ē-ən-,tāt, -ē-,en-\ *transitive verb* (circa 1704)
: DISORIENT
— **dis·ori·en·ta·tion** \,(,)di-,sòr-ē-ən-'tā-shən, -,sòr-, -ē-,en-\ *noun*

**dis·own** \,(,)di-'sōn\ *transitive verb* (1649)
**1** : to refuse to acknowledge as one's own
**2 a** : to repudiate any connection or identification with **b** : to deny the validity or authority of
— **dis·own·ment** \-mənt\ *noun*

**dis·par·age** \di-'spar-ij\ *transitive verb* -aged; -ag·ing [Middle English, to degrade by marriage below one's class, disparage,

from Middle French *desparagier* to marry below one's class, from Old French, from *des-* dis- + *parage* extraction, lineage, from *per* peer] (14th century)
**1** : to lower in rank or reputation : DEGRADE
**2** : to depreciate by indirect means (as invidious comparison) : speak slightingly about
*synonym* see DECRY
— **dis·par·age·ment** \-ij-mənt\ *noun*
— **dis·par·ag·er** *noun*
— **dis·par·ag·ing** *adjective*
— **dis·par·ag·ing·ly** \-ij-iŋ-lē\ *adverb*

**dis·pa·rate** \'dis-p(ə-)rət, di-'spar-ət\ *adjective* [Latin *disparatus*, past participle of *disparare* to separate, from *dis-* + *parare* to prepare — more at PARE] (15th century)
**1** : containing or made up of fundamentally different and often incongruous elements
**2** : markedly distinct in quality or character
*synonym* see DIFFERENT
— **dis·pa·rate·ly** *adverb*
— **dis·pa·rate·ness** *noun*
— **dis·par·i·ty** \di-'spar-ə-tē\ *noun*

**dis·part** \,(,)dis-'pärt\ *verb* [Italian & Latin; Italian *dispartire*, from Latin, from *dis-* + *partire* to divide — more at PART] (1590)
*archaic* : SEPARATE, DIVIDE

**dis·pas·sion** \,(,)dis-'pa-shən\ *noun* (1692)
: absence of passion : COOLNESS

**dis·pas·sion·ate** \-sh(ə-)nət\ *adjective* (1594)
: not influenced by strong feeling; *especially* : not affected by personal or emotional involvement ⟨a *dispassionate* critic⟩ ⟨a *dispassionate* approach to an issue⟩
*synonym* see FAIR
— **dis·pas·sion·ate·ly** *adverb*
— **dis·pas·sion·ate·ness** *noun*

**¹dis·patch** \di-'spach\ *verb* [Spanish *despachar* or Italian *dispacciare*, from Provençal *despachar* to get rid of, from Middle French *despeechier* to set free, from Old French, from *des-* dis- + *-peechier* (as in *empeechier* to hinder) — more at IMPEACH] (1517)
*transitive verb*
**1** : to send off or away with promptness or speed; *especially* : to send off on official business
**2 a** : to kill with quick efficiency **b** *obsolete* : DEPRIVE
**3** : to dispose of (as a task) rapidly or efficiently
**4** : DEFEAT 3
*intransitive verb*
*archaic* : to make haste : HURRY
*synonym* see KILL
— **dis·patch·er** *noun*

**²dis·patch** \di-'spach, 'dis-,pach\ *noun* (1537)
**1 a** : a message sent with speed; *especially* : an important official message sent by a diplomatic, military, or naval officer **b** : a news item filed by a correspondent
**2** : the act of dispatching: as **a** *obsolete* : DISMISSAL **b** : the act of killing **c** (1) : prompt settlement (as of an item of business) (2) : quick riddance **d** : a sending off : SHIPMENT
**3** : promptness and efficiency in performance or transmission ⟨done with *dispatch*⟩
*synonym* see HASTE

**dispatch case** *noun* (circa 1918)
: a case for carrying papers

**dis·pel** \di-'spel\ *transitive verb* **dis·pelled; dis·pel·ling** [Middle English, from Latin *dispellere*, from *dis-* + *pellere* to drive, beat — more at FELT] (15th century)
: to drive away by or as if by scattering : DISSIPATE ⟨*dispel* a rumor⟩
*synonym* see SCATTER

**dis·pens·able** \di-'spen(t)-sə-bəl\ *adjective* (1649)
: capable of being dispensed with
— **dis·pens·abil·i·ty** \-,spen(t)-sə-'bi-lə-tē\ *noun*

**dis·pen·sa·ry** \di-'spen(t)s-(ə-)rē\ *noun, plural* **-ries** (1699)

: a place where medicine or medical or dental treatment is dispensed

**dis·pen·sa·tion** \,dis-pən-'sā-shən, -,pen-\ *noun* (14th century)
**1 a** : a general state or ordering of things; *specifically* : a system of revealed commands and promises regulating human affairs **b** : a particular arrangement or provision especially of providence or nature
**2 a** : an exemption from a law or from an impediment, vow, or oath **b** : a formal authorization
**3 a** : the act of dispensing **b** : something dispensed or distributed
— **dis·pen·sa·tion·al** \-shnəl, -shə-nᵊl\ *adjective*

**dis·pen·sa·to·ry** \di-'spen(t)-sə-,tōr-ē, -,tòr-\ *noun, plural* **-ries** (1566)
: a medicinal formulary

**dis·pense** \di-'spen(t)s\ *verb* **dis·pensed; dis·pens·ing** [Middle English, from Medieval Latin & Latin; Medieval Latin *dispensare* to exempt, from Latin, to distribute, from *dis-* + *pensare* to weigh, frequentative of *pendere* to weigh, pay out — more at SPIN] (14th century)
*transitive verb*
**1 a** : to deal out in portions **b** : ADMINISTER ⟨*dispense* justice⟩
**2** : to give dispensation to : EXEMPT
**3** : to prepare and distribute (medication)
*intransitive verb*
*archaic* : to grant dispensation
*synonym* see DISTRIBUTE
— **dispense with 1** : to set aside : DISCARD ⟨*dispensing with* the usual introduction⟩
**2** : to do without ⟨could *dispense with* such a large staff⟩

**dis·pens·er** \-'spen(t)-sər\ *noun* (14th century)
: one that dispenses: as **a** : a container that extrudes, sprays, or feeds out in convenient units **b** : a usually mechanical device for vending merchandise

**dis·peo·ple** \,(,)dis-'pē-pəl\ *transitive verb* (15th century)
: DEPOPULATE

**dis·per·sal** \di-'spər-səl\ *noun* (1821)
: the act or result of dispersing; *especially* : the process or result of the spreading of organisms from one place to another

**dis·per·sant** \di-'spər-sənt\ *noun* (1941)
: a dispersing agent; *especially* : a substance for promoting the formation and stabilization of a dispersion of one substance in another
— **dispersant** *adjective*

**dis·perse** \di-'spərs\ *verb* **dis·persed; dis·pers·ing** [Middle English *dysparsen*, from Middle French *disperser*, from Latin *dispersus*, past participle of *dispergere* to scatter, from *dis-* + *spargere* to scatter — more at SPARK] (14th century)
*transitive verb*
**1 a** : to cause to break up ⟨police *dispersed* the crowd⟩ **b** : to cause to become spread widely **c** : to cause to evaporate or vanish ⟨sunlight *dispersing* the mist⟩
**2** : to spread or distribute from a fixed or constant source: as **a** *archaic* : DISSEMINATE **b** : to subject (as light) to dispersion **c** : to distribute (as fine particles) more or less evenly throughout a medium
*intransitive verb*
**1** : to break up in random fashion ⟨the crowd *dispersed* on request⟩
**2 a** : to become dispersed **b** : DISSIPATE, VANISH ⟨the fog *dispersed* toward morning⟩
*synonym* see SCATTER
— **dis·persed·ly** \-'spər-səd-lē, -'spərst-lē\ *adverb*

— **dis·pers·er** noun

— **dis·pers·ible** \-'spər-sə-bəl\ adjective

**dis·per·sion** \di-'spər-zhən, -shən\ noun (14th century)
**1** capitalized : DIASPORA 1a
**2** : the act or process of dispersing : the state of being dispersed
**3** : the scattering of the values of a frequency distribution from an average
**4** : the separation of light into colors by refraction or diffraction with formation of a spectrum; also : the separation of radiation into components in accordance with some varying characteristic (as energy)
**5 a** : a dispersed substance **b** : a system consisting of a dispersed substance and the medium in which it is dispersed : COLLOID 2b

**dis·per·sive** \-'spər-siv, -ziv\ adjective (1677)
**1** : of or relating to dispersion (a dispersive medium) (the dispersive power of a lens)
**2** : tending to disperse
— **dis·per·sive·ly** adverb
— **dis·per·sive·ness** noun

**dis·per·soid** \-'spər-,sȯid\ noun (1911)
: finely divided particles of one substance dispersed in another

**dis·pir·it** \(,)dis-'pir-ət\ transitive verb [dis- + spirit] (1647)
: to deprive of morale or enthusiasm
— **dis·pir·it·ed** adjective
— **dis·pir·it·ed·ly** adverb
— **dis·pir·it·ed·ness** noun

**dis·pit·eous** \di-'spi-tē-əs\ adjective [alteration of despiteous] (1803)
archaic : CRUEL

**dis·place** \(,)dis-'plās\ transitive verb [probably from Middle French desplacer, from des- dis- + place place] (1553)
**1 a** : to remove from the usual or proper place; specifically : to expel or force to flee from home or homeland **b** : to remove from an office, status, or job **c** obsolete : to drive out : BANISH
**2 a** : to move physically out of position (a floating object displaces water) **b** : to take the place of (as in a chemical reaction) : SUPPLANT
synonym see REPLACE
— **dis·place·able** \-'plā-sə-bəl\ adjective

**dis·place·ment** \di-'splā-smənt\ noun (1611)
**1** : the act or process of displacing : the state of being displaced
**2 a** : the volume or weight of a fluid (as water) displaced by a floating body (as a ship) of equal weight **b** : the difference between the initial position of something (as a body or geometric figure) and any later position **c** : the volume displaced by a piston (as in a pump or an engine) in a single stroke; also : the total volume so displaced by all the pistons in an internal combustion engine (as in an automobile)
**3 a** : the redirection of an emotion or impulse from its original object (as an idea or person) to another **b** : the substitution of another form of behavior for what is usual or expected especially when the usual response is nonadaptive

**dis·plant** \di-'splant\ transitive verb [Middle French desplanter, from des- dis- + planter to plant, from Late Latin plantare] (15th century)
**1** : DISPLACE, REMOVE
**2** : SUPPLANT

¹**dis·play** \di-'splā\ verb [Middle English, from Anglo-French despleer, desploier, literally, to unfold — more at DEPLOY] (14th century)
transitive verb
**1 a** : to put or spread before the view (display the flag) **b** : to make evident (displayed great skill) **c** : to exhibit ostentatiously (liked to display his erudition)
**2** obsolete : DESCRY
intransitive verb
**1** obsolete : SHOW OFF
**2** : to make a breeding display (penguins displayed and copulated)
synonym see SHOW

— **dis·play·able** \-'splā-ə-bəl\ adjective

²**display** noun, often attributive (1665)
**1 a** (1) : a setting or presentation of something in open view (a fireworks display) (2) : a clear sign or evidence : EXHIBITION (a display of courage) **b** : ostentatious show **c** : type, composition, or printing designed to catch the eye **d** : an eye-catching arrangement by which something is exhibited **e** : an electronic device (as a cathode-ray tube) that temporarily presents information in visual form; also : the visual information
**2** : a pattern of behavior exhibited especially by male birds in the breeding season

**dis·please** \(,)dis-'plēz\ verb [Middle English displesen, from Middle French desplaisir, modification of (assumed) Vulgar Latin displacēre, from Latin dis- + placēre to please — more at PLEASE] (14th century)
transitive verb
**1** : to incur the disapproval or dislike of especially by annoying (their gossip displeases her)
**2** : to be offensive to (abstract art displeases him)
intransitive verb
: to give displeasure (behavior calculated to displease)

**dis·plea·sure** \(,)dis-'ple-zhər, -'plā-\ noun (15th century)
**1** : the feeling of one that is displeased : DISFAVOR
**2** : DISCOMFORT, UNHAPPINESS
**3** archaic : OFFENSE, INJURY

**dis·plode** \di-'splōd\ verb **dis·plod·ed; dis·plod·ing** [Latin displodere, from dis- + plaudere to clap, applaud] (1667)
archaic : EXPLODE
— **dis·plo·sion** \-'splō-zhən\ noun

¹**dis·port** \di-'spōrt, -'spȯrt\ noun (14th century)
archaic : SPORT, PASTIME

²**disport** verb [Middle English, from Middle French desporter, from des- dis- + porter to carry, from Latin portare — more at FARE] (14th century)
transitive verb
**1** : DIVERT, AMUSE
**2** : DISPLAY
intransitive verb
: to amuse oneself in light or lively fashion : FROLIC
— **dis·port·ment** \-mənt\ noun

¹**dis·pos·able** \di-'spō-zə-bəl\ adjective (1643)
**1** : subject to or available for disposal; specifically : remaining to an individual after deduction of taxes (disposable income)
**2** : designed to be used once and then thrown away (disposable diapers)
— **dis·pos·abil·i·ty** \-,spō-zə-'bi-lə-tē\ noun

²**disposable** noun (1963)
: something that is disposable

**dis·pos·al** \di-'spō-zəl\ noun (1630)
**1** : the power or authority to dispose or make use of as one chooses (the car was at my disposal)
**2** : the act or process of disposing: as **a** : orderly placement or distribution **b** : REGULATION, ADMINISTRATION **c** : the act or action of presenting or bestowing something (disposal of favors) **d** : systematic destruction; especially : destruction or transformation of garbage
**3** [garbage disposal unit] : a device used to reduce waste matter (as by grinding)

¹**dis·pose** \di-'spōz\ verb **dis·posed; dis·pos·ing** [Middle English, from Middle French disposer, from Latin disponere to arrange (perfect indicative disposui), from dis- + ponere to put — more at POSITION] (14th century)
transitive verb
**1** : to give a tendency to : INCLINE (faulty diet disposes one to sickness)

**2 a** : to put in place : set in readiness : ARRANGE (disposing troops for withdrawal) **b** obsolete : REGULATE **c** : BESTOW
intransitive verb
**1** : to settle a matter finally
**2** obsolete : to come to terms
synonym see INCLINE
— **dis·pos·er** noun
— **dispose of 1** : to place, distribute, or arrange especially in an orderly way **2 a** : to transfer to the control of another (disposing of personal property to a total stranger) **b** (1) : to get rid of (how to dispose of toxic waste) (2) : to deal with conclusively (disposed of the matter efficiently)

²**dispose** noun (1590)
**1** obsolete : DISPOSAL
**2** obsolete **a** : DISPOSITION **b** : DEMEANOR

**dis·po·si·tion** \,dis-pə-'zi-shən\ noun [Middle English, from Middle French, from Latin disposition-, dispositio, from disponere] (14th century)
**1** : the act or the power of disposing or the state of being disposed: as **a** : ADMINISTRATION, CONTROL **b** (1) : final arrangement : SETTLEMENT (the disposition of the case) **c** (1) : transfer to the care or possession of another (2) : the power of such transferal **d** : orderly arrangement
**2 a** : prevailing tendency, mood, or inclination **b** : temperamental makeup **c** : the tendency of something to act in a certain manner under given circumstances ☆
— **dis·po·si·tion·al** \-'zish-nəl, -'zi-shə-n°l\ adjective

**dis·pos·i·tive** \di-'spä-zə-tiv\ adjective (1613)
: directed toward or effecting disposition (as of a case) (dispositive evidence)

**dis·pos·sess** \,dis-pə-'zes also -'ses\ transitive verb [Middle French despossesser, from des- dis- + possesser to possess] (1555)
: to put out of possession or occupancy (dispossessed the nobles of their land)
— **dis·pos·ses·sion** \-'ze-shən also -'se-\ noun
— **dis·pos·ses·sor** \-'ze-sər also -'se-\ noun

**dis·pos·sessed** adjective (15th century)
: deprived of homes, possessions, and security

**dis·po·sure** \di-'spō-zhər\ noun (1569)
archaic : DISPOSAL, DISPOSITION

**dis·praise** \(,)dis-'prāz\ transitive verb [Middle English dispraisen, from Middle French despreisier, from Old French, from des- dis- + preisier to praise] (13th century)
: to comment on with disapproval or censure
— **dispraise** noun
— **dis·prais·er** noun
— **dis·prais·ing·ly** \-'prā-ziŋ-lē\ adverb

**dispread** \di-'spred\ transitive verb (1590)
: to spread abroad or out

---

☆ **SYNONYMS**
**Disposition, temperament, temper, character, personality** mean the dominant quality or qualities distinguishing a person or group. DISPOSITION implies customary moods and attitude toward the life around one (a cheerful disposition). TEMPERAMENT implies a pattern of innate characteristics associated with one's specific physical and nervous organization (an artistic temperament). TEMPER implies the qualities acquired through experience that determine how a person or group meets difficulties or handles situations (a resilient temper). CHARACTER applies to the aggregate of moral qualities by which a person is judged apart from intelligence, competence, or special talents (strength of character). PERSONALITY applies to an aggregate of qualities that distinguish one as a person (a somber personality).

**dis·prize** \(ˌ)dis-ˈprīz\ *transitive verb* [Middle French *despriser,* from Old French *despreisier*] (15th century)
*archaic* : UNDERVALUE, SCORN
**dis·proof** \(ˌ)dis-ˈprüf\ *noun* (15th century)
**1** : the action of disproving
**2** : evidence that disproves
¹**dis·pro·por·tion** \ˌdis-prə-ˈpōr-shən, -ˈpȯr-\ *noun* (1555)
: lack of proportion, symmetry, or proper relation : DISPARITY; *also* : an instance of such disparity
— **dis·pro·por·tion·al** \-shnəl, -shə-nᵊl\ *adjective*
²**disproportion** *transitive verb* (1593)
: to make out of proportion : MISMATCH
**dis·pro·por·tion·ate** \-sh(ə-)nət\ *adjective* (1555)
: being out of proportion ⟨a *disproportionate* share⟩
— **dis·pro·por·tion·ate·ly** *adverb*
**dis·pro·por·tion·ation** \-ˌpōr-shə-ˈnā-shən, -ˌpȯr-\ *noun* (circa 1929)
: the transformation of a substance into two or more dissimilar substances usually by simultaneous oxidation and reduction
— **dis·pro·por·tion·ate** \-ˈpōr-shə-ˌnāt, -ˈpȯr-\ *intransitive verb*
**dis·prove** \(ˌ)dis-ˈprüv\ *transitive verb* [Middle English, from Middle French *desprover,* from *des-* dis- + *prover* to prove] (14th century)
: to prove to be false or wrong : REFUTE
— **dis·prov·able** \-ˈprü-və-bəl\ *adjective*
**dis·pu·tant** \di-ˈspyü-tᵊnt, ˈdis-pyə-tənt\ *noun* (1593)
: one that is engaged in a dispute
**dis·pu·ta·tion** \ˌdis-pyə-ˈtā-shən\ *noun* (14th century)
**1** : the action of disputing : verbal controversy ⟨continuous *disputation* between them⟩ ⟨ideological *disputations*⟩
**2** : an academic exercise in oral defense of a thesis by formal logic
**dis·pu·ta·tious** \-shəs\ *adjective* (1660)
**1 a** : inclined to dispute **b** : marked by disputation
**2** : provoking debate : CONTROVERSIAL
— **dis·pu·ta·tious·ly** *adverb*
— **dis·pu·ta·tious·ness** *noun*
¹**dis·pute** \di-ˈspyüt\ *verb* **dis·put·ed; dis·put·ing** [Middle English, from Old French *desputer,* from Latin *disputare* to discuss, from *dis-* + *putare* to think] (13th century)
*intransitive verb*
: to engage in argument : DEBATE; *especially* : to argue irritably or with irritating persistence
*transitive verb*
**1 a** : to make the subject of disputation **b** : to call into question ⟨her honesty was never *disputed*⟩
**2 a** : to struggle against : OPPOSE ⟨*disputed* the advance of the invaders⟩ **b** : to contend over ⟨both sides *disputed* the bridgehead⟩
— **dis·put·able** \di-ˈspyü-tə-bəl, ˈdis-pyə-\ *adjective*
— **dis·put·ably** \-blē\ *adverb*
— **dis·put·er** *noun*
²**dis·pute** \di-ˈspyüt, ˈdis-ˌpyüt\ *noun* (1608)
**1 a** : verbal controversy : DEBATE **b** : QUARREL
**2** *obsolete* : physical combat
**dis·qual·i·fi·ca·tion** \(ˌ)dis-ˌkwä-lə-fə-ˈkā-shən\ *noun* (1714)
**1** : something that disqualifies or incapacitates
**2** : the act of disqualifying : the state of being disqualified ⟨*disqualification* from office⟩
**dis·qual·i·fy** \(ˌ)dis-ˈkwä-lə-ˌfī\ *transitive verb* (1723)
**1** : to deprive of the required qualities, properties, or conditions : make unfit
**2** : to deprive of a power, right, or privilege
**3** : to make ineligible for a prize or for further competition because of violations of the rules
**dis·quan·ti·ty** \(ˌ)dis-ˈkwän-(t)ə-tē\ *transitive verb* (1605)

*obsolete* : DIMINISH, LESSEN
¹**dis·qui·et** \(ˌ)dis-ˈkwī-ət\ *transitive verb* (circa 1530)
: to take away the peace or tranquillity of : DISTURB, ALARM
*synonym* see DISCOMPOSE
— **dis·qui·et·ing** *adjective*
— **dis·qui·et·ing·ly** \-ˈkwī-ə-tiŋ-lē\ *adverb*
²**disquiet** *noun* (1581)
: lack of peace or tranquillity : ANXIETY
³**disquiet** *adjective* (1587)
*archaic* : UNEASY, DISQUIETED
— **dis·qui·et·ly** *adverb*
**dis·qui·etude** \(ˌ)dis-ˈkwī-ə-ˌt(y)üd\ *noun* (1709)
: ANXIETY, AGITATION
**dis·qui·si·tion** \ˌdis-kwə-ˈzi-shən\ *noun* [Latin *disquisition-, disquisitio,* from *disquirere* to investigate, from *dis-* + *quaerere* to seek] (1647)
: a formal inquiry into or discussion of a subject : DISCOURSE
**dis·rate** \(ˌ)dis-ˈrāt\ *transitive verb* (1811)
: to reduce in rank : DEMOTE
¹**dis·re·gard** \ˌdis-ri-ˈgärd\ *transitive verb* (1641)
: to pay no attention to : treat as unworthy of regard or notice
*synonym* see NEGLECT
²**disregard** *noun* (1665)
: the act of disregarding : the state of being disregarded : NEGLECT
— **dis·re·gard·ful** \-fəl\ *adjective*
**dis·re·lat·ed** \ˌdis-ri-ˈlā-təd\ *adjective* (1894)
: not related
**dis·re·la·tion** \-ˈlā-shən\ *noun* (1893)
: lack of a fitting or proportionate connection or relationship
¹**dis·rel·ish** \(ˌ)dis-ˈre-lish\ *transitive verb* (1604)
: to find unpalatable or distasteful
²**disrelish** *noun* (circa 1625)
: lack of relish : DISTASTE, DISLIKE
**dis·re·mem·ber** \ˌdis-ri-ˈmem-bər\ *transitive verb* (1815)
: FORGET
**dis·re·pair** \ˌdis-ri-ˈpar, -ˈper\ *noun* (1798)
: the state of being in need of repair ⟨a building fallen into *disrepair*⟩
**dis·rep·u·ta·ble** \(ˌ)dis-ˈre-pyə-tə-bəl\ *adjective* (1772)
: not reputable
— **dis·rep·u·ta·bil·i·ty** \(ˌ)dis-ˌre-pyə-tə-ˈbi-lə-tē\ *noun*
— **dis·rep·u·ta·ble·ness** \(ˌ)dis-ˈre-pyə-tə-bəl-nəs\ *noun*
— **dis·rep·u·ta·bly** \-blē\ *adverb*
**dis·re·pute** \ˌdis-ri-ˈpyüt\ *noun* (1653)
: lack or decline of good reputation : a state of being held in low esteem
*synonym* see DISGRACE
¹**dis·re·spect** \ˌdis-ri-ˈspekt\ *transitive verb* (1614)
: to have disrespect for
²**disrespect** *noun* (1631)
: lack of respect
— **dis·re·spect·ful** \-fəl\ *adjective*
— **dis·re·spect·ful·ly** \-fə-lē\ *adverb*
— **dis·re·spect·ful·ness** *noun*
**dis·re·spect·able** \ˌdis-ri-ˈspek-tə-bəl\ *adjective* (1813)
: not respectable
— **dis·re·spect·abil·i·ty** \-ˌspek-tə-ˈbi-lə-tē\ *noun*
**dis·robe** \(ˌ)dis-ˈrōb\ *verb* [Middle French *desrober,* from *des-* dis- + *robe* garment, from Old French] (1581)
*intransitive verb*
: to take off one's clothing
*transitive verb*
: to strip of clothing or covering
**dis·rupt** \dis-ˈrəpt\ *transitive verb* [Latin *disruptus,* past participle of *disrumpere,* from *dis-* + *rumpere* to break — more at REAVE] (1817)
**1 a** : to break apart : RUPTURE **b** : to throw into disorder ⟨agitators trying to *disrupt* the meeting⟩

**2** : to interrupt the normal course or unity of
— **dis·rupt·er** *noun*
— **dis·rup·tion** \-ˈrəp-shən\ *noun*
— **dis·rup·tive** \-ˈrəp-tiv\ *adjective*
— **dis·rup·tive·ly** *adverb*
— **dis·rup·tive·ness** *noun*
**diss** *variant of* DIS
**dis·sat·is·fac·tion** \(ˌ)di(s)-ˌsat-əs-ˈfak-shən\ *noun* (1640)
: the quality or state of being dissatisfied : DISCONTENT
**dis·sat·is·fac·to·ry** \-ˈfak-t(ə-)rē\ *adjective* (circa 1610)
: causing dissatisfaction
**dis·sat·is·fied** \(ˌ)di(s)-ˈsa-təs-ˌfīd\ *adjective* (1675)
: expressing or showing lack of satisfaction : not pleased or satisfied
**dis·sat·is·fy** \-ˌfī\ *transitive verb* (1666)
: to fail to satisfy : DISPLEASE
**dis·save** \(ˌ)di(s)-ˈsāv\ *intransitive verb* (1936)
: to use savings for current expenses
**dis·seat** \(ˌ)di(s)-ˈsēt\ *transitive verb* (1612)
*archaic* : UNSEAT
**dis·sect** \di-ˈsekt; ÷dī-ˈsekt, ÷ˈdī-\ *verb* [Latin *dissectus,* past participle of *dissecare* to cut apart, from *dis-* + *secare* to cut — more at SAW] (1607)
*transitive verb*
**1** : to separate into pieces : expose the several parts of (as an animal) for scientific examination
**2** : to analyze and interpret minutely
*intransitive verb*
: to make a dissection
*synonym* see ANALYZE
— **dis·sec·tor** \-ˈsek-tər\ *noun*
**dis·sect·ed** *adjective* (1652)
**1** : cut deeply into fine lobes ⟨a *dissected* leaf⟩
**2** : divided into hills and ridges (as by gorges) ⟨a *dissected* plateau⟩
**dis·sect·ing microscope** *noun* (circa 1897)
: a microscope with low magnification
**dis·sec·tion** \di-ˈsek-shən; ÷dī-ˈsek-, ÷ˈdī-\ *noun* (1605)
**1** : the act or process of dissecting : the state of being dissected
**2** : an anatomical specimen prepared by dissecting
**dis·seise** *or* **dis·seize** \(ˌ)di(s)-ˈsēz\ *transitive verb* **dis·seised** *or* **dis·seized; dis·seis·ing** *or* **dis·seiz·ing** [Middle English *disseisen,* from Medieval Latin *disseisiare* & Anglo-French *disseisir,* from Old French *dessaisir,* from *des-* dis- + *saisir* to put in possession of — more at SEIZE] (14th century)
: to deprive especially wrongfully of seisin : DISPOSSESS
— **dis·sei·sor** \-ˈsē-zər\ *noun*
**dis·sei·sin** *or* **dis·sei·zin** \-ˈsē-zᵊn\ *noun* [Middle English *dysseysyne,* from Anglo-French *disseisine,* from Old French *dessaisine,* from *des-* dis- + *saisine* seisin] (14th century)
: the act of disseising : the state of being disseised
**dis·sem·ble** \di-ˈsem-bəl\ *verb* **dis·sem·bled; dis·sem·bling** \-b(ə-)liŋ\ [Middle English *dissymblen,* alteration of *dissimulen,* from Middle French *dissimuler,* from Latin *dissimulare* — more at DISSIMULATE] (15th century)
*transitive verb*
**1** : to hide under a false appearance
**2** : to put on the appearance of : SIMULATE
*intransitive verb*
: to put on a false appearance : conceal facts, intentions, or feelings under some pretense
— **dis·sem·bler** \-b(ə-)lər\ *noun*

\ə\ abut \ᵊ\ kitten \ər\ further \a\ ash \ā\ ace \ä\ mop, mar \au̇\ out \ch\ chin \e\ bet \ē\ easy \g\ go \i\ hit \ī\ ice \j\ job \ŋ\ sing \ō\ go \ȯ\ law \ȯi\ boy \th\ thin \th\ the \ü\ loot \u̇\ foot \y\ yet \zh\ vision *see also* Guide to Pronunciation

**dis·sem·i·nate** \di-'se-mə-ˌnāt\ *transitive verb* **-nat·ed; -nat·ing** [Latin *disseminatus*, past participle of *disseminare*, from *dis-* + *seminare* to sow, from *semin-, semen* seed — more at SEMEN] (1603) **1 :** to spread abroad as though sowing seed ⟨*disseminate* ideas⟩ **2 :** to disperse throughout — **dis·sem·i·na·tion** \-ˌse-mə-'nā-shən\ *noun* — **dis·sem·i·na·tor** \-'se-mə-ˌnā-tər\ *noun*

**dis·sem·i·nat·ed** *adjective* (1876) **:** widely dispersed in a tissue, organ, or the entire body ⟨*disseminated* gonococcal disease⟩

**dis·sem·i·nule** \di-'sem-ə-ˌnyül\ *noun* (1904) **:** a part or organ (as a seed or spore) of a plant that ensures propagation

**dis·sen·sion** *also* **dis·sen·tion** \di-'sen(t)-shən\ *noun* [Middle English, from Middle French, from Latin *dissension-, dissensio,* from *dissentire*] (14th century) **:** DISAGREEMENT; *especially* **:** partisan and contentious quarreling
**synonym** see DISCORD

**dis·sen·sus** \(ˌ)di(s)-'sen(t)-səs\ *noun* [*dis-* + *consensus*] (1966) **:** difference of opinion

¹**dis·sent** \di-'sent\ *intransitive verb* [Middle English, from Latin *dissentire,* from *dis-* + *sentire* to feel — more at SENSE] (15th century) **1 :** to withhold assent **2 :** to differ in opinion

²**dissent** *noun* (1585) **:** difference of opinion: as **a :** religious nonconformity **b :** a justice's nonconcurrence with a decision of the majority — called also *dissenting opinion*

**dis·sent·er** \di-'sen-tər\ *noun* (1639) **1 :** one that dissents **2** *capitalized* **:** an English Nonconformist

**dis·sen·tient** \di-'sen(t)-sh(ē-)ənt\ *adjective* [Latin *dissentient-, dissentiens,* present participle of *dissentire*] (1651) **:** expressing dissent
— **dissentient** *noun*

**dis·sent·ing** \di-'sen-tiŋ\ *adjective, often capitalized* (1644) **:** of or relating to the English Nonconformists ⟨a *dissenting* church⟩ ⟨*dissenting* merchants⟩

**dis·sen·tious** \di-'sen(t)-shəs\ *adjective* (1560) **:** characterized by dissension or dissent

**dis·sep·i·ment** \di-'se-pə-mənt\ *noun* [Latin *dissaepimentum* partition, from *dissaepire* to divide, from *dis-* + *saepire* to fence in — more at SEPTUM] (circa 1727) **:** a dividing tissue **:** SEPTUM

**dis·sert** \di-'sərt\ *intransitive verb* [Latin *dissertus,* past participle of *disserere,* from *dis-* + *serere* to join, arrange — more at SERIES] (1657) **:** to speak or write at length

**dis·ser·tate** \'di-sər-ˌtāt\ *intransitive verb* **-tat·ed; -tat·ing** [Latin *dissertatus,* past participle of *dissertare,* from *dissertus*] (1766) **:** DISSERT; *also* **:** to write a dissertation
— **dis·ser·ta·tor** \-ˌtā-tər\ *noun*

**dis·ser·ta·tion** \ˌdi-sər-'tā-shən\ *noun* (1651) **:** an extended usually written treatment of a subject; *specifically* **:** one submitted for a doctorate
— **dis·ser·ta·tion·al** \-'tāsh-nəl, -'tā-shə-n°l\ *adjective*

**dis·serve** \(ˌ)di(s)-'sərv\ *transitive verb* (1629) **:** to serve badly or falsely **:** HARM

**dis·ser·vice** \(ˌ)di(s)-'sər-vəs\ *noun* (1599) **:** ill service **:** HARM; *also* **:** an unhelpful, unkind, or harmful act

**dis·ser·vice·able** \di(s)-'sər-və-sə-bəl\ *adjective* (1644) **:** COUNTERPRODUCTIVE

**dis·sev·er** \di-'se-vər\ *verb* [Middle English, from Old French *dessevrer,* from Late Latin *disseparare,* from Latin *dis-* + *separare* to separate] (13th century)

*transitive verb* **:** SEVER, SEPARATE
*intransitive verb* **:** to come apart **:** DISUNITE
— **dis·sev·er·ance** \-'se-v(ə-)rən(t)s\ *noun*
— **dis·sev·er·ment** \-'se-vər-mənt\ *noun*

**dis·si·dence** \'di-sə-dən(t)s\ *noun* (circa 1656) **:** DISSENT, DISAGREEMENT

**dis·si·dent** \-dənt\ *adjective* [Latin *dissident-, dissidens,* present participle of *dissidēre* to sit apart, disagree, from *dis-* + *sedēre* to sit — more at SIT] (1837) **:** disagreeing especially with an established religious or political system, organization, or belief
— **dissident** *noun*

**dis·sim·i·lar** \(ˌ)di(s)-'si-mə-lər, -'sim-lər\ *adjective* (1599) **:** UNLIKE
— **dis·sim·i·lar·i·ty** \(ˌ)di(s)-ˌsi-mə-'lar-ə-tē\ *noun*
— **dis·sim·i·lar·ly** \(')di(s)-'si-mə-lər-lē, -'sim-lər-\ *adverb*
— **dis·sim·i·lars** \-lərz\ *noun plural*

**dis·sim·i·late** \(ˌ)di-'si-mə-ˌlāt\ *intransitive verb* **-lat·ed; -lat·ing** [*dis-* + *-similate* (as in *assimilate*)] (1841) **:** to undergo dissimilation
— **dis·sim·i·la·to·ry** \-mə-lə-ˌtōr-ē, -ˌtòr-\ *adjective*

**dis·sim·i·la·tion** \(ˌ)di-ˌsi-mə-'lā-shən\ *noun* (circa 1874) **:** the change or omission of one of two identical or closely related sounds in a word

**dis·si·mil·i·tude** \ˌdi(s)-sə-'mi-lə-ˌtüd, -ˌtyüd\ *noun* [Latin *dissimilitudo,* from *dissimilis* unlike, from *dis-* + *similis* like — more at SAME] (15th century) **:** lack of resemblance

**dis·sim·u·late** \(ˌ)di-'sim-yə-ˌlāt\ *verb* **-lat·ed; -lat·ing** [Latin *dissimulatus,* past participle of *dissimulare,* from *dis-* + *simulare* to simulate] (15th century)
*transitive verb* **:** to hide under a false appearance ⟨smiled to *dissimulate* her urgency —Alice Glenday⟩
*intransitive verb* **:** DISSEMBLE
— **dis·sim·u·la·tion** \(ˌ)di-ˌsim-yə-'lā-shən\ *noun*
— **dis·sim·u·la·tor** \(')di-'sim-yə-ˌlā-tər\ *noun*

**dis·si·pate** \'di-sə-ˌpāt\ *verb* **-pat·ed; -pat·ing** [Latin *dissipatus,* past participle of *dissipare, dissupare,* from *dis-* + *supare* to throw] (15th century)
*transitive verb* **1 a :** to break up and drive off (as a crowd) **b :** to cause to spread thin or scatter and gradually vanish ⟨one's sympathy is eventually *dissipated* —Andrew Feinberg⟩ **c :** to lose (as heat or electricity) irrecoverably **2 :** to spend or use up wastefully or foolishly ⟨lifelong tendency to *dissipate* his gifts in travel and pleasure —Edmund Morris⟩ ⟨his fortune is *dissipated* in imprudent political adventures —John Butt⟩
*intransitive verb* **1 :** to break up and scatter or vanish **2 :** to be extravagant or dissolute in the pursuit of pleasure; *especially* **:** to drink to excess
**synonym** see SCATTER
— **dis·si·pat·er** *noun*

**dis·si·pat·ed** *adjective* (1744) **:** given to or marked by dissipation **:** DISSOLUTE
— **dis·si·pat·ed·ly** *adverb*
— **dis·si·pat·ed·ness** *noun*

**dis·si·pa·tion** \ˌdi-sə-'pā-shən\ *noun* (15th century) **1 :** the action or process of dissipating **:** the state of being dissipated: **a :** DISPERSION, DIFFUSION **b** *archaic* **:** DISSOLUTION, DISINTEGRATION **c :** wasteful expenditure **d :** intemperate living; *especially* **:** excessive drinking

**2 :** an act of self-indulgence; *especially* **:** one that is not harmful **:** AMUSEMENT

**dis·si·pa·tive** \'di-sə-ˌpā-tiv\ *adjective* (1684) **:** relating to dissipation especially of heat

**dis·so·cia·ble** \(ˌ)di-'sō-sh(ē-)ə-bəl, -sē-ə-\ *adjective* (1833) **:** SEPARABLE
— **dis·so·cia·bil·i·ty** \(ˌ)di-ˌsō-sh(ē)ə-'bi-lə-tē, -sē-ə-\ *noun*

**dis·so·cial** \(ˌ)di(s)-'sō-shəl\ *adjective* (1762) **:** UNSOCIAL, SELFISH

**dis·so·ci·ate** \(ˌ)di-'sō-shē-ˌāt, -sē-\ *verb* **-at·ed; -at·ing** [Latin *dissociatus,* past participle of *dissociare,* from *dis-* + *sociare* to join, from *socius* companion — more at SOCIAL] (1590)
*transitive verb* **1 :** to separate from association or union with another **2 :** DISUNITE; *specifically* **:** to subject to chemical dissociation
*intransitive verb* **1 :** to undergo dissociation **2 :** to mutate especially reversibly

**dis·so·ci·a·tion** \(ˌ)di-ˌsō-sē-'ā-shən, -shē-\ *noun* (1611) **1 :** the act or process of dissociating **:** the state of being dissociated: as **a :** the process by which a chemical combination breaks up into simpler constituents; *especially* **:** one that results from the action of energy (as heat) on a gas or of a solvent on a dissolved substance **b :** the separation of whole segments of the personality (as in multiple personality) or of discrete mental processes (as in the schizophrenias) from the mainstream of consciousness or of behavior **2 :** the property inherent in some biological stocks (as of certain bacteria) of differentiating into two or more distinct and relatively permanent strains; *also* **:** such a strain
— **dis·so·cia·tive** \(ˌ)di-'sō-shē-ˌā-tiv, -sē-, -shə-tiv\ *adjective*

**dis·sol·u·ble** \di-'säl-yə-bəl\ *adjective* [Latin *dissolubilis,* from *dissolvere* to dissolve] (1534) **:** capable of being dissolved or disintegrated

**dis·so·lute** \'di-sə-ˌlüt, -lət\ *adjective* [Latin *dissolutus,* from past participle of *dissolvere* to loosen, dissolve] (14th century) **:** lacking restraint; *especially* **:** marked by indulgence in things (as drink or promiscuous sex) deemed vices ⟨*dissolute* and degrading aspects of human nature —Wallace Fowlie⟩
— **dis·so·lute·ly** *adverb*
— **dis·so·lute·ness** *noun*

**dis·so·lu·tion** \ˌdi-sə-'lü-shən\ *noun* (14th century) **1 :** the act or process of dissolving: as **a :** separation into component parts **b** (1) **:** DECAY, DISINTEGRATION (2) **:** DEATH **c :** termination or destruction by breaking down, disrupting, or dispersing ⟨the *dissolution* of the republic⟩ **d :** the dissolving of an assembly or organization **e :** LIQUEFACTION **2 :** a dissolute act or practice

¹**dis·solve** \di-'zälv, -'zòlv *also* -'zäv *or* -'zòv\ *verb* [Middle English, from Latin *dissolvere,* from *dis-* + *solvere* to loosen — more at SOLVE] (14th century)
*transitive verb* **1 a :** to cause to disperse or disappear **:** DESTROY **b :** to separate into component parts **:** DISINTEGRATE **c :** to bring to an end **:** TERMINATE ⟨*dissolve* parliament⟩ **d :** ANNUL ⟨*dissolve* an injunction⟩ **2 a :** to cause to pass into solution ⟨*dissolve* sugar in water⟩ **b :** MELT, LIQUEFY **c :** to cause to be emotionally moved **d :** to cause to fade out in a dissolve **3** *archaic* **:** DETACH, LOOSEN **4 :** to clear up ⟨*dissolve* a problem⟩
*intransitive verb* **1 a :** to become dissipated or decomposed **b :** BREAK UP, DISPERSE **c :** to fade away

**2 a :** to become fluid **:** MELT **b :** to pass into solution **c :** to be overcome emotionally 〈*dissolved* into tears〉 **d :** to resolve itself as if by dissolution 〈hate *dissolved* into fear〉 **e :** to change by a dissolve 〈the scene *dissolves* to a Victorian parlor〉
— **dis·solv·able** \-'zäl-və-bəl, -'zȯl-\ *adjective*
— **dis·sol·vent** \-'zäl-vənt, -'zȯl-\ *noun or adjective*
— **dis·solv·er** *noun*

**²dissolve** *noun* (1916)
**:** a gradual superimposing of one motion-picture or television shot upon another on a screen

**dis·so·nance** \'di-sə-nən(t)s\ *noun* (15th century)
**1 a :** lack of agreement; *especially* **:** inconsistency between the beliefs one holds or between one's actions and one's beliefs — compare COGNITIVE DISSONANCE **b :** an instance of such inconsistency or disagreement
**2 :** a mingling of discordant sounds; *especially* **:** a clashing or unresolved musical interval or chord

**dis·so·nant** \-nənt\ *adjective* [Middle French or Latin; Middle French, from Latin *dissonant-, dissonans,* present participle of *dissonare* to be discordant, from *dis-* + *sonare* to sound — more at SOUND] (15th century)
**1 :** marked by dissonance **:** DISCORDANT
**2 :** INCONGRUOUS
**3 :** harmonically unresolved
— **dis·so·nant·ly** *adverb*

**dis·suade** \di-'swād\ *transitive verb* **dis·suad·ed; dis·suad·ing** [Middle French or Latin; Middle French *dissuader,* from Latin *dissuadēre,* from *dis-* + *suadēre* to urge — more at SWEET] (15th century)
**1 a :** to advise (a person) against something **b** *archaic* **:** to advise against (an action)
**2 :** to turn from something by persuasion
— **dis·suad·er** *noun*

**dis·sua·sion** \di-'swā-zhən\ *noun* [Middle French or Latin; Middle French, from Latin *dissuasion-, dissuasio,* from *dissuadēre*] (15th century)
**:** the action of dissuading

**dis·sua·sive** \di-'swā-siv, -ziv\ *adjective* (1609)
**:** tending to dissuade
— **dis·sua·sive·ly** *adverb*
— **dis·sua·sive·ness** *noun*

**dis·syl·la·ble** \'di-,si-lə-bəl, (,)di(s)-'si-; 'dī-,si-, (,)dī-'si-\ *variant of* DISYLLABLE

**dis·sym·me·try** \(,)di(s)-'si-mə-trē\ *noun* (1845)
**:** the absence of or the lack of symmetry
— **dis·sym·met·ric** \(,)di(s)-sə-'me-trik\ *adjective*

**¹dis·taff** \'dis-,taf\ *noun, plural* **distaffs** \-,tafs, -,tavz\ [Middle English *distaf,* from Old English *distæf,* from *dis-* (akin to Middle Low German *dise* bunch of flax) + *stæf* staff] (before 12th century)
**1 a :** a staff for holding the flax, tow, or wool in spinning **b :** woman's work or domain
**2 :** the female branch or side of a family ◆

**²distaff** *adjective* (circa 1633)
**:** MATERNAL 〈the *distaff* side of the family〉 — compare SPEAR; *also* **:** FEMALE 〈*distaff* executives〉

**dis·tain** \dis-'tān\ *transitive verb* [Middle English *disteynen,* from Middle French *desteindre* to take away the color of, from Old French, from *des- dis-* + *teindre* to dye, from Latin *tingere* to wet, dye — more at TINGE] (14th century)
**1** *archaic* **:** STAIN
**2** *archaic* **:** DISHONOR

distaff 1a

**dis·tal** \'dis-t°l\ *adjective* [*distant* + *-al*] (1808)
**1 :** situated away from the point of attachment or origin or a central point especially of the body — compare PROXIMAL
**2 :** of, relating to, or being the surface of a tooth that is next to the tooth behind it or that is farthest from the middle of the front of the jaw — compare MESIAL 2
— **dis·tal·ly** \-t°l-ē\ *adverb*

**distal convoluted tubule** *noun* (circa 1901)
**:** the convoluted portion of the vertebrate nephron that lies between the loop of Henle and the nonsecretory part of the nephron and that is concerned especially with the concentration of urine

**¹dis·tance** \'dis-tən(t)s\ *noun* (14th century)
**1** *obsolete* **:** DISCORD
**2 a :** separation in time **b :** the degree or amount of separation between two points, lines, surfaces, or objects **c** (1) **:** an extent of area or an advance along a route measured linearly (2) **:** an extent of space measured other than linearly 〈within walking *distance*〉 **d :** an extent of advance from a beginning **e :** EXPANSE **f** (1) **:** length of a race or contest 〈won at all *distances*〉 (2) **:** the full length (as of a prizefight or ball game) (3) **:** a long race 〈*distance* training〉
**3 :** the quality or state of being distant: as **a :** spatial remoteness **b :** personal and especially emotional separation; *also* **:** RESERVE, COLDNESS **c :** DIFFERENCE, DISPARITY
**4 :** a distant point or region
**5 a :** AESTHETIC DISTANCE **b :** capacity to observe dispassionately
— **go the distance** *also* **last the distance :** to complete a course of action

**²distance** *transitive verb* **dis·tanced; dis·tanc·ing** (1578)
**1 :** to place or keep at a distance
**2 :** to leave far behind **:** OUTSTRIP

**dis·tant** \'dis-tənt\ *adjective* [Middle English, from Middle French, from Latin *distant-, distans,* present participle of *distare* to stand apart, be distant, from *dis-* + *stare* to stand — more at STAND] (14th century)
**1 a :** separated in space **:** AWAY **b :** situated at a great distance **:** FAR-OFF **c :** separated by a great distance from each other **:** far apart **d :** far behind 〈finished a *distant* third〉
**2 :** separated in a relationship other than spatial 〈a *distant* cousin〉 〈the *distant* past〉
**3 :** different in kind
**4 :** reserved or aloof in personal relationship **:** COLD 〈was *distant* and distracted〉
**5 a :** going a long distance 〈*distant* voyages〉 **b :** concerned with remote things 〈*distant* thoughts〉
— **dis·tant·ly** *adverb*
— **dis·tant·ness** *noun*

**¹dis·taste** \(,)dis-'tāst\ (1592)
*transitive verb*
**1** *archaic* **:** to feel aversion to
**2** *archaic* **:** OFFEND, DISPLEASE
*intransitive verb*
*obsolete* **:** to have an offensive taste

**²distaste** *noun* (1598)
**1 a** *archaic* **:** dislike of food or drink **b :** AVERSION, DISINCLINATION 〈a *distaste* for opera〉
**2** *obsolete* **:** ANNOYANCE, DISCOMFORT

**dis·taste·ful** \(,)dis-'tāst-fəl\ *adjective* (1607)
**1 :** objectionable because offensive to one's personal taste **:** DISAGREEABLE
**2 :** unpleasant to the taste **:** LOATHSOME
— **dis·taste·ful·ly** \-fə-lē\ *adverb*
— **dis·taste·ful·ness** *noun*

**dis·tel·fink** \'dish-t°l-,fiŋk, 'dis-\ *noun* [Pennsylvania German *dischdelfink,* literally, goldfinch, from *dischdel* thistle + *fink* finch] (1939)
**:** a traditional Pennsylvania Dutch design motif in the form of a stylized bird

**¹dis·tem·per** \dis-'tem-pər\ *transitive verb* [Middle English *distempren,* from Late Latin

*distemperare* to temper badly, from Latin *dis-* + *temperare* to temper] (14th century)
**1 :** to throw out of order
**2** *archaic* **:** DERANGE, UNSETTLE

**²distemper** *noun* (circa 1555)
**1 :** bad humor or temper
**2 :** a disordered or abnormal bodily state especially of quadruped mammals: as **a :** a highly contagious virus disease especially of dogs marked by fever, leukopenia, and respiratory, gastrointestinal, and neurological symptoms **b :** STRANGLES **c :** PANLEUKOPENIA
**3 :** AILMENT, DISORDER 〈political *distemper*〉 〈intellectual *distempers*〉
— **dis·tem·per·ate** \-p(ə-)rət\ *adjective*

**³distemper** *noun* [obsolete *distemper,* verb, to dilute, mix to produce distemper, from Middle English, from Middle French *destemprer,* from Latin *dis-* + *temperare*] (1632)
**1 :** a process of painting in which the pigments are mixed with an emulsion of egg yolk, with size, or with white of egg as a vehicle and which is used for painting scenery and murals
**2 a :** the paint or the prepared ground used in the distemper process **b :** a painting done in distemper
**3 :** any of various water-based paints

**⁴distemper** *transitive verb* (circa 1873)
**:** to paint in or with distemper

**dis·tem·per·a·ture** \di-'stem-p(ə-)rə-,chùr, -pə(r)-, -chər, *chiefly Southern* -,t(y)ù(ə)r\ *noun* (1531)
**:** a disordered condition

**dis·tend** \di-'stend\ *verb* [Middle English, from Latin *distendere,* from *dis-* + *tendere* to stretch — more at THIN] (15th century)
*transitive verb*
**1 :** EXTEND
**2 :** to enlarge from internal pressure **:** SWELL
*intransitive verb*
**:** to become expanded
*synonym* see EXPAND

**dis·ten·si·ble** \-'sten(t)-sə-bəl\ *adjective* [*distens-* (from Latin *distensus,* past participle of *distendere*) + *-ible*] (circa 1828)
**:** capable of being distended
— **dis·ten·si·bil·i·ty** \-,sten(t)-sə-'bi-lə-tē\ *noun*

**dis·ten·sion** *or* **dis·ten·tion** \di-'sten(t)-shən\ *noun* [Latin *distention-, distentio,* from *distendere*] (15th century)
**:** the act of distending or the state of being distended especially unduly or abnormally

**dis·tich** \'dis-(,)tik\ *noun* [Latin *distichon,* from Greek, from neuter of *distichos* having two rows, from *di-* + *stichos* row, verse; akin to Greek *steichein* to go — more at STAIR] (1553)
**:** a strophic unit of two lines

**dis·ti·chous** \'dis-ti-kəs\ *adjective* [Late Latin *distichus,* from Greek *distichos*] (circa 1753)

---

◇ WORD HISTORY
**distaff** A distaff was originally a short staff that held a bundle of fibers, such as flax or wool, that were drawn and twisted into yarn or thread either by hand or with the aid of a spinning wheel. The job of spinning customarily fell to women, and since it was such a basic daily task, the distaff naturally came to be a symbol for women's work. This symbolic use of the word *distaff* dates back at least to the time of Chaucer. Eventually *distaff* came to be used figuratively for everything relating to the female domain and for women collectively. The women of a family became known as the *distaff* or the *distaff side*.

---

\ə\ abut \ᵊ\ kitten \ər\ **further** \a\ ash \ā\ ace
\ä\ mop, mar \aù\ **out** \ch\ chin \e\ bet \ē\ **easy**
\g\ go \i\ hit \ī\ ice \j\ job \ŋ\ sing \ō\ go
\ò\ law \òi\ boy \th\ thin \t͟h\ the \ü\ loot \ù\ foot
\y\ yet \zh\ vision    *see also* Guide to Pronunciation

: disposed in two vertical rows ⟨*distichous* leaves⟩

**dis·till** *also* **dis·til** \di-'stil\ *verb* **dis·tilled; dis·till·ing** [Middle English *distillen,* from Middle French *distiller,* from Late Latin *distillare,* alteration of Latin *destillare,* from *de-* + *stillare* to drip, from *stilla* drop] (14th century)
*transitive verb*
**1 :** to let fall, exude, or precipitate in drops or in a wet mist
**2 a :** to subject to or transform by distillation **b :** to obtain by or as if by distillation **c :** to extract the essence of **:** CONCENTRATE
*intransitive verb*
**1 a :** to fall or materialize in drops or in a fine moisture **b :** to appear slowly or in small quantities at a time
**2 a :** to undergo distillation **b :** to perform distillation

**dis·til·late** \'dis-tə-ˌlāt, -lət; di-'sti-lət\ *noun* (circa 1859)
**1 :** a liquid product condensed from vapor during distillation
**2 :** something concentrated or extracted as if by distilling

**dis·til·la·tion** \ˌdis-tə-'lā-shən\ *noun* (14th century)
**1 a :** the process of purifying a liquid by successive evaporation and condensation **b :** a process like distillation; *also* **:** an instance of distilling
**2 :** something distilled **:** DISTILLATE 2

**dis·till·er** \di-'sti-lər\ *noun* (1577)
**:** one that distills especially alcoholic liquors

**dis·till·ery** \di-'sti-lə-rē, -'stil-rē\ *noun, plural* **-er·ies** (1759)
**:** the works where distilling (as of alcoholic liquors) is done

**dis·tinct** \di-'stiŋ(k)t\ *adjective* [Middle English, from Middle French, from Latin *distinctus,* from past participle of *distinguere*] (14th century)
**1 :** distinguishable to the eye or mind as discrete **:** SEPARATE ⟨a *distinct* cultural group⟩ ⟨teaching as *distinct* from research⟩
**2 :** presenting a clear unmistakable impression ⟨a neat *distinct* handwriting⟩
**3** *archaic* **:** notably decorated
**4 a :** NOTABLE ⟨a *distinct* contribution to scholarship⟩ **b :** readily and unmistakably apprehended ⟨a *distinct* possibility of snow⟩ ⟨a *distinct* British accent⟩ ☆
— **dis·tinct·ly** \-'stiŋ(k)t-lē, -'stiŋ-klē\ *adverb*
— **dis·tinct·ness** \-'stiŋ(k)t-nəs, -'stiŋk-nəs\ *noun*

**dis·tinc·tion** \di-'stiŋ(k)-shən\ *noun* (13th century)
**1 a** *archaic* **:** DIVISION **b :** CLASS 4
**2 :** the distinguishing of a difference ⟨without *distinction* as to race, sex, or religion⟩; *also* **:** the difference distinguished ⟨the *distinction* between *imply* and *infer*⟩
**3 :** something that distinguishes ⟨regional *distinctions*⟩
**4 :** the quality or state of being distinguishable
**5 a :** the quality or state of being distinguished or worthy ⟨a politician of *distinction*⟩ **b :** special honor or recognition ⟨took a law degree with *distinction*⟩ **c :** achievement that sets one apart ⟨the *distinction* of winning the title⟩

**dis·tinc·tive** \di-'stiŋ(k)-tiv\ *adjective* (15th century)
**1 a :** serving to distinguish **b :** having or giving style or distinction
**2 :** capable of making a segment of utterance different in meaning as well as in sound from an otherwise identical utterance
*synonym* see CHARACTERISTIC
— **dis·tinc·tive·ly** *adverb*
— **dis·tinc·tive·ness** *noun*

**dis·tin·gué** \ˌdēs-ˌtaŋ-'gā, (ˌ)dis-; di-'staŋ-ˌ\ *adjective* [French, from past participle of *distinguer*] (1813)
**:** distinguished especially in manner or bearing

**dis·tin·guish** \di-'stiŋ-(g)wish\ *verb* [Middle French *distinguer,* from Latin *distinguere,* literally, to separate by pricking, from *dis-* + *-stinguere* (akin to Latin in*stigare* to urge on) — more at STICK] (1561)
*transitive verb*
**1 :** to perceive a difference in **:** mentally separate ⟨so alike they could not be *distinguished*⟩
**2 a :** to mark as separate or different **b :** to separate into kinds, classes, or categories **c :** to give prominence or distinction to ⟨*distinguished* herself in music⟩ **d :** CHARACTERIZE
**3 a :** DISCERN ⟨*distinguished* a light in the distance⟩ **b :** to single out **:** take special notice of
*intransitive verb*
**:** to perceive a difference
— **dis·tin·guish·abil·i·ty** \-ˌstiŋ-(g)wi-shə-'bi-lə-tē\ *noun*
— **dis·tin·guish·able** \-'stiŋ-(g)wi-shə-bəl\ *adjective*
— **dis·tin·guish·ably** \-blē\ *adverb*

**dis·tin·guished** *adjective* (1714)
**1 :** marked by eminence, distinction, or excellence
**2 :** befitting an eminent person
*synonym* see FAMOUS

**Distinguished Conduct Medal** *noun* (1862)
**:** a British military decoration awarded for distinguished conduct in the field

**Distinguished Flying Cross** *noun* (1918)
**1 :** a British military decoration awarded for acts of gallantry when flying in operations against an enemy
**2 :** a U.S. military decoration awarded for heroism or extraordinary achievement while participating in an aerial flight

**Distinguished Service Cross** *noun* (1914)
**1 :** a British military decoration awarded for distinguished service against the enemy
**2 :** a U.S. Army decoration awarded for extraordinary heroism during operations against an armed enemy

**Distinguished Service Medal** *noun* (1914)
**1 :** a British military decoration awarded for distinguished conduct in war
**2 :** a U.S. military decoration awarded for exceptionally meritorious service to the government in a wartime duty of great responsibility

**Distinguished Service Order** *noun* (1886)
**:** a British military decoration awarded for special services in action

**dis·tort** \di-'stȯrt\ *verb* [Latin *distortus,* past participle of *distorquēre,* from *dis-* + *torquēre* to twist — more at TORTURE] (circa 1586)
*transitive verb*
**1 :** to twist out of the true meaning or proportion ⟨*distorted* the facts⟩
**2 :** to twist out of a natural, normal, or original shape or condition ⟨a face *distorted* by pain⟩; *also* **:** to cause to be perceived unnaturally ⟨the new lights *distorted* colors⟩
**3 :** PERVERT
*intransitive verb*
**:** to become distorted; *also* **:** to cause a twisting from the true, natural, or normal
*synonym* see DEFORM
— **dis·tort·er** *noun*

**dis·tor·tion** \di-'stȯr-shən\ *noun* (1581)
**1 :** the act of distorting
**2 :** the quality or state of being distorted **:** a product of distorting: as **a :** a lack of proportionality in an image resulting from defects in the optical system **b :** falsified reproduction of an audio or video signal caused by change in the wave form of the original signal
— **dis·tor·tion·al** \-shnəl, -shə-nᵊl\ *adjective*

**¹dis·tract** \di-'strakt, 'dis-ˌtrakt\ *adjective* (14th century)
*archaic* **:** INSANE, MAD

**²dis·tract** \di-'strakt\ *transitive verb* [Middle English, from Latin *distractus,* past participle

of *distrahere,* literally, to draw apart, from *dis-* + *trahere* to draw] (14th century)
**1 a :** to turn aside **:** DIVERT **b :** to draw or direct (as one's attention) to a different object or in different directions at the same time
**2 :** to stir up or confuse with conflicting emotions or motives
*synonym* see PUZZLE
— **dis·tract·i·bil·i·ty** \-ˌstrak-tə-'bi-lə-tē\ *noun*
— **dis·tract·ible** *or* **dis·tract·able** \-'strak-tə-bəl\ *adjective*
— **dis·tract·ing·ly** \-tiŋ-lē\ *adverb*

**dis·tract·ed** *adjective* (1590)
**1 :** maddened or deranged especially by grief or anxiety
**2 :** mentally confused, troubled, or remote
— **dis·tract·ed·ly** *adverb*

**dis·trac·tion** \di-'strak-shən\ *noun* (15th century)
**1 :** the act of distracting or the state of being distracted; *especially* **:** mental confusion
**2 :** something that distracts; *especially* **:** AMUSEMENT
— **dis·trac·tive** \-'strak-tiv\ *adjective*

**dis·train** \di-'strān\ *verb* [Middle English *distreynen,* from Old French *destreindre,* from Medieval Latin *distringere,* from Latin, to draw apart, detain, from *dis-* + *stringere* to bind tight — more at STRAIN] (14th century)
*transitive verb*
**1 :** to force or compel to satisfy an obligation by means of a distress
**2 :** to seize by distress
*intransitive verb*
**:** to levy a distress
— **dis·train·able** \-'strā-nə-bəl\ *adjective*
— **dis·train·er** \-'strā-nər\ *or* **dis·train·or** \-'strā-nər, -ˌstrā-'nȯr\ *noun*

**dis·traint** \di-'strānt\ *noun* [*distrain* + *-t* (as in *constraint*)] (circa 1736)
**:** the act or action of distraining

**dis·trait** \di-'strā\ *adjective* [Middle English, from Old French *destrait,* from Latin *distractus*] (15th century)
**:** apprehensively divided or withdrawn in attention **:** DISTRACTED 2

**dis·traite** \di-'strāt\ *adjective* (15th century)
**:** DISTRAIT — used especially of women

**dis·traught** \dis-'trȯt\ *adjective* [Middle English, modification of Latin *distractus*] (14th century)
**1 :** agitated with doubt or mental conflict
**2 :** INSANE
— **dis·traught·ly** *adverb*

**¹dis·tress** \di-'stres\ *noun* [Middle English *destresse,* from Old French, from (assumed) Vulgar Latin *districtia,* from Latin *districtus,* past participle of *distringere*] (13th century)
**1 a :** seizure and detention of the goods of another as pledge or to obtain satisfaction of a claim by the sale of the goods seized **b :** something that is distrained
**2 a :** pain or suffering affecting the body, a bodily part, or the mind **:** TROUBLE ⟨gastric *distress*⟩ **b :** a painful situation **:** MISFORTUNE
**3 :** a state of danger or desperate need ⟨a ship in *distress*⟩ ☆

**²distress** *transitive verb* (14th century)
**1 :** to subject to great strain or difficulties

---

☆ SYNONYMS
**Distinct, separate, discrete** mean not being each and every one the same. DISTINCT indicates that something is distinguished by the mind or eye as being apart or different from others ⟨two *distinct* versions⟩. SEPARATE often stresses lack of connection or a difference in identity between two things ⟨*separate* rooms⟩. DISCRETE strongly emphasizes individuality and lack of connection ⟨broke the job down into *discrete* stages⟩. See in addition EVIDENT.

**2** *archaic* : to force or overcome by inflicting pain
**3** : to cause to worry or be troubled : UPSET
**4** : to mar (as clothing or wood) deliberately to give an effect of age
— **dis·tress·ing·ly** \-'stre-siŋ-lē\ *adverb*
³**distress** *adjective* (1926)
**1** : offered for sale at a loss ⟨*distress* merchandise⟩
**2** : involving distress goods ⟨a *distress* sale⟩
**dis·tress·ful** \di-'stres-fəl\ *adjective* (1591)
: causing distress : full of distress
— **dis·tress·ful·ly** \-fə-lē\ *adverb*
— **dis·tress·ful·ness** *noun*
**dis·trib·u·tary** \di-'stri-byə-,ter-ē\ *noun, plural* **-tar·ies** (1863)
: a river branch flowing away from the main stream
**dis·trib·ute** \di-'stri-byət, *British also* 'dis-tri-,byüt\ *verb* **-ut·ed; -ut·ing** [Middle English, from Latin *distributus*, past participle of *distribuere*, from *dis-* + *tribuere* to allot — more at TRIBUTE] (15th century)
*transitive verb*
**1** : to divide among several or many : APPORTION ⟨*distribute* expenses⟩
**2 a** : to spread out so as to cover something : SCATTER **b** : to give out or deliver especially to members of a group ⟨*distribute* newspapers⟩ ⟨*distribute* leaflets⟩ **c** : to place or position so as to be properly apportioned over or throughout an area ⟨200 pounds *distributed* on a 6-foot frame⟩ **d** : to use (a term) so as to convey information about every member of the class named ⟨the proposition "all men are mortal" *distributes* "man" but not "mortal"⟩
**3 a** : to divide or separate especially into kinds **b** : to return the units of (as typeset matter) to storage
**4** : to use in or as an operation so as to be mathematically distributive
*intransitive verb*
: to be mathematically distributive ⟨multiplication *distributes* over addition⟩ ☆
— **dis·trib·u·tee** \dis-,tri-byə-'tē\ *noun*
**dis·trib·ut·ed** *adjective* (1968)
**1** : characterized by a statistical distribution of a particular kind ⟨a normally *distributed* random variable⟩
**2** : of, relating to, or being a computer network in which at least some of the processing is done by the individual workstations and information is shared by and often stored at the workstations
**dis·tri·bu·tion** \,dis-trə-'byü-shən\ *noun* (14th century)
**1 a** : the act or process of distributing **b** : the apportionment by a court of the personal property of an intestate
**2 a** : the position, arrangement, or frequency of occurrence (as of the members of a group) over an area or throughout a space or unit of time **b** : the natural geographic range of an organism
**3 a** : something distributed **b** (1) : FREQUENCY DISTRIBUTION (2) : PROBABILITY FUNCTION (3) : PROBABILITY DENSITY FUNCTION 2
**4** : the pattern of branching and termination of a ramifying structure (as a nerve)
**5** : the marketing or merchandising of commodities
— **dis·tri·bu·tion·al** \-shnəl, -shə-n°l\ *adjective*
**distribution function** *noun* (circa 1909)
: a function that gives the probability that a random variable is less than or equal to the independent variable of the function
**dis·trib·u·tive** \di-'stri-byə-tiv\ *adjective* (15th century)
**1** : of or relating to distribution: as **a** : dealing a proper share to each of a group **b** : diffusing more or less evenly
**2** *of a word* : referring singly and without exception to the members of a group ⟨*each, either,* and *none* are *distributive*⟩

**3 a** : being an operation (as multiplication in $a(b + c) = ab + ac$) that produces the same result when operating on the whole mathematical expression as when operating on each part and collecting the results **b** : being or relating to a rule or property concerning a distributive operation ⟨the *distributive* property of multiplication with respect to addition⟩
— **dis·trib·u·tive·ly** *adverb*
— **dis·trib·u·tiv·i·ty** \-,stri-byə-'ti-və-tē\ *noun*
**dis·trib·u·tor** \di-'stri-byə-tər\ *noun* (1526)
**1** : one that distributes
**2** : one that markets a commodity; *especially* : WHOLESALER
**3** : an apparatus for directing the secondary current from the induction coil to the various spark plugs of an engine in their proper firing order
¹**dis·trict** \'dis-(,)trikt\ *noun, often attributive* [French, from Medieval Latin *districtus* jurisdiction, district, from *distringere* to distrain — more at DISTRAIN] (1611)
**1 a** : a territorial division (as for administrative or electoral purposes) **b** : the basic administrative unit for local government in Northern Ireland
**2** : an area, region, or section with a distinguishing character
²**district** *transitive verb* (1792)
: to divide or organize into districts
**district attorney** *noun* (1789)
: the prosecuting officer of a judicial district
**district court** *noun* (1789)
: a trial court that has jurisdiction over certain cases within a specific judicial district
¹**dis·trust** \(,)dis-'trəst\ *noun* (1513)
: the lack or absence of trust
²**distrust** *transitive verb* (1548)
: to have no trust or confidence in
**dis·trust·ful** \-'trəs(t)-fəl\ *adjective* (1589)
: having or showing distrust
— **dis·trust·ful·ly** \-fə-lē\ *adverb*
— **dis·trust·ful·ness** *noun*
**dis·turb** \di-'stərb\ *verb* [Middle English *disturben, destourben,* from Old French & Latin; Old French *destourber,* from Latin *disturbare,* from *dis-* + *turbare* to throw into disorder, from *turba* disorder — more at TURBID] (14th century)
*transitive verb*
**1 a** : to interfere with : INTERRUPT **b** : to alter the position or arrangement of **c** : to upset the natural and especially the ecological balance or relations of ⟨land *disturbed* by dumping⟩
**2 a** : to destroy the tranquillity or composure of **b** : to throw into disorder **c** : ALARM **d** : to put to inconvenience
*intransitive verb*
: to cause disturbance
*synonym* see DISCOMPOSE
— **dis·turb·er** *noun*
— **dis·turb·ing·ly** \-'stər-biŋ-lē\ *adverb*
**dis·tur·bance** \di-'stər-bən(t)s\ *noun* (13th century)
**1** : the act of disturbing : the state of being disturbed
**2** : a local variation from the average or normal wind conditions
**dis·turbed** *adjective* (1904)
: showing symptoms of emotional illness ⟨*disturbed* children⟩ ⟨*disturbed* behavior⟩
**di·sub·sti·tut·ed** \(,)dī-'səb-stə-,tü-təd, -,tyü-\ *adjective* (circa 1909)
: having two substituent atoms or groups in a molecule
**di·sul·fide** \(,)dī-'səl-,fīd\ *noun* (1872)
**1** : a compound containing two atoms of sulfur combined with an element or radical
**2** : an organic compound containing the bivalent group SS composed of two sulfur atoms
**di·sul·fi·ram** \dī-'səl-fə-,ram\ *noun* [*disulf*ide + *amyl*] (1952)
: a compound $C_{10}H_{20}N_2S_4$ that causes a severe physiological reaction to alcohol and is used especially in the treatment of alcoholism

**di·sul·fo·ton** \dī-'səl-fə-,tän\ *noun* [*di-* + *sulfo-* + *-ton* (probably from *thion-*)] (1965)
: an organophosphorus systemic insecticide $C_8H_{19}O_2PS_3$
**dis·union** \(,)dis-'yü-nyən, dish-\ *noun* (15th century)
**1** : the termination of union : SEPARATION
**2** : DISUNITY
— **dis·union·ist** \-nyə-nist\ *noun*
**dis·unite** \(,)dis-yü-'nīt, -yə-, dish-\ *transitive verb* (1598)
: DIVIDE, SEPARATE
**dis·uni·ty** \(,)dis-'yü-nə-tē, dish-\ *noun* (1632)
: lack of unity; *especially* : DISSENSION
¹**dis·use** \(,)dis-'yüz, dish-\ *transitive verb* (15th century)
: to discontinue the use or practice of
²**dis·use** \-'yüs\ *noun* (15th century)
: cessation of use or practice
**dis·util·i·ty** \(,)dis-yü-'ti-lə-tē, -yə-, dish-\ *noun* (1879)
: the state or fact of being counterproductive
¹**dis·val·ue** \(,)dis-'val-(,)yü, -yə-(w)\ *transitive verb* (1603)
**1** *archaic* : UNDERVALUE, DEPRECIATE
**2** : to consider of little value
²**disvalue** *noun* (1603)
**1** *obsolete* : DISREGARD, DISESTEEM
**2** : a negative value
**di·syl·la·ble** \'dī-,si-lə-bəl, (,)dī-'sil-; 'di-,sil-, (,)di(s)-'sil-\ *noun* [part translation of Middle French *dissilabe,* from Latin *disyllabus* having two syllables, from Greek *disyllabos,* from *di-* + *syllabē* syllable] (1589)
: a linguistic form consisting of two syllables
— **di·syl·lab·ic** \,dī-sə-'la-bik, ,di(s)-sə-\ *adjective*
**dit** \'dit\ *noun* [imitative] (1940)
: a dot in radio or telegraphic code
¹**ditch** \'dich\ *noun* [Middle English *dich,* from Old English *dīc* dike, ditch; akin to Middle High German *tīch* pond, dike] (before 12th century)

\ə\ abut \ᵊ\ kitten \ər\ further \a\ ash \ā\ ace
\ä\ mop, mar \aủ\ out \ch\ chin \e\ bet \ē\ easy
\g\ go \i\ hit \ī\ ice \j\ job \ŋ\ sing \ō\ go
\ỏ\ law \ỏi\ boy \th\ thin \t͟h\ the \ü\ loot \ủ\ foot
\y\ yet \zh\ vision *see also* Guide to Pronunciation

: a long narrow excavation dug in the earth (as for drainage)

²**ditch** (14th century)
*transitive verb*
**1 a :** to enclose with a ditch **b :** to dig a ditch in
**2 :** to make a forced landing of (an airplane) on water
**3 :** to get rid of **:** DISCARD
*intransitive verb*
**1 :** to dig a ditch
**2 :** to crash-land at sea

**ditch·dig·ger** \-₊di-gər\ *noun* (circa 1897)
**1 :** one that digs ditches
**2 :** one employed at menial and usually hard physical labor

**dite** \'dīt\ *noun* [variant of *doit*] (circa 1877)
*dialect* **:** MITE, BIT

¹**dith·er** \'di-thər\ *intransitive verb* **dith·ered; dith·er·ing** \-th(ə-)riŋ\ [Middle English *didderen*] (15th century)
**1 :** SHIVER, TREMBLE
**2 :** to act nervously or indecisively **:** VACILLATE
— **dith·er·er** \-thər-ər\ *noun*

²**dither** *noun* (1819)
**:** a highly nervous, excited, or agitated state **:** EXCITEMENT, CONFUSION
— **dith·ery** \'di-thə-rē\ *adjective*

**dithi-** *or* **dithio-** *combining form* [International Scientific Vocabulary *di-* + *thi-*]
**:** containing two atoms of sulfur usually in place of two oxygen atoms ⟨*dithio*carbamate⟩

**di·thio·car·ba·mate** \₊dī-₊thī-ō-'kär-bə-₊māt\ *noun* (1929)
**:** any of several sulfur analogues of the carbamates including some used as fungicides

**dith·y·ramb** \'di-thi-₊ram(b)\ *noun, plural* **-rambs** \-₊ramz\ [Greek *dithyrambos*] (1656)
**1 :** a usually short poem in an inspired wild irregular strain
**2 :** a statement or writing in an exalted or enthusiastic vein
— **dith·y·ram·bic** \₊di-thi-'ram-bik\ *adjective*
— **dith·y·ram·bi·cal·ly** \-bi-k(ə-)lē\ *adverb*

**di·tran·si·tive** \₊dī-'tran(t)-sə-tiv, -'tran-zə-\ *adjective* (1972)
**:** able to take both a direct and an indirect object ⟨a *ditransitive* verb⟩
— **ditransitive** *noun*

**dit·sy** *or* **dit·zy** \'dit-sē\ *adjective* **dits·i·er** *or* **ditz·i·er; -est** [origin unknown] (1973)
**:** eccentrically silly, giddy, or inane **:** DIZZY

**dit·ta·ny** \'di-t°n-ē\ *noun, plural* **-nies** [Middle English *ditoyne*, from Old French *ditayne*, from Latin *dictamnum*, from Greek *diktamnon*] (12th century)
**1 :** a pink-flowered herb (*Origanum dictamnus*) that is native to Crete
**2 :** an American herb (*Conila origanoides*) of the mint family that has much-branched stems

¹**dit·to** \'di-(₊)tō\ *noun, plural* **dittos** [Italian *ditto, detto*, past participle of *dire* to say, from Latin *dicere* — more at DICTION] (circa 1678)
**1 :** a thing mentioned previously or above — used to avoid repeating a word; often symbolized by inverted commas or apostrophes
**2 :** a ditto mark

²**ditto** *adjective* (1776)
**:** having the same characteristics **:** SIMILAR

³**ditto** *verb* (1837)
**1 :** to repeat the action or statement of
**2** [from *Ditto*, a trademark] **:** to copy (as printed matter) on a duplicator

⁴**ditto** *adverb* (circa 1864)
**:** as before or aforesaid **:** in the same manner

**dit·ty** \'di-tē\ *noun, plural* **ditties** [Middle English *ditee*, from Middle French *ditié* poem, from past participle of *ditier* to compose, from Latin *dictare* to dictate, compose] (14th century)
**:** an especially simple and unaffected song

**dit·ty bag** \'di-tē-\ *noun* [origin unknown] (circa 1860)

: a bag used especially by sailors to hold small articles (as needles and thread)

**ditty box** *noun* (circa 1880)
**:** a box used for the same purpose as a ditty bag

**ditz** \'dits\ *noun* (1982)
**:** a ditsy person

**di·ure·sis** \₊dī-yə-'rē-səs\ *noun, plural* **-ure·ses** \-₊sēz\ [New Latin] (circa 1681)
**:** an increased excretion of urine

**di·uret·ic** \₊dī-yə-'re-tik\ *adjective* [Middle English, from Middle French or Late Latin; Middle French *diuretique*, from Late Latin *diureticus*, from Greek *diourētikos*, from *diourein* to urinate, from *dia-* + *ourein* to urinate — more at URINE] (14th century)
**:** tending to increase the flow of urine
— **diuretic** *noun*
— **di·uret·i·cal·ly** \-ti-k(ə-)lē\ *adverb*

¹**di·ur·nal** \dī-'ər-n°l\ *adjective* [Middle English, from Latin *diurnalis* — more at JOURNAL] (14th century)
**1 a :** recurring every day ⟨*diurnal* tasks⟩ **b :** having a daily cycle ⟨*diurnal* tides⟩
**2 a :** of, relating to, or occurring in the daytime ⟨the city's *diurnal* noises⟩ **b :** active chiefly in the daytime ⟨*diurnal* animals⟩ **c :** opening during the day and closing at night ⟨*diurnal* flowers⟩
— **di·ur·nal·ly** \-n°l-ē\ *adverb*

²**diurnal** *noun* (1600)
**1** *archaic* **:** DIARY, DAYBOOK
**2 :** JOURNAL 2a

**di·u·ron** \'dī-yə-₊rän\ *noun* [*di*chlor- + *urea* + ¹*-on*] (1957)
**:** a persistent herbicide $C_9H_{10}Cl_2N_2O$ used especially to control annual weeds

**di·va** \'dē-və\ *noun, plural* **divas** *or* **di·ve** \-(₊)vā\ [Italian, literally, goddess, from Latin, feminine of *divus* divine, god — more at DEITY] (1883)
**:** PRIMA DONNA 1

**di·va·gate** \'dī-və-₊gāt, 'di-\ *intransitive verb* **-gat·ed; -gat·ing** [Late Latin *divagatus*, past participle of *divagari*, from Latin *dis-* + *vagari* to wander — more at VAGARY] (1599)
**:** to wander or stray from a course or subject **:** DIVERGE, DIGRESS
— **di·va·ga·tion** \₊dī-və-'gā-shən, ₊di-\ *noun*

**di·va·lent** \(₊)dī-'vā-lənt\ *adjective* (1869)
**:** having a chemical valence of two; *also* **:** bonded to two other atoms or groups

**di·van** \di-'van, 'dī-₊van, *especially in senses 1, 2, & 4 also* di-'vän, dī-'van\ *noun* [Turkish, from Persian *dīwān* account book] (1586)
**1 a :** the privy council of the Ottoman Empire **b :** COUNCIL
**2 :** a council chamber
**3 :** a large couch usually without back or arms often designed for use as a bed
**4 :** a collection of poems in Persian or Arabic usually by one author

**di·var·i·cate** \dī-'var-ə-₊kāt, də-\ *transitive verb* **-cat·ed; -cat·ing** [Latin *divaricatus*, past participle of *divaricare*, from *dis-* + *varicare* to straddle — more at PREVARICATE] (1673)
**:** to spread apart **:** branch off **:** DIVERGE

**di·var·i·ca·tion** \(₊)dī-₊var-ə-'kā-shən, də-\ *noun* (1578)
**1 :** the action, process, or fact of divaricating
**2 :** a divergence of opinion

¹**dive** \'dīv\ *verb* **dived** \'dīvd\ *or* **dove** \'dōv\; **dived** *also* **dove; div·ing** [Middle English *diven, duven*, from Old English *dyfan* to dip & *dūfan* to dive; akin to Old English *dyppan* to dip — more at DIP] (before 12th century)
*intransitive verb*
**1 a :** to plunge into water intentionally and especially headfirst; *also* **:** to execute a dive **b :** SUBMERGE
**2 a :** to come or drop down precipitously **:** PLUNGE 3 **b :** to plunge one's hand into something **c** *of an airplane* **:** to descend in a dive

**3 a :** to plunge into some matter or activity **b :** to plunge or dash for some place ⟨*diving* for cover⟩; *also* **:** to lunge especially in order to seize something ⟨*dove* for the ball⟩
*transitive verb*
**1 :** to thrust into something
**2 :** to cause to dive ▪

²**dive** *noun* (1700)
**1 :** the act or an instance of diving: as **a** (1) **:** a plunge into water executed in a prescribed manner (2) **:** a submerging of a submarine (3) **:** a steep descent of an airplane at greater than the maximum horizontal speed **b :** a sharp decline
**2 :** a disreputable entertainment establishment
**3 :** a faked knockout — usually used in the phrase *take a dive*
**4 :** an offensive play in football in which the ballcarrier plunges into the line for short yardage

**dive–bomb** \'dīv-₊bäm\ *transitive verb* (1935)
**:** to bomb from an airplane by making a steep dive toward the target before releasing the bomb
— **dive–bomb·er** *noun*

**div·er** \'dī-vər\ *noun* (1506)
**1 :** one that dives
**2 a :** a person who stays underwater for long periods by having air supplied from the surface or by carrying a supply of compressed air **b :** any of various birds that obtain food by diving in water; *especially* **:** LOON

**di·verge** \də-'vərj, dī-\ *verb* **di·verged; di·verg·ing** [Medieval Latin *divergere*, from Latin *dis-* + *vergere* to incline — more at WRENCH] (1665)
*intransitive verb*
**1 a :** to move or extend in different directions from a common point **:** draw apart ⟨*diverging* roads⟩ **b :** to become or be different in character or form **:** differ in opinion
**2 :** to turn aside from a path or course **:** DEVIATE
**3 :** to be mathematically divergent
*transitive verb*
**:** DEFLECT
*synonym* see SWERVE

**di·ver·gence** \-'vər-jən(t)s\ *noun* (1656)
**1 a :** a drawing apart (as of lines extending from a common center) **b :** DIFFERENCE, DISAGREEMENT **c :** the acquisition of dissimilar characters by related organisms in unlike environments
**2 :** a deviation from a course or standard
**3 :** the condition of being mathematically divergent

**di·ver·gen·cy** \-jən(t)-sē\ *noun, plural* **-cies** (1709)
**:** DIVERGENCE

**di·ver·gent** \-jənt\ *adjective* [Latin *divergent-, divergens*, present participle of *divergere*] (1696)
**1 a :** diverging from each other **b :** differing from each other or from a standard **:** DEVIANT ⟨the *divergent* interests of capital and labor⟩

---

☐ USAGE

**dive** *Dive*, which was originally a weak verb, developed a past tense *dove*, probably by analogy with verbs like *drive, drove*. *Dove* exists in some British dialects and has become the standard past tense especially in speech in some parts of Canada. In the U.S. *dived* and *dove* are both widespread in speech as past tense and past participle, with *dove* less common than *dived* in the south Midland area, and *dived* less common than *dove* in the Northern and north Midland areas. In writing, the past tense *dived* is usual in British English and somewhat more common in American English. *Dove* seems relatively rare as a past participle in writing.

**2 :** relating to or being an infinite sequence that does not have a limit or an infinite series whose partial sums do not have a limit
**3 :** causing divergence of rays ⟨a *divergent* lens⟩
*synonym* see DIFFERENT
— **di·ver·gent·ly** *adverb*
**di·vers** \'dī-vərz\ *adjective* [Middle English *divers, diverse*] (14th century)
**:** VARIOUS
**di·verse** \dī-'vərs, də-', 'dī-,\ *adjective* [Middle English *divers, diverse*, from Old French & Latin; Old French *divers*, from Latin *diversus*, from past participle of *divertere*] (14th century)
**1 :** differing from one another **:** UNLIKE
**2 :** composed of distinct or unlike elements or qualities
*synonym* see DIFFERENT
— **di·verse·ly** *adverb*
— **di·verse·ness** *noun*
**di·ver·si·fy** \də-'vər-sə-ˌfī, dī-\ *verb* **-fied; -fy·ing** (15th century)
*transitive verb*
**1 :** to make diverse **:** give variety to ⟨*diversify* a course of study⟩
**2 :** to balance (as an investment portfolio) defensively by dividing funds among securities of different industries or of different classes
**3 :** to increase the variety of the products of
*intransitive verb*
**1 :** to produce variety
**2 :** to engage in varied operations
— **di·ver·si·fi·ca·tion** \-ˌvər-sə-fə-'kā-shən\ *noun*
— **di·ver·si·fi·er** \-'vər-sə-ˌfī(-ə)r\ *noun*
**di·ver·sion** \də-'vər-zhən, dī-, -shən\ *noun* (1600)
**1 :** the act or an instance of diverting from a course, activity, or use **:** DEVIATION
**2 :** something that diverts or amuses **:** PASTIME
**3 :** an attack or feint that draws the attention and force of an enemy from the point of the principal operation
**di·ver·sion·ary** \də-'vər-zhə-ˌner-ē, dī-, -shə-\ *adjective* (1846)
**:** tending to draw attention away from the principal concern **:** being a diversion
**di·ver·sion·ist** \-zhə-nəst, -shə-\ *noun* (1937)
**1 :** one engaged in diversionary activities
**2 :** one characterized by political deviation
**di·ver·si·ty** \də-'vər-sə-tē, dī-\ *noun, plural* **-ties** (14th century)
**1 :** the condition of being diverse **:** VARIETY
**2 :** an instance of being diverse
**di·vert** \də-'vərt, dī-\ *verb* [Middle English, from Middle French & Latin; Middle French *divertir*, from Latin *divertere* to turn in opposite directions, from *dis-* + *vertere* to turn — more at WORTH] (15th century)
*intransitive verb*
**:** to turn aside **:** DEVIATE ⟨studied law but *diverted* to diplomacy⟩
*transitive verb*
**1 a :** to turn from one course or use to another **:** DEFLECT **b :** DISTRACT
**2 :** to give pleasure to especially by distracting the attention from what burdens or distresses
*synonym* see AMUSE
**di·ver·tic·u·li·tis** \ˌdī-vər-ˌti-kyə-'lī-təs\ *noun* [New Latin] (circa 1900)
**:** inflammation of a diverticulum
**di·ver·tic·u·lo·sis** \ˌdī-vər-ˌti-kyə-'lō-səs\ *noun* [New Latin] (1917)
**:** an intestinal disorder characterized by the presence of many diverticula
**di·ver·tic·u·lum** \ˌdī-vər-'ti-kyə-ləm\ *noun, plural* **-la** \-lə\ [New Latin, from Latin, bypath, probably alteration of *deverticulum*, from *devertere* to turn aside, from *de-* + *vertere*] (circa 1819)
**1 :** an abnormal pouch or sac opening from a hollow organ (as the intestine or bladder)
**2 :** a pocket or closed branch opening off a main passage
— **di·ver·tic·u·lar** \-kyə-lər\ *adjective*

**di·ver·ti·men·to** \di-ˌvər-tə-'men-(ˌ)tō, -ˌver-\ *noun, plural* **-men·ti** \-'men-(ˌ)tē\ *or* **-mentos** [Italian, literally, diversion, from *divertire* to divert, amuse, from Latin *divertere*] (1823)
**1 :** an instrumental chamber work in several movements usually light in character
**2 :** DIVERTISSEMENT 1
**di·ver·tisse·ment** \di-'vər-təs-mənt, -təz-, French dē-ver-tē-smäⁿ\ *noun, plural* **divertissements** \-mən(t)s, -smäⁿ(z)\ [French, literally, diversion, from *divertiss-* (stem of *divertir*)] (1728)
**1 :** a dance sequence or short ballet usually used as an interlude
**2 :** DIVERTIMENTO 1
**3 :** DIVERSION, ENTERTAINMENT
**Di·ves** \'dī-(ˌ)vēz\ *noun* [Middle English, from Latin, rich, rich man; misunderstood as a proper name in Luke 16:19] (14th century)
**:** a rich man
**di·vest** \dī-'vest, də-\ *transitive verb* [alteration of *devest*] (1563)
**1 a :** to deprive or dispossess especially of property, authority, or title **b :** to undress or strip especially of clothing, ornament, or equipment **c :** RID, FREE
**2 :** to take away from a person
— **di·vest·ment** \-'vest(t)-mənt\ *noun*
**di·ves·ti·ture** \dī-'ves-tə-ˌchùr, -chər, də-, *chiefly Southern* -t(y)ù(ə)r\ *noun* [*divest* + *-iture* (as in *investiture*)] (1601)
**1 :** the act of divesting
**2 :** the compulsory transfer of title or disposal of interests (as stock in a corporation) upon government order
¹**di·vide** \də-'vīd\ *verb* **di·vid·ed; di·vid·ing** [Middle English, from Latin *dividere*, from *dis-* + *-videre* to separate — more at WIDOW] (14th century)
*transitive verb*
**1 a :** to separate into two or more parts, areas, or groups **b :** to separate into classes, categories, or divisions **c :** CLEAVE, PART
**2 a :** to separate into portions and give out in shares **:** DISTRIBUTE **b :** to possess, enjoy, or make use of in common **c :** APPORTION
**3 a :** to cause to be separate, distinct, or apart from one another **b :** to separate into opposing sides or parties **c :** to cause (a parliamentary body) to vote by division
**4 a :** to subject (a number or quantity) to the operation of finding how many times it contains another number or quantity ⟨*divide* 42 by 14⟩ **b :** to be used as a divisor with respect to (a dividend) ⟨4 *divides* 16 evenly⟩ **c :** to use as a divisor — used with *into* ⟨*divide* 14 into 42⟩
*intransitive verb*
**1 :** to perform mathematical division
**2 a (1) :** to undergo replication, multiplication, fission, or separation into parts **(2) :** to branch out **b :** to become separated or disunited especially in opinion or interest
*synonym* see SEPARATE, DISTRIBUTE
— **di·vid·able** \-'vī-də-bəl\ *adjective*
²**divide** *noun* (1642)
**1 :** an act of dividing
**2 a :** a dividing ridge between drainage areas **:** WATERSHED **b :** a point or line of division
**di·vid·ed** *adjective* (14th century)
**1 a :** separated into parts or pieces **b** *of a leaf* **:** cut into distinct parts by incisions extending to the base or to the midrib **c :** having a barrier (as a guardrail) to separate lanes of traffic going in opposite directions ⟨a *divided* highway⟩
**2 a :** disagreeing with each other **:** DISUNITED **b :** directed or moved toward conflicting interests, states, or objects ⟨*divided* loyalties⟩
**3 :** separated by distance ⟨familiar objects from which she had never dreamed of being *divided* —James Joyce⟩
— **di·vid·ed·ly** \də-'vī-dəd-lē\ *adverb*
— **di·vid·ed·ness** \-nəs\ *noun*

**div·i·dend** \'di-və-ˌdend, -dənd\ *noun* [Middle English *divident*, from Latin *dividendus*, gerundive of *dividere*] (15th century)
**1 :** an individual share of something distributed: as **a :** a share in a pro rata distribution (as of profits) to stockholders **b :** a share of surplus allocated to a policyholder in a participating insurance policy
**2 a :** a resultant return or reward **b :** BONUS
**3 a :** a number to be divided **b :** a sum or fund to be divided and distributed
— **div·i·dend·less** \-ləs\ *adjective*
**di·vid·er** \də-'vī-dər\ *noun* (1534)
**1 :** one that divides
**2** *plural* **:** an instrument for measuring or marking (as in dividing lines)
**3 :** something serving as a partition between separate spaces within a larger area
**di·vi–di·vi** \ˌdē-vē-'dē-vē, ˌdi-vē-'dē-vē\ *noun* [American Spanish *dividivi*, probably from Cumanagoto (extinct Cariban language of northern Venezuela)] (circa 1837)
**:** a small leguminous tree (*Caesalpinia coriaria*) of tropical America with twisted astringent pods that contain a large proportion of tannin

dividers

**div·i·na·tion** \ˌdi-və-'nā-shən\ *noun* [Middle English *divinacioun*, from Latin *divination-, divinatio*, from *divinare*] (14th century)
**1 :** the art or practice that seeks to foresee or foretell future events or discover hidden knowledge usually by the interpretation of omens or by the aid of supernatural powers
**2 :** unusual insight **:** intuitive perception
— **di·vi·na·to·ry** \də-'vi-nə-ˌtōr-ē, də-'vī-nə-, 'di-və-nə-, -ˌtōr-\ *adjective*
¹**di·vine** \də-'vīn\ *adjective* **di·vin·er; -est** [Middle English *divin*, from Middle French, from Latin *divinus*, from *divus* god — more at DEITY] (14th century)
**1 a :** of, relating to, or proceeding directly from God or a god ⟨*divine* love⟩ **b :** being a deity ⟨the *divine* Savior⟩ **c :** directed to a deity ⟨*divine* worship⟩
**2 a :** supremely good **:** SUPERB ⟨the pie was *divine*⟩ **b :** HEAVENLY, GODLIKE
— **di·vine·ly** *adverb*
²**divine** *noun* [Middle English, from Medieval Latin *divinus*, from Latin, soothsayer, from *divinus*, adjective] (14th century)
**1 :** CLERGYMAN
**2 :** THEOLOGIAN
³**divine** *verb* **di·vined; di·vin·ing** [Middle English, from Middle French & Latin; Middle French *diviner*, from Latin *divinare*, from *divinus*, noun] (14th century)
*transitive verb*
**1 :** to discover intuitively **:** INFER
**2 :** to discover or locate (as water or minerals underground) usually by means of a divining rod
*intransitive verb*
**1 :** to practice divination **:** PROPHESY
**2 :** to perceive intuitively
*synonym* see FORESEE
**Divine Liturgy** *noun* (1870)
**:** the eucharistic rite of Eastern churches
**Divine Office** *noun* (15th century)
**:** the office for the canonical hours of prayer that priests and religious say daily
**di·vin·er** \də-'vī-nər\ *noun* (14th century)
**1 :** one who practices divination **:** SOOTHSAYER
**2 :** a person who divines the location of water or minerals
**divine right** *noun* (circa 1600)

\ə\ abut \ᵊ\ kitten \ər\ further \a\ ash \ā\ ace \ä\ mop, mar \aù\ out \ch\ chin \e\ bet \ē\ easy \g\ go \i\ hit \ī\ ice \j\ job \ŋ\ sing \ō\ go \ò\ law \òi\ boy \th\ thin \th\ the \ü\ loot \ù\ foot \y\ yet \zh\ vision *see also* Guide to Pronunciation

: the right of a sovereign to rule as set forth by the theory of government that holds that a monarch receives the right to rule directly from God and not from the people

**divine service** *noun* (14th century)
: a service of Christian worship; *specifically*
: such a service that is not sacramental in character

**diving beetle** *noun* ( circa 1889)
: any of various predatory aquatic beetles (family Dytiscidae) that breathe while submerged using air trapped under their elytra

**diving bell** *noun* (1661)
: a diving apparatus consisting of a container open only at the bottom and supplied with compressed air by a hose

**diving board** *noun* (1893)
: SPRINGBOARD 1

**diving duck** *noun* (1813)
: any of various ducks (as a bufflehead) that frequent deep waters and obtain their food by diving

**diving suit** *noun* (1908)
: a waterproof suit with a removable helmet that is worn by a diver who is supplied with air pumped through a tube

**divining rod** *noun* (1751)
: a forked rod believed to indicate the presence of water or minerals especially by dipping downward when held over a vein

**di·vin·i·ty** \də-'vi-nə-tē\ *noun, plural* **-ties** (14th century)
**1 :** THEOLOGY
**2 :** the quality or state of being divine
**3** *often capitalized* : a divine being: as **a :** GOD 1 **b** (1) : GOD 2 (2) : GODDESS
**4 :** fudge made of whipped egg whites, sugar, and nuts

**divinity school** *noun* (circa 1555)
: a professional school having a religious curriculum especially for ministerial candidates

**di·vis·i·ble** \də-'vi-zə-bəl\ *adjective* (15th century)
: capable of being divided
— **di·vis·i·bil·i·ty** \də-ˌvi-zə-'bi-lə-tē\ *noun*

**di·vi·sion** \də-'vi-zhən\ *noun* [Middle English, from Middle French, from Latin *division-, divisio,* from *dividere* to divide] (14th century)
**1 a :** the act or process of dividing **:** the state of being divided **b :** the act, process, or an instance of distributing among a number **:** DISTRIBUTION **c** *obsolete* **:** a method of arranging or disposing (as troops)
**2 :** one of the parts or groupings into which a whole is divided or is divisible
**3 :** the condition or an instance of being divided in opinion or interest **:** DISAGREEMENT, DISUNITY ⟨exploited the *divisions* between the two countries⟩
**4 a :** something that divides, separates, or marks off **b :** the act, process, or an instance of separating or keeping apart **:** SEPARATION
**5 :** the mathematical operation of dividing something
**6 a :** a self-contained major military unit capable of independent action **b :** a tactical military unit composed of headquarters and usually three to five brigades **c** (1) : the basic naval administrative unit (2) : a tactical subdivision of a squadron of ships **d :** a unit of the U.S. Air Force higher than a wing and lower than an air force
**7 a :** a portion of a territorial unit marked off for a particular purpose (as administrative or judicial functions) **b :** an administrative or operating unit of a governmental, business, or educational organization
**8 :** the physical separation into different lobbies of the members of a parliamentary body voting for and against a question
**9 :** plant propagation by dividing parts and planting segments capable of producing roots and shoots
**10 :** a group of organisms forming part of a larger group; *specifically* **:** a primary category of the plant kingdom

**11 :** a competitive class or category (as in boxing or wrestling)
*synonym* see PART
— **di·vi·sion·al** \-'vizh-nəl, -'vi-zhə-n°l\ *adjective*

**di·vi·sion·ism** \-'vi-zhə-ˌni-zəm\ *noun, often capitalized* (1901)
: POINTILLISM
— **di·vi·sion·ist** \-'vi-zhə-nəst\ *noun or adjective*

**division of labor** (1776)
: the breakdown of labor into its components and their distribution among different persons, groups, or machines to increase productive efficiency

**division sign** *noun* (circa 1934)
**1 :** the symbol ÷ used to indicate division
**2 :** the diagonal / used to indicate a fraction

**di·vi·sive** \də-'vī-siv *also* -'vi- *or* -ziv\ *adjective* (1642)
: creating disunity or dissension
— **di·vi·sive·ly** *adverb*
— **di·vi·sive·ness** *noun*

**di·vi·sor** \də-'vī-zər\ *noun* (15th century)
: the number by which a dividend is divided

**¹di·vorce** \də-'vōrs, -'vȯrs *also* dī-\ *noun* [Middle English *divorse,* from Middle French, from Latin *divortium,* from *divertere, divortere* to divert, to leave one's husband] (14th century)
**1 :** the action or an instance of legally dissolving a marriage
**2 :** SEPARATION, SEVERANCE

**²divorce** *verb* **di·vorced; di·vorc·ing** (15th century)
*transitive verb*
**1 a :** to end marriage with (one's spouse) by divorce **b :** to dissolve the marriage contract between
**2 :** to terminate an existing relationship or union **:** SEPARATE ⟨*divorce* church from state⟩
*intransitive verb*
: to obtain a divorce
*synonym* see SEPARATE
— **di·vorce·ment** \-'vōr-smənt, -'vȯr-\ *noun*

**di·vor·cé** \də-ˌvȯr-'sā, -ˌvȯr-, -'sē, -'vōr-, -'vȯr-\ *noun* (1877)
: a divorced man

**di·vor·cée** \də-ˌvōr-'sā, -ˌvȯr-, -'sē, -'vōr-, -'vȯr-\ *noun* [French, from feminine of *divorcé,* past participle of *divorcer* to divorce, from Middle French *divorse*] (1813)
: a divorced woman

**div·ot** \'di-vət\ *noun* [alteration of earlier Scots *devat,* from Middle English (Scots dialect) *duvat*] (1586)
**1** *Scottish* : a square of turf or sod
**2 :** a loose piece of turf (as one dug from a golf fairway in making a shot)

**di·vulge** \də-'vəlj, dī-\ *transitive verb* **di·vulged; di·vulg·ing** [Middle English, from Latin *divulgare,* from *dis-* + *vulgare* to make known, from *vulgus* mob] (15th century)
**1** *archaic* : to make public **:** PROCLAIM
**2 :** to make known (as a confidence or secret)
*synonym* see REVEAL
— **di·vul·gence** \-'vəl-jən(t)s\ *noun*

**div·vy** \'di-vē\ *transitive verb* **div·vied; div·vy·ing** [by shortening & alteration from *divide*] (1877)
: DIVIDE, SHARE — usually used with *up*

**Dix·ie** \'dik-sē\ *noun* [name for the Southern states in the song *Dixie* (1859) by Daniel D. Emmett] (1859)
: the Southern states of the U.S.

**Dix·ie·crat** \-ˌkrat\ *noun* (1948)
: a dissident Southern Democrat; *specifically*
: a supporter of a 1948 presidential ticket opposing the civil rights stand of the Democrats
— **Dix·ie·crat·ic** \ˌdik-sē-'kra-tik\ *adjective*

**Dix·ie·land** \-ˌland\ *noun* [probably from the *Original Dixieland Jazz Band*] (1927)
: jazz music in duple time usually played by a small band and characterized by ensemble and solo improvisation

**DIY** \ˌdē-(ˌ)ī-'wī\ *noun, often attributive* (1955)
*chiefly British* : DO-IT-YOURSELF

**di·zen** \'dī-z°n, 'di-\ *transitive verb* [earlier *disen* to dress a distaff with flax, from Middle Dutch] (1619)
*archaic* : BEDIZEN

**di·zy·got·ic** \ˌdī-(ˌ)zī-'gä-tik\ *also* **di·zy·gous** \(ˌ)dī-'zī-gəs\ *adjective* (1916)
*of twins* : FRATERNAL 2

**¹diz·zy** \'di-zē\ *adjective* **diz·zi·er; -est** [Middle English *disy,* from Old English *dysig* stupid; akin to Old High German *tusig* stupid] (before 12th century)
**1 :** FOOLISH, SILLY
**2 a :** having a whirling sensation in the head with a tendency to fall **b :** mentally confused
**3 a :** causing giddiness or mental confusion **b** : caused by or marked by giddiness **c :** extremely rapid
— **diz·zi·ly** \'di-zə-lē\ *adverb*
— **diz·zi·ness** \-zē-nəs\ *noun*

**²dizzy** *transitive verb* **diz·zied; diz·zy·ing** (1501)
**1 :** to make dizzy or giddy
**2 :** BEWILDER ⟨disasters that *dizzy* the mind⟩
— **diz·zy·ing·ly** \-zē-iŋ-lē\ *adverb*

**DJ** \'dē-ˌjā\ *noun, often not capitalized* (1950)
: DISC JOCKEY

**djel·la·ba** *also* **djel·la·bah** \jə-'lä-bə\ *noun* [French *djellaba,* from Arabic *jallābīya*] (1919)
: a long loose garment with full sleeves and a hood

**djin·ni** \'jē-nē\ *or* **djinn** *or* **djin** \'jin\ *variant of* JINNI

**dl-** \(ˌ)dē-'el, 'dē-\ *prefix*
**1** *also* **d,l-** : consisting of equal amounts of the dextro and levo forms of a specified compound ⟨*dl-*tartaric acid⟩
**2 :** consisting of equal amounts of the D- and L- forms of a specified compound ⟨DL-fructose⟩

**D layer** *noun* (circa 1934)
: a layer that may exist within the D region of the ionosphere; *also* : D REGION

**D–mark** \'dȯich-ˌmärk, 'doi-chə-\ *noun* (1948)
: DEUTSCHE MARK

**DME** \ˌdē-(ˌ)em-'ē\ *noun* [*d*istance *m*easuring *e*quipment] (1947)
: an electronic device that informs the pilot of an airplane of its distance from a particular ground station

**DMSO** \ˌdē-ˌem-ˌes-'ō\ *noun* (1964)
: DIMETHYL SULFOXIDE

**DMT** \ˌdē-(ˌ)em-'tē\ *noun* (circa 1966)
: DIMETHYLTRYPTAMINE

**DNA** \ˌdē-ˌen-'ā\ *noun* [*d*eoxyribo*n*ucleic *a*cid] (1944)
: any of various nucleic acids that are usually the molecular basis of heredity, are localized especially in cell nuclei, and are constructed of a double helix held together by hydrogen bonds between purine and pyrimidine bases

DNA: *A* molecular model: *1* hydrogen, *2* oxygen, *3* carbon in the helical phosphate ester chains, *4* carbon and nitrogen in the cross-linked purine and pyrimidine bases, *5* phosphorus; *B* double helix which project inward from two chains containing alternate links of deoxyribose and phosphate — compare RECOMBINANT DNA

**DNA fingerprinting** *noun* (1984)
: a method of identification (as for forensic purposes) by determining the sequence of base pairs in the DNA especially of a person
**— DNA fingerprint** *noun*

**DNA polymerase** *noun* (circa 1962)
: any of several polymerases that promote replication or repair of DNA usually using single-stranded DNA as a template

**DN·ase** \(,)dē-'en-,ās, -,āz\ *also* **DNA·ase** \(,)dē,en-'ā-,ās, -,āz\ *noun* (circa 1956)
: DEOXYRIBONUCLEASE

¹**do** \'dü, də-(w)\ *verb* **did** \'did, dəd\; **done** \'dən\; **do·ing** \'dü-iŋ\; **does** \'dəz\ [Middle English *don*, from Old English *dōn;* akin to Old High German *tuon* to do, Latin *-dere* to put, *facere* to make, do, Greek *tithenai* to place, set] (before 12th century)
*transitive verb*
**1** : to bring to pass : CARRY OUT
**2** : PUT — used chiefly in *do to death*
**3 a** : PERFORM, EXECUTE ⟨*do* some work⟩ ⟨*did* his duty⟩ **b** : COMMIT ⟨crimes *done* deliberately⟩
**4 a** : BRING ABOUT, EFFECT ⟨trying to *do* good⟩ ⟨*do* violence⟩ **b** : to give freely : PAY ⟨*do* honor to her memory⟩
**5** : to bring to an end : FINISH — used in the past participle ⟨the job is finally *done*⟩
**6** : to put forth : EXERT ⟨*did* her best to win the race⟩
**7 a** : to wear out especially by physical exertion : EXHAUST ⟨at the end of the race they were pretty well *done*⟩ **b** *British* : to attack physically : BEAT; *also* : KILL
**8** : to bring into existence : PRODUCE ⟨*do* a biography on the general⟩
**9** — used as a substitute verb especially to avoid repetition ⟨if you must make such a racket, *do* it somewhere else⟩
**10 a** : to play the role or character of **b** : MIMIC; *also* : to behave like ⟨*do* a Houdini and disappear⟩ **c** : to perform in or serve as producer of ⟨*do* a play⟩
**11** : to treat unfairly; *especially* : CHEAT ⟨*did* him out of his inheritance⟩
**12** : to treat or deal with in any way typically with the sense of preparation or with that of care or attention: **a** (1) : to put in order : CLEAN ⟨was *doing* the kitchen⟩ (2) : WASH ⟨*did* the dishes after supper⟩ **b** : to prepare for use or consumption; *especially* : COOK ⟨like my steak *done* rare⟩ **c** : SET, ARRANGE ⟨had her hair *done*⟩ **d** : to apply cosmetics to ⟨wanted to *do* her face before the party⟩ **e** : DECORATE, FURNISH ⟨*did* the living room in Early American⟩
**13** : to be engaged in the study or practice of ⟨*do* science⟩; *especially* : to work at as a vocation ⟨what to *do* after college⟩
**14 a** : to pass over (as distance) : TRAVERSE **b** : to travel at a speed of ⟨*doing* 55 on the turnpike⟩
**15** : TOUR ⟨*doing* 12 countries in 30 days⟩
**16** : to spend or serve out (a period of time) ⟨*did* ten years in prison⟩
**17** : to serve the needs of : SUIT, SUFFICE ⟨worms will *do* us for bait⟩
**18** : to approve especially by custom, opinion, or propriety ⟨you oughtn't to say a thing like that . . . it's not *done* —Dorothy Sayers⟩
**19** : to treat with respect to physical comforts ⟨*did* themselves well⟩
**20** : USE *transitive verb* 3 ⟨doesn't *do* drugs⟩
*intransitive verb*
**1** : ACT, BEHAVE ⟨*do* as I say⟩
**2 a** : GET ALONG, FARE ⟨*do* well in school⟩ **b** : to carry on business or affairs : MANAGE ⟨we can *do* without your help⟩
**3** : to take place : HAPPEN ⟨what's *doing* across the street⟩
**4** : to come to or make an end : FINISH — used in the past participle

**5** : to be active or busy ⟨let us then be up and *doing* —H. W. Longfellow⟩
**6** : to be adequate or sufficient : SERVE ⟨half of that will *do*⟩
**7** : to be fitting : conform to custom or propriety ⟨won't *do* to be late⟩
**8** — used as a substitute verb to avoid repetition ⟨wanted to run and play as children *do*⟩; used especially in British English following a modal auxiliary or perfective *have* ⟨a great many people had died, or would *do* —Bruce Chatwin⟩
**9** — used in the imperative after an imperative to add emphasis ⟨be quiet *do*⟩
*verbal auxiliary*
**1 a** — used with the infinitive without *to* to form present and past tenses in legal and parliamentary language ⟨*do* hereby bequeath⟩ and in poetry ⟨give what she *did* crave —Shakespeare⟩ **b** — used with the infinitive without *to* to form present and past tenses in declarative sentences with inverted word order ⟨fervently *do* we pray —Abraham Lincoln⟩, in interrogative sentences ⟨*did* you hear that⟩, and in negative sentences ⟨we *don't* know⟩ ⟨*don't* go⟩
**2** — used with the infinitive without *to* to form present and past tenses expressing emphasis ⟨I *do* say⟩ ⟨*do* be careful⟩
**— do·able** \'dü-ə-bəl\ *adjective*
**— do a number on** : to defeat or confound thoroughly especially by indirect or deceptive means
**— do away with 1** : to put an end to : ABOLISH **2** : to put to death : KILL
**— do by** : to deal with : TREAT
**— do for** *chiefly British* **1** : to attend to the wants and needs of : take care of **2** : to bring about the death or ruin of
**— do it** : to have sexual intercourse
**— do justice 1 a** : to act justly **b** : to treat fairly or adequately **c** : to show due appreciation for **2** : to acquit in a way worthy of one's abilities
**— do proud** : to give cause for pride or gratification
**— do the trick** : to produce a desired result
**— do with** : to make good use of : benefit by ⟨could *do* with a cup of coffee⟩
**— to do** : necessary to be done ⟨I've done my best and all's *to do* again —A. E. Housman⟩

²**do** \'dü\ *noun, plural* **dos** *or* **do's** \'düz\ (1599)
**1** *chiefly dialect* : FUSS, ADO
**2** *archaic* : DEED, DUTY
**3 a** : a festive get-together : AFFAIR, PARTY **b** *chiefly British* : BATTLE
**4** : a command or entreaty to do something ⟨a list of *dos* and don'ts⟩
**5** *British* : CHEAT, SWINDLE
**6** : HAIRDO

³**do** \'dō\ *noun* [Italian] (circa 1754)
: the 1st tone of the diatonic scale in solmization

**dob·bin** \'dä-bᵊn\ *noun* [*Dobbin*, nickname for *Robert*] (1596)
**1** : a farm horse
**2** : a quiet plodding horse

**dob·by** \'dä-bē\ *noun, plural* **dobbies** [perhaps from *Dobby*, nickname for *Robert*] (1878)
**1** : a loom attachment for weaving small figures
**2** : a fabric or figured weave made with a dobby

**Dobe** \'dōb\ *noun* (1946)
: DOBERMAN PINSCHER

**Do·ber·man pin·scher** \,dō-bər-mən-'pin-chər\ *noun* [German *Dobermann-pinscher*, from Ludwig *Dobermann*, 19th century German dog breeder + German *Pinscher*, a breed of hunting dog] (1917)

: any of a breed of short-haired medium-sized dogs of German origin — called also *Doberman*

**do·bra** \'dō-brə, 'dò-\ *noun* [Portuguese, from feminine of obsolete *dobro* double, from Latin *duplus* — more at DOUBLE] (1978)
**—** see MONEY table

**Do·bro** \'dō-(,)brō\ *trademark*
**—** used for an acoustic guitar having a metal resonator

**dob·son·fly** \'däb-sən-,flī\ *noun* [origin unknown] (circa 1904)
: a winged insect (family Corydalidae) that has very long slender mandibles in the male and a large carnivorous aquatic larva and that is now usually considered a neuropteran — compare HELLGRAMMITE

**doc** \'däk\ *noun* (circa 1850)
: DOCTOR

**do·cent** \'dō-sᵊnt, dō(t)-'sent\ *noun* [obsolete German (now *Dozent*), from Latin *docent-*, *docens*, present participle of *docēre*] (1880)
**1** : a college or university teacher or lecturer
**2** : a person who leads guided tours especially through a museum or art gallery

**do·ce·tic** \dō-'sē-tik, -'se-\ *adjective, often capitalized* [Late Greek *Dokētai* Docetists, from Greek *dokein* to seem — more at DECENT] (1846)
: of or relating to Docetism or the Docetists

**Do·ce·tism** \dō-'sē-,ti-zəm, 'dō-sə-\ *noun* (1846)
: a belief opposed as heresy in early Christianity that Christ only seemed to have a human body and to suffer and die on the cross
**— Do·ce·tist** \-'sē-tist, -sə-\ *noun*

**doch-an-dor·ris** *or* **doch-an-dor·is** \,däk-ən-'dòr-əs\ *noun* [Scottish Gaelic *deoch an doruis* & Irish *deoch an dorais*, literally, drink of the door] (1691)
*Scottish & Irish* : a parting drink : STIRRUP CUP

**doc·ile** \'dä-səl *also* -,sīl, *especially British* 'dō-,sīl\ *adjective* [Latin *docilis*, from *docēre* to teach; akin to Latin *decēre* to be fitting — more at DECENT] (15th century)
**1** : easily taught
**2** : easily led or managed : TRACTABLE
*synonym* see OBEDIENT
**— doc·ile·ly** \'dä-sə(l)-lē\ *adverb*
**— do·cil·i·ty** \dä-'si-lə-tē, dō-\ *noun*

¹**dock** \'däk\ *noun* [Middle English, from Old English *docce;* akin to Middle Dutch *docke* dock] (before 12th century)
**1** : any of a genus (*Rumex*) of the buckwheat family of coarse weedy plants that have long taproots and are sometimes used as potherbs
**2** : any of several usually broad-leaved weedy plants

²**dock** *noun* [Middle English *dok*, perhaps from Old English *-docca* (as in *fingirdocca* finger muscle); akin to Old High German *tocka* doll, Old Norse *dokka* bundle] (14th century)
**1** : the solid part of an animal's tail as distinguished from the hair
**2** : the part of an animal's tail left after it has been shortened

³**dock** *transitive verb* (14th century)
**1 a** : to cut off the end of a body part of; *specifically* : to remove part of the tail of **b** : to cut (as ears or a tail) short
**2 a** : to take away a part of : ABRIDGE **b** : to subject (as wages) to a deduction **c** : to penalize by depriving of a benefit ordinarily due; *especially* : to fine by a deduction of wages ⟨*docked* him for tardiness⟩

⁴**dock** *noun* [Middle English *dokke*, probably from Middle Dutch *docke*] (15th century)

**1 :** a usually artificial basin or enclosure for the reception of ships that is equipped with means for controlling the water height **2 :** the waterway extending between two piers for the reception of ships **3 :** a place (as a wharf or platform) for the loading or unloading of materials ■
**⁵dock** (1600) *transitive verb* **1 :** to haul or guide into a dock **2 :** to join (as two spacecraft) mechanically while in space *intransitive verb* **1 :** to come into dock **2 :** to become docked
**⁶dock** *noun* [Flemish *docke* cage] (1586) **:** the place in a criminal court where a prisoner stands or sits during trial — **in the dock :** on trial
**dock·age** \'dä-kij\ *noun* (1648) **1 :** a charge for the use of a dock **2 :** the docking of ships **3 :** docking facilities
**¹dock·er** \'dä-kər\ *noun* (1810) **:** one that docks the tails of animals
**²docker** *noun* (1887) **:** one connected with docks; *especially* **:** LONGSHOREMAN
**¹dock·et** \'dä-kət\ *noun* [Middle English *doggette*] (15th century) **1 :** a brief written summary of a document **:** ABSTRACT **2 a** (1) **:** a formal abridged record of the proceedings in a legal action (2) **:** a register of such records **b** (1) **:** a list of legal causes to be tried (2) **:** a calendar of business matters to be acted on **:** AGENDA **3 :** an identifying statement about a document placed on its outer surface or cover
**²docket** *transitive verb* (1615) **1 :** to place on the docket for legal action **2 :** to make a brief abstract of (as a legal matter) and inscribe it in a list **3 :** to inscribe (as a document) with an identifying statement
**dock·hand** \'däk-,hand\ *noun* (1920) **:** LONGSHOREMAN
**dock·land** \-,land\ *noun* (1904) *British* **:** the part of a port occupied by docks; *also* **:** a residential section adjacent to docks
**dock·mas·ter** \'däk-,mas-tər\ *noun* (1736) **:** a person in charge of a dock or marina or of the docking of ships
**dock·side** \-,sīd\ *noun, often attributive* (1887) **:** the shore or area adjacent to a dock
**dock·work·er** \-,wər-kər\ *noun* (1921) **:** LONGSHOREMAN
**dock·yard** \-,yärd\ *noun* (1704) **1 :** SHIPYARD **2** *British* **:** NAVY YARD
**¹doc·tor** \'däk-tər\ *noun* [Middle English *doctour* teacher, doctor, from Middle French & Medieval Latin; Middle French, from Medieval Latin *doctor,* from Latin, teacher, from *docēre* to teach — more at DOCILE] (14th century) **1 a :** an eminent theologian declared a sound expounder of doctrine by the Roman Catholic Church — called also *doctor of the church* **b :** a learned or authoritative teacher **c :** a person who has earned one of the highest academic degrees (as a PhD) conferred by a university **d :** a person awarded an honorary doctorate (as an LLD or Litt D) by a college or university **2 a :** one skilled or specializing in healing arts; *especially* **:** a physician, surgeon, dentist, or veterinarian who is licensed to practice **b :** MEDICINE MAN **3 a :** material added (as to food) to produce a desired effect **b :** a blade (as of metal) for spreading a coating or scraping a surface **4 :** a person who restores or repairs things — **doc·tor·al** \-t(ə-)rəl\ *adjective*

— **doc·tor·less** \-tər-ləs\ *adjective*
— **doc·tor·ship** \-,ship\ *noun*
**²doctor** *verb* **doc·tored; doc·tor·ing** \-t(ə-)riŋ\ (1712) *transitive verb* **1 a :** to give medical treatment to **b :** to restore to good condition **:** REPAIR ⟨*doctor* an old clock⟩ **2 a :** to adapt or modify for a desired end by alteration or special treatment ⟨*doctored* the play to suit the audience⟩ ⟨the drink was *doctored*⟩ **b :** to alter deceptively ⟨accused of *doctoring* the election returns⟩ *intransitive verb* **1 :** to practice medicine **2** *dialect* **:** to take medicine
**doc·tor·ate** \'däk-t(ə-)rət\ *noun* (1676) **:** the degree, title, or rank of a doctor
**¹doc·tri·naire** \,däk-trə-'nar, -'ner\ *noun* [French, from *doctrine*] (1831) **:** one who attempts to put into effect an abstract doctrine or theory with little or no regard for practical difficulties
**²doctrinaire** *adjective* (1834) **:** of, relating to, or characteristic of a doctrinaire **:** DOGMATIC *synonym* see DICTATORIAL — **doc·tri·nair·ism** \-'nar-,i-zəm, -'ner-\ *noun*
**doc·trin·al** \'däk-trə-n°l, *especially British* däk-'trī-\ *adjective* (15th century) **:** of, relating to, or preoccupied with doctrine — **doc·trin·al·ly** \-n°l-ē\ *adverb*
**doc·trine** \'däk-trən\ *noun* [Middle English, from Middle French & Latin; Middle French, from Latin *doctrina,* from *doctor*] (14th century) **1** *archaic* **:** TEACHING, INSTRUCTION **2 a :** something that is taught **b :** a principle or position or the body of principles in a branch of knowledge or system of belief **:** DOGMA **c :** a principle of law established through past decisions **d :** a statement of fundamental government policy especially in international relations
**docu·dra·ma** \'dä-kyə-,drä-mə, -,dra-\ *noun* [*documentary + drama*] (circa 1961) **:** a drama for television, motion pictures, or theater dealing freely with historical events especially of a recent and controversial nature
**¹doc·u·ment** \'dä-kyə-mənt\ *noun* [Middle English, from Middle French, from Late Latin & Latin; Late Latin *documentum* official paper, from Latin, lesson, proof, from *docēre* to teach — more at DOCILE] (15th century) **1 a** *archaic* **:** PROOF, EVIDENCE **b :** an original or official paper relied on as the basis, proof, or support of something **c :** something (as a photograph or a recording) that serves as evidence or proof **2 a :** a writing conveying information **b :** a material substance (as a coin or stone) having on it a representation of thoughts by means of some conventional mark or symbol **c :** DOCUMENTARY — **doc·u·men·tal** \,dä-kyə-'men-t°l\ *adjective*
**²doc·u·ment** \'dä-kyə-,ment\ *transitive verb* (1711) **1 :** to furnish documentary evidence of **2 :** to furnish with documents **3 a :** to provide with factual or substantial support for statements made or a hypothesis proposed; *especially* **:** to equip with exact references to authoritative supporting information **b** (1) **:** to construct or produce (as a movie or novel) with authentic situations or events (2) **:** to portray realistically **4 :** to furnish (a ship) with ship's papers — **doc·u·ment·able** \-,men-tə-bəl, ,däk-yə-'\ *adjective* — **doc·u·ment·er** \'dä-kyə-,men-tər\ *noun*
**doc·u·men·tal·ist** \,dä-kyə-'men-t°l-ist\ *noun* (1939) **:** a specialist in documentation

**doc·u·men·tar·i·an** \,dä-kyə-mən-'ter-ē-ən, -,men-\ *noun* [²*documentary*] (1943) **:** one who makes a documentary
**doc·u·men·ta·rist** \-'men-tə-rist\ *noun* [²*documentary*] (1949) **:** DOCUMENTARIAN
**¹doc·u·men·ta·ry** \,dä-kyə-'men-tə-rē, -'men-trē\ *adjective* (1802) **1 :** being or consisting of documents **:** contained or certified in writing ⟨*documentary* evidence⟩ **2 :** of, relating to, or employing documentation in literature or art; *broadly* **:** FACTUAL, OBJECTIVE ⟨a *documentary* film of the war⟩ — **doc·u·men·tar·i·ly** \-mən-'ter-ə-lē, -,men-\ *adverb*
**²documentary** *noun, plural* **-ries** (1935) **:** a documentary presentation (as a film or novel)
**doc·u·men·ta·tion** \,dä-kyə-mən-'tā-shən, -,men-\ *noun* (1884) **1 :** the act or an instance of furnishing or authenticating with documents **2 a :** the provision of documents in substantiation; *also* **:** documentary evidence **b** (1) **:** the use of historical documents (2) **:** conformity to historical or objective facts (3) **:** the provision of footnotes, appendices, or addenda referring to or containing documentary evidence **3 :** INFORMATION SCIENCE **4 :** the usually printed instructions, comments, and information for using a particular piece or system of computer software or hardware — **doc·u·men·ta·tion·al** \-shnəl, -shə-n°l\ *adjective*
**¹dod·der** \'dä-dər\ *noun* [Middle English *doder;* akin to Middle High German *toter* dodder, egg yolk] (13th century) **:** any of a genus (*Cuscuta*) of parasitic wiry twining vines of the morning-glory family that are deficient in chlorophyll and have tiny scales instead of leaves
**²dodder** *intransitive verb* **dod·dered; dod·der·ing** \'dä-d(ə-)riŋ\ [Middle English *dadiren*] (14th century) **1 :** to tremble or shake from weakness or age **2 :** to progress feebly and unsteadily ⟨was *doddering* down the walk⟩ — **dod·der·er** \-dər-ər\ *noun*
**dod·dered** \'dä-dərd\ *adjective* [probably alteration of *dodded,* from past participle of English dialect *dod* to lop, from Middle English *dodden*] (1697) **1 :** deprived of branches through age or decay ⟨a *doddered* oak⟩ **2 :** INFIRM, ENFEEBLED
**dod·der·ing** \'dä-d(ə-)riŋ\ *adjective* (1898) **:** FEEBLE, SENILE
**dod·dery** \-d(ə-)rē\ *adjective* (1866) **1 :** DODDERED 2 **2 :** DODDERING
**dodeca-** *or* **dodec-** *combining form* [Latin, from Greek *dōdeka-, dōdek-,* from *dōdeka, dyōdeka,* from *dyō, dyo* two + *deka* ten] **:** twelve ⟨*dodeca*phonic⟩

**do·deca·gon** \dō-'de-kə-ˌgän\ *noun* [Greek *dōdekagōnon*, from *dōdeka-* + *-gōnon* -gon] (circa 1658)
: a polygon of 12 angles and 12 sides

**do·deca·he·dron** \(ˌ)dō-ˌde-kə-'hē-drən\ *noun, plural* **-drons** *or* **-dra** \-drə\ [Greek *dōdekaedron*, from *dōdeka-* + *-edron* -hedron] (circa 1570)
: a solid having 12 plane faces
— **do·deca·he·dral** \-drəl\ *adjective*

**do·deca·phon·ic** \(ˌ)dō-ˌde-kə-'fä-nik\ *adjective* [*dodeca-* + *phon-* + *-ic*] (1949)
: TWELVE-TONE
— **do·deca·phon·i·cal·ly** \-ni-k(ə-)lē\ *adverb*
— **do·deca·pho·nist** \dō-'de-kə-fə-nist, -ˌfō-; ˌdō-di-'ka-fə-nist\ *noun*
— **do·deca·pho·ny** \-nē\ *noun*

**¹dodge** \'däj\ *noun* [origin unknown] (1575)
**1 a** : an artful device to evade, deceive, or trick **b** : EXPEDIENT
**2** : an act of evading by sudden bodily movement

**²dodge** *verb* **dodged; dodg·ing** (1680)
*transitive verb*
**1** : to evade (as a duty) usually indirectly or by trickery ⟨*dodged* the draft by leaving the country⟩ ⟨*dodged* questions⟩
**2 a** : to evade by a sudden or repeated shift of position **b** : to avoid an encounter with
*intransitive verb*
**1 a** : to make a sudden movement in a new direction (as to evade a blow) ⟨*dodged* behind the door⟩ **b** : to move to and fro or from place to place usually in an irregular course ⟨*dodged* through the crowd⟩
**2** : to evade a responsibility or duty especially by trickery or deceit

**dodge·ball** \'däj-ˌbȯl\ *noun* (circa 1922)
: a game in which players stand in a circle and try to hit opponents within the circle with a large inflated ball

**dodg·em** \'dä-jəm\ *noun, often capitalized* (1921)
: an amusement ride featuring bumper cars

**dodgem car** *noun* (1945)
: BUMPER CAR

**dodg·er** \'dä-jər\ *noun* (1568)
**1** : one that dodges; *especially* : one who uses tricky devices
**2** : a small leaflet : CIRCULAR
**3** : CORN DODGER
**4** : a usually canvas screen on a boat or ship that provides protection from spray

**dodg·ery** \'dä-jə-rē\ *noun, plural* **-er·ies** (1670)
: EVASION, TRICKERY

**dodgy** \'dä-jē\ *adjective* (1861)
**1** *chiefly British* : EVASIVE, TRICKY
**2** *chiefly British* : not sound, stable, or reliable : SHAKY
**3** *British* : requiring skill or care in handling; *also* : CHANCY, RISKY
— **dodg·i·ness** \-nəs\ *noun*

**do·do** \'dō-(ˌ)dō\ *noun, plural* **dodoes** *or* **dodos** [Portuguese *doudo*, from *doudo* silly, stupid] (1628)
**1 a** : an extinct heavy flightless bird (*Raphus cucullatus*, synonym *Didus ineptus*) of the island of Mauritius that is related to the pigeon and larger than a turkey **b** : an extinct bird of the island of Réunion similar to and apparently closely related to the dodo
**2 a** : one hopelessly behind the times **b** : a stupid person

*dodo 1a*

**do down** *transitive verb* (14th century)
*British* : to get the better of (as by trickery)

**doe** \'dō\ *noun, plural* **does** *or* **doe** [Middle English *do*, from Old English *dā*; akin to German dialect *tē* doe] (before 12th century)

: the adult female of various mammals (as a deer, rabbit, or kangaroo) of which the male is called buck

**doe—eyed** \'dō-ˌīd\ *adjective* (1933)
: having large innocent-looking eyes

**do·er** \'dü-ər\ *noun* (14th century)
: one that takes an active part ⟨a thinker or a *doer*⟩

**does** *present 3d singular of* DO, *plural of* DOE

**doe·skin** \'dō-ˌskin\ *noun* (15th century)
**1** : the skin of does or leather made of it; *also* : soft leather from sheep- or lambskins
**2** : a compact coating and sportswear fabric napped and felted for a smooth surface

**doesn't** \'də-z°nt\ (1860)
: does not

**do·est** \'dü-əst\ *archaic present 2d singular of* DO

**do·eth** \'dü-əth\ *archaic present 3d singular of* DO

**doff** \'däf, 'dȯf\ *transitive verb* [Middle English, from *don* to do + *of* off] (14th century)
**1 a** : to remove (an article of wear) from the body **b** : to take off (the hat) in greeting or as a sign of respect
**2** : to rid oneself of : put aside
— **doff one's hat to** *or* **doff one's cap to** : to show respect to : SALUTE

**¹dog** \'dȯg, 'däg\ *noun, often attributive* [Middle English, from Old English *docga*] (before 12th century)
**1 a** : CANID; *especially* : a highly variable domestic mammal (*Canis familiaris*) closely related to the common wolf (*Canis lupus*) **b** : a male dog; *also* : a male usually carnivorous mammal
**2 a** : a worthless person **b** : FELLOW, CHAP ⟨a lazy *dog*⟩ ⟨you lucky *dog*⟩
**3 a** : any of various usually simple mechanical devices for holding, gripping, or fastening that consist of a spike, bar, or hook **b** : ANDIRON
**4** : uncharacteristic or affected stylishness or dignity ⟨put on the *dog*⟩
**5** *capitalized* : either of the constellations Canis Major or Canis Minor
**6** *plural* : FEET
**7** *plural* : RUIN ⟨going to the *dogs*⟩
**8** : one inferior of its kind: as **a** : an investment not worth its price **b** : an undesirable piece of merchandise
**9** : an unattractive person and especially a girl or woman
**10** : HOT DOG 1
— **dog·like** \'dȯg-ˌlīk\ *adjective*

dog 1a: *1* pastern, *2* chest, *3* flews, *4* muzzle, *5* stop, *6* occiput, *7* leather, *8* crest, *9* withers, *10* loin, *11* point of rump, *12* hock *or* tarsus, *13* knee *or* stifle, *14* brisket, *15* elbow, *16* feathering

**²dog** *adjective* (14th century)
**1** : CANINE
**2** : SPURIOUS; *especially* : unlike that used by native speakers or writers ⟨*dog* Latin⟩ ⟨*dog* French⟩

**³dog** *transitive verb* **dogged** \'dȯgd, 'dägd\; **dog·ging** (1519)
**1 a** : to hunt or track like a hound **b** : to worry as if by pursuit with dogs : PLAGUE
**2** : to fasten with a dog

— **dog it** : to fail to do one's best : GOLD-BRICK

**⁴dog** *adverb* (circa 1552)
: EXTREMELY, UTTERLY ⟨*dog*-tired⟩

**dog and pony show** *noun* (1965)
: an often elaborate public relations or sales presentation

**dog·bane** \'dȯg-ˌbān\ *noun* (1597)
: any of a genus (*Apocynum* of the family Apocynaceae, the dogbane family) comprising chiefly tropical and often poisonous plants with milky juice and usually showy flowers

**dog biscuit** *noun* (circa 1858)
: a hard dry cracker for dogs

**dog·cart** \'dȯg-ˌkärt\ *noun* (1668)
**1** : a cart drawn by a dog
**2** : a light two-wheeled carriage with two transverse seats set back to back

**dog·catch·er** \-ˌka-chər, -ˌke-\ *noun* (1835)
: a community official assigned to catch and dispose of stray dogs

**dog collar** *noun* (1524)
**1** : a collar for a dog
**2** *slang* : CLERICAL COLLAR
**3** : a wide flexible snug-fitting necklace

**dog days** *noun plural* [from their being reckoned from the heliacal rising of the Dog Star (Sirius)] (1538)
**1** : the period between early July and early September when the hot sultry weather of summer usually occurs in the northern hemisphere
**2** : a period of stagnation or inactivity ◆

**dog·dom** \'dȯg-dəm\ *noun* (1854)
: the world of dogs or of dog fanciers

**doge** \'dōj\ *noun* [Italian dialect, from Latin *duc-, dux* leader — more at DUKE] (1549)
: the chief magistrate in the republics of Venice and Genoa

**dog-ear** \'dȯ-ˌgir\ *noun* (circa 1725)
: the turned-down corner of a page especially of a book
— **dog-ear** *transitive verb*

**dog-eared** \'dȯ-ˌgird\ *adjective* (1784)
**1** : having dog-ears ⟨a *dog-eared* book⟩
**2** : SHABBY, TIMEWORN ⟨a *dog-eared* resort⟩ ⟨*dog-eared* myths⟩

**dog-eat-dog** \ˌdȯ-ˌgēt-'dȯg\ *adjective* (1834)
: marked by ruthless self-interest ⟨*dog-eat-dog* competition⟩

**dog-face** \'dȯg-ˌfās\ *noun* (1941)
: SOLDIER; *especially* : INFANTRYMAN

**dog fennel** *noun* (14th century)
: a strong-scented chamomile (*Anthemis cotula*) of Europe and Asia naturalized along roadsides in the U.S.

**dog-fight** \'dȯg-ˌfīt\ *noun* (1656)

\ə\ abut \ᵊ\ kitten \ər\ further \a\ ash \ā\ ace \ä\ mop, mar \au̇\ out \ch\ chin \e\ bet \ē\ easy \g\ go \i\ hit \ī\ ice \j\ job \ŋ\ sing \ō\ go \ȯ\ law \ȯi\ boy \th\ thin \t̲h̲\ the \ü\ loot \u̇\ foot \y\ yet \zh\ vision    *see also* Guide to Pronunciation

**1** : a fight between dogs; *broadly* : a fiercely disputed contest
**2** : a fight between two or more fighter planes usually at close quarters
— **dogfight** *intransitive verb*
**dog·fish** \-₁fish\ *noun* (15th century)
: any of various usually small bottom-dwelling sharks (as of the families Squalidae, Carcharhinidae, and Scyliorhinidae) that often appear in schools near shore, prey chiefly on fish and invertebrates, and are a valuable food source
**dog·ged** \'do̊-gəd\ *adjective* (1653)
: marked by stubborn determination
*synonym* see OBSTINATE
— **dog·ged·ly** *adverb*
— **dog·ged·ness** *noun*
¹**dog·ger·el** \'do̊-g(ə-)rəl, 'dä-\ *adjective* [Middle English *dogerel*, probably diminutive of *dogge* dog] (14th century)
: loosely styled and irregular in measure especially for burlesque or comic effect; *also*
: marked by triviality or inferiority
²**doggerel** *noun* (1630)
: doggerel verse
**dog·gery** \'do̊-gə-rē\ *noun, plural* **-ger·ies** (1830)
: a cheap saloon : DIVE
**dog·gie bag** *or* **doggy bag** \'do̊-gē-\ *noun* [¹*doggy*; from the presumption that such leftovers are intended for a pet dog] (1963)
: a container for carrying home leftover food and especially meat from a restaurant meal
**dog·gish** \'do̊-gish\ *adjective* (15th century)
**1** : CANINE
**2** : stylish in a showy way
— **dog·gish·ly** *adverb*
— **dog·gish·ness** *noun*
**dog·go** \'do̊-(₁)gō\ *adverb* [probably from ¹*dog*] (1893)
: in hiding — used chiefly in the phrase *to lie doggo*
¹**dog·gone** \'däg-₁gän, 'do̊g-'go̊n\ *verb* **doggoned; dog·gon·ing** [euphemism for *God damn*] (1828)
: DAMN
²**dog·gone** *or* **dog·goned** \₁däg-₁gän(d), ₁do̊g-₁go̊n(d)\ *adjective or adverb* (1851)
: DAMNED
³**doggone** *noun* (1928)
: DAMN
¹**dog·gy** *or* **dog·gie** \'do̊-gē\ *noun, plural* **doggies** (1825)
: a small dog
²**dog·gy** \'do̊-gē\ *adjective* **dog·gi·er; -est** (1859)
**1** : concerned with or fond of dogs
**2** : resembling or suggestive of a dog ⟨*doggy* odor⟩
**3** : STYLISH, SHOWY
**4** : not worthy or profitable : INFERIOR
**dog·house** \'do̊g-₁haủs\ *noun* (1594)
: a shelter for a dog
— **in the doghouse** : in a state of disfavor
**do·gie** \'dō-gē\ *noun* [origin unknown] (1888)
*chiefly West* : a motherless calf in a range herd
**dog in the manger** [from the fable of the dog who prevented an ox from eating hay which he did not want himself] (1573)
: a person who selfishly withholds from others something useless to himself
¹**dog·leg** \'do̊g-₁leg, -₁lāg\ *adjective* (1889)
: crooked or bent like a dog's hind leg
²**dogleg** *noun* (circa 1909)
**1 a** : something having an abrupt angle **b** : a sharp bend (as in a road)
**2** : a golf hole having an angled fairway
³**dogleg** *intransitive verb* (1947)
: to proceed along a dogleg course ⟨the single narrow street that *doglegs* through town —Russ Leadabrand⟩
**dog·ma** \'do̊g-mə, 'däg-\ *noun, plural* **dogmas** *also* **dog·ma·ta** \-mə-tə\ [Latin *dogmat-, dogma*, from Greek, from *dokein* to seem — more at DECENT] (1638)

**1 a** : something held as an established opinion; *especially* : a definite authoritative tenet **b** : a code of such tenets ⟨pedagogical *dogma*⟩ **c** : a point of view or tenet put forth as authoritative without adequate grounds
**2** : a doctrine or body of doctrines concerning faith or morals formally stated and authoritatively proclaimed by a church
**dog·mat·ic** \do̊g-'ma-tik, däg-\ *also* **dog·mat·i·cal** \-ti-kəl\ *adjective* (circa 1681)
**1** : characterized by or given to the use of dogmatism ⟨a *dogmatic* critic⟩
**2** : of or relating to dogma
*synonym* see DICTATORIAL
— **dog·mat·i·cal·ly** \-ti-k(ə-)lē\ *adverb*
— **dog·mat·i·cal·ness** \-ti-kəl-nəs\ *noun*
**dog·mat·ics** \-tiks\ *noun plural but singular or plural in construction* (1845)
: a branch of theology that seeks to interpret the dogmas of a religious faith
**dogmatic theology** *noun* (1846)
: DOGMATICS
**dog·ma·tism** \'do̊g-mə-₁ti-zəm, 'däg-\ *noun* (1603)
**1** : positiveness in assertion of opinion especially when unwarranted or arrogant
**2** : a viewpoint or system of ideas based on insufficiently examined premises
**dog·ma·tist** \-mə-tist\ *noun* (1541)
: one who dogmatizes
**dog·ma·tize** \'do̊g-mə-₁tīz, 'däg-\ *verb* **-tized; -tiz·ing** [French *dogmatiser*, from Late Latin *dogmatizare*, from Greek *dogmatizein*, from *dogmat-, dogma*] (1611)
*intransitive verb*
: to speak or write dogmatically
*transitive verb*
: to state as a dogma or in a dogmatic manner
— **dog·ma·ti·za·tion** \₁do̊g-mə-tə-'zā-shən, ₁däg-\ *noun*
— **dog·ma·tiz·er** *noun*
**dog·nap** \'do̊g-₁nap\ *transitive verb* **-napped** *or* **-naped** \-₁napt\; **-nap·ping** *or* **-nap·ing** \-₁na-pin\ [¹*dog* + *-nap* (as in *kidnap*)] (1947)
: to steal (a dog) especially to obtain a reward for its return or to sell to a scientific laboratory
— **dog·nap·per** *or* **dog·nap·er** *noun*
**Do·gon** \'dō-₁gän\ *noun, plural* **Dogon** *or* **Dogons** (circa 1931)
**1** : a member of a people of Mali noted for their sculpture
**2** : the language of the Dogon
**do–good** \'dü-₁gủd\ *adjective* (1952)
: designed or disposed sometimes impractically and too zealously toward bettering the conditions under which others live
— **do–good·ism** \-₁i-zəm\ *noun*
**do–good·er** \-₁gủ-dər\ *noun* (1926)
: an earnest often naive humanitarian or reformer
— **do–good·ing** \-din\ *noun or adjective*
**dog paddle** *noun* (1904)
: an elementary swimming stroke in which the arms paddle in the water and the legs maintain a kicking motion
— **dog–pad·dle** *intransitive verb*
**dog rose** *noun* (circa 1597)
: a common European wild rose (*Rosa canina*)
**dogs·body** \'do̊gz-₁bä-dē\ *noun* [British naval slang *dogsbody* pudding made of peas, junior officer] (1922)
*chiefly British* : DRUDGE
**dog's chance** *noun* (1902)
: a bare chance in one's favor
**dog·sled** \'do̊g-₁sled\ *noun* (1810)
: a sled drawn by dogs
— **dogsled** *intransitive verb*
— **dog·sled·der** \-₁sle-dər\ *noun*
**Dog Star** *noun*
: SIRIUS
**dog tag** *noun* (1918)
: an identification tag (as for military personnel or pets)
**dog tick** *noun* (circa 1552)
: AMERICAN DOG TICK

**dog·tooth** \'do̊g-₁tüth\ *noun* (1552)
**1** : CANINE 1, EYETOOTH
**2** : an architectural ornament common in early English Gothic consisting usually of four leaves radiating from a raised point at the center
**3** *chiefly British* : HOUNDSTOOTH CHECK
**dogtooth violet** *noun* (1629)
: any of a genus (*Erythronium*) of small spring-flowering bulbous herbs of the lily family
¹**dog·trot** \'do̊g-₁trät\ *noun* (15th century)
**1** : a quick easy gait suggesting that of a dog
**2** *chiefly Southern & Midland* : a roofed passage similar to a breezeway; *especially* : one connecting two parts of a cabin

dogtooth 2

²**dogtrot** *intransitive verb* (circa 1900)
: to move or progress at a dogtrot
**dog·watch** \'do̊g-₁wäch\ *noun* (1700)
**1** : either of two watches of two hours on shipboard that extend from 4 to 6 and 6 to 8 p.m.
**2** : any of various night shifts; *especially* : the last shift
**dog·wood** \'do̊g-₁wủd\ *noun* (1617)
: any of various trees and shrubs (genus *Cornus* of the family Cornaceae, the dogwood family) with clusters of small flowers and often large white, pink, or red involucral bracts
**doi·ly** \'do̊i-lē\ *noun, plural* **doilies** [*Doily* or *Doyley* (flourished 1711) London draper] (1711)
**1** : a small napkin
**2** : a small often decorative mat
**do in** *transitive verb* (1905)
**1 a** : to bring about the defeat or destruction of; *also* : KILL **b** : EXHAUST, WEAR OUT
**2** : CHEAT
**do·ing** \'dü-in\ *noun* (14th century)
**1** : the act of performing or executing : ACTION ⟨that will take a great deal of *doing*⟩
**2** *plural* **a** : things that are done or that occur : GOINGS-ON ⟨everyday *doings*⟩ **b** : social activities
**doit** \'do̊it\ *noun* [Dutch *duit*; akin to Old Norse *thveiti* small coin, *thveita* to hew] (1592)
**1** : an old Dutch coin equal to about ⅛ stiver
**2** : TRIFLE 1
**do–it–your·self** \₁dü-ə-chər-'self, -tyər-\ *noun, often attributive* (1952)
: the activity of doing or making something (as in woodworking or home repair) without professional training or assistance; *broadly* : an activity in which one does something oneself or on one's own initiative
— **do–it–your·self·er** \-'sel-fər\ *noun*
**do·jo** \'dō-(₁)jō\ *noun, plural* **dojos** [Japanese *dōjō*, from *dō* way, art + *-jō* ground] (1942)
: a school for training in various arts of self-defense (as judo or karate)
**Dol·by** \'do̊l-bē, 'dōl-\ *trademark*
— used for an electronic device that eliminates noise from recorded sound or sound broadcast on FM radio
**dol·ce** \'dōl-(₁)chā\ *adjective or adverb* [Italian, literally, sweet, from Latin *dulcis* — more at DULCET] (circa 1847)
: SOFT, SMOOTH — used as a direction in music
**dol·ce far nien·te** \'dōl-chē-₁fär-nē-'en-tē\ *noun* [Italian, literally, sweet doing nothing] (1814)
: pleasant relaxation in carefree idleness
**dol·ce vi·ta** \₁dōl-chā-'vē-(₁)tä\ *noun* [Italian, literally, sweet life] (1961)
: a life of indolence and self-indulgence
**dol·drums** \'dōl-drəmz, 'däl-, 'do̊l-\ *noun plural* [probably akin to Old English *dol* foolish] (1811)
**1** : a spell of listlessness or despondency
**2** *often capitalized* : a part of the ocean near the equator abounding in calms, squalls, and light shifting winds

**3 :** a state or period of inactivity, stagnation, or slump

**¹dole** \'dōl\ *noun* [Middle English, from Old English *dāl* portion — more at DEAL] (before 12th century)
**1** *archaic* **:** one's allotted share, portion, or destiny
**2 a** (1) **:** a giving or distribution of food, money, or clothing to the needy (2) **:** a grant of government funds to the unemployed **b :** something distributed at intervals to the needy; *also* **:** HANDOUT 1 **c :** something portioned out bit by bit

**²dole** *transitive verb* **doled; dol·ing** (15th century)
**:** to give or distribute as a charity — usually used with *out*

**³dole** *noun* [Middle English *dol,* from Old French, from Late Latin *dolus,* alteration of Latin *dolor*] (13th century)
*archaic* **:** GRIEF, SORROW

**dole·ful** \'dōl-fəl\ *adjective* (13th century)
**1 :** causing grief or affliction ⟨a *doleful* loss⟩
**2 :** full of grief **:** CHEERLESS ⟨a *doleful* face⟩
**3 :** expressing grief **:** SAD ⟨a *doleful* melody⟩
— **dole·ful·ly** \-fə-lē\ *adverb*
— **dole·ful·ness** *noun*

**dole out** *transitive verb* (1749)
**1 :** to give or deliver in small portions
**2 :** DISH OUT
**synonym** see DISTRIBUTE

**dol·er·ite** \'dä-lə-ˌrīt\ *noun* [French *dolérite,* from Greek *doleros* deceitful, from *dolos* deceit; from its being easily mistaken for diorite] (1838)
**1 :** any of various coarse basalts
**2** *chiefly British* **:** DIABASE 3
— **dol·er·it·ic** \ˌdä-lə-'ri-tik\ *adjective*

**dole·some** \'dōl-səm\ *adjective* (1533)
**:** DOLEFUL

**dol·i·cho·ce·phal·ic** \ˌdä-li-kō-sə-'fa-lik\ *adjective* [New Latin *dolichocephalus* long-headed, from Greek *dolichos* long + *-kephalos,* from *kephalē* head — more at CEPHALIC] (1852)
**:** having a relatively long head with cephalic index of less than 75
— **dol·i·cho·ceph·a·ly** \-'se-fə-lē\ *noun*

**doll** \'däl, 'dȯl\ *noun* [probably from *Doll,* nickname for *Dorothy*] (circa 1700)
**1 :** a small-scale figure of a human being used especially as a child's plaything
**2 a** (1) **:** a pretty but often empty-headed young woman (2) **:** WOMAN **b :** DARLING, SWEETHEART **c :** an attractive person
— **doll·ish** \'dä-lish, 'dȯ-\ *adjective*
— **doll·ish·ly** *adverb*
— **doll·ish·ness** *noun*

**dol·lar** \'dä-lər\ *noun, often attributive* [Dutch or Low German *daler,* from German *Taler,* short for *Joachimstaler,* from Sankt *Joachimsthal,* Bohemia, where talers were first made] (1553)
**1 :** TALER
**2 :** any of numerous coins patterned after the taler (as a Spanish peso)
**3 a :** any of various basic monetary units (as in the U.S. and Canada) — see MONEY table **b :** a coin, note, or token representing one dollar
**4 :** RINGGIT ◆

**dollar cost averaging** *noun* (circa 1957)
**:** investment in a security at regular intervals of a uniform sum regardless of the price level in order to obtain an overall reduction in cost per unit — called also *dollar averaging*

**dollar–a–year** *adjective* (1918)
**:** compensated by a token salary usually for government service ⟨a *dollar-a-year* man⟩

**dollar day** *noun* (1949)
**:** a day on which special low prices are offered — often used in plural

**dollar diplomacy** *noun* (1910)
**1 :** diplomacy used by a country to promote its financial or commercial interests abroad

**2 :** diplomacy that seeks to strengthen the power of a country or effect its purposes in foreign relations by the use of its financial resources

**dollars–and–cents** \'dä-lər-zⁿ-'sen(t)s\ *adjective* (1899)
**:** dealing with or expressed in terms of money, sales, or profits

**dollar sign** *noun* (1881)
**:** a mark $ placed before a number to indicate that it stands for dollars — called also *dollar mark*

**doll·house** \'däl-ˌhaus, 'dȯl-\ *also* **doll's house** *or* **dolls' house** *noun* (1783)
**1 :** a child's small-scale toy house
**2 :** a dwelling so small as to suggest a house for dolls

**¹dol·lop** \'dä-ləp\ *noun* [origin unknown] (circa 1812)
**1** *chiefly British* **:** an indefinite often large quantity especially of something liquid ⟨out of heaven, as if a plug had been pulled, fell a jolly *dollop* of rain —E. M. Forster⟩
**2 :** a lump or glob of something soft or mushy ⟨top it with a *dollop* of jam⟩
**3 :** an amount given, spooned, or ladled out **:** PORTION ⟨hold out their mess tins for a *dollop* of gruel —Robert Craft⟩
**4 :** a small lump, portion, or amount ⟨want just a *dollop* of catsup⟩ ⟨a *dollop* of brandy after dinner⟩
**5 :** something added or served as if in dollops ⟨fantasy with a *dollop* of satire —Lee Rogow⟩ ⟨a delicious *dollop* of gossip —Leon Harris⟩

**²dollop** *transitive verb* (circa 1860)
**:** to serve or dispense in dollops

**doll up** (1906)
*transitive verb*
**1 :** to dress elegantly or extravagantly
**2 :** to make more attractive (as by addition of decorative details)
*intransitive verb*
**:** to get dolled up

**¹dol·ly** \'dä-lē, 'dȯ-lē\ *noun, plural* **dollies** (1790)
**1 :** DOLL
**2 :** a wooden-pronged instrument for beating and stirring clothes in the process of washing them in a tub
**3 :** a compact narrow-gauge railroad locomotive for moving construction trains and for switching
**4 a :** a platform on a roller or on wheels or casters for moving heavy objects **b :** a wheeled platform for a television or motion-picture camera

**²dolly** *verb* **dol·lied; dol·ly·ing** (1878)
*transitive verb*
**1 :** to treat with a dolly
**2 :** to move or convey on a dolly
*intransitive verb*
**:** to move a motion-picture or television camera about on a dolly while shooting a scene; *also of a camera* **:** to be moved on a dolly

**dol·ly bird** \'dä-lē-ˌbərd, 'dȯ-lē-\ *noun* (1964)
*British* **:** a pretty young woman

**dolly shot** *noun* (1933)
**:** TRACKING SHOT

**Dol·ly Var·den trout** \ˌdä-lē-'vär-dᵊn-\ *noun* [*Dolly Varden,* gaily dressed coquette in *Barnaby Rudge* (1841), novel by Charles Dickens] (circa 1876)
**:** a large char (*Salvelinus malma*) widespread in streams of western North America and Japan as well as in coastal salt waters — called also *Dolly Varden*

**dol·ma** \ˌdōl-'mä, 'dȯl-mə, 'däl-\ *noun, plural* **dolmas** *or* **dol·ma·des** \ˌdōl-'mä-(ˌ)thēz, dȯl-, däl-\ [Turkish, literally, something stuffed] (circa 1889)
**:** a stuffed grape leaf or vegetable shell

**dolman sleeve** *noun* [French *dolman* coat with dolman sleeves, from German *Dolman* or Hungarian *dolmány,* from Turkish *dolama,* a Turkish robe] (1934)

**:** a sleeve very wide at the armhole and tight at the wrist often cut in one piece with the bodice

**dol·men** \'dōl-mən, 'dȯl-, 'däl-\ *noun* [French, from Breton *tolmen,* from *tol* table + *men* stone] (1859)
**:** a prehistoric monument of two or more upright stones supporting a horizontal stone slab found especially in Britain and France and thought to be a tomb

**dolmen**

**do·lo·mite** \'dō-lə-ˌmīt, 'dä-\ *noun* [French, from Déodat de *Dolomieu* (died 1801) French geologist] (1794)
**1 :** a mineral $CaMg(CO_3)_2$ consisting of a calcium magnesium carbonate found in crystals and in extensive beds as a compact limestone
**2 :** a limestone or marble rich in magnesium carbonate
— **do·lo·mit·ic** \ˌdō-lə-'mi-tik, ˌdä-\ *adjective*

**do·lo·mi·ti·za·tion** \ˌdō-lə-mə-tə-'zā-shən, ˌdä-, -ˌmī-\ *noun* (1862)
**:** the process of converting into dolomite
— **do·lo·mi·tize** \'dō-lə-mə-ˌtīz, 'dä-\ *transitive verb*

**do·lor** \'dō-lər *also* 'dä-\ *noun* [Middle English *dolour,* from Middle French, from Latin *dolor* pain, grief, from *dolēre* to feel pain, grieve] (14th century)
**:** mental suffering or anguish **:** SORROW

**do·lor·ous** \'dō-lə-rəs *also* 'dä-\ *adjective* (15th century)
**:** causing, marked by, or expressing misery or grief
— **do·lor·ous·ly** *adverb*
— **do·lor·ous·ness** *noun*

**do·lour** *chiefly British variant of* DOLOR

**dol·phin** \'däl-fən, 'dȯl-\ *noun* [Middle English, from Middle French *dophin, daufin,* from Old French *dalfin,* from Old Provençal, from Medieval Latin *dalfinus,* alteration of Latin *delphinus,* from Greek *delphin-, delphis;* akin to Greek *delphys* womb, Sanskrit *garbha*] (14th century)

**dolphin 1a**

\ə\ abut \ᵊ\ kitten \ər\ further \a\ ash \ā\ ace
\ä\ mop, mar \au̇\ out \ch\ chin \e\ bet \ē\ easy
\g\ go \i\ hit \ī\ ice \j\ job \ŋ\ sing \ō\ go
\ȯ\ law \ȯi\ boy \th\ thin \t͟h\ the \ü\ loot \u̇\ foot
\y\ yet \zh\ vision *see also* Guide to Pronunciation

**1 a :** any of various small toothed whales (family Delphinidae) with the snout more or less elongated into a beak and the neck vertebrae partially fused **b :** PORPOISE 1
**2 :** either of two active pelagic bony food fishes (genus *Coryphaena* of the family Coryphaenidae) of tropical and temperate seas that are used for food — called also *dolphinfish*
**3** *capitalized* **:** DELPHINUS
**4 :** a spar or buoy for mooring boats; *also* **:** a cluster of closely driven piles used as a fender for a dock or as a mooring or guide for boats
**dolphin striker** *noun* (1833)
**:** a vertical spar under the end of the bowsprit of a sailboat to extend and support the martingale
**dolt** \'dōlt\ *noun* [probably akin to Old English *dol* foolish] (1553)
**:** a stupid person
— **dolt·ish** \'dōl-tish\ *adjective*
— **dolt·ish·ly** *adverb*
— **dolt·ish·ness** *noun*
**Dom** [Latin *dominus* master] (1716)
**1** \'däm\ — used as a title for some monks and canons regular
**2** \'dōⁿ\ — used as a title prefixed to the Christian name of a Portuguese or Brazilian man of rank
**-dom** \dəm\ *noun suffix* [Middle English, from Old English *-dōm; akin* to Old High German *-tuom* -dom, Old English *dōm* judgment — more at DOOM]
**1 a :** dignity **:** office ⟨duke*dom*⟩ **b :** realm **:** jurisdiction ⟨king*dom*⟩
**2 :** state or fact of being ⟨free*dom*⟩
**3 :** those having a (specified) office, occupation, interest, or character ⟨official*dom*⟩
**do·main** \dō-'mān, də-\ *noun* [Middle English *domayne*, from Middle French *domaine, demaine*, from Latin *dominium*, from *dominus*] (15th century)
**1 a :** complete and absolute ownership of land — compare EMINENT DOMAIN **b :** land so owned
**2 :** a territory over which dominion is exercised
**3 :** a region distinctively marked by some physical feature ⟨the *domain* of rushing streams, tall trees, and lakes⟩
**4 :** a sphere of knowledge, influence, or activity ⟨the *domain* of art⟩
**5 :** the set of elements to which a mathematical or logical variable is limited; *specifically* **:** the set on which a function is defined
**6 :** any of the small randomly oriented regions of uniform magnetization in a ferromagnetic substance
**7 :** INTEGRAL DOMAIN
¹**dome** \'dōm\ *noun* [French, Italian, & Latin; French *dôme* dome, cathedral, from Italian *duomo* cathedral, from Medieval Latin *domus* church, from Latin, house; akin to Greek *domos* house, Sanskrit *dam*] (1513)
**1** *archaic* **:** a stately building **:** MANSION
**2 :** a large hemispherical roof or ceiling
**3 :** a natural formation or structure that resembles the dome or cupola of a building
**4 :** a form of crystal composed of planes parallel to a lateral axis that meet above in a horizontal edge like a roof
**5 :** an upward fold in rock whose sides dip uniformly in all directions
**6 :** a roofed sports stadium
— **dom·al** \'dō-məl\ *adjective*
²**dome** *verb* **domed; dom·ing** (1876)
*transitive verb*
**1 :** to cover with a dome
**2 :** to form into a dome
*intransitive verb*
**:** to swell upward or outward like a dome
**Domes·day Book** \'dümz-,dā-, 'dōmz-\ *noun* [Middle English, from *domesday* doomsday] (1591)
**:** a record of a survey of English lands and landholdings made by order of William the Conqueror about 1086

¹**do·mes·tic** \də-'mes-tik\ *adjective* [Middle English, from Middle French *domestique*, from Latin *domesticus*, from *domus*] (15th century)
**1 a :** living near or about human habitations **b** **:** TAME, DOMESTICATED
**2 :** of, relating to, or originating within a country and especially one's own country ⟨*domestic* politics⟩ ⟨*domestic* wines⟩
**3 :** of or relating to the household or the family
**4 :** devoted to home duties and pleasures
**5 :** INDIGENOUS
— **do·mes·ti·cal·ly** \-ti-k(ə-)lē\ *adverb*
²**domestic** *noun* (1613)
**1 :** a household servant
**2 :** an article of domestic manufacture — usually used in plural
**domestic animal** *noun* (circa 1855)
**:** any of various animals (as the horse or sheep) domesticated so as to live and breed in a tame condition
¹**do·mes·ti·cate** \də-'mes-ti-,kāt\ *transitive verb* **-cat·ed; -cat·ing** (circa 1639)
**1 :** to bring into domestic use **:** ADOPT
**2 :** to adapt (an animal or plant) to life in intimate association with and to the advantage of humans
**3 :** to make domestic **:** fit for domestic life
**4 :** to bring to the level of ordinary people **:** FAMILIARIZE
— **do·mes·ti·ca·tion** \-,mes-ti-'kā-shən\ *noun*
²**do·mes·ti·cate** \-kət, -,kāt\ *noun* (1951)
**:** a domesticated animal or plant
**do·mes·tic·i·ty** \,dō-,mes-'ti-sə-tē, -məs-; ,dä-\ *noun, plural* **-ties** (1721)
**1 :** the quality or state of being domestic or domesticated
**2 :** domestic activities or life
**3** *plural* **:** domestic affairs
**domestic prelate** *noun* (1929)
**:** a priest having permanent honorary membership in the papal household
**domestic relations court** *noun* (circa 1939)
**:** COURT OF DOMESTIC RELATIONS
**domestic science** *noun* (1869)
**:** HOME ECONOMICS
**dom·i·cal** \'dō-mi-kəl, 'dä-\ *adjective* (1846)
**:** relating to, shaped like, or having a dome
¹**do·mi·cile** \'dä-mə-,sīl, 'dō-; 'dä-mə-sil\ *also* **dom·i·cil** \'däm-ə-səl\ *noun* [Middle English, from Middle French, from Latin *domicilium*, from *domus*] (15th century)
**1 :** a dwelling place **:** place of residence **:** HOME
**2 a :** a person's fixed, permanent, and principal home for legal purposes **b :** RESIDENCE 2b
²**domicile** *transitive verb* **-ciled; -cil·ing** (1809)
**:** to establish in or provide with a domicile
**do·mi·cil·i·ary** \,dä-mə-'si-lē-,er-ē, ,dō-\ *adjective* (1790)
**:** of, relating to, or constituting a domicile: as **a :** provided or taking place in the home ⟨*domiciliary* midwifery⟩ **b :** providing care and living space (as for disabled veterans)
**do·mi·cil·i·ate** \,dä-mə-'si-lē-,āt, ,dō-\ *verb* **-at·ed; -at·ing** [Latin *domicilium*] (1778)
*transitive verb*
**:** DOMICILE
*intransitive verb*
**:** RESIDE
— **do·mi·cil·i·a·tion** \-,si-lē-'ā-shən\ *noun*
**dom·i·nance** \'dä-mə-nən(t)s, 'däm-nən(t)s\ *noun* (1819)
**1 :** the fact or state of being dominant: as **a :** dominant position especially in a social hierarchy **b :** the property of one of a pair of alleles or traits that suppresses expression of the other in the heterozygous condition **c :** the influence or control over ecological communities exerted by a dominant

**2 :** functional asymmetry between a pair of bodily structures (as the right and left hands)
¹**dom·i·nant** \-nənt\ *adjective* [Middle French or Latin; Middle French, from Latin *dominant-, dominans*, present participle of *dominari*] (circa 1532)
**1 :** commanding, controlling, or prevailing over all others
**2 :** overlooking and commanding from a superior position
**3 :** of, relating to, or exerting ecological or genetic dominance
**4 :** being the one of a pair of bodily structures that is the more effective or predominant in action ⟨*dominant* eye⟩ ☆
— **dom·i·nant·ly** *adverb*
²**dominant** *noun* (1819)
**1 :** the fifth tone of a diatonic scale
**2 a :** a dominant genetic character or factor **b :** any of one or more kinds of organism (as a species) in an ecological community that exerts a controlling influence on the environment and thereby largely determines what other kinds of organisms are present **c :** a dominant individual in a social hierarchy
**dom·i·nate** \'dä-mə-,nāt\ *verb* **-nat·ed; -nat·ing** [Latin *dominatus*, past participle of *dominari*, from *dominus* master; akin to Latin *domus* house — more at DOME] (1611)
*transitive verb*
**1 :** RULE, CONTROL
**2 :** to exert the supreme determining or guiding influence on
**3 :** to overlook from a superior elevation or command because of superior height or position
**4 :** to have a commanding or preeminent place or position in ⟨name brands *dominate* the market⟩
*intransitive verb*
**1 :** to have or exert mastery, control, or preeminence
**2 :** to occupy a more elevated or superior position
— **dom·i·na·tive** \-,nā-tiv\ *adjective*
— **dom·i·na·tor** \-,nā-tər\ *noun*
**dom·i·na·tion** \,dä-mə-'nā-shən\ *noun* (14th century)
**1 :** supremacy or preeminence over another
**2 :** exercise of mastery or ruling power
**3 :** exercise of preponderant, governing, or controlling influence
**4** *plural* **:** DOMINION 3
**do·mi·na·trix** \,dä-mi-'nā-triks\ *noun, plural* **-trices** \-'nā-trə-sēz, -nə-'trī-sēz\ [Latin, feminine of *dominator*] (1971)
**:** a woman who physically and psychologically dominates and abuses her partner in sadomasochistic sex; *broadly* **:** a dominating woman
**dom·i·neer** \,dä-mə-'nir\ *verb* [Dutch *domineren*, from French *dominer*, from Latin *dominari*] (1591)
*intransitive verb*
**:** to exercise arbitrary or overbearing control

---

☆ **SYNONYMS**
**Dominant, predominant, paramount, preponderant** mean superior to all others in influence or importance. DOMINANT applies to something that is uppermost because ruling or controlling ⟨a *dominant* social class⟩. PREDOMINANT applies to something that exerts, often temporarily, the most marked influence ⟨a *predominant* emotion⟩. PARAMOUNT implies supremacy in importance, rank, or jurisdiction ⟨unemployment was the *paramount* issue in the campaign⟩. PREPONDERANT applies to an element or factor that outweighs all others in influence or effect ⟨*preponderant* evidence in her favor⟩.

*transitive verb*
: to tyrannize over
**dom·i·neer·ing** *adjective* (1588)
: inclined to domineer
**synonym** *see* MASTERFUL
— **dom·i·neer·ing·ly** \-iŋ-lē\ *adverb*
— **dom·i·neer·ing·ness** *noun*
**do·min·i·cal** \də-'mi-ni-kəl\ *adjective* [Late Latin *dominicalis*, from *dominicus* (*dies*) the Lord's day, from Latin *dominicus* of a lord, from *dominus* lord, master] (15th century)
**1** : of or relating to Jesus Christ as Lord
**2** : of or relating to the Lord's day
**Do·min·i·can** \də-'mi-ni-kən\ *noun* [Saint *Dominic*] (circa 1632)
: a member of a mendicant order of friars founded by Saint Dominic in 1215 and dedicated especially to preaching
— **Dominican** *adjective*
**dom·i·nick·er** \'dä-mə-,ne-kər, -,ni-\ *also* **dom·i·nick** \-(,)nik, -nek\ *noun, often capitalized* (1806)
: DOMINIQUE
**do·mi·nie** \1 *usually* 'dä-mə-nē, 2 *usually* 'dō-\ *noun* [Latin *domine*, vocative of *dominus*] (1612)
**1** *chiefly Scottish* : SCHOOLMASTER
**2** : CLERGYMAN
**do·min·ion** \də-'mi-nyən\ *noun* [Middle English *dominioun*, from Middle French *dominion*, modification of Latin *dominium*, from *dominus*] (14th century)
**1** : DOMAIN
**2** : supreme authority : SOVEREIGNTY
**3** *plural* : an order of angels — *see* CELESTIAL HIERARCHY
**4** *often capitalized* : a self-governing nation of the Commonwealth other than the United Kingdom that acknowledges the British monarch as chief of state
**5** : absolute ownership
**synonym** *see* POWER
**Dominion Day** *noun* (1867)
: CANADA DAY
**dom·i·nique** \'dä-mə-,nēk\ *noun* [*Dominique* (Dominica), one of the Windward islands, West Indies] (1849)
: any of an American breed of domestic fowl with a rose comb, yellow legs, and barred plumage; *broadly* : a barred fowl
**dom·i·no** \'dä-mə-,nō\ *noun, plural* **-noes** *or* **-nos** [French, probably from Latin (in the ritual formula *benedicamus Domino* let us bless the Lord)] (circa 1694)
**1 a** (1) : a long loose hooded cloak usually worn with a half mask as a masquerade costume (2) : a half mask worn over the eyes with a masquerade costume **b** : a person wearing a domino
**2 a** : a flat rectangular block (as of wood or plastic) whose face is divided into two equal parts that are blank or bear usually from one to six dots arranged as on dice faces **b** *plural but usually singular in construction* : any of several games played with a set of usually 28 dominoes
**3** : a member of a group (as of nations) expected to behave in accordance with the domino theory ◆
**domino effect** *noun* (1966)
: a cumulative effect produced when one event initiates a succession of similar events — compare RIPPLE EFFECT
**domino theory** *noun* [from the fact that if dominoes are stood on end one slightly behind the other, a slight push on the first will topple the others] (1965)
**1** : a theory that if one nation becomes Communist-controlled the neighboring nations will also become Communist-controlled
**2** : the theory that if one act or event is allowed to take place a series of similar acts or events will follow
**¹don** \'dän\ *transitive verb* **donned; donning** [Middle English, contraction of *do on*] (14th century)

**1** : to put on (an article of clothing)
**2** : to wrap oneself in : TAKE ON 3a
**²don** \'dän\ *noun* [Spanish, from Latin *dominus* master — more at DAME] (1523)
**1** : a Spanish nobleman or gentleman — used as a title prefixed to the Christian name
**2** *archaic* : a person of consequence : GRANDEE
**3** : a head, tutor, or fellow in a college of Oxford or Cambridge University; *broadly* : a college or university professor
**4** [Italian, title of respect, from *donno*, literally, lord, from Latin *dominus*] : a powerful Mafia leader
**do·na** \,dō-nə\ *noun* [Portuguese, from Latin *domina* lady — more at DAME] (circa 1897)
: a Portuguese or Brazilian woman of rank — used as a title prefixed to the Christian name
**do·ña** \'dō-nyə\ *noun* [Spanish, from Latin *domina*] (1622)
: a Spanish woman of rank — used as a title prefixed to the Christian name
**do·nate** \'dō-,nāt, dō-'\ *verb* **do·nat·ed; do·nat·ing** [back-formation from *donation*] (1785)
*transitive verb*
**1** : to make a gift of; *especially* : to contribute to a public or charitable cause
**2** : to transfer (as electrons) to another atom or molecule
*intransitive verb*
: to make a donation
**synonym** *see* GIVE
**do·na·tion** \dō-'nā-shən\ *noun* [Middle English *donatyowne*, from Latin *donation-, donatio*, from *donare* to present, from *donum* gift; akin to Latin *dare* to give — more at DATE] (15th century)
: the act or an instance of donating: as **a** : the making of a gift especially to a charity or public institution **b** : a free contribution : GIFT
**Do·na·tism** \'dō-nə-,ti-zəm, 'dä-\ *noun* [*Donatus*, 4th century bishop of Carthage] (1588)
: the doctrines of a Christian sect arising in North Africa in 311 and holding that sanctity is essential for the administration of sacraments and church membership
— **Do·na·tist** \-tist\ *noun*
**¹do·na·tive** \'dō-nə-tiv, 'dä-\ *noun* (15th century)
: a special gift or donation
**²do·na·tive** \*same or* 'dō-,nā-, dō-'\ *adjective* [Latin *donativus*, from *donatus*] (1559)
: of or relating to donation
**do·na·tor** \'dō-,nā-tər, dō-'\ *noun* (15th century)
: DONOR
**¹done** \'dən\ *past participle of* DO
**²done** *adjective* (14th century)
**1** : arrived at or brought to an end
**2** : doomed to failure, defeat, or death
**3** : gone by : OVER
**4** : physically exhausted
**5** : cooked sufficiently
**6** : conformable to social convention
**do·nee** \dō-'nē\ *noun* [*donor*] (1523)
: a recipient of a gift
**done for** \'dən-,fȯr\ *adjective* (1803)
**1** : sunk in defeat : BEATEN
**2** : mortally stricken : DOOMED
**done·ness** \'dən-nəs\ *noun* (1927)
: the condition of being cooked to the desired degree
**¹dong** \'dȯŋ, 'dän\ *noun* [origin unknown] (circa 1930)
: PENIS — usually considered vulgar
**²dong** *noun, plural* **dong** [Vietnamese *đồng*] (1948)
— *see* MONEY table
**don·jon** \'dän-jən, 'dən-\ *noun* [Middle English — more at DUNGEON] (14th century)
: a massive inner tower in a medieval castle
**word history** *see* DUNGEON
**Don Juan** \'dän-'(h)wän, *chiefly British & in poetry* dän-'jü-ən\ *noun* [Spanish]

**1** : a legendary Spaniard proverbial for his seduction of women
**2** : a captivating man known as a great lover or seducer of women
— **Don Juan·ism** \-'(h)wän-,i-zəm, -'jü-ə-,ni-\ *noun*

1 donjon

**don·key** \'däŋ-kē, 'dəŋ-, 'dȯŋ-\ *noun, plural* **donkeys** [origin unknown] (circa 1785)
**1** : the domestic ass (*Equus asinus*)
**2** : a stupid or obstinate person
**donkey engine** *noun* (1858)
**1** : a small usually portable auxiliary engine
**2** : a small locomotive used in switching
**donkey jacket** *noun* (1929)
*British* : a jacket of heavy material worn especially by laborers
**donkey's years** *noun plural* (1927)
*chiefly British* : a very long time
**don·key·work** \'däŋ-kē-,wərk, 'dəŋ-, 'dȯŋ-\ *noun* (1920)
: monotonous and routine work : DRUDGERY
**don·na** \'dä-nə, 'dȯ-\ *noun, plural* **don·ne** \-(,)nā\ [Italian, from Latin *domina*] (1740)
: an Italian woman especially of rank — used as a title prefixed to the Christian name
**don·née** \dȯ-'nā, (,)də-\ *noun, plural* **don·nées** \-'nā(z)\ [French, from feminine of *donné*, past participle of *donner* to give, from Latin *donare* to donate — more at DONATION] (1876)
: the set of assumptions on which a work of fiction or drama proceeds
**don·nick·er** *or* **don·ni·ker** \'dä-ni-kər\ *noun* [alteration of English dialect *dunnekin* toilet, cesspool] (circa 1931)
: TOILET 3a
**don·nish** \'dä-nish\ *adjective* (1848)
: of, relating to, or characteristic of a university don
— **don·nish·ly** *adverb*

\ə\ abut \ᵊ\ kitten \ər\ further \a\ ash \ā\ ace
\ä\ mop, mar \au̇\ out \ch\ chin \e\ bet \ē\ easy
\g\ go \i\ hit \ī\ ice \j\ job \ŋ\ sing \ō\ go
\ȯ\ law \ȯi\ boy \th\ thin \t͟h\ the \ü\ loot \u̇\ foot
\y\ yet \zh\ vision *see also* Guide to Pronunciation

— **don·nish·ness** *noun*

**don·ny·brook** \'dä-nē-ˌbru̇k\ *noun, often capitalized* [*Donnybrook* Fair, annual Irish event known for its brawls] (1852)
**1** : FREE-FOR-ALL, BRAWL
**2** : a usually public quarrel or dispute ◆

**do·nor** \'dō-nər, -ˌnȯr\ *noun* [Middle French *doneur*, from Latin *donator*, from *donare*] (15th century)
**1** : one that gives, donates, or presents something
**2** : one used as a source of biological material (as blood or an organ)
**3 a** : a compound capable of giving up a part (as an atom, chemical group, or subatomic particle) for combination with an acceptor **b** : an impurity added to a semiconductor to increase the number of mobile electrons

**¹do–noth·ing** \'dü-ˌnə-thiŋ\ *noun* (1579)
: a shiftless or lazy person

**²do–nothing** *adjective* (1832)
: marked by inactivity or failure to make positive progress
— **do–noth·ing·ism** \-ˌi-zəm\ *noun*

**Don Qui·xote** \ˌdän-kē-'(h)ō-tē, ˌdäŋ-; *chiefly British* dän-'kwik-sət\ *noun* [Spanish, hero of Cervantes' *Don Quixote*]
: an impractical idealist

**don·sie** *or* **don·sy** \'dän(t)-sē\ *adjective* [Scottish Gaelic *donas* evil, harm + English *-ie*] (1720)
**1** *dialect British* : UNLUCKY
**2** *Scottish* **a** : RESTIVE **b** : SAUCY
**3** *chiefly northern Midland* : slightly ill

**¹don't** \'dōnt\ (1639)
**1** : do not
**2** : does not ■

**²don't** \'dōnt\ *noun* (1894)
: a command or entreaty not to do something

**do·nut** \'dō-(ˌ)nət\ *variant of* DOUGHNUT

**doo·dad** \'dü-ˌdad\ *noun* [origin unknown] (1888)
**1** : an ornamental attachment or decoration
**2** : an often small article whose common name is unknown or forgotten : GADGET

**¹doo·dle** \'dü-dᵊl\ *verb* **doo·dled; doo·dling** \'dü-d(ᵊ)liŋ, 'dü-dᵊl-iŋ\ [perhaps from *doodle* (to ridicule)] (1936)
*intransitive verb*
**1** : to make a doodle
**2** : DAWDLE, TRIFLE
*transitive verb*
: to produce by doodling
— **doo·dler** \'düd-lər, 'dü-dᵊl-ər\ *noun*

**²doodle** *noun* (1937)
: an aimless or casual scribble, design, or sketch; *also* : a minor work

**doo·dle·bug** \'dü-dᵊl-ˌbəg\ *noun* [probably from *doodle* (fool) + *bug*] (circa 1866)
**1** : the larva of an ant lion; *also* : any of several other insects
**2** : a device (as a divining rod) used in attempting to locate underground gas, water, oil, or ores
**3** : BUZZ BOMB

**doodley–squat** *or* **doodly–squat** \'dü-dᵊl-ē-ˌskwät\ *noun* [perhaps from *doodle* + ⁴-*y* + *squat*, euphemism for *shit*] (1934)
: DIDDLY-SQUAT

**doo–doo** \'dü-(ˌ)dü\ *noun* [baby talk] (1948)
: EXCREMENT
— **in deep doo–doo** : in trouble

**doo·fus** \'dü-fəs, -fis\ *noun, plural* **doo·fus·es** \-fə-siz\ [perhaps alteration of ¹*goof*] (1970)
*slang* : a stupid, incompetent, or foolish person

**doo·hick·ey** \'dü-ˌhi-kē\ *noun, plural* **-hickeys** *also* **-hickies** [probably from *doo*dad + *hickey*] (1914)
: DOODAD 2

**¹doom** \'düm\ *noun* [Middle English, from Old English *dōm;* akin to Old High German *tuom* condition, state, Old English *dōn* to do] (before 12th century)

**1** : a law or ordinance especially in Anglo-Saxon England
**2 a** : JUDGMENT, DECISION; *especially* : a judicial condemnation or sentence **b** (1) : JUDGMENT 3a (2) : JUDGMENT DAY 1
**3 a** : DESTINY; *especially* : unhappy destiny **b** : DEATH, RUIN
**synonym** see FATE

**²doom** *transitive verb* (15th century)
**1** : to give judgment against : CONDEMN
**2 a** : to fix the fate of : DESTINE **b** : to make certain the failure or destruction of

**doom·ful** \'düm-fəl\ *adjective* (1586)
: presaging doom : OMINOUS
— **doom·ful·ly** \-fə-lē\ *adverb*

**doom·say·er** \'düm-ˌsā-ər\ *noun* (1953)
: one given to forebodings and predictions of impending calamity
— **doom·say·ing** \-ˌsā-iŋ\ *noun*

**dooms·day** \'dümz-ˌdā\ *noun, often attributive* (before 12th century)
: a day of final judgment

**dooms·day·er** \-ˌdā-ər, -ˌde(ə)r\ *noun* (1972)
: DOOMSAYER

**doom·ster** \'düm(p)-stər\ *noun* (15th century)
**1** : JUDGE
**2** : DOOMSAYER

**doomy** \'dü-mē\ *adjective* (1971)
: suggestive of doom : DOOMFUL
— **doom·i·ly** \'dü-mi-lē\ *adverb*

**door** \'dōr, 'dȯr\ *noun, often attributive* [Middle English *dure, dor*, from Old English *duru* door & *dor* gate; akin to Old High German *turi* door, Latin *fores*, Greek *thyra*] (before 12th century)
**1** : a usually swinging or sliding barrier by which an entry is closed and opened; *also* : a similar part of a piece of furniture
**2** : DOORWAY
**3** : a means of access or participation : OPPORTUNITY ⟨opens new *doors*⟩ ⟨*door* to success⟩
— **door·less** \-ləs\ *adjective*
— **at one's door** : as a charge against one as being responsible ⟨laid the blame *at our door*⟩

**door·bell** \'dōr-ˌbel, 'dȯr-\ *noun* (circa 1815)
: a bell or set of chimes to be rung usually by a push button at an outer door

**do–or–die** \'dü-ər-'dī, -ȯr-\ *adjective* (1879)
**1** : doggedly determined to reach one's objective : INDOMITABLE
**2** : presenting as the only alternatives complete success or complete ruin ⟨a *do-or-die* situation⟩

**door·jamb** \'dōr-ˌjam, 'dȯr-\ *noun* (1837)
: an upright piece forming the side of a door opening

**door·keep·er** \-ˌkē-pər\ *noun* (1535)
: a person who tends a door

**door·knob** \-ˌnäb\ *noun* (1846)
: a knob that releases a door latch

**door·man** \-ˌman, -mən\ *noun* (circa 1897)
: a usually uniformed attendant at the door of a building (as a hotel or apartment house)

**door·mat** \-ˌmat\ *noun* (1665)
**1** : a mat placed before or inside a door for wiping dirt from the shoes
**2** : one that submits without protest to abuse or indignities
**3** : a team that regularly finishes last

**door·nail** \-ˌnāl, -'nā(ə)l\ *noun* (14th century)
: a large-headed nail — used chiefly in the phrase *dead as a doornail*

**door·plate** \-ˌplāt\ *noun* (1823)
: a nameplate on a door

**door·post** \-ˌpōst\ *noun* (1535)
: DOORJAMB

**door prize** *noun* (1951)
: a prize awarded to the holder of a winning ticket passed out at the entrance to an entertainment or function

**door·sill** \'dōr-ˌsil, 'dȯr-\ *noun* (1587)
: SILL 1b

**door·step** \-ˌstep\ *noun* (1767)
: a step before an outer door

— **on one's doorstep** : close at hand; *especially* : too close to be overlooked

**door·stop** \-ˌstäp\ *noun* (circa 1895)
**1** : a device (as a wedge or weight) for holding a door open
**2** : a usually rubber-tipped device attached to a wall or floor to prevent damaging contact between an opened door and the wall

**door–to–door** \ˌdōr-tə-'dōr, ˌdȯr-tə-'dȯr\ *adjective* (1902)
: going or made by going to each house in a neighborhood ⟨*door-to-door* salesmen⟩ ⟨a *door-to-door* canvass⟩
— **door–to–door** *adverb*

**door·way** \'dōr-ˌwā, 'dȯr-\ *noun* (1799)
**1** : the opening that a door closes; *especially* : an entrance into a building or room
**2** : DOOR 3

**door·yard** \-ˌyärd\ *noun* (circa 1764)
: a yard next to the door of a house

**doo–wop** \'dü-ˌwäp\ *noun* [from nonsense syllables typical of the style] (1969)
: a vocal style of rock and roll characterized by the a cappella singing of nonsense syllables in rhythmical support of the melody

**doo·zy** *or* **doo·zie** \'dü-zē\ *also* **doo·zer** \-zər\ *noun, plural* **doozies** *or* **doozers** [perhaps alteration of *daisy*] (1916)
: an extraordinary one of its kind

**do·pa** \'dō-pə, -(ˌ)pä\ *noun* [International Scientific Vocabulary *d*ihydroxy- + *p*henylal*a*nine] (1917)
: an amino acid $C_9H_{11}NO_4$ that in the levorotatory form is found in the broad bean and is used in the treatment of Parkinson's disease

**do·pa·mine** \'dō-pə-ˌmēn\ *noun* [*dopa* + *amine*] (1959)

---

□ USAGE

**don't** *Don't* is the earliest attested contraction of *does not* and until about 1900 was the standard spoken form in the U.S. (it survived as spoken standard longer in British English). Dialect surveys find it more common in the speech of the less educated than in that of the educated; in those places (as the Midland and southern Atlantic seaboard regions) where it has lasted in educated speech, it is most common with older informants. Surveys of attitudes toward usage show it more widely disapproved in 1971 than it had been 40 years earlier. Its chief use in edited prose is in fiction for purposes of characterization. It is sometimes used consciously, like *ain't*, to gain an informal effect.

---

◇ WORD HISTORY

**donnybrook** Donnybrook, now a suburban district of Dublin, was once a village about a mile and a half from the city's center. From the year 1204 it was the site of a fair held annually in August, where working-class Dubliners would come to find whatever amusement they could afford. Horses were traded, and trinkets and food were sold from crude wattle booths and tents, with entertainment provided mainly by strolling pipers and dancers. By the end of the 18th century, the Donnybrook fair had become notorious for its rowdy brawls, fueled by the consumption of great quantities of liquor. Victorian Dublin became more conservative and temperance-minded, however, and both Catholic and evangelical clergymen campaigned to have the fair abolished. Though the fighting and drunkenness for which it was renowned had greatly subsided, the fair ended in 1855. By that time, nonetheless, *donnybrook* had acquired the generic sense in English that it still maintains.

: a monoamine $C_8H_{11}NO_2$ that is a decarboxylated form of dopa and that occurs especially as a neurotransmitter in the brain

**do·pa·mi·ner·gic** \ˌdō-pə-ˌmē-'nər-jik\ *adjective* (1970)
: relating to, participating in, or activated by dopamine or related substances

**dop·ant** \'dō-pənt\ *noun* [²*dope*] (1962)
: an impurity added usually in minute amounts to a pure substance to alter its properties

**¹dope** \'dōp\ *noun* [Dutch *doop* sauce, from *dopen* to dip; akin to Old English *dyppan* to dip] (1807)
**1 a :** a thick liquid or pasty preparation **b :** a preparation for giving a desired quality to a substance or surface
**2 :** absorbent or adsorbent material used in various manufacturing processes (as the making of dynamite)
**3 a** (1) **:** an illicit, habit-forming, or narcotic drug (2) **:** a preparation given to a racehorse to help or hinder its performance **b** *chiefly Southern* **:** a cola drink **c :** a stupid person
**4 :** information especially from a reliable source ⟨the inside *dope*⟩

**²dope** *verb* **doped; dop·ing** (1889)
*transitive verb*
**1 :** to treat or affect with dope; *especially* **:** to give a narcotic to
**2 :** FIGURE OUT — usually used with *out*
**3 :** to treat with a dopant
*intransitive verb*
: to take dope
— **dop·er** *noun*

**dope·head** \'dōp-ˌhed\ *noun* (1903)
: a drug addict

**dope·ster** \'dōp-stər\ *noun* (1907)
: a forecaster of the outcome of future events (as sports contests or elections)

**dop·ey** *also* **dopy** \'dō-pē\ *adjective* **dop·i·er; -est** (1896)
**1 a :** dulled by alcohol or a narcotic **b :** SLUGGISH, STUPEFIED
**2 :** STUPID, FATUOUS
— **dop·i·ness** *noun*

**dop·pel·gäng·er** *or* **dop·pel·gang·er** \'dä-pəl-ˌgaŋ-ər, -ˌgeŋ-, ˌdä-pəl-'\ *n* [German *Doppelgänger*, from *doppel-* double + *-gänger* goer] (1851)
**1 :** a ghostly counterpart of a living person
**2 a :** DOUBLE 2a **b :** ALTER EGO b **c :** a person who has the same name as another

**Dopp·ler** \'dä-plər\ *adjective* (1905)
: of, relating to, being, or utilizing a shift in frequency in accordance with the Doppler effect; *also* **:** of or relating to Doppler radar

**Doppler effect** *noun* [Christian J. *Doppler*] (1905)
: a change in the frequency with which waves (as sound or light) from a given source reach an observer when the source and the observer are in motion with respect to each other so that the frequency increases or decreases according to the speed at which the distance is decreasing or increasing

**Doppler radar** *noun* (1954)
: a radar system that utilizes the Doppler effect for measuring velocity

**Dor·cas** \'dòr-kəs\ *noun* [Greek *Dorkas*]
: a Christian woman of New Testament times who made clothing for the poor

**Do·ri·an** \'dōr-ē-ən, 'dòr-\ *noun* [Latin *Dorius* of Doris, from Greek *dōrios*, from *Dōris*, region of ancient Greece] (1662)
: a member of an ancient Hellenic race that completed the overthrow of Mycenaean civilization and settled especially in the Peloponnisos and Crete
— **Dorian** *adjective*

**¹Dor·ic** \'dòr-ik, 'där-\ *adjective* (1569)
**1 :** of, relating to, or characteristic of the Dorians
**2 :** belonging to the oldest and simplest Greek architectural order — see ORDER illustration
**3 :** of, relating to, or constituting Doric

**²Doric** *noun* (1837)

: a dialect of ancient Greek spoken especially in the Peloponnisos, Crete, Sicily, and southern Italy

**dork** \'dòrk\ *noun* [perhaps alteration of *dick*] (1972)
*slang* **:** NERD; *also* **:** JERK 4

**dorky** \'dòr-kē\ *adjective* **dork·i·er; -est** (1983)
*slang* **:** foolishly stupid **:** INEPT

**dorm** \'dòrm\ *noun* (1900)
: DORMITORY

**dor·man·cy** \'dòr-mən(t)-sē\ *noun* (1789)
: the quality or state of being dormant

**dor·mant** \'dòr-mənt\ *adjective* [Middle English, fixed, stationary, from Middle French, from present participle of *dormir* to sleep, from Latin *dormire*; akin to Sanskrit *drāti* he sleeps] (1500)
**1 :** represented on a coat of arms in a lying position with the head on the forepaws
**2 :** marked by a suspension of activity: as **a :** temporarily devoid of external activity ⟨a *dormant* volcano⟩ **b :** temporarily in abeyance yet capable of being activated
**3 a :** ASLEEP, INACTIVE **b :** having the faculties suspended **:** SLUGGISH **c :** having biological activity suspended: as (1) **:** being in a state of suspended animation (2) **:** not actively growing but protected (as by bud scales) from the environment — used of plant parts
**4 :** associated with, carried out, or applied during a period of dormancy ⟨*dormant* grafting⟩
**synonym** see LATENT

**dor·mer** \'dòr-mər\ *noun* [Middle French *dormeor* dormitory, from Latin *dormitorium*] (1592)
: a window set vertically in a structure projecting through a sloping roof; *also* **:** the roofed structure containing such a window

**dor·mie** *or* **dor·my** \'dòr-mē\ *adjective* [origin unknown] (1847)
: being ahead by as many holes in golf as remain to be played

**dor·mi·to·ry** \'dòr-mə-ˌtōr-ē, -ˌtòr-\ *noun, plural* **-ries** [Middle English, from Latin *dormitorium*, from *dormitus*, past participle of *dormire*] (15th century)
**1 :** a room for sleeping; *especially* **:** a large room containing numerous beds
**2 :** a residence hall providing rooms for individuals or for groups usually without private baths
**3** *chiefly British* **:** a residential community inhabited chiefly by commuters

**dor·mouse** \'dòr-ˌmaùs\ *noun, plural* **dor·mice** \-ˌmīs\ [Middle English *dormowse*, perhaps from Middle French *dormir* + Middle English *mous* mouse] (15th century)
: any of numerous small Old World rodents (families Gliridae and Seleviniidae) that are intermediate in form and behavior between mice and squirrels

**dor·nick** \'dòr-nik, 'dä-nik\ *noun* [probably from Irish *dornóg*] (1840)
: a stone small enough to throw; *also* **:** a large piece of rock

**do·ron·i·cum** \də-'rä-ni-kəm\ *noun* [New Latin, genus name, from Arabic *darūnaj*, a plant of this genus] (1892)
: any of a genus (*Doronicum*) of Eurasian perennial composite herbs including several cultivated for their showy yellow flower heads

**dorp** \'dòrp\ *noun* [Dutch, from Middle Dutch; akin to Old High German *dorf* village — more at THORP] (circa 1576)
: VILLAGE

**dors-** *or* **dorsi-** *or* **dorso-** *combining form* [Late Latin *dors-*, from Latin *dorsum*]
**1 :** back ⟨*dors*ad⟩
**2 :** dorsal and ⟨*dorso*lateral⟩

**dor·sad** \'dòr-ˌsad\ *adverb* (circa 1803)
: toward the back **:** DORSALLY

**¹dorsal** *variant of* DOSSAL

**²dor·sal** \'dòr-səl\ *adjective* [Late Latin *dorsalis*, from Latin *dorsum* back] (1727)

**1 :** relating to or situated near or on the back especially of an animal or of one of its parts
**2 :** ABAXIAL
— **dor·sal·ly** \-sə-lē\ *adverb*

**³dorsal** *noun* (1834)
: a dorsally located part; *especially* **:** a thoracic vertebra

**dorsal lip** *noun* (1940)
: the margin of the fold of blastula wall that delineates the dorsal limit of the blastopore, constitutes the primary organizer, and forms the point of origin of chordamesoderm

**dorsal root** *noun* (circa 1934)
: the one of the two roots of a spinal nerve that passes dorsally to the spinal cord and consists of sensory fibers

**Dor·set** \'dòr-sət\ *noun* (1891)
: any of a breed of domestic white-faced sheep originally developed in Dorset, England

**dor·si·ven·tral** \ˌdòr-si-'ven-trəl\ *adjective* (circa 1882)
**1 :** having distinct dorsal and ventral surfaces
**2 :** DORSOVENTRAL 1
— **dor·si·ven·tral·i·ty** \-ven-'tra-lə-tē\ *noun*
— **dor·si·ven·tral·ly** \-'ven-trə-lē\ *adverb*

**dor·so·lat·er·al** \ˌdòr-sō-'la-tə-rəl, -'la-trəl\ *adjective* (1835)
: of, relating to, or involving both the back and the sides

**dor·so·ven·tral** \-'ven-trəl\ *adjective* [International Scientific Vocabulary] (1870)
**1 :** relating to, involving, or extending along the axis joining the dorsal and ventral sides
**2 :** DORSIVENTRAL 1
— **dor·so·ven·tral·i·ty** \-ven-'tra-lə-tē\ *noun*
— **dor·so·ven·tral·ly** \-trə-lē\ *adverb*

**dor·sum** \'dòr-səm\ *noun, plural* **dor·sa** \-sə\ [Latin] (1840)
**1 :** the upper surface of an appendage or part
**2 :** BACK; *especially* **:** the entire dorsal surface of an animal

**do·ry** \'dōr-ē, 'dòr-\ *noun, plural* **dories** [Miskito *dóri* dugout] (1709)
: a flat-bottomed boat with high flaring sides, sharp bow, and deep V-shaped transom

**dos** *or* **do's** *plural of* ²DO

**dos·age** \'dō-sij\ *noun* (circa 1867)
**1 a :** the addition of an ingredient or the application of an agent in a measured dose **b :** the presence and relative representation or strength of a factor or agent
**2 a :** DOSE 2 **b** (1) **:** the giving of a dose (2) **:** regulation or determination of doses
**3 :** an exposure to some experience in or as if in measured portions

**¹dose** \'dōs\ *noun* [Middle English, from Middle French, from Late Latin *dosis*, from Greek, literally, act of giving, from *didonai* to give — more at DATE] (15th century)
**1 a :** the measured quantity of a therapeutic agent to be taken at one time **b :** the quantity of radiation administered or absorbed
**2 :** a portion of a substance added during a process
**3 :** something experienced as if in a prescribed or measured amount ⟨a daily *dose* of hard work⟩
**4 :** a gonorrheal infection

**²dose** *transitive verb* **dosed; dos·ing** (1654)
**1 :** to give a dose to; *especially* **:** to give medicine to
**2 :** to divide (as a medicine) into doses
**3 :** to treat with an application or agent

**do–si–do** \ˌdō-(ˌ)sē-'dō\ *noun, plural* **do–si–dos** [French *dos-à-dos* back to back] (1926)
: a square-dance figure: **a :** a figure in which the dancers pass each other right shoulder to right shoulder and circle each other back to

back **b :** a figure in which the woman moves in a figure circling first her partner and then the man on her right

**do·sim·e·ter** \dō-'si-mə-tər\ *noun* [Late Latin *dosis* + International Scientific Vocabulary *-meter*] (1938)
**:** a device for measuring doses of radiations (as X rays)
— **do·si·met·ric** \ˌdō-sə-'me-trik\ *adjective*
— **do·sim·e·try** \dō-'si-mə-trē\ *noun*

**¹doss** \'dȯs, 'däs\ *intransitive verb* [origin unknown] (circa 1785)
*chiefly British* **:** to sleep or bed down in a convenient place — usually used with *down*

**²doss** *noun* (circa 1789)
*chiefly British* **:** a crude or makeshift bed

**dos·sal** \'dä-səl\ *or* **dor·sal** \'dȯr-səl\ *or* **dos·sel** \'dä-səl\ *noun* [Medieval Latin *dossale, dorsale*, from neuter of Late Latin *dorsalis* dorsal] (1851)
**:** an ornamental cloth hung behind and above an altar

**doss–house** \'dȯs-ˌhaùs, 'däs-\ *noun* (1888)
*chiefly British* **:** a cheap rooming house or hotel

**dos·sier** \'dȯs-ˌyā, 'däs-; 'dȯ-sē-ˌā, 'dä-\ *noun* [French, bundle of documents labeled on the back, dossier, from *dos* back, from Latin *dorsum*] (1880)
**:** a file containing detailed records on a particular person or subject

**dost** \'dəst\ *archaic present 2d singular of* DO

**¹dot** \'dät\ *noun* [(assumed) Middle English, from Old English *dott* head of a boil; akin to Old High German *tutta* nipple] (1674)
**1 :** a small spot **:** SPECK
**2 a** (1) **:** a small point made with a pointed instrument ⟨a *dot* on the chart marked the ship's position⟩ (2) **:** a small round mark used in orthography or punctuation ⟨put a *dot* over the *i*⟩ **b :** a centered point used as a multiplication sign (as in 6 · 5 = 30) (1) **:** a point after a note or rest in music indicating augmentation of the time value by one half (2) **:** a point over or under a note indicating that it is to be played staccato
**3 :** a precise point especially in time ⟨arrived at six on the *dot*⟩
**4 :** a short click or buzz forming a letter or part of a letter (as in the Morse code)

**²dot** *verb* **dot·ted; dot·ting** (circa 1740)
*transitive verb*
**1 :** to mark with a dot
**2 :** to intersperse with dots or objects scattered at random ⟨boats *dotting* the lake⟩
*intransitive verb*
**:** to make a dot
— **dot·ter** *noun*

**³dot** \'dȯt\ *noun* [French, from Latin *dot-, dos* dowry] (1855)
**:** DOWRY 2

**dot·age** \'dō-tij\ *noun* [*dote*] (14th century)
**:** a state or period of senile decay marked by decline of mental poise and alertness

**do·tal** \'dō-t°l\ *adjective* [Latin *dotalis*, from *dot-, dos*] (1513)
**:** of or relating to a woman's marriage dowry

**dot·ard** \'dō-tərd\ *noun* (14th century)
**:** a person in his or her dotage

**dote** \'dōt\ *intransitive verb* **dot·ed; dot·ing** [Middle English; akin to Middle Low German *doten* to be foolish] (13th century)
**1 :** to exhibit mental decline of or like that of old age **:** be in one's dotage
**2 :** to be lavish or excessive in one's attention, fondness, or affection — used especially with *on* ⟨*doted* on her only grandchild⟩
— **dot·er** *noun*
— **dot·ing·ly** \'dō-tiŋ-lē\ *adverb*

**doth** \'dəth\ *archaic present 3d singular of* DO

**dot matrix** *noun* (1963)
**:** a pattern of dots in a grid from which alphanumeric characters can be formed ⟨a *dot matrix* printer⟩

**dot product** *noun* [¹*dot;* from its being commonly written *A · B*] (1901)
**:** SCALAR PRODUCT

**dotted swiss** *noun* (circa 1924)
**:** a sheer light muslin ornamented with evenly spaced raised dots

**dot·ter·el** \'dä-tə-rəl, 'dä-trəl\ *noun* [Middle English *dotrelle*, irregular from *doten* to dote] (15th century)
**:** a Eurasian plover (*Eudromias morinellus*) formerly common in England; *also* **:** any of various related plovers chiefly of eastern Asia, Australia, and South America

**dot·tle** \'dä-t°l, 'dȯ-\ *noun* [Middle English *dottel* plug, from (assumed) Middle English *dot*] (circa 1825)
**:** unburned and partially burned tobacco in the bowl of a pipe

**¹dot·ty** \'dä-tē\ *adjective* **dot·ti·er; -est** [alteration of Scots *dottle* fool, from Middle English *dotel*, from *doten*] (15th century)
**1 a :** mentally unbalanced **:** CRAZY **b :** amiably eccentric
**2 :** being obsessed or infatuated
**3 :** amusingly absurd **:** RIDICULOUS ⟨some sublimely *dotty* exchanges of letters⟩
— **dot·ti·ly** \'dä-t°l-ē\ *adverb*
— **dot·ti·ness** \'dä-tē-nəs\ *noun*

**²dotty** *adjective* (1812)
**:** composed of or marked by dots

**Dou·ay Version** \dü-'ā-\ *noun* [*Douay*, France] (1837)
**:** an English translation of the Vulgate used by Roman Catholics

**¹dou·ble** \'də-bəl\ *adjective* [Middle English, from Old French, from Latin *duplus* (akin to Greek *diploos*), from *duo* two + *-plus* multiplied by; akin to Old English *-feald* -fold — more at TWO, -FOLD] (13th century)
**1 :** having a twofold relation or character **:** DUAL
**2 :** consisting of two usually combined members or parts ⟨an egg with a *double* yolk⟩
**3 a :** being twice as great or as many ⟨*double* the number of expected applicants⟩ **b** *of a coin* **:** worth two of the specified amount ⟨a *double* eagle⟩ ⟨a *double* crown⟩
**4 :** marked by duplicity **:** DECEITFUL
**5 :** folded in two
**6 :** of extra size, strength, or value ⟨a *double* martini⟩
**7 :** having more than the normal number of floral leaves often at the expense of the sporophylls
**8** *of rhyme* **:** involving correspondence of two syllables (as in *exciting* and *inviting*)
**9 :** designed for the use of two persons ⟨a *double* room⟩ ⟨a *double* bed⟩
— **dou·ble·ness** *noun*

**²double** *verb* **dou·bled; dou·bling** \'də-b(ə-)liŋ\ (13th century)
*transitive verb*
**1 :** to make twice as great or as many: as **a :** to increase by adding an equal amount **b :** to amount to twice the number of **c :** to make a call in bridge that increases the value of odd tricks or undertricks at (an opponent's bid)
**2 a :** to make of two thicknesses **:** FOLD **b :** CLENCH ⟨*doubled* his fist⟩ **c :** to cause to stoop
**3 :** to avoid by doubling **:** ELUDE
**4 a :** to replace in a dramatic role **b :** to play (dramatic roles) by doubling
**5 a** (1) **:** to advance or score (a base runner) by a double (2) **:** to bring about the scoring of (a run) by a double **b :** to put out (a base runner) in completing a double play
*intransitive verb*
**1 a :** to become twice as much or as many **b :** to double a bid (as in bridge)
**2 a :** to turn sharply and suddenly; *especially* **:** to turn back on one's course **b :** to follow a circuitous course
**3 :** to become bent or folded usually in the middle — usually used with *up* ⟨she *doubled* up in pain⟩

**4 a :** to serve an additional purpose or perform an additional duty **b :** to play a dramatic role as a double
**5 :** to make a double in baseball
— **dou·bler** \-b(ə-)lər\ *noun*

**³double** *adverb* (14th century)
**1 :** to twice the extent or amount
**2 :** two together

**⁴double** *noun* (14th century)
**1 :** something twice the usual size, strength, speed, quantity, or value: as **a :** a double amount **b :** a base hit that enables the batter to reach second base
**2 :** one that is the counterpart of another **:** DUPLICATE: as **a :** a living person that closely resembles another living person **b :** WRAITH (1) **:** UNDERSTUDY (2) **:** one who resembles an actor and takes his or her place especially in scenes calling for special skills (3) **:** an actor who plays more than one role in a production
**3 a :** a sharp turn (as in running) **:** REVERSAL **b :** an evasive shift
**4 :** something consisting of two paired members: as **a :** FOLD **b :** a combined bet placed on two different contests **c :** two consecutive strikes in bowling
**5** *plural* **:** a game between two pairs of players
**6 :** an act of doubling in a card game
**7 :** a room (as in a hotel) for two guests — compare SINGLE 4

**double agent** *noun* (1935)
**:** a spy pretending to serve one government while actually serving another

**double bar** *noun* (circa 1674)
**:** two adjacent vertical lines or a heavy single line separating principal sections of a musical composition

**dou·ble–bar·rel** \ˌdə-bəl-'bar-əl\ *noun* (1811)
**:** a double-barreled gun

**dou·ble–bar·reled** \-əld\ *adjective* (1709)
**1** *of a firearm* **:** having two barrels mounted side by side or one beneath the other
**2 :** TWOFOLD; *especially* **:** having a double purpose ⟨asked a *double-barreled* question⟩

**double bass** *noun* (1752)
**:** the largest and lowest-pitched of the stringed instruments tuned in fourths
— **double bass·ist** \-'bā-sist\ *noun*

**double bassoon** *noun* (circa 1876)
**:** CONTRABASSOON

**double bill** *noun* (1917)
**:** a bill (as at a theater) offering two principal features

**double bind** *noun* (1956)
**:** a psychological predicament in which a person receives from a single source conflicting messages that allow no appropriate response to be made; *broadly* **:** DILEMMA 2

**double bass**

**dou·ble–blind** \ˌdə-bəl-'blīnd\ *adjective* (1950)
**:** of, relating to, or being an experimental procedure in which neither the subjects nor the experimenters know the makeup of the test and control groups during the actual course of the experiments — compare SINGLE-BLIND

**double boiler** *noun* (1879)
**:** a cooking utensil consisting of two saucepans fitting together so that the contents of the upper can be cooked or heated by boiling water in the lower

**double bond** *noun* (1889)
**:** a chemical bond in which two pairs of electrons are shared by two atoms in a molecule — compare SINGLE BOND, TRIPLE BOND

**dou·ble–breast·ed** \ˌdə-bəl-'bres-təd\ *adjective* (1701)
**1 :** having one half of the front lapped over the other and usually a double row of buttons

and a single row of buttonholes ⟨a *double-breasted* coat⟩ **2** : having a double-breasted coat ⟨a *double-breasted* suit⟩

**double-check** \ˌdə-bəl-'chek, 'də-bəl-ˌ\ (1944) *transitive verb* : to subject to a double check ⟨an article *double-checked* for accuracy⟩ *intransitive verb* : to make a double check

**double check** *noun* (1953) : a careful checking to determine accuracy, condition, or progress especially of something already checked

**dou·ble-clutch** \ˌdə-bəl-'kləch\ *intransitive verb* (1928) : to shift gears in an automotive vehicle by shifting into neutral and pumping the clutch before shifting to another gear

**dou·ble-crop** \ˌdə-bəl-'kräp\ *intransitive verb* (1918) : to grow two or more crops on the same land in the same season or at the same time

**dou·ble-cross** \ˌdə-bəl-'krós\ *transitive verb* (1903) : to deceive by double-dealing : BETRAY
— **dou·ble-cross·er** *noun*

**double cross** *noun* (1834) **1 a** : an act of winning or trying to win a fight or match after agreeing to lose it **b** : an act of betraying or cheating an associate **2** : a cross between first-generation hybrids of four separate inbred lines (as in the production of hybrid seed corn)

**double dagger** *noun* (1706) : the character ‡ used as a reference mark — called also *diesis*

**double date** *noun* (circa 1931) : a date participated in by two couples
— **dou·ble-date** *intransitive verb*

**¹dou·ble-deal·ing** \ˌdə-bəl-'dē-liŋ\ *noun* (1529) : action contradictory to a professed attitude : DUPLICITY
*synonym* see DECEPTION
— **dou·ble-deal·er** \-'dē-lər\ *noun*

**²double-dealing** *adjective* (1587) : given to or marked by duplicity

**dou·ble-deck** \ˌdə-bəl-ˌdek\ *or* **dou·ble-decked** \-'dekt\ *adjective* (1894) : having two decks, levels, or layers ⟨a *double-deck* bus⟩ ⟨a *double-deck* sandwich⟩

**dou·ble-deck·er** \-'de-kər\ *noun* (1835) : something that is double-deck

**dou·ble-dig·it** \ˌdə-bəl-'di-jət\ *adjective* (1959) : amounting to 10 percent or more ⟨*double-digit* inflation⟩ ⟨*double-digit* price increases⟩

**dou·ble-dip·per** \-'di-pər\ *noun* (circa 1974) : a person who collects both a government pension and a government salary
— **dou·ble-dip·ping** \-piŋ\ *noun*

**dou·ble-dome** \'də-bəl-ˌdōm\ *noun* (1938) : INTELLECTUAL

**double door** *noun* (1840) : an opening with two vertical doors that meet in the middle of the opening when closed
— compare DUTCH DOOR

**double dribble** *noun* (circa 1949) : an illegal action in basketball made when a player dribbles the ball with two hands simultaneously or continues to dribble after allowing the ball to come to rest in one or both hands

**double Dutch** *noun* (1876) **1** : unintelligible language : GIBBERISH **2** : the jumping of two jump ropes rotating in opposite directions simultaneously

**dou·ble-edged** \ˌdə-bəl-'ejd\ *adjective* (15th century) **1** : having two cutting edges **2 a** : having two components or aspects ⟨a spy with a *double-edged* mission⟩ **b** : capable of being taken in two ways ⟨a *double-edged* remark⟩

**double-edged sword** *noun* (15th century) : something that has or can have both favorable and unfavorable consequences ⟨freedom of expression . . . can be a *double-edged* sword —Linda Connors⟩

**dou·ble-end·ed** \ˌdə-bəl-'en-dəd\ *adjective* (circa 1874) : similar at both ends ⟨a *double-ended* bolt⟩

**dou·ble-end·er** \-dər\ *noun* (1864) : a ship or boat with bow and stern of similar shape

**dou·ble en·ten·dre** \'düb-ᵊl-än-'tä<sup>n</sup>d(-r°); 'də-bəl-än-'tänd(-rə)\ *noun, plural* **double entendres** \*same also* -'tä<sup>n</sup>z; -'tän-drəz\ [obsolete French, literally, double meaning] (1673) **1** : ambiguity of meaning arising from language that lends itself to more than one interpretation **2** : a word or expression capable of two interpretations with one usually risqué

**double entry** *noun* (1741) : a method of bookkeeping that recognizes both sides of a business transaction by debiting the amount of the transaction to one account and crediting it to another account so the total debits equal the total credits

**dou·ble-faced** \ˌdə-bəl-'fāst\ *adjective* (1577) **1** : HYPOCRITICAL, TWO-FACED **2 a** : having two faces or sides designed for use ⟨a *double-faced* bookshelf⟩ **b** *also* **dou·ble-face** \-'fās\ : finished on both sides : REVERSIBLE — used of fabric

**double fault** *noun* (circa 1909) : two consecutive serving faults in tennis that result in the loss of a point
— **dou·ble-fault** \ˌdə-bəl-'fólt\ *intransitive verb*

**double feature** *noun* (1928) : a movie program with two main films

**double fertilization** *noun* (circa 1909) : fertilization characteristic of seed plants in which one sperm nucleus fuses with the egg nucleus to form an embryo and another fuses with polar nuclei to form endosperm

**double genitive** *noun* (1824) : a syntactic construction in English in which possession is marked both by the preposition *of* and a noun or pronoun in the possessive case (as in "A friend of Bob's is a friend of mine") — called also *double possessive*

**double glazing** *noun* (1943) : two layers of glass set in a window to reduce heat flow in either direction

**Double Glouces·ter** \-'gläs-tər, -ˌglòs-\ *noun* [*Gloucester*, England] (1816) : a firm mild orange-colored English cheese similar to cheddar

**dou·ble-head·er** \ˌdə-bəl-'he-dər\ *noun* (1878) **1** : a train pulled by two locomotives **2** : two games, contests, or events held consecutively on the same program

**double helix** *noun* (1954) : a helix or spiral consisting of two strands in the surface of a cylinder that coil around its axis; *especially* : the structural arrangement of DNA in space that consists of paired polynucleotide strands stabilized by cross-links between purine and pyrimidine bases — compare ALPHA-HELIX, WATSON-CRICK MODEL
— **dou·ble-he·li·cal** \-'he-li-kəl, -'hē-\ *adjective*

**double-hung** \ˌdə-bəl-'həŋ\ *adjective* (1823) *of a window* : having an upper and a lower sash that can slide vertically past each other

**double hyphen** *noun* (1893) : a punctuation mark ⸗ used in place of a hyphen at the end of a line to indicate that the word so divided is normally hyphenated

**double indemnity** *noun* (1924) : a provision in a life-insurance or accident policy whereby the company agrees to pay twice the face of the contract in case of accidental death

**double jeopardy** *noun* (1910)

: the putting of a person on trial for an offense for which he or she has previously been put on trial under a valid charge : two adjudications for one offense

**dou·ble-joint·ed** \ˌdə-bəl-'jòin-təd\ *adjective* (1831) : having a joint that permits an exceptional degree of freedom of motion of the parts joined

**double knit** *noun* (1895) : a knitted fabric (as wool) made with a double set of needles to produce a double thickness of fabric with each thickness joined by interlocking stitches; *also* : an article of clothing made of such fabric

**double negative** *noun* (1827) : a now substandard syntactic construction containing two negatives and having a negative meaning ⟨"I didn't hear nothing" is a *double negative*⟩ ■

**dou·ble-park** \ˌdə-bəl-'pärk\ (1936) *transitive verb* : to park (a vehicle) beside a row of vehicles already parked parallel to the curb *intransitive verb* : to double-park a vehicle

**double play** *noun* (1867) : a play in baseball by which two players are put out

**dou·ble-quick** \'də-bəl-ˌkwik\ *noun* (1834) : DOUBLE TIME 1; *broadly* : a rapid pace
— **double-quick** *adjective or adverb*

**double reed** *noun* (1876) : two reeds bound together with a slight separation between them so that air passing through them causes them to beat against one another and that are used as a sound-

□ USAGE
**double negative** The grammarian Otto Jespersen once observed that although negation is very important to the meaning of the sentence, it is often marked in an almost inconspicuous way—perhaps only by an unstressed particle like *-n't*. Hence there has long been a tendency to strengthen the negative idea by adding more negative elements to the sentence. This multiple negation is known popularly as the *double negative*. Multiple negation occurs in Chaucer, and it continued in common use at least through Shakespeare's time ⟨no woman has; nor never none shall mistress be of it —*Twelfth Night*⟩ and the ordinary double negative into the early 18th century ⟨lost no time, nor abated no Diligence —Daniel DeFoe ⟨*Robinson Crusoe,* 1719⟩⟩. During the 18th century it began to drop out of use in writing but continued in familiar use—conversation and letters. Thus grammarians, seeing it in older literature but not in current literature, decided that it was obsolete. Later grammarians were content to call it wrong. More important than the strictures of the grammarians was the perception that it was associated with the lower classes, both rural and urban, and hence was a construction to be avoided by the socially ambitious. The current status of the double negative remains much the same, confined to the most familiar discourse of those who choose to use it ⟨as you know, Ez hasn't changed none —Archibald MacLeish ⟨letter⟩⟩ and used as an everyday form only in the speech of less educated people and of some educated people who are comfortable with it. It is not a prestige form, even though it may be used on occasion for effect ⟨the sailplane sure ain't no 747! —Susan Ochshorn ⟨*Saturday Rev.*⟩⟩.

\ə\ **abut** \ᵊ\ **kitten** \ər\ **further** \a\ **ash** \ā\ **ace** \ä\ **mop, mar** \aú\ **out** \ch\ **chin** \e\ **bet** \ē\ **easy** \g\ **go** \i\ **hit** \ī\ **ice** \j\ **job** \ŋ\ **sing** \ō\ **go** \ó\ **law** \ói\ **boy** \th\ **thin** \t͟h\ **the** \ü\ **loot** \ù\ **foot** \y\ **yet** \zh\ **vision** *see also* Guide to Pronunciation producing device in certain woodwind instruments (as members of the oboe family)

**double refraction** *noun* (1831)
: BIREFRINGENCE

**dou·ble–ring** \'də-bəl-,riŋ\ *adjective* (circa 1959)
: of or relating to a wedding ceremony in which each partner ceremonially gives the other a wedding ring while reciting vows

**double salt** *noun* (circa 1849)
: a salt (as an alum) yielding on hydrolysis two different cations or anions

**dou·ble–space** \,də-bəl-'spās\ (circa 1937) *transitive verb*
: to type (text) leaving alternate lines blank *intransitive verb*
: to type on every other line

**dou·ble·speak** \'də-bəl-,spēk\ *noun* (1952)
: language used to deceive usually through concealment or misrepresentation of truth; *also* : GOBBLEDYGOOK
— **dou·ble·speak·er** \-,spē-kər\ *noun*

**double standard** *noun* (1894)
**1** : BIMETALLISM
**2** : a set of principles that applies differently and usually more rigorously to one group of people or circumstances than to another; *especially* : a code of morals that applies more severe standards of sexual behavior to women than to men

**double star** *noun* (1781)
**1** : BINARY STAR
**2** : two stars in very nearly the same line of sight but actually physically separate

**dou·ble–stop** \,də-bəl-'stäp\ *transitive verb* (circa 1889)
: to produce two or more tones simultaneously on (as a violin)
— **double–stop** *noun*

**double sugar** *noun* (1956)
: DISACCHARIDE

**dou·blet** \'dəb-lət\ *noun* [Middle English, from Middle French, from *double*] (14th century)
**1** : a man's close-fitting jacket worn in Europe especially during the Renaissance
**2** : something consisting of two identical or similar parts: as **a** : a lens consisting of two components; *especially* : a handheld magnifier consisting of two lenses in a metal cylinder **b** : a spectrum line having two close components **c** : a domino with the same number of spots on each end
**3** : a set of two identical or similar things: as **a** : two thrown dice with the same number of spots on the upper face **b** : one of nine pairs of microtubules found in cilia and flagella
**4** : one of a pair; *specifically* : one of two or more words (as *guard* and *ward*) in the language derived by different routes of transmission from the same source

*doublet 1*

**dou·ble take** \'də-bəl-,tāk\ *noun* (1930)
: a delayed reaction to a surprising or significant situation after an initial failure to notice anything unusual — usually used in the phrase *do a double take*

**dou·ble–talk** \-,tök\ *noun* (1936)
**1** : language that appears to be earnest and meaningful but in fact is a mixture of sense and nonsense
**2** : inflated, involved, and often deliberately ambiguous language
— **dou·ble–talk** *intransitive verb*
— **dou·ble–talk·er** *noun*

**dou·ble–team** \-,tēm\ *transitive verb* (1860)
: to block or guard (an opponent) with two players at one time

**Double Ten** *noun* [translation of Chinese (Beijing) *shuāngshí*; from its being the tenth day of the tenth month] (1940)

: October 10 observed by the Republic of China in commemoration of the revolution of 1911

**dou·ble·think** \'də-bəl-,thiŋk\ *noun* (1949)
: a simultaneous belief in two contradictory ideas

**dou·ble–time** \'də-bəl-,tīm\ *intransitive verb* (1943)
: to move at double time

**double time** *noun* (1853)
**1** : a marching cadence of 180 36-inch steps per minute
**2** : payment of a worker at twice the regular wage rate

**dou·ble·ton** \'də-bəl-tən\ *noun* [*double* + *-ton* (as in *singleton*)] (circa 1894)
: two cards that are the only ones of their suit originally dealt to a player — compare SINGLETON 1, VOID 4

**dou·ble–tongue** \,də-bəl-'təŋ\ *intransitive verb* (circa 1900)
: to cause the tongue to alternate rapidly between the positions for *t* and *k* so as to produce a fast succession of detached notes on a wind instrument

**dou·ble–u** \as at w\ *noun* (1840)
: the letter *w*

**double up** *intransitive verb* (1789)
: to share accommodations designed for one

**double vision** *noun* (circa 1860)
: DIPLOPIA

**double whammy** *noun* (1951)
: a combination of two usually adverse forces, circumstances, or effects

**double–wide** \,də-bəl-'wīd\ *noun* (1970)
: a mobile home consisting of two units which have been fastened together along their length

**dou·bloon** \,də-'blün\ *noun* [Spanish *doblón*, augmentative of *dobla*, an old Spanish coin, from Latin *dupla*, feminine of *duplus* double — more at DOUBLE] (1622)
: an old gold coin of Spain and Spanish America

**dou·bly** \'də-b(ə-)lē\ *adverb* (15th century)
**1** : in a twofold manner
**2** : to twice the degree

**¹doubt** \'daút\ *verb* [alteration of Middle English *douten*, from Old French *douter* to doubt, from Latin *dubitare*; akin to Latin *dubius* dubious] (13th century) *transitive verb*
**1** *archaic* **a** : FEAR **b** : SUSPECT
**2** : to be in doubt about ⟨he *doubts* everyone's word⟩
**3 a** : to lack confidence in : DISTRUST ⟨find myself *doubting* him even when I know that he is honest —H. L. Mencken⟩ **b** : to consider unlikely ⟨I *doubt* if I can go⟩ *intransitive verb*
: to be uncertain
— **doubt·able** \'daú-tə-bəl\ *adjective*
— **doubt·er** *noun*
— **doubt·ing·ly** \-tiŋ-lē\ *adverb*

**²doubt** *noun* (13th century)
**1 a** : uncertainty of belief or opinion that often interferes with decision-making **b** : a deliberate suspension of judgment
**2** : a state of affairs giving rise to uncertainty, hesitation, or suspense
**3 a** : a lack of confidence : DISTRUST **b** : an inclination not to believe or accept
**synonym** see UNCERTAINTY
— **no doubt** : ¹DOUBTLESS

**doubt·ful** \'daút-fəl\ *adjective* (14th century)
**1** : giving rise to doubt : open to question ⟨it is *doubtful* that they ever knew what happened⟩
**2 a** : lacking a definite opinion, conviction, or determination ⟨they were *doubtful* about the advantages of the new system⟩ **b** : uncertain in outcome : UNDECIDED ⟨the outcome of the election remains *doubtful*⟩
**3** : marked by qualities that raise doubts about worth, honesty, or validity ⟨of *doubtful* repute⟩
☆
— **doubt·ful·ly** \-fə-lē\ *adverb*
— **doubt·ful·ness** *noun*

**doubting Thom·as** \-'tä-məs\ *noun* [Saint *Thomas*, apostle who doubted Jesus' resurrection until he had proof of it (John 20:24–29)] (1883)
: a habitually doubtful person

**¹doubt·less** \'daút-ləs\ *adverb* (14th century)
**1** : without doubt
**2** : PROBABLY

**²doubtless** *adjective* (14th century)
: free from doubt : CERTAIN
— **doubt·less·ly** *adverb*
— **doubt·less·ness** *noun*

**douce** \'düs\ *adjective* [Middle English, sweet, pleasant, from Middle French, from feminine of *douz*, from Latin *dulcis* sweet — more at DULCET] (1721)
*chiefly Scottish* : SOBER, SEDATE ⟨the *douce* faces of the mourners —L. J. A. Bell⟩
— **douce·ly** *adverb, chiefly Scottish*

**dou·ceur** \dü-'sər\ *noun* [French, pleasantness, from Late Latin *dulcor* sweetness, from Latin *dulcis*] (1763)
: a conciliatory gift

**douche** \'düsh\ *noun* [French, from Italian *doccia*, from *docciare* to douche, from *doccia* water pipe, probably back-formation from *doccione* conduit, from Latin *duction-, ductio* means of conveying water, from *ducere* to lead — more at TOW] (1766)
**1 a** : a jet or current especially of water directed against a part or into a cavity of the body **b** : an act of cleansing with a douche
**2** : a device for giving douches
**3** *British* : a rude awakening ⟨the icy *douche* (what he said about my work) —John Fowles⟩
— **douche** *verb*

**douche bag** *noun* (circa 1963)
*slang* : an unattractive or offensive person

**dough** \'dō\ *noun* [Middle English *dogh*, from Old English *dāg*; akin to Old High German *teic* dough, Latin *fingere* to shape, Greek *teichos* wall] (before 12th century)
**1** : a mixture that consists essentially of flour or meal and a liquid (as milk or water) and is stiff enough to knead or roll
**2** : something resembling dough especially in consistency
**3** : MONEY
**4** : DOUGHBOY
— **dough·like** \-,līk\ *adjective*

**dough box** *noun* (circa 1944)
: a rectangular wooden box mounted on legs that is used as a worktable and storage box

**dough·boy** \-,bói\ *noun* (1865)
: an American infantryman especially in World War I

**dough·face** \-,fās\ *noun* (1830)
: a Northern congressman not opposed to slavery in the South before or during the Civil War; *also* : a Northerner sympathetic to the South during the same period
— **dough–faced** \-'fāst\ *adjective*

**dough·nut** \-(,)nət\ *noun* (circa 1809)
**1** : a small usually ring-shaped cake fried in fat

☆ SYNONYMS
**Doubtful, dubious, problematic, questionable** mean not affording assurance of the worth, soundness, or certainty of something. DOUBTFUL implies little more than a lack of conviction or certainty ⟨*doubtful* about whether I said the right thing⟩. DUBIOUS stresses suspicion, mistrust, or hesitation ⟨*dubious* about the practicality of the scheme⟩. PROBLEMATIC applies especially to things whose existence, meaning, fulfillment, or realization is highly uncertain ⟨whether the project will ever be finished is *problematic*⟩. QUESTIONABLE may imply no more than the existence of doubt but usually suggests that the suspicions are well-grounded ⟨a man of *questionable* honesty⟩.

**2 :** something (as a mathematical torus) that resembles a doughnut especially in shape
— **dough·nut·like** \-,līk\ *adjective*

**dough·ty** \'daú-tē\ *adjective* **dough·ti·er; -est** [Middle English, from Old English *dohtig;* akin to Old High German *toug* is useful, Greek *teuchein* to make] (before 12th century)
**:** marked by fearless resolution **:** VALIANT
— **dough·ti·ly** \'daú-t°l-ē\ *adverb*
— **dough·ti·ness** \'daú-tē-nəs\ *noun*

**doughy** \'dō-ē\ *adjective* **dough·i·er; -est** (1601)
**:** resembling dough: as **a :** not thoroughly baked **b :** unhealthily pale **:** PASTY

**Doug·las fir** \,də-gləs-\ *noun* [David *Douglas* (died 1834) Scottish botanist] (1873)
**:** any of a genus (*Pseudotsuga*) of tall evergreen timber trees having thick bark, pitchy wood, and pendulous cones; *especially* **:** one (*P. menziesii* synonym *P. taxifolia*) of the western U.S.

**Dou·kho·bor** \'dü-kə-,bór\ *noun* [Russian *dukhobor, dukhoborets,* from *dukh* spirit + *borets* wrestler] (1876)
**:** a member of a Christian sect of 18th century Russian origin emphasizing the duty of obeying the inner light and rejecting church or civil authority

**do up** *transitive verb* (1666)
**1 :** to prepare (as by cleaning or repairing) for wear or use ⟨*do up* a shirt⟩
**2 a :** to wrap up ⟨*do up* a package⟩ **b :** PUT UP, CAN
**3 a :** to deck out **:** CLOTHE **b :** to furnish with something ornamental **:** DECORATE
**4 :** EXHAUST, WEAR OUT

**dour** \'dú(-ə)r, 'daú(-ə)r\ *adjective* [Middle English, from Latin *durus* hard — more at DURING] (14th century)
**1 :** STERN, HARSH
**2 :** OBSTINATE, UNYIELDING
**3 :** GLOOMY, SULLEN
— **dour·ly** *adverb*
— **dour·ness** *noun*

**dou·rou·cou·li** \,dúr-ə-'kü-lē\ *noun* [French, from an unidentified American Indian language of Venezuela] (1842)
**:** any of several small nocturnal monkeys (genus *Aotus*) of tropical America that have round heads, large eyes, and densely furred bodies

**¹douse** \'daús *also* 'daúz\ *verb* **doused; dous·ing** [perhaps from obsolete English *douse* (to smite)] (1600)
*transitive verb*
**1 :** to plunge into water
**2 a :** to throw a liquid on **:** DRENCH **b :** SLOSH
**3 :** EXTINGUISH ⟨*douse* the lights⟩
*intransitive verb*
**:** to fall or become plunged into water
— **dous·er** *noun*

**²douse** \'daús *also* 'daúz\ *noun* (1881)
**:** a heavy drenching

**³douse** \'düs, 'daús\ *noun* [origin unknown] (circa 1625)
*British* **:** BLOW, STROKE

**⁴douse** \'daús\ *transitive verb* **doused; dous·ing** (1627)
**1 a :** FURL ⟨*douse* a sail⟩ **b :** SLACKEN ⟨*douse* a rope⟩
**2 :** TAKE OFF, DOFF

**doux** \'dü\ *adjective* [French, literally, sweet, from Old French *douz* — more at DOUCE] (circa 1943)
*of champagne* **:** very sweet

**¹dove** \'dəv\ *noun* [Middle English, from (assumed) Old English *dūfe;* akin to Old High German *tūba* dove] (13th century)
**1 :** any of numerous pigeons; *especially* **:** a small wild pigeon
**2 :** a gentle woman or child
**3 :** one who takes a conciliatory attitude and advocates negotiations and compromise; *especially* **:** an opponent of war — compare HAWK
— **dov·ish** \'də-vish\ *adjective*
— **dov·ish·ness** *noun*

**²dove** \'dōv\ *past of* DIVE

**dove·cote** \'dəv-,kōt, -,kät\ *also* **dove·cot** \-,kät\ *noun* (15th century)
**1 :** a small compartmented raised house or box for domestic pigeons
**2 :** a settled or harmonious group or organization

**dove·kie** \'dəv-kē\ *noun* [diminutive of *dove*] (1821)
**:** a small short-billed auk (*Alle alle*) breeding on arctic coasts and ranging south in winter

**doven** *variant of* DAVEN

**Dover sole** *noun* [probably from *Dover,* England] (circa 1911)
**1 :** a common European sole (*Solea solea*) esteemed as a food fish
**2 :** a brownish blotched flatfish (*Microstomus pacificus*) of the Pacific coast of North America that is a market fish in California

**Do·ver's powder** \,dō-vərz-\ *noun* [Thomas *Dover* (died 1742) English physician] (1801)
**:** a powder of ipecac and opium and used as a pain reliever and diaphoretic

**¹dove·tail** \'dəv-,tāl\ *noun* (1573)
**:** something resembling a dove's tail; *especially* **:** a flaring tenon and a mortise into which it fits tightly making an interlocking joint between two pieces (as of wood)

**²dovetail** (circa 1656)
*transitive verb*
**1 a :** to join by means of dovetails **b :** to cut to a dovetail
**2 a :** to fit skillfully to form a whole **b :** to fit together with
*intransitive verb*
**:** to fit together into a whole

dovetail: *1* mortises, *2* tenons, *3* joint

**dow** \'daú\ *intransitive verb* **dought** \'daút\ *or* **dowed** \'daúd\; **dow·ing** [Middle English *dow, deih* have worth, am able, from Old English *dēah, dēag;* akin to Old High German *toug* is worthy, is useful — more at DOUGHTY] (before 12th century)
*chiefly Scottish* **:** to be able or capable

**Dow** \'daú\ *noun* (1949)
**:** DOW-JONES AVERAGE

**dow·a·ger** \'daú-i-jər\ *noun* [Middle French *douagiere,* from *douage* dower, from *douer* to endow, from Latin *dotare,* from *dot-, dos* gift, dower — more at DATE] (1530)
**1 :** a widow holding property or a title from her deceased husband
**2 :** a dignified elderly woman

**dowager's hump** *noun* (1948)
**:** an abnormal curvature of the upper back with round shoulders and stooped posture caused especially by bone loss and anterior compression of the vertebrae in osteoporosis

**¹dowdy** \'daú-dē\ *noun, plural* **dowd·ies** [diminutive of *dowd* (dowdy), from Middle English *doude*] (1581)
*archaic* **:** a dowdy woman

**²dowdy** *adjective* **dowd·i·er; -est** (1676)
**1 :** not neat or becoming in appearance **:** SHABBY
**2 a :** lacking smartness or taste **b :** OLD-FASHIONED
— **dowd·i·ly** \'daú-d°l-ē\ *adverb*
— **dowd·i·ness** \'daú-dē-nəs\ *noun*
— **dowdy·ish** \-ish\ *adjective*

**³dowdy** *noun* [origin unknown] (1936)
**:** PANDOWDY

**¹dow·el** \'daú(-ə)l\ *noun* [Middle English *dowle;* akin to Old High German *tubili* plug, Late Greek *typhos* wedge] (14th century)
**1 :** a pin fitting into a hole in an abutting piece to prevent motion or slipping; *also* **:** a round rod or stick used especially for cutting up into dowels
**2 :** a piece of wood driven into a wall so that other pieces can be nailed to it

**²dowel** *transitive verb* **-elled** *also* **-eled; -elling** *also* **-eling** (1713)
**:** to fasten by or furnish with dowels

**¹dow·er** \'daú(-ə)r\ *noun* [Middle English *dowere,* from Middle French *douaire,* modification of Medieval Latin *dotarium* — more at DOWRY] (14th century)
**1 :** the part of or interest in the real estate of a deceased husband given by law to his widow during her life — compare CURTESY
**2 :** DOWRY 2, 3

**²dower** *transitive verb* (1605)
**:** to supply with a dower or dowry **:** ENDOW

**dow·itch·er** \'daú-i-chər\ *noun, plural* **dow·itchers** *also* **dowitcher** [probably of Iroquoian origin; akin to Oneida *tawístawis* dowitcher] (1841)
**:** any of several long-billed wading birds (especially *Limnodromus griseus* and *L. scolopaceus* of the family Scolopacidae) related to the sandpipers

**Dow–Jones average** \,daú-'jōnz-\ *noun* [Charles H. *Dow* (died 1902) & Edward D. *Jones* (died 1920) American financial statisticians] (1922)
**:** an index of the relative price of securities

**¹down** \'daún\ *adverb* [Middle English *doun,* from Old English *dūne,* short for *adūne, of dūne,* from *a-* (from *of*), *of* off, from + *dūne,* dative of *dūn* hill] (before 12th century)
**1 a** (1) **:** toward or in a lower physical position (2) **:** to a lying or sitting position (3) **:** toward or to the ground, floor, or bottom **b :** as a down payment ⟨paid $10 *down*⟩ **c :** on paper ⟨put *down* what he says⟩
**2 :** in a direction that is the opposite of up: as **a :** SOUTHWARD **b :** to or toward a point away from the speaker or the speaker's point of reference
**3 :** to a lesser degree, level, or rate ⟨cool *down* tensions⟩
**4 :** to or toward a lower position in a series
**5 a :** to or in a lower or worse condition or status **b** — used to indicate completion ⟨dusted *down* the house⟩
**6 :** from a past time
**7 :** to or in a state of less activity or prominence
**8 :** to a concentrated state ⟨got the report *down* to three pages⟩
**9 :** into defeat ⟨voted the motion *down*⟩
— **down to the ground :** PERFECTLY, COMPLETELY ⟨that suits me *down to the ground*⟩

**²down** *preposition* (14th century)
**:** down along, around, through, toward, in, into, or on ⟨fell *down* the stairs⟩ ⟨*down* the years⟩

**³down** (1562)
*transitive verb*
**1 :** to cause to go or come down
**2 :** to cause (a football) to be out of play
**3 :** DEFEAT
*intransitive verb*
**:** to go down

**⁴down** *adjective* (circa 1565)
**1 a** (1) **:** occupying a low position; *specifically* **:** lying on the ground ⟨*down* timber⟩ (2) **:** directed or going downward ⟨attendance is *down*⟩ **b :** lower in price **c :** not being in play in football because of wholly stopped progress or because the officials stop the play **d :** defeated or trailing an opponent (as in points scored) ⟨*down* by two runs⟩ **e** *baseball* **:** OUT
**2 a :** reduced or low in activity or intensity ⟨a *down* economy⟩ **b :** not operating or able to function ⟨the computer is *down*⟩ **c :** DEPRESSED, DEJECTED; *also* **:** DEPRESSING ⟨a *down* movie⟩ **d :** SICK ⟨*down* with flu⟩

**3 :** DONE, FINISHED ⟨eight *down* and two to go⟩
**4 :** completely mastered ⟨had her lines *down*⟩ — often used with *pat*
**5** *slang* : COOL 7 ⟨a *down* dude⟩
**6 :** being a quark with an electric charge of −⅓, zero charm, and zero strangeness ⟨a *down* quark⟩ — compare ²UP 5
**7 :** being on record ⟨you're *down* for two tickets⟩
— **down on :** having a low opinion of or dislike for
⁵**down** *noun* (1710)
**1 :** DESCENT, DEPRESSION
**2 :** an instance of putting down
**3 a :** a complete play to advance the ball in football **b :** one of a series of four attempts in American football or three attempts in Canadian football to advance the ball 10 yards
**4** *chiefly British* : DISLIKE, GRUDGE
**5 :** DOWNER
⁶**down** *noun* [Middle English *doun* hill, from Old English *dūn*] (14th century)
**1 :** an undulating usually treeless upland with sparse soil — usually used in plural
**2** *often capitalized* : a sheep of any breed originating in the downs of southern England
⁷**down** *noun* [Middle English *doun*, from Old Norse *dūnn*] (14th century)
**1 :** a covering of soft fluffy feathers; *also* : these feathers
**2 :** something soft and fluffy like down
**down and dirty** *adjective or adverb* (1967)
**1 :** UNVARNISHED ⟨the *down and dirty* truth⟩
**2 :** made or done hastily : not revised or polished
**3 :** marked by fierce competition
**4 :** BAWDY
**5 :** SEEDY 2
**down–and–out** \ˌdaü-nən-'(d)aüt\ *adjective* (1901)
**1 :** DESTITUTE, IMPOVERISHED
**2 :** physically weakened or incapacitated
— **down–and–out** *or* **down–and–out·er** \-'(d)aüt-ər\ *noun*
**down–at–the–heels** \ˌdaü-nət-ₜhə-'hē(ə)lz, -nət-\ *or* **down–at–heel** \-nət-'hē(ə)l\ *also* **down–at–the–heel** \-thə-'hē(ə)l\ *or* **down–at–heels** \-nət-'hē(ə)lz\ *adjective* (1732)
**:** SHABBY
¹**down·beat** \'daün-ˌbēt\ *noun* (1876)
**1 :** the downward stroke of a conductor indicating the principally accented note of a measure of music; *also* : the first beat of a measure
**2 :** a decline in activity or prosperity
²**downbeat** *adjective* (1950)
**:** PESSIMISTIC, GLOOMY
**down–bow** \'daün-ˌbō\ *noun* (circa 1889)
**:** a stroke in playing a bowed instrument (as a violin) in which the bow is drawn across the strings from the frog to the tip
**down·burst** \-ˌbərst\ *noun* (1978)
**:** a powerful downdraft usually associated with a thunderstorm that strikes the ground and deflects in all directions and that constitutes a hazard especially for low-flying aircraft; *also* **:** MICROBURST
**down·cast** \'daün-ˌkast\ *adjective* (14th century)
**1 :** low in spirit : DEJECTED
**2 :** directed downward ⟨with *downcast* eyes⟩
**down·court** \-'kōrt, -'kòrt\ *adverb or adjective* (1952)
**:** in or into the opposite end of the court (as in basketball)
**down·draft** \-ˌdraft\ *noun* (1849)
**:** a downward current of gas (as air during a thunderstorm)
**down east** *adverb, often D&E capitalized* (1825)
**:** in or into the northeast coastal section of the U.S. and parts of the Maritime Provinces of Canada; *specifically* **:** in or into coastal Maine

— **down east** *adjective, often D&E capitalized*
**down–east·er** \daü-'nē-stər\ *noun, often D&E capitalized* (1827)
**:** one born or living down east
**down·er** \'daü-nər\ *noun* (1966)
**1 :** a depressant drug; *especially* **:** BARBITURATE
**2 :** someone or something depressing
**down·fall** \'daün-ˌfòl\ *noun* (13th century)
**1 a :** a sudden fall (as from power) **b :** a fall (as of snow or rain) especially when sudden or heavy
**2 :** something that causes a downfall (as of a person)
— **down·fall·en** \-ˌfò-lən\ *adjective*
**down·field** \-'fē(ə)ld\ *adverb or adjective* (1944)
**:** in or into the part of the field toward which the offensive team is headed
¹**down·grade** \'daün-ˌgrād\ *noun* (1858)
**1 :** a downward grade (as of a road)
**2 :** a descent toward an inferior state ⟨a career on the *downgrade*⟩
²**downgrade** *transitive verb* (1930)
**1 :** MINIMIZE, DEPRECIATE
**2 :** to lower in quality, value, status, or extent
**down·haul** \'daün-ˌhòl\ *noun* (1669)
**:** a rope or line for hauling down or holding down a sail or spar
**down·heart·ed** \-'här-təd\ *adjective* (circa 1774)
**:** DOWNCAST, DEJECTED
— **down·heart·ed·ly** *adverb*
— **down·heart·ed·ness** *noun*
¹**down·hill** \'daün-'hil\ *adverb* (14th century)
**1 :** toward the bottom of a hill
**2 :** toward a worsened or inferior state or level — used especially in the phrase *go downhill*
²**down·hill** \'daün-ˌhil\ *noun* (1591)
**1 :** a descending slope
**2 :** a skiing race against time down a trail — often used attributively
³**down·hill** \-ˌhil\ *adjective* (1727)
**1 :** sloping downhill
**2 :** closer to the bottom of an incline ⟨your *downhill* ski⟩
**3 :** not difficult : EASY ⟨after that problem the rest was *downhill*⟩
**4 :** progressively worse
**down·hill·er** \-hi-lər\ *noun* (1967)
**:** a downhill skier
**down–home** \'daün-ˌhōm\ *adjective* (1938)
**:** of, relating to, or having qualities (as informality and simplicity) associated with rural or small-town people especially of the Southern U.S. ⟨*down-home* country cooking⟩; *broadly* **:** SIMPLE, UNPRETENTIOUS
**down in the mouth** *adjective* (1649)
**:** DEJECTED 1
**down·land** \'daün-ˌland\ *noun* (before 12th century)
**:** ⁶DOWN 1
**down·link** \'daün-ˌliŋk\ *noun* (circa 1969)
**:** a communications channel for receiving transmissions from a spacecraft; *also* **:** such transmissions
**down·load** \'daün-ˌlōd\ *transitive verb* (1980)
**:** to transfer (data) from a usually large computer to the memory of another device (as a smaller computer)
— **down·load·able** \-ˌlō-də-bəl\ *adjective*
**down–market** \'daün-ˌmär-kət\ *adjective* (1970)
**:** relating or appealing to lower-income consumers
**down payment** *noun* (1926)
**:** a part of the full price paid at the time of purchase or delivery with the balance to be paid later; *broadly* **:** the first step in a process
**down·pipe** \'daün-ˌpīp\ *noun* (1858)
*British* **:** DOWNSPOUT
**down·play** \'daün-ˌplā\ *transitive verb* (1954)
**:** PLAY DOWN, DE-EMPHASIZE

**down·pour** \-ˌpōr, -ˌpòr\ *noun* (1811)
**:** a pouring or streaming downward; *especially* **:** a heavy rain
**down·range** \-'rānj\ *adverb* (1952)
**:** away from a launching site
¹**down·right** \-ˌrīt\ *adverb* (13th century)
**1** *archaic* **:** straight down
**2 :** ABSOLUTELY 1 ⟨*downright* handsome⟩ ⟨*downright* mean⟩
**3** *obsolete* **:** FORTHRIGHT
²**downright** *adjective* (1530)
**1** *archaic* **:** directed vertically downward
**2 :** OUTRIGHT, THOROUGH ⟨a *downright* lie⟩
**3 :** PLAIN, BLUNT ⟨stories he had heard of her *downright* tongue —Angus Wilson⟩
— **down·right·ly** *adverb*
— **down·right·ness** *noun*
**down·riv·er** \'daün-'ri-vər\ *adverb or adjective* (1852)
**:** toward or at a point nearer the mouth of a river
¹**down·scale** \'daün-ˌskāl\ *transitive verb* **down·scaled; down·scal·ing** (1945)
**:** to cut back in size or scope ⟨the recession forced us to *downscale* vacation plans⟩
²**downscale** *adjective* (circa 1966)
**:** lower in class, income, or quality
**down·shift** \-ˌshift\ *intransitive verb* (1955)
**:** to shift an automotive vehicle into a lower gear
— **downshift** *noun*
**down·side** \'daün-ˌsīd\ *noun* (1946)
**1 :** a downward trend (as of prices)
**2 :** a negative aspect ⟨the *downside* of fame⟩
**down·size** \'daün-ˌsīz\ (1975) *transitive verb*
**:** to reduce in size; *especially* **:** to design or produce in smaller size
*intransitive verb*
**:** to undergo a reduction in size
**down·slide** \'daün-ˌslīd\ *noun* (1926)
**:** a downward movement
**down·slope** \'daün-ˌslōp\ *adjective or adverb* (1928)
**:** toward the bottom of a slope
**down·spout** \'daün-ˌspaüt\ *noun* (circa 1896)
**:** a vertical pipe used to drain rainwater from a roof
**Down's syndrome** \'daün(z)-\ *noun* [J. L. H. *Down* (died 1896) English physician] (1961)
**:** a congenital condition characterized by moderate to severe mental retardation, slanting eyes, a broad short skull, broad hands with short fingers, and trisomy of the human chromosome numbered 21 — called also *Down's, Down syndrome*
¹**down·stage** \'daün-'stāj\ *adverb or adjective* (1898)
**1 :** toward or at the front of a theatrical stage
**2 :** toward a motion-picture or television camera
²**down·stage** \-ˌstāj\ *noun* (circa 1931)
**:** the part of a stage that is nearest the audience or camera
¹**down·stairs** \'daün-'starz, -'sterz\ *adverb* (1596)
**:** down the stairs **:** on or to a lower floor
²**down·stairs** \'daün-ˌstarz, -ˌsterz\ *adjective* (1819)
**:** situated on the main, lower, or ground floor of a building
³**down·stairs** \'daün-', 'daün-ˌ\ *noun plural but singular or plural in construction* (1843)
**:** the lower floor of a building
**down·state** \-ˌstāt\ *noun* (1909)
**:** the chiefly southerly sections of a state; *also* **:** the chiefly rural part of a state when the major metropolitan area is to the north
— **down·state** \-'stāt\ *adjective or adverb*
— **down·stat·er** \-'stā-tər\ *noun*
**down·stream** \'daün-'strēm\ *adverb or adjective* (1706)
**1 :** in the direction of or nearer to the mouth of a stream

**2 :** in or toward the latter stages of a usually industrial process or the stages (as marketing) after manufacture

**down·stroke** \-ˌstrōk\ *noun* (1852)
: a downward stroke

**down·swing** \-ˌswiŋ\ *noun* (1899)
**1 :** a downward swing
**2 :** DOWNTREND

**down–the–line** *adjective* (1940)
: COMPLETE ⟨a *down-the-line* union supporter⟩

**down·time** \ˈdaṅn-ˌtīm\ *noun* (1928)
**1 :** time during which production is stopped especially during setup for an operation or when making repairs
**2 :** break time between periods of work ⟨napping during our *downtime*⟩

**down–to–earth** \ˌdaṅn-tə-'(w)ərth\ *adjective* (1932)
**1 :** PRACTICAL ⟨*down-to-earth* traveling tips⟩
**2 :** UNPRETENTIOUS ⟨surprised to find the movie star so *down-to-earth*⟩

**down–to–the–wire** \ˈdaṅn-tə-thə-'wīr\ *adjective* (1952)
**:** full of suspense; *especially* **:** unsettled until the very end

**down·town** \ˌdaṅn-'taṅn, 'daṅn-ˌ\ *noun* (1851)
: the lower part of a city; *especially* **:** the main business district — often used attributively
— **downtown** \ˌdaṅn-'taṅn\ *adverb*
— **down·town·er** \-'taṅ-nər\ *noun*

**down·trend** \-ˌtrend\ *noun* (1926)
**:** a downturn especially in business and economic activity

**down·trod·den** \ˈdaṅn-'trä-d°n\ *adjective* (1595)
**:** suffering oppression

**down·turn** \-ˌtərn\ *noun* (1926)
**:** a downward turn especially toward a decline in business activity

**down under** *adverb or adjective, often D&U capitalized* (1886)
**:** to or in Australia or New Zealand

**¹down·ward** \ˈdaṅn-wərd\ *or* **down·wards** \-wərdz\ *adverb* (13th century)
**1 a :** from a higher to a lower place **b :** toward a direction that is the opposite of up
**2 :** from a higher to a lower condition
**3 a :** from an earlier time **b :** from an ancestor or predecessor

**²downward** *adjective* (circa 1552)
**1 :** moving or extending downward
**2 :** descending from a head, origin, or source
— **down·ward·ly** *adverb*
— **down·ward·ness** *noun*

**down·wash** \ˈdaṅn-ˌwȯsh, -ˌwäsh\ *noun* (1915)
**:** an airstream directed downward (as by an airfoil)

**down·wind** \ˈdaṅn-'wind\ *adverb or adjective* (1855)
**:** in the direction that the wind is blowing

**downy** \ˈdaṅ-nē\ *adjective* **down·i·er; -est** (1578)
**1 :** resembling a bird's down
**2 :** covered with down
**3 :** made of down
**4 :** SOFT, SOOTHING

**downy mildew** *noun* (1886)
**1 :** any of various parasitic lower fungi (family Peronosporaceae) that produce whitish masses of sporangiophores or conidiophores on the undersurface of the leaves of the host
**2 :** a plant disease caused by a downy mildew

**downy woodpecker** *noun* (1808)
**:** a small black-and-white woodpecker (*Dendrocopos pubescens*) of North America that has a white back and is smaller than the hairy woodpecker

**dow·ry** \ˈdaṅ(-ə)-rē\ *noun, plural* **dowries** [Middle English *dowarie*, from Anglo-French, irregular from Medieval Latin *dotarium*, from Latin *dot-, dos* gift, marriage portion — more at DATE] (14th century)
**1** *archaic* **:** DOWER 1

**2 :** the money, goods, or estate that a woman brings to her husband in marriage
**3 :** a gift of money or property by a man to or for his bride
**4 :** a natural talent

**dowsabel** *noun* [*Dowsabel*, feminine name] (circa 1652)
*obsolete* **:** SWEETHEART

**¹dowse** *variant of* DOUSE

**²dowse** \ˈdaüz\ *verb* **dowsed; dows·ing** [origin unknown] (1894)
*intransitive verb*
**:** to use a divining rod
*transitive verb*
**:** to find (as water) by dowsing

**dows·er** \ˈdaü-zər\ *noun* (1838)
**:** DIVINING ROD; *also* **:** a person who uses it

**dowsing rod** *noun* (1691)
**:** DIVINING ROD

**dox·ol·o·gy** \däk-'sä-lə-jē\ *noun, plural* **-gies** [Medieval Latin *doxologia*, from Late Greek, from Greek *doxa* opinion, glory (from *dokein* to seem, seem good) + *-logia* -logy — more at DECENT] (1649)
**:** a usually liturgical expression of praise to God

**doxo·ru·bi·cin** \ˌdäk-sə-'rü-bə-sən\ *noun* [*deoxy-* + *-orubicin* (as in *daunorubicin*)] (circa 1977)
**:** an antibiotic with broad antitumor activity that is obtained from a bacterium (*Streptomyces peucetius*) and is administered as the hydrochloride $C_{27}H_{29}NO_{11} \cdot HCl$

**doxy** *also* **dox·ie** \ˈdäk-sē\ *noun, plural* **dox·ies** [perhaps modification of obsolete Dutch *docke* doll, from Middle Dutch] (circa 1530)
**1 :** FLOOZY, PROSTITUTE
**2 :** MISTRESS 4a

**doxy·cy·cline** \ˌdäk-sə-'sī-ˌklēn\ *noun* [*deoxy-* + *tetracycline*] (1966)
**:** a broad-spectrum tetracycline antibiotic $C_{22}H_{24}N_2O_8$ with potent antibacterial activity that is often taken orally as a prophylactic against diarrhea by travelers

**doy·en** \ˈdȯi-ən, -ˌ(y)en; 'dwä-ˌyaⁿ(n)\ *noun* [French, from Late Latin *decanus* dean — more at DEAN] (1670)
**1 a :** the senior member of a body or group **b :** a person considered to be knowledgeable or uniquely skilled as a result of long experience in some field of endeavor
**2 :** the oldest example of a category

**doy·enne** \dȯi-'(y)en, dwä-'yen\ *noun* [French, feminine of *doyen*] (circa 1897)
**:** a woman who is a doyen

**doy·ley** *chiefly British variant of* DOILY

**¹doze** \ˈdōz\ *verb* **dozed; doz·ing** [probably of Scandinavian origin; akin to Old Norse *dūsa* to doze] (1693)
*transitive verb*
**:** to pass (as time) drowsily
*intransitive verb*
**1 a :** to sleep lightly **b :** to fall into a light sleep — usually used with *off*
**2 :** to be in a dull or stupefied condition
— **doze** *noun*
— **doz·er** *noun*

**²doze** *transitive verb* **dozed; doz·ing** [probably back-formation from *dozer* (bulldozer)] (1945)
**:** BULLDOZE 2
— **doz·er** *noun*

**doz·en** \ˈdə-z°n\ *noun, plural* **dozens** *or* **dozen** [Middle English *dozeine*, from Middle French *dozaine*, from *doze* twelve, from Latin *duodecim*, from *duo* two + *decem* ten — more at TWO, TEN] (13th century)
**1 :** a group of 12
**2 :** an indefinitely large number ⟨*dozens* of times⟩
**3** *plural but singular in construction* **:** a ritualized word game that consists of exchanging insults usually about the members of the opponent's family — used with *the*

— **dozen** *adjective*
— **doz·enth** \-z°n(t)th\ *adjective*

**dozy** \ˈdō-zē\ *adjective* **doz·i·er; -est** (1693)
**:** DROWSY, SLEEPY
— **doz·i·ly** \ˈdō-zə-lē\ *adverb*
— **doz·i·ness** *noun*

**DP** \ˌdē-'pē\ *noun, plural* **DP's** *or* **DPs** (circa 1944)
**:** a displaced person

**DPN** \ˌdē-ˌpē-'en\ *noun* [*d*iphospho*p*yridine *n*ucleotide] (1938)
**:** NAD

**¹drab** \ˈdrab\ *noun* [origin unknown] (circa 1515)
**1 :** SLATTERN
**2 :** PROSTITUTE

**²drab** *intransitive verb* **drabbed; drab·bing** (1602)
**:** to associate with prostitutes

**³drab** *noun* [Middle French *drap* cloth, from Late Latin *drappus*] (1541)
**1 :** any of various cloths of a dull brown or gray color
**2 a :** a light olive brown **b :** a dull, lifeless, or faded appearance or quality

**⁴drab** *adjective* **drab·ber; drab·best** (1686)
**1 a :** of the dull brown color of drab **b :** of the color drab
**2 :** characterized by dullness and monotony **:** CHEERLESS
— **drab·ly** *adverb*
— **drab·ness** *noun*

**⁵drab** *noun* [probably alteration of *drib*] (1828)
**:** a small amount — usually used in the phrase *dribs and drabs*

**drab·ble** \ˈdra-bəl\ *verb* **drab·bled; drab·bling** \-b(ə-)liŋ\ [Middle English *drabelen*; akin to Low German *drabbelen*] (15th century)
*transitive verb*
**:** DRAGGLE
*intransitive verb*
**:** to become wet and muddy

**dra·cae·na** \drə-'sē-nə\ *noun* [New Latin, from Late Latin, she-serpent, from Greek *drakaina*, feminine of *drakōn* serpent — more at DRAGON] (circa 1823)
**:** any of two genera (*Dracaena* and *Cordyline*) of Old World tropical shrubs or trees of the agave family that have naked branches ending in tufts of sword-shaped leaves and include some used as houseplants

**drachm** \ˈdram\ *noun* [alteration of Middle English *dragme* — more at DRAM] (14th century)
**1 :** DRACHMA
**2** *chiefly British* **:** DRAM

**drach·ma** \ˈdrak-mə\ *noun, plural* **drach·mas** *or* **drach·mai** \-ˌmī\ *or* **drach·mae** \-ˌ(ˌ)mē, -ˌmī\ [Latin, from Greek *drachmē* — more at DRAM] (1525)
**1 a :** any of various ancient Greek units of weight **b :** any of various modern units of weight; *especially* **:** DRAM 1
**2 a :** an ancient Greek silver coin equivalent to 6 obols **b** — see MONEY table

**Dra·co** \ˈdrā-(ˌ)kō\ *noun* [Latin (genitive *Draconis*), literally, dragon — more at DRAGON]
**:** a northern circumpolar constellation within which is the north pole of the ecliptic

**dra·co·ni·an** \drā-'kō-nē-ən, drə-\ *adjective, often capitalized* [Latin *Dracon-, Draco*, from Greek *Drakōn* Draco (Athenian lawgiver)] (1876)
**1 :** of, relating to, or characteristic of Draco or the severe code of laws held to have been framed by him

\ə\ abut \ᵊ\ kitten \ər\ further \a\ ash \ā\ ace \ä\ mop, mar \aú\ out \ch\ chin \e\ bet \ē\ easy \g\ go \i\ hit \ī\ ice \j\ job \ŋ\ sing \ō\ go \ȯ\ law \ȯi\ boy \th\ thin \t̲h\ the \ü\ loot \ü\ foot \y\ yet \zh\ vision *see also* Guide to Pronunciation

**2** : CRUEL; *also* : SEVERE ⟨*draconian* littering fines⟩ ◆

**¹dra·con·ic** \drə-'kä-nik\ *adjective* [Latin *dracon-, draco*] (1680)
: of or relating to a dragon

**²dra·con·ic** \drā-'kä-nik, drə-\ *adjective* (1708)
: DRACONIAN

**¹draft** \'draft, 'dràft\ *noun* [Middle English *draght;* akin to Old English *dragan* to draw — more at DRAW] (13th century)
**1** : the act of drawing a net; *also* : the quantity of fish taken at one drawing
**2 a** : the act or an instance of drinking or inhaling; *also* : the portion drunk or inhaled in one such act **b** : a portion poured out or mixed for drinking : DOSE
**3 a** : the force required to pull an implement **b** : load or load-pulling capacity
**4 a** : the act of moving loads by drawing or pulling : PULL **b** : a team of animals together with what they draw
**5 a** : DELINEATION, REPRESENTATION **b** : SCHEME, DESIGN **c** : a preliminary sketch, outline, or version ⟨the author's first *draft*⟩ ⟨a *draft* treaty⟩
**6** : the act, result, or plan of drawing out or stretching
**7 a** : the act of drawing (as from a cask) **b** : a portion of liquid so drawn ⟨a *draft* of ale⟩ **c** : draft beer ⟨a glass of *draft*⟩
**8** : the depth of water a ship draws especially when loaded
**9 a** (1) : a system for or act of selecting individuals from a group (as for compulsory military service) (2) : an act or process of selecting an individual (as for political candidacy) without his expressed consent **b** : a group of individuals selected especially by military draft **c** : a system whereby exclusive rights to selected new players are apportioned among professional teams
**10 a** : an order for the payment of money drawn by one person or bank on another **b** : the act or an instance of drawing from or making demands upon something : DEMAND
**11 a** : a current of air in a closed-in space ⟨felt a *draft*⟩ **b** : a device for regulating the flow of air (as in a fireplace)
**12** : ANGLE, TAPER; *specifically* : the taper given to a pattern or die so that the work can be easily withdrawn
**13** : a pocket of reduced air pressure behind a moving object; *also* : the use of such a draft to save energy
— **on draft** : ready to be drawn from a receptacle ⟨beer *on draft*⟩

**²draft** *adjective* (15th century)
**1** : used or adapted for drawing loads ⟨*draft* horses⟩
**2** : being or having been on draft ⟨drinking *draft* beer⟩

**³draft** (1714)
*transitive verb*
**1** : to select for some purpose: as **a** : to conscript for military service **b** : to select (a professional athlete) by draft
**2 a** : to draw the preliminary sketch, version, or plan of **b** : COMPOSE, PREPARE
**3** : to draw off or away ⟨water *drafted* by pumps⟩
**4** : to stay close behind (another racer) so as to take advantage of the reduced air pressure created by the leading racer
*intransitive verb*
**1** : to practice draftsmanship
**2** : to draft another racer (as in car or bike racing)
— **draft·able** \'draf-tə-bəl, 'dràf-\ *adjective*
— **draft·ee** \draf-'tē, dràf-\ *noun*
— **draft·er** \'draf-tər, 'dràf-\ *noun*

**draft board** *noun* (1953)
: a civilian board that registers, classifies, and selects men for compulsory military service

**drafts·man** \'draf(t)s-mən, 'dràf(t)-\ *noun* (1663)

**1** : a person who draws plans and sketches (as of machinery or structures)
**2** : a person who draws legal documents or other writings
**3** : an artist who excels in drawing
— **drafts·man·ship** \-,ship\ *noun*

**drafts·person** \'draf(t)s-,pər-s°n\ *noun* (1975)
: DRAFTSMAN 1

**drafty** \'draf-tē, 'dràf-\ *adjective* **draft·i·er; -est** (1846)
: exposed to or abounding in drafts of air
— **draft·i·ly** \-tə-lē\ *adverb*
— **draft·i·ness** \-tē-nəs\ *noun*

**¹drag** \'drag\ *noun* (14th century)
**1** : something used to drag with; *especially* : a device for dragging under water to detect or obtain objects
**2** : something that is dragged, pulled, or drawn along or over a surface: as **a** : HARROW **b** : a sledge for conveying heavy bodies **c** : CONVEYANCE
**3 a** : the act or an instance of dragging or drawing: as (1) : a drawing along or over a surface with effort or pressure (2) : motion effected with slowness or difficulty; *also* : the condition of having or seeming to have such motion (3) : a draw on a pipe, cigarette, or cigar; *also* : a draft of liquid **b** : a movement, inclination, or retardation caused by or as if by dragging **c** *slang* : influence securing special favor : PULL
**4 a** : something that retards motion or action **b** (1) : the retarding force acting on a body (as an airplane) moving through a fluid (as air) parallel and opposite to the direction of motion (2) : friction between engine parts; *also* : retardation due to friction **c** : BURDEN, ENCUMBRANCE ⟨the *drag* of population growth on living standards⟩ ⟨maturity is a *drag*⟩ **d** : one that is boring or gets in the way of enjoyment ⟨this sickly kid is going to be a social *drag* —Edmund Morris⟩
**5 a** : an object drawn over the ground to leave a scented trail **b** : a clog fastened to a trap to prevent the escape of a trapped animal
**6** : STREET, ROAD ⟨the main *drag*⟩
**7 a** : COSTUME, OUTFIT ⟨in Victorian *drag*⟩ **b** : clothing typical of one sex worn by a person of the opposite sex — often used in the phrase *in drag*
**8** : DRAG RACE

**²drag** *verb* **dragged; drag·ging** [Middle English *draggen,* from Old Norse *draga* — more at DRAW] (15th century)
*transitive verb*
**1 a** (1) : to draw slowly or heavily : HAUL (2) : to cause to move with painful or undue slowness or difficulty ⟨*dragging* the national anthem⟩ (3) : to cause to trail along a surface ⟨wandered off *dragging* the leash⟩ **b** (1) : to bring by or as if by force or compulsion ⟨had to *drag* her husband to the opera⟩ (2) : to extract by or as if by pulling **c** : PROTRACT ⟨*drag* a story out⟩
**2 a** : to explore with a drag **b** : to catch with a dragnet
**3** : to hit (a drag bunt) while moving toward first base
*intransitive verb*
**1** : to hang or lag behind
**2** : to fish or search with a drag
**3** : to trail along on the ground
**4** : to move or proceed laboriously or tediously ⟨the lawsuit *dragged* on for years⟩ ⟨was *dragging* after the long trip⟩
**5** : DRAW 4a ⟨*drag* on a cigarette⟩
**6** : to make a plucking or pulling movement
**7** : to participate in a drag race
— **drag·ging·ly** \'dra-giŋ-lē\ *adverb*
— **drag one's feet** *also* **drag one's heels** : to act in a deliberately slow or dilatory manner

**³drag** *adjective* (1887)
: of, being, involving, or intended for a person in drag ⟨a *drag* ball⟩

**drag bunt** *noun* (circa 1949)

: a bunt in baseball made by a left-handed batter by trailing the bat while moving toward first base; *broadly* : a bunt made with the object of getting on base safely rather than sacrificing

**drag coefficient** *noun* (circa 1942)
: a factor representing the drag acting on a body (as an automobile or airfoil)

**dra·gée** \dra-'zhā\ *noun* [French, from Middle French *dragie* — more at DREDGE] (1853)
**1** : a sugar-coated nut
**2** : a small silver-colored ball for decorating cakes

**drag·ger** \'dra-gər\ *noun* (circa 1500)
: one that drags; *specifically* : a fishing boat operating a trawl or dragnet

**drag·gle** \'dra-gəl\ *verb* **drag·gled; drag·gling** \-g(ə-)liŋ\ [frequentative of *drag*] (1513)
*transitive verb*
: to make wet and dirty by dragging
*intransitive verb*
**1** : to trail on the ground
**2** : STRAGGLE

**drag·gle–tail** \'dra-gəl-,tāl\ *noun* (1596)
: SLATTERN

**drag·gy** \'dra-gē\ *adjective* **drag·gi·er; -est** (15th century)
: SLUGGISH, DULL

**drag·line** \'drag-,līn\ *noun* (circa 1911)
**1** : a line used in or for dragging
**2** : an excavating machine in which the bucket is attached by cables and operates by being drawn toward the machine

**drag·net** \'drag-,net\ *noun* (circa 1541)
**1 a** : a net drawn along the bottom of a body of water **b** : a net used on the ground (as to capture small game)
**2** : a network of measures for apprehension (as of criminals)

**drag·o·man** \'dra-gə-mən\ *noun, plural* **-mans** *or* **-men** \-mən\ [Middle English *drogman,* from Middle French, from Old Italian *dragomanno,* from Middle Greek *dragomanos,* from Arabic *tarjumān,* from Aramaic *tūrĕĕmānā*] (14th century)
: an interpreter chiefly of Arabic, Turkish, or Persian employed especially in the Near East

**drag·on** \'dra-gən\ *noun* [Middle English, from Old French, from Latin *dracon-, draco* serpent, dragon, from Greek *drakōn* serpent; akin to Old English *torht* bright, Greek *derkesthai* to see, look at] (13th century)
**1** *archaic* : a huge serpent
**2** : a mythical animal usually represented as a monstrous winged and scaly serpent or saurian with a crested head and enormous claws
**3** : a violent, combative, or very strict person
**4** *capitalized* : DRACO
**5** : something or someone formidable or baneful
— **drag·on·ish** \-gə-nish\ *adjective*

**drag·on·et** \,dra-gə-'net, 'dra-gə-nət\ *noun* (14th century)
**1** : a little dragon

◇ **WORD HISTORY**
**draconian** According to ancient Athenian tradition, Draco was a lawgiver of the 7th century B.C., associated with the first commitment of Greek law to writing. Draco's code was famed for its harshness, as most criminal offenses required the death penalty. According to the 4th century orator Demades, the statutes were literally written in blood. Not many decades after Draco supposedly lived, the 6th century statesman Solon abolished all of Draco's punishments except those dealing with homicide. Modern scholars are unsure if Draco or his code ever actually existed, but in any event *draconian* remains in English as a synonym for "severe" in reference to laws or other measures taken by persons in a position of power.

**2 :** any of various small often brightly colored scaleless marine fishes constituting a family (Callionymidae); *especially* **:** a European fish (*Callionymus lyra*) sometimes used as food

**drag·on·fly** \'dra-gən-ˌflī\ *noun* (1626)
**:** any of a suborder (Anisoptera) of odonate insects that are larger and stouter than damselflies, hold the wings horizontal in repose, and have rectal gills during the naiad stage; *broadly* **:** ODONATE

dragonfly

**drag·on·head** \-ˌhed\ *noun* (1784)
**:** any of several mints (genus *Dracocephalum*) often grown for their showy flower heads; *especially* **:** a North American plant (*D. parviflorum*)

**dragon lady** *noun* [character in the comic strip "Terry and the Pirates" by Milton Caniff] (1973)
**:** an overbearing or tyrannical woman; *also* **:** a glamorous often mysterious woman

**dragon's blood** *noun* (1599)
**:** any of several resinous mostly dark-red plant products; *specifically* **:** a resin from the fruit of a palm (genus *Daemonorops*) used for coloring varnish and in photoengraving

**dragon's teeth** *noun plural* [from the dragon's teeth sown by Cadmus which sprang up as armed warriors who killed one another off] (1853)
**1 :** seeds of strife
**2 :** wedge-shaped concrete antitank barriers laid in multiple rows

**¹dra·goon** \drə-'gün, dra-\ *noun* [French *dragon* dragon, dragoon, from Middle French] (1622)
**:** a member of a European military unit formerly composed of heavily armed mounted troops

**²dragoon** *transitive verb* (1689)
**1 :** to subjugate or persecute by harsh use of troops
**2 :** to force or attempt to force into submission by violent measures **:** COERCE

**drag queen** *noun* (circa 1941)
**:** a male homosexual who dresses as a woman

**drag race** *noun* (1949)
**:** an acceleration contest between vehicles (as automobiles)
**— drag racing** *noun*

**drag·ster** \'drag-stər\ *noun* (circa 1954)
**1 :** a vehicle built or modified for use in a drag race
**2 :** one who participates in a drag race

**drag strip** *noun* (1952)
**:** the site of a drag race; *specifically* **:** a strip of pavement with a racing area at least ¼ mile long

**¹drain** \'drān\ *verb* [Middle English *draynen*, from Old English *drēahnian* — more at DRY] (before 12th century)
*transitive verb*
**1** *obsolete* **:** FILTER
**2 a :** to draw off (liquid) gradually or completely ⟨*drained* all the water out⟩ **b :** to cause the gradual disappearance of **c :** to exhaust physically or emotionally
**3 a :** to make gradually dry ⟨*drain* a swamp⟩ **b :** to carry away the surface water of ⟨the river that *drains* the valley⟩ **c :** to deplete or empty by or as if by drawing off by degrees or in increments **d :** to empty by drinking the contents of
**4 :** DROP 7c, SINK ⟨*drained* the putt⟩
*intransitive verb*
**1 a :** to flow off gradually **b :** to disappear gradually **:** DWINDLE
**2 :** to become emptied or freed of liquid by its flowing or dropping
**3 :** to discharge surface or surplus water

*synonym* see DEPLETE
**— drain·er** *noun*

**²drain** *noun* (1552)
**1 :** a means (as a pipe) by which usually liquid matter is drained
**2 a :** the act of draining **b :** a gradual outflow or withdrawal **:** DEPLETION
**3 :** something that causes depletion **:** BURDEN
**4 :** an electrode in a field-effect transistor toward which charge carriers move — compare GATE, SOURCE
**— down the drain :** to a state of being wasted or irretrievably lost

**drain·age** \'drā-nij\ *noun* (1652)
**1 :** the act, process, or mode of draining; *also* **:** something drained off
**2 :** a device for draining **:** DRAIN; *also* **:** a system of drains
**3 :** an area or district drained

**drain·pipe** \'drān-ˌpīp\ *noun* (1857)
**:** a pipe for drainage

**Draize test** \'drāz-\ *noun* [John H. *Draize* (born 1900) American pharmacologist] (1980)
**:** a test for harmfulness of chemicals to the human eye that involves dropping the test substance into one eye of a rabbit without anesthesia using the other eye as a control — called also *Draize eye test*

**drake** \'drāk\ *noun* [Middle English; akin to Old High German an*trahho* drake] (14th century)
**:** a male duck

**dram** \'dram\ *noun* [Middle English *dragme*, from Middle French & Late Latin; Middle French, dram, drachma, from Late Latin *dragma*, from Latin *drachma*, from Greek *drachmē*, literally, handful, from *drassesthai* to grasp] (14th century)
**1 a** — see WEIGHT table **b :** FLUID DRAM
**2 a :** a small portion of something to drink **b :** a small amount

**DRAM** \'dram *also* 'dē-ˌram\ *noun* [dynamic + *RAM* (random-access memory)] (1980)
**:** a computer memory chip that must be continuously supplied with power in order to retain data

**dra·ma** \'drä-mə, 'dra-\ *noun* [Late Latin *dramat-, drama*, from Greek, deed, drama, from *dran* to do, act] (1515)
**1 :** a composition in verse or prose intended to portray life or character or to tell a story usually involving conflicts and emotions through action and dialogue and typically designed for theatrical performance **:** PLAY — compare CLOSET DRAMA
**2 :** dramatic art, literature, or affairs
**3 a :** a state, situation, or series of events involving interesting or intense conflict of forces **b :** dramatic state, effect, or quality ⟨the *drama* of the courtroom proceedings⟩

**Dram·a·mine** \'dra-mə-ˌmēn\ *trademark*
— used for dimenhydrinate

**dra·mat·ic** \drə-'ma-tik\ *adjective* (1589)
**1 :** of or relating to the drama
**2 a :** suitable to or characteristic of the drama **b :** striking in appearance or effect
**3** *of an opera singer* **:** having a powerful voice and a declamatory style — compare LYRIC ☆
**— dra·mat·i·cal·ly** \-ti-k(ə-)lē\ *adverb*

**dramatic irony** *noun* (circa 1907)
**:** IRONY 3b

**dramatic monologue** *noun* (circa 1935)
**:** a literary work in which a character reveals himself in a monologue usually addressed to a second person

**dra·mat·ics** \drə-'ma-tiks\ *noun plural but singular or plural in construction* (1796)
**1 :** the study or practice of theatrical arts (as acting and stagecraft)
**2 :** dramatic behavior or expression

**dramatic unities** *noun plural* (circa 1922)
**:** the unities of time, place, and action that are observed in classical drama

**dramatisation, dramatise** *British variant of* DRAMATIZATION, DRAMATIZE

**dra·ma·tis per·so·nae** \ˌdra-mə-təs-pər-'sō-(ˌ)nē, ˌdrä-, -ˌnī\ *noun plural* [New Latin] (1730)
**1 :** the characters or actors in a drama
**2** *singular in construction* **:** a list of the characters or actors in a drama
**3 :** the participants in an event

**dra·ma·tist** \'dra-mə-tist, 'drä-\ *noun* (1678)
**:** PLAYWRIGHT

**dra·ma·ti·za·tion** \ˌdra-mə-tə-'zā-shən, ˌdrä-\ *noun* (1796)
**1 :** the action of dramatizing
**2 :** a dramatized version (as of a novel)

**dra·ma·tize** \'dra-mə-ˌtīz, 'drä-\ *verb* **-tized; -tiz·ing** (1783)
*transitive verb*
**1 :** to adapt (as a novel) for theatrical presentation
**2 :** to present or represent in a dramatic manner
*intransitive verb*
**1 :** to be suitable for dramatization
**2 :** to behave dramatically
**— dra·ma·tiz·able** \-ˌtī-zə-bəl\ *adjective*

**dra·ma·turge** *or* **dra·ma·turg** \'dra-mə-ˌtərj, 'drä-\ *noun* (1870)
**:** a specialist in dramaturgy

**dra·ma·tur·gy** \'dra-mə-ˌtər-jē, 'drä-\ *noun* [German *Dramaturgie*, from Greek *dramatourgia* dramatic composition, from *dramat-, drama* + *-ourgia* -urgy] (1801)
**:** the art or technique of dramatic composition and theatrical representation
**— dra·ma·tur·gic** \ˌdra-mə-'tər-jik, ˌdrä-\ *or* **dra·ma·tur·gi·cal** \-ji-kəl\ *adjective*
**— dra·ma·tur·gi·cal·ly** \-ji-k(ə-)lē\ *adverb*

**dra·me·dy** \'drä-mə-dē, 'dra-\ *noun* [blend of *drama* and *comedy*] (1978)
**:** a situation comedy having dramatic scenes

**dram·mock** \'dra-mək\ *noun* [Scottish Gaelic *dramag*] (1562)
*chiefly Scottish* **:** raw oatmeal mixed with cold water

**dram·shop** \'dram-ˌshäp\ *noun* (1725)
**:** BARROOM

**drank** *past and past participle of* DRINK

**¹drape** \'drāp\ *verb* **draped; drap·ing** [probably back-formation from *drapery*] (1847)
*transitive verb*
**1 :** to cover or adorn with or as if with folds of cloth
**2 :** to cause to hang or stretch out loosely or carelessly
**3 :** to arrange in flowing lines or folds
*intransitive verb*
**:** to become arranged in folds ⟨this silk *drapes* beautifully⟩

---

☆ **SYNONYMS**
**Dramatic, theatrical, histrionic, melodramatic** mean having a character or an effect like that of acted plays. DRAMATIC applies to situations in life and literature that stir the imagination and emotions deeply ⟨a *dramatic* meeting of world leaders⟩. THEATRICAL implies a crude appeal through artificiality or exaggeration in gesture or vocal expression ⟨a *theatrical* oration⟩. HISTRIONIC applies to tones, gestures, and motions and suggests a deliberate affectation or staginess ⟨a *histrionic* show of grief⟩. MELODRAMATIC suggests an exaggerated emotionalism or an inappropriate theatricalism ⟨made a *melodramatic* plea⟩.

---

\ə\ **abut** \ᵊ\ **kitten** \ər\ **further** \a\ **ash** \ā\ **ace**
\ä\ **mop, mar** \au̇\ **out** \ch\ **chin** \e\ **bet** \ē\ **easy**
\g\ **go** \i\ **hit** \ī\ **ice** \j\ **job** \ŋ\ **sing** \ō\ **go**
\ȯ\ **law** \ȯi\ **boy** \th\ **thin** \t͟h\ **the** \ü\ **loot** \u̇\ **foot**
\y\ **yet** \zh\ **vision** *see also* Guide to Pronunciation

— **drap·abil·i·ty** also **drape·abil·i·ty** \ˌdrā-pə-'bi-lə-tē\ noun
— **drap·able** also **drape·able** \'drā-pə-bəl\ adjective

²**drape** noun (1889)
**1** : arrangement in or of folds
**2 a** : a drapery especially for a window : CURTAIN **b** : a sterile covering used in an operating room — usually used in plural
**3** : the cut or hang of clothing
— **drap·ey** \'drā-pē\ adjective

**drap·er** \'drā-pər\ noun [Middle English, weaver, clothier, from Middle French drapier, from Old French, from drap cloth — more at DRAB] (14th century)
chiefly British : a dealer in cloth and sometimes also in clothing and dry goods

**drap·ery** \'drā-p(ə-)rē\ noun, plural -er·ies (14th century)
**1** British : DRY GOODS
**2 a** : a decorative piece of material usually hung in loose folds and arranged in a graceful design **b** : hangings of heavy fabric for use as a curtain
**3** : the draping or arranging of materials

**dras·tic** \'dras-tik\ adjective [Greek drastikos, from dran to do] (circa 1691)
**1** : acting rapidly or violently ⟨a drastic purgative⟩
**2** : extreme in effect or action : SEVERE ⟨drastic measures⟩
— **dras·ti·cal·ly** \-ti-k(ə-)lē\ adverb

**drat** \'drat\ verb **drat·ted**; **drat·ting** [probably euphemistic alteration of God rot] (1815)
: DAMN — used as a mild oath

**draught** \'draft\, **draughty** \'draf-tē\ chiefly British variant of DRAFT, DRAFTY

**draughts** \'draf(t)s\ noun plural but singular or plural in construction [Middle English draghtes, from plural of draght draft, move in chess] (15th century)
British : CHECKERS

**draughts·man** chiefly British variant of DRAFTSMAN

**Dra·vid·i·an** \drə-'vi-dē-ən\ noun [Sanskrit Drāviḍa] (1856)
**1** : a member of an ancient dark-skinned people of southern India
**2** : DRAVIDIAN LANGUAGES
— **Dravidian** adjective

**Dravidian languages** noun plural (1871)
: a language family of India, Sri Lanka, and Pakistan that includes Tamil, Telugu, Kannada, and Malayalam

¹**draw** \'dro\ verb **drew** \'drü\; **drawn** \'dron, 'drän\; **draw·ing** [Middle English drawen, dragen, from Old English dragan; akin to Old Norse draga to draw, drag] (before 12th century)
transitive verb
**1** : to cause to move continuously toward or after a force applied in advance : PULL ⟨draw your chair up by the fire⟩: as **a** : to move (as a covering) over or to one side ⟨draw the drapes⟩ **b** : to pull up or out of a receptacle or place where seated or carried ⟨draw water from the well⟩ ⟨drew a gun⟩; also : to cause to come out of a container ⟨draw water for a bath⟩
**2** : to cause to go in a certain direction (as by leading) ⟨drew him aside⟩
**3 a** : to bring by inducement or allure : ATTRACT ⟨honey draws flies⟩ **b** : to bring in or gather from a specified group or area ⟨a college that draws its students from many states⟩ **c** : BRING ON, PROVOKE ⟨drew enemy fire⟩ **d** : to bring out by way of response : ELICIT ⟨drew cheers from the audience⟩ **e** : to receive in the course of play ⟨the batter drew a walk⟩ ⟨draw a foul⟩
**4** : INHALE ⟨drew a deep breath⟩
**5 a** : to extract the essence from ⟨draw tea⟩ **b** : EVISCERATE ⟨plucking and drawing a goose before cooking⟩ **c** : to derive to one's benefit ⟨drew inspiration from the old masters⟩

**6** : to require (a specified depth) to float in ⟨a ship that draws 12 feet of water⟩
**7 a** : ACCUMULATE, GAIN ⟨drawing interest⟩ **b** : to take (money) from a place of deposit **c** : to use in making a cash demand ⟨drawing a check against his account⟩ **d** : to receive regularly or in due course ⟨draw a salary⟩
**8 a** : to take (cards) from a stack or from the dealer **b** : to receive or take at random ⟨drew a winning number⟩
**9** : to bend (a bow) by pulling back the string
**10** : to cause to shrink, contract, or tighten
**11** : to strike (a ball) so as to impart a backward spin
**12** : to leave (a contest) undecided : TIE
**13 a** (1) : to produce a likeness or representation of by making lines on a surface ⟨draw a picture⟩ ⟨draw a graph with chalk⟩ (2) : to give a portrayal of : DELINEATE ⟨a writer who draws characters well⟩ **b** : to write out in due form ⟨draw a will⟩ **c** : to design or describe in detail : FORMULATE ⟨draw comparisons⟩
**14** : to infer from evidence or premises ⟨draw a conclusion⟩
**15** : to spread or elongate (metal) by hammering or by pulling through dies; also : to shape (as plastic) by stretching or by pulling through dies
intransitive verb
**1** : to come or go steadily or gradually ⟨night draws near⟩
**2 a** : to move something by pulling ⟨drawing at the well⟩ **b** : to exert an attractive force ⟨the play is drawing well⟩
**3 a** : to pull back a bowstring **b** : to bring out a weapon ⟨drew, aimed, and fired⟩
**4 a** : to produce a draft ⟨the chimney draws well⟩ ⟨draw on a cigar⟩ **b** : to swell out in a wind ⟨all sails drawing⟩
**5 a** : to wrinkle or tighten up : SHRINK **b** : to change shape by pulling or stretching
**6** : to cause blood or pus to localize at one point
**7** : to create a likeness or a picture in outlines : SKETCH
**8** : to come out even in a contest
**9 a** : to make a written demand for payment of money on deposit **b** : to obtain resources (as of information) ⟨drawing from a common fund of knowledge⟩
— **draw·able** \-ə-bəl\ adjective
— **draw a bead on** : to take aim at
— **draw a blank** : to fail to gain a desired object (as information sought); also : to be unable to think of something
— **draw on** or **draw upon** : to use as a source of supply ⟨drawing on the whole community for support⟩
— **draw straws** : to decide or assign something by lottery in which straws of unequal length are used
— **draw the line** or **draw a line 1** : to fix an arbitrary boundary between things that tend to intermingle **2** : to fix a boundary excluding what one will not tolerate or engage in

²**draw** noun (1663)
**1** : the act or process of drawing: as **a** : a sucking pull on something held with the lips **b** : a removal of a handgun from its holster ⟨quick on the draw⟩ **c** : backward spin given to a ball by striking it below center — compare FOLLOW
**2** : something that is drawn: as **a** : a card drawn to replace a discard in poker **b** : a lot or chance drawn at random **c** : the movable part of a drawbridge
**3** : a contest left undecided or deadlocked : TIE
**4** : one that draws attention or patronage
**5 a** : the distance from the string to the back of a drawn bow **b** : the force required to draw a bow fully
**6** : a gully shallower than a ravine
**7** : the deal in draw poker to improve the players' hands after discarding

**8** : a football play that simulates a pass play so a runner can go straight up the middle past the pass rushers

**draw away** intransitive verb (1670)
: to move ahead (as of an opponent in a race)

**draw·back** \'dro-ˌbak\ noun (1697)
**1** : a refund of duties especially on an imported product subsequently exported or used to produce a product for export
**2** : an objectionable feature : DISADVANTAGE

**draw back** \dro-'bak\ intransitive verb (14th century)
: to avoid an issue or commitment

**draw·bar** \'dro-ˌbär\ noun (1839)
**1** : a railroad coupler
**2** : a beam across the rear of a vehicle (as a tractor) to which implements are hitched

**draw·bridge** \-ˌbrij\ noun (14th century)
: a bridge made to be raised up, let down, or drawn aside so as to permit or hinder passage

**draw·down** \-ˌdaun\ noun (1918)
**1** : a lowering of a water level (as in a reservoir)
**2 a** : the process of depleting **b** : REDUCTION

**draw down** \ˌdro-'daun\ transitive verb (1949)
: to deplete by using or spending

drawbridge

**draw·ee** \dro-'ē\ noun (1766)
: the party on which an order or bill of exchange is drawn

**draw·er** \'dro(-ə)r\ noun (14th century)
**1** : one that draws: as **a** : a person who draws liquor **b** : DRAFTSMAN **c** : one that draws a bill of exchange or order for payment or makes a promissory note
**2** : a sliding box or receptacle opened by pulling out and closed by pushing in
**3** plural : an article of clothing (as underwear) for the lower body
— **drawer·ful** \-ˌful\ noun

**draw in** (1558)
transitive verb
**1** : to cause or entice to enter or participate
**2** : to sketch roughly
intransitive verb
**1 a** : to draw to an end ⟨the day drew in⟩ **b** : to shorten seasonally ⟨the evenings are already drawing in⟩
**2** : to become more cautious or economical

**draw·ing** \'dro(-)iŋ\ noun (14th century)
**1** : an act or instance of drawing; especially : the process of deciding something by drawing lots
**2** : the art or technique of representing an object or outlining a figure, plan, or sketch by means of lines
**3** : something drawn or subject to drawing: as **a** : an amount drawn from a fund **b** : a representation formed by drawing : SKETCH

**drawing account** noun (1920)
: an account showing payments made to an employee in advance of actual earnings or for traveling expenses

**drawing board** noun (1725)
**1** : a board used as a base for drafting on paper
**2** : a planning stage ⟨a project still on the drawing board⟩

**drawing card** noun (1887)
: one that attracts attention or patronage

**drawing pin** noun (1859)
British : THUMBTACK

**drawing room** noun [short for withdrawing room] (1642)
**1 a** : a formal reception room **b** : a private room on a railroad passenger car with three berths and an enclosed toilet
**2** : a formal reception

**drawing table** *noun* (1706)
: a table with a surface adjustable for elevation and angle of incline
**draw·knife** \'drȯ-ˌnīf\ *noun* (1703)
: a woodworker's tool consisting of a blade with a handle at each end for use in shaving off surfaces
**¹drawl** \'drȯl\ *verb* [probably frequentative of *draw*] (1598)
*intransitive verb*
: to speak slowly with vowels greatly prolonged
*transitive verb*
: to utter in a slow lengthened tone
— **drawl·er** *noun*
— **drawl·ing·ly** \'drȯ-liŋ-lē\ *adverb*
**²drawl** *noun* (1760)
: a drawling manner of speaking
— **drawly** \'drȯ-lē\ *adjective*
**¹drawn** *past participle of* DRAW
**²drawn** \'drȯn, 'drän\ *adjective* (1613)
: showing the effects of tension, pain, or illness : HAGGARD
**drawn butter** *noun* (1826)
: melted clarified butter
**drawn-work** \'drȯn-ˌwȯrk\ *noun* (1595)
: decoration on cloth made by drawing out threads according to a pattern
**draw off** (13th century)
*transitive verb*
: REMOVE, WITHDRAW
*intransitive verb*
: to move apart or ahead
**draw on** (15th century)
*intransitive verb*
: APPROACH ⟨night *draws on*⟩
*transitive verb*
: BRING ON, CAUSE
**draw out** *transitive verb* (14th century)
**1** : REMOVE, EXTRACT
**2** : to extend beyond a minimum in time : PROTRACT 2
**3** : to cause to speak freely ⟨a reporter's ability to *draw* a person *out*⟩
**draw·plate** \'drȯ-ˌplāt\ *noun* (1832)
: a die with holes through which wires are drawn
**draw play** *noun* (1952)
: DRAW 8
**draw poker** *noun* (1849)
: poker in which each player is dealt five cards face down and after betting may get replacements for discards
**draw·shave** \'drȯ-ˌshāv\ *noun* (1828)
: DRAWKNIFE
**draw shot** *noun* (1897)
: a shot in billiards or pool made by hitting the cue ball with draw so it moves back after striking the object ball
**draw·string** \'drȯ-ˌstriŋ\ *noun* (1845)
: a string, cord, or tape inserted into hems or casings or laced through eyelets for use in closing a bag or controlling fullness in garments or curtains
**draw·tube** \-ˌtüb, -ˌtyüb\ *noun* (circa 1891)
: a telescoping tube (as for the eyepiece of a microscope)
**draw up** (1605)
*transitive verb*
**1** : to bring (as troops) into array
**2** : to prepare a draft or version of ⟨*draw up* plans⟩
**3** : to bring to a halt
**4** : to straighten (oneself) to an erect posture especially as an assertion of dignity or resentment
*intransitive verb*
: to come to a halt
**¹dray** \'drā\ *noun* [Middle English *draye*, a wheelless vehicle; akin to Old English *dræge* dragnet, *dragan* to pull — more at DRAW] (14th century)
: a vehicle used to haul goods; *especially* : a strong cart or wagon without sides
**²dray** *transitive verb* (1857)
: to haul on a dray : CART

**dray·age** \'drā-ij\ *noun* (1791)
: the work or cost of hauling by dray
**dray horse** *noun* (1709)
: a horse adapted for drawing heavy loads
**dray·man** \'drā-mən\ *noun* (1581)
: one whose work is hauling by dray
**¹dread** \'dred\ *verb* [Middle English *dreden*, from Old English *drǣdan*] (before 12th century)
*transitive verb*
**1 a** : to fear greatly **b** *archaic* : to regard with awe
**2** : to feel extreme reluctance to meet or face
*intransitive verb*
: to be apprehensive or fearful
**²dread** *noun* (13th century)
**1 a** : great fear especially in the face of impending evil **b** : extreme uneasiness in the face of a disagreeable prospect ⟨*dread* of a social blunder⟩ **c** *archaic* : AWE
**2** : one causing fear or awe
*synonym* see FEAR
**³dread** *adjective* (15th century)
**1** : causing great fear or anxiety
**2** : inspiring awe
**¹dread·ful** \'dred-fəl\ *adjective* (13th century)
**1 a** : inspiring dread : causing great and oppressive fear **b** : inspiring awe or reverence
**2** : extremely bad, distasteful, unpleasant, or shocking
**3** : EXTREME ⟨*dreadful* disorder⟩
— **dread·ful·ly** \-f(ə-)lē\ *adverb*
— **dread·ful·ness** \-fəl-nəs\ *noun*
**²dreadful** *noun* (1873)
: a cheap and sensational story or periodical
**dread·lock** \'dred-ˌläk\ *noun* (1960)
**1** : a narrow ropelike strand of hair formed by matting or braiding
**2** *plural* : a hairstyle consisting of dreadlocks
**dread·nought** \'dred-ˌnȯt, -ˌnät\ *noun* (1806)
**1** : a warm garment of thick cloth; *also* : the cloth
**2** [*Dreadnought*, British battleship] : BATTLESHIP
**3** : one that is among the largest or most powerful of its kind
**¹dream** \'drēm\ *noun, often attributive* [Middle English *dreem*, from Old English *drēam* noise, joy, and Old Norse *draumr* dream; akin to Old High German *troum* dream] (13th century)
**1** : a series of thoughts, images, or emotions occurring during sleep — compare REM SLEEP
**2** : an experience of waking life having the characteristics of a dream: as **a** : a visionary creation of the imagination : DAYDREAM **b** : a state of mind marked by abstraction or release from reality : REVERIE **c** : an object seen in a dreamlike state : VISION
**3** : something notable for its beauty, excellence, or enjoyable quality ⟨the new car is a *dream* to operate⟩
**4 a** : a strongly desired goal or purpose ⟨a *dream* of becoming president⟩ **b** : something that fully satisfies a wish : IDEAL ⟨a meal that was a gourmet's *dream*⟩ ◆
— **dream·ful** \-fəl\ *adjective*
— **dream·ful·ly** \-fə-lē\ *adverb*
— **dream·ful·ness** *noun*
— **dream·less** *adjective*
— **dream·less·ly** *adverb*
— **dream·less·ness** *noun*
— **dream·like** \'drēm-ˌlīk\ *adjective*
**²dream** *verb* **dreamed** \'drem(p)t, 'drēmd\ *or* **dreamt** \'drem(p)t\; **dream·ing** \'drē-miŋ\ (13th century)
*intransitive verb*
**1** : to have a dream
**2** : to indulge in daydreams or fantasies ⟨*dreaming* of a better future⟩
**3** : to appear tranquil or dreamy ⟨houses *dream* in leafy shadows —Gladys Taber⟩
*transitive verb*
**1** : to have a dream of
**2** : to consider as a possibility : IMAGINE

**3** : to pass (time) in reverie or inaction ⟨*dreaming* the hours away⟩
— **dream of** : to consider possible or fitting ⟨wouldn't *dream of* disturbing you⟩
**dream·er** \'drē-mər\ *noun* (14th century)
**1** : one that dreams
**2 a** : one who lives in a world of fancy and imagination **b** : one who has ideas or conceives projects regarded as impractical : VISIONARY
**dream·land** \'drēm-ˌland\ *noun* (circa 1834)
: an unreal delightful country existing only in imagination or in dreams : NEVER-NEVER LAND
**dream·time** \-ˌtīm\ *noun, often capitalized* (1896)
: the time of creation in the mythology of the Australian aborigines
**dream up** *transitive verb* (1941)
: to form in the mind : DEVISE, CONCOCT
**dream vision** *noun* (1906)
: a usually medieval poem having a framework in which the poet pictures himself as falling asleep and envisioning in his dream a series of allegorical people and events
**dream·world** \'drēm-ˌwərld\ *noun* (1817)
: a world of illusion or fantasy
**dreamy** \'drē-mē\ *adjective* **dream·i·er; -est** (1567)
**1 a** : full of dreams ⟨a *dreamy* night's sleep⟩ **b** : pleasantly abstracted from immediate reality
**2** : given to dreaming or fantasy ⟨a *dreamy* child⟩
**3 a** : suggestive of a dream in vague or visionary quality **b** : quiet and soothing **c** : DELIGHTFUL, IDEAL ⟨he's so handsome . . . real *dreamy* —Greg Foley⟩
— **dream·i·ly** \-mə-lē\ *adverb*
— **dream·i·ness** \-mē-nəs\ *noun*
**drear** \'drir\ *adjective* (1629)
: DREARY
— **drear** *noun*
**drea·ry** \'drir-ē\ *adjective* **drea·ri·er; -est** [Middle English *drery*, from Old English *drēorig* sad, bloody, from *drēor* gore; akin to Old High German *trūrēn* to be sad, Gothic *driusan* to fall] (before 12th century)
**1** : feeling, displaying, or reflecting listlessness or discouragement
**2** : having nothing likely to provide cheer, comfort, or interest : GLOOMY, DISMAL
— **drea·ri·ly** \'drir-ə-lē\ *adverb*
— **drea·ri·ness** \'drir-ē-nəs\ *noun*
**dreck** *also* **drek** \'drek\ *noun* [Yiddish *drek* & German *Dreck*, from Middle High German *drec*; akin to Old English *threax* rubbish] (1922)
: TRASH, RUBBISH

◇ WORD HISTORY
**dream** Not until the 13th century did *dream*, in the Middle English forms *drem* and *dreem*, appear in reference to images seen during sleep; however, the word itself is considerably older. In Old English *drēam* meant "joy, ecstasy" or "melody, music." Yet the shift in sense between Old and Middle English was not simply the result of an adaptation and specialization of the earlier senses. Rather it would appear that after the Scandinavian conquests and settlements in Britain of the 9th and 10th centuries, which had a major impact on the history of English, the Old Norse word *draumr*, referring to a dream during sleep, influenced the meaning of the similar and almost certainly related English word. By the end of the 14th century, the Old English meanings of the word had been entirely replaced.

\ə\ abut \ᵊ\ kitten \ər\ further \a\ ash \ā\ ace
\ä\ mop, mar \au̇\ out \ch\ chin \e\ bet \ē\ easy
\g\ go \i\ hit \ī\ ice \j\ job \ŋ\ sing \ō\ go
\ȯ\ law \ȯi\ boy \th\ thin \th\ the \ü\ loot \u̇\ foot
\y\ yet \zh\ vision *see also* Guide to Pronunciation

**¹dredge** \'drej\ *verb* **dredged; dredg·ing**
(1508)
*transitive verb*
**1 a :** to dig, gather, or pull out with or as if
with a dredge — often used with *up* **b :** to
deepen (as a waterway) with a dredging machine
**2 :** to bring to light by deep searching — often used with *up* ⟨*dredging* up memories⟩
*intransitive verb*
**1 :** to use a dredge
**2 :** to search deeply
— **dredg·er** *noun*

**²dredge** *noun* [perhaps from (assumed) Old
English *drecge;* akin to Old English *dræge*
dragnet, *dragan* to draw] (1602)
**1 :** an apparatus usually in the form of an oblong iron frame with an attached bag net used
especially for gathering fish and shellfish
**2 :** a machine for removing earth usually by
buckets on an endless chain or a suction tube
**3 :** a barge used in dredging

**³dredge** *transitive verb* **dredged; dredging** [obsolete *dredge,* noun, sweetmeat, from
Middle English *drage, drege,* from Middle
French *dragie,* modification of Latin *trage-
mata* sweetmeats, from Greek *tragēmata,* plural of *tragēma* sweetmeat, from *trōgein* to
gnaw] (1596)
**:** to coat (food) by sprinkling (as with flour)
— **dredg·er** *noun*

**dree** \'drē\ *transitive verb* **dreed; dree·ing**
[Middle English, from Old English *drēogan;*
akin to Gothic *driugan* to perform military
service] (before 12th century)
*chiefly Scottish* **:** ENDURE, SUFFER

**dreg** \'dreg\ *noun* [Middle English, from Old
Norse *dregg;* perhaps akin to Latin *fraces*
dregs of oil] (14th century)
**1 :** sediment contained in a liquid or precipitated from it **:** LEES — usually used in plural
**2 :** the most undesirable part — usually used
in plural
**3 :** the last remaining part **:** VESTIGE
— **dreg·gy** \'dre-gē\ *adjective*

**D region** *noun* (1930)
**:** the lowest part of the ionosphere occurring
approximately between 30 and 55 miles (50
and 90 kilometers) above the surface of the
earth

**dreich** \'drēk\ *adjective* [Middle English, of
Scandinavian origin; akin to Old Norse *drjūgr*
lasting] (1813)
*chiefly Scottish* **:** DREARY

**drei·del** *also* **dreidl** \'drā-d°l\ *noun* [Yiddish
*dreydl,* from *dreyen* to turn, from Middle High
German *dræjen,* from Old High German *drāen*
— more at THROW] (1926)
**1 :** a 4-sided toy marked with
Hebrew letters and spun like a
top in a game of chance
**2 :** a children's game of chance
played especially at Hanukkah
with a dreidel

**¹drench** \'drench\ *noun* (before
12th century)
**1 :** a poisonous or medicinal
drink; *specifically* **:** a large dose
of medicine mixed with liquid
and put down the throat of an animal
**2 a :** something that drenches **b :** a quantity
sufficient to drench or saturate

**²drench** *transitive verb* [Middle English, from
Old English *drencan;* akin to Old English
*drincan* to drink] (before 12th century)
**1 a** *archaic* **:** to force to drink **b :** to administer a drench to (an animal)
**2 :** to wet thoroughly (as by soaking or immersing in liquid)
**3 :** to soak or cover thoroughly with liquid
that falls or is precipitated
**4 :** to fill or cover completely as if by soaking
or precipitation ⟨was *drenched* in furs and diamonds —Richard Brautigan⟩
**synonym** see SOAK
— **drench·er** *noun*

dreidel 1

**¹dress** \'dres\ *verb* [Middle English, from
Middle French *dresser,* from Old French
*drecier,* from (assumed) Vulgar Latin *direc-
tiare,* from Latin *directus* direct, past participle
of *dirigere* to direct, from *dis-* + *regere* to lead
straight — more at RIGHT] (14th century)
*transitive verb*
**1 a :** to make or set straight **b :** to arrange (as
troops) in a straight line and at proper intervals
**2 :** to prepare for use or service; *specifically*
**:** to prepare for cooking or for the table
**3 :** to add decorative details or accessories to
**:** EMBELLISH
**4 a :** to put clothes on **b :** to provide with
clothing
**5** *archaic* **:** DRESS DOWN
**6 a :** to apply dressings or medicaments to **b**
(1) **:** to arrange (the hair) by combing, brushing, or curling (2) **:** to groom and curry (an animal) **c :** to kill and prepare for market or for
consumption — often used with *out* **d :** CULTI-
VATE, TEND; *especially* **:** to apply manure or
fertilizer to **e :** to put through a finishing process; *especially* **:** to trim and smooth the surface of (as lumber or stone)
*intransitive verb*
**1 a :** to put on clothing **b :** to put on or wear
formal, elaborate, or fancy clothes ⟨*dress* for
dinner⟩
**2** *of a food animal* **:** to weigh after being
dressed — often used with *out*
**3 :** to align oneself with the next soldier in a
line to make the line straight
— **dress ship :** to ornament a ship for a
celebration by hoisting national ensigns at the
mastheads and running a line of signal flags
and pennants from bow to stern

**²dress** *noun* (1606)
**1 :** APPAREL, CLOTHING
**2 :** an outer garment (as for a woman or girl)
usually consisting of a one-piece bodice and
skirt
**3 :** covering, adornment, or appearance appropriate or peculiar to a particular time
**4 :** a particular form of presentation **:** GUISE

**³dress** *adjective* (1767)
**1 :** suitable for a formal occasion
**2 :** requiring or permitting formal dress ⟨a
*dress* affair⟩
**3 :** relating to or used for a dress

**dres·sage** \drə-'säzh, dre-\ *noun, often attributive* [French, from *dresser* to train, drill, from
Middle French] (1936)
**:** the execution by a trained horse of precision
movements in response to barely perceptible
signals from its rider

**dress circle** *noun* (1825)
**:** the first or lowest curved tier of seats above
the main floor in a theater or opera house

**dress code** *noun* (1968)
**:** formally or socially imposed standards of
dress

**dress down** (circa 1897)
*transitive verb*
**:** to reprove severely
*intransitive verb*
**:** to dress casually especially for reasons of
fashion

**¹dress·er** \'dre-sər\ *noun* (15th century)
**1** *obsolete* **:** a table or sideboard for preparing
and serving food
**2 :** a cupboard to hold dishes and cooking
utensils
**3 :** a chest of drawers or bureau with a mirror

**²dresser** *noun* (1520)
**:** one that dresses ⟨a fashionable *dresser*⟩

**dresser set** *noun* (circa 1934)
**:** a set of toilet articles including hairbrush,
comb, and mirror for use at a dresser or dressing table

**dress·ing** *noun* (15th century)
**1 a :** the act or process of one who dresses **b**
**:** an instance of such act or process

**2 a :** a sauce for adding to a dish (as a salad)
**b :** a seasoned mixture usually used as a stuffing (as for poultry)
**3 a :** material (as ointment or gauze) applied
to cover a lesion **b :** fertilizing material (as
manure or compost)

**dres·sing–down** \,dre-siŋ-'daun\ *noun* (circa
1890)
**:** a severe reprimand

**dressing glass** *noun* (1714)
**:** a small mirror set to swing in a standing
frame and used at a dresser or dressing table

**dressing gown** *noun* (1777)
**:** a robe worn especially while dressing or
resting

**dressing room** *noun* (1675)
**:** a room used chiefly for dressing; *especially*
**:** a room in a theater for changing costumes
and makeup

**dressing table** *noun* (1692)
**:** a table often fitted with drawers and a mirror
in front of which one sits while dressing and
grooming oneself

**¹dress·mak·er** \'dres-,mā-kər\ *noun* (1803)
**:** one that makes dresses
— **dress·mak·ing** \-,mā-kiŋ\ *noun*

**²dressmaker** *adjective* (1904)
*of women's clothes* **:** having softness, rounded
lines, and intricate detailing ⟨a *dressmaker*
suit⟩

**dress rehearsal** *noun* (1828)
**1 :** a full rehearsal (as of a play) in costume
and with stage properties shortly before the
first performance
**2 :** a practice exercise for something to come
**:** DRY RUN

**dress shield** *noun* (1884)
**:** a pad worn inside a part of the clothing liable
to be soiled by perspiration (as at the underarm)

**dress shirt** *noun* (1892)
**:** a man's shirt especially for wear with
evening dress; *broadly* **:** a shirt suitable for
wear with a necktie

**dress uniform** *noun* (circa 1897)
**:** a uniform for formal wear

**dress up** (1674)
*transitive verb*
**1 a :** to attire in best or formal clothes **b :** to
attire in clothes suited to a particular role
**2 a :** to present in the most attractive or impressive light ⟨a fiasco *dressed up* as a tri-
umph⟩ **b :** to make more attractive, glamorous,
or fancy ⟨*dress up* a plain dessert with a rich
chocolate sauce⟩
*intransitive verb*
**:** to get dressed up

**dressy** \'dre-sē\ *adjective* **dress·i·er; -est**
(1768)
**1 :** showy in dress
**2 :** STYLISH, SMART
— **dress·i·ness** *noun*

**drew** *past of* DRAW

**Drey·fu·sard** \,drī-f(y)ə-'sär(d), ,drā-, -'zär(d)\
*noun* [French] (1898)
**:** a defender or partisan of Alfred Dreyfus

**drib** \'drib\ *noun* [probably back-formation
from *dribble & driblet*] (circa 1730)
**:** a small amount — usually used in the
phrase *dribs and drabs*

**¹drib·ble** \'dri-bəl\ *verb* **drib·bled; drib·
bling** \-(ə-)liŋ\ [frequentative of *drib* (to dribble)] (circa 1589)
*transitive verb*
**1 :** to issue sporadically and in small bits
**2 :** to let or cause to fall in drops little by little
**3 a :** to propel by successive slight taps or
bounces with hand, foot, or stick **b :** to hit (as
a baseball) so as to cause a slow bouncing
*intransitive verb*
**1 :** to fall or flow in drops or in a thin intermittent stream **:** TRICKLE
**2 :** to let saliva trickle from the corner of the
mouth **:** DROOL
**3 :** to come or issue in piecemeal or desultory
fashion

**4 a :** to dribble a ball or puck **b :** to proceed by dribbling **c** *of a ball* **:** to move with short bounces
— **drib·bler** \-b(ə-)lər\ *noun*
²**dribble** *noun* (circa 1680)
**1 :** a tiny or insignificant bit or quantity
**2 :** a small trickling stream or flow
**3 :** an act, instance, or manner of dribbling a ball or puck
— **drib·bly** \'dri-b(ə-)lē\ *adjective*
**drib·let** \'drib-lət\ *noun* (1678)
**1 :** a trifling or small sum or part
**2 :** a drop of liquid
**dried–up** \'drīd-,əp, ,drī-'\ *adjective* (1885)
**:** being wizened and shriveled
¹**drier** *comparative of* DRY
²**dri·er** *or* **dry·er** \'drī(-ə)r\ *noun* (1528)
**1 :** something that extracts or absorbs moisture
**2 :** a substance that accelerates drying (as of oils, paints, and printing inks)
**3** *usually* **dryer :** a device for drying
**driest** *superlative of* DRY
¹**drift** \'drift\ *noun* [Middle English; akin to Old English *drīfan* to drive — more at DRIVE] (14th century)
**1 a :** the act of driving something along **b :** the flow or the velocity of the current of a river or ocean stream
**2 :** something driven, propelled, or urged along or drawn together in a clump by or as if by a natural agency: as **a :** wind-driven snow, rain, cloud, dust, or smoke usually at or near the ground surface **b** (1) **:** a mass of matter (as sand) deposited together by or as if by wind or water (2) **:** a helter-skelter accumulation **c :** DROVE, FLOCK **d :** something (as driftwood) washed ashore **e :** rock debris deposited by natural agents; *specifically* **:** a deposit of clay, sand, gravel, and boulders transported by a glacier or by running water from a glacier
**3 a :** a general underlying design or tendency **b :** the underlying meaning, import, or purport of what is spoken or written
**4 :** something (as a tool) driven down upon or forced into a body
**5 :** the motion or action of drifting especially spatially and usually under external influence: as **a :** the lateral motion of an aircraft due to air currents **b :** an easy moderate more or less steady flow or sweep along a spatial course **c :** a gradual shift in attitude, opinion, or position **d :** an aimless course; *especially* **:** a foregoing of any attempt at direction or control **e :** a deviation from a true reproduction, representation, or reading
**6 a :** a nearly horizontal mine passageway driven on or parallel to the course of a vein or rock stratum **b :** a small crosscut in a mine connecting two larger tunnels
**7 a :** an assumed trend toward a general change in the structure of a language over a period of time **b :** GENETIC DRIFT **c :** a gradual change in the zero reading of an instrument or in any quantitative characteristic that is supposed to remain constant
**synonym** *see* TENDENCY
— **drifty** \'drif-tē\ *adjective*
²**drift** (circa 1600)
*intransitive verb*
**1 a :** to become driven or carried along (as by a current of water, wind, or air) **b :** to move or float smoothly and effortlessly
**2 a :** to move along a line of least resistance **b :** to move in a random or casual way **c :** to become carried along subject to no guidance or control ⟨the talk *drifted* from topic to topic⟩
**3 a :** to accumulate in a mass or become piled up in heaps by wind or water **b :** to become covered with a drift
**4 :** to vary or deviate from a set course or adjustment
*transitive verb*
**1 a :** to cause to be driven in a current **b** *West* **:** to drive (livestock) slowly especially to allow grazing

**2 a :** to pile in heaps **b :** to cover with drifts
— **drift·ing·ly** \'drif-tiŋ-lē\ *adverb*
**drift·age** \'drif-tij\ *noun* (1768)
**:** drifted material
**drift·er** \'drif-tər\ *noun* (1897)
**:** one that drifts; *especially* **:** one that travels or moves about aimlessly
**drift fence** *noun* (1907)
**:** a stretch of fence on rangeland especially in the western U.S. for preventing cattle from drifting from their home range
**drift net** *noun* (1848)
**:** a fishing net often miles in extent arranged to drift with the tide or current and buoyed up by floats or attached to a boat
**drift·wood** \'drift-,wùd\ *noun* (1633)
**1 :** wood drifted or floated by water
**2 :** FLOTSAM 2
¹**drill** \'dril\ *verb* [Dutch *drillen*] (1622)
*transitive verb*
**1 a :** to fix something in the mind or habit pattern of by repetitive instruction ⟨*drill* pupils in spelling⟩ **b :** to impart or communicate by repetition ⟨impossible to *drill* the simplest idea into some people⟩ **c :** to train or exercise in military drill
**2 a** (1) **:** to bore or drive a hole in (2) **:** to make by piercing action **b :** to shoot with or as if with a gun **c** (1) **:** to propel (as a ball) with force or accuracy ⟨*drilled* a single to right field⟩ (2) **:** to hit with force ⟨*drilled* the batter with the first pitch⟩
*intransitive verb*
**1 :** to make a hole with a drill
**2 :** to engage in an exercise
— **drill·abil·i·ty** \,dri-lə-'bi-lə-tē\ *noun*
— **drill·able** \-lə-bəl\ *adjective*
— **drill·er** \'dri-lər\ *noun*
²**drill** *noun* (1611)
**1 :** an instrument with an edged or pointed end for making holes in hard substances by revolving or by a succession of blows; *also* **:** a machine for operating such an instrument
**2 :** the act or exercise of training soldiers in marching and in executing prescribed movements with a weapon
**3 a :** a physical or mental exercise aimed at perfecting facility and skill especially by regular practice **b :** a formal exercise by a team of marchers **c** *chiefly British* **:** the approved or correct procedure for accomplishing something efficiently
**4 a :** a marine snail (*Urosalpinx cinerea*) destructive to oysters by boring through their shells and feeding on the soft parts **b :** any of several mollusks related to the drill
**5 :** a drilling sound
³**drill** *noun* [origin unknown] (1644)
**:** a western African baboon (*Papio leucophaeus* synonym *Mandrillus leucophaeus*) having a black face and brown coat and closely related to the typical mandrills
⁴**drill** *noun* [perhaps from *drill* (rill)] (1727)
**1 a :** a shallow furrow or trench into which seed is sown **b :** a row of seed sown in such a furrow
**2 :** a planting implement that makes holes or furrows, drops in the seed and sometimes fertilizer, and covers them with earth
⁵**drill** *transitive verb* (circa 1740)
**1 :** to sow (seeds) by dropping along a shallow furrow
**2 a :** to sow with seed or set with seedlings inserted in drills **b :** to distribute seed or fertilizer in by means of a drill
⁶**drill** *noun* [short for *drilling*] (1743)
**:** a durable cotton twilled fabric
**dril·ling** \'dri-liŋ\ *noun* [modification of German *Drillich*, from Middle High German *drilich* fabric woven with a threefold thread, from Old High German *drilīh* made up of three threads, from Latin *trilic-, trilix*, from *tri- + licium* thread] (1640)
**:** ⁶DRILL
**drill·mas·ter** \'dril-,mas-tər\ *noun* (1869)
**1 :** an instructor in military drill

**2 :** an instructor or director who maintains severe discipline and often stresses method and detail
**drill press** *noun* (circa 1864)
**:** an upright drilling machine in which the drill is pressed to the work by a hand lever or by power
**drill team** *noun* (1928)
**:** an exhibition marching team that engages in precision drill
**drily** *variant of* DRYLY
**D ring** \'dē-,riŋ\ *noun* (circa 1899)
**:** a usually metal ring having the shape of a capital D
¹**drink** \'driŋk\ *verb* **drank** \'draŋk\; **drunk** \'drəŋk\ *or* **drank; drink·ing** [Middle English, from Old English *drincan*; akin to Old High German *trinkan* to drink] (before 12th century)
*transitive verb*
**1 a :** SWALLOW, IMBIBE **b :** to take in or suck up **:** ABSORB ⟨*drinking* air into his lungs⟩ **c :** to take in or receive avidly — usually used with *in* ⟨*drank* in every word of the lecture⟩
**2 :** to join in a toast to ⟨I'll *drink* your good health⟩
**3 :** to bring to a specified state by drinking alcoholic beverages ⟨*drank* himself into oblivion⟩
*intransitive verb*
**1 a :** to take liquid into the mouth for swallowing **b :** to receive into one's consciousness
**2 :** to partake of alcoholic beverages
**3 :** to make or join in a toast ⟨I'll *drink* to that!⟩
²**drink** *noun* (before 12th century)
**1 a :** a liquid suitable for swallowing **b :** alcoholic beverages
**2 :** a draft or portion of liquid
**3 :** excessive consumption of alcoholic beverages
**4 :** a sizable body of water — used with *the*
¹**drink·able** \'driŋ-kə-bəl\ *adjective* (1611)
**:** suitable or safe for drinking
— **drink·abil·i·ty** \,driŋ-kə-'bi-lə-tē\ *noun*
²**drinkable** *noun* (1708)
**:** a liquid suitable for drinking **:** BEVERAGE
**drink·er** \'driŋ-kər\ *noun* (before 12th century)
**1 a :** one that drinks **b :** a person who drinks alcoholic beverages especially to a notable degree ⟨a heavy *drinker*⟩
**2 :** WATERER b
**drinking fountain** *noun* (1860)
**:** a fixture with nozzle that delivers a stream of water for drinking
**drinking song** *noun* (1597)
**:** a song on a convivial theme appropriate for a group engaged in social drinking
¹**drip** \'drip\ *verb* **dripped; drip·ping** [Middle English *drippen*, from Old English *dryppan*; akin to Old English *dropa* drop] (before 12th century)
*transitive verb*
**1 :** to let fall in drops
**2 :** to let out or seem to spill copiously ⟨her voice *dripping* sarcasm⟩
*intransitive verb*
**1 a :** to let fall drops of moisture or liquid **b :** to overflow with or as if with moisture ⟨a uniform *dripping* with gold braid⟩
**2 :** to fall in or as if in drops
**3 :** to waft or pass gently
— **drip·per** *noun*
²**drip** *noun* (1664)
**1 :** a part of a cornice or other member that projects to throw off rainwater; *also* **:** an overlapping metal strip or an underneath groove for the same purpose
**2 a :** a falling in drops **b :** liquid that falls, overflows, or is extruded in drops

| | | | | |
|---|---|---|---|---|
| \ə\ abut | \ᵊ\ kitten | \ər\ **further** | \a\ ash | \ā\ ace |
| \ä\ mop, mar | \aù\ **out** | \ch\ **chin** | \e\ bet | \ē\ **easy** |
| \g\ go | \i\ hit | \ī\ ice | \j\ job | \ŋ\ sing | \ō\ go |
| \ò\ law | \òi\ boy | \th\ **thin** | \th\ **the** | \ü\ loot | \ù\ **foot** |
| \y\ yet | \zh\ vision | *see also* Guide to Pronunciation | | |

**3 :** the sound made by or as if by falling drops
**4 :** a device for the administration of a fluid at a slow rate especially into a vein; *also* **:** a material so administered
**5 :** a dull or unattractive person
**³drip** *adjective* (1895)
**:** of, relating to, or being coffee made by letting boiling water drip slowly through finely ground coffee ⟨*drip* coffee⟩ ⟨a *drip* pot⟩
**¹drip–dry** \'drip-,drī\ (1953)
*intransitive verb*
**:** to dry with few or no wrinkles when hung wet
*transitive verb*
**:** to hang (as wet clothing) to drip-dry
**²drip–dry** *adjective* (1957)
**:** made of a washable fabric that drip-dries
**³drip–dry** *noun* (1959)
**:** a drip-dry garment
**drip·less** \'dri-pləs\ *adjective* (1887)
**:** designed not to drip ⟨*dripless* candles⟩
**drip·ping** \'dri-piŋ\ *noun* (15th century)
**:** fat and juices drawn from meat during cooking — often used in plural
**drip·py** \'dri-pē\ *adjective* **drip·pi·er; -est** (circa 1718)
**1 :** characterized by dripping; *especially* **:** RAINY, DRIZZLY
**2 :** MAWKISH 2
**drip·stone** \'drip-,stōn\ *noun* (circa 1818)
**1 :** a stone drip (as over a window)
**2 :** calcium carbonate in the form of stalactites or stalagmites
**¹drive** \'drīv\ *verb* **drove** \'drōv\; **driv·en** \'dri-vən\; **driv·ing** \'drī-viŋ\ [Middle English, from Old English *drīfan;* akin to Old High German *trīban* to drive] (before 12th century)
*transitive verb*
**1 a :** to frighten or prod (as game or cattle) into moving in a desired direction **b :** to go through (a district) driving game animals
**2 :** to carry on or through energetically ⟨*drives* a hard bargain⟩
**3 a :** to impart a forward motion to by physical force ⟨waves *drove* the boat ashore⟩ **b :** to repulse, remove, or cause to go by force, authority, or influence ⟨*drive* the enemy back⟩ **c :** to set or keep in motion or operation ⟨*drive* machinery by electricity⟩
**4 a :** to direct the motions and course of (a draft animal) **b :** to operate the mechanism and controls and direct the course of (as a vehicle) **c :** to convey in a vehicle **d :** to float (logs) down a stream
**5 a :** to exert inescapable or coercive pressure on **:** FORCE **b :** to compel to undergo or suffer a change (as in situation or emotional state) ⟨*drove* him crazy⟩ ⟨*drove* her out of business⟩ **c :** to urge relentlessly to continuous exertion ⟨the sergeant *drove* his recruits⟩ **d :** to press or force into an activity, course, or direction ⟨the drug habit *drives* addicts to steal⟩ **e :** to project, inject, or impress incisively ⟨*drove* her point home⟩
**6 :** to force (a passage) by pressing or digging
**7 a :** to propel (an object of play) swiftly **b :** to hit (a golf ball) from the tee especially with a driver; *also* **:** to drive a golf ball onto (a green) **c :** to cause (a run or runner) to be scored in baseball — usually used with *in*
**8 :** to give shape or impulse to ⟨factors that *drive* the business cycle⟩
*intransitive verb*
**1 a :** to dash, plunge, or surge ahead rapidly or violently **b :** to progress with strong momentum ⟨the rain was *driving* hard⟩
**2 a :** to operate a vehicle **b :** to have oneself carried in a vehicle
**3 :** to drive a golf ball
**synonym** SEE MOVE
— **driv·abil·i·ty** *also* **drive·abil·i·ty** \,drī-və-'bi-lə-tē\ *noun*
— **driv·able** *also* **drive·able** \'drī-və-bəl\ *adjective*
— **drive at :** to intend to express, convey, or accomplish ⟨did not understand what she was *driving* at —Eric Goldman⟩

**²drive** *noun, often attributive* (1785)
**1 :** an act of driving: **a :** a trip in a carriage or automobile **b :** a collection and driving together of animals; *also* **:** the animals gathered **c :** a driving of cattle or sheep overland **d :** a hunt or shoot in which the game is driven within the hunter's range **e :** the guiding of logs downstream to a mill; *also* **:** the floating logs amassed in a drive **f** (1) **:** the act or an instance of driving an object of play (as a golf ball) (2) **:** the flight of a ball
**2 a :** a private road **:** DRIVEWAY **b :** a public road for driving (as in a park)
**3 :** the state of being hurried and under pressure
**4 a :** a strong systematic group effort ⟨a fund-raising *drive*⟩ **b :** a sustained offensive effort ⟨the *drive* ended in a touchdown⟩
**5 a :** the means for giving motion to a machine or machine part **b :** the means by which the propulsive power of an automobile is applied to the road ⟨front wheel *drive*⟩ **c :** the means by which the propulsion of an automotive vehicle is controlled and directed ⟨left-hand *drive*⟩
**6 :** an offensive, aggressive, or expansionist move; *especially* **:** a strong military attack against enemy-held terrain
**7 a :** an urgent, basic, or instinctual need **:** a motivating physiological condition of an organism ⟨a sexual *drive*⟩ **b :** an impelling culturally acquired concern, interest, or longing **c :** dynamic quality
**8 :** a device for reading and writing on magnetic media (as tapes or disks)
**drive–by** \'drīv-,bī\ *adjective* (1986)
**:** carried out from a moving vehicle ⟨a *drive-by* shooting⟩
**¹drive–in** \'drī-,vin\ *noun* (1937)
**:** an establishment (as a theater or restaurant) so laid out that patrons can be accommodated while remaining in their automobiles
— **drive–in** *adjective*
**¹driv·el** \'dri-vəl\ *verb* **-eled** *or* **-elled; -el·ing** *or* **-el·ling** \-v(ə-)liŋ\ [Middle English, from Old English *dreflian;* perhaps akin to Old Norse *draf* malt dregs] (before 12th century)
*intransitive verb*
**1 :** to let saliva dribble from the mouth **:** SLAVER
**2 :** to talk stupidly and carelessly
*transitive verb*
**1 :** to utter in an infantile or imbecilic way
**2 :** to waste or fritter in a childish fashion
— **driv·el·er** \-v(ə-)lər\ *noun*
**²drivel** *noun* (14th century)
**1** *archaic* **:** DROOL 1
**2 :** NONSENSE
**drive·line** \'drīv-,līn\ *noun* (1949)
**:** DRIVETRAIN
**driv·en** *adjective* (1925)
**:** having a compulsive or urgent quality ⟨a *driven* sense of obligation⟩
— **driv·en·ness** \'dri-vən-nəs\ *noun*
**driv·er** \'drī-vər\ *noun* (14th century)
**:** one that drives: as **a :** COACHMAN **b :** the operator of a motor vehicle **c :** an implement (as a hammer) for driving **d :** a mechanical piece for imparting motion to another piece **e :** a golf wood with a nearly straight face used in driving **f :** an electronic circuit that supplies input to another electronic circuit; *also* **:** LOUDSPEAKER **g :** a piece of computer software that controls input and output operations
— **driv·er·less** \-ləs\ *adjective*
**driver ant** *noun* (1859)
**:** ARMY ANT; *specifically* **:** any of various African and Asian ants (*Dorylus* or related genera) that move in vast armies
**driver's license** *noun* (1926)
**:** a license issued under governmental authority that permits the holder to operate a motor vehicle
**driver's seat** *noun* (1923)
**:** the position of top authority or dominance

**drive·shaft** \'drīv-,shaft\ *noun* (1895)
**:** a shaft that transmits mechanical power
**drive time** *noun* (1966)
**:** a time during rush hour when radio audiences are swelled by commuters listening to car radios
**drive·train** \'drīv-,trān\ *noun* (1954)
**:** the parts (as the universal joint and the driveshaft) that connect the transmission with the driving axles of an automobile
**drive·way** \-,wā\ *noun* (1871)
**:** a private road giving access from a public way to a building on abutting grounds
**driv·ing** *adjective* (14th century)
**1 a :** communicating force ⟨a *driving* wheel⟩ **b :** exerting pressure ⟨a *driving* influence⟩
**2 a :** having great force ⟨a *driving* rain⟩ **b :** acting with vigor **:** ENERGETIC ⟨a hard-*driving* worker⟩
**driving range** *noun* (circa 1949)
**:** an area equipped with distance markers, clubs, balls, and tees for practicing golf drives
**¹driz·zle** \'dri-zəl\ *noun* (1554)
**:** a fine misty rain
— **driz·zly** \'driz-(ə-)lē\ *adjective*
**²drizzle** *verb* **driz·zled; driz·zling** \-z(ə-)liŋ\ [perhaps alteration of Middle English *drysnen* to fall, from Old English *-drysnian* to disappear; akin to Gothic *driusan* to fall] (1584)
*transitive verb*
**1 :** to shed or let fall in minute drops or particles
**2 :** to make wet with minute drops
*intransitive verb*
**:** to rain in very small drops or very lightly **:** SPRINKLE
— **driz·zling·ly** \-z(ə-)liŋ-lē\ *adverb*
**drogue** \'drōg\ *noun* [probably alteration of ¹*drag*] (1875)
**1 :** SEA ANCHOR
**2 a :** a cylindrical or funnel-shaped device towed as a target by an airplane **b :** a small parachute for stabilizing or decelerating something (as an astronaut's capsule) or for pulling a larger parachute out of stowage
**3 :** a funnel-shaped device which is attached to the end of a long flexible hose suspended from a tanker airplane in flight and into which the probe of another airplane is fitted so as to receive fuel from the tanker
**droit** \'drȯit, 'drwä\ *noun* [Middle English, from Middle French, from Medieval Latin *directum,* from Late Latin, neuter of *directus* just, from Latin, direct — more at DRESS] (15th century)
**:** a legal right
**droit du sei·gneur** \drwä-dœ-se-nʸœr\ *noun* [French, right of the lord] (1825)
**:** a supposed legal or customary right of a feudal lord to have sexual relations with a vassal's bride on her wedding night
**¹droll** \'drōl\ *adjective* [French *drôle,* from *drôle* scamp, from Middle French *drolle,* from Middle Dutch, imp] (1623)
**:** having a humorous, whimsical, or odd quality
— **droll·ness** *noun*
— **drol·ly** \'drō(l)-lē\ *adverb*
**²droll** *noun* (circa 1645)
**:** an amusing person **:** JESTER, COMEDIAN
**³droll** *intransitive verb* (1654)
*archaic* **:** to make fun **:** JEST, SPORT
**droll·ery** \'drōl-rē, 'drō-lə-\ *noun, plural* **-er·ies** (1597)
**1 :** something that is droll; *especially* **:** a comic picture or drawing
**2 :** the act or an instance of jesting or burlesquing
**3 :** whimsical humor
**-drome** \,drōm\ *noun combining form* [*hippodrome*]
**1 :** racecourse ⟨motor*drome*⟩
**2 :** large specially prepared place ⟨aero*drome*⟩
**drom·e·dary** \'drä-mə-,der-ē *also* 'drə-\ *noun, plural* **-dar·ies** [Middle English *dromedarie,*

from Old French *dromedaire*, from Late Latin *dromedarius*, from Latin *dromad-*, *dromas*, from Greek, running; akin to Greek *dramein* to run, *dromos* racecourse, Sanskrit *dramati* he runs about] (13th century)
: CAMEL 1a

**-dro·mous** \drə-məs\ *adjective combining form* [New Latin *-dromus*, from Greek *-dromos* (akin to Greek *dramein*)]
: running (cata*dromous*)

¹**drone** \ˈdrōn\ *noun* [Middle English, from Old English *drān;* akin to Old High German *treno* drone, Greek *thrēnos* dirge] (before 12th century)
**1** : the male of a bee (as the honeybee) that has no sting and gathers no honey
**2** : one that lives on the labors of others : PARASITE
**3** : an unmanned airplane, helicopter, or ship guided by remote control
**4** : DRUDGE

²**drone** *verb* **droned; dron·ing** (circa 1520)
*intransitive verb*
**1 a** : to make a sustained deep murmuring, humming, or buzzing sound **b** : to talk in a persistently dull or monotonous tone
**2** : to pass, proceed, or act in a dull, drowsy, or indifferent manner
*transitive verb*
**1** : to utter or pronounce with a drone
**2** : to pass or spend in dull or monotonous activity or in idleness
— **dron·er** *noun*
— **dron·ing·ly** \ˈdrō-niŋ-lē\ *adverb*

³**drone** *noun* (circa 1520)
**1** : a deep sustained or monotonous sound : HUM
**2** : an instrument or part of an instrument (as one of the fixed-pitch pipes of a bagpipe) that sounds a continuous unvarying tone
**3** : PEDAL POINT

¹**drool** \ˈdrü(-ə)l\ *verb* [perhaps alteration of *drivel*] (1802)
*intransitive verb*
**1 a** : to secrete saliva in anticipation of food **b** : DRIVEL 1
**2** : to make an effusive show of pleasure or often envious or covetous appreciation
**3** : to talk nonsense
*transitive verb*
: to express sentimentally or effusively

²**drool** *noun* (1869)
**1** : saliva trickling from the mouth
**2** : NONSENSE

¹**droop** \ˈdrüp\ *verb* [Middle English *drupen*, from Old Norse *drūpa;* akin to Old English *dropa* drop] (13th century)
*intransitive verb*
**1** : to hang or incline downward
**2** : to sink gradually
**3** : to become depressed or weakened : LANGUISH
*transitive verb*
: to let droop
— **droop·ing·ly** \ˈdrü-piŋ-lē\ *adverb*

²**droop** *noun* (1647)
: the condition or appearance of drooping

**droopy** \ˈdrü-pē\ *adjective* **droop·i·er; -est** (13th century)
**1** : GLOOMY
**2** : drooping or tending to droop

¹**drop** \ˈdräp\ *noun, often attributive* [Middle English, from Old English *dropa;* akin to Old High German *tropfo* drop] (before 12th century)
**1 a** (1) : the quantity of fluid that falls in one spherical mass (2) *plural* : a dose of medicine measured by drops; *especially* : a solution for dilating the pupil of the eye **b** : a minute quantity or degree of something nonmaterial or intangible **c** : a small quantity of drink **d** : the smallest practical unit of liquid measure
**2** : something that resembles a liquid drop: as **a** : a pendent ornament attached to a piece of jewelry; *also* : an earring with such a pendant **b** : a small globular cookie or candy

**3** [²*drop*] **a** : the act or an instance of dropping : FALL **b** : a decline in quantity or quality **c** : a descent by parachute; *also* : the people or equipment dropped by parachute **d** : a place or central depository to which something (as mail, money, or stolen property) is brought for distribution or transmission; *also* : the act of depositing something at such a place (made the *drop*)
**4 a** : the distance from a higher to a lower level or through which something drops **b** : a fall of electric potential
**5** : a slot into which something is to be dropped
**6** [²*drop*] : something that drops, hangs, or falls: as **a** : a movable plate that covers the keyhole of a lock **b** : an unframed piece of cloth stage scenery; *also* : DROP CURTAIN **c** : a hinged platform on a gallows **d** : a fallen fruit
**7** : the advantage of having an opponent covered with a firearm; *broadly* : ADVANTAGE, SUPERIORITY — usually used in the phrase *get the drop on*
— **at the drop of a hat** : as soon as the slightest provocation is given : IMMEDIATELY
— **drop in the bucket** : a part so small as to be negligible

²**drop** *verb* **dropped; drop·ping** (before 12th century)
*intransitive verb*
**1** : to fall in drops
**2 a** (1) : to fall unexpectedly or suddenly (2) : to descend from one line or level to another **b** : to fall in a state of collapse or death **c** *of a card* : to become played by reason of the obligation to follow suit **d** *of a ball* : to fall or roll into a hole or basket
**3** : to enter or pass as if without conscious effort of will into some state, condition, or activity (*dropped* into sleep)
**4 a** : to cease to be of concern : LAPSE (let the matter *drop*) **b** : to pass from view or notice : DISAPPEAR — often used with *out* (*drop* out of sight) **c** : to become less (production *dropped*) — often used with *off*
**5** : to move with a favoring wind or current — usually used with *down*
*transitive verb*
**1** : to let fall : cause to fall
**2 a** : GIVE UP 2, ABANDON (*drop* an idea) (*drop* the charges) **b** : DISCONTINUE (*dropped* what she was doing) **c** : to break off an association or connection with : DISMISS (*drop* a failing student)
**3 a** : to utter or mention in a casual way (*drop* a suggestion) (*drop* names) **b** : WRITE (*drop* us a line soon)
**4 a** : to lower or cause to descend from one level or position to another **b** : to cause to lessen or decrease : REDUCE (*dropped* his speed)
**5** *of an animal* : to give birth to
**6 a** : LOSE (*dropped* three games) (*dropped* $50 in a poker game) **b** : SPEND (*drop* $20 for lunch)
**7 a** : to bring down with a shot or a blow **b** : to cause (a high card) to fall **c** : to toss or roll into a hole or basket (*drop* a putt)
**8 a** : to deposit or deliver during a usually brief stop — usually used with *off* (*drop* the kids off at school) **b** : AIR-DROP
**9** : to cause (the voice) to be less loud
**10 a** : to leave (a letter representing a speech sound) unsounded (*drop* the g in *running*) **b** : to leave out in writing : OMIT
**11** : to draw from an external point (*drop* a perpendicular to the line)
**12** : to take (a drug) orally : SWALLOW (*drop* acid)
— **drop·pa·ble** \ˈdrä-pə-bəl\ *adjective*
— **drop behind** : to fail to keep up

**drop back** *intransitive verb* (1927)
**1** : RETREAT
**2** : to move straight back from the line of scrimmage (the quarterback *drops back* to pass)

**drop by** (circa 1905)
*intransitive verb*
: to pay a brief casual visit
*transitive verb*
: to visit casually or unexpectedly (*drop by* a friend's house)

**drop cloth** *noun* (circa 1928)
: a protective sheet (as of cloth or plastic) used especially by painters to cover floors and furniture

**drop curtain** *noun* (1832)
: a stage curtain that can be lowered and raised

**drop–dead** *adjective* (1970)
: sensationally striking, attractive, or impressive (a *drop-dead* evening gown)
— **drop–dead** *adverb*

**drop–forge** \ˈdräp-ˌfōrj, -ˌfȯrj\ *transitive verb* (1886)
: to forge between dies by means of a drop hammer or punch press
— **drop forger** *noun*

**drop front** *noun* (1925)
: a hinged cover on the front of a desk that may be lowered to provide a surface for writing

**drop hammer** *noun* (circa 1864)
: a power hammer raised and then released to drop (as on metal resting on an anvil or die)

**drop·head** \ˈdräp-ˌhed\ *noun, often attributive* (1932)
*British* : a convertible automobile

**drop–in** \ˈdräp-ˌin\ *noun* (1819)
**1** : a casual visit or brief stop
**2** : one who drops in : a casual visitor

**drop in** *intransitive verb* (circa 1600)
: to pay an unexpected or casual visit — often used with *on*

**drop·kick** \-ˌkik\ *noun* (1857)
: a kick made by dropping a ball to the ground and kicking it at the moment it starts to rebound

**drop–kick** \-ˌkik\ (circa 1909)
*intransitive verb*
: to make a dropkick
*transitive verb*
: to kick by means of a dropkick (*drop-kick* a ball) (*drop-kick* a field goal)
— **drop·kick·er** *noun*

**drop leaf** *noun* (1882)
: a hinged leaf on the side or end of a table that can be folded down

**drop·let** \ˈdräp-lət\ *noun* (1607)
: a tiny drop (as of a liquid)

**drop·light** \ˈdräp-ˌlīt\ *noun* (1890)
: an electric light suspended by a cord or on a portable extension

**drop–off** \ˈdräp-ˌȯf\ *noun* (1923)
**1** : a very steep or perpendicular descent
**2** : a marked dwindling or decline (a *drop-off* in attendance)

**drop off** \ˌdräp-ˈȯf\ *intransitive verb* (1820)
: to fall asleep

**drop·out** \ˈdräp-ˌaut\ *noun* (1930)
**1 a** : one who drops out of school **b** : one who drops out of conventional society **c** : one who abandons an attempt, activity, or chosen path (a corporate *dropout*)
**2** : a spot on a magnetic tape or disk from which data has disappeared

**drop out** \ˌdräp-ˈaut\ *intransitive verb* (1883)
: to withdraw from participation or membership : QUIT; *especially* : to withdraw from conventional society

**drop pass** *noun* (1949)
: a pass in ice hockey in which the passer skates past the puck leaving it for a teammate following close behind

**dropped** *adjective* (1953)

: designed to extend or begin lower than normal 〈a dress with a *dropped* waist〉 〈*dropped* shoulders〉

**dropped egg** *noun* (1824)
: a poached egg

**drop·per** \'drä-pər\ *noun* (circa 1700)
**1** : one that drops
**2** : a short glass tube fitted with a rubber bulb and used to measure liquids by drops — called also *eyedropper, medicine dropper*
— **drop·per·ful** \-,ful\ *noun*

**drop·ping** *noun* (14th century)
**1** : something dropped
**2** *plural* : DUNG

**drop seat** *noun* (1926)
**1** : a hinged seat (as in a taxi) that may be dropped down
**2** : a seat (as in an undergarment) that can be unbuttoned

**drop shot** *noun* (1908)
: a delicately hit shot (as in tennis or squash) that drops quickly after crossing the net or dies after hitting a wall

**drop·si·cal** \'dräp-si-kəl\ *adjective* (1678)
**1** : relating to or affected with dropsy
**2** : TURGID, SWOLLEN

**drop·sy** \'dräp-sē\ *noun* [Middle English *dropesie,* short for *ydropesie,* from Old French, from Latin *hydropisis,* modification of Greek *hydrōps,* from *hydōr* water — more at WATER] (13th century)
: EDEMA

**drop tank** *noun* (1943)
: an auxiliary fuel tank for airplanes that can be jettisoned when empty

**drop volley** *noun* (1907)
: a drop shot made on a volley in tennis

**drop zone** *noun* (circa 1943)
: the area in which troops, supplies, or equipment are to be air-dropped; *also* : the target on which a skydiver lands

**drosh·ky** \'dräsh-kē\ *also* **dros·ky** \'dräs-kē\ *noun, plural* **droshkies** *also* **droskies** [Russian *drozhki,* from *droga* pole of a wagon] (1808)
: any of various 2- or 4-wheeled carriages used especially in Russia

**dro·soph·i·la** \drō-'sä-fə-lə\ *noun* [New Latin, genus name, from Greek *drosos* dew + New Latin *-phila,* feminine of *-philus* -phil] (1910)
: any of a genus (*Drosophila*) of small two-winged flies used in genetic research

**dross** \'dräs, 'dros\ *noun* [Middle English *dros,* from Old English *drōs* dregs] (before 12th century)
**1** : the scum that forms on the surface of molten metal
**2** : waste or foreign matter : IMPURITY
**3** : something that is base, trivial, or inferior
— **drossy** \'drä-sē, 'drö-\ *adjective*

**drought** \'draut\ *also* **drouth** \'drauth\ *noun* [Middle English, from Old English *drūgath,* from *drūgian* to dry up; akin to Old English *drȳge* dry — more at DRY] (before 12th century)
**1** : a period of dryness especially when prolonged that causes extensive damage to crops or prevents their successful growth
**2** : a prolonged or chronic shortage or lack of something expected or desired
— **drought·i·ness** *noun*
— **droughty** \'drau-tē\ *adjective*

**¹drove** \'drōv\ *noun* [Middle English, from Old English *drāf,* from *drīfan* to drive — more at DRIVE] (before 12th century)
**1** : a group of animals driven or moving in a body
**2** : a large number : CROWD — usually used in plural especially with *in* 〈tourists arriving in *droves*〉 〈stayed away in *droves*〉

**²drove** *past of* DRIVE

**drov·er** \'drō-vər\ *noun* (15th century)
: one that drives cattle or sheep

**drown** \'draun\ *verb* **drowned** \'draund\; **drown·ing** \'drau-niŋ\ [Middle English *drounen*] (14th century)

*intransitive verb*
: to become drowned
*transitive verb*
**1 a** : to suffocate by submersion especially in water **b** : to submerge especially by a rise in the water level **c** : to soak, drench, or cover with a liquid
**2** : to engage (oneself) deeply and strenuously
**3** : to cause (a sound) not to be heard by making a loud noise — usually used with *out*
**4 a** : to drive out (as a sensation or an idea) 〈*drowned* his sorrows in liquor〉 **b** : OVERWHELM

**drownd** \'draund\ *nonstandard variant of* DROWN

**¹drowse** \'drauz\ *verb* **drowsed; drows·ing** [probably akin to Gothic *driusan* to fall — more at DREARY] (1573)
*intransitive verb*
**1** : to be inactive
**2** : to fall into a light slumber
*transitive verb*
**1** : to make drowsy or inactive
**2** : to pass (time) drowsily or in drowsing

**²drowse** *noun* (1814)
: the act or an instance of drowsing : DOZE

**drowsy** \'drau-zē\ *adjective* **drows·i·er; -est** (1530)
**1 a** : ready to fall asleep **b** : inducing or tending to induce sleep **c** : INDOLENT, LETHARGIC
**2** : giving the appearance of peaceful inactivity
— **drows·i·ly** \-zə-lē\ *adverb*
— **drows·i·ness** \-zē-nəs\ *noun*

**drub** \'drəb\ *verb* **drubbed; drub·bing** [perhaps from Arabic *ḍaraba*] (1634)
*transitive verb*
**1** : to beat severely
**2** : to abuse with words : BERATE
**3** : to defeat decisively
*intransitive verb*
: DRUM, STAMP
— **drub·ber** *noun*

**¹drudge** \'drəj\ *verb* **drudged; drudg·ing** [Middle English *druggen*] (14th century)
*intransitive verb*
: to do hard, menial, or monotonous work
*transitive verb*
: to force to do hard, menial, or monotonous work
— **drudg·er** *noun*

**²drudge** *noun* (15th century)
**1** : one who is obliged to do menial work
**2** : one whose work is routine and boring

**drudg·ery** \'drəj-rē, 'drə-jə-rē\ *noun, plural* **-er·ies** (1550)
: dull, irksome, and fatiguing work : uninspiring or menial labor
*synonym* see WORK

**drudg·ing** \'drə-jiŋ\ *adjective* (1548)
: MONOTONOUS, TIRING
— **drudg·ing·ly** \-jiŋ-lē\ *adverb*

**¹drug** \'drəg\ *noun* [Middle English *drogge*] (14th century)
**1 a** *obsolete* : a substance used in dyeing or chemical operations **b** : a substance used as a medication or in the preparation of medication **c** *according to the Food, Drug, and Cosmetic Act* (1) : a substance recognized in an official pharmacopoeia or formulary (2) : a substance intended for use in the diagnosis, cure, mitigation, treatment, or prevention of disease (3) : a substance other than food intended to affect the structure or function of the body (4) : a substance intended for use as a component of a medicine but not a device or a component, part, or accessory of a device
**2** : a commodity that is not salable or for which there is no demand — used in the phrase *drug on the market*
**3** : something and often an illegal substance that causes addiction, habituation, or a marked change in consciousness
— **drug·gy** *also* **drug·gie** \'drə-gē\ *adjective*

**²drug** *verb* **drugged; drug·ging** (1605)
*transitive verb*
**1** : to affect with a drug; *especially* : to stupefy by a narcotic drug
**2** : to administer a drug to
**3** : to lull or stupefy as if with a drug
*intransitive verb*
: to take drugs for narcotic effect

**³drug** *dialect past of* DRAG

**drug·get** \'drə-gət\ *noun* [Middle French *droguet,* diminutive of *drogue* trash, drug] (1580)
**1** : a wool or partly wool fabric formerly used for clothing
**2** : a coarse durable cloth used chiefly as a floor covering
**3** : a rug having a cotton warp and a wool filling

**drug·gie** *also* **drug·gy** \'drə-gē\ *noun, plural* **druggies** (1967)
: one who habitually uses drugs

**drug·gist** \'drə-gist\ *noun* (1611)
: one who sells or dispenses drugs and medicines: as **a** : PHARMACIST **b** : one who owns or manages a drugstore

**drug·mak·er** \'drəg-,mā-kər\ *noun* (1964)
: one that manufactures pharmaceuticals

**drug·store** \-,stōr, -,stȯr\ *noun* (1810)
: a retail store where medicines and miscellaneous articles are sold : PHARMACY

**drugstore cowboy** *noun* (1925)
**1** : one who wears cowboy clothes but has had no experience as a cowboy
**2** : one who loafs on street corners and in drugstores

**dru·id** \'drü-id\ *noun, often capitalized* [Latin *druides, druidae,* plural, from Gaulish *druides;* akin to Old Irish *druí* druid, and perhaps to Old English *trēow* tree] (1563)
: one of an ancient Celtic priesthood appearing in Irish and Welsh sagas and Christian legends as magicians and wizards
— **dru·id·ic** \drü-'i-dik\ *or* **dru·id·i·cal** \-di-kəl\ *adjective, often capitalized*

**dru·id·ism** \'drü-ə-,di-zəm\ *noun, often capitalized* (1715)
: the system of religion, philosophy, and instruction of the druids

**¹drum** \'drəm\ *noun* [probably from Dutch *trom;* akin to Middle High German *trumme* drum] (1539)
**1** : a percussion instrument consisting of a hollow shell or cylinder with a drumhead stretched over one or both ends that is beaten with the hands or with some implement (as a stick or wire brush)
**2** : TYMPANIC MEMBRANE

drum 1: *1* bass, *2* snare (orchestra), *3* snare (parade)

**3** : the sound of a drum; *also* : a sound similar to that of a drum
**4** : any of various bony fishes (family Sciaenidae) that make a drumming noise
**5** : something resembling a drum in shape: as **a** : a cylindrical machine or mechanical device or part **b** : a cylindrical container; *specifically* : a large usually metal container for liquids 〈a 55-gallon *drum*〉 **c** : a disk-shaped magazine for an automatic weapon
— **drum·like** \-,līk\ *adjective*

**²drum** *verb* **drummed; drum·ming** (1583)
*intransitive verb*
**1** : to make a succession of strokes or vibrations that produce sounds like drumbeats
**2** : to beat a drum
**3** : to throb or sound rhythmically
**4** : to stir up interest : SOLICIT
*transitive verb*
**1** : to summon or enlist by or as if by beating a drum 〈were *drummed* into service〉

**2 :** to dismiss ignominiously **:** EXPEL — usually used with *out*
**3 :** to drive or force by steady effort or reiteration ⟨*drummed* the speech into her head⟩
**4 a :** to strike or tap repeatedly **b :** to produce (rhythmic sounds) by such action
³**drum** *noun* [Scottish Gaelic *druim* back, ridge, from Old Irish *druimm*] (1725)
**1** *chiefly Scottish* **:** a long narrow hill or ridge
**2 :** DRUMLIN
**drum·beat** \'drəm-ˌbēt\ *noun* (1855)
**1 :** a stroke on a drum or its sound; *also* **:** a series of such strokes
**2 :** vociferous advocacy of a cause
**3 :** DRUMFIRE 2
— **drum·beat·er** \-ˌbē-tər\ *noun*
— **drum·beat·ing** \-tiŋ\ *noun*
**drum brake** *noun* (1950)
**:** a brake that operates by the friction of usually a pair of shoes pressing against the inner surface of the cylinder of a rotating drum — compare DISC BRAKE
**drum·fire** \'drəm-ˌfīr\ *noun* (1916)
**1 :** artillery firing so continuous as to sound like a drumroll
**2 :** something suggestive of drumfire in intensity **:** BARRAGE ⟨a *drumfire* of publicity⟩
**drum·head** \-ˌhed\ *noun* (1622)
**1 :** the material (as skin or plastic) stretched over one or both ends of a drum
**2 :** the top of a capstan that is pierced with sockets for the levers used in turning it
**drumhead court–martial** *noun* [from the use of a drumhead as a table] (1835)
**:** a summary court-martial that tries offenses on the battlefield
**drum·lin** \'drəm-lən\ *noun* [Irish *druim* back, ridge (from Old Irish *druimm*) + English -*lin* (alteration of -*ling*)] (circa 1833)
**:** an elongate or oval hill of glacial drift
**drum major** *noun* (1844)
**:** the leader of a marching band
**drum ma·jor·ette** \ˌdrəm-ˌmā-jə-'ret\ *noun* (1938)
**1 :** a girl or woman who leads a marching band
**2 :** a baton twirler who accompanies a marching band
**drum·mer** \'drə-mər\ *noun* (1580)
**1 a :** one that plays a drum **b** — used figuratively in expressions denoting an unconventional way of behaving or thinking ⟨march to a different *drummer*⟩
**2 :** TRAVELING SALESMAN
**drum·roll** \'drəm-ˌrōl\ *noun* (1887)
**:** a roll on a drum or its sound
**drum·stick** \-ˌstik\ *noun* (1589)
**1 :** a stick for beating a drum
**2 :** the segment of a fowl's leg between the thigh and tarsus
**drum up** *transitive verb* (1830)
**1 :** to bring about by persistent effort ⟨*drum up* some business⟩
**2 :** INVENT, ORIGINATE ⟨*drum up* a new method⟩
¹**drunk** *past participle of* DRINK
²**drunk** \'drəŋk\ *adjective* [Middle English *drunke*, alteration of *drunken*] (14th century)
**1 a :** having the faculties impaired by alcohol **b :** having a level of alcohol in the blood that exceeds a maximum prescribed by law ⟨legally *drunk*⟩
**2 :** dominated by an intense feeling ⟨*drunk* with rage⟩
**3 :** of, relating to, or caused by intoxication **:** DRUNKEN
³**drunk** *noun* (1779)
**1 :** a period of drinking to intoxication or of being intoxicated ⟨a 2-day *drunk*⟩
**2 :** one who is drunk; *especially* **:** DRUNKARD
**drunk·ard** \'drəŋ-kərd\ *noun* (15th century)
**:** one who is habitually drunk
**drunk·en** \'drəŋ-kən\ *adjective* [Middle English, from Old English *druncen*, from past participle of *drincan* to drink] (before 12th century)
**1 :** DRUNK 1 ⟨a *drunken* driver⟩

**2** *obsolete* **:** saturated with liquid
**3 a :** given to habitual excessive use of alcohol **b :** of, relating to, or characterized by intoxication ⟨they come from . . . broken homes, *drunken* homes —P. B. Gilliam⟩ **c :** resulting from or as if from intoxication ⟨a *drunken* brawl⟩
**4 :** unsteady or lurching as if from alcoholic intoxication
— **drunk·en·ly** *adverb*
— **drunk·en·ness** \-kən-nəs\ *noun*
**drunk tank** *noun* (1947)
**:** a large detention cell for arrested drunks
**dru·pa·ceous** \drü-'pā-shəs\ *adjective* (1822)
**1 :** of or relating to a drupe
**2 :** bearing drupes
**drupe** \'drüp\ *noun* [New Latin *drupa*, from Latin, overripe olive, from Greek *dryppa* olive] (circa 1753)
**:** a one-seeded indehiscent fruit having a hard bony endocarp, a fleshy mesocarp, and a thin exocarp that is flexible (as in the cherry) or dry and almost leathery (as in the almond)
**drupe·let** \'drü-plət\ *noun* (1880)
**:** a small drupe; *specifically* **:** one of the individual parts of an aggregate fruit (as the raspberry)
**druth·ers** \'drə-thərz\ *noun plural* [*druther*, alteration of *would rather*] (1875)
*dialect* **:** free choice **:** PREFERENCE — used especially in the phrase *if one had one's druthers*
**Druze** *or* **Druse** \'drüz\ *noun, plural* **Druze** *or* **Druzes** *or* **Druse** *or* **Druses** *often attributive* [Arabic *Durūz*, plural, from Muhammed ibn-Isma'īl al-*Darazīy* (died 1019) Muslim religious leader] (1786)
**:** a member of a religious sect originating among Muslims and centered in the mountains of Lebanon and Syria
¹**dry** \'drī\ *adjective* **dri·er** *also* **dry·er** \'drī-(-ə)r\; **dri·est** *also* **dry·est** \'drī-əst\ [Middle English, from Old English *drȳge*; akin to Old High German *truckan* dry, Old English *drēahnian* to drain] (before 12th century)
**1 a :** free or relatively free from a liquid and especially water **b :** not being in or under water ⟨*dry* land⟩ **c :** lacking precipitation or humidity ⟨*dry* climate⟩
**2 a :** characterized by exhaustion of a supply of liquid ⟨a *dry* well⟩ **b :** devoid of running water ⟨a *dry* ravine⟩ **c :** devoid of natural moisture ⟨my throat was *dry*⟩ **d :** no longer sticky or damp ⟨the paint is *dry*⟩ **e :** not giving milk ⟨a *dry* cow⟩ **f :** lacking freshness **:** STALE **g :** ANHYDROUS
**3 a :** marked by the absence or scantiness of secretions ⟨a *dry* cough⟩ **b :** not shedding or accompanied by tears ⟨a *dry* sob⟩
**4** *obsolete* **:** involving no bloodshed or drowning ⟨I would fain die a *dry* death —Shakespeare⟩
**5 a :** marked by the absence of alcoholic beverages ⟨a *dry* party⟩ **b :** prohibiting the manufacture or distribution of alcoholic beverages
**6 :** served or eaten without butter or margarine ⟨*dry* toast⟩
**7 a :** lacking sweetness **:** SEC ⟨*dry* champagne⟩ **b :** having all or most sugar fermented to alcohol ⟨a *dry* wine⟩ ⟨*dry* beer⟩
**8 a :** solid as opposed to liquid ⟨*dry* groceries⟩ **b :** reduced to powder or flakes **:** DEHYDRATED ⟨*dry* milk⟩
**9 :** functioning without lubrication ⟨a *dry* clutch⟩
**10** *of natural gas* **:** containing no recoverable hydrocarbon (as gasoline)
**11 :** requiring no liquid in preparation or operation ⟨a *dry* photocopying process⟩
**12 a :** not showing or communicating warmth, enthusiasm, or tender feeling **:** SEVERE ⟨a *dry* style of painting⟩ **b :** WEARISOME, UNINTERESTING ⟨*dry* passages of description⟩ **c :** lacking embellishment **:** PLAIN ⟨the *dry* facts⟩
**13 a :** not yielding what is expected or desired **:** UNPRODUCTIVE **b :** having no personal bias or emotional concern ⟨the *dry* light of reason⟩ **c :** RESERVED, ALOOF

**14 :** marked by matter-of-fact, ironic, or terse manner of expression ⟨*dry* wit⟩
**15 :** lacking smooth sound qualities ⟨a *dry* rasping voice⟩
**16 :** being a dry run ⟨a *dry* rehearsal⟩
— **dry·ish** \'drī-ish\ *adjective*
— **dry·ly** *adverb*
— **dry·ness** *noun*
²**dry** *verb* **dried; dry·ing** (before 12th century)
*transitive verb*
**:** to make dry
*intransitive verb*
**:** to become dry
— **dry·able** \'drī-ə-bəl\ *adjective*
³**dry** *noun, plural* **drys** (13th century)
**1 :** the condition of being dry **:** DRYNESS
**2 :** something dry; *especially* **:** a dry place
**3 :** PROHIBITIONIST
**dry·ad** \'drī-əd, -ˌad\ *noun* [Latin *dryad-, dryas*, from Greek, from *drys* tree — more at TREE] (14th century)
**:** WOOD NYMPH
**dry·as·dust** \'drī-əz-ˌdəst\ *adjective* (circa 1872)
**:** BORING
— **dryasdust** *noun*
**dry cell** *noun* (1893)
**:** a voltaic cell whose contents are not spillable — called also *dry battery*
**dry-clean** \'drī-ˌklēn\ (1817)
*transitive verb*
**:** to subject to dry cleaning
*intransitive verb*
**:** to undergo dry cleaning
— **dry-clean·able** \-'klē-nə-bəl\ *adjective*
**dry cleaner** *noun* (1897)
**:** one whose business is dry cleaning
**dry cleaning** *noun* (1897)
**1 :** the cleansing of fabrics with substantially nonaqueous organic solvents
**2 :** something that is dry-cleaned
**dry-dock** \'drī-ˌdäk\ *transitive verb* (1884)
**:** to place in a dry dock
**dry dock** *noun* (circa 1627)
**:** a dock that can be kept dry for use during the construction or repairing of ships
**dry·er** *variant of* DRIER
**dry-eyed** \'drī-ˌīd\ *adjective* (1667)
**1 :** not moved to tears or to empathy
**2 :** marked by the absence of sentimentalism or romanticism
**dry farming** *noun* (1878)
**:** farming on nonirrigated land with little rainfall that relies on moisture-conserving tillage and drought-resistant crops
— **dry-farm** *transitive verb*
— **dry farm** *noun*
— **dry farmer** *noun*
**dry fly** *noun* (1846)
**:** an artificial angling fly designed to float
**Dry·gas** \'drī-ˌgas\ *trademark*
— used for fuel-line antifreeze for motor vehicles
**dry goods** \'drī-ˌgu̇dz\ *noun plural* (1657)
**:** textiles, ready-to-wear clothing, and notions as distinguished especially from hardware and groceries
**dry hole** *noun* (1883)
**:** a well (as for gas or oil) that proves unproductive
**dry ice** *noun* (1925)
**:** solidified carbon dioxide
**drying oil** *noun* (circa 1865)
**:** an oil (as linseed oil) that changes readily to a hard tough elastic substance when exposed in a thin film to air
**dry·land** \'drī-ˌland\ *adjective* (1893)
**:** of, relating to, or being a relatively arid region ⟨a *dryland* wheat state⟩; *also* **:** of, adapted

to, practicing, or being agricultural methods (as dry farming) suited to such a region

**dry·lot** \'drī-,lät\ *noun* (1924)
**:** an enclosure of limited size usually bare of vegetation and used for fattening livestock

**dry measure** *noun* (1688)
**:** a series of units of capacity for dry commodities — see METRIC SYSTEM table, WEIGHT table

**dry mop** *noun* (1933)
**:** a long-handled mop for dusting floors

**dry–nurse** *transitive verb* (1581)
**1 :** to act as dry nurse to
**2 :** to give unnecessary supervision to

**dry nurse** *noun* (1598)
**:** a nurse who takes care of but does not breast-feed another woman's baby

**dryo·pith·e·cine** \,drī-ō-'pi-thə-,sīn\ *noun* [ultimately from Greek *drys* tree + *pithēkos* ape] (1948)
**:** any of a subfamily (Dryopithecinae) of Miocene and Pliocene Old World anthropoid apes sometimes regarded as ancestors of both man and modern anthropoids
— **dryopithecine** *adjective*

**dry out** *intransitive verb* (1892)
**:** to undergo an extended period of withdrawal from alcohol or drug use especially at a special clinic

**dry·point** \'drī-,point\ *noun* (1883)
**:** an engraving made with a steel or jeweled point directly into the metal plate without the use of acid as in etching; *also* **:** a print made from such an engraving

**dry–rot** (1870)
*transitive verb*
**:** to affect with dry rot
*intransitive verb*
**:** to become affected with dry rot

**dry rot** *noun* (1795)
**1 a :** a decay of seasoned timber caused by fungi that consume the cellulose of wood leaving a soft skeleton which is readily reduced to powder **b :** a fungal rot of plant tissue in which the affected areas are dry and often firmer than normal or more or less mummified
**2 :** a fungus causing dry rot
**3 :** decay from within caused especially by resistance to new forces

**dry run** *noun* (circa 1941)
**1 :** a practice exercise **:** REHEARSAL, TRIAL
**2 :** a practice firing without ammunition

**dry·salt·er** \'drī-,sȯl-tər\ *noun* (1707)
*British* **:** a dealer in crude dry chemicals and dyes
— **dry·salt·ery** \-tə-rē\ *noun, British*

**dry–shod** \'drī-,shäd\ *adjective* (15th century)
**:** having dry shoes or feet

**dry sink** *noun* (1951)
**:** a wooden cabinet with a tray top for holding a wash basin

**dry·stone** \'drī-,stōn\ *adjective* (circa 1702)
*chiefly British* **:** constructed of stone without the use of mortar as an adhesive ⟨a *drystone* wall⟩

**dry suit** *noun* (1955)
**:** a close-fitting air-insulated waterproof suit for divers

**dry up** (14th century)
*transitive verb*
**:** to cut off the supply of
*intransitive verb*
**1 :** to disappear as if by evaporation, draining, or cutting off of a source of supply
**2 :** to wither or die through gradual loss of vitality
**3 :** to stop talking

**dry·wall** \'drī-,wȯl\ *noun* (1952)
**:** PLASTERBOARD

**dry wash** *noun* (1872)
*West* **:** WASH 1d

**dry well** *noun* (circa 1942)
**:** a hole in the ground filled with gravel or rubble to receive drainage water and allow it to percolate away

**d.t.'s** \,dē-'tēz\ *noun plural, often D&T capitalized* (1858)

**:** DELIRIUM TREMENS

**¹du·al** \'dü(-ə)l\ *also* 'dyü-əl\ *adjective* [Latin *dualis*, from *duo* two — more at TWO] (1607)
**1** *of grammatical number* **:** denoting reference to two
**2 a :** consisting of two parts or elements or having two like parts **:** DOUBLE **b :** having a double character or nature
— **du·al·ly** \-ə(l)-lē\ *adverb*

**²dual** *noun* (1650)
**1 :** the dual number of a language
**2 :** a linguistic form in the dual

**dual carriageway** *noun* (1933)
*chiefly British* **:** a divided highway

**dual citizenship** *noun* (circa 1924)
**:** the status of an individual who is a citizen of two or more nations

**du·al·ism** \'dü-ə-,li-zəm\ *also* 'dyü-\ *noun* (1794)
**1 :** a theory that considers reality to consist of two irreducible elements or modes
**2 :** the quality or state of being dual or of having a dual nature
**3 a :** a doctrine that the universe is under the dominion of two opposing principles one of which is good and the other evil **b :** a view of human beings as constituted of two irreducible elements (as matter and spirit)
— **du·al·ist** \-list\ *noun*
— **du·al·is·tic** \,dü-ə-'lis-tik, ,dyü-\ *adjective*
— **du·al·is·ti·cal·ly** \-ti-k(ə-)lē\ *adverb*

**du·al·i·ty** \dü-'a-lə-tē\ *also* dyü-\ *noun, plural* **-ties** (15th century)
**:** DUALISM 2; *also* **:** DICHOTOMY

**du·al·ize** \'dü-ə-,līz\ *also* 'dyü-\ *transitive verb* **-ized; -iz·ing** (1838)
**:** to make dual

**dual–purpose** *adjective* (1904)
**:** having breed characteristics that serve two purposes ⟨*dual-purpose* cattle that supply milk and meat⟩

**¹dub** \'dəb\ *transitive verb* **dubbed; dub·bing** [Middle English *dubben*, from Old English *dubbian*; akin to Old Norse *dubba* to dub, Old High German *tubili* plug] (before 12th century)
**1 a :** to confer knighthood on **b :** to call by a distinctive title, epithet, or nickname
**2 :** to trim or remove the comb and wattles of
**3 a :** to hit (a golf ball) poorly **b :** to execute poorly
— **dub·ber** *noun*

**²dub** *noun* (1887)
**:** one who is inept or clumsy

**³dub** *noun* [Middle English (Scots dialect) *dubbe*] (15th century)
*chiefly Scottish* **:** POOL, PUDDLE

**⁴dub** *transitive verb* **dubbed; dub·bing** [by shortening & alteration from *double*] (1930)
**1 :** to add (sound effects or new dialogue) to a film or to a radio or television production — usually used with *in*
**2 :** to provide (a motion-picture film) with a new sound track and especially dialogue in a different language
**3 :** to make a new recording of (sound or videotape already recorded); *also* **:** to mix (recorded sound or videotape from different sources) into a single recording
— **dubber** *noun*

**⁵dub** *noun* (1974)
**:** Jamaican pop music in which audio effects and spoken or chanted words are imposed on an instrumental reggae background

**dub·bin** \'də-bən\ *also* **dub·bing** \-bən, -biŋ\ *noun* [*dubbing*, gerund of *dub* (to dress leather)] (1781)
**:** a dressing of oil and tallow for leather

**du·bi·ety** \du-'bī-ət-ē\ *also* dyü-\ *noun, plural* **-eties** [Late Latin *dubietas*, from Latin *dubius*] (1750)
**1 :** a usually hesitant uncertainty or doubt that tends to cause vacillation
**2 :** a matter of doubt
**synonym** see UNCERTAINTY

**du·bi·ous** \'dü-bē-əs *also* dyü-\ *adjective* [Latin *dubius*, from *dubare* to vacillate; akin to Latin *duo* two — more at TWO] (1548)
**1 :** giving rise to uncertainty: as **a :** of doubtful promise or outcome ⟨felt that our plan was a little *dubious*⟩ **b :** questionable or suspect as to true nature or quality ⟨the practice is of *dubious* legality⟩ ⟨the *dubious* honor of being the world's biggest polluter⟩
**2 :** unsettled in opinion **:** DOUBTFUL ⟨I was *dubious* about the plan⟩
**synonym** see DOUBTFUL
— **du·bi·ous·ly** *adverb*
— **du·bi·ous·ness** *noun*

**du·bi·ta·ble** \'dü-bə-tə-bəl\ *also* 'dyü-\ *adjective* [Latin *dubitabilis*, from *dubitare* to doubt — more at DOUBT] (circa 1616)
**:** open to doubt or question

**du·bi·ta·tion** \,d(y)ü-bə-'tā-shən\ *noun* (15th century)
*archaic* **:** DOUBT

**du·cal** \'dü-kəl\ *also* 'dyü-\ *adjective* [Middle English, from Middle French, from Late Latin *ducalis* of a leader, from Latin *duc-, dux* leader — more at DUKE] (15th century)
**:** of or relating to a duke or dukedom
— **du·cal·ly** \-kə-lē\ *adverb*

**duc·at** \'də-kət\ *noun* [Middle English, from Middle French, from Old Italian *ducato* coin with the doge's portrait on it, from *duca* doge, from Late Greek *douk-, doux* leader, from Latin *duc-, dux*] (14th century)
**1 :** a usually gold coin formerly used in various European countries
**2 :** TICKET 2

**du·ce** \'dü-(,)chā\ *noun* [Italian (*Il*) *Duce*, literally, the leader, title of Benito Mussolini, from Latin *duc-, dux*] (1923)
**:** LEADER — used especially for the leader of the Italian Fascist party

**Du·chenne** \dü-'shen, də-\ *also* **Du·chenne's** \-'shenz\ *adjective* [Guillaume Armand *Duchenne* (died 1875) French neurologist] (circa 1882)
**:** relating to or being a severe form of muscular dystrophy of males that affects the muscles of the pelvic and shoulder girdles and the pectoral muscles first and is inherited as a sex-linked recessive trait

**duch·ess** \'də-chəs\ *noun* [Middle English *duchesse*, from Middle French, from *duc* duke] (14th century)
**1 :** the wife or widow of a duke
**2 :** a woman who holds the rank of duke in her own right
**usage** see -ESS

**duchy** \'də-chē\ *noun, plural* **duch·ies** [Middle English *duche*, from Middle French *duché*, from *duc*] (14th century)
**1 :** the territory of a duke or duchess **:** DUKEDOM
**2 :** special domain

**¹duck** \'dək\ *noun, plural* **ducks** *often attributive* [Middle English *duk, doke*, from Old English *dūce*] (before 12th century)
**1** *or plural* **duck a :** any of various swimming birds (family Anatidae, the duck family) in which the neck and legs are short, the body more or less depressed, the bill often broad and flat, and the sexes almost always different from each other in plumage **b :** the flesh of any of these birds used as food
**2 :** a female duck — compare DRAKE
**3** *chiefly British* **:** DARLING — often used in plural but sing. in construction
**4 :** PERSON, CREATURE

**²duck** *verb* [Middle English *douken*; akin to Old High German *tūhhan* to dive, Old English *dūce* duck] (14th century)
*transitive verb*
**1 :** to thrust under water
**2 :** to lower (as the head) quickly **:** BOW
**3 :** AVOID, EVADE ⟨*duck* the issue⟩
*intransitive verb*
**1 a :** to plunge under the surface of water **b :** to descend suddenly **:** DIP

**2 a :** to lower the head or body suddenly **:** DODGE **b :** BOW, BOB **3 a :** to move quickly **b :** to evade a duty, question, or responsibility
— **duck·er** *noun*

³**duck** *noun* (1554)
: an instance of ducking

⁴**duck** *noun* [Dutch *doek* cloth; akin to Old High German *tuoh* cloth] (1640)
**1 :** a durable closely woven usually cotton fabric
**2** *plural* **:** light clothes and especially trousers made of duck

duck 1a (male): *1* bean, *2* bill, *3* nostril, *4* head, *5* eye, *6* auricular region, *7* neck, *8* cape, *9* shoulder, *10, 11* wing coverts, *12* saddle, *13* secondaries, *14* primaries, *15* rump, *16* drake feathers, *17* tail, *18* tail coverts, *19* down, *20* shank, *21* web, *22* breast, *23* wing front, *24* wing bow

**duck·bill** \'dək-ˌbil\ *noun* (1840)
**1 :** PLATYPUS
**2 :** HADROSAUR

**duck–billed dinosaur** *noun* (circa 1928)
: HADROSAUR

**duck–billed platypus** *also* **duckbill platypus** *noun* (1799)
: PLATYPUS

**duck·board** \-ˌbōrd, -ˌbȯrd\ *noun* (1917)
: a boardwalk or slatted flooring laid on a wet, muddy, or cold surface — usually used in plural

**duck call** *noun* (1872)
: a device for imitating the calls of ducks

**duck hook** *noun* (1973)
: a pronounced and unintended hook in golf

**ducking stool** *noun* (1597)
: a seat attached to a plank and formerly used to plunge culprits tied to it into water

**duck·ling** \'dək-liŋ, 'də-kliŋ\ *noun* (15th century)
: a young duck

**duck·pin** \-ˌpin\ *noun* (circa 1911)
**1 :** a small bowling pin shorter than a tenpin but proportionately wider at mid-diameter
**2** *plural but singular in construction* **:** a bowling game using duckpins

**ducks and drakes** *or* **duck and drake** *noun* (1583)
: the pastime of skimming flat stones or shells along the surface of calm water
— **play ducks and drakes with** *or* **make ducks and drakes of :** to use recklessly **:** SQUANDER ⟨*played ducks and drakes with his money*⟩

**duck soup** *noun* (1912)
: something easy to do

**duck·tail** \'dək-ˌtāl\ *noun* [from its resemblance to the tail of a duck] (1948)
: a hairstyle in which the hair on each side is slicked back to meet in a ridge at the back of the head

**duck·walk** \'dək-ˌwȯk\ *intransitive verb* (1950)
: to walk while in a crouch or full squatting position

**duck·weed** \'dək-ˌwēd\ *noun* (15th century)
: a small floating aquatic monocotyledonous plant (family Lemnaceae, the duckweed family)

ducktail

**ducky** \'də-kē\ *adjective* **duck·i·er; -est** (1897)
**1 :** DARLING, CUTE ⟨a *ducky* little tearoom⟩
**2 :** SATISFACTORY, FINE ⟨everything is just *ducky*⟩

¹**duct** \'dəkt\ *noun* [New Latin *ductus,* from Medieval Latin, aqueduct, from Latin, act of leading, from *ducere* to lead — more at TOW] (1667)
**1 :** a bodily tube or vessel especially when carrying the secretion of a gland
**2 a :** a pipe, tube, or channel that conveys a substance **b :** a pipe or tubular runway for carrying an electric power line, telephone cables, or other conductors
**3 a :** a continuous tube formed in plant tissue by a row of elongated cells that have lost their intervening end walls **b :** an elongated cavity (as a resin canal of a conifer) formed by disintegration or separation of cells
**4 :** a layer (as in the atmosphere or the ocean) which occurs under usually abnormal conditions and in which radio or sound waves are confined to a restricted path
— **duc·tal** \'dək-tᵊl\ *adjective*
— **duct·less** \'dək(t)-ləs\ *adjective*

²**duct** *transitive verb* (1936)
**1 :** to enclose in a duct
**2 :** to convey (as a gas) through a duct; *also* **:** to propagate (as radio waves) through a duct

**duc·tile** \'dək-tᵊl, -ˌtīl\ *adjective* [Middle French & Latin; Middle French, from Latin *ductilis,* from *ducere*] (14th century)
**1 :** capable of being drawn out or hammered thin ⟨*ductile* iron⟩
**2 :** easily led or influenced
**3 :** capable of being fashioned into a new form
**synonym** see PLASTIC
— **duc·til·i·ty** \ˌdək-'ti-lə-tē\ *noun*

**duct·ing** \'dək-tiŋ\ *noun* (1945)
: a system of ducts; *also* **:** the material composing a duct

**ductless gland** *noun* (circa 1852)
: ENDOCRINE GLAND

**duct tape** \'dək(t)-\ *noun* (1970)
: a wide silvery cloth adhesive tape designed for sealing joints in heating or air-conditioning ducts

**duct·ule** \'dək-(ˌ)chül\ *noun* (1883)
: a small duct

**duc·tus ar·te·ri·o·sus** \ˌdək-təs-är-ˌtir-ē-'ō-səs\ *noun* [New Latin, literally, arterial duct] (1811)
: a short broad vessel in the fetus that connects the pulmonary artery with the aorta and conducts most of the blood directly from the right ventricle to the aorta bypassing the lungs

**duct·work** \'dəkt-ˌwərk\ *noun* (1934)
: DUCTING

¹**dud** \'dəd\ *noun* [Middle English *dudde*] (1567)
**1** *plural* **a :** CLOTHING **b :** personal belongings
**2 a :** one that is ineffectual; *also* **:** FAILURE ⟨a box-office *dud*⟩ **b :** MISFIT
**3 :** a bomb or missile that fails to explode

²**dud** *adjective* (1903)
: of little or no worth **:** VALUELESS ⟨*dud* checks⟩

**dud·die** *or* **dud·dy** \'də-dē\ *adjective* (1718) *Scottish* **:** RAGGED, TATTERED

¹**dude** \'düd *also* 'dyüd\ *noun* [origin unknown] (1883)
**1 :** a man extremely fastidious in dress and manner **:** DANDY
**2 :** a city dweller unfamiliar with life on the range; *especially* **:** an Easterner in the West
**3 :** FELLOW, GUY
— **dud·ish** \'d(y)üd-ish\ *adjective*
— **dud·ish·ly** *adverb*

²**dude** *transitive verb* **dud·ed; dud·ing** (1899)
: DRESS UP — usually used with *up*

**du·deen** \dü-'dēn\ *noun* [Irish *dúidín,* diminutive of *dúd* pipe] (1841)
: a short tobacco pipe made of clay

**dude ranch** *noun* (1921)
: a vacation resort offering activities (as horseback riding) typical of western ranches

¹**dud·geon** \'də-jən\ *noun* [Middle English *dogeon,* from Anglo-French *digeon*] (15th century)

**1** *obsolete* **:** a wood used especially for dagger hilts
**2 a** *archaic* **:** a dagger with a handle of dudgeon **b** *obsolete* **:** a haft made of dudgeon

²**dudgeon** *noun* [origin unknown] (1573)
: a fit or state of indignation — often used in the phrase *in high dudgeon*
**synonym** see OFFENSE

¹**due** \'dü, 'dyü\ *adjective* [Middle English, from Middle French *deu,* past participle of *devoir* to owe, from Latin *debēre* — more at DEBT] (14th century)
**1 :** owed or owing as a debt
**2 a :** owed or owing as a natural or moral right ⟨everyone's right to dissent . . . is *due* the full protection of the Constitution —Nat Hentoff⟩ **b :** according to accepted notions or procedures **:** APPROPRIATE
**3 a :** satisfying or capable of satisfying a need, obligation, or duty **:** ADEQUATE **b :** REGULAR, LAWFUL ⟨*due* proof of loss⟩
**4 :** capable of being attributed **:** ASCRIBABLE — used with *to* ⟨this advance is partly *due* to a few men of genius —A. N. Whitehead⟩
**5 :** having reached the date at which payment is required **:** PAYABLE
**6 :** required or expected in the prescribed, normal, or logical course of events **:** SCHEDULED; *also* **:** expected to give birth
— **due·ness** *noun*

²**due** *noun* (15th century)
: something due or owed: as **a :** something that rightfully belongs to one **b :** a payment or obligation required by law or custom **:** DEBT **c** *plural* **:** FEES, CHARGES

³**due** *adverb* (1582)
**1 :** DIRECTLY, EXACTLY ⟨*due* north⟩
**2** *obsolete* **:** DULY

**due diligence** *noun* (1903)
: the care that a reasonable person exercises under the circumstances to avoid harm to other persons or their property

¹**du·el** \'dü-əl *also* 'dyü-\ *noun* [Middle English, from Medieval Latin *duellum,* from Old Latin, war] (15th century)
**1 :** a combat between two persons; *specifically* **:** a formal combat with weapons fought between two persons in the presence of witnesses
**2 :** a conflict between antagonistic persons, ideas, or forces; *also* **:** a hard-fought contest between two opponents

²**duel** *verb* **du·eled** *or* **du·elled; du·el·ing** *or* **du·el·ling** (circa 1645)
*intransitive verb*
: to fight a duel
*transitive verb*
: to encounter (an opponent) in a duel
— **du·el·er** *or* **du·el·ler** *noun*
— **du·el·ist** *or* **du·el·list** \'dü-ə-list\ *noun*

**du·el·lo** \d(y)ü-'e-(ˌ)lō\ *noun, plural* **-los** [Italian, from Medieval Latin *duellum*] (1588)
**1 :** the rules or practice of dueling
**2 :** DUEL

**du·en·de** \dü-'en-(ˌ)dā\ *noun* [Spanish dialect, charm, from Spanish, ghost, goblin, probably from *duen de casa,* from *dueño de casa* owner of a house] (1964)
: the power to attract through personal magnetism and charm

**du·en·na** \dü-'e-nə, 'dyü-\ *noun* [Spanish *dueña,* from Latin *domina* mistress — more at DAME] (1623)
**1 :** an elderly woman serving as governess and companion to the younger ladies in a Spanish or a Portuguese family
**2 :** CHAPERON
— **du·en·na·ship** \-ˌship\ *noun*

**due process** *noun* (1791)

\ə\ abut \ᵊ\ kitten \ər\ further \a\ ash \ā\ ace \ä\ mop, mar \aú\ out \ch\ chin \e\ bet \ē\ easy \g\ go \i\ hit \ī\ ice \j\ job \ŋ\ sing \ō\ go \ȯ\ law \ȯi\ boy \th\ thin \th\ the \ü\ loot \ú\ foot \y\ yet \zh\ vision *see also* Guide to Pronunciation

**1 :** a course of formal proceedings (as legal proceedings) carried out regularly and in accordance with established rules and principles — called also *procedural due process*
**2 :** a judicial requirement that enacted laws may not contain provisions that result in the unfair, arbitrary, or unreasonable treatment of an individual — called also *substantive due process*

**¹du·et** \dü-'et *also* dyü-\ *noun* [Italian *duetto,* diminutive of *duo*] (circa 1740)
**:** a composition for two performers
**²duet** *intransitive verb* **du·et·ted; du·et·ting** (1822)
**:** to perform a duet

**due to** *preposition* (1897)
**:** as a result of **:** BECAUSE OF ⟨*due to* the complaints of uptight parents . . . he lost his job —Herbert Gold⟩ ▪

**¹duff** \'dəf\ *noun* [English dialect, alteration of *dough*] (1816)
**1 :** a boiled or steamed pudding often containing dried fruit
**2 :** the partly decayed organic matter on the forest floor
**3 :** fine coal **:** SLACK
**²duff** *noun* [origin unknown] (circa 1888)
**:** BUTTOCKS ⟨get off your *duff*⟩
**³duff** *adjective* [*duff,* noun, something worthless, from ¹*duff*] (circa 1889)
*British* **:** INFERIOR, WORTHLESS

**duf·fel** *or* **duf·fle** \'də-fəl\ *noun* [Dutch *duffel,* from *Duffel,* Belgium] (1677)
**1 :** a coarse heavy woolen material with a thick nap
**2 :** transportable personal belongings, equipment, and supplies
**3 :** DUFFEL BAG
**4 :** DUFFLE COAT

**duffel bag** *noun* (1917)
**:** a large cylindrical fabric bag for personal belongings

**duf·fer** \'də-fər\ *noun* [perhaps from *duff,* noun, something worthless] (1756)
**1 a :** a peddler especially of cheap flashy articles **b :** something counterfeit or worthless
**2 :** an incompetent, ineffectual, or clumsy person; *especially* **:** a mediocre golfer
**3** *Australian* **:** a cattle rustler

**duffle coat** \'də-fəl-\ *or* **duffel coat** *noun* (1684)
**:** a heavy usually woolen medium-length coat with toggle fasteners and a hood

**¹dug** *past and past participle of* DIG
**²dug** \'dəg\ *noun* [perhaps of Scandinavian origin; akin to Old Swedish *dæggia* to suckle; akin to Old English *delu* nipple — more at FEMININE] (1530)
**:** UDDER; *also* **:** TEAT — usually used of a suckling animal; usually considered vulgar when used of a woman

**du·gong** \'dü-,gäŋ, -,góŋ\ *noun* [New Latin, genus name, modification of Malay *duyong* dugong] (1800)
**:** an aquatic herbivorous mammal of a monotypic genus (*Dugong*) that has a bilobed tail and in the male upper incisors altered into short tusks, is related to the manatee, and inhabits warm coastal regions — called also *sea cow*

dugong

**dug·out** \'dəg-,aůt\ *noun* (1819)
**1 :** a boat made by hollowing out a large log
**2 a :** a shelter dug in a hillside; *also* **:** a shelter dug in the ground and roofed with sod **b :** an area in the side of a trench for quarters, storage, or protection

**3 :** either of two low shelters on either side of and facing a baseball diamond that contain the players' benches

**dui·ker** \'dī-kər\ *noun* [Afrikaans, literally, diver, from *duik* to dive, from Middle Dutch *dūken;* akin to Old High German *tūhhan* to dive — more at DUCK] (1777)
**:** any of several small African antelopes comprising two genera (*Cephalophus* and *Sylvicapra*)

**duit** *variant of* DOIT

**du jour** \dü-'zhər, də-, -'zhùr, -'zhür\ *adjective* [French, literally, of the day] (1969)
**1 :** made for a particular day — used of an item not specified on the regular menu ⟨soup *du jour*⟩
**2 :** popular, fashionable, or prominent at a particular time ⟨the buzzword *du jour*⟩

**¹duke** \'dük *also* 'dyük\ *noun* [Middle English, from Old French *duc,* from Latin *duc-, dux,* from *ducere* to lead — more at TOW] (12th century)
**1 :** a sovereign male ruler of a continental European duchy
**2 :** a nobleman of the highest hereditary rank; *especially* **:** a member of the highest grade of the British peerage
**3** [probably from *dukes of York,* rhyming slang for *fork* (hand, fist)] *slang* **:** FIST, HAND — usually used in plural
— **duke·dom** \-dəm\ *noun*
**²duke** *intransitive verb* **duked; duk·ing** (circa 1947)
**:** FIGHT
— **duke it out :** to engage in a fight and especially a fistfight

**Du·kho·bor** *variant of* DOUKHOBOR

**dul·cet** \'dəl-sət\ *adjective* [Middle English *doucet,* from Middle French, from *douz* sweet, from Latin *dulcis;* perhaps akin to Greek *glykys* sweet] (14th century)
**1 :** sweet to the taste
**2 :** pleasing to the ear
**3 :** generally pleasing or agreeable
— **dul·cet·ly** *adverb*

**dul·ci·fy** \'dəl-sə-,fī\ *transitive verb* **-fied; -fy·ing** [Late Latin *dulcificare,* from Latin *dulcis*] (1599)
**1 :** to make sweet
**2 :** to make agreeable **:** MOLLIFY

**dul·ci·mer** \'dəl-sə-mər\ *noun* [Middle English *dowcemere,* from Middle French *doulcemer,* from Old Italian *dolcimelo,* from *dolce* sweet, from Latin *dulcis*] (15th century)
**1 :** a stringed instrument of trapezoidal shape played with light hammers held in the hands
**2** *or* **dul·ci·more** \-,mōr, -,mȯr\ **:** an American folk instrument with three or four strings stretched over an elongate fretted sound box that is held on the lap and played by plucking or strumming

**dul·ci·nea** \,dəl-sə-'nē-ə, -'si-nē-ə\ *noun* [Spanish, from *Dulcinea* del Toboso, beloved of Don Quixote] (1748)
**:** MISTRESS, SWEETHEART

**¹dull** \'dəl\ *adjective* [Middle English *dul;* akin to Old English *dol* foolish, Old Irish *dall* blind] (13th century)
**1 :** mentally slow **:** STUPID
**2 a :** slow in perception or sensibility **:** INSENSIBLE **b :** lacking zest or vivacity **:** LISTLESS
**3 :** slow in action **:** SLUGGISH
**4 a :** lacking in force, intensity, or sharpness **b :** not resonant or ringing ⟨a *dull* booming sound⟩
**5 :** lacking sharpness of edge or point
**6 :** lacking brilliance or luster
**7** *of a color* **:** low in saturation and low in lightness
**8 :** CLOUDY
**9 :** TEDIOUS, UNINTERESTING ☆
— **dull·ness** *or* **dul·ness** \'dəl-nəs\ *noun*
— **dul·ly** \'dəl(l)-lē\ *adverb*
**²dull** (13th century)
*transitive verb*
**:** to make dull

*intransitive verb*
**:** to become dull

**dull·ard** \'də-lərd\ *noun* (15th century)
**:** a stupid or unimaginative person

**dull·ish** \'də-lish\ *adjective* (14th century)
**:** somewhat dull
— **dull·ish·ly** *adverb*

**dulls·ville** \'dəlz-,vil\ *noun* (circa 1960)
**:** something or some place that is dull or boring; *also* **:** BOREDOM

**dulse** \'dəls\ *noun* [modification of Scottish Gaelic *duileasg;* akin to Welsh *delysg* dulse] (circa 1698)
**:** any of several coarse red seaweeds (especially *Palmaria palmata* synonym *Rhodymenia palmata*) found especially in northern latitudes and used as a food condiment

**du·ly** \'dü-lē *also* 'dyü-\ *adverb* (14th century)
**:** in a due manner or time **:** PROPERLY

**du·ma** \'dü-mə, -(,)mä\ *noun* [Russian, from Old Russian, council, thought, probably of Germanic origin; akin to Old English *dōm* judgment — more at DOOM] (circa 1870)
**:** a representative council in Russia; *especially,* *often capitalized* **:** the principal legislative assembly in czarist Russia

**¹dumb** \'dəm\ *adjective* [Middle English, from Old English; akin to Old High German *tumb* mute] (before 12th century)
**1 :** lacking the power of speech ⟨deaf and *dumb* from birth⟩ ⟨*dumb* animals⟩
**2 :** temporarily unable to speak (as from shock or astonishment) ⟨struck *dumb* with fear⟩
**3 :** not expressed in uttered words ⟨*dumb* grief⟩
**4 :** SILENT; *also* **:** TACITURN
**5 :** lacking some usual attribute or accompaniment; *especially* **:** having no means of self-propulsion ⟨*dumb* barge⟩
**6 a :** markedly lacking in intelligence **:** STUPID **b :** showing a lack of intelligence **c :** having little or no meaning — sometimes used in the phrase *dumb luck*
**7 :** not having the capability to process data ⟨*dumb* terminal⟩ — compare INTELLIGENT 3a ▪
*synonym* see STUPID
— **dumb·ly** \'dəm-lē\ *adverb*
— **dumb·ness** *noun*
**²dumb** *transitive verb* (1608)
**:** to make silent **:** DEADEN ⟨would lie around, *dumbed* by the drugs —Norman Mailer⟩

**dumb·bell** \'dəm-,bel\ *noun* (1785)

---

**1 :** a short bar with weights at each end that is used usually in pairs for exercise
**2 :** one that is dull and stupid
**dumb·cane** \'dəm-ˌkān\ *noun* [from the fact that chewing it causes the tongue and throat to swell] (1696)
**:** DIEFFENBACHIA
**dumb down** *transitive verb* (1980)
**:** to lower the level of difficulty and the intellectual content of (as a textbook)
**dumb·found** *or* **dum·found** \ˌdəm-'faund, 'dəm-ˌ\ *transitive verb* [dumb + -found (as in confound)] (1653)
**:** to confound briefly and usually with astonishment
**synonym** see PUZZLE
**dumb·foun·der** \-'faun-dər\ *transitive verb* (1710)
*British* **:** DUMBFOUND
**dumb·head** \'dəm-ˌhed\ *noun* [probably translation of German *dummkopf*] (1887)
*slang* **:** a stupid person **:** BLOCKHEAD
**dumb show** *noun* (1561)
**1 :** a part of a play presented in pantomime
**2 :** signs and gestures without words **:** PANTOMIME
**dumb·struck** \'dəm-ˌstrək\ *adjective* (1887)
**:** made silent by astonishment
**dumb·wait·er** \'dəm-ˌwā-tər, ˌdəm-'\ *noun* (1749)
**1 :** a portable serving table or stand
**2 :** a small elevator used for conveying food and dishes from one story of a building to another
**dum-dum** \'dəm-ˌdəm\ *noun* [*Dum Dum*, arsenal near Calcutta, India] (circa 1889)
**:** a bullet (as one with a hollow point) that expands more than usual upon hitting an object
**dum–dum** *noun* [reduplication of ¹*dumb*] (1928)
**:** a stupid person **:** DUMMY
**dum·ka** \'dúm-kə\ *noun, plural* **dum·ky** \-kē\ [Czech, elegy, from Ukrainian, diminutive of *duma* narrative folk poem, from Old Russian] (1895)
**:** a musical composition containing alternating sad and gay passages
**dumm·kopf** \'dúm-ˌkòpf\ *noun* [German, from *dumm* stupid + *Kopf* head] (1809)
**:** BLOCKHEAD
**¹dum·my** \'də-mē\ *noun, plural* **dummies** [¹*dumb* + ⁴-*y*] (1598)
**1 a :** one who is incapable of speaking **b :** one who is habitually silent **c :** one who is stupid
**2 a :** the exposed hand in bridge played by the declarer in addition to his own hand **b :** a bridge player whose hand is a dummy
**3 :** an imitation, copy, or likeness of something used as a substitute: as **a :** MANNEQUIN **b :** a stuffed figure or cylindrical bag used by football players for tackling and blocking practice **c :** a large puppet usually having movable features (as mouth and arms) manipulated by a ventriloquist **d** *chiefly British* **:** PACIFIER 2
**4 :** one seeming to act independently but in reality controlled by another
**5 a :** a mock-up of a proposed publication (as a book or magazine) **b :** a set of pages (as for a newspaper or magazine) with the position of text and artwork indicated for the printer
**²dummy** *adjective* (1846)
**1 a :** having the appearance of being real **:** ARTIFICIAL ⟨*dummy* foods in the display case⟩ **b :** existing in name only **:** FICTITIOUS ⟨*dummy* corporations⟩
**2 :** apparently acting for oneself while really acting for or at the direction of another ⟨a *dummy* director⟩
**³dummy** *transitive verb* **dum·mied; dum·my·ing** (1928)
**:** to make a dummy of (as a publication) — often used with *up* ⟨*dummied* up the front page⟩
**dummy up** *intransitive verb* (1926)
**:** to say nothing **:** CLAM UP

**dummy variable** *noun* (1957)
**:** an arbitrary mathematical symbol or variable that can be replaced by another without affecting the value of the expression in which it occurs
**du·mor·ti·er·ite** \dù-'mòr-tē-ə-ˌrīt *also* dyú-\ *noun* [French *dumortiérite*, from Eugène *Dumortier* (died 1876) French paleontologist] (1881)
**:** a bright blue or greenish blue mineral consisting of a silicate of aluminum and used especially for jewelry
**¹dump** \'dəmp\ *verb* [perhaps from Middle Dutch *dompen* to immerse, topple; akin to Old Norse *dumpa* to thump, fall suddenly] (14th century)
*transitive verb*
**1 a :** to let fall in or as if in a heap or mass **b :** to get rid of unceremoniously or irresponsibly **c :** JETTISON ⟨an airplane *dumping* gasoline⟩
**2** *slang* **:** to knock down **:** BEAT ⟨the man rushed out and *dumped* him —John Corry⟩
**3 :** to sell in quantity at a very low price; *specifically* **:** to sell abroad at less than the market price at home
**4 :** to copy (data in a computer's internal storage) to an external storage or output device
**5 :** to throw (as a pass) short and softly — often used with *off*
*intransitive verb*
**1 :** to fall abruptly **:** PLUNGE
**2 :** to dump refuse
— **dump·er** *noun*
— **dump on :** to treat disrespectfully; *especially* **:** BELITTLE, BAD-MOUTH
**²dump** *noun* (1784)
**1 a :** an accumulation of refuse and discarded materials **b :** a place where such materials are dumped
**2 a :** a quantity of reserve materials accumulated at one place **b :** a place where such materials are stored ⟨ammunition *dump*⟩
**3 :** a disorderly, slovenly, or objectionable place
**4 :** an instance of dumping data stored in a computer
**5 :** an act of defecation — usually used with *take*; often considered vulgar
**dump·ing** *noun* (1857)
**:** the act of one that dumps; *especially* **:** the selling of goods in quantity at below market price
**dumping ground** *noun* (1857)
**:** a place to which unwanted people or things are sent
**dump·ish** \'dəm-pish\ *adjective* [*dumps*] (1519)
**:** SAD, MELANCHOLY
**dump·ling** \'dəm-pliŋ\ *noun* [perhaps alteration of *lump*] (circa 1600)
**1 a :** a small mass of leavened dough cooked by boiling or steaming **b :** a usually baked dessert of fruit wrapped in dough
**2 :** something soft and rounded like a dumpling; *especially* **:** a short fat person or animal
**dumps** \'dəm(p)s\ *noun plural* [probably from Dutch *domp* haze, from Middle Dutch *damp* — more at DAMP] (1529)
**:** a gloomy state of mind **:** DESPONDENCY ⟨in the *dumps*⟩
**Dump·ster** \'dəm(p)-stər\ *trademark* — used for a large trash receptacle
**dump truck** *noun* (1930)
**:** an automotive truck for the transportation of bulk material that has a body which tilts to dump its contents
**dumpy** \'dəm-pē\ *adjective* **dump·i·er; -est** [English dialect *dump* (lump)] (1750)
**1 :** being short and thick in build **:** SQUAT
**2 :** SHABBY, DINGY
— **dump·i·ly** \-pə-lē\ *adverb*
— **dump·i·ness** \-pē-nəs\ *noun*
**dumpy level** *noun* (1838)

**:** a surveyor's level with a short telescope rigidly fixed and rotating only in a horizontal plane
**¹dun** \'dən\ *adjective* [Middle English, from Old English *dunn* — more at DUSK] (before 12th century)
**1 a :** having the color dun **b** *of a horse* **:** having a grayish yellow coat with black mane and tail
**2 :** marked by dullness and drabness
— **dun·ness** \'dən-nəs\ *noun*
**²dun** *noun* (14th century)
**1 :** a dun horse
**2 :** a variable color averaging a nearly neutral slightly brownish dark gray
**3 :** a subadult mayfly; *also* **:** an artificial fly tied to imitate such an insect
**³dun** *transitive verb* **dunned; dun·ning** [origin unknown] (circa 1626)
**1 :** to make persistent demands upon for payment
**2 :** PLAGUE, PESTER
**⁴dun** *noun* (1628)
**1 :** one who duns
**2 :** an urgent request; *especially* **:** a demand for payment
**Dun·can Phyfe** \ˌdən-kən-'fīf\ *adjective* (1926)
**:** of, relating to, or constituting furniture designed and built by or in the style of Duncan Phyfe
**dunce** \'dən(t)s\ *noun* [John *Duns* Scotus, whose once accepted writings were ridiculed in the 16th century] (1587)
**:** one who is slow-witted or stupid ◆
**dunce cap** *noun* (1840)
**:** a conical cap formerly used as a punishment for slow learners at school — called also *dunce's cap*
**dun·der·head** \'dən-dər-ˌhed\ *noun* [perhaps from Dutch *donder* thunder + English *head*; akin to Old High German *thonar* thunder — more at THUNDER] (circa 1625)
**:** DUNCE, BLOCKHEAD
— **dun·der·head·ed** \ˌdən-dər-'he-dəd\ *adjective*
**dun·drea·ries** \ˌdən-'drir-ēz\ *noun plural, often capitalized* [Lord *Dundreary*, character in the play *Our American Cousin* (1858), by Tom Taylor] (circa 1922)
**:** long flowing sideburns
**dune** \'dün *also* 'dyün\ *noun* [French, from Old French, from Middle Dutch; akin to Old English *dūn* down — more at DOWN] (1790)
**:** a hill or ridge of sand piled up by the wind

◇ **WORD HISTORY**
**dunce** The irony of *dunce* lies in the fact that this synonym for *dullard* is derived from the name of one of the most brilliant thinkers of the later Middle Ages. *Duns* was the name of a Scottish market town and the birthplace in the mid 13th century of John Duns Scotus, one of the luminaries of Scholasticism. So ingenious were the theological and metaphysical speculations of this thinker that he was given the epithet of *Doctor Subtilis* ("the Subtle Doctor"). His followers, who were known as *Scotists* or *dunsmen*, were a powerful conservative element in English universities through the 16th century. They tended to resist both the new learning of humanism and the complaints of church reformers. As a result, *dunsman* and the shorter form *duns* (later respelled as we have it today) became terms of opprobrium and scorn meaning first "sophist" or "pedant" and gradually taking on the modern sense "slow-witted person."

\ə\ abut \ᵊ\ kitten \ər\ further \a\ ash \ā\ ace \ä\ mop, mar \aú\ out \ch\ chin \e\ bet \ē\ easy \g\ go \i\ hit \ī\ ice \j\ job \ŋ\ sing \ō\ go \ò\ law \òi\ boy \th\ thin \t̲h̲\ the \ü\ loot \ú\ foot \y\ yet \zh\ vision *see also* Guide to Pronunciation

— **dune·like** \-₁līk\ *adjective*
**dune buggy** *noun* (1956)
: an off-road motor vehicle with oversize tires for use especially on sand
**dune·land** \'dün-₁land\ *noun* (1922)
: an area having many dunes
¹**dung** \'dəŋ\ *noun* [Middle English, from Old English; akin to Old Norse *dyngja* manure pile] (before 12th century)
**1** : the excrement of an animal : MANURE
**2** : something repulsive
— **dungy** \'dəŋ-ē\ *adjective*
²**dung** (before 12th century)
*transitive verb*
: to fertilize or dress with manure
*intransitive verb*
: DEFECATE
**dun·ga·ree** \₁dəŋ-gə-'rē, 'dəŋ-gə-₁\ *noun* [Hindi *dūgrī*] (1673)
**1** : a heavy coarse durable cotton twill woven from colored yarns; *specifically* : blue denim
**2** *plural* : clothes made usually of blue denim
**dung beetle** *noun* (circa 1634)
: a beetle (as a tumblebug) that rolls balls of dung in which to lay eggs and on which the larvae feed
**Dunge·ness crab** \₁dən-jə-₁nes-\ *noun* [*Dungeness*, village on the Strait of Juan de Fuca, Washington] (1925)
: a large edible crab (*Cancer magister*) of the Pacific coast of North America from Alaska to California
**dun·geon** \'dən-jən\ *noun* [Middle English *donjon*, from Middle French, from (assumed) Vulgar Latin *domnion-*, *domnio* keep, mastery, from Latin *dominus* lord — more at DOMINATE] (14th century)
**1** : DONJON
**2** : a dark usually underground prison or vault
◆
**dung·hill** \'dəŋ-₁hil\ *noun* (14th century)
**1** : a heap of dung
**2** : something (as a situation or condition) that is repulsive or degraded
**du·nite** \'dü-₁nīt, 'də-\ *noun* [Mount *Dun*, New Zealand] (circa 1868)
: a granitoid igneous rock consisting chiefly of olivine
— **du·nit·ic** \dü-'ni-tik, ₁də-\ *adjective*
¹**dunk** \'dəŋk\ *verb* [Pennsylvania German *dunke*, from Middle High German *dunken*, from Old High German *dunkōn* — more at TINGE] (1919)
*transitive verb*
**1** : to dip (as a piece of bread) into a beverage while eating
**2** : to dip or submerge temporarily in liquid
**3** : to throw (a basketball) into the basket from above the rim
*intransitive verb*
**1** : to submerge oneself in water
**2** : to make a dunk shot in basketball
²**dunk** *noun* (circa 1944)
: the act or action of dunking; *especially* : DUNK SHOT
**Dun·ker** \'dəŋ-kər\ *or* **Dun·kard** \-kərd\ *noun* [Pennsylvania German *Dunker*, from *dunke*] (1744)
: a member of the Church of the Brethren or any of several other originally German Baptist denominations practicing trine immersion and love feasts and refusing to take oaths or to perform military service
**Dun·kirk** \'dən-₁kərk, ₁dən-'\ *noun* [*Dunkirk* or *Dunkerque*, France, scene of the evacuation of Allied forces in 1940] (1941)
**1** : a retreat to avoid total defeat
**2** : a crisis situation that requires a desperate last effort to forestall certain failure ⟨a *Dunkirk* for U.S. foreign policy —*Time*⟩
**dunk shot** *noun* (circa 1961)
: a shot in basketball made by jumping high into the air and throwing the ball down through the basket

**dun·lin** \'dən-lən\ *noun, plural* **dunlins** *or* **dunlin** [¹*dun* + *-lin* (alteration of *-ling*)] (circa 1532)
: a small widely distributed sandpiper (*Calidris alpina*) largely cinnamon to rusty brown above and white below
**Dun·lop** \'dən-₁läp, ₁dən-'\ *noun* [*Dunlop*, Ayrshire, Scotland] (circa 1780)
: a Scottish cheese similar to cheddar
**dun·nage** \'də-nij\ *noun* [origin unknown] (15th century)
**1** : loose materials used to support and protect cargo in a ship's hold; *also* : padding in a shipping container
**2** : BAGGAGE
**duo** \'dü-(₁)ō *also* 'dyü-\ *noun, plural* **du·os** [Italian, from Latin, two — more at TWO] (1590)
**1** : DUET
**2** : PAIR 2
**duo-** *combining form* [Latin *duo*]
: two ⟨*duo*logue⟩
**duo·de·cil·lion** \₁dü-ō-di-'sil-yən, ₁dyü-\ *noun, often attributive* [Latin *duodecim* twelve + English *-illion* (as in *million*)] (1875)
— see NUMBER table
**duo·dec·i·mal** \₁dü-ə-'de-sə-məl, ₁dyü-\ *adjective* [Latin *duodecim* — more at DOZEN] (1727)
: of, relating to, or proceeding by twelve or the scale of twelves
— **duodecimal** *noun*
**duo·dec·i·mo** \-₁mō\ *noun, plural* **-mos** [Latin, ablative of *duodecimus* twelfth, from *duodecim*] (1658)
: TWELVEMO
**du·o·de·num** \₁dü-ə-'dē-nəm, dü-'ä-d°n-əm *also* (₁)dyü-\ *noun, plural* **-de·na** \-'dē-nə, -d°n-ə\ *or* **-denums** [Middle English, from Medieval Latin, from Latin *duodeni* twelve each, from *duodecim* twelve; from its length, about 12 fingers' breadth] (14th century)
: the first part of the small intestine extending from the pylorus to the jejunum
— **du·o·de·nal** \-'dē-n°l, -d°n-əl\ *adjective*
**duo·logue** \'dü-ə-₁lòg, -₁läg *also* 'dyü-\ *noun* (1864)
: a dialogue between two persons
**duo·mo** \'dwò-(₁)mō\ *noun, plural* **duomos** [Italian, from Latin *domus* house — more at DOME] (1549)
: CATHEDRAL
**du·op·o·ly** \dü-'ä-pə-lē *also* dyü-\ *noun, plural* **-lies** [*duo-* + *-poly* (as in *monopoly*)] (1920)
**1** : an oligopoly limited to two sellers
**2** : preponderant influence or control by two political powers
— **du·op·o·lis·tic** \-₁ä-pə-'lis-tik\ *adjective*
**dup** \'dəp\ *transitive verb* [contraction of *do up*] (1547)
*archaic* : OPEN
¹**dupe** \'düp *also* 'dyüp\ *noun* [French, from Middle French *duppe*, probably alteration of *huppe* hoopoe] (1681)
: one that is easily deceived or cheated : FOOL
²**dupe** *transitive verb* **duped; dup·ing** (1704)
: to make a dupe of ☆
— **dup·er** *noun*
³**dupe** *noun or verb* (circa 1900)
: DUPLICATE
**dup·ery** \'dü-pə-rē *also* 'dyü-\ *noun, plural* **-er·ies** (1759)
**1** : the condition of being duped
**2** : the act or practice of duping
**du·ple** \'dü-pəl *also* 'dyü-\ *adjective* [Latin *duplus* double — more at DOUBLE] (15th century)
**1** : having two elements
**2 a** : marked by two or a multiple of two beats per measure of music ⟨*duple* time⟩ **b** : of rhythm : consisting of a meter based on disyllabic feet
¹**du·plex** \'dü-₁pleks *also* 'dyü-\ *adjective* [Latin, from *duo* two + *-plex* -fold — more at TWO, -FOLD] (1567)

**1 a** : having two principal elements or parts : DOUBLE, TWOFOLD **b** : having complementary polynucleotide strands ⟨*duplex* DNA⟩
**2** : allowing telecommunication in opposite directions simultaneously
²**duplex** *transitive verb* (1833)
: to make duplex
³**duplex** *noun* (1922)
: something duplex: as **a** : a 2-family house **b** : DUPLEX APARTMENT **c** : a duplex molecule of DNA or of RNA and DNA
**duplex apartment** *noun* (circa 1925)
: an apartment having rooms on two floors
**du·plex·er** \'dü-₁plek-sər *also* 'dyü-\ *noun* (circa 1932)
: a switching device that permits alternate transmission and reception with the same radio antenna
¹**du·pli·cate** \'dü-pli-kət *also* 'dyü-\ *adjective* [Middle English, from Latin *duplicatus*, past participle of *duplicare* to double, from *duplic-*, *duplex*] (15th century)
**1** : consisting of or existing in two corresponding or identical parts or examples ⟨*duplicate* invoices⟩
**2** : being the same as another ⟨*duplicate* copies⟩
²**du·pli·cate** \'dü-pli-₁kāt *also* 'dyü-\ *verb* **-cat·ed; -cat·ing** (15th century)
*transitive verb*
**1** : to make double or twofold
**2 a** : to make a copy of ⟨a cell *duplicates* itself when it divides⟩ **b** : to produce something equal to ⟨trying to *duplicate* last year's success⟩ **c** : to do over or again often needlessly ⟨*duplicated* effort⟩
*intransitive verb*
: to become duplicated; *also* : REPEAT
— **du·pli·ca·tive** \-₁kā-tiv\ *adjective*
³**du·pli·cate** \-kət\ *noun* (1532)
**1 a** : either of two things exactly alike and usually produced at the same time or by the

☆ **SYNONYMS**
**Dupe, gull, trick, hoax** mean to deceive by underhanded means. DUPE suggests unwariness in the person deluded. GULL stresses credulousness or readiness to be imposed on (as through greed) on the part of the victim. TRICK implies an intent to delude by means of a ruse or fraud but does not always imply a vicious intent. HOAX implies the contriving of an elaborate or adroit imposture in order to deceive.

◇ **WORD HISTORY**
**dungeon** The word *dungeon*, in use in English since the 14th century, originally referred to the keep of a castle—the massive inner tower detached from the rest of the structure that was its most securely located and protected part. During its early history this word had about a dozen different spellings, but nowadays, in the sense of a castle's keep, the usual form is *donjon*. The donjon was the stronghold to which the garrison and residents of the castle retreated if the outer walls had been scaled or breached in a siege. The subterranean part of a donjon was called by the same word in the form *dungeon*, the usual spelling for this sense. This dark, damp chamber was used as a cell for the confinement of prisoners. Both *donjon* and *dungeon* are borrowed from Old French *donjon*, most likely the descendant of an unrecorded vernacular Latin form *domnio*, reflected in Medieval Latin renderings such as *dominionus* and *domnionus*, and ultimately a derivative of Latin *dominus* "lord." The underlying sense of *domnio* would have been "dominating tower," reflecting the relation between the keep and the rest of the castle.

same process **b** : an additional copy of something (as a book or stamp) already in a collection

**2** : one that resembles or corresponds to another : COUNTERPART

**3** : two identical copies — used in the phrase *in duplicate*

**synonym** see REPRODUCTION

**duplicate bridge** *noun* (1926)
: a tournament form of contract bridge in which identical deals are played in order to compare individual scores

**du·pli·ca·tion** \ˌdü-pli-ˈkā-shən *also* ˌdyü-\ *noun* (15th century)
**1 a** : the act or process of duplicating **b** : the quality or state of being duplicated
**2** : DUPLICATE, COUNTERPART
**3** : a part of a chromosome in which the genetic material is repeated; *also* : the process of forming a duplication

**du·pli·ca·tor** \ˈdü-pli-ˌkā-tər *also* ˈdyü-\ *noun* (1893)
: one that duplicates; *specifically* : a machine for making copies of graphic matter

**du·plic·i·tous** \dü-ˈpli-sə-təs *also* dyü-\ *adjective* (1928)
: marked by duplicity
— **du·plic·i·tous·ly** *adverb*

**du·plic·i·ty** \dü-ˈpli-sə-tē *also* dyü-\ *noun, plural* **-ties** [Middle English *duplicite*, from Middle French, from Late Latin *duplicitat-, duplicitas*, from Latin *duplex*] (15th century)
**1** : contradictory doubleness of thought, speech, or action; *especially* : the belying of one's true intentions by deceptive words or action
**2** : the quality or state of being double or twofold
**3** : the technically incorrect use of two or more distinct items (as claims, charges, or defenses) in a single legal action

**du·ra·ble** \ˈdu̇r-ə-bəl *also* ˈdyu̇r-\ *adjective* [Middle English, from Middle French, from Latin *durabilis*, from *durare* to last — more at DURING] (14th century)
: able to exist for a long time without significant deterioration; *also* : designed to be durable ⟨*durable* goods⟩

**synonym** see LASTING
— **du·ra·bil·i·ty** \ˌdu̇r-ə-ˈbi-lə-tē, ˌdyu̇r-\ *noun*
— **du·ra·ble·ness** \ˈdu̇r-ə-bəl-nəs, ˈdyu̇r-\ *noun*
— **du·ra·bly** \-blē\ *adverb*

**durable press** *noun* (1966)
: PERMANENT PRESS

**du·ra·bles** \ˈdu̇r-ə-bəlz *also* ˈdyu̇r-\ *noun plural* (1941)
: consumer goods (as vehicles and household appliances) that are typically used repeatedly over a period of years — called also *durable goods*

**du·ral·u·min** \du̇-ˈral-yə-mən *also* dyu̇-\ *noun* [from *Duralumin*, a trademark] (1910)
: a light strong alloy of aluminum, copper, manganese, and magnesium

**du·ra ma·ter** \ˈdu̇r-ə-ˌmā-tər, ˈdyu̇r-, -ˌmä-\ *noun* [Middle English, from Medieval Latin, literally, hard mother] (14th century)
: the tough fibrous membrane that envelops the brain and spinal cord external to the arachnoid and pia mater

**du·rance** \ˈdu̇r-ən(t)s *also* ˈdyu̇r-\ *noun* [Middle English, from Middle French, from *durer* to endure, from Latin *durare*] (15th century)
**1** *archaic* : ENDURANCE
**2** : restraint by or as if by physical force — usually used in the phrase *durance vile*

**du·ra·tion** \du̇-ˈrā-shən *also* dyu̇-\ *noun* (14th century)
**1** : continuance in time
**2** : the time during which something exists or lasts

**du·ra·tive** \ˈdu̇r-ə-tiv, ˈdyu̇r-\ *adjective* (1889)
: CONTINUATIVE
— **durative** *noun*

**dur·bar** \ˈdər-ˌbär, ˌdər-ˈ\ *noun* [Hindi *darbār*, from Persian, from *dar* door + *bār* admission, audience] (1609)
**1** : court held by an Indian prince
**2** : a formal reception held by an Indian prince or an African ruler

**du·ress** \du̇-ˈres *also* dyu̇-\ *noun* [Middle English *duresse*, from Middle French *duresce* hardness, severity, from Latin *duritia*, from *durus*] (15th century)
**1** : forcible restraint or restriction
**2** : compulsion by threat; *specifically* : unlawful constraint

**Dur·ham** \ˈdər-əm, ˈdə-rəm, ˈdu̇r-əm\ *noun* [County *Durham*, England] (1810)
: SHORTHORN

**Durham Rule** *noun* [Monte *Durham*, 20th century American litigant] (1955)
: a legal hypothesis under which a person is not judged responsible for a criminal act that is attributed to a mental disease or defect

**du·ri·an** \ˈdu̇r-ē-ən, -ē-ˌän *also* ˈdyu̇r-\ *noun* [Malay] (1588)
**1** : a large oval tasty but foul-smelling fruit with a prickly rind
**2** : an East Indian tree (*Durio zibethinus*) of the silk-cotton family that bears durians

**dur·ing** \ˈdu̇r-iŋ *also* ˈdyu̇r-\ *preposition* [Middle English, from present participle of *duren* to last, from Old French *durer*, from Latin *durare* to harden, endure, from *durus* hard; perhaps akin to Sanskrit *dāru* wood — more at TREE] (14th century)
**1** : throughout the duration of ⟨swims every day *during* the summer⟩
**2** : at a point in the course of ⟨was offered a job *during* a visit to the capital⟩

**dur·mast oak** \ˈdər-ˌmast-\ *noun* [perhaps alteration of *dun mast*, from ¹*dun* + *mast*] (1791)
: a European oak (*Quercus petraea*) valued especially for its dark heavy tough elastic wood and for its tannin-rich bark

**durn** \ˈdərn\, **durned** \ˈdərn(d)\ *variant of* DARN, DARNED

**du·ro** \ˈdu̇r-(ˌ)ō\ *noun, plural* **duros** [Spanish, short for *peso duro* hard peso] (1832)
: a Spanish or Spanish American peso or silver dollar

**du·roc** \ˈdu̇r-ˌäk *also* ˈdyu̇r-\ *noun, often capitalized* [*Duroc*, 19th century American stallion] (1883)
: any of a breed of large vigorous red American hogs

**du·rom·e·ter** \du̇-ˈrä-mə-tər *also* dyu̇-\ *noun* [Latin *durus* hard] (circa 1879)
: an instrument for measuring hardness

**dur·ra** *also* **du·ra** \ˈdu̇r-ə\ *noun* [Arabic *dhurah*] (1798)
: any of several grain sorghums widely grown in warm dry regions

**durst** \ˈdərst\ *archaic & dialect past of* DARE

**du·rum wheat** \ˈdu̇r-əm-, ˈdyu̇r-, ˈdər-əm-, ˈdə-rəm-\ *noun* [New Latin *durum*, from Latin, neuter of *durus* hard] (circa 1903)
: a wheat (*Triticum durum*) that yields a glutenous flour used especially in pasta — called also *durum*

**¹dusk** \ˈdəsk\ *adjective* [Middle English *dosk*, alteration of Old English *dox*; akin to Latin *fuscus* dark brown, Old English *dunn* dun, *dūst* dust] (13th century)
: DUSKY

**²dusk** (13th century)
*intransitive verb*
: to become dark
*transitive verb*
: to make dark or gloomy

**³dusk** *noun* (1622)
**1** : the darker part of twilight especially at night
**2** : darkness or semidarkness caused by the shutting out of light

**dusky** \ˈdəs-kē\ *adjective* **dusk·i·er; -est** (1558)

**1** : somewhat dark in color; *specifically* : having dark skin
**2** : marked by slight or deficient light : SHADOWY
— **dusk·i·ly** \-kə-lē\ *adverb*
— **dusk·i·ness** \-kē-nəs\ *noun*

**¹dust** \ˈdəst\ *noun* [Middle English, from Old English *dūst*; akin to Old High German *tunst* storm, and probably to Latin *fumus* smoke — more at FUME] (before 12th century)
**1** : fine particles of matter (as of earth)
**2** : the particles into which something disintegrates
**3 a** : something worthless **b** : a state of humiliation
**4 a** : the earth especially as a place of burial **b** : the surface of the ground
**5 a** : a cloud of dust **b** : CONFUSION, DISTURBANCE
**6** *archaic* : a single particle (as of earth)
**7** *British* : refuse ready for collection
— **dust·less** \-ləs\ *adjective*
— **dust·like** \-ˌlīk\ *adjective*

**²dust** (1530)
*transitive verb*
**1** *archaic* : to make dusty
**2** : to make free of dust
**3 a** : to sprinkle with fine particles **b** : to sprinkle in the form of dust
*intransitive verb*
**1** *of a bird* : to work dust into the feathers
**2** : to remove dust
**3** : to give off dust

**dust·bin** \ˈdəs(t)-ˌbin\ *noun* (1848)
**1** *British* : a can for trash or garbage
**2** : DUSTHEAP 2

**dust bowl** *noun* (1936)
: a region that suffers from prolonged droughts and dust storms

**dust·cov·er** \-ˌkə-vər\ *noun* (1899)
**1** : a cover (as of cloth or plastic) used to protect furniture or equipment from dust
**2** : DUST JACKET

**dust devil** *noun* (1888)
: a small whirlwind containing sand or dust

**dust·er** \ˈdəs-tər\ *noun* (1576)
**1** : one that removes dust
**2 a** (1) : a long lightweight overgarment to protect clothing from dust (2) : a long coat cut like a duster — called also *duster coat* **b** : a dress-length housecoat
**3** : one that scatters fine particles; *specifically* : a device for applying insecticidal or fungicidal dusts to crops
**4** : DUST STORM

**dust·heap** \ˈdəst-ˌ(h)ēp\ *noun* (1599)
**1** : a pile of refuse
**2** : a category of forgotten items ⟨the *dustheap* of history —*New Republic*⟩

**dust jacket** *noun* (1926)
: a paper cover for a book

**dust·man** \ˈdəs(t)-mən\ *noun* (1707)
*British* : a collector of trash or garbage

**dust mop** *noun* (1953)
: DRY MOP

**dust off** *transitive verb* (1940)
: to bring out or back to use again

**dust·pan** \ˈdəs(t)-ˌpan\ *noun* (1783)
: a shovel-shaped pan for sweepings

**dust storm** *noun* (1879)
**1** : a dust-laden whirlwind that moves across an arid region and is usually associated with hot dry air and marked by high electrical tension
**2** : strong winds bearing clouds of dust

**dust-up** \ˈdəs-ˌtəp\ *noun* (1897)
: ROW, FIGHT

**dust wrapper** *noun* (1932)
: DUST JACKET

**dusty** \'dəs-tē\ *adjective* **dust·i·er; -est** (13th century)
**1** : covered or abounding with dust
**2** : consisting of dust : POWDERY
**3** : resembling dust
**4** : lacking vitality : DRY ⟨*dusty* scholarship⟩
**5** *British* : UNSATISFACTORY — used especially in the phrases *dusty answer* and *not so dusty*
— **dust·i·ly** \'dəs-tə-lē\ *adverb*
— **dust·i·ness** \-tē-nəs\ *noun*
**dusty miller** *noun* (circa 1825)
: any of several plants having ashy-gray or white tomentose leaves; *especially* : an herbaceous artemisia (*Artemisia stelleriana*) with greyish foliage found along the eastern coast of the U.S.
**dutch** \'dəch\ *adverb, often capitalized* (1914)
: with each person paying his or her own way
¹**Dutch** \'dəch\ *adjective* [Middle English *Duch,* from Middle Dutch *duutsch;* akin to Old High German *diutisc* German, Old English *thēod* nation, Gothic *thiudisko* as a gentile, *thiuda* people, Oscan *touto* city] (14th century)
**1 a** *archaic* : of, relating to, or in any of the Germanic languages of Germany, Austria, Switzerland, and the Low Countries **b** : of, relating to, or in the Dutch of the Netherlands
**2 a** *archaic* : of or relating to the Germanic peoples of Germany, Austria, Switzerland, and the Low Countries **b** : of or relating to the Netherlands or its inhabitants **c** : ²GERMAN
**3** : of or relating to the Pennsylvania Dutch or their language
— **Dutch·ly** *adverb*
²**Dutch** *noun* (14th century)
**1 a** *archaic* (1) : any of the Germanic languages of Germany, Austria, Switzerland, and the Low Countries (2) : GERMAN 3 **b** : the Germanic language of the Netherlands
**2 Dutch** *plural* **a** *archaic* : the Germanic peoples of Germany, Austria, Switzerland, and the Low Countries **b** : GERMANS 2a, b **c** : the people of the Netherlands
**3** : PENNSYLVANIA DUTCH
**4** : DANDER ⟨her *Dutch* is up⟩
**5** : DISFAVOR, TROUBLE ⟨in *Dutch* with the boss⟩
**Dutch cheese** *noun* (1829)
*chiefly Northern* : COTTAGE CHEESE
**Dutch clover** *noun* (1800)
: WHITE CLOVER
**Dutch Colonial** *adjective* (1922)
: characterized by a gambrel roof with overhanging eaves
**Dutch courage** *noun* (1809)
: courage artificially stimulated especially by drink; *also* : drink taken for courage
**Dutch door** *noun* (circa 1890)
: a door divided horizontally so that the lower or upper part can be shut separately

**Dutch elm disease** *noun* (1927)
: a disease of elms caused by an ascomycetous fungus (*Ceratocystis ulmi*) and characterized by yellowing of the foliage, defoliation, and death
**Dutch hoe** *noun* (1744)
: SCUFFLE HOE

**Dutch door**

**dutch·man** \'dəch-mən\ *noun* (14th century)
**1** *capitalized* **a** *archaic* : a member of any of the Germanic peoples of Germany, Austria, Switzerland, and the Low Countries **b** : a native or inhabitant of the Netherlands **c** : a person of Dutch descent **d** : GERMAN 1a, b
**2** : a device for hiding or counteracting structural defects
**Dutch·man's-breech·es** \,dəch-mənz-'brich·əz\ *noun plural but singular or plural in construction* (1837)
: a spring-flowering herb (*Dicentra cucullaria*) of the fumitory family occurring in the eastern U.S. and having finely divided leaves and

cream-white double-spurred flowers
**Dutchman's-pipe** \-'pīp\ *noun, plural*
**Dutchman's-pipes** \-'pīps\ (1845)
: a vine (*Aristolochia durior*) with large leaves and early summer flowers having the tube of the calyx curved like the bowl of a pipe
**Dutch oven** *noun* (1769)
**1** : a metal shield for roasting before an open fire
**2** : a brick oven in which cooking is done by the preheated walls
**3 a** : a cast-iron kettle with a tight cover that is used for baking in an open fire **b** : a heavy pot with a tight-fitting domed cover
**Dutch roll** *noun* (1913)
: a combination of directional and lateral oscillation of an airplane
¹**dutch treat** *noun, often D capitalized* (1887)
: a meal or other entertainment for which each person pays his or her own way
²**dutch treat** *adverb, often D capitalized* (1942)
: DUTCH ⟨go *dutch treat*⟩
**Dutch uncle** *noun* (1837)
: one who admonishes sternly and bluntly
**du·te·ous** \'dü-tē-əs *also* 'dyü-\ *adjective* [irregular from *duty*] (1593)
: DUTIFUL, OBEDIENT
**du·ti·able** \'dü-tē-ə-bəl *also* 'dyü-\ *adjective* (1774)
: subject to a duty
**du·ti·ful** \'dü-ti-fəl *also* 'dyü-\ *adjective* (1552)
**1** : filled with or motivated by a sense of duty
**2** : proceeding from or expressive of a sense of duty
— **du·ti·ful·ly** \-f(ə-)lē\ *adverb*
— **du·ti·ful·ness** \-fəl-nəs\ *noun*
¹**du·ty** \'dü-tē *also* 'dyü-\ *noun, plural* **duties** [Middle English *duete,* from Anglo-French *dueté,* from Old French *deu* due] (13th century)
**1** : conduct due to parents and superiors : RESPECT
**2 a** : obligatory tasks, conduct, service, or functions that arise from one's position (as in life or in a group) **b** (1) : assigned service or business (2) : active military service (3) : a period of being on duty
**3 a** : a moral or legal obligation **b** : the force of moral obligation
**4** : TAX; *especially* : a tax on imports
**5 a** : WORK 1a **b** (1) : the service required (as of an electric machine) under specified conditions (2) : functional application : USE ⟨got double *duty* out of the trip⟩ (3) : use as a substitute ⟨making the word do *duty* for the thing —Edward Sapir⟩
**synonym** see FUNCTION, TASK
— **off duty** : free from assignment or responsibility
— **on duty** : engaged in or responsible for an assigned task or duty
²**duty** *adjective* (1806)
**1** : done as a duty
**2** : being on duty : assigned to specified tasks or functions ⟨the *duty* officer⟩
**duty-free** \,dü-tē-'frē, ,dyü-, 'dü-tē-,\ *adjective or adverb* (1689)
**1** : without payment of customs duties : free from duties ⟨imported *duty-free*⟩ ⟨*duty-free* goods⟩
**2** : relating to or selling duty-free goods ⟨a *duty-free* shop⟩
**du·um·vir** \dü-'əm-vər *also* dyü-\ *noun* [Latin, from *duum* (genitive of *duo* two) + *vir* man] (1600)
**1** : one of two Roman officers or magistrates constituting a board or court

**2** : one of two people jointly holding power
— **du·um·vi·rate** \-və-rət\ *noun*
**du·vet** \d(y)ü-'vā, 'd(y)ü-,\ *noun* [French] (1758)
: COMFORTER 2b
**duve·tyn** \'dü-və-,tēn, 'dyü-, 'dəv-,tēn\ *noun* [French *duvetine,* from *duvet* down, from Middle French, alteration of (assumed) Middle French *dumet,* diminutive of Old French *dun, dum* down, from Old Norse *dūnn* — more at DOWN] (1913)
: a smooth lustrous velvety fabric
**dux·elles** \,dük-'sel, (,)dü-'sel\ *noun* [Marquis Louis Chalon du Blé *d'Uxelles* (died 1658) French nobleman] (1877)
: a garnish or stuffing made especially of finely chopped sautéed mushrooms
¹**dwarf** \'dwórf\ *noun, plural* **dwarfs** \'dwórfs\ *also* **dwarves** \'dwórvz\ *often attributive* [Middle English *dwergh, dwerf,* from Old English *dweorg, dweorh;* akin to Old High German *twerg* dwarf] (before 12th century)
**1 a** : a person of unusually small stature; *especially* : one whose bodily proportions are abnormal **b** : an insignificant person
**2** : an animal or plant much below normal size
**3** : a small legendary manlike being who is usually misshapen and ugly and skilled as an artificer
**4** : a star (as the sun) of ordinary or low luminosity and relatively small mass and size
— **dwarf·ish** \'dwór-fish\ *adjective*
— **dwarf·ish·ly** *adverb*
— **dwarf·ish·ness** *noun*
— **dwarf·like** \'dwór-,flīk\ *adjective*
— **dwarf·ness** \'dwórf-nəs\ *noun*
²**dwarf** (circa 1626)
*transitive verb*
**1** : to restrict the growth of : STUNT
**2** : to cause to appear smaller or to seem inferior
*intransitive verb*
: to become smaller
³**dwarf** *adjective* (1664)
*of a plant* : low-growing in habit ⟨*dwarfer* forms of citrus⟩
**dwarf·ism** \'dwór-,fi-zəm\ *noun* (1865)
: the condition of stunted growth
**dweeb** \'dwēb\ *noun* [origin unknown] (1983)
*slang* : an unattractive, insignificant, or inept person
**dwell** \'dwel\ *intransitive verb* **dwelled** \'dweld, 'dwelt\ *or* **dwelt** \'dwelt\; **dwelling** [Middle English, from Old English *dwellan* to go astray, hinder; akin to Old High German *twellen* to tarry] (13th century)
**1** : to remain for a time
**2 a** : to live as a resident **b** : EXIST, LIE
**3 a** : to keep the attention directed — used with *on* or *upon* ⟨tried not to *dwell* on my fears⟩ **b** : to speak or write insistently — used with *on* or *upon* ⟨leering reviewers *dwelled* on a publicity photograph —James Atlas⟩
— **dwell·er** *noun*
**dwell·ing** *noun* (14th century)
: a shelter (as a house) in which people live
**dwin·dle** \'dwin-d°l\ *verb* **dwin·dled; dwin·dling** \-(d)liŋ, -d°l-iŋ\ [probably frequentative of *dwine* to waste away, from Middle English, from Old English *dwīnan;* akin to Old Norse *dvīna* to pine away, *deyja* to die — more at DIE] (1596)
*intransitive verb*
: to become steadily less : SHRINK
*transitive verb*
: to make steadily less
**synonym** see DECREASE
**DX** \(,)dē-'eks\ *noun* (circa 1924)
: DISTANCE — used of long-distance radio transmission
**dy-** *or* **dyo-** *combining form* [Late Latin, from Greek, from *dyo* — more at TWO]
: two ⟨*dyarchy*⟩
**dy·ad** \'dī-,ad, -əd\ *noun* [Late Latin *dyad-, dyas,* from Greek, from *dyo*] (1675)

*[illustration caption, top middle:]* **Dutchman's-breeches**

**1** : PAIR; *specifically* : two individuals (as husband and wife) maintaining a sociologically significant relationship
**2** : a meiotic chromosome after separation of the two homologous members of a tetrad
**3** : a mathematical operator indicated by writing the symbols of two vectors without a dot or cross between (as AB)
— **dy·ad·ic** \dī-'a-dik\ *adjective*
— **dy·ad·i·cal·ly** \-di-k(ə-)lē\ *adverb*
**dy·ad·ic** \dī-'a-dik\ *noun* (1884)
: a mathematical expression formed by addition or subtraction of dyads
**Dy·ak** *variant of* DAYAK
**dy·ar·chy** \'dī-,är-kē\ *noun, plural* **-chies** (1640)
: a government in which power is vested in two rulers or authorities
**dyb·buk** \'di-bək\ *noun, plural* **dyb·bu·kim** \,di-bu̇-'kēm\ *also* **dybbuks** [Late Hebrew *dibbūq*] (circa 1903)
: a wandering soul believed in Jewish folklore to enter and control a living body until exorcised by a religious rite
**¹dye** \'dī\ *noun* [Middle English *dehe,* from Old English *dēah, dēag*] (before 12th century)
**1** : color from dyeing
**2** : a soluble or insoluble coloring matter
**²dye** *verb* **dyed; dye·ing** (before 12th century)
*transitive verb*
**1** : to impart a new and often permanent color to especially by impregnating with a dye
**2** : to impart (a color) by dyeing ⟨*dyeing* blue on yellow⟩
*intransitive verb*
: to take up or impart color in dyeing
— **dye·abil·i·ty** \,dī-ə-'bi-lə-tē\ *noun*
— **dye·able** \'dī-ə-bəl\ *adjective*
— **dy·er** \'dī(-ə)r\ *noun*
**dyed–in–the–wool** \,dīd-ᵊn-thə-'wu̇l\ *adjective* (1580)
: THOROUGHGOING, UNCOMPROMISING ⟨a *dyed-in-the-wool* conservative⟩
**dye·stuff** \'dī-,stəf\ *noun* (1837)
: DYE 2
**dye·wood** \-,wu̇d\ *noun* (1699)
: a wood (as logwood or fustic) from which coloring matter is extracted for dyeing
**dying** *present participle of* DIE
**¹dyke** *chiefly British variant of* DIKE
**²dyke** \'dīk\ *noun* [origin unknown] (circa 1942)
: LESBIAN — often used disparagingly
— **dykey** \'dī-kē\ *adjective*
**¹dy·nam·ic** \dī-'na-mik\ *adjective* **·ia** [French *dynamique,* from Greek *dynamikos* powerful, from *dynamis* power, from *dynasthai* to be able] (1827)
**1** *also* **dy·nam·i·cal** \-mi-kəl\ **a** : of or relating to physical force or energy **b** : of or relating to dynamics
**2 a** : marked by usually continuous and productive activity or change ⟨a *dynamic* city⟩ **b** : ENERGETIC, FORCEFUL ⟨a *dynamic* personality⟩
**3** *of random-access memory* : requiring periodic refreshment of charge in order to retain data
— **dy·nam·i·cal·ly** \-mi-k(ə-)lē\ *adverb*
**²dynamic** *noun* (1879)
**1** : a dynamic force
**2** : DYNAMICS 2; *also* : an underlying cause of change or growth
**dynamic range** *noun* (1949)
: the ratio of the strongest to the weakest sound intensity that can be transmitted or reproduced by an audio or broadcasting system
**dy·nam·ics** \dī-'na-miks\ *noun plural but singular or plural in construction* (circa 1789)
**1** : a branch of mechanics that deals with forces and their relation primarily to the motion but sometimes also to the equilibrium of bodies
**2** : a pattern or process of change, growth, or activity ⟨population *dynamics*⟩

**3** : variation and contrast in force or intensity (as in music)
**dy·na·mism** \'dī-nə-,mi-zəm\ *noun* (circa 1857)
**1 a** : a theory that all phenomena (as matter or motion) can be explained as manifestations of force — compare MECHANISM **b** : DYNAMICS 2
**2** : a dynamic or expansionist quality
— **dy·na·mist** \-mist\ *noun*
— **dy·na·mis·tic** \,dī-nə-'mis-tik\ *adjective*
**¹dy·na·mite** \'dī-nə-,mīt\ *noun* (1867)
**1** : an explosive that is made of nitroglycerin absorbed in a porous material and that often contains ammonium nitrate or cellulose nitrate; *also* : an explosive (as a mixture of ammonium nitrate and nitrocellulose) that contains no nitroglycerin
**2** : one that has a powerful effect; *also* : something that has great potential to cause trouble or conflict
— **dy·na·mit·ic** \,dī-nə-'mi-tik\ *adjective*
**²dynamite** *transitive verb* **-mit·ed; -mit·ing** (1881)
**1** : to blow up with dynamite
**2** : to cause the failure or destruction of
— **dy·na·mit·er** *noun*
**³dynamite** *adjective* (1940)
: TERRIFIC, WONDERFUL
**dy·na·mo** \'dī-nə-,mō\ *noun, plural* **-mos** [short for *dynamoelectric machine*] (circa 1882)
**1** : GENERATOR 3
**2** : a forceful energetic individual
**dy·na·mom·e·ter** \,dī-nə-'mä-mə-tər\ *noun* [French *dynamomètre,* from Greek *dynamis* power + French *-mètre* -meter] (1810)
**1** : an instrument for measuring mechanical force
**2** : an apparatus for measuring mechanical power (as of an engine)
— **dy·na·mo·met·ric** \-mō-'me-trik\ *adjective*
— **dy·na·mom·e·try** \-'mä-mə-trē\ *noun*
**dy·na·mo·tor** \'dī-nə-,mō-tər\ *noun* [*dynamo* + *motor*] (1899)
: a motor generator combining the electric motor and generator
**dy·nast** \'dī-,nast, -nəst\ *noun* [Latin *dynastes,* from Greek *dynastēs,* from *dynasthai* to be able, have power] (1631)
: RULER 1
**dy·nas·ty** \'dī-nə-stē *also* -,nas-tē, *especially British* 'di-nə-stē\ *noun, plural* **-ties** (14th century)
**1** : a succession of rulers of the same line of descent
**2** : a powerful group or family that maintains its position for a considerable time
— **dy·nas·tic** \dī-'nas-tik\ *adjective*
— **dy·nas·ti·cal·ly** \-ti-k(ə-)lē\ *adverb*
**dy·na·tron** \'dī-nə-,trän\ *noun* [Greek *dynamis* power] (1918)
: a vacuum tube in which the secondary emission of electrons from the plate results in a decrease in the plate current as the plate voltage increases
**dyne** \'dīn\ *noun* [French, from Greek *dynamis*] (circa 1873)
: the unit of force in the centimeter-gram-second system equal to the force that would give a free mass of one gram an acceleration of one centimeter per second per second
**dy·ne·in** \'dī-nē-in\ *noun* [*dyne* (force) + *-in*] (1965)
: an ATPase that is associated especially with microtubules involved in the ciliary and flagellar movement of cells
**dy·node** \'dī-,nōd\ *noun* [Greek *dynamis*] (1939)
: an electrode in an electron tube that functions to produce secondary emission of electrons
**dys-** *prefix* [Middle English *dis-* bad, difficult, from Middle French & Latin; Middle French

*dis-,* from Latin *dys-,* from Greek; akin to Old English *tō-, te-* apart, Sanskrit *dus-* bad, difficult]
**1** : abnormal ⟨*dys*plasia⟩
**2** : difficult ⟨*dys*phagia⟩ — compare EU-
**3** : impaired ⟨*dys*function⟩
**4** : bad ⟨*dys*logistic⟩ — compare EU-
**dys·ar·thria** \dis-'sär-thrē-ə\ *noun* [New Latin, from *dys-* + *arthr-* + *-ia*] (1878)
: difficulty in articulating words due to disease of the central nervous system
**dys·cra·sia** \dis-'krā-zh(ē-)ə\ *noun* [New Latin, from Medieval Latin, bad mixture of humors, from Greek *dyskrasia,* from *dys-* + *krasis* mixture, from *kerannynai* to mix — more at CRATER] (14th century)
: an abnormal condition of the body and especially the blood
**dys·en·ter·ic** \,dis-sᵊn-'ter-ik\ *adjective* (1727)
: of or relating to dysentery
**dys·en·tery** \'dis-ᵊn-,ter-ē\ *noun, plural* **-ter·ies** [Middle English *dissenterie,* from Latin *dysenteria,* from Greek, from *dys-* + *enteron* intestine — more at INTER-] (14th century)
**1** : a disease characterized by severe diarrhea with passage of mucus and blood and usually caused by infection
**2** : DIARRHEA
**dys·func·tion** \(,)dis-'fəŋ(k)-shən\ *noun* (circa 1916)
: impaired or abnormal functioning
— **dys·func·tion·al** \-shnəl, -shə-nᵊl\ *adjective*
**dys·gen·e·sis** \(,)dis-'je-nə-səs\ *noun* [New Latin] (circa 1883)
: defective development especially of the gonads (as in Klinefelter's syndrome)
**dys·gen·ic** \(,)dis-'je-nik\ *adjective* (1912)
**1** : tending to promote survival of or reproduction by less well-adapted individuals (as the weak or diseased) especially at the expense of well-adapted individuals (as the strong or healthy) ⟨the *dysgenic* effect of war⟩
**2** : biologically defective or deficient
**dys·ki·ne·sia** \,dis-kə-'nē-zh(ē-)ə, -kī-\ *noun* [New Latin, from Greek *dyskinēsia* difficulty in moving, from *dys-* + *-kinesia,* from *kinēsis* motion, from *kinein* to move — more at HIGHT] (circa 1706)
: impairment of voluntary movements resulting in fragmented or jerky motions (as in Parkinson's disease) — compare TARDIVE DYSKINESIA
— **dys·ki·net·ic** \-'net-ik\ *adjective*
**dys·lex·ia** \dis-'lek-sē-ə\ *noun* [New Latin, from *dys-* + Greek *lexis* word, speech, from *legein* to say — more at LEGEND] (circa 1888)
: a disturbance of the ability to read; *broadly* : disturbance of the ability to use language
— **dys·lex·ic** \-sik\ *adjective or noun*
**dys·lo·gis·tic** \,dis-lə-'jis-tik\ *adjective* [*dys-* + *-logistic* (as in *eulogistic*)] (1812)
: UNCOMPLIMENTARY
— **dys·lo·gis·ti·cal·ly** \-ti-k(ə-)lē\ *adverb*
**dys·men·or·rhea** \(,)dis-,me-nə-'rē-ə\ *noun* [New Latin] (circa 1810)
: painful menstruation
— **dys·men·or·rhe·ic** \-'rē-ik\ *adjective*
**dys·pep·sia** \dis-'pep-shə, -sē-ə\ *noun* [Latin, from Greek, from *dys-* + *pepsis* digestion, from *peptein, pessein* to cook, digest — more at COOK] (circa 1706)
**1** : INDIGESTION
**2** : ill humor : DISGRUNTLEMENT
— **dys·pep·tic** \-'pep-tik\ *adjective or noun*
— **dys·pep·ti·cal·ly** \-ti-k(ə-)lē\ *adverb*
**dys·pha·gia** \dis-'fā-j(ē-)ə\ *noun* [New Latin] (1783)

: difficulty in swallowing

**dys·pha·sia** \dis-'fā-zh(ē-)ə\ *noun* [New Latin] (circa 1883)
: loss of or deficiency in the power to use or understand language as a result of injury to or disease of the brain
— **dys·pha·sic** \-'fā-zik\ *noun or adjective*

**dys·phe·mism** \'dis-fə-ˌmi-zəm\ *noun* [*dys-* + *-phemism* (as in *euphemism*)] (1884)
: the substitution of a disagreeable, offensive, or disparaging expression for an agreeable or inoffensive one; *also* : an expression so substituted
— **dys·phe·mis·tic** \ˌdis-fə-'mis-tik\ *adjective*

**dys·pho·nia** \dis-'fō-nē-ə\ *noun* [New Latin] (circa 1706)
: defective use of the voice

**dys·pho·ria** \dis-'fōr-ē-ə, -'fór-\ *noun* [New Latin, from Greek, from *dysphoros* hard to bear, from *dys-* + *pherein* to bear — more at BEAR] (circa 1842)
: a state of feeling unwell or unhappy
— **dys·phor·ic** \-'fór-ik, -'fär-\ *adjective*

**dys·pla·sia** \dis-'plā-zh(ē-)ə\ *noun* [New Latin] (circa 1923)
: abnormal growth or development (as of organs or cells); *broadly* : abnormal anatomic structure due to such growth
— **dys·plas·tic** \-'plas-tik\ *adjective*

**dys·pnea** \'dis(p)-nē-ə\ *noun* [Latin *dyspnoea*, from Greek *dyspnoia*, from *dyspnoos* short of breath, from *dys-* + *pnein* to breathe — more at SNEEZE] (circa 1681)
: difficult or labored respiration
— **dys·pne·ic** \-nē-ik\ *adjective*

**dyspnoea** *chiefly British variant of* DYSPNEA

**dys·pro·si·um** \dis-'prō-zē-əm, -zh(ē-)əm\ *noun* [New Latin, from Greek *dysprositos* hard to get at, from *dys-* + *prositos* approachable, from *prosienai* to approach, from *pros-* + *ienai* to go — more at ISSUE] (1886)
: an element of the rare-earth group that forms highly magnetic compounds — see ELEMENT table

**dys·rhyth·mia** \dis-'rith-mē-ə\ *noun* [New Latin, from *dys-* + Latin *rhythmus* rhythm] (circa 1909)
: an abnormal rhythm; *especially* : a disordered rhythm exhibited in a record of electrical activity of the brain or heart
— **dys·rhyth·mic** \-mik\ *adjective*

**dys·to·cia** \di-'stō-sh(ē-)ə\ *noun* [New Latin, from Greek *dystokia,* from *dys-* + *tokos* child-birth; akin to Greek *tiktein* to give birth to — more at THANE] (circa 1706)
: slow or difficult labor or delivery

**dys·to·pia** \(ˌ)dis-'tō-pē-ə\ *noun* [New Latin, from *dys-* + *-topia* (as in *utopia*)] (circa 1950)
**1** : an imaginary place where people lead dehumanized and often fearful lives
**2** : ANTI-UTOPIA 2
— **dys·to·pi·an** \-pē-ən\ *adjective*

**dys·tro·phic** \dis-'trō-fik\ *adjective* (1893)
**1 a** : relating to or caused by faulty nutrition **b** : relating to or affected with a dystrophy ⟨a *dystrophic* patient⟩
**2** *of a lake* : brownish with much dissolved humic matter, a sparse bottom fauna, and a high oxygen consumption

**dys·tro·phy** \'dis-trə-fē\ *noun, plural* **-phies** [New Latin *dystrophia,* from *dys-* + *-trophia* -trophy] (1901)
**1** : a condition produced by faulty nutrition
**2** : any myogenic atrophy; *especially* : MUSCULAR DYSTROPHY

**dys·uria** \dis-'yu̇r-ē-ə, dish-\ *noun* [New Latin, from Greek *dysouria,* from *dys-* + *-ouria* -uria] (14th century)
: difficult or painful discharge of urine — compare STRANGURY

# E

E *is the fifth letter of the English alphabet and of most alphabets that are closely related to it. It came through Latin from Etruscan and there from Greek, which took it from a Phoenician letter called* he, *representing a sound like English* h. *In Greek the letter, renamed* epsilon ("*simple e*"), *designated a short vowel equivalent to the* e *in English* end. *Although the corresponding long vowel (pronounced like the* a *in English* ale*) was indicated in Greek by the letter* eta (*see* H), *in Latin* E *was used for both the short and the long vowel. English* E *inherited these Latin phonetic values, but in Modern English "long"* e *has come to represent the sound of the letter* e *in* eve. *The small letterform of* e *developed in two main stages: first by a curving of the upright line of capital* E *so as to form a semicircle with the top and bottom bars* (ϵ); *next by the joining of the top curve and middle bar to form a crescent.*

**e** \'ē\ *noun, plural* **e's** *or* **es** \'ēz\ *often capitalized, often attributive* (before 12th century)
**1 a :** the 5th letter of the English alphabet **b :** a graphic representation of this letter **c :** a speech counterpart of orthographic *e*
**2 :** the 3d tone of a C-major scale
**3 :** a graphic device for reproducing the letter *e*
**4 :** one designated *e* especially as the 5th in order or class
**5 a :** a grade rating a student's work as poor and usually constituting a conditional pass **b :** a grade rating a student's work as failing **c :** one graded or rated with an E
**6 :** a transcendental number having a value to eight decimal places of 2.71828183 that is the base of natural logarithms
**7 :** something shaped like the letter E
**e-** \(')ē, i\ *prefix* [Middle English, from Old French & Latin; Old French, out, forth, away, from Latin, from *ex*-]
**1 :** missing : absent ⟨*edentulous*⟩
**2 :** away ⟨*eluviation*⟩
**¹each** \'ēch\ *adjective* [Middle English *ech*, from Old English *ǣlc*; akin to Old High German *iogilīh* each; both from a prehistoric West Germanic compound whose first and second constituents respectively are represented by Old English *ā* always and by Old English *gelīc* alike] (before 12th century)
**:** being one of two or more distinct individuals having a similar relation and often constituting an aggregate
**²each** *pronoun* (before 12th century)
**:** each one
**³each** *adverb* (before 12th century)
**:** to or for each : APIECE
**each other** *pronoun* (before 12th century)
**:** each of two or more in reciprocal action or relation ⟨looked at *each other* in surprise⟩ ■
**ea·ger** \'ē-gər\ *adjective* [Middle English *egre*, from Middle French *aigre*, from Latin *acer* — more at EDGE] (14th century)
**1 a** *archaic* **:** SHARP **b** *obsolete* **:** SOUR
**2 :** marked by enthusiastic or impatient desire or interest ☆
— **ea·ger·ly** *adverb*
— **ea·ger·ness** *noun*
**eager beaver** *noun* (1943)
**:** a person who is extremely zealous about performing duties and volunteering for more
**ea·gle** \'ē-gəl\ *noun* [Middle English *egle*, from Old French *aigle*, from Latin *aquila*] (13th century)
**1 :** any of various large diurnal birds of prey of the accipiter family noted for their strength, size, keenness of vision, and powers of flight
**2 a :** the eagle-bearing standard of the ancient Romans **b :** one of a pair of eagle-bearing silver insignia of rank worn by a military colonel or a navy captain

**3 :** a gold coin of the U.S. bearing an eagle on the reverse and usually having a value of ten dollars
**4 :** a golf score of two strokes less than par on a hole — compare BIRDIE
**5** *capitalized* [Fraternal Order of *Eagles*] **:** a member of a major fraternal order
**eagle eye** *noun* (1802)
**1 :** the ability to see or observe with exceptional keenness
**2 :** one that sees or observes keenly
— **eagle–eyed** \'ē-gəl-,īd\ *adjective*
**eagle ray** *noun* (circa 1856)
**:** any of several widely distributed large active stingrays (family Myliobatidae) with broad pectoral fins like wings
**Eagle Scout** *noun* (1913)
**1 :** a Boy Scout who has reached the highest level of achievement in scouting
**2 :** a straight-arrow and self-reliant man
**ea·glet** \'ē-glət\ *noun* (1572)
**:** a young eagle
**eal·dor·man** \'al-dər-mən\ *noun* [Old English — more at ALDERMAN] (before 12th century)
**:** the chief officer in a district (as a shire) in Anglo-Saxon England
**Eames chair** \'ēmz-, 'āmz-\ *noun* [Charles *Eames* (died 1978) American designer] (1946)
**:** any of several chairs designed by Charles Eames to fit the contours of the body and to be made from modern materials
**-ean** — see -AN
**¹ear** \'ir, ēr\ *noun* [Middle English *ere*, from Old English *ēare*; akin to Old High German *ōra* ear, Latin *auris*, Greek *ous*] (before 12th century)
**1 a :** the characteristic vertebrate organ of hearing and equilibrium consisting in the typical mammal of a sound-collecting outer ear separated by the tympanic membrane from a sound-transmitting middle ear that in turn is separated from a sensory inner ear by membranous fenestrae **b :** any of various organs capable of detecting vibratory motion
**2 :** the external ear of humans and most mammals
**3 a :** the sense or act of hearing **b :** acuity of hearing **c :** sensitivity to musical tone and pitch; *also* **:** the ability to retain and reproduce music that has been heard **d :** sensitivity to nuances of language especially as revealed in the command of verbal melody and rhythm or in the ability to render a spoken idiom accurately
**4 :** something resembling a mammalian ear in shape, position, or function: as **a :** a projecting part (as a lug or handle) **b :** either of a pair of tufts of lengthened feathers on the head of some birds
**5 a :** sympathetic attention **b :** ATTENTION, AWARENESS
**6 :** a space in the upper corner of the front

page of a periodical (as a newspaper) usually containing advertising for the periodical itself or a weather forecast
— **by ear :** without reference to or memorization of written music ⟨plays *by ear*⟩
— **in one ear and out the other :** through one's mind without making an impression ⟨everything you say to him goes *in one ear and out the other*⟩
— **on one's ear :** in or into a state of irritation, shock, or discord ⟨set the racing world *on its ear* by breaking the record⟩
— **up to one's ears :** deeply involved **:** heavily implicated ⟨*up to his ears* in shady deals⟩

**ear 1a:** *1* pinna, *2* lobe, *3* auditory meatus, *4* tympanic membrane, *5* eustachian tube, *6* auditory nerve, *7* cochlea, *8* semicircular canals, *9* stapes, *10* incus, *11* malleus, *12* bones of skull

**²ear** *noun* [Middle English *er*, from Old English *ēar*; akin to Old High German *ahir* ear, Old English *ecg* edge — more at EDGE] (before 12th century)
**:** the fruiting spike of a cereal (as wheat or Indian corn) including both the seeds and protective structures
**³ear** *intransitive verb* (14th century)
**:** to form ears in growing ⟨the rye should be *earing* up⟩
**ear·ache** \'ir-,āk\ *noun* (1789)
**:** an ache or pain in the ear
**ear candy** *noun* (1977)
**:** music that is pleasing to listen to but lacks depth

---

☆ **SYNONYMS**
**Eager, avid, keen, anxious, athirst** mean moved by a strong and urgent desire or interest. EAGER implies ardor and enthusiasm and sometimes impatience at delay or restraint ⟨*eager* to get started⟩. AVID adds to EAGER the implication of insatiability or greed ⟨*avid* for new thrills⟩. KEEN suggests intensity of interest and quick responsiveness in action ⟨*keen* on the latest fashions⟩. ANXIOUS emphasizes fear of frustration or failure or disappointment ⟨*anxious* not to make a social blunder⟩. ATHIRST stresses yearning but not necessarily readiness for action ⟨*athirst* for adventure⟩.

---

□ **USAGE**
**each other** Some handbooks and textbooks recommend that *each other* be restricted to reference to two and *one another* to reference to three or more. The distinction, while neat, is not observed in actual usage. *Each other* and *one another* are used interchangeably by good writers and have been since at least the sixteenth century.

---

\ə\ **abut** \ᵊ\ **kitten** \ər\ **further** \a\ **ash** \ā\ **ace**
\ä\ **mop, mar** \au̇\ **out** \ch\ **chin** \e\ **bet** \ē\ **easy**
\g\ **go** \i\ **hit** \ī\ **ice** \j\ **job** \ŋ\ **sing** \ō\ **go**
\ȯ\ **law** \ȯi\ **boy** \th\ **thin** \t̲h̲\ **the** \ü\ **loot** \u̇\ **foot**
\y\ **yet** \zh\ **vision** *see also* Guide to Pronunciation

**ear clip** *noun* (1945)
: an earring with a clip fastener

**ear·drop** \-,dräp\ *noun* (1720)
: EARRING; *especially* : one with a pendant

**ear·drum** \-,drəm\ *noun* (1645)
: TYMPANIC MEMBRANE

**eared** \'ird\ *adjective* (14th century)
: having ears especially of a specified kind or number ⟨a big-*eared* man⟩ ⟨golden-*eared* corn⟩

**eared seal** *noun* (1883)
: any of a family (Otariidae) of seals including the sea lions and fur seals and having independent mobile hind limbs and small well-developed external ears — compare HAIR SEAL

**ear·flap** \'ir-,flap\ *noun* (1907)
: a warm covering for the ears; *especially* : an extension on the lower edge of a cap that may be folded up or down

**ear·ful** \'ir-,fùl\ *noun* (1911)
**1** : an outpouring of news or gossip
**2** : an outpouring of anger, abuse, or complaint

**ear·ing** \'ir-iŋ\ *noun* [perhaps from ¹*ear*] (1626)
: a line used to fasten a corner of a sail to the yard or gaff or to haul a reef cringle to the yard

**earl** \'ər(-ə)l\ *noun* [Middle English *erl,* from Old English *eorl* warrior, nobleman; akin to Old Norse *jarl* warrior, nobleman] (12th century)
: a member of the British peerage ranking below a marquess and above a viscount
— **earl·dom** \-dəm\ *noun*

**earl marshal** *noun* (13th century)
: an officer of state in England serving chiefly as a royal attendant on ceremonial occasions, as marshal of state processions, and as head of the College of Arms

**ear·lobe** \'ir-,lōb\ *noun* (1859)
: the pendent part of the ear of humans or some fowls

**ear·lock** \-,läk\ *noun* (circa 1775)
: a curl of hair hanging in front of the ear

¹**ear·ly** \'ər-lē\ *adverb* **ear·li·er; -est** [Middle English *erly,* from Old English *ǣrlīce,* from *ǣr* early, soon — more at ERE] (before 12th century)
**1 a** : near the beginning of a period of time ⟨awoke *early* in the morning⟩ **b** : near the beginning of a course, process, or series ⟨*early* in his senatorial career⟩
**2 a** : before the usual or expected time **b** *archaic* : SOON **c** : sooner than related forms ⟨these apples bear *early*⟩

²**early** *adjective* **ear·li·er; -est** (13th century)
**1 a** : of, relating to, or occurring near the beginning of a period of time, a development, or a series **b** (1) : distant in past time (2) : PRIMITIVE
**2 a** : occurring before the usual or expected time **b** : occurring in the near future ⟨at your *earliest* convenience⟩ **c** : maturing or producing sooner than related forms ⟨an *early* peach⟩
— **ear·li·ness** *noun*

**Early American** *noun* (1895)
: a style (as of furniture, architecture, or fabric) originating in or characteristic of colonial America

**early bird** *noun* [from the proverb, "the early bird catches the worm"] (circa 1922)
**1** : an early riser
**2** : one that arrives early and especially before possible competitors

**early on** *adverb* (1928)
: at or during an early point or stage ⟨the reasons were obvious *early on* in the experiment⟩

**ear·ly·wood** \'ər-lē-,wùd\ *noun* (circa 1914)
: SPRINGWOOD

¹**ear·mark** \'ir-,märk\ *noun* (15th century)
**1** : a mark of identification on the ear of an animal

**2** : a distinguishing mark ⟨all the *earmarks* of poverty⟩

²**earmark** *transitive verb* (1591)
**1 a** : to mark (livestock) with an earmark **b** : to mark in a distinguishing manner
**2** : to designate (as funds) for a specific use or owner

**ear·muff** \'ir-,məf\ *noun* (1889)
: one of a pair of ear coverings connected by a flexible band and worn as protection against cold or noises

¹**earn** \'ərn\ *transitive verb* [Middle English *ernen,* from Old English *earnian;* akin to Old High German *arnōn* to reap, Czech *jeseň* autumn] (before 12th century)
**1 a** : to receive as return for effort and especially for work done or services rendered **b** : to bring in by way of return ⟨bonds *earning* 10% interest⟩
**2 a** : to come to be duly worthy of or entitled or suited to ⟨she *earned* a promotion⟩ **b** : to make worthy of or obtain for ⟨the suggestion *earned* him a promotion⟩
— **earn·er** *noun*

²**earn** *intransitive verb* [probably alteration of *yearn*] (1599)
*obsolete* : GRIEVE

**earned run** *noun* (1886)
: a run in baseball that scores without benefit of an error before the fielding team has had a chance to make the third putout of the inning

**earned run average** *noun* (1947)
: the average number of earned runs per game scored against a pitcher in baseball determined by dividing the total of earned runs scored against him by the total number of innings pitched and multiplying by nine

¹**ear·nest** \'ər-nəst\ *noun* [Middle English *ernest,* from Old English *eornost;* akin to Old High German *ernust* earnest] (before 12th century)
: a serious and intent mental state ⟨in *earnest*⟩

²**earnest** *adjective* (before 12th century)
**1** : characterized by or proceeding from an intense and serious state of mind
**2** : GRAVE, IMPORTANT
*synonym* see SERIOUS
— **ear·nest·ly** *adverb*
— **ear·nest·ness** \-nəs(t)-nəs\ *noun*

³**earnest** *noun* [Middle English *ernes, ernest,* from Old French *erres,* plural of *erre* earnest, from Latin *arra,* short for *arrabo,* from Greek *arrhabōn,* of Semitic origin; akin to Hebrew *'ērābhōn* pledge] (13th century)
**1** : something of value given by a buyer to a seller to bind a bargain
**2** : a token of what is to come : PLEDGE ◆

**earn·ings** \'ər-niŋz\ *noun plural* (1732)
**1** : something (as wages) earned
**2** : the balance of revenue after deduction of costs and expenses

**ear·phone** \'ir-,fōn\ *noun* (1924)
: a device that converts electrical energy into sound waves and is worn over or inserted into the ear

**ear pick** *noun* (14th century)
: a device often of precious metal for removing wax or foreign bodies from the ear

**ear·piece** \'ir-,pēs\ *noun* (1853)
**1** : a part of an instrument (as a stethoscope or hearing aid) which is applied to the ear; *especially* : EARPHONE
**2** : one of the two sidepieces that support eyeglasses by passing over or behind the ears

**ear·plug** \-,pləg\ *noun* (1904)
**1** : an ornament inserted in the lobe of the ear especially to distend it
**2** : a device of pliable material for insertion into the outer opening of the ear (as to keep out water or deaden sound)

**ear·ring** \'ir-(,)iŋ, -,riŋ\ *noun* (before 12th century)
: an ornament for the earlobe

**ear rot** *noun* (1926)

: a condition of Indian corn that is characterized by molding and decay of the ears and that is caused by fungi (genera *Diplodia, Fusarium,* or *Gibberella*)

**ear shell** *noun* (circa 1753)
: ABALONE

**ear·shot** \'ir-,shät\ *noun* (1607)
: the range within which the unaided voice may be heard

**ear·split·ting** \-,spli-tiŋ\ *adjective* (1884)
: distressingly loud or shrill
*synonym* see LOUD

¹**earth** \'ərth\ *noun* [Middle English *erthe,* from Old English *eorthe;* akin to Old High German *erda* earth, Greek *era*] (before 12th century)
**1** : the fragmental material composing part of the surface of the globe; *especially* : cultivable soil
**2** : the sphere of mortal life as distinguished from spheres of spirit life — compare HEAVEN, HELL
**3 a** : areas of land as distinguished from sea and air **b** : the solid footing formed of soil : GROUND
**4** *often capitalized* : the planet on which we live that is third in order from the sun — see PLANET table
**5 a** : the people of the planet Earth **b** : the mortal human body **c** : the pursuits, interests, and pleasures of earthly life as distinguished from spiritual concerns
**6** : the lair of a burrowing animal
**7** : an excessive amount of money — used with *the* ⟨real suede, which costs the *earth* to clean —Joanne Winship⟩
— **earth·like** \-,līk\ *adjective*
— **on earth** — used as an intensive ⟨to find out what *on earth* he was up to —Michael Holroyd⟩

²**earth** (1575)

---

□ USAGE

**early on** This adverb is sometimes objected to in American writing as an obtrusive Briticism. It is a relative newcomer to the language, having arisen in British English around 1928. It seems to have filled a need, however. It came into frequent use in American English in the late 1960s and is now well established on both sides of the Atlantic in both speech and writing.

---

◇ WORD HISTORY

**earnest** *Earnest money,* which is given to ensure the seriousness of a buyer's intent in a transaction, would seem to be money given "in earnest," but the third homograph *earnest,* the financial word, actually has no historical connection with the first homograph *earnest,* the one meaning "seriousness." As its etymology shows, the *earnest* given in a transaction has reached English through a centuries-long passage from one language to another. English borrowed the word from medieval French, which inherited it from ancient Rome. The Romans acquired the word, perhaps via the Etruscans, from the Greeks, who in turn had borrowed it from Semitic peoples of the eastern Mediterranean with whom they were in contact, such as the Phoenicians. The Semitic source of the Greek word is exactly paralleled by Biblical Hebrew *'ērābhōn,* a derivative of a verb *'ārabh* "pledge." The long trail of this word meaning "pledge in a bargain" shows us the remarkable continuity of mercantile customs first devised millennia ago, which have spread from culture to culture as each culture in its turn discovered the usefulness of its more sophisticated neighbor's business practices.

*transitive verb*
**1** : to drive to hiding in the earth
**2** : to draw soil about (plants) — often used with *up*
**3** *chiefly British* : GROUND 3
*intransitive verb*
*of a hunted animal* : to hide in the ground
**earth·born** \'ərth-ˌbȯrn\ *adjective* (1667)
**1** : born on this earth : MORTAL
**2** : associated with earthly life ⟨*earthborn* cares⟩
**earth·bound** \-ˌbau̇nd\ *adjective* (1605)
**1 a** : fast in or to the soil ⟨*earthbound* roots⟩ **b** : located on or restricted to land or to the surface of the earth
**2 a** : bound by earthly interests **b** : PEDESTRIAN, UNIMAGINATIVE
**earth color** *noun* (1931)
: EARTH TONE
**earth·en** \'ər-thən, -thən\ *adjective* (13th century)
**1** : made of earth
**2** : EARTHLY
**earth·en·ware** \-ˌwar, -ˌwer\ *noun* (1648)
: ceramic ware made of slightly porous opaque clay fired at low heat
**earth·i·ly** \'ər-thə-lē, -thə-\ *adverb* (1953)
: in an earthy manner
**earth·light** \'ərth-ˌlīt\ *noun* (1833)
: EARTHSHINE
**earth·ling** \'ərth-liŋ\ *noun* (1593)
**1** : an inhabitant of the earth
**2** : WORLDLING
**earth·ly** \'ərth-lē\ *adjective* (before 12th century)
**1 a** : characteristic of or belonging to this earth **b** : relating to man's actual life on this earth
**2** : POSSIBLE ⟨there is no *earthly* reason for such behavior⟩ ☆
— **earth·li·ness** *noun*
**earth mother** *noun, often E&M capitalized* (1902)
**1** : the earth viewed (as in primitive theology) as the divine source of terrestrial life
**2** : the embodiment of the female principle of fertility : a nurturing maternal woman
**earth·mov·er** \'ərth-ˌmü-vər\ *noun* (1941)
: a machine (as a bulldozer) for excavating, pushing, or transporting large quantities of earth (as in road building)
— **earth·mov·ing** \-ˌmü-viŋ\ *noun*
**earth·quake** \'ərth-ˌkwāk\ *noun* (14th century)
**1** : a shaking or trembling of the earth that is volcanic or tectonic in origin
**2** : UPHEAVAL 2
**earth·rise** \'ərth-ˌrīz\ *noun* (1968)
: the rising of the earth above the horizon of the moon as seen from lunar orbit
**earth science** *noun* (1939)
: any of the sciences (as geology, meteorology, or oceanography) that deal with the earth or with one or more of its parts — compare GEOSCIENCE
— **earth scientist** *noun*
**earth·shak·er** \'ərth-ˌshā-kər\ *noun* (1953)
: one that is earthshaking
**earth·shak·ing** \-kiŋ\ *adjective* (1948)
: of great importance : MOMENTOUS
— **earth·shak·ing·ly** \-kiŋ-lē\ *adverb*
**earth·shat·ter·ing** \'ərth-ˌsha-tə-riŋ\ *adjective* (1970)
: EARTHSHAKING
**earth–shel·tered** \'ərth-ˌshel-tərd\ *adjective* (1979)
: built partly or mostly underground ⟨an *earth-sheltered* house⟩
**earth·shine** \'ərth-ˌshīn\ *noun* (1876)
: sunlight reflected by the earth that illuminates the dark part of the moon — called also *earthlight*
**earth·star** \-ˌstär\ *noun* (1885)
: any of a genus (*Geastrum*) of globose basidiomycetous fungi with an outer peridium that splits into the shape of a star

**earth station** *noun* (1970)
: DISH 3a(2); *especially* : one used primarily for receiving and transmitting television signals
**earth tone** *noun* (1973)
: any of various rich colors containing some brown
**earth·ward** \-wərd\ *also* **earth·wards** \-wərdz\ *adverb* (14th century)
: toward the earth
**earth·work** \'ərth-ˌwərk\ *noun* (1633)
**1** : an embankment or other construction made of earth; *especially* : one used as a field fortification
**2** : the operations connected with excavations and embankments of earth
**3** : a work of art consisting of a portion of land modified by an artist
**earth·worm** \-ˌwərm\ *noun* (14th century)
: a terrestrial annelid worm (class Oligochaeta); *especially* : any of a family (Lumbricidae) of numerous widely distributed hermaphroditic worms that move through the soil by means of setae
**earthy** \'ər-thē, -thē\ *adjective* **earth·i·er; -est** (14th century)
**1 a** : of, relating to, or consisting of earth ⟨*earthy* creatures like worms⟩ **b** : suggestive of earth (as in texture, odor, or color) ⟨an *earthy* yellow⟩ **c** : rough, coarse, or plain in taste ⟨*earthy* flavors⟩
**2 a** *archaic* : EARTHLY, WORLDLY **b** : characteristic of or associated with mortal life on the earth ⟨prefers *earthy* to ethereal themes⟩
**3** : suggestive of plain or poor people or their ways: as **a** : PRACTICAL, DOWN-TO-EARTH ⟨*earthy* problems of daily life⟩ **b** : CRUDE, GROSS ⟨*earthy* humor⟩ **c** : plain and simple in style : UNSOPHISTICATED ⟨*earthy* peasant cookery⟩ ⟨*earthy* decor⟩ ⟨*earthy* clothes⟩
— **earth·i·ness** *noun*
**ear·wax** \'ir-ˌwaks\ *noun* (14th century)
: CERUMEN
**¹ear·wig** \-ˌwig\ *noun* [Middle English *erwigge*, from Old English *ēarwicga*, from *ēare* ear + *wicga* insect] (before 12th century)
: any of numerous insects (order Dermaptera) having slender many-jointed antennae and a pair of cerci resembling forceps at the end of the body
**²earwig** *transitive verb* **ear·wigged; ear·wig·ging** (1837)
: to annoy or attempt to influence by private talk
**ear·wit·ness** \'ir-'wit-nəs\ *noun* (1594)
: one who overhears something; *especially* : one who gives a report on what has been heard
**¹ease** \'ēz\ *noun* [Middle English *ese*, from Old French *aise* convenience, comfort, from Latin *adjacent-, adjacens* neighboring — more at ADJACENT] (13th century)
**1** : the state of being comfortable: as **a** : freedom from pain or discomfort **b** : freedom from care **c** : freedom from labor or difficulty **d** : freedom from embarrassment or constraint : NATURALNESS **e** : an easy fit
**2** : relief from discomfort or obligation
**3** : FACILITY, EFFORTLESSNESS
**4** : an act of easing or a state of being eased
— **ease·ful** \-fəl\ *adjective*
— **ease·ful·ly** \-fə-lē\ *adverb*
— **at ease 1** : free from pain or discomfort
**2 a** : free from restraint or formality **b** : standing silently (as in a military formation) with the feet apart, the right foot in place, and one or both hands behind the body — often used as a command
**²ease** *verb* **eased; eas·ing** (14th century)
*transitive verb*
**1** : to free from something that pains, disquiets, or burdens
**2** : to make less painful : ALLEVIATE ⟨*ease* his suffering⟩

**3 a** : to lessen the pressure or tension of especially by slackening, lifting, or shifting **b** : to maneuver gently or carefully **c** : to moderate or reduce especially in amount or intensity
**4** : to make less difficult ⟨*ease* credit⟩
**5 a** : to put the helm of (a ship) alee **b** : to let (a helm or rudder) come back a little after having been put hard over
*intransitive verb*
**1** : to give freedom or relief
**2** : to move or pass with freedom or with little resistance
**3** : MODERATE, SLACKEN
**ea·sel** \'ē-zəl\ *noun* [Dutch *ezel*, literally, ass, from Middle Dutch *esel*; akin to Old English *esol* ass; both from a prehistoric East Germanic-West Germanic word borrowed from Latin *asinus* ass] (1596)
: a frame for supporting something (as an artist's canvas) ◆
**ease·ment** \'ēz-mənt\ *noun* (14th century)
**1** : an act or means of easing or relieving (as from discomfort)
**2** : an interest in land owned by another that entitles its holder to a specific limited use or enjoyment
**eas·i·ly** \'ēz-lē, 'ē-zə-\ *adverb* (13th century)
**1** : in an easy manner : without difficulty
**2** : without question : by far
**3** : WELL 10b ⟨it could *easily* have been me⟩
**¹east** \'ēst\ *adverb* [Middle English *est*, from Old English *ēast;* akin to Old High German *ōstar* to the east, Latin *aurora* dawn, Greek *ēōs, heōs*] (before 12th century)
: to, toward, or in the east
**²east** *adjective* (before 12th century)
**1** : situated toward or at the east ⟨an *east* window⟩
**2** : coming from the east ⟨an *east* wind⟩
**³east** *noun* (before 12th century)
**1 a** : the general direction of sunrise : the direction toward the right of one facing north **b** : the compass point directly opposite to west
**2** *capitalized* **a** : regions lying to the east of a specified or implied point of orientation **b** : regions having a culture derived from ancient non-European especially Asian areas
**3** : the altar end of a church

---

\ə\ abut  \ᵊ\ kitten  \ər\ further  \a\ ash  \ā\ ace
\ä\ mop, mar  \au̇\ out  \ch\ chin  \e\ bet  \ē\ easy
\g\ go  \i\ hit  \ī\ ice  \j\ job  \ŋ\ sing  \ō\ go
\ȯ\ law  \ȯi\ boy  \th\ thin  \th\ the  \ü\ loot  \u̇\ foot
\y\ yet  \zh\ vision  *see also* Guide to Pronunciation

**4** *often capitalized* **a :** the one of four positions at 90-degree intervals that lies to the east or at the right of a diagram **b :** a person (as a bridge player) occupying this position in the course of a specified activity

**east·bound** \'ēs(t)-ˌbau̇nd\ *adjective* (1880)
: traveling or heading east

**east by north** (1594)
: a compass point that is one point north of due east : N78°45′E

**east by south** (14th century)
: a compass point that is one point south of due east : S78°45′E

**East Caribbean dollar** *noun* (circa 1974)
: the basic monetary unit shared by a number of islands of the British West Indies

**Eas·ter** \'ē-stər\ *noun* [Middle English *estre*, from Old English *ēastre;* akin to Old High German *ōstarun* (plural) Easter, Old English *ēast* east] (before 12th century)
: a feast that commemorates Christ's resurrection and is observed with variations of date due to different calendars on the first Sunday after the paschal full moon

## EASTER DATES

| YEAR | ASH WEDNESDAY | EASTER |
|---|---|---|
| 1993 | February 24 | April 11 |
| 1994 | February 16 | April 3 |
| 1995 | March 1 | April 16 |
| 1996 | February 21 | April 7 |
| 1997 | February 12 | March 30 |
| 1998 | February 25 | April 12 |
| 1999 | February 17 | April 4 |
| 2000 | March 8 | April 23 |
| 2001 | February 28 | April 15 |
| 2002 | February 13 | March 31 |
| 2003 | March 5 | April 20 |
| 2004 | February 25 | April 11 |
| 2005 | February 9 | March 27 |
| 2006 | March 1 | April 16 |
| 2007 | February 21 | April 8 |
| 2008 | February 6 | March 23 |
| 2009 | February 25 | April 12 |
| 2010 | February 17 | April 4 |
| 2011 | March 9 | April 24 |
| 2012 | February 22 | April 8 |

**Easter egg** *noun* (1804)
: an egg that is dyed and sometimes decorated and that is associated with the celebration of Easter

**Easter lily** *noun* (1877)
: any of several white cultivated lilies (especially *Lilium longiflorum*) that bloom in early spring

**¹east·er·ly** \'ē-stər-lē\ *adjective or adverb* [obsolete *easter* (eastern)] (1548)
**1 :** situated toward or belonging to the east ⟨the *easterly* shore of the lake⟩
**2 :** coming from the east ⟨an *easterly* storm⟩

**²easterly** *noun, plural* **-lies** (1901)
: a wind from the east

**Easter Monday** *noun* (14th century)
: the Monday after Easter observed as a legal holiday in some nations of the Commonwealth and in North Carolina

**east·ern** \'ē-stərn\ *adjective* [Middle English *estern*, from Old English *ēasterne;* akin to Old High German *ōstrōni* eastern, Old English *ēast* east] (before 12th century)
**1** *capitalized* : of, relating to, or characteristic of a region conventionally designated East
**2** *capitalized* **a :** of, relating to, or being the Christian churches originating in the church of the Eastern Roman Empire **b :** EASTERN ORTHODOX
**3 a :** lying toward the east **b :** coming from the east ⟨an *eastern* wind⟩
**— east·ern·most** \-ˌmōst\ *adjective*
**East·ern·er** \'ē-stə(r)-nər\ *noun* (1840)

: a native or inhabitant of the East; *especially* : a native or resident of the eastern part of the U.S.

**eastern hemisphere** *noun, often E&H capitalized* (1624)
: the half of the earth east of the Atlantic Ocean including Europe, Asia, Australia, and Africa

**Eastern Orthodox** *adjective* (1909)
: of or consisting of the Eastern churches that form a loose federation according primacy of honor to the patriarch of Constantinople and adhering to the decisions of the first seven ecumenical councils and to the Byzantine rite

**eastern time** *noun, often E capitalized* (1883)
: the time of the 5th time zone west of Greenwich that includes the eastern U.S. — see TIME ZONE illustration

**eastern white pine** *noun* (1925)
: WHITE PINE 1a

**Eas·ter·tide** \'ē-stər-ˌtīd\ *noun* [Middle English *estertide*, from Old English *ēastortīd*, from *ēastor* + *tīd* time — more at TIDE] (before 12th century)
: the period from Easter to Ascension Day, to Whitsunday, or to Trinity Sunday

**East Germanic** *noun* (circa 1901)
: a subdivision of the Germanic languages that includes Gothic — see INDO-EUROPEAN LANGUAGES table

**east·ing** \'ē-stiŋ\ *noun* (1628)
**1 :** easterly progress
**2 :** difference in longitude to the east from the last preceding point of reckoning

**east–northeast** *noun* (1725)
: a compass point that is two points north of due east : N67°30′E

**east–southeast** *noun* (1555)
: a compass point that is two points south of due east : S67°30′E

**¹east·ward** \'ēs-twərd\ *adverb or adjective* (before 12th century)
: toward the east
**— east·wards** \-twərdz\ *adverb*

**²eastward** *noun* (1582)
: eastward direction or part ⟨sail to the *eastward*⟩

**¹easy** \'ē-zē\ *adjective* **eas·i·er; -est** [Middle English *esy*, from Old French *aaisié*, past participle of *aaisier* to ease, from *a-* ad- (from Latin *ad-*) + *aise* ease] (13th century)
**1 a :** causing or involving little difficulty or discomfort ⟨within *easy* reach⟩ **b :** requiring or indicating little effort, thought, or reflection ⟨*easy* clichés⟩
**2 a :** not severe : LENIENT **b :** not steep or abrupt ⟨*easy* slopes⟩ **c :** not difficult to endure or undergo ⟨an *easy* penalty⟩ **d :** readily taken advantage of ⟨an *easy* target for takeovers⟩ **e** (1) **:** readily available : easily come by ⟨*easy* pickings⟩ (2) **:** plentiful in supply at low or declining interest rates ⟨*easy* money⟩ (3) **:** less in demand and usually lower in price ⟨bonds were *easier*⟩ **f :** PLEASANT ⟨*easy* listening⟩
**3 a :** marked by peace and comfort ⟨the *easy* life of a courtier⟩ **b :** not hurried or strenuous ⟨an *easy* pace⟩
**4 a :** free from pain, annoyance, or anxiety ⟨did all she could to make him *easier*⟩ **b :** marked by social ease ⟨an air of *easy* assurance⟩ **c :** EASYGOING ⟨an *easy* disposition⟩
**5 a :** giving ease, comfort, or relaxation ⟨*easy* chairs⟩ **b :** not burdensome or straitened ⟨bought on *easy* terms⟩ **c :** fitting comfortably : allowing freedom of movement ⟨*easy* jackets⟩ **d :** marked by ready facility ⟨an *easy* flowing style⟩ **e :** felt or attained to readily, naturally, and spontaneously ⟨an *easy* smile⟩
☆
**— eas·i·ness** *noun*

**²easy** *adverb* **eas·i·er; -est** (14th century)
**1 :** EASILY 1 ⟨promises come *easy*⟩
**2 a :** without undue speed or excitement ⟨take it *easy*⟩ **b :** in or with moderation ⟨go *easy* on the mustard⟩

**3 a :** without worry or care ⟨rest *easy*⟩ **b :** without a severe penalty ⟨got off *easy*⟩ **c :** without violent movement ⟨the boat rode *easy*⟩
**4 :** EASILY 2 ⟨cost $500 *easy*⟩

**easy·go·ing** \ˌē-zē-'gō-iŋ, -'gȯ(-)iŋ\ *adjective* (1674)
**1 a :** relaxed and casual in style or manner ⟨an *easygoing* boss⟩ **b :** morally lax
**2 :** UNHURRIED, COMFORTABLE ⟨an *easygoing* pace⟩
**— easy·go·ing·ness** *noun*

**easy mark** *noun* (circa 1896)
: one easily taken advantage of

**easy street** *noun* (1900)
: a situation with no worries

**easy virtue** *noun* (1809)
: sexually promiscuous behavior or habits ⟨ladies of *easy virtue*⟩

**¹eat** \'ēt\ *verb* **ate** \'āt, *dialect or British* 'et\; **eat·en** \'ē-tᵊn\; **eat·ing** [Middle English *eten*, from Old English *etan;* akin to Old High German *ezzan* to eat, Latin *edere*, Greek *edmenai*] (before 12th century)
*transitive verb*
**1 :** to take in through the mouth as food : ingest, chew, and swallow in turn
**2 a :** to destroy, consume, or waste by or as if by eating ⟨expenses *ate* up the profits⟩ **b :** to bear the expense of : take a loss on
**3 a :** to consume gradually : CORRODE **b :** to consume with vexation : BOTHER ⟨what's *eating* you now⟩
*intransitive verb*
**1 :** to take food or a meal
**2 :** to affect something by gradual destruction or consumption — usually used with *into*, *away*, or *at*
**— eat·er** *noun*
**— eat another's lunch :** to deprive of profit, dominance, or success
**— eat crow :** to accept what one has fought against
**— eat humble pie :** to apologize or retract under pressure
**— eat one's heart out 1 :** to grieve bitterly **2 :** to be jealous
**— eat one's words :** to retract what one has said
**— eat out of one's hand :** to accept the domination of another

**²eat** *noun* [Middle English *et*, from Old English *ǣt;* akin to Old High German *āz* food; derivative from the root of ¹*eat*] (before 12th century)
: something to eat : FOOD — usually used in plural

**¹eat·able** \'ē-tə-bəl\ *adjective* (14th century)
: fit or able to be eaten

**²eatable** *noun* (1672)
**1 :** something to eat
**2** *plural* : FOOD

**eat·ery** \'ē-tə-rē\ *noun, plural* **-er·ies** (1901)

---

☆ **SYNONYMS**
**Easy, facile, simple, light, effortless, smooth** mean not demanding effort or involving difficulty. EASY is applicable either to persons or things imposing tasks or to activity required by such tasks ⟨an *easy* college course⟩. FACILE often adds to EASY the connotation of undue haste or shallowness ⟨*facile* answers to complex questions⟩. SIMPLE stresses ease in understanding or dealing with because complication is absent ⟨a *simple* problem in arithmetic⟩. LIGHT stresses freedom from what is burdensome ⟨a *light* teaching load⟩. EFFORTLESS stresses the appearance of ease and usually implies the prior attainment of artistry or expertness ⟨moving with *effortless* grace⟩. SMOOTH stresses the absence or removal of all difficulties, hardships, or obstacles ⟨a *smooth* ride⟩. See in addition COMFORTABLE.

**: LUNCHEONETTE, RESTAURANT**

**eath** \'ēth\ *adverb or adjective* [Middle English *ethe,* from Old English *ēathe;* akin to Old High German *ōdi* easy] (before 12th century) *Scottish* : EASY

**eat·ing** \'ē-tiŋ\ *adjective* (15th century)
**1** : used for eating ⟨*eating* utensils⟩
**2** : suitable to eat ⟨the finest *eating* fish⟩; *also* : suitable to eat raw ⟨an *eating* apple⟩

**eau de co·logne** \ˌō-də-kə-'lōn\ *noun, plural* **eaux de cologne** \ˌō(z)d-ə-\ [French, literally, Cologne water, from *Cologne,* Germany] (1802)
**: COLOGNE**

**eau–de–vie** \ˌō-də-'vē\ *noun, plural* **eaux-de-vie** \ˌō(z)-də-\ [French, literally, water of life, translation of Medieval Latin *aqua vitae*] (1748)
: a clear brandy distilled from the fermented juice of fruit (as pears or raspberries)

**eaves** \'ēvz\ *noun plural* [Middle English *eves* (singular), from Old English *efes;* akin to Old High German *obasa* portico, Old English *ūp* up — more at UP] (before 12th century)
**1** : the lower border of a roof that overhangs the wall
**2** : a projecting edge (as of a hill)

**eaves·drop** \'ēvz-ˌdräp\ *intransitive verb* [probably back-formation from *eavesdropper,* literally, one standing under the drip from the eaves] (1606)
: to listen secretly to what is said in private ◆
— **eaves·drop·per** *noun*

**eaves trough** *noun* (1878)
**: GUTTER 1a**

**¹ebb** \'eb\ *noun* [Middle English *ebbe,* from Old English *ebba;* akin to Middle Dutch *ebbe* ebb, Old English *of* from — more at OF] (before 12th century)
**1** : the reflux of the tide toward the sea
**2** : a point or condition of decline ⟨our spirits were at a low *ebb*⟩

**²ebb** *intransitive verb* (before 12th century)
**1** : to recede from the flood
**2** : to fall from a higher to a lower level or from a better to a worse state
**synonym** see ABATE

**ebb tide** *noun* (1823)
**1** : the tide while ebbing or at ebb
**2** : a period or state of decline

**EBCDIC** \'ep-sə-ˌdik, 'eb-\ *noun* [extended *b*inary *c*oded *d*ecimal *i*nterchange *c*ode] (circa 1966)
: a code for representing alphanumeric information (as on magnetic tape)

**Ebo·la virus** \ē-'bō-lə, i-, e-\ *noun* [Ebola River, Zaire, site of an outbreak of the virus in 1976] (1977)
: an RNA-containing virus of African origin that causes an often fatal hemorrhagic fever — called also *Ebola*

**eb·on** \'e-bən\ *adjective* (15th century)
: EBONY

**eb·o·nite** \'e-bə-ˌnīt\ *noun* (1861)
: hard rubber especially when black

**eb·o·nize** \-ˌnīz\ *transitive verb* **-nized; -niz·ing** (circa 1828)
: to stain black in imitation of ebony

**¹eb·o·ny** \'e-bə-nē\ *noun, plural* **-nies** [probably from Late Latin *hebeninus* of ebony, from Greek *ebeninos,* from *ebenos* ebony, from Egyptian *hbnj*] (14th century)
**1** : a hard heavy wood yielded by various Old World tropical dicotyledonous trees (genus *Diospyros* of the family Ebonaceae, the ebony family)
**2 a** : a tree yielding ebony **b** : any of several trees yielding wood like ebony

**²ebony** *adjective* (1598)
**1** : made of or resembling ebony
**2** : BLACK, DARK

**ebul·lience** \i-'bùl-yən(t)s, -'bəl-\ *noun* (1749)
: the quality of lively or exuberant expression of thoughts or feelings : EXUBERANCE

**ebul·lien·cy** \-yən(t)-sē\ *noun* (1676)

**: EBULLIENCE**

**ebul·lient** \-yənt\ *adjective* [Latin *ebullient-, ebulliens,* present participle of *ebullire* to bubble out, from *e-* + *bullire* to bubble, boil — more at BOIL] (1599)
**1** : BOILING, AGITATED
**2** : characterized by ebullience
— **ebul·lient·ly** *adverb*

**eb·ul·li·tion** \ˌe-bə-'li-shən\ *noun* (1534)
**1** : a sudden violent outburst or display
**2** : the act, process, or state of boiling or bubbling up

**EB virus** \ˌē-'bē-\ *noun* (1968)
**: EPSTEIN-BARR VIRUS**

**¹ec·cen·tric** \ik-'sen-trik, ek-\ *adjective* [Middle English, from Medieval Latin *eccentricus,* from Greek *ekkentros,* from *ex* out of + *kentron* center] (circa 1630)
**1 a** : deviating from an established or usual pattern or style **b** : deviating from conventional or accepted usage or conduct especially in odd or whimsical ways
**2 a** : deviating from a circular path; *especially* : ELLIPTICAL 1 ⟨an *eccentric* orbit⟩ **b** : located elsewhere than at the geometrical center; *also* : having the axis or support so located ⟨an *eccentric* wheel⟩
**synonym** see STRANGE
— **ec·cen·tri·cal·ly** \-tri-k(ə-)lē\ *adverb*

**²eccentric** *noun* (1827)
**1** : a mechanical device consisting of a disk through which a shaft is keyed eccentrically and a circular strap which works freely round the rim of the disk for communicating its motion to one end of a rod whose other end is constrained to move in a straight line so as to produce reciprocating motion
**2** : an eccentric person

**ec·cen·tric·i·ty** \ˌek-(ˌ)sen-'tri-sə-tē\ *noun, plural* **-ties** (1545)
**1 a** : the quality or state of being eccentric **b** : deviation from an established pattern or norm; *especially* : odd or whimsical behavior
**2 a** : a mathematical constant that for a given conic section is the ratio of the distances from any point of the conic section to a focus and the corresponding directrix **b** : the eccentricity of an astronomical orbit used as a measure of its deviation from circularity

**ec·chy·mo·sis** \ˌe-ki-'mō-səs\ *noun, plural* **-mo·ses** \-ˌsēz\ [New Latin, from Greek *ekchymōsis,* from *ekchymousthai* to extravasate blood, from *ex-* + *chymos* juice — more at CHYME] (1541)
: the escape of blood into the tissues from ruptured blood vessels
— **ec·chy·mot·ic** \-'mä-tik\ *adjective*

**ecclesi-** *or* **ecclesio-** *combining form* [Middle English *ecclesi-,* from Late Latin *ecclesia,* from Greek *ekklēsia* assembly of citizens, church, from *ekkalein* to call forth, summon, from *ex-* + *kalein* to call — more at LOW] : church ⟨*ecclesiology*⟩

**ec·cle·si·al** \i-'klē-zē-əl, e-'klē-\ *adjective* (1641)
: of or relating to a church

**Ec·cle·si·as·tes** \i-ˌklē-zē-'as-(ˌ)tēz, e-ˌklē-\ *noun* [Greek *Ekklēsiastēs,* literally, preacher (translation of Hebrew *qōheleth*), from *ekklēsiastēs* member of an assembly, from *ekklēsia*]
: a book of wisdom literature in canonical Jewish and Christian Scripture — see BIBLE table

**¹ec·cle·si·as·tic** \-'as-tik\ *adjective* (15th century)
**: ECCLESIASTICAL**

**²ecclesiastic** *noun* (1651)
**: CLERGYMAN**

**ec·cle·si·as·ti·cal** \-ti-kəl\ *adjective* [Middle English, from Late Latin *ecclesiasticus,* from Late Greek *ekklēsiastikos,* from Greek, of an assembly of citizens, from *ekklēsiastēs*] (15th century)
**1** : of or relating to a church especially as an established institution
**2** : suitable for use in a church

— **ec·cle·si·as·ti·cal·ly** \-ti-k(ə-)lē\ *adverb*

**ec·cle·si·as·ti·cism** \-tə-ˌsi-zəm\ *noun* (circa 1859)
: excessive attachment to ecclesiastical forms and practices

**Ec·cle·si·as·ti·cus** \-ti-kəs\ *noun* [Late Latin, from *ecclesiasticus*]
: a didactic book included in the Protestant Apocrypha and as Sirach in the Roman Catholic canon of the Old Testament

**ec·cle·si·ol·o·gy** \i-ˌklē-zē-'ä-lə-jē, e-ˌklē-\ *noun, plural* **-gies** (circa 1837)
**1** : the study of church architecture and adornment
**2** : theological doctrine relating to the church
— **ec·cle·si·o·log·i·cal** \-zē-ə-'lä-ji-kəl\ *adjective*
— **ec·cle·si·ol·o·gist** \-zē-'ä-lə-jist\ *noun*

**ec·crine gland** \'e-krən-, -ˌkrīn-, -ˌkrēn-\ *noun* [Greek *ekkrinein* to secrete, from *ek-, ex-* out + *krinein* to separate — more at CERTAIN] (circa 1927)
: any of the rather small sweat glands in the human skin that produce a fluid secretion without removing cytoplasm from the secretory cells — called also *eccrine sweat gland*

**ec·dys·i·ast** \ek-'di-zē-ˌast, -ē-əst\ *noun* [Greek *ekdysis*] (1940)
**: STRIPTEASER**

**ec·dy·sis** \'ek-də-səs\ *noun, plural* **ec·dy·ses** \-də-ˌsēz\ [New Latin, from Greek *ekdysis* act of getting out, from *ekdyein* to strip, from *ex-* + *dyein* to enter, don] (circa 1854)
: the act of molting or shedding an outer cuticular layer (as in insects and crustaceans)

**ec·dy·sone** \'ek-də-ˌsōn\ *also* **ec·dy·son** \-ˌsän\ *noun* [International Scientific Vocabulary *ecdysis* + hormone] (1956)
: any of several arthropod hormones that in insects are produced by the prothoracic gland and that trigger molting and metamorphosis

**ece·sis** \i-'sē-səs, -'kē-\ *noun* [New Latin, from Greek *oikēsis* inhabitation, from *oikein* to inhabit — more at ECUMENICAL] (circa 1904)
: the establishment of a plant or animal in a new habitat

**echelle** \ā-'shel\ *noun* [French, literally, ladder, from Old French *eschele*] (1949)

◇ WORD HISTORY
**eavesdrop** The verb *eavesdrop* first appeared in the 17th century and is probably a back-formation from *eavesdropper,* which is attested in Middle English as *evesdropper* and is apparently a derivative of an earlier noun *evesdrop. Evesdrop,* and a related Old English word *yfesdrype,* occur very rarely and then only in law texts that refer to the ground below the eaves of a house on which rainwater drips. This use comes from an old sanction against building so close to the edge of one's property that water from the eaves falls on a neighbor's land. For a while the word *eavesdropper* too occurred mainly in legal contexts—persons snooping on others' conversations seem to have been considered a sort of public nuisance, like Peeping Toms—but less literal uses of *eavesdropper* and the verb *eavesdrop* appear in the 17th and 18th centuries. Today applications of the words to secret observation by satellite or electronic device are far removed from eaves, rainwater, or stealthy listening outside the walls of someone's house.

: a diffraction grating made by ruling a plane metallic mirror with lines having a relatively wide spacing

**¹ech·e·lon** \'e-shə-ˌlän\ *noun* [French *échelon*, literally, rung of a ladder, from Old French *eschelon*, from *eschele* ladder, from Late Latin *scala*] (1796)
**1 a** (1) **:** an arrangement of a body of troops with its units each somewhat to the left or right of the one in the rear like a series of steps (2) **:** a formation of units or individuals resembling such an echelon (3) **:** a flight formation in which each airplane flies at a certain elevation above or below and at a certain distance behind and to the right or left of the airplane ahead **b :** any of several military units in echelon formation
**2 a :** one of a series of levels or grades (as of leadership or responsibility) in an organization or field of activity **b :** a group of individuals at a particular level or grade in an organization

◆

**²echelon** (circa 1860)
*transitive verb*
**:** to form or arrange in an echelon
*intransitive verb*
**:** to take position in an echelon

**ech·e·ve·ria** \ˌe-chə-və-'rē-ə\ *noun* [New Latin, genus name, after Atanasio *Echeverría* (flourished 1771) Mexican botanical illustrator] (1883)
**:** any of a large genus (*Echeveria*) of tropical American succulent plants of the orpine family that have showy rosettes of often plushy basal leaves and axillary clusters of flowers with erect petals and that are often grown as ornamentals

**echid·na** \i-'kid-nə\ *noun* [New Latin, from Latin, viper, from Greek — more at OPHITIC] (1832)
**:** an oviparous spiny-coated toothless burrowing nocturnal monotreme mammal (*Tachyglossus aculeatus*) of Australia, Tasmania, and New Guinea that has a long extensile tongue and long heavy claws and that feeds chiefly on ants; *also* **:** a related mammal (*Zaglossus bruijni*) of New Guinea having a longer snout and shorter spines

echidna

**echin-** *or* **echino-** *combining form* [Latin, from Greek, from *echinos* sea urchin]
**1 :** prickle ⟨*echino*derm⟩
**2 :** sea urchin ⟨*echino*id⟩

**echi·no·coc·co·sis** \i-ˌkī-nə-kä-'kō-səs\ *noun, plural* **-co·ses** \-ˌsēz\ [New Latin] (1900)
**:** infestation with or disease caused by an echinococcus (as *Echinococcus granulosus*)

**echi·no·coc·cus** \i-ˌkī-nə-'kä-kəs\ *noun, plural* **-coc·ci** \-'käk-ˌ(s)ī, -'käk-ˌ(ˌ)s)ē\ [New Latin, genus name] (1839)
**:** any of a genus (*Echinococcus*) of tapeworms that alternate a minute adult living as a commensal in the intestine of carnivores with a hydatid larva invading tissues especially of the liver of cattle, sheep, swine, and humans and acting as a dangerous pathogen

**echi·no·derm** \i-'kī-nə-ˌdərm\ *noun* [New Latin *Echinodermata*, phylum name, from *echin-* + *-dermata* (from Greek *derma* skin)] (1835)
**:** any of a phylum (Echinodermata) of radially symmetrical coelomate marine animals including the starfishes, sea urchins, and related forms
**— echi·no·der·ma·tous** \-ˌkī-nə-'dər-mə-təs\ *adjective*

**echi·noid** \i-'kī-ˌnoid, 'e-kə-ˌnoid\ *noun* (1864)
**:** SEA URCHIN

**echi·nus** \i-'kī-nəs\ *noun, plural* **-ni** \-ˌnī\ [Middle English, from Latin, from Greek *echi-*

*nos* hedgehog, sea urchin — more at OPHITE] (14th century)
**1 :** SEA URCHIN
**2 a :** the rounded molding forming the bell of the capital in the Greek Doric order **b :** a similar member in other orders

**echi·uroid** \ˌe-ki-'yür-ˌoid\ *noun* [New Latin *Echiuroidea* or *Echiura*, ultimately from Greek *echis* viper + *oura* tail] (circa 1889)
**:** any of a taxon (class Echiuroidea or phylum Echiura) of marine worms of uncertain taxonomic affinities that have a sensitive but nonretractile proboscis above the mouth

**¹echo** \'e-(ˌ)kō\ *noun, plural* **ech·oes** *also* **echos** [Middle English *ecco*, from Middle French & Latin; Middle French *echo*, from Latin, from Greek *ēchō;* akin to Latin *vagire* to wail, Greek *ēchē* sound] (14th century)
**1 a :** the repetition of a sound caused by reflection of sound waves **b :** the sound due to such reflection
**2 a :** a repetition or imitation of another **:** REFLECTION **b :** REPERCUSSION, RESULT **c :** TRACE, VESTIGE **d :** RESPONSE
**3 :** one who closely imitates or repeats another's words, ideas, or acts
**4 :** a soft repetition of a musical phrase
**5 a :** the repetition of a received radio signal due especially to reflection of part of the wave from an ionized layer of the atmosphere **b** (1) **:** the reflection of transmitted radar signals by an object (2) **:** the visual indication of this reflection on a radarscope
**— echo·ey** \'e-ˌkō-ē\ *adjective*

**²echo** *verb* **ech·oed; echo·ing** \'e-(ˌ)kō-iŋ, 'e-kə-wiŋ\ (1596)
*intransitive verb*
**1 :** to resound with echoes
**2 :** to produce an echo
*transitive verb*
**1 :** REPEAT, IMITATE
**2 :** to send back (a sound) by the reflection of sound waves

**¹Echo** *noun* [Greek *Ēchō*]
**:** a nymph in Greek mythology who pines away for love of Narcissus until nothing is left of her but her voice

**²Echo** (circa 1952)
**—** a communications code word for the letter *e*

**echo·car·dio·gram** \ˌe-kō-'kär-dē-ə-ˌgram\ *noun* (1967)
**:** a visual record made by echocardiography

**echo·car·di·og·ra·phy** \-ˌkär-dē-'ä-grə-fē\ *noun, plural* **-phies** (1965)
**:** the use of ultrasound to examine the structure and functioning of the heart for abnormalities and disease
**— echo·car·di·og·raph·er** \-grə-fər\ *noun*
**— echo·car·dio·graph·ic** \-dē-ə-'gra-fik\ *adjective*

**echo chamber** *noun* (circa 1937)
**:** a room with sound-reflecting walls used for producing hollow or echoing sound effects

**echo·ic** \ə-'kō-ik, e-\ *adjective* (circa 1880)
**1 :** formed in imitation of some natural sound **:** ONOMATOPOEIC
**2 :** of or relating to an echo

**echo·la·lia** \ˌe-kō-'lā-lē-ə\ *noun* [New Latin] (circa 1885)
**:** the often pathological repetition of what is said by other people as if echoing them
**— echo·lal·ic** \-'la-lik\ *adjective*

**echo·lo·ca·tion** \ˌe-kō-lō-'kā-shən\ *noun* (circa 1944)
**:** a physiological process for locating distant or invisible objects (as prey) by means of sound waves reflected back to the emitter (as a bat) by the objects

**echo sounder** *noun* (1927)
**:** an instrument for determining the depth of a body of water or of an object below the surface by sound waves

**echo·vi·rus** \'e-kō-ˌvī-rəs\ *noun* [enteric *cyto*pathogenic *human orphan* + *virus*] (1955)

**:** any of a group of picornaviruses that are found in the gastrointestinal tract, that cause cytopathic changes in cells in tissue culture, and that are sometimes associated with respiratory ailments and meningitis

**éclair** \ā-'klar, i-, -'kler, 'ā-ˌ, 'ē-ˌ\ *noun* [French, literally, lightning] (1861)
**:** a usually chocolate-frosted oblong light pastry with whipped cream or custard filling

**éclair·cis·se·ment** \ā-kler-sēs-(ə-)mäⁿ\ *noun, plural* **-ments** \-mäⁿ(z)\ [French] (1667)
**:** a clearing up of something obscure **:** ENLIGHTENMENT

**eclamp·sia** \i-'klam(p)-sē-ə\ *noun* [New Latin, from Greek *eklampsis* sudden flashing, from *eklampein* to shine forth, from *ex-* out + *lampein* to shine] (circa 1860)
**:** a convulsive state; *especially* **:** an attack of convulsions during pregnancy or parturition
**— eclamp·tic** \-'klam(p)-tik\ *adjective*

**éclat** \ā-'klä, 'ā-ˌ\ *noun* [French, splinter, burst, *éclat*] (1672)
**1 :** ostentatious display **:** PUBLICITY
**2 :** dazzling effect **:** BRILLIANCE
**3 a :** brilliant or conspicuous success **b :** PRAISE, APPLAUSE

**¹eclec·tic** \e-'klek-tik, i-\ *adjective* [Greek *eklektikos*, from *eklegein* to select, from *ex-* out + *legein* to gather — more at LEGEND] (1683)
**1 :** selecting what may be best in various doctrines, methods, or styles
**2 :** composed of elements drawn from various sources; *also* **:** HETEROGENEOUS
**— eclec·ti·cal·ly** \-ti-k(ə-)lē\ *adverb*

**²eclectic** *noun* (1817)
**:** one who uses an eclectic method or approach

**eclec·ti·cism** \-'klek-tə-ˌsi-zəm\ *noun* (1798)
**1 :** the theory or practice of an eclectic method
**2 :** a mid-19th-century movement in architecture and design that revived the styles of various historical periods

**¹eclipse** \i-'klips\ *noun* [Middle English, from Old French, from Latin *eclipsis*, from Greek *ekleipsis*, from *ekleipein* to omit, fail, suffer eclipse, from *ex-* + *leipein* to leave — more at LOAN] (13th century)
**1 a :** the total or partial obscuring of one celestial body by another **b :** the passing into the shadow of a celestial body — compare OCCULTATION, TRANSIT
**2 :** a falling into obscurity or decline; *also* **:** the state of being eclipsed
**3 :** the state of being in eclipse plumage

**²eclipse** *transitive verb* **eclipsed; eclips·ing** (13th century)
**:** to cause an eclipse of: as **a :** OBSCURE, DARKEN **b :** to reduce in importance or repute **c :** SURPASS

eclipse 1a: *S* sun, *E* earth, *M* moon in solar
eclipse, *M*¹ moon in lunar eclipse

**eclipse plumage** *noun* (1906)
: comparatively dull plumage that is usually of
seasonal occurrence in birds exhibiting a distinct breeding plumage

¹**eclip·tic** \i-'klip-tik\ *adjective* [Middle English *ecliptik,* from Late Latin *ecliptica linea,*
literally, line of eclipses] (14th century)
: of or relating to the ecliptic or an eclipse

²**ecliptic** *noun* (15th century)
: the great circle of the celestial sphere that is
the apparent path of the sun among the stars or
of the earth as seen from the sun : the plane of
the earth's orbit extended to meet the celestial
sphere

**ec·logue** \'ek-ˌlȯg, -ˌläg\ *noun* [Middle English *eclog,* from Latin *Eclogae,* title of Virgil's pastorals, literally, selections, plural of
*ecloga,* from Greek *eklogē,* from *eklegein* to
select] (15th century)
: a poem in which shepherds converse

**eclo·sion** \i-'klō-zhən\ *noun* [French *éclosion,*
from *éclore* to hatch, from (assumed) Vulgar
Latin *excludere,* alteration of Latin *excludere*
to hatch out, exclude] (circa 1889)
*of an insect* : the act of emerging from the pupal case or hatching from the egg

**eco-** *combining form* [Late Latin *oeco-* household, from Greek *oik-, oiko-,* from *oikos* house
— more at VICINITY]
**1** : habitat or environment ⟨*eco*species⟩
**2** : ecological or environmental ⟨*eco*catastro-
phe⟩

**eco·ca·tas·tro·phe** \ē-(ˌ)kō-kə-'tas-trə-fē,
ˌe-(ˌ)kō-\ *noun* (1969)
: a major destructive upset in the balance of
nature especially when caused by the intervention of humans

**ecol·o·gy** \i-'kä-lə-jē, e-\ *noun, plural* **-gies**
[German *Ökologie,* from *öko-* eco- + *-logie*
-logy] (1873)
**1** : a branch of science concerned with the interrelationship of organisms and their environments
**2** : the totality or pattern of relations between
organisms and their environment
**3** : HUMAN ECOLOGY
— **eco·log·i·cal** \ˌē-kə-'lä-ji-kəl, ˌe-kə-\
*also* **eco·log·ic** \-jik\ *adjective*
— **eco·log·i·cal·ly** \-ji-k(ə-)lē\ *adverb*
— **ecol·o·gist** \i-'kä-lə-jist, e-\ *noun*

**econo·box** \i-'kä-nō-ˌbäks, ē-\ *noun* [*economical* + ²*box*] (1980)
: a small economical car

**econo·met·rics** \i-ˌkä-nə-'me-triks, ē-, ˌkä-\
*noun plural but singular in construction*
[blend of *economics* and *metric*] (1933)
: the application of statistical methods to the
study of economic data and problems
— **econo·met·ric** \-trik\ *adjective*
— **econo·met·ri·cal·ly** \-tri-k(ə-)lē\ *adverb*
— **econo·me·tri·cian** \-mə-'tri-shən\ *noun*
— **econo·met·rist** \-'me-trist\ *noun*

**eco·nom·ic** \ˌe-kə-'nä-mik, ˌē-kə-\ *adjective*
(1592)
**1** *archaic* : of or relating to a household or its
management
**2** : ECONOMICAL 2
**3 a** : of or relating to economics **b** : of, relating to, or based on the production, distribution, and consumption of goods and services **c**
: of or relating to an economy
**4** : having practical or industrial significance
or uses : affecting material resources

**5** : PROFITABLE ■

**eco·nom·i·cal** \-'nä-mi-kəl\ *adjective* (15th
century)
**1** *archaic* : ECONOMIC 1
**2** : marked by careful, efficient, and prudent
use of resources : THRIFTY
**3** : operating with little waste or at a saving
*synonym* see SPARING
— **eco·nom·i·cal·ly** \-mi-k(ə-)lē\ *adverb*

**economic rent** *noun* (1889)
: the return for the use of a factor in excess of
the minimum required to bring forth its service

**eco·nom·ics** \ˌe-kə-'nä-miks, ˌē-kə-\ *noun
plural but singular or plural in construction*
(1792)
**1** : a social science concerned chiefly with description and analysis of the production, distribution, and consumption of goods and services
**2** : economic aspect or significance

**economise** *British variant of* ECONOMIZE

**econ·o·mist** \i-'kä-nə-mist\ *noun* (1586)
**1** *archaic* : one who practices economy
**2** : a specialist in economics

**econ·o·mize** \-ˌmīz\ *verb* **-mized; -miz·ing**
(1820)
*intransitive verb*
: to practice economy : be frugal
*transitive verb*
: to use more economically : SAVE
— **econ·o·miz·er** *noun*

¹**econ·o·my** \i-'kä-nə-mē, ə-, ē-\ *noun, plural*
**-mies** [Middle French *yconomie,* from Medieval Latin *oeconomia,* from Greek *oikonomia,*
from *oikonomos* household manager, from *oikos* house + *nemein* to manage — more at VI-
CINITY, NIMBLE] (15th century)
**1** *archaic* : the management of household or
private affairs and especially expenses
**2 a** : thrifty and efficient use of material resources : frugality in expenditures; *also* : an
instance or a means of economizing : SAVING **b**
: efficient and concise use of nonmaterial resources (as effort, language, or motion)
**3** : the arrangement or mode of operation of
something : ORGANIZATION
**4** : the structure of economic life in a country,
area, or period; *specifically* : an economic system

²**economy** *adjective* (circa 1906)
: designed to save money ⟨*economy* cars⟩

**economy of scale** (1957)
: a reduction in unit costs brought about especially by increased size of production facilities
— usually used in plural

**eco·phys·i·ol·o·gy** \ˌē-kō-ˌfi-zē-'ä-lə-jē, ˌe-
kō-\ *noun* (1962)
: the science of the interrelationships between
the physiology of organisms and their environment
— **eco·phys·i·o·log·i·cal** \-ē-ə-'lä-ji-kəl\
*adjective*

**eco·spe·cies** \'ē-kō-ˌspē-(ˌ)shēz, 'e-kō-,
-(ˌ)sēz\ *noun, plural* **ecospecies** (1922)
: a subdivision of a cenospecies comparable
with a taxonomic species and composed of interbreeding individuals that are less capable of
fertile crosses with individuals of other subdivisions

**eco·sphere** \'ē-kō-ˌsfir, 'e-kō-\ *noun* (1953)
: the parts of the universe habitable by living
organisms; *especially* : BIOSPHERE 1

**eco·sys·tem** \-ˌsis-təm\ *noun* (1935)
: the complex of a community of organisms
and its environment functioning as an ecological unit in nature

**eco·tone** \'ē-kə-ˌtōn, 'e-kə-\ *noun* [*ec-* +
Greek *tonos* tension — more at TONE] (1904)
: a transition area between two adjacent ecological communities

**eco·tour·ism** \ˌē-kō-'tu̇r-ˌi-zəm, ˌe-kō-\ *noun*
(1989)
: the practice of touring natural habitats in a
manner meant to minimize ecological impact
— **eco·tour·ist** \-'tu̇r-ist\ *noun*

**eco·type** \'ē-kə-ˌtīp, 'e-\ *noun* (1922)
: a subdivision of an ecospecies that survives
as a distinct group through environmental selection and isolation and that is comparable
with a taxonomic subspecies
— **eco·typ·ic** \ˌē-kə-'ti-pik, ˌe-kə-\ *adjective*

**ecru** \'e-(ˌ)krü, 'ā-(ˌ)krü\ *noun* [French *écru,* literally, unbleached, raw, from Old French *es-
cru,* from *es-* completely (from Latin *ex-*) +
*cru* raw, from Latin *crudus* — more at RAW]
(1850)
: BEIGE 2
— **ecru** *adjective*

**ec·sta·sy** \'ek-stə-sē\ *noun, plural* **-sies**
[Middle English *extasie,* from Middle French,
from Late Latin *ecstasis,* from Greek *ekstasis,*
from *existanai* to derange, from *ex-* out +
*histanai* to cause to stand — more at EX-,
STAND] (14th century)
**1 a** : a state of being beyond reason and self-
control **b** *archaic* : SWOON
**2** : a state of overwhelming emotion; *especially* : rapturous delight
**3** : TRANCE; *especially* : a mystic or prophetic
trance
**4** : a synthetic amphetamine analogue
$C_{11}H_{15}NO_2$ used illicitly for its mood-
enhancing and hallucinogenic properties ☆

¹**ec·stat·ic** \ek-'sta-tik, ik-'sta-\ *adjective*
[Medieval Latin *ecstaticus,* from Greek *eksta-
tikos,* from *existanai*] (1590)
: of, relating to, or marked by ecstasy
— **ec·stat·i·cal·ly** \-'sta-ti-k(ə-)lē\ *adverb*

²**ecstatic** *noun* (1659)
• : one that is subject to ecstasies

**ect-** *or* **ecto-** *combining form* [New Latin,
from Greek *ekto-,* from *ektos,* from *ex* out —
more at EX-]
: outside : external ⟨*ecto*derm⟩ — compare
END-, EXO-

**ec·to·derm** \'ek-tə-ˌdərm\ *noun* [International
Scientific Vocabulary] (1861)
**1** : the outer cellular membrane of a diploblas-
tic animal (as a jellyfish)

---

☆ **SYNONYMS**
**Ecstasy, rapture, transport** mean intense exaltation of mind and feelings. ECSTA-
SY and RAPTURE both suggest a state of
trance or near immobility produced by an
overpowering emotion. ECSTASY may apply
to any strong emotion (as joy, fear, rage, adoration) ⟨religious *ecstasy*⟩. RAPTURE usually
implies intense bliss or beatitude ⟨in speechless *rapture*⟩. TRANSPORT applies to any
powerful emotion that lifts one out of oneself
and usually provokes vehement expression
or frenzied action ⟨in a *transport* of rage⟩.

---

□ **USAGE**
**economic** While orthoepists have disagreed for centuries over the first vowel of
*economic* and related words, common usage
has in that same time established both \ē\
and \e\ variants of *economic* as acceptable.
British speakers prefer the initial \ē\ vowel,
as they do in *ecumenical.* Americans are
split evenly on *economic,* but overwhelmingly
prefer initial \e\ in *ecumenical,* as they do
also in *estrogen* (spelled *oestrogen* in British
English and pronounced most often with initial \ē\). The variable vowel in these words
derives ultimately from the Greek diphthong
*oi,* which was pronounced \oi\ in ancient
times but is \ē\ in modern Greek.

---

\ə\ abut \ᵊ\ kitten \ər\ further \a\ ash \ā\ ace
\ä\ mop, mar \au̇\ out \ch\ chin \e\ bet \ē\ easy
\g\ go \i\ hit \ī\ ice \j\ job \ŋ\ sing \ō\ go
\ȯ\ law \ȯi\ boy \th\ thin \th\ the \ü\ loot \u̇\ foot
\y\ yet \zh\ vision *see also* Guide to Pronunciation

**2 a :** the outermost of the three primary germ layers of an embryo **b :** a tissue (as neural tissue) derived from this germ layer
— **ec·to·der·mal** \,ek-tə-'dər-məl\ *adjective*

**ec·to·morph** \'ek-tə-,mòrf\ *noun* [*ecto*derm + *-morph*] (1940)
**:** an ectomorphic individual

**ec·to·mor·phic** \,ek-tə-'mòr-fik\ *adjective* [*ecto*derm + *-morphic;* from the predominance in such types of structures developed from the ectoderm] (1940)
**1 :** of or relating to the component in W. H. Sheldon's classification of body types that measures the body's degree of slenderness, angularity, and fragility
**2 :** characterized by a light body build with slight muscular development

**-ec·to·my** \'ek-tə-mē\ *noun combining form* [New Latin *-ectomia,* from Greek *ektemnein* to cut out, from *ec-, ex-* out + *temnein* to cut — more at TOME]
**:** surgical removal ⟨gast*rectomy*⟩

**ec·to·par·a·site** \,ek-tō-'par-ə-,sīt\ *noun* [International Scientific Vocabulary] (1861)
**:** a parasite that lives on the exterior of its host
— **ec·to·par·a·sit·ic** \-,par-ə-'si-tik\ *adjective*

**ec·top·ic** \ek-'tä-pik\ *adjective* [Greek *ektopos* out of place, from *ex-* out + *topos* place] (1873)
**:** occurring in an abnormal position or in an unusual manner or form ⟨*ectopic* lesions⟩
— **ec·top·i·cal·ly** \-pi-k(ə-)lē\ *adverb*

**ectopic pregnancy** *noun* (1929)
**:** gestation elsewhere than in the uterus (as in a fallopian tube or in the peritoneal cavity)

**ec·to·plasm** \'ek-tə-,pla-zəm\ *noun* (1883)
**1 :** the outer relatively rigid granule-free layer of the cytoplasm usually held to be a gel reversibly convertible to a sol
**2 :** a substance held to produce spirit materialization and telekinesis
— **ec·to·plas·mic** \,ek-tə-'plaz-mik\ *adjective*

**ec·to·therm** \'ek-tə-,thərm\ *noun* (1945)
**:** a cold-blooded animal **:** POIKILOTHERM
— **ec·to·ther·mic** \,ek-tə-'thər-mik\ *adjective*

**ec·to·tro·phic** \,ek-tə-'trō-fik\ *adjective* (circa 1889)
*of a mycorrhiza* **:** growing in a close web on the surface of the associated root — compare ENDOTROPHIC

**¹ecu** \'ā-,kyü, ā-kū\ *noun, plural* **ecus** \-,kyüz, -kū\ [Middle French, literally, shield, from Old French *escu,* from Latin *scutum;* from the device of a shield on the coin — more at ESQUIRE] (circa 1593)
**:** any of various old French units of value; *also* **:** a coin representing an ecu

**²ecu** \,ē-(,)sē-'yü\ *noun, often E&C&U capitalized* [European Currency Unit (influenced by French *écu* ecu)] (1970)
**:** a money of account based on the currency units of members of the European Community

**ec·u·men·i·cal** \,e-kyə-'me-ni-kəl\ *adjective* [Late Latin *oecumenicus,* from Late Greek *oikoumenikos,* from Greek *oikoumenē* the inhabited world, from feminine of *oikoumenos,* present passive participle of *oikein* to inhabit, from *oikos* house — more at VICINITY] (circa 1587)
**1 :** worldwide or general in extent, influence, or application
**2 a :** of, relating to, or representing the whole of a body of churches **b :** promoting or tending toward worldwide Christian unity or cooperation
— **ec·u·men·i·cal·ly** \-k(ə-)lē\ *adverb*
*usage* see ECONOMIC

**ec·u·men·i·cal·ism** \-'me-ni-kə-,li-zəm\ *noun* (1888)
**:** ECUMENISM

**ecumenical patriarch** *noun* (1862)

**:** the patriarch of Constantinople as the dignitary given first honor in the Eastern Orthodox Church

**ec·u·men·i·cism** \,e-kyə-'me-nə-,si-zəm\ *noun* (1961)
**:** ECUMENISM
— **ec·u·men·i·cist** \-sist\ *noun*

**ec·u·me·nic·i·ty** \,e-kyə-mə-'ni-sə-tē, -me-\ *noun* (1840)
**:** the quality or state of being drawn close to others especially through Christian ecumenism

**ec·u·men·ics** \-'me-niks\ *noun plural but singular in construction* (circa 1937)
**:** the study of the nature, mission, problems, and strategy of the Christian church from the perspective of its ecumenical character

**ecu·me·nism** \e-'kyü-mə-,ni-zəm, i- *also* 'e-kyə- *or* ,e-kyə-'me-\ *noun* (1948)
**:** ecumenical principles and practices especially as shown among religious groups (as Christian denominations)
— **ecu·me·nist** \e-'kyü-mə-nist, i- *also* 'e-kyə-mə-nist *or* ,e-kyə-'me-nist\ *noun*

**ec·ze·ma** \ig-'zē-mə, 'eg-zə-mə, 'ek-sə-\ *noun* [New Latin, from Greek *ekzema,* from *ekzein* to erupt, from *ex-* out + *zein* to boil — more at EX-, YEAST] (circa 1753)
**:** an inflammatory condition of the skin characterized by redness, itching, and oozing vesicular lesions which become scaly, crusted, or hardened
— **ec·zem·a·tous** \ig-'ze-mə-təs\ *adjective*

**ed** \'ed\ *noun* (1954)
**:** EDUCATION ⟨driver's *ed*⟩ ⟨adult *ed*⟩

**¹-ed** \d *after a vowel or* b, g, j, l, m, n, ŋ, r, th, v, z, *or* zh; əd, id *after* d *or* t; t *after other sounds; exceptions are pronounced at their entries*\ *verb suffix or adjective suffix* [Middle English, from Old English *-ed, -od, -ad;* akin to Old High German *-t,* past participle ending, Latin *-tus,* Greek *-tos,* suffix forming verbals]
**1** — used to form the past participle of regular weak verbs ⟨end*ed*⟩ ⟨fad*ed*⟩ ⟨tri*ed*⟩ ⟨patt*ed*⟩
**2** — used to form adjectives of identical meaning from Latin-derived adjectives ending in *-ate* ⟨crenulat*ed*⟩
**3 a :** having **:** characterized by ⟨cultur*ed*⟩ ⟨two-legg*ed*⟩ **b :** having the characteristics of ⟨bigot*ed*⟩

**²-ed** *verb suffix* [Middle English *-ede, -de,* from Old English *-de, -ede, -ode, -ade;* akin to Old High German *-ta,* past ending (1st singular) and probably to Old High German *-t,* past participle ending]
— used to form the past tense of regular weak verbs ⟨judg*ed*⟩ ⟨denied*d*⟩ ⟨dropp*ed*⟩

**eda·cious** \i-'dā-shəs\ *adjective* [Latin *edac-, edax,* from *edere* to eat — more at EAT] (circa 1798)
**1** *archaic* **:** of or relating to eating
**2 :** VORACIOUS
— **edac·i·ty** \-'da-sə-tē\ *noun*

**Edam** \'ē-dəm, 'ē-,dam\ *noun* [*Edam,* Netherlands] (1836)
**:** a yellow pressed cheese of Dutch origin usually made in flattened balls and often coated with red wax

**edaph·ic** \i-'da-fik\ *adjective* [Greek *edaphos* bottom, ground] (circa 1900)
**1 :** of or relating to the soil
**2 :** resulting from or influenced by the soil rather than the climate — compare CLIMATIC 2
— **edaph·i·cal·ly** \-'da-fi-k(ə-)lē\ *adverb*

**edaphic climax** *noun* (circa 1934)
**:** an ecological climax resulting from soil factors and commonly persisting through cycles of climatic and physiographic change — compare CLIMATIC CLIMAX

**Ed·dic** \'e-dik\ *adjective* [Old Norse *Edda,* a 13th century collection of mythological, heroic, and aphoristic poetry] (1868)
**:** of, relating to, or resembling the Old Norse *Edda*

**¹ed·dy** \'e-dē\ *noun, plural* **eddies** [Middle English (Scots dialect) *ydy,* probably from Old Norse *itha*] (15th century)
**1 a :** a current of water or air running contrary to the main current; *especially* **:** a circular current **:** WHIRLPOOL **b :** something moving similarly
**2 :** a contrary or circular current (as of thought or policy)

**²eddy** *verb* **ed·died; ed·dy·ing** (1810)
*transitive verb*
**:** to cause to move in an eddy
*intransitive verb*
**:** to move in an eddy or in the manner of an eddy

**eddy current** *noun* (1887)
**:** an electric current induced by an alternating magnetic field

**edel·weiss** \'ā-d°l-,vīs, -,wīs\ *noun* [German, from *edel* noble + *weiss* white] (1862)
**:** a small alpine perennial composite herb (*Leontopodium alpinum*) of central and southeast Europe that has a dense woolly white pubescence

edelweiss

**ede·ma** \i-'dē-mə\ *noun* [New Latin, from Greek *oidēma* swelling, from *oidein* to swell; akin to Old English *ātor* poison] (15th century)
**1 :** an abnormal infiltration and excess accumulation of serous fluid in connective tissue or in a serous cavity — called also *dropsy*
**2 a :** watery swelling of plant organs or parts **b :** any of various plant diseases characterized by such swellings
— **edem·a·tous** \-'de-mə-təs\ *adjective*

**Eden** \'ē-d°n\ *noun* [Late Latin, from Hebrew *'Ēdhen*] (13th century)
**1 :** PARADISE 2
**2 :** the garden where according to the account in Genesis Adam and Eve first lived
— **Eden·ic** \i-'de-nik, ē-\ *adjective*

**¹eden·tate** \(,)ē-'den-,tāt\ *adjective* [Latin *edentatus,* past participle of *edentare* to make toothless, from *e-* + *dent-, dens* tooth — more at TOOTH] (1828)
**1 :** lacking teeth
**2 :** being an edentate

**²edentate** *noun* (1835)
**:** any of an order (Edentata) of mammals having few or no teeth and including the sloths, armadillos, and New World anteaters and formerly also the pangolins and the aardvark

**eden·tu·lous** \(,)ē-'den-chə-ləs\ *adjective* [Latin *edentulus,* from *e-* + *dent-, dens*] (1782)
**:** TOOTHLESS

**Ed·gar** \'ed-gər\ *noun* [*Edgar* Allan Poe, regarded as father of the detective story] (1947)
**:** a statuette awarded annually by a professional organization for notable achievement in mystery-novel writing

**¹edge** \'ej\ *noun* [Middle English *egge,* from Old English *ecg;* akin to Latin *acer* sharp, Greek *akmē* point] (before 12th century)
**1 a :** the cutting side of a blade **b :** the sharpness of a blade **c** (1) **:** FORCE, EFFECTIVENESS ⟨blunted the *edge* of the legislation⟩ (2) **:** vigor or energy especially of body ⟨maintains his hard *edge*⟩ **d** (1) **:** incisive or penetrating quality ⟨writing with a satirical *edge*⟩ (2) **:** a noticeably harsh or sharp quality ⟨her voice had an *edge* to it⟩ **e :** keenness of desire or enjoyment ⟨lost my competitive *edge*⟩ ⟨took the *edge* off our appetites⟩
**2 a :** the line where an object or area begins or ends **:** BORDER ⟨on the *edge* of a plain⟩ **b :** the narrow part adjacent to a border ⟨the *edge* of the deck⟩ **c :** a point near the beginning or the end; *especially* **:** BRINK, VERGE ⟨on the *edge* of disaster⟩ **d :** a favorable margin **:** ADVANTAGE ⟨has an *edge* on the competition⟩

**3 :** a line or line segment that is the intersection of two plane faces (as of a pyramid) or of two planes
— **edge·less** *adjective*
— **on edge :** ANXIOUS, NERVOUS
²**edge** *verb* **edged; edg·ing** (14th century)
*transitive verb*
**1 a :** to give an edge to **b :** to be on an edge of ⟨trees *edging* the lake⟩
**2 :** to move or force gradually ⟨*edged* him off the road⟩
**3 :** to incline (a ski) sideways so that one edge cuts into the snow
**4 :** to defeat by a small margin — often used with *out* ⟨*edged* out her opponent⟩
*intransitive verb*
**:** to advance by short moves
**edged** \'ejd, 'e-jid\ *adjective* (before 12th century)
**1 :** having a specified kind of edge, boundary, or border or a specified number of edges ⟨rough-*edged*⟩ ⟨two-*edged*⟩
**2 :** SHARP, CUTTING ⟨an *edged* knife⟩ ⟨an *edged* remark⟩
**edge effect** *noun* (1933)
**:** the effect of an abrupt transition between two quite different adjoining ecological communities on the numbers and kinds of organisms in the marginal habitat
**edge–grain** \'ej-,grān\ *or* **edge–grained** \'ej-,grānd\ *adjective* (1906)
**:** QUARTERSAWN
**edge in** *transitive verb* (1683)
**:** to work in **:** INTERPOLATE ⟨*edged in* a few remarks⟩
**edg·er** \'e-jər\ *noun* (1591)
**:** one that edges; *especially* **:** a tool used to trim the edge of a lawn along a sidewalk or curb
**edge tool** *noun* (14th century)
**:** a tool with a sharp cutting edge
**edge·ways** \'ej-,wāz\ *adverb* (1566)
*chiefly British* **:** SIDEWAYS
**edge·wise** \-,wīz\ *adverb* (1677)
**:** SIDEWAYS
**edg·ing** *noun* (1558)
**:** something that forms an edge or border
**edgy** \'e-jē\ *adjective* **edg·i·er; -est** (1775)
**1 :** having an edge **:** SHARP
**2 a :** being on edge **:** TENSE, IRRITABLE **b** **:** characterized by tension ⟨*edgy* negotiations⟩
— **edg·i·ly** \'e-jə-lē\ *adverb*
— **edg·i·ness** \'e-jē-nəs\ *noun*
**edh** \'eth\ *noun* [Icelandic *eth*] (1875)
**:** the letter ð used in Old English and in Icelandic to represent either of the fricatives \th\ or \th̲\ and in some phonetic alphabets to represent the fricative \th̲\
**ed·i·ble** \'e-də-bəl\ *adjective* [Late Latin *edibilis*, from Latin *edere* to eat — more at EAT] (1594)
**:** fit to be eaten **:** EATABLE
— **ed·i·bil·i·ty** \,e-də-'bi-lə-tē\ *noun*
— **edible** *noun*
— **ed·i·ble·ness** \'e-də-bəl-nəs\ *noun*
**edict** \'ē-,dikt\ *noun* [Middle English, from Latin *edictum*, from neuter of *edictus*, past participle of *edicere* to decree, from *e-* + *dicere* to say — more at DICTION] (14th century)
**1 :** a proclamation having the force of law
**2 :** ORDER, COMMAND ⟨we held firm to Grandmother's *edict* —M. F. K. Fisher⟩
— **edic·tal** \i-'dik-t°l\ *adjective*
**ed·i·fi·ca·tion** \,e-də-fə-'kā-shən\ *noun* (14th century)
**:** an act or process of edifying
**ed·i·fice** \'e-də-fəs\ *noun* [Middle English, from Middle French, from Latin *aedificium*, from *aedificare*] (14th century)
**1 :** BUILDING; *especially* **:** a large or massive structure
**2 :** a large abstract structure ⟨holds together the social *edifice* —R. H. Tawney⟩
**ed·i·fy** \'e-də-,fī\ *transitive verb* **-fied; -fy·ing** [Middle English, from Middle French *edifier*,

from Late Latin & Latin; Late Latin *aedificare* to instruct or improve spiritually, from Latin, to erect a house, from *aedes* temple, house; akin to Old English *ād* funeral pyre, Latin *aestas* summer] (14th century)
**1** *archaic* **a :** BUILD **b :** ESTABLISH
**2 :** to instruct and improve especially in moral and religious knowledge **:** UPLIFT; *also* **:** ENLIGHTEN 2, INFORM
¹**ed·it** \'e-dət\ *transitive verb* [back-formation from *editor*] (1791)
**1 a :** to prepare (as literary material) for publication or public presentation **b :** to assemble (as a moving picture or tape recording) by cutting and rearranging **c :** to alter, adapt, or refine especially to bring about conformity to a standard or to suit a particular purpose ⟨carefully *edited* the speech⟩
**2 :** to direct the publication of ⟨*edits* the daily newspaper⟩
**3 :** DELETE — usually used with *out*
— **ed·it·able** \'e-də-tə-bəl\ *adjective*
²**edit** *noun* (1955)
**:** an instance of editing
**edi·tion** \i-'di-shən\ *noun* [Middle French, from Latin *edition-, editio* publication, edition, from *edere* to bring forth, publish, from *e-* + *-dere* to put or *-dere* (from *dare* to give) — more at DO, DATE] (1555)
**1 a :** the form or version in which a text is published ⟨a paperback *edition*⟩ ⟨the German *edition*⟩ **b** (1) **:** the whole number of copies published at one time (2) **:** a usually special issue of a newspaper (as for a particular day or purpose) ⟨Sunday *edition*⟩ ⟨international *edition*⟩ (3) **:** one of the usually several issues of a newspaper in a single day ⟨city *edition*⟩ ⟨late *edition*⟩
**2 a :** one of the forms in which something is presented ⟨this year's *edition* of the annual charity ball⟩ **b :** the whole number of articles of one style put out at one time ⟨a limited *edition* of collectors' pieces⟩
**3 :** COPY, VERSION
**edi·tio prin·ceps** \ā-,di-tē-(,)ō-'prin-,keps, i-,di-shē-(,)ō-'prin-,seps\ *noun, plural* **edi·ti·o·nes prin·ci·pes** \ā-,di-tē-'ō-,nās-'prin-kə-,pās, i-,di-shē-'ō-(,)nēz-'prin(t)-sə-,pēz\ [New Latin, literally, first edition] (1802)
**:** the first printed edition especially of a work that circulated in manuscript before printing became common
**ed·i·tor** \'e-də-tər\ *noun* (1649)
**1 :** someone who edits especially as an occupation
**2 :** a device used in editing motion-picture film or magnetic tape
**3 :** a computer program that permits the user to create or modify data (as text or graphics) especially on a display screen
— **ed·i·tor·ship** \-,ship\ *noun*
¹**ed·i·to·ri·al** \,e-də-'tōr-ē-əl, -'tòr-\ *adjective* (1744)
**1 :** of or relating to an editor or editing ⟨an *editorial* office⟩
**2 :** being or resembling an editorial ⟨an *editorial* statement⟩
— **ed·i·to·ri·al·ly** \-ē-ə-lē\ *adverb*
²**editorial** *noun* (1830)
**:** a newspaper or magazine article that gives the opinions of the editors or publishers; *also* **:** an expression of opinion that resembles such an article ⟨a television *editorial*⟩
**ed·i·to·ri·al·ist** \-ē-ə-list\ *noun* (1901)
**:** a writer of editorials
**ed·i·to·ri·al·ize** \,e-də-'tōr-ē-ə-,līz, -'tòr-\ *intransitive verb* **-ized; -iz·ing** (1856)
**1 :** to express an opinion in the form of an editorial
**2 :** to introduce opinion into the reporting of facts
**3 :** to express an opinion (as on a controversial issue)
— **ed·i·to·ri·al·iza·tion** \-,tōr-ē-ə-lə-'zā-shən, -,tòr-\ *noun*
— **ed·i·to·ri·al·iz·er** *noun*

**editor in chief** *noun* (1873)
**:** an editor who heads an editorial staff
**ed·i·tress** \'e-də-trəs\ *noun* (1799)
**:** a woman who is an editor
**Edom·ite** \'ē-də-,mīt\ *noun* [*Edom* (Esau), ancestor of the Edomites] (1534)
**:** a member of a Semitic people living south of the Dead Sea in biblical times
**EDTA** \,ē-(,)dē-(,)tē-'ā\ *noun* [*e*thylene*d*iamine*t*etra*a*cetic acid] (1954)
**:** a white crystalline acid $C_{10}H_{16}N_2O_8$ used especially as a chelating agent and in medicine as an anticoagulant and in the treatment of lead poisoning
**ed·u·ca·ble** \'e-jə-kə-bəl\ *adjective* (1845)
**:** capable of being educated; *specifically* **:** capable of some degree of learning
— **ed·u·ca·bil·i·ty** \,e-jə-kə-'bi-lə-tē\ *noun*
**ed·u·cate** \'e-jə-,kāt\ *verb* **-cat·ed; -cat·ing** [Middle English, to rear, from Latin *educatus*, past participle of *educare* to rear, educate, from *educere* to lead forth — more at EDUCE] (15th century)
*transitive verb*
**1 a :** to provide schooling for **b :** to train by formal instruction and supervised practice especially in a skill, trade, or profession
**2 a :** to develop mentally, morally, or aesthetically especially by instruction **b :** to provide with information **:** INFORM
**3 :** to persuade or condition to feel, believe, or act in a desired way ⟨*educate* the public to support our position⟩
*intransitive verb*
**:** to educate a person or thing
**synonym** see TEACH
**ed·u·cat·ed** *adjective* (1588)
**1 :** having an education; *especially* **:** having an education beyond the average
**2 a :** giving evidence of training or practice **:** SKILLED **b :** befitting one that is educated ⟨*educated* taste⟩ **c :** based on some knowledge of fact ⟨an *educated* guess⟩
— **ed·u·cat·ed·ness** *noun*
**ed·u·ca·tion** \,e-jə-'kā-shən\ *noun* (1531)
**1 a :** the action or process of educating or of being educated; *also* **:** a stage of such a process **b :** the knowledge and development resulting from an educational process ⟨a man of little *education*⟩
**2 :** the field of study that deals mainly with methods of teaching and learning in schools
— **ed·u·ca·tion·al** \-shnəl, -shə-n°l\ *adjective*
— **ed·u·ca·tion·al·ly** \-ē\ *adverb*
**educational psychology** *noun* (1911)
**:** psychology concerned with human maturation, school learning, teaching methods, guidance, and evaluation of aptitude and progress by standardized tests
— **educational psychologist** *noun*
**educational television** *noun* (1951)
**1 :** television that provides instruction especially for students
**2 :** PUBLIC TELEVISION
**ed·u·ca·tion·ese** \,e-jə-,kā-shə-'nēz, -'nēs\ *noun* (1954)
**:** the jargon used especially by educational theorists
**ed·u·ca·tion·ist** \,e-jə-'kā-sh(ə-)nist\ *also* **ed·u·ca·tion·al·ist** \-shnə-list, -shə-n°l-ist\ *noun* (1829)
**1** *chiefly British* **:** a professional educator
**2 :** an educational theorist
**ed·u·ca·tive** \'e-jə-,kā-tiv\ *adjective* (1856)
**1 :** tending to educate **:** INSTRUCTIVE
**2 :** of or relating to education
**ed·u·ca·tor** \'e-jə-,kā-tər\ *noun* (1673)
**1 :** one skilled in teaching **:** TEACHER

**2 a :** a student of the theory and practice of education : EDUCATIONIST 2 **b :** an administrator in education

**educe** \i-'düs *also* -'dyüs\ *transitive verb* **educed; educ·ing** [Latin *educere* to draw out, from *e-* + *ducere* to lead — more at TOW] (1603)
**1 :** to bring out (as something latent)
**2 :** DEDUCE ☆
— **educ·ible** \-'dü-sə-bəl *also* -'dyü-\ *adjective*
— **educ·tion** \-'dək-shən\ *noun*

**educ·tor** \i-'dək-tər\ *noun* [Late Latin, one that leads out, from Latin *educere*] (1796)
**:** EJECTOR 2

**edul·co·rate** \i-'dəl-kə-ˌrāt\ *transitive verb* **-rat·ed; -rat·ing** [New Latin *edulcoratus,* past participle of *edulcorare,* from Latin *e-* + *dulcor* sweetness, from *dulcis* sweet — more at DULCET] (1641)
**:** to free from harshness (as of attitude) **:** SOFTEN

**ed·u·tain·ment** \ˌe-jə-'tān-mənt, ˌe-dyü-\ *noun* [*education* + enter*tainment*] (1973)
**:** a form of entertainment (as by games, films, or shows) that is designed to be educational

**Ed·war·di·an** \e-'dwär-dē-ən, -'dwȯr-\ *adjective* (1908)
**:** of, relating to, or characteristic of Edward VII of England or his age; *especially, of clothing* **:** marked by the hourglass silhouette for women and long narrow fitted suits and high collars for men
— **Edwardian** *noun*

**¹-ee** \'ē, ˌē, ē\ *noun suffix* [Middle English *-e,* from Middle French *-é,* from *-é,* past participle ending, from Latin *-atus*]
**1 :** recipient or beneficiary of (a specified action) ⟨appoint*ee*⟩ ⟨grant*ee*⟩
**2 :** person furnished with (a specified thing) ⟨patent*ee*⟩
**3 :** person that performs (a specified action) ⟨escap*ee*⟩

**²-ee** *noun suffix* [probably alteration of *-y*]
**1 :** one associated with ⟨barg*ee*⟩
**2 :** a particular especially small kind of ⟨boo*tee*⟩
**3 :** one resembling or suggestive of ⟨goa*tee*⟩

**eel** \'ē(ə)l\ *noun* [Middle English *ele,* from Old English *el;* akin to Old High German *āl* eel] (before 12th century)
**1 a :** any of numerous voracious elongate snakelike bony fishes (order Anguilliformes) that have a smooth

eel 1a

slimy skin, lack pelvic fins, and have the median fins confluent around the tail — compare AMERICAN EEL **b :** any of numerous other elongate fishes (as of the order Symbranchii)
**2 :** any of various nematodes
— **eel·like** \'ē(ə)l-ˌlīk\ *adjective*
— **eely** \'ē-lē\ *adjective*

**eel·grass** \'ē(ə)l-ˌgras\ *noun* (1790)
**1 :** a submerged long-leaved monocotyledonous marine plant (*Zostera marina*) of the eelgrass family that is abundant along the Atlantic coast and has stems used especially in woven products (as mats and hats)
**2 :** TAPE GRASS

**eel·pout** \-ˌpaut\ *noun* (before 12th century)
**1 :** any of various elongate tapered marine fishes (family Zoarcidae) usually living on the bottom of cold seas
**2 :** BURBOT

**eel·worm** \-ˌwərm\ *noun* (1888)
**:** a nematode worm; *especially* **:** any of various small free-living or plant-parasitic roundworms

**-een** \'ēn\ *noun suffix* [probably from *ratteen*]
**:** inferior fabric resembling (a specified fabric) **:** imitation ⟨velvet*een*⟩

**e'en** \'ēn\ *adverb* (circa 1553)

**:** EVEN

**-eer** \'ir\ *noun suffix* [Middle French *-ier,* from Latin *-arius* — more at -ARY]
**:** one that is concerned with professionally, conducts, or produces ⟨auction*eer*⟩ ⟨pamphle*teer*⟩ — often in words with derogatory meaning ⟨profit*eer*⟩

**e'er** \'er, 'ar\ *adverb* (13th century)

**:** EVER

**ee·rie** *also* **ee·ry** \'ir-ē, 'ēr-\ *adjective* **ee·ri·er; -est** [Middle English (northern dialect) *eri*] (14th century)
**1** *chiefly Scottish* **:** affected with fright **:** SCARED
**2 :** so mysterious, strange, or unexpected as to send a chill up the spine ⟨a coyote's *eerie* howl⟩ ⟨the similarities were *eerie*⟩; *also* **:** seemingly not of earthly origin ⟨the flames cast an *eerie* glow⟩
*synonym see* WEIRD
— **ee·ri·ly** \'ir-ə-lē, 'ēr-\ *adverb*
— **ee·ri·ness** \'ir-ē-nəs, 'ēr-\ *noun*

**ef** \'ef\ *noun* (before 12th century)
**:** the letter *f*

**ef·face** \i-'fās, e-\ *transitive verb* **ef·faced; ef·fac·ing** [Middle English, from Middle French *effacer,* from Old French *esfacier,* from *e-* + *face* face] (15th century)
**1 :** to eliminate or make indistinct by or as if by wearing away a surface ⟨coins with dates *effaced* by wear⟩; *also* **:** to cause to vanish ⟨daylight *effaced* the stars⟩
**2 :** to make (oneself) modestly or shyly inconspicuous
— **ef·face·able** \-'fā-sə-bəl\ *adjective*
— **ef·face·ment** \-'fā-smənt\ *noun*
— **ef·fac·er** *noun*

**¹ef·fect** \i-'fekt, e-, ē-\ *noun* [Middle English, from Middle French & Latin; Middle French, from Latin *effectus,* from *efficere* to bring about, from *ex-* + *facere* to make, do — more at DO] (14th century)
**1 a :** PURPORT, INTENT **b :** basic meaning **:** ESSENCE
**2 :** something that inevitably follows an antecedent (as a cause or agent)
**3 :** an outward sign **:** APPEARANCE
**4 :** ACCOMPLISHMENT, FULFILLMENT
**5 :** power to bring about a result **:** INFLUENCE ⟨the content itself of television . . . is therefore less important than its *effect* —*Current Biography*⟩
**6** *plural* **:** movable property **:** GOODS ⟨personal *effects*⟩
**7 a :** a distinctive impression ⟨the color gives the *effect* of being warm⟩ **b :** the creation of a desired impression ⟨her tears were purely for *effect*⟩ **c** (1) **:** something designed to produce a distinctive or desired impression — usually used in plural (2) *plural* **:** SPECIAL EFFECTS
**8 :** the quality or state of being operative **:** OPERATION ⟨the law goes into *effect* next week⟩
— **in effect :** in substance **:** VIRTUALLY ⟨the . . . committee agreed to what was *in effect* a reduction in the hourly wage —*Current Biography*⟩
— **to the effect :** with the meaning ⟨issued a statement *to the effect* that he would resign⟩

**²effect** *transitive verb* (1533)
**1 :** to cause to come into being
**2 a :** to bring about often by surmounting obstacles **:** ACCOMPLISH ⟨*effect* a settlement of a dispute⟩ **b :** to put into operation ⟨the duty of the legislature to *effect* the will of the citizens⟩
■
*synonym see* PERFORM

**¹ef·fec·tive** \i-'fek-tiv, e-, ē-\ *adjective* (14th century)
**1 a :** producing a decided, decisive, or desired effect **b :** IMPRESSIVE, STRIKING ⟨a gold lamé fabric studded with *effective* . . . precious stones —Stanley Marcus⟩
**2 :** ready for service or action ⟨*effective* manpower⟩
**3 :** ACTUAL ⟨the need to increase *effective* demand for goods⟩

**4 :** being in effect **:** OPERATIVE ⟨the tax becomes *effective* next year⟩
**5** *of a rate of interest* **:** equal to the rate of simple interest that yields the same amount when the interest is paid once at the end of the interest period as a quoted rate of interest does when calculated at compound interest over the same period — compare NOMINAL 4 ☆
— **ef·fec·tive·ness** *noun*
— **ef·fec·tiv·i·ty** \ˌe-ˌfek-'ti-və-tē, i-, ē-\ *noun*

**²effective** *noun* (1722)
**:** one that is effective; *especially* **:** a soldier equipped for duty

**ef·fec·tive·ly** \-lē\ *adverb* (circa 1536)
**1 :** in effect **:** VIRTUALLY
**2 :** in an effective manner

**ef·fec·tor** \i-'fek-tər, -ˌtȯr\ *noun* (1906)
**1 :** a bodily organ (as a gland or muscle) that becomes active in response to stimulation
**2 :** a substance (as an inducer or corepressor) that controls protein synthesis by combining allosterically with a genetic repressor

**ef·fec·tu·al** \i-'fek-chə(-wə)l, -'feksh-wəl\ *adjective* (14th century)
**:** producing or able to produce a desired effect
*synonym see* EFFECTIVE
— **ef·fec·tu·al·i·ty** \-ˌfek-chə-'wa-lə-tē\ *noun*
— **ef·fec·tu·al·ness** \-'fek-chə(-wə)l-nəs, -'feksh-wəl-\ *noun*

**ef·fec·tu·al·ly** \i-'fek-chə(-wə)-lē, -'fek-shwə-\ *adverb* (14th century)

**1 :** in an effectual manner
**2 :** with great effect **: COMPLETELY**

**ef·fec·tu·ate** \i-'fek-chə-ˌwāt\ *transitive verb* **-at·ed; -at·ing** (1580)
**: EFFECT 2**
— **ef·fec·tu·a·tion** \-ˌfek-chə-'wā-shən\ *noun*

**ef·fem·i·na·cy** \ə-'fe-mə-nə-sē\ *noun* (1602)
**:** the quality of being effeminate

**¹ef·fem·i·nate** \-nət\ *adjective* [Middle English, from Latin *effeminatus*, from past participle of *effeminare* to make effeminate, from *ex-* + *femina* woman — more at FEMININE] (15th century)
**1 :** having feminine qualities untypical of a man **:** not manly in appearance or manner
**2 :** marked by an unbecoming delicacy or overrefinement ⟨*effeminate* art⟩ ⟨an *effeminate* civilization⟩

**²effeminate** *noun* (1597)
**:** an effeminate person

**ef·fen·di** \e-'fen-dē, ə-\ *noun* [Turkish *efendi* master, from New Greek *aphentēs*, alteration of Greek *authentēs* — more at AUTHENTIC] (1614)
**:** a man of property, authority, or education in an eastern Mediterranean country

**ef·fer·ent** \'e-fər-ənt, -ˌfer-, 'ē-\ *adjective* [French *efférent*, from Latin *efferent-, efferens,* present participle of *efferre* to carry outward, from *ex-* + *ferre* to carry — more at BEAR] (1856)
**:** conducting outward from a part or organ; *specifically* **:** conveying nervous impulses to an effector — compare AFFERENT
— **efferent** *noun*
— **ef·fer·ent·ly** *adverb*

**ef·fer·vesce** \ˌe-fər-'ves\ *intransitive verb* **-vesced; -vesc·ing** [Latin *effervescere,* from *ex-* + *fervescere* to begin to boil, inchoative of *fervēre* to boil — more at BREW] (1784)
**1 :** to bubble, hiss, and foam as gas escapes
**2 :** to show liveliness or exhilaration
— **ef·fer·ves·cence** \-'ve-s°n(t)s\ *noun*
— **ef·fer·ves·cent** \-s°nt\ *adjective*
— **ef·fer·ves·cent·ly** *adverb*

**ef·fete** \e-'fēt, i-\ *adjective* [Latin *effetus,* from *ex-* + *fetus* fruitful — more at FEMININE] (1660)
**1 :** no longer fertile
**2 a :** having lost character, vitality, or strength ⟨the *effete* monarchies . . . of feudal Europe —G. M. Trevelyan⟩ **b :** marked by weakness or decadence ⟨the *effete* East⟩ **c :** soft or delicate from or as if from a pampered existence ⟨peddled . . . trendy tweeds to *effete* Easterners —William Helmer⟩ ⟨*effete* tenderfeet⟩; *also* **:** characteristic of an effete person ⟨a wool scarf . . . a bit *effete* on an outdoorsman —Nelson Bryant⟩
**3 :** EFFEMINATE 1 ⟨a good-humored, *effete* boy brought up by maiden aunts —Herman Wouk⟩
— **ef·fete·ly** *adverb*
— **ef·fete·ness** *noun*

**ef·fi·ca·cious** \ˌe-fə-'kā-shəs\ *adjective* [Latin *efficac-, efficax,* from *efficere*] (1528)
**:** having the power to produce a desired effect
**synonym** see EFFECTIVE
— **ef·fi·ca·cious·ly** *adverb*
— **ef·fi·ca·cious·ness** *noun*

**ef·fi·cac·i·ty** \ˌe-fə-'ka-sə-tē\ *noun* (15th century)
**: EFFICACY**

**ef·fi·ca·cy** \'e-fi-kə-sē\ *noun, plural* **-cies** (13th century)
**:** the power to produce an effect

**ef·fi·cien·cy** \i-'fi-shən-sē\ *noun, plural* **-cies** (1633)
**1 :** the quality or degree of being efficient
**2 a :** efficient operation **b** (1) **:** effective operation as measured by a comparison of production with cost (as in energy, time, and money) (2) **:** the ratio of the useful energy delivered by a dynamic system to the energy supplied to it
**3 :** EFFICIENCY APARTMENT

**efficiency apartment** *noun* (1930)
**:** a small usually furnished apartment with minimal kitchen and bath facilities

**efficiency expert** *noun* (1913)
**:** one who analyzes methods, procedures, and jobs in order to secure maximum efficiency — called also *efficiency engineer*

**ef·fi·cient** \i-'fi-shənt\ *adjective* [Middle English, from Middle French or Latin; Middle French, from Latin *efficient-, efficiens,* from present participle of *efficere*] (14th century)
**1 :** being or involving the immediate agent in producing an effect ⟨the *efficient* action of heat in changing water to steam⟩
**2 :** productive of desired effects; *especially* **:** productive without waste
**synonym** see EFFECTIVE
— **ef·fi·cient·ly** *adverb*

**ef·fi·gy** \'e-fə-jē\ *noun, plural* **-gies** [Middle French *effigie,* from Latin *effigies,* from *effingere* to form, from *ex-* + *fingere* to shape — more at DOUGH] (1539)
**:** an image or representation especially of a person; *especially* **:** a crude figure representing a hated person
— **in effigy :** publicly in the form of an effigy ⟨the football coach was burned *in effigy*⟩

**ef·flo·resce** \ˌe-flə-'res\ *intransitive verb* **-resced; -resc·ing** [Latin *efflorescere,* from *ex-* + *florescere* to begin to blossom — more at FLORESCENCE] (1775)
**1 :** to burst forth **: BLOOM**
**2 a :** to change to a powder from loss of water of crystallization **b :** to form or become covered with a powdery crust ⟨bricks may *effloresce* owing to the deposition of soluble salts⟩

**ef·flo·res·cence** \-'re-s°n(t)s\ *noun* (1626)
**1 a :** the action or process of developing and unfolding as if coming into flower **: BLOSSOMING** ⟨periods of . . . intellectual and artistic *efflorescence* —Julian Huxley⟩ **b :** an instance of such development **c :** fullness of manifestation **: CULMINATION**
**2 :** the period or state of flowering
**3 :** the process or product of efflorescing chemically
— **ef·flo·res·cent** \-s°nt\ *adjective*

**ef·flu·ence** \'e-ˌflü-ən(t)s; e-'flü-, ə-'\ *noun* (1603)
**1 :** something that flows out
**2 :** an action or process of flowing out

**¹ef·flu·ent** \-ənt\ *adjective* [Latin *effluent-, effluens,* present participle of *effluere* to flow out, from *ex-* + *fluere* to flow — more at FLUID] (1726)
**:** flowing out **: EMANATING, OUTGOING** ⟨an *effluent* river⟩

**²effluent** *noun* (1859)
**:** something that flows out: as **a :** an outflowing branch of a main stream or lake **b :** waste material (as smoke, liquid industrial refuse, or sewage) discharged into the environment especially when serving as a pollutant

**ef·flu·vi·um** \e-'flü-vē-əm\ *also* **ef·flu·via** \-vē-ə\ *noun, plural* **-via** *or* **-vi·ums** [Latin *effluvium* act of flowing out, from *effluere*] (1651)
**1 :** an invisible emanation; *especially* **:** an offensive exhalation or smell
**2 :** a by-product especially in the form of waste

**ef·flux** \'e-ˌfləks\ *noun* [Medieval Latin *effluxus,* from *effluere*] (1647)
**1 :** something given off in or as if in a stream
**2 a :** EFFLUENCE 2 **b :** a passing away **: EXPIRATION**
— **ef·flux·ion** \e-'flək-shən\ *noun*

**ef·fort** \'e-fərt, -ˌfōrt\ *noun* [Middle English, from Middle French, from Old French *esfort,* from *esforcier* to force, from *ex-* + *forcier* to force] (15th century)
**1 :** conscious exertion of power **:** hard work
**2 :** a serious attempt **: TRY**
**3 :** something produced by exertion or trying ⟨the novel was her most ambitious *effort*⟩

**4 :** effective force as distinguished from the possible resistance called into action by such a force
**5 :** the total work done to achieve a particular end ⟨the war *effort*⟩

**ef·fort·ful** \-fərt-fəl\ *adjective* (circa 1895)
**:** showing or requiring effort
— **ef·fort·ful·ly** \-fə-lē\ *adverb*
— **ef·fort·ful·ness** \-fəl-nəs\ *noun*

**ef·fort·less** \-fərt-ləs\ *adjective* (1801)
**:** showing or requiring little or no effort
**synonym** see EASY
— **ef·fort·less·ly** *adverb*
— **ef·fort·less·ness** *noun*

**ef·fron·tery** \i-'frən-tə-rē, e-\ *noun, plural* **-ter·ies** [French *effronterie,* ultimately from Medieval Latin *effront-, effrons* shameless, from Latin *ex-* + *front-, frons* forehead] (1697)
**:** shameless boldness **: INSOLENCE**
**synonym** see TEMERITY

**ef·ful·gence** \i-'fùl-jən(t)s, e-, -'fəl-\ *noun* [Late Latin *effulgentia,* from Latin *effulgent-, effulgens,* present participle of *effulgēre* to shine forth, from *ex-* + *fulgēre* to shine — more at FULGENT] (1667)
**:** radiant splendor **: BRILLIANCE**
— **ef·ful·gent** \-jənt\ *adjective*

**¹ef·fuse** \i-'fyüz, e-\ *verb* **ef·fused; ef·fus·ing** [Latin *effusus,* past participle of *effundere,* from *ex-* + *fundere* to pour — more at FOUND] (1526)
*transitive verb*
**:** to pour out (a liquid)
*intransitive verb*
**:** to flow out **: EMANATE**

**²ef·fuse** \-'fyüs\ *adjective* (circa 1530)
**: DIFFUSE;** *specifically* **:** spread out flat without definite form ⟨*effuse* lichens⟩

**ef·fu·sion** \i-'fyü-zhən, e-\ *noun* (15th century)
**1 :** an act of effusing
**2 :** unrestrained expression of words or feelings ⟨greeted her with great *effusion* —Olive H. Prouty⟩
**3 a** (1) **:** the escape of a fluid from anatomical vessels by rupture or exudation (2) **:** the flow of a gas through an aperture whose diameter is small as compared with the distance between the molecules of the gas **b :** the fluid that escapes

**ef·fu·sive** \i-'fyü-siv, e-, -ziv\ *adjective* (1662)
**1 :** excessively demonstrative
**2 :** *archaic* **:** pouring freely
**3 :** characterized or formed by a nonexplosive outpouring of lava ⟨*effusive* rocks⟩
— **ef·fu·sive·ly** *adverb*
— **ef·fu·sive·ness** *noun*

**Ef·ik** \'e-fik\ *noun* (1849)
**1 :** a member of a people of southeastern Nigeria
**2 :** the language of the Efik people

**eft** \'eft\ *noun* [Middle English *evete, ewte,* from Old English *efete*] (before 12th century)
**: NEWT;** *especially* **:** the terrestrial phase of a predominantly aquatic newt

**eft·soons** \eft-'sünz\ *adverb* [Middle English *eftsones,* alteration of Old English *eftsōna,* from Old English *eft* after + *sōna* soon; akin to Old English *æfter* after] (before 12th century)
*archaic* **:** soon after

**egad** \i-'gad\ *or* **egads** \-'gadz\ *interjection* [probably euphemism for *oh God*] (1673)
— used as a mild oath

**egal** \'ē-gəl\ *adjective* [Middle English, from Middle French, from Latin *aequalis*] (14th century)
*obsolete* **: EQUAL**

\ə\ **abut** \ᵊ\ **kitten** \ər\ **further** \a\ **ash** \ā\ **ace**
\ä\ **mop, mar** \aù\ **out** \ch\ **chin** \e\ **bet** \ē\ **easy**
\g\ **go** \i\ **hit** \ī\ **ice** \j\ **job** \ŋ\ **sing** \ō\ **go**
\ò\ **law** \òi\ **boy** \th\ **thin** \ṯẖ\ **the** \ü\ **loot** \ù\ **foot**
\y\ **yet** \zh\ **vision** *see also* Guide to Pronunciation

**egal·i·tar·i·an** \i-ˌga-lə-'ter-ē-ən\ *adjective* [French *égalitaire*, from *égalité* equality, from Latin *aequalitat-, aequalitas*, from *aequalis* equal] (1885)
: asserting, promoting, or marked by egalitarianism
— **egalitarian** *noun*
**egal·i·tar·i·an·ism** \-ē-ə-ˌni-zəm\ *noun* (1905)
**1** : a belief in human equality especially with respect to social, political, and economic rights and privileges
**2** : a social philosophy advocating the removal of inequalities among people
**éga·li·té** \ā-gä-lē-tā\ *noun* [French] (1794)
: social or political equality
**Ege·ria** \i-'jir-ē-ə\ *noun* [Latin, a nymph who advised the legendary Roman king Numa Pompilius] (1621)
: a woman adviser or companion
**eges·ta** \i-'jes-tə\ *noun plural* [New Latin, from Latin, neuter plural of *egestus*] (1727)
: something egested
**eges·tion** \i-'jes(h)-chən\ *noun* [Middle English *egestioun*, from Middle French or Latin; Middle French *egestion*, from Latin *egestion-, egestio* to carry outside, discharge, from *egerere* to carry outside, discharge, from *e-* + *gerere* to carry] (1547)
: the act or process of discharging undigested or waste material from a cell or organism; *specifically* : DEFECATION
— **egest** \i-'jest\ *transitive verb*
— **eges·tive** \-'jes-tiv\ *adjective*
**¹egg** \'eg, 'āg\ *transitive verb* [Middle English, from Old Norse *eggja*; akin to Old English *ecg* edge — more at EDGE] (13th century)
: to incite to action — usually used with *on* ⟨*egged* the mob on to riot⟩
**²egg** *noun, often attributive* [Middle English *egge*, from Old Norse *egg*; akin to Old English *ǣg* egg, Latin *ovum*, Greek *ōion*] (14th century)
**1 a** : the hard-shelled reproductive body produced by a bird and especially by the common domestic chicken; *also* : its contents used as food **b** : an animal reproductive body consisting of an ovum together with its nutritive and protective envelopes and having the capacity to develop into a new individual capable of independent existence **c** : OVUM
**2** : something resembling an egg
**3** : PERSON, SORT ⟨a good *egg*⟩
— **egg·less** *adjective*
— **eggy** \-gē\ *adjective*
— **egg on one's face** : a state of embarrassment or humiliation
**³egg** *transitive verb* (1833)
**1** : to cover with egg
**2** : to pelt with eggs
**egg and dart** *noun* (circa 1864)
: a carved ornamental design in relief consisting of an egg-shaped figure alternating with a figure somewhat like an elongated javelin or arrowhead
**egg·beat·er** \'eg-ˌbē-tər, 'āg-\ *noun* (1828)
**1** : a hand-operated kitchen utensil used for beating, stirring, or whipping; *especially* : a rotary device for these purposes
**2** : HELICOPTER
**egg case** *noun* (1847)
: a protective case enclosing eggs : OOTHECA — called also *egg capsule*
**egg cell** *noun* (1880)
: OVUM
**egg cream** *noun* (1954)

egg 1a: *1* shell, *2* shell membrane, *3* egg membrane, *4* air space, *5* chalaza, *6* albumen or white layers, *7* yolk layers, *8* blastodisc, *9* vitelline membrane

: a drink consisting of milk, a flavoring syrup, and soda water
**egg·cup** \'eg-ˌkəp, 'āg-\ *noun* (1773)
: a cup for holding an egg that is to be eaten from the shell
**egg·head** \-ˌhed\ *noun, often attributive* (1952)
: INTELLECTUAL, HIGHBROW
**egg·head·ed** \-'he-dəd\ *adjective* (1938)
: having the characteristics of an egghead
— **egg·head·ed·ness** *noun*
**egg·nog** \-ˌnäg\ *noun* (circa 1775)
: a drink consisting of eggs beaten with sugar, milk or cream, and often alcoholic liquor
**egg·plant** \-ˌplant\ *noun* (1767)
**1 a** : a widely cultivated perennial herb (*Solanum melongena*) of the nightshade family yielding edible fruit **b** : the usually smooth ovoid fruit of the eggplant
**2** : a dark grayish or blackish purple
**egg roll** *noun* (1947)
: a thin egg-dough casing filled with minced vegetables and often bits of meat (as shrimp or chicken) and usually deep-fried
**eggs Ben·e·dict** \-'be-nə-ˌdikt\ *noun plural but singular or plural in construction* [probably from the name *Benedict*] (1898)
: poached eggs and broiled ham placed on toasted halves of English muffin and covered with hollandaise
**¹egg·shell** \'eg-ˌshel, 'āg-\ *noun* (14th century)
**1** : the hard exterior covering of an egg
**2** : something resembling an eggshell especially in fragility
**²eggshell** *adjective* (1835)
**1** : thin and fragile
**2** : slightly glossy
**3** : yellowish white
**egg timer** *noun* (1884)
: a small sandglass for timing the boiling of eggs
**egg tooth** *noun* (1893)
: a hard sharp prominence on the beak of an unhatched bird or the nose of an unhatched reptile that is used to break through the eggshell
**egis** \'ē-jəs\ *variant of* AEGIS
**eg·lan·tine** \'e-glən-ˌtīn, -ˌtēn\ *noun* [Middle English *eglentyn*, from Middle French *aiglent*, from (assumed) Vulgar Latin *aculentum*, from Latin *acus* needle; akin to Latin *acer* sharp — more at EDGE] (14th century)
: SWEETBRIER
**eglo·mi·se** *also* **églo·mi·sé** \ˌā-glə-(ˌ)mē-'zā, ˌe-; 'ā-glə-(ˌ)mē-, ˌe'-\ *adjective* [French, past participle of *églomiser* to decorate a glass panel by painting on its back, from Jean-Baptiste *Glomy* (died 1786) French decorator] (1877)
: made of glass on the back of which is a painted picture that shows through ⟨a clock with *eglomise* panels⟩
**ego** \'ē-(ˌ)gō *also* 'e-\ *noun, plural* **egos** [New Latin, from Latin, I — more at I] (1789)
**1** : the self especially as contrasted with another self or the world
**2 a** : EGOTISM 2 **b** : SELF-ESTEEM 1
**3** : the one of the three divisions of the psyche in psychoanalytic theory that serves as the organized conscious mediator between the person and reality especially by functioning both in the perception of and adaptation to reality — compare ID, SUPEREGO
— **ego·less** *adjective*
**ego·cen·tric** \ˌē-gō-'sen-trik *also* ˌe-\ *adjective* (1894)
**1** : concerned with the individual rather than society
**2** : taking the ego as the starting point in philosophy
**3 a** : limited in outlook or concern to one's own activities or needs **b** : SELF-CENTERED, SELFISH
— **egocentric** *noun*
— **ego·cen·tri·cal·ly** \-tri-k(ə-)lē\ *adverb*

— **ego·cen·tric·i·ty** \-ˌsen-'tri-sə-tē\ *noun*
— **ego·cen·trism** \-'sen-ˌtri-zəm\ *noun*
**ego ideal** *noun* (1922)
: the standards, ideals, and ambitions that according to psychoanalytic theory are assimilated from the superego
**ego·ism** \'ē-gə-ˌwi-zəm *also* 'e-\ *noun* (1785)
**1 a** : a doctrine that individual self-interest is the actual motive of all conscious action **b** : a doctrine that individual self-interest is the valid end of all actions
**2** : excessive concern for oneself with or without exaggerated feelings of self-importance — compare EGOTISM 2
**ego·ist** \-wist\ *noun* (1785)
**1** : a believer in egoism
**2** : an egocentric or egotistic person
— **ego·is·tic** \ˌē-gə-'wis-tik *also* ˌe-\ *also* **ego·is·ti·cal** \-ti-kəl\ *adjective*
— **ego·is·ti·cal·ly** \-ti-k(ə-)lē\ *adverb*
**egoistic hedonism** *noun* (1874)
: the ethical theory that achieving one's own happiness is the proper goal of all conduct
**ego·ma·nia** \ˌē-gō-'mā-nē-ə, -nyə\ *noun* (1825)
: the quality or state of being extremely egocentric
— **ego·ma·ni·ac** \-nē-ˌak\ *noun*
— **ego·ma·ni·a·cal** \-mə-'nī-ə-kəl\ *adjective*
— **ego·ma·ni·a·cal·ly** \-k(ə-)lē\ *adverb*
**ego·tism** \'ē-gə-ˌti-zəm *also* 'e-\ *noun* [Latin *ego* + English *-tism* (as in *idiotism*)] (1714)
**1 a** : excessive use of the first person singular personal pronoun **b** : the practice of talking about oneself too much
**2** : an exaggerated sense of self-importance : CONCEIT — compare EGOISM 2
— **ego·tist** \-tist\ *noun*
— **ego·tis·tic** \-'tis-tik\ *or* **ego·tis·ti·cal** \-'tis-ti-kəl\ *adjective*
— **ego·tis·ti·cal·ly** \-k(ə-)lē\ *adverb*
**ego trip** *noun* (1967)
: an act or course of action that enhances and satisfies one's ego
— **ego–trip** *intransitive verb*
— **ego–trip·per** *noun*
**egre·gious** \i-'grē-jəs\ *adjective* [Latin *egregius*, from *e-* + *greg-, grex* herd — more at GREGARIOUS] (circa 1534)
**1** *archaic* : DISTINGUISHED
**2** : CONSPICUOUS; *especially* : conspicuously bad : FLAGRANT ⟨an *egregious* mistake⟩ ◆
— **egre·gious·ly** *adverb*
— **egre·gious·ness** *noun*
**¹egress** \'ē-ˌgres\ *noun* [Latin *egressus*, from *egressus*, past participle of *egredi* to go out, from *e-* + *gradi* to go — more at GRADE] (1538)
**1** : the action or right of going or coming out
**2** : a place or means of going out : EXIT
**²egress** \ē-'gres\ *intransitive verb* (1578)
: to go or come out

**egres·sion** \ē-'gre-shən\ *noun* (15th century)
: EGRESS, EMERGENCE

**egret** \'ē-grət, -,gret *also* i-'gret, 'eg-rət\ *noun*
[Middle English, from Middle French *aigrette*,
from Old Provençal *aigreta*, of Germanic origin; akin to Old High German *heigaro* heron]
(14th century)
: any of various
herons that bear
long plumes dur-
ing the breeding
season

egret

¹**Egyp·tian** \i-
'jip-shən\ *adjec-
tive* (14th centu-
ry)
: of, relating to,
or characteristic
of Egypt or the
Egyptians
²**Egyptian** *noun* (14th century)
**1** : a native or inhabitant of Egypt
**2** : the Afro-Asiatic language of the ancient
Egyptians from earliest times to about the 3d
century A.D.
**3** *often not capitalized* : a typeface having little contrast between thick and thin strokes and
squared serifs
**Egyptian alfalfa weevil** *noun* (1943)
: an Old World weevil (*Hypera brunneipennis*)
established in western North America where it
feeds on alfalfa and various clovers
**Egyptian clover** *noun* (circa 1900)
: BERSEEM
**Egyptian cotton** *noun* (1877)
: a fine long-staple often somewhat brownish
cotton grown chiefly in Egypt
**Egyp·tol·o·gy** \,ē-(,)jip-'tä-lə-jē\ *noun* (1862)
: the study of Egyptian antiquities
— **Egyp·to·log·i·cal** \-tə-'lä-jə-kəl\ *adjective*
— **Egyp·tol·o·gist** \-'tä-lə-jist\ *noun*
**eh** \'ā, 'e, 'a(i), *also with* h *preceding and/or
with nasalization*\ *interjection* [Middle English
*ey*] (13th century)
— used to ask for confirmation or repetition
or to express inquiry; used especially in Canadian English in anticipation of the listener's or
reader's agreement
**ei·cos·a·noid** \ī-'kō-sə-,nȯid\ *noun* [*eicosa-*
containing 20 atoms (from Greek *eikosa-*
twenty, from *eikosi*) + *-noic*, suffix used in
names of fatty acids (from *-ane* + *-oic*) + ¹*-oid*
— more at VIGESIMAL] (1980)
: any of a class of compounds (as the prostaglandins) derived from polyunsaturated acids
(as arachidonic acid) and involved in cellular
activity
**ei·der** \'ī-dər\ *noun* [Dutch, German, or Swedish, from Icelandic *æthur*, from Old Norse
*æthr*] (1743)
**1** : any of several large northern sea ducks
(genera *Somateria* and *Polystica*) having fine
soft down that is used by the female for lining
the nest — called also *eider duck*
**2** : EIDERDOWN 1
**ei·der·down** \-,daun\ *noun* [probably from
German *Eiderdaune*, from Icelandic *æthar-
dūnn*, from *æthur* + *dūnn* ⁷down] (1774)
**1** : the down of the eider
**2** : a comforter filled with eiderdown
**3** : a soft lightweight clothing fabric knitted or
woven and napped on one or both sides
**ei·det·ic** \ī-'de-tik\ *adjective* [Greek *eidētikos*
of a form, from *eidos* form — more at WISE]
(circa 1924)
: marked by or involving extraordinarily accurate and vivid recall especially of visual images ⟨an *eidetic* memory⟩
— **ei·det·i·cal·ly** \-ti-k(ə-)lē\ *adverb*
**ei·do·lon** \ī-'dō-lən\ *noun, plural* **-lons** \-lənz\
*or* **-la** \-lə\ [Greek *eidōlon* — more at IDOL]
(1828)
**1** : an unsubstantial image : PHANTOM
**2** : IDEAL

**ei·gen·mode** \'ī-gən-,mōd\ *noun* [*eigen-* (as
in *eigenvector*) + ¹*mode*]
: a normal mode of vibration of an oscillating
system
**ei·gen·val·ue** \'ī-gən-,val-(,)yü, -yə(-w)\ *noun*
[part translation of German *Eigenwert*, from
*eigen* own, peculiar + *Wert* value] (1927)
: a scalar associated with a given linear transformation of a vector space and having the
property that there is some nonzero vector
which when multiplied by the scalar is equal
to the vector obtained by letting the transformation operate on the vector; *especially* : a
root of the characteristic equation of a matrix
**ei·gen·vec·tor** \-,vek-tər\ *noun* [International
Scientific Vocabulary *eigen-* (from German
*eigen*) + *vector*] (1941)
: a nonzero vector that is mapped by a given
linear transformation of a vector space onto a
vector that is the product of a scalar multiplied
by the original vector — called also *characteristic vector*
**eight** \'āt\ *noun* [Middle English *eighte*, from
*eighte*, adjective, from Old English *eahta*;
akin to Old High German *ahto* eight, Latin
*octo*, Greek *oktō*] (before 12th century)
**1** — see NUMBER table
**2** : the eighth in a set or series ⟨the *eight* of
spades⟩
**3** : something having eight units or members:
as **a** : an 8-oared racing boat or its crew **b** : an
8-cylinder engine or automobile
— **eight** *adjective*
— **eight** *pronoun, plural in construction*
**eight ball** *noun* (1932)
**1** : a black pool ball numbered 8
**2** : MISFIT
— **behind the eight ball** : in a highly disadvantageous position
**eigh·teen** \(')ā(t)-'tēn\ *noun* [Middle English
*eightetene*, adjective, from Old English *eahtatīene*, from *eahta* + *-tīene*; akin to Old English
*tīen* ten] (before 12th century)
— see NUMBER table
— **eighteen** *adjective*
— **eighteen** *pronoun, plural in construction*
— **eigh·teenth** \-'tēn(t)th\ *adjective or
noun*
**18–wheel·er** *or* **eigh·teen–wheel·er**
\,ā(t)-(,)tēn-'wē-lər\ *noun* (1976)
: a trucking rig consisting of a tractor and a
trailer and typically having eighteen wheels
**eight·fold** \'āt-,fōld, -'fōld\ *adjective* (before
12th century)
**1** : having eight units or members
**2** : being eight times as great or as many
— **eight·fold** \-'fōld\ *adverb*
**eightfold way** *noun* (1961)
: a unified theoretical scheme for classifying
the relationship among strongly interacting elementary particles on the basis of isospin and
hypercharge
**eighth** \'āt*th*, 'ā*th*\ *noun, plural* **eighths**
\'āt(th)s, 'ā*th*s\ (1557)
**1** — see NUMBER table
**2** : OCTAVE
— **eighth** *adjective or adverb*
**eighth note** *noun* (circa 1864)
: a musical note with the time value of ⅛ of a
whole note — see NOTE illustration
**eighth rest** *noun* (circa 1890)
: a musical rest corresponding in time value to
an eighth note — see REST illustration
**800 number** \,āt-'hən-drəd-, -dərd-\ *noun*
(1979)
: a toll-free telephone number for long-
distance calls (as to a business) that is prefixed
by the number 800
**eight·pen·ny nail** \,āt-,pe-nē-\ *noun* [from its
original price per hundred] (15th century)
: a nail typically 2½ inches (6.35 centimeters)
long
**eighty** \'ā-tē\ *noun, plural* **eight·ies** [Middle
English *eighty*, adjective, from Old English
*eahtatig*, short for *hundeahtatig*, noun, group

of eighty, from *hund-*, literally, hundred +
*eahta* eight + *-tig* group of ten; akin to Old
English *tīen* ten] (before 12th century)
**1** — see NUMBER table
**2** *plural* : the numbers 80 to 89; *specifically*
: the years 80 to 89 in a lifetime or century
— **eight·i·eth** \'ā-tē-əth\ *adjective or noun*
— **eighty** *adjective*
— **eighty** *pronoun, plural in construction*
**eighty–six** *or* **86** \,ā-tē-'siks\ *transitive verb*
[probably rhyming slang for ³*nix*] (1967)
*slang* : to refuse to serve (a customer); *also*
: to get rid of : THROW OUT
**ein·korn** \'īn-,kȯrn\ *noun* [German, from Old
High German, from *ein* one + *korn* grain —
more at ONE, CORN] (circa 1901)
: a one-grained wheat (*Triticum monococcum*)
sometimes considered the most primitive
wheat and grown especially in poor soils in
central Europe — called also *einkorn wheat*
**ein·stei·ni·um** \īn-'stī-nē-əm\ *noun* [New
Latin, from Albert *Einstein*] (1955)
: a radioactive element produced artificially
— see ELEMENT table
**ei·re·nic** *chiefly British variant of* IRENIC
**eis·ege·sis** \,ī-sə-'jē-səs, 'ī-sə-,\ *noun, plural*
**-ege·ses** \-,sēz\ [Greek *eis* into (akin to
Greek *en* in) + English ex*egesis* — more at
IN] (1892)
: the interpretation of a text (as of the Bible)
by reading into it one's own ideas — compare EXEGESIS
**ei·stedd·fod** \ī-'steth-,vȯd, ā-\ *noun, plural*
**-fods** \-,vȯdz\ *or* **-fod·au** \-,steth-'vȯ-,dī\
[Welsh, literally, session, from *eistedd* to sit +
*bod* being] (1822)
: a usually Welsh competitive festival of the
arts especially in poetry and singing
— **ei·stedd·fod·ic** \,ī-,steth-'vȯ-dik, ,ā-\
*adjective*
**eis·wein** \'īs-,wīn, -,vīn\ *noun, often capitalized* [German, from *Eis* ice + *Wein* wine]
(1967)
: a sweet German wine made from grapes that
have frozen on the vine
¹**ei·ther** \'ē-thər *also* 'ī-\ *adjective* [Middle English, from Old English *æghwæther* both,
each, from *ā* always + *ge-*, collective prefix +
*hwæther* which of two, whether — more at
AYE, CO-] (before 12th century)
**1** : being the one and the other of two : EACH
⟨flowers blooming on *either* side of the walk⟩
**2** : being the one or the other of two ⟨take *either* road⟩ ■
²**either** *pronoun* (before 12th century)
: the one or the other
³**either** *conjunction* (before 12th century)
— used as a function word before two or
more coordinate words, phrases, or clauses
joined usually by *or* to indicate that what immediately follows is the first of two or more
alternatives

\ə\ abut  \ᵊ\ kitten  \ər\ further  \a\ ash  \ā\ ace
\ä\ mop, mar  \aú\ out  \ch\ chin  \e\ bet  \ē\ easy
\g\ go  \i\ hit  \ī\ ice  \j\ job  \ŋ\ sing  \ō\ go
\ȯ\ law  \ȯi\ boy  \th\ thin  \t̷h\ the  \ü\ loot  \ú\ foot
\y\ yet  \zh\ vision  *see also* Guide to Pronunciation

**⁴either** *adverb* (15th century)
**1** : LIKEWISE, MOREOVER — used for emphasis after a negative ⟨not smart or handsome *either*⟩
**2** : for that matter — used for emphasis after an alternative following a question or conditional clause especially where negation is implied ⟨who answers for the Irish parliament? or army *either*? —Robert Browning⟩
**¹ei·ther–or** \ˌē-thə-ˈrȯr *also* ˌī-\ *noun* (1922)
: an unavoidable choice or exclusive division between only two alternatives
**²either–or** *adjective* (1926)
: of or marked by either-or : BLACK-AND-WHITE
**¹ejac·u·late** \i-ˈja-kyə-ˌlāt\ *verb* **-lat·ed; -lat·ing** [Latin *ejaculatus*, past participle of *ejaculari* to throw out, from *e-* + *jaculari* to throw, from *jaculum* dart, from *jacere* to throw — more at JET] (1578)
*transitive verb*
**1** : to eject from a living body; *specifically* : to eject (semen) in orgasm
**2** : to utter suddenly and vehemently
*intransitive verb*
: to eject a fluid
— **ejac·u·la·tor** \-ˌlā-tər\ *noun*
**²ejac·u·late** \-lət\ *noun* (1927)
: the semen released by one ejaculation
**ejac·u·la·tion** \i-ˌja-kyə-ˈlā-shən\ *noun* (1603)
**1** : an act of ejaculating; *specifically* : a sudden discharging of a fluid from a duct
**2** : something ejaculated; *especially* : a short sudden emotional utterance
**ejac·u·la·to·ry** \i-ˈja-kyə-lə-ˌtōr-ē, -ˌtȯr-\ *adjective* (1644)
**1** : marked by or given to vocal ejaculation
**2** : casting or throwing out; *specifically* : associated with or concerned in physiological ejaculation ⟨*ejaculatory* vessels⟩
**ejaculatory duct** *noun* (1751)
: a duct through which semen is ejaculated; *specifically* : either of the paired ducts in the human male that are formed by the junction of the duct from the seminal vesicle with the vas deferens and that pass through the prostate to empty into the urethra by means of a small opening
**eject** \i-ˈjekt\ *transitive verb* [Middle English, from Latin *ejectus*, past participle of *eicere*, from *e-* + *jacere*] (15th century)
**1 a** : to drive out especially by physical force
**b** : to evict from property
**2** : to throw out or off from within ⟨*ejects* the empty cartridges⟩ ☆
— **eject·able** \-ˈjek-tə-bəl\ *adjective*
— **ejec·tion** \-ˈjek-shən\ *noun*
— **ejec·tive** \-ˈjek-tiv\ *adjective*
**ejec·ta** \i-ˈjek-tə\ *noun plural but singular or plural in construction* [New Latin, from Latin, neuter plural of *ejectus*] (1886)
: material thrown out (as from a volcano)
**ejection seat** *noun* (1945)
: an emergency escape seat for propelling an occupant out and away from an airplane
**eject·ment** \i-ˈjek(t)-mənt\ *noun* (1523)
**1** : the act or an instance of ejecting : DISPOSSESSION
**2** : an action for the recovery of possession of real property and damages and costs
**ejec·tor** \i-ˈjek-tər\ *noun* (1640)
**1** : one that ejects; *especially* : a mechanism of a firearm that ejects an empty cartridge
**2** : a jet pump for withdrawing a gas, fluid, or powdery substance from a space
**eka-** \ˌe-kə, ˌā-kə\ *combining form* [International Scientific Vocabulary, from Sanskrit *eka* one — more at ONE]
: standing or assumed to stand next in order beyond (a specified element) in the same family of the periodic table — in names of chemical elements especially when not yet discovered ⟨*eka*-lead is the hypothetical element 114⟩

**¹eke** \ˈēk\ *adverb* [Middle English, from Old English *ēac;* akin to Old High German *ouh* also, Latin *aut* or, Greek *au* again] (before 12th century)
*archaic* : ALSO
**²eke** *transitive verb* **eked; ek·ing** [Middle English, from Old English *īecan, ēcan;* akin to Old High German *ouhhōn* to add, Latin *augēre* to increase, Greek *auxein*] (before 12th century)
**1** *archaic* : INCREASE, LENGTHEN
**2** : to get with great difficulty — usually used with *out* ⟨*eke* out a living⟩
**eke out** *transitive verb* (1596)
**1** : to make up for the deficiencies of : SUPPLEMENT ⟨*eked out* his income by getting a second job⟩
**2** : to make (a supply) last by economy
**ekis·tics** \i-ˈkis-tiks\ *noun plural but singular in construction* [New Greek *oikistikē*, from feminine of *oikistikos* of settlement, from Greek, from *oikizein* to settle, colonize, from *oikos* house — more at VICINITY] (1958)
: a science dealing with human settlements and drawing on the research and experience of professionals in various fields (as architecture, engineering, city planning, and sociology)
— **ekis·tic** \-tik\ *adjective*
**Ek·man dredge** \ˈek-mən-\ *noun* [probably from V. W. *Ekman* (died 1954) Swedish oceanographer] (1948)
: a dredge that has opposable jaws operated by a messenger traveling down a cable to release a spring catch and that is used in ecology for sampling the bottom of a body of water
**ekue·le** \ā-ˈkwā-(ˌ)lā\ *also* **ek·pwe·le** \ek-ˈpwā-lā\ *noun, plural* **ekuele** *also* **ekpweles** [Fang (Bantu language of western equatorial Africa)] (circa 1973)
: the basic monetary unit of Equatorial Guinea 1975–85
**¹el** \ˈel\ *noun* (14th century)
: the letter *l*
**²el** *noun, often capitalized* (circa 1906)
: an urban railway that operates chiefly on an elevated structure; *also* : a train belonging to such a railway
**¹elab·o·rate** \i-ˈla-b(ə-)rət\ *adjective* [Latin *elaboratus*, from past participle of *elaborare* to work out, acquire by labor, from *e-* + *laborare* to work — more at LABORATORY] (1592)
**1** : planned or carried out with great care ⟨took *elaborate* precautions⟩
**2** : marked by complexity, fullness of detail, or ornateness ⟨*elaborate* prose⟩
— **elab·o·rate·ly** *adverb*
— **elab·o·rate·ness** *noun*
**²elab·o·rate** \i-ˈla-bə-ˌrāt\ *verb* **-rat·ed; -rat·ing** (1611)
*transitive verb*
**1** : to produce by labor
**2** : to build up (as complex organic compounds) from simple ingredients
**3** : to work out in detail : DEVELOP
*intransitive verb*
**1** : to become elaborate
**2** : to expand something in detail ⟨would you care to *elaborate* on that statement⟩
— **elab·o·ra·tion** \-ˌla-bə-ˈrā-shən\ *noun*
— **elab·o·ra·tive** \-ˈla-bə-ˌrā-tiv\ *adjective*
**Elaine** \i-ˈlān\ *noun*
: any of several women in Arthurian legend; *especially* : one who dies for unrequited love of Lancelot
**Elam·ite** \ˈē-lə-ˌmīt\ *noun* (1874)
: a language of unknown affinities used in Elam approximately from the 25th to the 4th centuries B.C.
**élan** \ā-ˈlä[n]\ *noun* [French, from Middle French *eslan* rush, from (*s'*)*eslancer* to rush, from *ex-* + *lancer* to hurl — more at LANCE] (1864)
: vigorous spirit or enthusiasm
**eland** \ˈē-lənd, -ˌland\ *noun, plural* **eland** *also* **elands** [Afrikaans, elk, from Dutch, from obsolete German *Elend*, probably from obsolete

Lithuanian *ellenis;* akin to Old High German *elaho* elk — more at ELK] (1600)
: either of two large African antelopes (*Tragelaphus oryx* and *T. derbianus*) bovine in form with short spirally twisted horns in both sexes

eland

**élan vi·tal** \ā-lä[n]-vē-tál\ *noun* [French] (1907)
: the vital force or impulse of life; *especially* : a creative principle held by Bergson to be immanent in all organisms and responsible for evolution
**el·a·pid** \ˈe-lə-pəd\ *noun* [New Latin *Elap-, Elaps*, genus of snakes, from Middle Greek, a fish, alteration of Greek *elops*] (1885)
: any of a family (Elapidae) of venomous snakes with grooved fangs
**¹elapse** \i-ˈlaps\ *intransitive verb* **elapsed; elaps·ing** [Latin *elapsus*, past participle of *elabi*, from *e-* + *labi* to slip — more at SLEEP] (1644)
: to slip or glide away : PASS ⟨four years *elapsed* before he returned⟩
**²elapse** *noun* (circa 1677)
: PASSAGE ⟨returned after an *elapse* of 15 years⟩
**elapsed time** *noun* (circa 1909)
: the actual time taken (as by a boat or automobile in traveling over a racecourse)
**elas·mo·branch** \i-ˈlaz-mə-ˌbraŋk\ *noun, plural* **-branchs** [ultimately from Greek *elasmos* metal plate (from *elaunein*) + *branchia* gills] (1872)
: any of a subclass (Elasmobranchii) of cartilaginous fishes that have five to seven lateral to ventral gill openings on each side and that comprise the sharks, rays, skates, and extinct related fishes
— **elasmobranch** *adjective*
**elas·tase** \i-ˈlas-ˌtās, -ˌtāz\ *noun* [*elastin* + *-ase*] (1949)
: an enzyme especially of pancreatic juice that digests elastin
**¹elas·tic** \i-ˈlas-tik\ *adjective* [New Latin *elasticus*, from Late Greek *elastos* ductile, beaten, from Greek *elaunein* to drive, beat out; probably akin to Greek *ēlythe* he went, Old Irish *luid*] (1674)
**1 a** *of a solid* : capable of recovering size and shape after deformation **b** : being a collision between particles in which the total kinetic energy of the particles remains unchanged
**2** : capable of recovering quickly especially from depression or disappointment
**3** : capable of being easily stretched or expanded and resuming former shape : FLEXIBLE
**4 a** : capable of ready change or easy expansion or contraction : not rigid or constricted **b** : receptive to new ideas : ADAPTABLE ☆
— **elas·ti·cal·ly** \-ti-k(ə-)lē\ *adverb*

☆ SYNONYMS
**Eject, expel, oust, evict** mean to drive or force out. EJECT carries an especially strong implication of throwing or thrusting out from within as a physical action ⟨*ejected* an obnoxious patron from the bar⟩. EXPEL stresses a thrusting out or driving away especially permanently which need not be physical ⟨a student *expelled* from college⟩. OUST implies removal or dispossession by power of the law or by force or compulsion ⟨got the sheriff to *oust* the squatters⟩. EVICT chiefly applies to turning out of house and home ⟨*evicted* for nonpayment of rent⟩.

**²elastic** *noun* (1847)
**1 a :** easily stretched rubber usually prepared in cords, strings, or bands **b :** RUBBER BAND
**2 a :** an elastic fabric usually made of yarns containing rubber **b :** something made from this fabric

**elastic fiber** *noun* (1849)
**:** a thick very elastic smooth yellowish anastomosing fiber of connective tissue that contains elastin

**elas·tic·i·ty** \i-ˌlas-'ti-sə-tē, ˌē-ˌlas-, -'tis-tē\ *noun, plural* **-ties** (1664)
**:** the quality or state of being elastic: as **a :** the capability of a strained body to recover its size and shape after deformation **:** SPRINGINESS **b :** RESILIENCE 2 **c :** the quality of being adaptable

**elas·ti·cized** \i-'las-tə-ˌsīzd\ *adjective* (circa 1909)
**:** made with elastic thread or inserts

**elastic limit** *noun* (1898)
**:** the greatest stress that an elastic solid can sustain without undergoing permanent deformation

**elastic modulus** *noun* (1904)
**:** the ratio of the stress in a body to the corresponding strain

**elastic scattering** *noun* (1933)
**:** a scattering of particles as the result of an elastic collision

**elas·tin** \i-'las-tən\ *noun* [International Scientific Vocabulary, from New Latin *elasticus*] (1875)
**:** a protein that is similar to collagen and is the chief constituent of elastic fibers

**elas·to·mer** \-tə-mər\ *noun* [*elas*tic + *-o-* + *-mer*] (circa 1939)
**:** any of various elastic substances resembling rubber ⟨polyvinyl *elastomers*⟩
— **elas·to·mer·ic** \i-ˌlas-tə-'mer-ik\ *adjective*

**¹elate** \i-'lāt\ *transitive verb* **elat·ed; elat·ing** [Latin *elatus* (past participle of *efferre* to carry out, elevate), from e- + *latus*, past participle of *ferre* to carry — more at TOLERATE, BEAR] (circa 1619)
**:** to fill with joy or pride

**²elate** *adjective* (1647)
**:** ELATED

**elat·ed** *adjective* (circa 1619)
**:** marked by high spirits **:** EXULTANT
— **elat·ed·ly** *adverb*
— **elat·ed·ness** *noun*

**el·a·ter** \'e-lə-tər\ *noun* [New Latin, from Greek *elatēr* driver, from *elaunein* to drive] (1830)
**:** a plant structure functioning in the distribution of spores: as **a :** one of the elongated filaments among the spores in the capsule of a liverwort **b :** one of the filamentous appendages of the spores in the scouring rushes

**elat·er·ite** \i-'la-tə-ˌrīt\ *noun* [German *Elaterit*, from Greek *elatēr*] (1826)
**:** a dark brown elastic mineral resin occurring in soft flexible masses

**ela·tion** \i-'lā-shən\ *noun* (14th century)
**1 :** the quality or state of being elated
**2 :** pathological euphoria

**E layer** *noun* (1933)
**:** a layer of the ionosphere occurring about 65 miles (110 kilometers) above the earth's surface during daylight hours that is capable of reflecting shortwave frequencies

**El·ba** \'el-bə\ *noun* [Elba (Mediterranean island), residence of Napoléon Bonaparte after his first abdication May 14, 1814 to Feb. 26, 1815] (1924)
**:** a place or state of exile

**¹el·bow** \'el-ˌbō\ *noun* [Middle English *elbowe*, from Old English *elboga*, from el- (akin to *eln* ell) + Old English *boga* bow — more at ELL, BOW] (before 12th century)
**1 a :** the joint of the human arm **b :** a corresponding joint in the anterior limb of a lower vertebrate

**2 :** something (as macaroni or an angular pipe fitting) resembling an elbow
— **at one's elbow :** at one's side
— **out at elbows** *or* **out at the elbows**
**1 :** shabbily dressed **2 :** short of funds

**²elbow** (1605)
*transitive verb*
**1 a :** to push with the elbow **:** JOSTLE **b :** to shove aside by pushing with or as if with the elbow
**2 :** to force (as one's way) by pushing with or as if with the elbow ⟨*elbowing* our way through the crowd⟩ ⟨*elbows* her way into the best social circles⟩
*intransitive verb*
**1 :** to advance by pushing with the elbow
**2 :** to make an angle **:** TURN

**elbow grease** *noun* (1672)
**:** vigorously applied physical labor **:** hard work

**el·bow·room** \'el-ˌbō-ˌrüm, -ˌrùm\ *noun* (circa 1540)
**1 a :** room for moving the elbows freely **b :** adequate space for work or operation ⟨the large house gives plenty of *elbowroom*⟩
**2 :** free scope ⟨*elbowroom* to try new ideas⟩

**el cheapo** \(ˌ)el-'chē-(ˌ)pō, 'el-\ *adjective* [Spanish *el* the + English *cheap* + Spanish *-o* (masculine noun ending)] (1969)
**:** CHEAP 3a, b

**eld** \'eld\ *noun* [Middle English, from Old English *ieldo*; akin to Old English *eald* old — more at OLD] (before 12th century)
**1 :** old age
**2** *archaic* **:** old times **:** ANTIQUITY

**¹el·der** \'el-dər\ *noun* [Middle English *eldre*, from Old English *ellærn*; perhaps akin to Old English *alor* alder — more at ALDER] (before 12th century)
**:** ELDERBERRY 2

**²elder** *adjective* [Middle English, from Old English *ieldra*, comparative of *eald* old] (before 12th century)
**1 :** of earlier birth or greater age ⟨his *elder* brother⟩
**2 :** of or relating to earlier times **:** FORMER
**3** *obsolete* **:** of or relating to a more advanced time of life
**4 :** prior or superior in rank, office, or validity

**³elder** *noun* (before 12th century)
**1 :** one living in an earlier period
**2 a :** one who is older **:** SENIOR ⟨a child trying to please her *elders*⟩ **b :** an aged person
**3 :** one having authority by virtue of age and experience ⟨the village *elders*⟩
**4 :** any of various officers of religious groups: as **a :** PRESBYTER 1 **b :** a permanent officer elected by a Presbyterian congregation and ordained to serve on the session and assist the pastor at communion **c :** MINISTER 2 **d :** a leader of the Shakers **e :** a Mormon ordained to the Melchizedek priesthood
— **el·der·ship** \-ˌship\ *noun*

**el·der·ber·ry** \'el-də(r)-ˌber-ē\ *noun* (1589)
**1 :** the edible black or red berrylike drupe of any of a genus (*Sambucus*) of shrubs or trees of the honeysuckle family bearing flat clusters of small white or pink flowers
**2 :** a tree or shrub bearing elderberries

**¹el·der·ly** \'el-dər-lē\ *adjective* (1611)
**1 a :** rather old; *especially* **:** being past middle age **b :** OLD-FASHIONED
**2 :** of, relating to, or characteristic of later life or elderly persons
— **el·der·li·ness** *noun*

**²elderly** *noun, plural* **-ly** *or* **-lies** (1865)
**:** an elderly person

**elder statesman** *noun* (1904)
**:** an eminent senior member of a group or organization; *especially* **:** a retired statesman who unofficially advises current leaders

**el·dest** \'el-dəst\ *adjective* (before 12th century)
**:** of the greatest age or seniority **:** OLDEST

**eldest hand** *noun* (1599)

**:** the card player who first receives cards in the deal

**El Do·ra·do** \ˌel-də-'rä-(ˌ)dō, -'rā-\ *noun* [Spanish, literally, the gilded one]
**1 :** a city or country of fabulous riches held by 16th century explorers to exist in South America
**2 :** a place of fabulous wealth or opportunity

**el·dress** \'el-drəs\ *noun* (1640)
**:** a woman elder especially of the Shakers

**el·dritch** \'el-drich\ *adjective* [perhaps from (assumed) Middle English *elfriche* fairyland, from Middle English *elf* + *riche* kingdom, from Old English *rīce* — more at RICH] (1508)
**:** WEIRD, EERIE

**El·e·at·ic** \ˌel-ē-'a-tik\ *adjective* [Latin *Eleaticus*, from Greek *Eleatikos*, from *Elea* (Velia), ancient town in southern Italy] (1695)
**:** of or relating to a school of Greek philosophers founded by Parmenides and developed by Zeno and marked by belief in the unity of being and the unreality of motion or change
— **Eleatic** *noun*
— **El·e·at·i·cism** \-'a-tə-ˌsi-zəm\ *noun*

**ele·cam·pane** \ˌe-li-ˌkam-'pān\ *noun* [Middle English *elena campana*, from Medieval Latin *enula campana*, literally, field elecampane, from *inula, enula* elecampane + *campana* of the field] (14th century)
**:** a large coarse European composite herb (*Inula helenium*) that has yellow ray flowers and is naturalized in the U.S.

**¹elect** \i-'lekt\ *adjective* [Middle English, from Latin *electus*, past participle of *eligere* to select, from e- + *legere* to choose — more at LEGEND] (15th century)
**1 :** carefully selected **:** CHOSEN
**2 :** chosen for salvation through divine mercy
**3 a :** chosen for office or position but not yet installed ⟨the president-*elect*⟩ **b :** chosen for marriage at some future time ⟨the bride-*elect*⟩

**²elect** *noun, plural* **elect** (15th century)
**1 :** one chosen or set apart (as by divine favor)
**2** *plural* **:** a select or exclusive group of people

**³elect** *verb* [Middle English, from Latin *electus*] (15th century)
*transitive verb*
**1 :** to select by vote for an office, position, or membership ⟨*elected* her class president⟩
**2 :** to make a selection of ⟨will *elect* an academic program⟩
**3 :** to choose (as a course of action) especially by preference ⟨might *elect* to sell the business⟩
*intransitive verb*
**:** to make a selection

**elect·able** \i-'lek-tə-bəl\ *adjective* (1879)
**:** capable of being elected (as to public office)

---

☆ **SYNONYMS**
**Elastic, resilient, springy, flexible, supple** mean able to endure strain without being permanently injured. ELASTIC implies the property of resisting deformation by stretching ⟨an *elastic* waistband⟩. RESILIENT implies the ability to recover shape quickly when the deforming force or pressure is removed ⟨a *resilient* innersole⟩. SPRINGY stresses both the ease with which something yields to pressure and the quickness of its return to original shape ⟨the cake is done when the top is *springy*⟩. FLEXIBLE applies to something which may or may not be resilient or elastic but which can be bent or folded without breaking ⟨*flexible* plastic tubing⟩. SUPPLE applies to something that can be readily bent, twisted, or folded without any sign of injury ⟨*supple* leather⟩.

---

\ə\ abut \°\ kitten \ər\ **further** \a\ ash \ā\ ace
\ä\ mop, mar \aù\ out \ch\ chin \e\ bet \ē\ easy
\g\ go \i\ hit \ī\ ice \j\ job \ŋ\ sing \ō\ go
\ò\ law \òi\ boy \th\ thin \t̲h̲\ the \ü\ loot \ù\ foot
\y\ yet \zh\ vision      *see also* Guide to Pronunciation

— **elect·abil·i·ty** \-ˌlek-tə-'bi-lə-tē\ *noun*
**elec·tion** \i-'lek-shən\ *noun* (13th century)
**1 a :** an act or process of electing **b :** the fact of being elected
**2 :** predestination to eternal life
**3 :** the right, power, or privilege of making a choice
**Election Day** *noun* (15th century)
**:** a day legally established for the election of public officials; *especially* **:** the first Tuesday after the first Monday in November in an even year designated for national elections in the U.S. and observed as a legal holiday in many states
**elec·tion·eer** \i-ˌlek-shə-'nir\ *intransitive verb* [*election* + *-eer* (as in *privateer,* verb)] (1789)
**:** to take an active part in an election; *specifically* **:** to work for the election of a candidate or party
— **elec·tion·eer·er** *noun*
¹**elec·tive** \i-'lek-tiv\ *adjective* (1531)
**1 a :** chosen or filled by popular election ⟨an *elective* official⟩ **b :** of or relating to election **c :** based on the right or principle of election ⟨the presidency is an *elective* office⟩
**2 a :** permitting a choice **:** OPTIONAL ⟨an *elective* course in school⟩ **b :** beneficial to the patient but not essential for survival ⟨*elective* surgery⟩
**3 a :** tending to operate on one substance rather than another ⟨*elective* absorption⟩ **b :** favorably inclined to one more than to another **:** SYMPATHETIC ⟨an *elective* affinity⟩
— **elec·tive·ly** *adverb*
— **elec·tive·ness** *noun*
²**elective** *noun* (1850)
**:** an elective course or subject
**elec·tor** \i-'lek-tər, -ˌtòr\ *noun* (15th century)
**1 :** one qualified to vote in an election
**2 :** one entitled to participate in an election: as
**a :** any of the German princes entitled to take part in choosing the Holy Roman Emperor
**b :** a member of the electoral college in the U.S.
**elec·tor·al** \i-'lek-t(ə-)rəl, ˌē-lek-'tòr-əl\ *adjective* (1675)
**1 :** of or relating to an elector ⟨the *electoral* vote⟩
**2 :** of or relating to election ⟨an *electoral* system⟩
— **elec·tor·al·ly** \-t(ə-)rə-lē, -'tòr-ə-lē\ *adverb*
**electoral college** *noun* (circa 1691)
**:** a body of electors; *especially* **:** one that elects the president and vice president of the U.S.
**elec·tor·ate** \i-'lek-t(ə-)rət\ *noun* (1675)
**1 :** the territory, jurisdiction, or dignity of a German elector
**2 :** a body of people entitled to vote
**electr-** *or* **electro-** *combining form* [New Latin *electricus*]
**1 a :** electricity ⟨*electro*meter⟩ **b :** electric ⟨*electro*de⟩ **:** electric and ⟨*electro*chemical⟩ **:** electrically ⟨*electro*positive⟩
**2 :** electrolytic ⟨*electro*analysis⟩
**3 :** electron ⟨*electro*philic⟩
**Elec·tra** \i-'lek-trə\ *noun* [Latin, from Greek *Ēlektra*]
**:** a sister of Orestes who aids him in killing their mother Clytemnestra
**Electra complex** *noun* (1913)
**:** the Oedipus complex when it occurs in a female
**elec·tress** \i-'lek-trəs\ *noun* (1618)
**:** the wife or widow of a German elector
**elec·tret** \i-'lek-trət, -ˌtret\ *noun* [*electricity* + *magnet*] (1885)
**:** a dielectric body in which a permanent state of electric polarization has been set up
¹**elec·tric** \i-'lek-trik, ē-\ *adjective* [New Latin *electricus* produced from amber by friction, electric, from Medieval Latin, of amber, from Latin *electrum* amber, electrum, from Greek *ēlektron;* akin to Greek *ēlektōr* beaming sun] (1675)

**1** *or* **elec·tri·cal** \-tri-kəl\ **:** of, relating to, or operated by electricity
**2 :** exciting as if by electric shock ⟨an *electric* performance⟩ ⟨an *electric* personality⟩; *also* **:** charged with strong emotion ⟨the room was *electric* with tension⟩
**3 a :** ELECTRONIC 3a **b :** amplifying sound by electronic means — used of a musical instrument ⟨an *electric* guitar⟩
**4 :** very bright ⟨*electric* blue⟩ ⟨*electric* orange⟩
— **elec·tri·cal·ly** \-tri-k(ə-)lē\ *adverb*
²**electric** *noun* (1646)
**1** *archaic* **:** a nonconductor of electricity used to excite or accumulate electricity
**2 :** something (as a light, automobile, or train) operated by electricity
**electrical storm** *noun* (1941)
**:** THUNDERSTORM — called also *electric storm*
**electric chair** *noun* (1889)
**1 :** a chair used in legal electrocution
**2 :** the penalty of death by electrocution
**electric eel** *noun* (1794)
**:** a large eel-shaped fish (*Electrophorus electricus*) of the Orinoco and Amazon basins that is capable of giving a severe shock with its electric organs
**electric eye** *noun* (1898)
**:** PHOTOELECTRIC CELL
**electric field** *noun* (circa 1889)
**:** a region associated with a distribution of electric charge or a varying magnetic field in which forces due to that charge or field act upon other electric charges
**elec·tri·cian** \i-ˌlek-'tri-shən, ē-ˌ\ *noun* (1869)
**:** one who installs, maintains, operates, or repairs electrical equipment
**elec·tric·i·ty** \i-ˌlek-'tri-sə-tē, ē-ˌ, -'tris-tē\ *noun, plural* **-ties** (1646)
**1 a :** a fundamental entity of nature consisting of negative and positive kinds, observable in the attractions and repulsions of bodies electrified by friction and in natural phenomena (as lightning or the aurora borealis), and usually utilized in the form of electric currents **b :** electric current or power
**2 :** a science that deals with the phenomena and laws of electricity
**3 :** keen contagious excitement
**electric organ** *noun* (1773)
**:** a specialized tract of tissue (as in the electric eel) in which electricity is generated
**electric ray** *noun* (1774)
**:** any of various round-bodied short-tailed rays (family Torpedinidae) of warm seas with a pair of electric organs
**elec·tri·fi·ca·tion** \i-ˌlek-trə-fə-'kā-shən, ē-ˌ\ *noun* (1748)
**1 :** an act or process of electrifying
**2 :** the state of being electrified
**elec·tri·fy** \i-'lek-trə-ˌfī, ē-'\ *transitive verb* **-fied; -fy·ing** (1745)
**1 a :** to charge with electricity **b** (1) **:** to equip for use of electric power (2) **:** to supply with electric power (3) **:** to amplify (music) electronically
**2 :** to excite intensely or suddenly as if by electric shock
**elec·tro·acous·tics** \i-ˌlek-trō-ə-'küs-tiks\ *noun plural but singular in construction* (1927)
**:** a science that deals with the transformation of acoustic energy into electric energy or vice versa
— **elec·tro·acous·tic** \-tik\ *adjective*
**elec·tro·anal·y·sis** \-ə-'na-lə-səs\ *noun* (1903)
**:** chemical analysis by electrolytic methods
— **elec·tro·an·a·lyt·i·cal** \-'lit-i-kəl\ *adjective*
**elec·tro·car·dio·gram** \-'kär-dē-ə-ˌgram\ *noun* (circa 1904)
**:** the tracing made by an electrocardiograph
**elec·tro·car·dio·graph** \-ˌgraf\ *noun* (1913)
**:** an instrument for recording the changes of electrical potential occurring during the heart-

beat used especially in diagnosing abnormalities of heart action
— **elec·tro·car·dio·graph·ic** \-ˌkär-dē-ə-'gra-fik\ *adjective*
— **elec·tro·car·dio·graph·i·cal·ly** \-fi-k(ə-)lē\ *adverb*
— **elec·tro·car·di·og·ra·phy** \-dē-'ä-grə-fē\ *noun*
**elec·tro·chem·is·try** \-'ke-mə-strē\ *noun* (1814)
**:** a science that deals with the relation of electricity to chemical changes and with the interconversion of chemical and electrical energy
— **elec·tro·chem·i·cal** \-'ke-mi-kəl\ *adjective*
— **elec·tro·chem·i·cal·ly** \-k(ə-)lē\ *adverb*
**elec·tro·con·vul·sive** \i-ˌlek-trō-kən-'vəl-siv\ *adjective* (1947)
**:** of, relating to, or involving convulsive response to electroshock ⟨*electroconvulsive* shocks⟩
**electroconvulsive therapy** *noun* (1948)
**:** ELECTROSHOCK THERAPY
**elec·tro·cor·ti·co·gram** \i-ˌlek-trō-'kòr-ti-kə-ˌgram\ *noun* (1939)
**:** an electroencephalogram made with the electrodes in direct contact with the brain
**elec·tro·cute** \i-'lek-trə-ˌkyüt\ *transitive verb* **-cut·ed; -cut·ing** [*electr-* + *-cute* (as in *execute*)] (1889)
**1 :** to execute (a criminal) by electricity
**2 :** to kill by electric shock
— **elec·tro·cu·tion** \-ˌlek-trə-'kyü-shən\ *noun*
**elec·trode** \i-'lek-ˌtrōd\ *noun* (1834)
**1 :** a conductor used to establish electrical contact with a nonmetallic part of a circuit
**2 :** an element in a semiconductor device (as a transistor) that emits or collects electrons or holes or controls their movements
¹**elec·tro·de·pos·it** \i-ˌlek-trō-di-'pä-zət\ *noun* (1864)
**:** a deposit formed in or at an electrode by electrolysis
²**electrodeposit** *transitive verb* (1882)
**:** to deposit (as a metal or rubber) by electrolysis
— **elec·tro·de·po·si·tion** \-ˌde-pə-'zi-shən, -ˌdē-pə-\ *noun*
**elec·tro·der·mal** \i-ˌlek-trō-'dər-məl\ *adjective* (1946)
**:** of or relating to electrical activity in or electrical properties of the skin
**elec·tro·des·ic·ca·tion** \i-ˌlek-trō-ˌde-si-'kā-shən\ *noun* (1919)
**:** the drying up of tissue by a high-frequency electric current applied with a needle-shaped electrode — called also *fulguration*
**elec·tro·di·al·y·sis** \i-ˌlek-trō-dī-'a-lə-səs\ *noun* (1921)
**:** dialysis accelerated by an electromotive force applied to electrodes adjacent to the membranes
— **elec·tro·di·a·lyt·ic** \-ˌdī-ə-'li-tik\ *adjective*
**elec·tro·dy·nam·ics** \-dī-'na-miks\ *noun plural but singular in construction* (1827)
**:** a branch of physics that deals with the effects arising from the interactions of electric currents with magnets, with other currents, or with themselves
— **elec·tro·dy·nam·ic** \-mik\ *adjective*
**elec·tro·dy·na·mom·e·ter** \-ˌdī-nə-'mä-mə-tər\ *noun* [International Scientific Vocabulary] (1876)
**:** an instrument that measures current by indicating the strength of the forces between a current flowing in fixed coils and one flowing in movable coils
**elec·tro·en·ceph·a·lo·gram** \-in-'se-f(ə-)lə-ˌgram\ *noun* [International Scientific Vocabulary] (1934)
**:** the tracing of brain waves made by an electroencephalograph

**elec·tro·en·ceph·a·lo·graph** \-ˌgraf\ *noun* [International Scientific Vocabulary] (1936) : an apparatus for detecting and recording brain waves
— **elec·tro·en·ceph·a·log·ra·pher** \-ˌse-fə-ˈlä-grə-fər\ *noun*
— **elec·tro·en·ceph·a·lo·graph·ic** \-ˌse-f(ə-)lə-ˈgra-fik\ *adjective*
— **elec·tro·en·ceph·a·lo·graph·i·cal·ly** \-fi-k(ə-)lē\ *adverb*
— **elec·tro·en·ceph·a·log·ra·phy** \-ˈlä-grə-fē\ *noun*

**elec·tro·fish·ing** \i-ˈlek-trō-ˌfi-shiŋ\ *noun* (1950) : the taking of fish by a system based on their tendency to respond positively to a source of direct electric current

**elec·tro·form** \i-ˈlek-trə-ˌfòrm\ *transitive verb* (1931) : to form (shaped articles) by electrodeposition on a mold
— **electroform** *noun*

**elec·tro·gen·ic** \i-ˌlek-trə-ˈje-nik\ *adjective* (circa 1891) : of or relating to the production of electrical activity in living tissue ⟨an *electrogenic* pump⟩
— **elec·tro·gen·e·sis** \-ˈje-nə-sis\ *noun*

**elec·tro·gram** \i-ˈlek-trə-ˌgram\ *noun* (circa 1935) : a tracing of the electrical potentials of a tissue (as the brain or heart) made by means of electrodes placed directly in the tissue instead of on the surface of the body

**elec·tro·hy·drau·lic** \i-ˌlek-trō-hī-ˈdrò-lik, -ˈdrä-\ *adjective* (1922) **1** : of or relating to a combination of electric and hydraulic mechanisms **2** : involving or produced by the action of very brief but powerful pulse discharges of electricity under a liquid resulting in the generation of shock waves and highly reactive chemical species ⟨an *electrohydraulic* effect⟩

**elec·tro·jet** \i-ˈlek-trə-ˌjet\ *noun* (1955) : an overhead concentration of electric current found in the regions of strong auroral displays and along the magnetic equator

**elec·tro·ki·net·ic** \i-ˌlek-trō-kə-ˈne-tik, -kī-\ *adjective* (1881) : of or relating to the motion of particles or liquids that results from or produces a difference of electric potential

**elec·tro·ki·net·ics** \-tiks\ *noun plural but singular in construction* (circa 1925) : a branch of physics dealing with the motion of electric currents or charged particles

**elec·tro·less** \i-ˈlek-ˌtrō-ləs, -trə-\ *adjective* (1947) : being or involving chemical deposition of metal instead of electrodeposition

**elec·trol·o·gist** \i-ˌlek-ˈträ-lə-jist\ *noun* [blend of *electrolysis* and *-logist* (from *-logy* + *-ist*)] (circa 1902) : one that removes hair, warts, moles, and birthmarks by means of an electric current applied to the body with a needle-shaped electrode
— **elec·trol·o·gy** \-lə-jē\ *noun*

**elec·tro·lu·mi·nes·cent** \i-ˌlek-trō-ˌlü-mə-ˈne-sᵊnt\ *adjective* (circa 1909) : of or relating to luminescence resulting from a high-frequency discharge through a gas or from application of an alternating current to a layer of phosphor
— **elec·tro·lu·mi·nes·cence** \-sᵊn(t)s\ *noun*

**elec·trol·y·sis** \i-ˌlek-ˈträ-lə-səs\ *noun* (1834) **1 a** : the producing of chemical changes by passage of an electric current through an electrolyte **b** : subjection to this action **2** : the destruction of hair roots with an electric current

**elec·tro·lyte** \i-ˈlek-trə-ˌlīt\ *noun* (1834) **1** : a nonmetallic electric conductor in which current is carried by the movement of ions

**2** : a substance that when dissolved in a suitable solvent or when fused becomes an ionic conductor

**elec·tro·lyt·ic** \i-ˌlek-trə-ˈli-tik\ *adjective* (1842) : of or relating to electrolysis or an electrolyte; *also* : involving, produced by, or used in electrolysis ⟨*electrolytic* cell⟩
— **elec·tro·lyt·i·cal·ly** \-ti-k(ə-)lē\ *adverb*

**elec·tro·lyze** \i-ˈlek-trə-ˌlīz\ *transitive verb* **-lyzed; -lyz·ing** (1834) : to subject to electrolysis

**elec·tro·mag·net** \i-ˌlek-trō-ˈmag-nət\ *noun* (1831) : a core of magnetic material surrounded by a coil of wire through which an electric current is passed to magnetize the core

**elec·tro·mag·net·ic** \-mag-ˈne-tik\ *adjective* (1821) : of, relating to, or produced by electromagnetism
— **elec·tro·mag·net·i·cal·ly** \-ti-k(ə-)lē\ *adverb*

**electromagnetic pulse** *noun* (1981) : high-intensity electromagnetic radiation generated by a nuclear blast high above the earth's surface and held to disrupt electronic and electrical systems

**electromagnetic radiation** *noun* (1939) : a series of electromagnetic waves

**electromagnetic spectrum** *noun* (circa 1934) : the entire range of wavelengths or frequencies of electromagnetic radiation extending from gamma rays to the longest radio waves and including visible light

**electromagnetic unit** *noun* (circa 1889) : any of a system of electrical units based primarily on the magnetic properties of electrical currents

**electromagnetic wave** *noun* (1908) : one of the waves that are propagated by simultaneous periodic variations of electric and magnetic field intensity and that include radio waves, infrared, visible light, ultraviolet, X rays, and gamma rays

**elec·tro·mag·ne·tism** \i-ˌlek-trō-ˈmag-nə-ˌti-zəm\ *noun* (1828) **1** : magnetism developed by a current of electricity **2 a** : a fundamental physical force that is responsible for interactions between charged particles which occur because of their charge and for the emission and absorption of photons, that is about 100 times weaker than the strong force, and that extends over infinite distances but is dominant over atomic and molecular distances — called also *electromagnetic force*; compare GRAVITY 3a(2), STRONG FORCE, WEAK FORCE **b** : a branch of physical science that deals with the physical relations between electricity and magnetism

**elec·tro·me·chan·i·cal** \-mə-ˈka-ni-kəl\ *adjective* (1888) : of, relating to, or being a mechanical process or device actuated or controlled electrically; *especially* : being a transducer for converting electrical energy to mechanical energy
— **elec·tro·me·chan·i·cal·ly** \-k(ə-)lē\ *adverb*

**elec·tro·met·al·lur·gy** \-ˈme-tᵊl-ˌər-jē, *especially British* -mə-ˈta-lər-\ *noun* (1840) : a branch of metallurgy that deals with the application of electric current either for electrolytic deposition or as a source of heat

**elec·trom·e·ter** \i-ˌlek-ˈträ-mə-tər\ *noun* (1749) : any of various instruments for detecting or measuring electric-potential differences or ionizing radiations by means of the forces of attraction or repulsion between charged bodies

**elec·tro·mo·tive force** \i-ˌlek-trō-ˌmō-tiv-, -trə-\ *noun* (1827) : something that moves or tends to move electricity : the potential difference derived from

an electrical source per unit quantity of electricity passing through the source (as a cell or generator)

**elec·tro·myo·gram** \i-ˌlek-trō-ˈmī-ə-ˌgram\ *noun* (1917) : a tracing made with an electromyograph

**elec·tro·myo·graph** \-ˌgraf\ *noun* [*electr-* + *my-* + *-graph*] (1948) : an instrument that converts the electrical activity associated with functioning skeletal muscle into a visual record or into sound and used to diagnose neuromuscular disorders and in biofeedback training
— **elec·tro·myo·graph·ic** \-ˌmī-ə-ˈgra-fik\ *adjective*
— **elec·tro·myo·graph·i·cal·ly** \-fi-k(ə-)lē\ *adverb*
— **elec·tro·my·og·ra·phy** \-mī-ˈä-grə-fē\ *noun*

**elec·tron** \i-ˈlek-ˌträn\ *noun* [*electr-* + ²*-on*] (1891) : an elementary particle consisting of a charge of negative electricity equal to about $1.602 \times 10^{-19}$ coulomb and having a mass when at rest of about $9.109534 \times 10^{-28}$ gram or about $1/1836$ that of a proton

**electron cloud** *noun* (1926) : the system of electrons surrounding the nucleus of an atom

**elec·tro·neg·a·tive** \i-ˌlek-trō-ˈne-gə-tiv\ *adjective* (1834) : having a tendency to attract electrons
— **elec·tro·neg·a·tiv·i·ty** \-ˌne-gə-ˈti-və-tē\ *noun*

**electron gas** *noun* (circa 1929) : a population of free electrons in a vacuum or in a metallic conductor

**electron gun** *noun* (1924) : an electron-emitting cathode and its surrounding assembly (as in a cathode-ray tube) for directing, controlling, and focusing a beam of electrons

**elec·tron·ic** \i-ˌlek-ˈträ-nik\ *adjective* (1902) **1** : of or relating to electrons **2** : of, relating to, or utilizing devices constructed or working by the methods or principles of electronics; *also* : implemented on or by means of a computer ⟨*electronic* food stamps⟩ ⟨*electronic* banking⟩ **3 a** : generating musical tones by electronic means ⟨an *electronic* organ⟩ **b** : of, relating to, or being music that consists of sounds electronically generated or modified **4** : of, relating to, or being a medium (as television) by which information is transmitted electronically ⟨*electronic* journalism⟩
— **elec·tron·i·cal·ly** \-ni-k(ə-)lē\ *adverb*

**electronic countermeasure** *noun* (1962) : the disruption of the operation of an enemy's equipment (as by jamming radio or radar signals)

**electronic mail** *noun* (1977) : messages sent and received electronically (as between terminals linked by telephone lines or microwave relays)

**electronic publishing** *noun* (1980) : publishing in which information is distributed by means of a computer network or is produced in a format for use with a computer

**elec·tron·ics** \i-ˌlek-ˈträ-niks\ *noun plural* (1910) **1** *singular in construction* : a branch of physics that deals with the emission, behavior, and effects of electrons (as in electron tubes and transistors) and with electronic devices **2** : electronic devices or equipment

**electron lens** *noun* (1931) : a device for focusing a beam of electrons by means of an electric or a magnetic field

**electron micrograph** *noun* (1934)

**:** a micrograph made with an electron microscope

— **electron micrography** \-mī-'krä-grə-fē\ *noun*

**electron microscope** *noun* (1932)
**:** an electron-optical instrument in which a beam of electrons focused by means of an electron lens is used to produce an enlarged image of a minute object on a fluorescent screen or photographic plate
— **electron microscopist** *noun*
— **electron microscopy** *noun*

**electron multiplier** *noun* (1936)
**:** a device utilizing secondary emission of electrons for amplifying a current of electrons

**electron optics** *noun plural but singular in construction* (1916)
**:** a branch of physics in which the principles of optics are applied to beams of electrons
— **elec·tron–op·ti·cal** \i-,lek-,trän-'äp-ti-kəl\ *adjective*

**electron probe** *noun* (1962)
**:** a microprobe that uses an electron beam to induce X-ray emissions in a sample

**electron transport** *noun* (1951)
**:** the sequential transfer of electrons especially by cytochromes in cellular respiration from an oxidizable substrate to molecular oxygen by a series of oxidation-reduction reactions

**electron tube** *noun* (1922)
**:** an electronic device in which conduction by electrons takes place through a vacuum or a gaseous medium within a sealed glass or metal container and which has various uses based on the controlled flow of electrons

**electron volt** *noun* (1930)
**:** a unit of energy equal to the energy gained by an electron in passing from a point of low potential to a point one volt higher in potential
**:** $1.60 \times 10^{-19}$ joule

**elec·tro·oc·u·lo·gram** \i-,lek-trō-'ä-kyə-lə-,gram\ *noun* [*electr-* + Latin *oculus* eye + English *-gram* — more at EYE] (1947)
**:** a record of the standing voltage between the front and back of the eye that is correlated with eyeball movement (as in REM sleep) and obtained by electrodes placed on the skin near the eye

**elec·tro·oc·u·log·ra·phy** \-,ä-kyə-'lä-grə-fē\ *noun, plural* **-phies** (1951)
**:** the preparation and study of electrooculograms

**elec·tro–op·ti·cal** \i-,lek-trō-'äp-ti-kəl\ *or* **elec·tro–op·tic** \-'äp-tik\ *adjective* (1879)
**1 :** of or relating to electro-optics
**2 a :** relating to or being a change in the refractive index of a material due to an electric field ⟨*electro-optical* effect⟩ **b :** using or being a material that exhibits electro-optical properties ⟨an *electro-optical* crystal⟩
**3 :** relating to or being an electronic device for emitting, modulating, transmitting, or sensing light
— **elec·tro–op·ti·cal·ly** \-k(ə-)lē\ *adverb*

**elec·tro–op·tics** \-trō-'äp-tiks\ *noun plural* (circa 1889)
**1** *singular in construction* **:** a branch of physics that deals with the effects of an electric field on light traversing it
**2 :** electro-optical devices

**elec·tro·os·mo·sis** \i-,lek-trō-äz-'mō-səs, -äs-\ *noun* (1906)
**:** the movement of a liquid out of or through a porous material or a biological membrane under the influence of an electric field
— **elec·tro·os·mot·ic** \-'mä-tik\ *adjective*

**elec·tro·phe·ro·gram** \-trə-'fir-ə-,gram, -'fer-\ *noun* [*electr-* + *phero-* (from Greek *pherein* to carry) + *-gram*] (1951)
**:** ELECTROPHORETOGRAM

**elec·tro·phile** \i-'lek-trə-,fīl\ *noun* (1943)
**:** an electrophilic substance (as an electron-accepting reagent)

**elec·tro·phil·ic** \i-,lek-trə-'fi-lik\ *adjective* (1936)

**1** *of an atom, ion, or molecule* **:** having an affinity for electrons **:** being an electron acceptor
**2 :** involving an electrophilic species ⟨an *electrophilic* reaction⟩ — compare NUCLEOPHILIC
— **elec·tro·phi·lic·i·ty** \-trō-fi-'li-sə-tē\ *noun*

**elec·tro·pho·re·sis** \-trə-fə-'rē-səs\ *noun* [New Latin] (1911)
**:** the movement of suspended particles through a fluid or gel under the action of an electromotive force applied to electrodes in contact with the suspension
— **elec·tro·pho·rese** \-'rēs, -'rēz\ *transitive verb*
— **elec·tro·pho·ret·ic** \-'re-tik\ *adjective*
— **elec·tro·pho·ret·i·cal·ly** \-ti-k(ə-)lē\ *adverb*

**elec·tro·pho·reto·gram** \-'re-tə-,gram\ *noun* [*electrophoretic* + *-o-* + *-gram*] (1954)
**:** a record that consists of the separated components of a mixture (as of proteins) produced by electrophoresis in a supporting medium (as filter paper)

**elec·troph·o·rus** \i-,lek-'trä-fə-rəs\ *noun, plural* **-ri** \-,rī, -,rē\ [New Latin, from *electr-* + *-phorus* -phore] (1778)
**:** a device for producing electric charges consisting of a disk that is negatively electrified by friction and a metal plate that becomes charged by induction when placed on the disk

**elec·tro·pho·tog·ra·phy** \i-,lek-trō-fō-'tä-grə-fē\ *noun* (1894)
**:** photography in which images are produced by electrical means (as in xerography)
— **elec·tro·pho·to·graph·ic** \-trə-,fō-tə-'gra-fik\ *adjective*

**elec·tro·phys·i·ol·o·gy** \i-,lek-trō-,fi-zē-'ä-lə-jē\ *noun* (1838)
**1 :** physiology that is concerned with the electrical aspects of physiological phenomena
**2 :** electrical phenomena associated with a physiological process (as the function of a body or bodily part) ⟨*electrophysiology* of the eye⟩
— **elec·tro·phys·i·o·log·i·cal** \-zē-ə-'lä-ji-kəl\ *also* **elec·tro·phys·i·o·log·ic** \-jik\ *adjective*
— **elec·tro·phys·i·o·log·i·cal·ly** \-ji-k(ə-)lē\ *adverb*
— **elec·tro·phys·i·ol·o·gist** \-zē-'äl-ə-jist\ *noun*

**elec·tro·plate** \i-'lek-trə-,plāt\ *transitive verb* (circa 1859)
**:** to plate with an adherent continuous coating by electrodeposition

**elec·tro·pos·i·tive** \i-,lek-trō-'pä-zə-tiv, -'päz-tiv\ *adjective* (1834)
**:** having a tendency to release electrons

**elec·tro·ret·i·no·gram** \-'re-t°n-ə-,gram\ *noun* (1936)
**:** a graphic record of electrical activity of the retina used especially in the diagnosis of retinal conditions

**elec·tro·ret·i·no·graph** \-,graf\ *noun* (1962)
**:** an instrument for recording electrical activity in the retina
— **elec·tro·ret·i·no·graph·ic** \-,re-t°n-ə-'gra-fik\ *adjective*
— **elec·tro·ret·i·nog·ra·phy** \-t°n-'ä-grə-fē\ *noun*

**elec·tro·scope** \i-'lek-trə-,skōp\ *noun* [probably from French *électroscope*] (1810)
**:** any of various instruments for detecting the presence of an electric charge on a body, for determining whether the charge is positive or negative, or for indicating and measuring intensity of radiation

**elec·tro·shock** \-trō-,shäk\ *noun* (1941)
**1 :** ³SHOCK 5
**2 :** ELECTROSHOCK THERAPY

**electroshock therapy** *noun* (1942)
**:** the treatment of mental disorder and especially depression by the induction of unconsciousness and convulsions through the use of

an electric current now usually on an anesthetized patient — called also *electroconvulsive therapy*

**elec·tro·stat·ic** \i-,lek-trə-'sta-tik\ *adjective* [International Scientific Vocabulary] (1860)
**1 :** of or relating to static electricity or electrostatics
**2 :** of or relating to painting with a spray that utilizes electrically charged particles to ensure complete coating
— **elec·tro·stat·i·cal·ly** \-'sta-ti-k(ə-)lē\ *adverb*

**electrostatic generator** *noun* (circa 1931)
**:** VAN DE GRAAFF GENERATOR

**electrostatic precipitator** *noun* (1949)
**:** an electrostatic device in chimney flues that removes particles from escaping gases

**elec·tro·stat·ics** \i-,lek-trə-'sta-tiks\ *noun plural but singular in construction* (1827)
**:** physics that deals with phenomena due to attractions or repulsions of electric charges but not dependent upon their motion

**elec·tro·sur·gery** \i-,lek-trō-'sər-jə-rē\ *noun* (circa 1903)
**:** surgery by means of diathermy
— **elec·tro·sur·gi·cal** \-'sər-ji-kəl\ *adjective*

**elec·tro·ther·a·py** \-'ther-ə-pē\ *noun* (1881)
**:** treatment of disease by means of electricity (as in diathermy)

**elec·tro·ther·mal** \-'thər-məl\ *adjective* (1884)
**:** relating to or combining electricity and heat; *specifically* **:** relating to the generation of heat by electricity
— **elec·tro·ther·mal·ly** \-mə-lē\ *adverb*

**elec·tro·ton·ic** \i-,lek-trə-'tä-nik\ *adjective* (1832)
**1 :** of, induced by, relating to, or constituting electrotonus
**2 :** of, relating to, or being the spread of electrical activity through living tissue or cells in the absence of repeated action potentials ⟨an *electrotonic* junction between cells⟩
— **elec·tro·ton·i·cal·ly** \-ni-k(ə-)lē\ *adverb*

**elec·trot·o·nus** \i-,lek-'trä-t°n-əs\ *noun* [New Latin] (1878)
**:** the altered sensitivity of a nerve when a constant current of electricity passes through any part of it

**elec·tro·type** \i-'lek-trə-,tīp\ *noun* (1840)
**1 :** a duplicate printing surface made by an electroplating process
**2 :** a copy (as of a coin) made by an electroplating process
— **electrotype** *transitive verb*
— **elec·tro·typ·er** \-,tī-pər\ *noun*

**elec·tro·weak** \i-,lek-trō-,wēk\ *adjective* (1978)
**:** of, relating to, or being the unification of electromagnetism and the weak force

**elec·tro·win·ning** \i-'lek-trō-,wi-niŋ\ *noun* (1924)
**:** the recovery especially of metals from solutions by electrolysis

**elec·trum** \i-'lek-trəm\ *noun* [Middle English, from Latin — more at ELECTRIC] (14th century)
**:** a natural pale yellow alloy of gold and silver

**elec·tu·ary** \i-'lek-chə-,wer-ē\ *noun, plural* **-ar·ies** [Middle English *electuarie*, from Late Latin *electuarium*, probably from Greek *ekleikton*, from *ekleichein* to lick up, from *ex-* + *leichein* to lick — more at LICK] (14th century)
**:** CONFECTION 2b

**el·e·doi·sin** \,e-lə-'dȯi-s°n\ *noun* [irregular from New Latin *Eledone*, from Greek *eledōnē*, a kind of octopus] (1963)
**:** a small protein $C_{54}H_{85}N_{13}O_{15}S$ from the salivary glands of several octopuses (genus *Eledone*) that is a powerful vasodilator and hypotensive agent

**el·ee·mo·sy·nary** \ˌe-li-'mä-s°n-ˌer-ē, -'mō-; -'mä-z°n-\ *adjective* [Medieval Latin *eleemosynarius,* from Late Latin *eleemosyna* alms — more at ALMS] (circa 1616)
**:** of, relating to, or supported by charity

**el·e·gance** \'e-li-gən(t)s\ *noun* (circa 1510)
**1 a :** refined grace or dignified propriety **:** URBANITY **b :** tasteful richness of design or ornamentation ⟨the sumptuous *elegance* of the furnishings⟩ **c :** dignified gracefulness or restrained beauty of style **:** POLISH ⟨the essay is marked by lucidity, wit, and *elegance*⟩ **d :** scientific precision, neatness, and simplicity ⟨the *elegance* of a mathematical proof⟩
**2 :** something that is elegant

**el·e·gan·cy** \-gən(t)-sē\ *noun, plural* **-cies** (15th century)
**:** ELEGANCE

**el·e·gant** \'e-li-gənt\ *adjective* [Middle French or Latin; Middle French, from Latin *elegant-, elegans;* akin to Latin *eligere* to select — more at ELECT] (15th century)
**1 :** marked by elegance
**2 :** of a high grade or quality **:** SPLENDID ⟨*elegant* gems priced at hundreds of thousands of dollars⟩
*synonym* see CHOICE
**— el·e·gant·ly** *adverb*

**ele·gi·ac** \ˌe-lə-'jī-ək, -ˌak *also* i-'lē-jē-ˌak\ *also* **el·e·gi·a·cal** \ˌe-lə-'jī-ə-kəl\ *adjective* [Late Latin *elegiacus,* from Greek *elegeiakos,* from *elegeion*] (1542)
**1 a :** of, relating to, or consisting of two dactylic hexameter lines the second of which lacks the arsis in the third and sixth feet **b** (1) **:** written in or consisting of elegiac couplets (2) **:** noted for having written poetry in such couplets **c :** of or relating to the period in Greece about the seventh century B.C. when poetry written in such couplets flourished
**2 :** of, relating to, or comprising elegy or an elegy; *especially* **:** expressing sorrow often for something now past ⟨an *elegiac* lament for departed youth⟩
**— elegiac** *noun*
**— el·e·gi·a·cal·ly** \ˌe-lə-'jī-ə-k(ə-)lē\ *adverb*

**ele·git** \i-'lē-jət\ *noun* [Latin, literally, he has chosen, from *eligere*] (1504)
**:** a judicial writ of execution by which a defendant's goods and if necessary his or her lands are delivered for debt to the plaintiff until the debt is paid

**el·e·gize** \'e-lə-ˌjīz\ *verb* **-gized; -giz·ing** (1702)
*intransitive verb*
**:** to write an elegy
*transitive verb*
**:** to write an elegy on

**el·e·gy** \'e-lə-jē\ *noun, plural* **-gies** [Latin *elegia* poem in elegiac couplets, from Greek *elegeia, elegeion,* from *elegos* song of mourning] (1501)
**1 :** a poem in elegiac couplets
**2 a :** a song or poem expressing sorrow or lamentation especially for one who is dead **b :** something (as a speech) resembling such a song or poem
**3 a :** a pensive or reflective poem that is usually nostalgic or melancholy **b :** a short pensive musical composition

**el·e·ment** \'e-lə-mənt\ *noun* [Middle English, from Old French & Latin; Old French, from Latin *elementum*] (13th century)
**1 a :** any of the four substances air, water, fire, and earth formerly believed to compose the physical universe **b** *plural* **:** weather conditions; *especially* **:** violent or severe weather ⟨battling the *elements*⟩ **c :** the state or sphere natural or suited to a person or thing ⟨at school she was in her *element*⟩
**2 :** a constituent part: as **a** *plural* **:** the simplest principles of a subject of study **:** RUDIMENTS **b** (1) **:** a part of a geometric magnitude ⟨an infinitesimal *element* of volume⟩ (2) **:** a generator of a geometric figure; *also* **:** a line or

line segment contained in the surface of a cone or cylinder (3) **:** a basic member of a mathematical or logical class or set (4) **:** one of the individual entries in a mathematical matrix or determinant **c :** one of a number of distinct groups composing a larger group or community ⟨the criminal *element* in the city⟩ **d** (1) **:** one of the necessary data or values on which calculations or conclusions are based (2) **:** one of the factors determining the outcome of a process **e :** any of more than 100 fundamental substances that consist of atoms of only one kind and that singly or in combination constitute all matter **f :** a distinct part of a composite device **g :** a subdivision of a military unit
**3** *plural* **:** the bread and wine used in the Eucharist ☆

## CHEMICAL ELEMENTS

| ELEMENT | SYMBOL | ATOMIC NUMBER | ATOMIC WEIGHT (C = 12) |
|---|---|---|---|
| actinium | Ac | 89 | 227.0278 |
| aluminum | Al | 13 | 26.98154 |
| americium | Am | 95 | |
| antimony | Sb | 51 | 121.75 |
| argon | Ar | 18 | 39.948 |
| arsenic | As | 33 | 74.9216 |
| astatine | At | 85 | |
| barium | Ba | 56 | 137.33 |
| berkelium | Bk | 97 | |
| beryllium | Be | 4 | 9.01218 |
| bismuth | Bi | 83 | 208.9804 |
| bohrium | Bh | 107 | |
| boron | B | 5 | 10.81 |
| bromine | Br | 35 | 79.904 |
| cadmium | Cd | 48 | 112.41 |
| calcium | Ca | 20 | 40.08 |
| californium | Cf | 98 | |
| carbon | C | 6 | 12.011 |
| cerium | Ce | 58 | 140.12 |
| cesium | Cs | 55 | 132.9054 |
| chlorine | Cl | 17 | 35.453 |
| chromium | Cr | 24 | 51.996 |
| cobalt | Co | 27 | 58.9332 |
| copper | Cu | 29 | 63.546 |
| curium | Cm | 96 | |
| dubnium | Db | 105 | |
| dysprosium | Dy | 66 | 162.50 |
| einsteinium | Es | 99 | |
| erbium | Er | 68 | 167.26 |
| europium | Eu | 63 | 151.96 |
| fermium | Fm | 100 | |
| fluorine | F | 9 | 18.998403 |
| francium | Fr | 87 | |
| gadolinium | Gd | 64 | 157.25 |
| gallium | Ga | 31 | 69.72 |
| germanium | Ge | 32 | 72.59 |
| gold | Au | 79 | 196.9665 |
| hafnium | Hf | 72 | 178.49 |
| hassium | Hs | 108 | |
| helium | He | 2 | 4.00260 |
| holmium | Ho | 67 | 164.9304 |
| hydrogen | H | 1 | 1.0079 |
| indium | In | 49 | 114.82 |
| iodine | I | 53 | 126.9045 |
| iridium | Ir | 77 | 192.22 |
| iron | Fe | 26 | 55.847 |
| krypton | Kr | 36 | 83.80 |
| lanthanum | La | 57 | 138.9055 |
| lawrencium | Lr | 103 | |
| lead | Pb | 82 | 207.2 |
| lithium | Li | 3 | 6.941 |
| lutetium | Lu | 71 | 174.967 |
| magnesium | Mg | 12 | 24.305 |
| manganese | Mn | 25 | 54.9380 |
| meitnerium | Mt | 109 | |
| mendelevium | Md | 101 | |
| mercury | Hg | 80 | 200.59 |
| molybdenum | Mo | 42 | 95.94 |
| neodymium | Nd | 60 | 144.24 |
| neon | Ne | 10 | 20.179 |
| neptunium | Np | 93 | 237.0482 |
| nickel | Ni | 28 | 58.69 |
| niobium | Nb | 41 | 92.9064 |
| nitrogen | N | 7 | 14.0067 |

| ELEMENT | SYMBOL | ATOMIC NUMBER | ATOMIC WEIGHT (C = 12) |
|---|---|---|---|
| nobelium | No | 102 | |
| osmium | Os | 76 | 190.2 |
| oxygen | O | 8 | 15.9994 |
| palladium | Pd | 46 | 106.42 |
| phosphorus | P | 15 | 30.97376 |
| platinum | Pt | 78 | 195.08 |
| plutonium | Pu | 94 | |
| polonium | Po | 84 | |
| potassium | K | 19 | 39.0983 |
| praseodymium | Pr | 59 | 140.9077 |
| promethium | Pm | 61 | |
| protactinium | Pa | 91 | 231.0359 |
| radium | Ra | 88 | 226.0254 |
| radon | Rn | 86 | |
| rhenium | Re | 75 | 186.207 |
| rhodium | Rh | 45 | 102.9055 |
| rubidium | Rb | 37 | 85.4678 |
| ruthenium | Ru | 44 | 101.07 |
| rutherfordium | Rf | 104 | |
| samarium | Sm | 62 | 150.36 |
| scandium | Sc | 21 | 44.9559 |
| seaborgium | Sg | 106 | |
| selenium | Se | 34 | 78.96 |
| silicon | Si | 14 | 28.0855 |
| silver | Ag | 47 | 107.868 |
| sodium | Na | 11 | 22.98977 |
| strontium | Sr | 38 | 87.62 |
| sulfur | S | 16 | 32.06 |
| tantalum | Ta | 73 | 180.9479 |
| technetium | Tc | 43 | |
| tellurium | Te | 52 | 127.60 |
| terbium | Tb | 65 | 158.9254 |
| thallium | Tl | 81 | 204.383 |
| thorium | Th | 90 | 232.0381 |
| thulium | Tm | 69 | 168.9342 |
| tin | Sn | 50 | 118.69 |
| titanium | Ti | 22 | 47.88 |
| tungsten | W | 74 | 183.85 |
| uranium | U | 92 | 238.0289 |
| vanadium | V | 23 | 50.9415 |
| xenon | Xe | 54 | 131.29 |
| ytterbium | Yb | 70 | 173.04 |
| yttrium | Y | 39 | 88.9059 |
| zinc | Zn | 30 | 65.38 |
| zirconium | Zr | 40 | 91.22 |

**el·e·men·tal** \ˌe-lə-'men-t°l\ *adjective* (15th century)
**1 a :** of, relating to, or being an element; *specifically* **:** existing as an uncombined chemical element **b** (1) **:** of, relating to, or being the basic or essential constituent of something **:** FUNDAMENTAL ⟨*elemental* biological needs⟩ (2) **:** SIMPLE, UNCOMPLICATED ⟨*elemental* food⟩ **c**

☆ SYNONYMS
**Element, component, constituent, ingredient** mean one of the parts of a compound or complex whole. ELEMENT applies to any such part and often connotes irreducible simplicity ⟨the basic *elements* of geometry⟩. COMPONENT and CONSTITUENT may designate any of the substances (whether elements or compounds) or the qualities that enter into the makeup of a complex product; COMPONENT stresses its separate entity or distinguishable character ⟨the *components* of a stereo system⟩. CONSTITUENT stresses its essential and formative character ⟨the *constituents* of a chemical compound⟩. INGREDIENT applies to any of the substances which when combined form a particular mixture (as a medicine or alloy) ⟨the *ingredients* of a cocktail⟩.

\ə\ **abut** \ᵊ\ **kitten** \ər\ **further** \a\ **ash** \ā\ **ace** \ä\ **mop, mar** \aú\ **out** \ch\ **chin** \e\ **bet** \ē\ **easy** \g\ **go** \i\ **hit** \ī\ **ice** \j\ **job** \ŋ\ **sing** \ō\ **go** \ò\ **law** \òi\ **boy** \th\ **thin** \th\ **the** \ü\ **loot** \ú\ **foot** \y\ **yet** \zh\ **vision** *see also* Guide to Pronunciation

**:** of, relating to, or dealing with the rudiments of something **:** ELEMENTARY ⟨taught *elemental* crafts to the children⟩ **d :** forming an integral part **:** INHERENT ⟨an *elemental* sense of rhythm⟩ **2 :** of, relating to, or resembling a great force of nature ⟨the rains come with *elemental* violence⟩ ⟨*elemental* passions⟩
— **elemental** *noun*
— **el·e·men·tal·ly** \-t°l-ē\ *adverb*
**el·e·men·ta·ry** \,e-lə-'men-tə-rē, -'men-trē\ *adjective* (14th century)
**1 a :** of, relating to, or dealing with the simplest elements or principles of something ⟨avoids the most *elementary* decision-making⟩ **b :** of or relating to an elementary school ⟨an *elementary* curriculum⟩
**2 :** ELEMENTAL 1a, 1b
**3 :** ELEMENTAL 2
— **el·e·men·ta·ri·ly** \-,men-'ter-ə-lē, -'men-trə-lē\ *adverb*
— **el·e·men·ta·ri·ness** \-'men-tə-rē-nəs, -'men-trē-\ *noun*

**elementary particle** *noun* (1934)
**:** any of the particles of which matter and energy are composed or which mediate the fundamental forces of nature; *especially* **:** one whose existence has not been attributed to the combination of other more fundamental entities

**elementary school** *noun* (1841)
**:** a school including usually the first four to the first eight grades and often a kindergarten
**el·e·mi** \'e-lə-mē\ *noun* [New Latin *elimi*, probably from Arabic *al lāmi* the elemi] (1543)
**:** any of various fragrant oleoresins obtained from tropical trees (family Burseraceae) and used chiefly in varnishes, lacquers, and printing inks
**elen·chus** \i-'leŋ-kəs\ *noun, plural* **-chi** \-,kī, -(,)kē\ [Latin, from Greek *elenchos*] (1663)
**:** REFUTATION; *especially* **:** one in syllogistic form
**el·e·phant** \'e-lə-fənt\ *noun, plural* **elephants** *also* **elephant** *often attributive* [Middle English, from Middle French & Latin; Middle French *olifant*, from Latin *elephantus*, from Greek *elephant-, elephas*] (14th century)
**1 :** any of a family (Elephantidae, the elephant family) of thickset usually extremely large nearly hairless herbivorous mammals that have a snout elongated into a muscular trunk and two incisors in the upper jaw developed especially in the male into large ivory tusks and that include two living forms and various extinct relatives: as **a :** a tall large-eared mammal (*Loxodonta africana*) of tropical Africa — called also *African elephant* **b :** a relatively small-eared mammal (*Elephas maximus*) of forests of southeastern Asia — called also *Asian elephant, Indian elephant*
**2 :** an animal or fossil related to the elephants
**3 :** one that is uncommonly large or hard to manage

elephant: *1* African, *2* Asian

**elephant bird** *noun* (circa 1889)
**:** AEPYORNIS
**elephant grass** *noun* (1832)
**1 :** an Old World cattail (*Typha elephantina*) used especially in making baskets

**2 :** NAPIER GRASS
**el·e·phan·ti·a·sis** \,e-lə-fən-'tī-ə-səs, -,fan-\ *noun, plural* **-a·ses** \-,sēz\ [New Latin, from Latin, a kind of leprosy, from Greek, from *elephant-, elephas*] (1581)
**1 :** enlargement and thickening of tissues; *specifically* **:** the enormous enlargement of a limb or the scrotum caused by obstruction of lymphatics by filarial worms (especially *Wuchereria bancrofti*)
**2 :** an undesirable usually enormous growth, enlargement, or overdevelopment ⟨*elephantiasis* of intellect and atrophy of emotion — Michael Lerner⟩
**el·e·phan·tine** \,e-lə-'fan-,tēn, -,tīn, 'e-lə-fən-\ *adjective* (1610)
**1 a :** having enormous size or strength **:** MASSIVE **b :** CLUMSY, PONDEROUS ⟨*elephantine* verse⟩
**2 :** of or relating to an elephant
**elephant seal** *noun* (1841)
**:** either of two very large seals (genus *Mirounga* of the family Phocidae) characterized by a long inflatable proboscis: **a :** one (*M. angustirostris*) found in Pacific coastal waters from southeastern Alaska to Baja California **b :** one (*M. leonina*) found in coastal waters of subantarctic islands and Patagonia
**El·eu·sin·i·an** \,el-yù-'si-nē-ən\ *adjective* (1611)
**:** of or relating to ancient Eleusis or to the religious mysteries celebrated there in worship of Demeter and Persephone
**¹el·e·vate** \'e-lə-,vāt, -vət\ *adjective* (14th century)
*archaic* **:** ELEVATED
**²el·e·vate** \-,vāt\ *verb* **-vat·ed; -vat·ing** [Middle English, from Latin *elevatus*, past participle of *elevare*, from *e-* + *levare* to raise — more at LEVER] (15th century)
*transitive verb*
**1 :** to lift up **:** RAISE
**2 :** to raise in rank or status **:** EXALT
**3 :** to improve morally, intellectually, or culturally
**4 :** to raise the spirits of **:** ELATE
*intransitive verb*
**:** to become elevated **:** RISE ⟨his voice *elevated* to a shout⟩
*synonym* see LIFT
**¹el·e·vat·ed** \-,vā-təd\ *adjective* (1553)
**1 a :** raised especially above the ground or other surface ⟨an *elevated* highway⟩ **b :** increased especially abnormally (as in degree or amount) ⟨*elevated* blood pressure⟩
**2 a :** being morally or intellectually on a high plane ⟨*elevated* conversation⟩ **b :** FORMAL, DIGNIFIED ⟨*elevated* diction⟩
**3 :** exhilarated in mood or feeling
**²elevated** *noun* (1881)
**:** ²EL
**el·e·va·tion** \,e-lə-'vā-shən\ *noun* (14th century)
**1 :** the height to which something is elevated: as **a :** the angular distance of something (as a celestial object) above the horizon **b :** the degree to which a gun is aimed above the horizon **c :** the height above the level of the sea **:** ALTITUDE
**2 :** a ballet dancer's or a skater's leap and seeming suspension in the air; *also* **:** the ability to achieve an elevation
**3 :** an act or instance of elevating
**4 :** something that is elevated: as **a :** an elevated place **b :** a swelling especially on the skin
**5 :** the quality or state of being elevated
**6 :** a geometrical projection (as of a building) on a vertical plane
*synonym* see HEIGHT
**el·e·va·tor** \'e-lə-,vā-tər\ *noun* (1646)
**1 :** one that raises or lifts something up: as **a :** an endless belt or chain conveyor with cleats, scoops, or buckets for raising material **b :** a cage or platform and its hoisting machinery for conveying people or things to different levels **c :** GRAIN ELEVATOR

**2 :** a movable auxiliary airfoil usually attached to the tail plane of an airplane for controlling pitch — see AIRPLANE illustration
**elevator music** *noun* (1979)
**:** instrumental arrangements of popular songs often piped in (as in an elevator or retail store)
**elev·en** \i-'le-vən\ *noun* [Middle English *enleven*, from *enleven*, adjective, from Old English *endleofan*, from *end-* (alteration of *ān* one) + *-leofan;* akin to Old English *lēon* to lend — more at ONE, LOAN] (before 12th century)
**1** — see NUMBER table
**2 :** the 11th in a set or series
**3 :** something having 11 units or members; *especially* **:** a football team
— **eleven** *adjective*
— **eleven** *pronoun, plural in construction*
— **elev·enth** \-vən(t)th\ *adjective or noun*
**eleven–plus** \i-,le-vən-'pləs\ *noun* (1955)
*British* **:** an examination taken by schoolchildren between the ages of 11 and 12 that determines the type of secondary education to which they are assigned
**elev·ens·es** \-vən-zəz\ *noun plural but sometimes singular in construction* [double plural of *eleven* (o'clock)] (circa 1819)
*British* **:** light refreshment (as a snack) taken in the middle of the morning
**eleventh hour** *noun* (1826)
**:** the latest possible time ⟨still making changes at the *eleventh hour*⟩
**el·e·von** \'e-lə-,vän\ *noun* [*elev*ator + ail*eron*] (1944)
**:** an airplane control surface that combines the functions of elevator and aileron
**elf** \'elf\ *noun, plural* **elves** \'elvz\ [Middle English, from Old English *ælf;* akin to Old Norse *alfr* elf & perhaps to Latin *albus* white — more at ALB] (before 12th century)
**1 :** a small often mischievous fairy
**2 :** a small lively creature; *also* **:** a usually lively mischievous or malicious person
— **elf·ish** \'el-fish\ *adjective*
— **elf·ish·ly** *adverb*
**elf·in** \'el-fən\ *adjective* [irregular from *elf*] (1596)
**1 a :** of, relating to, or produced by an elf **b :** resembling an elf especially in its tiny size ⟨*elfin* portions⟩
**2 :** having an otherworldly or magical quality or charm
**elf·lock** \'elf-,läk\ *noun* (1592)
**:** hair matted as if by elves — usually used in plural
**elf owl** *noun* (1887)
**:** a very small insectivorous owl (*Micrathene whitneyi*) of the Southwestern U.S. and Mexico that often roosts and nests in giant cacti
**el·hi** \(,)el-'hī\ *adjective* [*el*ementary (school) + *hi*gh (school)] (circa 1948)
**:** of, relating to, or designed for use in grades 1 to 12
**Eli** \'ē-,lī\ *noun* [Hebrew *‘Ēlī*]
**:** a judge and priest of Israel who according to the account in I Samuel was entrusted with the care of the boy Samuel
**Eli·as** \i-'lī-əs\ *noun* [Late Latin, from Greek *Elías*, from Hebrew *Ēlīyāh*]
**:** ELIJAH
**elic·it** \i-'li-sət\ *transitive verb* [Latin *elicitus*, past participle of *elicere*, from *e-* + *lacere* to allure] (1605)
**1 :** to draw forth or bring out (something latent or potential) ⟨hypnotism *elicited* his hidden fears⟩
**2 :** to call forth or draw out (as information or a response) ⟨her performance *elicited* wild applause⟩
*synonym* see EDUCE
— **elic·i·ta·tion** \i-,li-sə-'tā-shən, ,ē-\ *noun*
— **elic·i·tor** \i-'li-sə-tər\ *noun*
**elide** \i-'līd\ *transitive verb* **elid·ed; elid·ing** [Latin *elidere* to strike out, from *e-* + *laedere* to injure by striking] (1796)

**1 a :** to suppress or alter (as a vowel or syllable) by elision **b :** to strike out (as a written word)
**2 a :** to leave out of consideration **:** OMIT **b :** CURTAIL, ABRIDGE

**el·i·gi·ble** \'e-lə-jə-bəl\ *adjective* [Middle English, from Middle French & Late Latin; Middle French, from Late Latin *eligibilis*, from Latin *eligere* to choose — more at ELECT] (15th century)
**1 a :** qualified to be chosen **:** ENTITLED ⟨*eligible* to retire⟩ **b :** permitted under football rules to catch a forward pass ⟨an *eligible* receiver⟩
**2 :** worthy of being chosen **:** DESIRABLE ⟨an *eligible* young bachelor⟩
— **el·i·gi·bil·i·ty** \ˌe-lə-jə-'bi-lə-tē\ *noun*
— **eligible** *noun*
— **el·i·gi·bly** \'e-lə-jə-blē\ *adverb*

**Eli·jah** \i-'lī-jə\ *noun* [Hebrew *Ēlīyāh*]
**:** a Hebrew prophet of the 9th century B.C. who according to the account in I Kings championed the worship of Jehovah as against Baal

**elim·i·nate** \i-'li-mə-ˌnāt\ *transitive verb* **-nat·ed; -nat·ing** [Latin *eliminatus*, past participle of *eliminare*, from *e-* + *limin-, limen* threshold] (1568)
**1 a :** to cast out or get rid of **:** REMOVE, ERADICATE ⟨the need to *eliminate* poverty⟩ **b :** to set aside as unimportant **:** IGNORE
**2 :** to expel (as waste) from the living body
**3 :** to cause (as an unknown) to disappear by combining two or more mathematical equations
— **elim·i·na·tive** \-'li-mə-ˌnā-tiv\ *adjective*
— **elim·i·na·tor** \-ˌnā-tər\ *noun*

**elim·i·na·tion** \i-ˌli-mə-'nā-shən\ *noun, often attributive* (1627)
**:** the act, process, or an instance of eliminating or discharging: as **a :** the act of discharging or excreting waste products from the body **b :** the removal from a molecule of the constituents of a simpler molecule ⟨ethylene is formed by the *elimination* of water from ethanol⟩ — compare ADDITION 4

**ELISA** \ē-'lī-sə, -zə\ *noun* (1978)
**:** ENZYME-LINKED IMMUNOSORBENT ASSAY

**Eli·sha** \i-'lī-shə\ *noun* [Hebrew *Ēlīshāʿ*]
**:** a Hebrew prophet and disciple and successor of Elijah

**eli·sion** \i-'li-zhən\ *noun* [Late Latin *elision-, elisio,* from Latin *elidere*] (1581)
**1 a :** the use of a speech form that lacks a final or initial sound which a variant speech form has (as *'s* instead of *is* in *there's*) **b :** the omission of an unstressed vowel or syllable in a verse to achieve a uniform metrical pattern
**2 :** the act or an instance of omitting something **:** OMISSION

**elite** \ā-'lēt, i-, ē-\ *noun* [French *élite*, from Old French *eslite*, from feminine of *eslit*, past participle of *eslire* to choose, from Latin *eligere*] (1823)
**1 a** *singular or plural in construction* **:** the choice part **:** CREAM ⟨the *elite* of the entertainment world⟩ **b** *singular or plural in construction* **:** the best of a class ⟨superachievers who dominate the computer *elite* —Marilyn Chase⟩ **c** *singular or plural in construction* **:** the socially superior part of society ⟨how the *elite* live —A P World⟩ ⟨how the French-speaking *elite* . . . was changing —*Economist*⟩ **d :** a group of persons who by virtue of position or education exercise much power or influence ⟨members of the ruling *elite*⟩ ⟨the intellectual *elites* of the country⟩ **e :** a member of such an elite — usually used in plural ⟨the *elites* . . ., pursuing their studies in Europe —Robert Wernick⟩
**2 :** a typewriter type providing 12 characters to the linear inch
— **elite** *adjective*

**élite, élitism** *chiefly British variant of* ELITE, ELITISM

**elit·ism** \ā-'lē-ˌti-zəm, i-, ē-\ *noun* (1947)
**1 :** leadership or rule by an elite

**2 :** the selectivity of the elite; *especially* **:** SNOBBERY 1 ⟨*elitism* in choosing new members⟩
**3 :** consciousness of being or belonging to an elite
— **elit·ist** \-'lē-tist\ *noun or adjective*

**elix·ir** \i-'lik-sər\ *noun* [Middle English, from Medieval Latin, from Arabic *al-iksīr* the elixir, from *al* the + *iksīr* elixir, probably from Greek *xērion* desiccative powder, from *xēros* dry] (14th century)
**1 a** (1) **:** a substance held capable of changing base metals into gold (2) **:** a substance held capable of prolonging life indefinitely **b** (1) **:** CURE-ALL (2) **:** a medicinal concoction
**2 :** a sweetened liquid usually containing alcohol that is used in medication either for its medicinal ingredients or as a flavoring
**3 :** the essential principle

**Eliz·a·be·than** \i-ˌli-zə-'bē-thən\ *adjective* (1807)
**:** of, relating to, or characteristic of Elizabeth I of England or her reign
— **Elizabethan** *noun*

**elk** \'elk\ *noun, plural* **elks** [Middle English, probably from Old English *eolh;* akin to Old High German *elaho* elk, Greek *elaphos* deer] (before 12th century)
**1** *plural usually* **elk a :** MOOSE 1 — used for one of the Old World **b :** a large gregarious deer (*Cervus elaphus*) of North America, Europe, Asia, and northwestern Africa — called also *red deer, wapiti* **c :** any of various large Asian deer
**2 :** soft tanned rugged leather
**3** *capitalized* [Benevolent and Protective Order of *Elks*] **:** a member of a major benevolent and fraternal order

**elk·hound** \'elk-ˌhaund, 'el-ˌkaund\ *noun* (1889)
**:** NORWEGIAN ELKHOUND

**¹ell** \'el\ *noun* [Middle English *eln,* from Old English; akin to Old High German *elina* ell, Latin *ulna* forearm, Greek *ōlenē* elbow, Sanskrit *aratni*] (before 12th century)
**:** a former English unit of length (as for cloth) equal to 45 inches (about 1.14 meters); *also* **:** any of various units of length used similarly

**²ell** *noun* [alteration of ¹*el*] (1773)
**1 :** an extension at right angles to the length of a building
**2 :** an elbow in a pipe or conduit

**el·lag·ic acid** \ə-'la-jik-, e-\ *noun* [French *ellagique,* from *ellag,* anagram of *galle* gall] (1810)
**:** a crystalline phenolic compound $C_{14}H_6O_8$ with two lactone groupings that is obtained especially from oak galls and some tannins and is used medicinally as a hemostatic

**el·lipse** \i-'lips, e-\ *noun* [Greek *elleipsis*] (circa 1753)
**1 a :** OVAL **b :** a closed plane curve generated by a point moving in such a way that the sums of its distances from two fixed points is a constant **:** a plane section of a right circular cone that is a closed curve
**2 :** ELLIPSIS

ellipse 1b: *F, F'* foci; *P, P', P"* any point on the curve; $FP + PF' = FP'' + P''F' = FP' + P'F'$

**el·lip·sis** \i-'lip-səs, e-\ *noun, plural* **el·lip·ses** \-ˌsēz\ [Latin, from Greek *elleipsis* ellipsis, ellipse, from *elleipein* to leave out, fall short, from *en* in + *leipein* to leave — more at IN, LOAN] (1540)
**1 a :** the omission of one or more words that are obviously understood but that must be supplied to make a construction grammatically complete **b :** a sudden leap from one topic to another
**2 :** marks or a mark (as . . . or *** or —) indicating an omission (of words) or a pause

**el·lip·soid** \i-'lip-ˌsoid, e-\ *noun* (1721)

**:** a surface all plane sections of which are ellipses or circles
— **el·lip·soi·dal** \i-ˌlip-'soi-dºl, (ˌ)e-\ *also* **ellipsoid** *adjective*

**el·lip·ti·cal** \i-'lip-ti-kəl, e-\ *or* **el·lip·tic** \-tik\ *adjective* [Greek *elleiptikos* defective, marked by ellipsis, from *elleipein*] (1656)
**1 :** of, relating to, or shaped like an ellipse
**2 a :** of, relating to, or marked by ellipsis or an ellipsis **b** (1) **:** of, relating to, or marked by extreme economy of speech or writing (2) **:** of or relating to deliberate obscurity (as of literary or conversational style)
— **el·lip·ti·cal·ly** \-ti-k(ə-)lē\ *adverb*

**elliptical galaxy** *noun* (1948)
**:** a galaxy that has a generally elliptical shape and that has no apparent internal structure or spiral arms — called also *elliptical*; compare SPIRAL GALAXY

**el·lip·tic·i·ty** \i-ˌlip-'ti-sə-tē, (ˌ)e-\ *noun* (1753)
**:** deviation of an ellipse or a spheroid from the form of a circle or a sphere

**elm** \'elm\ *noun* [Middle English, from Old English; akin to Old High German *elme* elm, Latin *ulmus*] (before 12th century)
**1 :** any of a genus (*Ulmus* of the family Ulmaceae, the elm family) comprising large trees with alternate stipulate leaves and small apetalous flowers
**2 :** the wood of an elm

**elm bark beetle** *noun* (circa 1909)
**:** either of two beetles (family Scolytidae) that are vectors for the fungus causing Dutch elm disease: **a :** one (*Hylurgopinus rufipes*) native to eastern North America **b :** one (*Scolytus multistriatus*) introduced from Europe into eastern North America

**elm leaf beetle** *noun* (1881)
**:** a small orange-yellow black-striped Old World chrysomelid beetle (*Pyrrhalta luteola*) that in the larval and adult stage is a leaf-eating pest of elms in eastern North America

**El Ni·ño** \el-'nē-nyō\ *noun, plural* **El Niños** [Spanish, literally, the child (i.e., the Christ child); from the appearance of the flow at the Christmas season] (1925)
**:** an irregularly occurring flow of unusually warm surface water along the western coast of South America that is accompanied by abnormally high rainfall in usually arid areas and that prevents upwelling of nutrient-rich cold deep water causing a decline in the regional fish population

**el·o·cu·tion** \ˌe-lə-'kyü-shən\ *noun* [Middle English *elocucioun,* from Latin *elocution-, elocutio,* from *eloqui*] (15th century)
**1 :** a style of speaking especially in public
**2 :** the art of effective public speaking
— **el·o·cu·tion·ary** \-shə-ˌner-ē\ *adjective*
— **el·o·cu·tion·ist** \-sh(ə-)nist\ *noun*

**elo·dea** \i-'lō-dē-ə\ *noun* [New Latin, genus name, from Greek *helōdēs* marshy, from *helos* marsh; akin to Sanskrit *saras* pond] (circa 1868)
**:** any of a small American genus (*Elodea*) of submerged aquatic monocotyledonous herbs

**eloign** \i-'loin\ *transitive verb* [Middle English *eloynen,* from Middle French *esloigner,* from Old French, from *es-* ex- (from Latin *ex-*) + *loing* (adverb) far, from Latin *longe,* from *longus* long] (15th century)
**1** *archaic* **:** to take (oneself) far away
**2** *archaic* **:** to remove to a distant or unknown place **:** CONCEAL

**¹elon·gate** \i-'loŋ-ˌgāt, (ˌ)ē-, 'ē-ˌ\ *verb* **-gat·ed; -gat·ing** [Late Latin *elongatus,* past participle of *elongare,* to withdraw, from Latin *e-* + *longus*] (1578)
*transitive verb*

\ə\ abut \ᵊ\ kitten \ər\ further \a\ ash \ā\ ace
\ä\ mop, mar \au\ out \ch\ chin \e\ bet \ē\ easy
\g\ go \h\ hit \ī\ ice \j\ job \ŋ\ sing \ō\ go
\o\ law \oi\ boy \th\ thin \th\ the \ü\ loot \u\ foot
\y\ yet \zh\ vision *see also* Guide to Pronunciation

**:** to extend the length of
*intransitive verb*
**:** to grow in length
²**elongate** *or* **elon·gat·ed** *adjective* (1751)
**1 :** stretched out
**2 :** SLENDER
**elon·ga·tion** \(ˌ)ē-ˌlȯŋ-'gā-shən\ *noun* (14th century)
**1 :** the angular distance of a celestial body from another around which it revolves or from a particular point in the sky
**2 a :** the state of being elongated or lengthened; *also* **:** the process of growing or increasing in length **b :** something that is elongated
**elope** \i-'lōp\ *intransitive verb* **eloped; elop·ing** [Anglo-French *aloper*] (1628)
**1 :** to slip away **:** ESCAPE
**2 a :** to run away from one's husband with a lover **b :** to run away secretly with the intention of getting married usually without parental consent
**— elope·ment** \-'lōp-mənt\ *noun*
**— elop·er** *noun*
**el·o·quence** \'e-lə-kwən(t)s\ *noun* (14th century)
**1 :** discourse marked by force and persuasiveness; *also* **:** the art or power of using such discourse
**2 :** the quality of forceful or persuasive expressiveness
**el·o·quent** \-kwənt\ *adjective* [Middle English, from Middle French, from Latin *eloquent-, eloquens,* from present participle of *eloqui* to speak out, from *e-* + *loqui* to speak] (14th century)
**1 :** marked by forceful and fluent expression ⟨an *eloquent* preacher⟩
**2 :** vividly or movingly expressive or revealing ⟨an *eloquent* monument⟩
**— el·o·quent·ly** *adverb*
¹**else** \'el(t)s\ *adverb* [Middle English *elles,* from Old English; akin to Latin *alius* other, *alter* other of two, Greek *allos* other] (before 12th century)
**1 a :** in a different manner or place or at a different time ⟨how *else* could he have acted⟩ ⟨here and nowhere *else*⟩ **b :** in an additional manner or place or at an additional time ⟨where *else* is gold found⟩
**2 :** if not **:** OTHERWISE ⟨leave or *else* you'll be sorry⟩ — used absolutely to express a threat ⟨do what I tell you or *else*⟩
²**else** *adjective* (before 12th century)
**:** OTHER **a :** being different in identity ⟨it must have been somebody *else*⟩ **b :** being in addition ⟨what *else* did he say⟩
**else·where** \-ˌ(h)wer, -ˌ(h)war\ *adverb* [Middle English *elleswher,* from Old English *elles hwær*] (before 12th century)
**:** in or to another place ⟨took my business *elsewhere*⟩
**el·u·ant** *or* **el·u·ent** \'el-yə-wənt\ *noun* [Latin *eluent-, eluens,* present participle of *eluere*] (1941)
**:** a solvent used in eluting
**el·u·ate** \'el-yə-wət, -ˌwāt\ *noun* [Latin *eluere* + English ¹*-ate*] (1932)
**:** the washings obtained by eluting
**elu·ci·date** \i-'lü-sə-ˌdāt\ *verb* **-dat·ed; -dat·ing** [Late Latin *elucidatus,* past participle of *elucidare,* from Latin *e-* + *lucidus* lucid] (circa 1568)
*transitive verb*
**:** to make lucid especially by explanation or analysis
*intransitive verb*
**:** to give a clarifying explanation
**synonym** see EXPLAIN
**— elu·ci·da·tion** \-ˌlü-sə-'dā-shən\ *noun*
**— elu·ci·da·tive** \-'lü-sə-ˌdā-tiv\ *adjective*
**— elu·ci·da·tor** \-ˌdā-tər\ *noun*
**elu·cu·brate** \i-'lü-k(y)ə-ˌbrāt\ *transitive verb* **-brat·ed; -brat·ing** [Latin *elucubratus,* past participle of *elucubrare* to work on far into the night, from *e-* + *lucubrare* to work by lamplight — more at LUCUBRATION] (circa 1623)

**:** to work out or express by studious effort
**— elu·cu·bra·tion** \-ˌlü-k(y)ə-'brā-shən\ *noun*
**elude** \ē-'lüd\ *transitive verb* **elud·ed; elud·ing** [Latin *eludere,* from *e-* + *ludere* to play — more at LUDICROUS] (1667)
**1 :** to avoid adroitly **:** EVADE ⟨the mice *eluded* the traps⟩ ⟨managed to *elude* capture⟩
**2 :** to escape the perception, understanding, or grasp of ⟨subtlety simply *eludes* them⟩ ⟨victory continued to *elude* us⟩
**3 :** DEFY 4 ⟨it *eludes* explanation⟩
**synonym** see ESCAPE
**Elul** \e-'lül\ *noun* [Hebrew *Ĕlūl*] (1535)
**:** the 12th month of the civil year or the 6th month of the ecclesiastical year in the Jewish calendar — see MONTH table
**elu·sion** \ē-'lü-zhən\ *noun* [Medieval Latin *elusion-, elusio,* from Late Latin, deception, from Latin *eludere*] (1617)
**:** an act of eluding
**elu·sive** \ē-'lü-siv, -'lü-ziv\ *adjective* (1719)
**:** tending to elude: as **a :** tending to evade grasp or pursuit **b :** hard to comprehend or define ⟨an *elusive* concept⟩ **c :** hard to isolate or identify ⟨a haunting *elusive* aroma⟩
**— elu·sive·ly** *adverb*
**— elu·sive·ness** *noun*
**elute** \ē-'lüt\ *transitive verb* **elut·ed; elut·ing** [Latin *elutus,* past participle of *eluere* to wash out, from *e-* + *lavere* to wash — more at LYE] (1731)
**:** EXTRACT; *specifically* **:** to remove (adsorbed material) from an adsorbent by means of a solvent
**— elu·tion** \-'lü-shən\ *noun*
**elu·tri·ate** \ē-'lü-trē-ˌāt\ *transitive verb* **-at·ed; -at·ing** [Latin *elutriatus,* past participle of *elutriare* to put in a vat, perhaps from (assumed) *elutrum* vat, from Greek *elytron* reservoir, literally, covering] (circa 1727)
**:** to purify, separate, or remove by washing
**— elu·tri·a·tion** \ē-ˌlü-trē-'ā-shən\ *noun*
**— elu·tri·a·tor** \ē-'lü-trē-ˌā-tər\ *noun*
**elu·vi·a·tion** \(ˌ)ē-ˌlü-vē-'ā-shən\ *noun* [*eluvial* of eluviation (from *e-* + *-luvial*—as in *alluvial*) + *-ation*] (1899)
**:** the transportation of dissolved or suspended material within the soil by the movement of water when rainfall exceeds evaporation
**— elu·vi·al** \ē-'lü-vē-əl\ *adjective*
**— elu·vi·at·ed** \-'lü-vē-ā-təd\ *adjective*
**el·ver** \'el-vər\ *noun* [alteration of *eelfare* (migration of eels)] (circa 1640)
**:** a young eel
**elves** *plural of* ELF
**el·vish** \'el-vish\ *adjective* (13th century)
**1 :** of or relating to elves
**2 :** MISCHIEVOUS
**ely·sian** \i-'li-zhən\ *adjective, often capitalized* (1579)
**1 :** of or relating to Elysium
**2 :** BLISSFUL, DELIGHTFUL
**elysian fields** *noun plural, often E capitalized* (1579)
**:** ELYSIUM
**Ely·si·um** \i-'li-zhē-əm, -zē-\ *noun, plural* **-si·ums** *or* **-sia** \-zhē-ə, -zē-\ [Latin, from Greek *Ēlysion*]
**1 :** the abode of the blessed after death in classical mythology
**2 :** PARADISE 2
**el·y·tron** \'e-lə-ˌträn\ *noun, plural* **-tra** \-trə\ [New Latin, from Greek, sheath, wing cover, from *eilyein* to roll, wrap — more at VOLUBLE] (1774)
**:** one of the anterior wings in beetles and some other insects that serve to protect the posterior pair of functional wings
**em** \'em\ *noun* (13th century)
**1 :** the letter *m*
**2 :** the width of a piece of type about as wide as it is tall used as a unit of measure of typeset matter
**em-** — see EN-

'**em** \əm; *after* p,b,f, *or* v *often* °m\ *pronoun* [Middle English *hem,* from Old English *heom, him,* dative plural of *hē* he] (before 12th century)
**:** THEM
**ema·ci·ate** \i-'mā-shē-ˌāt\ *verb* **-at·ed; -at·ing** [Latin *emaciatus,* past participle of *emaciare,* from *e-* + *macies* leanness, from *macer* lean — more at MEAGER] (1646)
*intransitive verb*
**:** to waste away physically
*transitive verb*
**1 :** to cause to lose flesh so as to become very thin
**2 :** to make feeble
**— ema·ci·a·tion** \-ˌmā-s(h)ē-'ā-shən\ *noun*
**E-mail** \'ē-ˌmāl\ *noun* (1982)
**:** ELECTRONIC MAIL
**emalangeni** *plural of* LILANGENI
**em·a·nate** \'e-mə-ˌnāt\ *verb* **-nat·ed; -nat·ing** [Latin *emanatus,* past participle of *emanare,* from *e-* + *manare* to flow] (1756)
*intransitive verb*
**:** to come out from a source
*transitive verb*
**:** EMIT
**synonym** see SPRING
**em·a·na·tion** \ˌe-mə-'nā-shən\ *noun* (1570)
**1 a :** the action of emanating **b :** the origination of the world by a series of hierarchically descending radiations from the Godhead through intermediate stages to matter
**2 a :** something that emanates or is produced by emanation **:** EFFLUENCE **b :** an isotope of radon produced by radioactive disintegration ⟨radium *emanation*⟩
**— em·a·na·tive** \'e-mə-ˌnā-tiv\ *adjective*
**eman·ci·pate** \i-'man(t)-sə-ˌpāt\ *transitive verb* **-pat·ed; -pat·ing** [Latin *emancipatus,* past participle of *emancipare,* from *e-* + *mancipare* to transfer ownership of, from *mancip-, manceps* contractor, from *manus* hand + *capere* to take — more at MANUAL, HEAVE] (1613)
**1 :** to free from restraint, control, or the power of another; *especially* **:** to free from bondage
**2 :** to release from paternal care and responsibility and make sui juris
**3 :** to free from any controlling influence (as traditional mores or beliefs)
**synonym** see FREE
**— eman·ci·pa·tor** \-ˌpā-tər\ *noun*
**eman·ci·pa·tion** \i-ˌman(t)-sə-'pā-shən\ *noun* (1631)
**:** the act or process of emancipating
**— eman·ci·pa·tion·ist** \-sh(ə-)nist\ *noun*
**emar·gin·ate** \(ˌ)ē-'mär-jə-nət, -ˌnāt\ *adjective* [Latin *emarginatus,* past participle of *emarginare* to deprive of a margin, from *e-* + *margin-, margo* margin] (1794)
**:** having the margin notched
**— emar·gi·na·tion** \(ˌ)ē-ˌmär-jə-'nā-shən\ *noun*
**emas·cu·late** \i-'mas-kyə-ˌlāt\ *transitive verb* **-lat·ed; -lat·ing** [Latin *emasculatus,* past participle of *emasculare,* from *e-* + *masculus* male — more at MALE] (1607)
**1 :** to deprive of strength, vigor, or spirit **:** WEAKEN
**2 :** to deprive of virility or procreative power **:** CASTRATE
**3 :** to remove the androecium of (a flower) in the process of artificial cross-pollination
**synonym** see UNNERVE
**— emas·cu·late** \-lət\ *adjective*
**— emas·cu·la·tion** \-ˌmas-kyə-'lā-shən\ *noun*
**— emas·cu·la·tor** \-'mas-kyə-ˌlā-tər\ *noun*
**em·balm** \im-'bä(l)m, *New England also* -'bàm\ *transitive verb* [Middle English *embaumen,* from Middle French *embaumer,* from Old French *embasmer,* from *en-* + *basme* balm — more at BALM] (14th century)
**1 :** to treat (a dead body) so as to protect from decay
**2 :** to fill with sweet odors **:** PERFUME

**3 :** to protect from decay or oblivion **:** PRE-SERVE
**4 :** to fix in a static condition
— **em·balm·er** noun
— **em·balm·ment** \-'bä(l)m-mənt, -'bȧm-\ noun

**em·bank** \im-'baŋk\ transitive verb (1576)
**:** to enclose or confine by an embankment

**em·bank·ment** \-mənt\ noun (1786)
**1 :** a raised structure to hold back water or to carry a roadway
**2 :** the action of embanking

**em·bar·ca·de·ro** \(ˌ)em-ˌbär-kə-'der-(ˌ)ō\ noun, plural **-ros** [Spanish, from embarcado, past participle of embarcar to embark, from em- (from Latin in-) + barca bark, from Late Latin] (1846)
West **:** a landing place especially on an inland waterway

**¹em·bar·go** \im-'bär-(ˌ)gō\ noun, plural **-goes** [Spanish, from embargar to bar, from (assumed) Vulgar Latin imbarricare, from Latin in- + (assumed) Vulgar Latin barra bar] (1593)
**1 :** an order of a government prohibiting the departure of commercial ships from its ports
**2 :** a legal prohibition on commerce ⟨an embargo on arms shipments⟩
**3 :** STOPPAGE, IMPEDIMENT; especially **:** PROHIBITION ⟨I lay no embargo on anybody's words —Jane Austen⟩
**4 :** an order by a common carrier or public regulatory agency prohibiting or restricting freight transportation

**²embargo** transitive verb **-goed; -go·ing** (1755)
**:** to place an embargo on

**em·bark** \im-'bärk\ verb [Middle French embarquer, from Old Provençal embarcar, from em- (from Latin in-) + barca bark] (1533)
intransitive verb
**1 :** to go on board a vehicle for transportation
**2 :** to make a start ⟨embarked on a new career⟩
transitive verb
**1 :** to cause to go on board (as a boat or airplane)
**2 :** to engage, enlist, or invest in an enterprise
— **em·bar·ka·tion** \ˌem-ˌbär-'kā-shən, -bər-\ noun
— **em·bark·ment** \im-'bärk-mənt\ noun

**em·bar·rass** \im-'bar-əs\ transitive verb [French embarrasser, from Spanish embarazar, from Portuguese embaraçar, from em- (from Latin in-) + baraça noose] (1672)
**1 a :** to place in doubt, perplexity, or difficulties **b :** to involve in financial difficulties **c :** to cause to experience a state of self-conscious distress ⟨bawdy stories embarrassed him⟩
**2 a :** to hamper the movement of **b :** HINDER, IMPEDE
**3 :** to make intricate **:** COMPLICATE
**4 :** to impair the activity of (a bodily function) or the function of (a bodily part) ⟨digestion embarrassed by overeating⟩ ☆
— **em·bar·rass·able** \-sə-bəl\ adjective
**em·bar·rassed·ly** \-əst-lē, -ə-səd-lē\ adverb (1883)
**:** with embarrassment
**em·bar·rass·ing·ly** \-ə-siŋ-lē\ adverb (circa 1864)
**:** to an embarrassing degree **:** so as to cause embarrassment
**em·bar·rass·ment** \im-'bar-ə-smənt\ noun (1729)
**1 a :** something that embarrasses **:** IMPEDIMENT **b :** an excessive quantity from which to select — used especially in the phrase embarrassment of riches
**2 :** the state of being embarrassed: as **a :** confusion or disturbance of mind **b :** difficulty arising from the want of money to pay debts **c :** difficulty in functioning as a result of disease ⟨cardiac embarrassment⟩

**em·bas·sage** \'em-bə-sij\ noun (1526)

**1 :** the message or commission entrusted to an ambassador
**2** archaic **:** EMBASSY

**em·bas·sy** \'em-bə-sē\ noun, plural **-sies** [Middle French ambassee, ultimately of Germanic origin; akin to Old High German ambaht service] (1534)
**1 :** a body of diplomatic representatives; specifically **:** one headed by an ambassador
**2 a :** the function or position of an ambassador **b :** a mission abroad undertaken officially especially by an ambassador
**3 :** EMBASSAGE 1
**4 :** the official residence and offices of an ambassador

**em·bat·tle** \im-'bat-ᵊl\ transitive verb **em·bat·tled; em·bat·tling** \-'bat-liŋ, -tᵊl-iŋ\ [Middle English embatailen, from Middle French embatailler, from en- + batailler to battle] (14th century)
**1 :** to arrange in order of battle **:** prepare for battle
**2 :** FORTIFY

**em·bat·tled** adjective (15th century)
**1 a :** ready to fight **:** prepared to give battle ⟨here once the embattled farmers stood —R. W. Emerson⟩ **b :** engaged in battle, conflict, or controversy ⟨an embattled official accused of extortion⟩
**2 a :** being a site of battle, conflict, or controversy ⟨the embattled capital⟩ **b :** characterized by conflict or controversy ⟨his . . . often embattled experience as an educator —Nat Hentoff⟩

**em·bat·tle·ment** \im-'ba-tᵊl-mənt\ noun (15th century)
**1 :** BATTLEMENT
**2 :** the state of being embattled

**em·bay** \im-'bā\ transitive verb (1600)
**:** to trap or catch in or as if in a bay ⟨an embayed sailing ship⟩

**em·bay·ment** \im-'bā-mənt\ noun (1815)
**1 :** formation of a bay
**2 :** a bay or a conformation resembling a bay

**Emb·den** \'em-dən\ noun [Emden, Germany] (1903)
**:** a breed of large white domestic geese with an orange bill and deep orange shanks and toes

**em·bed** \im-'bed\ verb **em·bed·ded; em·bed·ding** (circa 1794)
transitive verb
**1 a :** to enclose closely in or as if in a matrix ⟨fossils embedded in stone⟩ **b :** to make something an integral part of ⟨the prejudices embedded in our language⟩ **c :** to prepare (a microscopy specimen) for sectioning by infiltrating with and enclosing in a supporting substance
**2 :** to surround closely ⟨a sweet pulp embeds the plum seed⟩
intransitive verb
**:** to become embedded
— **em·bed·ment** \-'bed-mənt\ noun

**em·bed·ded** \im-'be-dəd\ adjective (1961)
**:** occurring as a grammatical constituent (as a verb phrase or clause) within a like constituent
— **em·bed·ding** \-diŋ\ noun

**em·bel·lish** \im-'be-lish\ transitive verb [Middle English, from Middle French embeliss-, stem of embelir, from en- + bel beautiful — more at BEAUTY] (14th century)
**1 :** to make beautiful with ornamentation **:** DECORATE
**2 :** to heighten the attractiveness of by adding ornamental details **:** ENHANCE ⟨embellished our account of the trip⟩
synonym see ADORN
— **em·bel·lish·er** noun

**em·bel·lish·ment** \-lish-mənt\ noun (1591)
**1 :** the act or process of embellishing
**2 :** something serving to embellish
**3 :** ORNAMENT 5

**em·ber** \'em-bər\ noun [Middle English eymere, from Old Norse eimyrja; akin to Old

English ǣmerge ashes, Latin urere to burn] (14th century)
**1 :** a glowing fragment (as of coal) from a fire; especially **:** one smoldering in ashes
**2** plural **:** the smoldering remains of a fire
**3** plural **:** slowly dying or fading emotions, memories, ideas, or responses still capable of being revived

**ember day** \'em-bər-\ noun [Middle English, from Old English ymbrendæg, from ymbrene circuit, anniversary + dæg day] (before 12th century)
**:** a Wednesday, Friday, or Saturday following the first Sunday in Lent, Whitsunday, September 14, or December 13 set apart for fasting and prayer in Western churches

**em·bez·zle** \im-'be-zəl\ transitive verb **em·bez·zled; em·bez·zling** \-(ə-)liŋ\ [Middle English embesilen, from Anglo-French embeseiller, from Middle French en- + besillier to destroy] (15th century)
**:** to appropriate (as property entrusted to one's care) fraudulently to one's own use
— **em·bez·zle·ment** \-zəl-mənt\ noun
— **em·bez·zler** \-z(ə-)lər\ noun

**em·bit·ter** \im-'bi-tər\ transitive verb (15th century)
**1 :** to excite bitter feelings in
**2 :** to make bitter
— **em·bit·ter·ment** \-mənt\ noun

**¹em·blaze** \im-'blāz\ transitive verb **em·blazed; em·blaz·ing** (15th century)
**1 :** to illuminate especially by a blaze
**2 :** to set ablaze

**²emblaze** transitive verb **em·blazed; em·blaz·ing** [en- + blaze (to blazon)] (1593)
**1** archaic **:** EMBLAZON 1
**2 :** to adorn sumptuously ⟨with gems and golden luster rich emblazed —John Milton⟩

**em·bla·zon** \im-'blā-zᵊn\ transitive verb **em·bla·zoned; em·bla·zon·ing** \-'blāz-niŋ, -'blā-zᵊn-iŋ\ (1589)
**1 a :** to inscribe or adorn with or as if with heraldic bearings or devices **b :** to inscribe (as heraldic bearings) on a surface
**2 :** CELEBRATE, EXTOL ⟨have his . . . deeds emblazoned by a poet —Thomas Nash⟩
— **em·bla·zon·er** \-'blāz-nər, -zᵊn-ər\ noun
— **em·bla·zon·ment** \-'blā-zᵊn-mənt\ noun

**em·bla·zon·ry** \-zᵊn-rē\ noun (1667)
**1 :** emblazoned figures **:** brilliant decoration
**2 :** the act or art of emblazoning

**¹em·blem** \'em-bləm\ noun [Middle English, from Latin emblema inlaid work, from Greek emblēmat-, emblēma, from emballein to insert, from en- + ballein to throw — more at DEVIL] (15th century)

---

---

\ə\ **abut** \ᵊ\ **kitten** \ər\ **further** \a\ **ash** \ā\ **ace**
\ä\ **mop, mar** \au̇\ **out** \ch\ **chin** \e\ **bet** \ē\ **easy**
\g\ **go** \i\ **hit** \ī\ **ice** \j\ **job** \ŋ\ **sing** \ō\ **go**
\ȯ\ **law** \ȯi\ **boy** \th\ **thin** \t̲h\ **the** \ü\ **loot** \u̇\ **foot**
\y\ **yet** \zh\ **vision** see also Guide to Pronunciation

**1 :** a picture with a motto or set of verses intended as a moral lesson
**2 :** an object or the figure of an object symbolizing and suggesting another object or an idea
**3 a :** a symbolic object used as a heraldic device **b :** a device, symbol, or figure adopted and used as an identifying mark
**²emblem** *transitive verb* (1584)
**:** EMBLEMATIZE
**em·blem·at·ic** \,em-blə-'ma-tik\ *also* **em·blem·at·i·cal** \-ti-kəl\ *adjective* (1645)
**:** of, relating to, or constituting an emblem
**:** SYMBOLIC, REPRESENTATIVE
— **em·blem·at·i·cal·ly** \-ti-k(ə-)lē\ *adverb*
**em·blem·a·tize** \em-'ble-mə-,tīz\ *transitive verb* **-tized; -tiz·ing** (1615)
**:** to represent by or as if by an emblem **:** SYMBOLIZE
**em·ble·ments** \'em-blə-mən(t)s\ *noun plural* [Middle English *emblayment*, from Middle French *emblaement*, from *emblaer* to sow with grain, from *en-* + *blee* grain, of Germanic origin; akin to Old English *blæd* fruit, growth, leaf — more at BLADE] (15th century)
**:** crops from annual cultivation legally belonging to the tenant
**em·bod·i·ment** \im-'bä-di-mənt\ *noun* (1828)
**1 :** one that embodies something ⟨the *embodiment* of all our hopes⟩
**2 :** the act of embodying **:** the state of being embodied
**em·body** \im-'bä-dē\ *transitive verb* **em·bod·ied; em·body·ing** (circa 1548)
**1 :** to give a body to (a spirit) **:** INCARNATE
**2 a :** to deprive of spirituality **b :** to make concrete and perceptible
**3 :** to cause to become a body or part of a body **:** INCORPORATE
**4 :** to represent in human or animal form **:** PERSONIFY ⟨men who greatly *embodied* the idealism of American life —A. M. Schlesinger (born 1917)⟩
— **em·bod·i·er** *noun*
**em·bold·en** \im-'bōl-dən\ *transitive verb* (15th century)
**:** to instill with boldness or courage
**em·bo·lec·to·my** \,em-bə-'lek-tə-mē\ *noun, plural* **-mies** (1923)
**:** surgical removal of an embolus
**em·bol·ic** \em-'bä-lik, im-\ *adjective* (1866)
**:** of or relating to an embolus or embolism
**em·bo·lism** \'em-bə-,li-zəm\ *noun* [Middle English *embolisme*, from Medieval Latin *embolismus*, from Greek *embol-* (from *emballein* to insert, intercalate) — more at EMBLEM] (14th century)
**1 :** the insertion of one or more days in a calendar **:** INTERCALATION
**2 a :** the sudden obstruction of a blood vessel by an embolus **b :** EMBOLUS
— **em·bo·lis·mic** \,em-bə-'liz-mik\ *adjective*
**em·bo·li·za·tion** \,em-bə-lə-'zā-shən\ *noun* (1942)
**:** the process or state in which a blood vessel or organ is obstructed by the lodgment of a material mass (as an embolus)
**em·bo·lus** \'em-bə-ləs\ *noun, plural* **-li** \-,lī\ [New Latin, from Greek *embolos* wedge-shaped object, stopper, from *emballein*] (1855)
**:** an abnormal particle (as an air bubble) circulating in the blood — compare THROMBUS
**em·bon·point** \äⁿ-bōⁿ-pwäⁿ\ *noun* [French, from Middle French, from *en bon point* in good condition] (1670)
**:** plumpness of person **:** STOUTNESS
**em·bos·om** \im-'bu̇-zəm *also* -'bü-\ *transitive verb* (circa 1590)
**1** *archaic* **:** to take into or place in the bosom
**2 :** to shelter closely **:** ENCLOSE ⟨his house *embosomed* in the grove —Alexander Pope⟩
**¹em·boss** \im-'bäs, -'bȯs\ *transitive verb* [Middle English *embosen* to become exhausted from being hunted, ultimately from Middle French *bois* woods] (14th century)

*archaic* **:** to drive (as a hunted animal) to bay or to exhaustion
**²emboss** *transitive verb* [Middle English *embosen*, from Middle French *embocer*, from *en-* + *boce* boss] (15th century)
**1 :** to raise the surface of into bosses; *especially* **:** to ornament with raised work
**2 :** to raise in relief from a surface
**3 :** ADORN, EMBELLISH
— **em·boss·able** \-'bä-sə-bəl, -'bȯ-\ *adjective*
— **em·boss·er** \-sər\ *noun*
— **em·boss·ment** \-mənt\ *noun*
**em·bou·chure** \'äm-bu̇-,shu̇r, ,äm-bu̇-'\ *noun* [French, from (*s'*)*emboucher* to flow into, from *en-* + *bouche* mouth — more at DEBOUCH] (1760)
**1 :** the position and use of the lips, tongue, and teeth in playing a wind instrument
**2 :** the mouthpiece of a musical instrument
**em·bour·geoise·ment** \em-'bu̇rzh-,wäz-mənt, äm-; äⁿ-bu̇rzh-wáz-mäⁿ\ *noun* [French, from *embourgeoiser* to make bourgeois, from *em-* + *bourgeois*] (1937)
**:** a shift to bourgeois values and practices
**em·bowed** \im-'bōd\ *adjective* (15th century)
**:** bent like a bow **:** ARCHED
**em·bow·el** \im-'bau̇-(ə)l\ *transitive verb* **-eled** *or* **-elled; -el·ing** *or* **-el·ling** (1521)
**1 :** DISEMBOWEL
**2** *obsolete* **:** ENCLOSE
**em·bow·er** \im-'bau̇-(ə)r\ *transitive verb* (1580)
**:** to shelter or enclose in or as if in a bower ⟨like a rose *embowered* in its own green leaves —P. B. Shelley⟩
**¹em·brace** \im-'brās\ *verb* **em·braced; em·brac·ing** [Middle English, from Middle French *embracer*, from Old French *embracier*, from *en-* + *brace* two arms — more at BRACE] (14th century)
*transitive verb*
**1 a :** to clasp in the arms **:** HUG **b :** CHERISH, LOVE
**2 :** ENCIRCLE, ENCLOSE
**3 a :** to take up especially readily or gladly ⟨*embrace* a cause⟩ **b :** to avail oneself of **:** WELCOME ⟨*embraced* the opportunity to study further⟩
**4 a :** to take in or include as a part, item, or element of a more inclusive whole ⟨charity *embraces* all acts that contribute to human welfare⟩ **b :** to be equal or equivalent to ⟨his assets *embraced* $10⟩
*intransitive verb*
**:** to participate in an embrace
**synonym** see ADOPT, INCLUDE
— **em·brace·able** \-'brā-sə-bəl\ *adjective*
— **em·brace·ment** \-'brā-smənt\ *noun*
— **em·brac·er** *noun*
— **em·brac·ing·ly** \-'brā-siŋ-lē\ *adverb*
**²embrace** *noun* (1592)
**1 :** a close encircling with the arms and pressure to the bosom especially as a sign of affection **:** HUG
**2 :** GRIP, ENCIRCLEMENT ⟨in the *embrace* of terror⟩
**3 :** ACCEPTANCE ⟨her *embrace* of new ideas⟩
**em·bra·ceor** \im-'brā-sər\ *noun* [Anglo-French, from Middle French *embraseor* instigator, from *embraser* to set on fire, from *en-* + *brase, brese* live coals] (15th century)
**:** one guilty of embracery
**em·brac·ery** \im-'brā-sə-rē\ *noun, plural* **-er·ies** [Middle English, from Anglo-French *embraceor*] (15th century)
**:** an attempt to influence a jury corruptly
**em·brac·ive** \-'brā-siv\ *adjective* (1855)
**1 :** disposed to embrace
**2 :** INCLUSIVE, COMPREHENSIVE
**em·bran·gle** \im-'braŋ-gəl\ *transitive verb* **-gled; -gling** \-g(ə-)liŋ\ [*en-* + *brangle* (squabble)] (1664)
**:** EMBROIL
— **em·bran·gle·ment** \-gəl-mənt\ *noun*

**em·bra·sure** \im-'brā-zhər\ *noun* [French, from obsolete *embraser* to widen an opening] (1702)
**1 :** an opening with sides flaring outward in a wall or parapet of a fortification usually for allowing the firing of cannon
**2 :** a recess of a door or window
**em·brit·tle** \im-'bri-t°l\ *verb* **-brit·tled; -brit·tling** \-'brit-liŋ, -t°l-iŋ\ (1902)
*transitive verb*
**:** to make brittle
*intransitive verb*
**:** to become brittle
— **em·brit·tle·ment** \-'brit-t°l-mənt\ *noun*

*E* embrasure 2

**em·bro·ca·tion** \,em-brə-'kā-shən\ *noun* [Middle English *embrocacioun*, from Middle French *embrocacion*, from Medieval Latin *embrocation-, embrocatio*, from Late Latin *embrocare* to rub with lotion, from Greek *embroche* lotion, from *en-* + *brechein* to wet] (15th century)
**:** LINIMENT
**em·broi·der** \im-'brȯi-dər\ *verb* **em·broi·dered; em·broi·der·ing** \-d(ə-)riŋ\ [Middle English *embroderen*, from Middle French *embroder*, from *en-* + *broder* to embroider, of Germanic origin; akin to Old English *brord* point, *byrst* bristle] (14th century)
*transitive verb*
**1 a :** to ornament with needlework **b :** to form with needlework
**2 :** to elaborate on **:** EMBELLISH
*intransitive verb*
**1 :** to make embroidery
**2 :** to provide embellishments **:** ELABORATE
— **em·broi·der·er** \-'brȯi-dər-ər\ *noun*
**em·broi·dery** \im-'brȯi-d(ə-)rē\ *noun, plural* **-der·ies** (14th century)
**1 a :** the art or process of forming decorative designs with hand or machine needlework **b :** a design or decoration formed by or as if by embroidery **c :** an object decorated with embroidery
**2 :** elaboration by use of decorative and often fictitious detail
**3 :** something pleasing or desirable but unimportant ⟨considered the humanities mere educational *embroidery*⟩
**em·broil** \im-'brȯi(ə)l\ *transitive verb* [French *embrouiller*, from Middle French, from *en-* + *brouiller* to broil] (1603)
**1 :** to throw into disorder or confusion
**2 :** to involve in conflict or difficulties
— **em·broil·ment** \-mənt\ *noun*
**em·brown** \im-'brau̇n\ *transitive verb* (1667)
**1 :** DARKEN
**2 :** to cause to turn brown
**embrue** *variant of* IMBRUE
**embry-** *or* **embryo-** *combining form* [Late Latin, from Greek, from *embryon*]
**:** embryo ⟨*embryo*geny⟩
**em·bryo** \'em-brē-,ō\ *noun, plural* **em·bry·os** [Medieval Latin *embryon-, embryo*, from Greek *embryon*, from *en-* + *bryein* to swell; akin to Greek *bryon* catkin] (1548)
**1 a** *archaic* **:** a vertebrate at any stage of development prior to birth or hatching **b :** an animal in the early stages of growth and differentiation that are characterized by cleavage, the laying down of fundamental tissues, and the formation of primitive organs and organ systems; *especially* **:** the developing human individual from the time of implantation to the end of the eighth week after conception
**2 :** the young sporophyte of a seed plant usually comprising a rudimentary plant with plumule, radicle, and cotyledons
**3 a :** something as yet undeveloped **b :** a beginning or undeveloped state of something

⟨productions seen in *embryo* during their out-of-town tryout period —Henry Hewes⟩

**em·bry·o·gen·e·sis** \,em-brē-ō-'je-nə-səs\ *noun* (1830)
: the formation and development of the embryo
— **em·bryo·ge·net·ic** \-jə-'ne-tik\ *adjective*

**em·bry·og·e·ny** \,em-brē-'ä-jə-nē\ *noun, plural* **-nies** (1835)
: EMBRYOGENESIS
— **em·bryo·gen·ic** \-brē-ō-'je-nik\ *adjective*

**em·bry·oid** \'em-brē-,ȯid\ *noun* (circa 1927)
: a mass of plant or animal tissue that resembles an embryo
— **embryoid** *adjective*

**em·bry·ol·o·gy** \,em-brē-'ä-lə-jē\ *noun* [French *embryologie*] (circa 1847)
**1** : a branch of biology dealing with embryos and their development
**2** : the features and phenomena exhibited in the formation and development of an embryo
— **em·bry·o·log·i·cal** \-brē-ə-'lä-ji-kəl\ *adjective*
— **em·bry·o·log·i·cal·ly** \-ji-k(ə-)lē\ *adverb*
— **em·bry·ol·o·gist** \-brē-'ä-lə-jist\ *noun*

**embryon-** *or* **embryoni-** *combining form* [Medieval Latin *embryon-, embryo*]
: embryo ⟨*embryonic*⟩

**em·bry·o·nal** \em-'brī-ə-n°l\ *adjective* (1652)
: EMBRYONIC 1

**em·bry·o·nat·ed** \'em-brē-ə-,nā-təd\ *adjective* (1687)
: having an embryo

**em·bry·on·ic** \,em-brē-'ä-nik\ *adjective* (circa 1841)
**1** : of or relating to an embryo
**2** : being in an early stage of development : INCIPIENT, RUDIMENTARY
— **em·bry·on·i·cal·ly** \-ni-k(ə-)lē\ *adverb*

**embryonic disk** *noun* (circa 1938)
**1 a** : BLASTODISC **b** : BLASTODERM
**2** : the part of the inner cell mass of a blastocyst from which the embryo of a placental mammal develops — called also *embryonic shield*

**embryonic membrane** *noun* (1947)
: a structure (as the amnion) that derives from the fertilized ovum but does not form a part of the embryo

**em·bryo·phyte** \'em-brē-ə-,fīt\ *noun* (circa 1909)
: any of a subkingdom (Embryophyta) of plants in which the embryo is retained within maternal tissue and which include the bryophytes and tracheophytes

**embryo sac** *noun* (1872)
: the female gametophyte of a seed plant consisting of a thin-walled sac within the nucellus that contains the egg nucleus and other nuclei which give rise to endosperm on fertilization

**embryo transfer** *noun* (1969)
: a procedure used especially in animal breeding in which an embryo from a superovulated female is removed and reimplanted in the uterus of another female — called also *embryo transplant*

**¹em·cee** \,em-'sē\ *noun* [*MC*] (circa 1933)
: MASTER OF CEREMONIES

**²emcee** *verb* **em·ceed; em·cee·ing** (1937)
*transitive verb*
: to act as master of ceremonies of
*intransitive verb*
: to act as master of ceremonies

**-eme** \ēm\ *noun suffix* [French *-ème* (from *phonème* speech sound, phoneme)]
: significantly distinctive unit of language structure ⟨tax*eme*⟩

**emend** \ē-'mend\ *transitive verb* [Middle English, from Latin *emendare* — more at AMEND] (15th century)
: to correct usually by textual alterations
**synonym** see CORRECT

— **emend·able** \-'men-də-bəl\ *adjective*
— **emend·er** *noun*

**emen·da·tion** \,ē-,men-'dā-shən; ,e-mən-, e-,men-\ *noun* (1536)
**1** : the act or practice of emending
**2** : an alteration designed to correct or improve

**¹em·er·ald** \'em-rəld, 'e-mə-\ *noun* [Middle English *emeralde*, from Middle French *esmeralde*, from (assumed) Vulgar Latin *smaralda*, from Latin *smaragdus*, from Greek *smaragdos*] (14th century)
**1** : a rich green variety of beryl prized as a gemstone
**2** : any of various green gemstones (as synthetic corundum or demantoid)

**²emerald** *adjective* (1508)
: brightly or richly green

**emerald cut** *noun* (1926)
: a rectangular cut for a gem having a series of parallel facets on each side and at each corner

**emerald green** *noun* (1646)
**1** : a clear bright green resembling that of the emerald
**2** : any of various strong greens

**emerge** \i-'mərj\ *intransitive verb* **emerged; emerg·ing** [Latin *emergere*, from *e-* + *mergere* to plunge — more at MERGE] (1563)
**1** : to become manifest
**2** : to rise from or as if from an enveloping fluid : come out into view
**3** : to rise from an obscure or inferior position or condition
**4** : to come into being through evolution

**emer·gence** \i-'mər-jən(t)s\ *noun* (1704)
**1** : the act or an instance of emerging
**2** : any of various superficial outgrowths of plant tissue usually formed from both epidermis and immediately underlying tissues
**3** : penetration of the soil surface by a newly germinated plant

**emer·gen·cy** \i-'mər-jənt-sē\ *noun, plural* **-cies** *often attributive* (circa 1631)
**1** : an unforeseen combination of circumstances or the resulting state that calls for immediate action
**2** : an urgent need for assistance or relief ⟨the governor declared a state of *emergency* after the flood⟩
**synonym** see JUNCTURE

**emergency brake** *noun* (1900)
: a brake (as on an automobile) that can be used for stopping in the event of failure of the main brakes and to keep the vehicle from rolling when parked

**emergency medical technician** *noun* (1980)
: EMT

**emergency room** *noun* (1964)
: a hospital room or area staffed and equipped for the reception and treatment of persons requiring immediate medical care

**¹emer·gent** \i-'mər-jənt\ *adjective* [Middle English, from Latin *emergent-, emergens*, present participle of *emergere*] (1593)
**1 a** : arising unexpectedly **b** : calling for prompt action : URGENT
**2** : rising out of or as if out of a fluid
**3** : arising as a natural or logical consequence
**4** : newly formed or prominent

**²emergent** *noun* (1620)
**1** : something emergent
**2 a** : a tree that rises above the surrounding forest **b** : a plant rooted in shallow water and having most of the vegetative growth above water

**emergent evolution** *noun* (1923)
: evolution that according to some theories involves the appearance of new characters and qualities at complex levels of organization (as the cell or organism) which cannot be predicted solely from the study of less complex levels (as the atom or molecule) — compare CREATIVE EVOLUTION

**emerg·ing** *adjective* (1646)
: EMERGENT 4 ⟨the *emerging* nations of Africa⟩

**emer·i·ta** \i-'mer-ə-tə\ *adjective* [Latin, feminine of *emeritus*] (1928)
: EMERITUS — used of a woman ⟨Professor *Emerita* Mary Smith⟩

**¹emer·i·tus** \i-'mer-ə-təs\ *noun, plural* **-i·ti** \-ə-,tī, -,tē\ (1750)
: one retired from professional life but permitted to retain as an honorary title the rank of the last office held

**²emeritus** *adjective* [Latin, past participle of *emereri* to serve out one's term, from *e-* + *mereri, merēre* to earn, deserve, serve — more at MERIT] (1794)
**1** : holding after retirement an honorary title corresponding to that held last during active service
**2** : retired from an office or position ⟨professor *emeritus*⟩ — converted to *emeriti* after a plural ⟨professors *emeriti*⟩

**emersed** \(,)ē-'mərst\ *adjective* (1686)
: standing out of or rising above a surface (as of a fluid) ⟨*emersed* aquatic weeds⟩

**emer·sion** \(,)ē-'mər-zhən, -shən\ *noun* [Latin *emersus*, past participle of *emergere*] (1633)
: an act of emerging : EMERGENCE

**em·ery** \'em-rē, 'e-mə-\ *noun, plural* **em·er·ies** *often attributive* [Middle English, from Middle French *emeri*, from Old Italian *smiriglio*, from Medieval Latin *smiriglum*, from Greek *smyrid-, smyris*] (15th century)
: a dark granular mineral that consists essentially of corundum and is used for grinding and polishing; *also* : a hard abrasive powder

**emery board** *noun* (1725)
: a cardboard nail file covered with emery

**eme·sis** \'e-mə-səs, i-'mē-\ *noun, plural* **eme·ses** \-,sēz\ [New Latin, from Greek, from *emein*] (circa 1847)
: an act or instance of vomiting

**emet·ic** \i-'me-tik\ *noun* [Latin *emetica*, from Greek *emetikē*, from feminine of *emetikos* causing vomiting, from *emein* to vomit — more at VOMIT] (1657)
: an agent that induces vomiting
— **emetic** *adjective*
— **emet·i·cal·ly** \-ti-k(ə-)lē\ *adverb*

**em·e·tine** \'e-mə-,tēn\ *noun* (1819)
: an amorphous alkaloid $C_{29}H_{40}N_2O_4$ extracted from ipecac root and used as an emetic and expectorant

**émeute** \ā-'mœt\ *noun, plural* **émeutes** \same\ [French, from Old French *esmeute* act of starting, from feminine of *esmeut*, past participle of *esmovoir* to start — more at EMOTION] (1782)
: UPRISING

**emf** \,ē-(,)em-'ef\ *noun* [*electromotive force*] (1868)
: POTENTIAL DIFFERENCE

**-emia** \'ē-mē-ə\ *noun combining form* [New Latin *-emia, -aemia*, from Greek *-aimia*, from *haima* blood]
**1** : condition of having (such) blood ⟨leuk*emia*⟩
**2** : condition of having (a specified thing) in the blood ⟨ur*emia*⟩

**emic** \'ē-mik\ *adjective* [phon*emic*] (1954)
: of, relating to, or involving analysis of linguistic or behavioral phenomena in terms of the internal structural or functional elements of a particular system — compare ETIC

**¹em·i·grant** \'e-mi-grənt\ *noun* (1754)
**1** : one who emigrates
**2** : a migrant plant or animal

**²emigrant** *adjective* (1794)
: departing or having departed from a country to settle elsewhere

**em·i·grate** \'e-mə-,grāt\ *intransitive verb* **-grat·ed; -grat·ing** [Latin *emigratus*, past

\ə\ abut \ᵊ\ kitten \ər\ further \a\ ash \ā\ ace
\ä\ mop, mar \au̇\ out \ch\ chin \e\ bet \ē\ easy
\g\ go \i\ hit \ī\ ice \j\ job \ŋ\ sing \ō\ go
\ȯ\ law \ȯi\ boy \th\ thin \t͟h\ the \ü\ loot \u̇\ foot
\y\ yet \zh\ vision    *see also* Guide to Pronunciation

participle of *emigrare*, from *e-* + *migrare* to migrate] (1778)
**:** to leave one's place of residence or country to live elsewhere
— **em·i·gra·tion** \ˌe-mə-ˈgrā-shən\ *noun*
**émi·gré** *also* **emi·gre** \ˈe-mi-ˌgrā, ˌe-mi-ˈ\ *noun, often attributive* [French *émigré*, from past participle of *émigrer* to emigrate, from Latin *emigrare*] (1792)
**:** EMIGRANT; *especially* **:** a person forced to emigrate for political reasons
**em·i·nence** \ˈe-mə-nən(t)s\ *noun* (15th century)
**1 :** a position of prominence or superiority
**2 :** one that is eminent, prominent, or lofty: as **a :** an anatomical protuberance (as on a bone) **b :** a person of high rank or attainments — often used as a title for a cardinal **c :** a natural elevation
**émi·nence grise** \ā-mē-näⁿs-grēz\ *noun, plural* **éminences grises** \same\ [French, literally, gray eminence, nickname of Père Joseph (François du Tremblay) (died 1638) French monk and diplomat, confidant of Cardinal Richelieu who was known as *Éminence Rouge* red eminence; from the colors of their respective habits] (1925)
**:** a confidential agent; *especially* **:** one exercising unsuspected or unofficial power
**em·i·nen·cy** \ˈe-mə-nən(t)-sē\ *noun, plural* **-cies** (1605)
*archaic* **:** EMINENCE
**em·i·nent** \ˈe-mə-nənt\ *adjective* [Middle English, from Middle French or Latin; Middle French, from Latin *eminent-, eminens*, present participle of *eminēre* to stand out, from *e-* + *-minēre*; akin to Latin *mont-, mons* mountain — more at MOUNT] (15th century)
**1 :** standing out so as to be readily perceived or noted **:** CONSPICUOUS
**2 :** jutting out **:** PROJECTING
**3 :** exhibiting eminence especially in standing above others in some quality or position **:** PROMINENT
*synonym* see FAMOUS
**eminent domain** *noun* (1783)
**:** a right of a government to take private property for public use by virtue of the superior dominion of the sovereign power over all lands within its jurisdiction
**em·i·nent·ly** \-lē\ *adverb* (1641)
**:** to a high degree **:** VERY ⟨*eminently* worthy⟩ ⟨an *eminently* sensible plan⟩
**emir** \i-ˈmir, ā-\ *noun* [Arabic *amīr* commander] (1595)
**:** a ruler, chief, or commander in Islamic countries
**emir·ate** \ˈe-mə-rət, -ˌrāt\ *noun* (1863)
**:** the state or jurisdiction of an emir
**em·is·sary** \ˈe-mə-ˌser-ē\ *noun, plural* **-saries** [Latin *emissarius*, from *emissus*, past participle of *emittere*] (1616)
**1 :** one designated as the agent of another **:** REPRESENTATIVE
**2 :** a secret agent
**emis·sion** \ē-ˈmi-shən\ *noun* (1607)
**1 a :** an act or instance of emitting **:** EMANATION **b** *archaic* **:** PUBLICATION **c :** a putting into circulation
**2 a :** something sent forth by emitting: as (1) **:** electromagnetic waves radiated by an antenna or a celestial body (2) **:** substances discharged into the air (as by a smokestack or an automobile gasoline engine) **b :** EFFLUVIUM
— **emis·sive** \-ˈmi-siv\ *adjective*
**emis·siv·i·ty** \ˌe-mə-ˈsi-və-tē, ˌē-ˌmi-ˈsiv-\ *noun, plural* **-ties** (1880)
**:** the relative power of a surface to emit heat by radiation **:** the ratio of the radiant energy emitted by a surface to that emitted by a blackbody at the same temperature
**emit** \ē-ˈmit\ *transitive verb* **emit·ted; emit·ting** [Latin *emittere* to send out, from *e-* + *mittere* to send] (1626)
**1 a :** to throw or give off or out (as light) **b :** to send out **:** EJECT

**2 a :** to issue with authority; *especially* **:** to put (as money) into circulation **b** *obsolete* **:** PUBLISH
**3 :** to give utterance or voice to ⟨*emitted* a groan⟩
— **emit·ter** *noun*
**emit·tance** \ē-ˈmi-tᵊn(t)s\ *noun* (1940)
**1 :** the energy radiated by the surface of a body per second per unit area
**2 :** EMISSIVITY
**Emmanuel** *variant of* IMMANUEL
**em·men·a·gogue** \ə-ˈme-nə-ˌgäg, e-\ *noun* [Greek *emmēna* menses (from neuter plural of *emmēnos* monthly, from *en-* + *mēn* month) + English *-agogue* — more at MOON] (circa 1732)
**:** an agent that promotes the menstrual discharge
**Em·men·ta·ler** *or* **Em·men·tha·ler** \ˈe-mən-ˌtä-lər\ *or* **Em·men·tal** *or* **Em·men·thal** \-ˌtäl\ *noun* [German, from *Emmental*, Switzerland] (1902)
**:** SWISS CHEESE
**em·mer** \ˈe-mər\ *noun* [German, from Old High German *amari*] (circa 1900)
**:** a wheat (*Triticum dicoccum*) having spikelets with two hard red kernels that remain in the glumes after threshing; *broadly* **:** a tetraploid wheat — called also *emmer wheat*
**em·met** \ˈe-mət\ *noun* [Middle English *emete*, from Old English *æmette* ant — more at ANT] (before 12th century)
*chiefly dialect* **:** ANT
**Em·my** \ˈe-mē\ *noun, plural* **Emmys** [from alteration of *Immy*, nickname for *image orthicon* (a camera tube used in television)] (1949)
**:** a statuette awarded annually by a professional organization for notable achievement in television
**em·o·din** \ˈe-mə-dən\ *noun* [International Scientific Vocabulary *emodi-* (from New Latin *Rheum emodi*, species of rhubarb) + *-in*] (1858)
**:** an orange crystalline phenolic compound $C_{15}H_{10}O_5$ that is obtained from plants (as rhubarb and cascara buckthorn) and is used as a laxative
**¹emol·lient** \i-ˈmäl-yənt\ *adjective* [Latin *emollient-, emolliens*, present participle of *emollire* to soften, from *e-* + *mollis* soft — more at MOLLIFY] (circa 1640)
**1 :** making soft or supple; *also* **:** soothing especially to the skin or mucous membrane
**2 :** making less intense or harsh **:** MOLLIFYING ⟨soothe us in our agonies with *emollient* words —H. L. Mencken⟩
**²emollient** *noun* (1656)
**:** something that softens or soothes
**emol·u·ment** \i-ˈmäl-yə-mənt\ *noun* [Middle English, from Latin *emolumentum* advantage, from *emolere* to produce by grinding, from *e-* + *molere* to grind — more at MEAL] (15th century)
**1 :** the returns arising from office or employment usually in the form of compensation or perquisites
**2** *archaic* **:** ADVANTAGE
**emote** \i-ˈmōt\ *intransitive verb* **emot·ed; emot·ing** [back-formation from *emotion*] (1917)
**:** to give expression to emotion especially in or as if in acting
**emo·tion** \i-ˈmō-shən\ *noun* [Middle French, from *emouvoir* to stir up, from Old French *esmovoir*, from Latin *emovēre* to remove, displace, from *e-* + *movēre* to move] (1579)
**1 a** *obsolete* **:** DISTURBANCE **b :** EXCITEMENT
**2 a :** the affective aspect of consciousness **:** FEELING **b :** a state of feeling **c :** a psychic and physical reaction (as anger or fear) subjectively experienced as strong feeling and physiologically involving changes that prepare the body for immediate vigorous action
*synonym* see FEELING
**emo·tion·al** \-shnəl, -shə-nᵊl\ *adjective* (1834)

**1 :** of or relating to emotion ⟨an *emotional* disorder⟩
**2 :** dominated by or prone to emotion ⟨an *emotional* person⟩
**3 :** appealing to or arousing emotion ⟨an *emotional* sermon⟩
**4 :** markedly aroused or agitated in feeling or sensibilities ⟨gets *emotional* at weddings⟩
— **emo·tion·al·i·ty** \-ˌmō-shə-ˈna-lə-tē\ *noun*
— **emo·tion·al·ly** \-ˈmō-shnə-lē, -shə-nᵊl-ē\ *adverb*
**emo·tion·al·ism** \i-ˈmō-shnə-ˌli-zəm, -shə-nᵊl-ˌiz-\ *noun* (1865)
**1 :** a tendency to regard things emotionally
**2 :** undue indulgence in or display of emotion
**emo·tion·al·ist** \-shnə-list, -shə-nᵊl-ist\ *noun* (circa 1866)
**1 :** one who bases a theory or policy on an emotional conviction
**2 :** one prone to emotionalism
— **emo·tion·al·is·tic** \-ˌmō-shnə-ˈlis-tik, -shə-nᵊl-ˈis-\ *adjective*
**emo·tion·al·ize** \i-ˈmō-shnə-ˌlīz, -shə-nᵊl-ˌīz\ *transitive verb* **-ized; -iz·ing** (1879)
**:** to give an emotional quality to
**emo·tion·less** \i-ˈmō-shən-ləs\ *adjective* (1862)
**:** showing, having, or expressing no emotion
— **emo·tion·less·ness** *noun*
— **emo·tion·less·ly** *adverb*
**emo·tive** \i-ˈmō-tiv\ *adjective* (1830)
**1 :** of or relating to the emotions
**2 :** appealing to or expressing emotion ⟨the *emotive* use of language⟩
— **emo·tive·ly** *adverb*
— **emo·tiv·i·ty** \ˌi-ˌmō-ˈti-və-tē, ˌē-ˌmō-\ *noun*
**em·pa·na·da** \ˌem-pə-ˈnä-də\ *noun* [American Spanish, from Spanish, feminine of *empanado*, past participle of *empanar* to bread, from *em-* (from Latin *in-*) + *pan* bread, from Latin *panis* — more at FOOD] (circa 1922)
**:** a turnover with a sweet or savory filling
**empanel** *variant of* IMPANEL
**em·pa·thet·ic** \ˌem-pə-ˈthe-tik\ *adjective* (1932)
**:** EMPATHIC
— **em·pa·thet·i·cal·ly** \-ti-k(ə-)lē\ *adverb*
**em·path·ic** \em-ˈpa-thik, im-\ *adjective* (1909)
**:** involving, eliciting, characterized by, or based on empathy
— **em·path·i·cal·ly** \-thi-k(ə-)lē\ *adverb*
**em·pa·thise** *British variant of* EMPATHIZE
**em·pa·thize** \ˈem-pə-ˌthīz\ *intransitive verb* **-thized; -thiz·ing** (circa 1921)
**:** to experience empathy ⟨adults unable to *empathize* with a child's frustrations⟩
**em·pa·thy** \ˈem-pə-thē\ *noun* [Greek *empatheia*, literally, passion, from *empathēs* emotional, from *em-* + *pathos* feelings, emotion — more at PATHOS] (1904)
**1 :** the imaginative projection of a subjective state into an object so that the object appears to be infused with it
**2 :** the action of understanding, being aware of, being sensitive to, and vicariously experiencing the feelings, thoughts, and experience of another of either the past or present without having the feelings, thoughts, and experience fully communicated in an objectively explicit manner; *also* **:** the capacity for this
**em·pen·nage** \ˌäm-pə-ˈnäzh, ˌem-\ *noun* [French, feathers of an arrow, empennage, from *empenner* to feather an arrow, from *em-* ¹en- + *penne* feather, from Middle French — more at PEN] (1909)
**:** the tail assembly of an airplane
**em·per·or** \ˈem-pər-ər, -prər\ *noun* [Middle English, from Old French *empereor*, from Latin *imperator*, literally, commander, from *imperare* to command, from *in-* + *parare* to prepare, order — more at PARE] (13th century)
**:** the sovereign or supreme male monarch of an empire
— **em·per·or·ship** \-ˌship\ *noun*

**emperor penguin** *noun* (1885)
: a penguin (*Aptenodytes forsteri*) that is the largest known and that is noted for its habit of brooding the egg or young between the feet and a fold of abdominal skin resembling a pouch

**em·pery** \'em-p(ə-)rē\ *noun, plural* **em·per·ies** [Middle English *emperie*, from Old French, from *emperer* to command, from Latin *imperare*] (13th century)
: wide dominion : EMPIRE

**em·pha·sise** *British variant of* EMPHASIZE

**em·pha·sis** \'em(p)-fə-səs\ *noun, plural* **-pha·ses** \-,sēz\ [Latin, from Greek, exposition, emphasis, from *emphainein* to indicate, from *en-* + *phainein* to show — more at FANCY] (1573)
**1 a** : force or intensity of expression that gives impressiveness or importance to something **b** : a particular prominence given in reading or speaking to one or more words or syllables
**2** : special consideration of or stress or insistence on something

**em·pha·size** \'em(p)-fə-,sīz\ *transitive verb* **-sized; -siz·ing** (circa 1806)
: to place emphasis on : STRESS ⟨*emphasized* the need for reform⟩

**em·phat·ic** \im-'fa-tik, em-\ *adjective* [Greek *emphatikos*, from *emphainein*] (circa 1708)
**1** : uttered with or marked by emphasis
**2** : tending to express oneself in forceful speech or to take decisive action
**3** : attracting special attention
**4** : constituting or belonging to a set of tense forms in English consisting of the auxiliary *do* followed by an infinitive without *to* that are used to facilitate rhetorical inversion or to emphasize something
— **em·phat·i·cal·ly** \-'fa-ti-k(ə-)lē\ *adverb*

**em·phy·se·ma** \,em(p)-fə-'zē-mə, -'sē-\ *noun* [New Latin, from Greek *emphysēma*, from *emphysan* to inflate, from *em-* ²en- + *physan* to blow, from *physa* breath — more at PUSTULE] (1661)
: a condition characterized by air-filled expansions of body tissues; *specifically* : a condition of the lung marked by abnormal dilation of its air spaces and distension of its walls and frequently by impairment of heart action
— **em·phy·se·ma·tous** \-'ze-mə-təs, -'se-, -'zē-, -'sē-\ *adjective*
— **em·phy·se·mic** \-'zē-mik, -'sē-\ *adjective*

**em·pire** \'em-,pīr\ *noun* [Middle English, from Old French *empire, empirie*, from Latin *imperium* absolute authority, empire, from *imperare*] (14th century)
**1 a** (1) : a major political unit having a territory of great extent or a number of territories or peoples under a single sovereign authority; *especially* : one having an emperor as chief of state (2) : the territory of such a political unit **b** : something resembling a political empire; *especially* : an extensive territory or enterprise under single domination or control
**2** : imperial sovereignty, rule, or dominion

**Em·pire** \'äm-,pir, 'em-,pīr\ *adjective* [French, from (*le premier*) *Empire* the first Empire of France] (1869)
: of, relating to, or characteristic of a style (as of clothing or furniture) popular in early 19th century France

**Em·pire Day** \'em-,pīr-\ *noun* (1902)
: COMMONWEALTH DAY — used before the official adoption of *Commonwealth Day* in 1958

**em·pir·ic** \im-'pir-ik, em-\ *noun* [Latin *empiricus*, from Greek *empeirikos* doctor relying on experience alone, from *empeiria* experience, from *em-* ²en- + *peiran* to attempt — more at FEAR] (1562)
**1** : CHARLATAN 2
**2** : one who relies on practical experience

**em·pir·i·cal** \-i-kəl\ *also* **em·pir·ic** \-ik\ *adjective* (1569)
**1** : originating in or based on observation or experience ⟨*empirical* data⟩

**2** : relying on experience or observation alone often without due regard for system and theory
**3** : capable of being verified or disproved by observation or experiment ⟨*empirical* laws⟩
**4** : of or relating to empiricism
— **em·pir·i·cal·ly** \-i-k(ə-)lē\ *adverb*

**empirical formula** *noun* (1885)
: a chemical formula showing the simplest ratio of elements in a compound rather than the total number of atoms in the molecule ⟨$CH_2O$ is the *empirical formula* for glucose⟩

**em·pir·i·cism** \im-'pir-ə-,si-zəm, em-\ *noun* (1657)
**1 a** : a former school of medical practice founded on experience without the aid of science or theory **b** : QUACKERY, CHARLATANRY
**2 a** : the practice of relying on observation and experiment especially in the natural sciences **b** : a tenet arrived at empirically
**3** : a theory that all knowledge originates in experience
— **em·pir·i·cist** \-sist\ *noun*

**em·place** \im-'plās\ *transitive verb* [back-formation from *emplacement*] (1865)
: to put into position ⟨missiles *emplaced* around the city⟩

**em·place·ment** \-'plā-smənt\ *noun* [French, from Middle French *emplacer* to emplace, from *en-* + *place*] (1802)
**1** : the situation or location of something
**2** : a prepared position for weapons or military equipment ⟨radar *emplacements*⟩
**3** : a putting into position : PLACEMENT

**em·plane** \im-'plān\ *variant of* ENPLANE

**¹em·ploy** \im-'plói, em-\ *transitive verb* [Middle English *emploien*, from Middle French *emploier*, from Latin *implicare* to enfold, involve, implicate, from *in-* + *plicare* to fold — more at PLY] (15th century)
**1 a** : to make use of (someone or something inactive) ⟨*employ* a pen for sketching⟩ **b** : to use (as time) advantageously **c** (1) : to use or engage the services of (2) : to provide with a job that pays wages or a salary
**2** : to devote to or direct toward a particular activity or person ⟨*employed* all her energies to help the poor⟩
*synonym* see USE
— **em·ploy·er** *noun*

**²em·ploy** \im-'plói, 'im-,, 'em-\ *noun* (1666)
**1 a** : USE, PURPOSE **b** : OCCUPATION, JOB
**2** : the state of being employed ⟨in the government's *employ*⟩

**¹em·ploy·able** \im-'plói-ə-bəl\ *adjective* (1593)
: capable of being employed
— **em·ploy·abil·i·ty** \-,plói-ə-'bi-lə-tē\ *noun*

**²employable** *noun* (1934)
: one who is employable

**em·ploy·ee** *or* **em·ploye** \im-,plói(i)-'ē, (,)em-; im-'plói(i)-,ē, em-\ *noun* (1822)
: one employed by another usually for wages or salary and in a position below the executive level

**em·ploy·ment** \im-'plói-mənt\ *noun* (15th century)
**1** : USE, PURPOSE
**2 a** : activity in which one engages or is employed **b** : an instance of such activity
**3** : the act of employing : the state of being employed
*synonym* see WORK

**employment agency** *noun* (1888)
: an agency whose business is to find jobs for people seeking them or to find people to fill jobs that are open

**em·poi·son** \im-'pói-z°n\ *transitive verb* [Middle English *empoysonen*, from Middle French *empoisoner*, from *en-* + *poison* poison, from Old French] (14th century)
**1** *archaic* : POISON
**2** : EMBITTER ⟨a look of *empoisoned* acceptance —Saul Bellow⟩
— **em·poi·son·ment** \-mənt\ *noun*

**em·po·ri·um** \im-'pór-ē-əm, em-, -'pór-\ *noun, plural* **-ri·ums** *also* **-ria** \-ē-ə\ [Latin, from Greek *emporion*, from *emporos* traveler, trader, from *em-* ²en- + *poros* passage, journey — more at FARE] (1586)
**1 a** : a place of trade; *especially* : a commercial center **b** : a retail outlet ⟨a hardware *emporium*⟩ ⟨a pizza *emporium*⟩
**2** : a store carrying a diversity of merchandise

**em·pow·er** \im-'paú(-ə)r\ *transitive verb* (1648)
**1** : to give official authority or legal power to
**2** : ENABLE 1a
**3** : to promote the self-actualization or influence of ⟨women's movement has been inspiring and *empowering* women —Ron Hansen⟩
— **em·pow·er·ment** \-mənt\ *noun*

**em·press** \'em-prəs\ *noun* [Middle English *emperesse*, from Old French, feminine of *empereor* emperor] (12th century)
**1** : the wife or widow of an emperor
**2** : a woman who is the sovereign or supreme monarch of an empire

**em·presse·ment** \ä<sup>n</sup>-pres-mä<sup>n</sup>\ *noun* [French, from (*s'*)*empresser* to hurry, from *en-* + *presser* to press] (1709)
: demonstrative warmth or cordiality

**em·prise** \im-'prīz\ *noun* [Middle English, from Middle French, from Old French, from *emprendre* to undertake, from (assumed) Vulgar Latin *imprehendere*, from Latin *in-* + *prehendere* to seize — more at GET] (13th century)
: an adventurous, daring, or chivalric enterprise

**¹emp·ty** \'em(p)-tē\ *adjective* **emp·ti·er; -est** [Middle English, from Old English *æmettig* unoccupied, from *æmetta* leisure, perhaps from *æ-* without + *-metta* (probably akin to *mōtan* to have to) — more at MUST] (before 12th century)
**1 a** : containing nothing **b** : not occupied or inhabited **c** : UNFREQUENTED **d** : not pregnant ⟨*empty* heifer⟩ **e** : NULL 4a ⟨the *empty* set⟩
**2 a** : lacking reality, substance, meaning, or value : HOLLOW ⟨an *empty* pleasure⟩ **b** : destitute of effect or force **c** : devoid of sense : FOOLISH
**3** : HUNGRY
**4 a** : IDLE ⟨*empty* hours⟩ **b** : having no purpose or result : USELESS
**5** : marked by the absence of human life, activity, or comfort ☆
— **emp·ti·ly** \-tə-lē\ *adverb*
— **emp·ti·ness** \-tē-nəs\ *noun*

**²empty** *verb* **emp·tied; emp·ty·ing** (1555) *transitive verb*
**1 a** : to make empty : remove the contents of **b** : DEPRIVE, DIVEST **c** : to discharge (itself) of contents **d** : to fire (a repeating firearm) until empty

---

☆ **SYNONYMS**
**Empty, vacant, blank, void, vacuous**
mean lacking contents which could or should be present. EMPTY suggests a complete absence of contents ⟨an *empty* bucket⟩. VACANT suggests an absence of appropriate contents or occupants ⟨a *vacant* apartment⟩. BLANK stresses the absence of any significant, relieving, or intelligible features on a surface ⟨a *blank* wall⟩. VOID suggests absolute emptiness as far as the mind or senses can determine ⟨a statement *void* of meaning⟩. VACUOUS suggests the emptiness of a vacuum and especially the lack of intelligence or significance ⟨a *vacuous* facial expression⟩. See in addition VAIN.

---

\ə\ abut \ᵊ\ kitten \ər\ further \a\ ash \ā\ ace \ä\ mop, mar \aú\ out \ch\ chin \e\ bet \ē\ easy \g\ go \i\ hit \ī\ ice \j\ job \ŋ\ sing \ō\ go \ó\ law \ói\ boy \th\ thin \th\ the \ü\ loot \ú\ foot \y\ yet \zh\ vision *see also* Guide to Pronunciation

**2 :** to remove from what holds or encloses ⟨*empty* the grain from sacks⟩
*intransitive verb*
**1 :** to become empty
**2 :** to discharge contents ⟨the river *empties* into the ocean⟩

³**empty** *noun, plural* **emp·ties** (1535)
**:** something (as a container) that is empty

**emp·ty–hand·ed** \ˌem(p)-tē-ˈhan-dəd\ *adjective* (1589)
**1 :** having or bringing nothing
**2 :** having acquired or gained nothing ⟨came back *empty-handed*⟩

**emp·ty–head·ed** \-ˈhe-dəd\ *adjective* (1650)
**:** SCATTERBRAINED

**empty nest·er** \-ˈnes-tər\ *noun* (1962)
**:** a parent whose children have grown and moved away from home

**emp·ty–nest syndrome** \ˌem(p)-tē-ˈnest-\ *noun* (1972)
**:** the emotional letdown experienced by an empty nester

**em·pur·ple** \im-ˈpər-pəl\ *verb* **em·pur·pled; em·pur·pling** \-ˈpər-p(ə-)liŋ\ (1590)
*transitive verb*
**:** to tinge or color purple
*intransitive verb*
**:** to become purple

**em·py·ema** \ˌem-ˌpī-ˈē-mə\ *noun, plural* **-ema·ta** \-mə-tə\ *or* **-emas** [Late Latin, from Greek *empyēma*, from *empyein* to suppurate, from *em-* ²*en-* + *pyon* pus — more at FOUL] (circa 1605)
**:** the presence of pus in a bodily cavity
**— em·py·emic** \-mik\ *adjective*

**em·py·re·al** \ˌem-ˌpī-ˈrē-əl, -pə-; em-ˈpir-ē-əl, -ˈpī-rē-\ *adjective* [Late Latin *empyrius, empyreus*, from Late Greek *empyrios*, from Greek *em-* ²*en-* + *pyr* fire] (15th century)
**1 :** of or relating to the empyrean **:** CELESTIAL
**2 :** SUBLIME

¹**em·py·re·an** \-ən\ *adjective* (15th century)
**:** EMPYREAL

²**empyrean** *noun* (circa 1610)
**1 a :** the highest heaven or heavenly sphere in ancient and medieval cosmology usually consisting of fire or light **b :** the true and ultimate heavenly paradise
**2 :** FIRMAMENT, HEAVENS
**3 :** an ideal place or state

**EMT** \ˌē-(ˌ)em-ˈtē\ *noun* [emergency medical technician] (1972)
**:** a specially trained medical technician licensed to provide basic emergency services before and during transportation to a hospital — compare PARAMEDIC 2

**emu** \ˈē-(ˌ)myü\ *noun* [modification of Portuguese *ema* cassowary] (1656)
**1 :** any of various tall flightless birds (as the rhea)
**2 :** a swift-running Australian bird (*Dromaius novae-hollandiae*) with undeveloped wings that is related to and smaller than the ostrich

emu 2

¹**em·u·late** \ˈem-yə-ˌlāt\ *transitive verb* **-lat·ed; -lat·ing** [Latin *aemulatus*, past participle of *aemulari*, from *aemulus* rivaling] (1582)
**1 a :** to strive to equal or excel **b :** IMITATE; *especially* **:** to imitate by means of an emulator
**2 :** to equal or approach equality with

²**em·u·late** \-lət\ *adjective* (1602)
*obsolete* **:** EMULOUS 1b ⟨pricked on by a most *emulate* pride —Shakespeare⟩

**em·u·la·tion** \ˌem-yə-ˈlā-shən\ *noun* (1542)
**1** *obsolete* **:** ambitious or envious rivalry
**2 :** ambition or endeavor to equal or excel others (as in achievement)
**3 a :** IMITATION **b :** the use of or technique of using an emulator

**— em·u·la·tive** \ˈem-yə-ˌlā-tiv\ *adjective*
**— em·u·la·tive·ly** *adverb*

**em·u·la·tor** \ˈem-yə-ˌlā-tər\ *noun* (1589)
**1 :** one that emulates
**2 :** hardware or software that permits programs written for one computer to be run on another usually newer computer

**em·u·lous** \ˈem-yə-ləs\ *adjective* (1535)
**1 a :** inspired by or deriving from a desire to emulate **b :** ambitious or eager to emulate
**2** *obsolete* **:** JEALOUS
**— em·u·lous·ly** *adverb*
**— em·u·lous·ness** *noun*

**emul·si·fi·er** \i-ˈməl-sə-ˌfī(-ə)r\ *noun* (1888)
**:** one that emulsifies; *especially* **:** a surface-active agent (as a soap) promoting the formation and stabilization of an emulsion

**emul·si·fy** \-ˌfī\ *transitive verb* **-fied; -fy·ing** (1859)
**:** to disperse (as an oil) in an emulsion; *also* **:** to convert (two or more immiscible liquids) into an emulsion
**— emul·si·fi·able** \i-ˈməl-sə-ˌfī-ə-bəl\ *adjective*
**— emul·si·fi·ca·tion** \i-ˌməl-sə-fə-ˈkā-shən\ *noun*

**emul·sion** \i-ˈməl-shən\ *noun* [New Latin *emulsion-, emulsio*, from Latin *emulgēre* to milk out, from *e-* + *mulgēre* to milk; akin to Old English *melcan* to milk, Greek *amelgein*] (1612)
**1 a :** a system (as fat in milk) consisting of a liquid dispersed with or without an emulsifier in an immiscible liquid usually in droplets of larger than colloidal size **b :** the state of such a system
**2 :** SUSPENSION 2b(3); *especially* **:** a suspension of a sensitive silver salt or a mixture of silver halides in a viscous medium (as a gelatin solution) forming a coating on photographic plates, film, or paper

**emul·soid** \i-ˈməl-ˌsȯid\ *noun* (circa 1909)
**1 :** a colloidal system consisting of a liquid dispersed in a liquid
**2 :** a lyophilic sol (as a gelatin solution)
**— emul·soi·dal** \-ˌməl-ˈsȯi-dᵊl\ *adjective*

**en** \ˈen\ *noun* (1792)
**1 :** the width of a piece of type half the width of an em
**2 :** the letter *n*

¹**en-** *also* **em-** \in *also* en; *sometimes only in* is *shown when* en *is infrequent*\ *prefix* [Middle English, from Old French, from Latin *in-, im-*, from *in*]
**1 :** put into or onto ⟨*en*throne⟩ **:** cover with ⟨*en*shroud⟩ **:** go into or onto ⟨*en*plane⟩ — in verbs formed from nouns
**2 :** cause to be ⟨*en*slave⟩ — in verbs formed from adjectives or nouns
**3 :** provide with ⟨*em*power⟩ — in verbs formed from nouns
**4 :** so as to cover ⟨*en*wrap⟩ **:** thoroughly ⟨*en*tangle⟩ — in verbs formed from verbs; in all senses usually *em-* before *b*, *m*, or *p*

²**en-** *also* **em-** *prefix* [Middle English, from Latin, from Greek, from *en* in — more at IN]
**:** in **:** within ⟨*en*zootic⟩ — usually *em-* before *b*, *m*, or *p* ⟨*em*pathy⟩

³**en-** *combining form* [International Scientific Vocabulary, from *-ene*]
**:** chemically unsaturated; *especially* **:** having one double bond ⟨*en*amine⟩

¹**-en** \ən, ⁿn\ *also* **-n** \n\ *adjective suffix* [Middle English, from Old English; akin to Old High German *-īn* made of, Latin *-īnus* of or belonging to, Greek *-inos* made of, of or belonging to]
**:** made of **:** consisting of ⟨earth*en*⟩ ⟨leather*n*⟩

²**-en** *verb suffix* [Middle English *-nen*, from Old English *-nian*; akin to Old High German *-inōn* *-en*]
**1 a :** cause to be ⟨sharp*en*⟩ **b :** cause to have ⟨length*en*⟩
**2 a :** come to be ⟨steep*en*⟩ **b :** come to have ⟨length*en*⟩

**en·able** \i-ˈnā-bəl\ *transitive verb* **en·abled; en·abling** \-b(ə-)liŋ\ (15th century)
**1 a :** to provide with the means or opportunity ⟨training that *enables* people to earn a living⟩ **b :** to make possible, practical, or easy **c :** to cause to operate ⟨software that *enables* the keyboard⟩
**2 :** to give legal power, capacity, or sanction to ⟨a law *enabling* admission of a state⟩

**en·act** \i-ˈnakt\ *transitive verb* (15th century)
**1 :** to establish by legal and authoritative act; *specifically* **:** to make (as a bill) into law
**2 :** ACT OUT ⟨*enact* a role⟩
**— en·ac·tor** \-ˈnak-tər\ *noun*

**en·act·ment** \-ˈnak(t)-mənt\ *noun* (1817)
**1 :** the act of enacting **:** the state of being enacted
**2 :** something (as a law) that has been enacted

¹**enam·el** \i-ˈna-məl\ *transitive verb* **-eled** *or* **-elled; -el·ing** *or* **-el·ling** \-ˈnam-liŋ, -ˈna-mə-\ [Middle English, from Middle French *enamailler*, from *en-* + *esmail* enamel, of Germanic origin; akin to Old High German *smelzan* to melt — more at SMELT] (14th century)
**1 :** to cover, inlay, or decorate with enamel
**2 :** to beautify with a colorful surface
**3 :** to form a glossy surface on (as paper, leather, or cloth)
**— enam·el·er** *noun*
**— enam·el·ist** \-mə-list\ *noun*

²**enamel** *noun* (15th century)
**1 :** a usually opaque vitreous composition applied by fusion to the surface of metal, glass, or pottery
**2 :** a surface or outer covering that resembles enamel
**3 a :** something that is enameled **b :** ENAMELWARE
**4 :** a cosmetic intended to give a smooth or glossy appearance
**5 :** a hard calcareous substance that forms a thin layer capping the teeth — see TOOTH illustration
**6 :** a paint that flows out to a smooth coat when applied and that dries with a glossy appearance

**enam·el·ware** \i-ˈna-məl-ˌwar, -ˌwer\ *noun* (1903)
**:** metalware (as kitchen utensils) coated with enamel

**en·amine** \ˈe-nə-ˌmēn, ˈē-\ *noun* (1942)
**:** an amine containing the double bond linkage C=C—N

**en·am·or** \i-ˈna-mər\ *transitive verb* **-ored; -or·ing** \-mə-riŋ, -ˈnam-riŋ\ [Middle English *enamouren*, from Middle French *enamourer*, from *en-* + *amour* love — more at AMOUR] (14th century)
**1 :** to inflame with love — usually used in the passive with *of*
**2 :** FASCINATE 2b — usually used in the passive with *of* or *with*

**en·am·our** *chiefly British variant of* ENAMOR

**en·an·tio·mer** \i-ˈnan-tē-ə-mər\ *noun* [Greek *enantios* + English *-mer*] (circa 1929)
**:** either of a pair of chemical compounds whose molecular structures have a mirror-image relationship to each other
**— en·an·tio·mer·ic** \-ˌnan-tē-ə-ˈmer-ik\ *adjective*

**en·an·tio·morph** \i-ˈnan-tē-ə-ˌmȯrf\ *noun* [Greek *enantios* opposite (from *enanti* facing, from *en* in + *anti* against) + International Scientific Vocabulary *-morph* -morph] (1885)
**:** ENANTIOMER; *also* **:** either of a pair of crystals (as of quartz) that are structural mirror images
**— en·an·tio·mor·phic** \-ˌnan-tē-ə-ˈmȯr-fik\ *adjective*
**— en·an·tio·mor·phism** \-ˈmȯr-ˌfi-zəm\ *noun*
**— en·an·tio·mor·phous** \-ˈmȯr-fəs\ *adjective*

**ena·tion** \i-ˈnā-shən\ *noun* [Latin *enatus*, past participle of *enasci* to rise out of, from *e-* + *nasci* to be born — more at NATION] (circa 1842)

: an outgrowth from the surface of an organ ⟨a plant virus forming *enations* on leaves⟩

**en banc** \äⁿ-'bäⁿ\ *adverb or adjective* [French, on the bench] (1863)
: in full court : with full judiciary authority

**en bloc** \äⁿ-'bläk\ *adverb or adjective* [French] (1861)
: as a whole : in a mass

**en bro·chette** \,äⁿ-brō-'shet\ *adjective* [French] (circa 1909)
*of food* : cooked or served on a skewer ⟨shrimp *en brochette*⟩

**en·cae·nia** \en-'sē-nyə\ *noun plural but singular or plural in construction, often capitalized* [New Latin, from Latin, dedication festival, from Greek *enkainia*, from *en* + *kainos* new — more at RECENT] (1691)
: an annual university ceremony (as at Oxford) of commemoration with recital of poems and essays and conferring of degrees

**en·cage** \in-'kāj, en-\ *transitive verb* (1593)
: CAGE 1

**en·camp** \in-'kamp, en-\ (1568)
*transitive verb*
: to place or establish in a camp
*intransitive verb*
: to set up or occupy a camp

**en·camp·ment** \-mənt\ *noun* (1598)
**1 a** : the place where a group (as a body of troops) is encamped **b** : the individuals that make up an encampment
**2** : the act of encamping : the state of being encamped

**en·cap·su·late** \in-'kap-sə-,lāt, en-\ *verb* **-lat·ed; -lat·ing** (1876)
*transitive verb*
**1** : to enclose in or as if in a capsule ⟨a pilot *encapsulated* in the cockpit⟩
**2** : EPITOMIZE, SUMMARIZE ⟨*encapsulate* an era in an aphorism⟩
*intransitive verb*
: to become encapsulated
— **en·cap·su·la·tion** \-,kap-sə-'lā-shən\ *noun*

**en·cap·su·lat·ed** *adjective* (1894)
**1** : surrounded by a gelatinous or membranous envelope ⟨*encapsulated* water bacteria⟩
**2** : CONDENSED

**en·cap·sule** \in-'kap-səl, -(,)sül, en-\ *transitive verb* **-suled; -sul·ing** (1877)
: ENCAPSULATE

**en·case** \in-'kās, en-\ *transitive verb* (1633)
: to enclose in or as if in a case

**en·case·ment** \in-'kā-smənt, en-\ *noun* (1741)
: the act or process of encasing : the state of being encased; *also* : CASE, COVERING

**en·cash** \in-'kash, en-\ *transitive verb* (1861) *British* : CASH
— **en·cash·able** \-'ka-shə-bəl\ *adjective, chiefly British*
— **en·cash·ment** \-mənt\ *noun, chiefly British*

**en·caus·tic** \in-'kȯ-stik\ *noun* [*encaustic*, adjective, from Latin *encausticus*, from Greek *enkaustikos*, from *enkaiein* to burn in, from *en-* + *kaiein* to burn] (1601)
**1** : a paint made from pigment mixed with melted beeswax and resin and after application fixed by heat
**2** : the method involving the use of encaustic; *also* : a work produced by this method
— **encaustic** *adjective*

**-ence** \ən(t)s, ⁿ(t)s\ *noun suffix* [Middle English, from Old French, from Latin *-entia*, from *-ent-*, *-ens*, present participle ending + *-ia* ²-y]
**1** : action or process ⟨emerg*ence*⟩ : instance of an action or process ⟨refer*ence*⟩
**2** : quality or state ⟨despond*ence*⟩

**¹en·ceinte** \äⁿ(n)-'sant\ *adjective* [Middle French, perhaps from (assumed) Vulgar Latin *incenta*, alteration of Latin *incient-*, *inciens* being with young, modification of Greek *enkyos* pregnant, from *en-* + *kyein* to be pregnant — more at CYME] (1599)

: PREGNANT 3

**²enceinte** *noun* [French, from Old French, enclosing wall, from *enceindre* to surround, from Latin *incingere*, from *in-* + *cingere* to gird — more at CINCTURE] (circa 1708)
: a line of fortification enclosing a castle or town; *also* : the area so enclosed

**encephal-** *or* **encephalo-** *combining form* [French *encéphal-*, from Greek *enkephal-*, from *enkephalos*, from *en-* + *kephalē* head — more at CEPHALIC]
: brain ⟨*encephal*itis⟩ ⟨*encephalo*myocarditis⟩

**en·ceph·a·li·tis** \in-,se-fə-'lī-təs\ *noun, plural* **-lit·i·des** \-'li-tə-,dēz\ (1843)
: inflammation of the brain
— **en·ceph·a·lit·ic** \-'li-tik\ *adjective*

**en·ceph·a·li·to·gen·ic** \-,lī-tə-'je-nik\ *adjective* (1923)
: tending to cause encephalitis ⟨an *encephalitogenic* virus⟩
— **en·ceph·a·li·to·gen** \-'lī-tə-jən, -,jen\ *noun*

**en·ceph·a·lo·gram** \in-'se-fə-lə-,gram\ *noun* (1928)
: an X-ray picture of the brain made by encephalography

**en·ceph·a·lo·graph** \-,graf\ *noun* (1928)
**1** : ENCEPHALOGRAM
**2** : ELECTROENCEPHALOGRAPH

**en·ceph·a·log·ra·phy** \in-,se-fə-'lä-grə-fē\ *noun* (1922)
: roentgenography of the brain after the cerebrospinal fluid has been replaced by a gas (as air)

**en·ceph·a·lo·my·eli·tis** \in-,se-fə-lō-,mī-ə-'lī-təs\ *noun, plural* **-elit·i·des** \-ə-'li-tə-,dēz\ [New Latin] (1908)
: concurrent inflammation of the brain and spinal cord; *specifically* : any of several virus diseases of horses

**en·ceph·a·lo·myo·car·di·tis** \-,mī-ə-kär-'dī-təs\ *noun* [New Latin] (1947)
: an acute febrile virus disease characterized by degeneration and inflammation of skeletal and cardiac muscle and lesions of the central nervous system

**en·ceph·a·lon** \in-'se-fə-,län, -lən\ *noun, plural* **-la** \-lə\ [New Latin, from Greek *enkephalos*] (1741)
: the vertebrate brain

**en·ceph·a·lop·a·thy** \in-,se-fə-'lä-pə-thē\ *noun* (1866)
: a disease of the brain; *especially* : one involving alterations of brain structure
— **en·ceph·a·lo·path·ic** \-lə-'pa-thik\ *adjective*

**en·chain** \in-'chān\ *transitive verb* [Middle English *encheynen*, from Middle French *enchainer*, from Old French, from *en-* + *chaeine* chain] (14th century)
: to bind or hold with or as if with chains
— **en·chain·ment** \-mənt\ *noun*

**en·chant** \in-'chant, en-\ *transitive verb* [Middle English, from Middle French *enchanter*, from Latin *incantare*, from *in-* + *cantare* to sing — more at CHANT] (14th century)
**1** : to influence by or as if by charms and incantation : BEWITCH
**2** : to attract and move deeply : rouse to ecstatic admiration ⟨the scene *enchanted* her to the point of tears —Elinor Wylie⟩
**synonym** *see* ATTRACT

**en·chant·er** *noun* (13th century)
: one that enchants; *especially* : SORCERER

**en·chant·ing** *adjective* (1606)
: CHARMING
— **en·chant·ing·ly** \-'chan-tiŋ-lē\ *adverb*

**en·chant·ment** \in-'chant-mənt, en-\ *noun* (13th century)
**1 a** : the act or art of enchanting **b** : the quality or state of being enchanted
**2** : something that enchants

**en·chant·ress** \in-'chan-trəs, en-\ *noun* (14th century)
**1** : a woman who practices magic : SORCERESS
**2** : a fascinating woman

**en·chase** \in-'chās\ *transitive verb* [Middle English, to emboss, from Middle French *enchasser* to enshrine, set, from *en-* + *chasse* reliquary, from Latin *capsa* case — more at CASE] (15th century)
**1** : ORNAMENT: as **a** : to cut or carve in relief **b** : INLAY
**2** : SET ⟨*enchase* a gem⟩

**en·chi·la·da** \,en-chə-'lä-də\ *noun* [American Spanish, from feminine of *enchilado*, past participle of *enchilar* to season with chili, from Spanish *en-* ¹*en-* + *chile* chili] (1887)
**1** : a rolled filled tortilla covered with chili sauce and usually baked
**2** : SCHMEAR, BALL OF WAX ⟨the whole *enchilada*⟩

**en·chi·rid·i·on** \,en-,kī-'ri-dē-ən, -,ki-\ *noun, plural* **-rid·ia** \-dē-ə\ [Late Latin, from Greek *encheiridion*, from *en* in + *cheir* hand — more at IN, CHIR-] (15th century)
: HANDBOOK, MANUAL

**-en·chy·ma** \'eŋ-kə-mə\ *noun combining form, plural* **-en·chy·ma·ta** \en-'ki-mə-tə, -'kī-mə-\ *or* **-enchymas** [New Latin, from *parenchyma*]
: cellular tissue ⟨coll*enchyma*⟩

**en·ci·pher** \in-'sī-fər, en-\ *transitive verb* (1577)
: to convert (a message) into cipher
— **en·ci·pher·er** \-fər-ər\ *noun*
— **en·ci·pher·ment** \-fər-mənt\ *noun*

**en·cir·cle** \in-'sər-kəl, en-\ *transitive verb* [Middle English *enserclen*] (15th century)
**1** : to form a circle around : SURROUND
**2** : to pass completely around
— **en·cir·cle·ment** \-mənt\ *noun*

**en clair** \äⁿ-'kler\ *adverb or adjective* [French, in clear] (circa 1897)
: in plain language ⟨a message sent *en clair*⟩

**en·clasp** \in-'klasp, en-\ *transitive verb* (1596)
: to seize and hold : EMBRACE

**en·clave** \'en-,klāv, ÷'än-,klāv, ÷'äŋ-\ *noun* [French, from Middle French, from *enclaver* to enclose, from (assumed) Vulgar Latin *inclavare* to lock up, from Latin *in-* + *clavis* key — more at CLAVICLE] (1868)
: a distinct territorial, cultural, or social unit enclosed within or as if within foreign territory ⟨ethnic *enclaves*⟩

**en·clit·ic** \en-'kli-tik\ *noun* [Late Latin *encliticus*, from Greek *enklitikos*, from *enklinesthai* to lean on, from *en-* + *klinein* to lean — more at LEAN] (circa 1663)
: a clitic that is associated with a preceding word
— **enclitic** *adjective*

**en·close** \in-'klōz, en-\ *transitive verb* [Middle English, probably from *enclos* enclosed, from Middle French, past participle of *enclore* to enclose, from (assumed) Vulgar Latin *inclaudere*, alteration of Latin *includere* — more at INCLUDE] (14th century)
**1 a** (1) : to close in : SURROUND ⟨*enclose* a porch with glass⟩ (2) : to fence off (common land) for individual use **b** : to hold in : CONFINE
**2** : to include along with something else in a parcel or envelope ⟨a check is *enclosed* herewith⟩

**en·clo·sure** \in-'klō-zhər, en-\ *noun* (15th century)
**1** : the act or action of enclosing : the quality or state of being enclosed
**2** : something that encloses
**3** : something enclosed ⟨a letter with two *enclosures*⟩

**en·code** \in-'kōd, en-\ *transitive verb* (circa 1919)

**1 :** to convert (as a body of information) from one system of communication into another; *especially* **:** to convert (a message) into code **2 :** to specify the genetic code for

— **en·cod·er** *noun*

**en·co·mi·ast** \en-'kō-mē-ˌast, -mē-əst\ *noun* [Greek *enkōmiastēs,* from *enkōmiazein* to praise, from *enkōmion*] (1610)
**:** one that praises **:** EULOGIST

— **en·co·mi·as·tic** \-ˌkō-mē-'as-tik\ *adjective*

**en·co·mi·um** \en-'kō-mē-əm\ *noun, plural* **-mi·ums** *or* **-mia** \-mē-ə\ [Latin, from Greek *enkōmion,* from *en* in + *kōmos* revel, celebration] (1589)
**:** glowing and warmly enthusiastic praise; *also* **:** an expression of this ☆

**en·com·pass** \in-'kəm-pəs, en- *also* -'käm-\ *transitive verb* [Middle English] (14th century)
**1 a :** to form a circle about **:** ENCLOSE **b** *obsolete* **:** to go completely around **2 a :** ENVELOP **b :** INCLUDE ⟨a plan that *encompasses* a number of aims⟩ **3 :** BRING ABOUT, ACCOMPLISH ⟨*encompass* a task⟩

— **en·com·pass·ment** \-pə-smənt\ *noun*

**¹en·core** \'än-ˌkōr, -ˌkȯr\ *noun* [French, still, again] (1712)
**:** a demand for repetition or reappearance made by an audience; *also* **:** a reappearance or additional performance in response to such a demand

**²encore** *transitive verb* **en·cored; en·cor·ing** (1748)
**:** to request an encore of or by

**¹en·coun·ter** \in-'kaun-tər, en-\ *verb* **en·coun·tered; en·coun·ter·ing** \-'kaun-t(ə-)riŋ\ [Middle English *encountren,* from Middle French *encontrer,* from Medieval Latin *incontrare,* from Late Latin *incontra* toward, from Latin *in-* + *contra* against — more at COUNTER] (14th century)
*transitive verb*
**1 a :** to meet as an adversary or enemy **b :** to engage in conflict with **2 :** to come upon face-to-face **3 :** to come upon especially unexpectedly
*intransitive verb*
**:** to meet especially by chance

**²encounter** *noun* (14th century)
**1 a :** a meeting especially between hostile factions or persons **b :** a sudden often violent clash **:** COMBAT **2 a :** a chance meeting **b :** a direct often momentary meeting **3 :** a coming into the vicinity of a celestial body ⟨the Martian *encounter* of a spacecraft⟩

**encounter group** *noun* (1967)
**:** a usually unstructured group that seeks to develop the capacity of the individual to express feelings and to form emotional ties by unrestrained confrontation of individuals

**en·cour·age** \in-'kər-ij, -'kə-rij, en-\ *transitive verb* **-aged; -ag·ing** [Middle English *encoragen,* from Middle French *encoragier,* from Old French, from *en-* + *corage* courage] (15th century)
**1 :** to inspire with courage, spirit, or hope **:** HEARTEN **2 :** to spur on **:** STIMULATE **3 :** to give help or patronage to **:** FOSTER ☆
*synonym* see HEARTEN

— **en·cour·ag·er** *noun*

**en·cour·age·ment** \-ij-mənt, -rij-\ *noun* (1568)
**1 :** the act of encouraging **:** the state of being encouraged **2 :** something that encourages

**en·cour·ag·ing** \-i-jiŋ, -ri-jiŋ\ *adjective* (1593)
**:** giving hope or promise **:** INSPIRITING

— **en·cour·ag·ing·ly** \-jiŋ-lē\ *adverb*

**en·crim·son** \in-'krim-zən\ *transitive verb* (1597)
**:** to make or dye crimson

**en·croach** \in-'krōch, en-\ *intransitive verb* [Middle English *encrochen* to get, seize, from Middle French *encrochier,* from Old French, from *en-* + *croc, croche* hook — more at CROCHET] (circa 1534)
**1 :** to enter by gradual steps or by stealth into the possessions or rights of another **2 :** to advance beyond the usual or proper limits ⟨the gradually *encroaching* sea⟩
*synonym* see TRESPASS

— **en·croach·er** *noun*

— **en·croach·ment** \-'krōch-mənt\ *noun*

**en·crust** \in-'krəst, iŋ-\ *verb* [probably from Latin *incrustare,* from *in-* + *crusta* crust] (1641)
*transitive verb*
**:** to cover, line, or overlay with or as if with a crust
*intransitive verb*
**:** to form a crust

**en·crus·ta·tion** \(ˌ)in-ˌkrəs-'tā-shən, ˌen-\ *variant of* INCRUSTATION

**en·crypt** \in-'kript, en-\ *transitive verb* [*en-* + *crypt-* (as in *cryptogram*)] (1944)
**1 :** ENCIPHER **2 :** ENCODE 1

— **en·cryp·tion** \-'krip-shən\ *noun*

**en·cum·ber** \in-'kəm-bər\ *transitive verb* **-cum·bered; -cum·ber·ing** \-b(ə-)riŋ\ [Middle English *encombren,* from Middle French *encombrer,* from Old French, from *en-* + (assumed) Old French *combre* dam, weir] (14th century)
**1 :** WEIGH DOWN, BURDEN **2 :** to impede or hamper the function or activity of **:** HINDER **3 :** to burden with a legal claim (as a mortgage) ⟨*encumber* an estate⟩

**en·cum·brance** \in-'kəm-brən(t)s\ *noun* (1535)
**1 :** something that encumbers **:** IMPEDIMENT **2 :** a claim (as a mortgage) against property

**en·cum·branc·er** \-brən(t)-sər\ *noun* (1858)
**:** one that holds an encumbrance

**-en·cy** \ən(t)-sē, ᵊn(t)-\ *noun suffix* [Middle English *-encie,* from Latin *-entia* — more at -ENCE]
**:** quality or state ⟨despond*ency*⟩

**¹en·cyc·li·cal** \in-'si-kli-kəl, en-\ *adjective* [Late Latin *encyclicus,* from Greek *enkyklios* circular, general, from *en* in + *kyklos* circle — more at IN, WHEEL] (1647)
**:** addressed to all the individuals of a group **:** GENERAL

**²encyclical** *noun* (1837)
**:** an encyclical letter; *specifically* **:** a papal letter to the bishops of the church as a whole or to those in one country

**en·cy·clo·pe·dia** *also* **en·cy·clo·pae·dia** \in-ˌsī-klə-'pē-dē-ə\ *noun* [Medieval Latin *encyclopaedia* course of general education, from Greek *enkyklios* + *paideia* education, child rearing, from *paid-, pais* child — more at FEW] (1644)
**:** a work that contains information on all branches of knowledge or treats comprehensively a particular branch of knowledge usually in articles arranged alphabetically often by subject

**en·cy·clo·pe·dic** *also* **en·cy·clo·pae·dic** \-'pē-dik\ *adjective* (1824)
**:** of, relating to, or suggestive of an encyclopedia or its methods of treating or covering a subject **:** COMPREHENSIVE ⟨an *encyclopedic* mind⟩ ⟨an *encyclopedic* collection of armor⟩

— **en·cy·clo·pe·di·cal·ly** \-di-k(ə-)lē\ *adverb*

**en·cy·clo·pe·dism** \-'pē-ˌdi-zəm\ *noun* (1833)
**:** the quality or state of being encyclopedic

**en·cy·clo·pe·dist** \-'pē-dist\ *noun* (1651)
**1 :** one who compiles or writes for an encyclopedia **2** *often capitalized* **:** one of the writers of a French encyclopedia (1751–80) who were

identified with the Enlightenment and advocated deism and scientific rationalism

**en·cyst** \in-'sist, en-\ (1845)
*transitive verb*
**:** to enclose in a cyst
*intransitive verb*
**:** to form or become enclosed in a cyst

— **en·cyst·ment** \-'sis(t)-mənt\ *noun*

**¹end** \'end\ *noun* [Middle English *ende,* from Old English; akin to Old High German *enti* end, Latin *ante* before, Greek *anti* against] (before 12th century)
**1 a :** the part of an area that lies at the boundary **b** (1) **:** a point that marks the extent of something (2) **:** the point where something ceases to exist ⟨world without *end*⟩ **c :** the extreme or last part lengthwise **:** TIP **d :** the terminal unit of something spatial that is marked off by units **e :** a player stationed at the extremity of a line (as in football) **2 a :** cessation of a course of action, pursuit, or activity **b :** DEATH, DESTRUCTION **c** (1) **:** the ultimate state (2) **:** RESULT, ISSUE **3 :** something incomplete, fragmentary, or undersized **:** REMNANT **4 a :** an outcome worked toward **:** PURPOSE ⟨the *end* of poetry is to be poetry —R. P. Warren⟩ **b :** the object by virtue of or for the sake of which an event takes place **5 a :** a share in an undertaking ⟨kept your *end* up⟩ **b :** a particular operation or aspect of an undertaking or organization ⟨the sales *end* of the business⟩ **6 :** something that is extreme **:** ULTIMATE — used with *the* **7 :** a period of action or turn in any of various sports events (as archery or lawn bowling)
*synonym* see INTENTION

— **end·ed** \'en-dəd\ *adjective*

— **in the end :** AFTER ALL, ULTIMATELY

— **no end :** EXCEEDINGLY

— **on end :** without a stop or letup ⟨it rained for days *on end*⟩

**²end** (before 12th century)
*transitive verb*
**1 a :** to bring to an end **b :** DESTROY **2 :** to make up the end of
*intransitive verb*

---

☆ SYNONYMS

**Encomium, eulogy, panegyric, tribute, citation** mean a formal expression of praise. ENCOMIUM implies enthusiasm and warmth in praising a person or a thing. EULOGY applies to a prepared speech or writing extolling the virtues and services of a person. PANEGYRIC suggests an elaborate often poetic compliment. TRIBUTE implies deeply felt praise conveyed either through words or through a significant act. CITATION applies to the formal praise accompanying the mention of a person in a military dispatch or in awarding an honorary degree.

**Encourage, inspirit, hearten, embolden** mean to fill with courage or strength of purpose. ENCOURAGE suggests the raising of one's confidence especially by an external agency ⟨the teacher's praise *encouraged* the students to greater efforts⟩. INSPIRIT, somewhat literary, implies instilling life, energy, courage, or vigor into something ⟨patriots *inspirited* the people to resist⟩. HEARTEN implies the lifting of dispiritedness or despondency by an infusion of fresh courage or zeal ⟨a hospital patient *heartened* by good news⟩. EMBOLDEN implies the giving of courage sufficient to overcome timidity or reluctance ⟨*emboldened* by her first success, she tried an even more difficult climb⟩.

**1 a :** to come to an end **b :** to reach a specified ultimate rank or situation — usually used with *up* ⟨*ended* up as a colonel⟩
**2 :** DIE
**synonym** see CLOSE

**³end** *adjective* (13th century)
**:** FINAL. ULTIMATE ⟨*end* results⟩ ⟨*end* markets⟩ ⟨*end* product⟩

**⁴end** *transitive verb* [probably alteration of English dialect *in* (to harvest)] (1607)
*dialect English* **:** to put (grain or hay) into a barn or stack

**end-** *or* **endo-** *combining form* [French, from Greek, from *endon* within; akin to Greek *en* in, Old Latin *indu*, Hittite *andan* within — more at IN]
**1 :** within : inside ⟨*endo*skeleton⟩ — compare ECT-, EXO-
**2 :** taking in ⟨*endo*thermic⟩

**en·dam·age** \in-'da-mij\ *transitive verb* [Middle English] (14th century)
**:** to cause loss or damage to

**end·amoe·ba** \ˌen-də-'mē-bə\ *noun* [New Latin, genus name] (circa 1879)
**:** any of a genus (*Endamoeba*) comprising amoebas parasitic in the intestines of insects — compare ENTAMOEBA

**en·dan·ger** \in-'dān-jər\ *verb* **-dan·gered; -dan·ger·ing** \-'dānj-riŋ, -'dān-jə-\ (1509)
*transitive verb*
**:** to bring into danger or peril
*intransitive verb*
**:** to create a dangerous situation ⟨driving to *endanger*⟩
— **en·dan·ger·ment** \-'dān-jər-mənt\ *noun*

**en·dan·gered** *adjective* (1964)
**:** being or relating to an endangered species ⟨an *endangered* bird⟩ ⟨put on the *endangered* list⟩

**endangered species** *noun* (1964)
**:** a species threatened with extinction; *broadly* **:** anyone or anything whose continued existence is threatened

**en·darch** \'en-ˌdärk\ *adjective* (circa 1900)
**:** formed or taking place from inner cells outward ⟨*endarch* xylem⟩

**end around** *noun* (1926)
**:** a football play in which an offensive end comes behind the line of scrimmage to take a handoff and attempts to carry the ball around the opposite flank

**end·ar·ter·ec·to·my** \ˌen-ˌdär-tə-'rek-tə-mē\ *noun, plural* **-mies** [New Latin *endarterium* intima of an artery (from *end-* + *arteria* artery) + English *-ectomy*] (1950)
**:** surgical removal of the inner layer of an artery when thickened and atheromatous or occluded (as by intimal plaques)

**end·brain** \'en(d)-ˌbrān\ *noun* (1927)
**:** TELENCEPHALON

**end brush** *noun* (circa 1891)
**:** END PLATE

**en·dear** \in-'dir\ *transitive verb* (1580)
**1** *obsolete* **:** to make higher in cost, value, or estimation
**2 :** to cause to become beloved or admired
— **en·dear·ing·ly** \-iŋ-lē\ *adverb*

**en·dear·ment** \in-'dir-mənt\ *noun* (1610)
**1 :** a word or an act (as a caress) expressing affection
**2 :** the act or process of endearing

**¹en·deav·or** \in-'de-vər\ *verb* **en·deav·ored; en·deav·or·ing** \-v(ə-)riŋ\ [Middle English *endeveren* to exert oneself, from *en-* + *dever* duty — more at DEVOIR] (15th century)
*transitive verb*
**1** *archaic* **:** to strive to achieve or reach
**2 :** to attempt (as the fulfillment of an obligation) by exertion of effort ⟨*endeavors* to finish the race⟩
*intransitive verb*
**:** to work with set purpose
**synonym** see ATTEMPT

**²endeavor** *noun* (15th century)
**1 :** serious determined effort

**2 :** activity directed toward a goal : ENTERPRISE ⟨fields of *endeavor*⟩

**en·deav·our** *chiefly British variant of* ENDEAVOR

**¹en·dem·ic** \en-'de-mik, in-\ *adjective* [French *endémique*, from *endémie* endemic disease, from Greek *endēmia* action of dwelling, from *endēmos* endemic, from *en* in + *dēmos* people, populace — more at DEMAGOGUE] (1759)
**1 a :** belonging or native to a particular people or country **b :** characteristic of or prevalent in a particular field, area, or environment ⟨problems *endemic* to translation⟩ ⟨the self-indulgence *endemic* in the film industry⟩
**2 :** restricted or peculiar to a locality or region ⟨*endemic* diseases⟩ ⟨an *endemic* species⟩
**synonym** see NATIVE
— **en·dem·i·cal·ly** \-'de-mi-k(ə-)lē\ *adverb*
— **en·de·mic·i·ty** \ˌen-ˌde-'mi-sə-tē, -də-'mi-\ *noun*
— **en·de·mism** \'en-də-ˌmi-zəm\ *noun*

**²endemic** *noun* (1926)
**:** an endemic organism

**end·er·gon·ic** \ˌen-ˌdər-'gä-nik\ *adjective* [*end-* + Greek *ergon* work — more at WORK] (1940)
**:** ENDOTHERMIC 1 ⟨an *endergonic* biochemical reaction⟩

**end·ex·ine** \(ˌ)en-'dek-ˌsēn, -ˌsīn\ *noun* (1947)
**:** an inner membranous layer of the exine

**end·game** \'en(d)-ˌgām\ *noun* (1884)
**:** the stage of a chess game after major reduction of forces; *also* **:** the final stages of some action

**end·ing** \'en-diŋ\ *noun* (before 12th century)
**:** something that constitutes an end: as **a :** CONCLUSION **b :** one or more letters or syllables added to a word base especially in inflection

**endite** *variant of* INDITE

**en·dive** \'en-ˌdīv, än-'dēv\ *noun* [Middle English, from Middle French, from Late Latin *endivia*, from Late Greek *entybion*, from Latin *intubus*] (14th century)
**1 :** an annual or biennial composite herb (*Cichorium endivia*) widely cultivated as a salad plant — called also *escarole*
**2 :** the developing crown of chicory when blanched for use as a vegetable or in salads by growing in darkness or semidarkness

**end·leaf** \'end-ˌlēf\ *noun* (1888)
**:** ENDPAPER

**end·less** \'en(d)-ləs\ *adjective* (before 12th century)
**1 :** being or seeming to be without end ⟨an *endless* speech⟩
**2 :** extremely numerous ⟨all the multiplied, *endless*, nameless iniquities —Edmund Burke⟩
**3 :** joined at the ends ⟨an *endless* chain⟩
— **end·less·ly** *adverb*
— **end·less·ness** *noun*

**end line** *noun* (1893)
**:** a line marking an end or boundary especially of a playing area: as **a :** a line at either end of a football field 10 yards beyond and parallel to the goal line **b :** a line at either end of a court (as in basketball or tennis) perpendicular to the sidelines

**end·long** \'end-ˌlȯŋ\ *adverb* [Middle English *endelong*, alteration of *andlong*, from Old English *andlang* along, from *andlang*, preposition — more at ALONG] (13th century)
*archaic* **:** LENGTHWISE

**end man** *noun* (1865)
**:** a man at each end of the line of performers in a minstrel show who engages in comic repartee with the interlocutor

**end·most** \'en(d)-ˌmōst\ *adjective* (before 12th century)
**:** situated at the very end

**end·note** \'en(d)-ˌnōt\ *noun* (1926)
**:** a note placed at the end of the text

**en·do·bi·ot·ic** \ˌen-dō-ˌbī-'ä-tik, -bē-\ *adjective* [International Scientific Vocabulary] (circa 1900)

**:** dwelling within the cells or tissues of a host ⟨*endobiotic* fungi⟩

**en·do·car·di·al** \ˌen-dō-'kär-dē-əl\ *adjective* (circa 1849)
**1 :** situated within the heart
**2 :** of or relating to the endocardium

**en·do·car·di·tis** \-ˌkär-'dī-təs\ *noun* [New Latin] (circa 1839)
**:** inflammation of the lining of the heart and its valves

**en·do·car·di·um** \-'kär-dē-əm\ *noun, plural* **-dia** \-dē-ə\ [New Latin, from *end-* + Greek *kardia* heart] (circa 1864)
**:** a thin serous membrane lining the cavities of the heart

**en·do·carp** \'en-də-ˌkärp\ *noun* [French *endocarpe*] (1830)
**:** the inner layer of the pericarp of a fruit (as an apple or orange) when it consists of two or more layers of different texture or consistency

**en·do·cast** \'en-dō-ˌkast\ *noun* (1949)
**:** ENDOCRANIAL CAST

**en·do·chon·dral** \ˌen-də-'kän-drəl\ *adjective* (1882)
**:** relating to, formed by, or being ossification that takes place from centers arising in cartilage and involves deposition of lime salts in the cartilage matrix followed by secondary absorption and replacement by true bony tissue

endocarp (cross section of a cherry): *1* exocarp, *2* mesocarp, *3* endocarp, *4* seed; *1, 2,* and *3* together form the pericarp

**en·do·cra·ni·al cast** \ˌen-də-ˌkrā-nē-əl-\ *noun* (1923)
**:** a cast of the cranial cavity showing the approximate shape of the brain

**¹en·do·crine** \'en-də-krən, -ˌkrīn, -ˌkrēn\ *adjective* [International Scientific Vocabulary *end-* + Greek *krinein* to separate — more at CERTAIN] (circa 1911)
**1 :** secreting internally; *specifically* **:** producing secretions that are distributed in the body by way of the bloodstream ⟨an *endocrine* system⟩
**2 :** of, relating to, affecting, or resembling an endocrine gland or secretion ⟨*endocrine* tumors⟩

**²endocrine** *noun* (1922)
**1 :** HORMONE
**2 :** ENDOCRINE GLAND

**endocrine gland** *noun* (1914)
**:** a gland (as the thyroid or the pituitary) that produces an endocrine secretion — called also *ductless gland*

**en·do·cri·no·log·ic** \ˌen-də-ˌkri-nᵊl-'ä-jik, -ˌkrī-, -ˌkrē-\ *or* **en·do·cri·no·log·i·cal** \-ji-kəl\ *adjective* (circa 1934)
**:** involving or relating to the endocrine glands or secretions or to endocrinology

**en·do·cri·nol·o·gy** \ˌen-də-kri-'nä-lə-jē, -ˌkrī-\ *noun* [International Scientific Vocabulary] (circa 1913)
**:** a science dealing with the endocrine glands
— **en·do·cri·nol·o·gist** \-jist\ *noun*

**en·do·cy·to·sis** \-sī-'tō-səs\ *noun* [New Latin, from *end-* + *-cytosis* (as in *phagocytosis*)] (1963)
**:** incorporation of substances into a cell by phagocytosis or pinocytosis
— **en·do·cy·tot·ic** \-'tä-tik\ *adjective*

**en·do·derm** \'en-də-ˌdərm\ *noun* [French *endoderme*, from *end-* + Greek *derma* skin — more at DERM-] (1861)
**:** the innermost of the germ layers of an embryo that is the source of the epithelium of the

\ə\ abut \ᵊ\ kitten \ər\ further \a\ ash \ā\ ace \ä\ mop, mar \aů\ out \ch\ chin \e\ bet \ē\ easy \g\ go \i\ hit \ī\ ice \j\ job \ŋ\ sing \ō\ go \ȯ\ law \ȯi\ boy \th\ thin \th̲\ the \ü\ loot \ů\ foot \y\ yet \zh\ vision *see also* Guide to Pronunciation digestive tract and its derivatives; *also* : a tissue that is derived from this germ layer — compare HYPOBLAST

— **en·do·der·mal** \,en-də-'dər-məl\ *adjective*

**en·do·der·mis** \,en-də-'dər-məs\ *noun* [New Latin] (1884)
: the innermost tissue of the cortex in many roots and stems

**end·odon·tics** \-'dän-tiks\ *noun plural but singular in construction* [end- + odont- + -ics] (1946)
: a branch of dentistry concerned with diseases of the pulp

— **end·odon·tic** \-'dän-tik\ *adjective*

— **end·odon·ti·cal·ly** \-'dän-ti-k(ə-)lē\ *adverb*

— **end·odon·tist** \-'dän-tist\ *noun*

**en·do·en·zyme** \,en-dō-'en-,zīm\ *noun* [International Scientific Vocabulary] (circa 1909)
: an enzyme that functions inside the cell

**en·do·er·gic** \,en-dō-'ər-jik\ *adjective* (1940)
: absorbing energy : ENDOTHERMIC ⟨*endoergic* nuclear reactions⟩

**en·dog·a·my** \en-'dä-gə-mē\ *noun* (1865)
: marriage within a specific group as required by custom or law

— **en·dog·a·mous** \-məs\ *adjective*

**en·do·gen·ic** \,en-də-'je-nik\ *adjective* (circa 1904)
**1** : of or relating to metamorphism taking place within a planet or moon
**2** : ENDOGENOUS

**en·dog·e·nous** \en-'dä-jə-nəs\ *adjective* (1830)
**1** : growing or produced by growth from deep tissue ⟨*endogenous* plant roots⟩
**2 a** : caused by factors inside the organism or system ⟨an *endogenous* psychic depression⟩ ⟨*endogenous* business cycles⟩ **b** : produced or synthesized within the organism or system ⟨an *endogenous* hormone⟩

— **en·dog·e·nous·ly** *adverb*

**en·do·lith·ic** \,en-də-'li-thik\ *adjective* (1886)
: living within or penetrating deeply into stony substances (as rocks, coral, or mollusk shells) ⟨*endolithic* lichens⟩

**en·do·lymph** \'en-də-,lim(p)f\ *noun* [International Scientific Vocabulary] (circa 1839)
: the watery fluid in the membranous labyrinth of the ear

— **en·do·lym·phat·ic** \,en-də-lim-'fa-tik\ *adjective*

**en·do·me·tri·osis** \,en-dō-,mē-trē-'ō-səs\ *noun* [New Latin] (1925)
: the presence and growth of functioning endometrial tissue in places other than the uterus that often results in severe pain and infertility

**en·do·me·tri·tis** \,en-dō-mə-'trī-təs\ *noun* [New Latin] (1872)
: inflammation of the endometrium

**en·do·me·tri·um** \-'mē-trē-əm\ *noun, plural* **-tria** \-trē-ə\ [New Latin, from *end-* + Greek *mētra* uterus, from *mētr-, mētēr* mother — more at MOTHER] (circa 1882)
: the mucous membrane lining the uterus

— **en·do·me·tri·al** \-trē-əl\ *adjective*

**en·do·mi·to·sis** \-mī-'tō-səs\ *noun* [New Latin] (1942)
: division of chromosomes not followed by nuclear division that results in an increased number of chromosomes in the cell

— **en·do·mi·tot·ic** \-mī-'tä-tik\ *adjective*

**en·do·mix·is** \-'mik-səs\ *noun* [New Latin, from *end-* + Greek *mixis* act of mixing, from *mignynai* to mix — more at MIX] (1914)
: a periodic nuclear reorganization in ciliated protozoans

**en·do·morph** \'en-də-,mȯrf\ *noun* [*endo*derm + *-morph*] (1940)
: an endomorphic individual

**en·do·mor·phic** \,en-də-'mȯr-fik\ *adjective* [*endo*derm + *-morphic*; from the predominance in such types of structures developed from the endoderm] (1940)

**1** : of or relating to the component in W. H. Sheldon's classification of body types that measures the massiveness of the digestive viscera and the body's degree of roundedness and softness
**2** : having a heavy rounded body build often with a marked tendency to become fat

— **en·do·mor·phy** \'en-də-,mȯr-fē\ *noun*

**en·do·mor·phism** \,en-də-'mȯr-fi-zəm\ *noun* (1909)
: a homomorphism that maps a mathematical set into itself — compare ISOMORPHISM

**en·do·nu·cle·ase** \,en-dō-'nü-klē-,ās, -,āz, -'nyü-\ *noun* (1962)
: an enzyme that breaks down a nucleotide chain into two or more shorter chains by cleaving it at points not adjacent to the end — compare EXONUCLEASE

**en·do·nu·cleo·lyt·ic** \-,nü-klē-ō-'li-tik, -,nyü-\ *adjective* [*end-* + *nucleo-* + *-lytic*] (1967)
: cleaving a nucleotide chain at an internal point ⟨*endonucleolytic* nicks⟩

**en·do·par·a·site** \-'par-ə-,sīt\ *noun* [International Scientific Vocabulary] (circa 1882)
: a parasite that lives in the internal organs or tissues of its host

— **en·do·par·a·sit·ic** \-,par-ə-'si-tik\ *adjective*

— **en·do·par·a·sit·ism** \-'par-ə-,sī-,ti-zəm, -sə-,ti-\ *noun*

**en·do·pep·ti·dase** \-'pep-tə-,dās, -,dāz\ *noun* (1936)
: any of a group of enzymes that hydrolyze peptide bonds within the long chains of protein molecules : PROTEASE — compare EXOPEPTIDASE

**en·do·per·ox·ide** \-pə-'räk-,sīd\ *noun* (1962)
: any of various biosynthetic intermediates in the formation of prostaglandins

**en·do·phyte** \'en-də-,fīt\ *noun* [International Scientific Vocabulary] (1854)
: a plant living within another plant

— **en·do·phyt·ic** \,en-də-'fi-tik\ *adjective*

**en·do·plasm** \'en-də-,pla-zəm\ *noun* [International Scientific Vocabulary] (1882)
: the inner relatively fluid part of the cytoplasm

— **en·do·plas·mic** \,en-də-'plaz-mik\ *adjective*

**endoplasmic reticulum** *noun* (1947)
: a system of interconnected vesicular and lamellar cytoplasmic membranes that functions especially in the transport of materials within the cell and that is studded with ribosomes in some places — see CELL illustration

**en·dop·o·dite** \en-'dä-pə-,dīt\ *noun* [International Scientific Vocabulary] (1870)
: the mesial or internal branch of a typical limb of a crustacean

**en·do·poly·ploidy** \,en-dō-'pä-li-,plȯi-dē\ *noun* (1940)
: a polyploid state in which the chromosomes have divided repeatedly without subsequent division of the nucleus or cell

— **en·do·poly·ploid** \-,plȯid\ *adjective*

**end organ** *noun* (1878)
: a structure forming the end of a neural path and consisting of an effector or a receptor with its associated nerve terminations

**en·dor·phin** \en-'dȯr-fən\ *noun* [International Scientific Vocabulary *end*ogenous + *mor*phine] (1976)
: any of a group of proteins with potent analgesic properties that occur naturally in the brain — compare ENKEPHALIN

**en·dorse** \in-'dȯrs, en-\ *transitive verb* **endorsed; en·dors·ing** [alteration of obsolete *endoss*, from Middle English *endosen*, from Middle French *endosser*, from Old French, to put on the back, from *en-* + *dos* back, from Latin *dorsum*] (1581)
**1 a** : to write on the back of; *especially* : to sign one's name as payee on the back of (a check) in order to obtain the cash or credit

represented on the face **b** : to inscribe (one's signature) on a check, bill, or note **c** : to inscribe (as an official document) with a title or memorandum **d** : to make over to another (the value represented in a check, bill, or note) by inscribing one's name on the document **e** : to acknowledge receipt of (a sum specified) by one's signature on a document
**2** : to approve openly ⟨*endorse* an idea⟩; *especially* : to express support or approval of publicly and definitely ⟨*endorse* a mayoral candidate⟩

*synonym* see APPROVE

— **en·dors·able** \-'dȯr-sə-bəl\ *adjective*

— **en·dors·ee** \in-,dȯr-'sē, ,en-\ *noun*

— **en·dors·er** \in-'dȯr-sər\ *noun*

**en·dorse·ment** \in-'dȯr-smənt, en-\ *noun* (1547)
**1** : the act or process of endorsing
**2 a** : something that is written in the process of endorsing **b** : a provision added to an insurance contract altering its scope or application
**3** : SANCTION, APPROVAL

**en·do·scope** \'en-də-,skōp\ *noun* [International Scientific Vocabulary] (1861)
: an instrument for visualizing the interior of a hollow organ (as the rectum or urethra)

— **en·dos·co·py** \en-'däs-kə-pē\ *noun*

**en·do·scop·ic** \,en-də-'skä-pik\ *adjective* (1861)
: of, relating to, or performed by means of an endoscope or endoscopy

— **en·do·scop·i·cal·ly** \-pi-k(ə-)lē\ *adverb*

**en·do·skel·e·ton** \,en-dō-'ske-lə-t°n\ *noun* (circa 1847)
: an internal skeleton or supporting framework in an animal

— **en·do·skel·e·tal** \-lə-t°l\ *adjective*

**en·do·sperm** \'en-dō-,spərm\ *noun* [French *endosperme*, from *end-* + Greek *sperma* seed — more at SPERM] (circa 1850)
: a nutritive tissue in seed plants formed within the embryo sac

**endosperm nucleus** *noun* (circa 1902)
: the triploid nucleus formed in the embryo sac of a seed plant by fusion of a sperm nucleus with two polar nuclei or with a nucleus formed by the prior fusion of the polar nuclei

**en·do·spore** \'en-dō-,spōr, -,spȯr\ *noun* [International Scientific Vocabulary] (1875)
: an asexual spore developed within the cell especially in bacteria

**end·os·te·al** \en-'däs-tē-əl\ *adjective* (circa 1868)
**1** : of or relating to the endosteum
**2** : located within bone or cartilage

— **end·os·te·al·ly** *adverb*

**end·os·te·um** \en-'däs-tē-əm\ *noun, plural* **-tea** \-tē-ə\ [New Latin, from *end-* + Greek *osteon* bone — more at OSSEOUS] (circa 1881)
: the layer of vascular connective tissue lining the medullary cavities of bone

**en·do·style** \'en-dō-,stīl\ *noun* [International Scientific Vocabulary *end-* + Greek *stylos* pillar — more at STEER] (1854)
: a pair of parallel longitudinal folds projecting into the pharyngeal cavity and bounding a furrow lined with glandular ciliated cells in lower chordates (as the tunicates)

**en·do·sul·fan** \,en-də-'səl-fən, -,fan\ *noun* [*endo-* + *sulf-* + ³-*an*] (1962)
: a brownish crystalline insecticide $C_9H_6Cl_6O_3S$ that is used in the control of numerous crop insects and some mites

**en·do·sym·bi·o·sis** \,en-dō-,sim-bī-'ō-səs, -bē-\ *noun* (circa 1940)
: symbiosis in which a symbiont dwells within the body of its symbiotic partner

— **en·do·sym·bi·ont** \-'sim-bī-,änt, -bē-\ *noun*

— **en·do·sym·bi·ot·ic** \-,sim-bī-'ä-tik, -bē-\ *adjective*

**en·do·the·ci·um** \,en-dō-'thē-s(h)ē-əm\ *noun, plural* **-cia** \-s(h)ē-ə\ [New Latin] (1832)

: the inner lining of a mature anther

**en·do·the·li·o·ma** \-,thē-lē-'ō-mə\ *noun, plural* **-o·mas** *or* **-o·ma·ta** \-mə-tə\ [New Latin] (1880)
: a tumor developing from endothelial tissue

**en·do·the·li·um** \,en-də-'thē-lē-əm\ *noun, plural* **-lia** \-lē-ə\ [New Latin, from *end-* + *-thelium* (as in *epithelium*)] (1872)
**1** : an epithelium of mesodermal origin composed of a single layer of thin flattened cells that lines internal body cavities
**2** : the inner layer of the seed coat of some plants
— **en·do·the·li·al** \-lē-əl\ *adjective*

**en·do·therm** \'en-dō-,thərm\ *noun* (1946)
: a warm-blooded animal

**en·do·ther·mic** \,en-də-'thər-mik\ *adjective* [International Scientific Vocabulary] (1884)
**1** : characterized by or formed with absorption of heat
**2** : WARM-BLOODED

**en·do·ther·my** \'en-də-,thər-mē\ *noun* (1922)
: physiological regulation of body temperature by metabolic means; *especially* : the property or state of being warm-blooded

**en·do·tox·in** \,en-dō-'tak-sən\ *noun* [International Scientific Vocabulary] (1904)
: a toxin of internal origin; *specifically* : a poisonous substance present in bacteria (as the causative agent of typhoid fever) but separable from the cell body only on its disintegration
— **en·do·tox·ic** \-sik\ *adjective*

**en·do·tra·che·al** \-'trā-kē-əl\ *adjective* (1910)
**1** : placed within the trachea ⟨an *endotracheal* tube⟩
**2** : applied or effected through the trachea

**en·do·tro·phic** \,en-də-'trō-fik\ *adjective* (1899)
*of a mycorrhiza* : penetrating into the associated root and ramifying between the cells — compare ECTOTROPHIC

**en·dow** \in-'daù, en-\ *transitive verb* [Middle English, from Anglo-French *endouer*, from Middle French *en-* + *douer* to endow, from Latin *dotare*, from *dot-, dos* gift, dowry — more at DATE] (15th century)
**1** : to furnish with an income; *especially* : to make a grant of money providing for the continuing support or maintenance of ⟨*endow* a hospital⟩
**2** : to furnish with a dower
**3** : to provide with something freely or naturally ⟨*endowed* with a good sense of humor⟩

**en·dow·ment** \-mənt\ *noun* (15th century)
**1** : the act or process of endowing
**2** : something that is endowed; *specifically* : the part of an institution's income derived from donations
**3** : natural capacity, power, or ability

**end·pa·per** \'en(d)-,pā-pər\ *noun* (1818)
: a once-folded sheet of paper having one leaf pasted flat against the inside of the front or back cover of a book and the other pasted at the base to the first or last page

**end plate** *noun* (1878)
: a complex terminal treelike branching of a motor nerve cell

**end point** *noun* (1899)
**1** : a point marking the completion of a process or stage of a process; *especially* : a point in a titration at which a definite effect (as a color change) is observed
**2** *usually* **end·point** : either of two points or values that mark the ends of a line segment or interval; *also* : a point that marks the end of a ray

**en·drin** \'en-drən\ *noun* [*end-* + dield*rin*] (1952)
: a chlorinated hydrocarbon insecticide $C_{12}H_8Cl_6O$ that is a stereoisomer of dieldrin and resembles dieldrin in toxicity

**end run** *noun* (1902)
**1** : a football play in which the ballcarrier attempts to run wide around the end of the line; *specifically* : SWEEP 3e

**2** : an evasive trick or maneuver

**end-stopped** \'en(d)-,stäpt\ *adjective* (1877)
: marked by a logical or rhetorical pause at the end ⟨an *end-stopped* line of verse⟩ — compare RUN-ON

**end table** *noun* (1851)
: a small table usually about the height of the arm of a chair that is used beside a larger piece of furniture (as a sofa)

**en·due** \in-'dü, -'dyü, en-\ *transitive verb* **en·dued; en·du·ing** [Middle English, from Middle French *enduire* to bring in, introduce, from Latin *inducere* — more at INDUCE] (15th century)
**1** : PROVIDE, ENDOW
**2** : IMBUE, TRANSFUSE
**3** [Middle English *induen;* influenced by Latin *induere* to put on] : PUT ON, DON

**en·dur·able** \in-'dur-ə-bəl, -'dyur-, en-\ *adjective* (1800)
: capable of being endured : BEARABLE
— **en·dur·ably** \-blē\ *adverb*

**en·dur·ance** \in-'dur-ən(t)s, -'dyur-, en-\ *noun* (15th century)
**1** : PERMANENCE, DURATION
**2** : the ability to withstand hardship or adversity; *especially* : the ability to sustain a prolonged stressful effort or activity ⟨a marathon runner's *endurance*⟩
**3** : the act or an instance of enduring or suffering ⟨*endurance* of many hardships⟩

**en·dure** \in-'dur, -'dyur, en-\ *verb* **en·dured; en·dur·ing** [Middle English, from Middle French *endurer*, from (assumed) Vulgar Latin *indurare*, from Latin, to harden, from *in-* + *durare* to harden, endure — more at DURING] (14th century)
*transitive verb*
**1** : to undergo (as a hardship) especially without giving in : SUFFER
**2** : to regard with acceptance or tolerance ⟨could not *endure* noisy children⟩
*intransitive verb*
**1** : to continue in the same state : LAST
**2** : to remain firm under suffering or misfortune without yielding
*synonym* see BEAR, CONTINUE

**en·dur·ing** *adjective* (15th century)
: LASTING, DURABLE
— **en·dur·ing·ly** \-'d(y)ur-iŋ-lē\ *adverb*
— **en·dur·ing·ness** *noun*

**en·duro** \in-'dur-(,)ō, -'dyur-\ *noun, plural* **en·dur·os** [*endurance* + *-o* (Italian or Spanish masculine noun ending)] (1935)
: a long race (as for automobiles or motorcycles) stressing endurance rather than speed

**end user** *noun* (circa 1945)
: the ultimate consumer of a finished product

**end·ways** \'en-,dwāz\ *adverb or adjective* (circa 1608)
**1** : in or toward the direction of the ends : LENGTHWISE ⟨*endways* pressure⟩
**2** : with the end forward (as toward the observer)
**3** : on end : UPRIGHT ⟨boxes set *endways*⟩

**end·wise** \'en-,dwīz\ *adverb or adjective* (1657)
: ENDWAYS

**En·dym·i·on** \en-'di-mē-ən\ *noun* [Latin, from Greek *Endymiōn*]
: a beautiful youth loved by Selene in Greek mythology

**end zone** *noun* (circa 1916)
: the area at either end of a football field between the goal line and the end line

**-ene** \,ēn\ *noun suffix* [International Scientific Vocabulary, from Greek *-ēnē,* feminine of *-ēnos,* adjective suffix]
: unsaturated carbon compound ⟨benz*ene*⟩; *especially* : carbon compound with one double bond ⟨ethyl*ene*⟩

**en·e·ma** \'e-nə-mə\ *noun, plural* **enemas** *also* **ene·ma·ta** \,e-nə-'mä-tə, 'e-nə-mə-tə\ [Late Latin, from Greek, from *enienai* to inject, from *en-* + *hienai* to send — more at JET] (15th century)

**1** : the injection of liquid into the intestine by way of the anus
**2** : material for injection as an enema

**en·e·my** \'e-nə-mē\ *noun, plural* **-mies** [Middle English *enemi*, from Old French, from Latin *inimicus*, from *in-* [1]*in-* + *amicus* friend — more at AMIABLE] (13th century)
**1** : one that is antagonistic to another; *especially* : one seeking to injure, overthrow, or confound an opponent
**2** : something harmful or deadly
**3 a** : a military adversary **b** : a hostile unit or force

**en·er·get·ic** \,e-nər-'je-tik\ *adjective* [Greek *energētikos*, from *energein* to be active, from *energos*] (1651)
**1** : operating with or marked by vigor or effect
**2** : marked by energy : STRENUOUS
**3** : of or relating to energy ⟨*energetic* equation⟩
*synonym* see VIGOROUS
— **en·er·get·i·cal·ly** \-ti-k(ə-)lē\ *adverb*

**en·er·get·ics** \-tiks\ *noun plural but singular in construction* (1855)
**1** : a branch of mechanics that deals primarily with energy and its transformations
**2** : the total energy relations and transformations of a physical, chemical, or biological system ⟨the *energetics* of an ecological community⟩

**en·er·gise** *British variant of* ENERGIZE

**en·er·gize** \'e-nər-,jīz\ *verb* **-gized; -giz·ing** (1752)
*intransitive verb*
: to put forth energy : ACT
*transitive verb*
**1** : to make energetic, vigorous, or active
**2** : to impart energy to
**3** : to apply voltage to
— **en·er·gi·za·tion** \,e-nər-,jī-'zā-shən\ *noun*
— **en·er·giz·er** *noun*

**en·er·gy** \'e-nər-jē\ *noun, plural* **-gies** [Late Latin *energia*, from Greek *energeia* activity, from *energos* active, from *en* in + *ergon* work — more at WORK] (1599)
**1 a** : dynamic quality ⟨narrative *energy*⟩ **b** : the capacity of acting or being active ⟨intellectual *energy*⟩
**2** : vigorous exertion of power : EFFORT ⟨investing time and *energy*⟩
**3** : the capacity for doing work
**4** : usable power (as heat or electricity); *also* : the resources for producing such power
*synonym* see POWER

**energy level** *noun* (1910)
: one of the stable states of constant energy that may be assumed by a physical system — used especially of the quantum states of electrons in atoms and of nuclei; called also *energy state*

**¹en·er·vate** \i-'nər-vət\ *adjective* (1603)
: lacking physical, mental, or moral vigor : ENERVATED

**²en·er·vate** \'e-nər-,vāt\ *transitive verb* **-vat·ed; -vat·ing** [Latin *enervatus*, past participle of *enervare*, from *e-* + *nervus* sinew — more at NERVE] (1614)
**1** : to reduce the mental or moral vigor of
**2** : to lessen the vitality or strength of
*synonym* see UNNERVE
— **en·er·va·tion** \,e-nər-'vā-shən\ *noun*

**en·fant ter·ri·ble** \äⁿ-fäⁿ-te-rēblᵉ\ *noun, plural* **enfants terribles** \*same*\ [French, literally, terrifying child] (1851)
**1 a** : a child whose inopportune remarks cause embarrassment **b** : a person known for shocking remarks or outrageous behavior

---

**2 :** a usually young and successful person who is strikingly unorthodox, innovative, or avant=garde

**en·fee·ble** \in-'fē-bəl, en-\ *transitive verb* **en·fee·bled; en·fee·bling** \-b(ə-)liŋ\ [Middle English *enfeblen,* from Middle French *enfeblir,* from Old French, from *en-* + *feble* feeble] (14th century)
**:** to make feeble **:** deprive of strength
**synonym** see WEAKEN
— **en·fee·ble·ment** \-bəl-mənt\ *noun*

**en·feoff** \in-'fef, -'fēf, en-\ *transitive verb* [Middle English *enfeoffen,* from Anglo-French *enfeoffer,* from Old French *en-* + *fief* fief] (15th century)
**:** to invest with a fief or fee
— **en·feoff·ment** \-mənt\ *noun*

**en·fet·ter** \in-'fe-tər, en-\ *transitive verb* (1599)
**:** to bind in fetters **:** ENCHAIN

**en·fe·ver** \in-'fē-vər, en-\ *transitive verb* (1647)
**:** FEVER

**En·field rifle** \'en-,fēld-\ *noun* [*Enfield,* England] (1854)
**:** a .30 caliber bolt-action repeating rifle used by U.S. and British troops in World War I

**¹en·fi·lade** \'en-fə-,lād, -,läd\ *noun* [French, from *enfiler* to thread, enfilade, from Old French, to thread, from *en-* + *fil* thread — more at FILE] (circa 1730)
**1 :** an interconnected group of rooms arranged usually in a row with each room opening into the next
**2 :** gunfire directed from a flanking position along the length of an enemy battle line

**²enfilade** *transitive verb* **-lad·ed; -lad·ing** (1706)
**:** to rake or be in a position to rake with gunfire in a lengthwise direction

**enflame** *variant of* INFLAME

**en·fleu·rage** \,äⁿ-,flər-'äzh\ *noun* [French, from *enfleurer* to saturate with the perfume of flowers, from *en-* ¹en- + *fleur* flower, from Old French *flor* — more at FLOWER] (1855)
**:** a process of extracting perfumes by exposing absorbents to the exhalations of flowers

**en·fold** \in-'fōld, en-\ *transitive verb* (circa 1674)
**1 a :** to cover with or as if with folds **:** ENVELOP **b :** to surround with a covering **:** CONTAIN
**2 :** to clasp within the arms **:** EMBRACE

**en·force** \in-'fōrs, -'fȯrs, en-\ *transitive verb* [Middle English, from Middle French *enforcier,* from Old French, from *en-* + *force* force] (14th century)
**1 :** to give force to **:** STRENGTHEN
**2 :** to urge with energy
**3 :** CONSTRAIN, COMPEL
**4** *obsolete* **:** to effect or gain by force
**5 :** to carry out effectively ⟨*enforce* laws⟩
— **en·force·abil·i·ty** \-,fōr-sə-'bi-lə-tē, -,fȯr-\ *noun*
— **en·force·able** \-'fōr-sə-bəl, -'fȯr-\ *adjective*
— **en·force·ment** \-'fōr-smənt, -'fȯr-\ *noun*

**en·forc·er** \in-'fōr-sər, -'fȯr-\ *noun* (1580)
**1 :** one that enforces
**2 a :** a violent criminal employed by a crime syndicate; *especially* **:** HIT MAN 1 **b :** an aggressive player (as in ice hockey) known for rough play and fighting

**en·frame** \in-'frām\ *transitive verb* (1848)
**:** FRAME 6
— **en·frame·ment** \-'frām-mənt\ *noun*

**en·fran·chise** \in-'fran-,chīz, en-\ *transitive verb* **-chised; -chis·ing** [Middle English, from Middle French *enfranchiss-,* stem of *enfranchir,* from Old French, from *en-* + *franc* free — more at FRANK] (15th century)
**1 :** to set free (as from slavery)
**2 :** to endow with a franchise: as **a :** to admit to the privileges of a citizen and especially to the right of suffrage **b :** to admit (a municipality) to political privileges or rights

— **en·fran·chise·ment** \-,chīz-mənt, -chəz-\ *noun*

**en·gage** \in-'gāj, en-\ *verb* **en·gaged; en·gag·ing** [Middle English, from Middle French *engagier,* from Old French, from *en-* + *gage* token, gage] (15th century)
*transitive verb*
**1 :** to offer (as one's word) as security for a debt or cause
**2 a** *obsolete* **:** to entangle or entrap in or as if in a snare or bog **b :** to attract and hold by influence or power **c :** to interlock with **:** MESH; *also* **:** to cause (mechanical parts) to mesh
**3 :** to bind (as oneself) to do something; *especially* **:** to bind by a pledge to marry
**4 a :** to provide occupation for **:** INVOLVE ⟨*engage* him in a new project⟩ **b :** to arrange to obtain the use or services of **:** HIRE
**5 a :** to hold the attention of **:** ENGROSS ⟨her work *engages* her completely⟩ **b :** to induce to participate ⟨*engaged* the shy boy in conversation⟩
**6 a :** to enter into contest with **b :** to bring together or interlock (weapons)
**7 :** to deal with especially at length
*intransitive verb*
**1 a :** to pledge oneself **:** PROMISE **b :** GUARANTEE ⟨he *engages* for the honesty of his brother⟩
**2 a :** to begin and carry on an enterprise or activity ⟨*engaged* in trade for a number of years⟩ **b :** to take part **:** PARTICIPATE ⟨at college she *engaged* in gymnastics⟩
**3 :** to enter into conflict
**4 :** to come together and interlock (as of machinery parts) **:** be or become in gear

**en·ga·gé** \,äⁿ-,gä-'zhā\ *adjective* [French, past participle of *engager* to engage, from Middle French *engagier*] (1946)
**:** committed to or supportive of a cause

**en·gaged** \in-'gājd, en-\ *adjective* (1665)
**1 :** involved in activity **:** OCCUPIED
**2 :** pledged to be married **:** BETROTHED
**3 :** greatly interested **:** COMMITTED
**4 :** involved especially in a hostile encounter
**5 :** partly embedded in a wall ⟨an *engaged* column⟩
**6 :** being in gear **:** MESHED

**en·gage·ment** \in-'gāj-mənt, en-\ *noun* (1601)
**1 a :** an arrangement to meet or be present at a specified time and place ⟨a dinner *engagement*⟩ **b :** a job or period of employment especially as a performer
**2 :** something that engages **:** PLEDGE
**3 a :** the act of engaging **:** the state of being engaged **b :** emotional involvement or commitment ⟨seesaws between obsessive *engagement* and ambiguous detachment —Gary Taylor⟩ **c :** BETROTHAL
**4 :** the state of being in gear
**5 :** a hostile encounter between military forces

**en·gag·ing** *adjective* (1673)
**:** tending to draw favorable attention **:** ATTRACTIVE
— **en·gag·ing·ly** \-'gā-jiŋ-lē\ *adverb*

**en·gar·land** \in-'gär-lənd, en-\ *transitive verb* (1581)
**:** to adorn with or as if with a garland

**En·gel·mann spruce** \'en-gəl-mən-\ *noun* [George *Engelmann* (died 1884) American botanist] (1908)
**:** a large spruce (*Picea engelmannii*) of the Rocky mountain region and British Columbia that yields a light-colored wood

**en·gen·der** \in-'jen-dər, en-\ *verb* **en·gendered; en·gen·der·ing** \-d(ə-)riŋ\ [Middle English *engendren,* from Middle French *engendrer,* from Latin *ingenerare,* from *in-* + *generare* to generate] (14th century)
*transitive verb*
**1 :** BEGET, PROCREATE
**2 :** to cause to exist or to develop **:** PRODUCE ⟨angry words *engender* strife⟩
*intransitive verb*
**:** to assume form **:** ORIGINATE

**en·gild** \in-'gild, en-\ *transitive verb* (15th century)
**:** to make bright with or as if with light

**¹en·gine** \'en-jən\ *noun* [Middle English *engin,* from Middle French, from Latin *ingenium* natural disposition, talent, from *in-* + *gignere* to beget — more at KIN] (13th century)
**1** *obsolete* **a :** INGENUITY **b :** evil contrivance **:** WILE
**2 :** something used to effect a purpose **:** AGENT, INSTRUMENT ⟨mournful and terrible *engine* of horror and of crime —E. A. Poe⟩
**3 a :** a mechanical tool: as (1) **:** an instrument or machine of war (2) *obsolete* **:** a torture implement **b :** MACHINERY **c :** any of various mechanical appliances — often used in combination ⟨fire *engine*⟩
**4 :** a machine for converting any of various forms of energy into mechanical force and motion; *also* **:** a mechanism or object that serves as an energy source ⟨black holes may be the *engines* for quasars⟩
**5 :** a railroad locomotive

**²engine** *transitive verb* **en·gined; en·gin·ing** (1868)
**:** to equip with engines

**engine driver** *noun* (1828)
*British* **:** ENGINEER 4

**¹en·gi·neer** \,en-jə-'nir\ *noun* [alteration of earlier *enginer,* from Middle English, alteration of *enginour,* from Middle French *engigneur,* from Old French *enginier* to contrive, from *engin*] (14th century)
**1 :** a member of a military group devoted to engineering work
**2 :** a crafty schemer **:** PLOTTER
**3 a :** a designer or builder of engines **b :** a person who is trained in or follows as a profession a branch of engineering **c :** a person who carries through an enterprise by skillful or artful contrivance
**4 :** a person who runs or supervises an engine or an apparatus

**²engineer** *transitive verb* (1843)
**1 :** to lay out, construct, or manage as an engineer
**2 a :** to contrive or plan out usually with more or less subtle skill and craft **b :** to guide the course of
**3 :** to modify or produce by genetic engineering ⟨grain crops *engineered* to require fewer nutrients and produce higher yields⟩
**synonym** see GUIDE

**en·gi·neer·ing** *noun* (1720)
**1 :** the activities or function of an engineer
**2 a :** the application of science and mathematics by which the properties of matter and the sources of energy in nature are made useful to people **b :** the design and manufacture of complex products ⟨software *engineering*⟩
**3 :** calculated manipulation or direction (as of behavior) ⟨social *engineering*⟩ — compare GENETIC ENGINEERING

**en·gine·ry** \'en-jən-rē\ *noun* (1641)
**:** instruments of war

**en·gird** \in-'gərd, en-\ *transitive verb* (1566)
*archaic* **:** GIRD, ENCOMPASS

**en·gir·dle** \in-'gər-d°l, en-\ *transitive verb* (1602)
**:** to encircle with or as if with a girdle

**¹En·glish** \'iŋ-glish, 'iŋ-lish\ *adjective* [Middle English, from Old English *englisc,* from *Engle* (plural) Angles] (before 12th century)
**:** of, relating to, or characteristic of England, the English people, or the English language
— **En·glish·ness** *noun*

**²English** *noun* (before 12th century)
**1 a :** the language of the people of England and the U.S. and many areas now or formerly under British control **b :** a particular variety of English distinguished by peculiarities (as of pronunciation) **c :** English language, literature, or composition when a subject of study
**2** *plural in construction* **:** the people of England

**3 a :** an English translation **b :** idiomatic or intelligible English
**4 :** spin around the vertical axis deliberately imparted to a ball that is driven or rolled — compare DRAW, FOLLOW; BODY ENGLISH

³**English** *transitive verb* (14th century)
**1 :** to translate into English
**2 :** to adopt into English **:** ANGLICIZE

**English breakfast** *noun* (1807)
**1 :** a substantial breakfast (as of eggs, ham or bacon, toast, and cereal)
**2 :** CONGOU; *broadly* **:** any similar black tea

**English cocker spaniel** *noun* (1948)
**:** any of a breed of spaniels that have square muzzles, wide well-developed noses, and distinctive heads which are ideally half muzzle and half skull with the forehead and skull arched and slightly flattened

English cocker spaniel

**English daisy** *noun* (circa 1890)
**:** DAISY 1a

**English foxhound** *noun* (1929)
**:** any of a breed of medium-sized foxhounds developed in England and characterized by a muscular body, bi- or tri-colored short coat, and lightly fringed tail

**English horn** *noun* [translation of Italian *corno inglese*] (1838)
**:** a double-reed woodwind instrument resembling the oboe in design and having a longer tube and a range a fifth lower than that of the oboe

**English ivy** *noun* (1624)
**:** IVY 1

**En·glish·man** \'iŋ-glish-mən, 'iŋ-lish-\ *noun* (before 12th century)
**:** a native or inhabitant of England

**English muffin** *noun* (1902)
**:** bread dough rolled and cut into rounds, baked on a griddle, and split and toasted just before eating

**English pea** *noun* (1634)
*Southern* **:** PEA 1a, b

**En·glish·ry** \'iŋ-glish-rē, 'iŋ-lish-\ *noun* (1620)
**:** the state, fact, or quality of being English **:** ENGLISHNESS

**English saddle** *noun* (1817)
**:** a saddle with long side bars, steel cantle and pommel, no horn, and a leather seat supported by webbing stretched between the saddlebow and cantle — see SADDLE illustration

**English setter** *noun* (1859)
**:** any of a breed of dogs often trained as bird dogs and characterized by a moderately long flat silky coat of white or white with color and by feathering on the tail and legs

**English shepherd** *noun* (1950)
**:** any of a breed of vigorous medium-sized working dogs with a long and glossy black coat usually with tan to brown markings that was developed in England for herding sheep and cattle

**English sonnet** *noun* (circa 1903)
**:** a sonnet consisting of three quatrains and a couplet with a rhyme scheme of *abab cdcd efef gg* — called also *Shakespearean sonnet*

**English sparrow** *noun* (1876)
**:** HOUSE SPARROW

**English springer spaniel** *noun* (1929)
**:** any of a breed of springer spaniels having a muscular build and a moderately long silky coat usually of black and white or liver and white hair — called also *English springer*

**English system** *noun* (1927)
**:** the foot-pound-second system of units

**English toy spaniel** *noun* (circa 1934)
**:** any of a breed of small blocky spaniels with well-rounded upper skull projecting forward toward the short turned-up nose

**English walnut** *noun* (1772)
**:** a Eurasian walnut (*Juglans regia*) valued for its large edible nut and its hard richly figured wood; *also* **:** its nut

English toy spaniel

**En·glish·wom·an** \'iŋ-glish-,wu̇-mən *also* 'iŋ-lish-\ *noun* (15th century)
**:** a woman of English birth, nationality, or origin

**English yew** *noun* (circa 1930)
**:** YEW 1a(1)

**en·gorge** \in-'gȯrj, en-\ *verb* [Middle French *engorgier*, from Old French, to devour, from *en-* + *gorge* throat — more at GORGE] (1515)
*transitive verb*
**:** GORGE, GLUT; *especially* **:** to fill with blood to the point of congestion
*intransitive verb*
**:** to suck blood to the limit of body capacity
— **en·gorge·ment** \-mənt\ *noun*

**en·graft** \in-'graft, en-\ *transitive verb* (1585)
**1 :** to join or fasten as if by grafting
**2 :** GRAFT 1, 3 (*engrafted* embryonic gill tissue into the back)
— **en·graft·ment** \-'graf(t)-mənt\ *noun*

**en·grailed** \in-'grāld, en-\ *adjective* [Middle English *engreled*, from Middle French *engreslé*, from *en-* + *gresle* slender, from Latin *gracilis*] (15th century)
**1 :** indented with small concave curves (an *engrailed* heraldic bordure)
**2 :** made of or bordered by a circle of raised dots (an *engrailed* coin)

**en·grain** \in-'grān\ *transitive verb* (circa 1641)
**:** INGRAIN

**en·gram** *also* **en·gramme** \'en-,gram\ *noun* [International Scientific Vocabulary] (1908)
**:** a hypothetical change in neural tissue postulated in order to account for persistence of memory

**en·grave** \in-'grāv, en-\ *transitive verb* **en·graved; en·grav·ing** [Middle French *engraver*, from *en-* + *graver* to grave, of Germanic origin; akin to Old English *grafan* to grave] (1509)
**1 a :** to form by incision (as on wood or metal) **b :** to impress deeply as if with a graver (the incident was *engraved* in his memory)
**2 a :** to cut figures, letters, or designs on for printing; *also* **:** to print from an engraved plate **b :** PHOTOENGRAVE
— **en·grav·er** *noun*

**en·grav·ing** *noun* (1601)
**1 :** the act or process of one that engraves
**2 :** something that is engraved: as **a :** an engraved printing surface **b :** engraved work
**3 :** an impression from an engraved printing surface

**en·gross** \in-'grōs, en-\ *transitive verb* [Middle English, from Anglo-French *engrosser*, probably from Medieval Latin *ingrossare*, from Latin *in* + Medieval Latin *grossa* large handwriting, from Latin, feminine of *grossus* thick] (15th century)
**1 a :** to copy or write in a large hand **b :** to prepare the usually final handwritten or printed text of (an official document)
**2** [Middle English, from Middle French *en gros* in large quantities] **a :** to purchase large quantities of (as for speculation) **b** *archaic* **:** AMASS, COLLECT **c :** to take or engage the whole attention of **:** occupy completely (ideas that have *engrossed* the minds of scholars for generations)
— **en·gross·er** *noun*

**en·gross·ing** \-'grō-siŋ\ *adjective* (1820)
**:** taking up the attention completely **:** ABSORBING
— **en·gross·ing·ly** \-siŋ-lē\ *adverb*

**en·gross·ment** \in-'grō-smənt, en-\ *noun* (1526)

**1 :** the act of engrossing
**2 :** the state of being absorbed or occupied **:** PREOCCUPATION

**en·gulf** \in-'gəlf, en-\ *transitive verb* (1555)
**1 :** to flow over and enclose **:** OVERWHELM (the mounting seas threatened to *engulf* the island)
**2 :** to take in (food) by or as if by flowing over and enclosing
— **en·gulf·ment** \-mənt\ *noun*

**en·ha·lo** \in-'hā-(,)lō, en-\ *transitive verb* (1842)
**:** to surround with or as if with a halo

**en·hance** \in-'han(t)s, en-\ *transitive verb* **en·hanced; en·hanc·ing** [Middle English *enhauncen*, from Anglo-French *enhauncer*, alteration of Old French *enhaucier*, from (assumed) Vulgar Latin *inaltiare*, from Latin *in* + *altus* high — more at OLD] (13th century)
**1** *obsolete* **:** RAISE
**2 :** HEIGHTEN, INCREASE; *especially* **:** to increase or improve in value, quality, desirability, or attractiveness
— **en·hance·ment** \-'han(t)-smənt\ *noun*

**enhanced recovery** *noun* (1970)
**:** the extraction of oil from a nearly exhausted well by methods more costly and complex than waterflooding alone

**en·hanc·er** \in-'han(t)-sər, en-\ *noun* (14th century)
**1 :** one that enhances
**2 :** a nucleotide sequence that increases the rate of genetic transcription by preferentially increasing the activity of the nearest promoter on the same DNA molecule

**en·har·mon·ic** \,en-(,)här-'mä-nik\ *adjective* [French *enharmonique*, from Middle French, of a scale employing quarter tones, from Greek *enarmonios*, from *en* in + *harmonia* harmony, scale] (1794)
**:** of, relating to, or being notes that are written differently (as A flat and G sharp) but sound the same in the tempered scale
— **en·har·mon·i·cal·ly** \-ni-k(ə-)lē\ *adverb*

**enig·ma** \i-'nig-mə, e-\ *noun* [Latin *aenigma*, from Greek *ainigmat-, ainigma*, from *ainissesthai* to speak in riddles, from *ainos* fable] (15th century)
**1 :** an obscure speech or writing
**2 :** something hard to understand or explain
**3 :** an inscrutable or mysterious person
*synonym* see MYSTERY

**enig·mat·ic** \,e-(,)nig-'ma-tik *also* ,ē-(,)nig-\ *also* **enig·mat·i·cal** \-ti-kəl\ *adjective* (1677)
**:** of, relating to, or resembling an enigma **:** MYSTERIOUS
*synonym* see OBSCURE
— **enig·mat·i·cal·ly** \-ti-k(ə-)lē\ *adverb*

**en·isle** \in-'ī(ə)l, en-\ *transitive verb* (1612)
**1 :** to place apart **:** ISOLATE
**2 :** to make an island of

**en·jamb·ment** \in-'jam-mənt\ *or* **en·jambe·ment** \*same or* äⁿ-zhäⁿb-mäⁿ\ *noun* [French *enjambement*, from Middle French, encroachment, from *enjamber* to straddle, encroach on, from *en-* + *jambe* leg — more at JAMB] (1839)
**:** the running over of a sentence from one verse or couplet into another so that closely related words fall in different lines — compare RUN-ON

**en·join** \in-'jȯin, en-\ *transitive verb* [Middle English, from Old French *enjoindre*, from Latin *injungere*, from *in-* + *jungere* to join — more at YOKE] (13th century)
**1 :** to direct or impose by authoritative order or with urgent admonition (*enjoined* us to be careful)

\ə\ **abut** \ᵊ\ **kitten** \ər\ **further** \a\ **ash** \ā\ **ace** \ä\ **mop, mar** \au̇\ **out** \ch\ **chin** \e\ **bet** \ē\ **easy** \g\ **go** \i\ **hit** \ī\ **ice** \j\ **job** \ŋ\ **sing** \ō\ **go** \ȯ\ **law** \ȯi\ **boy** \th\ **thin** \t̲h̲\ **the** \ü\ **loot** \u̇\ **foot** \y\ **yet** \zh\ **vision** *see also* Guide to Pronunciation

**2 a :** FORBID, PROHIBIT ⟨was *enjoined* by conscience from telling a lie⟩ **b :** to prohibit by a judicial order **:** put an injunction on ⟨a book had been *enjoined* prior to publication —David Margolick⟩
*synonym* see COMMAND
**en·joy** \in-'jȯi, en-\ *verb* [Middle English *enjoie*, from Middle French *enjoir*, from Old French, from *en-* + *joir* to enjoy, from Latin *gaudēre* to rejoice — more at JOY] (15th century)
*intransitive verb*
**:** to have a good time
*transitive verb*
**1 :** to have for one's use, benefit, or lot **:** EXPERIENCE ⟨*enjoyed* great success⟩
**2 :** to take pleasure or satisfaction in
— **en·joy·able** \-ə-bəl\ *adjective*
— **en·joy·able·ness** *noun*
— **en·joy·ably** \-blē\ *adverb*
— **en·joy·er** *noun*
— **enjoy oneself :** to have a good time
**en·joy·ment** \in-'jȯi-mənt\ *noun* (1553)
**1 a :** the action or state of enjoying **b :** possession and use ⟨the *enjoyment* of civic rights⟩
**2 :** something that gives keen satisfaction
**en·keph·a·lin** \in-'ke-fə-lən, -ˌ(ˌ)lin, en-\ *noun* [*enkephal-* (alteration of *encephal-*) + *-in*] (1975)
**:** either of two pentapeptides with opiate and analgesic activity that occur naturally in the brain and have a marked affinity for opiate receptors — compare ENDORPHIN
**en·kin·dle** \in-'kin-dᵊl, en-\ (1542)
*transitive verb*
**1 :** to set (as fuel) on fire
**2 :** to make bright and glowing
*intransitive verb*
**:** to take fire **:** FLAME
**en·lace** \in-'lās, en-\ *transitive verb* [Middle English, from Middle French *enlacier*, from Old French, from *en-* + *lacier* to lace] (14th century)
**1 :** ENCIRCLE, ENFOLD
**2 :** ENTWINE, INTERLACE
**en·lace·ment** \in-'lā-smənt, en-\ *noun* (1830)
**1 :** the process or result of interlacing
**2 :** a pattern of interlacing elements
**en·large** \in-'lärj, en-\ *verb* **en·larged; en·larg·ing** [Middle English, from Middle French *enlargier*, from Old French, from *en-* + *large* large, abundant] (14th century)
*transitive verb*
**1 :** to make larger **:** EXTEND
**2 :** to give greater scope to **:** EXPAND
**3 :** to set free (as a captive)
*intransitive verb*
**1 :** to grow larger
**2 :** to speak or write at length **:** ELABORATE ⟨let me *enlarge* upon that point⟩
*synonym* see INCREASE
— **en·large·able** \-'lär-jə-bəl\ *adjective*
— **en·larg·er** *noun*
**en·large·ment** \in-'lärj-mənt, en-\ *noun* (1540)
**1 :** an act or instance of enlarging **:** the state of being enlarged
**2 :** a photographic print larger than the negative that is made by projecting the negative image through a lens onto a photographic printing surface
**en·light·en** \in-'lī-tᵊn, en-\ *transitive verb* **en·light·ened; en·light·en·ing** \-'līt-niŋ, -ᵊn-iŋ\ (1587)
**1** *archaic* **:** ILLUMINATE
**2 a :** to furnish knowledge to **:** INSTRUCT **b :** to give spiritual insight to
**en·light·ened** *adjective* (1652)
**1 :** freed from ignorance and misinformation ⟨an *enlightened* people⟩
**2 :** based on full comprehension of the problems involved ⟨issued an *enlightened* ruling⟩
**en·light·en·ment** \in-'lī-tᵊn-mənt, en-\ *noun* (1669)
**1 :** the act or means of enlightening **:** the state of being enlightened

**2** *capitalized* **:** a philosophic movement of the 18th century marked by a rejection of traditional social, religious, and political ideas and an emphasis on rationalism — used with *the*
**3** *Buddhism* **:** a final blessed state marked by the absence of desire or suffering
**en·list** \in-'list, en-\ (1599)
*transitive verb*
**1 a :** to secure the support and aid of **:** employ in advancing an interest ⟨*enlist* all the available resources⟩ ⟨*enlist* the community in an experiment⟩ **b :** to win over **:** ATTRACT ⟨trying to *enlist* my sympathies⟩
**2 :** to engage (a person) for duty in the armed forces
*intransitive verb*
**1 :** to enroll oneself in the armed forces
**2 :** to participate heartily (as in a cause, drive, or crusade)
— **en·list·ee** \-ˌlis-'tē, -'lis-tē\ *noun*
— **en·list·ment** \-'lis(t)-mənt\ *noun*
**en·list·ed** \-'lis-təd\ *adjective* (1724)
**:** of, relating to, or constituting the part of a military or naval force below commissioned or warrant officers
**enlisted man** *noun* (1724)
**:** a man or woman in the armed forces ranking below a commissioned or warrant officer; *specifically* **:** one ranking below a noncommissioned officer or petty officer
**en·liv·en** \in-'lī-vən, en-\ *transitive verb* (1604)
**:** to give life, action, or spirit to **:** ANIMATE
*synonym* see QUICKEN
**en masse** \äⁿ(n)-'mas, -'mäs, en-\ *adverb* [French] (1795)
**:** in a body **:** as a whole
**en·mesh** \in-'mesh, en-\ *transitive verb* (1604)
**:** to catch or entangle in or as if in meshes
— **en·mesh·ment** \-mənt\ *noun*
**en·mi·ty** \'en-mə-tē\ *noun, plural* **-ties** [Middle English *enmite*, from Middle French *enemité*, from Old French *enemisté*, from *enemi* enemy] (13th century)
**:** positive, active, and typically mutual hatred or ill will ☆
**en·ne·ad** \'e-nē-ˌad\ *noun* [Greek *ennead-, enneas*, from *ennea* nine — more at NINE] (1550)
**:** a group of nine
**en·no·ble** \in-'nō-bəl, e-'nō-\ *transitive verb* **en·no·bled; en·no·bling** \-b(ə-)liŋ\ [Middle English *ennobelen*, from Middle French *ennoblir*, from Old French, from *en-* + *noble* noble] (15th century)
**1 :** to make noble **:** ELEVATE ⟨seemed *ennobled* by suffering⟩
**2 :** to raise to the rank of nobility
— **en·no·ble·ment** \-bəl-mənt\ *noun*
**en·nui** \ˌän-'wē\ *noun* [French, from Old French *enui* annoyance, from *enuier* to annoy — more at ANNOY] (1732)
**:** a feeling of weariness and dissatisfaction **:** BOREDOM
**Enoch** \'ē-nək, -nik\ *noun* [Greek *Enōch*, from Hebrew *Ḥănōkh*]
**:** an Old Testament patriarch and father of Methuselah
**eno·ki·da·ke** \e-ˌnō-kē-'dä-kē\ *noun* [Japanese *enokitake*, from *enoki* Chinese hackberry (*Celtis sinensis*) + *take* mushroom] (1983)
**:** ENOKI MUSHROOM
**enoki mushroom** \e-'nō-kē-\ *noun* [Japanese *enoki*] (circa 1977)
**:** a small white edible mushroom (*Flammulina velutipes* synonym *Collybia velutipes* of the family Agaricaceae) — called also *enoki*
**enol** \'ē-ˌnȯl, -ˌnōl\ *noun* [International Scientific Vocabulary *ene-* (from *-ene*) + *-ol*] (1904)
**:** an organic compound that contains a hydroxyl group bonded to a carbon atom having a double bond and that is usually characterized by the grouping $C=C(OH)$
— **eno·lic** \ē-'nō-lik, -'nä-lik\ *adjective*
**eno·lase** \'ē-nə-ˌlās, -ˌlāz\ *noun* [International Scientific Vocabulary *enol* + *-ase*] (1942)

**:** a crystalline enzyme that is found especially in muscle and yeast and is important in the metabolism of carbohydrates
**enol·o·gy** \ē-'nä-lə-jē\ *noun* [Greek *oinos* wine + English *-logy* — more at WINE] (1814)
**:** a science that deals with wine and wine making
— **eno·log·i·cal** \ˌē-nə-'lä-ji-kəl\ *adjective*
— **enol·o·gist** \ē-'nä-lə-jist\ *noun*
**enor·mi·ty** \i-'nȯr-mə-tē\ *noun, plural* **-ties** (15th century)
**1 :** an outrageous, improper, vicious, or immoral act ⟨the *enormities* of state power —Susan Sontag⟩ ⟨other *enormities* too juvenile to mention —Richard Freedman⟩
**2 :** the quality or state of being immoderate, monstrous, or outrageous; *especially* **:** great wickedness ⟨the *enormity* of the crimes committed during the Third Reich —G. A. Craig⟩
**3 :** the quality or state of being huge **:** IMMENSITY
**4 :** a quality of momentous importance ☐
**enor·mous** \i-'nȯr-məs, ē-\ *adjective* [Latin *enormis*, from *e, ex* out of + *norma* rule] (1531)
**1 a** *archaic* **:** ABNORMAL, INORDINATE **b :** exceedingly wicked **:** SHOCKING ⟨an *enormous* sin⟩

---

☆ SYNONYMS
**Enmity, hostility, antipathy, antagonism, animosity, rancor, animus** mean deep-seated dislike or ill will. ENMITY suggests positive hatred which may be open or concealed ⟨an unspoken *enmity*⟩. HOSTILITY suggests an enmity showing itself in attacks or aggression ⟨*hostility* between the two nations⟩. ANTIPATHY and ANTAGONISM imply a natural or logical basis for one's hatred or dislike, ANTIPATHY suggesting repugnance, a desire to avoid or reject, and ANTAGONISM suggesting a clash of temperaments leading readily to hostility ⟨a natural *antipathy* for self-seekers⟩ ⟨*antagonism* between the brothers⟩. ANIMOSITY suggests intense ill will and vindictiveness that threaten to kindle hostility ⟨*animosity* that led to revenge⟩. RANCOR is especially applied to bitter brooding over a wrong ⟨*rancor* filled every line of his letters⟩. ANIMUS adds to animosity the implication of strong prejudice ⟨objections devoid of personal *animus*⟩.

---

☐ USAGE
**enormity** *Enormity*, some people insist, is improperly used to denote large size. They insist on *enormousness* for this meaning, and would limit *enormity* to the meaning "great wickedness." Those who urge such a limitation may not recognize the subtlety with which *enormity* is actually used. It regularly denotes a considerable departure from the expected or normal ⟨they awakened; they sat up; and then the *enormity* of their situation burst upon them. "How did the fire start?" —John Steinbeck⟩. When used to denote large size, either literal or figurative, it usually suggests something so large as to seem overwhelming ⟨no intermediate zone of study. Either the *enormity* of the desert or the sight of a tiny flower —Paul Theroux⟩ ⟨the *enormity* of the task of teachers in slum schools —J. B. Conant⟩ and may even be used to suggest both great size and deviation from morality ⟨the *enormity* of existing stockpiles of atomic weapons —*New Republic*⟩. It can also emphasize the momentousness of what has happened ⟨the sombre *enormity* of the Russian Revolution —George Steiner⟩ or of its consequences ⟨perceived as no one in the family could the *enormity* of the misfortune —E. L. Doctorow⟩.

**2** : marked by extraordinarily great size, number, or degree; *especially* : exceeding usual bounds or accepted notions ☆
— **enor·mous·ly** *adverb*
— **enor·mous·ness** *noun*

**eno·sis** \i-'nō-səs\ *noun* [New Greek *henōsis*, from Greek, union, from *henoun* to unite, from *hen-, heis* one — more at SAME] (1928) : a movement to secure the political union of Greece and Cyprus

**¹enough** \i-'nəf; *after* t, d, s, z *often* ᵊn-'əf\ *adjective* [Middle English *ynough*, from Old English *genōg* (akin to Old High German *ginuog* enough), from *ge-* (perfective prefix) + *-nōg*; akin to Latin *nancisci* to get, Greek *enenkein* to carry — more at CO-] (before 12th century) : occurring in such quantity, quality, or scope as to fully meet demands, needs, or expectations
*synonym* see SUFFICIENT

**²enough** *adverb* (before 12th century)
**1** : in or to a degree or quantity that satisfies or that is sufficient or necessary for satisfaction : SUFFICIENTLY
**2** : FULLY, QUITE
**3** : in a tolerable degree

**³enough** *pronoun* (before 12th century) : a sufficient number, quantity, or amount ⟨*enough* were present to constitute a quorum⟩ ⟨had *enough* of their foolishness⟩

**enounce** \ē-'naun(t)s\ *transitive verb* **enounced; enounc·ing** [French *énoncer*, from Latin *enuntiare* to report — more at ENUNCIATE] (1805)
**1** : to set forth or state (as a proposition)
**2** : to pronounce distinctly : ARTICULATE

**enow** \i-'naù, i-'nō\ *adverb or adjective* [Middle English *inow*, from Old English *genōg*] (before 12th century)
*archaic* : ENOUGH

**en pas·sant** \,äⁿ-,pä-'säⁿ, -pə-\ *adverb* [French] (1665)
**1** : in passing
**2** — used in chess of the capture of a pawn as it makes a first move of two squares by an enemy pawn that threatens the first of these squares

**en·plane** \in-'plān, en-\ *intransitive verb* (1941) : to board an airplane

**en prise** \äⁿ-'prēz\ *adjective* [French, literally, engaged, within grasp] (1899)
*of a chess piece* : exposed to capture

**en·quire** \in-'kwīr\, **en·qui·ry** \'in-,kwīr-ē, in-'; 'in-kwə-rē, iŋ-\ *variant of* INQUIRE, INQUIRY

**en·rage** \in-'rāj, en-\ *transitive verb* [Middle French *enrager* to become mad, from Old French *enragier*, from *en-* + *rage* rage] (1589) : to fill with rage : ANGER

**en·rapt** \in-'rapt, en-\ *adjective* (1606) : wholly absorbed with rapture

**en·rap·ture** \in-'rap-chər, en-\ *transitive verb* **en·rap·tured; en·rap·tur·ing** \-'rap-chə-riŋ, -'rap-shriŋ\ (1740) : to fill with delight

**en·reg·is·ter** \in-'re-jə-stər, en-\ *transitive verb* [Middle French *enregistrer*, from Old French, from *en-* + *registre* register] (1523) : to put on record : REGISTER

**en·rich** \in-'rich, en-\ *transitive verb* [Middle English, from Middle French *enrichir*, from Old French, from *en-* + *riche* rich] (14th century) : to make rich or richer especially by the addition or increase of some desirable quality, attribute, or ingredient ⟨the experience will *enrich* your life⟩: as **a** : to add beauty to : ADORN **b** : to enhance the taste of ⟨butter will *enrich* the sauce⟩ **c** : to make (a soil) more fertile **d** : to improve the nutritive value of (a food) by adding nutrients (as vitamins or amino acids) and especially by restoring part of the nutrients lost in processing ⟨*enriched* flour⟩ **e** : to process so as to add or increase the proportion of a desirable ingredient ⟨*enriched* uranium⟩ ⟨*enriched* natural gas⟩

— **en·rich·er** *noun*
— **en·rich·ment** \-'rich-mənt\ *noun*

**en·robe** \in-'rōb, en-\ *transitive verb* (1593)
**1** : to cover with or as if with a robe
**2** : COAT 2

**en·roll** *or* **en·rol** \in-'rōl, en-\ *verb* **en·rolled; en·roll·ing** [Middle English, from Middle French *enroller*, from *en-* + *rolle* roll, register] (14th century)
*transitive verb*
**1** : to insert, register, or enter in a list, catalog, or roll ⟨the school *enrolls* about 800 pupils⟩
**2** : to prepare a final perfect copy of (a bill passed by a legislature) in written or printed form
**3** : to roll or wrap up
*intransitive verb*
: to enroll oneself or cause oneself to be enrolled ⟨we *enrolled* in the history course⟩
— **en·roll·ee** \-rō-'lē\ *noun*
— **en·roll·ment** \-'rōl-mənt\ *noun*

**en·root** \in-'rüt, -'rüt\ *transitive verb* [Middle English] (15th century)
: ESTABLISH, IMPLANT

**en route** \äⁿ(n)-'rüt, en-, in-, -'raut\ *adverb or adjective* [French] (1779)
: on or along the way ⟨he reads *en route*⟩ ⟨arrived early despite *en route* delays⟩

**en·sam·ple** \in-'sam-pəl\ *noun* [Middle English, from Middle French *ensample*, example] (13th century)
*archaic* : EXAMPLE, INSTANCE

**en·san·guine** \in-'saŋ-gwən\ *transitive verb* **-guined; -guin·ing** (1667)
**1** : to make bloody
**2** : CRIMSON

**en·sconce** \in-'skän(t)s\ *transitive verb* **en·sconced; en·sconc·ing** [*en-* + ²*sconce*] (1598)
**1** : SHELTER, CONCEAL
**2** : ESTABLISH, SETTLE ⟨*ensconced* in a new job⟩

**¹en·sem·ble** \än-'säm-bəl, äⁿ-\ *noun* [French, from *ensemble* together, from Latin *insimul* at the same time, from *in-* + *simul* at the same time — more at SAME] (1750)
: a group producing a single effect: as **a** : concerted music of two or more parts **b** : a complete costume of harmonizing or complementary clothing and accessories **c** (1) : the musicians engaged in the performance of a musical ensemble (2) : a group of supporting players, singers, or dancers; *especially* : CORPS DE BALLET

**²ensemble** *adjective* (circa 1911)
: emphasizing the roles of all performers as a whole rather than a star performance ⟨*ensemble* acting⟩

**en·serf** \in-'sərf, en-\ *transitive verb* (1882)
: to make a serf of : deprive of liberty and personal rights
— **en·serf·ment** \-mənt\ *noun*

**en·sheathe** \in-'shēth, en-\ *transitive verb* (1593)
: to cover with or as if with a sheath

**en·shrine** \in-'shrīn, en-, *especially Southern* -'srīn\ *transitive verb* [Middle English] (14th century)
**1** : to enclose in or as if in a shrine
**2** : to preserve or cherish as sacred
— **en·shrine·ment** \-mənt\ *noun*

**en·shri·nee** \in-'shrī-nē, -,shrī-'nē, en-\ *noun* (1968)
: a person inducted into a Hall of Fame

**en·shroud** \in-'shraud, en-, *especially Southern* -'sraud\ *transitive verb* (1583)
: to cover or enclose with or as if with a shroud

**en·si·form** \'en(t)-sə-,form\ *adjective* [French *ensiforme*, from Latin *ensis* sword + French *-forme* -form; akin to Sanskrit *asi* sword] (1541)
: having sharp edges and tapering to a slender point ⟨*ensiform* leaves of the gladiolus⟩ — see LEAF illustration

**en·sign** \'en(t)-sən, *also* 'en-,sīn *for 1, 2, & 3a*\ *noun* [Middle English *ensigne*, from Middle French *enseigne*, from Latin *insignia* insignia, flags] (15th century)
**1** : a flag that is flown (as by a ship) as the symbol of nationality and that may also be flown with a distinctive badge added to its design
**2 a** : a badge of office, rank, or power **b** : EMBLEM, SIGN
**3 a** : an infantry officer of what was formerly the lowest commissioned rank **b** : a commissioned officer in the navy or coast guard ranking above a chief warrant officer and below a lieutenant junior grade

**en·si·lage** \'en(t)-s(ə-)lij, *for 1 also* in-'sī-lij\ *noun* [French, from *ensiler* to ensile, from *en-* + *silo* silo, from Spanish] (1876)
**1** : the process of preserving fodder by ensiling
**2** : SILAGE

**en·sile** \en-'sī(ə)l, in-\ *transitive verb* **en·siled; en·sil·ing** (1883)
: to prepare and store (fodder) for silage

**en·sky** \in-'skī, en-\ *transitive verb* (1603)
: EXALT

**en·slave** \in-'slāv, en-\ *transitive verb* (1630)
: to reduce to or as if to slavery : SUBJUGATE
— **en·slave·ment** \-mənt\ *noun*
— **en·slav·er** *noun*

**en·snare** \in-'snar, -'sner, en-\ *transitive verb* (1576)
: to take in or as if in a snare
*synonym* see CATCH

**en·snarl** \in-'snär(-)l, en-\ *transitive verb* (1593)
: to involve in a snarl

**en·sor·cell** *or* **en·sor·cel** \in-'sor-səl\ *transitive verb* **-celled** *or* **-celed; -cell·ing** *or* **-cel·ing** [Middle French *ensorceler*, alteration of Old French *ensorcerer*, from *en-* + *-sorcerer*, from *sorcier* sorcerer — more at SORCERY] (circa 1541)
: BEWITCH, ENCHANT
— **en·sor·cell·ment** \-mənt\ *noun*

**en·soul** \in-'sōl, en-\ *transitive verb* (1605)
: to endow or imbue with a soul

**en·sphere** \in-'sfir, en-\ *transitive verb* (1612)
: to enclose in or as if in a sphere

**en·sue** \in-'sü, en-\ *verb* **en·sued; en·su·ing** [Middle English, from Middle French *ensuivre*, from Old French, from *en-* + *suivre* to follow — more at SUE] (14th century)
*transitive verb*
: to strive to attain : PURSUE ⟨I wander, seeking peace, and *ensuing* it —Rupert Brooke⟩
*intransitive verb*
: to take place afterward or as a result
*synonym* see FOLLOW

---

☆ **SYNONYMS**
**Enormous, immense, huge, vast, gigantic, colossal, mammoth** mean exceedingly large. ENORMOUS and IMMENSE both suggest an exceeding of all ordinary bounds in size or amount or degree, but ENORMOUS often adds an implication of abnormality or monstrousness ⟨an *enormous* expense⟩ ⟨an *immense* shopping mall⟩. HUGE commonly suggests an immensity of bulk or amount ⟨incurred a *huge* debt⟩. VAST usually suggests immensity of extent ⟨the *vast* Russian steppes⟩. GIGANTIC stresses the contrast with the size of others of the same kind ⟨a *gigantic* sports stadium⟩. COLOSSAL applies especially to a human creation of stupendous or incredible dimensions ⟨a *colossal* statue of Lincoln⟩. MAMMOTH suggests both hugeness and ponderousness of bulk ⟨a *mammoth* boulder⟩.

---

\ə\ **abut** \ᵊ\ **kitten** \ər\ **further** \a\ **ash** \ā\ **ace**
\ä\ **mop, mar** \aù\ **out** \ch\ **chin** \e\ **bet** \ē\ **easy**
\g\ **go** \i\ **hit** \ī\ **ice** \j\ **job** \ŋ\ **sing** \ō\ **go**
\ȯ\ **law** \ȯi\ **boy** \th\ **thin** \t͟h\ **the** \ü\ **loot** \ù\ **foot**
\y\ **yet** \zh\ **vision** *see also* Guide to Pronunciation

**en suite** \äⁿ-'swēt\ *adverb or adjective* [French] (1818)
**:** so as to form a suite **:** CONNECTED ⟨bathroom *en suite*⟩; *also* **:** so as to make a matching set
**en·sure** \in-'shùr\ *transitive verb* **en·sured; en·sur·ing** [Middle English, from Anglo-French *enseurer*, probably alteration of Old French *aseûrer* — more at ASSURE] (circa 1704)
**:** to make sure, certain, or safe **:** GUARANTEE ☆
**en·swathe** \in-'swäth, -'swòth, -'swäth, en-\ *transitive verb* (1597)
**:** to enfold or enclose with or as if with a covering **:** SWATHE
**ent-** *or* **ento-** *combining form* [New Latin, from Greek *entos* within; akin to Latin *intus* within, Greek *en* in — more at IN]
**:** inner **:** within ⟨*ento*derm⟩
**en·tab·la·ture** \in-'ta-blə-,chùr, -chər, -,t(y)ùr\ *noun* [obsolete French, modification of Italian *intavolatura*, from *intavolare* to put on a board or table, from *in-* (from Latin) + *tavola* board, table, from Latin *tabula*] (1611)
**:** a horizontal part in classical architecture that rests on the columns and consists of architrave, frieze, and cornice

*1 entablature,*
*2 cornice, 3 frieze,*
*4 architrave*

¹**en·tail** \in-'tā(ə)l, en-\ *transitive verb* [Middle English *entailen, entaillen,* from ¹*en-* + *taile, taille* limitation — more at TAIL] (14th century)
**1 :** to restrict (property) by limiting the inheritance to the owner's lineal descendants or to a particular class thereof
**2 a :** to confer, assign, or transmit as if by entail **:** FASTEN ⟨*entailed* on them indelible disgrace —Robert Browning⟩ **b :** to fix (a person) permanently in some condition or status ⟨*entail* him and his heirs unto the crown —Shakespeare⟩
**3 :** to impose, involve, or imply as a necessary accompaniment or result ⟨the project will *entail* considerable expense⟩
— **en·tail·er** \-'tā-lər\ *noun*
— **en·tail·ment** \-'tāl-mənt\ *noun*
²**en·tail** \'en-,tāl, in-'tā(ə)l\ *noun* (14th century)
**1 a :** an entailing especially of lands **b :** an entailed estate
**2 :** something transmitted as if by entail
**ent·amoe·ba** \,en-tə-'mē-bə\ *noun* [New Latin] (1914)
**:** any of a genus (*Entamoeba*) comprising various amoebas parasitic in vertebrates and including one (*E. histolytica*) that causes amebic dysentery in humans — compare ENDAMOEBA
**en·tan·gle** \in-'taŋ-gəl, en-\ *transitive verb* (15th century)
**1 a :** to wrap or twist together **:** INTERWEAVE **b : ENSNARE**
**2 a :** to involve in a perplexing or troublesome situation ⟨became *entangled* in a lawsuit⟩ **b :** to make complicated ⟨the story is *entangled* with legends⟩
— **en·tan·gler** \-g(ə-)lər\ *noun*
**en·tan·gle·ment** \in-'taŋ-gəl-mənt, en-\ *noun* (1535)
**1 a :** the action of entangling **:** the state of being entangled **b :** something that entangles, confuses, or ensnares
**2 :** the condition of being deeply involved
**en·ta·sis** \'en-tə-sis\ *noun, plural* **-ta·ses** \-tə-,sēz\ [Greek, literally, distension, stretching, from *enteinen* to stretch tight (from *en-* + ²*en-* + *teinein* to stretch) — more at THIN] (1664)
**:** a slight convexity especially in the shaft of a column

**en·tel·e·chy** \en-'te-lə-kē, in-\ *noun, plural* **-chies** [Late Latin *entelechia,* from Greek *entelecheia,* from *enteles* complete (from *en-* ²*en-* + *telos* end) + *echein* to have — more at WHEEL, SCHEME] (1603)
**1 :** the actualization of form-giving cause as contrasted with potential existence
**2 :** a hypothetical agency not demonstrable by scientific methods that in some vitalist doctrines is considered an inherent regulating and directing force in the development and functioning of an organism
**en·tente** \än-'tänt\ *noun* [French, from Old French, intent, understanding — more at INTENT] (1854)
**1 :** an international understanding providing for a common course of action
**2** [French *entente cordiale*] **:** a coalition of parties to an entente
**en·tente cor·diale** \(')än-'tänt-,kòr-'dyäl\ *noun* [French, literally, cordial understanding] (1844)
**1 :** ENTENTE 1
**2 :** a friendly agreement or working relationship
**en·ter** \'en-tər\ *verb* **en·tered; en·ter·ing** \'en-t(ə-)riŋ\ [Middle English *entren,* from Old French *entrer,* from Latin *intrare,* from *intra* within; akin to Latin *inter* between — more at INTER-] (13th century)
*intransitive verb*
**1 :** to go or come in
**2 :** to come or gain admission into a group **:** JOIN — often used with *into*
**3 a :** to make a beginning ⟨*entering* upon a career⟩ **b :** to begin to consider a subject — usually used with *into* or *upon*
**4 :** to go upon land for the purpose of taking possession
**5 :** to play a part **:** be a factor ⟨other considerations *enter* when money is involved⟩
*transitive verb*
**1 :** to come or go into ⟨*enter* a room⟩
**2 :** INSCRIBE, REGISTER ⟨*enter* the names of qualified voters⟩
**3 :** to cause to be received or admitted ⟨*enter* a child at a school⟩
**4 :** to put in **:** INSERT ⟨*enter* the new data into the computer⟩
**5 a :** to make a beginning in ⟨*enter* politics⟩ **b :** to go into (a particular period of time) ⟨*enter* middle age⟩
**6 :** to become a member of or an active participant in ⟨*enter* the university⟩ ⟨*enter* a race⟩
**7 :** to make report of (a ship or its cargo) to customs authorities
**8 :** to place in proper form before a court of law or upon record ⟨*enter* a writ⟩
**9 :** to go into or upon and take actual possession of (as land)
**10 :** to put formally on record ⟨*entering* a complaint⟩ ☆
— **en·ter·able** \'en-t(ə-)rə-bəl\ *adjective*
— **enter into 1 :** to make oneself a party to or in ⟨*enter into* an agreement⟩ **2 :** to form or be part of ⟨your prejudices shouldn't *enter into* it⟩ **3 :** to participate or share in ⟨*enter into* the spirit of the occasion⟩
— **enter the lists :** to engage in a fight or struggle
**enter-** *or* **entero-** *combining form* [Greek, from *enteron* — more at INTER-]
**:** intestine ⟨*enter*itis⟩
**en·ter·al** \'en-tə-rəl\ *adjective* (1903)
**:** ENTERIC
— **en·ter·al·ly** \-rə-lē\ *adverb*
**en·ter·ic** \en-'ter-ik, in-\ *adjective* (circa 1859)
**1 :** of or relating to the intestines; *broadly* **:** ALIMENTARY
**2 :** of, relating to, or being a medicinal preparation treated to pass through the stomach unaltered and disintegrate in the intestines
**en·ter·i·tis** \,en-tə-'rī-təs\ *noun* (1808)
**1 :** inflammation of the intestines and especially of the human ileum

**2 :** a disease of domestic animals (as panleucopenia of cats) marked by enteritis and diarrhea
**en·tero·bac·te·ri·um** \,en-tə-rō-bak-'tir-ē-əm\ *noun* [New Latin]
**:** any of a family (Enterobacteriaceae) of gram-negative straight rod bacteria (as a salmonella or a colon bacillus) that ferment glucose and include saprophytes as well as some serious plant and animal pathogens
— **en·tero·bac·te·ri·al** \-ē-əl\ *adjective*
**en·tero·bi·a·sis** \-'bī-ə-səs\ *noun, plural* **-a·ses** \-,sēz\ [New Latin, from *Enterobius,* genus name (from Greek *enter-* + *bios* mode of life) + *-iasis*] (circa 1927)
**:** infestation with or disease caused by pinworms (genus *Enterobius*) that occurs especially in children
**en·tero·chro·maf·fin** \-'krō-mə-fən\ *adjective* (circa 1941)
**:** of or relating to epithelial cells of the intestinal mucosa that stain especially with chromium salts and usually contain serotonin
**en·tero·coc·cus** \-'kä-kəs\ *noun, plural* **-coc·ci** \-'käk-,(s)ī, -'käk-,(,)(s)ē\ [New Latin, genus name] (1908)
**:** STREPTOCOCCUS; *especially* **:** a streptococcus (as *Streptococcus faecalis*) normally present in the intestine
— **en·tero·coc·cal** \-'kä-kəl\ *adjective*
**en·tero·coele** *or* **en·tero·coel** \'en-tə-rō-,sēl\ *noun* (1877)
**:** a coelom originating by outgrowth from the archenteron
— **en·tero·coe·lous** \,en-tə-rō-'sē-ləs\ *adjective*
— **en·tero·coe·lic** \-lik\ *adjective*
**en·tero·co·li·tis** \,en-tə-rō-kə-'lī-təs\ *noun* [New Latin] (circa 1857)
**:** enteritis affecting both the large and small intestine
**en·tero·gas·trone** \-'gas-,trōn\ *noun* [*enter-* + *gastr-* + *-one* (as in *hormone*)] (circa 1930)
**:** a hormone that is produced by the duodenal mucosa and has an inhibitory action on gastric motility and secretion
**en·tero·ki·nase** \,en-tə-rō-'kī-,nās, -,nāz\ *noun* [International Scientific Vocabulary] (circa 1902)
**:** an enzyme especially of the upper intestinal mucosa that activates trypsinogen by converting it to trypsin
**en·ter·on** \'en-tə-,rän, -rən\ *noun* [New Latin, from Greek, intestine — more at INTER-] (circa 1842)

: the alimentary canal or system — used especially of the embryo

**en·tero·patho·gen·ic** \,en-tə-rō-,pa-thə-'je-nik\ *adjective* (1961)
: tending to produce disease in the intestinal tract ⟨*enteropathogenic* bacteria⟩

**en·ter·op·a·thy** \,en-tə-'rä-pə-thē\ *noun* (circa 1889)
: a disease of the intestinal tract

**en·ter·os·to·my** \,en-tə-'räs-tə-mē\ *noun, plural* **-mies** [International Scientific Vocabulary] (1878)
: a surgical formation of an opening into the intestine through the abdominal wall
— **en·ter·os·to·mal** \-tə-məl\ *adjective*

**en·tero·tox·in** \,en-tə-rō-'täk-sən\ *noun* (circa 1928)
: a toxin that is produced by microorganisms (as some staphylococci) and causes gastrointestinal symptoms (as in some forms of food poisoning or cholera)

**en·tero·vi·rus** \-'vī-rəs\ *noun* [New Latin] (1957)
: any of a group of picornaviruses (as the poliomyelitis virus) that typically occur in the gastrointestinal tract but may be involved in respiratory ailments, meningitis, and neurological disorders
— **en·tero·vi·ral** \-rəl\ *adjective*

**en·ter·prise** \'en-tə(r)-,prīz\ *noun* [Middle English, from Middle French, from Old French *entreprendre* to undertake, from *entre-* inter- + *prendre* to take — more at PRIZE] (15th century)
**1** : a project or undertaking that is especially difficult, complicated, or risky
**2** : readiness to engage in daring action : INITIATIVE
**3 a** : a unit of economic organization or activity; *especially* : a business organization **b** : a systematic purposeful activity ⟨agriculture is the main economic *enterprise* among these people⟩

**en·ter·pris·er** \-,prī-zər\ *noun* (1523)
: ENTREPRENEUR

**en·ter·pris·ing** \-,prī-ziŋ\ *adjective* (1611)
: marked by an independent energetic spirit and by readiness to undertake or experiment

**en·ter·tain** \,en-tər-'tān\ *verb* [Middle English *entertinen*, from Middle French *entretenir*, from *entre-* inter- + *tenir* to hold — more at TENABLE] (15th century)
*transitive verb*
**1 a** *archaic* : MAINTAIN **b** *obsolete* : RECEIVE
**2** : to show hospitality to
**3 a** : to keep, hold, or maintain in the mind ⟨I *entertain* grave doubts about her sincerity⟩ **b** : to receive and take into consideration ⟨refused to *entertain* our plea⟩
**4** : to provide entertainment for
**5** : to play against (an opposing team) on one's home field or court
*intransitive verb*
: to provide entertainment especially for guests
**synonym** see AMUSE
— **en·ter·tain·er** *noun*

**en·ter·tain·ing** *adjective* (1568)
: providing entertainment : DIVERTING
— **en·ter·tain·ing·ly** \-'tā-niŋ-lē\ *adverb*

**en·ter·tain·ment** \,en-tər-'tān-mənt\ *noun* (15th century)
**1** : the act of entertaining
**2 a** *archaic* : MAINTENANCE, PROVISION **b** *obsolete* : EMPLOYMENT
**3** : something diverting or engaging: as **a** : a public performance **b** : a usually light comic or adventure novel

**en·thal·py** \'en-,thal-pē, en-\ *noun* [*en-* + Greek *thalpein* to heat] (circa 1924)
: the sum of the internal energy of a body and the product of its volume multiplied by the pressure

**en·thrall** *or* **en·thral** \in-'thról, en-\ *transitive verb* **en·thralled; en·thrall·ing** [Middle English] (15th century)

**1** : to hold in or reduce to slavery
**2** : to hold spellbound : CHARM
— **en·thrall·ment** \-'thról-mənt\ *noun*

**en·throne** \in-'thrōn, en-\ *transitive verb* (1606)
**1 a** : to seat ceremonially on a throne **b** : to seat in a place associated with a position of authority or influence
**2** : to assign supreme virtue or value to : EXALT
— **en·throne·ment** \-mənt\ *noun*

**en·thuse** \in-'thüz, en-, *also* -'thyüz\ *verb* **en·thused; en·thus·ing** [back-formation from *enthusiasm*] (1827)
*transitive verb*
**1** : to make enthusiastic
**2** : to express with enthusiasm
*intransitive verb*
: to show enthusiasm ⟨a splendid performance, and I was *enthusing* over it —Julian Huxley⟩
□

**en·thu·si·asm** \in-'thü-zē-,a-zəm, en-, *also* -'thyü-\ *noun* [Greek *enthousiasmos*, from *enthousiazein* to be inspired, irregular from *entheos* inspired, from *en-* + *theos* god] (1603)
**1 a** : belief in special revelations of the Holy Spirit **b** : religious fanaticism
**2 a** : strong excitement of feeling : ARDOR **b** : something inspiring zeal or fervor ◆
**synonym** see PASSION

**en·thu·si·ast** \-,ast, -əst\ *noun* (1570)
: a person filled with enthusiasm: as **a** : one who is ardently attached to a cause, object, or pursuit ⟨a sports car *enthusiast*⟩ **b** : one who tends to become ardently absorbed in an interest

**en·thu·si·as·tic** \in-,thü-zē-'as-tik, en-, *also* -,thyü-\ *adjective* (1603)
: filled with or marked by enthusiasm
— **en·thu·si·as·ti·cal·ly** \-ti-k(ə-)lē\ *adverb*

**en·thy·meme** \'en(t)-thi-,mēm\ *noun* [Latin *enthymema*, from Greek *enthymēma*, from *enthymeisthai* to keep in mind, from *en-* + *thymos* mind, soul] (1552)
: a syllogism in which one of the premises is implicit

**en·tice** \in-'tīs, en-\ *transitive verb* **en·ticed; en·tic·ing** [Middle English, from Middle French *enticier*, from (assumed) Vulgar Latin *intitiare*, from Latin *in-* + *titio* firebrand] (14th century)
: to attract artfully or adroitly or by arousing hope or desire : TEMPT
**synonym** see LURE
— **en·tice·ment** \-'tī-smənt\ *noun*
— **en·tic·ing·ly** \-'tī-siŋ-lē\ *adverb*

**¹en·tire** \in-'tīr, 'en-\ *adjective* [Middle English, from Middle French *entir*, from Latin *integer*, literally, untouched, from *in-* + *tangere* to touch — more at TANGENT] (14th century)
**1** : having no element or part left out : WHOLE ⟨was alone the *entire* day⟩
**2** : complete in degree : TOTAL ⟨their *entire* devotion to their family⟩
**3 a** : consisting of one piece **b** : HOMOGENEOUS, UNMIXED **c** : INTACT ⟨strove to keep the collection *entire*⟩
**4** : not castrated
**5** : having the margin continuous or free from indentations ⟨an *entire* leaf⟩
**synonym** see WHOLE, PERFECT
— **entire** *adverb*
— **en·tire·ness** *noun*

**²entire** *noun* (1597)
**1** *archaic* : the whole : ENTIRETY
**2** : STALLION

**en·tire·ly** *adverb* (14th century)
**1** : to the full or entire extent : COMPLETELY ⟨I agree *entirely*⟩ ⟨you are *entirely* welcome⟩
**2** : to the exclusion of others : SOLELY ⟨*entirely* by my own efforts⟩

**en·tire·ty** \in-'tī-rə-tē, -'tī(-ə)r-tē\ *noun, plural* **-ties** (1548)
**1** : the state of being entire or complete
**2** : SUM TOTAL, WHOLE

**en·ti·tle** \in-'tī-t°l, en-\ *transitive verb* **en·ti·tled; en·ti·tling** \-'tīt-liŋ, -°l-iŋ\ [Middle English, from Middle French *entituler*, from Late Latin *intitulare*, from Latin *in-* + *titulus* title] (14th century)
**1** : to give a title to : DESIGNATE
**2** : to furnish with proper grounds for seeking or claiming something ⟨this ticket *entitles* the bearer to free admission⟩

**en·ti·tle·ment** \-'tī-t°l-mənt\ *noun* (1944)
**1 a** : the state or condition of being entitled : RIGHT **b** : a right to benefits specified especially by law or contract
**2** : a government program providing benefits to members of a specified group; *also* : funds supporting or distributed by such a program

**en·ti·ty** \'en-tə-tē, 'e-nə-\ *noun, plural* **-ties** [Medieval Latin *entitas*, from Latin *ent-, ens* existing thing, from coined present participle of *esse* to be — more at IS] (1596)
**1 a** : BEING, EXISTENCE; *especially* : independent, separate, or self-contained existence **b** : the existence of a thing as contrasted with its attributes
**2** : something that has separate and distinct existence and objective or conceptual reality

**ento-** — see ENT-

**en·to·derm** \'en-tə-,dərm\ *noun* (1879)
: ENDODERM
— **en·to·der·mal** \,en-tə-'dər-məl\ *adjective*
— **en·to·der·mic** \-mik\ *adjective*

**en·toil** \in-'tói(ə)l\ *transitive verb* (1581)
: ENTRAP, ENMESH

**entom-** *or* **entomo-** *combining form* [French, from Greek *entomon*]
: insect ⟨*entomo*phagous⟩

**en·tomb** \in-'tüm, en-\ *transitive verb* [Middle English *entoumben*, from Middle French *entomber*, from *en-* + *tombe* tomb] (1576)

□ **USAGE**
**enthuse** *Enthuse* is apparently American in origin, although the earliest known example of its use occurs in a letter written in 1827 by a young Scotsman who spent about two years in the Pacific Northwest. It has been disapproved since about 1870. Current evidence shows it to be flourishing nonetheless on both sides of the Atlantic especially in journalistic prose.

◇ **WORD HISTORY**
**enthusiasm** In Greek *theos* means "god" and *entheos* or *enthous* means "inspired or possessed by a god." Hence, the noun *enthousiasmos*, the source of our *enthusiasm*, literally means "inspiration or possession by a god." It was in this sense that *enthusiasm* was first used when it made its appearance in English in the 17th century. Shortly thereafter, the word also took on a secular dimension, coming to be used of any very strong emotion, such as the fervor that the greatest poetry can inspire. For a time *enthusiasm* took on negative connotations, being applied specifically to the display of religious emotion associated with dissenters from the Church of England such as the Methodists, a display considered unseemly by members of the established church. By the 18th century *enthusiasm* was increasingly being used in nonreligious contexts. In the process it lost its suggestion of excess and acquired the neutral or positive sense of "ardent zeal for a cause or subject."

\ə\ **abut** \°\ **kitten** \ər\ **further** \a\ **ash** \ā\ **ace**
\ä\ **mop, mar** \au̇\ **out** \ch\ **chin** \e\ **bet** \ē\ **easy**
\g\ **go** \i\ **hit** \ī\ **ice** \j\ **job** \ŋ\ **sing** \ō\ **go**
\ò\ **law** \òi\ **boy** \th\ **thin** \th\ **the** \ü\ **loot** \u̇\ **foot**
\y\ **yet** \zh\ **vision** *see also* Guide to Pronunciation

**1 :** to deposit in a tomb **:** BURY
**2 :** to serve as a tomb for

**en·tomb·ment** \-'tüm-mənt\ *noun*
**en·to·mo·fau·na** \,en-tə-mō-'fo-nə, -'fä-\ *noun* [New Latin] (1951)
**:** a fauna of insects **:** the insects of an environment or region
**en·to·mol·o·gy** \,en-tə-'mä-lə-jē\ *noun* [French *entomologie*, from Greek *entomon* insect (from neuter of *entomos* cut up, from *en-* + *temnein* to cut) + French *-logie* -logy — more at TOME] (1766)
**:** a branch of zoology that deals with insects
— **en·to·mo·log·i·cal** \-mə-'lä-ji-kəl\ *adjective*
— **en·to·mo·log·i·cal·ly** \-k(ə-)lē\ *adverb*
— **en·to·mol·o·gist** \,en-tə-'mä-lə-jist\ *noun*
**en·to·moph·a·gous** \,en-tə-'mä-fə-gəs\ *adjective* (1847)
**:** feeding on insects
**en·to·moph·i·lous** \,en-tə-'mä-fə-ləs\ *adjective* (1880)
**:** normally pollinated by insects — compare ZOOPHILIC
— **en·to·moph·i·ly** \-lē\ *noun*
**en·to·proct** \'en-tə-,präkt\ *noun* [ultimately from *ent-* + Greek *prōktos* anus] (1940)
**:** any of a phylum (Entoprocta) of animals that are very similar to bryozoans but lack a true coelom and have the anus located near the mouth inside a crown of tentacles
**en·tou·rage** \,än-tu-'räzh\ *noun* [French, from Middle French, from *entourer* to surround, from *entour* around, from *en* in (from Latin *in*) + *tour* circuit — more at TURN] (1834)
**1 :** one's attendants or associates
**2 :** SURROUNDINGS
**en·tr'acte** \'ä<sup>n</sup>(n)-,trakt, -,träkt, ä<sup>n</sup>(n)-'-\ *noun* [French, from *entre-* inter- + *acte* act] (circa 1842)
**1 :** a dance, piece of music, or interlude performed between two acts of a play
**2 :** the interval between two acts of a play
**en·trails** \'en-,trālz, -trəlz\ *noun plural* [Middle English *entrailles*, from Middle French, from Medieval Latin *intralia*, alteration of Latin *interanea*, plural of *interaneum* intestine, from neuter of *interaneus* interior] (14th century)
**1 :** BOWELS, VISCERA; *broadly* **:** internal parts
**2 :** the inner workings of something ⟨the *entrails* of the movie industry⟩
**¹en·train** \in-'trān\ *transitive verb* [Middle French *entrainer*, from *en-* + *trainer* to draw, drag — more at TRAIN] (1568)
**1 :** to draw along with or after oneself
**2 :** to draw in and transport (as solid particles or gas) by the flow of a fluid
**3 :** to incorporate (air bubbles) into concrete
**4 :** to determine or modify the phase or period of ⟨circadian rhythms *entrained* by a light cycle⟩
— **en·train·er** *noun*
— **en·train·ment** \-'trān-mənt\ *noun*
**²entrain** (1881)
*transitive verb*
**:** to put aboard a train
*intransitive verb*
**:** to go aboard a train
**¹en·trance** \'en-trən(t)s\ *noun* (15th century)
**1 :** power or permission to enter **:** ADMISSION
**2 :** the act of entering
**3 :** the means or place of entry
**4 :** the point at which a voice or instrument part begins in ensemble music
**5 :** the first appearance of an actor in a scene
**²en·trance** \in-'tran(t)s, en-\ *transitive verb*
**en·tranced; en·tranc·ing** (1593)
**1 :** to carry away with delight, wonder, or rapture
**2 :** to put into a trance
— **en·trance·ment** \-'tran(t)-smənt\ *noun*
**en·trance·way** \'en-trən(t)s-,wā\ *noun* (1865)
**:** ENTRYWAY
**en·trant** \'en-trənt\ *noun* (1635)

**:** one that enters; *especially* **:** one that enters a contest
**en·trap** \in-'trap, en-\ *transitive verb* [Middle French *entraper*, from *en-* + *trape* trap] (1534)
**1 :** to catch in or as if in a trap
**2 :** to lure into a compromising statement or act
*synonym* see CATCH
**en·trap·ment** \-mənt\ *noun* (1597)
**1 a :** the action or process of entrapping **b** **:** the condition of being entrapped
**2 :** the action of luring an individual into committing a crime in order to prosecute the person for it
**en·treat** \in-'trēt, en-\ *verb* [Middle English *entreten*, from Middle French *entraitier*, from *en-* + *traitier* to treat] (14th century)
*intransitive verb*
**1** *obsolete* **a :** NEGOTIATE **b :** INTERCEDE
**2 :** to make an earnest request **:** PLEAD
*transitive verb*
**1 :** to plead with especially in order to persuade **:** ask urgently ⟨*entreated* his boss for another chance⟩
**2** *archaic* **:** to deal with **:** TREAT
*synonym* see BEG
— **en·treat·ing·ly** \-'trē-tiŋ-lē\ *adverb*
— **en·treat·ment** \-mənt\ *noun*
**en·treaty** \-'trē-tē\ *noun, plural* **-treat·ies** (15th century)
**:** an act of entreating **:** PLEA
**en·tre·chat** \'ä<sup>n</sup>(n)-trə-,shä\ *noun* [French, modification of Italian (*capriola*) *intrecciata*, literally, intertwined caper] (1775)
**:** a leap in which a ballet dancer repeatedly crosses the legs and sometimes beats them together
**en·tre·côte** *also* **en·tre·cote** \'ä<sup>n</sup>(n)-trə-,kōt\ *noun* [French *entrecôte*, from *entre-* inter- + *côte* rib, from Latin *costa* — more at INTER-, COAST] (1841)
**:** a steak cut from between the ribs
**en·trée** *or* **en·tree** \'än-,trā *also* än-'\ *noun* [French *entrée*, from Old French — more at ENTRY] (1761)
**1 a :** the act or manner of entering **:** ENTRANCE **b :** freedom of entry or access
**2 :** the main course of a meal in the U.S. ◆
**en·tre·mets** \as singular ,ä<sup>n</sup>(n)-trə-'mā, as plural -'mā(z)\ *noun plural but singular or plural in construction* [Middle English, from Middle French, from Old French *entremes*, from Latin *intermissus*, past participle of *intermittere* to intermit] (15th century)
**:** dishes served in addition to the main course of a meal; *especially* **:** DESSERT
**en·trench** \in-'trench, en-\ (1555)
*transitive verb*
**1 a :** to place within or surround with a trench especially for defense **b :** to place (oneself) in a strong defensive position **c :** to establish solidly ⟨*entrenched* themselves in the business⟩
**2 :** to cut into **:** FURROW; *specifically* **:** to erode downward so as to form a trench
*intransitive verb*
**1 :** to dig or occupy a trench for defensive purposes
**2 :** to enter upon or take over something unfairly, improperly, or unlawfully **:** ENCROACH — used with *on* or *upon*
— **en·trench·ment** \-mənt\ *noun*
**en·tre·pôt** \'ä<sup>n</sup>(n)-trə-,pō\ *noun* [French, from Middle French *entrepost*, from *entreposer* to put between, from *entre-* inter- + *poser* to pose, put] (1758)
**:** an intermediary center of trade and transshipment
**en·tre·pre·neur** \,ä<sup>n</sup>-trə-p(r)ə-'nər, -'n(y)ur\ *noun* [French, from Old French, from *entreprendre* to undertake — more at ENTERPRISE] (1852)
**:** one who organizes, manages, and assumes the risks of a business or enterprise
— **en·tre·pre·neur·ial** \-'n(y)ur-ē-əl, -'nər-\ *adjective*

— **en·tre·pre·neur·ial·ism** \-ē-ə-li-zəm\ *noun*
— **en·tre·pre·neur·ial·ly** \-ē-ə-lē\ *adverb*
— **en·tre·pre·neur·ship** \-'nər-,ship, -'n(y)ur-\ *noun*
**en·tre·sol** \'ä<sup>n</sup>(n)-trə-,säl, -,sol\ *noun* [French, from Spanish *entresuelo*, from *entre* between + *suelo* level, from (assumed) Vulgar Latin *sola*, from Latin *solea* sandal, sole, sill — more at SOLE] (1711)
**:** MEZZANINE
**en·tro·pi·on** \en-'trō-pē-,än, -pē-ən\ *noun* [New Latin, from *en-* ²*en-* + *ectropion* turning out of the eyelid, from Greek *ektropion*, from *ektrepein* to turn out, from *ex-* out + *trepein* to turn] (circa 1860)
**:** the inversion or turning inward of the border of the eyelid against the eyeball
**en·tro·py** \'en-trə-pē\ *noun, plural* **-pies** [International Scientific Vocabulary ²*en-* + Greek *tropē* change, literally, turn, from *trepein* to turn] (1875)
**1 :** a measure of the unavailable energy in a closed thermodynamic system that is also usually considered to be a measure of the system's disorder and that is a property of the system's state and is related to it in such a manner that a reversible change in heat in the system produces a change in the measure which varies directly with the heat change and inversely with the absolute temperature at which the change takes place; *broadly* **:** the degree of disorder or uncertainty in a system
**2 a :** the degradation of the matter and energy in the universe to an ultimate state of inert uniformity **b :** a process of degradation or running down or a trend to disorder
**3 :** CHAOS, DISORGANIZATION, RANDOMNESS
— **en·tro·pic** \en-'trō-pik, -'trä-pik\ *adjective*
— **en·tro·pi·cal·ly** \-pi-k(ə-)lē\ *adverb*
**en·trust** \in-'trəst, en-\ *transitive verb* (1602)
**1 :** to confer a trust on; *especially* **:** to deliver something in trust to
**2 :** to commit to another with confidence
*synonym* see COMMIT
— **en·trust·ment** \-'trəs(t)-mənt\ *noun*
**en·try** \'en-trē\ *noun, plural* **entries** [Middle English *entre*, from Old French *entree*, from feminine of *entré*, past participle of *entrer* to enter] (13th century)
**1 :** the right or privilege of entering **:** ENTRÉE
**2 :** the act of entering **:** ENTRANCE
**3 :** a place of entrance: as **a :** VESTIBULE, PASSAGE **b :** DOOR, GATE

---

◇ WORD HISTORY

**entrée**, which signifies the main course of a meal in the U.S., is in fact the French word for "entry." The culinary sense of *entrée* can be traced back to 18th century Britain. In those days a formal dinner could be a gastronomic marathon. In addition to the principal courses of soup, fish, meat, and dessert, there would be an impressive array of side dishes, not to mention the salad and cheese courses. Between the fish and meat courses would come a small dish concocted of several ingredients and often garnished and sauced. Because this secondary dish immediately preceded the centerpiece of the whole meal—typically a roast—it was called the *entrée*, being, in effect, the "entrance" to the really important part of the meal. As Anglo-American dining habits changed, meals gradually diminished in their elaborateness; fewer and simpler courses were served. In the U.S. the course following the appetizer course continued to be known as the *entrée*, even if it did turn out to be a roast. Perhaps the continued preference for *entrée* in menu terminology lay in the fact that it was obviously French, and anything French was considered to have prestige.

**4 a :** the act of making or entering a record **b** : something entered: as (1) : a record or notation of an occurrence, transaction, or proceeding (2) : a descriptive record (as in a card catalog or an index) (3) : HEADWORD (4) : a headword with its definition or identification (5) : VOCABULARY ENTRY
**5 :** a person, thing, or group entered in a contest

**en·try–lev·el** \'en-trē-ˌle-vəl\ *adjective* (1975) : of or being at the lowest level of a hierarchy ⟨*entry-level* jobs⟩

**en·try·way** \-trē-ˌwā\ *noun* (1746) : a passage for entrance

**entry word** *noun* (circa 1908) : HEADWORD

**en·twine** \in-'twīn, en-\ (1590) *transitive verb* : to twine together or around *intransitive verb* : to become twisted or twined

**en·twist** \in-'twist, en-\ *transitive verb* (1590) : ENTWINE

**enu·cle·ate** \(ˌ)ē-'nü-klē-ˌāt, -'nyü-\ *transitive verb* **-at·ed; -at·ing** [Latin *enucleatus,* past participle of *enucleare,* literally, to remove the kernel from, from *e-* + *nucleus* kernel — more at NUCLEUS] (1548)
**1** *archaic* : EXPLAIN
**2 :** to deprive of a nucleus
**3 :** to remove without cutting into ⟨*enucleate* a tumor⟩ ⟨*enucleate* the eyeball⟩
— **enu·cle·ation** \(ˌ)ē-ˌn(y)ü-klē-'ā-shən\ *noun*

**enu·mer·a·ble** \i-'n(y)üm-rə-bəl, -'n(y)ü-mə-\ *adjective* (circa 1889) : DENUMERABLE
— **enu·mer·a·bil·i·ty** \-ˌn(y)üm-rə-'bi-lə-tē, -'n(y)ü-mə-\ *noun*

**enu·mer·ate** \i-'n(y)ü-mə-ˌrāt\ *transitive verb* **-at·ed; -at·ing** [Latin *enumeratus,* past participle of *enumerare,* from *e-* + *numerare* to count, from *numerus* number] (1616)
**1 :** to ascertain the number of : COUNT
**2 :** to specify one after another : LIST
— **enu·mer·a·tion** \-ˌn(y)ü-mə-'rā-shən\ *noun*
— **enu·mer·a·tive** \-'n(y)ü-mə-ˌrā-tiv, -'n(y)üm-rə-, -'n(y)ü-mə-rə-\ *adjective*

**enu·mer·a·tor** \-'n(y)ü-mə-ˌrā-tər\ *noun* (1856) : one that enumerates; *especially* : a census taker

**enun·ci·ate** \ē-'nən(t)-sē-ˌāt\ *verb* **-at·ed; -at·ing** [Latin *enuntiatus,* past participle of *enuntiare* to report, declare, from *e-* + *nuntiare* to report — more at ANNOUNCE] (1623) *transitive verb*
**1 a :** to make a definite or explicit statement of **b** : ANNOUNCE, PROCLAIM ⟨*enunciated* the new policy⟩
**2 :** ARTICULATE, PRONOUNCE ⟨*enunciate* all the syllables⟩ *intransitive verb* : to utter articulate sounds
— **enun·ci·a·ble** \-'nən(t)-sē-ə-bəl, -'nənch(ē-)ə-\ *adjective*
— **enun·ci·a·tion** \-ˌnən(t)-sē-'ā-shən\ *noun*
— **enun·ci·a·tor** \-'nən(t)-sē-ˌā-tər\ *noun*

**enure** *variant of* INURE

**en·ure·sis** \ˌen-yü-'rē-səs\ *noun* [New Latin, from Greek *enourein* to urinate in, wet the bed, from *en-* + *ourein* to urinate — more at URINE] (circa 1800) : the involuntary discharge of urine : incontinence of urine
— **en·uret·ic** \-'re-tik\ *adjective or noun*

**en·vel·op** \in-'ve-ləp, en-\ *transitive verb* [Middle English *envolupen,* from Middle French *envoluper, enveloper,* from Old French *envoloper,* from *en-* + *voloper* to wrap] (14th century)
**1 :** to enclose or enfold completely with or as if with a covering
**2 :** to mount an attack on (an enemy's flank)

— **en·vel·op·ment** \-mənt\ *noun*

**en·ve·lope** \'en-və-ˌlōp, ÷'än-\ *noun* (circa 1714)
**1 :** a flat usually paper container (as for a letter)
**2 :** something that envelops : WRAPPER ⟨the *envelope* of air around the earth⟩
**3 a :** the outer covering of an aerostat **b** : the bag containing the gas in a balloon or airship
**4 :** a natural enclosing covering (as a membrane, shell, or integument)
**5 a :** a curve tangent to each of a family of curves **b** : a surface tangent to each of a family of surfaces
**6 :** a set of performance limits (as of an aircraft) that may not be safely exceeded; *also* : the set of operating parameters that exists within these limits ◻

**en·ven·om** \in-'ve-nəm, en-\ *transitive verb* [Middle English *envenimen,* from Old French *envenimer,* from *en-* + *venim* venom] (13th century)
**1 :** to make poisonous
**2 :** EMBITTER

**en·ven·om·iza·tion** \in-ˌve-nə-mə-'zā-shən, en-\ *noun* (1960) : a poisoning caused by a bite or sting

**en·vi·able** \'en-vē-ə-bəl\ *adjective* (1602) : highly desirable
— **en·vi·able·ness** *noun*
— **en·vi·ably** \-blē\ *adverb*

**en·vi·er** \'en-vē-ər\ *noun* (15th century) : one that envies

**en·vi·ous** \'en-vē-əs\ *adjective* (13th century)
**1 :** feeling or showing envy ⟨*envious* of their neighbor's new car⟩ ⟨*envious* looks⟩
**2** *archaic* **a :** EMULOUS **b** : ENVIABLE
— **en·vi·ous·ly** *adverb*
— **en·vi·ous·ness** *noun*

**en·vi·ron** \in-'vī-rən, -'vī-(ə)rn\ *transitive verb* [Middle English *environen,* from Middle French *environner,* from *environ* around, from *en* in (from Latin *in*) + *viron* circle, from *virer* to turn — more at VEER] (14th century) : ENCIRCLE, SURROUND

**en·vi·ron·ment** \in-'vī-rə(n)-mənt, -'vī(-ə)r(n)-\ *noun* (1827)
**1 :** the circumstances, objects, or conditions by which one is surrounded
**2 a :** the complex of physical, chemical, and biotic factors (as climate, soil, and living things) that act upon an organism or an ecological community and ultimately determine its form and survival **b** : the aggregate of social and cultural conditions that influence the life of an individual or community
**3 :** the position or characteristic position of a linguistic element in a sequence
*synonym see* BACKGROUND
— **en·vi·ron·men·tal** \-ˌvī-rə(n)-'men-tᵊl, -ˌvī(-ə)r(n)-\ *adjective*
— **en·vi·ron·men·tal·ly** \-tᵊl-ē\ *adverb*

**en·vi·ron·men·tal·ism** \-ˌvī-rə(n)-'men-tᵊl-ˌi-zəm, -ˌvī(-ə)r(n)-\ *noun* (circa 1922)
**1 :** a theory that views environment rather than heredity as the important factor in the development and especially the cultural and intellectual development of an individual or group
**2 :** advocacy of the preservation or improvement of the natural environment; *especially* : the movement to control pollution

**en·vi·ron·men·tal·ist** \-tᵊl-əst\ *noun* (1916)
**1 :** an advocate of environmentalism
**2 :** one concerned about environmental quality especially of the human environment with respect to the control of pollution

**en·vi·rons** \in-'vī-rənz, -'vī-(ə)rnz\ *noun plural* (1665)
**1 :** the districts around a city
**2 a :** environing things : SURROUNDINGS **b** : an adjoining region or space : VICINITY

**en·vis·age** \in-'vi-zij, en-\ *transitive verb* **-aged; -ag·ing** [French *envisager,* from *en-* + *visage* face] (1837)
**1 :** to view or regard in a certain way ⟨*envisages* the slum as a hotbed of crime⟩

**2 :** to have a mental picture of especially in advance of realization ⟨*envisages* an entirely new system of education⟩
*synonym see* THINK

**en·vi·sion** \in-'vi-zhən, en-\ *transitive verb* (1919) : to picture to oneself ⟨*envisions* a career dedicated to promoting peace⟩
*synonym see* THINK

**en·voi** *or* **en·voy** \'en-ˌvoi, 'än-\ *noun* [Middle English *envoye,* from Middle French *envoi,* literally, message, from Old French *envei,* from *envoier* to send on one's way, from (assumed) Vulgar Latin *inviare,* from Latin *in-* + *via* way — more at WAY] (14th century) : the usually explanatory or commendatory concluding remarks to a poem, essay, or book; *especially* : a short final stanza of a ballade serving as a summary or dedication

**en·voy** \'en-ˌvoi, ÷'än-\ *noun* [French *envoyé,* from past participle of *envoyer* to send, from Old French *envoier*] (1635)
**1 a :** a minister plenipotentiary accredited to a foreign government who ranks between an ambassador and a minister resident — called also *envoy extraordinary* **b** : a person delegated to represent one government in its dealings with another
**2 :** MESSENGER, REPRESENTATIVE

**¹en·vy** \'en-vē\ *noun, plural* **envies** [Middle English *envie,* from Old French, from Latin *invidia,* from *invidus* envious, from *invidēre* to look askance at, envy, from *in-* + *vidēre* to see — more at WIT] (13th century)
**1 :** painful or resentful awareness of an advantage enjoyed by another joined with a desire to possess the same advantage
**2** *obsolete* : MALICE
**3 :** an object of envious notice or feeling ⟨his new car made him the *envy* of his friends⟩

**²envy** *verb* **en·vied; en·vy·ing** (14th century) *transitive verb*
**1 :** to feel envy toward or on account of
**2** *obsolete* : BEGRUDGE *intransitive verb*
*obsolete* : to feel or show envy
— **en·vy·ing·ly** \-vē-iŋ-lē\ *adverb*

**en·wheel** \in-'hwē(ə)l, -'wē(ə)l, en-\ *transitive verb* (1604) *obsolete* : ENCIRCLE

**en·wind** \in-'wīnd, en-\ *transitive verb* **en·wound** \-'waùnd\; **en·wind·ing** (1850) : to wind in or about : ENFOLD

**en·womb** \in-'wüm, en-\ *transitive verb* (circa 1591) : to shut up as if in a womb

**en·wrap** \in-'rap, en-\ *transitive verb* (14th century)
**1 :** to wrap in a covering : ENFOLD
**2 a :** ENVELOP **b** : to preoccupy or absorb mentally : ENGROSS

**en·wreathe** \in-'rēth, en-\ *transitive verb* (15th century)

---

---

\ə\ abut \ᵊ\ kitten \ər\ further \a\ ash \ā\ ace
\ä\ mop, mar \aù\ out \ch\ chin \e\ bet \ē\ easy
\g\ go \i\ hit \ī\ ice \j\ job \ŋ\ sing \ō\ go
\o\ law \oi\ boy \th\ thin \th\ the \ü\ loot \ù\ foot
\y\ yet \zh\ vision *see also* Guide to Pronunciation

: to encircle with or as if with a wreath **:** EN-
VELOP

**en·zo·ot·ic** \en-zə-'wä-tik\ *adjective* [en- +
epi*zootic*] (1882)
*of animal diseases* **:** peculiar to or constantly
present in a locality
— **enzootic** *noun*

**en·zy·mat·ic** \en-zə-'ma-tik\ *also* **en·zy-
mic** \en-'zī-mik\ *adjective* (1900)
**:** of, relating to, or produced by an enzyme
— **en·zy·mat·i·cal·ly** \en-zə-'ma-ti-
k(ə-)lē\ *also* **en·zy·mi·cal·ly** \en-'zī-mi-
k(ə-)lē\ *adverb*

**en·zyme** \'en-,zīm\ *noun* [German *Enzym*,
from Middle Greek *enzymos* leavened, from
Greek *en-* + *zymē* leaven — more at JUICE]
(1881)
**:** any of numerous complex proteins that are
produced by living cells and catalyze specific
biochemical reactions at body temperatures

**enzyme–linked immunosorbent assay**
*noun* (1977)
**:** a quantitative in vitro test for an antibody or
antigen in which the test material is adsorbed
on a surface and exposed to a complex of an
enzyme linked to an antibody specific for the
substance being tested for with a positive result indicated by a treatment yielding a color
in proportion to the amount of antigen or antibody in the test material — called also *ELISA*

**en·zy·mol·o·gy** \en-,zī-'mä-lə-jē, -zə-\ *noun*
[International Scientific Vocabulary] (circa
1900)
**:** a branch of biochemistry that deals with enzymes, their nature, activity, and significance
— **en·zy·mol·o·gist** \-jist\ *noun*

**eo-** *combining form* [Greek *ēō-* dawn, from *ēos*
— more at EAST]
**:** earliest **:** oldest ⟨*eo*lithic⟩

**Eo·cene** \'ē-ə-,sēn\ *adjective* (1831)
**:** of, relating to, or being an epoch of the Tertiary between the Paleocene and the Oligocene
or the corresponding system of rocks — see
GEOLOGIC TIME table
— **Eocene** *noun*

**eo·hip·pus** \,ē-ō-'hi-pəs\ *noun* [New Latin,
from *eo-* + Greek *hippos* horse — more at
EQUINE] (circa 1879)
**:** any of a genus (*Hyracotherium* synonym *Eohippus*) of very small primitive horses from
the Lower Eocene having four-toed forefeet
and three-toed hind feet — called also *dawn
horse*

**eo·lian** \ē-'ō-lē-ən, -'ōl-yən\ *adjective* [Latin
*Aeolus*, Aeolus] (1853)
**:** borne, deposited, produced, or eroded by the
wind

**eo·lith** \'ē-ə-,lith\ *noun* (1895)
**:** a very crudely chipped flint

**Eo·lith·ic** \,ē-ə-'li-thik\ *adjective* (1890)
**:** of or relating to the early period of the Stone
Age marked by the use of eoliths

**eon** \'ē-ən, 'ē-,än\ *variant of* AEON

**eo no·mi·ne** \,ē-ō-'nä-mə-nē\ [Latin] (1627)
**:** by or under that name

**Eos** \'ē-,äs\ *noun* [Greek *Ēōs*]
**:** the Greek goddess of dawn — compare AU-
RORA

**eo·sin** \'ē-ə-sən\ *also* **eo·sine** \-sən, -,sēn\
*noun* [International Scientific Vocabulary,
from Greek *ēos* dawn] (1866)
**1 :** a red fluorescent dye $C_{20}H_8Br_4O_5$ obtained
by the action of bromine on fluorescein and
used especially in cosmetics and as a toner;
*also* **:** its red to brown sodium or potassium
salt used especially as a biological stain for
cytoplasmic structures
**2 :** any of several dyes related to eosin

**¹eo·sin·o·phil** \,ē-ə-'si-nə-,fil\ *adjective* (circa
1882)
**:** EOSINOPHILIC 1

**²eosinophil** \-'fil\ *noun* (circa 1900)
**:** a white blood cell or other granulocyte with
cytoplasmic inclusions readily stained by
eosin

**eo·sin·o·phil·ia** \-,si-nə-'fi-lē-ə\ *noun* [New
Latin] (circa 1903)
**:** abnormal increase in the number of eosinophils in the blood that is characteristic of allergic states and various parasitic infections

**eo·sin·o·phil·ic** \-,si-nə-'fi-lik\ *adjective* (circa 1900)
**1 :** staining readily with eosin
**2 :** of, relating to, or characterized by eosino-
philia

**epact** \'ē-,pakt, 'e-,pakt\ *noun* [Middle French
*epacte*, from Late Latin *epacta*, from Greek
*epaktē*, from *epagein* to bring in, intercalate,
from *epi-* + *agein* to drive — more at AGENT]
(1588)
**:** a period added to harmonize the lunar with
the solar calendar

**ep·ar·chy** \'e-,pär-kē\ *noun, plural* **-chies**
[Greek *eparchia* province, from *eparchos* prefect, from *epi-* + *archos* ruler — more at
ARCH-] (1796)
**:** a diocese of an Eastern church

**ep·au·let** *also* **ep·au·lette** \,e-pə-'let; 'e-pə-
,let, -lət\ *noun* [French *épaulette*, diminutive
of *épaule* shoulder, from Late Latin *spatula*
shoulder blade, spoon, diminutive of Latin
*spatha* spoon, sword — more at SPADE]
(1783)
**:** something that ornaments or protects the
shoulder: as **a :** an ornamental fringed shoulder
pad formerly worn as
part of a military uni-
form **b :** an ornamental
strip or loop sewn across
the shoulder of a dress
or coat
— **ep·au·let·ted** \,e-
pə-'le-təd, 'e-pə-,\ *adjective*

*E* **epaulet**

**ep·a·zote** \'e-pə-,zōt\ *noun* [Mexican Spanish,
from Nahuatl *epazōtl*] (1946)
**:** WORMSEED b

**épée** \'e-,pā, ā-'pā\ *noun* [French, from Latin
*spatha*] (1889)
**1 :** a fencing or dueling sword having a bowl-
shaped guard and a rigid blade of triangular
section with no cutting edge that tapers to a
sharp point blunted for fencing — compare
⁴FOIL 1, SABER
**2 :** the art or sport of fencing with the épée

**épée·ist** \-ist\ *noun* (1910)
**:** one who fences with an épée

**ep·ei·rog·e·ny** \,e-,pī-'rä-jə-nē\ *noun, plural*
**-nies** [Greek *ēpeiros* mainland, continent +
English *-geny*] (1890)
**:** the deformation of the earth's crust by which
the broader features of relief are produced
— **epei·ro·gen·ic** \i-,pī-rə-'je-nik\ *adjective*
— **epei·ro·gen·i·cal·ly** \-ni-k(ə-)lē\ *adverb*

**epen·the·sis** \i-'pen(t)-thə-səs, e-\ *noun, plural* **-the·ses** \-,sēz\ [Late Latin, from Greek,
from *epentithenai* to insert a letter, from *epi-*
+ *entithenai* to put in, from *en-* + *tithenai* to
put — more at DO] (1543)
**:** the insertion or development of a sound or
letter in the body of a word (as \ə\ in \'a-thə-
,lēt\ *athlete*)
— **ep·en·thet·ic** \,e-pən-'the-tik\ *adjective*

**epergne** \i-'pərn, ā-\ *noun* [probably from
French *épargne* saving] (1761)
**:** an often ornate tiered centerpiece consisting
typically of a frame of wrought metal (as silver or gold) bearing dishes, vases, or candle
holders or a combination of these

**ep·ex·e·ge·sis** \,e-,pek-sə-'jē-səs, plural* **-ge·ses** \-,sēz\ [Greek *epexēgesis*, from
*epi-* + *exēgēsis* exegesis] (circa 1577)
**:** additional explanation or explanatory matter
— **ep·ex·e·get·i·cal** \-'je-ti-kəl\ *or* **ep-
ex·e·get·ic** \-'je-tik\ *adjective*
— **ep·ex·e·get·i·cal·ly** \-'je-ti-k(ə-)lē\ *adverb*

**ephah** \'ē-fə, 'e-fə\ *noun* [Middle English *ephi*,
from Late Latin, from Hebrew *ēphāh*, from
Egyptian *'pt*] (1611)
**:** an ancient Hebrew unit of dry measure equal
to ¹⁄₁₀ homer or a little over a bushel

**ephebe** \'e-,fēb, i-'fēb\ *noun* [Latin *ephebus*]
(1880)
**:** EPHEBUS; *also* **:** a young man **:** YOUTH

**ephe·bic** \i-'fē-bik\ *adjective* (1865)
**:** of, relating to, or characteristic of an ephebe
or ephebus

**ephe·bus** \i-'fē-bəs, e-\ *noun, plural* **-bi** \-,bī\
[Latin, from Greek *ephēbos*, from *epi-* + *hēbē*
youth, puberty] (1697)
**:** a youth of ancient Greece; *especially* **:** an
Athenian 18 or 19 years old in training for full
citizenship

**ephe·dra** \i-'fe-drə, 'e-fə-drə\ *noun* [New Latin, genus name, from Latin, equisetum, from
Greek, from *ephedros* sitting upon, from *epi-*
+ *hedra* seat — more at SIT] (circa 1889)
**:** any of a large genus (*Ephedra* of the family
Gnetaceae) of jointed nearly leafless desert
shrubs with the leaves reduced to scales at the
nodes

**ephed·rine** \i-'fe-drən, *British also* 'e-fə-drən\
*noun* [New Latin *Ephedra*] (1889)
**:** a crystalline alkaloid $C_{10}H_{15}NO$ extracted
from Chinese ephedras or synthesized and
used in the form of a salt for relief of hay fever, asthma, and nasal congestion

**ephem·era** \i-'fe-mər-ə, -'fem-rə\ *noun, plural* **ephemera** *also* **ephem·er·ae** \-mər-ē,
-,rē\ *or* **ephemeras** [New Latin, from Greek
*ephēmera*, neuter plural of *ephēmeros*] (1751)
**1 :** something of no lasting significance —
usually used in plural
**2** *ephemera plural* **:** collectibles (as posters,
broadsides, and tickets) not intended to have
lasting value

**¹ephem·er·al** \i-'fem-rəl, -'fēm-; -'fe-mə-,
-'fē-\ *adjective* [Greek *ephēmeros* lasting a
day, daily, from *epi-* + *hēmera* day] (1576)
**1 :** lasting one day only ⟨an *ephemeral* fever⟩
**2 :** lasting a very short time ⟨*ephemeral*
pleasures⟩
**synonym** see TRANSIENT
— **ephem·er·al·ly** \-rə-lē\ *adverb*

**²ephemeral** *noun* (1817)
**:** something ephemeral; *specifically* **:** a plant
that grows, flowers, and dies in a few days

**ephem·er·al·i·ty** \i-,fe-mə-'ra-lə-tē, -,fē-\
*noun, plural* **-ties** (1822)
**1 :** the quality or state of being ephemeral
**2** *plural* **:** ephemeral things

**ephem·er·id** \i-'fe-mə-rəd\ *noun* [ultimately
from Greek *ephēmeron*] (1872)
**:** MAYFLY

**ephem·er·is** \-mə-rəs\ *noun, plural* **eph·e-
mer·i·des** \,e-fə-'mer-ə-,dēz\ [Latin, diary,
ephemeris, from Greek *ephēmeris*, from
*ephēmeros*] (1508)
**:** a tabular statement of the assigned places of
a celestial body for regular intervals

**ephemeris time** *noun* (1950)
**:** a uniform measure of time defined by the orbital motions of the planets

**Ephe·sians** \i-'fē-zhənz\ *noun plural but singular in construction* [short for *Epistle to the
Ephesians*]
**:** a letter addressed to early Christians and included as a book in the New Testament —
see BIBLE table

**eph·od** \'e-,fäd, 'ē-,fäd\ *noun* [Middle English,
from Late Latin, from Hebrew *ēphōdh*] (14th
century)
**1 :** a linen apron worn in ancient Hebrew rites;
*especially* **:** a vestment for the high priest
**2 :** an ancient Hebrew instrument of priestly
divination

**eph·or** \'e-fər, -,fòr\ *noun* [Latin *ephorus*, from
Greek *ephoros*, from *ephoran* to oversee, from
*epi-* + *horan* to see — more at WARY] (1579)
**1 :** one of five ancient Spartan magistrates
having power over the king

**2** : a government official in modern Greece; *especially* : one who oversees public works

— **eph·or·ate** \'e-fə-ˌrāt\ *noun*

**Ephra·im** \'ē-frē-əm\ *noun* [Hebrew *Ephrayim*]

: a son of Joseph and the traditional eponymous ancestor of one of the tribes of Israel

**Ephra·im·ite** \-frē-ə-ˌmīt\ *noun* (1611)

**1** : a member of the Hebrew tribe of Ephraim

**2** : a native or inhabitant of the biblical northern kingdom of Israel

**epi-** *or* **ep-** *prefix* [Middle English, from Middle French & Latin; Middle French, from Latin, from Greek, from *epi* on, at, besides, after; akin to Old English *eof*ot crime]

**1** : upon ⟨*epi*phyte⟩ : besides ⟨*epi*phenomenon⟩ : attached to ⟨*epi*didymis⟩ : over ⟨*epi*center⟩ : outer ⟨*epi*blast⟩ : after ⟨*epi*genesis⟩

**2 a** : chemical entity related to (such) another ⟨*epi*mer⟩ **b** : chemical entity distinguished from (such) another by having a bridge connection ⟨*epi*chlorohydrin⟩

**epi·blast** \'e-pə-ˌblast\ *noun* (1875)

: the outer layer of the blastoderm : ECTODERM

— **epi·blas·tic** \ˌe-pə-'blas-tik\ *adjective*

**epib·o·ly** \i-'pi-bə-lē\ *noun, plural* **-lies** [Greek *epibolē* addition, from *epiballein* to throw on, from *epi* + *ballein* to throw — more at DEVIL] (1875)

: the growing of one part about another; *especially* : such growth of the dorsal lip area during gastrulation

— **ep·i·bol·ic** \ˌe-pə-'bä-lik\ *adjective*

**¹ep·ic** \'e-pik\ *adjective* [Latin *epicus*, from Greek *epikos*, from *epos* word, speech, poem — more at VOICE] (1589)

**1** : of, relating to, or having the characteristics of an epic

**2 a** : extending beyond the usual or ordinary especially in size or scope ⟨his genius was *epic* —*Times Literary Supplement*⟩ **b** : HEROIC

— **ep·i·cal** \-pi-kəl\ *adjective*

— **ep·i·cal·ly** \-pi-k(ə-)lē\ *adverb*

**²epic** *noun* (1706)

**1** : a long narrative poem in elevated style recounting the deeds of a legendary or historical hero ⟨the *Iliad* and the *Odyssey* are *epics*⟩

**2** : a work of art (as a novel or drama) that resembles or suggests an epic

**3** : a series of events or body of legend or tradition thought to form the proper subject of an epic ⟨the winning of the West was a great American *epic*⟩

**epi·ca·lyx** \ˌe-pi-'kā-liks *also* -'ka-liks\ *noun* (1870)

: an involucre resembling the calyx but consisting of a whorl of bracts that is exterior to the calyx or results from the union of the sepal appendages

**epi·can·thic fold** \ˌe-pə-'kan(t)-thik\ *noun* [New Latin *epicanthus* epicanthic fold, from *epi-* + *canthus* canthus] (1913)

: a prolongation of a fold of the skin of the upper eyelid over the inner angle or both angles of the eye

**epi·car·di·um** \ˌe-pə-'kär-dē-əm\ *noun, plural* **-dia** \-dē-ə\ [New Latin] (circa 1865)

: the visceral part of the pericardium that closely envelops the heart

— **epi·car·di·al** \-dē-əl\ *adjective*

**epi·carp** \'e-pi-ˌkärp\ *noun* [French *épicarpe*, from *épi-* epi- + *-carpe* -carp] (1835)

: EXOCARP

**ep·i·cene** \'e-pə-ˌsēn\ *adjective* [Middle English, from Latin *epicoenus*, from Greek *epikoinos*, from *epi-* + *koinos* common — more at CO-] (15th century)

**1** *of a noun* : having but one form to indicate either sex

**2 a** : having characteristics typical of the other sex : INTERSEXUAL **b** : EFFEMINATE

**3** : lacking characteristics of either sex

— **epicene** *noun*

— **ep·i·cen·ism** \-ˌsē-ˌni-zəm, ˌe-pə-'\ *noun*

**epi·cen·ter** \'e-pi-ˌsen-tər\ *noun* [New Latin *epicentrum*, from *epi-* + Latin *centrum* center] (1887)

**1** : the part of the earth's surface directly above the focus of an earthquake — compare HYPOCENTER 1

**2** : CENTER 2a, b, c ⟨the *epicenter* of world finance⟩

— **epi·cen·tral** \ˌe-pi-'sen-trəl\ *adjective*

**epi·chlo·ro·hy·drin** \ˌe-pi-ˌklōr-ə-'hī-drən, -ˌklor-\ *noun* (circa 1891)

: a volatile liquid toxic epoxide C₃H₅ClO having a chloroform odor and used especially in making epoxy resins and rubbers

**epi·con·ti·nen·tal** \ˌe-pi-ˌkän-t³n-'en-t³l\ *adjective* (1900)

: lying upon a continent or a continental shelf ⟨*epicontinental* seas⟩

**epi·cot·yl** \'e-pi-ˌkä-t³l\ *noun* [*epi-* + *cotyledon*] (1880)

: the portion of the axis of a plant embryo or seedling above the cotyledonary node

**ep·i·crit·ic** \ˌe-pə-'kri-tik\ *adjective* [Greek *epikritikos* determinative, from *epikrinein* to decide, from *epi-* + *krinein* to judge — more at CERTAIN] (circa 1905)

: of, relating to, being, or mediating cutaneous sensory reception marked by accurate discrimination between small degrees of sensation

**epic simile** *noun* (1931)

: an extended simile that is used typically in epic poetry to intensify the heroic stature of the subject

**epi·cure** \'e-pi-ˌkyūr\ *noun* [*Epicurus*] (1565)

**1** *archaic* : one devoted to sensual pleasure : SYBARITE

**2** : one with sensitive and discriminating tastes especially in food or wine ☆ ◆

**epi·cu·re·an** \ˌe-pi-kyū-'rē-ən, -'kyūr-ē-\ *adjective* (1586)

**1** *capitalized* : of or relating to Epicurus or Epicureanism

**2** : of, relating to, or suited to an epicure

**Epicurean** *noun* (14th century)

**1** : a follower of Epicurus

**2** *often not capitalized* : EPICURE 2

**ep·i·cu·re·an·ism** \-ə-ˌni-zəm\ *noun* (circa 1751)

**1** *capitalized* **a** : the philosophy of Epicurus who subscribed to a hedonistic ethics that considered an imperturbable emotional calm the highest good and whose followers held intellectual pleasures superior to transient sensualism **b** : a mode of life in consonance with Epicureanism

**2** : EPICURISM

**ep·i·cur·ism** \'e-pi-ˌkyūr-ˌi-zəm, ˌe-pi-'\ *noun* (1586)

: the practices or tastes of an epicure or an epicurean

**epi·cu·ti·cle** \ˌe-pi-'kyū-ti-kəl\ *noun* (1929)

: an outermost waxy layer of the insect exoskeleton

— **epi·cu·tic·u·lar** \-kyū-'ti-kyə-lər\ *adjective*

**epi·cy·cle** \'e-pə-ˌsī-kəl\ *noun* [Middle English *epicicle*, from Late Latin *epicyclus*, from Greek *epikyklos*, from *epi-* + *kyklos* circle — more at WHEEL] (14th century)

**1** *in Ptolemaic astronomy* : a circle in which a planet moves and which has a center that is itself carried around at the same time on the circumference of a larger circle

**2** : a process going on within a larger one

— **epi·cy·clic** \ˌe-pə-'sī-klik, -'si-klik\ *adjective*

**epicyclic train** *noun* (circa 1890)

: a train (as of gear wheels) designed to have one or more parts travel around the circumference of another fixed or revolving part

**epi·cy·cloid** \ˌe-pə-'sī-ˌklȯid\ *noun* (circa 1755)

: a curve traced by a point on a circle that rolls on the outside of a fixed circle

— **epi·cy·cloi·dal** \-sī-'klȯi-d³l\ *adjective*

**epicycloid** *E*, traced by point *P*, on circle *R*, rolling on fixed circle *F*

**¹ep·i·dem·ic** \ˌe-pə-'de-mik\ *adjective* [French *épidémique*, from Middle French, from *epidemie*, noun, epidemic, from Late Latin *epidemia*, from Greek *epidēmia* visit, epidemic, from *epidēmos* visiting, epidemic, from *epi-* + *dēmos* people — more at DEMAGOGUE] (1603)

**1** : affecting or tending to affect a disproportionately large number of individuals within a population, community, or region at the same time ⟨typhoid was *epidemic*⟩

**2 a** : excessively prevalent **b** : CONTAGIOUS 4 ⟨*epidemic* laughter⟩

**3** : of, relating to, or constituting an epidemic ⟨the practice had reached *epidemic* proportions⟩

— **ep·i·dem·i·cal** \-'de-mi-kəl\ *adjective*

— **ep·i·dem·i·cal·ly** \-'de-mi-k(ə-)lē\ *adverb*

— **ep·i·de·mic·i·ty** \-də-'mi-sə-tē\ *noun*

**²epidemic** *noun* (1799)

**1** : an outbreak of epidemic disease

**2** : an outbreak or product of sudden rapid spread, growth, or development; *specifically* : a natural population suddenly and greatly enlarged

**ep·i·de·mi·ol·o·gy** \ˌe-pə-ˌdē-mē-'ä-lə-jē, -ˌde-mē-\ *noun* [Late Latin *epidemia* + International Scientific Vocabulary *-logy*] (circa 1860)

---

**1 :** a branch of medical science that deals with the incidence, distribution, and control of disease in a population
**2 :** the sum of the factors controlling the presence or absence of a disease or pathogen
— **ep·i·de·mi·o·log·i·cal** \-ˌdē-mē-ə-'lä-ji-kəl, -ˌde-mē-\ *also* **ep·i·de·mi·o·log·ic** \-jik\ *adjective*
— **ep·i·de·mi·o·log·i·cal·ly** \-ji-k(ə-)lē\ *adverb*
— **ep·i·de·mi·ol·o·gist** \-ˌdē-mē-'ä-lə-jist, -ˌde-mē-\ *noun*
**ep·i·den·drum** \ˌe-pə-'den-drəm\ *noun* [New Latin, from Greek *epi-* + *dendron* tree — more at DENDR-] (1791)
**:** any of a large genus (*Epidendrum*) of chiefly epiphytic orchids found especially in tropical America
**epi·der·mal** \ˌe-pə-'dər-məl\ *also* **epi·der·mic** \-mik\ *adjective* (1816)
**:** of, relating to, or arising from the epidermis
**epidermal growth factor** *noun* (1966)
**:** a polypeptide hormone that stimulates cell proliferation
**epi·der·mis** \ˌe-pə-'dər-məs\ *noun* [Late Latin, from Greek, from *epi-* + *derma* skin — more at DERM-] (1626)
**1 a :** the outer epithelial layer of the external integument of the animal body that is derived from the embryonic epiblast; *specifically* **:** the outer nonsensitive and nonvascular layer of the skin of a vertebrate that overlies the dermis **b :** any of various animal integuments
**2 :** a thin surface layer of tissue in higher plants formed by growth of a primary meristem
**epi·der·moid** \-ˌmóid\ *adjective* (1836)
**:** resembling epidermis or epidermal cells **:** made up of elements like those of epidermis 〈*epidermoid* cancer of the lung〉
**epi·dia·scope** \ˌe-pə-'dī-ə-ˌskōp\ *noun* [International Scientific Vocabulary] (1903)
**1 :** a projector for images of both opaque objects and transparencies
**2 :** EPISCOPE
**ep·i·did·y·mis** \ˌe-pə-'di-də-məs\ *noun, plural* **-mi·des** \-mə-ˌdēz\ [New Latin, from Greek, from *epi-* + *didymos* testicle, twin, from *dyo* two — more at TWO] (1610)
**:** a system of ductules emerging posteriorly from the testis that holds sperm during maturation and that forms a tangled mass before uniting into a single coiled duct which is continuous with the vas deferens
— **ep·i·did·y·mal** \-məl\ *adjective*
**epi·did·y·mi·tis** \ˌe-pə-ˌdi-də-'mī-təs\ *noun* [New Latin] (1852)
**:** inflammation of the epididymis
**ep·i·dote** \'e-pə-ˌdōt\ *noun* [French *épidote*, from Greek *epididonai* to give in addition, from *epi-* + *didonai* to give — more at DATE] (1808)
**:** a yellowish green mineral Ca₂(Al,Fe)₃Si₃O₁₂OH usually occurring in grains or columnar masses and sometimes used as a gemstone
**epi·du·ral** \ˌe-pi-'d(y)úr-əl\ *adjective* (1882)
**:** situated upon or administered outside the dura mater 〈*epidural* anesthesia〉 〈*epidural* structures〉
**epi·fau·na** \-'fò-nə, -'fä-\ *noun* [New Latin] (circa 1914)
**:** benthic fauna living on the substrate (as a hard sea floor) or on other organisms — compare INFAUNA
— **epi·fau·nal** \-'fò-nᵊl, -'fä-\ *adjective*
**epi·gas·tric** \ˌe-pi-'gas-trik\ *adjective* (circa 1678)
**1 :** lying upon or over the stomach
**2 a :** of, relating to, supplying, or draining the anterior walls of the abdomen **b :** of or relating to the abdominal region
**epi·ge·al** \ˌe-pi-'jē-əl\ *or* **epi·ge·an** \-'jē-ən\ *also* **epi·ge·ous** \-'jē-əs\ *or* **epi·ge·ic** \-'jē-ik\ *adjective* [Greek *epigaios* upon the earth, from *epi-* + *gaia* earth] (1861)

**1** *of a cotyledon* **:** forced above ground by elongation of the hypocotyl
**2 :** marked by the production of epigeal cotyledons 〈*epigeal* germination〉
**3 :** living on or near the surface of the ground; *also* **:** relating to or being the environment near the surface of the ground
**epi·gen·e·sis** \ˌe-pə-'je-nə-səs\ *noun* [New Latin] (1798)
**1 :** development of a plant or animal from an egg or spore through a series of processes in which unorganized cell masses differentiate into organs and organ systems; *also* **:** the theory that plant and animal development proceeds in this way — compare PREFORMATION 2
**2 :** change in the mineral character of a rock owing to outside influences
**epi·ge·net·ic** \-jə-'ne-tik\ *adjective* (1883)
**1 :** of, relating to, or produced by the chain of developmental processes in epigenesis that lead from genotype to phenotype after the initial action of the genes
**2** *of a deposit or structure* **:** formed after the laying down of the enclosing rock
— **epi·ge·net·i·cal·ly** \-'ne-ti-k(ə-)lē\ *adverb*
**epi·glot·tal** \ˌe-pə-'glä-tᵊl\ *also* **epi·glot·tic** \-'glä-tik\ *adjective* (1926)
**:** of, relating to, or produced with the aid of the epiglottis
**epi·glot·tis** \-'glä-təs\ *noun* [New Latin, from Greek *epiglōttis*, from *epi-* + *glōttis* glottis] (1615)
**:** a thin plate of flexible cartilage in front of the glottis that folds back over and protects the glottis during swallowing
**ep·i·gone** \'e-pə-ˌgōn\ *noun* [German, from Latin *epigonus* successor, from Greek *epigonos*, from *epigignesthai* to be born after, from *epi-* + *gignesthai* to be born — more at KIN] (1865)
**:** FOLLOWER, DISCIPLE; *also* **:** an inferior imitator
— **ep·i·gon·ic** \ˌe-pə-'gä-nik\ *or* **epig·o·nous** \i-'pi-gə-nəs, e-\ *adjective*
— **epig·o·nism** \-'pi-gə-ˌni-zəm\ *noun*
**epig·o·nus** \i-'pi-gə-nəs, e-\ *noun, plural* **-ni** \-ˌnī, -ˌnē\ [Latin] (1922)
**:** EPIGONE — usually used in plural
**ep·i·gram** \'e-pə-ˌgram\ *noun* [Middle English *epigrame*, from Latin *epigrammat-*, *epigramma*, from Greek, from *epigraphein* to write on, inscribe, from *epi-* + *graphein* to write — more at CARVE] (15th century)
**1 :** a concise poem dealing pointedly and often satirically with a single thought or event and often ending with an ingenious turn of thought
**2 :** a terse, sage, or witty and often paradoxical saying
**3 :** epigrammatic expression
— **ep·i·gram·ma·tism** \ˌe-pə-'gra-mə-ˌti-zəm\ *noun*
— **ep·i·gram·ma·tist** \-'gra-mə-tist\ *noun*
**ep·i·gram·mat·ic** \ˌe-pə-grə-'ma-tik\ *adjective* (circa 1704)
**1 :** of, relating to, or resembling an epigram
**2 :** marked by or given to the use of epigrams
— **ep·i·gram·mat·i·cal·ly** \-'ma-ti-k(ə-)lē\ *adverb*
**ep·i·gram·ma·tize** \-'gra-mə-ˌtīz\ *verb* **-tized; -tiz·ing** (1691)
*transitive verb*
**1 :** to express in the form of an epigram
**2 :** to make an epigram about
*intransitive verb*
**:** to make an epigram
— **ep·i·gram·ma·tiz·er** *noun*
**ep·i·graph** \'e-pə-ˌgraf\ *noun* [Greek *epigraphē*, from *epigraphein*] (1624)
**1 :** an engraved inscription
**2 :** a quotation set at the beginning of a literary work or one of its divisions to suggest its theme
**epig·ra·pher** \i-'pi-grə-fər, e-\ *noun* (1887)
**:** EPIGRAPHIST

**epi·graph·ic** \ˌe-pə-'gra-fik\ *also* **epi·graph·i·cal** \-fi-kəl\ *adjective* (1858)
**:** of or relating to epigraphs or epigraphy
— **epi·graph·i·cal·ly** \-fi-k(ə-)lē\ *adverb*
**epig·ra·phist** \i-'pi-grə-fist, e-\ *noun* (circa 1864)
**:** a specialist in epigraphy
**epig·ra·phy** \-fē\ *noun* (1851)
**1 :** EPIGRAPHS, INSCRIPTIONS
**2 :** the study of inscriptions; *especially* **:** the deciphering of ancient inscriptions
**epig·y·nous** \i-'pi-jə-nəs, e-\ *adjective* (1830)
**1** *of a floral organ* **:** adnate to the surface of the ovary and appearing to grow from the top of it
**2 :** having epigynous floral organs
— **epig·y·ny** \-nē\ *noun*
**ep·i·la·tion** \ˌe-pə-'lā-shən\ *noun* [French *épilation*, from *épiler* to remove hair, from *é-* e- + Latin *pilus* hair — more at PILE] (1878)
**:** the loss or removal of hair
**ep·i·lep·sy** \'e-pə-ˌlep-sē\ *noun, plural* **-sies** [Middle French *epilepsie*, from Late Latin *epilepsia*, from Greek *epilēpsia*, from *epilambanein* to seize, from *epi-* + *lambanein* to take, seize — more at LATCH] (1543)
**:** any of various disorders marked by disturbed electrical rhythms of the central nervous system and typically manifested by convulsive attacks usually with clouding of consciousness
**epilept-** *or* **epilepti-** *or* **epilepto-** *combining form* [Greek *epilēpt-*, from *epilēptos* seized by epilepsy, from *epilambanein*]
**:** epilepsy 〈*epileptoid*〉
**ep·i·lep·tic** \ˌe-pə-'lep-tik\ *adjective* (1605)
**:** relating to, affected with, or having the characteristics of epilepsy
— **epileptic** *noun*
— **ep·i·lep·ti·cal·ly** \-ti-k(ə-)lē\ *adverb*
**ep·i·lep·ti·form** \-'lep-tə-ˌfórm\ *adjective* (circa 1859)
**:** resembling that of epilepsy 〈an *epileptiform* convulsion〉
**ep·i·lep·to·gen·ic** \-ˌlep-tə-'je-nik\ *adjective* (circa 1882)
**:** inducing or tending to induce epilepsy 〈an *epileptogenic* drug〉
**ep·i·lep·toid** \-'lep-ˌtóid\ *adjective* (circa 1860)
**1 :** EPILEPTIFORM
**2 :** exhibiting symptoms resembling those of epilepsy 〈the *epileptoid* person〉
**epi·lim·ni·on** \ˌe-pə-'lim-nē-ˌän, -nē-ən\ *noun* [New Latin, from *epi-* + Greek *limnion*, diminutive of *limnē* marshy lake — more at LIMNETIC] (circa 1910)
**:** the water layer overlying the thermocline of a lake
**ep·i·logue** *also* **ep·i·log** \'e-pə-ˌlóg, -ˌläg\ *noun* [Middle English *epiloge*, from Middle French *epilogue*, from Latin *epilogus*, from Greek *epilogos*, from *epilegein* to say in addition, from *epi-* + *legein* to say — more at LEGEND] (15th century)
**1 :** a concluding section that rounds out the design of a literary work
**2 a :** a speech often in verse addressed to the audience by an actor at the end of a play; *also* **:** the actor speaking such an epilogue **b :** the final scene of a play that comments on or summarizes the main action
**3 :** the concluding section of a musical composition **:** CODA
**epi·mer** \'e-pi-mər\ *noun* [*epi-* + isomer] (circa 1911)
**:** either of the stereoisomers of a sugar or sugar derivative that differ in the arrangement of the hydrogen atom and the hydroxyl group on the first asymmetric carbon atom of a chain
— **epi·mer·ic** \ˌe-pi-'mer-ik\ *adjective*
**epim·er·ase** \i-'pi-mə-ˌrās, e-, -ˌrāz\ *noun* (1960)
**:** any of various isomerases that catalyze the inversion of asymmetric groups in a substrate with several centers of asymmetry

**epi·my·si·um** \\,e-pə-'mi-zhē-əm, -zē-\\ *noun*, *plural* **-sia** \\-zhē-ə, -zē-ə\\ [New Latin, irregular from *epi-* + Greek *mys* mouse, muscle — more at MOUSE] (1900)
: the external connective-tissue sheath of a muscle

**epi·nas·ty** \\'e-pə-,nas-tē\\ *noun* [International Scientific Vocabulary *epi-* + Greek *nastos* close-pressed (from *nassein* to press) + International Scientific Vocabulary ²-y] (1880)
: a nastic movement in which a plant part (as a flower petal) is bent outward and often downward

**epi·neph·rine** *also* **epi·neph·rin** \\,e-pə-'ne-frən\\ *noun* [International Scientific Vocabulary *epi-* + Greek *nephros* kidney — more at NEPHRITIS] (1899)
: a colorless crystalline feebly basic sympathomimetic hormone $C_9H_{13}NO_3$ that is the principal blood-pressure raising hormone secreted by the adrenal medulla and is used medicinally especially as a heart stimulant, a vasoconstrictor in controlling hemorrhages of the skin, and a muscle relaxant in bronchial asthma — called also *adrenaline*

**epi·neu·ri·um** \\,e-pə-'n(y)ùr-ē-əm\\ *noun* [New Latin] (circa 1882)
: the external connective-tissue sheath of a nerve trunk

**epi·pe·lag·ic** \\,e-pi-pə-'la-jik\\ *adjective* (1940)
: of, relating to, or constituting the part of the oceanic zone into which enough light penetrates for photosynthesis

**ep·i·phan·ic** \\,e-pə-'fa-nik\\ *adjective* (1951)
: of or having the character of an epiphany

**epiph·a·nous** \\i-'pi-fə-nəs\\ *adjective* (1823)
: EPIPHANIC

**epiph·a·ny** \\i-'pi-fə-nē\\ *noun*, *plural* **-nies** [Middle English *epiphanie*, from Middle French, from Late Latin *epiphania*, from Late Greek, plural, probably alteration of Greek *epiphaneia* appearance, manifestation, from *epiphainein* to manifest, from *epi-* + *phainein* to show — more at FANCY] (14th century)
**1** *capitalized* : January 6 observed as a church festival in commemoration of the coming of the Magi as the first manifestation of Christ to the Gentiles or in the Eastern Church in commemoration of the baptism of Christ
**2** : an appearance or manifestation especially of a divine being
**3 a** (1) : a usually sudden manifestation or perception of the essential nature or meaning of something (2) : an intuitive grasp of reality through something (as an event) usually simple and striking (3) : an illuminating discovery **b** : a revealing scene or moment

**epi·phe·nom·e·nal** \\,e-pi-fi-'nä-mə-n°l\\ *adjective* (1899)
: of or relating to an epiphenomenon : DERIVATIVE
— **epi·phe·nom·e·nal·ly** \\-n°l-ē\\ *adverb*
**epi·phe·nom·e·nal·ism** \\-n°l-,i-zəm\\ *noun* (1899)
: a doctrine that mental processes are epiphenomena of brain processes

**epi·phe·nom·e·non** \\-'nä-mə-,nän, -nən\\ *noun*, *plural* **-na** \\-,nä, -nə\\ (circa 1706)
: a secondary phenomenon accompanying another and caused by it

**ep·i·phragm** \\'e-pə-,fram\\ *noun* [Greek *epiphragma* covering] (circa 1854)
: a closing membrane or septum (as of a snail shell or a moss capsule)

**epiph·y·se·al** \\i-,pi-fə-'sē-əl\\ *also* **epi·phys·i·al** \\,e-pə-'fi-zē-əl\\ *adjective* (1842)
: of or relating to an epiphysis

**epiph·y·sis** \\i-'pi-fə-səs\\ *noun*, *plural* **-y·ses** \\-,sēz\\ [New Latin, from Greek, growth, from *epiphyesthai* to grow on, from *epi-* + *phyesthai* to grow, middle voice of *phyein* to bring forth — more at BE] (1634)

**1** : a part or process of a bone that ossifies separately and later becomes ankylosed to the main part of the bone; *especially* : an end of a long bone
**2** : PINEAL GLAND

**epi·phyte** \\'e-pə-,fīt\\ *noun* (circa 1847)
: a plant that derives its moisture and nutrients from the air and rain and grows usually on another plant

**epi·phyt·ic** \\,e-pə-'fi-tik\\ *adjective* (1830)
**1** : of, relating to, or being an epiphyte
**2** : living on the surface of plants
— **epi·phyt·i·cal·ly** \\-'fi-ti-k(ə-)lē\\ *adverb*
— **epi·phyt·ism** \\'e-pə-,fi-,ti-zəm\\ *noun*

**ep·i·phy·tol·o·gy** \\,e-pə-,fī-'tä-lə-jē\\ *noun* [*epiphytotic* + *-logy*] (1940)
**1** : a science that deals with character, ecology, and causes of outbreak of plant diseases
**2** : the sum of the factors controlling the occurrence of a disease or pathogen of plants

**ep·i·phy·tot·ic** \\-'tä-tik\\ *adjective* [*epi-* + *-phyte* + *-otic* (as in *epizootic*)] (circa 1899)
: of, relating to, or being a plant disease that tends to recur sporadically and to affect large numbers of susceptible plants
— **epiphytotic** *noun*

**epis·cia** \\i-'pi-sh(ē-)ə\\ *noun* [New Latin, from Greek *episkios* shaded, from *epi-* + *skia* shadow — more at SHINE] (circa 1868)
: any of a genus (*Episcia*) of tropical American herbs that have hairy foliage and are related to the African violet

**epis·co·pa·cy** \\i-'pis-kə-pə-sē\\ *noun*, *plural* **-cies** (1647)
**1** : government of the church by bishops or by a hierarchy
**2** : EPISCOPATE

**epis·co·pal** \\i-'pis-kə-pəl, -bəl\\ *adjective* [Middle English, from Late Latin *episcopalis*, from *episcopus* bishop — more at BISHOP] (15th century)
**1** : of or relating to a bishop
**2** : of, having, or constituting government by bishops
**3** *capitalized* : of or relating to the Protestant Episcopal Church representing the Anglican communion in the U.S.
— **epis·co·pal·ly** \\-p(ə-)lē\\ *adverb*

**Episcopal** *noun* (1752)
: EPISCOPALIAN

**Epis·co·pa·lian** \\i-,pis-kə-'pāl-yən\\ *noun* (1690)
**1** : an adherent of the episcopal form of church government
**2** : a member of an episcopal church (as the Protestant Episcopal Church)
— **Episcopalian** *adjective*
— **Epis·co·pa·lian·ism** \\-yə-,ni-zəm\\ *noun*

**epis·co·pate** \\i-'pis-kə-pət, -,pāt\\ *noun* (1641)
**1** : the rank, office, or term of bishop
**2** : DIOCESE
**3** : the body of bishops (as in a country)

**epi·scope** \\'e-pə-,skōp\\ *noun* [International Scientific Vocabulary] (circa 1909)
: a projector for images of opaque objects (as photographs)

**epi·si·ot·o·my** \\i-,pi-zē-'ä-tə-mē, -,pē-\\ *noun* [International Scientific Vocabulary *episio-* vulva (from Greek *epision* pubic region) + *-tomy*] (1878)
: surgical enlargement of the vulval orifice for obstetrical purposes during parturition

**ep·i·sode** \\'e-pə-,sōd *also* -,zōd\\ *noun* [Greek *epeisodion*, from neuter of *epeisodios* coming in besides, from *epi-* + *eisodios* coming in, from *eis* into (akin to Greek *en* in) + *hodos* road, journey — more at IN] (1678)
**1** : a usually brief unit of action in a dramatic or literary work: as **a** : the part of an ancient Greek tragedy between two choric songs **b** : a developed situation that is integral to but separable from a continuous narrative : INCIDENT **c** : one of a series of loosely connected stories

or scenes **d** : the part of a serial presented at one performance
**2** : an event that is distinctive and separate although part of a larger series
**3** : a digressive subdivision in a musical composition
*synonym* see OCCURRENCE

**ep·i·sod·ic** \\,e-pə-'sä-dik *also* -'zä-\\ *also* **ep·i·sod·i·cal** \\-di-kəl\\ *adjective* (1711)
**1** : made up of separate especially loosely connected episodes
**2** : having the form of an episode
**3** : of or limited in duration or significance to a particular episode : TEMPORARY ⟨may be able to establish whether the sea-floor spreading is continuous or *episodic* —A. I. Hammond⟩
**4** : occurring, appearing, or changing at usually irregular intervals : OCCASIONAL ⟨an *episodic* illness⟩
— **ep·i·sod·i·cal·ly** \\-di-k(ə-)lē\\ *adverb*

**epi·some** \\'e-pə-,sōm, -,zōm\\ *noun* (circa 1931)
: a genetic determinant (as the DNA of some bacteriophages) that can replicate autonomously in bacterial cytoplasm or as an integral part of the chromosomes
— **epi·som·al** \\,e-pə-'sō-məl, -'zō-\\ *adjective*
— **epi·som·al·ly** \\-mə-lē\\ *adverb*

**epis·ta·sis** \\i-'pis-tə-səs\\ *noun*, *plural* **-ta·ses** \\-,sēz\\ [New Latin, from Greek, act of stopping, from *ephistanai* to stop, from *epi-* + *histanai* to cause to stand — more at STAND] (circa 1917)
: suppression of the effect of a gene by a nonallelic gene
— **ep·i·stat·ic** \\,e-pə-'sta-tik\\ *adjective*

**ep·i·stax·is** \\,e-pə-'stak-səs\\ *noun*, *plural* **-stax·es** \\-,sēz\\ [New Latin, from Greek, from *epistazein* to drip on, to bleed at the nose again, from *epi-* + *stazein* to drip] (1793)
: NOSEBLEED

**ep·i·ste·mic** \\,e-pə-'stē-mik, -'ste-mik\\ *adjective* (1922)
: of or relating to knowledge or knowing : COGNITIVE
— **ep·i·ste·mi·cal·ly** \\-mi-k(ə-)lē\\ *adverb*

**epis·te·mol·o·gy** \\i-,pis-tə-'mä-lə-jē\\ *noun* [Greek *epistēmē* knowledge, from *epistanai* to understand, know, from *epi-* + *histanai* to cause to stand — more at STAND] (circa 1856)
: the study or a theory of the nature and grounds of knowledge especially with reference to its limits and validity
— **epis·te·mo·log·i·cal** \\-mə-'lä-ji-kəl\\ *adjective*
— **epis·te·mo·log·i·cal·ly** \\-k(ə-)lē\\ *adverb*
— **epis·te·mol·o·gist** \\-'mä-lə-jist\\ *noun*

**epis·tle** \\i-'pi-səl\\ *noun* [Middle English, letter, Epistle, from Old French, from Latin *epistula*, *epistola* letter, from Greek *epistolē* message, letter, from *epistellein* to send to, from *epi-* + *stellein* to send] (13th century)
**1** *capitalized* **a** : one of the letters adopted as books of the New Testament **b** : a liturgical lection usually from one of the New Testament Epistles
**2 a** : LETTER; *especially* : a formal or elegant letter **b** : a composition in the form of a letter
— **epis·tler** \\-'pi-sə-lər\\ *noun*

¹**epis·to·lary** \\i-'pis-tə-,ler-ē, ,e-pi-'stó-lə-rē\\ *adjective* (circa 1656)
**1** : of, relating to, or suitable to a letter
**2** : contained in or carried on by letters ⟨an endless sequence of . . . *epistolary* love affairs —*Times Literary Supplement*⟩
**3** : written in the form of a series of letters ⟨*epistolary* novel⟩

---

\\ə\\ abut \\ᵊ\\ kitten \\ər\\ further \\a\\ ash \\ā\\ ace
\\ä\\ mop, mar \\aù\\ out \\ch\\ chin \\e\\ bet \\ē\\ easy
\\g\\ go \\i\\ hit \\ī\\ ice \\j\\ job \\ŋ\\ sing \\ō\\ go
\\ò\\ law \\òi\\ boy \\th\\ thin \\th\\ the \\ü\\ loot \\ù\\ foot
\\y\\ yet \\zh\\ vision *see also* Guide to Pronunciation

**²epistolary** *noun, plural* **-lar·ies** (circa 1900)
**:** a lectionary containing a body of liturgical epistles

**epis·to·ler** \i-'pis-tə-lər\ *noun* (1530)
**:** the reader of the liturgical Epistle especially in Anglican churches

**ep·i·stome** \'e-pə-ˌstōm\ *noun* [New Latin *epistoma*] (1852)
**:** any of several structures or regions situated above or covering the mouth of various invertebrates

**epis·tro·phe** \i-'pis-trə-(ˌ)fē\ *noun* [Greek *epistrophē*, literally, turning about, from *epi-* + *strophē* turning — more at STROPHE] (circa 1584)
**:** repetition of a word or expression at the end of successive phrases, clauses, sentences, or verses especially for rhetorical or poetic effect (as Lincoln's "of the people, by the people, for the people") — compare ANAPHORA

**ep·i·taph** \'e-pə-ˌtaf\ *noun* [Middle English *epitaphe*, from Middle French & Medieval Latin; Middle French, from Medieval Latin *epi taphium*, from Latin, funeral oration, from Greek *epitaphion*, from *epi-* + *taphos* tomb, funeral] (14th century)
**1 :** an inscription on or at a tomb or a grave in memory of the one buried there
**2 :** a brief statement commemorating or epitomizing a deceased person or something past
— **ep·i·taph·ial** \ˌe-pə-'ta-fē-əl\ *adjective*
— **ep·i·taph·ic** \-'ta-fik\ *adjective*

**epit·a·sis** \i-'pi-tə-səs\ *noun, plural* **-a·ses** \-ˌsēz\ [Greek, increased intensity, from *epiteinein* to stretch tighter, from *epi-* + *teinein* to stretch — more at THIN] (1589)
**:** the part of a play developing the main action and leading to the catastrophe

**ep·i·taxy** \'e-pə-ˌtak-sē\ *noun* [International Scientific Vocabulary] (circa 1931)
**:** the growth on a crystalline substrate of a crystalline substance that mimics the orientation of the substrate
— **ep·i·tax·i·al** \ˌe-pə-'tak-sē-əl\ *adjective*
— **ep·i·tax·i·al·ly** \-sē-ə-lē\ *adverb*

**ep·i·tha·la·mi·um** \ˌe-pə-thə-'lā-mē-əm\ *or* **ep·i·tha·la·mi·on** \-mē-ən\ *noun, plural* **-mi·ums** *or* **-mia** \-mē-ə\ [Latin & Greek; Latin *epithalamium*, from Greek *epithalamion*, from *epi-* + *thalamos* room, bridal chamber; perhaps akin to Greek *tholos* rotunda] (circa 1589)
**:** a song or poem in honor of a bride and bridegroom
— **ep·i·tha·lam·ic** \-'la-mik\ *adjective*

**ep·i·the·li·al** \ˌe-pə-'thē-lē-əl\ *adjective* (1845)
**:** of or relating to epithelium

**ep·i·the·li·oid** \-lē-ˌȯid\ *adjective* (1878)
**:** resembling epithelium ⟨*epithelioid* cells⟩

**ep·i·the·li·o·ma** \-ˌthē-lē-'ō-mə\ *noun* (1872)
**:** a tumor derived from epithelial tissue
— **ep·i·the·li·o·ma·tous** \-mə-təs\ *adjective*

**ep·i·the·li·um** \ˌe-pə-'thē-lē-əm\ *noun, plural* **-lia** \-lē-ə\ [New Latin, from *epi-* + Greek *thēlē* nipple — more at FEMININE] (1748)
**1 :** a membranous cellular tissue that covers a free surface or lines a tube or cavity of an animal body and serves especially to enclose and protect the other parts of the body, to produce secretions and excretions, and to function in assimilation
**2 :** a usually thin layer of parenchyma that lines a cavity or tube of a plant

**ep·i·the·li·za·tion** \ˌe-pə-ˌthē-lə-'zā-shən\ *or* **ep·i·the·li·al·iza·tion** \-ˌthē-lē-ə-\ *noun* (circa 1934)
**:** the process of becoming covered with or converted to epithelium
— **ep·i·the·lize** \ˌe-pə-'thē-ˌlīz\ *or* **ep·i·the·li·al·ize** \-'thē-lē-ə-ˌlīz\ *transitive verb*

**ep·i·thet** \'e-pə-ˌthet *also* -thət\ *noun* [Latin *epitheton*, from Greek, from neuter of *epithe-*

*tos* added, from *epitithenai* to put on, add, from *epi-* + *tithenai* to put — more at DO] (1579)
**1 a :** a characterizing word or phrase accompanying or occurring in place of the name of a person or thing **b :** a disparaging or abusive word or phrase **c :** the part of a taxonomic name identifying a subordinate unit within a genus
**2** *obsolete* **:** EXPRESSION
— **ep·i·thet·ic** \ˌe-pə-'the-tik\ *or* **ep·i·thet·i·cal** \-ti-kəl\ *adjective*

**epit·o·me** \i-'pi-tə-mē\ *noun* [Latin, from Greek *epitomē*, from *epitemnein* to cut short, from *epi-* + *temnein* to cut — more at TOME] (1520)
**1 a :** a summary of a written work **b :** a brief presentation or statement of something
**2 :** a typical or ideal example **:** EMBODIMENT ⟨the British monarchy itself is the *epitome* of tradition —Richard Joseph⟩
**3 :** brief or miniature form — usually used with *in*
— **ep·i·tom·ic** \ˌe-pə-'tä-mik\ *or* **ep·i·tom·i·cal** \-mi-kəl\ *adjective*

**epit·o·mise** *British variant of* EPITOMIZE

**epit·o·mize** \-ˌmīz\ *transitive verb* **-mized; -miz·ing** (1594)
**1 :** to make or give an epitome of
**2 :** to serve as the typical or ideal example of

**epi·tope** \'e-pə-ˌtōp\ *noun* [International Scientific Vocabulary, from *epi-* + Greek *topos* place] (1960)
**:** a molecular region on the surface of an antigen capable of eliciting an immune response and of combining with the specific antibody produced by such a response — called also *determinant, antigenic determinant*

**epi·zo·ic** \ˌe-pə-'zō-ik\ *adjective* (circa 1857)
**:** living upon the body of an animal ⟨an *epizoic* plant⟩
— **epi·zo·ite** \-ˌīt\ *noun*

**epi·zo·ot·ic** \ˌe-pə-zə-'wä-tik\ *noun* [French *épizootique*, from *épizootie* such an outbreak, from *épi-* (as in *épidemie* epidemic) + Greek *zōiotēs* animal nature, from *zōē* life — more at QUICK] (1748)
**:** an outbreak of disease affecting many animals of one kind at the same time; *also* **:** the disease itself
— **epizootic** *adjective*

**epi·zo·ot·i·ol·o·gy** \ˌe-pə-zə-ˌwä-tē-'ä-lə-jē\ *noun* (1910)
**1 :** the sum of the factors controlling the occurrence of a disease or pathogen of animals
**2 :** a science that deals with the character, ecology, and causes of outbreaks of animal diseases
— **epi·zo·oti·o·log·i·cal** \-zə-ˌwä-tē-ə-'lä-ji-kəl\ *also* **epi·zo·oti·o·log·ic** \-jik\ *adjective*

**ep·och** \'e-pək, 'e-ˌpäk, *US also & British usually* 'ē-ˌpäk\ *noun* [Medieval Latin *epocha*, from Greek *epochē* cessation, fixed point, from *epechein* to pause, hold back, from *epi-* + *echein* to hold — more at SCHEME] (1614)
**1 a :** an event or a time marked by an event that begins a new period or development **b :** a memorable event or date
**2 a :** an extended period of time usually characterized by a distinctive development or by a memorable series of events **b :** a division of geologic time less than a period and greater than an age
**3 :** an instant of time or a date selected as a point of reference (as in astronomy)
**synonym** see PERIOD

**ep·och·al** \'e-pə-kəl, 'e-ˌpä-kəl\ *adjective* (1685)
**1 :** of or relating to an epoch
**2 :** uniquely or highly significant **:** MOMENTOUS ⟨during his three *epochal* years in the assembly —C. G. Bowers⟩; *also* **:** UNPARALLELED ⟨*epochal* stupidity⟩
— **ep·och·al·ly** *adverb*

**ep·ode** \'e-ˌpōd\ *noun* [Latin *epodos*, from Greek *epōidos*, from *epōidos* sung or said after, from *epi-* + *aidein* to sing — more at ODE] (1598)
**1 :** a lyric poem in which a long verse is followed by a shorter one
**2 :** the third part of a triadic Greek ode following the strophe and the antistrophe

**ep·onym** \'e-pə-ˌnim\ *noun* [Greek *epōnymos*, from *epōnymos* eponymous, from *epi-* + *onyma* name — more at NAME] (1846)
**1 :** one for whom or which something is or is believed to be named
**2 :** a name (as of a drug or a disease) based on or derived from an eponym
— **ep·onym·ic** \ˌe-pə-'ni-mik\ *adjective*

**epon·y·mous** \i-'pä-nə-məs, e-\ *adjective* (1846)
**:** of, relating to, or being an eponym

**epon·y·my** \-mē\ *noun, plural* **-mies** (1865)
**:** the explanation of a proper name (as of a town or tribe) by supposing a fictitious eponym

**ep·o·pee** \'e-pə-ˌpē\ *noun* [French *épopée*, from Greek *epopoiia*, from *epos* + *poiein* to make — more at POET] (1697)
**:** EPIC; *especially* **:** an epic poem

**ep·os** \'e-ˌpäs\ *noun* [Greek, word, epic poem — more at VOICE] (circa 1828)
**1 :** EPIC
**2 :** a number of poems that treat an epic theme but are not formally united

**ep·ox·i·da·tion** \(ˌ)e-ˌpäk-sə-'dā-shən\ *noun* (1944)
**:** a conversion of a usually unsaturated compound into an epoxide

**ep·ox·ide** \(ˌ)e-'päk-ˌsīd\ *noun* (1930)
**:** an epoxy compound

**ep·ox·i·dize** \(ˌ)e-'päk-sə-ˌdīz\ *transitive verb* **-dized; -diz·ing** (1945)
**:** to convert into an epoxide ⟨*epoxidized* esters⟩

**¹ep·oxy** \i-'päk-sē\ *adjective* [*epi-* + *oxy*] (1916)
**1 :** containing oxygen attached to two different atoms already united in some other way; *specifically* **:** containing a 3-membered ring consisting of one oxygen and two carbon atoms
**2 :** of or relating to an epoxide

**²epoxy** *transitive verb* **ep·ox·ied** *or* **ep·oxyed; ep·oxy·ing** (1966)
**:** to glue with epoxy resin

**epoxy resin** *noun* (1950)
**:** a flexible usually thermosetting resin made by copolymerization of an epoxide with another compound having two hydroxyl groups and used chiefly in coatings and adhesives — called also *epoxy*

**EPROM** \'ē-ˌpräm\ *noun* [erasable programmable read-only memory] (1977)
**:** a programmable read-only memory that can be erased usually by exposure to ultraviolet radiation

**ep·si·lon** \'ep-sə-ˌlän, -lən\ *noun* [Greek *e psi lon*, literally, simple e] (15th century)
**1 :** the 5th letter of the Greek alphabet — see ALPHABET table
**2 :** an arbitrarily small positive quantity in mathematical analysis
— **ep·si·lon·ic** \ˌep-sə-'lä-nik\ *adjective*

**Ep·som salt** \'ep-səm-\ *noun* (1770)
**:** EPSOM SALTS

**Epsom salts** *noun plural but singular in construction* [*Epsom*, England] (1876)
**:** a bitter colorless or white crystalline salt $MgSO_4 \cdot 7H_2O$ that is a hydrated magnesium sulfate with cathartic properties

**Ep·stein–Barr virus** \ˌep-ˌstīn-'bär-\ *noun* [Michael Anthony *Epstein* (born 1921) and Y. M. *Barr* (born 1932) English pathologists] (1968)
**:** a herpesvirus that causes infectious mononucleosis and is associated with Burkitt's lymphoma and nasopharyngeal carcinoma

**equa·ble** \'e-kwə-bəl, 'ē-\ *adjective* · [Latin *aequabilis,* from *aequare* to make level or equal, from *aequus*] (1677)
**1** : marked by lack of variation or change : UNIFORM
**2** : marked by lack of noticeable, unpleasant, or extreme variation or inequality
*synonym* see STEADY
— **equa·bil·i·ty** \,e-kwə-'bi-lə-tē, ,ē-\ *noun*
— **equa·ble·ness** \'e-kwə-bəl-nəs, 'ē-\ *noun*
— **equa·bly** \-blē\ *adverb*

**¹equal** \'ē-kwəl\ *adjective* [Middle English, from Latin *aequalis,* from *aequus* level, equal] (14th century)
**1 a** (1) : of the same measure, quantity, amount, or number as another (2) : identical in mathematical value or logical denotation : EQUIVALENT **b** : like in quality, nature, or status **c** : like for each member of a group, class, or society ⟨provide *equal* employment opportunities⟩
**2** : regarding or affecting all objects in the same way : IMPARTIAL
**3** : free from extremes: as **a** : tranquil in mind or mood **b** : not showing variation in appearance, structure, or proportion
**4 a** : capable of meeting the requirements of a situation or a task **b** : SUITABLE ⟨bored with work not *equal* to his abilities⟩
*synonym* see SAME

**²equal** *transitive verb* **equaled** *or* **equalled;** **equal·ing** *or* **equal·ling** (1590)
**1** : to be equal to; *especially* : to be identical in value to
**2** *archaic* : EQUALIZE
**3** : to make or produce something equal to

**³equal** *noun* (1753)
**1** : one that is equal ⟨insists that women can be absolute *equals* with men —Anne Bernays⟩
**2** : an equal quantity

**equal–area** *adjective* (circa 1929)
*of a map projection* : maintaining constant ratio of size between quadrilaterals formed by the meridians and parallels and the quadrilaterals of the globe thereby preserving true areal extent of forms represented

**equal·ise, equal·is·er** *British variant of* EQUALIZE, EQUALIZER

**equal·i·tar·i·an** \i-,kwä-lə-'ter-ē-ən\ *adjective or noun* (1799)
: EGALITARIAN
— **equal·i·tar·i·an·ism** \-ē-ə-,ni-zəm\ *noun*

**equal·i·ty** \i-'kwä-lə-tē\ *noun, plural* **-ties** (15th century)
**1** : the quality or state of being equal
**2** : EQUATION 2a

**equal·ize** \'ē-kwə-,līz\ *verb* **-ized; -iz·ing** (1622)
*transitive verb*
**1** : to make equal
**2 a** : to compensate for **b** : to make uniform; *especially* : to distribute evenly or uniformly ⟨*equalize* the tax burden⟩ **c** : to adjust or correct the frequency characteristics of (an electronic signal) by restoring to their original level high frequencies that have been attenuated
*intransitive verb*
*chiefly British* : to tie the score
— **equal·iza·tion** \,ē-kwə-lə-'zā-shən\ *noun*

**equal·iz·er** \-,lī-zər\ *noun* (1792)
: one that equalizes: as **a** : a score that ties a game **b** : an electronic device (as in a sound-reproducing system) used to adjust response to different audio frequencies

**equal·ly** \'ē-kwə-lē\ *adverb* (14th century)
**1** : in an equal or uniform manner : EVENLY
**2** : to an equal degree ⟨respected *equally* by young and old⟩

**equal opportunity employer** *noun* (1963)
: an employer who agrees not to discriminate against any employee or job applicant because of race, color, religion, national origin, sex, physical or mental handicap, or age

**equal sign** *noun* (circa 1909)
: a sign = indicating mathematical or logical equivalence — called also *equality sign,* *equals sign*

**equa·nim·i·ty** \,ē-kwə-'ni-mə-tē, ,e-kwə-\ *noun, plural* **-ties** [Latin *aequanimitas,* from *aequo animo* with even mind] (circa 1616)
**1** : evenness of mind especially under stress
**2** : right disposition : BALANCE ☆

**equate** \i-'kwāt, 'ē-\ *verb* **equat·ed; equat·ing** [Middle English, from Latin *aequatus,* past participle of *aequare*] (15th century)
*transitive verb*
**1 a** : to make equal : EQUALIZE **b** : to make such an allowance or correction in as will reduce to a common standard or obtain a correct result
**2** : to treat, represent, or regard as equal, equivalent, or comparable ⟨*equates* disagreement with disloyalty⟩
*intransitive verb*
: to correspond as equal

**equa·tion** \i-'kwā-zhən *also* -shən\ *noun* (14th century)
**1 a** : the act or process of equating **b** (1) : an element affecting a process : FACTOR (2) : a complex of variable factors **c** : a state of being equated; *specifically* : a state of close association or identification ⟨bring governmental enterprises and payment for them into immediate *equation* —R. G. Tugwell⟩
**2 a** : a usually formal statement of the equality or equivalence of mathematical or logical expressions **b** : an expression representing a chemical reaction quantitatively by means of chemical symbols

**equa·tion·al** \i-'kwāzh-nəl, -'kwā-zhə-nᵊl *also* -'kwāsh-\ *adjective* (1864)
**1** : of, using, or involving equation or equations
**2** : dividing into two equal parts — used especially of the mitotic cell division usually following reduction in meiosis
— **equa·tion·al·ly** *adverb*

**equation of time** (1726)
: the difference between apparent time and mean time usually expressed as a correction which is to be added to apparent time to give local mean time

**equa·tor** \i-'kwā-tər, 'ē-\ *noun* [Middle English, from Medieval Latin *aequator,* literally, equalizer, from Latin *aequare*] (14th century)
**1** : the great circle of the celestial sphere whose plane is perpendicular to the axis of the earth
**2** : a great circle of the earth or a celestial body that is everywhere equally distant from the two poles and divides the surface into the northern and southern hemispheres
**3 a** : a circle or circular band dividing the surface of a body into two usually equal and symmetrical parts **b** : EQUATORIAL PLANE ⟨the *equator* of a dividing cell⟩
**4** : GREAT CIRCLE

**equa·to·ri·al** \,ē-kwə-'tōr-ē-əl, ,e-kwə-, -'tȯr-\ *adjective* (1664)
**1 a** : of, relating to, or located at the equator or an equator; *also* : being in the plane of the equator ⟨a satellite in *equatorial* orbit⟩ **b** : of, originating in, or suggesting the region around the geographic equator
**2 a** : being or having a support that includes two axles at right angles to each other with one parallel to the earth's axis of rotation ⟨an *equatorial* telescope⟩ **b** : extending in a direction essentially in the plane of a cyclic structure (as of cyclohexane) ⟨*equatorial* hydrogens⟩ — compare AXIAL

**equatorial plane** *noun* (circa 1892)
: the plane perpendicular to the spindle of a dividing cell and midway between the poles

**equatorial plate** *noun* (1887)
**1** : METAPHASE PLATE
**2** : EQUATORIAL PLANE

**equa·tor·ward** \i-'kwā-tər-wərd\ *adverb or adjective* (1875)
: toward or near the equator ⟨currents flowing *equatorward*⟩ ⟨*equatorward* winds⟩

**equer·ry** \'e-kwə-rē, i-'kwer-ē\ *noun, plural* **-ries** [obsolete *escuirie,* *equerry* stable, from Middle French *escuirie* office of a squire, stable, from *escuier* squire — more at ESQUIRE] (1591)
**1** : an officer of a prince or noble charged with the care of horses
**2** : an officer of the British royal household in personal attendance on the sovereign or a member of the royal family

**¹eques·tri·an** \i-'kwes-trē-ən\ *adjective* [Latin *equestr-, equester* of a horseman, from *eques* horseman, from *equus* horse — more at EQUINE] (circa 1681)
**1 a** : of, relating to, or featuring horseback riding **b** *archaic* : riding on horseback : MOUNTED **c** : representing a person on horseback ⟨an *equestrian* statue⟩
**2** : of, relating to, or composed of knights

**²equestrian** *noun* (1791)
: one who rides on horseback

**eques·tri·enne** \i-,kwes-trē-'en\ *noun* [²*equestrian* + *-enne* (as in *tragedienne*)] (circa 1864)
: a female rider on horseback

**equi-** *combining form* [Middle English, from Middle French, from Latin *aequi-,* from *aequus* equal]
: equal ⟨*equi*poise⟩ : equally ⟨*equi*probable⟩

**equi·an·gu·lar** \,ē-kwi-'aŋ-gyə-lər, ,e-kwi-\ *adjective* (1660)
: having all or corresponding angles equal ⟨mutually *equiangular* parallelograms⟩

**equi·ca·lor·ic** \,ē-kwə-kə-'lȯr-ik, ,e-kwə-, -'lär-\ *adjective* (1940)
: capable of yielding equal amounts of energy in the body ⟨*equicaloric* diets⟩

**equid** \'e-,kwid, 'ē-\ *noun* [New Latin *Equidae,* family name, from *Equus,* genus name, from Latin, horse] (circa 1889)
: any of a family (Equidae) of perissodactyl mammals consisting of the horses, asses, zebras, and extinct related animals

**equi·dis·tant** \,ē-kwə-'dis-tənt, ,e-kwə-\ *adjective* [Middle French or Late Latin; Middle French, from Late Latin *aequidistant-, aequidistans,* from Latin *aequi- + distant-, distans,* present participle of *distare* to stand apart — more at DISTANT] (1593)
**1** : equally distant
**2** : representing map distances true to scale in all directions
— **equi·dis·tant·ly** *adverb*

**equi·lat·er·al** \,ē-kwə-'la-tə-rəl, ,e-kwə-, -'la-trəl\ *adjective* [Late Latin *aequilateralis,* from Latin *aequi- + later-, latus* side — more at LATERAL] (1570)
**1** : having all sides equal ⟨an *equilateral* triangle⟩ ⟨an *equilateral* polygon⟩ — see TRIANGLE illustration

---

☆ **SYNONYMS**
**Equanimity, composure, sangfroid**
mean evenness of mind under stress. EQUANIMITY suggests a habit of mind that is only rarely disturbed under great strain ⟨accepted her troubles with *equanimity*⟩. COMPOSURE implies the controlling of emotional or mental agitation by an effort of will or as a matter of habit ⟨maintaining his *composure* even under hostile questioning⟩. SANGFROID implies great coolness and steadiness under strain ⟨handled the situation with professional *sangfroid*⟩.

---

\ə\ **abut** \ᵊ\ **kitten** \ər\ **further** \a\ **ash** \ā\ **ace**
\ä\ **mop, mar** \aú\ **out** \ch\ **chin** \e\ **bet** \ē\ **easy**
\g\ **go** \i\ **hit** \ī\ **ice** \j\ **job** \ŋ\ **sing** \ō\ **go**
\ȯ\ **law** \ȯi\ **boy** \th\ **thin** \th\ **the** \ü\ **loot** \ú\ **foot**
\y\ **yet** \zh\ **vision** *see also* Guide to Pronunciation

**2 :** having all the faces equal ⟨an *equilateral* polyhedron⟩

**equilateral hyperbola** *noun* (1880)
**:** a hyperbola with its asymptotes at right angles

**equil·i·brant** \i-'kwi-lə-brənt, ē-, *also* ˌē-kwə-'li-brənt\ *noun* (1883)
**:** a force that will balance one or more unbalanced forces

**equil·i·brate** \i-'kwi-lə-ˌbrāt\ *verb* **-brat·ed; -brat·ing** (1635)
*transitive verb*
**:** to bring into or keep in equilibrium **:** BALANCE
*intransitive verb*
**:** to bring about, come to, or be in equilibrium
**— equil·i·bra·tion** \-ˌkwi-lə-'brā-shən\ *noun*
**— equil·i·bra·tor** \-'kwi-lə-ˌbrā-tər\ *noun*
**— equil·i·bra·to·ry** \-brə-ˌtȯr-ē, -ˌtȯr-\ *adjective*

**equi·li·brist** \ˌē-kwə-'li-brist, ˌe-kwə-; i-'kwi-lə-brist\ *noun* (1760)
**:** one (as a rope dancer) who performs difficult feats of balancing
**— equil·i·bris·tic** \i-ˌkwi-lə-'bris-tik\ *adjective*

**equi·lib·ri·um** \ˌē-kwə-'li-brē-əm, ˌe-kwə-\ *noun, plural* **-ri·ums** *or* **-ria** \-brē-ə\ [Latin *aequilibrium,* from *aequilibris* being in equilibrium, from *aequi-* + *libra* weight, balance] (1608)
**1 a :** a state of intellectual or emotional balance **:** POISE **b :** a state of adjustment between opposing or divergent influences or elements
**2 :** a state of balance between opposing forces or actions that is either static (as in a body acted on by forces whose resultant is zero) or dynamic (as in a reversible chemical reaction when the velocities in both directions are equal)
**3 :** BALANCE 6a

**equilibrium constant** *noun* (1929)
**:** a number that expresses the relationship between the amounts of products and reactants present at equilibrium in a reversible chemical reaction at a given temperature

**equi·mo·lar** \-'mō-lər\ *adjective* (circa 1909)
**1 :** of or relating to an equal number of moles ⟨an *equimolar* mixture⟩
**2 :** having equal molar concentration

**equine** \'ē-ˌkwīn, 'e-ˌkwīn\ *adjective* [Latin *equinus,* from *equus* horse; akin to Old English *eoh* horse, Greek *hippos,* Sanskrit *aśva*] (1778)
**:** of, relating to, or resembling a horse or the horse family
**— equine** *noun*
**— equine·ly** *adverb*

**¹equi·noc·tial** \ˌē-kwə-'näk-shəl, ˌe-kwə-\ *adjective* (1545)
**1 :** relating to an equinox or to a state or the time of equal day and night
**2 :** relating to the regions or climate on or near the equator
**3 :** relating to the time when the sun passes an equinoctial point

**²equinoctial** *noun* (1527)
**1 :** EQUATOR 1
**2 :** an equinoctial storm

**equi·nox** \'ē-kwə-ˌnäks, 'e-kwə-\ *noun* [Middle English, from Middle French or Medieval Latin; Middle French *equinoxe,* from Medieval Latin *equinoxium,* alteration of Latin *aequinoctium,* from *aequi-* equi- + *noct-, nox* night — more at NIGHT] (14th century)
**1 :** either of the two points on the celestial sphere where the celestial equator intersects the ecliptic
**2 :** either of the two times each year (as about March 21 and September 23) when the sun crosses the equator and day and night are everywhere of equal length

**equip** \i-'kwip\ *transitive verb* **equipped; equip·ping** [Middle French *equiper,* from

Old French *esciper,* of Germanic origin; akin to Old English *scip* ship] (1523)
**1 :** to furnish for service or action by appropriate provisioning
**2 :** DRESS, ARRAY
**3 :** to make ready **:** PREPARE
**synonym** *see* FURNISH

**equi·page** \'e-kwə-pij\ *noun* (1579)
**1 a :** material or articles used in equipment **:** OUTFIT **b** *archaic* (1) **:** a set of small articles (as for table service) (2) **:** ETUI **c :** TRAPPINGS
**2** *archaic* **:** RETINUE
**3 :** a horse-drawn carriage with its servants; *also* **:** such a carriage alone

**equip·ment** \i-'kwip-mənt\ *noun* (1717)
**1 a :** the set of articles or physical resources serving to equip a person or thing: as (1) **:** the implements used in an operation or activity **:** APPARATUS (2) **:** all the fixed assets other than land and buildings of a business enterprise (3) **:** the rolling stock of a railway **b :** a piece of such equipment
**2 a :** the equipping of a person or thing **b :** the state of being equipped
**3 :** mental or emotional traits or resources **:** ENDOWMENT

**¹equi·poise** \'e-kwə-ˌpȯiz, 'ē-\ *noun* (1658)
**1 :** a state of equilibrium
**2 :** COUNTERBALANCE

**²equipoise** *transitive verb* (1664)
**1 :** to serve as an equipoise to
**2 :** to put or hold in equipoise

**equi·pol·lence** \ˌē-kwə-'pä-lən(t)s, ˌe-kwə-\ *noun* (15th century)
**:** the quality of being equipollent

**equi·pol·lent** \-lənt\ *adjective* [Middle English, from Middle French, from Latin *aequipollent-, aequipollens,* from *aequi-* equi- + *pollent-, pollens,* present participle of *pollēre* to be able] (15th century)
**1 :** equal in force, power, or validity
**2 :** the same in effect or signification
**— equipollent** *noun*
**— equi·pol·lent·ly** *adverb*

**equi·pon·der·ant** \-'pän-d(ə-)rənt\ *adjective* [Medieval Latin *aequiponderant-, aequiponderans,* present participle of *aequiponderare,* from Latin *aequi-* + *ponderare* to weigh — more at PONDER] (1630)
**:** evenly balanced

**equi·po·ten·tial** \ˌē-kwə-pə-'ten(t)-shəl, ˌe-kwə-\ *adjective* (circa 1865)
**:** having the same potential **:** of uniform potential throughout ⟨*equipotential* points⟩

**equi·prob·a·ble** \-'prä-bə-bəl\ *adjective* (1921)
**:** having the same degree of logical or mathematical probability ⟨*equiprobable* alternatives⟩

**eq·ui·se·tum** \ˌe-kwə-'sē-təm\ *noun, plural* **-se·tums** *or* **-se·ta** \-'sē-tə\ [New Latin, from Latin *equisaetum* horsetail plant, from *equus* horse + *saeta* bristle] (1830)
**:** any of a genus (*Equisetum*) of lower tracheophytes comprising perennial plants that spread by creeping rhizomes and have leaves reduced to nodal sheaths on the hollow jointed ribbed shoots — called *also* horsetail, scouring rush

equisetum: *1* vegetative plant, *2* fertile plant

**equi·ta·ble** \'e-kwə-tə-bəl\ *adjective* (1646)
**1 :** having or exhibiting equity **:** dealing fairly and equally with all concerned
**2 :** existing or valid in equity as distinguished from law
**synonym** *see* FAIR

**— eq·ui·ta·bil·i·ty** \ˌe-kwə-tə-'bi-lə-tē\ *noun*
**— eq·ui·ta·ble·ness** \'e-kwə-tə-bəl-nəs\ *noun*
**— eq·ui·ta·bly** \-blē\ *adverb*

**eq·ui·ta·tion** \ˌe-kwə-'tā-shən\ *noun* [Middle French, from Latin *equitation-, equitatio,* from *equitare* to ride on horseback, from *equit-, eques* horseman, from *equus* horse] (1562)
**:** the act or art of riding on horseback

**eq·ui·ty** \'e-kwə-tē\ *noun, plural* **-ties** [Middle English *equite,* from Middle French *equité,* from Latin *aequitat-, aequitas,* from *aequus* equal, fair] (14th century)
**1 a :** justice according to natural law or right; *specifically* **:** freedom from bias or favoritism **b :** something that is equitable
**2 a :** a system of law originating in the English chancery and comprising a settled and formal body of legal and procedural rules and doctrines that supplement, aid, or override common and statute law and are designed to protect rights and enforce duties fixed by substantive law **b :** trial or remedial justice under or by the rules and doctrines of equity **c :** a body of legal doctrines and rules developed to enlarge, supplement, or override a narrow rigid system of law
**3 a :** a right, claim, or interest existing or valid in equity **b :** the money value of a property or of an interest in a property in excess of claims or liens against it **c :** a risk interest or ownership right in property **d :** the common stock of a corporation

**equity capital** *noun* (1942)
**:** VENTURE CAPITAL

**equiv·a·lence** \i-'kwiv-lən(t)s, -'kwi-və-\ *noun* (circa 1541)
**1 a :** the state or property of being equivalent **b :** the relation holding between two statements if they are either both true or both false so that to affirm one and to deny the other would result in a contradiction
**2 :** a presentation of terms as equivalent
**3 :** equality in metrical value of a regular foot and one in which there are substitutions

**equivalence class** *noun* (1952)
**:** a set for which an equivalence relation holds between every pair of elements

**equivalence relation** *noun* (circa 1949)
**:** a relation (as equality) between elements of a set (as the real numbers) that is symmetric, reflexive, and transitive and for any two elements either holds or does not hold

**equiv·a·len·cy** \i-'kwiv-lən(t)-sē, -'kwi-və-\ *noun, plural* **-cies** (1535)
**1 :** EQUIVALENCE
**2 :** a level of achievement equivalent to completion of an educational or training program ⟨a high school *equivalency* certificate⟩

**equiv·a·lent** \-lənt\ *adjective* [Middle English, from Middle French or Late Latin; Middle French, from Late Latin *aequivalent-, aequivalens,* present participle of *aequivalēre* to have equal power, from Latin *aequi-* + *valēre* to be strong — more at WIELD] (15th century)
**1 :** equal in force, amount, or value; *also* **:** equal in area or volume but not admitting of superposition ⟨a square *equivalent* to a triangle⟩
**2 a :** like in signification or import **b :** having logical equivalence ⟨*equivalent* statements⟩
**3 :** corresponding or virtually identical especially in effect or function
**4** *obsolete* **:** equal in might or authority
**5 :** having the same chemical combining capacity ⟨*equivalent* quantities of two elements⟩
**6 a :** having the same solution set ⟨*equivalent* equations⟩ **b :** capable of being placed in one-to-one correspondence ⟨*equivalent* sets⟩ **c :** related by an equivalence relation
**synonym** *see* SAME
**— equivalent** *noun*
**— equiv·a·lent·ly** *adverb*

**equivalent weight** *noun* (1904)
: the mass of a substance especially in grams that combines with or is chemically equivalent to eight grams of oxygen or one gram of hydrogen : the atomic or molecular weight divided by the valence

**equiv·o·cal** \i-'kwi-və-kəl\ *adjective* [Late Latin *aequivocus*, from *aequi-* equi- + *voc-*, *vox* voice — more at VOICE] (1599)
**1 a** : subject to two or more interpretations and usually used to mislead or confuse **b** : uncertain as an indication or sign
**2 a** : of uncertain nature or classification **b** : of uncertain disposition toward a person or thing : UNDECIDED **c** : of doubtful advantage, genuineness, or moral rectitude ⟨*equivocal* behavior⟩
**synonym** see OBSCURE
— **equiv·o·cal·i·ty** \-,kwi-və-'ka-lə-tē\ *noun*
— **equiv·o·cal·ly** \-'kwi-və-k(ə-)lē\ *adverb*
— **equiv·o·cal·ness** \-kəl-nəs\ *noun*

**equiv·o·cate** \i-'kwi-və-,kāt\ *intransitive verb* **-cat·ed; -cat·ing** (1590)
**1** : to use equivocal language especially with intent to deceive
**2** : to avoid committing oneself in what one says
**synonym** see LIE
— **equiv·o·ca·tion** \-,kwi-və-'kā-shən\ *noun*
— **equiv·o·ca·tor** \-'kwi-və-,kā-tər\ *noun*

**equi·voque** *also* **equi·voke** \'e-kwə-,vōk, 'ē-\ *noun* [French *équivoque*, from *équivoque* equivocal, from Late Latin *aequivocus*] (1599)
**1** : an equivocal word or phrase; *specifically* : PUN
**2 a** : double meaning **b** : WORDPLAY

**¹-er** \ər; *after some vowels, often* r; *after* ŋ, *usually* gər\ *adjective suffix or adverb suffix* [Middle English *-er, -ere, -re,* from Old English *-ra* (in adjectives), *-or* (in adverbs); akin to Old High German *-iro,* adjective comparative suffix, Latin *-ior,* Greek *-iōn*]
— used to form the comparative degree of adjectives and adverbs of one syllable ⟨hott*er*⟩ ⟨dri*er*⟩ and of some adjectives and adverbs of two syllables ⟨complet*er*⟩ and sometimes of longer ones ⟨beautiful*er*⟩

**²-er** \ər; *after some vowels, often* r\ *also* **-ier** \ē-ər, yər\ *or* **-yer** \yər\ *noun suffix* [Middle English *-er, -ere, -ier, -iere;* partly from Old English *-ere* (from Latin *-arius*); partly from Old French *-ier, -iere,* from Latin *-arius, -aria, -arium* -ary; partly from Middle French *-ere,* from Latin *-ator* -or — more at -ARY, -OR]
**1 a** : person occupationally connected with ⟨hatt*er*⟩ ⟨furri*er*⟩ ⟨law*yer*⟩ **b** : person or thing belonging to or associated with ⟨head*er*⟩ ⟨old-tim*er*⟩ **c** : native of : resident of ⟨cottag*er*⟩ ⟨New York*er*⟩ **d** : one that has ⟨three-deck*er*⟩ **e** : one that produces or yields ⟨pork*er*⟩
**2 a** : one that does or performs (a specified action) ⟨report*er*⟩ — sometimes added to both elements of a compound ⟨build*er*-upp*er*⟩ **b** : one that is a suitable object of (a specified action) ⟨broil*er*⟩
**3** : one that is ⟨foreign*er*⟩ — in all senses *-yer* in a few words after *w, -ier* in a few other words, otherwise *-er*

**era** \'ir-ə, 'er-ə, 'ē-rə\ *noun* [Late Latin *aera,* from Latin, counters, plural of *aer-, aes* copper, money — more at ORE] (1615)
**1 a** : a fixed point in time from which a series of years is reckoned **b** : a memorable or important date or event; *especially* : one that begins a new period in the history of a person or thing
**2** : a system of chronological notation computed from a given date as basis
**3 a** : a period identified by some prominent figure or characteristic feature **b** : a stage in development; *especially* : one of the four major divisions of geologic time ⟨Paleozoic *era*⟩
**synonym** see PERIOD

**erad·i·cate** \i-'ra-də-,kāt\ *transitive verb* **-cat·ed; -cat·ing** [Latin *eradicatus,* past participle of *eradicare,* from *e-* + *radic-, radix* root — more at ROOT] (1578)
**1** : to pull up by the roots
**2** : to do away with as completely as if by pulling up by the roots ⟨programs to *eradicate* illiteracy⟩
**synonym** see EXTERMINATE
— **erad·i·ca·ble** \-'ra-di-kə-bəl\ *adjective*
— **erad·i·ca·tion** \-,ra-də-'kā-shən\ *noun*
— **erad·i·ca·tor** \-,kā-tər\ *noun*

**erase** \i-'rās, *British* -'rāz\ *verb* **erased; eras·ing** [Latin *erasus,* past participle of *eradere,* from *e-* + *radere* to scratch, scrape — more at RODENT] (1605)
*transitive verb*
**1 a** : to rub or scrape out (as written, painted, or engraved letters) **b** : to remove (recorded matter) from a magnetic medium; *also* : to remove recorded matter from ⟨*erase* a videotape⟩ **c** : to delete from a computer storage device
**2 a** : to remove from existence or memory as if by erasing **b** : to nullify the effect or force of
*intransitive verb*
: to yield to being erased
— **eras·abil·i·ty** \-,rā-sə-'bi-lə-tē\ *noun*
— **eras·able** \-'rā-sə-bəl\ *adjective*

**eras·er** \i-'rā-sər\ *noun* (1790)
: one that erases; *especially* : a device (as a piece of rubber, or a felt pad) used to erase marks (as of ink or chalk)

**Eras·tian** \i-'ras-tē-ən, -'ras-chən\ *adjective* [Thomas *Erastus* (died 1583) Swiss physician and Zwinglian theologian] (1839)
: of, characterized by, or advocating the doctrine of state supremacy in ecclesiastical affairs
— **Erastian** *noun*
— **Eras·tian·ism** \-,ni-zəm\ *noun*

**era·sure** \i-'rā-shər *also* -zhər\ *noun* (1734)
: an act or instance of erasing

**Er·a·to** \'er-ə-,tō\ *noun* [Greek *Eratō*]
: the Greek Muse of lyric and love poetry

**er·bi·um** \'ər-bē-əm\ *noun* [New Latin, from *Ytterby,* Sweden] (1843)
: a metallic element of the rare-earth group that occurs with yttrium — see ELEMENT table

**¹ere** \'er, 'ar\ *preposition* [Middle English *er,* from Old English *ær,* from *ær,* adverb, early, soon; akin to Old High German *ēr* earlier, Greek *ēri* early] (before 12th century)
: ²BEFORE 2 ⟨contrived *ere* the beginning of the world —Norman Douglas⟩

**²ere** *conjunction* (before 12th century)
: ³BEFORE

**Er·e·bus** \'er-ə-bəs\ *noun* [Latin, from Greek *Erebos*]
**1** : a personification of darkness in Greek mythology
**2** : a place of darkness in the underworld on the way to Hades

**¹erect** \i-'rekt\ *adjective* [Middle English, from Latin *erectus,* past participle of *erigere* to erect, from *e-* + *regere* to lead straight, guide — more at RIGHT] (14th century)
**1 a** : vertical in position; *also* : not spread out or decumbent ⟨an *erect* plant stem⟩ **b** : standing up or out from the body ⟨*erect* hairs⟩ **c** : characterized by firm or rigid straightness in bodily posture ⟨an *erect* bearing⟩
**2** *archaic* : directed upward
**3** *obsolete* : ALERT, WATCHFUL
**4** : being in a state of physiological erection
— **erect·ly** \-'rek-(t)lē\ *adverb*
— **erect·ness** \-'rek(t)-nəs\ *noun*

**²erect** *transitive verb* (15th century)
**1 a** (1) : to put up by the fitting together of materials or parts : BUILD (2) : to fix in an upright position (3) : to cause to stand up or stand out **b** *archaic* : to direct upward **c** : to change (an image) from an inverted to a normal position
**2** : to elevate in status
**3** : SET UP, ESTABLISH
**4** *obsolete* : ENCOURAGE, EMBOLDEN
**5** : to draw or construct (as a perpendicular or figure) upon a given base
— **erect·able** \-'rek-tə-bəl\ *adjective*

**erec·tile** \i-'rek-t²l, -,tīl\ *adjective* (1830)
: capable of becoming erect ⟨*erectile* tissue⟩ — compare CAVERNOUS 1b
— **erec·til·i·ty** \-,rek-'ti-lə-tē\ *noun*

**erec·tion** \i-'rek-shən\ *noun* (15th century)
**1 a** : the state marked by firm turgid form and erect position of a previously flaccid bodily part containing cavernous tissue when that tissue becomes dilated with blood **b** : an occurrence of such a state in the penis or clitoris
**2** : the act or process of erecting something : CONSTRUCTION
**3** : something erected

**erec·tor** \i-'rek-tər\ *noun* (1538)
: one that erects; *especially* : a muscle that raises or keeps a part erect

**Erector** *trademark*
— used for a metal toy construction set

**E region** *noun* (1930)
: the part of the ionosphere occurring between 55 and 80 miles (90 and 130 kilometers) above the surface of the earth and containing the daytime E layer and the sporadic E layer

**ere·long** \er-'lóŋ, ar-\ *adverb* (1577)
*archaic* : before long : SOON

**er·e·mite** \'er-ə-,mīt\ *noun* [Middle English — more at HERMIT] (13th century)
: HERMIT; *especially* : a religious recluse
— **er·e·mit·ic** \,er-ə-'mi-tik\ *or* **er·e·mit·i·cal** \-ti-kəl\ *adjective*
— **er·e·mit·ism** \'er-ə-,mī-,ti-zəm\ *noun*

**er·em·urus** \,er-ə-'myúr-əs\ *noun, plural* **-uri** \-'myúr-,ī\ [New Latin, from Greek *erēmos* solitary + *oura* tail — more at ASS] (1829)
: any of a genus (*Eremurus*) of perennial herbs of the lily family that produce tall racemes of showy blooms — called also *foxtail lily*

**ere·now** \er-'naú, ar-\ *adverb* (14th century)
: before now : HERETOFORE

**erep·sin** \i-'rep-sən\ *noun* [International Scientific Vocabulary *er-* (probably from Latin *eripere* to snatch away, from *e-* + *rapere* to seize) + *pepsin* — more at RAPID] (1902)
: a proteolytic fraction obtained especially from the intestinal juice and known to be a mixture of exopeptidases

**er·e·thism** \'er-ə-,thi-zəm\ *noun* [French *éréthisme,* from Greek *erethismos* irritation, from *erethizein* to irritate; akin to Greek *ornynai* to rouse — more at ORIENT] (1800)
: abnormal irritability or responsiveness to stimulation

**ere·while** \er-'(h)wī(ə)l, ar-\ *also* **ere·whiles** \-'(h)wī(ə)lz\ *adverb* (13th century)
*archaic* : HERETOFORE

**erg** \'ərg\ *noun* [Greek *ergon* work — more at WORK] (circa 1873)
: a centimeter-gram-second unit of work equal to the work done by a force of one dyne acting through a distance of one centimeter and equivalent to $10^{-7}$ joule

**erg-** *or* **ergo-** *combining form* [Greek, from *ergon*]
: work ⟨*ergo*meter⟩

**er·gas·tic** \(,)ər-'gas-tik\ *adjective* [Greek *ergastikos* able to work, from *ergazesthai* to work, from *ergon* work] (circa 1896)
: constituting the nonliving by-products of protoplasmic activity ⟨*ergastic* substances⟩

**er·gas·to·plasm** \-tə-,pla-zəm\ *noun* [International Scientific Vocabulary] (1902)
: ribosome-studded endoplasmic reticulum
— **er·gas·to·plas·mic** \-,gas-tə-'plaz-mik\ *adjective*

---

\ə\ abut \ᵊ\ kitten \ər\ further \a\ ash \ā\ ace
\ä\ mop, mar \aú\ out \ch\ chin \e\ bet \ē\ easy
\g\ go \i\ hit \ī\ ice \j\ job \ŋ\ sing \ō\ go
\ó\ law \ói\ boy \th\ thin \t̶h\ the \ü\ loot \ú\ foot
\y\ yet \zh\ vision *see also* Guide to Pronunciation

**er·ga·tive** \'ər-gə-tiv\ *adjective* [Greek *ergatēs* worker, from *ergon* work] (1939)
**:** of, relating to, or being a language (as Inuit or Georgian) in which the objects of transitive verbs and subjects of intransitive verbs are typically marked by the same linguistic forms; *also* **:** being an inflectional morpheme that typically marks the subject of a transitive verb in an ergative language

**-er·gic** \(ˌ)ər-jik\ *adjective combining form* [*-ergy* work (from Late Latin *-ergia*, from Greek, from *ergon* work) + *-ic* — more at WORK]
**:** exhibiting or stimulating activity of ⟨dopaminergic⟩

**er·go** \'ər-(ˌ)gō, 'ər-\ *adverb* [Middle English, from Latin, from Old Latin, because of, from (assumed) Old Latin *e rogo* from the direction (of)] (14th century)
**:** THEREFORE, HENCE

**ergo-** *combining form* [French, from *ergot*]
**:** ergot ⟨*ergosterol*⟩

**er·go·dic** \(ˌ)ər-'gä-dik, -'gō-\ *adjective* [International Scientific Vocabulary *erg-* + *-ode*] (1926)
**1 :** of or relating to a process in which every sequence or sizable sample is equally representative of the whole (as in regard to a statistical parameter)
**2 :** involving or relating to the probability that any state will recur; *especially* **:** having zero probability that any state will never recur
— **er·go·dic·i·ty** \ˌər-gə-'di-sə-tē\ *noun*

**er·go·graph** \'ər-gə-ˌgraf\ *noun* [International Scientific Vocabulary] (1892)
**:** an apparatus for measuring the work capacity of a muscle

**er·gom·e·ter** \(ˌ)ər-'gä-mə-tər\ *noun* (circa 1879)
**:** an apparatus for measuring the work performed (as by a person exercising); *also* **:** an exercise machine equipped with an ergometer
— **er·go·met·ric** \ˌər-gə-'me-trik\ *adjective*

**er·go·nom·ics** \ˌər-gə-'nä-miks\ *noun plural but singular or plural in construction* [*erg-* + *-nomics* (as in *economics*)] (1949)
**:** an applied science concerned with designing and arranging things people use so that the people and things interact most efficiently and safely — called also *human engineering*
— **er·go·nom·ic** \-mik\ *adjective*
— **er·go·nom·i·cal·ly** \-mi-k(ə-)lē\ *adverb*
— **er·gon·o·mist** \(ˌ)ər-'gä-nə-mist\ *noun*

**er·go·no·vine** \ˌər-gə-'nō-ˌvēn\ *noun* [*ergo-* + Latin *novus* new — more at NEW] (circa 1936)
**:** an alkaloid $C_{19}H_{23}N_3O_2$ from ergot with similar pharmacological action but reduced toxicity

**er·gos·ter·ol** \(ˌ)ər-'gäs-tə-ˌról, -ˌról\ *noun* [International Scientific Vocabulary] (1906)
**:** a crystalline steroid alcohol $C_{28}H_{44}O$ that occurs especially in yeast, molds, and ergot and is converted by ultraviolet irradiation ultimately into vitamin $D_2$

**er·got** \'ər-gət, -ˌgät\ *noun* [French, literally, cock's spur] (1683)
**1 :** the black or dark purple sclerotium of fungi (genus *Claviceps*) that occurs as a club-shaped body replacing the seed of a grass (as rye); *also* **:** a fungus bearing ergots
**2 :** a disease of rye and other cereals caused by an ergot fungus
**3 a :** the dried sclerotia of an ergot fungus grown on rye and containing several alkaloids (as ergonovine and ergotamine) **b :** any of such alkaloids used medicinally for their contractile effect on smooth muscle (as of peripheral arterioles)
— **er·got·ic** \(ˌ)ər-'gä-tik\ *adjective*

**er·got·a·mine** \(ˌ)ər-'gä-tə-ˌmēn\ *noun* [International Scientific Vocabulary] (1921)
**:** an alkaloid $C_{33}H_{35}N_5O_5$ from ergot that is used chiefly in the form of its tartrate especially in treating migraine

**er·got·ism** \'ər-gə-ˌti-zəm\ *noun* (circa 1841)
**:** a toxic condition produced by eating grain, grain products (as rye bread), or grasses infected with ergot fungus or by chronic excessive use of an ergot drug

**er·got·ized** \-ˌtīzd\ *adjective* (1860)
**:** infected with ergot ⟨*ergotized* grain⟩; *also* **:** poisoned by ergot ⟨*ergotized* cattle⟩

**er·i·ca** \'er-i-kə\ *noun* [New Latin, from Latin *erice* heather, from Greek *ereikē* — more at BRIER] (1826)
**:** any of a large genus (*Erica*) of the heath family of low much-branched evergreen shrubs

**er·i·ca·ceous** \ˌer-ə-'kā-shəs\ *adjective* (circa 1859)
**:** of, relating to, or being a heath or the heath family

**er·i·coid** \'er-ə-ˌkóid\ *adjective* (circa 1900)
**:** resembling heath ⟨*ericoid* foliage⟩

**Erie** \'ir-ē, 'ēr-ē\ *noun* (circa 1909)
**1 :** a member of an American Indian people living south of Lake Erie in the 17th century
**2 :** the extinct and probably Iroquoian language of the Erie people

**erig·er·on** \ə-'ri-jə-ˌrän\ *noun* [New Latin, from Latin, groundsel, from Greek *ērigerōn*, from *ēri* early + *gerōn* old man; from the hoary down of some species — more at ERE, GERONT-] (1601)
**:** any of a widely distributed genus (*Erigeron*) of composite herbs with flower heads that resemble asters but have fewer and narrower involucral bracts

**Er·i·nys** \i-'ri-nəs, -'rī-\ *noun, plural* **Erin·y·es** \-'ri-nē-ˌēz\ [Greek] (1590)
**:** FURY 2a

**er·i·o·phy·id** \ˌer-ē-'ä-fē-əd, -ē-ə-'fī-əd\ *noun* [ultimately from Greek *erion* wool + *phyē* growth; akin to Greek *physis* growth — more at PHYSICS] (1942)
**:** any of a large family (Eriophyidae) of minute plant-feeding mites that have two pairs of legs placed far anterior and lack a respiratory system
— **eriophyid** *adjective*

**¹eris·tic** \i-'ris-tik, e-\ *also* **eris·ti·cal** \-ti-kəl\ *adjective* [Greek *eristikos* fond of wrangling, from *erizein* to wrangle, from *eris* strife] (1637)
**:** characterized by disputatious and often subtle and specious reasoning
— **eris·ti·cal·ly** \-ti-k(ə-)lē\ *adverb*

**²eristic** *noun* (1659)
**1 :** a person devoted to logical disputation
**2 :** the art or practice of disputation and polemics

**Er·len·mey·er flask** \ˌər-lən-ˌmī-(ə)r-, ˌer-lən-\ *noun* [Emil *Erlenmeyer*] (circa 1890)
**:** a flat-bottomed conical laboratory flask

**er·mine** \'ər-mən\ *noun, plural* **ermines** [Middle English, from Old French, of Germanic origin; akin to Old High German *harmo* weasel] (12th century)
**1** *or plural* **ermine a :** any of several weasels whose coats become white in winter usually with black on the tip of the tail; *especially* **:** a short-tailed weasel (*Mustela erminea*) of the forests and tundra of Eurasia and North America **b :** the white fur of the ermine
**2 :** a rank or office whose ceremonial or official robe is ornamented with ermine

ermine 1a: winter coat

**er·mined** \-mənd\ *adjective* (15th century)
**:** clothed or adorned with ermine

**erne** \'ərn, 'ern\ *noun* [Middle English, from Old English *earn;* akin to Old High German *arn* eagle, Greek *ornis* bird] (before 12th century)
**:** EAGLE; *especially* **:** a long-winged sea eagle (*Haliäetus albicilla*) with a short white wedge-shaped tail

**erode** \i-'rōd\ *verb* **erod·ed; erod·ing** [Latin *erodere* to eat away, from *e-* + *rodere* to gnaw — more at RODENT] (1612)
*transitive verb*
**1 :** to diminish or destroy by degrees: **a :** to eat into or away by slow destruction of substance (as by acid, infection, or cancer) **b :** to wear away by the action of water, wind, or glacial ice **c :** to cause to deteriorate or disappear as if by eating or wearing away ⟨inflation *eroding* buying power⟩
**2 :** to produce or form by eroding ⟨glaciers *erode* U-shaped valleys⟩
*intransitive verb*
**:** to undergo erosion
— **erod·ibil·i·ty** \-ˌrō-də-'bi-lə-tē\ *noun*
— **erod·ible** \-'rō-də-bəl\ *adjective*

**erog·e·nous** \i-'rä-jə-nəs\ *adjective* [Greek *erōs* + English *-genous, -genic*] (circa 1889)
**1 :** producing sexual excitement or libidinal gratification when stimulated **:** sexually sensitive
**2 :** of, relating to, or arousing sexual feelings

**Eros** \'er-ˌäs, 'ir-\ *noun* [Greek *Erōs*, from *erōs* sexual love; akin to Greek *erasthai* to love, desire]
**1 :** the Greek god of erotic love — compare CUPID
**2 :** the sum of life-preserving instincts that are manifested as impulses to gratify basic needs, as sublimated impulses, and as impulses to protect and preserve the body and mind — compare DEATH INSTINCT
**3 a :** love conceived in the philosophy of Plato as a fundamental creative impulse having a sensual element **b** *often not capitalized* **:** erotic love or desire

**erose** \i-'rōs\ *adjective* [Latin *erosus*, past participle of *erodere*] (1793)
**:** IRREGULAR, UNEVEN; *specifically* **:** having the margin irregularly notched as if gnawed ⟨an *erose* leaf⟩

**ero·sion** \i-'rō-zhən\ *noun* (1541)
**1 a :** the action or process of eroding **b :** the state of being eroded
**2 :** an instance or product of erosive action
— **ero·sion·al** \-'rōzh-nəl, -'rō-zhə-n°l\ *adjective*
— **ero·sion·al·ly** \-ē\ *adverb*

**ero·sive** \i-'rō-siv, -ziv\ *adjective* (1830)
**:** tending to erode or to induce or permit erosion
— **ero·sive·ness** *noun*
— **ero·siv·i·ty** \i-ˌrō-'si-və-tē\ *noun*

**erot·ic** \i-'rä-tik\ *also* **erot·i·cal** \-ti-kəl\ *adjective* [Greek *erōtikos*, from *erōt-, erōs*] (1651)
**1 :** of, devoted to, or tending to arouse sexual love or desire ⟨*erotic* art⟩
**2 :** strongly marked or affected by sexual desire ◆

— **erotic** *noun*
— **erot·i·cal·ly** \-ti-k(ə-)lē\ *adverb*
**erot·i·ca** \i-'rä-ti-kə\ *noun plural but singular or plural in construction* [New Latin, from Greek *erōtika*, neuter plural of *erōtikos*] (1854)
**1** : literary or artistic works having an erotic theme or quality
**2** : depictions of things erotic
**erot·i·cism** \i-'rä-tə-ˌsi-zəm\ *noun* (1881)
**1** : an erotic theme or quality
**2** : a state of sexual arousal
**3** : insistent sexual impulse or desire
— **erot·i·cist** \-sist\ *noun*
**erot·i·cize** \-ˌsīz\ *transitive verb* **-cized; -ciz·ing** (circa 1914)
: to make erotic
— **erot·i·ci·za·tion** \i-ˌrä-tə-sə-'zā-shən\ *noun*
**er·o·tism** \'er-ə-ˌti-zəm\ *noun* (1849)
: EROTICISM
**er·o·tize** \'er-ə-ˌtīz\ *transitive verb* **-tized; -tiz·ing** (1936)
: to invest with erotic significance or sexual feeling
— **er·o·ti·za·tion** \ˌer-ə-tə-'zā-shən\ *noun*
**eroto-** *combining form* [New Latin, from Greek *erōto-*, from *erot-, eros*]
: sexual desire ⟨*erotogenic*⟩
**ero·to·gen·ic** \i-ˌrō-tə-'je-nik, -ˌrä-\ *adjective* (circa 1909)
: EROGENOUS
**err** \'er, 'ər\ *intransitive verb* [Middle English, from Middle French *errer*, from Latin *errare* to wander, err; akin to Old English *ierre* wandering, angry, Old Norse *rās* race — more at RACE] (14th century)
**1** *archaic* : STRAY
**2 a** : to make a mistake **b** : to violate an accepted standard of conduct □
**er·ran·cy** \'er-ən(t)-sē\ *noun, plural* **-cies** (1621)
: the state or an instance of erring
**er·rand** \'er-ənd\ *noun* [Middle English *erend* message, business, from Old English *ærend*; akin to Old High German *ārunti* message] (before 12th century)
**1** *archaic* **a** : an oral message entrusted to a person **b** : EMBASSY, MISSION
**2 a** : a short trip taken to attend to some business often for another ⟨was on an *errand* for his mother⟩ **b** : the object or purpose of such a trip
**er·rant** \'er-ənt\ *adjective* [Middle English *erraunt*, from Middle French *errant*, present participle of *errer* to err & *errer* to travel, from Late Latin *iterare*, from Latin *iter* road, journey — more at ITINERANT] (14th century)
**1** : traveling or given to traveling ⟨an *errant* knight⟩
**2 a** : straying outside the proper path or bounds ⟨an *errant* calf⟩ **b** : moving about aimlessly or irregularly ⟨an *errant* breeze⟩ **c** : deviating from a standard (as of truth or propriety) ⟨an *errant* child⟩ **d** : FALLIBLE
— **errant** *noun*
— **er·rant·ly** *adverb*
**er·rant·ry** \'er-ən-trē\ *noun, plural* **-ries** (1654)
: the quality, condition, or fact of wandering; *especially* : a roving in search of chivalrous adventure
**er·ra·ta** \e-'rä-tə, -'rā-, -'ra-\ *noun* [Latin, plural of *erratum*] (1589)
: a list of corrigenda; *also* : a page bearing such a list
**¹er·rat·ic** \ir-'a-tik\ *adjective* [Middle English, from Middle French or Latin; Middle French *erratique*, from Latin *erraticus*, from *erratus*, past participle of *errare*] (14th century)
**1 a** : having no fixed course : WANDERING ⟨an *erratic* comet⟩ **b** *archaic* : NOMADIC
**2** : transported from an original resting place especially by a glacier ⟨an *erratic* boulder⟩
**3 a** : characterized by lack of consistency, regularity, or uniformity **b** : deviating from what is ordinary or standard : ECCENTRIC ⟨an *erratic* genius⟩

**synonym** *see* STRANGE
— **er·rat·i·cal** \-ti-kəl\ *adjective*
— **er·rat·i·cal·ly** \-ti-k(ə-)lē\ *adverb*
— **er·rat·i·cism** \-'a-tə-ˌsi-zəm\ *noun*
**²erratic** *noun* (circa 1623)
: one that is erratic; *especially* : an erratic boulder or block of rock
**er·ra·tum** \e-'rä-təm, -'rā-, -'ra-\ *noun, plural* **-ta** \-tə\ [Latin, from neuter of *erratus*] (1589)
: ERROR; *especially* : CORRIGENDUM
**er·ro·ne·ous** \i-'rō-nē-əs, e-'rō-\ *adjective* [Middle English, from Latin *erroneus*, from *erron-, erro* wanderer, from *errare*] (15th century)
**1** : containing or characterized by error : MISTAKEN ⟨*erroneous* assumptions⟩
**2** *archaic* : WANDERING
— **er·ro·ne·ous·ly** *adverb*
— **er·ro·ne·ous·ness** *noun*
**er·ror** \'er-ər\ *noun* [Middle English *errour*, from Middle French, from Latin *error*, from *errare*] (13th century)
**1 a** : an act or condition of ignorant or imprudent deviation from a code of behavior **b** : an act involving an unintentional deviation from truth or accuracy **c** : an act that through ignorance, deficiency, or accident departs from or fails to achieve what should be done: as (1) : a defensive misplay other than a wild pitch or passed ball made by a baseball player when normal play would have resulted in an out or prevented an advance by a base runner (2) : the failure of a player (as in tennis) to make a successful return of a ball during play **d** : a mistake in the proceedings of a court of record in matters of law or of fact
**2 a** : the quality or state of erring **b** *Christian Science* : illusion about the nature of reality that is the cause of human suffering : the contradiction of truth **c** : an instance of false belief
**3** : something produced by mistake; *especially* : a postage stamp exhibiting a consistent flaw (as a wrong color) in its manufacture
**4 a** : the difference between an observed or calculated value and a true value; *specifically* : variation in measurements, calculations, or observations of a quantity due to mistakes or to uncontrollable factors **b** : the amount of deviation from a standard or specification
**5** : a deficiency or imperfection in structure or function ⟨an *error* of metabolism⟩ ☆
— **er·ror·less** \'er-ər-ləs\ *adjective*
**er·satz** \'er-ˌsäts, -ˌzäts, er-'; 'ər-ˌsats\ *adjective* [German *ersatz-*, from *Ersatz*, noun, substitute] (1875)
: being a usually artificial and inferior substitute or imitation ⟨*ersatz* turf⟩ ⟨*ersatz* intellectuals⟩
— **ersatz** *noun*
**Erse** \'ərs\ *noun* [Middle English (Scots) *Erisch*, adjective, Irish, alteration of *Irish*] (15th century)
**1** : SCOTTISH GAELIC
**2** : IRISH GAELIC
— **Erse** *adjective*
**erst** \'ərst\ *adverb* [Middle English *erest* earliest, formerly, from Old English *ærest*, superlative of *ær* early — more at ERE] (12th century)
*archaic* : ERSTWHILE
**¹erst·while** \'ərst-ˌ(h)wīl\ *adverb* (1569)
: in the past : FORMERLY ⟨cultures, *erstwhile* unknown to each other —Robert Plank⟩
**²erstwhile** *adjective* (1903)
: FORMER, PREVIOUS ⟨her *erstwhile* students⟩
**eru·cic acid** \i-'rü-sik-\ *noun* [New Latin *Eruca*, genus of herbs, from Latin, colewort] (1869)
: a crystalline fatty acid $C_{22}H_{42}O_2$ found in the form of glycerides in rapeseed oil
**eruct** \i-'rəkt\ *verb* [Latin *eructare*, frequentative of *erugere* to belch, disgorge; akin to Old English *rocettan* to belch, Greek *ereugesthai*] (1666)

: BELCH
**eruc·ta·tion** \i-ˌrək-'tā-shən, ˌē-\ *noun* (15th century)
: an act or instance of belching
**er·u·dite** \'er-ə-ˌdīt, 'er-yə-\ *adjective* [Middle English *erudit*, from Latin *eruditus*, from past participle of *erudire* to instruct, from *e- + rudis* rude, ignorant] (15th century)
: possessing or displaying erudition : LEARNED ⟨an *erudite* scholar⟩
— **er·u·dite·ly** *adverb*
**er·u·di·tion** \ˌer-ə-'di-shən, ˌer-yə-\ *noun* (15th century)
: extensive knowledge acquired chiefly from books : profound, recondite, or bookish learning
**synonym** *see* KNOWLEDGE
**erum·pent** \i-'rəm-pənt\ *adjective* [Latin *erumpent-, erumpens*, present participle of *erumpere*] (1650)
: bursting forth ⟨*erumpent* fungi⟩
**erupt** \i-'rəpt\ *verb* [Latin *eruptus*, past participle of *erumpere* to burst forth, from *e- + rumpere* to break — more at REAVE] (1657)
*intransitive verb*
**1 a** (1) : to burst from limits or restraint (2) *of a tooth* : to emerge through the gum **b** : to force out or release suddenly and often violently something (as lava or steam) that is pent up **c** : to become active or violent especially suddenly
**2** : to break out with or as if with a skin eruption

---

☆ SYNONYMS
**Error, mistake, blunder, slip, lapse** mean a departure from what is true, right, or proper. ERROR suggests the existence of a standard or guide and a straying from the right course through failure to make effective use of this ⟨procedural *errors*⟩. MISTAKE implies misconception or inadvertence and usually expresses less criticism than *error* ⟨dialed the wrong number by *mistake*⟩. BLUNDER regularly imputes stupidity or ignorance as a cause and connotes some degree of blame ⟨diplomatic *blunders*⟩. SLIP stresses inadvertence or accident and applies especially to trivial but embarrassing mistakes ⟨a *slip* of the tongue⟩. LAPSE stresses forgetfulness, weakness, or inattention as a cause ⟨a *lapse* in judgment⟩.

---

□ USAGE
**err** The sound of the letter *r* often colors a preceding vowel in English, so that the originally distinct vowels of *curt, word, bird,* and *were* are now pronounced the same. Originally *err* and *error* had the same first vowel, but over time *err* developed the pronunciation \'ər\ as well. Commentators have expressed a visceral dislike for the original pronunciation \'er\; perhaps they believe that once usage has established a new pronunciation for a word that there can be no going back. By this reasoning, though, we should embrace the once established innovative pronunciations of *gold* \'gu̇ld\ and *Rome* \'rüm\ (as seen in Shakespeare's pun on *Rome* and *room* in *Julius Caesar* I.ii.156). For these two words the English language has returned to the older forms, and no sound reason prevents us from accepting again the \'er\ pronunciation of *err*, which is today also the more common variant in American speech.

---

\ə\ abut  \ᵊ\ kitten  \ər\ further  \a\ ash  \ā\ ace
\ä\ mop, mar  \au̇\ out  \ch\ chin  \e\ bet  \ē\ easy
\g\ go  \i\ hit  \ī\ ice  \j\ job  \ŋ\ sing  \ō\ go
\ȯ\ law  \ȯi\ boy  \th\ thin  \th\ the  \ü\ loot  \u̇\ foot
\y\ yet  \zh\ vision  *see also* Guide to Pronunciation

*transitive verb*
: to force out or release usually suddenly and violently
— **erupt·ible** \-'rəp-tə-bəl\ *adjective*
— **erup·tive** \-tiv\ *adjective*
— **erup·tive·ly** *adverb*
**erup·tion** \i-'rəp-shən\ *noun* (1555)
**1 a** : an act, process, or instance of erupting **b** : the breaking out of a rash on the skin or mucous membrane
**2** : a product of erupting (as a skin rash)
**-ery** \(ə-)rē\ *noun suffix, plural* **-er·ies** [Middle English *-erie*, from Old French, from *-ier -er* + *-ie -y*]
**1** : qualities collectively : character : -NESS ⟨snobb*ery*⟩
**2** : art : practice ⟨quack*ery*⟩
**3** : place of doing, keeping, producing, or selling (the thing specified) ⟨fish*ery*⟩ ⟨bak*ery*⟩
**4** : collection : aggregate ⟨fin*ery*⟩
**5** : state or condition ⟨slav*ery*⟩
**eryn·go** \i-'riŋ-(,)gō\ *noun, plural* **-goes** *or* **-gos** [modification of Latin *eryngion* sea holly, from Greek *ēryngion*] (1543)
**1** : any of various plants (genus *Eryngium*) of the carrot family that have elongate spinulose-margined leaves and flowers in dense bracted heads
**2** *obsolete* : candied root of the sea holly made to be used as an aphrodisiac
**ery·sip·e·las** \,er-ə-'si-p(ə-)ləs, ,ir-\ *noun* [Middle English *erisipila*, from Latin *erysipelas*, from Greek, from *erysi-* (probably akin to Greek *erythros* red) + *-pelas* (probably akin to Latin *pellis* skin) — more at RED, FELL] (14th century)
: an acute febrile disease associated with intense edematous local inflammation of the skin and subcutaneous tissues caused by a hemolytic streptococcus
**er·y·the·ma** \,er-ə-'thē-mə\ *noun* [New Latin, from Greek *erythēma*, from *erythainein* to redden, from *erythros*] (circa 1783)
: abnormal redness of the skin due to capillary congestion
— **er·y·them·a·tous** \-'the-mə-təs\ *adjective*
**er·y·thor·bate** \,er-ə-'thor-,bāt\ *noun* (1963)
: a salt of erythorbic acid that is used in foods as an antioxidant
**er·y·thor·bic acid** \-,thor-bik-\ *noun* [*erythr-* + *ascorbic acid*] (1963)
: a diastereoisomer of ascorbic acid with optical activity
**erythr-** *or* **erythro-** *combining form* [Greek, from *erythros* — more at RED]
**1** : red ⟨*erythro*cyte⟩
**2** : erythrocyte ⟨*erythro*id⟩
**er·y·thre·mia** \,er-ə-'thrē-mē-ə\ *noun* [New Latin] (1908)
: POLYCYTHEMIA VERA
**er·y·thrism** \'er-ə-,thri-zəm\ *noun* (1864)
: a condition marked by exceptional prevalence of red pigmentation (as in skin or hair)
— **er·y·thris·tic** \,er-ə-'thris-tik\ *also* **er·y·thris·mal** \-'thriz-məl\ *adjective*
**er·y·thrite** \'er-ə-,thrīt\ *noun* (1844)
: a usually rose-colored mineral consisting of a hydrous cobalt arsenate occurring especially in monoclinic crystals
**eryth·ro·blast** \i-'rith-rə-,blast\ *noun* [International Scientific Vocabulary] (circa 1890)
: a polychromatic nucleated cell of red marrow that synthesizes hemoglobin and that is an intermediate in the initial stage of red blood cell formation; *broadly* : a cell ancestral to red blood cells
— **eryth·ro·blas·tic** \-,rith-rə-'blas-tik\ *adjective*
**eryth·ro·blas·to·sis** \i-,rith-rə-,blas-'tō-səs\ *noun, plural* **-to·ses** \-,sēz\ [New Latin] (circa 1923)
: abnormal presence of erythroblasts in the circulating blood; *especially* : ERYTHROBLASTOSIS FETALIS

**erythroblastosis fe·ta·lis** \-fi-'ta-ləs\ *noun* [New Latin, fetal erythroblastosis] (circa 1934)
: a hemolytic disease of the fetus and newborn that occurs when the system of an Rh-negative mother produces antibodies to an antigen in the blood of an Rh-positive fetus which cross the placenta and destroy fetal erythrocytes and that is characterized by an increase in circulating erythroblasts and by jaundice
**eryth·ro·cyte** \i-'rith-rə-,sīt\ *noun* [International Scientific Vocabulary] (circa 1894)
: RED BLOOD CELL
— **eryth·ro·cyt·ic** \-,rith-rə-'si-tik\ *adjective*
**ery·throid** \i-'rith-,roid, 'er-ə-,throid\ *adjective* (1927)
: relating to erythrocytes or their precursors
**eryth·ro·my·cin** \i-,rith-rə-'mī-s°n\ *noun* (1952)
: a broad-spectrum antibiotic $C_{37}H_{67}NO_{13}$ produced by an actinomycete (*Streptomyces erythreus*)
**eryth·ro·poi·e·sis** \i-,rith-rō-,pói-'ē-səs\ *noun* [New Latin, from *erythr-* + Greek *poiēsis* creation — more at POESY] (1918)
: the production of red blood cells (as from the bone marrow)
— **eryth·ro·poi·et·ic** \-'e-tik\ *adjective*
**eryth·ro·poi·e·tin** \-'pói-ə-t°n\ *noun* (1948)
: a hormonal substance that is formed especially in the kidney and stimulates red blood cell formation
**eryth·ro·sin** \i-'rith-rə-sən\ *also* **eryth·ro·sine** \-sən, -,sēn\ *noun* [International Scientific Vocabulary *erythr-* + *eosin*] (circa 1882)
: any of several dyes made from fluorescein that yield reddish shades
**¹-es** \əz, iz *after* s, z, sh, ch; z *after* v *or a vowel*\ *noun plural suffix* [Middle English *-es, -s* — more at ¹-S]
— used to form the plural of most nouns that end in *s* ⟨glass*es*⟩, *z* ⟨fuzz*es*⟩, *sh* ⟨bush*es*⟩, *ch* ⟨peach*es*⟩, or a final *y* that changes to *i* ⟨lad*ies*⟩ and of some nouns ending in *f* that changes to *v* ⟨loav*es*⟩; compare ¹-S
**²-es** *verb suffix* [Middle English — more at ³-S]
— used to form the third person singular present of most verbs that end in *s* ⟨bless*es*⟩, *z* ⟨fizz*es*⟩, *sh* ⟨hush*es*⟩, *ch* ⟨catch*es*⟩, or a final *y* that changes to *i* ⟨defi*es*⟩; compare ³-S
**Esau** \'ē-(,)sò\ *noun* [Latin, from Greek *Esau*, from Hebrew *'Ēsāw*]
: the elder son of Isaac and Rebekah who sold his birthright to his twin brother Jacob
**es·ca·drille** \'es-kə-,dril, -,drē\ *noun* [French, flotilla, escadrille, from Spanish *escuadrilla*, diminutive of *escuadra* squadron, squad — more at SQUAD] (1912)
: a unit of a European air command containing usually six airplanes
**es·ca·lade** \'es-kə-,lād, -,läd\ *noun* [French, from Italian *scalata*, from *scalare* to scale, from *scala* ladder, from Late Latin — more at SCALE] (1598)
: an act of scaling especially the walls of a fortification
— **escalade** *transitive verb*
— **es·ca·lad·er** *noun*
**es·ca·late** \'es-kə-,lāt, ÷-kyə-\ *verb* **-lat·ed; -lat·ing** [back-formation from *escalator*] (1944)
*intransitive verb*
: to increase in extent, volume, number, amount, intensity, or scope ⟨a little war threatens to *escalate* into a huge ugly one —Arnold Abrams⟩
*transitive verb*
: EXPAND 2
— **es·ca·la·tion** \,es-kə-'lā-shən, ÷-kyə-\ *noun*
— **es·ca·la·to·ry** \'es-kə-lə-,tōr-ē, -,tòr-, ÷-kyə-\ *adjective*
**¹es·ca·la·tor** \'es-kə-,lā-tər, ÷-kyə-\ *noun* [from *Escalator*, a trademark] (1900)

**1 a** : a power-driven set of stairs arranged like an endless belt that ascend or descend continuously **b** : an upward course suggestive of an escalator ⟨a never-stopping *escalator* of economic progress —D. W. Brogan⟩
**2** : an escalator clause or provision
**²escalator** *adjective* (1930)
: providing for a periodic proportional upward or downward adjustment (as of prices or wages) ⟨an *escalator* arrangement tying the base pay . . . to living costs —*N. Y. Times*⟩
**es·cal·lop** \is-'kä-ləp, -'ka-\ *variant of* SCALLOP
**es·ca·pade** \'es-kə-,pād\ *noun* [French, action of escaping, from Spanish *escapada*, from *escapar* to escape, from (assumed) Vulgar Latin *excappare*] (1672)
: a usually adventurous action that runs counter to approved or conventional conduct
**¹es·cape** \is-'kāp, es-, *dialect* iks-'kāp\ *verb* **es·caped; es·cap·ing** [Middle English, from Old North French *escaper*, from (assumed) Vulgar Latin *excappare*, from Latin *ex-* + Late Latin *cappa* head covering, cloak] (13th century)
*intransitive verb*
**1 a** : to get away (as by flight) ⟨*escaped* from prison⟩ **b** : to issue from confinement ⟨gas is *escaping*⟩ **c** *of a plant* : to run wild from cultivation
**2** : to avoid a threatening evil
*transitive verb*
**1** : to get free of : break away from ⟨*escape* the jungle⟩ ⟨*escape* the solar system⟩
**2** : to get or stay out of the way of : AVOID
**3** : to fail to be noticed or recallable by ⟨his name *escapes* me⟩
**4 a** : to issue from **b** : to be uttered involuntarily by ☆
— **es·cap·er** *noun*
**²escape** *noun* (14th century)
**1** : an act or instance of escaping: as **a** : flight from confinement **b** : evasion of something undesirable **c** : leakage or outflow especially of a fluid **d** : distraction or relief from routine or reality
**2** : a means of escape
**3** : a cultivated plant run wild
**³escape** *adjective* (1817)
**1** : providing a means of escape ⟨*escape* literature⟩
**2** : providing a means of evading a regulation, claim, or commitment ⟨an *escape* clause in a contract⟩
**escape artist** *noun* (1943)
: one (as a performer or criminal) unusually adept at escaping from confinement
**es·cap·ee** \is-,kā-'pē, ,es-(,)kā-, ,es-kə-\ *noun* (circa 1866)
: one that has escaped; *especially* : an escaped prisoner

---

☆ **SYNONYMS**
**Escape, avoid, evade, elude, shun, eschew** mean to get away or keep away from something. ESCAPE stresses the fact of getting away or being passed by not necessarily through effort or by conscious intent ⟨nothing *escapes* her sharp eyes⟩. AVOID stresses forethought and caution in keeping clear of danger or difficulty ⟨try to *avoid* past errors⟩. EVADE implies adroitness, ingenuity, or lack of scruple in escaping or avoiding ⟨*evaded* the question by changing the subject⟩. ELUDE implies a slippery or baffling quality in the person or thing that escapes ⟨what she sees in him *eludes* me⟩. SHUN often implies an avoiding as a matter of habitual practice or policy and may imply repugnance or abhorrence ⟨you have *shunned* your responsibilities⟩. ESCHEW implies an avoiding or abstaining from as unwise or distasteful ⟨a playwright who *eschews* melodrama⟩.

**escape hatch** *noun* (1925)
**1 :** a hatch providing an emergency exit from an enclosed space
**2 :** a means of evading a difficulty, dilemma, or responsibility
**escape mechanism** *noun* (1927)
**:** a mode of behavior or thinking adopted to evade unpleasant facts or responsibilities
**es·cape·ment** \is-'kāp-mənt\ *noun* (1779)
**1 a :** a device in a timepiece which controls the motion of the train of wheelwork and through which the energy of the power source is delivered to the pendulum or balance by means of impulses that permit a tooth to escape from a pallet at regular intervals **b :** a ratchet device (as the spacing mechanism of a typewriter) that permits motion in one direction only in equal steps

escapement 1a

**2 a :** the act of escaping **b :** a way of escape
**:** VENT
**escape velocity** *noun* (1934)
**:** the minimum velocity that a moving body (as a rocket) must have to escape from the gravitational field of a celestial body (as the earth) and move outward into space
**es·cap·ism** \is-'kā-ˌpi-zəm\ *noun* (1933)
**:** habitual diversion of the mind to purely imaginative activity or entertainment as an escape from reality or routine
  — **es·cap·ist** \-pist\ *adjective or noun*
**es·cap·ol·o·gy** \is-ˌkā-'pä-lə-jē, ˌes-(ˌ)\ *noun* (1939)
**:** the art or practice of escaping
  — **es·cap·ol·o·gist** \-jist\ *noun*
**es·car·got** \ˌes-ˌkär-'gō\ *noun, plural* **-gots** \-'gō(z)\ [French, snail, from Middle French, from Old Provençal *escaragol*] (circa 1892)
**:** a snail prepared for use as food
**es·ca·role** \'es-kə-ˌrōl\ *noun* [French, from Late Latin *escariola*, from Latin *escarius* of food, from *esca* food, from *edere* to eat — more at EAT] (1897)
**:** ENDIVE 1
**es·carp·ment** \i-'skärp-mənt\ *noun* [French *escarpement*, from *escarper* to scarp, from Middle French, from *escarpe* scarp, from Old Italian *scarpa* — more at SCARP] (circa 1802)
**1 :** a steep slope in front of a fortification
**2 :** a long cliff or steep slope separating two comparatively level or more gently sloping surfaces and resulting from erosion or faulting
**-es·cence** \'e-sᵊn(t)s\ *noun suffix* [Middle French, from Latin *-escentia*, from *-escent-, -escens* + *-ia* -y]
**:** state or process of becoming ⟨obsol*escence*⟩
**-es·cent** \'e-sᵊnt\ *adjective suffix* [Middle French, from Latin *-escent-, -escens,* present participle suffix of inchoative verbs in *-escere*]
**1 :** beginning **:** beginning to be **:** slightly ⟨frut*escent*⟩
**2 :** reflecting or emitting light (in a specified way) ⟨opal*escent*⟩
**es·char** \'es-ˌkär\ *noun* [Middle English *escare* — more at SCAR] (1543)
**:** a scab formed especially after a burn
**es·cha·rot·ic** \ˌes-kə-'rä-tik\ *adjective* [French or Late Latin; French *escharotique,* from Late Latin *escharoticus,* from Greek *escharōtikos,* from *escharoun* to form an eschar, from *eschara* eschar] (1612)
**:** producing an eschar
  — **escharotic** *noun*
**es·cha·to·log·i·cal** \(ˌ)es-ˌka-tᵊl-'ä-ji-kəl, ˌes-kə-\ *adjective* (1854)
**1 :** of or relating to eschatology or an eschatology
**2 :** of or relating to the end of the world or the events associated with it in eschatology
  — **es·cha·to·log·i·cal·ly** \-ji-k(ə-)lē\ *adverb*
**es·cha·tol·o·gy** \ˌes-kə-'tä-lə-jē\ *noun, plural* **-gies** [Greek *eschatos* last, farthest] (1844)

**1 :** a branch of theology concerned with the final events in the history of the world or of mankind
**2 :** a belief concerning death, the end of the world, or the ultimate destiny of mankind; *specifically* **:** any of various Christian doctrines concerning the Second Coming, the resurrection of the dead, or the Last Judgment
**¹es·cheat** \is-'chēt, ish-'chēt\ *noun* [Middle English *eschete,* from Old French, reversion of property, from *escheoir* to fall, devolve, from (assumed) Vulgar Latin *excadēre,* from Latin *ex-* + (assumed) Vulgar Latin *cadēre* to fall, from Latin *cadere* — more at CHANCE] (14th century)
**1 :** escheated property
**2 a :** the reversion of lands in English feudal law to the lord of the fee when there are no heirs capable of inheriting under the original grant **b :** the reversion of property to the crown in England or to the state in the U.S. when there are no legal heirs
**²escheat** (14th century)
*transitive verb*
**:** to cause to revert by escheat
*intransitive verb*
**:** to revert by escheat
  — **es·cheat·able** \-'chē-tə-bəl\ *adjective*
**es·chew** \e-'shü, i-; es-'chü, is-; *also* e-'skyü\ *transitive verb* [Middle English, from Middle French *eschiuver,* of Germanic origin; akin to Old High German *sciuhen* to frighten off — more at SHY] (14th century)
**:** to avoid habitually especially on moral or practical grounds **:** SHUN
**synonym** see ESCAPE
  — **es·chew·al** \-əl\ *noun*
**es·co·lar** \ˌes-kə-'lär\ *noun, plural* **escolar** *or* **escolars** [Spanish, literally, scholar, from Medieval Latin *scholaris* — more at SCHOLAR] (circa 1890)
**:** a large widely distributed rough-scaled fish (*Lepidocybium flavobrunneum*) that resembles a mackerel
**¹es·cort** \'es-ˌkȯrt\ *noun* [French *escorte,* from Italian *scorta,* from *scorgere* to guide, from (assumed) Vulgar Latin *excorrigere,* from Latin *ex-* + *corrigere* to make straight, correct — more at CORRECT] (1745)
**1 a (1) :** a person or group of persons accompanying another to give protection or as a courtesy **(2) :** the man who goes on a date with a woman **b :** a protective screen of warships or fighter planes or a single ship or plane used to fend off enemy attack from one or more vulnerable craft
**2 :** accompaniment by a person or an armed protector (as a ship)
**²es·cort** \is-'kȯrt, es-, 'es-ˌ\ *transitive verb* (1708)
**:** to accompany as an escort
**es·cot** \is-'kät\ *transitive verb* [Middle French *escoter,* from *escot* contribution, of Germanic origin; akin to Old Norse *skot* contribution, shot — more at SHOT] (1602)
*obsolete* **:** SUPPORT, MAINTAIN
**es·cri·toire** \'es-krə-ˌtwär\ *noun* [obsolete French, writing desk, scriptorium, from Medieval Latin *scriptorium*] (1694)
**:** a writing table or desk; *specifically* **:** SECRETARY 4b
**¹es·crow** \'es-ˌkrō, es-'\ *noun* [Middle French *escroue* scroll — more at SCROLL] (1594)
**1 :** a deed, a bond, money, or a piece of property held in trust by a third party to be turned over to the grantee only upon fulfillment of a condition
**2 :** a fund or deposit designed to serve as an escrow
  — **in escrow :** in trust as an escrow ⟨had $1000 *in escrow* to pay taxes⟩
**²es·crow** \es-'krō, 'es-ˌ\ *transitive verb* (1949)
**:** to place in escrow
**es·cu·do** \is-'kü-(ˌ)dō\ *noun, plural* **-dos** [Spanish & Portuguese, literally, shield, from Latin *scutum*] (circa 1821)

**1 :** any of various former gold or silver coins of Hispanic countries
**2 —** see MONEY table
**3 :** the basic monetary unit of Chile between 1960 and 1975
**4 :** the peso of Guinea-Bissau
**es·cu·lent** \'es-kyə-lənt\ *adjective* [Latin *esculentus,* from *esca* food, from *edere* to eat — more at EAT] (1626)
**:** EDIBLE
  — **esculent** *noun*
**es·cutch·eon** \is-'kə-chən\ *noun* [Middle English *escochon,* from Middle French *escuchon,* from (assumed) Vulgar Latin *scution-, scutio,* from Latin *scutum* shield — more at ESQUIRE] (15th century)
**1 :** a defined area on which armorial bearings are displayed and which usually consists of a shield
**2 :** a protective or ornamental plate or flange (as around a keyhole)
**3 :** the part of a ship's stern on which the name is displayed
**Es·dras** \'ez-drəs\ *noun* [Late Latin, from Greek, from Hebrew *'Ezrā*]
**1 :** either of two books of the Roman Catholic canon of the Old Testament: **a :** EZRA 2 **b :** NEHEMIAH 2
**2 :** either of two uncanonical books of Scripture included in the Protestant Apocrypha — see BIBLE table
**¹-ese** \'ēz, 'ēs\ *adjective suffix* [Portuguese *-ês* & Italian *-ese,* from Latin *-ensis*]
**:** of, relating to, or originating in (a certain place or country) ⟨Japan*ese*⟩
**²-ese** *noun suffix, plural* **-ese**
**1 :** native or resident of (a specified place or country) ⟨Chin*ese*⟩
**2 a :** language of (a particular place, country, or nationality) ⟨Siam*ese*⟩ **b :** speech, literary style, or diction peculiar to (a specified place, person, or group) — usually in words applied in depreciation ⟨journal*ese*⟩
**es·em·plas·tic** \ˌe-ˌsem-'plas-tik, -səm-\ *adjective* [Greek *es hen* into one + English *plastic*] (1817)
**:** shaping or having the power to shape disparate things into a unified whole ⟨the *esemplastic* power of the poetic imagination —W. H. Gardner⟩
**es·er·ine** \'e-sə-ˌrēn\ *noun* [French *ésérine*] (1879)
**:** PHYSOSTIGMINE
**es·ker** \'es-kər\ *noun* [Irish *eiscir* ridge] (1848)
**:** a long narrow ridge or mound of sand, gravel, and boulders deposited by a stream flowing on, within, or beneath a stagnant glacier
**Es·ki·mo** \'es-kə-ˌmō\ *noun* [obsolete *Esquimawe,* probably from Spanish *esquimao,* from Montagnais (Algonquian language of eastern Canada) *aiachkime8* Micmac, Eskimo; probably akin to modern Montagnais *assime'w* she laces a snowshoe, Ojibwa *aškime'*] (1584)
**1** *plural* **Eskimo** *or* **Eskimos :** a member of a group of peoples of northern Canada, Greenland, Alaska, and eastern Siberia
**2 :** any of the languages of the Eskimo peoples
  — **Es·ki·mo·an** \ˌes-kə-'mō-ən\ *adjective*
**Eskimo curlew** *noun* (1813)
**:** an extremely rare New World curlew (*Numenius borealis*) that breeds in northern North America and winters in South America

Eskimo curlew

**Eskimo dog** *noun* (1774)
: a sled dog of American origin

**ESOP** \ē-,es-(,)ō-'pē, 'ē-,säp\ *noun* [employee *s*tock *o*wnership *p*lan] (1975)
: a program by which a corporation's employees acquire its capital stock

**esoph·a·gus** \i-'sä-fə-gəs\ *noun, plural* **-gi** \-,gī, -,jī\ [Middle English *ysophagus,* from Greek *oisophagos,* from *oisein* to be going to carry + *phagein* to eat — more at BAKSHEESH] (14th century)
: a muscular tube that in humans is about nine inches long and passes from the pharynx down the neck between the trachea and the spinal column and behind the left bronchus where it pierces the diaphragm slightly to the left of the middle line and joins the cardiac end of the stomach
— **esoph·a·ge·al** \i-,sä-fə-'jē-əl\ *adjective*

**es·o·ter·ic** \,e-sə-'ter-ik\ *adjective* [Late Latin *esotericus,* from Greek *esōterikos,* from *esōterō,* comparative of *eisō, esō* within, from *eis* into; akin to Greek *en* in — more at IN] (circa 1660)
**1 a :** designed for or understood by the specially initiated alone ⟨a body of *esoteric* legal doctrine —B. N. Cardozo⟩ **b :** of or relating to knowledge that is restricted to a small group
**2 a :** limited to a small circle ⟨*esoteric* pursuits⟩ **b :** PRIVATE, CONFIDENTIAL ⟨an *esoteric* purpose⟩
— **es·o·ter·i·cal·ly** \-i-k(ə-)lē\ *adverb*

**es·o·ter·i·ca** \-i-kə\ *noun plural* [New Latin, from Greek *esōterika,* neuter plural of *esōterikos*] (circa 1929)
: esoteric items

**es·o·ter·i·cism** \-'ter-ə-,si-zəm\ *noun* (1846)
**1 :** esoteric doctrines or practices
**2 :** the quality or state of being esoteric

**ESP** \,ē-,es-'pē\ *noun* [*e*xtra*s*ensory *p*erception] (1934)
: EXTRASENSORY PERCEPTION

**es·pa·drille** \'es-pə-,dril\ *noun* [French, alteration of *espardille,* ultimately from Latin *spartum*] (1892)
: a sandal usually having a fabric upper and a flexible sole

**¹es·pal·ier** \is-'pal-yər, -,yā\ *noun* [French, ultimately from Italian *spalla* shoulder, from Late Latin *spatula* shoulder blade — more at EPAULET] (1662)
**1 :** a plant (as a fruit tree) trained to grow flat against a support (as a wall)
**2 :** a railing or trellis on which fruit trees or shrubs are trained to grow flat

**²espalier** *transitive verb* (1810)
**1 :** to train as an espalier
**2 :** to furnish with an espalier

**es·par·to** \is-'pär-(,)tō\ *noun, plural* **-tos** [Spanish, from Latin *spartum,* from Greek *sparton* — more at SPIRE] (1845)
**1 :** either of two Spanish and Algerian grasses (*Stipa tenacissima* and *Lygeum spartum*) used especially to make cordage, shoes, and paper — called also *esparto grass*
**2 :** the fiber of esparto

**es·pe·cial** \is-'pe-shəl\ *adjective* [Middle English, from Middle French — more at SPECIAL] (14th century)
: being distinctive: as **a :** directed toward a particular individual, group, or end ⟨sent *especial* greetings to his son⟩ ⟨took *especial* care to speak clearly⟩ **b :** of special note or importance : unusually great or significant ⟨a decision of *especial* relevance⟩ **c :** highly distinctive or personal : PECULIAR ⟨had an *especial* dislike for music⟩ **d :** CLOSE, INTIMATE ⟨his *especial* crony⟩ **e :** SPECIFIC, PARTICULAR ⟨had no *especial* destination in mind⟩
**synonym** see SPECIAL
— **in especial :** in particular

**es·pe·cial·ly** \is-'pesh-lē, -'pe-shə-\ *adverb* (15th century)
**1 :** SPECIALLY 1

**2 a :** in particular : PARTICULARLY ⟨food seems cheaper, *especially* meats⟩ **b :** for a particular purpose ⟨built *especially* for research⟩
**3 —** used as an intensive ⟨an *especially* good essay⟩ ⟨nothing *especially* radical in the remarks⟩

**es·per·ance** \'es-p(ə-)rən(t)s\ *noun* [Middle English *esperaunce,* from Middle French *esperance*] (15th century)
*obsolete :* HOPE, EXPECTATION

**Es·pe·ran·to** \,es-pə-'rän-(,)tō, -'ran-(,)tō\ *noun* [Dr. *Esperanto,* pseudonym of L. L. Zamenhof (died 1917) Polish oculist, its inventor] (1892)
: an artificial international language based as far as possible on words common to the chief European languages
— **Es·pe·ran·tist** \-'rän-tist, -'ran-\ *noun or adjective*

**es·pi·al** \is-'pī(-ə)l\ *noun* (14th century)
**1 :** OBSERVATION
**2 :** an act of noticing : DISCOVERY

**es·piè·gle** \es-pyegl^\ *adjective* [French, after *Ulespiegle* (Till Eulenspiegel), peasant prankster] (1816)
: FROLICSOME, ROGUISH

**es·piè·gle·rie** \es-pyeg-lə-rē\ *noun* [French, from *espiègle*] (1816)
: the quality or state of being roguish or frolicsome

**es·pi·o·nage** \'es-pē-ə-,näzh, -,näj, -nij, *Canadian also* -,nazh; ,es-pē-ə-'näzh; is-'pē-ə-nij\ *noun* [French *espionnage,* from Middle French *espionner* to spy, from *espion* spy, from Old Italian *spione,* from *spia,* of Germanic origin; akin to Old High German *spehōn* to spy — more at SPY] (1793)
: the practice of spying or using spies to obtain information about the plans and activities especially of a foreign government or a competing company ⟨industrial *espionage*⟩

**es·pla·nade** \'es-plə-,näd, ,es-plə-' *also* -'näd *or* -,näd\ *noun* [Middle French, from Italian *spianata,* from *spianare* to level, from Latin *explanare* — more at EXPLAIN] (1591)
: a level open stretch of paved or grassy ground; *especially :* one designed for walking or driving along a shore

**es·pous·al** \is-'pau̇-zəl *also* -səl\ *noun* (14th century)
**1 a :** BETROTHAL **b :** WEDDING **c :** MARRIAGE
**2 :** a taking up or adopting of a cause or belief

**es·pouse** \is-'pau̇z *also* -'pau̇s\ *transitive verb*
**es·poused; es·pous·ing** [Middle English, from Middle French *espouser,* from Late Latin *sponsare* to betroth, from Latin *sponsus* betrothed — more at SPOUSE] (15th century)
**1 :** MARRY
**2 :** to take up and support as a cause : become attached to
**synonym** see ADOPT
— **es·pous·er** *noun*

**es·pres·so** \e-'spre-(,)sō\ *noun, plural* **-sos** [Italian (*caffè*) espresso, literally, pressed out coffee] (1945)
**1 :** coffee brewed by forcing steam through finely ground darkly roasted coffee beans
**2 :** a cup of espresso

**es·prit** \is-'prē\ *noun* [French, from Latin *spiritus* spirit] (1591)
**1 :** vivacious cleverness or wit
**2 :** ESPRIT DE CORPS

**es·prit de corps** \is-,prē-də-'kȯr, -'kȯr\ *noun* [French] (1780)
: the common spirit existing in the members of a group and inspiring enthusiasm, devotion, and strong regard for the honor of the group

**es·py** \is-'pī\ *transitive verb* **es·pied; es·py·ing** [Middle English *espien,* from Old French *espier* — more at SPY] (14th century)
: to catch sight of ⟨among the several horses . . . she *espied* the white mustang —Zane Grey⟩

**-esque** \'esk\ *adjective suffix* [French, from Italian *-esco,* of Germanic origin; akin to Old High German *-isc* -ish — more at -ISH]

: in the manner or style of : like ⟨statu*esque*⟩

**Es·qui·mau** \'es-kə-,mō\ *noun, plural* **Esquimau** *or* **Es·qui·maux** \-,mō(z)\ [French, from Montagnais (Algonquian language)] (1744)
: ESKIMO

**es·quire** \'es-,kwīr, is-'\ *noun* [Middle English, from Middle French *escuier* squire, from Late Latin *scutarius,* from Latin *scutum* shield; akin to Old Irish *sciath* shield] (15th century)
**1 :** a member of the English gentry ranking below a knight
**2 :** a candidate for knighthood serving as shield bearer and attendant to a knight
**3 —** used as a title of courtesy usually placed in its abbreviated form after the surname ⟨John R. Smith, *Esq.*⟩
**4** *archaic :* a landed proprietor ◆

**ess** \'es\ *noun* (1540)
**1 :** the letter *s*
**2 :** something resembling the letter *S* in shape; *especially :* an S-shaped curve in a road

**-ess** \əs, is *also* ,es\ *noun suffix* [Middle English *-esse,* from Old French, from Late Latin *-issa,* from Greek]
: female ⟨giant*ess*⟩ □

**¹es·say** \e-'sā, ə-'sā, 'e-,sā\ *transitive verb* (14th century)
**1 :** to put to a test
**2 :** to make an often tentative or experimental effort to perform : TRY
**synonym** see ATTEMPT
— **es·say·er** *noun*

**²es·say** \'e-,sā; *senses 1, 2 & 4 also* e-'sā\ *noun* [Middle English, from Middle French *essai,* ultimately from Late Latin *exagium* act of weighing, from *ex-* + *agere* to drive — more at AGENT] (14th century)
**1 :** TRIAL, TEST
**2 a :** EFFORT, ATTEMPT; *especially :* an initial tentative effort **b :** the result or product of an attempt
**3 a :** an analytic or interpretative literary composition usually dealing with its subject from a limited or personal point of view **b :** something resembling such a composition ⟨a photographic *essay*⟩
**4 :** a proof of an unaccepted design for a stamp or piece of paper money

**es·say·ist** \'e-,sā-ist\ *noun* (1601)
: a writer of essays

**es·say·is·tic** \,e-(,)sā-'is-tik\ *adjective* (1862)
**1 :** of or relating to an essay or an essayist
**2 :** resembling an essay in quality or character

**essay question** *noun* (1947)

---

◇ WORD HISTORY

**esquire** The word *esquire* in its oldest senses, "young candidate for knighthood" and "member of the English gentry ranking below a knight in social precedence," has been less common than the shortened form *squire* since Middle English. It is only as an abbreviated title placed after a person's name that *esquire* maintains a curious sort of afterlife in English, even in the United States, where there have never been knights or gentry. This peculiar usage came about because the technical stipulations for members of the gentry who could be styled *esquire,* as established by 17th century lawyers and antiquaries, were so complex and so loosely observed that the title became practically equivalent to "gentleman." (The title *knight* never became similarly nebulous because since the 16th century knighthood has been an honor specifically bestowed on individuals by the British sovereign, and not hereditary.) In America, *esquire* is less common than in Britain, persisting mainly among attorneys, who use it, chiefly in the form of its abbreviation *Esq.,* when referring to or addressing each other in writing.

**:** an examination question that requires an answer in a sentence, paragraph, or short composition

**es·sence** \'e-s°n(t)s\ *noun* [Middle English, from Middle French & Latin; Middle French, from Latin *essentia,* from *esse* to be — more at IS] (14th century)
**1 a :** the permanent as contrasted with the accidental element of being **b :** the individual, real, or ultimate nature of a thing especially as opposed to its existence **c :** the properties or attributes by means of which something can be placed in its proper class or identified as being what it is
**2 :** something that exists **:** ENTITY
**3 a** (1) **:** a volatile substance or constituent (as of perfume) (2) **:** a constituent or derivative possessing the special qualities (as of a plant or drug) in concentrated form; *also* **:** a preparation of such an essence or a synthetic substitute **b :** ODOR, PERFUME
**4 :** one that possesses or exhibits a quality in abundance as if in concentrated form ⟨she was the *essence* of punctuality⟩
**— in essence :** in or by its very nature **:** ESSENTIALLY, BASICALLY ⟨was *in essence* an honest person⟩
**— of the essence :** of the utmost importance ⟨time is *of the essence*⟩

**Es·sene** \i-'sēn, 'e-,sēn\ *noun* [Greek *Essēnos*] (1553)
**:** a member of a monastic brotherhood of Jews in Palestine from the 2d century B.C. to the 2d century A.D.
**— Es·se·ni·an** \i-'sē-nē-ən, e-'se-\ *or* **Es·se·nic** \-'se-nik, -'sē-nik\ *adjective*
**— Es·se·nism** \-'sē-,ni-zəm\ *noun*

**¹es·sen·tial** \i-'sen(t)-shəl\ *adjective* (14th century)
**1 :** of, relating to, or constituting essence **:** INHERENT
**2 :** of the utmost importance **:** BASIC, INDISPENSABLE, NECESSARY ⟨*essential* foods⟩ ⟨an *essential* requirement for admission to college⟩
**3 :** IDIOPATHIC ⟨*essential* disease⟩ ☆
**— es·sen·tial·ly** \-'sench-lē, -'sen-chə-\ *adverb*
**— es·sen·tial·ness** \-'sen-chəl-nəs\ *noun*

**²essential** *noun* (15th century)
**1 :** something basic ⟨the *essentials* of astronomy⟩
**2 :** something necessary, indispensable, or unavoidable

**essential amino acid** *noun* (1935)
**:** an amino acid (as lysine) required for normal health and growth, manufactured in the body in insufficient quantities or not at all, and usually supplied by dietary protein

**es·sen·tial·ism** \-,li-zəm\ *noun* (1927)
**1 :** an educational theory that ideas and skills basic to a culture should be taught to all alike by time-tested methods — compare PROGRESSIVISM
**2 :** a philosophical theory ascribing ultimate reality to essence embodied in a thing perceptible to the senses — compare NOMINALISM
**— es·sen·tial·ist** \-list\ *adjective or noun*

**es·sen·ti·al·i·ty** \i-,sen(t)-shē-'a-lə-tē\ *noun,* *plural* **-ties** (1616)
**1 a :** essential nature **:** ESSENCE **b :** an essential quality, property, or aspect
**2 :** the quality or state of being essential ⟨the *essentiality* of freedom and justice —P. G. Hoffman⟩

**es·sen·tial·ize** \i-'sen(t)-shə-,līz\ *transitive verb* **-ized; -iz·ing** (1913)
**:** to express or formulate in essential form **:** reduce to essentials

**essential oil** *noun* (1674)
**:** any of a class of volatile oils that give plants their characteristic odors and are used especially in perfumes and flavorings — compare FIXED OIL

**es·soin** \i-'sȯin\ *noun* [Middle English *essoine,* from Middle French, from Old French, from *essoinier* to offer an essoin, from *es-* ex-

+ *soine* legal excuse, of Germanic origin; akin to Old Saxon *sunnea* denial, Old English *sōth* truth — more at SOOTH] (14th century)
**1 :** an excuse for not appearing in an English law court at the appointed time
**2** *obsolete* **:** EXCUSE, DELAY

**es·so·nite** \'e-s°n-,īt\ *noun* [French, from Greek *hēsson* inferior; from its being less hard than true hyacinth] (1820)
**:** a yellow to brown garnet

**¹-est** \əst, ist\ *adjective suffix or adverb suffix* [Middle English, from Old English *-st, -est, -ost;* akin to Old High German *-isto* (adjective superlative suffix), Greek *-istos*]
— used to form the superlative degree of adjectives and adverbs of one syllable ⟨fatt*est*⟩ ⟨lat*est*⟩, of some adjectives and adverbs of two syllables ⟨lucki*est*⟩ ⟨often*est*⟩, and less often of longer ones ⟨beggarli*est*⟩

**²-est** \əst, ist\ *or* **-st** \st\ *verb suffix* [Middle English, from Old English *-est, -ast, -st;* akin to Old High German *-ist, -ōst, -ēst,* 2d singular ending]
— used to form the archaic 2d person singular of English verbs (with *thou*) ⟨did*st*⟩

**es·tab·lish** \is-'ta-blish\ *transitive verb* [Middle English *establissen,* from Middle French *establiss-,* stem of *establir,* from Latin *stabilire,* from *stabilis* stable] (14th century)
**1 :** to institute (as a law) permanently by enactment or agreement
**2** *obsolete* **:** SETTLE 7
**3 a :** to make firm or stable **b :** to introduce and cause to grow and multiply ⟨*establish* grass on pasturelands⟩
**4 a :** to bring into existence **:** FOUND ⟨*established* a republic⟩ **b :** BRING ABOUT, EFFECT ⟨*established* friendly relations⟩
**5 a :** to put on a firm basis **:** SET UP ⟨*establish* his son in business⟩ **b :** to put into a favorable position **c :** to gain full recognition or acceptance of ⟨the role *established* her as a star⟩
**6 :** to make (a church) a national or state institution
**7 :** to put beyond doubt **:** PROVE ⟨*established* my innocence⟩
**— es·tab·lish·able** \-shə-bəl\ *adjective*
**— es·tab·lish·er** \-shər\ *noun*

**established church** *noun* (1731)
**:** a church recognized by law as the official church of a nation or state and supported by civil authority

**es·tab·lish·ment** \is-'ta-blish-mənt\ *noun* (15th century)
**1 :** something established: as **a :** a settled arrangement; *especially* **:** a code of laws **b :** ESTABLISHED CHURCH **c :** a permanent civil or military organization **d :** a place of business or residence with its furnishings and staff **e :** a public or private institution
**2 :** an established order of society: as **a** *often capitalized* **:** a group of social, economic, and political leaders who form a ruling class (as of a nation) **b** *often capitalized* **:** a controlling group ⟨the literary *establishment*⟩
**3 a :** the act of establishing **b :** the state of being established

**es·tab·lish·men·tar·i·an** \is-,ta-blish-mən-'ter-ē-ən, -,men-\ *adjective* (1847)
**:** of, relating to, or favoring the social or political establishment
**— establishmentarian** *noun*
**— es·tab·lish·men·tar·i·an·ism** \-ē-ə-,ni-zəm\ *noun*

**es·ta·mi·net** \e-stá-mē-nā\ *noun,* *plural* **-nets** \-nā(z)\ [French] (1814)
**:** a small café

**es·tate** \is-'tāt\ *noun* [Middle English *estat,* from Old French — more at STATE] (13th century)
**1 :** STATE, CONDITION
**2 :** social standing or rank especially of a high order
**3 :** a social or political class; *specifically* **:** one of the great classes (as the nobility, the clergy,

and the commons) formerly vested with distinct political powers
**4 a :** the degree, quality, nature, and extent of one's interest in land or other property **b** (1) **:** POSSESSIONS, PROPERTY; *especially* **:** a person's property in land and tenements ⟨a man of small *estate*⟩ (2) **:** the assets and liabilities left by a person at death **c :** a landed property usually with a large house on it **d** *British* **:** PROJECT 4
**5** *British* **:** STATION WAGON

**estate agent** *noun* (1880)
*British* **:** a real estate broker or manager

**estate car** *noun* (1950)
*British* **:** STATION WAGON

**estate tax** *noun* (1928)
**:** an excise in the form of a percentage of the net estate that is levied on the privilege of an

---

☆ **SYNONYMS**
**Essential, fundamental, vital, cardinal** mean so important as to be indispensable. ESSENTIAL implies belonging to the very nature of a thing and therefore being incapable of removal without destroying the thing itself or its character ⟨conflict is *essential* in drama⟩. FUNDAMENTAL applies to something that is a foundation without which an entire system or complex whole would collapse ⟨*fundamental* principles of algebra⟩. VITAL suggests something that is necessary to a thing's continued existence or operation ⟨cut off from *vital* supplies⟩. CARDINAL suggests something on which an outcome turns or depends ⟨a *cardinal* rule in buying a home⟩.

---

□ **USAGE**
**-ess** In 1865 Sara Josepha Hale, self-styled editress of *Godey's Lady's Book,* proposed for use a list of more than 50 terms ending in *-ess* that she thought would lend dignity to women and their work. We are not sure if her plea for the use of these words had any effect on late 19th century usage, but the male commentators of that time mostly disapproved the forms. In the 20th century, attitudes have become no more nearly unanimous. A few male commentators have looked on the forms with approval, if not with the evangelistic fervor of Mrs. Hale, but more, both men and women, find them objectionable in some way. Of course some words with this ending, like *lioness* or *duchess* or *goddess,* have never been in dispute. But actual users always have the final say. If *stewardess* is falling into disuse, it is probably due as much to the increased number of male flight attendants as to language attitudes. *Poetess,* which has been dismissed as archaic or disused since the 18th century, is still used, but in historical reference; it does not appear to be applied to contemporary writers. *Mayoress* and *manageress,* which look a bit strange to American eyes, are quite common in British English. *Actress* and *waitress* are still in common use. *Priestess* in its first sense generally refers to ancient or pagan religions; its second sense, "a woman regarded as a leader," is still in common use, often in such phrases as *high priestess of fashion.* These are a few of the *-ess* words that have been commented on. You can assume that any *-ess* word entered in this dictionary is in current acceptable use unless it bears a warning label or usage note.

---

\ə\ abut  \°\ kitten  \ər\ further  \a\ ash  \ā\ ace
\ä\ mop, mar  \au̇\ out  \ch\ chin  \e\ bet  \ē\ easy
\g\ go  \i\ hit  \ī\ ice  \j\ job  \ŋ\ sing  \ō\ go
\ȯ\ law  \ȯi\ boy  \th\ thin  \t͟h\ the  \ü\ loot  \u̇\ foot
\y\ yet  \zh\ vision  *see also* Guide to Pronunciation

owner of property of transmitting the property to others after his or her death — compare INHERITANCE TAX 1

**¹es·teem** \is-'tēm\ *noun* (14th century)
**1** *archaic* : WORTH, VALUE
**2** *archaic* : OPINION, JUDGMENT
**3** : the regard in which one is held; *especially* : high regard ⟨the *esteem* we all feel for her⟩
**²esteem** *transitive verb* [Middle English *estemen* to estimate, from Middle French *estimer*, from Latin *aestimare*] (15th century)
**1** *archaic* : APPRAISE
**2 a** : to view as : CONSIDER ⟨*esteem* it a privilege⟩ **b** : THINK, BELIEVE
**3** : to set a high value on : regard highly and prize accordingly
**synonym** see REGARD
**es·ter** \'es-tər\ *noun* [German, from *Essigäther* ethyl acetate, from *Essig* vinegar + *Äther* ether] (circa 1852)
: any of a class of often fragrant compounds that can be represented by the formula RCOOR' and that are usually formed by the reaction between an acid and an alcohol with elimination of water
**es·ter·ase** \'es-tə-ˌrās, -ˌrāz\ *noun* (1910)
: an enzyme that accelerates the hydrolysis or synthesis of esters
**es·ter·i·fy** \e-'ster-ə-ˌfī\ *transitive verb* **-fied; -fy·ing** (circa 1905)
: to convert into an ester
— **es·ter·i·fi·ca·tion** \-ˌster-ə-fə-'kā-shən\ *noun*
**Es·ther** \'es-tər\ *noun* [Latin, from Hebrew *Estēr*]
**1** : the Jewish heroine of the Old Testament book of Esther
**2** : a narrative book of canonical Jewish and Christian Scripture — see BIBLE table
**es·thete, es·thet·ic, es·the·ti·cian, es·the·ti·cism** *variant of* AESTHETE, AESTHETIC, AESTHETICIAN, AESTHETICISM
**es·ti·ma·ble** \'es-tə-mə-bəl\ *adjective* (15th century)
**1** : capable of being estimated
**2** *archaic* : VALUABLE
**3** : worthy of esteem
— **es·ti·ma·ble·ness** *noun*
— **es·ti·ma·bly** \-blē\ *adverb*
**¹es·ti·mate** \'es-tə-ˌmāt\ *transitive verb* **-mat·ed; -mat·ing** [Latin *aestimatus*, past participle of *aestimare* to value, estimate] (circa 1532)
**1** *archaic* **a** : ESTEEM **b** : APPRAISE
**2 a** : to judge tentatively or approximately the value, worth, or significance of **b** : to determine roughly the size, extent, or nature of **c** : to produce a statement of the approximate cost of
**3** : JUDGE, CONCLUDE ☆
— **es·ti·ma·tive** \-ˌmā-tiv\ *adjective*
**²es·ti·mate** \'es-tə-mət\ *noun* (1563)
**1** : the act of appraising or valuing : CALCULATION
**2** : an opinion or judgment of the nature, character, or quality of a person or thing ⟨had a high *estimate* of his abilities⟩
**3 a** : a rough or approximate calculation **b** : a numerical value obtained from a statistical sample and assigned to a population parameter
**4** : a statement of the cost of work to be done
**es·ti·ma·tion** \ˌes-tə-'mā-shən\ *noun* (14th century)
**1** : JUDGMENT, OPINION
**2 a** : the act of estimating something **b** : the value, amount, or size arrived at in an estimate
**3** : ESTEEM, HONOR
**es·ti·ma·tor** \'es-tə-ˌmā-tər\ *noun* (1611)
**1** : one that estimates
**2** : ESTIMATE 3b; *also* : a statistical function whose value for a sample furnishes an estimate of a population parameter
**es·ti·val** \'es-tə-vəl\ *adjective* [Middle English, from Middle French or Latin; Middle French, from Latin *aestivalis*, from *aestivus* of

summer, from *aestas* summer — more at EDIFY] (14th century)
: of or relating to the summer
**es·ti·vate** \-ˌvāt\ *intransitive verb* **-vat·ed; -vat·ing** (1626)
**1** : to spend the summer usually at one place
**2** : to pass the summer in a state of torpor — compare HIBERNATE
**es·ti·va·tion** \ˌes-tə-'vā-shən\ *noun* (1625)
: the state of one that estivates
**Es·to·nian** \e-'stō-nē-ən, -nyən\ *noun* (1795)
**1** : a native or inhabitant of Estonia
**2** : the Finno-Ugric language of the Estonian people
— **Estonian** *adjective*
**es·top** \e-'stäp\ *transitive verb* **es·topped; es·top·ping** [Middle English *estoppen*, from Middle French *estouper*, from (assumed) Vulgar Latin *stuppare* to stop with a tow — more at STOP] (15th century)
**1** *archaic* : to stop up
**2** : BAR; *specifically* : to impede by estoppel
**es·top·pel** \e-'stä-pəl\ *noun* [probably from Middle French *estoupail* bung, from *estouper*] (1531)
: a legal bar to alleging or denying a fact because of one's own previous actions or words to the contrary
**estr-** or **estro-** *combining form*
: estrus ⟨*estrogen*⟩
**es·tra·di·ol** \ˌes-trə-'dī-ˌól, -ˌōl\ *noun* [International Scientific Vocabulary *estra-* (from *estrane* parent compound of estradiol, from New Latin *estrus* + English *-ane*) + *di-* + ¹*-ol*] (1934)
: an estrogenic hormone that is a phenolic steroid alcohol $C_{18}H_{24}O_2$ usually made synthetically and that is often used combined as an ester especially in treating menopausal symptoms
**es·tral cycle** \'es-trəl-\ *noun* (1941)
: ESTROUS CYCLE
**es·trange** \is-'trānj\ *transitive verb* **es·tranged; es·trang·ing** [Middle English, from Middle French *estranger*, from Medieval Latin *extraneare*, from Latin *extraneus* strange — more at STRANGE] (15th century)
**1** : to remove from customary environment or associations
**2** : to arouse especially mutual enmity or indifference in where there had formerly been love, affection, or friendliness : ALIENATE ☆
— **es·trange·ment** \-'trānj-mənt\ *noun*
— **es·trang·er** *noun*
**¹es·tray** \is-'trā\ *noun* (circa 1523)
: STRAY 1
**²estray** *intransitive verb* [Middle French *estraier*] (1572)
*archaic* : STRAY
**es·tri·ol** \'es-ˌtrī-ˌól, e-'strī-, -ˌōl\ *noun* [*estrane* + *tri-* + ¹*-ol*] (1933)
: a crystalline estrogenic hormone that is a glycol $C_{18}H_{24}O_3$ usually obtained from the urine of pregnant women
**es·tro·gen** \'es-trə-jən\ *noun* [New Latin *estrus* + International Scientific Vocabulary *-o-* + *-gen*] (1927)
: a substance (as a sex hormone) tending to promote estrus and stimulate the development of female secondary sex characteristics
**usage** see ECONOMIC
**es·tro·gen·ic** \ˌes-trə-'je-nik\ *adjective* (1930)
**1** : promoting estrus
**2** : of, relating to, caused by, or being an estrogen
— **es·tro·gen·i·cal·ly** \-ni-k(ə-)lē\ *adverb*
**es·trone** \'es-ˌtrōn\ *noun* [*estrane*] (1933)
: an estrogenic hormone that is a ketone $C_{18}H_{22}O_2$ usually obtained from the urine of pregnant females and used similarly to estradiol
**es·trous** \'es-trəs\ *adjective* (1900)
**1** : of, relating to, or characteristic of estrus
**2** : being in heat
**estrous cycle** *noun* (1900)

: the correlated phenomena of the endocrine and generative systems of a female mammal from the beginning of one period of estrus to the beginning of the next — called also *estral cycle, estrus cycle*
**es·tru·al** \'es-trə-wəl\ *adjective* (circa 1857)
: ESTROUS
**es·trus** \'es-trəs\ *noun* [New Latin, from Latin *oestrus* gadfly, frenzy, from Greek *oistros* — more at IRE] (circa 1890)
: a regularly recurrent state of sexual excitability during which the female of most mammals will accept the male and is capable of conceiving : HEAT; *also* : a single occurrence of this state
**es·tu·ar·i·al** \ˌes-chə-'wer-ē-əl, ˌesh-\ *adjective* (1883)
: ESTUARINE
**es·tu·a·rine** \'es-chə-(wə-)ˌrīn, -ˌrēn, -ˌrin, 'esh-\ *adjective* (1846)
: of, relating to, or formed in an estuary ⟨*estuarine* currents⟩ ⟨*estuarine* animals⟩
**es·tu·ary** \'es-chə-ˌwer-ē, 'esh-\ *noun, plural* **-ar·ies** [Latin *aestuarium*, from *aestus* boiling, tide; akin to Latin *aestas* summer — more at EDIFY] (1538)
: a water passage where the tide meets a river current; *especially* : an arm of the sea at the lower end of a river
**esu·ri·ence** \i-'sur-ē-ən(t)s, -'zur-\ *noun* (1825)
: the quality or state of being esurient
**esu·ri·ent** \-ənt\ *adjective* [Latin *esurient-, esuriens*, present participle of *esurire* to be hungry; akin to Latin *edere* to eat — more at EAT] (circa 1672)
: HUNGRY, GREEDY
— **esu·ri·ent·ly** *adverb*
**et** \'et\ *dialect past and past participle of* EAT
**¹-et** \'et, ˌet, ət, it\ *noun suffix* [Middle English, from Old French *-et*, masculine, & *-ete*, feminine, from Late Latin *-itus* & *-ita*]
: small one ⟨baron*et*⟩ ⟨cellar*et*⟩

---

☆ **SYNONYMS**
**Estimate, appraise, evaluate, value, rate, assess** mean to judge something with respect to its worth or significance. ESTIMATE implies a judgment, considered or casual, that precedes or takes the place of actual measuring or counting or testing out ⟨*estimated* the crowd at two hundred⟩. APPRAISE commonly implies the fixing by an expert of the monetary worth of a thing, but it may be used of any critical judgment ⟨having their house *appraised*⟩. EVALUATE suggests an attempt to determine relative or intrinsic worth in terms other than monetary ⟨*evaluate* a student's work⟩. VALUE equals APPRAISE but without implying expertness of judgment ⟨a watercolor *valued* by the donor at $500⟩. RATE adds to ESTIMATE the notion of placing a thing according to a scale of values ⟨a highly *rated* restaurant⟩. ASSESS implies a critical appraisal for the purpose of understanding or interpreting, or as a guide in taking action ⟨officials are trying to *assess* the damage⟩.

**Estrange, alienate, disaffect** mean to cause one to break a bond of affection or loyalty. ESTRANGE implies the development of indifference or hostility with consequent separation or divorcement ⟨his *estranged* wife⟩. ALIENATE may or may not suggest separation but always implies loss of affection or interest ⟨managed to *alienate* all his coworkers⟩. DISAFFECT refers especially to those from whom loyalty is expected and stresses the effects (as rebellion or discontent) of alienation without actual separation ⟨conservatives were *disaffected* by the new tax⟩.

**²-et** *noun suffix* [*duet*]
**:** group 〈*octet*〉

**eta** \'ā-tə, *chiefly British* 'ē-tə\ *noun* [Middle English, from Late Latin, from Greek *ēta*, of Semitic origin; akin to Hebrew *ḥēth* heth] (15th century)
**:** the 7th letter of the Greek alphabet — see ALPHABET table

**éta·gère** *or* **eta·gere** \ˌā-ˌtä-'zher, -tə-\ *noun* [French, from Middle French *estagiere*, from *estage* floor of a building, station, from Old French — more at STAGE] (1851)
**:** a piece of furniture consisting of a set of open shelves for displaying small objects and sometimes having an enclosed cabinet as a base

étagère

**et alia** \(ˌ)et-'ä-l(ē-)yə, -'ā-, -'a-\ [Latin] (1953)
**:** and others

**eta·mine** \'ā-tə-ˌmēn\ *noun* [French *étamine*] (1714)
**:** a light cotton or worsted fabric with an open mesh

**etat·ism** \ā-'tä-ˌti-zəm\ *noun* [French *étatisme*, from *état* state, from Old French *estat* — more at STATE] (1923)
**:** STATE SOCIALISM
— **etat·ist** \-'tä-tist\ *adjective*

**et·cet·era** \et-'se-tə-rə, -'se-trə *also* it-, ÷ek-, ÷ik-\ *noun* (1656)
**1 :** a number of unspecified additional persons or things
**2** *plural* **:** unspecified additional items **:** ODDS AND ENDS

**et cet·era** \*same*\ [Latin] (12th century)
**:** and others especially of the same kind **:** and so forth

**¹etch** \'ech\ *verb* [Dutch *etsen*, from German *ätzen* to etch, corrode, from Old High German *azzen* to feed; akin to Old High German *ezzan* to eat — more at EAT] (1634)
*transitive verb*
**1 a :** to produce (as a pattern or design) on a hard material by eating into the material's surface (as by acid or laser beam) **b :** to subject to such etching
**2 :** to delineate or impress clearly 〈scenes *etched* in our minds〉 〈pain was *etched* on his features〉
*intransitive verb*
**:** to practice etching
— **etch·er** *noun*

**²etch** *noun* (1896)
**1 :** the action or effect of etching a surface
**2 :** a chemical agent used in etching

**etch·ant** \'e-chənt\ *noun* (1904)
**:** ETCH 2

**etch·ing** *noun* (1634)
**1 a :** the action or process of etching **b :** the art of producing pictures or designs by printing from an etched metal plate
**2 a :** an etched design **b :** an impression from an etched plate

**¹eter·nal** \i-'tər-nᵊl\ *adjective* [Middle English, from Middle French, from Late Latin *aeternalis*, from Latin *aeternus* eternal, from *aevum* age, eternity — more at AYE] (14th century)
**1 a :** having infinite duration **:** EVERLASTING **b :** of or relating to eternity **c :** characterized by abiding fellowship with God 〈good teacher, what must I do to inherit *eternal* life? —Mark 10:17 (Revised Standard Version)〉
**2 a :** continued without intermission **:** PERPETUAL **b :** seemingly endless
**3** *archaic* **:** INFERNAL 〈some *eternal* villain . . . devised this slander —Shakespeare〉
**4 :** valid or existing at all times **:** TIMELESS 〈*eternal* verities〉
— **eter·nal·ize** \-nᵊl-ˌīz\ *transitive verb*

— **eter·nal·ly** \-nᵊl-ē\ *adverb*
— **eter·nal·ness** *noun*

**²eternal** *noun* (1582)
**1** *capitalized* **:** GOD 1 — used with *the*
**2 :** something eternal

**eterne** \i-'tərn\ *adjective* [Middle English, from Middle French, from Latin *aeternus*] (14th century)
*archaic* **:** ETERNAL

**eter·ni·ty** \i-'tər-nə-tē\ *noun, plural* **-ties** [Middle English *eternite*, from Middle French *eternité*, from Latin *aeternitat-, aeternitas*, from *aeternus*] (14th century)
**1 :** the quality or state of being eternal
**2 :** infinite time
**3** *plural* **:** AGE 3b
**4 :** the state after death **:** IMMORTALITY
**5 :** a seemingly endless or immeasurable time

**eter·nize** \i-'tər-ˌnīz\ *transitive verb* **-nized; -niz·ing** (1580)
**1 a :** to make eternal **b :** to prolong indefinitely
**2 :** IMMORTALIZE
— **eter·ni·za·tion** \-ˌtər-nə-'zā-shən\ *noun*

**Ete·sian** \i-'tē-zhən\ *adjective* [Latin *etesius*, from Greek *etēsios*, from *etos* year — more at WETHER] (1601)
**:** recurring annually — used of summer winds that blow over the Mediterranean
— **Etesian** *noun*

**eth** \'eth\ *variant of* EDH

**eth-** *combining form* [International Scientific Vocabulary]
**:** ethyl 〈*ethene*〉

**¹-eth** \əth, ith\ *or* **-th** \th\ *verb suffix* [Middle English, from Old English *-eth, -ath, -th*; akin to Old High German *-it, -ōt, -ēt*, 3d singular ending, Latin *-t, -it*]
— used to form the archaic third person singular present of verbs 〈do*eth*〉

**²-eth** — see -TH

**eth·a·cryn·ic acid** \ˌe-thə-ˌkri-nik-\ *noun* [perhaps from *eth-* + *ac*etic + *but*yryl + *phe*nol] (1964)
**:** a potent synthetic diuretic $C_{13}H_{12}Cl_2O_4$ used especially in the treatment of edema

**eth·am·bu·tol** \e-'tham-byu̇-ˌtȯl, -ˌtōl\ *noun* [*eth*ylene + *am*ine + *butanol*] (1965)
**:** a compound $C_{10}H_{24}N_2O_2$ used especially in the treatment of tuberculosis

**eth·ane** \'e-ˌthān, *British usually* 'ē-\ *noun* [International Scientific Vocabulary, from *ethyl*] (1873)
**:** a colorless odorless gaseous alkane $C_2H_6$ found in natural gas and used as a fuel

**eth·a·nol** \'e-thə-ˌnȯl, -ˌnōl, *British also* 'ē-\ *noun* (1900)
**:** a colorless volatile flammable liquid $C_2H_5OH$ that is the intoxicating agent in liquors and is also used as a solvent — called also *ethyl alcohol, grain alcohol*

**eth·a·nol·amine** \ˌe-thə-'nä-lə-ˌmēn, -'nō-, *British also* ˌē-\ *noun* (1897)
**:** a colorless liquid amino alcohol $C_2H_7NO$ used especially as a solvent in the synthesis of detergents and in gas purification

**eth·ene** \'e-ˌthēn\ *noun* (1873)
**:** ETHYLENE

**eth·e·phon** \'e-thə-ˌfän\ *noun* [*ethyl* + *phos*phonic acid (a dibasic organic acid)] (1971)
**:** a synthetic plant growth regulator $C_2H_6ClO_3P$ that induces flowering and abscission by promoting the release of ethylene and has been used to cause early ripening (as of apples on the tree)

**ether** \'ē-thər\ *noun* [Middle English, from Latin *aether*, from Greek *aithēr*, from *aithein* to ignite, blaze; akin to Old English *ād* pyre — more at EDIFY] (14th century)
**1 a :** the rarefied element formerly believed to fill the upper regions of space **b :** the upper regions of space **:** HEAVENS
**2 a :** a medium that in the wave theory of light permeates all space and transmits transverse waves **b :** AIRWAVES

**3 a :** a light volatile flammable liquid $C_4H_{10}O$ used chiefly as a solvent and anesthetic **b :** any of various organic compounds characterized by an oxygen atom attached to two carbon atoms
— **ethe·ric** \i-'ther-ik, -'thir-\ *adjective*

**ethe·re·al** \i-'thir-ē-əl\ *adjective* (1513)
**1 a :** of or relating to the regions beyond the earth **b :** CELESTIAL, HEAVENLY **c :** UNWORLDLY, SPIRITUAL
**2 a :** lacking material substance **:** IMMATERIAL, INTANGIBLE **b :** marked by unusual delicacy or refinement 〈this smallest, most *ethereal*, and daintiest of birds —William Beebe〉
**3 :** relating to, containing, or resembling a chemical ether
— **ethe·re·al·i·ty** \-ˌthir-ē-'a-lə-tē\ *noun*
— **ethe·re·al·iza·tion** \-ē-ə-lə-'zā-shən\ *noun*
— **ethe·re·al·ize** \-'thir-ē-ə-ˌlīz\ *transitive verb*
— **ethe·re·al·ly** \-ē-ə-lē\ *adverb*
— **ethe·re·al·ness** *noun*

**ether extract** *noun* (circa 1900)
**:** the part of a complex organic material that is soluble in ether and consists chiefly of fats and fatty acids

**ether·ize** \'ē-thə-ˌrīz\ *transitive verb* **-ized; -iz·ing** (1853)
**1 :** to treat or anesthetize with ether
**2 :** to make numb as if by anesthetizing
— **ether·iza·tion** \ˌē-thə-rə-'zā-shən\ *noun*
— **ether·iz·er** *noun*

**eth·ic** \'e-thik\ *noun* [Middle English *ethik*, from Middle French *ethique*, from Latin *ethice*, from Greek *ēthikē*, from *ēthikos*] (14th century)
**1** *plural but singular or plural in construction* **:** the discipline dealing with what is good and bad and with moral duty and obligation
**2 a :** a set of moral principles or values **b :** a theory or system of moral values 〈the present-day materialistic *ethic*〉 **c** *plural but singular or plural in construction* **:** the principles of conduct governing an individual or a group 〈professional *ethics*〉 **d :** a guiding philosophy

**eth·i·cal** \'e-thi-kəl\ *also* **eth·ic** \-thik\ *adjective* [Middle English *etik*, from Latin *ethicus*, from Greek *ēthikos*, from *ēthos* character — more at SIB] (1607)
**1 :** of or relating to ethics
**2 :** involving or expressing moral approval or disapproval
**3 :** conforming to accepted professional standards of conduct
**4** *of a drug* **:** restricted to sale only on a doctor's prescription
*synonym* see MORAL
— **eth·i·cal·i·ty** \ˌe-thə-'ka-lə-tē\ *noun*
— **eth·i·cal·ly** \'e-thi-k(ə-)lē\ *adverb*
— **eth·i·cal·ness** \-kəl-nəs\ *noun*

**ethi·cian** \e-'thi-shən\ *noun* (1629)
**:** ETHICIST

**eth·i·cist** \'e-thə-sist\ *noun* (circa 1890)
**:** a specialist in ethics

**ethid·i·um bromide** \e-'thi-dē-əm-\ *noun* [*ethyl* + *-id* + *-ium*] (1963)
**:** a biological dye used especially to block nucleic acid synthesis (as in mitochondria) and to destroy trypanosomes

**ethinyl** *variant of* ETHYNYL
— used especially in pharmacology

**ethinyl estradiol** *noun* (1939)
**:** a very potent synthetic estrogen $C_{20}H_{24}O_2$ used orally

**eth·i·on** \'e-thē-ˌän\ *noun* [blend of *eth-* and *thion-*] (circa 1960)
**:** an organophosphate $C_9H_{22}O_4P_2S_4$ used as a pesticide

---

\ə\ abut \ᵊ\ kitten \ər\ further \a\ ash \ā\ ace
\ä\ mop, mar \au̇\ out \ch\ chin \e\ bet \ē\ easy
\g\ go \i\ hit \ī\ ice \j\ job \ŋ\ sing \ō\ go
\ȯ\ law \ȯi\ boy \th\ thin \th\ the \ü\ loot \u̇\ foot
\y\ yet \zh\ vision *see also* Guide to Pronunciation

**eth·i·on·amide** \‚e-thē-'ä-nə-‚mīd\ *noun* (1960)
**:** a compound $C_8H_{10}N_2S$ used against mycobacteria (as in tuberculosis and leprosy)

**ethi·o·nine** \e-'thī-ə-‚nēn\ *noun* (1938)
**:** an amino acid $C_6H_{13}NO_2S$ that is the ethyl homologue of methionine and is biologically antagonistic to methionine

**Ethi·op** \'ē-thē-‚äp\ *or* **Ethi·ope** \-‚ōp\ *noun* [Middle English *Ethiope*, from Latin *Aethiops*, from Greek *Aithiops*] (13th century)
*archaic* **:** ETHIOPIAN

**¹Ethi·o·pi·an** \‚ē-thē-'ō-pē-ən\ *noun* (13th century)
**1 :** a member of any of the mythical or actual peoples usually described by the ancient Greeks as dark-skinned and living far to the south
**2** *archaic* **:** a black person
**3 :** a native or inhabitant of Ethiopia

**²Ethiopian** *adjective* (1578)
**1 :** of, relating to, or characteristic of the inhabitants or the country of Ethiopia
**2 :** of, relating to, or being the biogeographic region that includes Africa south of the Sahara, southern Arabia, and sometimes Madagascar and the adjacent islands

**¹Ethi·o·pic** \-'ä-pik, -'ō-pik\ *adjective* (1654)
**1 :** ETHIOPIAN
**2 a :** of, relating to, or constituting Ethiopic **b :** of, relating to, or constituting a group of related Semitic languages spoken in Ethiopia

**²Ethiopic** *noun* (1677)
**1 :** a Semitic language formerly spoken in Ethiopia and still used as the liturgical language of the Christian church in Ethiopia
**2 :** the Ethiopic group of Semitic languages

**eth·moid** \'eth-‚mȯid\ *noun* [French *ethmoïde*, from Greek *ēthmoeidēs*, literally, like a strainer, from *ēthmos* strainer] (1842)
**:** a light spongy cubical bone forming much of the walls of the nasal cavity and part of those of the orbits
— **ethmoid** \*same*\ *or* **eth·moi·dal** \(‚)eth-'mȯi-d°l\ *adjective*

**¹eth·nic** \'eth-nik\ *adjective* [Middle English, from Late Latin *ethnicus*, from Greek *ethnikos* national, gentile, from *ethnos* nation, people; akin to Greek *ēthos* custom — more at SIB] (15th century)
**1 :** HEATHEN
**2 a :** of or relating to large groups of people classed according to common racial, national, tribal, religious, linguistic, or cultural origin or background ⟨*ethnic* minorities⟩ ⟨*ethnic* enclaves⟩ **b :** being a member of an ethnic group **c :** of, relating to, or characteristic of ethnics ⟨*ethnic* neighborhoods⟩ ⟨*ethnic* foods⟩

**²ethnic** *noun* (1941)
**:** a member of an ethnic group; *especially* **:** a member of a minority group who retains the customs, language, or social views of the group

**eth·ni·cal** \'eth-ni-kəl\ *adjective* (15th century)
**1 :** ETHNIC
**2 :** of or relating to ethnology : ETHNOLOGIC
— **eth·ni·cal·ly** \-k(ə-)lē\ *adverb*

**ethnic cleansing** *noun* (1992)
**:** the expulsion, imprisonment, or killing of ethnic minorities by a dominant majority group

**eth·nic·i·ty** \eth-'ni-sə-tē\ *noun* (1950)
**:** ethnic quality or affiliation

**ethno-** *combining form* [French, from Greek *ethno-, ethn-,* from *ethnos*]
**:** race : people : cultural group ⟨*ethno*centric⟩

**eth·no·bot·a·ny** \‚eth-nō-'bä-t°n-ē, -'bät-nē\ *noun* (1890)
**:** the plant lore of a race or people; *also* **:** the systematic study of such lore
— **eth·no·bo·tan·i·cal** \-bə-'ta-ni-kəl\ *adjective*
— **eth·no·bot·a·nist** \-'bä-t°n-ist, -'bät-nist\ *noun*

**eth·no·cen·tric** \‚eth-nō-'sen-trik\ *adjective* (1900)
**:** characterized by or based on the attitude that one's own group is superior
— **eth·no·cen·tric·i·ty** \-sen-'tri-sə-tē\ *noun*
— **eth·no·cen·trism** \-'sen-‚tri-zəm\ *noun*

**eth·nog·ra·phy** \eth-'nä-grə-fē\ *noun* [French *ethnographie*, from *ethno-* + *-graphie* -graphy] (1834)
**:** the study and systematic recording of human cultures; *also* **:** a descriptive work produced from such research
— **eth·nog·ra·pher** \-fər\ *noun*
— **eth·no·graph·ic** \‚eth-nə-'gra-fik\ *or* **eth·no·graph·i·cal** \-fi-kəl\ *adjective*
— **eth·no·graph·i·cal·ly** \-fi-k(ə-)lē\ *adverb*

**eth·no·his·to·ry** \‚eth-nō-'his-t(ə-)rē\ *noun* (1943)
**:** a study of the development of cultures
— **eth·no·his·to·ri·an** \-(h)is-'tȯr-ē-ən, -'tȯr-, -'tär-\ *noun*
— **eth·no·his·to·ric** \-(h)is-'tȯr-ik, -'tär-\ *or* **eth·no·his·to·ri·cal** \-i-kəl\ *adjective*

**eth·nol·o·gy** \eth-'nä-lə-jē\ *noun* (circa 1828)
**1 :** a science that deals with the division of human beings into races and their origin, distribution, relations, and characteristics
**2 :** anthropology dealing chiefly with the comparative and analytical study of cultures : CULTURAL ANTHROPOLOGY
— **eth·no·log·i·cal** \‚eth-nə-'lä-ji-kəl\ *also* **eth·no·log·ic** \-jik\ *adjective*
— **eth·nol·o·gist** \eth-'nä-lə-jist\ *noun*

**eth·no·meth·od·ol·o·gy** \‚eth-nō-‚me-thə-'dä-lə-jē\ *noun* (1967)
**:** a branch of sociology dealing with nonspecialists' commonsense understanding of the structure and organization of society
— **eth·no·meth·od·ol·o·gist** \-'dä-lə-jist\ *noun*

**eth·no·mu·si·col·o·gy** \‚eth-nō-‚myü-zi-'kä-lə-jē\ *noun* (1950)
**1 :** the study of music that is outside the European art tradition
**2 :** the study of music in a sociocultural context
— **eth·no·mu·si·co·log·i·cal** \-kə-'lä-ji-kəl\ *adjective*
— **eth·no·mu·si·col·o·gist** \-'kä-lə-jist\ *noun*

**eth·no·sci·ence** \'eth-nō-‚sī-ən(t)s\ *noun* (1961)
**:** the nature lore (as folk taxonomy of plants and animals) of primitive peoples

**ethol·o·gy** \ē-'thä-lə-jē\ *noun* (circa 1843)
**1 :** a branch of knowledge dealing with human ethos and with its formation and evolution
**2 :** the scientific and objective study of animal behavior especially under natural conditions
— **etho·log·i·cal** \‚ē-thə-'lä-ji-kəl, ‚e-thə-\ *adjective*
— **ethol·o·gist** \ē-'thä-lə-jist\ *noun*

**ethos** \'ē-‚thäs\ *noun* [New Latin, from Greek *ēthos* custom, character — more at SIB] (1851)
**:** the distinguishing character, sentiment, moral nature, or guiding beliefs of a person, group, or institution

**eth·oxy** \e-'thäk-sē\ *adjective* (circa 1909)
**:** relating to or containing the univalent group $CH_3CH_2O-$ composed of ethyl united with oxygen

**eth·yl** \'e-thəl\ *noun* [German *Ethyl* (now *Äthyl*), from *Äther* ether + *-yl*] (1838)
**:** a univalent hydrocarbon group $CH_3CH_2-$
— **eth·yl·ic** \e-'thi-lik\ *adjective*

**ethyl acetate** *noun* (1874)
**:** a colorless fragrant volatile flammable liquid ester $C_4H_8O_2$ used especially as a solvent

**ethyl alcohol** *noun* (1869)
**:** ETHANOL

**eth·yl·ben·zene** \‚e-thil-'ben-‚zēn\ *noun* [International Scientific Vocabulary] (1873)
**:** a liquid hydrocarbon $C_8H_{10}$ that is made usually from benzene and ethylene and is used chiefly in the manufacture of styrene

**ethyl cellulose** *noun* (1936)
**:** any of various thermoplastic substances used especially in plastics and lacquers

**ethyl chloride** *noun* (circa 1891)
**:** a colorless pungent flammable gaseous or volatile liquid $C_2H_5Cl$ used especially as a local surface anesthetic

**eth·yl·ene** \'e-thə-‚lēn\ *noun* (circa 1852)
**1 :** a colorless flammable gaseous unsaturated hydrocarbon $C_2H_4$ that is found in coal gas, can be produced by pyrolysis of petroleum hydrocarbons, and occurs in plants functioning especially as a natural growth regulator that promotes the ripening of fruit
**2 :** a divalent hydrocarbon group $C_2H_4$ derived from ethane
— **eth·yl·en·ic** \‚e-thə-'lē-nik, -'le-nik\ *adjective*

**eth·yl·ene·di·amine·tet·ra·ac·e·tate** \‚e-thə-‚lēn-‚dī-ə-‚mēn-‚te-trə-'a-sə-‚tāt, -dī-‚a-mən-\ *noun* (1954)
**:** a salt of EDTA

**eth·yl·ene·di·amine·tet·ra·ace·tic acid** \-(ə-)'sē-tik-\ *noun* (1942)
**:** EDTA

**ethylene di·bro·mide** \-(‚)dī-'brō-‚mīd\ *noun* (circa 1929)
**:** a colorless toxic liquid compound $C_2H_4Br_2$ that is used chiefly as a fuel additive in leaded gasolines, that has been found to be strongly carcinogenic in laboratory animals, and that was used formerly in the U.S. as an agricultural pesticide — abbreviation *EDB*

**ethylene glycol** *noun* (1901)
**:** a thick liquid diol $C_2H_6O_2$ used especially as an antifreeze and in making polyester fibers

**ethylene oxide** *noun* (1898)
**:** a colorless flammable toxic compound $C_2H_4O$ used especially in synthesis (as of ethylene glycol) and in sterilization and fumigation

**ethyl ether** *noun* (1878)
**:** ETHER 3a

**eth·yne** \'e-‚thīn, e-'\ *noun* [*ethyl* + *²-ine*] (circa 1929)
**:** ACETYLENE

**ethy·nyl** \e-'thī-n°l, 'e-thə-‚nil\ *noun* (1929)
**:** a univalent unsaturated group $HC≡C-$ derived from acetylene by removal of one hydrogen atom

**et·ic** \'e-tik\ *adjective* [phonetic] (1954)
**:** of, relating to, or having linguistic or behavioral characteristics considered without regard to their structural significance — compare EMIC

**-et·ic** \'e-tik\ *adjective suffix* [Latin & Greek; Latin *-eticus*, from Greek *-etikos, -ētikos,* from *-etos, -ētos,* ending of certain verbals]
**:** -IC ⟨limn*etic*⟩ — often in adjectives corresponding to nouns ending in *-esis* ⟨gen*etic*⟩

**eti·o·late** \'ē-tē-ə-‚lāt\ *transitive verb* **-lat·ed; -lat·ing** [French *étioler*] (1791)
**1 :** to bleach and alter the natural development of (a green plant) by excluding sunlight
**2 a :** to make pale **b :** to deprive of natural vigor : make feeble
— **eti·o·la·tion** \‚ē-tē-ə-'lā-shən\ *noun*

**eti·o·log·ic** \‚ē-tē-ə-'lä-jik\ *or* **eti·o·log·i·cal** \-ji-kəl\ *adjective* (circa 1753)
**1 :** assigning or seeking to assign a cause
**2 :** of or relating to etiology
— **eti·o·log·i·cal·ly** \-ji-k(ə-)lē\ *adverb*

**eti·ol·o·gy** \‚ē-tē-'ä-lə-jē\ *noun, plural* **-gies** [Medieval Latin *aetiologia* statement of causes, from Greek *aitiologia,* from *aitia* cause] (circa 1555)
**1 :** CAUSE, ORIGIN; *specifically* **:** all of the causes of a disease or abnormal condition
**2 :** a branch of knowledge concerned with causes; *specifically* **:** a branch of medical science concerned with the causes and origins of diseases

**et·i·quette** \'e-ti-kət, -,ket\ *noun* [French *étiquette,* literally, ticket — more at TICKET] (1750)
: the conduct or procedure required by good breeding or prescribed by authority to be observed in social or official life ◆

**Eton collar** \'ē-t°n-\ *noun* [*Eton* College, English public school] (1887)
: a large stiff turnover collar

**Eto·ni·an** \ē-'tō-nē-ən\ *noun* (circa 1770)
: a student or former student of Eton College
— **Etonian** *adjective*

**Eton jacket** *noun* (1881)
: a short black jacket with long sleeves, wide lapels, and an open front

**étouf·fée** *also* **etouf·fee** \,ā-tü-'fā\ *noun* [Louisiana French, from French *à l'étouffée* braised, from feminine of *étouffer,* past participle of *étouffer* to smother, from Old French *estofer,* alteration of *estoper* to plug up — more at ESTOP] (circa 1933)
: a Cajun stew of shellfish or chicken served over rice

**Etru·ri·an** \i-'trür-ē-ən\ *noun* (1623)
: ETRUSCAN
— **Etrurian** *adjective*

**¹Etrus·can** \i-'trəs-kən\ *adjective* [Latin *etruscus;* akin to Latin *Etruria,* ancient country] (1706)
: of, relating to, or characteristic of Etruria, the Etruscans, or the Etruscan language

**²Etruscan** *noun* (1773)
**1** : the language of the Etruscans which is of unknown affiliation
**2** : a native or inhabitant of ancient Etruria

**-ette** \'et, ,et, ət, it\ *noun suffix* [Middle English, from Middle French, feminine diminutive suffix, from Old French *-ete* — more at -ET]
**1** : little one ⟨kitchen*ette*⟩
**2** : female ⟨farmer*ette*⟩

**étude** \'ā-,tüd, -,tyüd\ *noun* [French, literally, study, from Middle French *estude, estudie,* from Old French — more at STUDY] (circa 1837)
**1** : a piece of music for the practice of a point of technique
**2** : a composition built on a technical motive but played for its artistic value

**etui** \ā-'twē, 'ā-,\ *noun, plural* **etuis** [French *étui*] (1611)
: a small ornamental case

**et·y·mol·o·gise** *British variant of* ETYMOLOGIZE

**et·y·mol·o·gist** \,e-tə-'mä-lə-jist\ *noun* (1635)
: a specialist in etymology

**et·y·mol·o·gize** \-,jīz\ *verb* **-gized; -giz·ing** (1530)
*transitive verb*
: to discover, formulate, or state an etymology for
*intransitive verb*
: to study or formulate etymologies

**et·y·mol·o·gy** \-jē\ *noun, plural* **-gies** [Middle English *ethimologie,* from Latin *etymologia,* from Greek, from *etymon* + *-logia* -logy] (14th century)
**1** : the history of a linguistic form (as a word) shown by tracing its development since its earliest recorded occurrence in the language where it is found, by tracing its transmission from one language to another, by analyzing it into its component parts, by identifying its cognates in other languages, or by tracing it and its cognates to a common ancestral form in an ancestral language
**2** : a branch of linguistics concerned with etymologies
— **et·y·mo·log·i·cal** \-mə-'lä-ji-kəl\ *adjective*
— **et·y·mo·log·i·cal·ly** \-k(ə-)lē\ *adverb*

**et·y·mon** \'e-tə-,män\ *noun, plural* **-ma** \-mə\ *also* **-mons** [Latin, from Greek, literal meaning of a word according to its origin, from *ety-*

*mos* true; akin to Greek *eteos* true — more at SOOTH] (circa 1576)
**1 a** : an earlier form of a word in the same language or an ancestral language **b** : a word in a foreign language that is the source of a particular loanword
**2** : a word or morpheme from which words are formed by composition or derivation

**eu-** *combining form* [Middle English, from Latin, from Greek, from *eu* well, from neuter of *eys* good; perhaps akin to Latin *esse* to be]
**1 a** : well ⟨*euclase*⟩ — compare DYS-
**b** : good ⟨*eudaemonism*⟩ — compare DYS-
**2** : true ⟨*euchromatin*⟩

**eu·ca·lypt** \'yü-kə-,lipt\ *noun* (1885)
: EUCALYPTUS

**eu·ca·lyp·tol** *also* **eu·ca·lyp·tole** \,yü-kə-'lip-,tól, -,tōl\ *noun* (1879)
: CINEOLE

**eu·ca·lyp·tus** \,yü-kə-'lip-təs\ *noun, plural* **-ti** \-,tī, -,tē\ *or* **-tus·es** [New Latin, genus name, from *eu-* + Greek *kalyptos* covered, from *kalyptein* to conceal; from the conical covering of the buds — more at HELL] (1801)
: any of a genus (*Eucalyptus*) of mostly Australian evergreen trees or rarely shrubs of the myrtle family that have rigid entire leaves and umbellate flowers and are widely cultivated for their gums, resins, oils, and woods

**eu·cary·ote** *variant of* EUKARYOTE

**Eu·cha·rist** \'yü-k(ə-)rəst\ *noun* [Middle English *eukarist,* from Middle French *eucariste,* from Late Latin *eucharistia,* from Greek, Eucharist, gratitude, from *eucharistos* grateful, from *eu-* + *charizesthai* to show favor, from *charis* favor, grace, gratitude; akin to Greek *chairein* to rejoice — more at YEARN] (14th century)
**1** : COMMUNION 2a
**2** *Christian Science* : spiritual communion with God
— **eu·cha·ris·tic** \,yü-kə-'ris-tik\ *adjective, often capitalized*

**¹eu·chre** \'yü-kər\ *noun* [origin unknown] (1841)
: a card game in which each player is dealt five cards and the player making trump must take three tricks to win a hand

**²euchre** *transitive verb* **eu·chred; eu·chring** \-k(ə-)riŋ\ (1847)
**1** : to prevent from winning three tricks in euchre
**2** : CHEAT, TRICK ⟨*euchred* out of their life savings —Pete Martin⟩

**eu·chro·ma·tin** \(,)yü-'krō-mə-tən\ *noun* [International Scientific Vocabulary] (1932)
: the genetically active portion of chromatin that is largely composed of genes
— **eu·chro·mat·ic** \,yü-krō-'ma-tik\ *adjective*

**eu·clase** \'yü-,klās, -,klāz\ *noun* [French, from *eu-* (from Latin) + Greek *klasis* breaking, from *klan* to break] (1804)
: a mineral that consists of a brittle silicate of beryllium and aluminum in pale-yellow, green, or blue prismatic crystals and is used especially as a gemstone

**eu·clid·e·an** *also* **eu·clid·i·an** \yü-'kli-dē-ən\ *adjective, often capitalized* (1660)
: of, relating to, or based on the geometry of Euclid or a geometry with similar axioms

**Euclidean algorithm** *noun* (circa 1955)
: a method of finding the greatest common divisor of two numbers by dividing the larger by the smaller, the smaller by the remainder, the first remainder by the second remainder, and so on until exact division is obtained whence the greatest common divisor is the exact divisor — called also *Euclid's algorithm*

**euclidean geometry** *noun, often E capitalized* (circa 1865)
**1** : geometry based on Euclid's axioms
**2** : the geometry of a euclidean space

**euclidean space** *noun, often E capitalized* (1883)

: a space in which Euclid's axioms and definitions (as of straight and parallel lines and angles of plane triangles) apply

**eu·crite** \'yü-,krīt\ *noun* [German *Eukrit,* from Greek *eukritos* easily discerned, from *eu-* + *kritos* separated, from *krinein* to separate — more at CERTAIN] (circa 1899)
**1** : a stony meteorite composed essentially of plagioclase and pigeonite
**2** : a rock consisting of a very basic gabbro
— **eu·crit·ic** \yü-'kri-tik\ *adjective*

**eu·dae·mo·nism** \yü-'dē-mə-,ni-zəm\ *or* **eu·dai·mo·nism** \-'dī-\ *noun* [Greek *eudaimonia* happiness, from *eudaimōn* having a good attendant spirit, happy, from *eu-* + *daimōn* spirit — more at DEMON] (1827)
: a theory that the highest ethical goal is happiness and personal well-being
— **eu·dae·mo·nist** \-nist\ *noun*
— **eu·dae·mo·nis·tic** \-,dē-mə-'nis-tik\ *adjective*

**eu·di·om·e·ter** \,yü-dē-'ä-mə-tər\ *noun* [modification of Italian *eudiometro,* from Greek *eudia* fair weather (from *eu-* + *-dia* weather—akin to Latin *dies* day) + Italian *-metro* -meter, from Greek *metron* measure] (1777)
: an instrument for the volumetric measurement and analysis of gases
— **eu·di·o·met·ric** \,yü-dē-ə-'me-trik\ *adjective*
— **eu·di·o·met·ri·cal·ly** \-tri-k(ə-)lē\ *adverb*

**eu·gen·ic** \yú-'je-nik\ *adjective* [Greek *eugenēs* wellborn, from *eu-* + *-genēs* born — more at -GEN] (1883)
**1** : relating to or fitted for the production of good offspring
**2** : of or relating to eugenics
— **eu·gen·i·cal·ly** \-ni-k(ə-)lē\ *adverb*

**eu·gen·i·cist** \-'je-nə-sist\ *noun* (circa 1909)
: a student or advocate of eugenics

**eu·gen·ics** \yú-'je-niks\ *noun plural but singular or plural in construction* (1883)
: a science that deals with the improvement (as by control of human mating) of hereditary qualities of a race or breed

**eu·gen·ist** \yú-'je-nist\ *noun* (1908)
: EUGENICIST

---

◇ **WORD HISTORY**
**etiquette**  The Middle French word *estiquette* or *etiquette* denoted a label attached to something, such as a bundle of documents, for description or identification; it was a derivative of a medieval French verb *estichier* or *estiquier* "to stick or attach" (itself ultimately borrowed from a verb akin to Modern English *stick* and *stitch* in the old Germanic language called Frankish). Middle French *etiquette* is the source of the English word *ticket,* and Modern French *étiquette* still retains the primary meaning "label." In the 16th century, the court of the Spanish king and Holy Roman Emperor Charles V borrowed Middle French *etiquette* as Spanish *etiqueta* to denote the written protocols describing order of precedence and other aspects of correct courtly behavior. The *etiqueta* eventually became the court ceremonies themselves as well as the documents that described them. Under the influence of Spanish, French *étiquette* also acquired the meaning "proper court behavior" and in the 18th century was borrowed into English. It then expanded in sense to cover all sorts of proper behavior required by society.

---

\ə\ abut \ᵊ\ kitten \ər\ further \a\ ash \ā\ ace
\ä\ mop, mar \aú\ out \ch\ chin \e\ bet \ē\ easy
\g\ go \i\ hit \ī\ ice \j\ job \ŋ\ sing \ō\ go
\ó\ law \ói\ boy \th\ thin \ṭh\ the \ü\ loot \ú\ foot
\y\ yet \zh\ vision *see also* Guide to Pronunciation

**eu·ge·nol** \'yü-jə-ˌnȯl, -ˌnōl\ *noun* [International Scientific Vocabulary *eugen*-, from New Latin *Eugenia*, genus of tropical trees] (1886) **:** a colorless aromatic liquid phenol $C_{10}H_{12}O_2$ found especially in clove oil and used commercially in flavors and perfumes and in dentistry as an analgesic

**eu·geo·syn·cline** \(ˌ)yü-ˌjē-ō-'sin-ˌklīn\ *noun* (1944) **:** a narrow rapidly subsiding geosyncline usually with volcanic materials mingled with clastic sediments — **eu·geo·syn·cli·nal** \-(ˌ)sin-'klī-nᵊl\ *adjective*

**eu·gle·na** \yü-'glē-nə\ *noun* [New Latin, genus name, from *eu*- + Greek *glēnē* eyeball, socket of a joint] (circa 1889) **:** any of a genus (*Euglena*) of green freshwater flagellates often classed as algae

**eu·gle·noid** \-ˌnȯid\ *noun* (1885) **:** any of a taxon (Euglenoidina or Euglenophyta) of varied flagellates (as a euglena) that are typically green or colorless stigma-bearing solitary organisms with one or two flagella emerging from a well-defined gullet — **euglenoid** *adjective*

**euglenoid movement** *noun* (1940) **:** writhing usually nonprogressive protoplasmic movement of plastic-bodied euglenoid flagellates

**eu·glob·u·lin** \yü-'glä-byə-lən\ *noun* [International Scientific Vocabulary] (1904) **:** a simple protein that does not dissolve in pure water

**eu·he·mer·ism** \yü-'hē-mə-ˌri-zəm, -'he-mə-\ *noun* [*Euhemerus*, 4th century B.C. Greek mythographer] (1846) **:** interpretation of myths as traditional accounts of historical persons and events — **eu·he·mer·ist** \-rist\ *noun* — **eu·he·mer·is·tic** \-ˌhē-mə-'ris-tik, -ˌhe-mə-\ *adjective*

**eu·kary·ote** \(ˌ)yü-'kar-ē-ˌōt, -ē-ət\ *noun* [New Latin *Eukaryotes*, proposed subdivision of protists, from *eu*- + *kary*- + *-otes*, plural noun suffix, from Greek *-ōtos* — more at -OTIC] (1943) **:** an organism composed of one or more cells containing visibly evident nuclei and organelles — compare PROKARYOTE — **eu·kary·ot·ic** \-ˌkar-ē-'ä-tik\ *adjective*

**eu·la·chon** \'yü-lə-ˌkän, -li-kən\ *noun, plural* **eulachon** *or* **eulachons** [Chinook Jargon *ulâkân*] (1807) **:** an anadromous marine food fish (*Thaleichthys pacificus*) of the north Pacific coast related to the smelt — called also *candlefish*

**eulogise** *British variant of* EULOGIZE

**eu·lo·gist** \'yü-lə-jist\ *noun* (1808) **:** one who eulogizes

**eu·lo·gi·um** \yü-'lō-jē-əm\ *noun, plural* **-gia** \-jē-ə\ *or* **-gi·ums** [Medieval Latin] (1621) **:** EULOGY

**eu·lo·gize** \'yü-lə-ˌjīz\ *transitive verb* **-gized; -giz·ing** (1810) **:** to speak or write in high praise of **:** EXTOL — **eu·lo·giz·er** *noun*

**eu·lo·gy** \'yü-lə-jē\ *noun, plural* **-gies** [Middle English *euloge*, from Medieval Latin *eulogium*, from Greek *eulogia* praise, from *eu*- + *-logia* -logy] (15th century) **1 :** a commendatory formal statement or set oration **2 :** high praise **synonym** *see* ENCOMIUM — **eu·lo·gis·tic** \ˌyü-lə-'jis-tik\ *adjective* — **eu·lo·gis·ti·cal·ly** \-ti-k(ə-)lē\ *adverb*

**Eu·men·i·des** \yü-'me-nə-ˌdēz\ *noun plural* [Latin, from Greek, literally, the gracious ones] **:** the Furies in Greek mythology

**eu·nuch** \'yü-nək, -nik\ *noun* [Middle English *eunuk*, from Latin *eunuchus*, from Greek *eunouchos*, from *eunē* bed + *echein* to have,

have charge of — more at SCHEME] (15th century) **1 :** a castrated man placed in charge of a harem or employed as a chamberlain in a palace **2 :** a man or boy deprived of the testes or external genitals **3 :** one that lacks virility or power ⟨political *eunuchs*⟩ — **eu·nuch·ism** \-nə-ˌki-zəm, -ni-\ *noun*

**eu·nuch·oid** \-nə-ˌkȯid, -ni-\ *noun* (1906) **:** a sexually deficient individual; *especially* **:** one lacking in sexual differentiation and tending toward the intersex state — **eunuchoid** *adjective*

**eu·on·y·mus** \yü-'ä-nə-məs\ *noun* [New Latin, genus name, from Latin *euonymos* spindle tree, from Greek *euōnymos*, from *euōnymos* having an auspicious name, from *eu*- + *onyma* name — more at NAME] (1767) **:** SPINDLE TREE

**eu·pa·trid** \yü-'pa-trəd, 'yü-pə-\ *noun, plural* **eu·pat·ri·dae** \yü-'pa-trə-ˌdē\ *often capitalized* [Greek *eupatridēs*, from *eu*- + *patr*-, *patēr* father — more at FATHER] (1836) **:** one of the hereditary aristocrats of ancient Athens

**eu·pep·tic** \yü-'pep-tik\ *adjective* (1831) **1 :** of, relating to, or having good digestion **2 :** CHEERFUL, OPTIMISTIC

**eu·phau·si·id** \yü-'fȯ-zē-əd\ *noun* [New Latin *Euphausia*, genus of crustaceans] (circa 1893) **:** any of an order (Euphausiacea) of small usually luminescent malacostracan crustaceans that resemble shrimps and in some areas form an important element in marine plankton — **euphausiid** *adjective*

**euphemise** *British variant of* EUPHEMIZE

**eu·phe·mism** \'yü-fə-ˌmi-zəm\ *noun* [Greek *euphēmismos*, from *euphēmos* auspicious, sounding good, from *eu*- + *phēmē* speech, from *phanai* to speak — more at BAN] (circa 1681) **:** the substitution of an agreeable or inoffensive expression for one that may offend or suggest something unpleasant; *also* **:** the expression so substituted — **eu·phe·mist** \-mist\ *noun* — **eu·phe·mis·tic** \ˌyü-fə-'mis-tik\ *adjective* — **eu·phe·mis·ti·cal·ly** \-ti-k(ə-)lē\ *adverb*

**eu·phe·mize** \'yü-fə-ˌmīz\ *transitive verb* **-mized; -miz·ing** (1857) **:** to express or describe euphemistically ⟨*euphemize* death⟩ — **eu·phe·miz·er** \-ˌmī-zər\ *noun*

**eu·phen·ics** \yü-'fe-niks\ *noun plural but singular in construction* [*eu*- + *phen*- (from *phenotype*) + *-ics*; after English *genotype* : *eugenics*] (1963) **:** a science that deals with the biological improvement of human beings after birth — **eu·phen·ic** \-nik\ *adjective*

**eu·pho·ni·ous** \yü-'fō-nē-əs\ *adjective* (1774) **:** pleasing to the ear — **eu·pho·ni·ous·ly** *adverb* — **eu·pho·ni·ous·ness** *noun*

**eu·pho·ni·um** \yü-'fō-nē-əm\ *noun* [Greek *euphōnos* + English *-ium* (as in *harmonium*)] (1865) **:** a brass instrument smaller than but resembling a tuba and having a range from B flat below the bass staff upward for three octaves

**eu·pho·ny** \'yü-fə-nē\ *noun, plural* **-nies** [French *euphonie*, from Late Latin *euphonia*, from Greek *euphōnia*, from *euphōnos* sweet-voiced, musical, from *eu*- + *phōnē* voice — more at BAN] (circa 1616)

**1 :** pleasing or sweet sound; *especially* **:** the acoustic effect produced by words so formed or combined as to please the ear **2 :** a harmonious succession of words having a pleasing sound — **eu·phon·ic** \yü-'fä-nik\ *adjective* — **eu·phon·i·cal·ly** \-ni-k(ə-)lē\ *adverb*

**eu·phor·bia** \yü-'fȯr-bē-ə\ *noun* [New Latin, alteration of Latin *euphorbea*, from *Euphorbus*, 1st century A.D. Greek physician] (14th century) **:** any of a large genus (*Euphorbia* of the family Euphorbiaceae) of plants that have a milky juice and flowers lacking a calyx and included in an involucre which surrounds a group of several staminate flowers and a central pistillate flower with 3-lobed pistils; *broadly* **:** SPURGE

**eu·pho·ria** \yü-'fōr-ē-ə, -'fȯr-\ *noun* [New Latin, from Greek, from *euphoros* healthy, from *eu*- + *pherein* to bear — more at BEAR] (circa 1751) **:** a feeling of well-being or elation — **eu·phor·ic** \-'fȯr-ik, -'fär-\ *adjective* — **eu·phor·i·cal·ly** \-i-k(ə-)lē\ *adverb*

**eu·pho·ri·ant** \yü-'fōr-ē-ənt, -'fȯr-\ *noun* (1947) **:** a drug that tends to induce euphoria — **euphoriant** *adjective*

**eu·pho·tic** \yü-'fō-tik\ *adjective* [International Scientific Vocabulary] (1909) **:** of, relating to, or constituting the upper layers of a body of water into which sufficient light penetrates to permit growth of green plants

**Eu·phros·y·ne** \yü-'frä-sᵊn-(ˌ)ē, -zᵊn-\ *noun* [Latin, from Greek *Euphrosynē*] **:** one of the three Graces

**eu·phu·ism** \'yü-fyə-ˌwi-zəm\ *noun* [*Euphues*, character in prose romances by John Lyly] (1592) **1 :** an elegant Elizabethan literary style marked by excessive use of balance, antithesis, and alliteration and by frequent use of similes drawn from mythology and nature **2 :** artificial elegance of language — **eu·phu·ist** \-wist\ *noun* — **eu·phu·is·tic** \ˌyü-fyə-'wis-tik\ *adjective* — **eu·phu·is·ti·cal·ly** \-ti-k(ə-)lē\ *adverb*

**eu·ploid** \'yü-ˌplȯid\ *adjective* [International Scientific Vocabulary] (1926) **:** having a chromosome number that is an exact multiple of the monoploid number — compare ANEUPLOID — **euploid** *noun* — **eu·ploi·dy** \-ˌplȯi-dē\ *noun*

**eup·nea** *also* **eup·noea** \yüp-'nē-ə\ *noun* [New Latin, from Greek *eupnoia*, from *eupnous* breathing freely, from *eu*- + *pnein* to breathe — more at SNEEZE] (circa 1706) **:** normal respiration — **eup·ne·ic** \-'nē-ik\ *adjective*

**Eur-** *or* **Euro-** *combining form* [*Europe*] **:** European and ⟨*Euramerican*⟩ **:** European ⟨*Eurocentric*⟩ **:** western European ⟨*Eurocommunism*⟩ **:** of the European Communities ⟨*Eurocrat*⟩

**Eur·amer·i·can** \ˌyür-ə-'mer-ə-kən\ *or* **Eu·ro–Amer·i·can** \ˌyür-ō-ə-'mer-\ *adjective* (1941) **:** common to Europe and America

**Eur·asian** \yü-'rā-zhən, -shən\ *adjective* (1844) **1 :** of a mixed European and Asian origin **2 :** of or relating to Europe and Asia — **Eurasian** *noun*

**eu·re·ka** \yü-'rē-kə\ *interjection* [Greek *heurēka* I have found, from *heuriskein* to find; from the exclamation attributed to Archimedes on discovering a method for determining the purity of gold — more at HEURISTIC] (1603)

euphonium

— used to express triumph on a discovery ◆

**eu·ro** \'yuṙ-(ˌ)ō\ *noun, plural* **euros** [Adnyamadhanha (Australian aboriginal language of South Australia) *yuru*] (1855)
: WALLAROO

**Eu·ro·bond** \'yuṙ-ō-ˌbänd\ *noun* (1966)
: a bond of a U.S. corporation that is sold outside the U.S. and that is denominated and paid for in dollars and yields interest in dollars

**Eu·ro·cen·tric** \ˌyuṙ-ə-'sen-trik\ *adjective* (1963)
: centered on Europe or the Europeans; *especially* : reflecting a tendency to interpret the world in terms of western and especially European values and experiences
— **Eu·ro·cen·trism** \-ˌtri-zəm\ *noun*

**Eu·ro·com·mu·nism** \ˌyuṙ-ō-'käm-yə-ˌni-zəm\ *noun* (1976)
: the communism especially of western European Communist parties that is marked by a willingness to reach power through coalitions and by independence from Soviet leadership
— **Eu·ro·com·mu·nist** *noun or adjective*

**Eu·ro·crat** \'yuṙ-ə-ˌkrat\ *noun* (1961)
: a staff member of the administrative commission of the European Communities

**Eu·ro·cur·ren·cy** \ˌyuṙ-ō-'kər-ən-sē, -'kə-rən-\ *noun* (1963)
: moneys (as of the U.S. and Japan) held outside their countries of origin and used in the money markets of Europe

**Eu·ro·dol·lar** \'yuṙ-ō-ˌdä-lər\ *noun* (1960)
: a U.S. dollar held as Eurocurrency

**Eu·ro·pa** \yu̇-'rō-pə\ *noun* [Latin, from Greek *Eurōpē*]
: a Phoenician princess carried off by Zeus in the form of a white bull and by him mother of Minos, Rhadamanthus, and Sarpedon

**¹Eu·ro·pe·an** \ˌyuṙ-ə-'pē-ən, -'pēn\ *adjective* (1603)
: of, relating to, or characteristic of the continent of Europe or its people
— **Eu·ro·pe·an·iza·tion** \-ˌpē-ə-nə-'zā-shən\ *noun*
— **Eu·ro·pe·an·ize** \-'pē-ə-ˌnīz\ *transitive verb*

**²European** *noun* (1632)
**1** : a native or inhabitant of Europe
**2** : a person of European descent

**European bison** *noun* (1860)
: WISENT

**European chafer** *noun* (1947)
: an Old World beetle (*Rhizotragus majalis* synonym *Amphimallon majalis*) established in parts of eastern North America where its larva is a destructive pest on the roots of turf grasses

**European corn borer** *noun* (1920)
: an Old World moth (*Ostrinia nubilalis*) that is widespread in eastern North America where its larva is a major pest especially in the stems and crowns of Indian corn, dahlias, and potatoes

**European plan** *noun* (1834)
: a hotel plan whereby the daily rates cover only the cost of the room — compare AMERICAN PLAN

**European red mite** *noun* (1940)
: a small bright or brownish red oval mite (*Panonychus ulmi*) that is a destructive orchard pest

**eu·ro·pi·um** \yu̇-'rō-pē-əm\ *noun* [New Latin, from *Europa* Europe] (1901)
: a bivalent and trivalent metallic element of the rare-earth group found in monazite sand — see ELEMENT table

**Eu·ro·po·cen·tric** \yu̇-ˌrō-pə-'sen-trik\ *adjective* (1926)
: EUROCENTRIC
— **Eu·ro·po·cen·trism** \-ˌtri-zəm\ *noun*

**eury-** *combining form* [New Latin, from Greek, from *eurys;* akin to Sanskrit *uru* broad, wide]
: broad : wide ⟨*euryhaline*⟩

**eu·ry·bath·ic** \ˌyuṙ-i-'ba-thik\ *adjective* [*eury-* + Greek *bathos* depth] (1902)

: capable of living on the bottom in both deep and shallow water

**Eu·ryd·i·ce** \yu̇-'ri-də-(ˌ)sē\ *noun* [Latin, from Greek *Eurydikē*]
: the wife of Orpheus whom he attempts to bring back from Hades

**eu·ry·ha·line** \ˌyuṙ-i-'hā-ˌlīn, -'ha-\ *adjective* [International Scientific Vocabulary *eury-* + Greek *halinos* of salt, from *hals* salt — more at SALT] (1888)
: able to live in waters of a wide range of salinity ⟨*euryhaline* crabs⟩

**eu·ryp·ter·id** \yu̇-'rip-tə-rəd\ *noun* [ultimately from Greek *eury-* + *pteron* wing — more at FEATHER] (1871)
: any of an order (Eurypterida) of usually large aquatic Paleozoic arthropods related to the horseshoe crabs
— **eurypterid** *adjective*

**eu·ry·ther·mal** \ˌyuṙ-i-'thər-məl\ *adjective* [International Scientific Vocabulary] (1881)
: tolerating a wide range of temperature ⟨*eurythermal* animals⟩

**eu·ry·ther·mic** \-mik\ *adjective* [International Scientific Vocabulary] (1903)
: EURYTHERMAL

**eu·ry·ther·mous** \-məs\ *adjective* [International Scientific Vocabulary] (1940)
: EURYTHERMAL

**eu·ryth·mic** *or* **eu·rhyth·mic** \yu̇-'rith-mik\ *adjective* (1921)
**1** : HARMONIOUS
**2** : of or relating to eurythmy or eurythmics

**eu·ryth·mics** *or* **eu·rhyth·mics** \-miks\ *noun plural but singular or plural in construction* (1912)
: the art of harmonious bodily movement especially through expressive timed movements in response to improvised music

**eu·ryth·my** *or* **eu·rhyth·my** \-mē\ *noun* [German *Eurhythmie,* from Latin *eurythmia* rhythmical movement, from Greek, from *eurythmos* rhythmical, from *eu-* + *rhythmos* rhythm] (1949)
: a system of harmonious body movement to the rhythm of spoken words

**eu·ry·top·ic** \ˌyuṙ-i-'tä-pik\ *adjective* [International Scientific Vocabulary *eury-* + Greek *topos* place] (circa 1945)
: tolerant of wide variation in one or more physical factors of the environment

**eu·sta·chian tube** \yu̇-'stā-sh(ē-)ən- *also* -'stā-kē-ən-\ *noun, often E capitalized* [Bartolommeo *Eustachio*] (1741)
: a bony and cartilaginous tube connecting the middle ear with the nasopharynx and equalizing air pressure on both sides of the tympanic membrane — called also *auditory tube;* see EAR illustration

**eu·stat·ic** \yu̇-'sta-tik\ *adjective* [International Scientific Vocabulary] (1906)
: relating to or characterized by worldwide change of sea level

**eu·stele** \'yü-ˌstēl, yu̇-'stē-lē\ *noun* (circa 1920)
: a stele typical of dicotyledonous plants that consists of vascular bundles of xylem and phloem strands with parenchymal cells between the bundles

**eu·tec·tic** \yu̇-'tek-tik\ *adjective* [Greek *eutēktos* easily melted, from *eu-* + *tēktos* melted, from *tēkein* to melt — more at THAW] (1884)
**1** *of an alloy or solution* : having the lowest melting point possible
**2** : of or relating to a eutectic alloy or solution or its melting or freezing point
— **eutectic** *noun*
— **eu·tec·toid** \-ˌtȯid\ *adjective or noun*

**Eu·ter·pe** \yu̇-'tər-pē\ *noun* [Latin, from Greek *Euterpē*]
: the Greek Muse of music

**eu·tha·na·sia** \ˌyü-thə-'nā-zh(ē-)ə\ *noun* [Greek, easy death, from *euthanatos,* from *eu-* + *thanatos* death — more at THANATOS] (1869)

: the act or practice of killing or permitting the death of hopelessly sick or injured individuals (as persons or domestic animals) in a relatively painless way for reasons of mercy
— **eu·tha·na·sic** \-zik, -sik\ *adjective*

**eu·than·a·tize** \yü-'tha-nə-ˌtīz\ *also* **eu·tha·nize** \'yü-thə-ˌnīz\ *transitive verb* **-tized** *also* **-nized; -tiz·ing** *also* **-niz·ing** [Greek *euthanatos*] (1873)
: to subject to euthanasia

**eu·then·ics** \yu̇-'the-niks\ *noun plural but singular or plural in construction* [Greek *euthenein* to thrive, from *eu-* + *thenein*] (1905)
: a science that deals with development of human well-being by improvement of living conditions
— **eu·the·nist** \yu̇-'the-nist, 'yü-thə-\ *noun*

**eu·the·ri·an** \yü-'thir-ē-ən\ *adjective* [ultimately from New Latin *eu-* + Greek *thērion* beast — more at TREACLE] (1880)
: of or relating to a major division (Eutheria) of mammals comprising the placental mammals
— **eutherian** *noun*

**eu·thy·roid** \(ˌ)yü-'thī-ˌrȯid\ *adjective* (1924)
: characterized by normal thyroid function

**eu·tro·phic** \yu̇-'trō-fik\ *adjective* [probably from German *Eutroph* eutrophic, from Greek *eutrophos* well-nourished, nourishing, from *eu-* + *trephein* to nourish] (1928)
*of a body of water* : characterized by the state resulting from eutrophication — compare MESOTROPHIC, OLIGOTROPHIC
— **eu·tro·phy** \'yü-trə-fē\ *noun*

**eu·tro·phi·ca·tion** \yu̇-ˌtrō-fə-'kā-shən, ˌyü-trə-fə-\ *noun* (1946)
: the process by which a body of water becomes enriched in dissolved nutrients (as phosphates) that stimulate the growth of aquatic plant life usually resulting in the depletion of dissolved oxygen

**evac·u·ate** \i-'va-kyə-ˌwāt\ *verb* **-at·ed; -at·ing** [Middle English, to draw off morbid humors, from Latin *evacuatus,* past participle of *evacuare* to empty, from *e-* + *vacuus* empty] (15th century)
*transitive verb*
**1** : to remove the contents of : EMPTY
**2** : to discharge from the body as waste : VOID
**3** : to remove something (as gas or water) from especially by pumping

---

◇ **WORD HISTORY**

**eureka**  When people make an unexpected discovery or have a sudden flash of inspiration, a traditional response is an exclamation of "Eureka!" Whether they know it or not, the elated discoverers are reenacting a legendary event in the life of the Greek mathematician and mechanical inventor Archimedes (ca. 287–212 B.C.). While wrestling with the problem of how to determine the purity of gold, he made the sudden realization that the buoyancy of an object placed in water is equal in magnitude to the weight of the water displaced by the object. According to the most popular and elaborate version of the legend, he made this discovery while at a public bathhouse, whereupon he leapt out of his bath, exclaimed *"Heurēka! Heurēka!"* ("I have found (it)") and ran naked through the streets of Syracuse all the way home. The absence of a contemporary source for the anecdote has done nothing to diminish its popularity over the centuries.

---

**4 a :** to remove especially from a military zone or dangerous area **b :** to withdraw from military occupation of **c :** VACATE ⟨were ordered to *evacuate* the building⟩
*intransitive verb*
**1 :** to withdraw from a place in an organized way especially for protection
**2 :** to pass urine or feces from the body
— **evac·u·a·tive** \-ˌwā-tiv\ *adjective*
**evac·u·a·tion** \i-ˌva-kyə-'wā-shən\ *noun* (14th century)
**1 :** the act or process of evacuating
**2 :** something evacuated or discharged
**evac·u·ee** \i-ˌva-kyə-'wē\ *noun* (1918)
**:** an evacuated person
**evade** \i-'vād\ *verb* **evad·ed; evad·ing** [Middle French & Latin; Middle French *evader*, from Latin *evadere*, from *e-* + *vadere* to go, walk — more at WADE] (1513)
*intransitive verb*
**1 :** to slip away
**2 :** to take refuge in evasion
*transitive verb*
**1 :** to elude by dexterity or stratagem
**2 a :** to avoid facing up to ⟨*evaded* the real issues⟩ **b :** to avoid the performance of **:** DODGE, CIRCUMVENT; *especially* **:** to fail to pay (taxes)
**c :** to avoid answering directly **:** turn aside
**3 :** to be elusive to **:** BAFFLE ⟨the simple, personal meaning *evaded* them —C. D. Lewis⟩
*synonym* see ESCAPE
— **evad·able** \-'vā-də-bəl\ *adjective*
— **evad·er** *noun*
**evag·i·na·tion** \i-ˌva-jə-'nā-shən\ *noun* [Late Latin *evagination-, evaginatio*, act of unsheathing, from Latin *evaginatus*, past participle of *evaginare* to unsheathe, from *e-* + *vagina* sheath] (circa 1676)
**1 :** an act or instance of everting
**2 :** a product of eversion **:** OUTGROWTH
**eval·u·ate** \i-'val-yə-ˌwāt\ *transitive verb* **-at·ed; -at·ing** [back-formation from *evaluation*] (1842)
**1 :** to determine or fix the value of
**2 :** to determine the significance, worth, or condition of usually by careful appraisal and study
*synonym* see ESTIMATE
— **eval·u·a·tion** \-ˌval-yə-'wā-shən\ *noun*
— **eval·u·a·tive** \-'val-yə-ˌwā-tiv\ *adjective*
— **eval·u·a·tor** \-ˌwā-tər\ *noun*
**ev·a·nesce** \ˌe-və-'nes\ *intransitive verb* **-nesced; -nesc·ing** [Latin *evanescere* — more at VANISH] (1822)
**:** to dissipate like vapor
**ev·a·nes·cence** \ˌe-və-'ne-sᵊn(t)s\ *noun* (1751)
**1 :** the process or fact of evanescing
**2 :** evanescent quality
**ev·a·nes·cent** \-sᵊnt\ *adjective* [Latin *evanescent-, evanescens*, present participle of *evanescere*] (1717)
**:** tending to vanish like vapor
*synonym* see TRANSIENT
**¹evan·gel** \i-'van-jəl\ *noun* [Middle English *evangile*, from Middle French, from Late Latin *evangelium*, from Greek *euangelion* good news, gospel, from *euangelos* bringing good news, from *eu-* + *angelos* messenger] (14th century)
**:** GOSPEL
**²evangel** *noun* (1614)
**:** EVANGELIST
**evan·gel·i·cal** \ˌē-ˌvan-'je-li-kəl, ˌe-vən-\ *also* **evan·gel·ic** \-ik\ *adjective* (1531)
**1 :** of, relating to, or being in agreement with the Christian gospel especially as it is presented in the four Gospels
**2 :** PROTESTANT
**3 :** emphasizing salvation by faith in the atoning death of Jesus Christ through personal conversion, the authority of Scripture, and the importance of preaching as contrasted with ritual

**4 a** *capitalized* **:** of or relating to the Evangelical Church in Germany **b** *often capitalized* **:** of, adhering to, or marked by fundamentalism **:** FUNDAMENTALIST **c** *often capitalized* **:** LOW CHURCH
**5 :** marked by militant or crusading zeal **:** EVANGELISTIC ⟨the *evangelical* ardor of the movement's leaders —Amos Vogel⟩
— **Evan·gel·i·cal·ism** \-li-kə-ˌli-zəm\ *noun*
— **evan·gel·i·cal·ly** \-li-k(ə-)lē\ *adverb*
**Evangelical** *noun* (1532)
**:** one holding evangelical principles or belonging to an evangelical party or church
**evan·ge·lism** \i-'van-jə-ˌli-zəm\ *noun* (circa 1626)
**1 :** the winning or revival of personal commitments to Christ
**2 :** militant or crusading zeal
— **evan·ge·lis·tic** \-ˌvan-jə-'lis-tik\ *adjective*
— **evan·ge·lis·ti·cal·ly** \-ti-k(ə-)lē\ *adverb*
**evan·ge·list** \i-'van-jə-list\ *noun* (13th century)
**1** *often capitalized* **:** a writer of any of the four Gospels
**2 :** a person who evangelizes; *specifically* **:** a Protestant minister or layman who preaches at special services
**evan·ge·lize** \i-'van-jə-ˌlīz\ *verb* **-lized; -liz·ing** (14th century)
*transitive verb*
**1 :** to preach the gospel to
**2 :** to convert to Christianity
*intransitive verb*
**:** to preach the gospel
— **evan·ge·li·za·tion** \-ˌvan-jə-lə-'zā-shən\ *noun*
**evap·o·rate** \i-'va-p(ə-)ˌrāt\ *verb* **-rat·ed; -rat·ing** [Middle English, from Latin *evaporatus*, past participle of *evaporare*, from *e-* + *vapor* steam, vapor] (15th century)
*transitive verb*
**1 a :** to convert into vapor; *also* **:** to dissipate or draw off in vapor or fumes **b :** to deposit (as a metal) in the form of a film by sublimation
**2 a :** to expel moisture from **b :** EXPEL ⟨*evaporate* electrons from a hot wire⟩
*intransitive verb*
**1 a :** to pass off in vapor or in invisible minute particles **b** (1) **:** to pass off or away **:** DISAPPEAR ⟨my despair *evaporated* —J. F. Wharton⟩ (2) **:** to diminish quickly
**2 :** to give forth vapor
— **evap·o·ra·tion** \-ˌva-pə-'rā-shən\ *noun*
— **evap·o·ra·tive** \-'va-pə-ˌrā-tiv\ *adjective*
— **evap·o·ra·tor** \-'va-pə-ˌrā-tər\ *noun*
**evaporated milk** *noun* (1870)
**:** unsweetened milk concentrated by partial evaporation
**evap·o·rite** \i-'va-pə-ˌrīt\ *noun* [*evapor*ation + *-ite*] (1924)
**:** a sedimentary rock (as gypsum) that originates by evaporation of seawater in an enclosed basin
— **evap·o·rit·ic** \-ˌva-pə-'ri-tik\ *adjective*
**evapo·trans·pi·ra·tion** \i-ˌva-pō-ˌtran(t)-spə-'rā-shən\ *noun* [*evapor*ation + *transpira*tion] (1938)
**:** loss of water from the soil both by evaporation and by transpiration from the plants growing thereon
**eva·sion** \i-'vā-zhən\ *noun* [Middle English, from Middle French or Late Latin; Middle French, from Late Latin *evasion-, evasio*, from Latin *evadere* to evade] (15th century)
**1 :** a means of evading **:** DODGE
**2 :** the act or an instance of evading **:** ESCAPE ⟨suspected of tax *evasion*⟩
**eva·sive** \i-'vā-siv, -ziv\ *adjective* (1725)
**:** tending or intended to evade **:** EQUIVOCAL ⟨*evasive* answers⟩
— **eva·sive·ly** *adverb*
— **eva·sive·ness** *noun*

**eve** \'ēv\ *noun* [Middle English *eve, even*] (13th century)
**1 :** EVENING
**2 :** the evening or the day before a special day
**3 :** the period immediately preceding
**Eve** \'ēv\ *noun* [Old English *Ēfe*, from Late Latin *Eva*, from Hebrew *Ḥawwāh*]
**:** the first woman and wife of Adam
**¹even** \'ē-vən\ *noun* [Middle English *even, eve*, from Old English *ǣfen*] (before 12th century)
*archaic* **:** EVENING
**²even** \'ē-vən, -bᵊm\ *adjective* [Middle English, from Old English *efen*; akin to Old High German *eban* even] (before 12th century)
**1 a :** having a horizontal surface **:** FLAT ⟨*even* ground⟩ **b :** being without break, indentation, or irregularity **:** SMOOTH **c :** being in the same plane or line
**2 a :** free from variation **:** UNIFORM ⟨his disposition was *even*⟩ **b :** LEVEL 4
**3 a :** EQUAL, FAIR ⟨an *even* exchange⟩ **b** (1) **:** leaving nothing due on either side **:** SQUARE ⟨we will not be *even* until you repay my visit⟩ (2) **:** fully revenged **c :** being in equilibrium **:** BALANCED; *specifically* **:** showing neither profit nor loss **d** *obsolete* **:** CANDID
**4 a :** being any of the integers (as −2, 0, and +2) that are exactly divisible by two **b :** marked by an even number **c :** being a mathematical function such that $f(x) = f(-x)$ where the value remains unchanged if the sign of the independent variable is reversed
**5 :** EXACT, PRECISE ⟨an *even* dollar⟩
**6 :** as likely as not **:** FIFTY-FIFTY ⟨an *even* chance of winning⟩
*synonym* see LEVEL, STEADY
— **even·ly** *adverb*
— **even·ness** \-vən-nəs\ *noun*
— **on an even keel** *also* **on even keel**
**:** in a sound or stable condition
**³even** *adverb* [Middle English, from Old English *efne*, from *efen*, adjective] (before 12th century)
**1 a :** EXACTLY, PRECISELY **b :** to a degree that extends **:** FULLY, QUITE ⟨faithful *even* unto death⟩ **c :** at the very time
**2 a :** used as an intensive to emphasize the identity or character of something ⟨he looked content, *even* happy⟩ **b** — used as an intensive to stress an extreme or highly unlikely condition or instance ⟨so simple *even* a child can do it⟩ **c** — used as an intensive to stress the comparative degree ⟨he did *even* better⟩ **d** — used as an intensive to indicate a small or minimum amount ⟨didn't *even* try⟩
**⁴even** *verb* **evened; even·ing** \'ēv-niŋ, 'ē-və-\ (13th century)
*transitive verb*
**:** to make even
*intransitive verb*
**:** to become even
— **even·er** \-nər\ *noun*
**even·fall** \'ē-vən-ˌfȯl\ *noun* (1814)
**:** the beginning of evening **:** DUSK
**even·hand·ed** \ˌē-vən-'han-dəd\ *adjective* (1605)
**:** FAIR, IMPARTIAL
— **even·hand·ed·ly** *adverb*
— **even·hand·ed·ness** *noun*
**¹eve·ning** \'ēv-niŋ\ *noun, often attributive* [Middle English, from Old English *ǣfnung*, from *ǣfnian* to grow toward evening, from *ǣfen* evening; akin to Old High German *āband* evening and perhaps to Greek *epi* on] (before 12th century)
**1 a :** the latter part and close of the day and early part of the night **b** *chiefly Southern & Midland* **:** AFTERNOON **c :** the period from sunset or the evening meal to bedtime
**2 :** the latter portion
**3 :** the period of an evening's entertainment
**²evening** *adjective* (1797)
**:** suitable for formal or semiformal evening social occasions ⟨*evening* dress⟩ ⟨*evening* clothes⟩

**evening prayer** *noun, often E&P capitalized* (1598)
: the daily evening office of the Anglican liturgy

**evening primrose** *noun* (1806)
: any of several dicotyledonous plants of a family (Onagraceae, the evening-primrose family) and especially of the type genus (*Oenothera*); *especially* : a coarse biennial herb (*O. biennis*) with yellow flowers that open in the evening

**eve·nings** \'ēv-niŋz\ *adverb* (1652)
: in the evening repeatedly : on any evening ⟨goes bowling *evenings*⟩

**evening star** *noun* (1535)
**1** : a bright planet (as Venus) seen especially in the western sky at or after sunset
**2** : a planet that rises before midnight

**even money** *noun* (1891)
: a situation in wagering in which the odds are even

**even permutation** *noun* (circa 1932)
: a permutation that is produced by the successive application of an even number of interchanges of pairs of elements

**even so** *adverb* (1948)
: in spite of that : NEVERTHELESS

**even·song** \'ē-vən-,sȯŋ\ *noun, often capitalized* [Middle English, from Old English *ǣfensang*, from *ǣfen* evening + *sang* song] (before 12th century)
**1** : VESPERS 1
**2** : EVENING PRAYER

**event** \i-'vent\ *noun* [Middle French or Latin; Middle French, from Latin *eventus*, from *evenire* to happen, from *e-* + *venire* to come — more at COME] (1573)
**1 a** *archaic* : OUTCOME **b** : the final outcome or determination of a legal action **c** : a postulated outcome, condition, or eventuality ⟨in the *event* that I am not there, call the house⟩
**2 a** : something that happens : OCCURRENCE **b** : a noteworthy happening **c** : a social occasion or activity
**3** : any of the contests in a program of sports
**4** : the fundamental entity of observed physical reality represented by a point designated by three coordinates of place and one of time in the space-time continuum postulated by the theory of relativity
**5** : a subset of the possible outcomes of an experiment
*synonym* see OCCURRENCE
— **event·less** \-ləs\ *adjective*
— **at all events** : in any case
— **in any event** : in any case
— **in the event** *British* : as it turns out

**event·ful** \i-'vent-fəl\ *adjective* (1600)
**1** : full of or rich in events
**2** : MOMENTOUS
— **event·ful·ly** \-fə-lē\ *adverb*
— **event·ful·ness** *noun*

**event horizon** *noun* (1969)
: the surface of a black hole : the boundary of a black hole at which the escape velocity equals the speed of light and beyond which nothing can escape from within it

**even·tide** \'ē-vən-,tīd\ *noun* (before 12th century)
: the time of evening : EVENING

**even·tu·al** \i-'ven(t)-sh(ə-)wəl, -'ven-chəl\ *adjective* (1683)
**1** *archaic* : CONTINGENT, CONDITIONAL
**2** : taking place at an unspecified later time : ultimately resulting ⟨they counted on our *eventual* success⟩
*synonym* see LAST

**even·tu·al·i·ty** \i-,ven-chə-'wa-lə-tē\ *noun, plural* **-ties** (1759)
: a possible event or outcome : POSSIBILITY

**even·tu·al·ly** \-ē\ *adverb* (1680)
: at an unspecified later time : in the end

**even·tu·ate** \i-'ven-chə-,wāt\ *intransitive verb* **-at·ed; -at·ing** (1789)
: to come out finally : RESULT, COME ABOUT

**ev·er** \'e-vər\ *adverb* [Middle English, from Old English *ǣfre*] (before 12th century)
**1** : ALWAYS ⟨*ever* striving to improve⟩ ⟨the *ever*-increasing population⟩
**2 a** : at any time ⟨more than *ever* before⟩ **b** : in any way ⟨how can I *ever* thank you⟩
**3** — used as an intensive ⟨looks *ever* so angry⟩ ⟨am I *ever* happy to see you⟩

**ev·er·bloom·ing** \,e-vər-'blü-miŋ\ *adjective* (circa 1891)
: blooming more or less continuously throughout the growing season

**ev·er·dur·ing** \,e-vər-'dùr-iŋ, -'dyùr-\ *adjective* (15th century)
*archaic* : EVERLASTING

**ev·er·glade** \'e-vər-,glād\ *noun* [the *Everglades*, Fla.] (1823)
: a swampy grassland especially in southern Florida usually containing saw grass and at least seasonally covered by slowly moving water — usually used in plural

**¹ev·er·green** \'e-vər-,grēn\ *noun* (1644)
**1** : an evergreen plant; *also* : CONIFER
**2** *plural* : twigs and branches of evergreen plants used for decoration
**3** : something that retains its freshness, interest, or popularity

**²evergreen** *adjective* (1671)
**1** : having foliage that remains green and functional through more than one growing season — compare DECIDUOUS 1
**2** : retaining freshness or interest : PERENNIAL

**evergreen oak** *noun* (circa 1682)
: any of various oaks (as a live oak, a holm oak, or a tan oak) with foliage that persists for two years so that the plant is more or less continuously green

**¹ev·er·last·ing** \,e-vər-'las-tiŋ\ *adjective* (13th century)
**1** : lasting or enduring through all time : ETERNAL
**2 a** (1) : continuing long or indefinitely (2) : having or being flowers or foliage that retain form or color for a long time when dried **b** : tediously persistent ⟨the *everlasting* sympathy-seeker who demands attention —H. A. Overstreet⟩
**3** : wearing indefinitely
— **ev·er·last·ing·ly** \-tiŋ-lē\ *adverb*
— **ev·er·last·ing·ness** *noun*

**²everlasting** *noun* (14th century)
**1** : ETERNITY ⟨from *everlasting*⟩
**2** *capitalized* : GOD 1 — used with *the*
**3 a** : any of several chiefly composite plants (as cudweed) with flowers that can be dried without loss of form or color — compare PEARLY EVERLASTING **b** : the flower of an everlasting

**ev·er·more** \,e-vər-'mōr, -'mȯr\ *adverb* (13th century)
**1** : FOREVER, ALWAYS
**2** : in the future

**ever·sion** \i-'vər-zhən, -shən\ *noun* (1751)
**1** : the act of turning inside out : the state of being turned inside out ⟨*eversion* of the bladder⟩
**2** : the condition (as of the foot) of being turned or rotated outward
— **ever·si·ble** \-'vər-sə-bəl\ *adjective*

**evert** \i-'vərt\ *transitive verb* [Latin *evertere*, from *e-* + *vertere* to turn — more at WORTH] (1538)
**1** : OVERTHROW, UPSET
**2** : to subject to eversion

**ev·ery** \'ev-rē\ *adjective* [Middle English *everich, every,* from Old English *ǣfre ǣlc,* from *ǣfre* ever + *ǣlc* each] (before 12th century)
**1 a** : being each individual or part of a group without exception **b** : being each in a series or succession ⟨*every* few days⟩
**2** *obsolete* : being all taken severally
**3** : being each within a range of possibilities ⟨was given *every* chance⟩
**4** : COMPLETE, ENTIRE ⟨we have *every* confidence in her⟩

— **every now and then** *or* **every now and again** *or* **every so often** : at intervals
: OCCASIONALLY

**ev·ery·body** \'ev-ri-,bə-dē, -,bä-\ *pronoun* (1530)
: every person : EVERYONE ▪

**ev·ery·day** \,ev-rē-'dā\ *adjective* (circa 1623)
: encountered or used routinely or typically
: ORDINARY ⟨*everyday* clothes⟩
— **ev·ery·day·ness** \-'dā-nəs\ *noun*

**ev·ery·man** \'ev-rē-,man\ *noun, often capitalized* [*Everyman*, allegorical character in *The Summoning of Everyman*, 15th century English morality play] (1906)
: the typical or ordinary person

**ev·ery·one** \-(,)wən\ *pronoun* (13th century)
: EVERYBODY
*usage* see EVERYBODY

**ev·ery·place** \-,plās\ *adverb* (circa 1917)
: EVERYWHERE

**ev·ery·thing** \'ev-rē-,thiŋ\ *pronoun* (14th century)
**1 a** : all that exists **b** : all that relates to the subject
**2** : all that is important ⟨you mean *everything* to me⟩
**3** : all sorts of other things — used to indicate related but unspecified events, facts, or conditions ⟨all the pains and colds and *everything* —E. B. White⟩

**ev·ery·where** \'ev-rē-,(h)wer, -,(h)war\ *adverb* (13th century)
: in every place or part

**every which way** *adverb* [probably by folk etymology from Middle English *everich way* every way] (1824)
**1** : in every direction
**2** : in a disorderly manner : IRREGULARLY ⟨toys scattered about *every which way*⟩

**ev·ery·wom·an** \'ev-rē-,wù-mən\ *noun, often capitalized* [after *everyman*] (1945)
: the typical or ordinary woman

**evict** \i-'vikt\ *transitive verb* [Late Latin *evictus*, past participle of *evincere*, from Latin, to vanquish, win a point — more at EVINCE] (15th century)

\ə\ abut \ᵊ\ kitten \ər\ further \a\ ash \ā\ ace
\ä\ mop, mar \aù\ out \ch\ chin \e\ bet \ē\ easy
\g\ go \i\ hit \ī\ ice \j\ job \ŋ\ sing \ō\ go
\ȯ\ law \ȯi\ boy \th\ thin \t͟h\ the \ü\ loot \ù\ foot
\y\ yet \zh\ vision  *see also* Guide to Pronunciation

**1 a :** to recover (property) from a person by legal process **b :** to put (a tenant) out by legal process
**2 :** to force out **:** EXPEL
**synonym** see EJECT
— **evic·tion** \-'vik-shən\ *noun*
— **evic·tor** \-'vik-tər\ *noun*

**evict·ee** \i-ˌvik-'tē\ *noun* (1879)
**:** an evicted person

**¹ev·i·dence** \'e-və-dən(t)s, -və-ˌden(t)s\ *noun* (14th century)
**1 a :** an outward sign **:** INDICATION **b :** something that furnishes proof **:** TESTIMONY; *specifically* **:** something legally submitted to a tribunal to ascertain the truth of a matter
**2 :** one who bears witness; *especially* **:** one who voluntarily confesses a crime and testifies for the prosecution against his accomplices
— **in evidence 1 :** to be seen **:** CONSPICUOUS ⟨trim lawns . . . are everywhere *in evidence* —*American Guide Series: North Carolina*⟩ **2 :** as evidence

**²evidence** *transitive verb* **-denced; -dencing** (circa 1610)
**:** to offer evidence of **:** PROVE, EVINCE
**synonym** see SHOW

**ev·i·dent** \'e-və-dənt, -və-ˌdent\ *adjective* [Middle English, from Middle French, from Latin *evident-, evidens*, from *e-* + *vident-, videns*, present participle of *vidēre* to see — more at WIT] (14th century)
**:** clear to the vision or understanding ☆

**ev·i·den·tial** \ˌe-və-'den(t)-shəl\ *adjective* (1641)
**:** EVIDENTIARY 1
— **ev·i·den·tial·ly** *adverb*

**ev·i·den·tia·ry** \ˌe-və-'den-chə-rē, -chē-ˌer-ē\ *adjective* (1810)
**1 :** being, relating to, or affording evidence ⟨photographs of *evidentiary* value⟩
**2 :** conducted so that evidence may be presented ⟨an *evidentiary* hearing⟩

**ev·i·dent·ly** \'e-və-dənt-lē, -ə-ˌdent-, *especially for 2 often* ˌev-ə-'dent-\ *adverb* (1690)
**1 :** in an evident manner **:** CLEARLY, OBVIOUSLY ⟨any style . . . so *evidently* bad or second-rate —T. S. Eliot⟩
**2 :** on the basis of available evidence ⟨he was born . . . *evidently* in Texas —Robert Coughlan⟩

**¹evil** \'ē-vəl, *British often & US also* 'ē-(ˌ)vil\ *adjective* **evil·er** *or* **evil·ler; evil·est** *or* **evil·lest** [Middle English, from Old English *yfel;* akin to Old High German *ubil* evil] (before 12th century)
**1 a :** morally reprehensible **:** SINFUL, WICKED ⟨an *evil* impulse⟩ **b :** arising from actual or imputed bad character or conduct ⟨a man of *evil* reputation⟩
**2 a** *archaic* **:** INFERIOR **b :** causing discomfort or repulsion **:** OFFENSIVE ⟨an *evil* odor⟩ **c :** DISAGREEABLE ⟨woke late and in an *evil* temper⟩
**3 a :** causing harm **:** PERNICIOUS ⟨the *evil* institution of slavery⟩ **b :** marked by misfortune **:** UNLUCKY
— **evil** *adverb, archaic*
— **evil·ly** \-(l)ē\ *adverb*
— **evil·ness** \-nəs\ *noun*

**²evil** *noun* (before 12th century)
**1 a :** the fact of suffering, misfortune, and wrongdoing **b :** a cosmic evil force
**2 :** something that brings sorrow, distress, or calamity

**evil·do·er** \ˌē-vəl-'dü-ər\ *noun* (14th century)
**:** one who does evil

**evil·do·ing** \-'dü-iŋ\ *noun* (14th century)
**:** the act or action of doing evil

**evil eye** *noun* (before 12th century)
**:** an eye or glance held capable of inflicting harm; *also* **:** a person believed to have such an eye or glance

**evil-mind·ed** \ˌē-vəl-'mīn-dəd, -vil-\ *adjective* (1531)
**:** having an evil disposition or evil thoughts
— **evil-mind·ed·ly** *adverb*
— **evil-mind·ed·ness** *noun*

**evince** \i-'vin(t)s\ *transitive verb* **evinced; evinc·ing** [Latin *evincere* to vanquish, win a point, from *e-* + *vincere* to conquer — more at VICTOR] (1621)
**1 :** to constitute outward evidence of
**2 :** to display clearly **:** REVEAL
**synonym** see SHOW
— **evinc·ible** \-'vin(t)-sə-bəl\ *adjective*

**evis·cer·ate** \i-'vi-sə-ˌrāt\ *verb* **-at·ed; -at·ing** [Latin *evisceratus*, past participle of *eviscerare*, from *e-* + *viscera* viscera] (1621)
*transitive verb*
**1 a :** to take out the entrails of **:** DISEMBOWEL **b :** to deprive of vital content or force
**2 :** to remove an organ from (a patient) or the contents of (an organ)
*intransitive verb*
**:** to protrude through a surgical incision or suffer protrusion of a part through an incision
— **evis·cer·a·tion** \-ˌvi-sə-'rā-shən\ *noun*

**ev·i·ta·ble** \'e-və-tə-bəl\ *adjective* [Latin *evitabilis*, from *evitare* to avoid, from *e-* + *vitare* to shun] (1502)
**:** capable of being avoided

**evo·ca·ble** \'e-və-kə-bəl, i-'vō-kə-\ *adjective* (1886)
**:** capable of being evoked

**evo·ca·tion** \ˌē-vō-'kā-shən, ˌe-və-\ *noun* [Latin *evocation-, evocatio*, from *evocare*] (1633)
**1 :** the act or fact of evoking **:** SUMMONING: as **a :** the summoning of a spirit **b :** imaginative recreation ⟨an *evocation* of the past⟩
**2 :** INDUCTION 4e
— **evo·ca·tor** \'ē-vō-ˌkā-tər, 'e-və-\ *noun*

**evoc·a·tive** \i-'vä-kə-tiv\ *adjective* (1657)
**:** evoking or tending to evoke an especially emotional response ⟨settings . . . so *evocative* that they bring tears to the eyes —Eric Malpass⟩
— **evoc·a·tive·ly** *adverb*
— **evoc·a·tive·ness** *noun*

**evoke** \i-'vōk\ *transitive verb* **evoked; evok·ing** [French *évoquer*, from Latin *evocare*, from *e-* + *vocare* to call — more at VOCATION] (circa 1626)
**1 :** to call forth or up: as **a :** CONJURE 2a ⟨*evoke* evil spirits⟩ **b :** to cite especially with approval or for support **:** INVOKE **c :** to bring to mind or recollection ⟨this place *evokes* memories⟩
**2 :** to recreate imaginatively
**synonym** see EDUCE

**evo·lute** \'e-və-ˌlüt *also* 'ē-və-\ *noun* (circa 1736)
**:** the locus of the center of curvature or the envelope of the normals of a curve

**evo·lu·tion** \ˌe-və-'lü-shən, ˌē-və-\ *noun* [Latin *evolution-, evolutio* unrolling, from *evolvere*] (1622)
**1 :** one of a set of prescribed movements
**2 a :** a process of change in a certain direction **:** UNFOLDING **b :** the action or an instance of forming and giving something off **:** EMISSION **c** (1) **:** a process of continuous change from a lower, simpler, or worse to a higher, more complex, or better state **:** GROWTH (2) **:** a process of gradual and relatively peaceful social, political, and economic advance **d :** something evolved
**3 :** the process of working out or developing
**4 a :** the historical development of a biological group (as a race or species) **:** PHYLOGENY **b :** a theory that the various types of animals and plants have their origin in other preexisting types and that the distinguishable differences are due to modifications in successive generations
**5 :** the extraction of a mathematical root
**6 :** a process in which the whole universe is a progression of interrelated phenomena
— **evo·lu·tion·ari·ly** \-shə-ˌner-ə-lē\ *adverb*
— **evo·lu·tion·ary** \-shə-ˌner-ē\ *adjective*
— **evo·lu·tion·ism** \-shə-ˌni-zəm\ *noun*
— **evo·lu·tion·ist** \-sh(ə-)nist\ *noun or adjective*

**evolve** \i-'välv, -'vȯlv, ē- *also* -'väv *or* -'vȯv\ *verb* **evolved; evolv·ing** [Latin *evolvere* to unroll, from *e-* + *volvere* to roll — more at VOLUBLE] (1641)
*transitive verb*
**1 :** EMIT
**2 a :** DERIVE, EDUCE **b :** to produce by natural evolutionary processes **c :** DEVELOP, WORK OUT ⟨*evolve* social, political, and literary philosophies —L. W. Doob⟩
*intransitive verb*
**:** to undergo evolutionary change
— **evolv·able** \-'väl-və-bəl, -'vȯl- *also* -'vä-və- *or* -'vȯ-və-\ *adj*
— **evolve·ment** \-'välv-mənt, -'vȯlv- *also* -'väv- *or* -'vȯv-\ *noun*

**evul·sion** \i-'vəl-shən\ *noun* [Latin *evulsion-, evulsio*, from *evellere* to pluck out, from *e-* + *vellere* to pluck — more at VULNERABLE] (circa 1611)
**:** EXTRACTION

**ev·zone** \'ev-ˌzōn\ *noun* [New Greek *euzōnos*, from Greek, active, literally, well girt, from *eu-* + *zōnē* girdle — more at ZONE] (1897)
**:** a member of a select Greek infantry unit often serving as a palace guard

**ewe** \'yü, *in rural dials also* 'yō\ *noun* [Middle English, from Old English *ēowu;* akin to Old High German *ouwi* ewe, Latin *ovis* sheep, Greek *ois*] (before 12th century)
**:** the female of the sheep especially when mature; *also* **:** the female of various related animals

**Ewe** \'ā-ˌwā, 'ā-ˌvā\ *noun, plural* **Ewe** *also* **Ewes** (1861)
**:** a people of Ghana and Togo speaking a Kwa language; *also* **:** the language itself

**ewe–neck** \-'nek\ *noun* (1820)
**:** a thin neck with a concave arch occurring as a defect in dogs and horses
— **ewe–necked** \-'nekt\ *adjective*

**ew·er** \'yü-ər, 'yú(-ə)r\ *noun* [Middle English, from Anglo-French, from Old French *evier*, from Latin *aquarium* water source, neuter of *aquarius* of water, from *aqua* water — more at ISLAND] (14th century)
**:** a vase-shaped pitcher or jug

**Ew·ing's sarcoma** \'yü-iŋz-\ *noun* [James *Ewing* (died 1943) American pathologist] (1951)

ewer

---

☆ SYNONYMS
**Evident, manifest, patent, distinct, obvious, apparent, plain, clear** mean readily perceived or apprehended. EVIDENT implies presence of visible signs that lead one to a definite conclusion ⟨an *evident* fondness for sweets⟩. MANIFEST implies an external display so evident that little or no inference is required ⟨*manifest* hostility⟩. PATENT applies to a cause, effect, or significant feature that is clear and unmistakable once attention has been directed to it ⟨*patent* defects⟩. DISTINCT implies such sharpness of outline or definition that no unusual effort to see or hear or comprehend is required ⟨a *distinct* refusal⟩. OBVIOUS implies such ease in discovering that it often suggests conspicuousness or little need for perspicacity in the observer ⟨the *obvious* solution⟩. APPARENT is very close to EVIDENT except that it may imply more conscious exercise of inference ⟨for no *apparent* reason⟩. PLAIN suggests lack of intricacy, complexity, or elaboration ⟨her feelings about him are *plain*⟩. CLEAR implies an absence of anything that confuses the mind or obscures the pattern ⟨a *clear* explanation⟩.

: a tumor that invades the shaft of a long bone and that tends to recur but rarely metastasizes

**¹ex** \(ˌ)eks\ *preposition* [Latin] (circa 1755)
**1 :** out of : FROM: as **a :** from a specified place or source **b :** from a specified dam ⟨a promising calf by Eric XVI *ex* Heatherbell⟩
**2 :** free from : WITHOUT: as **a :** without an indicated value or right — used especially of securities **b :** free of charges precedent to removal from the specified place with purchaser to provide means of subsequent transportation ⟨*ex* dock⟩ ◆

**²ex** *noun* [¹*ex-*] (1827)
: one that formerly held a specified position or place; *especially* : a former spouse

**³ex** *noun* (circa 1889)
: the letter *x*

**¹ex-** \e also occurs in this prefix where only i is shown below (as in "express") and ks sometimes occurs where only gz is shown (as in "exact")\ *prefix* [Middle English, from Old French & Latin; Old French, from Latin (also, prefix with perfective and causative value), from *ex* out of, from; akin to Greek *ex, ex-* out of, from Old Church Slavonic *iz*]
**1 :** out of : outside ⟨*ex*clave⟩
**2 :** not ⟨*ex*stipulate⟩
**3** \(ˌ)eks, ˈeks\ [Middle English, from Late Latin, from Latin] : former ⟨*ex*-president⟩

**²ex-** — see EXO-

**exa-** *combining form* [International Scientific Vocabulary, modification of Greek *hexa-* hexa-]
: quintillion ⟨*exa*joules⟩

**ex·ac·er·bate** \ig-ˈza-sər-ˌbāt\ *transitive verb* **-bat·ed; -bat·ing** [Latin *exacerbatus*, past participle of *exacerbare*, from *ex-* + *acerbus* harsh, bitter, from *acer* sharp — more at EDGE] (1660)
: to make more violent, bitter, or severe ⟨the proposed shutdown . . . would *exacerbate* unemployment problems —*Science*⟩
— **ex·ac·er·ba·tion** \-ˌza-sər-ˈbā-shən\ *noun*

**¹ex·act** \ig-ˈzakt\ *transitive verb* [Middle English, to require as payment, from Latin *exactus*, past participle of *exigere* to drive out, demand, measure, from *ex-* + *agere* to drive — more at AGENT] (1564)
**1 :** to call for forcibly or urgently and obtain ⟨from them has been *exacted* the ultimate sacrifice —D. D. Eisenhower⟩
**2 :** to call for as necessary or desirable
*synonym* see DEMAND
— **ex·act·able** \-ˈzak-tə-bəl\ *adjective*
— **ex·ac·tor** *also* **ex·act·er** \-ˈzak-tər\ *noun*

**²exact** *adjective* [Latin *exactus*] (1533)
**1 :** exhibiting or marked by strict, particular, and complete accordance with fact or a standard
**2 :** marked by thorough consideration or minute measurement of small factual details
*synonym* see CORRECT
— **ex·act·ness** \-ˈzak(t)-nəs\ *noun*

**ex·ac·ta** \ig-ˈzak-tə\ *noun* [American Spanish (*quiniela*) *exacta* exact quiniela] (1964)
: PERFECTA

**exact differential** *noun* (1825)
: a differential expression of the form $X_1dx_1 + \ldots + X_ndx_n$ where the $X$'s are the partial derivatives of a function $f(x_1, \ldots, x_n)$ with respect to $x_1, \ldots, x_n$ respectively

**ex·act·ing** \ig-ˈzak-tiŋ\ *adjective* (1634)
**1 :** tryingly or unremittingly severe in making demands
**2 :** requiring careful attention and precision
*synonym* see ONEROUS
— **ex·act·ing·ly** \-tiŋ-lē\ *adverb*
— **ex·act·ing·ness** *noun*

**ex·ac·tion** \ig-ˈzak-shən\ *noun* (15th century)
**1 a :** the act or process of exacting **b :** EXTORTION
**2 :** something exacted; *especially* : a fee, reward, or contribution demanded or levied with severity or injustice

**ex·ac·ti·tude** \ig-ˈzak-tə-ˌtüd, -ˌtyüd\ *noun* (1734)
: the quality or an instance of being exact : EXACTNESS

**ex·act·ly** \ig-ˈzak-(t)lē\ *adverb* (1612)
**1 a :** in a manner or measure or to a degree or number that strictly conforms to a fact or condition ⟨it's *exactly* 3 o'clock⟩ ⟨these two pieces are *exactly* the same size⟩ **b :** in every respect : ALTOGETHER, ENTIRELY ⟨that was *exactly* the wrong thing to do⟩ ⟨not *exactly* what I had in mind⟩
**2 :** quite so — used to express agreement

**exact science** *noun* (1843)
: a science (as physics, chemistry, or astronomy) whose laws are capable of accurate quantitative expression

**ex·ag·ger·ate** \ig-ˈza-jə-ˌrāt\ *verb* **-at·ed; -at·ing** [Latin *exaggeratus*, past participle of *exaggerare*, literally, to heap up, from *ex-* + *agger* heap, from *aggerere* to carry toward, from *ad-* + *gerere* to carry] (circa 1587)
*transitive verb*
**1 :** to enlarge beyond bounds or the truth : OVERSTATE ⟨a friend *exaggerates* a man's virtues —Joseph Addison⟩
**2 :** to enlarge or increase especially beyond the normal : OVEREMPHASIZE
*intransitive verb*
: to make an overstatement
— **ex·ag·ger·at·ed·ly** *adverb*
— **ex·ag·ger·at·ed·ness** *noun*
— **ex·ag·ger·a·tion** \-ˌza-jə-ˈrā-shən\ *noun*
— **ex·ag·ger·a·tive** \-ˈza-jə-ˌrā-tiv, -ˈzaj-rə-, -ˈza-jə-\ *adjective*
— **ex·ag·ger·a·tor** \-ˈza-jə-ˌrā-tər\ *noun*
— **ex·ag·ger·a·to·ry** \-ˈzaj-rə-ˌtōr-ē, -ˌtȯr-, -ˈza-jə-\ *adjective*

**ex·alt** \ig-ˈzȯlt\ *verb* [Middle English, from Middle French & Latin; Middle French *exalter*, from Latin *exaltare*, from *ex-* + *altus* high — more at OLD] (15th century)
*transitive verb*
**1 :** to raise in rank, power, or character
**2 :** to elevate by praise or in estimation : GLORIFY
**3** *obsolete* : ELATE
**4 :** to raise high : ELEVATE
**5 :** to enhance the activity of : INTENSIFY ⟨rousing and *exalting* the imagination —George Eliot⟩
*intransitive verb*
: to induce exaltation
— **ex·alt·ed·ly** *adverb*
— **ex·alt·er** *noun*

**ex·al·ta·tion** \ˌeg-ˌzȯl-ˈtā-shən, ˌek-ˌsȯl-\ *noun* (14th century)
**1 :** an act of exalting : the state of being exalted
**2 :** an excessively intensified sense of well-being, power, or importance
**3 :** an increase in degree or intensity ⟨*exaltation* of virulence of a virus⟩

**ex·am** \ig-ˈzam\ *noun* (1877)
: EXAMINATION

**ex·a·men** \ig-ˈzā-mən\ *noun* [Latin, tongue of a balance, examination, from *exigere* — more at EXACT] (1606)
**1 :** EXAMINATION
**2 :** a critical study

**ex·am·i·nant** \-ˈza-mə-nənt\ *noun* (1588)
**1 :** EXAMINEE
**2 :** one who examines : EXAMINER

**ex·am·i·na·tion** \ig-ˌza-mə-ˈnā-shən\ *noun* (14th century)
**1 :** the act or process of examining : the state of being examined
**2 :** an exercise designed to examine progress or test qualification or knowledge
**3 :** a formal interrogation
— **ex·am·i·na·tion·al** \-shnəl, -shə-nᵊl\ *adjective*

**ex·am·ine** \ig-ˈza-mən\ *verb* **ex·am·ined; ex·am·in·ing** \-ˈzam-niŋ, -ˈza-mə-\ [Middle English, from Middle French *examiner*, from Latin *examinare*, from *examen*] (14th century)
*transitive verb*
**1 a :** to inspect closely **b :** to test the condition of **c :** to inquire into carefully : INVESTIGATE
**2 a :** to interrogate closely ⟨*examine* a prisoner⟩ **b :** to test by questioning in order to determine progress, fitness, or knowledge
*intransitive verb*
: to make or give an examination
*synonym* see SCRUTINIZE
— **ex·am·in·able** \-ˈza-mə-nə-bəl\ *adjective*
— **ex·am·in·er** \-ˈzam-nər, -ˈza-mə-\ *noun*

**ex·am·in·ee** \ig-ˌza-mə-ˈnē\ *noun* (1788)
: a person who is examined

**¹ex·am·ple** \ig-ˈzam-pəl\ *noun* [Middle English, from Middle French, from Latin *exemplum*, from *eximere* to take out, from *ex-* + *emere* to take — more at REDEEM] (14th century)
**1 :** one that serves as a pattern to be imitated or not to be imitated ⟨a good *example*⟩ ⟨a bad *example*⟩
**2 :** a punishment inflicted on someone as a warning to others; *also* : an individual so punished
**3 :** one (as an item or incident) that is representative of all of a group or type
**4 :** a parallel or closely similar case especially when serving as a precedent or model
**5 :** an instance (as a problem to be solved) serving to illustrate a rule or precept or to act as an exercise in the application of a rule
*synonym* see INSTANCE, MODEL
— **for example** \fər-ig-ˈzam-pəl, frig-\ **:** as an example ⟨there are many sources of air pollution; exhaust fumes, *for example*⟩

**²example** *transitive verb* **ex·am·pled; ex·am·pling** \-p(ə-)liŋ\ (15th century)
**1 :** to serve as an example of
**2** *archaic* : to be or set an example to

**ex·an·i·mate** \eg-ˈza-nə-mət\ *adjective* [Latin *exanimatus*, past participle of *exanimare* to deprive of life or spirit, from *ex-* + *anima* breath, soul — more at ANIMATE] (circa 1534)
**1 :** lacking animation : SPIRITLESS
**2 :** being or appearing lifeless

**ex·an·them** \eg-ˈzan(t)-thəm, ˈek-ˌsan-ˌthem\ *also* **ex·an·the·ma** \ˌeg-ˌzan-ˈthē-mə\ *noun, plural* **-thems** *also* **-them·a·ta** \ˌeg-ˌzan-ˈthe-mə-tə\ *or* **-themas** [Late Latin *exanthema*, from Greek *exanthēma*, from *exanthein* to bloom, break out, from *ex-* + *anthos* flower — more at ANTHOLOGY] (1656)

---

◇ **WORD HISTORY**
**ex** The word *ex* meaning "former spouse" is clearly a shortening of *ex-wife* or *ex-husband*, but the origin of the prefix *ex-* that forms these words is less straightforward. In Latin, both the prefix *ex-* and the preposition *ex* meant "out of, from." The preposition took on the meaning "from being, having formerly been" in phrases describing a man's office and the office he had previously held. For example, *ex assessore praefectus praetorii* meant "prefect of the Praetorian Guard, having formerly held the office of assessor" (literally, "out of assessor, prefect of the Praetorian Guard"). Because of phrases of this type, *ex* in the sense "having formerly been" came to be used in Late Latin simply as a prefix, in words like *exconsul* "person who was formerly consul." Although *ex-* in this meaning has been used sporadically in English since the late Middle Ages, coinages such as *ex-president* and *ex-wife* did not become common until the 19th century.

---

\ə\ abut \ᵊ\ kitten \ər\ further \a\ ash \ā\ ace
\ä\ mop, mar \aů\ out \ch\ chin \e\ bet \ē\ easy
\g\ go \i\ hit \ī\ ice \j\ job \ŋ\ sing \ō\ go
\ȯ\ law \ȯi\ boy \th\ thin \t͟h\ the \ü\ loot \ů\ foot
\y\ yet \zh\ vision *see also* Guide to Pronunciation

: an eruptive disease (as measles) or its symptomatic eruption

— **ex·an·them·a·tous** \,eg-,zan-'the-mə-təs\ *or* **ex·an·the·mat·ic** \-,zan-thə-'ma-tik\ *adjective*

¹**ex·arch** \'ek-,särk\ *noun* [Late Latin *exarchus*, from Late Greek *exarchos*, from Greek, leader, from *exarchein* to begin, take the lead, from *ex-* + *archein* to rule, begin — more at ARCH-] (1588)
**1** : a Byzantine viceroy
**2** : an Eastern bishop ranking below a patriarch and above a metropolitan; *specifically* : the head of an independent church
— **ex·ar·chal** \ek-'sär-kəl\ *adjective*
— **ex·arch·ate** \'ek-,sär-kət\ *noun*
— **ex·ar·chy** \'ek-,sär-kē\ *noun*

²**exarch** *adjective* [*exo-* + *-arch*] (1891)
: formed or taking place from the periphery toward the center ⟨*exarch* xylem⟩

¹**ex·as·per·ate** \ig-'zas-pə-,rāt\ *transitive verb* **-at·ed; -at·ing** [Latin *exasperatus*, past participle of *exasperare*, from *ex-* + *asper* rough — more at ASPERITY] (1534)
**1 a** : to excite the anger of : ENRAGE **b** : to cause irritation or annoyance to
**2** *obsolete* : to make more grievous : AGGRAVATE
**synonym** see IRRITATE
— **ex·as·per·at·ed·ly** *adverb*
— **ex·as·per·at·ing·ly** *adverb*

²**ex·as·per·ate** \-p(ə-)rət\ *adjective* (1541)
**1** : irritated or annoyed especially to the point of injudicious action : EXASPERATED
**2** : roughened with irregular prickles or elevations ⟨*exasperate* seed coats⟩

**ex·as·per·a·tion** \ig-,zas-pə-'rā-shən\ *noun* (1547)
**1** : the state of being exasperated
**2** : the act or an instance of exasperating

**Ex·cal·i·bur** \ek-'ska-lə-bər\ *noun* [Middle English *Excalaber*, from Old French *Escalibor*, from Medieval Latin *Caliburnus*]
: the sword of King Arthur

**ex ca·the·dra** \,eks-kə-'thē-drə\ *adverb or adjective* [New Latin, literally, from the chair] (1818)
: by virtue of or in the exercise of one's office or position ⟨*ex cathedra* pronouncements⟩

**ex·ca·vate** \'ek-skə-,vāt\ *verb* **-vat·ed; -vat·ing** [Latin *excavatus*, past participle of *excavare*, from *ex-* + *cavare* to make hollow — more at CAVATINA] (1599)
*transitive verb*
**1** : to form a cavity or hole in
**2** : to form by hollowing out
**3** : to dig out and remove
**4** : to expose to view by or as if by digging away a covering ⟨*excavate* the remains of a temple⟩ ⟨another writer whose work I *excavated* —William Zinsser⟩
*intransitive verb*
: to make excavations

**ex·ca·va·tion** \,ek-skə-'vā-shən\ *noun* (circa 1611)
**1** : the action or process of excavating
**2** : a cavity formed by cutting, digging, or scooping
— **ex·ca·va·tion·al** \-shnəl, -shə-n°l\ *adjective*

**ex·ca·va·tor** \'ek-skə-,vā-tər\ *noun* (circa 1815)
: one that excavates; *especially* : a power-operated shovel

**ex·ceed** \ik-'sēd\ *verb* [Middle English *exceden*, from Middle French *exceder*, from Latin *excedere*, from *ex-* + *cedere* to go] (14th century)
*transitive verb*
**1** : to extend outside of ⟨the river will *exceed* its banks⟩
**2** : to be greater than or superior to
**3** : to go beyond a limit set by ⟨*exceeded* his authority⟩
*intransitive verb*
**1** *obsolete* : OVERDO

**2** : PREDOMINATE ☆

**ex·ceed·ing** *adjective* (15th century)
: exceptional in amount, quality, or degree

**ex·ceed·ing·ly** \-'sē-diŋ-lē\ *also* **ex·ceed·ing** *adverb* (1535)
: to an extreme degree : EXTREMELY

**ex·cel** \ik-'sel\ *verb* **ex·celled; ex·cel·ling** [Middle English *excellen*, from Latin *excellere*, from *ex-* + *-cellere* to rise, project; akin to Latin *collis* hill — more at HILL] (15th century)
*transitive verb*
: to be superior to : surpass in accomplishment or achievement
*intransitive verb*
: to be distinguishable by superiority : surpass others ⟨*excel* in sports⟩ ⟨*excelled* at lipreading⟩
**synonym** see EXCEED

**ex·cel·lence** \'ek-s(ə-)lən(t)s\ *noun* (14th century)
**1** : the quality of being excellent
**2** : an excellent or valuable quality : VIRTUE
**3** : EXCELLENCY 2

**ex·cel·len·cy** \-s(ə-)lən(t)-sē\ *noun, plural* **-cies** (15th century)
**1** : EXCELLENCE; *especially* : outstanding or valuable quality — usually used in plural ⟨so crammed, as he thinks, with *excellencies* —Shakespeare⟩
**2** — used as a title for high dignitaries of state (as a governor or an ambassador) or church (as a Roman Catholic archbishop or bishop)

**ex·cel·lent** \'ek-s(ə-)lənt\ *adjective* [Middle English, from Middle French, from Latin *excellent-*, *excellens*, from present participle of *excellere*] (14th century)
**1** *archaic* : SUPERIOR
**2** : very good of its kind : eminently good : FIRST-CLASS
— **ex·cel·lent·ly** *adverb*

**ex·cel·si·or** \ik-'sel-sē-ər, -ôr\ *noun* [trade name, from Latin, higher, comparative of *excelsus* high, from past participle of *excellere*] (1868)
: fine curled wood shavings used especially for packing fragile items

¹**ex·cept** \ik-'sept\ *also* **ex·cept·ing** \-'sep-tiŋ\ *preposition* (14th century)
: with the exclusion or exception of ⟨daily *except* Sundays⟩

²**except** *verb* [Middle English, from Middle French *excepter*, from Latin *exceptare*, from *exceptus*, past participle of *excipere* to take out, except, from *ex-* + *capere* to take — more at HEAVE] (14th century)
*transitive verb*
: to take or leave out from a number or a whole : EXCLUDE
*intransitive verb*
: to take exception : OBJECT
— **ex·cep·tive** \-'sep-təv\ *adjective*

³**except** *also* **excepting** *conjunction* (15th century)
**1** : on any other condition than that : UNLESS ⟨*except* you repent⟩
**2** : with this exception, namely ⟨was inaccessible *except* by boat⟩
**3** : ONLY — often followed by *that* ⟨I would go *except* that it's too far⟩

**except for** *preposition* (1842)
**1** : with the exception of ⟨everyone was gone *except for* me⟩
**2** : were it not for ⟨*except for* you I would be dead⟩

**ex·cep·tion** \ik-'sep-shən\ *noun* (14th century)
**1** : the act of excepting : EXCLUSION
**2** : one that is excepted; *especially* : a case to which a rule does not apply
**3** : QUESTION, OBJECTION ⟨witnesses whose authority is beyond *exception* —T. B. Macaulay⟩
**4** : an oral or written legal objection

**ex·cep·tion·able** \ik-'sep-sh(ə)nə-bəl\ *adjective* (1691)

: being likely to cause objection : OBJECTIONABLE ⟨visitors even drink the *exceptionable* beer —W. D. Howells⟩
— **ex·cep·tion·abil·i·ty** \-,sep-sh(ə)nə-'bi-lə-tē\ *noun*
— **ex·cep·tion·ably** \-'sep-sh(ə)nə-blē\ *adverb*

**ex·cep·tion·al** \ik-'sep-shnəl, -shə-n°l\ *adjective* (circa 1846)
**1** : forming an exception : RARE ⟨an *exceptional* number of rainy days⟩
**2** : better than average : SUPERIOR ⟨*exceptional* skill⟩
**3** : deviating from the norm: as **a** : having above or below average intelligence **b** : physically handicapped
— **ex·cep·tion·al·i·ty** \-,sep-shə-'na-lə-tē\ *noun*
— **ex·cep·tion·al·ness** *noun*

**ex·cep·tion·al·ism** \ik-'sep-shnə-,li-zəm, -shə-n°l-,i-\ *noun* (1937)
: the condition of being different from the norm; *also* : a theory expounding the exceptionalism especially of a nation or region

**ex·cep·tion·al·ly** \ik-'sep-shnə-lē, -shə-n°l-ē\ *adverb* (1848)
: in an exceptional manner : to an exceptional degree; *especially* : more than average or usual ⟨an *exceptionally* difficult task⟩

¹**ex·cerpt** \ek-'sərpt, eg-'zərpt, 'ek-,, 'eg-,\ *transitive verb* [Latin *excerptus*, past participle of *excerpere*, from *ex-* + *carpere* to gather, pluck — more at HARVEST] (15th century)
**1** : to select (a passage) for quoting : EXTRACT
**2** : to take or publish extracts from (as a book)
— **ex·cerp·tor** *or* **ex·cerpt·er** *noun*
— **ex·cerp·tion** \ek-'sərp-shən, eg-'zərp-\ *noun*

²**ex·cerpt** \'ek-,sərpt, 'eg-,zərpt\ *noun* (1627)
: a passage (as from a book or musical composition) selected, performed, or copied : EXTRACT

¹**ex·cess** \ik-'ses, 'ek-,\ *noun* [Middle English, from Middle French or Late Latin; Middle French *exces*, from Late Latin *excessus*, from Latin, departure, projection, from *excedere* to exceed] (14th century)
**1 a** : the state or an instance of surpassing usual, proper, or specified limits : SUPERFLUITY
**b** : the amount or degree by which one thing or quantity exceeds another ⟨an *excess* of 10 bushels⟩
**2** : undue or immoderate indulgence : INTEMPERANCE; *also* : an act or instance of intemperance ⟨prevent *excesses* and abuses by newly created local powers —Albert Shanker⟩
— **in excess of** : to an amount or degree beyond : OVER

²**excess** *adjective* (15th century)
: more than the usual, proper, or specified amount

³**excess** *transitive verb* (1974)
: to eliminate the position of ⟨*excessed* several teachers because of budget cutbacks⟩

---

☆ **SYNONYMS**
**Exceed, surpass, transcend, excel, outdo, outstrip** mean to go or be beyond a stated or implied limit, measure, or degree. EXCEED implies going beyond a limit set by authority or established by custom or by prior achievement ⟨*exceed* the speed limit⟩. SURPASS suggests superiority in quality, merit, or skill ⟨the book *surpassed* our expectations⟩. TRANSCEND implies a rising or extending notably above or beyond ordinary limits ⟨*transcended* the values of their culture⟩. EXCEL implies preeminence in achievement or quality and may suggest superiority to all others ⟨*excels* in mathematics⟩. OUTDO applies to a bettering or exceeding what has been done before ⟨*outdid* herself this time⟩. OUTSTRIP suggests surpassing in a race or competition ⟨*outstripped* other firms in sales⟩.

**ex·ces·sive** \ik-'se-siv\ *adjective* (14th century)
: exceeding what is usual, proper, necessary, or normal ☆
— **ex·ces·sive·ly** *adverb*
— **ex·ces·sive·ness** *noun*

¹**ex·change** \iks-'chānj, 'eks-\ *noun, often attributive* [Middle English *exchaunge*, from Middle French *eschange*, from *eschangier* to exchange, from (assumed) Vulgar Latin *excambiare*, from Latin *ex-* + *cambiare* to exchange — more at CHANGE] (14th century)
**1** : the act of giving or taking one thing in return for another : TRADE ⟨an *exchange* of prisoners⟩
**2 a** : the act or process of substituting one thing for another **b** : reciprocal giving and receiving
**3** : something offered, given, or received in an exchange
**4 a** : funds payable currently at a distant point either in a foreign currency or in domestic currency **b** (1) : interchange or conversion of the money of two countries or of current and uncurrent money with allowance for difference in value (2) : EXCHANGE RATE (3) : the amount of the difference in value between two currencies or between values of a particular currency at two places **c** : instruments (as checks or bills of exchange) presented in a clearinghouse for settlement
**5** : a place where things or services are exchanged: as **a** : an organized market or center for trading in securities or commodities **b** : a store or shop specializing in merchandise usually of a particular type **c** : a cooperative store or society **d** : a central office in which telephone lines are connected to permit communication
— **in exchange** : as a substitute

²**exchange** *verb* **ex·changed; ex·chang·ing** (15th century)
*transitive verb*
**1 a** : to part with, give, or transfer in consideration of something received as an equivalent **b** : to have replaced by other merchandise ⟨*exchanged* the shirt for one in a larger size⟩
**2** : to part with for a substitute ⟨*exchanging* future security for immediate pleasure⟩
**3** : to give and receive reciprocally ⟨*exchange* gifts⟩
*intransitive verb*
**1** : to pass or become received in exchange
**2** : to engage in an exchange
— **ex·change·abil·i·ty** \iks-,chān-jə-'bi-lə-tē\ *noun*
— **ex·change·able** \iks-'chān-jə-bəl\ *adjective*
— **ex·chang·er** \iks-'chān-jər, eks-,\ *noun*

**exchange rate** *noun* (1896)
: the ratio at which the principal unit of two currencies may be traded

**exchange student** *noun* (circa 1930)
: a student from one country received into an institution in another country in exchange for one sent to an institution in the home country of the first

**Ex·chang·ite** \iks-'chān-,jīt\ *noun* [*(National) Exchange (club)*] (circa 1934)
: a member of a major national service club

**ex·che·quer** \'eks-,che-kər, iks-'\ *noun* [Middle English *escheker*, from Anglo-French, from Old French *eschequier* chessboard, counting table — more at CHECKER] (14th century)
**1** *capitalized* : a department or office of state in medieval England charged with the collection and management of the royal revenue and judicial determination of all revenue causes
**2** *capitalized* : a former superior court having jurisdiction in England and Wales primarily over revenue matters and now merged with King's Bench
**3** *often capitalized* **a** : the department or office of state in Great Britain and Northern Ireland charged with the receipt and care of the na-

tional revenue **b** : the national banking account of this realm
**4** : TREASURY; *especially* : a national or royal treasury
**5** : pecuniary resources : FUNDS

**ex·ci·mer laser** \'ek-si-,mər-\ *noun* [*excited* + *dimer*] (1973)
: a laser that uses a noble-gas halide to generate radiation usually in the ultraviolet region of the spectrum

**ex·cip·i·ent** \ik-'si-pē-ənt\ *noun* [Latin *excipient-, excipiens*, present participle of *excipere* to take out, take up — more at EXCEPT] (1753)
: a usually inert substance (as gum arabic or starch) that forms a vehicle (as for a drug)

**ex·ci·ple** \'ek-sə-pəl\ *noun* [New Latin *excipulum*, from Latin, receptacle, from *excipere*] (circa 1866)
: a saucer-shaped rim around the hymenium of various lichens

**ex·cis·able** \'ek-,sī-zə-bəl, -,sī-sə-, ek-'\ *adjective* (1689)
: subject to excise

¹**ex·cise** \'ek-,sīz, -,sīs\ *noun* [obsolete Dutch *excijs* (now *accijns*), from Middle Dutch, probably modification of Old French *assise* session, assessment — more at ASSIZE] (15th century)
**1** : an internal tax levied on the manufacture, sale, or consumption of a commodity
**2** : any of various taxes on privileges often assessed in the form of a license or fee

²**ex·cise** \'ek-,sīz, -,sīs, ik-'sīz\ *transitive verb* **ex·cised; ex·cis·ing** (1652)
: to impose an excise on

³**ex·cise** \ik-'sīz\ *transitive verb* **ex·cised; ex·cis·ing** [Latin *excisus*, past participle of *excidere*, from *ex-* + *caedere* to cut] (1634)
: to remove by or as if by excision

**ex·cise·man** \'ek-,sīz-mən, -,sīs-, -,man, ek-'\ *noun* (1647)
: an officer who inspects and rates articles liable to excise under British law

**ex·ci·sion** \ik-'si-zhən\ *noun* [Middle English *excysion*, from Middle French *excision*, from Latin *excision-, excisio*, from *excidere*] (1541)
: the act or procedure of removing by or as if by cutting out; *especially* : surgical removal or resection
— **ex·ci·sion·al** \-'sizh-nəl, -zh°n-əl\ *adjective*

**ex·cit·able** \ik-'sī-tə-bəl\ *adjective* (1609)
**1** : capable of being readily roused into action or a state of excitement or irritability
**2** : capable of being activated by and reacting to stimuli
— **ex·cit·abil·i·ty** \-,sī-tə-'bi-lə-tē\ *noun*
— **ex·cit·able·ness** \-'sī-tə-bəl-nəs\ *noun*

**ex·ci·tant** \ik-'sī-t°nt, 'ek-sə-tənt\ *adjective* (1607)
: tending to excite or augment ⟨*excitant* drugs⟩
— **excitant** *noun*

**ex·ci·ta·tion** \,ek-,sī-'tā-shən, ,ek-sə-\ *noun* (14th century)
: EXCITEMENT; *especially* : the disturbed or altered condition resulting from stimulation of an individual, organ, tissue, or cell

**ex·cit·ative** \ik-'sī-tə-tiv\ *adjective* (15th century)
: tending to induce excitation (as of a neuron) ⟨*excitative* substances⟩

**ex·cit·ato·ry** \ik-'sī-tə-,tōr-ē, -,tòr-\ *adjective* (1803)
: exhibiting, resulting from, related to, or producing excitement or excitation ⟨*excitatory* nerve fibers⟩

**ex·cite** \ik-'sīt, ek-\ *transitive verb* **ex·cit·ed; ex·cit·ing** [Middle English, from Middle French *exciter*, from Latin *excitare*, from *ex-* + *citare* to rouse — more at CITE] (14th century)
**1 a** : to call to activity **b** : to rouse to an emotional response ⟨scenes to *excite* the hardest

man to pity⟩ **c** : to arouse (as a strong emotional response) by appropriate stimuli ⟨*excite* enthusiasm for the new regime —Arthur Knight⟩
**2 a** : ENERGIZE ⟨*excite* an electromagnet⟩ **b** : to produce a magnetic field in ⟨*excite* a dynamo⟩
**3** : to increase the activity of (as a living organism) : STIMULATE
**4** : to raise (as an atomic nucleus, an atom, or a molecule) to a higher energy level
**synonym** see PROVOKE
— **ex·cit·ed·ly** \-'sī-təd-lē\ *adverb*

**excited state** *noun* (1927)
: a state of a physical system (as an atomic nucleus, an atom, or a molecule) that is higher in energy than the ground state

**ex·cite·ment** \ik-'sīt-mənt\ *noun* (1604)
**1** : something that excites or rouses
**2** : the action of exciting : the state of being excited

**ex·cit·er** \ik-'sī-tər\ *noun* (14th century)
**1** : one that excites
**2 a** : a generator or battery that supplies the electric current used to produce the magnetic field in another generator or motor **b** : an electrical oscillator that generates the carrier frequency (as for a radio transmitter)

**ex·cit·ing** \ik-'sī-tiŋ\ *adjective* (circa 1811)
: producing excitement
— **ex·cit·ing·ly** \-iŋ-lē\ *adverb*

**ex·ci·ton** \'ek-sə-,tän, -,sī-\ *noun* [International Scientific Vocabulary *excitation* + ²*-on*] (1936)
: a mobile combination of an electron and a hole in an excited crystal (as of a semiconductor)
— **ex·ci·ton·ic** \,ek-sə-'tä-nik, -,sī-\ *adjective*

**ex·ci·tor** \ik-'sī-tər\ *noun* (1816)
: an afferent nerve arousing increased action of the part that it supplies

**ex·claim** \iks-'klām\ *verb* [Middle French *exclamer*, from Latin *exclamare*, from *ex-* + *clamare* to cry out — more at CLAIM] (circa 1570)
*intransitive verb*
**1** : to cry out or speak in strong or sudden emotion ⟨*exclaimed* in delight⟩
**2** : to speak loudly or vehemently ⟨*exclaimed* against immorality⟩
*transitive verb*
: to utter sharply, passionately, or vehemently : PROCLAIM
— **ex·claim·er** *noun*

**ex·cla·ma·tion** \,eks-klə-'mā-shən\ *noun* (14th century)
**1** : a sharp or sudden utterance

---

☆ SYNONYMS
**Excessive, immoderate, inordinate, extravagant, exorbitant, extreme** mean going beyond a normal limit. EXCESSIVE implies an amount or degree too great to be reasonable or acceptable ⟨*excessive* punishment⟩. IMMODERATE implies lack of desirable or necessary restraint ⟨*immoderate* spending⟩. INORDINATE implies an exceeding of the limits dictated by reason or good judgment ⟨*inordinate* pride⟩. EXTRAVAGANT implies an indifference to restraints imposed by truth, prudence, or good taste ⟨*extravagant* claims for the product⟩. EXORBITANT implies a departure from accepted standards regarding amount or degree ⟨*exorbitant* prices⟩. EXTREME may imply an approach to the farthest limit possible or conceivable but commonly means only to a notably high degree ⟨*extreme* shyness⟩.

---

\ə\ abut \ᵊ\ kitten \ər\ further \a\ ash \ā\ ace
\ä\ mop, mar \aù\ out \ch\ chin \e\ bet \ē\ easy
\g\ go \i\ hit \ī\ ice \j\ job \ŋ\ sing \ō\ go
\ò\ law \òi\ boy \th\ thin \th\ the \ü\ loot \ù\ foot
\y\ yet \zh\ vision *see also* Guide to Pronunciation

**2 :** vehement expression of protest or complaint

**exclamation point** *noun* (1824)
**:** a mark ! used especially after an interjection or exclamation to indicate forceful utterance or strong feeling — called also *exclamation mark*

**ex·clam·a·to·ry** \iks-'kla-mə-ˌtōr-ē, -ˌtȯr-\ *adjective* (1593)
**:** containing, expressing, using, or relating to exclamation ⟨an *exclamatory* phrase⟩

**ex·clave** \'eks-ˌklāv, -ˌkläv\ *noun* [*ex-* + *-clave* (as in *enclave*)] (1888)
**:** a portion of a country separated from the main part and constituting an enclave in respect to the surrounding territory

**ex·clud·able** *or* **ex·clud·ible** \iks-'klü-də-bəl\ *adjective* (1916)
**:** subject to exclusion ⟨*excludable* income⟩
— **ex·clud·abil·i·ty** \-ˌklü-də-'bi-lə-tē\ *noun*

**ex·clude** \iks-'klüd\ *transitive verb* **ex·clud·ed; ex·clud·ing** [Middle English, from Latin *excludere,* from *ex-* + *claudere* to close — more at CLOSE] (14th century)
**1 a :** to prevent or restrict the entrance of **b :** to bar from participation, consideration, or inclusion
**2 :** to expel or bar especially from a place or position previously occupied
— **ex·clud·er** *noun*

**ex·clu·sion** \iks-'klü-zhən\ *noun* [Latin *exclusion-, exclusio,* from *excludere*] (15th century)
**1 :** the act or an instance of excluding
**2 :** the state of being excluded
— **ex·clu·sion·ary** \-zhə-ˌner-ē\ *adjective*

**exclusionary rule** *noun* (1964)
**:** a legal rule that bars unlawfully obtained evidence from being used in court proceedings

**ex·clu·sion·ist** \iks-'klüzh-nist, -'klü-zhə-\ *noun* (1822)
**:** one who would exclude another from some right or privilege
— **exclusionist** *adjective*

**exclusion principle** *noun* (1926)
**:** a principle in physics: no two particles (as electrons) in an atom or molecule can have the same set of quantum numbers

**¹ex·clu·sive** \iks-'klü-siv, -ziv\ *adjective* (1515)
**1 a :** excluding or having power to exclude **b :** limiting or limited to possession, control, or use by a single individual or group
**2 a :** excluding others from participation **b :** snobbishly aloof
**3 a :** accepting or soliciting only a socially restricted patronage (as of the upper class) **b :** STYLISH, FASHIONABLE **c :** restricted in distribution, use, or appeal because of expense
**4 a :** SINGLE, SOLE ⟨*exclusive* jurisdiction⟩ **b :** WHOLE, UNDIVIDED ⟨his *exclusive* attention⟩
— **ex·clu·sive·ly** *adverb*
— **ex·clu·sive·ness** *noun*

**²exclusive** *noun* (15th century)
**:** something exclusive: as **a :** a newspaper story at first released to or printed by only one newspaper **b :** an exclusive right (as to sell a particular product in a certain area)

**exclusive disjunction** *noun* (1942)
**:** a compound proposition in logic that is true when one and only one of its constituent statements is true — see TRUTH TABLE table

**exclusive of** *preposition* (1762)
**:** not taking into account ⟨there were four of us *exclusive of* the guide⟩

**ex·clu·siv·ism** \iks-'klü-sə-ˌvi-zəm, -'klü-zə-\ *noun* (circa 1834)
**:** the practice of excluding or of being exclusive
— **ex·clu·siv·ist** \-vist\ *noun or adjective*

**ex·clu·siv·i·ty** \ˌeks-ˌklü-'si-və-tē, iks-, -'zi-\ *noun, plural* **-ties** (1926)
**1 :** the quality or state of being exclusive
**2 :** exclusive rights or services

**ex·cog·i·tate** \ek-'skä-jə-ˌtāt\ *transitive verb* [Latin *excogitatus,* past participle of *excogitare,* from *ex-* + *cogitare* to cogitate] (circa 1530)
**:** to think out : DEVISE
— **ex·cog·i·ta·tion** \(ˌ)ek-ˌskä-jə-'tā-shən\ *noun*
— **ex·cog·i·ta·tive** \ek-'skä-jə-ˌtā-tiv\ *adjective*

**¹ex·com·mu·ni·cate** \ˌek-skə-'myü-nə-ˌkāt\ *transitive verb* [Middle English, from Late Latin *excommunicatus,* past participle of *excommunicare,* from Latin *ex-* + Late Latin *communicare* to communicate] (15th century)
**:** to subject to excommunication
— **ex·com·mu·ni·ca·tor** \-ˌkā-tər\ *noun*

**²ex·com·mu·ni·cate** \-ni-kət\ *adjective* (1551)
**:** excluded from the rites of the church : EXCOMMUNICATED
— **excommunicate** *noun*

**ex·com·mu·ni·ca·tion** \-ˌmyü-nə-'kā-shən\ *noun* (15th century)
**1 :** an ecclesiastical censure depriving a person of the rights of church membership
**2 :** exclusion from fellowship in a group or community
— **ex·com·mu·ni·ca·tive** \-'myü-nə-ˌkā-tiv, -ni-kət-\ *adjective*

**ex·co·ri·ate** \ek-'skōr-ē-ˌāt, -'skȯr-\ *transitive verb* **-at·ed; -at·ing** [Middle English, from Late Latin *excoriatus,* past participle of *excoriare,* from Latin *ex-* + *corium* skin, hide — more at CUIRASS] (15th century)
**1 :** to wear off the skin of : ABRADE
**2 :** to censure scathingly
— **ex·co·ri·a·tion** \(ˌ)ek-ˌskōr-ē-'ā-shən, -ˌskȯr-\ *noun*

**ex·cre·ment** \'ek-skrə-mənt\ *noun* [Latin *excrementum,* from *excernere*] (1533)
**:** waste matter discharged from the body; *especially* **:** waste (as feces) discharged from the alimentary canal
— **ex·cre·men·tal** \ˌek-skrə-'men-t°l\ *adjective*
— **ex·cre·men·ti·tious** \-ˌmen-'ti-shəs, -mən-\ *adjective*

**ex·cres·cence** \ik-'skre-s°n(t)s, ek-\ *noun* (15th century)
**1 :** a projection or outgrowth especially when abnormal ⟨warty *excrescences* in the colon⟩
**2 :** a disfiguring, extraneous, or unwanted mark or part : BLOT

**ex·cres·cen·cy** \-s°n-sē\ *noun, plural* **-cies** (1545)
**:** EXCRESCENCE

**ex·cres·cent** \-s°nt\ *adjective* [Latin *excrescent-, excrescens,* present participle of *excrescere* to grow out, from *ex-* + *crescere* to grow — more at CRESCENT] (1633)
**1 :** forming an abnormal, excessive, or useless outgrowth
**2 :** of, relating to, or constituting epenthesis
— **ex·cres·cent·ly** *adverb*

**ex·cre·ta** \ik-'skrē-tə\ *noun plural* [New Latin, from Latin, neuter plural of *excretus*] (1857)
**:** waste matter eliminated or separated from an organism; *especially* **:** EXCRETIONS
— **ex·cre·tal** \-'skrē-t°l\ *adjective*

**ex·crete** \ik-'skrēt\ *transitive verb* **ex·cret·ed; ex·cret·ing** [Latin *excretus,* past participle of *excernere* to sift out, discharge, from *ex-* + *cernere* to sift — more at CERTAIN] (1620)
**:** to separate and eliminate or discharge (waste) from the blood or tissues or from the active protoplasm
— **ex·cret·er** *noun*

**ex·cre·tion** \ik-'skrē-shən\ *noun* (1603)
**1 :** the act or process of excreting
**2 :** something excreted; *especially* **:** metabolic waste products (as urea and carbon dioxide) that are eliminated from the body and differ from a secretion in not being produced to perform a useful function

**ex·cre·to·ry** \'ek-skrə-ˌtōr-ē, -ˌtȯr-\ *adjective* (circa 1681)
**:** of, relating to, or functioning in excretion ⟨*excretory* ducts⟩

**ex·cru·ci·ate** \ik-'skrü-shē-ˌāt\ *transitive verb* **-at·ed; -at·ing** [Latin *excruciatus,* past participle of *excruciare,* from *ex-* + *cruciare* to crucify, from *cruc-, crux* cross] (circa 1570)
**1 :** to inflict intense pain on : TORTURE
**2 :** to subject to intense mental distress
— **ex·cru·ci·a·tion** \-ˌskrü-shē-'ā-shən, -sē-\ *noun*

**ex·cru·ci·at·ing** *adjective* (1599)
**1 :** causing great pain or anguish : AGONIZING ⟨the nation's most *excruciating* dilemma —W. H. Ferry⟩
**2 :** very intense : EXTREME ⟨*excruciating* pain⟩
— **ex·cru·ci·at·ing·ly** \-ˌā-tiŋ-lē\ *adverb*

**ex·cul·pate** \'ek-(ˌ)skəl-ˌpāt, (ˌ)ek-'\ *transitive verb* **-pat·ed; -pat·ing** [Medieval Latin *exculpatus,* past participle of *exculpare,* from Latin *ex-* + *culpa* blame] (circa 1681)
**:** to clear from alleged fault or guilt ☆
— **ex·cul·pa·tion** \ˌek-(ˌ)skəl-'pā-shən\ *noun*

**ex·cul·pa·to·ry** \ek-'skəl-pə-ˌtōr-ē, -ˌtȯr-\ *adjective* (1781)
**:** tending or serving to exculpate

**ex·cur·rent** \(ˌ)ek-'skər-ənt, -'skə-rənt\ *adjective* [Latin *excurrent-, excurrens,* present participle of *excurrere* to run out, extend, from *ex-* + *currere* to run — more at CAR] (1826)
**1 :** characterized by a current that flows outward ⟨*excurrent* canals of a sponge⟩
**2 a :** having the axis prolonged to form an undivided main stem or trunk (as in conifers) — compare DELIQUESCENT 2 **b :** projecting beyond the apex — used especially of the midrib of a mucronate leaf

**ex·cur·sion** \ik-'skər-zhən\ *noun* [Latin *excursion-, excursio,* from *excurrere*] (1587)
**1 a :** a going out or forth : EXPEDITION **b** (1) **:** a usually brief pleasure trip (2) **:** a trip at special reduced rates
**2 :** deviation from a direct, definite, or proper course; *especially* **:** DIGRESSION ⟨needless *excursions* into abstruse theory⟩
**3 a :** a movement outward and back or from a mean position or axis; *also* **:** the distance traversed : AMPLITUDE ⟨the *excursion* of a piston⟩ **b :** one complete movement of expansion and contraction of the lungs and their membranes (as in breathing)

**ex·cur·sion·ist** \-'skərzh-nist, -'skər-zhə-\ *noun* (1830)
**:** a person who goes on an excursion

**ex·cur·sive** \-'skər-siv\ *adjective* (1749)
**:** constituting a digression : characterized by digression
— **ex·cur·sive·ly** *adverb*

— **ex·cur·sive·ness** *noun*

**ex·cur·sus** \ik-'skər-səs\ *noun, plural* **ex·cur·sus·es** *also* **ex·cur·sus** \-səs, -ˌsüs\ [Latin, digression, from *excurrere*] (1803)
: an appendix or digression that contains further exposition of some point or topic

**ex·cu·sa·to·ry** \ik-'skyü-zə-ˌtōr-ē, -ˌtȯr-\ *adjective* (1535)
: making or containing excuse

¹**ex·cuse** \ik-'skyüz, *imperatively often* 'skyüz\ *transitive verb* **ex·cused; ex·cus·ing** [Middle English, from Old French *excuser*, from Latin *excusare*, from *ex-* + *causa* cause, explanation] (13th century)
**1 a :** to make apology for **b :** to try to remove blame from
**2 :** to forgive entirely or disregard as of trivial import : regard as excusable ⟨graciously *excused* his tardiness⟩
**3 a :** to grant exemption or release to ⟨was *excused* from jury duty⟩ **b :** to allow to leave ⟨*excused* the class⟩
**4 :** to serve as excuse for : JUSTIFY ⟨nothing can *excuse* such neglect⟩ ☆
— **ex·cus·able** \ik-'skyü-zə-bəl\ *adjective*
— **ex·cus·able·ness** *noun*
— **ex·cus·ably** \-blē\ *adverb*
— **ex·cus·er** *noun*

²**ex·cuse** \ik-'skyüs\ *noun* (14th century)
**1 :** the act of excusing
**2 a :** something offered as justification or as grounds for being excused **b** *plural* : an expression of regret for failure to do something **c :** a note of explanation of an absence
**3 :** JUSTIFICATION, REASON
**synonym** see APOLOGY

**ex–di·rec·to·ry** \ˌeks-də-'rek-t(ə-)rē, -dī-\ *adjective* [Latin *ex* out of — more at EX-] (1936)
*British* : not listed in a telephone book : UNLISTED

**ex·ec** \ig-'zek\ *noun* (1896)
**1 :** EXECUTIVE OFFICER
**2 :** EXECUTIVE

**ex·e·cra·ble** \'ek-si-krə-bəl\ *adjective* (14th century)
**1 :** deserving to be execrated : DETESTABLE ⟨*execrable* crimes⟩
**2 :** very bad : WRETCHED ⟨*execrable* hotel food⟩
— **ex·e·cra·ble·ness** *noun*
— **ex·e·cra·bly** \-blē\ *adverb*

**ex·e·crate** \'ek-sə-ˌkrāt\ *transitive verb* **-crat·ed; -crat·ing** [Latin *exsecratus*, past participle of *exsecrari* to put under a curse, from *ex* + *sacr-, sacer* sacred] (1561)
**1 :** to declare to be evil or detestable : DENOUNCE
**2 :** to detest utterly
— **ex·e·cra·tive** \-ˌkrā-tiv\ *adjective*
— **ex·e·cra·tor** \-ˌkrā-tər\ *noun*

**ex·e·cra·tion** \ˌek-sə-'krā-shən\ *noun* (14th century)
**1 :** the act of cursing or denouncing; *also* : the curse so uttered
**2 :** an object of curses : something detested

**ex·ec·u·tant** \ig-'ze-k(y)ə-tənt\ *noun* (1858)
: one who executes or performs; *especially* : one skilled in the technique of an art : PERFORMER

**ex·e·cute** \'ek-si-ˌkyüt\ *verb* **-cut·ed; -cut·ing** [Middle English, from Middle French *executer*, back-formation from *execution*] (14th century)
*transitive verb*
**1 :** to carry out fully : put completely into effect ⟨*execute* a command⟩
**2 :** to do what is provided or required by ⟨*execute* a decree⟩
**3 :** to put to death especially in compliance with a legal sentence
**4 :** to make or produce (as a work of art) especially by carrying out a design
**5 :** to perform what is required to give validity to ⟨*execute* a deed⟩
**6 :** PLAY ⟨*execute* a piece of music⟩

*intransitive verb*
**1 :** to perform properly or skillfully the fundamentals of a sport or of a particular play ⟨never had a team *execute* better —Bobby Knight⟩
**2 :** to perform indicated tasks according to encoded instructions — used of a computer program or routine
**synonym** see KILL, PERFORM
— **ex·e·cut·able** \-ˌkyü-tə-bəl\ *adjective*

**ex·e·cu·tion** \ˌek-si-'kyü-shən\ *noun* [Middle English, from Middle French, from Latin *exsecution-, exsecutio,* from *exsequi* to execute, from *ex-* + *sequi* to follow — more at SUE] (14th century)
**1 :** the act or process of executing : PERFORMANCE
**2 :** a putting to death especially as a legal penalty
**3 :** the process of enforcing a legal judgment (as against a debtor); *also* : a judicial writ directing such enforcement
**4 :** the act or mode or result of performance
**5** *archaic* : effective or destructive action ⟨his brandished steel, which smoked with bloody *execution* —Shakespeare⟩ — usually used with *do* ⟨as soon as day came, we went out to see what *execution* we had done —Daniel Defoe⟩

**ex·e·cu·tion·er** \-sh(ə-)nər\ *noun* (1536)
: one who executes; *especially* : one who puts to death

¹**ex·ec·u·tive** \ig-'ze-k(y)ə-tiv\ *adjective* (1649)
**1 a :** of or relating to the execution of the laws and the conduct of public and national affairs **b :** belonging to the branch of government that is charged with such powers as diplomatic representation, superintendence of the execution of the laws, and appointment of officials and that usually has some power over legislation (as through veto) — compare JUDICIAL, LEGISLATIVE
**2 a :** designed for or relating to execution or carrying into effect ⟨*executive* board⟩ **b :** having administrative or managerial responsibility ⟨*executive* director⟩
**3 :** of or relating to an executive ⟨the *executive* offices⟩

²**executive** *noun* (1774)
**1 :** the executive branch of a government; *also* : the person or persons who constitute the executive magistracy of a state
**2 :** a directing or controlling office of an organization
**3 :** one that exercises administrative or managerial control

**executive agreement** *noun* (1942)
: an agreement between the U.S. and a foreign government made by the executive branch of the government either alone or with Congressional approval and dealing usually with routine matters

**executive council** *noun* (1778)
**1 :** a council constituted to advise or share in the functions of a political executive
**2 :** a council that exercises supreme executive power

**executive officer** *noun* (1881)
: the officer second in command of a military or naval organization

**executive order** *noun* (1883)
: REGULATION 2b

**executive privilege** *noun* (1940)
: exemption from legally enforced disclosure of communications within the executive branch of government when such disclosure would adversely affect the functions and decision-making processes of the executive branch

**executive secretary** *noun* (1950)
: a secretary having administrative duties; *especially* : an official responsible for administering the activities and business affairs of an organization

**executive session** *noun* (1840)

: a usually closed session (as of a legislative body) that functions as an executive council (as of the U.S. Senate when considering appointments or the ratification of treaties)

**ex·ec·u·tor** \ig-'ze-k(y)ə-tər *or in sense 1* 'ek-sə-ˌkyü-\ *noun* [Middle English, from Old French, from Latin *exsecutor,* from *exsequi*] (13th century)
**1 a :** one who executes something **b** *obsolete* : EXECUTIONER
**2 a :** the person appointed by a testator to execute a will **b :** LITERARY EXECUTOR
— **ex·ec·u·to·ri·al** \ig-ˌze-k(y)ə-'tōr-ē-əl, -'tȯr-\ *adjective*

**ex·ec·u·to·ry** \ig-'ze-k(y)ə-ˌtōr-ē, -ˌtȯr-\ *adjective* (1592)
**1 :** designed or of such a nature as to be executed in time to come or to take effect on a future contingency
**2 :** relating to administration

**ex·ec·u·trix** \ig-'ze-k(y)ə-(ˌ)triks\ *noun, plural* **ex·ec·u·tri·ces** \-ˌze-k(y)ə-'trī-(ˌ)sēz\ *or* **ex·ec·u·trix·es** \-'ze-k(y)ə-ˌtrik-səz\ (15th century)
: a woman who is an executor

**ex·e·dra** \'ek-sə-drə\ *noun, plural* **-drae** \-ˌdrē, -ˌdrī\ [Latin, from Greek, from *ex-* + *hedra* seat — more at SIT] (1706)
**1 :** a room (as in a temple or house) in ancient Greece and Rome used for conversation and formed by an open or columned recess often semicircular in shape and furnished with seats
**2 :** a large outdoor nearly semicircular seat with a solid back

**ex·e·ge·sis** \ˌek-sə-'jē-səs, 'ek-sə-ˌ\ *noun, plural* **-ge·ses** \-'jē-(ˌ)sēz\ [New Latin, from Greek *exēgēsis,* from *exēgeisthai* to explain, interpret, from *ex-* + *hēgeisthai* to lead — more at SEEK] (1619)
: EXPOSITION, EXPLANATION; *especially* : an explanation or critical interpretation of a text

**ex·e·gete** \'ek-sə-ˌjēt\ *noun* [Greek *exēgētēs,* from *exēgeisthai*] (circa 1736)
: one who practices exegesis

**ex·e·get·i·cal** \ˌek-sə-'je-ti-kəl\ *also* **ex·e·get·ic** \-tik\ *adjective* [Greek *exēgētikos,* from *exēgeisthai*] (1623)
: of or relating to exegesis : EXPLANATORY

**ex·e·get·ist** \-'jē-tist, -'je-\ *noun* (1848)
: EXEGETE

**ex·em·plar** \ig-'zem-ˌplär, -plər, eg-\ *noun* [Middle English, from Latin, from *exemplum* example] (15th century)

---

☆ **SYNONYMS**
**Excuse, condone, pardon, forgive** mean to exact neither punishment nor redress. EXCUSE may refer to specific acts especially in social or conventional situations or the person responsible for these ⟨*excuse* an interruption⟩ ⟨*excused* them for interrupting⟩. Often the term implies extenuating circumstances ⟨injustice *excuses* strong responses⟩. CONDONE implies that one overlooks without censure behavior (as dishonesty or violence) that involves a serious breach of a moral, ethical, or legal code, and the term may refer to the behavior or to the agent responsible for it ⟨a society that *condones* alcohol but not narcotics⟩. PARDON implies that one remits a penalty due for an admitted or established offense ⟨*pardon* a criminal⟩. FORGIVE implies that one gives up all claim to requital and to resentment or vengeful feelings ⟨could not *forgive* their rudeness⟩.

---

\ə\ **abut** \ᵊ\ **kitten** \ər\ **further** \a\ **ash** \ā\ **ace** \ä\ **mop, mar** \aù\ **out** \ch\ **chin** \e\ **bet** \ē\ **easy** \g\ **go** \i\ **hit** \ī\ **ice** \j\ **job** \ŋ\ **sing** \ō\ **go** \ȯ\ **law** \ȯi\ **boy** \th\ **thin** \th\ **the** \ü\ **loot** \ù\ **foot** \y\ **yet** \zh\ **vision** *see also* Guide to Pronunciation

: one that serves as a model or example: as **a** : an ideal model **b** : a typical or standard specimen **c** : a copy of a book or writing **d** : IDEA 1a
**synonym** see MODEL

**ex·em·pla·ry** \ig-'zem-plə-rē\ *adjective* (1589)
**1 a** : serving as a pattern **b** : deserving imitation : COMMENDABLE ⟨his courage was *exemplary*⟩; *also* : deserving imitation because of excellence ⟨they serve *exemplary* pastries —G. V. Higgins⟩
**2** : serving as a warning : MONITORY
**3** : serving as an example, instance, or illustration
— **ex·em·plar·i·ly** \,eg-,zem-'pler-ə-lē\ *adverb*
— **ex·em·pla·ri·ness** \ig-'zem-plə-rē-nəs\ *noun*
— **ex·em·plar·i·ty** \,eg-,zem-'plar-ə-tē\ *noun*

**ex·em·pli·fi·ca·tion** \ig-,zem-plə-fə-'kā-shən\ *noun* (1510)
**1 a** : the act or process of exemplifying **b** : EXAMPLE, CASE IN POINT
**2** : an exemplified copy of a document

**ex·em·pli·fy** \ig-'zem-plə-,fī\ *transitive verb* **-fied; -fy·ing** [Middle English *exemplifien*, from Middle French *exemplifier*, from Medieval Latin *exemplificare*, from Latin *exemplum*] (15th century)
**1** : to show or illustrate by example
**2** : to make an attested copy or transcript of (a document) under seal
**3 a** : to be an instance of or serve as an example : EMBODY **b** : to be typical of

**ex·em·pli gra·tia** \ig-,zem-(,)plē-'grä-tē-,ä, -'grä-sh(ē-)ə\ *adverb* [Latin] (1602)
: for example

**ex·em·plum** \ig-'zem-pləm, eg-\ *noun, plural* **-pla** \-plə\ [Latin] (1890)
**1** : EXAMPLE, MODEL
**2** : an anecdote or short narrative used to point a moral or sustain an argument

**¹ex·empt** \ig-'zem(p)t\ *adjective* [Middle English, from Latin *exemptus*, past participle of *eximere* to take out — more at EXAMPLE] (14th century)
**1** *obsolete* : set apart
**2** : free or released from some liability or requirement to which others are subject ⟨was *exempt* from jury duty⟩ ⟨the estate was *exempt* from taxes⟩

**²exempt** *transitive verb* (15th century)
**1** : to release or deliver from some liability or requirement to which others are subject : EXCUSE ⟨a man *exempted* from military service⟩
**2** *obsolete* : to set apart

**³exempt** *noun* (1670)
: one exempted or freed from duty

**ex·emp·tion** \ig-'zem(p)-shən\ *noun* (14th century)
**1** : the act of exempting or state of being exempt : IMMUNITY
**2** : one that exempts or is exempted; *especially* : a source or amount of income exempted from taxation

**ex·en·ter·ate** \ig-'zen-tə-,rāt\ *transitive verb* **-at·ed; -at·ing** [Latin *exenteratus*, past participle of *exenterare* to disembowel, modification of Greek *exenterizein*, from *ex-* + *enteron* intestine — more at INTER-] (1607)
: to remove the contents of (as the orbit or pelvis)
— **ex·en·ter·a·tion** \-,zen-tə-'rā-shən\ *noun*

**¹ex·er·cise** \'ek-sər-,sīz\ *noun* [Middle English, from Middle French *exercice*, from Latin *exercitium*, from *exercitare* to train, exercise, frequentative of *exercēre* to train, occupy, from *ex-* + *arcēre* to enclose, hold off — more at ARK] (14th century)

**1 a** : the act of bringing into play or realizing in action : USE **b** : the discharge of an official function or professional occupation **c** : the act or an instance of carrying out the terms of an agreement (as an option)
**2 a** : regular or repeated use of a faculty or bodily organ **b** : bodily exertion for the sake of developing and maintaining physical fitness
**3** : something performed or practiced in order to develop, improve, or display a specific power or skill ⟨arithmetic *exercises*⟩
**4** : a performance having a strongly marked secondary or ulterior aspect ⟨party politics has always been an *exercise* in compromise —H. S. Ashmore⟩
**5 a** : a maneuver, operation, or drill carried out for training and discipline **b** *plural* : a program including speeches, announcements of awards and honors, and various traditional practices of secular or religious character ⟨commencement *exercises*⟩

**²exercise** *verb* **-cised; -cis·ing** (14th century)
*transitive verb*
**1 a** : to make effective in action : USE ⟨didn't *exercise* good judgment⟩ **b** : to bring to bear : EXERT ⟨*exercise* influence⟩ **c** : to implement the terms of (as an option)
**2 a** : to use repeatedly in order to strengthen or develop **b** : to train (as troops) by drills and maneuvers **c** : to put through exercises ⟨*exercise* the horses⟩
**3 a** : to engage the attention and effort of **b** : to cause anxiety, alarm, or indignation in ⟨the issues *exercising* voters this year⟩
*intransitive verb*
: to take exercise
— **ex·er·cis·able** \-,sī-zə-bəl\ *adjective*

**ex·er·cis·er** \'ek-sər-,sī-zər\ *noun* (1552)
**1** : one that exercises
**2** : an apparatus for use in physical exercise

**ex·er·ci·ta·tion** \ig-,zər-sə-'tā-shən\ *noun* [Middle English *exercitacioun*, from Latin *exercitation-, exercitatio*, from *exercitare*] (14th century)
: EXERCISE

**Ex·er·cy·cle** \'ek-sər-,sī-kəl\ *trademark*
— used for a stationary bicycle

**ex·er·gon·ic** \,ek-(,)sər-'gä-nik\ *adjective* [*exo-* + Greek *ergon* work — more at WORK] (1940)
: EXOTHERMIC ⟨an *exergonic* biochemical reaction⟩

**ex·ergue** \'ek-,sərg, 'eg-,zərg\ *noun* [French, from New Latin *exergum*, from Greek *ex* out of + *ergon* work] (1697)
: a space on a coin, token, or medal usually on the reverse below the central part of the design

**ex·ert** \ig-'zərt\ *transitive verb* [Latin *exsertus*, past participle of *exserere* to thrust out, from *ex-* + *serere* to join — more at SERIES] (1681)
**1 a** : to put forth (as strength) **b** : to put (oneself) into action or to a tiring effort
**2** : to bring to bear especially with sustained effort or lasting effect
**3** : EMPLOY, WIELD ⟨*exerted* her leadership abilities intelligently⟩

**ex·er·tion** \ig-'zər-shən\ *noun* (1677)
: the act or an instance of exerting; *especially* : a laborious or perceptible effort

**ex·e·unt** \'ek-sē-(,)ənt, -,ünt\ [Latin, they go out, from *exire* to go out — more at EXIT] (15th century)
— used as a stage direction to specify that all or certain named characters leave the stage

**ex·fo·li·ate** \(,)eks-'fō-lē-,āt\ *verb* **-at·ed; -at·ing** [Late Latin *exfoliatus*, past participle of *exfoliare* to strip of leaves, from Latin *ex-* + *folium* leaf — more at BLADE] (1612)
*transitive verb*
**1** : to cast off in scales, laminae, or splinters
**2** : to remove the surface of in scales or laminae
**3** : to spread or extend by or as if by opening out leaves
*intransitive verb*

**1** : to split into or give off scales, laminae, or body cells
**2** : to come off in thin layers or scales
**3** : to grow by or as if by producing or unfolding leaves
— **ex·fo·li·a·tion** \(,)eks-,fō-lē-'ā-shən\ *noun*
— **ex·fo·li·a·tive** \eks-'fō-lē-,ā-tiv\ *adjective*

**ex gra·tia** \(,)eks-'grä-sh(ē-)ə\ *adjective or adverb* [New Latin] (1769)
: as a favor : not compelled by legal right ⟨*ex gratia* pension payments⟩

**ex·hal·ant** *or* **ex·hal·ent** \eks-'hā-lənt, ek-'sā-\ *adjective* (1771)
: bearing out or outward : EMISSIVE ⟨an *exhalant* siphon of a clam⟩

**ex·ha·la·tion** \,eks-hə-'lā-shən, ,ek-sə-\ *noun* (14th century)
**1** : something exhaled or given off : EMANATION
**2** : an act of exhaling

**ex·hale** \eks-'hā(ə)l, ek-'sā(ə)l\ *verb* **exhaled; ex·hal·ing** [Middle English *exalen*, from Latin *exhalare*, from *ex-* + *halare* to breathe] (14th century)
*intransitive verb*
**1** : to rise or be given off as vapor
**2** : to emit breath or vapor
*transitive verb*
**1 a** : to breathe out **b** : to give forth (gaseous matter) : EMIT
**2** *archaic* : to cause to be emitted in vapor

**¹ex·haust** \ig-'zȯst\ *verb* [Latin *exhaustus*, past participle of *exhaurire*, from *ex-* + *haurire* to draw; akin to Middle High German *œsen* to empty, Greek *auein* to take] (1533)
*transitive verb*
**1 a** : to consume entirely : USE UP ⟨*exhausted* our funds in a week⟩ **b** : to tire extremely or completely ⟨*exhausted* by overwork⟩ **c** : to deprive of a valuable quality or constituent ⟨*exhaust* a photographic developer⟩ ⟨*exhaust* a soil of fertility⟩
**2 a** : to draw off or let out completely **b** : to empty by drawing off the contents; *specifically* : to create a vacuum in
**3 a** : to develop (a subject) completely **b** : to try out the whole number of ⟨*exhausted* all the possibilities⟩
*intransitive verb*
: DISCHARGE, EMPTY ⟨the engine *exhausts* through the muffler⟩
**synonym** see DEPLETE, TIRE
— **ex·haust·er** *noun*
— **ex·haust·ibil·i·ty** \-,zȯ-stə-'bi-lə-tē\ *noun*
— **ex·haust·ible** \-'zȯ-stə-bəl\ *adjective*

**²exhaust** *noun* (1848)
**1 a** : the escape of used gas or vapor from an engine **b** : the gas or vapor thus escaping
**2 a** : the conduit through which used gases escape **b** : an arrangement for removing fumes, dusts, or odors from an enclosure
**3** : EXHAUSTION

**ex·haus·tion** \ig-'zȯs-chən\ *noun* (1646)
: the act or process of exhausting : the state of being exhausted

**ex·haus·tive** \ig-'zȯ-stiv\ *adjective* (1786)
: testing all possibilities or considering all elements : THOROUGH ⟨conducted an *exhaustive* investigation⟩
— **ex·haus·tive·ly** *adverb*
— **ex·haus·tive·ness** *noun*
— **ex·haus·tiv·i·ty** \-,zȯ-'sti-və-tē\ *noun*

**ex·haust·less** \ig-'zȯst-ləs\ *adjective* (1712)
: not to be exhausted : INEXHAUSTIBLE
— **ex·haust·less·ly** *adverb*
— **ex·haust·less·ness** *noun*

**¹ex·hib·it** \ig-'zi-bət\ *verb* [Middle English, from Latin *exhibitus*, past participle of *exhibēre*, from *ex-* + *habēre* to have, hold — more at GIVE] (15th century)
*transitive verb*

**exhibit** 639 **ex libris**

**1 :** to submit (as a document) to a court or officer in course of proceedings; *also* **:** to present or offer officially or in legal form
**2 :** to present to view: as **a :** to show or display outwardly especially by visible signs or actions ⟨*exhibited* no fear⟩ **b :** to have as a readily discernible quality or feature ⟨in all cultures we know, men *exhibit* an aesthetic sense —H. J. Muller⟩ **c :** to show publicly especially for purposes of competition or demonstration
*intransitive verb*
**:** to display something for public inspection
**synonym** see SHOW
— **ex·hib·i·tive** \-bə-tiv\ *adjective*
— **ex·hib·i·tor** \-bə-tər\ *noun*
— **ex·hib·i·to·ry** \-bə-₁tōr-ē, -₁tòr-\ *adjective*

²**exhibit** *noun* (1626)
**1 :** a document or material object produced and identified in court or before an examiner for use as evidence
**2 :** something exhibited
**3 :** an act or instance of exhibiting

**ex·hi·bi·tion** \₁ek-sə-'bi-shən\ *noun* (14th century)
**1 :** an act or instance of exhibiting
**2** *British* **:** a grant drawn from the funds of a school or university to help maintain a student
**3 :** a public showing (as of works of art, objects of manufacture, or athletic skill) ⟨a one-man *exhibition*⟩ ⟨an *exhibition* game⟩

**ex·hi·bi·tion·er** \-'bish-nər, -'bi-shə-\ *noun* (1679)
*British* **:** one who holds a grant from a school or university

**ex·hi·bi·tion·ism** \-'bi-shə-₁ni-zəm\ *noun* (1893)
**1 a :** a perversion marked by a tendency to indecent exposure **b :** an act of such exposure **2 :** the act or practice of behaving so as to attract attention to oneself
— **ex·hi·bi·tion·ist** \-'bish-nist, -'bi-shə-\ *noun or adjective*
— **ex·hi·bi·tion·is·tic** \-₁bi-shə-'nis-tik\ *adjective*
— **ex·hi·bi·tion·is·ti·cal·ly** \-ti-k(ə-)lē\ *adverb*

**ex·hil·a·rate** \ig-'zi-lə-₁rāt\ *transitive verb* **-rat·ed; -rat·ing** [Latin *exhilaratus*, past participle of *exhilarare*, from *ex-* + *hilarare* to gladden, from *hilarus* cheerful — more at HILARIOUS] (1540)
**1 a :** to make cheerful **b :** ENLIVEN, EXCITE
**2 :** REFRESH, STIMULATE
— **ex·hil·a·rat·ing·ly** \ig-'zi-lə-₁rā-tiŋ-lē\ *adverb*
— **ex·hil·a·ra·tive** \-₁rā-tiv\ *adjective*

**ex·hil·a·ra·tion** \ig-₁zi-lə-'rā-shən\ *noun* (circa 1626)
**1 :** the action of exhilarating
**2 :** the feeling or the state of being exhilarated

**ex·hort** \ig-'zòrt\ *verb* [Middle English, from Middle French *exhorter*, from Latin *exhortari*, from *ex-* + *hortari* to incite — more at YEARN] (15th century)
*transitive verb*
**:** to incite by argument or advice **:** urge strongly
*intransitive verb*
**:** to give warnings or advice **:** make urgent appeals
— **ex·hort·er** *noun*

**ex·hor·ta·tion** \₁ek-₁sòr-'tā-shən, -sər-; ₁eg-₁zòr-, -zər-\ *noun* (14th century)
**1 :** an act or instance of exhorting
**2 :** language intended to incite and encourage

**ex·hor·ta·tive** \ig-'zòr-tə-tiv\ *adjective* (15th century)
**:** serving to exhort

**ex·hor·ta·to·ry** \-tə-₁tōr-ē, -₁tòr-\ *adjective* (15th century)
**:** using exhortation **:** EXHORTATIVE ⟨an *exhortatory* appeal⟩

**ex·hume** \ig-'züm, igz-'yüm, iks-'(h)yüm\ *transitive verb* **ex·humed; ex·hum·ing**

[French or Medieval Latin; French *exhumer*, from Medieval Latin *exhumare*, from Latin *ex* out of + *humus* earth — more at EX-, HUMBLE] (15th century)
**1 :** DISINTER
**2 :** to bring back from neglect or obscurity
— **ex·hu·ma·tion** \₁eks-(h)yü-'mā-shən, ₁eg-zü-, ₁egz-yü-\ *noun*
— **ex·hum·er** \ig-'zü-mər, igz-'yü-, iks-'(h)yü-\ *noun*

**ex hy·po·the·si** \₁eks-hī-'pä-thə-₁sī\ *adverb* [New Latin, from a hypothesis] (1603)
**:** according to assumptions made **:** by hypothesis ⟨regard . . . all elites as *ex hypothesi* incompatible with democracy —P. G. J. Pulzer⟩

**ex·i·gence** \'ek-sə-jən(t)s\ *noun* (15th century)
**:** EXIGENCY

**ex·i·gen·cy** \'ek-sə-jən(t)-sē, ig-'zi-jən(t)-\ *noun, plural* **-cies** (1581)
**1 :** that which is required in a particular situation — usually used in plural
**2 a :** the quality or state of being exigent **b :** a state of affairs that makes urgent demands ⟨a leader must act in any sudden *exigency*⟩
**synonym** see JUNCTURE

**ex·i·gent** \'ek-sə-jənt\ *adjective* [Latin *exigent-, exigens*, present participle of *exigere* to demand — more at EXACT] (1629)
**1 :** requiring immediate aid or action
**2 :** requiring or calling for much **:** DEMANDING
— **ex·i·gent·ly** *adverb*

**ex·i·gu·i·ty** \₁eg-zi-'gyü-ə-tē\ *noun, plural* **-ities** (circa 1626)
**:** the quality or state of being exiguous **:** SCANTINESS

**ex·ig·u·ous** \ig-'zi-gyə-wəs\ *adjective* [Latin *exiguus*, from *exigere*] (1651)
**:** excessively scanty **:** INADEQUATE ⟨wrest an *exiguous* existence from the land⟩ ⟨*exiguous* evidence⟩
— **ex·ig·u·ous·ly** *adverb*
— **ex·ig·u·ous·ness** *noun*

¹**ex·ile** \'eg-₁zīl, 'ek-₁sīl\ *noun* [Middle English *exil*, from Middle French, from Latin *exilium* from *exul, exsul* an exile] (14th century)
**1 a :** the state or a period of forced absence from one's country or home **b :** the state or a period of voluntary absence from one's country or home
**2 :** a person who is in exile
— **ex·il·ic** \eg-'zi-lik\ *adjective*

²**exile** *transitive verb* **ex·iled; ex·il·ing** (14th century)
**:** to banish or expel from one's own country or home
**synonym** see BANISH

**ex·im·i·ous** \eg-'zi-mē-əs\ *adjective* [Latin *eximius*, from *eximere* to take out — more at EXAMPLE] (1547)
*archaic* **:** CHOICE, EXCELLENT

**ex·ine** \'ek-₁sēn, -₁sīn\ *noun* [International Scientific Vocabulary *ex-* + *in-* fibrous tissue, from Greek *in-, is* tendon] (circa 1884)
**:** the outer of the two major layers forming the walls of some spores and especially pollen grains

**ex·ist** \ig-'zist\ *intransitive verb* [Latin *exsistere* to come into being, exist, from *ex-* + *sistere* to stand, stop; akin to Latin *stare* to stand — more at STAND] (1602)
**1 a :** to have real being whether material or spiritual ⟨did unicorns *exist*⟩ ⟨the largest galaxy known to *exist*⟩ **b :** to have being in a specified place or with respect to understood limitations or conditions ⟨strange ideas *existed* in his mind⟩
**2 :** to continue to be ⟨racism still *exists* in society⟩
**3 a :** to have life or the functions of vitality ⟨we cannot *exist* without oxygen⟩ **b :** to live at an inferior level or under adverse circumstances ⟨the hungry *existing* from day to day⟩

**ex·is·tence** \ig-'zis-tən(t)s\ *noun* (14th century)

**1 a** *obsolete* **:** reality as opposed to appearance **b :** reality as presented in experience **c** (1) **:** the totality of existent things (2) **:** a particular being ⟨all the fair *existences* of heaven —John Keats⟩ **d :** sentient or living being **:** LIFE
**2 a :** the state or fact of having being especially independently of human consciousness and as contrasted with nonexistence **b :** the manner of being that is common to every mode of being **c :** being with respect to a limiting condition or under a particular aspect
**3 :** continued or repeated manifestation

**ex·is·tent** \-tənt\ *adjective* [Latin *exsistent-, exsistens*, present participle of *exsistere*] (1561)
**1 :** having being **:** EXISTING
**2 :** existing now **:** PRESENT
— **existent** *noun*

**ex·is·ten·tial** \₁eg-(₁)zis-'ten(t)-shəl, ₁ek-(₁)sis-\ *adjective* (1693)
**1 :** of, relating to, or affirming existence ⟨*existential* propositions⟩
**2 a :** grounded in existence or the experience of existence **:** EMPIRICAL **b :** having being in time and space
**3** [translation of Danish *eksistentiel* & German *existential*] **:** EXISTENTIALIST
— **ex·is·ten·tial·ly** *adverb*

**ex·is·ten·tial·ism** \-'ten(t)-shə-₁li-zəm\ *noun* (1941)
**:** a chiefly 20th century philosophical movement embracing diverse doctrines but centering on analysis of individual existence in an unfathomable universe and the plight of the individual who must assume ultimate responsibility for his acts of free will without any certain knowledge of what is right or wrong or good or bad

¹**ex·is·ten·tial·ist** \-list\ *noun* (1942)
**:** an adherent of existentialism

²**existentialist** *adjective* (1946)
**:** of or relating to existentialism or existentialists
— **ex·is·ten·tial·is·tic** \-₁ten(t)-shə-'lis-tik\ *adjective*
— **ex·is·ten·tial·is·ti·cal·ly** \-ti-k(ə-)lē\ *adverb*

**existential quantifier** *noun* (1940)
**:** a quantifier (as *for some* in "for some $x$, $2x + 5 = 8$") that asserts that there exists at least one value of a variable — called also *existential operator*

¹**ex·it** \'eg-zət, 'ek-sət\ [Latin, he goes out, from *exire* to go out, from *ex-* + *ire* to go — more at ISSUE] (1538)
— used as a stage direction to specify who goes off stage

²**exit** *noun* [Latin *exitus*, from *exire*] (1588)
**1** [¹*exit*] **:** a departure from a stage
**2 a :** the act of going out or going away **b :** DEATH
**3 :** a way out of an enclosed place or space
**4 :** one of the designated points of departure from an expressway
— **ex·it·less** *adjective*

³**exit** (1607)
*intransitive verb*
**1 :** to go out or away **:** DEPART
**2 :** DIE
*transitive verb*
**:** LEAVE 3a

**exit poll** *noun* (1980)
**:** a poll taken (as by news media) of voters leaving the voting place that is usually used for predicting the winners
— **exit polling** *noun*

**ex li·bris** \eks-'lē-brəs, -₁brēs\ *noun, plural* **ex libris** [New Latin, from the books; used before the owner's name on bookplates] (1880)
**:** BOOKPLATE

\ə\ abut \ᵊ\ kitten \ər\ further \a\ ash \ā\ ace \ä\ mop, mar \aú\ out \ch\ chin \e\ bet \ē\ easy \g\ go \i\ hit \ī\ ice \j\ job \ŋ\ sing \ō\ go \ò\ law \òi\ boy \th\ thin \t̲h̲\ the \ü\ loot \ú\ foot \y\ yet \zh\ vision *see also* Guide to Pronunciation

**Ex·moor** \'ek-,muṙ, -,smōr, -,smȯr\ *noun* [*Exmoor*, England] (1808)

**1 :** any of a breed of horned sheep of Devonshire in England valued especially for mutton **2 :** any of a breed of hardy ponies native to the Exmoor district and having a mealy-colored muzzle

Exmoor 1

**ex ni·hi·lo** \(,)eks-'nē-(h)ə-,lō, -'ni-, -'nī-\ *adverb or adjective* [Latin] (1580)
**:** from or out of nothing ⟨creation *ex nihilo*⟩

**exo-** *or* **ex-** *combining form* [Greek *exō* out, outside, from *ex* out of — more at EX-]
**1 :** outside ⟨*exogamy*⟩ **:** outer ⟨*exoskeleton*⟩ — compare ECT-, END-
**2 :** turning out ⟨*exoergic*⟩

**exo·bi·ol·o·gy** \,ek-sō-bī-'ä-lə-jē\ *noun* (1960)
**:** a branch of biology concerned with the search for life outside the earth and with the effects of extraterrestrial environments on living organisms
— **exo·bi·o·log·i·cal** \-,bī-ə-'lä-ji-kəl\ *adjective*
— **exo·bi·ol·o·gist** \-bī-'ä-lə-jist\ *noun*

**exo·carp** \'ek-sō-,kärp\ *noun* [International Scientific Vocabulary] (circa 1845)
**:** the outermost layer of the pericarp of a fruit — see ENDOCARP illustration

**exo·crine** \'ek-sə-krən, -,krīn, -,krēn\ *adjective* [International Scientific Vocabulary *exo-* + Greek *krinein* to separate — more at CERTAIN] (circa 1911)
**:** producing, being, or relating to a secretion that is released outside its source ⟨*exocrine* pancreatic cells⟩

**exocrine gland** *noun* (circa 1927)
**:** a gland (as a salivary gland or part of the pancreas) that releases a secretion external to or at the surface of an organ by means of a canal or duct

**exo·cy·clic** \,ek-sō-'sī-klik, -'si-\ *adjective* (1888)
**:** situated outside of a ring in a chemical structure

**exo·cy·to·sis** \,ek-sō-sī-'tō-səs\ *noun, plural* **-to·ses** \-,sēz\ [New Latin, from *exo-* + *cyt-* + *-osis*] (1963)
**:** the release of cellular substances (as secretory products) contained in cell vesicles by fusion of the vesicular membrane with the plasma membrane and subsequent release of the contents to the exterior of the cell
— **exo·cy·tot·ic** \-'tä-tik\ *adjective*

**exo·der·mis** \,ek-sō-'dər-məs\ *noun* [New Latin] (circa 1900)
**:** a layer of the outer living cortical cells of plants that takes over the functions of the epidermis in roots lacking secondary thickening

**ex·odon·tia** \,ek-sə-'dän(t)-sh(ē-)ə\ *noun* [New Latin, from *ex-* + *-odontia*] (1913)
**:** a branch of dentistry that deals with the extraction of teeth
— **ex·odon·tist** \-'dän-tist\ *noun*

**ex·o·dus** \'ek-sə-dəs, 'eg-zə-\ *noun* [Latin, from Greek *Exodos*, literally, road out, from *ex-* + *hodos* road] (15th century)
**1** *capitalized* **:** the mainly narrative second book of canonical Jewish and Christian Scripture — see BIBLE table
**2 :** a mass departure **:** EMIGRATION

**exo·en·zyme** \,ek-sō-'en-,zīm\ *noun* [International Scientific Vocabulary] (circa 1923)
**:** an extracellular enzyme

**exo·er·gic** \,ek-sō-'ər-jik\ *adjective* (1942)
**:** releasing energy **:** EXOTHERMIC

**exo·eryth·ro·cyt·ic** \,ek-sō-i-,ri-thrə-'si-tik\ *adjective* (1942)

**:** occurring outside the red blood cells — used especially of stages of malaria parasites

**ex of·fi·cio** \,ek-sə-'fi-shē-,ō, -sē-\ *adverb or adjective* [Late Latin] (1533)
**:** by virtue or because of an office ⟨the Vice President serves *ex officio* as president of the Senate⟩

**ex·og·a·my** \ek-'sä-gə-mē\ *noun, plural* **-mies** (1865)
**:** marriage outside of a specific group especially as required by custom or law
— **ex·og·a·mous** \ek-'sä-gə-məs\ *or* **exo·gam·ic** \,ek-sə-'ga-mik\ *adjective*

**ex·og·e·nous** \ek-'sä-jə-nəs\ *adjective* [French *exogène* exogenous, from *exo-* + *-gène* (from Greek *-genēs* born) — more at -GEN] (1830)
**1 :** produced by growth from superficial tissue ⟨*exogenous* roots produced by leaves⟩
**2 a :** caused by factors (as food or a traumatic factor) or an agent (as a disease-producing organism) from outside the organism or system ⟨*exogenous* obesity⟩ ⟨*exogenous* psychic depression⟩ **b :** introduced from or produced outside the organism or system; *specifically* **:** not synthesized within the organism or system
— **ex·og·e·nous·ly** *adverb*

**ex·on** \'ek-,sän\ *noun* [expressed sequence + [2]*-on*] (circa 1978)
**:** a polynucleotide sequence in a nucleic acid that codes information for protein synthesis and that is copied and spliced together with other such sequences to form messenger RNA — compare INTRON
— **ex·on·ic** \ek-'sä-nik\ *adjective*

**ex·on·er·ate** \ig-'zä-nə-,rāt, eg-\ *transitive verb* **-at·ed; -at·ing** [Middle English, from Latin *exoneratus*, past participle of *exonerare* to unburden, from *ex-* + *oner-, onus* load] (1524)
**1 :** to relieve of a responsibility, obligation, or hardship
**2 :** to clear from accusation or blame
**synonym** see EXCULPATE
— **ex·on·er·a·tion** \-,zä-nə-'rā-shən\ *noun*
— **ex·on·er·a·tive** \-'zä-nə-,rā-tiv\ *adjective*

**exo·nu·cle·ase** \,ek-sō-'nü-klē-,ās, -'nyü-, -,āz\ *noun* (1963)
**:** an enzyme that breaks down a nucleic acid by removing nucleotides one by one from the end of a chain — compare ENDONUCLEASE

**exo·nu·mia** \,ek-sə-'nü-mē-ə, -'nyü-\ *noun plural* [New Latin, from *exo-* + English numismatic + New Latin *-ia*] (1966)
**:** numismatic items (as tokens, medals, or scrip) other than coins and paper money

**exo·pep·ti·dase** \-'pep-tə-,dās, -,dāz\ *noun* (1936)
**:** any of a group of enzymes that hydrolyze peptide bonds formed by the terminal amino acids of peptide chains **:** PEPTIDASE — compare ENDOPEPTIDASE

**ex·oph·thal·mos** *also* **ex·oph·thal·mus** \,ek-säf-'thal-məs, -səf-, -säp-\ *noun* [New Latin, from Greek *exophthalmos* having prominent eyes, from *ex* out + *ophthalmos* eye; akin to Greek *ōps* eye — more at EYE] (1872)
**:** abnormal protrusion of the eyeball
— **ex·oph·thal·mic** \-mik\ *adjective*

**ex·or·bi·tance** \ig-'zȯr-bə-tən(t)s\ *noun* (1611)
**1 :** an exorbitant action or procedure; *especially* **:** excessive or gross deviation from rule, right, or propriety
**2 :** the tendency or disposition to be exorbitant

**ex·or·bi·tant** \-tənt\ *adjective* [Middle English, from Middle French, from Late Latin *exorbitant-, exorbitans*, present participle of *exorbitare* to deviate, from Latin *ex-* + *orbita* track of a wheel, rut, from *orbis* disk, hoop] (15th century)
**1 :** not coming within the scope of the law
**2 :** exceeding in intensity, quality, amount, or size the customary or appropriate limits
**synonym** see EXCESSIVE

**— ex·or·bi·tant·ly** *adverb*

**ex·or·cise** *also* **ex·or·cize** \'ek-,sȯr-,sīz, -sər-\ *transitive verb* **-cised** *also* **-cized; -cis·ing** *also* **-ciz·ing** [Middle English, from Middle French *exorciser*, from Late Latin *exorcizare*, from Greek *exorkizein*, from *ex-* + *horkizein* to bind by oath, adjure, from *horkos* oath] (1539)
**1 a :** to expel (an evil spirit) by adjuration **b :** to get rid of (something troublesome, menacing, or oppressive)
**2 :** to free of an evil spirit
— **ex·or·cis·er** *noun*

**ex·or·cism** \-,si-zəm\ *noun* (14th century)
**1 :** the act or practice of exorcising
**2 :** a spell or formula used in exorcising
— **ex·or·cist** \-,sist, -səst\ *noun*
— **ex·or·cis·tic** \,ek-,sȯr-'sis-tik, -sər-\ *or* **ex·or·cis·ti·cal** \-ti-kəl\ *adjective*

**ex·or·di·um** \eg-'zȯr-dē-əm\ *noun, plural* **-diums** *or* **-dia** \-dē-ə\ [Latin, from *exordiri* to begin, from *ex-* + *ordiri* to begin — more at ORDER] (1577)
**:** a beginning or introduction especially to a discourse or composition
— **ex·or·di·al** \-dē-əl\ *adjective*

**exo·skel·e·ton** \,ek-sō-'ske-lə-t°n\ *noun* (1847)
**1 :** an external supportive covering of an animal (as an arthropod)
**2 :** bony or horny parts of a vertebrate produced from epidermal tissues
— **exo·skel·e·tal** \-lə-t°l\ *adjective*

**exo·sphere** \'ek-sō-,sfir\ *noun* [International Scientific Vocabulary] (1949)
**:** the outer fringe region of the atmosphere of the earth or a planet
— **exo·spher·ic** \,ek-sō-'sfir-ik, -'sfer-\ *adjective*

**exo·spore** \'ek-sə-,spōr, -,spȯr\ *noun* [International Scientific Vocabulary] (1859)
**:** an asexual spore cut off from a parent sporophore by the formation of septa

**ex·os·to·sis** \,ek-(,)säs-'tō-səs\ *noun, plural* **-to·ses** \-,sēz\ [New Latin, from Greek *exostōsis*, from *ex* out of + *osteon* bone — more at EX-, OSSEOUS] (1736)
**:** a spur or bony outgrowth from a bone or the root of a tooth

**ex·o·ter·ic** \,ek-sə-'ter-ik\ *adjective* [Latin & Greek; Latin *exotericus*, from Greek *exōterikos*, literally, external, from *exōterō* more outside, comparative of *exō* outside — more at EXO-] (1660)
**1 a :** suitable to be imparted to the public ⟨the *exoteric* doctrine⟩ — compare ESOTERIC **b :** belonging to the outer or less initiate circle
**2 :** relating to the outside **:** EXTERNAL
— **ex·o·ter·i·cal·ly** \-i-k(ə-)lē\ *adverb*

**exo·ther·mal** \,ek-sō-'thər-məl\ (1906)
**:** EXOTHERMIC
— **exo·ther·mal·ly** \-mə-lē\ *adverb*

**exo·ther·mic** \-mik\ *adjective* [International Scientific Vocabulary] (1884)
**:** characterized by or formed with evolution of heat
— **exo·ther·mi·cal·ly** \-mi-k(ə-)lē\ *adverb*
— **exo·ther·mi·ci·ty** \-,thər-'mis-ə-tē\ *noun*

[1]**ex·ot·ic** \ig-'zä-tik\ *adjective* [Latin *exoticus*, from Greek *exōtikos*, from *exō*] (1599)
**1 :** introduced from another country **:** not native to the place where found
**2** *archaic* **:** FOREIGN, ALIEN
**3 :** strikingly, excitingly, or mysteriously different or unusual
**4 :** of or relating to striptease ⟨*exotic* dancing⟩
— **ex·ot·i·cal·ly** \-ti-k(ə-)lē\ *adverb*
— **ex·ot·ic·ness** \-tik-nəs\ *noun*

[2]**exotic** *noun* (1645)
**1 :** one (as a plant or animal) that is exotic
**2 :** STRIPTEASER

**ex·ot·i·ca** \ig-'zä-ti-kə\ *noun plural* [New Latin, from Latin, neuter plural of *exoticus*] (1876)

: things excitingly different or unusual; *especially* : literary or artistic items having an exotic theme or nature

**ex·ot·i·cism** \ig-'zä-tə-,si-zəm\ *also* **ex·o·tism** \'eg-zə-,ti-zəm, 'ek-sə-\ *noun* (1827)
: the quality or state of being exotic

**exo·tox·in** \ek-sō-'täk-sən\ *noun* [International Scientific Vocabulary] (1920)
: a soluble poisonous substance produced during growth of a microorganism and released into the surrounding medium

**ex·pand** \ik-'spand\ *verb* [Middle English *expaunden*, from Latin *expandere*, from *ex-* + *pandere* to spread — more at FATHOM] (15th century)
*transitive verb*
**1 :** to open up : UNFOLD
**2 :** to increase the extent, number, volume, or scope of : ENLARGE
**3 a :** to express at length or in greater detail **b** : to write out in full ⟨*expand* all abbreviations⟩ **c :** to subject to mathematical expansion ⟨*expand* a function in a power series⟩
*intransitive verb*
**1 :** to open out : SPREAD
**2 :** to increase in extent, number, volume, or scope
**3 :** to speak or write fully or in detail ⟨*expanded* on the theme⟩
**4 :** to feel generous or optimistic ☆
— **ex·pand·abil·i·ty** \-,span-də-'bi-lə-tē\ *noun*
— **ex·pand·able** \-'span-də-bəl\ *adjective*

**ex·pand·ed** *adjective* (1875)
*of a typeface* : EXTENDED

**expanded metal** *noun* (1890)
: sheet metal cut and expanded into a lattice and used especially as lath

**expanded plastic** *noun* (1945)
: lightweight cellular plastic used especially as insulation and protective packing material — called also *foamed plastic, plastic foam*

**ex·pand·er** \ik-'span-dər\ *noun* (1862)
: one that expands; *specifically* : any of several colloidal substances (as dextran) of high molecular weight used as a blood or plasma substitute for increasing the blood volume

**ex·panse** \ik-'span(t)s\ *noun* [New Latin *expansum*, from Latin, neuter of *expansus*, past participle of *expandere*] (1667)
**1 :** FIRMAMENT
**2 :** great extent of something spread out ⟨an *expanse* of calm ocean⟩

**ex·pan·si·ble** \ik-'span(t)-sə-bəl\ *adjective* (circa 1691)
: capable of being expanded
— **ex·pan·si·bil·i·ty** \-,span(t)-sə-'bi-lə-tē\ *noun*

**ex·pan·sion** \ik-'span(t)-shən\ *noun* (1611)
**1 :** EXPANSE
**2 :** the act or process of expanding ⟨territorial *expansion*⟩
**3 :** the quality or state of being expanded
**4 :** the increase in volume of working fluid (as steam) in an engine cylinder after cutoff or in an internal combustion engine after explosion
**5 a :** an expanded part **b** : something that results from an act of expanding ⟨the book is an *expansion* of a lecture series⟩
**6 :** the result of carrying out an indicated mathematical operation : the expression of a function in the form of a series
— **ex·pan·sion·al** \-'panch-nəl, -chə-n³l\ *adjective*

**ex·pan·sion·ary** \ik-'span(t)-shə-,ner-ē\ *adjective* (1936)
: tending toward expansion ⟨an *expansionary* economy⟩

**ex·pan·sion·ism** \ik-'span-(t)-shə-,ni-zəm\ *noun* (1899)
: a policy or practice of expansion and especially of territorial expansion by a nation
— **ex·pan·sion·ist** \-'span(t)-sh(ə-)nist\ *noun*
— **expansionist** *also* **ex·pan·sion·is·tic** \-,span(t)-shə-'nis-tik\ *adjective*

**ex·pan·sive** \ik-'span(t)-siv\ *adjective* (1651)
**1 :** having a capacity or a tendency to expand
**2 :** causing or tending to cause expansion
**3 a :** characterized by high spirits, generosity, or readiness to talk : OPEN ⟨grew *expansive* after dinner⟩ **b** : marked by or indicative of exaggerated euphoria and delusions of self-importance ⟨an *expansive* patient⟩
**4 :** marked by expansion; *especially* : having a great expanse or extent : SIZABLE, EXTENSIVE
**5 :** characterized by richness, abundance, or magnificence ⟨*expansive* living⟩
— **ex·pan·sive·ly** *adverb*
— **ex·pan·sive·ness** *noun*

**ex·pan·siv·i·ty** \,ek-,span-'si-və-tē, ik-\ *noun* (1837)
: the quality or state of being expansive; *especially* : the capacity to expand

**ex par·te** \(,)eks-'pär-tē\ *adverb or adjective* [Medieval Latin] (1672)
**1 :** on or from one side or party only — used of legal proceedings
**2 :** from a one-sided or partisan point of view

**ex·pat** \'eks-,pat\ *noun* (1962)
*chiefly British* : an expatriate person : EXPATRIATE

**ex·pa·ti·ate** \ek-'spā-shē-,āt\ *intransitive verb* **-at·ed; -at·ing** [Latin *exspatiatus*, past participle of *exspatiari* to wander, digress, from *ex-* + *spatium* space, course] (1538)
**1 :** to move about freely or at will : WANDER
**2 :** to speak or write at length or in detail ⟨*expatiating* upon the value of the fabric —Thomas Hardy⟩
— **ex·pa·ti·a·tion** \(,)ek-,spā-shē-'ā-shən\ *noun*

**¹ex·pa·tri·ate** \ek-'spā-trē-,āt\ *verb* **-at·ed; -at·ing** [Medieval Latin *expatriatus*, past participle of *expatriare* to leave one's own country, from Latin *ex-* + *patria* native country, from feminine of *patrius* of a father, from *patr-, pater* father — more at FATHER] (1784)
*transitive verb*
**1 :** to withdraw (oneself) from residence in or allegiance to one's native country
**2 :** BANISH, EXILE
*intransitive verb*
: to leave one's native country to live elsewhere; *also* : to renounce allegiance to one's native country
— **ex·pa·tri·ate** \-,āt, -ət\ *noun*
— **ex·pa·tri·a·tion** \(,)ek-,spā-trē-'ā-shən\ *noun*

**²ex·pa·tri·ate** \ek-'spā-trē-ət, -trē-,āt\ *adjective* (1812)
: living in a foreign land

**ex·pa·tri·a·tism** \ek-'spā-trē-ə-,ti-zəm\ *noun* (1937)
: the fact or state of being an expatriate

**ex·pect** \ik-'spekt\ *verb* [Latin *exspectare* to look forward to, from *ex-* + *spectare* to look at, from *spectus*, past participle of *specere* to look — more at SPY] (1560)
*intransitive verb*
**1** *archaic* : WAIT, STAY
**2 :** to look forward
**3 :** to be pregnant : await the birth of one's child — used in progressive tenses ⟨she's *expecting* next month⟩
*transitive verb*
**1** *archaic* : AWAIT
**2 :** SUPPOSE, THINK
**3 :** to anticipate or look forward to the coming or occurrence of ⟨we *expect* them any minute now⟩ ⟨*expected* a telephone call⟩
**4 a :** to consider probable or certain ⟨*expect* to be forgiven⟩ ⟨*expect* that things will improve⟩ **b :** to consider reasonable, due, or necessary ⟨*expected* hard work from the students⟩ **c :** to consider bound in duty or obligated ⟨they *expect* you to pay your bills⟩ ☆
— **ex·pect·able** \-'spek-tə-bəl\ *adjective*
— **ex·pect·ably** \-blē\ *adverb*
— **ex·pect·ed·ly** *adverb*
— **ex·pect·ed·ness** *noun*

**ex·pec·tance** \ik-'spek-tən(t)s\ *noun* (1603)

: EXPECTANCY

**ex·pec·tan·cy** \-tən(t)-sē\ *noun, plural* **-cies** (1600)
**1 a :** the act, action, or state of expecting **b** : the state of being expected
**2 a :** something expected **b** : the expected amount (as of the number of years of life) based on statistical probability ⟨life *expectancy*⟩

**¹ex·pec·tant** \-tənt\ *adjective* (14th century)
**1 :** characterized by expectation
**2 :** expecting the birth of a child ⟨*expectant* mothers⟩
— **ex·pec·tant·ly** *adverb*

**²expectant** *noun* (1628)
: one who is looking forward to something

**ex·pec·ta·tion** \,ek-,spek-'tā-shən, ik-\ *noun* (1540)
**1 :** the act or state of expecting : ANTICIPATION
**2 a :** something expected ⟨not up to *expectations*⟩ **b :** basis for expecting : ASSURANCE ⟨they have every *expectation* of success⟩ **c :** prospects of inheritance — usually used in plural
**3 :** the state of being expected
**4 a :** EXPECTANCY 2b **b :** EXPECTED VALUE
— **ex·pec·ta·tion·al** \-'tā-shə-n³l, -shnəl\ *adjective*

**ex·pec·ta·tive** \ik-'spek-tə-tiv\ *adjective* (15th century)
: of, relating to, or constituting an object of expectation

**expected value** *noun* (1947)
**1 :** the sum of the values of a random variable with each value multiplied by its probability of occurrence
**2 :** the integral of the product of a probability density function of a continuous random variable and the random variable itself when taken over all possible values of the variable

**ex·pec·to·rant** \ik-'spek-t(ə-)rənt\ *noun* (1782)

---

☆ **SYNONYMS**
**Expand, amplify, swell, distend, inflate, dilate** mean to increase in size or volume. EXPAND may apply whether the increase comes from within or without and regardless of manner (as growth, unfolding, addition of parts). AMPLIFY implies the extension or enlargement of something inadequate. SWELL implies gradual expansion beyond a thing's original or normal limits. DISTEND implies outward extension caused by pressure from within. INFLATE implies expanding by introduction of air or something insubstantial and suggests a resulting vulnerability and liability to sudden collapse. DILATE applies especially to expansion of circumference.

**Expect, hope, look** mean to await some occurrence or outcome. EXPECT implies a high degree of certainty and usually involves the idea of preparing or envisioning ⟨*expects* to be finished by Tuesday⟩. HOPE implies little certainty but suggests confidence or assurance in the possibility that what one desires or longs for will happen ⟨*hopes* to find a job soon⟩. LOOK, with *to*, implies assurance that expectations will be fulfilled ⟨*looks* to a tidy profit from the sale⟩; with *for* it implies less assurance and suggests an attitude of expectancy and watchfulness ⟨*look* for rain when the wind shifts to the northeast⟩.

---

\ə\ abut \ᵊ\ kitten \ər\ further \a\ ash \ā\ ace
\ä\ mop, mar \aú\ out \ch\ chin \e\ bet \ē\ easy
\g\ go \i\ hit \ī\ ice \j\ job \ŋ\ sing \ō\ go
\ó\ law \ói\ boy \th\ thin \t̷h\ the \ü\ loot \ú\ foot
\y\ yet \zh\ vision *see also* Guide to Pronunciation

: an agent that promotes the discharge or expulsion of mucus from the respiratory tract; *broadly* : an antitussive agent
— **expectorant** *adjective*

**ex·pec·to·rate** \-tə-ˌrāt\ *verb* **-rat·ed; -rat·ing** [Latin *expectoratus*, past participle of *expectorare* to banish from the mind (taken to mean literally "to expel from the chest"), from *ex-* + *pector-, pectus* breast, soul — more at PECTORAL] (1601)
*transitive verb*
**1** : to eject from the throat or lungs by coughing or hawking and spitting
**2** : SPIT
*intransitive verb*
**1** : to discharge matter from the throat or lungs by coughing or hawking and spitting
**2** : SPIT
— **ex·pec·to·ra·tion** \-ˌspek-tə-ˈrā-shən\ *noun*

**ex·pe·di·ence** \ik-ˈspē-dē-ən(t)s\ *noun* (1593) : EXPEDIENCY

**ex·pe·di·en·cy** \-dən-sē\ *noun, plural* **-cies** (1612)
**1** : the quality or state of being suited to the end in view : SUITABILITY, FITNESS
**2** *obsolete* **a** : HASTE, DISPATCH **b** : an enterprise requiring haste or caution
**3** : adherence to expedient means and methods ⟨put more emphasis on *expediency* than on principle —W. H. Jones⟩
**4** : a means of achieving a particular end : EXPEDIENT
— **ex·pe·di·en·tial** \-ˌspē-dē-ˈen-chəl\ *adjective*

¹**ex·pe·di·ent** \ik-ˈspē-dē-ənt\ *adjective* [Middle English, from Middle French or Latin; Middle French, from Latin *expedient-, expediens*, present participle of *expedire* to extricate, prepare, be useful, from *ex-* + *ped-, pes* foot — more at FOOT] (14th century)
**1** : suitable for achieving a particular end in a given circumstance
**2** : characterized by concern with what is opportune; *especially* : governed by self-interest
☆
— **ex·pe·di·ent·ly** *adverb*

²**expedient** *noun* (1653)
: something expedient : a temporary means to an end
**synonym** see RESOURCE

**ex·pe·dite** \ˈek-spə-ˌdīt\ *transitive verb* **-dit·ed; -dit·ing** [Latin *expeditus*, past participle of *expedire*] (15th century)
**1** : to execute promptly
**2** : to accelerate the process or progress of : speed up
**3** : ISSUE, DISPATCH

**ex·pe·dit·er** *also* **ex·pe·di·tor** \-ˌdī-tər\ *noun* (1891)
: one that expedites; *specifically* : one employed to ensure efficient movement of goods or supplies in a business

**ex·pe·di·tion** \ˌek-spə-ˈdi-shən\ *noun* (15th century)
**1 a** : a journey or excursion undertaken for a specific purpose **b** : the group of persons making such a journey
**2** : efficient promptness : SPEED
**3** : a sending or setting forth
**synonym** see HASTE

**ex·pe·di·tion·ary** \-ˈdi-shə-ˌner-ē\ *adjective* (1817)
: of, relating to, or being an expedition; *also* : sent on military service abroad ⟨an *expeditionary* force⟩

**ex·pe·di·tious** \ˌek-spə-ˈdi-shəs\ *adjective* (1559)
: characterized by or acting promptly and efficiently
**synonym** see FAST
— **ex·pe·di·tious·ly** *adverb*
— **ex·pe·di·tious·ness** *noun*

**ex·pel** \ik-ˈspel\ *transitive verb* **ex·pelled; ex·pel·ling** [Middle English *expellen*, from

Latin *expellere*, from *ex-* + *pellere* to drive — more at FELT] (14th century)
**1** : to force out : EJECT ⟨*expelled* the smoke from her lungs⟩
**2** : to force to leave (as a place or organization) by official action : take away rights or privileges of membership ⟨*expelled* from college⟩
**synonym** see EJECT
— **ex·pel·la·ble** \-ˈspe-lə-bəl\ *adjective*

**ex·pel·lee** \ˌek-ˌspe-ˈlē, ik-\ *noun* (1888)
: a person who is expelled especially from a native or adopted country

**ex·pend** \ik-ˈspend\ *transitive verb* [Middle English, from Latin *expendere* to weigh out, expend, from *ex-* + *pendere* to weigh — more at SPIN] (15th century)
**1** : to pay out : SPEND ⟨the social services upon which public revenue is *expended* —J. A. Hobson⟩
**2** : to make use of for a specific purpose : UTILIZE ⟨projects on which they *expended* great energy⟩; *also* : USE UP
— **ex·pend·er** *noun*

¹**ex·pend·able** \ik-ˈspen-də-bəl\ *adjective* (1805)
: that may be expended: as **a** : normally used up or consumed in service ⟨*expendable* supplies like pencils and paper⟩ **b** : more easily or economically replaced than rescued, salvaged, or protected
— **ex·pend·abil·i·ty** \-ˌspen-də-ˈbi-lə-tē\ *noun*

²**expendable** *noun* (1942)
: one that is expendable — usually used in plural

**ex·pen·di·ture** \ik-ˈspen-di-chər, -də-ˌchür, -də-ˌt(y)ùr\ *noun* [irregular from *expend*] (1769)
**1** : the act or process of expending ⟨an *expenditure* of energy⟩
**2** : something expended : DISBURSEMENT, EXPENSE ⟨income should exceed *expenditures*⟩

¹**ex·pense** \ik-ˈspen(t)s\ *noun* [Middle English, from Anglo-French or Late Latin; Anglo-French, from Late Latin *expensa*, from Latin, feminine of *expensus*, past participle of *expendere*] (14th century)
**1** *archaic* : the act or an instance of expending : EXPENDITURE
**2 a** : something expended to secure a benefit or bring about a result **b** : financial burden or outlay : COST ⟨built the monument at their own *expense*⟩ **c** : an item of business outlay chargeable against revenue for a specific period
**3** : a cause or occasion of expenditure ⟨an estate is a great *expense*⟩
**4** : a loss, detriment, or embarrassment that results from some action or gain : SACRIFICE ⟨everyone had a good laugh at my *expense*⟩ — usually used in the phrase *at the expense of* ⟨develop a boy's physique at the *expense* of his intelligence —Bertrand Russell⟩

²**expense** *transitive verb* **ex·pensed; ex·pens·ing** (circa 1909)
**1** : to charge with expenses
**2 a** : to charge to an expense account **b** : to write off as an expense

**expense account** *noun* (1872)
: an account of expenses reimbursable to an employee; *also* : the right of charging expenses to such an account

**ex·pen·sive** \ik-ˈspen(t)-siv\ *adjective* (1634)
**1** : involving high cost or sacrifice ⟨an *expensive* hobby⟩
**2 a** : commanding a high price and especially one that is not based on intrinsic worth or is beyond a prospective buyer's means **b** : characterized by high prices ⟨*expensive* shops⟩
— **ex·pen·sive·ly** *adverb*
— **ex·pen·sive·ness** *noun*

¹**ex·pe·ri·ence** \ik-ˈspir-ē-ən(t)s\ *noun* [Middle English, from Middle French, from Latin *experientia* act of trying, from *experient-, experiens*, present participle of *experiri* to try,

from *ex-* + *-periri* (akin to *periculum* attempt) — more at FEAR] (14th century)
**1 a** : direct observation of or participation in events as a basis of knowledge **b** : the fact or state of having been affected by or gained knowledge through direct observation or participation
**2 a** : practical knowledge, skill, or practice derived from direct observation of or participation in events or in a particular activity **b** : the length of such participation ⟨has 10 years *experience* in the job⟩
**3 a** : the conscious events that make up an individual life **b** : the events that make up the conscious past of a community or nation or mankind generally
**4** : something personally encountered, undergone, or lived through
**5** : the act or process of directly perceiving events or reality

²**experience** *transitive verb* **-enced; -enc·ing** (1580)
**1** : to learn by experience ⟨I have *experienced* that a landscape and the sky unfold the deepest beauty —Nathaniel Hawthorne⟩
**2** : to have experience of : UNDERGO ⟨*experienced* severe hardships as a child⟩

**ex·pe·ri·enced** \-ən(t)st\ *adjective* (1576)
: made skillful or wise through experience : PRACTICED ⟨an *experienced* driver⟩

**ex·pe·ri·en·tial** \ik-ˌspir-ē-ˈen(t)-shəl\ *adjective* (1816)
: relating to, derived from, or providing experience : EMPIRICAL ⟨*experiential* knowledge⟩ ⟨*experiential* lessons⟩
— **ex·pe·ri·en·tial·ly** \-ˈen(t)-sh(ə-)lē\ *adverb*

¹**ex·per·i·ment** \ik-ˈsper-ə-mənt *also* -ˈspir-\ *noun* [Middle English, from Middle French, from Latin *experimentum*, from *experiri*] (14th century)
**1 a** : TEST, TRIAL ⟨make another *experiment* of his suspicion —Shakespeare⟩ **b** : a tentative procedure or policy **c** : an operation carried out under controlled conditions in order to discover an unknown effect or law, to test or establish a hypothesis, or to illustrate a known law
**2** *obsolete* : EXPERIENCE
**3** : the process of testing : EXPERIMENTATION

²**ex·per·i·ment** \-ˌment\ *intransitive verb* (1787)
: to carry out experiments : try out a new procedure, idea, or activity
— **ex·per·i·men·ta·tion** \ik-ˌsper-ə-mən-ˈtā-shən, -ˌmen- *also* -ˌspir-\ *noun*
— **ex·per·i·ment·er** \-ˈsper-ə-ˌmen-tər *also* -ˈspir-\ *noun*

**ex·per·i·men·tal** \ik-ˌsper-ə-ˈmen-tᵊl *also* -ˌspir-\ *adjective* (15th century)
**1** : of, relating to, or based on experience or experiment
**2 a** : serving the ends of or used as a means of experimentation ⟨an *experimental* school⟩ **b** : relating to or having the characteristics of experiment : TENTATIVE ⟨still in the *experimental* stage⟩
— **ex·per·i·men·tal·ly** \-tᵊl-ē\ *adverb*

**ex·per·i·men·tal·ism** \-tᵊl-ˌi-zəm\ *noun* (circa 1834)

☆ SYNONYMS
**Expedient, politic, advisable** mean dictated by practical or prudent motives. EXPEDIENT usually implies what is immediately advantageous without regard for ethics or consistent principles ⟨a politically *expedient* decision⟩. POLITIC stresses judiciousness and tactical value but usually implies some lack of candor or sincerity ⟨a *politic* show of interest⟩. ADVISABLE applies to what is practical, prudent, or advantageous but lacks the derogatory implication of EXPEDIENT and POLITIC ⟨sometimes it's *advisable* to say nothing⟩.

: reliance on or advocacy of experimental or empirical principles and procedures; *specifically*
: INSTRUMENTALISM

**ex·per·i·men·tal·ist** \-t°l-əst\ *noun* (1762)
: one who experiments; *specifically* : a person conducting scientific experiments

**experiment station** *noun* (1874)
: an establishment for scientific research (as in agriculture) where experiments are carried out, studies of practical application are made, and information is disseminated

¹**ex·pert** \'ek-ˌspərt, ik-'\ *adjective* [Middle English, from Middle French & Latin; Middle French, from Latin *expertus,* from past participle of *experiri*] (14th century)
**1** *obsolete* : EXPERIENCED
**2** : having, involving, or displaying special skill or knowledge derived from training or experience
**synonym** see PROFICIENT
— **ex·pert·ly** *adverb*
— **ex·pert·ness** *noun*

²**ex·pert** \'ek-ˌspərt\ *noun* [French, from *expert,* adjective] (1535)
: one with the special skill or knowledge representing mastery of a particular subject

³**ex·pert** \'ek-ˌspərt\ *intransitive verb* (circa 1889)
: to serve as an expert

**ex·per·tise** \ˌek-(ˌ)spər-'tēz, -'tēs\ *noun* [French, from Middle French, expertness, from *expert*] (1868)
**1** : expert opinion or commentary
**2** : the skill of an expert

**ex·pert·ism** \'ek-ˌspər-ˌti-zəm\ *noun* (1886)
: EXPERTISE 2

**ex·pert·ize** \'ek-spər-ˌtīz\ *verb* **-ized; -iz·ing** (1889)
*intransitive verb*
: to give a professional opinion usually after careful study
*transitive verb*
: to examine and give expert judgment on

**expert system** *noun* (1977)
: computer software that attempts to mimic the reasoning of a human specialist

**ex·pi·ate** \'ek-spē-ˌāt\ *verb* **-at·ed; -at·ing** [Latin *expiatus,* past participle of *expiare* to atone for, from *ex-* + *piare* to atone for, appease, from *pius* faithful, pious] (1594)
*transitive verb*
**1** *obsolete* : to put an end to
**2 a** : to extinguish the guilt incurred by **b** : to make amends for ⟨permission to *expiate* their offences by their assiduous labours —Francis Bacon⟩
*intransitive verb*
: to make expiation
— **ex·pi·a·ble** \'ek-spē-ə-bəl\ *adjective*
— **ex·pi·a·tor** \-spē-ˌā-tər\ *noun*

**ex·pi·a·tion** \ˌek-spē-'ā-shən\ *noun* (15th century)
**1** : the act of making atonement
**2** : the means by which atonement is made

**ex·pi·a·to·ry** \'ek-spē-ə-ˌtōr-ē, -ˌtȯr-\ *adjective* (15th century)
: serving to expiate

**ex·pi·ra·tion** \ˌek-spə-'rā-shən\ *noun* (1526)
**1 a** : the last emission of breath : DEATH **b** (1) : the act or process of releasing air from the lungs through the nose or mouth (2) : the escape of carbon dioxide from the body protoplasm (as through the blood and lungs or by diffusion)
**2** : the fact of coming to an end or the point at which something ends : TERMINATION

**ex·pi·ra·to·ry** \ik-'spī-rə-ˌtōr-ē, ek-', -ˌtȯr-; 'ek-sp(ə-)rə-\ *adjective* (circa 1847)
: of, relating to, or employed in the expiration of air from the lungs

**ex·pire** \ik-'spīr, *oftenest for intransitive verb* 3 *and transitive verb* 2 ek-\ *verb* **ex·pired; ex·pir·ing** [Middle English, from Middle French or Latin; Middle French *expirer,* from Latin *exspirare,* from *ex-* + *spirare* to breathe] (14th century)

*intransitive verb*
**1** : to breathe one's last breath : DIE
**2** : to come to an end
**3** : to emit the breath
*transitive verb*
**1** *obsolete* : CONCLUDE
**2** : to breathe out from or as if from the lungs
**3** *archaic* : EMIT

**ex·pi·ry** \ik-'spīr-ē, 'ek-spə-rē\ *noun, plural* **-ries** (1752)
: EXPIRATION: as **a** : exhalation of breath **b** : DEATH **c** : TERMINATION; *especially* : the termination of a time or period fixed by law, contract, or agreement

**ex·plain** \ik-'splān\ *verb* [Middle English *explanen,* from Latin *explanare,* literally, to make level, from *ex-* + *planus* level, flat — more at FLOOR] (15th century)
*transitive verb*
**1 a** : to make known **b** : to make plain or understandable ⟨footnotes that *explain* the terms⟩
**2** : to give the reason for or cause of
**3** : to show the logical development or relationships of
*intransitive verb*
: to make something plain or understandable ☆
— **ex·plain·able** \-'splā-nə-bəl\ *adjective*
— **ex·plain·er** *noun*
— **explain oneself** : to clarify one's statements or the reasons for one's conduct

**explain away** *transitive verb* (1704)
**1** : to get rid of by or as if by explanation
**2** : to minimize the significance of by or as if by explanation

**ex·pla·na·tion** \ˌek-splə-'nā-shən\ *noun* (14th century)
**1** : the act or process of explaining
**2** : something that explains ⟨gave no *explanation*⟩

**ex·plan·a·tive** \ik-'spla-nə-tiv\ *adjective* (circa 1616)
: EXPLANATORY
— **ex·plan·a·tive·ly** *adverb*

**ex·plan·a·to·ry** \ik-'spla-nə-ˌtōr-ē, -ˌtȯr-\ *adjective* (1618)
: serving to explain ⟨*explanatory* notes⟩
— **ex·plan·a·to·ri·ly** \-ˌspla-nə-'tōr-ə-lē, -'tȯr-\ *adverb*

¹**ex·plant** \(ˌ)ek-'splant\ *transitive verb* [*ex-* + *-plant* (as in *implant*)] (1915)
: to remove (living tissue) especially to a medium for tissue culture
— **ex·plan·ta·tion** \ˌek-ˌsplan-'tā-shən\ *noun*

²**ex·plant** \'ek-ˌsplant\ *noun* (1917)
: living tissue removed from an organism and placed in a medium for tissue culture

¹**ex·ple·tive** \'ek-splə-tiv\ *noun* (1612)
**1 a** : a syllable, word, or phrase inserted to fill a vacancy (as in a sentence or a metrical line) without adding to the sense; *especially* : a word (as *it* in "make it clear which you prefer") that occupies the position of the subject or object of a verb in normal English word order and anticipates a subsequent word or phrase that supplies the needed meaningful content **b** : an exclamatory word or phrase; *especially* : one that is obscene or profane
**2** : one that serves to fill out or as a filling

²**expletive** *adjective* [Late Latin *expletivus,* from Latin *expletus,* past participle of *explēre* to fill out, from *ex-* + *plēre* to fill — more at FULL] (1666)
**1** : serving to fill up ⟨*expletive* phrases⟩
**2** : marked by the use of expletives

**ex·ple·to·ry** \'ek-splə-ˌtōr-ē, -ˌtȯr-\ *adjective* (1672)
: EXPLETIVE

**ex·pli·ca·ble** \ek-'spli-kə-bəl, 'ek-(ˌ)splik-\ *adjective* (1556)
: capable of being explained
— **ex·pli·ca·bly** \-blē\ *adverb*

**ex·pli·cate** \'ek-splə-ˌkāt\ *transitive verb* **-cat·ed; -cat·ing** [Latin *explicatus,* past

participle of *explicare,* literally, to unfold, from *ex-* + *plicare* to fold — more at PLY] (1531)
**1** : to give a detailed explanation of
**2** : to develop the implications of : analyze logically
**synonym** see EXPLAIN
— **ex·pli·ca·tion** \ˌek-splə-'kā-shən\ *noun*
— **ex·pli·ca·tor** \'ek-splə-ˌkā-tər\ *noun*

**ex·pli·ca·tion de texte** \ek-splē-kä-syōⁿ-də-tekst\ *noun, plural* **explications de texte** \*same*\ [French, literally, explanation of text] (1935)
: a method of literary criticism involving a detailed analysis of a work

**ex·pli·ca·tive** \ek-'spli-kə-tiv, 'ek-splə-ˌkāt-\ *adjective* (1649)
: serving to explicate; *specifically* : serving to explain logically what is contained in the subject ⟨an *explicative* proposition⟩
— **ex·pli·ca·tive·ly** *adverb*

**ex·pli·ca·to·ry** \ek-'spli-kə-ˌtōr-ē, 'ek-(ˌ)spli-, -ˌtȯr-\ *adjective* (1625)
: EXPLICATIVE

**ex·plic·it** \ik-'spli-sət\ *adjective* [French or Medieval Latin; French *explicite,* from Medieval Latin *explicitus,* from Latin, past participle of *explicare*] (circa 1609)
**1 a** : fully revealed or expressed without vagueness, implication, or ambiguity : leaving no question as to meaning or intent ⟨*explicit* instructions⟩ **b** : open in the depiction of nudity or sexuality ⟨*explicit* books and films⟩
**2** : fully developed or formulated ⟨an *explicit* plan⟩ ⟨an *explicit* notion of our objective⟩
**3** : unambiguous in expression ⟨was very *explicit* on how we are to behave⟩
**4** *of a mathematical function* : defined by an expression containing only independent variables — compare IMPLICIT 1c ☆
— **ex·plic·it·ly** *adverb*
— **ex·plic·it·ness** *noun*

**ex·plode** \ik-'splōd\ *verb* **ex·plod·ed; ex·plod·ing** [Latin *explodere* to drive off the

---

☆ **SYNONYMS**
**Explain, expound, explicate, elucidate, interpret** mean to make something clear or understandable. EXPLAIN implies a making plain or intelligible what is not immediately obvious or entirely known ⟨*explain* the rules⟩. EXPOUND implies a careful often elaborate explanation ⟨*expounding* a scientific theory⟩. EXPLICATE adds the idea of a developed or detailed analysis ⟨*explicate* a poem⟩. ELUCIDATE stresses the throwing of light upon as by offering details or motives previously unclear or only implicit ⟨*elucidate* an obscure passage⟩. INTERPRET adds to EXPLAIN the need for imagination or sympathy or special knowledge in dealing with something ⟨*interpreting* a work of art⟩.

**Explicit, definite, express, specific** mean perfectly clear in meaning. EXPLICIT implies such verbal plainness and distinctness that there is no need for inference and no room for difficulty in understanding ⟨*explicit* instructions⟩. DEFINITE stresses precise, clear statement or arrangement that leaves no doubt or indecision ⟨the law is *definite* in such cases⟩. EXPRESS implies both explicitness and direct and positive utterance ⟨her *express* wishes⟩. SPECIFIC applies to what is precisely and fully treated in detail or particular ⟨two *specific* criticisms⟩.

---

stage by clapping, from *ex-* + *plaudere* to clap] (circa 1611)
*transitive verb*
**1** *archaic* **:** to drive from the stage by noisy disapproval
**2 :** to bring into disrepute or discredit ⟨*explode* a theory⟩
**3 :** to cause to explode or burst noisily ⟨*explode* a bomb⟩
*intransitive verb*
**1 :** to burst forth with sudden violence or noise from internal energy: as **a :** to undergo a rapid chemical or nuclear reaction with the production of noise, heat, and violent expansion of gases ⟨dynamite *explodes*⟩ **b :** to burst violently as a result of pressure from within
**2 a :** to give forth a sudden strong and noisy outburst of emotion ⟨*exploded* in anger⟩ **b :** to move with sudden speed and force ⟨*exploded* from the starting gate⟩
**3 :** to increase rapidly ⟨the population of the city *exploded*⟩ ◆
— **ex·plod·er** *noun*

**ex·plod·ed** *adjective* (1944)
**:** showing the parts separated but in correct relationship to each other ⟨an *exploded* view of a carburetor⟩

**¹ex·ploit** \'ek-₁sploit, ik-'-\ *noun* [Middle English, outcome, success, from Middle French, from Latin *explicitum*, neuter of *explicitus*, past participle] (circa 1538)
**:** DEED, ACT; *especially* **:** a notable or heroic act
*synonym* see FEAT

**²ex·ploit** \ik-'sploit, 'ek-₁\ *transitive verb* (1838)
**1 :** to make productive use of **:** UTILIZE ⟨*exploiting* your talents⟩ ⟨*exploit* your opponent's weakness⟩
**2 :** to make use of meanly or unjustly for one's own advantage ⟨*exploiting* migrant farm workers⟩
— **ex·ploit·able** \-'sploi-tə-bəl\ *adjective*
— **ex·ploit·er** *noun*

**ex·ploi·ta·tion** \₁ek-₁sploi-'tā-shən\ *noun* (1803)
**:** an act or instance of exploiting ⟨*exploitation* of natural resources⟩ ⟨*exploitation* of immigrant laborers⟩ ⟨clever *exploitation* of the system⟩

**ex·ploit·a·tive** \ik-'sploi-tə-tiv, 'ek-₁sploi-\ *adjective* (1885)
**:** exploiting or tending to exploit; *especially* **:** unfairly or cynically using another person or group for profit or advantage ⟨*exploitative* terms of employment⟩ ⟨an *exploitative* film⟩
— **ex·ploit·a·tive·ly** *adverb*

**ex·ploit·ive** \ik-'sploi-tiv\ *adjective* (1921)
**:** EXPLOITATIVE

**ex·plo·ra·tion** \₁ek-splə-'rā-shən, -₁splȯ-\ *noun* (1537)
**:** the act or an instance of exploring
— **ex·plo·ra·tion·al** \-shnəl, -shə-n°l\ *adjective*

**ex·plor·ative** \ik-'splȯr-ə-tiv, -'splȯr-\ *adjective* (1738)
**:** EXPLORATORY
— **ex·plor·ative·ly** *adverb*

**ex·plor·a·to·ry** \-ə-₁tȯr-ē, -₁tȯr-\ *adjective* (1620)
**:** of, relating to, or being exploration ⟨*exploratory* surgery⟩ ⟨*exploratory* drilling for oil⟩

**ex·plore** \ik-'splȯr, -'splȯr\ *verb* **ex·plored**; **ex·plor·ing** [Latin *explorare*, from *ex-* + *plorare* to cry out] (1585)
*transitive verb*
**1 a :** to investigate, study, or analyze **:** look into ⟨*explore* the relationship between social class and learning ability⟩ — sometimes used with indirect questions ⟨to *explore* where ethical issues arise —R. T. Blackburn⟩ **b :** to become familiar with by testing or experimenting ⟨*explore* new cuisines⟩
**2 :** to travel over (new territory) for adventure or discovery
**3 :** to examine minutely especially for diagnostic purposes ⟨*explore* the wound⟩

*intransitive verb*
**:** to make or conduct a systematic search ⟨*explore* for oil⟩

**ex·plor·er** \ik-'splȯr-ər, -'splȯr-\ *noun* (1685)
**1 :** one that explores; *especially* **:** a person who travels in search of geographical or scientific information
**2** *capitalized* **:** a member of a coed scouting program of the Boy Scouts of America for young people ages 14 to 20 focusing on career awareness

**ex·plo·sion** \ik-'splō-zhən\ *noun* [Latin *explosion-, explosio* act of driving off by clapping, from *explodere*] (circa 1616)
**1 :** the act or an instance of exploding ⟨injured in a laboratory *explosion*⟩
**2 :** a large-scale, rapid, or spectacular expansion or bursting out or forth ⟨the *explosion* of suburbia⟩ ⟨an *explosion* of red hair⟩
**3 :** the release of occluded breath that occurs in one kind of articulation of stop consonants

**¹ex·plo·sive** \ik-'splō-siv, -ziv\ *adjective* (1667)
**1 a :** relating to, characterized by, or operated by explosion ⟨an *explosive* hatch⟩ **b :** resulting from or as if from an explosion ⟨*explosive* population growth⟩
**2 a :** tending to explode ⟨an *explosive* person⟩ **b :** likely to erupt in or produce hostile reaction or violence ⟨an *explosive* ghetto situation⟩
— **ex·plo·sive·ly** *adverb*
— **ex·plo·sive·ness** *noun*

**²explosive** *noun* (1874)
**1 :** an explosive substance
**2 :** a consonant characterized by explosion in its articulation when it occurs in certain environments **:** STOP

**ex·po** \'ek-(₁)spō\ *noun, plural* **expos** (1913)
**:** EXPOSITION 3

**ex·po·nent** \ik-'spō-nənt, 'ek-₁\ *noun* [Latin *exponent-, exponens*, present participle of *exponere*] (1706)
**1 :** a symbol written above and to the right of a mathematical expression to indicate the operation of raising to a power
**2 a :** one that expounds or interprets **b :** one that champions, practices, or exemplifies

**ex·po·nen·tial** \₁ek-spə-'nen-chəl\ *adjective* (1704)
**1 :** of or relating to an exponent
**2 :** involving a variable in an exponent ⟨$10^x$ is an *exponential* expression⟩
**3 :** expressible or approximately expressible by an exponential function; *especially* **:** characterized by or being an extremely rapid increase (as in size or extent) ⟨an *exponential* growth rate⟩
— **ex·po·nen·tial·ly** \-'nench-(ə-)lē\ *adverb*

**exponential function** *noun* (circa 1890)
**:** a mathematical function in which an independent variable appears in one of the exponents — called also *exponential*

**ex·po·nen·ti·a·tion** \₁ek-spə-₁nen(t)-shē-'ā-shən\ *noun* (1903)
**:** the act or process of raising a quantity to a power — called also *involution*

**¹ex·port** \ek-'spōrt, -'spȯrt, 'ek-₁\ *verb* [Middle English, from Latin *exportare*, from *ex-* + *portare* to carry — more at FARE] (15th century)
*transitive verb*
**1 :** to carry away **:** REMOVE
**2 :** to carry or send (as a commodity) to some other place (as another country)
*intransitive verb*
**:** to export something abroad
— **ex·port·abil·i·ty** \(₁)ek-₁spȯr-tə-'bi-lə-tē, -₁spȯr-\ *noun*
— **ex·port·able** \ek-'spȯr-tə-bəl, -'spȯr-, 'ek-₁\ *adjective*

**²ex·port** \'ek-₁spōrt, -₁spȯrt\ *noun* (1690)
**1 :** something exported; *specifically* **:** a commodity conveyed from one country or region to another for purposes of trade
**2 :** the act of exporting **:** EXPORTATION ⟨the *export* of wheat⟩

**³ex·port** \'ek-₁\ *adjective* (1795)
**:** of or relating to exportation or exports ⟨*export* duties⟩

**ex·por·ta·tion** \₁ek-₁spȯr-'tā-shən, -₁spȯr-, -spər-\ *noun* (1641)
**:** the act of exporting; *also* **:** a commodity exported

**ex·port·er** \ek-'spōr-tər, -'spȯr-, 'ek-₁\ *noun* (1691)
**:** one that exports; *specifically* **:** a wholesaler who sells to merchants or industrial consumers in foreign countries

**ex·pose** \ik-'spōz\ *transitive verb* **ex·posed**; **ex·pos·ing** [Middle English, from Middle French *exposer*, from Latin *exponere* to set forth, explain (perfect indicative *exposui*), from *ex-* + *ponere* to put, place — more at POSITION] (15th century)
**1 a :** to deprive of shelter, protection, or care **:** subject to risk from a harmful action or condition ⟨*expose* troops needlessly⟩ ⟨has not yet been *exposed* to measles⟩ **b :** to submit or make accessible to a particular action or influence ⟨*expose* children to good books⟩; *especially* **:** to subject (a sensitive photographic film, plate, or paper) to radiant energy **c :** to abandon (an infant) especially by leaving in the open
**2 a :** to make known **:** bring to light (as something shameful) **b :** to disclose the faults or crimes of ⟨*expose* a murderer⟩
**3 :** to cause to be visible or open to view **:** DISPLAY: as **a :** to offer publicly for sale **b :** to exhibit for public veneration **c :** to reveal the face of (a playing card) or the cards of (a player's hand) **d :** to engage in indecent exposure of (oneself)
*synonym* see SHOW
— **ex·pos·er** *noun*

**ex·po·sé** *also* **ex·po·se** \₁ek-spō-'zā, -spə-\ *noun* [French *exposé*, from past participle of *exposer*] (1803)
**1 :** a formal statement of facts
**2 :** an exposure of something discreditable ⟨a newspaper *exposé* of government corruption⟩

**ex·posed** \ik-'spōzd\ *adjective* (circa 1623)
**1 :** open to view
**2 :** not shielded or protected; *also* **:** not insulated ⟨an *exposed* electric wire⟩
*synonym* see LIABLE

**ex·pos·it** \ik-'spä-zət\ *transitive verb* [Latin *expositus*, past participle of *exponere*] (1882)
**:** EXPOUND

**ex·po·si·tion** \₁ek-spə-'zi-shən\ *noun* (14th century)
**1 :** a setting forth of the meaning or purpose (as of a writing)
**2 a :** discourse or an example of it designed to convey information or explain what is difficult to understand **b** (1) **:** the first part of a musical composition in sonata form in which the thematic material of the movement is presented (2) **:** the opening section of a fugue
**3 :** a public exhibition or show

---

◇ WORD HISTORY
**explode** A modern audience often expresses its disapproval of a performer or performance by hissing. But in ancient Rome a customary expression of audience disapproval was loud clapping, sometimes expressly intended to drive the performer from the stage. The Latin verb meaning "to drive off by clapping" was *explodere*, a compound of *ex-*, meaning "out of, from" and *plaudere*, meaning "to clap." *Explodere* was, of course, the source of English *explode*, which initially also meant "to drive from the stage by a noisy expression of dislike." This sense is no longer current, but the senses that have replaced it have kept the notion either of dismissal and rejection or of a loud, violent burst.

**— ex·po·si·tion·al** \-'zish-nəl, -'zi-shə-nᵊl\ *adjective*

**ex·pos·i·tive** \ik-'spä-zə-tiv\ *adjective* (15th century)
**:** DESCRIPTIVE, EXPOSITORY

**ex·pos·i·tor** \-zə-tər\ *noun* [Middle English *expositour*, from Middle French *expositeur*, from Late Latin *expositor*, from Latin *exponere*] (14th century)
**:** a person who explains **:** COMMENTATOR

**ex·pos·i·to·ry** \-zə-,tōr-ē, -,tȯr-\ *adjective* (1628)
**:** of, relating to, or containing exposition ⟨*expository* writing⟩

**¹ex post fac·to** \,eks-,pōs(t)-'fak-(,)tō\ *adverb* [Late Latin, literally, from a thing done afterward] (1621)
**:** after the fact **:** RETROACTIVELY

**²ex post facto** *adjective* (1787)
**:** done, made, or formulated after the fact **:** RETROACTIVE ⟨*ex post facto* approval⟩ ⟨*ex post facto* laws⟩

**ex·pos·tu·late** \ik-'späs-chə-,lāt\ *verb* [Latin *expostulatus*, past participle of *expostulare* to demand, dispute, from *ex-* + *postulare* to ask for — more at POSTULATE] (1573)
*transitive verb*
*obsolete* **:** DISCUSS, EXAMINE
*intransitive verb*
**:** to reason earnestly with a person for purposes of dissuasion or remonstrance

**ex·pos·tu·la·tion** \-,späs-chə-'lā-shən\ *noun* (1540)
**:** an act or an instance of expostulating
**— ex·pos·tu·la·to·ry** \-'späs-chə-lə-,tōr-ē, -,tȯr-\ *adjective*

**ex·po·sure** \ik-'spō-zhər\ *noun* (1606)
**1 :** the fact or condition of being exposed: as **a :** the condition of being presented to view or made known ⟨a politician seeks a lot of *exposure*⟩ **b :** the condition of being unprotected especially from severe weather ⟨died of *exposure*⟩ **c :** the condition of being subject to some effect or influence ⟨risk *exposure* to the flu⟩ **d :** the condition of being at risk of financial loss; *also* **:** an amount at risk
**2 :** the act or an instance of exposing: as **a :** disclosure of something secret ⟨tried to prevent *exposure* of their past⟩ **b :** the treating of sensitized material (as film) to controlled amounts of radiant energy; *also* **:** the amount of such energy or length of such treatment ⟨a 3-second *exposure*⟩
**3 a :** the manner of being exposed **b :** the position (as of a house) with respect to weather influences or compass points ⟨a room with a southern *exposure*⟩
**4 :** a piece or section of sensitized material (as film) on which an exposure is or can be made ⟨36 *exposures* per roll⟩

**exposure meter** *noun* (1891)
**:** a device for indicating correct photographic exposure under varying conditions of illumination

**ex·pound** \ik-'spaund\ *verb* [Middle English, from Middle French *expondre*, from Latin *exponere* to explain — more at EXPOSE] (14th century)
*transitive verb*
**1 a :** to set forth **:** STATE **b :** to defend with argument
**2 :** to explain by setting forth in careful and often elaborate detail ⟨*expound* a law⟩
*intransitive verb*
**:** to make a statement **:** COMMENT
*synonym* see EXPLAIN
**— ex·pound·er** *noun*

**¹ex·press** \ik-'spres\ *adjective* [Middle English, from Middle French *expres*, from Latin *expressus*, past participle of *exprimere* to press out, express, from *ex-* + *premere* to press — more at PRESS] (14th century)
**1 a :** directly, firmly, and explicitly stated ⟨my *express* orders⟩ **b :** EXACT, PRECISE

**2 a :** designed for or adapted to its purpose **b :** of a particular sort **:** SPECIFIC ⟨for that *express* purpose⟩
**3 a :** traveling at high speed; *specifically* **:** traveling with few or no stops along the way ⟨*express* train⟩ **b :** adapted or suitable for travel at high speed ⟨an *express* highway⟩ **c** *British* **:** designated to be delivered without delay by special messenger
*synonym* see EXPLICIT

**²express** *adverb* (14th century)
**1** *obsolete* **:** EXPRESSLY
**2 :** by express ⟨delivered *express*⟩

**³express** *noun* (1619)
**1 a** *British* **:** a messenger sent on a special errand **b** *British* **:** a dispatch conveyed by a special messenger **c** (1) **:** a system for the prompt and safe transportation of parcels, money, or goods at rates higher than standard freight charges (2) **:** a company operating such a merchandise freight service **d** *British* **:** SPECIAL DELIVERY
**2 :** an express vehicle

**⁴express** *transitive verb* [Middle English, from Middle French & Latin; Middle French *expresser*, from Old French, from *expres*, adjective, from Latin *expressus*, past participle] (14th century)
**1 a :** DELINEATE, DEPICT **b :** to represent in words **:** STATE **c :** to give or convey a true impression of **:** SHOW, REFLECT **d :** to make known the opinions or feelings of (oneself) **e :** to give expression to the artistic or creative impulses or abilities of (oneself) **f :** to represent by a sign or symbol **:** SYMBOLIZE
**2 a :** to force out (as the juice of a fruit) by pressure **b :** to subject to pressure so as to extract something
**3 :** to send by express
**4 :** to cause (a gene) to manifest its effects in the phenotype ☆
**— ex·press·er** *noun*
**— ex·press·ible** \-ə-bəl\ *adjective*

**ex·press·age** \ik-'spre-sij\ *noun* (1857)
**:** a carrying of parcels by express; *also* **:** a charge for such carrying

**ex·pres·sion** \ik-'spre-shən\ *noun* (15th century)
**1 a :** an act, process, or instance of representing in a medium (as words) **:** UTTERANCE ⟨freedom of *expression*⟩ **b** (1) **:** something that manifests, embodies, or symbolizes something else ⟨this gift is an *expression* of my admiration for you⟩ (2) **:** a significant word or phrase (3) **:** a mathematical or logical symbol or a meaningful combination of symbols (4) **:** the detectable effect of a gene; *also* **:** EXPRESSIVITY 1
**2 a :** a mode, means, or use of significant representation or symbolism; *especially* **:** felicitous or vivid indication or depiction of mood or sentiment ⟨read the poem with *expression*⟩ **b** (1) **:** the quality or fact of being expressive (2) **:** facial aspect or vocal intonation as indicative of feeling
**3 :** an act or product of pressing out
**— ex·pres·sion·al** \-'spresh-nəl, -'spre-shə-nᵊl\ *adjective*

**ex·pres·sion·ism** \ik-'spre-shə-,ni-zəm\ *noun, often capitalized* (circa 1901)
**:** a theory or practice in art of seeking to depict the subjective emotions and responses that objects and events arouse in the artist
**— ex·pres·sion·ist** \-'spre-shə-nist\ *noun or adjective, often capitalized*
**— ex·pres·sion·is·tic** \-,spre-shə-'nis-tik\ *adjective*
**— ex·pres·sion·is·ti·cal·ly** \-ti-k(ə-)lē\ *adverb*

**ex·pres·sion·less** \ik-'spre-shən-ləs\ *adjective* (1831)
**:** lacking expression ⟨an *expressionless* face⟩
**— ex·pres·sion·less·ly** *adverb*
**— ex·pres·sion·less·ness** *noun*

**ex·pres·sive** \ik-'spre-siv\ *adjective* (15th century)

**1 :** of or relating to expression ⟨the *expressive* function of language⟩
**2 :** serving to express, utter, or represent ⟨foul and novel terms *expressive* of rage —H. G. Wells⟩
**3 :** effectively conveying meaning or feeling ⟨an *expressive* silence⟩ ⟨*expressive* line drawings⟩
**— ex·pres·sive·ly** *adverb*
**— ex·pres·sive·ness** *noun*

**ex·pres·siv·i·ty** \,ek-,spre-'si-və-tē\ *noun, plural* **-ties** (1934)
**1 :** the relative capacity of a gene to affect the phenotype of the organism of which it is a part
**2 :** the quality of being expressive

**ex·press·ly** \ik-'spres-lē\ *adverb* (14th century)
**1 :** in an express manner **:** EXPLICITLY ⟨*expressly* rejected the proposal⟩
**2 :** for the express purpose **:** PARTICULARLY, SPECIFICALLY ⟨made *expressly* for me⟩

**Express Mail** *service mark*
**—** used for overnight delivery of mail

**ex·press·man** \ik-'spres-,man, -mən\ *noun* (1839)
**:** a person employed in the express business

**ex·pres·so** \ik-'spre-(,)sō\ *variant of* ESPRESSO

**ex·press·way** \ik-'spres-,wā\ *noun* (1944)
**:** a high-speed divided highway for through traffic with access partially or fully controlled

**ex·pro·pri·ate** \ek-'sprō-prē-,āt\ *transitive verb* **-at·ed; -at·ing** [Medieval Latin *expropriatus*, past participle of *expropriare*, from Latin *ex-* + *proprius* own] (1611)
**1 :** to deprive of possession or proprietary rights
**2 :** to transfer (the property of another) to one's own possession
**— ex·pro·pri·a·tor** \-,ā-tər\ *noun*

**ex·pro·pri·a·tion** \(,)ek-,sprō-prē-'ā-shən\ *noun* (15th century)
**:** the act of expropriating or the state of being expropriated; *specifically* **:** the action of the state in taking or modifying the property rights of an individual in the exercise of its sovereignty

**ex·pulse** \ik-'spəls\ *transitive verb* **expulsed; ex·puls·ing** (15th century)
**:** EXPEL

**ex·pul·sion** \ik-'spəl-shən\ *noun* [Middle English, from Latin *expulsion-, expulsio,* from *expellere* to expel] (15th century)
**:** the act of expelling **:** the state of being expelled
**— ex·pul·sive** \-'spəl-siv\ *adjective*

---

---

\ə\ **abut** \ᵊ\ **kitten** \ər\ **further** \a\ **ash** \ā\ **ace**
\ä\ **mop, mar** \aü\ **out** \ch\ **chin** \e\ **bet** \ē\ **easy**
\g\ **go** \i\ **hit** \ī\ **ice** \j\ **job** \ŋ\ **sing** \ō\ **go**
\ȯ\ **law** \ȯi\ **boy** \th\ **thin** \t̷h\ **the** \ü\ **loot** \u̇\ **foot**
\y\ **yet** \zh\ **vision** *see also* Guide to Pronunciation

**ex·punc·tion** \ik-'spəŋ(k)-shən\ *noun* [Latin *expungere*] (1606)
: the act of expunging : the state of being expunged : ERASURE

**ex·punge** \ik-'spənj\ *transitive verb* **ex·punged; ex·pung·ing** [Latin *expungere* to mark for deletion by dots, from *ex-* + *pungere* to prick — more at PUNGENT] (1602)
**1** : to strike out, obliterate, or mark for deletion
**2** : to efface completely : DESTROY
— **ex·pung·er** *noun*

**ex·pur·gate** \'ek-spər-,gāt\ *transitive verb* **-gat·ed; -gat·ing** [Latin *expurgatus*, past participle of *expurgare*, from *ex-* + *purgare* to purge] (1678)
: to cleanse of something morally harmful, offensive, or erroneous; *especially* : to expunge objectionable parts from before publication or presentation ⟨an *expurgated* edition of the letters⟩
— **ex·pur·ga·tion** \,ek-spər-'gā-shən\ *noun*
— **ex·pur·ga·tor** \'ek-spər-,gā-tər\ *noun*

**ex·pur·ga·to·ri·al** \(,)ek-,spər-gə-'tōr-ē-əl, -'tȯr-\ *adjective* (1807)
: relating to expurgation or an expurgator : EXPURGATORY

**ex·pur·ga·to·ry** \ek-'spər-gə-,tōr-ē, -,tȯr-\ *adjective* (1625)
: serving to purify from something morally harmful, offensive, or erroneous

**¹ex·qui·site** \ek-'skwi-zət, 'ek-(,)\ *adjective* [Middle English *exquisit*, from Latin *exquisitus*, past participle of *exquirere* to search out, from *ex-* + *quaerere* to seek] (15th century)
**1** : carefully selected : CHOICE
**2** *archaic* : ACCURATE
**3 a** : marked by flawless craftsmanship or by beautiful, ingenious, delicate, or elaborate execution **b** : marked by nice discrimination, deep sensitivity, or subtle understanding ⟨*exquisite* taste⟩ **c** : ACCOMPLISHED, PERFECTED ⟨an *exquisite* gentleman⟩
**4 a** : pleasing through beauty, fitness, or perfection ⟨an *exquisite* white blossom⟩ **b** : ACUTE, INTENSE ⟨*exquisite* pain⟩ **c** : having uncommon or esoteric appeal ◆
**synonym** see CHOICE
— **ex·qui·site·ly** *adverb*
— **ex·qui·site·ness** *noun*

**²exquisite** *noun* (1819)
: one who is overly fastidious in dress or ornament

**ex·san·gui·na·tion** \(,)ek(s)-,saŋ-gwə-'nā-shən\ *noun* [Latin *exsanguinatus* drained of blood, from *ex-* + *sanguin-, sanguis* blood] (circa 1909)
: the action or process of draining or losing blood
— **ex·san·gui·nate** \ek(s)-'saŋ-gwə-,nāt\ *transitive verb*

**ex·scind** \ek-'sind\ *transitive verb* [Latin *exscindere*, from *ex-* + *scindere* to cut, tear — more at SHED] (1662)
: to cut off or out : EXCISE

**ex·sert** \ek-'sərt\ *transitive verb* [Latin *exsertus*, past participle of *exserere* — more at EXERT] (1836)
: to thrust out
— **ex·ser·tile** \-'sər-t°l, -'sər-,tīl\ *adjective*
— **ex·ser·tion** \-'sər-shən\ *noun*

**ex·sert·ed** *adjective* (1816)
: projecting beyond an enclosing organ or part

**ex·sic·cate** \'ek-si-,kāt\ *transitive verb* **-cat·ed; -cat·ing** [Middle English, from Latin *exsiccatus*, past participle of *exsiccare*, from *ex-* + *siccare* to dry, from *siccus* dry — more at SACK] (15th century)
: to remove moisture from : DRY
— **ex·sic·ca·tion** \,ek-si-'kā-shən\ *noun*

**ex·so·lu·tion** \,ek-sə-'lü-shən\ *noun* (1929)
: the process of separating or precipitating from a solid crystalline phase

**ex·tant** \'ek-stənt; ek-'stant, 'ek-,\ *adjective* [Latin *exstant-, exstans*, present participle of

*exstare* to stand out, be in existence, from *ex-* + *stare* to stand — more at STAND] (1545)
**1** *archaic* : standing out or above
**2 a** : currently or actually existing ⟨the most charming writer *extant* —G. W. Johnson⟩ **b** : not destroyed or lost ⟨*extant* manuscripts⟩

**ex·tem·po·ral** \ek-'stem-p(ə-)rəl\ *adjective* [Latin *extemporalis*, from *ex tempore*] (1570)
*archaic* : EXTEMPORANEOUS
— **ex·tem·po·ral·ly** \-ē\ *adverb*

**ex·tem·po·ra·ne·ity** \(,)ek-,stem-pə-rə-'nē-ə-tē, -'nā-\ *noun* (1937)
: the quality or state of being extemporaneous

**ex·tem·po·ra·ne·ous** \(,)ek-,stem-pə-'rā-nē-əs\ *adjective* [Late Latin *extemporaneus*, from Latin *ex tempore*] (1673)
**1 a** (1) : composed, performed, or uttered on the spur of the moment : IMPROMPTU (2) : carefully prepared but delivered without notes or text **b** : skilled at or given to extemporaneous utterance **c** : happening suddenly and often unexpectedly and usually without clearly known causes or relationships ⟨a great deal of criminal and delinquent behavior is . . . *extemporaneous* —W. C. Reckless⟩
**2** : provided, made, or put to use as an expedient : MAKESHIFT
— **ex·tem·po·ra·ne·ous·ly** *adverb*
— **ex·tem·po·ra·ne·ous·ness** *noun*

**ex·tem·po·rary** \ik-'stem-pə-,rer-ē\ *adjective* (1596)
: EXTEMPORANEOUS
— **ex·tem·po·rar·i·ly** \-,stem-pə-'rer-ə-lē\ *adverb*

**ex·tem·po·re** \ik-'stem-pə-(,)rē\ *adverb or adjective* [Latin *ex tempore*, from *ex* + *tempore*, ablative of *tempus* time] (1553)
: in an extemporaneous manner ⟨speaking *extempore*⟩

**ex·tem·por·i·sa·tion, ex·tem·po·rise**
*British variant of* EXTEMPORIZATION, EXTEMPORIZE

**ex·tem·po·ri·za·tion** \ik-,stem-pə-rə-'zā-shən\ *noun* (circa 1860)
**1** : the act of extemporizing : IMPROVISATION
**2** : something extemporized

**ex·tem·po·rize** \ik-'stem-pə-,rīz\ *verb* **-rized; -riz·ing** (1644)
*intransitive verb*
**1** : to do something extemporaneously : IMPROVISE; *especially* : to speak extemporaneously
**2** : to get along in a makeshift manner
*transitive verb*
: to compose, perform, or utter extemporaneously : IMPROVISE
— **ex·tem·po·riz·er** *noun*

**ex·tend** \ik-'stend\ *verb* [Middle English, from Middle French or Latin; Middle French *estendre*, from Latin *extendere*, from *ex-* + *tendere* to stretch — more at THIN] (14th century)
*transitive verb*
**1** : to spread or stretch forth : UNBEND ⟨*extended* both her arms⟩
**2 a** : to stretch out to fullest length **b** : to cause (as a horse) to move at full stride **c** : to exert (oneself) to full capacity ⟨could work long and hard without seeming to *extend* himself⟩ **d** (1) : to increase the bulk of (as by adding a cheaper substance or a modifier) (2) : ADULTERATE
**3** [Middle English, from Medieval Latin *extendere* (from Latin) or Anglo-French *estendre*, from Old French] **a** *British* : to take possession of (as lands) by a writ of extent **b** *obsolete* : to take by force
**4 a** : to make the offer of : PROFFER ⟨*extending* aid to the needy⟩ **b** : to make available ⟨*extending* credit to customers⟩
**5 a** : to cause to reach (as in distance or scope) ⟨national authority was *extended* over new territories⟩ **b** : to cause to be longer : PROLONG ⟨*extend* the side of a triangle⟩ ⟨*extended* their visit another day⟩; *also* : to prolong the time of payment of **c** : ADVANCE, FURTHER ⟨*extending* her potential through job training⟩

**6 a** : to cause to be of greater area or volume : ENLARGE **b** : to increase the scope, meaning, or application of : BROADEN ⟨beauty, I suppose, opens the heart, *extends* the consciousness —Algernon Blackwood⟩ **c** *archaic* : EXAGGERATE
*intransitive verb*
**1** : to stretch out in distance, space, or time : REACH ⟨their jurisdiction *extended* over the whole area⟩
**2** : to reach in scope or application ⟨his concern *extends* beyond mere business to real service to his customers⟩ ☆
— **ex·tend·abil·i·ty** \-,sten-də-'bi-lə-tē\ *noun*
— **ex·tend·able** *also* **ex·tend·ible** \-'sten-də-bəl\ *adjective*

**ex·tend·ed** *adjective* (15th century)
**1** : drawn out in length especially of time ⟨an *extended* visit⟩
**2 a** : fully stretched out ⟨an *extended* battle line⟩ **b** *of a horse's gait* : performed with a greatly lengthened stride but without a break —, compare COLLECTED **c** : INTENSIVE ⟨*extended* efforts⟩
**3** : having spatial magnitude : being larger than a point ⟨an *extended* source of light⟩
**4** : EXTENSIVE 1 ⟨made available *extended* information —Ruth G. Strickland⟩
**5** : DERIVATIVE 1, SECONDARY 2a ⟨an *extended* sense of a word⟩
**6** *of a typeface* : having a wider face than that of a standard typeface
— **ex·tend·ed·ly** *adverb*
— **ex·tend·ed·ness** *noun*

**extended family** *noun* (circa 1935)
: a family that includes in one household near relatives in addition to a nuclear family

**ex·tend·er** \ik-'sten-dər\ *noun* (1611)
: one that extends: as **a** : a substance added to a product especially in the capacity of a diluent, adulterant, or modifier **b** : an added ingredient used to increase the bulk of a food (as soup or meat)

**ex·ten·si·ble** \ik-'sten(t)-sə-bəl\ *adjective* (1611)
: capable of being extended
— **ex·ten·si·bil·i·ty** \-,sten(t)-sə-'bi-lə-tē\ *noun*

**ex·ten·sile** \ik-'sten(t)-səl, -'sten-,sīl\ *adjective* (1744)
: EXTENSIBLE

**ex·ten·sion** \ik-'sten(t)-shən\ *noun* [Middle English, from Middle French or Late Latin; Middle French, from Late Latin *extension-, extensio*, from Latin *extendere*] (15th century)

---

☆ **SYNONYMS**
**Extend, lengthen, prolong, protract** mean to draw out or add to so as to increase in length. EXTEND and LENGTHEN imply a drawing out in space or time but EXTEND may also imply increase in width, scope, area, or range ⟨*extend* a vacation⟩ ⟨*extend* welfare services⟩ ⟨*lengthen* a skirt⟩ ⟨*lengthen* the workweek⟩. PROLONG suggests chiefly increase in duration especially beyond usual limits ⟨*prolonged* illness⟩. PROTRACT adds to PROLONG implications of needlessness, vexation, or indefiniteness ⟨*protracted* litigation⟩.

---

◇ WORD HISTORY
**exquisite** The source of English *exquisite* is the Latin verb *exquirere*, which meant "to ask about" or "to seek." The past participle of this verb, *exquisitus*, came to be used as an adjective, eventually acquiring not just the meaning of "sought out" but also "sought out with care"—in other words, "choice." This was the sense that was adopted into Middle English as *exquisit* and from which the modern senses of *exquisite* have developed.

**1 a :** the action of extending **:** state of being extended **b :** an enlargement in scope or operation ⟨tools are *extensions* of human hands⟩ **2 a :** the total range over which something extends **:** COMPASS **b :** DENOTATION 4 **3 a :** the stretching of a fractured or dislocated limb so as to restore it to its natural position **b :** an unbending movement around a joint in a limb (as the knee or elbow) that increases the angle between the bones of the limb at the joint — compare FLEXION 4a **4 :** a property whereby something occupies space **5 :** an increase in length of time; *specifically* **:** an increase in time allowed under agreement or concession ⟨was granted an *extension*⟩ **6 :** a program that geographically extends the educational resources of an institution by special arrangements (as correspondence courses) to persons otherwise unable to take advantage of such resources **7 a :** a part constituting an addition **b :** a section or line segment forming an additional length **c :** an extra telephone connected to the principal line **8 :** a mathematical set (as a field or group) that includes a given and similar set as a subset

**extension agent** *noun* (1949)
**:** COUNTY AGENT

**ex·ten·sion·al** \ik-'stench-nəl, -'sten(t)-shə-nºl\ *adjective* (1647)
**1 :** of, relating to, or marked by extension; *specifically* **:** DENOTATIVE
**2 :** concerned with objective reality
— **ex·ten·sion·al·i·ty** \-,sten(t)-shə-'na-lə-tē\ *noun*
— **ex·ten·sion·al·ly** \-'stench-nə-lē, -'sten(t)-shə-nºl-ē\ *adverb*

**extension cord** *noun* (1946)
**:** an electric cord fitted with a plug at one end and a receptacle at the other

**ex·ten·si·ty** \ik-'sten(t)-sə-tē\ *noun, plural* **-ties** (circa 1834)
**1 a :** the quality of having extension **b :** degree of extension **:** RANGE
**2 :** an attribute of sensation whereby space or size is perceived

**ex·ten·sive** \ik-'sten(t)-siv\ *adjective* (1605)
**1 :** having wide or considerable extent ⟨*extensive* reading⟩
**2 :** EXTENSIONAL
**3 :** of, relating to, or constituting farming in which large areas of land are utilized with minimum outlay and labor
— **ex·ten·sive·ly** *adverb*
— **ex·ten·sive·ness** *noun*

**ex·ten·som·e·ter** \,ek-,sten-'sä-mə-tər\ *noun* [*extension* + -*o-* + -*meter*] (1887)
**:** an instrument for measuring minute deformations of test specimens caused by tension, compression, bending, or twisting

**ex·ten·sor** \ik-'sten(t)-sər\ *noun* (1713)
**:** a muscle serving to extend a bodily part (as a limb)

**ex·tent** \ik-'stent\ *noun* [Middle English, from Anglo-French & Middle French; Anglo-French *extente* land valuation, from Middle French, area, surveying of land, from *extendre, estendre* to extend] (14th century)
**1** *archaic* **:** valuation (as of land) in Great Britain especially for taxation
**2 a :** seizure (as of land) in execution of a writ of extent in Great Britain **:** the condition of being so seized **b :** a writ giving to a creditor temporary possession of his debtor's property
**3 a :** the range over which something extends **:** SCOPE ⟨the *extent* of her jurisdiction⟩ **b :** the point, degree, or limit to which something extends ⟨using talents to the greatest *extent*⟩ **c :** the amount of space or surface that something occupies or the distance over which it extends ⟨MAGNITUDE ⟨the *extent* of the forest⟩

**ex·ten·u·ate** \ik-'sten-yə-,wāt\ *transitive verb* **-at·ed; -at·ing** [Latin *extenuatus*, past parti-

ciple of *extenuare*, from *ex-* + *tenuis* thin — more at THIN] (1529)
**1 a** *archaic* **:** to make light of **b :** to lessen or to try to lessen the seriousness or extent of by making partial excuses **:** MITIGATE **c** *obsolete* **:** DISPARAGE
**2 a** *archaic* **:** to make thin or emaciated **b :** to lessen the strength or effect of
— **ex·ten·u·a·tor** \-,wā-tər\ *noun*
— **ex·ten·u·a·to·ry** \-wə-,tōr-ē, -,tór-\ *adjective*

**ex·ten·u·a·tion** \ik-,sten-yə-'wā-shən\ *noun* (circa 1543)
**1 :** the act of extenuating or state of being extenuated; *especially* **:** partial justification
**2 :** something extenuating; *especially* **:** a partial excuse

**¹ex·te·ri·or** \ek-'stir-ē-ər\ *adjective* [Latin, comparative of *exter, exterus* being on the outside, foreign, from *ex*] (1528)
**1 :** being on an outside surface **:** situated on the outside
**2 :** observable by outward signs ⟨his *exterior* quietness is belied by an occasional nervous twitch —*Current Biography*⟩
**3 :** suitable for use on outside surfaces
— **ex·te·ri·or·ly** *adverb*

**²exterior** *noun* (1591)
**1 a :** an exterior part or surface **:** OUTSIDE **b :** outward manner or appearance
**2 :** a representation (as on stage or film) of an outdoor scene; *also* **:** a scene filmed outdoors

**exterior angle** *noun* (circa 1864)
**1 :** the angle between a side of a polygon and an extended adjacent side
**2 :** an angle formed by a transversal as it cuts one of two lines and situated on the outside of the line

*ega, egb, fhc, fhd*
**exterior angle 2**

**ex·te·ri·or·ise** *British variant of* EXTERIORIZE
**ex·te·ri·or·i·ty** \(,)ek-,stir-ē-'ór-ə-tē, -'är-\ *noun* (1611)
**:** the quality or state of being exterior or exteriorized **:** EXTERNALITY

**ex·te·ri·or·ize** \ek-'stir-ē-ə-,rīz\ *transitive verb* **-ized; -iz·ing** (1879)
**1 :** EXTERNALIZE
**2 :** to bring out of the body (as for surgery)
— **ex·te·ri·or·iza·tion** \-,stir-ē-ə-rə-'zā-shən\ *noun*

**ex·ter·mi·nate** \ik-'stər-mə-,nāt\ *transitive verb* **-nat·ed; -nat·ing** [Latin *exterminatus*, past participle of *exterminare*, from *ex-* + *terminus* boundary — more at TERM] (1591)
**:** to get rid of completely usually by killing off ⟨*exterminate* crabgrass from a lawn⟩ ☆
— **ex·ter·mi·na·tion** \-,stər-mə-'nā-shən\ *noun*
— **ex·ter·mi·na·tor** \-'stər-mə-,nā-tər\ *noun*

**ex·ter·mi·na·to·ry** \ik-'stər-mə-nə-,tōr-ē, -,tór-\ *adjective* (1790)
**:** of, relating to, or marked by extermination

**ex·ter·mine** \ik-'stər-mən\ *transitive verb* **-mined; -min·ing** (1539)
*obsolete* **:** EXTERMINATE

**¹ex·tern** \ek-'stərn, 'ek-,\ *adjective* [Middle French or Latin; Middle French *externe*, from Latin *externus*] (1530)
*archaic* **:** EXTERNAL

**²ex·tern** *also* **ex·terne** \'ek-,stərn\ *noun* (circa 1610)
**:** a person connected with an institution but not living or boarding in it; *specifically* **:** a nonresident doctor or medical student at a hospital

**¹ex·ter·nal** \ek-'stər-nºl\ *adjective* [Latin *externus* external, from *exter*] (1556)
**1 a :** capable of being perceived outwardly ⟨*external* signs of a disease⟩ ⟨*external* reality⟩ **b :** having merely the outward appearance of something **:** SUPERFICIAL (2) **:** not intrinsic or essential ⟨*external* circumstances⟩

**2 a :** of, relating to, or connected with the outside or an outer part **b :** applied or applicable to the outside
**3 a** (1) **:** situated outside, apart, or beyond; *specifically* **:** situated near or toward the surface of the body (2) **:** arising or acting from outside ⟨*external* force⟩ **b :** of or relating to dealings or relationships with foreign countries **c :** having existence independent of the mind ⟨*external* reality⟩
— **ex·ter·nal·ly** \-nºl-ē\ *adverb*

**²external** *noun* (circa 1635)
**:** something that is external: as **a :** an outer part **b :** an external feature or aspect — usually used in plural

**external combustion engine** *noun* (1915)
**:** a heat engine (as a steam engine) that derives its heat from fuel consumed outside the engine cylinder

**external degree** *noun* (1928)
**:** a degree conferred on a student who has not attended the university but has passed the qualifying examination

**ex·ter·nal·isa·tion, ex·ter·nal·ise** *British variant of* EXTERNALIZATION, EXTERNALIZE
**ex·ter·nal·ism** \ek-'stər-nºl-,i-zəm\ *noun* (1856)
**1 :** attention to externals; *especially* **:** excessive preoccupation with externals
**2 :** EXTERNALITY 1

**ex·ter·nal·i·ty** \,ek-,stər-'na-lə-tē\ *noun, plural* **-ties** (1673)
**1 :** the quality or state of being external or externalized
**2 :** something that is external
**3 :** a secondary or unintended consequence ⟨pollution and other *externalities* of manufacturing⟩

**ex·ter·nal·iza·tion** \ek-,stər-nºl-ə-'zā-shən\ *noun* (1803)
**1 a :** the action or process of externalizing **b :** the quality or state of being externalized
**2 :** something externalized **:** EMBODIMENT

**ex·ter·nal·ize** \ek-'stər-nºl-,īz\ *transitive verb* **-ized; -iz·ing** (1852)
**1 :** to make external or externally manifest
**2 :** to attribute to causes outside the self **:** RATIONALIZE

**external respiration** *noun* (1940)
**:** exchange of gases between the external environment and a distributing system of the animal body (as the lungs of higher vertebrates or the tracheal tubes of insects) or between the alveoli of the lungs and the blood — compare INTERNAL RESPIRATION

**ex·tern·ship** \'ek-,stərn-,ship\ *noun* (1945)
**:** a training program that is part of a course of study of an educational institution and is taken in private business

---

☆ **SYNONYMS**
**Exterminate, extirpate, eradicate, uproot** mean to effect the destruction or abolition of something. EXTERMINATE implies complete and immediate extinction by killing off all individuals ⟨*exterminate* cockroaches⟩. EXTIRPATE implies extinction of a race, family, species, or sometimes an idea or doctrine by destruction or removal of its means of propagation ⟨many species have been *extirpated* from the area⟩. ERADICATE implies the driving out or elimination of something that has established itself ⟨a campaign to *eradicate* illiteracy⟩. UPROOT implies a forcible or violent removal and stresses displacement or dislodgment rather than immediate destruction ⟨the war *uprooted* thousands⟩.

---

\ə\ abut  \ᵊ\ kitten  \ər\ further  \a\ ash  \ā\ ace
\ä\ mop, mar  \aú\ out  \ch\ chin  \e\ bet  \ē\ easy
\g\ go  \i\ hit  \ī\ ice  \j\ job  \ŋ\ sing  \ō\ go
\ò\ law  \òi\ boy  \th\ thin  \t̲h̲\ the  \ü\ loot  \ú\ foot
\y\ yet  \zh\ vision  *see also* Guide to Pronunciation

**ex·tero·cep·tive** \ek-stə-rō-'sep-tiv\ *adjective* [*exterior* + *-o-* + *-ceptive* (as in *receptive*)] (circa 1921)
**:** activated by, relating to, or being stimuli received by an organism from outside
**ex·tero·cep·tor** \-tər\ *noun* (1906)
**:** a sense organ excited by exteroceptive stimuli

**ex·ter·ri·to·ri·al** \ek-,ster-ə-'tōr-ē-əl, -'tȯr-\ *adjective* (circa 1880)
**:** EXTRATERRITORIAL
— **ex·ter·ri·to·ri·al·i·ty** \-,tōr-ē-'a-lə-tē, -,tȯr-\ *noun*

**¹ex·tinct** \ik-'stiŋ(k)t, 'ek-,\ *adjective* [Middle English, from Latin *exstinctus,* past participle of *exstinguere*] (15th century)
**1 a :** no longer burning **b :** no longer active ⟨an *extinct* volcano⟩
**2 :** no longer existing ⟨an *extinct* animal⟩
**3 a :** gone out of use **:** SUPERSEDED **b :** having no qualified claimant ⟨an *extinct* title⟩

**²extinct** *transitive verb* (15th century)
*archaic* **:** EXTINGUISH

**ex·tinc·tion** \ik-'stiŋ(k)-shən\ *noun* (15th century)
**1 :** the act of making extinct or causing to be extinguished
**2 :** the condition or fact of being extinct or extinguished; *also* **:** the process of becoming extinct ⟨*extinction* of a species⟩
**3 :** the process of eliminating or reducing a conditioned response by not reinforcing it

**extinction coefficient** *noun* (1902)
**:** a measure of the rate of diminution of transmitted light via scattering and absorption for a medium

**ex·tinc·tive** \ik-'stiŋ(k)-tiv\ *adjective* (1600)
**:** tending or serving to extinguish or make extinct

**ex·tin·guish** \ik-'stiŋ-(g)wish\ *transitive verb* [Latin *exstinguere* (from *ex-* + *stinguere* to extinguish) + English *-ish* (as in *abolish*); akin to Latin *instigare* to incite — more at STICK] (1551)
**1 a :** to cause to cease burning **:** QUENCH **b** (1) **:** to bring to an end **:** make an end of ⟨hope for their safety was slowly *extinguished*⟩ (2) **:** to reduce to silence or ineffectiveness **c :** to cause extinction of (a conditioned response) **d :** to dim the brightness of **:** ECLIPSE
**2 a :** to cause to be void **:** NULLIFY ⟨*extinguish* a claim⟩ **b :** to get rid of usually by payment ⟨*extinguish* a debt⟩
— **ex·tin·guish·able** \-(g)wi-shə-bəl\ *adjective*
— **ex·tin·guish·er** \-shər\ *noun*
— **ex·tin·guish·ment** \-mənt\ *noun*

**ex·tir·pate** \'ek-stər-,pāt\ *transitive verb* **-pat·ed; -pat·ing** [Latin *exstirpatus,* past participle of *exstirpare,* from *ex-* + *stirp-, stirps* trunk, root — more at TORPID] (1535)
**1 a :** to destroy completely **:** WIPE OUT **b :** to pull up by the root
**2 :** to cut out by surgery
*synonym* see EXTERMINATE
— **ex·tir·pa·tion** \,ek-stər-'pā-shən\ *noun*
— **ex·tir·pa·tor** \'ek-stər-,pā-tər\ *noun*

**ex·tol** *also* **ex·toll** \ik-'stōl\ *transitive verb* **ex·tolled; ex·tol·ling** [Middle English, from Latin *extollere,* from *ex-* + *tollere* to lift up — more at TOLERATE] (15th century)
**:** to praise highly **:** GLORIFY
— **ex·tol·ler** *noun*
— **ex·tol·ment** \-'stōl-mənt\ *noun*

**ex·tort** \ik-'stȯrt\ *transitive verb* [Latin *extortus,* past participle of *extorquēre* to wrench out, extort, from *ex-* + *torquēre* to twist — more at TORTURE] (1529)
**:** to obtain from a person by force, intimidation, or undue or illegal power **:** WRING; *also*
**:** to gain especially by ingenuity or compelling argument
*synonym* see EDUCE
— **ex·tort·er** *noun*
— **ex·tor·tive** \-'stȯr-tiv\ *adjective*

**ex·tor·tion** \ik-'stȯr-shən\ *noun* (14th century)
**1 :** the act or practice of extorting especially money or other property; *especially* **:** the offense committed by an official engaging in such practice
**2 :** something extorted; *especially* **:** a gross overcharge
— **ex·tor·tion·er** \-sh(ə-)nər\ *noun*
— **ex·tor·tion·ist** \-sh(ə-)nist\ *noun*

**ex·tor·tion·ary** \-shə-,ner-ē\ *adjective* (1805)
*archaic* **:** EXTORTIONATE 1

**ex·tor·tion·ate** \ik-'stȯr-sh(ə-)nət\ *adjective* (1789)
**1 :** characterized by extortion
**2 :** EXCESSIVE, EXORBITANT ⟨*extortionate* prices⟩
— **ex·tor·tion·ate·ly** *adverb*

**¹ex·tra** \'ek-strə\ *adjective* [probably short for *extraordinary*] (1776)
**1 a :** more than is due, usual, or necessary **:** ADDITIONAL ⟨*extra* work⟩ **b :** subject to an additional charge ⟨room service is *extra*⟩
**2 :** SUPERIOR ⟨*extra* quality⟩

**²extra** *noun* (1793)
**1 :** one that is extra or additional: as **a :** a special edition of a newspaper **b :** an added charge **c :** an additional worker; *specifically* **:** one hired to act in a group scene in a motion picture or stage production
**2 :** something of superior quality or grade

**³extra** *adverb* (1823)
**:** beyond the usual size, extent, or degree ⟨*extra* large⟩

**extra-** *prefix* [Middle English, from Latin, from *extra,* adverb & preposition, outside, except, beyond, from *exter* being on the outside — more at EXTERIOR]
**:** outside **:** beyond ⟨*extrajudicial*⟩

**extra–base hit** *noun* (circa 1949)
**:** a hit in baseball that lets the batter take more than one base

**ex·tra·cel·lu·lar** \,ek-strə-'sel-yə-lər\ *adjective* (1867)
**:** situated or occurring outside a cell or the cells of the body ⟨*extracellular* digestion⟩ ⟨*extracellular* enzymes⟩
— **ex·tra·cel·lu·lar·ly** *adverb*

**ex·tra·chro·mo·som·al** \-,krō-mə-'sō-məl, -'zō-\ *adjective* (1940)
**:** situated or controlled by factors outside the chromosome ⟨*extrachromosomal* inheritance⟩

**ex·tra·cor·po·re·al** \-kȯr-'pōr-ē-əl, -'pȯr-\ *adjective* (1865)
**:** occurring or based outside the living body ⟨heart surgery employing *extracorporeal* circulation⟩
— **ex·tra·cor·po·re·al·ly** \-ē-ə-lē\ *adverb*

**ex·tra·cra·ni·al** \-'krā-nē-əl\ *adjective* (circa 1884)
**:** situated or occurring outside the cranium

**¹ex·tract** \ik-'strakt, *oftenest in sense 5* 'ek-,\ *transitive verb* [Middle English, from Latin *extractus,* past participle of *extrahere,* from *ex-* + *trahere* to draw] (15th century)
**1 a :** to draw forth (as by research) ⟨*extract* data⟩ **b :** to pull or take out forcibly ⟨*extracted* a wisdom tooth⟩ **c :** to obtain by much effort from someone unwilling ⟨*extracted* a confession⟩
**2 :** to withdraw (as a juice or fraction) by physical or chemical process; *also* **:** to treat with a solvent so as to remove a soluble substance
**3 :** to separate (a metal) from an ore
**4 :** to determine (a mathematical root) by calculation
**5 :** to select (excerpts) and copy out or cite
*synonym* see EDUCE
— **ex·tract·abil·i·ty** \ik-,strak-tə-'bi-lə-tē, (,)ek-\ *noun*
— **ex·tract·able** \ik-'strak-tə-bəl, 'ek-,\ *adjective*

**²ex·tract** \'ek-,strakt\ *noun* (15th century)
**1 :** a selection from a writing or discourse **:** EXCERPT

**2 :** a product (as an essence or concentrate) prepared by extracting; *especially* **:** a solution (as in alcohol) of essential constituents of a complex material (as meat or an aromatic plant)

**ex·trac·tion** \ik-'strak-shən\ *noun* (15th century)
**1 :** the act or process of extracting something
**2 :** ANCESTRY, ORIGIN
**3 :** something extracted

**¹ex·trac·tive** \ik-'strak-tiv, 'ek-,\ *adjective* (1599)
**1 a :** of, relating to, or involving extraction **b :** tending toward or resulting in withdrawal of natural resources by extraction with no provision for replenishment ⟨*extractive* agriculture⟩
**2 :** capable of being extracted
— **ex·trac·tive·ly** *adverb*

**²extractive** *noun* (1847)
**:** something extracted or extractable **:** EXTRACT

**ex·trac·tor** \ik-'strak-tər\ *noun* (1611)
**:** one that extracts; *especially* **:** the mechanism in a firearm that dislodges a spent cartridge from the chamber

**ex·tra·cur·ric·u·lar** \,ek-strə-kə-'ri-kyə-lər\ *adjective* (1925)
**1 :** not falling within the scope of a regular curriculum; *specifically* **:** of or relating to officially or semiofficially approved and usually organized student activities (as athletics) connected with school and usually carrying no academic credit
**2 a :** lying outside one's regular duties or routine **b :** EXTRAMARITAL
— **extracurricular** *noun*

**ex·tra·dit·able** \'ek-strə-,dī-tə-bəl\ *adjective* (1881)
**1 :** subject or liable to extradition
**2 :** making one liable to extradition ⟨an *extraditable* offense⟩

**ex·tra·dite** \'ek-strə-,dīt\ *transitive verb* **-dit·ed; -dit·ing** [back-formation from *extradition*] (1864)
**1 :** to deliver up to extradition
**2 :** to obtain the extradition of

**ex·tra·di·tion** \,ek-strə-'di-shən\ *noun* [French, from *ex-* + Latin *tradition-, traditio* act of handing over — more at TREASON] (1839)
**:** the surrender of an alleged criminal usually under the provisions of a treaty or statute by one authority (as a state) to another having jurisdiction to try the charge

**ex·tra·dos** \'ek-strə-,däs, -,dō; ek-'strā-,däs\ *noun, plural* **-dos·es** \-,dä-səz\ *or* **-dos** \-,dōz, -,däs\ [French, from Latin *extra* + French *dos* back — more at DOSSIER] (1772)
**:** the exterior curve of an arch — see ARCH illustration

**ex·tra·em·bry·on·ic** \,ek-strə-,em-brē-'ä-nik\ *adjective* (circa 1903)
**:** situated outside the embryo; *especially* **:** developed from the zygote but not part of the embryo ⟨*extraembryonic* membranes⟩

**ex·tra·ga·lac·tic** \,ek-strə-gə-'lak-tik\ *adjective* [International Scientific Vocabulary] (1851)
**:** lying or coming from outside the Milky Way; *also* **:** of or relating to extragalactic space ⟨*extragalactic* astronomy⟩

**ex·tra·he·pat·ic** \-hi-'pa-tik\ *adjective* (circa 1923)
**:** situated or originating outside the liver

**ex·tra·ju·di·cial** \-jü-'di-shəl\ *adjective* (1630)
**1 a :** not forming a valid part of regular legal proceedings ⟨an *extrajudicial* investigation⟩ **b :** delivered without legal authority **:** PRIVATE 2a(2) ⟨the judge's *extrajudicial* statements⟩
**2 :** done in contravention of due process of law ⟨an *extrajudicial* execution⟩
— **ex·tra·ju·di·cial·ly** \-'dish-lē, -'di-shə-\ *adverb*

**ex·tra·le·gal** \,ek-strə-'lē-gəl\ *adjective* (1644)
**:** not regulated or sanctioned by law

— **ex·tra·le·gal·ly** \-gə-lē\ *adverb*

**ex·tra·lim·it·al** \-'li-mə-t°l\ *adjective* (1874)
: not present in a given area — used of kinds of organisms (as species)

**ex·tra·lin·guis·tic** \-liŋ-'gwis-tik\ *adjective* (1927)
: lying outside the province of linguistics
— **ex·tra·lin·guis·ti·cal·ly** \-ti-kə-lē\ *adverb*

**ex·tra·lit·er·ary** \-'li-tə-,rer-ē\ *adjective* (1945)
: lying outside the field of literature

**ex·tral·i·ty** \ek-'stra-lə-tē\ *noun* [by contraction] (1925)
: EXTRATERRITORIALITY

**ex·tra·log·i·cal** \,ek-strə-'lä-ji-kəl\ *adjective* (1833)
: not guided or determined by considerations of logic

**ex·tra·mar·i·tal** \,ek-strə-'mar-ə-t°l\ *adjective* (1925)
: of, relating to, or being sexual intercourse between a married person and someone other than his or her spouse : ADULTEROUS

**ex·tra·mun·dane** \,ek-strə-'mən-,dān, -'mən-,dān\ *adjective* [Late Latin *extramundanus,* from Latin *extra* + *mundus* the world] (1665)
: situated in or relating to a region beyond the material world

**ex·tra·mu·ral** \-'myu̇r-əl\ *adjective* (1854)
**1** : existing or functioning outside or beyond the walls, boundaries, or precincts of an organized unit (as a school or hospital)
**2** *chiefly British* : of, relating to, or taking part in extension courses or facilities
— **ex·tra·mu·ral·ly** \-ə-lē\ *adverb*

**ex·tra·mu·si·cal** \-'myü-zi-kəl\ *adjective* (1923)
: lying outside the province of music

**ex·tra·ne·ous** \ek-'strā-nē-əs\ *adjective* [Latin *extraneus* — more at STRANGE] (1638)
**1** : existing on or coming from the outside
**2 a** : not forming an essential or vital part ⟨*extraneous* ornamentation⟩ **b** : having no relevance ⟨an *extraneous* digression⟩
**3** : being a number obtained in solving an equation that is not a solution of the equation ⟨*extraneous* roots⟩
**synonym** *see* EXTRINSIC
— **ex·tra·ne·ous·ly** *adverb*
— **ex·tra·ne·ous·ness** *noun*

**ex·tra·nu·cle·ar** \,ek-strə-'nü-klē-ər, -'nyü-, ÷-kyə-lər\ *adjective* (1887)
**1** : situated in or affecting the parts of a cell external to the nucleus : CYTOPLASMIC
**2** : situated outside the nucleus of an atom

**ex·tra·oc·u·lar muscle** \,ek-strə-'ä-kyə-lər\ *noun* (1939)
: any of six small voluntary muscles that pass between the eyeball and the orbit and control the movement of the eyeball in relation to the orbit

**ex·traor·di·naire** \ik-,strȯ(r)-d°n-'er, ek-\ *adjective* [French] (1940)
: EXTRAORDINARY — used postpositively ⟨a chef *extraordinaire*⟩

**ex·traor·di·nary** \ik-'strȯr-d°n-,er-ē, ,ek-strə-'ȯr-\ *adjective* [Middle English *extraordinarie,* from Latin *extraordinarius,* from *extra ordinem* out of course, from *extra* + *ordinem,* accusative of *ordin-, ordo* order] (15th century)
**1 a** : going beyond what is usual, regular, or customary ⟨*extraordinary* powers⟩ **b** : exceptional to a very marked extent ⟨*extraordinary* beauty⟩ **c** *of a financial transaction* : NONRECURRING
**2** : employed for or sent on a special function or service ⟨an ambassador *extraordinary*⟩
— **ex·traor·di·nari·ly** \ik-,strȯr-d°n-'er-ə-lē, ,ek-strə-,ȯr-\ *adverb*
— **ex·traor·di·nari·ness** \ik-'strȯr-d°n-,er-ē-nəs, ,ek-strə-'ȯr-\ *noun*

**extra point** *noun* (circa 1949)
: a point gained on a conversion in football

**ex·trap·o·late** \ik-'stra-pə-,lāt\ *verb* **-lat·ed; -lat·ing** [Latin *extra* outside + English *-polate* (as in *interpolate*) — more at EXTRA-] (1874)
*transitive verb*
**1** : to infer (values of a variable in an unobserved interval) from values within an already observed interval
**2 a** : to project, extend, or expand (known data or experience) into an area not known or experienced so as to arrive at a usually conjectural knowledge of the unknown area ⟨*extrapolates* present trends to construct an image of the future⟩ **b** : to predict by projecting past experience or known data ⟨*extrapolate* public sentiment on one issue from known public reaction on others⟩
*intransitive verb*
: to perform the act or process of extrapolating
— **ex·trap·o·la·tion** \-,stra-pə-'lā-shən\ *noun*
— **ex·trap·o·la·tive** \-'stra-pə-,lā-tiv\ *adjective*
— **ex·trap·o·la·tor** \-,lā-tər\ *noun*

**ex·tra·py·ra·mi·dal** \,ek-strə-pə-'ra-mə-d°l, -,pir-ə-'mi-d°l\ *adjective* (circa 1902)
: situated outside of and especially involving descending nerve tracts other than the pyramidal tracts

**ex·tra·sen·so·ry** \,ek-strə-'sen(t)s-rē, -'sen(t)-sə-\ *adjective* (1934)
: residing beyond or outside the ordinary senses

**extrasensory perception** *noun* (1934)
: perception (as in telepathy, clairvoyance, and precognition) that involves awareness of information about events external to the self not gained through the senses and not deducible from previous experience — called also *ESP*

**ex·tra·sys·to·le** \-'sis-tə-(,)lē\ *noun* [New Latin] (circa 1900)
: a premature beat of one of the chambers of the heart that leads to momentary arrhythmia

**¹ex·tra·ter·res·tri·al** \-tə-'res-trē-əl, -'res(h)-chəl\ *adjective* (1868)
: originating, existing, or occurring outside the earth or its atmosphere ⟨*extraterrestrial* life⟩

**²extraterrestrial** *noun* (1960)
: an extraterrestrial being

**ex·tra·ter·ri·to·ri·al** \-,ter-ə-'tȯr-ē-əl, -'tȯr-\ *adjective* (1869)
: existing or taking place outside the territorial limits of a jurisdiction

**ex·tra·ter·ri·to·ri·al·i·ty** \-,tȯr-ē-'a-lə-tē, -,tȯr-\ *noun* (1836)
: exemption from the application or jurisdiction of local law or tribunals

**ex·tra·tex·tu·al** \,ek-strə-'teks-chə-wəl, -chəl\ *adjective* (1960)
: of, relating to, or being something outside a literary text

**ex·tra·trop·i·cal cyclone** \,ek-strə-'trä-pi-kəl-\ *noun* (1923)
: a cyclone in the middle latitudes often being 1500 miles (2400 kilometers) in diameter and usually containing a cold front that extends toward the equator for hundreds of miles

**ex·tra·uter·ine** \,ek-strə-'yü-tə-rən, -,rīn\ *adjective* (1709)
: situated or occurring outside the uterus ⟨*extrauterine* pregnancy⟩

**ex·trav·a·gance** \ik-'stra-vi-gən(t)s\ *noun* (1650)
**1 a** : an instance of excess or prodigality; *specifically* : an excessive outlay of money **b** : something extravagant
**2** : the quality or fact of being extravagant

**ex·trav·a·gan·cy** \-gən(t)-sē\ *noun, plural* **-cies** (1625)
: EXTRAVAGANCE

**ex·trav·a·gant** \ik-'stra-vi-gənt\ *adjective* [Middle English, from Middle French, from Medieval Latin *extravagant-, extravagans,* from Latin *extra-* + *vagant-, vagans,* present participle of *vagari* to wander about, from *vagus* wandering] (15th century)

**1 a** *obsolete* : STRANGE, CURIOUS **b** *archaic* : WANDERING
**2 a** : exceeding the limits of reason or necessity ⟨*extravagant* claims⟩ **b** : lacking in moderation, balance, and restraint ⟨*extravagant* praise⟩
**c** : extremely or excessively elaborate
**3 a** : spending much more than necessary **b** : PROFUSE, LAVISH
**4** : unreasonably high in price ◆
**synonym** *see* EXCESSIVE
— **ex·trav·a·gant·ly** *adverb*

**ex·trav·a·gan·za** \ik-,stra-və-'gan-zə\ *noun* [Italian *extravaganza,* literally, extravagance, from *estravagante* extravagant, from Medieval Latin *extravagant-, extravagans*] (1754)
**1** : a literary or musical work marked by extreme freedom of style and structure and usually by elements of burlesque or parody
**2** : a lavish or spectacular show or event
**3** : something extravagant

**ex·trav·a·gate** \ik-'stra-və-,gāt\ *intransitive verb* **-gat·ed; -gat·ing** (circa 1755)
*archaic* : to go beyond proper limits

**ex·trav·a·sate** \ik-'stra-və-,sāt, -,zāt\ *verb* **-sat·ed; -sat·ing** [Latin *extra* + *vas* vessel] (1668)
*transitive verb*
: to force out or cause to escape from a proper vessel or channel
*intransitive verb*
: to pass by infiltration or effusion from a proper vessel or channel (as a blood vessel) into surrounding tissue
— **ex·trav·a·sa·tion** \-,stra-və-'sā-shən, -,zā-\ *noun*

**ex·tra·vas·cu·lar** \,ek-strə-'vas-kyə-lər\ *adjective* (1804)
: not occurring or contained in body vessels ⟨*extravascular* tissue fluids⟩

**ex·tra·ve·hic·u·lar** \-vē-'hi-kyə-lər\ *adjective* (1965)
: taking place outside a vehicle (as a spacecraft) ⟨*extravehicular* activity⟩

**¹ex·treme** \ik-'strēm\ *adjective* [Middle English, from Middle French, from Latin *extremus,* superlative of *exter, exterus* being on the outside — more at EXTERIOR] (15th century)
**1 a** : existing in a very high degree ⟨*extreme* poverty⟩ **b** : going to great or exaggerated lengths : RADICAL ⟨went on an *extreme* diet⟩ **c** : exceeding the ordinary, usual, or expected ⟨*extreme* weather conditions⟩
**2** *archaic* : LAST
**3** : situated at the farthest possible point from a center ⟨the country's *extreme* north⟩
**4 a** : most advanced or thoroughgoing ⟨the *extreme* political left⟩ **b** : MAXIMUM
**synonym** *see* EXCESSIVE

◇ **WORD HISTORY**

**extravagant** A person who buys an extravagant gift has in all likelihood strayed quite far from the amount originally budgeted for the purchase. The notion of wandering far afield actually is inherent in the word *extravagant,* which comes from a word in Medieval Latin. *Extravagans* is formed from the Latin prefix *extra-* "outside" or "beyond" and the verb *vagari* "to wander about." Originally *extravagant* was used literally of things that wandered beyond their usual confines. In Shakespeare's *Hamlet* the restless ghost of Hamlet's father is spoken of as an "extravagant and erring spirit." From this literal use of *extravagant,* the extended meanings "exceeding the limits of reason or necessity" and "lacking in moderation, balance, and restraint" developed.

\ə\ abut \°\ kitten \ər\ further \a\ ash \ā\ ace
\ä\ mop, mar \au̇\ out \ch\ chin \e\ bet \ē\ easy
\g\ go \i\ hit \ī\ ice \j\ job \ŋ\ sing \ō\ go
\ȯ\ law \ȯi\ boy \th\ thin \th\ the \ü\ loot \u̇\ foot
\y\ yet \zh\ vision *see also* Guide to Pronunciation

— **ex·treme·ness** *noun*

**²extreme** *noun* (1555)
**1 a :** something situated at or marking one end or the other of a range ⟨*extremes* of heat and cold⟩ **b :** the first term or the last term of a mathematical proportion **c :** the major term or minor term of a syllogism
**2 a :** a very pronounced or excessive degree **b :** highest degree **:** MAXIMUM
**3 :** an extreme measure or expedient ⟨going to *extremes*⟩
— **in the extreme :** to the greatest possible extent

**ex·treme·ly** *adverb* (1531)
**1 :** in an extreme manner
**2 :** to an extreme extent

**extremely high frequency** *noun* (1952)
**:** a radio frequency in the highest range of the radio spectrum — see RADIO FREQUENCY table

**extremely low frequency** *noun* (1966)
**:** a radio frequency in the lowest range of the radio spectrum — see RADIO FREQUENCY table

**extreme unction** \ik-ˌstrēm-ˈəŋ(k)-shən, ˌek-(ˌ)strēm-\ *noun* (15th century)
**:** a sacrament in which a priest anoints and prays for the recovery and salvation of a critically ill or injured person

**ex·trem·ism** \ik-ˈstrē-ˌmi-zəm\ *noun* (1865)
**1 :** the quality or state of being extreme
**2 :** advocacy of extreme political measures **:** RADICALISM
— **ex·trem·ist** \-mist\ *noun or adjective*

**ex·trem·i·ty** \ik-ˈstre-mə-tē\ *noun, plural* **-ties** (14th century)
**1 a :** the farthest or most remote part, section, or point **b :** a limb of the body; *especially* **:** a human hand or foot
**2 a :** extreme danger or critical need **b :** a moment marked by imminent destruction or death
**3 a :** an intense degree ⟨the *extremity* of his participation —*Saturday Review*⟩ **b :** the utmost degree (as of emotion or pain)
**4 :** a drastic or desperate act or measure ⟨driven to *extremities*⟩

**ex·tre·mum** \ik-ˈstrē-məm\ *noun, plural* **-ma** \-mə\ [New Latin, from Latin, neuter of *extremus*] (1904)
**:** a maximum or a minimum of a mathematical function — called also *extreme value*

**ex·tri·cate** \ˈek-strə-ˌkāt\ *transitive verb* **-cat·ed; -cat·ing** [Latin *extricatus*, past participle of *extricare*, from *ex-* + *tricae* trifles, perplexities] (1614)
**1 a** *archaic* **:** UNRAVEL **b :** to distinguish from a related thing
**2 :** to free or remove from an entanglement or difficulty ☆
— **ex·tri·ca·ble** \ik-ˈstri-kə-bəl, ek-ˈ, ˈek-(ˌ)\ *adjective*
— **ex·tri·ca·tion** \ˌek-strə-ˈkā-shən\ *noun*

**ex·trin·sic** \ek-ˈstrin-zik, -ˈstrin(t)-sik\ *adjective* [French & Late Latin; French *extrinsèque*, from Late Latin *extrinsecus*, from Latin, adverb, from without; akin to Latin *exter* outward and to Latin *sequi* to follow — more at EXTERIOR, SUE] (1613)
**1 a :** not forming part of or belonging to a thing **:** EXTRANEOUS **b :** originating from or on the outside; *especially* **:** originating outside a part and acting upon the part as a whole ⟨*extrinsic* muscles of the tongue⟩
**2 :** EXTERNAL ☆
— **ex·trin·si·cal·ly** \-zi-k(ə-)lē, -si-\ *adverb*

**extrinsic factor** *noun* (1938)
**:** VITAMIN B₁₂

**extro-** *prefix* [alteration of Latin *extra-*]
**:** outward ⟨*extrovert*⟩ — compare INTRO-

**ex·trorse** \ˈek-ˌstrȯrs\ *adjective* [probably from (assumed) New Latin *extrorsus*, from Late Latin, adverb, outward, from Latin *extra-* + *-orsus* (as in *introrsus*)] (1858)
**:** facing outward ⟨an *extrorse* anther⟩

**ex·tro·ver·sion** *or* **ex·tra·ver·sion** \ˌek-strə-ˈvər-zhən, -shən\ *noun* [German *Extraver-*

*sion*, from Latin *extra-* + *versus*, past participle of *vertere* to turn — more at WORTH] (1915)
**:** the act, state, or habit of being predominantly concerned with and obtaining gratification from what is outside the self

**ex·tro·vert** *also* **ex·tra·vert** \ˈek-strə-ˌvərt\ *noun* [modification of German *extravertiert*, from Latin *extra-* + *vertere*] (1918)
**:** one whose personality is characterized by extroversion; *broadly* **:** a gregarious and unreserved person
— **extrovert** *also* **extravert** *adjective*
— **ex·tro·vert·ed** *also* **ex·tra·vert·ed** \-ˌvər-təd, ek-strə-ˈvər-\ *adjective*

**ex·trude** \ik-ˈstrüd\ *verb* **ex·trud·ed; ex·trud·ing** [Latin *extrudere*, from *ex-* + *trudere* to thrust — more at THREAT] (1566)
*transitive verb*
**1 :** to force, press, or push out
**2 :** to shape (as metal or plastic) by forcing through a die
*intransitive verb*
**:** to become extruded
— **ex·trud·abil·i·ty** \-ˌstrü-də-ˈbi-lə-tē\ *noun*
— **ex·trud·able** \-ˈstrü-də-bəl\ *adjective*
— **ex·trud·er** \-ˈstrü-dər\ *noun*

**ex·tru·sion** \ik-ˈstrü-zhən\ *noun* [Medieval Latin *extrusion-, extrusio*, from Latin *extrudere*] (1540)
**:** the act or process of extruding; *also* **:** a form or product produced by this process

**ex·tru·sive** \ik-ˈstrü-siv, -ziv\ *adjective* (1816)
**:** relating to or formed by geological extrusion from the earth in a molten state or as volcanic ash

**ex·u·ber·ance** \ig-ˈzü-b(ə-)rən(t)s\ *noun* (1631)
**1 :** the quality or state of being exuberant
**2 :** an exuberant act or expression

**ex·u·ber·ant** \-b(ə-)rənt\ *adjective* [Middle English, from Middle French, from Latin *exuberant-, exuberans*, present participle of *exuberare* to be abundant, from *ex-* + *uber* fruitful, from *uber* udder — more at UDDER] (15th century)
**1 :** extreme or excessive in degree, size, or extent
**2 a :** joyously unrestrained and enthusiastic **b :** unrestrained or elaborate especially in style **:** FLAMBOYANT ⟨*exuberant* architecture⟩
**3 :** produced in extreme abundance **:** PLENTIFUL
**synonym** see PROFUSE
— **ex·u·ber·ant·ly** *adverb*

**ex·u·ber·ate** \-bə-ˌrāt\ *intransitive verb* **-at·ed; -at·ing** (15th century)
**1** *archaic* **:** to have something in abundance **:** OVERFLOW
**2 :** to become exuberant **:** show exuberance ⟨*exuberated* over his victory⟩

**ex·u·date** \ˈek-s(y)ù-ˌdāt, -shù-\ *noun* (1876)
**:** exuded matter

**ex·u·da·tion** \ˌek-s(y)ù-ˈdā-shən, -shù-\ *noun* (1612)
**1 :** the process of exuding
**2 :** EXUDATE
— **ex·u·da·tive** \ig-ˈzü-də-tiv; ˈek-s(y)ù-ˌdā-tiv, -shù-\ *adjective*

**ex·ude** \ig-ˈzüd\ *verb* **ex·ud·ed; ex·ud·ing** [Latin *exsudare*, from *ex-* + *sudare* to sweat — more at SWEAT] (1574)
*intransitive verb*
**1 :** to ooze out
**2 :** to undergo diffusion
*transitive verb*
**1 :** to cause to ooze or spread out in all directions
**2 :** to display conspicuously or abundantly ⟨*exudes* charm⟩

**ex·ult** \ig-ˈzəlt\ *intransitive verb* [Middle French *exulter*, from Latin *exsultare*, literally, to leap up, from *ex-* + *saltare* to leap — more at SALTATION] (1570)
**1** *obsolete* **:** to leap for joy

**2 :** to be extremely joyful **:** REJOICE
— **ex·ult·ing·ly** \-ˈzəl-tiŋ-lē\ *adverb*

**ex·ul·tance** \ig-ˈzəl-t⁰n(t)s\ *noun* (1650)
**:** EXULTATION

**ex·ul·tan·cy** \-ˈzəl-t⁰n(t)-sē\ *noun* (1621)
**:** EXULTATION

**ex·ul·tant** \ig-ˈzəl-t⁰nt\ *adjective* (1653)
**:** filled with or expressing great joy or triumph **:** JUBILANT
— **ex·ul·tant·ly** *adverb*

**ex·ul·ta·tion** \ˌek-(ˌ)səl-ˈtā-shən, ˌeg-(ˌ)zəl-\ *noun* (15th century)
**:** the act of exulting **:** the state of being exultant

**ex·urb** \ˈek-ˌsərb, ˈeg-ˌzərb\ *noun* [*ex-* + suburb] (1955)
**:** a region or settlement that lies outside a city and usually beyond its suburbs and that often is inhabited chiefly by well-to-do families
— **ex·ur·ban** \ek-ˈsər-bən; eg-ˈzər-, ig-\ *adjective*

**ex·ur·ban·ite** \ek-ˈsər-bə-ˌnīt; eg-ˈzər-, ig-\ *noun* (1955)
**:** one who lives in an exurb

**ex·ur·bia** \-bē-ə\ *noun* (1955)
**:** the generalized region of exurbs

**ex·u·vi·ae** \ig-ˈzü-vē-ˌē, -vē-ˌī\ *noun plural* [Latin, from *exuere* to take off, from *ex-* + *-uere* to put on; akin to Old Church Slavonic *obuti* to put on (footwear)] (1653)
**:** sloughed off natural animal coverings (as the skins of snakes)
— **ex·u·vi·al** \-vē-əl\ *adjective*

**ex·u·vi·a·tion** \-ˌzü-vē-ˈā-shən\ *noun* (1839)
**:** the process of molting

**¹ex-vo·to** \(ˌ)eks-ˈvō-(ˌ)tō\ *noun, plural* **ex-votos** [Latin *ex voto* according to a vow] (1787)
**:** a votive offering

**²ex-voto** *adjective* (1823)
**:** VOTIVE

**-ey** — see -Y

**ey·as** \ˈī-əs\ *noun* [Middle English, alteration (by incorrect division of *a neias*) of *neias*, from Middle French *niais* fresh from the nest,

---

☆ **SYNONYMS**
**Extricate, disentangle, untangle, disencumber, disembarrass** mean to free from what binds or holds back. EXTRICATE implies the use of care or ingenuity in freeing from a difficult position or situation ⟨*extricated* himself from financial difficulties⟩. DISENTANGLE and UNTANGLE suggest painstaking separation of a thing from other things ⟨*disentangling* fact from fiction⟩ ⟨*untangle* a web of deceit⟩. DISENCUMBER implies a release from something that clogs or weighs down ⟨an article *disencumbered* of jargon⟩. DISEMBARRASS suggests a release from something that impedes or hinders ⟨*disembarrassed* herself of her advisers⟩.

**Extrinsic, extraneous, foreign, alien** mean external to a thing, its essential nature, or its original character. EXTRINSIC applies to what is distinctly outside the thing in question or is not contained in or derived from its essential nature ⟨sentimental value that is *extrinsic* to the house's market value⟩. EXTRANEOUS applies to what is on or comes from the outside and may or may not be capable of becoming an essential part ⟨arguments *extraneous* to the issue⟩. FOREIGN applies to what is so different as to be rejected or repelled or to be incapable of becoming assimilated ⟨techniques *foreign* to French cuisine⟩. ALIEN is stronger than FOREIGN in suggesting opposition, repugnance, or irreconcilability ⟨a practice totally *alien* to her nature⟩.

from (assumed) Vulgar Latin *nidax* nestling, from Latin *nidus* nest — more at NEST] (15th century)

: an unfledged bird; *specifically* : a nestling hawk

¹**eye** \ˈī\ *noun* [Middle English, from Old English *ēage;* akin to Old High German *ouga* eye, Latin *oculus,* Greek *ōps* eye, face, Sanskrit *akṣi* eye] (before 12th century)

**1 a :** an organ of sight; *especially* : a nearly spherical hollow organ that is lined with a sensitive retina, is lodged in a bony orbit in the skull, is the vertebrate organ of sight, and is normally paired **b** : all the visible structures within and surrounding the orbit and including eyelids, eyelashes, and eyebrows **c** (1) : the faculty of

eye 1a: *1* optic nerve, *2* blind spot, *3* fovea, *4* sclera, *5* choroid, *6* retina, *7* ciliary body, *8* posterior chamber, *9* anterior chamber, *10* cornea, *11* lens, *12* iris, *13* suspensory ligament, *14* conjunctiva, *15* vitreous humor

seeing with eyes (2) : the faculty of intellectual or aesthetic perception or appreciation ⟨an *eye* for beauty⟩ **d** : LOOK, GLANCE ⟨cast an eager *eye*⟩ **e** (1) : an attentive look ⟨kept an *eye* on his valuables⟩ (2) : ATTENTION, NOTICE ⟨caught his *eye*⟩ (3) : close observation : SCRUTINY ⟨works under the *eye* of her boss⟩ ⟨in the public *eye*⟩ **f** : POINT OF VIEW, JUDGMENT ⟨beauty is in the *eye* of the beholder⟩ — often used in plural ⟨an offender in the *eyes* of the law⟩ **g** : VIEW 5 ⟨with an *eye* to the future⟩

**2** : something having an appearance suggestive of an eye: as **a** : the hole through the head of a needle **b** : a usually circular marking (as on a peacock's tail) **c** : LOOP; *especially* : a loop or catch to receive a hook **d** : an undeveloped bud (as on a potato) **e** : an area like a hole in the center of a tropical cyclone marked by only light winds or complete calm with no precipitation **f** : the center of a flower especially when differently colored or marked; *specifically* : the disk of a composite **g** (1) : a triangular piece of beef cut from between the top and bottom of a round (2) : the chief muscle of a chop (3) : a compact mass of muscular tissue usually embedded in fat in a rib or loin cut of meat **h** : a device (as a photoelectric cell) that functions in a manner analogous to human vision

**3** : something central : CENTER ⟨the *eye* of the problem —Norman Mailer⟩

**4** : the direction from which the wind is blowing

— **eye·less** \ˈī-ləs\ *adjective*
— **eye·like** \-ˌlīk\ *adjective*
— **an eye for an eye** : retribution in kind
— **my eye** — used to express mild disagreement or sometimes surprise ⟨a diamond, *my eye!* That's glass⟩

²**eye** *verb* **eyed; eye·ing** *or* **ey·ing** (15th century)
*transitive verb*
**1 a** : to fix the eyes on : look at **b** : to watch closely
**2** : to furnish with an eye
*intransitive verb*
*obsolete* : SEEM, LOOK
— **ey·er** \ˈī(-ə)r\ *noun*

¹**eye·ball** \ˈī-ˌbȯl\ *noun* (1590)
: the more or less globular capsule of the vertebrate eye formed by the sclera and cornea together with their contained structures

²**eyeball** *transitive verb* (1901)
: to look at intently

³**eyeball** *adjective* (1971)
: based on observation ⟨*eyeball* judgment⟩

**eyeball–to–eyeball** *adverb or adjective* (1962)
: FACE-TO-FACE

**eye bank** *noun* (1944)
: a storage place for human corneas from the newly dead for transplanting to the eyes of those blind through corneal defects

**eye·bar** \ˈī-ˌbär\ *noun* (circa 1889)
: a metal bar having a closed loop at one or both ends

**eye·bolt** \ˈī-ˈbōlt\ *noun* (1769)
: a bolt with a looped head

**eye·bright** \ˈī-ˌbrīt\ *noun* (1533)
: any of a genus (*Euphrasia*) of herbs of the snapdragon family with opposite toothed or cut leaves

**eye·brow** \ˈī-ˌbraủ\ *noun* (15th century)
: the ridge over the eye or the hair growing on it

**eyebrow pencil** *noun* (1881)
: a cosmetic pencil for the eyebrows

**eye–catch·er** \ˈī-ˌka-chər, -ˌke-\ *noun* (1923)
: something that arrests the eye
— **eye–catch·ing** \-chiŋ\ *adjective*
— **eye–catch·ing·ly** \-chiŋ-lē\ *adverb*

**eye chart** *noun* (1943)
: a chart read at a fixed distance for purposes of testing sight; *especially* : one with rows of letters or objects of decreasing size

**eye contact** *noun* (1955)
: visual contact with another person's eyes

**eye·cup** \ˈī-ˌkəp\ *noun* (circa 1874)
**1** : a small oval cup with a rim curved to fit the orbit of the eye used for applying liquid remedies to the eyes
**2** : OPTIC CUP
**3** : a usually rubber cup at the eyepiece of an optical instrument (as binoculars) for keeping out extraneous light

**eyed** \ˈīd\ *adjective* (14th century)
: having an eye or eyes especially of a specified kind or number — often used in combination ⟨an almond-*eyed* girl⟩

**eyed·ness** \ˈīd-nəs\ *noun* [-*eyed* (as in *right-eyed, left-eyed*)] (1924)
: preference for the use of one eye instead of the other (as in using a monocular microscope)

**eye·drop·per** \ˈī-ˌdrä-pər\ *noun* (1937)
: DROPPER 2

**eye·drops** \-ˌdräps\ *noun plural* (1926)
: a medicated solution for the eyes applied in drops

**eye·ful** \ˈī-ˌfůl\ *noun* (circa 1864)
**1** : a full or completely satisfying view
**2** : one that is visually attractive; *especially* : a strikingly beautiful woman

**eye·glass** \ˈī-ˌglas\ *noun* (1664)
**1 a** : EYEPIECE **b** : a lens worn to aid vision; *specifically* : MONOCLE **c** *plural* : GLASSES, SPECTACLES
**2** : EYECUP 1

**eye·hole** \ˈī-ˌhōl\ *noun* (1637)
**1** : ¹ORBIT
**2** : PEEPHOLE

**eye·lash** \ˈī-ˌlash\ *noun* (1752)
**1** : the fringe of hair edging the eyelid — usually used in plural
**2** : a single hair of the eyelashes

**eye lens** *noun* (1871)
: the lens nearest the eye in an eyepiece

**eye·let** \ˈī-lət\ *noun* [alteration of Middle English *oilet,* from Middle French *oillet,* diminutive of *oil* eye, from Latin *oculus*] (14th century)
**1 a** : a small hole designed to receive a cord or used for decoration (as in embroidery) **b** : a small typically metal ring to reinforce an eyelet : GROMMET
**2** : PEEPHOLE, LOOPHOLE

**eye·lid** \ˈī-ˌlid\ *noun* (13th century)
: either of the movable folds of skin and muscle that can be closed over the eyeball

**eye·lin·er** \ˈī-ˌlī-nər\ *noun* (1947)
: makeup used to emphasize the contour of the eyes

**ey·en** \ˈī(-ə)n\ *archaic plural of* EYE

**eye–open·er** \ˈī-ˌōp-nər, -ˌō-pə-\ *noun* (1818)
**1** : a drink intended to wake one up
**2** : something startling, surprising, or enlightening
— **eye–open·ing** \-niŋ\ *adjective*

**eye·piece** \ˈī-ˌpēs\ *noun* (1790)
: the lens or combination of lenses at the eye end of an optical instrument

**eye·pop·per** \ˈī-ˌpä-pər\ *noun* (1941)
: something that excites, astonishes, or attracts the eye
— **eye–pop·ping** \-ˌpä-piŋ\ *adjective*

**eye rhyme** *noun* (1871)
: an imperfect rhyme that appears to have identical vowel sounds from similarity of spelling (as *move* and *love*)

**eye·shade** \ˈī-ˌshād\ *noun* (1845)
: a visor that shields the eyes from strong light and is fastened on with a headband

**eye shadow** *noun* (1930)
: a cosmetic cream or powder in one of various colors that is applied to the eyelids to accent the eyes

**eye·shot** \ˈī-ˌshät\ *noun* (1599)
: the range of the eye : VIEW

**eye·sight** \ˈī-ˌsīt\ *noun* (13th century)
**1** : SIGHT 4a
**2** *archaic* : OBSERVATION 1

**eye socket** *noun* (circa 1844)
: ¹ORBIT

**eyes only** *adjective* (1972)
: to be read by only the person addressed

**eye·sore** \ˈī-ˌsōr, -ˌsȯr\ *noun* (1530)
: something offensive to view

**eye·spot** \ˈī-ˌspät\ *noun* (1877)
**1 a** : a simple visual organ of pigment or pigmented cells covering a sensory termination : OCELLUS **b** : a small pigmented body of various unicellular algae
**2** : a spot of color
**3** : any of several fungal diseases of plants characterized by yellowish oval lesions on the leaves and stem; *especially* : a disease of various grasses (as sugarcane) caused by a fungus (*Helminthosporium sacchari*)

**eye·stalk** \ˈī-ˌstȯk\ *noun* (1854)
: one of the movable peduncles bearing an eye at the tip in a decapod crustacean

**eye·strain** \ˈī-ˌstrān\ *noun* (1874)
: weariness or a strained state of the eye

**eye·strings** \ˈī-ˌstriŋz\ *noun plural* (1590)
*obsolete* : organic eye attachments formerly believed to break at death or blindness

**eye·tooth** \ˈī-ˈtüth\ *noun* (circa 1545)
: a canine tooth of the upper jaw

**eye view** *noun* (circa 1771)
: POINT OF VIEW ⟨an alien *eye view*⟩

**eye·wash** \ˈī-ˌwȯsh, -ˌwäsh\ *noun* (circa 1859)
**1** : an eye lotion
**2** : misleading or deceptive statements, actions, or procedures

**eye·wear** \ˈī-ˌwar, -ˌwer\ *noun* (1926)
: corrective or protective devices (as glasses or contact lenses) for the eyes

**eye·wink** \ˈī-ˌwiŋk\ *noun* (1598)
: LOOK, GLANCE

**eye·wit·ness** \ˈī-ˈwit-nəs\ *noun* (1539)
: one who sees an occurrence or an object; *especially* : one who gives a report on what he or she has seen

**eyre** \ˈar, ˈer\ *noun* [Middle English *eire,* from Anglo-French, from Old French *erre* trip, from *errer* to travel — more at ERRANT] (14th century)
: a circuit traveled by an itinerant justice in medieval England or the court he presided over

**ey·rie** \ˈir-ē, *or same as* AERIE\ *variant of* AERIE

**ey·rir** \'ā-ˌrir\ *noun, plural* **au·rar** \'au̇-ˌrär, 'œi-\ [Icelandic, from Old Norse, money (in plural), probably from Latin *aureus* a gold coin] (circa 1927)
— see *krona* at MONEY table

**Eze·chiel** \i-'zē-kyəl, -kē-əl\ *noun* [Late Latin]
: EZEKIEL

**Eze·kiel** \i-'zē-kyəl, -kē-əl\ *noun* [Late Latin *Ezechiel,* from Hebrew *Yĕḥezqēl*]
**1 :** a Hebrew priest and prophet of the 6th century B.C.
**2 :** a prophetic book of canonical Jewish and Christian Scripture written by Ezekiel — see BIBLE table

**Ez·ra** \'ez-rə\ *noun* [Late Latin, from Hebrew *'Ezrā*]
**1 :** a Hebrew priest, scribe, and reformer of Judaism of the 5th century B.C. in Babylon and Jerusalem
**2 :** a narrative book of canonical Jewish and Christian Scripture — see BIBLE table

# F

F *is the sixth letter of the English, Latin, and early Greek alphabets. Corresponding to the Phoenician wāw, which represented a bilabial fricative, a consonant with a sound somewhat like that of a breathy English* w, *it came into Greek as* digamma *(written "Ϝ"). This letter dropped out of Classical Greek but was preserved in western Greek alphabets, from which it passed into Etruscan, taking there the value of a voiceless labiodental fricative with the sound of* f *in English* flag. *Latin adopted both the Etruscan letterform and pronunciation of* f, *which has the same phonetic value in English, except in the word* of *and its compounds, where it is voiced (pronounced with vibrating vocal cords). Small* f *evolved from the capital form through lengthening of the upright stem, shortening of the top and middle horizontal bars, and rounding of the top bar.*

---

**f** \'ef\ *noun, plural* **f's** *or* **fs** \'efs\ *often capitalized, often attributive* (before 12th century)
**1 a :** the 6th letter of the English alphabet **b :** a graphic representation of this letter **c :** a speech counterpart of orthographic *f*
**2 :** the 4th tone of a C-major scale
**3 :** a graphic device for reproducing the letter *f*
**4 :** one designated *f* especially as the 6th in order or class
**5 a :** a grade rating a student's work as failing **b :** one graded or rated with an F
**6 :** something shaped like the letter F
**fa** \'fä\ *noun* [Middle English, from Medieval Latin, from the syllable sung to this note in a medieval hymn to Saint John the Baptist] (13th century)
**:** the 4th tone of the diatonic scale in solmization
**Fa·bi·an** \'fā-bē-ən\ *adjective* (1777)
**1 a :** of, relating to, or in the manner of the Roman general Quintus Fabius Maximus known for his defeat of Hannibal in the Second Punic War by the avoidance of decisive contests **b :** CAUTIOUS, DILATORY
**2** [the *Fabian* Society; from the members' belief in slow rather than revolutionary change in government] **:** of, relating to, or being a society of socialists organized in England in 1884 to spread socialist principles gradually
**— Fabian** *noun*
**— Fa·bi·an·ism** \-ə-,ni-zəm\ *noun*
**¹fa·ble** \'fā-bəl\ *noun* [Middle English, from Middle French, from Latin *fabula* conversation, story, play, from *fari* to speak — more at BAN] (14th century)
**:** a fictitious narrative or statement: as **a :** a legendary story of supernatural happenings **b :** a narration intended to enforce a useful truth; *especially* **:** one in which animals speak and act like human beings **c :** FALSEHOOD, LIE
**²fable** *verb* **fa·bled; fa·bling** \-b(ə-)liŋ\ (14th century)
*intransitive verb*
*archaic* **:** to tell fables
*transitive verb*
**:** to talk or write about as if true
**— fa·bler** \-b(ə-)lər\ *noun*
**fa·bled** \'fā-bəld\ *adjective* (1606)
**1 :** FICTITIOUS
**2 :** told or celebrated in fables
**3 :** RENOWNED, FAMOUS
**fab·li·au** \'fa-blē-,ō\ *noun, plural* **-aux** \-,ō(z)\ [French, from Old French, diminutive of *fable*] (1804)
**:** a short, usually comic, frankly coarse, and often cynical tale in verse popular especially in the 12th and 13th centuries
**fab·ric** \'fa-brik\ *noun* [Middle French *fabrique*, from Latin *fabrica* workshop, structure] (15th century)
**1 a :** STRUCTURE, BUILDING **b :** underlying structure **:** FRAMEWORK ⟨the *fabric* of society⟩

**2 :** an act of constructing **:** ERECTION; *specifically* **:** the construction and maintenance of a church building
**3 a :** structural plan or style of construction **b :** TEXTURE, QUALITY — used chiefly of textiles **c :** the arrangement of physical components (as of soil) in relation to each other
**4 a :** CLOTH 1a **b :** a material that resembles cloth
**5 :** the appearance or pattern produced by the shapes and arrangement of the crystal grains in a rock
**fab·ri·cant** \'fa-bri-kənt\ *noun* (1757)
**:** MANUFACTURER
**fab·ri·cate** \'fa-bri-,kāt\ *transitive verb* **-cated; -cat·ing** [Middle English, from Latin *fabricatus*, past participle of *fabricari*, from *fabrica*] (15th century)
**1 a :** INVENT, CREATE **b :** to make up for the purpose of deception
**2 :** CONSTRUCT, MANUFACTURE; *specifically* **:** to construct from diverse and usually standardized parts
**— fab·ri·ca·tor** \'fa-bri-,kā-tər\ *noun*
**fab·ri·ca·tion** \,fa-bri-'kā-shən\ *noun* (15th century)
**1 :** the act or process of fabricating
**2 :** a product of fabrication; *especially* **:** LIE, FALSEHOOD
**fabric softener** *noun* (1965)
**:** a product used to make laundered fabrics softer and fluffier
**fab·u·lar** \'fa-byə-lər\ *adjective* (1684)
**:** of, relating to, or having the form of a fable
**fab·u·list** \'fa-byə-list\ *noun* (1593)
**1 :** a creator or writer of fables
**2 :** LIAR
**— fabulist** *or* **fab·u·lis·tic** \,fa-byə-'lis-tik\ *adjective*
**fab·u·lous** \'fa-byə-ləs\ *adjective* [Middle English, from Latin *fabulosus*, from *fabula*] (15th century)
**1 a :** resembling or suggesting a fable **:** of an incredible, astonishing, or exaggerated nature ⟨*fabulous* wealth⟩ **b :** WONDERFUL, MARVELOUS ⟨had a *fabulous* time⟩
**2 :** told in or based on fable
**synonym** see FICTITIOUS
**— fab·u·lous·ly** *adverb*
**— fab·u·lous·ness** *noun*
**fa·cade** *also* **fa·çade** \fə-'säd\ *noun* [French *façade*, from Italian *facciata*, from *faccia* face, from (assumed) Vulgar Latin *facia*] (circa 1681)

**facade 1**

**1 :** the front of a building; *also* **:** any face of a building given special architectural treatment ⟨a museum's east *facade*⟩
**2 :** a false, superficial, or artificial appearance or effect
**¹face** \'fās\ *noun, often attributive* [Middle English, from Old French, from (assumed) Vulgar Latin *facia*, from Latin *facies* make, form, face, from *facere* to make, do — more at DO] (13th century)
**1 a :** the front part of the human head including the chin, mouth, nose, cheeks, eyes, and usually the forehead **b :** the face as a means of identification **:** COUNTENANCE ⟨would know that *face* anywhere⟩
**2** *archaic* **:** PRESENCE, SIGHT
**3 a :** facial expression **b :** GRIMACE **c :** MAKEUP 3a(1)
**4 a :** outward appearance ⟨suspicious on the *face* of it⟩ **b :** DISGUISE, PRETENSE **c** (1) **:** ASSURANCE, CONFIDENCE ⟨maintaining a firm *face* in spite of adversity⟩ (2) **:** EFFRONTERY ⟨how anyone could have the *face* to ask that question⟩ **d :** DIGNITY, PRESTIGE ⟨afraid to lose *face*⟩
**5 :** SURFACE: **a** (1) **:** a front, upper, or outer surface (2) **:** the front of something having two or four sides (3) **:** FACADE (4) **:** an exposed surface of rock (5) **:** any of the plane surfaces that bound a geometric solid **b :** a surface specially prepared: as (1) **:** the principal dressed surface (as of a disk) (2) **:** the right side (as of cloth or leather) (3) **:** an inscribed, printed, or marked side **c** (1) **:** the surface (as of type) that receives the ink and transfers it to the paper (2) **:** a style of type
**6 :** the end or wall of a mine tunnel, drift, or excavation at which work is progressing
**7 :** FACE VALUE
**8 :** PERSON ⟨lots of new *faces* around here⟩
**— in the face of** *also* **in face of :** face-to-face with **:** DESPITE ⟨succeed *in the face of* great difficulties⟩
**— to one's face :** in one's presence or so that one is fully aware of what is going on **:** FRANKLY
**²face** *verb* **faced; fac·ing** (15th century)
*transitive verb*
**1 :** to confront impudently
**2 a :** to line near the edge especially with a different material **b :** to cover the front or surface of ⟨*faced* the building with marble⟩
**3 :** to meet face-to-face or in competition
**4 a :** to stand or sit with the face toward **b :** to have the front oriented toward ⟨a house *facing* the park⟩
**5 a :** to recognize and deal with straightforwardly ⟨*face* the facts⟩ **b :** to master by confronting with determination — used with *down* ⟨*faced* down his critics⟩
**6 a :** to have as a prospect **:** be confronted by ⟨*face* a grim future⟩ **b :** to be a prospect or a source of concern for ⟨the problems that *face* us⟩ **c :** to bring face-to-face ⟨he was *faced* with ruin⟩
**7 :** to make the surface of (as a stone) flat or smooth
**8 :** to cause (troops) to face in a particular direction on command
*intransitive verb*
**1 :** to have the face or front turned in a specified direction
**2 :** to turn the face in a specified direction
**— face the music :** to meet an unpleasant situation, a danger, or the consequences of one's actions
**face angle** *noun* (1913)
**:** an angle formed by two edges of a polyhedral angle
**face card** *noun* (1826)
**:** a king, queen, or jack in a deck of cards

\ə\ abut \ᵊ\ kitten \ər\ further \a\ ash \ā\ ace
\ä\ mop, mar \au̇\ out \ch\ chin \e\ bet \ē\ easy
\g\ go \i\ hit \ī\ ice \j\ job \ŋ\ sing \ō\ go
\o̊\ law \o̊i\ boy \th\ thin \t̶h̶\ the \ü\ loot \u̇\ foot
\y\ yet \zh\ vision    *see also* Guide to Pronunciation

**face·cen·tered** \'fās-ˌsen-tərd\ *adjective* (1913)
: relating to or being a crystal space lattice in which each cubic unit cell has an atom at the center and at the corners of each face — compare BODY-CENTERED

**face·cloth** \'fās-ˌklȯth\ *noun* (1602)
: WASHCLOTH

**face cord** *noun* (circa 1926)
: a unit of wood cut for fuel equal to a stack 4 × 8 feet with lengths of pieces from about 12 to 16 inches

**-faced** \ˌfāst\ *adjective combining form*
: having (such) a face or (so many) faces ⟨rosy-*faced*⟩ ⟨two-*faced*⟩

**face·down** \ˌfās-'daȯn\ *adverb* (1949)
: with the face down ⟨sliding *facedown*⟩

**face fly** *noun* (1961)
: a European fly (*Musca autumnalis*) that is similar to the housefly, is widely established in North America, and causes distress to livestock by clustering about the face

**face·less** \'fās-ləs\ *adjective* (1596)
1 : lacking a face
2 a : lacking character or individuality : NONDESCRIPT ⟨the *faceless* masses⟩ b : not identified : ANONYMOUS ⟨a *faceless* accuser⟩
— **face·less·ness** *noun*

**face-lift** \'fās-ˌlift\ *noun* (1934)
1 : a cosmetic operation for removal of facial defects (as wrinkles) typical of aging
2 : an alteration, restoration, or restyling (as of a building) intended especially to modernize
— **face-lift** *transitive verb*

**face mask** *noun* (1906)
: a mask covering the face (as in football or scuba diving) : MASK 3

**face-off** \'fās-ˌȯf\ *noun* (1896)
1 : a method of beginning play (as in hockey or lacrosse) in which two opponents face each other and attempt to gain control of a puck or ball dropped between them
2 : CONFRONTATION

**face·plate** \'fās-ˌplāt\ *noun* (1841)
1 : a disk fixed with its face at right angles to the live spindle of a lathe for the attachment of the work
2 a : a protective plate for a machine or device b : a protective cover for the human face (as of a diver)
3 : the glass front of a cathode-ray tube on which the image is seen

**fac·er** \'fā-sər\ *noun* (15th century)
1 : one that faces
2 *British* : a sudden often stunning check or obstacle

**face-sav·er** \'fā(s)-ˌsā-vər\ *noun* (1923)
: something (as a compromise) that saves face
— **face-sav·ing** \-ˌsā-viŋ\ *adjective or noun*

**fac·et** \'fa-sət\ *noun* [French *facette*, diminutive of *face*] (1625)
1 : a small plane surface (as on a cut gem)
2 : any of the definable aspects that make up a subject (as of contemplation) or an object (as of consideration)
3 : the external corneal surface of an ommatidium
4 : a smooth flat circumscribed anatomical surface (as of a bone)
— **fac·et·ed** *or* **fac·et·ted** \'fa-sə-təd\ *adjective*

**fa·cete** \fə-'sēt\ *adjective* [Latin *facetus*] (1603)
*archaic* : FACETIOUS, WITTY

**fa·ce·ti·ae** \fə-'sē-shē-ˌē, -ˌī\ *noun plural* [Latin, from plural of *facetia* jest, from *facetus* elegant, witty] (1529)
: witty or humorous writings or sayings

**fa·ce·tious** \fə-'sē-shəs\ *adjective* [Middle French *facetieux*, from *facetie* jest, from Latin *facetia*] (1599)
1 : joking or jesting often inappropriately : WAGGISH ⟨just being *facetious*⟩

2 : meant to be humorous or funny : not serious ⟨a *facetious* remark⟩
**synonym** see WITTY
— **fa·ce·tious·ly** *adverb*
— **fa·ce·tious·ness** *noun*

**face-to-face** *adverb or adjective* (14th century)
1 : within each other's sight or presence ⟨met and talked *face-to-face*⟩ ⟨a *face-to-face* consultation⟩
2 : in or into direct contact or confrontation ⟨came *face-to-face* with the problem⟩

**face-up** \'fā-'səp\ *adverb* (1897)
: with the face up

**face up** *intransitive verb* (1920)
: to confront or deal directly with someone or something previously avoided — usually used with *to* ⟨*faced up* to the situation⟩

**face value** *noun* (1876)
1 : the value indicated on the face (as of a postage stamp or a stock certificate)
2 : the apparent value or significance ⟨if their remarks may be taken at *face value*⟩

**facia** *variant of* FASCIA

**¹fa·cial** \'fā-shəl\ *adjective* (circa 1818)
1 : of or relating to the face
2 : concerned with or used in improving the appearance of the face
— **fa·cial·ly** \-shə-lē\ *adverb*

**²facial** *noun* (1914)
: a facial treatment

**facial index** *noun* (circa 1889)
: the ratio of the breadth of the face to its length multiplied by 100

**facial nerve** *noun* (circa 1818)
: either of the 7th pair of cranial nerves that supply motor fibers especially to the muscles of the face and jaw and sensory and parasympathetic fibers to the tongue, palate, and fauces

**-fa·cient** \'fā-shənt\ *adjective combining form* [Latin *-facient-*, *-faciens* (as in *calefacient-*, *calefaciens* making warm, present participle of *calefacere* to warm)]
: making : causing ⟨somni*facient*⟩

**fa·cies** \'fā-sh(ē-)ˌēz\ *noun, plural* **facies** [New Latin, from Latin, face] (circa 1736)
1 : an appearance and expression of the face characteristic of a particular condition especially when abnormal ⟨adenoid *facies*⟩
2 : general appearance ⟨a plant species with a particularly distinct *facies*⟩
3 : a part of a rock or group of rocks that differs from the whole formation (as in composition, age, or fossil content)

**fac·ile** \'fa-səl\ *adjective* [Middle French, from Latin *facilis*, from *facere* to do — more at DO] (15th century)
1 a (1) : easily accomplished or attained ⟨a *facile* victory⟩ (2) : SPECIOUS, SUPERFICIAL ⟨I am not concerned . . . with offering any *facile* solution for so complex a problem —T. S. Eliot⟩ b : used or comprehended with ease c : readily manifested and often lacking sincerity or depth ⟨*facile* tears⟩
2 *archaic* : mild or pleasing in manner or disposition
3 a : READY, FLUENT ⟨*facile* prose⟩ b : POISED, ASSURED
**synonym** see EASY
— **fac·ile·ly** \-sə(l)-lē\ *adverb*
— **fac·ile·ness** \-səl-nəs\ *noun*

**fa·cil·i·tate** \fə-'si-lə-ˌtāt\ *transitive verb* **-tat·ed; -tat·ing** (1611)
: to make easier : help bring about ⟨*facilitate* economic recovery⟩
— **fa·cil·i·ta·tive** \-ˌtā-tiv\ *adjective*
— **fa·cil·i·ta·tor** \-ˌtā-tər\ *noun*

**fa·cil·i·ta·tion** \fə-ˌsi-lə-'tā-shən\ *noun* (1619)
1 : the act of facilitating : the state of being facilitated
2 a : the lowering of the threshold for reflex conduction along a particular neural pathway especially from repeated use of that pathway b : the increasing of the ease or intensity of a response by repeated stimulation

**fa·cil·i·ta·to·ry** \fə-'si-lə-tə-ˌtȯr-ē, -ˌtȯr-\ *adjective* (1944)
: inducing or involved in facilitation especially of a reflex action

**fa·cil·i·ty** \fə-'si-lə-tē\ *noun, plural* **-ties** (1531)
1 : the quality of being easily performed
2 : ease in performance : APTITUDE
3 : readiness of compliance
4 (1) : something that makes an action, operation, or course of conduct easier — usually used in plural ⟨*facilities* for study⟩ (2) : LAVATORY 2 — often used in plural b : something (as a hospital) that is built, installed, or established to serve a particular purpose

**fac·ing** \'fā-siŋ\ *noun* (1566)
1 a : a lining at the edge especially of a garment b *plural* : the collar, cuffs, and trimmings of a uniform coat
2 : an ornamental or protective layer
3 : material for facing

**fac·sim·i·le** \fak-'si-mə-lē\ *noun* [Latin *fac simile* make similar] (1691)
1 : an exact copy
2 : a system of transmitting and reproducing graphic matter (as printing or still pictures) by means of signals sent over telephone lines
**synonym** see REPRODUCTION

**fact** \'fakt\ *noun* [Latin *factum*, from neuter of *factus*, past participle of *facere*] (15th century)
1 : a thing done: as a *obsolete* : FEAT b : CRIME ⟨accessory after the *fact*⟩ c *archaic* : ACTION
2 *archaic* : PERFORMANCE, DOING
3 : the quality of being actual : ACTUALITY ⟨a question of *fact* hinges on evidence⟩
4 a : something that has actual existence ⟨space exploration is now a *fact*⟩ b : an actual occurrence ⟨prove the *fact* of damage⟩
5 : a piece of information presented as having objective reality
— **in fact** : in truth

**fact finder** *noun* (1926)
: one that tries to determine the realities of a case, situation, or relationship; *especially* : an impartial examiner designated by a government agency to appraise the facts underlying a particular matter (as a labor dispute)
— **fact-find·ing** *noun or adjective*

**fac·tic·i·ty** \fak-'ti-sə-tē\ *noun* [French or German; French *facticité*, from German *Faktizität*, from *Factum* fact, from Latin *factum*] (1945)
: the quality or state of being a fact

**fac·tion** \'fak-shən\ *noun* [Middle French & Latin; Middle French, from Latin *faction-*, *factio* act of making, faction — more at FASHION] (1509)
1 : a party or group (as within a government) that is often contentious or self-seeking : CLIQUE
2 : party spirit especially when marked by dissension
— **fac·tion·al** \-shnəl, -shə-n°l\ *adjective*
— **fac·tion·al·ism** \-shnə-ˌli-zəm, -shə-n°l-ˌiz-\ *noun*
— **fac·tion·al·ly** \-ē\ *adverb*

**-fac·tion** \'fak-shən\ *noun combining form* [Middle English *-faccioun*, from Middle French & Latin; Middle French *-faction*, from Latin *-faction-*, *-factio* (as in *satisfaction-*, *satisfactio* satisfaction)]
: making : -FICATION ⟨petri*faction*⟩

**fac·tious** \'fak-shəs\ *adjective* [Middle French or Latin; Middle French *factieux*, from Latin *factiosus*, from *factio*] (1532)
: of or relating to faction: as a : caused by faction ⟨*factious* disputes⟩ b : inclined to faction or the formation of factions c : SEDITIOUS
— **fac·tious·ly** *adverb*
— **fac·tious·ness** *noun*

**fac·ti·tious** \fak-'ti-shəs\ *adjective* [Latin *facticius*, from *factus*, past participle of *facere* to make, do — more at DO] (1646)
1 : produced by humans rather than by natural forces

**2 a :** formed by or adapted to an artificial or conventional standard **b :** produced by special effort : SHAM ⟨created a *factitious* demand by spreading rumors of shortage⟩
— **fac·ti·tious·ly** *adverb*
— **fac·ti·tious·ness** *noun*

**fac·ti·tive** \'fak-tə-tiv\ *adjective* [probably from Latin *factitare* to do habitually, frequentative of *facere*] (1846)
: of, relating to, or being a transitive verb that in some constructions requires an objective complement as well as an object
— **fac·ti·tive·ly** *adverb*

**-fac·tive** \'fak-tiv\ *adjective combining form* [Middle French *-factif*, from *-faction*]
: making : causing ⟨putre*factive*⟩

**fact of life** (1854)
**1 :** something that exists and must be taken into consideration
**2** *plural* **:** the fundamental physiological processes and behavior involved in sex and reproduction

**fac·toid** \'fak-ˌtȯid\ *noun* (1973)
**1 :** an invented fact believed to be true because of its appearance in print
**2 :** a brief and usually trivial news item

**¹fac·tor** \'fak-tər\ *noun* [Middle English, from Middle French *facteur*, from Latin *factor* doer, from *facere*] (15th century)
**1 :** one who acts or transacts business for another: as **a :** BROKER 1b **b :** one that lends money to producers and dealers (as on the security of accounts receivable)
**2 a** (1) **:** one that actively contributes to the production of a result : INGREDIENT ⟨price wasn't a *factor* in the decision⟩ (2) **:** a substance that functions in or promotes the function of a particular physiological process or bodily system **b :** a good or service used in the process of production
**3 :** GENE
**4 a :** any of the numbers or symbols in mathematics that when multiplied together form a product; *also* **:** a number or symbol that divides another number or symbol **b :** a quantity by which a given quantity is multiplied or divided in order to indicate a difference in measurement ⟨costs increased by a *factor* of 10⟩
— **fac·tor·ship** \-ˌship\ *noun*

**²factor** *verb* **fac·tored; fac·tor·ing** \-t(ə-)riŋ\ (1621)
*intransitive verb*
: to work as a factor
*transitive verb*
**1 :** to resolve into factors
**2 a :** to include or admit as a factor — used with *in* or *into* ⟨*factor* inflation into our calculations⟩ **b :** to exclude as a factor — used with *out*
— **fac·tor·able** \-t(ə-)rə-bəl\ *adjective*

**fac·tor·age** \-t(ə-)rij\ *noun* (1613)
**1 :** the charges made by a factor for services
**2 :** the business of a factor

**factor analysis** *noun* (1931)
: the analytical process of transforming statistical data (as measurements) into linear combinations of usually independent variables
— **factor analytic** *adjective*

**factor VIII** \-'āt\ *noun* (1954)
: a glycoprotein of blood plasma that is essential for blood clotting and is absent or inactive in hemophilia — called also *antihemophilic factor*

**factor group** *noun* (1897)
: QUOTIENT GROUP

**¹fac·to·ri·al** \fak-'tōr-ē-əl, -'tȯr-\ *adjective* (1837)
: of, relating to, or being a factor or a factorial

**²factorial** *noun* (1869)
**1 :** the product of all the positive integers from 1 to *n* — symbol *n*!
**2 :** the quantity *0!* arbitrarily defined as equal to 1

**fac·tor·iza·tion** \ˌfak-tə-rə-'zā-shən\ *noun* (1886)

: the operation of resolving a quantity into factors; *also* **:** a product obtained by factorization
— **fac·tor·ize** \'fak-tə-ˌrīz\ *transitive verb*

**fac·to·ry** \'fak-t(ə-)rē\ *noun, plural* **-ries** (1582)
**1 :** a station where resident factors trade
**2 a :** a building or set of buildings with facilities for manufacturing **b :** the seat of some kind of production ⟨the vice *factories* of the slums⟩
— **fac·to·ry·like** \-ˌlīk\ *adjective*

**factory ship** *noun* (1927)
: a ship equipped to process a whale or fish catch at sea

**fac·to·tum** \fak-'tō-təm\ *noun* [New Latin, literally, do everything, from Latin *fac* (imperative of *facere* do) + *totum* everything] (1566)
**1 :** a person having many diverse activities or responsibilities
**2 :** a general servant

**fac·tu·al** \'fak-chə-wəl, -chəl, 'faksh-wəl\ *adjective* [*fact* + *-ual* (as in *actual*)] (circa 1834)
**1 :** of or relating to facts
**2 :** restricted to or based on fact
— **fac·tu·al·i·ty** \ˌfak-chə-'wa-lə-tē\ *noun*
— **fac·tu·al·ly** \'fak-chə-wə-lē, -chə-lē, 'faksh-wə-\ *adverb*
— **fac·tu·al·ness** *noun*

**fac·tu·al·ism** \'fak-chə-wə-ˌli-zəm, -chə-ˌli-, 'faksh-wə-\ *noun* (1936)
: adherence or dedication to facts
— **fac·tu·al·ist** \-list\ *noun*

**fac·ture** \'fak-chər\ *noun* [Middle English, from Middle French, from Latin *factura* action of making, from *factus*] (15th century)
: the manner in which something (as an artistic work) is made : EXECUTION

**fac·u·la** \'fa-kyə-lə\ *noun, plural* **-lae** \-ˌlē, -ˌlī\ [New Latin, from Latin, diminutive of *fac-, fax* torch] (1706)
: any of the bright regions of the sun's photosphere seen most easily near the sun's edge

**fac·ul·ta·tive** \'fa-kəl-ˌtā-tiv, *British* -tə-tiv\ *adjective* (1820)
**1 a :** of or relating to the grant of permission, authority, or privilege ⟨*facultative* legislation⟩ **b :** OPTIONAL
**2 :** of or relating to a mental faculty
**3 a :** taking place under some conditions but not under others ⟨*facultative* diapause⟩ **b :** exhibiting an indicated lifestyle under some environmental conditions but not under others ⟨*facultative* anaerobes⟩
— **fac·ul·ta·tive·ly** *adverb*

**fac·ul·ty** \'fa-kəl-tē\ *noun, plural* **-ties** [Middle English *faculte*, from Middle French *faculté*, from Medieval Latin & Latin; Medieval Latin *facultat-, facultas* branch of learning or teaching, from Latin, ability, abundance, from *facilis* facile] (14th century)
**1 :** ABILITY, POWER: as **a :** innate or acquired ability to act or do **b :** an inherent capability, power, or function ⟨the *faculty* of hearing⟩ **c :** any of the powers of the mind formerly held by psychologists to form a basis for the explanation of all mental phenomena **d :** natural aptitude ⟨has a *faculty* for saying the right things⟩
**2 a :** a branch of teaching or learning in an educational institution **b** *archaic* **:** something in which one is trained or qualified
**3 a :** the members of a profession **b :** the teaching and administrative staff and those members of the administration having academic rank in an educational institution **c :** faculty *plural* **:** faculty members ⟨many *faculty* were present⟩
**4 :** power, authority, or prerogative given or conferred
*synonym* see GIFT

**fad** \'fad\ *noun* [origin unknown] (1867)
: a practice or interest followed for a time with exaggerated zeal : CRAZE
*synonym* see FASHION
— **fad·dish** \'fa-dish\ *adjective*
— **fad·dish·ness** *noun*

**fad·dism** \'fa-ˌdi-zəm\ *noun*
**fad·dist** \'fa-dist\ *noun*
**fad·dy** \-dē\ *adjective*

**FAD** \ˌef-ˌā-'dē\ *noun* (1944)
: FLAVIN ADENINE DINUCLEOTIDE

**¹fade** \'fād\ *verb* **fad·ed; fad·ing** [Middle English, from Middle French *fader*, from *fade* feeble, insipid, from (assumed) Vulgar Latin *fatidus*, alteration of Latin *fatuus* fatuous, insipid] (14th century)
*intransitive verb*
**1 :** to lose freshness, strength, or vitality : WITHER
**2 :** to lose freshness or brilliance of color
**3 :** to sink away : VANISH
**4 :** to change gradually in loudness, strength, or visibility — used of a motion-picture image or of an electronics signal and usually with *in* or *out*
**5** *of an automobile brake* **:** to lose braking power gradually
**6 :** to move back from the line of scrimmage — used of a quarterback
*transitive verb*
: to cause to fade
— **fad·er** *noun*

**²fade** *noun* (1918)
**1 a :** FADE-OUT **b :** a gradual changing of one picture to another in a motion-picture or television sequence
**2 :** a fading of an automobile brake
**3 :** a slight to moderate and usually intentional slice in golf

**³fade** \'fād\ *adjective* [Middle English, from Middle French] (15th century)
: INSIPID, COMMONPLACE

**fade·away** \'fā-də-ˌwā\ *noun* (1909)
**1 a :** SCREWBALL 1 **b :** a slide in which a base runner throws his body sideways to avoid the tag
**2 :** an act or instance of fading away

**fade–in** \'fā-ˌdin\ *noun* (1917)
: a gradual increase in a motion-picture or television image's visibility at the beginning of a sequence

**fade·less** \'fād-ləs\ *adjective* (1652)
: not susceptible to fading

**fade–out** \'fā-ˌdau̇t\ *noun* (1917)
: an act or instance of fading out; *especially* **:** a gradual decrease in a motion-picture or television image's visibility at the end of a sequence

**fa·do** \'fä-(ˌ)thü, 'fa-\ *noun, plural* **fados** [Portuguese, literally, fate, from Latin *fatum*] (1902)
: a plaintive Portuguese folk song

**fae·cal, fae·ces** *variant of* FECAL, FECES

**fa·e·na** \fä-'ā-(ˌ)nä\ *noun* [Spanish, literally, task, from obsolete Catalan, from Latin *facienda* things to be done, from *facere* to do — more at DO] (1927)
: a series of final passes leading to the kill made by the matador in a bullfight

**fa·er·ie** *also* **fa·ery** \'fā-(ə-)rē, 'far-ē, 'fer-ē\ *noun, plural* **fa·er·ies** [Middle French *faerie* — more at FAIRY] (1590)
**1 :** FAIRYLAND
**2 :** FAIRY
— **faery** *adjective*

**Faer·o·ese** \ˌfar-ə-'wēz, ˌfer-, -'wēs\ *noun, plural* **Faeroese** (1855)
**1 :** a member of the people inhabiting the Faeroes
**2 :** the North Germanic language of the Faeroese people
— **Faeroese** *adjective*

**Faf·nir** \'fäv-nər, 'fäf-, -ˌnir\ *noun* [Old Norse *Fáfnir*]
: a dragon in Norse mythology that guards the Nibelungs' gold hoard until slain by Sigurd

---

\ə\ abut \ᵊ\ kitten \ər\ further \a\ ash \ā\ ace
\ä\ mop, mar \au̇\ out \ch\ chin \e\ bet \ē\ easy
\g\ go \i\ hit \ī\ ice \j\ job \ŋ\ sing \ō\ go
\ȯ\ law \ȯi\ boy \th\ thin \t͟h\ the \ü\ loot \u̇\ foot
\y\ yet \zh\ vision *see also* Guide to Pronunciation

**¹fag** \'fag\ *verb* **fagged; fag·ging** [obsolete *fag* to droop, perhaps from *fag* (fag end)] (1772)
*intransitive verb*
**1** : to work hard : TOIL
**2** : to act as a fag especially in an English public school ⟨*fagging* for older boys during his first year⟩
*transitive verb*
: to tire by strenuous activity : EXHAUST
**synonym** see TIRE
**²fag** *noun* (1780)
**1** *chiefly British* : TOIL, DRUDGERY
**2 a** : an English public-school boy who acts as servant to an older schoolmate **b** : DRUDGE
**³fag** *noun* [*fag end*] (circa 1888)
: CIGARETTE
**⁴fag** *noun* [probably by shortening] (circa 1931)
: FAGGOT — usually used disparagingly
— **fag·gy** \'fa-gē\ *adjective*
**fag end** *noun* [earlier *fag*, from Middle English *fagge* flap] (1613)
**1 a** : a poor or worn-out end : REMNANT **b** : the extreme end
**2 a** : the last part or coarser end of a web of cloth **b** : the untwisted end of a rope
**fag·got** \'fa-gət\ *noun* [origin unknown] (1914)
: a male homosexual — usually used disparagingly
— **fag·got·ry** \-gə-trē\ *noun*
— **fag·goty** \-gə-tē\ *adjective*
**fa·gin** \'fā-gən\ *noun, often capitalized* [*Fagin*, character in Charles Dickens' *Oliver Twist* (1839)] (1847)
: an adult who instructs others (as children) in crime
**¹fag·ot** *or* **fag·got** \'fa-gət\ *noun* [Middle English *fagot*, from Middle French] (14th century)
: BUNDLE: as **a** : a bundle of sticks **b** : a bundle of pieces of wrought iron to be shaped by rolling or hammering at high temperature
**²fagot** *or* **faggot** *transitive verb* (circa 1598)
: to make a fagot of : bind together into a bundle ⟨*fagoted* sticks⟩
**fag·ot·ing** *or* **fag·got·ing** *noun* (1885)
**1** : an embroidery produced by pulling out horizontal threads from a fabric and tying the remaining cross threads into groups of an hourglass shape

fagoting 1

**2** : an openwork stitch joining hemmed edges
**Fahr·en·heit** \'far-ən-ˌhīt, 'fer-\ *adjective* [Gabriel D. *Fahrenheit*] (1753)
: relating or conforming to a thermometric scale on which under standard atmospheric pressure the boiling point of water is at 212 degrees above the zero of the scale, the freezing point is at 32 degrees above zero, and the zero point approximates the temperature produced by mixing equal quantities by weight of snow and common salt — abbreviation *F* ◆
**fa·ience** *or* **fa·ïence** \fī-'än(t)s, fī-, -'äns\ *noun* [French, from *Faenza*, Italy] (1714)
: earthenware decorated with opaque colored glazes
**¹fail** \'fā(ə)l\ *verb* [Middle English *failen*, from Old French *faillir*, from (assumed) Vulgar Latin *fallire*, alteration of Latin *fallere* to deceive, disappoint] (13th century)
*intransitive verb*
**1 a** : to lose strength : WEAKEN ⟨her health was *failing*⟩ **b** : to fade or die away ⟨until our family line *fails*⟩ **c** : to stop functioning ⟨the patient's heart *failed*⟩
**2 a** : to fall short ⟨*failed* in his duty⟩ **b** : to be or become absent or inadequate ⟨the water supply *failed*⟩ **c** : to be unsuccessful (as in passing an examination) **d** : to become bankrupt or insolvent

*transitive verb*
**1 a** : to disappoint the expectations or trust of ⟨her friends *failed* her⟩ **b** : to miss performing an expected service or function for ⟨his wit *failed* him⟩
**2** : to be deficient in : LACK ⟨never *failed* an invincible courage —Douglas MacArthur⟩
**3** : to leave undone : NEGLECT ⟨*fail* to lock the door⟩
**4 a** : to be unsuccessful in passing (as a test) **b** : to grade (as a student) as not passing
— **fail·ing·ly** \'fā-liŋ-lē\ *adverb*
**²fail** *noun* (13th century)
**1** : FAILURE — usually used in the phrase *without fail*
**2** : a failure (as by a security dealer) to deliver or receive securities within a prescribed period after purchase or sale
**¹fail·ing** \'fā-liŋ\ *noun* (1590)
: a usually slight or insignificant defect in character, conduct, or ability
**synonym** see FAULT
**²failing** *preposition* (1810)
: in absence or default of ⟨*failing* specific instructions, use your own judgment⟩
**faille** \'fī(ə)l\ *noun* [French, from Old French] (1869)
: a somewhat shiny closely woven silk, rayon, or cotton fabric characterized by slight ribs in the weft
**fail-safe** \'fā(ə)l-ˌsāf\ *adjective* (1946)
**1** : incorporating some feature for automatically counteracting the effect of an anticipated possible source of failure
**2** : being or relating to a safeguard that prevents continuing on a bombing mission according to a preconceived plan
**3** : having no chance of failure : infallibly problem-free
**fail·ure** \'fā(ə)l-yər\ *noun* [alteration of earlier *failer*, from Anglo-French, from Old French *faillir* to fail] (1643)
**1 a** : omission of occurrence or performance; *specifically* : a failing to perform a duty or expected action **b** : a state of inability to perform a normal function ⟨kidney *failure*⟩ — compare HEART FAILURE **c** : a fracturing or giving way under stress ⟨structural *failure*⟩
**2 a** : lack of success **b** : a failing in business : BANKRUPTCY
**3 a** : a falling short : DEFICIENCY ⟨a crop *failure*⟩ **b** : DETERIORATION, DECAY
**4** : one that has failed
**¹fain** \'fān\ *adjective* [Middle English *fagen, fayn*, from Old English *fægen*; akin to Old Norse *fegiun* happy, Old English *fæger* fair] (before 12th century)
**1** *archaic* : HAPPY, PLEASED
**2** *archaic* : INCLINED, DESIROUS
**3 a** : WILLING ⟨he was very *fain*, for the young widow was "altogether fair and lovely . . . ." —Amy Kelly⟩ **b** : being obliged or constrained ⟨COMPELLED ⟨Great Britain was *fain* to devote its whole energy . . . to the business of slaying and being slain —G. M. Trevelyan⟩
**²fain** *adverb* (12th century)
**1** : with pleasure : GLADLY ⟨a speech of fire that *fain* would blaze —Michael Billington⟩
**2 a** : by preference ⟨knew it, too, though he would *fain* not admit it publicly —John Lukacs⟩ **b** : by desire ⟨I would *fain* consult you —W. S. Gilbert⟩
**¹fai·né·ant** \fā-nā-'äⁿ, *noun, plural* **fainéants** \-'äⁿ(z)\ [French, from Middle French *fait-nient*, literally, does nothing, by folk etymology from *faignant*, from present participle of *faindre, feindre* to feign] (1619)
: an irresponsible idler
**²fai·né·ant** \fā-nā-'äⁿ\ *or* **fai·ne·ant** \'fā-nē-ənt\ *adjective* (1855)
: idle and ineffectual : INDOLENT
**¹faint** \'fānt\ *adjective* [Middle English *faint, feint*, from Middle French, from past participle

of *faindre, feindre* to feign, shirk — more at FEIGN] (14th century)
**1** : lacking courage and spirit : COWARDLY
**2** : weak, dizzy, and likely to faint
**3** : lacking strength or vigor : performed, offered, or accomplished weakly or languidly
**4** : producing a sensation of faintness : OPPRESSIVE ⟨the *faint* atmosphere of a tropical port⟩
**5** : lacking distinctness : DIM
— **faint·ish** \'fān-tish\ *adjective*
— **faint·ish·ness** *noun*
— **faint·ly** *adverb*
— **faint·ness** *noun*
**²faint** *intransitive verb* (14th century)
**1** *archaic* : to lose courage or spirit
**2** *archaic* : to become weak
**3** : to lose consciousness because of a temporary decrease in the blood supply to the brain
**³faint** *noun* (1808)
: the physiological action of fainting; *also* : the resulting condition : SYNCOPE 1
**faint·heart·ed** \'fānt-'här-təd\ *adjective* (15th century)
: lacking courage or resolution : TIMID
— **faint·heart·ed·ly** *adverb*
— **faint·heart·ed·ness** *noun*
**¹fair** \'far, 'fer\ *adjective* [Middle English *fager, fair*, from Old English *fæger*; akin to Old High German *fagar* beautiful] (before 12th century)
**1** : pleasing to the eye or mind especially because of fresh, charming, or flawless quality
**2** : superficially pleasing : SPECIOUS ⟨she trusted his *fair* promises⟩
**3 a** : CLEAN, PURE ⟨*fair* sparkling water⟩ **b** : CLEAR, LEGIBLE
**4** : not stormy or foul : FINE ⟨*fair* weather⟩
**5** : AMPLE ⟨a *fair* estate⟩
**6 a** : marked by impartiality and honesty : free from self-interest, prejudice, or favoritism ⟨a very *fair* person to do business with⟩ **b** (1) : conforming with the established rules : ALLOWED (2) : consonant with merit or importance : DUE ⟨a *fair* share⟩ **c** : open to legitimate pursuit, attack, or ridicule ⟨*fair* game⟩
**7 a** : PROMISING, LIKELY ⟨in a *fair* way to win⟩ **b** : favorable to a ship's course ⟨a *fair* wind⟩
**8** *archaic* : free of obstacles
**9** : not dark : BLOND
**10** : sufficient but not ample : ADEQUATE ⟨a *fair* understanding of the work⟩
**11** : being such to the utmost : UTTER ⟨a *fair* treat to watch him —*New Republic*⟩ ☆
— **fair·ness** *noun*
**²fair** *noun* (before 12th century)
**1** *obsolete* : BEAUTY, FAIRNESS
**2** : something that is fair or fortunate
**3** *archaic* : WOMAN; *especially* : SWEETHEART
— **for fair** : to the greatest extent or degree : FULLY ⟨the rush is on *for fair*⟩
— **no fair** : something that is not according to the rules ⟨that's *no fair*⟩
**³fair** *adverb* (before 12th century)
*chiefly British* : FAIRLY 5
**⁴fair** (1836)
*intransitive verb*
*of the weather* : CLEAR

◇ WORD HISTORY
**Fahrenheit** The Fahrenheit scale memorializes the German physicist Daniel Gabriel Fahrenheit (1686–1736). Fahrenheit devoted his career to the making of precision scientific instruments. In 1709 he developed an alcohol thermometer, superseding it with a mercury thermometer in 1714. His most important achievement was his development, from the work of Olaus Roemer, of the thermometric scale that bears his name.

*transitive verb*
: to join so that the external surfaces blend smoothly

**⁵fair** *noun* [Middle English *feire,* from Old French, fair, from Late Latin *festal day,* from Latin *feria* weekday, fair, from Late Latin, festal day, from Latin *feriae* (plural) holidays — more at FEAST] (13th century)
**1** : a gathering of buyers and sellers at a particular place and time for trade
**2 a** : a competitive exhibition (as of farm products) usually with accompanying entertainment and amusements **b** : an exhibition designed to acquaint prospective buyers or the general public with a product
**3** : a sale of assorted articles usually for a charitable purpose

**fair ball** *noun* (1856)
: a batted baseball that lands within the foul lines or that is within the foul lines when bounding to the outfield past first or third base or when going beyond the outfield for a home run

**fair catch** *noun* (circa 1876)
: a catch of a kicked football by a player who gives a prescribed signal, may not advance the ball, and may not be tackled

**fair copy** *noun* (1709)
: a neat and exact copy especially of a corrected draft

**fair·ground** \'far-ˌgraund, 'fer-\ *noun* (1741)
: an area where outdoor fairs, circuses, or exhibitions are held — often used in plural with singular construction ⟨what a spot for a *fairgrounds* —W. L. Gresham⟩

**fair–haired** \'far-'hard, 'fer-'herd\ *adjective* (1909)
: specially favored : WHITE-HEADED — used especially in the phrase *fair-haired boy*

**¹fair·ing** \'far-iŋ, 'fer-\ *noun* (1574)
**1** *British* **a** : a present bought or given at a fair **b** : GIFT
**2** *British* : ³DESERT 2

**²fairing** *noun* (1914)
: a member or structure whose primary function is to produce a smooth outline and to reduce drag (as on an airplane)

**fair·ish** \'far-ish, 'fer-\ *adjective* (1611)
: fairly good ⟨a *fairish* wage for those days⟩
— **fair·ish·ly** *adverb*

**Fair Isle** *noun* (1851)
: a style of knitting originating in the Shetland Islands that is characterized by bands of multicolored geometric patterns; *also* : an article of clothing knitted in this style

**fair·lead** \'far-ˌlēd, 'fer-\ *noun* (circa 1841)
**1** *also* **fair·lead·er** \-ˌlē-dər\ : a block, ring, or strip of plank with holes that serves as a guide for the running rigging or any ship's rope and keeps it from chafing
**2** : a course of running ship's rope that avoids all chafing

**fair·ly** \'far-lē, 'fer-\ *adverb* (12th century)
**1** : in a handsome manner ⟨a table *fairly* set⟩
**2** *obsolete* **a** : in a gentle manner : QUIETLY **b** : in a courteous manner
**3** : in a manner of speaking ⟨*fairly* bursting with pride⟩
**4 a** : in a proper or legal manner ⟨*fairly* priced stocks⟩ **b** : without bias or distortion : IMPARTIALLY ⟨a story told *fairly* and objectively⟩
**5** : to a full degree or extent : PLAINLY, DISTINCTLY ⟨had *fairly* caught sight of him⟩
**6** : RATHER 5, MODERATELY ⟨a *fairly* easy job⟩

**fair market value** *noun* (1901)
: a price at which both buyers and sellers are willing to do business

**fair–mind·ed** \'far-ˌmīn-dəd, 'fer-\ *adjective* (1874)
: marked by impartiality and honesty : JUST, UNPREJUDICED
— **fair–mind·ed·ness** *noun*

**fairness doctrine** *noun* (1967)
: a tenet of licensed broadcasting that ensures a reasonable opportunity for the airing of conflicting viewpoints on controversial issues

**fair play** *noun* (1595)
: equitable or impartial treatment : JUSTICE

**fair shake** *noun* (1830)
: a fair chance or fair treatment ⟨give the negative side a *fair shake* —S. L. Payne⟩

**fair–spo·ken** \'far-ˌspō-kən, 'fer-\ *adjective* (15th century)
: pleasant and courteous in speech ⟨a *fairspoken* youth⟩

**fair–trade** \'far-'trād, 'fer-\ *transitive verb* (1947)
: to market (a commodity) in compliance with the provisions of a fair-trade agreement
— **fair trade** *noun*
— **fair trader** *noun*

**fair–trade agreement** *noun* (1937)
: an agreement between a producer and a seller that commodities bearing a trademark, label, or brand name belonging to the producer be sold at or above a specified price

**fair·way** \'far-ˌwā, 'fer-\ *noun* (1584)
**1 a** : a navigable part of a river, bay, or harbor **b** : an open path or space
**2** : the closely mowed part of a golf course between a tee and a green

**fair–weather** *adjective* (1736)
**1** : loyal only during a time of success ⟨a *fairweather* friend⟩
**2** : suitable for or done during fair weather ⟨a *fair-weather* sail⟩

**fairy** \'far-ē, 'fer-\ *noun, plural* **fair·ies** [Middle English *fairie* fairyland, fairy people, from Old French *faerie,* from *feie, fee* fairy, from Latin *Fata,* goddess of fate, from *fatum* fate] (14th century)
**1** : a mythical being of folklore and romance usually having diminutive human form and magic powers
**2** : a male homosexual — usually used disparagingly
— **fairy** *adjective*
— **fairy·like** \-ˌlīk\ *adjective*

**fairy godmother** *noun* (1851)
: a generous friend or benefactor

**fairy·ism** \-ˌi-zəm\ *noun* (1715)
*archaic* : the power to enchant

**fairy·land** \-ˌland\ *noun* (1590)
**1** : the land of fairies
**2** : a place of delicate beauty or magical charm

**fairy ring** *noun* [from the folk belief that such rings were dancing places of the fairies] (1599)
**1** : a ring of basidiomycetous mushrooms produced at the periphery of a body of mycelium which has grown outward from an initial growth point; *also* : a ring of luxuriant vegetation especially when associated with these mushrooms
**2** : a mushroom (especially *Marasmius oreades*) that commonly grows in fairy rings

**fairy shrimp** *noun* (1857)
: any of several delicate transparent freshwater branchiopod crustaceans (order Anostraca)

**fairy–tale** *adjective* (1924)
: characteristic of or suitable to a fairy tale; *especially* : marked by seemingly unreal beauty, perfection, luck, or happiness

**fairy tale** *noun* (1749)
**1** : a story (as for children) involving fantastic forces and beings (as fairies, wizards, and goblins) — called also *fairy story*
**2** : a made-up story usually designed to mislead

**fait ac·com·pli** \ˌfā-tə-ˌkäm-'plē, 'fe-, 'fe-ˌta-, -kō<sup>n</sup>(m)-\, *British usually* -'käm-(ˌ)plē\ *noun, plural* **faits accomplis** \*same, or* -'plēz\ [French, accomplished fact] (1845)
: a thing accomplished and presumably irreversible

**¹faith** \'fāth\ *noun, plural* **faiths** \'fāths, *sometimes* 'fāthz\ [Middle English *feith,* from Old French *feid, foi,* from Latin *fides;* akin to Latin *fidere* to trust — more at BIDE] (13th century)
**1 a** : allegiance to duty or a person : LOYALTY **b** (1) : fidelity to one's promises (2) : sincerity of intentions
**2 a** (1) : belief and trust in and loyalty to God (2) : belief in the traditional doctrines of a religion **b** (1) : firm belief in something for which there is no proof (2) : complete trust
**3** : something that is believed especially with strong conviction; *especially* : a system of religious beliefs ◆
**synonym** see BELIEF
— **in faith** : without doubt or question : VERILY

**²faith** *transitive verb* (15th century)
*archaic* : BELIEVE, TRUST

**¹faith·ful** \'fāth-fəl\ *adjective* (14th century)
**1** *obsolete* : full of faith
**2** : steadfast in affection or allegiance : LOYAL
**3** : firm in adherence to promises or in observance of duty : CONSCIENTIOUS
**4** : given with strong assurance : BINDING ⟨*faithful* promise⟩

\ə\ **abut** \ᵊ\ **kitten** \ər\ **further** \a\ **ash** \ā\ **ace** \ä\ **mop, mar** \aú\ **out** \ch\ **chin** \e\ **bet** \ē\ **easy** \g\ **go** \i\ **hit** \ī\ **ice** \j\ **job** \ŋ\ **sing** \ō\ **go** \ȯ\ **law** \ȯi\ **boy** \th\ **thin** \ṯh\ **the** \ü\ **loot** \ú\ **foot** \y\ **yet** \zh\ **vision** *see also* Guide to Pronunciation

**5 :** true to the facts, to a standard, or to an original ⟨a *faithful* copy⟩ ☆
— **faith·ful·ly** \-fə-lē\ *adverb*
— **faith·ful·ness** *noun*

²**faithful** *noun* (1558)
**1** *plural in construction* **a :** church members in full communion and good standing — used with the **b :** the body of believers in Islam — used with *the*
**2** *plural* **faithful** *or* **faithfuls :** one who is faithful; *especially* **:** a loyal follower, member, or fan ⟨party *faithfuls*⟩

**faith healing** *noun* (1885)
**:** a method of treating diseases by prayer and exercise of faith in God
— **faith healer** *noun*

**faith·less** \'fāth-ləs\ *adjective* (14th century)
**1 :** not true to allegiance or duty **:** TREACHEROUS, DISLOYAL ⟨a *faithless* servant⟩
**2 :** not to be relied on **:** UNTRUSTWORTHY ⟨a *faithless* tool⟩ ☆
— **faith·less·ly** *adverb*
— **faith·less·ness** *noun*

**fai·tour** \'fā-tər\ *noun* [Middle English, from Anglo-French, from Old French *faitor* perpetrator, from Latin *factor* doer — more at FACTOR] (14th century)
*archaic* **:** CHEAT, IMPOSTER

**fa·ji·ta** \fə-'hē-tə, fä-\ *noun* [American Spanish, diminutive of Spanish *faja* sash, belt, probably from Catalan *faixa*, from Latin *fascia* band — more at FASCIA] (1984)
**:** a marinated strip usually of beef or chicken grilled or broiled and served usually with a flour tortilla and various savory fillings — usually used in plural

¹**fake** \'fāk\ *transitive verb* **faked; fak·ing** [Middle English] (15th century)
**:** to coil in fakes

²**fake** *noun* (1627)
**:** one loop of a coil (as of ship's rope or a fire hose) coiled free for running

³**fake** *adjective* [origin unknown] (1775)
**:** COUNTERFEIT, SHAM

⁴**fake** *noun* (1827)
**:** one that is not what it purports to be: as **a :** a worthless imitation passed off as genuine **b :** IMPOSTOR, CHARLATAN **c :** a simulated movement in a sports contest (as a pretended kick, pass, or jump or a quick movement in one direction before going in another) designed to deceive an opponent **d :** a device or apparatus used by a magician to achieve the illusion of magic in a trick
**synonym** see IMPOSTURE

⁵**fake** *verb* **faked; fak·ing** (1851)
*transitive verb*
**1 :** to alter, manipulate, or treat so as to give a spuriously genuine appearance to **:** DOCTOR ⟨*faked* the lab results⟩
**2 :** COUNTERFEIT, SIMULATE, CONCOCT
**3 :** to deceive (an opponent) in a sports contest by means of a fake
**4 :** IMPROVISE, AD-LIB ⟨whistle a few bars . . . and I'll *fake* the rest —Robert Sylvester⟩
*intransitive verb*
**1 :** to engage in faking something **:** PRETEND
**2 :** to give a fake to an opponent
— **fak·er** *noun*
— **fak·ery** \'fā-k(ə-)rē\ *noun*

**fake out** *transitive verb* (1968)
**:** to deliberately mislead **:** FOOL, TRICK

**fa·kir** *noun* [Arabic *faqīr*, literally, poor man] (1609)
**1** \fə-'kir, fä-, fa-; 'fā-kər\ **a :** a Muslim mendicant **:** DERVISH **b :** an itinerant Hindu ascetic or wonder-worker
**2** \'fā-kər\ **:** IMPOSTOR; *especially* **:** SWINDLER

**fa la** \fä-'lä\ *noun* [*fa-la*, meaningless syllables often occurring in its refrain] (1597)
**:** a 16th and 17th century part-song

**fa·la·fel** \fə-'lä-fəl\ *noun, plural* **falafel** [Arabic *falāfil*] (1950)
**:** a spicy mixture of ground vegetables (as chick-peas or fava beans) formed into balls or patties and then fried

**Fa·lan·gist** \fə-'lan-jist, 'fä-\ *noun* [Spanish *falangista*, from *Falange española* Spanish Phalanx, a fascist organization] (1936)
**:** a member of the fascist political party governing Spain after the civil war of 1936–39

**Fa·la·sha** \fə-'lä-shə\ *noun, plural* **-sha** *or* **-shas** [Amharic *fälaša*] (1710)
**:** a member of a people of highland Ethiopia who practice a variety of Judaism

**fal·cate** \'fal-,kāt, 'fòl-\ *adjective* [Latin *falcatus*, from *falc-, falx* sickle, scythe] (1826)
**:** hooked or curved like a sickle

**fal·chion** \'fòl-chən\ *noun* [Middle English *fauchoun*, from Middle French *fauchon*, from *fauchier* to mow, from (assumed) Vulgar Latin *falcare*, from Latin *falc-, falx*] (14th century)
**1 :** a broad-bladed slightly curved sword of medieval times
**2** *archaic* **:** SWORD

**fal·ci·form** \'fal-sə-,fòrm, 'fòl-\ *adjective* [Latin *falc-, falx* + English *-iform*] (1766)
**:** having the shape of a falcon or sickle

**fal·con** \'fal-kən, 'fòl- *also* 'fò-kən\ *noun* [Middle English, from Old French, from Late Latin *falcon-, falco*, probably from Latin *falc-, falx*] (13th century)
**1 :** any of various hawks trained for use in falconry; *especially* **:** PEREGRINE — used technically only of a female; compare TIERCEL
**2 :** any of various hawks (family Falconidae) that have long pointed wings, a long tail, and a notched beak and that usually inhabit open areas

falcon 1: *1* hood, *2* jess, *3* gauntlet

**fal·con·er** \-kə-nər\ *noun* (14th century)
**:** a person who breeds, trains, or hunts with hawks

**fal·con·et** \,fal-kə-'net, ,fòl- *also* ,fò-\ *noun* (1559)
**1 :** a very small cannon used in the 16th and 17th centuries
**2 :** any of several very small falcons (genera *Microhierax, Prolihierax,* and *Spiziapteryx*)

**fal·con·gen·tle** \-kən-'jen-t°l\ *noun* [Middle English *faucon gentil* peregrine falcon, from Middle French, literally, noble falcon] (15th century)
**:** the female peregrine falcon

**fal·co·nine** \'fal-kə-,nīn, 'fòl- *also* 'fò-\ *adjective* (circa 1889)
**:** of or resembling a falcon ⟨a *falconine* face⟩

**fal·con·ry** \'fal-kən-rē, 'fòl- *also* 'fò-kən-\ *noun* (1575)
**1 :** the art of training hawks to hunt in cooperation with a person
**2 :** the sport of hunting with hawks

**fal·de·ral** \'fäl-də-,räl\ *variant of* FOLDEROL

**fald·stool** \'fòl(d)-,stül\ *noun* [Medieval Latin *faldistolium,* of Germanic origin; akin to Old High German *faltstuol* folding chair, from *falt* (akin to Old High German *faldan* to fold) + *stuol* chair — more at FOLD, STOOL] (1603)
**1:** a foldingstool or chair; *specifically* **:** one used by a bishop
**2 :** a folding stool or small desk at which one kneels during devotions; *especially* **:** one used by the sovereigns of England at their coronation
**3 :** the desk from which the litany is read in Anglican churches

faldstool 1

¹**fall** \'fòl\ *verb* **fell** \'fel\; **fall·en** \'fò-lən\; **fall·ing** [Middle English, from Old English *feallan;* akin to Old High German *fallan* to fall and perhaps to Lithuanian *pulti*] (before 12th century)

*intransitive verb*
**1 a :** to descend freely by the force of gravity **b :** to hang freely ⟨her hair *falls* over her shoulders⟩ **c :** to drop oneself to a lower position ⟨*fell* to his knees⟩ **d :** to come or go as if by falling ⟨darkness *falls* early in the winter⟩
**2 :** to become born — usually used of lambs
**3 a :** to become lower in degree or level ⟨the temperature *fell* 10°⟩ **b :** to drop in pitch or volume ⟨their voices *fell* to a whisper⟩ **c :** ISSUE 1a,b ⟨wisdom that *fell* from his lips⟩ **d :** to become lowered ⟨her eyes *fell*⟩
**4 a :** to leave an erect position suddenly and involuntarily ⟨slipped and *fell* on the ice⟩ **b :** to enter as if unawares **:** STUMBLE, STRAY ⟨*fell* into error⟩ **c :** to drop down wounded or dead; *especially* **:** to die in battle **d :** to suffer military capture ⟨after a long siege the city *fell*⟩ **e :** to lose office ⟨the party *fell* from power⟩ **f :** to suffer ruin, defeat, or failure ⟨the deal *fell* through⟩
**5 :** to commit an immoral act; *especially* **:** to lose one's chastity
**6 a :** to move or extend in a downward direction ⟨the land *falls* away to the east⟩ **b :** SUBSIDE, ABATE ⟨the wind is *falling*⟩ **c :** to decline in quality, activity, or quantity ⟨production *fell* off⟩ **d :** to lose weight — used with *off* or *away* **e :** to assume a look of shame, disappointment, or dejection ⟨his face *fell*⟩ **f :** to decline in financial value or price ⟨stocks *fell* sharply⟩
**7 a :** to occur at a certain time **b :** to come by chance ⟨*fell* in with a fast crowd⟩ **c :** to come or pass by lot, assignment, or inheritance **:** DEVOLVE ⟨it *fell* to him to break the news⟩ **d :** to have a certain or proper position, place, or station ⟨the accent *falls* on the second syllable⟩

**8 :** to come within the limits, scope, or jurisdiction of something ⟨this word *falls* into the class of verbs⟩
**9 :** to pass suddenly and passively into a state of body or mind or a new state or condition ⟨*fall* asleep⟩ ⟨*fall* in love⟩
**10 :** to set about heartily or actively ⟨*fell* to work⟩
**11 :** STRIKE, IMPINGE ⟨music *falling* on the ear⟩
*transitive verb*
**:** FELL 1
— **fall apart 1 :** DISINTEGRATE **2 :** to succumb to mental or emotional stress : BREAK DOWN
— **fall behind 1 :** to lag behind **2 :** to be in arrears
— **fall between two stools :** to fail because of inability to choose between or reconcile two alternative or conflicting courses of action
— **fall flat :** to produce no response or result ⟨the joke *fell flat*⟩
— **fall for 1 :** to fall in love with **2 :** to become a victim of ⟨*fell for* the trick⟩
— **fall foul :** to have a quarrel : CLASH — often used with *of*
— **fall from grace :** BACKSLIDE 1
— **fall home :** to curve inward; used of the timbers or upper parts of a ship's side
— **fall into line :** to comply with a certain course of action
— **fall on** *or* **fall upon :** to meet with ⟨*fell on* hard times⟩
— **fall over oneself** *or* **fall over backward :** to display excessive eagerness
— **fall short 1 :** to be deficient **2 :** to fail to attain something (as a goal or target)

²**fall** *noun* (13th century)
**1 :** the act of falling by the force of gravity
**2 a :** a falling out, off, or away : DROPPING ⟨the *fall* of leaves⟩ ⟨a *fall* of snow⟩ **b :** the season when leaves fall from trees : AUTUMN **c :** a thing or quantity that falls or has fallen ⟨a *fall* of rock at the base of the cliff⟩; *especially* **:** one or more meteorites or their fragments that have fallen together **d** (1) **:** BIRTH (2) **:** the quantity born — usually used of lambs
**3 a :** a costume decoration of lace or thin fabric arranged to hang loosely and gracefully **b :** a very wide turned-down collar worn in the 17th century **c :** the part of a turnover collar from the crease to the outer edge **d :** a wide front flap on trousers (as those worn by sailors) **e :** the freely hanging lower edge of the skirt of a coat **f :** one of the three outer and often drooping segments of the flower of an iris **g :** long hair overhanging the face of dogs of some breeds **h :** a usually long straight portion of hair that is attached to a person's own hair
**4 :** a hoisting-tackle rope or chain; *especially* **:** the part of it to which the power is applied
**5 a :** loss of greatness : COLLAPSE ⟨the *fall* of the Roman Empire⟩ **b :** the surrender or capture of a besieged place ⟨the *fall* of Troy⟩ **c :** lapse or departure from innocence or goodness **d :** loss of a woman's chastity
**6 a :** the downward slope (as of a hill) : DECLIVITY **b :** a precipitous descent of water : WATERFALL — usually used in plural but sing. or plural in construction **c :** a musical cadence **d :** a falling-pitch intonation in speech
**7 :** a decrease in size, quantity, degree, or value
**8 a :** the distance which something falls **b :** INCLINATION, PITCH
**9 a :** the act of felling something **b :** the quantity of trees cut down **c** (1) **:** an act of forcing a wrestler's shoulders to the mat for a specified time (as one second) (2) **:** a bout of wrestling
**10** *Scottish* **:** DESTINY, LOT

³**fall** *adjective* (1677)
**:** of, relating to, or suitable for autumn ⟨a new *fall* coat⟩

**fal·la·cious** \fə-'lā-shəs\ *adjective* (1509)
**1 :** embodying a fallacy

**2 :** tending to deceive or mislead : DELUSIVE
— **fal·la·cious·ly** *adverb*
— **fal·la·cious·ness** *noun*
**fal·la·cy** \'fa-lə-sē\ *noun, plural* **-cies** [Latin *fallacia*, from *fallac-, fallax* deceitful, from *fallere* to deceive] (14th century)
**1 a** *obsolete* **:** GUILE, TRICKERY **b :** deceptive appearance : DECEPTION
**2 a :** a false or mistaken idea ⟨popular *fallacies*⟩ **b :** erroneous character : ERRONEOUSNESS
**3 :** an often plausible argument using false or invalid inference

**fal·lal** \fa-'lal, 'fa(l)-,lal\ *noun* [perhaps alteration of *falbala* furbelow, from French, from French dialect *ferbelà, farbélla*] (circa 1706)
**:** a fancy ornament especially in dress
— **fal·lal·ery** \fa-'la-lə-rē\ *noun*

**fall armyworm** *noun* (1881)
**:** a migratory American moth (*Spodoptera frugiperda*) that is especially destructive to small grains and grasses as a larva

**fall·away** \'fo-lə-,wā\ *adjective* (1966)
**:** made while moving away from the basket in basketball ⟨a *fallaway* jumper⟩
— **fallaway** *noun*

**fall away** *intransitive verb* (1535)
**1 a :** to withdraw friendship or support **b :** to renounce one's faith
**2 a :** to diminish gradually in size **b :** to drift off a course

**fall·back** \'fol-,bak\ *noun* (1851)
**1 :** something on which one can fall back : RESERVE
**2 :** a falling back : RETREAT
**3 :** something that falls back ⟨the *fallback* from an explosion⟩

**fall back** *intransitive verb* (1607)
**:** RETREAT, RECEDE
— **fall back on** *or* **fall back upon :** to have recourse to ⟨had to *fall back on* their reserves⟩

**fall down** *intransitive verb* (1873)
**:** to fail to meet expectations or requirements ⟨*fell down* on the job⟩

**fall·er** \'fo-lər\ *noun* (1677)
**1 :** a machine part that acts by falling
**2 :** a logger who fells trees

**fall·fish** \'fol-,fish\ *noun* (circa 1811)
**:** a common cyprinid fish (*Semotilus corporalis*) of the streams of northeastern North America

**fall guy** *noun* (1906)
**1 :** one that is easily duped
**2 :** SCAPEGOAT

**fal·li·bil·i·ty** \,fa-lə-'bi-lə-tē\ *noun* (1634)
**:** liability to err

**fal·li·ble** \'fa-lə-bəl\ *adjective* [Middle English, from Medieval Latin *fallibilis*, from Latin *fallere*] (15th century)
**1 :** liable to be erroneous ⟨a *fallible* generalization⟩
**2 :** capable of making a mistake ⟨all men are *fallible*⟩
— **fal·li·bly** \-blē\ *adverb*

**fall in** *intransitive verb* (1719)
**1 :** to sink inward ⟨the roof *fell in*⟩
**2 :** to take one's proper place in a military formation
— **fall in with 1 :** to concur with ⟨had to *fall in with* her wishes⟩ **2 :** to harmonize with ⟨it *falls in* exactly *with* my views⟩

**falling diphthong** *noun* (1888)
**:** a diphthong (as \òi\ in \'nòiz\ *noise*) composed of a vowel followed by a less sonorous glide

**fall·ing–out** \,fo-liŋ-'aut\ *noun, plural* **fallings–out** *or* **falling–outs** (1568)
**:** an instance of falling out : QUARREL

**falling rhythm** *noun* (1918)
**:** rhythm with stress occurring regularly on the first syllable of each foot — compare RISING RHYTHM

**falling star** *noun* (1563)
**:** METEOR 2a

**fall line** *noun* (1882)

**1 :** a line joining the waterfalls on numerous rivers that marks the point where each river descends from the upland to the lowland and the limit of the navigability of each river
**2 :** the natural downhill course (as for skiing) between two points on a slope

**fall-off** \'fo-,lof\ *noun* (1880)
**:** a decline especially in quantity or quality ⟨a *falloff* in exports⟩ ⟨a *falloff* of light intensity⟩

**fall off** *intransitive verb* (1613)
**1 :** TREND 1b
**2** *of a ship* **:** to deviate to leeward of the point to which the bow was directed

**fal·lo·pi·an tube** \fə-'lō-pē-ən-\ *noun, often F capitalized* [Gabriel *Fallopius* (died 1562) Italian anatomist] (circa 1706)
**:** either of the pair of tubes conducting the egg from the ovary to the uterus

**fall·out** \'fo-,laut\ *noun* (1949)
**1 a :** the often radioactive particles stirred up by or resulting from a nuclear explosion and descending through the atmosphere; *also* **:** other polluting particles (as volcanic ash) descending likewise **b :** descent (as of fallout) through the atmosphere
**2 :** a secondary and often lingering effect, result, or set of consequences ⟨have to take a position and accept the political *fallout* —Andy Logan⟩

**fall out** *intransitive verb* (15th century)
**1 :** QUARREL; *also* **:** to cut off relations over a quarrel ⟨former friends who have *fallen out*⟩
**2 :** TURN OUT, HAPPEN ⟨expected to be in the States . . . , but things *fell out* otherwise —Mark Twain⟩
**3 a :** to leave one's place in the ranks **b :** to leave a building in order to take one's place in a military formation

¹**fal·low** \'fa-(,)lō, -lə(-w)\ *adjective* [Middle English *falow*, from Old English *fealu*; akin to Old High German *falo* pale, fallow, Latin *pallēre* to be pale, Greek *polios* gray] (before 12th century)
**:** of a light yellowish brown color

²**fallow** *noun* [Middle English *falwe, falow*, from Old English *fealg* — more at FELLY] (before 12th century)
**1 :** usually cultivated land that is allowed to lie idle during the growing season
**2** *obsolete* **:** plowed land
**3 :** the state or period of being fallow
**4 :** the tilling of land without sowing it for a season

³**fallow** *transitive verb* (15th century)
**:** to plow, harrow, and break up (land) without seeding to destroy weeds and conserve soil moisture

⁴**fallow** *adjective* (15th century)
**1 :** left untilled or unsown after plowing
**2 :** DORMANT, INACTIVE — used especially in the phrase *to lie fallow* ⟨at this very moment there are probably important inventions lying *fallow* —Harper's⟩
— **fal·low·ness** *noun*

**fallow deer** *noun* [¹*fallow*] (15th century)
**:** a deer (*Cervus dama* synonym *Dama dama*) of variable color with broad antlers and typically a yellow-brown coat spotted with white in the summer that was originally found in Europe and Asia Minor but has been introduced elsewhere

**fallow deer**

**fall to** *intransitive verb* (1593)

: to begin doing something (as working or eating) especially vigorously — often used in invitation or command

**¹false** \'fôls\ *adjective* **fals·er; fals·est** [Middle English *fals,* from Old French & Latin; Old French, from Latin *falsus,* from past participle of *fallere* to deceive] (12th century)
**1 :** not genuine ⟨*false* documents⟩ ⟨*false* teeth⟩ **2 a :** intentionally untrue ⟨*false* testimony⟩ **b :** adjusted or made so as to deceive ⟨*false* scales⟩ ⟨a trunk with a *false* bottom⟩ **c :** intended or tending to mislead ⟨a *false* promise⟩ **3 :** not true ⟨*false* concepts⟩ **4 a :** not faithful or loyal : TREACHEROUS ⟨a *false* friend⟩ **b :** lacking naturalness or sincerity ⟨*false* sympathy⟩ **5 a :** not essential or permanent — used of parts of a structure that are temporary or supplemental **b :** fitting over a main part to strengthen it, to protect it, or to disguise its appearance ⟨a *false* ceiling⟩ **6 :** inaccurate in pitch ⟨a *false* note⟩ **7 a :** based on mistaken ideas ⟨*false* pride⟩ **b :** inconsistent with the facts ⟨a *false* position⟩ ⟨a *false* sense of security⟩ **8 :** threateningly sudden or deceptive ⟨don't make a *false* move⟩
**synonym** see FAITHLESS
— **false·ly** *adverb*
— **false·ness** *noun*

**²false** *adverb* (13th century)
**:** in a false or faithless manner : TREACHEROUSLY ⟨his friends played him *false*⟩

**false alarm** *noun* (1579)
**1 :** one causing alarm or excitement that proves to be unfounded **2 :** an alarm (as a fire or burglar alarm) that is set off needlessly

**false arrest** *noun* (1926)
**:** an arrest not justifiable under law

**false color** *noun* (1968)
**:** color in an image (as a photograph) of an object that does not actually appear in the object but is used to enhance, contrast, or distinguish details which are evident solely or chiefly from differences in the absorption and reflection of electromagnetic radiation at wavelengths outside the visual spectrum

**false·hood** \'fôls-,hu̇d\ *noun* (13th century)
**1 :** an untrue statement : LIE **2 :** absence of truth or accuracy **3 :** the practice of lying : MENDACITY

**false imprisonment** *noun* (14th century)
**:** imprisonment of a person contrary to law

**false mi·ter·wort** \-'mī-tər-,wərt, -,wȯrt\ *noun* [*miterwort* from the resemblance of the plant's capsule to a bishop's miter] (1868)
**:** FOAMFLOWER

**false morel** *noun* (1942)
**:** any of a genus (*Gyromitra*) of fungi that are often poisonous and have a cap with convolutions resembling a brain

**false pregnancy** *noun* (circa 1860)
**:** PSEUDOCYESIS, PSEUDOPREGNANCY

**false rib** *noun* (15th century)
**:** a rib whose cartilages unite indirectly or not at all with the sternum — compare FLOATING RIB

**false Solomon's seal** *noun* (circa 1856)
**:** any of a genus (*Smilacina*) of herbs of the lily family that differ from Solomon's seal in having flowers in a terminal raceme or panicle — called also *false Solomonseal*

**false start** *noun* (1815)
**1 :** a premature start (as of a race) **2 :** an unsuccessful attempt to begin something (as a career)

**¹fal·set·to** \fôl-'se-(,)tō\ *noun, plural* **-tos** [Italian, from diminutive of *falso* false, from Latin *falsus*] (1774)
**1 :** an artificially high voice; *especially* **:** an artificially produced singing voice that overlaps and extends above the range of the full voice especially of a tenor **2 :** a singer who uses falsetto

**²falsetto** *adverb* (1940)

: in falsetto

**false·work** \'fôls-,wərk\ *noun* (circa 1874)
**:** temporary construction work on which a main work is wholly or partly built and supported until the main work is strong enough to support itself

**fals·ie** \'fôl-sē\ *noun* (circa 1943)
**:** an artificial addition to a bodily part worn to enhance appearance; *specifically* **:** a breast-shaped usually fabric or rubber cup used to pad a brassiere — usually used in plural

**fal·si·fy** \'fôl-sə-,fī\ *verb* **-fied; -fy·ing** [Middle English *falsifien,* from Middle French *falsifier,* from Medieval Latin *falsificare,* from Latin *falsus*] (15th century)
*transitive verb*
**1 :** to prove or declare false **2 :** to make false: as **a :** to make false by mutilation or addition ⟨the accounts were *falsified* to conceal a theft⟩ **b :** to represent falsely : MISREPRESENT **3 :** to prove unsound by experience
*intransitive verb*
**:** to tell lies : LIE
— **fal·si·fi·abil·i·ty** \,fôl-sə-,fī-ə-'bi-lə-tē\ *noun*
— **fal·si·fi·able** \-'fī-ə-bəl\ *adjective*
— **fal·si·fi·ca·tion** \,fôl-sə-fə-'kā-shən\ *noun*
— **fal·si·fi·er** \'fôl-sə-,fī(-ə)r\ *noun*

**fal·si·ty** \'fôl-sə-tē\ *noun, plural* **-ties** (13th century)
**1 :** something false : LIE **2 :** the quality or state of being false

**Fal·staff** \'fôl-,staf\ *noun*
**:** a fat, convivial, roguish character in Shakespeare's *Merry Wives of Windsor* and *Henry IV*
— **Fal·staff·ian** \fôl-'sta-fē-ən\ *adjective*

**¹fal·ter** \'fôl-tər\ *verb* **fal·tered; fal·ter·ing** \-t(ə-)riŋ\ [Middle English] (14th century)
*intransitive verb*
**1 a :** to walk unsteadily : STUMBLE **b :** to give way : TOTTER ⟨could feel my legs *faltering*⟩ **c :** to move waveringly or hesitatingly **2 :** to speak brokenly or weakly : STAMMER **3 a :** to hesitate in purpose or action : WAVER **b :** to lose drive or effectiveness ⟨the business was *faltering*⟩
*transitive verb*
**:** to utter hesitatingly or brokenly
**synonym** see HESITATE
— **fal·ter·er** \-tər-ər\ *noun*
— **fal·ter·ing·ly** \-t(ə-)riŋ-lē\ *adverb*

**²falter** *noun* (1834)
**:** an act or instance of faltering

**¹fame** \'fām\ *noun* [Middle English, from Old French, from Latin *fama* report, fame; akin to Latin *fari* to speak — more at BAN] (13th century)
**1 a :** public estimation : REPUTATION **b :** popular acclaim : RENOWN **2** *archaic* **:** RUMOR

**²fame** *transitive verb* **famed; fam·ing** (14th century)
**1** *archaic* **:** REPORT, REPUTE **2 :** to make famous

**famed** \'fāmd\ *adjective* (circa 1533)
**:** known widely and well : FAMOUS

**fa·mil·ial** \fə-'mil-yəl, -'mi-lē-əl\ *adjective* [French, from Latin *familia*] (circa 1900)
**1 :** tending to occur in more members of a family than expected by chance alone ⟨a *familial* disorder⟩ **2 :** of, relating to, or suggestive of a family

**¹fa·mil·iar** \fə-'mil-yər\ *noun* (13th century)
**1 :** a member of the household of a high official **2 :** one that is familiar; *especially* **:** an intimate associate : COMPANION **3 :** a spirit often embodied in an animal and held to attend and serve or guard a person **4 a :** one who is well acquainted with something **b :** one who frequents a place

**²familiar** *adjective* [Middle English *familier,* from Middle French, from Latin *familiaris,* from *familia*] (14th century)

**1 :** closely acquainted : INTIMATE ⟨a *familiar* family friend⟩ **2** *obsolete* **:** AFFABLE, SOCIABLE **3 a :** of or relating to a family ⟨remembering past *familiar* celebrations⟩ **b :** frequented by families ⟨a *familiar* resort⟩ **4 a :** being free and easy ⟨the *familiar* association of old friends⟩ **b :** marked by informality ⟨a *familiar* essay⟩ **c :** overly free and unrestrained : PRESUMPTUOUS ⟨grossly *familiar* behavior⟩ **d :** moderately tame ⟨*familiar* animals⟩ **5 a :** frequently seen or experienced : easily recognized ⟨a *familiar* theme⟩ **b :** of everyday occurrence **c :** possibly known but imperfectly remembered ⟨her face looked *familiar*⟩ **6 :** having personal or intimate knowledge — used with *with* ⟨*familiar* with the facts of the case⟩
**synonym** see COMMON
— **fa·mil·iar·ly** *adverb*
— **fa·mil·iar·ness** *noun*

**fa·mil·iar·ise** *British variant of* FAMILIARIZE

**fa·mil·iar·i·ty** \fə-,mi-lē-'(y)ar-ə-tē, -,mil-'yar-\ *noun, plural* **-ties** (13th century)
**1 a :** the quality or state of being familiar **b :** a state of close relationship : INTIMACY **2 a :** absence of ceremony : INFORMALITY **b :** an unduly informal act or expression : IMPROPRIETY **c :** a sexual liberty **3 :** close acquaintance with something ⟨my *familiarity* with American history⟩

**fa·mil·iar·ize** \fə-'mil-yə-,rīz\ *transitive verb* **-ized; -iz·ing** (1608)
**1 :** to make known or familiar ⟨Shakespeare . . . *familiarizes* the wonderful —Samuel Johnson⟩ **2 :** to make well acquainted ⟨*familiarize* students with good literature⟩
— **fa·mil·iar·iza·tion** \-,mil-yə-rə-'zā-shən\ *noun*

**familiar spirit** *noun* (1565)
**1 :** a spirit or demon that serves or prompts an individual **2 :** the spirit of a dead person invoked by a medium to advise or prophesy

**fam·i·lism** \'fa-mə-,li-zəm\ *noun* (1925)
**:** a social pattern in which the family assumes a position of ascendance over individual interests
— **fam·i·lis·tic** \,fa-mə-'lis-tik\ *adjective*

**fa·mille rose** \fə-'mē-\ *noun* [French, literally, rose family] (circa 1898)
**:** Chinese porcelain in the decoration of which a rose color predominates

**fa·mille verte** \fə-'mē-'vert\ *noun* [French, literally, green family] (1872)
**:** Chinese porcelain in the decoration of which green predominates

**¹fam·i·ly** \'fam-lē, 'fa-mə-\ *noun, plural* **-lies** [Middle English *familie,* from Latin *familia* household (including servants as well as kin of the householder), from *famulus* servant] (15th century)
**1 :** a group of individuals living under one roof and usually under one head : HOUSEHOLD **2 a :** a group of persons of common ancestry : CLAN **b :** a people or group of peoples regarded as deriving from a common stock : RACE **3 a :** a group of people united by certain convictions or a common affiliation : FELLOWSHIP **b :** the staff of a high official (as the President) **4 :** a group of things related by common characteristics: as **a :** a closely related series of elements or chemical compounds **b :** a group of soils that have similar profiles and include one or more series **c :** a group of related languages descended from a single ancestral language **5 a :** the basic unit in society traditionally consisting of two parents rearing their own or adopted children; *also* **:** any of various social units differing from but regarded as equivalent to the traditional family ⟨a single-parent *family*⟩ **b :** spouse and children ⟨want to spend more time with my *family*⟩

**6 a :** a group of related plants or animals forming a category ranking above a genus and below an order and usually comprising several to many genera **b** *in livestock breeding* (1) : the descendants or line of a particular individual especially of some outstanding female (2) : an identifiable strain within a breed
**7 :** a set of curves or surfaces whose equations differ only in parameters
**8 :** a unit of a crime syndicate (as the Mafia) operating within a geographical area

²**family** *adjective* (1602)
**1 :** of or relating to a family
**2 :** designed or suitable for both children and adults ⟨*family* restaurants⟩ ⟨*family* movies⟩

**family Bible** *noun* (1740)
: a large Bible usually having special pages for recording births, marriages, and deaths

**family court** *noun* (circa 1931)
: COURT OF DOMESTIC RELATIONS

**family doctor** *noun* (1846)
**1 :** a doctor regularly consulted by a family
**2 :** a doctor specializing in family practice

**family jewels** *noun plural* (circa 1946)
*slang* : a man's testicles

**family man** *noun* (1856)
**1 :** a man with a wife and children dependent on him
**2 :** a responsible man of domestic habits

**family name** *noun* (1699)
: SURNAME 2

**family physician** *noun* (1807)
: FAMILY DOCTOR

**family planning** *noun* (1939)
: planning intended to determine the number and spacing of one's children through birth control

**family practice** *noun* (1969)
: a medical practice or specialty which provides continuing general medical care for the individual and family — called also *family medicine*

**family practitioner** *noun* (1846)
: FAMILY DOCTOR

**family room** *noun* (1853)
: a large room designed as a recreation center for members of a family

**family style** *adverb or adjective* (1932)
: with the food placed on the table in serving dishes from which those eating may help themselves

**family tree** *noun* (1807)
**1 :** a genealogical diagram
**2 :** GENEALOGY

**family way** *noun* (1796)
: condition of being pregnant — used with *in* and *the* or *a* ⟨she is in a *family way*⟩

**fam·ine** \'fa-mən\ *noun* [Middle English, from Middle French, from *faim* hunger, from Latin *fames*] (14th century)
**1 :** an extreme scarcity of food
**2** *archaic* : STARVATION
**3** *archaic* : a ravenous appetite
**4 :** a great shortage

**fam·ish** \'fa-mish\ *verb* [Middle English, probably alteration of *famen*, from Middle French *afamer*, from (assumed) Vulgar Latin *affamare*, from Latin *ad-* + *fames*] (15th century)
*transitive verb*
**1 :** to cause to suffer severely from hunger
**2** *archaic* : to cause to starve to death
*intransitive verb*
**1** *archaic* : STARVE
**2 :** to suffer for lack of something necessary ⟨a moment when French poetry in particular was *famishing* for such invention — T. S. Eliot⟩
— **fam·ish·ment** \-mənt\ *noun*

**fam·ished** \'fa-misht\ *adjective* (15th century)
: intensely hungry; *also* : NEEDY

**fa·mous** \'fā-məs\ *adjective* [Middle English, from Middle French *fameux*, from Latin *famosus*, from *fama* fame] (14th century)
**1 a :** widely known **b :** honored for achievement
**2 :** EXCELLENT, FIRST-RATE ⟨*famous* weather for a walk⟩ ☆

— **fa·mous·ness** *noun*
**fa·mous·ly** *adverb* (1579)
**1 :** in a celebrated manner
**2 :** in a superlative fashion
**3 :** to an unusual degree : VERY

**fam·u·lus** \'fam-yə-ləs\ *noun, plural* **-li** \-,lī, -,lē\ [German, assistant to a professor, from Latin, servant] (1837)
: a private secretary or attendant

¹**fan** \'fan\ *noun* [Middle English, from Old English *fann*, from Latin *vannus* — more at WINNOW] (before 12th century)
**1 :** any of various devices for winnowing grain
**2 :** an instrument for producing a current of air: as **a :** a device for cooling the person that is usually shaped like a segment of a circle and is composed of material (as feathers or paper) mounted on thin rods or slats moving about a pivot so that the device may be closed compactly when not in use **b :** a device that consists of a series of vanes radiating from a hub rotated on its axle by a motor **c** *slang* : an airplane propeller
**3 a :** something resembling an open fan **b :** a gently sloping fan-shaped body of detritus; *especially* : ALLUVIAL FAN
— **fan·like** \-,līk\ *adjective*

²**fan** *verb* **fanned; fan·ning** (before 12th century)
*transitive verb*
**1 a :** to drive away the chaff of (grain) by means of a current of air **b :** to eliminate (as chaff) by winnowing
**2 :** to move or impel (air) with a fan
**3 :** to blow or breathe upon ⟨the breeze *fanning* her hair⟩
**4 a :** to direct a current of air upon with a fan **b :** to stir up to activity as if by fanning : STIMULATE ⟨*fanning* the fires of nationalism⟩
**5** *archaic* : WAVE
**6** *slang* : SPANK
**7 :** to spread like a fan ⟨the peacock *fanned* his tail⟩
**8 :** to strike (a batter) out in baseball
**9 :** to fire a series of shots from (a single-action revolver) by holding the trigger back and successively striking the hammer to the rear with the free hand
*intransitive verb*
**1 :** to move like a fan : FLUTTER
**2 :** to spread like a fan — often used with *out* ⟨deputies *fanning* out on the hunt⟩
**3 :** STRIKE OUT 3
— **fan·ner** \'fa-nər\ *noun*

³**fan** *noun* [probably short for *fanatic*] (1682)
**1 :** an enthusiastic devotee (as of a sport or a performing art) usually as a spectator
**2 :** an ardent admirer or enthusiast (as of a celebrity or a pursuit) ⟨science-fiction *fans*⟩
*word history* see FANATIC

**fa·nat·ic** \fə-'na-tik\ *or* **fa·nat·i·cal** \-ti-kəl\ *adjective* [Latin *fanaticus* inspired by a deity, frenzied, from *fanum* temple — more at FEAST] (1550)
: marked by excessive enthusiasm and often intense uncritical devotion ⟨they're *fanatic* about politics⟩ ◆
— **fanatic** *noun*
— **fa·nat·i·cal·ly** \fə-'na-ti-k(ə-)lē\ *adverb*
— **fa·nat·i·cal·ness** \-kəl-nəs\ *noun*

**fa·nat·i·cism** \fə-'na-tə-,si-zəm\ *noun* (1652)
: fanatic outlook or behavior

**fa·nat·i·cize** \-,sīz\ *transitive verb* **-cized; -ciz·ing** (1812)
: to cause to become fanatic

**fan·ci·er** \'fan(t)-sē-ər\ *noun* (1765)
**1 :** one that has a special liking or interest
**2 :** a person who breeds or grows a particular animal or plant for points of excellence ⟨a pigeon *fancier*⟩

**fan·ci·ful** \'fan(t)-si-fəl\ *adjective* (circa 1627)
**1 :** marked by fancy or unrestrained imagination rather than by reason and experience ⟨a *fanciful* person⟩
**2 :** existing in fancy only ⟨a *fanciful* notion⟩

**3 :** marked by or as if by fancy or whim ⟨gave their children *fanciful* names⟩
*synonym* see IMAGINARY
— **fan·ci·ful·ly** \-f(ə-)lē\ *adverb*
— **fan·ci·ful·ness** \-fəl-nəs\ *noun*

**fan·ci·fy** \'fan(t)-sə-,fī\ *transitive verb* **-fied; -fy·ing** (1890)
: to make ornate, elaborate, or fancy ⟨a *fancified* hamburger⟩

¹**fan·cy** \'fan(t)-sē\ *transitive verb* **fan·cied; fan·cy·ing** (14th century)
**1 :** to have a fancy for : LIKE
**2 :** to form a conception of : IMAGINE ⟨*fancy* our embarrassment⟩
**3 a :** to believe mistakenly or without evidence **b :** to believe without being certain ⟨she *fancied* she had met him before⟩
**4 :** to visualize or interpret as ⟨*fancied* myself a child again⟩
*synonym* see THINK

²**fancy** *noun, plural* **fancies** [Middle English *fantasie, fantsy* fantasy, fancy, from Middle French *fantasie*, from Latin *phantasia*, from

---

☆ **SYNONYMS**
**Famous, renowned, celebrated, noted, notorious, distinguished, eminent, illustrious** mean known far and wide. FAMOUS implies little more than the fact of being, sometimes briefly, widely and popularly known ⟨a *famous* actress⟩. RENOWNED implies more glory and acclamation ⟨one of the most *renowned* figures in sports history⟩. CELEBRATED implies notice and attention especially in print ⟨the most *celebrated* beauty of her day⟩. NOTED suggests well-deserved public attention ⟨the *noted* mystery writer⟩. NOTORIOUS frequently adds to FAMOUS an implication of questionableness or evil ⟨a *notorious* gangster⟩. DISTINGUISHED implies acknowledged excellence or superiority ⟨a *distinguished* scientist who won the Nobel Prize⟩. EMINENT implies even greater conspicuousness for outstanding quality or character ⟨the country's most *eminent* writers⟩. ILLUSTRIOUS stresses enduring honor and glory attached to a deed or person ⟨our *illustrious* national heroes⟩.

---

◇ **WORD HISTORY**
**fanatic** In Latin the adjective *fanaticus,* a derivative of *fanum* "consecrated space, temple," meant literally "pertaining to a temple," though more common was the sense "inspired by a deity, frenzied." With the latter meaning the word was borrowed into English as *fanatic* in the 16th century. In the following century the word as both adjective and noun was applied to adherents of more radical Protestant sects who espoused their beliefs—in the view of the conservative mainstream who belonged to the Church of England—with excessive zeal, acting as if they were divinely inspired. Eventually *fanatic* became a more general negative label for extreme partisans of dubious causes, and in the 19th and 20th centuries has been associated as much with politics as religion. The word *fan* is probably a shortening of *fanatic;* it occurs in a single text in the 17th century (in the curious spellings *phann* and *fann*), but was in all likelihood formed anew in 19th century American English, where it first appears in reference to enthusiastic devotees of local sports teams—still a frequent usage of the word.

---

\ə\ abut \ᵊ\ kitten \ər\ further \a\ ash \ā\ ace
\ä\ mop, mar \aů\ out \ch\ chin \e\ bet \ē\ easy
\g\ go \i\ hit \ī\ ice \j\ job \ŋ\ sing \ō\ go
\ò\ law \òi\ boy \th\ thin \t̲h̲\ the \ü\ loot \ů\ foot
\y\ yet \zh\ vision *see also* Guide to Pronunciation

Greek, appearance, imagination, from *phantazein* to present to the mind (middle voice, to imagine), from *phainein* to show; akin to Old English geb*ō*ned polished, Greek *phōs* light] (15th century)
**1 a :** a liking formed by caprice rather than reason **:** INCLINATION ⟨took a *fancy* to the strange little animal⟩ **b :** amorous fondness **:** LOVE
**2 a :** NOTION, WHIM **b :** an image or representation of something formed in the mind
**3** *archaic* **:** fantastic quality or state
**4 a :** imagination especially of a capricious or delusive sort **b :** the power of conception and representation used in artistic expression (as by a poet)
**5 :** TASTE, JUDGMENT
**6 a :** devotees of some particular art, practice, or amusement **b :** the object of interest of such a fancy; *especially* **:** ²BOXING
**³fancy** *adjective* **fan·ci·er; -est** (1646)
**1 :** dependent or based on fancy **:** WHIMSICAL
**2 a** (1) **:** not plain **:** ORNAMENTAL ⟨a *fancy* hairdo⟩ (2) **:** SWANKY 2, POSH ⟨a *fancy* restaurant⟩ **b** (1) **:** of particular excellence or highest grade ⟨*fancy* tuna⟩ (2) **:** IMPRESSIVE ⟨posted some *fancy* numbers⟩ **c** *of an animal or plant* **:** bred especially for bizarre or ornamental qualities that lack practical utility
**3 :** based on conceptions of the fancy ⟨*fancy* sketches⟩
**4 a :** dealing in fancy goods **b :** EXTRAVAGANT ⟨paying *fancy* prices⟩
**5 :** executed with technical skill and style ⟨*fancy* footwork⟩ ⟨*fancy* diving⟩
**6 :** PARTI-COLOR ⟨*fancy* carnations⟩
— **fan·ci·ly** \'fan(t)-sə-lē\ *adverb*
— **fan·ci·ness** \-sē-nəs\ *noun*
**fancy–dan** \'fan(t)-sē-'dan, -,dan\ *adjective, often D capitalized* (1938)
**:** SHOWY 2, FANCY
**fancy Dan** *noun, often F capitalized* (circa 1943)
**:** one given to flamboyant display especially of technique or dress
**fancy dress** *noun* (1770)
**:** a costume (as for a masquerade) chosen to suit the wearer's fancy
**fan·cy–free** \,fan(t)-sē-'frē\ *adjective* (1590)
**1 :** free from amorous attachment or engagement
**2 :** free to imagine or fancy
**fancy man** *noun* (circa 1811)
**:** a woman's paramour; *also* **:** PIMP
**fancy–pants** *adjective* (1945)
**:** overly elegant or refined **:** LA-DI-DA
**fancy up** *transitive verb* (1934)
**:** to add superficial adornment to
**fancy woman** *noun* (1812)
**:** a woman of questionable morals; *specifically* **:** PROSTITUTE
**fan·cy·work** \'fan(t)-sē-,wərk\ *noun* (1810)
**:** decorative needlework
**fan·dan·go** \fan-'daŋ-(,)gō\ *noun, plural* **-gos** [Spanish] (1774)
**1 :** a lively Spanish or Spanish-American dance in triple time that is usually performed by a man and a woman to the accompaniment of guitar and castanets; *also* **:** music for this dance
**2 :** TOMFOOLERY
**fan·dom** \'fan-dəm\ *noun* (1903)
**:** all the fans (as of a sport)
**fane** \'fān\ *noun* [Middle English, from Latin *fanum* — more at FEAST] (15th century)
**1 :** TEMPLE
**2 :** CHURCH
**fan·fare** \'fan-,far, -,fer\ *noun* [French] (1676)
**1 :** a showy outward display
**2 :** a short and lively sounding of trumpets
**fan·far·o·nade** \,fan-,far-ə-'nād, -'näd\ *noun* [French *fanfaronnade*, from Spanish *fanfarronada*, from *fanfarrón* braggart] (1652)
**:** empty boasting **:** BLUSTER
**fan·fold** \'fan-,fōld\ *noun* (1925)

**:** paper (as business forms or tape) made from a web and folded like a fan lengthwise and sometimes crosswise
— **fanfold** *transitive verb*
**fang** \'faŋ\ *noun* [Middle English, that which is taken, from Old English; akin to Old High German *fang* seizure, Old English *fōn* to seize — more at PACT] (1555)
**1 a :** a long sharp tooth: as (1) **:** one by which an animal's prey is seized and held or torn (2) **:** one of the long hollow or grooved and often erectile teeth of a venomous snake **b :** one of the chelicerae of a spider at the tip of which a poison gland opens
**2 :** the root of a tooth or one of the processes or prongs into which a root divides
**3 :** a projecting tooth or prong
— **fanged** \'faŋd\ *adjective*
**Fang** \'faŋ, 'fäŋ\ *also* **Fan** \'fan, 'fän\ *noun, plural* **Fang** *or* **Fangs** *also* **Fan** *or* **Fans** (1861)
**1 :** a member of a Bantu-speaking people of northern Gabon, mainland Equatorial Guinea, and southern Cameroon
**2 :** the language of the Fang people
**fan–jet** \'fan-,jet\ *noun* (1962)
**:** a jet engine having a fan that operates in a duct and draws in extra air whose compression and expulsion provide extra thrust; *also* **:** an airplane powered by a fan-jet engine
**fan letter** *noun* (1932)
**:** a letter sent to a public figure by an admirer
**fan·light** \'fan-,līt\ *noun* (1819)
**:** a semicircular window with radiating bars like the ribs of a fan that is placed over a door or window
**fan mail** *noun* (1924)
**:** FAN LETTERS
**fan·ny** \'fa-nē\ *noun, plural* **fannies** [perhaps from *Fanny*, nickname of *Frances*] (1928)
**1 :** BUTTOCKS
**2** *slang British* **:** VULVA
**fanny pack** *noun* (1967)
**:** a pack for carrying personal articles that straps to the waist
**fan·tab·u·lous** \fan-'ta-byə-ləs\ *adjective* [blend of *fantastic* and *fabulous*] (1959)
*slang* **:** marvelously good
**fan·tail** \'fan-,tāl\ *noun* (1728)
**1 :** a fan-shaped tail or end
**2 :** a domestic pigeon having a broad rounded tail often with 30 or 40 feathers
**3 :** an architectural part resembling a fan
**4 :** a counter or after overhang of a ship shaped like a duck's bill
**fan–tan** \'fan-,tan\ *noun* [Chinese (Guangdong) *fāantāan*] (1878)
**1 :** a Chinese gambling game in which the banker divides a pile of objects (as beans) into fours and players bet on what number will be left at the end of the count
**2 :** a card game in which players must build in sequence upon sevens and attempt to be the first one out of cards
**fan·ta·sia** \fan-'tā-zhə, -z(h)ē-ə; ,fan-tə-'zē-ə\ *noun* [Italian, literally, fancy, from Latin *phantasia* — more at FANCY] (1724)
**1 :** a free usually instrumental composition not in strict form
**2 a :** a work (as a poem or play) in which the author's fancy roves unrestricted **b :** something possessing grotesque, bizarre, or unreal qualities
**fan·ta·sie** \,fan-tə-'zē, ,fän-\ *noun* [German *Phantasie*, from Latin *phantasia*] (circa 1859)
**:** FANTASIA
**fan·ta·sied** \'fan-tə-sēd, -zēd\ *adjective* (1561)
**1 :** existing only in the imagination **:** FANCIED
**2** *obsolete* **:** full of fancies or strange whims
**fan·ta·sise** *British variant of* FANTASIZE
**fan·ta·sist** \-sist, -zist\ *noun* (1896)
**:** one who creates fantasias or fantasies
**fan·ta·size** \-,sīz\ *verb* **-sized; -siz·ing** (1926)
*intransitive verb*

**:** to indulge in reverie **:** create or develop imaginative and often fantastic views or ideas ⟨doing things I'd *fantasized* about in my sheltered childhood —Diane Arbus⟩
*transitive verb*
**:** to portray in the mind **:** FANCY ⟨likes to *fantasize* herself as very wealthy⟩
— **fan·ta·siz·er** \-,sī-zər\ *noun*
**fan·tasm** *variant of* PHANTASM
**fan·tast** \'fan-,tast\ *noun* [German, from Medieval Latin *fantasta*, probably back-formation from Late Latin *phantasticus*] (1588)
**1 :** VISIONARY
**2 :** a fantastic or eccentric person
**3 :** FANTASIST
**¹fan·tas·tic** \fan-'tas-tik, fən-\ *also* **fan·tas·ti·cal** \-ti-kəl\ *adjective* [Middle English *fantastic, fantastical*, from Middle French & Late Latin; Middle French *fantastique*, from Late Latin *phantasticus*, from Greek *phantastikos* producing mental images, from *phantazein* to present to the mind] (14th century)
**1 a :** based on fantasy **:** not real **b :** conceived or seemingly conceived by unrestrained fancy **c :** so extreme as to challenge belief **:** UNBELIEVABLE; *broadly* **:** exceedingly large or great
**2 :** marked by extravagant fantasy or extreme individuality **:** ECCENTRIC
**3** *fantastic* **:** EXCELLENT, SUPERLATIVE ⟨a *fantastic* dinner⟩ ☆
— **fan·tas·ti·cal·i·ty** \(,)fan-,tas-tə-'ka-lə-tē, fən-\ *noun*
— **fan·tas·ti·cal·ness** \-'tas-tə-kəl-nəs\ *noun*
**²fantastic** *noun* (1598)
**:** ECCENTRIC 2
**fan·tas·ti·cal·ly** \fan-'tas-ti-k(ə-)lē, fən-\ *adverb* (1543)
**1 :** in a fantastic manner
**2 :** to a fantastic degree **:** EXTREMELY ⟨*fantastically* expensive clothes⟩
**fan·tas·ti·cate** \fan-'tas-tə-,kāt, fən-\ *transitive verb* **-cat·ed; -cat·ing** (1600)
**:** to make fantastic
— **fan·tas·ti·ca·tion** \(,)fan-,tas-tə-'kā-shən, fən-\ *noun*
**fan·tas·ti·co** \fan-'tas-ti-,kō, fən-\ *noun, plural* **-coes** [Italian, fantastic (adjective), from Late Latin *phantasticus*] (1596)
**:** a ridiculously fantastic individual
**¹fan·ta·sy** \'fan-tə-sē, -zē\ *noun, plural* **-sies** [Middle English *fantasie* — more at FANCY] (14th century)
**1** *obsolete* **:** HALLUCINATION
**2 :** FANCY; *especially* **:** the free play of creative imagination
**3 :** a creation of the imaginative faculty whether expressed or merely conceived: as **a** **:** a fanciful design or invention **b :** a chimerical or fantastic notion **c :** FANTASIA 1 **d :** imaginative fiction featuring especially strange settings and grotesque characters — called also *fantasy fiction*
**4 :** CAPRICE

---

☆ **SYNONYMS**
**Fantastic, bizarre, grotesque** mean conceived, made, or carried out without adherence to truth or reality. FANTASTIC may connote unrestrained extravagance in conception or merely ingenuity of decorative invention ⟨dreamed up *fantastic* rumors to spread⟩. BIZARRE applies to the sensationally queer or strange and implies violence of contrast or incongruity of combination ⟨a *bizarre* medieval castle built in the heart of a modern city⟩. GROTESQUE may apply to what is conventionally ugly but artistically effective or it may connote ludicrous awkwardness or incongruity often with sinister or tragic overtones ⟨*grotesque* statues adorn the cathedral⟩ ⟨though grief-stricken, she made a *grotesque* attempt at a smile⟩. See in addition IMAGINARY.

**5 :** the power or process of creating especially unrealistic or improbable mental images in response to psychological need ⟨an object of *fantasy*⟩; *also* **:** a mental image or a series of mental images (as a daydream) so created ⟨sexual *fantasies* of adolescence⟩
**6 :** a coin usually not intended for circulation as currency and often issued by a dubious authority (as a government-in-exile)
²**fantasy** *verb* **-sied; -sy·ing** (15th century)
**:** FANTASIZE
**fan·ta·sy·land** \-ˌland\ *noun* (1967)
**:** an imaginary or ideal place or situation
**fan·toc·ci·ni** \ˌfän-tə-ˈchē-nē, ˌfan-\ *noun plural* [Italian, plural of *fantoccino*, diminutive of *fantoccio* doll, augmentative of *fante* child, from Latin *infant-, infans* infant] (1771)
**:** a puppet show using puppets operated by strings or mechanical devices; *also* **:** such puppets
**fan·tod** \ˈfan-ˌtäd\ *noun* [perhaps alteration of English dialect *fantigue, fanteeg*] (1839)
**1** *plural* **a :** a state of irritability and tension **b :** FIDGETS
**2 :** an emotional outburst **:** FIT
**fan·tom** *variant of* PHANTOM
**fan vault** *noun* (circa 1901)
**:** a Gothic vault in which the ribs from each springer spread out like the vanes of a fan
— **fan vaulting** *noun*
**fan·wise** \ˈfan-ˌwīz\ *adverb or adjective* (1882)
**:** in the manner or position of the slats of an open fan ⟨boats anchored *fanwise* at the pier⟩
**fan·zine** \ˈfan-ˌzēn\ *noun* [³*fan* + maga*zine*] (1949)
**:** a magazine written by and for fans especially of science fiction or fantasy writing
¹**far** \ˈfär\ *adverb* **far·ther** \-thər\ *or* **fur·ther** \ˈfor-\; **far·thest** *or* **fur·thest** \-thəst\ [Middle English *fer*, from Old English *feorr*; akin to Old High German *ferro* far, Old English *faran* to go — more at FARE] (before 12th century)
**1 :** at or to a considerable distance in space ⟨wandered *far* from home⟩
**2 a :** to a great extent **:** MUCH ⟨*far* better methods⟩ **b :** by a broad interval **:** WIDELY ⟨the *far* distant future⟩
**3 :** to or at a definite distance, point, or degree ⟨as *far* as I know⟩
**4 :** to an advanced point or extent ⟨a bright student will go *far*⟩ ⟨worked *far* into the night⟩
**5 :** at a considerable distance in time ⟨not *far* from the year 1870⟩
— **by far :** far and away ⟨is *by far* the best runner⟩
— **far be it from :** it would be inappropriate or impossible for ⟨*far be it from* God, that he should do wickedness —Job 34:10 (Authorized Version)⟩
— **far from :** of a distinctly different and especially opposite quality than ⟨the trip was *far from* a failure⟩
— **how far :** to what extent, degree, or distance ⟨didn't know *how far* to trust them⟩
— **so far :** to a certain extent, degree, or distance ⟨when the water rose *so far*, the villagers sought higher ground⟩ **2 :** up to the present ⟨has written just one novel *so far*⟩
— **thus far :** so far ⟨*thus far* our findings have been negative⟩
²**far** *adjective* **farther** *or* **further; farthest** *or* **furthest** (before 12th century)
**1 a :** remote in space **b :** distinctly different in quality or relationship **c :** remote in time
**2 a :** LONG ⟨a *far* journey⟩ **b :** of notable extent **:** COMPREHENSIVE ⟨a man of *far* vision⟩
**3 :** the more distant of two
**4 :** EXTREME ⟨the *far* left⟩ ⟨a *far* right political organization⟩
**far·ad** \ˈfar-ˌad, ˈfar-əd\ *noun* [Michael *Faraday*] (1873)
**:** the unit of capacitance equal to the capacitance of a capacitor between whose plates

there appears a potential of one volt when it is charged by one coulomb of electricity
**far·a·day** \ˈfar-ə-ˌdā, -ə-dē\ *noun* [Michael *Faraday*] (1904)
**:** the quantity of electricity transferred in electrolysis per equivalent weight of an element or ion equal to about 96,500 coulombs
**fa·rad·ic** \fə-ˈra-dik, fa-ˈra-\ *also* **far·a·da·ic** \ˌfar-ə-ˈdā-ik\ *adjective* (1875)
**:** of or relating to an asymmetric alternating current of electricity produced by an induction coil ⟨*faradic* stimulation of the muscles⟩
**far·a·dism** \ˈfar-ə-ˌdi-zəm\ *noun* (1876)
**:** the application of a faradic current of electricity (as for therapeutic purposes)
**far and away** *adverb* (1852)
**:** by a considerable margin ⟨was *far and away* the better team⟩
**far·an·dole** \ˈfar-ən-ˌdōl\ *noun* [French *farandole*, from Provençal *farandoulo*] (1863)
**1 :** a lively Provençal dance in which men and women hold hands, form a chain, and follow a leader through a serpentine course
**2 :** music in sextuple time for a farandole
**far and wide** *adverb* (before 12th century)
**:** in every direction **:** EVERYWHERE ⟨searched *far and wide*⟩
**far·away** \ˈfär-ə-ˌwä\ *adjective* (1735)
**1 :** lying at a great distance **:** REMOTE
**2 :** DREAMY, ABSTRACTED ⟨a *faraway* look in her eyes⟩
¹**farce** \ˈfärs\ *transitive verb* **farced; farc·ing** [Middle English *farsen*, from Middle French *farcir*, from Latin *farcire*] (14th century)
**1 :** STUFF
**2 :** to improve as if by stuffing ◆
²**farce** *noun* [Middle English *farse*, from Middle French *farce*, from (assumed) Vulgar Latin *farsa*, from Latin, feminine of *farsus*, past participle of *farcire*] (14th century)
**1 :** a savory stuffing **:** FORCEMEAT
**2 :** a light dramatic composition marked by broadly satirical comedy and improbable plot
**3 :** the broad humor characteristic of farce or pretense
**4 a :** ridiculous or empty show **b :** MOCKERY ⟨the enforcement of this law became a *farce*⟩
**far·ceur** \fär-ˈsər\ *noun* [French, from Middle French, from *farcer* to joke, from Old French, from *farce*] (1781)
**1 :** JOKER, WAG
**2 :** a writer or actor of farce
**far·ci** *or* **far·cie** \fär-ˈsē\ *adjective* [French, from past participle of *farcir*] (1903)
**:** stuffed especially with forcemeat ⟨oysters *farci*⟩
**far·ci·cal** \ˈfär-si-kəl\ *adjective* (1716)
**1 :** of, relating to, or resembling farce **:** LUDICROUS
**2 :** laughably inept **:** ABSURD
— **far·ci·cal·i·ty** \ˌfär-sə-ˈka-lə-tē\ *noun*
— **far·ci·cal·ly** \ˈfär-si-k(ə-)lē\ *adverb*
**far·cy** \ˈfär-sē\ *noun* [Middle English *farsin, farsi*, from Middle French *farcin*, from Late Latin *farcimen*, from Latin, sausage, from *farcire*] (15th century)
**:** GLANDERS; *especially* **:** cutaneous glanders
**fard** \ˈfärd\ *transitive verb* [Middle English, from Middle French *farder*, of Germanic origin; akin to Old High German *faro* colored — more at PERCH] (15th century)
**1 :** to paint (the face) with cosmetics
**2** *archaic* **:** to gloss over
— **fard** *noun, archaic*
**far·del** \ˈfär-dᵊl\ *noun* [Middle English, from Middle French, probably from Arabic *fardah*] (14th century)
**1 :** BUNDLE
**2 :** BURDEN
¹**fare** \ˈfar, ˈfer\ *intransitive verb* **fared; far·ing** [Middle English *faren*, from Old English *faran*; akin to Old High German *faran* to go, Latin *portare* to carry, Greek *peran* to pass through, *poros* passage, journey] (before 12th century)

**1 :** GO, TRAVEL
**2 :** GET ALONG, SUCCEED ⟨how did you *fare* on your exam?⟩
**3 :** EAT, DINE
²**fare** *noun* [Middle English, journey, passage, supply of food, from Old English *faru, fær*; akin to Old English *faran* to go] (15th century)
**1 a :** range of food **:** DIET **b :** material provided for use, consumption, or enjoyment
**2 a :** the price charged to transport a person **b :** a paying passenger on a public conveyance
**fare-thee-well** \ˈfar-(ˌ)thē-ˌwel, ˈfer-\ *also* **fare-you-well** \-yə-, -yü-, -yē-\ *noun* (1884)
**1 :** the utmost degree ⟨researched the story to a *fare-thee-well*⟩
**2 :** a state of perfection ⟨imitated the speaker's pompous manner to a *fare-thee-well*⟩
¹**fare·well** \far-ˈwel, fer-\ *verb imperative* (14th century)
**:** get along well — used interjectionally to or by one departing
²**farewell** *noun* (14th century)
**1 :** a wish of well-being at parting **:** GOOD-BYE
**2 a :** an act of departure **:** LEAVE-TAKING **b :** a formal occasion honoring a person about to leave or retire
³**fare·well** *transitive verb* (1580)
*chiefly Australian & New Zealand* **:** to bid farewell to
⁴**fare·well** \ˈfar-ˌwel, ˈfer-\ *adjective* (1669)
**:** of or relating to leave-taking **:** FINAL ⟨a *farewell* appearance⟩
**far·fel** *or* **far·fal** \ˈfär-fəl\ *noun* [Yiddish *farfl* (plural), from Middle High German *varveln* noodles, noodle soup] (1892)
**:** noodles in the form of small pellets or granules
**far-fetched** \ˈfär-ˈfecht\ *adjective* (1583)
**1 :** brought from a remote time or place
**2 :** not easily or naturally deduced or introduced ⟨a *far-fetched* story⟩
— **far-fetched·ness** \-ˈfech(t)-nəs, -ˈfe-chəd-nəs\ *noun*
**far-flung** \-ˈfləŋ\ *adjective* (1895)
**1 :** widely spread or distributed ⟨a *far-flung* empire⟩
**2 :** REMOTE ⟨a *far-flung* correspondent⟩
**fa·ri·na** \fə-ˈrē-nə\ *noun* [Latin, meal, flour, from *far* spelt — more at BARLEY] (14th century)

---

◇ **WORD HISTORY**
**farce** When *farce* first appeared in English, its connection was with cooking, not comedy. In the 14th century English adopted *farce* (spelling it *farse* until the 18th century) from French, retaining its original meaning of "stuffing or forcemeat." The comedic sense of *farce* in English dates back to the 16th century, when England imported a kind of knockabout comedy that was already well-established in France and Italy. This dramatic genre had its origins in the 13th century practice of interlarding or "stuffing" Latin liturgical texts with explanatory passages in the vernacular. By the 15th century the practice arose of inserting unscripted buffoonery into performances of religious plays. Such farces, which included clowning, acrobatics, reversal of social roles, and indecency, soon developed into a distinct dramatic genre, a kind of broad comedy with a slapstick element. Since its introduction into England, farce in one guise or another has continued its popularity into the age of television.

---

\ə\ abut \ᵊ\ kitten \ər\ further \a\ ash \ā\ ace \ä\ mop, mar \au̇\ out \ch\ chin \e\ bet \ē\ easy \g\ go \i\ hit \ī\ ice \j\ job \ŋ\ sing \ō\ go \o̊\ law \o̊i\ boy \th\ thin \th\ the \ü\ loot \u̇\ foot \y\ yet \zh\ vision *see also* Guide to Pronunciation

**1 :** a fine meal of vegetable matter (as cereal grains) used chiefly for puddings or as a breakfast cereal
**2 :** any of various powdery or mealy substances

**far·i·na·ceous** \ˌfar-ə-'nā-shəs\ adjective (1646)
**1 :** having a mealy texture or surface
**2 :** containing or rich in starch

**far·in·fra·red** \ˌfär-ˌin-frə-'red\ adjective (1923)
**:** of or relating to the longer wavelengths of radiation in the infrared spectrum and especially to those between 10 and 1000 micrometers

**fa·ri·nha** \fə-'rēn-yə\ noun [Portuguese, flour, cassava meal, from Latin farina] (1726)
**:** cassava meal

**far·kle·ber·ry** \'fär-kəl-ˌber-ē\ noun [origin unknown] (1765)
**:** a shrub or small tree (Vaccinium arboreum) of the heath family of the southeastern U.S. having a black berry with stony seeds

**farl** \'fär(-ə)l\ noun [contraction of Scots fardel, literally, fourth part, from Middle English (Scots), from ferde del; from ferde fourth + del part] (1686)
Scottish **:** a small thin triangular cake or biscuit made especially with oatmeal or wheat flour

**¹farm** \'färm\ noun, often attributive [Middle English ferme rent, lease, from Old French, lease, from fermer to fix, make a contract, from Latin firmare to make firm, from firmus firm] (14th century)
**1** obsolete **:** a sum or due fixed in amount and payable at fixed intervals
**2 :** a letting out of revenues or taxes for a fixed sum to one authorized to collect and retain them
**3 :** a district or division of a country leased out for the collection of government revenues
**4 :** a tract of land devoted to agricultural purposes
**5 a :** a plot of land devoted to the raising of animals and especially domestic livestock **b :** a tract of water reserved for the artificial cultivation of some aquatic life form
**6 :** a minor-league team (as in baseball) associated with a major-league team as a subsidiary
**7 :** an area containing a number of similar structures (as radio antennas or storage tanks)

**²farm** (15th century)
transitive verb
**1** obsolete **:** RENT
**2 :** to collect and take the fees or profits of (an occupation or business) on payment of a fixed sum
**3 :** to give up (as an estate or a business) to another on condition of receiving in return a fixed sum
**4 a :** to devote to agriculture **b :** to manage and cultivate as a farm **c :** to grow or cultivate in quantity ⟨farm trees for fuel⟩ ⟨farm salmon⟩
intransitive verb
**:** to engage in raising crops, animals, or fish

**farm·er** \'fär-mər\ noun (14th century)
**1 :** a person who pays a fixed sum for some privilege or source of income
**2 :** a person who cultivates land or crops or raises animals or fish
**3 :** YOKEL, BUMPKIN

**farmer cheese** noun (1949)
**:** a pressed unripened cheese similar to but drier and firmer than cottage cheese

**farm·er·ette** \ˌfär-mə-'ret\ noun (1902)
**:** a woman who is a farmer or farmhand

**farmer's lung** noun (1945)
**:** an acute pulmonary disorder characterized by sudden onset, fever, cough, expectoration, and breathlessness that results from the inhalation of dust from moldy hay or straw

**farm·hand** \'färm-ˌhand\ noun (1843)
**1 :** a farm laborer; especially **:** a hired laborer on a farm

**2 :** a player on a farm team

**farm·house** \-ˌhaůs\ noun (1598)
**:** a dwelling on a farm

**farm·ing** noun (1733)
**:** the practice of agriculture or aquaculture

**farm·land** \'färm-ˌland\ noun (1638)
**:** land used or suitable for farming

**farm out** transitive verb (1607)
**1 :** to turn over (as a job) for performance by another usually under contract
**2 a :** to put (as children) into the hands of another for care **b :** to send (as a baseball player) to a farm team
**3 :** to exhaust (land) by farming especially by continuously raising one crop

**farm·stead** \'färm-ˌsted\ noun (1807)
**:** the buildings and adjacent service areas of a farm; broadly **:** a farm with its buildings

**farm·wife** \'färm-ˌwīf\ noun (1880)
**:** a farmer's wife

**farm·work·er** \'färm-ˌwər-kər\ noun (1946)
**:** FARMHAND 1
— **farm·work** \-ˌwərk\ noun

**farm·yard** \-ˌyärd\ noun (1748)
**:** land around or enclosed by farm buildings; especially **:** BARNYARD

**faro** \'far-(ˌ)ō, 'fer-\ noun, plural **far·os** [probably alteration of earlier pharaoh, translation of French pharaon] (circa 1735)
**:** a gambling game in which players bet on cards drawn from a dealing box

**Faro·ese** variant of FAEROESE

**far-off** \'fär-ˌôf\ adjective (15th century)
**:** remote in time or space

**fa·rouche** \fə-'rüsh\ adjective [French, wild, shy, from Late Latin forasticus living outside, from Latin foras outdoors; akin to Latin fores door — more at DOOR] (1765)
**1 :** WILD
**2 :** marked by shyness and lack of social graces

**far-out** \'fär-ˌaůt\ adjective (1954)
**:** marked by a considerable departure from the conventional or traditional ⟨far-out clothes⟩
— **far-out·ness** noun

**far·rag·i·nous** \fə-'ra-jə-nəs\ adjective (1615)
**:** consisting of a farrago

**far·ra·go** \fə-'rä-(ˌ)gō, -'rā-\ noun, plural **-goes** [Latin farragin-, farrago mixed fodder, mixture, from far spelt — more at BARLEY] (1632)
**:** a confused mixture **:** HODGEPODGE

**far-reach·ing** \'fär-ˌrē-chiṇ\ adjective (1824)
**:** having a wide range or effect

**far-red** \-'red\ adjective (1951)
**:** NEAR-INFRARED

**far·ri·er** \'far-ē-ər\ noun [alteration of Middle English ferrour, from Middle French ferrour blacksmith, from Old French ferreor, from ferrer to fit with iron, from (assumed) Vulgar Latin ferrare, from Latin ferrum iron] (15th century)
**:** a person who shoes horses

**¹far·row** \'far-(ˌ)ō, -ə(-w)\ verb [Middle English farwen, from (assumed) Old English feargian, from Old English fearh young pig; akin to Old High German farah young pig, Latin porcus pig] (13th century)
transitive verb
**:** to give birth to (a farrow)
intransitive verb
of swine **:** to bring forth young — often used with down

**²farrow** noun (1577)
**1 :** a litter of pigs
**2 :** an act of farrowing

**³farrow** adjective [Middle English (Scots) ferow] (15th century)
of a cow **:** not pregnant

**far-see·ing** \'fär-ˌsē-iṇ\ adjective (1837)
**:** FARSIGHTED 1

**Far·si** \'fär-sē\ noun [Persian fārsī, from Fārs Persia] (1878)
**:** PERSIAN 2b

**far·side** noun (15th century)

**:** the farther side; especially **:** the side of the moon away from the earth
— **on the far side of :** BEYOND ⟨just on the far side of 40⟩

**far·sight·ed** \'fär-ˌsī-təd\ adjective (1609)
**1 a :** seeing or able to see to a great distance **b :** having or showing foresight or good judgment **:** SAGACIOUS
**2 :** affected with hyperopia
— **far·sight·ed·ly** adverb

**far·sight·ed·ness** noun (circa 1829)
**1 :** the quality or state of being farsighted
**2 :** HYPEROPIA

**¹fart** \'färt\ intransitive verb [Middle English ferten, farten; akin to Old High German ferzan to break wind, Old Norse freta, Greek perdesthai, Sanskrit pardate he breaks wind] (13th century)
**:** to expel intestinal gas from the anus — often considered vulgar

**²fart** noun (14th century)
**1 :** an expulsion of intestinal gas — often considered vulgar
**2 :** a foolish or contemptible person ⟨couldn't stand the old fart⟩ — seldom in polite use

**¹far·ther** \'fär-thər\ adverb [Middle English ferther, alteration of further] (14th century)
**1 :** at or to a greater distance or more advanced point ⟨got no farther than the first page⟩ ⟨nothing could be farther from the truth⟩
**2 :** to a greater degree or extent ⟨see to it that I do not have to act any farther in the matter —Bernard DeVoto⟩ ▪

**²farther** adjective (14th century)
**1 :** more distant **:** REMOTER ⟨the farther side of town⟩
**2 :** FURTHER 2 ⟨clearing his throat preparatory to farther revelations —Edith Wharton⟩

**far·ther·most** \-ˌmōst\ adjective (15th century)
**:** most distant **:** FARTHEST

**¹far·thest** \'fär-thəst\ adjective (14th century)
**:** most distant especially in space or time

**²farthest** adverb (15th century)
**1 :** to or at the greatest distance in space or time ⟨who can jump the farthest⟩
**2 :** to the most advanced point ⟨goes farthest toward answering the question⟩
**3 :** by the greatest degree or extent **:** MOST ⟨the painting farthest removed from reality⟩

**far·thing** \'fär-thiṇ\ noun [Middle English ferthing, from Old English fēorthung (akin to Middle High German vierdunc fourth part), from Old English fēortha fourth] (before 12th century)
**1 a :** a former British monetary unit equal to ¼ of a penny **b :** a coin representing this unit
**2 :** something of small value **:** MITE

**far·thin·gale** \'fär-thən-ˌgāl, -thiṇ-\ noun [modification of Middle French verdugale, from Old Spanish verdugado, from verdugo young shoot of a tree, from verde green, from Latin viridis — more at VERDANT] (1552)

---

□ USAGE

**farther** Farther and further have been used more or less interchangeably throughout most of their history, but currently they are showing signs of diverging. As adverbs they continue to be used interchangeably whenever spatial, temporal, or metaphorical distance is involved. But where there is no notion of distance, further is used (our techniques can be further refined). Further is also used as a sentence modifier (further, the workshop participants were scarcely optimistic —L. B. Mayhew), but farther is not. A polarizing process appears to be taking place in their adjective use. Farther is taking over the meaning of distance (the farther shore) and further the meaning of addition (needed no further invitation).

: a support (as of hoops) worn especially in the 16th century beneath a skirt to expand it at the hipline

**far ultraviolet** *adjective* (1947)
: of, relating to, or being the shortest wavelengths of radiation in the ultraviolet spectrum and especially those between 100 and 300 nanometers

**fas·ces** \'fas-ˌēz\ *noun plural but singular or plural in construction* [Latin, from plural of *fascis* bundle; akin to Latin *fascia*] (1598)
: a bundle of rods and among them an ax with projecting blade borne before ancient Roman magistrates as a badge of authority

**fas·cia** \1 & 3 are usually 'fā-sh(ē-)ə, 2 is usually 'fa-\ *noun, plural* **-ci·ae** \-shē-ˌē\ *or* **-cias** [Italian, from Latin, band, bandage; akin to Middle Irish *basc* necklace] (1563)
**1 :** a flat usually horizontal member of a building having the form of a flat band or broad fillet: as **a :** a flat piece used as a molding **b :** a horizontal piece (as a board) covering the joint between the top of a wall and the projecting eaves — called also *fascia board* **c :** a nameplate over the front of a shop
**2 :** a sheet of connective tissue covering or binding together body structures; *also* : tissue of this character
**3** *or* **fa·cia** \'fā-sh(ē-)ə\ *British* : the dashboard of an automobile
— **fas·cial** \'fa-sh(ē-)əl\ *adjective*

**fas·ci·at·ed** \'fa-shē-ˌā-təd\ *adjective* (circa 1835)
**1 :** exhibiting fasciation
**2 :** arranged in fascicles

**fas·ci·a·tion** \ˌfa-s(h)ē-'ā-shən\ *noun* (1677)
: a malformation of plant stems commonly manifested as enlargement and flattening as if several stems were fused

**fas·ci·cle** \'fa-si-kəl\ *noun* [Latin *fasciculus*, diminutive of *fascis*] (15th century)
**1 :** a small or slender bundle (as of pine needles or nerve fibers)
**2 :** one of the divisions of a book published in parts
— **fas·ci·cled** \-kəld\ *adjective*

**fas·cic·u·lar** \fə-'si-kyə-lər, fa-\ *adjective* (1816)
: of, relating to, or consisting of fascicles or fasciculi
— **fas·cic·u·lar·ly** *adverb*

**fas·cic·u·late** \-lət\ *also* **fas·cic·u·lat·ed** \-ˌlā-təd\ *adjective* (1794)
: FASCICULAR

**fas·cic·u·la·tion** \fə-ˌsi-kyə-'lā-shən, fa-\ *noun* (1938)
: muscular twitching involving the simultaneous contraction of contiguous groups of muscle fibers

**fas·ci·cule** \'fa-si-ˌkyü\ *noun* [French, from Latin *fasciculus*] (1880)
: FASCICLE 2

**fas·cic·u·lus** \fə-'si-kyə-ləs, fa-\ *noun, plural* **-li** \-ˌlī\ [New Latin, from Latin] (1713)
**1 :** a slender bundle of anatomical fibers
**2 :** FASCICLE 2

**fas·ci·nate** \'fa-s°n-ˌāt\ *verb* **fas·ci·nat·ed; fas·ci·nat·ing** \'fas-ˌnā-tiŋ, 'fa-s°n-ˌā-\ [Latin *fascinatus*, past participle of *fascinare*, from *fascinum* evil spell] (1598)
*transitive verb*
**1** *obsolete* : BEWITCH
**2 a :** to transfix and hold spellbound by an irresistible power ⟨believed that the serpent could *fascinate* its prey⟩ **b :** to command the interest of : ALLURE ⟨was *fascinated* by carnivals⟩
*intransitive verb*
: to be irresistibly attractive ⟨the novel's flamboyant cover *fascinates*⟩ ◆
**synonym** see ATTRACT

**fas·ci·nat·ing** *adjective* (1648)

: extremely interesting or charming : CAPTIVATING
— **fas·ci·nat·ing·ly** \-ˌā-tiŋ-lē\ *adverb*

**fas·ci·na·tion** \ˌfa-s°n-'ā-shən\ *noun* (1605)
**1 a :** the quality or power of fascinating **b** : something fascinating
**2 :** the state of being fascinated

**fas·ci·na·tor** \'fa-s°n-ˌā-tər\ *noun* (1750)
**1 :** one that fascinates
**2 :** a woman's lightweight head scarf usually of crochet or lace

**fas·cine** \fa-'sēn, fə-\ *noun* [French, from Latin *fascina*, from *fascis*] (circa 1688)
: a long bundle of sticks of wood bound together and used for such purposes as filling ditches and making revetments for riverbanks

**fas·ci·o·li·a·sis** \fə-ˌsē-ə-'lī-ə-səs, -ˌsī-\ *noun, plural* **-a·ses** \-ˌsēz\ [New Latin, from *Fasciola*, genus of flukes + *-iasis*] (1890)
: infestation with or disease caused by liver flukes (genus *Fasciola*)

**fas·cism** \'fa-ˌshi-zəm *also* 'fa-ˌsi-\ *noun* [Italian *fascismo*, from *fascio* bundle, fasces, group, from Latin *fascis* bundle & *fasces* fasces] (1921)
**1** *often capitalized* : a political philosophy, movement, or regime (as that of the Fascisti) that exalts nation and often race above the individual and that stands for a centralized autocratic government headed by a dictatorial leader, severe economic and social regimentation, and forcible suppression of opposition
**2 :** a tendency toward or actual exercise of strong autocratic or dictatorial control ⟨early instances of army *fascism* and brutality —J. W. Aldridge⟩ ◆
— **fas·cist** \-shist *also* -sist\ *noun or adjective, often capitalized*
— **fas·cis·tic** \fa-'shis-tik *also* -'sis-\ *adjective, often capitalized*
— **fas·cis·ti·cal·ly** \-ti-k(ə-)lē\ *adverb, often capitalized*

**Fa·sci·sta** \fä-'shē-(ˌ)stä\ *noun, plural* **-sti** \-(ˌ)stē\ [Italian, from *fascio*] (1921)
: a member of an Italian political organization under Mussolini governing Italy 1922–1943 according to the principles of fascism

**fash** \'fash\ *verb* [Middle French *fascher*, from (assumed) Vulgar Latin *fastidiare* to disgust, from Latin *fastidium* disgust — more at FASTIDIOUS] (1533)
*chiefly Scottish* : VEX
— **fash** *noun, chiefly Scottish*

**¹fash·ion** \'fa-sh°n\ *noun* [Middle English *facioun*, *fasoun* shape, manner, from Middle French *façon*, from Latin *faction-*, *factio* act of making, faction, from *facere* to make — more at DO] (14th century)
**1 a :** the make or form of something **b** *archaic* : KIND, SORT
**2 a :** a distinctive or peculiar and often habitual manner or way ⟨he will, after his sour *fashion*, tell you —Shakespeare⟩ **b :** mode of action or operation ⟨assembled in an orderly *fashion*⟩
**3 a :** a prevailing custom, usage, or style **b** (1) : the prevailing style (as in dress) during a particular time (2) : a garment in such a style ⟨always wears the latest *fashions*⟩ **c :** social standing or prominence especially as signalized by dress or conduct ⟨men and women of *fashion*⟩ ☆
— **after a fashion** : in an approximate or rough way ⟨became an artist *after a fashion*⟩

**²fashion** *transitive verb* **fash·ioned; fash·ion·ing** \'fash-niŋ, 'fa-sh°n-iŋ\ (15th century)
**1 a :** to give shape or form to : MOLD **b :** ALTER, TRANSFORM **c :** to mold into a particular character by influencing or training **d :** to make or construct usually with the use of imagination and ingenuity ⟨*fashion* a lamp from an old churn⟩
**2 :** FIT, ADAPT
**3** *obsolete* : CONTRIVE
— **fash·ion·er** \'fash-nər, 'fa-sh°n-ər\ *noun*

☆ SYNONYMS
**Fashion, style, mode, vogue, fad, rage, craze** mean the usage accepted by those who want to be up-to-date. FASHION is the most general term and applies to any way of dressing, behaving, writing, or performing that is favored at any one time or place ⟨the current *fashion*⟩. STYLE often implies a distinctive fashion adopted by people of taste ⟨a media baron used to traveling in *style*⟩. MODE suggests the fashion of the moment among those anxious to appear elegant and sophisticated ⟨slim bodies are the *mode* at this resort⟩. VOGUE stresses the wide acceptance of a fashion ⟨short skirts are back in *vogue*⟩. FAD suggests caprice in taking up or in dropping a fashion ⟨last year's *fad* is over⟩. RAGE and CRAZE stress intense enthusiasm in adopting a fad ⟨Cajun food was the *rage* nearly everywhere for a time⟩ ⟨crossword puzzles once seemed just a passing *craze* but have lasted⟩. See in addition METHOD.

◇ WORD HISTORY
**fascinate** The word *fascinate* has its roots in a world where witchcraft and enchantment were taken much more seriously than they are in our time. Synonyms such as *bewitch* and *charm* have a magical side that is still apparent enough from the literal meanings of the words themselves, but this aspect of *fascinate* is clear only if we look at its etymology. In Latin the verb *fascinare* meant "to cast a spell on, bewitch" and was a derivative of a noun *fascinum*. The original meaning of *fascinum* seems to have been "bewitchment," though this usage is very sparsely attested. More frequently *fascinum* referred to a sort of counter charm, an amulet worn around the neck to avert the evil eye. *Fascinum* is similar in sound to Greek *baskanos* "malicious" (with derivatives such as *baskanein* "to avert the evil eye" and *baskanion* "charm, amulet"), but the ultimate source of both words is uncertain.

**fascism** The words *fascism* and *fascist* have long been associated with the Fascisti of Benito Mussolini and the bundle of rods called *fasces*, which the Fascisti adopted as a symbol of authoritarianism. However, Mussolini did not introduce the word *fascista* when his black-shirted organization, the *Fasci di combattimento*, was organized in 1919, nor did the fasces have any direct connection with the origin of *fascista*. In Italian, the word *fascio* (plural *fasci*) means literally "bundle," and figuratively "group." From at least 1872 *fascio* was used in the names of labor and agrarian unions, and in October 1914 a political coalition was formed called the *Fascio rivoluzionario d'azione internazionalista* ("revolutionary group for international action"), which advocated Italian participation in World War I on the side of the Allies. Members of this group were first called *fascisti* in January 1915. Although Mussolini was closely associated with this interventionist movement, it had no direct link with the postwar *Fasci di combattimento*, and in 1919 the word *fascista* was already in political circulation. Of course, it is to the Fascisti in their 1919 incarnation—who seized power in Italy three years later—that we owe the customary meanings of our *fascism* and *fascist*.

\ə\ abut \ᵊ\ kitten \ər\ further \a\ ash \ā\ ace \ä\ mop, mar \au̇\ out \ch\ chin \e\ bet \ē\ easy \g\ go \i\ hit \ī\ ice \j\ job \ŋ\ sing \ō\ go \ȯ\ law \ȯi\ boy \th\ thin \t͟h\ the \ü\ loot \u̇\ foot \y\ yet \zh\ vision *see also* Guide to Pronunciation

**¹fash·ion·able** \'fash-nə-bəl, 'fa-sh°n-ə-\ *adjective* (1606)
**1 :** conforming to the custom, fashion, or established mode
**2 :** of or relating to the world of fashion
— **fash·ion·abil·i·ty** \,fash-nə-'bi-lə-tē, ,fa-sh°n-ə-\ *noun*
— **fash·ion·able·ness** \'fash-nə-bəl-nəs, 'fa-shə-\ *noun*
— **fash·ion·ably** \-blē\ *adverb*
**²fashionable** *noun* (circa 1800)
**:** a fashionable person
**fash·ion·mon·ger** \'fa-sh°n-,mäŋ-gər, -,məŋ-\ *noun* (1599)
**:** one that studies, imitates, or sets the fashion
**fashion plate** *noun* (1851)
**1 :** an illustration of a clothing style
**2 :** a person who dresses in the latest fashions
**¹fast** \'fast\ *adjective* [Middle English, from Old English *fæst*; akin to Old High German *festi* firm, Old Norse *fastr*, Armenian *hast*] (before 12th century)
**1 a :** firmly fixed ⟨roots *fast* in the ground⟩ **b :** tightly shut ⟨the drawers were *fast*⟩ **c :** adhering firmly **d :** not easily freed **:** STUCK ⟨a ball *fast* in the mouth of the cannon⟩ **e :** STABLE ⟨movable items were made *fast* to the deck⟩
**2 :** firmly loyal ⟨became *fast* friends⟩
**3 a :** characterized by quick motion, operation, or effect: (1) **:** moving or able to move rapidly **:** SWIFT (2) **:** taking a comparatively short time (3) **:** imparting quickness of motion ⟨a *fast* bowler⟩ (4) **:** accomplished quickly (5) **:** agile of mind; *especially* **:** quick to learn ⟨a class for *fast* students⟩ **b :** conducive to rapidity of play or action **c** (1) *of a timepiece or weighing device* **:** indicating in advance of what is correct (2) **:** according to or being daylight saving time **d :** contributing to a shortening of exposure time ⟨*fast* film⟩ **e :** acquired with unusually little effort and often by shady or dishonest methods ⟨had a keen eye for a *fast* buck —R. A. Keith⟩
**4 a :** securely attached ⟨a rope *fast* to the wharf⟩ **b :** TENACIOUS ⟨a *fast* hold on her purse⟩
**5 a** *archaic* **:** sound asleep **b** *of sleep* **:** not easily disturbed
**6 :** not fading or changing color readily
**7 a :** WILD ⟨a pretty *fast* crowd⟩ **b :** sexually promiscuous
**8 :** resistant to change (as from destructive action or fading) ⟨*fast* dyes⟩ — often used in combination ⟨sun*fast*⟩ ⟨acid-*fast* bacteria⟩ ☆
**²fast** *adverb* (before 12th century)
**1 :** in a firm or fixed manner ⟨stuck *fast*⟩
**2 :** in a sound manner **:** DEEPLY ⟨*fast* asleep⟩
**3 a :** in a rapid manner **:** QUICKLY **b :** in quick succession ⟨kaleidoscopic impressions that come so thick and *fast* —M. B. Tucker⟩
**4 :** in a reckless or dissipated manner
**5 :** ahead of a correct time or schedule
**6** *archaic* **:** CLOSE, NEAR
**³fast** *intransitive verb* [Middle English, from Old English *fæstan*] (before 12th century)
**1 :** to abstain from food
**2 :** to eat sparingly or abstain from some foods
**⁴fast** *noun* (before 12th century)
**1 :** the practice of fasting
**2 :** a time of fasting
**⁵fast** *noun* [alteration of Middle English *fest*, from Old Norse *festr* rope, mooring cable, from *fastr* firm] (15th century)
**:** something that fastens (as a mooring line) or holds a fastening
**fast and loose** *adverb* (1557)
**1 :** in a reckless or irresponsible manner ⟨played *fast and loose* with the public purse strings —Paul Stuewe⟩
**2 :** in a craftily deceitful way ⟨manipulated evidence . . . and played *fast and loose* with the truth —C. V. Woodward⟩
**fast·back** \'fas(t)-,bak\ *noun* (1954)
**:** an automobile with a roof having a long curving downward slope to the rear; *also* **:** the back of such an automobile
**fast·ball** \'fas(t)-,bȯl\ *noun* (1912)

**:** a baseball pitch thrown at full speed and often rising slightly as it nears the plate
— **fast·ball·er** \-,bȯ-lər\ *noun*
**fast break** *noun* (circa 1949)
**:** a quick offensive drive toward a goal (as in basketball) in an attempt to score before the opponent's defense is set up
— **fast-break** *intransitive verb*
**fas·ten** \'fa-s°n\ *verb* **fas·tened; fas·ten·ing** \'fas-niŋ, 'fa-s°n-iŋ\ [Middle English *fastnen*, from Old English *fæstnian* to make fast; akin to Old High German *festinōn* to make fast, Old English *fæst* fast] (before 12th century)
*transitive verb*
**1 a :** to attach especially by pinning, tying, or nailing **b :** to make fast and secure **c :** to fix firmly or securely **d :** to secure against opening
**2 :** to fix or set steadily ⟨*fastened* her attention on the main problem⟩
**3 :** to take a firm grip with ⟨the dog *fastened* its teeth in the shoe⟩
**4 a :** to attach (oneself) persistently and usually objectionably **b :** IMPOSE ⟨*fastened* the blame on the wrong person⟩
*intransitive verb*
**1 :** to become fast or fixed
**2 a :** to take a firm grip or hold **b :** to focus attention ☆
— **fas·ten·er** \'fas-nər, 'fa-s°n-ər\ *noun*
**fas·ten·ing** *noun* (12th century)
**:** something that fastens **:** FASTENER
**fast-food** \'fas(t)-,füd\ *adjective* (1951)
**1 :** of, relating to, or specializing in food that can be prepared and served quickly ⟨a *fast-food* restaurant⟩
**2 :** designed for ready availability, use, or consumption and with little consideration given to quality or significance ⟨*fast-food* TV programming⟩
— **fast food** *noun*
**¹fast-for·ward** \,fas(t)-'fȯr-wərd\ *noun, often attributive* (1948)
**1 :** a function of a tape player by which the tape is advanced at a higher speed than when it is playing normally
**2 :** a state or an instance of rapid advancement ⟨put her career in *fast-forward*⟩
**²fast-forward** (1974)
*transitive verb*
**1 :** to advance (a magnetic tape) using the fast-forward of a tape player
**2 :** to bypass (as a commercial) by fast-forwarding
*intransitive verb*
**1 :** to advance a magnetic tape using the fast-forward
**2 :** to proceed rapidly forward especially in time ⟨*fast-forward* to the future⟩
**fas·tid·i·ous** \fa-'sti-dē-əs, fə-\ *adjective* [Middle English, from Latin *fastidiosus*, from *fastidium* disgust, probably from *fastus* arrogance (probably akin to Latin *fastigium* top) + *taedium* irksomeness — more at TEDIUM] (15th century)
**1** *archaic* **:** SCORNFUL
**2 a :** having high and often capricious standards **:** difficult to please ⟨critics . . . so *fastidious* that they can talk only to a small circle of initiates —Granville Hicks⟩ **b :** showing or demanding excessive delicacy or care **c :** reflecting a meticulous, sensitive, or demanding attitude ⟨*fastidious* workmanship⟩
**3 :** having complex nutritional requirements ⟨*fastidious* microorganisms⟩
— **fas·tid·i·ous·ly** *adverb*
— **fas·tid·i·ous·ness** *noun*
**fas·ti·gi·ate** \fa-'sti-jē-ət\ *adjective* [probably from (assumed) New Latin *fastigiatus*, from Latin *fastigium* — more at BRISTLE] (1662)
**:** narrowing toward the top; *especially* **:** having upright usually clustered branches ⟨*fastigiate* trees⟩
**fast lane** *noun* (1966)

**1 :** a traffic lane intended for vehicles traveling at higher speeds
**2 :** a way of life marked by a fast pace and usually the pursuit of immediate gratification
**3 :** FAST TRACK
— **fast-lane** *adjective*
**fast·ness** \'fas(t)-nəs\ *noun* (before 12th century)
**1 :** the quality or state of being fast: as **a :** the quality or state of being fixed **b :** the quality or state of being swift **c :** colorfast quality **d :** resistance (as of an organism) to the action of a usually toxic substance
**2 a :** a fortified or secure place **b :** a remote and secluded place ⟨vacationed in their mountain *fastness*⟩
**Fast of Esther** (1887)
**:** a Jewish fast day observed the day before Purim in commemoration of a fast proclaimed by Queen Esther
**fast-talk** \'fas(t)-,tȯk\ *transitive verb* (1946)
**:** to influence or persuade by fluent, facile, and usually deceptive or tricky talk ⟨*fast-talked* him into buying a lemon⟩
**¹fast-track** \'fas(t)-,trak\ *adjective* (1967)
**1 :** of, relating to, or moving along a fast track ⟨*fast-track* executives⟩
**2 :** of, relating to, or being a construction procedure in which work on a building begins before designs are completed
**²fast-track** *transitive verb* (1971)
**:** to speed up the processing, production, or construction of in order to meet a goal
— **fast-track·er** *noun*
**fast track** *noun* (1980)
**:** a course leading to rapid advancement or success
**fast-twitch** \'fas(t)-,twich\ *adjective* (1970)
**:** of, relating to, or being muscle fiber that contracts quickly especially during brief high-intensity physical activity requiring strength — compare SLOW-TWITCH
**fas·tu·ous** \'fas-chə-wəs\ *adjective* [Latin *fastuosus*, from *fastus* arrogance] (1638)
**1 :** HAUGHTY, ARROGANT ⟨a *fastuous* air of finality —Carl Van Vechten⟩

---

☆ **SYNONYMS**
**Fast, rapid, swift, fleet, quick, speedy, hasty, expeditious** mean moving, proceeding, or acting with celerity. FAST and RAPID are very close in meaning, but FAST applies particularly to the thing that moves ⟨*fast* horses⟩ and RAPID to the movement itself ⟨*rapid* current⟩. SWIFT suggests great rapidity coupled with ease of movement ⟨returned the ball with one *swift* stroke⟩. FLEET adds the implication of lightness and nimbleness ⟨*fleet* runners⟩. QUICK suggests promptness and the taking of little time ⟨a *quick* wit⟩. SPEEDY implies quickness of successful accomplishment ⟨*speedy* delivery of mail⟩ and may also suggest unusual velocity. HASTY suggests hurry and precipitousness and often connotes carelessness ⟨a *hasty* inspection⟩. EXPEDITIOUS suggests efficiency together with rapidity of accomplishment ⟨the *expeditious* handling of an order⟩.

**Fasten, fix, attach, affix** mean to make something stay firmly in place. FASTEN implies an action such as tying, buttoning, nailing, locking, or otherwise securing ⟨*fasten* the reins to a post⟩. FIX usually implies a driving in, implanting, or embedding ⟨*fixed* the stake in the ground⟩. ATTACH suggests a connecting or uniting by a bond, link, or tie in order to keep things together ⟨*attach* the W-2 form here⟩. AFFIX implies an imposing of one thing on another by gluing, impressing, or nailing ⟨*affix* your address label here⟩.

**2** : OSTENTATIOUS, SHOWY ⟨disdained *fastuous* ceremonies⟩

**¹fat** \'fat\ *adjective* **fat·ter; fat·test** [Middle English, from Old English *fætt,* past participle of *fætan* to cram; akin to Old High German *feizit* fat] (before 12th century)
**1** : notable for having an unusual amount of fat: **a** : PLUMP **b** : OBESE **c** *of a meat animal* : fattened for market **d** *of food* : OILY, GREASY
**2 a** : well filled out : THICK, BIG ⟨a *fat* book⟩ **b** : full in tone and quality : RICH ⟨a gorgeous *fat* bass voice —*Irish Digest*⟩ **c** : well stocked ⟨a *fat* larder⟩ **d** : PROSPEROUS, WEALTHY ⟨grew *fat* on the war —*Time*⟩ **e** : being substantial and impressive ⟨a *fat* bank account⟩
**3 a** : richly rewarding or profitable ⟨a *fat* part in a movie⟩ ⟨a *fat* contract⟩ **b** : practically non-existent ⟨a *fat* chance⟩
**4** : PRODUCTIVE, FERTILE ⟨a *fat* year for crops⟩
**5** : STUPID, FOOLISH
**6** : being swollen ⟨got a *fat* lip from the fight⟩
**7** *of a baseball pitch* : easy to hit
— **fat·ness** *noun*

**²fat** *transitive verb* **fat·ted; fat·ting** (before 12th century)
: to make fat : FATTEN

**³fat** *noun* (14th century)
**1** : animal tissue consisting chiefly of cells distended with greasy or oily matter
**2 a** : oily or greasy matter making up the bulk of adipose tissue and often abundant in seeds **b** : any of numerous compounds of carbon, hydrogen, and oxygen that are glycerides of fatty acids, are the chief constituents of plant and animal fat, are a major class of energy-rich food, and are soluble in organic solvents but not in water **c** : a solid or semisolid fat as distinguished from an oil
**3** : the best or richest part
**4** : OBESITY
**5** : something in excess : SUPERFLUITY ⟨trim the *fat* from the news operation —Ray Olson⟩
— **fat·less** \-ləs\ *adjective*

**fa·tal** \'fā-t°l\ *adjective* [Middle English, from Middle French & Latin; Middle French, from Latin *fatalis,* from *fatum*] (14th century)
**1** *obsolete* : FATED
**2** : FATEFUL ⟨a *fatal* hour⟩
**3 a** : of or relating to fate **b** : resembling fate in proceeding according to a fixed sequence **c** : determining one's fate
**4 a** : causing death **b** : bringing ruin ☐
*synonym* see DEADLY

**fa·tal·ism** \-ˌi-zəm\ *noun* (1678)
: a doctrine that events are fixed in advance so that human beings are powerless to change them; *also* : a belief in or attitude determined by this doctrine
— **fa·tal·ist** \-ist\ *noun*
— **fa·tal·is·tic** \ˌfā-t°l-'is-tik\ *adjective*
— **fa·tal·is·ti·cal·ly** \-ti-k(ə-)lē\ *adverb*

**fa·tal·i·ty** \fā-'ta-lə-tē, fə-\ *noun, plural* **-ties** [Middle English, from Middle French *fatalité,* from Late Latin *fatalitat-, fatalitas,* from Latin *fatalis*] (15th century)
**1 a** : the quality or state of causing death or destruction **b** : the quality or condition of being destined for disaster
**2** : something established by fate
**3 a** : FATE 1 **b** : FATALISM
**4** : the agent or agency of fate
**5 a** : death resulting from a disaster **b** : one that experiences a fatal outcome

**fa·tal·ly** \'fā-t°l-ē\ *adverb* (15th century)
**1** : in a way determined by fate
**2** : in a manner suggesting fate or an act of fate: as **a** : in a manner resulting in death : MORTALLY ⟨*fatally* wounded⟩ **b** : beyond repair : IRREVOCABLY **c** : in a manner resulting in ruin or evil ⟨it is *fatally* easy to pass off our prejudices as our opinions —W. F. Hambly⟩ **d** : in a manner that cannot be easily resisted ⟨thinks she is *fatally* attractive —J. W. Krutch⟩

**fa·ta mor·ga·na** \ˌfä-tə-mòr-'gä-nə, -'ga-\ *noun* [Italian, literally, Morgan le Fay (sorceress of Arthurian legend)] (1818)

: MIRAGE

**fat·back** \'fat-ˌbak\ *noun* (1903)
: the strip of fat from the back of a hog carcass usually cured by drying and salting

**fat body** *noun* (1869)
: a fatty tissue especially of nearly mature insect larvae that serves as a food reserve

**fat cat** *noun* (1928)
**1 a** : a wealthy contributor to a political campaign fund **b** : a wealthy and privileged person **c** : BIG SHOT
**2** : a lethargic complacent person
— **fat–cat** \'fat-ˌkat\ *adjective*

**fat cell** *noun* (1845)
: one of the fat-laden cells making up adipose tissue

**fat depot** *noun* (1946)
: ADIPOSE TISSUE

**¹fate** \'fāt\ *noun* [Middle English, from Middle French or Latin; Middle French, from Latin *fatum,* literally, what has been spoken, from neuter of *fatus,* past participle of *fari* to speak — more at BAN] (14th century)
**1** : the principle or determining cause or will by which things in general are believed to come to be as they are or events to happen as they do : DESTINY
**2 a** : an inevitable and often adverse outcome, condition, or end **b** : DISASTER; *especially* : DEATH
**3 a** : final outcome **b** : the expected result of normal development ⟨prospective *fate* of embryonic cells⟩
**4** *plural, capitalized* : the three goddesses who determine the course of human life in classical mythology ☆

**²fate** *transitive verb* **fat·ed; fat·ing** (1601)
: DESTINE; *also* : DOOM

**fat·ed** *adjective* (circa 1606)
: decreed, controlled, or marked by fate

**fate·ful** \'fāt-fəl\ *adjective* (circa 1720)
**1** : having a quality of ominous prophecy ⟨a *fateful* remark⟩
**2 a** : involving momentous consequences : DECISIVE ⟨made his *fateful* decision to declare war —W. L. Shirer⟩ **b** : DEADLY, CATASTROPHIC
**3** : controlled by fate : FOREORDAINED
*synonym* see OMINOUS
*usage* see FATAL
— **fate·ful·ly** \-fə-lē\ *adverb*
— **fate·ful·ness** *noun*

**fat farm** *noun* (1969)
: a health spa that specializes in weight reduction

**fat·head** \'fat-ˌhed\ *noun* (1842)
: a stupid person
— **fat·head·ed** \-'he-dəd\ *adjective*
— **fat·head·ed·ly** *adverb*
— **fat·head·ed·ness** *noun*

**¹fa·ther** \'fä-thər, 'fà-\ *noun* [Middle English *fader,* from Old English *fæder;* akin to Old High German *fater* father, Latin *pater,* Greek *patēr*] (before 12th century)
**1 a** : a man who has begotten a child; *also* : SIRE 3 **b** *capitalized* (1) : GOD 1 (2) : the first person of the Trinity
**2** : FOREFATHER
**3 a** : one related to another in a way suggesting that of father to child **b** : an old man — used as a respectful form of address
**4** *often capitalized* : a pre-Scholastic Christian writer accepted by the church as an authoritative witness to its teaching and practice — called also *church father*
**5 a** : one that originates or institutes ⟨the *father* of modern science⟩ **b** : SOURCE ⟨the sun, the *father* of warmth and light —Lena M. Whitney⟩ **c** : PROTOTYPE
**6** : a priest of the regular clergy; *broadly* : PRIEST — used especially as a title
**7** : one of the leading men (as of a city) — usually used in plural
— **fa·ther·hood** \-ˌhud\ *noun*
— **fa·ther·less** \-ləs\ *adjective*
— **fa·ther·like** \-ˌlīk\ *adjective or adverb*

**²father** *verb* **fa·thered; fa·ther·ing** \'fäth-riŋ, 'fàth-; 'fä-thə-, 'fà-\ (15th century)
*transitive verb*
**1 a** : BEGET **b** : to make oneself the founder, producer, or author of ⟨*fathered* the improvement plan⟩ **c** : to accept responsibility for
**2 a** : to fix the paternity or origin of **b** : to place responsibility for the origin or cause of ⟨collected gossip and *fathered* it on responsible men —J. A. Williamson⟩
**3** : FOIST, IMPOSE
*intransitive verb*
: to care for or look after someone as a father might

**Father Christmas** *noun*
*British* : SANTA CLAUS

**father figure** *noun* (1934)
: one often of particular power or influence who serves as an emotional substitute for a father

**father image** *noun* (1937)
: an idealization of one's father often projected onto someone to whom one looks for guidance and protection

**father-in-law** \'fä-thə-rən-ˌlo, -thərn-ˌlo, 'fà-\ *noun, plural* **fa·thers–in–law** \-thər-zən-\ (14th century)

---

☆ **SYNONYMS**
**Fate, destiny, lot, portion, doom** mean a predetermined state or end. FATE implies an inevitable and usually an adverse outcome ⟨the *fate* of the submarine is unknown⟩. DESTINY implies something foreordained and often suggests a great or noble course or end ⟨the country's *destiny* to be a model of liberty to the world⟩. LOT and PORTION imply a distribution by fate or destiny, LOT suggesting blind chance ⟨it was her *lot* to die childless⟩, PORTION implying the apportioning of good and evil ⟨remorse was his daily *portion*⟩. DOOM distinctly implies a grim or calamitous fate ⟨if the rebellion fails, his *doom* is certain⟩.

---

☐ **USAGE**
**fatal** *Fatal* and *fateful* have long shared a meaning ⟨a *fatal* or *fateful* day⟩ and in the second half of the 20th century a curious opinion has grown up that *fatal* ought to be restricted to its fourth sense and its second sense abandoned to *fateful.* The purpose of this newly imposed distinction is presumably to tidy up the language and to reduce confusion. But these uses seem plain enough ⟨at Pearl Harbor on the *fatal* day —David McCullough⟩ ⟨weeping when she thinks of the *fatal* moment when they first met —Samuel Eliot Morison⟩. Here, as in most similar uses of *fatal,* the direction of the portent is toward evil or the undesirable. *Fateful* may be used in a less ominous way ⟨the day when the *fateful* letter from the college admission office is due —James B. Conant⟩. Sometimes *fatal* is similarly used ⟨when the *fatal* call comes over the public address system—"Jones, city desk"—Jones can feel his colleagues thinking as he walks past them, "I hope he gets a lousy assignment . . ." —Robert Darnton⟩. *Fatal* doesn't share its sense "causing death or destruction" ⟨a *fatal* shooting⟩. This sense is also used frequently with weakened force ⟨tediousness is the most *fatal* of all faults —Samuel Johnson⟩ ⟨to assume that the listeners know all about it already . . . is a *fatal* mistake —George Bernard Shaw⟩.

---

**1 :** the father of one's spouse
**2** *archaic* **:** STEPFATHER
**fa·ther·land** \'fä-thər-,land, 'fä-\ *noun* (12th century)
**1 :** the native land or country of one's father or ancestors
**2 :** one's native land or country
**fa·ther·ly** \'fä-thər-lē, 'fä-\ *adjective* (15th century)
**1 :** of, relating to, or befitting a father ⟨*fatherly* responsibilities⟩
**2 :** resembling a father (as in affection or care) ⟨a *fatherly* old man⟩
— **fa·ther·li·ness** \-lē-nəs\ *noun*
— **fatherly** *adverb*
**Father's Day** *noun* (1927)
**:** the third Sunday in June appointed for the honoring of fathers
**¹fath·om** \'fa-thəm\ *noun* [Middle English *fadme*, from Old English *fæthm* outstretched arms, length of the outstretched arms; akin to Old Norse *fathmr* fathom, Latin *patēre* to be open, *pandere* to spread out, Greek *petannynai*] (before 12th century)
**1 :** a unit of length equal to six feet (1.83 meters) used especially for measuring the depth of water
**2 :** COMPREHENSION
**²fathom** (1607)
*intransitive verb*
**1 :** PROBE
**2 :** to take soundings
*transitive verb*
**1 :** to measure by a sounding line
**2 :** to penetrate and come to understand ⟨couldn't *fathom* the problem⟩
— **fath·om·able** \'fa-thə-mə-bəl\ *adjective*
**Fa·thom·e·ter** \fa-'thä-mə-tər, 'fa-thə-,mē-\ *trademark*
— used for a sonic depth finder
**fath·om·less** \'fa-thəm-ləs\ *adjective* (1638)
**:** incapable of being fathomed
— **fath·om·less·ly** *adverb*
— **fath·om·less·ness** *noun*
**fa·tid·ic** \fā-'ti-dik, fə-\ *or* **fa·tid·i·cal** \-di-kəl\ *adjective* [Latin *fatidicus*, from *fatum* fate + *dicere* to say — more at DICTION] (1607)
**:** of or relating to prophecy
**fa·ti·ga·ble** \fə-'tē-gə-bəl, 'fa-ti-gə-\ *adjective* (1608)
**:** susceptible to fatigue
— **fa·ti·ga·bil·i·ty** \fə-,tē-gə-'bi-lə-tē, ,fa-ti-gə-\ *noun*
**¹fa·tigue** \fə-'tēg\ *noun* [French, from Middle French, from *fatiguer* to fatigue, from Latin *fatigare*; akin to Latin af*fatim* sufficiently] (1669)
**1 a :** LABOR **b :** manual or menial work performed by military personnel **c** *plural* **:** the uniform or work clothing worn on fatigue and in the field
**2 a :** weariness or exhaustion from labor, exertion, or stress **b :** the temporary loss of power to respond induced in a sensory receptor or motor end organ by continued stimulation
**3 :** the tendency of a material to break under repeated stress
**²fatigue** *verb* **fa·tigued; fa·tigu·ing** (1693)
*transitive verb*
**1 :** to weary with labor or exertion
**2 :** to induce a condition of fatigue in
*intransitive verb*
**:** to suffer fatigue
**synonym** see TIRE
— **fa·tigu·ing·ly** \-'tē-giŋ-lē\ *adverb*
**³fatigue** *adjective* (1774)
**1 :** consisting of, done, or used in fatigue ⟨*fatigue* detail⟩
**2 :** belonging to fatigues ⟨a *fatigue* cap⟩
**fat·ling** \'fat-liŋ\ *noun* (circa 1534)
**:** a young animal fattened for slaughter
**fat·ly** *adverb* (15th century)
**1 :** RICHLY
**2 :** in the manner of one that is fat ⟨waddled *fatly*⟩

**3 :** in a smug manner **:** COMPLACENTLY ⟨snickered *fatly*⟩
**fats·hed·era** \fats-'he-d(ə-)rə, 'fat-'se-\ *noun* [New Latin *Fatsia*, genus of shrubs + *Hedera*, genus of vines (from Latin, ivy)] (1948)
**:** a vigorous upright hybrid ornamental foliage plant (*Hedera helix* × *Aralia elata*) with glossy deeply lobed palmate leaves
**fat·so** \'fat-(,)sō\ *noun, plural* **fat·soes** [probably from *Fats*, nickname for a fat person + *-o*] (1944)
**:** a fat person — often used disparagingly
**fat·stock** \-,stäk\ *noun* (1880)
*chiefly British* **:** livestock that is fat and ready for market
**fat–tailed sheep** \'fat-,tāld-\ *noun* (1842)
**:** a coarse-wooled mutton sheep that has great quantities of fat on each side of the tail bones
**fat·ten** \'fa-tⁿn\ *verb* **fat·tened; fat·ten·ing** \'fat-niŋ, 'fa-tⁿn-iŋ\ (1552)
*transitive verb*
**1 a :** to make fat, fleshy, or plump; *especially* **:** to feed (as a stock animal) for slaughter **b :** to make more substantial
**2 :** to make fertile
*intransitive verb*
**:** to become fat
— **fat·ten·er** \'fat-nər, 'fa-tⁿn-ər\ *noun*
**fat·tish** \'fa-tish\ *adjective* (14th century)
**:** somewhat fat
**¹fat·ty** \'fa-tē\ *adjective* **fat·ti·er; -est** (14th century)
**1 :** containing fat especially in unusual amounts; *also* **:** unduly stout **:** CORPULENT
**2 :** GREASY
**3 :** derived from or chemically related to fat
— **fat·ti·ness** *noun*
**²fatty** *noun, plural* **fat·ties** (1797)
**:** one that is fat; *especially* **:** an overweight person
**fatty acid** *noun* (circa 1872)
**1 :** any of numerous saturated aliphatic monocarboxylic acids $C_nH_{2n+1}COOH$ (as acetic acid) including many that occur naturally usually in the form of esters in fats, waxes, and essential oils
**2 :** any of the saturated or unsaturated monocarboxylic acids (as palmitic acid) usually with an even number of carbon atoms that occur naturally in the form of glycerides in fats and fatty oils
**fa·tu·ity** \fə-'tü-ət-ē, fa-, -'chü-, -'tyü-\ *noun, plural* **-ities** [Middle French *fatuité* foolishness, from Latin *fatuitat-, fatuitas*, from *fatuus*] (1538)
**1 a :** something foolish or stupid **b :** STUPIDITY, FOOLISHNESS
**2** *archaic* **:** IMBECILITY, DEMENTIA
**fat·u·ous** \'fa-chü-əs, -tyü-\ *adjective* [Latin *fatuus* foolish] (1633)
**:** complacently or inanely foolish **:** SILLY
**synonym** see SIMPLE
— **fat·u·ous·ly** *adverb*
— **fat·u·ous·ness** *noun*
**fat·wa** \'fɔt-wə\ *noun* [Arabic *fatwā*] (1947)
**:** a legal opinion or decree handed down by an Islamic religious leader
**fat–wit·ted** \'fat-,wi-təd\ *adjective* (1596)
**:** STUPID, IDIOTIC
**fat·wood** \'fat-,wùd\ *noun* (1904)
*chiefly Southern* **:** LIGHTWOOD
**fau·bourg** \fō-'bùr\ *noun* [Middle English *fabour*, from Middle French *fauxbourg*, alteration of *forsbourg*, from Old French *forsborc*, from *fors* outside + *borc* town — more at BOURG] (15th century)
**1 :** SUBURB; *especially* **:** a suburb of a French city
**2 :** a city quarter
**fau·ces** \'fɔ-,sēz\ *noun plural but singular or plural in construction* [Latin, plural, throat, *fauces*] (1541)
**:** the narrow passage from the mouth to the pharynx situated between the soft palate and the base of the tongue
— **fau·cial** \'fɔ-shəl\ *adjective*

**fau·cet** \'fɔ-sət, 'fäs-\ *noun* [Middle English, bung, faucet, from Middle French *fausset* bung, perhaps from *fausser* to damage, from Late Latin *falsare* to falsify, from Latin *falsus* false] (15th century)
**:** a fixture for drawing or regulating the flow of liquid especially from a pipe
**faugh** \*a strong p-sound or lip trill; often read as* 'fò(k)\ *interjection* (1542)
— used to express contempt, disgust, or abhorrence
**¹fault** \'fòlt, *in poetry also* 'fòt\ *noun* [Middle English *faute*, from Middle French, from (assumed) Vulgar Latin *fallita*, from feminine of *fallitus*, past participle of Latin *fallere* to deceive, disappoint] (14th century)
**1** *obsolete* **:** LACK
**2 a :** WEAKNESS, FAILING; *especially* **:** a moral weakness less serious than a vice **b :** a physical or intellectual imperfection or impairment **:** DEFECT **c :** an error especially in service in a net or racket game

**fault 5:** *1* fault with displaced strata *a, b, c, d, e; 2* scarp

**3 a :** MISDEMEANOR **b :** MISTAKE
**4 :** responsibility for wrongdoing or failure ⟨the accident was the driver's *fault*⟩
**5 :** a fracture in the crust of a planet (as the earth) or moon accompanied by a displacement of one side of the fracture with respect to the other usually in a direction parallel to the fracture ☆
— **at fault 1 :** unable to find the scent and continue chase **2 :** open to blame **:** RESPONSIBLE ⟨couldn't determine who was really *at fault*⟩
— **to a fault :** to an excessive degree ⟨precise *to a fault*⟩
**²fault** (15th century)
*intransitive verb*
**1 :** to commit a fault **:** ERR
**2 :** to fracture so as to produce a geologic fault
*transitive verb*
**1 :** to find a fault in ⟨easy to praise this book and to *fault* it —H. G. Roepke⟩
**2 :** to produce a geologic fault in
**3 :** BLAME, CENSURE ⟨can't *fault* them for not coming⟩
**fault–find·er** \'fòlt-,fīn-dər\ *noun* (1561)
**:** one given to faultfinding
**¹fault–find·ing** \-diŋ\ *adjective* (1622)
**:** disposed to find fault **:** captiously critical
**synonym** see CRITICAL
**²faultfinding** *noun* (1626)
**:** petty, nagging, or unreasonable criticism
**fault·less** \'fòlt-ləs\ *adjective* (14th century)
**:** having no fault **:** IRREPROACHABLE ⟨*faultless* workmanship⟩
— **fault·less·ly** *adverb*
— **fault·less·ness** *noun*

---

**☆ SYNONYMS**
**Fault, failing, frailty, foible, vice** mean an imperfection or weakness of character. FAULT implies a failure, not necessarily culpable, to reach some standard of perfection in disposition, action, or habit ⟨a writer of many virtues and few *faults*⟩. FAILING suggests a minor shortcoming in character ⟨being late is a *failing* of mine⟩. FRAILTY implies a general or chronic proneness to yield to temptation ⟨human *frailties*⟩. FOIBLE applies to a harmless or endearing weakness or idiosyncrasy ⟨an eccentric's charming *foibles*⟩. VICE can be a general term for any imperfection or weakness, but it often suggests violation of a moral code or the giving of offense to the moral sensibilities of others ⟨compulsive gambling was his *vice*⟩.

**fault line** *noun* (1869)
: something resembling a fault : SPLIT, RIFT ⟨a major conceptual *fault line* in foreign policy —Morton Kondracke⟩

**faulty** \'fȯl-tē\ *adjective* **fault·i·er; -est** (14th century)
: marked by fault or defect : IMPERFECT
— **fault·i·ly** \-tə-lē\ *adverb*
— **fault·i·ness** \-tē-nəs\ *noun*

**faun** \'fȯn, 'fän\ *noun* [Middle English, from Latin *faunus*, from *Faunus*] (14th century)
: a figure in Roman mythology similar to but gentler than the satyr

**fau·na** \'fȯ-nə, 'fä-\ *noun, plural* **faunas** *also* **fau·nae** \-,nē, -,nī\ [New Latin, from Latin *Fauna*, sister of Faunus] (1771)
: animal life; *especially* : the animals characteristic of a region, period, or special environment — compare FLORA
— **fau·nal** \-n°l\ *adjective*
— **fau·nal·ly** \-n°l-ē\ *adverb*

**fau·nis·tic** \fȯ-'nis-tik, fä-\ *adjective* (1881)
: of or relating to zoogeography : FAUNAL
— **fau·nis·ti·cal·ly** \-ti-k(ə-)lē\ *adverb*

**Fau·nus** \'fȯ-nəs, 'fä-\ *noun* [Latin]
: the Roman god of animals

**Faust** \'faůst\ *or* **Fau·stus** \'faů-stəs, 'fȯ-\ *noun* [German]
: a magician of German legend who enters into a compact with the devil

**Faust·ian** \'faů-stē-ən, 'fȯ-\ *adjective* (1876)
: of, relating to, resembling, or suggesting Faust; *especially* : made or done for present gain without regard for future cost or consequences ⟨a *Faustian* bargain⟩

**faute de mieux** \,fōt-də-'myœ(r), -'myœ\ *adverb* [French] (1766)
: for lack of something better or more desirable ⟨sherry made him dopey but he drank it *faute de mieux* —F. T. Marsh⟩

**fau·teuil** \fō-'tœy; 'fō-,til\ *noun, plural* **fau·teuils** \fō-'tœy; -,tilz\ [French, from Old French *faudestuel*, of Germanic origin; akin to Old High German *faltistuol* folding chair — more at FALDSTOOL] (1744)
: ARMCHAIR; *especially* : an upholstered chair with open arms

**¹fauve** \'fōv\ *noun, often capitalized* [French, literally, wild animal, from *fauve* tawny, wild, from Old French *falve* tawny, of Germanic origin; akin to Old High German *falo* fallow — more at FALLOW] (1931)
: a painter practicing fauvism : FAUVIST

**²fauve** *adjective* (1945)
**1** *often capitalized* : of or relating to the fauves
**2** : vivid in color

**fau·vism** \'fō-,vi-zəm\ *noun, often capitalized* (1922)
: a movement in painting typified by the work of Matisse and characterized by vivid colors, free treatment of form, and a resulting vibrant and decorative effect
— **fau·vist** \-vist\ *noun, often capitalized*

**faux** \'fō\ *adjective* [French, false] (1975)
: IMITATION, ERSATZ ⟨*faux* marble⟩

**faux pas** \'fō-,pä, fō-'\ *noun, plural* **faux pas** \-,pä(z), -'pä(z)\ [French, literally, false step] (1676)
: BLUNDER; *especially* : a social blunder

**fa·va** \'fä-və\ *noun* [Italian, from Latin *faba* bean] (1928)
: BROAD BEAN — called also *fava bean*

**fave** \'fāv\ *noun* (1938)
: FAVORITE 1
— **fave** *adjective*

**fa·ve·la** *also* **fa·vel·la** \fə-'ve-lə\ *noun* [Brazilian Portuguese *favela*, perhaps from *Favela*, hill outside Rio de Janeiro] (1946)
: a settlement of jerry-built shacks lying on the outskirts of a Brazilian city

**fa·vism** \'fä-,vi-zəm\ *noun* (circa 1927)
: a hereditary condition especially of males of Mediterranean descent that involves a severe allergic reaction to the broad bean or its pollen

which is characterized by hemolytic anemia, fever, and jaundice

**fa·vo·ni·an** \fə-'vō-nē-ən\ *adjective* [Latin *favonianus*, from *Favonius*, the west wind] (circa 1681)
: of or relating to the west wind : MILD

**¹fa·vor** \'fā-vər\ *noun* [Middle English, friendly regard, attractiveness, from Old French *favor* friendly regard, from Latin, from *favēre* to be favorable; perhaps akin to Old High German *gouma* attention, Old Church Slavonic *gověti* to revere] (14th century)
**1 a** (1) : friendly regard shown toward another especially by a superior (2) : approving consideration or attention : APPROBATION **b** : PARTIALITY **c** *archaic* : LENIENCY **d** *archaic* : PERMISSION **e** : POPULARITY
**2** *archaic* **a** : APPEARANCE **b** (1) : FACE (2) : a facial feature
**3 a** : gracious kindness; *also* : an act of such kindness **b** *archaic* : AID, ASSISTANCE **c** *plural* : effort in one's behalf or interest : ATTENTION
**4 a** : a token of love (as a ribbon) usually worn conspicuously **b** : a small gift or decorative item given out at a party **c** : BADGE
**5 a** : a special privilege or right granted or conceded **b** : sexual privileges — usually used in plural
**6** *archaic* : LETTER
**7** : BEHALF, INTEREST
— **in favor of 1 a** : in accord or sympathy with **b** : for the acquittal of ⟨a verdict *in favor of* the accused⟩ **c** : in support of **2** : to the order of **3** : in order to choose : out of preference for ⟨turned down the scholarship *in favor of* a pro career⟩
— **in one's favor 1** : in one's good graces **2** : to one's advantage ⟨the odds were *in my favor*⟩
— **out of favor** : UNPOPULAR, DISLIKED ⟨was *out of favor* with his neighbors⟩

**²favor** *transitive verb* **fa·vored; fa·vor·ing** \'fā-v(ə-)riŋ\ (14th century)
**1 a** : to regard or treat with favor **b** (1) : to do a kindness for : OBLIGE (2) : ENDOW **c** : to treat gently or carefully ⟨*favored* his injured leg⟩
**2** : to show partiality toward : PREFER
**3 a** : to give support or confirmation to : SUSTAIN **b** : to afford advantages for success to : FACILITATE ⟨good weather *favored* the outing⟩
**4** : to bear a resemblance to ⟨he *favors* his father⟩
— **fa·vor·er** \'fā-vər-ər\ *noun*

**fa·vor·able** \'fā-v(ə-)rə-bəl, 'fā-vər-bəl\ *adjective* (14th century)
**1 a** : disposed to favor : PARTIAL **b** : expressing approval : COMMENDATORY **c** : giving a result that is in one's favor ⟨a *favorable* comparison⟩ **d** : AFFIRMATIVE
**2** : winning approval : PLEASING
**3 a** : tending to promote or facilitate : ADVANTAGEOUS ⟨*favorable* wind⟩ **b** : marked by success ☆
— **fa·vor·able·ness** *noun*
— **fa·vor·ably** \-blē\ *adverb*

**fa·vored** \'fā-vərd\ *adjective* (15th century)
**1** : having an appearance or features of a particular kind ⟨hard-*favored*⟩
**2** : endowed with special advantages or gifts
**3** : providing preferential treatment

**¹fa·vor·ite** \'fā-v(ə-)rət, 'fā-vərt, *chiefly dialect* 'fā-və-,rīt\ *noun* [Italian *favorito*, past participle of *favorire* to favor, from *favore* favor, from Latin *favor*] (1583)
**1** : one that is treated or regarded with special favor or liking; *especially* : one unusually loved, trusted, or provided with favors by a person of high rank or authority
**2** : a competitor judged most likely to win

**²favorite** *adjective* (1711)
: constituting a favorite; *especially* : markedly popular

**favorite son** *noun* (1788)
**1** : one favored by the delegates of his state as presidential candidate at a national political convention

**2** : a famous person who is popular with hometown people

**fa·vor·it·ism** \'fā-v(ə-)rə-,ti-zəm, 'fā-vər-\ *noun* (1763)
**1** : the showing of special favor : PARTIALITY
**2** : the state or fact of being a favorite

**fa·vour** *chiefly British variant of* FAVOR

**fa·vus** \'fā-vəs\ *noun* [New Latin, from Latin, honeycomb] (circa 1543)
: a contagious skin disease caused by a fungus (as *Trichophyton schoenleinii*) and occurring in humans and many domestic animals and fowls

**¹fawn** \'fȯn, 'fän\ *intransitive verb* [Middle English *faunen*, from Old English *fagnian* to rejoice, from *fægen*, *fagan* glad — more at FAIN] (13th century)
**1** : to show affection — used especially of a dog
**2** : to court favor by a cringing or flattering manner ☆
— **fawn·er** *noun*
— **fawn·ing·ly** \'fȯ-niŋ-lē, 'fä-\ *adverb*

**²fawn** *noun* [Middle English *foun*, from Middle French *feon*, *faon* young of an animal, from (assumed) Vulgar Latin *feton-*, *feto*, from Latin *fetus* offspring — more at FETUS] (14th century)
**1** : a young deer; *especially* : one still unweaned or retaining a distinctive baby coat
**2** : KID 1
**3** : a light grayish brown

**fawn lily** *noun* (circa 1894)
: DOGTOOTH VIOLET

**fawny** \'fȯ-nē, 'fä-\ *adjective* (1849)
: of a color approximating fawn

**fax** \'faks\ *noun* [by shortening & alteration] (1948)
**1** : FACSIMILE 2
**2** : a machine used to send or receive facsimile communications
**3** : a facsimile communication
— **fax** *transitive verb*

**¹fay** \'fā\ *verb* [Middle English *feien*, from Old English *fēgan*; akin to Old High German *fuogen* to fit, Latin *pangere* to fasten — more at PACT] (before 12th century)

\ə\ abut \ᵊ\ kitten \ər\ further \a\ ash \ā\ ace \ä\ mop, mar \aů\ out \ch\ chin \e\ bet \ē\ easy \g\ go \i\ hit \ī\ ice \j\ job \ŋ\ sing \ō\ go \ȯ\ law \ȯi\ boy \th\ thin \t̲h̲\ the \ü\ loot \ů\ foot \y\ yet \zh\ vision *see also* Guide to Pronunciation

: to fit or join closely or tightly

**²fay** *noun* [Middle English *fai, fei,* from Old French *feid, fei* — more at FAITH] (13th century)
*obsolete* : FAITH

**³fay** *noun* [Middle English *faie,* from Middle French *feie, fee* — more at FAIRY] (14th century)
: FAIRY, ELF

**⁴fay** *adjective* (14th century)
: resembling an elf

**⁵fay** *noun* (1927)
: OFAY

**faze** \'fāz\ *transitive verb* **fazed; faz·ing** [alteration of *feeze* (to drive away, frighten), from Middle English *fesen,* from Old English *fēsian* to drive away] (1830)
: to disturb the composure of : DISCONCERT, DAUNT ⟨nothing *fazed* her⟩

**F clef** *noun* (1596)
: BASS CLEF

**F distribution** *noun* [Sir Ronald *F*isher (died 1962) English geneticist and statistician] (1947)
: a probability density function that is used especially in analysis of variance and is a function of the ratio of two independent random variables each of which has a chi-square distribution and is divided by its number of degrees of freedom

**fe·al·ty** \'fē(-ə)l-tē\ *noun, plural* **-ties** [alteration of Middle English *feute,* from Old French *feelté, fealté,* from Latin *fidelitat-, fidelitas* — more at FIDELITY] (14th century)
**1 a** : the fidelity of a vassal or feudal tenant to his lord **b** : the obligation of such fidelity
**2** : intense fidelity
*synonym* see FIDELITY

**¹fear** \'fir\ (before 12th century)
*transitive verb*
**1** *archaic* : FRIGHTEN
**2** *archaic* : to feel fear in (oneself)
**3** : to have a reverential awe of ⟨*fear* God⟩
**4** : to be afraid of : expect with alarm
*intransitive verb*
: to be afraid or apprehensive
— **fear·er** *noun*

**²fear** *noun* [Middle English *fer,* from Old English *fǣr* sudden danger; akin to Latin *periculum* attempt, peril, Greek *peiran* to attempt] (12th century)
**1 a** : an unpleasant often strong emotion caused by anticipation or awareness of danger **b** (1) : an instance of this emotion (2) : a state marked by this emotion
**2** : anxious concern : SOLICITUDE
**3** : profound reverence and awe especially toward God
**4** : reason for alarm : DANGER ☆

**fear·ful** \'fir-fəl\ *adjective* (14th century)
**1** : causing or likely to cause fear, fright, or alarm especially because of dangerous quality ⟨a *fearful* storm⟩
**2 a** : full of fear **b** : indicating or arising from fear ⟨a *fearful* glance⟩ **c** : inclined to fear : TIMOROUS
**3** : very great or bad — used as an intensive ⟨a *fearful* waste⟩ ⟨*fearful* slum conditions⟩ ☆
— **fear·ful·ly** \-f(ə-)lē\ *adverb*
— **fear·ful·ness** \-fəl-nəs\ *noun*

**fear·less** \'fir-ləs\ *adjective* (1591)
: free from fear : BRAVE
— **fear·less·ly** *adverb*
— **fear·less·ness** *noun*

**fear·some** \'fir-səm\ *adjective* (1768)
**1** : causing fear
**2** : TIMID, TIMOROUS
— **fear·some·ly** *adverb*
— **fear·some·ness** *noun*

**fea·si·ble** \'fē-zə-bəl\ *adjective* [Middle English *faisible,* from Middle French, from *fais-,* stem of *faire* to make, do, from Latin *facere* — more at DO] (15th century)
**1** : capable of being done or carried out ⟨a *feasible* plan⟩

**2** : capable of being used or dealt with successfully : SUITABLE
**3** : REASONABLE, LIKELY
*synonym* see POSSIBLE
— **fea·si·bil·i·ty** \ˌfē-zə-'bi-lə-tē\ *noun*
— **fea·si·bly** \'fē-zə-blē\ *adverb*

**¹feast** \'fēst\ *noun* [Middle English *feste* festival, feast, from Middle French, from Latin *festa,* plural of *festum* festival, from neuter of *festus* solemn, festal; akin to Latin *feriae* holidays, *fanum* temple] (13th century)
**1 a** : an elaborate meal often accompanied by a ceremony or entertainment : BANQUET **b** : something that gives unusual or abundant pleasure
**2** : a periodic religious observance commemorating an event or honoring a deity, person, or thing

**²feast** (14th century)
*intransitive verb*
**1** : to take part in a feast
**2** : to enjoy some unusual pleasure or delight
*transitive verb*
**1** : to give a feast for
**2** : DELIGHT, GRATIFY
— **feast·er** *noun*

**Feast of Tabernacles** (14th century)
: SUKKOTH

**¹feat** \'fēt\ *noun* [Middle English *fait,* from Middle French, from Latin *factum,* from neuter of *factus,* past participle of *facere* to make, do — more at DO] (14th century)
**1** : ACT, DEED
**2 a** : a deed notable especially for courage **b** : an act or product of skill, endurance, or ingenuity ☆

**²feat** *adjective* [Middle English *fete, fayt,* from Middle French *fait,* past participle of *faire*] (15th century)
**1** *archaic* : BECOMING, NEAT
**2** *archaic* : SMART, DEXTEROUS

**¹feath·er** \'fe-thər\ *noun* [Middle English *fether,* from Old English; akin to Old High German *federa* wing, Latin *petere* to go to, seek, Greek *petesthai* to fly, *piptein* to fall, *pteron* wing] (before 12th century)
**1 a** : any of the light horny epidermal outgrowths that form the external covering of the body of birds and that consist of a shaft bearing on each side a series of barbs which bear barbules which in turn bear barbicels commonly ending in hooked hamuli and interlocking with the barbules of an adjacent barb to link the barbs into a continuous vane **b** : PLUME **c** : the vane of an arrow
**2 a** : PLUMAGE **b** : KIND, NATURE ⟨birds of a *feather* flock together⟩ **c** : ATTIRE, DRESS **d** : CONDITION, MOOD
**3** : FEATHERING 2
**4** : a projecting strip, rib, fin, or flange
**5** : a feathery flaw in the eye or in a precious stone
**6** : the act of feathering an oar
— **feath·ered** \-thərd\ *adjective*
— **feath·er·less** *adjective*
— **a feather in one's cap** : a mark of distinction : HONOR

**²feather** *verb* **feath·ered; feath·er·ing** \'feth-riŋ, 'fe-thə-\ (13th century)
*transitive verb*
**1 a** : to furnish (as an arrow) with a feather **b** : to cover, clothe, or adorn with or as if with feathers

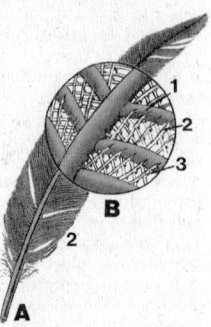

feather 1a: *A: 1* quill, *2* vane; *B: 1* barb, *2* barbule, *3* barbicel with hamulus

**2 a** : to turn (an oar blade) almost horizontal when lifting from the water at the end of a stroke to reduce air resistance **b** (1) : to change the angle of (airplane propeller blades) so that the chords become approximately parallel to the line of flight; *also* : to change the angle of airplane propeller blades of (an engine) in such a manner (2) : to change the angle of (a rotor blade of a rotorcraft) periodically in forward flight
**3** : to reduce the edge of to a featheredge
**4** : to cut (as air) with or as if with a wing
**5** : to join by a tongue and groove
*intransitive verb*
**1** : to grow or form feathers
**2** : to have or take on the appearance of a feather or something feathered
**3** : to soak in and spread : BLUR — used of ink or a printed impression
**4** : to feather an oar or an airplane propeller blade
— **feather one's nest** : to provide for oneself especially while in a position of trust

**¹feath·er·bed** \'fe-thər-ˌbed\ *adjective* (1938)
: calling for, sanctioning, or resulting from featherbedding

**²featherbed** (1949)
*intransitive verb*
**1 a** : to require that more workers be hired than are needed **b** : to limit production under a featherbed rule
**2** : to do featherbed work or put in time under a featherbed rule
*transitive verb*
**1** : to bring under a featherbed rule
**2** : to assist (as an industry) by government aid

**feather bed** *noun* (before 12th century)
**1** : a feather mattress
**2** : a bed having a feather mattress

**feath·er·bed·ding** *noun* (1921)

---

☆ **SYNONYMS**

**Fear, dread, fright, alarm, panic, terror, trepidation** mean painful agitation in the presence or anticipation of danger. FEAR is the most general term and implies anxiety and usually loss of courage ⟨*fear* of the unknown⟩. DREAD usually adds the idea of intense reluctance to face or meet a person or situation and suggests aversion as well as anxiety ⟨faced the meeting with *dread*⟩. FRIGHT implies the shock of sudden, startling fear ⟨*fright* at being awakened suddenly⟩. ALARM suggests a sudden and intense awareness of immediate danger ⟨view the situation with *alarm*⟩. PANIC implies unreasoning and overmastering fear causing hysterical activity ⟨the news caused widespread *panic*⟩. TERROR implies the most extreme degree of fear ⟨immobilized with *terror*⟩. TREPIDATION adds to DREAD the implications of timidity, trembling, and hesitation ⟨raised the subject with *trepidation*⟩.

**Fearful, apprehensive, afraid** mean disturbed by fear. FEARFUL implies often a timorous or worrying temperament ⟨the child is *fearful* of loud noises⟩. APPREHENSIVE suggests a state of mind and implies a premonition of evil or danger ⟨*apprehensive* of being found out⟩. AFRAID often suggests weakness or cowardice and regularly implies inhibition of action or utterance ⟨*afraid* to speak the truth⟩.

**Feat, exploit, achievement** mean a remarkable deed. FEAT implies strength or dexterity or daring ⟨an acrobatic *feat*⟩. EXPLOIT suggests an adventurous or heroic act ⟨his *exploits* as a spy⟩. ACHIEVEMENT implies hard-won success in the face of difficulty or opposition ⟨her *achievements* as a chemist⟩.

: the requiring of an employer usually under a union rule or safety statute to hire more employees than are needed or to limit production

**feath·er·brain** \-ˌbrān\ *noun* (1839)
: a foolish scatterbrained person
— **feath·er·brained** \-ˌbrānd\ *adjective*

**feath·er·edge** \'fe-thə-ˌrej, ˌfe-thə-'\ *noun* (1616)
: a very thin sharp edge; *especially* : one that is easily broken or bent over
— **featheredge** *transitive verb*

**feath·er·head** \'fe-thər-ˌhed\ *noun* (1831)
: FEATHERBRAIN
— **feath·er·head·ed** \ˌfe-thər-'he-dəd\ *adjective*

**feath·er·ing** \'feth-riŋ, 'fe-thə-\ *noun* (1721)
**1** : a covering of feathers : PLUMAGE
**2** : a fringe of hair (as on the legs of a dog) — see DOG illustration

**feath·er·light** \'fe-thər-'līt\ *adjective* (circa 1837)
: extremely light

**feather star** *noun* (1862)
: any of an order (Comatulida) of free-swimming stalkless crinoids

**feath·er·stitch** \'fe-thər-ˌstich\ *noun* (1835)
: an embroidery stitch consisting of a line of diagonal blanket stitches worked alternately to the left and right
— **featherstitch** *verb*

**feath·er·weight** \-ˌwāt\ *noun, often attributive* (1812)
**1** : one that is very light in weight; *especially* : a boxer in a weight division having a maximum limit of 126 pounds for professionals and 125 pounds for amateurs — compare BANTAMWEIGHT, LIGHTWEIGHT
**2** : LIGHTWEIGHT 2

**featherstitch**

**feath·ery** \'feth-rē, 'fe-thə-\ *adjective* (1580)
: resembling, suggesting, or covered with feathers; *especially* : extremely light

**¹feat·ly** \'fēt-lē\ *adverb* [Middle English *fetly*, from *fete* feat (adjective)] (14th century)
**1** : in a graceful manner : NIMBLY
**2** : in a suitable manner : PROPERLY
**3** : with skill and ingenuity

**²featly** *adjective* (1801)
: GRACEFUL, NEAT

**¹fea·ture** \'fē-chər\ *noun* [Middle English *feture*, from Middle French, from Latin *factura* act of making, from *factus*, past participle of *facere* to make — more at DO] (14th century)
**1 a** : the structure, form, or appearance especially of a person **b** *obsolete* : physical beauty
**2 a** : the makeup or appearance of the face or its parts **b** : a part of the face : LINEAMENT
**3 a** : a prominent part or characteristic **b** : any of the properties (as voice or gender) that are characteristic of a grammatical element (as a phoneme or morpheme); *especially* : one that is distinctive
**4** : a special attraction: as **a** : the principal motion picture shown on a program with other pictures **b** : a featured article, story, or department in a newspaper or magazine **c** : something offered to the public or advertised as particularly attractive
— **fea·ture·less** \-ləs\ *adjective*

**²feature** *verb* **fea·tured; fea·tur·ing** \'fēch-riŋ, 'fē-chə-\ (circa 1755)
*transitive verb*
**1** *chiefly dialect* : to resemble in features
**2** : to picture or portray in the mind : IMAGINE
**3 a** : to give special prominence to **b** : to have as a characteristic or feature
*intransitive verb*
: to play an important part

**fea·tured** \'fē-chərd\ *adjective* (15th century)
**1** : having facial features of a particular kind — used in combination ⟨a heavy-*featured* lout⟩
**2** : displayed, advertised, or presented as a special attraction

**fea·tur·ette** \'fē-chə-ˌret, ˌfē-chə-'\ *noun* (1940)
: a short film

**feaze** \'fēz, 'fāz\ *variant of* FAZE

**febri-** *combining form* [Late Latin, from Latin *febris*]
: fever ⟨*febrific*⟩

**fe·brif·ic** \fi-'brif-ik\ *adjective* (1710)
*archaic* : FEVERISH

**feb·ri·fuge** \'fe-brə-ˌfyüj\ *noun* [French *fébrifuge*, probably from (assumed) New Latin *febrifuga*, from Late Latin *febrifuga, febrifugia* centaury, from *febri-* + Late Latin *-fuga* -fuge] (1686)
: ANTIPYRETIC
— **febrifuge** *adjective*

**fe·brile** \'fe-ˌbrīl also 'fē-\ *adjective* [Medieval Latin *febrilis*, from Latin *febris* fever] (1651)
: FEVERISH

**Feb·ru·ary** \÷'fe-b(y)ə-ˌwer-ē, 'fe-brə-\ *noun, plural* **-ar·ies** *or* **-ar·ys** [Middle English *Februarie*, from Old English *Februarius*, from Latin, from *Februa*, plural, feast of purification] (before 12th century)
: the 2d month of the Gregorian calendar ◻

**fe·cal** \'fē-kəl\ *adjective* (1541)
: of, relating to, or constituting feces

**fe·ces** \'fē-(ˌ)sēz\ *noun plural* [Middle English, from Latin *faec-, faex* (singular) dregs] (14th century)
: bodily waste discharged through the anus : EXCREMENT

**feck·less** \'fek-ləs\ *adjective* [Scots, from *feck* effect, majority, from Middle English (Scots) *fek*, alteration of Middle English *effect*] (circa 1585)
**1** : WEAK, INEFFECTIVE
**2** : WORTHLESS, IRRESPONSIBLE
— **feck·less·ly** *adverb*
— **feck·less·ness** *noun*

**feck·ly** \'fek-lē\ *adverb* [*feck* + *-ly*] (1768)
*chiefly Scottish* : ALMOST, NEARLY

**fec·u·lent** \'fe-kyə-lənt\ *adjective* [Middle English, from Latin *faeculentus*, from *faec-, faex*] (15th century)
: foul with impurities : FECAL
— **fec·u·lence** \-lən(t)s\ *noun*

**fe·cund** \'fe-kənd, 'fē-\ *adjective* [Middle English, from Middle French *fecond*, from Latin *fecundus* — more at FEMININE] (15th century)
**1** : fruitful in offspring or vegetation : PROLIFIC
**2** : intellectually productive or inventive to a marked degree
**synonym** see FERTILE
— **fe·cun·di·ty** \fi-'kən-də-tē, fe-\ *noun*

**fe·cun·date** \'fe-kən-ˌdāt, 'fē-\ *transitive verb* **-dat·ed; -dat·ing** [Latin *fecundatus*, past participle of *fecundare*, from *fecundus*] (circa 1631)
**1** : to make fecund
**2** : IMPREGNATE
— **fe·cun·da·tion** \ˌfe-kən-'dā-shən, ˌfē-\ *noun*

**fed** \'fed\ *noun, often capitalized* (1916)
: a federal agent, officer, or official — usually used in plural

**fe·da·yee** \fi-ˌda-'(y)ē, -ˌdä-\ *noun, plural* **fe·da·yeen** \-'(y)ēn\ [Arabic *fidā'ī*, literally, one who sacrifices himself] (1955)
: a member of an Arab commando group operating especially against Israel — usually used in plural

**fed·er·al** \'fe-d(ə-)rəl\ *adjective* [Latin *foeder-, foedus* compact, league; akin to Latin *fidere* to trust — more at BIDE] (1660)
**1** *archaic* : of or relating to a compact or treaty
**2 a** : formed by a compact between political units that surrender their individual sovereignty to a central authority but retain limited residuary powers of government **b** : of or constituting a form of government in which power is distributed between a central authority and a number of constituent territorial units **c** : of or relating to the central government of a federa-

tion as distinguished from the governments of the constituent units
**3** *capitalized* : advocating or friendly to the principle of a federal government with strong centralized powers; *especially* : of or relating to the American Federalists
**4** *often capitalized* : of, relating to, or loyal to the federal government or the Union armies of the U.S. in the American Civil War
**5** *capitalized* : being or belonging to a style of architecture and decoration current in the U.S. following the Revolution
— **fed·er·al·ly** \-d(ə-)rə-lē\ *adverb*

**Federal** *noun* (1861)
**1** : a supporter of the U.S. government in the Civil War; *especially* : a soldier in the federal armies
**2** : FED — usually used in plural

**federal case** *noun* (1955)
: BIG DEAL ⟨don't make a *federal case* out of it⟩

**federal court** *noun* (1789)
: a court established by a federal government; *especially* : one established under the constitution and laws of the U.S.

**federal district** *noun* (circa 1934)
: a district set apart as the seat of the central government of a federation

**federal district court** *noun* (1948)
: a district trial court of law and equity that hears cases under federal jurisdiction

**fed·er·al·ese** \ˌfe-d(ə-)rə-'lēz, -'lēs; 'fe-d(ə-)rə-ˌ\ *noun* (1944)
: BUREAUCRATESE

**federal funds** *noun plural* (1950)
: reserve funds lent overnight by one Federal Reserve bank to another

**fed·er·al·ism** \'fe-d(ə-)rə-ˌli-zəm\ *noun* (1789)
**1 a** *often capitalized* : the distribution of power in an organization (as a government) between a central authority and the constituent units — compare CENTRALISM **b** : support or advocacy of this principle
**2** *capitalized* : Federalist principles

**fed·er·al·ist** \-list\ *noun* (1787)
**1** : an advocate of federalism: as **a** *often capitalized* : an advocate of a federal union between the American colonies after the Revolution and of the adoption of the U.S. Constitution **b** *often capitalized* : WORLD FEDERALIST
**2** *capitalized* : a member of a major political party in the early years of the U.S. favoring a strong centralized national government
— **federalist** *adjective, often capitalized*

**fed·er·al·iza·tion** \ˌfe-d(ə-)rə-lə-'zā-shən\ *noun* (circa 1860)
**1** : the act of federalizing
**2** : the state of being federalized

**fed·er·al·ize** \'fe-d(ə-)rə-ˌlīz\ *transitive verb* **-ized; -iz·ing** (1801)
**1** : to unite in or under a federal system
**2** : to bring under the jurisdiction of a federal government

◻ **USAGE**
**February** Dissimilation may occur when a word contains two identical or closely related sounds, resulting in the change or loss of one of them. This happens regularly in *February*, which is more often pronounced \'fe-b(y)ə-ˌwer-ē\ than \'fe-brə-ˌwer-ē\, though all of these variants are in frequent use and widely accepted. The \y\ heard from many speakers is not an intrusion but rather a common pronunciation of the vowel *u* after a consonant, as in *January* and *annual*.

**Federal Reserve bank** *noun* (1914)
: one of 12 reserve banks set up under the Federal Reserve Act to hold reserves and discount commercial paper for affiliated banks in their respective districts

¹**fed·er·ate** \'fe-d(ə-)rət\ *adjective* [Latin *foederatus*, from *foeder-, foedus*] (1710)
: united in an alliance or federation : FEDERATED

²**fed·er·ate** \'fe-də-,rāt\ *transitive verb* **-at·ed; -at·ing** (1837)
: to join in a federation

**federated church** *noun* (circa 1926)
: a local church uniting two or more congregations that maintain different denominational ties — compare UNION CHURCH

**fed·er·a·tion** \,fe-də-'rā-shən\ *noun* (1791)
**1** : something formed by federation: as **a** : a federal government **b** : a union of organizations
**2** : the act of federating; *especially* : the forming of a federal union

**fed·er·a·tive** \'fe-də-,rā-tiv, 'fe-d(ə-)rə-\ *adjective* (1690)
: FEDERAL
— **fed·er·a·tive·ly** *adverb*

**fe·do·ra** \fi-'dōr-ə, -'dȯr-\ *noun* [*Fédora* (1882), drama by V. Sardou] (1895)
: a low soft felt hat with the crown creased lengthwise ◆

**fed up** *adjective* (1900)
: tired, sated, or disgusted beyond endurance

¹**fee** \'fē\ *noun* [Middle English, from Middle French *fé, fief,* from Old French, of Germanic origin; akin to Old English *feoh* cattle, property, Old High German *fihu* cattle; akin to Latin *pecus* cattle, *pecunia* money] (14th century)
**1 a** (1) : an estate in land held in feudal law from a lord on condition of homage and service (2) : a piece of land so held **b** : an inherited or heritable estate in land
**2 a** : a fixed charge **b** : a sum paid or charged for a service
— **in fee** : in absolute and legal possession

²**fee** *transitive verb* **feed; fee·ing** (15th century)
**1** *chiefly Scottish* : HIRE
**2** : ⁹TIP 2

**fee·ble** \'fē-bəl\ *adjective* **fee·bler** \-b(ə-)lər\; **fee·blest** \-b(ə-)ləst\ [Middle English *feble,* from Old French, from Latin *flebilis* lamentable, wretched, from *flēre* to weep — more at BLEAT] (12th century)
**1 a** : markedly lacking in strength **b** : indicating weakness
**2 a** : deficient in qualities or resources that indicate vigor, authority, force, or efficiency **b** : INADEQUATE, INFERIOR
**synonym** see WEAK
— **fee·ble·ness** \-bəl-nəs\ *noun*
— **fee·bly** \-blē\ *adverb*

**fee·ble·mind·ed** \,fē-bəl-'mīn-dəd\ *adjective* (1534)
**1** *obsolete* : IRRESOLUTE, VACILLATING
**2** : mentally deficient
**3** : FOOLISH, STUPID
— **fee·ble·mind·ed·ly** *adverb*
— **fee·ble·mind·ed·ness** *noun*

**fee·blish** \'fē-b(ə-)lish\ *adjective* (1674)
: somewhat feeble

¹**feed** \'fēd\ *verb* **fed** \'fed\; **feed·ing** [Middle English *feden,* from Old English *fēdan;* akin to Old English *fōda* food — more at FOOD] (before 12th century)
*transitive verb*
**1 a** : to give food to **b** : to give as food
**2 a** : to furnish something essential to the growth, sustenance, maintenance, or operation of **b** : to supply (material to be operated on) to a machine
**3** : to produce or provide food for
**4 a** : SATISFY, GRATIFY **b** : SUPPORT, ENCOURAGE
**5 a** (1) : to supply for use or consumption (2) : CHANNEL, ROUTE **b** (1) : to supply (a signal) to an electronic circuit (2) : to send (as by wire or satellite) to a transmitting station for broadcast

**6** : to supply (a fellow actor) with cues and situations that make a role more effective
**7** : to pass a ball or puck to (a teammate) especially for a shot at the goal
*intransitive verb*
**1 a** : to consume food : EAT **b** : PREY — used with *on, upon,* or *off*
**2** : to become nourished or satisfied or sustained as if by food
**3 a** : to become channeled or directed **b** : to move into a machine or opening in order to be used or processed

²**feed** *noun* (1576)
**1 a** : an act of eating **b** : MEAL; *especially* : a large meal
**2 a** : food for livestock; *specifically* : a mixture or preparation for feeding livestock **b** : the amount given at each feeding
**3 a** : material supplied (as to a furnace or machine) **b** : a mechanism by which the action of feeding is effected **c** : the motion or process of carrying forward the material to be operated upon (as in a machine) **d** : the process of feeding a television program (as to a local station)
**4** : the action of passing a ball or puck to a team member who is in position to score

**feed·back** \'fēd-,bak\ *noun* (1920)
**1** : the return to the input of a part of the output of a machine, system, or process (as for producing changes in an electronic circuit that improve performance or in an automatic control device that provide self-corrective action)
**2 a** : the partial reversion of the effects of a process to its source or to a preceding stage **b** : the transmission of evaluative or corrective information to the original or controlling source about an action, event, or process; *also* : the information so transmitted

**feedback inhibition** *noun* (1960)
: inhibition of an enzyme controlling an early stage of a series of biochemical reactions by the end product when it reaches a critical concentration

**feed dog** *noun* (circa 1939)
: a notched piece of metal on a sewing machine that feeds material into position under the needle

**feed·er** \'fē-dər\ *noun* (14th century)
**1** : one that feeds: as **a** : one that fattens livestock for slaughter **b** : a device or apparatus for supplying food
**2** : one that eats or takes nourishment; *especially* : an animal being fattened or one suitable for fattening
**3 a** : one that supplies, replenishes, or connects **b** : TRIBUTARY **c** : a heavy wire conductor supplying electricity at some point of an electric distribution system (as from a substation) **d** : BRANCH; *especially* : a branch transportation line **e** : FEEDER ROAD

**feeder road** *noun* (1938)
: a road that provides access to a major artery

**feeding frenzy** *noun* (1973)
: a frenzy of eating; *also* : the excited pursuit of something by a group

**feed·lot** \'fēd-,lät\ *noun* (1889)
: a plot of land on which livestock are fattened for market

**feed·stock** \-,stäk\ *noun* (1932)
: raw material supplied to a machine or processing plant

**feed·stuff** \-,stəf\ *noun* (1856)
: FEED 2a; *also* : any of the constituent nutrients of an animal ration

¹**feel** \'fē(ə)l\ *verb* **felt** \'felt\; **feel·ing** [Middle English *felen,* from Old English *fēlan;* akin to Old High German *fuolen* to feel, Latin *palpare* to caress] (before 12th century)
*transitive verb*
**1 a** : to handle or touch in order to examine, test, or explore some quality **b** : to perceive by a physical sensation coming from discrete end organs (as of the skin or muscles)
**2 a** : to undergo passive experience of **b** : to have one's sensibilities markedly affected by

**3** : to ascertain by cautious trial — usually used with *out*
**4 a** : to be aware of by instinct or inference **b** : BELIEVE, THINK
*intransitive verb*
**1 a** : to receive or be able to receive a tactile sensation **b** : to search for something by using the sense of touch
**2 a** : to be conscious of an inward impression, state of mind, or physical condition **b** : to have a marked sentiment or opinion ⟨*feels* strongly about it⟩
**3** : SEEM ⟨it *feels* like spring today⟩
**4** : to have sympathy or pity ⟨I *feel* for you⟩
— **feel like** : to have an inclination for ⟨*feel like* a walk?⟩

²**feel** *noun* (13th century)
**1** : SENSATION, FEELING
**2** : the sense of touch
**3 a** : the quality of a thing as imparted through or as if through touch **b** : typical or peculiar quality or atmosphere; *also* : an awareness of such a quality or atmosphere
**4** : intuitive knowledge or ability

**feel·er** \'fē-lər\ *noun* (1526)
: one that feels: as **a** : a tactile process (as a tentacle) of an animal **b** : something (as a proposal) ventured to ascertain the views of others

**feeler gauge** *noun* (1925)
: a thin metal strip or wire of known thickness used as a gauge

**feel–good** \'fē(ə)l-,gu̇d\ *adjective* (1978)
: relating to or promoting an often specious sense of satisfaction or well-being

¹**feel·ing** \'fē-liŋ\ *noun* (12th century)
**1 a** (1) : the one of the basic physical senses of which the skin contains the chief end organs and of which the sensations of touch and temperature are characteristic : TOUCH (2) : a sensation experienced through this sense **b** : generalized bodily consciousness or sensation **c** : appreciative or responsive awareness or recognition
**2 a** : an emotional state or reaction ⟨had a kindly *feeling* toward the child⟩ **b** *plural* : susceptibility to impression : SENSITIVITY ⟨the remark hurt her *feelings*⟩
**3 a** : the undifferentiated background of one's awareness considered apart from any identifiable sensation, perception, or thought **b** : the overall quality of one's awareness **c** : conscious recognition : SENSE
**4 a** : often unreasoned opinion or belief : SENTIMENT **b** : PRESENTIMENT

◇ WORD HISTORY
**fedora** The hat known as a *fedora* is generally thought to have some connection with *Fédora,* a melodrama by the French playwright Victorien Sardou (1831–1908), though the exact nature of the connection has yet to be established. Sardou, a popular dramatist in the 19th century, though now nearly forgotten except by literary and theater historians, premiered *Fédora* in 1882, with the celebrated actress Sarah Bernhardt in the title role of Fédora Romanoff, a Russian princess. There is some evidence that the long plume worn by Bernhardt in the play made an impression on Parisian fashion, but the word *fédora,* if it was used for the plume in French, did not survive. Sardou's play ran successfully in New York in 1883 with the American actress Fanny Davenport in the title role. Sometime afterward, *fedora* found its way into American English as a name for a man's soft felt hat, with no obvious link to either Sarah Bernhardt's or Fanny Davenport's headgear. By 1895 the word appeared in a Montgomery Ward catalog—clearly a sign that the hat style had entered mainstream American fashion.

**5 :** capacity to respond emotionally especially with the higher emotions
**6 :** the character ascribed to something **:** ATMOSPHERE
**7 a :** the quality of a work of art that conveys the emotion of the artist **b :** sympathetic aesthetic response
**8 :** FEEL 4 ☆
²**feeling** *adjective* (14th century)
**1 a :** SENTIENT, SENSITIVE **b :** easily moved emotionally
**2** *obsolete* **:** deeply felt
**3 :** expressing emotion or sensitivity
— **feel·ing·ly** \-liŋ-lē\ *adverb*
— **feel·ing·ness** *noun*
**feel up** *transitive verb* (1930)
**:** to touch or fondle (someone) for sexual pleasure
**fee simple** *noun, plural* **fees simple** (14th century)
**:** a fee without limitation to any class of heirs or restrictions on transfer of ownership
**fee splitting** *noun* (1943)
**:** payment by a specialist (as a doctor or a lawyer) of a part of his fee to the person who made the referral
**feet** *plural of* FOOT
**fee tail** *noun, plural* **fees tail** (15th century)
**:** a fee limited to a particular class of heirs
**feet-first** \ˌfēt-ˈfərst\ *adverb* (circa 1901)
**:** with the feet foremost
**feet of clay** [from the feet of the idol in Daniel 2:33] (1814)
**:** a flaw of character that is usually not readily apparent
**feeze** \ˈfēz, ˈfāz\ *noun* [Middle English *veze*, from *fesen, vesen* to drive away — more at FAZE] (14th century)
**1** *chiefly dialect* **:** RUSH
**2** *dialect* **:** a state of alarm or excitement
**Feh·ling's solution** \ˈfā-liŋ(z)-\ *noun* [Hermann *Fehling* (died 1885) German chemist] (1873)
**:** a blue solution of Rochelle salt and copper sulfate used as an oxidizing agent in a test for sugars and aldehydes
**feign** \ˈfān\ *verb* [Middle English, from Old French *feign-*, stem of *feindre*, from Latin *fingere* to shape, feign — more at DOUGH] (13th century)
*intransitive verb*
**:** PRETEND, DISSEMBLE
*transitive verb*
**1 a :** to give a false appearance of **:** induce as a false impression ⟨*feign* death⟩ **b :** to assert as if true **:** PRETEND
**2** *archaic* **a :** INVENT, IMAGINE **b :** to give fictional representation to
**3** *obsolete* **:** DISGUISE, CONCEAL
**synonym** see ASSUME
— **feign·er** *noun*
**feigned** *adjective* (14th century)
**1 :** FICTITIOUS
**2 :** not genuine or real
**fei·joa** \fā-ˈyō-ə, -ˈhō-ə\ *noun* [New Latin, genus name, from João da Silva *Feijó* (died 1824) Brazilian naturalist] (1898)
**:** the green edible fruit of a shrub or small tree (*Feijoa sellowiana*) of the myrtle family that is native to South America and is grown commercially especially in New Zealand; *also* **:** the tree or shrub
¹**feint** \ˈfānt\ *noun* [French *feinte*, from Old French, from *feint*, past participle of *feindre*] (1679)
**:** something feigned; *specifically* **:** a mock blow or attack on or toward one part in order to distract attention from the point one really intends to attack
**synonym** see TRICK
²**feint** (1810)
*intransitive verb*
**:** to make a feint
*transitive verb*
**1 :** to lure or deceive with a feint
**2 :** to make a pretense of

**fei·rie** \ˈfē-rē\ *adjective* [Middle English (Scots) *fery*, from Middle English *fere* strong, from Old English *fēre* able to go; akin to Old English *faran* to travel, fare] (before 12th century)
*Scottish* **:** NIMBLE, STRONG
**feist** \ˈfīst\ *noun* [obsolete *fisting hound*, from obsolete *fist* (to break wind)] (1770)
*chiefly dialect* **:** a small dog
**feisty** \ˈfī-stē\ *adjective* **feist·i·er; -est** (1896)
**1** *chiefly Southern & Midland* **a :** full of nervous energy **:** FIDGETY **b :** being touchy and quarrelsome **c :** being frisky and exuberant
**2 :** having or showing a lively aggressiveness **:** SPUNKY ◆
— **feist·i·ness** *noun*
**fe·la·fel** \fə-ˈlä-fəl\ *variant of* FALAFEL
**feld·sher** \ˈfel(d)-shər\ *noun* [Russian *fel'dsher*, from German *Feldscher, Feldscherer* field surgeon, from *Feld* field + *Scherer* barber, surgeon] (1877)
**:** a medical or surgical practitioner without full professional qualifications or status in some east European countries and especially Russia
**feld·spar** \ˈfel(d)-ˌspär\ *noun* [modification of obsolete German *Feldspath* (now *Feldspat*), from German *Feld* field + obsolete German *Spath* (now *Spat*) spar] (1772)
**:** any of a group of crystalline minerals that consist of aluminum silicates with either potassium, sodium, calcium, or barium and that are an essential constituent of nearly all crystalline rocks
**feld·spath·ic** \fel(d)-ˈspa-thik\ *adjective* [*feldspath* (variant of *feldspar*), from obsolete German] (circa 1828)
**:** relating to or containing feldspar — used especially of a porcelain glaze
**fe·li·cif·ic** \ˌfē-lə-ˈsi-fik\ *adjective* [Latin *felic-, felix*] (1865)
**:** causing or intended to cause happiness
**felicific calculus** *noun* (1945)
**:** a method of determining the rightness of an action by balancing the probable pleasures and pains that it would produce
¹**fe·lic·i·tate** \fi-ˈli-sə-ˌtāt\ *adjective* [Late Latin *felicitatus*, past participle of *felicitare* to make happy, from Latin *felicitas*] (1605)
*obsolete* **:** made happy
²**felicitate** *transitive verb* **-tat·ed; -tat·ing** (1628)
**1** *archaic* **:** to make happy
**2 a :** to consider happy or fortunate **b :** to offer congratulations to
— **fe·lic·i·ta·tion** \-ˌli-sə-ˈtā-shən\ *noun*
— **fe·lic·i·ta·tor** \-ˈli-sə-ˌtā-tər\ *noun*
**fe·lic·i·tous** \fi-ˈli-sə-təs\ *adjective* (1789)
**1 :** very well suited or expressed **:** APT ⟨a *felicitous* remark⟩
**2 :** PLEASANT, DELIGHTFUL
**synonym** see FIT
— **fe·lic·i·tous·ly** *adverb*
— **fe·lic·i·tous·ness** *noun*
**fe·lic·i·ty** \fi-ˈli-sə-tē\ *noun, plural* **-ties** [Middle English *felicite*, from Middle French *félicité*, from Latin *felicitat-, felicitas*, from *felic-, felix* fruitful, happy — more at FEMININE] (14th century)
**1 a :** the quality or state of being happy; *especially* **:** great happiness **b :** an instance of happiness
**2 :** something that causes happiness
**3 :** a pleasing manner or quality especially in art or language
**4 :** an apt expression
**fe·lid** \ˈfē-ləd\ *noun* [New Latin *Felidae*, family name, from *Felis*, genus of cats, from Latin, cat] (circa 1889)
**:** CAT 1b
— **felid** *adjective*
**fe·line** \ˈfē-ˌlīn\ *adjective* [Latin *felinus*, from *felis*] (1681)
**1 :** of, relating to, or affecting cats or the cat family

**2 :** resembling a cat: as **a :** sleekly graceful **b :** SLY, TREACHEROUS **c :** STEALTHY
— **feline** *noun*
— **fe·line·ly** *adverb*
— **fe·lin·i·ty** \fē-ˈli-nə-tē\ *noun*
**feline distemper** *noun* (1942)
**:** PANLEUKOPENIA
**feline panleukopenia** *noun* (circa 1943)
**:** PANLEUKOPENIA
¹**fell** \ˈfel\ *noun* [Middle English, from Old English; akin to Old High German *fel* skin, Latin *pellis*] (before 12th century)
**1 :** SKIN, HIDE, PELT
**2 :** a thin tough membrane covering a carcass directly under the hide
²**fell** *transitive verb* [Middle English, from Old English *fellan*; akin to Old English *feallan* to fall — more at FALL] (before 12th century)
**1 a :** to cut, knock, or bring down **b :** KILL
**2 :** to sew (a seam) by folding one raw edge under the other and sewing flat on the wrong side
— **fell·able** \ˈfe-lə-bəl\ *adjective*
— **fell·er** *noun*
³**fell** *past of* FALL
⁴**fell** *adjective* [Middle English *fel*, from Middle French, from Old French — more at FELON] (14th century)

---

---

---

\ə\ abut \ᵊ\ kitten \ər\ further \a\ ash \ā\ ace
\ä\ mop, mar \aù\ out \ch\ chin \e\ bet \ē\ easy
\g\ go \i\ hit \ī\ ice \j\ job \ŋ\ sing \ō\ go
\ò\ law \òi\ boy \th\ thin \t͟h\ the \ü\ loot \ù\ foot
\y\ yet \zh\ vision *see also* Guide to Pronunciation

**1 a :** FIERCE, CRUEL, TERRIBLE **b :** SINISTER, MALEVOLENT ⟨a *fell* purpose⟩ **c :** very destructive **:** DEADLY ⟨a *fell* disease⟩
**2** *Scottish* **:** SHARP, PUNGENT
— **fell·ness** *noun*
— **fel·ly** \'fel-lē\ *adverb*
— **at one fell swoop** *or* **in one fell swoop :** all at once; *also* **:** with a single concentrated effort

**⁵fell** *noun* [Middle English, from Old Norse *fell, fjall* mountain; akin to Old High German *felis* rock] (14th century)
*dialect British* **:** a high barren field or moor

**fel·lah** \'fe-lə, fə-'lä\ *noun, plural* **fel·la·hin** *or* **fel·la·heen** \,fel-ə-'hēn, fə-,lä-'hēn\ [Arabic *fallāḥ*] (1743)
**:** a peasant or agricultural laborer in an Arab country (as Egypt)

**fel·late** \'fe-,lāt, fə-'lāt\ *verb* **fel·lat·ed; fel·lat·ing** [back-formation from *fellatio*] (1948)
*transitive verb*
**:** to perform fellatio on
*intransitive verb*
**:** to fellate someone
— **fel·la·tor** \-,lā-tər, -'lā-tər\ *noun*

**fel·la·tio** \fə-'lā-shē-,ō, fe-\ *also* **fel·la·tion** \-'lā-shən\ *noun* [New Latin *fellation-, fellatio*, from Latin *felare, fellare*, literally, to suck — more at FEMININE] (circa 1893)
**:** oral stimulation of the penis

**fell·mon·ger** \'fel-,məŋ-gər, -,mäŋ-\ *noun* [¹*fell*] (1530)
*British* **:** one who removes hair or wool from hides in preparation for leather making
— **fell·mon·gered** \-gərd\ *adjective, British*
— **fell·mon·ger·ing** \-g(ə-)riŋ\ *noun, British*
— **fell·mon·gery** \-g(ə-)rē\ *noun, British*

**fel·low** \'fe-(,)lō, -lə(-w)\ *noun, often attributive* [Middle English *felawe*, from Old English *fēolaga*, from Old Norse *fēlagi*, from *fēlag* partnership, from *fē* cattle, money + *lag* act of laying] (before 12th century)
**1 :** COMRADE, ASSOCIATE
**2 a :** an equal in rank, power, or character **:** PEER **b :** one of a pair **:** MATE
**3 :** a member of a group having common characteristics; *specifically* **:** a member of an incorporated literary or scientific society
**4 a** *obsolete* **:** a person of one of the lower social classes **b :** a worthless man or boy **c :** MAN, BOY **d :** BOYFRIEND, BEAU
**5 :** an incorporated member of a college or collegiate foundation especially in a British university
**6 :** a person appointed to a position granting a stipend and allowing for advanced study or research ◇

**fellow feeling** *noun* (1712)
**:** a feeling of community of interest or of mutual understanding

**fel·low·ly** \-lō-lē, -lə-lē\ *adjective* (13th century)
**:** SOCIABLE
— **fellowly** *adverb*

**fel·low·man** \,fe-lō-'man, -lə-\ *noun* (1667)
**:** a kindred human being

**fellow servant** *noun* (1900)
**:** an employee working with another employee under such circumstances that each one if negligent may expose the other to harm which the employer cannot reasonably be expected to guard against or be held legally liable for

**¹fel·low·ship** \'fe-lə-,ship, -lō-\ *noun* (before 12th century)
**1 :** COMPANIONSHIP, COMPANY
**2 a :** community of interest, activity, feeling, or experience **b :** the state of being a fellow or associate
**3 :** a company of equals or friends **:** ASSOCIATION
**4 :** the quality or state of being comradely
**5** *obsolete* **:** MEMBERSHIP, PARTNERSHIP

**6 a :** the position of a fellow (as of a university) **b :** the stipend of a fellow **c :** a foundation for the providing of such a stipend

**²fellowship** *verb* **-shipped** *also* **-shiped** \-,shipt\; **-ship·ping** *also* **-ship·ing** \-,shi-piŋ\ (14th century)
*intransitive verb*
**:** to join in fellowship especially with a church member
*transitive verb*
**:** to admit to fellowship (as in a church)

**fellow traveler** *noun* [translation of Russian *poputchik*] (1925)
**:** one that sympathizes with and often furthers the ideals and program of an organized group (as the Communist party) without membership in the group or regular participation in its activities
— **fel·low–trav·el·ing** *adjective*

**fel·ly** \'fe-lē\ *or* **fel·loe** \-(,)lō\ *noun, plural* **fellies** *or* **felloes** [Middle English *fely, felive*, from Old English *felg;* akin to Old High German *felga* felly, Old English *fealg* piece of plowed land] (before 12th century)
**:** the exterior rim or a segment of the rim of a wheel supported by the spokes

**felo–de–se** \,fe-lō-də-'sā, -'sē\ *noun, plural* **fe·lo·nes–de–se** \fə-,lō-(,)nēz-də-\ *or* **felos–de–se** \,fe-lōz-də-\ [Medieval Latin *felo de se, fello de se*, literally, evildoer in respect to oneself] (1607)
**1 :** one who deliberately kills himself or who dies from the effects of his commission of an unlawful malicious act
**2 :** an act of deliberate self-destruction **:** SUICIDE

**¹fel·on** \'fe-lən\ *noun* [Middle English, from Middle French *felon, fel* evildoer, probably of Germanic origin; akin to Old High German *fillen* to beat, whip, *fel* skin — more at FELL] (13th century)
**1 :** one who has committed a felony
**2** *archaic* **:** VILLAIN
**3 :** WHITLOW

**²felon** *adjective* (13th century)
**1** *archaic* **a :** CRUEL **b :** EVIL
**2** *archaic* **:** WILD

**fe·lo·ni·ous** \fə-'lō-nē-əs\ *adjective* (1575)
**1** *archaic* **:** very evil **:** VILLAINOUS
**2 :** of, relating to, or having the nature of a felony
— **fe·lo·ni·ous·ly** *adverb*
— **fe·lo·ni·ous·ness** *noun*

**fel·on·ry** \'fe-lən-rē\ *noun* (1837)
**:** FELONS; *especially* **:** the convict population of a penal colony

**fel·o·ny** \'fe-lə-nē\ *noun, plural* **-nies** (14th century)
**1 :** an act on the part of a feudal vassal involving the forfeiture of his fee
**2 a :** a grave crime formerly differing from a misdemeanor under English common law by involving forfeiture in addition to any other punishment **b :** a grave crime declared to be a felony by the common law or by statute regardless of the punishment actually imposed **c :** a crime declared a felony by statute because of the punishment imposed **d :** a crime for which the punishment in federal law may be death or imprisonment for more than one year

**fel·site** \'fel-,sīt\ *noun* [*felspar* + *-ite*] (1794)
**:** a dense igneous rock consisting almost entirely of feldspar and quartz
— **fel·sit·ic** \fel-'si-tik\ *adjective*

**fel·spar** *chiefly British variant of* FELDSPAR

**¹felt** \'felt\ *noun* [Middle English, from Old English; akin to Old High German *filz* felt, Latin *pellere* to drive, beat] (before 12th century)
**1 a :** a cloth made of wool and fur often mixed with natural or synthetic fibers through the action of heat, moisture, chemicals, and pressure **b :** a firm woven cloth of wool or cotton heavily napped and shrunk
**2 :** an article made of felt

**3 :** a material resembling felt: as **a :** a heavy paper of organic or asbestos fibers impregnated with asphalt and used in building construction **b :** semirigid pressed fiber insulation used in building
— **felt·like** *adjective*

**²felt** *transitive verb* (14th century)
**1 :** to make out of or cover with felt
**2 :** to cause to adhere and mat together
**3 :** to make into felt or a similar substance

**³felt** *past and past participle of* FEEL

**felt·ing** \'fel-tiŋ\ *noun* (1686)
**1 :** the process of making felt
**2 :** FELT

**fe·luc·ca** \fə-'lü-kə, -'lə-kə\ *noun* [Italian *feluca*] (1615)
**:** a narrow fast lateen-rigged sailing vessel chiefly of the Mediterranean area

felucca

**¹fe·male** \'fē-,māl\ *adjective* (14th century)
**1 a :** of, relating to, or being the sex that bears young or produces eggs **b :** PISTILLATE
**2 :** having some quality (as gentleness) associated with the female sex
**3 :** designed with a hollow or groove into which a corresponding male part fits ⟨*female* coupling of a hose⟩ ◇
— **fe·male·ness** *noun*

**²female** *noun* [Middle English, alteration of *femel, femelle*, from Middle French & Medieval Latin; Middle French *femelle*, from Medieval Latin *femella*, from Latin, girl, diminutive of *femina*] (14th century)
**1 a :** a female person **:** WOMAN, GIRL **b :** an individual that bears young or produces large usually immobile gametes (as eggs) that are fertilized by small usually motile gametes of a male
**2 :** a pistillate plant

◇ WORD HISTORY
**fellow** *Fellow* is one of a significant number of words—from *law* and *outlaw* in the social sphere to *egg* and *sky* in the everyday world—that English owes to the Scandinavian conquests and settlement of Britain in the 9th and 10th centuries. *Fēolaga*, the late Old English ancestor of *fellow*, was borrowed from Old Norse *fēlagi*, literally, a "fee-layer," that is, someone who put down property, typically in the form of livestock or money in a joint venture with another person, for trade or some other common goal. This sense, which we might render more loosely as "partner" or "business associate," has been lost in Modern English, but *fellow* over the course of centuries has acquired a wide variety of other meanings, one of the most common now being simply "male person."

**female** In the 14th century *female* first appears in Middle English as one spelling alongside others such as *femel* and *femelle*. All are borrowed, through medieval French, from Latin *femella* "young woman, girl," a diminutive of *femina* "woman." French *femelle* had no etymological connection to English *male*, but the phonetic similarity of the words and the fact that "male" and "female" are naturally paired concepts led English speakers to reshape the French word to make it look more similar to *male*. This process reflects the simple operation of folk etymology, that is, the alteration of less familiar words in the direction of more familiar ones.

**¹fem·i·nine** \'fe-mə-nən\ *adjective* [Middle English, from Middle French *feminin,* from Latin *femininus,* from *femina* woman; akin to Old English *delu* nipple, Latin *filius* son, *felix, fetus,* & *fecundus* fruitful, *felare* to suck, Greek *thēlē* nipple] (14th century)
**1** : FEMALE 1a
**2** : characteristic of or appropriate or unique to women
**3** : of, relating to, or constituting the gender that ordinarily includes most words or grammatical forms referring to females ⟨a *feminine* noun⟩
**4 a** : being an unstressed and usually hypermetric final syllable ⟨*feminine* ending⟩ **b** *of rhyme* : having an unstressed final syllable **c** : having the final chord occurring on a weak beat ⟨music in *feminine* cadences⟩
— **fem·i·nine·ly** *adverb*
— **fem·i·nine·ness** \-nə(n)-nəs\ *noun*
**²feminine** *noun* (15th century)
**1 a** : a noun, pronoun, adjective, or inflectional form or class of the feminine gender **b** : the feminine gender
**2** : the female principle ⟨eternal *feminine*⟩
**fem·i·nin·i·ty** \ˌfe-mə-'ni-nə-tē\ *noun* (14th century)
**1** : the quality or nature of the female sex
**2** : EFFEMINACY
**3** : WOMEN, WOMANKIND
**fem·i·nise** *British variant of* FEMINIZE
**fem·i·nism** \'fe-mə-ˌni-zəm\ *noun* (1895)
**1** : the theory of the political, economic, and social equality of the sexes
**2** : organized activity on behalf of women's rights and interests
— **fem·i·nist** \-nist\ *noun or adjective*
— **fem·i·nis·tic** \ˌfe-mə-'nis-tik\ *adjective*
**fe·min·i·ty** \fe-'mi-nə-tē, fə-\ *noun* (14th century)
: FEMININITY
**fem·i·nize** \'fe-mə-ˌnīz\ *transitive verb* **-nized; -niz·ing** (1652)
**1** : to give a feminine quality to
**2** : to cause (a male or castrate) to take on feminine characters (as by implantation of ovaries or administration of estrogenic substances)
— **fem·i·ni·za·tion** \ˌfe-mə-nə-'zā-shən\ *noun*
**femme** *also* **fem** \'fem\ *noun* [probably from French *femme* woman, from Latin *femina*] (1958)
: a lesbian who plays the female role in a homosexual relationship
**femme fa·tale** \ˌfem-fə-'tal, ˌfam-, -'täl\ *noun, plural* **femmes fa·tales** \-'tal(z), -'täl(z)\ [French, literally, disastrous woman] (1912)
**1** : a seductive woman who lures men into dangerous or compromising situations
**2** : a woman who attracts men by an aura of charm and mystery
**fem·o·ral** \'fe-mə-rəl, 'fem-rəl\ *adjective* (circa 1771)
: of or relating to the femur or thigh
**femoral artery** *noun* (circa 1771)
: the chief artery of the thigh lying in its anterior inner part
**fem·to-** \ˌfem(p)-tō\ *combining form* [International Scientific Vocabulary, from Danish or Norwegian *femten* fifteen, from Old Norse *fimmtān;* akin to Old English *fiftēne* fifteen]
: one quadrillionth ($10^{-15}$) part of ⟨*femtosecond*⟩
**fem·to·sec·ond** \'fem(p)-tə-ˌse-kənd, -kənt, -tō-\ *noun* (1976)
: one quadrillionth of a second
**fe·mur** \'fē-mər\ *noun, plural* **fe·murs** *or* **fem·o·ra** \'fe-mə-rə, 'fem-rə\ [New Latin *femor-, femur,* from Latin, thigh] (circa 1771)
**1** : the proximal bone of the hind or lower limb — called also *thighbone*
**2** : the segment of an insect's leg that is third from the body

**¹fen** \'fen\ *noun* [Middle English, from Old English *fenn;* akin to Old High German *fenna* fen, Sanskrit *paṅka* mud] (before 12th century)
: low land covered wholly or partly with water unless artificially drained
**²fen** \'fən\ *noun, plural* **fen** [Chinese (Beijing) *fēn*] (1916)
— see *yuan* at MONEY table
**¹fence** \'fen(t)s\ *noun, often attributive* [Middle English *fens,* short for *defens* defense] (14th century)
**1** *archaic* : a means of protection : DEFENSE
**2** : a barrier intended to prevent escape or intrusion or to mark a boundary; *especially* : such a barrier made of posts and wire or boards
**3** : FENCING 1
**4 a** : a receiver of stolen goods **b** : a place where stolen goods are bought
— **fence·less** \-ləs\ *adjective*
— **fence·less·ness** *noun*
— **on the fence** : in a position of neutrality or indecision
**²fence** *verb* **fenced; fenc·ing** (15th century)
*transitive verb*
**1 a** : to enclose with a fence **b** (1) : to keep in or out with a fence (2) : to ward off
**2** : to provide a defense for
**3** : to sell (stolen property) to a fence
*intransitive verb*
**1 a** : to practice fencing **b** (1) : to use tactics of attack and defense resembling those of fencing (2) : to parry arguments by shifting ground
**2** *archaic* : to provide protection
— **fenc·er** *noun*
**fence–mend·ing** \'fen(t)s-ˌmen-diŋ\ *noun* (1947)
: the rehabilitating of a deteriorated political relationship
**fence·row** \'fen(t)s-ˌrō\ *noun* (1842)
: the land occupied by a fence including the uncultivated area on each side
**fence–sit·ting** \'fen(t)s-ˌsi-tiŋ\ *noun* (1904)
: a state of indecision or neutrality with respect to conflicting positions
— **fence–sit·ter** *noun*
**fenc·ing** *noun* (1581)
**1** : the art or practice of attack and defense with the foil, épee, or saber
**2 a** (1) : FENCE 2 (2) : the fences of a property or region **b** : material used for building fences
**¹fend** \'fend\ *verb* [Middle English *fenden,* short for *defenden*] (14th century)
*transitive verb*
**1** : DEFEND
**2** : to keep or ward off : REPEL — often used with *off*
**3** *dialect British* : to provide for : SUPPORT
*intransitive verb*
**1** *dialect British* : to make an effort : STRUGGLE
**2 a** : to try to get along without help : SHIFT ⟨had to *fend* for themselves⟩ **b** : to provide a livelihood
**²fend** *noun* (1721)
*chiefly Scottish* : an effort or attempt especially for oneself
**fend·er** \'fen-dər\ *noun* (13th century)
: a device that protects: as **a** (1) : a cushion (as foam rubber or a wood float) between a boat and a dock or between two boats that lessens shock and prevents chafing (2) : a pile or a row or cluster of piles placed to protect a dock or bridge pier from damage by ships or floating objects **b** : RAILING **c** : a device in front of locomotives and streetcars to lessen injury to animals or pedestrians in case of collision **d** : a guard over the wheel of a motor vehicle **e** : a low metal frame or a screen before an open fireplace **f** : an oblong or triangular shield of leather attached to the stirrup leather of a saddle to protect a rider's legs
— **fend·ered** \-dərd\ *adjective*

— **fend·er·less** *adjective*
**fender bender** *noun* (circa 1962)
: a minor automobile accident
**fe·nes·tra** \fə-'nes-trə\ *noun, plural* **-trae** \-ˌtrē, -ˌtrī\ [New Latin, from Latin, window] (circa 1737)
**1** : a small anatomical opening (as in a bone): as **a** : an oval opening between the middle ear and the vestibule having the base of the stapes or columella attached to its membrane — called also *fenestra ova·lis* \-ō-'vā-ləs\, *fenestra ves·tib·u·li* \-ves-'ti-byə-ˌ)lē\, *oval window* **b** : a round opening between the middle ear and the cochlea — called also *fenestra cochleae, fenestra ro·tun·da* \-rō-'tən-də\, *round window*
**2** : an opening cut in bone
— **fe·nes·tral** \-trəl\ *adjective*
**fe·nes·trate** \fə-'nes-ˌtrāt, 'fe-nə-ˌstrāt\ *adjective* [Latin *fenestratus,* from *fenestra*] (1835)
: FENESTRATED
**fen·es·trat·ed** \'fe-nə-ˌstrā-təd\ *adjective* (circa 1852)
: having one or more openings or pores ⟨*fenestrated* blood capillaries⟩
**fen·es·tra·tion** \ˌfe-nə-'strā-shən\ *noun* (1846)
**1** : the arrangement, proportioning, and design of windows and doors in a building
**2** : an opening in a surface (as a wall or membrane)
**3** : the operation of cutting an opening in the bony labyrinth between the inner ear and tympanum to replace natural fenestrae that are not functional
**Fe·ni·an** \'fē-nē-ən\ *noun* [Irish *féinne,* plural of *fiann,* legendary band of Irish warriors] (1816)
**1** : a member of a legendary band of warriors defending Ireland in the 2d and 3d centuries A.D.
**2** : a member of a secret 19th century Irish and Irish-American organization dedicated to the overthrow of British rule in Ireland
— **Fenian** *adjective*
— **Fe·ni·an·ism** \-ə-ˌni-zəm\ *noun*
**fen·land** \'fen-ˌland\ *noun* (before 12th century)
: an area of low often marshy ground
**fen·nec** \'fe-nik\ *noun* [Arabic *fanak*] (1790)
: a small pale-fawn fox (*Vulpes zerda* synonym *Fennecus zerda*) with large ears that inhabits the deserts of northern Africa and Arabia
**fen·nel** \'fe-nᵊl\ *noun* [Middle English *fenel,* from Old English *finugl,* from (assumed) Vulgar Latin *fenuculum,* from Latin *feniculum* fennel, irregular diminutive of *fenum* hay] (before 12th century)
: a perennial European herb (*Foeniculum vulgare*) of the carrot family introduced into North America and cultivated for its foliage and aromatic seeds
**fen·ny** \'fe-nē\ *adjective* (before 12th century)
**1** : having the characteristics of a fen : BOGGY
**2** *archaic* : peculiar to or found in a fen
**fenu·greek** \'fen-yə-ˌgrēk\ *noun* [Middle English *fenugrek,* from Middle French *fenugrec,* from Latin *fenum Graecum,* literally, Greek hay] (14th century)
: a leguminous annual Asian herb (*Trigonella foenumgraecum*) with aromatic seeds
**feoff·ee** \fe-'fē, fē-'fē\ *noun* (15th century)
: one to whom a feoffment is made
**feoff·ment** \'fef-mənt, 'fēf-\ *noun* [Middle English *feoffement,* from Anglo-French, from *feoffer* to invest with a fee, from Old French *fief* fee] (14th century)
: the granting of a fee

| | | | | |
|---|---|---|---|---|
| \ə\ abut | \ᵊ\ kitten | \ər\ further | \a\ ash | \ā\ ace |
| \ä\ mop, mar | \au̇\ out | \ch\ chin | \e\ bet | \ē\ easy |
| \g\ go | \i\ hit | \ī\ ice | \j\ job | \ŋ\ sing | \ō\ go |
| \o̊\ law | \o̊i\ boy | \th\ thin | \ṯẖ\ the | \ü\ loot | \u̇\ foot |
| \y\ yet | \zh\ vision | | *see also* Guide to Pronunciation | |

**feof·for** \'fe-fər, 'fē-; fe-'fȯr, fē-\ *or* **feoff·er** \'fef-ər, 'fēf-\ *noun* (15th century)
: one who makes a feoffment

**-fer** \fər\ *noun combining form* [French & Latin; French *-fère,* from Latin *-fer* bearing, one that bears, from *ferre* to carry — more at BEAR]
: one that bears ⟨aqui*fer*⟩

**fe·rae na·tu·rae** \'fer-ī-nə-'tùr-ī\ *adjective* [Latin, of a wild nature] (circa 1661)
: wild by nature and not usually tamed

**fe·ral** \'fir-əl, 'fer-\ *adjective* [Medieval Latin *feralis,* from Latin *fera* wild animal, from feminine of *ferus* wild — more at FIERCE] (1604)
**1** : of, relating to, or suggestive of a wild beast : SAVAGE
**2 a** : not domesticated or cultivated : WILD **b** : having escaped from domestication and become wild
*synonym* see BRUTAL

**fer–de–lance** \'fer-dᵊl-'an(t)s, -'än(t)s\ *noun, plural* **fer–de–lance** [French, literally, lance iron, spearhead] (1880)
: a large extremely venomous pit viper (*Bothrops atrox*) of Central and South America

**fere** \'fir\ *noun* [Middle English, from Old English *gefēra;* akin to Old English *faran* to go, travel — more at FARE] (before 12th century)
**1** *archaic* : COMPANION, COMRADE
**2** *archaic* : SPOUSE

**¹fe·ria** \'fir-ē-ə, 'fer-\ *noun* [Medieval Latin — more at FAIR] (15th century)
: a weekday of a church calendar on which no feast falls
— **fe·ri·al** \-ē-əl\ *adjective*

**²fe·ria** \'fer-ē-ə, -ē-,ä\ *noun* [Spanish, fair, market, from Medieval Latin — more at FAIR] (1844)
: an Hispanic market festival often in observance of a religious holiday

**fe·rine** \'fir-,īn\ *adjective* [Latin *ferinus,* from *fera*] (1640)
: FERAL

**fer·i·ty** \'fer-ət-ē\ *noun, plural* **-ties** [Latin *feritas,* from *ferus*] (1534)
*archaic* : the quality or state of being feral; *also* : BARBARITY

**fer·lie** *also* **fer·ly** \'fer-lē\ *noun, plural* **fer·lies** [Middle English, from *ferly* strange, from Old English *fǣrlic* unexpected, from *fær* sudden danger — more at FEAR] (13th century)
*Scottish* : WONDER

**fer·ma·ta** \fer-'mä-tə\ *noun* [Italian, literally, stop, from *fermare* to stop, from Latin *firmare* to make firm] (circa 1859)
: a prolongation at the discretion of the performer of a musical note, chord, or rest beyond its given time value; *also* : the sign ⌒ denoting such a prolongation — called also *hold*

**¹fer·ment** \(,)fər-'ment\ *(14th century)*
*intransitive verb*
**1** : to undergo fermentation
**2** : to be in a state of agitation or intense activity
*transitive verb*
**1** : to cause to undergo fermentation
**2** : to work up (as into a state of agitation) : FOMENT ⟨quick-spreading rumors *fermented* the city and violence soon broke out⟩
— **fer·ment·able** \-'men-tə-bəl\ *adjective*

**²fer·ment** \'fər-,ment *also* (,)fər-'\ *noun* [Middle English, from Latin *fermentum* yeast — more at BARM] (15th century)
**1 a** : a living organism (as a yeast) that causes fermentation by virtue of its enzymes **b** : ENZYME
**2 a** : a state of unrest : AGITATION **b** : a process of active often disorderly development ⟨the great period of creative *ferment* in literature —William Barrett⟩

**fer·men·ta·tion** \,fər-mən-'tā-shən, -,men-\ *noun* (1601)
**1 a** : a chemical change with effervescence **b** : an enzymatically controlled anaerobic break-

down of an energy-rich compound (as a carbohydrate to carbon dioxide and alcohol or to an organic acid); *broadly* : an enzymatically controlled transformation of an organic compound
**2** : FERMENT 2

**fer·men·ta·tive** \(,)fər-'men-tə-tiv\ *adjective* (1661)
**1** : causing or producing a substance that causes fermentation ⟨*fermentative* organisms⟩
**2** : of, relating to, or produced by fermentation

**fer·men·ter** \(,)fər-'men-tər\ *noun* (1918)
**1** : an organism that causes fermentation
**2** *or* **fer·men·tor** : an apparatus for carrying out fermentation

**fer·mi** \'fer-(,)mē, 'fər-\ *noun* [Enrico *Fermi*] (1955)
: a unit of length equal to $10^{-13}$ centimeter

**fer·mi·on** \'fer-mē-,än, 'fər-\ *noun* [Enrico *Fermi* + English ²*-on*] (1947)
: a particle (as an electron, proton, or neutron) whose spin quantum number is an odd multiple of ½ — compare BOSON

**fer·mi·um** \'fer-mē-əm, 'fər-\ *noun* [Enrico *Fermi*] (1955)
: a radioactive metallic element artificially produced (as by bombardment of plutonium with neutrons) — see ELEMENT table

**fern** \'fərn\ *noun* [Middle English, from Old English *fearn;* akin to Old High German *farn* fern, Sanskrit *parṇa* wing, leaf] (before 12th century)
: any of a large class (Filicopsida) of flowerless spore-producing vascular plants; *especially* : any of an order (Filicales) of homosporous plants possessing roots, stems, and leaflike fronds
— **fern·like** \-,līk\ *adjective*
— **ferny** \'fər-nē\ *adjective*

**fern bar** *noun* (1976)
: a bar or restaurant fashionably decorated with green plants and especially ferns

**fern·ery** \'fər-nə-rē\ *noun, plural* **-er·ies** (1840)
**1** : a place or stand where ferns grow
**2** : a collection of growing ferns

**fern seed** *noun* (1596)
: the dustlike asexual spores of ferns formerly thought to be seeds and believed to make the possessor invisible

**fe·ro·cious** \fə-'rō-shəs\ *adjective* [Latin *feroc-, ferox,* literally, fierce looking, from *ferus* + *-oc-, -ox* (akin to Greek *ōps* eye) — more at EYE] (1646)
**1** : exhibiting or given to extreme fierceness and unrestrained violence and brutality
**2** : extremely intense ⟨*ferocious* heat⟩
*synonym* see FIERCE
— **fe·ro·cious·ly** *adverb*
— **fe·ro·cious·ness** *noun*

**fe·roc·i·ty** \fə-'rä-sə-tē\ *noun* (1606)
: the quality or state of being ferocious

**-ferous** *adjective combining form* [Middle English, from Middle French & Latin; Middle French *-fere* -fer, from Latin *-fer*]
: bearing : producing ⟨carboni*ferous*⟩

**fer·re·dox·in** \,fer-ə-'däk-sən\ *noun* [Latin *ferrum* + English *redox* + *-in*] (1962)
: any of a group of iron-containing plant proteins that function as electron carriers in photosynthetic organisms and in some anaerobic bacteria

**¹fer·ret** \'fer-ət\ *noun* [Middle English *furet, ferret,* from Middle French *furet,* from (assumed) Vulgar Latin *furittus,* literally, little thief, diminutive of Latin *fur* thief — more at FURTIVE] (14th century)
**1** : a partially domesticated usually albino European polecat that is sometimes classed as a separate species (*Mustela furo*)
**2** : an active and persistent searcher ◆
— **fer·rety** \-ə-tē\ *adjective*

**²ferret** (15th century)
*intransitive verb*
**1** : to hunt with ferrets
**2** : to search about
*transitive verb*

**1 a** (1) : to hunt (as rabbits) with ferrets (2) : to force out of hiding : FLUSH **b** : to find and bring to light by searching — usually used with *out* ⟨*ferret* out the answers⟩
**2** : HARRY, WORRY
— **fer·ret·er** *noun*

**³ferret** *noun* [probably modification of Italian *fioretti* floss silk, from plural of *fioretto,* diminutive of *fiore* flower, from Latin *flor-, flos* — more at BLOW] (1649)
: a narrow cotton, silk, or wool tape — called also *ferreting*

**ferri-** *combining form* [Latin, from *ferrum*]
**1** : iron ⟨*ferri*ferous⟩
**2** : ferric iron ⟨*ferri*cyanide⟩

**fer·ri·age** \'fer-ē-ij\ *noun* [Middle English] (14th century)
**1** : the fare paid for a ferry passage
**2** : the act or business of transporting by ferry

**fer·ric** \'fer-ik\ *adjective* (1799)
**1** : of, relating to, or containing iron
**2** : being or containing iron usually with a valence of three

**ferric ammonium citrate** *noun* (circa 1924)
: a complex salt containing varying amounts of iron and used especially for making blueprints

**ferric chloride** *noun* (1885)
: a deliquescent dark salt $FeCl_3$ that readily hydrates to the yellow-orange form and that is used in sewage treatment and as an astringent

**ferric hydroxide** *noun* (1885)
: a hydrate $Fe_2O_3 \cdot nH_2O$ of ferric oxide that is capable of acting both as a base and as a weak acid

**ferric oxide** *noun* (1882)
: the red or black oxide of iron $Fe_2O_3$ found in nature as hematite and as rust and also obtained synthetically and used as a pigment and for polishing

**fer·ri·cy·a·nide** \,fer-ī-'sī-ə-,nīd, ,fer-i-\ *noun* [International Scientific Vocabulary] (1845)
**1** : the trivalent anion $Fe(CN)_6^{3-}$
**2** : a compound containing the ferricyanide anion; *especially* : the red salt $K_3Fe(CN)_6$ used in making blue pigments

**fer·rif·er·ous** \fə-'ri-f(ə-)rəs, fe-\ *adjective* (1811)
: containing or yielding iron

**fer·ri·mag·net·ic** \'fer-,ī-mag-'ne-tik, ,fer-i-\ *adjective* (1951)
: of or relating to a substance (as ferrite) characterized by magnetization in which one group of magnetic ions is polarized in a direction opposite to the other
— **fer·ri·mag·net** \'fer-,ī-,mag-nət, 'fer-i-\ *noun*
— **fer·ri·mag·net·i·cal·ly** \'fer-,ī-mag-'ne-ti-k(ə-)lē, ,fer-i-\ *adverb*
— **fer·ri·mag·ne·tism** \-'mag-nə-,ti-zəm\ *noun*

**Fer·ris wheel** \'fer-əs-\ *noun* [G. W. G. *Ferris* (died 1896) American engineer] (1893)

◇ WORD HISTORY
**ferret** The *ferret* is a partially domesticated breed of the European polecat. For centuries the ferret has been used in Europe in hunting rats and sometimes rabbits. But both the wild polecat and his domestic relative have rather bad reputations, especially as poultry thieves. The polecat's name (Middle English *polcat*) is of uncertain origin, but one suggestion is that it may be a compound of Middle French *pol* (or *poul*) "cock," and Middle English *cat.* And the ferret is a "little thief": Middle English *ferret* (or *furet* ) comes from Middle French *furet,* which ultimately goes back to Latin *fur* "thief." The sport of ferreting out rodents and rabbits gives us the common modern sense of the verb *ferret,* "to find and bring to light by searching."

: an amusement device consisting of a large upright power-driven wheel carrying seats that remain horizontal around its rim

**fer·rite** \'fer-ˌīt\ *noun* (1851)
**1 :** any of several magnetic substances that consist essentially of ferric oxide combined with the oxides of one or more metals (as manganese, nickel, or zinc), have high magnetic permeability and high electrical resistivity, and are used especially in electronic devices
**2 :** a solid solution in which alpha iron is the solvent
— **fer·rit·ic** \fə-'ri-tik, fe-\ *adjective*

**fer·ri·tin** \'fer-ə-t°n\ *noun* [International Scientific Vocabulary, alteration of *ferratin*, iron-containing protein, from Latin *ferrat*us bound with iron (from *ferrum*) + International Scientific Vocabulary *-in*] (1937)
**:** a crystalline iron-containing protein that functions in the storage of iron and is found especially in the liver and spleen

**ferro-** *combining form* [Medieval Latin, from Latin *ferrum*]
**1 :** iron ⟨*ferro*concrete⟩
**2 :** ferrous iron ⟨*ferro*cyanide⟩

**fer·ro·ce·ment** \ˌfer-ō-si-'ment\ *noun* (1956)
**:** a building material made of thin cement slabs reinforced with steel mesh

**fer·ro·cene** \'fer-ō-ˌsēn\ *noun* [*ferro-* + *cycl-* + *-ene*] (1952)
**:** a crystalline stable organometallic coordination compound $(C_5H_5)_2Fe$; *also* **:** an analogous compound with a heavy metal (as chromium)

**fer·ro·con·crete** \ˌfer-ō-'kän-ˌkrēt, -ˌkän-'\ *noun* (1900)
**:** REINFORCED CONCRETE

**fer·ro·cy·a·nide** \-'sī-ə-ˌnīd\ *noun* (circa 1826)
**1 :** the tetravalent anion $Fe(CN)_6^{4-}$
**2 :** a compound containing the ferrocyanide anion; *especially* **:** the salt $K_4Fe(CN)_6$ used in making blue pigments (as Prussian blue)

**fer·ro·elec·tric** \ˌfer-ō-i-'lek-trik\ *adjective* (1935)
**:** of or relating to crystalline substances having spontaneous electric polarization reversible by an electric field
— **ferroelectric** *noun*
— **fer·ro·elec·tric·i·ty** \-ˌlek-'tri-sə-tē, -'tris-tē\ *noun*

**fer·ro·mag·ne·sian** \-mag-'nē-zhən, -shən\ *adjective* (1899)
**:** containing iron and magnesium ⟨*ferromagnesian* minerals⟩

**fer·ro·mag·net·ic** \-'ne-tik\ *adjective* (1896)
**:** of or relating to substances with an abnormally high magnetic permeability, a definite saturation point, and appreciable residual magnetism and hysteresis
— **fer·ro·mag·net** \'fer-ə-ˌmag-nət\ *noun*
— **fer·ro·mag·ne·tism** \ˌfer-ō-'mag-nə-ˌti-zəm\ *noun*

**fer·ro·man·ga·nese** \-'maŋ-gə-ˌnēz, -ˌnēs\ *noun* (1864)
**:** an alloy of iron and manganese containing usually about 80 percent manganese and used in the manufacture of steel

**fer·ro·sil·i·con** \-'si-li-kən, -lə-ˌkän\ *noun* (1882)
**:** an alloy of iron and silicon containing 15 to 95 percent silicon and used for deoxidizing molten steel and making silicon steel and high-silicon cast iron

**fer·ro·type** \'fer-ə-ˌtīp\ *noun* (1844)
**1 :** a positive photograph made by a collodion process on a thin iron plate having a darkened surface
**2 :** the process by which a ferrotype is made

**fer·rous** \'fer-əs\ *adjective* [New Latin *ferrosus*, from Latin *ferrum*] (1865)
**1 :** of, relating to, or containing iron
**2 :** being or containing divalent iron

**ferrous oxide** *noun* (1873)
**:** a black easily oxidizable powder FeO that is the monoxide of iron

**ferrous sulfate** *noun* (1865)
**:** a salt $FeSO_4$; *especially* **:** COPPERAS

**fer·ru·gi·nous** \fə-'rü-jə-nəs, fe-\ *adjective* [Latin *ferrugineus, ferruginus,* from *ferrugin-, ferrugo* iron rust, from *ferrum*] (circa 1661)
**1 :** of, relating to, or containing iron ⟨a *ferruginous* soil⟩
**2 :** resembling iron rust in color

**fer·rule** \'fer-əl\ *noun* [alteration of Middle English *virole*, from Middle French, from Latin *viriola*, diminutive of *viria* bracelet, of Celtic origin; akin to Old Irish *fiar* oblique] (1611)
**1 :** a ring or cap usually of metal put around a slender shaft (as a cane or a tool handle) to strengthen it or prevent splitting
**2 :** a usually metal sleeve used especially for joining or binding one part to another (as pipe sections or the bristles and handle of a brush)
— **fer·ruled** *adjective*

**¹fer·ry** \'fer-ē\ *verb* **fer·ried; fer·ry·ing** [Middle English *ferien*, from Old English *ferian* to carry, convey; akin to Old English *faran* to go — more at FARE] (before 12th century)
*transitive verb*
**1 a :** to carry by boat over a body of water **b :** to cross by a ferry
**2 a :** to convey (as by aircraft or motor vehicle) from one place to another **:** TRANSPORT **b :** to fly (an airplane) from the factory or other shipping point to a designated delivery point or from one base to another
*intransitive verb*
**:** to cross water in a boat

**²ferry** *noun, plural* **fer·ries** (15th century)
**1 :** a place where persons or things are carried across a body of water (as a river) in a boat
**2 :** FERRYBOAT
**3 :** a franchise or right to operate a ferry service across a body of water
**4 :** an organized service and route for flying airplanes especially across a sea or continent for delivery to the user

**fer·ry·boat** \'fer-ē-ˌbōt\ *noun* (15th century)
**:** a boat used to ferry passengers, vehicles, or goods

**fer·ry·man** \-mən\ *noun* (15th century)
**:** a person who operates a ferry

**fer·tile** \'fər-t°l\ *adjective* [Middle English, from Middle French & Latin; Middle French, from Latin *fertilis*, from *ferre* to carry, bear — more at BEAR] (15th century)
**1 a :** producing or bearing fruit in great quantities **:** PRODUCTIVE **b :** characterized by great resourcefulness of thought or imagination **:** INVENTIVE ⟨a *fertile* mind⟩ **c** *obsolete* **:** PLENTIFUL
**2 a** (1) **:** capable of sustaining abundant plant growth ⟨*fertile* soil⟩ (2) **:** affording abundant possibilities for development ⟨a *fertile* area for research⟩ **b :** capable of growing or developing ⟨*fertile* egg⟩ **c** (1) **:** capable of producing fruit (2) *of an anther* **:** containing pollen (3) **:** developing spores or spore-bearing organs **d :** capable of breeding or reproducing
**3 :** capable of being converted into fissionable material ⟨*fertile* uranium 238⟩ ☆
— **fer·tile·ly** \-t°l-(l)ē\ *adverb*
— **fer·tile·ness** \-t°l-nəs\ *noun*

**fer·til·i·ty** \(ˌ)fər-'ti-lə-tē\ *noun* (15th century)
**1 :** the quality or state of being fertile
**2 :** the birthrate of a population

**fer·til·iza·tion** \ˌfər-t°l-ə-'zā-shən\ *noun* (circa 1787)
**:** an act or process of making fertile: as **a :** the application of fertilizer **b** (1) **:** an act or process of fecundation, insemination, or pollination — not used technically (2) **:** the process of union of two gametes whereby the somatic chromosome number is restored and the development of a new individual is initiated

**fertilization membrane** *noun* (1931)
**:** a resistant membranous layer in eggs of many animals that forms following fertilization by the thickening and separation of the vitelline membrane from the cell surface and that prevents multiple fertilization

**fer·til·ize** \'fər-t°l-ˌīz\ *transitive verb* **-ized; -iz·ing** (1648)
**:** to make fertile: as **a :** to apply a fertilizer to ⟨*fertilize* land⟩ **b :** to cause the fertilization of
— **fer·til·iz·able** \-ˌī-zə-bəl\ *adjective*

**fer·til·iz·er** \-ˌī-zər\ *noun* (circa 1661)
**:** one that fertilizes; *specifically* **:** a substance (as manure or a chemical mixture) used to make soil more fertile

**fer·ule** \'fer-əl\ *also* **fer·u·la** \'fer-(y)ə-lə\ *noun* [Latin *ferula* giant fennel, ferule] (1580)
**1 :** an instrument (as a flat piece of wood like a ruler) used to punish children
**2 :** school discipline

**fe·ru·lic acid** \fə-'rü-lik-\ *noun* [*ferula*] (1876)
**:** a white crystalline acid that is structurally related to vanillin and is obtained especially from plant sources (as aspen bark)

**fer·ven·cy** \'fər-vən(t)-sē\ *noun, plural* **-cies** (15th century)
**:** FERVOR

**fer·vent** \'fər-vənt\ *adjective* [Middle English, from Middle French & Latin; Middle French, from Latin *fervent-, fervens,* present participle of *fervēre* to boil, froth — more at BARM] (14th century)
**1 :** very hot **:** GLOWING
**2 :** exhibiting or marked by great intensity of feeling **:** ZEALOUS ⟨*fervent* prayers⟩
*synonym* see IMPASSIONED
— **fer·vent·ly** *adverb*

**fer·vid** \'fər-vəd\ *adjective* [Latin *fervidus,* from *fervēre*] (1599)
**1 :** very hot **:** BURNING
**2 :** marked by often extreme fervor ⟨a *fervid* crusader⟩
*synonym* see IMPASSIONED
— **fer·vid·ly** *adverb*
— **fer·vid·ness** *noun*

**fer·vor** \'fər-vər\ *noun* [Middle English *fervour,* from Middle French & Latin; Middle French *ferveur,* from Latin *fervor,* from *fervēre*] (14th century)
**1 :** intensity of feeling or expression ⟨booing and cheering with almost equal *fervor* —Alan Rich⟩
**2 :** intense heat
*synonym* see PASSION

**fer·vour** *chiefly British variant of* FERVOR

**fes·cen·nine** \'fe-s°n-ˌīn, -ˌēn\ *adjective* [Latin *fescennini* (*versus*), ribald songs sung at rustic weddings, probably from *Fescinninus* of Fescennium, from *Fescennium,* town in Etruria] (1601)
**:** SCURRILOUS, OBSCENE

**fes·cue** \'fes-(ˌ)kyü\ *noun* [Middle English *festu* stalk, straw, from Middle French, from Late Latin *festucum,* from Latin *festuca*] (1513)
**1 :** a small pointer (as a stick) used to point out letters to children learning to read

---

☆ **SYNONYMS**

**Fertile, fecund, fruitful, prolific** mean producing or capable of producing offspring or fruit. FERTILE implies the power to reproduce in kind or to assist in reproduction and growth ⟨*fertile* soil⟩; applied figuratively, it suggests readiness of invention and development ⟨a *fertile* imagination⟩. FECUND emphasizes abundance or rapidity in bearing fruit or offspring ⟨a *fecund* herd⟩. FRUITFUL adds to FERTILE and FECUND the implication of desirable or useful results ⟨*fruitful* research⟩. PROLIFIC stresses rapidity of spreading or multiplying by or as if by natural reproduction ⟨a *prolific* writer⟩.

---

\ə\ abut \ᵊ\ kitten \ər\ further \a\ ash \ā\ ace
\ä\ mop, mar \aù\ out \ch\ chin \e\ bet \ē\ easy
\g\ go \i\ hit \ī\ ice \j\ job \ŋ\ sing \ō\ go
\ò\ law \òi\ boy \th\ thin \t̠h\ the \ü\ loot \ù\ foot
\y\ yet \zh\ vision *see also* Guide to Pronunciation

**2 :** any of a genus (*Festuca*) of tufted perennial grasses with panicled spikelets

**fescue foot** *noun* (1949)
: a disease of the feet of cattle resembling ergotism that is associated with feeding on fescue grass and especially tall fescue

¹**fess** *also* **fesse** \'fes\ *noun* [Middle English *fesse*, from Middle French *faisse*, from Latin *fascia* band — more at FASCIA] (15th century)
**1 :** a broad horizontal bar across the middle of a heraldic field
**2 :** the center point of an armorial escutcheon

²**fess** \'fes\ *intransitive verb* [short for *confess*] (1840)
: to own up : CONFESS — usually used with *up*

**-fest** \,fest\ *noun combining form* [German, from *Fest* celebration, from Latin *festum* — more at FEAST]
: meeting or occasion marked by (such) activity ⟨song*fest*⟩

**fes·tal** \'fes-t°l\ *adjective* [Latin *festum*] (15th century)
: of or relating to a feast or festival : FESTIVE
— **fes·tal·ly** \-t°l-ē\ *adverb*

¹**fes·ter** \'fes-tər\ *noun* [Middle English, from Middle French *festre*, from Latin *fistula* pipe, fistulous ulcer] (14th century)
: a suppurating sore : PUSTULE

²**fester** *verb* **fes·tered; fes·ter·ing** \-t(ə-)riŋ\ (14th century)
*intransitive verb*
**1 :** to generate pus
**2 :** PUTREFY, ROT
**3 a :** to cause increasing poisoning, irritation, or bitterness : RANKLE ⟨dissent *festered* unchecked⟩ **b :** to undergo or exist in a state of progressive deterioration ⟨allowed slums to *fester*⟩
*transitive verb*
: to make inflamed or corrupt

¹**fes·ti·nate** \'fes-tə-,nāt\ *verb* **-nat·ed; -nat·ing** (1596)
: HASTEN

²**fes·ti·nate** \-nət, -,nāt\ *adjective* [Latin *festinatus*, past participle of *festinare* to hasten; perhaps akin to Middle Irish *bras* forceful, Welsh *brys* haste] (1605)
: HASTY
— **fes·ti·nate·ly** *adverb*

¹**fes·ti·val** \'fes-tə-vəl\ *adjective* [Middle English, from Middle French, from Latin *festivus* festive] (14th century)
: of, relating to, appropriate to, or set apart as a festival

²**festival** *noun* (1589)
**1 a :** a time of celebration marked by special observances **b :** FEAST 2
**2 :** a periodic season or program of cultural events or entertainment
**3 :** GAIETY, CONVIVIALITY

**fes·ti·val·go·er** \-,gō-(-ə)r\ *noun* (1959)
: one who attends a festival

**fes·tive** \'fes-tiv\ *adjective* [Latin *festivus*, from *festum*] (1651)
**1 :** of, relating to, or suitable for a feast or festival
**2 :** JOYFUL, GAY
— **fes·tive·ly** *adverb*
— **fes·tive·ness** *noun*

**fes·tiv·i·ty** \fes-'ti-və-tē, fəs-\ *noun, plural* **-ties** (14th century)
**1 :** FESTIVAL 1
**2 :** the quality or state of being festive : GAIETY
**3 :** festive activity

¹**fes·toon** \fes-'tün\ *noun* [French *feston*, from Italian *festone*, from *festa* festival, from Latin — more at FEAST] (1630)
**1 :** a decorative chain or strip hanging between two points
**2 :** a carved, molded, or painted ornament representing a decorative chain

²**festoon** *transitive verb* (1800)
**1 :** to hang or form festoons on
**2 :** to shape into festoons

**3 :** DECORATE, ADORN

**fes·toon·ery** \fes-'tü-nə-rē\ *noun* (1836)
: an arrangement of festoons

**Fest·schrift** \'fest(t)-,shrift\ *noun, plural* **Fest·schrif·ten** \-,shrif-tən\ *or* **Fest·schrifts** [German, from *Fest* celebration + *Schrift* writing] (1898)
: a volume of writings by different authors presented as a tribute or memorial especially to a scholar

**fe·ta** \'fe-tə, 'fe-,tä\ *noun, often capitalized* [New Greek (*tyri*) *pheta*, from *tyri* cheese + *pheta* slice, from Italian *fetta* — more at FETTUCCINE] (1940)
: a white moderately hard and crumbly Greek cheese made from sheep's or goat's milk and cured in brine

**fe·tal** \'fē-t°l\ *adjective* (1811)
: of, relating to, or being a fetus

**fetal alcohol syndrome** *noun* (1974)
: a highly variable group of birth defects including mental retardation, deficient growth, and defects of the skull, face, and brain that tend to occur in the infants of women who consume large amounts of alcohol during pregnancy

**fetal hemoglobin** *noun* (1950)
: a hemoglobin variant that predominates in the blood of a newborn and persists in increased proportions in some forms of anemia (as thalassemia)

**fetal position** *noun* (1963)
: a position (as of a sleeping person) in which the body lies on one side, curled up with the arms and legs drawn up toward the chest and the head bowed forward

¹**fetch** \'fech\ *verb* [Middle English *fecchen*, from Old English *fetian, feccan*; perhaps akin to Old English *fōt* foot — more at FOOT] (before 12th century)
*transitive verb*
**1 a :** to go or come after and bring or take back **b :** DERIVE, DEDUCE
**2 a :** to cause to come **b :** to bring in (as a price) : REALIZE **c :** INTEREST, ATTRACT
**3 a :** to give (a blow) by striking : DEAL **b** *chiefly dialect* **:** BRING ABOUT, ACCOMPLISH **c** (1) **:** to take in (as a breath) : DRAW (2) **:** to bring forth (as a sound) : HEAVE ⟨*fetch* a sigh⟩
**4 a :** to reach by sailing especially against the wind or tide **b :** to arrive at : REACH
*intransitive verb*
**1 :** to get and bring something; *specifically* **:** to retrieve killed game
**2 :** to take a roundabout way : CIRCLE
**3 a :** to hold a course on a body of water **b :** VEER
— **fetch·er** *noun*

²**fetch** *noun* (circa 1530)
**1 :** TRICK, STRATAGEM
**2 :** an act or instance of fetching
**3 a :** the distance along open water or land over which the wind blows **b :** the distance traversed by waves without obstruction

³**fetch** *noun* [origin unknown] (circa 1787)
: DOPPELGÄNGER 1

**fetch·ing** \'fe-chiŋ\ *adjective* (1880)
: ATTRACTIVE, PLEASING
— **fetch·ing·ly** \-chiŋ-lē\ *adverb*

**fetch up** (1599)
*transitive verb*
**1 :** to bring up or out : PRODUCE
**2 :** to make up (as lost time)
**3 :** to bring to a stop
*intransitive verb*
: to reach a standstill, stopping place, or goal
: end up ⟨may have *fetched up* running a village store —Geoffrey Household⟩

¹**fete** *or* **fête** \'fāt, 'fet\ *noun* [Middle English *fete*, from Middle French, from Old French *feste* — more at FEAST] (15th century)
**1 :** FESTIVAL
**2 a :** a lavish often outdoor entertainment **b :** a large elaborate party

²**fete** *or* **fête** *transitive verb* **fet·ed** *or* **fêt·ed; fet·ing** *or* **fêt·ing** (1819)

**1 :** to honor or commemorate with a fete
**2 :** to pay high honor to

**fête cham·pê·tre** \,fāt-,shäⁿ(m)-'petr°, ,fet-\ *noun, plural* **fêtes champêtres** \*same*\ [French, literally, rural festival] (1774)
: an outdoor entertainment

**fe·ti·cide** \'fē-tə-,sīd\ *noun* (circa 1844)
: the act of causing the death of a fetus

**fet·id** \'fe-təd, *especially British* 'fē-tid\ *adjective* [Middle English, from Latin *foetidus*, from *foetēre* to stink] (15th century)
: having a heavy offensive smell
**synonym** see MALODOROUS
— **fet·id·ly** *adverb*
— **fet·id·ness** *noun*

**fe·tish** *also* **fe·tich** \'fe-tish *also* 'fē-\ *noun* [French & Portuguese; French *fétiche*, from Portuguese *feitiço*, from *feitiço* artificial, false, from Latin *facticius* factitious] (1613)
**1 a :** an object (as a small stone carving of an animal) believed to have magical power to protect or aid its owner; *broadly* **:** a material object regarded with superstitious or extravagant trust or reverence **b :** an object of irrational reverence or obsessive devotion : PREPOSSESSION **c :** an object or bodily part whose real or fantasied presence is psychologically necessary for sexual gratification and that is an object of fixation to the extent that it may interfere with complete sexual expression
**2 :** a rite or cult of fetish worshipers
**3 :** FIXATION ◆

**fe·tish·ism** *also* **fe·tich·ism** \-tish-,i-zəm\ *noun* (1801)
**1 :** belief in magical fetishes
**2 :** extravagant irrational devotion
**3 :** the pathological displacement of erotic interest and satisfaction to a fetish
— **fe·tish·ist** \-tish-ist\ *noun*
— **fe·tish·is·tic** \,fe-ti-'shis-tik *also* ,fē-\ *adjective*
— **fe·tish·is·ti·cal·ly** \-ti-k(ə-)lē\ *adverb*

**fet·lock** \'fet-,läk\ *noun* [Middle English *fitlok, fetlak*; akin to Old English *fōt* foot] (14th century)
**1 a :** a projection bearing a tuft of hair on the back of the leg above the hoof of a horse or similar animal — see HORSE illustration **b :** the tuft of hair itself
**2 :** the joint of the limb at the fetlock

**feto-** *or* **feti-** *combining form* [New Latin *fetus*]
: fetus ⟨*feti*cide⟩

**fe·tol·o·gy** \fē-'tä-lə-jē\ *noun* (1965)

---

◇ WORD HISTORY
**fetish**   The Portuguese word *feitiço* "charm, amulet" is descended from Latin *facticius* "made, artificial," a derivative of *facere* "to make, do." These Latin words are also the source of English *factitious*. When in the 15th century the Portuguese began to encounter and soon enslave peoples of West Africa, they applied *feitiço* to African religious objects, whether natural or man-made. English borrowed this word in the 17th century, at first directly from Portuguese (in spellings such as *fetisso*). Later it was borrowed again through French *fétiche*, itself ultimately from Portuguese, which gave rise to the current English form *fetish*. Both in English and other languages that borrowed it, the meaning of the word was extended to any object thought to be irrationally or obsessively worshiped. *Fetish* was given new life when it was used at the end of the 19th century by Havelock Ellis, a pioneering student of human sexuality, to refer to objects of displaced sexual obsession, and the term was adopted by psychoanalytic theorists such as Sigmund Freud, who first used the German equivalent *Fetisch* in 1905.

: a branch of medical science concerned with the study and treatment of the fetus in the uterus

— **fe·tol·o·gist** \-jist\ *noun*

**fe·to·pro·tein** \ˌfē-tō-'prō-ˌtēn, -'prō-tē-ən\ *noun* (1965)
: any of several fetal antigens present in the adult in some abnormal conditions

**fe·tor** \'fē-tər, 'fē-ˌtȯr\ *noun* [Middle English *fetoure*, from Latin *foetor*, from *foetēre*] (15th century)
: a strong offensive smell **: STENCH**

**fe·tos·co·py** \fē-'täs-kə-pē\ *noun, plural* **-pies** (1971)
: examination of the pregnant uterus by means of a fiber-optic tube

— **fe·to·scope** \'fē-tə-ˌskōp\ *noun*

**¹fet·ter** \'fe-tər\ *noun* [Middle English *feter*, from Old English; akin to Old English *fōt* foot] (before 12th century)
**1 :** a chain or shackle for the feet
**2 :** something that confines **: RESTRAINT**

**²fetter** *transitive verb* (before 12th century)
**1 :** to put fetters on **: SHACKLE**
**2 :** to restrain from motion, action, or progress
**synonym** see HAMPER

**¹fet·tle** \'fe-t°l\ *noun* (1740)
: state or condition of health, fitness, wholeness, spirit, or form — often used in the phrase *in fine fettle*

**²fettle** *transitive verb* **fet·tled; fet·tling** \'fet-liŋ, 'fe-t°l-iŋ\ [Middle English *fetlen* to shape, prepare; perhaps akin to Old English *fæt* vessel — more at VAT] (1881)
: to cover or line the hearth of (as a reverberatory furnace) with loose material (as sand or gravel)

**fet·tuc·ci·ne** *or* **fet·tuc·ci·ni** *or* **fet·tu·ci·ne** *or* **fet·tu·ci·ni** \ˌfe-tə-'chē-nē\ *noun plural but singular or plural in construction* [Italian, plural of *fettuccina*, diminutive of *fettuccia* small slice, ribbon, diminutive of *fetta* slice, probably alteration of (assumed) *offetta*, from *offa* flour cake, from Latin] (1912)
: pasta in the form of narrow ribbons; *also* **:** a dish of which fettuccine forms the base

**fettuccine Al·fre·do** \-ˌ(ˌ)al-'frā-(ˌ)dō, -ˌ(ˌ)äl-\ *noun* [from *Alfredo all'Augusteo*, restaurant in Rome where it originated] (1961)
: a dish consisting of fettuccine with butter, Parmesan cheese, cream, and seasonings — called also *fettuccine all'Alfredo* \-ˌal-(ˌ)al-, -ˌäl-(ˌ)äl-\

**fe·tus** \'fē-təs\ *noun* [Middle English, from Latin, act of bearing young, offspring; akin to Latin *fetus* newly delivered, fruitful — more at FEMININE] (14th century)
: an unborn or unhatched vertebrate especially after attaining the basic structural plan of its kind; *specifically* **:** a developing human from usually three months after conception to birth

**¹feud** \'fyüd\ *noun* [alteration of Middle English *feide*, from Middle French, of Germanic origin; akin to Old High German *fēhida* hostility, feud, Old English *fāh* hostile — more at FOE] (15th century)
: a mutual enmity or quarrel that is often prolonged or inveterate; *especially* **:** a lasting state of hostilities between families or clans marked by violent attacks for revenge

— **feud** *intransitive verb*

**²feud** *noun* [Medieval Latin *feodum, feudum*, of Germanic origin; akin to Old English *feoh* cattle, property — more at FEE] (1614)
**:** FEE 1a

**feu·dal** \'fyü-d°l\ *adjective* (1612)
**1 :** of, relating to, or having the characteristics of a medieval fee
**2 :** of, relating to, or suggestive of feudalism ⟨*feudal* law⟩

— **feu·dal·ly** \-d°l-ē\ *adverb*

**feu·dal·ism** \'fyü-d°l-ˌi-zəm\ *noun* (circa 1818)
**1 :** the system of political organization prevailing in Europe from the 9th to about the 15th centuries having as its basis the relation

of lord to vassal with all land held in fee and as chief characteristics homage, the service of tenants under arms and in court, wardship, and forfeiture
**2 :** any of various political or social systems similar to medieval feudalism

— **feu·dal·ist** \-d°l-ist\ *noun*
— **feu·dal·is·tic** \ˌfyü-d°l-'is-tik\ *adjective*

**feu·dal·i·ty** \fyü-'da-lə-tē\ *noun, plural* **-ties** (1790)
**1 :** the quality or state of being feudal
**2 :** a feudal holding, domain, or concentration of power

**feu·dal·ize** \'fyü-d°l-ˌīz\ *transitive verb* **-ized; -iz·ing** (1828)
: to make feudal

— **feu·dal·iza·tion** \ˌfyü-d°l-ə-'zā-shən\ *noun*

**¹feu·da·to·ry** \'fyü-də-ˌtōr-ē, -ˌtȯr-\ *adjective* [Medieval Latin *feudatorius*, from *feudatus*, past participle of *feudare* to enfeoff, from *feudum*] (1592)
**1 :** owing feudal allegiance
**2 :** being under the overlordship of a foreign state

**²feudatory** *noun, plural* **-ries** (1644)
**1 :** a dependent lordship **: FEE**
**2 :** one holding lands by feudal tenure

**¹feud·ist** \'fyü-dist\ *noun* (1607)
: a specialist in feudal law

**²feudist** *noun* (1901)
: one who feuds

**feuil·le·ton** \ˌfə-yə-'tōⁿ, ˌfər-, ˌfœ-\ *noun* [French, from *feuillet* sheet of paper, from Old French *foillet*, diminutive of *foille* leaf — more at FOIL] (1845)
**1 :** part of a European newspaper or magazine devoted to material designed to entertain the general reader
**2 :** something (as an installment of a novel) printed in a feuilleton
**3 a :** a novel printed in installments **b :** a work of fiction catering to popular taste
**4 :** a short literary composition often having a familiar tone and reminiscent content

— **feuil·le·ton·ism** \-'tō(ⁿ)-ˌni-zəm\ *noun*
— **feuil·le·ton·ist** \-nist\ *noun*

**Feul·gen** \'fȯil-gən\ *adjective* (1928)
: of, relating to, utilizing, or staining by the Feulgen reaction ⟨positive *Feulgen* mitochondria⟩

**Feulgen reaction** *noun* [Robert *Feulgen* (died 1955) German physiologist] (1928)
: the development of a brilliant purple color by DNA in a microscopic preparation stained with a modified Schiff's reagent

**¹fe·ver** \'fē-vər\ *noun* [Middle English, from Old English *fēfer*, from Latin *febris*] (before 12th century)
**1 a :** a rise of body temperature above the normal **b :** any of various diseases of which fever is a prominent symptom
**2 a :** a state of heightened or intense emotion or activity **b :** a contagious usually transient enthusiasm **: CRAZE**

**²fever** *verb* **fe·vered; fe·ver·ing** \'fē-v(ə-)riŋ\ (1606)
*transitive verb*
: to throw into a fever **: AGITATE**
*intransitive verb*
: to contract or be in a fever **:** become feverish

**fever blister** *noun* (circa 1860)
**: COLD SORE**

**fe·ver·few** \'fē-vər-ˌfyü\ *noun* [Middle English, from Old English *feferfuge*, from Late Latin *febrifugia* centaury — more at FEBRIFUGE] (15th century)
: a perennial European composite herb (*Chrysanthemum parthenium*) widely cultivated as an ornamental

**fe·ver·ish** \'fē-v(ə-)rish\ *adjective* (14th century)
**1 a :** tending to cause fever **b :** having the symptoms of a fever **c :** indicating or relating to fever

**2 :** marked by intense emotion, activity, or instability

— **fe·ver·ish·ly** *adverb*
— **fe·ver·ish·ness** *noun*

**fe·ver·ous** \'fē-v(ə-)rəs\ *adjective* (14th century)
**: FEVERISH**

**fever pitch** *noun* (1915)
: a state of intense excitement and agitation

**fever tree** *noun* (1868)
: any of several shrubs or trees that are thought to indicate regions free from fever or that yield remedies for fever; *especially* **:** an African acacia (*Acacia xanthlophloea*)

**fe·ver·wort** \'fē-vər-ˌwərt, -ˌwȯrt\ *noun* (circa 1814)
: a coarse American herb (*Triosteum perfoliatum*) of the honeysuckle family — called also *horse gentian*

**¹few** \'fyü\ *pronoun, plural in construction* [Middle English *fewe*, pronoun & adjective, from Old English *fēawa*; akin to Old High German *fō* little, Latin *paucus* little, *pauper* poor, Greek *paid-, pais* child, Sanskrit *putra* son] (before 12th century)
**:** not many persons or things ⟨*few* were present⟩ ⟨*few* of his stories are true⟩

**²few** *adjective* (before 12th century)
**1 :** consisting of or amounting to only a small number ⟨one of our *few* pleasures⟩
**2 :** at least some but indeterminately small in number — used with *a* ⟨caught a *few* fish⟩

— **few·ness** *noun*
— **few and far between :** few in number and infrequently met **: RARE**

**³few** *noun, plural in construction* (before 12th century)
**1 :** a small number of units or individuals ⟨a *few* of them⟩
**2 :** a special limited number ⟨the discriminating *few*⟩

**¹few·er** \'fyü-ər, 'fyu̇r\ *pronoun, plural in construction* (before 12th century)
**:** a smaller number of persons or things

**²fewer** *adjective, comparative of* FEW
**usage** see LESS

**few·trils** \'fyü-trəlz\ *noun plural* [origin unknown] (circa 1750)
*dialect English* **:** things of little value **: TRIFLES**

**fey** \'fā\ *adjective* [Middle English *feye*, from Old English *fæge*; akin to Old High German *feigi* fey and perhaps to Old English *fāh* hostile, outlawed — more at FOE] (before 12th century)
**1 a** *chiefly Scottish* **:** fated to die **: DOOMED b :** marked by a foreboding of death or calamity
**2 a :** able to see into the future **: VISIONARY b :** marked by an otherworldly air or attitude **c :** CRAZY, TOUCHED
**3 a :** PRECIOUS 3 **b :** UNCONVENTIONAL, CAMPY

— **fey·ly** *adverb*
— **fey·ness** *noun*

**fez** \'fez\ *noun, plural* **fez·zes** *also* **fez·es** [French, from *Fez*, Morocco] (circa 1803)
: a brimless cone-shaped flat-crowned hat that usually has a tassel, is usually made of red felt, and is worn especially by men in eastern Mediterranean countries

— **fezzed** \'fezd\ *adjective*

fez

**fi·acre** \fē-'äkᵣ\ *noun, plural* **fi·acres** \same, *or* -'äk-rəz\ [French, from the Hotel Saint *Fiacre*, Paris] (1699)
: a small hackney coach

**fi·an·cé** \ˌfē-ˌän-'sā, fē-'än-ˌ\ *noun* [French, from Middle French, from past participle of *fiancer* to promise, betroth, from

Old French *fiancier,* from *fiance* promise, trust, from *fier* to trust, from (assumed) Vulgar Latin *fidare,* alteration of Latin *fidere* — more at BIDE] (1864)
**:** a man engaged to be married

**fi·an·cée** \ˌfē-ˌän-'sā, fē-'än-\ *noun* [French, feminine of *fiancé*] (1853)
**:** a woman engaged to be married

**fi·an·chet·to** \ˌfē-ən-'ke-(ˌ)tō, -'che-\ *verb* [*fianchetto* (an opening in chess), from Italian, diminutive of *fianco* side, flank, from Old French *flanc* — more at FLANK] (1927) *transitive verb*
**:** to develop (a bishop) in a chess game to the second square on the adjacent knight's file *intransitive verb*
**:** to fianchetto a bishop in a chess game

**¹fi·as·co** \fē-'as-(ˌ)kō *also* -'äs-\ *noun, plural* **-coes** [French, from Italian, from *fare fiasco,* literally, to make a bottle] (circa 1854)
**:** a complete failure ◆

**²fi·as·co** \fē-'äs-(ˌ)kō, -'as-\ *noun, plural* **-coes** *also* **fi·as·chi** \-(ˌ)kē\ [Italian, from Late Latin *flasco* bottle — more at FLASK] (1887)
**:** BOTTLE, FLASK; *especially* **:** a bulbous long-necked straw-covered bottle for wine

**fi·at** \'fē-ət, -ˌat, -ˌät; 'fī-ət, -ˌat\ *noun* [Latin, let it be done, 3d singular present subjunctive of *fieri* to become, be done — more at BE] (circa 1631)
**1 :** a command or act of will that creates something without or as if without further effort
**2 :** an authoritative determination **:** DICTATE ⟨a *fiat* of conscience⟩
**3 :** an authoritative or arbitrary order **:** DECREE ⟨government by *fiat*⟩

**fiat money** *noun* (1876)
**:** money (as paper currency) not convertible into coin or specie of equivalent value

**¹fib** \'fib\ *noun* [perhaps by shortening & alteration from *fable*] (1611)
**:** a trivial or childish lie

**²fib** *intransitive verb* **fibbed; fib·bing** (1690)
**:** to tell a fib
**synonym** see LIE
— **fib·ber** *noun*

**³fib** *verb* **fibbed; fib·bing** [origin unknown] (circa 1665)
*British* **:** BEAT, PUMMEL

**fi·ber** *or* **fi·bre** \'fī-bər\ *noun* [French *fibre,* from Latin *fibra*] (1540)
**1 :** a thread or a structure or object resembling a thread: as **a** (1) **:** a slender root (as of a grass) (2) **:** an elongated tapering thick-walled plant cell void at maturity that imparts elasticity, flexibility, and tensile strength **b** (1) **:** a strand of nerve tissue **:** AXON, DENDRITE (2) **:** one of the filaments composing most of the intercellular matrix of connective tissue (3) **:** one of the elongated contractile cells of muscle tissue **c :** a slender and greatly elongated natural or synthetic filament (as of wool, cotton, asbestos, gold, glass, or rayon) typically capable of being spun into yarn **d :** indigestible material in human food that stimulates the intestine to peristalsis — called also *bulk, roughage*
**2 :** material made of fibers; *especially* **:** VULCANIZED FIBER
**3 a :** an element that gives texture or substance **b :** basic toughness **:** STRENGTH, FORTITUDE **c :** essential structure or character ⟨the very *fiber* of a person's being⟩
— **fi·bered** \-bərd\ *adjective*

**fi·ber·board** *also* **fi·bre·board** \-ˌbōrd, -ˌbȯrd\ *noun* (1897)
**:** a material made by compressing fibers (as of wood) into stiff sheets; *also* **:** PAPERBOARD

**fi·ber·fill** *also* **fi·bre·fill** \-ˌfil\ *noun* (1962)
**:** synthetic fibers used as a filling material (as for cushions)

**¹fi·ber·glass** *also* **fi·bre·glass** \-ˌglas\ *noun* (1937)

**1 :** glass in fibrous form used in making various products (as glass wool for insulation)
**2 :** a composite structural material of plastic and fiberglass

**²fiberglass** *transitive verb* (1967)
**:** to protect or repair by the application of fiberglass

**fi·ber·ize** \'fī-bə-ˌrīz\ *transitive verb* **-ized; -iz·ing** (1925)
**:** to make or break down into fibers
— **fi·ber·iza·tion** \ˌfī-b(ə-)rə-'zā-shən\ *noun*

**fi·ber–op·tic** \'fī-bə-ˌräp-tik\ *adjective* (1961)
**:** of, relating to, or using fiber optics

**fiber optics** *noun plural* (1956)
**1 :** thin transparent fibers of glass or plastic that are enclosed by material of a lower index of refraction and that transmit light throughout their length by internal reflections; *also* **:** a bundle of such fibers used in an instrument (as for viewing body cavities)
**2** *singular in construction* **:** the technique of the use of fiber optics

**fi·ber·scope** \'fī-bər-ˌskōp\ *noun* (1954)
**:** a flexible instrument utilizing fiber optics and used for examination of inaccessible areas

**Fi·bo·nac·ci number** \ˌfē-bə-ˌnä-chē-, ˌfi-bə-\ *noun* [Leonardo *Fibonacci* (died *about* 1250) Italian mathematician] (1914)
**:** an integer in the infinite sequence 1, 1, 2, 3, 5, 8, 13, . . . of which the first two terms are 1 and 1 and each succeeding term is the sum of the two immediately preceding

**fibr-** *or* **fibro-** *combining form* [Latin *fibra*]
**:** fiber **:** fibrous tissue ⟨*fibroid*⟩ **:** fibrous and ⟨*fibrovascular*⟩

**fi·branne** \'fī-ˌbran, fī-'\ *noun* [French, viscose rayon, from *fibre*] (1941)
**:** a fabric made of spun-rayon yarn

**fi·bril** \'fī-brəl, 'fi-\ *noun* [New Latin *fibrilla,* diminutive of Latin *fibra*] (1664)
**:** a small filament or fiber: as **a :** ROOT HAIR **b** (1) **:** one of the fine threads into which a striated muscle fiber can be longitudinally split (2) **:** NEUROFIBRIL
— **fi·bril·lar** \'fi-brə-lər, 'fī-\ *adjective*

**fi·bril·late** \'fi-brə-ˌlāt, 'fī-\ *verb* **-lat·ed; -lat·ing** (circa 1847) *intransitive verb*
**:** to undergo or exhibit fibrillation *transitive verb*
**:** to cause to undergo fibrillation

**fi·bril·la·tion** \ˌfi-brə-'lā-shən, ˌfī-\ *noun* (1845)
**1 :** an act or process of forming fibers or fibrils
**2 a :** a muscular twitching involving individual muscle fibers acting without coordination **b :** very rapid irregular contractions of the muscle fibers of the heart resulting in a lack of synchronism between heartbeat and pulse

**fi·brin** \'fī-brən\ *noun* (1800)
**:** a white insoluble fibrous protein formed from fibrinogen by the action of thrombin especially in the clotting of blood

**fi·brin·o·gen** \fī-'bri-nə-jən\ *noun* [International Scientific Vocabulary] (1872)
**:** a plasma protein that is produced in the liver and is converted into fibrin during blood clot formation

**fi·bri·noid** \'fī-brə-ˌnȯid, 'fī-\ *noun, often attributive* (1910)
**:** a homogeneous acidophilic refractile material that somewhat resembles fibrin and is formed in the walls of blood vessels and in connective tissue in some pathological conditions and normally in the placenta

**fi·bri·no·ly·sin** \ˌfī-brə-nᵊl-'ī-sᵊn\ *noun* [International Scientific Vocabulary] (1915)
**:** any of several proteolytic enzymes that promote the dissolution of blood clots; *especially* **:** PLASMIN

**fi·bri·no·ly·sis** \-'ī-səs, -brə-'nä-lə-səs\ *noun* [New Latin] (1907)

**:** the usually enzymatic breakdown of fibrin
— **fi·bri·no·lyt·ic** \-brə-nᵊl-'i-tik\ *adjective*

**fi·bri·no·pep·tide** \ˌfī-brə-nō-'pep-ˌtīd\ *noun* (1960)
**:** any of the vertebrate polypeptides that are cleaved from fibrinogen by thrombin during blood clot formation

**fi·bro·blast** \'fī-brə-ˌblast, 'fi-\ *noun* [International Scientific Vocabulary] (1876)
**:** a connective-tissue cell of mesenchymal origin that secretes proteins and especially molecular collagen from which the extracellular fibrillar matrix of connective tissue forms
— **fi·bro·blas·tic** \ˌfī-brə-'blas-tik, ˌfi-\ *adjective*

**fi·bro·cys·tic** \ˌfī-brə-'sis-tik, ˌfi-\ *adjective* (1854)
**:** characterized by the presence or development of fibrous tissue and cysts

**¹fi·broid** \'fī-ˌbrȯid, 'fi-\ *adjective* (1852)
**:** resembling, forming, or consisting of fibrous tissue

**²fibroid** *noun* (circa 1860)
**:** a benign tumor that consists of fibrous and muscular tissue and occurs especially in the uterine wall

**fi·bro·in** \'fī-brə-wən, 'fi-\ *noun* [French *fibroïne,* from *fibr-* + *-ine* -in] (1878)
**:** an insoluble protein comprising the filaments of the raw silk fiber

**fi·bro·ma** \fī-'brō-mə\ *noun, plural* **-mas** *also* **-ma·ta** \-mə-tə\ (circa 1849)
**:** a benign tumor consisting mainly of fibrous tissue
— **fi·bro·ma·tous** \-mə-təs\ *adjective*

**fi·bro·nec·tin** \ˌfī-brə-'nek-tən\ *noun* [*fibr-* + Latin *nectere* to tie, bind + English *-in*] (1976)
**:** any of a group of glycoproteins of cell surfaces, blood plasma, and connective tissue that promote cellular adhesion and migration

**fi·bro·sar·co·ma** \ˌfī-brə-sär-'kō-mə, ˌfi-\ *noun* (1878)
**:** a sarcoma of relatively low malignancy consisting chiefly of spindle-shaped cells that tend to form collagenous fibrils

**fi·bro·sis** \fī-'brō-səs\ *noun* [New Latin] (1873)
**:** a condition marked by increase of interstitial fibrous tissue
— **fi·brot·ic** \-'brä-tik\ *adjective*

**fi·bro·si·tis** \ˌfī-brə-'sī-təs, ˌfi-\ *noun* [New Latin, from *fibrosus* fibrous, from International Scientific Vocabulary *fibrous*] (1904)

: a rheumatic disorder of fibrous tissue

**fi·brous** \'fī-brəs\ *adjective* [modification of French *fibreux*, from *fibre* fiber] (1626)
**1 a :** containing, consisting of, or resembling fibers **b :** characterized by fibrosis **c :** capable of being separated into fibers ⟨a *fibrous* mineral⟩
**2 :** TOUGH, SINEWY ⟨*fibrous* texture⟩

**fibrous root** *noun* (1626)
: a root (as in most grasses) that has no prominent central axis and that branches in all directions

**fi·bro·vas·cu·lar** \'fī-brō-'vas-kyə-lər, ‚fī-\ *adjective* (1845)
: having or consisting of fibers and conducting cells

**fibrovascular bundle** *noun* (circa 1889)
: VASCULAR BUNDLE

**fib·u·la** \'fi-byə-lə\ *noun, plural* **-lae** \-lē, -lī\ *or* **-las** [Latin, pin, clasp; akin to Latin *figere* to fasten] (1615)
**1 :** the outer and usually smaller of the two bones between the knee and ankle in the hind or lower limbs of vertebrates
**2 :** a clasp resembling a safety pin used especially by the ancient Greeks and Romans
— **fib·u·lar** \-lər\ *adjective*

**fibula 2**

**-fic** \fik\ *adjective suffix* [Middle French & Latin; Middle French *-fique*, from Latin *-ficus*, from *facere* to make — more at DO]
: making : causing ⟨felici*fic*⟩

**-fi·ca·tion** \fə-'kā-shən\ *noun combining form* [Middle English *-ficacioun*, from Middle French & Latin; Middle French *-fication*, from Latin *-fication-, -ficatio*, from *-ficare* to make, from *-ficus*]
: making : production ⟨rei*fication*⟩

**fice** \'fīs\ *variant of* FEIST

**fiche** \'fēsh *also* 'fish\ *noun, plural* **fiche** *also* **fiches** (1951)
: MICROFICHE

**fi·chu** \'fi-(‚)shü, 'fē-\ *noun* [French, from past participle of *ficher* to stick in, throw on, from (assumed) Vulgar Latin *figicare*, from Latin *figere* to fasten, pierce] (1803)
: a woman's light triangular scarf that is draped over the shoulders and fastened in front or worn to fill in a low neckline

**fi·cin** \'fī-s°n\ *noun* [Latin *ficus* fig] (1930)
: a protease obtained from the latex of fig trees and used as an anthelmintic and protein digestive

**fick·le** \'fi-kəl\ *adjective* [Middle English *fikel* deceitful, inconstant, from Old English *ficol* deceitful; akin to Old English *beficlan* to deceive, and probably to Old English *fāh* hostile — more at FOE] (13th century)
: marked by lack of steadfastness, constancy, or stability : given to erratic changeableness
**synonym** see INCONSTANT
— **fick·le·ness** *noun*
— **fick·ly** \'fi-k(ə-)lē\ *adverb*

**fi·co** \'fē-(‚)kō\ *noun, plural* **ficoes** [obsolete *fico*, obscene gesture of contempt, modification of Italian *fica* fig, vulva, gesture of contempt, from (assumed) Vulgar Latin *fica* fig — more at FIG] (1598)
*archaic* : FIG 2

**fic·tile** \'fik-t°l, -‚tīl\ *adjective* [Latin *fictilis* molded of clay, from *fingere*] (1626)
**1** *archaic* : PLASTIC 2a
**2 :** of or relating to pottery
**3 :** MALLEABLE 2a

**fic·tion** \'fik-shən\ *noun* [Middle English *ficcioun*, from Middle French *fiction*, from Latin *fiction-, fictio* act of fashioning, fiction, from *fingere* to shape, fashion, feign — more at DOUGH] (14th century)
**1 a :** something invented by the imagination

or feigned; *specifically* : an invented story **b** : fictitious literature (as novels or short stories) **c :** a work of fiction; *especially* : NOVEL
**2 a :** an assumption of a possibility as a fact irrespective of the question of its truth ⟨a legal *fiction*⟩ **b :** a useful illusion or pretense
**3 :** the action of feigning or of creating with the imagination
— **fic·tion·al** \-shnəl, -shə-n°l\ *adjective*
— **fic·tion·al·i·ty** \‚fik-shə-'na-lə-tē\ *noun*
— **fic·tion·al·ly** \'fik-shnə-lē, -shə-n°l-ē\ *adverb*

**fictionalise** *British variant of* FICTIONALIZE
**fic·tion·al·ize** \'fik-shnə-‚līz, -shə-n°l-‚īz\ *transitive verb* **-ized; -iz·ing** (1918)
: to make into or treat in the manner of fiction ⟨*fictionalize* a biography⟩
— **fic·tion·al·iza·tion** \‚fik-shnə-lə-'zā-shən, -shə-n°l-ə-\ *noun*

**fic·tion·eer** \‚fik-shə-'nir\ *noun* (1923)
: one who writes fiction especially in quantity and without high standards
— **fic·tion·eer·ing** *noun*

**fic·tion·ist** \'fik-sh(ə-)nist\ *noun* (1829)
: a writer of fiction; *especially* : NOVELIST
**fic·tion·ize** \'fik-shə-‚nīz\ *transitive verb* **-ized; -iz·ing** (1831)
: FICTIONALIZE
— **fic·tion·iza·tion** \‚fik-shə-nə-'zā-shən\ *noun*

**fic·ti·tious** \fik-'ti-shəs\ *adjective* [Latin *ficticius* artificial, feigned, from *fictus*] (1634)
**1 :** of, relating to, or characteristic of fiction : IMAGINARY
**2 a :** conventionally or hypothetically assumed or accepted ⟨a *fictitious* concept⟩ **b** *of a name* : FALSE, ASSUMED
**3 :** not genuinely felt ☆
— **fic·ti·tious·ly** *adverb*
— **fic·ti·tious·ness** *noun*

**fic·tive** \'fik-tiv\ *adjective* (1612)
**1 :** not genuine : FEIGNED
**2 :** of, relating to, or capable of imaginative creation
**3 :** of, relating to, or having the characteristics of fiction : FICTIONAL
— **fic·tive·ly** *adverb*
— **fic·tive·ness** *noun*

**fi·cus** \'fī-kəs\ *noun, plural* **ficus** *or* **fi·cus·es** [New Latin, from Latin, fig] (1864)
: FIG 1b

**fid** \'fid\ *noun* [origin unknown] (1615)
: a tapered usually wooden pin used in opening the strands of a rope

**-fid** \fəd\ *adjective combining form* [Latin *-fidus*, from *findere* to split — more at BITE]
: divided into (so many) parts or (such) parts ⟨pinnati*fid*⟩

**¹fid·dle** \'fi-d°l\ *noun* [Middle English *fidel*, from (assumed) Old English *fithele*, probably from Medieval Latin *vitula*] (13th century)
**1 :** VIOLIN
**2 :** a device (as a slat, rack, or light railing) to keep dishes from sliding off a table aboard ship
**3 :** FIDDLESTICKS — used as an interjection
**4** [²*fiddle*] *chiefly British* : SWINDLE

**²fiddle** *verb* **fid·dled; fid·dling** \'fid-liŋ, 'fi-d°l-iŋ\ (14th century)
*intransitive verb*
**1 :** to play on a fiddle
**2 a :** to move the hands or fingers restlessly **b :** to spend time in aimless or fruitless activity : PUTTER, TINKER ⟨*fiddled* around with the engine for hours⟩ **c :** MEDDLE, TAMPER
*transitive verb*
**1 :** to play (as a tune) on a fiddle
**2 :** CHEAT, SWINDLE
**3 :** to alter or manipulate deceptively for fraudulent gain ⟨accountants *fiddling* the books —Stanley Cohen⟩
— **fid·dler** \'fid-lər, 'fi-d°l-ər\ *noun*

**fiddle away** *transitive verb* (1667)
: to fritter away ⟨*fiddling away* the time⟩

**fid·dle–back** \'fi-d°l-‚bak\ *noun* (1890)
: something resembling a fiddle

**fid·dle–fad·dle** \'fi-d°l-‚fa-d°l\ *noun* [reduplication of *fiddle* (fiddlesticks)] (1577)
: NONSENSE — often used as an interjection

**fid·dle–foot·ed** \‚fi-d°l-'fù-təd\ *adjective* (1941)
**1 :** SKITTISH, JUMPY ⟨a *fiddle-footed* horse⟩
**2 :** prone to wander ⟨the nameless *fiddle-footed* drifters, the shifty riders who traveled the back trails —Luke Short⟩

**fid·dle·head** \'fi-d°l-‚hed\ *noun* (1882)
: one of the young unfurling fronds of some ferns that are often eaten as greens

**fiddler crab** *noun* (1843)
: any of a genus (*Uca*) of burrowing crabs in which the male has one claw that is greatly enlarged

**fiddler crab**

**fid·dle·stick** \'fi-d°l-‚stik\ *noun* (15th century)
**1 :** a violin bow
**2 a :** something of little value : TRIFLE ⟨didn't care a *fiddlestick* for that⟩ **b** *plural* : NONSENSE — used as an interjection

**fid·dling** \'fid-liŋ, -lən\ *adjective* (1652)
: TRIFLING, PETTY ⟨a *fiddling* excuse⟩

**fid·dly** \'fi-d°l-ē\ *adjective* (1926)
*chiefly British* : requiring close attention to detail : FUSSY

**fi·de·ism** \'fē-(‚)dā-‚i-zəm\ *noun* [probably from French *fidéisme*, from Latin *fides*] (1885)
: reliance on faith rather than reason in pursuit of religious truth
— **fi·de·ist** \-‚dā-ist\ *noun*
— **fi·de·is·tic** \‚fē-(‚)dā-'is-tik\ *adjective*

**Fi·del·is·ta** \‚fē-d°l-'ē-stə\ *noun* [American Spanish, from *Fidel* Castro + *-ista* -ist] (1960)
: an adherent of Castroism

**fi·del·i·ty** \fə-'de-lə-tē, fī-\ *noun, plural* **-ties** [Middle English *fidelite*, from Middle French *fidelité*, from Latin *fidelitat-, fidelitas*, from *fidelis* faithful, from *fides* faith, from *fidere* to trust — more at BIDE] (15th century)
**1 a :** the quality or state of being faithful **b :** accuracy in details : EXACTNESS
**2 :** the degree to which an electronic device (as a record player, radio, or television) accu-

---

☆ **SYNONYMS**

**Fictitious, fabulous, legendary, mythical, apocryphal** mean having the nature of something imagined or invented. FICTITIOUS implies fabrication and suggests artificiality or contrivance more than deliberate falsification or deception ⟨*fictitious* characters⟩. FABULOUS stresses the marvelous or incredible character of something without necessarily implying impossibility or actual nonexistence ⟨a land of *fabulous* riches⟩. LEGENDARY suggests the elaboration of invented details and distortion of historical facts produced by popular tradition ⟨the *legendary* exploits of Davy Crockett⟩. MYTHICAL implies a purely fanciful explanation of facts or the creation of beings and events out of the imagination ⟨*mythical* creatures⟩. APOCRYPHAL implies an unknown or dubious source or origin or may imply that the thing itself is dubious or inaccurate ⟨a book that repeats many *apocryphal* stories⟩.

---

rately reproduces its effect (as sound or picture) ☆

**fidge** \'fij\ *intransitive verb* **fidged; fidg·ing** [probably alteration of English dialect *fitch*, from Middle English *fichen*] (1575) *chiefly Scottish* **:** FIDGET

¹**fidg·et** \'fi-jət\ *noun* [irregular from *fidge*] (1674)
**1 :** uneasiness or restlessness as shown by nervous movements — usually used in plural
**2** [²*fidget*] **:** one that fidgets

²**fidget** (1754)
*intransitive verb*
**:** to move or act restlessly or nervously
*transitive verb*
**:** to cause to move or act nervously

**fidg·ety** \'fi-jə-tē\ *adjective* (circa 1736)
**1 :** inclined to fidget
**2 :** making unnecessary fuss **:** FUSSY
— **fidg·et·i·ness** *noun*

**fi·do** \'fī-(,)dō\ *noun, plural* **fidos** [freaks + irregulars + defects + oddities] (1967)
**:** a coin having a minting error

**fi·du·cial** \fə-'dü-shəl, -'dyü-, fī-\ *adjective* (1571)
**1 :** taken as standard of reference ⟨a *fiducial* mark⟩
**2 :** founded on faith or trust
**3 :** having the nature of a trust **:** FIDUCIARY
— **fi·du·cial·ly** \-shə-lē\ *adverb*

¹**fi·du·cia·ry** \-'dü-shē-,er-ē, -shə-rē, -'dyü-\ *noun, plural* **-ries** (1631)
**:** one that holds a fiduciary relation or acts in a fiduciary capacity

²**fiduciary** *adjective* [Latin *fiduciarius,* from *fiducia* confidence, trust, from *fidere*] (circa 1641)
**:** of, relating to, or involving a confidence or trust: as **a :** held or founded in trust or confidence **b :** holding in trust **c :** depending on public confidence for value or currency ⟨*fiduciary* fiat money⟩

**fie** \'fī\ *interjection* [Middle English *fī,* from Old French] (14th century)
— used to express disgust or disapproval

**fief** \'fēf\ *noun* [French, from Old French — more at FEE] (circa 1611)
**1 :** a feudal estate **:** FEE
**2 :** something over which one has rights or exercises control ⟨a politician's *fief*⟩
— **fief·dom** \-dəm\ *noun*

¹**field** \'fē(ə)ld\ *noun* [Middle English, from Old English *feld;* akin to Old High German *feld* field, Old English *flōr* floor — more at FLOOR] (before 12th century)
**1 a** (1) **:** an open land area free of woods and buildings (2) **:** an area of land marked by the presence of particular objects or features ⟨dune *field*⟩ **b** (1) **:** an area of cleared enclosed land used for cultivation or pasture ⟨a *field* of wheat⟩ (2) **:** land containing a natural resource (3) **:** AIRFIELD **c :** the place where a battle is fought; *also* **:** BATTLE **d :** a large unbroken expanse (as of ice)
**2 a :** an area or division of an activity **b :** the sphere of practical operation outside a base (as a laboratory, office, or factory) ⟨geologists working in the *field*⟩ **c :** an area for military exercises or maneuvers **d** (1) **:** an area constructed, equipped, or marked for sports (2) **:** the portion of an indoor or outdoor sports area within the running track on which field events are held (3) **:** any of the three sections of a baseball outfield ⟨hits to all *fields*⟩
**3 :** a space on which something is drawn or projected: as **a :** the space on the surface of a coin, medal, or seal that does not contain the design **b :** the ground of each division in a flag **c :** the whole surface of an escutcheon
**4 :** the individuals that make up all or part of the participants in a sports activity; *especially* **:** all participants with the exception of the favorite or the winner in a contest where more than two are entered
**5 :** the area visible through the lens of an optical instrument

**6 a :** a region or space in which a given effect (as magnetism) exists **b :** a region of embryonic tissue capable of a particular type of differentiation ⟨a morphogenetic *field*⟩
**7 :** a set of mathematical elements that is subject to two binary operations the second of which is distributive relative to the first and that constitutes a commutative group under the first operation and also under the second if the zero or unit element under the first is omitted
**8 :** a complex of forces that serve as causative agents in human behavior
**9 :** a series of drain tiles and an absorption area for septic-tank overflow
**10 :** a particular area (as of a record in a database) in which the same type of information is regularly recorded

²**field** *adjective* (12th century)
**:** of or relating to a field: as **a :** growing in or inhabiting the fields or open country **b :** made, conducted, or used in the field **c :** operating or active in the field

³**field** (1823)
*transitive verb*
**1 a :** to catch or pick up (a batted ball) and usually throw to a teammate **b :** to take care of or respond to (as a telephone call or a request) **c :** to give an impromptu answer or solution to ⟨the senator *fielded* the reporters' questions⟩
**2 :** to put into the field ⟨*field* an army⟩ ⟨*field* a team⟩; *also* **:** to enter in competition
*intransitive verb*
**:** to play as a fielder

**field artillery** *noun* (1644)
**:** artillery other than antiaircraft artillery used with armies in the field

**field bed** *noun* (1926)
**:** a four-poster with a canopy arched at the center

**field corn** *noun* (1856)
**:** an Indian corn (as dent corn or flint corn) with starchy kernels grown for feeding stock or for market grain

**field crop** *noun* (1860)
**:** an agricultural crop (as hay, grain, or cotton) grown on large areas

**field day** *noun* (1747)
**1 a :** a day for military exercises or maneuvers **b :** an outdoor meeting or social gathering **c :** a day of sports and athletic competition
**2 :** a time of extraordinary pleasure or opportunity ⟨TV had a *field day* with the scandal⟩

**field–ef·fect transistor** \'fēl-də-,fekt-\ *noun* (1959)
**:** a transistor in which the output current is controlled by a variable electric field

**field·er** \'fēl-dər\ *noun* (1832)
**:** one that fields; *especially* **:** a defensive player stationed in the field (as in baseball)

**fielder's choice** *noun* (1902)
**:** a situation in baseball in which a batter reaches base safely because the fielder attempts to put out another base runner on the play

**field event** *noun* (1899)
**:** an event (as weight-throwing or jumping) in a track-and-field meet other than a race

**field·fare** \'fē(ə)l(d)-,far, -,fer\ *noun* [Middle English *feldefare,* from Old English, from *feld* + *-fare;* probably akin to Old English *fara* companion; akin to Old English *faran* to go — more at FARE] (before 12th century)
**:** a medium-sized Eurasian thrush (*Turdus pilaris*) with an ash-colored head and chestnut wings

**field glass** *noun* (1836)
**:** a binocular without prisms especially for use outdoors — usually used in plural

**field goal** *noun* (1902)
**1 :** a score of three points in football made by drop-kicking or place-kicking the ball over the crossbar from ordinary play
**2 :** a goal in basketball made while the ball is in play

**field grade** *noun* (1944)
**:** the rank of a field officer

**field guide** *noun* (1934)
**:** a manual for identifying natural objects, flora, or fauna in the field

**field hand** *noun* (1826)
**:** an outdoor farm laborer

**field hockey** *noun* (1903)
**:** a game played on a turfed field between two teams of 11 players each whose object is to direct a ball into the opponent's goal with a hockey stick

**field house** *noun* (1895)
**1 :** a building at an athletic field for housing equipment or providing dressing facilities
**2 :** a building enclosing a large area suitable for various forms of athletics and usually providing seats for spectators

**fielding average** *noun* (1947)
**:** the average (as of a baseball fielder) determined by dividing the number of putouts and assists by the number of chances — compare BATTING AVERAGE

**field judge** *noun* (circa 1929)
**:** a football official whose duties include covering action on kicks and forward passes and timing intermission periods and time-outs

**field lens** *noun* (1837)
**:** the lens in a compound eyepiece that is nearer the objective

**field magnet** *noun* (1883)
**:** a magnet for producing and maintaining a magnetic field especially in a generator or electric motor

**field marshal** *noun* (1614)
**:** the highest ranking military officer (as in the British army)

**field mouse** *noun* (15th century)
**:** any of various mice and voles that inhabit fields

**field officer** *noun* (1656)
**:** a commissioned officer in the army, air force, or marine corps of the rank of colonel, lieutenant colonel, or major — compare COMPANY OFFICER, GENERAL OFFICER

**field of force** (1850)
**:** FIELD 6a

**field of honor** (1824)
**1 :** BATTLEFIELD
**2 :** a place where a duel is fought

**field of view** (circa 1816)
**:** FIELD 5

**field of vision** (1862)
**:** VISUAL FIELD

**field pea** *noun* (1709)
**:** a small-seeded pea (*Pisum sativum* variety *arvense*) widely grown for forage and food

**field·piece** \'fē(ə)l(d)-,pēs\ *noun* (1590)
**:** a gun or howitzer for use in the field

**field spaniel** *noun* (1867)
**:** any of a breed of medium-sized hunting and retrieving spaniels that have a flat dense usually black, liver, red, or roan coat

**field·stone** \'fē(ə)l(d)-,stōn\ *noun* (1799)
**:** stone (as in building) in usually unaltered form as taken from the field

---

☆ SYNONYMS
**Fidelity, allegiance, fealty, loyalty, devotion, piety** mean faithfulness to something to which one is bound by pledge or duty. FIDELITY implies strict and continuing faithfulness to an obligation, trust, or duty ⟨marital *fidelity*⟩. ALLEGIANCE suggests an adherence like that of citizens to their country ⟨pledging *allegiance*⟩. FEALTY implies a fidelity acknowledged by the individual and as compelling as a sworn vow ⟨*fealty* to the truth⟩. LOYALTY implies a faithfulness that is steadfast in the face of any temptation to renounce, desert, or betray ⟨valued the *loyalty* of his friends⟩. DEVOTION stresses zeal and service amounting to self-dedication ⟨a painter's *devotion* to her art⟩. PIETY stresses fidelity to obligations regarded as natural and fundamental ⟨filial *piety*⟩.

**field·strip** \-ˌstrip\ *transitive verb* (1947)
: to take apart (a weapon) to the extent authorized for routine cleaning, lubrication, and minor repairs
**field–test** \-ˌtest\ *transitive verb* (1948)
: to test (as a procedure or product) in a natural environment
— **field test** *noun*
**field theory** *noun* (1901)
: a detailed mathematical description of the assumed physical properties of a region under some influence (as gravitation)
**field trial** *noun* (1895)
**1** : a trial of sporting dogs in actual performance
**2** : a trial of a new product in actual situations for which it is intended
**field trip** *noun* (1926)
: a visit (as to a factory, farm, or museum) made (as by students and a teacher) for purposes of firsthand observation
**field winding** *noun* (1893)
: the winding of a field magnet
**field·work** \ˈfē(ə)l-ˌdwərk\ *noun* (1819)
**1** : a temporary fortification thrown up by an army in the field
**2** : work done in the field (as by students) to gain practical experience and knowledge through firsthand observation
**3** : the gathering of anthropological or sociological data through the interviewing and observation of subjects in the field
— **field·work·er** *noun*
**fiend** \ˈfēnd\ *noun* [Middle English, from Old English *fēond*; akin to Old High German *fīant* enemy, Sanskrit *pīyati* he scorns] (before 12th century)
**1 a** : DEVIL 1 **b** : DEMON **c** : a person of great wickedness or maliciousness
**2** : a person extremely devoted to a pursuit or study : FANATIC ⟨a golf *fiend*⟩
**3** : ADDICT 1 ⟨a dope *fiend*⟩
**4** : WIZARD 3 ⟨a *fiend* at mathematics⟩
**fiend·ish** \ˈfēn-dish\ *adjective* (1529)
**1** : perversely diabolical ⟨took a *fiendish* pleasure in hurting people⟩
**2** : extremely cruel or wicked
**3** : excessively bad, unpleasant, or difficult ⟨*fiendish* weather⟩
— **fiend·ish·ly** *adverb*
— **fiend·ish·ness** *noun*
**fierce** \ˈfirs\ *adjective* **fierc·er**; **fierc·est** [Middle English *fiers*, from Middle French, from Latin *ferus* wild, savage; akin to Greek *thēr* wild animal] (14th century)
**1 a** : violently hostile or aggressive in temperament **b** : given to fighting or killing : PUGNACIOUS
**2 a** : marked by unrestrained zeal or vehemence ⟨a *fierce* argument⟩ **b** : extremely vexatious, disappointing, or intense ⟨*fierce* pain⟩
**3** : furiously active or determined ⟨make a *fierce* effort⟩
**4** : wild or menacing in appearance ☆
— **fierce·ly** *adverb*
— **fierce·ness** *noun*
**fi·eri fa·cias** \ˌfī-(ə)rē-ˈfā-sh(ē-)əs\ *noun* [Latin, cause (it) to be done] (15th century)
: a writ authorizing the sheriff to obtain satisfaction of a judgment in debt or damages from the goods and chattels of the defendant
**fi·ery** \ˈfī-(ə)-rē\ *adjective* **fi·er·i·er**; **-est** [Middle English, from *fire, fier* fire] (13th century)
**1 a** : consisting of fire **b** : BURNING, BLAZING **c** : using or carried out with fire **d** : liable to catch fire or explode : FLAMMABLE ⟨a *fiery* vapor⟩
**2 a** : hot like a fire **b** (1) : being in an inflamed state or condition ⟨a *fiery* boil⟩ (2) : feverish and flushed ⟨a *fiery* forehead⟩
**3** : of the color of fire : RED ⟨a *fiery* sunset⟩
**4** : full of or exuding emotion or spirit ⟨a *fiery* sermon⟩ **b** : easily provoked : IRRITABLE
— **fi·eri·ly** \ˈfī-rə-lē\ *adverb*
— **fi·eri·ness** \ˈfī-rē-nəs\ *noun*

— **fiery** *adverb*
**fi·es·ta** \fē-ˈes-tə\ *noun* [Spanish, from Latin *festa* — more at FEAST] (1844)
: FESTIVAL; *specifically* : a saint's day celebrated in Spain and Latin America with processions and dances
**fife** \ˈfīf\ *noun* [German *Pfeife* pipe, fife, from Old High German *pfīfa*, from (assumed) Vulgar Latin *pipa* pipe — more at PIPE] (1539)
: a small transverse flute with six to eight finger holes and usually no keys
**fife rail** *noun* (circa 1800)
: a rail about the mast near the deck to which rigging is belayed
**fif·teen** \ˌfif-ˈtēn, ˈfif-ˌ\ *noun* [Middle English *fiftene*, adjective, from Old English *fīftēne*, from *fīf* five + *-tīene* (akin to Old English *tīen* ten) — more at FIVE, TEN] (before 12th century)
**1** — see NUMBER table
**2** : the first point scored by a side in a game of tennis — called also *five*
— **fifteen** *adjective*
— **fifteen** *pronoun, plural in construction*
— **fif·teenth** \-ˈtēn(t)th, -ˌtēn(t)th\ *adjective or noun*
**fifth** \ˈfith, ˈfif(t)th, ˈfift\ *noun, plural* **fifths** \ˈfiths, ˈfif(t)ths, ˈfif(t)s\ (before 12th century)
**1** — see NUMBER table
**2 a** : the musical interval embracing five diatonic degrees **b** : a tone at this interval; *specifically* : DOMINANT 1 **c** : the harmonic combination of two tones at this interval
**3** : a unit of measure for liquor equal to one fifth of a U.S. gallon (0.757 liter)
**4** *capitalized* : the Fifth Amendment of the U.S. Constitution
— **fifth** *adjective or adverb*
— **fifth·ly** *adverb*
**fifth column** *noun* [name applied to rebel sympathizers in Madrid in 1936 when four rebel columns advanced on the city] (1936)
: a group of secret sympathizers or supporters of an enemy that engage in espionage or sabotage within defense lines or national borders
◆
— **fifth col·um·nism** \-ˈkä-ləm-ˌ(n)i-zəm\ *noun*
— **fifth col·um·nist** \-(n)ist\ *noun*
**fifth wheel** *noun* (circa 1874)
**1 a** : a horizontal wheel or segment of a wheel that consists of two parts rotating on each other above the fore axle of a carriage and that forms support to prevent tipping **b** : a similar coupling between tractor and trailer of a semitrailer
**2** : one that is superfluous, unnecessary, or burdensome
**fif·ty** \ˈfif-tē\ *noun, plural* **fifties** [Middle English, from *fifty*, adjective, from Old English *fīftig*, from *fīftig*, noun, group of 50, from *fīf* five + *-tig* group of ten; akin to *tīen* ten] (before 12th century)
**1** — see NUMBER table
**2** *plural* : the numbers 50 to 59; *specifically* : the years 50 to 59 in a lifetime or century
**3** : a 50-dollar bill
— **fif·ti·eth** \-tē-əth\ *adjective or noun*
— **fifty** *adjective*
— **fifty** *pronoun, plural in construction*
— **fif·ty·ish** \-tē-ish\ *adjective*
**fif·ty–fif·ty** \ˌfif-tē-ˈfif-tē\ *adjective* (1913)
**1** : shared, assumed, or borne equally ⟨a *fifty-fifty* proposition⟩
**2** : half favorable and half unfavorable ⟨a *fifty-fifty* chance⟩
— **fifty–fifty** *adverb*
**¹fig** \ˈfig\ *noun* [Middle English *fige*, from Old French, from Old Provençal *figa*, from (assumed) Vulgar Latin *fica*, from Latin *ficus* fig tree, fig] (13th century)
**1 a** : an oblong or pear-

**fig 1: leaves and fruit**

shaped fruit that is a syconium **b** : any of a genus (*Ficus*) of trees of the mulberry family bearing fruits that are syconia; *especially* : a widely cultivated tree (*F. carica*) that produces edible figs
**2** : a worthless trifle : the least bit ⟨doesn't care a *fig*⟩
**²fig** *noun* [*fig*, verb (to adorn)] (1835)
: DRESS, ARRAY ⟨a young woman in dazzling royal full *fig* —Mollie Panter-Downes⟩
**¹fight** \ˈfīt\ *verb* **fought** \ˈfȯt\; **fight·ing** [Middle English, from Old English *feohtan*; akin to Old High German *fehtan* to fight and perhaps to Latin *pectere* to comb — more at PECTINATE] (before 12th century)
*intransitive verb*
**1 a** : to contend in battle or physical combat; *especially* : to strive to overcome a person by blows or weapons **b** : to engage in boxing
**2** : to put forth a determined effort
*transitive verb*
**1 a** (1) : to contend against in or as if in battle or physical combat (2) : to box against in the

---

☆ SYNONYMS
**Fierce, ferocious, barbarous, savage, cruel** mean showing fury or malignity in looks or actions. FIERCE applies to humans and animals that inspire terror because of their wild and menacing aspect or fury in attack ⟨*fierce* warriors⟩. FEROCIOUS implies extreme fierceness and unrestrained violence and brutality ⟨a *ferocious* dog⟩. BARBAROUS implies a ferocity or mercilessness regarded as unworthy of civilized people ⟨*barbarous* treatment of prisoners⟩. SAVAGE implies the absence of inhibitions restraining civilized people filled with rage, lust, or other violent passion ⟨a *savage* criminal⟩. CRUEL implies indifference to suffering and even positive pleasure in inflicting it ⟨the *cruel* jokes of schoolboys⟩.

---

◇ WORD HISTORY
**fifth column** *Fifth column* apparently first appeared in English in *New York Times* dispatches by William Carney, a correspondent reporting on the Spanish Civil War. On October 16, 1936, Carney mentioned raids in Republican-held Madrid that "apparently were instigated by a recent broadcast over the Rebel radio station by General Emilio Mola. He stated he was counting on four columns of troops outside Madrid and another column of persons hiding within the city who would join the invaders as soon as they entered the capital." Carney was accurately reflecting the fact that Spanish *quinta columna* "fifth column" was an epithet for subversive Nationalist ("Rebel") elements in the city. But subsequent literature on the war makes no mention of a radio broadcast by Mola, which Carney himself seems not to have heard, and Nationalist biographies of Mola do not attribute the phrase to him. In fact, the first documented use of *quinta columna* was on October 2, in a newspaper article by the Communist leader "La Pasionaria" (Dolores Ibárruri). The phrase may actually have been a propaganda invention of the Republicans attributed to Mola in order to justify reprisals against supposed Nationalist supporters in Madrid. In any event, *fifth column* soon became an international catchphrase for a conspiracy of traitors within one's own camp.

---

\ə\ **abut** \ᵊ\ **kitten** \ər\ **further** \a\ **ash** \ā\ **ace**
\ä\ **mop, mar** \au̇\ **out** \ch\ **chin** \e\ **bet** \ē\ **easy**
\g\ **go** \i\ **hit** \ī\ **ice** \j\ **job** \ŋ\ **sing** \ō\ **go**
\ȯ\ **law** \ȯi\ **boy** \th\ **thin** \t͟h\ **the** \ü\ **loot** \u̇\ **foot**
\y\ **yet** \zh\ **vision** *see also* Guide to Pronunciation

ring **b** (1) **:** to attempt to prevent the success or effectiveness of ⟨the company *fought* the takeover attempt⟩ (2) **:** to oppose the passage or development of ⟨*fight* a bill in Congress⟩ **2 a :** WAGE, CARRY ON ⟨*fight* a battle⟩ **b :** to take part in (as a boxing match) **3 :** to struggle to endure or surmount ⟨*fight* a cold⟩ **4 a :** to gain by struggle ⟨*fights* his way through⟩ **b :** to resolve by struggle ⟨*fought* out their differences in court⟩ **5 a :** to manage (a ship) in a battle or storm **b :** to cause to struggle or contend **c :** to manage in an unnecessarily rough or awkward manner
— **fight shy of :** to avoid facing or meeting
**²fight** *noun* (before 12th century) **1 a :** a hostile encounter **:** BATTLE, COMBAT **b :** a boxing match **c :** a verbal disagreement **:** ARGUMENT **2 :** a struggle for a goal or an objective ⟨a *fight* for justice⟩ **3 :** strength or disposition for fighting **:** PUGNACITY ⟨still full of *fight*⟩

**fight·er** \'fī-tər\ *noun* (13th century) **:** one that fights: as **a** (1) **:** WARRIOR, SOLDIER (2) **:** a pugnacious or game individual (3) **:** ¹BOXER 1 **b :** an airplane of high speed and maneuverability with armament designed to destroy enemy aircraft

**fight·er-bomb·er** \-'bä-mər\ *noun* (1936) **:** a fighter aircraft fitted to carry bombs and rockets in addition to its normal armament

**fighting chair** *noun* (1950) **:** a chair from which a salt-water angler plays a hooked fish

**fighting chance** *noun* (1889) **:** a chance that may be realized by a struggle ⟨the patient had a *fighting chance* to live⟩

**fighting word** *noun* (1917) **:** a word likely to provoke a fight

**fight song** *noun* (1954) **:** a song used to inspire enthusiasm usually during an athletic competition

**fig leaf** *noun* (14th century) **1 :** the leaf of a fig tree **2** [from the use by Adam and Eve of fig leaves to cover their nakedness after eating the forbidden fruit (Genesis 3:7)] **:** something that conceals or camouflages usually inadequately or dishonestly

**fig marigold** *noun* (1731) **:** any of several herbs (genus *Mesembryanthemum*) of the carpetweed family with showy white or pink flowers

**fig·ment** \'fig-mənt\ *noun* [Middle English, from Latin *figmentum*, from *fingere* to shape — more at DOUGH] (15th century) **:** something made up or contrived

**fig·ur·al** \'fi-g(y)ə-rəl\ *adjective* (1813) **:** of, relating to, or consisting of human or animal figures ⟨a *figural* composition⟩

**fig·u·ra·tion** \,fi-g(y)ə-'rā-shən\ *noun* (14th century) **1 :** FORM, OUTLINE **2 :** the act or process of creating or providing a figure **3 :** an act or instance of representation in figures and shapes ⟨cubism was explained as a synthesis of colored *figurations* of objects —Janet Flanner⟩ **4 :** ornamentation of a musical passage by using decorative and usually repetitive figures

**fig·u·ra·tive** \'fi-g(y)ə-rə-tiv\ *adjective* (14th century) **1 a :** representing by a figure or resemblance **:** EMBLEMATIC **b :** of or relating to representation of form or figure in art ⟨*figurative* sculpture⟩ **2 a :** expressing one thing in terms normally denoting another with which it may be regarded as analogous **:** METAPHORICAL ⟨*figurative* language⟩ **b :** characterized by figures of speech ⟨a *figurative* description⟩
— **fig·u·ra·tive·ly** *adverb*
— **fig·u·ra·tive·ness** *noun*

**¹fig·ure** \'fi-gyər, *British & often US* 'fi-gər\ *noun* [Middle English, from Old French, from Latin *figura*, from *fingere*] (13th century) **1 a :** a number symbol **:** NUMERAL, DIGIT ⟨a salary running into six *figures*⟩ **b** *plural* **:** arithmetical calculations ⟨good at *figures*⟩ **c :** a written or printed character **d :** value especially as expressed in numbers **:** SUM, PRICE ⟨sold at a low *figure*⟩ **2 a :** a geometric form (as a line, triangle, or sphere) especially when considered as a set of geometric elements (as points) in space of a given number of dimensions ⟨a square is a plane *figure*⟩ **b :** bodily shape or form especially of a person ⟨a slender *figure*⟩ **c :** an object noticeable only as a shape or form ⟨*figures* moving in the dusk⟩ **3 a :** the graphic representation of a form especially of a person or geometric entity **b :** a diagram or pictorial illustration of textual matter **4 :** a person, thing, or action representative of another **5 a :** FIGURE OF SPEECH **b :** an intentional deviation from the ordinary form or syntactical relation of words **6 :** the form of a syllogism with respect to the relative position of the middle term **7 :** an often repetitive pattern or design in a manufactured article (as cloth) or natural product (as wood) ⟨a polka-dot *figure*⟩ **8 :** appearance made **:** impression produced ⟨the couple cut quite a *figure*⟩ **9 a :** a series of movements in a dance **b :** an outline representation of a form traced by a series of evolutions (as with skates on an ice surface or by an airplane in the air) **10 :** a prominent personality **:** PERSONAGE ⟨great *figures* of history⟩ **11 :** a short coherent group of notes or chords that may constitute part of a phrase, theme, or composition

**²figure** *verb* **fig·ured; fig·ur·ing** \'fi-gyə-riŋ, 'fi-g(ə-)riŋ\ (14th century) *transitive verb* **1 :** to represent by or as if by a figure or outline **2 :** to decorate with a pattern; *also* **:** to write figures over or under (the bass) in order to indicate the accompanying chords **3 :** to indicate or represent by numerals **4 a :** CALCULATE **b :** CONCLUDE, DECIDE ⟨*figured* there was no use in further effort⟩ **c :** REGARD, CONSIDER **d :** to appear likely ⟨*figures* to win⟩ *intransitive verb* **1 a :** to be or appear important or conspicuous **b :** to be involved or implicated ⟨*figured* in a robbery⟩ **2 :** to perform a figure in dancing **3 :** COMPUTE, CALCULATE **4 :** to seem rational, normal, or expected ⟨that *figures*⟩
— **fig·ur·er** \-g(y)ər-ər\ *noun*
— **figure on 1 :** to take into consideration ⟨*figuring* on the extra income⟩ **2 :** to rely on **3 :** PLAN ⟨I *figure on* going into town⟩

**fig·ured** \-g(y)ərd\ *adjective* (15th century) **1 :** adorned with, formed into, or marked with a figure ⟨*figured* muslin⟩ ⟨*figured* wood⟩ **2 :** being represented **:** PORTRAYED **3 :** indicated by figures

**figured bass** *noun* (1801) **:** CONTINUO

**figure eight** *noun* (1887) **:** something resembling the Arabic numeral eight in form or shape: as **a :** a small knot — see KNOT illustration **b :** an embroidery stitch **c :** a dance pattern **d :** a skater's figure — called also *figure-of-eight*

**fig·ure·head** \'fi-g(y)ər-,hed\ *noun* (1765) **1 :** the figure on a ship's bow **2 :** a head or chief in name only

**figure in** *transitive verb* (circa 1934) **:** to include especially in a reckoning

**figure of merit** (circa 1865) **:** a numerical quantity based on one or more characteristics of a system or device that represents a measure of efficiency or effectiveness

**figure of speech** (1824) **:** a form of expression (as a simile or metaphor) used to convey meaning or heighten effect often by comparing or identifying one thing with another that has a meaning or connotation familiar to the reader or listener

**figure out** *transitive verb* (1833) **1 :** DISCOVER, DETERMINE ⟨try to *figure out* a way to do it⟩ **2 :** SOLVE, FATHOM ⟨*figure out* a problem⟩

**figure skating** *noun* (1852) **:** skating characterized by the performance of various jumps, spins, and dance movements and formerly by the tracing of prescribed figures
— **figure skater** *noun*

**fig·u·rine** \,fi-g(y)ə-'rēn\ *noun* [French, from Italian *figurina*, diminutive of *figura* figure, from Latin — more at FIGURE] (1854) **:** a small carved or molded figure **:** STATUETTE

**fig wasp** *noun* (1883) **:** a minute wasp (*Blastophaga psenes* of the family Agaontidae) that breeds in the caprifig and is the agent of caprification; *broadly* **:** any wasp of the same family

**fig·wort** \'fig-,wərt, -,wôrt\ *noun* (1548) **:** any of a genus (*Scrophularia*) of chiefly herbaceous plants of the snapdragon family with leaves having no stipules, an irregular bilabiate corolla, and a 2-celled ovary

**Fi·ji·an** \'fē-(,)jē-ən, fi-\ *noun* (1809) **1 :** a member of a Melanesian people of Fiji **2 :** the Austronesian language of the Fijians
— **Fijian** *adjective*

**fil·a·ment** \'fi-lə-mənt\ *noun* [Middle French, from Medieval Latin *filamentum*, from Late Latin *filare* to spin — more at FILE] (1594) **:** a single thread or a thin flexible threadlike object, process, or appendage: as **a :** a tenuous conductor (as of carbon or metal) made incandescent by the passage of an electric current; *specifically* **:** a cathode in the form of a metal wire in an electron tube **b** (1) **:** a thin and fine elongated constituent part of a gill (2) **:** an elongated thin series of cells attached one to another or a very long thin cylindrical single cell (as of some algae, fungi, or bacteria) **c :** the anther-bearing stalk of a stamen — see FLOWER illustration
— **fil·a·men·ta·ry** \,fil-ə-'men-t(ə-)rē\ *adjective*
— **fil·a·men·tous** \-'men-təs\ *adjective*

**fi·lar** \'fī-lər\ *adjective* [Latin *filum* thread] (circa 1859) **:** of or relating to a thread or line; *especially* **:** having threads across the field of view ⟨a *filar* eyepiece⟩

**fi·lar·ia** \fə-'lar-ē-ə, -'ler-\ *noun, plural* **-i·ae** \-ē-,ē, -ē-,ī\ [New Latin, genus name, from Latin *filum*] (1834) **:** any of numerous slender filamentous nematodes (*Filaria* and related genera) that as adults are parasites in the blood or tissues of mammals and as larvae usually develop in biting insects
— **fi·lar·i·al** \-ē-əl\ *adjective*
— **fi·lar·i·id** \-ē-əd\ *adjective or noun*

**fil·a·ri·a·sis** \,fil-ə-'rī-ə-səs\ *noun, plural* **-a·ses** \-,sēz\ [New Latin] (1879) **:** infestation with or disease caused by filariae

**fil·a·ture** \'fil-ə-,chú(ə)r, -,chər, -,t(y)ú(ə)r\ *noun* [French, from Late Latin *filatus*, past participle of *filare*] (1759) **:** a factory where silk is reeled

**fil·bert** \'fil-bərt\ *noun* [Middle English, from Anglo-French *philber*, from Saint *Philibert* (died 684) Frankish abbot whose feast day falls in the nutting season] (14th century) **1 :** either of two European hazels (*Corylus avellana* and *C. maxima*); *also* **:** the sweet thick-shelled nut of the filbert

**2 :** HAZELNUT ◆

**filch** \'filch\ *transitive verb* [Middle English] (1561)
: to appropriate furtively or casually ⟨*filch* a cookie⟩
**synonym** see STEAL

**¹file** \'fī(ə)l\ *noun* [Middle English, from Old English *fēol;* akin to Old High German *fīla* file] (before 12th century)
**1 :** a tool usually of hardened steel with cutting ridges for forming or smoothing surfaces especially of metal
**2 :** a shrewd or crafty person

**²file** *transitive verb* **filed; fil·ing** (13th century)
: to rub, smooth, or cut away with or as if with a file

**³file** *transitive verb* **filed; fil·ing** [Middle English, from Old English *fȳlan,* from *fūl* foul] (before 12th century)
*chiefly dialect* **:** DEFILE, CORRUPT

**⁴file** *verb* **filed; fil·ing** [Middle English, from Middle French *filer* to string documents on a string or wire, from *fil* thread, from Old French, from Latin *filum;* akin to Armenian *ǰil* sinew] (15th century)
*transitive verb*
**1 :** to arrange in order for preservation and reference ⟨*file* letters⟩
**2 a :** to place among official records as prescribed by law ⟨*file* a mortgage⟩ **b :** to send (copy) to a newspaper ⟨*filed* a story⟩ **c :** to return to the office of the clerk of a court without action on the merits
**3 :** to initiate (as a legal action) through proper formal procedure ⟨threatened to *file* charges⟩
*intransitive verb*
**1 :** to register as a candidate especially in a primary election
**2 :** to place items in a file
— **fil·er** \'fī-lər\ *noun*

**⁵file** *noun* (1525)
**1 :** a device (as a folder, case, or cabinet) by means of which papers are kept in order
**2 a** *archaic* **:** ROLL, LIST **b :** a collection of papers or publications usually arranged or classified **c** (1) **:** a collection of related data records (as for a computer) (2) **:** a complete collection of data (as text or a program) treated by a computer as a unit especially for purposes of input and output
— **on file :** in or as if in a file for ready reference

**⁶file** *noun* [Middle French, from *filer* to spin, from Late Latin *filare,* from Latin *filum*] (1598)
**1 :** a row of persons, animals, or things arranged one behind the other
**2 :** any of the rows of squares that extend across a chessboard from one player's side to the other player's side

**⁷file** *intransitive verb* **filed; fil·ing** (1616)
: to march or proceed in file

**filé** *also* **file** \fə-'lā, (,)fē-'lā, 'fē-(,)lā\ *noun* [Louisiana French, from French, past participle of *filer* to twist, spin] (1806)
: powdered young leaves of sassafras used to thicken soups or stews

**file clerk** *noun* (1919)
: a clerk who works on files

**file·fish** \'fī(ə)l-,fish\ *noun* (1814)
: any of various bony fishes (order Tetraodontiformes and especially genera *Aluterus, Cantherhines,* and *Monacanthus* of the family Balistidae) with rough granular leathery skins

**fi·let** \fi-'lā\ *noun* [French, literally, net] (1881)
: a lace with a square mesh and geometric designs

**fi·let mi·gnon** \,fi-(,)lā-mēn-'yōⁿ, fi-,lā-\ *noun, plural* **filets mignons** \,fi-(,)lā-mēn-'yōⁿz, fi-,lā-\ [French, literally, dainty fillet] (1906)
: a thick slice of beef cut from the narrow end of a beef tenderloin

**fili-** *or* **filo-** *combining form* [Latin *filum*]
**:** thread ⟨*filiform*⟩

**fil·ial** \'fi-lē-əl, 'fil-yəl\ *adjective* [Middle English, from Late Latin *filialis,* from Latin *filius* son — more at FEMININE] (14th century)
**1 :** of, relating to, or befitting a son or daughter ⟨*filial* obedience⟩
**2 :** having or assuming the relation of a child or offspring
— **fil·ial·ly** \-lē-ə-lē, -yə-lē\ *adverb*

**filial generation** *noun* (1909)
: a generation in a breeding experiment that is successive to a mating between parents of two distinctively different but usually relatively pure genotypes

**fil·i·a·tion** \,fi-lē-'ā-shən\ *noun* (15th century)
**1 a :** filial relationship especially of a son to his father **b :** the adjudication of paternity
**2 a :** descent or derivation especially from a culture or language **b :** the act or process of determining such relationship

**¹fil·i·bus·ter** \'fi-lə-,bəs-tər\ *noun* [Spanish *filibustero,* literally, freebooter] (1851)
**1 :** an irregular military adventurer; *specifically* **:** an American engaged in fomenting insurrections in Latin America in the mid-19th century
**2** [²filibuster] **a :** the use of extreme dilatory tactics in an attempt to delay or prevent action especially in a legislative assembly **b :** an instance of this practice ◆

**²filibuster** *verb* **-tered; -ter·ing** \-t(ə-)riŋ\ (1853)
*intransitive verb*
**1 :** to carry out insurrectionist activities in a foreign country
**2 :** to engage in a filibuster
*transitive verb*
: to subject to a filibuster
— **fil·i·bus·ter·er** \-tər-ər\ *noun*

**fi·li·form** \'fi-lə-,form, 'fī-\ *adjective* (1757)
: shaped like a filament

**¹fil·i·gree** \'fi-lə-,grē\ *noun* [modification of French *filigrane,* from Italian *filigrana,* from Latin *filum* + *granum* grain — more at CORN] (1693)
**1 :** ornamental work especially of fine wire of gold, silver, or copper applied chiefly to gold and silver surfaces

**filigree 2a**

**2 a :** ornamental openwork of delicate or intricate design **b :** a pattern or design resembling such openwork ⟨a *filigree* of frost⟩ **c :** ORNAMENTATION, EMBELLISHMENT ⟨writings . . . heavy with late Victorian *filigree* —Jack Beatty⟩

**²filigree** *transitive verb* **fil·i·greed; fil·i·gree·ing** (1831)
: to adorn with or as if with filigree

**fil·ing** \'fī-liŋ\ *noun* (14th century)
**1 :** an act or instance of using a file
**2 :** a fragment rubbed off in filing ⟨iron *filings*⟩

**fil·io·pi·etis·tic** \'fi-lē-ō-,pī-ə-'tis-tik\ *adjective* [*filial* + *-o-* + *pietistic*] (1893)
: of or relating to an often excessive veneration of ancestors or tradition

**Fil·i·pi·na** \,fi-lə-'pē-nə\ *noun* [Spanish] (1899)
: a Filipino girl or woman

**Fil·i·pi·no** \-'pē-(,)nō\ *noun, plural* **Filipinos** [Spanish] (circa 1889)
**1 :** a native of the Philippine islands
**2 :** a citizen of the Republic of the Philippines
— **Filipino** *adjective*

**¹fill** \'fil\ *verb* [Middle English, from Old English *fyllan;* akin to Old English *full* full] (before 12th century)
*transitive verb*
**1 a :** to put into as much as can be held or conveniently contained ⟨*fill* a cup with water⟩

**b :** to supply with a full complement ⟨the class is already *filled*⟩ **c** (1) **:** to cause to swell or billow ⟨wind *filled* the sails⟩ (2) **:** to trim (a sail) to catch the wind **d :** to raise the level of with *fill* ⟨*filled* land⟩ **e :** to repair the cavities of (teeth) **f :** to stop up **:** OBSTRUCT, PLUG ⟨wreckage *filled* the channel⟩ **g :** to stop up the interstices, crevices, or pores of (as cloth, wood, or leather) with a foreign substance
**2 a :** FEED, SATIATE **b :** SATISFY, FULFILL ⟨*fills* all requirements⟩ **c :** MAKE OUT, COMPLETE — used with *out* or *in* ⟨*fill* out a form⟩ ⟨*fill* in the blanks⟩ **d :** to draw the playing cards necessary to complete (as a straight or flush in poker)
**3 a :** to occupy the whole of ⟨smoke *filled* the room⟩ **b :** to spread through **c :** to make full ⟨a mind *filled* with fantasies⟩
**4 a :** to possess and perform the duties of **:** HOLD ⟨*fill* an office⟩ **b :** to place a person in ⟨*fill* a vacancy⟩
**5 :** to supply as directed ⟨*fill* a prescription⟩
**6 :** to cover the surface of with a layer of precious metal
*intransitive verb*
: to become full
— **fill one's shoes :** to take over one's job, position, or responsibilities

**²fill** *noun* (before 12th century)
**1 :** a full supply; *especially* **:** a quantity that satisfies or satiates ⟨eat your *fill*⟩
**2 :** something that fills: as **a :** material used to fill a receptacle, cavity, passage, or low place

| | | | |
|---|---|---|---|
| \ə\ abut | \ᵊ\ kitten | \ər\ **further** | \a\ ash | \ā\ ace |
| \ä\ mop, mar | \aú\ out | \ch\ chin | \e\ bet | \ē\ **easy** |
| \g\ go | \i\ hit | \ī\ ice | \j\ job | \ŋ\ sing | \ō\ go |
| \ò\ law | \òi\ boy | \th\ thin | \th\ the | \ü\ loot | \ù\ foot |
| \y\ yet | \zh\ vision | | *see also* Guide to Pronunciation |

**b :** a bit of instrumental music that fills the pauses between phrases (as of a vocalist or soloist)

**fill away** *intransitive verb* (1840)
**1 :** to trim a sail to catch the wind
**2 :** to proceed on the course especially after being brought up in the wind

¹**fill·er** \'fi-lər\ *noun* (15th century)
**:** one that fills: as **a :** a substance added to a product (as to increase bulk, weight, viscosity, opacity, or strength) **b :** a composition used to fill the pores and grain especially of a wood surface before painting or varnishing **c :** a piece used to cover or fill in a space between two parts of a structure **d :** tobacco used to form the core of a cigar **e :** material used to fill extra space in a column or page of a newspaper or magazine **f :** a pack of paper for a loose-leaf notebook **g :** a sound, word, or phrase (as "you know?") used to fill pauses in speaking

²**fil·ler** \'fi-,ler\ *noun, plural* **fillers** *or* **filler** [Hungarian *fillér*] (1904)
— see *forint* at MONEY table

¹**fil·let** \'fi-lət, *in sense 2b also* fi-'lā, 'fi-(,)lā\ *also* **fi·let** \fi-'lā, 'fi-(,)lā\ *noun* [Middle English *filet*, from Middle French, diminutive of *fil* thread — more at FILE] (14th century)
**1 :** a ribbon or narrow strip of material used especially as a headband
**2 a :** a thin narrow strip of material **b :** a piece or slice of boneless meat or fish; *especially* **:** the tenderloin of beef
**3 a :** a concave junction formed where two surfaces meet (as at an angle) **b :** a strip that gives a rounded appearance to such a junction; *also* **:** a strip to reinforce the corner where two surfaces meet
**4 :** a narrow flat architectural member: **a :** a flat molding separating others — see BASE illustration **b :** the space between two flutings in a shaft

²**fil·let** \'fi-lət, *in sense 2 also* fi-'lā, 'fi-(,)lā\ *transitive verb* (1604)
**1 :** to bind, furnish, or adorn with or as if with a fillet
**2 :** to cut into fillets

**fillet weld** *noun* (1926)
**:** a weld of approximately triangular cross section used to join two pieces especially perpendicularly

**fill-in** \'fil-,in\ *noun* (1917)
**:** someone or something that fills in

**fill in** (1840)
*transitive verb*
**1 :** to give necessary or recently acquired information to ⟨I'll *fill* you *in*⟩
**2 :** to enrich (as a design) with detail
*intransitive verb*
**:** to fill a vacancy usually temporarily

**fill·ing** \'fi-liŋ\ *noun* (14th century)
**1 :** an act or instance of filling
**2 :** something used to fill a cavity, container, or depression
**3 :** something that completes: as **a :** the yarn interlacing the warp in a fabric; *also* **:** yarn for the shuttle **b :** a food mixture used to fill pastry or sandwiches

**filling station** *noun* (1921)
**:** SERVICE STATION 1

¹**fil·lip** \'fi-ləp\ *transitive verb* [probably of imitative origin] (15th century)
**1 a :** to make a filliping motion with **b :** to strike or tap with a fillip ⟨*filliped* him on the nose⟩
**2 :** to project quickly by or as if by a fillip ⟨*fillip* crumbs off the table⟩
**3 :** STIMULATE ⟨with this to *fillip* his spirits —Robert Westerby⟩

²**fillip** *noun* (1519)
**1 a :** a blow or gesture made by the sudden forcible straightening of a finger curled up against the thumb **b :** a short sharp blow **:** BUFFET
**2 :** something tending to arouse or excite: as **a :** STIMULUS ⟨just the *fillip* my confidence need-

ed⟩ ⟨lent a *fillip* of danger to the sport⟩ **b :** a trivial addition **:** EMBELLISHMENT ⟨showy *fillips* of language⟩ **c :** a significant and often unexpected development **:** WRINKLE ⟨plot twists and *fillips*⟩

**fill out** *intransitive verb* (1888)
**:** to put on flesh

**fill–up** \'fil-,əp\ *noun* (1853)
**:** an action or instance of filling up something (as a gas tank)

**fil·ly** \'fi-lē\ *noun, plural* **fillies** [Middle English *fyly*, from Old Norse *fylja*; akin to Old English *fola* foal] (15th century)
**1 :** a young female horse usually of less than four years
**2 :** a young woman **:** GIRL

¹**film** \'film, *Southern also* 'fi(ə)m\ *noun, often attributive* [Middle English *filme*, from Old English *filmen*; akin to Greek *pelma* sole of the foot, Old English *fell* skin — more at FELL] (before 12th century)
**1 a :** a thin skin or membranous covering **:** PELLICLE **b :** an abnormal growth on or in the eye
**2 :** a thin covering or coating ⟨a *film* of ice⟩
**3 a :** an exceedingly thin layer **:** LAMINA **b** (1) **:** a thin flexible transparent sheet (as of plastic) used especially as a wrapping (2) **:** such a sheet of cellulose acetate or nitrocellulose coated with a radiation-sensitive emulsion for taking photographs
**4 :** MOTION PICTURE

²**film** (1602)
*transitive verb*
**1 :** to cover with or as if with a film
**2 :** to make a motion picture of or from ⟨*film* a scene⟩
*intransitive verb*
**1 :** to become covered or obscured with or as if with a film
**2 :** to make a motion picture
— **film·able** \'fil-mə-bəl\ *adjective*

**film badge** *noun* (1945)
**:** a small pack of sensitive photographic film worn as a badge for indicating exposure to radiation

**film·dom** \'film-dəm\ *noun* (1914)
**:** the motion-picture industry

**film·go·er** \-,gō(-ə)r\ *noun* (1919)
**:** one who frequently attends films

**film·ic** \'fil-mik\ *adjective* (circa 1930)
**:** of, relating to, or resembling motion pictures
— **film·i·cal·ly** \-mi-k(ə-)lē\ *adverb*

**film·land** \'film-,land\ *noun* (1913)
**:** FILMDOM

**film·mak·er** \'film-,mā-kər\ *noun* (1908)
**:** one who makes motion pictures

**film·mak·ing** \-,mā-kiŋ\ *noun* (1913)
**:** the making of motion pictures

**film noir** \-'nwär\ *noun* [French, literally, black film] (1958)
**:** a type of crime film featuring cynical malevolent characters in a sleazy setting and an ominous atmosphere that is conveyed by shadowy photography and foreboding background music; *also* **:** a film of this type

**film·og·ra·phy** \fil-'mä-grə-fē\ *noun, plural* **-phies** [*film* + *-ography* (as in *bibliography*)] (1962)
**:** a list of motion pictures featuring the work of a prominent film figure or relating to a particular topic

**film·set·ting** \'film-,se-tiŋ\ *noun* (1954)
**:** PHOTOCOMPOSITION
— **film·set** *adjective*
— **filmset** *transitive verb*
— **film·set·ter** *noun*

**film·strip** \'film-,strip\ *noun* (1930)
**:** a strip of film bearing a sequence of images for projection as still pictures

**filmy** \'fil-mē\ *adjective* **film·i·er; -est** (1604)
**1 :** of, resembling, or composed of film **:** GAUZY ⟨*filmy* draperies⟩
**2 :** covered with a haze or film
— **film·i·ly** \-mə-lē\ *adverb*
— **film·i·ness** \-mē-nəs\ *noun*

**filo** *also* **fil·lo** *variant of* PHYLLO
**filo-** — see FILI-

**fils** \'fils\ *noun, plural* **fils** [Arabic] (1931)
— see *dinar, dirham, rial* at MONEY table

¹**fil·ter** \'fil-tər\ *noun* [Middle English *filtre*, from Medieval Latin *filtrum* piece of felt used as a filter, of Germanic origin; akin to Old High German *filz* felt — more at FELT] (1563)
**1 a :** a porous article or mass (as of paper or sand) through which a gas or liquid is passed to separate out matter in suspension **b :** something that has the effect of a filter
**2 :** an apparatus containing a filter medium
**3 a :** a device or material for suppressing or minimizing waves or oscillations of certain frequencies (as of electricity, light, or sound) **b :** a transparent material (as colored glass) that absorbs light of certain wavelengths or colors selectively and is used for modifying light that reaches a sensitized photographic material — called also *color filter*

²**filter** *verb* **fil·tered; fil·ter·ing** \-t(ə-)riŋ\ (1576)
*transitive verb*
**1 :** to subject to the action of a filter
**2 :** to remove by means of a filter
*intransitive verb*
**1 :** to pass or move through or as if through a filter
**2 :** to come or go in small units over a period of time ⟨people began *filtering* in⟩

**fil·ter·able** *also* **fil·tra·ble** \'fil-t(ə-)rə-bəl\ *adjective* (1908)
**:** capable of being filtered or of passing through a filter
— **fil·ter·abil·i·ty** \,fil-t(ə-)rə-'bi-lə-tē\ *noun*

**filterable virus** *noun* (1911)
**:** any of the infectious agents that pass through a filter of diatomite or unglazed porcelain with the filtrate and remain virulent and that include the viruses as presently understood and various other groups (as the mycoplasmas and rickettsias) which were originally considered viruses before their cellular nature was established

**filter bed** *noun* (circa 1874)
**:** a sand or gravel bed for filtering water or sewage

**filter feeder** *noun* (1928)
**:** an animal that obtains its food by filtering organic matter or minute organisms from a current of water that passes through some part of its system

**filter paper** *noun* (circa 1846)
**:** porous unsized paper used especially for filtering

**filter tip** *noun* (1932)
**:** a cigar or cigarette tip designed to filter the smoke before it enters the smoker's mouth; *also* **:** a cigar or cigarette provided with such a tip
— **fil·ter–tipped** \,fil-tər-'tipt\ *adjective*

**filth** \'filth\ *noun* [Middle English, from Old English *fȳlth*, from *fūl* foul] (before 12th century)
**1 :** foul or putrid matter; *especially* **:** loathsome dirt or refuse
**2 a :** moral corruption or defilement **b :** something that tends to corrupt or defile

**filthy** \'fil-thē\ *adjective* **filth·i·er; -est** (14th century)
**1 :** covered with or containing filth **:** offensively dirty
**2 a :** UNDERHAND, VILE **b :** OBSCENE
**synonym** see DIRTY
— **filth·i·ly** \-thə-lē\ *adverb*
— **filth·i·ness** \-thē-nəs\ *noun*

**fil·trate** \'fil-,trāt\ *noun* (circa 1846)
**:** material that has passed through a filter

**fil·tra·tion** \fil-'trā-shən\ *noun* (1605)
**1 :** the process of filtering
**2 :** the process of passing through or as if through a filter; *also* **:** DIFFUSION

**fim·bria** \'fim-brē-ə\ *noun, plural* **-bri·ae** \-brē-ē, -ī\ [New Latin, from Latin, fringe] (1752)
: a bordering fringe especially at the entrance of the fallopian tubes
— **fim·bri·al** \-brē-əl\ *adjective*
**fim·bri·at·ed** \'fim-brē-ˌā-təd\ *also* **fim·bri·ate** \-ˌāt\ *adjective* (15th century)
: having the edge or extremity bordered by slender processes : FRINGED
— **fim·bri·a·tion** \ˌfim-brē-'ā-shən\ *noun*
**¹fin** \'fin\ *noun* [Middle English *finn,* from Old English] (before 12th century)
**1** : an external membranous process of an aquatic animal (as a fish) used in propelling or guiding the body — see FISH illustration
**2** : something resembling a fin: as **a** : HAND, ARM **b** (1) : an appendage of a boat (as a submarine) (2) : an airfoil attached to an airplane for directional stability **c** : FLIPPER 1b **d** : any of the projecting ribs on a radiator or an engine cylinder
— **fin·like** \-ˌlīk\ *adjective*
— **finned** \'find\ *adjective*
**²fin** *verb* **finned; fin·ning** (1933)
*transitive verb*
: to equip with fins
*intransitive verb*
**1** : to show the fins above the water
**2** : to move through the water propelled by fins
**³fin** *noun* [Yiddish *finf* five, from Middle High German, from Old High German — more at FIVE] (1925)
*slang* : a 5-dollar bill
**fi·na·gle** \fə-'nā-gəl\ *verb* **fi·na·gled; fi·na·gling** \-g(ə-)liŋ\ [perhaps alteration of *fainaigue* (to renege)] (circa 1924)
*transitive verb*
**1** : to obtain by indirect or involved means
**2** : to obtain by trickery
*intransitive verb*
: to use devious or dishonest methods to achieve one's ends
— **fi·na·gler** \-g(ə-)lər\ *noun*
**¹fi·nal** \'fī-nᵊl\ *adjective* [Middle English, from Middle French, from Latin *finalis,* from *finis* boundary, end] (14th century)
**1 a** : not to be altered or undone ⟨all sales are *final*⟩ **b** : of or relating to a concluding court action or proceeding ⟨*final* decree⟩
**2** : coming at the end : being the last in a series, process, or progress ⟨the *final* chapter⟩
**3** : of or relating to the ultimate purpose or result of a process ⟨our *final* goal⟩
**synonym** see LAST
— **fi·nal·ly** \'fī-nᵊl-ē, 'fīn-lē\ *adverb*
**²final** *noun* (1609)
: something that is final: as **a** : a deciding match, game, heat, or trial — usually used in plural **b** : the last examination in a course — often used in plural
**fi·na·le** \fə-'na-lē, fi-'nä-\ *noun* [Italian, from *finale,* adjective, final, from Latin *finalis*] (1783)
: the close or termination of something: as **a** : the last section of an instrumental musical composition **b** : the closing part, scene, or number in a public performance **c** : the last and often climactic event or item in a sequence
**fi·nal·ise** *British variant of* FINALIZE
**fi·nal·ist** \'fī-nᵊl-ist\ *noun* (1898)
: a contestant in the finals of a competition
**fi·nal·i·ty** \fī-'na-lə-tē, fə-\ *noun, plural* **-ties** (1833)
**1 a** : the character or condition of being final, settled, irrevocable, or complete **b** : the condition of being at an ultimate point especially of development or authority
**2** : something final; *especially* : a fundamental fact, action, or belief
**fi·nal·ize** \'fī-nᵊl-ˌīz\ *transitive verb* **-ized; -iz·ing** (1901)

**1** : to put in final or finished form ⟨soon my conclusion will be *finalized* —D. D. Eisenhower⟩
**2** : to give final approval to ⟨*finalizing* the papers prepared . . . by his staff —*Newsweek*⟩
□
— **fi·nal·iza·tion** \ˌfī-nᵊl-ə-'zā-shən\ *noun*
**final solution** *noun, often F&S capitalized* (1947)
: the Nazi program for extermination of all Jews in Europe
**¹fi·nance** \fə-'nan(t)s, 'fī-ˌ, fī-'\ *noun* [Middle English, payment, ransom, from Middle French, from *finer* to end, pay, from *fin* end — more at FINE] (1739)
**1** *plural* : money or other liquid resources of a government, business, group, or individual
**2** : the system that includes the circulation of money, the granting of credit, the making of investments, and the provision of banking facilities
**3** : the science or study of the management of funds
**4** : the obtaining of funds or capital : FINANCING □
**²finance** *transitive verb* **fi·nanced; fi·nanc·ing** (1866)
**1 a** : to raise or provide funds or capital for ⟨*finance* a new house⟩ **b** : to furnish with necessary funds ⟨*finance* a son through college⟩
**2** : to sell something to on credit
**finance company** *noun* (circa 1924)
: a company that makes usually small short-term loans usually to individuals
**fi·nan·cial** \fə-'nan(t)-shəl, fī-\ *adjective* (1769)
: relating to finance or financiers
— **fi·nan·cial·ly** \-'nan(t)-sh(ə-)lē\ *adverb*
**fi·nan·cier** \ˌfi-nən-'sir; fə-ˌnan-, ˌfī-\ *noun* (1618)
**1** : one who specializes in raising and expending public moneys
**2** : one who deals with finance and investment on a large scale
**fi·nanc·ing** *noun* (1827)
: the act or process or an instance of raising or providing funds; *also* : the funds thus raised or provided
**fin·back** \'fin-ˌbak\ *noun* (1725)
: FIN WHALE
**finch** \'finch\ *noun* [Middle English *finc,* from Old English *finc;* akin to Old High German *fincho* finch and perhaps to Greek *spiza* chaffinch] (before 12th century)
: any of numerous songbirds (especially families Fringillidae, Estrildidae, and Emberizidae) having a short stout usually conical bill adapted for crushing seeds — compare BUNTING, CROSSBILL, GOLDFINCH, GROSBEAK, LINNET, SPARROW
**¹find** \'find\ *verb* **found** \'faund\; **find·ing** [Middle English, from Old English *findan;* akin to Old High German *findan* to find, Latin *pont-, pons* bridge, Greek *pontos* sea, Sanskrit *patha* way, course] (before 12th century)
*transitive verb*
**1 a** : to come upon often accidentally : ENCOUNTER **b** : to meet with (a particular reception) ⟨hoped to *find* favor⟩
**2 a** : to come upon by searching or effort ⟨must *find* a suitable person for the job⟩ **b** : to discover by study or experiment ⟨*find* an answer⟩ **c** : to obtain by effort or management ⟨*find* the time to study⟩ **d** : ATTAIN, REACH ⟨the bullet *found* its mark⟩
**3 a** : to discover by the intellect or the feelings : EXPERIENCE ⟨*find* much pleasure in your company⟩ **b** : to perceive (oneself) to be in a certain place or condition **c** : to gain or regain the use or power of ⟨trying to *find* his tongue⟩ **d** : to bring (oneself) to a realization of one's powers or of one's proper sphere of activity ⟨must help the student to *find* himself as an individual —N. M. Pusey⟩

**4 a** : PROVIDE, SUPPLY **b** : to furnish (room and board) especially as a condition of employment
**5** : to determine and make a statement about ⟨*find* a verdict⟩ ⟨*found* her guilty⟩
*intransitive verb*
: to determine a case judicially by a verdict ⟨*find* for the defendant⟩
— **find·able** \'fīn-də-bəl\ *adjective*
— **find fault** : to criticize unfavorably
**²find** *noun* (1825)
**1** : an act or instance of finding
**2** : something found: as **a** : a valuable discovery ⟨an archaeological *find*⟩ **b** : a person whose ability proves to be unexpectedly good
**find·er** \'fīn-dər\ *noun* (14th century)
**1** : one that finds
**2** : a small astronomical telescope of low power and wide field attached to a larger telescope for finding an object
**3** : VIEWFINDER
**fin de siè·cle** \ˌfan-də-sē-'e-kᵊl; faⁿ-də-syeklᵊ\ *adjective* [French, end of the century] (1890)
: of, relating to, or characteristic of the close of the 19th century and especially its literary and artistic climate of sophistication, world-weariness, and fashionable despair
**find·ing** \'fīn-diŋ\ *noun* (14th century)
**1 a** : the act of one that finds **b** : FIND 2
**2** *plural* : small tools and supplies used by an artisan (as a dressmaker, jeweler, or shoemaker)
**3 a** : the result of a judicial examination or inquiry **b** : the results of an investigation — usually used in plural
**find out** (13th century)
*transitive verb*
**1** : to learn by study, observation, or search : DISCOVER
**2 a** : to catch in an offense (as a crime) ⟨the culprits were soon *found out*⟩ **b** : to ascertain the true character or identity of ⟨the informer was *found out*⟩
*intransitive verb*
: to discover, learn, or verify something ⟨I don't know, but I'll *find out* for you⟩
**¹fine** \'fīn\ *noun* [Middle English, from Old French *fin,* from Latin *finis* boundary, end] (13th century)
**1** *obsolete* : END, CONCLUSION

\ə\ **abut** \ᵊ\ **kitten** \ər\ **further** \a\ **ash** \ā\ **ace**
\ä\ **mop, mar** \aù\ **out** \ch\ **chin** \e\ **bet** \ē\ **easy**
\g\ **go** \i\ **hit** \ī\ **ice** \j\ **job** \ŋ\ **sing** \ō\ **go**
\ò\ **law** \òi\ **boy** \th\ **thin** \t͟h\ **the** \ü\ **loot** \ù\ **foot**
\y\ **yet** \zh\ **vision** *see also* Guide to Pronunciation

**2 :** a compromise of a fictitious suit used as a form of conveyance of lands
**3 a :** a sum imposed as punishment for an offense **b :** a forfeiture or penalty paid to an injured party in a civil action
**— in fine :** in short
²**fine** *transitive verb* **fined; fin·ing** (1559)
: to impose a fine on : punish by a fine
³**fine** *adjective* **fin·er; fin·est** [Middle English *fin,* from Old French, from Latin *finis,* noun, end, limit] (13th century)
**1 :** free from impurity **b** *of a metal* : having a stated proportion of pure metal in the composition expressed in parts per thousand ⟨a gold coin .9166 *fine*⟩
**2 a** (1) **:** very thin in gauge or texture ⟨*fine* thread⟩ (2) **:** not coarse ⟨*fine* sand⟩ (3) **:** very small ⟨*fine* print⟩ (4) **:** KEEN ⟨a knife with a *fine* edge⟩ (5) **:** very precise or accurate ⟨a *fine* adjustment⟩ ⟨trying to be too *fine* with his pitches⟩ **b :** physically trained or hardened close to the limit of efficiency — used of an athlete or animal
**3 :** delicate, subtle, or sensitive in quality, perception, or discrimination ⟨a *fine* distinction⟩
**4 :** superior in kind, quality, or appearance **:** EXCELLENT ⟨a *fine* job⟩ ⟨a *fine* day⟩ ⟨*fine* wines⟩
**5 a :** ORNATE 1 ⟨*fine* writing⟩ **b :** marked by or affecting elegance or refinement ⟨*fine* manners⟩
**6 a :** very well ⟨feel *fine*⟩ **b :** ALL RIGHT ⟨that's *fine* with me⟩
**7 :** used as an intensive ⟨the leader, in a *fine* frenzy, beheaded one of his wives —Brian Crozier⟩
**— fine·ness** \ˈfīn-nəs\ *noun*
⁴**fine** *adverb* (14th century)
**1 :** FINELY: as **a :** very well **b :** ALL RIGHT
**2 :** with a very narrow margin of time or space ⟨she had not intended to cut her escape so *fine* —Melinda Beck *et al.*⟩
⁵**fine** *verb* **fined; fin·ing** (14th century)
*transitive verb*
**1 :** PURIFY, CLARIFY ⟨*fine* and filter wine⟩
**2 :** to make finer in quality or size
*intransitive verb*
**1 :** to become pure or clear ⟨the ale will *fine*⟩
**2 :** to become smaller in lines or proportions
⁶**fi·ne** \ˈfē-(ˌ)nā\ *noun* [Italian, from Latin *finis* end] (circa 1798)
**:** END — used as a direction in music to mark the closing point after a repeat
**fine art** *noun* (1767)
**1 a :** art (as painting, sculpture, or music) concerned primarily with the creation of beautiful objects — usually used in plural **b :** objects of fine art
**2 :** an activity requiring a fine skill
**fine·ly** \ˈfīn-lē\ *adverb* (14th century)
**:** in a fine manner: as **a :** extremely well : EXCELLENTLY ⟨plays the hero very *finely* —*New Yorker*⟩ **b :** with close discrimination : PRECISELY **c :** with delicacy or subtlety : SENSITIVELY ⟨a leader *finely* attuned to the needs of the people⟩ **d :** MINUTELY ⟨*finely* ground meal⟩
**fine print** *noun* (1951)
**:** something thoroughly and often deliberately obscure; *especially* **:** a part of an agreement or document spelling out restrictions and limitations often in small type or obscure language
**fin·ery** \ˈfīn-rē, ˈfī-nə-\ *noun, plural* **-er·ies** (1680)
**:** ORNAMENT, DECORATION; *especially* **:** dressy or showy clothing and jewels
**fines** \ˈfīnz\ *noun plural* [³*fine*] (circa 1903)
**:** finely crushed or powdered material (as ore); *also* **:** very small particles in a mixture of various sizes
**fines herbes** \fēn-ˈzerb, fē-ˈnerb\ *noun plural* [French, literally, fine herbs] (1846)
**:** a mixture of herbs used as a seasoning or garnish
**fine·spun** \ˈfīn-ˈspən\ *adjective* (1647)

**:** developed with extreme care or delicacy; *also* **:** developed in excessively fine or subtle detail
¹**fi·nesse** \fə-ˈnes\ *noun* [Middle English, from Middle French, from *fin*] (1528)
**1 :** refinement or delicacy of workmanship, structure, or texture
**2 :** skillful handling of a situation : adroit maneuvering
**3 :** the withholding of one's highest card or trump in the hope that a lower card will take the trick because the only opposing higher card is in the hand of an opponent who has already played
²**finesse** *verb* **fi·nessed; fi·ness·ing** (1746)
*intransitive verb*
**:** to make a finesse in playing cards
*transitive verb*
**1 :** to play (a card) in a finesse
**2 a :** to bring about or manage by adroit maneuvering ⟨*finesse* his way through tight places —Marquis James⟩ **b :** EVADE, TRICK
**fin·est** \ˈfī-nəst\ *noun, plural in construction* [superlative of ³*fine*] (1951)
**:** POLICE OFFICERS — usually used with the possessive form of a city or area ⟨the city's *finest*⟩
**fine structure** *noun* (1935)
**:** microscopic structure of a biological entity or one of its parts especially as studied in preparations for the electron microscope
**— fine structural** *adjective*
**fine–tooth comb** \ˈfīn-ˌtüth-\ *noun* (1839)
**1 :** a comb with close-set teeth used especially for clearing parasites or foreign matter from the hair
**2 :** an attitude or system of thorough searching or scrutinizing ⟨went over the report with a *fine-tooth comb*⟩
**fine–tune** \ˈfīn-ˈtün\ *transitive verb* (1967)
**1 a :** to adjust precisely so as to bring to the highest level of performance or effectiveness ⟨*fine-tune* a TV set⟩ ⟨*fine-tune* the format⟩ **b :** to improve through minor alteration or revision ⟨*fine-tune* the temperature of the room⟩
**2 :** to stabilize (an economy) by small-scale fiscal and monetary manipulations
**fin·fish** \ˈfin-ˌfish\ *noun* (circa 1890)
**:** FISH 1b — compare SHELLFISH
¹**fin·ger** \ˈfin-gər\ *noun* [Middle English, from Old English; akin to Old High German *fingar* finger] (before 12th century)
**1 :** any of the five terminating members of the hand **:** a digit of the forelimb; *especially* **:** one other than the thumb
**2 a :** something that resembles a finger ⟨a narrow *finger* of land⟩ **b :** a part of a glove into which a finger is inserted **c :** a projecting piece (as a pawl for a ratchet) brought into contact with an object to affect its motion
**3 :** the breadth of a finger
**4 :** INTEREST, SHARE — often used in the phrase *have a finger in the pie*
**5 :** BIRD 10 — usually used with *the*
**— fin·ger·like** \-ˌlīk\ *adjective*
²**finger** *verb* **fin·gered; fin·ger·ing** \-g(ə-)riŋ\ (15th century)
*transitive verb*
**1 :** to touch or feel with the fingers
**2 a :** to play (a musical instrument) with the fingers **b :** to play (as notes or chords) with a specific fingering **c :** to mark the notes of (a music score) as a guide in playing
**3 :** to point out : IDENTIFY
**4 :** to extend into or penetrate in the shape of a finger
*intransitive verb*
**1 :** to touch or handle something
**2 a :** to use the fingers in playing a musical instrument **b :** to have a certain fingering — used of a musical instrument
**3 :** to extend in the shape or manner of a finger
**fin·ger·board** \ˈfin-gər-ˌbōrd, -ˌbord\ *noun* (circa 1672)

**:** the part of a stringed instrument against which the fingers press the strings to vary the pitch — see VIOLIN illustration
**finger bowl** *noun* (circa 1860)
**:** a small water bowl for rinsing the fingers at the table
**fin·gered** \ˈfin-gərd\ *adjective* (circa 1529)
**1 :** having fingers especially of a specified kind or number — used in combination ⟨stubby-*fingered*⟩ ⟨five-*fingered*⟩
**2 :** having projections or processes like fingers ⟨the *fingered* roots of giant trees⟩
**finger food** *noun* (1928)
**:** a food that is to be held with the fingers for eating
**fin·ger·hold** \ˈfin-gər-ˌhōld\ *noun* (1909)
**1 :** a hold or place of support for the fingers
**2 :** a tenuous hold or support
**finger hole** *noun* (1854)
**1 :** any of several holes in the side of a wind instrument (as a recorder) which may be covered or left open by the fingers to change the pitch of the tone
**2 :** a hole (as in a telephone dial or a bowling ball) into which the finger is placed to provide a grip
**fin·ger·ing** \ˈfin-g(ə-)riŋ\ *noun* (14th century)
**1 a :** the act or method of using the fingers in playing an instrument **b :** the marking (as by figures on a musical score) of the method of fingering
**2 :** the act or process of handling or touching with the fingers
**fin·ger·ling** \ˈfin-gər-liŋ\ *noun* (1836)
**:** a small fish especially up to one year of age
**fin·ger·nail** \ˈfin-gər-ˌnāl, ˌfin-gər-ˈnā(ə)l\ *noun* (13th century)
**:** the nail of a finger
**finger painting** *noun* (1937)
**:** a technique of spreading pigment on wet paper chiefly with the fingers; *also* **:** a picture so produced
**fin·ger·pick·ing** \ˈfin-gər-ˌpi-kiŋ\ *noun* (1969)
**:** a method of playing a stringed instrument (as a guitar) with the thumb and tips of the fingers rather than with a pick
**— fin·ger·pick** *verb*
**fin·ger·point·ing** \-ˌpoin-tiŋ\ *noun* (1949)
**:** the act of making explicit and often unfair accusations of blame
**fin·ger·post** \ˈfin-gər-ˌpōst\ *noun* (1785)
**1 :** a post bearing one or more signs often terminating in a pointing finger
**2 :** something serving as a guide to understanding or knowledge
**fin·ger·print** \-ˌprint\ *noun* (1859)
**1 :** the impression of a fingertip on any surface; *also* **:** an ink impression of the lines upon the fingertip taken for the purpose of identification
**2 :** something that identifies: as **a :** a trait, trace, or characteristic revealing origin or responsibility **b :** analytical evidence (as a spectrogram) that characterizes an object or substance; *especially* **:** the chromatogram or electrophoretogram obtained by cleaving a protein by enzymatic action and subjecting the resulting collection of peptides to two-dimensional chromatography or electrophoresis
**— fingerprint** *transitive verb*
**— fin·ger·print·ing** *noun*

fingerprint 1: *1* arch, *2* loop, *3* whorl, *4* composite

**finger spelling** *noun* (1918)
: communication by signs made with the fingers — called also *dactylology*

**¹fin·ger·tip** \-ˌtip\ *noun* (1842)
**1** : the tip of a finger
**2** : a protective covering for the end of a finger

**— at one's fingertips** : instantly or readily available

**²fingertip** *adjective* (1926)
**1** : readily accessible : being within easy reach ⟨*fingertip* information⟩ ⟨*fingertip* controls⟩
**2** : extending from head or shoulders to mid-thigh — used of clothing

**finger wave** *noun* (circa 1934)
: a method of setting hair by dampening with water or wave solution and forming waves or curls with the fingers and a comb

**fin·i·al** \'fi-nē-əl\ *noun* [Middle English, from *final*, *finial* final] (15th century)
**1** : a usually foliated ornament forming an upper extremity especially in Gothic architecture
**2** : a crowning ornament or detail (as a decorative knob)

**fin·i·cal** \'fi-ni-kəl\ *adjective* [probably from ³*fine*] (1592)
: FINICKY
**— fin·i·cal·ly** \-k(ə-)lē\ *adverb*
**— fin·i·cal·ness** \-kəl-nəs\ *noun*

**fin·ick·ing** \-kiŋ, -kən\ *adjective* [alteration of *finical*] (1661)
: FINICKY

**fin·icky** \'fi-ni-kē\ *adjective* [alteration of *finicking*] (circa 1825)
**1** : extremely or excessively nice, exacting, or meticulous in taste or standards
**2** : requiring much care, precision, or attentive effort ⟨a *finicky* recipe⟩
**— fin·ick·i·ness** *noun*

**fi·nis** \'fi-nəs, 'fī-nəs; fə-'nē\ *noun* [Middle English, from Latin] (15th century)
: END, CONCLUSION

**¹fin·ish** \'fi-nish\ *verb* [Middle English *finisshen*, from Middle French *finiss-*, stem of *finir*, from Latin *finire*, from *finis*] (14th century)
*intransitive verb*
**1 a** : to come to an end : TERMINATE **b** : END 1b
**2 a** : to come to the end of a course, task, or undertaking **b** : to end relations — used with *with* ⟨decided to *finish* with him for good⟩
**3** : to end a competition in a specified manner or position ⟨*finished* third in the race⟩
*transitive verb*
**1 a** : to bring to an end : TERMINATE ⟨*finished* the speech and sat down⟩ **b** : to use or dispose of entirely ⟨her sandwich *finished* the loaf⟩
**2 a** : to bring to completion or issue ⟨hope to *finish* their new home before winter⟩ **b** : to provide with a finish; *especially* : to put a final coat or surface on ⟨*finish* a table with varnish⟩
**3 a** : to defeat or ruin utterly and finally ⟨the scandal *finished* his career⟩ **b** : to bring about the death of
**synonym** see CLOSE
**— fin·ish·er** *noun*

**²finish** *noun* (1779)
**1** : something that completes or perfects: as **a** : the fine or decorative work required for a building or one of its parts **b** : a finishing material used in painting **c** : the final treatment or coating of a surface **d** : the taste in the mouth after swallowing a beverage (as wine)
**2 a** : final stage : END **b** : the cause of one's ruin
**3** : the result or product of a finishing process
**4** : the quality or state of being perfected

**fin·ished** *adjective* (1709)
: marked by the highest quality : CONSUMMATE

**finishing school** *noun* (circa 1837)
: a private school for girls that emphasizes cultural studies and prepares students especially for social activities

**finish line** *noun* (1899)
: a line marking the end of a racecourse

**fi·nite** \'fī-ˌnīt\ *adjective* [Middle English *finit*, from Latin *finitus*, past participle of *finire*] (15th century)
**1 a** : having definite or definable limits ⟨*finite* number of possibilities⟩ **b** : having a limited nature or existence ⟨*finite* beings⟩
**2** : completely determinable in theory or in fact by counting, measurement, or thought ⟨the *finite* velocity of light⟩
**3 a** : less than an arbitrary positive integer and greater than the negative of that integer **b** : having a finite number of elements ⟨a *finite* set⟩
**4** : of, relating to, or being a verb or verb form that can function as a predicate or as the initial element of one and that is limited (as in tense, person, and number)
**— finite** *noun*
**— fi·nite·ly** *adverb*
**— fi·nite·ness** *noun*

**finite difference** *noun* (1807)
: any of a sequence of differences obtained by incrementing successively the dependent variable of a function by a fixed amount; *especially* : any of such differences obtained from a polynomial function using successive integral values of its dependent variable

**fi·ni·tude** \'fī-nə-ˌtüd, -ˌtyüd, 'fin-ə-\ *noun* (1644)
: finite quality or state

**¹fink** \'fiŋk\ *noun* [origin unknown] (1903)
**1** : one who is disapproved of or is held in contempt
**2** : STRIKEBREAKER
**3** : INFORMER 2

**²fink** *intransitive verb* (circa 1925)
: to turn informer : SQUEAL

**fink out** *intransitive verb* (1956)
: BACK OUT, COP OUT

**Fin·land·isa·tion** *British variant of* FINLANDIZATION

**Fin·land·iza·tion** \ˌfin-lən-də-'zā-shən, ˌ()fin-ˌlan-\ *noun* [*Finland*] (1969)
: a foreign policy of neutrality under the influence of the Soviet Union; *also* : the conversion to such a policy
**— Fin·land·ize** \'fin-lən-ˌdīz, ()fin-'lan-\ *transitive verb*

**Finn** \'fin\ *noun* [Swedish *Finne*] (before 12th century)
**1** : a member of a people speaking Finnish or a Finnic language
**2 a** : a native or inhabitant of Finland **b** : one who is of Finnish descent

**fin·nan had·die** \ˌfi-nən-'ha-dē\ *noun* [alteration of *findon haddock*, from *Findon*, village in Scotland] (1811)
: smoked haddock — called also *finnan haddock*

**Finn·ic** \'fi-nik\ *adjective* (1668)
**1** : of or relating to the Finns
**2** : of, relating to, or constituting the branch of the Finno-Ugric subfamily that includes Finnish, Estonian, and Lapp

**¹Finn·ish** \'fi-nish\ *adjective* (1699)
: of, relating to, or characteristic of Finland, the Finns, or Finnish

**²Finnish** *noun* (circa 1845)
: a Finno-Ugric language spoken in Finland, Karelia, and small areas of Sweden and Norway

**Fin·no–Ugri·an** \ˌfi-()nō-'(y)ü-grē-ən\ *adjective* (1880)
: FINNO-UGRIC
**— Finno–Ugrian** *noun*

**Fin·no–Ugric** \ˌfi-nō-'(y)ü-grik\ *adjective* (1879)
**1** : of, relating to, or constituting a subfamily of the Uralic family of languages comprising various languages spoken in Hungary, Lapland, Finland, Estonia, and parts of western Russia
**2** : of or relating to any of the peoples speaking Finno-Ugric languages
**— Finno–Ugric** *noun*

**fin·ny** \'fi-nē\ *adjective* (1590)
**1** : provided with or characterized by fins
**2** : relating to or being fish

**fino** \'fē-()nō\ *noun, plural* **finos** [Spanish, from *fino* fine, from *fin* end, from Latin *finis*] (1846)
: a very dry Spanish sherry

**fin whale** *noun* (1885)
: a baleen whale (*Balaenoptera physalus*) that attains a length of over 60 feet (18.3 meters) and is found in arctic to tropical waters worldwide — called also *finback*

**fin whale**

**fiord** *variant of* FJORD

**fio·ri·tu·ra** \fē-ˌȯr-ə-'tür-ə\ *noun, plural* **-tu·re** \-'tür-ē\ [Italian, literally, flowering, from *fiorito*, past participle of *fiorire* to flower, from (assumed) Vulgar Latin *florire* — more at FLOURISH] (1841)
: ORNAMENT 5

**fip·ple flute** \'fi-pəl-\ *noun* [origin unknown] (1911)
: any of a group of wind instruments (as a flageolet or recorder) having a straight tubular shape, a whistle mouthpiece, and finger holes

**fir** \'fər\ *noun* [Middle English, from Old English *fyrh*; akin to Old High German *forha* fir, Latin *quercus* oak] (before 12th century)
**1** : any of a genus (*Abies*) of north temperate evergreen trees of the pine family that have flattish leaves, circular leaf scars, and erect female cones and are valued for their wood; *also* : any of various conifers (as the Douglas fir) of other genera
**2** : the wood of a fir

**¹fire** \'fīr\ *noun, often attributive* [Middle English, from Old English *fȳr*; akin to Old High German *fiur* fire, Greek *pyr*] (before 12th century)
**1 a** (1) : the phenomenon of combustion manifested in light, flame, and heat (2) : one of the four elements of the alchemists **b** (1) : burning passion : ARDOR (2) : liveliness of imagination : INSPIRATION
**2 a** : fuel in a state of combustion (as on a hearth) **b** *British* : a small gas or electric space heater
**3 a** : a destructive burning (as of a building) **b** (1) : death or torture by fire (2) : severe trial or ordeal
**4** : BRILLIANCY, LUMINOSITY ⟨the *fire* of a gem⟩
**5 a** : the firing of weapons (as firearms, artillery, or missiles) **b** : intense verbal attack or criticism **c** : a rapidly delivered series (as of remarks)
**— fire·less** \-ləs\ *adjective*
**— on fire 1** : being consumed by fire : AFLAME **2** : EAGER, BURNING
**— under fire 1** : exposed to fire from an enemy's weapons **2** : under attack

**²fire** *verb* **fired; fir·ing** (13th century)
*transitive verb*
**1 a** : to set on fire : KINDLE; *also* : IGNITE ⟨*fire* a rocket engine⟩ **b** (1) : to give life or spirit to : INSPIRE (2) : to fill with passion or enthusiasm — often used with *up* **c** : to light up as if by fire **d** : to cause to start operating — usually used with *up*
**2 a** : to drive out or away by or as if by fire **b** : to dismiss from a position

**3 a** (1) : to cause to explode : DETONATE (2) : to propel from or as if from a gun : DISCHARGE, LAUNCH ⟨*fire* a rocket⟩ (3) : SHOOT 1b ⟨*fire* a gun⟩ (4) : to score (a number) in a game or contest **b** : to throw with speed or force ⟨*fired* the ball to first base⟩ ⟨*fire* a left jab⟩ **c** : to utter with force and rapidity
**4** : to apply fire or fuel to: as **a** : to process by applying heat **b** : to feed or serve the fire of ~ *intransitive verb*
**1 a** : to take fire : KINDLE, IGNITE **b** : to begin operation : START ⟨the engine *fired*⟩ **c** : to operate especially as the result of the application of an electrical impulse ⟨the spark plug *fires*⟩
**2 a** : to become irritated or angry — often used with *up* **b** : to become filled with excitement or enthusiasm
**3 a** : to discharge a firearm **b** : to emit or let fly an object
**4** : to tend a fire
**5** : to transmit a nerve impulse
— **fire·able** \'fīr-ə-bəl, 'fī-rə-\ *adjective*
— **fir·er** *noun*
**fire and brimstone** *noun* (13th century)
: the torments suffered by sinners in hell
— **fire–and–brimstone** *adjective*
**fire ant** *noun* (1796)
: any of a genus (*Solenopsis*) of fiercely stinging omnivorous ants; *especially* : IMPORTED FIRE ANT
**fire·arm** \'fīr-ˌärm\ *noun* (1646)
: a weapon from which a shot is discharged by gunpowder — usually used of small arms
**fire away** *intransitive verb* (1840)
: to speak without hesitation — usually used as an imperative
**fire·back** \-ˌbak\ *noun* (1847)
: an often decorated cast-iron plate lining the back wall of a fireplace
**fire·ball** \'fīr-ˌból\ *noun* (1555)
**1** : a ball of fire; *also* : something resembling such a ball ⟨the primordial *fireball* associated with the beginning of the universe —*Scientific American*⟩
**2** : a brilliant meteor that may trail bright sparks
**3** : the highly luminous cloud of vapor and dust created by a nuclear explosion
**4** : a highly energetic person
**fire·ball·er** \-ˌbó-lər\ *noun* (1946)
: a baseball pitcher known for throwing fastballs
— **fire·ball·ing** \-liŋ\ *adjective*
**fire·base** \-ˌbās\ *noun* (1968)
: a secured site from which field artillery can lay down interdicting fire
**fire blight** *noun* (1817)
: a destructive infectious disease especially of apples, pears, and related fruits caused by a bacterium (*Erwinia amylovora*)
**fire·boat** \'fīr-ˌbōt\ *noun* (1849)
: a ship equipped with fire-fighting apparatus
**fire·bomb** \-ˌbäm\ *noun* (1895)
: an incendiary bomb
— **firebomb** *transitive verb*
**fire·box** \-ˌbäks\ *noun* (1791)
**1** : a chamber (as of a furnace or steam boiler) that contains a fire
**2** : a box containing an apparatus for transmitting an alarm to a fire station
**fire·brand** \-ˌbrand\ *noun* (13th century)
**1** : a piece of burning wood
**2** : one that creates unrest or strife (as in aggressively promoting a cause) : AGITATOR
**fire·brat** \-ˌbrat\ *noun* (1895)
: a wingless insect (*Thermobia domestica*) related to the silverfish and found in warm moist places
**fire·break** \-ˌbrāk\ *noun* (1841)
: a barrier of cleared or plowed land intended to check a forest or grass fire
**fire·breath·ing** \-ˌbrē-thiŋ\ *adjective* (1933)
: intimidatingly or violently aggressive in speech and manner ⟨a *fire-breathing* orator⟩

**fire·brick** \-ˌbrik\ *noun* (1793)
: a refractory brick capable of sustaining high temperatures that is used especially for lining furnaces or fireplaces
**fire brigade** *noun* (1838)
: a body of firefighters: as **a** : a usually private or temporary fire-fighting organization **b** *British* : FIRE DEPARTMENT
**fire·bug** \'fīr-ˌbəg\ *noun* (1872)
: INCENDIARY, PYROMANIAC
**fire chief** *noun* (1889)
: the head of a fire department
**fire·clay** \-ˌklā\ *noun* (1819)
: clay capable of withstanding high temperatures that is used especially for firebrick and crucibles
**fire control** *noun* (1864)
: the planning, preparation, and delivery of fire on targets
**fire·crack·er** \'fīr-ˌkra-kər\ *noun* (1829)
: a usually paper cylinder containing an explosive and a fuse and set off to make a noise
**fired** \'fīrd\ *adjective* (1889)
: using a specified fuel — usually used in combination ⟨oil-*fired* power plant⟩
**fire·damp** \'fīr-ˌdamp\ *noun* (1677)
: a combustible mine gas that consists chiefly of methane; *also* : the explosive mixture of this gas with air
**fire department** *noun* (1825)
**1** : an organization for preventing or extinguishing fires; *especially* : a government division (as in a municipality) having these duties
**2** : the members of a fire department
**fire·dog** \-ˌdóg\ *noun* (1792)
*chiefly Southern & Midland* : ANDIRON
**fire·drake** \'fīr-ˌdrāk\ *noun* [Middle English *firdrake*, from Old English *fȳrdraca*, from *fȳr* + *draca* dragon, from Latin *draco* — more at DRAGON] (before 12th century)
: a fire-breathing dragon especially in Germanic mythology
**fire drill** *noun* (circa 1890)
: a practice drill in extinguishing fires or in the conduct and manner of exit in case of fire
**fire–eat·er** \'fīr-ˌē-tər\ *noun* (1672)
**1** : a performer who pretends to eat fire
**2 a** : a violent or pugnacious person **b** : a person who displays very militant or aggressive partisanship
**fire–eat·ing** \-ˌē-tiŋ\ *adjective* (1819)
: violent or highly militant in disposition, bearing, or policy ⟨a *fire-eating* radical⟩
**fire engine** *noun* (circa 1680)
: a usually mobile apparatus for directing an extinguishing agent upon fires; *especially* : FIRE TRUCK
**fire–en·gine red** \'fīr-ˌen-jən-\ *noun* (1954)
: a bright red
**fire escape** *noun* (1788)
: a device for escape from a burning building; *especially* : a metal stairway attached to the outside of a building
**fire extinguisher** *noun* (1849)
: a portable or wheeled apparatus for putting out small fires by ejecting extinguishing chemicals
**fire·fight** \'fīr-ˌfīt\ *noun* (1899)
**1 a** : a usually brief intense exchange of fire between opposing military units **b** : a hostile confrontation that involves gunfire
**2** : SKIRMISH 2b
**fire·fight·er** \-ˌfī-tər\ *noun* (1903)
: a person who fights fires : FIREMAN 2
— **fire fighting** *noun*
**fire·fly** \-ˌflī\ *noun* (1658)
: any of various winged nocturnal beetles (especially family Lampyridae) that produce a bright soft intermittent light by oxidation of luciferin especially for courtship purposes
**fire·guard** \-ˌgärd\ *noun* (1833)
**1** : a person who watches for the outbreak of fire; *also* : a person whose duty is to extinguish fires
**2** : FIRE SCREEN
**3** : FIREBREAK

**fire hall** *noun* (1881)
*chiefly Canadian* : FIRE STATION
**fire·house** \'fīr-ˌhaús\ *noun* (1901)
: FIRE STATION
**fire irons** *noun plural* (1648)
: utensils (as tongs) for tending a fire especially in a fireplace
**fire·light** \'fīr-ˌlīt\ *noun* (before 12th century)
: the light of a fire (as in a fireplace)
— **fire·lit** \-ˌlit\ *adjective*
**fire·lock** \-ˌläk\ *noun* (1547)
**1** : a gun's lock employing a slow match to ignite the powder charge; *also* : a gun having such a lock
**2 a** : FLINTLOCK **b** : WHEEL LOCK
**fire·man** \-mən\ *noun* (14th century)
**1** : a person who tends or feeds fires : STOKER
**2** : a member of a fire department : FIREFIGHTER
**3** : an enlisted man in the navy who works with engineering machinery
**4** : a relief pitcher in baseball
**fire·man·ic** \-ˌma-nik\ *adjective* [fireman + ¹-*ic*] (1902)
: of or relating to firefighters or fire fighting
**fire off** *transitive verb* (1888)
: to write and send usually in haste or anger ⟨*fired off* a memo⟩
**fire opal** *noun* (1816)
: GIRASOLE 2
**fire·place** \'fīr-ˌplās\ *noun* (1698)
**1** : a framed opening made in a chimney to hold an open fire : HEARTH; *also* : a metal container with a smoke pipe used for the same purpose
**2** : an outdoor structure of brick, stone, or metal for an open fire
— **fire·placed** \-ˌplāst\ *adjective*
**fire·plug** \-ˌpləg\ *noun* (1713)
: HYDRANT
**fire·pot** \-ˌpät\ *noun* (1627)
**1** : a clay pot filled with combustibles formerly used as a missile in war
**2** : a vessel used in Oriental cuisine for cooking foods in broth at the table; *also* : the food cooked in it
**fire·pow·er** \-ˌpaú(-ə)r\ *noun* (1913)
**1 a** : the capacity (as of a military unit) to deliver effective fire on a target **b** : effective fire
**2 a** : effective power or force ⟨intellectual *firepower*⟩ **b** : the scoring action or potential of a team or player
¹**fire·proof** \-ˌprüf\ *adjective* (circa 1638)
: proof against or resistant to fire
²**fireproof** *transitive verb* (1867)
: to make fireproof
**fire sale** *noun* (1891)
: a sale of merchandise damaged in a fire; *also* : a sale at very low prices
**fire screen** *noun* (15th century)
: a protective screen before a fireplace
**fire ship** *noun* (1588)
: a ship carrying combustibles or explosives sent among the enemy's ships or works to set them on fire
¹**fire·side** \'fīr-ˌsīd\ *noun* (1563)
**1** : a place near the fire or hearth
**2** : HOME
²**fireside** *adjective* (1740)
: having an informal or intimate quality ⟨a *fireside* chat⟩
**fire station** *noun* (1877)
: a building housing fire apparatus and usually firefighters
**fire·stone** \'fīr-ˌstōn\ *noun* (before 12th century)
**1** : pyrite formerly used for striking fire; *also* : FLINT
**2** : a stone that will endure high heat
**fire–stop** \-ˌstäp\ *noun* (1897)
: material used to close open parts especially of a building for preventing the spread of fire
— **fire–stop** *transitive verb*
**fire·storm** \-ˌstórm\ *noun* (1945)
**1** : a large usually stationary fire characterized by very high temperatures in which the central

column of rising heated air induces strong inward winds which supply oxygen to the fire
**2** : a sudden or violent outburst ⟨a *firestorm* of public protest⟩

**fire·thorn** \-,thȯrn\ *noun* (circa 1900)
: any of a genus (*Pyracantha*) of usually thorny ornamental shrubs of the rose family; *especially* : a European semievergreen shrub (*P. coccinea*) with orange-red berries

**fire tower** *noun* (1827)
: a tower (as in a forest) from which a watch for fires is maintained

**fire·trap** \'fīr-,trap\ *noun* (1881)
: a place (as a building) apt to catch on fire or difficult to escape from in case of fire

**fire truck** *noun* (1935)
: an automotive vehicle equipped with fire-fighting apparatus

**fire wall** *noun* (1759)
: a wall constructed to prevent the spread of fire

**fire·wa·ter** \'fīr-,wȯ-tər, -,wä-\ *noun* (1817)
: strong alcoholic liquor

**fire·weed** \-,wēd\ *noun* (1784)
: any of several plants that grow especially in clearings or burned districts: as **a** : a weedy composite (*Erechtites hieracifolia*) of the eastern U.S. and Canada that has clusters of brush-shaped flower heads with no ray flowers **b** : a tall perennial (*Epilobium angustifolium*) of the evening-primrose family that has long spikes of pinkish purple flowers and is an important honey plant in some areas — called also *willow herb*

**fire·wood** \-,wu̇d\ *noun* (14th century)
: wood used for fuel

**fire·work** \-,wərk\ *noun* (1575)
**1** : a device for producing a striking display by the combustion of explosive or flammable compositions
**2** *plural* : a display of fireworks
**3** *plural* **a** : a display of temper or intense conflict **b** : a spectacular display ⟨the *fireworks* of autumn leaves⟩

**fir·ing** \'fīr-iŋ\ *noun* (14th century)
**1** : the act or process of one that fires
**2** : the process of maturing ceramic products by the application of heat

**firing line** *noun* (1881)
**1** : a line from which fire is delivered against a target
**2** : the forefront of an activity — used especially in the phrase *on the firing line*

**firing pin** *noun* (1874)
: the pin that strikes the cartridge primer in the breech mechanism of a firearm

**firing squad** *noun* (1904)
**1** : a detachment detailed to fire volleys over the grave of one buried with military honors
**2** : a detachment detailed to carry out a sentence of death by shooting

**fir·kin** \'fər-kən\ *noun* [Middle English, ultimately from Middle Dutch *veerdel* fourth, from *veer* four; akin to Old English *fēower* — more at FOUR] (14th century)
**1** : a small wooden vessel or cask
**2** : any of various British units of capacity usually equal to ¼ barrel

**¹firm** \'fərm\ *adjective* [Middle English *ferm*, from Middle French, from Latin *firmus*; akin to Greek *thronos* chair, throne] (14th century)
**1 a** : securely or solidly fixed in place **b** : not weak or uncertain : VIGOROUS **c** : having a solid or compact structure that resists stress or pressure
**2 a** (1) : not subject to change or revision (2) : not subject to price weakness : STEADY **b** : not easily moved or disturbed : STEADFAST **c** : WELL-FOUNDED
**3** : indicating firmness or resolution ⟨a *firm* mouth⟩
— **firm·ly** *adverb*
— **firm·ness** *noun*

**²firm** *adverb* (14th century)
: in a firm manner : STEADFASTLY, FIXEDLY

**³firm** (14th century)
*transitive verb*
**1 a** : to make secure or fast : TIGHTEN ⟨*firming* her grip on the racquet⟩ — often used with *up* **b** : to make solid or compact ⟨*firm* the soil⟩
**2** : to put into final form : SETTLE ⟨*firm* a contract⟩ ⟨*firm* up plans⟩
**3** : to give additional support to : STRENGTHEN — usually used with *up*
*intransitive verb*
**1** : to become firm : HARDEN — often used with *up*
**2** : to recover from a decline : IMPROVE ⟨the market is *firming*⟩

**⁴firm** *noun* [German *Firma*, from Italian, signature, ultimately from Latin *firmare* to make firm, confirm, from *firmus*] (1744)
**1** : the name or title under which a company transacts business
**2** : a partnership of two or more persons that is not recognized as a legal person distinct from the members composing it
**3** : a business unit or enterprise

**fir·ma·ment** \'fər-mə-mənt\ *noun* [Middle English, from Late Latin & Latin; Late Latin *firmamentum*, from Latin, support, from *firmare*] (13th century)
**1** : the vault or arch of the sky : HEAVENS
**2** *obsolete* : BASIS
**3** : the field or sphere of an interest or activity ⟨the international fashion *firmament*⟩
— **fir·ma·men·tal** \,fər-mə-'men-t²l\ *adjective*

**fir·mer chisel** \'fər-mər-\ *noun* [French *fermoir* chisel, alteration of Middle French *formoir*, from *former* to form, from Old French *forme* form] (1823)
: a woodworking chisel with a thin flat blade

**firm·ware** \'fərm-,war, -,wer\ *noun* (1967)
: computer programs contained permanently in a hardware device (as a read-only memory)

**firn** \'firn\ *noun* [German, from Old High German *firni* old; akin to Old English *faran*] (1853)
: NÉVÉ

**¹first** \'fərst\ *adjective* [Middle English, from Old English *fyrst*; akin to Old High German *furist* first, Old English *faran* to go — more at FARE] (before 12th century)
: preceding all others in time, order, or importance: as **a** : EARLIEST **b** : being the lowest forward gear or speed of a motor vehicle **c** : having the highest or most prominent part among a group of similar voices or instruments ⟨*first* tenor⟩ ⟨*first* violins⟩

**²first** *adverb* (before 12th century)
**1 a** : before another in time, space, or importance **b** : in the first place — often used with *of all* **c** : for the first time
**2** : in preference to something else : SOONER

**³first** *noun* (13th century)
**1** — see NUMBER table
**2** : something that is first: as **a** : the first occurrence or item of a kind **b** : the first forward gear or speed of a motor vehicle **c** : the highest or chief voice or instrument of a group **d** : an article of commerce of the finest grade **e** : the winning or highest place in a competition, examination, or contest
**3** : FIRST BASE
— **at first** : at the beginning : INITIALLY

**first aid** *noun* (1882)
: emergency care or treatment given to an ill or injured person before regular medical aid can be obtained

**first base** *noun* (1845)
**1** : the base that must be touched first by a base runner in baseball
**2** : the player position for defending the area around first base
**3** : the first step or stage in a course of action ⟨plans never got to *first base*⟩
— **first base·man** \-'bā-smən\ *noun*

**first·born** \'fərs(t)-'bȯrn\ *adjective* (14th century)
: first brought forth : ELDEST

— **firstborn** *noun*

**first cause** *noun* (14th century)
: the self-created ultimate source of all being

**first–class** \'fərs(t)-'klas\ *adjective* (circa 1838)
**1** : of or relating to first class
**2** : of the highest quality ⟨a *first-class* meal⟩
— **first–class** *adverb*

**first class** *noun* (1750)
: the first or highest group in a classification: as **a** : the highest of usually three classes of travel accommodations **b** : a class of mail that comprises letters, postcards, or matter sealed against inspection

**first cousin** *noun* (1661)
: COUSIN 1a

**first day cover** *noun* (1932)
: a philatelic cover franked with a newly issued postage stamp and postmarked on the first day of issue at a city officially chosen for first day sale

**first–degree burn** *noun* (circa 1929)
: a mild burn characterized by heat, pain, and reddening of the burned surface but not exhibiting blistering or charring of tissues

**first down** *noun* (1897)
**1** : the first of a series of usually four downs in which a football team must net a 10-yard gain to retain possession of the ball
**2** : a gain of a total of 10 or more yards within usually four downs giving the team the right to start a new series of downs

**first edition** *noun* (circa 1828)
: the copies of a literary work first printed from the same type and issued at the same time; *also* : a single copy from a first edition

**first estate** *noun, often F&E capitalized* (1935)
: the first of the traditional political estates; *specifically* : CLERGY

**first floor** *noun* (15th century)
**1** : GROUND FLOOR 1
**2** *chiefly British* : the floor next above the ground floor

**first–fruits** \'fərs(t)-'früts\ *noun plural* (14th century)
**1** : the earliest gathered fruits offered to the Deity in acknowledgment of the gift of fruitfulness
**2** : the earliest products or results of an endeavor

**first·hand** \'fərst-'hand\ *adjective* (1748)
: obtained by, coming from, or being direct personal observation or experience ⟨a *firsthand* account of the war⟩
— **firsthand** *adverb*

**first lady** *noun, often F&L capitalized* (1834)
**1** : the wife or hostess of the chief executive of a country or jurisdiction
**2** : the leading woman of an art or profession

**first lieutenant** *noun* (1782)
**1** : a commissioned officer in the army, air force, or marine corps ranking above a second lieutenant and below a captain
**2** : a naval officer responsible for a ship's upkeep

**first·ling** \'fərst-liŋ\ *noun* (1535)
**1** : the first of a class or kind
**2** : the first produce or result of something

**first·ly** \-lē\ *adverb* (circa 1532)
: in the first place : FIRST

**first mortgage** *noun* (1855)
: a mortgage that has priority as a lien over all mortgages and liens except those imposed by law

**first name** *noun* (13th century)
: the name that stands first in one's full name

**first night** *noun* (1711)

: the night on which a theatrical production is first performed at a given place; *also* **:** the performance itself

**first–night·er** \'fərs(t)-'nī-tər\ *noun* (1882)
: a spectator at a first-night performance

**first off** *adverb* (1880)
: in the first place : before anything else

**first offender** *noun* (1849)
: one convicted of an offense for the first time

**first papers** *noun plural* (1912)
: papers declaring intention filed by an applicant for citizenship as the first step in the naturalization process

**first person** *noun* (1520)
**1 a :** a set of linguistic forms (as verb forms, pronouns, and inflectional affixes) referring to the speaker or writer of the utterance in which they occur **b :** a linguistic form belonging to such a set **c :** reference of a linguistic form to the speaker or writer of the utterance in which it occurs
**2 :** a style of discourse marked by general use of verbs and pronouns of the first person

**¹first–rate** \'fərs(t)-'rāt\ *adjective* (1671)
: of the first order of size, importance, or quality
— **first–rate·ness** *noun*
— **first–rat·er** \-'rā-tər\ *noun*

**²first–rate** *adverb* (1844)
: very well ⟨is getting along *first-rate*, now —Mark Twain⟩

**First Reader** *noun* (1895)
: a Christian Scientist chosen to conduct meetings for a specified time and specifically to read aloud from the writings of Mary Baker Eddy

**first reading** *noun* (circa 1703)
: the first submitting of a bill before a quorum of a legislative assembly usually by title or number only

**first–run** \'fərs(t)-'rən\ *adjective* (1912)
: available for public viewing for the first time ⟨*first-run* movies⟩; *also* **:** exhibiting first-run movies ⟨*first-run* theaters⟩

**first sergeant** *noun* (circa 1860)
**1 :** a noncommissioned officer serving as the chief assistant to the commander of a military unit (as a company or squadron)
**2 :** the rank of a first sergeant; *specifically* **:** a rank in the army above a platoon sergeant and below a command sergeant major and in the marine corps above a gunnery sergeant and below a sergeant major

**first strike** *noun* (1960)
: a preemptive nuclear attack
— **first–strike** *adjective*

**first–string** \'fərs(t)-'striŋ\ *adjective* (1917)
**1 :** being a regular as distinguished from a substitute (as on a team)
**2 :** FIRST-RATE

**first water** *noun* (1753)
**1 :** the purest luster — used of gems
**2 :** the highest grade, degree, or quality

**first world** *noun, often F&W capitalized* [after *third world*] (1967)
: the highly developed industrialized nations often considered the westernized countries of the world

**firth** \'fərth\ *noun* [Middle English, from Old Norse *fjǫrthr* — more at FORD] (14th century)
: ESTUARY

**fisc** \'fisk\ *noun* [Latin *fiscus*] (1598)
: a state or royal treasury

**¹fis·cal** \'fis-kəl\ *adjective* [Latin *fiscalis,* from *fiscus* basket, treasury] (1563)
**1 :** of or relating to taxation, public revenues, or public debt ⟨*fiscal* policy⟩
**2 :** of or relating to financial matters
— **fis·cal·ly** \-kə-lē\ *adverb*

**²fiscal** *noun* (1929)
**1 :** REVENUE STAMP
**2 :** FISCAL YEAR

**fiscal year** *noun* (1843)
: an accounting period of 12 months

**¹fish** \'fish\ *noun, plural* **fish** *or* **fish·es** *often attributive* [Middle English, from Old English *fisc;* akin to Old High German *fisc* fish, Latin *piscis*] (before 12th century)
**1 a :** an aquatic animal — usually used in combination ⟨star*fish*⟩ ⟨cuttle*fish*⟩ **b :** any of numerous cold-blooded strictly aquatic craniate vertebrates that include the bony fishes and usually the cartilaginous and jawless fishes and that have typically an elongated somewhat spindle-shaped body terminating in a broad caudal fin, limbs in the form of fins when present at all, and a 2-chambered heart by which blood is sent through thoracic gills to be oxygenated
**2 :** the flesh of fish used as food
**3 a :** a person who is caught or is wanted (as in a criminal investigation) **b :** FELLOW, PERSON ⟨an odd *fish*⟩ **c :** SUCKER 5a
**4 :** something that resembles a fish: as **a** *plural, capitalized* **:** PISCES 1, 2a **b :** TORPEDO 2b
— **fish·less** \'fish-ləs\ *adjective*
— **fish·like** \-,līk\ *adjective*
— **fish out of water :** a person who is in an unnatural or uncomfortable sphere or situation
— **fish to fry :** concerns or interests to pursue — usually used with *other*
— **neither fish nor fowl :** one that does not belong to a particular class or category

fish 1b: *1* mandible, *2* nasal opening, *3* eye, *4* cheek, *5* operculum, *6* dorsal fins, *7* lateral line, *8* caudal fin, *9* scales, *10* anal fin, *11* anus, *12* pectoral fin, *13* pelvic fin, *14* maxilla, *15* premaxilla, *16* upper jaw

**²fish** (before 12th century)
*intransitive verb*
**1 :** to attempt to catch fish
**2 :** to seek something by roundabout means ⟨*fishing* for a compliment⟩
**3 a :** to search for something underwater ⟨*fish* for pearls⟩ **b :** to engage in a search by groping or feeling ⟨*fishing* around in her purse for her keys⟩
*transitive verb*
**1 a :** to try to catch fish in **b :** to fish with : use (as a boat, net, or bait) in fishing
**2 a :** to go fishing for ⟨*fish* salmon⟩ **b :** to pull or draw as if fishing ⟨*fished* the ball from under the car⟩ ⟨*fish* wires through a conduit⟩
— **fish·abil·i·ty** \,fi-shə-'bi-lə-tē\ *noun*
— **fish·able** \'fi-shə-bəl\ *adjective*
— **fish or cut bait :** to make a choice between alternatives

**fish–and–chips** \,fi-shᵊn-'chips\ *noun plural* (1876)
: fried fish and french fried potatoes

**fish·bowl** \'fish-,bōl\ *noun* (1906)
**1 :** a bowl for the keeping of live fish
**2 :** a place or condition that affords no privacy

**fish cake** *noun* (1854)
: a round fried cake made of shredded fish and mashed potato

**fish duck** *noun* (1858)
: MERGANSER

**fish·er** \'fi-shər\ *noun* (before 12th century)
**1 :** one that fishes
**2 a :** a large dark brown North American carnivorous mammal (*Martes pennanti*) related to the weasels **b :** the fur or pelt of this animal

**fish·er·folk** \'fi-shər-,fōk\ *noun plural* (1854)
: people who fish especially for a living

**fish·er·man** \-mən\ *noun* (15th century)
**1 :** one who engages in fishing as an occupation or for pleasure
**2 :** a ship used in commercial fishing

**fisherman's bend** *noun* (1823)
: a knot made by passing the end twice round a spar or through a ring and then back under both turns — see KNOT illustration

**fish·er·wo·man** \'fi-shər-,wu̇-mən\ *noun* (1816)
: a woman who fishes as an occupation or for pleasure

**fish·ery** \'fi-shə-rē\ *noun, plural* **-er·ies** (1528)
**1 :** the occupation, industry, or season of taking fish or other sea animals (as sponges, shrimp, or seals) **:** FISHING
**2 :** a place for catching fish or taking other sea animals
**3 :** a fishing establishment; *also* **:** its fishermen
**4 :** the legal right to take fish at a particular place or in particular waters
**5 :** the technology of fishery — usually used in plural

**fish–eye** \'fish-,ī\ *adjective* (1943)
: being, having, or produced by a wide-angle photographic lens that has a highly curved protruding front, that covers an angle of about 180 degrees, and that gives a circular image

**fish farm** *noun* (1865)
: a commercial facility for raising aquatic animals for human food
— **fish–farm** \'fish-,färm\ *transitive verb*

**fish finger** *noun* (1962)
*British* **:** FISH STICK

**fish fry** *noun* (1824)
**1 :** a picnic or supper featuring fried fish
**2 :** fried fish

**fish hawk** *noun* (1709)
: OSPREY 1

**fish·hook** \'fish-,hu̇k\ *noun* (14th century)
: a usually barbed hook for catching fish

**fish·ing** *noun* (13th century)
**1 :** the sport or business of catching fish
**2 :** a place for catching fish

**fishing expedition** *noun* (circa 1925)
**1 :** a legal interrogation or examination to discover information for a later proceeding
**2 :** an investigation that does not stick to a stated objective but hopes to uncover incriminating or newsworthy evidence

**fish ladder** *noun* (1865)
: a series of pools arranged like steps by which fish can pass over a dam in going upstream

**fish meal** *noun* (1854)
: ground dried fish and fish waste used as fertilizer and animal food

**fish·mong·er** \'fish-,mäŋ-gər, -,məŋ-\ *noun* (15th century)
*chiefly British* **:** a fish dealer

**fish·net** \-,net\ *noun* (before 12th century)
**1 :** netting fitted with floats and weights or a supporting frame for catching fish
**2 :** a coarse open-mesh fabric

**fish out** *transitive verb* (1892)
: to exhaust the supply of fish in by fishing

**fish·plate** \-,plāt\ *noun* (1855)
: a steel plate used to lap a butt joint

**fish·pond** \-,pänd\ *noun* (14th century)
: a pond stocked with fish

**fish protein concentrate** *noun* (1961)
: a protein-rich food additive made from ground whole fish

**fish stick** *noun* (1953)
: a small elongated breaded fillet of fish

**fish story** *noun* [from the traditional exaggeration by fishermen of the size of fish almost caught] (1819)
: an extravagant or incredible story

**fish·tail** \'fish-,tāl\ *intransitive verb* (1927)
**1 :** to swing the tail of an airplane from side to side to reduce speed especially when landing
**2 :** to have the rear end slide from side to side out of control while moving forward ⟨the car *fishtailed* on the icy curve⟩

**fish·way** \-ˌwā\ *noun* (1845)
: a contrivance for enabling fish to pass around a fall or dam in a stream; *specifically*
: FISH LADDER

**fish·wife** \-ˌwīf\ *noun* [Middle English] (15th century)
**1** : a woman who sells fish
**2** : a vulgar abusive woman

**fishy** \'fi-shē\ *adjective* **fish·i·er; -est** (15th century)
**1** : of or resembling fish especially in taste or odor
**2** : creating doubt or suspicion : QUESTIONABLE

**fis·sile** \'fi-səl, 'fi-ˌsīl\ *adjective* [Latin *fissilis*, from *findere*] (1661)
**1** : capable of being split or divided in the direction of the grain or along natural planes of cleavage ⟨*fissile* wood⟩ ⟨*fissile* crystals⟩
**2** : capable of undergoing fission
— **fis·sil·i·ty** \fi-'si-lə-tē\ *noun*

**¹fis·sion** \'fi-shən, -zhən\ *noun* [Latin *fission-, fissio*, from *findere* to split — more at BITE] (circa 1617)
**1** : a splitting or breaking up into parts
**2** : reproduction by spontaneous division of the body into two or more parts each of which grows into a complete organism
**3** : the splitting of an atomic nucleus resulting in the release of large amounts of energy
— **fis·sion·al** \-ⁿl\ *adjective*

**²fission** (1929)
*intransitive verb*
: to undergo fission
*transitive verb*
: to cause to undergo fission

**fis·sion·able** \'fi-shən-ə-bəl, -zhən-; 'fish-nə-, 'fizh-\ *adjective* (1945)
: FISSILE 2
— **fis·sion·abil·i·ty** \ˌfi-shən-ə-'bi-lə-tē, -zhən-; ˌfish-nə-, ˌfizh-\ *noun*
— **fissionable** *noun*

**fis·sip·a·rous** \fi-'si-p(ə-)rəs\ *adjective* [Latin *fissus*, past participle of *findere* + English *-parous*] (1874)
: tending to break up into parts : DIVISIVE
— **fis·sip·a·rous·ness** *noun*

**¹fis·sure** \'fi-shər\ *noun* [Middle English, from Middle French, from Latin *fissura*, from *fissus*] (14th century)
**1** : a narrow opening or crack of considerable length and depth usually occurring from some breaking or parting
**2 a** : a natural cleft between body parts or in the substance of an organ **b** : a break or slit in tissue usually at the junction of skin and mucous membrane
**3** : a separation or disagreement in thought or viewpoint : SCHISM ⟨*fissures* in a political party⟩

**²fissure** *verb* **fis·sured; fis·sur·ing** (1656)
*transitive verb*
: to break into fissures : CLEAVE
*intransitive verb*
: CRACK, DIVIDE

**¹fist** \'fist\ *noun* [Middle English, from Old English *fÿst*; akin to Old High German *fūst* fist, Polish *pięść*, and probably to Old English *fīf* five] (before 12th century)
**1** : the hand clenched with the fingers doubled into the palm and the thumb doubled inward across the fingers
**2** : the hand closed as in grasping : CLUTCH
**3** : INDEX 5

**²fist** *transitive verb* (1607)
**1** : to grip with the fist : HANDLE
**2** : to clench into a fist

**-fist·ed** \'fis-təd\ *combining form*
: having (such or so many) fists ⟨two-*fisted*⟩ ⟨tight*fisted*⟩

**fist·fight** \'fist-ˌfīt\ *noun* (1603)
: a usually spontaneous fight with bare fists

**fist·ful** \-ˌfůl\ *noun* (1611)
**1** : HANDFUL ⟨a *fistful* of coins⟩
**2** : a considerable number or amount ⟨a whole *fistful* of musicians —Thomas Lask⟩

**fist·ic** \'fis-tik\ *adjective* (1806)

: of or relating to boxing or to fighting with the fists

**fist·i·cuffs** \'fis-ti-ˌkəfs\ *noun plural* [alteration of *fisty cuff*, from *fisty* (fistic) + *cuff*] (1605)
: a fight with the fists

**fist·note** \'fis(t)-ˌnōt\ *noun* (circa 1934)
: matter in a text to which attention is directed by means of an index mark

**fis·tu·la** \'fis(h)-chə-lə\ *noun, plural* **-las** *or* **-lae** \-ˌlē, -ˌlī\ [Middle English, from Latin, pipe, fistula] (14th century)
: an abnormal passage leading from an abscess or hollow organ to the body surface or from one hollow organ to another and permitting passage of fluids or secretions

**fis·tu·lous** \-ləs\ *adjective* (15th century)
**1** : of, relating to, or having the form or nature of a fistula
**2** : hollow like a pipe or reed

**fistulous withers** *noun plural but singular or plural in construction* (circa 1900)
: a deep-seated chronic inflammation of the withers of the horse in which bloody fluid is discharged

**¹fit** \'fit\ *noun* [Middle English, from Old English *fitt*; akin to Old Saxon *fittea* division of a poem, Old High German *fizza* skein] (before 12th century)
*archaic* : a division of a poem or song

**²fit** *adjective* **fit·ter; fit·test** [Middle English; akin to Middle English *fitten*] (14th century)
**1 a** (1) : adapted to an end or design : suitable by nature or by art (2) : adapted to the environment so as to be capable of surviving **b** : acceptable from a particular viewpoint (as of competence or morality) : PROPER ⟨a movie *fit* for the whole family⟩
**2 a** : put into a suitable state : made ready ⟨get the house *fit* for company⟩ **b** : being in such a state as to be or seem ready to do or suffer something ⟨fair *fit* to cry I was —Bryan MacMahon⟩ ⟨laughing *fit* to burst⟩
**3** : sound physically and mentally : HEALTHY ☆
— **fit·ly** *adverb*
— **fit to be tied** : extremely angry or irritated
— **fit to kill** : in a striking manner ⟨dressed *fit to kill*⟩

**³fit** *noun* [Middle English, from Old English *fitt* strife] (circa 1541)
**1 a** : a sudden violent attack of a disease (as epilepsy) especially when marked by convulsions or unconsciousness : PAROXYSM **b** : a sudden but transient attack of a physical disturbance
**2** : a sudden burst or flurry (as of activity) ⟨cleaned the whole house in a *fit* of efficiency⟩
**3** : an emotional reaction (as in anger or frustration) ⟨has a *fit* when I show up late⟩
— **by fits** *or* **by fits and starts** *or* **in fits and starts** : in an impulsive and irregular manner

**⁴fit** *verb* **fit·ted** *also* **fit; fit·ting** [Middle English *fitten* to marshal troops, from or akin to Middle Dutch *vitten* to be suitable; akin to Old High German *fizza* skein] (15th century)
*transitive verb*
**1 a** : to be suitable for or to : harmonize with **b** *archaic* : to be seemly or proper for ⟨it *fits* us then to be as provident as fear may teach us —Shakespeare⟩
**2 a** : to conform correctly to the shape or size of ⟨it doesn't *fit* me anymore⟩ **b** (1) : to insert or adjust until correctly in place ⟨*fit* the mechanism into the box⟩ (2) : to make or adjust to the right shape and size ⟨*fitting* the jacket to the customer⟩ (3) : to measure for determining the specifications of something to be worn by ⟨*fitted* him for a new suit⟩ **c** : to make a place or room for : ACCOMMODATE
**3** : to be in agreement or accord with ⟨the theory *fits* all the facts⟩
**4 a** : to put into a condition of readiness **b** : to cause to conform to or suit something

**5** : SUPPLY, EQUIP ⟨*fitted* the ship with new engines⟩ — often used with *out*
**6** : to adjust (a smooth curve of a specified type) to a given set of points
*intransitive verb*
**1** *archaic* : to be seemly, proper, or suitable
**2** : to conform to a particular shape or size; *also* : to be accommodated ⟨will we all *fit* into the car?⟩
**3** : to be in harmony or accord : BELONG — often used with *in*
— **fit·ter** *noun*

**⁵fit** *noun* (1823)
: the fact, condition, or manner of fitting or being fitted: as **a** : the way clothing fits the wearer **b** : the degree of closeness between surfaces in an assembly of parts **c** : GOODNESS OF FIT

**⁶fit** *dialect past and past participle of* FIGHT

**fitch** \'fich\ *or* **fitch·ew** \'fich-(ˌ)ü\ *noun* [Middle English *fiche, ficheux*, from Middle French or Middle Dutch; Middle French *fichau*, from Middle Dutch *vitsau*] (15th century)
**1** : POLECAT 1
**2** : the fur or pelt of the polecat

**fitch·et** \'fi-chət\ *noun* (1535)
: POLECAT 1

**fit·ful** \'fit-fəl\ *adjective* (1592)
**1** *obsolete* : characterized by fits or paroxysms
**2** : having an erratic or intermittent character : IRREGULAR ☆
— **fit·ful·ly** \-fə-lē\ *adverb*
— **fit·ful·ness** *noun*

**fit·ment** \'fit-mənt\ *noun* [⁴fit] (1851)
*chiefly British* : FURNISHING 2, FIXTURE, CABINETRY — usually used in plural

**fit·ness** \'fit-nəs\ *noun* (1580)
**1** : the quality or state of being fit
**2** : the capacity of an organism to survive and transmit its genotype to reproductive offspring as compared to competing organisms; *also* : the contribution of an allele or genotype to

☆ **SYNONYMS**
**Fit, suitable, meet, proper, appropriate, fitting, apt, happy, felicitous** mean right with respect to some end, need, use, or circumstance. FIT stresses adaptability and sometimes special readiness for use or action ⟨*fit* for battle⟩. SUITABLE implies an answering to requirements or demands ⟨clothes *suitable* for camping⟩. MEET suggests a just proportioning ⟨*meet* payment⟩. PROPER suggests a suitability through essential nature or accordance with custom ⟨*proper* acknowledgement⟩. APPROPRIATE implies eminent or distinctive fitness ⟨an *appropriate* gift⟩. FITTING implies harmony of mood or tone ⟨a *fitting* end⟩. APT connotes a fitness marked by nicety and discrimination ⟨*apt* quotations⟩. HAPPY suggests what is effectively or successfully appropriate ⟨a *happy* choice of words⟩. FELICITOUS suggests an aptness that is opportune, telling, or graceful ⟨a *felicitous* phrase⟩.

**Fitful, spasmodic, convulsive** mean lacking steadiness or regularity in movement. FITFUL implies intermittence, a succession of starts and stops or risings and fallings ⟨*fitful* sleep⟩. SPASMODIC adds to FITFUL the implication of rapid or violent activity alternating with inactivity ⟨*spasmodic* growth⟩. CONVULSIVE suggests the breaking of regularity or quiet by uncontrolled movement ⟨*convulsive* shocks⟩.

\ə\ abut \ᵊ\ kitten \ər\ further \a\ ash \ā\ ace \ä\ mop, mar \au̇\ out \ch\ chin \e\ bet \ē\ easy \g\ go \i\ hit \ī\ ice \j\ job \ŋ\ sing \ō\ go \ȯ\ law \ȯi\ boy \th\ thin \t̶h̶\ the \ü\ loot \u̇\ foot \y\ yet \zh\ vision *see also* Guide to Pronunciation the gene pool of subsequent generations as compared to that of other alleles or genotypes

**fit·ted** \'fi-təd\ *adjective* (circa 1666)
**1** : FIT, SUITABLE
**2** : shaped for a precise fit ⟨a *fitted* sheet⟩; *especially* : shaped to conform to the lines of the body ⟨a *fitted* shirt⟩

¹**fit·ting** \'fi-tiŋ\ *adjective* (15th century)
: of a kind appropriate to the situation : SUITABLE
**synonym** see FIT
— **fit·ting·ly** \-tiŋ-lē\ *adverb*
— **fit·ting·ness** *noun*

²**fitting** *noun* (1607)
**1** : an action or act of one that fits; *specifically* : a trying on of clothes which are in the process of being made or altered
**2** : a small often standardized part ⟨an electrical *fitting*⟩

**five** \'fīv\ *noun* [Middle English, from *five*, adjective, from Old English *fīf*; akin to Old High German *finf* five, Latin *quinque*, Greek *pente*] (before 12th century)
**1** — see NUMBER table
**2** *plural* : a British handball game
**3** : the fifth in a set or series ⟨the *five* of clubs⟩
**4** : something having five units or members; *especially* : a basketball team
**5** : a 5-dollar bill
**6** : FIFTEEN 2
— **five** *adjective*
— **five** *pronoun, plural in construction*

**five-and-ten** \ˌfī-vən-'ten\ *noun* [from the fact that all articles in such stores were formerly priced at either 5 or 10 cents] (1880)
: a retail store that carries chiefly inexpensive merchandise (as notions and household goods) — called also *five-and-dime*

**five–fin·ger** \'fīv-ˌfiŋ-gər\ *noun* (before 12th century)
: CINQUEFOIL 1

**five·fold** \'fīv-ˌfōld, -'fōld\ *adjective* (before 12th century)
**1** : having five units or members
**2** : being five times as great or as many
— **five·fold** \-'fōld\ *adverb*

**five of a kind** (1897)
: four cards of the same rank plus a wild card in one hand — see POKER illustration

**fiv·er** \'fī-vər\ *noun* (1843)
**1** *slang* : a 5-dollar bill
**2** *British* : a 5-pound note

**five-spice powder** \'fīv-ˌspīs-\ *noun* (1970)
: a blend of spices typically including anise, pepper, fennel, cloves, and cinnamon that is used in Chinese cooking

**five-star** \'fīv-'stär\ *adjective* (1913)
: of first class or quality

¹**fix** \'fiks\ *verb* [Middle English, from Latin *fixus*, past participle of *figere* to fasten; akin to Lithuanian *dygti* to sprout, break through] (14th century)
*transitive verb*
**1 a** : to make firm, stable, or stationary **b** : to give a permanent or final form to: as (1) : to change into a stable compound or available form ⟨bacteria that *fix* nitrogen⟩ (2) : to kill, harden, and preserve for microscopic study (3) : to make the image of (a photographic film) permanent by removing unused salts **c** : AFFIX, ATTACH
**2 a** : to hold or direct steadily ⟨*fixes* his eyes on the horizon⟩ **b** : to capture the attention of ⟨*fixed* her with a stare⟩
**3 a** : to set or place definitely : ESTABLISH **b** : to make an accurate determination of : DISCOVER ⟨*fixing* our location on the chart⟩ **c** : ASSIGN ⟨*fix* the blame⟩
**4** : to set in order : ADJUST
**5** : to get ready : PREPARE ⟨*fix* lunch⟩
**6 a** : REPAIR, MEND ⟨*fix* the clock⟩ **b** : RESTORE, CURE ⟨the doctor *fixed* him up⟩ **c** : SPAY, CASTRATE
**7 a** : to get even with **b** : to influence the actions, outcome, or effect of by improper or illegal methods ⟨the race had been *fixed*⟩

*intransitive verb*
**1** : to become firm, stable, or fixed
**2** : to get set : be on the verge ⟨we're *fixing* to leave soon⟩
**3** : to direct one's attention or efforts : FOCUS; *also* : DECIDE, SETTLE — usually used with *on*
**synonym** see FASTEN
— **fix·able** \'fik-sə-bəl\ *adjective*

²**fix** *noun* (1809)
**1** : a position of difficulty or embarrassment : PREDICAMENT
**2 a** : the position (as of a ship) determined by bearings, observations, or radio; *also* : a determination of one's position **b** : an accurate determination or understanding especially by observation or analysis
**3** : an act or instance of improper or illegal fixing ⟨the *fix* was in⟩
**4** : a supply or dose of something strongly desired or craved; *especially* : a shot of a narcotic
**5** : FIXATION
**6** : something that fixes or restores ⟨a quick *fix*⟩

**fix·ate** \'fik-ˌsāt\ *verb* **fix·at·ed; fix·at·ing** (1885)
*transitive verb*
**1** : to make fixed, stationary, or unchanging
**2** : to focus one's gaze on
**3** : to direct (the libido) toward an infantile form of gratification
*intransitive verb*
**1** : to focus or concentrate one's gaze or attention intently or obsessively
**2** : to undergo arrestment at a stage of development

**fix·at·ed** *adjective* (1926)
: arrested in development or adjustment; *especially* : arrested at a pregenital level of psychosexual development

**fix·a·tion** \fik-'sā-shən\ *noun* (14th century)
: the act, process, or result of fixing, fixating, or becoming fixated: as **a** : a persistent concentration of libidinal energies upon objects characteristic of psychosexual stages of development preceding the genital stage **b** : stereotyped behavior (as in response to frustration) **c** : an obsessive or unhealthy preoccupation or attachment

**fix·a·tive** \'fik-sə-tiv\ *noun* (circa 1859)
: something that fixes or sets: as **a** : a substance added to a perfume especially to prevent too rapid evaporation **b** : a substance used to fix living tissue **c** : a varnish used especially for the protection of drawings (as in pastel or charcoal)
— **fixative** *adjective*

**fixed** \'fikst\ *adjective* (14th century)
**1 a** : securely placed or fastened : STATIONARY **b** (1) : NONVOLATILE (2) : formed into a chemical compound **c** (1) : not subject to change or fluctuation ⟨a *fixed* income⟩ (2) : firmly set in the mind ⟨a *fixed* idea⟩ (3) : having a final or crystallized form or character (4) : recurring on the same date from year to year ⟨*fixed* holidays⟩ **d** : IMMOBILE, CONCENTRATED ⟨a *fixed* stare⟩
**2** : supplied with something (as money) needed ⟨comfortably *fixed*⟩
— **fixed·ly** \'fik-səd-lē, 'fiks-tlē\ *adverb*
— **fixed·ness** \'fik-səd-nəs, 'fiks(t)-nəs\ *noun*

**fixed charge** *noun* (circa 1901)
: a regularly recurring expense (as rent, taxes, or interest) that must be met when due

**fixed oil** *noun* (circa 1800)
: a nonvolatile oil; *especially* : a fatty oil — compare ESSENTIAL OIL

**fixed-point** *adjective* (1960)
: involving or being a mathematical notation (as in a decimal system) in which the point separating whole numbers and fractions is fixed — compare FLOATING-POINT

**fixed star** *noun* (1561)

: a star so distant that its motion can be measured only by very precise observations over long periods

**fix·er** \'fik-sər\ *noun* (1849)
: one that fixes: as **a** : one who intervenes to enable a person to circumvent the law or obtain a political favor **b** : one who adjusts matters or disputes by negotiation **c** : ²HYPO

**fix·ing** \-siŋ\ *noun* (1605)
**1** : the act or process of one that fixes
**2** *plural* \often -sənz\ : customary accompaniments : TRIMMINGS ⟨a turkey dinner with all the *fixings*⟩

**fix·i·ty** \'fik-sə-tē\ *noun, plural* **-ties** (1666)
**1** : the quality or state of being fixed or stable
**2** : something that is fixed

**fix·ture** \'fiks-chər\ *noun* [modification of Late Latin *fixura*, from Latin *fixus*] (1598)
**1** : the act or process of fixing : the state of being fixed
**2 a** : something that is fixed or attached (as to a building) as a permanent appendage or as a structural part ⟨a plumbing *fixture*⟩ **b** : a device for supporting work during machining **c** : an item of movable property so incorporated into real property that it may be regarded as legally a part of it
**3** : a familiar or invariably present element or feature in some particular setting; *especially* : a person long associated with a place or activity
**4** : a settled date or time especially for a sporting or festive event; *also* : such an event especially as a regularly scheduled affair

**fix up** *transitive verb* (1831)
**1** : REFURBISH ⟨*fix* up the attic⟩
**2** : to set right : SETTLE ⟨*fixed* up their dispute⟩
**3** : to provide with something needed or wanted; *especially* : to arrange a date for

¹**fizz** \'fiz\ *intransitive verb* [probably of imitative origin] (1685)
**1** : to make a hissing or sputtering sound : EFFERVESCE
**2** : to show excitement or exhilaration

²**fizz** *noun* (1842)
**1 a** : a hissing sound **b** : SPIRIT, LIVELINESS
**2** : an effervescent beverage
— **fizzy** \'fi-zē\ *adjective*

¹**fiz·zle** \'fi-zəl\ *intransitive verb* **fiz·zled; fiz·zling** \-z(ə-)liŋ\ [probably alteration of *fist* (to break wind)] (circa 1841)
**1** : FIZZ
**2** : to fail or end feebly especially after a promising start — often used with *out*

²**fizzle** *noun* (1842)
: an abortive effort : FAILURE

**fjord** \fē-'ord, 'fē-ˌ; 'fyord\ *noun* [Norwegian *fjord*, from Old Norse *fjorthr* — more at FORD] (1674)
: a narrow inlet of the sea between cliffs or steep slopes

**flab** \'flab\ *noun* [back-formation from *flabby*] (1951)
: soft flabby body tissue

**flab·ber·gast** \'fla-bər-ˌgast\ *transitive verb* [origin unknown] (1772)
: to overwhelm with shock, surprise, or wonder : DUMBFOUND
**synonym** see SURPRISE
— **flab·ber·gast·ing·ly** \-ˌgas-tiŋ-lē\ *adverb*

**flab·by** \'fla-bē\ *adjective* **flab·bi·er; -est** [alteration of *flappy*] (1697)
**1** : lacking resilience or firmness : FLACCID
**2** : weak and ineffective : FEEBLE
— **flab·bi·ly** \'fla-bə-lē\ *adverb*
— **flab·bi·ness** \'fla-bē-nəs\ *noun*

fjord

**fla·bel·late** \flə-'be-lət, 'fla-bə-,lāt\ *adjective* [Latin *flabellum* fan] (1819)
: shaped like a fan
**fla·bel·li·form** \flə-'be-lə-,fȯrm\ *adjective* (1777)
: FLABELLATE
**flac·cid** \÷'fla-səd *also* 'flak-səd\ *adjective* [Latin *flaccidus*, from *flaccus* flabby] (1620)
**1 a** : not firm or stiff; *also* : lacking normal or youthful firmness *(flaccid* muscles) **b** *of a plant part* : deficient in turgor
**2** : lacking vigor or force *(flaccid* leadership)
— **flac·cid·i·ty** \fla(k)-'si-də-tē\ *noun*
— **flac·cid·ly** \'fla(k)-səd-lē\ *adverb*
**¹flack** \'flak\ *noun* [origin unknown] (1939)
: one who provides publicity; *especially*
: PRESS AGENT
— **flack·ery** \'fla-k(ə-)rē\ *noun*
**²flack** *variant of* FLAK
**³flack** *intransitive verb* (1965)
: to provide publicity : engage in press-agentry
**fla·con** \'fla-kən, -,kän; fla-'kō<sup>n</sup>\ *noun* [French, from Middle French, bottle — more at FLAGON] (1824)
: a small usually ornamental bottle with a tight cap
**¹flag** \'flag *also* 'fläg\ *noun* [Middle English *flagge* reed, rush] (14th century)
: any of various monocotyledonous plants with long ensiform leaves: as **a** : IRIS; *especially* : a wild iris **b** : SWEET FLAG
**²flag** *noun, often attributive* [perhaps from ¹*flag*] (1530)
**1** : a usually rectangular piece of fabric of distinctive design that is used as a symbol (as of a nation), as a signaling device, or as a decoration
**2 a** : the tail of some dogs (as a setter or hound); *also* : the long hair fringing a dog's tail **b** : the tail of a deer
**3 a** : something used like a flag to signal or attract attention **b** : one of the cross strokes of a musical note less than a quarter note in value
**4** : something represented by a flag: as **a** : FLAGSHIP **b** : an admiral functioning in his office of command **c** : NATIONALITY; *especially* : the nationality of registration of a ship or aircraft
**³flag** *transitive verb* **flagged; flag·ging** (1856)
**1** : to signal with or as if with a flag; *especially* : to signal to stop *(flagged* the train) — often used with *down*
**2** : to put a flag on (as for identification)
**3** : to call a penalty on : PENALIZE (a lineman *flagged* for being offside)
**⁴flag** *intransitive verb* **flagged; flag·ging** [probably from ²*flag*] (1545)
**1** : to hang loose without stiffness
**2 a** : to become unsteady, feeble, or spiritless **b** : to decline in interest or attraction
**⁵flag** *noun* [Middle English *flagge* turf, from Old Norse *flaga* slab; akin to Old English *flōh* chip] (1604)
: a hard evenly stratified stone that splits into flat pieces suitable for paving; *also* : a piece of such stone
**⁶flag** *transitive verb* **flagged; flag·ging** (1615)
: to lay (as a pavement) with flags
**flag day** *noun* (1894)
**1** *F&D capitalized* : June 14 observed in various states in commemoration of the adoption in 1777 of the official U.S. flag
**2** *British* : a day on which charitable contributions are solicited in exchange for small flags
**fla·gel·lant** \'fla-jə-lənt, flə-'je-lənt\ *noun* (circa 1587)
**1** : a person who scourges himself as a public penance
**2** : a person who responds sexually to being beaten by or to beating another person
— **flagellant** *adjective*
— **fla·gel·lant·ism** \-lən-,ti-zəm\ *noun*
**fla·gel·lar** \flə-'je-lər, 'fla-jə-lər\ *adjective* (circa 1889)

: of or relating to a flagellum
**¹flag·el·late** \'fla-jə-,lāt\ *transitive verb* **-lat·ed; -lat·ing** [Latin *flagellatus*, past participle of *flagellare*, from *flagellum*, diminutive of *flagrum* whip; perhaps akin to Old Norse *blaka* to wave] (circa 1623)
**1** : WHIP, SCOURGE
**2** : to drive or punish as if by whipping
**²fla·gel·late** \'fla-jə-lət, -,lāt; flə-'je-lət\ *adjective* [New Latin *flagellatus*, from *flagellum*] (circa 1859)
**1 a** *or* **flag·el·lat·ed** \'fla-jə-,lā-təd\ : having flagella **b** : shaped like a flagellum
**2** : of, relating to, or caused by flagellates *(flagellate* diarrhea)
**³flagellate** \*same as* ²\ *noun* [New Latin *Flagellata*, class of unicellular organisms, from neuter plural of *flagellatus*] (1879)
: a flagellate protozoan or alga
**flag·el·la·tion** \,fla-jə-'lā-shən\ *noun* (15th century)
: the act or practice of flagellating; *especially* : the practice of a flagellant
**fla·gel·lin** \flə-'je-lən\ *noun* [*flagell*um + ¹-*in*] (1955)
: a polymeric protein that is the chief constituent of bacterial flagella and is responsible for the specificity of their flagellar antigens
**fla·gel·lum** \flə-'je-ləm\ *noun, plural* **-la** \-lə\ *also* **-lums** [New Latin, from Latin, whip, shoot of a plant] (1852)
: any of various elongated filiform appendages of plants or animals: as **a** : the slender distal part of an antenna **b** : a long tapering process that projects singly or in groups from a cell and is the primary organ of motion of many microorganisms
**¹fla·geo·let** \,fla-jə-'let, -'lā\ *noun* [French, from Old French *flajolet*, from *flajol* flute, from (assumed) Vulgar Latin *flabeolum*, from Latin *flare* to blow — more at BLOW] (1659)
: a small fipple flute resembling the treble recorder
**²flageolet** *noun* [French, diminutive of *flageolle* kidney bean, modification of Italian *fagiolo*, from Latin *phaseolus* — more at FRIJOLE] (1877)
: a green kidney bean used in French cuisine
**flag football** *noun* (1954)
: a variation of football in which a player must remove a flag attached to the ballcarrier's clothing to stop the play
**flag·ging** \'fla-giŋ, *also* 'flā-\ *adjective* (1545)
**1** : LANGUID, WEAK
**2** : becoming progressively less : DWINDLING
— **flag·ging·ly** \-giŋ-lē\ *adverb*
**fla·gi·tious** \flə-'ji-shəs\ *adjective* [Middle English *flagicious*, from Latin *flagitiosus*, from *flagitium* shameful thing] (14th century)
: marked by scandalous crime or vice : VILLAINOUS
— **fla·gi·tious·ly** *adverb*
— **fla·gi·tious·ness** *noun*
**flag·man** \'flag-mən\ *noun* (1832)
: a person who signals with a flag
**flag of convenience** (1956)
: registry of a merchant ship under a foreign flag in order to profit from less restrictive regulations
**flag officer** *noun* [from his being entitled to display a flag with one or more stars indicating his rank] (1665)
: any of the officers in the navy or coast guard above captain — compare GENERAL OFFICER
**flag of truce** (1627)
: a white flag carried or displayed to an enemy as an invitation to conference or parley
**flag·on** \'fla-gən\ *noun* [Middle English, from Middle French *flascon, flacon* bottle, from Late Latin *flascon-, flasco* — more at FLASK] (15th century)
**1 a** : a large usually metal or pottery vessel (as for wine) with handle and spout and often a lid **b** : a large bulging short-necked bottle
**2** : the contents of a flagon
**flag·pole** \'flag-,pōl\ *noun* (1884)

: a pole on which to raise a flag
**fla·grance** \'flā-grən(t)s *also* 'fla-\ *noun* (circa 1615)
: FLAGRANCY
**fla·gran·cy** \'flā-grən(t)-sē *also* 'fla-\ *noun* (1599)
: the quality or state of being flagrant
**flag rank** *noun* (1894)
: the rank of a flag officer
**fla·grant** \'flā-grənt *also* 'fla-\ *adjective* [Latin *flagrant-, flagrans*, present participle of *flagrare* to burn — more at BLACK] (1513)
**1** *archaic* : fiery hot : BURNING
**2** : conspicuously offensive *(flagrant* errors); *especially* : so obviously inconsistent with what is right or proper as to appear to be a flouting of law or morality *(flagrant* violations of human rights) ☆
— **fla·grant·ly** *adverb*
**fla·gran·te de·lic·to** \flə-,grän-tē-di-'lik-(,)tō, -,gran-\ *adverb or adjective* [Medieval Latin, literally, while the crime is blazing] (1826)
**1** : in the very act of committing a misdeed
: RED-HANDED; *also* : in the midst of sexual activity
**flag·ship** \'flag-,ship\ *noun* (1672)
**1** : the ship that carries the commander of a fleet or subdivision of a fleet and flies his flag
**2** : the finest, largest, or most important one of a series, network, or chain
**flag·staff** \-,staf\ *noun* (circa 1613)
: a staff on which a flag is hoisted
**flag·stick** \-,stik\ *noun* (1926)
: a staff for a flag marking the location of the cup on a golf putting green
**flag·stone** \-,stōn\ *noun* (1730)
: ⁵FLAG
**flag stop** *noun* (1941)
: a point at which a vehicle in public transportation stops only on prearrangement or signal
**flag–wav·er** \'flag-,wā-vər\ *noun* (1894)
**1** : one who is intensely and conspicuously patriotic
**2** : one who waves a flag in signaling
**3** : a song intended to rouse patriotic sentiment
**flag–wav·ing** \-viŋ\ *noun* (1892)
: passionate appeal to patriotic or partisan sentiment : CHAUVINISM
**¹flail** \'flā(ə)l\ *noun* [Middle English *fleil, flail,* partly from (assumed) Old English *flegel* (whence Old English *fligel*), from Late Latin *flagellum* flail, from Latin, whip & partly from Middle French *flaiel*, from Late Latin *flagellum* — more at FLAGELLATE] (before 12th century)

flagon 1a

\ə\ abut \ᵊ\ kitten \ər\ further \a\ ash \ā\ ace
\ä\ mop, mar \au̇\ out \ch\ chin \e\ bet \ē\ easy
\g\ go \i\ hit \ī\ ice \j\ job \ŋ\ sing \ō\ go
\ȯ\ law \ȯi\ boy \th\ thin \t͟h\ the \ü\ loot \u̇\ foot
\y\ yet \zh\ vision *see also* Guide to Pronunciation

: a hand threshing implement consisting of a wooden handle at the end of which a stouter and shorter stick is so hung as to swing freely

²**flail** (15th century)
*transitive verb*
**1 a :** to strike with or as if with a flail ⟨arms *flailing* the water⟩ **b :** to move, swing, or beat as if wielding a flail ⟨*flailing* a club to drive away the insects⟩
**2 :** to thresh (grain) with a flail
*intransitive verb*
: to move, swing, or beat like a flail

**flair** \'flar, 'fler\ *noun* [French, literally, sense of smell, from Old French, odor, from *flairier* to give off an odor, from Late Latin *flagrare*, alteration of Latin *fragrare*] (1881)
**1 :** a skill or instinctive ability to appreciate or make good use of something : TALENT ⟨a *flair* for color⟩; *also* : INCLINATION, TENDENCY ⟨a *flair* for the dramatic⟩
**2 :** a uniquely attractive quality : STYLE ⟨fashionable dresses with a *flair* all their own⟩

**flak** \'flak\ *noun, plural* **flak** [German, from *Fliegerabwehrkanonen*, from *Flieger* flyer + *Abwehr* defense + *Kanonen* cannons] (1938)
**1 :** antiaircraft guns
**2 :** the bursting shells fired from flak
**3 :** CRITICISM, OPPOSITION

¹**flake** \'flāk\ *noun* [Middle English, of Scandinavian origin; akin to Norwegian *flak* disk] (14th century)
**1 :** a small loose mass or bit ⟨snow *flakes*⟩
**2 :** a thin flattened piece or layer : CHIP
**3** *slang* : COCAINE

²**flake** *verb* **flaked; flak·ing** (1627)
*intransitive verb*
: to separate into flakes; *also* : to peel in flakes
*transitive verb*
**1 :** to form or break into flakes : CHIP
**2 :** to cover with or as if with flakes
— **flak·er** *noun*

³**flake** *noun* [Middle English, hurdle, from Old Norse *flaki*] (1623)
: a stage, platform, or tray for drying fish or produce

⁴**flake** *noun* [perhaps from *flake out*] (1964)
: a person who is flaky : ODDBALL

**flake out** *intransitive verb* [probably from dialect *flake* to lie, bask] (1939)
**1** *slang* : to fall asleep
**2** *slang* : to be overcome especially by exhaustion

**flake tool** *noun* (circa 1947)
: a Stone-Age tool that is a flake of stone struck off from a larger piece

**flak jacket** *noun* (1950)
: a jacket containing metal plates for protection against flak; *broadly* : a bulletproof vest
— called also *flak vest*

¹**flaky** *also* **flak·ey** \'flā-kē\ *adjective* **flak·i·er; -est** (1580)
**1 :** consisting of flakes ⟨*flaky* snow⟩
**2 :** tending to flake ⟨a *flaky* crust⟩
— **flak·i·ness** *noun*

²**flaky** *adjective* **flak·i·er; -est** [⁴*flake*] (circa 1963)
: markedly odd or unconventional : OFFBEAT, WACKY
— **flak·i·ness** *noun*

**flam** \'flam\ *noun* [probably imitative] (1819)
: a drumbeat of two strokes of which the first is a very quick grace note

¹**flam·bé** \fläm-'bā, flä°-\ *adjective* [French *flambé*, from past participle of *flamber* to flame, singe, from Old French, from *flambe* flame] (1914)
: dressed or served covered with flaming liquor — usually used postpositively ⟨crepes suzette *flambé*⟩

²**flambé** *transitive verb* **flam·béed; flam·bé·ing** (circa 1946)
: to douse with a liquor (as brandy, rum, or cognac) and ignite

**flam·beau** \'flam-,bō\ *noun, plural* **flam·beaux** \-,bōz\ *or* **flambeaus** [French, from Middle French, from *flambe* flame] (1632)

: a flaming torch; *broadly* : TORCH

**flam·boy·ance** \flam-'bȯi-ən(t)s\ *noun* (1891)
: the quality or state of being flamboyant

**flam·boy·an·cy** \-ən(t)-sē\ *noun* (circa 1889)
: FLAMBOYANCE

¹**flam·boy·ant** \-ənt\ *adjective* [French, from present participle of *flamboyer* to flame, from Old French, from *flambe*] (1832)
**1** *often capitalized* : characterized by waving curves suggesting flames ⟨*flamboyant* tracery⟩ ⟨*flamboyant* architecture⟩
**2 :** marked by or given to strikingly elaborate or colorful display or behavior
— **flam·boy·ant·ly** *adverb*

²**flamboyant** *noun* (1879)
: ROYAL POINCIANA

¹**flame** \'flām\ *noun* [Middle English *flaume, flaumbe*, from Middle French *flamme*, from Latin *flamma* & *flambe*, from Old French, from *flamble*, from Latin *flammula*, diminutive of *flamma* flame; akin to Latin *flagrare* to burn — more at BLACK] (14th century)
**1 :** the glowing gaseous part of a fire
**2 a :** a state of blazing combustion ⟨the car burst into *flame*⟩ **b :** a condition or appearance suggesting a flame or burning: as (1) : burning zeal or passion (2) : a strong reddish orange color
**3 :** BRILLIANCE, BRIGHTNESS
**4 :** SWEETHEART
**5 :** an angry, hostile, or abusive electronic message

²**flame** *verb* **flamed; flam·ing** (14th century)
*intransitive verb*
**1 :** to burn with a flame : BLAZE
**2 a :** to burst or break out violently or passionately ⟨*flaming* with indignation⟩ **b :** to send an angry, hostile, or abusive electronic message
**3 :** to shine brightly : GLOW ⟨color *flaming* up in her cheeks⟩
*transitive verb*
**1 :** to send or convey by means of flame ⟨*flame* a message by signal fires⟩
**2 :** to treat or affect with flame: as **a :** to sear, sterilize, or destroy by fire **b :** FLAMBÉ
**3 :** to send an angry, hostile, or abusive electronic message to or about
— **flam·er** *noun*

**flame cell** *noun* (1888)
: a hollow cell that has a tuft of vibratile cilia and is part of some lower invertebrate excretory systems (as of a flatworm)

**fla·men** \'flā-mən\ *noun, plural* **flamens** *or* **flam·i·nes** \'fla-mə-,nēz\ [Middle English *flamin*, from Latin *flamin-, flamen*] (14th century)
: a priest especially in ancient Rome

**fla·men·co** \flə-'meŋ-(,)kō\ *noun, plural* **-cos** [Spanish, from *flamenco* of the Gypsies, literally, Flemish, from Middle Dutch *Vlaminc* Fleming] (1896)
**1 :** a vigorous rhythmic dance style of the Andalusian Gypsies; *also* : a dance in flamenco style
**2 :** music or song suitable to accompany a flamenco dance ◆

**flame-out** \'flā-,maut\ *noun* (1950)
**1 :** the unintentional cessation of operation of a jet airplane engine
**2 :** a sudden or spectacular failure
**3 :** a person whose successful career ends abruptly

**flame photometer** *noun* (1945)
: a spectrophotometer in which a spray of metallic salts in solution is vaporized in a very hot flame and subjected to quantitative analysis by measuring the intensities of the spectral lines of the metals present
— **flame photometric** *adjective*
— **flame photometry** *noun*

**flame-proof** \'flām-,prüf\ *adjective* (1886)
: resistant to damage or burning on contact with flame
— **flameproof** *transitive verb*

— **flame·proof·er** *noun*

**flame–retardant** *adjective* (1947)
: made or treated so as to resist burning

**flame stitch** *noun* (1936)
: a needlepoint stitch that produces a pattern resembling flames

**flame·throw·er** \-,thrō(-ə)r\ *noun* (1917)
**1 :** a device that expels from a nozzle a burning stream of liquid or semiliquid fuel under pressure
**2 :** a pitcher who throws hard : a fastball pitcher

**flame tree** *noun* (1860)
: any of several trees or shrubs with showy scarlet or yellow flowers: as **a :** a tree (*Brachychiton acerifolium* of the family Sterculiaceae) of southern Australia with panicles of brilliant scarlet flowers **b :** ROYAL POINCIANA

**flam·ing** \'flā-miŋ\ *adjective* (14th century)
**1 :** resembling or suggesting a flame in color, brilliance, or wavy outline ⟨the *flaming* sunset sky⟩ ⟨*flaming* red hair⟩
**2 :** being on fire : BLAZING
**3 :** INTENSE, PASSIONATE ⟨*flaming* youth⟩
**4 :** — used as an intensive ⟨you *flaming* idiot⟩
— **flam·ing·ly** \-miŋ-lē\ *adverb*

**fla·min·go** \flə-'miŋ-(,)gō\ *noun, plural* **-gos** *also* **-goes** [obsolete Spanish *flamengo* (now *flamenco*), literally, Fleming, German (conventionally), thought of as ruddy-complexioned)] (1565)
: any of several large aquatic birds (family Phoenicopteridae) with long legs and neck, webbed feet, a broad lamellate bill resembling that of a duck but abruptly bent downward, and usually rosy-white plumage with scarlet wing coverts and black wing quills

**flam·ma·bil·i·ty** \,fla-mə-'bi-lə-tē\ *noun* (1646)
: ability to support combustion; *especially* : a high capacity for combustion

flamingo

**flam·ma·ble** \'fla-mə-bəl\ *adjective* [Latin *flammare* to flame, set on fire, from *flamma*] (1813)

◇ **WORD HISTORY**
**flamenco** The Spanish word *flamenco* means literally "Flemish," and its usage in the sense "Gypsy-like," especially in reference to a distinctive song, dance, and guitar-music style of Andalusia, has inspired a number of hypotheses. It has been speculated that Gypsies were called *flamenco* because they reached Spain in the 16th century via Germany or Flanders, or that *flamenco* became a derogatory epithet for any foreigner because certain Flemish courtiers of the Spanish king and Holy Roman Emperor Charles V were much disliked in Spain. These notions of such an early origin for the "Gypsy-like" sense of *flamenco* all look implausible in light of the fact that this meaning is unattested in Spanish before 1870. In the later 19th century *flamenco* also meant "jaunty, cocky" and, in reference to women, "provocatively attractive," and the suggestion has been made that "Gypsy-like" is a secondary development from these senses. In any event, a direct connection between the senses "Flemish" and "Gypsy-like" has not been demonstrated. The ordinary Spanish word for "Gypsy" is *gitano*, which, like English *Gypsy*, is altered from a word meaning "Egyptian."

: capable of being easily ignited and of burning quickly
— **flammable** *noun*

**flan** \'flan, 'flä<sup>n</sup>(n)\ *noun* [French, from Old French *flaon,* from Late Latin *fladon-, flado* flat cake, of Germanic origin; akin to Old High German *flado* flat cake] (1846)
**1 a :** an open pie containing any of various sweet or savory fillings **b :** custard baked with a caramel glaze
**2 :** the metal disk of a coin, token, or medal as distinguished from the design and lettering stamped on it

**fla·neur** \flä-'nər\ *noun* [French *flâneur*] (1854)
: an idle man-about-town

**¹flange** \'flanj\ *noun* [perhaps alteration of *flanch* (a curving charge on a heraldic shield)] (circa 1735)
**1 :** a rib or rim for strength, for guiding, or for attachment to another object ⟨a *flange* on a pipe⟩ ⟨a *flange* on a wheel⟩
**2 :** a projecting edge of cloth used for decoration on clothing ⟨a jacket with *flange* shoulders⟩

**²flange** *transitive verb* **flanged; flang·ing** (circa 1859)
: to furnish with a flange

**¹flank** \'flaŋk\ *noun* [Middle English, from Old French *flanc,* of Germanic origin; akin to Old High German *hlanca* loin, flank — more at LANK] (before 12th century)
**1 a :** the fleshy part of the side between the ribs and the hip; *broadly* : the side of a quadruped **b :** a cut of meat from this part of an animal — see BEEF illustration
**2 a :** SIDE **b :** the right or left of a formation
**3 :** the area along either side of a heraldic shield

**²flank** *transitive verb* (1596)
**1 :** to protect a flank of
**2 :** to attack or threaten the flank of ⟨as a body of troops⟩
**3 a :** to be situated at the side of; *especially* : to be situated on both sides of ⟨a road *flanked* with linden trees⟩ **b :** to place something on each side of

**flan·ken** \'fläŋ-kən\ *noun* [Yiddish, plural of *flank,* literally, flank, ultimately from Old French *flanc*] (1950)
: beef flank cooked especially by boiling

**flank·er** \'flaŋ-kər\ *noun* (1940)
: a football player stationed wide of the formation slightly behind the line of scrimmage as a pass receiver — called also *flanker back*

**flank steak** *noun* (1902)
: a pear-shaped muscle of the beef flank; *also* : a steak cut from this muscle — see BEEF illustration

**flan·nel** \'fla-n°l\ *noun* [Middle English *flaunneol* woolen cloth or garment] (1503)
**1 a :** a soft twilled wool or worsted fabric with a loose texture and a slightly napped surface **b :** a napped cotton fabric of soft yarns simulating the texture of wool flannel **c :** a stout cotton fabric usually napped on one side
**2** *plural* **a :** flannel underwear **b :** outer garments of flannel; *especially* : men's trousers
**3** *British* : WASHCLOTH
**4** *British* : flattering or evasive talk; *also* : NONSENSE, RUBBISH
— **flannel** *adjective*
— **flan·nel·ly** \-n°l-ē\ *adjective*

**flan·nel·ette** \,fla-n°l-'et\ *noun* (circa 1882)
: a lightweight cotton flannel

**flan·nel·mouthed** \'fla-n°l-,mauṫht, -,maúṫhd\ *adjective* (circa 1893)
**1 :** speaking indistinctly
**2 :** speaking in a tricky or ingratiating way

**¹flap** \'flap\ *noun* [Middle English *flappe*] (14th century)
**1 :** a stroke with something broad : SLAP
**2** *obsolete* : something broad and flat used for striking
**3 :** something that is broad, limber, or flat and usually thin and that hangs loose or projects

freely: as **a :** a piece on a garment that hangs free **b :** a part of a book jacket that folds under the book's cover **c :** a piece of tissue partly severed from its place of origin for use in surgical grafting **d :** an extended part forming the closure (as of an envelope or carton)
**4 :** the motion of something broad and limber (as a sail or wing)
**5 :** a movable auxiliary airfoil usually attached to an airplane wing's trailing edge to increase lift or drag — see AIRPLANE illustration
**6 a :** a state of excitement or agitation : TIZZY, UPROAR **b :** something (as an incident or remark) that generates an uproar
**7 :** a consonant (as the sound \d\ in *ladder* and \t\ in *latter*) characterized by a single rapid contact of the tongue or lower lip against another point in the mouth — called also *tap*

**²flap** *verb* **flapped; flap·ping** (14th century)
*transitive verb*
**1 :** to beat with or as if with a flap
**2 :** to toss sharply : FLING
**3 :** to move or cause to move in flaps
*intransitive verb*
**1 :** to sway loosely usually with a noise of striking and especially when moved by wind
**2 a :** to beat or pulsate wings or something suggesting wings **b :** to progress by flapping **c :** to flutter ineffectively
**3 :** to talk foolishly and persistently

**flap·doo·dle** \'flap-,dü-d°l\ *noun* [origin unknown] (1878)
: NONSENSE

**flap·jack** \-,jak\ *noun* (circa 1600)
: PANCAKE

**flap·pa·ble** \'fla-pə-bəl\ *adjective* (1968)
: easily upset

**flap·per** \'fla-pər\ *noun* (circa 1570)
**1 a :** one that flaps **b :** something used in flapping or striking **c :** FLIPPER 1
**2 :** a young woman; *specifically* : a young woman of the period of World War I and the following decade who showed freedom from conventions (as in conduct)

**flap·py** \'fla-pē\ *adjective* (1905)
: flapping or tending to flap

**¹flare** \'flar, 'fler\ *verb* **flared; flar·ing** [origin unknown] (circa 1700)
*intransitive verb*
**1 a :** to burn with an unsteady flame **b :** to stream in the wind
**2 a :** to shine with a sudden light ⟨a match *flares* in the darkness⟩ **b** (1) : to become suddenly excited or angry — usually used with *up* (2) : to break out or intensify usually suddenly or violently — often used with *up* ⟨fighting *flared* up after a two-week lull⟩ **c :** to express strong emotion (as anger) ⟨*flaring* out at such abuses⟩
**3 :** to open or spread outward ⟨the pants *flare* at the bottom⟩
*transitive verb*
**1 :** to display conspicuously ⟨*flaring* her scarf to attract attention⟩
**2 :** to cause to flare ⟨the breeze *flares* the candle⟩
**3 :** to signal with a flare or by flaring
**4 :** to burn (a jet of waste gas) in the open air

**²flare** *noun* (1814)
**1 :** an unsteady glaring light
**2 a :** a fire or blaze of light used especially to signal, illuminate, or attract attention; *also* : a device or composition used to produce such a flare **b :** SOLAR FLARE; *also* : a sudden increase and decrease in the brightness of a star often amounting to a difference of several magnitudes
**3 :** a sudden outburst (as of excitement or anger)
**4 a :** a spreading outward; *also* : a place or part that spreads **b :** an area of skin flush
**5 :** light resulting from reflection (as between lens surfaces) or an effect of this light (as a fogged or dense area in a photographic negative)

**flare–up** \-,əp\ *noun* (1839)

**1 :** a sudden outburst or intensification
**2 :** a sudden bursting (as of a smoldering fire) into flame or light

**flar·ing** \'flar-iŋ, 'fler-\ *adjective* (1593)
**1 :** opening or spreading outward ⟨*flaring* nostrils⟩
**2 a :** flaming or as if flaming brightly or unsteadily **b :** GAUDY ⟨a *flaring* resort hotel⟩
— **flar·ing·ly** \-iŋ-lē\ *adverb*

**¹flash** \'flash\ *verb* [Middle English *flaschen,* of imitative origin] (13th century)
*intransitive verb*
**1 :** RUSH, DASH — used of flowing water
**2 :** to break forth in or like a sudden flame or flare
**3 a :** to appear suddenly ⟨an idea *flashes* into her mind⟩ **b :** to move with great speed ⟨the days *flash* by⟩
**4 a :** to break forth or out so as to make a sudden display ⟨the sun *flashed* from behind a cloud⟩ **b :** to act or speak vehemently and suddenly especially in anger
**5 a :** to give off light suddenly or in transient bursts **b :** to glow or gleam especially with animation or passion ⟨her eyes *flashed* with anger⟩
**6 :** to change suddenly or violently into vapor ⟨hot water *flashing* to steam under reduced pressure⟩
**7 :** to expose one's genitals usually suddenly and briefly in public
**8 :** to have sudden insight — often used with *on*
*transitive verb*
**1 a** *archaic* : SPLASH **b :** to fill by a sudden inflow of water
**2 a :** to cause the sudden appearance of (light) **b :** to cause to burst violently into flame **c** (1) : to cause (light) to reflect (2) : to cause (as a mirror) to reflect light (3) : to cause (a lamp) to flash **d :** to convey by means of flashes of light
**3 a :** to make known or cause to appear with great speed ⟨*flash* a message on the screen⟩ **b :** to display obtrusively and ostentatiously ⟨always *flashing* a roll of bills⟩ **c :** to expose to view suddenly and briefly ⟨*flashed* a badge⟩
**4 :** to cover with or form into a thin layer: as **a :** to protect against rain by covering with sheet metal or a substitute **b :** to coat (as glass) with a thin layer (as of metal or a differently colored glass)
**5 :** to subject (an exposed photographic negative or positive) to a supplementary uniform exposure to light before development in order to modify detail or tone ☆

**²flash** *noun* (1566)

---

☆ SYNONYMS

**Flash, gleam, glint, sparkle, glitter, glisten, glimmer, shimmer** mean to send forth light. FLASH implies a sudden and transient outburst of bright light ⟨lightning *flashed*⟩. GLEAM suggests a steady light seen through an obscuring medium or against a dark background ⟨lights *gleamed* in the valley⟩. GLINT implies a cold glancing light ⟨*glinting* steel⟩. SPARKLE suggests innumerable moving points of bright light ⟨the *sparkling* waters of the gulf⟩. GLITTER connotes a brilliant sparkling or gleaming ⟨*glittering* diamonds⟩. GLISTEN applies to the soft sparkle from a wet or oily surface ⟨*glistening* rain-drenched sidewalks⟩. GLIMMER suggests a faint or wavering gleam ⟨a distant *glimmering* light⟩. SHIMMER implies a soft tremulous gleaming or a blurred reflection ⟨a *shimmering* satin dress⟩.

---

\ə\ abut \ᵊ\ kitten \ər\ **further** \a\ ash \ā\ ace
\ä\ mop, mar \aú\ out \ch\ chin \e\ bet \ē\ **easy**
\g\ go \i\ hit \ī\ ice \j\ job \ŋ\ sing \ō\ go
\ó\ law \ói\ boy \th\ thin \t̲h̲\ the \ü\ loot \ú\ foot
\y\ yet \zh\ vision    *see also* Guide to Pronunciation

**1 a :** a sudden burst of light **b :** a movement of a flag in signaling
**2 :** a sudden and often brilliant burst ⟨a *flash* of wit⟩
**3 :** a brief time ⟨I'll be back in a *flash*⟩
**4 a :** SHOW, DISPLAY; *especially* **:** a vulgar ostentatious display **b** *archaic* **:** a showy ostentatious person **c :** one that attracts notice; *especially* **:** an outstanding athlete **d :** PIZZAZZ
**5** *obsolete* **:** thieves' slang
**6 :** something flashed: as **a :** GLIMPSE, LOOK **b :** SMILE **c :** a first brief news report **d :** FLASHLIGHT 1,2 **e :** a quick-spreading flame or momentary intense outburst of radiant heat **f :** a device for producing a brief and very bright flash of light for taking photographs
**7 :** RUSH 7a
**8 :** the rapid conversion of a liquid into vapor
³**flash** *adjective* (circa 1700)
**1 a :** FLASHY, SHOWY **b :** of, relating to, or characteristic of flashy people or things ⟨*flash* behavior⟩ **c :** of, relating to, or characteristic of persons considered social outcasts ⟨*flash* language⟩
**2 a :** of sudden origin and short duration ⟨a *flash* fire⟩ **b :** involving very brief exposure to an intense altering agent (as heat or cold) ⟨*flash* drying of milk⟩ ⟨*flash* freezing of food⟩
**flash·back** \'flash-,bak\ *noun* (1903)
**1 :** a recession of flame to an unwanted position (as into a blowpipe)
**2 a :** interruption of chronological sequence (as in a film or literary work) by interjection of events of earlier occurrence; *also* **:** an instance of flashback **b :** a past incident recurring vividly in the mind
**flash back** *intransitive verb* (1944)
**1 :** to focus one's mind on or vividly remember a past time or incident — usually used with *to*
**2 :** to employ a flashback (as in a film) — usually used with *to*
**flash·board** \-,bōrd, -,bȯrd\ *noun* (circa 1774)
**:** one or more boards projecting above the top of a dam to increase the depth of the water
**flash·bulb** \-,bəlb\ *noun* (1935)
**:** an electric bulb that can be used only once to produce a brief and very bright flash of light for taking photographs
**flash card** *noun* (1923)
**:** a card bearing words, numbers, or pictures that is briefly displayed (as by a teacher to a class) usually as a learning aid
**flash·cube** \'flash-,kyüb\ *noun* (1965)
**:** a cubical device incorporating four flashbulbs
**flash·er** \'fla-shər\ *noun* (1686)
**:** one that flashes: as **a :** a light (as a traffic signal or automobile light) that catches the attention by flashing **b :** a device for automatically flashing a light **c :** an exhibitionist who flashes
**flash flood** *noun* (1940)
**:** a local flood of great volume and short duration generally resulting from heavy rainfall in the immediate vicinity
**— flash flood** *verb*
**flash–for·ward** \'flash-'fȯr-wərd\ *noun* (1949)
**:** interruption of chronological sequence (as in a film or literary work) by interjection of events of future occurrence; *also* **:** an instance of flash-forward
**flash–gun** \-,gən\ *noun* (1925)
**:** a device for producing a bright flash of light for photography
**flash·ing** \'fla-shiŋ\ *noun* (1742)
**:** sheet metal used in waterproofing (as at roof valleys or hips or the angle between a chimney and a roof)
**flash in the pan** [from the firing of the priming in the pan of a flintlock musket without discharging the piece] (1901)
**1 :** a sudden spasmodic effort that accomplishes nothing
**2 :** one that appears promising but turns out to be disappointing or worthless

**flash·lamp** \'flash-,lamp\ *noun* (1890)
**:** a lamp for producing a brief but intense flash of light (as for taking photographs)
**flash·light** \'flash-,līt\ *noun* (1886)
**1 a :** a sudden bright artificial light used in taking photographic pictures **b :** a photograph taken by such a light
**2 :** a small battery-operated portable electric light
**flash·over** \-,ō-vər\ *noun* (1892)
**1 :** an abnormal electrical discharge (as through the air to the ground from a high potential source or between two conducting portions of a structure)
**2 :** the sudden spread of flame over an area when it becomes heated to the flash point
**flash point** *noun* (1878)
**1 :** the lowest temperature at which vapors above a volatile combustible substance ignite in air when exposed to flame
**2 :** a point at which someone or something bursts suddenly into action or being
**3 :** TINDERBOX 2
**flash·tube** \'flash-,t(y)üb\ *noun* (1945)
**:** a gas discharge tube that produces very brief intense flashes of light and is used especially in photography
**flashy** \'fla-shē\ *adjective* **flash·i·er; -est** (circa 1598)
**1** *chiefly dialect* **:** lacking in substance or flavor **:** INSIPID
**2 :** momentarily dazzling
**3 a :** superficially attractive or impressive **b :** ostentatious or showy often beyond the bounds of good taste; *especially* **:** marked by gaudy brightness
*synonym* see GAUDY
**— flash·i·ly** \'fla-shə-lē\ *adverb*
**— flash·i·ness** \'fla-shē-nəs\ *noun*
**flask** \'flask, flàsk\ *noun* [Middle French *flasque* powder flask, ultimately from Late Latin *flascon-, flasco* bottle, probably of Germanic origin; akin to Old High German *flaska* bottle] (1549)
**:** a container often somewhat narrowed toward the outlet and often fitted with a closure: as **a :** a broad flattened necked vessel used especially to carry alcoholic beverages on the person **b** *British* **:** VACUUM BOTTLE
¹**flat** \'flat\ *adjective* **flat·ter; flat·test** [Middle English, from Old Norse *flatr;* akin to Old High German *flaz* flat, and probably Greek *platys* broad — more at PLACE] (14th century)
**1 a :** lying at full length or spread out upon the ground **:** PROSTRATE **b :** utterly ruined or destroyed **c :** resting with a surface against something
**2 a :** having a continuous horizontal surface **b :** being or characterized by a horizontal line or tracing without peaks or depressions ⟨a *flat* EEG⟩
**3 :** having a relatively smooth or even surface
**4 :** arranged or laid out so as to be level or even
**5 a :** having the major surfaces essentially parallel and distinctly greater than the minor surfaces ⟨a *flat* piece of wood⟩ **b** *of a heel* **:** very low and broad
**6 a :** clearly unmistakable **:** DOWNRIGHT ⟨a *flat* denial⟩ **b** (1) **:** not varying **:** FIXED ⟨a *flat* rate⟩ (2) **:** having no fraction either lacking or in excess **:** EXACT ⟨in a *flat* 10 seconds⟩ (3) *of a frequency response* **:** not varying significantly throughout its range
**7 a :** lacking in animation, zest, or vigor **:** DULL ⟨life seemed *flat* without her⟩ **b :** lacking flavor **:** TASTELESS **c :** lacking effervescence or sparkle ⟨*flat* ginger ale⟩ **d :** commercially inactive; *also* **:** characterized by no significant rise or decline from one period to another ⟨sales were *flat*⟩ **e** *of a tire* **:** lacking air **:** DEFLATED **f** *chiefly British, of a battery* **:** DEAD 3c, DISCHARGED

**8 a** (1) *of a tone* **:** lowered a half step in pitch (2) **:** lower than the proper pitch **b** *of the vowel a* **:** pronounced as in *bad* or *bat*
**9 a :** having a low trajectory **b** *of a tennis stroke* **:** made so as to give little or no spin to the ball
**10** *of a sail* **:** TAUT
**11 a :** uniform in hue or shade **b :** having little or no illusion of depth **c** *of a photograph or negative* **:** lacking contrast **d** *of lighting conditions* **:** lacking shadows or contours **e :** free from gloss ⟨a *flat* paint⟩ **f :** TWO-DIMENSIONAL 2
**12 :** of, relating to, or used in competition on the flat ⟨a *flat* horse⟩
*synonym* see LEVEL, INSIPID
**— flat·ly** *adverb*
**— flat·ness** *noun*
**— flat·tish** \'fla-tish\ *adjective*
²**flat** *noun* (14th century)
**1 a :** a level surface of land — usually used in plural ⟨sagebrush *flats*⟩ ⟨tidal *flats*⟩ **b :** a stretch of land without obstacles; *especially* **:** a track or course for a flat race — usually used with *the* ⟨has won twice on the *flat*⟩
**2 :** a flat part or surface ⟨the *flat* of one's hand⟩
**3 a :** a musical note or tone one half step lower than a specified note or tone **b :** a character ♭ on a line or space of the musical staff indicating a half step drop in pitch
**4 :** something flat: as **a :** a shallow container for shipping produce **b :** a shallow box in which seedlings are started **c :** a flat piece of theatrical scenery **d :** a shoe or slipper having a flat heel or no heel
**5** *chiefly British* **:** an apartment on one floor
**6 :** a deflated tire
**7 :** the area to either side of an offensive football formation
³**flat** *adverb* (1531)
**1 :** in a flat manner **:** DIRECTLY, POSITIVELY
**2 :** in a complete manner **:** ABSOLUTELY ⟨*flat* broke⟩
**3 :** below the proper musical pitch
**4 :** without interest charge; *especially* **:** without allowance or charge for accrued interest ⟨bonds sold *flat*⟩
⁴**flat** *verb* **flat·ted; flat·ting** (circa 1604)
*transitive verb*
**1 :** FLATTEN
**2 :** to lower in pitch especially by a half step
*intransitive verb*
**:** to sing or play below the true pitch
¹**flat·bed** \'flat-,bed\ *adjective* (1892)
**:** having a horizontal bed on which the work rests ⟨a *flatbed* printing press⟩ ⟨a *flatbed* plotter⟩
²**flatbed** *noun* (1944)
**:** a motortruck or trailer with a body in the form of a platform or shallow box
**flat·boat** \-,bōt\ *noun* (1660)
**:** a boat with a flat bottom and square ends used for transportation of bulky freight especially in shallow waters
**flat·car** \-,kär\ *noun* (1881)
**:** a railroad freight car without permanent raised sides, ends, or covering
**flat–coated retriever** \'flat-,kō-təd-\ *noun* (1929)
**:** any of an English breed of medium-sized sporting dogs that have a dense smooth black or liver-colored coat
**flat–earth·er** \,flat-'ər-thər\ *also* **flat–earth·ist** \-'thist\ *noun* (1926)
**:** a person who believes that the Earth is flat
**flat·fish** \'flat-,fish\ *noun* (1710)
**:** any of an order (Heterosomata) of marine typically bottom-dwelling bony fishes (as the halibuts, flounders, turbots, and soles) that as adults swim on one side of the laterally compressed body and have both eyes on the upper side
**flat·foot** \-,fut (*always so in sense 3*), ,flat-'\ *noun, plural* **flat·feet** \-,fēt, -'fēt\ (1860)

**1 :** a condition in which the arch of the instep is flattened so that the entire sole rests upon the ground **2 :** a foot affected with flatfoot **3 a** *or plural* **flatfoots** *slang* **:** POLICE OFFICER; *especially* **:** a patrolman walking a regular beat **b** *slang* **:** SAILOR

¹**flat·foot·ed** \'flat-ˌfu̇-təd, ˌflat-\ *adjective* (1601)
**1 :** affected with flatfoot; *broadly* **:** walking with a dragging or shambling gait **2 a :** firm and well balanced on the feet **b :** free from reservation **:** FORTHRIGHT ⟨had an honest *flat-footed* way of saying a thing⟩ **3 :** not ready **:** UNPREPARED — used chiefly in the phrase *catch one flat-footed* **4 :** proceeding in a plodding or unimaginative way **:** PEDESTRIAN ⟨*flat-footed* prose⟩
— **flat·foot·ed·ly** *adverb*
— **flat·foot·ed·ness** *noun*

²**flat-footed** *adverb* (1828)
**1 :** in an open and determined manner **:** FLATLY **2 :** with the feet flat on a surface (as the ground)

**flat–hat** \'flat-ˌhat\ *intransitive verb* [from an alleged incident in which a pedestrian's hat was crushed by a low-flying plane] (1940)
**:** to fly low in an airplane in a reckless manner **:** HEDGEHOP
— **flat–hat·ter** *noun*

**Flat·head** \-ˌhed\ *noun, plural* **Flatheads** *or* **Flathead** (1709)
**1 :** a member of any of several North American Indian peoples that practiced head-flattening **2 :** an American Indian people of Montana **3** *not capitalized* **:** any of a family (Platycephalidae) of mostly Australian and East Indian marine food fishes that resemble sculpins

**flat·head catfish** \'flat-ˌhed-\ *noun* (1945)
**:** a large yellowish brown-mottled catfish (*Pylodictis olivaris*) of the central and Gulf states of the U.S.

**flat·iron** \'flat-ˌī(-ə)rn\ *noun* (1744)
**:** IRON 2c

**flat·land** \'flat-ˌland\ *noun* (1735)
**1 :** a region in which the land is predominantly flat — usually used in plural **2 :** land that lacks significant variation in elevation
— **flat·land·er** \-ˌlan-dər\ *noun*

**flat·let** \'flat-lət\ *noun* (1925)
*British* **:** EFFICIENCY APARTMENT

**flat·ling** \'flat-liŋ\ *or* **flat·lings** \-liŋz\ *adverb* (15th century)
*dialect British* **:** with a flat side or edge

**flat·mate** \'flat-ˌmāt\ *noun* (1955)
*chiefly British* **:** one of two or more persons sharing the same flat

**flat–out** \'flat-ˌau̇t\ *adjective* (1906)
**1 :** being or going at maximum effort or speed **2 :** OUT-AND-OUT, DOWNRIGHT ⟨it was a *flat-out* lie⟩

**flat out** *adverb* (1932)
**1 :** in a blunt and direct manner **:** OPENLY ⟨called *flat out* for revolution —*National Review*⟩ **2 :** at top speed or peak performance ⟨the car does 180 m.p.h. *flat out*⟩ **3** *usually* **flat–out :** to the greatest degree **:** COMPLETELY — usually used as an intensive ⟨is just *flat-out* confusing⟩

**flat–picking** \'flat-ˌpi-kiŋ\ *noun* (1970)
**:** a method of playing a stringed instrument (as a guitar) with a plectrum held between the thumb and forefinger

**flat race** *noun* (1848)
**:** a race (as for horses) on a level course without obstacles (as hurdles) — compare STEEPLECHASE
— **flat racing** *noun*

**flat·ten** \'fla-t°n\ *verb* **flat·tened; flat·ten·ing** \'flat-niŋ, 'fla-tə-\ (1630)
*transitive verb*

**:** to make flat: as **a :** to make level or smooth **b :** to knock down; *also* **:** to defeat decisively **c :** to make dull or uninspired — often used with *out* **d :** to make (as paint) lusterless **e :** to stabilize especially at a lower level
*intransitive verb*
**:** to become flat or flatter: as **a :** to become dull or spiritless **b :** to extend in or into a flat position or form **c :** to become uniform or stabilized often at a new lower level — usually used with *out*
— **flat·ten·er** \-nər\ *noun*

¹**flat·ter** \'fla-tər\ *verb* [Middle English *flateren*, from Old French *flater* to lick, flatter, of Germanic origin; akin to Old High German *flaz* flat] (13th century)
*transitive verb*
**1 :** to praise excessively especially from motives of self-interest **2 a** *archaic* **:** BEGUILE **4 b :** to encourage or gratify especially with the assurance that something is right ⟨I *flatter* myself that my interpretation is correct⟩ **3 a :** to portray too favorably ⟨the portrait *flatters* him⟩ **b :** to display to advantage ⟨candlelight often *flatters* the face⟩
*intransitive verb*
**:** to use flattery
— **flat·ter·er** \-tər-ər\ *noun*
— **flat·ter·ing·ly** \-tə-riŋ-lē\ *adverb*

²**flatter** *noun* (1714)
**:** one that flattens; *especially* **:** a flat-faced swage used in smithing

**flat·tery** \'fla-tə-rē\ *noun, plural* **-ter·ies** (14th century)
**1 a :** the act or practice of flattering **b** (1) **:** something that flatters (2) **:** insincere or excessive praise **2** *obsolete* **:** a pleasing self-deception

**flat·top** \'flat-ˌtäp\ *noun* (1940)
**:** something with a flat or flattened upper surface: as **a :** AIRCRAFT CARRIER **b :** a modified crew cut

**flat·u·lence** \'fla-chə-lən(t)s\ *noun* (1711)
**:** the quality or state of being flatulent

**flat·u·len·cy** \-lən(t)-sē\ *noun* (1660)
**:** FLATULENCE

**flat·u·lent** \-lənt\ *adjective* [Middle French, from Latin *flatus* act of blowing, wind, from *flare* to blow — more at BLOW] (1599)
**1 a :** marked by or affected with gas generated in the intestine or stomach **b :** likely to cause gas **2 :** pompously or portentously overblown **:** INFLATED
— **flat·u·lent·ly** *adverb*

**fla·tus** \'flā-təs\ *noun* [Latin, act of blowing, act of breaking wind] (1651)
**:** gas generated in the stomach or bowels

**flat·ware** \'flat-ˌwar, -ˌwer\ *noun* (1851)
**:** tableware more or less flat and usually formed or cast in a single piece; *especially* **:** eating and serving utensils (as knives, forks, and spoons) — compare HOLLOWWARE

**flat·ways** \-ˌwāz\ *adverb* (1692)
**:** FLATWISE

**flat·wise** \-ˌwīz\ *adverb* (1601)
**:** with the flat surface presented in some expressed or implied position

**flat·work** \-ˌwərk\ *noun* (1925)
**:** laundry that can be finished mechanically and does not require hand ironing

**flat·worm** \-ˌwərm\ *noun* (circa 1889)
**:** PLATYHELMINTH; *especially* **:** TURBELLARIAN

**flaunt** \'flȯnt, 'flänt\ *verb* [perhaps of Scandinavian origin; akin to Old Norse *flana* to rush around — more at PLANET] (1566)
*intransitive verb*
**1 :** to display or obtrude oneself to public notice **2 :** to wave or flutter showily ⟨the flag *flaunts* in the breeze⟩
*transitive verb*
**1 :** to display ostentatiously or impudently **:** PARADE ⟨*flaunting* his superiority⟩

**2 :** to treat contemptuously ⟨*flaunted* the rules —Louis Untermeyer⟩ ∎
**synonym** see SHOW
— **flaunt** *noun*
— **flaunt·ing·ly** \'flȯn-tiŋ-lē, 'flän-\ *adverb*
— **flaunty** \-tē\ *adjective*

**flau·tist** \'flȯ-tist, 'flau̇-\ *noun* [Italian *flautista,* from *flauto* flute, from Old Provençal *flaut*] (1860)
**:** FLUTIST

**fla·va·none** \'flā-və-ˌnōn\ *noun* [Latin *flavus* + International Scientific Vocabulary *-ane* + *-one*] (1949)
**:** a colorless crystalline ketone $C_{15}H_{12}O_2$; *also* **:** any of the derivatives of this ketone many of which occur in plants often in the form of glycosides

**fla·vin** \'flā-vən\ *noun* [International Scientific Vocabulary, from Latin *flavus* yellow — more at BLUE] (1933)
**:** any of a class of yellow water-soluble nitrogenous pigments derived from isoalloxazine and occurring in the form of nucleotides as coenzymes of flavoproteins; *especially* **:** RIBOFLAVIN

**flavin adenine dinucleotide** *noun* (1960)
**:** a coenzyme $C_{27}H_{33}N_9O_{15}P_2$ of some flavoproteins

**fla·vine** \'flā-ˌvēn\ *noun* [International Scientific Vocabulary, from Latin *flavus*] (circa 1853)
**:** any of a series of yellow acridine dyes (as acriflavine) often used medicinally for their antiseptic properties

**flavin mononucleotide** *noun* (circa 1953)
**:** FMN

**fla·vone** \'flā-ˌvōn\ *noun* [International Scientific Vocabulary, from Latin *flavus*] (1897)
**:** a colorless crystalline ketone $C_{15}H_{10}O_2$ found in the leaves, stems, and seed capsules of many primroses; *also* **:** any of the derivatives of this ketone many of which occur as yellow plant pigments in the form of glycosides and are used as dyestuffs

**fla·vo·noid** \'flā-və-ˌnȯid\ *noun* [*flavone* + *-oid*] (1947)
**:** any of a group of aromatic compounds that includes many common pigments (as the anthocyanins and flavones)

**fla·vo·nol** \'flā-və-ˌnȯl, -ˌnōl\ *noun* (1898)
**:** any of various hydroxy derivatives of flavone

**fla·vo·pro·tein** \ˌflā-vō-'prō-ˌtēn, -'prō-tē-ən\ *noun* [International Scientific Vocabulary *flavin* + *-o-* + *protein*] (1934)

---

☐ **USAGE**

**flaunt**  Although transitive sense 2 of *flaunt* undoubtedly arose from confusion with *flout,* the contexts in which it appears cannot be called substandard ⟨meting out punishment to the occasional mavericks who operate rigged games, tolerate rowdyism, or otherwise *flaunt* the law —Oscar Lewis⟩ ⟨observed with horror the *flaunting* of their authority in the suburbs, where men . . . put up buildings that had no place at all in a Christian commonwealth —Marchette Chute⟩ ⟨in our profession . . . very rarely do we publicly chastise a colleague who has *flaunted* our most basic principles —R. T. Blackburn, *AAUP Bulletin*⟩. If you use it, however, you should be aware that many people will consider it a mistake. Use of *flout* in the sense of *flaunt* 1 is found occasionally ⟨"The proper pronunciation," the blonde said, *flouting* her refined upbringing, "is pree feeks" —Mike Royko⟩.

---

\ə\ abut  \ᵊ\ kitten  \ər\ further  \a\ ash  \ā\ ace
\ä\ mop, mar  \au̇\ out  \ch\ chin  \e\ bet  \ē\ easy
\g\ go  \i\ hit  \ī\ ice  \j\ job  \ŋ\ sing  \ō\ go
\ȯ\ law  \ȯi\ boy  \th\ thin  \t͟h\ the  \ü\ loot  \u̇\ foot
\y\ yet  \zh\ vision   *see also* Guide to Pronunciation

: a dehydrogenase that contains a flavin and often a metal and plays a major role in biological oxidations

**¹fla·vor** \'flā-vər\ *noun* [Middle English, from Middle French *flaor, flavor,* from (assumed) Vulgar Latin *flator,* alteration of Latin *flatus* breath, act of blowing — more at FLATULENT] (14th century)
**1 a** *archaic* : ODOR, FRAGRANCE **b** : the quality of something that affects the sense of taste **c** : the blend of taste and smell sensations evoked by a substance in the mouth ⟨the *flavor* of apples⟩
**2** : a substance that flavors ⟨artificial *flavors*⟩
**3** : characteristic or predominant quality ⟨the ethnic *flavor* of a neighborhood⟩
**4 a** : VARIETY 3a **b** : a property that distinguishes different types of elementary particles (as quarks and neutrinos); *also* : any of the different types of particles that are distinguished by flavor
— **fla·vored** \-vərd\ *adjective*
— **fla·vor·ful** \-vər-fəl\ *adjective*
— **fla·vor·ful·ly** \-fə-lē\ *adverb*
— **fla·vor·less** \-vər-ləs\ *adjective*
— **fla·vor·some** \-səm\ *adjective*

**²flavor** *transitive verb* **fla·vored; fla·vor·ing** \'flā-v(ə-)riŋ\ (1542)
: to give or add flavor to

**fla·vor·ing** *noun* (1845)
: FLAVOR 2

**fla·vor·ist** \'flā-vər-ist\ *noun* (1964)
: a specialist in the creation of artificial flavors

**fla·vour** *chiefly British variant of* FLAVOR

**¹flaw** \'flȯ\ *noun* [of Scandinavian origin; akin to Norwegian *flaga* gust] (1513)
**1** : a sudden brief burst of wind; *also* : a spell of stormy weather
**2** *obsolete* : an outburst especially of passion

**²flaw** *noun* [Middle English, flake, probably of Scandinavian origin; akin to Swedish *flaga* flake, flaw; akin to Old English *flōh* flat stone] (1586)
**1 a** : a defect in physical structure or form **b** : an imperfection or weakness and especially one that detracts from the whole or hinders effectiveness ⟨vanity was the *flaw* in his character⟩ ⟨a *flaw* in the book's plot⟩
**2** *obsolete* : FRAGMENT
— **flawed** \'flȯd\ *adjective*
— **flaw·less** \-ləs\ *adjective*
— **flaw·less·ly** *adverb*
— **flaw·less·ness** *noun*

**³flaw** (1610)
*transitive verb*
: to make flaws in : MAR
*intransitive verb*
: to become defective

**flax** \'flaks\ *noun, often attributive* [Middle English, from Old English *fleax;* akin to Old High German *flahs* flax, Latin *plectere* to braid — more at PLY] (before 12th century)
**1** : any of a genus (*Linum* of the family Linaceae, the flax family) of herbs; *especially* : a slender erect annual (*Linum usitatissimum*) with blue flowers commonly cultivated for its bast fiber and seed
**2** : the fiber of the flax plant especially when prepared for spinning
**3** : any of several plants resembling flax

**flax·en** \'flak-sən\ *adjective* (15th century)
**1** : made of flax
**2** : resembling flax especially in pale soft strawy color ⟨*flaxen* hair⟩

**flax·seed** \'flak(s)-,sēd\ *noun* (1562)
: the seed of flax used as a source of oil and medicinally as a demulcent and emollient

**flaxy** \'flak-sē\ *adjective* **flax·i·er; -est** (1634)
: resembling flax especially in texture

**flay** \'flā\ *transitive verb* [Middle English *flen,* from Old English *flēan;* akin to Old Norse *flā* to flay, Lithuanian *plešti* to tear] (before 12th century)
**1** : to strip off the skin or surface of : SKIN
**2** : to criticize harshly : EXCORIATE

**3** : LASH 1b ⟨the wind whipped up to gale fury, *flaying* his face —Richard Kent⟩

**F layer** *noun* (1928)
: the highest and most densely ionized regular layer of the ionosphere occurring at night within the F region

**flea** \'flē\ *noun* [Middle English *fle,* from Old English *flēa;* akin to Old High German *flōh* flea] (before 12th century)
: any of an order (Siphonaptera) of small wingless bloodsucking insects that have a hard laterally compressed body and legs adapted to leaping and that feed on warm-blooded animals
— **flea in one's ear** : REBUKE ⟨sent him away with a *flea in his ear*⟩

**flea·bag** \'flē-,bag\ *noun* (1839)
: an inferior hotel or rooming house

**flea·bane** \-,bān\ *noun* (1548)
: any of various composite plants (as of the genus *Erigeron*) that were once believed to drive away fleas

**flea beetle** *noun* (1842)
: any of a subfamily (Alticinae, especially genera *Alticia* and *Epitrix*) of small chrysomelid beetles with legs adapted for leaping that feed on foliage and sometimes serve as vectors of virus diseases of plants

**flea·bite** \'flē-,bīt\ *noun* (circa 1570)
**1** : the bite of a flea; *also* : the red spot caused by such a bite
**2** : a trifling pain or annoyance

**flea–bit·ten** \-,bi-tᵊn\ *adjective* (1570)
**1** *of a horse* : having a white or gray coat flecked with a darker color
**2** : bitten by or infested with fleas

**flea collar** *noun* (1953)
: a collar for animals (as dogs and cats) that contains insecticide for killing fleas

**flea–flick·er** \-,fli-kər\ *noun* (1927)
: any of various deceptive football plays in which the ball is quickly transferred between players (as by a lateral) before or after a forward pass

**flea·hop·per** \-,hä-pər\ *noun* (1902)
: any of various small jumping bugs that feed on cultivated plants

**flea market** *noun* [translation of French *Marché aux Puces,* a market in Paris] (1922)
: a usually open-air market for secondhand articles and antiques

**flea·pit** \-,pit\ *noun* (1937)
*British* : a dilapidated building usually housing a movie theater

**flea·wort** \'flē-,wərt, -,wȯrt\ *noun* (before 12th century)
: any of three Old World plantains (especially *Plantago psyllium*) whose seeds are sometimes used as a mild laxative — compare PSYLLIUM SEED

**flèche** \'flāsh, 'flesh\ *noun* [French, literally, arrow, from Old French *fleche,* of Germanic origin; akin to Middle Dutch *vlieke* arrow, Old English *flēogan* to fly] (1848)
: SPIRE; *especially* : a slender spire above the intersection of the nave and transepts of a church

**flé·chette** \flā-'shet, fle-\ *noun* [French, from diminutive of *flèche* arrow] (1915)
: a small dart-shaped projectile that is clustered in an explosive warhead, dropped as a missile from an airplane, or fired from a handheld gun

**¹fleck** \'flek\ *transitive verb* [back-formation from *flecked* spotted, from Middle English, probably from Old Norse *flekkōttr,* from *flekkr* spot] (14th century)
**1** : STREAK, SPOT ⟨whitecaps *flecked* the blue sea⟩
**2** : to color as if by sprinkling with flecks ⟨his wit is *flecked* with sarcasm —James Atlas⟩

**²fleck** *noun* (1598)
**1** : SPOT, MARK ⟨a brown tweed with *flecks* of yellow⟩
**2** : FLAKE, PARTICLE ⟨*flecks* of snow drifted down⟩

**fledge** \'flej\ *verb* **fledged; fledg·ing** [*fledge* capable of flying, from Middle English *flegge,* from Old English *-flycge;* akin to Old High German *flucki* capable of flying, Old English *flēogan* to fly — more at FLY] (1566)
*intransitive verb*
*of a bird* : to acquire the feathers necessary for flight or independent activity
*transitive verb*
**1** : to rear until ready for flight or independent activity
**2** : to cover with or as if with feathers or down
**3** : to furnish (as an arrow) with feathers

**fledg·ling** \'flej-liŋ\ *noun* (1830)
**1** : a young bird just fledged
**2** : an immature or inexperienced person
**3** : one that is new ⟨a *fledgling* company⟩

**flee** \'flē\ *verb* **fled** \'fled\; **flee·ing** [Middle English *flen,* from Old English *flēon;* akin to Old High German *fliohan* to flee] (before 12th century)
*intransitive verb*
**1 a** : to run away often from danger or evil : FLY **b** : to hurry toward a place of security
**2** : to pass away swiftly : VANISH
*transitive verb*
: to run away from : SHUN

**¹fleece** \'flēs\ *noun* [Middle English *flees,* from Old English *flēos;* akin to Middle High German *vlius* fleece and perhaps to Latin *pluma* feather, down] (before 12th century)
**1 a** : the coat of wool covering a wool-bearing animal (as a sheep) **b** : the wool obtained from a sheep at one shearing
**2 a** : any of various soft or woolly coverings **b** : a soft bulky deep-piled knitted or woven fabric used chiefly for clothing

**²fleece** *transitive verb* **fleeced; fleec·ing** (1537)
**1 a** : to strip of money or property by fraud or extortion **b** : to charge excessively for goods or services
**2** : to remove the fleece from : SHEAR
**3** : to dot or cover with fleecy masses

**fleeced** \'flēst\ *adjective* (1580)
**1** : covered with or as if with a fleece
**2** *of a textile* : having a soft nap

**fleech** \'flēch\ *verb* [Middle English (Scots) *flechen*] (14th century)
*dialect* : COAX, WHEEDLE

**fleecy** \'flē-sē\ *adjective* **fleec·i·er; -est** (1590)
: covered with, made of, or resembling fleece ⟨a *fleecy* winter coat⟩

**¹fleer** \'flir\ *intransitive verb* [Middle English *fleryen,* of Scandinavian origin; akin to Norwegian *flire* to giggle] (15th century)
: to laugh or grimace in a coarse derisive manner : SNEER
*synonym* see SCOFF
— **fleer·ing·ly** \-iŋ-lē\ *adverb*

**²fleer** *noun* (1604)
: a word or look of derision or mockery

**¹fleet** \'flēt\ *verb* [Middle English *fleten,* from Old English *flēotan* to float, Old High German *fliozzan* to float, Old English *flōwan* to flow] (before 12th century)
*intransitive verb*
**1** *obsolete* : DRIFT
**2 a** *archaic* : FLOW **b** : to fade away : VANISH
**3** [³*fleet*] : to fly swiftly
*transitive verb*
: to cause (time) to pass usually quickly or imperceptibly

**²fleet** *noun* [Middle English *flete,* from Old English *flēot* ship, from *flēotan*] (13th century)
**1** : a number of warships under a single command; *specifically* : an organization of ships and aircraft under the command of a flag officer
**2** : GROUP 2a, b; *especially* : a group (as of ships, planes, or trucks) operated under unified control

**³fleet** *adjective* [probably from ¹*fleet*] (circa 1529)
**1** : swift in motion : NIMBLE

**2** : EVANESCENT, FLEETING
*synonym* see FAST
— **fleet·ly** *adverb*
— **fleet·ness** *noun*
**fleet admiral** *noun* (1946)
: an admiral of the highest rank in the navy whose insignia is five stars
**fleet–foot·ed** \-ˌfu̇-təd\ *adjective* (circa 1743)
: able to run fast
**fleet·ing** *adjective* (1563)
: passing swiftly : TRANSITORY
*synonym* see TRANSIENT
— **fleet·ing·ly** \ˈflē-tiŋ-lē\ *adverb*
— **fleet·ing·ness** *noun*
**Fleet Street** \ˈflēt-\ *noun* [*Fleet Street*, London, England, center of the London newspaper district] (1882)
: the London press
**flei·shig** \ˈflā-shik\ *adjective* [Yiddish *fleyshik*, from Middle High German *vleischic* meaty, from *vleisch* flesh, meat, from Old High German *fleisk*] (1943)
: made of, prepared with, or used for meat or meat products — compare MILCHIG, PAREVE
**Flem·ing** \ˈfle-miŋ\ *noun* [Middle English, from Middle Dutch *Vlaminc* (akin to Middle Dutch *Vlander* Flanders)] (12th century)
: a member of the Germanic people inhabiting northern Belgium and a small section of northern France
**¹Flem·ish** \ˈfle-mish\ *adjective* (14th century)
: of, relating to, or characteristic of Flanders or the Flemings or their language
**²Flemish** *noun* (circa 1741)
**1** : the Germanic language of the Flemings that is made up of dialects of Dutch
**2** *plural in construction* : FLEMINGS
**Flemish giant** *noun* (1898)
: any of a breed of very large solid-colored rabbits probably of Belgian origin
**flense** \ˈflen(t)s\ *transitive verb* **flensed; flens·ing** [Dutch *flensen* or Danish & Norwegian *flense*] (1820)
: to strip (as a whale) of blubber or skin
**¹flesh** \ˈflesh\ *noun* [Middle English, from Old English *flǣsc*; akin to Old High German *fleisk* flesh and perhaps to Old Norse *flā* to flay — more at FLAY] (before 12th century)
**1 a** : the soft parts of the body of an animal and especially of a vertebrate; *especially* : the parts composed chiefly of skeletal muscle as distinguished from visceral structures, bone, and integuments **b** : sleek well-fatted condition of body **c** : SKIN
**2 a** : edible parts of an animal **b** : flesh of a mammal or fowl eaten as food
**3 a** : the physical nature of human beings ⟨the spirit indeed is willing, but the *flesh* is weak —Matthew 26:41 (Authorized Version)⟩ **b** : HUMAN NATURE
**4 a** : human beings : MANKIND **b** : living beings **c** : STOCK, KINDRED
**5** : a fleshy plant part used as food; *also* : the fleshy part of a fruit
**6** *Christian Science* : an illusion that matter has sensation
**7** : SUBSTANCE ⟨insights buried in the *flesh* of the narrative —Jan Carew⟩
— **in the flesh** : in person and alive
**²flesh** (1530)
*transitive verb*
**1** : to initiate or habituate especially by giving a foretaste
**2** *archaic* : GRATIFY
**3** : to clothe or cover with or as if with flesh; *broadly* : to give substance to — usually used with *out*
**4** : to free from flesh
*intransitive verb*
: to become fleshy — often used with *up* or *out*
**flesh and blood** *noun* (before 12th century)
**1** : corporeal nature as composed of flesh and of blood
**2** : near kindred — used chiefly in the phrase *one's own flesh and blood*

**3** : SUBSTANCE, REALITY
**fleshed** \ˈflesht\ *adjective* (15th century)
: having flesh especially of a specified kind — often used in combination ⟨pink-*fleshed*⟩ ⟨thick-*fleshed*⟩
**flesh fly** *noun* (14th century)
: a dipteran fly whose maggots feed on flesh; *especially* : any of a family (Sarcophagidae) of flies some of which cause myiasis
**flesh·ings** \ˈfle-shiŋz\ *noun plural* (1860)
: material removed in fleshing a hide
**flesh·ly** \ˈflesh-lē\ *adjective* (before 12th century)
**1 a** : CORPOREAL, BODILY **b** : of, relating to, or characterized by indulgence of bodily appetites; *especially* : LASCIVIOUS ⟨*fleshly* desires⟩ **c** : not spiritual : WORLDLY
**2** : FLESHY, PLUMP
**3** : having a sensuous quality ⟨*fleshly* art⟩
*synonym* see CARNAL
**flesh·ment** \ˈflesh-mənt\ *noun* [²*flesh*] (1605)
*obsolete* : excitement associated with a successful beginning
**flesh out** *transitive verb* (1886)
: to make fuller or more nearly complete ⟨museums *fleshing* out their collections with borrowed works⟩
— **fleshed–out** *adjective*
**flesh·pot** \ˈflesh-ˌpät\ *noun* (1592)
**1** *plural* : bodily comfort : LUXURY
**2** : a place of lascivious entertainment — usually used in plural
**flesh wound** *noun* (circa 1674)
: an injury involving penetration of the body musculature without damage to bones or internal organs
**fleshy** \ˈfle-shē\ *adjective* **flesh·i·er; -est** (14th century)
**1 a** : marked by, consisting of, or resembling flesh **b** : marked by abundant flesh; *especially* : CORPULENT
**2 a** : SUCCULENT, PULPY ⟨the *fleshy* texture of a melon⟩ **b** : not thin, dry, or membranous ⟨*fleshy* fungi⟩
— **flesh·i·ness** *noun*
**fleshy fruit** *noun* (1929)
: a fruit (as a berry, drupe, or pome) consisting largely of soft succulent tissue
**fletch** \ˈflech\ *transitive verb* [back-formation from *fletcher*] (circa 1656)
: FEATHER ⟨*fletch* an arrow⟩
**fletch·er** \ˈfle-chər\ *noun* [Middle English *fleccher*, from Old French *flechier*, from *fleche* arrow — more at FLÈCHE] (14th century)
: a maker of arrows
**fletch·ing** \-chiŋ\ *noun* (circa 1930)
: the feathers on an arrow; *also* : the arrangement of such feathers
**fleur de coin** \ˌflər-də-ˈkwaⁿ\ *adjective* [French *à fleur de coin*, literally, with the bloom of the die] (circa 1889)
: being in the preserved mint condition
**fleur–de–lis** *or* **fleur–de–lys** \ˌflər-dᵊl-ˈē, ˌflu̇r-\ *noun, plural* **fleurs–de–lis** *or* **fleur–de–lis** *or* **fleurs–de–lys** *or* **fleur–de–lys** \ˌflər-dᵊl-ˈē(z), ˌflu̇r-\ [Middle English *flourdelis*, from Middle French *flor de lis*, literally, lily flower] (14th century)
**1** : IRIS 3
**2** : a conventionalized iris in artistic design and heraldry
**fleu·ry** \ˈflu̇r-ē\ *adjective* [alteration of Middle English *flory*, from Old French *floré*, from *flor* flower — more at FLOWER] (15th century)
*of a heraldic cross* : having the ends of the arms broadening out into the heads of fleurs-de-lis — see CROSS illustration
**flew** *past of* FLY
**flews** \ˈflüz\ *noun plural* [origin unknown] (1575)

fleur-de-lis 2

: the pendulous lateral parts of a dog's upper lip — see DOG illustration
**¹flex** \ˈfleks\ *verb* [Latin *flexus*, past participle of *flectere* to bend] (circa 1521)
*transitive verb*
**1** : to bend especially repeatedly
**2 a** : to move muscles so as to cause flexion of (a joint) **b** : to move or tense (a muscle) by contraction
*intransitive verb*
: BEND
— **flex one's muscles** : to demonstrate one's strength ⟨an exaggerated need to *flex his* political *muscles* —J. P. Lash⟩
**²flex** *noun* [short for *flexible cord*] (1905)
*chiefly British* : an electric cord
**³flex** *noun* (circa 1934)
: an act or instance of flexing
**flex·i·ble** \ˈflek-sə-bəl\ *adjective* (15th century)
**1** : capable of being flexed : PLIANT
**2** : yielding to influence : TRACTABLE
**3** : characterized by a ready capability to adapt to new, different, or changing requirements ⟨a *flexible* foreign policy⟩ ⟨a *flexible* schedule⟩
*synonym* see ELASTIC
— **flex·i·bil·i·ty** \ˌflek-sə-ˈbi-lə-tē\ *noun*
— **flex·i·bly** \ˈflek-sə-blē\ *adverb*
**flex·ile** \ˈflek-səl, -ˌsīl\ *adjective* (1633)
: FLEXIBLE
**flex·ion** \ˈflek-shən\ *noun* [Latin *flexion-, flexio*, from *flectere*] (1615)
**1** : the act of flexing or bending
**2** : a part bent : BEND
**3** : INFLECTION 3
**4 a** : a bending movement around a joint in a limb (as the knee or elbow) that decreases the angle between the bones of the limb at the joint — compare EXTENSION 3b **b** : a forward raising of the arm or leg by a movement at the shoulder or hip joint
**flex·og·ra·phy** \flek-ˈsä-grə-fē\ *noun* [*flex*ible + *-o-* + *-graphy*] (1954)
: a process of rotary letterpress printing using flexible plates and fast-drying inks
— **flexo·graph·ic** \ˌflek-sə-ˈgra-fik\ *adjective*
— **flexo·graph·i·cal·ly** \-fi-k(ə-)lē\ *adverb*
**flex·or** \ˈflek-sər, -ˌsȯr\ *noun* (1615)
: a muscle serving to bend a body part (as a limb)
**flex·time** \ˈflek-ˌstīm\ *or* **flexi·time** \ˈflek-si-ˌtīm\ *noun* (1972)
: a system that allows employees to choose their own times for starting and finishing work within a broad range of available hours
**flex·u·ous** \ˈflek-sh(ə-)wəs\ *adjective* [Latin *flexuosus*, from *flexus* bend, from *flectere*] (1605)
**1** : having curves, turns, or windings
**2** : lithe or fluid in action or movement
**flex·ur·al** \ˈflek-sh(ə-)rəl\ *adjective* (1879)
**1** : of, relating to, or resulting from flexure
**2** : characterized by flexure
**flex·ure** \ˈflek-shər\ *noun* (1592)
**1** : the quality or state of being flexed : FLEXION
**2** : TURN, BEND, FOLD
**fley** \ˈflā\ *transitive verb* [Middle English *flayen*, from Old English *āflēgan*, from *ā-*, perfective prefix + *-flēgan* to put to flight] (13th century)
*Scottish* : FRIGHTEN
**flib·ber·ti·gib·bet** \ˌfli-bər-tē-ˈji-bət\ *noun* [Middle English *flepergebet*] (15th century)
: a silly flighty person
— **flib·ber·ti·gib·bety** \-bə-tē\ *adjective*
**flic** \ˈflēk\ *noun* [French] (1899)
: a French police officer

\ə\ abut \ᵊ\ kitten \ər\ further \a\ ash \ā\ ace
\ä\ mop, mar \au̇\ out \ch\ chin \e\ bet \ē\ easy
\g\ go \i\ hit \ī\ ice \j\ job \ŋ\ sing \ō\ go
\ȯ\ law \ȯi\ boy \th\ thin \t͟h\ the \ü\ loot \u̇\ foot
\y\ yet \zh\ vision    *see also* Guide to Pronunciation

**¹flick** \'flik\ *noun* [imitative] (15th century)
**1 :** a light sharp jerky stroke or movement
**2 :** a sound produced by a flick
**3 :** FLICKER 1
**²flick** (1816)
*transitive verb*
**1 a :** to move or propel with or as if with a flick ⟨*flicked* her hair back over her shoulder⟩ ⟨*flick* a switch⟩ **b :** to activate, deactivate, or change by or as if by flicking a switch ⟨*flick* on a cigarette lighter⟩ ⟨*flick* off the radio⟩
**2 a :** to strike lightly with a quick sharp motion ⟨*flicked* the horse with a whip⟩ **b :** to remove with light blows ⟨*flicked* an ash off her sleeve⟩
*intransitive verb*
**1 :** to go or pass quickly or abruptly ⟨a bird *flicked* by⟩ ⟨*flicking* through some papers⟩
**2 :** to direct flicks at something
**³flick** *noun* [short for ²*flicker*] (1926)
**:** MOVIE
**¹flick·er** \'fli-kər\ *verb* **flick·ered; flick·er·ing** \-k(ə-)riŋ\ [Middle English *flikeren,* from Old English *flicorian*] (before 12th century)
*intransitive verb*
**1 :** to move irregularly or unsteadily **:** FLUTTER
**2 :** to burn or shine fitfully or with a fluctuating light
**3 :** to appear briefly
*transitive verb*
**1 :** to cause to flicker
**2 :** to produce by flickering
— **flick·er·ing·ly** \-k(ə-)riŋ-lē\ *adverb*
**²flicker** *noun* (1849)
**1 a :** an act of flickering **b :** a sudden brief movement **c :** a momentary quickening ⟨a *flicker* of anger⟩ **d :** a slight indication **:** HINT ⟨a *flicker* of recognition⟩
**2 :** a wavering light
**3 :** MOVIE — often used in plural
— **flick·ery** \'fli-k(ə-)rē\ *adjective*
**³flicker** *noun* [probably imitative of its call] (1809)
**:** a large barred and spotted North American woodpecker (*Colaptes auratus*) with a brown back that commonly forages on the ground for ants — compare RED-SHAFTED FLICKER, YELLOW-SHAFTED FLICKER
**flick-knife** \'flik-,nīf\ *noun* (1957)
*British* **:** SWITCHBLADE
**flied** *past and past participle of* ³FLY
**fli·er** \'flī(-ə)r\ *noun* (15th century)
**1 :** one that flies; *specifically* **:** AIRMAN
**2 :** a reckless or speculative venture — usually used in the phrase *take a flier*
**3** *usually* **fly·er :** an advertising circular
**¹flight** \'flīt\ *noun, often attributive* [Middle English, from Old English *flyht;* akin to Middle Dutch *vlucht* flight, Old English *flēogan* to fly] (before 12th century)
**1 a :** an act or instance of passing through the air by the use of wings ⟨the *flight* of a bee⟩ **b :** the ability to fly ⟨*flight* is natural to birds⟩
**2 a :** a passing through the air or through space outside the earth's atmosphere ⟨*flight* of an arrow⟩ ⟨*flight* of a rocket to the moon⟩ **b :** the distance covered in such a flight **c :** swift movement
**3 a :** a trip made by or in an airplane or spacecraft **b :** a scheduled airplane trip
**4 :** a group of similar beings or objects flying through the air together
**5 :** a brilliant, imaginative, or unrestrained exercise or display ⟨a *flight* of fancy⟩
**6 a :** a continuous series of stairs from one landing or floor to another **b :** a series (as of terraces or conveyors) resembling a flight of stairs
**7 :** a unit of the U.S. Air Force below a squadron
— **flight·less** \-ləs\ *adjective*
**²flight** (1873)
*intransitive verb*
**:** to rise, settle, or fly in a flock ⟨geese *flighting* on the marsh⟩

*transitive verb*
**:** ¹FLUSH
**³flight** *noun* [Middle English *fluht, fliht;* akin to Old High German *fluht* flight, Old English *flēon* to flee] (13th century)
**:** an act or instance of running away
**flight attendant** *noun* (1947)
**:** a person who attends passengers on an airplane
**flight bag** *noun* [¹*flight*] (1943)
**1 :** a lightweight traveling bag with zippered outside pockets
**2 :** a small canvas satchel
**flight deck** *noun* (1924)
**1 :** the uppermost complete deck of an aircraft carrier
**2 :** the forward compartment in some airplanes
**flight engineer** *noun* (1938)
**:** a flight crewman responsible for mechanical operation
**flight feather** *noun* (1735)
**:** one of the quills of a bird's wing or tail that support it in flight — compare CONTOUR FEATHER
**flight lieutenant** *noun* (1914)
**:** a commissioned officer in the British air force who ranks with a captain in the army
**flight line** *noun* (1943)
**:** a parking and servicing area for airplanes
**flight path** *noun* (1911)
**:** the path in the air or space made or followed by something (as a particle, an airplane, or a spacecraft) in flight
**flight pay** *noun* (1928)
**:** an additional allowance paid to military personnel who take part in regular authorized aircraft flights
**flight plan** *noun* (circa 1936)
**:** a usually written statement (as by a pilot) of the details of an intended flight (as of an airplane or spacecraft) usually filed with an authority
**flight recorder** *noun* (1939)
**:** a crashworthy instrument for recording flight data (as airspeed and altitude)
**flight suit** *noun* (1944)
**:** a usually one-piece garment especially of fire-resistant fabric worn especially by military aircrews
**flight surgeon** *noun* (1925)
**:** a military medical officer trained in aerospace medicine
**flight–test** \'flīt-,test\ *transitive verb* (1930)
**:** to test (as an airplane or spacecraft) in flight
**flighty** \'flī-tē\ *adjective* **flight·i·er; -est** (1552)
**1 :** SWIFT
**2 :** lacking stability or steadiness: **a :** easily upset **:** VOLATILE ⟨a *flighty* temper⟩ **b :** easily excited **:** SKITTISH ⟨a *flighty* horse⟩ **c :** CAPRICIOUS, SILLY
— **flight·i·ly** \'flī-tᵊl-ē\ *adverb*
— **flight·i·ness** \'flī-tē-nəs\ *noun*
**¹flim·flam** \'flim-,flam\ *noun* [probably of Scandinavian origin; akin to Old Norse *flim* mockery] (circa 1538)
**1 :** DECEPTION, FRAUD
**2 :** deceptive nonsense
**²flimflam** *transitive verb* **flim·flammed; flim·flam·ming** (1660)
**:** to subject to a flimflam
— **flim·flam·mer** *noun*
— **flim·flam·mery** \-,fla-mə-rē\ *noun*
**¹flim·sy** \'flim-zē\ *adjective* **flim·si·er; -est** [perhaps alteration of ¹*film* + -*sy* (as in *tricksy*)] (1702)
**1 a :** lacking in physical strength or substance ⟨*flimsy* silks⟩ **b :** of inferior materials and workmanship
**2 :** having little worth or plausibility
— **flim·si·ly** \-zə-lē\ *adverb*
— **flim·si·ness** \-zē-nəs\ *noun*
**²flimsy** *noun, plural* **flim·sies** (1857)

*chiefly British* **:** a lightweight paper used especially for multiple copies; *also* **:** a document printed on flimsy
**flinch** \'flinch\ *intransitive verb* [Middle French *flenchir* to bend, of Germanic origin; akin to Middle High German *lenken* to bend, Old High German *hlanca* flank — more at LANK] (1579)
**:** to withdraw or shrink from or as if from pain **:** WINCE; *also* **:** to tense the muscles involuntarily in anticipation of discomfort
**synonym** see RECOIL
— **flinch** *noun*
— **flinch·er** *noun*
**flin·ders** \'flin-dərz\ *noun plural* [Middle English *flendris*] (15th century)
**:** SPLINTERS, FRAGMENTS
**¹fling** \'fliŋ\ *verb* **flung** \'fləŋ\; **fling·ing** \'fliŋ-iŋ\ [Middle English, perhaps of Scandinavian origin; akin to Old Norse *flengja* to whip] (14th century)
*intransitive verb*
**1 :** to move in a brusque or headlong manner ⟨*flung* out of the room in a rage⟩
**2** *of an animal* **:** to kick or plunge vigorously
**3** *Scottish* **:** CAPER
*transitive verb*
**1 a :** to throw forcefully, impetuously, or casually ⟨*flung* herself down on the sofa⟩ ⟨clothes were *flung* on the floor⟩ **b :** to cast as if by throwing ⟨*flung* off all restraint⟩
**2 :** to place or send suddenly and unceremoniously ⟨was arrested and *flung* into prison⟩
**3 :** to give unrestrainedly ⟨*flung* himself into music⟩
**synonym** see THROW
— **fling·er** \'fliŋ-ər\ *noun*
**²fling** *noun* (1589)
**1 :** an act or instance of flinging
**2 a :** a casual try or involvement **b :** a casual or brief love affair
**3 :** a period devoted to self-indulgence
**flint** \'flint\ *noun* [Middle English, from Old English; akin to Old High German *flins* pebble, hard stone] (before 12th century)
**1 :** a massive hard quartz that produces a spark when struck by steel
**2 :** an implement of flint used in prehistoric cultures
**3 a :** a piece of flint **b :** a material used for producing a spark; *especially* **:** an alloy (as of iron and cerium) used in lighters
**4 :** something resembling flint in hardness
— **flint·like** \-,līk\ *adjective*
**flint corn** *noun* (1705)
**:** an Indian corn (*Zea mays indurata*) having hard horny usually rounded kernels with the soft endosperm enclosed by a hard outer layer
**flint glass** *noun* (1683)
**:** heavy brilliant glass that contains lead oxide, has a relatively high index of refraction, and is used in lenses and prisms
**flint·lock** \'flint-,läk\ *noun* (1683)
**1 :** a lock for a gun or pistol having a flint in the hammer for striking a spark to ignite the charge
**2 :** a firearm fitted with a flintlock
**flinty** \'flin-tē\ *adjective* **flint·i·er; -est** (1536)
**1 :** resembling flint; *especially* **:** STERN, UNYIELDING
**2 :** composed of or covered with flint
— **flint·i·ly** \'flin-tᵊl-ē\ *adverb*
— **flint·i·ness** \'flin-tē-nəs\ *noun*
**¹flip** \'flip\ *verb* **flipped; flip·ping** [probably imitative] (1616)
*transitive verb*
**1 :** to toss so as to cause to turn over in the air ⟨*flip* a coin⟩; *also* **:** TOSS ⟨*flip* me the ball⟩ ⟨*flip* one end of the scarf over your shoulder⟩
**2 a :** to cause to turn and especially to turn over ⟨*flipped* the car⟩ ⟨*flipping* the pages of⟩ **b :** to move with a small quick motion ⟨*flip* a switch⟩
*intransitive verb*

**1 :** to make a twitching or flicking movement ⟨the fish *flipped* and flopped on the deck⟩; *also* **:** to change from one position to another and especially turn over ⟨the car *flipped*⟩
**2 :** LEAF 2 ⟨*flipped* through the pages⟩
**3** *slang* **a :** to lose one's mind or composure — often used with *out* **b :** to become very enthusiastic
**²flip** *noun* (1695)
**1 :** a mixed drink usually consisting of a sweetened spiced liquor with beaten eggs
**2 :** an act or instance of flipping
**3 :** the motion used in flipping
**4 :** a somersault especially in the air
**³flip** *adjective* (circa 1847)
**:** FLIPPANT, IMPERTINENT
**flip-flop** \'flip-ˌfläp\ *noun* (1600)
**1 :** the sound or motion of something flapping loosely
**2 a :** a backward handspring **b :** a sudden reversal (as of direction or point of view)
**3 :** a usually electronic device or a circuit (as in a computer) capable of assuming either of two stable states
**4 :** a rubber sandal loosely fastened to the foot by a thong
**— flip-flop** *intransitive verb*
**flip-pan-cy** \'fli-pən(t)-sē\ *noun, plural* **-cies** (1746)
**:** unbecoming levity or pertness especially in respect to grave or sacred matters
**flip-pant** \'fli-pənt\ *adjective* [probably from ¹*flip*] (1605)
**1** *archaic* **:** GLIB, TALKATIVE
**2 :** lacking proper respect or seriousness
**— flip-pant-ly** *adverb*
**flip-per** \'fli-pər\ *noun* (1822)
**1 a :** a broad flat limb (as of a seal or cetacean) adapted for swimming **b :** a flat rubber shoe with the front expanded into a paddle used in skin diving
**2 :** one that flips
**flip-py** \'fli-pē\ *adjective* (1967)
**:** loose and flaring at the bottom ⟨a *flippy* skirt⟩
**flip side** *noun* (1949)
**1 :** the reverse and usually less popular side of a phonograph record
**2 :** a reverse or opposite side, aspect, or result ⟨the *flip side* of deficient saving . . . is overconsumption —R. S. Gay⟩
**¹flirt** \'flərt\ *verb* [origin unknown] (1583)
*transitive verb*
**1 :** FLICK
**2 :** to move in a jerky manner
*intransitive verb*
**1 :** to move erratically **:** FLIT
**2 a :** to behave amorously without serious intent **b :** to show superficial or casual interest or liking ⟨*flirted* with the idea⟩; *also* **:** EXPERIMENT ⟨a novelist *flirting* with poetry⟩
**3 :** to come close to — used with *with* ⟨the temperature *flirted* with 100°⟩
**synonym** see TRIFLE
**— flir-ta-tion** \ˌflər-'tā-shən\ *noun*
**— flirt-er** *noun*
**— flirty** \'flər-tē\ *adjective*
**²flirt** *noun* (circa 1590)
**1 :** an act or instance of flirting
**2 :** a person who flirts
**flir-ta-tious** \ˌflər-'tā-shəs\ *adjective* (1834)
**:** inclined to flirt **:** COQUETTISH
**— flir-ta-tious-ly** *adverb*
**— flir-ta-tious-ness** *noun*
**flit** \'flit\ *intransitive verb* **flit-ted; flit-ting** [Middle English *flitten*, of Scandinavian origin; akin to Old Norse *flytjask* to move, Old English *flēotan* to float] (13th century)
**1 :** to pass quickly or abruptly from one place or condition to another
**2** *archaic* **:** ALTER, SHIFT
**3 :** to move in an erratic fluttering manner
**— flit** *noun*
**flitch** \'flich\ *noun* [Middle English *flicche*, from Old English *flicce;* akin to Old High German *fleisk* flesh — more at FLESH] (before 12th century)

**1 :** a side of cured meat; *especially* **:** a side of bacon
**2 a :** a longitudinal section of a log **b :** a bundle of sheets of veneer laid together in sequence
**¹flit-ter** \'fli-tər\ *intransitive verb* [frequentative of *flit*] (1534)
**:** FLUTTER, FLICKER
**²flitter** *noun* (1554)
**:** one that flits
**fliv-ver** \'fli-vər\ *noun* [origin unknown] (1910)
**:** a small cheap usually old automobile
**¹float** \'flōt\ *noun* [Middle English *flote* boat, float, from Old English *flota* ship; akin to Old High German *flōz* raft, stream, Old English *flēotan* to float — more at FLEET] (before 12th century)
**1 :** an act or instance of floating
**2 :** something that floats in or on the surface of a fluid: as **a :** a device (as a cork) buoying up the baited end of a fishing line **b :** a floating platform anchored near a shoreline for use by swimmers or boats **c :** a hollow ball that floats at the end of a lever in a cistern, tank, or boiler and regulates the liquid level **d :** a sac containing air or gas and buoying up the body of a plant or animal — compare PNEUMATOPHORE 1 **e :** a watertight structure giving an airplane buoyancy on water
**3 :** a tool or apparatus for smoothing a surface (as of wet concrete)
**4 :** a government grant of a fixed amount of land not yet located by survey out of a larger specific tract
**5 a :** a vehicle with a platform used to carry an exhibit in a parade **b :** the vehicle and exhibit together
**6 a :** an amount of money represented by checks outstanding and in process of collection **b :** the time between a transaction (as the writing of a check or a purchase on credit) and the actual withdrawal of funds to cover it **c :** the volume of a company's shares available for active trading in the auction market
**7 :** a soft drink with ice cream floating in it
**— floaty** \'flō-tē\ *adjective*
**²float** (before 12th century)
*intransitive verb*
**1 :** to rest on the surface of or be suspended in a fluid
**2 a :** to drift on or through or as if on or through a fluid ⟨yellow leaves *floated* down⟩ **b :** WANDER
**3** *of a currency* **:** to find a level in the international exchange market in response to the law of supply and demand and without any restrictive effect of artificial support or control
*transitive verb*
**1 a :** to cause to float in or on the surface of a fluid **b :** to cause to float as if in a fluid
**2 :** FLOOD ⟨*float* a cranberry bog⟩
**3 :** to smooth (as plaster or cement) with a float
**4 a :** to put forth (as a proposal) for acceptance **b :** to place (an issue of securities) on the market **c :** to obtain money for the establishment or development of (an enterprise) by issuing and selling securities **d :** NEGOTIATE ⟨*float* a loan⟩
**floa-ta-tion** *variant of* FLOTATION
**float-er** \'flō-tər\ *noun* (1717)
**1 a :** one that floats **b :** a person who floats something
**2 :** a person who votes illegally in various polling places
**3 a :** a person without a permanent residence or regular employment **b :** a worker who moves from job to job; *especially* **:** one without fixed duties
**4 :** a policy insuring specific items of personal property (as jewelry or art)
**float glass** *noun* (1959)
**:** flat glass produced by solidifying molten glass on the surface of a bath of molten tin
**float-ing** *adjective* (1600)

**1 :** buoyed on or in a fluid
**2 :** located out of the normal position ⟨a *floating* kidney⟩
**3 a :** continually drifting or changing position ⟨the *floating* population⟩ **b :** not presently committed or invested ⟨*floating* capital⟩ **c :** short-term and usually not funded ⟨*floating* debt⟩ **d :** having no fixed value or rate ⟨*floating* currencies⟩ ⟨*floating* interest rates⟩
**4 :** connected or constructed so as to operate and adjust smoothly ⟨a *floating* axle⟩
**floating dock** *noun* (1866)
**:** a dock that floats on the water and can be partly submerged to permit entry of a ship and raised to keep the ship high and dry — called also *floating drydock*
**floating island** *noun* (1771)
**:** a dessert consisting of custard with floating masses of beaten egg whites
**floating–point** *adjective* (1948)
**:** expressed in, using, or being a mathematical notation in which a number is represented (as in a computer display) by an integer or a decimal fraction multiplied by a power of the number base indicated by an exponent (as in 4.52E2 for 452) — compare FIXED-POINT
**floating rib** *noun* (1831)
**:** a rib (as one of either of the last two pairs in humans) that has no attachment to the sternum — compare FALSE RIB
**float-plane** \'flōt-ˌplān\ *noun* (1922)
**:** a seaplane supported on the water by one or more floats
**floc** \'fläk\ *noun* [short for *floccule*] (1921)
**:** a flocculent mass formed by the aggregation of a number of fine suspended particles
**floc-cu-late** \'flä-kyə-ˌlāt\ *verb* **-lat-ed; -lat-ing** (1877)
*transitive verb*
**:** to cause to aggregate into a flocculent mass ⟨*flocculate* clay⟩
*intransitive verb*
**:** to become flocculent
**— floc-cu-lant** \-lənt\ *noun*
**— floc-cu-la-tion** \ˌflä-kyə-'lā-shən\ *noun*
**— floc-cu-la-tor** \'flä-kyə-ˌlā-tər\ *noun*
**floc-cule** \'flä-(ˌ)kyü(ə)l\ *noun* [Late Latin *flocculus*] (circa 1846)
**:** FLOC
**floc-cu-lent** \-lənt\ *adjective* [Latin *flocc*us + English *-ulent*] (1800)
**1 :** resembling wool especially in loose fluffy organization
**2 :** made up of flocs or floccules ⟨a *flocculent* precipitate⟩
**floc-cu-lus** \-ləs\ *noun, plural* **-li** \-ˌlī, -ˌlē\ [Late Latin, diminutive of Latin *floccus* tuft of wool] (1799)
**1 :** a small loosely aggregated mass
**2 :** a bright or dark patch on the sun
**¹flock** \'fläk\ *noun* [Middle English, from Old English *flocc* crowd, band; akin to Old Norse *flokkr* crowd, band] (13th century)
**1 :** a group of birds or mammals assembled or herded together
**2 :** a group under the guidance of a leader; *especially* **:** a church congregation
**3 :** a large number ⟨a *flock* of tourists⟩
**²flock** *intransitive verb* (14th century)
**:** to gather or move in a flock ⟨they *flocked* to the beach⟩
**³flock** *noun* [Middle English *flok,* from Old French *floc,* from Latin *floccus*] (13th century)
**1 :** a tuft of wool or cotton fiber
**2 :** woolen or cotton refuse used for stuffing furniture and mattresses
**3 :** very short or pulverized fiber used especially to form a velvety pattern on cloth or paper or a protective covering on metal
**4 :** FLOC

\ə\ abut \ᵊ\ kitten \ər\ further \a\ ash \ā\ ace
\ä\ mop, mar \au̇\ out \ch\ chin \e\ bet \ē\ easy
\g\ go \i\ hit \ī\ ice \j\ job \ŋ\ sing \ō\ go
\ȯ\ law \ȯi\ boy \th\ thin \t͟h\ the \ü\ loot \u̇\ foot
\y\ yet \zh\ vision *see also* Guide to Pronunciation

**⁴flock** *transitive verb* (1530)
**1** : to fill with flock
**2** : to decorate with flock
**flock·ing** \'flä-kiŋ\ *noun* (circa 1874)
: a design in flock
**floe** \'flō\ *noun* [probably from Norwegian *flo* flat layer] (1817)
**1** : floating ice formed in a large sheet on the surface of a body of water
**2** : ICE FLOE
**flog** \'fläg\ *verb* **flogged; flog·ging** [perhaps modification of Latin *flagellare* to whip — more at FLAGELLATE] (circa 1676)
*transitive verb*
**1 a** : to beat with or as if with a rod or whip **b** : to criticize harshly
**2** : to force or urge into action : DRIVE
**3 a** *chiefly British* : to sell (as stolen goods) illegally ⟨*flogged* their employers' petrol to ordinary motorists —*Economist*⟩ **b** : SELL 7 ⟨traveled by horse, *flogging* encyclopedias —Robert Darnton⟩ **c** : to promote aggressively : PLUG ⟨flying around the world *flogging* your movies —Peter Bogdanovich⟩
**4** *British* : STEAL 1
*intransitive verb*
**1** : FLAP, FLUTTER ⟨sails *flogging*⟩
**2** *British* : to move along with difficulty : SLOG
— **flog·ger** *noun*
**flo·ka·ti** \flō-'kä-tē\ *noun* [New Greek *phlokatē*] (1967)
: a hand-woven Greek woolen rug with a thick shaggy pile
**¹flood** \'fləd\ *noun* [Middle English, from Old English *flōd;* akin to Old High German *fluot* flood, Old English *flōwan* to flow] (before 12th century)
**1 a** : a rising and overflowing of a body of water especially onto normally dry land; *also* : a condition of overflowing ⟨rivers in *flood*⟩ **b** *capitalized* : a flood described in the Bible as covering the earth in the time of Noah
**2** : the flowing in of the tide
**3** : an overwhelming quantity or volume; *also* : a state of abundant flow or volume ⟨a debate in full *flood*⟩
**4** : FLOODLIGHT
**²flood** (1663)
*transitive verb*
**1** : to cover with a flood : INUNDATE
**2 a** : to fill abundantly or excessively ⟨*flood* the market⟩ **b** : to supply to (the carburetor of an internal combustion engine) an excess of fuel so that engine operation is hampered
*intransitive verb*
**1** : to pour forth, go, or come in a flood
**2** : to become filled with a flood
— **flood·er** *noun*
**flood·gate** \'fləd-,gāt\ *noun* [Middle English *flodgate*] (13th century)
**1** : a gate for shutting out, admitting, or releasing a body of water : SLUICE
**2** : something serving to restrain an outburst ⟨opened the *floodgates*⟩
**¹flood·light** \-,līt\ *transitive verb* **-lit** \-,lit\ *also* **-light·ed; -light·ing** (1923)
: to illuminate by means of one or more floodlights
**²floodlight** *noun* (1924)
**1 a** : artificial illumination in a broad beam **b** : a source of such illumination
**2** : a lighting unit for projecting a beam of light
**flood·plain** \'fləd-,plān\ *noun* (1873)
**1** : level land that may be submerged by floodwaters
**2** : a plain built up by stream deposition
**flood tide** *noun* (1719)
**1** : a rising tide
**2 a** : an overwhelming quantity **b** : a high point : PEAK
**flood·wa·ter** \-,wȯ-tər, -,wä-\ *noun* (1791)
: the water of a flood
**flood·way** \-,wā\ *noun* (1928)
: a channel for diverting floodwaters

**floo·ey** \'flü-ē\ *adjective* [origin unknown] (1920)
: AWRY, ASKEW ⟨go *flooey*⟩
**¹floor** \'flōr, 'flȯr\ *noun, often attributive* [Middle English *flor*, from Old English *flōr;* akin to Old High German *fluor* meadow, Latin *planus* level, and perhaps to Greek *planasthai* to wander] (before 12th century)
**1** : the level base of a room
**2 a** : the lower inside surface of a hollow structure (as a cave or bodily part) **b** : a ground surface ⟨the ocean *floor*⟩
**3 a** : a structure dividing a building into stories; *also* : STORY **b** : the occupants of such a floor
**4** : the surface of a structure on which one travels ⟨the *floor* of a bridge⟩
**5 a** : a main level space (as in a stock exchange or legislative chamber) distinguished from a platform or gallery **b** : the members of an assembly ⟨took questions from the *floor*⟩ **c** : the right to address an assembly ⟨the senator from Utah has the *floor*⟩
**6** : a lower limit : BASE
— **floored** *adjective*
**²floor** *transitive verb* (15th century)
**1** : to cover with a floor or flooring
**2 a** : to knock or bring down **b** : FLABBERGAST, DUMBFOUND
**3** : to press (the accelerator of a vehicle) to the floorboard; *also* : to accelerate rapidly ⟨*floored* the van⟩
— **floor·er** *noun*
**floor·board** \'flōr-,bōrd, 'flȯr-,bȯrd\ *noun* (1881)
**1** : a board in a floor
**2** : the floor of an automobile
**floor·cloth** \-,klȯth\ *noun, plural* **-cloths** \-,klȯthz, -,klȯths\ (1746)
: a usually decorated heavy cloth (as of canvas) used for a floor covering
**floor exercise** *noun* (1961)
: an event in gymnastics competition consisting of various ballet and tumbling movements (as jumps, somersaults, and handstands) performed without apparatus
**floor·ing** \'flōr-iŋ, 'flȯr-\ *noun* (1624)
**1** : FLOOR, BASE
**2** : material for floors
**floor lamp** *noun* (1892)
: a tall lamp that stands on the floor
**floor leader** *noun* (1899)
: a member of a legislative body chosen by a party to have charge of its organization and strategy on the floor
**floor–length** *adjective* (1939)
: reaching to the floor ⟨a *floor-length* gown⟩
**floor manager** *noun* (1887)
: a person who directs something from the floor (as of a nominating convention)
**floor show** *noun* (1927)
: a series of acts presented in a nightclub
**floor–through** \'flōr-,thrü, 'flȯr-\ *noun* (1967)
: an apartment that occupies an entire floor of a building
**floor·walk·er** \'flōr-,wȯ-kər, 'flȯr-\ *noun* (1876)
: a person employed in a retail store to oversee the salespeople and aid customers
**floo·zy** *or* **floo·zie** \'flü-zē\ *noun, plural* **floozies** [origin unknown] (1911)
: a usually young woman of loose morals
**¹flop** \'fläp\ *verb* **flopped; flop·ping** [alteration of ²flap] (1602)
*intransitive verb*
**1** : to swing or move loosely : FLAP
**2** : to throw or move oneself in a heavy, clumsy, or relaxed manner ⟨*flopped* into the chair⟩
**3** : to change or turn suddenly
**4** : to go to bed ⟨a place to *flop* at night⟩
**5** : to fail completely ⟨the play *flopped*⟩
*transitive verb*
: to move or drop heavily or noisily : cause to flop ⟨*flopped* the bundles down⟩ ⟨*flop* the rag over⟩
— **flop·per** *noun*

**²flop** *adverb* (1728)
: RIGHT, SQUARELY ⟨fell *flop* on my face⟩
**³flop** *noun* (1823)
**1** : an act or sound of flopping
**2** : a complete failure
**3** *slang* : a place to sleep; *especially* : FLOPHOUSE
**4** : DUNG ⟨cow *flop*⟩; *also* : a piece of dung
**flop·house** \'fläp-,haůs\ *noun* (1916)
: a cheap rooming house or hotel
**¹flop·py** \'flä-pē\ *adjective* **flop·pi·er; -est** (1858)
: tending to flop; *especially* : being both soft and flexible
— **flop·pi·ly** \'flä-pə-lē\ *adverb*
— **flop·pi·ness** \'flä-pē-nəs\ *noun*
**²floppy** *noun, plural* **-pies** (1974)
: FLOPPY DISK
**floppy disk** *noun* (1972)
: a small flexible plastic disk coated with magnetic material on which data for a computer can be stored
**flo·ra** \'flōr-ə, 'flȯr-\ *noun, plural* **floras** *also* **flo·rae** \'flōr-,ē, 'flȯr-, -,ī\ [New Latin, from Latin *Flora*, Roman goddess of flowers, from Latin *flor-, flos*] (1777)
**1** : a treatise on or list of the plants of an area or period
**2** : plant or bacterial life; *especially* : such life characteristic of a region, period, or special environment ⟨fossil *flora*⟩ ⟨intestinal *flora*⟩ — compare FAUNA
**¹flo·ral** \'flōr-əl, 'flȯr-\ *adjective* [Latin *flor-, flos* flower — more at BLOW] (1753)
: of or relating to flowers or a flora
**²floral** *noun* (1897)
: a design, pattern, or picture in which flowers predominate
**floral envelope** *noun* (circa 1829)
: PERIANTH
**Flor·ence flask** \'flȯr-ən(t)s-, 'flär-\ *noun* [*Florence*, Italy; from the use of flasks of this shape for certain Italian wines] (1744)
: a round usually flat-bottomed laboratory vessel with a long neck
**Flor·en·tine** \'flȯr-ən-,tēn, 'flär-, -tīn\ *adjective* [Medieval Latin *Florentinus*] (1597)
**1 a** : of or relating to Florence, Italy **b** : MACHIAVELLIAN ⟨*Florentine* politics⟩
**2** : served or dressed with spinach ⟨poached eggs *Florentine*⟩
**3** : having a matte brushed finish ⟨*Florentine* gold⟩
**flo·res·cence** \flȯ-'re-s°n(t)s, flə-\ *noun* [New Latin *florescentia*, from Latin *florescent-, florescens*, present participle of *florescere*, inchoative of *florēre* to blossom, flourish — more at FLOURISH] (1793)
: a state or period of flourishing
— **flo·res·cent** \-s°nt\ *adjective*
**flo·ret** \'flōr-ət, 'flȯr-\ *noun* [Middle English *flourette*, from Middle French *flouret*, diminutive of *flour* flower] (1671)
**1** : a small flower; *especially* : one of the small flowers forming the head of a composite plant
**2** : a cluster of flower buds separated from a head especially when used as food ⟨cauliflower *florets*⟩
**flori-** *combining form* [Latin, from *flor-, flos*]
: flower or flowers ⟨*floriculture*⟩
**flo·ri·at·ed** \'flōr-ē-,ā-təd, 'flȯr-\ *adjective* (1845)
: having floral ornaments or a floral form
— **flo·ri·a·tion** \,flōr-ē-'ā-shən, ,flȯr-\ *noun*
**flo·ri·bun·da** \,flōr-ə-'bən-də, ,flȯr-\ *noun* [New Latin, feminine of *floribundus* flowering freely] (1898)
: any of various bush roses with large flowers in open clusters that derive from crosses of polyantha and tea roses
**flo·ri·cul·ture** \'flōr-ə-,kəl-chər, 'flȯr-\ *noun* (1822)
: the cultivation and management of ornamental and especially flowering plants

— **flo·ri·cul·tur·al** \ˌflōr-ə-'kəlch-rəl, -'kəl-chə-, ˌflȯr-\ *adjective*
— **flo·ri·cul·tur·ist** \-rist\ *noun*

**flor·id** \'flȯr-əd, 'flär-\ *adjective* [Latin *floridus* blooming, flowery, from *florēre*] (circa 1656) **1 a** *obsolete* : covered with flowers **b** : very flowery in style : ORNATE ⟨*florid* prose⟩ ⟨*florid* declamations⟩; *also* : having a florid style ⟨a *florid* writer⟩ **c** : elaborately decorated ⟨*florid* interior⟩ **2 a** : tinged with red : RUDDY ⟨a *florid* complexion⟩ **b** : marked by emotional or sexual fervor ⟨a *florid* secret life⟩ ⟨a *florid* sensibility⟩ **3** *archaic* : HEALTHY **4** : fully developed : manifesting a complete and typical clinical syndrome ⟨the *florid* stage of a disease⟩
— **flo·rid·i·ty** \flə-'ri-də-tē, flȯ-\ *noun*
— **flor·id·ly** \'flȯr-əd-lē, 'flär-\ *adverb*
— **flor·id·ness** \-nəs\ *noun*

**flo·rif·er·ous** \flȯ-'ri-f(ə-)rəs\ *adjective* [Latin *florifer*, from *flori-* + *-fer* fer] (1678) : bearing flowers; *especially* : blooming freely
— **flo·rif·er·ous·ness** *noun*

**flo·ri·gen** \'flȯr-ə-jən, 'flär-\ *noun* [International Scientific Vocabulary] (1936) : a hormone or hormonal agent that promotes flowering
— **flo·ri·gen·ic** \ˌflȯr-ə-'je-nik, ˌflär-\ *adjective*

**flo·ri·le·gium** \ˌflȯr-ə-'lē-j(ē-)əm, ˌflär-\ *noun*, *plural* **-gia** \-j(ē-)ə\ [New Latin, from Latin *florilegus* culling flowers, from *flori-* + *legere* to gather — more at LEGEND] (1647) : a volume of writings : ANTHOLOGY

**flo·rin** \'flȯr-ən, 'flär-, 'flōr-\ *noun* [Middle English, from Middle French, from Old Italian *fiorino*, from *fiore* flower, from Latin *flor-*, *flos*; from the lily on the coins] (14th century) **1 a** : an old gold coin first struck at Florence in 1252 **b** : any of various European gold coins patterned after the Florentine florin **2 a** : a British silver coin worth two shillings **b** : any of several similar coins issued in Commonwealth countries **3** : GULDEN **4** : FORINT

**flo·rist** \'flōr-ist, 'flȯr-, 'flär-\ *noun* (1623) : one who sells or grows for sale flowers and ornamental plants
— **flo·rist·ry** \-ə-strē\ *noun*

**flo·ris·tic** \flȯ-'ris-tik\ *adjective* (1898) : of or relating to flowers, a flora, or the phytogeographical study of plants and plant groups
— **flo·ris·ti·cal·ly** \-ti-k(ə-)lē\ *adverb*

**flo·ru·it** \'flȯr-(y)ə-wət, 'flär-\ *noun* [Latin, he flourished, from *florēre* to flourish] (1843) : a period of flourishing (as of a person or movement)

**¹floss** \'fläs, 'flȯs\ *noun* [probably modification of French *floche* soft, weak (of silk fiber), from Gascon, from Latin *fluxus*, literally, loose, flowing, past participle of *fluere* to flow — more at FLUID] (1759) **1 a** : soft thread of silk or mercerized cotton for embroidery **b** : DENTAL FLOSS **2** : fluffy fibrous material

**²floss** (1974) *transitive verb* : to use dental floss on *intransitive verb* : to use dental floss

**flossy** \'flä-sē, 'flȯ-\ *adjective* **floss·i·er; -est** (1839) **1** : of, relating to, or having the characteristics of floss **2** : stylish or glamorous especially at first impression ⟨*flossy* new hotels⟩
— **floss·i·ly** \'flä-sə-lē\ *adverb*

**flo·ta** \'flō-tə\ *noun* [Spanish] (1527) : a fleet of Spanish ships

**flo·ta·tion** \flō-'tā-shən\ *noun* [²*float*] (1806) **1** : the act, process, or state of floating **2** : an act or instance of financing (as an issue of stock)

**3** : the separation of the particles of a mass of pulverized ore according to their relative capacity for floating on a given liquid; *also* : any of various similar processes involving the relative capacity of materials for floating **4** : the ability (as of a tire or snowshoes) to stay on the surface of soft ground or snow

**flo·til·la** \flō-'ti-lə\ *noun* [Spanish, diminutive of *flota* fleet, from Old French *flote*, from Old Norse *floti*; akin to Old English *flota* ship, fleet — more at FLOAT] (1711) **1** : a fleet of ships or boats; *especially* : a navy organizational unit consisting of two or more squadrons of small warships **2** : an indefinite large number ⟨a *flotilla* of changes⟩

**flot·sam** \'flät-səm\ *noun* [Anglo-French *floteson*, from Old French *floter* to float, of Germanic origin; akin to Old English *flotian* to float, *flota* ship] (circa 1607) **1** : floating wreckage of a ship or its cargo; *broadly* : floating debris **2 a** : a floating population (as of emigrants or castaways) **b** : an accumulation of miscellaneous or unimportant stuff

**¹flounce** \'flaun(t)s\ *intransitive verb* **flounced; flounc·ing** [perhaps of Scandinavian origin; akin to Norwegian *flunsa* to hurry] (1542) **1 a** : to move with exaggerated jerky or bouncy motions ⟨*flounced* about the room, jerking her shoulders, gesticulating —Agatha Christie⟩; *also* : to move so as to draw attention to oneself ⟨*flounced* into the lobby⟩ **b** : to go with sudden determination ⟨*flounced* out of the room in a huff⟩ **2** : FLOUNDER, STRUGGLE

**²flounce** *noun* (1583) : an act or instance of flouncing
— **flouncy** \'flaun(t)-sē\ *adjective*

**³flounce** *transitive verb* **flounced; flounc·ing** [alteration of earlier *frounce*, from Middle English *frouncen* to curl] (1711) : to trim with flounces

**⁴flounce** *noun* (1713) : a strip of fabric attached by one edge; *also* : a wide ruffle
— **flouncy** \'flaun(t)-sē\ *adjective*

**flounc·ing** \'flaun(t)-sin\ *noun* (1865) : material used for flounces

**¹floun·der** \'flaun-dər\ *noun*, *plural* **flounder** or **flounders** [Middle English, from Anglo-French *floundre*, of Scandinavian origin; akin to Old Norse *flythra* flounder] (15th century) : FLATFISH; *especially* : a fish of either of two families (Pleuronectidae and Bothidae) that include important marine food fishes

**²flounder** *intransitive verb* **floun·dered; floun·der·ing** \-d(ə-)rin\ [probably alteration of *founder*] (1592) **1** : to struggle to move or obtain footing : thrash about wildly **2** : to proceed or act clumsily or ineffectually

**¹flour** \'flaur\ *noun* [Middle English — more at FLOWER] (13th century) **1** : finely ground meal of wheat usually largely freed from bran; *also* : a similar meal of another material (as a cereal grain, an edible seed, or dried processed fish) **2** : a fine soft powder
— **flour·less** *adjective*
— **floury** \-ē\ *adjective*

**²flour** (circa 1657) *transitive verb* : to coat with or as if with flour *intransitive verb* : to break up into particles

**¹flour·ish** \'flər-ish, 'flə-rish\ *verb* [Middle English *florisshen*, from Middle French *floriss-*, stem of *florir*, from (assumed) Vulgar Latin *florire*, alteration of Latin *florēre*, from *flor-*, *flos* flower] (14th century) *intransitive verb* **1** : to grow luxuriantly : THRIVE **2 a** : to achieve success : PROSPER **b** : to be in a state of activity or production ⟨*flourished*

around 1850⟩ **c** : to reach a height of development or influence **3** : to make bold and sweeping gestures *transitive verb* : to wield with dramatic gestures : BRANDISH *synonym* see SWING
— **flour·ish·er** *noun*
— **flour·ish·ing·ly** \-i-shin-lē\ *adverb*

**²flourish** *noun* (1597) **1 a** : a period of thriving **b** : a luxuriant growth or profusion ⟨a *flourish* of white hair⟩ ⟨a springtime *flourish* of color⟩ **2 a** : a florid bit of speech or writing ⟨rhetorical *flourishes*⟩ **b** : an ornamental stroke in writing or printing **c** : a decorative or finishing detail ⟨a house with clever little *flourishes*⟩ **3** : FANFARE **4** : an act or instance of brandishing or waving **5** : showiness in the doing of something ⟨opened the door with a *flourish*⟩ **6** : a sudden burst (as of activity) ⟨the week ends with a *flourish* of tests⟩

**¹flout** \'flaut\ *verb* [probably from Middle English *flouten* to play the flute, from *floute* flute] (1551) *transitive verb* : to treat with contemptuous disregard : SCORN ⟨*flouting* the rules⟩ *intransitive verb* : to indulge in scornful behavior *synonym* see SCOFF *usage* see FLAUNT
— **flout·er** *noun*

**²flout** *noun* (circa 1570) : JEER

**¹flow** \'flō\ *verb* [Middle English, from Old English *flōwan*; akin to Old High German *flouwen* to rinse, wash, Latin *pluere* to rain, Greek *plein* to sail, float] (before 12th century) *intransitive verb* **1 a** (1) : to issue or move in a stream (2) : CIRCULATE **b** : to move with a continual change of place among the constituent particles ⟨molasses *flows* slowly⟩ **2** : RISE ⟨the tide ebbs and *flows*⟩ **3** : ABOUND **4 a** : to proceed smoothly and readily ⟨conversation *flowed* easily⟩ **b** : to have a smooth continuity **5** : to hang loose and billowing **6** : to derive from a source : COME ⟨the wealth that *flows* from trade⟩ **7** : to deform under stress without cracking or rupturing — used especially of minerals and rocks **8** : MENSTRUATE *transitive verb* **1** : to cause to flow **2** : to discharge in a flow *synonym* see SPRING
— **flow·ing·ly** \-in-lē\ *adverb*

**²flow** *noun* (15th century) **1** : an act of flowing **2** : FLOOD 1a, 2 **3 a** : a smooth uninterrupted movement or progress ⟨a *flow* of information⟩ **b** : STREAM; *also* : a mass of material which has flowed when molten ⟨an old lava *flow*⟩ **c** : the direction of movement or development ⟨go with the *flow*⟩ **4** : the quantity that flows in a certain time **5** : MENSTRUATION **6 a** : the motion characteristic of fluids **b** : a continuous transfer of energy

**flow·age** \'flō-ij\ *noun* (1830) **1 a** : an overflowing onto adjacent land **b** : a body of water formed by overflowing or damming **c** : floodwater especially of a stream

---

\ə\ abut \ᵊ\ kitten \ər\ further \a\ ash \ā\ ace \ä\ mop, mar \au̇\ out \ch\ chin \e\ bet \ē\ easy \g\ go \i\ hit \ī\ ice \j\ job \ŋ\ sing \ō\ go \ȯ\ law \ȯi\ boy \th\ thin \t͟h\ the \ü\ loot \u̇\ foot \y\ yet \zh\ vision *see also* Guide to Pronunciation

**2 :** gradual deformation of a body of plastic solid (as rock) by intermolecular shear

**flow·chart** \-ˌchärt\ *noun* (1920)
: a diagram that shows step-by-step progression through a procedure or system especially using connecting lines and a set of conventional symbols
— **flow·chart·ing** \-ˌchär-tiŋ\ *noun*

**flow cy·tom·e·try** \-sī-'tä-mə-trē\ *noun* (1978)
: a technique for identifying and sorting cells and their components (as DNA) by staining with a fluorescent dye and detecting the fluorescence usually by laser beam illumination

**flow diagram** *noun* (1943)
: FLOWCHART

¹**flow·er** \'flau̇(-ə)r\ *noun* [Middle English *flour* flower, best of anything, flour, from Old French *flor, flour,* from Latin *flor-, flos* — more at BLOW] (13th century)
**1 a :** BLOSSOM, IN-
FLORESCENCE **b :** a
shoot of the sporo-
phyte of a higher
plant that is modi-
fied for reproduc-
tion and consists
of a shortened axis
bearing modified
leaves; *especially*
: one of a seed
plant differentiated
into a calyx, corol-
la, stamens, and
carpels **c :** a plant
cultivated for its
blossoms

cross section of flower 1b:
*1* filament, *2* anther, *3* stigma, *4* style, *5* petal, *6* ovary, *7* sepal, *8* pedicel,
*9* stamen, *10* pistil,
*11* perianth

**2 a :** the best part or example ⟨the *flower* of our youth⟩ **b :** the finest most vigorous period **c :** a state of blooming or flourishing ⟨in full *flower*⟩
**3** *plural* **:** a finely divided powder produced especially by condensation or sublimation ⟨*flowers* of sulfur⟩
— **flow·ered** \'flau̇(-ə)rd\ *adjective*
— **flow·er·ful** \'flau̇(-ə)r-fəl\ *adjective*
— **flow·er·less** \-ləs\ *adjective*
— **flow·er·like** \-ˌlīk\ *adjective*

²**flower** (13th century)
*intransitive verb*
**1 a :** DEVELOP ⟨*flowered* into young womanhood⟩ **b :** FLOURISH
**2 :** to produce flowers **:** BLOSSOM
*transitive verb*
**1 :** to cause to bear flowers
**2 :** to decorate with flowers or floral designs
— **flow·er·er** \'flau̇(-ə)r-ər\ *noun*

**flow·er·age** \'flau̇(-ə)r-ij\ *noun* (1840)
: a flowering process, state, or condition

**flower bud** *noun* (1828)
: a plant bud that produces only a flower

**flower bug** *noun* (circa 1889)
: any of various small mostly black-and-white predaceous bugs (family Anthocoridae) that frequent flowers and feed on pest insects (as aphids and thrips)

**flower child** *noun* (1967)
: a hippie who advocates love, beauty, and peace

**flow·er·et** *also* **flow·er·ette** \'flau̇(-ə)r-ət\ *noun* (15th century)
: FLORET 1

**flower girl** *noun* (1925)
: a little girl who carries flowers at a wedding

**flower head** *noun* (1845)
: a capitulum (as of a composite) having sessile flowers so arranged that the whole inflorescence looks like a single flower

**flowering dogwood** *noun* (1843)
: a common spring-flowering white-bracted dogwood (*Cornus florida*)

**flowering plant** *noun* (1745)
: ANGIOSPERM

**flower people** *noun plural* (1967)
: FLOWER CHILDREN

**flow·er·pot** \'flau̇(-ə)r-ˌpät\ *noun* (1598)
: a pot in which to grow plants

**flow·ery** \'flau̇(-ə)r-ē\ *adjective* (14th century)
**1 :** of, relating to, or resembling flowers
**2 :** marked by or given to rhetorical elegance
— **flow·er·i·ly** \'flau̇(-ə)r-ə-lē\ *adverb*
— **flow·er·i·ness** *noun*

**flow·me·ter** \'flō-ˌmē-tər\ *noun* (1915)
: an instrument for measuring one or more properties (as velocity or pressure) of a flow (as of a liquid in a pipe)

¹**flown** \'flōn\ *past participle of* FLY

²**flown** *adjective* [archaic past participle of ¹*flow*] (1626)
: filled to excess

**flow sheet** *noun* (1912)
: FLOWCHART

**flow·stone** \'flō-ˌstōn\ *noun* (1925)
: calcite deposited by a thin sheet of flowing water usually along the walls or floor of a cave

**flu** \'flü\ *noun* [by shortening] (1839)
**1 :** INFLUENZA
**2 :** any of several virus diseases marked especially by respiratory symptoms

¹**flub** \'fləb\ *verb* **flubbed; flub·bing** [origin unknown] (1904)
*transitive verb*
: to make a mess of **:** BOTCH ⟨*flubbed* my lines⟩
*intransitive verb*
: BLUNDER

²**flub** *noun* (1948)
: an act or instance of flubbing

**flub·dub** \'fləb-ˌdəb\ *noun* [origin unknown] (1888)
: BUNKUM, BALDERDASH

**fluc·tu·ant** \'flək-chə-wənt\ *adjective* (1560)
**1 :** moving in waves
**2 :** VARIABLE, UNSTABLE
**3 :** being movable and compressible ⟨a *fluctuant* abscess⟩

**fluc·tu·ate** \'flək-chə-ˌwāt\ *verb* **-at·ed; -at·ing** [Latin *fluctuatus,* past participle of *fluctuare,* from *fluctus* flow, wave, from *fluere* — more at FLUID] (1634)
*intransitive verb*
**1 :** to shift back and forth uncertainly
**2 :** to ebb and flow in waves
*transitive verb*
: to cause to fluctuate
*synonym* see SWING
— **fluc·tu·a·tion** \ˌflək-chə-'wā-shən\ *noun*
— **fluc·tu·a·tion·al** \-'wā-shnəl, -shə-nᵊl\ *adjective*

**flue** \'flü\ *noun* [origin unknown] (1582)
: an enclosed passageway for directing a current: as **a :** a channel in a chimney for conveying flame and smoke to the outer air **b :** a pipe for conveying flame and hot gases around or through water in a steam boiler **c :** an air channel leading to the lip of a wind instrument **d :** FLUE PIPE

**flue–cured** \-ˌkyu̇rd\ *adjective* (1905)
: cured with heat transmitted through a flue without exposure to smoke or fumes ⟨*flue-cured* tobacco⟩

**flu·en·cy** \'flü-ən(t)-sē\ *noun* (1636)
: the quality or state of being fluent

**flu·ent** \'flü-ənt\ *adjective* [Latin *fluent-, fluens,* present participle of *fluere*] (1599)
**1 a :** capable of flowing **:** FLUID **b :** capable of moving with ease and grace ⟨the *fluent* body of a dancer⟩
**2 a :** ready or facile in speech ⟨*fluent* in Spanish⟩ **b :** effortlessly smooth and rapid **:** POLISHED ⟨a *fluent* performance⟩
— **flu·ent·ly** *adverb*

**flue pipe** *noun* (1852)
: an organ pipe whose tone is produced by an air current striking the lip and causing the air within to vibrate — compare REED PIPE

**flue stop** *noun* (1855)
: an organ stop made up of flue pipes

¹**fluff** \'fləf\ *noun* [perhaps blend of *flue* (fluff) and *puff*] (1790)
**1 :** NAP, DOWN

**2 :** something fluffy
**3 :** something inconsequential
**4 :** BLUNDER; *especially* **:** an actor's lapse of memory

²**fluff** (1875)
*intransitive verb*
**1 :** to become fluffy
**2 :** to make a mistake; *especially* **:** to forget or bungle one's lines in a play
*transitive verb*
**1 :** to make fluffy
**2 a :** to spoil by a mistake **:** BOTCH **b :** to deliver badly or forget ⟨one's lines⟩ in a play

**fluffy** \'flə-fē\ *adjective* **fluff·i·er; -est** (circa 1825)
**1 a :** covered with or resembling fluff **b :** being light and soft or airy ⟨a *fluffy* omelet⟩
**2 :** lacking in meaning or substance **:** SUPERFICIAL 2c
— **fluff·i·ly** \'flə-fə-lē\ *adverb*
— **fluff·i·ness** \'flə-fē-nəs\ *noun*

**flü·gel·horn** *or* **flue·gel·horn** \'flü-gəl-ˌhȯrn, 'flü-\ *noun* [German, from *Flügel* wing, flank + *Horn* horn; from its use to signal the flanking drivers in a battue] (1854)
: a valved brass instrument resembling a cornet but having a larger bore
— **flü·gel·horn·ist** \-ˌhȯr-nist\ *noun*

¹**flu·id** \'flü-əd\ *adjective* [French or Latin; French *fluide,* from Latin *fluidus,* from *fluere* to flow; akin to Greek *phlyzein* to boil over] (1603)
**1 a :** having particles that easily move and change their relative position without a separation of the mass and that easily yield to pressure **:** capable of flowing **b :** subject to change or movement ⟨boundaries became *fluid*⟩
**2 :** characterized by or employing a smooth easy style ⟨the ballerina's *fluid* movements⟩
**3 a :** available for a different use **b :** LIQUID 4 ⟨*fluid* assets⟩
— **flu·id·ly** *adverb*
— **flu·id·ness** *noun*

²**fluid** *noun* (1661)
: a substance (as a liquid or gas) tending to flow or conform to the outline of its container
— **flu·id·al** \'flü-ə-dᵊl\ *adjective*
— **flu·id·al·ly** \-dᵊl-ē\ *adverb*

**fluid dram** *or* **flu·i·dram** \ˌflü-ə(d)-'dram\ *noun* (circa 1860)
: a unit of liquid capacity equal to ⅛ fluid ounce — see WEIGHT table

**flu·id·ex·tract** \ˌflü-ə-'dek-ˌstrakt\ *noun* (1851)
: an alcohol preparation of a vegetable drug containing the active constituents of one gram of the dry drug in each milliliter

**flu·id·ic** \flü-'i-dik\ *adjective* (1960)
: of, relating to, or being a device (as an amplifier or control) that depends for operation on the pressures and flows of a fluid in precisely shaped channels
— **fluidic** *noun*
— **flu·id·ics** \-diks\ *noun plural but singular in construction*

**flu·id·i·ty** \flü-'i-də-tē\ *noun* (1603)
**1 :** the quality or state of being fluid
**2 :** the physical property of a substance that enables it to flow

**flu·id·ize** \'flü-ə-ˌdīz\ *transitive verb* **-ized; -iz·ing** (circa 1855)
**1 :** to cause to flow like a fluid
**2 :** to suspend (as solid particles) in a rapidly moving stream of gas or vapor to induce flowing motion of the whole
— **flu·id·iza·tion** \ˌflü-ə-də-'zā-shən\ *noun*
— **flu·id·iz·er** \'flü-ə-ˌdī-zər\ *noun*

**fluidized bed** *noun* (1949)
: a bed of small solid particles (as in a coal burning furnace) suspended and kept in motion by an upward flow of a fluid (as a gas) — called also *fluid bed*

**fluid mechanics** *noun plural but singular or plural in construction* (1937)
: a branch of mechanics dealing with the properties of liquids and gases

**fluid ounce** *noun* (circa 1860)
**1** : a U.S. unit of liquid capacity equal to ¹⁄₁₆ pint — see WEIGHT table
**2** : a British unit of liquid capacity equal to ¹⁄₂₀ pint — see WEIGHT table

¹**fluke** \'flük\ *noun* [Middle English, from Old English *flōc*; akin to Old English *flōh* chip, Old High German *flah* smooth, Greek *plax* flat surface, and probably to Old English *flōr* floor — more at FLOOR] (before 12th century)
**1** : FLATFISH
**2** : a flattened digenetic trematode worm; *broadly* : TREMATODE — compare LIVER FLUKE

²**fluke** *noun* [perhaps from ¹*fluke*] (1561)
**1** : the part of an anchor that fastens in the ground — see ANCHOR illustration
**2** : one of the lobes of a whale's tail

³**fluke** *noun* [origin unknown] (1857)
**1** : an accidentally successful stroke at billiards or pool
**2** : a stroke of luck ⟨the discovery was a *fluke*⟩

**fluky** *also* **fluk·ey** \'flü-kē\ *adjective* **fluk·i·er; -est** (1867)
**1** : happening by or depending on chance
**2** : being unsteady or uncertain — used especially of wind

**flume** \'flüm\ *noun* [probably from Middle English *flum* river, from Old French, from Latin *flumen*, from *fluere* — more at FLUID] (1748)
**1** : an inclined channel for conveying water (as for power)
**2** : a ravine or gorge with a stream running through it

**flum·mery** \'fləm-rē, 'flə-mə-\ *noun, plural* **-mer·ies** [Welsh *llymru*] (1623)
**1 a** : a soft jelly or porridge made with flour or meal **b** : any of several sweet desserts
**2** : MUMMERY, MUMBO JUMBO

**flum·mox** \'flə-məks, -miks\ *transitive verb* [origin unknown] (1837)
: CONFUSE

¹**flump** \'fləmp\ [imitative] (1816)
*intransitive verb*
: to move or fall suddenly and heavily ⟨*flumped* down into the chair⟩
*transitive verb*
: to place or drop with a flump

²**flump** *noun* (1832)
: a dull heavy sound (as of a fall)

**flung** *past and past participle of* FLING

¹**flunk** \'fləŋk\ *verb* [perhaps blend of *flinch* and *funk*] (1823)
*intransitive verb*
: to fail especially in an examination or course
*transitive verb*
**1** : to give a failing grade to
**2** : to get a failing grade in
— **flunk·er** *noun*

²**flunk** *noun* (1846)
: an act or instance of flunking

**flunk out** (1920)
*intransitive verb*
: to be dismissed from a school or college for failure
*transitive verb*
: to dismiss from a school or college for failure

**flun·ky** *or* **flun·key** \'fləŋ-kē\ *noun, plural* **flunkies** *or* **flunkeys** [Scots, of unknown origin] (circa 1782)
**1 a** : a liveried servant **b** : one performing menial or miscellaneous duties
**2** : YES-MAN

**flu·o·cin·o·lone ac·e·to·nide** \,flü-ə-'si-n°l-,ōn-,a-sə-'tō-,nīd\ *noun* [*fluor-* + *-cinolone*, probably alteration of *-nisolone* (as in *prednisolone*)] (1963)
: a glucocorticoid steroid $C_{24}H_{30}F_2O_6$ used especially as an anti-inflammatory agent in the treatment of skin diseases

**flu·or** \'flü-,or, 'flü-ər\ *noun* [New Latin, mineral belonging to a group used as fluxes and including fluorite, from Latin, flow, from *fluere* — more at FLUID] (1661)
: FLUORITE

**fluor-** *or* **fluoro-** *combining form* [French]
**1** : fluorine ⟨*fluoride*⟩
**2** *also* **fluori-** : fluorescence ⟨*fluoroscope*⟩ ⟨*fluorimeter*⟩

**fluo·resce** \flù-'res, flō-, flò-\ *intransitive verb* **-resced; -resc·ing** [back-formation from *fluorescence*] (1874)
: to produce, undergo, or exhibit fluorescence
— **fluo·resc·er** *noun*

**fluo·res·ce·in** \-'re-sē-ən\ *noun* (1876)
: a yellow or red crystalline dye $C_{20}H_{12}O_5$ with a bright yellow-green fluorescence in alkaline solution

**fluo·res·cence** \-'re-s°n(t)s\ *noun* [*fluorspar* + opal*escence*] (1852)
: luminescence that is caused by the absorption of radiation at one wavelength followed by nearly immediate reradiation usually at a different wavelength and that ceases almost immediately when the incident radiation stops; *also* : the radiation emitted — compare PHOSPHORESCENCE

**fluo·res·cent** \-s°nt\ *adjective* (1853)
**1** : having or relating to fluorescence
**2** : bright and glowing as a result of fluorescence ⟨*fluorescent* inks⟩; *broadly* : very bright in color
— **fluorescent** *noun*

**fluorescent lamp** *noun* (1896)
: a tubular electric lamp having a coating of fluorescent material on its inner surface and containing mercury vapor whose bombardment by electrons from the cathode provides ultraviolet light which causes the material to emit visible light

**fluo·ri·date** \'flùr-ə-,dāt, 'flōr-, 'flòr-\ *transitive verb* **-dat·ed; -dat·ing** (1949)
: to add a fluoride to (as drinking water) to reduce tooth decay
— **fluo·ri·da·tion** \,flùr-ə-'dā-shən, ,flōr-, ,flòr-\ *noun*

**fluo·ride** \'flōr-,īd, 'flùr-\ *noun, often attributive* (1826)
**1** : a compound of fluorine
**2** : the monovalent anion of fluorine

**fluo·ri·nate** \'flōr-ə-,nāt, 'flōr-, 'flùr-\ *transitive verb* **-nat·ed; -nat·ing** (circa 1929)
: to treat or cause to combine with fluorine or a compound of fluorine
— **fluo·ri·na·tion** \,flōr-ə-'nā-shən, ,flōr-, ,flùr-\ *noun*

**fluo·rine** \'flùr-,ēn, 'flōr-, 'flòr-\ *noun* [French, from New Latin *fluor*] (1813)
: a nonmetallic halogen element that is isolated as a pale yellowish flammable irritating toxic diatomic gas — see ELEMENT table

**fluo·rite** \'flùr-,īt, 'flōr-, 'flòr-\ *noun* [Italian, from New Latin *fluor*] (1868)
: a transparent or translucent mineral of different colors that consists of the fluoride of calcium and is used as a flux and in the making of opalescent and opaque glasses

**fluo·ro·car·bon** \,flùr-ō-'kär-bən, ,flōr-, ,flòr-\ *noun* (1937)
: any of various chemically inert compounds containing carbon and fluorine used chiefly as lubricants, refrigerants, nonstick coatings, and formerly aerosol propellants and in making resins and plastics; *also* : CHLOROFLUOROCARBON

**fluo·ro·chrome** \'flùr-ə-,krōm, ,flōr-, ,flòr-\ *noun* (1943)
: any of various fluorescent substances used in biological staining to produce fluorescence in a specimen

**fluo·rog·ra·phy** \flù-'rä-grə-fē, flō-, flō-\ *noun* (1941)
: PHOTOFLUOROGRAPHY
— **flu·o·ro·graph·ic** \,flùr-ə-'gra-fik, ,flōr-, ,flòr-\ *adjective*

**fluo·rom·e·ter** \flù-'rä-mə-tər, flō-, flō-\ *or* **fluo·rim·e·ter** \-'ri-\ *noun* (1897)
: an instrument for measuring fluorescence and related phenomena (as intensity of radiation)

— **fluo·ro·met·ric** *or* **fluo·ri·met·ric** \,flùr-ə-'me-trik, ,flōr-, ,flòr-\ *adjective*
— **fluo·rom·e·try** \flù-'rä-mə-trē, flō-, flō-\ *or* **fluo·rim·e·try** \-'ri-\ *noun*

¹**fluo·ro·scope** \'flùr-ə-,skōp, 'flōr-, 'flòr-\ *noun* [International Scientific Vocabulary] (1896)
: an instrument used for observing the internal structure of an opaque object (as the living body) by means of X rays
— **fluo·ro·scop·ic** \,flùr-ə-'skä-pik, ,flōr-, ,flòr-\ *adjective*
— **fluo·ro·scop·i·cal·ly** \-pi-k(ə-)lē\ *adverb*
— **fluo·ros·co·pist** \flù-'räs-kə-pist, flō-, flō-\ *noun*
— **fluo·ros·co·py** \-pē\ *noun*

²**fluoroscope** *transitive verb* **-scoped; -scop·ing** (1898)
: to examine by fluoroscopy

**fluo·ro·sis** \flù-'rō-səs, flō-\ *noun* [New Latin] (1927)
: an abnormal condition (as mottling of the teeth) caused by fluorine or its compounds
— **fluo·rot·ic** \-'rä-tik\ *adjective*

**fluo·ro·ura·cil** \,flùr-ō-'yùr-ə-,sil, -,səl, ,flōr-, ,flòr-\ *noun* [*fluor-* + *uracil*] (circa 1958)
: a fluorine-containing pyrimidine base $C_4H_3FN_2O_2$ used to treat some kinds of cancer

**fluor·spar** \'flùr-,spär, 'flōr-, 'flòr-\ *noun* (1794)
: FLUORITE

**flu·phen·azine** \flü-'fe-nə-,zēn\ *noun* [*fluor-* + *phenazine*] (circa 1960)
: a tranquilizing compound $C_{22}H_{26}F_3OS$ used especially combined as a salt

¹**flur·ry** \'flər-ē, 'flə-rē\ *noun, plural* **flurries** [probably from *flurr* (to throw scatteringly)] (1686)
**1 a** : a gust of wind **b** : a brief light snowfall
**2 a** : a brief period of commotion or excitement **b** : a sudden occurrence of many things at once : BARRAGE 2 ⟨a *flurry* of insults⟩
**3** : a brief advance or decline in prices : a short-lived outburst of trading activity

²**flurry** *verb* **flur·ried; flur·ry·ing** (1757)
*transitive verb*
: to cause to become agitated and confused
*intransitive verb*
: to move in an agitated or confused manner

¹**flush** \'fləsh\ *verb* [Middle English *flusshen*] (13th century)
*intransitive verb*
: to take wing suddenly
*transitive verb*
**1** : to cause (a bird) to flush
**2** : to expose or chase from a place of concealment ⟨*flushed* the boys from their hiding place⟩

²**flush** *noun* [Middle French *flus, fluz*, from Latin *fluxus* flow, flux] (circa 1529)
**1** : a hand of playing cards all of the same suit; *specifically* : a poker hand containing five cards of the same suit but not in sequence — see POKER illustration
**2** : a series of three or more slalom gates set vertically on a slope

³**flush** *noun* [perhaps modification of Latin *fluxus*] (1529)
**1** : a sudden flow (as of water); *also* : a rinsing or cleansing with or as if with a flush of water
**2 a** : a sudden increase or expansion; *especially* : sudden and usually abundant new plant growth **b** : a surge of emotion ⟨felt a *flush* of anger at the insult⟩
**3 a** : a tinge of red : BLUSH **b** : a fresh and vigorous state ⟨in the first *flush* of womanhood⟩
**4** : a transitory sensation of extreme heat — compare HOT FLASH

---

**⁴flush** (1548)
*intransitive verb*
**1 :** to flow and spread suddenly and freely
**2 a :** to glow brightly **b :** BLUSH
**3 :** to produce new growth ⟨the plants *flush* twice during the year⟩
*transitive verb*
**1 a :** to cause to flow **b :** to pour liquid over or through; *especially* : to cleanse or wash out with or as if with a rush of liquid ⟨*flush* the toilet⟩ ⟨*flush* the lungs with air⟩
**2 :** INFLAME, EXCITE — usually used passively ⟨*flushed* with pride⟩
**3 :** to cause to blush
**⁵flush** *adjective* (1594)
**1 a :** of a ruddy healthy color **b :** full of life and vigor : LUSTY
**2 a :** filled to overflowing **b :** AFFLUENT
**3 :** readily available : ABUNDANT
**4 a :** having or forming a continuous plane or unbroken surface ⟨*flush* paneling⟩ **b :** directly abutting or immediately adjacent: as (1) : set even with an edge of a type page or column : having no indention (2) : arranged edge to edge so as to fit snugly
**— flush·ness** *noun*
**⁶flush** *adverb* (1700)
**1 :** in a flush manner
**2 :** SQUARELY ⟨hit him *flush* on the chin⟩
**⁷flush** *transitive verb* (circa 1842)
**:** to make flush ⟨*flush* the headings on a page⟩
**flush·able** \'flə-shə-bəl\ *adjective* (1973)
**:** suitable for disposal by flushing down a toilet
**¹flus·ter** \'fləs-tər\ *verb* **flus·tered; flus·ter·ing** \-t(ə-)riŋ\ [probably of Scandinavian origin; akin to Icelandic *flaustur* hurry] (1604)
*transitive verb*
**1 :** to make tipsy
**2 :** to put into a state of agitated confusion : UPSET
*intransitive verb*
**:** to move or behave in an agitated or confused manner
**synonym** see DISCOMPOSE
**— flus·tered·ly** *adverb*
**²fluster** *noun* (1728)
**:** a state of agitated confusion
**¹flute** \'flüt\ *noun* [Middle English *floute*, from Middle French *fleute*, from Old French *flaüte*, probably from Old Provençal *flaut*] (14th century)
**1 a :** RECORDER 3 **b :** a keyed woodwind instrument consisting of a cylindrical tube which is stopped at one end and which has a side hole over which air is blown to produce the tone

flute 1b

and having a range from middle C upward for three octaves
**2 :** something long and slender: as **a :** a tall slender wineglass **b :** a grooved pleat (as on a hat brim)
**3 :** a rounded groove; *specifically* : one of the vertical parallel grooves on a classical architectural column
**— flute·like** \-,līk\ *adjective*
**— fluty** *or* **flut·ey** \'flü-tē\ *adjective*
**²flute** *verb* **flut·ed; flut·ing** (14th century)
*intransitive verb*
**1 :** to play a flute
**2 :** to produce a flutelike sound
*transitive verb*
**1 :** to utter with a flutelike sound
**2 :** to form flutes in
**— flut·er** *noun*
**flut·ed** *adjective* (1611)
**:** having or marked by grooves
**flut·ing** \'flü-tiŋ\ *noun* (1611)
**1 :** a series of flutes ⟨the *fluting* of a column⟩
**2 :** fluted material
**flut·ist** \'flü-tist\ *noun* (1603)

**:** one who plays a flute
**¹flut·ter** \'flə-tər\ *verb* [Middle English *floteren* to float, flutter, from Old English *floterian*, frequentative of *flotian* to float; akin to Old English *flēotan* to float — more at FLEET] (before 12th century)
*intransitive verb*
**1 :** to flap the wings rapidly
**2 a :** to move with quick wavering or flapping motions **b :** to vibrate in irregular spasms
**3 :** to move about or behave in an agitated aimless manner
*transitive verb*
**:** to cause to flutter
**— flut·ter·er** \-tər-ər\ *noun*
**— flut·tery** \-tə-rē\ *adjective*
**²flutter** *noun* (1641)
**1 :** an act of fluttering
**2 a :** a state of nervous confusion or excitement **b :** FLURRY, COMMOTION **c :** abnormal spasmodic fluttering of a body part ⟨treatment of atrial *flutter*⟩
**3 a :** a distortion in reproduced sound similar to but of a higher pitch than wow **b :** fluctuation in the brightness of a television image
**4 :** an unwanted oscillation (as of an aileron or a bridge) set up by natural forces
**5** *chiefly British* : a small speculative venture or gamble
**flut·ter·board** \'flə-tər-,bȯrd, -,bȯrd\ *noun* (1950)
**:** a rectangular board used by swimmers in practicing leg strokes
**flutter kick** *noun* (circa 1934)
**:** an alternating whipping motion of the legs used in various swimming styles (as the crawl)
**flutter sleeve** *noun* (1973)
**:** a loose-fitting tapered sleeve falling in folds over the upper arm
**flu·vi·al** \'flü-vē-əl\ *adjective* [Latin *fluvialis*, from *fluvius* river, from *fluere*] (14th century)
**1 :** of, relating to, or living in a stream or river
**2 :** produced by the action of a stream
**flu·vi·a·tile** \'flü-vē-ə-,tīl\ *adjective* [Middle French, from Latin *fluviatilis*, from *fluvius*] (1599)
**:** FLUVIAL
**¹flux** \'fləks\ *noun* [Middle English, from Middle French & Medieval Latin; Middle French, from Medieval Latin *fluxus*, from Latin, flow, from *fluere* to flow — more at FLUID] (14th century)
**1 :** a flowing of fluid from the body; *especially* : an excessive abnormal discharge from the bowels
**2 :** a continuous moving on or passing by (as of a stream)
**3 :** a continued flow : FLOOD
**4 a :** INFLUX **b :** CHANGE, FLUCTUATION ⟨in a state of *flux*⟩
**5 :** a substance used to promote fusion (as of metals or minerals); *especially* : one (as rosin) applied to surfaces to be joined by soldering, brazing, or welding to clean and free them from oxide and promote their union
**6 :** the rate of transfer of fluid, particles, or energy across a given surface
**²flux** (15th century)
*transitive verb*
**1 :** to cause to become fluid
**2 :** to treat with a flux
*intransitive verb*
**:** to become fluid : FUSE
**flux·gate** \'fləks-,gāt\ *noun* (1944)
**:** a device used to indicate the direction and intensity of the magnetic field (as on a planet)
**flux·ion** \'flək-shən\ *noun* (1599)
**1 :** the action of flowing or changing; *also* : something subjected to such action
**2 :** DERIVATIVE 3 — compare METHOD OF FLUXIONS
**— flux·ion·al** \-shnəl, -shə-nᵊl\ *adjective*
**¹fly** \'flī\ *verb* **flew** \'flü\; **flown** \'flōn\; **fly·ing** [Middle English *flien*, from Old English *flēogan*; akin to Old High German *fliogan* to

fly and probably Old English *flōwan* to flow] (before 12th century)
*intransitive verb*
**1 a :** to move in or pass through the air with wings **b :** to move through the air or before the wind or through outer space **c :** to float, wave, or soar in the air ⟨flags *flying* at half-mast⟩
**2 a :** to take flight : FLEE **b :** to fade and disappear : VANISH
**3 a :** to move, pass, or spread quickly ⟨rumors were *flying*⟩ **b :** to be moved with sudden extreme emotion ⟨*flew* into a rage⟩ **c :** to seem to pass quickly ⟨the time simply *flew*⟩
**4 :** to become expended or dissipated rapidly
**5 :** to operate or travel in an airplane or spacecraft
**6 :** to work successfully : win popular acceptance ⟨knew . . . a pure human-rights approach would not *fly* —Charles Brydon⟩
*transitive verb*
**1 a :** to cause to fly, float, or hang in the air ⟨*flying* a kite⟩ **b :** to operate (as a balloon, aircraft, rocket, or spacecraft) in flight **c :** to journey over or through by flying
**2 a :** to flee or escape from **b :** AVOID, SHUN
**3 :** to transport by aircraft or spacecraft
**— fly at :** to assail suddenly and violently
**— fly blind :** to fly an airplane solely by instruments
**— fly high :** to be elated
**— fly in the face of** *or* **fly in the teeth of :** to stand or act forthrightly or brazenly in defiance or contradiction of
**²fly** *noun, plural* **flies** (before 12th century)
**1 :** the action or process of flying : FLIGHT
**2 a :** a device consisting of two or more radial vanes capable of rotating on a spindle to act as a fan or to govern the speed of clockwork or very light machinery **b :** FLYWHEEL
**3** *plural* : the space over a theater stage where scenery and equipment can be hung
**4 :** something attached by one edge: as **a :** a garment closing concealed by a fold of cloth extending over the fastener **b** (1) : the length of an extended flag from its staff or support (2) : the outer or loose end of a flag
**5 :** a baseball hit high into the air
**6 :** FLYLEAF
**7 :** a sheet of material (as canvas) that is attachable to a tent for use as a double top or as a rooflike extension
**8 :** a football pass pattern in which the receiver runs straight downfield
**— on the fly 1 :** in motion : BUSY **2 :** while still in the air : without the ball bouncing ⟨the home run carried 450 feet *on the fly*⟩
**³fly** *intransitive verb* **flied; fly·ing** (1893)
**:** to hit a fly in baseball
**⁴fly** *noun, plural* **flies** [Middle English *flie*, from Old English *flēoge*; akin to Old High German *flioga* fly, Old English *flēogan* to fly] (before 12th century)
**1 :** a winged insect — used chiefly in combination ⟨may*flies*⟩ ⟨butter*fly*⟩
**2 a :** any of a large order (Diptera) of winged or rarely wingless insects (as the housefly, mosquito, or gnat) that have segmented often headless, eyeless, and legless larvae, the anterior wings functional, and the posterior wings reduced to halteres **b :** a large stout-bodied fly
**3 :** a fishhook dressed (as with feathers or tinsel) to suggest an insect
**— fly in the ointment :** a detracting factor or element
**⁵fly** *adjective* [probably from ¹*fly*] (1811)
*chiefly British* : KEEN, ARTFUL
**fly·able** \'flī-ə-bəl\ *adjective* (circa 1909)
**:** suitable for flying or for being flown
**fly agaric** *noun* (1788)
**:** a poisonous mushroom (*Amanita muscaria*) with a usually bright red cap
**fly ash** *noun* (1931)
**:** fine solid particles of ashes, dust, and soot carried out from burning fuel (as coal or oil) by the draft

**fly·away** \'flī-ə-ˌwā\ *adjective* (1844)
**1** : loose and flowing especially because of unconfined fullness at the back ⟨a *flyaway* jacket⟩
**2** : of, relating to, or being an aircraft that is ready to fly ⟨a *flyaway* price⟩

**fly ball** *noun* (1865)
: ²FLY 5

¹**fly·blow** \-ˌblō\ *transitive verb* **-blew; -blown** [⁴*fly* + ¹*blow*] (1603)
**1** : TAINT, CONTAMINATE
**2** : to deposit eggs or young larvae of a flesh fly or blowfly in

²**flyblow** *noun* (1825)
: FLY-STRIKE

**fly·blown** \'flī-ˌblōn\ *adjective* (circa 1529)
**1 a** : not pure : TAINTED ⟨a world *flyblown* with the vices of irresponsible power —V. L. Parrington⟩ **b** : not bright and new : SEEDY, MOTH-EATEN **c** : TRITE, HACKNEYED ⟨a long list of *flyblown* metaphors —*Horizon*⟩
**2 a** : infested with eggs or young larvae of a flesh fly or blowfly **b** : covered with flyspecks

**fly·boat** \-ˌbōt\ *noun* [modification of Dutch *vlieboot,* from *Vlie,* channel between North Sea & Wadden Zee + *boot* boat] (1577)
: any of various fast boats

**fly·boy** \'flī-ˌbȯi\ *noun* (1946)
: a member of the air force; *broadly* : an aircraft pilot

**fly·bridge** \'flī-ˌbrij\ *noun* (1965)
: an open deck on a cabin cruiser located above the bridge on the cabin roof and usually having a duplicate set of navigating equipment

**fly·by** \'flī-ˌbī\ *noun, plural* **flybys** (1953)
**1** : a prearranged usually low-altitude flight by one or more airplanes over a public gathering (as an air show)
**2 a** : a flight of a spacecraft past a celestial body (as Mars) close enough to obtain scientific data **b** : a spacecraft that makes a flyby

¹**fly–by–night** \'flī-bī-ˌnīt\ *noun* (1822)
**1** : one that seeks to evade responsibilities and especially creditors by flight
**2** : one without established reputation or standing; *especially* : a shaky business enterprise

²**fly–by–night** *adjective* (1914)
**1** : given to making a quick profit usually by shady or irresponsible acts
**2** : TRANSITORY, PASSING ⟨*fly-by-night* fashions⟩

**fly–by–night·er** \ˌflī-bī-ˈnī-tər\ *noun* (1946)
: FLY-BY-NIGHT

**fly–by–wire** \'flī-bī-ˌwīr\ *adjective* (1968)
: of, relating to, being, or utilizing a flight-control system in which controls are operated electrically rather than mechanically

**fly casting** *noun* (circa 1889)
: the casting of artificial flies in fly-fishing or as a competitive sport

**fly·catch·er** \'flī-ˌka-chər, -ˌke-\ *noun* (1678)
: any of various passerine birds (families Muscicapidae and Tyrannidae) that feed on insects taken on the wing

**fly dope** *noun* (1897)
: an insect repellent

**fly·er** *variant of* FLIER

**fly fisherman** *noun* (1886)
: an angler who uses the technique of fly-fishing

**fly–fish·ing** \'flī-ˌfi-shiŋ\ *noun* (1653)
: a method of fishing in which an artificial fly is cast by use of a fly rod, a reel, and a relatively heavy oiled or treated line

**fly front** *noun* (1893)
: a concealed closing on the front of a coat, skirt, shirt, dress, or pants
— **fly–front** \'flī-ˌfrənt\ *adjective*

**fly gallery** *noun* (1888)
: a narrow raised platform at the side of a theater stage from which flying scenery lines are operated

¹**fly·ing** \'flī-iŋ\ *adjective* (before 12th century)
**1 a** : moving or capable of moving in the air **b** : moving or made by moving rapidly ⟨*flying* feet⟩ ⟨a *flying* leap⟩ **c** : very brief

**2** : intended for ready movement or action ⟨a *flying* squad car⟩
**3** : having stylized wings — used especially of livestock brand marks
**4** : of or relating to the operation of aircraft ⟨a *flying* club⟩
**5** : traversed or to be traversed (as in speed-record trials) after a running start ⟨a *flying* kilometer⟩
— **with flying colors** : with complete or eminent success

²**flying** *noun* (1548)
**1** : travel by air
**2** : the operation of an aircraft or spacecraft

**flying boat** *noun* (1913)
: a seaplane with a hull designed for floating

**flying bomb** *noun* (1944)
*chiefly British* : BUZZ BOMB

**flying bridge** *noun* (circa 1909)
**1** : the highest navigational bridge on a ship
**2** : FLYBRIDGE

**flying buttress** *noun* (1669)
: a masonry structure that typically consists of a straight inclined bar carried on an arch and a solid pier or buttress against which it abuts and that receives the thrust of a roof or vault

**Flying Dutchman** *noun*
**1** : a legendary Dutch mariner condemned to sail the seas until Judgment Day
**2** : a spectral ship that according to legend haunts the seas near the Cape of Good Hope

**flying fish** *noun* (circa 1511)
: any of numerous fishes (family Exocoetidae) chiefly of tropical and warm seas that are capable of long gliding flights out of water by spreading their large pectoral fins like wings

**flying fox** *noun* (1759)
: FRUIT BAT

**flying gurnard** *noun* (1884)
: any of several marine fishes (family Dactylopteridae) that resemble gurnards and have large pectoral fins allowing them to glide above the water for short distances

**flying jib** *noun* (1711)
: a sail outside the jib on an extension of the jibboom — see SAIL illustration

**flying lemur** *noun* (1883)
: either of two East Indian or Philippine arboreal nocturnal mammals (*Cynocephalus volans* and *C. variegatus*) that are about the size of a cat, that make long gliding leaps using a broad fold of skin on each side attached to and extending between the limbs, and that are placed in a separate order (Dermoptera)

**flying machine** *noun* (1736)
: an apparatus for navigating the air

**flying mare** *noun* (1754)
: a wrestling maneuver in which the aggressor seizes his opponent's wrist, turns about, and jerks him over his back

**flying officer** *noun* (1913)
: a commissioned officer in the British air force who ranks with a first lieutenant in the army

**flying saucer** *noun* (1947)
: any of various unidentified flying objects usually described as being saucer-shaped or disk-shaped

**flying spot** *noun* (1933)
: a spot of light moved over a surface (as one bearing printing or an image) so that light reflected from or transmitted by different parts of the surface is translated into electrical signals for transmission (as in television or computers)

**1 flying buttress**

**flying squad** *noun* (1927)
: a usually small standby group of people ready to move or act swiftly; *especially* : a police unit formed to respond quickly in an emergency

**flying squirrel** *noun* (1624)
: either of two small nocturnal North American squirrels (*Glaucomys volans* and *G. sabrinus*) with folds of skin connecting the forelegs and hind legs that enable it to make long gliding leaps; *also* : any of various squirrels that possess a patagium

**flying start** *noun* (1851)
**1** : a start in racing in which the participants are already moving when they cross the starting line or receive the starting signal
**2** : a favorable start of something

**flying wedge** *noun* (1909)
: a moving formation (as of guards or police) resembling a wedge

**fly·leaf** \'flī-ˌlēf\ *noun, plural* **fly·leaves** \-ˌlēvz\ (1832)
: one of the free endpapers of a book

**fly·man** \-mən, -ˌman\ *noun* (1883)
: a worker in the flies of a theater who manipulates curtains and scenery

**fly net** *noun* (before 12th century)
: a net to exclude or keep off insects (as from a harness horse)

**fly·over** \'flī-ˌō-vər\ *noun* (1931)
**1** : FLYBY 1
**2** *British* : OVERPASS

**fly·pa·per** \-ˌpā-pər\ *noun* (1847)
: paper coated with a sticky often poisonous substance for killing flies

**fly·past** \-ˌpast\ *noun* (1914)
*chiefly British* : FLYBY 1

**fly rod** *noun* (1684)
: a light springy fishing rod used in fly casting

**flysch** \'flish\ *noun* [German dialect] (1853)
: a thick and extensive deposit largely of sandstone that is formed in a geosyncline adjacent to a rising mountain belt and is especially common in the Alpine region of Europe

**fly sheet** *noun* (1833)
**1** : a small loose advertising sheet : HANDBILL
**2** : a sheet of a folder, booklet, or catalog giving directions for the use of or information about the material that follows

**fly·speck** \'flī-ˌspek\ *noun* (circa 1847)
**1** : a speck made by fly excrement
**2** : something small and insignificant
— **flyspeck** *transitive verb*

**fly–strike** \-ˌstrīk\ *noun* (1940)
: infestation with fly maggots
— **fly–struck** \-ˌstrək\ *adjective*

**fly–swat·ter** \-ˌswä-tər\ *noun* (1917)
: a device for killing insects that consists of a flat piece of perforated rubber or plastic or fine-mesh wire netting attached to a handle

**fly·ti·er** \'flī-ˌtī-(ə)r\ *noun* [*fly* + *tier* (one that ties)] (1881)
: a person who makes flies for fishing

**flyt·ing** \'flī-tiŋ\ *noun* [Scots, literally, contention, gerund of *flyte* to contend, argue, from Middle English *fliten,* from Old English *flītan;* akin to Old High German *flīzan* to argue] (1508)
: a dispute or exchange of personal abuse in verse form

**fly·way** \'flī-ˌwā\ *noun* (1891)
: an established air route of migratory birds

**fly·weight** \-ˌwāt\ *noun* (1911)
: a boxer in a weight division having a maximum limit of 112 pounds — compare BANTAMWEIGHT

**fly·wheel** \-ˌhwēl, -ˌwēl\ *noun* (1784)
: a heavy wheel for opposing and moderating by its inertia any fluctuation of speed in the machinery with which it revolves; *also* : a

similar wheel used for storing kinetic energy (as for motive power)

**fly whisk** *noun* (1841)
: a whisk for brushing away flies

**FM** \'ef-,em\ *noun, often attributive* [*frequency modulation*] (1940)
: a broadcasting system using frequency modulation; *also* : a radio receiver of such a system

**FMN** \,ef-,em-'en\ *noun* [*flavin mononucleotide*] (circa 1953)
: a yellow crystalline phosphoric ester $C_{17}H_{21}N_4O_9P$ of riboflavin that is a coenzyme of several flavoprotein enzymes

**f-num·ber** \'ef-,nəm-bər\ *noun* [*focal length*] (circa 1903)
**1** : the ratio of the focal length to the aperture in an optical system
**2** : a number following the symbol f/ that expresses the effectiveness of the aperture of a camera lens in relation to brightness of image so that the smaller the number the brighter the image and therefore the shorter the exposure required

**¹foal** \'fōl\ *noun* [Middle English *fole*, from Old English *fola*; akin to Latin *pullus* young of an animal, Greek *pais* child — more at FEW] (before 12th century)
: a young animal of the horse family; *especially* : one under one year
— **in foal** : PREGNANT 3

**²foal** *intransitive verb* (14th century)
: to give birth to a foal

**¹foam** \'fōm\ *noun* [Middle English *fome*, from Old English *fām*; akin to Old High German *feim* foam, Latin *spuma* foam, *pumex* pumice] (before 12th century)
**1** : a light frothy mass of fine bubbles formed in or on the surface of a liquid: as **a** : a frothy mass formed in salivating or sweating **b** : a stabilized froth produced chemically or mechanically and used especially in fighting oil fires **c** : a material in a lightweight cellular form resulting from introduction of gas bubbles during manufacture
**2** : SEA
**3** : something resembling foam
— **foam·less** \-ləs\ *adjective*

**²foam** (before 12th century)
*intransitive verb*
**1 a** : to produce or form foam **b** : to froth at the mouth especially in anger; *broadly* : to be angry
**2** : to gush out in foam
**3** : to become covered with or as if with foam ⟨streets . . . *foaming* with life —Thomas Wolfe⟩
*transitive verb*
**1** : to cause to foam; *specifically* : to cause air bubbles to form in
**2** : to convert (as a plastic) into a foam
— **foam·able** \'fō-mə-bəl\ *adjective*
— **foam·er** \fō-mər\ *noun*

**foamed plastic** *noun* (1945)
: EXPANDED PLASTIC

**foam·flow·er** \'fōm-,flau̇(-ə)r\ *noun* (1895)
: an American woodland spring-flowering herb (*Tiarella cordifolia*) that has white flowers with very long stamens and no stem leaves — called also *false miterwort*

**foam rubber** *noun* (circa 1939)
: spongy rubber of fine texture made from latex by foaming (as by whipping) before vulcanization

**foamy** \'fō-mē\ *adjective* **foam·i·er; -est** (before 12th century)
**1** : covered with foam : FROTHY
**2** : full of, consisting of, or resembling foam
— **foam·i·ly** \-mə-lē\ *adverb*
— **foam·i·ness** \-mē-nəs\ *noun*

**¹fob** \'fäb\ *transitive verb* **fobbed; fob·bing** [Middle English *fobben*] (14th century)
*archaic* : DECEIVE, CHEAT

**²fob** *noun* [perhaps akin to German dialect *Fuppe* pocket] (1653)
**1** : WATCH POCKET

**2** : a short strap, ribbon, or chain attached especially to a pocket watch
**3** : an ornament attached to a fob chain

**fob off** *transitive verb* (1597)
**1** : to put off with a trick, excuse, or inferior substitute
**2** : to pass or offer (something spurious) as genuine
**3** : to put aside ⟨now *fob off* what once they would have welcomed eagerly —Walter Lippmann⟩

**fo·cac·cia** \fō-'kä-ch(ē-)ə\ *noun* [Italian, from Late Latin *focacia* (neuter plural), from Latin *focus* hearth] (1969)
: a flat Italian bread typically seasoned with herbs and olive oil

**fo·cal** \'fō-kəl\ *adjective* (1693)
: of, relating to, being, or having a focus
— **fo·cal·ly** \-kə-lē\ *adverb*

**focal infection** *noun* (circa 1923)
: a persistent bacterial infection of some organ or region; *especially* : one causing symptoms elsewhere in the body

**fo·cal·ize** \'fō-kə-,līz\ *verb* **-ized; -iz·ing** (1845)
*transitive verb*
**1** : to bring to a focus
**2** : LOCALIZE
*intransitive verb*
**1** : to come to a focus : CONCENTRATE
**2** : LOCALIZE
— **fo·cal·iza·tion** \,fō-kə-lə-'zā-shən\ *noun*

**focal length** *noun* (1753)
: the distance of a focus from the surface of a lens or curved mirror

**focal plane** *noun* (1889)
: a plane that is perpendicular to the axis of a lens or mirror and passes through the focus

**focal point** *noun* (1713)
: FOCUS 1a, 5a

**focal ratio** *noun* (1926)
: F-NUMBER

**fo'c'sle** *variant of* FORECASTLE

**¹fo·cus** \'fō-kəs\ *noun, plural* **fo·ci** \'fō-,sī *also* -,kī\ *also* **fo·cus·es** [New Latin, from Latin, hearth] (1644)
**1 a** : a point at which rays (as of light, heat, or sound) converge or from which they diverge or appear to diverge; *specifically* : the point where the geometrical lines or their prolongations conforming to the rays diverging from or converging toward another point intersect and give rise to an image after reflection by a mirror or refraction by a lens or optical system **b** : a point of convergence of a beam of particles (as electrons)
**2 a** : FOCAL LENGTH **b** : adjustment for distinct vision; *also* : the area that may be seen distinctly or resolved into a clear image **c** : a state or condition permitting clear perception or understanding ⟨tried to bring the issues into *focus*⟩ **d** : DIRECTION 6c
**3** : one of the fixed points that with the corresponding directrix defines a conic section
**4** : a localized area of disease or the chief site of a generalized disease or infection
**5 a** : a center of activity, attraction, or attention ⟨the *focus* of the meeting was drug abuse⟩ **b** : a point of concentration
**6** : the place of origin of an earthquake or moonquake
**7** : directed attention : EMPHASIS ◆
— **fo·cus·less** \-ləs\ *adjective*
— **in focus** : having or giving the proper sharpness of outline due to good focusing
— **out of focus** : not in focus

**²focus** *verb* **fo·cused** *also* **fo·cussed; fo·cus·ing** *also* **fo·cus·sing** (1775)
*transitive verb*
**1 a** : to bring into focus **b** : to adjust the focus of (as the eye or a lens)
**2** : to cause to be concentrated ⟨*focused* their attention on the most urgent problems⟩
**3** : to bring (as light rays) to a focus : CONCENTRATE

*intransitive verb*
**1** : to come to a focus : CONVERGE
**2** : to adjust one's eye or a camera to a particular range
**3** : to concentrate attention or effort
— **fo·cus·able** \-kə-sə-bəl\ *adjective*
— **fo·cus·er** *noun*

**fod·der** \'fä-dər\ *noun* [Middle English, from Old English *fōdor*; akin to Old High German *fuotar* food — more at FOOD] (before 12th century)
**1** : something fed to domestic animals; *especially* : coarse food for cattle, horses, or sheep
**2** : inferior or readily available material used to supply a heavy demand ⟨routine entertainment *fodder*⟩ ⟨*fodder* for gossip columnists⟩
— **fodder** *transitive verb*

**fod·gel** \'fä-jəl\ *adjective* [origin unknown] (1724)
*Scottish* : BUXOM

**foe** \'fō\ *noun* [Middle English *fo*, from Old English *fāh*, from *fāh*, adjective, hostile; akin to Old High German gi*fēh* hostile] (before 12th century)
**1** : one who has personal enmity for another
**2 a** : an enemy in war **b** : ADVERSARY, OPPONENT
**3** : one who opposes on principle ⟨a *foe* of needless expenditures⟩
**4** : something prejudicial or injurious

**foehn** *or* **föhn** \'fə(r)n, 'fēn, 'fān\ *noun* [German *Föhn*] (1861)
: a warm dry wind blowing down the side of a mountain

**foe·man** \'fō-mən\ *noun* (before 12th century)
: FOE 2

**foe·tal, foe·tus** *chiefly British variant of* FE·TAL, FETUS

**foe·tid** *variant of* FETID

**foeto-** *or* **foeti-** *chiefly British variant of* FETO-

**¹fog** \'fȯg, fäg\ *noun* [probably of Scandinavian origin; akin to Danish *fog* spray, shower] (1544)
**1 a** : vapor condensed to fine particles of water suspended in the lower atmosphere that differs from cloud only in being near the ground **b** : a fine spray or a foam for fire fighting
**2** : a murky condition of the atmosphere or a substance causing it
**3 a** : a state of confusion or bewilderment **b** : something that confuses or obscures ⟨hid behind a *fog* of rhetoric⟩
**4** : cloudiness or partial opacity in a developed photographic image caused by chemical action or stray radiation
— **fog·less** \-ləs\ *adjective*

**²fog** *verb* **fogged; fog·ging** (1599)
*transitive verb*

◇ WORD HISTORY
**focus** The Latin word *focus* meant "hearth, fireplace." In the spoken Latin of the Roman Empire, the word must have shifted to the more general meaning "fire" and then ousted the literary Latin word *ignis*. It is the sense "fire" that we see reflected in the Romance languages, where the offspring of *focus* include Italian *fuoco*, Spanish *fuego*, French *feu*, and Romanian *foc*. In the scientific Latin of treatises written in the 17th century, the classical Latin word *focus* reappears, used to refer to the point at which rays of light refracted by a lens converge. Because rays of sunlight when directed by a magnifying glass can produce enough heat to burn paper, a word meaning "fireplace" is quite appropriate metaphorically to describe their convergence point. From this optical sense of *focus* have arisen more extended senses in English such as "point of concentration" or "emphasis."

**1 :** to cover, envelop, or suffuse with or as if with fog ⟨*fog* the barns with pesticide⟩
**2 :** to make obscure or confusing ⟨accusations which *fogged* the real issues⟩
**3 :** to make confused
**4 :** to produce fog on (as a photographic film) during development
*intransitive verb*
**1 :** to become covered or thick with fog
**2 a :** to become blurred by a covering of fog or mist **b :** to become indistinct through exposure to light or radiation
**fog·bound** \ˈfȯg-ˌbau̇nd, ˈfäg-\ *adjective* (circa 1855)
**1 :** unable to move because of fog ⟨*fogbound* ship⟩
**2 :** covered with or surrounded by fog ⟨*fogbound* coast⟩
**fog·bow** \-ˌbō\ *noun* (1831)
**:** a nebulous arc or circle of white or yellowish light sometimes seen in fog
**fog·gage** \ˈfȯ-gij, ˈfä-\ *noun* [Scots, from Middle English (Scots) *fogage*, from Anglo Latin *fogagium*, from Middle English *fogge* second growth of grass + Medieval Latin *-agium* -age] (1786)
*Scottish* **:** a second growth of grass
**fog·gy** \ˈfȯ-gē, ˈfä-\ *adjective* **fog·gi·er; -est** (15th century)
**1 a :** filled or abounding with fog **b :** covered or made opaque by moisture or grime
**2 :** blurred or obscured as if by fog ⟨hadn't the *foggiest* notion⟩
— **fog·gi·ly** \ˈfȯ-gə-lē, ˈfä-\ *adverb*
— **fog·gi·ness** \ˈfȯ-gē-nəs, ˈfä-\ *noun*
**Foggy Bottom** *noun* [*Foggy Bottom*, district in Washington, D.C.] (1951)
**:** the U.S. Department of State
**fog·horn** \ˈfȯg-ˌhȯrn, ˈfäg-\ *noun* (1858)
**1 :** a horn (as on a ship) sounded in a fog to give warning
**2 :** a loud hoarse voice
**fo·gy** *also* **fo·gey** \ˈfō-gē\ *noun, plural* **fo·gies** *also* **fogeys** [origin unknown] (1780)
**:** a person with old-fashioned ideas — usually used with *old*
— **fo·gy·ish** \-gē-ish\ *adjective*
— **fo·gy·ism** \-gē-ˌi-zəm\ *noun*
**foi·ble** \ˈfȯi-bəl\ *noun* [obsolete French (now *faible*), from obsolete *foible* weak, from Old French *feble* feeble] (circa 1648)
**1 :** the part of a sword or foil blade between the middle and point
**2 :** a minor flaw or shortcoming in character or behavior **:** WEAKNESS
*synonym* see FAULT
**foie gras** \ˈfwä-ˈgrä\ *noun* [French, literally, fat liver] (1818)
**:** the fatted liver of an animal and especially of a goose usually served as a pâté
**¹foil** \ˈfȯi(ə)l\ *transitive verb* [Middle English, to trample, full cloth, from Middle French *fouler* — more at FULL] (14th century)
**1** *obsolete* **:** TRAMPLE
**2 a :** to prevent from attaining an end **:** DEFEAT **b :** to bring to naught **:** THWART
*synonym* see FRUSTRATE
**²foil** *noun* [Middle English, leaf, from Middle French *foille* (from Latin *folia*, plural of *folium*) & *foil*, from Latin *folium* — more at BLADE] (14th century)
**1 :** very thin sheet metal ⟨aluminum *foil*⟩
**2 :** a thin piece of material (as metal) put under an inferior or paste stone to add color or brilliance
**3 :** someone or something that serves as a contrast to another ⟨acted as a *foil* for a comedian⟩
**4 a :** an indentation between cusps in Gothic tracery **b :** one of several arcs that enclose a complex figure
**5 :** HYDROFOIL 1
**³foil** *noun* (15th century)
**1** *archaic* **:** DEFEAT
**2** *archaic* **:** the track or trail of an animal

**⁴foil** *noun* [origin unknown] (1594)
**1 :** a light fencing sword having a usually circular guard and a flexible blade of rectangular section tapering to a blunted point — compare ÉPÉE, SABER
**2 :** the art or sport of fencing with the foil — often used in plural
**⁵foil** *transitive verb* (1611)
**1 :** to back or cover with foil
**2 :** to enhance by contrast
**foiled** \ˈfȯi(ə)ld\ *adjective* (1835)
**:** ornamented with foils ⟨a *foiled* arch⟩
**foils·man** \ˈfȯi(ə)lz-mən\ *noun* (1927)
**:** one who fences with a foil
**¹foin** \ˈfȯin\ *intransitive verb* [Middle English, from *foin* fork for spearing fish, from Middle French *foisne*] (14th century)
*archaic* **:** to thrust with a pointed weapon **:** LUNGE
**²foin** *noun* (15th century)
*archaic* **:** a pass in fencing **:** LUNGE
**foi·son** \ˈfȯi-zᵊn\ *noun* [Middle English *foisoun*, from Middle French *foison*, from Latin *fusion-, fusio* pouring, effusion — more at FUSION] (14th century)
**1** *archaic* **:** rich harvest
**2** *chiefly Scottish* **:** physical energy or strength
**3** *plural, obsolete* **:** RESOURCES
**foist** \ˈfȯist\ *transitive verb* [probably from obsolete Dutch *vuisten* to take into one's hand, from Middle Dutch *vuysten*, from *vuyst* fist; akin to Old English *fȳst* fist] (circa 1587)
**1 a :** to introduce or insert surreptitiously or without warrant **b :** to force another to accept especially by stealth or deceit
**2 :** to pass off as genuine or worthy ⟨*foist* costly and valueless products on the public —Jonathan Spivak⟩
**fo·la·cin** \ˈfō-lə-sən\ *noun* [*folic acid* + *-in*] (1949)
**:** FOLIC ACID
**fo·late** \ˈfō-ˌlāt\ *noun* (1951)
**:** FOLIC ACID
**¹fold** \ˈfōld\ *noun* [Middle English, from Old English *falod*; akin to Old Saxon *faled* enclosure] (before 12th century)
**1 :** an enclosure for sheep
**2 a :** a flock of sheep **b :** a group of people or institutions that share a common faith, belief, activity, or enthusiasm
**²fold** *transitive verb* (before 12th century)
**:** to pen up or confine (as sheep) in a fold
**³fold** *verb* [Middle English, from Old English *fealdan*; akin to Old High German *faldan* to fold, Greek *diplasios* twofold] (before 12th century)
*transitive verb*
**1 :** to lay one part over another part of ⟨*fold* a letter⟩
**2 :** to reduce the length or bulk of by doubling over ⟨*fold* a tent⟩
**3 :** to clasp together **:** ENTWINE ⟨*fold* the hands⟩
**4 :** to clasp or enwrap closely **:** EMBRACE
**5 :** to bend (as a layer of rock) into folds
**6 a :** to incorporate (a food ingredient) into a mixture by repeated gentle overturnings without stirring or beating **b :** to incorporate closely
**7 a :** to concede defeat by withdrawing (one's cards) from play (as in poker) **b :** to bring to an end
*intransitive verb*
**1 :** to become doubled or pleated
**2 :** to fail completely **:** COLLAPSE; *especially* **:** to go out of business
**3 :** to fold one's cards (as in poker)
— **fold·able** \ˈfōl-də-bəl\ *adjective*
**⁴fold** *noun* (13th century)
**1 :** a part doubled or laid over another part **:** PLEAT
**2 :** something that is folded together or that enfolds
**3 a :** a bend or flexure produced in rock by forces operative after the depositing or consolidation of the rock **b** *chiefly British* **:** an undulation in the landscape

**4 :** a margin apparently formed by the doubling upon itself of a flat anatomical structure (as a membrane)
**5 :** a crease made by folding something (as a newspaper)
**-fold** \ˌfōld, ˈfōld\ *suffix* [Middle English, from Old English *-feald*; akin to Old High German *-falt* -fold, Latin *-plex, -plus*, Old English *fealdan*]
**1 :** multiplied by (a specified number) **:** times — in adjectives ⟨a six*fold* increase⟩ and adverbs ⟨repay you ten*fold*⟩
**2 :** having (so many) parts ⟨three*fold* aspect of the problem⟩
**fold·away** \ˈfōl-də-ˌwā\ *adjective* (1948)
**:** designed to be folded for storage or portability ⟨*foldaway* doors⟩ ⟨*foldaway* bed⟩ ⟨a *foldaway* table⟩
**fold·boat** \ˈfōl(d)-ˌbōt\ *noun* [translation of German *Faltboot*] (1938)
**:** a small collapsible canoe made of rubberized sailcloth stretched over a framework
**fold·er** \ˈfōl-dər\ *noun* (1552)
**1 :** one that folds
**2 :** a folded printed circular
**3 :** a folded cover or large envelope for holding or filing loose papers
**fol·de·rol** \ˈfäl-də-ˌräl\ *noun* [*fol-de-rol*, a nonsense refrain in songs] (1820)
**1 :** a useless ornament or accessory **:** TRIFLE
**2 :** NONSENSE
**fold·ing** \ˈfōl-diŋ\ *adjective* (15th century)
**:** capable of being folded into a more compact shape ⟨*folding* chairs⟩ ⟨a *folding* door⟩
**folding money** *noun* (circa 1930)
**:** PAPER MONEY
**fold·out** \ˈfōl-ˌdau̇t\ *noun, often attributive* (1950)
**:** a folded leaf in a publication (as a book) that is larger in some dimension than the page ⟨a *foldout* map⟩
**fo·li·a·ceous** \ˌfō-lē-ˈā-shəs\ *adjective* [Latin *foliaceus*, from *folium* leaf + *-aceus* -aceous] (1658)
**:** of, relating to, or resembling an ordinary green leaf as distinguished from a modified leaf (as a petal, bract, or scale)
**fo·li·age** \ˈfō-lē-ij *also* -lyij; ÷ˈfō-lij, ÷ˈfȯi-lij\ *noun* [Middle French *fuellage*, from *foille* leaf — more at FOIL] (1598)
**1 :** a representation of leaves, flowers, and branches for architectural ornamentation
**2 :** the aggregate of leaves of one or more plants
**3 :** a cluster of leaves, flowers, and branches
▢
— **fo·li·aged** \-lē-ijd *also* -lyijd; ÷ˈfō-lijd, ÷ˈfȯi-\ *adjective*
**foliage plant** *noun* (1862)
**:** a plant grown primarily for its decorative foliage
**fo·li·ar** \ˈfō-lē-ər\ *adjective* [French *foliaire*, from Latin *folium* leaf + French *-aire* -ar] (circa 1859)

▢ USAGE
**foliage** The disyllabic pronunciation \ˈfō-lij\ is very common. Some commentators insist that *foliage* requires a trisyllabic pronunciation because of its spelling, but words of a similar pattern such as *carriage* and *marriage* do not fall under their prescription. The pronunciation \ˈfȯi-lij\ is disapproved because it suggests the transposition of the *l* and *i* in the spelling. It is not as common as \ˈfō-lij\ and may be associated with the nonstandard spelling *foilage*.

\ə\ abut \ᵊ\ kitten \ər\ further \a\ ash \ā\ ace
\ä\ mop, mar \au̇\ out \ch\ chin \e\ bet \ē\ easy
\g\ go \i\ hit \ī\ ice \j\ job \ŋ\ sing \ō\ go
\ȯ\ law \ȯi\ boy \th\ thin \th\ the \ü\ loot \u̇\ foot
\y\ yet \zh\ vision *see also* Guide to Pronunciation

**:** of, relating to, or applied to leaves ⟨*foliar* sprays⟩

**fo·li·ate** \'fō-lē-ət, -,āt\ *adjective* [Latin *foliatus* leafy, from *folium* leaf — more at BLADE] (circa 1658)
**1 :** shaped like a leaf ⟨a *foliate* sponge⟩
**2 :** FOLIATED

**fo·li·at·ed** \-,ā-təd\ *adjective* (1650)
**1 :** composed of or separable into layers ⟨a *foliated* rock⟩
**2 :** ornamented with foils or a leaf design

**fo·li·a·tion** \,fō-lē-'ā-shən\ *noun* (circa 1623)
**1 a :** the process of forming into a leaf **b :** the state of being in leaf **c :** VERNATION
**2 :** the numbering of the leaves of a manuscript or early printed book
**3 a :** ornamentation with foliage **b :** a decoration resembling a leaf
**4 :** the enrichment of an opening by foils
**5 :** foliated texture

**fo·lic acid** \,fō-lik-\ *noun* [Latin *folium*] (1941)
**:** a crystalline vitamin $C_{19}H_{19}N_7O_6$ of the B complex that is used especially in the treatment of nutritional anemias — called also *pteroylglutamic acid*

**fo·lie à deux** \fȯ-lē-à-dœ̄, ,fä-lē-,ä-'də(r)\ *noun* [French, literally, double madness] (circa 1892)
**:** the presence of the same or similar delusional ideas in two persons closely associated with one another

¹**fo·lio** \'fō-lē-,ō\ *noun, plural* **fo·li·os** [Middle English, from Latin, ablative of *folium*] (1447)
**1 a :** a leaf especially of a manuscript or book **b :** a leaf number **c :** a page number **d :** an identifying reference in accounting used in posting
**2 a :** a sheet of paper folded once **b :** a case or folder for loose papers
**3 a :** the size of a piece of paper cut two from a sheet; *also :* paper or a page of this size **b :** a book printed on folio pages **c :** a book of the largest size
**4 :** a certain number of words taken as a unit or division in a document for purposes of measurement or reference

²**folio** *transitive verb* (1858)
**:** to put a serial number on each leaf or page of

**fo·li·ose** \'fō-lē-,ōs\ *adjective* [Latin *foliosus* leafy] (1758)
**:** having a flat, thin, and usually lobed thallus attached to the substratum ⟨*foliose* lichens⟩ — compare CRUSTOSE, FRUTICOSE

¹**folk** \'fōk\ *noun, plural* **folk** *or* **folks** [Middle English, from Old English *folc;* akin to Old High German *folc* people] (before 12th century)
**1** *archaic :* a group of kindred tribes forming a nation **:** PEOPLE
**2 :** the great proportion of the members of a people that determines the group character and that tends to preserve its characteristic form of civilization and its customs, arts and crafts, legends, traditions, and superstitions from generation to generation
**3** *plural :* a certain kind, class, or group of people ⟨old *folks*⟩ ⟨just plain *folk*⟩ ⟨country *folk*⟩ ⟨media *folk*⟩
**4** *folks plural :* people generally
**5** *folks plural :* the persons of one's own family; *especially :* PARENTS

²**folk** *adjective* (before 12th century)
**1 :** originating or traditional with the common people of a country or region and typically reflecting their lifestyle ⟨*folk* hero⟩ ⟨*folk* music⟩
**2 :** of or relating to the common people or to the study of the common people ⟨*folk* sociology⟩

**folk etymology** *noun* (1882)
**:** the transformation of words so as to give them an apparent relationship to other better-known or better-understood words (as in the change of Spanish *cucaracha* to English *cockroach*)

¹**folk·ie** *also* **folky** \'fō-kē\ *noun, plural* **folk·ies** (1965)
**:** a folk singer or instrumentalist

²**folkie** *or* **folky** *adjective* (1965)
**:** of or relating to folk music

**folk·ish** \'fō-kish\ *adjective* (1938)
**:** FOLKLIKE
— **folk·ish·ness** *noun*

**folk·life** \'fōk-,līf\ *noun* (1864)
**:** the traditions, activities, skills, and products (as handicrafts) of a particular people or group

**folk·like** \'fō-,klīk\ *adjective* (1939)
**:** having a folk character

**folk·lore** \'fōk-,klōr, -,klȯr\ *noun* (1846)
**1 :** traditional customs, tales, sayings, dances, or art forms preserved among a people
**2 :** a branch of knowledge that deals with folklore
**3 :** an often unsupported notion, story, or saying that is widely circulated
— **folk·lor·ic** \-,klȯr-ik, -,klȯr-\ *adjective*
— **folk·lor·ish** \-ish\ *adjective*
— **folk·lor·ist** \-ist\ *noun*
— **folk·lor·is·tic** \,fō-klȯr-'is-tik, -,klȯr-\ *adjective*

**folk mass** *noun* (1966)
**:** a mass in which traditional liturgical music is replaced by folk music

**folk medicine** *noun* (1878)
**:** traditional medicine as practiced nonprofessionally especially by people isolated from modern medical services and usually involving the use of plant-derived remedies on an empirical basis

**folk·moot** \'fōk-,müt\ *or* **folk·mote** \-,mōt\ *noun* [alteration of Old English *folcmōt, folcgemōt,* from *folc* people + *mōt, gemōt* meeting —, more at MOOT] (before 12th century)
**:** a general assembly of the people (as of a shire) in early England

**folk·sing·er** \-,siŋ-ər\ *noun* (1884)
**:** one who sings folk songs or sings in a style associated with folk songs
— **folk·sing·ing** \-,siŋ-iŋ\ *noun*

**folk song** *noun* (1847)
**:** a traditional or composed song typically characterized by stanzaic form, refrain, and simplicity of melody

**folksy** \'fōk-sē\ *adjective* **folks·i·er; -est** (1852)
**1 :** SOCIABLE, FRIENDLY
**2 :** informal, casual, or familiar in manner or style ⟨*folksy* humor⟩
— **folks·i·ly** \-sə-lē\ *adverb*
— **folks·i·ness** \-sē-nəs\ *noun*

**folk·tale** \'fōk-,tāl\ *noun* (1852)
**:** a characteristically anonymous, timeless, and placeless tale circulated orally among a people

**folk·way** \'fō-,kwā\ *noun* (circa 1906)
**:** a mode of thinking, feeling, or acting common to a given group of people; *especially :* a traditional social custom

**fol·li·cle** \'fä-li-kəl\ *noun* [New Latin *folliculus,* from Latin, diminutive of *follis* bag — more at FOOL] (1646)
**1 a :** a small anatomical cavity or deep narrow-mouthed depression **b :** a small lymph node **c :** a vesicle in the mammalian ovary that contains a developing egg surrounded by a covering of cells; *especially :* GRAAFIAN FOLLICLE
**2 :** a dry dehiscent one-celled many-seeded fruit (as of the milkweed) that has a single carpel and opens along one suture
— **fol·lic·u·lar** \fə-'li-kyə-lər, fä-\ *adjective*

**follicle mite** *noun* (1925)
**:** any of several minute mites (genus *Demodex*) parasitic in hair follicles

**follicle–stimulating hormone** *noun* (circa 1943)
**:** a hormone produced by the anterior lobe of the pituitary gland that stimulates the growth of the ovum-containing follicles in the ovary and activates sperm-forming cells

**fol·lic·u·li·tis** \fə-,li-kyə-'lī-təs\ *noun* [New Latin, from *folliculus* + *-itis*] (circa 1860)
**:** inflammation of one or more follicles especially of the hair

¹**fol·low** \'fä-(,)lō, -lə(-w)\ *verb* [Middle English *folwen,* from Old English *folgian;* akin to Old High German *folgēnoun* to follow] (before 12th century)
*transitive verb*
**1 :** to go, proceed, or come after ⟨*followed* the guide⟩
**2 a :** to engage in as a calling or way of life **:** PURSUE ⟨wheat-growing is generally *followed* here⟩ **b :** to walk or proceed along ⟨*follow* a path⟩
**3 a :** to be or act in accordance with ⟨*follow* directions⟩ **b :** to accept as authority **:** OBEY ⟨*followed* his conscience⟩
**4 a :** to pursue in an effort to overtake **b :** to seek to attain ⟨*follow* knowledge⟩
**5 :** to come into existence or take place as a result or consequence of ⟨disaster *followed* the blunder⟩
**6 a :** to come or take place after in time, sequence, or order **b :** to cause to be followed ⟨*followed* dinner with a liqueur⟩
**7 :** to copy after **:** IMITATE
**8 a :** to watch steadily ⟨*followed* the flight of the ball⟩ **b :** to keep the mind on ⟨*follow* a speech⟩ **c :** to attend closely to **:** keep abreast of ⟨*followed* his career with interest⟩ **d :** to understand the sense or logic of (as a line of thought)
*intransitive verb*
**1 :** to go or come after a person or thing in place, time, or sequence
**2 :** to result or occur as a consequence, effect, or inference ☆
— **as follows :** as comes next — used impersonally
— **follow one's nose 1 :** to go in a straight or obvious course **2 :** to proceed without plan or reflection **:** obey one's instincts
— **follow suit 1 :** to play a card of the same suit as the card led **2 :** to follow an example set

²**follow** *noun* (1870)
**1 :** the act or process of following
**2 :** forward spin given to a ball by striking it above center — compare DRAW, ENGLISH

**fol·low·er** \'fä-lə-wər\ *noun* (before 12th century)
**1 a :** one in the service of another **:** RETAINER **b :** one that follows the opinions or teachings of another **c :** one that imitates another
**2** *archaic :* one that chases
**3 :** a sheet added to the first sheet of an indenture or other deed
**4 :** a machine part that receives motion from another part
**5 :** a spring-loaded plate at the bottom of a firearm's magazine that angles cartridges for proper insertion into the chamber

---

☆ SYNONYMS
**Follow, succeed, ensue, supervene** mean to come after something or someone. FOLLOW may apply to a coming after in time, position, or logical sequence ⟨speeches *followed* the dinner⟩. SUCCEED implies a coming after immediately in a sequence determined by natural order, inheritance, election, or laws of rank ⟨she *succeeded* her father as head of the business⟩. ENSUE commonly suggests a logical consequence or naturally expected development ⟨after the talk a general discussion *ensued*⟩. SUPERVENE suggests the following or beginning of something unforeseen or unpredictable ⟨*supervening* events brought unhappiness to him⟩. See in addition CHASE.

**6 :** FAN, DEVOTEE ☆

**fol·low·er·ship** \-,ship\ *noun* (circa 1928)
**1 :** FOLLOWING
**2 :** the capacity or willingness to follow a leader

**¹fol·low·ing** \'fä-lə-wiŋ\ *adjective* (15th century)
**1 :** being next in order or time ⟨the *following* day⟩
**2 :** listed or shown next ⟨trains will leave at the *following* times⟩

**²following** *noun* (15th century)
**:** a group of followers, adherents, or partisans

**³following** *preposition* (circa 1926)
**:** SUBSEQUENT TO ⟨*following* the lecture tea was served⟩

**fol·low–on** \'fä-lə-,wȯn, -,wän\ *adjective* (1960)
**:** being or relating to something that follows as a natural or logical consequence, development, or progression
**— follow–on** *noun*

**follow out** *transitive verb* (1762)
**1 :** to follow to the end or to a conclusion
**2 :** CARRY OUT, EXECUTE ⟨*followed out* their orders⟩

**follow shot** *noun* (circa 1909)
**1 :** a shot in billiards or pool made by striking the cue ball above its center to cause it to continue forward after striking the object ball
**2 :** a camera shot in which the camera follows the movement of the subject

**fol·low–through** \'fä-lō-,thrü, ,fä-lō-', -lə-\ *noun* (circa 1899)
**1 :** the act or an instance of following through
**2 :** the part of the stroke following the striking of a ball

**follow through** *intransitive verb* (1895)
**1 :** to continue a stroke or motion to the end of its arc
**2 :** to press on in an activity or process especially to a conclusion

**¹fol·low–up** \'fä-lə-,wəp\ *noun* (1916)
**1 a :** the act or an instance of following up **b :** something that follows up
**2 :** maintenance of contact with or reexamination of a person (as a patient) especially following treatment
**3 :** a news story presenting new information on a story published earlier

**²follow–up** *adjective* (1912)
**1 :** of, relating to, or being something that follows up ⟨*follow-up* action by the police —Frank Faulkner⟩
**2 :** done, conducted, or administered in the course of following up persons ⟨*follow-up* care for discharged hospital patients⟩

**follow up** (1792)
*transitive verb*
**1 :** to follow with something similar, related, or supplementary ⟨*following up* his convictions with action —G. P. Merrill⟩
**2 :** to maintain contact with (a person) so as to monitor the effects of earlier activities or treatments
**3 :** to pursue in an effort to take further action ⟨the police *follow up* leads⟩
*intransitive verb*
**:** to take appropriate action ⟨*follow up* on complaints⟩

**fol·ly** \'fä-lē\ *noun, plural* **follies** [Middle English *folie*, from Old French, from *fol* fool] (13th century)
**1 :** lack of good sense or normal prudence and foresight
**2 a :** criminally or tragically foolish actions or conduct **b** *obsolete* **:** EVIL, WICKEDNESS; *especially* **:** lewd behavior
**3 :** a foolish act or idea
**4 :** an excessively costly or unprofitable undertaking
**5 :** an often extravagant picturesque building erected to suit a fanciful taste

**Fol·som** \'fōl-səm\ *adjective* [*Folsom*, town in New Mexico] (1928)

**:** of, relating to, or characteristic of a prehistoric culture of North America on the east side of the Rocky Mountains that is characterized by flint projectile points having a concave base with side projections and a longitudinal groove on each face

**fo·ment** \'fō-,ment, fō-'\ *transitive verb* [Middle English *fomenten* to apply a warm substance to, from Late Latin *fomentare*, from Latin *fomentum* compress, from *fovēre* to heat, soothe; akin to Lithuanian *degti* to burn, Sanskrit *dahati* it burns] (circa 1613)
**:** to promote the growth or development of **:** ROUSE, INCITE ⟨*foment* a rebellion⟩
**synonym** see INCITE
**— fo·ment·er** *noun*

**fo·men·ta·tion** \,fō-mən-'tā-shən, -,men-\ *noun* (14th century)
**1 a :** the application of hot moist substances to the body to ease pain **b :** the material so applied
**2 :** the act of fomenting **:** INSTIGATION

**¹fond** \'fänd\ *adjective* [Middle English, from *fonne* fool] (14th century)
**1 :** FOOLISH, SILLY ⟨*fond* pride⟩
**2 a :** prizing highly **:** DESIROUS ⟨*fond* of praise⟩ **b :** having an affection or liking — used with *of* ⟨*fond* of music⟩
**3 a :** foolishly tender **:** INDULGENT ⟨a *fond* mother⟩ **b :** AFFECTIONATE, LOVING ⟨absence makes the heart grow *fonder*⟩
**4 :** cherished with great affection **:** doted on ⟨our *fondest* hopes⟩

**²fond** *intransitive verb* (1530)
*obsolete* **:** to lavish affection **:** DOTE

**³fond** \'fō\ *noun, plural* **fonds** \'fō(z)\ [French, from Latin *fundus* bottom, piece of property — more at BOTTOM] (1664)
**1 :** BACKGROUND, BASIS
**2** *obsolete* **:** FUND

**fon·dant** \'fän-dənt\ *noun* [French, from present participle of *fondre* to melt — more at FOUND] (1877)
**1 :** a soft creamy preparation of sugar, water, and flavorings that is used as a basis for candies or icings
**2 :** a candy consisting chiefly of fondant

**fon·dle** \'fän-dəl\ *verb* **fon·dled; fon·dling** \-(d)liŋ, -dəl-iŋ\ [frequentative of obsolete *fond* to fondle] (1694)
*transitive verb*
**1** *obsolete* **:** PAMPER
**2 :** to handle tenderly, lovingly, or lingeringly **:** CARESS
*intransitive verb*
**:** to show affection or desire by caressing
**— fon·dler** \-(d)lər, -dəl-ər\ *noun*

**fond·ly** \'fän-(d)lē\ *adverb* (14th century)
**1** *archaic* **:** in a foolish manner **:** FOOLISHLY
**2 :** in a fond manner **:** AFFECTIONATELY
**3 :** in a willingly credulous manner ⟨it would stun, I *fondly* hoped, the reader —Annie Dillard⟩

**fond·ness** \'fän(d)-nəs\ *noun* (14th century)
**1** *obsolete* **:** FOOLISHNESS, FOLLY
**2 :** tender affection
**3 :** APPETITE, RELISH ⟨had a *fondness* for argument⟩

**fon·due** *also* **fon·du** \fän-'dü, -'dyü, 'fän-\ *noun* [French *fondue*, from feminine of *fondu*, past participle of *fondre* to melt] (1878)
**1 a** (1) **:** a preparation of melted cheese (as Swiss cheese and Gruyère) usually flavored with white wine and kirsch (2) **:** a dish that consists of small pieces of food (as meat or fruit) cooked in or dipped into a hot liquid ⟨beef *fondue*⟩ ⟨chocolate *fondue*⟩ **b :** a chafing dish in which fondue is made
**2 :** a dish similar to a soufflé usually made with cheese and bread crumbs

**F₁ layer** \'ef-'wən-\ *noun* (1933)
**:** the lower of the two layers into which the F region of the ionosphere splits in the daytime that occurs at varying heights from about 80 to 120 miles (130 to 200 kilometers) above the earth's surface

**¹font** \'fänt\ *noun* [Middle English, from Old English, from Late Latin *font-, fons,* from Latin, fountain] (before 12th century)
**1 a :** a receptacle for baptismal water **b :** a receptacle for holy water **c :** a receptacle for various liquids
**2 :** SOURCE, FOUNTAIN ⟨a *font* of information⟩
**— font·al** \'fän-tᵊl\ *adjective*

**²font** *noun* [Middle French *fonte* act of founding, from (assumed) Vulgar Latin *fundita*, feminine of *funditus*, past participle of Latin *fundere* to found, pour — more at FOUND] (circa 1688)
**:** an assortment or set of type all of one size and style

**fon·ta·nel** *or* **fon·ta·nelle** \,fän-tᵊn-'el, 'fän-tᵊn-,\ *noun* [Middle English *fontinelle* a bodily hollow or pit, from Middle French *fontenele*, diminutive of *fontaine* fountain] (1741)
**:** a membrane-covered opening in bone or between bones; *specifically* **:** any of the spaces closed by membranous structures between the uncompleted angles of the parietal bones and the neighboring bones of a fetal or young skull

**fon·ti·na** \fän-'tē-nə\ *noun, often capitalized* [Italian] (1938)
**:** a cheese that is semisoft to hard in texture and mild to medium sharp in flavor

**food** \'füd\ *noun, often attributive* [Middle English *fode*, from Old English *fōda;* akin to Old High German *fuotar* food, fodder, Latin *panis* bread, *pascere* to feed] (before 12th century)
**1 a :** material consisting essentially of protein, carbohydrate, and fat used in the body of an organism to sustain growth, repair, and vital processes and to furnish energy; *also* **:** such food together with supplementary substances (as minerals, vitamins, and condiments) **b :** inorganic substances absorbed by plants in gaseous form or in water solution
**2 :** nutriment in solid form
**3 :** something that nourishes, sustains, or supplies ⟨*food* for thought⟩
**— food·less** \-ləs\ *adjective*
**— food·less·ness** *noun*

**food chain** *noun* (1926)
**:** an arrangement of the organisms of an ecological community according to the order of predation in which each uses the next usually lower member as a food source

**food·ie** \'fü-dē\ *noun* (1982)
**:** a person having an avid interest in the latest food fads

**foo dog** \'fü-\ *noun, often F capitalized* [Chinese (Beijing) *fó* Buddha; from the use of such figures in ceramic or stone as guardians of Buddhist temples] (1953)
**:** a mythical lion-dog used as a decorative motif in Far Eastern art

**food poisoning** *noun* (1887)
**:** an acute gastrointestinal disorder caused by bacteria or their toxic products or by chemical residues in food

**food processor** *noun* (1974)

---

☆ **SYNONYMS**
**Follower, adherent, disciple, partisan** mean one who gives full loyalty and support to another. FOLLOWER may apply to people who attach themselves either to the person or beliefs of another ⟨an evangelist and his *followers*⟩. ADHERENT suggests a close and persistent attachment ⟨*adherents* to Marxism⟩. DISCIPLE implies a devoted allegiance to the teachings of one chosen as a master ⟨*disciples* of Gandhi⟩. PARTISAN suggests a zealous often prejudiced attachment ⟨*partisans* of the President⟩.

---

\ə\ **abut** \ᵊ\ **kitten** \ər\ **further** \a\ **ash** \ā\ **ace** \ä\ **mop, mar** \au̇\ **out** \ch\ **chin** \e\ **bet** \ē\ **easy** \g\ **go** \i\ **hit** \ī\ **ice** \j\ **job** \ŋ\ **sing** \ō\ **go** \ȯ\ **law** \ȯi\ **boy** \th\ **thin** \t̲h̲\ **the** \ü\ **loot** \u̇\ **foot** \y\ **yet** \zh\ **vision** *see also* Guide to Pronunciation

: an electric kitchen appliance with a set of interchangeable blades revolving inside a container

**food pyramid** *noun* (1949)
: an ecological hierarchy of food relationships in which a chief predator is at the top, each level preys on the next lower level, and usually green plants are at the bottom

**food stamp** *noun* (1940)
: a government-issued coupon that is sold or given to low-income persons and is redeemable for food

**food·stuff** \'füd-,stəf\ *noun* (1872)
: a substance with food value; *specifically* : the raw material of food before or after processing

**food vacuole** *noun* (circa 1889)
: a membrane-bound vacuole (as in an amoeba) in which ingested food is digested — see AMOEBA illustration

**food·ways** \'füd-,wāz\ *noun plural* (1946)
: the eating habits and culinary practices of a people, region, or historical period

**food web** *noun* (1949)
: the totality of interacting food chains in an ecological community

**foo·fa·raw** \'fü-fə-,ró\ *noun* [origin unknown] (1934)
**1** : frills and flashy finery
**2** : a disturbance or to-do over a trifle : FUSS

¹**fool** \'fül\ *noun* [Middle English, from Old French *fol*, from Late Latin *follis*, from Latin, bellows, bag; akin to Old High German *bolla* blister, *balg* bag — more at BELLY] (13th century)
**1** : a person lacking in judgment or prudence
**2 a** : a retainer formerly kept in great households to provide casual entertainment and commonly dressed in motley with cap, bells, and bauble **b** : one who is victimized or made to appear foolish : DUPE
**3 a** : a harmlessly deranged person or one lacking in common powers of understanding **b** : one with a marked propensity or fondness for something ⟨a dancing *fool*⟩ ⟨a *fool* for candy⟩
**4** : a cold dessert of pureed fruit mixed with whipped cream or custard

²**fool** *adjective* (13th century)
: FOOLISH, SILLY ⟨barking its *fool* head off⟩

³**fool** (1593)
*intransitive verb*
**1 a** : to behave foolishly ⟨why old men *fool* and children calculate —Shakespeare⟩ — often used with *around* **b** : to meddle, tamper, or experiment especially thoughtlessly or ignorantly ⟨don't *fool* with that gun⟩ — often used with *around*
**2 a** : to play or improvise a comic role **b** : to speak in jest : JOKE ⟨I was only *fooling*⟩
**3** : to contend or fight without serious intent or with less than full strength : TOY ⟨a dangerous man to *fool* with⟩
*transitive verb*
**1** : to make a fool of : DECEIVE
**2** *obsolete* : INFATUATE
**3** : to spend on trifles or without advantage : FRITTER — used with *away*

**fool around** *intransitive verb* (1837)
**1** : to spend time idly, aimlessly, or frivolously
**2** : to engage in casual sexual activity

**fool·ery** \'fül-rē, 'fü-lə-\ *noun, plural* **-er·ies** (1552)
**1** : a foolish act, utterance, or belief
**2** : foolish behavior

**fool·har·dy** \'fül-,här-dē\ *adjective* (13th century)
: foolishly adventurous and bold : RASH
**synonym** see ADVENTUROUS
— **fool·har·di·ly** \-,här-d°l-ē\ *adverb*
— **fool·har·di·ness** \-,här-dē-nəs\ *noun*

**fool·ish** \'fü-lish\ *adjective* (13th century)
**1** : lacking in sense, judgment, or discretion
**2 a** : ABSURD, RIDICULOUS **b** : marked by a loss of composure : NONPLUSSED, ABASHED
**3** : INSIGNIFICANT, TRIFLING, HUMBLE
**synonym** see SIMPLE

— **fool·ish·ly** *adverb*
**fool·ish·ness** *noun* (15th century)
**1** : foolish behavior : FOLLY
**2** : a foolish act or idea

**fool·proof** \'fül-,prüf\ *adjective* (1902)
: so simple, plain, or reliable as to leave no opportunity for error, misuse, or failure ⟨a *foolproof* plan⟩

**fools·cap** *also* **fool's cap** \'fül-,skap\ *noun* (1632)
**1** : a cap or hood usually with bells worn by jesters
**2** : a conical cap for slow or lazy students
**3** *usually* **foolscap** [from the watermark of a foolscap formerly applied to such paper] : a size of paper formerly standard in Great Britain; *broadly* : a piece of writing paper

**fool's gold** *noun* (1872)
: PYRITE; *broadly* : any of various pyritic minerals resembling gold

foolscap 1

**fool's paradise** *noun* (15th century)
: a state of delusory happiness

**fool's parsley** *noun* (1755)
: a poisonous European weed (*Aethusa cynapium*) of the carrot family that resembles parsley and is naturalized in the northern U.S. and southern Canada

¹**foot** \'fut\ *noun, plural* **feet** \'fēt\ *also* **foot** [Middle English *fot*, from Old English *fōt*; akin to Old High German *fuot* foot, Latin *ped-, pes*, Greek *pod-, pous*] (before 12th century)
**1** : the terminal part of the vertebrate leg upon which an individual stands
**2** : an invertebrate organ of locomotion or attachment; *especially* : a ventral muscular surface or process of a mollusk — see CLAM illustration
**3** : any of various units of length based on the length of the human foot; *especially* : a unit equal to ⅓ yard and comprising 12 inches — plural *foot* used between a number and a noun ⟨a 10-*foot* pole⟩; plural *feet* or *foot* used between a number and an adjective ⟨6 *feet* tall⟩; see WEIGHT table
**4** : the basic unit of verse meter consisting of any of various fixed combinations or groups of stressed and unstressed or long and short syllables
**5 a** : motion or power of walking or running : STEP ⟨fleet of *foot*⟩ **b** : SPEED, SWIFTNESS ⟨showed early *foot*⟩
**6** : something resembling a foot in position or use: as **a** : the lower end of the leg of a chair or table **b** (1) : the basal portion of the sporogonium in mosses (2) : a specialized outgrowth by which the embryonic sporophyte of many ferns and related plants and some seed plants absorbs nourishment from the gametophyte **c** : a piece on a sewing machine that presses the cloth against the feed
**7** *foot plural, chiefly British* : INFANTRY
**8** : the lower edge (as of a sail)
**9** : the lowest part : BOTTOM ⟨the *foot* of the hill⟩
**10 a** : the end that is lower or opposite the head ⟨the *foot* of the bed⟩ **b** : the part (as of a stocking) that covers the foot
**11 foots** *plural but singular or plural in construction* : material deposited especially in aging or refining : DREGS
**12 foots** *plural* : FOOTLIGHTS
— **at one's feet** : under one's spell or influence
— **foot in the door** : the initial step toward a goal
— **off one's feet** : in a sitting or lying position
— **on foot** : by walking or running ⟨tour the campus *on foot*⟩
— **on one's feet 1** : in a standing position
**2** : in an established position or state **3** : in a

recovered condition (as from illness) ⟨back *on my feet*⟩ **4** : in an extemporaneous manner : while in action ⟨good debaters can think *on their feet*⟩
— **to one's feet** : to a standing position ⟨brought the crowd *to its feet*⟩

²**foot** (15th century)
*intransitive verb*
**1** : DANCE
**2** : to go on foot
**3** *of a sailboat* : to make speed : MOVE
*transitive verb*
**1 a** : to perform the movements of (a dance) **b** : to walk, run, or dance on, over, or through
**2** *archaic* **a** : KICK **b** : REJECT
**3** *archaic* : ESTABLISH
**4 a** : to add up **b** : to pay or stand credit for ⟨*foot* the bill⟩
**5** : to make or renew the foot of (as a stocking)

**foot·age** \'fu-tij\ *noun* (1892)
: length or quantity expressed in feet: as **a** : BOARD FEET **b** : the total number of running feet of motion-picture film used (as for a scene or subject); *also* : the material contained on such footage

**foot–and–mouth disease** *noun* (1862)
: an acute contagious febrile virus disease especially of cloven-footed animals marked by ulcerating vesicles in the mouth, about the hooves, and on the udder and teats — called also *foot-and-mouth, hoof-and-mouth disease*

**foot·ball** \'fut-,ból\ *noun* (15th century)
**1** : any of several games played between two teams on a rectangular field having two goalposts at each end and whose object is to get the ball over a goal line or between goalposts by running, passing, or kicking: as **a** *British* : SOCCER **b** *British* : RUGBY **c** : an American game played between two teams of 11 players each in which the ball is in possession of one side at a time and is advanced by running or passing **d** *Australian* : AUSTRALIAN RULES FOOTBALL **e** *Canadian* : CANADIAN FOOTBALL
**2 a** : an inflated oval ball used in the game of football **b** *British* : a soccer ball
**3** : something treated roughly especially as the subject of a prolonged dispute ⟨the issue became a political *football* in Congress⟩
— **foot·ball·er** \-,bó-lər\ *noun*

**foot·bath** \'fut-,bath, -,bäth\ *noun* (1599)
: a bath (as at the entrance to an indoor swimming pool) for cleansing, warming, or disinfecting the feet

**foot·board** \'fut-,bórd, -,bòrd\ *noun* (1766)
**1** : a narrow platform on which to stand or brace the feet
**2** : a board forming the foot of a bed

**foot·boy** \-,bói\ *noun* (1590)
: a serving boy : PAGE, ATTENDANT

**foot·bridge** \'fut-,brij\ *noun* (14th century)
: a bridge for pedestrians

**foot–can·dle** \-'kan-d°l\ *noun* (1906)
: a unit of illuminance on a surface that is everywhere one foot from a uniform point source of light of one candle and equal to one lumen per square foot

**foot·cloth** \-,klóth\ *noun* (14th century)
**1** *archaic* : an ornamental cloth draped over the back of a horse to reach the ground on each side
**2** : CARPET

**foot·drag·ger** \-,dra-gər\ *noun* (1957)
: one who engages in foot-dragging

**foot–drag·ging** \-,dra-giŋ\ *noun* (1952)
: failure to act with the necessary promptness or vigor

**foot·ed** \'fu-təd\ *adjective* (14th century)
: having a foot or feet especially of a specified kind or number — often used in combination ⟨a four-*footed* animal⟩

**foot·er** \'fu-tər\ *noun* (1608)
*archaic* : PEDESTRIAN

**-foot·er** \'fu-tər\ *noun combining form*
: one that is a specified number of feet in height, length, or breadth ⟨a six-*footer*⟩

**foot·fall** \'fut-,fol\ *noun* (1610)
: the sound of a footstep

**foot fault** *noun* (1886)
: an infraction of the service rules (as in tennis, racquetball, or volleyball) that results from illegal placement of the server's feet
— **foot-fault** \'fut-,folt\ *intransitive verb*

**foot·gear** \'fut-,gir\ *noun* (1837)
: FOOTWEAR

**foot·hill** \-,hil\ *noun* (1850)
**1** : a hill at the foot of higher hills
**2** *plural* : a hilly region at the base of a mountain range

**foot·hold** \-,hōld\ *noun* (1625)
**1** : a hold for the feet : FOOTING
**2** : a position usable as a base for further advance

**foot·ing** \'fu-tiŋ\ *noun* (14th century)
**1** : a stable position or placing of the feet
**2** : a surface or its condition with respect to one walking or running on it; *especially* : the condition of a racetrack
**3** : the act of moving on foot : STEP, TREAD
**4 a** : a place or space for standing : FOOTHOLD **b** : established position : STATUS; *especially* : position or rank in relation to others ⟨they all started off on an equal *footing*⟩
**5** : BASIS
**6** : terms of social intercourse
**7** : an enlargement at the lower end of a foundation wall, pier, or column to distribute the load
**8** : the sum of a column of figures

**foot·lam·bert** \'fut-,lam-bərt\ *noun* (1925)
: a unit of luminance equal to the luminance of a perfectly diffusing surface that emits or reflects one lumen per square foot

**foo·tle** \'fü-t³l\ *intransitive verb* **foo·tled**; **foo·tling** \-t³l-iŋ, 'füt-liŋ\ [alteration of *footer* (to footle)] (1892)
**1** : to talk or act foolishly
**2** : to waste time : TRIFLE, FOOL
— **footle** *noun*
— **foo·tler** \-t³l-ər, 'füt-lər\ *noun*

**foot·less** \'fut-ləs\ *adjective* (14th century)
**1 a** : having no feet **b** : lacking foundation : UNSUBSTANTIAL
**2** : STUPID, INEPT
— **foot·less·ly** *adverb*
— **foot·less·ness** *noun*

**foot·lights** \-,līts\ *noun plural* (circa 1839)
**1** : a row of lights set across the front of a stage floor
**2** : the stage as a profession

**foo·tling** \'fü-t³l-iŋ, 'füt-liŋ\ *adjective* [*footle*] (circa 1897)
**1** : lacking judgment or ability : INEPT ⟨*footling* amateurs who understand nothing —E. R. Bentley⟩
**2** : lacking use or value : TRIVIAL

**foot·lock·er** \'fut-,lä-kər\ *noun* (circa 1942)
: a small trunk designed to be placed at the foot of a bed (as in a barracks)

**foot·loose** \-,lüs\ *adjective* (1873)
: having no ties : free to move about

**foot·man** \-mən\ *noun* (14th century)
**1 a** *archaic* : a traveler on foot : PEDESTRIAN **b** : INFANTRYMAN
**2 a** : a servant in livery formerly attending a rider or required to run in front of his master's carriage **b** : a servant who serves at table, tends the door, and runs errands

**foot·mark** \-,märk\ *noun* (1826)
: FOOTPRINT

**¹foot·note** \-,nōt\ *noun* (1822)
**1** : a note of reference, explanation, or comment usually placed below the text on a printed page
**2** : something that is subordinately related to a larger event or work : COMMENTARY ⟨that biography is an illuminating *footnote* to our times⟩

**²footnote** *transitive verb* (1864)
: to furnish with a footnote : ANNOTATE

**foot·pace** \'fut-,pās\ *noun* (1538)
**1** : a walking pace
**2** : PLATFORM, DAIS

**¹foot·pad** \-,pad\ *noun* [*foot* + *pad* (highwayman)] (1683)
: one who robs a pedestrian

**²footpad** *noun* [*foot* + ¹*pad*] (1966)
: a flattish foot on the leg of a spacecraft for distributing weight to minimize sinking into a surface

**foot·path** \'fut-,path, -,pàth\ *noun* (1526)
: a narrow path for pedestrians

**foot–pound** \-'paůnd\ *noun, plural* **foot–pounds** (1850)
: a unit of work equal to the work done by a force of one pound acting through a distance of one foot in the direction of the force

**foot–pound–second** *adjective* (1892)
: being or relating to a system of units based upon the foot as the unit of length, the pound as the unit of weight and the second as the unit of time — abbreviation *fps*

**foot·print** \'fut-,print\ *noun* (1552)
**1** : an impression of the foot on a surface
**2** : the area on a surface covered by something ⟨a tire with a wide *footprint*⟩ ⟨the *footprint* of a laser beam on the surface of a planet⟩

**foot·race** \-,rās\ *noun* (1663)
: a race run by humans on foot

**foot·rest** \-,rest\ *noun* (1861)
: a support for the feet

**foot·rope** \-,rōp\ *noun* (1772)
**1** : the part of a boltrope sewed to the lower edge of a sail
**2** : a rope rigged below a yard for men to stand on

**foot rot** *noun* (1807)
**1** : a progressive inflammation of the feet of sheep or cattle that is associated with bacterial infection
**2** : a plant disease marked by rot of the stem near the ground

**foot·sie** *or* **foot·sy** \'fut-sē\ *noun* [diminutive of ¹*foot*] (1944)
**1** : a furtive flirtatious caressing with the feet (as under a table)
**2** : a usually surreptitious cooperation or negotiation with someone supposed hostile to one's own interests — usually used with *play*

**foot·slog** \'fut-,släg\ *intransitive verb* (1899)
: to march or tramp through mud
— **foot·slog·ger** *noun*

**foot soldier** *noun* (1622)
: INFANTRYMAN

**foot·sore** \'fut-,sōr, -,sòr\ *adjective* (1719)
: having sore or tender feet (as from much walking)
— **foot·sore·ness** *noun*

**foot·step** \-,step\ *noun* (13th century)
**1** : the mark of the foot : TRACK
**2 a** : TREAD **b** : distance covered by a step : PACE
**3** : a step on which to ascend or descend
**4** : a way of life, conduct, or action ⟨followed in his father's *footsteps*⟩

**foot·stone** \-,stōn\ *noun* (1724)
: a stone placed at the foot of a grave

**foot·stool** \-,stül\ *noun* (1530)
: a low stool used to support the feet

**foot·wall** \-,wòl\ *noun* (1860)
**1** : the lower underlying wall of a vein, ore deposit, or coal seam in a mine
**2** : the lower wall of an inclined fault

**foot·way** \-,wā\ *noun* (15th century)
: a narrow way or path for pedestrians

**foot·wear** \-,war, -,wer\ *noun* (1881)
: wearing apparel (as shoes or boots) for the feet

**foot·work** \-,wərk\ *noun* (1895)
**1** : the management of the feet (as in boxing); *also* : the work done with them
**2** : the activity of moving from place to place ⟨the investigation entailed a lot of *footwork*⟩
**3** : active and adroit maneuvering to achieve an end ⟨fancy political *footwork*⟩

**¹foo·zle** \'fü-zəl\ *noun* (1890)
: an act of foozling; *especially* : a bungling golf stroke

**²foozle** *transitive verb* **foo·zled**; **foo·zling** \'füz-liŋ, 'fü-zə-\ [perhaps from German dialect *fuseln* to work carelessly] (1892)
: to manage or play awkwardly : BUNGLE

**¹fop** \'fäp\ *noun* [Middle English; akin to Middle English *fobben* to deceive, Middle High German *voppen*] (15th century)
**1** *obsolete* : a foolish or silly person
**2** : a man who is devoted to or vain about his appearance or dress : COXCOMB, DANDY

**²fop** *transitive verb* **fopped**; **fop·ping** (1602)
*obsolete* : FOOL, DUPE

**fop·pery** \'fä-p(ə-)rē\ *noun, plural* **-per·ies** (1546)
**1** : foolish character or action : FOLLY
**2** : the behavior or dress of a fop

**fop·pish** \'fä-pish\ *adjective* (1599)
**1** *obsolete* : FOOLISH, SILLY
**2 a** : characteristic of a fop ⟨a *foppish* dressing gown⟩ **b** : behaving or dressing in the manner of a fop
— **fop·pish·ly** *adverb*
— **fop·pish·ness** *noun*

**¹for** \fər, (')fòr, *Southern also* (')fär\ *preposition* [Middle English, from Old English; akin to Latin *per* through, *prae* before, *pro* before, for, ahead, Greek *pro*, Old English *faran* to go — more at FARE] (before 12th century)
**1 a** — used as a function word to indicate purpose ⟨a grant *for* studying medicine⟩ **b** — used as a function word to indicate an intended goal ⟨left *for* home⟩ ⟨acted *for* the best⟩ **c** — used as a function word to indicate the object or recipient of a perception, desire, or activity ⟨now *for* a good rest⟩ ⟨run *for* your life⟩ ⟨an eye *for* a bargain⟩
**2 a** : as being or constituting ⟨taken *for* a fool⟩ ⟨eggs *for* breakfast⟩ **b** — used as a function word to indicate an actual or implied enumeration or selection ⟨*for* one thing, the price is too high⟩
**3** : because of ⟨can't sleep *for* the heat⟩
**4** — used as a function word to indicate suitability or fitness ⟨it is not *for* you to choose⟩ ⟨ready *for* action⟩
**5 a** : in place of ⟨go to the store *for* me⟩ **b** (1) : on behalf of : REPRESENTING ⟨speaks *for* the court⟩ (2) : in favor of ⟨all *for* the plan⟩
**6** : in spite of — usually used with *all* ⟨*for* all his large size, he moves gracefully⟩
**7** : with respect to : CONCERNING ⟨a stickler *for* detail⟩ ⟨heavy *for* its size⟩
**8 a** — used as a function word to indicate equivalence in exchange ⟨$10 *for* a hat⟩, equality in number or quantity ⟨point *for* point⟩, or correspondence or correlation ⟨*for* every one that works, you'll find five that don't⟩ **b** — used as a function word to indicate number of attempts ⟨0 *for* 4⟩
**9** — used as a function word to indicate duration of time or extent of space ⟨gone *for* two days⟩
**10** : in honor of : AFTER ⟨named *for* her grandmother⟩

**²for** *conjunction* (12th century)
: for the reason that : on this ground : BECAUSE

**for-** *prefix* [Middle English, from Old English; akin to Old High German *far-* for-, Old English *for*]
**1** : so as to involve prohibition, exclusion, omission, failure, neglect, or refusal ⟨*for*bid⟩
**2** : destructively or detrimentally ⟨*for*do⟩
**3** : completely : excessively : to exhaustion : to pieces ⟨*for*spent⟩

**fora** *plural of* FORUM

**¹for·age** \'fòr-ij, 'fär-\ *noun* [Middle English, from Old French, from *forre* fodder, of Germanic origin; akin to Old High German *fuotar* food, fodder — more at FOOD] (14th century)

**1 :** food for animals especially when taken by browsing or grazing
**2** [²forage] **:** the act of foraging **:** search for provisions

²**forage** verb **for·aged; for·ag·ing** (15th century)
transitive verb
**1 :** to strip of provisions **:** collect forage from
**2 :** to secure by foraging ⟨foraged a chicken for the feast⟩
intransitive verb
**1 :** to wander in search of forage or food
**2 :** to secure forage (as for horses) by stripping the country
**3 :** RAVAGE, RAID
**4 :** to make a search **:** RUMMAGE
— **for·ag·er** noun

**fo·ram** \'fōr-əm, 'fȯr-\ noun (1927)
**:** FORAMINIFER

**fo·ra·men** \fə-'rā-mən\ noun, plural **fo·ram·i·na** \-'ra-mə-nə\ or **fo·ra·mens** \-'rā-mənz\ [Latin foramin-, foramen, from forare to bore — more at BORE] (1671)
**:** a small opening, perforation, or orifice **:** FENESTRA
— **fo·ram·i·nal** \fə-'ra-mə-n°l\ or **fo·ram·i·nous** \-mə-nəs\ adjective

**fo·ra·men mag·num** \fə-,rā-mən-'mag-nəm\ noun [New Latin, literally, large opening] (1860)
**:** the opening in the skull through which the spinal cord passes to become the medulla oblongata

**foramen ova·le** \-ō-'va-lē, -'vä-, -'vā-\ noun [New Latin, literally, oval opening] (circa 1860)
**:** an opening in the septum between the two atria of the heart that is normally present only in the fetus

**for·a·min·i·fer** \,fȯr-ə-'mi-nə-fər, ,fär-\ noun (circa 1842)
**:** any of an order (Foraminifera) of large chiefly marine rhizopod protozoans usually having calcareous shells that often are perforated with minute holes for protrusion of slender pseudopodia and form the bulk of chalk and nummulitic limestone
— **fo·ra·mi·nif·er·al** \fə-,ra-mə-'ni-f(ə-)rəl, ,fȯr-ə-mə-'ni-, ,fär-\ adjective

**fo·ra·mi·nif·era** \fə-,ra-mə-'ni-f(ə-)rə, ,fȯr-ə-mə-'ni-, ,fär-\ noun plural [New Latin, from Latin foramin-, foramen + -fera, neuter plural of -fer -fer] (circa 1836)
**:** organisms that are foraminifers

**fo·ra·mi·nif·er·an** \-f(ə-)rən\ noun (1920)
**:** FORAMINIFER

**for and** conjunction (circa 1529)
obsolete **:** and also

**for·as·much as** \'fȯr-əz-,mə-chəz\ conjunction (13th century)
**:** in view of the fact that

¹**for·ay** \'fȯr-,ā, 'fär-, -ē also fȯ-'rā or fə-\ verb [Middle English forrayen, from Middle French forrer, from forre fodder — more at FORAGE] (14th century)
transitive verb
archaic **:** to ravage in search of spoils **:** PILLAGE
intransitive verb
**:** to make a raid or brief invasion ⟨forayed into enemy territory⟩
— **for·ay·er** noun

²**foray** noun (14th century)
**1 :** a sudden or irregular invasion or attack for war or spoils **:** RAID
**2 :** a brief excursion or attempt especially outside one's accustomed sphere ⟨the novelist's foray into nonfiction⟩

**forb** \'fȯrb\ noun [Greek phorbē fodder, food, from pherbein to graze] (1924)
**:** an herb other than grass

¹**for·bear** \fȯr-'bar, fər-, -'ber\ verb **-bore** \-'bōr, -'bȯr\; **-borne** \-'bōrn, -'bȯrn\; **-bear·ing** [Middle English forberen, from Old English forberan to endure, do without, from for- + beran to bear] (before 12th century)
transitive verb
**1** obsolete **:** to do without
**2 :** to hold oneself back from especially with an effort
**3** obsolete **:** to leave alone **:** SHUN ⟨forbear his presence —Shakespeare⟩
intransitive verb
**1 :** HOLD BACK, ABSTAIN ⟨can write with ease what I forbear to read —Flannery O'Connor⟩
**2 :** to control oneself when provoked **:** be patient
— **for·bear·er** noun

²**forbear** variant of FOREBEAR

**for·bear·ance** \fȯr-'bar-ən(t)s, fər-, -'ber-\ noun (1576)
**1 :** a refraining from the enforcement of something (as a debt, right, or obligation) that is due
**2 :** the act of forbearing **:** PATIENCE
**3 :** the quality of being forbearing **:** LENIENCY

¹**for·bid** \fər-'bid, fȯr-\ transitive verb **-bade** \-'bad, -'bād\ also **-bad** \-'bad\; **-bid·den** \-'bi-d°n\; **-bid·ding** [Middle English forbidden, from Old English forbēodan, from for- + bēodan to bid — more at BID] (before 12th century)
**1 :** to proscribe from or as if from the position of one in authority **:** command against ⟨the law forbids stores to sell liquor to minors⟩ ⟨her mother forbids her to go⟩
**2 :** to hinder or prevent as if by an effectual command ⟨space forbids further treatment here⟩ ☆
— **for·bid·der** noun

²**forbid** adjective (1606)
archaic **:** ACCURSED ⟨he shall live a man forbid —Shakespeare⟩

**for·bid·dance** \fər-'bi-d°n(t)s, fȯr-\ noun (circa 1611)
**:** the act of forbidding

**for·bid·den** \-'bi-d°n\ adjective (13th century)
**1 :** not permitted or allowed
**2 :** not conforming to the usual selection principles — used of quantum phenomena ⟨forbidden transition⟩ ⟨forbidden radiation⟩ ⟨forbidden spectral line⟩

**forbidden fruit** noun [from the forbidden fruit of the Garden of Eden in Genesis 3:2–19] (1662)
**:** an immoral or illegal pleasure

**for·bid·ding** adjective (1712)
**1 :** such as to make approach or passage difficult or impossible ⟨forbidding walls⟩
**2 :** DISAGREEABLE, REPELLENT ⟨a forbidding task⟩
**3 :** GRIM, MENACING ⟨a dark forbidding sky⟩
— **for·bid·ding·ly** \-'bi-diŋ-lē\ adverb

**forbode** variant of FOREBODE

¹**for·by** or **for·bye** \fȯr-'bī\ preposition [Middle English forby, preposition & adverb, from fore- + by] (14th century)
**1** archaic **a :** PAST **b :** NEAR
**2** chiefly Scottish **:** BESIDES

²**forby** or **forbye** adverb (1590)
chiefly Scottish **:** BESIDES **:** in addition

¹**force** \'fōrs, 'fȯrs\ noun [Middle English, from Middle French, from (assumed) Vulgar Latin fortia, from Latin fortis strong] (14th century)
**1 a (1) :** strength or energy exerted or brought to bear **:** cause of motion or change **:** active power ⟨the forces of nature⟩ ⟨the motivating force in her life⟩ **(2)** usually capitalized **:** used with a number to indicate the strength of the wind according to the Beaufort scale ⟨a Force 10 hurricane⟩ **b :** moral or mental strength **:** capacity to persuade or convince ⟨the force of the argument⟩
**2 a :** military strength **b (1) :** a body (as of troops or ships) assigned to a military purpose **(2)** plural **:** the whole military strength (as of a nation) **c :** a body of persons or things available for a particular end ⟨a labor force⟩ ⟨the missile force⟩ **d :** an individual or group having the power of effective action ⟨join forces to prevent violence⟩ ⟨a force in politics⟩ **e** often capitalized **:** POLICE FORCE — usually used with the
**3 :** violence, compulsion, or constraint exerted upon or against a person or thing
**4 a :** an agency or influence that if applied to a free body results chiefly in an acceleration of the body and sometimes in elastic deformation and other effects **b :** any of the natural influences (as electromagnetism, gravity, the strong force, and the weak force) that exist especially between particles and determine the structure of the universe
**5 :** the quality of conveying impressions intensely in writing or speech
synonym see POWER
— **force·less** \-ləs\ adjective
— **in force 1 :** in great numbers ⟨picnickers were out in force⟩ **2 :** VALID, OPERATIVE ⟨the ban remains in force⟩

²**force** transitive verb **forced; forc·ing** (14th century)
**1 :** to do violence to; especially **:** RAPE
**2 :** to compel by physical, moral, or intellectual means
**3 :** to make or cause especially through natural or logical necessity ⟨forced to admit my error⟩
**4 a :** to press, drive, attain to, or effect against resistance or inertia ⟨force your way through⟩ **b :** to impose or thrust urgently, importunately, or inexorably ⟨force unwanted attentions on a woman⟩
**5 :** to achieve or win by strength in struggle or violence: as **a :** to win one's way into ⟨force a castle⟩ ⟨forced the mountain passes⟩ **b :** to break open or through ⟨force a lock⟩
**6 a :** to raise or accelerate to the utmost ⟨forcing the pace⟩ **b :** to produce only with unnatural or unwilling effort ⟨forced a smile⟩ **c :** to wrench, strain, or use (language) with marked unnaturalness and lack of ease
**7 a :** to hasten the rate of progress or growth of **b :** to bring (as plants) to maturity out of the normal season ⟨forcing lilies for Easter⟩
**8 :** to induce (as a particular bid or play by another player) in a card game by some conventional act, play, bid, or response
**9 a :** to cause (a runner in baseball) to be put out on a force-out **b :** to cause (a run) to be scored in baseball by giving a base on balls when the bases are full ☆
— **forc·er** noun
— **force one's hand :** to cause one to act precipitously **:** force one to reveal one's purpose or intention

**forced** \'fōrst, 'fȯrst\ adjective (circa 1537)
**1 :** compelled by force or necessity **:** INVOLUNTARY ⟨a forced landing⟩
**2 :** done or produced with effort, exertion, or pressure ⟨a forced laugh⟩
— **forc·ed·ly** \'fōr-səd-lē, 'fȯr-\ adverb

**force–feed** transitive verb **-fed; -feed·ing** (1901)
**1 :** to feed (as an animal) by forcible administration of food

---

☆ **SYNONYMS**
**Forbid, prohibit, interdict, inhibit** mean to debar one from doing something or to order that something not be done. FORBID implies that the order is from one in authority and that obedience is expected ⟨smoking is forbidden in the building⟩. PROHIBIT suggests the issuing of laws, statutes, or regulations ⟨prohibited the sale of liquor⟩. INTERDICT implies prohibition by civil or ecclesiastical authority usually for a given time or a declared purpose ⟨practices interdicted by the church⟩. INHIBIT implies the imposition of restraints or restrictions that amount to prohibitions, not only by authority but also by the exigencies of the time or situation ⟨conditions inhibiting the growth of free trade⟩.

**2** : to force to take in ⟨*force-feed* students the classics⟩ — also used with a single object ⟨*force-feed* the classics to students⟩ ⟨*force-feed* students with the classics⟩

**force·ful** \'fōrs-fəl, 'fȯrs-\ *adjective* (1571)
: possessing or filled with force : EFFECTIVE
— **force·ful·ly** \-fə-lē\ *adverb*
— **force·ful·ness** *noun*

**force ma·jeure** \ˌfȯr-smä-'zhər, ˌfȯr-, -smə-\ *noun* [French, superior force] (1883)
**1** : superior or irresistible force
**2** : an event or effect that cannot be reasonably anticipated or controlled — compare ACT OF GOD

**force·meat** \'fōrs-ˌmēt, 'fȯrs-\ *noun* [*force* (alteration of ²*farce*) + *meat*] (circa 1688)
: finely chopped and highly seasoned meat or fish that is either served alone or used as a stuffing — called also *farce*

**force of habit** (circa 1925)
: behavior made involuntary or automatic by repeated practice

**force of nature** (1981)
: FORCE 4b

**force-out** \'fōrs-ˌaut, 'fȯrs-\ *noun* (1896)
: a play in baseball in which a runner is put out by being forced to advance to the next base but failing to do so safely

**force play** *noun* (1912)
: FORCE-OUT

**for·ceps** \'fȯr-səps, -ˌseps\ *noun, plural* **for·ceps** [Latin, tongs, perhaps from *formus* warm + *capere* to take — more at THERM, HEAVE] (1634)
: an instrument for grasping, holding firmly, or exerting traction upon objects especially for delicate operations (as by jewelers or surgeons)
— **for·ceps·like** \-ˌlīk\ *adjective*

**force pump** *noun* (1659)
: a pump with a solid piston for drawing and forcing through valves a liquid (as water) to a considerable height above the pump or under a considerable pressure

**forc·ible** \'fōr-sə-bəl, 'fȯr-\ *adjective* (15th century)
**1** : effected by force used against opposition or resistance
**2** : characterized by force, efficiency, or energy : POWERFUL
— **forc·ible·ness** *noun*
— **forc·ibly** \-blē\ *adverb*

**¹ford** \'fōrd, 'fȯrd\ *noun* [Middle English, from Old English; akin to Old Norse *fjorthr* fjord, Latin *portus* port, Old English *faran* to go — more at FARE] (before 12th century)
: a shallow part of a body of water that may be crossed by wading

**²ford** *transitive verb* (1614)
: to cross (a body of water) by wading
— **ford·able** \'fōr-də-bəl, 'fȯr-\ *adjective*

**for·do** \fȯr-'dü, fōr-\ *transitive verb* **-did** \-'did\; **-done** \-'dən\; **-do·ing** \-'dü-iŋ\ [Middle English *fordon*, from Old English *fordōn*, from *for-* + *dōn* to do] (before 12th century)
**1** *archaic* : to do away with : DESTROY
**2** : to overcome with fatigue — used only as past participle ⟨quite *fordone* with the heat⟩

**¹fore** \'fōr, 'fȯr\ *adverb* [Middle English, from Old English; akin to Old English *for*] (before 12th century)
**1** *obsolete* : at an earlier time or period
**2** : in, toward, or adjacent to the front : FORWARD

**²fore** *also* **'fore** *preposition* (before 12th century)
**1** *chiefly dialect* : BEFORE
**2** : in the presence of

**³fore** *adjective* [*fore-*] (15th century)
**1** : situated in front of something else : FORWARD
**2** : prior in order of occurrence : FORMER

**⁴fore** *noun* (1842)
: something that occupies a front position
— **to the fore** : in or into a position of prominence : FORWARD

**⁵fore** *interjection* [probably short for *before*] (circa 1878)
— used by a golfer to warn anyone within range of the probable line of flight of the ball

**fore-** *combining form* [Middle English *for-, fore-*, from Old English *fore-*, from *fore*, adverb]
**1 a** : earlier : beforehand ⟨*foresee*⟩ **b** : occurring earlier : occurring beforehand ⟨*foreshock*⟩
**2 a** : situated at the front : in front ⟨*foreleg*⟩ **b** : front part of (something specified) ⟨*forearm*⟩ **c** : foremast

**fore-and-aft** \ˌfōr-ə-'naft, ˌfȯr-\ *adjective* (1820)
**1** : lying, running, or acting in the general line of the length of a construction (as a ship or a house) : LONGITUDINAL
**2** : having no square sails

**fore and aft** *adverb* (circa 1618)
**1** : lengthwise of a ship : from stem to stern
**2** : in, at, or toward both the bow and stern
**3** : in or at the front and back or the beginning and end

**fore-and-aft·er** \-'naf-tər\ *noun* (1823)
: a ship with a fore-and-aft rig; *especially* : SCHOONER

**fore-and-aft rig** *noun* (1879)
: a sailing-ship rig in which most or all of the sails are not attached to yards but are bent to gaffs or set on the masts or on stays in a fore-and-aft line

**¹fore·arm** \(ˌ)fōr-'ärm, (ˌ)fȯr-\ *transitive verb* (1592)
: to arm in advance : PREPARE

**²fore·arm** \'fōr-ˌärm, 'fȯr-\ *noun* (1741)
: the part of the arm between the elbow and the wrist; *also* : the corresponding part in other vertebrates

**fore·bay** \'fōr-ˌbā, 'fȯr-\ *noun* (1770)
: a reservoir or canal from which water is taken to run equipment (as a waterwheel or turbine)

**fore·bear** \-ˌbar, -ˌber\ *noun* [Middle English (Scots), from *fore-* + *-bear* (from *been* to be)] (15th century)
: ANCESTOR, FOREFATHER; *also* : PRECURSOR — usually used in plural

**fore·bode** \(ˌ)fōr-'bōd, (ˌ)fȯr-\ (1603)
*transitive verb*
**1** : to have an inward conviction of (as coming ill or misfortune)
**2** : FORETELL, PORTEND
*intransitive verb*
: AUGUR, PREDICT
— **fore·bod·er** *noun*

**¹fore·bod·ing** \-'bō-diŋ\ *noun* (14th century)
: the act of one who forebodes; *also* : an omen, prediction, or presentiment especially of coming evil : PORTENT

**²foreboding** *adjective* (1679)
: indicative of or marked by foreboding
— **fore·bod·ing·ly** \-diŋ-lē\ *adverb*
— **fore·bod·ing·ness** *noun*

**fore·brain** \'fōr-ˌbrān, 'fȯr-\ *noun* (1879)
: the anterior of the three primary divisions of the developing vertebrate brain or the corresponding part of the adult brain that includes especially the cerebral hemispheres, the thalamus, and the hypothalamus and that especially in higher vertebrates is the main control center for sensory and associative information processing, visceral functions, and voluntary motor functions — called also *prosencephalon*; compare DIENCEPHALON, TELENCEPHALON

**fore·cad·die** \-ˌka-dē\ *noun* (1792)
: a golf caddie who is stationed in the fairway and who indicates the position of balls on the course

**¹fore·cast** \-ˌkast; fōr-'kast, fȯr-'\ *verb* **forecast** *also* **fore·cast·ed; fore·cast·ing** (15th century)
*transitive verb*
**1 a** : to calculate or predict (some future event or condition) usually as a result of study and analysis of available pertinent data; *especially* : to predict (weather conditions) on the basis

of correlated meteorological observations **b** : to indicate as likely to occur
**2** : to serve as a forecast of : PRESAGE ⟨such events may *forecast* peace⟩
*intransitive verb*
: to calculate the future
**synonym** *see* FORETELL
— **fore·cast·able** \-ˌkas-tə-bəl\ *adjective*
— **fore·cast·er** *noun*

**²fore·cast** \'fōr-ˌkast, 'fȯr-\ *noun* (circa 1541)
**1** *archaic* : foresight of consequences and provision against them : FORETHOUGHT
**2** : a prophecy, estimate, or prediction of a future happening or condition

**fore·cas·tle** \'fōk-səl; 'fōr-ˌka-səl, 'fȯr-\ *noun* (15th century)
**1** : the forward part of the upper deck of a ship
**2** : the crew's quarters usually in a ship's bow

**fore·check** \'fōr-ˌchek, 'fȯr-\ *intransitive verb* (1951)
: to check an opponent in ice hockey in his own defensive zone
— **fore·check·er** \-ˌche-kər\ *noun*

**fore·close** \(ˌ)fōr-'klōz, (ˌ)fȯr-\ *verb* [Middle English, from Middle French *forclos*, past participle of *forclore*, from *fors* outside (from Latin *foris*) + *clore* to close — more at FORUM] (15th century)
*transitive verb*
**1** : to shut out : PRECLUDE
**2** : to hold exclusively
**3** : to deal with or close in advance
**4** : to subject to foreclosure proceedings
*intransitive verb*
: to foreclose a mortgage

**fore·clo·sure** \-'klō-zhər\ *noun* (1728)
: an act or instance of foreclosing; *specifically* : a legal proceeding that bars or extinguishes a mortgagor's right of redeeming a mortgaged estate

**fore·court** \'fōr-ˌkōrt, 'fȯr-, -ˌkȯrt\ *noun* (1535)
**1** : an open court in front of a building
**2** : the area near the net in a court game

**fore·deck** \'fōr-ˌdek, 'fȯr-\ *noun* (1565)
: the forepart of a ship's main deck

**fore·do** *variant of* FORDO

**fore·doom** \(ˌ)fōr-'düm, (ˌ)fȯr-\ *transitive verb* (1603)
: DOOM 2

**fore·face** \'fōr-ˌfās, 'fȯr-\ *noun* (1545)
: the part of the head of a quadruped that is in front of the eyes

**fore·fa·ther** \-ˌfä-thər, -ˌfȧ-\ *noun* (14th century)
**1** : ANCESTOR 1a
**2** : a person of an earlier period and common heritage

---

☆ SYNONYMS

**Force, compel, coerce, constrain, oblige** mean to make someone or something yield. FORCE is the general term and implies the overcoming of resistance by the exertion of strength, power, or duress ⟨*forced* to flee for their lives⟩. COMPEL typically suggests overcoming of resistance or unwillingness by an irresistible force ⟨*compelled* to admit my mistake⟩. COERCE suggests overcoming resistance or unwillingness by actual or threatened violence or pressure ⟨*coerced* into signing over the rights⟩. CONSTRAIN suggests the effect of a force or circumstance that limits freedom of action or choice ⟨*constrained* by conscience⟩. OBLIGE implies the constraint of necessity, law, or duty ⟨felt *obliged* to go⟩.

---

\ə\ **abut** \ᵊ\ **kitten** \ər\ **further** \a\ **ash** \ā\ **ace**
\ä\ **mop, mar** \au̇\ **out** \ch\ **chin** \e\ **bet** \ē\ **easy**
\g\ **go** \i\ **hit** \ī\ **ice** \j\ **job** \ŋ\ **sing** \ō\ **go**
\ȯ\ **law** \ȯi\ **boy** \th\ **thin** \th\ **the** \ü\ **loot** \u̇\ **foot**
\y\ **yet** \zh\ **vision**   *see also* Guide to Pronunciation

**fore·feel** \(ˌ)fōr-ˈfēl, (ˌ)fòr-\ *transitive verb* **-felt** \-ˈfelt\; **-feel·ing** (1580)
**:** to have a presentiment of
**fore·fend** *variant of* FORFEND
**fore·fin·ger** \ˈfōr-ˌfiŋ-gər, ˈfòr-\ *noun* (15th century)
**:** the finger next to the thumb — called also *index finger*
**fore·foot** \-ˌfùt\ *noun* (14th century)
**1 a :** one of the anterior feet especially of a quadruped **b :** the front part of the human foot **2 :** the forward part of a ship where the stem and keel meet
**fore·front** \-ˌfrənt\ *noun* (15th century)
**:** the foremost part or place
**fore·gath·er** *variant of* FORGATHER
**¹fore·go** \fōr-ˈgō, fòr-\ *transitive verb* **-went** \-ˈwent\; **-gone** \-ˈgòn *also* -ˈgän\; **-go·ing** \-ˈgō-iŋ, -ˈgó(-)iŋ\ (before 12th century)
**:** to go before **:** PRECEDE
— **fore·go·er** \-ˈgō(-ə)r\ *noun*
**²forego** *variant of* FORGO
**fore·go·ing** \-ˈgō-iŋ, -ˈgó(-)iŋ\ *adjective* (15th century)
**:** listed, mentioned, or occurring before ⟨the *foregoing* statement can be proven⟩
**synonym** see PRECEDING
**fore·gone** \ˈfōr-ˌgòn, ˈfòr- *also* -ˌgän\ *adjective* (circa 1600)
**:** PREVIOUS, PAST
**foregone conclusion** *noun* (1604)
**1 :** a conclusion that has preceded argument or examination **2 :** an inevitable result **:** CERTAINTY ⟨the victory was a *foregone conclusion*⟩
**¹fore·ground** \ˈfōr-ˌgraùnd, ˈfòr-\ *noun* (1695)
**1 :** the part of a scene or representation that is nearest to and in front of the spectator **2 :** a position of prominence **:** FOREFRONT
**²foreground** *transitive verb* (1892)
**:** to bring to the foreground; *especially* **:** to give prominence or emphasis to
**fore·gut** \ˈfōr-ˌgət, ˈfòr-\ *noun* (circa 1889)
**:** the anterior part of the alimentary canal of a vertebrate embryo that develops into the pharynx, esophagus, stomach, and extreme anterior part of the intestine
**¹fore·hand** \-ˌhand\ *noun* (1557)
**1** *archaic* **:** superior position **:** ADVANTAGE **2 :** the part of a horse that is before the rider **3 :** a forehand stroke (as in tennis or racquets); *also* **:** the side on which such strokes are made

**forehand 3**

**²forehand** *adjective* (1599)
**1** *obsolete* **:** done or given in advance **:** PRIOR **2 :** made with the palm of the hand turned in the direction in which the hand is moving ⟨a *forehand* tennis stroke⟩
**³forehand** *adverb* (1925)
**:** with a forehand stroke
**fore·hand·ed** \(ˌ)fōr-ˈhan-dəd, (ˌ)fòr-\ *adjective* (1650)
**1 a :** mindful of the future **:** PRUDENT **b :** WELL-TO-DO **2 :** FOREHAND 2
— **fore·hand·ed·ly** *adverb*
— **fore·hand·ed·ness** *noun*
**fore·head** \ˈfär-əd, ˈfòr-; ˈfōr-ˌhed, ˈfòr- *also* -ˌed\ *noun* (before 12th century)
**1 :** the part of the face above the eyes **2 :** the front or forepart of something ⟨flames in the *forehead* of the morning sky —John Milton⟩
**fore·hoof** \ˈfōr-ˌhùf, ˈfòr-, -ˌhüf\ *noun* (1770)
**:** the hoof of a forefoot
**for·eign** \ˈfòr-ən, ˈfär-\ *adjective* [Middle English *forein,* from Old French, from Late Latin *foranus* on the outside, from Latin *foris* outside — more at FORUM] (13th century)

**1 :** situated outside a place or country; *especially* **:** situated outside one's own country **2 :** born in, belonging to, or characteristic of some place or country other than the one under consideration **3 :** of, relating to, or proceeding from some other person or material thing than the one under consideration **4 :** alien in character **:** not connected or pertinent **5 :** related to or dealing with other nations **6 :** occurring in an abnormal situation in the living body and often introduced from outside **7 :** not being within the jurisdiction of a political unit (as a state)
**synonym** see EXTRINSIC
— **for·eign·ness** \-ən-nəs\ *noun*
**foreign affairs** *noun plural* (1611)
**:** matters having to do with international relations and with the interests of the home country in foreign countries
**foreign aid** *noun* (1949)
**:** assistance (as economic aid) provided by one nation to another
**foreign bill** *noun* (1682)
**:** a bill of exchange that is not both drawn and payable within a particular jurisdiction
**for·eign-born** \ˌfòr-ən-ˈbòrn, ˌfär-\ *adjective* (1856)
**:** foreign by birth
**foreign correspondent** *noun* (1948)
**:** a correspondent employed to send news or comment from a foreign country
**for·eign·er** \ˈfòr-ə-nər, ˈfär-\ *noun* (15th century)
**1 :** a person belonging to or owing allegiance to a foreign country **2** *chiefly dialect* **:** one not native to a place or community **:** STRANGER 1c
**foreign exchange** *noun* (1691)
**1 :** a process of settling accounts or debts between persons residing in different countries **2 :** foreign currency or current short-term credit instruments payable in such currency
**for·eign·ism** \ˈfòr-ə-ˌni-zəm, ˈfär-\ *noun* (1855)
**:** something peculiar to a foreign language or people; *specifically* **:** a foreign idiom or custom
**foreign minister** *noun* (1709)
**:** a governmental minister for foreign affairs
**foreign office** *noun* (1859)
**:** a government office (as a ministry) that deals with foreign affairs
**foreign policy** *noun* (1859)
**:** the policy of a sovereign state in its interaction with other sovereign states
**foreign service** *noun* (1927)
**:** the field force of a foreign office comprising diplomatic and consular personnel
**¹fore·judge** \fər-ˈjəj, fōr-, fòr-\ *transitive verb* [Middle English *forjuggen,* from Middle French *forjugier,* from *fors* outside (from Latin *foris*) + *jugier* to judge] (15th century)
**:** to expel, oust, or put out by judgment of a court
**²fore·judge** \(ˌ)fōr-ˈjəj, (ˌ)fòr-\ *transitive verb* (1561)
**:** PREJUDGE
**fore·know** \(ˌ)fōr-ˈnō, (ˌ)fòr-\ *transitive verb* **-knew** \-ˈnü, -ˈnyü\; **-known** \-ˈnōn\; **-know·ing** (14th century)
**:** to have previous knowledge of **:** known beforehand especially by paranormal means or by revelation
**synonym** see FORESEE
— **fore·knowl·edge** \-ˈnä-lij\ *noun*
**fore·la·dy** \ˈfōr-ˌlā-dē, ˈfòr-\ *noun* (circa 1889)
**:** FOREWOMAN
**fore·land** \ˈfōr-lənd, ˈfòr-\ *noun* (14th century)
**:** PROMONTORY, HEADLAND
**fore·leg** \ˈfōr-ˌleg, ˈfòr-, -ˌlāg\ *noun* (15th century)
**:** a front leg
**fore·limb** \-ˌlim\ *noun* (circa 1796)

**:** a limb (as an arm, wing, fin, or leg) that is situated anteriorly ⟨the *forelimb* of a bat⟩
**fore·lock** \-ˌläk\ *noun* (1589)
**:** a lock of hair growing from the front of the head
**fore·man** \ˈfōr-mən, ˈfòr-\ *noun* (15th century)
**:** a first or chief person: as **a :** a member of a jury who acts as chairman and spokesman **b** (1) **:** a chief and often specially trained worker who works with and commonly leads a gang or crew (2) **:** a person in charge of a group of workers, a particular operation, or a section of a plant
— **fore·man·ship** \-ˌship\ *noun*
**fore·mast** \ˈfōr-ˌmast, ˈfòr-, -məst\ *noun* (1582)
**:** the mast nearest the bow of a ship
**¹fore·most** \-ˌmōst\ *adjective* [Middle English *formest,* from Old English, superlative of *forma* first; akin to Old High German *fruma* advantage, Old English *fore* fore] (before 12th century)
**1 :** first in a series or progression **2 :** of first rank or position **:** PREEMINENT
**²foremost** *adverb* (before 12th century)
**1 :** in the first place **2 :** most importantly ⟨first and *foremost*⟩
**fore·moth·er** \ˈfōr-ˌmə-thər, ˈfòr-\ *noun* (1582)
**:** a female ancestor
**fore·name** \-ˌnām\ *noun* (1533)
**:** a name that precedes one's surname
**fore·named** \-ˌnāmd\ *adjective* (13th century)
**:** named previously **:** AFORESAID
**fore·noon** \ˈfōr-ˌnün, ˈfòr-ˌ, fōr-ˈ, fòr-ˈ\ *noun* (15th century)
**:** the early part of the day ending with noon **:** MORNING
**¹fo·ren·sic** \fə-ˈren(t)-sik, -ˈren-zik\ *adjective* [Latin *forensis* public, forensic, from *forum* forum] (1659)
**1 :** belonging to, used in, or suitable to courts of judicature or to public discussion and debate **2 :** ARGUMENTATIVE, RHETORICAL **3 :** relating to or dealing with the application of scientific knowledge to legal problems ⟨*forensic* medicine⟩ ⟨*forensic* science⟩ ⟨*forensic* pathologist⟩ ⟨*forensic* experts⟩
— **fo·ren·si·cal·ly** \-si-k(ə-)lē, -zi-\ *adverb*
**²forensic** *noun* (1814)
**1 :** an argumentative exercise **2** *plural but singular or plural in construction* **:** the art or study of argumentative discourse
**fore·or·dain** \ˌfōr-òr-ˈdān, ˌfòr-\ *transitive verb* (15th century)
**:** to dispose or appoint in advance **:** PREDESTINE
— **fore·or·di·na·tion** \-ˌòr-dᵊn-ˈā-shən\ *noun*
**fore·part** \ˈfōr-ˌpärt, ˈfòr-\ *noun* (14th century)
**1 :** the anterior part of something **2 :** the earlier part of a period of time
**fore·passed** *or* **fore·past** \-ˌpast\ *adjective* (1557)
**:** BYGONE
**fore·paw** \-ˌpò\ *noun* (1825)
**:** the paw of a foreleg
**fore·peak** \-ˌpēk\ *noun* (1693)
**:** the extreme forward lower compartment or tank usually used for trimming or storage in a ship
**fore·play** \-ˌplā\ *noun* (1929)
**1 :** erotic stimulation preceding sexual intercourse **2 :** action or behavior that precedes an event
**fore·quar·ter** \-ˌkwò(r)-tər, -ˌkòr-\ *noun* (15th century)
**:** the front half of a lateral half of the body or carcass of a quadruped ⟨a *forequarter* of beef⟩
**fore·reach** \fōr-ˈrēch, fòr-\ (1644)
*intransitive verb*
*of a ship* **:** to gain ground in tacking
*transitive verb*
**:** to gain on or go ahead of (a ship) when close-hauled

**fore·run** \-'rən\ *transitive verb* **-ran** \-'ran\; **-run; -run·ning** (before 12th century) **1** : to run before **2** : to come before as a token of something to follow **3** FORESTALL, ANTICIPATE

**fore·run·ner** \'fōr-ˌrə-nər, 'fȯr-\ *noun* (13th century) **1** : one that precedes and indicates the approach of another: as **a** : a premonitory sign or symptom **b** : a skier who runs the course before the start of a race **2** : PREDECESSOR, ANCESTOR ☆

**fore·said** \-ˌsed\ *adjective* (before 12th century) *archaic* : AFORESAID

**fore·sail** \'fōr-ˌsāl, 'fȯr-, -səl\ *noun* (15th century) **1** : the lowest sail set on the foremast of a square-rigged ship or schooner — see SAIL illustration **2** : the sole or principal headsail (as of a sloop, cutter, or schooner)

**fore·see** \fōr-'sē, fȯr-\ *transitive verb* **-saw** \-'sȯ\; **-seen** \-'sēn\; **-see·ing** (before 12th century) : to see (as a development) beforehand ☆ — **fore·seer** \-'sē-ər, fȯr-, -'si-(ə)r\ *noun*

**fore·see·able** \-'sē-ə-bəl\ *adjective* (1804) **1** : being such as may be reasonably anticipated ⟨*foreseeable* problems⟩ **2** : lying within the range for which forecasts are possible ⟨in the *foreseeable* future⟩ — **fore·see·abil·i·ty** \-ˌsē-ə-'bi-lə-tē\ *noun*

**fore·shad·ow** \-'sha-(ˌ)dō, -də(-w)\ *transitive verb* (1577) : to represent, indicate, or typify beforehand : PREFIGURE — **fore·shad·ow·er** \-də-wər\ *noun*

**fore·shank** \'fōr-ˌshaŋk, 'fȯr-\ *noun* (1924) : the upper part of the foreleg of cattle; *also* : meat cut from this part

**fore·sheet** \-ˌshēt\ *noun* (1667) **1** : one of the sheets of a foresail **2** *plural* : the forward part of an open boat

**fore·shock** \-ˌshäk\ *noun* (1902) : any of the usually minor tremors commonly preceding the principal shock of an earthquake

**fore·shore** \-ˌshōr, -ˌshȯr\ *noun* (1764) **1** : a strip of land margining a body of water **2** : the part of a seashore between high-water and low-water marks

**fore·short·en** \fōr-'shȯr-t°n, fȯr-\ *transitive verb* (1606) **1** : to shorten by proportionately contracting in the direction of depth so that an illusion of projection or extension in space is obtained **2** : to make more compact : ABRIDGE, SHORTEN

**fore·side** \'fōr-ˌsīd, 'fȯr-\ *noun* (14th century) : the front side or part : FRONT

**fore·sight** \'fōr-ˌsīt, 'fȯr-\ *noun* (14th century) **1** : an act or the power of foreseeing : PRESCIENCE **2** : provident care : PRUDENCE ⟨had the *foresight* to invest his money wisely⟩ **3** : an act of looking forward; *also* : a view forward — **fore·sight·ed** \-ˌsī-təd\ *adjective* — **fore·sight·ed·ly** *adverb* — **fore·sight·ed·ness** *noun* — **fore·sight·ful** \-ˌsīt-fəl\ *adjective*

**fore·skin** \-ˌskin\ *noun* (1535) : a fold of skin that covers the glans of the penis — called also *prepuce*

**fore·speak** \fōr-'spēk, fȯr-\ *transitive verb* **-spoke** \-'spōk\; **-spo·ken** \-'spō-kən\; **-speak·ing** (14th century) **1** : FORETELL, PREDICT **2** : to arrange for in advance

**¹for·est** \'fȯr-əst, 'fär-\ *noun, often attributive* [Middle English, from Old French, from Late Latin *forestis* (*silva*) unenclosed (woodland), from Latin *foris* outside — more at FORUM] (13th century) **1** : a dense growth of trees and underbrush covering a large tract

**2** : a tract of wooded land in England formerly owned by the sovereign and used for game **3** : something resembling a forest especially in profusion ⟨a *forest* of microphones⟩ — **for·est·al** \-əs-t°l\ *or* **fo·res·tial** \fə-'res-tē-əl, fȯ-, -'res(h)-chəl\ *adjective* — **for·est·ed** \'fȯr-ə-stəd, 'fär-\ *adjective*

**²forest** *transitive verb* (circa 1828) : to cover with trees or forest — **for·es·ta·tion** \ˌfȯr-ə-'stā-shən, ˌfär-\ *noun*

**fore·stage** \'fōr-ˌstāj, 'fȯr-\ *noun* (1923) : APRON 2e

**fore·stall** \fōr-'stȯl, fȯr-\ *transitive verb* [Middle English, from *forstall* act of waylaying, from Old English *foresteall*, from *fore-* + *steall* position, stall] (before 12th century) **1** : to prevent the normal trading in by buying or diverting goods or by persuading persons to raise prices **2** *archaic* : INTERCEPT **3** *obsolete* : OBSTRUCT, BESET **4** : to exclude, hinder, or prevent by prior occupation or measures **5** : to get ahead of : ANTICIPATE *synonym* see PREVENT — **fore·stall·er** *noun* — **fore·stall·ment** \-'stȯl-mənt\ *noun*

**fore·stay** \'fōr-ˌstā, 'fȯr-\ *noun* (13th century) : a stay from the foremast to the foredeck or bow of a ship

**fore·stay·sail** \-ˌsāl, -səl\ *noun* (1742) : the triangular aftermost headsail of a schooner, ketch, or yawl set on the forestay — see SAIL illustration

**for·est·er** \'fȯr-ə-stər, 'fär-\ *noun* [Middle English *forster, forester*, from Old French *forestier*, from *forest*] (14th century) **1** : a person trained in forestry **2** : an inhabitant of a forest **3** : any of various woodland moths (family Agaristidae) **4** *capitalized* : a member of a major benevolent and fraternal order

**forest floor** *noun* (1849) : the richly organic layer of soil and debris characteristic of forested land

**forest green** *noun* (1810) : a dark yellowish or moderate olive green

**for·est·land** \'fȯr-əst-ˌland, 'fär-\ *noun* (1649) : land covered with forest or reserved for the growth of forests

**forest ranger** *noun* (1830) : an officer charged with the patrolling and guarding of a forest; *especially* : one in charge of the management and protection of a portion of a public forest

**for·est·ry** \'fȯr-ə-strē, 'fär-\ *noun* (1823) **1** : FORESTLAND **2 a** : the science of developing, caring for, or cultivating forests **b** : the management of growing timber

**forest tent caterpillar** *noun* (1854) : a moth (*Malacosoma disstria* of the family Lasiocampidae) whose orange-marked larva is a tent caterpillar and a serious defoliator of deciduous trees

**foreswear, foresworn** *variant of* FORSWEAR, FORSWORN

**¹fore·taste** \'fōr-ˌtāst, 'fȯr-\ *noun* (15th century) **1** : a small anticipatory sample **2** : an advance indication or warning *synonym* see PROSPECT

**²fore·taste** \fōr-'tāst, fȯr-', 'fōr-ˌ, 'fȯr-\ *transitive verb* (15th century) : to taste beforehand : ANTICIPATE

**fore·tell** \fōr-'tel, fȯr-\ *transitive verb* **-told** \-'tōld\; **-tell·ing** (14th century) : to tell beforehand : PREDICT ☆ — **fore·tell·er** *noun*

**¹fore·thought** \'fōr-ˌthȯt, 'fȯr-\ *noun* (14th century) **1** : a thinking or planning out in advance : PREMEDITATION **2** : consideration for the future

**²forethought** *adjective* (15th century) *archaic* : AFORETHOUGHT

**fore·thought·ful** \-fəl\ *adjective* (1809) : full of or having forethought — **fore·thought·ful·ly** \-fə-lē\ *adverb* — **fore·thought·ful·ness** *noun*

**fore·time** \'fōr-ˌtīm, 'fȯr-\ *noun* (circa 1540) : former or past time : the time before the present

**¹fore·to·ken** \'fōr-ˌtō-kən, 'fȯr-\ *noun* (before 12th century) : a premonitory sign

**²fore·to·ken** \fōr-'tō-kən, fȯr-\ *transitive verb* **fore·to·kened; fore·to·ken·ing** \-'tōk-niŋ, -'tō-kə-\ (15th century) : to indicate or warn of in advance

**fore·top** \'fōr-ˌtäp, 'fȯr-; -təp\ *noun* (1509) : the platform at the head of a ship's foremast

**fore·top·man** \'fōr-ˌtäp-mən, 'fȯr-; -təp-\ *noun* (1816) : a sailor on duty on the foremast and above

**fore–top·mast** \'fōr-ˌtäp-məst, 'fȯr-; -təp-ˌmast\ *noun* (1626)

---

☆ **SYNONYMS**

**Forerunner, precursor, harbinger, herald** mean one that goes before or announces the coming of another. FORERUNNER is applicable to anything that serves as a sign or presage ⟨the blockade was the *forerunner* of war⟩. PRECURSOR applies to a person or thing paving the way for the success or accomplishment of another ⟨18th-century poets like Burns were *precursors* of the Romantics⟩. HARBINGER and HERALD both apply, chiefly figuratively, to one that proclaims or announces the coming or arrival of a notable event ⟨their early victory was the *harbinger* of a winning season⟩ ⟨the *herald* of a new age in medicine⟩.

**Foresee, foreknow, divine, anticipate** mean to know beforehand. FORESEE implies nothing about how the knowledge is derived and may apply to ordinary reasoning and experience ⟨economists should have *foreseen* the recession⟩. FOREKNOW usually implies supernatural assistance, as through revelation ⟨if only we could *foreknow* our own destinies⟩. DIVINE adds to FORESEE the suggestion of exceptional wisdom or discernment ⟨was able to *divine* Europe's rapid recovery from the war⟩. ANTICIPATE implies taking action about or responding emotionally to something before it happens ⟨the waiter *anticipated* our every need⟩.

**Foretell, predict, forecast, prophesy, prognosticate** mean to tell beforehand. FORETELL applies to the telling of the coming of a future event by any procedure or any source of information ⟨seers *foretold* the calamity⟩. PREDICT commonly implies inference from facts or accepted laws of nature ⟨astronomers *predicted* an eclipse⟩. FORECAST adds the implication of anticipating eventualities and differs from PREDICT in being usually concerned with probabilities rather than certainties ⟨*forecast* snow⟩. PROPHESY connotes inspired or mystic knowledge of the future especially as the fulfilling of divine threats or promises ⟨*prophesying* a new messiah⟩. PROGNOSTICATE is used less often than the other words; it may suggest learned or skilled interpretation, but more often it is simply a colorful substitute for PREDICT or PROPHESY ⟨*prognosticating* the future⟩.

---

\ə\ abut \°\ kitten \ər\ further \a\ ash \ā\ ace \ä\ mop, mar \au̇\ out \ch\ chin \e\ bet \ē\ easy \g\ go \i\ hit \ī\ ice \j\ job \ŋ\ sing \ō\ go \ȯ\ law \ȯi\ boy \th\ thin \t̲h̲\ the \ü\ loot \u̇\ foot \y\ yet \zh\ vision *see also* Guide to Pronunciation

**:** a mast next above the foremast

**¹for·ev·er** \fə-'rev-ər, fȯ-; *Southern often* fə-'e-və\ *adverb* (1629)
**1 :** for a limitless time ⟨wants to live *forever*⟩ **2 :** at all times **:** CONTINUALLY ⟨is *forever* making bad puns⟩

**²forever** *noun* (1858)
**:** a seemingly interminable time **:** excessively long ⟨it took her *forever* to find the answer⟩

**for·ev·er·more** \-,re-və(r)-'mȯr, -'mȯr\ *adverb* (1837)
**:** FOREVER 1

**for·ev·er·ness** \-'re-vər-nəs\ *noun* (1945)
**:** ETERNITY

**fore·warn** \fȯr-'wȯrn, fȯr-\ *transitive verb* (14th century)
**:** to warn in advance

**fore·wing** \'fȯr-,wiŋ, 'fȯr-\ *noun* (circa 1889)
**:** either of the anterior wings of a 4-winged insect

**fore·wom·an** \'fȯr-,wu̇-mən, 'fȯr-\ *noun* (1709)
**:** a woman who is a foreman

**fore·word** \'fȯr-(,)wərd, 'fȯr-\ *noun* (1842)
**:** prefatory comments (as for a book) especially when written by someone other than the author

**fore·worn** *archaic variant of* FORWORN
**¹for·feit** \'fȯr-fət\ *noun* [Middle English *forfait,* from Middle French, from past participle of *forfaire* to commit a crime, forfeit, from *fors* outside (from Latin *foris*) + *faire* to do, from Latin *facere* — more at FORUM, DO] (14th century)
**1 :** something forfeited or subject to being forfeited (as for a crime, offense, or neglect of duty) **:** PENALTY **2 :** forfeiture especially of civil rights **3 a :** something deposited (as for making a mistake in a game) and then redeemed on payment of a fine **b** *plural* **:** a game in which forfeits are exacted

**²forfeit** *transitive verb* (14th century)
**1 :** to lose or lose the right to by some error, offense, or crime **2 :** to subject to confiscation as a forfeit
**— for·feit·able** \-fə-tə-bəl\ *adjective*
**— for·feit·er** *noun*

**³forfeit** *adjective* (14th century)
**:** forfeited or subject to forfeiture

**for·fei·ture** \'fȯr-fə-,chu̇r, -chər, -,t(y)u̇r\ *noun* (14th century)
**1 :** the act of forfeiting **:** the loss of property or money because of a breach of a legal obligation **2 :** something (as money or property) that is forfeited **:** PENALTY

**for·fend** \fȯr-'fend, fȯr-\ *transitive verb* (14th century)
**1 a** *archaic* **:** FORBID **b :** to ward off **:** PREVENT **2 :** PROTECT, PRESERVE

**for·gath·er** \fȯr-'ga-thər, fȯr-\ *intransitive verb* (1513)
**1 :** to come together **:** ASSEMBLE **2 :** to meet someone usually by chance

**¹forge** \'fȯrj, 'fȯrj\ *noun* [Middle English, from Old French, from Latin *fabrica,* from *fabr-, faber* smith] (13th century)
**1 :** a furnace or a shop with its furnace where metal is heated and wrought **:** SMITHY **2 :** a workshop where wrought iron is produced or where iron is made malleable

**²forge** *verb* **forged; forg·ing** (14th century)
*transitive verb*
**1 a :** to form (as metal) by heating and hammering **b :** to form (metal) by a mechanical or hydraulic press with or without heat **2 :** to make or imitate falsely especially with intent to defraud **:** COUNTERFEIT **3 :** to form or bring into being especially by an expenditure of effort ⟨working to *forge* party unity⟩
*intransitive verb*
**1 :** to work at a forge **2 :** to commit forgery

**— forge·abil·i·ty** \,fȯr-jə-'bi-lə-tē, ,fȯr-\ *noun*
**— forge·able** \'fȯr-jə-bəl, 'fȯr-\ *adjective*
**³forge** *intransitive verb* **forged; forg·ing** [origin unknown] (1611)
**1 :** to move forward slowly and steadily ⟨the ship *forged* ahead through heavy seas⟩ **2 :** to move with a sudden increase of speed and power ⟨*forged* into the lead⟩ ⟨*forged* ahead in marketing the product⟩

**forg·er** \'fȯr-jər, 'fȯr-\ *noun* [²*forge*] (14th century)
**1 :** one that forges metals **2 a :** one that falsifies; *especially* **:** a creator of false tales **b :** a person guilty of forgery

**forg·ery** \'fȯrj-rē, 'fȯrj-; 'fȯr-jə-, 'fȯr-\ *noun, plural* **-er·ies** (1583)
**1** *archaic* **:** INVENTION **2 :** something forged **3 :** an act of forging; *especially* **:** the crime of falsely and fraudulently making or altering a document (as a check)

**for·get** \fər-'get, fȯr-\ *verb* **-got** \-'gät\; **-got·ten** \-'gä-t³n\ *or* **-got; -get·ting** [Middle English, from Old English *forgietan,* from *for- + -gietan* (akin to Old Norse *geta* to get)] (before 12th century)
*transitive verb*
**1 a :** to lose the remembrance of **:** be unable to think of or recall ⟨I *forget* his name⟩ **b** *obsolete* **:** to cease from doing **2 :** to treat with inattention or disregard ⟨*forgot* their old friends⟩ **3 :** to disregard intentionally **:** OVERLOOK — usually used in the imperative ⟨*forget* it⟩
*intransitive verb*
**1 :** to cease remembering or noticing ⟨*forgive* and *forget*⟩ **2 :** to fail to become mindful at the proper time ⟨*forget* about paying the bill⟩
*synonym* see NEGLECT
**— for·get·ter** *noun*
**— forget oneself :** to lose one's dignity, temper, or self-control

**for·get·ful** \-'get-fəl\ *adjective* (14th century)
**1 :** likely to forget **2 :** characterized by negligent failure to remember **:** NEGLECTFUL **3 :** inducing oblivion ⟨*forgetful* sleep⟩
**— for·get·ful·ly** \-fə-lē\ *adverb*
**— for·get·ful·ness** *noun*

**for·ge·tive** \'fȯr-jə-tiv, 'fȯr-\ *adjective* [probably from ²*forge* + *-tive* (as in *inventive*)] (1597)
*archaic* **:** INVENTIVE, IMAGINATIVE

**for·get—me—not** \fər-'get-mē-,nät, fȯr-\ *noun* (1532)
**:** any of a genus (*Myosotis*) of small herbs of the borage family having bright-blue or white flowers usually arranged in a curving spike

**for·get·ta·ble** \fər-'ge-tə-bəl, fȯr-\ *adjective* (1845)
**:** fit or likely to be forgotten ⟨a *forgettable* movie⟩

**forg·ing** \'fȯr-jiŋ, 'fȯr-\ *noun* (14th century)
**1 :** the art or process of forging **2 :** a piece of forged work **3 :** FORGERY 3

**for·give** \fər-'giv, fȯr-\ *verb* **-gave** \-'gāv\; **-giv·en** \-'gi-vən\; **-giv·ing** [Middle English, from Old English *forgifan,* from *for- + gifan* to give] (before 12th century)
*transitive verb*
**1 a :** to give up resentment of or claim to requital for ⟨*forgive* an insult⟩ **b :** to grant relief from payment of ⟨*forgive* a debt⟩ **2 :** to cease to feel resentment against (an offender) **:** PARDON ⟨*forgive* one's enemies⟩
*intransitive verb*
**:** to grant forgiveness
*synonym* see EXCUSE
**— for·giv·able** \-'gi-və-bəl\ *adjective*
**— for·giv·ably** \-blē\ *adverb*
**— for·giv·er** *noun*

**for·give·ness** \-'giv-nəs\ *noun* (before 12th century)

**:** the act of forgiving

**for·giv·ing** *adjective* (1690)
**1 :** willing or able to forgive **2 :** allowing room for error or weakness ⟨designed to be a *forgiving* tennis racquet⟩
**— for·giv·ing·ly** \-'gi-viŋ-lē\ *adverb*
**— for·giv·ing·ness** *noun*

**for·go** \fȯr-'gō, fȯr-\ *transitive verb* **-went** \-'went\; **-gone** \-'gȯn *also* -'gän\; **-go·ing** \-'gō-iŋ, -'gȯ(-)iŋ\ [Middle English, from Old English *forgān* to pass by, forgo, from *for- + gān* to go] (before 12th century)
**1 :** to give up the enjoyment or advantage of **:** do without **2** *archaic* **:** FORSAKE
**— for·go·er** \-'gō(-ə)r\ *noun*

**forgotten man** *noun* (1925)
**:** a person or category of persons that receives less attention than is merited

**for instance** \fə-'rin(t)-stənts, 'frin(t)-\ *noun* (1959)
**:** EXAMPLE ⟨I'll give you a *for instance*⟩

**fo·rint** \'fȯr-,int\ *noun, plural* **forints** *also* **forint** [Hungarian] (circa 1916)
**—** see MONEY table

**for·judge** *variant of* FOREJUDGE
**¹fork** \'fȯrk\ *noun* [Middle English *forke,* from Old English & Old North French; Old English *forca* & Old North French *forque,* from Latin *furca*] (before 12th century)
**1 :** an implement with two or more prongs used especially for taking up (as in eating), pitching, or digging **2 :** a forked part, tool, or piece of equipment **3 a :** a division into branches or the place where something divides into branches **b :** CONFLUENCE **4 :** one of the branches into which something forks **5 :** an attack by one chess piece (as a knight) on two pieces simultaneously
**— fork·ful** \-,fu̇l\ *noun*

**²fork** (15th century)
*intransitive verb*
**1 :** to divide into two or more branches ⟨where the road *forks*⟩ **2 a :** to use or work with a fork **b :** to turn into a fork
*transitive verb*
**1 :** to give the form of a fork to ⟨*forking* her fingers⟩ **2 :** to attack (two chessmen) simultaneously **3 :** to raise, pitch, dig, or work with a fork ⟨*fork* hay⟩ **4 :** PAY, CONTRIBUTE — used with *over, out,* or *up* ⟨had to *fork* over $5000⟩
**— fork·er** *noun*

**fork·ball** \'fȯrk-,bȯl\ *noun* (1936)
**:** a baseball pitch in which the ball is gripped between the forked index and middle fingers

**forked** \'fȯrkt, 'fȯr-kəd\ *adjective* (13th century)
**1 :** resembling a fork especially in having one end divided into two or more branches or points ⟨*forked* lightning⟩ **2 :** shaped like a fork or having a forked part ⟨a *forked* road⟩

**forked tongue** *noun* (1836)
**:** intent to mislead or deceive — usually used in the phrase *to speak with forked tongue*

**fork·lift** \'fȯr-,klift\ *noun* (1944)
**:** a self-propelled machine for hoisting and transporting heavy objects by means of steel fingers inserted under the load

**fork—ten·der** \'fȯrk-'ten-dər\ *adjective* (1973)
**:** tender enough to be easily pierced or cut with a fork ⟨*fork-tender* filet mignon⟩

**forky** \'fȯr-kē\ *adjective* **fork·i·er; -est** (1697)
**:** FORKED ⟨a *forky* beard⟩

**for·lorn** \fər-'lȯrn, fȯr-\ *adjective* [Middle English *forloren,* from Old English, past participle of *forlēosan* to lose, from *for- + lēosan* to lose — more at LOSE] (before 12th century)

**1 a :** BEREFT, FORSAKEN 〈left quite *forlorn* of hope〉 **b :** sad and lonely because of isolation or desertion **:** DESOLATE
**2 :** being in poor condition **:** MISERABLE, WRETCHED 〈*forlorn* tumbledown buildings〉
**3 :** nearly hopeless 〈a *forlorn* attempt〉
*synonym* see ALONE
— **for·lorn·ly** *adverb*
— **for·lorn·ness** \-'lòrn-nəs\ *noun*
**forlorn hope** *noun* [by folk etymology from Dutch *verloren hoop,* literally, lost band] (1579)
**1 :** a body of men selected to perform a perilous service
**2 :** a desperate or extremely difficult enterprise
**¹form** \'fòrm\ *noun* [Middle English *forme,* from Old French, from Latin *forma* form, beauty] (13th century)
**1 a :** the shape and structure of something as distinguished from its material **b :** a body (as of a person) especially in its external appearance or as distinguished from the face **:** FIGURE **c** *archaic* **:** BEAUTY
**2 :** the essential nature of a thing as distinguished from its matter: as **a :** IDEA 1a **b :** the component of a thing that determines its kind
**3 a :** established method of expression or proceeding **:** procedure according to rule or rote **b :** a prescribed and set order of words **:** FORMULA 〈the *form* of the marriage service〉
**4 :** a printed or typed document with blank spaces for insertion of required or requested information 〈tax *forms*〉
**5 a** (1) **:** conduct regulated by extraneous controls (as of custom or etiquette) **:** CEREMONY (2) **:** show without substance **b :** manner or conduct as tested by a prescribed or accepted standard 〈rudeness is simply bad *form*〉 **c :** manner or style of performing or accomplishing according to recognized standards of technique 〈a strong swimmer but weak on *form*〉
**6 a :** the resting place or nest of a hare **b :** a long seat **:** BENCH
**7 a :** a supporting frame model of the human figure or part (as the torso) of the human figure usually used for displaying apparel **b :** a proportioned and often adjustable model for fitting clothes **c :** a mold in which concrete is placed to set
**8 :** the printing type or other matter arranged and secured in a chase ready for printing
**9 a :** one of the different modes of existence, action, or manifestation of a particular thing or substance **:** KIND 〈one *form* of respiratory disorder〉 〈a *form* of art〉 **b :** a distinguishable group of organisms **c :** LINGUISTIC FORM **d :** one of the different aspects a word may take as a result of inflection or change of spelling or pronunciation 〈verbal *forms*〉 **e :** a mathematical expression of a particular type 〈a bilinear *form*〉 〈a polynomial *form*〉
**10 a** (1) **:** orderly method of arrangement (as in the presentation of ideas) **:** manner of coordinating elements (as of an artistic production or course of reasoning) (2) **:** a particular kind or instance of such arrangement 〈the sonnet is a poetical *form*〉 **b :** PATTERN, SCHEMA 〈arguments of the same logical *form*〉 **c :** the structural element, plan, or design of a work of art — compare CONTENT 2c **d :** a visible and measurable unit defined by a contour **:** a bounded surface or volume
**11 :** a grade in a British school or in some American private schools
**12 a** (1) **:** the past performance of a race horse (2) **:** RACING FORM **b :** known ability to perform 〈a singer at the top of her *form*〉 **c :** condition suitable for performing (as in athletic competition) 〈back on *form*〉
**²form** (13th century)
*transitive verb*
**1 a :** to give a particular shape to **:** shape or mold into a certain state or after a particular model 〈*form* the dough into a ball〉 〈a state

*formed* along republican lines〉 **b :** to arrange themselves in 〈the dancers *formed* a line〉 **c :** to model by instruction and discipline 〈a mind *formed* by classical education〉
**2 :** to give form or shape to **:** FASHION, CONSTRUCT
**3 :** to serve to make up or constitute **:** be an essential or basic element of
**4 :** DEVELOP, ACQUIRE 〈*form* a habit〉
**5 :** to arrange in order **:** DRAW UP
**6 a :** to assume an inflection so as to produce (as a tense) 〈*forms* the past in *-ed*〉 **b :** to combine to make (a compound word)
*intransitive verb*
**1 :** to become formed or shaped
**2 :** to take form **:** come into existence **:** ARISE
**3 :** to take on a definite form, shape, or arrangement
— **form·abil·i·ty** \ˌfòr-mə-'bi-lə-tē\ *noun*
— **form·able** \'fòr-mə-bəl\ *adjective*
— **form on :** to take up a formation next to
**form-** *or* **formo-** *combining form* [*formic*] **:** formic acid 〈*formate*〉
**-form** \ˌfòrm\ *adjective combining form* [Middle French & Latin; Middle French *-forme,* from Latin *-formis,* from *forma*] **:** in the form or shape of **:** resembling 〈filiform〉
**¹for·mal** \'fòr-məl\ *adjective* [Middle English, from Middle French or Latin; Middle French, from Latin *formalis,* from *forma*] (14th century)
**1 a :** belonging to or constituting the form or essence of a thing 〈*formal* cause〉 **b :** relating to or involving the outward form, structure, relationships, or arrangement of elements rather than content 〈*formal* logic〉 〈*formal* style of painting〉 〈*formal* approach to comparative linguistics〉
**2 a :** following or according with established form, custom, or rule 〈lacked *formal* schooling〉 〈a *formal* dinner party〉 〈*formal* attire〉 **b :** done in due or lawful form 〈a *formal* contract〉 〈received *formal* recognition〉
**3 a :** characterized by punctilious respect for form **:** METHODICAL 〈very *formal* in all his dealings〉 **b :** rigidly ceremonious **:** PRIM
**4 :** having the appearance without the substance 〈*formal* Christians who go to church only at Easter〉
*synonym* see CEREMONIAL
— **for·mal·ly** \-mə-lē\ *adverb*
— **for·mal·ness** *noun*
**²formal** *noun* (1605)
**:** something (as a dance or a dress) formal in character
**³formal** *adjective* [*formula* + ¹*-al*] (circa 1934) **:** ³MOLAR
**form·al·de·hyde** \fòr-'mal-də-ˌhīd, fər-\ *noun* [International Scientific Vocabulary *form-* + *aldehyde*] (1872)
**:** a colorless pungent irritating gas $CH_2O$ used chiefly as a disinfectant and preservative and in chemical synthesis
**for·ma·lin** \'fòr-mə-lən, -ˌlēn\ *noun* [*Formalin,* a trademark] (1893)
**:** a clear aqueous solution of formaldehyde containing a small amount of methanol
**for·mal·ise** *British variant of* FORMALIZE
**for·mal·ism** \'fòr-mə-ˌli-zəm\ *noun* (circa 1840)
**1 :** the practice or the doctrine of strict adherence to prescribed or external forms (as in religion or art); *also* **:** an instance of this
**2 :** marked attention to arrangement, style, or artistic means (as in art or literature) usually with corresponding de-emphasis of content
— **for·mal·ist** \-list\ *noun or adjective*
— **for·mal·is·tic** \ˌfòr-mə-'lis-tik\ *adjective*
**for·mal·i·ty** \fòr-'ma-lə-tē\ *noun, plural* **-ties** (1597)
**1 :** compliance with formal or conventional rules **:** CEREMONY
**2 :** the quality or state of being formal
**3 :** an established form or procedure that is required or conventional

**for·mal·ize** \'fòr-mə-ˌlīz\ *transitive verb* **-ized; -iz·ing** (1646)
**1 :** to give a certain or definite form to **:** SHAPE
**2 a :** to make formal **b :** to give formal status or approval to
— **for·mal·iz·able** \-ˌlī-zə-bəl\ *adjective*
— **for·mal·iza·tion** \ˌfòr-mə-lə-'zā-shən\ *noun*
— **for·mal·iz·er** \'fòr-mə-ˌlī-zər\ *noun*
**form·am·ide** \fòr-'ma-ˌmīd; 'fòr-mə-ˌmīd, -məd\ *noun* (1852)
**:** a colorless hygroscopic liquid $CHONH_2$ used chiefly as a solvent
**for·mant** \'fòr-mənt, -ˌmant\ *noun* (1901)
**:** a characteristic component of the quality of a speech sound; *specifically* **:** any of several resonance bands held to determine the phonetic quality of a vowel
**¹for·mat** \'fòr-ˌmat\ *noun* [French or German; French, from German, from Latin *formatus,* past participle of *formare* to form, from *forma*] (1840)
**1 :** the shape, size, and general makeup (as of something printed)
**2 :** general plan of organization, arrangement, or choice of material (as for a television show)
**²format** *transitive verb* **for·mat·ted; for·mat·ting** (1964)
**:** to arrange (as material to be printed or stored data) in a particular format
— **for·mat·ter** *noun*
**for·mate** \'fòr-ˌmāt\ *noun* (1807)
**:** a salt or ester of formic acid
**for·ma·tion** \fòr-'mā-shən\ *noun* (15th century)
**1 :** an act of giving form or shape to something or of taking form **:** DEVELOPMENT
**2 :** something that is formed 〈new word *formations*〉
**3 :** the manner in which a thing is formed **:** STRUCTURE 〈the peculiar *formation* of the heart〉
**4 :** the largest unit in an ecological community comprising two or more associations and their precursors 〈grassland *formation*〉
**5 a :** any igneous, sedimentary, or metamorphic rock represented as a unit **b :** any sedimentary bed or consecutive series of beds sufficiently homogeneous or distinctive to be a unit
**6 :** an arrangement of a body or group of persons or things in some prescribed manner or for a particular purpose
**¹for·ma·tive** \'fòr-mə-tiv\ *adjective* (15th century)
**1 a :** giving or capable of giving form **:** CONSTRUCTIVE 〈a *formative* influence〉 **b :** used in word formation or inflection
**2 :** capable of alteration by growth and development; *also* **:** producing new cells and tissues
**3 :** of, relating to, or characterized by formative effects or formation 〈*formative* years〉
— **for·ma·tive·ly** *adverb*
**²formative** *noun* (1816)
**:** the element (as a suffix) in a word that serves to give the word appropriate form and is not part of the base
**form class** *noun* (1921)
**:** a class of linguistic forms that can be used in the same position in a construction and that have one or more morphological or syntactical features in common
**form–critical** *adjective* (1933)
**:** based on or applying form criticism
**form criticism** *noun* (1928)
**:** a method of criticism for determining the sources and historicity of biblical writings through analysis of the writings in terms of ancient literary forms and oral traditions (as love poems, parables, and proverbs)

---

\ə\ **abut** \ᵊ\ **kitten** \ər\ **further** \a\ **ash** \ā\ **ace**
\ä\ **mop, mar** \aù\ **out** \ch\ **chin** \e\ **bet** \ē\ **easy**
\g\ **go** \i\ **hit** \ī\ **ice** \j\ **job** \ŋ\ **sing** \ō\ **go**
\ò\ **law** \òi\ **boy** \th\ **thin** \t̲h̲\ **the** \ü\ **loot** \ù\ **foot**
\y\ **yet** \zh\ **vision** *see also* Guide to Pronunciation

— **form critic** *noun*

**forme** \'fòm, 'fòrm\ *noun* (15th century)
*British* : FORM 8

**formed** \'fòrmd\ *adjective* (1605)
: organized in a way characteristic of living matter ⟨mitochondria are *formed* bodies of the cell⟩

**for·mée** \'fòr-ˌmā, fòr-'\ *adjective* [French, feminine past participle of *former* to form, from Latin *formare*] (15th century)
*of a heraldic cross* : having the arms narrow at the center and expanding toward the ends — see CROSS illustration

**¹for·mer** \'fòr-mər\ *adjective* [Middle English, from *forme* first, from Old English *forma* — more at FOREMOST] (12th century)
**1 a** : coming before in time **b** : of, relating to, or occurring in the past ⟨*former* correspondence⟩
**2** : preceding in place or arrangement : FOREGOING ⟨*former* part of the chapter⟩
**3** : first in order of two or more things cited or understood ⟨of the two given, the *former* spelling is more common⟩ ⟨of the two spellings, the *former* is more common⟩
**4** : having been previously : ONETIME ⟨a *former* athlete⟩
**synonym** see PRECEDING

**²form·er** \'fòr-mər\ *noun* (14th century)
**1** : one that forms
**2** *chiefly British* : a member of a school form — usually used in combination ⟨sixth *former*⟩

**for·mer·ly** \'fòr-mə(r)-lē\ *adverb* (1534)
**1** : at an earlier time : PREVIOUSLY
**2** *obsolete* : just before

**form·fit·ting** \'fòrm-ˌfi-tiŋ\ *adjective* (1897)
: conforming to the outline of the body : fitting snugly ⟨a *formfitting* sweater⟩

**form·ful** \'fòrm-fəl\ *adjective* (1832)
: exhibiting or notable for form

**form genus** *noun* (1873)
: an artificial taxonomic category established for organisms (as imperfect fungi) of obscure true relationships

**For·mi·ca** \fòr-'mī-kə, fər-\ *trademark*
— used for any of various laminated plastic products used especially for surface finish

**for·mic acid** \'fòr-mik-\ *noun* [irregular from Latin *formica* ant — more at PISMIRE] (1791)
: a colorless pungent fuming vesicant liquid acid $CH_2O_2$ found especially in ants and in many plants and used chiefly in dyeing and finishing textiles

**for·mi·cary** \'fòr-mə-ˌker-ē\ *noun, plural* **-car·ies** [Medieval Latin *formicarium*, from Latin *formica*] (1816)
: an ant nest

**for·mi·da·ble** \'fòr-mə-də-bəl; fòr-'mi-, fər-'mi-\ *adjective* [Middle English, from Latin *formidabilis*, from *formidare* to fear, from *formido* terror, bogey; akin to Greek *mormō* bogey] (15th century)
**1** : causing fear, dread, or apprehension ⟨a *formidable* prospect⟩
**2** : having qualities that discourage approach or attack
**3** : tending to inspire awe or wonder
— **for·mi·da·bil·i·ty** \ˌfòr-mə-də-'bi-lə-tē; fòr-ˌmi-, fər-\ *noun*
— **for·mi·da·ble·ness** \'fòr-mə-də-bəl-nəs; fòr-'mi-, fər-\ *noun*
— **for·mi·da·bly** \-blē\ *adverb*

**form·less** \'fòrm-ləs\ *adjective* (1591)
**1** : having no regular form or shape
**2** : lacking order or arrangement
**3** : having no physical existence
— **form·less·ly** *adverb*
— **form·less·ness** *noun*

**form letter** *noun* (1909)
**1** : a letter on a subject of frequent recurrence that can be sent to different people without essential change except in the address
**2** : a letter for mass circulation that is printed in many copies and has a very general salutation (as *Dear Friend*)

**formo-** — see FORM-

**¹for·mu·la** \'fòr-myə-lə\ *noun, plural* **-las** *or* **-lae** \-ˌlē, -ˌlī\ [Latin, diminutive of *forma* form] (1618)
**1 a** : a set form of words for use in a ceremony or ritual **b** : a conventionalized statement intended to express some fundamental truth or principle especially as a basis for negotiation or action
**2 a** (1) : RECIPE (2) : PRESCRIPTION **b** : a milk mixture or substitute for feeding an infant
**3 a** : a general fact, rule, or principle expressed in usually mathematical symbols **b** : a symbolic expression of the chemical composition or constitution of a substance **c** : a group of symbols (as letters and numbers) associated to express concisely facts or data (as the number and kinds of teeth in the jaw) **d** : a combination of signs in a logical calculus
**4** : a customary or set form or method allowing little room for originality
— **for·mu·la·ic** \ˌfòr-myə-'lā-ik\ *adjective*
— **for·mu·la·ical·ly** \-'lā-ə-k(ə-)lē\ *adverb*

**²formula** *adjective* (1927)
: of, relating to, or being an open-wheel open-cockpit rear-engine racing car conforming to prescribed specifications as to size, weight, and engine displacement

**for·mu·la·rize** \'fòr-myə-lə-ˌrīz\ *transitive verb* **-rized; -riz·ing** (1852)
: to state in or reduce to a formula : FORMULATE
— **for·mu·la·ri·za·tion** \ˌfòr-myə-lə-rə-'zā-shən\ *noun*
— **for·mu·la·riz·er** \'fòr-myə-lə-ˌrī-zər\ *noun*

**for·mu·lary** \'fòr-myə-ˌler-ē\ *noun, plural* **-lar·ies** (1541)
**1** : a collection of prescribed forms (as oaths or prayers)
**2** : FORMULA 1
**3** : a book listing medicinal substances and formulas
— **formulary** *adjective*

**for·mu·late** \'fòr-myə-ˌlāt\ *transitive verb* **-lat·ed; -lat·ing** (1860)
**1 a** : to reduce to or express in a formula **b** : to put into a systematized statement or expression **c** : DEVISE ⟨*formulate* a policy⟩
**2 a** : to develop a formula for the preparation of (as a soap or plastic) **b** : to prepare according to a formula
— **for·mu·la·tor** \-ˌlā-tər\ *noun*

**for·mu·la·tion** \ˌfòr-myə-'lā-shən\ *noun* (1876)
: an act or the product of formulating

**formula weight** *noun* (circa 1920)
: MOLECULAR WEIGHT — used especially of ionic compounds

**for·mu·lize** \'fòr-myə-ˌlīz\ *transitive verb* **-lized; -liz·ing** (1842)
: FORMULATE 1

**form word** *noun* (1875)
: FUNCTION WORD

**form·work** \'fòrm-ˌwərk\ *noun* (1918)
: a set of forms in place to hold wet concrete until it sets

**for·myl** \'fòr-ˌmil\ *noun* [International Scientific Vocabulary] (circa 1859)
: the radical HCO of formic acid that is also characteristic of aldehydes

**for·ni·cate** \'fòr-nə-ˌkāt\ *verb* **-cat·ed; -cat·ing** [Late Latin *fornicatus*, past participle of *fornicare* to have intercourse with prostitutes, from Latin *fornic-, fornix* arch, vault, brothel] (1552)
*intransitive verb*
: to commit fornication
*transitive verb*
: to commit fornication with
— **for·ni·ca·tor** \-ˌkā-tər\ *noun*

**for·ni·ca·tion** \ˌfòr-nə-'kā-shən\ *noun* (14th century)
: consensual sexual intercourse between two persons not married to each other — compare ADULTERY

**for·nix** \'fòr-niks\ *noun, plural* **for·ni·ces** \-nə-ˌsēz\ [New Latin, from Latin] (1681)
: an anatomical arch or fold

**for·rad·er** *also* **for·rard·er** \'fär-ə-dər\ *adverb* [English dialect, comparative of English *forward*] (1888)
*chiefly British* : further ahead

**for·sake** \fər-'sāk, fòr-\ *transitive verb* **for·sook** \-'sůk\; **for·sak·en** \-'sā-kən\; **for·sak·ing** [Middle English, from Old English *forsacan*, from *for-* + *sacan* to dispute; akin to Old English *sacu* action at law — more at SAKE] (before 12th century)
: to renounce or turn away from entirely ⟨friends have *forsaken* her⟩ ⟨*forsook* the theater for politics⟩
**synonym** see ABANDON

**for·sooth** \fər-'sůth\ *adverb* [Middle English *for soth*, from Old English *forsōth*, from *for* + *sōth* sooth] (before 12th century)
: in truth : INDEED — often used to imply contempt or doubt

**for·spent** \fər-'spent, fòr-\ *adjective* (1563)
*archaic* : WORN-OUT, EXHAUSTED

**for·swear** \fòr-'swar, fòr-, -'swer\ *verb* **-swore** \-'swōr, -'swòr\; **-sworn** \-'swōrn, -'swòrn\; **-swear·ing** [Middle English *forsweren*, from Old English *forswerian*, from *for-* + *swerian* to swear] (before 12th century)
*transitive verb*
**1** : to make a liar of (oneself) under or as if under oath
**2 a** : to reject or renounce under oath **b** : to renounce earnestly
**3** : to deny under oath
*intransitive verb*
: to swear falsely
**synonym** see ABJURE

**for·sworn** \-'swōrn, -'swòrn\ *adjective* (before 12th century)
**1** : guilty of perjury
**2** : marked by perjury

**for·syth·ia** \fər-'si-thē-ə, *chiefly British* -'sī-\ *noun* [New Latin, genus name, from William Forsyth (died 1804) British botanist] (circa 1814)
: any of a genus (*Forsythia*) of ornamental shrubs of the olive family with opposite leaves and yellow bell-shaped flowers appearing before the leaves in early spring

**forsythia**

**fort** \'fòrt, 'fòrt\ *noun* [Middle English *forte*, from Middle French *fort*, from *fort*, adjective, strong, from Latin *fortis*] (15th century)
**1** : a strong or fortified place; *especially* : a fortified place occupied only by troops and surrounded with such works as a ditch, rampart, and parapet : FORTIFICATION
**2** : a permanent army post — often used in place names

**for·ta·lice** \'fòr-t°l-əs\ *noun* [Middle English, from Medieval Latin *fortalitia* — more at FORTRESS] (15th century)
**1** *archaic* : FORTRESS
**2** *archaic* : a small fort

**¹forte** \'fòrt, 'fòrt; *2 is often* 'fòr-ˌtā *or* fòr-'tā *or* 'fòr-tē\ *noun* [French *fort*, from *fort*, adjective, strong] (circa 1648)
**1** : the part of a sword or foil blade that is between the middle and the hilt and that is the strongest part of the blade
**2** : one's strong point ◼

**²for·te** \'fòr-ˌtā, 'fòr-tē\ *adverb or adjective* [Italian, from *forte* strong, from Latin *fortis*] (circa 1724)
: LOUD — used as a direction in music

**³for·te** \'fòr-ˌtā, 'fòr-tē\ *noun* (1759)
: a tone or passage played forte

**for·te·pia·no** \ˌfòr-ˌtā-pē-'a-(ˌ)nō *also* -'ä-(ˌ)nō\ *noun* [French or Italian; French, from Italian, from *forte* loud + *piano* soft] (1771)

: an early form of the piano originating in the 18th and early 19th centuries and having a smaller range and softer timbre than a modern piano

**word history** see PIANO

**for·te·pi·a·no** \ˌfȯr-ˌtā-pē-'ä-(ˌ)nō, ˌfȯr-tē-\ *adverb or adjective* (circa 1889)
: loud then immediately soft — used as a direction in music

**¹forth** \'fōrth, 'fȯrth\ *adverb* [Middle English, from Old English; akin to Old English *for*] (before 12th century)
**1** : onward in time, place, or order : FORWARD ⟨from that day *forth*⟩
**2** : out into notice or view ⟨put *forth* leaves⟩
**3** *obsolete* : AWAY, ABROAD

**²forth** *preposition* (circa 1577)
*archaic* : forth from : OUT OF

**forth·com·ing** \fōrth-'kə-miŋ, fȯrth-; 'fōrth-ˌ, 'fȯrth-\ *adjective* [obsolete *forthcome* (to come forth)] (circa 1532)
**1** : being about to appear or to be produced or made available ⟨the *forthcoming* holidays⟩ ⟨your *forthcoming* novel⟩ ⟨funds are *forthcoming*⟩
**2 a** : RESPONSIVE, OUTGOING ⟨a *forthcoming* and courteous man⟩ **b** : characterized by openness, candidness, and forthrightness ⟨not *forthcoming* about his memories of medical school —Mark Kramer⟩

**forth of** *preposition* (13th century)
*archaic* : out from : OUT OF

**¹forth·right** \'fȯr-ˌthrīt, 'fȯrth-\ *adverb* [Middle English, from Old English *forthriht*, from *forth* + *riht* right] (before 12th century)
**1** *archaic* **a** : directly forward **b** : without hesitation : FRANKLY
**2** *archaic* : at once

**²forthright** *adjective* (before 12th century)
**1** *archaic* : proceeding straight on
**2** : free from ambiguity or evasiveness : going straight to the point ⟨a *forthright* critic⟩ ⟨was *forthright* in appraising the problem⟩
**3** : notably simple in style or quality ⟨*forthright* furniture⟩
— **forth·right·ly** *adverb*
— **forth·right·ness** *noun*

**³forthright** *noun* (1606)
*archaic* : a straight path

**forth·with** \(ˌ)fōrth-'with, (ˌ)fȯrth- *also* -'with\ *adverb* (14th century)
: IMMEDIATELY

**for·ti·fi·ca·tion** \ˌfȯr-tə-fə-'kā-shən\ *noun* (15th century)
**1** : an act or process of fortifying
**2** : something that fortifies, defends, or strengthens; *especially* : works erected to defend a place or position

**fortified wine** *noun* (1906)
: a wine (as sherry) to which alcohol usually in the form of grape brandy has been added during or after fermentation

**for·ti·fi·er** \'fȯr-tə-ˌfī-(ə)r\ *noun* (circa 1552)
: one that fortifies

**for·ti·fy** \-ˌfī\ *verb* **-fied; -fy·ing** [Middle English *fortifien*, from Middle French *fortifier*, from Late Latin *fortificare*, from Latin *fortis* strong] (15th century)
*transitive verb*
: to make strong: as **a** : to strengthen and secure (as a town) by forts or batteries **b** : to give physical strength, courage, or endurance to **c** : to add mental or moral strength to : ENCOURAGE ⟨*fortified* by prayer⟩ **d** : to add material to for strengthening or enriching
*intransitive verb*
: to erect fortifications

**for·tis** \'fȯr-təs\ *adjective* [New Latin, from Latin, strong] (1897)
: produced with relatively great articulatory tenseness and strong expiration ⟨\t\ in *toe* is *fortis*, \d\ in *doe* is lenis⟩

**¹for·tis·si·mo** \fȯr-'ti-sə-ˌmō\ *adverb or adjective* [Italian, superlative of *forte*] (1724)
: very loud — used especially as a direction in music

**²fortissimo** *noun, plural* **-mos** *or* **-mi** \-ˌmē\ (1856)
: a very loud passage, sound, or tone

**for·ti·tude** \'fȯr-tə-ˌtüd, -ˌtyüd\ *noun* [Middle English, from Latin *fortitudin-, fortitudo*, from *fortis*] (12th century)
**1** : strength of mind that enables a person to encounter danger or bear pain or adversity with courage
**2** *obsolete* : STRENGTH

**fort·night** \'fȯrt-ˌnīt, 'fȯrt-\ *noun* [Middle English *fourtenight*, alteration of *fourtene night*, from Old English *fēowertȳne niht* fourteen nights] (before 12th century)
: a period of 14 days : two weeks

**¹fort·night·ly** \-lē\ *adjective* (1800)
: occurring or appearing once in a fortnight

**²fortnightly** *adverb* (1820)
: once in a fortnight : every fortnight

**³fortnightly** *noun, plural* **-lies** (1940)
: a publication issued fortnightly

**FOR·TRAN** *or* **For·tran** \'fȯr-ˌtran\ *noun* [*formula translation*] (1956)
: a computer programming language that resembles algebra in its notation and is widely used for scientific applications

**for·tress** \'fȯr-trəs\ *noun* [Middle English *forteresse*, from Middle French *forteresce*, from Medieval Latin *fortalitia*, from Latin *fortis* strong] (14th century)
: a fortified place : STRONGHOLD; *especially* : a large and permanent fortification sometimes including a town
— **for·tress·like** \-ˌlīk\ *adjective*

**for·tu·itous** \fȯr-'tü-ə-təs, -'tyü-, fər-\ *adjective* [Latin *fortuitus*; akin to Latin *fort-, fors*] (1653)
**1** : occurring by chance
**2 a** : FORTUNATE, LUCKY ⟨from a cost standpoint, the company's timing is *fortuitous* —*Business Week*⟩ **b** : coming or happening by a lucky chance ⟨belted down the stairs, and there was a *fortuitous* train —Doris Lessing⟩ ☐
**synonym** see ACCIDENTAL
— **for·tu·itous·ly** *adverb*
— **for·tu·itous·ness** *noun*

**for·tu·ity** \-ə-tē\ *noun, plural* **-ities** (circa 1747)
**1** : the quality or state of being fortuitous
**2** : a chance event or occurrence

**for·tu·nate** \'fȯrch-nət, 'fȯr-chə-\ *adjective* (14th century)
**1** : bringing some good thing not forseen as certain : AUSPICIOUS
**2** : receiving some unexpected good
**synonym** see LUCKY
— **for·tu·nate·ness** *noun*

**for·tu·nate·ly** \-lē\ *adverb* (1548)
**1** : in a fortunate manner
**2** : it is fortunate

**¹for·tune** \'fȯr-chən\ *noun* [Middle English, from Middle French, from Latin *fortuna*; akin to Latin *fort-, fors* chance, luck, and perhaps to *ferre* to carry — more at BEAR] (14th century)
**1** *often capitalized* : a hypothetical force or personified power that unpredictably determines events and issues favorably or unfavorably
**2** *obsolete* : ACCIDENT, INCIDENT
**3 a** : prosperity attained partly through luck : SUCCESS **b** : LUCK 1 **c** *plural* : the turns and courses of luck accompanying one's progress (as through life) ⟨her *fortunes* varied but she never gave up⟩
**4** : DESTINY, FATE ⟨can tell your *fortune*⟩; *also* : a prediction of fortune
**5 a** : RICHES, WEALTH ⟨a man of *fortune*⟩ **b** : a store of material possessions ⟨the family *fortune*⟩ **c** : a very large sum of money ⟨spent a *fortune* redecorating⟩

**²fortune** *verb* **for·tuned; for·tun·ing** (14th century)
*transitive verb*
**1** *obsolete* : to give good or bad fortune to

**2** *archaic* : to endow with a fortune
*intransitive verb*
*archaic* : HAPPEN, CHANCE

**fortune cookie** *noun* (1962)
: a thin cookie folded to contain a slip of paper on which is printed a fortune, proverb, or humorous statement

**fortune hunter** *noun* (1689)
: a person who seeks wealth especially by marriage

**for·tune–tell·er** \-ˌte-lər\ *noun* (1590)
: one that professes to foretell future events
— **for·tune–tell·ing** \-liŋ\ *noun or adjective*

**for·ty** \'fȯr-tē\ *noun, plural* **forties** [Middle English *fourty*, adjective, from Old English *fēowertig*, from *fēowertig* group of 40, from *fēower* four + *-tig* group of 10; akin to Old English *tīen* ten] (before 12th century)
**1** — see NUMBER table
**2** *plural* : the numbers 40 to 49; *specifically* : the years 40 to 49 in a lifetime or century
**3** : the third point scored by a side in a game of tennis
— **for·ti·eth** \'fȯr-tē-əth\ *adjective or noun*
— **forty** *adjective*
— **forty** *pronoun, plural in construction*
— **for·ty·ish** \-tē-ish\ *adjective*

**for·ty–five** \ˌfȯr-tē-'fīv\ *noun* (1904)
**1** — see NUMBER table
**2** : a .45 caliber handgun — usually written .45
**3** : a phonograph record designed to be played at 45 revolutions per minute — usually written 45
— **forty–five** *adjective*
— **forty–five** *pronoun, plural in construction*

**Forty Hours** *noun plural but singular or plural in construction* (1759)
: a Roman Catholic devotion in which the churches of a diocese in two-day turns have the Blessed Sacrament exposed on the altar for continuous daytime veneration

**for·ty–nin·er** \ˌfȯr-tē-'nī-nər\ *noun* (1853)
: one taking part in the rush to California for gold in 1849

**forty winks** *noun plural but singular or plural in construction* (1872)
: a short sleep : NAP

---

☐ **USAGE**

**forte** In *forte* we have a word derived from French that in its "strong point" sense has no entirely satisfactory pronunciation. Usage writers have denigrated \'fȯr-ˌtā\ and \'fȯr-tē\ because they reflect the influence of the Italian-derived ²*forte*. Their recommended pronunciation \'fȯrt\, however, does not exactly reflect French either: the French would write the word *le fort* and would rhyme it with English *for*. So you can take your choice, knowing that someone somewhere will dislike whichever variant you choose. All are standard, however. In British English \'fȯ-ˌtā\ and \'fȯt\ predominate; \'fȯr-ˌtā\ and fȯr-'tā\ are probably the most frequent pronunciations in American English.

**fortuitous** Sense 2a has been influenced in meaning by *fortunate*. It has been in standard if not elevated use for some 70 years, but is still disdained by some critics. Sense 2b, a blend of 1 and 2a, is virtually unnoticed by the critics. Sense 1 is the only sense commonly used in negative constructions.

---

| | | |
|---|---|---|
| \ə\ abut | \ᵊ\ kitten | \ər\ **further** | \a\ ash | \ā\ ace |
| \ä\ mop, mar | \au̇\ out | \ch\ chin | \e\ bet | \ē\ easy |
| \g\ go | \i\ hit | \ī\ ice | \j\ job | \ŋ\ sing | \ō\ go |
| \ȯ\ law | \ȯi\ boy | \th\ thin | \t͟h\ the | \ü\ loot | \u̇\ foot |
| \y\ yet | \zh\ vision | *see also* Guide to Pronunciation |

**fo·rum** \'fōr-əm, 'for-\ *noun, plural* **forums** *also* **fo·ra** \-ə\ [Latin; akin to Latin *foris* outside, *fores* door — more at DOOR] (15th century) **1 a :** the marketplace or public place of an ancient Roman city forming the center of judicial and public business **b :** a public meeting place for open discussion **c :** a medium (as a newspaper) of open discussion or expression of ideas **2 :** a judicial body or assembly : COURT **3 a :** a public meeting or lecture involving audience discussion **b :** a program (as on radio or television) involving discussion of a problem usually by several authorities

**¹for·ward** \'for-wərd, *also* 'fō- *or* 'fò-, *Southern also* 'fär-\ *adjective* [Middle English, from Old English *foreweard*, from *fore-* + *-weard* -ward] (before 12th century) **1 a :** near, being at, or belonging to the forepart **b :** situated in advance **2 a :** strongly inclined : READY **b :** lacking modesty or reserve : BRASH **3 :** notably advanced or developed : PRECOCIOUS **4 :** moving, tending, or leading toward a position in front; *also* : moving toward an opponent's goal **5 a :** advocating an advanced policy in the direction of what is considered progress **b :** EXTREME, RADICAL **6 :** of, relating to, or getting ready for the future ⟨*forward* buying of produce⟩
— **for·ward·ly** *adverb*
— **for·ward·ness** *noun*
**²forward** *adverb* (before 12th century) **:** to or toward what is ahead or in front ⟨from that time *forward*⟩ ⟨moved slowly *forward*⟩
**³forward** *transitive verb* (1596) **1 :** to help onward : PROMOTE ⟨*forwarded* his friend's career⟩ **2 a :** to send forward : TRANSMIT ⟨will *forward* the goods on receipt of your check⟩ **b :** to send or ship onward from an intermediate post or station in transit ⟨*forward* mail⟩
**synonym** see ADVANCE
**⁴forward** *noun* (1879) **:** a player who plays at the front of his team's formation near the goal at which his team is attempting to score
**for·ward·er** \-wər-dər\ *noun* (1549) **:** one that forwards; *especially* : an agent who performs services (as receiving, transshipping, or delivering) designed to move goods to their destination
**for·ward–look·ing** \'for-wərd-,lu̇-kiŋ\ *adjective* (1800) **:** concerned with or planning for the future
**forward pass** *noun* (1903) **:** a pass (as in football) made in the direction of the opponents' goal
**for·wards** \'for-wərdz\ *adverb* (15th century) **:** FORWARD
**for·worn** \fər-'worn, -'wȯrn\ *adjective* (1528) *archaic* **:** WORN-OUT
**for·zan·do** \fort-'sän-(,)dō\ *adjective or adverb* [Italian] (circa 1828) **:** SFORZANDO
**¹fos·sa** \'fä-sə\ *noun, plural* **fos·sae** \-,sē, -,sī\ [New Latin, from Latin, ditch] (1771) **:** an anatomical pit, groove, or depression
**²fossa** *noun* [Malagasy] (1838) **:** a slender lithe carnivorous mammal (*Cryptoprocta ferox*) of Madagascar that resembles a cat especially in having retractile claws but is usually considered a viverrid
**fosse** *or* **foss** \'fäs\ *noun* [Middle English *fosse*, from Old French, from Latin *fossa*, from feminine of *fossus*] (15th century) **:** DITCH, MOAT
**fos·sick** \'fä-sik\ *verb* [English dialect *fossick* to ferret out] (1852) *intransitive verb* **1** *Australian & New Zealand* **:** to search for gold or gemstones typically by picking over abandoned workings

**2** *chiefly Australian & New Zealand* **:** to search about **:** RUMMAGE
*transitive verb*
*chiefly Australian & New Zealand* **:** to search for by or as if by rummaging **:** ferret out
— **fos·sick·er** *noun, chiefly Australian & New Zealand*
**¹fos·sil** \'fä-səl\ *adjective* [Latin *fossilis* obtained by digging, from *fodere* to dig — more at BED] (1665) **1 :** preserved from a past geologic age ⟨*fossil* plants⟩ ⟨*fossil* water in an underground reservoir⟩ **2 :** being or resembling a fossil **3 :** of or relating to fossil fuel
**²fossil** *noun* (1736) **1 :** a remnant, impression, or trace of an organism of past geologic ages that has been preserved in the earth's crust — compare LIVING FOSSIL **2 a :** one whose views are outmoded : FOGY **b :** something (as a theory) that has become rigidly fixed **3 :** an old word or word element preserved only by idiom (as *fro* in *to and fro*)
**fossil fuel** *noun* (1835) **:** a fuel (as coal, oil, or natural gas) that is formed in the earth from plant or animal remains
— **fos·sil–fueled** \-,fyü(-ə)ld\ *adjective*
**fos·sil·if·er·ous** \,fä-sə-'li-f(ə-)rəs\ *adjective* (circa 1846) **:** containing fossils
**fos·sil·ise** *chiefly British variant of* FOSSILIZE
**fos·sil·ize** \'fä-sə-,līz\ *verb* **-ized; -iz·ing** (1794) *transitive verb* **1 :** to convert into a fossil **2 :** to make outmoded, rigid, or fixed *intransitive verb* **:** to become changed into a fossil
— **fos·sil·iza·tion** \'fä-sə-lə-'zā-shən\ *noun*
**fos·so·ri·al** \fä-'sor-ē-əl, -'sȯr-\ *adjective* [Medieval Latin *fossorius* used for digging, from Latin *fossor* digger, from *fodere*] (1837) **:** adapted to digging ⟨a *fossorial* foot⟩
**¹fos·ter** \'fȯs-tər, 'fäs-\ *adjective* [Middle English, from Old English *fōstor-*, from *fōstor* food, feeding; akin to Old English *fōda* food] (before 12th century) **:** affording, receiving, or sharing nurture or parental care though not related by blood or legal ties
**²foster** *transitive verb* **fos·tered; fos·ter·ing** \-t(ə-)riŋ\ (12th century) **1 :** to give parental care to : NURTURE **2 :** to promote the growth or development of **:** ENCOURAGE
— **fos·ter·er** \-tər-ər\ *noun*
**fos·ter·age** \-tə-rij\ *noun* (1614) **1 :** the act of fostering **2 :** a custom once prevalent in Ireland, Wales, and Scotland of entrusting one's child to foster parents to be brought up
**foster home** *noun* (1886) **:** a household in which an orphaned, neglected, or delinquent child is placed for care
**fos·ter·ling** \-tər-liŋ\ *noun* (before 12th century) **:** a foster child
**fou** \'fü\ *adjective* [Middle English (Scots) *fow* full, from Middle English *full*] (1535) *Scottish* **:** DRUNK 1a
**Fou·cault pendulum** \,fü-'kō-\ *noun* [J.B.L. *Foucault*] (1931) **:** a freely swinging pendulum that consists of a heavy weight hung by a long wire and that swings in a constant direction which appears to change showing that the earth rotates
**fouet·té** \(,)fwe-'tā\ *noun* [French, from past participle of *fouetter* to whip, from Middle French *fouet* whip, from Old French, from *fou* beech, from Latin *fagus* — more at BEECH] (1830) **:** a quick whipping movement of the raised leg in ballet usually accompanying a pirouette

**fought** *past and past participle of* FIGHT
**¹foul** \'fau̇(-ə)l\ *adjective* [Middle English, from Old English *fūl*; akin to Old High German *fūl* rotten, Latin *pus* pus, *putēre* to stink, Greek *pyon* pus] (before 12th century) **1 a :** offensive to the senses : LOATHSOME **b :** filled or covered with offensive matter **2 :** full of dirt or mud **3 a :** morally or spiritually odious : DETESTABLE ⟨a *foul* crime⟩ **b :** notably unpleasant or distressing : WRETCHED, HORRID ⟨in a *foul* mood⟩ **4 :** OBSCENE, ABUSIVE ⟨*foul* language⟩ **5 a :** being wet and stormy **b :** obstructive to navigation ⟨a *foul* tide⟩ **6** *dialect British* **:** HOMELY, UGLY **7 a :** TREACHEROUS, DISHONORABLE ⟨fair means or *foul*⟩ **b :** constituting an infringement of rules in a game or sport ⟨a *foul* blow in boxing⟩ **8 :** containing marked-up corrections ⟨*foul* manuscript⟩ ⟨*foul* proofs⟩ **9 :** encrusted, clogged, or choked with a foreign substance ⟨the chimney was *foul* and smoked badly⟩ **10 :** being odorous and impure : POLLUTED ⟨*foul* air⟩ **11 :** placed in a situation that impedes physical movement **:** ENTANGLED **12 :** being outside the foul lines in baseball
**synonym** see DIRTY
— **foul·ly** \'fau̇(l)-lē\ *adverb*
— **foul·ness** *noun*
**²foul** *noun* (before 12th century) **1** *archaic* **:** something foul **2 :** an entanglement or collision especially in angling or sailing **3 a :** an infringement of the rules in a game or sport **b :** FREE THROW **4 :** FOUL BALL
**³foul** (before 12th century) *intransitive verb* **1 :** to become or be foul: as **a :** DECOMPOSE, ROT **b :** to become encrusted, clogged, or choked with a foreign substance **c :** to become entangled or come into collision **2 :** to commit a violation of the rules in a sport or game **3 :** to hit a foul ball *transitive verb* **1 :** to make foul: as **a :** to make dirty : POLLUTE **b :** to tangle or come into collision with **c :** to encrust with a foreign substance ⟨a ship's bottom *fouled* with barnacles⟩ **d :** OBSTRUCT, BLOCK **2 :** DISHONOR, DISCREDIT **3 :** to commit a foul against **4 :** to hit (a baseball) foul
**⁴foul** *adverb* (13th century) **:** in a foul manner **:** so as to be foul
**fou·lard** \fu̇-'lärd\ *noun* [French] (1830) **1 a :** a lightweight plain-woven or twilled silk usually decorated with a printed pattern **b :** an imitation of this fabric **2 :** an article of clothing made of foulard
**foul ball** *noun* (1860) **:** a baseball batted into foul territory
**foul·brood** \'fau̇l-,brüd\ *noun* (1863) **:** a destructive disease of honeybee larvae caused by bacteria (as *Bacillus larvae*)
**foul·ing** *noun* (14th century) **:** DEPOSIT, INCRUSTATION ⟨*fouling* on a ship's bottom⟩
**foul line** *noun* (1878) **1 :** either of two straight lines extending from the rear corner of home plate through the outer corners of first and third base respectively and prolonged to the boundary of a baseball field **2 :** a line across a bowling alley that a player must not step over when delivering the ball **3 :** either of two lines on a basketball court parallel to and 15 feet from the backboards behind which a player must stand while shooting a free throw
**foul–mouthed** \'fau̇l-,mau̇thd, -,mau̇tht\ *adjective* (1596)

: given to the use of obscene, profane, or abusive language

**foul out** *intransitive verb* (1948)
: to be put out of a basketball game for exceeding the number of fouls permitted

**foul play** *noun* (15th century)
: VIOLENCE; *especially* : MURDER

**foul shot** *noun* (circa 1949)
: FREE THROW

**foul tip** *noun* [¹*foul* + *tip* (tap)] (1870)
: a pitched ball in baseball that is slightly deflected by the bat; *specifically* : a tipped pitch legally caught by the catcher and counting as a full strike with the ball remaining in play

**foul-up** \'faùl-ˌəp\ *noun* (1950)
**1** : a state of confusion or an error caused by ineptitude, carelessness, or mismanagement ⟨*foul-ups* in transportation⟩
**2** : a mechanical difficulty

**foul up** (1947)
*transitive verb*
**1** : to make dirty : CONTAMINATE
**2** : to spoil by making mistakes or using poor judgment : CONFUSE
**3** : ENTANGLE, BLOCK ⟨*fouled up* communications⟩
*intransitive verb*
: to cause a foul-up : BUNGLE ⟨it was his fault. He had *fouled up* —Pat Frank⟩

**¹found** \'faùnd\ *past and past participle of* FIND

**²found** *adjective* (1793)
**1** : having all usual, standard, or reasonably expected equipment ⟨the boat comes fully *found*, ready to go —*Holiday*⟩
**2** : presented as or incorporated into an artistic work essentially as found ⟨sculpture of fabric, wood, and other *found* materials —Hilton Kramer⟩

**³found** *noun* (1830)
: free food and lodging in addition to wages ⟨they're paid $175 a month and *found* —*New Yorker*⟩

**⁴found** *transitive verb* [Middle English, from Old French *fonder*, from Latin *fundare*, from *fundus* bottom — more at BOTTOM] (13th century)
**1** : to take the first steps in building
**2** : to set or ground on something solid : BASE
**3** : to establish (as an institution) often with provision for future maintenance

**⁵found** *transitive verb* [Middle French *fondre* to pour, melt, from Latin *fundere*; akin to Old English *gēotan* to pour, Greek *chein*] (1562)
: to melt (as metal) and pour into a mold

**foun·da·tion** \faùn-'dā-shən\ *noun* (14th century)
**1** : the act of founding
**2** : a basis (as a tenet, principle, or axiom) upon which something stands or is supported ⟨the *foundations* of geometry⟩ ⟨the rumor is without *foundation* in fact⟩
**3 a** : funds given for the permanent support of an institution : ENDOWMENT **b** : an organization or institution established by endowment with provision for future maintenance
**4** : an underlying base or support; *especially* : the whole masonry substructure of a building
**5 a** : a body or ground upon which something is built up or overlaid **b** : a woman's supporting undergarment : CORSET **c** : a cosmetic usually used as a base for makeup
— **foun·da·tion·al** \-shnəl, -shə-nᵊl\ *adjective*
— **foun·da·tion·al·ly** *adverb*
— **foun·da·tion·less** \-shən-ləs\ *adjective*

**foundation stone** *noun* (1651)
**1** : BASIS, GROUNDWORK
**2** : a stone in the foundation of a building; *especially* : such a stone laid with public ceremony — compare CORNERSTONE

**¹found·er** \'faùn-dər\ *noun* [⁴*found*] (14th century)
: one that founds or establishes

**²foun·der** \'faùn-dər\ *verb* **foun·dered**; **foun·der·ing** \-d(ə-)riŋ\ [Middle English

*foundren* to send to the bottom, collapse, from Middle French *fondrer*, ultimately from Latin *fundus*] (14th century)
*intransitive verb*
**1** : to become disabled; *especially* : to go lame
**2** : to give way : COLLAPSE
**3** : to sink below the surface of the water
**4** : to come to grief : FAIL
*transitive verb*
: to disable (an animal) especially by excessive feeding

**³foun·der** *noun* (circa 1547)
: LAMINITIS

**⁴found·er** *noun* [⁵*found*] (15th century)
: one that founds metal; *especially* : TYPEFOUNDER

**founding father** *noun* (1914)
**1** : an originator of an institution or movement : FOUNDER
**2** *often both Fs capitalized* : a leading figure in the founding of the U.S.; *specifically* : a member of the American Constitutional Convention of 1787

**found·ling** \'faùn(d)-liŋ\ *noun* (14th century)
: an infant found after its unknown parents have abandoned it

**found object** *noun* (1950)
: OBJET TROUVÉ

**found poem** *noun* (1966)
: a poem consisting of words found in a non-poetic context (as a product label) and usually broken into lines that convey a verse rhythm

**found·ry** \'faùn-drē\ *noun, plural* **foundries** (1536)
**1** : an establishment where founding is carried on
**2** : the act, process, or art of casting metals

**¹fount** \'faùnt\ *noun* [Middle English, from Middle French *font*, from Latin *font-, fons*] (15th century)
: FOUNTAIN, SOURCE

**²fount** \'fänt, 'faùnt\ *noun* [French *fonte*, from Middle French — more at FONT] (circa 1683)
*British* : a type font

**¹foun·tain** \'faùn-t°n\ *noun* [Middle English, from Middle French *fontaine*, from Late Latin *fontana*, from Latin, feminine of *fontanus* of a spring, from *font-, fons*] (14th century)
**1** : the source from which something proceeds or is supplied
**2** : a spring of water issuing from the earth
**3** : an artificially produced jet of water; *also* : the structure from which it rises
**4** : a reservoir containing a liquid that can be drawn off as needed
**5** : SODA FOUNTAIN 2

**²fountain** (1903)
*intransitive verb*
: to flow or spout like a fountain
*transitive verb*
: to cause to flow like a fountain

**foun·tain·head** \-ˌhed\ *noun* (1585)
**1** : a spring that is the source of a stream
**2** : principal source : ORIGIN

**fountain pen** *noun* (1710)
: a pen containing a reservoir that automatically feeds the writing point with ink

**four** \'fōr, 'fòr\ *noun* [Middle English, from *four* adjective, from Old English *fēower*; akin to Old High German *fior* four, Latin *quattuor*, Greek *tessares, tettares*] (before 12th century)
**1** — see NUMBER table
**2** : the fourth in a set or series ⟨the *four* of hearts⟩
**3** : something having four units or members: as **a** : a 4-oared racing shell or its crew **b** : a 4-cylinder engine or automobile
— **four** *adjective*
— **four** *pronoun, plural in construction*

**four–bag·ger** \-ˌba-gər\ *noun* (1926)
: HOME RUN

**four–ball** \-ˌbòl\ *adjective* (1904)
: relating to or being a golf match in which the best individual score of one partnership is matched against the best individual score of another partnership for each hole

**four·chée** \fùr-'shā\ *adjective* [French (feminine), literally, forked] (1706)
*of a heraldic cross* : having the end of each arm forked — see CROSS illustration

**four–dimensional** *adjective* (1880)
: relating to or having four dimensions ⟨*four-dimensional* space-time continuum⟩; *especially* : consisting of or relating to elements requiring four coordinates to determine them

**four·dri·nier** \ˌfōr-drə-'nir, ˌfòr-; fùr-'dri-nē-ər, fōr-, fòr-\ *noun, often capitalized* [Henry & Sealy *Fourdrinier*] (1839)
: a machine for making paper in an endless web

**four–eyed** \'fōr-ˌīd, 'fòr-\ *adjective* (1926)
: wearing glasses

**4–F** \'fōr-'ef, 'fòr-\ *noun* (1944)
: classification as unfit for military service; *also* : a person having this classification

**four–flush** *intransitive verb* (1896)
: to bluff in poker holding a four flush; *broadly* : to make a false claim : BLUFF
— **four–flush·er** \-'flə-shər\ *noun*

**four flush** *noun* (1887)
: four cards of the same suit in a 5-card poker hand

**four–fold** \'fōr-ˌfōld, 'fòr-, -'fōld\ *adjective* [Middle English, from Old English *fēowerfeald*, from *fēower* + *-feald* -fold] (before 12th century)
**1** : being four times as great or as many
**2** : having four units or members
— **four·fold** \-'fōld\ *adverb*

**four–foot·ed** \-'fù-təd\ *adjective* (14th century)
: having four feet : QUADRUPED

**four·gon** \fùr-'gō^n\ *noun, plural* **fourgons** \-'gō^n(z)\ [French] (1848)
: a wagon for carrying baggage

**4–H** \'fōr-'āch, 'fòr-\ *adjective* [from the fourfold aim of improving the head, heart, hands, and health] (1926)
: of or relating to a program set up by the U.S. Department of Agriculture originally in rural areas to help young people become productive citizens by instructing them in useful skills (as in agriculture, animal husbandry, and carpentry), community service, and personal development
— **4–H'·er** *also* **4–H·er** \-'ā-chər\ *noun*

**four–hand** \'fōr-ˌhand, 'fòr-\ *adjective* (circa 1909)
: FOUR-HANDED

**four–hand·ed** \-'han-dəd\ *adjective* (1824)
**1** : engaged in by four persons ⟨a *four-handed* card game⟩
**2** : designed for four hands ⟨a *four-handed* musical composition⟩

**Four Horsemen** *noun plural* [from the apocalyptic vision in Revelation 6:2–8] (1918)
: war, famine, pestilence, and death personified as the four major plagues of mankind

**Four Hundred** *or* **400** *noun* (1888)
: the exclusive social set of a community — used with *the*

**Fou·ri·er analysis** \ˌfùr-ē-ˌā-\ *noun* [Baron J.B.J. *Fourier* (died 1830) French geometrician & physicist] (circa 1928)
: the process of using the terms of a Fourier series to find a function that approximates periodic data

**Fou·ri·er·ism** \'fùr-ē-ə-ˌri-zəm, -ē-ˌā-ˌi-\ *noun* [French *fouriérisme*, from F.M.C. *Fourier*] (1843)
: a system for reorganizing society into cooperative communities of small self-sustaining groups
— **Fou·ri·er·ist** \-ē-ə-rist, -ē-ˌā-ist\ *noun*

**Fou·ri·er series** \'fùr-ē-ˌā-\ *noun* [Baron J.B.J. *Fourier*] (1877)

: an infinite series in which the terms are constants multiplied by sine or cosine functions of integer multiples of the variable and which is used in the analysis of periodic functions

**Fourier's theorem** *noun* (1834)
: a theorem in mathematics: under suitable conditions any periodic function can be represented by a Fourier series

**Fourier transform** *noun* (1923)
: any of various functions (as $F(u)$) that under suitable conditions can be obtained from given functions (as $f(x)$) by multiplying by $e^{iux}$ and integrating over all values of $x$ and that in scientific instrumentation describe the dependence of the average of a series of measurements (as of a spectrum) on a quantity of interest (as brightness) especially of a very small magnitude — called also *Fourier transformation*

**four-in-hand** \'fōr-ən-ˌhand, 'fȯr-\ *noun* (1793)
**1 a :** a team of four horses driven by one person **b :** a vehicle drawn by such a team
**2 :** a necktie tied in a slipknot with long ends overlapping vertically in front

**four-letter** *adjective* (1897)
: of, relating to, or being four-letter words

**four-letter word** *noun* (1897)
: any of a group of vulgar or obscene words typically made up of four letters

**four-line octave** *noun* [from the four accent marks appended to the letters representing its notes] (1931)
: the musical octave that begins on the third C above middle C — see PITCH illustration

**four-o'clock** \'fōr-ə-ˌkläk, 'fȯr-\ *noun* (1756)
: any of a genus (*Mirabilis*) of chiefly American annual or perennial herbs (family Nyctaginaceae, the four-o'clock family) having apetalous flowers with a showy involucre simulating a calyx; *especially* **:** a garden plant (*M. jalapa*) with fragrant yellow, red, or white flowers opening late in the afternoon

**four of a kind** (circa 1934)
: four cards of the same rank in one hand — see POKER illustration

**four-plex** \'fōr-ˌpleks, 'fȯr-\ *noun* (1952)
: a building that contains four separate apartments

**four-post-er** \ˌfōr-'pō-stər, ˌfȯr-\ *noun* (1836)
: a bed with tall often carved corner posts originally designed to support curtains or a canopy

four-poster

**four-ra-gère** \ˌfür-ə-'zher\ *noun* [French, from feminine of *fourrager* of forage, from *fourrage* forage] (1919)
: a braided cord worn usually around the left shoulder; *especially* **:** such a cord awarded as a decoration to a military unit

**four-score** \'fōr-'skōr, 'fȯr-'skȯr\ *adjective* (13th century)
: being four times twenty **:** EIGHTY

**four-some** \'fōr-səm, 'fȯr-\ *noun* (14th century)
**1 a :** a group of four persons or things **:** QUARTET **b :** two couples
**2 :** a golf match in which two players compete against two others with players on each side taking turns playing one ball; *broadly* **:** any golf match involving four players

**four-square** \-'skwär, -'skwer\ *adjective* (14th century)
**1 :** SQUARE
**2 :** marked by boldness and conviction **:** FORTHRIGHT
— **foursquare** *adverb*

**four-star** \-'stär\ *adjective* [from the number of asterisks used to denote relative excellence in guidebooks] (1921)

: of a superior degree of excellence ⟨a *four-star* French restaurant⟩

**four-teen** \fōr-'tēn, fȯr-; 'fōr(t)-ˌtēn, 'fȯr(t)-\ *noun* [Middle English *fourtene*, from Old English *fēowertīene*, from *fēowertīene*, adjective, from *fēower* + *-tīene*; akin to Old English *tīen* ten] (before 12th century)
— see NUMBER table
— **fourteen** *adjective*
— **fourteen** *pronoun*, plural in construction
— **four-teenth** \-'tēn(t)th; -ˌtēn(t)th\ *adjective or noun*

**four-teen-er** \-'tē-nər\ *noun* (1884)
: a verse consisting of 14 syllables or especially of 7 iambic feet

**fourth** \'fōrth, 'fȯrth\ *noun*, *plural* **fourths** \'fōr(th)s, 'fȯr(th)s\ (before 12th century)
**1** — see NUMBER table
**2 a :** a musical interval embracing four tones of the diatonic scale **b :** a tone at this interval; *specifically* **:** SUBDOMINANT 1 **c :** the harmonic combination of two tones a fourth apart
**3 :** the 4th forward gear or speed of a motor vehicle
**4** *capitalized* **:** INDEPENDENCE DAY — used with *the*
— **fourth** *adjective or adverb*
— **fourth-ly** *adverb*

**fourth class** *noun* (1862)
**1 :** a class or group ranking fourth in a series
**2 :** a class of mail in the U.S. that comprises merchandise and non-second-class printed matter and is not sealed against inspection

**fourth dimension** *noun* (1875)
**1 :** a dimension in addition to length, breadth, and depth; *specifically* **:** a coordinate in addition to three rectangular coordinates especially when interpreted as the time coordinate in a space-time continuum
**2 :** something outside the range of ordinary experience
— **fourth-dimensional** *adjective*

**fourth estate** *noun*, *often F&E capitalized* (1752)
: the public press ◆

**Fourth of July** (1779)
**:** INDEPENDENCE DAY

**fourth world** *noun*, *often F&W capitalized* (1974)
: a group of nations especially in Africa and Asia characterized by extremely low per capita income and an absence of valuable natural resources

**four-way** \'fōr-ˌwā, 'fȯr-\ *adjective* (1824)
**1 :** allowing or affecting passage in any of four directions
**2 :** including four participants

**four-wheel** \'fōr-ˌhwēl, 'fȯr-, -ˌwēl\ *or* **four-wheeled** \-ˌhwē(ə)ld, -ˌwē(ə)ld\ *adjective* (1740)
**1 :** having four wheels
**2 :** acting on or by means of four wheels of an automotive vehicle ⟨*four-wheel* drive⟩

**four-wheel-er** \-ˌhwē-lər, -ˌwē-\ *noun* (1846)
: a vehicle with four wheels

**fo-vea** \'fō-vē-ə\ *noun*, *plural* **fo-ve-ae** \-vē-ˌē, -vē-ˌī\ [New Latin, from Latin, pit] (1849)
**1 :** a small fossa
**2 :** a small rodless area of the retina that affords acute vision — see EYE illustration
— **fo-ve-al** \-vē-əl\ *adjective*
— **fo-ve-ate** \-vē-ˌāt, -ət\ *adjective*

**fovea cen-tra-lis** \-sen-'tra-ləs, -'trä-, -'trā-\ *noun* [New Latin, central fovea] (1858)
**:** FOVEA 2

**fowl** \'faù(ə)l\ *noun*, *plural* **fowl** *or* **fowls** [Middle English *foul*, from Old English *fugel*; akin to Old High German *fogal* bird, and probably to Old English *flēogan* to fly — more at FLY] (before 12th century)
**1 :** a bird of any kind — compare WATERFOWL, WILDFOWL
**2 a :** a cock or hen of the domestic chicken (*Gallus gallus*); *especially* **:** an adult hen **b**

: any of several domesticated or wild gallinaceous birds — compare GUINEA FOWL, JUNGLE FOWL
**3 :** the meat of fowls used as food

**fowl** *intransitive verb* (before 12th century)
: to seek, catch, or kill wildfowl
— **fowl-er** *noun*

**fowling piece** *noun* (1596)
: a shotgun for shooting birds or small quadrupeds

**fox** \'fäks\ *noun*, *plural* **fox-es** *also* **fox** *often attributive* [Middle English, from Old English; akin to Old High German *fuhs* fox and perhaps to Sanskrit *puccha* tail] (before 12th century)
**1 a :** any of various carnivorous mammals (especially genus *Vulpes*) of the dog family related to but smaller than wolves with shorter legs, more pointed muzzle, large erect ears, and long bushy tail **b :** the fur of a fox
**2 :** a clever crafty person
**3** *archaic* **:** SWORD
**4** *capitalized* **:** a member of an American Indian people formerly living in what is now Wisconsin
**5 :** a good-looking young woman or man
**word history** see VIXEN

**fox** *transitive verb* (1611)
**1** *obsolete* **:** INTOXICATE
**2 a :** to trick by ingenuity or cunning **:** OUTWIT
**b :** BAFFLE

**foxed** \'fäkst\ *adjective* (1847)
: discolored with yellowish brown stains

**fox fire** *noun* (15th century)
: an eerie phosphorescent light (as of decaying wood); *also* **:** a luminous fungus (as *Armillaria mellea*) that causes decaying wood to glow

**fox-glove** \'fäks-ˌgləv\ *noun* (before 12th century)
: any of a genus (*Digitalis*) of erect herbs of the snapdragon family; *especially* **:** a common European biennial or perennial (*D. purpurea*) cultivated for its showy racemes of dotted white or purple tubular flowers and as a source of digitalis

**fox grape** *noun* (1657)
: any of several native grapes (especially *Vitis labrusca*) of eastern North America with sour or musky fruit

**fox-hole** \'fäks-ˌhōl\ *noun* (1919)
: a pit dug usually hastily for individual cover from enemy fire

**fox-hound** \-ˌhaùnd\ *noun* (circa 1763)
: any of various large swift powerful hounds of great endurance used in hunting foxes and developed to form several breeds and many distinctive strains — compare AMERICAN FOXHOUND, ENGLISH FOXHOUND

**fox-hunt-er** \-ˌhən-tər\ *noun* (1692)
**1 :** one who engages in foxhunting
**2 :** HUNTER 1c

**fox-hunt-ing** \-ˌhən-tiŋ\ *noun* (1674)
: a pastime in which participants on horseback ride over the countryside following a pack of hounds on the trail of a fox
— **fox-hunt** \-ˌhənt\ *intransitive verb*

**fox-tail** \'fäks-ˌtāl\ *noun* (14th century)

**1 a :** the tail of a fox **b :** something resembling the tail of a fox
**2 :** any of several grasses (especially genera *Alopecurus, Hordeum,* and *Setaria*) with spikes resembling brushes — called also *foxtail grass*

**foxtail lily** *noun* (1946)
**:** EREMURUS

**foxtail millet** *noun* (circa 1899)
**:** a coarse drought-resistant but frost-sensitive annual grass (*Setaria italica*) grown for grain, hay, and forage

**fox terrier** *noun* (1823)
**:** any of a smooth-haired or a wirehaired breed of small lively terriers formerly used to dig out foxes

fox terrier

**Fox·trot** \'fäks-ˌträt\ (1952)
— a communications code word for the letter *f*

**¹fox–trot** \'fäks-ˌträt\ *noun* (1872)
**1 :** a short broken slow trotting gait in which the hind foot of the horse hits the ground a trifle before the diagonally opposite forefoot
**2 :** a ballroom dance in duple time that includes slow walking steps, quick running steps, and the step of the two-step

**²fox–trot** *intransitive verb* (1916)
**:** to dance the fox-trot

**foxy** \'fäk-sē\ *adjective* **fox·i·er; -est** (1528)
**1 :** resembling or suggestive of a fox ⟨a narrow *foxy* face⟩: as **a :** cunningly shrewd **b :** of a warm reddish brown color ⟨*foxy* eyebrows⟩
**2 :** having a sharp brisk flavor ⟨*foxy* grapes⟩
**3 :** physically attractive ⟨a *foxy* lady⟩
*synonym* see SLY
— **fox·i·ly** \'fäk-sə-lē\ *adverb*
— **fox·i·ness** \-sē-nəs\ *noun*

**foy** \'fȯi\ *noun* [Dutch dialect *fooi* feast at end of the harvest] (circa 1645)
*chiefly Scottish* **:** a farewell feast or gift

**foy·er** \'fȯi-(ə)r, 'fȯi-ˌ(y)ā *also* 'fwä-ˌyā\ *noun* [French, literally, fireplace, from (assumed) Vulgar Latin *focarium,* from Latin *focus* hearth] (1859)
**:** an anteroom or lobby especially of a theater; *also* **:** an entrance hallway **:** VESTIBULE

**Fra** \'frä\ *noun* [Italian, short for *frate,* from Latin *frater* — more at BROTHER] (circa 1890)
— used as a title equivalent to *brother* preceding the name of an Italian monk or friar

**fra·cas** \'frä-kəs, 'frā-, *British* 'fra-ˌkä\ *noun, plural* **fra·cas·es** \-kə-səz\ *or British* **frac·as** \-ˌkäz\ [French, din, row, from Italian *fracasso,* from *fracassare* to shatter] (1727)
**:** a noisy quarrel **:** BRAWL

**frac·tal** \'frak-t³l\ *noun* [French *fractale,* from Latin *fractus* broken, uneven (past participle of *frangere* to break) + French *-ale -al* (noun suffix)] (1975)
**:** any of various extremely irregular curves or shapes for which any suitably chosen part is similar in shape to a given larger or smaller part when magnified or reduced to the same size
— **fractal** *adjective*

**fract·ed** \'frak-təd\ *adjective* [Latin *fractus*] (1547)
*obsolete* **:** BROKEN

**frac·tion** \'frak-shən\ *noun* [Middle English *fraccioun,* from Late Latin *fraction-, fractio*

act of breaking, from Latin *frangere* to break — more at BREAK] (14th century)
**1 a :** a numerical representation (as ¾, ⅝, 3.234) indicating the quotient of two numbers **b** (1) **:** a piece broken off **:** FRAGMENT (2) **:** a discrete unit **:** PORTION
**2 :** one of several portions (as of a distillate) separable by fractionation
**3 :** BIT, LITTLE ⟨a *fraction* closer⟩

**frac·tion·al** \-shnəl, -shə-n³l\ *adjective* (1675)
**1 :** of, relating to, or being a fraction
**2 :** of, relating to, or being fractional currency
**3 :** relatively small **:** INCONSIDERABLE
**4 :** of, relating to, or involving a process for separating components of a mixture through differences in physical or chemical properties ⟨*fractional* distillation⟩
— **frac·tion·al·ly** *adverb*

**fractional currency** *noun* (1862)
**1 :** paper money in denominations of less than one dollar issued by the U.S. 1863–76
**2 :** currency in denominations less than the basic monetary unit

**frac·tion·al·ize** \'frak-shnə-ˌlīz, -shə-n³l-ˌīz\ *transitive verb* **-ized; -iz·ing** (1924)
**:** to break up into parts or sections
— **frac·tion·al·iza·tion** \ˌfrak-shnə-lə-'zā-shən, -shə-n³l-ə-'zā-\ *noun*

**frac·tion·ate** \'frak-shə-ˌnāt\ *transitive verb* **-at·ed; -at·ing** (1867)
**1 :** to separate (as a mixture) into different portions
**2 :** to divide or break up
— **frac·tion·ation** \ˌfrak-shə-'nā-shən\ *noun*
— **frac·tion·ator** \'frak-shə-ˌnā-tər\ *noun*

**frac·tious** \'frak-shəs\ *adjective* [*fraction* (discord) + *-ous*] (1725)
**1 :** tending to be troublesome **:** UNRULY
**2 :** QUARRELSOME, IRRITABLE
— **frac·tious·ly** *adverb*
— **frac·tious·ness** *noun*

**¹frac·ture** \'frak-chər, -shər\ *noun* [Middle English, from Latin *fractura,* from *fractus*] (15th century)
**1 :** the result of fracturing **:** BREAK
**2 a :** the act or process of breaking or the state of being broken; *especially* **:** the breaking of hard tissue (as bone) **b :** the rupture (as by tearing) of soft tissue ⟨kidney *fracture*⟩
**3 :** the general appearance of a freshly broken surface of a mineral

**²fracture** *verb* **frac·tured; frac·tur·ing** \-chə-riŋ, -shriŋ\ (1612)
*transitive verb*
**1 a :** to cause a fracture in **:** BREAK ⟨*fracture* a rib⟩ **b :** RUPTURE, TEAR
**2 a :** to damage or destroy as if by rupturing **b :** to cause great disorder in **c :** to break up **:** FRACTIONATE **d :** to go beyond the limits of (as rules) **:** VIOLATE ⟨*fractured* the English language with malaprops —Goodman Ace⟩
*intransitive verb*
**:** to undergo fracture

**fracture zone** *noun* (1946)
**:** an area of suboceanic crust characterized by fractures

**frae** \'frā\ *preposition* [Middle English (northern) *fra, frae,* from Old Norse *frā;* akin to Old English *fram* from] (1700)
*Scottish* **:** FROM

**frag·ile** \'fra-jəl, -ˌjīl\ *adjective* [Middle French, from Latin *fragilis* — more at FRAIL] (1607)
**1 a :** easily broken or destroyed **b :** constitutionally delicate **:** lacking in physical vigor
**2 :** TENUOUS, SLIGHT ☆
— **fra·gil·i·ty** \frə-'ji-lə-tē\ *noun*

**¹frag·ment** \'frag-mənt\ *noun* [Middle English, from Latin *fragmentum,* from *frangere* to break — more at BREAK] (15th century)
**:** a part broken off, detached, or incomplete
*synonym* see PART

**²frag·ment** \-ˌment\ (1818)
*intransitive verb*
**:** to fall to pieces

*transitive verb*
**:** to break up or apart into fragments

**frag·men·tal** \frag-'men-t³l\ *adjective* (1798)
**:** FRAGMENTARY
— **frag·men·tal·ly** \-t³l-ē\ *adverb*

**frag·men·tary** \'frag-mən-ˌter-ē\ *adjective* (1611)
**:** consisting of fragments **:** INCOMPLETE
— **frag·men·tari·ly** \ˌfrag-mən-'ter-ə-lē\ *adverb*
— **frag·men·tari·ness** \-ter-ē-nəs\ *noun*

**frag·men·ta·tion** \ˌfrag-mən-'tā-shən, -ˌmen-\ *noun* (1881)
**1 :** the act or process of fragmenting or making fragmentary
**2 :** the state of being fragmented or fragmentary
— **frag·men·tate** \'frag-mən-ˌtāt\ *verb*

**fragmentation bomb** *noun* (1918)
**:** a bomb or shell whose relatively thick casing is splintered upon explosion and thrown in fragments in all directions

**frag·men·tize** \'frag-mən-ˌtīz\ *transitive verb* **-tized; -tiz·ing** (1815)
**:** FRAGMENT

**fra·grance** \'frā-grən(t)s\ *noun* (1667)
**1 a :** a sweet or delicate odor (as of fresh flowers, pine trees, or perfume) **b :** something (as a perfume) compounded to give off a sweet or pleasant odor
**2 :** the quality or state of having a sweet odor ☆

**fra·gran·cy** \-grən(t)-sē\ *noun* (1578)
**:** FRAGRANCE

**fra·grant** \'frā-grənt\ *adjective* [Middle English, from Latin *fragrant-, fragrans,* from present participle of *fragrare* to be fragrant] (15th century)
**:** marked by fragrance
*synonym* see ODOROUS
— **fra·grant·ly** *adverb*

**frail** \'frā(ə)l\ *adjective* [Middle English, from Middle French *fraile,* from Latin *fragilis* fragile, from *frangere*] (14th century)
**1 :** easily led into evil ⟨*frail* humanity⟩
**2 :** easily broken or destroyed **:** FRAGILE
**3 a :** physically weak **b :** SLIGHT, UNSUBSTANTIAL
*synonym* see WEAK

---

☆ SYNONYMS
**Fragile, frangible, brittle, crisp, friable** mean breaking easily. FRAGILE implies extreme delicacy of material or construction and need for careful handling ⟨a *fragile* antique chair⟩. FRANGIBLE implies susceptibility to being broken without implying weakness or delicacy ⟨*frangible* stone used for paving⟩. BRITTLE implies hardness together with lack of elasticity or flexibility or toughness ⟨patients with *brittle* bones⟩. CRISP implies a firmness and brittleness desirable especially in some foods ⟨*crisp* lettuce⟩. FRIABLE applies to substances that are easily crumbled or pulverized ⟨*friable* soil⟩. See in addition WEAK.

**Fragrance, perfume, scent, redolence** mean a sweet or pleasant odor. FRAGRANCE suggests the odors of flowers or other growing things ⟨the *fragrance* of pine⟩. PERFUME may suggest a stronger or heavier odor ⟨the *perfume* of lilacs⟩. SCENT is very close to PERFUME but of wider application because more neutral in connotation ⟨*scent*-free soaps⟩. REDOLENCE implies a mixture of fragrant or pungent odors ⟨the *redolence* of a forest after a rain⟩.

---

— **frail·ly** \'frā(ə)(l)-lē\ adverb

— **frail·ness** noun

**frail·ty** \'frā(-ə)l-tē\ noun, plural **frailties** (14th century)
**1** : the quality or state of being frail
**2** : a fault due to weakness especially of moral character
**synonym** see FAULT

**fraise** \'frāz\ noun [French] (1775)
: an obstacle of pointed stakes driven into the ramparts of a fortification in a horizontal or inclined position

**Frak·tur** also **Frac·tur** \fräk-'tùr\ noun [German, from Latin fractura fracture] (1904)
**1** : a German style of black letter
**2** often not capitalized : a Pennsylvania German document (as a birth or wedding certificate) that is written in calligraphy and illuminated with decorative motifs (as tulips, birds, and scrolls)

**fram·be·sia** \fram-'bē-zh(ē-)ə\ noun [New Latin, from French framboise raspberry; from the appearance of the lesions] (1803)
: YAWS

**fram·boise** \frä<sup>n</sup>-'bwäz\ noun [French, literally, raspberry, from Old French, of Germanic origin; akin to Dutch braambes blackberry, literally, bramble berry, Old High German brāmberi — more at BROOM, BERRY] (circa 1945)
: a brandy or liqueur made from raspberries.

**¹frame** \'frām\ verb **framed**; **fram·ing** [Middle English, to benefit, construct, from Old English framian to benefit, make progress; akin to Old Norse fram forward, Old English fram from] (14th century)
transitive verb
**1** : to construct by fitting and uniting the parts of the skeleton of (a structure)
**2 a** : PLAN, CONTRIVE ⟨framed a new method of achieving their purpose⟩ **b** : SHAPE, CONSTRUCT **c** : to give expression to : FORMULATE **d** : to draw up (as a document)
**3 a** : to devise falsely (as a criminal charge) **b** : to contrive the evidence against (an innocent person) so that a verdict of guilty is assured **c** : FIX 7b
**4** : to fit or adjust especially to something or for an end : ARRANGE
**5** obsolete : PRODUCE
**6** : to enclose in a frame; also : to enclose as if in a frame
intransitive verb
**1** archaic : PROCEED, GO
**2** obsolete : MANAGE
— **fram·able** or **frame·able** \'frā-mə-bəl\ adjective
— **fram·er** noun

**²frame** noun (14th century)
**1 a** : something composed of parts fitted together and united **b** : the physical makeup of an animal and especially a human body : PHYSIQUE, FIGURE
**2 a** : the constructional system that gives shape or strength (as to a building); also : a frame dwelling **b** : such a skeleton not filled in or covered
**3** obsolete : the act or manner of framing
**4 a** : a machine built upon or within a framework ⟨a spinning frame⟩ **b** : an open case or structure made for admitting, enclosing, or supporting something ⟨a window frame⟩ **c** (1) : a part of a pair of glasses that holds one of the lenses (2) plural : that part of a pair of glasses other than the lenses **d** : a structural unit in an automobile chassis supported on the axles and supporting the rest of the chassis and the body
**5 a** : an enclosing border **b** : the matter or area enclosed in such a border: as (1) : one of the squares in which scores for each round are recorded (as in bowling); also : a round in bowling (2) : an individual drawing in a comic strip usually enclosed by a bordering line (3) : one picture of the series on a length of film (4) : a complete image for display (as on a television

set) **c** : an inning in baseball **d** (1) : FRAMEWORK 1a (2) : CONTEXT, FRAME OF REFERENCE **e** : an event that forms the background for the action of a novel or play
**6** : FRAME-UP

**³frame** adjective (1775)
: having a wood frame ⟨frame houses⟩

**frame of mind** (1665)
: mental attitude or outlook : MOOD

**frame of reference** (1897)
**1** : an arbitrary set of axes with reference to which the position or motion of something is described or physical laws are formulated
**2** : a set of ideas, conditions, or assumptions that determine how something will be approached, perceived, or understood ⟨a Marxian frame of reference⟩

**frame·shift** \'frām-,shift\ adjective (1967)
: relating to, being, or causing a mutation in which a number of nucleotides not divisible by three is inserted or deleted so as to change the reading frame of some triplet codons during genetic translation
— **frameshift** noun

**frame-up** \'frā-,məp\ noun (1889)
**1** : an act or series of actions in which someone is framed
**2** : an action that is framed

**frame·work** \'frām-,wərk\ noun (1644)
**1 a** : a basic conceptional structure (as of ideas) ⟨the framework of the constitution⟩ **b** : a skeletal, openwork, or structural frame
**2** : FRAME OF REFERENCE
**3** : the larger branches of a tree that determine its shape

**fram·ing** \'frā-miŋ\ noun (1703)
: FRAME, FRAMEWORK

**franc** \'fraŋk\ noun [French] (14th century)
— see MONEY table

**¹fran·chise** \'fran-,chīz\ noun [Middle English, from Middle French, from franchir to free, from Old French franc free — more at FRANK] (14th century)
**1** : freedom or immunity from some burden or restriction vested in a person or group
**2 a** : a special privilege granted to an individual or group; especially : the right to be and exercise the powers of a corporation **b** : a constitutional or statutory right or privilege; especially : the right to vote **c** (1) : the right or license granted to an individual or group to market a company's goods or services in a particular territory; also : a business granted such a right or license (2) : the territory involved in such a right
**3 a** : the right of membership in a professional sports league **b** : a team and its operating organization having such membership

**²franchise** transitive verb **fran·chised**; **fran·chis·ing** (14th century)
**1** archaic : FREE
**2** : to grant a franchise to

**fran·chi·see** \,fran-chī-'zē, -chə-\ noun (1954)
: one granted a franchise

**fran·chis·er** \'fran-,chī-zər\ noun [in sense 1, from ¹franchise; in sense 2, from ²franchise] (1843)
**1** : FRANCHISEE
**2** : FRANCHISOR

**fran·chi·sor** \,fran-,chī-'zòr, -chə-\ noun [²franchise + ¹-or] (1967)
: one that grants a franchise

**Fran·cis·can** \fran-'sis-kən\ noun [Medieval Latin Franciscus Francis] (1599)
: a member of the Order of Friars Minor founded by Saint Francis of Assisi in 1209 and dedicated especially to preaching, missions, and charities
— **Franciscan** adjective

**fran·ci·um** \'fran(t)-sē-əm\ noun [New Latin, from France] (1946)
: a radioactive element of the alkali-metal group discovered as a disintegration product of actinium and obtained artificially by the

bombardment of thorium with protons — see ELEMENT table

**Franco-** combining form [Medieval Latin, from Francus Frenchman, from Late Latin, Frank]
**1** : French and ⟨Franco-American⟩
**2** : French ⟨Francophile⟩

**Fran·co-Amer·i·can** \,fran-kō-ə-'mer-ə-kən\ noun (1859)
: an American of French or especially French-Canadian descent
— **Franco–American** adjective

**fran·co·lin** \'fran-k(ə-)lən\ noun [French, from Italian francolino] (1653)
: any of a genus (Francolinus) of partridges of southern Asia and Africa

**Fran·co·phile** \'fran-kə-,fīl, -kō-\ or **Fran·co·phil** \-,fil\ adjective (1889)
: markedly friendly to France or French culture
— **Francophile** noun
— **Fran·co·phil·ia** \,fran-kə-'fi-lē-ə, -lyə, -kō-\ noun

**Fran·co·phobe** \-,fōb\ adjective (1891)
: marked by a fear or strong dislike of France or French culture or customs
— **Francophobe** noun
— **Fran·co·pho·bia** \,fran-kə-'fō-bē-ə, -kō-\ noun

**fran·co·phone** \-,fōn\ adjective, often capitalized (1962)
: of, having, or belonging to a population using French as its first or sometimes second language
— **Francophone** noun

**franc-ti·reur** \,frä<sup>n</sup>-(,)tē-'rər\ noun [French, from franc free + tireur shooter] (1808)
: a civilian fighter or sniper

**fran·gi·ble** \'fran-jə-bəl\ adjective [Middle English, from Middle French & Medieval Latin; Middle French, from Medieval Latin frangibilis, from Latin frangere to break — more at BREAK] (15th century)
: readily or easily broken
**synonym** see FRAGILE
— **fran·gi·bil·i·ty** \,fran-jə-'bi-lə-tē\ noun

**fran·gi·pane** \'fran-jə-,pān, frä<sup>n</sup>-zhē-'pán\ noun [French, frangipani (perfume), fragipane, from Italian] (1858)
: a custard usually flavored with almonds

**fran·gi·pa·ni** also **fran·gi·pan·ni** \,fran-jə-'pa-nē, -'pä-\ noun, plural **-pani** also **-panni** [modification of Italian frangipane, from Muzio Frangipane, 16th century Italian nobleman] (1676)
**1** : a perfume derived from or imitating the odor of the flower of a frangipani (Plumeria rubra)
**2** : any of a genus (Plumeria) of shrubs or small trees of the dogbane family that are native to the American tropics and widely cultivated as ornamentals

**fran·glais** \frä<sup>n</sup>-'glä\ noun, often capitalized [French, blend of français French and anglais English] (1964)
: French marked by a considerable number of borrowings from English

**¹frank** \'fraŋk\ adjective [Middle English, free, from Old French franc, from Medieval Latin francus, from Late Latin Francus Frank] (1548)
**1** : marked by free, forthright, and sincere expression ⟨a frank reply⟩
**2 a** : unmistakably evident ⟨frank materialism⟩ **b** : clinically evident and unmistakable ⟨frank pus⟩ ☆ ◆
— **frank·ness** noun

**²frank** transitive verb (1708)
**1 a** : to mark (a piece of mail) with an official signature or sign indicating the right of the sender to free mailing **b** : to mail free **c** : to affix to (mail) a stamp or a marking indicating the payment of postage
**2** : to enable to pass or go freely or easily
— **frank·able** \'fraŋ-kə-bəl\ adjective
— **frank·er** noun

**³frank** *noun* (1713)
**1 a :** the signature of the sender on a piece of franked mail serving in place of a postage stamp **b :** a mark or stamp on a piece of mail indicating postage paíd **c :** a franked envelope **2 :** the privilege of sending mail free of charge
**⁴frank** *noun* (1904)
**:** FRANKFURTER
**Frank** \'fraŋk\ *noun* [Middle English, partly from Old English *Franca;* partly from Old French *Franc,* from Late Latin *Francus,* of Germanic origin; akin to Old High German *Franko* Frank, Old English *Franca*] (before 12th century)
**:** a member of a West Germanic people that entered the Roman provinces in A.D. 253, occupied the Netherlands and most of Gaul, and established themselves along the Rhine
**Fran·ken·stein** \'fraŋ-kən-ˌstīn *also* -ˌstēn\ *noun*
**1 a :** the title character in Mary W. Shelley's novel *Frankenstein* who creates a monster by which he is eventually killed **b :** a monster in the shape of a man especially in popularized versions of the Frankenstein story **2 :** a monstrous creation; *especially :* a work or agency that ruins its originator
— **Fran·ken·stein·ian** \ˌfraŋ-kən-'stī-nē-ən, -'sti-\ *adjective*
**frank·furt·er** \'fraŋk-fə(r)t-ər, -ˌfərt-\ *or* **frank·furt** \-fərt\ *noun* [German *Frankfurter* of Frankfurt, from *Frankfurt am Main,* Germany] (1894)
**:** a cured cooked sausage (as of beef or beef and pork) that may be skinless or stuffed in a casing
**frank·in·cense** \'fraŋ-kən-ˌsen(t)s\ *noun* [Middle English *fraunk encense,* from Old French *franc encens,* from *franc* (perhaps in sense "of high quality") + *encens* incense] (14th century)
**:** a fragrant gum resin from trees of a genus (*Boswellia* of the family Burseraceae) of Somalia and southern coastal Arabia that is an important incense resin and was used in ancient times in religious rites and in embalming
**¹Frank·ish** \'fraŋ-kish\ *adjective* (14th century)
**:** of or relating to the Franks
**²Frankish** *noun* (1863)
**:** the Germanic language of the Franks
**frank·lin** \'fraŋ-klən\ *noun* [Middle English *frankeleyn,* from Anglo-French *fraunclein,* from Old French *franc*] (14th century)
**:** a medieval English landowner of free but not noble birth
**frank·lin·ite** \-klə-ˌnīt\ *noun* [*Franklin,* N.J.] (1820)
**:** a black slightly magnetic mineral consisting of an oxide of iron and zinc
**Frank·lin stove** \'fraŋ-klən-\ *noun* [Benjamin Franklin, its inventor] (1787)
**:** a metal heating stove resembling an open fireplace but designed to be set out in a room
**frank·ly** \'fraŋ-klē\ *adverb* (1537)
**1 :** in a frank manner
**2 :** in truth **:** INDEED
**usage** *see* HOPEFULLY

**Franklin stove**

**frank·pledge** \'fraŋk-ˌplej\ *noun* [Middle English *frankeplegge,* from Anglo-French *fraunc plege* (probably translation of Middle English *friborg* peace pledge), from *fraunc* free (from Old French *franc*) + *plege* pledge] (15th century)
**:** an Anglo-Saxon system under which each adult male member of a tithing was responsible for the good conduct of the others; *also* **:** the member himself or the tithing

**fran·tic** \'fran-tik\ *adjective* [Middle English *frenetik, frantik* — more at FRENETIC] (14th century)
**1 a** *archaic* **:** mentally deranged **b :** emotionally out of control ⟨*frantic* with anger and frustration⟩
**2 :** marked by fast and nervous, disordered, or anxiety-driven activity ⟨made a *frantic* search for the lost child⟩
— **fran·ti·cal·ly** \-ti-k(ə-)lē\ *adverb*
— **fran·tic·ness** \-tik-nəs\ *noun*
**frap** \'frap\ *transitive verb* **frapped; frapping** [Middle English, to strike, beat, from Middle French *fraper*] (1548)
**:** to draw tight (as with ropes or cables) ⟨*frap* a sail⟩
**¹frap·pé** \fra-'pā\ *adjective* [French, from past participle of *frapper* to strike, chill, from Middle French *fraper* to strike] (1848)
**:** chilled or partly frozen
**²frap·pé** \fra-'pā\ *or* **frappe** \'frap, fra-'pā\ *noun* (1903)
**1 a :** a partly frozen drink (as of fruit juice) **b :** a liqueur served over shaved ice
**2 :** a thick milk shake
**Fra·ser fir** \'frā-zər-\ *noun* [John *Fraser* (died 1811) British botanist] (1897)
**:** a southern Appalachian fir (*Abies fraseri*) that resembles the balsam fir
**frass** \'fras\ *noun* [German, insect damage, literally, eating away, from Old High German *vrāz* food, from *frezzan* to devour — more at FRET] (1854)
**:** debris or excrement produced by insects
**frat** \'frat\ *noun* (circa 1895)
**:** FRATERNITY 1c
**fra·ter·nal** \frə-'tər-nᵊl\ *adjective* [Middle English, from Medieval Latin *fraternalis,* from Latin *fraternus,* from *frater* brother — more at BROTHER] (15th century)
**1 a :** of, relating to, or involving brothers **b :** of, relating to, or being a fraternity or society ⟨a *fraternal* order⟩
**2 :** derived from two ova **:** DIZYGOTIC ⟨*fraternal* twins⟩
**3 :** FRIENDLY, BROTHERLY
— **fra·ter·nal·ism** \-nᵊl-ˌiz-əm\ *noun*
— **fra·ter·nal·ly** \-nᵊl-ē\ *adverb*
**fra·ter·ni·ty** \frə-'tər-nə-tē\ *noun, plural* **-ties** (14th century)
**1 :** a group of people associated or formally organized for a common purpose, interest, or pleasure: as **a :** a fraternal order **b :** GUILD **c :** a men's student organization formed chiefly for social purposes having secret rites and a name consisting of Greek letters **d :** a student organization for scholastic, professional, or extracurricular activities ⟨a debating *fraternity*⟩
**2 :** the quality or state of being brothers **:** BROTHERLINESS
**3 :** persons of the same class, profession, character, or tastes ⟨the racetrack *fraternity*⟩
**frat·er·nize** \'fra-tər-ˌnīz\ *intransitive verb* **-nized; -niz·ing** (1611)
**1 :** to associate or mingle as brothers or on fraternal terms
**2 a :** to associate on close terms with members of a hostile group especially when contrary to military orders **b :** to be friendly or amiable
— **frat·er·ni·za·tion** \ˌfra-tər-nə-'zā-shən\ *noun*
— **frat·er·niz·er** \'fra-tər-ˌnī-zər\ *noun*
**frat·ri·cide** \'fra-trə-ˌsīd\ *noun* [in sense 1, from Middle English, from Middle French or Latin; Middle French, from Latin *fratricida,* from *fratr-, frater* brother + *-cida* -cide; in sense 2, from Middle French or Latin; Middle French, from Latin *fratricidium,* from *fratr-, frater* + *-cidium* -cide] (15th century)
**1 :** one that murders or kills his or her own brother or sister or an individual (as a countryman) having a relationship like that of a brother or sister
**2 :** the act of a fratricide
— **frat·ri·cid·al** \ˌfra-trə-'sī-dᵊl\ *adjective*

**Frau** \'fraủ\ *noun, plural* **Frau·en** \'fraủ(-ə)n\ [German, woman, wife, from Old High German *frouwa* mistress, lady; akin to Old English *frēa* lord, Old High German *fruma* advantage — more at FOREMOST] (circa 1813)
**:** a German married woman **:** WIFE — used as a title equivalent to *Mrs.*
**fraud** \'fród\ *noun* [Middle English *fraude,* from Middle French, from Latin *fraud-, fraus*] (14th century)
**1 a :** DECEIT, TRICKERY; *specifically :* intentional perversion of truth in order to induce another to part with something of value or to surrender a legal right **b :** an act of deceiving or misrepresenting **:** TRICK
**2 a :** a person who is not what he or she pretends to be **:** IMPOSTOR; *also :* one who defrauds **:** CHEAT **b :** one that is not what it seems or is represented to be
**synonym** *see* DECEPTION, IMPOSTURE
**fraud·u·lence** \'fró-jə-lən(t)s\ *noun* (1601)
**:** the quality or state of being fraudulent
**fraud·u·lent** \-lənt\ *adjective* (15th century)
**:** characterized by, based on, or done by fraud **:** DECEITFUL
— **fraud·u·lent·ly** *adverb*
— **fraud·u·lent·ness** *noun*
**¹fraught** \'frȯt\ *noun* [Middle English, freight, load, from Middle Dutch or Middle Low German *vracht, vrecht*] (14th century)
*chiefly Scottish* **:** LOAD, CARGO

---

☆ **SYNONYMS**
**Frank, candid, open, plain** mean showing willingness to tell what one feels or thinks. FRANK stresses lack of shyness or secretiveness or of evasiveness from considerations of tact or expedience ⟨*frank* discussions⟩. CANDID suggests expression marked by sincerity and honesty especially in offering unwelcome criticism or opinion ⟨a *candid* appraisal⟩. OPEN implies frankness but suggests more indiscretion than FRANK and less earnestness than CANDID ⟨*open* in saying what they think⟩. PLAIN suggests outspokenness and freedom from affectation or subtlety in expression ⟨*plain* talk⟩.

---

◇ **WORD HISTORY**
**frank** In the 5th century A.D. members of a group of Germanic tribes known collectively as the Franks migrated from the lower Rhine into the northern part of Roman Gaul. The region they settled, which was expanded and unified under their king Clovis (died around 511), was by the 7th century called *Francia* and would eventually become modern France. The Franks tended to merge with existing Gallo-Roman culture, and by the 8th century the Medieval Latin word *Francus* "Frank" had largely lost its ethnic sense and meant any inhabitant of *Francia,* whether of Frankish or Gallo-Roman ancestry, who was free, that is, not a slave or bondsman. From the noun *francus* "freeman" a corresponding adjective *francus* was formed with the meaning "free." Assimilated into the vernacular of Frankish Gaul, the adjective became *franc* in Old French and subsequently developed a wide range of extended senses, including "free of further charges or duties" (hence, ultimately, the English verb *frank*) and "expressing oneself freely, sincere" (hence the English adjective *frank*).

---

\ə\ abut \ᵊ\ kitten \ər\ **further** \a\ ash \ā\ ace
\ä\ mop, mar \aủ\ **out** \ch\ chin \e\ bet \ē\ easy
\g\ go \i\ hit \ī\ ice \j\ job \ŋ\ sing \ō\ go
\ȯ\ law \ȯi\ boy \th\ thin \t̲h̲\ the \ü\ loot \ủ\ foot
\y\ yet \zh\ vision *see also* Guide to Pronunciation

²**fraught** *transitive verb* **fraught·ed** *or* **fraught; fraught·ing** [Middle English *fraughten*, from ¹*fraught*] (14th century) *chiefly Scottish* : LOAD, FREIGHT

³**fraught** \'frȯt\ *adjective* [Middle English, from past participle of *fraughten*] (14th century)
**1** *archaic* **a** : LADEN **b** : well supplied or provided
**2** : full of or accompanied by something specified — used with *with* ⟨a situation *fraught* with danger⟩
**3** *chiefly British* : causing or characterized by emotional distress or tension : UNEASY

**fräu·lein** \'frȯi-,līn\ *noun* [German, diminutive of *Frau*] (circa 1689)
**1** *capitalized* : an unmarried German woman — used as a title equivalent to *Miss*
**2** : a German governess

**frax·i·nel·la** \,frak-sə-'ne-lə\ *noun* [New Latin, diminutive of Latin *fraxinus* ash tree — more at BIRCH] (1664)
: a Eurasian perennial herb (*Dictamnus albus*) of the rue family with flowers that exhale a flammable vapor in hot weather — called also *gas plant*

¹**fray** \'frā\ *transitive verb* [Middle English *fraien*, short for *affraien* to affray] (14th century)
*archaic* : SCARE; *also* : to frighten away

²**fray** *noun* (14th century)
: a usually disorderly or protracted fight, struggle, or dispute

³**fray** *verb* [Middle English *fraien*, from Middle French *froyer, frayer* to rub, from Latin *fricare* — more at FRICTION] (15th century)
*transitive verb*
**1 a** : to wear (as an edge of cloth) by or as if by rubbing : FRET **b** : to separate the threads at the edge of
**2** : STRAIN, IRRITATE ⟨tempers became a bit *frayed*⟩
*intransitive verb*
**1** : to wear out or into shreds
**2** : to show signs of strain ⟨*fraying* nerves⟩

⁴**fray** *noun* (1630)
: a raveled place or worn spot (as on fabric)

**fray·ing** *noun* (1637)
: something rubbed or worn off by fraying

¹**fraz·zle** \'fra-zəl\ *verb* **fraz·zled; fraz·zling** \'fraz-liŋ, 'fra-zə-\ [alteration of English dialect *fazle* (to tangle, fray)] (circa 1825)
*transitive verb*
**1** : ³FRAY
**2 a** : to put in a state of extreme physical or nervous fatigue **b** : UPSET
*intransitive verb*
: to become frazzled

²**frazzle** *noun* (1865)
**1** : the state of being frazzled
**2** : a condition of fatigue or nervous exhaustion ⟨worn to a *frazzle*⟩

¹**freak** \'frēk\ *noun* [origin unknown] (1563)
**1 a** : a sudden and odd or seemingly pointless idea or turn of the mind **b** : a seemingly capricious action or event
**2** *archaic* : a whimsical quality or disposition
**3** : one that is markedly unusual or abnormal: as **a** : a person or animal with a physical oddity who appears in a circus sideshow **b** *slang* (1) : a sexual deviate (2) : a person who uses an illicit drug **c** : HIPPIE **d** : an atypical postage stamp usually caused by a unique defect in paper (as a crease) or a unique event in the manufacturing process (as a speck of dirt on the plate) that does not produce a constant or systematic effect
**4** : an ardent enthusiast ⟨film *freaks*⟩

²**freak** *adjective* (circa 1887)
: having the character of a freak ⟨a *freak* accident⟩

³**freak** (1965)
*intransitive verb*
**1** : to withdraw from reality especially by taking drugs — often used with *out*

**2** : to experience nightmarish hallucinations as a result of taking drugs — often used with *out*
**3 a** : to behave irrationally or unconventionally under the influence of drugs — often used with *out* **b** : to react with extreme or irrational distress or discomposure — often used with *out*
*transitive verb*
**1** : to put under the influence of a psychedelic drug — often used with *out*
**2** : to make greatly distressed, astonished, or discomposed — often used with *out* ⟨the news *freaked* them out⟩
— **freaked** *adjective*
— **freaked–out** *adjective*

⁴**freak** *transitive verb* [perhaps from or akin to ¹*freckle*] (1637)
: to streak especially with color ⟨silver and mother-of-pearl *freaking* the intense azure —Robert Bridges (died 1930)⟩

**freak·ing** \'frē-kən, -kiŋ\ *adjective or adverb* [euphemism for *frigging* or *fucking*] (1963)
: DAMNED — used as an intensive

**freak·ish** \'frē-kish\ *adjective* (1653)
**1** : WHIMSICAL, CAPRICIOUS
**2** : markedly strange or abnormal
— **freak·ish·ly** *adverb*
— **freak·ish·ness** *noun*

**freak of nature** (1883)
: FREAK 3a

**freak–out** \'frē-,kaut\ *noun* (1966)
**1** : an act or instance of freaking out
**2** : a gathering of hippies

**freak show** *noun* (1887)
: an exhibition (as a sideshow) featuring freaks of nature

**freaky** \'frē-kē\ *adjective* **freak·i·er; -est** (1824)
: FREAKISH
— **freak·i·ness** *noun*

¹**freck·le** \'fre-kəl\ *noun* [Middle English *freken, frekel*, of Scandinavian origin; akin to Old Norse *freknōttr* freckled] (14th century)
: any of the small brownish spots in the skin usually due to precipitation of pigment that increase in number and intensity on exposure to sunlight
— **freck·ly** \'fre-k(ə-)lē\ *adjective*

²**freckle** *verb* **freck·led; freck·ling** \'fre-k(ə-)liŋ\ (1613)
*transitive verb*
: to sprinkle or mark with freckles or small spots
*intransitive verb*
: to become marked with freckles

¹**free** \'frē\ *adjective* **fre·er; fre·est** [Middle English, from Old English *frēo*; akin to Old High German *frī* free, Welsh *rhydd*, Sanskrit *priya* own, dear] (before 12th century)
**1 a** : having the legal and political rights of a citizen **b** : enjoying civil and political liberty ⟨*free* citizens⟩ **c** : enjoying political independence or freedom from outside domination **d** : enjoying personal freedom : not subject to the control or domination of another
**2 a** : not determined by anything beyond its own nature or being : choosing or capable of choosing for itself **b** : determined by the choice of the actor or performer ⟨*free* actions⟩ **c** : made, done, or given voluntarily or spontaneously
**3 a** : relieved from or lacking something unpleasant or burdensome ⟨*free* from pain⟩ ⟨a speech *free* of political rhetoric⟩ **b** : not bound, confined, or detained by force
**4 a** : having no trade restrictions **b** : not subject to government regulation **c** *of foreign exchange* : not subject to restriction or official control
**5 a** : having no obligations (as to work) or commitments ⟨I'll be *free* this evening⟩ **b** : not taken up with commitments or obligations ⟨a *free* evening⟩
**6** : having a scope not restricted by qualification ⟨a *free* variable⟩

**7 a** (1) : not obstructed or impeded : CLEAR (2) : not being used or occupied ⟨waved with his *free* hand⟩ **b** : not hampered or restricted in its normal operation
**8 a** : not fastened ⟨the *free* end of the rope⟩ **b** : not confined to a particular position or place; *also* : not having a specific opponent to cover in football ⟨a *free* safety⟩ **c** : capable of moving or turning in any direction ⟨a *free* particle⟩ **d** : performed without apparatus ⟨*free* tumbling⟩ **e** : done with artificial aids (as pitons) used only for protection against falling and not for support ⟨a *free* climb⟩
**9 a** : not parsimonious ⟨*free* spending⟩ **b** : OUTSPOKEN **c** : availing oneself of something without stint **d** : FRANK, OPEN **e** : overly familiar or forward in action or attitude **f** : LICENTIOUS
**10** : not costing or charging anything
**11 a** (1) : not united with, attached to, combined with, or mixed with something else : SEPARATE ⟨*free* ores⟩ ⟨a *free* surface of a bodily part⟩ (2) : FREESTANDING ⟨a *free* column⟩ **b** : chemically uncombined ⟨*free* oxygen⟩ ⟨*free* acids⟩ **c** : not permanently attached but able to move about ⟨a *free* electron in a metal⟩ **d** : capable of being used alone as a meaningful linguistic form ⟨the word *hats* is a *free* form⟩ — compare ⁵BOUND 7
**12 a** : not literal or exact ⟨*free* translation⟩ **b** : not restricted by or conforming to conventional forms ⟨*free* skating⟩
**13** : FAVORABLE — used of a wind blowing from a direction more than six points from dead ahead
**14** : not allowing slavery
**15** : open to all comers ☆ ▣
— **free·ness** \-nəs\ *noun*
— **for free** : without charge

---

☆ **SYNONYMS**
**Free, independent, sovereign, autonomous** mean not subject to the rule or control of another. FREE stresses the complete absence of external rule and the full right to make all of one's own decisions ⟨you're *free* to do as you like⟩. INDEPENDENT implies a standing alone; applied to a state it implies lack of connection with any other having power to interfere with its citizens, laws, or policies ⟨the colony's struggle to become *independent*⟩. SOVEREIGN stresses the absence of a superior power and implies supremacy within a thing's own domain or sphere ⟨separate and *sovereign* armed services⟩. AUTONOMOUS stresses independence in matters pertaining to self-government ⟨in this denomination each congregation is regarded as *autonomous*⟩.

---

☐ **USAGE**
**free** The idiomatic phrase *for free* apparently came into common use only in the early 1940s—our earliest printed evidence is from 1942—and it was no sooner popular than it was censured. The earliest complaint appeared barely six months after the earliest printed citation. Ever since, the critics have been denigrating the phrase, and others have kept on using it. One reason for the phrase's usefulness is that the preposition provides a little space between *free* and the preceding text ⟨it seemed best to find a way to live *for free* then —Jane Harriman⟩. In this example the *for* eliminates the ambiguous *live free*. But in many instances no potential ambiguity is involved; people seem to use the phrase simply because it sounds right to them. This American idiom is well established in speech and in general prose, but it is not used in writing of high solemnity.

²**free** *transitive verb* **freed; free·ing** (before 12th century)
**1 a** : to cause to be free **b** : to relieve or rid of what restrains, confines, restricts, or embarrasses ⟨*free* a person from debt⟩ **c** : DISENTANGLE, CLEAR
**2** *obsolete* : BANISH ☆
— **fre·er** *noun*
³**free** *adverb* (1559)
**1** : in a free manner
**2** : without charge
**3** : with the wind more than six points from dead ahead ⟨sailing *free*⟩
**free agent** *noun* (1955)
: a professional athlete (as a baseball player) who is free to negotiate a contract with any team
— **free agency** *noun*
**free alongside ship** *adverb or adjective* (circa 1903)
: with delivery at the side of the ship free of charges and the buyer's liability then beginning
**free and easy** *adjective* (1699)
**1** : marked by informality and lack of constraint ⟨the *free and easy*, open-air life of the plains —Allan Murray⟩
**2** : not observant of strict demands ⟨too *free and easy* in accepting political contributions⟩
— **free–and–eas·i·ness** \ˌfrē-ən-'(d)ē-zē-nəs\ *noun*
— **free and easy** *adverb*
**free association** *noun* (1899)
**1 a** : the expression (as by speaking or writing) of the content of consciousness without censorship as an aid in gaining access to unconscious processes especially in psychoanalysis **b** : the reporting of the first thought that comes to mind in response to a given stimulus (as a word)
**2** : an idea or image elicited by free association
**3** : a method using free association
— **free–as·so·ci·ate** \ˌfrē-ə-'sō-s(h)ē-ˌāt\ *intransitive verb*
— **free–as·so·ci·at·ive** \-s(h)ē-ˌā-tiv, -shə-tiv\ *adjective*
¹**free-base** \'frē-ˌbās\ (1980)
*intransitive verb*
: to prepare or use freebase cocaine
*transitive verb*
: to prepare or use (cocaine) as freebase
— **free·bas·er** *noun*
²**freebase** *noun* (1980)
: cocaine freed from impurities by treatment (as with ether) and heated to produce vapors for inhalation or smoked as crack
**free beach** *noun* (1975)
: a beach at which nudity is permitted
**free·bie** *or* **free·bee** \'frē-bē\ *noun* [by alteration from obsolete *freeby* gratis, irregular from *free*] (1942)
: something (as a theater ticket) given without charge
**free·board** \'frē-ˌbōrd, -ˌbȯrd\ *noun* (1726)
**1** : the distance between the waterline and the main deck or weather deck of a ship or between the level of the water and the upper edge of the side of a small boat
**2** : the height above the recorded high-water mark of a structure (as a dam) associated with the water
**free·boo·ter** \'frē-ˌbü-tər\ *noun* [by folk etymology from Dutch *vrijbuiter*, from *vrijbuit* plunder, from *vrij* free + *buit* booty] (1570)
: PIRATE, PLUNDERER
— **free·boot** \-ˌbüt\ *intransitive verb*
**free·born** \'frē-'bȯrn\ *adjective* (13th century)
**1** : not born in vassalage or slavery
**2** : of, relating to, or befitting one that is freeborn
**free diver** *noun* (1953)
: one who engages in skin diving
— **free diving** *noun*
**freed·man** \'frēd-mən, -ˌman\ *noun* (1601)
: a man freed from slavery

**free·dom** \'frē-dəm\ *noun* (before 12th century)
**1** : the quality or state of being free: as **a** : the absence of necessity, coercion, or constraint in choice or action **b** : liberation from slavery or restraint or from the power of another : INDEPENDENCE **c** : the quality or state of being exempt or released usually from something onerous ⟨*freedom* from care⟩ **d** : EASE, FACILITY ⟨spoke the language with *freedom*⟩ **e** : the quality of being frank, open, or outspoken ⟨answered with *freedom*⟩ **f** : improper familiarity **g** : boldness of conception or execution **h** : unrestricted use ⟨gave him the *freedom* of their home⟩
**2 a** : a political right **b** : FRANCHISE, PRIVILEGE ☆
**freedom of the seas** (1917)
: the right of a merchant ship to travel any waters except territorial waters either in peace or war
**freedom ride** *noun, often F&R capitalized* (1961)
: a ride made by civil rights workers through states of the southern U.S. to ascertain whether public facilities (as bus terminals) are desegregated
— **freedom rider** *noun*
**freed·wom·an** \'frēd-ˌwu̇-mən\ *noun* (1866)
: a woman freed from slavery
**free–elec·tron laser** \'frē-i-'lek-ˌträn-\ *noun* (1979)
: a laser that can be tuned over a wide range of frequencies and that produces electromagnetic radiation by the motion of electrons moving at relativistic velocities in a magnetic field
**free enterprise** *noun* (1890)
: freedom of private business to organize and operate for profit in a competitive system without interference by government beyond regulation necessary to protect public interest and keep the national economy in balance
**free enterpriser** *noun* (1943)
: a supporter or advocate of free enterprise
**free fall** *noun* (1919)
**1** : the condition of unrestrained motion in a gravitational field; *also* : such motion
**2 a** : the part of a parachute jump before the parachute opens **b** : a rapid and continuing drop or decline ⟨a *free fall* in stock prices⟩
— **free–fall** *intransitive verb*
**free–fire zone** \'frē-ˌfīr-\ *noun* (1967)
: a combat area in which any moving thing is a legitimate target
**free–float·ing** \-'flō-tiŋ\ *adjective* (1921)
**1 a** : floating freely ⟨*free-floating* vegetation⟩ **b** : lacking specific attachment, direction, or purpose ⟨*free-floating* ideas⟩
**2** : felt as an emotion without apparent cause ⟨*free-floating* anxiety⟩
**free–flow·ing** \-'flō-iŋ\ *adjective* (1920)
: characterized by easy freedom in movement, progression, or style ⟨a *free-flowing* essay⟩
**free–for–all** \'frē-fə-ˌrȯl\ *noun* (1881)
: a competition, dispute, or fight open to all comers and usually with no rules : BRAWL
— **free–for–all** *adjective*
**free–form** \'frē-ˌfȯrm\ *adjective* (1950)
**1** : having or being an irregular or asymmetrical shape or design ⟨*free-form* furniture⟩
**2** : FREE 12b ⟨*free-form* dancing⟩
**free·hand** \'frē-ˌhand\ *adjective* (circa 1862)
: done without mechanical aids or devices ⟨*freehand* drawing⟩
— **freehand** *adverb*
**free hand** \-'hand\ *noun* (1929)
: freedom of action or decision
**free·hand·ed** \'frē-'han-dəd\ *adjective* (circa 1656)
: GENEROUS, OPENHANDED
— **free·hand·ed·ly** *adverb*
— **free·hand·ed·ness** *noun*
**free·heart·ed** \-'här-təd\ *adjective* (14th century)
**1** : FRANK, UNRESERVED
**2** : GENEROUS

— **free·heart·ed·ly** *adverb*
**free·hold** \'frē-ˌhōld\ *noun* (15th century)
**1** : a tenure of real property by which an estate of inheritance in fee simple or fee tail or an estate for life is held; *also* : an estate held by such tenure — compare FEE 1
**2** *British* : an estate held in fee simple
— **freehold** *adjective or adverb*
— **free·hold·er** \-ˌhōl-dər\ *noun*
**free kick** *noun* (1882)
: a kick (as in football, soccer, or rugby) with which an opponent may not interfere; *especially* : such a kick in any direction awarded because of an infraction of the rules by an opponent
¹**free·lance** \'frē-ˌlan(t)s\ *noun* (1820)
**1 a** *usually* **free lance** : a mercenary soldier especially of the Middle Ages : CONDOTTIERE **b** : a person who acts independently without being affiliated with or authorized by an organization
**2** : a person who pursues a profession without a long-term commitment to any one employer
²**freelance** *adjective* (1901)
**1 a** : of, relating to, or being a freelance : INDEPENDENT ⟨a *freelance* photographer⟩ ⟨*freelance* fees⟩ **b** : done by a freelance ⟨*freelance* reviewing⟩ ⟨*freelance* jobs⟩
**2** : not sponsored by an organization ⟨*freelance* terrorists⟩ ⟨a *freelance* demonstration⟩
— **freelance** *adverb*
³**freelance** (1902)
*intransitive verb*
: to act or work as a freelance
*transitive verb*
: to produce as a freelance ⟨*freelancing* magazine articles⟩
**free·lanc·er** \'frē-ˌlan(t)-sər\ *noun* (1937)
: FREELANCE 1b, 2
**free–liv·ing** \'frē-'li-viŋ\ *adjective* (1818)
**1** : marked by more than usual freedom in the gratification of appetites

---

☆ **SYNONYMS**
**Free, release, liberate, emancipate, manumit** mean to set loose from restraint or constraint. FREE implies a usually permanent removal from whatever binds, confines, entangles, or oppresses ⟨*freed* the animals from their cages⟩. RELEASE suggests a setting loose from confinement, restraint, or a state of pressure or tension, often without implication of permanent liberation ⟨*released* his anger on a punching bag⟩. LIBERATE stresses particularly the resulting state of liberty ⟨*liberated* their country from the tyrant⟩. EMANCIPATE implies the liberation of a person from subjection or domination ⟨labor-saving devices *emancipated* us from household drudgery⟩. MANUMIT implies emancipation from slavery ⟨the document *manumitted* the slaves⟩.

**Freedom, liberty, license** mean the power or condition of acting without compulsion. FREEDOM has a broad range of application from total absence of restraint to merely a sense of not being unduly hampered or frustrated ⟨*freedom* of the press⟩. LIBERTY suggests release from former restraint or compulsion ⟨the released prisoner had difficulty adjusting to his new *liberty*⟩. LICENSE implies freedom specially granted or conceded and may connote an abuse of freedom ⟨freedom without responsibility may degenerate into *license*⟩.

---

\ə\ abut \ᵊ\ kitten \ər\ further \a\ ash \ā\ ace
\ä\ mop, mar \au̇\ out \ch\ chin \e\ bet \ē\ easy
\g\ go \i\ hit \ī\ ice \j\ job \ŋ\ sing \ō\ go
\ȯ\ law \ȯi\ boy \th\ thin \t̲h̲\ the \ü\ loot \u̇\ foot
\y\ yet \zh\ vision    *see also* Guide to Pronunciation

**2 a :** not fixed to the substrate but capable of motility ⟨a *free-living* protozoan⟩ **b :** being metabolically independent **:** neither parasitic nor symbiotic

**free·load** \-,lōd\ *intransitive verb* (circa 1934) **:** to impose upon another's generosity or hospitality without sharing in the cost or responsibility involved **:** SPONGE
— **free·load·er** *noun*

**free love** *noun* (1822)
**1 :** the practice of living openly with one of the opposite sex without marriage
**2 :** sexual relations without any commitments by either partner

**free lunch** *noun* (1975)
**:** something one does not have to pay for; *also* **:** FREE RIDE

**free·ly** \'frē-lē\ *adverb* (before 12th century)
**:** in a free manner: as **a :** of one's own accord ⟨left home *freely*⟩ **b :** with freedom from external control ⟨a *freely* elected government⟩ **c :** without restraint or reservation ⟨spent *freely* on clothes⟩ **d :** without hindrance ⟨a gate swinging *freely*⟩ ⟨currencies are *freely* convertible⟩ **e :** not strictly following a model, convention, or rule ⟨*freely* translated⟩

**free·man** \'frē-mən, -,man\ *noun* (before 12th century)
**1 :** one enjoying civil or political liberty
**2 :** one having the full rights of a citizen

**free market** *noun* (1907)
**:** an economic market operating by free competition

**free–mar·ke·teer** \'frē-,mär-kə-'tir\ *noun* (1954)
**:** a proponent of a free-market economy

**free·mar·tin** \'frē-,mär-t°n\ *noun* [origin unknown] (1681)
**:** a sexually imperfect usually sterile female calf twinborn with a male

**Free·ma·son** \-'mā-s°n\ *noun* (1646)
**:** a member of a major fraternal organization called Free and Accepted Masons or Ancient Free and Accepted Masons that has certain secret rituals

**free·ma·son·ry** \-rē\ *noun* (1741)
**1** *capitalized* **:** the principles, institutions, or practices of Freemasons — called also *Masonry*
**2 :** natural fellowship based on some common experience

**free on board** *adverb or adjective* (1924)
**:** without charge for delivery to and placing on board a carrier at a specified point

**free port** *noun* (1711)
**:** an enclosed port or section of a port where goods are received and shipped free of customs duty

**freer** *comparative of* FREE

**free radical** *noun* (1900)
**:** an especially reactive atom or group of atoms that has one or more unpaired electrons

**free–range** \'frē-,rānj\ *adjective* (1912)
**:** allowed to range and forage with relative freedom ⟨*free-range* chickens⟩; *also* **:** of, relating to, or produced by free-range poultry ⟨*free-range* eggs⟩

**free reed** *noun* (1855)
**:** a reed in a musical instrument (as a harmonium) that vibrates in an air opening just large enough to allow the reed to move freely — compare BEATING REED

**free rein** *noun* (1952)
**:** unrestricted liberty of action or decision

**free ride** *noun* (1899)
**:** a benefit obtained at another's expense or without the usual cost or effort
— **free ride** *intransitive verb*
— **free rider** *noun*

**free safety** *noun* (1973)
**:** a safety in football who has no particular receiver to cover in a man-to-man defense

**free·sia** \'frē-zh(ē-)ə, -zē-ə\ *noun* [New Latin, from F. H. T. *Freese* (died 1876) German physician] (circa 1882)

**:** any of a genus (*Freesia*) of the iris family of sweet-scented African herbs with red, pink, white, or yellow flowers

**free–soil** *adjective* (1846)
**1 :** characterized by free soil ⟨*free-soil* states⟩
**2** *F&S capitalized* **:** opposing the extension of slavery into U.S. territories and the admission of slave states into the Union prior to the Civil War; *specifically* **:** of, relating to, or constituting a minor U.S. political party having these aims
— **Free–Soil·er** \-'sȯi-lər\ *noun*
— **Free–Soil·ism** \-'sȯi(ə)-,li-zəm\ *noun*

**free soil** *noun* (1848)
**:** U.S. territory where prior to the Civil War slavery was prohibited

**free–spo·ken** \'frē-'spō-kən\ *adjective* (1625)
**:** speaking freely **:** OUTSPOKEN

**freest** *superlative of* FREE

**free–stand·ing** \'frē-'stan-diŋ\ *adjective* (1876)
**1 :** standing alone or on its own foundation free of support or attachment ⟨a *freestanding* wall⟩
**2 :** being independent; *especially* **:** not part of or affiliated with another organization ⟨a *freestanding* clinic⟩ ⟨a *freestanding* city⟩ ⟨a *freestanding* computer store⟩

**Free State** *noun* (1819)
**:** a state of the U.S. in which slavery was prohibited before the Civil War

**free·stone** \'frē-,stōn\ *noun* (13th century)
**1 :** a stone that may be cut freely without splitting
**2 a :** a fruit stone to which the flesh does not cling **b :** a fruit having such a stone

**free·style** \'frē-,stīl\ *noun, often attributive* (circa 1934)
**1 :** a competition in which the contestant is given more latitude than in related events; *especially* **:** swimming competition in which the swimmer may use any stroke
**2 :** CRAWL 2
— **free·styl·er** *noun*

**free–swim·ming** \-'swi-miŋ\ *adjective* (circa 1890)
**:** able to swim about **:** not attached ⟨the *free-swimming* larva of the barnacle⟩

**free–swing·ing** \-'swiŋ-iŋ\ *adjective* (1949)
**:** bold, forthright, and heedless of personal consequences ⟨a *free-swinging* soldier of fortune —Will Herberg⟩

**free–tailed bat** \'frē-,tāld-\ *noun* (1895)
**:** any of a family (Molossidae) of bats characterized by a tail that projects beyond the posterior part of the flight membrane and found in warm regions of the world

**free·think·er** \-'thiŋ-kər\ *noun* (1692)
**:** one that forms opinions on the basis of reason independently of authority; *especially* **:** one who doubts or denies religious dogma
— **free·think·ing** \-kiŋ\ *noun or adjective*

**free thought** *noun* (1711)
**:** unorthodox attitudes or beliefs; *specifically* **:** 18th century deism

**free throw** *noun* (circa 1929)
**:** an unhindered shot in basketball made from behind a set line and awarded because of a foul by an opponent

**free throw lane** *noun* (circa 1929)
**:** a 12 or 16 foot wide lane on a basketball court that extends from underneath the goal to a line 15 feet in front of the backboard and that players may not enter during a free throw

**free trade** *noun* (1823)
**:** trade based on the unrestricted international exchange of goods with tariffs used only as a source of revenue

**free trader** *noun* (1832)
**:** one that practices or advocates free trade

**free verse** *noun* (1908)
**:** verse whose meter is irregular in some respect or whose rhythm is not metrical

**free·way** \'frē-,wā\ *noun* (1930)
**1 :** an expressway with fully controlled access
**2 :** a toll-free highway

**¹free·wheel** \-'(h)wē(ə)l\ *noun* (1930)

**1 :** a clutch fitted in the rear hub of a bicycle that permits the rear wheel to run on free from the rear sprocket when the pedals are stopped
**2 :** a power-transmission system in a motor vehicle with a device that permits the propeller shaft to run freely when its speed is greater than that of the engine shaft

**²freewheel** *intransitive verb* (1903)
**1 :** to roll along freely independent of a gear
**2 :** to move, live, or play freely or irresponsibly
— **free·wheel·er** *noun*

**free·wheel·ing** \,frē-'hwē-liŋ, -'wē-\ *adjective* (1931)
**:** free and loose in form or manner: as **a :** heedless of social norms or niceties ⟨the raider style of his *freewheeling* father —Garry Wills⟩ **b :** not repressed or restrained ⟨*freewheeling* promiscuity⟩ ⟨a *freewheeling* competitive spirit⟩ ⟨a *freewheeling* vocabulary⟩ **c :** not bound by formal rules, procedures, or guidelines ⟨a *freewheeling* investigation⟩ ⟨*freewheeling* improvisation⟩ **d :** loose and undisciplined **:** not defensive ⟨a *freewheeling* style of hockey⟩
— **free·wheel·ing·ly** *adverb*

**free·will** \'frē-,wil\ *adjective* (1535)
**:** VOLUNTARY, SPONTANEOUS

**free will** *noun* (13th century)
**1 :** voluntary choice or decision ⟨I do this of my own *free will*⟩
**2 :** freedom of humans to make choices that are not determined by prior causes or by divine intervention

**Freewill Baptist** *noun* (1732)
**:** a member of a Baptist group holding to Arminian doctrine and practicing open communion

**free world** *noun, often F&W capitalized* (1949)
**:** the part of the world where democracy and capitalism or moderate socialism rather than totalitarian or Communist political and economic systems prevail

**free–writ·ing** \'frē-'rī-tiŋ\ *noun* (1980)
**:** automatic writing done especially as a classroom exercise

**¹freeze** \'frēz\ *verb* **froze** \'frōz\; **fro·zen** \'frō-z°n\; **freez·ing** [Middle English *fresen,* from Old English *frēosan;* akin to Old High German *friosan* to freeze, Latin *pruina* hoarfrost, Old English *frost* frost] (before 12th century)
*intransitive verb*
**1 a :** to become congealed into ice by cold **b :** to solidify as a result of abstraction of heat **c :** to withstand freezing ⟨the bread *freezes* well⟩
**2 :** to become chilled with cold ⟨almost *froze* to death⟩
**3 :** to adhere solidly by or as if by freezing ⟨pressure caused the metals to *freeze*⟩
**4 :** to become fixed or motionless; *especially* **:** to become incapable of acting or speaking
**5 :** to become clogged with ice ⟨the water pipes *froze*⟩
*transitive verb*
**1 a :** to harden into ice **b :** to convert from a liquid to a solid by cold
**2 :** to make extremely cold **:** CHILL
**3 a :** to act on usually destructively by frost **b :** to anesthetize by cold
**4 :** to cause to grip tightly or remain in immovable contact
**5 a :** to cause to become fixed, immovable, unavailable, or unalterable ⟨*freeze* interest rates⟩ **b :** to immobilize by governmental regulation the expenditure, withdrawal, or exchange of ⟨*freeze* foreign assets⟩ **c :** to render motionless ⟨a fake *froze* the defender⟩
**6 :** to attempt to retain continuous possession of (a ball or puck) without an attempt to score usually in order to protect a small lead
— **freez·ing·ly** *adverb*

**²freeze** *noun* (15th century)
**1 a :** an act or instance of freezing **b :** the state of being frozen

**2 :** a state of weather marked by low temperature especially when below the freezing point
**3 :** a halt in the production, testing, and deployment of military weapons ⟨a nuclear *freeze*⟩

**freeze–dried** \-'drīd\ *adjective* (1946)
**:** being in a state produced by or as if by freeze-drying

**freeze–dry** \-'drī\ *transitive verb* (1949)
**:** to dry (as food) in a frozen state under high vacuum especially for preservation

**freeze–etch·ing** \'frē-,ze-chiŋ\ *noun* (1968)
**:** preparation of a specimen (as of tissue) for electron microscopic examination by freezing, fracturing along natural structural lines, and preparing a replica (as by simultaneous vapor deposition of carbon and platinum) — **freeze–etch** \-'zech\ *adjective* — **freeze–etched** \-'zecht\ *adjective*

**freeze fracture** *noun* (1973)
**:** FREEZE-ETCHING

**freeze–frame** \'frēz-'frām\ *noun* (1948)
**1 a :** a frame of a motion-picture film that is repeated so as to give the illusion of a static picture **b :** a static picture produced from a videodisc or videotape recording
**2 :** something resembling a freeze-frame especially in unchanging quality

**freeze out** *transitive verb* (1861)
**:** EXCLUDE — **freeze–out** \'frē-,zaut\ *noun*

**freez·er** \'frē-zər\ *noun* (1847)
**:** one that freezes or keeps cool; *especially* **:** a compartment, room, or device for freezing food or keeping it frozen

**freezer burn** *noun* (1926)
**:** light-colored spots developed in frozen foods as a result of surface evaporation and drying when inadequately wrapped or packaged

**freezing point** *noun* (1747)
**:** the temperature at which a liquid solidifies

**free zone** *noun* (1900)
**:** an area within which goods may be received and stored without payment of duty

**F region** *noun* (1923)
**:** the highest region of the ionosphere occurring from 80 miles (130 kilometers) to more than 300 miles (500 kilometers)

**¹freight** \'frāt\ *noun, often attributive* [Middle English, from Middle Dutch or Middle Low German *vracht, vrecht*] (15th century)
**1 a :** the compensation paid for the transportation of goods **b :** COST ⟨help pay the *freight*⟩
**2 a :** goods to be shipped **:** CARGO **b :** LOAD, BURDEN **c :** MEANING 3, SIGNIFICANCE
**3 a :** the ordinary transportation of goods by a common carrier and distinguished from express **b :** a train designed or used for such transportation

**²freight** *transitive verb* (15th century)
**1 a :** to load with goods for transportation **b :** BURDEN, CHARGE ⟨*freighted* with memories⟩
**2 :** to transport or ship by freight

**freight·age** \'frā-tij\ *noun* (1694)
**:** FREIGHT

**freight·er** \-tər\ *noun* (1622)
**1 :** one that loads or charters and loads a ship
**2 :** SHIPPER
**3 :** a ship or airplane used chiefly to carry freight

**frem·i·tus** \'fre-mə-təs\ *noun* [New Latin, from Latin, murmur, from *fremere* to murmur; akin to Old English *bremman* to roar] (1879)
**:** a sensation felt by a hand placed on a part of the body (as the chest) that vibrates during speech

**french** \'french\ *transitive verb, often capitalized* (1941)
**1 :** to trim the meat from the end of the bone of (as a chop)
**2 :** to cut (green beans) in thin lengthwise strips before cooking

**¹French** \'french\ *adjective* [Middle English, from Old English *frencisc*, from *Franca* Frank] (before 12th century)
**1 :** of, relating to, or characteristic of France, its people, or their language

**2 :** of or relating to the overseas descendents of the French people — **French·ness** *noun*

**²French** *noun* (12th century)
**1 :** a Romance language that developed out of the Vulgar Latin spoken in northern and central Transalpine Gaul and that became the literary and official language of France
**2** *plural in construction* **:** the French people
**3 :** strong language ⟨pardon my *French*⟩

**French bean** *noun* (1632)
**1** *chiefly British* **:** a bean (as a green bean) of which the whole young pod is eaten
**2** *chiefly British* **:** KIDNEY BEAN 2

**French bread** *noun* (15th century)
**:** a crusty white bread baked usually in long thin loaves

**French bulldog** *noun* (1875)
**:** any of a breed of small compact heavy-boned dogs developed in France and having erect ears

**French Canadian** *noun* (1758)
**:** one of the descendants of French settlers in Lower Canada — **French–Canadian** *adjective*

**French chalk** *noun* (circa 1728)
**:** a soft white granular variety of steatite used especially for drawing lines on cloth and for removing grease in dry cleaning

**French cuff** *noun* (1916)
**:** a soft double cuff that is made by turning back half of a wide cuff band and fastening with cuff links

**french curve** *noun, often F capitalized* (1885)
**:** a curved piece of flat often plastic material used as a guide in drawing curves

**French door** *noun* (1923)
**:** a door with rectangular glass panes extending the full length; *also* **:** FRENCH WINDOW

**French dressing** *noun* (1876)
**1 :** a salad dressing made with oil and vinegar or lemon juice, and spices
**2 :** a commercial salad dressing that is tomato-flavored and of creamy consistency

**¹french fry** *noun, often 1st F capitalized* (1918)
**:** a strip of potato fried in deep fat — usually used in plural

**²french fry** *transitive verb, often 1st F capitalized* (circa 1930)
**:** to fry (as strips of potato) in deep fat until brown

**French horn** *noun* (1682)
**:** a circular valved brass instrument having a conical bore, a funnel-shaped mouthpiece, and a usual range from B below the bass staff upward for more than three octaves

**french·ify** \'fren-chə-,fī\ *transitive verb* **-ified; -ify·ing** *often capitalized* (1592)
**:** to make French in qualities, traits, or typical practices — **french·i·fi·ca·tion** \,fren-chə-fi-'kā-shən\ *noun, often capitalized*

**French kiss** *noun* (circa 1923)
**:** an open-mouth kiss usually involving tongue-to-tongue contact — **French–kiss** *verb*

**French leave** *noun* [from an 18th century French custom of leaving a reception without taking leave of the host or hostess] (1771)
**:** an informal, hasty, or secret departure

**French letter** *noun* (circa 1856)
*chiefly British* **:** CONDOM

**French·man** \'french-mən\ *noun* (before 12th century)
**1 :** a native or inhabitant of France
**2 :** one who is of French descent

**French pastry** *noun* (1922)

**:** a rich pastry filled especially with custard or fruit

**French provincial** *noun, often P capitalized* (1945)
**:** a style of furniture, architecture, or fabric originating in or characteristic of the 17th and 18th century French provinces

**French seam** *noun* (circa 1890)
**:** a strong seam stitched on both sides of the fabric to enclose all raw edges

**French telephone** *noun* (1932)
**:** HANDSET

**French toast** *noun* (1871)
**:** bread dipped in a mixture of egg and milk and sautéed

**French window** *noun* (1801)
**:** a pair of casement windows that reaches to the floor, opens in the middle, and is placed in an exterior wall

**French·wom·an** \'french-,wu̇-mən\ *noun* (1593)
**1 :** a woman who is a native or inhabitant of France
**2 :** a woman of French descent

**fre·net·ic** \fri-'ne-tik\ *adjective* [Middle English *frenetik* insane, from Middle French *frenetique*, from Latin *phreneticus*, modification of Greek *phrenitikos*, from *phrenitis* inflammation of the brain, from *phren-, phrēn* diaphragm, mind] (14th century)
**:** FRENZIED, FRANTIC — **fre·net·i·cal·ly** \-ti-k(ə-)lē\ *adverb* — **fre·net·i·cism** \-'ne-tə-,si-zəm\ *noun*

**fren·u·lum** \'fren-yə-ləm\ *noun, plural* **-la** \-lə\ [New Latin, diminutive of Latin *frenum*] (circa 1706)
**1 :** a connecting fold of membrane serving to support or restrain a part (as the tongue)
**2 :** a bristle or group of bristles on the front edge of the posterior wings of some lepidoptera that unites the wings by interlocking with the retinaculum of the forewings

**fre·num** \'frē-nəm\ *noun, plural* **frenums** *or* **fre·na** \-nə\ [New Latin, from Latin, bridle, reins, and bit; probably akin to Latin *frendere* to grind — more at GRIND] (1741)
**:** FRENULUM 1

**fren·zied** \'fren-zēd\ *adjective* (1796)
**:** marked by frenzy — **fren·zied·ly** *adverb*

**¹fren·zy** \'fren-zē\ *noun, plural* **frenzies** [Middle English *frenesie*, from Middle French, from Medieval Latin *phrenesia*, alteration of Latin *phrenesis*, from *phreneticus*] (14th century)
**1 a :** a temporary madness **b :** a violent mental or emotional agitation
**2 :** intense usually wild and often disorderly compulsive or agitated activity

**²frenzy** *transitive verb* **fren·zied; fren·zy·ing** (1791)
**:** to affect with frenzy

**Fre·on** \'frē-,än\ *trademark*
— used for any of various nonflammable fluorocarbons used as refrigerants and as propellants for aerosols

**fre·quence** \'frē-kwən(t)s\ *noun* (1603)
**:** FREQUENCY

**fre·quen·cy** \'frē-kwən(t)-sē\ *noun, plural* **-cies** (1600)
**1 :** the fact or condition of occurring frequently
**2 a :** the number of times that a periodic function repeats the same sequence of values during a unit variation of the independent variable
**b :** the number of individuals in a single class when objects are classified according to variations in a set of one or more specified attributes

**French horn**

**3 :** the number of repetitions of a periodic process in a unit of time: as **a :** the number of complete alternations per second of an alternating current **b :** the number of complete oscillations per second of energy (as sound or electromagnetic radiation) in the form of waves

**frequency distribution** *noun* (1895)
**:** an arrangement of statistical data that exhibits the frequency of the occurrence of the values of a variable

**frequency modulation** *noun* (1922)
**:** modulation of the frequency of the carrier wave in accordance with speech or a signal; *also* **:** FM

**frequency response** *noun* (1926)
**:** the ability of a device (as an audio amplifier) to handle the frequencies applied to it; *also* **:** a graph representing this ability

**¹fre·quent** \frē-'kwent, 'frē-kwənt\ *transitive verb* (15th century)
**1 :** to associate with, be in, or resort to often or habitually
**2** *archaic* **:** to read systematically or habitually
— **fre·quen·ta·tion** \,frē-,kwen-'tā-shən, -kwən-\ *noun*
— **fre·quent·er** *noun*

**²fre·quent** \'frē-kwənt\ *adjective* [Middle English, ample, from Middle French or Latin; Middle French, crowded, from Latin *frequent-, frequens*] (1531)
**1 a :** COMMON, USUAL **b :** happening at short intervals **:** often repeated or occurring
**2** *obsolete* **:** FULL, THRONGED
**3 :** HABITUAL, PERSISTENT
**4** *archaic* **:** INTIMATE, FAMILIAR
— **fre·quent·ness** *noun*

**fre·quen·ta·tive** \frē-'kwen-tə-tiv\ *adjective* (1533)
**:** denoting repeated or recurrent action or state — used of a verb aspect, verb form, or meaning
— **frequentative** *noun*

**fre·quent·ly** \'frē-kwənt-lē\ *adverb* (1531)
**:** at frequent or short intervals

**fres·co** \'fres-(,)kō\ *noun, plural* **frescoes** [Italian, from *fresco* fresh, of Germanic origin; akin to Old High German *frisc* fresh] (1598)
**1 :** the art of painting on freshly spread moist lime plaster with water-based pigments
**2 :** a painting executed in fresco ◆
— **fresco** *transitive verb*

**¹fresh** \'fresh\ *adjective* [Middle English, from Old French *freis*, of Germanic origin; akin to Old High German *frisc* fresh, Old English *fersc* fresh] (13th century)
**1 a :** having its original qualities unimpaired: as (1) **:** full of or renewed in vigor **:** REFRESHED ⟨rose *fresh* from a good night's sleep⟩ (2) **:** not stale, sour, or decayed ⟨*fresh* bread⟩ (3) **:** not faded ⟨the lessons remain *fresh* in her memory⟩ (4) **:** not worn or rumpled ⟨a *fresh* white shirt⟩ **b :** not altered by processing ⟨*fresh* vegetables⟩
**2 a :** not salt **b** (1) **:** free from taint **:** PURE ⟨*fresh* air⟩ (2) *of wind* **:** moderately strong
**3 a** (1) **:** experienced, made, or received newly or anew ⟨form *fresh* friendships⟩ (2) **:** ADDITIONAL, ANOTHER ⟨a *fresh* start⟩ **b :** ORIGINAL, VIVID ⟨a *fresh* portrayal⟩ **c :** lacking experience **:** RAW **d :** newly or just come or arrived ⟨*fresh* from school⟩ **e :** having the milk flow recently established ⟨a *fresh* cow⟩
**4** [probably by folk etymology from German *frech*] **:** disposed to take liberties **:** IMPUDENT
*synonym* see NEW
— **fresh·ly** *adverb*
— **fresh·ness** *noun*

**²fresh** *adverb* (14th century)
**:** just recently **:** NEWLY ⟨we're *fresh* out of eggs⟩ ⟨*fresh* caught fish⟩

**³fresh** *noun* (1538)
**1 :** an increased flow or rush (as of water) **:** FRESHET
**2** *archaic* **:** a stream, spring, or pool of freshwater

**fresh breeze** *noun* (circa 1881)

**:** wind having a speed of 19 to 24 miles per hour (30 to 38 kilometers per hour) — see BEAUFORT SCALE table

**fresh·en** \'fre-shən\ *verb* **fresh·ened; fresh·en·ing** \-sh(ə-)niŋ\ (1697)
*intransitive verb*
**1 :** to grow or become fresh: as **a** *of wind* **:** to increase in strength **b :** to become fresh in appearance or vitality — usually used with *up* ⟨*freshen* up with a shower⟩
**2** *of a milk animal* **:** to begin lactating
*transitive verb*
**:** to make fresh; *also* **:** REFRESH, REVIVE
— **fresh·en·er** \-sh(ə-)nər\ *noun*

**fresh·et** \'fre-shət\ *noun* (1596)
**1** *archaic* **:** STREAM 1
**2 a :** a great rise or overflowing of a stream caused by heavy rains or melted snow **b :** something resembling or suggesting a freshet ⟨a *freshet* of visitors⟩

**fresh gale** *noun* (1582)
**:** wind having a speed of 39 to 46 miles per hour (62 to 74 kilometers per hour) — see BEAUFORT SCALE table

**fresh·man** \'fresh-mən\ *noun, often attributive* (1550)
**1 :** a first-year student
**2 :** BEGINNER, NEWCOMER

**¹fresh·wa·ter** \'fresh-'wȯ-tər, -'wä-\ *noun* (14th century)
**:** water that is not salty especially when considered as a natural resource

**²freshwater** *adjective* (1528)
**1 :** of, relating to, being, or living in freshwater
**2 :** accustomed to navigating only in inland waters ⟨a *freshwater* sailor⟩; *also* **:** UNSKILLED
**3 :** inland and usually provincial ⟨a *freshwater* college⟩

**freshwater drum** *noun* (1879)
**:** a croaker (*Aplodinotus grunniens*) of the Great Lakes and Mississippi valley that may attain a weight of 50 pounds (23 kilograms) or more — called also *sheepshead, white perch*

**freshwater pearl** *noun* (1918)
**:** a usually very small pearl produced by a freshwater mollusk

**Fres·nel lens** \'frez-nəl-, frā-'nel-\ *noun* [Augustin J. *Fresnel*] (circa 1884)
**:** a lens that has a surface consisting of a concentric series of simple lens sections so that a thin lens with a short focal length and large diameter is possible and that is used especially for spotlights

**¹fret** \'fret\ *verb* **fret·ted; fret·ting** [Middle English, to devour, fret, from Old English *fretan* to devour; akin to Old High German *frezzan* to devour, *ezzan* to eat — more at EAT] (12th century)
*transitive verb*
**1 a :** to eat or gnaw into **:** CORRODE; *also* **:** FRAY **b :** RUB, CHAFE **c :** to make by wearing away a substance ⟨the stream *fretted* a channel⟩
**2 :** to cause to suffer emotional strain **:** VEX
**3 :** to pass (as time) in fretting
**4 :** AGITATE, RIPPLE
*intransitive verb*
**1 a :** to eat into something **b :** to affect something as if by gnawing or biting **c :** GRATE
**2 a :** WEAR, CORRODE **b :** CHAFE **c :** FRAY 1
**3 a :** to become vexed or worried **b** *of running water* **:** to become agitated

**²fret** *noun* (15th century)
**1 a :** the action of wearing away **:** EROSION **b :** a worn or eroded spot
**2 :** an agitation of mind **:** IRRITATION

**³fret** *transitive verb* **fret·ted; fret·ting** [Middle English, back-formation from *fret, fretted* adorned, interwoven, from Middle French *freté*, from Old French, past participle of *freter, ferter* to tie, bind, probably from (assumed) Vulgar Latin *firmitare*, from Latin *firmus* firm] (14th century)
**1 a :** to decorate with interlaced designs **b :** to form a pattern upon

**2 :** to enrich with embossed or pierced carved patterns

**⁴fret** *noun* (14th century)
**1 :** an ornamental network; *especially* **:** a medieval metallic or jeweled net for a woman's headdress
**2 :** an ornament or ornamental work often in relief consisting of small straight bars intersecting one another in right or oblique angles

fret 2

**⁵fret** *noun* [perhaps from Middle French *frete* ferrule, from *freter*] (circa 1500)
**:** one of a series of ridges fixed across the fingerboard of a stringed musical instrument (as a guitar)
— **fret·less** *adjective*
— **fret·ted** *adjective*

**⁶fret** *transitive verb* **fret·ted; fret·ting** (1602)
**:** to press (the strings of a stringed instrument) against the frets

**fret·ful** \'fret-fəl\ *adjective* (1602)
**:** disposed to fret **:** IRRITABLE
— **fret·ful·ly** \-fə-lē\ *adverb*
— **fret·ful·ness** *noun*

**fret·saw** \'fret-,sȯ\ *noun* (1865)
**:** a narrow-bladed fine-toothed saw held under tension in a frame and used for cutting curved outlines

**fret·work** \-,wərk\ *noun* (1601)
**1 :** decoration consisting of work adorned with frets
**2 :** ornamental openwork or work in relief

**Freud·ian** \'frȯi-dē-ən\ *adjective* (1910)
**:** of, relating to, or according with the psychoanalytic theories or practices of Freud ◆
— **Freudian** *noun*
— **Freud·ian·ism** \-ə-,ni-zəm\ *noun*

**Freudian slip** *noun* (1953)

: a slip of the tongue that is motivated by and reveals some unconscious aspect of the mind

**Frey** \'frā\ *noun* [Old Norse *Freyr*]
: the Norse god of fertility, crops, peace, and prosperity

**Freya** \'frā-ə\ *noun* [Old Norse *Freyja*]
: the Norse goddess of love and beauty

**fri·a·ble** \'frī-ə-bəl\ *adjective* [Middle French or Latin; Middle French, from Latin *friabilis*, from *friare* to crumble — more at FRICTION] (1563)
: easily crumbled or pulverized ⟨*friable* soil⟩
**synonym** see FRAGILE
— **fri·a·bil·i·ty** \ˌfrī-ə-'bi-lə-tē\ *noun*

**fri·ar** \'frī(-ə)r\ *noun* [Middle English *frere, fryer*, from Old French *frere*, literally, brother, from Latin *fratr-, frater* — more at BROTHER] (13th century)
: a member of a mendicant order

**fri·ar·ly** \-lē\ *adjective* (1549)
: resembling a friar : relating to friars

**friar's lantern** *noun* (1632)
*obsolete* : IGNIS FATUUS

**fri·ary** \'frī(-ə)r-ē\ *noun, plural* **-ar·ies** (1538)
: a monastery of friars

**¹frib·ble** \'fri-bəl\ *verb* **frib·bled; frib·bling** \-b(ə-)liŋ\ [origin unknown] (1633)
*intransitive verb*
**1** : TRIFLE
**2** *obsolete* : DODDER
*transitive verb*
: to trifle or fool away

**²fribble** *noun* (1664)
: a frivolous person, thing, or idea : TRIFLER
— **frib·ble** *adjective*

**fric·an·deau** \'fri-kən-ˌdō\ *noun* [French, from Middle French, probably from *fricasser* + *-ande* (as in *viande* meat) + *-eau*, noun suffix] (1706)
: larded veal roasted and glazed in its own juices

**¹fric·as·see** *also* **fric·as·sée** \'fri-kə-ˌsē, ˌfri-kə-'\ *noun* [Middle French, from feminine of *fricassé*, past participle of *fricasser* to fricassee] (1568)
: a dish of cut-up pieces of meat (as chicken) stewed in stock and served in a white sauce

**²fricassee** *transitive verb* **-seed; -see·ing** (1657)
: to cook as a fricassee

**fric·a·tive** \'fri-kə-tiv\ *noun* [Latin *fricatus*, past participle of *fricare*] (1863)
: a consonant characterized by frictional passage of the expired breath through a narrowing at some point in the vocal tract
— **fricative** *adjective*

**fric·tion** \'frik-shən\ *noun* [Middle English, from Middle French or Latin; Middle French, from Latin *friction-, frictio*, from *fricare* to rub; akin to Latin *friare* to crumble, and perhaps to Sanskrit *bhrīṇanti* they injure] (1704)
**1 a** : the rubbing of one body against another **b** : the force that resists relative motion between two bodies in contact
**2** : the clashing between two persons or parties of opposed views : DISAGREEMENT
— **fric·tion·less** \-ləs\ *adjective*
— **fric·tion·less·ly** *adverb*

**fric·tion·al** \'frik-shnəl, -shə-nᵊl\ *adjective* (1850)
**1** : of or relating to friction
**2** : moved or produced by friction
— **fric·tion·al·ly** *adverb*

**friction clutch** *noun* (circa 1842)
: a clutch in which connection is made through sliding friction

**friction drive** *noun* (1907)
: a power-transmission system that transmits motion by surface friction instead of teeth

**friction tape** *noun* (1920)
: a usually cloth tape impregnated with water-resistant insulating material and an adhesive and used especially to protect, insulate, and support electrical conductors

**Fri·day** \'frī-dē, -(ˌ)dā\ *noun* [Middle English, from Old English *frīgedæg* (akin to Old High

German *frīatag* Friday), from (assumed) *Frīg* Frigga + *dæg* day, prehistoric translation of Latin *dies Veneris* Venus' day] (before 12th century)
: the sixth day of the week
— **Fri·days** \-dēz, -(ˌ)dāz\ *adverb*

**fridge** *also* **frig** \'frij\ *noun* [by shortening & alteration] (1926)
: REFRIGERATOR

**fried** \'frīd\ *adjective* (1926)
: INTOXICATED

**fried·cake** \'frīd-ˌkāk\ *noun* (1839)
: DOUGHNUT, CRULLER

**¹friend** \'frend\ *noun* [Middle English *frend*, from Old English *frēond*; akin to Old High German *friunt* friend, Old English *frēon* to love, *frēo* free] (before 12th century)
**1 a** : one attached to another by affection or esteem **b** : ACQUAINTANCE
**2 a** : one that is not hostile **b** : one that is of the same nation, party, or group
**3** : one that favors or promotes something (as a charity)
**4** : a favored companion
**5** *capitalized* : a member of a Christian sect that stresses Inner Light, rejects sacraments and an ordained ministry, and opposes war — called also *Quaker*
— **friend·less** \'fren(d)-ləs\ *adjective*
— **friend·less·ness** *noun*
— **be friends with** : to have a friendship or friendly relationship with
— **make friends with** : to establish a friendship or friendly relations with

**²friend** *transitive verb* (13th century)
: to act as the friend of : BEFRIEND

**¹friend·ly** \'fren(d)-lē\ *adjective* **friend·li·er; -est** (before 12th century)
**1** : of, relating to, or befitting a friend: as **a** : showing kindly interest and goodwill **b** : not hostile ⟨a *friendly* merger offer⟩; *also* : involving or coming from actions of one's own forces ⟨*friendly* fire⟩ **c** : CHEERFUL, COMFORTING ⟨the *friendly* glow of the fire⟩
**2** : serving a beneficial or helpful purpose
**3** : easy to use or understand ⟨*friendly* computer software⟩
**synonym** see AMICABLE
— **friend·li·ly** \'fren(d)-lə-lē\ *adverb*
— **friend·li·ness** *noun*

**²friendly** *adverb* (before 12th century)
: in a friendly manner : AMICABLY

**³friendly** *noun, plural* **friendlies** (1861)
**1** : one that is friendly; *especially* : a native who is friendly to settlers or invaders
**2** *British* : a match between sports teams and especially international teams that has no connection with league or championship play

**friendly society** *noun* (1703)
*British* : a mutual association for providing life and health insurance and old-age pension benefits to members

**friend of the court** (1944)
: AMICUS CURIAE

**friend·ship** \'fren(d)-ˌship\ *noun* (before 12th century)
**1** : the state of being friends
**2** : the quality or state of being friendly : FRIENDLINESS
**3** *obsolete* : AID

**fri·er** *variant of* FRYER

**Frie·sian** \'frē-zhən\ *noun* [variant of *Frisian*] (1923)
*chiefly British* : HOLSTEIN

**¹frieze** \'frēz *or* frē-'zā\ *noun* [Middle English *frise*, from Middle French, from Middle Dutch *vriese*] (15th century)
**1** : a heavy durable coarse wool and shoddy fabric with a rough surface
**2** : a pile surface of uncut loops or of patterned cut and uncut loops

**²frieze** \'frēz\ *noun* [Middle French *frise*, perhaps from Medieval Latin *phrygium, frisium* embroidered cloth, from Latin *phrygium*, from neuter of *Phrygius* Phrygian, from *Phrygia*] (1563)

**1** : the part of an entablature between the architrave and the cornice — see ENTABLATURE illustration
**2** : a sculptured or richly ornamented band (as on a building or piece of furniture)
**3** : a band, line, or series suggesting a frieze ⟨a constant *frieze* of visitors wound its way around the . . . ruins —Mollie Panter-Downes⟩
— **frieze·like** *adjective*

**frig** \'frig\ *intransitive verb* **frigged; frig·ging** [Middle English *fryggen* to wriggle] (1598)
: COPULATE — usually considered vulgar; sometimes used in present participle as a meaningless intensive

**frig·ate** \'fri-gət\ *noun* [Middle French, from Old Italian *fregata*] (1585)
**1** : a light boat propelled originally by oars but later by sails
**2** : a square-rigged war vessel intermediate between a corvette and a ship of the line
**3** : a warship that is smaller than a destroyer

**frigate bird** *noun* (1738)
: any of a family (Fregatidae) of tropical seabirds having a forked tail and large wingspans that are noted for aggressively taking food from other birds

**Frig·ga** \'fri-gə\ *noun* [Old Norse *Frigg*]
: the wife of Odin and Norse goddess of married love and of the hearth

**¹fright** \'frīt\ *noun* [Middle English, from Old English *fyrhto, fryhto*; akin to Old High German *forhta* fear] (before 12th century)
**1** : fear excited by sudden danger : ALARM
**2** : something strange, ugly, or shocking
**synonym** see FEAR

**²fright** *transitive verb* (before 12th century)
: to alarm suddenly : FRIGHTEN

**fright·en** \'frī-tᵊn\ *verb* **fright·ened; fright·en·ing** \'frī-tᵊn-iŋ, 'frīt-niŋ\ (1666)
*transitive verb*
**1** : to make afraid : TERRIFY
**2** : to drive or force by frightening ⟨*frightened* the boy into confessing⟩
*intransitive verb*
: to become frightened
— **fright·en·ing·ly** \-tᵊn-iŋ-lē, -niŋ-lē\ *adverb*

**fright·ful** \'frīt-fəl\ *adjective* (1607)
**1** : causing intense fear or alarm : TERRIFYING
**2** : startling especially in being bad or objectionable ⟨a *frightful* novel⟩
**3** : EXTREME ⟨*frightful* thirst⟩
— **fright·ful·ly** \-fə-lē\ *adverb*
— **fright·ful·ness** *noun*

**fright wig** *noun* (1886)
: a wig with hair that stands out from the head

**frig·id** \'fri-jəd\ *adjective* [Latin *frigidus*, from *frigēre* to be cold; akin to Latin *frigus* frost, cold, Greek *rhigos*] (1622)
**1 a** : intensely cold **b** : lacking warmth or ardor : INDIFFERENT
**2** : lacking imaginative qualities : INSIPID
**3 a** : abnormally averse to sexual intercourse — used especially of women **b** *of a female* : unable to achieve orgasm during sexual intercourse
— **frig·id·ly** *adverb*
— **frig·id·ness** *noun*

**Frig·i·daire** \ˌfri-jə-'dar, -'der\ *trademark*
— used for a mechanical refrigerator

**fri·gid·i·ty** \fri-'ji-də-tē\ *noun* (15th century)
: the quality or state of being frigid; *specifically* : marked or abnormal sexual indifference especially in a woman

**frigid zone** *noun* (1622)
: the area or region between the arctic circle and the north pole or between the antarctic circle and the south pole

---

\ə\ **abut** \ᵊ\ **kitten** \ər\ **further** \a\ **ash** \ā\ **ace** \ä\ **mop, mar** \au̇\ **out** \ch\ **chin** \e\ **bet** \ē\ **easy** \g\ **go** \i\ **hit** \ī\ **ice** \j\ **job** \ŋ\ **sing** \ō\ **go** \ȯ\ **law** \ȯi\ **boy** \th\ **thin** \t̲h̲\ **the** \ü\ **loot** \u̇\ **foot** \y\ **yet** \zh\ **vision** *see also* Guide to Pronunciation

**frig·o·rif·ic** \\,fri-gə-'ri-fik\ *adjective* [Latin *frigorificus*, from *frigor-*, *frigus* frost] (1667) : causing cold : CHILLING

**fri·jo·le** \frē-'hō-lē\ *also* **fri·jol** \frē-'hōl, 'frē-,\ *noun, plural* **fri·jo·les** \frē-'hō-lēz, 'frē-,\ [American Spanish *frijol*, from Spanish, kidney bean, from earlier *fesol, fresol*, probably modification of Galician *feijoo*, from Latin *phaseolus*, diminutive of *phaselus* cowpea, from Greek *phasēlos*] (1577) : any of various beans used in Mexican style cooking — usually used in plural

¹**frill** \'fril\ *transitive verb* (1574) : to provide or decorate with a frill

²**frill** *noun* [perhaps from Flemish *frul*] (1591) **1 a** : a gathered, pleated, or bias-cut fabric edging used on clothing **b** : a strip of paper curled at one end and rolled to be slipped over the bone end (as of a chop) in serving **2** : a ruff of hair or feathers or a bony projection about the neck of an animal **3 a** : AFFECTATION, AIR — usually used in plural ⟨an honest . . . man who had no *frills*, . . . no nonsense about him —W. A. White⟩ **b** : something decorative or useful and desirable but not essential : LUXURY
— **frilly** \'fri-lē\ *adjective*

¹**fringe** \'frinj\ *noun, often attributive* [Middle English *frenge*, from Middle French, from (assumed) Vulgar Latin *frimbia*, from Latin *fimbriae* (plural)] (14th century) **1** : an ornamental border consisting of short straight or twisted threads or strips hanging from cut or raveled edges or from a separate band **2 a** : something resembling a fringe : EDGE, PERIPHERY — often used in plural ⟨operated on the *fringes* of the law⟩ **b** : one of various light or dark bands produced by the interference or diffraction of light **c** : an area bordering a putting green on a golf course with grass trimmed longer than on the green itself **3 a** : something that is marginal, additional, or secondary to some activity, process, or subject **b** : a group with marginal or extremist views **c** : FRINGE BENEFIT
— **fringy** \'frin-jē\ *adjective*

²**fringe** *transitive verb* **fringed; fring·ing** \'frin-jiŋ\ (15th century) **1** : to furnish or adorn with a fringe **2** : to serve as a fringe for : BORDER

**fringe area** *noun* (1950) : a region in which reception from a given broadcasting station is weak or subject to serious distortion

**fringe benefit** *noun* (1948) **1** : an employment benefit (as a pension, a paid holiday, or health insurance) granted by an employer that has a monetary value but does not affect basic wage rates **2** : any additional benefit

**fringe tree** *noun* (circa 1730) : a small tree (*Chionanthus virginicus*) of the olive family that has clusters of white flowers and is native to the southern U.S. but is widely cultivated as an ornamental

**frip·pery** \'fri-p(ə-)rē\ *noun, plural* **-per·ies** [Middle French *friperie*, alteration of Old French *freperie*, from *frepe* old garment] (1568) **1** *obsolete* **a** : cast-off clothes **b** *archaic* : a place where old clothes are sold **2 a** : FINERY; *also* : an elegant or showy garment **b** : something showy, frivolous, or nonessential : LUXURY, TRIFLE **c** : OSTENTATION; *especially* : something foolish or affectedly elegant

**Fris·bee** \'friz-bē\ *trademark*
— used for a plastic disk several inches in diameter sailed between players by a flip of the wrist

**fri·sé** \frē-'zā\ *noun* [French, from past participle of *friser* to curl] (1884) : ¹FRIEZE

**Frise aileron** \'frēz-\ *noun* [Leslie George Frise (born 1897) English engineer] (circa 1934) : an aileron having a nose portion projecting ahead of the hinge axis and a lower surface in line with the lower surface of the wing

**fri·seur** \frē-'zər\ *noun* [French, from *friser*] (1750) : HAIRDRESSER

¹**Fri·sian** \'fri-zhən, 'frē-\ *adjective* [Latin *Frisius* Frisian; akin to Old English *Frīsa, Frēsa* a Frisian] (1598) : of, relating to, or characteristic of Friesland, the Frisians, or Frisian

²**Frisian** *noun* (1601) **1** : a member of a people that inhabit principally the Netherlands province of Friesland and the Frisian islands in the North Sea **2** : the Germanic language of the Frisian people

¹**frisk** \'frisk\ *verb* [obsolete *frisk* (lively)] (1519) *intransitive verb* : to leap, skip, or dance in a lively or playful way : GAMBOL *transitive verb* : to search (a person) for something (as a concealed weapon) by running the hand rapidly over the clothing and through the pockets
— **frisk·er** *noun*

²**frisk** *noun* (1525) **1 a** *archaic* : CAPER **b** : GAMBOL, ROMP **c** : DIVERSION **2** : an act of frisking

**fris·ket** \'fris-kət\ *noun* [French *frisquette*, from Middle French] (circa 1898) : a masking device or material used especially in printing or graphic arts

**frisky** \'fris-kē\ *adjective* **frisk·i·er; -est** (circa 1500) : inclined to frisk : PLAYFUL; *also* : LIVELY
— **frisk·i·ly** \'fris-kə-lē\ *adverb*
— **frisk·i·ness** \-kē-nəs\ *noun*

**fris·son** \frē-'sōⁿ\ *noun, plural* **frissons** \-'sōⁿ(z)\ [French, shiver, from Old French *friçon*, from Late Latin *friction-, frictio*, from Latin, literally, friction (taken in Late Latin as derivative of *frigēre* to be cold)] (1777) : a brief moment of emotional excitement : SHUDDER, THRILL

¹**frit** \'frit\ *noun* [Italian *fritta*, from feminine of *fritto*, past participle of *friggere* to fry, from Latin *frigere* to roast — more at FRY] (1662) **1** : the calcined or partly fused materials of which glass is made **2** : any of various chemically complex glasses used ground especially to introduce soluble or unstable ingredients into glazes or enamels

²**frit** *transitive verb* **frit·ted; frit·ting** (1832) **1** : to prepare (materials for glass) by heat : FUSE **2** : to convert into a frit

**frith** \'frith\ *noun* (14th century) *archaic* : ESTUARY

**frit·il·lar·ia** \,fri-tᵊl-'er-ē-ə, -'ar-\ *noun* [New Latin, from Latin *fritillus* dice cup; from the markings of the petals] : any of a widespread genus (*Fritillaria*) of bulbous herbs of the lily family with variably colored and often mottled or checkered flowers

**frit·il·lary** \'fri-tᵊl-,er-ē\ *noun, plural* **-lar·ies** [New Latin *fritillaria*] (1633) **1** : FRITILLARIA **2** : any of numerous nymphalid butterflies (*Argynnis, Speyeria*, and related genera) that usually are orange with black spots on the upper side of both wings and silver spotted on the underside of the hind wing

**frit·ta·ta** \frē-'tä-tə\ *noun* [Italian, from *fritto*] (1931)

: an unfolded omelet often containing chopped vegetables or meats

**frit·ted** *adjective* [²*frit*] (1879) : being porous glass made of sintered powdered glass or fiberglass

¹**frit·ter** \'fri-tər\ *noun* [Middle English *fritour*, from Middle French *friture*, from (assumed) Vulgar Latin *frictura*, from Latin *frictus*, past participle of *frigere* to roast] (14th century) : a small mass of fried or sautéed batter often containing fruit or meat

²**fritter** *verb* [*fritter*, noun (fragment, shred)] (1728) *transitive verb* **1** : to spend or waste bit by bit, on trifles, or without commensurate return — usually used with *away* **2** : to break into small fragments *intransitive verb* : DISSIPATE, DWINDLE
— **frit·ter·er** \-tər-ər\ *noun*

**frit·to mi·sto** \'frē-(,)tō-'mē-(,)stō\ *noun* [Italian, literally, mixed fried (food)] (1903) : small morsels of meat, seafood, or vegetables coated with batter and deep fried

**fritz** \'fritz\ *noun* [origin unknown] (1902) : a state of disorder or disrepair — used in the phrase *on the fritz*

**friv·ol** \'fri-vᵊl\ *intransitive verb* **-oled** *or* **-olled; -ol·ing** *or* **-ol·ling** \-vᵊl-iŋ, -və-liŋ\ [back-formation from *frivolous*] (1866) : to act frivolously : TRIFLE
— **friv·ol·er** *or* **friv·ol·ler** \-vᵊl-ər, -və-lər\ *noun*

**friv·ol·i·ty** \fri-'vä-lə-tē\ *noun, plural* **-ties** (1796) **1** : the quality or state of being frivolous **2** : a frivolous act or thing

**friv·o·lous** \'fri-vᵊl-əs, -və-ləs\ *adjective* [Middle English, from Latin *frivolus*] (15th century) **1 a** : of little weight or importance **b** : having no sound basis (as in fact or law) ⟨a *frivolous* lawsuit⟩ **2 a** : lacking in seriousness **b** : marked by unbecoming levity
— **friv·o·lous·ly** *adverb*
— **friv·o·lous·ness** *noun*

¹**frizz** \'friz\ *verb* [French *friser*] (1660) *transitive verb* : to form into small tight curls *intransitive verb* *of hair* : to form a mass of tight curls

²**frizz** *noun* (1668) **1** : a tight curl **2** : hair that is tightly curled

³**frizz** *verb* [alteration of ¹*fry*] (1835) *transitive verb* : to fry or sear with a sizzling noise *intransitive verb* : SIZZLE

¹**friz·zle** \'fri-zᵊl\ *verb* **friz·zled; friz·zling** \-zᵊl-iŋ, -zə-liŋ\ [probably akin to Old Frisian *frīsle* curl] (1573) : FRIZZ, CURL

²**frizzle** *noun* (1613) : a crisp curl

³**frizzle** *verb* **friz·zled; friz·zling** [¹*fry* + *sizzle*] (1839) *transitive verb* **1** : to fry until crisp and curled **2** : BURN, SCORCH *intransitive verb* : to cook with a sizzling noise

**frizzy** \'fri-zē\ *adjective* **frizz·i·er; -est** (circa 1864) : tightly curled
— **frizz·i·ness** *noun*

¹**fro** \frə, 'frō\ *preposition* [Middle English, from Old Norse *frā*; akin to Old English *fram* from] (13th century) *dialect British* : FROM

²**fro** \'frō\ *adverb* (14th century) : BACK, AWAY — used in the phrase *to and fro*

fritillaria

**¹frock** \'fräk\ *noun* [Middle English *frok,* from Middle French *froc,* of Germanic origin; akin to Old High German *hroch* mantle, coat] (14th century)
**1** : an outer garment worn by monks and friars : HABIT
**2** : an outer garment worn chiefly by men: **a** : a long loose mantle **b** : a workman's outer shirt; *especially* : SMOCK FROCK **c** : a woolen jersey worn especially by sailors
**3** : a woman's dress
**²frock** *transitive verb* (1828)
**1** : to clothe in a frock
**2** : to make a cleric of
**frock coat** *noun* (1823)
: a man's knee-length usually double-breasted coat
**froe** \'frō\ *noun* [perhaps alteration of obsolete *froward* turned away, from Middle English; from the position of the handle] (1574)
: a cleaving tool for splitting cask staves and shingles from the block
**frog** \'frȯg, 'fräg\ *noun* [Middle English *frogge,* from Old English *frogga;* akin to Old High German *frosk* frog; senses 2, 3, 5, 7, 8 unclearly derived & perhaps of distinct origin] (before 12th century)
**1** : any of various smooth-skinned web-footed largely aquatic tailless agile leaping amphibians (as a ranid) — compare TOAD
**2** : the triangular elastic horny pad in the middle of the sole of the foot of a horse — see HOOF illustration
**3 a** : a loop attached to a belt to hold a weapon or tool **b** : an ornamental braiding for fastening the front of a garment that consists of a button and a loop through which it passes
**4** *often capitalized* : FRENCHMAN — usually taken to be offensive
**5** : a device permitting the wheels on one rail of a track to cross an intersecting rail
**6** : a condition in the throat that produces hoarseness ⟨had a *frog* in his throat⟩
**7** : the nut of a violin bow
**8** : a small holder (as of metal, glass, or plastic) with perforations or spikes for holding flowers in place in a bowl or vase
**frog·eye** \-ˌī\ *noun* (circa 1909)
: any of numerous leaf diseases characterized by concentric rings about the diseased spots
**frog·hop·per** \-ˌhä-pər\ *noun* (1711)
: SPITTLEBUG
**frog kick** *noun* (1940)
: a breaststroke kick executed with the knees turned outward and the legs separated and then swung together
**frog·man** \'frȯg-ˌman, 'fräg-, -mən\ *noun* (1945)
: a person equipped (as with face mask, flippers, and air supply) for extended periods of underwater swimming; *especially* : a person so equipped for military reconnaissance and demolition
**frog–march** \-ˌmärch\ *transitive verb* (1923)
: to seize from behind roughly and forcefully propel forward ⟨*frog-marched* him out the door⟩
**frog spit** *noun* (circa 1825)
: CUCKOO SPIT 1
**¹frol·ic** \'frä-lik\ *adjective* [Dutch *vroolijk,* from Middle Dutch *vrolijc,* from *vro* happy; akin to Old High German *frō* happy] (1538)
: full of fun : MERRY
**²frolic** *intransitive verb* **frol·icked; frol·ick·ing** (1593)
**1** : to amuse oneself : make merry
**2** : to play and run about happily : ROMP
**³frolic** *noun* (1616)
**1** : a playful or mischievous action
**2 a** : an occasion or scene of fun : PARTY **b** : FUN, MERRIMENT
**frol·ic·some** \'frä-lik-səm\ *adjective* (1699)
: full of gaiety : SPORTIVE, PLAYFUL
**from** \'frəm, 'främ *also* fəm\ *preposition* [Middle English, from Old English *from, fram;* akin to Old High German *fram,* adverb, forth,

away, Old English *faran* to go — more at FARE] (before 12th century)
**1** — used as a function word to indicate a starting point of a physical movement or a starting point in measuring or reckoning or in a statement of limits ⟨came here *from* the city⟩ ⟨a week *from* today⟩ ⟨cost *from* $5 to $10⟩
**2** — used as a function word to indicate physical separation or an act or condition of removal, abstention, exclusion, release, subtraction, or differentiation ⟨protection *from* the sun⟩ ⟨relief *from* anxiety⟩
**3** — used as a function word to indicate the source, cause, agent, or basis ⟨we conclude *from* this⟩ ⟨a call *from* my lawyer⟩ ⟨inherited a love of music *from* his father⟩ ⟨worked hard *from* necessity⟩
**frond** \'fränd\ *noun* [Latin *frond-, frons* foliage] (1785)
**1** : a large leaf (especially of a palm or fern) usually with many divisions
**2** : a thallus or thalloid shoot (as of a lichen or seaweed) resembling a leaf
**— frond·ed** \'frän-dəd\ *adjective*
**fron·deur** \frōⁿ-'dər\ *noun* [French, literally, slinger, participant in a 17th century revolt in which the rebels were compared to schoolboys using slings only when the teacher was not looking] (1798)
: REBEL, MALCONTENT
**¹front** \'frənt\ *noun* [Middle English, from Old French, from Latin *front-, frons*] (13th century)
**1 a** : FOREHEAD; *also* : the whole face **b** : external and often feigned appearance especially in the face of danger or adversity
**2 a** (1) : VANGUARD (2) : a line of battle (3) : a zone of conflict between armies **b** (1) : a stand on an issue : POLICY (2) : an area of activity (as study or debate) ⟨progress on the educational *front*⟩ (3) : a movement linking divergent elements to achieve common objectives; *especially* : a political coalition
**3** : a side of a building; *especially* : the side that contains the principal entrance
**4 a** : the forward part or surface **b** (1) : FRONTAGE (2) : a beach promenade at a seaside resort **c** : DICKEY 1a **d** : the boundary between two dissimilar air masses
**5** *archaic* : BEGINNING
**6 a** (1) : a position ahead of a person or of the foremost part of a thing (2) — used as a call by a hotel desk clerk in summoning a bellhop **b** : a position of leadership or superiority
**7 a** : a person, group, or thing used to mask the identity or true character or activity of the actual controlling agent **b** : a person who serves as the nominal head or spokesman of an enterprise or group to lend it prestige
**— in front of** : directly before or ahead of
**— out front** : in the audience
**²front** (1523)
*intransitive verb*
**1** : to have the front or principal side adjacent to something; *also* : to have frontage on something ⟨a ten-acre plot *fronting* on a lake —*Current Biography*⟩
**2** : to serve as a front ⟨*fronting* for special interests⟩
*transitive verb*
**1 a** : CONFRONT ⟨went to the woods because I wished . . . to *front* only the essential facts of life —H. D. Thoreau⟩ **b** : to appear before ⟨daily *fronted* him in some fresh splendor —Alfred Tennyson⟩
**2 a** : to be in front of ⟨lawn *fronting* the house⟩ **b** : to be the leader of (a musical group) ⟨appeared as a soloist and *fronted* bands⟩
**3** : to face toward or have frontage on ⟨the house *fronts* the street⟩
**4** : to supply a front to ⟨*fronted* the building with bricks⟩
**5 a** : to articulate (a sound) with the tongue farther forward **b** : to move (a word or phrase) to the beginning of a sentence

**6** *basketball* : to play in front of (an opposing player) rather than between the player and the basket
**³front** *adjective* (1600)
**1 a** : of, relating to, or situated at the front **b** : acting as a front ⟨*front* company⟩
**2** : articulated at or toward the front of the oral passage ⟨*front* vowels⟩
**3** : constituting the first nine holes of an 18-hole golf course
**— front** *adverb*
**front·age** \'frən-tij\ *noun* (1622)
**1 a** : a piece of land that lies adjacent (as to a street or the ocean) **b** : the land between the front of a building and the street **c** : the length of a frontage
**2** : the act or fact of facing a given way
**3** : the front side of a building
**frontage road** *noun* (1949)
: a local street that parallels an expressway or through street and that provides access to property near the expressway — called also *service road*
**¹fron·tal** \'frən-tᵊl\ *noun* (14th century)
**1** [Middle English *frontel,* from Medieval Latin *frontellum,* diminutive of Latin *front-, frons*] : a cloth hanging over the front of an altar
**2** : FACADE 1
**²frontal** *adjective* [New Latin *frontalis,* from Latin *front-, frons*] (1656)
**1** : of, relating to, or adjacent to the forehead or the frontal bone
**2 a** : of, relating to, or situated at the front **b** : directed against the front or at the main point or issue : DIRECT ⟨*frontal* assault⟩
**3** : parallel to the main axis of the body and at right angles to the sagittal plane
**4** : of or relating to a meteorological front
**— fron·tal·ly** \-tᵊl-ē\ *adverb*
**frontal bone** *noun* (1741)
: a bone that forms the forehead and roofs over most of the orbits and nasal cavity and that at birth consists of two halves separated by a suture
**fron·tal·i·ty** \ˌfrən-'ta-lə-tē\ *noun* (1905)
**1** *sculpture* : a schematic composition of the front view that is complete without lateral movement
**2** *painting* : the depiction of an object, figure, or scene in a plane parallel to the plane of the picture surface
**frontal lobe** *noun* (1879)
: the anterior division of each cerebral hemisphere
**front and center** *adverb* (1951)
: in or to the forefront of activity or consideration
**front bench** *noun* (circa 1889)
: either of the two benches nearest the chair in a British legislature (as the House of Commons) occupied by government and opposition leaders; *also* : the leaders themselves — compare BACKBENCH
**— front–bench·er** \-'ben-chər\ *noun*
**front burner** *noun* (1973)
: the condition of being in active consideration or development — compare BACK BURNER
**front·court** \'frənt-ˌkȯrt, -'kȯrt\ *noun* (circa 1949)
: a basketball team's offensive half of the court; *also* : the positions of forward and center on a basketball team
**front dive** *noun* (circa 1934)
: a dive from a position facing the water
**front–end** *adjective* (1962)
: relating to or required at the beginning of an undertaking ⟨no *front-end* charge at the time of investment⟩
**front end** *noun* (1973)

: a unit in a computer system devoted to controlling the data communications link between terminals and the main computer and often to the preliminary processing of data

**front–end load** *noun* (1962)
: the part of the total commission and expenses taken out of early payments under a contract plan for the periodic purchase of investment-company shares

**front–end loader** *noun* (1954)
: a usually wheeled vehicle with a hydraulically operated scoop in front for excavating and loading loose material — called also *front loader*

**fron·tier** \ˌfrən-'tir, 'frən-ˌ, frän-', 'frän-ˌ\ *noun* [Middle English *fronter*, from Middle French *frontiere*, from *front*] (15th century)
**1 a** : a border between two countries **b** *obsolete* : a stronghold on a frontier
**2 a** : a region that forms the margin of settled or developed territory **b** : the farthermost limits of knowledge or achievement in a particular subject **c** : a line of division between different or opposed things ⟨the *frontiers* separating science and the humanities —R. W. Clark⟩ **d** : a new field for exploitative or developmental activity
— **frontier** *adjective*

**fron·tiers·man** \ˌfrən-'tirz-mən, frän-\ *noun* (1782)
: one who lives or works on a frontier

**fron·tis·piece** \'frən-tə-ˌspēs\ *noun* [Middle French *frontispice*, from Late Latin *frontispicium* facade, from Latin *front-, frons* + *-i-* + *specere* to look at — more at SPY] (circa 1598)
**1 a** : the principal front of a building **b** : a decorated pediment over a portico or window
**2** : an illustration preceding and usually facing the title page of a book or magazine ◆

**front·less** \'frənt-ləs\ *adjective* (1605)
*archaic* : SHAMELESS

**front·let** \-lət\ *noun* [Middle English *frontlette*, from Middle French *frontelet*, diminutive of *frontel*, from Latin *frontale*, from *front-, frons*] (15th century)
**1** : a band or phylactery worn on the forehead
**2** : the forehead especially of an animal

**front·line** \'frənt-ˌlīn\ *adjective* (1915)
**1** : relating to, being, or involved in a front line ⟨*frontline* ambulances⟩
**2** : FIRST-RATE ⟨*frontline* teachers⟩; *also* : FIRST-STRING ⟨*frontline* goalie⟩

**front line** *noun* (1917)
**1 a** : a military line formed by the most advanced tactical combat units; *also* : FRONT 2a(2) **b** : an area of potential or actual conflict or struggle
**2** : the most advanced, responsible, or visible position in a field or activity

**front–load** *transitive verb* (1976)
: to assign costs or benefits to the early stages of (as a contract, project, or time period)

**front man** *noun* (1927)
**1** : a person serving as a front or figurehead
**2** : the lead performer in a musical group

**front matter** *noun* (circa 1909)
: matter preceding the main text of a book

**front money** *noun* (circa 1928)
: money that is paid in advance for a promised service or product

**fronto–** *combining form* ['front]
: boundary of an air mass ⟨*fronto*genesis⟩

**front office** *noun, often attributive* (1900)
: the policy-making officials of an organization

**front·o·gen·e·sis** \ˌfrən-tō-'je-nə-səs\ *noun* [New Latin] (1931)
: the coming together into a distinct front of two dissimilar air masses that commonly react upon each other to induce cloud and precipitation

**front·ol·y·sis** \ˌfrən-'tä-lə-səs\ *noun* [New Latin] (circa 1938)
: a process tending to destroy a meteorological front

**fron·ton** \'frän-ˌtän\ *noun* [Spanish *frontón* gable, wall of a pelota court, fronton, from augmentative of *frente* forehead, from Latin *front-, frons*] (1896)
: a jai alai arena

**¹front–page** \'frənt-'pāj\ *adjective* (1917)
: printed on the front page of a newspaper; *also* : very newsworthy

**²front–page** *transitive verb* (1929)
: to print or report on the front page

**front room** *noun* (1853)
: LIVING ROOM, PARLOR

**front–run·ner** \'frənt-ˌrə-nər\ *noun* (1914)
**1** : a contestant who runs best when in the lead
**2** : a leading contestant in or as if in a rivalry or competition ⟨a political *front-runner*⟩ ⟨dubbed . . . *front-runner* for the title of "worst Senator" —Edward Roeder⟩

**front·ward** \'frənt-wərd\ *or* **front·wards** \-wərdz\ *adverb or adjective* (1865)
: toward the front

**frore** \'frōr, 'frȯr\ *adjective* [Middle English *froren*, from Old English, past participle of *frēosan* to freeze] (13th century)
: FROSTY, FROZEN

**frosh** \'fräsh\ *noun, plural* **frosh** [by shortening & alteration] (1915)
: FRESHMAN

**¹frost** \'frȯst\ *noun* [Middle English, from Old English; akin to Old High German *frost* — more at FREEZE] (before 12th century)
**1 a** : the process of freezing **b** : a covering of minute ice crystals on a cold surface; *also* : ice particles formed from a gas **c** : the temperature that causes freezing
**2 a** : coldness of deportment or temperament : an indifferent, reserved, or unfriendly manner **b** : FAILURE ⟨the play was . . . a most dreadful *frost* —Arnold Bennett⟩

**²frost** (1635)
*transitive verb*
**1 a** : to cover with or as if with frost; *especially* : to put icing on (cake) **b** : to produce a fine-grained slightly roughened surface on (as metal or glass)
**2** : to injure or kill (as plants) by frost
**3** : to make angry or irritated ⟨your attitude really *frosts* me⟩
*intransitive verb*
: to become frosted

**¹frost·bite** \'frȯs(t)-ˌbīt\ *transitive verb* **-bit** \-ˌbit\; **-bit·ten** \-ˌbi-t°n\; **-bit·ing** \-ˌbī-tiŋ\ (1601)
: to affect or injure by frost or frostbite

**²frostbite** *noun* (1813)
: the freezing or the local effect of a partial freezing of some part of the body

**³frostbite** *adjective* (1953)
: done in cold weather ⟨*frostbite* sailing⟩; *also* : of or relating to cold-weather sailing ⟨*frostbite* sailors⟩

**frost·bit·ing** \-ˌbī-tiŋ\ *noun* (1965)
: the sport of sailing in cold weather

**frost·ed** \'frȯ-stəd\ *adjective* (1947)
: having undergone frosting ⟨*frosted* hair⟩

**frost heave** *noun* (1941)
: an upthrust of ground or pavement caused by freezing of moist soil — called also *frost heaving*

**frost·ing** \'frȯ-stiŋ\ *noun* (1858)
**1 a** : ICING **b** : TRIMMING, ORNAMENTATION
**2** : lusterless finish of metal or glass : MAT; *also* : a white finish produced on glass (as by etching)
**3** : the lightening (as by chemicals) of small strands of hair throughout the entire head to produce a two-tone effect — compare STREAKING

**frost·work** \'frȯs(t)-ˌwərk\ *noun* (1729)
: the figures that moisture sometimes forms in freezing (as on a windowpane)

**frosty** \'frȯ-stē\ *adjective* **frost·i·er; -est** (before 12th century)
**1 a** : attended with or producing frost : FREEZING **b** : briskly cold : CHILLY

**2** : covered or appearing as if covered with frost : HOARY ⟨a man of 65, with *frosty* eyebrows and hair —Nan Robertson⟩
**3** : marked by coolness or extreme reserve in manner ⟨his smile was distinctly *frosty* —Erle Stanley Gardner⟩
— **frost·i·ly** \-stə-lē\ *adverb*
— **frost·i·ness** \-stē-nəs\ *noun*

**¹froth** \'frȯth\ *noun, plural* **froths** \'frȯths, 'frȯthz\ [Middle English, from Old Norse *frotha*; akin to Old English *āfrēothan* to froth] (14th century)
**1 a** : bubbles formed in or on a liquid : FOAM **b** : a foamy slaver sometimes accompanying disease or exhaustion
**2** : something resembling froth (as in being unsubstantial, worthless, or light and airy)

**²froth** \'frȯth, 'frȯth\ (14th century)
*intransitive verb*
**1** : to foam at the mouth
**2** : to throw froth out or up
**3** : to become covered with or as if with froth ⟨whole groves *froth* with nodding blossoms —Amy Lovejoy⟩
*transitive verb*
**1** : to cause to foam
**2** : to cover with froth
**3** : VENT, VOICE

**frothy** \'frȯ-thē, -thē\ *adjective* **froth·i·er; -est** (15th century)
**1** : full of or consisting of froth
**2 a** : gaily frivolous or light in content or treatment : INSUBSTANTIAL ⟨a *frothy* comedy⟩ **b** : made of light thin material
— **froth·i·ly** \-thə-lē, -thə-\ *adverb*
— **froth·i·ness** \-thē-nəs, -thē-\ *noun*

**frot·tage** \frȯ-'täzh\ *noun* [French, from *frotter* to rub] (1935)
: the technique of creating a design by rubbing (as with a pencil) over an object placed underneath the paper; *also* : a composition so made

**frou·frou** \'frü-ˌfrü\ *noun* [French, of imitative origin] (1870)
**1** : a rustling especially of a woman's skirts
**2** : showy or frilly ornamentation

**frow** \'frō\ *variant of* FROE

**fro·ward** \'frō-(w)ərd\ *adjective* [Middle English, turned away, froward, from *fro* from + *-ward* -ward] (13th century)
**1** : habitually disposed to disobedience and opposition
**2** *archaic* : ADVERSE
— **fro·ward·ly** *adverb*
— **fro·ward·ness** *noun*

**¹frown** \'fraůn\ *verb* [Middle English *frounen*, from Middle French *froigner* to snort, frown, of Celtic origin; akin to Welsh *ffroen* nostril, Old Irish *srón* nose] (14th century)
*intransitive verb*

**1 :** to contract the brow in displeasure or concentration
**2 :** to give evidence of displeasure or disapproval by or as if by facial expression ⟨critics *frown* on the idea⟩
*transitive verb*
**:** to show displeasure with or disapproval of especially by facial expression
— **frown·er** *noun*
— **frown·ing·ly** \'fraủ-niŋ-lē\ *adverb*
²**frown** *noun* (1581)
**1 :** an expression of displeasure
**2 :** a wrinkling of the brow in displeasure or concentration
**frows·ty** \'fraủ-stē\ *adjective* **frowst·i·er; -est** [alteration of *frowsy*] (1865)
**1** *chiefly British* **:** MUSTY
**2** *chiefly British* **:** FROWSY 2
**frow·sy** *or* **frow·zy** \'fraủ-zē\ *adjective* **frow·si·er** *or* **frow·zi·er; -est** [origin unknown] (1681)
**1 :** MUSTY, STALE ⟨a *frowsy* smell of stale beer and stale smoke —W. S. Maugham⟩
**2 :** having a slovenly or uncared-for appearance ⟨a couple of *frowsy* stuffed chairs —R. M. Williams⟩
**froze** *past of* FREEZE
**fro·zen** \'frō-z°n\ *adjective* (14th century)
**1 a :** treated, affected, or crusted over by freezing **b :** subject to long and severe cold ⟨*frozen* north⟩
**2 a :** incapable of being changed, moved, or undone **:** FIXED; *specifically* **:** debarred by official action from movement or from change in status ⟨*frozen* wages⟩ **b :** not available for present use ⟨*frozen* capital⟩ **c** (1) **:** drained or incapable of emotion (2) **:** expressing or characterized by cold unfriendliness
— **fro·zen·ly** *adverb*
— **fro·zen·ness** \-z°n-(n)əs\ *noun*
**fruc·ti·fi·ca·tion** \,frək-tə-fə-'kā-shən, ,frúk-\ *noun* (1764)
**:** the reproductive organs or fruit of a plant; *especially* **:** SPOROPHORE
**fruc·ti·fy** \'frək-tə-,fī, 'frúk-\ *verb* **-fied; -fy·ing** [Middle English *fructifien*, from Middle French *fructifier*, from Latin *fructificare*, from *fructus* fruit] (14th century)
*intransitive verb*
**:** to bear fruit ⟨its seeds shall *fructify* —Amy Lowell⟩ ⟨no partnership can *fructify* without candor on both sides —D. M. Ogilvy⟩
*transitive verb*
**:** to make fruitful or productive
**fruc·tose** \'frək-,tōs, 'frúk-, 'frúk-, -,tōz\ *noun* (circa 1864)
**1 :** an optically active sugar $C_6H_{12}O_6$ that differs from glucose in having a ketonic rather than aldehydic carbonyl group
**2 :** the very sweet soluble levorotatory D-form of fructose that occurs especially in fruit juices and honey — called also *levulose*
**fruc·tu·ous** \'frək-chə-wəs, 'frúk-\ *adjective* (14th century)
**:** FRUITFUL ⟨a *fructuous* land⟩
**fru·gal** \'frü-gəl\ *adjective* [Middle French or Latin; Middle French, from Latin *frugalis* virtuous, frugal, from *frug-, frux* fruit, value; akin to Latin *frui* to enjoy] (1598)
**:** characterized by or reflecting economy in the use of resources
*synonym see* SPARING
— **fru·gal·i·ty** \frü-'ga-lə-tē\ *noun*
— **fru·gal·ly** \'frü-gə-lē\ *adverb*
**fru·giv·o·rous** \frü-'ji-və-rəs\ *adjective* [Latin *frug-, frux* + English *-vorous*] (1713)
**:** feeding on fruit
— **fru·gi·vore** \'frü-ji-,vōr, -,vȯr\ *noun*
¹**fruit** \'früt\ *noun, often attributive* [Middle English, from Old French, from Latin *fructus* fruit, use, from *frui* to enjoy, have the use of — more at BROOK] (12th century)
**1 a :** a product of plant growth (as grain, vegetables, or cotton) ⟨the *fruits* of the field⟩ **b** (1) **:** the usually edible reproductive body of a seed plant; *especially* **:** one having a sweet

pulp associated with the seed ⟨the *fruit* of the tree⟩ (2) **:** a succulent plant part (as the petioles of a rhubarb plant) used chiefly in a dessert or sweet course **c :** a dish, quantity, or diet of fruits ⟨live on *fruit*⟩ **d :** a product of fertilization in a plant with its modified envelopes or appendages; *specifically* **:** the ripened ovary of a seed plant and its contents **e :** the flavor or aroma of fresh fruit in mature wine
**2 :** OFFSPRING, PROGENY
**3 a :** the state of bearing fruit ⟨a tree in *fruit*⟩ **b :** the effect or consequence of an action or operation **:** PRODUCT, RESULT ⟨the *fruits* of our labor⟩
**4 :** a male homosexual — often used disparagingly
— **fruit·ed** \'frü-təd\ *adjective*
²**fruit** (14th century)
*intransitive verb*
**:** to bear fruit
*transitive verb*
**:** to cause to bear fruit
**fruit·age** \'frü-tij\ *noun* (15th century)
**1 a :** FRUIT **b :** the condition or process of bearing fruit
**2 :** the product or result of an action
**frui·tar·i·an** \(,)frü(t)-'ter-ē-ən\ *noun* (1893)
**:** a person who lives on fruit
**fruit bat** *noun* (1877)
**:** any of a family (Pteropodidae of the suborder Megachiroptera) of often large tropical and subtropical Old World bats that feed on ripe fruit, pollen, and nectar and that usually use visual navigation rather than echolocation — called also *flying fox*

**fruit bat**

**fruit·cake** \'früt-,kāk\ *noun* (1848)
**1 :** a rich cake containing nuts, dried or candied fruits, and spices
**2 :** NUT 6a
**fruit·er·er** \'frü-tər-ər\ *noun* [Middle English, modification of Middle French *fruitier*, from *fruit*] (15th century)
*chiefly British* **:** a person who deals in fruit
**fruit fly** *noun* (circa 1753)
**:** any of various small dipteran flies (as a drosophila) whose larvae feed on fruit or decaying vegetable matter
**fruit·ful** \'früt-fəl\ *adjective* (14th century)
**1 a :** yielding or producing fruit **b :** conducive to an abundant yield
**2 :** abundantly productive
*synonym see* FERTILE
— **fruit·ful·ly** \-fə-lē\ *adverb*
— **fruit·ful·ness** *noun*
**fruiting body** *noun* (1918)
**:** a plant organ specialized for producing spores; *especially* **:** SPOROPHORE
**fru·ition** \frü-'i-shən\ *noun* [Middle English *fruicioun*, from Middle French or Late Latin; Middle French *fruition*, from Late Latin *fruition-, fruitio*, from *frui*] (15th century)
**1 :** pleasurable use or possession **:** ENJOYMENT
**2 a :** the state of bearing fruit **b :** REALIZATION
**fruit·less** \'früt-ləs\ *adjective* (14th century)
**1 :** UNSUCCESSFUL
**2 :** lacking or not bearing fruit
*synonym see* FUTILE
— **fruit·less·ly** *adverb*
— **fruit·less·ness** *noun*
**fruit·let** \-lət\ *noun* (1882)
**1 :** a small fruit
**2 :** a unit of a collective fruit
**fruit machine** *noun* (1933)
*British* **:** SLOT MACHINE 2
**fruit sugar** *noun* (circa 1889)
**:** FRUCTOSE 2
**fruit·wood** \'früt-,wúd\ *noun, often attributive* (1927)

**:** the wood of a fruit tree (as the apple, cherry, or pear) ⟨*fruitwood* furniture⟩
**fruity** \'frü-tē\ *adjective* **fruit·i·er; -est** (1657)
**1 a :** relating to, made with, or resembling fruit **b :** having the flavor or aroma of ripe fruit
**2 a :** extremely effective, interesting, or enjoyable **b :** sweet or sentimental especially to excess **c** *of a voice* **:** rich and deep
**3** *slang* **:** CRAZY, SILLY **b :** HOMOSEXUAL — often used disparagingly
— **fruit·i·ness** *noun*
**fru·men·ty** \'frü-mən-tē\ *noun, plural* **-ties** [Middle English, from Middle French *frumentee*, from *frument* grain, from Latin *frumentum*, from *frui* to enjoy — more at BROOK] (14th century)
**:** a dish of wheat boiled in milk and usually sweetened and spiced
**frump** \'frəmp\ *noun* [probably from *frumple* (to wrinkle)] (1817)
**1 :** a dowdy unattractive girl or woman
**2 :** a staid, drab, old-fashioned person
**frump·ish** \'frəm-pish\ *adjective* (circa 1847)
**:** DOWDY, DRAB
**frumpy** \'frəm-pē\ *adjective* **frump·i·er; -est** (circa 1840)
**:** DOWDY, DRAB
¹**frus·trate** \'frəs-,trāt\ *transitive verb* **frus·trat·ed; frus·trat·ing** [Middle English, from Latin *frustratus*, past participle of *frustrare* to deceive, frustrate, from *frustra* in error, in vain] (15th century)
**1 a :** to balk or defeat in an endeavor **b :** to induce feelings of discouragement
**2 a** (1) **:** to make ineffectual **:** bring to nothing (2) **:** IMPEDE, OBSTRUCT **b :** to make invalid or of no effect ☆
²**frustrate** *adjective* (15th century)
**:** characterized by frustration
**frus·trat·ing** \-,trā-tiŋ\ *adjective* (1871)
**:** tending to produce or characterized by frustration
— **frus·trat·ing·ly** \-tiŋ-lē\ *adverb*
**frus·tra·tion** \(,)frəs-'trā-shən\ *noun* (1555)
**1 :** the act of frustrating
**2 a :** the state or an instance of being frustrated **b :** a deep chronic sense or state of insecurity and dissatisfaction arising from unresolved problems or unfulfilled needs
**3 :** something that frustrates
**frus·tule** \'frəs-(,)chü(ə)l, -(,)t(y)ü(ə)l\ *noun* [French, from Latin *frustulum*, diminutive of *frustum*] (1857)
**:** the 2-valved siliceous shell of a diatom
**frus·tum** \'frəs-təm\ *noun, plural* **frustums** *or* **frus·ta** \-tə\ [New Latin, from Latin, piece, bit — more at BRUISE] (1658)

---

☆ **SYNONYMS**
**Frustrate, thwart, foil, baffle, balk** mean to check or defeat another's plan or block achievement of a goal. FRUSTRATE implies making vain or ineffectual all efforts however vigorous or persistent ⟨*frustrated* attempts at government reform⟩. THWART suggests frustration or checking by crossing or opposing ⟨the army *thwarted* his attempt at a coup⟩. FOIL implies checking or defeating so as to discourage further effort ⟨*foiled* by her parents, he stopped trying to see her⟩. BAFFLE implies frustration by confusing or puzzling ⟨*baffled* by the maze of rules and regulations⟩. BALK suggests the interposing of obstacles or hindrances ⟨officials felt that legal restrictions had *balked* their efforts to control crime⟩.

---

\ə\ **abut** \°\ **kitten** \ər\ **further** \a\ **ash** \ā\ **ace** \ä\ **mop, mar** \aú\ **out** \ch\ **chin** \e\ **bet** \ē\ **easy** \g\ **go** \i\ **hit** \ī\ **ice** \j\ **job** \ŋ\ **sing** \ō\ **go** \ȯ\ **law** \ȯi\ **boy** \th\ **thin** \t͟h\ **the** \ü\ **loot** \ú\ **foot** \y\ **yet** \zh\ **vision** *see also* Guide to Pronunciation

: the basal part of a solid cone or pyramid formed by cutting off the top by a plane parallel to the base; *also* : the part of a solid intersected between two usually parallel planes

**fru·tes·cent** \frü-'te-s°nt\ *adjective* [Latin *frutex* + English *-escent*] (1709)
: having or approaching the habit or appearance of a shrub : SHRUBBY

**fru·ti·cose** \'frü-ti-ˌkōs\ *adjective* [Latin *fruticosus,* from *frutic-, frutex* shrub] (1882)
: having a shrubby often branched thallus that grows perpendicular to the substrate ⟨*fruticose* lichens⟩ — compare CRUSTOSE, FOLIOSE

**¹fry** \'frī\ *verb* **fried; fry·ing** [Middle English *frien,* from Old French *frire,* from Latin *frigere* to roast; akin to Greek *phrygein* to roast, fry, Sanskrit *bhṛjjati* he roasts] (13th century)
*transitive verb*
: to cook in a pan or on a griddle over heat especially with the use of fat
*intransitive verb*
**1** : to undergo frying
**2** : to get very hot or burn as if being fried ⟨bodies *frying* on the beach⟩

**²fry** *noun, plural* **fries** (1833)
**1** : a social gathering or picnic where food is fried and eaten ⟨a fish *fry*⟩
**2 a** : a dish of something fried **b** : FRENCH FRY — usually used in plural

**³fry** *noun, plural* **fry** [Middle English, probably from Old North French *fri,* from Old French *frier, froyer* to rub, spawn — more at FRAY] (14th century)
**1 a** : recently hatched or juvenile fishes **b** : the young of other animals
**2** : very small adult fishes
**3** : members of a group or class : INDIVIDUALS ⟨small *fry*⟩ ⟨a great part of the earth is peopled with these *fry* —Katherine Mansfield⟩

**fry bread** *noun* (1950)
: quick bread cooked (as by American Indians) by deep-frying

**fry·er** \'frī-(ə)r\ *noun* (1851)
: something intended for or used in frying: as
**a** : a young chicken; *especially* : one weighing 2½ to 4 pounds (1.1 to 1.8 kilograms) when dressed **b** : a deep utensil for frying foods

**frying pan** *noun* (14th century)
: a metal pan with a handle that is used for frying foods — called also *fry pan*
**— out of the frying pan into the fire**
: clear of one difficulty only to fall into a greater one

**fry–up** \'frī-ˌəp\ *noun* (1967)
*British* : a dish or meal of fried food

**f–stop** \'ef-ˌstäp\ *noun* (1946)
: a camera lens aperture setting indicated by an f-number

**F₂ layer** \'ef-'tü-\ *noun* (1933)
: the upper of the two layers into which the F region of the ionosphere splits in the daytime at varying heights from about 120 miles (200 kilometers) to more than 300 miles (500 kilometers) above the earth

**fubsy** \'fəb-zē\ *adjective* [obsolete English *fubs* (chubby person)] (1780)
: chubby and somewhat squat

**fuch·sia** \'fyü-shə\ *noun* [New Latin, from Leonhard *Fuchs* (died 1566) German botanist] (1846)
**1** : any of a genus (*Fuchsia*) of decorative shrubs of the evening-primrose family having showy nodding flowers usually in deep pinks, reds, and purples
**2** : a vivid reddish purple

**fuch·sin** *or* **fuch·sine** \'fyük-sən, -ˌsēn\ *noun* [French *fuchsine,* probably from New Latin *Fuchsia;* from its color] (1865)
: a dye that is produced by oxidation of a mixture of aniline and toluidines and yields a brilliant bluish red

fuchsia 1

**¹fuck** \'fək\ *verb* [akin to Dutch *fokken* to breed (cattle), Swedish dialect *fokka* to copulate] (15th century)
*intransitive verb*
**1** : COPULATE — usually considered obscene; sometimes used in the present participle as a meaningless intensive
**2** : MESS 3 — used with *with;* usually considered vulgar
*transitive verb*
**1** : to engage in coitus with — usually considered obscene; sometimes used interjectionally with an object (as a personal or reflexive pronoun) to express anger, contempt, or disgust
**2** : to deal with unfairly or harshly : CHEAT, SCREW — usually considered vulgar

**²fuck** *noun* (1680)
**1** : an act of copulation — usually considered obscene
**2** : a sexual partner — usually considered obscene
**3 a** : DAMN 2 — usually considered vulgar **b** — used especially with *the* as a meaningless intensive; usually considered vulgar ⟨what the *fuck* do they want from me⟩

**fucked–up** \'fək-'təp\ *adjective* (1966)
: thoroughly confused or disordered — usually considered vulgar

**fuck·er** \'fə-kər\ *noun* (1598)
: one that fucks — often used as a generalized term of abuse; usually considered vulgar

**fuck off** *intransitive verb* (1929)
: SCRAM — usually used as a command; usually considered vulgar

**fuck up** (1951)
*intransitive verb*
: to act foolishly or stupidly : BLUNDER — usually considered vulgar
*transitive verb*
: to ruin or spoil especially through stupidity or carelessness : BUNGLE — usually considered vulgar
**— fuck·up** \'fək-ˌəp\ *noun*

**¹fu·coid** \'fyü-ˌkȯid\ *adjective* [New Latin *Fucus,* from Latin] (1839)
: relating to or resembling the rockweeds

**²fucoid** *noun* (circa 1841)
: a fucoid seaweed or fossil

**fu·cose** \'fyü-ˌkōs, -ˌkōz\ *noun* [International Scientific Vocabulary *fuc-* (from Latin *fucus*) + *-ose*] (circa 1909)
: an aldose sugar that occurs in bound form in the dextrorotatory form in various glycosides and in the levorotatory form in some brown algae and in mammalian polysaccharides typical of some blood groups

**fu·co·xan·thin** \ˌfyü-kō-'zan-thən\ *noun* (1873)
: a brown carotenoid pigment $C_{40}H_{60}O_6$ occurring especially in the chloroplasts of brown algae

**fu·cus** \'fyü-kəs\ *noun* [Latin, seaweed, archil, dye obtained from archil, from Greek *phykos*] (1599)
**1** *obsolete* : a face paint
**2** [New Latin, genus name, from Latin] : any of a genus (*Fucus*) of cartilaginous brown algae used in the kelp industry; *broadly* : any of various brown algae

**fud** \'fəd\ *noun* (1913)
: FUDDY-DUDDY

**fud·dle** \'fə-d°l\ *verb* **fud·dled; fud·dling** \'fəd-liŋ, 'fə-d°l-iŋ\ [origin unknown] (1588)
*intransitive verb*
: BOOZE, TIPPLE
*transitive verb*
**1** : to make drunk : INTOXICATE
**2** : to make confused : MUDDLE

**fud·dy–dud·dy** \'fə-dē-ˌdə-dē\ *noun, plural* **-dies** [origin unknown] (circa 1904)
: one that is old-fashioned, unimaginative, or conservative
**— fuddy–duddy** *adjective*

**¹fudge** \'fəj\ *verb* **fudged; fudg·ing** [origin unknown] (1674)
*transitive verb*
**1 a** : to devise as a substitute : FAKE **b** : FALSIFY ⟨*fudged* the figures⟩
**2** : to fail to come to grips with : DODGE ⟨*fudged* the issue⟩
*intransitive verb*
**1** : to exceed the proper bounds or limits of something ⟨feel that the author has *fudged* a little on the . . . rules for crime fiction —*Newsweek*⟩; *also* : CHEAT ⟨*fudging* on an exam⟩
**2** : to fail to perform as expected
**3** : to avoid commitment : HEDGE ⟨the government's tendency to *fudge* on delicate matters of policy —Claire Sterling⟩

**²fudge** *noun* (1766)
**1** : foolish nonsense — often used interjectionally to express annoyance, disappointment, or disbelief
**2** : a soft creamy candy made typically of sugar, milk, butter, and flavoring
**3** : something that is fudged; *especially* : a bending of rules or a compromise

**fudge factor** *noun* (1962)
: an arbitrary mathematical term inserted into a calculation in order to arrive at an expected solution or to allow for errors especially of underestimation; *broadly* : any arbitrary unspecified factor

**fu dog** *often* F *capitalized, variant of* FOO DOG

**¹fu·el** \'fyü-(ə)l\ *noun, often attributive* [Middle English *fewel,* from Old French *fouaille,* from (assumed) Vulgar Latin *focalia,* from Latin *focus* hearth] (13th century)
**1 a** : a material used to produce heat or power by burning **b** : nutritive material **c** : a material from which atomic energy can be liberated especially in a reactor
**2** : a source of sustenance or incentive : REINFORCEMENT

**²fuel** *verb* **-eled** *or* **-elled; -el·ing** *or* **-el·ling** (1592)
*transitive verb*
**1** : to provide with fuel
**2** : SUPPORT, STIMULATE ⟨movement is *fueled* by massive grants-in-aid —Allen Schick⟩
*intransitive verb*
: to take in fuel — often used with *up*

**fuel cell** *noun* (1922)
: a device that continuously changes the chemical energy of a fuel (as hydrogen) and an oxidant directly into electrical energy

**fuel oil** *noun* (1893)
: an oil that is used for fuel and that usually has a higher flash point than kerosene

**fuel·wood** \'fyü-(ə)l-ˌwu̇d\ *noun* (14th century)
: wood grown or used for fuel

**¹fug** \'fəg\ *noun* [perhaps alteration of ¹*fog*] (1888)
: the stuffy atmosphere of a poorly ventilated space; *also* : a stuffy or malodorous emanation
**— fug·gy** \'fə-gē\ *adjective*

**²fug** *verb* **fugged; fug·ging** (circa 1889)
*intransitive verb*
: to loll indoors in a stuffy atmosphere
*transitive verb*
: to make stuffy and odorous

**fu·ga·cious** \fyü-'gā-shəs\ *adjective* [Latin *fugac-, fugax,* from *fugere*] (1634)
**1** : lasting a short time : EVANESCENT
**2** : disappearing before the usual time — used chiefly of plant parts (as stipules) other than floral organs

**fu·gac·i·ty** \fyü-'ga-sə-tē\ *noun* [*fugacious*] (circa 1929)
: the vapor pressure of a vapor assumed to be an ideal gas obtained by correcting the determined vapor pressure and useful as a measure of the escaping tendency of a substance from a heterogeneous system

**fu·gal** \'fyü-gəl\ *adjective* (1854)
: of, relating to, or being in the style of a musical fugue
**— fu·gal·ly** \-gə-lē\ *adverb*

**-fuge** *noun combining form* [French, from Late Latin *-fuga,* from Latin *fugare* to put to flight, from *fuga*]
: one that drives away ⟨febri*fuge*⟩

**¹fu·gi·tive** \'fyü-jə-tiv\ *adjective* [Middle English, from Middle French & Latin; Middle French *fugitif,* from Latin *fugitivus,* from *fugitus,* past participle of *fugere* to flee; akin to Greek *pheugein* to flee] (14th century)
**1 :** running away or intending flight ⟨*fugitive* slave⟩ ⟨*fugitive* debtor⟩
**2 :** moving from place to place : WANDERING
**3 a :** being of short duration **b :** difficult to grasp or retain : ELUSIVE **c :** likely to evaporate, deteriorate, change, fade, or disappear ⟨dyed with *fugitive* colors⟩
**4 :** being of transient interest ⟨*fugitive* essays⟩
*synonym* see TRANSIENT
— **fu·gi·tive·ly** *adverb*
— **fu·gi·tive·ness** *noun*

**²fugitive** *noun* (14th century)
**1 :** a person who flees or tries to escape; *especially* : REFUGEE
**2 :** something elusive or hard to find

**fu·gle·man** \'fyü-gəl-mən\ *noun* [modification of German *Flügelmann,* from *Flügel* wing + *Mann* man] (1804)
**1 :** a trained soldier formerly posted in front of a line of soldiers at drill to serve as a model in their exercises
**2 :** one at the head or forefront of a group or movement

**fu·gu** \'f(y)ü-(ˌ)gü\ *noun* [Japanese] (1909)
: any of various very poisonous puffers (sense 2a) that contain tetrodotoxin and that are used as food in Japan after the toxin-containing organs are removed

**fugue** \'fyüg\ *noun* [probably from Italian *fuga* flight, fugue, from Latin, flight, from *fugere*] (1597)
**1 a :** a musical composition in which one or two themes are repeated or imitated by successively entering voices and contrapuntally developed in a continuous interweaving of the voice parts **b :** something that resembles a fugue especially in interweaving repetitive elements
**2 :** a disturbed state of consciousness in which the one affected seems to perform acts in full awareness but upon recovery cannot recollect the deeds
— **fugue** *verb*
— **fu·gu·ist** \'fyü-gist\ *noun*

**füh·rer** *or* **sueh·rer** \'fyùr-ər, 'fir-\ *noun* [German (*der*) *Führer,* literally, the leader (title assumed by Adolf Hitler), from Middle High German *vüerer,* from *vüeren* to lead, bear, from Old High German *fuoren* to lead; akin to Old English *faran* to go — more at FARE] (1934)
: LEADER 2; *especially* : TYRANT

**fu·ji** \'fü-(ˌ)jē\ *noun* [*Fuji,* mountain in Japan] (1925)
: a spun silk clothing fabric in plain weave originally made in Japan

**¹-ful** *adjective suffix, sometimes* **-ful·er** *sometimes* **-ful·lest** [Middle English, from Old English, from *full,* adjective]
**1 :** full of ⟨pride*ful*⟩
**2 :** characterized by ⟨peace*ful*⟩
**3 :** having the qualities of ⟨master*ful*⟩
**4 :** tending, given, or liable to ⟨help*ful*⟩

**²-ful** *noun suffix*
: number or quantity that fills or would fill ⟨room*ful*⟩ ▯

**Fu·la** *or* **Fu·lah** \'fü-lə\ *noun, plural* **Fula** *or* **Fulas** *or* **Fulah** *or* **Fulahs** (1832)
**1 :** a member of a mainly pastoral African people dispersed over savanna and desert from Senegal to eastern Sudan
**2 :** the language of the Fula people

**Fu·la·ni** \'fü-ˌlä-nē, fü-'\ *noun, plural* **-ni** *or* **-nis** (1860)
**1 :** FULA 1; *especially* : the Fula of northern Nigeria and adjacent areas
**2 :** FULA 2

**ful·crum** \'fùl-krəm, 'fəl-\ *noun, plural* **ful·crums** *or* **ful·cra** \-krə\ [Late Latin, from Latin, bedpost, from *fulcire* to prop — more at BALK] (1674)
**1 a :** PROP; *specifically* : the support about which a lever turns **b :** one that supplies capability for action
**2 :** a part of an animal that serves as a hinge or support

**ful·fill** *or* **ful·fil** \fù(l)-'fil *also* fə(l)-\ *transitive verb* **ful·filled; ful·fill·ing** [Middle English *fulfillen,* from Old English *fullfyllan,* from *full* + *fyllan* to fill] (before 12th century)
**1** *archaic* : to make full : FILL ⟨her subtle, warm, and golden breath . . . *fulfills* him with beatitude —Alfred Tennyson⟩
**2 a :** to put into effect : EXECUTE **b :** to bring to an end **c :** to measure up to : SATISFY
**3 a :** to convert into reality **b :** to develop the full potentialities of
*synonym* see PERFORM
— **ful·fill·er** *noun*
— **ful·fill·ment** \-mənt\ *noun*

**ful·gent** \'fùl-jənt, 'fəl-\ *adjective* [Middle English, from Latin *fulgent-, fulgens,* present participle of *fulgēre* to shine; akin to Latin *flagrare* to burn — more at BLACK] (15th century)
: dazzlingly bright : RADIANT
— **ful·gent·ly** *adverb*

**ful·gu·rant** \'fùl-g(y)ə-rənt, 'fùl-jə-, 'fəl-\ *adjective* (1647)
: flashing like lightning; *also* : BRILLIANT

**ful·gu·ra·tion** \ˌfùl-g(y)ə-'rā-shən, ˌfùl-jə-, fəl-\ *noun* [Latin *fulguration-, fulguratio* sheet lightning, from *fulgurare* to flash with lightning, from *fulgur* lightning, from *fulgēre*] (1633)
**1 :** the act or process of flashing like lightning
**2 :** ELECTRODESICCATION
— **ful·gu·rate** \'fùl-g(y)ə-ˌrāt, 'fùl-jə-, 'fəl-\ *transitive verb*

**ful·gu·rite** \'fùl-g(y)ə-ˌrīt, 'fùl-jə-, 'fəl-\ *noun* [International Scientific Vocabulary, from Latin *fulgur*] (1834)
: an often tubular vitrified crust produced by the fusion of sand or rock by lightning

**ful·gu·rous** \-rəs\ *adjective* [Latin *fulgur*] (1865)
: flashing with lightning

**ful·ham** \'fù-ləm\ *noun* [alteration of earlier *fullan,* perhaps from ¹*full* + ³*one*] (circa 1592)
*archaic* : a loaded die

**fu·lig·i·nous** \fyù-'li-jə-nəs\ *adjective* [Late Latin *fuliginosus,* from Latin *fuligin-, fuligo* soot; akin to Lithuanian *dūlis* cloud, vapor, and probably to Latin *fumus* smoke — more at FUME] (1621)
**1 a :** SOOTY **b :** OBSCURE, MURKY
**2 :** having a dark or dusky color
— **fu·lig·i·nous·ly** *adverb*

**¹full** \'fùl *also* 'fəl\ *adjective* [Middle English, from Old English; akin to Old High German *fol* full, Latin *plenus* full, *plēre* to fill, Greek *plērēs* full, *plēthein* to be full] (before 12th century)
**1 :** containing as much or as many as is possible or normal ⟨a bin *full* of corn⟩
**2 a :** complete especially in detail, number, or duration ⟨a *full* report⟩ ⟨my *full* share⟩ ⟨gone a *full* hour⟩ **b :** lacking restraint, check, or qualification ⟨*full* retreat⟩ ⟨*full* support⟩ **c :** having all distinguishing characteristics : enjoying all authorized rights and privileges ⟨*full* member⟩ ⟨*full* professor⟩ **d :** not lacking in any essential : PERFECT ⟨in *full* control of your senses⟩
**3 a :** being at the highest or greatest degree : MAXIMUM ⟨*full* speed⟩ ⟨*full* strength⟩ **b :** being at the height of development ⟨*full* bloom⟩
**4 :** rounded in outline ⟨a *full* figure⟩
**5 a :** possessing or containing a great number or amount — used with *of* ⟨a room *full* of pictures⟩ ⟨*full* of hope⟩ **b :** having an abundance of material especially in the form of gathered, pleated, or flared parts ⟨a *full* skirt⟩ **c :** rich in experience ⟨a *full* life⟩

**6 a :** satisfied especially with food or drink **b :** large enough to satisfy ⟨a *full* meal⟩
**7** *archaic* : completely weary
**8 :** having both parents in common ⟨*full* sisters⟩
**9 :** having volume or depth of sound ⟨*full* tones⟩
**10 :** completely occupied especially with a thought or plan ⟨*full* of their own concerns⟩
**11 :** possessing a rich or pronounced quality ⟨a food of *full* flavor⟩ ☆
— **full·ness** *also* **ful·ness** \'fùl-nəs\ *noun*
— **full of it** : not to be believed

**²full** *adverb* (before 12th century)
**1 a :** VERY, EXTREMELY ⟨knew *full* well they had lied to me⟩ **b :** ENTIRELY ⟨swung *full* around —Morley Callaghan⟩
**2 :** STRAIGHT, SQUARELY ⟨got hit *full* in the face⟩
**3 —** used as an intensive ⟨wound up winning by a *full* four strokes —William Johnson⟩

**³full** *noun* ⟨14th century⟩
**1 a :** the highest or fullest state or degree ⟨the *full* of the moon⟩ **b :** the utmost extent ⟨enjoy to the *full*⟩
**2 :** the requisite or complete amount ⟨paid in *full*⟩

**⁴full** (1794)
*intransitive verb*
*of the moon* : to become full
*transitive verb*
: to make full in sewing

**⁵full** *transitive verb* [Middle English, from Middle French *fouler* to trample under foot, from Medieval Latin *fullare* to walk, trample, full, from Latin *fullo* fuller] (14th century)
: to shrink and thicken (woolen cloth) by moistening, heating, and pressing

**full·back** \'fùl-ˌbak\ *noun* (1887)
**1 :** an offensive football back used primarily for line plunges and blocking

---

☆ **SYNONYMS**
**Full, complete, plenary, replete** mean containing all that is wanted or needed or possible. FULL implies the presence or inclusion of everything that is wanted or required by something or that can be held, contained, or attained by it ⟨a *full* schedule⟩. COMPLETE applies when all that is needed is present ⟨a *complete* picture of the situation⟩. PLENARY adds to COMPLETE the implication of fullness without qualification ⟨given *plenary* power⟩. REPLETE implies being filled to the brim or to satiety ⟨*replete* with delightful details⟩.

---

□ **USAGE**
**-ful** Nouns ending in *-ful,* like *cupful* and *spoonful,* regularly form the plural by adding *-s* at the end: *cupfuls, spoonfuls.* But these words have long been a puzzle to the public. Part of the problem stems from the fact that most were originally two words with the noun pluralized—many people will recall the nursery rhyme and its "yes sir, yes sir, three bags full." Another factor is that many people remember having been taught that internal pluralization was correct, although we have not yet found a schoolbook giving such a prescription. The result of the continuing uncertainty is the existence of less frequent variants such as *cupsful* and *teaspoonsful.* These variants are not wrong, but most people use *cupfuls* and *teaspoonfuls.*

---

\ə\ **abut** \ᵊ\ **kitten** \ər\ **further** \a\ **ash** \ā\ **ace**
\ä\ **mop, mar** \aù\ **out** \ch\ **chin** \e\ **bet** \ē\ **easy**
\g\ **go** \i\ **hit** \ī\ **ice** \j\ **job** \ŋ\ **sing** \ō\ **go**
\ò\ **law** \òi\ **boy** \th\ **thin** \th\ **the** \ü\ **loot** \ù\ **foot**
\y\ **yet** \zh\ **vision**    *see also* Guide to Pronunciation

**2 :** a primarily defensive player usually stationed nearest the defended goal (as in soccer or field hockey)

**full blast** *adverb* (1909)
**:** at full capacity **:** with great intensity

¹**full–blood** \'ful-ˌbləd\ *adjective* (1812)
**:** FULL-BLOODED 1

²**full–blood** *noun* (1846)
**:** a full-blooded individual

**full–blood·ed** \'ful-ˌblə-dəd\ *adjective* (1774)
**1 :** of unmixed ancestry **:** PUREBRED
**2 :** FLORID, RUDDY ⟨of *full-blooded* face⟩
**3 :** FORCEFUL ⟨*full-blooded* prose style⟩
**4 a :** lacking no particulars **:** GENUINE **b :** containing fullness of substance **:** RICH
**— full–blood·ed·ness** *noun*

**full–blown** \-'blōn\ *adjective* (1601)
**1 a :** fully mature **b :** being at the height of bloom **c :** FULL-FLEDGED
**2 :** possessing all the usual or necessary features ⟨a general philosophy, if not a *full-blown* ideology, is emerging —W. H. Jones⟩

**full–bod·ied** \-ˌbä-dēd\ *adjective* (1686)
**1 :** having a large body
**2** *of a beverage* **:** imparting to the palate the general impression of substantial weight and rich texture
**3 :** having importance, significance, or meaningfulness ⟨*full-bodied* study of literature⟩

**full circle** *adverb* (1879)
**:** through a series of developments that lead back to the original source, position, or situation or to a complete reversal of the original position — usually used in the phrase *come full circle*

**full–dress** *adjective* (1761)
**:** involving attention to every detail in preparation or execution ⟨a *full-dress* rehearsal⟩ ⟨a *full-dress* investigation⟩

**full dress** *noun* (1790)
**:** the style of dress prescribed for ceremonial or formal social occasions

¹**full·er** \'fu̇-lər\ *noun* [Middle English, from Old English *fullere*, from Latin *fullo*] (before 12th century)
**:** one that fulls cloth

²**full·er** \'fu̇-lər\ *noun* [*fuller* (to form a groove in)] (circa 1864)
**:** a blacksmithing hammer for grooving and spreading iron

**full·er·ene** \ˌfu̇-lə-ˈrēn\ *noun* [R. Buckminster *Fuller*; from the resemblance of the molecules to the geodesic domes designed by Fuller] (1988)
**:** any of a class of closed hollow aromatic carbon compounds that are made up of twelve pentagonal and differing numbers of hexagonal faces

**fuller's earth** *noun* [¹*fuller*; from its earlier use as fulling agent] (15th century)
**:** an earthy substance that consists chiefly of clay mineral but lacks plasticity and that is used as an adsorbent, a filter medium, and a carrier for catalysts

**full·er's teasel** *noun* (15th century)
**:** TEASEL 1a

**full–fash·ioned** \'fu̇l-'fa-shənd\ *adjective* (1883)
**:** employing or produced by a knitting process for shaping to conform to body lines ⟨*full-fashioned* hosiery⟩

**full–fledged** \-'flejd\ *adjective* (1883)
**1 :** fully developed **:** TOTAL, COMPLETE ⟨a *full-fledged* war⟩
**2 :** having attained complete status ⟨*full-fledged* lawyer⟩

**full house** *noun* (1887)
**:** a poker hand containing three of a kind and a pair — see POKER illustration

**full–length** \'fu̇l-ˌleŋ(k)th\ *adjective* (1760)
**1 :** showing or adapted to the entire length especially of the human figure ⟨a *full-length* mirror⟩ ⟨a *full-length* dress⟩
**2 :** having a length as great as that which is normal or standard for an object of its kind ⟨a *full-length* play⟩

**full marks** *noun plural* (1916)
*chiefly British* **:** due credit or commendation

**full moon** *noun* (before 12th century)
**:** the moon with its whole apparent disk illuminated

**full–mouthed** \'fu̇l-'maủthd, -'maủtht\ *adjective* (1577)
**1 :** having a full complement of teeth ⟨*full-mouthed* ewes⟩
**2 :** uttered loudly

**full nelson** *noun* (circa 1922)
**:** a wrestling hold gained from behind an opponent by thrusting the arms under the opponent's arms and clasping the hands behind the opponent's head — compare HALF NELSON

**full–out** \-ˌaủt\ *adjective* (14th century)
**:** COMPLETE, TOTAL

**full–scale** \-ˌskā(ə)l\ *adjective* (1933)
**1 :** identical to an original in proportion and size ⟨*full-scale* drawing⟩
**2 a :** involving full use of available resources ⟨a *full-scale* biography⟩ ⟨*full-scale* war⟩ **b :** TOTAL, COMPLETE ⟨a *full-scale* musical renaissance —*Current Biography*⟩

**full–ser·vice** \'fu̇l-'sər-vəs\ *adjective* (1957)
**:** providing comprehensive service of a particular kind ⟨a *full-service* bank⟩

**full–size** \-ˌsīz\ *adjective* (1832)
**1 :** having the usual or normal size of its kind
**2 :** having the dimensions 54 inches by 75 inches (about 1.4 by 1.9 meters) — used of a bed; compare KING-SIZE, QUEEN-SIZE, TWIN-SIZE

**full stop** *noun* (1596)
**:** PERIOD 5a

**full tilt** *adverb* [³*tilt*] (1600)
**:** at high speed

**full–time** *adjective* (1898)
**1 :** employed for or involving full time ⟨*full-time* employees⟩
**2 :** devoting one's full attention and energies to something ⟨a *full-time* gambler⟩
**— full–time** *adverb*

**full time** *noun* (1898)
**:** the amount of time considered the normal or standard amount for working during a given period

**full–tim·er** \'fu̇l-'tī-mər\ *noun* (1864)
**:** a person who works full-time

**ful·ly** \'fu̇(l)-lē\ *adverb* (before 12th century)
**1 :** in a full manner or degree **:** COMPLETELY
**2 :** at least ⟨*fully* nine tenths of us⟩
*usage* see PLENTY

**ful·mar** \'fu̇l-mər, -ˌmär\ *noun* [of Scandinavian origin; akin to Old Norse *fūlmār* fulmar, from *fūll* foul + *mār* gull — more at MEW] (1698)
**:** a seabird (*Fulmarus glacialis*) of colder northern seas closely related to the petrels; *also* **:** a related bird (*F. glacialoides*) of circumpolar distribution in colder southern seas

**ful·mi·nant** \'fu̇l-mə-nənt, 'fəl-\ *adjective* (1602)
**:** FULMINATING 3

¹**ful·mi·nate** \-ˌnāt\ *verb* **-nat·ed; -nat·ing** [Middle English, from Medieval Latin *fulminatus*, past participle of *fulminare*, from Latin, to strike (of lightning), from *fulmin-, fulmen* lightning; akin to Latin *flagrare* to burn — more at BLACK] (15th century)
*transitive verb*
**:** to utter or send out with denunciation
*intransitive verb*
**:** to send forth censures or invectives
**— ful·mi·na·tion** \ˌfu̇l-mə-ˈnā-shən, ˌfəl-\ *noun*

²**fulminate** *noun* [*fulminic acid*, from Latin *fulmin-, fulmen*] (1826)
**:** an often explosive salt (as mercury fulminate) containing the group −CNO

**ful·mi·nat·ing** *adjective* (1626)
**1 :** hurling denunciations or menaces
**2 :** EXPLOSIVE
**3 :** coming on suddenly with great severity

**ful·mine** \'fu̇l-mən, 'fəl-\ *verb* (1590)
*archaic* **:** FULMINATE

**ful·some** \'fu̇l-səm\ *adjective* [Middle English *fulsom* copious, cloying, from *full* + *-som* -some] (13th century)
**1 a :** characterized by abundance **:** COPIOUS ⟨describes in *fulsome* detail —G. N. Shuster⟩ ⟨*fulsome* bird life. The feeder overcrowded —Maxine Kumin⟩ **b :** generous in amount, extent, or spirit ⟨the passengers were *fulsome* in praise of the plane's crew —Don Oliver⟩ ⟨a *fulsome* victory for the far left —Bruce Rothwell⟩ ⟨the greetings have been *fulsome*, the farewells tender —Simon Gray⟩ **c :** being full and well developed ⟨she was in generally *fulsome*, limpid voice —Thor Eckert, Jr.⟩
**2 :** aesthetically, morally, or generally offensive ⟨*fulsome* lies and nauseous flattery —William Congreve⟩ ⟨the devil take thee for a . . . *fulsome* rogue —George Villiers⟩
**3 :** exceeding the bounds of good taste **:** OVERDONE ⟨the *fulsome* chromium glitter of the escalators dominating the central hall —Lewis Mumford⟩
**4 :** excessively complimentary or flattering **:** EFFUSIVE ⟨an admiration whose extent I did not express, lest I be thought *fulsome* —A. J. Liebling⟩ ◼
**— ful·some·ly** *adverb*
**— ful·some·ness** *noun*

**ful·vous** \'fu̇l-vəs, 'fəl-\ *adjective* [Latin *fulvus*; perhaps akin to Latin *flavus* yellow — more at BLUE] (1664)
**:** of a dull brownish yellow **:** TAWNY

**Fu Man·chu mustache** \ˌfü-(ˌ)man-'chü-\ *noun* [*Fu Manchu*, Chinese villain in stories by "Sax Rohmer" (A. S. Ward) (died 1955)] (1968)
**:** a long mustache with ends that turn down to the chin

**fu·ma·rase** \'fyü-mə-ˌrās, -ˌrāz\ *noun* (1936)
**:** an enzyme that catalyzes the interconversion (as in the Krebs cycle) of fumaric acid and malic acid or their salts

**fu·ma·rate** \-ˌrāt\ *noun* (1864)
**:** a salt or ester of fumaric acid

**fu·mar·ic acid** \fyu̇-'mar-ik-\ *noun* [International Scientific Vocabulary, from New Latin *Fumaria*, genus of herbs, from Late Latin *fumitory*, from Latin *fumus*] (1864)
**:** a crystalline acid $C_4H_4O_4$ found in various plants or made synthetically and used especially in making resins

**fu·ma·role** \'fyü-mə-ˌrōl\ *noun* [Italian *fumarola*, from Italian dialect (Neapolitan), from Late Latin *fumariolum* vent, from Latin *fumarium* smoke chamber for aging wine, from *fumus*] (1811)
**:** a hole in a volcanic region from which hot gases and vapors issue
**— fu·ma·rol·ic** \ˌfyü-mə-'rō-lik\ *adjective*

¹**fum·ble** \'fəm-bəl\ *verb* **fum·bled; fum·bling** \-b(ə-)liŋ\ [probably of Scandinavian origin; akin to Swedish *fumla* to fumble] (1534)
*intransitive verb*

**1 a :** to grope for or handle something clumsily or aimlessly **b :** to make awkward attempts to do or find something ⟨*fumbled* in his pocket for a coin⟩ **c :** to search by trial and error **d :** BLUNDER
**2 :** to feel one's way or move awkwardly
**3 a :** to drop or juggle or fail to play cleanly a grounder **b :** to lose hold of a football while handling or running with it
*transitive verb*
**1 :** to bring about by clumsy manipulation
**2 a :** to feel or handle clumsily **b :** to deal with in a blundering way : BUNGLE
**3 :** to make (one's way) in a clumsy manner
**4 a :** MISPLAY ⟨*fumble* a grounder⟩ **b :** to lose hold of (a football) while handling or running
— **fum·bler** \-b(ə-)lər\ *noun*
— **fum·bling·ly** \-b(ə-)liŋ-lē\ *adverb*
²**fumble** *noun* (1634)
**1 :** an act or instance of fumbling
**2 :** a fumbled ball
¹**fume** \'fyüm\ *noun* [Middle English, from Middle French *fum*, from Latin *fumus;* akin to Old High German *toumen* to be fragrant, Sanskrit *dhūma* smoke, Old Church Slavonic *dymŭ*] (14th century)
**1 a :** a smoke, vapor, or gas especially when irritating or offensive ⟨engine exhaust *fumes*⟩ **b :** an often noxious suspension of particles in a gas (as air)
**2 :** something (as an emotion) that impairs one's reasoning ⟨sometimes his head gets a little hot with the *fumes* of patriotism —Matthew Arnold⟩
**3 :** a state of excited irritation or anger — usually used in the phrase *in a fume*
— **fumy** \'fyü-mē\ *adjective*
²**fume** *verb* **fumed; fum·ing** (14th century)
*transitive verb*
**1 :** to expose to or treat with fumes
**2 :** to give off in fumes ⟨*fuming* thick black smoke⟩
**3 :** to utter while in a state of excited irritation or anger
*intransitive verb*
**1 a :** to emit fumes **b :** to be in a state of excited irritation or anger ⟨fretted and *fumed* over the delay⟩
**2 :** to rise in or as if in fumes
**fu·met** \fyü-'mā, 'fyü-mət\ *noun* [French, literally, pleasant aroma (of meat cooking), from Middle French, from *fumer* to give off smoke or steam, from Latin *fumare,* from *fumus*] (1906)
**:** a reduced and seasoned fish, meat, or vegetable stock
**fu·mi·gant** \'fyü-mi-gənt\ *noun* (1890)
**:** a substance used in fumigating
**fu·mi·gate** \'fyü-mə-ˌgāt\ *transitive verb* **-gat·ed; -gat·ing** [Latin *fumigatus,* past participle of *fumigare,* from *fumus* + *-igare* (akin to Latin *agere* to drive) — more at AGENT] (1781)
**:** to apply smoke, vapor, or gas to especially for the purpose of disinfecting or of destroying pests
— **fu·mi·ga·tion** \ˌfyü-mə-'gā-shən\ *noun*
— **fu·mi·ga·tor** \'fyü-mə-ˌgā-tər\ *noun*
**fu·mi·to·ry** \'fyü-mə-ˌtōr-ē, -ˌtȯr-\ *noun* [Middle English *fumeterre,* from Middle French, from Medieval Latin *fumus terrae,* literally, smoke of the earth, from Latin *fumus* + *terrae,* genitive of *terra* earth — more at TERRACE] (14th century)
**:** any of a genus (*Fumaria* of the family Fumariaceae, the fumitory family) of erect or climbing herbs; *especially* : a common European herb (*F. officinalis*)
¹**fun** \'fən\ *noun* [English dialect *fun* to hoax, perhaps alteration of Middle English *fonnen,* from *fonne* dupe] (1727)
**1 :** what provides amusement or enjoyment; *specifically* : playful often boisterous action or speech ⟨full of *fun*⟩
**2 :** a mood for finding or making amusement ⟨all in *fun*⟩

**3 a :** AMUSEMENT, ENJOYMENT ⟨sickness takes all the *fun* out of life⟩ **b :** derisive jest : SPORT, RIDICULE ⟨a figure of *fun*⟩
**4 :** violent or excited activity or argument ⟨let a snake loose in the classroom; then the *fun* began⟩ ☆
²**fun** *intransitive verb* **funned; fun·ning** (1833)
**:** to indulge in banter or play : JOKE
³**fun** *adjective, sometimes* **fun·ner;** *sometimes* **fun·nest** (circa 1846)
**1 :** providing entertainment, amusement, or enjoyment ⟨a *fun* party⟩ ⟨a *fun* person to be with⟩
**2 :** full of fun : PLEASANT ⟨a *fun* night⟩ ⟨have a *fun* time⟩
**fu·nam·bu·lism** \fyü-'nam-byə-ˌli-zəm\ *noun* [Latin *funambulus* ropewalker, from *funis* rope + *ambulare* to walk] (1824)
**1 :** tightrope walking
**2 :** a show especially of mental agility
— **fu·nam·bu·list** \-list\ *noun*
**fun and games** *noun plural but singular or plural in construction* (1920)
**:** light amusement
¹**func·tion** \'fəŋ(k)-shən\ *noun* [Latin *function-, functio* performance, from *fungi* to perform; probably akin to Sanskrit *bhuṅkte* he enjoys] (1533)
**1 :** professional or official position : OCCUPATION
**2 :** the action for which a person or thing is specially fitted or used or for which a thing exists : PURPOSE
**3 :** any of a group of related actions contributing to a larger action; *especially* : the normal and specific contribution of a bodily part to the economy of a living organism
**4 :** an official or formal ceremony or social gathering
**5 a :** a mathematical correspondence that assigns exactly one element of one set to each element of the same or another set **b :** a variable (as a quality, trait, or measurement) that depends on and varies with another ⟨height is a *function* of age⟩; *also* : RESULT ⟨illnesses that are a *function* of stress⟩
**6 :** characteristic behavior of a chemical compound due to a particular reactive unit; *also* : FUNCTIONAL GROUP
**7 :** a computer subroutine; *specifically* : one that performs a calculation with variables provided by a program and supplies the program with a single result ☆
— **func·tion·less** \-ləs\ *adjective*
²**function** *intransitive verb* **func·tioned; func·tion·ing** \-sh(ə-)niŋ\ (1856)
**1 :** to have a function : SERVE ⟨an attributive noun *functions* as an adjective⟩
**2 :** to carry on a function or be in action : OPERATE ⟨a government *functions* through numerous divisions⟩
**func·tion·al** \'fəŋ(k)-shnəl, -shə-nᵊl\ *adjective* (1631)
**1 a :** of, connected with, or being a function **b :** affecting physiological or psychological functions but not organic structure ⟨*functional* heart disease⟩
**2 :** used to contribute to the development or maintenance of a larger whole ⟨*functional* and practical school courses⟩; *also* : designed or developed chiefly from the point of view of use ⟨*functional* clothing⟩
**3 :** performing or able to perform a regular function
— **func·tion·al·i·ty** \ˌfəŋ(k)-shə-'na-lə-tē\ *noun*
— **func·tion·al·ly** \'fəŋ(k)-shnə-lē, -shə-nᵊl-ē\ *adverb*
**functional calculus** *noun* (1933)
**:** PREDICATE CALCULUS
**functional group** *noun* (1943)
**:** a characteristic reactive unit of a chemical compound especially in organic chemistry
**functional illiterate** *noun* (1946)

**:** a person having had some schooling but not meeting a minimum standard of literacy
— **functionally illiterate** *adjective*
**func·tion·al·ism** \'fəŋ(k)-shnə-ˌli-zəm, -shə-nᵊl-ˌi-\ *noun* (1914)
**1 :** a philosophy of design (as in architecture) holding that form should be adapted to use, material, and structure
**2 :** a theory that stresses the interdependence of the patterns and institutions of a society and their interaction in maintaining cultural and social unity
**3 :** a doctrine or practice that emphasizes practical utility or functional relations
— **func·tion·al·ist** \-shnə-list, -shə-nᵊl-ist\ *noun*
— **functionalist** *or* **func·tion·al·is·tic** \ˌfəŋ(k)-shnə-'lis-tik, -shə-nᵊl-'is-\ *adjective*
**functional shift** *noun* (1942)
**:** the process by which a word or form comes to be used in another grammatical function
**func·tion·ary** \'fəŋ(k)-shə-ˌner-ē\ *noun, plural* **-ar·ies** (1791)
**1 :** one who serves in a certain function
**2 :** one holding office in a government or political party
**function word** *noun* (1940)
**:** a word (as a preposition, auxiliary verb, or conjunction) expressing primarily grammatical relationship
**func·tor** \'fəŋ(k)-tər\ *noun* (1935)
**:** something that performs a function or an operation
¹**fund** \'fənd\ *noun* [Latin *fundus* bottom, country estate — more at BOTTOM] (1694)

---

☆ SYNONYMS
**Fun, jest, sport, game, play** mean action or speech that provides amusement or arouses laughter. FUN usually implies laughter or gaiety but may imply merely a lack of serious or ulterior purpose ⟨played cards just for *fun*⟩. JEST implies lack of earnestness in what is said or done and may suggest a hoaxing or teasing ⟨hurt by remarks said only in *jest*⟩. SPORT applies especially to the arousing of laughter against someone ⟨teasing begun in *sport* led to anger⟩. GAME is close to SPORT, and often stresses mischievous or malicious fun ⟨made *game* of their poor relations⟩. PLAY stresses the opposition to *earnest* without implying any element of malice or mischief ⟨pretended to strangle his brother in *play*⟩.

**Function, office, duty, province** mean the acts or operations expected of a person or thing. FUNCTION implies a definite end or purpose that the one in question serves or a particular kind of work it is intended to perform ⟨the *function* of language is two-fold: to communicate emotion and to give information —Aldous Huxley⟩. OFFICE is typically applied to the function or service expected of a person by reason of his trade or profession or his special relationship to others ⟨they exercise the *offices* of the judge, the priest, the counsellor —W. E. Gladstone⟩. DUTY applies to a task or responsibility imposed by one's occupation, rank, status, or calling ⟨it is the judicial *duty* of the court, to examine the whole case —R. B. Taney⟩. PROVINCE applies to a function, office, or duty that naturally or logically falls to one ⟨nursing does not belong to a man; it is not his *province* —Jane Austen⟩.

---

\ə\ abut \ᵊ\ kitten \ər\ further \a\ ash \ā\ ace
\ä\ mop, mar \au̇\ out \ch\ chin \e\ bet \ē\ easy
\g\ go \i\ hit \ī\ ice \j\ job \ŋ\ sing \ō\ go
\ȯ\ law \ȯi\ boy \th\ thin \t̲h̲\ the \ü\ loot \u̇\ foot
\y\ yet \zh\ vision *see also* Guide to Pronunciation

**1 a :** a sum of money or other resources whose principal or interest is set apart for a specific objective **b :** money on deposit on which checks or drafts can be drawn — usually used in plural **c :** CAPITAL **d** *plural* **:** the stock of the British national debt — usually used with *the*
**2 :** an available quantity of material or intangible resources **:** SUPPLY
**3** *plural* **:** available pecuniary resources
**4 :** an organization administering a special fund

²**fund** *transitive verb* (1789)
**1 a :** to make provision of resources for discharging the interest or principal of **b :** to provide funds for ⟨a science program federally *funded*⟩
**2 :** to place in a fund **:** ACCUMULATE
**3 :** to convert into a debt that is payable either at a distant date or at no definite date and that bears a fixed interest ⟨*fund* a floating debt⟩

**fun·da·ment** \'fən-də-mənt\ *noun* [Middle English, from Old French *fondement*, from Latin *fundamentum*, from *fundare* to found, from *fundus*] (13th century)
**1 :** an underlying ground, theory, or principle
**2 a :** BUTTOCKS **b :** ANUS
**3 :** the part of a land surface that has not been altered by human activities

¹**fun·da·men·tal** \,fən-də-'men-t°l\ *adjective* (15th century)
**1 a :** serving as an original or generating source **:** PRIMARY ⟨a discovery *fundamental* to modern computers⟩ **b :** serving as a basis supporting existence or determining essential structure or function **:** BASIC
**2 a :** of or relating to essential structure, function, or facts **:** RADICAL ⟨*fundamental* change⟩; *also* **:** of or dealing with general principles rather than practical application ⟨*fundamental* science⟩ **b :** adhering to fundamentalism
**3 :** of, relating to, or produced by the lowest component of a complex vibration
**4 :** of central importance **:** PRINCIPAL ⟨*fundamental* purpose⟩
**5 :** belonging to one's innate or ingrained characteristics **:** DEEP-ROOTED ⟨her *fundamental* good humor⟩
**synonym** see ESSENTIAL
**— fun·da·men·tal·ly** \-t°l-ē\ *adverb*

²**fundamental** *noun* (1637)
**1 :** something fundamental; *especially* **:** one of the minimum constituents without which a thing or a system would not be what it is
**2 a :** the principal musical tone produced by vibration (as of a string or column of air) on which a series of higher harmonics is based **b :** the root of a chord
**3 :** the harmonic component of a complex wave that has the lowest frequency and commonly the greatest amplitude

**fundamental group** *noun* (1957)
**:** a set that is a subset of all paths defined on a set of points each pair of which is joined by a path and that is the quotient group of the group of all paths beginning and ending with a given point

**fun·da·men·tal·ism** \-t°l-,i-zəm\ *noun* (1922)
**1 a** *often capitalized* **:** a movement in 20th century Protestantism emphasizing the literally interpreted Bible as fundamental to Christian life and teaching **b :** the beliefs of this movement **c :** adherence to such beliefs
**2 :** a movement or attitude stressing strict and literal adherence to a set of basic principles
**— fun·da·men·tal·ist** \-t°l-ist\ *noun*
**— fundamentalist** *or* **fun·da·men·tal·is·tic** \-,men-t°l-'is-tik\ *adjective*

**fundamental law** *noun* (circa 1914)
**:** the organic or basic law of a political unit as distinguished from legislative acts; *specifically* **:** CONSTITUTION

**fundamental particle** *noun* (1947)
**:** ELEMENTARY PARTICLE

**fun·dic** \'fən-dik\ *adjective* (circa 1927)

**:** of or relating to a fundus

**fund–rais·er** \'fən-,drā-zər\ *noun* (1957)
**1 :** a person employed to raise funds
**2 :** a social event (as a cocktail party) held for the purpose of raising funds

**fund–rais·ing** \-ziŋ\ *noun, often attributive* (1940)
**:** the organized activity of raising funds (as for an institution or political cause)

**fun·dus** \'fən-dəs\ *noun, plural* **fun·di** \-,dī, -,dē\ [New Latin, from Latin, bottom] (1764)
**:** the bottom of or part opposite the aperture of the internal surface of a hollow organ: as **a :** the greater curvature of the stomach **b :** the lower back part of the bladder **c :** the large upper end of the uterus **d :** the part of the eye opposite the pupil

¹**fu·ner·al** \'fyün-rəl, 'fyü-nə-\ *adjective* [Middle English, from Late Latin *funeralis*, from Latin *funer-, funus* funeral (noun)] (14th century)
**1 :** of, relating to, or constituting a funeral
**2 :** FUNEREAL 2

²**funeral** *noun* [Middle English *funerelles* (plural), from Middle French *funerailles*, from Medieval Latin *funeralia* (plural), from Late Latin, neuter plural of *funeralis*, adjective] (circa 1512)
**1 :** the observances held for a dead person usually before burial or cremation
**2** *chiefly dialect* **:** a funeral sermon
**3 :** a funeral procession
**4 :** an end of something's existence
**5 :** a matter of concern to one **:** WORRY ⟨if you flunk, that's your *funeral*⟩

**funeral director** *noun* (1886)
**:** one whose profession is the management of funerals and who is usually an embalmer

**funeral home** *noun* (1926)
**:** an establishment with facilities for the preparation of the dead for burial or cremation, for the viewing of the body, and for funerals — called also *funeral parlor*

**fu·ner·ary** \'fyü-nə-,rer-ē\ *adjective* (circa 1693)
**:** of, used for, or associated with burial ⟨a pharaoh's *funerary* chamber⟩

**fu·ne·re·al** \fyù-'nir-ē-əl\ *adjective* [Latin *funereus*, from *funer-, funus*] (1725)
**1 :** of or relating to a funeral
**2 :** befitting or suggesting a funeral (as in solemnity)
**— fu·ne·re·al·ly** \-ə-lē\ *adverb*

**fun·fair** \'fən-,far, -,fer\ *noun* (1925)
*chiefly British* **:** AMUSEMENT PARK

**fun·gal** \'fəŋ-gəl\ *adjective* (1835)
**1 :** of, relating to, or having the characteristics of fungi
**2 :** caused by a fungus

**fungi-** *combining form* [Latin *fungus*]
**:** fungus ⟨*fungi*form⟩

¹**fun·gi·ble** \'fən-jə-bəl\ *noun* (circa 1765)
**:** something that is fungible — usually used in plural

²**fungible** *adjective* [New Latin *fungibilis*, from Latin *fungi* to perform — more at FUNCTION] (1818)
**1 :** being of such a nature that one part or quantity may be replaced by another equal part or quantity in the satisfaction of an obligation ⟨oil, wheat, and lumber are *fungible* commodities⟩
**2 :** INTERCHANGEABLE
**— fun·gi·bil·i·ty** \,fən-jə-'bi-lə-tē\ *noun*

**fun·gi·cid·al** \,fən-jə-'sī-d°l, ,fəŋ-gə-\ *adjective* (1905)
**:** ANTIFUNGAL
**— fun·gi·cid·al·ly** \-d°l-ē\ *adverb*

**fun·gi·cide** \'fən-jə-,sīd, 'fəŋ-gə-\ *noun* [International Scientific Vocabulary] (1889)
**:** an agent that destroys fungi or inhibits their growth

**fun·gi·form** \'fən-jə-,form, 'fəŋ-gə-\ *adjective* (1823)
**:** shaped like a mushroom

**fun·gi·stat·ic** \,fən-jə-'sta-tik\ *adjective* (1922)
**:** inhibiting the growth of fungi without destroying them

**fun·go** \'fəŋ-(,)gō\ *noun, plural* **fungoes** [origin unknown] (circa 1867)
**1 :** a fly ball hit especially for practice fielding by a player who tosses a ball in the air and hits it as it comes down
**2 :** FUNGO BAT

**fungo bat** *noun* (1926)
**:** a long thin bat used for hitting fungoes

**fun·goid** \'fən-,goid\ *adjective* (circa 1836)
**:** resembling, characteristic of, caused by, or being a fungus ⟨*fungoid* growth⟩
**— fungoid** *noun*

**fun·gous** \'fən-gəs\ *adjective* (15th century)
**:** FUNGAL

**fun·gus** \'fən-gəs\ *noun, plural* **fun·gi** \'fən-,jī, 'fəŋ-,gī\ *also* **fun·gus·es** \'fən-gə-səz\ *often attributive* [Latin] (1527)
**:** any of a major group (Fungi) of saprophytic and parasitic spore-producing organisms usually classified as plants that lack chlorophyll and include molds, rusts, mildews, smuts, mushrooms, and yeasts

**fun house** *noun* (1948)
**:** a building in an amusement park that contains various devices designed to startle or amuse

¹**fu·nic·u·lar** \fyù-'ni-kyə-lər, fə-\ *adjective* [Latin *funiculus*] (1664)
**1 :** having the form of or associated with a cord usually under tension
**2** [New Latin *funiculus*] **:** of, relating to, or being a funiculus
**3 :** of, relating to, or being a funicular ⟨a *funicular* system⟩

²**funicular** *noun* (1911)
**:** a cable railway ascending a mountain; *especially* **:** one in which an ascending car counterbalances a descending car

**fu·nic·u·lus** \-ləs\ *noun, plural* **-li** \-,lī, -,lē\ [New Latin, from Latin, diminutive of *funis* rope] (1826)
**1 :** a bodily structure suggesting a cord; *especially* **:** a bundle of nerve fibers
**2 :** the stalk of a plant ovule

¹**funk** \'fəŋk\ (circa 1739)
*intransitive verb*
**:** to become frightened and shrink back
*transitive verb*
**1 :** to be afraid of **:** DREAD
**2 :** to shrink from undertaking or facing

²**funk** *noun* [probably from obsolete Flemish *fonck*] (1743)
**1 a :** a state of paralyzing fear **b :** a depressed state of mind
**2 :** one that funks **:** COWARD

³**funk** *noun* [back-formation from ²*funky*] (1959)
**1 :** music that combines traditional forms of black music (as blues, gospel, or soul) and is characterized by a strong backbeat
**2 :** the quality or state of being funky ⟨jeans . . . have lost much of their *funk* —Tom Wolfe⟩

**funk hole** *noun* (1900)
**1 :** DUGOUT 2
**2 :** a place of safe retreat

**fun·kia** \'fən-kē-ə, 'fùŋ-\ *noun* [New Latin, genus name, from C. H. *Funck* (died 1839) German botanist] (1839)
**:** PLANTAIN LILY

¹**funky** \'fən-kē\ *adjective* (1845)
**:** being in a funk **:** PANICKY

²**funky** *adjective* **funk·i·er; -est** [*funk* (offensive odor)] (circa 1899)
**1 :** having an offensive odor **:** FOUL
**2 :** having an earthy unsophisticated style and feeling; *especially* **:** having the style and feeling of older black American music (as blues or gospel) or of funk ⟨a slick, heavy beat that is unmistakably contemporary and irresistibly *funky* —Jay Cocks⟩

**3 a** : odd or quaint in appearance or feeling **b** : lacking style or taste **c** : unconventionally stylish : HIP ◆
— **funk·i·ness** noun

**¹fun·nel** \'fə-n°l\ noun [Middle English fonel, from Old Provençal fonilh, from Medieval Latin fundibulum, short for Latin infundibulum, from infundere to pour in, from in- + fundere to pour — more at FOUND] (15th century)
**1 a** : a utensil that is usually a hollow cone with a tube extending from the smaller end and that is designed to catch and direct a downward flow **b** : something shaped like a funnel
**2** : a stack or flue for the escape of smoke or for ventilation (as on a ship)

**²funnel** verb **-neled** also **-nelled; -nel·ing** also **-nel·ling** (1594)
intransitive verb
**1** : to have or take the shape of a funnel
**2** : to pass through or as if through a funnel or conduit
transitive verb
**1** : to form in the shape of a funnel ⟨funneled his hands and shouted through them⟩
**2** : to move to a focal point or into a conduit or central channel ⟨contributions were funneled into one account⟩

**funnel cloud** noun (circa 1909)
: a funnel-shaped cloud that projects from the base of a thundercloud and that often betokens the formation of a tornado; also : TORNADO 2b

**fun·nel·form** \'fə-n°l-ˌfȯrm\ adjective (circa 1828)
: INFUNDIBULIFORM

**¹fun·ny** \'fə-nē\ adjective **fun·ni·er; -est** (1756)
**1 a** : affording light mirth and laughter : AMUSING **b** : seeking or intended to amuse : FACETIOUS
**2** : differing from the ordinary in a suspicious, perplexing, quaint, or eccentric way : PECULIAR — often used as a sentence modifier ⟨funny, things didn't turn out the way we planned⟩
**3** : involving trickery or deception ⟨told his prisoner not to try anything funny⟩
— **fun·ni·ly** \'fə-n°l-ē\ adverb
— **fun·ni·ness** \'fə-nē-nəs\ noun
— **funny** adverb

**²funny** noun, plural **funnies** (1852)
**1** : one that is funny; especially : JOKE
**2** plural : comic strips or the comic section of a periodical — usually used with the

**funny bone** noun [from the tingling felt when it is struck] (1840)
**1** : the place at the back of the elbow where the ulnar nerve rests against a prominence of the humerus
**2** : a sense of humor

**funny book** noun (1947)
: COMIC BOOK

**funny car** noun (1969)
: a specialized dragster that has a one-piece molded body resembling the body of a mass-produced car

**funny farm** noun (1963)
slang : a psychiatric hospital

**fun·ny·man** \'fə-nē-ˌman\ noun (1852)
: COMEDIAN 2, HUMORIST

**funny money** noun (1943)
**1** : artificially inflated currency
**2** : counterfeit money

**funny paper** noun (1924)
: a comic section of a newspaper

**¹fur** \'fər\ verb **furred; fur·ring** [Middle English furren, from Middle French fourrer, from Old French forrer, from fuerre sheath, of Germanic origin; akin to Old High German fuotar sheath; akin to Greek pōma lid, cover, Sanskrit pāti he protects] (14th century)
transitive verb
**1** : to cover, line, trim, or clothe with fur
**2** : to coat or clog as if with fur
**3** : to apply furring to

intransitive verb
: to become coated or clogged as if with fur ◆

**²fur** noun, often attributive (14th century)
**1** : a piece of the dressed pelt of an animal used to make, trim, or line wearing apparel
**2** : an article of clothing made of or with fur
**3** : the hairy coat of a mammal especially when fine, soft, and thick; also : such a coat with the skin
**4** : a coating resembling fur: as **a** : a coat of epithelial debris on the tongue **b** : the thick pile of a fabric
— **fur·less** \'fər-ləs\ adjective

**fu·ran** \'fyu̇r-ˌan, fyu̇-'ran\ also **fu·rane** \'fyu̇r-ˌān, fyu̇-'rān\ noun [International Scientific Vocabulary, from furfural] (1894)
: a flammable liquid $C_4H_4O$ that is obtained from wood oils of pines or made synthetically and is used especially in organic synthesis; also : a derivative of furan

**fu·ra·nose** \'fyu̇r-ə-ˌnōs, -ˌnōz\ noun (1927)
: a sugar having an oxygen-containing ring of five atoms

**fu·ran·o·side** \fyu̇-'ra-nə-ˌsīd\ noun (1932)
: a glycoside containing the ring characteristic of furanose

**fu·ra·zol·i·done** \ˌfyu̇r-ə-'zä-lə-ˌdōn\ noun [furfural + azole + -ide + -one] (1955)
: an antimicrobial drug $C_8H_7N_3O_5$ used against bacteria and some protozoa especially in infections of the gastrointestinal tract

**fur·bear·er** \'fər-ˌbar-ər, -ˌber-\ noun (1875)
: an animal that bears fur especially of a commercially desired quality

**fur·be·low** \'fər-bə-ˌlō\ noun [by folk etymology from French dialect farbella] (1706)
**1** : a pleated or gathered piece of material; especially : a flounce on women's clothing
**2** : something that suggests a furbelow especially in being showy or superfluous
— **furbelow** transitive verb

**fur·bish** \'fər-bish\ transitive verb [Middle English furbisshen, from Middle French fourbiss-, stem of fourbir, of Germanic origin; akin to Old High German furben to polish] (14th century)
**1** : to make lustrous : POLISH
**2** : to give a new look to : RENOVATE — often used with up
— **fur·bish·er** noun

**fur·ca·tion** \ˌfər-'kā-shən\ noun [Medieval Latin furcation-, furcatio, from furcare to branch, from Latin furca fork] (1646)
**1** : something that is branched : FORK
**2** : the act or process of branching

**fur·cu·la** \'fər-kyə-lə\ noun, plural **-lae** \-ˌlē, -ˌlī\ [New Latin, from Latin, forked prop, diminutive of furca] (1859)
: a forked process or part: as **a** : WISHBONE **b** : the forked leaping appendage arising from the fourth abdominal segment of a springtail

**fur·fu·ral** \'fər-f(y)ə-ˌral\ noun [Latin furfur bran + International Scientific Vocabulary ³-al] (1879)
: a liquid aldehyde $C_5H_4O_2$ of penetrating odor that is usually made from plant materials and used especially in making furan or phenolic resins and as a solvent

**fu·ri·oso** \ˌfyu̇r-ē-'ō-(ˌ)sō, -(ˌ)zō\ adverb or adjective [Italian, literally, furious] (circa 1823)
: with great force or vigor — used as a direction in music

**fu·ri·ous** \'fyu̇r-ē-əs\ adjective [Middle English, from Middle French furieus, from Latin furiosus, from furia madness, fury] (14th century)
**1 a** (1) : exhibiting or goaded by anger (2) : indicative of or proceeding from anger **b** : giving a stormy or turbulent appearance ⟨furious bursts of flame⟩ **c** : marked by noise, excitement, activity, or rapidity
**2** : INTENSE 1a ⟨the furious growth of tropical vegetation⟩
— **fu·ri·ous·ly** adverb

**¹furl** \'fər(-ə)l\ verb [Middle French ferler, from Old North French ferlier to tie tightly, from Old French fer, ferm tight (from Latin firmus firm) + lier to tie, from Latin ligare — more at LIGATURE] (1556)
transitive verb
: to wrap or roll (as a sail or a flag) close to or around something
intransitive verb
: to curl or fold as in being furled

**²furl** noun (1643)
**1** : a furled coil
**2** : the act of furling

**fur·long** \'fər-ˌlȯŋ\ noun [Middle English, from Old English furlang, from furh furrow + lang long] (14th century)
: a unit of distance equal to 220 yards (about 201 meters)

**¹fur·lough** \'fər-(ˌ)lō\ noun [Dutch verlof, literally, permission, from Middle Dutch, from ver- for- + lof permission; akin to Middle High German loube permission — more at FOR-, LEAVE] (1625)
: a leave of absence from duty granted especially to a soldier; also : a document authorizing such a leave of absence

**²furlough** transitive verb (1781)
**1** : to grant a furlough to

---

◇ **WORD HISTORY**

**funky** The word funk, meaning "foul odor," first appears in the language of 17th century seamen—as near as we can judge from the small amount of evidence available—and in the 18th century it is found in dictionaries of London street talk. Henceforth it vanishes on the far side of the Atlantic but begins to surface in records of regional speech in the U.S. during the 19th century. Funk has been well-documented in African-American vernacular, and it may be part of the common lexical heritage of African varieties of English in the New World, to judge by the parallel record of funk, meaning "inferior (and thus, foul-smelling) tobacco" in Jamaican English. The derivative funky "foul-smelling" took on new life when its use was extended by black jazzmen to an earthy, blues-based style that developed in the 1950s, and funky in African-American vernacular began to be used as a term of approbation. In the 1960s funky entered mainstream American English, usually with the meaning "odd, eccentric," in either a positive or negative way, though its application has fluctuated in a way that makes the word difficult to define and its future difficult to predict.

**fur** Though we think of fur as physically part of the animal that wears it—and as something the animal has its entire life with any luck—the history of the word fur begins with clothing rather than animals. Middle English furre "fur trim or lining for a garment" was shortened from the synonymous word furrour or derived from a verb furren "to trim or line (a garment) with animal skin." This verb was borrowed from medieval French fourrer, with the identical meaning, itself a derivative of fuerre "sheath, wrapper," which referred to the lining of a garment providing a sort of warm wrapper for its wearer. The odyssey from "wrapper" to "line with something warm" to "lining material" to "pelt cut from a dead animal" to "coat of a live animal" is a long one, though each step along the way is easily grasped.

---

\ə\ abut \ᵊ\ kitten \ər\ further \a\ ash \ā\ ace
\ä\ mop, mar \au̇\ out \ch\ chin \e\ bet \ē\ easy
\g\ go \i\ hit \ī\ ice \j\ job \ŋ\ sing \ō\ go
\ȯ\ law \ȯi\ boy \th\ thin \th\ the \ü\ loot \u̇\ foot
\y\ yet \zh\ vision    see also Guide to Pronunciation

**2 :** to lay off from work

**fur·mi·ty** \'fər-mə-tē\ *variant of* FRUMENTY

**fur·nace** \'fər-nəs\ *noun* [Middle English *furnas*, from Old French *fornaise*, from Latin *fornac-*, *fornax*; akin to Latin *formus* warm — more at THERM] (13th century)
**:** an enclosed structure in which heat is produced (as for heating a house or for reducing ore)

**fur·nish** \'fər-nish\ *transitive verb* [Middle English *furnisshen*, from Middle French *fourniss-*, stem of *fournir* to complete, equip, of Germanic origin; akin to Old High German *frummen* to further, *fruma* advantage — more at FOREMOST] (15th century)
**1 :** to provide with what is needed; *especially* **:** to equip with furniture
**2 :** SUPPLY, GIVE ⟨*furnished* food and shelter for the refugees⟩ ☆
— **fur·nish·er** *noun*

**fur·nish·ing** *noun* (1594)
**1 :** an article or accessory of dress — usually used in plural
**2 :** an object that tends to increase comfort or utility; *especially* **:** an article of furniture for the interior of a building — usually used in plural

**fur·ni·ture** \'fər-ni-chər\ *noun* [Middle French *fourniture*, from *fournir*] (1542)
**:** equipment that is necessary, useful, or desirable: as **a** *archaic* **:** the trappings of a horse **b :** movable articles used in readying an area (as a room or patio) for occupancy or use

**furniture beetle** *noun* (1925)
**:** a widespread deathwatch beetle (*Anobium punctatum*) noted for boring in and damaging furniture and seasoned wood

**fu·ror** \'fyúr-,ór, -,ōr, -ər\ *noun* [Middle French & Latin; Middle French, from Latin, from *furere* to rage] (15th century)
**1 :** an angry or maniacal fit **:** RAGE
**2 :** FURY 4
**3 :** a fashionable craze **:** VOGUE
**4 a :** furious or hectic activity **b :** an outburst of public excitement or indignation **:** UPROAR

**fu·rore** \'fyùr-,ór, -,ór, *especially British* fyù-'rò-ri\ *noun* [Italian, from Latin *furor*] (1790)
**1 :** FUROR 4b
**2 :** FUROR 3

**fu·ro·se·mide** \fyú-'rō-sə-,mīd\ *noun* [*furfural* + *-o-* + *sulf-* + *-emide*, probably alteration of *amide*] (1965)
**:** a powerful diuretic $C_{12}H_{11}ClN_2O_5S$ used especially to treat edema

**furred** \'fərd\ *adjective* [Middle English] (14th century)
**1 :** lined, trimmed, or faced with fur
**2 :** coated as if with fur; *specifically* **:** having a coating consisting chiefly of mucus and dead epithelial cells ⟨a *furred* tongue⟩
**3 :** bearing or wearing fur
**4 :** provided with furring ⟨*furred* wall⟩

**fur·ri·er** \'fər-ē-ər, 'fə-rē-\ *noun* [alteration of Middle English *furrer*, from Anglo-French *furrere*, from Old French *forrer* to fur — more at FUR] (14th century)
**1 :** a fur dealer
**2 a :** one that dresses furs **b :** one that makes, repairs, alters, or cleans fur garments

**fur·ri·ery** \-ə-rē\ *noun* (circa 1864)
**1 :** the fur business
**2 :** fur craftsmanship

**fur·rin·er** \'fər-ə-nər\ *noun* [alteration of *foreigner*] (1849)
**:** FOREIGNER 2 — used to represent a dialectal pronunciation

**fur·ring** \'fər-iŋ\ *noun* (14th century)
**1 :** a fur trimming or lining
**2 a :** the application of thin wood, brick, or metal to joists, studs, or walls to form a level surface (as for attaching wallboard) or an air space **b :** the material used in this process

**¹fur·row** \'fər-(,)ō, 'fə-(,)rō\ *noun* [Middle English *furgh*, *forow*, from Old English *furh*;

akin to Old High German *furuh* furrow, Latin *porca*] (before 12th century)
**1 a :** a trench in the earth made by a plow **b :** plowed land **:** FIELD
**2 :** something that resembles the track of a plow: as **a :** a marked narrow depression **:** GROOVE **b :** a deep wrinkle ⟨*furrows* in his brow⟩

**²furrow** (15th century)
*transitive verb*
**:** to make furrows, grooves, wrinkles, or lines in
*intransitive verb*
**:** to make or form furrows, grooves, wrinkles, or lines

**fur·ry** \'fər-ē\ *adjective* **fur·ri·er; -est** (circa 1674)
**1 :** consisting of or resembling fur ⟨animals with *furry* coats⟩
**2 :** covered with fur
**3 :** thick in quality ⟨spoke with a *furry* voice⟩

**fur seal** *noun* (1775)
**:** any of two genera (*Callorhinus* and *Arctocephalus*) of eared seals that have a double coat with a dense soft underfur

**¹fur·ther** \'fər-thər\ *adverb* [Middle English, from Old English *furthor* (akin to Old High German *furthar* further), comparative, from the base of Old English *forth* forth] (before 12th century)
**1 :** FARTHER 1 ⟨my ponies are tired, and I have *further* to go —Thomas Hardy⟩
**2 :** in addition **:** MOREOVER
**3 :** to a greater degree or extent ⟨*further* annoyed by a second intrusion⟩
*usage* see FARTHER

**²further** *transitive verb* **fur·thered; fur·ther·ing** \'fərth-riŋ, 'fər-thə-\ (before 12th century)
**:** to help forward **:** PROMOTE
*synonym* see ADVANCE
— **fur·ther·er** \'fər-thər-ər\ *noun*

**³further** *adjective* (13th century)
**1 :** FARTHER 1 ⟨rode . . . across the valley and up the *further* slopes —T. E. Lawrence⟩
**2 :** going or extending beyond **:** ADDITIONAL ⟨*further* volumes⟩ ⟨*further* education⟩
*usage* see FARTHER

**fur·ther·ance** \'fərth-rən(t)s, 'fər-thə-\ *noun* (15th century)
**:** the act of furthering **:** ADVANCEMENT

**further education** *noun* (1937)
*British* **:** ADULT EDUCATION

**fur·ther·more** \'fər-thə(r)-,mōr, -,mór\ *adverb* (13th century)
**:** in addition to what precedes **:** BESIDES

**fur·ther·most** \-thər-,mōst\ *adjective* (15th century)
**:** most distant **:** FARTHEST

**fur·thest** \'fər-thəst\ *adverb or adjective* (14th century)
**:** FARTHEST

**fur·tive** \'fər-tiv\ *adjective* [French or Latin; French *furtif*, from Latin *furtivus*, from *furtum* theft, from *fur* thief, from or akin to Greek *phōr* thief, *pherein* to carry — more at BEAR] (1612)
**1 a :** done by stealth **:** SURREPTITIOUS **b :** expressive of stealth **:** SLY ⟨had a *furtive* look about him⟩
**2 :** obtained underhandedly **:** STOLEN
*synonym* see SECRET
— **fur·tive·ly** *adverb*
— **fur·tive·ness** *noun*

**fu·run·cle** \'fyùr-,əŋ-kəl\ *noun* [Latin *furunculus* petty thief, boil, diminutive of *furon-*, *furo* ferret, thief, from *fur*] (1676)
**:** ²BOIL

**fu·run·cu·lo·sis** \fyù-,rəŋ-kyə-'lō-səs\ *noun*, *plural* **-lo·ses** \-,sēz\ [New Latin] (1886)
**1 :** the condition of having or tending to develop multiple furuncles
**2 :** a highly infectious disease of various salmonoid fishes (as trout) that is caused by a

bacterium (*Bacterium salmonicida*) and is especially virulent in dense fish populations (as in hatcheries)

**fu·ry** \'fyúr-ē\ *noun*, *plural* **furies** [Middle English *furie*, from Middle French & Latin; Middle French, from Latin *furia*, from *furere* to rage] (14th century)
**1 :** intense, disordered, and often destructive rage
**2 a** *capitalized* **:** any of the avenging deities in Greek mythology who torment criminals and inflict plagues **b :** an avenging spirit **c :** one who resembles an avenging spirit; *especially* **:** a spiteful woman
**3 :** extreme fierceness or violence
**4 :** a state of inspired exaltation **:** FRENZY ◆
*synonym* see ANGER

**furze** \'fərz\ *noun* [Middle English *firse*, from Old English *fyrs*; akin to Russian *pyreĭ* quack grass, Greek *pyros* wheat] (before 12th century)
**:** GORSE
— **furzy** \'fər-zē\ *adjective*

**fus·cous** \'fəs-kəs\ *adjective* [Latin *fuscus* — more at DUSK] (1662)
**:** of any of several colors averaging a brownish gray

**¹fuse** \'fyüz\ *verb* **fused; fus·ing** [Latin *fusus*, past participle of *fundere* to pour, melt — more at FOUND] (1592)
*transitive verb*
**1 :** to reduce to a liquid or plastic state by heat
**2 :** to blend thoroughly by or as if by melting together **:** COMBINE ⟨in her richest work she *fuses* comedy and tragedy —T. A. Gullason⟩
**3 :** to stitch by applying heat and pressure with or without the use of an adhesive
*intransitive verb*
**1 a :** to become fluid with heat **b** *British* **:** to fail because of the blowing of a fuse
**2 :** to become blended or joined by or as if by melting together
*synonym* see MIX

**²fuse** *noun* (1884)
**:** an electrical safety device consisting of or including a wire or strip of fusible metal that

---

---

melts and interrupts the circuit when the current exceeds a particular amperage

**³fuse** *noun* [Italian *fuso* spindle, from Latin *fusus*, of unknown origin] (1644)
**1** : a continuous train of a combustible substance enclosed in a cord or cable for setting off an explosive charge by transmitting fire to it
**2** *usually* **fuze** : a mechanical or electrical detonating device for setting off the bursting charge of a projectile, bomb, or torpedo

**⁴fuse** *or* **fuze** \'fyüz\ *transitive verb* **fused** *or* **fuzed**; **fus·ing** *or* **fuz·ing** (1802)
: to equip with a fuse

**fused quartz** *noun* (1925)
: QUARTZ GLASS — called also *fused silica*

**fu·see** \fyü-'zē\ *noun* [French *fusée*, literally, spindleful of yarn, from Old French, from *fus* spindle, from Latin *fusus*] (1622)
**1** : a conical spirally grooved pulley in a timepiece from which a cord or chain unwinds onto a barrel containing the spring and which by its increasing diameter compensates for the lessening power of the spring
**2** : a red signal flare used especially for protecting stalled trains and trucks

**fu·se·lage** \'fyü-sə-,läzh, -zə-\ *noun* [French, from *fuselé* spindle-shaped, from Middle French, from *fusel*, diminutive of *fus*] (1909)
: the central body portion of an aircraft designed to accommodate the crew and the passengers or cargo — see AIRPLANE illustration

**fu·sel oil** \'fyü-zəl-\ *noun* [German *Fusel* bad liquor] (1850)
: an acrid oily liquid occurring in insufficiently distilled alcoholic liquors, consisting chiefly of amyl alcohol, and used especially as a source of alcohols and as a solvent

**fus·ible** \'fyü-zə-bəl\ *adjective* (14th century)
: capable of being fused and especially liquefied by heat ⟨*fusible* alloy⟩
— **fus·ibil·i·ty** \,fyü-zə-'bi-lə-tē\ *noun*

**fu·si·form** \'fyü-zə-,fórm\ *adjective* [Latin *fusus* spindle] (1746)
: tapering toward each end ⟨*fusiform* bacteria⟩

**¹fu·sil** \'fyü-zəl\ *or* **fu·sile** \'fyü-zəl, -,zīl\ *adjective* [Middle English, from Latin *fusilis*, from *fundere*] (14th century)
**1** *archaic* **a** : made by melting and pouring into forms : CAST **b** : liquefied by heat
**2** *archaic* : FUSIBLE

**²fusil** *noun* [French, literally, steel for striking fire, from Old French *foisil*, from (assumed) Vulgar Latin *focilis*, from Late Latin *focus* fire — more at FUEL] (1680)
: a light flintlock musket

**fu·sil·ier** *or* **fu·sil·eer** \,fyü-zə-'lir\ *noun* [French *fusilier*, from *fusil*] (1680)
**1** : a soldier armed with a fusil
**2** : a member of a British regiment formerly armed with fusils

**fu·sil·lade** \'fyü-sə-,läd, -,lād, ,fyü-sə-', -zə-\ *noun* [French, from *fusiller* to shoot, from *fusil*] (1801)
**1 a** : a number of shots fired simultaneously or in rapid succession **b** : something that gives the effect of a fusillade ⟨a *fusillade* of rocks and bottles⟩
**2** : a spirited outburst especially of criticism

**fu·sil·li** \fyü-'si-lē, -'sē\ *noun* [Italian, plural of *fusillo*, from Italian dialect (southern Italy), diminutive of *fuso* spindle, from Latin *fusus*] (1948)
: spiral-shaped pasta

**fu·sion** \'fyü-zhⁿn\ *noun, often attributive* [Latin *fusion-, fusio*, from *fundere*] (1555)
**1** : the act or process of liquefying or rendering plastic by heat
**2** : a union by or as if by melting: as **a** : a merging of diverse, distinct, or separate elements into a unified whole **b** : a political partnership : COALITION **c** : popular music combining different styles (as jazz and rock)

**3** : the union of atomic nuclei to form heavier nuclei resulting in the release of enormous quantities of energy when certain light elements unite

**fu·sion·ist** \'fyü-zhⁿn-ist\ *noun* (1851)
: a person involved in a political fusion or in nuclear or musical fusion

**¹fuss** \'fəs\ *noun* [origin unknown] (1701)
**1 a** : needless bustle or excitement : COMMOTION **b** : a show of flattering attention ⟨made a big *fuss* over his favorite niece⟩
**2 a** : a state of agitation especially over a trivial matter **b** : OBJECTION, PROTEST **c** : an often petty controversy or quarrel ⟨ended up having a pretty good *fuss* with my wife —Mac Hyman⟩

**²fuss** (1792)
*intransitive verb*
**1 a** : to create or be in a state of restless activity; *especially* : to shower flattering attentions ⟨*fussing* over the grandchildren⟩ **b** : to pay close or undue attention to small details ⟨*fussed* with her hair⟩
**2 a** : to become upset : WORRY **b** : to express annoyance or pique : COMPLAIN
*transitive verb*
: AGITATE, UPSET
— **fuss·er** *noun*

**fuss·bud·get** \'fəs-,bə-jət\ *noun* (circa 1904)
: one who fusses or is fussy especially about trifles
— **fuss·bud·gety** \-jə-tē\ *adjective*

**fuss·pot** \'fəs-,pät\ *noun* (1921)
: FUSSBUDGET

**fussy** \'fə-sē\ *adjective* **fuss·i·er; -est** (1831)
**1** : easily upset : IRRITABLE
**2** : overly decorative ⟨a *fussy* wallpaper pattern⟩
**3 a** : requiring or giving close attention to details ⟨*fussy* bookkeeping procedures⟩ **b** : revealing a sometimes extreme concern for niceties : FASTIDIOUS, PICKY
— **fuss·i·ly** \'fə-sə-lē\ *adverb*
— **fuss·i·ness** \'fə-sē-nəs\ *noun*

**fus·tian** \'fəs-chən\ *noun* [Middle English, from Old French *fustaine*, from Medieval Latin *fustaneum*, perhaps from *fustis* tree trunk, from Latin, club] (13th century)
**1 a** : a strong cotton and linen fabric **b** : a class of cotton fabrics usually having a pile face and twill weave
**2** : highflown or affected writing or speech; *broadly* : anything highflown or affected in style
— **fus·tian** *adjective*

**fus·tic** \'fəs-tik\ *noun* [Middle English *fustyk* smoke tree, from Middle French *fustoc*, from Arabic *fustuq*, from Greek *pistakē* pistachio tree — more at PISTACHIO] (15th century)
: the wood of a tropical American tree (*Chlorophora tinctoria*) of the mulberry family that yields a yellow dye; *also* : any of several similar dyewoods

**fus·ti·gate** \'fəs-tə-,gāt\ *transitive verb* **-gat·ed; -gat·ing** [Late Latin *fustigatus*, past participle of *fustigare*, from Latin *fustis* + *-igare* (as in *fumigare* to fumigate)] (circa 1661)
**1** : CUDGEL
**2** : to criticize severely
— **fus·ti·ga·tion** \,fəs-tə-'gā-shən\ *noun*

**fus·ty** \'fəs-tē\ *adjective* **fus·ti·er; -est** [Middle English, from *fust* wine cask, from Middle French, club, cask, from Latin *fustis*] (14th century)
**1** *British* : impaired by age or dampness : MOLDY
**2** : saturated with dust and stale odors : MUSTY
**3** : rigidly old-fashioned or reactionary
*synonym* see MALODOROUS
— **fus·ti·ly** \-tə-lē\ *adverb*
— **fus·ti·ness** \-tē-nəs\ *noun*

**fu·su·li·nid** \,fyü-zə-'lī-nid, -'lē-, -'li-\ *noun* [New Latin *Fusulinidae*, from *Fusulina*, a genus, from Latin *fusus* spindle + *-ulus* -ule + New Latin *-ina*, diminutive suffix] (1941)

: any of a family (Fusulinidae) of extinct marine foraminifers

**fu·thark** \'fü-,thärk\ *also* **fu·thorc** *or* **fu·thork** \-,thórk\ *noun* [from the first six letters, f, u, þ (th), o (or a), r, c (=k)] (1851)
: the runic alphabet — see RUNE illustration

**fu·tile** \'fyü-tⁿl, 'fyü-,tīl\ *adjective* [Middle French or Latin; Middle French, from Latin *futilis* brittle, pointless, probably from *fu-* (akin to *fundere* to pour) — more at FOUND] (circa 1555)
**1** : serving no useful purpose : completely ineffective ⟨efforts to convince him were *futile*⟩
**2** : occupied with trifles : FRIVOLOUS ☆
— **fu·tile·ly** \-tⁿl-(l)ē, -,tīl-lē\ *adverb*
— **fu·tile·ness** \-tⁿl-nəs, -,tīl-nəs\ *noun*

**fu·til·i·tar·i·an** \,fyü-,ti-lə-'ter-ē-ən, ,fyü-\ *noun* [blend of *futile* and *utilitarian*] (1827)
: one who believes that human striving is futile
— **futilitarian** *adjective*
— **fu·til·i·tar·i·an·ism** \-ē-ə-,ni-zəm\ *noun*

**fu·til·i·ty** \fyü-'ti-lə-tē\ *noun, plural* **-ties** (1623)
**1** : the quality or state of being futile : USELESSNESS
**2** : a useless act or gesture ⟨the *futilities* of debate for its own sake —W. A. White⟩

**fu·ton** \'fü-,tän\ *noun, plural* **futons** *also* **fu·ton** [Japanese] (1876)
: a usually cotton-filled mattress used on the floor or in a frame as a bed

**fut·tock** \'fə-tək\ *noun* [Middle English *votek, futtek*] (13th century)
: one of the curved timbers scarfed together to form the lower part of the compound rib of a ship

**futtock shroud** *noun* (1840)
: a short iron rod connecting the topmast rigging with the lower mast

**¹fu·ture** \'fyü-chər\ *adjective* [Middle English, from Middle French & Latin; Middle French *futur*, from Latin *futurus* about to be — more at BE] (14th century)
**1** : that is to be; *specifically* : existing after death
**2** : of, relating to, or constituting a verb tense expressive of time yet to come
**3** : existing or occurring at a later time ⟨met his *future* wife⟩

**²future** *noun* (15th century)
**1 a** : time that is to come **b** : what is going to happen
**2** : an expectation of advancement or progressive development
**3** : something (as a bulk commodity) bought for future acceptance or sold for future delivery — usually used in plural ⟨grain *futures*⟩
**4 a** : the future tense of a language **b** : a verb form in the future tense

**fu·ture·less** \'fyü-chər-ləs\ *adjective* (1863)
: having no future
— **fu·ture·less·ness** *noun*

**future perfect** *adjective* (circa 1898)

---

☆ **SYNONYMS**
**Futile, vain, fruitless** mean producing no result. FUTILE may connote completeness of failure or unwisdom of undertaking ⟨resistance had proved so *futile* that surrender was the only choice left⟩. VAIN usually implies simple failure to achieve a desired result ⟨a *vain* attempt to get the car started⟩. FRUITLESS comes close to VAIN but often suggests long and arduous effort or severe disappointment ⟨*fruitless* efforts to obtain a lasting peace⟩.

---

\ə\ abut \ⁿ\ kitten \ər\ further \a\ ash \ā\ ace
\ä\ mop, mar \aú\ out \ch\ chin \e\ bet \ē\ easy
\g\ go \i\ hit \ī\ ice \j\ job \ŋ\ sing \ō\ go
\ó\ law \ói\ boy \th\ thin \th̷\ the \ü\ loot \ú\ foot
\y\ yet \zh\ vision *see also* Guide to Pronunciation

**:** of, relating to, or constituting a verb tense that is traditionally formed in English with *will have* and *shall have* and that expresses completion of an action by a specified time that is yet to come
— **future perfect** *noun*
**future shock** *noun* (1965)
**:** the physical and psychological distress suffered by one who is unable to cope with the rapidity of social and technological changes
**fu·tur·ism** \'fyü-chə-ˌri-zəm\ *noun* (1909)
**1 :** a movement in art, music, and literature begun in Italy about 1909 and marked especially by an effort to give formal expression to the dynamic energy and movement of mechanical processes
**2 :** a point of view that finds meaning or fulfillment in the future rather than in the past or present
**fu·tur·ist** \'fyü-chə-rist\ *noun* (1911)
**1 :** one who advocates or practices futurism
**2 :** one who studies and predicts the future especially on the basis of current trends
— **futurist** *adjective*
**fu·tur·is·tic** \ˌfyü-chə-'ris-tik\ *adjective* (1915)
**:** of, relating to, or characteristic of the future, futurism, or futurology; *also* **:** very modern
— **fu·tur·is·ti·cal·ly** \-ti-k(ə-)lē\ *adverb*
**fu·tur·is·tics** \-tiks\ *noun plural but singular in construction* (1969)

**:** FUTUROLOGY
**fu·tu·ri·ty** \fyü-'tür-ə-tē, -'tyür-, -'chür-\ *noun, plural* **-ties** (1604)
**1 :** time to come **:** FUTURE
**2 :** the quality or state of being future
**3** *plural* **:** future events or prospects
**4 a :** a horse race usually for two-year-olds in which the competitors are nominated at birth or before **b :** a race or competition for which entries are made well in advance of the event
**fu·tur·ol·o·gy** \ˌfyü-chə-'rä-lə-jē\ *noun* (1946)
**:** a study that deals with future possibilities based on current trends
— **fu·tur·olog·i·cal** \-rə-'lä-ji-kəl\ *adjective*
— **fu·tur·olo·gist** \-'rä-lə-jist\ *noun*
**futz** \'fəts\ *intransitive verb* [perhaps part modification, part translation of Yiddish *arumfartsn zikh*, literally, to fart around] (1932)
*slang* **:** FOOL AROUND 1 — often used with *around* ⟨*futz* around without producing any worthwhile music —John Koegel⟩
**fuze, fu·zee** *variant of* FUSE, FUSEE
**¹fuzz** \'fəz\ *noun* [probably back-formation from *fuzzy*] (1674)
**1 :** fine light particles or fibers (as of down or fluff)
**2 :** a blurred effect
**²fuzz** (circa 1702)
*intransitive verb*

**1 :** to fly off in or become covered with fluffy particles
**2 :** to become blurred ⟨her frame of reference *fuzzing* at the edges —Jane O'Reilly⟩
*transitive verb*
**1 :** to make fuzzy
**2 :** to envelop in a haze **:** BLUR
**³fuzz** *noun* [origin unknown] (1927)
**:** POLICE; *also* **:** a police officer
**fuzzy** \'fə-zē\ *adjective* **fuzz·i·er; -est** [perhaps from Low German *fussig* loose, spongy] (1713)
**1 :** marked by or giving a suggestion of fuzz ⟨a *fuzzy* covering of felt⟩
**2 :** lacking in clarity or definition ⟨moving the camera causes *fuzzy* photos⟩ ⟨*fuzzy* thinking⟩
— **fuzz·i·ly** \'fə-zə-lē\ *adverb*
— **fuzz·i·ness** \'fə-zē-nəs\ *noun*
**-fy** \ˌfī\ *verb suffix* [Middle English *-fien*, from Old French *-fier*, from Latin *-ficare*, from *-ficus* *-fic*]
**1 :** make **:** form into ⟨dandi*fy*⟩
**2 :** invest with the attributes of **:** make similar to ⟨citi*fy*⟩
**fyce** \'fīs\ *variant of* FEIST
**fyke** \'fīk\ *noun* [Dutch *fuik*] (1832)
**:** a long bag net kept open by hoops
**fyl·fot** \'fil-ˌfät\ *noun* [Middle English, device used to fill the lower part of a painted glass window (from a conjectural manuscript reading)] (1842)
**:** SWASTIKA

**G** *is the seventh letter of the English alphabet and of most modern alphabets closely related to that of English. It came from Latin, where it was introduced to distinguish the voiced velar stop (the sound of g in go) from the corresponding voiceless stop (the sound of k in king), both of which had until then been represented by C. In Modern English, g represents two chief sounds, commonly called "hard g" and "soft g." The former, as in go, was the earlier sound, the latter, equivalent to j, as in gem, appears chiefly in words from Latin and Old French. The small g developed from a late Roman form of the capital letter that had a short curved flourish extending below the line (Ꮆ). The upper half of the letter closed to form a full oval, while the tail below the line also closed to form a loop (g or ɡ).*

**g** \'jē\ *noun, plural* **g's** *or* **gs** \'jēz\ *often capitalized, often attributive* (before 12th century)
**1 a :** the 7th letter of the English alphabet **b :** a graphic representation of this letter **c :** a speech counterpart of orthographic *g*
**2 :** the 5th tone of a C-major scale
**3 :** a graphic device for reproducing the letter *g*
**4 :** one designated *g* especially as the 7th in order or class
**5** [gravity] **:** ACCELERATION OF GRAVITY; *also* **:** a unit of force equal to the force exerted by gravity on a body at rest and used to indicate the force to which a body is subjected when accelerated
**6** [grand] *slang* **:** a sum of $1000
**7 :** something shaped like the letter G

**G** *certification mark*
— used to certify that a motion picture is of such a nature that persons of all ages may be allowed admission; compare NC-17, PG, PG-13, R

**¹gab** \'gab\ *intransitive verb* **gabbed; gab-bing** [probably short for *gabble*] (1786)
**:** to talk in a rapid or thoughtless manner **:** CHATTER
— **gab·ber** *noun*
**²gab** *noun* (1790)
**:** TALK; *especially* **:** idle talk
**³gab** *noun* (1939)
**:** GABARDINE 2

**gab·ar·dine** \'ga-bər-ˌdēn\ *noun* [Middle French *gaverdine*] (1520)
**1 :** GABERDINE 1
**2 a :** a firm hard-finish durable fabric (as of wool or rayon) twilled with diagonal ribs on the right side **b :** a garment of gabardine

**gab·ble** \'ga-bəl\ *verb* **gab·bled; gab·bling** \-b(ə-)liŋ\ [probably of imitative origin] (1577)
*intransitive verb*
**1 :** to talk fast or foolishly **:** JABBER
**2 :** to utter inarticulate or animal sounds
*transitive verb*
**:** to say with incoherent rapidity **:** BABBLE
— **gabble** *noun*
— **gab·bler** \-b(ə-)lər\ *noun*

**gab·bro** \'ga-(ˌ)brō\ *noun, plural* **gabbros** [Italian, probably modification of Latin *glaber* smooth — more at GLAD] (circa 1828)
**:** a granular igneous rock composed essentially of calcic plagioclase, a ferromagnesian mineral, and accessory minerals
— **gab·bro·ic** \ga-'brō-ik\ *adjective*

**gab·by** \'ga-bē\ *adjective* **gab·bi·er; -est** (1719)
**:** TALKATIVE, GARRULOUS

**ga·belle** \gə-'bel\ *noun* [Middle English, from Middle French, from Old Italian *gabella* tax, from Arabic *qabālah*] (15th century)
**:** a tax on salt levied in France prior to 1790

**gab·er·dine** \'ga-bər-ˌdēn\ *noun* [Middle French *gaverdine*] (1520)

**1 :** a long loose outer garment worn in medieval times and associated especially with Jews since the 16th century
**2 :** GABARDINE 2

**gab·fest** \'gab-ˌfest\ *noun* (1897)
**1 :** an informal gathering for general talk ⟨political *gabfests*⟩
**2 :** an extended conversation

**ga·bi·on** \'gā-bē-ən, 'ga-\ *noun* [Middle French, from Old Italian *gabbione*, literally, large cage, augmentative of *gabbia* cage, from Latin *cavea* — more at CAGE] (1579)
**:** a basket or cage filled with earth or rocks and used especially in building a support or abutment

**ga·ble** \'gā-bəl\ *noun* [Middle English, from Middle French, of Germanic origin; akin to Old Norse *gafl* gable — more at CEPHALIC] (14th century)
**1 a :** the vertical triangular end of a building from cornice or eaves to ridge **b :** the similar end of a gambrel roof **c :** the end wall of a building
**2 :** a triangular part or structure
— **ga·bled** \-bəld\ *adjective*

*1 gable 1a*

**gable roof** *noun* (1850)
**:** a double-sloping roof that forms a gable at each end

**gab·oon** \ga-'bün, gə-\ *noun* [alteration of ¹*gob* + *-oon* (as in *spittoon*)] (1929)
*dialect* **:** SPITTOON

**Ga·bri·el** \'gā-brē-əl\ *noun* [Hebrew *Gabhrī'ēl*]
**:** one of the four archangels named in Hebrew tradition

**ga·by** \'gā-bē\ *noun, plural* **gabies** [perhaps of Scandinavian origin; akin to Old Norse *gapa* to gape — more at GAPE] (circa 1796)
*dialect chiefly English* **:** SIMPLETON

**¹gad** \'gad\ *noun* [Middle English, spike, from Old Norse *gaddr*; akin to Old English *geard* rod — more at YARD] (1671)
**1 :** a chisel or pointed iron or steel bar for loosening ore or rock
**2** *chiefly dialect* **:** a long stick

**²gad** *intransitive verb* **gad·ded; gad·ding** [Middle English *gadden*] (15th century)
**:** to be on the go without a specific aim or purpose — usually used with *about*

**³gad** *interjection* [euphemism for *God*] (1608)
— used as a mild oath

**Gad** \'gad\ *noun* [Hebrew *Gādh*]
**:** a son of Jacob and the traditional eponymous ancestor of one of the tribes of Israel
— **Gad·ite** \'ga-ˌdīt\ *noun*

**gad·about** \'ga-də-ˌbaút\ *noun* (1837)
**:** a person who flits about in social activity
— **gadabout** *adjective*

**gad·a·rene** \'ga-də-ˌrēn\ *adjective, often capitalized* [from the demon-possessed *Gadarene* swine in Matthew 8:28 that rushed into the sea] (1922)
**:** HEADLONG, PRECIPITATE ⟨a *gadarene* rush to the cities⟩

**gad·fly** \'gad-ˌflī\ *noun* [¹*gad*] (1626)
**1 :** any of various flies (as a horsefly, botfly, or warble fly) that bite or annoy livestock
**2 :** a person who stimulates or annoys especially by persistent criticism

**gad·get** \'ga-jət\ *noun* [origin unknown] (1886)
**:** an often small mechanical or electronic device with a practical use but often thought of as a novelty
— **gad·ge·teer** \ˌga-jə-'tir\ *noun*
— **gad·get·ry** \'ga-jə-trē\ *noun*
— **gad·gety** \-jə-tē\ *adjective*

**ga·doid** \'gā-ˌdoid, 'ga-\ *adjective* [New Latin *Gadus*, genus of fishes, from Greek *gados*, a fish] (circa 1842)
**:** resembling or related to the cods
— **gadoid** *noun*

**gad·o·lin·ite** \'ga-d°l-ə-ˌnīt\ *noun* [German *Gadolinit*, from Johann *Gadolin* (died 1852) Finnish chemist] (1802)
**:** a black or brown mineral that is a source of rare earths and consists of a silicate of iron, beryllium, yttrium, cerium, and erbium

**gad·o·lin·i·um** \ˌga-də-'li-nē-əm\ *noun* [New Latin, from J. *Gadolin*] (1886)
**:** a magnetic metallic element of the rare-earth group occurring in combination in gadolinite and several other minerals — see ELEMENT table

**ga·droon** \gə-'drün\ *noun* [French *godron* round plait, gadroon] (circa 1724)
**1 :** the ornamental notching or carving of a rounded molding
**2 :** a short often oval fluting or reeding used in decoration
— **gadroon** *transitive verb*
— **ga·droon·ing** *noun*

**gad·wall** \'gad-ˌwȯl\ *noun, plural* **gadwalls** *or* **gadwall** [origin unknown] (1666)
**:** a grayish brown medium-sized dabbling duck (*Anas strepera*)

**gad·zook·ery** \gad-'zü-kə-rē, -'zù-\ *noun* (1955)
*British* **:** the use of archaisms (as in a historical novel)

**gad·zooks** \gad-'züks, -'züks\ *interjection, often capitalized* [perhaps from *God's hooks*, the nails of the Crucifixion] (1694)
*archaic* — used as a mild oath

**Gaea** \'jē-ə\ *noun* [Greek *Gaia*]
**:** the Greek earth goddess and mother of the Titans

**Gael** \'gā(ə)l\ *noun* [Scottish Gaelic *Gàidheal* & Irish *Gaedheal*] (1753)
**1 :** a Scottish Highlander
**2 :** a Celtic especially Gaelic-speaking inhabitant of Ireland, Scotland, or the Isle of Man
— **Gael·dom** \-dəm\ *noun*

**Gael·ic** \'gā-lik, 'ga-, 'gä-\ *adjective* [Scottish Gaelic *Gàidhlig* the Scottish Gaelic language, from *Gàidheal* Gaelic] (1741)
**1 :** of or relating to the Gaels and especially the Celtic Highlanders of Scotland
**2 :** of, relating to, or constituting the Goidelic speech of the Celts in Ireland, the Isle of Man, and the Scottish Highlands
— **Gaelic** *noun*

**Gael·tacht** \'gā(ə)l-təkt\ *noun* [Irish, from *Gaelic*, spelling variant of *Gaedheal* Irishman, Gael] (1929)
**:** any of the Irish-speaking regions remaining in Ireland

**¹gaff** \'gaf\ *noun* [French *gaffe,* from Provençal *gaf*] (circa 1656)
**1 a :** a spear or spearhead for taking fish or turtles **b :** a handled hook for holding or lifting heavy fish **c :** a metal spur for a gamecock **d :** a butcher's hook **e :** a climbing iron or its steel point used by a telephone lineman **2 :** the spar on which the head of a fore-and-aft sail is extended
**3 :** GAFFE

**²gaff** *transitive verb* (1844)
**1 :** to strike or secure with a gaff
**2 :** to fit (a gamecock) with a gaff

**³gaff** *noun* [origin unknown] (1812)
*British* **:** a cheap theater or music hall

**⁴gaff** *noun* [origin unknown] (1896)
**1 a :** something painful or difficult to bear **:** ORDEAL — usually used in the phrase *stand the gaff; especially* **:** persistent raillery or criticism **b :** rough treatment **:** ABUSE
**2 a :** HOAX, FRAUD **b :** GIMMICK, TRICK

**⁵gaff** *transitive verb* (1933)
**1 :** DECEIVE, TRICK; *also* **:** FLEECE
**2 :** to fix for the purpose of cheating ⟨*gaff* the dice⟩

**gaffe** \'gaf\ *noun* [French, gaff, gaffe] (1909)
**:** a social or diplomatic blunder

**gaf·fer** \'ga-fər\ *noun* [alteration of *godfather*] (1575)
**1 :** an old man — compare GAMMER
**2** *British* **a :** FOREMAN, OVERSEER **b :** EMPLOYER
**3 :** a head glassblower
**4 :** a lighting electrician on a motion-picture or television set

**gaff-top·sail** \'gaf-'täp-,sāl, -səl\ *noun* (1794)
**:** a usually triangular topsail with its foot extended upon the gaff — see SAIL illustration

**¹gag** \'gag\ *verb* **gagged; gag·ging** [Middle English *gaggen* to strangle, of imitative origin] (1509)
*transitive verb*
**1 a :** to restrict use of the mouth of by inserting a gag **b :** to prevent from exercising freedom of speech or expression **c :** to pry or hold open with a gag
**2 :** to provide or write quips or pranks for ⟨*gag* a show⟩
**3 :** to choke or cause to retch
*intransitive verb*
**1 a :** CHOKE; *also* **:** to suffer a throat spasm that makes swallowing or breathing difficult **b** **:** RETCH
**2 :** to be unable to endure something **:** BALK
**3 :** to make quips
— **gag·ger** *noun*

**²gag** *noun* (1553)
**1 :** something thrust into the mouth to keep it open or to prevent speech or outcry
**2 :** an official check or restraint on debate or free speech ⟨a *gag* order⟩ ⟨a *gag* rule⟩
**3 :** a laugh-provoking remark or act
**4 :** PRANK, TRICK

**ga·ga** \'gä-(,)gä\ *adjective* [French, from *gaga* fool, of imitative origin] (1920)
**1 :** CRAZY, FOOLISH
**2 :** marked by wild enthusiasm **:** INFATUATED, DOTING

**ga·ga·ku** \gä-'gä-(,)kü\ *noun* [Japanese, from *ga* elegance + *gaku* music] (1929)
**:** the ancient court music of Japan

**¹gage** \'gāj\ *noun* [Middle English, from Middle French, of Germanic origin; akin to Old High German *wetti* pledge — more at WED] (14th century)
**1 :** a token of defiance; *specifically* **:** a glove or cap cast on the ground to be taken up by an opponent as a pledge of combat
**2 :** something deposited as a pledge of performance

**²gage** *transitive verb* (15th century)
**1** *archaic* **:** PLEDGE
**2** *archaic* **:** STAKE, RISK

**³gage** *variant of* GAUGE

**⁴gage** *noun* (1847)
**:** GREENGAGE

**gag·gle** \'ga-gəl\ *noun* [Middle English *gagyll,* from *gagelen* to cackle] (15th century)
**1 :** FLOCK; *especially* **:** a flock of geese when not in flight — compare SKEIN
**2 :** AGGREGATION, CLUSTER ⟨a *gaggle* of reporters and photographers⟩

**gag·man** \'gag-,man\ *noun* (1928)
**1 :** a gag writer
**2 :** COMEDIAN 2

**gag·ster** \'gag-stər\ *noun* (1935)
**:** GAGMAN; *also* **:** one who plays practical jokes

**gahn·ite** \'gä-,nīt\ *noun* [German *Gahnit,* from J. G. *Gahn* (died 1818) Swedish chemist] (circa 1808)
**:** a usually dark green mineral consisting of an oxide of zinc and aluminum

**gai·ety** \'gā-ə-tē\ *noun, plural* **-eties** [French *gaieté*] (1634)
**1 :** MERRYMAKING; *also* **:** festive activity — often used in plural
**2 :** high spirits **:** MERRIMENT
**3 :** ELEGANCE, FINERY

**gai·jin** \'gī-(,)jēn, -(,)jin\ *noun, plural* **gaijin** [Japanese, from *gai-* outer, foreign + *-jin* person] (1964)
**:** a foreigner in Japan

**gail·lar·dia** \gə-'lär-d(ē-)ə\ *noun* [New Latin, from *Gaillard* de Marentonneau, 18th century French botanist] (1888)
**:** any of a genus (*Gaillardia*) of chiefly western American composite herbs with showy flower heads

**gai·ly** \'gā-lē\ *adverb* (14th century)
**:** in a gay manner **:** marked by gaiety

**¹gain** \'gān\ *noun* [Middle English *gayne,* from Middle French *gaigne, gain,* from Old French *gaaigne, gaaing,* from *gaaignier* to till, earn, gain, of Germanic origin; akin to Old High German *weidanōn* to hunt for food, Old English *wāth* pursuit, hunt] (14th century)
**1 :** resources or advantage acquired or increased **:** PROFIT ⟨made substantial *gains* last year⟩
**2 :** the act or process of gaining
**3 a :** an increase in amount, magnitude, or degree ⟨a *gain* in efficiency⟩ **b :** the increase (as of voltage or signal intensity) caused by an amplifier; *especially* **:** the ratio of output over input **c :** the signal-gathering ability of an antenna

**²gain** (14th century)
*transitive verb*
**1 a :** to acquire or get possession of usually by industry, merit, or craft ⟨*gain* an advantage⟩ ⟨he stood to *gain* a fortune⟩ **b :** to win in competition or conflict ⟨the troops *gained* enemy territory⟩ **c** (1) **:** to arrive at **:** REACH, ATTAIN ⟨*gained* the river that night⟩ (2) **:** TRAVERSE, COVER ⟨*gained* 10 yards on the play⟩ **d :** to get by a natural development or process ⟨*gain* strength⟩ **e :** to establish a specific relationship with ⟨*gain* a friend⟩
**2 a :** to make an increase of (a specified amount) ⟨*gained* 3% in the past month⟩ **b :** to increase in (a particular quality) ⟨*gain* momentum⟩
**3 :** to win to one's side **:** PERSUADE ⟨*gain* adherents to a cause⟩
**4 :** to cause to be obtained or given **:** ATTRACT ⟨*gain* attention⟩
**5** *of a timepiece* **:** to run fast by the amount of ⟨the clock *gains* a minute a day⟩
*intransitive verb*
**1 :** to get advantage **:** PROFIT ⟨hoped to *gain* by the deal⟩
**2 a :** INCREASE ⟨the day was *gaining* in warmth⟩ **b :** to increase in weight **c :** to improve in health or ability
**3** *of a timepiece* **:** to run fast
**4 :** to get closer to something pursued — usually used with *on* or *upon*
— **gain·er** *noun*
— **gain ground** **:** to make progress

**gain·ful** \'gān-fəl\ *adjective* (1555)
**:** productive of gain **:** PROFITABLE ⟨*gainful* employment⟩

— **gain·ful·ly** \-fə-lē\ *adverb*
— **gain·ful·ness** *noun*

**gain·giv·ing** \'gān-,gi-viŋ, ,gān-'\ *noun* [*gain-* (against) + *giving*] (1602)
*archaic* **:** MISGIVING

**gain·say** \,gān-'sā\ *transitive verb* **-said** \-'sād, -'sed\; **-say·ing** \-'sā-iŋ\; **-says** \-'sāz, -'sez\ [Middle English *gainsayen,* from *gain-* against (from Old English *gēan-*) + *sayen* to say — more at AGAIN] (14th century)
**1 :** to declare to be untrue or invalid
**2 :** CONTRADICT, OPPOSE
*synonym* see DENY
— **gain·say·er** *noun*

**¹gait** \'gāt\ *noun* [Middle English *gait, gate* gate, way] (1509)
**1 :** a manner of walking or moving on foot
**2 :** a sequence of foot movements (as a walk, trot, pace, or canter) by which a horse or a dog moves forward
**3 :** a manner or rate of movement or progress ⟨the leisurely *gait* of summer⟩

**²gait** (circa 1900)
*transitive verb*
**1 :** to train (a horse or a dog) to use a particular gait or set of gaits
**2 :** to lead (a show dog) before a judge to display carriage and movement
*intransitive verb*
**:** to walk with a particular gait

**gait·ed** \'gā-təd\ *adjective* (1588)
**:** having a particular gait or so many gaits ⟨slow-*gaited*⟩ ⟨a *gaited* horse⟩

**gai·ter** \'gā-tər\ *noun* [French *guêtre*] (1775)
**1 :** a cloth or leather leg covering reaching from the instep to above the ankle or to mid-calf or knee
**2 a :** an overshoe with fabric upper **b :** an ankle-high shoe with elastic gores in the sides

**¹gal** \'gal\ *noun* [by alteration] (1795)
**:** GIRL, WOMAN

**²gal** *noun* [*Galileo* Galilei] (1914)
**:** a unit of acceleration equivalent to one centimeter per second per second — used especially for values of gravity

**ga·la** \'gā-lə, 'ga-, 'gä-\ *noun* [Italian, from Middle French *gale* festivity, pleasure — more at GALLANT] (1777)
**:** a festive celebration; *especially* **:** a public entertainment marking a special occasion
— **gala** *adjective*

**ga·la·bia** *or* **ga·la·bi·eh** *or* **ga·la·bi·ya** \gə-'lä-b(ē-)ə\ *noun* [Arabic dialect (Egyptian) *gallābīyah*] (1725)
**:** DJELLABA

**galact-** *or* **galacto-** *combining form* [Latin *galact-,* from Greek *galakt-, galakto-,* from *galakt-, gala*]
**1 :** milk ⟨*galact*orrhea⟩
**2 :** related to galactose ⟨*galacto*semia⟩

**ga·lac·tic** \gə-'lak-tik\ *adjective* (1839)
**1 :** of or relating to a galaxy and especially the Milky Way galaxy
**2 :** HUGE ⟨a *galactic* sum of money⟩

**ga·lac·tor·rhea** \gə-,lak-tə-'rē-ə\ *noun* (circa 1860)
**:** a spontaneous flow of milk from the nipple

**ga·lac·tos·amine** \gə-,lak-'tō-sə-,mēn, -zə-\ *noun* (1900)
**:** an amino derivative $C_6H_{13}O_5N$ of galactose that occurs in cartilage

**ga·lac·tose** \gə-'lak-,tōs, -,tōz\ *noun* [French, from *galact-*] (1869)
**:** a sugar $C_6H_{12}O_6$ less soluble and less sweet than glucose

**ga·lac·to·semia** \gə-,lak-tə-'sē-mē-ə\ *noun* (1934)
**:** an inherited metabolic disorder in which galactose accumulates in the blood due to deficiency of an enzyme catalyzing its conversion to glucose
— **ga·lac·to·semic** \-mik\ *adjective*

**ga·lac·to·si·dase** \gə-,lak-'tō-sə-,dās, -zə-,dāz\ *noun* (1917)
**:** an enzyme (as lactase) that hydrolyzes a galactoside

**ga·lac·to·side** \gə-'lak-tə-ˌsīd\ *noun* (1862)
: a glycoside that yields galactose on hydrolysis

**ga·lac·to·syl** \gə-'lak-tə-ˌsil\ *noun* (1950)
: a glycosyl radical $C_6H_{11}O_5$ that is derived from galactose

**ga·lact·uron·ic acid** \gə-ˌlak-tù-'rä-nik-, -tyü-\ *noun* [International Scientific Vocabulary] (1917)
: a crystalline aldehyde-acid $C_6H_{10}O_7$ that occurs especially in polymerized form in pectin

**ga·la·go** \gə-'lä-(ˌ)gō, -'lä-\ *noun, plural* **-gos** [New Latin, perhaps from Wolof *golokh* monkey] (circa 1848)
: any of several small active nocturnal arboreal African primates (*Galago* and related genera) with large eyes, long ears, a long tail, and elongated hind limbs that enable them to leap with great agility — called also *bush baby*

**ga·lah** \gə-'lä\ *noun* [Yuwaalaraay (Australian aboriginal language of northern New South Wales) *gilaa*] (1862)
: a showy Australian cockatoo (*Eolophus roseicapillus*) that is a pest in wheat-growing areas and is often kept as a cage bird

galago

**Gal·a·had** \'ga-lə-ˌhad\ *noun*
**1** : the knight of the Round Table who successfully seeks the Holy Grail
**2** : one who is pure, noble, and unselfish

**gal·an·tine** \'ga-lən-ˌtēn\ *noun* [French, from Old French *galentine, galatine* fish sauce, from Medieval Latin *galatina*, probably from Latin *gelatus*, past participle of *gelare* to congeal, freeze — more at COLD] (1725)
: a cold dish consisting of boned meat or fish that has been stuffed, poached, and covered with aspic

**Gal·a·tea** \ˌga-lə-'tē-ə\ *noun* [Latin, from Greek *Galateia*]
: a female figure sculpted by Pygmalion and given life by Aphrodite in fulfillment of his prayer

**Ga·la·tians** \gə-'lā-shənz\ *noun plural but singular in construction*
: an argumentative letter of Saint Paul written to the Christians of Galatia and included as a book in the New Testament — see BIBLE table

**gal·a·vant** *variant of* GALLIVANT

**ga·lax** \'gā-ˌlaks\ *noun* [New Latin] (circa 1753)
: an evergreen herb (*Galax urceolata* synonym *G. aphylla* of the order Diapensiales) of the southeastern U.S. that has glossy leaves and is related to the heaths (order Ericales)

**gal·axy** \'ga-lək-sē\ *noun, plural* **-ax·ies** [Middle English *galaxie, galaxias*, from Late Latin *galaxias*, from Greek, from *galakt-, gala* milk; akin to Latin *lac* milk] (14th century)
**1 a** *often capitalized* : MILKY WAY GALAXY — used with *the* **b** : any of the very large groups of stars and associated matter that are found throughout the universe
**2** : an assemblage of brilliant or notable persons or things ⟨a *galaxy* of artists⟩ ◆

**gal·ba·num** \'gal-bə-nəm, 'ġól-\ *noun* [Middle English, from Latin, from Greek *chalbanē*, of Semitic origin; akin to Hebrew *ḥelbĕnāh* galbanum] (14th century)
: a yellowish to green or brown aromatic bitter gum resin derived from several Asian plants (as *Ferula galbaniflua*) and used in incense

**gale** \'gā(ə)l\ *noun* [origin unknown] (circa 1547)
**1 a** : a strong current of air: (1) : a wind from 32 to 63 miles per hour (about 51 to 101 kilometers per hour) (2) : FRESH GALE — see BEAUFORT SCALE table **b** *archaic* : BREEZE
**2** : an emotional outburst ⟨*gales* of laughter⟩

**ga·lea** \'gā-lē-ə\ *noun* [New Latin, from Latin, helmet] (1834)
: an anatomical part suggesting a helmet: as **a** : the upper lip of the corolla of a mint **b** : the outer or lateral lobe of the maxilla in mandibulate insects
— **ga·le·ate** \-lē-ˌāt\ *adjective*

**ga·le·na** \gə-'lē-nə\ *noun* [Latin, lead ore] (1671)
: a bluish gray mineral with metallic luster consisting of lead sulfide, showing highly perfect cubic cleavage, and constituting the principal ore of lead

**ga·len·i·cal** \gə-'le-ni-kəl, gā-\ *noun* [*Galen* + $^1$-*ic* + $^1$-*al*] (1768)
: a medicine prepared by extracting one or more active constituents of a plant

**ga·lère** \ga-'ler\ *noun* [French, galley, from Middle French, from Catalan *galera*, from Middle Greek *galea*] (1756)
: a group of people having an attribute in common

**gal Friday** *noun* (1958)
: GIRL FRIDAY

**Gal·i·le·an** \ˌga-lə-'lē-ən, -'lā-\ *adjective* (circa 1751)
: of, relating to, or discovered by Galileo Galilei

**gal·i·lee** \'ga-lə-ˌlē\ *noun* [Anglo-French, from Medieval Latin *galilaea*, probably from *Galilaea* Galilee, from Latin] (15th century)
: a chapel or porch at the entrance of an English church

**gal·in·gale** \'ga-lən-ˌgāl, -liŋ-\ *noun* [Middle English, a kind of ginger, from Middle French *galingal*, from Arabic *khalanjān*] (1578)
: an Old World sedge (*Cyperus longus*) that is used for papermaking and basket-weaving and has an aromatic root; *broadly* : any of various other sedges of the same genus

**gal·i·ot** *variant of* GALLIOT

**¹gall** \'ġól\ *noun* [Middle English, from Old English *gealla*; akin to Greek *cholē, cholos* gall, wrath, Old English *geolu* yellow — more at YELLOW] (before 12th century)
**1 a** : BILE; *especially* : bile obtained from an animal and used in the arts or medicine **b** : something bitter to endure **c** : bitterness of spirit : RANCOR
**2** : brazen boldness coupled with impudent assurance and insolence
*synonym* see TEMERITY

**²gall** *noun* [Middle English *galle*, from Old English *gealla*, from Latin *galla* gallnut] (before 12th century)
**1 a** : a skin sore caused by chronic irritation **b** : a cause or state of exasperation
**2** *archaic* : FLAW

**³gall** (14th century)
*transitive verb*
**1** : to fret and wear away by friction : CHAFE ⟨the loose saddle *galled* the horse's back⟩ ⟨the *galling* of a metal bearing⟩
**2** : IRRITATE, VEX ⟨sarcasm *galls* her⟩
*intransitive verb*
**1** : to become sore or worn by rubbing
**2** : SEIZE 2

**⁴gall** *noun* [Middle English *galle*, from Middle French, from Latin *galla*] (14th century)
: a swelling of plant tissue usually due to fungi or insect parasites and sometimes forming an important source of tannin

**Gal·la** \'ga-lə\ *noun, plural* **Galla** *or* **Gallas** (1875)
: OROMO

**gal·la·mine tri·eth·io·dide** \'ga-lə-ˌmēn-ˌtrī-ə,e-'thī-ə-ˌdīd\ *noun* [pyrogallol + *amine* + *triethyl* + *iodide*] (1951)
: a substituted ammonium salt $C_{30}H_{60}I_3N_3O_3$ that is used to produce muscle relaxation especially during anesthesia — called also *gallamine*

**¹gal·lant** \gə-'lant, gə-'länt, 'ga-lənt\ *noun* (14th century)
**1** : a young man of fashion
**2 a** : LADIES' MAN **b** : SUITOR **c** : PARAMOUR

**²gal·lant** \'ga-lənt *(usually in sense 2)*; gə-'lant, gə-'länt *(usually in sense 3)*\ *adjective* [Middle English *galaunt*, from Middle French *galant*, from present participle of *galer* to have a good time, from *gale* pleasure, of Germanic origin; akin to Old English *wela* weal — more at WEAL] (15th century)
**1** : showy in dress or bearing : SMART
**2 a** : SPLENDID, STATELY ⟨a *gallant* ship⟩ **b** : SPIRITED, BRAVE ⟨*gallant* efforts against the enemy⟩ **c** : nobly chivalrous and often self-sacrificing
**3** : courteously and elaborately attentive especially to ladies
*synonym* see CIVIL
— **gal·lant·ly** *adverb*

**³gal·lant** \gə-'lant, -'länt\ (1672)
*transitive verb*
**1** : to pay court to (a lady) : ATTEND ⟨used to *gallant* her in his youth —Washington Irving⟩
**2** *obsolete* : to manipulate (a fan) in a modish manner
*intransitive verb*
: to pay court to ladies

**gal·lant·ry** \'ga-lən-trē\ *noun, plural* **-ries** (1613)
**1** *archaic* : gallant appearance
**2 a** : an act of marked courtesy **b** : courteous attention to a lady **c** : amorous attention or pursuit
**3** : spirited and conspicuous bravery

**gal·late** \'ga-ˌlāt, 'ġó-\ *noun* (1794)
: a salt or ester of gallic acid

**gall·blad·der** \'ġól-ˌbla-dər\ *noun* (1676)
: a membranous muscular sac in which bile from the liver is stored

**gal·le·ass** \'ga-lē-əs\ *noun* [Middle French *galeasse*, from Old French *galie* galley] (1544)
: a large fast galley used especially as a warship by Mediterranean countries in the 16th and 17th centuries and having both sails and oars but usually propelled chiefly by rowing

**gal·le·on** \'ga-lē-ən\ *noun* [Old Spanish *galeón*, from Middle French *galion*, from Old French *galie*] (1529)
: a heavy square-rigged sailing ship of the 15th to early 18th centuries used for war or commerce especially by the Spanish

galleon

---

◇ **WORD HISTORY**
**galaxy**   The earliest known use in English of the words *galaxy* and *Milky Way* is in the following lines from a poem by Geoffrey Chaucer called *The House of Fame*, written sometime before 1385: "Se yonder, loo, the Galaxie, /Which men clepeth the Milky Wey,/ For hit is whit." (See yonder, lo, the galaxy, which they call the Milky Way, because it is white.) These lines make it clear that *Milky Way*, at least, was a term popular in England before that time, though how early it was in use is impossible to say. The idea of the whiteness of the Milky Way being similar to that of milk is considerably older than the English language, however, for *galaxy* is borrowed through Latin from Greek *galaxias*, a derivative of *gala* "milk." Not until the 19th century was *galaxy* used as a generic term for other star systems as well as the one in which we live, and to distinguish our galaxy from others the name *Milky Way* has proved useful in English.

---

\ə\ abut \ᵊ\ kitten \ər\ further \a\ ash \ā\ ace
\ä\ mop, mar \au̇\ out \ch\ chin \e\ bet \ē\ easy
\g\ go \i\ hit \ī\ ice \j\ job \ŋ\ sing \ō\ go
\ò\ law \òi\ boy \th\ thin \t̷h\ the \ü\ loot \u̇\ foot
\y\ yet \zh\ vision   *see also* Guide to Pronunciation

**gal·le·ria** \ˌga-lə-'rē-ə\ noun [Italian, gallery, from Medieval Latin galeria] (circa 1901)
: a roofed and usually glass-enclosed promenade or court (as at a mall)

**gal·lery** \'ga-lə-rē, 'gal-rē\ noun, plural **-ler·ies** [Middle English galerie, from Medieval Latin galeria, probably alteration of galilaea galilee] (15th century)
**1 a :** a roofed promenade : COLONNADE **b** : CORRIDOR
**2 a :** an outdoor balcony **b** Southern & Midland : PORCH, VERANDA **c** : a platform at the quarters or stern of a ship
**3 a :** a long and narrow passage, apartment, or corridor **b** : a subterranean passageway in a cave or military mining system; also : a working drift or level in mining **c** : an underground passage made by a mole or ant or a passage made in wood by an insect
**4 a :** a room or building devoted to the exhibition of works of art **b** : an institution or business exhibiting or dealing in works of art **c** : COLLECTION, AGGREGATION ⟨the rich gallery of characters in this novel —H. S. Canby⟩
**5 a :** a structure projecting from one or more interior walls of an auditorium to accommodate additional people; especially : the highest balcony in a theater commonly having the cheapest seats **b** : the part of a theater audience seated in the top gallery **c** : the undiscriminating general public **d** : the spectators at a tennis or golf match
**6 :** a small ornamental barrier or railing (as along the edge of a table or shelf)
**7 :** a photographer's studio
— **gal·ler·ied** \-rēd\ adjective
— **gal·lery·ite** \-rē-ˌīt\ noun

**gallery forest** noun (1920)
: a forest growing along a watercourse in a region otherwise devoid of trees

**gal·lery-go·er** \'ga-lə-rē-ˌgō(-ə)r, 'gal-rē-\ noun (1888)
: one who frequently goes to art galleries

**ga·lle·ta** \gə-'ye-tə, gī-'e-tə\ noun [Spanish, hardtack] (1872)
: either of two perennial forage grasses (Hilaria rigida and H. jamesii) used for hay in the southwestern U.S. and in Mexico

**gal·ley** \'ga-lē\ noun, plural **galleys** [Middle English galeie, from Old French galie, galee, ultimately from Middle Greek galea] (13th century)
**1 :** a ship or boat propelled solely or chiefly by oars: as **a** : a long low ship used for war and trading especially in the Mediterranean Sea from the Middle Ages to the 19th century; also : GALLEASS **b** : a warship of classical antiquity — compare BIREME, TRIREME **c** : a large open boat (as a gig) formerly used in England
**2 :** the kitchen and cooking apparatus especially of a ship or airplane
**3 a :** an oblong tray to hold especially a single column of set type **b** : a proof of typeset matter especially in a single column before being made into pages

**gal·ley-west** \ˌga-lē-'west\ adverb [probably alteration of English dialect collywest (badly askew)] (1875)
: into destruction or confusion ⟨was knocked galley-west⟩

**gall·fly** \'gòl-ˌflī\ noun (circa 1834)
: an insect (as a gall wasp) that deposits its eggs in plants causing the formation of galls in which the larvae feed

**¹gal·liard** \'gal-yərd\ adjective [Middle English gaillard, from Middle French] (14th century)
archaic : GAY, LIVELY

**²galliard** noun (1533)
: a sprightly dance with five steps to a phrase popular in the 16th and 17th centuries

**Gal·lic** \'ga-lik\ adjective [Latin Gallicus, from Gallia Gaul] (1672)
: of or relating to Gaul or France

**gallic acid** \'ga-lik-, 'gò-lik-\ noun [French gallique, from galle gall] (1791)
: a white crystalline acid $C_7H_6O_5$ found widely in plants or combined in tannins and used especially in dyes and as a photographic developer

**Gal·li·can** \'ga-li-kən\ adjective (14th century)
**1 :** GALLIC
**2** often not capitalized : of or relating to Gallicanism
— **Gallican** noun

**Gal·li·can·ism** \-kə-ˌni-zəm\ noun (1858)
: a movement originating in France and advocating administrative independence from papal control for the Roman Catholic Church in each nation

**gal·li·cism** \'ga-lə-ˌsi-zəm\ noun, often capitalized (circa 1656)
**1 :** a characteristic French idiom or expression appearing in another language
**2 :** a French trait

**gal·li·cize** \-ˌsīz\ transitive verb **-cized; -ciz·ing** often capitalized (1773)
: to cause to conform to a French mode or idiom
— **gal·li·ci·za·tion** \ˌga-lə-sə-'zā-shən\ noun, often capitalized

**gal·li·gas·kins** \ˌga-li-'gas-kənz\ noun plural [probably modification of Middle French garguesques, from Old Spanish greguescos, from griego Greek, from Latin Graecus] (1577)
**1 a :** loose wide hose or breeches worn in the 16th and 17th centuries **b** : very loose trousers
**2** dialect chiefly British : LEGGINGS

**gal·li·mau·fry** \ˌga-lə-'mò-frē\ noun, plural **-fries** [Middle French galimafree stew] (circa 1556)
: HODGEPODGE ⟨a gallimaufry of opinions⟩

**gal·li·na·ceous** \ˌga-lə-'nā-shəs\ adjective [Latin gallinaceus of domestic fowl, from gallina hen, from gallus cock] (1783)
: of or relating to an order (Galliformes) of heavy-bodied largely terrestrial birds including the pheasants, turkeys, grouse, and the common domestic fowl

**gall·ing** \'gò-liŋ\ adjective [³gall] (1583)
: markedly irritating : VEXING ⟨a most galling defeat⟩
— **gall·ing·ly** \-liŋ-lē\ adverb

**gal·li·nip·per** \'ga-lə-ˌni-pər\ noun [origin unknown] (1709)
chiefly Southern & Midland : any of various insects (as a large mosquito or crane fly)

**gal·li·nule** \'ga-lə-ˌnü(ə)l, -ˌnyü(ə)l\ noun [New Latin Gallinula, genus of birds, from Latin, pullet, diminutive of gallina] (1776)
: any of several aquatic birds of the rail family with long thin feet and a platelike frontal area on the head; especially : one (Gallinula chloropus) widespread in the New World, Eurasia, and Africa that has a largely red bill, red frontal area on the head, and a white band on the flanks

**gal·li·ot** \'ga-lē-ət\ noun [Middle English galiote, from Middle French, from Medieval Latin galeota, diminutive of galea galley, from Middle Greek] (14th century)
**1 :** a small swift galley formerly used in the Mediterranean
**2** [Dutch galjoot, from Middle French galiote] : a long narrow shallow-draft Dutch merchant sailing ship

**gal·li·pot** \'ga-li-ˌpät\ noun [Middle English galy pott] (15th century)
**1 :** a small usually ceramic vessel
**2** archaic : DRUGGIST

**gal·li·um** \'ga-lē-əm\ noun [New Latin, from Latin gallus cock (intended as translation of surname of Paul Lecoq de Boisbaudran (died 1912) French chemist)] (1875)
: a rare bluish white metallic element that is hard and brittle at low temperatures but melts just above room temperature and expands on freezing — see ELEMENT table

**gallium arsenide** noun (circa 1961)

: a synthetic compound GaAs used especially as a semiconducting material

**gal·li·vant** \'ga-lə-ˌvant\ intransitive verb [perhaps alteration of ³gallant] (1823)
**1 :** to go about usually ostentatiously or indiscreetly with members of the opposite sex
**2 :** to travel, roam, or move about for pleasure

**gall midge** noun (circa 1889)
: any of numerous minute dipteran flies (family Cecidomyiidae) most of which cause gall formation in plants

**gall mite** noun (1881)
: any of various minute 4-legged mites (family Eriophyidae) that form galls on plants

**gall·nut** \'gòl-ˌnət\ noun [⁴gall] (1572)
: a gall resembling a nut

**gal·lon** \'ga-lən\ noun [Middle English galon, a liquid measure, from Old North French, from Medieval Latin galeta pail, a liquid measure] (13th century)
: a unit of liquid capacity equal to 231 cubic inches or four quarts — see WEIGHT table

**gal·lon·age** \'ga-lə-nij\ noun (circa 1909)
: amount in gallons

**gal·loon** \gə-'lün\ noun [French galon] (1604)
: a narrow trimming (as of lace, embroidery, or braid with metallic threads) having both edges scalloped

**¹gal·lop** \'ga-ləp\ (15th century)
intransitive verb
**1 :** to progress or ride at a gallop
**2 :** to run fast
transitive verb
**1 :** to cause to gallop
**2 :** to transport at a gallop
— **gal·lop·er** noun

**²gallop** noun [Middle French galop] (1523)
**1 :** a bounding gait of a quadruped; specifically : a fast natural 3-beat gait of the horse — compare ³CANTER, RUN
**2 :** a ride or run at a gallop
**3 :** a stretch of land suitable for galloping horses
**4 :** a rapid or hasty progression or pace

**gal·lo·pade** \ˌga-lə-'pād, -'päd\ noun (1831)
: GALOP

**Gal·lo·phile** \'ga-lə-ˌfīl\ adjective [Latin Gallus Gaul + English -phile] (1923)
: FRANCOPHILE
— **Gallophile** noun

**gal·lop·ing** adjective (1642)
: progressing, developing, or increasing rapidly ⟨galloping inflation⟩ ⟨a galloping farce⟩ ⟨galloping alcoholism⟩

**Gal·lo·way** \'ga-lə-ˌwā\ noun [Galloway, Scotland] (1805)
: any of a breed of hardy medium-sized hornless chiefly black beef cattle native to southwestern Scotland

**gal·low·glass** \'ga-lō-ˌglas\ noun [alteration of Irish gallóglach, from gall foreigner + óglach young man, warrior] (circa 1515)
**1 :** a mercenary or retainer of an Irish chief
**2 :** an armed Irish foot soldier

**¹gal·lows** \'ga-(ˌ)lōz, -ləz, in sense 3 also -ləs\ noun, plural **gallows** or **gal·lows·es** [Middle English galwes, plural of galwe, from Old English gealga; akin to Old Norse gelgja pole, stake, Armenian jalk twig] (before 12th century)
**1 a :** a frame usually of two upright posts and a transverse beam from which criminals are hanged — called also gallows tree **b** : the punishment of hanging
**2 :** a structure consisting of an upright frame with a crosspiece
**3 :** SUSPENDER 2a

**²gallows** adjective (15th century)
: deserving the gallows

**gallows bird** noun (circa 1785)
: a person who deserves hanging

**gallows humor** noun (1901)
: humor that makes fun of a life-threatening, disastrous, or terrifying situation

**gall·stone** \'gòl-ˌstōn\ noun (1758)

: a calculus formed in the gallbladder or biliary passages

**gal·lus** \'ga-ləs\ *noun* [alteration of ¹*gallows*] (1836)
: SUSPENDER 2a — usually used in plural

**gal·lused** \'ga-ləst\ *adjective* (1927)
: wearing galluses

**gall wasp** *noun* (1879)
: any of a family (Cynipidae) of hymenopterous gallflies

**gal·ly** \'ga-lē\ *transitive verb* **gal·lied; gal·ly·ing** [origin unknown] (1605)
*chiefly dialect* : FRIGHTEN, TERRIFY

**Ga·lois theory** \(ˌ)gal-'wä-, 'gal-ˌwä-\ *noun* [Évariste *Galois*] (1893)
: a part of the theory of mathematical groups concerned especially with the conditions under which a solution to a polynomial equation with coefficients in a given mathematical field can be obtained in the field by the repetition of operations and the extraction of nth roots

**ga·loot** \gə-'lüt\ *noun* [origin unknown] (1866)
*slang* : FELLOW; *especially* : one who is strange or foolish

**ga·lop** \'ga-ləp, ga-'lō\ *noun* [French] (1831)
: a lively dance in duple measure; *also* : the music of a galop

**ga·lore** \gə-'lōr, -'lȯr\ *adjective* [Irish *go leor* enough] (1628)
: ABUNDANT, PLENTIFUL — used postpositively ⟨bargains *galore*⟩

**ga·losh** \gə-'läsh\ *noun* [Middle English *galoche,* from Middle French] (14th century)
**1** *obsolete* : a shoe with a heavy sole
**2** : a high overshoe worn especially in snow and slush
— **ga·loshed** \-'läsht\ *adjective*

**ga·lumph** \gə-'ləm(p)f\ *intransitive verb* [probably alteration of ¹*gallop*] (1872)
: to move with a clumsy heavy tread

**gal·van·ic** \gal-'va-nik\ *adjective* (1797)
**1** : of, relating to, or producing a direct current of electricity ⟨a *galvanic* cell⟩
**2 a** : having an electric effect : intensely exciting ⟨a *galvanic* performance⟩ **b** : produced as if by an electric shock ⟨had a *galvanic* effect on the audience⟩
— **gal·van·i·cal·ly** \-ni-k(ə-)lē\ *adverb*

**galvanic skin response** *noun* (1942)
: a change in the electrical resistance of the skin that is a physiochemical response to an emotional change

**gal·va·nise** *British variant of* GALVANIZE

**gal·va·nism** \'gal-və-ˌni-zəm\ *noun* [French or Italian; French *galvanisme,* from Italian *galvanismo,* from Luigi *Galvani*] (1797)
**1** : a direct current of electricity especially when produced by chemical action
**2** : the therapeutic use of direct electric current
**3** : vital or forceful activity

**gal·va·nize** \'gal-və-ˌnīz\ *verb* **-nized; -niz·ing** (1802)
*transitive verb*
**1 a** : to subject to the action of an electric current especially for the purpose of stimulating physiologically ⟨*galvanize* a muscle⟩ **b** : to stimulate or excite as if by an electric shock ⟨an issue that would *galvanize* public opinion⟩
**2** : to coat (iron or steel) with zinc; *especially* : to immerse in molten zinc to produce a coating of zinc-iron alloy
*intransitive verb*
: to react as if stimulated by an electric shock ⟨they *galvanized* into action⟩
— **gal·va·ni·za·tion** \ˌgal-və-nə-'zā-shən\ *noun*
— **gal·va·niz·er** \'gal-və-ˌnī-zər\ *noun*

**galvano-** *combining form* [*galvanic*]
: galvanic current ⟨*galvano*meter⟩

**gal·va·nom·e·ter** \ˌgal-və-'nä-mə-tər\ *noun* (1802)
: an instrument for detecting or measuring a small electric current by movements of a magnetic needle or of a coil in a magnetic field
— **gal·va·no·met·ric** \-nō-'me-trik\ *adjective*

**gal·va·no·scope** \gal-'va-nə-ˌskōp, 'gal-və-nə-\ *noun* (1832)
: an instrument for detecting the presence and direction of an electric current by the deflection of a magnetic needle

**¹gam** \'gam\ *noun* [probably ultimately from Lingua Franca *gamba* leg, from Italian, from Late Latin] (1781)
*slang* : LEG

**²gam** *noun* [perhaps short for obsolete *gammon* (talk)] (1846)
**1** : a visit or friendly conversation at sea or ashore especially between whalers
**2** : a school of whales

**³gam** *verb* **gammed; gam·ming** (1849)
*intransitive verb*
: to engage in a gam
*transitive verb*
**1** : to have a gam with
**2** : to spend or pass (as time) talking

**gam-** *or* **gamo-** *combining form* [New Latin, from Greek, marriage, from *gamos,* from *gamein* to marry]
: united : joined ⟨*gamo*petalous⟩

**gama grass** \'ga-mə-\ *noun* [probably alteration of *grama*] (1833)
: a tall coarse American grass (*Tripsacum dactyloides*) valuable for forage

**ga·may** \ga-'mā, 'ga-ˌmā\ *noun, often capitalized* [French, from *Gamay,* village in Burgundy] (circa 1941)
: a light dry red table wine made from the same grape used for French Beaujolais ⟨*gamay* rosé⟩

**gam·ba** \'gäm-bə, 'gam-\ *noun* (1598)
: VIOLA DA GAMBA

**¹gam·ba·do** \gam-'bā-(ˌ)dō\ *noun, plural* **-does** *also* **-dos** [perhaps modification of Italian *gambale,* from *gamba* leg] (circa 1656)
: a horseman's legging

**²gambado** *noun, plural* **-does** *also* **-dos** [modification of French *gambade* — more at GAMBOL] (1820)
**1** : a spring of a horse
**2** : CAPER, GAMBOL

**gam·bier** *also* **gam·bir** \'gam-ˌbir\ *noun* [Malay *gambir*] (1830)
: a yellowish catechu that is obtained from a Malayan woody vine (*Uncaria gambir*) of the madder family and is used for chewing with the betel nut and for tanning and dyeing

**gam·bit** \'gam-bət\ *noun* [Italian *gambetto,* literally, act of tripping someone, from *gamba* leg, from Late Latin *gamba, camba,* from Greek *kampē* bend; probably akin to Gothic *hamfs* maimed, Lithuanian *kampas* corner] (1656)
**1** : a chess opening in which a player risks one or more minor pieces to gain an advantage in position
**2 a** (1) : a remark intended to start a conversation or make a telling point (2) : TOPIC **b** : a calculated move : STRATAGEM

**¹gam·ble** \'gam-bəl\ *verb* **gam·bled; gam·bling** \-b(ə-)liŋ\ [probably back-formation from *gambler,* probably alteration of obsolete *gamner,* from obsolete *gamen* (to play)] (circa 1775)
*intransitive verb*
**1 a** : to play a game for money or property **b** : to bet on an uncertain outcome
**2** : to stake something on a contingency : take a chance
*transitive verb*
**1** : to risk by gambling : WAGER
**2** : VENTURE, HAZARD
— **gam·bler** \-blər\ *noun*

**²gamble** *noun* (1823)
**1 a** : an act having an element of risk **b** : something chancy
**2** : the playing of a game of chance for stakes

**gam·boge** \gam-'bōj, -'büzh\ *noun* [New Latin *gambogium,* alteration of *cambugium,* from or akin to Portuguese *Camboja* Cambodia] (1712)

**1** : an orange to brown gum resin from southeast Asian trees (genus *Garcinia*) of the Saint-John's-wort family that is used as a yellow pigment and cathartic
**2** : a strong yellow

**¹gam·bol** \'gam-bəl\ *intransitive verb* **-boled** *or* **-bolled; -bol·ing** *or* **-bol·ling** \-bə-liŋ *also* -bliŋ\ (1508)
: to skip about in play : FRISK, FROLIC

**²gambol** *noun* [modification of Middle French *gambade* spring of a horse, gambol, probably from Old Provençal *camba* leg, from Late Latin] (circa 1510)
: a skipping or leaping about in play

**gam·brel** \'gam-brəl\ *noun* [Old North French *gamberel,* from *gambe* leg, from Late Latin *gamba*] (1547)
: a stick or iron for suspending slaughtered animals

**gambrel roof** *noun* (1765)
: a roof with a lower steeper slope and an upper less steep one on each of its two sides — see ROOF illustration

**gam·bu·sia** \gam-'bü-zh(ē-)ə, -'byü-\ *noun* [New Latin, modification of American Spanish *gambusino* gambusia] (circa 1889)
: any of a genus (*Gambusia*) of live-bearers (family Poeciliidae) introduced as exterminators of mosquito larvae in warm fresh waters

**¹game** \'gām\ *noun* [Middle English, from Old English *gamen;* akin to Old High German *gaman* amusement] (before 12th century)
**1 a** (1) : activity engaged in for diversion or amusement : PLAY (2) : the equipment for a game **b** : often derisive or mocking jesting : FUN, SPORT ⟨make *game* of a nervous player⟩
**2 a** : a procedure or strategy for gaining an end : TACTIC **b** : an illegal or shady scheme or maneuver : RACKET
**3 a** (1) : a physical or mental competition conducted according to rules with the participants in direct opposition to each other (2) : a division of a larger contest (3) : the number of points necessary to win (4) : points scored in certain card games (as in all fours) by a player whose cards count up the highest (5) : the manner of playing in a contest (6) : the set of rules governing a game (7) : a particular aspect or phase of play in a game or sport ⟨a football team's kicking *game*⟩ **b** *plural* : organized athletics **c** (1) : a field of gainful activity : LINE ⟨the newspaper *game*⟩ (2) : any activity undertaken or regarded as a contest involving rivalry, strategy, or struggle ⟨the dating *game*⟩ ⟨the *game* of politics⟩; *also* : the course or period of such an activity ⟨got into aviation early in the *game*⟩ (3) : area of expertise : SPECIALTY 3 ⟨comedy is not my *game*⟩
**4 a** (1) : animals under pursuit or taken in hunting; *especially* : wild animals hunted for sport or food (2) : the flesh of game animals **b** *archaic* : PLUCK **c** : a target or object especially of ridicule or attack — often used in the phrase *fair game*
*synonym* see FUN
— **game·like** \-ˌlīk\ *adjective*

**²game** *verb* **gamed; gam·ing** (1529)
*intransitive verb*
: to play for a stake
*transitive verb*
*archaic* : to lose or squander by gambling

**³game** *adjective* (1610)
**1 a** : having or showing a resolute unyielding spirit ⟨*game* to the end⟩ **b** : willing or ready to proceed ⟨were *game* for anything⟩
**2** : of or relating to game ⟨*game* laws⟩
— **game·ly** *adverb*
— **game·ness** *noun*

**⁴game** *adjective* [origin unknown] (circa 1787)
: LAME ⟨a *game* leg⟩

**game ball** *noun* (1966)
: a ball (as a football) presented to a player or coach in recognition of an outstanding contribution to a team victory

**game bird** *noun* (1866)
: a bird that may be legally hunted according to the laws especially of a state of the U.S.

**game·cock** \'gām-,käk\ *noun* (1677)
: a rooster of the domestic chicken trained for fighting

**game fish** *noun* (1862)
**1** : a fish of a family (Salmonidae) including salmons, trouts, chars, and whitefishes
**2** : SPORT FISH; *especially* : a fish made a legal catch by law

**game·keep·er** \'gām-,kē-pər\ *noun* (circa 1671)
: a person in charge of the breeding and protection of game animals or birds on a private preserve

**gam·elan** \'ga-mə-,lan\ *noun* [Javanese] (1817)
: an Indonesian orchestra made up especially of percussion instruments (as gongs, xylophones, and drums)

**game of chance** (circa 1925)
: a game (as a dice game) in which chance rather than skill determines the outcome

**game plan** *noun* (1941)
: a strategy for achieving an objective

**game point** *noun* (circa 1949)
: a situation (as in tennis) in which one player will win the game by winning the next point; *also* : the point itself

**gam·er** \'gā-mər\ *noun* (circa 1630)
: a player who is game; *especially* : an athlete who relishes competition

**game show** *noun* (1958)
: a television program on which contestants compete for prizes in a game (as a quiz)

**games·man** \'gāmz-mən, -,man\ *noun* (1947)
: one who practices gamesmanship; *also* : one who plays games

**games·man·ship** \'gāmz-mən-,ship\ *noun* (1947)
**1** : the art or practice of winning games by questionable expedients without actually violating the rules
**2** : the use of ethically dubious methods to gain an objective ◆

**game·some** \'gām-səm\ *adjective* [Middle English] (14th century)
: MERRY, FROLICSOME
— **game·some·ly** *adverb*
— **game·some·ness** *noun*

**game·ster** \'gām-stər\ *noun* (1553)
: one who plays games; *especially* : GAMBLER

**gamet-** *or* **gameto-** *combining form* [New Latin, from *gameta*]
: gamete ⟨*gametophore*⟩

**gam·etan·gi·um** \,ga-mə-'tan-jē-əm\ *noun*, *plural* **-gia** \-jē-ə\ [New Latin, from *gamet-* + Greek *angeion* vessel — more at ANGI-] (1886)
: a cell or organ in which gametes are developed

**gam·ete** \'ga-,mēt *also* gə-'mēt\ *noun* [New Latin *gameta*, from Greek *gametēs* husband, from *gamein* to marry] (1886)
: a mature male or female germ cell usually possessing a haploid chromosome set and capable of initiating formation of a new diploid individual by fusion with a gamete of the opposite sex
— **ga·met·ic** \gə-'me-tik, -'mē-\ *adjective*
— **ga·met·i·cal·ly** \-ti-k(ə-)lē\ *adverb*

**game theory** *noun* (1949)
: the analysis of a situation involving conflicting interests (as in business or military strategy) in terms of gains and losses among opposing players
— **game theorist** *noun*

**ga·me·to·cyte** \gə-'mē-tə-,sīt\ *noun* [International Scientific Vocabulary] (1899)
: a cell (as of a protozoan causing malaria) that divides to produce gametes

**ga·me·to·gen·e·sis** \gə-,mē-tə-'je-nə-səs, ,ga-mə-tə-\ *noun* [New Latin] (circa 1900)
: the production of gametes
— **ga·me·to·gen·ic** \-'je-nik\ *or* **gam·etog·e·nous** \,ga-mə-'tä-jə-nəs\ *adjective*

**ga·me·to·phore** \gə-'mē-tə-,fōr, -,fȯr\ *noun* (1895)
: a modified branch (as of a moss) bearing gametangia

**ga·me·to·phyte** \gə-'mē-tə-,fīt\ *noun* [International Scientific Vocabulary] (circa 1889)
: the individual or generation of a plant exhibiting alternation of generations that bears sex organs — compare SPOROPHYTE
— **ga·me·to·phyt·ic** \-,mē-tə-'fi-tik\ *adjective*

**-gamic** *adjective combining form* [International Scientific Vocabulary, from Greek *-gamos* -gamous]
: having (such) reproductive organs ⟨cleisto*gamic*⟩

**gam·in** \'ga-mən\ *noun* [French] (1840)
**1** : a boy who hangs around on the streets
: URCHIN
**2** : GAMINE 2

**¹ga·mine** \ga-'mēn, 'ga-,mēn\ *noun* [French, feminine of *gamin*] (1889)
**1** : a girl who hangs around on the streets
**2** : a small playfully mischievous girl

**²gamine** *adjective* (1925)
: of, relating to, or suggesting a gamine

**gam·ing** \'gā-miŋ\ *noun* (1501)
**1** : the practice of gambling
**2** : the playing of games that simulate actual conditions (as of business or war) especially for training or testing purposes

**¹gam·ma** \'ga-mə\ *noun* [Middle English, from Late Latin, from Greek, of Semitic origin; akin to Hebrew *gīmel* gimel] (15th century)
**1** : the 3d letter of the Greek alphabet — see ALPHABET table
**2** : the degree of contrast of a developed photographic image or of a television image
**3** : a unit of magnetic flux density equal to one nanotesla
**4** : GAMMA RAY — usually used as the attributive form of gamma ray ⟨*gamma* counter⟩
**5** : MICROGRAM

**²gamma** *adjective* (1896)
**1** : of, relating to, or being one of three or more closely related chemical substances
**2** : third in position in the structure of an organic molecule from a particular group or atom — symbol γ

**gam·ma–ami·no·bu·tyr·ic acid** \,ga-mə-ə-,mē-(,)nō-byü-'tir-ik-, ,ga-mə-,a-mə-(,)nō-\ *noun* (1957)
: an amino acid $C_4H_9NO_2$ that is a neurotransmitter in the central nervous system

**gamma camera** *noun* (1964)
: a camera that detects the radiation from a radioactive tracer injected into the body and is used especially in medical diagnostic scanning

**gamma globulin** *noun* (1937)
**1 a** : a protein fraction of blood rich in antibodies **b** : a sterile solution of gamma globulin from pooled human blood administered especially for passive immunity against measles, German measles, infectious hepatitis, or poliomyelitis
**2** : any of numerous globulins of blood plasma or serum that have less electrophoretic mobility at alkaline pH than serum albumins, alpha globulins, or beta globulins and that include most antibodies — compare ANTIBODY

**gamma radiation** *noun* (1904)
: radiation composed of gamma rays

**gamma ray** *noun* (1903)
: a photon emitted spontaneously by a radioactive substance; *also* : a high-energy photon — usually used in plural

**gam·mer** \'ga-mər\ *noun* [alteration of *godmother*] (1575)
*archaic* : an old woman — compare GAFFER

**¹gam·mon** \'ga-mən\ *noun* [Middle English, from Old North French *gambon* ham, from *gambe* leg — more at GAM] (15th century)
**1** *chiefly British* : HAM 2
**2** *chiefly British* **a** : a side of bacon **b** : the lower end of a side of bacon

**²gammon** *noun* [perhaps alteration of Middle English *gamen* game] (circa 1734)
**1** *archaic* : BACKGAMMON
**2** : the winning of a backgammon game before the loser removes any men from the board

**³gammon** *transitive verb* (1735)
: to beat by scoring a gammon

**⁴gammon** (1789)
*intransitive verb*
**1** : to talk gammon
**2** : PRETEND, FEIGN
*transitive verb*
: DECEIVE, FOOL

**⁵gammon** *noun* [obsolete *gammon* (talk)] (1805)
: talk intended to deceive : HUMBUG

**gam·my** \'ga-mē\ *adjective* [perhaps from ⁴*game*] (1870)
*British* : LAME, GAME

**gamo-** — see GAM-

**gamo·pet·al·ous** \,ga-mə-'pe-t°l-əs\ *adjective* (1830)
: having the corolla composed of united petals ⟨the morning glory is *gamopetalous*⟩

**-gamous** *adjective combining form* [Greek *-gamos*, from *gamos* marriage, from *gamein* to marry]
**1** : characterized by having or practicing (such) a marriage or (such or so many) marriages ⟨exo*gamous*⟩
**2** : -GAMIC ⟨hetero*gamous*⟩

**gamp** \'gamp\ *noun* [Sarah *Gamp*, nurse with a large umbrella in *Martin Chuzzlewit* by Charles Dickens] (1864)
*British* : a large umbrella

**gam·ut** \'ga-mət\ *noun* [Medieval Latin *gamma*, lowest note of a medieval scale (from Late Latin, 3d letter of the Greek alphabet) + *ut* ut] (15th century)
**1** : the whole series of recognized musical notes

**2 :** an entire range or series ⟨ran the *gamut* from praise to contempt⟩ ◆
*synonym* see RANGE
**gamy** *or* **gam·ey** \'gā-mē\ *adjective* **gam·i·er; -est** (1844)
**1 :** BRAVE, PLUCKY — used especially of animals
**2 a :** having the flavor of game; *especially* **:** having the flavor of game near tainting **b :** SMELLY
**3 a :** SORDID, SCANDALOUS ⟨gave us all the *gamy* details⟩ **b :** CORRUPT, DISREPUTABLE ⟨a *gamy* character⟩ **c :** sexually suggestive **:** RACY ⟨*gamy* witticisms⟩
— **gam·i·ly** \-mə-lē\ *adverb*
— **gam·i·ness** \-mē-nəs\ *noun*
**-gamy** *noun combining form* [Middle English *-gamie*, from Late Latin *-gamia*, from Greek, from *gamein* to marry]
**1 :** marriage ⟨exo*gamy*⟩
**2 :** union for propagation or reproduction ⟨allo*gamy*⟩
**3 :** possession of (such) reproductive organs or (such) a mode of fertilization ⟨cleisto*gamy*⟩
**gan** *past of* GIN
**ga·nache** \(ˌ)gä-'näsh, gə-\ *noun* [French, literally, jowl, from Italian *ganascia*, modification of Greek *gnathos* jaw — more at -GNATHOUS] (1977)
**:** a sweet creamy chocolate mixture used especially as a filling or frosting
**Gan·da** \'gan-də, 'gän-\ *noun, plural* **Ganda** *or* **Gandas** (1934)
**1 :** a member of a Bantu-speaking people of Uganda
**2 :** LUGANDA
**¹gan·der** \'gan-dər\ *noun* [Middle English, from Old English *gandra;* akin to Old English *gōs* goose] (before 12th century)
**1 :** the adult male goose
**2 :** SIMPLETON
**²gander** *noun* [probably from ¹*gander;* from the outstretched neck of a person craning to look at something] (circa 1914)
**:** LOOK, GLANCE ⟨take a *gander*⟩
**gan·dy dancer** \'gan-dē-\ *noun* [origin unknown] (1923)
**1 :** a laborer in a railroad section gang
**2 :** an itinerant or seasonal laborer ◆
**ga·nef** \'gä-nəf\ *noun* [Yiddish, from Hebrew *gannābh* thief] (1923)
*slang* **:** THIEF, RASCAL
**Ga·ne·lon** \ˌga-nᵊl-'ōⁿ\ *noun* [French]
**:** the traitor in the Charlemagne romances who is responsible for the death of Roland
**¹gang** \'gaŋ\ *intransitive verb* [Middle English, from Old English *gangan;* akin to Lithuanian *žengti* to stride] (before 12th century)
*Scottish* **:** GO
**²gang** *noun* [Middle English, walking, journey, from Old English; akin to Old English *gangan*] (15th century)
**1 a** (1) **:** a set of articles **:** OUTFIT ⟨a *gang* of oars⟩ (2) **:** a combination of similar implements or devices arranged for convenience to act together ⟨a *gang* of saws⟩ **b :** GROUP: as **:** (1) **:** a group of persons working together (2) **:** a group of persons working to unlawful or antisocial ends; *especially* **:** a band of antisocial adolescents
**2 :** a group of persons having informal and usually close social relations
**³gang** (1856)
*transitive verb*
**1 a :** to assemble or operate simultaneously as a group **b :** to arrange in or produce as a gang
**2 :** to attack in a gang
*intransitive verb*
**:** to move or act as a gang
**gang bang** *noun* (1950)
**1 :** copulation by several persons in succession with the same passive partner — often considered vulgar
**2 :** GANG RAPE — often considered vulgar
— **gang–bang** *verb*

**gang–bang·er** \'gaŋ-ˌbaŋ-ər\ *noun* (circa 1972)
**:** a member of a street gang
**gang–bust·er** \'gaŋ-ˌbəs-tər\ *noun* (1940)
**:** one engaged in the aggressive breakup of organized criminal gangs
— **like gangbusters :** with great or excessive force or aggressiveness ⟨came on *like gangbusters*⟩; *also* **:** with great speed or success ⟨making money *like gangbusters* —Martha Hume⟩
**gangbusters** *also* **gangbuster** *adjective* (1971)
**:** outstandingly excellent or successful ⟨doesn't make her a *gangbusters* . . . player —Tim Allis⟩
— **gangbusters** *adverb*
**gang·er** \'gaŋ-ər\ *noun* (1849)
*British* **:** the foreman of a gang of workers
**gang hook** *noun* (circa 1934)
**:** two or three fishhooks with their shanks joined together
**gang·land** \'gaŋ-ˌland, -lənd\ *noun, often attributive* (1912)
**:** the world of organized crime
**gan·gling** \'gaŋ-gliŋ, -glən\ *adjective* [perhaps alteration of Scots *gangrel* vagrant, lanky person] (circa 1825)
**:** loosely and awkwardly built **:** LANKY
**gan·gli·on** \'gaŋ-glē-ən\ *noun, plural* **-glia** \-glē-ə\ *also* **-gli·ons** [Late Latin, from Greek] (circa 1681)
**1 :** a small cystic tumor connected either with a joint membrane or tendon sheath
**2 a :** a mass of nerve tissue containing nerve cells external to the brain or spinal cord; *also* **:** NUCLEUS 2b **b :** something likened to a nerve ganglion
— **gan·gli·on·at·ed** \'gaŋ-glē-ə-ˌnā-təd\ *adjective*
— **gan·gli·on·ic** \ˌgaŋ-glē-'ä-nik\ *adjective*
**gan·gli·o·side** \'gaŋ-glē-ə-ˌsīd\ *noun* [International Scientific Vocabulary *ganglion* + ²*-ose* + *-ide*] (1943)
**:** any of a group of glycolipids that yield a hexose sugar on hydrolysis and are found especially in the plasma membrane of cells of the gray matter
**gan·gly** \'gaŋ-glē\ *adjective* **gan·gli·er; -est** (1872)
**:** GANGLING
**gang·plank** \'gaŋ-ˌplaŋk\ *noun* (1846)
**:** a movable bridge used in boarding or leaving a ship at a pier
**gang·plow** \-ˌplaủ\ *noun* (1850)
**:** a plow designed to turn two or more furrows at one time
**gang rape** *noun* (1968)
**:** rape of one person by several attackers in succession
— **gang–rape** *transitive verb*
**gang·rel** \'gaŋ-(ə-)rəl\ *noun* [Middle English, from *gangen* to go, from Old English *gangan*] (14th century)
*Scottish* **:** VAGRANT
**¹gan·grene** \'gaŋ-ˌgrēn, gaŋ-', 'gan-ˌ, gan-'\ *noun* [Latin *gangraena*, from Greek *gangraina;* akin to Greek *gran* to gnaw] (1543)
**1 :** local death of soft tissues due to loss of blood supply
**2 :** pervasive decay or corruption **:** ROT ⟨moral *gangrene*⟩
— **gan·gre·nous** \'gaŋ-grə-nəs\ *adjective*
**²gangrene** *verb* **gan·grened; gan·gren·ing** (1607)
*transitive verb*
**:** to make gangrenous
*intransitive verb*
**:** to become gangrenous
**gang·ster** \'gaŋ-stər\ *noun* (1896)
**:** a member of a gang of criminals **:** RACKETEER
— **gang·ster·dom** \-dəm\ *noun*
— **gang·ster·ish** \-stə-rish\ *adjective*
— **gang·ster·ism** \-stə-ˌri-zəm\ *noun*
**gang–tackle** \'gaŋ-ˌta-kəl\ *transitive verb* (1951)

**:** to bring down (a ballcarrier in football) with several tacklers
**gangue** \'gaŋ\ *noun* [French, from German *Gang* vein of metal, from Old High German, act of going] (1809)
**:** the worthless rock or vein matter in which valuable metals or minerals occur
**gang up** *intransitive verb* (1925)
**1 :** to make a joint assault ⟨*ganged up* on him and beat him up⟩
**2 :** to combine for a specific purpose ⟨*ganged up* to raise prices⟩
**3 :** to exert group pressure ⟨the class *ganged up* against the teacher⟩
**gang·way** \'gaŋ-ˌwā\ *noun* (before 12th century)
**1 :** PASSAGEWAY; *especially* **:** a temporary way of planks
**2 a :** either of the sides of the upper deck of a ship **b :** the opening by which a ship is boarded **c :** GANGPLANK
**3** *British* **:** AISLE
**4 a :** a cross aisle dividing the front benches from the backbenches in the British House of Commons **b :** an aisle in the British House of Commons that separates government and opposition benches
**5 :** a clear passage through a crowd — often used as an interjection

**gan·is·ter** also **gan·nis·ter** \'ga-nə-stər\ noun [origin unknown] (1811)
: a fine-grained quartzite used in the manufacture of refractory brick

**gan·ja** \'gän-jə, 'gan-\ noun [Hindi gā̃jā, from Sanskrit gañjā hemp] (1689)
: a potent and selected preparation of marijuana used especially for smoking; broadly : MARIJUANA

**gan·net** \'ga-nət\ noun, plural **gannets** also **gannet** [Middle English ganet, from Old English ganot; akin to Old English gōs goose] (before 12th century)
: any of a genus (Morus of the family Sulidae) of large fish-eating seabirds that breed in colonies chiefly on offshore islands

**¹gan·oid** \'ga-ˌnȯid\ adjective [ultimately from Greek ganos brightness; akin to Greek gēthein to rejoice — more at JOY] (circa 1847)
: of, having, or being fish scales consisting of bone and an outer shiny layer resembling enamel; also : relating to or being fish with ganoid scales

**²ganoid** noun (circa 1839)
: a fish (as a sturgeon or gar) with ganoid scales

**gante·lope** or **gant·lope** \'gant-ˌlōp\ noun [modification of Swedish gatlopp, from Old Swedish gatulop, from gata road + lop course] (1646)
archaic : ²GAUNTLET

**gant·let** \'gȯnt-lət, 'gänt-\ variant of GAUNTLET

**gan·try** \'gan-trē\ noun, plural **gantries** [perhaps modification of Old North French gantier, from Latin cantherius trellis] (circa 1574)
**1** : a frame for supporting barrels
**2** : a frame structure raised on side supports so as to span over or around something: as **a** : a platform made to carry a traveling crane and supported by towers or side frames running on parallel tracks; also : a movable structure with platforms at different levels used for erecting and servicing rockets before launching **b** : a structure spanning several railroad tracks and displaying signals for each

**Gan·y·mede** \'ga-ni-ˌmēd\ noun [Latin Ganymedes, from Greek Ganymēdēs]
: a beautiful youth in classical mythology carried off to Olympus to be the cupbearer of the gods

**gaol** \'jā(ə)l\, **gaol·er** \'jā-lər\ chiefly British variant of JAIL, JAILER

**¹gap** \'gap\ noun [Middle English, from Old Norse, chasm, hole; akin to Old Norse gapa to gape] (14th century)
**1 a** : a break in a barrier (as a wall, hedge, or line of military defense) **b** : an assailable position
**2 a** : a mountain pass **b** : RAVINE
**3** : SPARK GAP
**4 a** : a separation in space **b** : an incomplete or deficient area ⟨a gap in her knowledge⟩
**5** : a break in continuity : HIATUS
**6** : a break in the vascular cylinder of a plant where a vascular trace departs from the central cylinder
**7** : lack of balance : DISPARITY ⟨the gap between imports and exports⟩
**8** : a wide difference in character or attitude ⟨the generation gap⟩
**9** : a problem caused by some disparity ⟨a communication gap⟩ ⟨credibility gap⟩
— **gap·py** \'ga-pē\ adjective

**²gap** verb **gapped; gap·ping** (1879)
transitive verb
**1** : to make an opening in
**2** : to adjust the space between the electrodes of (a spark plug)
intransitive verb
: to fall or stand open

**¹gape** \'gāp sometimes 'gap\ intransitive verb **gaped; gap·ing** [Middle English, from Old Norse gapa; perhaps akin to Latin hiare to gape, yawn — more at YAWN] (13th century)
**1 a** : to open the mouth wide **b** : to open or part widely ⟨holes gaped in the pavement⟩

**2** : to gaze stupidly or in openmouthed surprise or wonder
**3** : YAWN
— **gap·ing·ly** \'gā-piŋ-lē, 'ga-piŋ-\ adverb

**²gape** noun (1535)
**1** : an act of gaping: **a** : YAWN **b** : an openmouthed stare
**2** : an unfilled space or extent
**3 a** : the median margin-to-margin length of the open mouth **b** : the line along which the mandibles of a bird close **c** : the width of an opening
**4** plural but singular in construction **a** : a disease of birds and especially young birds in which gapeworms invade and irritate the trachea **b** : a fit of yawning

**gap·er** \'gā-pər sometimes 'ga-pər\ noun (circa 1637)
**1** : one that gapes
**2** : any of several large sluggish burrowing clams (families Myacidae and Mactridae) including several used for food

**gape·worm** \'gāp-ˌwərm sometimes 'gap-\ noun (1873)
: a nematode worm (Syngamus trachea) that causes gapes in birds

**gap·ing** \'gā-piŋ\ adjective (1588)
: wide open ⟨a gaping hole⟩

**gap junction** noun (1967)
: an area of contact between adjacent cells characterized by modification of the cell membranes for intercellular communication or transfer of low molecular-weight substances

**gapped scale** noun (1910)
: a musical scale derived from a larger system of tones by omitting certain tones

**gap–toothed** \'gap-ˌtütht\ adjective (1567)
: having gaps between the teeth

**¹gar** \'gär\ interjection [euphemism for God] (1598)
— used as a mild oath in the phrase by gar

**²gar** noun [short for garfish] (1765)
: any of various fishes that have an elongate body resembling that of a pike and long and narrow jaws: as **a** : NEEDLEFISH 1 **b** : any of several predaceous North American freshwater bony fishes (family Lepisosteidae) with heavy ganoid scales

**¹ga·rage** \gə-'räzh, -'räj; chiefly New England -'razh, -'raj; Canadian also -'razh, -'raj; British usually 'gar-(ˌ)äzh, -(ˌ)äj\ noun [French, act of docking, garage, from garer to dock, of Germanic origin; akin to Old High German biwarōn to protect — more at WARE] (1902)
: a shelter or repair shop for automotive vehicles

**²garage** transitive verb **ga·raged; ga·rag·ing** (1905)
: to keep or put in a garage

**ga·rage·man** \-ˌman\ noun (1919)
: one who works in a garage

**garage sale** noun (1964)
: a sale of used household or personal articles (as furniture, tools, or clothing) held on the seller's own premises

**ga·ram ma·sa·la** \gä-ˌräm-mə-'sä-lə\ noun [Hindi garam masālā, literally, hot spices] (1970)
: a pungent and aromatic mixture of ground spices used in Indian cooking

**Ga·rand rifle** \gə-'rand-, 'gar-ənd-\ noun [John C. Garand] (1931)
: M1 RIFLE

**¹garb** \'gärb\ noun [Middle French or Old Italian; Middle French garbe graceful contour, grace, from Old Italian garbo grace] (1599)
**1** obsolete : FASHION, MANNER
**2 a** : a style of apparel **b** : outward form : APPEARANCE

**²garb** transitive verb (1846)
: to cover with or as if with clothing ⟨garbed in T-shirt and blue jeans⟩

**gar·bage** \'gär-bij\ noun [Middle English, offal] (15th century)
**1 a** : food waste **b** : discarded or useless material

**2 a** : TRASH 1b **b** : inaccurate or useless data

**gar·bage·man** \-ˌman\ noun (1888)
: one who collects and hauls away garbage

**gar·ban·zo** \gär-'bän-(ˌ)zō, also -'ban-\ noun, plural **-zos** [Spanish] (1759)
: CHICKPEA

**garbanzo bean** noun (1944)
: CHICKPEA

**¹gar·ble** \'gär-bəl\ transitive verb **gar·bled; gar·bling** \-b(ə-)liŋ\ [Middle English garbelen, from Old Italian garbellare to sift, from Arabic gharbala, from Late Latin cribellare, from cribellum sieve; akin to Latin cernere to sift — more at CERTAIN] (15th century)
**1** archaic : CULL
**2** : to sift impurities from
**3 a** : to so alter or distort as to create a wrong impression or change the meaning ⟨garble a story⟩ **b** : to introduce textual error into (a message) by inaccurate encipherment, transmission, or decipherment
— **gar·bler** \-b(ə-)lər\ noun

**²garble** noun (1502)
**1** : the impurities removed from spices in sifting
**2** : an act or an instance of garbling

**gar·board** \'gär-ˌbōrd, -ˌbȯrd\ noun [obsolete Dutch gaarboord] (1627)
: the strake next to a ship's keel

**gar·boil** \-ˌbȯil\ noun [Middle French garbouil, from Old Italian garbuglio] (1548)
archaic : a confused disordered state : TURMOIL

**gar·çon** \gär-'sōⁿ\ noun, plural **garçons** \-'sōⁿ(z)\ [French, boy, servant, from Old French, of Germanic origin; akin to Old High German hrechjo fugitive — more at WRETCH] (1788)
: WAITER

**garde–man·ger** \ˌgärd-ˌmäⁿ-'zhä\ noun, plural **garde–mangers** \-'zhä(z)\ [French, literally, one who keeps food] (1928)
: a cook who specializes in the preparation of cold foods (as meats, fish, and salads)

**¹gar·den** \'gär-dᵊn\ noun [Middle English gardin, from Old North French, of Germanic origin; akin to Old High German gart enclosure — more at YARD] (13th century)
**1 a** : a plot of ground where herbs, fruits, flowers, or vegetables are cultivated **b** : a rich well-cultivated region **c** : a container (as a window box) planted with usually a variety of small plants
**2 a** : a public recreation area or park usually ornamented with plants and trees ⟨a botanical garden⟩ **b** : an open-air eating or drinking place **c** : a large hall for public entertainment
— **gar·den·ful** \-ˌfül\ noun

**²garden** verb **gar·dened; gar·den·ing** \'gär-dᵊn-iŋ, 'gärd-niŋ\ (1577)
intransitive verb
: to lay out or work in a garden
transitive verb
**1** : to make into a garden
**2** : to ornament with gardens
— **gar·den·er** \'gär-dᵊn-ər, 'gärd-nər\ noun

**³garden** adjective (1622)
**1** : of, relating to, used in, or frequenting a garden
**2 a** : of a kind grown in the open as distinguished from one more delicate ⟨garden plant⟩ **b** : commonly found : GARDEN-VARIETY

**garden apartment** noun (1946)
: a multiple-unit low-rise dwelling having considerable lawn or garden space

**garden city** noun (1898)
: a planned residential community with park and planted areas

**garden cress** noun (1577)
: an annual herb (Lepidium sativum) of the mustard family sometimes cultivated for its pungent basal leaves

**garden heliotrope** noun (circa 1902)

: a tall rhizomatous Old World valerian (*Valeriana officinalis*) widely cultivated for its fragrant tiny flowers and for its roots which yield the drug valerian

**gar·de·nia** \gär-'dē-nyə\ *noun* [New Latin, from Alexander *Garden* (died 1791) Scottish naturalist] (1760)
: any of a large genus (*Gardenia*) of Old World tropical trees and shrubs of the madder family with showy fragrant white or yellow flowers

**Garden of Eden** (1535)
: EDEN

**garden rocket** *noun* (1832)
: ARUGULA

**garden–variety** *adjective* (1928)
: ORDINARY, COMMONPLACE

**garde·robe** \'gär-ˌdrōb\ *noun* [Middle English, from Middle French; akin to Old North French *warderobe* wardrobe] (15th century)
**1** : a wardrobe or its contents
**2** : a private room : BEDROOM
**3** : PRIVY 1

**gar·dy·loo** \ˌgär-dē-'lü\ *interjection* [perhaps from French *garde à l'eau!* look out for the water!] (1622)
— used in Edinburgh as a warning cry when it was customary to throw slops from the windows into the streets

**Gar·eth** \'gar-əth\ *noun*
: a knight of the Round Table and nephew of King Arthur

**gar·fish** \'gär-ˌfish\ *noun* [Middle English *garfysshe*] (15th century)
: GAR

**Gar·gan·tua** \gär-'gan(t)-sh(ə-)wə\ *noun* [French]
: a gigantic king in Rabelais' *Gargantua* having a great capacity for food and drink

**gar·gan·tuan** \-wən\ *adjective, often capitalized* [*Gargantua*] (1596)
: of tremendous size or volume : GIGANTIC, COLOSSAL ⟨*gargantuan* waterfalls⟩

**¹gar·gle** \'gär-gəl\ *verb* **gar·gled; gar·gling** \-g(ə-)liŋ\ [Middle French *gargouiller*, of imitative origin] (1527)
*transitive verb*
**1 a** : to hold (a liquid) in the mouth or throat and agitate with air from the lungs **b** : to cleanse or disinfect (the oral cavity) in this manner
**2** : to utter with a gargling sound
*intransitive verb*
**1** : to use a gargle
**2** : to speak or sing as if gargling

**²gargle** *noun* (1657)
**1** : a liquid used in gargling
**2** : a sound or a like that of gargling

**gar·goyle** \'gär-ˌgóil\ *noun* [Middle English *gargoyl*, from Middle French *gargouille*; akin to Middle French *gargouiller*] (13th century)
**1 a** : a spout in the form of a grotesque human or animal figure projecting from a roof gutter to throw rainwater clear of a building **b** : a grotesquely carved figure
**2** : a person with an ugly face
— **gar·goyled** \-ˌgóild\ *adjective*

**gargoyle 1a**

**gar·i·bal·di** \ˌgar-ə-'bȯl-dē\ *noun* (1862)
: a woman's blouse copied from the red shirt worn by the Italian patriot Garibaldi

**ga·rigue** \gə-'rēg\ *noun* [French] (1896)
: a low open scrubland with many evergreen shrubs, low trees, aromatic herbs, and bunchgrasses found in poor or dry soil in the Mediterranean region

**gar·ish** \'gar-ish, 'ger-\ *adjective* [origin unknown] (1545)
**1** : clothed in vivid colors
**2 a** : excessively vivid : FLASHY **b** : offensively or distressingly bright : GLARING

**3** : tastelessly showy
*synonym* see GAUDY
— **gar·ish·ly** *adverb*
— **gar·ish·ness** *noun*

**¹gar·land** \'gär-lənd\ *noun* [Middle English, from Middle French *garlande*] (14th century)
**1** : WREATH, CHAPLET
**2** : ANTHOLOGY, COLLECTION

**²garland** *transitive verb* (15th century)
**1** : to form into a garland
**2** : to adorn with or as if with a garland

**gar·lic** \'gär-lik\ *noun* [Middle English *garlek*, from Old English *gārlēac*, from *gār* spear + *lēac* leek — more at GORE] (before 12th century)
**1** : a European bulbous herb (*Allium sativum*) of the lily family widely cultivated for its pungent compound bulbs much used in cookery; *broadly* : any plant of the same genus
**2** : a bulb of garlic
— **gar·licky** \-li-kē\ *adjective*

**gar·licked** \'gär-likt\ *adjective* (1950)
: containing or prepared with garlic

**garlic salt** *noun* (1927)
: a seasoning of ground dried garlic and salt

**¹gar·ment** \'gär-mənt\ *noun* [Middle English, from Middle French *garnement*, from Old French, from *garnir* to equip — more at GARNISH] (14th century)
: an article of clothing

**²garment** *transitive verb* (1547)
: to clothe with or as if with a garment

**garment bag** *noun* (1927)
: a bag used by travelers that folds in half and has a center handle for easy carrying

**¹gar·ner** \'gär-nər\ *noun* [Middle English, from Old French *gernier, grenier*, from Latin *granarium*, from *granum* grain — more at CORN] (12th century)
**1 a** : GRANARY **b** : a grain bin
**2** : something that is collected : ACCUMULATION

**²garner** *transitive verb* **gar·nered; gar·ner·ing** \'gärn-riŋ, 'gär-nə-\ (14th century)
**1 a** : to gather into storage **b** : to deposit as if in a granary ⟨volumes in which he has *garnered* the fruits of his lifetime labors —Reinhold Niebuhr⟩
**2 a** : to acquire by effort : EARN **b** : ACCUMULATE, COLLECT

**gar·net** \'gär-nət\ *noun* [Middle English *grenat*, from Middle French, from *grenat*, adjective, red like a pomegranate, from (*pomme*) *grenate* pomegranate] (14th century)
**1** : a brittle and more or less transparent usually red silicate mineral that has a vitreous luster, occurs mainly in crystals but also in massive form and in grains, is found commonly in gneiss and mica schist, and is used as a semiprecious stone and as an abrasive
**2** : a variable color averaging a dark red
— **gar·net·if·er·ous** \ˌgär-nə-'ti-f(ə-)rəs\ *adjective*

**garnet paper** *noun* (circa 1902)
: an abrasive paper with crushed garnet as the abrasive

**gar·ni·er·ite** \'gär-nē-ə-ˌrīt\ *noun* [Jules *Garnier* (died 1904) French geologist] (1875)
: a soft mineral consisting of hydrous nickel magnesium silicate and constituting an important ore of nickel

**¹gar·nish** \'gär-nish\ *transitive verb* [Middle English, from Middle French *garniss-*, stem of *garnir* to warn, equip, garnish, of Germanic origin; akin to Old High German *warnōn* to take heed — more at WARN] (14th century)
**1 a** : DECORATE, EMBELLISH **b** : to add decorative or savory touches to (food or drink)
**2** : to equip with accessories : FURNISH
**3** : GARNISHEE
*synonym* see ADORN

**²garnish** *noun* (1596)
**1** : EMBELLISHMENT, ORNAMENT
**2** : something (as lemon wedges or parsley) used to garnish food or drink

**3 a** : an unauthorized fee formerly extorted from a new inmate of an English jail **b** : a similar payment required of a new worker

**¹gar·nish·ee** \ˌgär-nə-'shē\ *noun* (1627)
: a person who is served with a legal process of garnishment

**²garnishee** *transitive verb* **-eed; -ee·ing** (circa 1876)
**1** : to serve with a garnishment
**2** : to take (as a debtor's wages) by legal authority

**gar·nish·ment** \'gär-nish-mənt\ *noun* (1550)
**1** : GARNISH
**2** : a legal summons or warning concerning the attachment of property to satisfy a debt
**3** : a stoppage of a specified sum from wages to satisfy a creditor

**gar·ni·ture** \'gär-ni-chər, -nə-ˌchùr\ *noun* [Middle French, equipment, alteration of Old French *garnesture*, from *garnir*] (1667)
**1** : EMBELLISHMENT, TRIMMING
**2** : a set of decorative objects (as vases, urns, or clocks)

**gar·pike** \'gär-ˌpīk\ *noun* (1776)
: GAR b

**gar·ret** \'gar-ət\ *noun* [Middle English *garette* watchtower, from Middle French *garite* watchtower, refuge, from Old French *garir*] (14th century)
: a room or unfinished part of a house just under the roof

**¹gar·ri·son** \'gar-ə-sən\ *noun* [Middle English *garisoun* protection, from Old French *garison*, from *garir* to protect, of Germanic origin; akin to Old High German *werien* to defend — more at WEIR] (15th century)
**1** : a military post; *especially* : a permanent military installation
**2** : the troops stationed at a garrison

**²garrison** *transitive verb* **gar·ri·soned; gar·ri·son·ing** \'gar-ə-s(ə-)niŋ\ (1569)
**1** : to station troops in
**2 a** : to assign as a garrison **b** : to occupy with troops

**garrison cap** *noun* (1944)
: a visorless folding cap worn as part of a military uniform — compare SERVICE CAP

**Gar·ri·son finish** \'gar-ə-sən-\ *noun* [probably from Edward "Snapper" *Garrison*, 19th century American jockey] (1935)
: a finish in which the winner comes from behind at the end

**garrison house** *noun* (1676)
**1** : a house fortified against Indian attack
**2** : BLOCKHOUSE
**3** : a house having the second story overhanging the first in the front

**garrison state** *noun* (1937)
: a state organized to serve primarily its own need for military security; *also* : a state maintained by military power

**gar·ron** \'gar-ən, gə-'rän\ *noun* [Irish *gearrán* & Scottish Gaelic *gearran*, gelding] (1540)
*Scottish & Irish* : a small sturdy workhorse

**¹gar·rote** *or* **ga·rotte** \gə-'rät, -'rōt; 'gar-ət\ *noun* [Spanish *garrote*] (1622)
**1 a** : a method of execution by strangulation **b** : the apparatus used
**2** : an implement (as a wire with a handle at each end) for strangulation

**²garrote** *or* **garotte** *transitive verb* **gar·rot·ed** *or* **ga·rott·ed; gar·rot·ing** *or* **ga·rott·ing** (1851)
: to strangle with or as if with a garrote
— **gar·rot·er** *noun*

**gar·ru·li·ty** \gə-'rü-lə-tē, ga-\ *noun* (1581)
: the quality or state of being garrulous

**gar·ru·lous** \'gar-ə-ləs *also* 'gar-yə-\ *adjective* [Latin *garrulus*, from *garrire* to chatter — more at CARE] (circa 1611)

\ə\ abut \ˀ\ kitten \ər\ further \a\ ash \ā\ ace
\ä\ mop, mar \aù\ out \ch\ chin \e\ bet \ē\ easy
\g\ go \i\ hit \ī\ ice \j\ job \ŋ\ sing \ō\ go
\ò\ law \òi\ boy \th\ thin \th\ the \ü\ loot \ù\ foot
\y\ yet \zh\ vision *see also* Guide to Pronunciation

**1** : given to prosy, rambling, or tedious loquacity : pointlessly or annoyingly talkative **2** : WORDY 1 ⟨*garrulous* speeches⟩
**synonym** see TALKATIVE
— **gar·ru·lous·ly** *adverb*
— **gar·ru·lous·ness** *noun*

¹**gar·ter** \'gär-tər\ *noun* [Middle English, from Old North French *gartier,* from *garet* bend of the knee, of Celtic origin; akin to Welsh *gar* shank] (14th century)
**1 a** : a band worn to hold up a stocking or sock **b** : a band worn to hold up a shirt sleeve **c** : a strap hanging from a girdle or corset to support a stocking
**2** *capitalized* **a** : the British Order of the Garter; *also* : the blue velvet garter that is its badge **b** : membership in the order

²**garter** *transitive verb* (15th century)
: to support with or as if with a garter

**garter snake** *noun* (1769)
: any of a genus (*Thamnophis*) of harmless viviparous American snakes with longitudinal stripes on the back

**garth** \'gärth\ *noun* [Middle English, from Old Norse *garthr* yard; akin to Old High German *gart* enclosure — more at YARD] (14th century)
: a small yard or enclosure : CLOSE

**gar·vey** \'gär-vē\ *noun, plural* **garveys** [probably from the name *Garvey*] (circa 1896)
: a small scow especially of the New Jersey coast

¹**gas** \'gas\ *noun, plural* **gas·es** *also* **gas·ses** [New Latin, alteration of Latin *chaos* space, chaos] (1779)
**1** : a fluid (as air) that has neither independent shape nor volume but tends to expand indefinitely
**2 a** : a combustible gas or gaseous mixture for fuel or lighting; *especially* : NATURAL GAS **b** : a gaseous product of digestion; *also* : discomfort from this **c** : a gas or gaseous mixture used to produce anesthesia **d** : a substance that can be used to produce a poisonous, asphyxiating, or irritant atmosphere
**3** : empty talk : BOMBAST
**4** : GASOLINE; *also* : the accelerator pedal of an automotive vehicle
**5** : driving force : ENERGY ⟨I was young, and full of *gas* —H. L. Mencken⟩ ⟨ran out of *gas* in the seventh inning⟩
**6** *slang* : something that gives pleasure : DELIGHT ⟨the party was a *gas*⟩

²**gas** *verb* **gassed; gas·sing** (1852)
*intransitive verb*
**1** : to talk idly or garrulously
**2** : to give off gas
**3** : to fill the tank (as of an automobile) with gasoline — usually used with *up*
*transitive verb*
**1** : to supply with gas or especially gasoline ⟨*gas* up the car⟩
**2 a** : to treat chemically with gas **b** : to poison or otherwise affect adversely with gas
**3** *slang* : to please greatly

**gas·bag** \'gas-,bag\ *noun* (1827)
**1** : a bag for holding gas
**2** : an idle or garrulous talker

**gas chamber** *noun* (1945)
: a chamber in which prisoners are executed by poison gas

**gas chromatograph** *noun* (1958)
: an instrument used to separate a sample into components in gas chromatography

**gas chromatography** *noun* (1952)
: chromatography in which the sample mixture is vaporized and injected into a stream of carrier gas (as nitrogen or helium) moving through a column containing a stationary phase composed of a liquid or particulate solid and is separated into its component compounds according to their affinity for the stationary phase
— **gas chromatographic** *adjective*

**gas·con** \'gas-kən\ *noun* (14th century)

**1** *capitalized* **a** : a native of Gascony **b** : the Romance speech of Gascony
**2** : a boastful swaggering person
— **Gascon** *adjective*

**gas·co·nade** \,gas-kə-'nād\ *noun* [French *gasconnade,* from *gasconner* to boast, from *gascon* gascon, boaster] (1709)
: BRAVADO, BOASTING
— **gasconade** *intransitive verb*
— **gas·con·ad·er** *noun*

**gas·eous** \'ga-sē-əs, 'ga-shəs\ *adjective* (1799)
**1** : having the form of or being gas; *also* : of or relating to gases
**2 a** : lacking substance or solidity **b** : GASSY 3 ⟨trick phrases and *gaseous* circumlocutions —Edwin Newman⟩
— **gas·eous·ness** *noun*

**gas fitter** *noun* (circa 1858)
: a worker who installs or repairs gas pipes and appliances

**gas gangrene** *noun* (1914)
: progressive gangrene marked by impregnation of the dead and dying tissue with gas and caused by one or more toxin-producing clostridia

**gas–guz·zler** \'gas-'gəz-lər, -'gə-zə-\ *noun* (1973)
: a usually large automobile that gets relatively poor mileage
— **gas–guz·zling** \-liŋ\ *adjective*

¹**gash** \'gash\ *noun* (1548)
**1** : a deep long cut in flesh
**2** : a deep narrow depression or cut ⟨cut a *gash* through the forest⟩ ⟨a *gash* in the hull⟩

²**gash** *verb* [alteration of Middle English *garsen,* from Old North French *garser,* from (assumed) Vulgar Latin *charissare,* from Greek *charassein* to scratch, engrave] (1570)
*transitive verb*
: to make a gash in
*intransitive verb*
: to make a gash : CUT

³**gash** *adjective* [origin unknown] (1706)
**1** *chiefly Scottish* : KNOWING, WITTY
**2** *chiefly Scottish* : well-dressed : TRIM

**gas·hold·er** \'gas-,hōl-dər\ *noun* (1802)
: a container for gas; *especially* : a huge cylindrical tank for storing fuel gas under pressure

**gas·house** \-,haus\ *noun* (1880)
: GASWORKS

**gas·i·fi·ca·tion** \,ga-sə-fə-'kā-shən\ *noun* (1812)
: conversion into gas; *especially* : conversion of coal into natural gas

**gas·i·fy** \'ga-sə-,fī\ *verb* **-i·fied; -i·fy·ing** (circa 1828)
*transitive verb*
: to convert into gas ⟨*gasify* coal⟩
*intransitive verb*
: to become gaseous
— **gas·i·fi·er** \'ga-sə-,fī(-ə)r\ *noun*

**gas·ket** \'gas-kət\ *noun* [perhaps modification of French *garcette*] (circa 1889)
: a material (as rubber) or a member (as an O-ring) used to make a joint fluid-tight

**gas·kin** \'gas-kən\ *noun* [probably short for *galligaskins*] (1573)
**1** *plural, obsolete* : HOSE, BREECHES
**2** : a part of the hind leg of a quadruped between the stifle and the hock — see HORSE illustration

**gas·light** \'gas-,līt, -'līt\ *noun* (1808)
**1** : light made by burning illuminating gas
**2** : a gas flame or gas lighting fixture

**gas–liquid chromatography** *noun* (1952)
: gas chromatography in which the stationary phase is a liquid
— **gas–liquid chromatographic** *adjective*

**gas·lit** \-,lit, -'lit\ *adjective* (1837)
: illuminated by gaslight

**gas log** *noun* (1885)
: a hollow perforated imitation log used as a gas burner in a fireplace

**gas mask** *noun* (1915)

: a mask connected to a chemical air filter and used to protect the face and lungs from toxic gases; *broadly* : RESPIRATOR 1

**gas·o·gene** \'ga-sə-,jēn\ *noun* [French *gazogène,* from *gaz* gas (from New Latin *gas*) + *-o-* + *-gène* -gen] (circa 1853)
**1** : a portable apparatus for carbonating liquids
**2** : an apparatus carried by a vehicle to produce gas for fuel by partial burning of charcoal or wood

**gas·o·hol** \'ga-sə-,hol\ *noun* [blend of *gasoline* and *alcohol*] (1977)
: a fuel consisting of a blend usually of 10 percent ethyl alcohol and 90 percent gasoline

**gas oil** *noun* (1901)
: a hydrocarbon oil used as a fuel oil; *especially* : a petroleum distillate intermediate in boiling range and viscosity between kerosene and lubricating oil

**gas·olier** \,ga-sə-'lir\ *noun* [alteration of *gaselier,* from *gas* + *-elier* (as in *chandelier*)] (1905)
: a gaslight chandelier

**gas·o·line** *also* **gas·o·lene** \'ga-sə-,lēn, ,ga-sə-'\ *also* -zə-\ *noun* [¹*gas* + ²*-ol* + ²*-ine* or *-ene*] (1865)
: a volatile flammable liquid hydrocarbon mixture used as a fuel especially for internal combustion engines and usually blended from several products of natural gas and petroleum
— **gas·o·lin·ic** \,ga-sə-'lē-nik, -'li-\ *adjective*

**gas·om·e·ter** \ga-'sä-mə-tər\ *noun* [French *gazomètre,* from *gaz* + *-o-* + *-mètre* -meter] (1808)
**1** : GASHOLDER
**2** : a laboratory apparatus for holding and measuring gases

**gas–operated** *adjective* (1944)
*of a firearm* : using part of the force of expanding propellant gases to operate the action

**gasp** \'gasp\ *verb* [Middle English; akin to Old Norse *geispa* to yawn] (14th century)
*intransitive verb*
**1** : to catch the breath convulsively and audibly (as with shock)
**2** : to breathe laboriously
*transitive verb*
: to utter in a gasping manner
— **gasp** *noun*

**gasp·er** \'gäs-pə(r)\ *noun* (1914)
*slang British* : CIGARETTE

**gas plant** *noun* (circa 1909)
: FRAXINELLA

**gas ring** *noun* (1901)
: a ring-shaped portable gas burner for cooking

**gassed** \'gast\ *adjective* (circa 1925)
: DRUNK 1

**gas·ser** \'ga-sər\ *noun* (circa 1944)
*slang* : something outstanding

**gas station** *noun* (1925)
: SERVICE STATION 1

**gas·sy** \'ga-sē\ *adjective* **gas·si·er; -est** (1757)
**1** : full of or containing gas
**2** : having the characteristics of gas
**3** : characterized by many words but little content : emptily verbose
— **gas·si·ly** \'ga-sə-lē\ *adverb*
— **gas·si·ness** *noun*

**gast** \'gast\ *transitive verb* [Middle English, from *gast, gost* ghost — more at GHOST] (14th century)
*obsolete* : SCARE ⟨*gasted* by the noise I made, full suddenly he fled —Shakespeare⟩

**Gast·ar·beit·er** \'gast-(,)är-,bī-tər\ *noun, plural* **Gastarbeiter** *also* **Gastarbeiters** [German, from *Gast* guest + *Arbeiter* worker] (1970)
: a foreign worker especially in Germany

**gas·ter** \'gas-tər\ *noun* [Greek *gastēr*] (circa 1909)
: the enlarged part of the abdomen behind the pedicel in hymenopterous insects (as ants)

**gas·tight** \'gas-'tīt\ adjective (1831)
: impervious to gas
— **gas·tight·ness** noun

**gast·ness** \'gas(t)-nəs\ noun (14th century)
obsolete : FRIGHT, TERROR

**gastr-** or **gastro-** also **gastri-** combining form [Greek, from gastr-, gastēr]
1 : stomach ⟨gastrectomy⟩
2 : gastric and ⟨gastrointestinal⟩

**gas·trea** also **gas·traea** \ga-'strē-ə\ noun [New Latin, from Greek gastr-, gastēr] (1879)
: a hypothetical metazoan ancestral form corresponding in organization to a simple invaginated gastrula

**gas·trec·to·my** \ga-'strek-tə-mē\ noun, plural **-mies** [International Scientific Vocabulary] (1886)
: surgical removal of all or part of the stomach

**gas·tric** \'gas-trik\ adjective [Greek gastr-, gastēr; alteration of (assumed) Greek grastēr, from Greek gran to gnaw, eat] (1656)
: of or relating to the stomach

**gastric gland** noun (1900)
: any of various glands in the walls of the stomach that secrete gastric juice

**gastric juice** noun (circa 1736)
: a thin watery acid digestive fluid secreted by glands in the mucous membrane of the stomach

**gastric ulcer** noun (circa 1910)
: a peptic ulcer situated in the stomach

**gas·trin** \'gas-trən\ noun (1905)
: any of various polypeptide hormones that are secreted by the gastric mucosa and induce secretion of gastric juice

**gas·tri·tis** \ga-'strī-təs\ noun (1806)
: inflammation especially of the mucous membrane of the stomach

**gas·troc·ne·mi·us** \,gas-(,)träk-'nē-mē-əs, -trək-\ noun, plural **-mii** \-mē-,ī\ [New Latin, from Greek gastroknēmē calf of the leg, from gastr- + knēmē shank — more at HAM] (1676)
: the largest and most superficial muscle of the calf of the leg arising by two heads from the condyles of the femur and attaching to a tendon that becomes part of the Achilles tendon

**gas·tro·du·o·de·nal** \,gas-trō-,d(y)ü-ə-'dē-nᵊl, -d(y)ü-'ä-dᵊn-əl\ adjective (1854)
: of, relating to, or involving the stomach and the duodenum

**gas·tro·en·ter·i·tis** \,gas-trō-,en-tə-'rī-təs\ noun (circa 1829)
: inflammation of the lining membrane of the stomach and the intestines

**gas·tro·en·ter·ol·o·gy** \-,en-tə-'rä-lə-jē\ noun [International Scientific Vocabulary] (circa 1904)
: a branch of medicine concerned with the structure, functions, diseases, and pathology of the stomach and intestines
— **gas·tro·en·ter·o·log·i·cal** \-rə-'lä-ji-kəl\ adjective
— **gas·tro·en·ter·ol·o·gist** \-,en-tə-'rä-lə-jist\ noun

**gas·tro·esoph·a·ge·al** \'gas-trō-i-,sä-fə-'jē-əl\ adjective (circa 1909)
: of, relating to, or involving the stomach and esophagus

**gas·tro·in·tes·ti·nal** \,gas-trō-in-'tes-tə-nᵊl, -'tes(t)-nəl\ adjective (1831)
: of, relating to, affecting, or including both stomach and intestine ⟨gastrointestinal tract⟩

**gas·tro·lith** \'gas-trə-,lith\ noun (1854)
: a stone or pebble ingested by an animal and functioning to grind food in gastric digestion

**gas·tro·nome** \'gas-trə-,nōm\ noun [French, back-formation from gastronomie] (1823)
: a lover of good food; especially : one with a serious interest in gastronomy
**synonym** see EPICURE

**gas·tro·nom·i·cal·ly** \,gas-trə-'nä-mi-k(ə-)lē\ adverb (1875)
1 : from the standpoint of gastronomy ⟨gastronomically fashionable⟩

2 : toward gastronomy ⟨gastronomically inclined⟩

**gas·tron·o·mist** \ga-'strä-nə-mist\ noun (1825)
: GASTRONOME

**gas·tron·o·my** \-mē\ noun [French gastronomie, from Greek Gastronomia, title of a 4th century B.C. poem, from gastro- gastr- + -nomia -nomy] (1814)
1 : the art or science of good eating
2 : culinary customs or style
— **gas·tro·nom·ic** \,gas-trə-'nä-mik\ also **gas·tro·nom·i·cal** \-mi-kəl\ adjective

**gas·tro·pod** \'gas-trə-,päd\ noun [New Latin Gastropoda, class name] (1826)
: any of a large class (Gastropoda) of mollusks (as snails and slugs) usually with a univalve shell or none and a distinct head bearing sensory organs
— **gastropod** adjective

**gas·tro·scope** \'gas-trə-,skōp\ noun [International Scientific Vocabulary] (1888)
: an instrument for viewing the interior of the stomach
— **gas·tro·scop·ic** \,gas-trə-'skä-pik\ adjective
— **gas·tros·co·pist** \ga-'sträs-kə-pist\ noun
— **gas·tros·co·py** \-pē\ noun

**gas·tro·trich** \'gas-trə-,trik\ noun [ultimately from Greek gastr- + trich-, thrix hair — more at TRICH-] (1940)
: any of a phylum (Gastrotricha) of minute aquatic pseudocoelomate animals that usually have a spiny or scaly cuticle and cilia on the ventral surface

**gas·tro·vas·cu·lar** \,gas-trō-'vas-kyə-lər\ adjective [International Scientific Vocabulary] (1876)
: functioning in both digestion and circulation ⟨the gastrovascular cavity of a coelenterate⟩

**gas·tru·la** \'gas-trə-lə\ noun, plural **-las** or **-lae** \-,lē, -,lī\ [New Latin, from gastr-] (1877)
: an early metazoan embryo in which the ectoderm, mesoderm, and endoderm are established either by invagination of the blastula (as in fish and amphibians) to form a multilayered cellular cup with a blastopore opening into the archenteron or by differentiation of the blastodisc (as in reptiles, birds, and mammals) and inward cellular migration — compare BLASTULA, MORULA
— **gas·tru·lar** \-lər\ adjective

**gas·tru·la·tion** \,gas-trə-'lā-shən\ noun (1879)
: the process of becoming or of forming a gastrula
— **gas·tru·late** \'gas-trə-,lāt\ intransitive verb

**gas turbine** noun (1904)
: an internal combustion engine in which expanding gases from the combustion chamber drive the blades of a turbine

**gas·works** \'gas-,wərks\ noun plural but singular or plural in construction (1819)
: a plant for manufacturing gas and especially illuminating gas

¹**gat** \'gat\ archaic past of GET

²**gat** noun [probably from Dutch, literally, hole; akin to Old English geat gate] (1723)
: a natural or artificial channel or passage

³**gat** noun [short for Gatling gun] (1904)
slang : HANDGUN

¹**gate** \'gāt\ noun [Middle English, from Old English geat; akin to Old Norse gat opening] (before 12th century)
1 : an opening in a wall or fence
2 : a city or castle entrance often with defensive structures (as towers)
3 **a** : the frame or door that closes a gate **b** : a movable barrier (as at a grade crossing)

4 **a** : a means of entrance or exit **b** : STARTING GATE **c** : an area (as at a railroad station or an airport) for departure or arrival **d** : a space between two markers through which a competitor must pass in the course of a slalom race
5 **a** : a door, valve, or other device for controlling the passage especially of a fluid **b** (1) : an electronic switch that allows or prevents the flow of current in a circuit (2) : an electrode in a field-effect transistor that modulates the current flowing through the transistor according to the voltage applied to the electrode — compare DRAIN, SOURCE **c** : a device (as in a computer) that outputs a signal when specified input conditions are met ⟨logic gate⟩ **d** : a molecular mechanism controlling the flow of a fluid, ion, or molecule through a channel especially in a cell membrane
6 slang : DISMISSAL ⟨gave him the gate⟩
7 : the total admission receipts or the number of spectators (as at a sports event)

²**gate** transitive verb **gat·ed**; **gat·ing** (1835)
1 British : to punish by confinement to a campus or dormitory
2 : to supply with a gate
3 : to control by means of a gate

³**gate** noun [Middle English, from Old Norse gata road; akin to Old High German gazza road] (13th century)
1 archaic : WAY, PATH
2 dialect : METHOD, STYLE

**-gate** \,gāt\ noun combining form [Watergate]
: usually political scandal often involving the concealment of wrongdoing ⟨Irangate⟩

**gâ·teau** or **ga·teau** \(,)gä-'tō\ noun, plural **gâ·teaux** or **ga·teaux** \-'tō(z)\ also **ga·teaus** [French, from Old French gastel, probably of Germanic origin; akin to Old English wist sustenance, food] (1845)
1 : food baked and served in the form of a cake ⟨eggplant gâteau⟩
2 : a rich or fancy cake

**gate–crash·er** \'gāt-,kra-shər\ noun (1921)
: a person who enters, attends, or participates without ticket or invitation
— **gate–crash** verb

**gate·fold** \-,fōld\ noun (1946)
: FOLDOUT; especially : one with a single fold that opens out like a gate

**gate·house** \-,haus\ noun (14th century)
: a building or house connected or associated with a gate

**gate·keep·er** \-,kē-pər\ noun (1572)
1 : one that tends or guards a gate
2 : a person who controls access
— **gate·keep·ing** \-piŋ\ adjective

**gate-leg table** \'gāt-,leg-, -,lāg-\ noun (1926)
: a table with drop leaves supported by movable paired legs

**gate·post** \'gāt-,pōst\ noun (1522)
: the post to which a gate is hung or the one against which it closes

**gate·way** \-,wā\ noun (1707)
1 : an opening for a gate
2 : GATE 4a

gateleg table

¹**gath·er** \'ga-thər also 'ge-\ verb **gath·ered**; **gath·er·ing** \'gath-riŋ, 'ga-thə-\ [Middle English gaderen, from Old English gaderian; akin to Sanskrit gadhya what one clings to — more at GOOD] (before 12th century)
transitive verb
1 : to bring together : COLLECT ⟨tried to gather a crowd⟩ ⟨gathered firewood⟩

\ə\ abut \ᵊ\ kitten \ər\ further \a\ ash \ā\ ace \ä\ mop, mar \au̇\ out \ch\ chin \e\ bet \ē\ easy \g\ go \i\ hit \ī\ ice \j\ job \ŋ\ sing \ō\ go \ȯ\ law \ȯi\ boy \th\ thin \th\ the \ü\ loot \u̇\ foot \y\ yet \zh\ vision    see also Guide to Pronunciation

**2 a :** PICK, HARVEST ⟨*gather* flowers⟩ **b :** to pick up or accumulate as if by harvesting ⟨*gathering* ideas for the project⟩ **c :** to assemble (the signatures of a book) in sequence for binding
**3 :** to serve as a center of attraction for
**4 :** to effect the collection of (as tax)
**5 a :** to summon up ⟨*gathered* his courage⟩ **b :** to gain by gradual increase **:** ACCUMULATE ⟨*gather* speed⟩ **c :** to prepare (as oneself) by mustering strength
**6 :** to reach a conclusion often intuitively from hints or through inferences ⟨I *gather* that you want to leave⟩
**7 a :** to pull (fabric) along a line of stitching so as to draw into puckers **b :** to draw about or close to something ⟨*gathering* her cloak about her⟩ **c :** to bring together the parts of **d :** to haul in
*intransitive verb*
**1 a :** to come together in a body **b :** to cluster around a focus of attraction
**2 a :** to swell and fill with pus **b :** GROW, INCREASE ☆
— **gath·er·er** \-thər-ər\ *noun*
**²gather** *noun* (1555)
**1 :** something gathered: as **a :** a puckering in cloth made by gathering **b :** a mass of molten glass collected for use in glassblowing
**2 :** an act or instance of gathering
**gath·er·ing** *noun* (before 12th century)
**1 :** ASSEMBLY, MEETING
**2 :** a suppurating swelling **:** ABCESS
**3 :** the collecting of food or raw materials from the wild
**4 :** COLLECTION, COMPILATION
**5 :** a gather in cloth
**Gat·ling gun** \'gat-liŋ-\ *noun* [Richard J. *Gatling* (died 1903) American inventor] (1867)
**:** a machine gun with a revolving cluster of barrels fired once each per revolution
**ga·tor** \'gā-tər\ *noun* (1844)
**:** ALLIGATOR
**gauche** \'gōsh\ *adjective, sometimes* **gauch·er** *sometimes* **gauch·est** [French, literally, left] (1751)
**1 a :** lacking social experience or grace; *also* **:** not tactful **:** CRUDE ⟨it would be *gauche* to mention the subject⟩ **b :** crudely made or done ⟨a *gauche* turn of phrase⟩
**2 :** not planar ⟨*gauche* conformation of molecules⟩
*synonym* see AWKWARD
— **gauche·ly** *adverb*
— **gauche·ness** *noun*
**gau·che·rie** \ˌgō-sh(ə-)'rē\ *noun* [French] (1826)
**:** a tactless or awkward act
**Gau·cher's disease** \ˌ(ˌ)gō-'shäz-\ *noun* [Philippe C. E. *Gaucher* (died 1918) French physician] (1902)
**:** a rare hereditary disorder of lipid metabolism caused by an enzyme deficiency and characterized by enlargement of the spleen and neurological impairment
**gau·cho** \'gaù-(ˌ)chō\ *noun, plural* **gauchos** [American Spanish] (1824)
**:** a cowboy of the South American pampas
**gaud** \'gòd, 'gäd\ *noun* [Middle English *gaude*] (15th century)
**:** ORNAMENT, TRINKET
**gaud·ery** \'gò-də-rē, 'gä-\ *noun* (circa 1598)
**:** showy ornamentation; *especially* **:** personal finery
**¹gau·dy** \'gò-dē, 'gä-\ *adjective* **gaud·i·er; -est** (1582)
**1 :** ostentatiously or tastelessly ornamented
**2 :** marked by dazzling brilliance, showiness, or extravagance ⟨*gaudy* praise⟩ ☆
— **gaud·i·ly** \'gò-dᵊl-ē, 'gä-\ *adverb*
— **gaud·i·ness** \'gò-dē-nəs, 'gä-\ *noun*
**²gaudy** *noun, plural* **gaudies** [probably from Latin *gaudium* joy — more at JOY] (1651)
**:** a feast or entertainment especially in the form of an annual college dinner at a British university

**gauf·fer** \'gä-fər, 'gó-, 'gō-\ *variant of* GOFFER
**¹gauge** \'gāj\ *noun* [Middle English *gauge*, from Old North French] (15th century)
**1 a :** a measurement (as of linear dimension) according to some standard or system: as (1) **:** the distance between the rails of a railroad (2) **:** the size of a shotgun barrel's inner diameter nominally expressed as the number of lead balls each just fitting that diameter required to make a pound ⟨a 12-*gauge* shotgun⟩ (3) **:** the thickness of a thin material (as sheet metal or plastic film) (4) **:** the diameter of a slender object (as wire or a hypodermic needle) (5) **:** the fineness of a knitted fabric expressed by the number of loops per unit width **b :** DIMENSIONS, SIZE **c :** MEASURE 1 ⟨surveys are a *gauge* of public sentiment⟩
**2 :** an instrument for or a means of measuring or testing: as **a :** an instrument for measuring a dimension or for testing mechanical accuracy **b :** an instrument with a graduated scale or dial for measuring or indicating quantity
**3 :** relative position of a ship with reference to another ship and the wind
**4 :** a function introduced into a field equation to produce a convenient form of the equation but having no observable physical consequences
*synonym* see STANDARD
**²gauge** *transitive verb* **gauged; gaug·ing** (15th century)
**1 a :** to measure precisely the size, dimensions, or other measurable quantity of **b :** to determine the capacity or contents of **c :** ESTIMATE, JUDGE ⟨hard to *gauge* his moods⟩
**2 a :** to check for conformity to specifications or limits **b :** to measure off or set out
**gauged** \'gājd\ *adjective* (1823)
*of masonry* **:** dressed to size
**gaug·er** \'gā-jər\ *noun* (15th century)
**1 :** one that gauges
**2** *chiefly British* **:** an exciseman who inspects dutiable bulk goods
**gauge theory** *noun* (1925)
**:** any of several theories in physics that explain the transmission of a fundamental force between two interacting particles by the exchange of an elementary particle
**Gaul** \'gòl\ *noun* (1625)
**1 :** a Celt of ancient Gaul
**2 :** FRENCHMAN
**¹Gaul·ish** \'gò-lish\ *adjective* (1659)
**:** of or relating to the Gauls or their language or land
**²Gaulish** *noun* (1668)
**:** the Celtic language of the ancient Gauls — see INDO-EUROPEAN LANGUAGES table
**Gaull·ism** \'gō-ˌli-zəm, 'gò-\ *noun* [Charles de *Gaulle*] (1943)
**1 :** a French political movement during World War II led by Charles de Gaulle in opposition to the Vichy regime
**2 :** a postwar French political movement led by Charles de Gaulle
— **Gaull·ist** \-list\ *adjective or noun*
**gault** \'gòlt\ *noun* [probably of Scandinavian origin; akin to Old Norse *gald* hard-packed snow] (1575)
*chiefly British* **:** a heavy thick clay soil
**gaum** \'gòm, 'gäm\ *transitive verb* [origin unknown] (1796)
*dialect* **:** SMUDGE, SMEAR
**gaunt** \'gònt, 'gänt\ *adjective* [Middle English] (15th century)
**1 :** excessively thin and angular ⟨a long *gaunt* face⟩
**2 :** BARREN, DESOLATE
*synonym* see LEAN
— **gaunt·ly** *adverb*
— **gaunt·ness** *noun*
**¹gaunt·let** \'gònt-lət, 'gänt-\ *noun* [Middle English, from Middle French *gantelet*, diminutive of *gant* glove, of Germanic origin; akin to Middle Dutch *want* glove, Old Norse *vǫttr*] (15th century)

**1 :** a glove worn with medieval armor to protect the hand
**2 :** any of various protective gloves used especially in industry
**3 :** an open challenge (as to combat) — used in phrases like *throw down the gauntlet*
**4 :** a dress glove extending above the wrist
— **gaunt·let·ed** \-lə-təd\ *adjective*
**²gauntlet** *noun* [by folk etymology from *gantelope*] (1661)
**1 :** a severe trial **:** ORDEAL ⟨ran the *gauntlet* of criticism and censure⟩
**2 a :** a double file of men facing each other and armed with clubs or other weapons with which to strike at an individual who is made to run between them — used with *run* **b :** a line (as of guards or well-wishers)
**gaur** \'gaùr\ *noun* [Hindi, from Sanskrit *gaura*; akin to Sanskrit *go* bull, cow — more at COW] (1806)
**:** a large wild ox (*Bos gaurus*) of India and southeast Asia with a broad forehead and short thick curved horns

gaur

**gauss** \'gaùs\ *noun, plural* **gauss** *also* **gauss·es** [Karl F. *Gauss*] (1882)
**:** the centimeter-gram-second unit of magnetic flux density that is equal to $1 \times 10^{-4}$ tesla
**Gauss·ian** \'gaù-sē-ən\ *adjective* [Karl F. *Gauss*] (1905)
**:** being or having the shape of a Gaussian curve or a Gaussian distribution
**Gaussian curve** *noun* (1905)
**:** NORMAL CURVE
**Gaussian distribution** *noun* (1905)
**:** NORMAL DISTRIBUTION
**gauze** \'gòz\ *noun* [Middle French *gaze*] (1561)
**1 a :** a thin often transparent fabric used chiefly for clothing or draperies **b :** a loosely woven cotton surgical dressing **c :** a firm woven fabric of metal or plastic filaments
**2 :** HAZE

---

☆ **SYNONYMS**
**Gather, collect, assemble, congregate** mean to come or bring together into a group, mass, or unit. GATHER is the most general term for bringing or coming together from a spread-out or scattered state ⟨a crowd quickly *gathered*⟩. COLLECT often implies careful selection or orderly arrangement ⟨*collected* books on gardening⟩. ASSEMBLE implies an ordered union or organization of persons or things often for a definite purpose ⟨experts *assembled* for a conference⟩. CONGREGATE implies a spontaneous flocking together into a crowd or huddle ⟨*congregating* under shelter in a storm⟩. See in addition INFER.

**Gaudy, tawdry, garish, flashy, meretricious** mean vulgarly or cheaply showy. GAUDY implies a tasteless use of overly bright, often clashing colors or excessive ornamentation ⟨circus performers in *gaudy* costumes⟩. TAWDRY applies to what is at once gaudy and cheap and sleazy ⟨*tawdry* saloons⟩. GARISH describes what is distressingly or offensively bright ⟨*garish* neon signs⟩. FLASHY implies an effect of brilliance quickly and easily seen to be shallow or vulgar ⟨a *flashy* nightclub act⟩. MERETRICIOUS stresses falsity and may describe a tawdry show that beckons with a false allure or promise ⟨a *meretricious* wasteland of casinos and bars⟩.

— **gauze·like** \-ˌlīk\ *adjective*
— **gauz·i·ly** \ˈgȯ-zə-lē\ *adverb*
— **gauzy** \-zē\ *adjective*
**ga·vage** \gə-ˈväzh, gä-\ *noun* [French, from *gaver* to stuff, force-feed, from Middle French dialect (Picardy) *gave* gullet, crop] (1889)
: introduction of material into the stomach by a tube
**gave** *past of* GIVE
¹**gav·el** \ˈga-vəl\ *noun* [Middle English, from Old English *gafol*; akin to Old English *giefan* to give] (before 12th century)
: rent or tribute in medieval England
²**gavel** *noun* [origin unknown] (circa 1859)
: a mallet used (as by a presiding officer or auctioneer) for commanding attention or confirming an action (as a vote or sale)
³**gavel** *transitive verb* **-eled** *or* **-elled; -el·ing** *or* **-el·ling** \ˈgav-liŋ, ˈga-və-\ (1925)
: to bring or force by use of a gavel ⟨*gaveled* the audience to silence⟩
**gav·el·kind** \ˈga-vəl-ˌkīnd\ *noun* [Middle English *gavelkynde*, from ¹*gavel* + *kinde* kind] (14th century)
: a tenure of land existing chiefly in Kent from Anglo-Saxon times until 1925 and providing for division of an intestate's estate equally among the sons or other heirs
**gavel–to–gavel** *adjective* (1968)
: extending from the beginning to the end of a meeting or session ⟨*gavel-to-gavel* television coverage⟩
**ga·vi·al** \ˈgä-vē-əl\ *noun* [French, modification of Bengali *ghāṛiyal* or Hindi *ghaṛyal*, from Sanskrit *ghaṇṭika* crocodilian] (circa 1825)
: a large long-snouted crocodilian (*Gavialis gangeticus*) of India
**ga·votte** \gə-ˈvät\ *noun* [French, from Middle French, from Old Provençal *gavoto*, from *gavot* Alpine dweller] (1696)
**1** : a dance of French peasant origin marked by the raising rather than sliding of the feet
**2** : a tune for the gavotte in moderately quick ¼ time
— **gavotte** *intransitive verb*
**Ga·wain** \gə-ˈwän, ˈgä-ˌwän, ˈgaú-ən\ *noun*
: a knight of the Round Table and nephew of King Arthur
¹**gawk** \ˈgȯk\ *noun* [probably from English dialect *gawk* (left-handed)] (1757)
: a clumsy stupid person : LOUT
²**gawk** *intransitive verb* [perhaps alteration of obsolete *gaw* (to stare)] (1785)
: to gape or stare stupidly
— **gawk·er** *noun*
**gawk·ish** \ˈgȯ-kish\ *adjective* (1876)
: GAWKY
— **gawk·ish·ly** *adverb*
— **gawk·ish·ness** *noun*
**gawky** \ˈgȯ-kē\ *adjective* **gawk·i·er; -est** (1759)
: AWKWARD, CLUMSY ⟨a *gawky* adolescent⟩
— **gawk·i·ly** \-kə-lē\ *adverb*
— **gawky** *noun*
**gawp** \ˈgȯp, ˈgäp\ *intransitive verb* [English dialect *gawp* to yawn, gape, from obsolete *galp*, from Middle English] (1855)
*chiefly British* : GAWK
— **gawp·er** \ˈgȯ-pər, ˈgä-\ *noun*
¹**gay** \ˈgā\ *adjective* [Middle English, from Middle French *gai*] (14th century)
**1 a** : happily excited : MERRY **b** : keenly alive and exuberant : having or inducing high spirits ⟨abandoned a sober traditional style for one more timely and *gay*⟩
**2 a** : BRIGHT, LIVELY ⟨*gay* sunny meadows⟩ **b** : brilliant in color
**3** : given to social pleasures; *also* : LICENTIOUS
**4 a** : HOMOSEXUAL **b** : of, relating to, or used by homosexuals ⟨the *gay* rights movement⟩ ⟨a *gay* bar⟩
**synonym** see LIVELY
— **gay** *adverb*
— **gay·ness** *noun*
²**gay** *noun* (1953)
: HOMOSEXUAL

**gay·ety, gay·ly** *variant of* GAIETY, GAILY
**ga·za·nia** \gə-ˈzā-nē-ə, -nyə\ *noun* [New Latin, from Theodorus *Gaza* (died 1478) Greek scholar] (1813)
: any of a genus (*Gazania*) of South African composite herbs often cultivated for their brightly colored flowers
**ga·zar** \gə-ˈzär\ *noun* [origin unknown] (1967)
: a silk organza
¹**gaze** \ˈgāz\ *intransitive verb* **gazed; gaz·ing** [Middle English] (14th century)
: to fix the eyes in a steady and intent look and often with eagerness or studious attention
— **gaz·er** *noun*
²**gaze** *noun* (1566)
: a fixed intent look
**ga·ze·bo** \gə-ˈzē-(ˌ)bō *also* -ˈzä-\ *noun, plural* **-bos** [perhaps from ¹*gaze* + Latin *-ebo* (as in *videbo* I shall see)] (1752)
**1** : BELVEDERE
**2** : a freestanding roofed structure usually open on the sides
**gaze·hound** \ˈgāz-ˌhaúnd\ *noun* (1610)
: a dog that hunts by sight rather than by scent; *especially* : GREYHOUND
**ga·zelle** \gə-ˈzel\ *noun, plural* **gazelles** *also* **gazelle** [French, from Middle French, from Arabic *ghazāl*] (1600)
: any of numerous small to medium graceful and swift African and Asian antelopes (*Gazella* and related genera)

gazelle

¹**ga·zette** \gə-ˈzet\ *noun* [French, from Italian *gazzetta*] (circa 1598)
**1** : NEWSPAPER
**2** : an official journal
**3** *British* : an announcement in an official gazette
²**gazette** *transitive verb* **ga·zett·ed; ga·zett·ing** (1678)
**1** *chiefly British* : to announce or publish in a gazette
**2** *British* : to announce the appointment or status of in an official gazette
**gaz·et·teer** \ˌga-zə-ˈtir\ *noun* (1611)
**1** *archaic* : JOURNALIST, PUBLICIST
**2** [*The Gazetteer's: or, Newsman's Interpreter*, a geographical index edited by Laurence Echard] : a geographical dictionary; *also* : a book in which a subject is treated especially in regard to geographic distribution and regional specialization
**gaz·o·gene** \ˈga-zə-ˌjēn\ *variant of* GASOGENE
**gaz·pa·cho** \gəz-ˈpä-(ˌ)chō, gə-ˈspä-\ *noun, plural* **-chos** [Spanish] (1845)
: a spicy soup that is usually made from chopped raw vegetables (as tomato, onion, pepper, and cucumber) and that is served cold
**GB** \ˌjē-ˈbē\ *noun* [code name] (1961)
: SARIN
**G clef** *noun* (1596)
: TREBLE CLEF
**ge-** *or* **geo-** *combining form* [Middle English *geo-*, from Middle French & Latin; Middle French, from Latin, from Greek *gē-*, *geō-*, from *gē*]
**1** : earth : ground : soil ⟨*ge*anticline⟩ ⟨*geo*phyte⟩
**2** : geographic : geography and ⟨*geo*politics⟩
**ge·an·ti·cline** \jē-ˈan-ti-ˌklīn\ *noun* (1889)
: a great upward flexure of the earth's crust
— *compare* GEOSYNCLINE
¹**gear** \ˈgir\ *noun* [Middle English *gere*, from Old Norse *gervi, gǫrvi*; akin to Old English *gearwe* equipment, clothing, *gearu* ready — more at YARE] (14th century)
**1 a** : CLOTHING, GARMENTS **b** : movable property : GOODS
**2** : EQUIPMENT, PARAPHERNALIA ⟨fishing *gear*⟩

**3 a** : the rigging of a ship or boat **b** : the harness especially of horses
**4** *dialect chiefly British* : absurd talk : NONSENSE
**5** *dialect chiefly British* : DOINGS
**6 a** (1) : a mechanism that performs a specific function in a complete machine ⟨steering *gear*⟩ (2) : a toothed wheel (3) : working relation, position, order, or adjustment ⟨got her career in *gear*⟩ **b** : one of two or more adjustments of a transmission (as of a bicycle or motor vehicle) that determine mechanical advantage, relative speed, and direction of travel
— **gear·less** \-ləs\ *adjective*
²**gear** (1851)
*transitive verb*
**1 a** : to provide (as machinery) with gearing **b** : to connect by gearing
**2 a** : to make ready for effective operation **b** : to adjust so as to match, blend with, or satisfy something ⟨*gearing* wages to productivity⟩
*intransitive verb*
**1 a** *British, of machinery* : to be in gear : MESH **b** : SHIFT 1c ⟨*gear* down⟩
**2 a** : to become adjusted so as to match, blend, or harmonize
**gear·box** \ˈgir-ˌbäks\ *noun* (1887)
**1** : GEARING 2
**2** : TRANSMISSION 3
**gear·change** \-ˌchānj\ *noun* (1927)
*British* : GEARSHIFT
**gear·ing** \ˈgir-iŋ\ *noun* (1833)
**1** : the act or process of providing or fitting with gears
**2** : the parts by which motion is transmitted from one portion of machinery to another; *especially* : a train of gears
**gear·shift** \ˈgir-ˌshift\ *noun* (1926)
: a mechanism by which the transmission gears in a power-transmission system are engaged and disengaged; *also* : a lever for controlling such a mechanism
**gear up** *intransitive verb* (1951)
: to get ready ⟨the team is *gearing up* for the big game⟩
**gear·wheel** \ˈgir-ˌhwēl, -ˌwēl\ *noun* (circa 1874)
: GEAR 6a(2)
**Geat** \ˈgēt, ˈgä-ət, ˈyaət\ *noun* [Old English *Gēat*] (before 12th century)
: a member of a Scandinavian people of southern Sweden to which the legendary hero Beowulf belonged
— **Geat·ish** \ˈgē-tish, ˈgä-, ˈyaə-\ *adjective*
**gecko** \ˈge-(ˌ)kō\ *noun, plural* **geck·os** *or* **geck·oes** [perhaps from Malay dialect *ge?kok*] (1774)
: any of numerous small harmless chiefly tropical and nocturnal insectivorous lizards (family Gekkonidae)

gecko

**ge·dank·en·ex·per·i·ment** \gə-ˈdäŋ-kən-ik-ˌsper-ə-mənt *also* -ˌspir-\ *noun* [German, from *Gedanke* thought + *Experiment* experiment] (1941)
: an experiment carried out in thought only
¹**gee** \ˈjē\ *verb* [origin unknown] (1628)
*verb imperative*
— used as a direction to turn to the right or move ahead; compare ⁵HAW
*intransitive verb*
**geed; gee·ing** : to turn to the right side
²**gee** *interjection* [euphemism for *Jesus*] (1895)
— used as an introductory expletive or to express surprise or enthusiasm

---

\ə\ abut \ᵊ\ kitten \ər\ further \a\ ash \ā\ ace
\ä\ mop, mar \aú\ out \ch\ chin \e\ bet \ē\ easy
\g\ go \i\ hit \ī\ ice \j\ job \ŋ\ sing \ō\ go
\ȯ\ law \ȯi\ boy \th\ thin \t͟h\ the \ü\ loot \ú\ foot
\y\ yet \zh\ vision *see also* Guide to Pronunciation

**³gee** *noun* (1926)
**1** : the letter *g*
**2** [*grand*] *slang* : a thousand dollars
**gee·gaw** \'jē-(,)gȯ, 'gē-\ *variant of* GEWGAW
**geek** \'gēk\ *noun* [probably from English dialect *geek, geck* fool, from Low German *geck,* from Middle Low German] (1914)
**1** : a person often of an intellectual bent who is disapproved of
**2** : a carnival performer often billed as a wild man whose act usually includes biting the head off a live chicken or snake
— **geeky** \'gē-kē\ *adjective*
**geese** *plural of* GOOSE
**gee-whiz** \'jē-,hwiz, -,wiz\ *adjective* (1934)
**1** : designed to arouse wonder or excitement or to amplify the merits or significance of something especially by the use of clever or sensational language ⟨play-by-play specialists who wallow in *gee-whiz* banality —Jack Gould⟩
**2** : marked by spectacular or astonishing qualities or achievement ⟨*gee-whiz* technology⟩
**3** : characterized by wide-eyed enthusiasm, excitement, and wonder
**gee whiz** \(,)jē-'\ *interjection* (1885)
: ²GEE
**geez** *variant of* JEEZ
**Ge·ez** \gē-'ez; 'gē-(,)ez, 'gā-\ *noun* (1790)
: a Semitic language formerly spoken in Ethiopia and still used as the liturgical language of the Christian church in Ethiopia
**gee·zer** \'gē-zər\ *noun* [probably alteration of Scots *guiser* (one in disguise)] (1885)
: a queer, odd, or eccentric person — used especially of elderly men
**ge·fil·te fish** \gə-'fil-tə-\ *noun* [Yiddish, literally, stuffed fish] (1892)
: balls or cakes of seasoned minced fish usually simmered in a fish stock or baked in a tomato sauce
**ge·gen·schein** \'gā-gən-,shīn\ *noun, often capitalized* [German, from *gegen* against, counter- + *Schein* shine] (1880)
: a faint light about 20° across on the celestial sphere opposite the sun probably caused by backscatter of sunlight by solar-system dust
**Ge·hen·na** \gi-'he-nə\ *noun* [Late Latin, from Greek *Geenna,* from Hebrew *Gē' Hinnōm,* literally, valley of Hinnom] (1594)
**1** : a place or state of misery
**2** : HELL 1a(2)
**Gei·ger counter** \'gī-gər-\ *noun* [Hans Geiger (died 1945) German physicist] (1924)
: an instrument for detecting the presence and intensity of radiations (as cosmic rays or particles from a radioactive substance) by means of the ionizing effect on an enclosed gas which results in a pulse that is amplified and fed to a device giving a visible or audible indication ◆
**Gei·ger–Mül·ler counter** \-'myü-lər, -'mi-, -'mə-\ *noun* [W. *Müller,* 20th century German physicist] (1932)
: GEIGER COUNTER
**gei·sha** \'gā-shə, *also* 'gē-\ *noun, plural* **geisha** *or* **geishas** [Japanese, from *gei* art + *-sha* person] (1887)
: a Japanese girl or woman who is trained to provide entertaining and lighthearted company especially for a man or a group of men
**¹gel** \'jel\ *noun* [*gelatin*] (1899)
**1** : a colloid in a more solid form than a sol; *broadly* : JELLY 2
**2** : a thin colored transparent sheet used over a stage light to color it
**3** : a gelatinous preparation used in styling hair
**²gel** *intransitive verb* **gelled; gel·ling** (1917)
: to change into or take on the form of a gel
: SET
— **gel·able** \'je-lə-bəl\ *adjective*
**gel·a·da baboon** \'je-lə-də, 'ge-; jə-'lä-də-\ *noun* [Amharic *č̣ällada*] (1878)
: a large long-haired primate (*Theropithecus gelada*) of Ethiopia related to the baboon — called also *gelada*

**ge·län·de·sprung** \gə-'len-də-,shprûn, -,sprûn\ *noun* [German, from *Gelände* open fields + *Sprung* jump] (1931)
: a jump usually over an obstacle in skiing that is made from a low crouch with the aid of both ski poles
**gel·ate** \'je-,lāt\ *intransitive verb* **gel·at·ed; gel·at·ing** (1915)
: GEL
**gel·a·tin** *also* **gel·a·tine** \'je-lə-tᵊn\ *noun* [French *gélatine* edible jelly, gelatin, from Italian *gelatina,* from *gelato,* past participle of *gelare* to freeze, from Latin — more at COLD] (1800)
**1** : glutinous material obtained from animal tissues by boiling; *especially* : a colloidal protein used as a food, in photography, and in medicine
**2 a** : any of various substances (as agar) resembling gelatin **b** : an edible jelly made with gelatin
**3** : GEL 2
**ge·la·ti·ni·za·tion** \jə-,la-tᵊn-ə-'zā-shən, ,je-lə-tᵊn-\ *noun* (1843)
: the process of converting into a gelatinous form or into a jelly
— **ge·la·ti·nize** \jə-'la-tᵊn-,īz, 'je-lə-tᵊn-\ *verb*
**ge·lat·i·nous** \jə-'lat-nəs, -'la-tᵊn-əs\ *adjective* (1766)
**1** : resembling gelatin or jelly : VISCOUS ⟨a *gelatinous* precipitate⟩
**2** : of, relating to, or containing gelatin
— **ge·lat·i·nous·ly** *adverb*
— **ge·lat·i·nous·ness** *noun*
**¹ge·la·tion** \ji-'lā-shən\ *noun* [Latin *gelation-, gelatio,* from *gelare*] (1854)
: the action or process of freezing
**²gel·ation** \je-'lā-shən\ *noun* [¹*gel* + *-ation*] (1915)
: the formation of a gel from a sol
**ge·la·to** \je-'lä-(,)tō\ *noun, plural* **-ti** \-tē\ *also* **-tos** [Italian, literally, frozen] (1929)
: a soft rich ice cream containing little or no air
**¹geld** \'geld\ *transitive verb* [Middle English, from Old Norse *gelda;* akin to Old English *gelde* sterile] (14th century)
**1** : CASTRATE
**2** : to deprive of a natural or essential part ⟨sick of workingmen being *gelded* of their natural expression —*Atlantic*⟩
**²geld** *noun* [Old English *gield, geld* service, tribute; akin to Old English *gieldan* to pay, yield — more at YIELD] (1610)
: the crown tax paid under Anglo-Saxon and Norman kings
**geld·ing** \'gel-diŋ\ *noun* [Middle English, from Old Norse *geldingr,* from *gelda*] (14th century)
**1** : a castrated animal; *specifically* : a castrated male horse
**2** *archaic* : EUNUCH
**ge·lée** \zhə-'lā\ *noun* [French, jelly, from Middle French — more at JELLY] (1966)
: a cosmetic gel
**gel electrophoresis** *noun* (1960)
: electrophoresis in which molecules (as proteins and nucleic acids) migrate through a gel and especially a polyacrylamide gel and separate into bands according to size
**gel·id** \'je-ləd\ *adjective* [Latin *gelidus,* from *gelu* frost, cold — more at COLD] (1599)
: extremely cold : ICY ⟨*gelid* water⟩ ⟨a man of *gelid* reserve —*New Yorker*⟩
— **ge·lid·i·ty** \jə-'li-də-tē, je-\ *noun*
— **gel·id·ly** \'je-ləd-lē\ *adverb*
**gel·ig·nite** \'je-lig-,nīt\ *noun* [*gelatin* + Latin *ignis* fire + English *-ite* — more at IGNEOUS] (1889)
: a dynamite in which the adsorbent base is largely potassium nitrate or a similar nitrate usually with some wood pulp
**gel·lant** \'je-lənt\ *noun* (1956)
: a substance used to produce gelling

**gel permeation chromatography** *noun* (1966)
: chromatography in which macromolecules (as polymers) in a solution are separated by size on a column packed with a gel (as of polystyrene)
**gelt** \'gelt\ *noun* [Dutch & German *geld* & Yiddish *gelt;* all akin to Old English *geld* ²*geld*] (circa 1529)
: MONEY
**¹gem** \'jem\ *noun* [Middle English *gemme,* from Middle French, from Latin *gemma* bud, gem] (14th century)
**1 a** : JEWEL **b** : a precious or sometimes semiprecious stone cut and polished for ornament
**2 a** : something prized especially for great beauty or perfection **b** : a highly prized or well-beloved person
**3** : MUFFIN
**²gem** *transitive verb* **gemmed; gem·ming** (1610)
: to adorn with or as if with gems
**Ge·ma·ra** \gə-'mär-ə, -'mȯr-\ *noun* [Aramaic *gĕmārā* completion] (1613)
: a commentary on the Mishnah forming the second part of the Talmud
— **Ge·ma·ric** \-ik\ *adjective*
— **Ge·ma·rist** \-ist\ *noun*
**ge·mein·schaft** \gə-'mīn-,shäft\ *noun* [German, community, from *gemein* common, general (from Old High German *gimeini*) + *-schaft* -ship — more at MEAN] (1937)
: a spontaneously arising organic social relationship characterized by strong reciprocal bonds of sentiment and kinship within a common tradition; *also* : a community or society characterized by this relationship — compare GESELLSCHAFT
**gem·i·nal** \'je-mə-nᵊl\ *adjective* [Latin *geminus* twin] (1967)
: relating to or characterized by two usually similar substituents on the same atom
— **gem·i·nal·ly** \-nᵊl-ē\ *adverb*
**¹gem·i·nate** \'je-mə-nət, -,nāt\ *adjective* [Latin *geminatus,* past participle of *geminare* to double, from *geminus* twin] (15th century)
**1** : arranged in pairs : DUPLICATE
**2** : being a sequence of identical speech sounds (as in *meanness* or Italian *notte* \'nȯt-te\ "night")
**²gem·i·nate** \-,nāt\ *verb* **-nat·ed; -nat·ing** (1637)
*transitive verb*
: to make geminate
*intransitive verb*
: to be or become geminate
— **gem·i·na·tion** \,je-mə-'nā-shən\ *noun*
**Gem·i·ni** \'je-mə-(,)nē, -,nī; 'ge-mə-,nē\ *noun plural but singular in construction* [Latin (genitive *Geminorum*), literally, the twins (Castor and Pollux)]
**1** : the 3d zodiacal constellation pictorially represented as the twins Castor and Pollux sitting together and located on the opposite side of the Milky Way from Taurus and Orion

◇ WORD HISTORY
**Geiger counter** The Geiger counter is named after the German physicist Hans Wilhelm Geiger (1882–1945). Geiger is credited with significant research on atomic theory, radioactivity, and cosmic rays. He developed a number of techniques and instruments for the detection of individual charged particles. With the British physicist Ernest Rutherford he developed in 1908 the first radiation counter, an instrument that counted alpha particles. Aided by fellow German physicist Walther Müller, he introduced an improved version of the Geiger counter in 1928. The Geiger-Müller counter marked the introduction of modern electrical devices into radiation research.

**2 a :** the 3d sign of the zodiac in astrology — see ZODIAC table **b :** one born under the sign of Gemini

**gem·ma** \'je-mə\ *noun, plural* **gem·mae** \-,mē\ [Latin] (1830)
**:** BUD; *broadly* **:** an asexual reproductive body that becomes detached from a parent plant

**gem·ma·tion** \je-'mā-shən\ *noun* (circa 1839)
**:** reproduction by gemmae

**gem·mule** \'jem-(,)yü(ə)l\ *noun* [French, from Latin *gemmula,* diminutive of *gemma*] (circa 1841)
**:** a small bud: **a :** a theoretical particle proposed in the theory of pangenesis that is shed by a somatic cell and contains all the information necessary to reproduce that cell type (as in an offspring) **b :** a reproductive bud produced by freshwater and some marine sponges that consists of a usually hardened aggregate of cells

**gem·my** \'je-mē\ *adjective* (15th century)
**1 :** having the characteristics desired in a gemstone
**2 :** BRIGHT, GLITTERING

**gem·ol·o·gist** *also* **gem·mol·o·gist** \je-'mä-lə-jist, jə-\ *noun* (1931)
**:** a specialist in gems; *specifically* **:** one who appraises gems

**gem·ol·o·gy** *or* **gem·mol·o·gy** \-jē\ *noun* [Latin *gemma* gem] (1811)
**:** the science of gems
— **gem·olog·i·cal** \,je-mə-'lä-ji-kəl\ *adjective*

**ge·mot** *or* **ge·mote** \gə-'mōt, yə-\ *noun* [Old English *gemōt,* from *ge-* (perfective prefix) + *mōt* assembly — more at CO-, MOOT] (before 12th century)
**:** a judicial or legislative assembly in Anglo-Saxon England

**gems·bok** \'gemz-,bäk\ *noun* [Afrikaans, from German *Gemsbock* male chamois, from *Gems* chamois + *Bock* male goat] (1777)
**:** a large and strikingly marked oryx (*Oryx ga-zella*) formerly abundant in southern Africa

**gem·stone** \'jem-,stōn\ *noun* (before 12th century)
**:** a mineral or petrified material that when cut and polished can be used in jewelry

**ge·müt·lich** \gə-'mu̇t-lik, -'müt-lik\ *adjective* [German, from Middle High German *gemüetlich* pleasant, from *gemüete* mentality, mind] (1852)
**:** agreeably pleasant **:** COMFORTABLE

gemsbok

**ge·müt·lich·keit** \gə-'mu̇t-lik-,kīt, -'müt-lik-\ *noun* [German, from *gemütlich* + *-keit,* alteration of *-heit* -hood] (1892)
**:** CORDIALITY, FRIENDLINESS

**gen** \'jen\ *noun* [perhaps from *gen*eral information] (1940)
*chiefly British* **:** INFORMATION 2a

**¹gen-** *or* **geno-** *combining form* [Greek *genos* birth, race, kind — more at KIN]
**1 :** race (*geno*cide)
**2 :** genus (*geno*type)

**²gen-** *or* **geno-** *combining form*
**:** gene (*geno*me)

**-gen** *also* **-gene** *noun combining form* [French *-gène,* from Greek *-genēs* born; akin to Greek *genos* birth]
**1 :** producer (andro*gen*)
**2 :** one that is (so) produced (culti*gen*)

**gen·darme** \'zhän-,därm *also* 'jän-\ *noun* [French, from Middle French, back-formation from *gensdarmes,* plural of *gent d'armes,* literally, armed people] (1796)
**1 :** a member of a body of soldiers especially in France serving as an armed police force for the maintenance of public order
**2 :** POLICE OFFICER

**gen·dar·mer·ie** *or* **gen·dar·mery** \zhän-'där-mə-rē, jän-\ *noun, plural* **-mer·ies** [French *gendarmerie,* from *gendarme*] (circa 1796)
**:** a body of gendarmes

**¹gen·der** \'jen-dər\ *noun* [Middle English *gendre,* from Middle French *genre, gendre,* from Latin *gener-, genus* birth, race, kind, gender — more at KIN] (14th century)
**1 a :** a subclass within a grammatical class (as noun, pronoun, adjective, or verb) of a language that is partly arbitrary but also partly based on distinguishable characteristics (as shape, social rank, manner of existence, or sex) and that determines agreement with and selection of other words or grammatical forms **b :** membership of a word or a grammatical form in such a subclass **c :** an inflectional form showing membership in such a subclass
**2 a :** SEX (the feminine *gender*) **b :** the behavioral, cultural, or psychological traits typically associated with one sex ▪

**²gender** *verb* **gen·dered; gen·der·ing** \-d(ə-)riŋ\ [Middle English *gendren,* from Middle French *gendrer,* from Latin *generare* — more at GENERATE] (14th century)
**:** ENGENDER

**gender bender** *noun* (1980)
**:** a person who dresses and behaves like a member of the opposite sex
— **gender–bending** *adjective or noun*

**gen·dered** \'jen-dərd\ *adjective* (1972)
**:** reflecting the experience, prejudices, or orientations of one sex more than the other (*gendered* language)

**gene** \'jēn\ *noun* [German *Gen,* short for *Pangen,* from *pan-* + *-gen*] (1911)
**:** a specific sequence of nucleotides in DNA or RNA that is located in the germ plasm usually on a chromosome and that is the functional unit of inheritance controlling the transmission and expression of one or more traits by specifying the structure of a particular polypeptide and especially a protein or controlling the function of other genetic material

**ge·ne·al·o·gist** \,jē-nē-'ä-lə-jist *also* -'a-lə- *also* ,je-nē-\ *noun* (1605)
**:** a person who traces or studies the descent of persons or families

**ge·ne·al·o·gy** \-jē\ *noun, plural* **-gies** [Middle English *genealogie,* from Middle French, from Late Latin *genealogia,* from Greek, from *genea* race, family + *-logia* -logy; akin to Greek *genos* race] (14th century)
**1 :** an account of the descent of a person, family, or group from an ancestor or from older forms
**2 :** regular descent of a person, family, or group of organisms from a progenitor or older form **:** PEDIGREE
**3 :** the study of family pedigrees
— **ge·ne·a·log·i·cal** \,jē-nē-ə-'lä-ji-kəl, ,je-nē-\ *adjective*
— **ge·ne·a·log·i·cal·ly** \-k(ə-)lē\ *adverb*

**gene amplification** *noun* (1968)
**:** replication and especially massive replication (as in the polymerase chain reaction) of the genetic material in part of a genome

**gene conversion** *noun* (1955)
**:** a genetic process in which a heterozygote with one damaged strand of DNA produces gametes in an aberrant allelic ratio (as 3:1) instead of the normal 1:1 Mendelian ratio due to repair of the damaged strand with genetic material complementary to the other strand

**gene flow** *noun* (1947)
**:** the passage and establishment of genes typical of one breeding population into the gene pool of another by hybridization and backcrossing

**gene frequency** *noun* (1930)
**:** the ratio of the number of a specified allele in a population to the total of all alleles at its genetic locus

**gene mutation** *noun* (1927)
**:** POINT MUTATION

**gene pool** *noun* (1946)
**:** the collection of genes of all the individuals in an interbreeding population

**genera** *plural of* GENUS

**gen·er·a·ble** \'jen-rə-bəl, 'je-nə-\ *adjective* (15th century)
**:** capable of being generated

**¹gen·er·al** \'jen-rəl, 'je-nə-\ *adjective* [Middle English, from Middle French, from Latin *generalis,* from *gener-, genus* kind, class — more at KIN] (14th century)
**1 :** involving, applicable to, or affecting the whole
**2 :** involving, relating to, or applicable to every member of a class, kind, or group (the *general* equation of a straight line)
**3 :** not confined by specialization or careful limitation
**4 :** belonging to the common nature of a group of like individuals **:** GENERIC
**5 a :** applicable to or characteristic of the majority of individuals involved **:** PREVALENT **b :** concerned or dealing with universal rather than particular aspects
**6 :** relating to, determined by, or concerned with main elements rather than limited details (bearing a *general* resemblance to the original)
**7 :** holding superior rank or taking precedence over others similarly titled (the *general* manager)

**²general** *noun* (14th century)
**1 :** something (as a concept, principle, or statement) that involves or is applicable to the whole
**2 :** SUPERIOR GENERAL
**3** *archaic* **:** the general public **:** PEOPLE
**4 a :** GENERAL OFFICER **b :** a commissioned officer in the army, air force, or marine corps who ranks above a lieutenant general and whose insignia is four stars — compare ADMIRAL
— **in general :** for the most part **:** GENERALLY

□ USAGE
**gender** "Until very recently, this was a purely grammatical term" writes a 1986 commentator. In fact, sense 2 is of just about the same age as sense 1—they both go back to the 1380s. But sense 2 has not had a great deal of use until recently. The 19th century examples that we have do not show the sense used in contexts of high seriousness (what a pity nature had not been of the masculine instead of the feminine *gender* —Washington Irving (*Salmagundi*)) (black divinities of the feminine *gender*—Charles Dickens (*A Tale of Two Cities*)) (a timid tender feminine *gender*—W. S. Gilbert (*The Grand Duke*)). Turn-of-the-century dictionaries labeled such use *jocular* or *humorous.* But by the middle of the 20th century, usage had changed and the old labels were no longer appropriate. Since the 1970s there has been a great increase in use, particularly in political and social reference, as opposed to biological reference (escapes the restrictions of *gender* by achieving power as a newspaper publisher —Justin Kaplan) (*gender* knows no double standard in Chinese sport —Frank Deford). It can be used for purposes of contrast (writers of either *gender* and any sexual preference —George Garrett). Sense 2 is often used attributively (*gender* identity) (*gender* differences) (the *gender* gap—the pattern of women voting differently from men —Nancy J. Walker) (the view that *gender* domination is as inevitable as tyranny —Virginia Held).

\ə\ **abut** \ᵊ\ **kitten** \ər\ **further** \a\ **ash** \ā\ **ace**
\ä\ **mop, mar** \au̇\ **out** \ch\ **chin** \e\ **bet** \ē\ **easy**
\g\ **go** \i\ **hit** \ī\ **ice** \j\ **job** \ŋ\ **sing** \ō\ **go**
\ȯ\ **law** \ȯi\ **boy** \th\ **thin** \t̲h̲\ **the** \ü\ **loot** \u̇\ **foot**
\y\ **yet** \zh\ **vision** *see also* Guide to Pronunciation

**general admission** *noun* (circa 1949)
**:** a fee paid for admission to a usually unreserved seating area (as in an auditorium or stadium)

**general agent** *noun* (1835)
**1 :** one employed to transact generally all legal business entrusted to him by his principal
**2 :** an insurance company agent working within a specified area

**general assembly** *noun* (1619)
**1 :** the highest governing body in a religious denomination (as the United Presbyterian Church)
**2 :** a legislative assembly; *especially* **:** a U.S. state legislature
**3** *G&A capitalized* **:** the supreme deliberative body of the United Nations

**general aviation** *noun* (1966)
**:** the operation of civilian aircraft not under the control of a common carrier; *also* **:** such aircraft collectively

**General Court** *noun* (1629)
**:** a legislative assembly; *specifically* **:** the state legislature in Massachusetts and New Hampshire

**general delivery** *noun* (1846)
**:** a department of a post office that handles the delivery of mail at a post office window to persons who call for it

**general election** *noun* (1716)
**:** an election usually held at regular intervals in which candidates are elected in all or most constituencies of a nation or state

**gen·er·al·isa·tion, gen·er·al·ise, gen·er·al·ised** *British variant of* GENERALIZATION, GENERALIZE, GENERALIZED

**gen·er·a·lis·si·mo** \ˌjen-rə-ˈli-sə-ˌmō, ˌje-nə-\ *noun, plural* **-mos** [Italian, from *generale* general] (1621)
**:** the chief commander of an army

**gen·er·al·ist** \ˈjen-rə-list, ˈje-nə-\ *noun* (1611)
**:** one whose skills, interests, or habits are varied or unspecialized

**gen·er·al·i·ty** \ˌje-nə-ˈra-lə-tē\ *noun, plural* **-ties** (15th century)
**1 :** the quality or state of being general
**2 a :** GENERALIZATION 2 **b :** a vague or inadequate statement
**3 :** the greatest part **:** BULK ⟨the *generality* of the population⟩

**gen·er·al·iza·tion** \ˌjen-rə-lə-ˈzā-shən, ˌje-nə-\ *noun* (1761)
**1 :** the act or process of generalizing
**2 :** a general statement, law, principle, or proposition
**3 :** the act or process whereby a response is made to a stimulus similar to but not identical with a reference stimulus

**gen·er·al·ize** \ˈjen-rə-ˌlīz, ˈje-nə-\ *verb* **-ized; -iz·ing** (circa 1751)
*transitive verb*
**1 :** to give a general form to
**2 a :** to derive or induce (a general conception or principle) from particulars **b :** to draw a general conclusion from
**3 :** to give general applicability to ⟨*generalize* a law⟩; *also* **:** to make indefinite
*intransitive verb*
**1 :** to form generalizations; *also* **:** to make vague or indefinite statements
**2 :** to spread or extend throughout the body
— **gen·er·al·iz·abil·i·ty** \ˌjen-rə-ˌlī-zə-ˈbi-lə-tē, ˌje-nə-\ *noun*
— **gen·er·al·iz·able** \-ˌlī-zə-bəl\ *adjective*
— **gen·er·al·iz·er** *noun*

**gen·er·al·ized** *adjective* (circa 1843)
**:** made general; *especially* **:** not highly differentiated biologically nor strictly adapted to a particular environment

**gen·er·al·ly** \ˈjen-rə-lē, ˈje-nə-, ˈje-nər-lē\ *adverb* (14th century)
**:** in a general manner: as **a :** in disregard of specific instances and with regard to an overall picture ⟨*generally* speaking⟩ **b :** as a rule **:** USUALLY

**general officer** *noun* (1681)

**:** any of the officers in the army, air force, or marine corps above colonel — compare COMPANY OFFICER, FIELD OFFICER, FLAG OFFICER

**general of the air force** (1949)
**:** a general of the highest rank in the air force whose insignia is five stars

**general of the army** (1945)
**:** a general of the highest rank in the army whose insignia is five stars

**general paresis** *noun* (1874)
**:** insanity caused by syphilitic alteration of the brain that leads to dementia and paralysis — called also *general paralysis of the insane*

**general partner** *noun* (1887)
**:** a partner whose liability for partnership debts and obligations is unlimited

**general practitioner** *noun* (circa 1885)
**:** a physician or veterinarian whose practice is not limited to a specialty; *broadly* **:** GENERALIST

**general–purpose** *adjective* (1894)
**:** suitable to be used for two or more basic purposes

**general quarters** *noun plural* (1902)
**:** a condition of maximum readiness of a warship for action

**general relativity** *noun* (1916)
**:** RELATIVITY 3b

**general semantics** *noun plural but singular or plural in construction* (1933)
**:** a doctrine and educational discipline intended to improve habits of response of human beings to their environment and one another especially by training in the more critical use of words and other symbols

**gen·er·al·ship** \ˈjen-rəl-ˌship, ˈje-nə-\ *noun* (1610)
**1 :** office or tenure of office of a general
**2 :** LEADERSHIP
**3 :** military skill in a high commander

**general store** *noun* (1835)
**:** a retail store located usually in a small or rural community that carries a wide variety of goods including groceries but is not divided into departments

**general theory of relativity** (1921)
**:** RELATIVITY 3b

**general will** *noun* (circa 1902)
**:** the collective will of a community that is the embodiment or expression of its common interest

**gen·er·ate** \ˈje-nə-ˌrāt\ *transitive verb* **-at·ed; -at·ing** [Latin *generatus*, past participle of *generare*, from *gener-, genus* descent, birth — more at KIN] (1509)
**1 :** to bring into existence: as **a :** PROCREATE, BEGET **b :** to originate by a vital, chemical, or physical process **:** PRODUCE ⟨*generate* electricity⟩
**2 :** to be the cause of (a situation, action, or state of mind) ⟨these stories . . . *generate* a good deal of psychological suspense —*Atlantic*⟩
**3 :** to define or originate (as a mathematical or linguistic set or structure) by the application of one or more rules or operations; *especially* **:** to trace out (as a curve) by a moving point or trace out (as a surface) by a moving curve

**gen·er·a·tion** \ˌje-nə-ˈrā-shən\ *noun* (14th century)
**1 a :** a body of living beings constituting a single step in the line of descent from an ancestor **b :** a group of individuals born and living contemporaneously **c :** a group of individuals having contemporaneously a status (as that of students in a school) which each one holds only for a limited period **d :** a type or class of objects usually developed from an earlier type ⟨first of the . . . new *generation* of powerful supersonic fighters —Kenneth Koyen⟩
**2 a :** the action or process of producing offspring **:** PROCREATION **b :** the process of coming or bringing into being ⟨*generation* of income⟩ **c :** origination by a generating process **:** PRODUCTION; *especially* **:** formation of a geometric figure by motion of another

**3 :** the average span of time between the birth of parents and that of their offspring
— **gen·er·a·tion·al** \-shnəl, -shə-nᵊl\ *adjective*
— **gen·er·a·tion·al·ly** \-shnə-lē, shə-nᵊl-ē\ *adverb*

**gen·er·a·tive** \ˈjen-rə-tiv, ˈje-nə-, -ˌrā-tiv\ *adjective* (14th century)
**:** having the power or function of generating, originating, producing, or reproducing

**generative cell** *noun* (circa 1892)
**:** a sexual reproductive cell **:** GAMETE

**generative grammar** \*usually* ˈje-nə-rə-tiv-\ *noun* (1959)
**1 :** a description in the form of an ordered set of rules for producing the grammatical sentences of a language
**2 :** TRANSFORMATIONAL GRAMMAR

**generative nucleus** *noun* (circa 1892)
**:** the one of the two nuclei resulting from the first division in the pollen grain of a seed plant that gives rise to sperm nuclei — compare TUBE NUCLEUS

**generative semantics** \*usually* ˈje-nə-rə-tiv-\ *noun plural but usually singular in construction* (1970)
**:** a description of a language emphasizing a semantic deep structure that is logical in form, that provides syntactic structure, and that is related to surface structure by transformations

**gen·er·a·tor** \ˈje-nə-ˌrā-tər\ *noun* (1646)
**1 :** one that generates
**2 :** an apparatus in which vapor or gas is formed
**3 :** a machine by which mechanical energy is changed into electrical energy
**4 :** a mathematical entity that when subjected to one or more operations yields another mathematical entity or its elements; *specifically* **:** GENERATRIX

**gen·er·a·trix** \ˌje-nə-ˈrā-triks\ *noun, plural* **-era·tri·ces** \-trə-ˌsēz, -ə-rə-ˈtrī-(ˌ)sēz\ (1840)
**:** a point, line, or surface whose motion generates a line, surface, or solid

**¹ge·ner·ic** \jə-ˈner-ik\ *adjective* [French *générique*, from Latin *gener-, genus* birth, kind, class] (1676)
**1 a :** relating to or characteristic of a whole group or class **:** GENERAL **b :** being or having a nonproprietary name **c :** having no particularly distinctive quality or application
**2 :** relating to or having the rank of a biological genus
— **ge·ner·i·cal·ly** \-i-k(ə-)lē\ *adverb*
— **ge·ner·ic·ness** *noun*

**²generic** *noun* (1967)
**:** a generic product (as a drug)

**gen·er·os·i·ty** \ˌje-nə-ˈrä-sə-tē, -ˈräs-tē\ *noun, plural* **-ties** (circa 1616)
**1 a :** the quality or fact of being generous **b :** a generous act
**2 :** ABUNDANCE

**gen·er·ous** \ˈjen-rəs, ˈje-nə-\ *adjective* [Middle French or Latin; Middle French *genereus*, from Latin *generosus*, from *gener-, genus*] (1588)
**1** *archaic* **:** HIGHBORN
**2 a :** characterized by a noble or forbearing spirit **:** MAGNANIMOUS, KINDLY **b :** liberal in giving **:** OPENHANDED **c :** marked by abundance or ample proportions **:** COPIOUS
*synonym* see LIBERAL
— **gen·er·ous·ly** *adverb*
— **gen·er·ous·ness** *noun*

**gen·e·sis** \ˈje-nə-səs\ *noun, plural* **-e·ses** \-ˌsēz\ [Latin, from Greek, from *gignesthai* to be born — more at KIN] (circa 1604)
**:** the origin or coming into being of something

**Genesis** *noun* [Greek]
**:** the mainly narrative first book of canonical Jewish and Christian Scriptures — see BIBLE table

**gene–splic·ing** \'jēn-,splī-siŋ\ *noun* (circa 1978)
: any of various techniques by which recombinant DNA is produced and made to function in an organism

**gen·et** \'je-nət\ *noun* [Middle English *genete*, from Middle French, from Arabic *jarnayṭ*] (15th century)
: any of a genus (*Genetta*) of small Old World usually carnivorous mammals related to the civets and having retractile claws, spotted or striped fur, and a ringed tail

**gene therapy** *noun* (1974)
: the insertion of normal or genetically altered genes into cells usually to replace defective genes especially in the treatment of genetic disorders

**ge·net·ic** \jə-'ne-tik\ *also* **ge·net·i·cal** \-ti-kəl\ *adjective* [*genesis*] (1831)
**1** : relating to or determined by the origin, development, or causal antecedents of something
**2 a** : of, relating to, or involving genetics **b** : GENIC
— **ge·net·i·cal·ly** \-ti-k(ə-)lē\ *adverb*

**-ge·net·ic** *adjective combining form*
: -GENIC 1, 2 ⟨psycho*genetic*⟩

**genetic code** *noun* (1961)
: the biochemical basis of heredity consisting of codons in DNA and RNA that determine the specific amino acid sequence in proteins and appear to be uniform for all known forms of life

**genetic counseling** *noun* (1968)
: medical education of affected individuals and the general public concerning inherited disorders

**genetic drift** *noun* (1945)
: random changes in gene frequency especially in small populations when leading to preservation or extinction of particular genes

**genetic engineering** *noun* (1966)
: the directed alteration of genetic material by intervention in genetic processes; *especially* : GENE-SPLICING
— **genetically engineered** *adjective*
— **genetic engineer** *noun*

**genetic map** *noun* (circa 1960)
: MAP 3

**genetic marker** *noun* (1950)
: a usually dominant gene or trait that serves especially to identify genes or traits linked with it

**ge·net·ics** \jə-'ne-tiks\ *noun plural but singular in construction* (1905)
**1** : a branch of biology that deals with the heredity and variation of organisms
**2** : the genetic makeup and phenomena of an organism, type, group, or condition
— **ge·net·i·cist** \-'ne-tə-sist\ *noun*

**ge·ne·va** \jə-'nē-və\ *noun* [modification of obsolete Dutch *genever* (now *jenever*), literally, juniper, from Middle Dutch, from Old French *geneivre*, ultimately from Latin *juniperus*] (1706)
: a highly aromatic bitter gin originally made in the Netherlands

**Ge·ne·va bands** \jə-'nē-və-\ *noun plural* [*Geneva*, Switzerland; from their use by the Calvinist clergy of Geneva] (1882)
: two strips of white cloth suspended from the front of a clerical collar and sometimes used by Protestant clergymen — called also *Geneva tabs*

**Geneva convention** *noun* (1880)
: one of a series of agreements concerning the treatment of prisoners of war and of the sick, wounded, and dead in battle first made at Geneva, Switzerland in 1864 and subsequently accepted in later revisions by most nations

Geneva bands

**Geneva cross** *noun* [from its adoption by the Geneva convention] (circa 1889)
: RED CROSS

**Geneva gown** *noun* [from its use by the Calvinist clergy of Geneva] (1820)
: a loose large-sleeved black academic gown widely used as a vestment by members of the Protestant clergy

**Ge·ne·van** \jə-'nē-vən\ *adjective* (1573)
**1** : of or relating to Geneva, Switzerland
**2** : of or relating to Calvinism
— **Genevan** *noun*

¹**ge·nial** \'jēn-yəl, 'jē-nē-əl\ *adjective* [Latin *genialis*, from *genius*] (1566)
**1** : of or relating to marriage or generation ⟨the *genial* bed —John Milton⟩
**2** *obsolete* : INBORN, NATIVE
**3 a** : favorable to growth or comfort : MILD ⟨*genial* sunshine⟩ **b** : marked by or diffusing sympathy or friendliness ⟨your *genial* host⟩
**4** : displaying or marked by genius
*synonym* see GRACIOUS
— **ge·nial·i·ty** \,jē-nē-'a-lə-tē, jēn-'yal-\ *noun*
— **ge·nial·ly** \'jēn-yə-lē\ *adverb*

²**ge·ni·al** \ji-'nī(-ə)l\ *adjective* [Greek *geneion* chin, from *genys* jaw — more at CHIN] (1831)
: of or relating to the chin

**gen·ic** \'jē-nik, 'je-\ *adjective* (1918)
: of, relating to, or being a gene
— **gen·i·cal·ly** \-ni-k(ə-)lē\ *adverb*

**-gen·ic** *adjective combining form* [International Scientific Vocabulary *-gen* & *-geny* + *-ic*]
**1** : producing : forming ⟨carcino*genic*⟩
**2** : produced by : formed from ⟨bio*genic*⟩
**3** [*photogenic*] : suitable for production or reproduction by (such) a medium ⟨tele*genic*⟩

**ge·nic·u·late** \jə-'ni-kyə-lət\ *or* **ge·nic·u·lat·ed** \-,lā-təd\ *adjective* [Latin *geniculatus*, from *geniculum*, diminutive of *genu* knee — more at KNEE] (1657)
: bent abruptly at an angle like a bent knee

**ge·nie** \'jē-nē\ *noun, plural* **ge·nies** *also* **ge·nii** \'jē-nē(-,ī)\ [French *génie*, from Arabic *jinnīy*] (1748)
**1** : JINNI 1
**2** : a magic spirit believed to take human form and serve the person who calls it

**gen·i·tal** \'je-nə-t°l\ *adjective* [Middle English, from Latin *genitalis*, from *genitus*, past participle of *gignere* to beget — more at KIN] (14th century)
**1** : GENERATIVE
**2** : of, relating to, or being a sexual organ
**3** : of, relating to, or characterized by the stage of psychosexual development in psychoanalytic theory during which oral and anal impulses are subordinated to adaptive interpersonal mechanisms
— **gen·i·tal·ly** \-tə-lē\ *adverb*

**genital herpes** *noun* (1968)
: herpes simplex of the type typically affecting the genitalia

**gen·i·ta·lia** \,je-nə-'tāl-yə\ *noun plural* [Latin, from neuter plural of *genitalis*] (1876)
: the organs of the reproductive system; *especially* : the external genital organs
— **gen·i·ta·lic** \-'ta-lik, -'tā-\ *adjective*

**gen·i·tals** \'je-nə-t°lz\ *noun plural* (14th century)
: GENITALIA

**gen·i·ti·val** \,je-nə-'tī-vəl\ *adjective* (1818)
: of, relating to, or formed with or from the genitive case
— **gen·i·ti·val·ly** \-və-lē\ *adverb*

**gen·i·tive** \'je-nə-tiv\ *adjective* [Middle English, from Latin *genetivus, genitivus*, literally, of generation (erroneous translation of Greek *genikos* genitive), from *genitus*] (14th century)
**1** : of, relating to, or constituting a grammatical case marking typically a relationship of possessor or source — compare POSSESSIVE
**2** : expressing a relationship that in some inflected languages is often marked by a genitive case — used especially of English prepositional phrases introduced by *of*

— **genitive** *noun*

**genito-** *combining form* [*genital*]
: genital and ⟨*genito*urinary⟩

**gen·i·to·uri·nary** \,je-nə-tō-'yūr-ə-,ner-ē\ *adjective* (circa 1836)
: of or relating to the genital and urinary organs or functions

**gen·i·ture** \'je-nə-,chùr, -chər, -,t(y)ùr\ *noun* (15th century)
: NATIVITY, BIRTH

**ge·nius** \'jēn-yəs, 'jē-nē-əs\ *noun, plural* **ge·nius·es** *or* **ge·nii** \-nē-,ī\ [Latin, tutelary spirit, natural inclinations, from *gignere* to beget] (1513)
**1 a** *plural* **genii** : an attendant spirit of a person or place **b** *plural usually* **genii** : a person who influences another for good or bad
**2** : a strong leaning or inclination : PENCHANT
**3 a** : a peculiar, distinctive, or identifying character or spirit **b** : the associations and traditions of a place **c** : a personification or embodiment especially of a quality or condition
**4** *plural usually* **genii** : SPIRIT, JINNI
**5** *plural usually* **geniuses a** : a single strongly marked capacity or aptitude ⟨had a *genius* for getting along with boys —Mary Ross⟩ **b** : extraordinary intellectual power especially as manifested in creative activity **c** : a person endowed with transcendent mental superiority; *especially* : a person with a very high intelligence quotient ◆
*synonym* see GIFT

**genius lo·ci** \-'lō-,sī, -,kē\ *noun* [Latin] (1605)
**1** : the pervading spirit of a place
**2** : a tutelary deity of a place

**geno-** — see GEN-

**gen·oa** \'je-nə-wə\ *noun* [*Genoa*, Italy] (1932)
: a large jib that overlaps the mainsail and is used especially in racing

**geno·cide** \'je-nə-,sīd\ *noun* (1944)
: the deliberate and systematic destruction of a racial, political, or cultural group
— **geno·cid·al** \,je-nə-'sī-d°l\ *adjective*

**ge·noise** *or* **gé·noise** \zhā-'nwäz\ *noun* [French *génoise*, from feminine of *génois* of Genoa, Italy] (1931)

◇ **WORD HISTORY**
**genius** For the Romans, *genius* was something between "soul" and "life," a spirit resident in every male human during his lifetime, with a counterpart in women called the *juno*. Originally, the *genius* seems to have resided only in the *paterfamilias*, the head of an extended family, for whom it was the expression of his procreative potency, in line with the etymological link between *genius* and the verbal base *gen-* (as in *gignere* "to beget" and *genitor* "parent"). The *genius* was thought of as the personification of a person's natural desires and so was used in phrases such as *indulgere genio* "to indulge oneself" (literally, "to indulge one's genius"). Corporate entities, such as military units, as well as places, were thought of as having their own *genius*. In late Roman religious belief, *genius* was detached from the individual and regarded as a tutelary spirit who presided over a person's well-being. The English word *genius*, borrowed from Latin in the 16th century, has drawn to some degree on several nuances of the Latin word and added complexities of its own. The sense "extraordinary intellectual power" arose in the 18th century, influenced in part by the meanings of French *génie*, itself descended from Latin *genius*.

**:** a sponge cake containing butter and leavened by stiffly beaten eggs

**ge·nome** \'jē-ˌnōm\ *noun* [German *Genom*, from *Gen* gene + -*om* (as in *Chromosom* chromosome)] (1930)
**:** one haploid set of chromosomes with the genes they contain; *broadly* **:** the genetic material of an organism
— **ge·no·mic** \ji-'nō-mik, -'nä-\ *adjective*
**ge·no·type** \'jē-nə-ˌtīp, 'je-\ *noun* (1897)
**1** [International Scientific Vocabulary ¹*gen-*] **:** TYPE SPECIES
**2** [International Scientific Vocabulary ²*gen-*] **:** all or part of the genetic constitution of an individual or group — compare PHENOTYPE
— **ge·no·typ·ic** \ˌjē-nə-'ti-pik, ˌje-\ *also* **ge·no·typ·i·cal** \-pi-kəl\ *adjective*
— **ge·no·typ·i·cal·ly** \-pi-k(ə-)lē\ *adverb*
**-genous** *adjective combining form* [-*gen* + -*ous*]
**1 :** producing **:** yielding ⟨erogenous⟩
**2 :** having (such) an origin ⟨terrigenous⟩
**genre** \'zhän-rə, 'zhä-; 'zhäⁿr; 'jän-rə\ *noun* [French, from Middle French, kind, gender — more at GENDER] (1770)
**1 :** a category of artistic, musical, or literary composition characterized by a particular style, form, or content
**2 :** KIND, SORT
**3 :** painting that depicts scenes or events from everyday life usually realistically
**gen·ro** \'gen-'rō\ *noun plural, often capitalized* [Japanese *genrō*] (1876)
**:** the elder statesmen of Japan who formerly advised the emperor
**gens** \'jenz, 'gen(t)s\ *noun, plural* **gen·tes** \'jen-ˌtēz, 'gen-ˌtās\ [Latin *gent-, gens* — more at GENTLE] (1847)
**1 :** a Roman clan embracing the families of the same stock in the male line with the members having a common name and worshiping a common ancestor
**2 :** CLAN; *especially* **:** a patrilineal clan
**3 :** a distinguishable group of related organisms
**¹gent** \'jent\ *adjective* [Middle English, noble, graceful, from Old French, from Latin *genitus*, past participle of *gignere* to beget — more at KIN] (13th century)
*archaic* **:** PRETTY, GRACEFUL
**²gent** *noun* (1564)
**:** GENTLEMAN
**gen·ta·mi·cin** \ˌjen-tə-'mī-s⁰n\ *noun* [alteration of earlier *gentamycin*, from *genti*an violet + kan*amycin*; from the color of the actinomycete] (1963)
**:** a broad-spectrum antibiotic that is derived from an actinomycete (*Micromonospora purpurea* or *M. echinospora*) and is extensively used as the sulfate in treating infections especially of the urinary tract
**gen·teel** \jen-'tē(ə)l\ *adjective* [Middle French *gentil* gentle] (1599)
**1 a :** having an aristocratic quality or flavor **:** STYLISH **b :** of or relating to the gentry or upper class **c :** elegant or graceful in manner, appearance, or shape **d :** free from vulgarity or rudeness **:** POLITE
**2 a :** maintaining or striving to maintain the appearance of superior or middle-class social status or respectability **b** (1) **:** marked by false delicacy, prudery, or affectation (2) **:** conventionally or insipidly pretty ⟨timid and *genteel* artistic style⟩
— **gen·teel·ly** \-'tē(ə)l-lē\ *adverb*
— **gen·teel·ness** *noun*
**gen·teel·ism** \-'tē(ə)l-ˌli-zəm\ *noun* (1926)
**:** a word believed by its user to be more polite or less vulgar than a common synonym; *also* **:** the use of genteelisms
**gen·tian** \'jen(t)-shən\ *noun* [Middle English *gencian*, from Middle French *gentiane*, from Latin *gentiana*] (14th century)
**1 :** any of numerous herbs (family Gentianaceae, the gentian family, and especially genus

*Gentiana*) with opposite smooth leaves and showy usually blue flowers
**2 :** the rhizome and roots of a yellow-flowered gentian (*Gentiana lutea*) of southern Europe that is used as a tonic, stomachic, and flavoring in vermouth
**gentian violet** *noun, often G&V capitalized* (1897)
**:** any of several dyes or dye mixtures consisting of one or more methyl derivatives of pararosaniline; *especially* **:** a dark green or greenish mixture used especially as a bactericide, fungicide, and anthelmintic
**¹gen·tile** \'jen-ˌtīl\ *noun* [Middle English, from Late Latin *gentilis*, from Latin *gent-, gens* nation] (14th century)
**1** *often capitalized* **:** a person of a non-Jewish nation or of non-Jewish faith; *especially* **:** a Christian as distinguished from a Jew
**2 :** HEATHEN, PAGAN
**3** *often capitalized* **:** a non-Mormon ◆
**²gentile** *adjective* (15th century)
**1** *often capitalized* **a :** of or relating to the nations at large as distinguished from the Jews; *also* **:** of or relating to Christians as distinguished from the Jews **b :** of or relating to non-Mormons
**2 :** HEATHEN, PAGAN
**3** [Latin *gentilis*] **:** relating to a tribe or clan
**gen·ti·lesse** \ˌjen-t⁰l-'es\ *noun* [Middle English, from Middle French, from *gentil*] (14th century)
**:** decorum of conduct befitting a member of the gentry
**gen·til·i·ty** \jen-'ti-lə-tē\ *noun, plural* **-ties** (14th century)
**1 a :** the condition of belonging to the gentry **b :** GENTLEFOLK, GENTRY
**2 a** (1) **:** decorum of conduct **:** COURTESY (2) **:** attitudes or activity marked by false delicacy, prudery, or affectation **b :** superior social status or prestige evidenced by manners, possessions, or mode of life
**¹gen·tle** \'jen-t⁰l\ *adjective* **gen·tler** \'jent-lər, -t⁰l-ər\; **gen·tlest** \'jent-ləst, -t⁰l-əst\ [Middle English *gentil*, from Old French, from Latin *gentilis* of a gens, of one's family, from *gent-, gens* gens, nation; akin to Latin *gignere* to beget — more at KIN] (13th century)
**1 a :** belonging to a family of high social station **b** *archaic* **:** CHIVALROUS **c :** HONORABLE, DISTINGUISHED; *specifically* **:** of or relating to a gentleman **d :** KIND, AMIABLE — used especially in address as a complimentary epithet ⟨*gentle* reader⟩ **e :** suited to a person of high social station
**2 a :** TRACTABLE, DOCILE **b :** free from harshness, sternness, or violence
**3 :** SOFT, DELICATE
**4 :** MODERATE
— **gent·ly** \'jent-lē\ *adverb*
**²gentle** *noun* (14th century)
**:** a person of gentle birth or status
**³gentle** *verb* **gen·tled; gen·tling** \'jent-liŋ, 'jen-t⁰l-iŋ\ (14th century)
*transitive verb*
**1 :** to raise from the commonalty **:** ENNOBLE
**2 a :** to make gentler **b :** to make (an animal) tame and docile **c :** MOLLIFY, PLACATE **d :** to stroke soothingly **:** PET
*intransitive verb*
**:** to become gentle ⟨the wind *gentled*⟩
**gentle breeze** *noun* (circa 1881)
**:** wind having a speed of 8 to 12 miles per hour (about 13 to 19 kilometers per hour) — see BEAUFORT SCALE table
**gen·tle·folk** \'jen-t⁰l-ˌfōk\ *also* **gen·tle·folks** \-ˌfōks\ *noun plural* (1594)
**:** persons of gentle or good family and breeding
**gen·tle·man** \'jen-t⁰l-mən, 'je-n⁰l-, *in rapid speech also* 'jen-tə-mən, 'je-nə-\ *noun, often attributive* [Middle English *gentilman*] (12th century)

**1 a :** a man of noble or gentle birth **b :** a man belonging to the landed gentry **c** (1) **:** a man who combines gentle birth or rank with chivalrous qualities (2) **:** a man whose conduct conforms to a high standard of propriety or correct behavior **d** (1) **:** a man of independent means who does not engage in any occupation or profession for gain (2) **:** a man who does not engage in a menial occupation or in manual labor for gain
**2 :** VALET — often used in the phrase *gentleman's gentleman*
**3 :** a man of any social class or condition — often used in a courteous reference ⟨show this *gentleman* to a seat⟩ or usually in the plural in address ⟨ladies and *gentlemen*⟩
— **gen·tle·man·like** \-mən-ˌlīk\ *adjective*
— **gen·tle·man·like·ness** *noun*
**gentleman–at–arms** *noun, plural* **gentlemen–at–arms** (1859)
**:** one of a military corps of 40 gentlemen who attend the British sovereign on state occasions
**gentleman–commoner** *noun, plural* **gentlemen–commoners** (1687)
**:** any of a privileged class of commoners formerly required to pay higher fees than ordinary commoners at the universities of Oxford and Cambridge
**gentleman farmer** *noun, plural* **gentlemen farmers** (1749)
**:** a man who farms mainly for pleasure rather than for profit
**gen·tle·man·ly** \-lē\ *adjective* (15th century)
**:** characteristic of or having the character of a gentleman
— **gen·tle·man·li·ness** *noun*
**gentleman of fortune** (1883)
**:** ADVENTURER
**gentleman's agreement** *or* **gentlemen's agreement** *noun* (1886)
**:** an agreement secured only by the honor of the participants
**gen·tle·ness** \'jen-t⁰l-nəs\ *noun* (14th century)
**:** the quality or state of being gentle; *especially* **:** mildness of manners or disposition
**gen·tle·per·son** \'jen-t⁰l-ˌpər-s⁰n\ *noun* (1943)
**:** a gentleman or lady
**gentle sex** *noun* (1583)
**:** the female sex **:** women in general
**gen·tle·wom·an** \'jen-t⁰l-ˌwu̇-mən\ *noun* (13th century)
**1 a :** a woman of noble or gentle birth **b :** a woman attendant upon a lady of rank
**2 :** a woman of refined manners or good breeding **:** LADY

---

◇ WORD HISTORY
**gentile** The Latin word *gens*, from the same Indo-European root as English *kin*, originally denoted a Roman clan, that is, a group of people sharing—either as a matter of legend or in reality—a common male ancestor. Early on, however, *gens*, especially in the plural *gentes*, was extended to any non-Roman people who, like the members of the clan, were ultimately all related to each other. Thus, it also meant simply "people, nation." The derived adjective *gentilis* meant accordingly both "of a clan" and "of a people, native." In the later Latin of the Christian church, *gentes* was used to translate Greek *ta ethnē* "the pagan peoples, those who were not the people of God." *Ta ethnē* in turn was a translation of Hebrew *goyim* in the Septuagint, the Greek translation of Jewish scripture. Correspondingly, the adjective *gentilis* was used in church Latin to mean "pagan" or "non-Jewish," the latter being the usual sense of English *gentile*, borrowed from Latin in the 14th century.

**Gen·too** \'jen-(,)tü\ *noun, plural* **Gentoos** [Portuguese *gentio,* literally, gentile, from Late Latin *gentilis*] (1638)
*archaic* : HINDU

**gen·too penguin** \'jen-(,)tü-\ *noun* [perhaps from *Gentoo*] (1860)
: a penguin (*Pygoscelis papua*) of Antarctica and nearby islands with a gray back and throat, white underparts, and white spots above the eyes — called also *gentoo*

**gen·trice** \'jen-trəs\ *noun* [Middle English *gentrise,* from Old French *genterise,* alteration of *gentelise,* from *gentil* gentle] (14th century)
*archaic* : gentility of birth : RANK

**gen·tri·fi·ca·tion** \,jen-trə-fə-'kā-shən\ *noun* (1964)
: the process of renewal and rebuilding accompanying the influx of middle-class or affluent people into deteriorating areas that often displaces earlier usually poorer residents

**gen·tri·fy** \'jen-trə-,fī\ *verb* **-fied; -fying** (1972)
*transitive verb*
: to attempt or accomplish the gentrification of
*intransitive verb*
: to become gentrified
— **gen·tri·fi·er** \-,fī(-ə)r\ *noun*

**gen·try** \'jen-trē\ *noun, plural* **gentries** [Middle English *gentrie,* alteration of *gentrise*] (14th century)
**1 a** *obsolete* : the qualities appropriate to a person of gentle birth; *especially* : COURTESY **b** : the condition or rank of a gentleman
**2 a** : upper or ruling class : ARISTOCRACY **b** : a class whose members are entitled to bear a coat of arms though not of noble rank; *especially* : the landed proprietors having such status
**3** : people of a specified class or kind : FOLKS ⟨no real heroes or heroines among the academic *gentry* —R. G. Hanvey⟩

**gents** \'jen(t)s\ *noun, often capitalized* (1938)
*chiefly British* : MEN'S ROOM

**gen·u·flect** \'jen-yə-,flekt\ *intransitive verb* [Late Latin *genuflectere,* from Latin *genu* knee + *flectere* to bend — more at KNEE] (1630)
**1 a** : to bend the knee **b** : to touch the knee to the floor or ground especially in worship
**2** : to be servilely obedient or respectful
— **gen·u·flec·tion** \,jen-yə-'flek-shən\ *noun*

**gen·u·ine** \'jen-yə-wən, -(,)win, ÷-,wīn\ *adjective* [Latin *genuinus* innate, genuine; akin to Latin *gignere* to beget — more at KIN] (circa 1639)
**1 a** : actually having the reputed or apparent qualities or character ⟨*genuine* vintage wines⟩ **b** : actually produced by or proceeding from the alleged source or author ⟨the signature is *genuine*⟩ **c** : sincerely and honestly felt or experienced ⟨a deep and *genuine* love⟩ **d** : ACTUAL, TRUE ⟨a *genuine* improvement⟩
**2** : free from hypocrisy or pretense : SINCERE ☐
*synonym* see AUTHENTIC
— **gen·u·ine·ly** *adverb*
— **gen·u·ine·ness** \-wə(n)-nəs\ *noun*

**ge·nus** \'jē-nəs, 'je-\ *noun, plural* **gen·era** \'je-nə-rə\ [Latin *gener-, genus* birth, race, kind — more at KIN] (1551)
**1** : a class, kind, or group marked by common characteristics or by one common characteristic; *specifically* : a category of biological classification ranking between the family and the species, comprising structurally or phylogenetically related species or an isolated species exhibiting unusual differentiation, and being designated by a Latin or latinized capitalized singular noun
**2** : a class of objects divided into several subordinate species
*word history* see SPICE

**-geny** *noun combining form* [Greek *-geneia* act of being born, from *-genēs* born — more at -GEN]
: generation : production ⟨phylo*geny*⟩

**geo-** — see GE-

**geo·bot·a·ny** \,jē-ō-'bä-tᵊn-ē, -'bät-nē\ *noun* (1904)
: PHYTOGEOGRAPHY
— **geo·bo·tan·i·cal** \-bə-'ta-ni-kəl\ *also* **geo·bo·tan·ic** \-'nik\ *adjective*
— **geo·bot·a·nist** \-'bä-tᵊn-ist, -'bät-nist\ *noun*

**geo·cen·tric** \,jē-ō-'sen-trik\ *adjective* (1686)
**1 a** : relating to, measured from, or as if observed from the earth's center — compare TOPOCENTRIC **b** : having or relating to the earth as center — compare HELIOCENTRIC
**2** : taking or based on the earth as the center of perspective and valuation
— **geo·cen·tri·cal·ly** \-tri-k(ə-)lē\ *adverb*

**geo·chem·is·try** \,jē-ō-'ke-mə-strē\ *noun* (1902)
**1** : a science that deals with the chemical composition of and chemical changes in the solid matter of the earth or a celestial body (as the moon)
**2** : the related chemical and geological properties of a substance
— **geo·chem·i·cal** \-'ke-mi-kəl\ *adjective*
— **geo·chem·i·cal·ly** \-k(ə-)lē\ *adverb*
— **geo·chem·ist** \-'ke-mist\ *noun*

**geo·chro·nol·o·gy** \-krə-'nä-lə-jē\ *noun* (1893)
**1** : the chronology of the past as indicated by geologic data
**2** : the study of geochronology
— **geo·chro·no·log·i·cal** \-,krä-nᵊl-'ä-ji-kəl, -,krō-\ *also* **geo·chro·no·log·ic** \-'ä-jik\ *adjective*
— **geo·chro·no·log·i·cal·ly** \-ji-k(ə-)lē\ *adverb*
— **geo·chro·nol·o·gist** \-krə-'nä-lə-jist\ *noun*

**ge·ode** \'jē-,ōd\ *noun* [Latin *geodes,* a gem, from Greek *geōdēs* earthlike, from *gē* earth] (circa 1732)
**1** : a nodule of stone having a cavity lined with crystals or mineral matter
**2** : the cavity in a geode

**¹geo·de·sic** \,jē-ə-'de-sik, -'dē-, -zik\ *adjective* (1821)
**1** : GEODETIC
**2** : made of light straight structural elements mostly in tension ⟨a *geodesic* dome⟩

**²geodesic** *noun* (1883)
: the shortest line between two points that lies in a given surface

**ge·od·e·sy** \jē-'ä-də-sē\ *noun* [Greek *geōdaisia,* from *geō-* ge- + *daiesthai* to divide — more at TIDE] (1570)
: a branch of applied mathematics concerned with the determination of the size and shape of the earth and the exact positions of points on its surface and with the description of variations of its gravity field
— **ge·od·e·sist** \-də-sist\ *noun*

**geo·det·ic** \,jē-ə-'de-tik\ *also* **geo·det·i·cal** \-ti-kəl\ *adjective* [*geodesy;* after such pairs as *heresy : heretic*] (circa 1828)
: of, relating to, or determined by geodesy

**geodetic survey** *noun* (1880)
: a survey of a large land area in which corrections are made for the curvature of the earth's surface

**Geo·dim·e·ter** \,jē-ə-'di-mə-tər\ *trademark*
— used for an electronic-optical device that measures distance using the velocity of light

**geo·duck** \'gü-ē-,dək\ *noun* [Lushootseed (Salishan language of the Puget Sound region) *gʷídəq*] (1883)
: a large edible clam (*Panopea abrupta* synonym *P. generosa*) of the Pacific coast that sometimes weighs over five pounds

**ge·og·ra·pher** \jē-'ä-grə-fər\ *noun* (1542)
: a specialist in geography

**geo·graph·ic** \,jē-ə-'gra-fik\ *or* **geo·graph·i·cal** \-fi-kəl\ *adjective* (1559)
**1** : of or relating to geography
**2** : belonging to or characteristic of a particular region
— **geo·graph·i·cal·ly** \-fi-k(ə-)lē\ *adverb*

**geographical mile** *noun* (1823)
: NAUTICAL MILE a

**ge·og·ra·phy** \jē-'ä-grə-fē\ *noun, plural* **-phies** [Latin *geographia,* from Greek *geōgraphia,* from *geōgraphein* to describe the earth's surface, from *geō-* + *graphein* to write — more at CARVE] (15th century)
**1** : a science that deals with the description, distribution, and interaction of the diverse physical, biological, and cultural features of the earth's surface
**2** : the geographic features of an area
**3** : a treatise on geography
**4** : a delineation or systematic arrangement of constituent elements : CONFIGURATION ⟨the philosophers . . . have tried to construct *geographies* of human reason —*Times Literary Supplement*⟩

**geo·hy·drol·o·gy** \,jē-ō-hī-'drä-lə-jē\ *noun* (circa 1909)
: a science that deals with the character, source, and mode of occurrence of underground water
— **geo·hy·dro·log·ic** \-,hī-drə-'lä-jik\ *adjective*
— **geo·hy·drol·o·gist** \-hī-'drä-lə-jist\ *noun*

**ge·oid** \'jē-,oid\ *noun* [German, from Greek *geoeidēs* earthlike, from *gē*] (1881)
: the surface within or around the earth that is everywhere normal to the direction of gravity and coincides with mean sea level in the oceans
— **ge·oi·dal** \jē-'oi-dᵊl\ *adjective*

**geo·log·ic** \,jē-ə-'lä-jik\ *or* **geo·log·i·cal** \-ji-kəl\ *adjective* (1791)
: of, relating to, or based on geology
— **geo·log·i·cal·ly** \-ji-k(ə-)lē\ *adverb*

**geologic time** *noun* (1861)
: the long period of time occupied by the earth's geologic history
▶ The Geologic Time table is on page 768.

**ge·ol·o·gize** \jē-'ä-lə-,jīz\ *intransitive verb* **-gized; -giz·ing** (1831)
: to study geology or make geologic investigations

**ge·ol·o·gy** \jē-'ä-lə-jē\ *noun, plural* **-gies** [New Latin *geologia,* from *ge-* + *-logia* -logy] (1735)
**1 a** : a science that deals with the history of the earth and its life especially as recorded in rocks **b** : a study of the solid matter of a celestial body (as the moon)
**2** : geologic features
**3** : a treatise on geology
— **ge·ol·o·gist** \-jist\ *noun*

**geo·mag·net·ic** \,jē-ō-mag-'ne-tik\ *adjective* (1904)
: of or relating to terrestrial magnetism
— **geo·mag·net·i·cal·ly** \-ti-k(ə-)lē\ *adverb*
— **geo·mag·ne·tism** \-'mag-nə-,ti-zəm\ *noun*

**geomagnetic storm** *noun* (1941)
: MAGNETIC STORM

---

☐ USAGE

**genuine** The objection which some commentators make to the pronunciation \'jen-yə-,wīn\ is perhaps occasioned by the fact that it is more frequent among those with less schooling. However, this variant is heard in the speech of cultured or highly educated speakers sufficiently frequently for it to be recognized as a widespread pronunciation at all social levels. This variant was recorded as early as 1890 and appears to be simply a long-standing spelling pronunciation.

---

\ə\ abut \ᵊ\ kitten \ər\ further \a\ ash \ā\ ace
\ä\ mop, mar \au̇\ out \ch\ chin \e\ bet \ē\ easy
\g\ go \i\ hit \ī\ ice \j\ job \ŋ\ sing \ō\ go
\ȯ\ law \ȯi\ boy \th\ thin \tẖ\ the \ü\ loot \u̇\ foot
\y\ yet \zh\ vision    *see also* Guide to Pronunciation

# GEOLOGIC TIME

| EON | ERA | PERIODS AND SYSTEMS | EPOCHS AND SERIES | BEGINNING OF INTERVAL* | BIOLOGICAL FORMS |
|---|---|---|---|---|---|
| Phanerozoic | Cenozoic | Quaternary | Holocene | 0.01 | |
| | | | Pleistocene | 1.6 | Earliest humans |
| | | Tertiary | Pliocene | 5 | |
| | | | Miocene | 24 | Earliest hominids |
| | | | Oligocene | 37 | |
| | | | Eocene | 58 | Earliest grasses |
| | | | Paleocene | 65 | Earliest large mammals |
| | | Cretaceous-Tertiary boundary (65 million years ago): extinction of dinosaurs | | | |
| | Mesozoic | Cretaceous | Upper | 98 | |
| | | | Lower | 144 | Earliest flowering plants; dinosaurs in ascendance |
| | | Jurassic | | 208 | Earliest birds & mammals |
| | | Triassic | | 245 | Age of Dinosaurs begins |
| | Paleozoic | Permian | | 286 | |
| | | Carboniferous | | | |
| | | Pennsylvanian | | 320 | Earliest reptiles |
| | | Mississippian | | 360 | Earliest winged insects |
| | | Devonian | | 408 | Earliest vascular plants (as ferns & mosses) & amphibians |
| | | Silurian | | 438 | Earliest land plants & insects |
| | | Ordovician | | 505 | Earliest corals |
| | | Cambrian | | 570 | Earliest fish |
| Proterozoic | Precambrian | | | 2500 | Earliest colonial algae & soft-bodied invertebrates |
| Archean | | | | 4000 | Life appears: earliest algae & primitive bacteria |

*In millions of years before the present

**geo·man·cy** \'jē-ə-,man(t)-sē\ *noun* [Middle English *geomancie*, from Middle French, from Medieval Latin *geomantia*, from Late Greek *geōmanteia*, from Greek *geō-* + *-manteia* -mancy] (14th century)
**:** divination by means of figures or lines or geographic features
— **geo·man·cer** \-sər\ *noun*
— **geo·man·tic** \,jē-ə-'man-tik\ *adjective*
**ge·om·e·ter** \jē-'ä-mə-tər\ *noun* (15th century)
**1 :** a specialist in geometry
**2 :** GEOMETRID
**geo·met·ric** \,jē-ə-'me-trik\ *or* **geo·met·ri·cal** \-'me-tri-kəl\ *adjective* (14th century)
**1 a :** of, relating to, or according to the methods or principles of geometry **b :** increasing in a geometric progression ⟨*geometric* population growth⟩

**2** *capitalized* **:** of or relating to a style of ancient Greek pottery characterized by geometric decorative motifs
**3 a :** utilizing rectilinear or simple curvilinear motifs or outlines in design **b :** of or relating to art based on simple geometric shapes (as straight lines, circles, or squares) ⟨*geometric* abstractions⟩
— **geo·met·ri·cal·ly** \-tri-k(ə-)lē\ *adverb*
**geo·me·tri·cian** \(,)jē-ä-mə-'tri-shən, ,jē-ə-mə-\ *noun* (15th century)
**:** GEOMETER 1
**geometric mean** *noun* (circa 1901)
**:** the nth root of the product of *n* numbers; *specifically* **:** a number that is the second term of three consecutive terms of a geometric progression ⟨the *geometric mean* of 9 and 4 is 6⟩
**geometric progression** *noun* (circa 1856)
**:** a sequence (as 1, ½, ¼) in which the ratio of a term to its predecessor is always the same

— called also *geometrical progression, geometric sequence*
**geo·met·rics** \,jē-ə-'me-triks\ *noun plural* (1977)
**:** decorative patterns or designs based on geometric shapes
**geometric series** *noun* (circa 1909)
**:** a series (as $1 + x + x^2 + x^3 + \dots$) whose terms form a geometric progression
**geo·me·trid** \jē-'ä-mə-trəd, ,jē-ə-'me-trəd\ *noun* [ultimately from Greek *geōmetrēs* geometer, from *geōmetrein*] (1876)
**:** any of a family (Geometridae) of usually medium-sized moths with large wings and larvae that are loopers
— **geometrid** *adjective*
**ge·om·e·trise** *British variant of* GEOMETRIZE
**ge·om·e·trize** \jē-'ä-mə-,trīz\ *verb* **-trized; -triz·ing** (1603)
*intransitive verb*
**:** to work by or as if by geometric methods or laws
*transitive verb*
**1 :** to represent geometrically
**2 :** to make conform to geometric principles and laws
— **ge·om·e·tri·za·tion** \-,ä-mə-trə-'zā-shən\ *noun*
**ge·om·e·try** \jē-'ä-mə-trē\ *noun, plural* **-tries** [Middle English *geometrie*, from Middle French, from Latin *geometria*, from Greek *geōmetria*, from *geōmetrein* to measure the earth, from *geō-* ge- + *metron* measure — more at MEASURE] (14th century)
**1 a :** a branch of mathematics that deals with the measurement, properties, and relationships of points, lines, angles, surfaces, and solids; *broadly* **:** the study of properties of given elements that remain invariant under specified transformations **b :** a particular type or system of geometry
**2 a :** CONFIGURATION **b :** surface shape
**3 :** an arrangement of objects or parts that suggests geometric figures
**geo·mor·phic** \,jē-ə-'mȯr-fik\ *adjective* (1893)
**:** GEOMORPHOLOGICAL
**geo·mor·pho·log·i·cal** \-mȯr-fə-'lä-ji-kəl\ *adjective* (1896)
**:** of or relating to the form or surface features of the earth or other celestial body (as the moon)
**geo·mor·phol·o·gy** \-mȯr-'fä-lə-jē\ *noun, plural* **-gies** [International Scientific Vocabulary] (1893)
**1 :** a science that deals with the relief features of the earth or of another celestial body (as the moon) and seeks a genetic interpretation of them
**2 :** the features dealt with in geomorphology
— **geo·mor·phol·o·gist** \-mȯr-'fä-lə-jist\ *noun*
**ge·oph·a·gy** \jē-'ä-fə-jē\ *noun* [International Scientific Vocabulary] (1850)
**:** a practice in rural or preindustrial societies of eating earthy substances (as clay) to augment a scanty or mineral-deficient diet — compare ¹PICA
**geo·phone** \'jē-ə-,fōn\ *noun* (1919)
**:** an instrument for detecting vibrations passing through rocks, soil, or ice
**geo·phys·ics** \,jē-ə-'fi-ziks\ *noun plural but singular or plural in construction* [International Scientific Vocabulary] (circa 1889)
**:** a branch of earth science dealing with the physical processes and phenomena occurring especially in the earth and in its vicinity
— **geo·phys·i·cal** \-zi-kəl\ *adjective*
— **geo·phys·i·cal·ly** \-zi-k(ə-)lē\ *adverb*
— **geo·phys·i·cist** \-'fi-zə-sist\ *noun*
**geo·phyte** \'jē-ə-,fīt\ *noun* (circa 1900)
**:** a perennial plant that bears its perennating buds below the surface of the soil
**geo·pol·i·ti·cian** \,jē-ō-,pä-lə-'ti-shən\ *noun* (1941)
**:** a specialist in geopolitics

**geo·pol·i·tics** \-'pä-lə-,tiks\ *noun plural but singular in construction* (1904)
**1** : a study of the influence of such factors as geography, economics, and demography on the politics and especially the foreign policy of a state
**2** : a governmental policy guided by geopolitics
**3** : a combination of political and geographic factors relating to something (as a state or particular resources)
— **geo·po·lit·i·cal** \-pə-'li-ti-kəl\ *adjective*
— **geo·po·lit·i·cal·ly** \-ti-k(ə-)lē\ *adverb*
**geo·pres·sured** \,jē-ō-'pre-shərd\ *adjective* (1968)
: subjected to great pressure from geologic forces ⟨*geopressured* methane⟩
**Geor·die** \'jȯr-dē\ *noun* [from *Geordie,* diminutive of the name *George*] (1866)
*chiefly British* : an inhabitant of Newcastle upon Tyne or its environs; *also* : the dialect of English spoken by Geordies
**George** \'jȯrj\ *noun* [Saint *George*] (1506)
**1** : either of two of the insignia of the British Order of the Garter
**2** : a British coin bearing the image of Saint George
**geor·gette** \jȯr-'jet\ *noun* [from *Georgette,* a trademark] (1915)
: a sheer crepe woven from hard-twisted yarns to produce a dull pebbly surface
¹**Geor·gian** \'jȯr-jən\ *noun* (15th century)
**1** : a native or inhabitant of Georgia in the Caucasus
**2** : the language of the Georgian people
²**Georgian** *adjective* (1607)
: of, relating to, or constituting Georgia in the Caucasus, the Georgians, or Georgian
³**Georgian** *noun* (1741)
: a native or resident of the state of Georgia
⁴**Georgian** *adjective* (1762)
: of, relating to, or characteristic of the state of Georgia or its people
⁵**Georgian** *adjective* (circa 1855)
**1** : of, relating to, or characteristic of the reigns of the first four Georges of Great Britain
**2** : of, relating to, or characteristic of the reign of George V of Great Britain
⁶**Georgian** *noun* (1901)
**1** : one belonging to either of the Georgian periods; *especially* : a poet of the second decade of the 20th century
**2** : Georgian taste or style especially in architecture
¹**geor·gic** \'jȯr-jik\ *noun* [the *Georgics,* poem by Virgil, from Latin *georgicus*] (1513)
: a poem dealing with agriculture
²**georgic** *adjective* [Latin *georgicus,* from Greek *geōrgikos,* from *geōrgos* farmer, from *geō-* ge- + *ergon* work — more at WORK] (circa 1720)
: of or relating to agriculture
**geo·sci·ence** \,jē-ō-'sī-ən(t)s\ *noun* (1942)
**1** : the sciences (as geology, geophysics, and geochemistry) dealing with the earth
**2** : any of the geosciences — compare EARTH SCIENCE
— **geo·sci·en·tist** \-ən-tist\ *noun*
**geo·sta·tion·ary** \-'stā-shə-,ner-ē\ *adjective* (1961)
: being or having an equatorial orbit requiring an angular velocity the same as that of the earth so that the position of a satellite in such an orbit is fixed with respect to the earth
**geo·strat·e·gy** \-'stra-tə-jē\ *noun* (1942)
**1** : a branch of geopolitics that deals with strategy
**2** : the combination of geopolitical and strategic factors characterizing a particular geographic region
**3** : the use by a government of strategy based on geopolitics
— **geo·stra·te·gic** \-strə-'tē-jik\ *adjective*
— **geo·strat·e·gist** \-'stra-tə-jist\ *noun*

**geo·stroph·ic** \,jē-ə-'strä-fik\ *adjective* [ge- + Greek *strophikos* turned, from *strophē* turning — more at STROPHE] (1916)
: of, relating to, or arising from the Coriolis force
— **geo·stroph·i·cal·ly** \-fi-k(ə-)lē\ *adverb*
**geo·syn·chro·nous** \,jē-ō-'siŋ-krə-nəs, -'sin-\ *adjective* (1968)
: GEOSTATIONARY
**geo·syn·cline** \-'sin-,klīn\ *noun* (1895)
: a great downward flexure of the earth's crust — compare GEANTICLINE
— **geo·syn·cli·nal** \-,sin-'klī-nəl\ *adjective*
**geo·tac·tic** \,jē-ō-'tak-tik\ *adjective* (1899)
: of or relating to geotaxis
**geo·tax·is** \-'tak-səs\ *noun* [New Latin] (1899)
: a taxis in which the force of gravity is the directive factor
**geo·tech·ni·cal** \-'tek-ni-kəl\ *adjective* (1967)
: of or relating to geotechnical engineering
**geotechnical engineering** *noun* (1974)
: a science that deals with the application of geology to engineering
**geo·tec·ton·ic** \-tek-'tä-nik\ *adjective* (1882)
: of or relating to the form, arrangement, and structure of rock masses of the earth's crust resulting from folding or faulting
— **geo·tec·ton·i·cal·ly** \-ni-k(ə-)lē\ *adverb*
**geo·ther·mal** \-'thər-məl\ *adjective* [International Scientific Vocabulary] (1875)
: of, relating to, or utilizing the heat of the earth's interior; *also* : produced or permeated by such heat ⟨*geothermal* steam⟩ ⟨*geothermal* region⟩
— **geo·ther·mal·ly** \-mə-lē\ *adverb*
**geo·tro·pic** \,jē-ə-'trō-pik, -'trä-\ *adjective* (1875)
: of or relating to geotropism
— **geo·tro·pi·cal·ly** \-'trō-pi-k(ə-)lē, -'trä-\ *adverb*
**ge·ot·ro·pism** \jē-'ä-trə-,pi-zəm\ *noun* [International Scientific Vocabulary] (1875)
: a tropism (as of plant roots) in which gravity is the orienting factor
**ge·rah** \'gir-ə\ *noun* [Hebrew *gērāh*] (1530)
: an ancient Hebrew unit of weight equal to 1/20 shekel
**ge·ra·ni·ol** \jə-'rā-nē-,ȯl, -,ōl\ *noun* [International Scientific Vocabulary, from New Latin *Geranium*] (1871)
: a fragrant liquid unsaturated alcohol $C_{10}H_{18}O$ used chiefly in perfumes and soap
**ge·ra·ni·um** \jə-'rā-nē-əm, -nyəm\ *noun* [New Latin, from Latin, geranium, from Greek *geranion,* from diminutive of *geranos* crane — more at CRANE] (1548)
**1** : any of a widely distributed genus (*Geranium* of the family Geraniaceae, the geranium family) of plants having regular usually white, pink, or purple flowers with elongated styles and glands that alternate with the petals
**2** : PELARGONIUM
**3** : a vivid or strong red
**ge·rar·dia** \jə-'rär-dē-ə\ *noun* [New Latin, from John *Gerard* (died 1612) English botanist] (1851)
: any of a genus (*Agalinis* synonym *Gerardia*) of often root-parasitic herbs of the snapdragon family having pink, purple, or yellow flowers
**ger·bera** \'gər-bə-rə, 'jər-\ *noun* [New Latin, from Traugott *Gerber* (died 1743) German naturalist] (1889)
: any of a genus (*Gerbera*) of Old World composite herbs having basal tufted leaves and showy heads of yellow, pink, or orange flowers with prominent rays
**ger·bil** *also* **ger·bille** \'jər-bəl\ *noun* [French *gerbille,* from New Latin *Gerbillus,* diminutive of *gerboa, jerboa* jerboa] (1849)
: any of numerous Old World burrowing desert rodents (*Gerbillus* and related genera) with long hind legs adapted for leaping

**ge·rent** \'jir-ənt\ *noun* [Latin *gerent-, gerens,* present participle of *gerere* to bear, carry on] (1576)
: one that rules or manages
**ge·re·nuk** \'ger-ə-,nu̇k, gə-'re-nək\ *noun, plural* **gerenuk** *or* **gerenuks** [Somali *gáránúug*] (1895)
: a large-eyed antelope (*Litocranius walleri*) of eastern Africa with a long neck and limbs

gerenuk

**ger·fal·con** *variant of* GYRFALCON
¹**ge·ri·at·ric** \,jer-ē-'a-trik, jir-\ *noun* (1909)
**1** *plural but singular in construction* : a branch of medicine that deals with the problems and diseases of old age and aging people — compare GERONTOLOGY
**2** : an aged person
²**geriatric** *adjective* [Greek *gēras* old age + English *-iatric*] (1926)
**1 a** : of or relating to geriatrics or the process of aging **b** : of, relating to, or appropriate for elderly people ⟨the *geriatric* set⟩
**2 a** : OLD, ELDERLY ⟨a *geriatric* dachshund⟩ **b** : being old and outmoded ⟨*geriatric* airplanes⟩
**ger·i·a·tri·cian** \,jer-ē-ə-'tri-shən, ,jir-\ *noun* (1926)
: a specialist in geriatrics
**germ** \'jərm\ *noun* [French *germe,* from Latin *germin-, germen,* from *gignere* to beget — more at KIN] (1644)
**1 a** : a small mass of living substance capable of developing into an organism or one of its parts **b** : the embryo with the scutellum of a cereal grain that is usually separated from the starchy endosperm during milling
**2** : something that initiates development or serves as an origin: RUDIMENTS, BEGINNING
**3** : MICROORGANISM; *especially* : a microorganism causing disease
¹**ger·man** \'jər-mən\ *adjective* [Middle English *germain,* from Middle French, from Latin *germanus* having the same parents, from *germen*] (14th century)
: having the same parents or the same grandparents on either the maternal or paternal side — usually used after the noun which it modifies and joined to it by a hyphen ⟨brother-*german*⟩ ⟨cousin-*german*⟩
²**german** *noun* (15th century)
*obsolete* : a near relative
¹**Ger·man** \'jər-mən\ *noun* [Middle English, from Medieval Latin *Germanus,* from Latin] (14th century)
**1** : a member of any of the Germanic peoples inhabiting western Europe in Roman times
**2 a** : a native or inhabitant of Germany **b** : a person of German descent **c** : one whose native language is German and who is a native of a country other than Germany
**3 a** : the Germanic language spoken mainly in Germany, Austria, and parts of Switzerland **b** : the literary and official language of Germany
**4** *often not capitalized* **a** : a dance consisting of intricate figures that are improvised and intermingled with waltzes **b** *chiefly Midland* : a dancing party; *specifically* : one at which the german is danced
²**German** *adjective* (1552)
: of, relating to, or characteristic of Germany, the Germans, or German
**German cockroach** *noun* (1896)
: a small active winged cockroach (*Blattella germanica*) probably of African origin that is a

common household pest in the U.S. — called also *Croton bug*

**ger·man·der** \(ˌ)jər-'man-dər\ *noun* [ultimately from Greek *chamaidrys,* from *chamai* on the ground + *drys* tree — more at HUMBLE, TREE] (15th century)
: any of a genus (*Teucrium*) of plants of the mint family with flowers having four exserted stamens, a short corolla tube, and a prominent lower lip

**ger·mane** \(ˌ)jər-'mān\ *adjective* [Middle English *germain,* literally, having the same parents, from Middle French] (14th century)
**1** *obsolete* : closely akin
**2** : being at once relevant and appropriate : FITTING ⟨omit details that are not *germane* to the discussion⟩
**synonym** see RELEVANT
— **ger·mane·ly** *adverb*

**¹Ger·man·ic** \(ˌ)jər-'ma-nik\ *adjective* (1633)
**1** : GERMAN
**2** : of, relating to, or characteristic of the Germanic-speaking peoples
**3** : of, relating to, or constituting Germanic

**²Germanic** *noun* (1892)
: a branch of the Indo-European language family containing English, German, Dutch, Afrikaans, Flemish, Frisian, the Scandinavian languages, and Gothic — see INDO-EUROPEAN LANGUAGES table

**Ger·man·ism** \'jər-mə-ˌni-zəm\ *noun* (1611)
**1** : a characteristic feature of German occurring in another language
**2** : partiality for Germany or German customs
**3** : the practices or objectives characteristic of the Germans

**Ger·man·ist** \-nist\ *noun* (1831)
: a specialist in German or Germanic language, literature, or culture

**ger·ma·ni·um** \(ˌ)jər-'mā-nē-əm\ *noun* [New Latin, from Medieval Latin *Germania* Germany] (1886)
: a grayish white hard brittle metalloid element that resembles silicon and is used as a semiconductor — see ELEMENT table

**ger·man·ize** \'jər-mə-ˌnīz\ *verb* **-ized; -iz·ing** *often capitalized* (1598)
*transitive verb*
**1** *archaic* : to translate into German
**2** : to cause to acquire German characteristics
*intransitive verb*
: to have or acquire German customs or leanings
— **ger·man·iza·tion** \ˌjər-mə-nə-'zā-shən\ *noun, often capitalized*

**German measles** *noun plural but singular or plural in construction* (circa 1875)
: an acute contagious virus disease that is milder than typical measles but is damaging to the fetus when occurring early in pregnancy

**Ger·mano-** *combining form*
: German ⟨*Germano*phile⟩

**¹Ger·mano·phile** \(ˌ)jər-'ma-nə-ˌfīl\ *adjective* (1898)
: approving or favoring the German people and their institutions and customs

**²Germanophile** *noun* (1911)
: one that is Germanophile

**German shepherd** *noun* (1926)
: any of a breed of working dogs of German origin that are intelligent and responsive and are often used in police work and as guide dogs for the blind — called also *Alsatian*

**German shorthaired pointer** *noun* (1931)
: any of a breed of gundogs of German origin that have a liver or liver and white coat

**German silver** *noun* (1830)
: a silver-white alloy of copper, zinc, and nickel

**German wirehaired pointer** *noun* (circa 1964)
: any of a breed of gundogs of German origin that have a liver or liver and white flat-lying wiry coat

**germ cell** *noun* (circa 1855)

: a gamete (as an egg or sperm cell) or one of its antecedent cells

**ger·men** \'jər-mən\ *noun* [Latin] (1605)
*archaic* : GERM 1a, 2

**germ-free** \'jərm-ˌfrē\ *adjective* (1926)
: free of microorganisms : AXENIC

**ger·mi·cid·al** \ˌjər-mə-'sī-d°l\ *adjective* (circa 1888)
: of or relating to a germicide; *also* : destroying germs

**ger·mi·cide** \'jər-mə-ˌsīd\ *noun* (1881)
: an agent that destroys germs

**ger·mi·na·bil·i·ty** \ˌjər-mə-nə-'bi-lə-tē\ *noun* (1896)
: the capacity to germinate

**ger·mi·nal** \'jərm-nəl, 'jer-mə-n°l\ *adjective* [French, from Latin *germin-, germen* — more at GERM] (1808)
**1 a** : being in the earliest stage of development **b** : CREATIVE, PRODUCTIVE
**2** : of, relating to, or having the characteristics of a germ cell or early embryo
— **ger·mi·nal·ly** *adverb*

**germinal vesicle** *noun* (circa 1856)
: the enlarged nucleus of the egg before completion of meiosis

**ger·mi·nate** \'jər-mə-ˌnāt\ *verb* **-nat·ed; -nat·ing** [Latin *germinatus,* past participle of *germinare* to sprout, from *germin-, germen* bud, germ] (1610)
*transitive verb*
: to cause to sprout or develop
*intransitive verb*
**1** : to come into being : EVOLVE ⟨before Western civilization began to *germinate* —A. L. Kroeber⟩
**2** : to begin to grow : SPROUT
— **ger·mi·na·tion** \ˌjər-mə-'nā-shən\ *noun*
— **ger·mi·na·tive** \'jər-mə-ˌnā-tiv, -mə-nə-\ *adjective*

**germ layer** *noun* (1879)
: any of the three primary layers of cells differentiated in most embryos during and immediately following gastrulation

**germ plasm** *noun* (1889)
**1** : germ cells and their precursors serving as the bearers of heredity and being fundamentally independent of other cells
**2** : the hereditary material of the germ cells : GENES

**germ-proof** \'jərm-ˌprüf\ *adjective* (1902)
: impervious to the penetration or action of germs

**germ theory** *noun* (1871)
: a theory in medicine: infections, contagious diseases, and various other conditions result from the action of microorganisms

**germ warfare** *noun* (1938)
: the use of harmful microorganisms (as bacteria) as weapons in war

**germy** \'jər-mē\ *adjective* **germ·i·er; -est** (1912)
: full of germs

**geront-** *or* **geronto-** *combining form* [French *géront-, géronto-,* from Greek *geront-, geronto-,* from *geront-, gerōn* old man; akin to Greek *gēras* old age, Sanskrit *jarati* he grows old]
: aged one : old age ⟨*geronto*logy⟩

**ge·ron·tic** \jə-'rän-tik\ *adjective* (1885)
: of or relating to decadence or old age

**ger·on·toc·ra·cy** \ˌjer-ən-'tä-krə-sē\ *noun, plural* **-cies** [French *gérontocratie,* from *géronto-* *geront-* + *-cratie* *-cracy*] (1830)
: rule by elders; *specifically* : a form of social organization in which a group of old men or a council of elders dominates or exercises control
— **ge·ron·to·crat** \jə-'rän-tə-ˌkrat\ *noun*
— **ge·ron·to·crat·ic** \-ˌrän-tə-'kra-tik\ *adjective*

**ger·on·tol·o·gy** \ˌjer-ən-'tä-lə-jē\ *noun* [International Scientific Vocabulary] (1903)
: the comprehensive study of aging and the problems of the aged — compare GERIATRIC 1

— **ge·ron·to·log·i·cal** \jə-ˌrän-t°l-'ä-ji-kəl\ *also* **ge·ron·to·log·ic** \-jik\ *adjective*
— **ger·on·tol·o·gist** \ˌjer-ən-'tä-lə-jist\ *noun*

**ge·ron·to·mor·phic** \jə-ˌrän-tə-'mor-fik\ *adjective* (1939)
: characterized by physical specialization most fully developed in the aged male of a species ⟨*gerontomorphic* traits⟩

**¹ger·ry·man·der** \'jer-ē-ˌman-dər, *also* 'ger-; *originally* 'ger-\ *noun* [Elbridge *Gerry* + sala*mander;* from the shape of an election district formed during Gerry's governorship of Mass.] (1812)
**1** : the act or method of gerrymandering
**2** : a district or pattern of districts varying greatly in size or population as a result of gerrymandering ◆

**²gerrymander** *transitive verb* **-dered; -der·ing** \(-d(ə-)riŋ\ (1812)
**1** : to divide (a territorial unit) into election districts to give one political party an electoral majority in a large number of districts while concentrating the voting strength of the opposition in as few districts as possible
**2** : to divide (an area) into political units to give special advantages to one group ⟨*gerrymander* a school district⟩

**ger·und** \'jer-ənd\ *noun* [Late Latin *gerundium,* from Latin *gerundus,* gerundive of *gerere* to bear, carry on] (1513)
**1** : a verbal noun in Latin that expresses generalized or uncompleted action
**2** : any of several linguistic forms analogous to the Latin gerund in languages other than Latin; *especially* : the English verbal noun in *-ing* that has the function of a substantive and at the same time shows the verbal features of tense, voice, and capacity to take adverbial qualifiers and to govern objects ▪

**ge·run·dive** \jə-'rən-div\ *noun* (15th century)
**1** : the Latin future passive participle that functions as the verbal adjective, that expresses the fitness or necessity of the action to be performed, and that has the same suffix as the gerund
**2** : a verbal adjective in a language other than Latin analogous to the gerundive

**ge·sell·schaft** \gə-'zel-ˌshäft\ *noun* [German, companionship, society] (1887)
: a rationally developed mechanistic type of social relationship characterized by impersonally contracted associations between persons;

---

◇ **WORD HISTORY**

**gerrymander** Elbridge Gerry (1744–1814), a Massachusetts politician who signed the Declaration of Independence and was a U.S. vice president, is now chiefly remembered for a bit of political flimflam. As a Democratic-Republican, Gerry was twice elected to the governorship of Massachusetts. His second administration achieved notoriety because of a measure of February 11, 1812, that has since become known as the "Gerrymander Bill." Its purpose was to redistrict the state in such a way as to give the Democratic-Republicans a majority in the state senate. During the ensuing election campaign a member of the opposition Federalists sketched an animal's head, wings, and claws onto an outline of one irregularly shaped senatorial district in Essex County. The fancied resemblance of the resulting image to the mythical salamander inspired the coinage *gerrymander.* This caricature of the district as a winged monster—with Gerry's profile superimposed upon its back—was widely reproduced, and *gerrymander* immediately caught on, at first applied to the caricature itself and then to the actual act of redistricting in such a way as to favor the party in power. Before long it was being used as a verb, too.

*also* **:** a community or society characterized by this relationship — compare GEMEINSCHAFT

**ges·ne·ri·ad** \ges-'nir-ē-,ad\ *noun* [New Latin *Gesneria*, genus name, from Konrad *Gesner* (died 1565) Swiss naturalist] (circa 1925)
**:** any of a family (Gesneriaceae) of tropical herbs (as an African violet or gloxinia) with chiefly opposite leaves and highly zygomorphic flowers

**ges·so** \'je-(,)sō\ *noun, plural* **gessoes** [Italian, literally, gypsum, from Latin *gypsum*] (1596)
**1 :** plaster of paris or gypsum prepared with glue for use in painting or making bas-reliefs
**2 :** a paste prepared by mixing whiting with size or glue and spread upon a surface to fit it for painting or gilding
— **ges·soed** \-(,)sōd\ *adjective*

**gest** *or* **geste** \'jest\ *noun* [Middle English *geste* — more at JEST] (13th century)
**1 :** a tale of adventures; *especially* **:** a romance in verse
**2 :** ADVENTURE, EXPLOIT

**ge·stalt** \gə-'stält, -'shtält, -'stölt, -'shtölt\ *noun, plural* **ge·stalt·en** \-'stäl-t°n, -'shtäl-, -'stöl-, -'shtöl-\ *or* **gestalts** [German, literally, shape, form] (1922)
**:** a structure, configuration, or pattern of physical, biological, or psychological phenomena so integrated as to constitute a functional unit with properties not derivable by summation of its parts

**ge·stalt·ist** \-'stäl-tist, -'shtäl-, -'stöl-, -'shtöl-\ *noun, often capitalized* (1931)
**:** a specialist in Gestalt psychology

**Gestalt psychology** *noun* (1927)
**:** the study of perception and behavior from the standpoint of an individual's response to configurational wholes with stress on the uniformity of psychological and physiological events and rejection of analysis into discrete events of stimulus, percept, and response

**ge·sta·po** \gə-'stä-(,)pō\ *noun, plural* **-pos** [German, from *Geheime Staatspolizei*, literally, secret state police] (1934)
**:** a secret-police organization employing underhanded and terrorist methods against persons suspected of disloyalty

**ges·tate** \'jes-,tāt\ *verb* **ges·tat·ed; ges·tat·ing** [back-formation from *gestation*] (1866)
*transitive verb*
**1 :** to carry in the uterus during pregnancy
**2 :** to conceive and gradually develop in the mind
*intransitive verb*
**:** to be in the process of gestation

**ges·ta·tion** \je-'stā-shən\ *noun* [Latin *gestation-, gestatio*, from *gestare* to bear, frequentative of *gerere* to bear] (1615)
**1 :** the carrying of young in the uterus **:** PREGNANCY
**2 :** conception and development especially in the mind
— **ges·ta·tion·al** \-shnəl, -shə-n°l\ *adjective*

**geste** *also* **gest** \'jest\ *noun* [Middle French *geste*, from Latin *gestus*, from *gerere*] (14th century)
**1** *archaic* **:** DEPORTMENT
**2** *archaic* **:** GESTURE

**ges·tic** \'jes-tik\ *adjective* (1764)
**:** relating to or consisting of bodily movements or gestures

**ges·tic·u·lant** \je-'sti-kyə-lənt\ *adjective* (1877)
**:** making gesticulations ⟨the little wiry man *gesticulant* and wild —William Faulkner⟩

**ges·tic·u·late** \je-'sti-kyə-,lāt\ *intransitive verb* **-lat·ed; -lat·ing** [Latin *gesticulatus*, past participle of *gesticulari*, from (assumed) Latin *gesticulus*, diminutive of Latin *gestus*] (circa 1609)
**:** to make gestures especially when speaking
— **ges·tic·u·la·tive** \je-'sti-kyə-,lā-tiv\ *adjective*

**— ges·tic·u·la·tor** \-,lā-tər\ *noun*
**— ges·tic·u·la·to·ry** \-lə-,tōr-ē, -,tȯr-\ *adjective*

**ges·tic·u·la·tion** \je-,sti-kyə-'lā-shən\ *noun* (15th century)
**1 :** the act of making gestures
**2 :** GESTURE; *especially* **:** an expressive gesture made in showing strong feeling or in enforcing an argument

**¹ges·ture** \'jes-chər, 'jesh-\ *noun* [Middle English, from Medieval Latin *gestura* mode of action, from Latin *gestus*, past participle of *gerere*] (15th century)
**1** *archaic* **:** CARRIAGE, BEARING
**2 :** a movement usually of the body or limbs that expresses or emphasizes an idea, sentiment, or attitude
**3 :** the use of motions of the limbs or body as a means of expression
**4 :** something said or done by way of formality or courtesy, as a symbol or token, or for its effect on the attitudes of others ⟨a political *gesture* to draw popular support —V. L. Parrington⟩
— **ges·tur·al** \-chə-rəl\ *adjective*
— **ges·tur·al·ly** \-chə-rə-lē\ *adverb*

**²gesture** *verb* **ges·tured; ges·tur·ing** (1542)
*intransitive verb*
**:** to make a gesture
*transitive verb*
**:** to express or direct by a gesture

**gesture language** *noun* (1865)
**:** communication by gestures; *especially* **:** SIGN LANGUAGE — called also *gestural language*

**ge·sund·heit** \gə-'zunt-,hīt\ *interjection* [German, literally, health, from *gesund* healthy (from Old High German *gisunt*) + *-heit* -hood — more at SOUND] (1914)
— used to wish good health especially to one who has just sneezed

**¹get** \'get, ÷'git\ *verb* **got** \'gät\; **got** *or* **got·ten** \'gä-t°n\; **get·ting** [Middle English, from Old Norse *geta* to get, beget; akin to Old English bi*gietan* to beget, Latin pre*hendere* to seize, grasp, Greek *chandanein* to hold, contain] (13th century)
*transitive verb*
**1 a :** to gain possession of **b :** to receive as a return **:** EARN ⟨he *got* a bad reputation for carelessness⟩
**2 a :** to obtain by concession or entreaty ⟨*get* your mother's permission to go⟩ **b :** to become affected by (a disease or bodily condition) **:** CATCH ⟨*got* measles from his sister⟩
**3 a :** to seek out and obtain ⟨hoped to *get* dinner at the inn⟩ **b :** to obtain and bring where wanted or needed ⟨*get* a pencil from the desk⟩
**4 :** BEGET
**5 a :** to cause to come or go ⟨quickly *got* his luggage through customs⟩ **b :** to cause to move ⟨*get* it out of the house⟩ **c :** to cause to be in a certain position or condition ⟨*got* his feet wet⟩ **d :** to make ready **:** PREPARE ⟨*get* breakfast⟩
**6 a :** to be subjected to ⟨*got* a bad fall⟩ **b :** to receive by way of punishment **c :** to suffer a specified injury ⟨*got* my nose broken⟩
**7 a :** to achieve as a result of military activity **b :** to obtain or receive by way of benefit or advantage ⟨he *got* little for his trouble⟩ ⟨*get* the better of an enemy⟩
**8 a :** SEIZE **b :** OVERCOME **c :** to have an emotional effect on ⟨the final scene always *gets* me⟩ **d :** IRRITATE ⟨the delays were starting to *get* her⟩ **e :** PUZZLE **f :** to take vengeance on; *specifically* **:** KILL **g :** HIT
**9 :** to prevail on **:** CAUSE ⟨finally *got* them to tidy up their room⟩
**10 a :** HAVE — used in the present perfect tense form with present meaning ⟨I've *got* no money⟩ **b :** to have as an obligation or necessity — used in the present perfect tense form with present meaning ⟨you have *got* to come⟩

**11 a :** to find out by calculation ⟨*get* the answer to a problem⟩ **b :** MEMORIZE ⟨*got* the verse by heart⟩ **c :** HEAR **d :** UNDERSTAND
**12 :** to establish communication with
**13 :** to put out in baseball
**14 :** DELIVER 6b ⟨the car *gets* 20 miles to the gallon⟩
*intransitive verb*

□ USAGE
**gerund** A question discussed in many grammars and handbooks is whether the possessive case of a noun or pronoun must be used before a gerund: must it be "I approve of Pat's going" only or is "I approve of Pat going" also acceptable? Actually both forms have been used side by side for many centuries. When grammarians first discovered this fact in the 18th century, they were perplexed; it never occurred to them that there could be two right ways of doing anything—one of them must be wrong. The 18th century grammarians disagreed as to which was right, but 20th century handbooks opt for the possessive and disapprove the objective pronoun and the common-case noun. Historical grammarians have in the meantime been studying the evidence, and they have discovered that certain circumstances influence the choice of the common (or objective) case or the possessive case. If the gerund is certainly a noun, as in Samuel Pepys' "and thence to Jacob Hall's dancing on the ropes" —where *dancing* could be replaced by the noun *performance*—the possessive is always used. Unfortunately, clear-cut noun gerunds are relatively uncommon; most gerunds seem to be more verblike. Verblike gerunds can take either the possessive case or the common (or objective) case, but again subtle influences are at work. Pronouns, for instance, are more often possessive (if you don't mind *my saying* so) ⟨no chance of *its being* ignored⟩, but if the pronoun is linked to a noun in the common case, the objective is usual ⟨they joked about my brother and *me liking* rice pudding⟩. Words intervening between the pronoun and the gerund can also trigger the objective case ⟨I don't understand *you*, of all people, *complaining*⟩. The objective case may also be felt to be more emphatic ⟨I can't imagine *me letting* that happen⟩. These same considerations can bring on the common case of nouns ⟨imagine *John*, of all people, *being* frightened⟩. Nouns appear to be somewhat more evenly divided between possessive and common case ⟨afraid of the *money's being* wasted⟩ ⟨seemed pleased at the *book being* out of print⟩. But the possessive is usually not used after nouns ending in an \s\ sound ⟨afraid of the *house being* robbed⟩. Some plurals without final -s are used in the common case because the possessive simply sounds wrong ⟨whatever is responsible for my *feet swelling*⟩. Using the common case permits the addition of a parallel construction with the gerund omitted ⟨was sorry to see *Tom getting* all the credit and Paul none⟩. Some words lack a possessive form ⟨never dreamed of *there being* a different way to do it⟩. And the more informal, the more conversational the context, the less likely is the possessive. All of these constructions are standard English, and when there is no reason prompting one form or the other, the choice is open.

\ə\ abut \ᵊ\ kitten \ər\ further \a\ ash \ā\ ace
\ä\ mop, mar \au̇\ out \ch\ chin \e\ bet \ē\ easy
\g\ go \i\ hit \ī\ ice \j\ job \ŋ\ sing \ō\ go
\ȯ\ law \ȯi\ boy \th\ thin \th\ the \ü\ loot \u̇\ foot
\y\ yet \zh\ vision *see also* Guide to Pronunciation

**1 a :** to succeed in coming or going **:** to bring or move oneself ⟨*get* away to the country⟩ ⟨*got* into the car⟩ **b :** to reach or enter into a certain condition ⟨*got* to sleep after midnight⟩ **c :** to make progress ⟨hasn't *gotten* far with the essay⟩
**2 :** to acquire wealth
**3 a :** to be able ⟨never *got* to go to college⟩ **b :** to come to be — often used with following present participle ⟨*got* talking about old times⟩
**4 a :** to succeed in becoming **:** BECOME ⟨how to *get* clear of all the debts I owe —Shakespeare⟩ **b :** to become involved ⟨people who *get* into trouble with the law⟩
**5 :** to leave immediately ⟨told them to *get*⟩
*verbal auxiliary*
— used with the past participle of transitive verbs as a passive voice auxiliary ⟨they *got* caught in the act⟩ ◻
— **get a bead on :** to gain a precise and telling knowledge or understanding of ⟨*got a bead on* his motives⟩
— **get after :** to pursue with exhortation, reprimand, or attack
— **get ahead :** to achieve success ⟨determined to *get ahead* in life⟩
— **get a move on :** HURRY
— **get at 1 :** to reach effectively **2 :** to influence corruptly **:** BRIBE **3 :** to turn one's attention to **4 :** to try to prove or make clear ⟨what is he *getting at*⟩
— **get away with :** to avoid criticism or punishment for or the consequences of ⟨as a reprehensible act⟩
— **get cracking :** to make a start **:** get going ⟨ought to *get cracking* on that assignment⟩
— **get even :** to get revenge
— **get even with :** to repay in kind
— **get going :** to make a start
— **get into :** to become strongly involved with or deeply interested in
— **get it :** to receive a scolding or punishment
— **get it on 1 :** to become enthusiastic, energetic, or excited **2 :** to engage in sexual intercourse
— **get on :** to produce an unfortunate effect on ⟨the noise *got on* my nerves⟩
— **get one's act together 1 :** to put one's life, thoughts, or emotions in order **:** cease to be confused or misdirected **2 :** to begin to function in a skillful or efficient manner ⟨the company finally *got its act together*⟩
— **get one's goat :** to make one angry or annoyed
— **get over 1 a :** OVERCOME, SURMOUNT **b :** to recover from **c :** to reconcile oneself to **:** become accustomed to **2 :** to move or travel across
— **get somewhere :** to be successful
— **get there :** to be successful
— **get through :** to reach the end of **:** COMPLETE
— **get to 1 a :** BEGIN ⟨*gets to* worrying over nothing at all⟩ **b :** to be ready to begin or deal with ⟨I'll *get to* the accounts as soon as I can⟩ **2 :** to have an effect on: as **a :** INFLUENCE **b :** BOTHER
— **get together 1 :** to bring together **:** ACCUMULATE **2 :** to come together **:** ASSEMBLE, MEET **3 :** to reach agreement
— **get wind of :** to become aware of
— **get with it :** to become alert or aware **:** show sophisticated consciousness
²**get** \'get\ *noun* (14th century)
**1 a :** something begotten: (1) **:** OFFSPRING (2) **:** the entire progeny of a male animal **b :** LINEAGE
**2 :** a return of a difficult shot in a game (as tennis)
³**get** \'get\ *noun, plural* **git·tin** \gē-'tēn, 'gi-tin\ [Late Hebrew *gēṭ*] (1892)
**1 :** a document of release from obligation in Jewish law; *specifically* **:** a bill of divorce
**2 :** a religious divorce by Jewish law

**ge·ta** \'ge-(ˌ)tä, -tə\ *noun, plural* **geta** *or* **ge-tas** [Japanese] (1884)
**:** a Japanese wooden clog for outdoor wear

geta

**get about** *intransitive verb* (1816)
**1 :** to become current **:** CIRCULATE
**2 :** to be up and about **:** begin to walk ⟨able to *get about* again⟩
**get across** (1913)
*intransitive verb*
**:** to become clear or convincing
*transitive verb*
**:** to make clear or convincing ⟨we couldn't *get* our point *across*⟩
**get along** *intransitive verb* (1768)
**1 a :** to proceed toward a destination **:** PROGRESS **b :** to approach an advanced stage; *especially* **:** to approach old age
**2 :** to meet one's needs **:** MANAGE ⟨we *got along* on a minimum of clothing⟩
**3 :** to be or remain on congenial terms
**get around** (1875)
*transitive verb*
**1 :** CIRCUMVENT, EVADE
**2 :** to get the better of
*intransitive verb*
**1 a :** to find or take the necessary time or effort — used with *to* **b :** to give attention or consideration — used with *to*
**2 :** to go from place to place
**3 :** to become known or current ⟨word *got around* that he was resigning⟩
**get·at·able** \get-'a-tə-bəl\ *adjective* (1799)
**:** ACCESSIBLE, APPROACHABLE
**get·away** \'ge-tə-ˌwā\ *noun* (1890)
**1 :** an act or instance of getting away: as **a :** ESCAPE **b :** START
**2 :** a place suitable for a vacation
**3 :** a vacation especially of brief duration
**get back** (1605)
*intransitive verb*
**1 :** to come or go again to a person, place, or condition **:** RETURN, REVERT ⟨*getting back* to the main topic of the lecture⟩
**2 :** to gain revenge **:** RETALIATE — used with *at*
*transitive verb*
**:** to regain possession of **:** RECOVER
**get by** *intransitive verb* (1908)
**1 :** to succeed with the least possible effort or accomplishment
**2 :** to make ends meet **:** SURVIVE
**3 :** to proceed without being discovered, criticized, or punished
**get down** (1757)
*intransitive verb*
**1 :** to alight especially from a vehicle **:** DESCEND
**2 :** to give one's attention or consideration — used with *to* ⟨*get down* to business⟩
*transitive verb*
**1 :** to cause to be physically, mentally, or emotionally exhausted **:** DEPRESS ⟨the weather was *getting* her *down*⟩
**2 :** to manage to swallow
**3 :** to commit to writing **:** DESCRIBE
**get–go** \'git-ˌgō, 'get-\ *noun* (1980)
**:** the very beginning — used in the phrase *from the get-go* ⟨didn't like me from the *get-go*⟩
**Geth·sem·a·ne** \geth-'se-mə-nē\ *noun* [Greek *Gethsēmanē*]
**1 :** the garden outside Jerusalem mentioned in Mark 14 as the scene of the agony and arrest of Jesus
**2 :** a place or occasion of great mental or spiritual suffering
**get in** (circa 1533)
*intransitive verb*
**1 a :** ENTER **b :** ARRIVE
**2 a :** to become friendly **b :** to become involved
**3 :** to become accepted for membership or chosen for office

*transitive verb*
**1 :** to succeed in doing, making, or delivering
**2 :** to include in one's schedule
**3 :** INVOLVE 2a, b
**get off** (1640)
*intransitive verb*
**1 :** to avoid the most serious consequences of a dangerous situation or punishment ⟨*got off* with a light sentence⟩
**2 :** START, LEAVE ⟨*got off* on the trip early⟩
**3 :** to leave work with permission or as scheduled
**4 :** to get high on a drug
**5 :** to experience orgasm
**6 :** to experience great pleasure — often used with *on*
*transitive verb*
**1 :** to secure the release of or procure a modified penalty for ⟨his lawyers *got* him *off*⟩
**2 a :** UTTER ⟨*get off* a joke⟩ **b :** to write and send
**3 :** to succeed in doing, making, or delivering
**4 :** to cause to get off
**get on** *intransitive verb* (1816)
**1 :** GET ALONG ⟨was *getting on* in years⟩ ⟨*got on* well with the boss⟩ ⟨*get on* with the game⟩
**2 :** to gain knowledge or understanding ⟨*got on* to the racket⟩
**get out** (14th century)
*intransitive verb*
**1 :** LEAVE, ESCAPE ⟨doubted that he would *get out* alive⟩
**2 :** to become known **:** leak out ⟨their secret *got out*⟩
*transitive verb*
**1 :** to cause to leave or escape
**2 :** to bring before the public; *especially* **:** PUBLISH
**get round** *intransitive verb* (1748)
**:** GET AROUND
**get·ter** \'ge-tər\ *noun* (15th century)
**1 :** one that gets
**2 :** a substance introduced into a vacuum tube or electric lamp to remove traces of gas
**get through** *intransitive verb* (1694)
**1 :** to reach a destination
**2 :** to gain approval or a desired outcome
**3 a :** to make something clear **b :** to complete a communications connection
**get–to·geth·er** \'get-tə-ˌge-thər\ *noun* (1911)
**:** MEETING; *especially* **:** an informal social gathering
**get·up** \'get-ˌəp\ *noun* (1847)
**1 :** OUTFIT, COSTUME
**2 :** general composition or structure
**get up** (14th century)
*intransitive verb*
**1 a :** to arise from bed **b :** to rise to one's feet **c :** CLIMB, ASCEND
**2 :** to go ahead or faster — used in the imperative as a command especially to driven animals
*transitive verb*
**1 :** to make preparations for **:** ORGANIZE ⟨*got up* a party for the newcomers⟩
**2 :** to arrange as to external appearance **:** DRESS
**3 :** to acquire a knowledge of
**4 :** to create in oneself ⟨cannot *get up* the courage to tell them⟩

◻ USAGE
**get** The pronunciation \'git\ has been noted as a feature of some British and American dialects since the 16th century. In the phonetic spelling of his own speech Benjamin Franklin records *git*. However, since at least 1687 American grammarians and teachers have disapproved this pronunciation. It nonetheless remains in widespread and unpredictable use in many dialects, often, but not exclusively, when *get* is a passive auxiliary (as in *get married*) or an imperative (as in *get up!*).

**get–up–and–go** \\,get-,əp-°n-'gō, ,git-, -°m-, -°ŋ-\ *noun* (1906)
: ENERGY, DRIVE

**ge·um** \\'jē-əm\ *noun* [Latin] (circa 1548)
: AVENS

**gew·gaw** \\'g(y)ü-(,)gȯ\ *noun* [origin unknown] (circa 1529)
: a showy trifle : BAUBLE, TRINKET

**ge·würz·tra·mi·ner** \\gə-'vu̇rt,stra-mə-nər, -'vȯrt-, -,strä; -strə-'mē-nər\ *noun, often capitalized* [German, variety of grape, from *Gewürz* spice + *Traminer*, variety of grape, from *Tramin* (Termeno, Italy) (circa 1950)
: a light dry Alsatian white wine with a spicy bouquet; *also* : a similar wine made elsewhere

**gey** \\'gā\ *adverb* [alteration of *gay*, adverb] (1796)
*chiefly Scottish* : VERY, QUITE

**gey·ser** \\'gī-zər, *British sometimes* 'gā- *or* 'gē- *for 1 &* usually 'gē- *for 2*\ *noun* [Icelandic *Geysir*, hot spring in Iceland, from *geysa* to rush forth, from Old Norse; akin to Old English *gēotan* to pour — more at FOUND] (1780)
**1** : a spring that throws forth intermittent jets of heated water and steam
**2** *British* : an apparatus for heating water rapidly with a gas flame (as for a bath)

**gey·ser·ite** \\-zə-,rīt\ *noun* [French *geysérite*, from *geyser*, from Icelandic *Geysir*] (circa 1814)
: a hydrous silica that constitutes one variety of opal and is deposited around some hot springs and geysers in white or grayish concretions

**g–fac·tor** \\'jē-,fak-tər\ *noun* (1942)
: GYROMAGNETIC RATIO

**gha·ri·al** \\'ger-ē-əl\ *noun* [Hindi *ghaṛyāl*] (circa 1809)
: GAVIAL

**ghar·ry** \\'gar-ē, 'gär-\ *noun, plural* **gharries** [Hindi *gāṛī*] (1810)
: a horse-drawn cab used especially in India and Egypt

**ghast** \\'gast\ *adjective* (1622)
*archaic* : GHASTLY

**ghast·ful** \\-fəl\ *adjective* (14th century)
*archaic* : FRIGHTFUL
— **ghast·ful·ly** *adverb, archaic*

**ghast·ly** \\'gast-lē\ *adjective* **ghast·li·er; -est** [Middle English *gastly*, from *gasten* to terrify — more at GAST] (14th century)
**1 a** : terrifyingly horrible to the senses : FRIGHTENING ⟨a *ghastly* crime⟩ **b** : intensely unpleasant, disagreeable, or objectionable ⟨such a life seems *ghastly* in its emptiness and sterility —Aldous Huxley⟩
**2** : resembling a ghost
**3** *obsolete* : filled with fear
**4** : very great ⟨*ghastly* mistake⟩ ☆
— **ghast·li·ness** *noun*
— **ghastly** *adverb*

**ghat** \\'gȯt, 'gät\ *noun* [Hindi *ghāṭ*, from Sanskrit *ghaṭṭa*] (1783)
: a broad flight of steps that is situated on an Indian riverbank and that provides access to the water especially for bathing

**ghee** *or* **ghi** \\'gē\ *noun* [Hindi *ghī*, from Sanskrit *ghṛta*] (1665)
: a semifluid clarified butter made especially in India

**gher·kin** \\'gər-kən\ *noun* [Dutch *gurken*, plural of *gurk* cucumber, ultimately from Middle Greek *agouros*] (1661)
**1** : a small prickly fruit used for pickling; *also* : the slender annual vine (*Cucumis anguria*) of the gourd family that bears it
**2** : the immature fruit of the cucumber

**¹ghet·to** \\'ge-(,)tō\ *noun, plural* **ghettos** *also* **ghettoes** [Italian, from Venetian dialect *ghèto* island where Jews were forced to live, literally, foundry (located on the island), from *ghetàr* to cast, from Latin *jactare* to throw — more at JET] (1611)
**1** : a quarter of a city in which Jews were formerly required to live

**2** : a quarter of a city in which members of a minority group live especially because of social, legal, or economic pressure
**3 a** : an isolated group ⟨a geriatric *ghetto*⟩ **b** : a situation that resembles a ghetto especially in conferring inferior status or limiting opportunity ⟨stuck in daytime TV's *ghetto*⟩ ◆

**²ghetto** *transitive verb* (1936)
: GHETTOIZE

**ghetto blaster** *noun* (1983)
: BOOM BOX

**ghet·to·ize** \\'ge-tō-,īz\ *transitive verb* **-ized; -iz·ing** (1939)
: to isolate in or as if in a ghetto
— **ghet·to·iza·tion** \\,ge-tō-ə-'zā-shən\ *noun*

**Ghib·el·line** \\'gi-bə-,lēn, -,līn, -lən\ *noun* [Italian *Ghibellino*] (1573)
: a member of an aristocratic political party in medieval Italy supporting the authority of the German emperors — compare GUELF

**ghib·li** \\'gib-lē\ *noun* [Arabic dialect *giblī* south wind, from Arabic *qiblī* southern] (1942)
: a hot desert wind of northern Africa

**ghil·lie** *variant of* GILLIE

**¹ghost** \\'gōst\ *noun* [Middle English *gost, gast*, from Old English *gāst*; akin to Old High German *geist* spirit, Sanskrit *heḍa* anger] (before 12th century)
**1** : the seat of life or intelligence : SOUL ⟨give up the *ghost*⟩
**2** : a disembodied soul; *especially* : the soul of a dead person believed to be an inhabitant of the unseen world or to appear to the living in bodily likeness
**3** : SPIRIT, DEMON
**4 a** : a faint shadowy trace ⟨a *ghost* of a smile⟩ **b** : the least bit ⟨not a *ghost* of a chance⟩
**5** : a false image in a photographic negative or on a television screen caused especially by reflection
**6** : one who ghostwrites
**7** : a red blood cell that has lost its hemoglobin ◆
— **ghost·like** \\-,līk\ *adjective*
— **ghosty** \\'gō-stē\ *adjective*

**²ghost** (1606)
*transitive verb*
**1** : to haunt like a ghost
**2** : GHOSTWRITE
*intransitive verb*
**1 a** : to move silently like a ghost **b** : to sail quietly in light winds
**2** : GHOSTWRITE

**Ghost Dance** *noun* (1890)
: a group dance of a late 19th century American Indian messianic cult believed to promote the return of the dead and the restoration of traditional ways of life

**ghost·ing** *noun* (circa 1957)
: a false image on a television screen; *also* : the formation of such images

**ghost·ly** \\'gōst-lē\ *adjective* **ghost·li·er; -est** (before 12th century)
**1** : of or relating to the soul : SPIRITUAL
**2** : of, relating to, or having the characteristics of a ghost : SPECTRAL
— **ghost·li·ness** *noun*
— **ghostly** *adverb*

**ghost story** *noun* (1819)
**1** : a story about ghosts
**2** : a tale based on imagination rather than fact

**ghost town** *noun* (1931)
: a once-flourishing town wholly or nearly deserted usually as a result of the exhaustion of some natural resource

**ghost word** *noun* (1886)
: a word form never in established usage

**ghost·write** \\'gōs(t)-,rīt\ *verb* **-wrote** \\-,rōt\; **-writ·ten** \\-,ri-t°n\ [back-formation from *ghostwriter*] (1927)
*intransitive verb*
: to write for and in the name of another

◇ **WORD HISTORY**

**ghetto** The etymology of Italian *ghetto* was formerly the subject of much speculation; among many hypotheses were suggestions that it had been shortened from Italian *borghetto*, a diminutive of *borgo* "small town, suburb," or that it had developed from Talmudic Hebrew *gēṭ* "document of release." Today there is little doubt on historical and linguistic grounds that the word comes from an Italian dialect form *ghèto* "foundry." A foundry for cannons was once located on an island forming part of Venice, where in 1516 the Venetians restricted Jewish residence. The word *ghèto* became the name for the quarter and was borrowed into standard Tuscan-based Italian as *ghetto*, with the generic meaning "quarter of a city where Jews are forced to live." From there it passed into most of the languages of Europe. The word took on its darkest connotations during World War II, when Nazi imprisonment of Jews in sectors of Warsaw, Łódź, and other Polish cities led to thousands of deaths through malnutrition and disease. Since the late 19th century, the reference of *ghetto* has been extended to crowded urban districts where other ethnic or racial groups have been confined by poverty and prejudice, and this is probably its most frequent current use.

**ghost** English *ghost* is descended directly from Old English *gāst*, which meant "soul" or "spirit." These senses now survive mainly in the idiom *to give up the ghost*, and in the Christian epithet *Holy Ghost* for the third person of the Trinity. Not untypically for English, a loanword, *spirit* (from Latin *spiritus*), fills in for the primary sense of an old native word that later developed a very restricted sense. *Ghost* now usually alludes to the spirit of a dead person that supposedly appears to the living in its bodily likeness—a meaning not attested in English before the 14th century. This situation contrasts with the history of German *Geist*, an exact cognate of *ghost*, which from Old High German to the present has retained its primary sense, "spirit." The peculiar spelling of English *ghost* with an initial *gh*, which did not become general until the end of the 16th century, was apparently introduced by the 15th century English printer and translator William Caxton. Having lived in the Low Countries for many years, Caxton most likely adopted the *gh* from Middle Dutch *gheest*, another Germanic cognate of *ghost*.

*transitive verb*
**:** to write (as a speech) for another who is the presumed author
— **ghost·writ·er** *noun*
**ghoul** \'gül\ *noun* [Arabic *ghūl*] (1786)
**1 :** a legendary evil being that robs graves and feeds on corpses
**2 :** one suggestive of a ghoul
— **ghoul·ish** \'gü-lish\ *adjective*
— **ghoul·ish·ly** *adverb*
— **ghoul·ish·ness** *noun*
**ghou·lie** \'gü-lē\ *noun* (1928)
**:** GHOUL 1
**¹GI** \,jē-'ī\ *adjective* [galvanized *iron*; from abbreviation used in listing such articles as garbage cans, but taken as abbreviation for *government issue*] (circa 1935)
**1 :** provided by an official U.S. military supply department ⟨*GI* shoes⟩
**2 :** of, relating to, or characteristic of U.S. military personnel
**3 :** conforming to military regulations or customs ⟨a *GI* haircut⟩
**²GI** *noun, plural* **GIs** *or* **GI's** \-'īz\ (1943)
**:** a member or former member of the U.S. armed forces; *especially* **:** a man enlisted in the army
**³GI** *adverb* (1949)
**:** in a strictly regulation manner
**⁴GI** *transitive verb* **GI'd** \-'īd\; **GI'·ing** \-'ī-iŋ\ (1951)
**:** to clean thoroughly (as floors) in preparation for or as if for a military inspection
**¹gi·ant** \'jī-ənt\ *noun* [Middle English *giaunt*, from Old French *geant*, from Latin *gigant-*, *gigas*, from Greek] (14th century)
**1 :** a legendary humanlike being of great stature and strength
**2 a :** a living being of great size **b :** a person of extraordinary powers
**3 :** something unusually large or powerful
— **gi·ant·like** \-,līk\ *adjective*
**²giant** *adjective* (15th century)
**:** having extremely large size, proportion, or power
**giant anteater** *noun* (1940)
**:** a large bushy-tailed anteater (*Myrmecophaga tridactyla*) of Central and South America
**giant cactus** *noun* (circa 1884)
**:** SAGUARO
**giant clam** *noun* (circa 1889)
**:** a very large clam (*Tridacna gigas*) found on the coral reefs of the Indian and Pacific oceans that sometimes weighs more than 500 pounds (227 kilograms)
**gi·ant·ess** \'jī-ən-təs\ *noun* (14th century)
**:** a female giant
**gi·ant·ism** \'jī-ən-,ti-zəm\ *noun* (1639)
**1 :** the quality or state of being a giant ⟨*giantism* in industry⟩
**2 :** GIGANTISM 2
**giant panda** *noun* (1920)
**:** a large black-and-white mammal (*Ailuropoda melanoleuca*) of chiefly central China now usually classified with the bears (family Ursidae) — see PANDA illustration
**giant reed** *noun* (1851)
**:** a tall European grass (*Arundo donax*) with woody stems used especially in making organ reeds, baskets, and shelters
**giant schnauzer** *noun* (circa 1934)
**:** any of a breed of powerful heavyset schnauzers that attain a height of 23½ to 27½ inches (60 to 70 centimeters)
**giant sequoia** *noun* (circa 1931)
**:** BIG TREE
**giant slalom** *noun* (1952)
**:** a slalom race for skiers on a longer and steeper course than that used for the regular slalom
**giant squid** *noun* (circa 1890)
**:** any of a genus (*Architeuthis*) of extremely large squids that include the largest mollusks known
**giant star** *noun* (1912)
**:** a star of great luminosity and of large mass

**giant tortoise** *noun* (circa 1909)
**:** any of various large long-lived herbivorous land tortoises (genus *Geochelone*) formerly common on the islands of the western Indian Ocean and on the Galapagos Islands
**giant water bug** *noun* (1901)
**:** any of a family (Belostomatidae and especially genus *Lethocerus*) of very large predatory bugs capable of inflicting a painful bite
**giaour** \'jaù(-ə)r\ *noun* [French, from Italian dialect (Venetian) *giaur*, from Turkish *gâvur*, from Persian *gawr*] (1564)
**:** one outside the Islamic faith **:** INFIDEL 2a
**giar·di·a·sis** \,(,)jē-,är-'dī-ə-səs, jē-ər-, jär-\ *noun, plural* **-a·ses** \-,sēz\ [New Latin, from *Giardia*, from Alfred M. *Giard* (died 1908) French biologist] (1919)
**:** infestation with or disease caused by a flagellate protozoan (genus *Giardia* and especially *G. lamblia* in humans) that is often characterized by diarrhea
**¹gib** \'gib\ *noun* [Middle English, from *Gib*, nickname for *Gilbert*] (1561)
**:** a male cat; *specifically* **:** a castrated male cat
**²gib** *noun* [origin unknown] (1795)
**:** a plate of metal or other material machined to hold other parts in place, to afford a bearing surface, or to provide means for overcoming looseness
**gib·ber** \'ji-bər\ *intransitive verb* **gib·bered**; **gib·ber·ing** \-b(ə-)riŋ\ [imitative] (1604)
**:** to speak rapidly, inarticulately, and often foolishly
— **gibber** *noun*
**gib·ber·el·lic acid** \,ji-bə-'re-lik-\ *noun* (1954)
**:** a crystalline acid $C_{19}H_{22}O_6$ that is a gibberellin used especially in the malting of barley
**gib·ber·el·lin** \-'re-lən\ *noun* [New Latin *Gibberella fujikoroi*, fungus from which it was first isolated] (1939)
**:** any of several growth-regulating plant hormones that promote cell elongation and activity of the cambium, induce parthenocarpy, and stimulate synthesis of nucleic acids and proteins
**gib·ber·ish** \'ji-b(ə-)rish, 'gi-\ *noun* [probably from *gibber*] (circa 1554)
**:** unintelligible or meaningless language: **a :** a technical or esoteric language **b :** pretentious or needlessly obscure language
**¹gib·bet** \'ji-bət\ *noun* [Middle English *gibet*, from Old French] (13th century)
**1 :** GALLOWS
**2 :** an upright post with a projecting arm for hanging the bodies of executed criminals as a warning
**²gibbet** *transitive verb* (1646)
**1 a :** to expose to infamy or public scorn **b :** to hang on a gibbet
**2 :** to execute by hanging on a gibbet
**gib·bon** \'gi-bən\ *noun* [French] (1774)
**:** any of a genus (*Hylobates*) of brachiating tailless apes of southeastern Asia that are the smallest and most arboreal anthropoid apes
**gib·bos·i·ty** \ji-'bä-sə-tē, gi-\ *noun, plural* **-ties** (14th century)
**:** PROTUBERANCE, SWELLING
**gib·bous** \'ji-bəs, 'gi-\ *adjective* [Middle English, from Middle French *gibbeux*, from Late Latin *gibbosus* humpbacked, from Latin *gibbus* hump] (14th century)
**1 a :** marked by convexity or swelling **b** *of the moon or a planet* **:** seen with more than half but not all of the apparent disk illuminated
**2 :** having a hump **:** HUMPBACKED
**gibe** \'jīb\ *verb* **gibed; gib·ing** [perhaps from Middle French *giber* to shake, handle roughly] (1567)

gibbon

*intransitive verb*
**:** to utter taunting words
*transitive verb*
**:** to deride or tease with taunting words
**synonym** see SCOFF
— **gibe** *noun*
— **gib·er** *noun*
**gib·lets** \'jib-ləts *also* 'gib-\ *noun plural* [Middle English *gibelet* entrails, garbage, from Middle French, stew of wildfowl] (15th century)
**:** the edible viscera of a fowl
**Gi·bral·tar** \jə-'brȯl-tər\ *noun* [*Gibraltar*, fortress in the British colony of Gibraltar] (1856)
**:** an impregnable stronghold
**Gib·son** \'gib-sən\ *noun* [from the name *Gibson*] (1948)
**:** a martini garnished with a cocktail onion
**Gibson girl** *adjective* [Charles D. *Gibson*] (1936)
**:** of or relating to a style especially in women's clothing characterized by high necks, full sleeves, and wasp waists
**gid** \'gid\ *noun* [back-formation from *giddy*] (1601)
**:** a disease especially of sheep caused by the larva of a tapeworm (*Multiceps multiceps*) in the brain
**gid·dap** \gi-'dap, -'dəp\ *also* **gid·dy·ap** \,gi-dē-'ap, -'əp\ *verb imperative* [alteration of *get up*] (circa 1897)
**:** a command to a horse to go ahead or go faster
**¹gid·dy** \'gi-dē\ *adjective* **gid·di·er; -est** [Middle English *gidy* mad, foolish, from Old English *gydig* possessed, mad; akin to Old English *god* god] (14th century)
**1 a :** DIZZY ⟨*giddy* from the unaccustomed exercise⟩ **b :** causing dizziness ⟨a *giddy* height⟩ **c :** whirling rapidly
**2 a :** lightheartedly silly **:** FRIVOLOUS **b :** joyfully elated **:** EUPHORIC ◆
— **gid·di·ly** \'gi-d°l-ē\ *adverb*
— **gid·di·ness** \'gi-dē-nəs\ *noun*
**²giddy** *verb* **gid·died; gid·dy·ing** (1602)
*transitive verb*
**:** to make giddy
*intransitive verb*
**:** to become giddy
**Gid·e·on** \'gi-dē-ən\ *noun* [Hebrew *Gidh'ōn*] (1)
**1 :** an early Hebrew hero noted for his defeat of the Midianites
**2 :** a member of an interdenominational organization whose activities include the placing of Bibles in hotel rooms
**gie** \'gē\ *chiefly Scottish variant of* GIVE

◇ **WORD HISTORY**

**giddy** Before the nature of mental illness began to be understood, the cause of insanity was long thought to be possession by spirits or demons. Old English *gidig* or *gydig* "insane" meant literally "possessed by a spirit" and was an adjectival derivative in prehistoric Old English of the noun that would become Old English and Modern English *god*. *Gidy*, the Middle English outcome of Old English *gydig*, retained overtones of madness, but its meaning tended more toward "foolish, stupid." Only a small semantic sidestep was then required to produce the sense "dizzy," which was first recorded at the end of the 14th century. By the 17th century, the new meaning of *giddy*, as it had come to be spelled, had produced several extended senses, including "causing dizziness" and "rapidly whirling." These meanings are still in use, as is the sense "lightheartedly or exuberantly silly," which first occurred in the middle of the 16th century and which combines elements of both the "foolish" and "dizzy" senses.

**Gi·em·sa stain** \gē-'em-zə-\ *noun* [Gustav *Giemsa* (died 1948) German chemotherapist] (circa 1909)
: a stain consisting of eosin and a blue dye and used chiefly in the differential staining of blood films — called also *Giemsa, Giemsa's stain*

**¹gift** \'gift\ *noun* [Middle English, from Old Norse, something given, talent; akin to Old English *giefan* to give] (12th century)
**1** : a notable capacity, talent, or endowment
**2** : something voluntarily transferred by one person to another without compensation
**3** : the act, right, or power of giving ☆

**²gift** *transitive verb* (circa 1550)
**1** : to endow with some power, quality, or attribute
**2** : PRESENT ⟨generously *gifted* us with a copy —*Saturday Review*⟩

**gift certificate** *noun* (1942)
: a certificate entitling the recipient to purchase goods or services in the establishment of the issuer to the amount specified

**gift·ed** \'gif-təd\ *adjective* (1644)
**1** : having great natural ability : TALENTED ⟨*gifted* children⟩
**2** : revealing a special gift ⟨*gifted* voices⟩
— **gift·ed·ly** *adverb*
— **gift·ed·ness** *noun*

**gift of gab** (circa 1890)
: the ability to talk glibly and persuasively

**gift of tongues** [from the gifts of the Spirit in 1 Corinthians 12:1–13] (1560)
: the charismatic gift of ecstatic speech

**gift·ware** \'gift-,war, -,wer\ *noun* (1904)
: wares or goods suitable for gifts

**gift wrap** *transitive verb* (1936)
: to wrap (merchandise intended as a gift) decoratively

**¹gig** \'gig\ *noun* [Middle English -*gyge* (in *whyrlegyge* whirligig), of unknown origin] (1570)
**1** : something that whirls or is whirled: as **a** *obsolete* : TOP, WHIRLIGIG **b** : a 3-digit selection in a numbers game
**2** : a person of odd or grotesque appearance
**3 a** : a long light ship's boat **b** : a rowboat designed for speed rather than for work
**4** : a light two-wheeled one-horse carriage

**²gig** *intransitive verb* **gigged; gig·ging** (1807)
: to travel in a gig

**³gig** *noun* [short for earlier *fizgig, fishgig,* of unknown origin] (1722)
**1** : a pronged spear for catching fish
**2** : an arrangement of hooks to be drawn through a school of fish in order to hook their bodies

**⁴gig** *verb* **gigged; gig·ging** (1803)
*transitive verb*
**1** : to spear with a gig
**2 a** *chiefly West* : SPUR, JAB **b** : GOAD, PROVOKE
*intransitive verb*
: to fish with a gig

**⁵gig** *noun* [origin unknown] (1926)
: a job usually for a specified time; *especially* : an entertainer's engagement

**⁶gig** *intransitive verb* **gigged; gig·ging** (1939)
: to work as a musician ⟨*gigged* with various bands —*Downbeat*⟩

**⁷gig** *noun* [origin unknown] (circa 1941)
: a military demerit

**⁸gig** *transitive verb* **gigged; gig·ging** (circa 1941)
: to give a military gig to

**giga-** \'ji-gə, 'gi-\ *combining form* [International Scientific Vocabulary, from Greek *gigas* giant]
: billion ⟨*giga*hertz⟩ ⟨*giga*watt⟩

**giga·bit** \-,bit\ *noun* (1970)
: a unit of information equal to one billion bits

**giga·byte** \-,bīt\ *noun* (1975)
: 1,073,741,824 bytes

**giga·hertz** \-,hərts, -,herts\ *noun* (1964)
: a unit of frequency equal to one billion hertz

**gi·gan·tesque** \,jī-,gan-'tesk, -gən-\ *adjective* (1821)
: of enormous or grotesquely large proportions

**gi·gan·tic** \jī-'gan-tik, jə-\ *adjective* [Greek *gigantikos*, from *gigant-, gigas* giant] (1651)
: exceeding the usual or expected (as in size, force, or prominence) ⟨a man of *gigantic* stature⟩ ⟨made a last *gigantic* effort⟩ ⟨*gigantic* industrial combines⟩
**synonym** see ENORMOUS
— **gi·gan·ti·cal·ly** \-ti-k(ə-)lē\ *adverb*

**gi·gan·tism** \jī-'gan-,ti-zəm, jə-; 'jī-gən-\ *noun* (circa 1885)
**1** : GIANTISM 1
**2** : development to abnormally large size
**3** : excessive vegetative growth often accompanied by the inhibiting of reproduction

**gi·gas** \'jī-gəs\ *adjective* [New Latin, from Latin, giant, from Greek] (1915)
*of a polyploid plant* : having thicker stem, taller growth, darker thicker leaves, and larger flowers and seeds than a corresponding diploid

**giga·watt** \'ji-gə-,wät, 'gi-\ *noun* (circa 1962)
: a unit of power equal to one billion watts

**¹gig·gle** \'gi-gəl\ *verb* **gig·gled; gig·gling** \-g(ə-)liŋ\ [imitative] (1509)
*intransitive verb*
: to laugh with repeated short catches of the breath
*transitive verb*
: to utter with a giggle
— **gig·gler** \-g(ə-)lər\ *noun*
— **gig·gling·ly** \-g(ə-)liŋ-lē\ *adverb*
— **gig·gly** \-g(ə-)lē\ *adjective*

**²giggle** *noun* (circa 1677)
**1** : the act of giggling
**2** *chiefly British* : a source of amusement

**gig·o·lo** \'ji-gə-,lō, 'zhi-\ *noun, plural* **-los** [French] (1922)
**1** : a man supported by a woman usually in return for his attentions
**2** : a professional dancing partner or male escort

**gi·got** \'ji-gət, zhē-'gō\ *noun, plural* **gi·gots** \-gəts, -'gō(z)\ [Middle French, diminutive of *gigue* fiddle; from its shape — more at JIG] (1526)
**1** : a leg of meat (as lamb) especially when cooked
**2** : a leg-of-mutton sleeve

**gigue** \'zhēg\ *noun* [French, from English *jig*] (1685)
: a lively dance movement (as of a suite) having compound triple rhythm and composed in fugal style

**Gi·la monster** \'hē-lə-\ *noun* [*Gila* River, Ariz.] (1877)
: a large orange and black venomous lizard (*Heloderma suspectum*) of the southwestern U.S.; *also* : a related lizard (*H. horridum*) of Mexico

**Gila monster**

**gil·bert** \'gil-bərt\ *noun* [William *Gilbert*] (1893)
: the centimeter-gram-second unit of magnetomotive force equivalent to 10÷4π ampere-turn

**¹gild** \'gild\ *transitive verb* **gild·ed** \'gil-dəd\ *or* **gilt** \'gilt\; **gild·ing** [Middle English, from Old English *gyldan*; akin to Old English *gold* gold] (14th century)
**1** : to overlay with or as if with a thin covering of gold
**2 a** : to give money to **b** : to give an attractive but often deceptive appearance to **c** *archaic* : to make bloody
— **gild·er** *noun*
— **gild the lily** : to add unnecessary ornamentation to something beautiful in its own right

**²gild** *variant of* GUILD

**Gil·ga·mesh** \'gil-gə-,mesh\

: a legendary Sumerian king and hero of the *Gilgamesh Epic*

**¹gill** \'jil\ *noun* [Middle English *gille*, from Medieval Latin *gillus*, from Late Latin *gillo, gello* water pot] (14th century)
— see WEIGHT table

**²gill** \'gil\ *noun* [Middle English *gile*, of Scandinavian origin; akin to Swedish *gäl* gill, Old Norse *gjǫlnar* lips; akin to Greek *chelynē* lip, jawbone] (14th century)
**1** : an organ (as of a fish) for obtaining oxygen from water
**2 a** : WATTLE 2 **b** : the flesh under or about the chin or jaws — usually used in plural **c** : one of the radiating plates forming the undersurface of the cap of a mushroom fungus
— **gilled** \'gild\ *adjective*
— **to the gills** : as full as possible

**³gill** \'gil\ (1884)
*transitive verb*
: GILLNET
*intransitive verb*
*of fish* : to become entangled in a gill net
— **gill·er** *noun*

**⁴gill** \'gil\ *noun* [Middle English *gille*, from Old Norse *gil*; akin to Old High German *gil* hernia] (14th century)
**1** *British* : RAVINE
**2** *British* : a narrow stream or rivulet

**⁵gill** \'jil\ *noun, often capitalized* [Middle English, from *Gill*, nickname for *Gillian*] (15th century)
: GIRL, SWEETHEART

**gill arch** *noun* (1879)
**1** : any of the bony or cartilaginous arches or curved bars extending dorsoventrally and placed one behind the other on each side of the pharynx and supporting the gills of fishes and amphibians
**2** : any of the rudimentary ridges in the embryos of all higher vertebrates that correspond to the gill arches

**gill cleft** *noun* (circa 1889)
: GILL SLIT 1, 2

**gill cover** *noun* (1776)
: OPERCULUM 1b

**¹gil·lie** \'gi-lē\ *noun* [Scottish Gaelic *gille* & Irish *giolla* youth, gillie] (1705)
**1** : a male attendant on a Scottish Highland chief; *broadly* : ATTENDANT
**2** *chiefly Scottish & Irish* : a fishing and hunting guide
**3** : a shoe with a low top and decorative lacing

**²gillie** *intransitive verb* **gil·lied; gil·ly·ing** (1900)

---

---

\ə\ abut \ᵊ\ kitten \ər\ further \a\ ash \ā\ ace \ä\ mop, mar \au̇\ out \ch\ chin \e\ bet \ē\ easy \g\ go \i\ hit \ī\ ice \j\ job \ŋ\ sing \ō\ go \ȯ\ law \ȯi\ boy \th\ thin \t͟h\ the \ü\ loot \u̇\ foot \y\ yet \zh\ vision    *see also* Guide to Pronunciation

: to serve as a gillie

**gill·net** \'gil-ˌnet\ *transitive verb* (1949)
: to catch (fish) with a gill net

**gill net** *noun* (1796)
: a flat net suspended vertically in the water with meshes that allow the head of a fish to pass but entangle it as it seeks to withdraw

**gill·net·ter** \-ˌne-tər\ *noun* (circa 1889)
: a boat equipped for or engaged in fishing with gill nets; *also* : a person who fishes with a gill net

**gill raker** *noun* (1880)
: any of the bony processes on a gill arch that divert solid substances away from the gills

**gill slit** *noun* (1854)
**1** : any of the openings or clefts between the gill arches in vertebrates that breathe by gills through which water taken in at the mouth passes to the exterior and so bathes the gills
**2** : any of the rudimentary grooves in the neck region of the embryos of air-breathing vertebrates that correspond to the gill slits
**3** : the external opening to the cavity containing the gills when a protective covering of the gills is present

**gil·ly·flow·er** \'ji-lē-ˌflaů(-ə)r\ *noun* [by folk etymology from Middle English *gilofre* clove, from Middle French *girofle, gilofre,* from Latin *caryophyllum,* from Greek *karyophyllon,* from *karyon* nut + *phyllon* leaf — more at CAREEN, BLADE] (1551)
: CARNATION 2

**Gil·son·ite** \'gil-sə-ˌnīt\ *trademark*
— used for uintaite

**¹gilt** \'gilt\ *adjective* [Middle English, from past participle of *gilden* to gild] (14th century)
: covered with gold or gilt : of the color of gold

**²gilt** *noun* (15th century)
**1** : gold or something that resembles gold laid on a surface
**2** *slang* : MONEY
**3** : superficial brilliance
**4** : a bond issued by the government of the United Kingdom

**³gilt** *noun* [Middle English *gylte,* from Old Norse *gyltr;* akin to Old English *gelde* sterile — more at GELD] (14th century)
: a young female swine

**gilt–edged** \'gilt-ˌejd\ *or* **gilt–edge** \-ˈej\ *adjective* (1818)
**1** : having a gilt edge
**2** : of the best quality or rating ⟨*gilt-edged* securities⟩

**¹gim·bal** \'gim-bəl, 'jim-\ *noun* [alteration of obsolete *gemel* (double ring)] (1780)
: a device that permits a body to incline freely in any direction or suspends it so that it will remain level when its support is tipped — usually used in plural; called also *gimbal ring*

**²gimbal** *transitive verb* **-balled** *or* **-baled;** **-bal·ling** *or* **-bal·ing** (1875)
: to provide with or support on gimbals

**gim·crack** \'jim-ˌkrak\ *noun* [origin unknown] (1676)
: a showy object of little use or value : GEWGAW
— **gimcrack** *adjective*
— **gim·crack·ery** \-ˌkra-k(ə-)rē\ *noun*

**gim·el** \'gi-məl\ *noun* [Hebrew *gīmel*] (1828)
: the 3d letter of the Hebrew alphabet — see ALPHABET table

**¹gim·let** \'gim-lət\ *noun* [Middle English, from Middle French *guimbelet,* probably modification of Middle Dutch *wimmelkijn,* from *wimmel* wimble] (14th century)
: a small tool with a screw point, grooved shank, and cross handle for boring holes

**²gimlet** *adjective* (1752)
: having a piercing or penetrating quality

**³gimlet** *transitive verb* (1840)
: to pierce as if with a gimlet

gimlet

**⁴gimlet** *noun* [probably from ¹*gimlet*] (1928)
: a drink consisting of sweetened lime juice and gin or vodka and sometimes carbonated or plain water

**gim·let–eyed** \-ˈīd\ *adjective* (1752)
: SHARP-SIGHTED

**gim·mal** \'gi-məl, 'ji-\ *noun* [alteration of obsolete *gemel* (double ring)] (1598)
**1** *plural* : joined work (as in a clock) whose parts move within each other
**2** : a pair or series of interlocked rings

**gim·me** \'gi-mē\ *noun, plural* **gimmes** [from *gimme,* contraction of *give me*] (1982)
: something easily achieved or won especially in a contest

**¹gim·mick** \'gi-mik\ *noun* [origin unknown] (circa 1926)
**1 a** : a mechanical device for secretly and dishonestly controlling gambling apparatus **b** : an ingenious or novel mechanical device : GADGET
**2 a** : an important feature that is not immediately apparent : CATCH ⟨what's the *gimmick* . . . what's in it for you —Maxwell Griffith⟩ **b** : an ingenious and usually new scheme or angle
— **gim·micky** \-mi-kē\ *adjective*

**²gimmick** *transitive verb* (1928)
**1** : to alter or influence by means of a gimmick
**2** : to provide with a gimmick — often used with *up*

**gim·mick·ry** \'gi-mi-krē\ *noun, plural* **-ries** (1948)
: an array or profusion of gimmicks; *also* : use of gimmicks

**¹gimp** \'gimp\ *noun* [perhaps from Dutch] (1664)
: an ornamental flat braid or round cord used as a trimming

**²gimp** *noun* [perhaps from *gimp* (fish line strengthened with wire)] (1901)
: SPIRIT, VIM

**³gimp** *noun* [origin unknown] (1929)
**1** : CRIPPLE
**2** : LIMP ⟨walks with a *gimp* —Damon Runyon⟩
— **gimpy** \'gim-pē\ *adjective*

**⁴gimp** *intransitive verb* (1948)
: LIMP, HOBBLE ⟨*gimping* up the stairs⟩

**¹gin** \'gin\ *verb* **gan** \'gan\; **gin·ning** [Middle English *ginnen,* short for *beginnen*] (13th century)
*archaic* : BEGIN

**²gin** \'jin\ *noun* [Middle English *gin,* modification of Old French *engin* — more at ENGINE] (13th century)
: any of various tools or mechanical devices: as **a** : a snare or trap for game **b** : COTTON GIN

**³gin** \'jin\ *transitive verb* **ginned; gin·ning** (circa 1625)
**1** : SNARE
**2** : to separate (cotton fiber) from seeds and waste material
— **gin·ner** *noun*

**⁴gin** \'gin\ *conjunction* [perhaps by contraction from dialect *gif* if + *an* if] (1580)
*dialect* : IF

**⁵gin** \'jin\ *noun* [by shortening & alteration from *geneva*] (1714)
**1** : a colorless alcoholic beverage made from distilled or redistilled neutral grain spirits flavored with juniper berries and aromatics (as anise and caraway seeds)
**2 a** : GIN RUMMY **b** : the act of laying down a full hand of matched cards in gin rummy ◆
— **gin·ny** \'jin-ē\ *adjective*

**¹gin·ger** \'jin-jər\ *noun* [Middle English, from Old English *gingifer,* from Medieval Latin *gingiber,* alteration of Latin *zingiber,* from Greek *zingiberi,* ultimately from Pali *singivēra*] (before 12th century)
**1 a** (1) : a thickened pungent aromatic rhizome that is used as a spice and sometimes

medicinally (2) : the spice usually prepared by drying and grinding ginger **b** : any of a genus (*Zingiber* of the family Zingiberaceae, the ginger family) of herbs with pungent aromatic rhizomes; *especially* : a widely cultivated tropical herb (*Z. officinale*) that supplies most of the ginger of commerce
**2** : high spirit : PEP ⟨the *ginger* to care hard and work hard —Willa Cather⟩
**3** : a strong brown
— **gin·gery** \'jinj-rē, 'jin-jə-\ *adjective*

**²ginger** *transitive verb* **gin·gered; gin·ger·ing** \'jinj-riŋ, 'jin-jə-\ (1849)
: to make lively : pep up ⟨*ginger* up the tourist trade —*N.Y. Times*⟩

**ginger ale** *noun* (1886)
: a sweetened carbonated nonalcoholic beverage flavored mainly with ginger extract

**ginger beer** *noun* (1809)
: a sweetened carbonated nonalcoholic beverage heavily flavored with ginger or capsicum or both

**gin·ger·bread** \'jin-jər-ˌbred\ *noun* (15th century)
**1** : a cake whose ingredients include molasses and ginger
**2** [from the fancy shapes and gilding formerly often applied to gingerbread] : lavish or superfluous ornament especially in architecture
— **gingerbread** *adjective*
— **gin·ger·bread·ed** \-ˌbre-dəd\ *adjective*
— **gin·ger·bready** \-dē\ *adjective*

**ginger group** *noun* (1925)
*chiefly British* : a group that serves as an energizing force within a larger body (as a political party)

**gin·ger·ly** \'jin-jər-lē\ *adjective* [perhaps from ¹*ginger*] (1594)
: very cautious or careful
— **gin·ger·li·ness** *noun*
— **gingerly** *adverb*

**ginger nut** *noun* (1842)
*British* : GINGERSNAP

**gin·ger·root** \'jin-jər-ˌ(r)üt, -ˌ(r)ůt\ *noun* (1831)
: GINGER 1a(1)

**gin·ger·snap** \-ˌsnap\ *noun* (1805)
: a thin brittle cookie sweetened with molasses and flavored with ginger

**ging·ham** \'giŋ-əm\ *noun* [modification of Malay *genggang* striped cloth] (1615)
: a clothing fabric usually of yarn-dyed cotton in plain weave

**gin·gi·va** \'jin-jə-və, jin-ˈjī-\ *noun, plural* **-vae** \-ˌvē\ [Latin] (circa 1889)
: ¹GUM
— **gin·gi·val** \'jin-jə-vəl\ *adjective*

---

◇ WORD HISTORY

**gin** *Genever* (now spelled with an initial *j*) was the Dutch word for a drink made of distilled spirits and flavored with juniper berries. Ultimately it came from Latin *juniperus* by way of Middle Dutch and Old French. Both the word and the beverage were introduced into Britain around the end of the 17th century, probably by soldiers returning from wars in the Low Countries. In its new land, however, the word was influenced by the similar-sounding name of a city in Switzerland, and thus the earliest name for the drink is *geneva,* which appeared in print in 1706. The creation of new words by clipping longer words to a monosyllable was as popular in 18th century English as it is today, and so a shortened form *gin* arose, to designate not only the Dutch drink but also a similar liquor made in Britain, not necessarily flavored with juniper but remarkably popular. So popular did it become, in fact, that gin drinking among the poorer classes became a major social problem. The epidemic proportions of this menace are long past, but the liquor and its clipped name are still with us.

**gin·gi·vec·to·my** \ˌjin-jə-'vek-tə-mē\ *noun,*
*plural* **-mies** (circa 1927)
: the excision of a portion of the gingiva
**gin·gi·vi·tis** \ˌjin-jə-'vī-təs\ *noun* (1874)
: inflammation of the gums
**gink** \'giŋk\ *noun* [origin unknown] (1908)
*slang* : PERSON, GUY
**gink·go** *also* **ging·ko** \'giŋ-(ˌ)kō *also* 'giŋk-
(ˌ)gō\ *noun, plural* **ginkgoes** *or* **ginkgos**
[New Latin *Ginkgo,* from Japanese *ginkyō*]
(1773)
: a gymnospermous tree (*Ginkgo biloba*) of
eastern China that is widely grown as an ornamental or shade tree and has fan-shaped leaves
and yellow fruit
**gin mill** *noun* (1865)
: BAR, SALOON
**gin rummy** *noun* [⁵*gin*] (1941)
: a rummy game for two players in which each
player is dealt 10 cards and in which a player
may win a hand by matching all the cards in it
or may end play when the unmatched cards
count up to 10 points or less
**gin·seng** \'jin-ˌseŋ, -ˌsiŋ\ *noun* [Chinese
(Beijing) *rénshēn*] (1654)
**1 a** : a Chinese perennial herb (*Panax schin-
seng* of the family Araliaceae, the ginseng
family) having 5-foliolate leaves, scarlet berries, and an aromatic root valued especially locally as a medicine **b** : any of several plants
related to ginseng; *espe-
cially* : a North American
herb (*P. quinquefolius*)
**2** : the root of a ginseng
**Gip·sy** *chiefly British*
variant of GYPSY
**gi·raffe** \jə-'raf\ *noun,*
*plural* **giraffes** [Italian
*giraffa,* from Arabic
*zirāfah*] (circa 1600)
**1** *or plural* **giraffe** : a
large fleet African rumi-
nant mammal (*Giraffa
camelopardalis*) that is
the tallest of living quadrupeds and has a very
long neck and a short
coat with dark blotches
separated by pale lines
**2** *capitalized* : CAMELOP-
ARDALIS
— **gi·raff·ish** \-'ra-
fish\ *adjective*

*giraffe 1*

**gir·an·dole** \'jir-ən-ˌdōl\ *noun* [French & Italian; French, from Italian *girandola,* from *girare* to turn, from Late Latin *gyrare,* from Latin *gyrus* gyre] (1749)
**1** : a radiating and showy
composition (as a cluster of
skyrockets fired together)
**2** : an ornamental branched
candlestick
**3** : a pendant earring usually with three ornaments
hanging from a central
piece
**gir·a·sole** *also* **gir·a·
sol** \'jir-ə-ˌsōl, -ˌsōl, -ˌsäl\
*noun* [Italian *girasole* sunflower, from *girare* + *sole*
sun, from Latin *sol* —
more at SOLAR] (circa
1586)
**1** : JERUSALEM ARTICHOKE
**2** *usually* **girasol** : an opal of varying color
that gives out fiery reflections in bright light
**¹gird** \'gərd\ *verb* **gird·ed** \'gər-dəd\ *or* **girt**
\'gərt\; **gird·ing** [Middle English, from Old
English *gyrdan;* akin to Old English *geard*
yard — more at YARD] (before 12th century)
*transitive verb*
**1 a** : to encircle or bind with a flexible band
(as a belt) **b** : to make fast (as a sword by a
belt or clothing with a cord) **c** : SURROUND

**2** : PROVIDE, EQUIP; *especially* : to invest with
the sword of knighthood
**3** : to prepare (oneself) for action
*intransitive verb*
: to prepare for action
— **gird one's loins** : to prepare for action
: muster up one's resources
**²gird** *verb* [Middle English, to strike, thrust]
(1546)
*intransitive verb*
: GIBE, RAIL
*transitive verb*
: to sneer at : MOCK
**³gird** *noun* (1566)
: a sarcastic remark
**gird·er** \'gər-dər\ *noun* [¹*gird*] (1611)
: a horizontal main structural member (as in a
building or bridge) that supports vertical loads
and that consists of a single piece or of more
than one piece bound together
**¹gir·dle** \'gər-dᵊl\ *noun* [Middle English *girdel,*
from Old English *gyrdel;* akin to Old High
German *gurtil* girdle, Old English *gyrdan* to
gird] (before 12th century)
**1** : something that encircles or confines: as a
: an article of dress encircling the body usually at the waist **b** : a woman's close-fitting undergarment often boned and usually elasticized that extends from the waist to below the
hips **c** (1) : PECTORAL GIRDLE (2) : PELVIC GIR-
DLE
**2** : the edge of a brilliant that is grasped by the
setting
**²girdle** *transitive verb* **gir·dled; gir·dling**
\'gər-dᵊl-iŋ\ (1582)
**1** : to encircle with or as if with a girdle
**2** : to cut away the bark and cambium in a
ring around (a plant) usually to kill by interrupting the circulation of water and nutrients
**3** : to move around : CIRCLE (*girdled* the
world)
**girl** \'gər(-ə)l\ *noun* [Middle English *gurle,*
*girle* young person of either sex] (14th century)
**1 a** : a female child **b** : a young unmarried
woman **c** : a single or married woman of any
age — sometimes taken to be offensive
**2 a** : SWEETHEART **b** : a female servant or employee — sometimes taken to be offensive **c**
: DAUGHTER ◆
— **girl·hood** \-ˌhùd\ *noun*
**girl Friday** *noun* [*girl* + *Friday* (as in *man
Friday*)] (1940)
: a female assistant (as in an office) entrusted
with a wide variety of tasks
**girl·friend** \'gər(-ə)l-ˌfrend\ *noun* (1859)
**1** : a female friend
**2** : a frequent or regular female companion of
a boy or man
**3** : MISTRESS 4a
**Girl Guide** *noun* (1909)
: a member of a worldwide scouting movement for girls 7 to 18 years of age that is
equivalent to the Girl Scouts in the U.S.
**girl·ie** *also* **girly** \'gər-lē\ *adjective* (1942)
: featuring scantily clothed women (*girlie*
magazines) (*girlie* show)
**girl·ish** \'gər-lish\ *adjective* (1565)
: of, relating to, or having the characteristics
of a girl or girlhood
— **girl·ish·ly** *adverb*
— **girl·ish·ness** *noun*
**Girl Scout** *noun* (1909)
: a member of any of the scouting programs of
the Girl Scouts of the United States of America for girls ages 5 through 17
**girn** \'girn\ *intransitive verb* [Middle English,
alteration of *grinnen* to grin, snarl] (12th century)
*chiefly Scottish* : SNARL
— **girn** *noun, chiefly Scottish*
**gi·ro** \'jir-(ˌ)ō, 'zhir-; 'jē-(ˌ)rō, 'zhē-, *especially*
*British* 'jī-\ *noun* [German, circulation (of currency), from Italian, from Latin *gyrus* gyre]
(1890)

: a service of many European banks that permits authorized direct transfer of funds among
account holders as well as conventional transfers by check
**gi·ron** *variant of* GYRON
**Gi·ron·din** \jə-'rän-din, zhə-\ *noun* [French,
from *girondin* of Gironde] (1837)
: GIRONDIST
**Gi·rond·ist** \-dist\ *noun* [French *girondiste,*
from *Gironde,* a political party, from *Gironde,*
department of France represented by its lead-
ers] (1795)
: a member of the moderate republican party
in the French legislative assembly in 1791
**girt** \'gərt\ *verb* [Middle English *girten,* alteration of *girden*] (15th century)
*transitive verb*
**1** : GIRD
**2** : to fasten by means of a girth
*intransitive verb*
: to measure in girth
**¹girth** \'gərth\ *noun* [Middle English, from Old
Norse *gjǫrth;* akin to Old English *gyrdan* to
gird] (13th century)
**1** : a band or strap that encircles the body of
an animal to fasten something (as a saddle) on
its back
**2 a** : a measure around a body (a man of more
than average *girth*) **b** : SIZE, DIMENSIONS
**²girth** *transitive verb* (15th century)
**1** : ENCIRCLE
**2** : to bind or fasten with a girth
**3** : to measure the girth of
**gi·sarme** \gi-'zärm\ *noun* [Middle English,
from Old French] (13th century)
: a medieval weapon consisting of a blade
mounted on a long staff and carried by foot
soldiers
**gist** \'jist\ *noun* [Anglo-French, it lies, from
Middle French, from *gesir* to lie, ultimately
from Latin *jacēre* — more at ADJACENT] (circa 1711)
**1** : the ground of a legal action
**2** : the main point or part : ESSENCE (the *gist* of
an argument)
**git** \'git\ *noun* [variant of *get,* term of abuse,
from ²*get*] (1943)
*British* : a foolish or worthless person

◇ WORD HISTORY
**girl** Words in European languages that
correspond to "boy" or "girl" are often of relatively recent origin and of obscure etymology,
having floated upwards into standard use
from the most colloquial and innovative varieties of speech. The English word *girl* is no
exception. It first appeared in Middle English,
about the end of the 13th century, in the
forms *gurle, gerle,* and *girle,* denoting a child
of either sex. Toward the end of the 14th
century it was applied specifically to a female, a sense that became dominant by
Shakespeare's time. Attempts have been
made to relate the Middle English word to
Old English *gierela, gerela* "apparel, banner."
The connection may be possible on semantic
grounds—witness the now fading English
use of *flapper* to mean "young woman"—but
it offers phonetic difficulties, as the expected
Old English ancestor of *girl* would more plausibly be an unattested *gyrela.* The word *girl*
shows a variety of dialect pronunciations in
Modern English, often with a dropped \r\
even in accents that do not normally lose \r\
before a consonant. One such form, *gal,* is
well-established in American English, though
now somewhat old-fashioned and restricted
in context.

**git–go** \'git-ˌgō\ *variant of* GET-GO

**git·tern** \'gi-tərn\ *noun* [Middle English *giterne*, from Middle French *guiterne*, modification of Old Spanish *guitarra* guitar] (14th century)
: a medieval guitar

¹**give** \'giv\ *verb* **gave** \'gāv\; **giv·en** \'gi-vən\; **giv·ing** [Middle English, of Scandinavian origin; akin to Old Swedish *giva* to give; akin to Old English *giefan, gifan* to give, and perhaps to Latin *habēre* to have, hold] (13th century)
*transitive verb*
**1** : to make a present of ⟨*give* a doll to a child⟩ **2 a** : to grant or bestow by formal action ⟨the law *gives* citizens the right to vote⟩ **b** : to accord or yield to another ⟨*gave* him her confidence⟩
**3 a** : to put into the possession of another for his use **b** (1) : to administer as a sacrament (2) : to administer as a medicine **c** : to commit to another as a trust or responsibility and usually for an expressed reason **d** : to transfer from one's authority or custody ⟨the sheriff *gave* the prisoner to the warden⟩ **e** : to execute and deliver ⟨all employees must *give* bond⟩ **f** : to convey to another ⟨*give* them my regards⟩
**4 a** : to offer to the action of another : PROFFER ⟨*gave* her his hand⟩ **b** : to yield (oneself) to a man in sexual intercourse
**5 a** : to present in public performance ⟨*give* a concert⟩ **b** : to present to view or observation ⟨*gave* the signal to start⟩
**6** : to provide by way of entertainment ⟨*give* a party⟩
**7** : to propose as a toast
**8 a** : to designate as a share or portion : ALLOT ⟨all the earth to thee and to thy race I *give* —John Milton⟩ **b** : to make assignment of (a name) **c** : to set forth as an actual or hypothetical datum ⟨*give* the dimensions of the room⟩ **d** : to attribute in thought or utterance : ASCRIBE ⟨*gave* the credit to you⟩
**9 a** : to yield as a product, consequence, or effect : PRODUCE ⟨cows *give* milk⟩ ⟨84 divided by 12 *gives* 7⟩ **b** : to bring forth : BEAR
**10 a** : to yield possession of by way of exchange : PAY **b** : to dispose of for a price : SELL
**11 a** : to deliver by some bodily action ⟨*gave* him a push⟩ **b** : to carry out (as a bodily movement) ⟨*gave* a cynical smile⟩ **c** : to inflict as punishment **d** : to award by formal verdict ⟨judgment was *given* against the plaintiff⟩
**12** : to offer for consideration, acceptance, or use ⟨*gives* no reason for his absence⟩
**13 a** : to suffer the loss of : SACRIFICE **b** : to offer as appropriate or due especially to something higher or more worthy ⟨*gave* his spirit to God⟩ **c** : to apply freely or fully : DEVOTE ⟨*gave* themselves to their work⟩ **d** : to offer as a pledge ⟨I *give* you my word⟩
**14 a** : to cause one to have or receive ⟨mountains always *gave* him pleasure⟩ **b** : to cause a person to catch by contagion, infection, or exposure
**15 a** : to allow one to have or take ⟨*give* me time⟩ **b** : to lead or attempt to lead — used with an infinitive ⟨you *gave* me to understand you'd be late⟩
**16** : to care to the extent of ⟨didn't *give* a hang⟩
*intransitive verb*
**1** : to make gifts or presents
**2 a** : to yield to physical force or strain **b** : to collapse from the application of force or pressure **c** : to undergo or submit to change ⟨for the strike to be settled, something has to *give*⟩
**3** : to afford a view or passage : OPEN
**4** : to enter wholeheartedly into an activity
**5** *slang* : GO ON, HAPPEN ⟨wants to know what *gives*⟩ ☆
— **give a good account of** : to acquit (oneself) well
— **give birth** : to have a baby ⟨*gave* birth last Thursday⟩

— **give birth to 1** : to produce as offspring ⟨*gave birth to* a son⟩ **2** : to be the source of
— **give chase** : to set off in pursuit
— **give ground** : to withdraw before superior force : RETREAT
— **give of** : to make available : provide generously ⟨freely *gave of* their time⟩
— **give or take** : as an estimate accurate within (an amount to be added or subtracted)
— **give place to** : to be replaced or succeeded by ⟨optimism *gave place to* worry⟩
— **give rise to** : to be the cause or source of : PRODUCE
— **give the gun** : to open the throttle of : speed up
— **give the lie to 1** : to accuse of falsehood **2** : to show to be false, inaccurate, or invalid
— **give tongue** *of hounds* : to begin barking on the scent
— **give way 1 a** : RETREAT **b** : to yield the right of way **2** : to yield oneself without restraint or control **3 a** : to yield to or as if to physical stress **b** : to yield to entreaty or insistence **4** : to yield place **5** : to begin to row

²**give** *noun* (1868)
**1** : capacity or tendency to yield to force or strain : FLEXIBILITY
**2** : the quality or state of being springy

**give–and–go** \ˌgiv-ən-'gō\ *noun* (1965)
: a play (as in basketball or hockey) in which a player passes to a teammate and immediately cuts toward the net or goal to receive a return pass

**give–and–take** \ˌgiv-ən-'tāk\ *noun* (1778)
**1** : the practice of making mutual concessions : COMPROMISE
**2** : a usually good-natured exchange (as of ideas or comments)

**give·away** \'gi-və-ˌwā\ *noun* (1882)
**1** : an unintentional revelation or betrayal
**2 a** : something given away free; *specifically* : PREMIUM 1d **b** : the act of giving something away free ⟨staging a promotional *giveaway*⟩
**3** : a radio or television program on which prizes are given away

**give away** *transitive verb* (14th century)
**1** : to make a present of
**2** : to deliver (a bride) ceremonially to the bridegroom at a wedding
**3 a** : BETRAY **b** : DISCLOSE, REVEAL
**4** : to give (as weight) by way of a handicap

**give·back** \'giv-ˌbak\ *noun* (1978)
: a previous gain (as an increase in wages or benefits) given back to management by workers (as in a labor contract)

**give back** (1548)
*intransitive verb*
: RETIRE, RETREAT
*transitive verb*
: to send in return or reply : RESTORE, RETURN

**give in** (1602)
*transitive verb*
: DELIVER, SUBMIT ⟨*gave in* his resignation⟩
*intransitive verb*
: to yield under insistence or entreaty : SURRENDER

¹**giv·en** \'gi-vən\ *adjective* (14th century)
**1** : PRONE, DISPOSED ⟨*given* to swearing⟩
**2** : presented as a gift : bestowed without compensation
**3** : PARTICULAR, SPECIFIED ⟨at a *given* time⟩
**4** *of an official document* : having been executed : DATED
**5** : immediately present in experience

²**given** *noun* (1879)
: something given; *especially* : something taken for granted : a basic condition or assumption

³**given** *preposition* (1904)
: in view of : CONSIDERING ⟨*given* what she knew about others' lives, how could she complain about her own? —Marilyn French⟩

**given name** *noun* (1827)
: a name that precedes one's surname; *especially* : FIRST NAME

**give off** (1831)
*transitive verb*
**1** : to send out as a branch
**2** : EMIT ⟨*give off* an unpleasant smell⟩
*intransitive verb*
: to branch off

**give out** (14th century)
*transitive verb*
**1 a** : DECLARE, PUBLISH ⟨*giving out* that the doctor . . . required a few days of complete rest —Charles Dickens⟩ **b** : to read aloud the words of (a hymn or psalm) for congregational singing
**2** : EMIT ⟨*gave out* a constant hum⟩
**3** : ISSUE ⟨*gave out* new uniforms⟩
*intransitive verb*
**1** : BREAK DOWN, FAIL
**2** : to become exhausted : COLLAPSE

**give over** (14th century)
*transitive verb*
**1** : CEASE
**2** : ENTRUST
**3 a** : to yield without restraint or control : ABANDON ⟨*gave* themselves *over* to laughter⟩ **b** : to set apart for a particular purpose or use
**4** *archaic* : to pronounce incurable
*intransitive verb*
*British* : to cease an activity : STOP ⟨told him to *give over* and let me alone —Brendan Behan⟩

**giv·er** \'gi-vər\ *noun* (14th century)
: one that gives : DONOR

**give up** (13th century)
*transitive verb*
**1** : to yield control or possession of : SURRENDER ⟨forced to *give up* his job⟩
**2** : to desist from : ABANDON ⟨refused to *give up* her efforts⟩
**3** : to declare incurable or insoluble
**4 a** : to abandon (oneself) to a particular feeling, influence, or activity ⟨*gave* himself *up* to despair⟩ **b** : to devote to a particular purpose or use
**5** : to despair of seeing ⟨we'd *given* you *up*⟩
**6** : to allow (a hit or run in baseball) while pitching
*intransitive verb*
: to cease doing or attempting something especially as an admission of defeat : QUIT — often used with *on* ⟨don't *give up* on the project⟩
— **give up the ghost** : to cease to live or function : DIE

**giz·mo** *also* **gis·mo** \'giz-(ˌ)mō\ *noun, plural* **gizmos** *also* **gismos** [origin unknown] (1943)
: GADGET

**giz·zard** \'gi-zərd\ *noun* [alteration of Middle English *giser*, from Old French *guisier, giser*, from Latin *gigeria* (plural) giblets] (1565)
**1 a** : the muscular enlargement of the alimentary canal of birds that has usually thick muscular walls and a tough horny lining for grinding the food and when the crop is present

---

☆ **SYNONYMS**
**Give, present, donate, bestow, confer, afford** mean to convey to another as a possession. GIVE, the general term, is applicable to any passing over of anything by any means ⟨*give* alms⟩ ⟨*gave* her a ride on a pony⟩ ⟨*give* my love to your mother⟩. PRESENT carries a note of formality and ceremony ⟨*present* an award⟩. DONATE is likely to imply a publicized giving (as to charity) ⟨*donate* a piano to the orphanage⟩. BESTOW implies the conveying of something as a gift and may suggest condescension on the part of the giver ⟨*bestow* unwanted advice⟩. CONFER implies a gracious giving (as of a favor or honor) ⟨*confer* an honorary degree⟩. AFFORD implies a giving or bestowing usually as a natural or legitimate consequence of the character of the giver ⟨the trees *afford* shade⟩ ⟨a development that *affords* us some hope⟩.

follows it and the proventriculus **b** : a thickened part of the alimentary canal in some animals (as an insect or an earthworm) that is similar in function to the crop of a bird
**2** : INNARDS
**gla·bel·la** \glə-'be-lə\ *noun, plural* **-bel·lae** \-'be-(ˌ)lē, -ˌlī\ [New Latin, from Latin, feminine of *glabellus* hairless, diminutive of *glaber*] (circa 1823)
: the smooth prominence between the eyebrows
— **gla·bel·lar** \-'be-lər\ *adjective*
**gla·bres·cent** \glā-'bres-s°nt\ *adjective* (1857)
**1** : somewhat glabrous
**2** : tending to become glabrous
**gla·brous** \'glā-brəs\ *adjective* [Latin *glabr-, glaber* smooth, bald — more at GLAD] (1640)
: SMOOTH; *especially* : having a surface without hairs or projections ⟨*glabrous* skin⟩ ⟨*glabrous* leaves⟩
**gla·cé** \gla-'sā\ *adjective* [French, from past participle of *glacer* to freeze, ice, glaze, from Latin *glaciare*, from *glacies*] (1847)
**1** : made or finished so as to have a smooth glossy surface ⟨*glacé* silk⟩
**2** *also* **gla·céed** \-'sād\ : coated with a glaze : CANDIED ⟨*glacé* cherries⟩
**gla·cial** \'glā-shəl\ *adjective* [Latin *glacialis*, from *glacies*] (1656)
**1 a** : extremely cold : FRIGID ⟨a *glacial* wind⟩ **b** : devoid of warmth and cordiality ⟨a *glacial* handshake⟩ **c** : coldly imperturbable ⟨maintained a *glacial* calm⟩
**2** : resembling ice in appearance ⟨*glacial* acetic acid⟩
**3 a** (1) : of, relating to, or being any of those parts of geologic time from Precambrian onward when a much larger portion of the earth was covered by glaciers than at present (2) *capitalized* : PLEISTOCENE **b** : of, relating to, or produced by glaciers **c** : suggestive of the very slow movement of glaciers ⟨progress on the bill has been *glacial*⟩
— **gla·cial·ly** \-shə-lē\ *adverb*
**gla·ci·ate** \'glā-shē-ˌāt, -sē-\ *transitive verb* **-at·ed; -at·ing** (circa 1623)
**1** : FREEZE
**2 a** : to subject to glacial action; *also* : to produce glacial effects in or on **b** : to cover with a glacier
— **gla·ci·a·tion** \ˌglā-shē-'ā-shən, -sē-\ *noun*
**gla·cier** \'glā-shər *also* -zhər, *especially British* 'gla-sē-ər *or* 'glā-sē-\ *noun* [French dialect, from Middle French dialect, from Middle French *glace* ice, from Latin *glacies*; akin to Latin *gelu* frost — more at COLD] (1744)
: a large body of ice moving slowly down a slope or valley or spreading outward on a land surface
**gla·ci·ol·o·gy** \ˌglā-shē-'ä-lə-jē, -sē-\ *noun* [Latin *glacies* + International Scientific Vocabulary *-logy*] (1889)
: any of the branches of science dealing with snow or ice accumulation, glaciation, or glacial epochs
— **gla·ci·o·log·i·cal** \-ə-'lä-ji-kəl\ *adjective*
— **gla·ci·ol·o·gist** \-'ä-lə-jist\ *noun*
**gla·cis** \gla-'sē, 'gla-sē\ *noun, plural* **glacis** \-'sēz, -sēz\ [French, from *glacer* to freeze, slide] (1672)
**1 a** : a gentle slope : INCLINE **b** : a slope that runs downward from a fortification
**2** : BUFFER STATE; *also* : BUFFER ZONE
**¹glad** \'glad\ *adjective* **glad·der; glad·dest** [Middle English, shining, glad, from Old English *glæd*; akin to Old High German *glat* shining, smooth, Latin *glaber* smooth, bald] (before 12th century)
**1** *archaic* : having a cheerful or happy disposition by nature
**2 a** : experiencing pleasure, joy, or delight : made happy **b** : made pleased, satisfied, or grateful — often used with *of* ⟨was *glad* of their help⟩ **c** : very willing ⟨*glad* to do it⟩

**3 a** : marked by, expressive of, or caused by happiness and joy ⟨a *glad* shout⟩ **b** : causing happiness and joy : PLEASANT ⟨*glad* tidings⟩
**4** : full of brightness and cheerfulness ⟨a *glad* spring morning⟩
— **glad·ly** *adverb*
— **glad·ness** *noun*
**²glad** *verb* **glad·ded; glad·ding** (before 12th century)
*archaic* : GLADDEN
**³glad** *noun* (1923)
: GLADIOLUS 1
**glad·den** \'gla-d°n\ *verb* **glad·dened; glad·den·ing** \'gla-d°n-iŋ\ (13th century)
*intransitive verb*
*archaic* : to be glad
*transitive verb*
: to make glad
**glade** \'glād\ *noun* [perhaps from ¹glad] (1529)
: an open space surrounded by woods
— **glady** \'glā-dē\ *adjective*
**glad–hand** \'glad-ˌhand\ (1903)
*transitive verb*
: to extend a glad hand to ⟨candidates *glad-handing* everyone they meet⟩
*intransitive verb*
: to extend a glad hand ⟨*glad-handing* as if he were running for mayor⟩
— **glad–hand·er** \'glad-ˌhan-dər\ *noun*
**glad hand** *noun* (circa 1895)
: a warm welcome or greeting often prompted by ulterior reasons
**glad·i·a·tor** \'gla-dē-ˌā-tər\ *noun* [Latin, from *gladius* sword, of Celtic origin; akin to Welsh *cleddyf* sword] (15th century)
**1** : a person engaged in a fight to the death as public entertainment for ancient Romans
**2** : a person engaging in a public fight or controversy
**3** : a trained fighter; *especially* : a professional boxer
— **glad·i·a·to·ri·al** \ˌgla-dē-ə-'tōr-ē-əl, -'tȯr-\ *adjective*
**glad·i·o·la** \ˌgla-dē-'ō-lə\ *noun* [back-formation from *gladiolus*, taken as a plural] (1926)
: GLADIOLUS 1
**glad·i·o·lus** \ˌgla-dē-'ō-ləs\ *noun, plural* **-li** \-(ˌ)lē, -ˌlī\ [New Latin, from Latin, gladiolus, from diminutive of *gladius*] (15th century)
**1** *or plural* **gladiolus** *also* **glad·i·o·lus·es** : any of a genus (*Gladiolus*) of chiefly African plants of the iris family with erect sword-shaped leaves and spikes of brilliantly colored irregular flowers arising from corms
**2** : the large middle portion of the sternum
**glad rags** *noun plural* (1896)
: dressy clothes
**glad·some** \'glad-səm\ *adjective* (14th century)
: giving or showing joy : CHEERFUL
— **glad·some·ly** *adverb*
— **glad·some·ness** *noun*
**glad·stone** \'glad-ˌstȯn, *chiefly British* -stən\ *noun, often capitalized* [W. E. *Gladstone*] (1889)
: a suitcase with flexible sides on a rigid frame that opens flat into two equal compartments — called also *gladstone bag*

gladiolus 1

**glai·kit** *or* **glai·ket** \'glā-kət\ *adjective* [Middle English (Scots) *glaikit*] (15th century)
*chiefly Scottish* : FOOLISH, GIDDY
**glair** *or* **glaire** \'glar, 'gler\ *noun* [Middle English *gleyre* egg white, from Middle French *glaire*, modification of (assumed) Vulgar Latin *claria*, from Latin *clarus* clear — more at CLEAR] (13th century)
**1** : a sizing liquid made from egg white

**2** : a viscid substance suggestive of an egg white
**glairy** \-ē\ *adjective* **glair·i·er; -est** (1662)
: having the characteristics of or overlaid with glair
**glaive** \'glāv\ *noun* [Middle English, from Middle French, javelin, sword, modification of Latin *gladius* sword] (15th century)
*archaic* : SWORD; *especially* : BROADSWORD
**glam·or·ise** *British variant of* GLAMORIZE
**glam·or·ize** *also* **glam·our·ize** \'gla-mə-ˌrīz\ *transitive verb* **-ized; -iz·ing** (1936)
**1** : to look upon or depict as glamorous : ROMANTICIZE ⟨the novel *glamorizes* war⟩
**2** : to make glamorous ⟨*glamorize* the living room⟩
— **glam·or·iza·tion** \ˌgla-mə-rə-'zā-shən\ *noun*
— **glam·or·iz·er** \'gla-mə-ˌrī-zər\ *noun*
**glam·or·ous** *also* **glam·our·ous** \'glam-rəs, 'gla-mə-\ *adjective* (1882)
: full of glamour
— **glam·or·ous·ly** *adverb*
— **glam·or·ous·ness** *noun*
**glam·our** *or* **glam·or** \'gla-mər\ *noun* [Scots *glamour*, alteration of English *grammar*; from the popular association of erudition with occult practices] (1715)
**1** : a magic spell ⟨the girls appeared to be under a *glamour* —Llewelyn Powys⟩
**2** : an exciting and often illusory and romantic attractiveness; *especially* : alluring or fascinating personal attraction — often used attributively ⟨*glamour* stock⟩ ⟨*glamour* boy⟩ ⟨*glamour* girl⟩ ◆
— **glamour** *transitive verb*
— **glam·our·less** \-ləs\ *adjective*
**glam·our–puss** \-ˌpús\ *noun* (1941)
: a glamorously attractive person
**¹glance** \'glan(t)s\ *verb* **glanced; glanc·ing** [Middle English *glencen, glenchen*] (15th century)
*intransitive verb*
**1** : to strike a surface obliquely so as to go off at an angle ⟨the bullet *glanced* off the wall⟩
**2 a** : to make sudden quick movements ⟨dragonflies *glancing* over the pond⟩ **b** : to flash or gleam with quick intermittent rays of light ⟨brooks *glancing* in the sun⟩

◇ WORD HISTORY
**glamour** In classical antiquity the Greek and Latin ancestors of the English word *grammar* were used in reference not only to the study of language but also to the study of literature. In the medieval period, Latin *grammatica* and its outcomes in other languages were extended to include learning in general. Since almost all learning was couched in a language not spoken or understood by the unschooled populace, it was commonly believed that subjects such as magic and astrology were included in *grammatica*. Scholars were sometimes regarded with awe and more than a little suspicion, and the Faust legend illustrates the popular intertwining of learning and alchemical studies with necromancy and the devil. This connection between grammar and the black arts was evident in a number of languages, and in Scotland by the 18th century a form of *grammar*, altered by dissimilation to *glamer* or *glamour*, meant "a magic spell." As *glamour* passed into more general English usage, it came to have its current meanings "an exciting and often deceptive attractiveness" and particularly "alluring personal attractiveness."

**3 :** to touch on a subject or refer to it briefly or indirectly ⟨the work *glances* at the customs of ancient cultures⟩
**4 a** *of the eyes* **:** to move swiftly from one thing to another **b :** to take a quick look at something ⟨*glanced* at his watch⟩
*transitive verb*
**1** *archaic* **a :** to take a quick look at **b :** to catch a glimpse of
**2 :** to give an oblique path of direction to: **a :** to throw or shoot so that the object glances from a surface **b** *archaic* **:** to aim (as an innuendo) indirectly **:** INSINUATE
— **glanc·er** *noun*

**²glance** *noun* (1503)
**1 a :** a quick intermittent flash or gleam **b** *archaic* **:** a sudden quick movement
**2 a** *archaic* **:** a rapid oblique movement **b :** a deflected impact or blow
**3 a :** a swift movement of the eyes **b :** a quick or cursory look
**4** *archaic* **a :** a brief satirical reference to something **:** GIBE **b :** ALLUSION
— **at first glance :** on first consideration ⟨*at first glance* the subject seems harmless enough⟩

**glanc·ing** \'glan(t)-siŋ\ *adjective* (circa 1541)
**1 :** hitting so as to glance off ⟨a *glancing* blow⟩
**2 :** INCIDENTAL, INDIRECT ⟨made *glancing* allusions to her past⟩
— **glanc·ing·ly** \-siŋ-lē\ *adverb*

**¹gland** \'gland\ *noun* [French *glande*, from Old French, glandular swelling on the neck, gland, ultimately from Latin *gland-*, *glans* acorn; akin to Greek *balanos* acorn] (1692)
**1 a :** a cell, group of cells, or organ of endothelial origin that selectively removes materials from the blood, concentrates or alters them, and secretes them for further use in the body or for elimination from the body **b :** any of various animal structures suggestive of glands though not secretory in function
**2 :** any of various secreting organs (as a nectary) of plants
— **gland·less** \'gland-ləs\ *adjective*

**²gland** *noun* [origin unknown] (1839)
**1 :** a device for preventing leakage of fluid past a joint in machinery
**2 :** the movable part of a stuffing box by which the packing is compressed

**glan·dered** \'glan-dərd\ *adjective* (1667)
**:** affected with glanders

**glan·ders** \-dərz\ *noun plural but singular or plural in construction* [Middle French *glandre* glandular swelling on the neck, from Latin *glandulae*, from plural of *glandula*, diminutive of *gland-*, *glans*] (1523)
**:** a contagious and destructive disease especially of horses caused by a bacterium (*Pseudomonas mallei* synonym *Actinobacillus mallei*) and characterized by caseating nodular lesions especially on the respiratory mucosae and lungs that tend to break down and form ulcers

**glan·du·lar** \'glan-jə-lər\ *adjective* (circa 1740)
**1 a :** of, relating to, or involving glands, gland cells, or their products **b :** having the characteristics or function of a gland
**2 a :** INNATE, INHERENT ⟨the almost *glandular* . . . instinct for adventure and romance —*Newsweek*⟩ **b :** PHYSICAL, SEXUAL
— **glan·du·lar·ly** *adverb*

**glandular fever** *noun* (1902)
**:** INFECTIOUS MONONUCLEOSIS

**glans** \'glanz\ *noun, plural* **glan·des** \'glan-,dēz\ [Latin *gland-*, *glans*, literally, acorn] (1650)
**1 :** a conical vascular body forming the extremity of the penis — called also *glans penis*
**2 :** a structure of the clitoris similar to the glans penis — called also *glans cli·to·ri·dis* \-klə-'tȯr-ə-dəs\

**¹glare** \'glar, 'gler\ *verb* **glared; glar·ing** [Middle English *glaren;* akin to Old English *glæs* glass] (13th century)
*intransitive verb*
**1 a :** to shine with a harsh uncomfortably brilliant light **b :** STAND OUT, OBTRUDE
**2 :** to stare angrily or fiercely
*transitive verb*
**1 :** to express (as hostility) by staring angrily
**2** *archaic* **:** to cause to be sharply reflected

**²glare** *noun* (15th century)
**1 a :** a harsh uncomfortably bright light ⟨the *glare* of a neon sign⟩ ⟨the *glare* of publicity⟩; *especially* **:** painfully bright sunlight **b :** cheap showy brilliance **:** GARISHNESS
**2 :** an angry or fierce stare
**3 :** a surface or sheet of smooth and slippery ice

**glar·ing** \'glar-iŋ, 'gler-\ *adjective* (14th century)
**1 :** having a fixed look of hostility, fierceness, or anger
**2 a :** shining with or reflecting an uncomfortably bright light **b** (1) **:** GARISH (2) **:** vulgarly ostentatious
**3 :** obtrusively and often painfully obvious ⟨a *glaring* error⟩
**synonym** see FLAGRANT
— **glar·ing·ly** \-iŋ-lē\ *adverb*
— **glar·ing·ness** *noun*

**glary** \'glar-ē, 'gler-\ *adjective* **glar·i·er; -est** (1632)
**:** having a dazzling brightness **:** GLARING

**glas·nost** \'glaz-(,)nōst, 'glas-, 'gläz-, 'gläs-\ *noun* [Russian *glasnost'*, literally, publicity, from *glasnyǐ* public, from *glas* voice, from Old Church Slavonic *glasŭ* — more at CALL] (1986)
**:** a Soviet policy permitting open discussion of political and social issues and freer dissemination of news and information

**¹glass** \'glas, 'glàs\ *noun, often attributive* [Middle English *glas*, from Old English *glæs;* akin to Old English *geolu* yellow — more at YELLOW] (before 12th century)
**1 :** any of various amorphous materials formed from a melt by cooling to rigidity without crystallization: as **a :** a usually transparent or translucent material consisting especially of a mixture of silicates **b :** a material (as obsidian) produced by fast cooling of magma
**2 a :** something made of glass: as (1) **:** TUMBLER; *also* **:** GLASSWARE (2) **:** MIRROR (3) **:** BAROMETER (4) **:** HOURGLASS (5) **:** BACKBOARD **b** (1) **:** an optical instrument or device that has one or more lenses and is designed to aid in the viewing of objects not readily seen (2) **:** FIELD GLASSES, BINOCULARS — usually used in plural **c** *plural* **:** a device used to correct defects of vision or to protect the eyes that consists typically of a pair of glass or plastic lenses and the frame by which they are held in place — called also *eyeglasses, spectacles*
**3 :** the quantity held by a glass container
**4 :** FIBERGLASS
— **glass·ful** \'glas-,fùl\ *noun*
— **glass·less** \'-ləs\ *adjective*

**²glass** (14th century)
*transitive verb*
**1 a :** to provide with glass **:** GLAZE 1 **b :** to enclose, case, or wall with glass ⟨the sunroom was *glassed* in⟩
**2 :** to make glassy
**3 a :** REFLECT **b :** to see mirrored
**4 :** to look at through an optical instrument (as binoculars)
*intransitive verb*
**:** ¹GLAZE 1

**glass·blow·ing** \-,blō-iŋ\ *noun* (circa 1829)
**:** the art of shaping a mass of glass that has been softened by heat by blowing air into it through a tube
— **glass·blow·er** \-,blō(-ə)r\ *noun*

**glass ceiling** *noun* (1986)

**:** an intangible barrier within the hierarchy of a company that prevents women or minorities from obtaining upper-level positions

**glass eye** *noun* (1687)
**1 :** an artificial eye made of glass
**2 :** an eye having a pale, whitish, or colorless iris
— **glass-eyed** \-,īd\ *adjective*

**glass fiber** *noun* (1882)
**:** FIBERGLASS

**glass harmonica** *noun* (circa 1909)
**:** a musical instrument consisting of a series of rotating glass bowls of differing sizes played by touching the dampened edges with a finger

**glass·house** \'glas-,haùs\ *noun* (14th century)
**1 :** a place where glass is made
**2** *chiefly British* **:** GREENHOUSE
**3** *British* **:** a military prison

**glass·ie** \'gla-sē\ *or* **glassy** *noun, plural* **glass·ies** (1887)
**:** a playing marble made of glass

**glass·ine** \gla-'sēn\ *noun* (1916)
**:** a thin dense transparent or semitransparent paper highly resistant to the passage of air and grease

**glass jaw** *noun* (1940)
**:** vulnerability (as of a boxer) to knockout punches

**glass·mak·er** \'glas-,mā-kər\ *noun* (1576)
**:** one that makes glass
— **glass·mak·ing** \-kiŋ\ *noun*

**glass·pa·per** \'gläs-,pā-pər\ *noun* (1815)
*British* **:** abrasive paper coated with pulverized glass and used like sandpaper
— **glasspaper** *verb*

**glass snake** *noun* (1709)
**:** any of a genus (*Ophisaurus*) of limbless snakelike lizards of the southern U.S., Eurasia, and Africa with a fragile tail that readily breaks into pieces

**glass sponge** *noun* (1875)
**:** any of a class (Hexactinellida synonym Hyalospongiae) of chiefly deep-water siliceous sponges with 6-rayed spicules and a skeleton often resembling glass when dried

**glass·ware** \'glas-,war, -,wer\ *noun* (1745)
**:** articles made of glass

**glass wool** *noun* (1879)
**:** glass fibers in a mass resembling wool and being used especially for thermal insulation and air filters

**glass·work** \'glas-,wərk\ *noun* (1611)
**1 a :** the manufacture of glass or glassware; *also* **:** glaziers' work **b** *plural* **:** GLASSHOUSE 1
**2 :** GLASSWARE
— **glass·work·er** \-,wər-kər\ *noun*

**glass·wort** \-,wərt, -,wȯrt\ *noun* [from its former use in the manufacture of glass] (1597)
**:** any of a genus (*Salicornia*) of woody jointed succulent herbs of the goosefoot family with leaves reduced to fleshy sheaths

**glassy** \'gla-sē\ *adjective* **glass·i·er; -est** (14th century)
**1 :** resembling or made of glass
**2 :** having little animation **:** DULL, LIFELESS ⟨*glassy* eyes⟩
— **glass·i·ly** \'gla-sə-lē\ *adverb*
— **glass·i·ness** \'gla-sē-nəs\ *noun*

**glassy-eyed** \-,īd\ *adjective* (1895)
**:** marked by or having glassy eyes

**Glau·ber's salt** \'glaù-bər(z)-\ *noun* [Johann R. *Glauber* (died 1668) German chemist] (1736)
**:** a colorless crystalline sulfate of sodium $Na_2SO_4 \cdot 10H_2O$ used especially in dyeing, as a cathartic, and in solar energy systems — called also *Glauber salt*; sometimes used in plural

**glau·co·ma** \glaù-'kō-mə, glȯ-\ *noun* [Latin, cataract, from Greek *glaukōma*, from *glaukoun* to have a cataract, from *glaukos*] (1885)
**:** a disease of the eye marked by increased pressure within the eyeball that can result in damage to the optic disk and gradual loss of vision

**glau·co·nite** \'glȯ-kə-ˌnīt\ *noun* [German *Glaukonit*, irregular from Greek *glaukos*] (1836)
: a mineral consisting of a dull green earthy iron potassium silicate occurring in greensand
— **glau·co·nit·ic** \ˌglȯ-kə-'ni-tik\ *adjective*

**glau·cous** \'glȯ-kəs\ *adjective* [Latin *glaucus*, from Greek *glaukos* gleaming, gray] (1671)
**1 a :** of a pale yellow-green color **b :** of a light bluish gray or bluish white color
**2 :** having a powdery or waxy coating that gives a frosted appearance and tends to rub off
— **glau·cous·ness** *noun*

**¹glaze** \'glāz\ *verb* **glazed; glaz·ing** [Middle English *glasen*, from *glas* glass] (14th century)
*transitive verb*
**1 :** to furnish or fit with glass
**2 a :** to coat with or as if with a glaze ⟨the storm *glazed* trees with ice⟩ **b :** to apply a glaze to ⟨*glaze* doughnuts⟩
**3 :** to give a smooth glossy surface to
*intransitive verb*
**1 :** to become glazed or glassy ⟨my eyes *glazed* over⟩
**2 :** to form a glaze
— **glaz·er** *noun*

**²glaze** *noun* (1752)
**1 :** a smooth slippery coating of thin ice
**2 a** (1) **:** a liquid preparation applied to food on which it forms a firm glossy coating (2) **:** a mixture mostly of oxides (as silica and alumina) applied to the surface of ceramic wares to form a moisture-impervious and often lustrous or ornamental coating **b :** a transparent or translucent color applied to modify the effect of a painted surface **c :** a smooth glossy or lustrous surface or finish
**3 :** a glassy film

**³glaze** *intransitive verb* **glazed; glaz·ing** [probably blend of *glare* and *gaze*] (1601)
*archaic* **:** STARE

**glazed** \'glāzd\ *adjective* (15th century)
**1 :** covered with or as if with a glassy film ⟨*glazed* eyes⟩
**2 :** marked by lack of expression

**gla·zier** \'glā-zhər, -zē-ər\ *noun* (14th century)
: one who sets glass
— **gla·ziery** \'glā-zh(ə-)rē, 'glā-zē-ə-rē\ *noun*

**glaz·ing** \'glā-ziŋ\ *noun* (1677)
**1 :** the action, process, or trade of fitting windows with glass
**2 a :** GLASSWORK **b :** GLAZE
**3 :** transparent material (as glass) used for windows

**¹gleam** \'glēm\ *noun* [Middle English *gleem*, from Old English *glǣm*; akin to Old English *geolu* yellow — more at YELLOW] (15th century)
**1 a :** a transient appearance of subdued or partly obscured light ⟨the *gleam* of dawn in the east⟩ **b** (1) **:** a small bright light ⟨the *gleam* of a match⟩ (2) **:** GLINT ⟨a *gleam* in his eyes⟩
**2 :** a brief or faint appearance ⟨a *gleam* of hope⟩
— **gleamy** \'glē-mē\ *adjective*

**²gleam** (1508)
*intransitive verb*
**1 :** to shine with or as if with subdued steady light or moderate brightness
**2 :** to appear briefly or faintly ⟨a light *gleamed* in the distance⟩
*transitive verb*
**:** to cause to gleam
**synonym** see FLASH

**glean** \'glēn\ *verb* [Middle English *glenen*, from Middle French *glener*, from Late Latin *glennare*, of Celtic origin; akin to Old Irish *doglenn* he selects] (14th century)
*intransitive verb*
**1 :** to gather grain or other produce left by reapers
**2 :** to gather information or material bit by bit
*transitive verb*

**1 a :** to pick up after a reaper **b :** to strip (as a field) of the leavings of reapers
**2 a :** to gather (as information) bit by bit **b :** to pick over in search of relevant material ⟨*gleaning* old files for information⟩
**3 :** FIND OUT
— **glean·able** \'glē-nə-bəl\ *adjective*
— **glean·er** *noun*

**glean·ings** \'glē-niŋz\ *noun plural* (15th century)
: things acquired by gleaning

**glebe** \'glēb\ *noun* [Latin *gleba* clod, land] (14th century)
**1** *archaic* **:** LAND; *specifically* **:** a plot of cultivated land
**2 :** land belonging or yielding revenue to a parish church or ecclesiastical benefice

**glede** \'glēd\ *noun* [Middle English, from Old English *glida;* akin to Old English *glīdan* to glide] (before 12th century)
: any of several birds of prey (as a kite of Europe)

**glee** \'glē\ *noun* [Middle English, from Old English *glēo* entertainment, music; akin to Old Norse *glȳ* joy, and perhaps to Greek *chleuē* joke] (before 12th century)
**1 :** exultant high-spirited joy **:** MERRIMENT
**2 :** a part-song for usually male voices

**glee club** *noun* (1844)
: a chorus organized for singing usually short pieces

**gleed** \'glēd\ *noun* [Middle English, from Old English *glēd;* akin to Old English *glōwan* to glow] (before 12th century)
*archaic* **:** a glowing coal

**glee·ful** \'glē-fəl\ *adjective* (1586)
**:** full of glee **:** MERRY
— **glee·ful·ly** \-fə-lē\ *adverb*
— **glee·ful·ness** *noun*

**gleek** \'glēk\ *intransitive verb* [origin unknown] (1590)
*archaic* **:** GIBE, JOKE

**glee·man** \'glē-mən\ *noun* [Middle English *gleman*, from Old English *glēoman*, from *glēo* + *man* man] (before 12th century)
**:** JONGLEUR

**glee·some** \'glē-səm\ *adjective* (1603)
*archaic* **:** GLEEFUL

**gleet** \'glēt\ *noun* [Middle English *glet* slimy or mucous matter, from Middle French *glete*, from Latin *glittus* viscous; akin to Latin *gluten* glue — more at CLAY] (14th century)
**:** a chronic inflammation (as gonorrhea) of a bodily orifice usually accompanied by an abnormal discharge; *also* **:** the discharge itself

**gleg** \'gleg\ *adjective* [Middle English, from Old Norse *gloggr* clear-sighted] (14th century)
*Scottish* **:** marked by quickness of perception or movement

**glei·za·tion** \glā-'zā-shən\ *noun* (1938)
**:** development of or conversion into gley

**glen** \'glen\ *noun* [Middle English (Scots), valley, from (assumed) Scottish Gaelic *glenn;* akin to Middle Irish *glend* valley] (15th century)
**:** a secluded narrow valley

**glen·gar·ry** \glen-'gar-ē\ *noun, plural* **-ries** *often capitalized* [*Glengarry*, valley in Scotland] (1845)
**:** a woolen cap of Scottish origin — called also **glengarry bonnet**

**glen plaid** \'glen-\ *noun* [short for *glenurquhart plaid*, from *Glen Urquhart*, valley in Inverness-shire, Scotland] (1926)
**:** a twill pattern of broken checks; *also* **:** a fabric woven in this pattern — called also **glen check**

**gley** \'glā\ *noun, often attributive* [Ukrainian *gleĭ* clayey earth; akin to Old English *clǣg* clay — more at CLAY] (1927)
**:** a sticky clay soil or soil layer formed under the surface of some waterlogged soils
— **gleyed** *adjective*

**gley·ing** \'glā-iŋ\ *noun* (1949)
**:** GLEIZATION

**glia** \'glē-ə, 'glī-ə\ *noun* [New Latin, from Middle Greek, glue — more at CLAY] (1891)
**:** NEUROGLIA
— **gli·al** \-əl\ *adjective*

**gli·a·din** \'glī-ə-dən\ *noun* [Italian *gliadina*, from Middle Greek *glia*] (circa 1828)
**:** PROLAMIN; *especially* **:** one obtained by alcoholic extraction of gluten from wheat and rye

**glib** \'glib\ *adjective* **glib·ber; glib·best** [probably modification of Low German *glibberig* slippery] (1593)
**1 a :** marked by ease and informality **:** NONCHALANT **b :** showing little forethought or preparation **:** OFFHAND ⟨*glib* answers⟩ **c :** lacking depth and substance **:** SUPERFICIAL ⟨*glib* solutions to knotty problems⟩
**2** *archaic* **:** SMOOTH, SLIPPERY
**3 :** marked by ease and fluency in speaking or writing often to the point of being insincere or deceitful ⟨a *glib* politician⟩
— **glib·ly** *adverb*
— **glib·ness** *noun*

**¹glide** \'glīd\ *verb* **glid·ed; glid·ing** [Middle English, from Old English *glīdan;* akin to Old High German *glītan* to glide] (before 12th century)
*intransitive verb*
**1 :** to move smoothly, continuously, and effortlessly ⟨swans *gliding* over the lake⟩
**2 :** to go or pass imperceptibly ⟨hours *glided* by⟩
**3 a** *of an airplane* **:** to descend gradually in controlled flight **b :** to fly in a glider
**4 :** to produce a glide (as in music or speech)
*transitive verb*
**:** to cause to glide

**²glide** *noun* (1596)
**1 :** the act or action of gliding
**2 :** a calm stretch of shallow water flowing smoothly
**3 :** PORTAMENTO
**4 a :** a less prominent vowel sound produced by the passing of the vocal organs to or from the articulatory position of a speech sound — compare DIPHTHONG **b :** SEMIVOWEL
**5 :** a device for facilitating movement of something; *especially* **:** a circular usually metal button attached to the bottom of furniture legs to provide a smooth surface

**glide path** *noun* (1936)
**:** GLIDE SLOPE

**glid·er** \'glī-dər\ *noun* (15th century)
**1 :** one that glides: as **a :** an aircraft similar to an airplane but without an engine **b :** a porch seat suspended from an upright framework
**2 :** something that aids gliding

**glide slope** *noun* (circa 1949)
**1 :** the proper path of descent for an aircraft preparing to land; *especially* **:** such a path indicated by a radio beam
**2 :** the radio beam that marks a glide slope

**glim** \'glim\ *noun* [perhaps short for ²*glimmer*] (circa 1700)
**:** something that furnishes light (as a lantern or candle); *also* **:** illumination given off by such a source

**¹glim·mer** \'gli-mər\ *intransitive verb* **glim·mered; glim·mer·ing** \'glim-riŋ, 'gli-mə-\ [Middle English *glimeren;* akin to Old English *glǣm* gleam] (15th century)
**1 a :** to shine faintly or unsteadily **b :** to give off a subdued unsteady reflection
**2 :** to appear indistinctly with a faintly luminous quality
**synonym** see FLASH

**²glimmer** *noun* (1590)
**1 a :** a feeble or intermittent light **b :** a subdued unsteady shining or sparkle

---

**2 a :** a dim perception or faint idea **:** INKLING **b :** HINT, SPARK ⟨a *glimmer* of intelligence⟩
**glim·mer·ing** *noun* (15th century)
**:** GLIMMER

**¹glimpse** \'glim(p)s\ *verb* **glimpsed; glimps·ing** [Middle English *glimsen;* akin to Middle High German *glimsen* to glimmer, Old English *glǣm* gleam] (14th century)
*intransitive verb*
**1** *archaic* **:** GLIMMER
**2 :** to look briefly
*transitive verb*
**:** to get a brief look at
— **glimps·er** *noun*
**²glimpse** *noun* (circa 1540)
**1** *archaic* **:** GLIMMER
**2 :** a fleeting view or look

**¹glint** \'glint\ *verb* [Middle English, to dart obliquely, glint, alteration of *glenten*, of Scandinavian origin; akin to Swedish dialect *glänta* to clear up; akin to Old High German *glanz* bright, Old English *geolu* yellow — more at YELLOW] (14th century)
*intransitive verb*
**1** *archaic* **:** to glance off an object **b** *of rays of light* **:** to be reflected at an angle from a surface
**2 :** to give off reflection in brilliant flashes; *also* **:** GLEAM
**3 :** to look quickly or briefly **:** GLANCE
**4 :** to appear briefly or faintly
*transitive verb*
**:** to cause to glint
**synonym** see FLASH
**²glint** *noun* (14th century)
**1 :** a tiny bright flash of light
**2 :** a brief or faint manifestation **:** GLIMMER ⟨a *glint* of recognition⟩; *also* **:** a trace of emotion expressed through the eyes ⟨a steely *glint* in his eye⟩

**glio·blas·to·ma** \ˌglī-ō-ˌbla-'stō-mə\ *noun, plural* **-mas** *or* **-ma·ta** \-mə-tə\ [New Latin, from *glia* neuroglia + *blast-* + *-oma*] (circa 1923)
**:** a malignant tumor of the central nervous system and usually of a cerebral hemisphere
**gli·o·ma** \glē-'ō-mə, glī-\ *noun, plural* **-mas** *or* **-ma·ta** \-mə-tə\ [New Latin, from *glia*] (1870)
**:** a tumor arising from neuroglia

**¹glis·sade** \gli-'säd, -'sād\ *intransitive verb* **glis·sad·ed; glis·sad·ing** [French, noun, slide, glissade, from *glisser* to slide, from Old French *glicier*, alteration of *glier*, of Germanic origin; akin to Old High German *glītan* to glide] (1837)
**1 :** to perform a ballet glissade
**2 :** to slide in a standing or squatting position down a snow-covered slope without the aid of skis
— **glis·sad·er** *noun*
**²glissade** *noun* (1843)
**1 :** a gliding step in ballet
**2 :** the action of glissading

**glis·san·do** \gli-'sän-(ˌ)dō\ *noun, plural* **-di** \-(ˌ)dē\ *or* **-dos** [probably modification of French *glissade*] (circa 1854)
**:** a rapid sliding up or down the musical scale

**¹glis·ten** \'gli-sᵊn\ *intransitive verb* **glis·tened; glis·ten·ing** \'gli-sᵊn-iŋ\ [Middle English *glistnen*, from Old English *glisnian;* akin to Old English *glisian* to glitter, *geolu* yellow — more at YELLOW] (before 12th century)
**:** to give off a sparkling or lustrous reflection of or as if of a moist or polished surface
**synonym** see FLASH
**²glisten** *noun* (1840)
**:** GLITTER, SPARKLE

**glis·ter** \'glis-tər\ *intransitive verb* **glistered; glis·ter·ing** \-t(ə-)riŋ\ [Middle English *glistren;* akin to Old English *glisian*] (14th century)
**:** GLITTER
— **glister** *noun*

**glitch** \'glich\ *noun* [perhaps from Yiddish *glitsh* slippery place, from *glitshn* (*zikh*) to slide, glide; akin to Old High German *glītan* to glide — more at GLIDE] (1962)
**1 a :** a usually minor malfunction ⟨a *glitch* in a spacecraft's fuel cell⟩; *also* **:** ²BUG 2 **b :** a minor problem that causes a temporary setback **:** SNAG
**2 :** a false or spurious electronic signal

**¹glit·ter** \'gli-tər\ *intransitive verb* [Middle English *gliteren*, from Old Norse *glitra;* akin to Old English *geolu* yellow] (14th century)
**1 a :** to shine by reflection with many small flashes of brilliant light **:** SPARKLE ⟨sequins *glittered* in the spotlight⟩ **b :** to shine with strong emotion **:** FLASH ⟨eyes *glittering* in anger⟩
**2 :** to be brilliantly attractive, lavish, or spectacular; *also* **:** to be superficially attractive or exciting
**synonym** see FLASH
— **glit·ter·ing·ly** \-tə-riŋ-lē\ *adverb*
**²glitter** *noun* (1602)
**1 a :** sparkling brilliance of something that glitters **b :** a bright usually superficial attractiveness **c :** the quality of being spectacular
**2 :** small glittering objects used for ornamentation
— **glit·tery** \'gli-tə-rē\ *adjective*

**glit·te·ra·ti** \ˌgli-tə-'rä-tē\ *noun plural* [blend of ²*glitter* and *literati*] (1940)
**:** CELEBRITIES, BEAUTIFUL PEOPLE

**glitter rock** *noun* (1973)
**:** rock music characterized by performers wearing glittering costumes and bizarre often grotesque makeup

**glitz** \'glits\ *noun* [perhaps modification of German *glitzern* to glitter, from Middle High German *glitzen;* akin to Old Norse *glitra* to glitter] (1971)
**:** extravagant showiness **:** GLITTER, OSTENTATION
— **glitzy** \'glit-sē\ *adjective*

**gloam** \'glōm\ *noun* [Scots *gloam* to become twilight, back-formation from *gloaming*] (circa 1821)
*archaic* **:** TWILIGHT
**gloam·ing** \'glō-miŋ\ *noun* [Middle English (Scots) *gloming*, from Old English *glōming*, from *glōm* twilight; akin to Old English *glōwan* to glow] (before 12th century)
**:** TWILIGHT, DUSK

**¹gloat** \'glōt\ *intransitive verb* [probably of Scandinavian origin; akin to Old Norse *glotta* to grin scornfully] (1676)
**1** *obsolete* **:** to look or glance admiringly or amorously
**2 :** to observe or think about something with triumphant and often malicious satisfaction, gratification, or delight ⟨*gloat* over an enemy's misfortune⟩
— **gloat·er** *noun*
— **gloat·ing·ly** *adverb*
**²gloat** *noun* (1899)
**:** the act or feeling of one who gloats

**glob** \'gläb\ *noun* [perhaps blend of *globe* and *blob*] (1900)
**1 :** a small drop **:** BLOB
**2 :** a usually large and rounded mass
— **glob·by** \'glä-bē\ *adjective*

**glob·al** \'glō-bəl\ *adjective* (1676)
**1 :** SPHERICAL
**2 :** of, relating to, or involving the entire world **:** WORLDWIDE ⟨*global* warfare⟩ ⟨a *global* system of communication⟩; *also* **:** of or relating to a celestial body (as the moon)
**3 :** of, relating to, or applying to a whole (as a mathematical function or a computer program) ⟨a *global* search of a file⟩
— **glob·al·ly** \'glō-bə-lē\ *adverb*
**glob·al·ise** *British variant of* GLOBALIZE
**glob·al·ism** \'glō-bə-ˌli-zəm\ *noun* (1943)
**:** a national policy of treating the whole world as a proper sphere for political influence — compare IMPERIALISM, INTERNATIONALISM
— **glob·al·ist** \-list\ *noun*

**glob·al·ize** \'glō-bə-ˌlīz\ *transitive verb* **-ized; -iz·ing** (1944)
**:** to make global; *especially* **:** to make worldwide in scope or application
— **glob·al·iza·tion** \ˌglō-bə-lə-'zā-shən\ *noun*

**global village** *noun* (1960)
**:** the world viewed as a community in which distance and isolation have been dramatically reduced by electronic media (as television)
**¹globe** \'glōb\ *noun* [Middle French, from Latin *globus*] (15th century)
**:** something spherical or rounded: as **a :** a spherical representation of the earth, a celestial body, or the heavens **b :** EARTH 4 **c :** ORB 5
**²globe** *transitive verb* **globed; glob·ing** (1641)
*archaic* **:** to form into a globe
**globe artichoke** *noun* (circa 1858)
**:** ARTICHOKE 1
**globe·fish** \'glōb-ˌfish\ *noun* (1668)
**:** PUFFER 2a
**globe·flow·er** \-ˌflau̇(-ə)r\ *noun* (1597)
**:** any of a genus (*Trollius*) of plants of the buttercup family with globose yellow flowers
**globe thistle** *noun* (1597)
**:** any of a genus (*Echinops*) of widely-cultivated Asian and Mediterranean composite herbs with spiky globose blue or white flowers
**globe–trot·ter** \-ˌträ-tər\ *noun* (1875)
**:** a person who travels widely
— **globe–trot·ting** \-ˌträ-tiŋ\ *noun or adjective*
**glo·bin** \'glō-bən\ *noun* [International Scientific Vocabulary, from *hemoglobin*] (1877)
**:** a colorless protein obtained by removal of heme from a conjugated protein and especially hemoglobin
**glo·boid** \'glō-ˌbȯid\ *adjective* (1887)
**:** shaped like a sphere
**glo·bose** \'glō-ˌbōs\ *adjective* (15th century)
**:** GLOBULAR 1a(1) ⟨*globose* pollen⟩
**glob·u·lar** \'glä-byə-lər, 1b is also 'glō-\ *adjective* [partly from Latin *globus* + English *-ular;* partly from Latin *globulus* + English *-ar*] (1654)
**1 a** (1) **:** having the shape of a globe or globule (2) **:** having a compact folded molecular structure ⟨*globular* proteins⟩ **b :** GLOBAL
**2 :** having or consisting of globules
**globular cluster** *noun* (1859)
**:** any of various approximately spherical clusters of gravitationally associated stars that typically populate galactic halos
**glob·ule** \'glä-(ˌ)byü(ə)l\ *noun* [French, from Latin *globulus*, diminutive of *globus*] (1661)
**:** a tiny globe or ball especially of a liquid ⟨*globules* of mercury⟩
**glob·u·lin** \'glä-byə-lən\ *noun* (1845)
**:** any of a class of simple proteins (as myosin) that are insoluble in pure water but are soluble in dilute salt solutions and that occur widely in plant and animal tissues — compare ALPHA GLOBULIN, BETA GLOBULIN, GAMMA GLOBULIN
**glo·chid·i·um** \glō-'ki-dē-əm\ *noun, plural* **-ia** \-dē-ə\ [New Latin, from Greek *glōchis* projecting point + New Latin *-idium*] (1882)
**:** the larva of a freshwater mussel (family Unionidae) that develops as an external parasite on fish
**glock·en·spiel** \'glä-kən-ˌspēl, -ˌshpēl\ *noun* [German, from *Glocke* bell + *Spiel* play] (circa 1834)
**:** a percussion instrument consisting of a series of graduated metal bars tuned to the chromatic scale and played with two hammers

**glogg** *or* **glögg** \'glu̇g, 'glüg\ *noun* [Swedish *glögg*, from *glödga* to burn, mull, from *glöd* glowing coal, from Old Norse *glōth;* akin to Old English *glēd* glowing coal — more at GLEED] (1927)

glockenspiel

**:** a hot spiced wine and liquor punch served in Scandinavian countries as a Christmas drink

**glom** \ˈgläm\ *transitive verb* **glommed; glom·ming** [alteration of English dialect *glaum* to grab] (1907)
**1 :** TAKE, STEAL
**2 :** SEIZE, CATCH
**— glom on to :** to grab hold of **:** appropriate to oneself

**glo·mer·u·lar** \glə-ˈmer-(y)ə-lər, glō-\ *adjective* (1885)
**:** of, relating to, or produced by a glomerulus ⟨*glomerular* nephritis⟩ ⟨*glomerular* capillaries⟩

**glom·er·ule** \ˈglä-mə-ˌrül, -mər-ˌyü(ə)l\ *noun* [New Latin *glomerulus*] (1793)
**:** a compacted cyme of almost sessile and usually small flowers

**glo·mer·u·lo·ne·phri·tis** \glä-ˌmer-(y)ə-lō-ni-ˈfrī-təs\ *noun, plural* **-phri·i·des** \-ˈfri-tə-ˌdēz\ (circa 1886)
**:** nephritis marked by inflammation of the capillaries of the renal glomeruli

**glo·mer·u·lus** \glə-ˈmer-(y)ə-ləs, glō-\ *noun, plural* **-li** \-ˌlī, -ˌlē\ [New Latin, glomerulus, glomerule, diminutive of Latin *glomer-, glomus* ball; akin to Latin *globus* globe] (1856)
**:** a small convoluted or intertwined mass; *especially* **:** a tuft of capillaries at the point of origin of each vertebrate nephron that passes a protein-free filtrate to the surrounding Bowman's capsule

**glo·mus** \ˈglō-məs\ *noun, plural* **glo·mera** \ˈglä-mə-rə, ˈglō-\ [New Latin, from Latin *glomer-, glomus*] (1903)
**:** a small arteriovenous anastomosis together with its supporting structures

**¹gloom** \ˈglüm\ *verb* [Middle English *gloumen*] (14th century)
*intransitive verb*
**1 :** to look, feel, or act sullen or despondent
**2 :** to be or become overcast
**3 :** to loom up dimly
*transitive verb*
**:** to make dark, murky, or somber **:** make gloomy

**²gloom** *noun* (1629)
**1 a :** partial or total darkness **b :** a dark or shadowy place
**2 a :** lowness of spirits **:** DEJECTION **b :** an atmosphere of despondency ⟨a *gloom* fell over the household⟩

**gloomy** \ˈglü-mē\ *adjective* **gloom·i·er; -est** (1588)
**1 a :** partially or totally dark; *especially* **:** dismally and depressingly dark ⟨*gloomy* weather⟩ **b :** having a frowning or scowling appearance **:** FORBIDDING ⟨a *gloomy* countenance⟩ **c :** low in spirits **:** MELANCHOLY
**2 a :** causing gloom **:** DEPRESSING ⟨a *gloomy* story⟩ ⟨a *gloomy* landscape⟩ **b :** lacking in promise or hopefulness **:** PESSIMISTIC ⟨*gloomy* prophecies⟩ ⟨a *gloomy* future⟩
*synonym* see SULLEN
**— gloom·i·ly** \-mə-lē\ *adverb*
**— gloom·i·ness** \-mē-nəs\ *noun*

**glop** \ˈgläp\ *noun* [origin unknown] (circa 1944)
**1 :** a thick semiliquid substance (as food) that is usually unattractive in appearance
**2 :** tasteless or worthless material
**— glop·py** \ˈglä-pē\ *adjective*

**Glo·ria** \ˈglȯr-ē-ə, ˈglȯr-\ *noun* [Latin, glory] (13th century)
**1 :** GLORIA IN EXCELSIS
**2 :** GLORIA PATRI

**Gloria in Ex·cel·sis** \-ˌin-eks-ˈchel-səs, -ek-ˈshel-\ [Late Latin, glory (be to God) on high] (14th century)
**:** a Christian liturgical hymn having the verse form of the Psalms

**Gloria Pa·tri** \-ˈpä-(ˌ)trē\ *noun* [Late Latin, glory (be) to the Father] (13th century)
**:** a 2-verse doxology to the Trinity

**glo·ri·fy** \ˈglȯr-ə-ˌfī, ˈglȯr-\ *transitive verb* **-fied; -fy·ing** [Middle English *glorifien*, from

Middle French *glorifier*, from Late Latin *glorificare*, from *gloria*] (14th century)
**1 a :** to make glorious by bestowing honor, praise, or admiration **b :** to elevate to celestial glory
**2 :** to light up brilliantly ⟨a large chandelier *glorifies* the whole room⟩
**3 a :** to represent as glorious **:** EXTOL ⟨a song *glorifying* romantic love⟩ **b :** to cause to be or seem to be better than the actual condition ⟨the new position is just a *glorified* version of the old stockroom job⟩
**4 :** to give glory to (as in worship)
**— glo·ri·fi·ca·tion** \ˌglȯr-ə-fə-ˈkā-shən, ˌglȯr-\ *noun*
**— glo·ri·fi·er** \ˈglȯr-ə-ˌfī(-ə)r, ˈglȯr-\ *noun*

**glo·ri·ous** \ˈglȯr-ē-əs, ˈglȯr-\ *adjective* [Middle English, from Old French & Latin; Old French *glorieus, glorios*, from Latin *gloriosus* glorious, vainglorious, from *gloria*] (13th century)
**1 a :** possessing or deserving glory **:** ILLUSTRIOUS **b :** entitling one to glory ⟨a *glorious* victory⟩
**2 :** marked by great beauty or splendor **:** MAGNIFICENT
**3 :** DELIGHTFUL, WONDERFUL ⟨had a *glorious* weekend⟩
*synonym* see SPLENDID
**— glo·ri·ous·ly** *adverb*
**— glo·ri·ous·ness** *noun*

**¹glo·ry** \ˈglȯr-ē, ˈglȯr-\ *noun, plural* **glories** [Middle English *glorie*, from Middle French & Latin; Middle French, from Latin *gloria*] (14th century)
**1 a :** praise, honor, or distinction extended by common consent **:** RENOWN **b :** worshipful praise, honor, and thanksgiving ⟨giving *glory* to God⟩
**2 a :** something that secures praise or renown ⟨the *glory* of a brilliant career⟩ **b :** a distinguished quality or asset
**3 a** (1) **:** great beauty and splendor **:** MAGNIFICENCE ⟨the *glory* that was Greece and the grandeur that was Rome —E. A. Poe⟩ (2) **:** something marked by beauty or resplendence ⟨a perfect *glory* of a day⟩ **b :** the splendor and beatific happiness of heaven; *broadly* **:** ETERNITY
**4 a :** a state of great gratification or exaltation ⟨when she's acting she's in her *glory*⟩ **b :** a height of prosperity or achievement
**5 :** a ring or spot of light: as **a :** AUREOLE **b :** CORONA 2a, b

**²glory** *intransitive verb* **glo·ried; glo·ry·ing** (14th century)
**:** to rejoice proudly — used with *in*

**³glory** *or* **glory be** *interjection* (1816)
**—** used to express surprise or delight

**glory-of-the-snow** *noun* (circa 1890)
**:** any of a genus (*Chionodoxa*) of hardy spring-flowering bulbous herbs of the lily family with narrow basal leaves and terminal racemes of blue, white, or pink flowers

**¹gloss** \ˈgläs, ˈglȯs\ *noun* [probably of Scandinavian origin; akin to Icelandic *glossa* to glow; akin to Old English *geolu* yellow] (1538)
**1 :** a surface luster or brightness **:** SHINE
**2 a :** a deceptively attractive appearance ⟨selfishness that had a *gloss* of humanitarianism about it⟩ **b :** bright often superficial attractiveness ⟨show-biz *gloss*⟩
**3 :** a transparent cosmetic preparation for adding shine and usually color to the lips

**²gloss** *transitive verb* (1656)
**1 a :** to mask the true nature of **:** give a deceptively attractive appearance to — used with *over* ⟨the misery was general, where not *glossed* over by liberal application of alcohol —Marston Bates⟩ **b :** to deal with (a subject or problem) too lightly or not at all — used with *over* ⟨*glosses* over scholarly controversies rather than confronting them head-on —John Israel⟩
**2 :** to give a gloss to

**³gloss** *noun* [alteration of *gloze*, from Middle English *glose*, from Middle French, from Me-

dieval Latin *glosa, glossa*, from Greek *glōssa, glōtta* tongue, language, obscure word; akin to Greek *glōchis* projecting point] (1548)
**1 a :** a brief explanation (as in the margin or between the lines of a text) of a difficult or obscure word or expression **b :** a false and often willfully misleading interpretation (as of a text)
**2 a :** GLOSSARY **b :** an interlinear translation **c :** a continuous commentary accompanying a text
**3 :** COMMENTARY, INTERPRETATION

**⁴gloss** *transitive verb* (1603)
**1 a :** to provide a gloss for **:** EXPLAIN, DEFINE **b :** INTERPRET
**2 :** to dispose of by false or perverse interpretation ⟨trying to *gloss* away the irrationalities of the universe —Irwin Edman⟩

**gloss-** *or* **glosso-** *combining form* [Latin, from Greek *glōss-, glōsso-*, from *glōssa*]
**1 :** tongue ⟨*glossitis*⟩
**2 :** language ⟨*glossolalia*⟩

**glos·sa** \ˈglä-sə, ˈglȯ-\ *noun, plural* **glos·sae** \-ˌsē, -ˌsī\ *also* **glossas** [New Latin, from Greek *glōssa*] (circa 1852)
**:** a tongue or lingual structure especially in an insect; *especially* **:** the median distal lobe of the labium of an insect

**glos·sa·rist** \ˈglä-sə-rist, ˈglȯ-\ *noun* (1774)
**:** GLOSSATOR

**glos·sa·ry** \-sə-rē\ *noun, plural* **-ries** (14th century)
**:** a collection of textual glosses or of specialized terms with their meanings
**— glos·sar·i·al** \glä-ˈsar-ē-əl, glȯ-, -ˈser-\ *adjective*

**glos·sa·tor** \ˈglä-ˌsā-tər, ˈglȯ-\ *noun* (14th century)
**1 :** one that makes textual glosses
**2 :** a compiler of a glossary

**glos·si·tis** \glä-ˈsī-təs, ˈglȯ-\ *noun* (circa 1834)
**:** inflammation of the tongue

**glos·sog·ra·pher** \glä-ˈsä-grə-fər, glȯ-\ *noun* [Greek *glōssographos*, from *glōssa* + *graphein* to write — more at CARVE] (1607)
**:** GLOSSATOR

**glos·so·la·lia** \ˌglä-sə-ˈlā-lē-ə, ˌglȯ-\ *noun* [New Latin] (1879)
**:** TONGUE 4c
**— glos·so·la·list** \-ˈlā-list\ *noun*

**glos·so·pha·ryn·geal nerve** \ˌglä-sō-ˌfarən-ˈjē-əl-, ˌglȯ-, -fə-ˈrin-j(ē-)əl-\ *noun* (circa 1823)
**:** either of the 9th pair of cranial nerves that are mixed nerves and supply chiefly the pharynx, posterior tongue, and parotid gland — called also *glossopharyngeal*

**¹glossy** \ˈglä-sē, ˈglȯ-\ *adjective* **gloss·i·er; -est** (1556)
**1 :** having a surface luster or brightness ⟨rich *glossy* leather⟩ ⟨*glossy* paper⟩
**2 :** attractive in an artificially opulent, sophisticated, or smoothly captivating manner **:** SLICK ⟨lots of *glossy* and phony chatter⟩
*synonym* see SLEEK
**— gloss·i·ly** \-sə-lē\ *adverb*
**— gloss·i·ness** \-sē-nəs\ *noun*

**²glossy** *noun, plural* **gloss·ies** (1928)
**1 :** a photograph printed on smooth shiny paper
**2** *chiefly British* **:** SLICK 3

**glott-** *or* **glotto-** *combining form* [Greek *glōtt-, glōtto-* tongue, from *glōssa, glōtta*]
**:** language ⟨*glotto*chronology⟩

**glot·tal** \ˈglä-tᵊl\ *adjective* (circa 1846)
**:** of, relating to, or produced in or by the glottis ⟨*glottal* constriction⟩

**glottal stop** *noun* (1888)
**:** the interruption of the breath stream during speech by closure of the glottis

---

\ə\ abut \ᵊ\ kitten \ər\ further \a\ ash \ā\ ace \ä\ mop, mar \aů\ out \ch\ chin \e\ bet \ē\ easy \g\ go \i\ hit \ī\ ice \j\ job \ŋ\ sing \ō\ go \ȯ\ law \ȯi\ boy \th\ thin \t͟h\ the \ü\ loot \ů\ foot \y\ yet \zh\ vision  *see also* Guide to Pronunciation

**glot·tis** \'glä-təs\ *noun, plural* **glot·tis·es** *or* **glot·ti·des** \-tə-ˌdēz\ [Greek *glōttid-, glōttis,* from *glōtta* tongue — more at GLOSS] (1578) **:** the elongated space between the vocal cords; *also* **:** the structures that surround this space — compare EPIGLOTTIS

**glot·to·chro·nol·o·gy** \ˌglä-tō-krə-'nä-lə-jē\ *noun* (1953) **:** a linguistic method that uses the rate of vocabulary replacement to estimate the date of divergence for distinct but genetically related languages — **glot·to·chro·no·log·i·cal** \-ˌkrä-n°l-'ä-ji-kəl, -ˌkrō-\ *adjective*

**glout** \'glüt, 'glaút\ *intransitive verb* [Middle English, probably of Scandinavian origin; akin to Old Norse *glotta* to grin scornfully] (14th century) *archaic* **:** FROWN, SCOWL

**¹glove** \'gləv\ *noun* [Middle English, from Old English *glōf;* akin to Old Norse *glōfi* glove] (before 12th century) **1 a :** a covering for the hand having separate sections for each of the fingers and the thumb and often extending part way up the arm **b :** ¹GAUNTLET 1, 3 **2 a :** a padded leather covering for the hand used in baseball to catch a thrown or batted ball; *specifically* **:** one having individual thumb and finger sections usually connected with a lacing or webbing — compare MITT (2) **:** fielding ability ⟨he's got a good *glove* at three positions and can pinch-hit —Casey Stengel⟩ **b :** BOXING GLOVE

**²glove** *transitive verb* **gloved; glov·ing** (15th century) **1 a :** to cover with or as if with a glove **b :** to furnish with gloves **2 :** to catch (a baseball) in one's gloved hand

**glove box** *noun* (1946) **1 :** GLOVE COMPARTMENT **2 :** a sealed protectively lined compartment having holes to which are attached gloves for use in handling dangerous materials inside the compartment

**glove compartment** *noun* (1939) **:** a small storage cabinet in the dashboard of an automobile

**glove leather** *noun* (1721) **:** a soft lightweight leather

**glov·er** \'glə-vər\ *noun* (14th century) **:** one that makes or sells gloves

**¹glow** \'glō\ *intransitive verb* [Middle English, from Old English *glōwan;* akin to Old English *geolu* yellow — more at YELLOW] (before 12th century) **1 a :** to shine with or as if with an intense heat ⟨embers *glowing* in the darkness⟩ **b** (1) **:** to have a rich warm typically ruddy color ⟨cheeks *glowing* with health⟩ (2) **:** FLUSH, BLUSH ⟨the children *glowed* with excitement⟩ **2 a :** to experience a sensation of or as if of heat ⟨*glowing* with rage⟩ **b :** to show exuberance or elation ⟨*glow* with pride⟩ — **glow·ing·ly** \-iŋ-lē\ *adverb*

**²glow** *noun* (1600) **1 :** brightness or warmth of color; *especially* **:** REDNESS **2 a :** warmth of feeling or emotion **b :** a sensation of warmth ⟨the drug produces a sustained *glow*⟩ **3 a :** the state of glowing with heat and light **b :** light such as is emitted by a solid body heated to luminosity **:** INCANDESCENCE

**glow discharge** *noun* (1844) **:** a luminous electrical discharge without sparks through a gas

**¹glow·er** \'glaú(-ə)r, ÷'glō(-ə)r\ *intransitive verb* [Middle English (Scots) *glowren;* perhaps of Scandinavian origin; akin to Norwegian dialect *glyra* to look askance, Icelandic *glossa* to glow — more at GLOSS] (15th century) **:** to look or stare with sullen annoyance or anger

**²glower** *noun* (1715)

**:** a sullen brooding look of annoyance or anger

**glow lamp** *noun* (1884) **:** a gas-discharge electric lamp in which most of the light proceeds from the glow of the gas near the cathode

**glow plug** *noun* (circa 1941) **:** a heating element in a diesel-engine cylinder to preheat the air and facilitate starting; *also* **:** a similar element for ignition in other internal-combustion engines

**glow·worm** \'glō-ˌwərm\ *noun* [Middle English] (14th century) **:** any of various luminous insect larvae or adults with wings rudimentary or lacking; *especially* **:** a larva or wingless female of a firefly (family Lampyridae) that emits light from the abdomen

**glox·in·ia** \gläk-'si-nē-ə\ *noun* [New Latin, from B. P. *Gloxin* 18th century German botanist] (circa 1820) **:** any of a genus (*Sinningia*) of Brazilian tuberous herbaceous gesneriads; *especially* **:** a plant (*S. speciosa*) widely cultivated for its showy bell-shaped or slipper-shaped flowers

gloxinia

**¹gloze** \'glōz\ *transitive verb* **glozed; gloz·ing** [Middle English *glosen* to gloss, flatter, from *glose* gloss] (14th century) *archaic* **:** ⁴GLOSS 1

**²gloze** *transitive verb* **glozed; gloz·ing** (14th century) **:** ²GLOSS 1 — often used with *over*

**gluc-** *or* **gluco-** *combining form* [International Scientific Vocabulary] **1 :** glucose ⟨*glucokinase*⟩ **2 :** related to or containing glucose ⟨*glucosamine*⟩

**glu·ca·gon** \'glü-kə-ˌgän\ *noun* [*gluc-* + *-agon* (perhaps from Greek *agōn,* present participle of *agein* to lead, drive) — more at AGENT] (1923) **:** a protein hormone that is produced especially by the islets of Langerhans and that promotes an increase in the sugar content of the blood by increasing the rate of glycogen breakdown in the liver

**glu·can** \'glü-ˌkan, -kən\ *noun* (1941) **:** a polysaccharide (as glycogen or cellulose) that is a polymer of glucose

**glu·co·cor·ti·coid** \ˌglü-kō-'kòr-ti-ˌkòid\ *noun* (1950) **:** any of a group of corticoids (as hydrocortisone) that are involved especially in carbohydrate, protein, and fat metabolism, that are anti-inflammatory and immunosuppressive, and that are used widely in medicine (as in the alleviation of the symptoms of rheumatoid arthritis) — compare MINERALOCORTICOID

**glu·co·ki·nase** \-'kī-ˌnās, -ˌnāz\ *noun* (1950) **:** a hexokinase found especially in the liver that catalyzes the phosphorylation of glucose

**glu·co·nate** \'glü-kə-ˌnāt\ *noun* (1884) **:** a salt or ester of gluconic acid

**glu·co·neo·gen·e·sis** \ˌglü-kə-ˌnē-ə-'je-nə-səs\ *noun* [New Latin] (1912) **:** formation of glucose within the animal body especially by the liver from substances (as fats and proteins) other than carbohydrates

**glu·con·ic acid** \(ˌ)glü-'kä-nik-\ *noun* [International Scientific Vocabulary, irregular from *glucose* + *-ic*] (1871) **:** a crystalline acid $C_6H_{12}O_7$ obtained by oxidation of glucose and used chiefly in cleaning metals

**glu·cos·amine** \glü-'kō-sə-ˌmēn, -zə-\ *noun* (1884) **:** an amino derivative $C_6H_{13}NO_5$ of glucose that occurs especially as a constituent of polysaccharides in animal supporting structures and some plant cell walls

**glu·cose** \'glü-ˌkōs, -ˌkōz\ *noun* [French, modification of Greek *gleukos* must, sweet wine; akin to Greek *glykys* sweet — more at DULCET] (1840) **1 :** an optically active sugar $C_6H_{12}O_6$ that has an aldehydic carbonyl group; *especially* **:** the sweet colorless soluble dextrorotatory form that occurs widely in nature and is the usual form in which carbohydrate is assimilated by animals **2 :** a light-colored syrup made from cornstarch

**glucose–1–phosphate** *noun* [from the position at which the phosphate group is attached] (1938) **:** an ester $C_6H_{13}O_9P$ that reacts in the presence of a phosphorylase with aldoses and ketoses to yield disaccharides or with itself in liver and muscle to yield glycogen and phosphoric acid

**glucose phosphate** *noun* (1912) **:** a phosphate ester of glucose: as **a :** GLUCOSE-1-PHOSPHATE **b :** GLUCOSE-6-PHOSPHATE

**glucose–6–phosphate** *noun* [from the position at which the phosphate group is attached] (1954) **:** an ester $C_6H_{13}O_9P$ that is formed from glucose and ATP in the presence of a glucokinase and that is an essential early stage in glucose metabolism

**glucose–6–phosphate dehydrogenase** *noun* (1954) **:** an enzyme found especially in red blood cells that dehydrogenates glucose-6-phosphate in a glucose degradation pathway alternative to the Krebs cycle

**glu·co·si·dase** \glü-'kō-sə-ˌdās, -zə-ˌdāz\ *noun* (circa 1926) **:** an enzyme (as maltase) that hydrolyzes a glucoside

**glu·co·side** \'glü-kə-ˌsīd\ *noun* (1855) **:** GLYCOSIDE; *especially* **:** a glycoside that yields glucose on hydrolysis — **glu·co·sid·ic** \ˌglü-kə-'si-dik\ *adjective*

**glu·cu·ron·ic acid** \ˌglü-kyə-'rä-nik-\ *noun* (1911) **:** a compound $C_6H_{10}O_7$ that occurs especially as a constituent of mucopolysaccharides (as hyaluronic acid) and combined as a glucuronide

**glu·cu·ron·i·dase** \-'rä-nə-ˌdās, -ˌdāz\ *noun* (1945) **:** an enzyme that hydrolyzes a glucuronide; *especially* **:** one that occurs widely (as in liver and spleen) and hydrolyzes the beta form of a glucuronide

**glu·cu·ro·nide** \glü-'kyùr-ə-ˌnīd\ *noun* (1934) **:** any of various derivatives of glucuronic acid that are formed especially as combinations with often toxic aromatic hydroxyl compounds and are excreted in the urine

**¹glue** \'glü\ *noun* [Middle English *glu,* from Middle French, from Late Latin *glut-, glus;* akin to Latin *gluten* glue — more at CLAY] (14th century) **1 a :** any of various strong adhesive substances; *especially* **:** a hard protein chiefly gelatinous substance that absorbs water to form a viscous solution with strong adhesive properties and that is obtained by cooking down collagenous materials (as hides or bones) **b :** a solution of glue used for sticking things together **2 :** something that binds together ⟨enough social *glue* . . . to satisfy the human desire for community —E. D. Hirsch, Jr.⟩ — **glu·ey** \'glü-ē\ *adjective* — **glu·i·ly** \'glü-ə-lē\ *adverb*

**²glue** *transitive verb* **glued; glu·ing** *also* **glue·ing** (14th century) **1 :** to cause to stick tightly with or as if with glue ⟨*gluing* the wings onto the model airplane⟩ ⟨used that war to *glue* together a frail story —Gloria Emerson⟩ **2 :** to fix (as the eyes) on an object steadily or with deep concentration ⟨kept his eyes *glued* to the TV screen⟩

**glum** \'gləm\ *adjective* **glum·mer; glum·mest** [akin to Middle English *gloumen* to gloom] (1547)
**1** : broodingly morose (became *glum* when they heard the news)
**2** : DREARY, GLOOMY ⟨a *glum* countenance⟩
**synonym** see SULLEN
— **glum·ly** *adverb*
— **glum·ness** *noun*

**glume** \'glüm\ *noun* [New Latin *gluma*, from Latin, hull, husk; akin to Latin *glubere* to peel — more at CLEAVE] (1789)
: a chaffy bract; *specifically* : either of two empty bracts at the base of the spikelet in grasses

**glu·on** \'glü-,än\ *noun* [¹*glue* + ²*-on*] (1971)
: a hypothetical neutral massless particle held to bind together quarks to form hadrons

**¹glut** \'glət\ *verb* **glut·ted; glut·ting** [Middle English *glouten*, probably from Middle French *gloutir* to swallow, from Latin *gluttire* — more at GLUTTON] (14th century)
*transitive verb*
**1** : to fill especially with food to satiety
**2** : to flood (the market) with goods so that supply exceeds demand
*intransitive verb*
: to eat gluttonously
**synonym** see SATIATE

**²glut** *noun* (circa 1546)
**1** : an excessive quantity : OVERSUPPLY
**2** *archaic* : the act or process of glutting

**³glut** *transitive verb* **glut·ted; glut·ting** [probably from obsolete *glut*, noun, swallow] (1600)
*archaic* : to swallow greedily

**glu·ta·mate** \'glü-tə-,māt\ *noun* (1876)
: a salt or ester of glutamic acid — compare MONOSODIUM GLUTAMATE

**glu·tam·ic acid** \(,)glü-'ta-mik-\ *noun* [International Scientific Vocabulary *gluten* + *amino* + *-ic*] (1871)
: a crystalline amino acid $C_5H_9NO_4$ widely distributed in plant and animal proteins

**glu·ta·min·ase** \'glü-tə-mə-,nās, glü-'ta-mə-, -,nāz\ *noun* (1938)
: an enzyme that hydrolyzes glutamine to glutamic acid and ammonia

**glu·ta·mine** \'glü-tə-,mēn\ *noun* [International Scientific Vocabulary *gluten* + *amine*] (circa 1885)
: a crystalline amino acid $C_5H_{10}N_2O_3$ that is found both free and in proteins in plants and animals and that yields glutamic acid and ammonia on hydrolysis

**glu·tar·al·de·hyde** \,glü-tə-'ral-də-,hīd\ *noun* [*glutaric* acid + *aldehyde*] (1951)
: a compound $C_5H_8O_2$ that contains two aldehyde groups and is used especially in tanning leather and in the fixation of biological tissues

**glu·tar·ic acid** \glü-'tar-ik-\ *noun* [probably from *gluten* + *-aric* (as in *tartaric acid*)] (circa 1885)
: a crystalline acid $C_5H_8O_4$ used especially in organic synthesis

**glu·ta·thi·one** \,glü-tə-'thī-,ōn\ *noun* [International Scientific Vocabulary *gluta-* (from *glutamic acid*) + *thi-* + *-one*] (1921)
: a peptide $C_{10}H_{17}N_3O_6S$ that contains one amino-acid residue each of glutamic acid, cysteine, and glycine, that occurs widely in plant and animal tissues, and that plays an important role in biological oxidation-reduction processes and as a coenzyme

**glu·te·al** \'glü-tē-əl, glü-'tē-\ *adjective* (1804)
: of or relating to the gluteus muscles

**glu·ten** \'glü-t⁰n\ *noun* [Latin *glutin-, gluten* glue — more at CLAY] (1803)
: a tenacious elastic protein substance especially of wheat flour that gives cohesiveness to dough
— **glu·ten·ous** \'glüt-nəs, 'glü-t⁰n-əs\ *adjective*

**glu·teth·i·mide** \glü-'te-thə-,mīd, -məd\ *noun* [*gluten* + *eth-* + *imide*] (1955)
: a sedative-hypnotic drug $C_{13}H_{15}NO_2$ that induces sleep with less depression of respiration than occurs with comparable doses of barbiturates

**glu·te·us** \'glü-tē-əs, glü-'tē-\ *noun, plural* **glu·tei** \'glü-tē-,ī, -tē-,ē; glü-'tē-,ī\ [New Latin *glutaeus, gluteus*, from Greek *gloutos* buttock — more at CLOUD] (circa 1681)
: any of the large muscles of the buttocks; *especially* : GLUTEUS MAXIMUS

**gluteus max·i·mus** \-'mak-sə-məs\ *noun, plural* **glutei max·i·mi** \-'mak-sə-,mī\ [New Latin, literally, largest gluteus] (1886)
: the outermost muscle of the three glutei found in each of the human buttocks

**glu·ti·nous** \'glüt-nəs, 'glü-t⁰n-əs\ *adjective* [Middle French or Latin; Middle French *glutineux*, from Latin *glutinosus*, from *glutin-, gluten*] (15th century)
: having the quality of glue : GUMMY
— **glu·ti·nous·ly** *adverb*

**glut·ton** \'glə-t⁰n\ *noun* [Middle English *glotoun*, from Old French *gloton*, from Latin *glutton-, glutto*; akin to Latin *gluttire* to swallow, *gula* throat, Old English *ceole*] (13th century)
**1 a** : one given habitually to greedy and voracious eating and drinking **b** : one that has a great capacity for accepting or enduring something ⟨a *glutton* for punishment⟩
**2** : WOLVERINE 1a

**glut·ton·ous** \'glət-nəs, 'glə-t⁰n-əs\ *adjective* (14th century)
: marked by or given to gluttony
**synonym** see VORACIOUS
— **glut·ton·ous·ly** *adverb*
— **glut·ton·ous·ness** *noun*

**glut·tony** \'glət-nē, 'glə-t⁰n-ē\ *noun, plural* **-ton·ies** (13th century)
**1** : excess in eating or drinking
**2** : greedy or excessive indulgence

**glyc-** *or* **glyco-** *combining form* [International Scientific Vocabulary, from Greek *glyk-* sweet, from *glykys*]
**1** : carbohydrate and especially sugar ⟨*glyco*protein⟩
**2** : glycine ⟨*glyc*yl⟩

**gly·can** \'glī-,kan\ *noun* (1953)
: POLYSACCHARIDE

**glyc·er·al·de·hyde** \,gli-sə-'ral-də-,hīd\ *noun* [*glyceric* acid + *aldehyde*] (1882)
: a sweet crystalline compound $C_3H_6O_3$ that is formed as an intermediate in carbohydrate metabolism by the breakdown of sugars and that yields glycerol on reduction

**gly·cer·ic acid** \gli-'ser-ik-\ *noun* [International Scientific Vocabulary, from *glycerin*] (circa 1864)
: a syrupy acid $C_3H_6O_4$ obtainable by oxidation of glycerol or glyceraldehyde

**glyc·er·ide** \'gli-sə-,rīd\ *noun* (circa 1864)
: an ester of glycerol especially with fatty acids
— **glyc·er·id·ic** \,gli-sə-'ri-dik\ *adjective*

**glyc·er·in** *or* **glyc·er·ine** \'glis-rən, 'gli-sə-\ *noun* [French *glycérine*, from Greek *glykeros* sweet; akin to Greek *glykys*] (1838)
: GLYCEROL

**glyc·er·in·ate** \'glis-rə-,nāt, 'gli-sə-\ *transitive verb* **-at·ed; -at·ing** (1897)
: to treat with or preserve in glycerin

**glyc·er·ol** \'gli-sə-,ról, -,rōl\ *noun* [*glycerin* + *-ol*] (1884)
: a sweet syrupy hygroscopic trihydroxy alcohol $C_3H_8O_3$ usually obtained by the saponification of fats and used especially as a solvent and plasticizer

**glyc·er·yl** \'glis-rəl, 'gli-sə-\ *noun* (1845)
: a radical derived from glycerol by removal of hydroxide; *especially* : a trivalent radical $CH_2CHCH_2$

**gly·cine** \'glī-,sēn, 'gli-s⁰n\ *noun* (1851)
: a sweet crystalline amino acid $C_2H_5NO_2$ obtained especially by hydrolysis of proteins

**gly·co·gen** \'glī-kə-jən\ *noun* (circa 1864)
: a white amorphous tasteless polysaccharide $(C_6H_{10}O_5)x$ that is the principal form in which carbohydrate is stored in animal tissues and especially muscle and liver tissue

**gly·co·gen·e·sis** \,glī-kə-'je-nə-səs\ *noun* [New Latin] (circa 1886)
: the formation and storage of glycogen

**gly·co·gen·ol·y·sis** \,glī-kə-jə-'nä-lə-səs\ *noun, plural* **-y·ses** \-,sēz\ [New Latin] (1909)
: the breakdown of glycogen especially to glucose in the animal body
— **gly·co·gen·o·lyt·ic** \-jə-n⁰l-'i-tik, -,je-\ *adjective*

**gly·col** \'glī-, kól, -,kōl\ *noun* [International Scientific Vocabulary *glyc-* + *-ol*] (1858)
: DIOL; *especially* : ETHYLENE GLYCOL

**gly·col·ic acid** *or* **gly·col·lic acid** \(,)glī-'kä-lik-\ *noun* [International Scientific Vocabulary *glycol* + ¹*-ic*] (1852)
: a translucent crystalline compound $C_2H_4O_3$ found especially in unripe grapes and sugar beets and used especially in textile and leather processing

**gly·co·lip·id** \,glī-kō-'li-pəd\ *noun* (1936)
: a lipid (as a ganglioside or a cerebroside) that contains a carbohydrate radical

**gly·col·y·sis** \glī-'kä-lə-səs\ *noun* [New Latin] (1892)
: the enzymatic breakdown of a carbohydrate (as glucose) by way of phosphate derivatives with the production of pyruvic or lactic acid and energy stored in high-energy phosphate bonds of ATP
— **gly·co·lyt·ic** \,glī-kə-'li-tik\ *adjective*

**gly·co·pep·tide** \,glī-kō-'pep-,tīd\ *noun* (1959)
: GLYCOPROTEIN

**gly·co·pro·tein** \-'prō-,tēn, -'prō-tē-ən\ *noun* (circa 1908)
: a conjugated protein in which the nonprotein group is a carbohydrate

**gly·cos·ami·no·gly·can** \,glī-kō-sə-,mē-nō-'glī-,kan, -kō-,sa-mə-nō-\ *noun* [*glyc-* + *hexosamine* (amine derived from a hexose) + *-o-* + *glycan*] (1962)
: any of various polysaccharides derived from an amino hexose that are constituents of mucoproteins, glycoproteins, and blood-group substances — called also *mucopolysaccharide*

**gly·co·si·dase** \glī-'kō-sə-,dās, -zə-,dāz\ *noun* (1944)
: an enzyme that catalyzes the hydrolysis of a bond joining a sugar of a glycoside to an alcohol or another sugar unit

**gly·co·side** \'glī-kə-,sīd\ *noun* [alteration of *glucoside*] (circa 1889)
: any of numerous sugar derivatives that contain a nonsugar group bonded to an oxygen or nitrogen atom and that on hydrolysis yield a sugar (as glucose)
— **gly·co·sid·ic** \,glī-kə-'si-dik\ *adjective*
— **gly·co·sid·i·cal·ly** \-di-k(ə-)lē\ *adverb*

**gly·cos·uria** \,glī-kō-'shùr-ē-ə, ,glī-kəs-'yùr-\ *noun* [New Latin, from International Scientific Vocabulary *glycose* glucose + New Latin *-uria*] (1860)
: the presence in the urine of abnormal amounts of sugar

**gly·co·syl** \'glī-kə-,sil\ *noun* [International Scientific Vocabulary *glycose* glucose] (1945)
: a univalent radical derived from a cyclic form of glucose by removal of the hemiacetal hydroxyl group

**gly·co·syl·a·tion** \,glī-kō-sə-'lā-shən\ *noun* (1946)
: the process of adding glycosyl groups to a protein to form a glycoprotein
— **gly·co·sy·late** \,glī-kō-'sī-,lāt\ *transitive verb*

---

\ə\ abut \ᵊ\ kitten \ər\ further \a\ ash \ā\ ace
\ä\ mop, mar \aù\ out \ch\ chin \e\ bet \ē\ easy
\g\ go \i\ hit \ī\ ice \j\ job \ŋ\ sing \ō\ go
\ò\ law \òi\ boy \th\ thin \th\ the \ü\ loot \ù\ foot
\y\ yet \zh\ vision *see also* Guide to Pronunciation

**gly·cyl** \'glī-səl\ *noun* (1901)
: the univalent acyl radical $NH_2CH_2CO-$ of glycine

**glyph** \'glif\ *noun* [Greek *glyphē* carved work, from *glyphein* to carve — more at CLEAVE] (1775)
**1** : an ornamental vertical groove especially in a Doric frieze
**2** : a symbolic figure or a character (as in the Mayan system of writing) usually incised or carved in relief
**3** : a symbol (as a curved arrow on a road sign) that conveys information nonverbally
— **glyph·ic** \'gli-fik\ *adjective*

**Glyp·tal** \'glip-t°l\ *trademark*
— used for an alkyd

**glyp·tic** \'glip-tik\ *noun* [probably from French *glyptique*, from Greek *glyptikē*, from *glyphein*] (circa 1818)
: the art or process of carving or engraving especially on gems

**G–man** \'jē-,man\ *noun* [probably from government *man*] (1928)
: a special agent of the Federal Bureau of Investigation

**gnar** *or* **gnarr** \'när\ *intransitive verb* **gnarred; gnar·ring** [imitative] (15th century)
: SNARL, GROWL

**¹gnarl** \'när(-ə)l\ *intransitive verb* [probably frequentative of *gnar*] (1593)
: SNARL, GROWL

**²gnarl** *transitive verb* [back-formation from *gnarled*] (1814)
: to twist into a state of deformity

**³gnarl** *noun* (1824)
: a hard protuberance with twisted grain on a tree

**gnarled** \'när(-ə)ld\ *adjective* [probably alteration of *knurled*] (1603)
**1** : full of knots or gnarls : KNOTTY ⟨*gnarled* hands⟩
**2** : crabbed in disposition, aspect, or character

**gnarly** \'när-lē\ *adjective* (1829)
**1** : GNARLED
**2** *slang* — used as a generalized term of approval or disparagement

**gnash** \'nash\ *transitive verb* [alteration of Middle English *gnasten*] (15th century)
: to strike or grind (as the teeth) together
— **gnash** *noun*

**gnat** \'nat\ *noun* [Middle English, from Old English *gnætt*; akin to Old English *gnagan* to gnaw] (before 12th century)
: any of various small usually biting dipteran flies
— **gnat·ty** \-ē\ *adjective*

**gnat·catch·er** \'nat-,ka-chər, -,ke-\ *noun* (1839)
: any of a genus (*Polioptila*) of several small North and South American insectivorous oscine birds

**gnath·ic** \'na-thik\ *or* **gna·thal** \'nā-thəl, 'na-\ *adjective* [Greek *gnathos* jaw] (1882)
: of or relating to the jaw

**-gnathous** *adjective combining form* [New Latin *-gnathus*, from Greek *gnathos*; akin to Greek *genys* jaw — more at CHIN]
: having (such) a jaw ⟨*prognathous*⟩

**gnaw** \'nö\ *verb* [Middle English *gnawen*, from Old English *gnagan*; akin to Old High German *gnagan* to gnaw] (before 12th century)
*transitive verb*
**1 a** : to bite or chew on with the teeth; *especially* : to wear away by persistent biting or nibbling ⟨a dog *gnawing* a bone⟩ **b** : to make by gnawing ⟨rats *gnawed* a hole⟩
**2 a** : to be a source of vexation to : PLAGUE ⟨anxiety always *gnawing* him⟩ **b** : to affect like gnawing ⟨hunger *gnawing* her vitals⟩
**3** : ERODE, CORRODE
*intransitive verb*
**1** : to bite or nibble persistently ⟨*gnawing* at his underlip⟩

**2** : to produce an effect of or as if of gnawing ⟨waves *gnawing* away at the cliffs⟩
— **gnaw·er** \'nö(-ə)r\ *noun*

**gneiss** \'nīs\ *noun* [German *Gneis*, alteration of Middle High German *gneiste* spark, from Old High German *gneisto*; akin to Old English *fȳrgnāst* spark] (1757)
: a foliated metamorphic rock corresponding in composition to a feldspathic plutonic rock (as granite)
— **gneiss·ic** \'nī-sik\ *adjective*
— **gneiss·oid** \-,sȯid\ *adjective*
— **gneiss·ose** \-,sōs\ *adjective*

**gnoc·chi** \'nȯ-kē, 'nyȯ-, 'nä-\ *noun plural* [Italian, plural of *gnocco*, from Italian dialect (Veneto), probably of Germanic origin; akin to Middle High German *knöchel* knuckle, *knoche* bone — more at KNUCKLE] (1891)
: dumplings usually made with potato or semolina and served with sauce

**¹gnome** \'nōm\ *noun* [Greek *gnōmē*, from *gignōskein* to know — more at KNOW] (1577)
: MAXIM, APHORISM

**²gnome** *noun* [French, from New Latin *gnomus*] (1712)
**1** : an ageless and often deformed dwarf of folklore who lives in the earth and usually guards treasure
**2** : an elemental being in the theory of Paracelsus that inhabits earth
— **gnome·like** \-,līk\ *adjective*
— **gnom·ish** \'nō-mish\ *adjective*

**gno·mic** \'nō-mik\ *adjective* (1815)
**1** : characterized by aphorism ⟨*gnomic* utterances⟩
**2** : given to the composition of gnomic writing ⟨a *gnomic* poet⟩

**gno·mon** \'nō-mən, -,män\ *noun* [Latin, from Greek *gnōmōn* interpreter, pointer on a sundial, from *gignōskein*] (1546)
**1** : an object that by the position or length of its shadow serves as an indicator especially of the hour of the day: as **a** : the pin of a sundial **b** : a column or shaft erected perpendicular to the horizon

*bcdefg* gnomon 2

**2** : the remainder of a parallelogram after the removal of a similar parallelogram containing one of its corners

**gno·sis** \'nō-səs\ *noun* [Greek *gnōsis*, literally, knowledge, from *gignōskein*] (1703)
: esoteric knowledge of spiritual truth held by the ancient Gnostics to be essential to salvation

**gnos·tic** \'näs-tik\ *noun, often capitalized* [Late Latin *gnosticus*, from Greek *gnōstikos* of knowledge, from *gignōskein*] (circa 1587)
: an adherent of gnosticism
— **gnostic** *adjective, often capitalized*

**gnos·ti·cism** \'näs-tə-,si-zəm\ *noun, often capitalized* (1664)
: the thought and practice especially of various cults of late pre-Christian and early Christian centuries distinguished by the conviction that matter is evil and that emancipation comes through gnosis

**gno·to·bi·ot·ic** \,nō-tō-bī-'ä-tik, -bē-\ *adjective* [Greek *gnōtos* known (from *gignōskein* to know) + *biotē* life, way of life — more at KNOW, BIOTA] (1949)
: of, relating to, living in, or being a controlled environment containing one or a few kinds of organisms; *also* : AXENIC
— **gno·to·bi·ot·i·cal·ly** \-ti-k(ə-)lē\ *adverb*

**gnu** \'nü *also* 'nyü\ *noun, plural* **gnu** *or* **gnus** [Khoikhoi *t'gnu*] (1777)
: either of two large African antelopes (*Connochaetes gnou* and *C. taurinus*) with a head like that of an ox, short mane, long tail, and horns in both sexes that curve downward and outward

**¹go** \'gō\ *verb* **went** \'went\; **gone** \'gȯn *also* 'gän\; **go·ing** \'gō-iŋ, 'gȯ(-)iŋ; "*going to*" in sense 13 is often 'gȱ-nə *or* 'gȯ-nə *or* 'gə-nə\; **goes** \'gȯz\ [Middle English *gon*, from Old English *gān*; akin to Old High German *gān* to go, Greek *kichanein* to reach, attain] (before 12th century)
*intransitive verb*

gnu

**1** : to move on a course : PROCEED ⟨*go* slow⟩ ⟨*went* by train⟩ — compare STOP
**2** : to move out of or away from a place expressed or implied : LEAVE, DEPART ⟨*went* from school to the party⟩ ⟨*going* away for vacation⟩
**3 a** : to take a certain course or follow a certain procedure ⟨reports *go* through channels to the president⟩ **b** : to pass by means of a process like journeying ⟨the message *went* by wire⟩ **c** : to proceed without delay and often in a thoughtless or reckless manner — used especially to intensify a complementary verb ⟨why did you *go* and spoil it⟩ ⟨*go* jump in a lake⟩ **d** (1) : to extend from point to point or in a certain direction ⟨the road *goes* to the lake⟩ (2) : to give access : LEAD ⟨that door *goes* to the cellar⟩
**4** *obsolete* : WALK
**5** : to be habitually in a certain state or condition ⟨*go* bareheaded⟩
**6 a** : to become lost, consumed, or spent ⟨our time has *gone*⟩ **b** : DIE **c** : to slip away : ELAPSE ⟨the evening *went* quickly⟩ **d** : to come to be given up or discarded ⟨these slums have to *go*⟩ **e** : to pass by sale ⟨*went* for a good price⟩ **f** : to become impaired or weakened ⟨his hearing started to *go*⟩ **g** : to give way especially under great force or pressure : BREAK ⟨the roof *went*⟩
**7 a** : to move along in a specified manner : FARE ⟨everything was *going* well⟩ **b** : to be in general or on an average ⟨cheap, as yachts *go*⟩ **c** : to be or become especially as the result of a contest ⟨the election *went* in her favor⟩ **d** : to turn out well : SUCCEED ⟨worked hard to make the party *go*⟩
**8 a** : to apply oneself ⟨*went* to work⟩ **b** : to put or subject oneself ⟨*went* to unnecessary expense⟩ **c** *chiefly Southern & Midland* : INTEND ⟨I didn't *go* to do it⟩
**9** : to have recourse to another for corroboration, vindication, or decision : RESORT ⟨*go* to court to recover damages⟩
**10 a** : to begin an action or motion ⟨here *goes*⟩ **b** : to maintain or perform a certain action or motion ⟨still *going* strong⟩ **c** : to function in the proper or expected manner : RUN ⟨the motor won't *go*⟩
**11** : to be known ⟨*goes* by an alias⟩
**12 a** : to act in accordance or harmony ⟨a good rule to *go* by⟩ **b** : to come to be determined ⟨dreams *go* by contraries⟩ **c** : to come to be applied or appropriated ⟨all proceeds *go* to charity⟩ **d** : to pass by award, assignment, or lot ⟨the prize *went* to a sophomore⟩ **e** (1) : to contribute to an end or result ⟨qualities that *go* to make a hero⟩ (2) : to be of advantage ⟨has a lot *going* for her⟩
**13** : to be about, intending, or expecting something — used in a progressive tense before an infinitive ⟨is *going* to leave town⟩
**14 a** : EXTEND ⟨his knowledge fails to *go* very deep⟩ **b** : to come or arrive at a certain state or condition ⟨*go* to sleep⟩ **c** : to come to be : BECOME ⟨the tire *went* flat⟩ — often used to express conversion to specified values or a specified state ⟨*gone* Hollywood⟩ ⟨*go* condo⟩ **d** : to undergo a change ⟨leaves *go* from green to red⟩
**15 a** : to be in phrasing or expression : READ ⟨as the story *goes*⟩ **b** : to be capable of being sung or played ⟨the tune *goes* like this⟩

**16 :** to be compatible, suitable, or becoming **:** HARMONIZE ⟨the tie *goes* with his suit⟩
**17 a :** to be capable of passing, extending, or being contained or inserted ⟨will these clothes *go* in your suitcase⟩ **b :** to have a usual or proper place or position **:** BELONG ⟨these books *go* on the top shelf⟩
**18 :** to have a tendency **:** CONDUCE ⟨it *goes* to show⟩
**19 a** (1) **:** to carry authority ⟨what she said *went*⟩ (2) **:** to be acceptable, satisfactory, or adequate ⟨anything *goes* here⟩ **b :** to hold true **:** be valid ⟨the rule *goes* for you, too⟩
**20 :** to empty the bladder or bowels
*transitive verb*
**1 :** to proceed along or according to **:** FOLLOW ⟨if I were *going* his way⟩ ⟨*went* the conventional route⟩
**2 :** to travel through or along **:** TRAVERSE ⟨*went* the length of the street⟩
**3 a :** to make a wager of **:** BET ⟨*go* a dollar on the outcome⟩ **b :** to make an offer of **:** BID ⟨willing to *go* $50 for the clock⟩
**4 a :** to assume the function or obligation of ⟨promised to *go* bail for his friend⟩ **b :** to participate to the extent of ⟨decided to *go* halves on the winnings⟩
**5 :** YIELD, WEIGH ⟨this fish *goes* ten pounds⟩
**6 a :** to put up with **:** TOLERATE ⟨couldn't *go* the noise⟩ **b :** AFFORD ⟨can't *go* the price⟩ **c :** ENJOY ⟨I could *go* a soda⟩
**7 a :** to cause (a characteristic sound) to occur ⟨the gun *went* bang⟩ **b :** SAY — used chiefly in oral narration of speech
**8 :** to engage in ⟨don't *go* telling everyone⟩
**9** *of a sports team or player* **:** to have a record of ⟨*went* 11-0 last season⟩
— **go·er** \'gō(-ə)r\ *noun*
— **go about :** to set about
— **go after :** to try to get **:** SEEK
— **go all the way 1 :** to enter into complete agreement **2 :** to engage in sexual intercourse
— **go at 1 a :** to make an attack on **b :** to make an approach to **2 :** UNDERTAKE
— **go back on 1 :** ABANDON **2 :** BETRAY **3 :** FAIL
— **go begging :** to be in little demand
— **go by the board 1 :** to be carried over a ship's side **2 :** to be discarded
— **go down the line :** to give wholehearted support
— **go easy :** to be sparing ⟨*go easy* with the sugar⟩ ⟨*go easy* on the kid⟩
— **go fly a kite :** to stop being an annoyance or disturbance ⟨told him to *go fly a kite*⟩
— **go for 1 :** to pass for or serve as **2 :** to try to secure or attain (as a goal) ⟨*go for* the prize⟩ **3 a :** FAVOR, ACCEPT ⟨cannot *go for* your idea⟩ **b :** to have an interest in or liking for ⟨she *went for* him in a big way —Chandler Brossard⟩ **4 :** ATTACK, ASSAIL ⟨my dog *went for* the intruder⟩
— **go for broke :** to put forth all one's strength or resources
— **go great guns :** to achieve great success
— **go hang :** to cease to be of interest or concern
— **go into :** to be contained in ⟨5 *goes into* 60 12 times⟩
— **go it 1 :** to behave in a reckless, excited, or impromptu manner **2 :** to proceed in a rapid or furious manner **3 :** to conduct one's affairs **:** ACT ⟨insists on *going it* alone⟩
— **go missing** *chiefly British* **:** to become lost **:** DISAPPEAR
— **go one better :** OUTDO, SURPASS
— **go over 1 :** EXAMINE **2 a :** REPEAT **b :** STUDY, REVIEW
— **go places :** to be on the way to success
— **go public 1** *of a close corporation* **:** to offer shares for sale to the general public **2 :** to make a public disclosure
— **go steady :** to date one person exclusively and frequently

— **go the vole :** to risk all for great gains
— **go through 1 :** to subject to thorough examination, consideration, or study **2 :** EXPERIENCE, UNDERGO **3 :** CARRY OUT, PERFORM ⟨*went through* his work in a daze⟩
— **go to bat for :** to give active support or assistance to **:** DEFEND, CHAMPION
— **go to bed with :** to have sexual intercourse with
— **go to one's head 1 :** to cause one to become confused, excited, or dizzy **2 :** to cause one to become conceited or overconfident
— **go to pieces :** to become shattered (as in nerves or health)
— **go to the mat :** to make an all-out combative effort (as in support of a position)
— **go to town 1 :** to work or act rapidly or efficiently **2 :** to be markedly successful **3 :** to indulge oneself excessively
— **go with 1 :** DATE **2 :** CHOOSE **2** ⟨*went with* an iron off the tee⟩
— **go without saying :** to be self-evident
— **go with the flow :** CONFORM **2b**
— **to go 1 :** still remaining ⟨ten minutes *to go*⟩ **2** *of prepared food* **:** sold for consumption off the premises

**²go** \'gō\ *noun, plural* **goes** (1727)
**1 :** the act or manner of going
**2 :** the height of fashion **:** RAGE ⟨elegant shawls labeled . . . "quite the *go*" —R. S. Surtees⟩
**3 :** an often unexpected turn of affairs **:** OCCURRENCE
**4 :** the quantity used or furnished at one time ⟨you can obtain a *go* of brandy for sixpence —C. B. Fairbanks⟩
**5 :** ENERGY, VIGOR
**6 a :** a turn in an activity (as a game) ⟨it's your *go*⟩ **b :** ATTEMPT, TRY ⟨have a *go* at painting⟩
**7 :** a spell of activity ⟨finished the job at one *go*⟩
**8 :** SUCCESS ⟨made a *go* of the business⟩
**9 :** permission to proceed **:** GO-AHEAD ⟨gave the astronauts a *go* for another orbit⟩
— **no go :** to no avail **:** USELESS
— **on the go :** constantly or restlessly active

**³go** *adjective* (1961)
**:** functioning properly **:** being in good and ready condition ⟨declared all systems *go*⟩

**⁴go** *noun, often capitalized* [Japanese] (1890)
**:** a Japanese game played between two players who alternately place black and white stones on a board checkered by 19 vertical lines and 19 horizontal lines in an attempt to enclose the larger area on the board

**¹goad** \'gōd\ *noun* [Middle English *gode*, from Old English *gād* spear, goad; akin to Langobardic *gaida* spear, and perhaps to Sanskrit *hinoti* he urges on] (before 12th century)
**1 a :** something that pricks like a goad **:** THORN **b :** something that urges or stimulates into action **:** SPUR
**2 :** a pointed rod used to urge on an animal
**synonym** see MOTIVE

**²goad** *transitive verb* (1579)
**1 :** to incite or rouse as if with a goad
**2 :** to drive (as cattle) with a goad

**¹go–ahead** \'gō-ə-ˌhed\ *adjective* (1834)
**1 :** marked by energy and enterprise **:** PROGRESSIVE ⟨a vigorous *go-ahead* company⟩
**2 :** indicating that one may proceed ⟨*go-ahead* signal⟩
**3 :** being a score that gives a team the lead in a game ⟨drove in the *go-ahead* run⟩

**²go–ahead** *noun* (1840)
**1 a :** ENERGY, SPIRIT ⟨had a great deal of courage and *go-ahead*⟩ **b :** one possessing go-ahead
**2 :** a sign, signal, or authority to proceed **:** GREEN LIGHT

**goal** \'gōl, *chiefly Northern especially in 1b & 3a also* 'gül\ *noun* [Middle English *gol* boundary, limit] (1531)

**1 a :** the terminal point of a race **b :** an area to be reached safely in children's games
**2 :** the end toward which effort is directed **:** AIM
**3 a :** an area or object toward which players in various games attempt to advance a ball or puck and usually through or into which it must go to score points **b :** the act or action of causing a ball or puck to go through or into such a goal **c :** the score resulting from such an act
**synonym** see INTENTION
— **goal** *intransitive verb*
— **goal·less** \'gō(l)-ləs\ *adjective*

**goal·ie** \'gō-lē\ *noun* (1921)
**:** GOALKEEPER

**goal·keep·er** \'gōl-ˌkē-pər\ *noun* (1658)
**:** a player who defends the goal in any of various games (as hockey, lacrosse, or soccer)

**goal kick** *noun* (1891)
**:** a free kick in soccer awarded to a defensive player when the ball is driven out of bounds over the end line by an opposing player

**goal line** *noun* (1867)
**:** a line at either end and usually running the width of a playing area on which a goal or goalpost is situated

**goal·mouth** \'gōl-ˌmau̇th\ *noun* (1882)
**:** the area directly in front of the goal (as in soccer or hockey)

**go along** *intransitive verb* (1602)
**1 :** to move along **:** PROCEED
**2 :** to go or travel as a companion
**3 :** to act in cooperation or express agreement ⟨*go along* with the crowd⟩

**goal·post** \'gōl-ˌpōst\ *noun* (1857)
**:** one of usually two vertical posts that with or without a crossbar constitute the goal in various games

**goal·tend·er** \'gōl-ˌten-dər\ *noun* (circa 1909)
**:** GOALKEEPER

**goal·tend·ing** \-diŋ\ *noun* (1968)
**1 :** the act of guarding a goal (as in hockey)
**2 :** a violation in basketball that involves touching or deflecting a ball that is on its downward path toward the basket or on or within the rim of the basket

**goal·ward** \'gōl-wərd\ *adverb or adjective* (1949)
**:** toward a goal

**go·an·na** \gō-'a-nə\ *noun* [alteration of *iguana*] (1831)
**:** any of several large Australian monitor lizards (genus *Varanus* of the family Varanidae)

**go–around** \'gō-ə-ˌrau̇nd\ *noun* (circa 1929)
**1 :** RUNAROUND ⟨gave me the *go-around*⟩
**2 a :** ROUND ⟨reached an agreement during the first *go-around*⟩ **b :** a heated argument or struggle ⟨had a real *go-around* with her about it⟩
**3 :** an act or instance of going around (as in an air traffic pattern)

**go around** *intransitive verb* (circa 1520)
**1 a :** to pass from place to place **:** go here and there **b :** to have currency **:** CIRCULATE ⟨an amusing story is *going around*⟩
**2 :** to satisfy demand **:** fill the need ⟨not enough jobs to *go around*⟩

**goat** \'gōt\ *noun, plural* **goats** [Middle English *gote*, from Old English *gāt*; akin to Old High German *geiz* goat, Old Norse *geit*, Latin *haedus* kid] (before 12th century)
**1 a** *or plural* **goat :** any of various hollow-horned ruminant mammals (especially of the genus *Capra*) related to the sheep but of lighter build and with backwardly arching horns, a short tail, and usually straight hair **b** *capitalized* **:** CAPRICORN
**2 :** a licentious man **:** LECHER
**3 :** SCAPEGOAT **2**
— **goat·ish** \'gō-tish\ *adjective*

\ə\ abut \ᵊ\ kitten \ər\ further \a\ ash \ā\ ace
\ä\ mop, mar \au̇\ out \ch\ chin \e\ bet \ē\ easy
\g\ go \i\ hit \ī\ ice \j\ job \ŋ\ sing \ō\ go
\ȯ\ law \ȯi\ boy \th\ thin \t͟h\ the \ü\ loot \u̇\ foot
\y\ yet \zh\ vision *see also* Guide to Pronunciation

— **goat·like** \-,līk\ *adjective*
**goat cheese** *noun* (1893)
: any of various cheeses made from goat's milk
**goa·tee** \gō-'tē\ *noun* [from its resemblance to the beard of a he-goat] (1844)
: a small pointed or tufted beard on a man's chin
— **goa·teed** \-'tēd\ *adjective*
**goat·fish** \'gōt-,fish\ *noun* (circa 1639)
: any of a family (Mullidae) of moderate-sized usually red or golden fishes with two barbels on the chin — called also *red mullet*
**goat·herd** \-,hərd\ *noun* [Middle English *gote-herd*, from Old English *gāthyrd*] (before 12th century)
: a person who tends goats
**goat·skin** \-,skin\ *noun* (14th century)
1 : the skin of a goat
2 : leather made from goatskin
**goat·suck·er** \-,sə-kər\ *noun* (1611)
: NIGHTJAR
¹**gob** \'gäb\ *noun* [Middle English *gobbe*, from Middle French *gobe* large piece of food, back-formation from *gobet*] (14th century)
1 : LUMP
2 : a large amount — usually used in plural ⟨*gobs* of money⟩
²**gob** \'gäb, 'gäb\ *noun* [probably from Scottish Gaelic, mouth & Irish, beak, pursed mouth] (circa 1550)
*chiefly British* : MOUTH
³**gob** \'gäb, 'gäb\ *noun* [origin unknown] (1915)
: SAILOR
**gob·bet** \'gä-bət\ *noun* [Middle English *gobet*, from Middle French, mouthful, piece] (14th century)
1 : a piece or portion (as of meat)
2 : LUMP, MASS
3 : a small fragment or extract ⟨a *gobbet* of information⟩
4 : a small quantity of liquid : DROP
¹**gob·ble** \'gä-bəl\ *transitive verb* **gob·bled; gob·bling** \-b(ə-)liŋ\ [probably irregular from ¹*gob*] (1601)
1 : to swallow or eat greedily
2 : to take eagerly — usually used with *up*
3 : to read rapidly or greedily — usually used with *up*
²**gobble** *intransitive verb* **gob·bled; gob·bling** \-b(ə-)liŋ\ [imitative] (1680)
1 : to make the natural guttural noise of a male turkey
2 : to make a sound resembling a gobble
— **gobble** *noun*
**gob·ble·dy·gook** *also* **gob·ble·de·gook** \'gä-bəl-dē-,gủk, -,gük\ *noun* [irregular from *gobble*, noun] (1944)
: wordy and generally unintelligible jargon
¹**gob·bler** \'gä-blər\ *noun* (circa 1737)
: a male turkey
²**gobbler** *noun* (circa 1755)
: one that gobbles
**Go·be·lin** \'gō-bə-lən, ,gō-bə-'laⁿ\ *adjective* [*Gobelin* dye and tapestry works, Paris, France] (1788)
: of, relating to, or characteristic of tapestry produced at the Gobelin works in Paris
— **Gobelin** *noun*
**go·be·tween** \'gō-bə-,twēn\ *noun* (1598)
: an intermediate agent : BROKER
**gob·let** \'gäb-lət\ *noun* [Middle English *gobelet*, from Middle French] (14th century)
1 *archaic* : a bowl-shaped drinking vessel without handles
2 : a drinking vessel (as of glass) with a foot and stem — compare TUMBLER
**goblet cell** *noun* [from its shape] (1878)
: a mucus-secreting epithelial cell (as of intestinal columnar epithelium) that is distended at the free end
**gob·lin** \'gäb-lən\ *noun* [Middle English *gobelin*, from Middle French, from Medieval Latin *gobelinus*, ultimately from Greek *kobalos* rogue] (14th century)

: an ugly or grotesque sprite that is mischievous and sometimes evil and malicious
**go·bo** \'gō-(,)bō\ *noun, plural* **gobos** *also* **goboes** [origin unknown] (circa 1930)
1 : a dark strip (as of wallboard) to shield a motion-picture or television camera from light
2 : a device to shield a microphone from sound
**go·by** \'gō-bē\ *noun, plural* **gobies** *also* **goby** [Latin *gobius* gudgeon, from Greek *kōbios*] (1769)
: any of numerous spiny-finned fishes (family Gobiidae) that usually have the pelvic fins united to form a ventral sucking disk

goby

**go by** *intransitive verb* (1508)
: PASS 3b ⟨as time *goes by*⟩
**go–cart** \'gō-,kärt\ *noun* (1689)
1 a : WALKER b : STROLLER
2 : HANDCART
3 : a light open carriage
¹**god** \'gäd *also* 'gȯd\ *noun* [Middle English, from Old English; akin to Old High German *got* god] (before 12th century)
1 *capitalized* : the supreme or ultimate reality: as a : the Being perfect in power, wisdom, and goodness who is worshipped as creator and ruler of the universe b *Christian Science* : the incorporeal divine Principle ruling over all as eternal Spirit : infinite Mind
2 : a being or object believed to have more than natural attributes and powers and to require human worship; *specifically* : one controlling a particular aspect or part of reality
3 : a person or thing of supreme value
4 : a powerful ruler
²**god** *transitive verb* **god·ded; god·ding** (1595)
: to treat as a god : IDOLIZE, DEIFY
**god–aw·ful** \'gä-'dȯ-fəl\ *adjective* [*god*damned + *awful*] (1878)
: extremely unpleasant or disagreeable : ABOMINABLE ⟨*god-awful* weather⟩
**god·child** \'gäd-,chīld *also* 'gȯd-\ *noun* (13th century)
: a person for whom another person becomes sponsor at baptism
¹**god·damn** *or* **god·dam** \'gä(d)-'dam\ *noun, often capitalized* (1640)
: DAMN ⟨they were in no mood to give a good *goddamn* about anything —Robert Lowry⟩
²**goddamn** *or* **goddam** *verb, often capitalized* (1928)
: DAMN
**god·damned** \,gä(d)-,damd\ *or* **god·damn** *or* **god·dam** \-,dam\ *adjective or adverb* (1918)
: DAMNED
**god·daugh·ter** \'gäd-,dȯ-tər *also* 'gȯd-\ *noun* (before 12th century)
: a female godchild
**god·dess** \'gä-dəs *also* 'gȯ-\ *noun* (14th century)
1 : a female god
2 : a woman whose great charm or beauty arouses adoration
*usage* see -ESS
**Go·del's theorem** \'gō-dəlz-, 'gȯr-, 'gœ-\ *noun* [Kurt Gödel (died 1978) American mathematician] (1933)
: a theorem in advanced logic: in any logical system as complex as or more complex than the arithmetic of the integers there can always be found either a statement which can be shown to be both true and false or a statement whose truth or falsity cannot be deduced from other statements in the system — called also *Godel's incompleteness theorem*
**go·det** \gō-'det, 'gō-,dā\ *noun, often attributive* [French, from *goder* to form creases, probably from *goderon* rounded pleat on a ruffle, gadroon] (1872)

: an inset of cloth placed in a seam to give fullness (as at the bottom of a skirt)
**go–dev·il** \'gō-,de-vəl\ *noun* (1852)
: any of various devices: as a : a cultivator with wooden runners b : a weight formerly dropped in a bored hole (as of an oil well) to set off an explosive c : a cleaning scraper propelled through a pipeline d : a handcar or small gasoline car used on a railroad e : a child's sled
¹**god·fa·ther** \'gäd-,fä-thər, -,fȧ-, *also* 'gȯd-\ *noun* (before 12th century)
1 : a man who sponsors a person at baptism
2 : one having a relation to someone or something analogous to that of a male sponsor to his godchild: as a : one that founds, supports, or inspires ⟨made him the *godfather* of a whole generation of rebels —*Times Literary Supplement*⟩ b : the leader of an organized crime syndicate
²**godfather** *transitive verb* (1780)
: to act as godfather to
**God–fear·ing** \-,fir-iŋ\ *adjective* (1835)
: having a reverent feeling toward God : DEVOUT
**god·for·sak·en** \-fər-,sā-kən\ *adjective* (1860)
1 : REMOTE, DESOLATE
2 : neglected and miserable in appearance or circumstances
**god·head** \-,hed\ *noun* [Middle English *godhed*, from *god* + *-hed* -hood; akin to Middle English *-hod* -hood] (13th century)
1 : divine nature or essence : DIVINITY
2 *capitalized* a : GOD 1 b : the nature of God especially as existing in three persons — used with *the*
**god·hood** \-,hủd\ *noun* [Middle English *godhod*, from Old English *godhād*, from *god* + *-hād* -hood] (1563)
: DIVINITY
**Go·di·va** \gə-'dī-və\ *noun*
: an English earl's wife who in legend rode naked through Coventry to save its citizens from a tax
**god·less** \'gäd-ləs *also* 'gȯd-\ *adjective* (1528)
: not acknowledging a deity or divine law
— **god·less·ness** *noun*
**god·like** \-,līk\ *adjective* (before 12th century)
: resembling or having the qualities of God or a god : DIVINE
— **god·like·ness** *noun*
**god·ling** \-liŋ\ *noun* (circa 1500)
: an inferior or local god
**god·ly** \-lē\ *adjective* **god·li·er; -est** (14th century)
1 : DIVINE
2 : PIOUS, DEVOUT
— **god·li·ness** *noun*
— **godly** *adverb, archaic*
**god·moth·er** \-,mə-thər\ *noun* (before 12th century)
: a woman who sponsors a person at baptism
**go·down** \'gō-,daủn\ *noun* [by folk etymology from Malay *gudang*] (1552)
: a warehouse in an oriental country
**go down** *intransitive verb* (14th century)
1 a : to go below the horizon : SET ⟨the sun *went down*⟩ b : to fall to or as if to the ground ⟨the plane *went down* in flames⟩ c : to become submerged ⟨the ship *went down* with all hands⟩
2 : to admit of being swallowed ⟨the medicine *went down* easily⟩
3 a : to find acceptance ⟨will the plan *go down* with the farmers⟩ b : to come to be remembered especially in posterity ⟨will he *go down* in history as a great president⟩
4 *British* : to leave a university
5 a : to undergo defeat or failure b *chiefly British* : to become incapacitated ⟨*went down* with . . . acute tonsillitis —Helen Cathcart⟩
6 *slang* : to take place : HAPPEN
— **go down on** : to perform fellatio or cunnilingus on
**god·par·ent** \'gäd-,par-ənt, -,per- *also* 'gȯd-\ *noun* (1865)

: a sponsor at baptism

**God's acre** *noun* (1617)
: CHURCHYARD

**god·send** \'gäd-,send *also* 'gȯd-\ *noun* [back-formation from *god-sent*] (1820)
: a desirable or needed thing or event that comes unexpectedly

**god·son** \-,sən\ *noun* (before 12th century)
: a male godchild

**God·speed** \-'spēd\ *noun* [Middle English *god speid*, from the phrase *God spede you* God prosper you] (15th century)
: a prosperous journey : SUCCESS ⟨bade him *Godspeed*⟩

**god·wit** \'gäd-,wit\ *noun* [origin unknown] (1552)
: any of a genus (*Limosa*) of wading birds that are related to the curlews and sandpipers and have a long slender slightly upturned or straight bill

**goes** *present 3d singular of* GO, *plural of* GO

**goe·thite** \'gə(r)-,tīt\ *noun* [German *Göthit*, from J. W. von *Goethe*] (circa 1823)
: a mineral that consists of an iron hydrogen oxide and is the commonest constituent of many forms of natural rust

**go·fer** \'gō-fər\ *noun* [alteration of *go for*] (1967)
: an employee whose duties include running errands

**gof·fer** \'gä-fər, 'gȯ-\ *transitive verb* [French *gaufrer*, from *gaufre* honeycomb, waffle, from Old French, of Germanic origin; akin to Middle Dutch *wafel* waffle] (1706)
: to crimp, plait, or flute (as linen or lace) especially with a heated iron
— **goffer** *noun*

**go-get·ter** \'gō-,ge-tər, -,ge-\ *noun* (1921)
: an aggressively enterprising person
— **go-get·ting** \-,ge-tiŋ\ *adjective or noun*

¹**gog·gle** \'gä-gᵊl\ *intransitive verb* **gog·gled; gog·gling** [Middle English *gogelen* to squint] (1616)
: to stare with wide or protuberant eyes
— **gog·gler** \'gä-gᵊl-ər\ *noun*

²**goggle** *adjective* (1540)
: PROTUBERANT, STARING ⟨*goggle* eyes⟩
— **gog·gly** \'gä-gᵊl-ē\ *adjective*

**gog·gle-eye** \'gä-gᵊl-,ī\ *noun* (1840)
**1** : ROCK BASS
**2** : WARMOUTH

**gog·gle-eyed** \-,īd\ *adjective* (1711)
: having bulging or rolling eyes

**gog·gles** \'gä-gᵊlz\ *noun plural* (1715)
: protective glasses set in a flexible frame (as of rubber or plastic) that fits snugly against the face
— **gog·gled** \-gᵊld\ *adjective*

**go-go** \'gō-(,)gō\ *adjective* [partly from *a-go-go*, partly from reduplication of ¹*go*] (1965)
**1 a** : employed to entertain in a disco ⟨*go-go* dancers⟩ **b** : of, relating to, or being a disco or the music or dances performed there
**2** : marked by spirited or aggressive action ⟨*go-go* baseball⟩
**3 a** : relating to or dealing in popular often speculative investment expected to yield high returns ⟨*go-go* mutual funds⟩ **b** : relating to, involved in, or marked by business growth and prosperity and aggressive efforts to turn a quick profit ⟨*go-go* bankers and entrepreneurs . . . who put together the megabuck deals —Ken Auletta⟩

¹**Goi·del·ic** \gȯi-'de-lik\ *adjective* [Middle Irish *Goídel* Gael, Irishman] (1896)
**1** : of, relating to, or characteristic of the Gaels
**2** : of, relating to, or constituting Goidelic

²**Goidelic** *noun* (1882)
: the branch of the Celtic languages that includes Irish, Scottish Gaelic, and Manx — see INDO-EUROPEAN LANGUAGES table

**go in** *intransitive verb* (1812)
**1** : to make an approach (as in attacking)

**2 a** : to take part in a game or contest **b** : to call the opening bet in poker : STAY
**3** *of a celestial body* : to become obscured by a cloud
**4** : to form a union or alliance : JOIN — often used with *with* ⟨asked the rest of us to *go in* with them⟩
— **go in for 1** : to give support to : ADVOCATE **2** : to have or show an interest in or a liking for **3** : to engage in : take part in

¹**go·ing** \'gō-iŋ, 'gȯ(-)iŋ\ *noun* (14th century)
**1** : an act or instance of going
**2** *plural* : BEHAVIOR, ACTIONS ⟨for his eyes are upon the ways of man, and he seeth all his *goings* —Job 34:21 (Authorized Version)⟩
**3** : the condition of the ground (as for walking)
**4** : advance toward an objective ⟨when the *going* gets tough⟩

²**going** *adjective* (14th century)
**1 a** : that goes — often used in combination ⟨easy*going*⟩ ⟨out*going*⟩ **b** : WORKING, MOVING ⟨everything was in *going* order⟩
**2** : LIVING, EXISTING ⟨the best novelist *going*⟩
**3** : CURRENT, PREVAILING ⟨*going* price⟩
**4** : conducting business with the expectation of indefinite continuance ⟨*going* concern⟩
— **going on** : drawing near to : APPROACHING ⟨is six years old *going on* seven⟩

**go·ing-over** \,gō-iŋ-'ō-vər, ,gȯ(-)iŋ-\ *noun, plural* **go·ings-over** (1872)
**1 a** : a severe scolding **b** : BEATING
**2** : a thorough examination or investigation

**go·ings-on** \,gō-iŋ-'zȯn, ,gȯ(-)iŋ-, -'zän\ *noun plural* (1775)
**1** : ACTIONS, EVENTS
**2** : irregular or reprehensible happenings or conduct ⟨titillating stories about the *goings-on* of the carefree millionaires —Eleanor Early⟩

**goi·ter** \'gȯi-tər\ *noun* [French *goitre*, from Middle French, back-formation from *goitron* throat, from (assumed) Vulgar Latin *guttrion-, guttrio*, from Latin *guttur*] (1625)
: an enlargement of the thyroid gland visible as a swelling of the front of the neck — compare HYPERTHYROIDISM, HYPOTHYROIDISM
— **goi·trous** \'gȯi-trəs, 'gȯi-tə-rəs\ *adjective*

**goi·tre** *chiefly British variant of* GOITER

**goi·tro·gen** \'gȯi-trə-jən\ *noun* [*goiter* + *-o-* + *-gen*] (1946)
: a substance (as thiourea or thiouracil) that induces goiter formation

**goi·tro·gen·ic** \,gȯi-trə-'je-nik\ *adjective* (1929)
: producing or tending to produce goiter
— **goi·tro·ge·nic·i·ty** \,gȯi-trə-jə-'ni-sə-tē\ *noun*

**Gol·con·da** \gäl-'kän-də\ *noun* [*Golconda*, India, famous for its diamonds] (1884)
: a rich mine; *broadly* : a source of great wealth

**gold** \'gōld\ *noun, often attributive* [Middle English, from Old English; akin to Old High German *gold* gold, Old English *geolu* yellow — more at YELLOW] (before 12th century)
**1** : a malleable ductile yellow metallic element that occurs chiefly free or in a few minerals and is used especially in coins, jewelry, and dentures — see ELEMENT table
**2 a** (1) : gold coins (2) : a gold piece **b** : MONEY **c** : GOLD STANDARD
**3** : a variable color averaging deep yellow
**4** : something resembling gold; *especially* : something valued as the finest of its kind ⟨a heart of *gold*⟩
**5** : a medal awarded as the top prize in a competition : a gold medal

¹**gold·brick** \'gōl(d)-,brik\ *noun* (1881)
**1 a** : a worthless brick that appears to be of gold **b** : something that appears to be valuable but is actually worthless
**2** : a person who shirks assigned work

²**goldbrick** (1902)
*transitive verb*

: SWINDLE
*intransitive verb*
: to shirk duty or responsibility

**gold-bug** \-,bəg\ *noun* (1878)
**1** : a supporter of the gold standard
**2** : a person who invests in or hoards gold

**gold coast** *noun, often G&C capitalized* (1877)
: an exclusive residential district

**gold digger** *noun* (1830)
**1** : one who digs for gold
**2** : a person who uses charm to extract money or gifts from others

**gold·en** \'gōl-dən\ *adjective* [Middle English] (13th century)
**1** : consisting of, relating to, or containing gold
**2 a** : being or having the color gold or the color of gold **b** : BLOND 1a
**3** : LUSTROUS, SHINING
**4** : of a high degree of excellence : SUPERB
**5** : PROSPEROUS, FLOURISHING ⟨*golden* days⟩
**6 a** : radiantly youthful and vigorous **b** : possessing talents that promise worldly success — often used with *boy* **c** : highly favored : POPULAR
**7** : FAVORABLE, ADVANTAGEOUS ⟨a *golden* opportunity⟩
**8** : of, relating to, or being a 50th anniversary or its celebration
**9** : MELLOW, RESONANT ⟨a smooth *golden* tenor⟩
— **gold·en·ly** *adverb*
— **gold·en·ness** \-də(n)-nəs\ *noun*

**golden age** *noun* (1555)
: a period of great happiness, prosperity, and achievement

**gold·en·ag·er** \'gōl-dən-'ā-jər\ *noun* (1961)
: an elderly and often retired person usually engaging in club activities

**golden al·ex·an·ders** \-,a-lig-'zan-dərz, -,e-lig-\ *noun plural but singular or plural in construction, often A capitalized* [Medieval Latin *alexandrum*] (circa 1923)
: a North American yellow-flowered perennial herb (*Zizia aurea*) of the carrot family occurring in moist woods and meadows; *also* : any of several related herbs

**golden–brown alga** *noun* (circa 1957)
: any of a division (Chrysophyta) of marine and freshwater algae (as diatoms) containing yellowish green to golden brown pigments that obscure the chlorophyll — called also *chrysophyte, golden alga*

**golden club** *noun* (1837)
: an American aquatic plant (*Orontium aquaticum*) of the arum family with a spadix of tiny yellow flowers

**golden eagle** *noun* (1839)
: a brown eagle (*Aquila chrysaetos*) of the northern hemisphere with gold-colored feathers on the back of the head and neck

**gold·en·eye** \'gōl-dən-,ī\ *noun* (circa 1678)
**1** : either of two diving ducks (genus *Bucephala*); *especially* : a large-headed swift-flying Holarctic diving duck (*B. clangula*) with the male having a green head and striking black and white markings
**2** : a lacewing (family Chrysopidae) with yellow eyes

golden eagle

**Golden Fleece** *noun* (14th century)

\ə\ abut \ᵊ\ kitten \ər\ further \a\ ash \ā\ ace \ä\ mop, mar \au̇\ out \ch\ chin \e\ bet \ē\ easy \g\ go \i\ hit \ī\ ice \j\ job \ŋ\ sing \ō\ go \ȯ\ law \ȯi\ boy \th\ thin \t̲h̲\ the \ü\ loot \u̇\ foot \y\ yet \zh\ vision    *see also* Guide to Pronunciation

: a fleece of gold placed by the king of Colchis in a dragon-guarded grove and recovered by the Argonauts

**golden glow** *noun* (1902)
: a tall branching composite herb (*Rudbeckia laciniata hortensia*) with showy yellow flower heads

**golden hamster** *noun* (1939)
: a small tawny hamster (*Mesocricetus auratus*) native to Asia Minor — called also *Syrian hamster*

**golden handshake** *noun* (1960)
: a generous severance agreement given especially as an inducement to early retirement

**Golden Horde** *noun* (1863)

golden hamster

: a body of Mongols that overran eastern Europe in the 13th century and dominated Russia until 1486

**golden lion tamarin** *noun* (1975)
: a marmoset (*Leontopithecus rosalia rosalia*) with a reddish gold coat and long mane that occurs in remnants of tropical forest in southeastern Brazil

**golden mean** *noun* (1587)
: the medium between extremes : MODERATION

**golden nematode** *noun* (1946)
: a small yellowish Old World nematode worm (*Globodera rostochiensis* synonym *Heterodera rostochiensis*) established locally as a pest of potatoes in eastern North America

**golden oldie** *noun* (1970)
: one that was a hit or favorite in the past

**golden parachute** *noun* (1981)
: a generous severance agreement for an executive in the event of a sudden dismissal (as because of a merger)

**golden plover** *noun* (1785)
: either of two gregarious plovers (genus *Pluvialis*); *especially* : one (*P. dominica*) that breeds in arctic America and Siberia and winters in Hawaii and the southern hemisphere

**gold·en·rain tree** \'gōl-dən-ˌrān-\ *noun* (1923)
: an Asian tree (*Koelreuteria paniculata* of the family Sapindaceae) that has a rounded crown with very long showy clusters of yellow flowers

**golden retriever** *noun* (1919)
: any of a breed of medium-sized retrievers having a flat moderately long golden coat

**gold·en·rod** \'gōl-dən-ˌräd\ *noun* (1568)
: any of numerous chiefly North American composite biennial or perennial plants (especially of the genus *Solidago*) with alternate leaves and heads of small yellow or sometimes white flowers often clustered in panicles

**golden rule** *noun* (1861)
**1** : a guiding principle
**2** *G&R capitalized* : a rule of ethical conduct referring to Matthew 7:12 and Luke 6:31: do to others as you would have them do to you

**gold·en·seal** \'gōl-dən-ˌsēl\ *noun* (1839)
: a perennial American herb (*Hydrastis canadensis*) of the buttercup family with large rounded leaves and a thick knotted yellow rootstock sometimes used in pharmacy

**golden section** *noun* (1875)
: a proportion (as one involving a line divided into two segments or the length and width of a rectangle and their sum) in which the ratio of the whole to the larger part is the same as the ratio of the larger part to the smaller

**golden shiner** *noun* (circa 1889)
: a common cyprinid fish (*Notemigonus crysoleucas*) of eastern North America having silvery sides with bright golden reflections

**golden syrup** *noun* (1860)
*chiefly British* : TREACLE 2b

**gold·field** \'gōl(d)-ˌfēld\ *noun* (1851)
: a gold-mining district

**gold–filled** \-'fild\ *adjective* (circa 1903)
: consisting of a base metal covered with a layer of gold (a *gold-filled* bracelet)

**gold·finch** \-ˌfinch\ *noun* (before 12th century)
**1** : a small Palearctic finch (*Carduelis carduelis*) with a red, white, and black head and yellow and black wings
**2** : any of three small American finches (genus *Carduelis* and especially *C. tristis*) having the breeding plumage of the male variably yellow with black markings on the wings, tail, and crown

**gold·fish** \-ˌfish\ *noun* (1791)
: a small usually golden yellow or orange cyprinid fish (*Carassius auratus*) often kept as an aquarium and pond fish

**goldfish bowl** *noun* (1935)
: a place or situation offering no privacy

**gold leaf** *noun* (circa 1741)
: an extremely thin sheet of gold that is used especially for gilding

**gold mine** *noun* (1833)
: a rich source of something desired

**gold of pleasure** (1597)
: a European herb (*Camelina sativa*) of the mustard family that is cultivated for its oil-rich seeds

**gold rush** *noun* (1876)
**1** : a rush to newly discovered goldfields in pursuit of riches
**2** : the headlong pursuit of sudden wealth in a new or lucrative field
— **gold rush·er** \-ˌrə-shər\ *noun*

**gold·smith** \'gōl(d)-ˌsmith\ *noun* (before 12th century)
: one who makes or deals in articles of gold

**gold standard** *noun* (1831)
: a monetary standard under which the basic unit of currency is defined by a stated quantity of gold and which is usually characterized by the coinage and circulation of gold, unrestricted convertibility of other money into gold, and the free export and import of gold for the settlement of international obligations

**gold·stone** \'gōl(d)-ˌstōn\ *noun* (circa 1889)
: aventurine glass spangled close and fine with particles of gold-colored material

**go·lem** \'gō-ləm, 'gói-, 'gä-\ *noun* [Yiddish *goylem*, from Hebrew *gōlem* shapeless mass] (1897)
**1** : an artificial human being in Hebrew folklore endowed with life
**2** : something or someone resembling a golem: as **a** : AUTOMATON **b** : BLOCKHEAD

**golf** \'gälf, 'gólf, 'gäf, 'góf *sometimes* 'gəlf\ *noun, often attributive* [Middle English (Scots)] (15th century)
: a game in which a player using special clubs attempts to sink a ball with as few strokes as possible into each of the 9 or 18 successive holes on a course ◻
— **golf** *intransitive verb*
— **golf·er** *noun*

**Golf** (1952)
— a communications code word for the letter *g*

**golf ball** *noun* (1545)
**1** : a small hard dimpled ball used in golf
**2** : the spherical printing element of an electric typewriter or printer

**golf cart** *noun* (1899)
**1** : a small cart for wheeling a golf bag around a golf course
**2** : a motorized cart for carrying golfers and their equipment over a golf course — called also *golf car*

**golf course** *noun* (1890)
: an area of land laid out for golf with a series of 9 or 18 holes each including tee, fairway,

and putting green and often one or more natural or artificial hazards — called also *golf links*

**Gol·gi** \'gól-(ˌ)jē\ *adjective* (1891)
: of or relating to the Golgi apparatus, Golgi bodies, or a method of staining nerve tissue (*Golgi* vesicles)

**Golgi apparatus** *noun* [Camillo *Golgi*] (1916)
: a cytoplasmic organelle that consists of a stack of smooth membranous saccules and associated vesicles and that is active in the modification and transport of proteins — called also *Golgi complex;* see CELL illustration

**Golgi body** *noun* (1925)
: GOLGI APPARATUS; *also* : DICTYOSOME

**go·liard** \'gōl-yərd, -ˌyärd\ *noun* [Middle English, from Middle French, goliard, glutton, from *gole* throat, from Latin *gula* — more at GLUTTON] (15th century)
: a wandering student of the 12th or 13th century given to the writing of satiric Latin verse and to convivial living and minstrelsy
— **go·liar·dic** \gōl-'yär-dik\ *adjective*

**Go·li·ath** \gə-'lī-əth\ *noun* [Hebrew *Golyath*]
**1** : a Philistine champion who in I Samuel 17 is killed by David
**2** : GIANT

**gol·li·wog** *also* **gol·ly·wog** *or* **gol·li·wogg** \'gä-lē-ˌwäg\ *noun* [*Golliwogg*, an animated doll in children's fiction by Bertha Upton (died 1912) American writer] (1895)
**1** : a grotesque black doll
**2** : a person resembling a golliwog

**gol·ly** \'gä-lē\ *interjection* [euphemism for *God*] (1775)
— used as a mild oath or to express surprise

**Go·mor·rah** \gə-'mór-ə\ *noun* [from *Gomorrah*, ancient city destroyed by God for its wickedness in Genesis 19] (1907)
: a place notorious for vice and corruption

**gon-** *or* **gono-** *combining form* [Greek, from *gonos* procreation, seed, from *gignesthai* to be born — more at KIN]
: sexual : generative : semen : seed (*gonocyte*)

**-gon** *noun combining form* [New Latin *-gonum*, from Greek *-gōnon*, from *gōnia* angle; akin to Greek *gony* knee — more at KNEE]
: figure having (so many) angles (decagon)

**go·nad** \'gō-ˌnad\ *noun* [New Latin *gonad-, gonas*, from Greek *gonos*] (1880)
: a reproductive gland (as an ovary or testis) that produces gametes
— **go·nad·al** \gō-'na-dᵊl\ *adjective*

**go·nad·ec·to·my** \ˌgō-nə-'dek-tə-mē\ *noun, plural* **-mies** (1915)
: surgical removal of an ovary or testis
— **go·nad·ec·to·mized** \-ˌmīzd\ *adjective*

**go·nad·o·trop·ic** \ˌgō-ˌna-də-'trä-pik\ *also* **go·nad·o·tro·phic** \-'trō-fik, -'trä-\ *adjective* (circa 1923)
: acting on or stimulating the gonads

**go·nad·o·tro·pin** \-'trō-pən\ *also* **go·nad·o·tro·phin** \-fən\ *noun* (1931)
: a gonadotropic hormone (as follicle-stimulating hormone)

**Gond** \'gänd\ *noun* (1801)
: a member of a Dravidian or pre-Dravidian people of central India

**Gondi** \'gän-dē\ *noun* (1855)

---

: the Dravidian language of the Gonds

**gon·do·la** \'gän-də-lə (*usual for sense 1*), gän-'dō-\ *noun* [Italian dialect (Venetian), probably from Middle Greek *kontoura* small vessel] (1549)

**1** : a long narrow flat-bottomed boat with a high prow and stern used on the canals of Venice

**2** : a heavy flat-bottomed boat used on New England rivers and on the Ohio and Mississippi rivers

gondola 1

**3** : a railroad car with no top, a flat bottom, and fixed sides that is used chiefly for hauling heavy bulk commodities

**4 a** : an elongated car attached to the underside of an airship **b** : an often spherical airtight enclosure suspended from a balloon for carrying passengers or instruments **c** : an enclosed car suspended from a cable and used for transporting passengers; *especially* : one used as a ski lift

**gon·do·lier** \ˌgän-də-'lir\ *noun* (1603)
: one who propels a gondola

**gone** \'gȯn *also* 'gän\ *adjective* [from past participle of *go*] (1598)

**1 a** : DEAD **b** : LOST, RUINED ⟨lost looks and *gone* faculties —Penelope Gilliatt⟩ **c** : characterized by sinking or dropping ⟨the empty or *gone* feeling in the abdomen so common in elevators —H. G. Armstrong⟩

**2 a** : INVOLVED, ABSORBED ⟨far *gone* in hysteria⟩ **b** : possessed with a strong attachment or a foolish or unreasoning love or desire : INFATUATED — often used with *on* ⟨was real *gone* on that man —Pete Martin⟩ **c** : PREGNANT ⟨she's six months *gone*⟩

**3** : PAST ⟨memories of *gone* summers —John Cheever⟩

**4** *slang* : GREAT ⟨a real *gone* fashion reporter —Inez Robb⟩

**G₁ phase** \ˌjē-'wən-\ *noun* [growth] (1966)
: the period in the cell cycle from the end of cell division to the beginning of DNA replication — compare G₂ PHASE, M PHASE, S PHASE

**gon·er** \'gȯ-nər *also* 'gä-nər\ *noun* (1854)
: one whose case is hopeless

**gon·fa·lon** \'gän-fə-ˌlän, -lən\ *noun* [Italian *gonfalone*] (1595)

**1** : the ensign of certain princes or states (as the medieval republics of Italy)

**2** : a flag that hangs from a crosspiece or frame

**gong** \'gäŋ, 'gȯŋ\ *noun* [Malay & Javanese, of imitative origin] (circa 1590)

**1** : a disk-shaped percussion instrument that produces a resounding tone when struck with a usually padded hammer

**2 a** : a saucer-shaped bell (as in a fire alarm) that is struck by a mechanical hammer **b** : a wire rod wound in a flat spiral for sounding the time or chime or alarm (as in a clock)

**3** *British* : MEDAL

— **gong** *intransitive verb*

**Gon·go·rism** \'gäŋ-gə-ˌri-zəm\ *noun* [Spanish *gongorismo*, from Luis de *Góngora* y Argote (died 1627) Spanish poet] (1813)
: a literary style characterized by studied obscurity and by the use of various ornate devices

— **gon·go·ris·tic** \ˌgäŋ-gə-'ris-tik\ *adjective*

**go·nid·i·um** \gō-'ni-dē-əm\ *noun, plural* **-ia** \-dē-ə\ [New Latin, from *gon-* + *-idium*] (1882)
: an asexual reproductive cell or group of cells especially in algae (as volvox)

**gon·if, gon·iff** \'gä-nəf\ *variant of* GANEF

**go·ni·om·e·ter** \ˌgō-nē-'ä-mə-tər\ *noun* [Greek *gōnia* angle] (1766)

**1** : an instrument for measuring angles

**2** : DIRECTION FINDER

— **go·nio·met·ric** \-nē-ə-'me-trik\ *adjective*

— **go·ni·om·e·try** \-nē-ə-'ä-mə-trē\ *noun*

**-gonium** *combining form* [New Latin, from Greek *gonos*]

**1** : germ cell ⟨spermato*gonium*⟩

**2** : reproductive structure of a plant or fungus ⟨oo*gonium*⟩

**gon·o·coc·cus** \ˌgä-nə-'kä-kəs\ *noun, plural* **-coc·ci** \-'käk-ˌsī, -(ˌ)sē; -'kä-ˌkī, -(ˌ)kē\ [New Latin] (1889)
: a pus-producing bacterium (*Neisseria gonorrhoeae*) that causes gonorrhea

— **gon·o·coc·cal** \-'kä-kəl\ *adjective*

**gon·o·cyte** \'gä-nə-ˌsīt\ *noun* [International Scientific Vocabulary] (1900)
: a cell that produces gametes; *especially* : GAMETOCYTE

**go–no–go** \'gō-'nō-ˌgō\ *adjective* (circa 1945)

**1** : being or relating to a required decision to continue or stop a course of action

**2** : being or relating to a point at which a go-no-go decision must be made

**gon·o·phore** \'gä-nə-ˌfōr, -ˌfȯr\ *noun* [International Scientific Vocabulary] (1859)
: an attached reproductive zooid of a hydroid colony

**gon·o·pore** \'gä-nə-ˌpōr, -ˌpȯr\ *noun* (1897)
: a genital pore in some invertebrates and especially some insects

**gon·or·rhea** \ˌgä-nə-'rē-ə\ *noun* [New Latin, from Late Latin, morbid loss of semen, from Greek *gonorrhoia*, from *gon-* + *-rrhoia* -rrhea] (circa 1526)
: a contagious inflammation of the genital mucous membrane caused by the gonococcus — called also *clap*

— **gon·or·rhe·al** \-'rē-əl\ *adjective*

**-gony** *noun combining form* [Latin *-gonia*, from Greek, from *gonos*]
: generation : reproduction : manner of coming into being ⟨iso*gony*⟩

**gon·zo** \'gän-(ˌ)zō\ *adjective* [origin unknown] (1971)
: idiosyncratically subjective but engagé ⟨*gonzo* journalism⟩; *also* : BIZARRE

**goo** \'gü\ *noun* [perhaps short for *burgoo*] (1900)

**1** : a viscid or sticky substance

**2** : sentimental tripe

— **goo·ey** \-ē\ *adjective*

— **goo·ey·ness** \-nəs\ *noun*

**goo·ber** \'gü-bər, 'gu̇-\ *noun* [of Bantu origin; akin to Kimbundu *ŋguba* peanut] (1833)
*Southern & Midland* : PEANUT

**¹good** \'gu̇d\ *adjective* **bet·ter** \'be-tər\; **best** \'best\ [Middle English, from Old English *gōd*; akin to Old High German *guot* good, Sanskrit *gadhya* what one clings to] (before 12th century)

**1 a** (1) : of a favorable character or tendency ⟨*good* news⟩ (2) : BOUNTIFUL, FERTILE ⟨*good* land⟩ (3) : HANDSOME, ATTRACTIVE ⟨*good* looks⟩ **b** (1) : SUITABLE, FIT ⟨*good* to eat⟩ (2) : free from injury or disease ⟨one *good* arm⟩ (3) : not depreciated ⟨bad money drives out *good*⟩ (4) : commercially sound ⟨a *good* risk⟩ (5) : that can be relied on ⟨*good* for another year⟩ ⟨*good* for a hundred dollars⟩ ⟨always *good* for a laugh⟩ (6) : PROFITABLE, ADVANTAGEOUS ⟨made a very *good* deal⟩ **c** (1) : AGREEABLE, PLEASANT ⟨had a *good* time⟩ (2) : SALUTARY, WHOLESOME ⟨*good* for a cold⟩ (3) : AMUSING, CLEVER ⟨a *good* joke⟩ **d** (1) : of a noticeably large size or quantity : CONSIDERABLE ⟨won by a *good* margin⟩ ⟨a *good* bit of the time⟩ (2) : FULL ⟨waited a *good* hour⟩ (3) — used as an intensive ⟨a

*good* many of us⟩ **e** (1) : WELL-FOUNDED, COGENT ⟨*good* reasons⟩ (2) : TRUE ⟨holds *good* for society at large⟩ (3) : deserving of respect : HONORABLE ⟨in *good* standing⟩ (4) : legally valid or effectual ⟨*good* title⟩ **f** (1) : ADEQUATE, SATISFACTORY ⟨*good* care⟩ — often used in faint praise ⟨his serve is only *good* —Frank Deford⟩ (2) : conforming to a standard ⟨*good* English⟩ (3) : CHOICE, DISCRIMINATING ⟨*good* taste⟩ (4) : containing less fat and being less tender than higher grades — used of meat and especially of beef

**2 a** (1) : VIRTUOUS, RIGHT, COMMENDABLE ⟨a *good* person⟩ ⟨*good* conduct⟩ (2) : KIND, BENEVOLENT ⟨*good* intentions⟩ **b** : UPPER-CLASS ⟨a *good* family⟩ **c** : COMPETENT, SKILLFUL ⟨a *good* doctor⟩ **d** (1) : LOYAL ⟨a *good* party man⟩ ⟨a *good* Catholic⟩ (2) : CLOSE ⟨a *good* friend⟩ **e** : free from infirmity or sorrow ⟨I feel *good*⟩ ▪

— **good·ish** \'gu̇-dish\ *adjective*

— **as good as** : in effect : VIRTUALLY ⟨as *good* as dead⟩

— **as good as gold 1** : of the highest worth or reliability ⟨his promise is as *good* as gold⟩ **2** : well-behaved ⟨the child was as *good* as gold⟩

— **good and** \ˌgu̇d-ᵊn\ : VERY, ENTIRELY ⟨was *good and* mad⟩

**²good** *noun* (before 12th century)

**1 a** : something that is good **b** (1) : something conforming to the moral order of the universe (2) : praiseworthy character : GOODNESS **c** : a good element or portion

**2 a** : advancement of prosperity or well-being ⟨the *good* of the community⟩ ⟨it's for your own *good*⟩ **b** : something useful or beneficial ⟨it's no *good* trying⟩

**3 a** : something that has economic utility or satisfies an economic want **b** *plural* : personal property having intrinsic value but usually excluding money, securities, and negotiable instruments **c** *plural* : CLOTH **d** *plural* : something manufactured or produced for sale : WARES, MERCHANDISE ⟨canned *goods*⟩ **e** *plural, British* : FREIGHT

**4** : good persons — used with *the*

**5** *plural* **a** : the qualities required to achieve an end **b** : proof of wrongdoing ⟨didn't have the *goods* on him —T. G. Cooke⟩

— **for good** *also* **for good and all** : FOREVER, PERMANENTLY

— **in good with** : in a favored position with

— **to the good 1** : for the best : BENEFICIAL ⟨efforts to restrict credit were all *to the good* —*Time*⟩ **2** : in a position of net gain or profit ⟨wound up $10 *to the good*⟩

**³good** *adverb* (13th century)

**1** : WELL ⟨he showed me how *good* I was doing —Herbert Gold⟩

□ **USAGE**

**good** An old notion that it is wrong to say "I feel good" in reference to health still occasionally appears in print. The origins of this notion, which goes back to the turn of the century, are obscure, but they seem to combine someone's idea that *good* should be reserved to describe virtue and uncertainty about whether an adverb or an adjective should follow *feel*. Today nearly everyone agrees that both *good* and *well* can be predicate adjectives after *feel*. Both are used to express good health, but *good* may connote good spirits in addition to good health.

**2** — used as an intensive ⟨a *good* 200 pounds⟩ ⟨a *good* long time⟩ ■

**good book** *noun, often G&B capitalized* (1860)
**:** BIBLE

**good-bye** *or* **good-by** \gu̇d-'bī, gə(d)-\ *noun* [alteration of *God be with you*] (circa 1580)
**1 :** a concluding remark or gesture at parting — often used interjectionally
**2 :** a taking of leave ⟨a tearful *good-bye*⟩ ◆

**good deal** *noun* (1881)
**:** a considerable quantity or extent **:** LOT ⟨knows a *good deal* about disease⟩ ⟨a *good deal* faster⟩

**good faith** *noun* (1893)
**:** honesty or lawfulness of purpose

**good fellow** *noun* (13th century)
**:** an affable companionable person
— **good-fel·low·ship** \'gu̇d-'fe-lō-,ship, -'fe-lə-\ *noun*

**good-for-noth·ing** \'gu̇d-fər-,nə-thiŋ\ *adjective* (1533)
**:** of no use or value
— **good-for-nothing** *noun*

**Good Friday** *noun* [from its special sanctity] (13th century)
**:** the Friday before Easter observed in churches as the anniversary of the crucifixion of Christ and in some states of the U.S. as a legal holiday

**good-heart·ed** \'gu̇d-'här-təd\ *adjective* (1552)
**:** having a kindly generous disposition
— **good-heart·ed·ly** *adverb*
— **good-heart·ed·ness** *noun*

**good-hu·mored** \-'(h)yü-mərd\ *adjective* (1662)
**:** GOOD-NATURED, CHEERFUL
— **good-hu·mored·ly** *adverb*
— **good-hu·mored·ness** *noun*

**good life** *noun* (1946)
**:** a life marked by a high standard of living

**good-look·ing** \'gu̇d-'lu̇-kiŋ\ *adjective* (1780)
**:** having a pleasing or attractive appearance
— **good-look·er** \-'lu̇-kər\ *noun*

**good·ly** \'gu̇d-lē\ *adjective* **good·li·er; -est** (before 12th century)
**1 :** pleasantly attractive
**2 :** significantly large **:** CONSIDERABLE ⟨a *goodly* number⟩

**good·man** \'gu̇d-mən\ *noun* (13th century)
**1** *archaic* **:** the master of a household
**2** *archaic* **:** MR.

**good-na·tured** \-'nā-chərd\ *adjective* (1577)
**:** of a pleasant cheerful cooperative disposition
**synonym** see AMIABLE
— **good-na·tured·ly** *adverb*
— **good-na·tured·ness** *noun*

**good-neighbor** *adjective* (1936)
**:** marked by principles of friendship, cooperation, and noninterference in the internal affairs of another country ⟨a *good-neighbor* policy⟩

**good·ness** \'gu̇d-nəs\ *noun* (before 12th century)
**1 :** the quality or state of being good
**2** — used interjectionally or in phrases especially to express mild surprise or shock ⟨oh, my *goodness*!⟩ ⟨*goodness* knows⟩
**3 :** the nutritious, flavorful, or beneficial part of something

**goodness of fit** (circa 1939)
**:** the conformity between an experimental result and theoretical expectation or between data and an approximating curve

**good offices** *noun plural* (1904)
**:** services as a mediator

**good old boy** *or* **good ol' boy** *or* **good ole boy** \'gu̇-dōl(d)-,bȯi\ *noun* (circa 1967)
**:** a usually white Southerner who conforms to the social behavior of his peers

**Good Samaritan** *noun* (1846)
**:** SAMARITAN 2

**good-tem·pered** \'gu̇d-'tem-pərd\ *adjective* (1768)
**:** not easily vexed
— **good-tem·pered·ly** *adverb*

— **good-tem·pered·ness** *noun*

**good-wife** \'gu̇d-,wīf\ *noun* (13th century)
**1** *archaic* **:** the mistress of a household
**2** *archaic* **:** MRS.

**good·will** \,gu̇d-'wil\ *noun* (before 12th century)
**1 a :** a kindly feeling of approval and support **:** benevolent interest or concern **b** (1) **:** the favor or prestige that a business has acquired beyond the mere value of what it sells (2) **:** the value of projected earnings increases of a business especially as part of its purchase price (3) **:** the value of other intangible assets (as tax credits) of a business especially as part of its purchase price
**2 a :** cheerful consent **b :** willing effort
— **good-willed** \-'wild\ *adjective*

**¹goody** \'gu̇-dē\ *noun* [alteration of *goodwife*] (1559)
*archaic* **:** a usually married woman of lowly station — used as a title preceding a surname

**²goody** *or* **good·ie** *noun, plural* **good·ies** (1756)
**1 :** something that is particularly attractive, pleasurable, good, or desirable
**2** *chiefly British* **:** one that is good; *especially* **:** an opponent of the villain (as in a motion picture)

**goody–goody** \,gu̇-dē-'gu̇-dē\ *adjective* (1871)
**:** affectedly or ingratiatingly good or proper
— **goody–goody** *noun*

**Goody Two-shoes** \'gu̇-dē-'tü-,shüz\ *noun, often S capitalized* [from *Goody Two-Shoes*, heroine of a children's story perhaps by Oliver Goldsmith] (1934)
**:** a person who is goody-goody; *also* **:** a person who is uncommonly good
— **goody–two–shoes** *adjective*

**¹goof** \'güf\ *noun* [probably alteration of English dialect *goff* (simpleton)] (1915)
**1 :** a silly or stupid person
**2 :** BLUNDER

**²goof** (1932)
*intransitive verb*
**1 a :** to spend time idly or foolishly — usually used with *off* **b :** to engage in playful activity — usually used with *around*
**2 :** to make a usually foolish or careless mistake **:** BLUNDER — often used with *up*
*transitive verb*
**:** to make a mess of **:** BUNGLE — usually used with *up*
— **goof on** *slang* **:** to make fun of **:** KID, PUT ON ⟨you're *goofing on* me, right?⟩

**goof·ball** \'güf-,bȯl\ *noun* (1950)
**1** *slang* **:** a barbiturate sleeping pill
**2 :** a goofy person

**go off** *intransitive verb* (1579)
**1 :** EXPLODE
**2 :** to burst forth or break out suddenly or noisily
**3 :** to go forth, out, or away **:** LEAVE
**4 :** to undergo decline or deterioration
**5 :** to follow the expected or desired course **:** PROCEED ⟨the party *went off* well⟩
**6 :** to make a characteristic noise **:** SOUND
— **go off the deep end 1 :** to enter recklessly on a course **2 :** to become very much excited

**goof-off** \'gü-,fȯf\ *noun* (1953)
**:** one who evades work or responsibility

**goofy** \'gü-fē\ *adjective* **goof·i·er; -est** (1921)
**:** being crazy, ridiculous, or mildly ludicrous **:** SILLY
— **goof·i·ly** \-fə-lē\ *adverb*
— **goof·i·ness** \-fē-nəs\ *noun*

**goo·gly-eyed** \'gü-glē-,īd\ *adjective* [by alteration] (1926)
**:** GOGGLE-EYED

**goo·gol** \'gü-,gȯl\ *noun* [coined by Milton Sirotta (born about 1929) nephew of Edward Kasner (died 1955) American mathematician] (1938)

**:** the figure 1 followed by 100 zeroes equal to $10^{100}$ ◆

**goo·gol·plex** \-,pleks\ *noun* (1938)
**:** the figure 1 followed by a googol of zeroes equal to

$$10^{googol} \text{ or } 10^{10^{100}}$$

**¹goo-goo** \'gü-(,)gü\ *adjective* [perhaps alteration of *²goggle*] (1900)
**:** LOVING, ENTICING — used chiefly in the phrase *goo-goo eyes*

**²goo-goo** *noun, plural* **goo-goos** [from *good government*] (1912)
**:** a member or advocate of a political reform movement

**¹gook** \'gük\ *noun* [origin unknown] (1935)
**:** a nonwhite or non-American person; *specifically* **:** ASIAN — usually used disparagingly

**²gook** \'gu̇k, 'gük\ *variant of* GUCK

**goon** \'gün\ *noun* [probably short for English dialect *gooney* (simpleton)] (1921)
**1 :** a stupid person
**2 :** a man hired to terrorize or eliminate opponents

**go on** *intransitive verb* (15th century)

□ USAGE
**good** Adverbial *good* has been under attack from the schoolroom since the 19th century. Insistence on *well* rather than *good* has resulted in a split in connotation: *well* is standard, neutral, and colorless, while *good* is emotionally charged and emphatic. This makes *good* the adverb of choice in sports ⟨"I'm seeing the ball real *good*" is what you hear —Roger Angell⟩. In such contexts as ⟨listen up. And listen *good* —Alex Karras⟩ ⟨lets fly with his tomatoes before they can flee. He gets Clarence *good* —Charles Dickinson⟩ *good* cannot be adequately replaced by *well*. Adverbial *good* is primarily a spoken form; in writing it occurs in reported and fictional speech and in generally familiar or informal contexts.

◇ WORD HISTORY
**good-bye** In Spanish *adios* and French *adieu* "farewell, good-bye," we see an explicit wish that the person addressed should be in the care of God (*dios, dieu*). The same sentiment lies at the origin of *good-bye*, which comes from the phrase *God be with you*. Gradually eroded over time, it appears in such versions as *God be wy you* (in the 16th century), *God b'y you* (a century later), and numerous other versions before settling into *good-bye* in the 19th century, the final form buttressed by the example of *good night* and *good day*. *Good-bye* was further shortened simply to *bye*, at which point reduction could scarcely proceed further. To some speakers, indeed, this meager monosyllable seemed in need of fattening, so they produced the reduplication *bye-bye*.

**googol** A *googol* is a very big number whose name was coined by a small boy. In the late 1930s American mathematician Edward Kasner (1878–1955) found himself working with numbers as large as 1 followed by a hundred zeroes. While it is possible to write this number, using scientific notation, simply as $10^{100}$, Kasner felt that having a name for it would facilitate discussing it. According to his own account, he asked his nine-year-old nephew Milton Sirotta to supply a name, promising that he would indeed use the word. Milton produced *googol*, Kasner kept his promise, and the word was accepted in the mathematical community.

**1 a :** to continue on or as if on a journey ⟨life *goes on*⟩ ⟨*went on* to greater things⟩ **b :** to keep on **: CONTINUE** ⟨*went on* smoking⟩ **c :** PROCEED ⟨*went on* to win the election⟩
**2 :** to take place **: HAPPEN** ⟨what's *going on*⟩
**3 :** to talk especially in an effusive manner ⟨the way people *go on* about their ancestors —Hamilton Basso⟩

**goo·ney** *or* **goo·ny** \'gü-nē\ *noun, plural* **gooneys** *or* **goonies** [probably from English dialect *gooney* (simpleton)] (1895)
**:** BLACK-FOOTED ALBATROSS; *broadly* **:** ALBATROSS

**goop** \'güp\ *noun* [probably alteration of *goo*] (circa 1958)
**:** GOO, GUNK

**goo·san·der** \gü-'san-dər\ *noun* [origin unknown] (1766)
**:** the common merganser (*Mergus merganser*) of the northern hemisphere

**¹goose** \'güs\ *noun, plural* **geese** \'gēs\ [Middle English *gos*, from Old English *gōs*; akin to Old High German *gans* goose, Latin *anser*, Greek *chēn*] (before 12th century)
**1 a :** any of numerous large waterfowl (family Anatidae) that are intermediate between the swans and ducks and have long necks, feathered lores, and reticulate tarsi **b :** a female goose as distinguished from a gander
**2 :** SIMPLETON, DOLT
**3** *plural* **goos·es :** a tailor's smoothing iron with a gooseneck handle
**4** *plural* **goos·es :** a poke between the buttocks

**²goose** *transitive verb* **goosed; goos·ing** (circa 1880)
**1 :** to poke between the buttocks with an upward thrust
**2 :** to increase the activity, speed, power, intensity, or amount of **: SPUR** ⟨an effort to *goose* newsstand sales⟩

**goose·ber·ry** \'güs-,ber-ē, 'güz-, -b(ə-)rē, *chiefly British* 'güz-\ *noun* (1573)
**1 a :** the acid usually prickly fruit of any of several shrubs (genus *Ribes*) of the saxifrage family **b :** a shrub bearing gooseberries
**2 :** CURRANT 2

**goose bumps** *noun plural* (1933)
**:** a roughness of the skin produced by erection of its papillae especially from cold, fear, or a sudden feeling of excitement

gooseberry: leaves and fruit

**goose egg** *noun* (1866)
**:** ZERO, NOTHING; *especially* **:** a score of zero in a game or contest

**goose·fish** \'güs-,fish\ *noun* (1807)
**:** any of a family (Lophiidae) of pediculate fishes with a large flattened head, a fringe of flaps along each side of the lower jaw, head, and body, and a long stalk on the head with a flap of flesh at the tip for attracting prey; *especially* **:** MONKFISH

**goose·flesh** \'güs-,flesh\ *noun* (circa 1810)
**:** GOOSE BUMPS

**goose·foot** \-,fut\ *noun, plural* **goose·foots** (1548)
**:** any of a genus (*Chenopodium*) or family (Chenopodiaceae, the goosefoot family) of glabrous herbs with utricular fruit

**goose·grass** \-,gras\ *noun* (1530)
**1 :** CLEAVERS
**2 :** YARD GRASS

**goose·neck** \'güs-,nek\ *noun, often attributive* (1688)
**1 :** something (as a flexible jointed metal pipe) curved like the neck of a goose or U-shaped
**2 :** a truck trailer (as for transporting livestock) with a projecting front end designed to attach to the bed of a pickup truck
**— goose·necked** \-,nekt\ *adjective*

**goose pimples** *noun plural* (circa 1889)
**:** GOOSE BUMPS

**goose–step** \'güs-,step\ *intransitive verb* (1879)
**1 :** to march in a goose step
**2 :** to practice an unthinking conformity

**goose step** *noun* (1806)
**:** a straight-legged stiff-kneed step used by troops of some armies when passing in review

**goos·ey** \'gü-sē\ *adjective* **goos·i·er; -est** (1811)
**1 :** resembling a goose
**2 a :** affected with goose bumps **: SCARED b :** very nervous **c :** reacting strongly when goosed or startled

**go out** *intransitive verb* (before 12th century)
**1 a :** to go forth, abroad, or outdoors; *specifically* **:** to leave one's house **b** (1) **:** to take the field as a soldier (2) **:** to participate as a principal in a duel **c :** to travel as or as if a colonist or immigrant **d :** to work away from home
**2 a :** to come to an end **b :** to give up office **: RESIGN c :** to become obsolete or unfashionable **d** (1) **:** to play the last card of one's hand (2) **:** to reach or exceed the total number of points required for game in cards
**3 :** to take part in social activities
**4 :** to go on strike
**5 :** BREAK, COLLAPSE
**6 :** to become a candidate ⟨*went out* for the football team⟩

**go over** *intransitive verb* (1645)
**1 :** to go on a journey
**2 :** to become converted
**3 :** to receive approval **: SUCCEED** ⟨his plan *went over* well⟩

**¹go·pher** \'gō-fər\ *noun* [origin unknown] (1791)
**1 :** a burrowing land tortoise (*Gopherus polyphemus*) of the southern U.S.; *broadly* **:** any of several related land tortoises — called also *gopher tortoise*
**2 a :** any of a family (Geomyidae) of burrowing rodents of western North America, Central America, and the southern U.S. that are the size of a large rat and have large cheek pouches opening beside the mouth — called also *pocket gopher* **b :** any of several small ground squirrels (genus *Citellus*) of the prairie region of North America closely related to the chipmunks
**3 :** GOPHER BALL

**²gopher** *variant of* GOFER

**gopher ball** *noun* (circa 1949)
**:** a pitched baseball hit for a home run

**gopher snake** *noun* (1837)
**1 :** INDIGO SNAKE
**2 :** BULL SNAKE

**Gor·di·an knot** \'gor-dē-ən-\ *noun*
**1 :** an intricate problem; *especially* **:** a problem insoluble in its own terms — usually used in the phrase *cut the Gordian knot*
**2 :** a knot tied by Gordius, king of Phrygia, held to be capable of being untied only by the future ruler of Asia, and cut by Alexander the Great with his sword

**Gor·don setter** \'gor-d°n-\ *noun* [Alexander, 4th Duke of *Gordon* (died 1827) Scottish sportsman] (1865)
**:** any of a breed of large bird dogs that have a long flat black-and-tan coat

**¹gore** \'gōr, 'gor\ *noun* [Middle English, from Old English *gāra*; akin to Old English *gār* spear, and perhaps to Greek *chaion* shepherd's staff] (before 12th century)
**1 :** a small usually triangular piece of land
**2 a :** a tapering or triangular piece (as of cloth in a skirt) **b :** an elastic gusset for providing a snug fit in a shoe

**²gore** *transitive verb* **gored; gor·ing** (1548)

Gordon setter

**1 :** to cut into a tapering triangular form
**2 :** to provide with a gore

**³gore** *transitive verb* **gored; gor·ing** [Middle English] (15th century)
**:** to pierce or wound with something pointed (as a horn or knife) ⟨*gored* by a bull⟩

**⁴gore** *noun* [Middle English, filth, from Old English *gor*] (1563)
**:** BLOOD; *especially* **:** clotted blood

**¹gorge** \'gorj\ *noun* [Middle English, from Middle French, from Late Latin *gurga*, alteration of *gurges*, from Latin, whirlpool — more at VORACIOUS] (14th century)
**1 :** THROAT — often used with *rise* to indicate revulsion accompanied by a sensation of constriction ⟨my *gorge* rises at the sight of blood⟩
**2 a :** a hawk's crop **b :** STOMACH, BELLY
**3 :** the entrance into an outwork (as a bastion) of a fort
**4 :** a narrow passage through land; *especially* **:** a narrow steep-walled canyon or part of a canyon
**5 :** a primitive device used instead of a fishhook that consists of an object (as a piece of bone attached in the middle of a line) easy to swallow but difficult to eject
**6 :** a mass choking a passage ⟨a river dammed by an ice *gorge*⟩
**7 :** the line on the front of a coat or jacket formed by the crease of the lapel and collar

**²gorge** *verb* **gorged; gorg·ing** (14th century)
*intransitive verb*
**:** to eat greedily or to repletion
*transitive verb*
**1 a :** to stuff to capacity **: GLUT b :** to fill completely or to the point of distension ⟨veins *gorged* with blood⟩
**2 :** to consume greedily
**synonym** *see* SATIATE
**— gorg·er** *noun*

**³gorge** *noun* (1854)
**:** the act or an instance of gorging

**gor·geous** \'gor-jəs\ *adjective* [Middle English *gorgayse*, from Middle French *gorgias* elegant, from *gorgias* wimple, from *gorge* gorget] (15th century)
**:** splendidly or showily brilliant or magnificent
**synonym** *see* SPLENDID
**— gor·geous·ly** *adverb*
**— gor·geous·ness** *noun*

**gor·get** \'gor-jət\ *noun* [Middle English, from Middle French, from *gorge*] (15th century)
**1 :** a piece of armor protecting the throat — see ARMOR illustration
**2 a :** an ornamental collar **b :** a part of a wimple covering the throat and shoulders

**gor·gon** \'gor-gən\ *noun* [Latin *Gorgon-, Gorgo*, from Greek *Gorgōn*]
**1** *capitalized* **:** any of three snake-haired sisters in Greek mythology whose appearance turns the beholder to stone
**2 :** an ugly or repulsive woman
**— Gor·go·ni·an** \gor-'gō-nē-ən\ *adjective*

**gor·go·ni·an** \gor-'gō-nē-ən\ *noun* [New Latin *Gorgonia*, a coral genus, from Latin, coral, from *Gorgon-, Gorgo*] (1835)
**:** any of an order (Gorgonacea) of colonial anthozoans with a usually horny and branching axial skeleton
**— gorgonian** *adjective*

**gor·gon·ize** \'gor-gə-,nīz\ *transitive verb* **-ized; -iz·ing** (1609)
**:** to have a paralyzing or mesmerizing effect on **: STUPEFY, PETRIFY**

**Gor·gon·zo·la** \,gor-gən-'zō-lə\ *noun* [Italian, from *Gorgonzola*, Italy] (1878)
**:** a pungent blue cheese of Italian origin

**go·ril·la** \gə-'ri-lə\ *noun* [New Latin, from Greek *Gorillai*, plural, a tribe of hairy women

\ə\ abut \ᵊ\ kitten \ər\ further \a\ ash \ā\ ace \ä\ mop, mar \aú\ out \ch\ chin \e\ bet \ē\ easy \g\ go \i\ hit \ī\ ice \j\ job \ŋ\ sing \ō\ go \o\ law \oi\ boy \th\ thin \t͟h\ the \ü\ loot \ú\ foot \y\ yet \zh\ vision  *see also* Guide to Pronunciation mentioned in an account of a voyage around Africa) (1847)

**1 :** an anthropoid ape (*Gorilla gorilla*) of western equatorial Africa related to the chimpanzee but less erect and much larger

**2 a :** an ugly or brutal man **b :** THUG, GOON ◆

**gor·man·dise** *chiefly British variant of* GORMANDIZE

**gor·man·dize** \ˈgȯr-mən-ˌdīz\ *verb* **-dized; -diz·ing** [*gormand*, alteration of *gourmand*] (1548)

*intransitive verb*
**:** to eat gluttonously or ravenously
*transitive verb*
**:** to eat greedily **:** DEVOUR
— **gor·man·diz·er** *noun*

**gorm·less** \ˈgȯrm-ləs\ *adjective* [alteration of English dialect *gaumless*, from *gaum* attention, understanding (from Middle English *gome*, from Old Norse *gaum, gaumr*) + *-less*] (1883)

*chiefly British* **:** lacking intelligence **:** STUPID

**go–round** \ˈgō-ˌraund\ *noun* (1891)
**:** GO-AROUND

**gorp** \ˈgȯrp\ *noun* [origin unknown] (1968)
**:** a snack consisting of high-energy food (as raisins and nuts)

**gorse** \ˈgȯrs\ *noun* [Middle English *gorst*, from Old English; akin to Old High German *gersta* barley, Latin *hordeum*] (before 12th century)
**:** a spiny yellow-flowered European shrub (*Ulex europaeus*) of the legume family; *broadly* **:** any of several related plants (genera *Ulex* and *Genista*)
— **gorsy** \ˈgȯr-sē\ *adjective*

**gory** \ˈgōr-ē, ˈgȯr-\ *adjective* **gor·i·er; -est** (15th century)
**1 :** covered with gore **:** BLOODSTAINED
**2 :** BLOODCURDLING, SENSATIONAL ⟨wanted to hear the *gory* details⟩
*synonym see* BLOODY

**gosh** \ˈgäsh, ˈgȯsh\ *interjection* [euphemism for *God*] (1757)
— used as a mild oath or to express surprise

**gos·hawk** \ˈgäs-ˌhȯk\ *noun* [Middle English *goshawke*, from Old English *gōshafoc*, from *gōs* goose + *hafoc* hawk] (before 12th century)
**:** any of several long-tailed accipitrine hawks with short rounded wings; *especially* **:** a hawk (*Accipiter gentilis*) of the northern parts of both the Old and the New World that is larger than a crow and has a white stripe above and behind the eye

**gos·ling** \ˈgäz-liŋ, ˈgȯz-, -lən\ *noun* [Middle English, from *gos* goose] (14th century)
**1 :** a young goose
**2 :** a foolish or callow person

**go–slow** \ˌgō-ˈslō\ *noun* (1926)
*British* **:** SLOWDOWN

**¹gos·pel** \ˈgäs-pəl\ *noun* [Middle English, from Old English *gōdspel* (translation of Late Latin *evangelium*), from *gōd* good + *spell* tale — more at SPELL] (before 12th century)
**1** *often capitalized* **:** the message concerning Christ, the kingdom of God, and salvation **b** *capitalized* **:** one of the first four New Testament books telling of the life, death, and resurrection of Jesus Christ; *also* **:** a similar apocryphal book **c :** an interpretation of the Christian message ⟨the social *gospel*⟩
**2** *capitalized* **:** a lection from one of the New Testament Gospels
**3 :** the message or teachings of a religious teacher
**4 :** something accepted as infallible truth or as a guiding principle ⟨the *gospel* of conservation —R. M. Hodesh⟩
**5 :** gospel music

**²gospel** *adjective* (before 12th century)
**1 a :** having a basis in or being in accordance with the gospel **:** EVANGELICAL ⟨ordained to the *gospel* ministry —*Christian Century*⟩ **b :** marked by special or fervid emphasis on the gospel ⟨a *gospel* meeting⟩

**2 :** of, relating to, or being religious songs of American origin associated with evangelism and popular devotion and marked by simple melody and harmony and elements of folk songs and blues

**gos·pel·er** *or* **gos·pel·ler** \ˈgäs-p(ə-)lər\ *noun* (1506)
**1 :** one who reads or sings the liturgical Gospel
**2 :** one who preaches or propounds a gospel

**gospel side** *noun, often G capitalized* [from the custom of reading the Gospel from this side] (1891)
**:** the left side of an altar or chancel as one faces it

**¹gos·sa·mer** \ˈgä-sə-mər *also* ˈgäz-mər, ˈgä-zə-\ *noun* [Middle English *gossomer*, from *gos* goose + *somer* summer] (14th century)
**1 :** a film of cobwebs floating in air in calm clear weather
**2 :** something light, delicate, or insubstantial ⟨the *gossamer* of youth's dreams —Andrea Parke⟩
— **gos·sa·mery** \-mə-rē\ *adjective*

**²gossamer** *adjective* (circa 1807)
**:** extremely light, delicate, or tenuous

**gos·san** \ˈgä-sᵊn\ *noun* [Cornish *gossen*, from *gōs* blood] (1776)
**:** decomposed rock or vein material of reddish or rusty color that results from oxidized pyrites

**¹gos·sip** \ˈgä-səp\ *noun* [Middle English *gossib*, from Old English *godsibb*, from *god* + *sibb* kinsman, from *sibb* related — more at SIB] (before 12th century)
**1 a :** *dialect British* **:** GODPARENT **b :** COMPANION, CRONY **c :** a person who habitually reveals personal or sensational facts about others
**2 a :** rumor or report of an intimate nature **b** **:** a chatty talk **c :** the subject matter of gossip ◆
— **gos·sip·ry** \-sə-prē\ *noun*

**²gossip** *intransitive verb* (1627)
**:** to relate gossip
— **gos·sip·er** *noun*

**gos·sip·mon·ger** \ˈgä-səp-ˌməŋ-gər, -ˌmäŋ-\ *noun* (1836)
**:** a person who starts or spreads gossip

**gos·sipy** \ˈgä-sə-pē\ *adjective* (1818)
**:** characterized by, full of, or given to gossip ⟨a *gossipy* letter⟩ ⟨*gossipy* neighbors⟩

**gos·sy·pol** \ˈgä-sə-ˌpȯl, -ˌpōl\ *noun* [International Scientific Vocabulary, ultimately from Latin *gossypion* cotton] (1899)
**:** a toxic phenolic pigment $C_{30}H_{30}O_8$ in cottonseed

**got** *past and past participle of* GET

**Goth** \ˈgäth\ *noun* [Middle English *Gothes, Gotes* (plural), partly from Old English *Gotan* (plural); partly from Late Latin *Gothi* (plural)] (14th century)
**:** a member of a Germanic people that overran the Roman Empire in the early centuries of the Christian era

**¹Goth·ic** \ˈgä-thik\ *adjective* (1591)
**1 a :** of, relating to, or resembling the Goths, their civilization, or their language **b :** TEUTONIC, GERMANIC **c :** MEDIEVAL **d :** UNCOUTH, BARBAROUS
**2 a :** of, relating to, or having the characteristics of a style of architecture developed in northern France and spreading through western Europe from the middle of the 12th century to the early 16th century that is characterized by the converging of weights and strains at isolated points upon slender vertical piers and counterbalancing buttresses and by pointed arches and vaulting **b :** of or relating to an architectural style reflecting the influence of the medieval Gothic
**3** *often not capitalized* **:** of or relating to a style of fiction characterized by the use of desolate or remote settings and macabre, mysterious, or violent incidents
— **goth·i·cal·ly** \-thi-k(ə-)lē\ *adverb*
— **Goth·ic·ness** \-thik-nəs\ *noun*

**²Gothic** *noun* (1691)
**1 a :** BLACK LETTER **b :** SANS SERIF
**2 :** Gothic art style or decoration; *specifically* **:** the Gothic architectural style
**3 :** the East Germanic language of the Goths — see INDO-EUROPEAN LANGUAGES table
**4** *often not capitalized* **:** a work of fiction in the gothic style

**Gothic arch** *noun* (1739)
**:** a pointed arch; *especially* **:** one with a joint instead of a keystone at its apex

**Goth·i·cism** \ˈgä-thə-ˌsi-zəm\ *noun* (1710)
**1 :** barbarous lack of taste or elegance
**2 :** conformity to or practice of Gothic style
— **Goth·i·cist** \-sist\ *noun*

**goth·i·cize** \-ˌsīz\ *transitive verb* **-cized; -ciz·ing** *often capitalized* (1712)
**:** to make Gothic

**Goth·ick** *chiefly British variant of* GOTHIC

**Gothic Revival** *noun* (1869)
**:** an artistic style or movement of the 18th and 19th centuries inspired by and imitative of the Gothic style especially in architecture

**go through** *intransitive verb* (1513)
**1 :** to continue firmly or obstinately to the end ⟨I was *going through* with it if it killed me —A. W. Long⟩
**2 a :** to receive approval or sanction **:** PASS **b** **:** to come to a desired or satisfactory conclusion

---

◇ WORD HISTORY

**gorilla** In the sixth or early fifth century B.C., the Carthaginian navigator Hanno made a voyage around the west coast of Africa, perhaps sailing as far as Sherbro Island in modern Sierra Leone. An account of his journey was inscribed on tablets that have since disappeared, though a Greek translation survives. Near the furthest point on their voyage Hanno and his men came upon an island "full of wild people, the greater part of whom were females, hairy on their bodies, whom our interpreters called Gorillas. We pursued them, but could not capture the males . . . but we captured three females, who, biting and scratching their captors, refused to go along with them. We killed and skinned them and brought the skins to Carthage." Whether Hanno actually saw a species of anthropoid ape or something else we will never know, but when the gorilla of western equatorial Africa was first described scientifically in 1847, it was given the Latin name *Troglodytes gorilla*. This binomial was superseded by *Gorilla gorilla*, and the vernacular name of the animal in English and other European languages has become simply *gorilla*.

**gossip** In Old English *sibb* occurs as a noun meaning "kinship" and as an adjective meaning "related by blood or kinship." By the 11th century a compound had been formed from the noun *sibb* prefixed by *god*, the predecessor of Modern English *god*. A *godsibb*, therefore, was a person spiritually related to another, specifically by being a sponsor at baptism. Today we would call such a person a *godmother* or *godfather*, using *god* in the same way. By the 14th century the *d* had begun to disappear, and *godsibb* developed into *gossib* and then, through devoicing of the final consonant, to *gossip*, the form that is still current. The meaning, too, had begun to change, and the sense of *gossip* as a close friend or comrade developed alongside the sense of a godparent. Since close friends naturally talk about family and other friends, it was only a short step to the *gossip* of today, a person no longer necessarily friend, relative, or sponsor, but someone filled with irresistible tidbits of rumor.

**go to** *intransitive verb* (15th century)
**1** *archaic* — used interjectionally as an exhortation ⟨and they said one to another, *go to, let us make brick* —Genesis 11:3 (Authorized Version)⟩
**2** *archaic* — used interjectionally to express disapproval or disbelief ⟨*go to, go to;* you have known what you should not —Shakespeare⟩
**gotten** *past participle of* GET
**Göt·ter·däm·mer·ung** \,gə(r)-tər-'de-mə-,rùŋ, -'da-\ *noun* [German, literally, twilight of the gods, from *Götter* (plural of *Gott* god) + *Dämmerung* twilight] (1909)
**:** a collapse (as of a society or regime) marked by catastrophic violence and disorder
**gouache** \'gwäsh\ *noun* [French, from Italian *guazzo*, literally, puddle, probably from Latin *aquatio* watering place, from *aquari* to fetch water, from *aqua* water — more at ISLAND] (1882)
**1 :** a method of painting with opaque watercolors
**2 a :** a picture painted by gouache **b :** the pigment used in gouache
**Gou·da** \'gü-də\ *noun* [*Gouda*, Netherlands] (1885)
**:** a mild cheese of Dutch origin that is similar to Edam but contains more fat
¹**gouge** \'gaúj\ *noun* [Middle English *gowge*, from Middle French *gouge*, from Late Latin *gulbia*, of Celtic origin; akin to Old Irish *gulban* beak, sting] (14th century)
**1 :** a chisel with a concavo-convex cross section
**2 a :** the act of gouging **b :** a groove or cavity scooped out
**3 :** an excessive or improper exaction **:** EXTORTION
²**gouge** *transitive verb* **gouged; goug·ing** (1570)
**1 :** to scoop out with or as if with a gouge
**2 a :** to force out (an eye) with the thumb **b :** to thrust the thumb into the eye of
**3 :** to subject to extortion or undue exaction **:** OVERCHARGE
— **goug·er** *noun*
**gou·lash** \'gü-,läsh, -,lash\ *noun* [Hungarian *gulyás*, short for *gulyáshús*, literally, herdsman's meat] (1866)
**1 :** a stew made with meat (as beef), assorted vegetables, and paprika
**2 :** a round in bridge played with hands produced by a redistribution of previously dealt cards
**3 :** a mixture of heterogeneous elements **:** JUMBLE
**go under** *intransitive verb* (1848)
**:** to be overwhelmed, destroyed, or defeated **:** FAIL
**go up** *intransitive verb* (15th century)
**1** *chiefly British* **:** to attend a university
**2** *of an actor* **:** to become confused
— **go up in flames** **:** BURN
— **go up in smoke** **:** to be destroyed by or as if by burning
**gou·ra·mi** \gü-'rä-mē\ *noun, plural* **-mi** *or* **-mis** *also* **-mies** [Malay dialect (Java), from Javanese *graméh*] (1878)
**:** any of numerous African and Asian tropical freshwater fishes (order Perciformes): as **a :** a large Asian food fish (*Osphronemus goramy*, family Osphronemidae) **b :** any of various small fishes (families Belontiidae and Helostomatidae) often kept in aquariums
**gourd** \'gòrd, 'gòrd, 'gùrd\ *noun* [Middle English *gourde*, from Middle French, from Latin *cucurbita*] (14th century)
**1 :** any of a family (Cucurbitaceae, the gourd family) of chiefly herbaceous tendril-bearing vines including the cucumber, melon, squash, and pumpkin
**2 :** the fruit of a gourd **:** PEPO; *especially* **:** any of various hard-rinded inedible fruits of plants

of two genera (*Lagenaria* and *Cucurbita*) often used for ornament or for vessels and utensils
— **out of one's gourd** *also* **off one's gourd :** CRAZY
**gourde** \'gùrd\ *noun* [American French] (circa 1858)
— see MONEY table
**gour·mand** \'gùr-,mänd, -mənd\ *noun* [Middle English, from Middle French *gourmant*] (15th century)
**1 :** one who is excessively fond of eating and drinking
**2 :** one who is heartily interested in good food and drink
*synonym* see EPICURE
— **gour·mand·ism** \'gùr-,män-,di-zəm, -mən-\ *noun*
— **gour·man·dize** \-,dīz\ *intransitive verb*
**gour·man·dise** \,gùr-män-'dēz\ *noun* [French, from Middle French, from *gourmand*] (15th century)
**:** appreciation of or interest in good food and drink **:** GOURMANDISM
**gour·met** \'gùr-,mā, gùr-'\ *noun* [French, from Middle French, alteration of *gromet* boy servant, vintner's assistant, probably ultimately from Middle English *grom* groom] (1820)
**:** a connoisseur of food and drink; *broadly* **:** CONNOISSEUR 2 ⟨a film *gourmet*⟩
*synonym* see EPICURE
— **gourmet** *adjective*
**gout** \'gaùt\ *noun* [Middle English *goute*, from Old French, gout, drop, from Latin *gutta* drop] (13th century)
**1 :** a metabolic disease marked by a painful inflammation of the joints, deposits of urates in and around the joints, and usually an excessive amount of uric acid in the blood
**2 :** a mass or aggregate especially of something fluid often gushing or bursting forth
— **gouty** \-ē\ *adjective*
**gov·ern** \'gə-vərn\ *verb* [Middle English, from Old French *governer*, from Latin *gubernare* to steer, govern, from Greek *kybernan*] (14th century)
*transitive verb*
**1 a :** to exercise continuous sovereign authority over; *especially* **:** to control and direct the making and administration of policy in **b :** to rule without sovereign power and usually without having the authority to determine basic policy
**2 a** *archaic* **:** MANIPULATE **b :** to control the speed of (as a machine) especially by automatic means
**3 a :** to control, direct, or strongly influence the actions and conduct of **b :** to exert a determining or guiding influence in or over ⟨income must *govern* expenditure⟩ **c :** to hold in check **:** RESTRAIN
**4 :** to require (a word) to be in a certain case
**5 :** to serve as a precedent or deciding principle for ⟨customs that *govern* human decisions⟩
*intransitive verb*
**1 :** to prevail or have decisive influence **:** CONTROL
**2 :** to exercise authority
— **gov·ern·able** \-vər-nə-bəl\ *adjective*
**gov·er·nance** \'gə-vər-nən(t)s\ *noun* (14th century)
**:** GOVERNMENT
**gov·ern·ess** \'gə-vər-nəs\ *noun* (15th century)
**1 :** a woman who governs
**2 :** a woman entrusted with the care and supervision of a child especially in a private household
**gov·ern·essy** \'gə-vər-ni-sē\ *adjective* (1872)
**:** characteristic of or resembling a governess (as in primness)
**gov·ern·ment** \'gə-vər(n)-mənt, -və-mənt; 'gə-b°m-ənt, -v°m-\ *noun, often attributive* (14th century)
**1 :** the act or process of governing; *specifically* **:** authoritative direction or control

**2** *obsolete* **:** moral conduct or behavior **:** DISCRETION
**3 a :** the office, authority, or function of governing **b** *obsolete* **:** the term during which a governing official holds office
**4 :** the continuous exercise of authority over and the performance of functions for a political unit **:** RULE
**5 a :** the organization, machinery, or agency through which a political unit exercises authority and performs functions and which is usually classified according to the distribution of power within it **b :** the complex of political institutions, laws, and customs through which the function of governing is carried out
**6 :** the body of persons that constitutes the governing authority of a political unit or organization: as **a :** the officials comprising the governing body of a political unit and constituting the organization as an active agency **b** *capitalized* **:** the executive branch of the U.S. federal government **c** *capitalized* **:** a small group of persons holding simultaneously the principal political executive offices of a nation or other political unit and being responsible for the direction and supervision of public affairs: (1) **:** such a group in a parliamentary system constituted by the cabinet or by the ministry (2) **:** ADMINISTRATION 4b
**7 :** POLITICAL SCIENCE
— **gov·ern·men·tal** \,gə-vər(n)-'men-t°l\ *adjective*
— **gov·ern·men·tal·ize** \-t°l-,īz\ *transitive verb*
— **gov·ern·men·tal·ly** \-t°l-ē\ *adverb*
**gov·ern·men·tal·ism** \,gə-vər(n)-'men-t°l-,i-zəm\ *noun* (1848)
**1 :** a theory advocating extension of the sphere and degree of government activity
**2 :** the tendency toward extension of the role of government
— **gov·ern·men·tal·ist** \-t°l-ist\ *noun*
**gov·ern·men·tese** \,gə-vər-mən-'tēz\ *noun* (1944)
**:** jargon held to be characteristic of government officials
**gov·er·nor** \'gə-v°n-ər *also* 'gə-vər-nər\ *noun* (14th century)
**1 :** one that governs: as **a :** one that exercises authority especially over an area or group **b :** an official elected or appointed to act as ruler, chief executive, or nominal head of a political unit **c :** COMMANDING OFFICER **d :** the managing director and usually the principal officer of an institution or organization **e :** a member of a group that directs or controls an institution or society
**2 :** TUTOR
**3 a** *slang* **:** one looked upon as governing **b :** MISTER, SIR — usually used as a term of address
**4 a :** an attachment to a machine (as a gasoline engine) for automatic control or limitation of speed **b :** a device giving automatic control (as of pressure or temperature)
— **gov·er·nor·ate** \-ət, -,āt\ *noun*
**governor–general** *noun, plural* **governors–general** *or* **governor–generals** (1586)
**:** a governor of high rank; *especially* **:** one who governs a large territory or has deputy governors under him
**gov·er·nor·ship** \'gə-v°n-ər-,ship *also* 'gə-vər-nər-\ *noun* (1658)
**1 :** the office of governor
**2 :** the period of incumbency of a governor
**gow·an** \'gaù-ən\ *noun* [probably alteration of Middle English *gollan*] (1570)
*chiefly Scottish* **:** DAISY 1; *broadly* **:** a white or yellow field flower

\ə\ abut  \°\ kitten  \ər\ further  \a\ ash  \ā\ ace
\ä\ mop, mar  \aú\ out  \ch\ chin  \e\ bet  \ē\ easy
\g\ go  \i\ hit  \ī\ ice  \j\ job  \ŋ\ sing  \ō\ go
\ò\ law  \òi\ boy  \th\ thin  \t͟h\ the  \ü\ loot  \ú\ foot
\y\ yet  \zh\ vision   *see also* Guide to Pronunciation

— **gow·any** \-ə-nē\ *adjective, chiefly Scottish*

**gown** \ˈgaün\ *noun* [Middle English, from Middle French *goune*, from Late Latin *gunna*, a fur or leather garment] (14th century) **1 a :** a loose flowing outer garment formerly worn by men **b :** a distinctive robe worn by a professional or academic person **c :** a woman's dress **d** (1) **:** DRESSING GOWN (2) **:** NIGHTGOWN **e :** a coverall worn in an operating room **2 :** the body of students and faculty of a college or university ⟨rivalry between town and *gown*⟩
— **gown** *transitive verb*

**gowns·man** \ˈgaünz-mən\ *noun* (1627) **:** a professional or academic person

**goy** \ˈgȯi\ *noun, plural* **goy·im** \ˈgȯi-əm\ *also* **goys** [Yiddish, from Hebrew *gōy* people, nation] (1841) **:** GENTILE 1 — sometimes used disparagingly
— **goy·ish** \ˈgȯi-ish\ *adjective*

**graaf·ian follicle** \ˌgrä-fē-ən-, ˌgra-\ *noun, often G capitalized* [Regnier de *Graaf* (died 1673) Dutch anatomist] (1883) **:** a liquid-filled cavity in a mammalian ovary containing a mature egg before ovulation

**¹grab** \ˈgrab\ *verb* **grabbed; grab·bing** [obsolete Dutch or Low German *grabben*] (circa 1581)
*transitive verb*
**1 :** to take or seize by or as if by a sudden motion or grasp ⟨*grab* up an ax⟩ ⟨*grabbed* the opportunity⟩ ⟨*grab* attention⟩ **2 :** to obtain unscrupulously ⟨*grab* public lands⟩ **3 :** to take hastily ⟨*grab* a bite to eat⟩ ⟨*grab* a cab⟩ **4 a :** to seize the attention of ⟨the technique of *grabbing* an audience —Pauline Kael⟩ **b :** to impress favorably and deeply
*intransitive verb*
**:** to make a grab
**synonym** see TAKE
— **grab·ber** *noun*

**²grab** *adjective* (1608) **1 :** intended to be grabbed ⟨a *grab* rail⟩ **2 :** taken at random ⟨*grab* samples of rocks⟩

**³grab** *noun* (1777) **1 a :** something grabbed **b :** a sudden snatch **c :** an unlawful or unscrupulous seizure **2** *chiefly British* **a :** a device for clutching an object **b :** CLAMSHELL
— **up for grabs :** available for anyone to take, win, or settle

**grab bag** *noun* (1855) **1 :** a receptacle (as a bag) containing small articles which are to be drawn (as at a party or fair) without being seen **2 :** a miscellaneous collection **:** POTPOURRI

**grab·ble** \ˈgra-bəl\ *intransitive verb* **grab·bled; grab·bling** \-b(ə-)liŋ\ [Dutch *grabbelen*, from Middle Dutch, frequentative of *grabben*] (circa 1580) **1 :** to search with the hand **:** GROPE **2 :** to lie or fall prone **:** SPRAWL
— **grab·bler** \-b(ə-)lər\ *noun*

**grab·by** \ˈgra-bē\ *adjective* **grab·bi·er; -est** (1910) **1 :** tending to grab **:** GRASPING, GREEDY **2 :** having the power to grab the attention ⟨*grabby* previews⟩

**gra·ben** \ˈgrä-bən\ *noun* [German, ditch, from Old High German *grabo*, from *graban* to dig — more at GRAVE] (1896) **:** a depressed segment of the crust of the earth or a celestial body (as the moon) bounded on at least two sides by faults

**¹grace** \ˈgrās\ *noun* [Middle English, from Old French, from Latin *gratia* favor, charm, thanks, from *gratus* pleasing, grateful; akin to Sanskrit *gṛṇāti* he praises] (12th century) **1 a :** unmerited divine assistance given humans for their regeneration or sanctification **b :** a virtue coming from God **c :** a state of sanctification enjoyed through divine grace

**2 a :** APPROVAL, FAVOR ⟨stayed in his good *graces*⟩ **b** *archaic* **:** MERCY, PARDON **c :** a special favor **:** PRIVILEGE ⟨each in his place, by right, not *grace*, shall rule his heritage —Rudyard Kipling⟩ **d :** disposition to or an act or instance of kindness, courtesy, or clemency **e :** a temporary exemption **:** REPRIEVE **3 a :** a charming or attractive trait or characteristic **b :** a pleasingly graceful appearance or effect **:** CHARM **c :** ease and suppleness of movement or bearing **4** — used as a title of address or reference for a duke, a duchess, or an archbishop **5 :** a short prayer at a meal asking a blessing or giving thanks **6** *plural, capitalized* **:** three sister goddesses in Greek mythology who are the givers of charm and beauty **7 :** a musical trill, turn, or appoggiatura **8 a :** sense of propriety or right ⟨had the *grace* not to run for elective office —Calvin Trillin⟩ **b :** the quality or state of being considerate or thoughtful
**synonym** see MERCY

**²grace** *transitive verb* **graced; grac·ing** (1585) **1 :** to confer dignity or honor on **2 :** ADORN, EMBELLISH ⟨graveled walks *graced* with statues —J. A. Michener⟩

**grace·ful** \ˈgrās-fəl\ *adjective* (circa 1586) **:** displaying grace in form or action **:** pleasing or attractive in line, proportion, or movement
— **grace·ful·ly** \-fə-lē\ *adverb*
— **grace·ful·ness** *noun*

**grace·less** \ˈgrā-sləs\ *adjective* (14th century) **1 :** lacking in divine grace **:** IMMORAL, UNREGENERATE **2 a :** lacking a sense of propriety **b :** devoid of attractive qualities **3 :** artistically inept or unbeautiful
— **grace·less·ly** *adverb*
— **grace·less·ness** *noun*

**grace note** *noun* (circa 1823) **1 :** a musical note added as an ornament; *especially* **:** APPOGGIATURA **2 :** a small addition or embellishment

**grace period** *noun* (1945) **:** a period of time beyond a due date during which a financial obligation may be met without penalty or cancellation

**grac·ile** \ˈgra-səl, -ˌsīl\ *adjective* [Latin *gracilis*] (1623) **1 :** SLENDER, SLIGHT **2 :** GRACEFUL **3 :** relating to, resembling, or being any of the primitive relatively small slender hominids (genus *Australopithecus*) characterized especially by molars and incisors of similar size that are adapted to an omnivorous diet — compare ROBUST
— **grac·ile·ness** *noun*
— **gra·cil·i·ty** \gra-ˈsi-lə-tē\ *noun*

**gra·ci·o·so** \ˌgrä-sē-ˈō-(ˌ)sō, -(ˌ)zō\ *noun, plural* **-sos** [Spanish, from *gracioso*, adjective, agreeable, amusing, from Latin *gratiosus*] (1749) **:** a buffoon in Spanish comedy

**gra·cious** \ˈgrā-shəs\ *adjective* [Middle English, from Middle French *gracieus*, from Latin *gratiosus* enjoying favor, agreeable, from *gratia*] (14th century) **1 a** *obsolete* **:** GODLY **b** *archaic* **:** PLEASING, ACCEPTABLE **2 a :** marked by kindness and courtesy **b :** GRACEFUL **c :** marked by tact and delicacy **:** URBANE **d :** characterized by charm, good taste, generosity of spirit, and the tasteful leisure of wealth and good breeding ⟨*gracious* living⟩ **3 :** MERCIFUL, COMPASSIONATE — used conventionally of royalty and high nobility ☆
— **gra·cious·ly** *adverb*
— **gra·cious·ness** *noun*

**grack·le** \ˈgra-kəl\ *noun* [New Latin *Gracula*, genus name, alteration of Latin *graculus* jackdaw] (1772)

**1 :** any of a genus (*Quiscalus* of the family Icteridae) of large American blackbirds having iridescent black plumage **2 :** any of various Asian starlings (as the hill mynahs)

**¹grad** \ˈgrad\ *noun or adjective* [ by shortening] (circa 1871) **:** GRADUATE

**²grad** *noun* [French *grade* degree, from Latin *gradus*] (1898) **:** one hundredth of a right angle

**gra·da·tion** \grā-ˈdā-shən, grə-\ *noun* (1549) **1 a :** a series forming successive stages **b :** a step or place in an ordered scale **2 :** an advance by regular degrees **3 :** a gradual passing from one tint or shade to another **4 :** the act or process of grading **5 :** ABLAUT
— **gra·da·tion·al** \-shnəl, -shə-nᵊl\ *adjective*
— **gra·da·tion·al·ly** *adverb*

**¹grade** \ˈgrād\ *noun* [French, from Latin *gradus* step, degree, from Latin *gradi* to step, go; akin to Lithuanian *gridyti* to go, wander] (1796) **1 a** (1) **:** a stage in a process (2) **:** a position in a scale of ranks or qualities **b :** a degree of severity in illness ⟨*grade* III carcinoma⟩ **c :** a class organized for the work of a particular year of a school course **d :** a military or naval rank **2 a :** a class of things of the same stage or degree **b :** a mark indicating a degree of accomplishment in school **c :** a standard of food quality **3 a :** the degree of inclination of a road or slope; *also* **:** a sloping road **b :** a datum or reference level; *especially* **:** ground level **4 :** a domestic animal with one parent purebred and the other of inferior breeding **5** *plural* **:** the elementary school system
— **grade·less** \-ləs\ *adjective*

**²grade** *verb* **grad·ed; grad·ing** (1659)
*transitive verb*
**1 a :** to arrange in grades **:** SORT **b :** to arrange in a scale or series **c :** to assign to a grade or assign a grade to **2 :** to level off to a smooth horizontal or sloping surface
*intransitive verb*
**1 a :** to form a series **b :** BLEND **2 :** to be of a particular grade
— **grad·able** \ˈgrā-də-bəl\ *adjective*

**³grade** *adjective* (1852) **:** being, involving, or yielding domestic animals of improved but not pure stock ⟨*grade* ewes⟩ ⟨*grade* breeding⟩

**-grade** \ˌgrād\ *adjective combining form* [French, from Latin *-gradus*, from *gradi*] **:** walking ⟨planti*grade*⟩

**grade crossing** *noun* (circa 1890) **:** a crossing of highways, railroad tracks, or pedestrian walks or combinations of these on the same level

**grade point** *noun* (1951)

---

: one of the points assigned to each course credit (as in a college) in accordance with the letter grade earned in the course — called also *quality point*

**grade point average** *noun* (1966)
: the average obtained by dividing the total number of grade points earned by the total number of credits attempted — called also *quality point average*

**grad·er** \'grā-dər\ *noun* (1832)
**1** : one that grades
**2** : a machine for leveling earth
**3** : a pupil in a school grade ⟨a fifth *grader*⟩

**grade school** *noun* (1869)
: ELEMENTARY SCHOOL
— **grade–school·er** \'grād-ˌskü-lər\ *noun*

**grade separation** *noun* (circa 1949)
: a highway or railroad crossing using an underpass or overpass

**grade up** *transitive verb* (1903)
: to improve by breeding females to purebred males

**gra·di·ent** \'grā-dē-ənt\ *noun* [Latin *gradient-, gradiens,* present participle of *gradi*] (1835)
**1 a** : the rate of regular or graded ascent or descent : INCLINATION **b** : a part sloping upward or downward
**2** : change in the value of a quantity (as temperature, pressure, or concentration) with change in a given variable and especially per unit distance in a specified direction
**3** : the vector sum of the partial derivatives with respect to the three coordinate variables *x, y,* and *z* of a scalar quantity whose value varies from point to point
**4** : a graded difference in physiological activity along an axis (as of the body or an embryonic field)
**5** : change in response with distance from the stimulus

**gra·di·om·e·ter** \ˌgrā-dē-'ä-mə-tər\ *noun* [*gradient* + *-o-* + *-meter*] (1899)
: an instrument for measuring the gradient of a physical quantity (as the earth's magnetic field)

**¹grad·u·al** \'gra-jə-wəl, -jəl, 'graj-wəl\ *noun, often capitalized* [Middle English, from Medieval Latin *graduale,* from Latin *gradus* step, from its being sung on the steps of the altar] (15th century)
**1** : a book containing the choral parts of the Mass
**2** : a pair of verses (as from the Psalms) proper after the Epistle in the Mass

**²gradual** *adjective* [Medieval Latin *gradualis,* from Latin *gradus*] (1692)
**1** : proceeding by steps or degrees
**2** : moving, changing, or developing by fine or often imperceptible degrees
— **grad·u·al·ly** *adverb*
— **grad·u·al·ness** *noun*

**grad·u·al·ism** \-jə-wə-ˌli-zəm, -jə-ˌli-\ *noun* (1835)
**1** : the policy of approaching a desired end by gradual stages
**2** : the evolution of new species by gradual accumulation of small genetic changes over long periods of time; *also* : a theory or model of evolution emphasizing this — compare PUNCTUATED EQUILIBRIUM
— **grad·u·al·ist** \-list\ *noun or adjective*

**grad·u·and** \ˌgra-jə-'wand\ *noun* [Medieval Latin *graduandus,* gerundive of *graduare*] (1882)
*British* : one about to graduate : a candidate for a degree

**¹grad·u·ate** \'gra-jə-wət, -ˌwät, 'graj-wət\ *noun* (15th century)
**1** : a holder of an academic degree or diploma
**2** : a graduated cup, cylinder, or flask

**²graduate** *adjective* (15th century)
**1** : holding an academic degree or diploma
**2** : of, relating to, or engaged in studies beyond the first or bachelor's degree ⟨*graduate* school⟩ ⟨*graduate* student⟩

**³grad·u·ate** \'gra-jə-ˌwāt\ *verb* **-at·ed; -at·ing** [Medieval Latin *graduare,* from Latin *gradus* step, degree] (15th century)
*transitive verb*
**1 a** : to grant an academic degree or diploma to **b** : to be graduated from
**2 a** : to mark with degrees of measurement **b** : to divide into grades or intervals
**3** : to admit to a particular standing or grade
*intransitive verb*
**1** : to receive an academic degree or diploma
**2** : to pass from one stage of experience, proficiency, or prestige to a usually higher one
**3** : to change gradually ◻
— **grad·u·a·tor** \-ˌwā-tər\ *noun*

**grad·u·at·ed** *adjective* (1861)
*of a tax* : increasing in rate with increase in taxable base : PROGRESSIVE ⟨*graduated* income tax⟩

**graduated cylinder** *noun* (1948)
: a tall narrow container with a volume scale used especially for measuring liquids

**grad·u·a·tion** \ˌgra-jə-'wā-shən\ *noun* (1594)
**1** : a mark on an instrument or vessel indicating degrees or quantity; *also* : these marks
**2 a** : the award or acceptance of an academic degree or diploma **b** : COMMENCEMENT
**3** : arrangement in degrees or ranks

**Graeco-** — see GRECO-

**graf·fi·to** \grə-'fē-(ˌ)tō, gra-, grä-\ *noun, plural* **-ti** \-(ˌ)tē\ [Italian, incised inscription, from *graffiare* to scratch, probably from *grafio* stylus, from Latin *graphium*] (1851)
: an inscription or drawing made on some public surface (as a rock or wall); *also* : a message or slogan written as or as if as a graffito ◻
— **graf·fi·tist** \-'fē-tist\ *noun*

**¹graft** \'graft\ *noun* [Middle English *graffe, grafte,* from Middle French *grafe,* from Medieval Latin *graphium,* from Latin, stylus, from Greek *grapheion,* from *graphein* to write — more at CARVE] (14th century)
**1 a** : a grafted plant **b** : SCION 1 **c** : the point of insertion of a scion upon a stock
**2 a** : the act of grafting **b** : something grafted; *specifically* : living tissue used in grafting

**²graft** (14th century)
*transitive verb*
**1 a** : to cause (a scion) to unite with a stock; *also* : to unite (plants or scion and stock) to form a graft **b** : to propagate (a plant) by grafting
**2 a** : to join or unite as if by grafting **b** : to attach (a chemical unit) to a main molecular chain
**3** : to implant (living tissue) surgically
*intransitive verb*
**1** : to become grafted
**2** : to perform grafting
— **graft·er** *noun*

**³graft** *noun* [English dialect *graft,* verb, to work, perhaps alteration of ¹*grave* (to dig)] (1853)
*chiefly British* : WORK, LABOR

**⁴graft** [origin unknown] (1859)
*transitive verb*
: to get (illicit gain) by graft
*intransitive verb*
: to practice graft

**⁵graft** *noun* (1865)
: the acquisition of gain (as money) in dishonest or questionable ways; *also* : illegal or unfair gain

**graft·age** \'graf-tij\ *noun* (circa 1895)
: the principles and practice of grafting

**graft–versus–host** *adjective* (1972)
: relating to or being the bodily condition that results when cells from a tissue or organ transplant mount an immunological attack against the cells or tissues of the host

**gra·ham cracker** \'gram-, 'grā-əm-\ *noun* [*graham flour*] (1882)
: a slightly sweet cracker made of whole wheat flour

**graham flour** *noun* [Sylvester *Graham* (died 1851) American dietary reformer] (1834)
: whole wheat flour

**grail** \'grā(ə)l\ *noun* [Middle English *graal,* from Middle French, bowl, grail, from Medieval Latin *gradalis*]
**1** *capitalized* : the cup or platter used according to medieval legend by Christ at the Last Supper and thereafter the object of knightly quests
**2** : the object of an extended or difficult quest

**¹grain** \'grān\ *noun* [Middle English, partly from Middle French *grain* cereal grain, from Latin *granum;* partly from Middle French *graine* seed, kermes, from Latin *grana,* plural of *granum* — more at CORN] (14th century)
**1 a** (1) *obsolete* : a single small hard seed (2) : a seed or fruit of a cereal grass : CARYOPSIS **b** : the seeds or fruits of various food plants including the cereal grasses and in commercial and statutory usage other plants (as the soybean) **c** : plants producing grain
**2 a** (1) : a small hard particle or crystal (2) : any of the particles produced in a photographic material by its development; *also* : the size of such grains in the aggregate (3) : an individual crystal in a metal **b** : a minute portion or particle **c** : the least amount possible ⟨a *grain* of truth⟩
**3 a** : kermes or a scarlet dye made from it **b** : cochineal or a brilliant scarlet dye made from it **c** : a fast dye **d** *archaic* : COLOR, TINT
**4 a** : a granulated surface or appearance **b** : the outer or hair side of a skin or hide
**5** : a unit of weight based on the weight of a grain of wheat taken as an average of the weight of grains from the middle of the ear — see WEIGHT table
**6 a** : the stratification of the wood fibers in a piece of wood **b** : a texture due to constituent particles or fibers ⟨the *grain* of a rock⟩ **c** : the direction of threads in cloth
**7** : tactile quality
**8 a** : natural disposition : TEMPER ⟨against my *grain*⟩ **b** : a basic or characteristic quality ⟨doctrines . . . very much in the American *grain* —R. W. Noland⟩
— **grained** \'grānd\ *adjective*

**²grain** (1530)
*transitive verb*
**1** : INGRAIN

graft 1c:
*a* scion, *b* stock

◻ USAGE

**graduate** In the 19th century the transitive sense (1a) was prescribed; the intransitive (I *graduated* from college) was condemned. The intransitive prevailed nonetheless, and today it is the sense likely to be prescribed and the newer transitive (sense 1b) the one condemned. All three are standard. The intransitive is currently the most common, the new transitive the least common.

**graffito** The plural *graffiti* is sometimes used with a singular verb as a mass noun ⟨the *graffiti* is being covered with fresh paint —*Springfield (Mass.) Union*⟩ ⟨*graffiti* comes in various styles —S. K. Oberbeck⟩ but this use is not yet as well established as the mass-noun use of *data.* Use of *graffiti* as a singular count noun is still quite rare and is not standard.

**2** : to form into grains : GRANULATE
**3** : to paint in imitation of the grain of wood or stone
**4** : to feed with grain
*intransitive verb*
: to become granular : GRANULATE
— **grain·er** *noun*
**grain alcohol** *noun* (1889)
: ETHANOL
**grain elevator** *noun* (1852)
: a building for elevating, storing, discharging, and sometimes processing grain
**grain·field** \'grān-ˌfēld\ *noun* (circa 1818)
: a field where grain is grown
**grain of salt** (1647)
: a skeptical attitude
**grains of paradise** (15th century)
: the pungent seeds of a West African plant (*Aframomum melegueta*) of the ginger family that are used as a spice
**grain sorghum** *noun* (1920)
: any of several sorghums cultivated primarily for grain — compare SORGO
**grainy** \'grā-nē\ *adjective* **grain·i·er; -est** (15th century)
**1** : resembling or having some characteristic of grain : not smooth or fine
**2** *of a photograph* : appearing to be composed of grain-like particles
— **grain·i·ness** *noun*
**¹gram** \'gram\ *noun* [obsolete Portuguese (now spelled *grão*), grain, from Latin *granum*] (1702)
: any of several leguminous plants (as a chickpea) grown especially for their seed; *also* : their seeds
**²gram** \'gram\ *noun* [French *gramme*, from Late Latin *gramma*, a small weight, from Greek *grammat-, gramma* letter, writing, a small weight, from *graphein* to write — more at CARVE] (1810)
**1** : a metric unit of mass equal to ¹/₁₀₀₀ kilogram and nearly equal to the mass of one cubic centimeter of water at its maximum density — see METRIC SYSTEM table
**2** : the weight of a gram under standard gravity
**³gram** *noun* [by shortening & alteration] (circa 1934)
: GRANDMOTHER
**-gram** \ˌgram\ *noun combining form* [Latin *-gramma*, from Greek, from *gramma*]
: drawing : writing : record ⟨chrono*gram*⟩ ⟨tele*gram*⟩
**grama** \'gra-mə\ *noun* [Spanish, from Latin *gramina*, plural of *gramen* grass] (1828)
: any of several pasture grasses (genus *Bouteloua*) of the western U.S.
**gram–atomic weight** *noun* (1927)
: the mass of one mole of an element equal in grams to the atomic weight — called also *gram-atom*
**gram calorie** *noun* (1902)
: CALORIE 1a
**gram equivalent** *noun* (circa 1897)
: the quantity of an element, group, or compound that has a mass in grams equal to the equivalent weight
**gra·mer·cy** \grə-'mər-sē\ *interjection* [Middle English *grand mercy*, from Middle French *grand merci* great thanks] (14th century)
*archaic* — used to express gratitude or surprise
**gram·i·ci·din** \ˌgra-mə-'sī-dᵊn\ *noun* [*gram-positive + -i- + -cide + -in*] (1940)
: any of several toxic crystalline polypeptide antibiotics produced by a soil bacterium (*Bacillus brevis*) and used against gram-positive bacteria in local infections
**gra·min·e·ous** \grə-'mi-nē-əs\ *adjective* [Latin *gramineus*, from *gramin-, gramen* grass] (circa 1658)
: of or relating to a grass
**gram·i·niv·o·rous** \ˌgra-mə-'ni-v(ə-)rəs\ *adjective* [Latin *gramin-, gramen*] (1739)

: feeding on grass or the seeds of grass ⟨*graminivorous* locusts⟩ ⟨*graminivorous* birds⟩
**gram·mar** \'gra-mər\ *noun* [Middle English *gramere*, from Middle French *gramaire*, modification of Latin *grammatica*, from Greek *grammatikē*, from feminine of *grammatikos* of letters, from *grammat-, gramma* — more at GRAM] (14th century)
**1 a** : the study of the classes of words, their inflections, and their functions and relations in the sentence **b** : a study of what is to be preferred and what avoided in inflection and syntax
**2 a** : the characteristic system of inflections and syntax of a language **b** : a system of rules that defines the grammatical structure of a language
**3 a** : a grammar textbook **b** : speech or writing evaluated according to its conformity to grammatical rules
**4** : the principles or rules of an art, science, or technique ⟨a *grammar* of the theater⟩
*word history* see GLAMOUR
— **gram·mar·i·an** \grə-'mer-ē-ən, -'mar-\ *noun*
**grammar school** *noun* (14th century)
**1 a** : a secondary school emphasizing Latin and Greek in preparation for college **b** : a British college preparatory school
**2** : a school intermediate between primary school and high school
**3** : ELEMENTARY SCHOOL
**gram·mat·i·cal** \grə-'ma-ti-kəl\ *adjective* (1530)
**1** : of or relating to grammar
**2** : conforming to the rules of grammar
— **gram·mat·i·cal·i·ty** \-ˌma-tə-'ka-lə-tē\ *noun*
— **gram·mat·i·cal·ly** \-'ma-ti-k(ə-)lē\ *adverb*
— **gram·mat·i·cal·ness** \-kəl-nəs\ *noun*
**grammatical meaning** *noun* (1769)
: the part of meaning that varies from one inflectional form to another (as from *plays* to *played* to *playing*) — compare LEXICAL MEANING
**gramme** *chiefly British variant of* ²GRAM
**gram molecular weight** *noun* (circa 1902)
: the mass of one mole of a compound equal in grams to the molecular weight — called also *gram-molecule*
**Gram·my** \'gra-mē\ *service mark*
— used for the annual presentation of a statuette for notable achievement in the recording industry
**gram–neg·a·tive** \'gram-'ne-gə-tiv\ *adjective* (1907)
: not holding the purple dye when stained by Gram's stain — used chiefly of bacteria
**gram·o·phone** \'gra-mə-ˌfōn\ *noun* [from *Gramophone*, a trademark] (1887)
: PHONOGRAPH
**gramp** \'gramp\ *or* **gramps** \'gram(p)s\ *noun, plural* **gramps** [by shortening & alteration] (circa 1900)
: GRANDFATHER
**gram–pos·i·tive** \'gram-'pä-zə-tiv, -'päz-tiv\ *adjective* (1907)
: holding the purple dye when stained by Gram's stain — used chiefly of bacteria
**gram·pus** \'gram-pəs\ *noun* [alteration of Middle English *graspey, grapay*, from Middle French *graspeis*, from *gras* fat (from Latin *crassus*) + *peis* fish, from Latin *piscis* — more at CRASS, FISH] (circa 1529)
**1** : a dolphin (*Grampus griseus*) of temperate and tropical seas; *also* : any of various small cetaceans
**2** : the giant whip scorpion (*Mastigoproctus giganteus*) of the southern U.S.
**Gram's stain** \'gramz-\ *or* **Gram stain** \'gram-\ *noun* [Hans C. J. *Gram* (died 1938) Danish physician] (1903)
**1** : a method for the differential staining of bacteria by treatment with a watery solution of iodine and the iodide of potassium after stain-

ing with a triphenylmethane dye (as crystal violet) — called also *Gram's method*
**2** : the chemicals used in Gram's stain
**gram–vari·able** \'gram-'ver-ē-ə-bəl, -'var-\ *adjective* (1956)
: staining irregularly or inconsistently by Gram's stain
**grana** *plural of* GRANUM
**gran·a·dil·la** \ˌgran-ə-'di-lə, -'dē-(y)ə\ *noun* [Spanish, diminutive of *granada* pomegranate, from Late Latin *granata* — more at GRENADE] (1613)
: the oblong fruit of various passionflowers (especially *Passiflora quadrangularis* of tropical America) used as a dessert; *also* : a plant that produces granadillas
**gra·na·ry** \'grā-nə-rē, 'gra-\ *noun, plural* **-ries** [Latin *granarium*, from *granum* grain] (1530)
**1 a** : a storehouse for threshed grain **b** : a region producing grain in abundance
**2** : a chief source or storehouse
**¹grand** \'grand\ *adjective* [Middle French, large, great, grand, from Latin *grandis*] (1584)
**1 a** : having more importance than others : FOREMOST **b** : having higher rank than others bearing the same general designation ⟨the *grand* champion⟩
**2 a** : INCLUSIVE, COMPREHENSIVE ⟨the *grand* total of all money paid out⟩ **b** : DEFINITIVE, INCONTROVERTIBLE ⟨*grand* example⟩
**3** : CHIEF, PRINCIPAL
**4** : large and striking in size, scope, extent, or conception ⟨*grand* design⟩
**5 a** : LAVISH, SUMPTUOUS ⟨a *grand* celebration⟩ **b** : marked by a regal form and dignity **c** : fine or imposing in appearance or impression **d** : LOFTY, SUBLIME ⟨writing in the *grand* style⟩
**6 a** : pretending to social superiority : SUPERCILIOUS **b** : intended to impress ⟨a person of *grand* gestures⟩
**7** : very good : WONDERFUL ⟨a *grand* time⟩ ☆
— **grand·ly** \'gran(d)lē\ *adverb*
— **grand·ness** \'gran(d)-nəs\ *noun*
**²grand** *noun* (1840)
**1** : GRAND PIANO
**2** *slang* : a thousand dollars
**gran·dam** \'gran-ˌdam, -dəm\ *noun* [Middle English *graundam*, from Anglo-French *graund dame*, literally, great lady] (13th century)
**1** *or* **gran·dame** \-ˌdām\ **a** : GRANDMOTHER **b** : an old woman
**2** *or* **gran·dam** \-ˌdam, -dəm\ : a dam's or sire's dam — used of an animal
**grand·aunt** \'gran-ˌdant, -'dànt\ *noun* (1826)
: the aunt of one's father or mother — called also *great-aunt*
**grand·ba·by** \'gran(d)-ˌbā-bē\ *noun* (1916)
: an infant grandchild
**grand·child** \-ˌchīld\ *noun* (1587)
: the child of one's son or daughter

**grand·dad** *or* **gran·dad** \'gran-ˌdad\ *noun* (1782)
: GRANDFATHER

**grand·dad·dy** \-ˌda-dē\ *also* **gran·dad·dy** *noun* (1769)
**1** : GRANDFATHER
**2** : one that is the first, earliest, or most venerable of its kind

**grand·daugh·ter** \-ˌdȯ-tər\ *noun* (1611)
: the daughter of one's son or daughter

**grand duchess** *noun* (circa 1757)
**1** : a woman who rules a grand duchy in her own right
**2** : the wife or widow of a grand duke

**grand duchy** *noun* (1835)
: the territory or dominion of a grand duke or grand duchess

**grand duke** *noun* (circa 1693)
**1** : the sovereign duke of any of various European states
**2** : a male descendant of a Russian czar in the male line

**grande dame** \'grän-ˈdäm, ˌgräⁿd-ˈdàm\ *noun*, *plural* **grandes dames** \-ˈdäm(z), -ˈdàm(z)\ *also* **grande dames** \*same*\ [French, literally, great lady] (1775)
: a usually elderly woman of great prestige or ability

**gran·dee** \gran-ˈdē\ *noun* [Spanish *grande*, from *grande*, adjective, large, great, from Latin *grandis*] (1598)
: a man of elevated rank or station; *especially* : a Spanish or Portuguese nobleman of the first rank

**gran·deur** \'gran-jər, -ˌjür, -ˌd(y)ür, -d(y)ər\ *noun* [Middle English, from Middle French, from *grand*] (1600)
**1** : the quality or state of being grand : MAGNIFICENCE ⟨the glory that was Greece and the *grandeur* that was Rome —E. A. Poe⟩
**2** : an instance or example of grandeur

¹**grand·fa·ther** \'gran(d)-ˌfä-ᵺər, -ˌfä-\ *noun* (15th century)
: the father of one's father or mother; *also* : ANCESTOR 1a
— **grand·fa·ther·ly** \-lē\ *adjective*

²**grandfather** *transitive verb* (1972)
: to permit to continue under a grandfather clause

**grandfather clause** *noun* (1900)
: a clause creating an exemption based on circumstances previously existing; *especially* : a provision in several southern state constitutions designed to enfranchise poor whites and disfranchise Negroes by waiving high voting requirements for descendants of men voting before 1867

**grandfather clock** *noun* [from the song *My Grandfather's Clock* (1876) by Henry C. Work (died 1884) American songwriter] (1909)
: a tall pendulum clock that stands on the floor — called also *grandfather, grandfather's clock*

**grand finale** *noun* (1800)
: a climactic finale (as of an opera)

**grand fir** *noun* (1897)
: a lofty fir tree (*Abies grandis*) of the northwestern Pacific coastal region of North America with cylindrical greenish cones and soft wood

**Grand Gui·gnol** \ˌgrä°-gēn-ˈyȯl, -ˈyōl\ *noun* [*Le Grand Guignol*, small theater in Montmartre, Paris, specializing in such performances] (1908)
: dramatic entertainment featuring the gruesome or horrible ◆
— **Grand Guignol** *adjective*

**gran·di·flo·ra** \ˌgran-də-ˈflȯr-ə, -ˈflȯr-\ *noun* [New Latin, from Latin *grandis* great + *flor-, flos* flower — more at BLOW] (1944)
: a bush rose derived from crosses of floribunda and hybrid tea roses and characterized by production of blooms both singly and in clusters on the same plant

**gran·dil·o·quence** \gran-ˈdi-lə-kwən(t)s\ *noun* [probably from Middle French, from Latin *grandiloquus* using lofty language, from *grandis* + *loqui* to speak] (1589)
: a lofty, extravagantly colorful, pompous, or bombastic style, manner, or quality especially in language
— **gran·dil·o·quent** \-kwənt\ *adjective*
— **gran·dil·o·quent·ly** *adverb*

**gran·di·ose** \'gran-dē-ˌōs, ˌgran-dē-ˈ\ *adjective* [French, from Italian *grandioso*, from *grande* great, from Latin *grandis*] (1840)
**1** : characterized by affectation of grandeur or splendor or by absurd exaggeration
**2** : impressive because of uncommon largeness, scope, effect, or grandeur
*synonym* see GRAND
— **gran·di·ose·ly** *adverb*
— **gran·di·ose·ness** *noun*
— **gran·di·os·i·ty** \ˌgran-dē-ˈä-sə-tē\ *noun*

**gran·di·o·so** \ˌgrän-dē-ˈō-(ˌ)sō, ˌgran-, -(ˌ)zō\ *adverb or adjective* [Italian] (circa 1859)
: in a broad and noble style — used as a direction in music

**grand jury** *noun* (15th century)
: a jury that examines accusations against persons charged with crime and if the evidence warrants makes formal charges on which the accused persons are later tried
— **grand juror** *noun*

**grand·kid** \'gran(d)-ˌkid\ *noun* (1927)
: GRANDCHILD

**Grand Lama** *noun* (1807)
: DALAI LAMA

**grand larceny** *noun* (1828)
: larceny of property of a value greater than that fixed as constituting petit larceny

**grand·ma** \'gran(d)-ˌmä, -ˌmȯ; 'gra-ˌmä, -ˌmȯ\ *noun* (1867)
: GRANDMOTHER

**grand mal** \'gran(d)-ˌmäl, 'gräⁿ-ˌmäl, -ˌmal; 'gran(d)-ˌmal\ *noun* [French, literally, great illness] (1897)
: severe epilepsy

**grand manner** *noun* (1775)
: an elevated or grand style (as in music or literature)

**grand march** *noun* (1898)
: an opening ceremony at a ball that consists of a march participated in by all the guests

**grand marshal** *noun* (1951)
: a person honored as the ceremonial marshal of a parade

**grand master** *noun* (1724)
**1** : the chief officer of a principal lodge in various fraternal orders (as Freemasonry)
**2** : an expert player (as of chess) who has consistently scored high in international competition

**grand·moth·er** \'gran(d)-ˌmə-ᵺər\ *noun* (15th century)
: the mother of one's father or mother; *also* : a female ancestor
— **grand·moth·er·ly** \-lē\ *adjective*

**grand·neph·ew** \'gran(d)-ˈnef-(ˌ)yü, *chiefly British* -ˈnev-\ *noun* (circa 1639)
: a grandson of one's brother or sister

**grand·niece** \-ˈnēs\ *noun* (circa 1830)
: a granddaughter of one's brother or sister

**grand old man** *noun* (1860)
: a venerated practitioner or former practitioner of an art, profession, or sport ⟨the *grand old man* of jazz⟩

**grand opera** *noun* (1803)
: opera in which the plot is serious or tragic and the entire text is set to music

**grand·pa** \'gran(d)-ˌpä, -ˌpȯ; 'gram-ˌpä, -ˌpȯ\ *noun* (circa 1889)
: GRANDFATHER

**grand·par·ent** \'gran(d)-ˌpar-ənt, -ˌper-\ *noun* (1830)
: a parent of one's father or mother

**grand·pa·ren·tal** \ˌgran(d)-pə-ˈren-t°l\ *adjective*
— **grand·par·ent·hood** \'gran(d)-ˈpar-ent-ˌhủd, -ˈper-\ *noun*

**grand piano** *noun* (1834)
: a piano with horizontal frame and strings — compare UPRIGHT PIANO

**grand prix** \ˈgräⁿ-ˈprē\ *noun*, *plural* **grand prix** *also* **grands prix** \-ˈprē(z)\ *often G&P capitalized* [French *Grand Prix de Paris*, an international horse race established 1863, literally, grand prize of Paris] (1863)
**1** : the highest level of international equestrian competition; *also* : a contest at this level
**2** : one of a series of international formula car races

**grand·sire** \'gran(d)-ˌsīr\ *noun* [Middle English] (14th century)
**1** *or* **grand·sir** \'gran(t)-sər\ *dialect* : GRANDFATHER
**2** *archaic* : FOREFATHER
**3** *archaic* : an aged man
**4** : a dam's or sire's sire — used of an animal

**grand slam** *noun* (1814)
**1** : the winning of all the tricks in one hand of a card game (as bridge)
**2** : a clean sweep or total success; *specifically* : the winning of all the major or specified tournaments on a tour ⟨twice won the tennis *grand slam*⟩
**3** : a home run made with the bases loaded
— **grand–slam** *adjective*

**grand·son** \'gran(d)-ˌsən\ *noun* (1586)
: the son of one's son or daughter

¹**grand·stand** \-ˌstand\ *noun* (1834)
**1** : a usually roofed stand for spectators at a racecourse or stadium
**2** : AUDIENCE

²**grandstand** *adjective* (1893)
: done for show or to impress onlookers ⟨a *grandstand* play⟩

³**grandstand** *intransitive verb* (circa 1917)
: to play or act so as to impress onlookers
— **grand·stand·er** *noun*

**grand theft** *noun* (circa 1930)
: GRAND LARCENY

**grand tour** *noun* (1670)
**1** : an extended tour of the Continent that was formerly a usual part of the education of young British gentlemen
**2** : an extensive and usually educational tour

---

◇ **WORD HISTORY**
**Grand Guignol** Long before cinematic violence became explicit, the Grand-Guignol theater in the Montmartre district of Paris presented to audiences graphic depictions of stabbings, assaults with sulphuric acid, and assorted other mayhem. Founded in 1895 as the Théâtre Salon, it adopted its better-known name and characteristic formula in 1897. On a single night's bill, one-act light comedies alternated with dramas of horror, the latter featuring cleverly arranged (for the time) special effects and plenty of gore. *Guignol* in French denotes both "hand puppet" and, as a proper noun, the leading character in a tradition of children's puppet theater, but aside from the uniformity of repertoire there was nothing puppetlike about the Grand-Guignol. The theater remained a Parisian attraction until 1962, when it finally closed, having outlived an era when stage violence could provide a real shock.

---

\ə\ abut \ᵊ\ kitten \ər\ further \a\ ash \ā\ ace
\ä\ mop, mar \aủ\ out \ch\ chin \e\ bet \ē\ easy
\g\ go \i\ hit \ī\ ice \j\ job \ŋ\ sing \ō\ go
\ȯ\ law \ȯi\ boy \th\ thin \ᵺ\ the \ü\ loot \ủ\ foot
\y\ yet \zh\ vision *see also* Guide to Pronunciation

**grand touring car** *noun* (1970)
: a usually 2-passenger coupe

**grand·un·cle**
\'gran-ˌdəŋ-kəl\
*noun* (15th century)
: an uncle of one's father or mother

grand touring car

**grand unified theory** *noun* (1978)
: any of several theories that seek to unite in a single mathematical framework the electromagnetic and weak forces with the strong force or with the strong force and gravity — called also *grand unification theory*

**grange** \'grānj\ *noun* [Middle English, from Middle French, from Medieval Latin *granica*, from Latin *granum* grain] (14th century)
**1** *archaic* : GRANARY, BARN
**2** : FARM; *especially* : a farmhouse with outbuildings
**3** *capitalized* : one of the lodges of a national fraternal association originally made up of farmers; *also* : the association itself

**grang·er** \'grān-jər\ *noun* (1873)
**1** *capitalized* : a member of a Grange
**2** *chiefly West* : FARMER, HOMESTEADER

**grang·er·ism** \'grān-jə-ˌri-zəm\ *noun* (1875)
: the policy or methods of the grangers

**gra·ni·ta** \grə-'nē-tə\ *noun* [Italian, from feminine of *granito*, past participle of *granire*] (1869)
: a coarse-textured ice confection typically made from fruit

**gran·ite** \'gra-nət\ *noun* [Italian *granito*, from past participle of *granire* to granulate, from *grano* grain, from Latin *granum*] (1646)
**1** : a very hard natural igneous rock formation of visibly crystalline texture formed essentially of quartz and orthoclase or microcline and used especially for building and for monuments
**2** : unyielding firmness or endurance ⟨the cold *granite* of Puritan formalism —V. L. Parrington⟩
— **gran·ite·like** \-ˌlīk\ *adjective*
— **gra·nit·ic** \gra-'ni-tik\ *adjective*
— **gran·it·oid** \'gra-nə-ˌtȯid\ *adjective*

**gran·ite·ware** \'gra-nət-ˌwar, -ˌwer\ *noun* (1878)
: ironware with grayish or bluish mottled enamel

**gra·niv·o·rous** \grə-'niv-rəs, grā-, -'ni-və-\ *adjective* [Latin *granum* grain] (1646)
: feeding on seeds or grain ⟨*granivorous* rodents⟩

**gran·ny** *or* **gran·nie** \'gra-nē\ *noun, plural* **grannies** [by shortening & alteration] (1663)
**1 a** : GRANDMOTHER **b** : a fussy person
**2** *chiefly Southern & south Midland* : MIDWIFE

**granny dress** *noun* (1909)
: a long loose-fitting dress usually with high neck and long sleeves

**granny glasses** *noun plural* (1966)
: spectacles with usually small oval, round, or square lenses and metal frames

**granny knot** *noun* (1853)
: an insecure knot often made instead of a square knot — see KNOT illustration

**Granny Smith** \-'smith\ *noun* [Maria Ann Smith (died 1870) who cultivated it near Sydney, Australia] (1895)
: a tart green apple of Australian origin

**grano-** *combining form* [German, from *granit*, from Italian *granito*]
: granite : granitic ⟨*grano*diorite⟩

**grano·di·o·rite** \ˌgra-nō-'dī-ə-ˌrīt\ *noun* (1893)
: a granular intrusive quartzose igneous rock intermediate between granite and quartz-containing diorite with plagioclase predominant over orthoclase
— **grano·di·o·rit·ic** \-ˌdī-ə-'ri-tik\ *adjective*

**gra·no·la** \grə-'nō-lə\ *noun* [from *Granola*, a trademark] (1970)
: a mixture typically of rolled oats and various added ingredients (as brown sugar, raisins, coconut, and nuts) that is eaten especially for breakfast or as a snack

**grano·lith·ic** \ˌgra-nə-'li-thik\ *adjective* (1881)
: relating to or composed of a mixture of crushed granite and cement

**grano·phyre** \'gran-ə-ˌfī(-ə)r\ *noun* [International Scientific Vocabulary, from *grano-* + French *-phyre* (as in *porphyre* porphyry)] (1882)
: a porphyritic igneous rock chiefly of feldspar and quartz with granular groundmass
— **grano·phyr·ic** \ˌgran-ə-'fir-ik\ *adjective*

**¹grant** \'grant\ *transitive verb* [Middle English, from Old French *creanter, graanter*, from (assumed) Vulgar Latin *credentare*, from Latin *credent-, credens*, present participle of *credere* to believe — more at CREED] (13th century)
**1 a** : to consent to carry out for a person : allow fulfillment of ⟨*grant* a request⟩ **b** : to permit as a right, privilege, or favor ⟨luggage allowances *granted* to passengers⟩
**2** : to bestow or transfer formally ⟨*grant* a scholarship to a student⟩; *specifically* : to give the possession or title of by a deed
**3 a** : to be willing to concede **b** : to assume to be true ⟨*granting* that you are correct, you may find it hard to prove your point⟩ ☆
— **grant·able** \'gran-tə-bəl\ *adjective*
— **grant·er** \-tər\ *noun*
— **grant·or** \'gran-tər, -ˌtȯr; gran-'tȯr\ *noun*

**²grant** *noun* (13th century)
**1** : the act of granting
**2** : something granted; *especially* : a gift (as of land or money) for a particular purpose
**3 a** : a transfer of property by deed or writing **b** : the instrument by which such a transfer is made; *also* : the property so transferred
**4** : a minor territorial division of Maine, New Hampshire, or Vermont originally granted by the state to an individual or institution

**grant·ee** \gran-'tē\ *noun* (15th century)
: one to whom a grant is made

**grant-in-aid** \ˌgran-tᵊn-'ād\ *noun, plural* **grants-in-aid** \ˌgran(t)s-\ (1851)
**1** : a grant or subsidy for public funds paid by a central to a local government in aid of a public undertaking
**2** : a grant or subsidy to a school or individual for an educational or artistic project

**grants·man** \'gran(t)s-mən\ *noun* (1966)
: a specialist in grantsmanship

**grants·man·ship** \-ˌship\ *noun* [*grants* + *-manship*] (1961)
: the art of obtaining grants (as for research)
***word history*** see GAMESMANSHIP

**granul-** *or* **granuli-** *or* **granulo-** *combining form* [Late Latin *granulum*]
: granule ⟨*granulo*cyte⟩

**gran·u·lar** \'gran-yə-lər\ *adjective* (1794)
: consisting of or appearing to consist of granules : GRAINY
— **gran·u·lar·i·ty** \ˌgran-yə-'lar-ə-tē\ *noun*

**gran·u·late** \'gran-yə-ˌlāt\ *verb* **-lat·ed; -lat·ing** (1666)
*transitive verb*
: to form or crystallize into grains or granules
*intransitive verb*
: to form granulations ⟨an open *granulating* wound⟩
— **gran·u·la·tor** \-ˌlā-tər\ *noun*

**gran·u·la·tion** \ˌgran-yə-'lā-shən\ *noun* (1612)
**1** : the act or process of granulating : the condition of being granulated
**2** : one of the minute red granules of new capillaries formed on the surface of a wound in healing
**3** : GRANULE 2

**granulation tissue** *noun* (1873)
: tissue made up of granulations that temporarily replaces lost tissue in a wound

**gran·ule** \'gran-(ˌ)yü(ə)l\ *noun* [Late Latin *granulum*, diminutive of Latin *granum* grain] (1652)
**1** : a small particle; *especially* : one of numerous particles forming a larger unit
**2** : any of the small short-lived brilliant spots on the sun's photosphere

**gran·u·lite** \'gran-yə-ˌlīt\ *noun* (1849)
: a granular metamorphic rock consisting mainly of feldspar and quartz
— **gran·u·lit·ic** \ˌgran-yə-'li-tik\ *adjective*

**gran·u·lo·cyte** \'gran-yə-lō-ˌsīt\ *noun* [International Scientific Vocabulary] (1906)
: a polymorphonuclear white blood cell with granule-containing cytoplasm
— **gran·u·lo·cyt·ic** \ˌgran-yə-lō-'si-tik\ *adjective*

**gran·u·lo·cy·to·poi·e·sis** \ˌgran-yə-lō-ˌsī-tə-ˌpȯi-'ē-səs\ *noun* [New Latin] (1944)
: the formation of blood granulocytes typically in the bone marrow

**gran·u·lo·ma** \ˌgran-yə-'lō-mə\ *noun, plural* **-mas** *or* **-ma·ta** \-mə-tə\ (1861)
: a mass or nodule of chronically inflamed tissue with granulations that is usually associated with an infective process
— **gran·u·lo·ma·tous** \-mə-təs\ *adjective*

**granuloma in·gui·na·le** \-ˌiŋ-gwə-'na-lē, -'nä-, -'nā-\ *noun* [New Latin, literally, inguinal granuloma] (1918)
: a sexually transmitted disease characterized by ulceration and formation of granulations on the genitalia and in the groin area and caused by a bacterium (*Calymmatobacterium granulomatis*, synonym *Donovania granulomatis*)

**gran·u·lo·sa cell** \ˌgran-yə-'lō-sə-\ *noun* [New Latin *granulosa*, from feminine of *granulosus* granulose] (1936)
: one of the estrogen-secreting cells of the epithelial lining of a graafian follicle or its follicular precursor

**gran·u·lose** \'gran-yə-ˌlōs\ *adjective* (1852)
: GRANULAR; *especially* : having the surface roughened with granules

**gran·u·lo·sis** \ˌgran-yə-'lō-səs\ *noun, plural* **-lo·ses** \-ˌsēz\ [New Latin] (1949)
: a virus disease of insect larvae distinguished by the presence of minute granular inclusions in infected cells

**gra·num** \'grā-nəm\ *noun, plural* **gra·na** \-nə\ [New Latin, from Latin, grain — more at CORN] (1894)
: one of the lamellar stacks of chlorophyll-containing thylakoids found in plant chloroplasts

**grape** \'grāp\ *noun, often attributive* [Middle English, from Old French *crape, grape* hook, grape stalk, bunch of grapes, grape, of Germanic origin; akin to Old High German *krāpfo* hook] (14th century)
**1** : a smooth-skinned juicy greenish white to deep red or purple berry eaten dried or fresh as a fruit or fermented to produce wine

---

☆ **SYNONYMS**
**Grant, concede, vouchsafe, accord, award** mean to give as a favor or a right. GRANT implies giving to a claimant or petitioner something that could be withheld ⟨*granted* them a new hearing⟩. CONCEDE implies yielding something reluctantly in response to a rightful or compelling claim ⟨even her critics *concede* she can be charming⟩. VOUCHSAFE implies granting something as a courtesy or an act of gracious condescension ⟨*vouchsafed* the secret to only a few chosen disciples⟩. ACCORD implies giving to another what is due or proper ⟨*accorded* all the honors befitting a head of state⟩. AWARD implies giving what is deserved or merited usually after a careful weighing of pertinent factors ⟨*awarded* the company a huge defense contract⟩.

**2 :** any of numerous woody vines (genus *Vitis* of the family Vitaceae, the grape family) that usually climb by tendrils, produce clustered fruits that are grapes, and are nearly cosmopolitan in cultivation
**3 :** GRAPESHOT
— **grape·like** \-ˌlīk\ *adjective*
**grape·fruit** \ˈgrāp-ˌfrüt\ *noun* (1814)
**1** *plural* **grapefruit** *or* **grapefruits :** a large citrus fruit with a bitter yellow rind and inner skin and a highly flavored somewhat acid juicy pulp
**2 :** a small roundheaded tree (*Citrus paradisi*) that produces grapefruit
**grape hyacinth** *noun* (1733)
**:** any of several small bulbous spring-flowering herbs (genus *Muscari*) of the lily family with racemes of usually blue flowers
**grape·shot** \ˈgrāp-ˌshät\ *noun* (1747)
**:** an antipersonnel weapon consisting of a cluster of small iron balls shot from a cannon
**grape sugar** *noun* (1831)
**:** DEXTROSE
**grape·vine** \ˈgrāp-ˌvīn\ *noun* (circa 1736)
**1 :** GRAPE 2
**2 a :** an informal person-to-person means of circulating information or gossip ⟨heard about the meeting through the *grapevine*⟩ **b :** a secret source of information
**¹graph** \ˈgraf\ *noun* [short for *graphic formula*] (1886)
**1 :** the collection of all points whose coordinates satisfy a given relation (as a function)
**2 :** a diagram (as a series of one or more points, lines, line segments, curves, or areas) that represents the variation of a variable in comparison with that of one or more other variables
**²graph** *transitive verb* (1898)
**1 :** to represent by a graph
**2 :** to plot on a graph
**³graph** *noun* [probably from -*graph*] (1933)
**1 :** a written or printed representation of a basic unit of speech (as a phoneme or syllable); *especially* **:** GRAPHEME 2
**2 :** a single occurrence of a letter of an alphabet in any of its various shapes
**-graph** \ˌgraf\ *noun combining form* [Middle French -*graphe*, from Latin -*graphum*, from Greek -*graphon*, from neuter of -*graphos* written, from *graphein* to write — more at CARVE]
**1 :** something written or drawn ⟨mono*graph*⟩
**2** [French -*graphe*, from Late Latin -*graphus*] **:** instrument for making or transmitting records or images ⟨chrono*graph*⟩
**graph·eme** \ˈgra-ˌfēm\ *noun* (1935)
**1 :** the set of units of a writing system (as letters and letter combinations) that represent a phoneme
**2 :** a unit (as a letter) of a writing system
— **gra·phe·mic** \gra-ˈfē-mik\ *adjective*
— **gra·phe·mi·cal·ly** \-mi-k(ə-)lē\ *adverb*
**gra·phe·mics** \gra-ˈfē-miks\ *noun plural but singular or plural in construction* (1951)
**:** the study and analysis of a writing system in terms of graphemes
**¹graph·ic** \ˈgra-fik\ *also* **graph·i·cal** \-fi-kəl\ *adjective* [Latin *graphicus*, from Greek *graphikos*, from *graphein*] (1637)
**1 :** formed by writing, drawing, or engraving
**2** *usually* **graphic a :** marked by clear lifelike or vividly realistic description **b :** vividly or plainly shown or described
**3 a :** of or relating to the pictorial arts; *also* **:** PICTORIAL **b :** of, relating to, or involving such reproductive methods as those of engraving, etching, lithography, photography, serigraphy, and woodcut **c :** of or relating to the art of printing **d :** relating or according to graphics
**4** *usually* **graphical :** of, relating to, or represented by a graph

**5 :** of or relating to the written or printed word or the symbols or devices used in writing or printing to represent sound or convey meaning ☆
— **graph·i·cal·ly** \-fi-k(ə-)lē\ *adverb*
— **graph·ic·ness** \-fik-nəs\ *noun*
**²graphic** *noun* (1944)
**1 a :** a product of graphic art **b** *plural* **:** the graphic media
**2 a :** a graphic representation (as a picture, map, or graph) used especially for illustration **b** *plural but singular or plural in construction* **:** the art or science of drawing a representation of an object on a two-dimensional surface according to mathematical rules of projection
**3** *plural but singular or plural in construction* **:** the process whereby a computer displays graphics on a CRT and an operator can manipulate them (as with a light pen)
**4 :** a printed message superimposed on a television picture
**-graphic** *or* **-graphical** *adjective combining form* [Late Latin -*graphicus*, from Greek -*graphikos*, from -*graphikos*]
**:** written or transmitted in a (specified) way ⟨stylo*graphic*⟩
**graphic arts** *noun plural* (1882)
**:** the fine and applied arts of representation, decoration, and writing or printing on flat surfaces together with the techniques and crafts associated with them
**graphic design** *noun* (1956)
**:** the art or profession of using design elements (as typography and images) to convey information or create an effect; *also* **:** a product of this art
— **graphic designer** *noun*
**graphic equalizer** *noun* (1969)
**:** an electronic device for adjusting the frequency response of an audio system by means of a number of slides each of which controls the response for a band centered on a particular frequency
**graphic novel** *noun* (1978)
**:** a fictional story for adults that is presented in comic-strip format and published as a book
**graphics tablet** *noun* (1980)
**:** a device by which pictorial information is entered into a computer in a manner similar to drawing
**graph·ite** \ˈgra-ˌfīt\ *noun* [German *Graphit*, from Greek *graphein* to write] (1796)
**1 :** a soft black lustrous form of carbon that conducts electricity and is used in lead pencils and electrolytic anodes, as a lubricant, and as a moderator in nuclear reactors
**2 :** a composite material in which carbon fibers are the reinforcing material
— **gra·phit·ic** \gra-ˈfi-tik\ *adjective*
**graph·i·tize** \ˈgra-fə-ˌtīz, -ˌfīt-ˌīz\ *transitive verb* **-tized; -tiz·ing** (1899)
**:** to convert into graphite
— **graph·i·tiz·able** \-ˌtī-zə-bəl, -ˌfīt-ˌīz-\ *adjective*
— **graph·i·ti·za·tion** \ˌgra-fə-tə-ˈzā-shən, -ˌfī-\ *noun*
**grapho-** *combining form* [French, from Middle French, from Greek, from *graphē*, from *graphein* to write]
**:** writing ⟨*grapholect*⟩
**graph·o·lect** \ˈgra-fə-ˌlekt\ *noun* [*grapho-* + -*lect* (as in *dialect*)] (1977)
**:** a standard written language
**gra·phol·o·gist** \gra-ˈfä-lə-jist\ *noun* (1885)
**:** a specialist in graphology
**gra·phol·o·gy** \-jē\ *noun* [French *graphologie*, from *grapho-* + -*logie* -logy] (1886)
**:** the study of handwriting especially for the purpose of character analysis
— **graph·o·log·i·cal** \ˌgra-fə-ˈlä-ji-kəl\ *adjective*
**graph paper** *noun* (1927)
**:** paper ruled for drawing graphs
**-graphy** *noun combining form* [Latin -*graphia*, from Greek, from *graphein*]

**1 :** writing or representation in a (specified) manner or by a (specified) means or of a (specified) object ⟨steno*graphy*⟩ ⟨photogra*phy*⟩
**2 :** writing on a (specified) subject or in a (specified) field ⟨hagio*graphy*⟩
**grap·nel** \ˈgrap-nᵊl\ *noun* [Middle English *grapenel*, from (assumed) Middle French *grapinel*, diminutive of *grapin*, diminutive of *grape* hook — more at GRAPE] (14th century)
**:** a small anchor with usually four or five flukes used in dragging or grappling operations and for anchoring a dory or skiff — see ANCHOR illustration
**grap·pa** \ˈgrä-pə\ *noun* [Italian, from Italian dialect, grape stalk, of Germanic origin; akin to Old High German *krāpfo* hook] (circa 1893)
**:** a dry colorless brandy distilled from fermented grape pomace
**¹grap·ple** \ˈgra-pəl\ *noun* [Old French *grappelle*, diminutive of *grape* hook — more at GRAPE] (1601)
**1 a :** the act or an instance of grappling **b :** a hand-to-hand struggle **c :** a contest for superiority or mastery
**2 :** a bucket similar to a clamshell but usually having more jaws
**²grapple** *verb* **grap·pled; grap·pling** \ˈgra-p(ə-)liŋ\ (1530)
*transitive verb*
**1 :** to seize with or as if with a grapple
**2 :** to come to grips with **:** WRESTLE
**3 :** to bind closely
*intransitive verb*
**1 :** to make a ship fast with a grappling iron
**2 :** to come to grips
**3 :** to use a grapple
— **grap·pler** \-p(ə-)lər\ *noun*
**grap·pling** *noun* (1582)
**1 :** GRAPNEL
**2 :** GRAPPLING IRON
**grappling iron** *noun* (1538)
**:** a hooked iron for anchoring a boat, grappling ships to each other, or recovering sunken objects — called also *grappling hook*
**grap·to·lite** \ˈgrap-tə-ˌlīt\ *noun* [Greek *graptos* painted (from *graphein* to write, paint) + English -*lite* — more at CARVE] (1841)
**:** any of numerous extinct fossil colonial Paleozoic animals (group Graptolitoidea) with zooids in cups along a chitinous support
**grapy** *or* **grap·ey** \ˈgrā-pē\ *adjective* **grap·i·er; -est** (1594)
**:** of or relating to grapes; *especially, of wine* **:** having the taste or aroma of fresh grapes
— **grap·i·ness** \-nəs\ *noun*
**¹grasp** \ˈgrasp\ *verb* [Middle English *graspen*] (14th century)
*intransitive verb*
**:** to make the motion of seizing **:** CLUTCH
*transitive verb*
**1 :** to take or seize eagerly
**2 :** to clasp or embrace especially with the fingers or arms

☆ **SYNONYMS**
**Graphic, vivid, picturesque** mean giving a clear visual impression in words. GRAPHIC stresses the evoking of a clear lifelike picture ⟨a *graphic* account of combat⟩. VIVID suggests an impressing on the mind of the vigorous aliveness of something ⟨a *vivid* re-creation of an exciting event⟩. PICTURESQUE suggests the presentation of a striking or effective picture composed of features notable for their distinctness and charm ⟨a *picturesque* account of his travels⟩.

\ə\ abut \ᵊ\ kitten \ər\ further \a\ ash \ā\ ace \ä\ mop, mar \aü\ out \ch\ chin \e\ bet \ē\ easy \g\ go \i\ hit \ī\ ice \j\ job \ŋ\ sing \ō\ go \ò\ law \òi\ boy \th\ thin \th\ the \ü\ loot \u̇\ foot \y\ yet \zh\ vision *see also* Guide to Pronunciation

**3 :** to lay hold of with the mind **:** COMPREHEND
**synonym** see TAKE
— **grasp·able** \'gras-pə-bəl\ *adjective*
— **grasp·er** *noun*
— **grasp at straws :** to reach for or try anything in desperation
— **grasp the nettle :** to act boldly
²**grasp** *noun* (1561)
**1 a :** HANDLE **b :** EMBRACE
**2 :** HOLD, CONTROL
**3 a :** the reach of the arms **b :** the power of seizing and holding or attaining
**4 :** mental hold or comprehension especially when broad
**grasp·ing** *adjective* (1748)
**:** desiring material possessions urgently and excessively and often to the point of ruthlessness
**synonym** see COVETOUS
— **grasp·ing·ly** \'gras-piŋ-lē\ *adverb*
— **grasp·ing·ness** *noun*
¹**grass** \'gras\ *noun, often attributive* [Middle English *gras*, from Old English *græs*; akin to Old High German *gras* grass, Old English *grōwan* to grow] (before 12th century)
**1 :** herbage suitable or used for grazing animals
**2 :** any of a large family (Gramineae) of monocotyledonous mostly herbaceous plants with jointed stems, slender sheathing leaves, and flowers borne in spikelets of bracts
**3 :** land (as a lawn or a turf racetrack) covered with growing grass ⟨keep off the *grass*⟩ ⟨the horse had never won on *grass*⟩
**4** *plural* **:** leaves or plants of grass
**5 :** a state or place of retirement ⟨put out to *grass*⟩
**6** [short for *grasshopper*, rhyming slang for *copper*] *slang British* **:** a police informer
**7 :** electronic noise on a radarscope that takes the form of vertical lines resembling lawn grass
**8 :** MARIJUANA
— **grass·less** \-ləs\ *adjective*
— **grass·like** \-,līk\ *adjective*
²**grass** (circa 1500)
*transitive verb*
**1 :** to feed (livestock) on grass sometimes without grain or other concentrates
**2 :** to cover with grass; *especially* **:** to seed to grass
*intransitive verb*
**1 :** to produce grass
**2** *slang British* **:** INFORM 2 — often used with *on*
**grass carp** *noun* (1885)
**:** an herbivorous cyprinid fish (*Ctenopharyngodon idella*) of Russia and mainland China that has been introduced elsewhere to control aquatic weeds — called also *white amur*
**grass cloth** *noun* (1857)
**:** a lustrous plain textile of usually loosely woven fibers
**grass court** *noun* (1883)
**:** a tennis court with a grass surface
**grass·hop·per** \'gras-,hä-pər\ *noun* (14th century)
**1 :** any of numerous plant-eating orthopterous insects (Acrididae, Tettigoniidae, and some related families) having the hind legs adapted for leaping and sometimes engaging in migratory flights in which whole regions may be stripped of vegetation
**2 :** a cocktail made with crème de menthe, crème de cacao, and light cream
**grass·land** \-,land\ *noun* (1682)
**1 :** farmland occupied chiefly by forage plants and especially grasses
**2 a :** land on which the natural dominant plant forms are grasses and forbs **b :** an ecological community in which the characteristic plants are grasses
**grass·roots** \'gras-,rüts, -,rùts\ *also* **grass·root** \-,rüt, -,rùt\ *adjective* (1907)
**1 :** BASIC, FUNDAMENTAL ⟨the *grassroots* factor in deciding to buy a house⟩

**2 :** being, originating, or operating in or at the grass roots ⟨a *grassroots* organization⟩ ⟨*grassroots* political support⟩
**3 :** not adapted from or added to an existing facility or operation **:** totally new ⟨a *grassroots* refinery⟩
**grass roots** *noun plural but singular or plural in construction, often attributive* (1901)
**1 :** the very foundation or source
**2 :** the basic level of society or of an organization especially as viewed from higher or more centralized positions of power
**grass tree** *noun* (1802)
**:** any of a genus (*Xanthorrhoea*) of Australian plants of the lily family with a thick woody trunk bearing a cluster of stiff linear leaves and a terminal spike of small flowers
**grass widow** *noun* (1528)
**1** *chiefly dialect* **a :** a discarded mistress **b :** a woman who has had an illegitimate child
**2 a :** a woman whose husband is temporarily away from her **b :** a woman divorced or separated from her husband
**grass widower** *noun* (1862)
**1 :** a man divorced or separated from his wife
**2 :** a man whose wife is temporarily away from him
**grassy** \'gra-sē\ *adjective* **grass·i·er; -est** (15th century)
**1 a :** covered or abounding with grass ⟨*grassy* lawns⟩ **b :** having a flavor or odor of grass ⟨*grassy* tea⟩ ⟨wine with a *grassy* bouquet⟩
**2 :** resembling grass especially in color
**grat** *past of* GREET
¹**grate** \'grāt\ *verb* **grat·ed; grat·ing** [Middle English, from Middle French *grater* to scratch, of Germanic origin; akin to Old High German *krazzōn* to scratch] (14th century)
*transitive verb*
**1** *archaic* **:** ABRADE
**2 :** to reduce to small particles by rubbing on something rough ⟨*grate* cheese⟩
**3 :** FRET, IRRITATE
**4 a :** to gnash or grind noisily **b :** to cause to make a rasping sound **c :** to utter in a harsh voice
*intransitive verb*
**1 :** to rub or rasp noisily
**2 :** to cause irritation **:** JAR ⟨dry, cerebral talk that tends to *grate* on the nerves —Hollis Alpert⟩
— **grat·er** *noun*
— **grat·ing·ly** \'grā-tiŋ-lē\ *adverb*
²**grate** *noun* [Middle English, from Medieval Latin *crata*, *grata* hurdle, alteration of Latin *cratis* — more at HURDLE] (14th century)
**1 a :** a barred frame for cooking over a fire **b :** a frame or bed of iron bars to hold a stove or furnace fire **c :** FIREPLACE
**2 :** GRATING 2
**3** *obsolete* **:** CAGE, PRISON
³**grate** *transitive verb* **grat·ed; grat·ing** (1547)
**:** to furnish with a grate
**grate·ful** \'grāt-fəl\ *adjective* [obsolete *grate* pleasing, thankful, from Latin *gratus* — more at GRACE] (1552)
**1 a :** appreciative of benefits received **b :** expressing gratitude
**2 a :** affording pleasure or contentment **:** PLEASING **b :** pleasing by reason of comfort supplied or discomfort alleviated
— **grate·ful·ly** \-fə-lē\ *adverb*
— **grate·ful·ness** *noun*
**grat·i·cule** \'gra-tə-,kyü(ə)l\ *noun* [French, from Latin *craticula* fine latticework, diminutive of *cratis* wickerwork, hurdle] (1914)
**1 :** RETICLE
**2 :** the network of lines of latitude and longitude upon which a map is drawn
**grat·i·fi·ca·tion** \,gra-tə-fə-'kā-shən\ *noun* (1576)
**1 :** REWARD, RECOMPENSE; *especially* **:** GRATUITY
**2 :** the act of gratifying **:** the state of being gratified

**3 :** a source of satisfaction or pleasure
**grat·i·fy** \'gra-tə-,fī\ *transitive verb* **-fied; -fying** [Middle French *gratifier*, from Latin *gratificari* to show kindness to, from *gratus* + *-ificari*, passive of *-ificare* -ify] (1539)
**1** *archaic* **:** REMUNERATE, REWARD
**2 :** to be a source of or give pleasure or satisfaction to ⟨it *gratified* him to have his wife wear jewels —Willa Cather⟩
**3 :** to give in to **:** INDULGE, SATISFY ⟨*gratify* a whim⟩
**grat·i·fy·ing** *adjective* (circa 1611)
**:** giving pleasure or satisfaction **:** PLEASING
— **grat·i·fy·ing·ly** \-iŋ-lē\ *adverb*
**gra·tin** \'gra-tᵊn, 'grä-\ *noun* [French, from Middle French, from *grater* to scratch] (1806)
**:** a brown crust formed on food that has been cooked au gratin; *also* **:** a dish so cooked
**2 :** UPPER CRUST (the *gratin* of London society)
**gra·ti·né** *or* **gra·ti·née** \,gra-tᵊn-'ā, ,grä-\ *adjective* [French, from past participle of *gratiner* to cook au gratin, from *gratin*] (1931)
**:** AU GRATIN
**gra·ti·née** *or* **gra·ti·nee** \,gra-tᵊn-'ā, ,grä-\ *transitive verb, past & past part* **gra·ti·néed** *or* **gra·ti·need** (1974)
**:** to cook au gratin
**grat·ing** \'grā-tiŋ\ *noun* (1626)
**1 :** a wooden or metal lattice used to close or floor any of various openings
**2 :** a partition, covering, or frame of parallel bars or crossbars
**3 :** a system of close equidistant and parallel lines or bars ruled on a polished surface to produce spectra by diffraction
**gra·tis** \'gra-təs, 'grä-\ *adverb or adjective* [Middle English, from Latin *gratiis*, *gratis*, from ablative plural of *gratia* favor — more at GRACE] (15th century)
**:** without charge or recompense **:** FREE
**grat·i·tude** \'gra-tə-,tüd, -,tyüd\ *noun* [Middle English, from Middle French or Medieval Latin; Middle French, from Medieval Latin *gratitudo*, from Latin *gratus* grateful] (1565)
**:** the state of being grateful **:** THANKFULNESS
**gra·tu·itous** \grə-'tü-ə-təs, -'tyü-\ *adjective* [Latin *gratuitus*, from *gratus*] (1656)
**1 a :** given unearned or without recompense **b :** not involving a return benefit, compensation, or consideration **c :** costing nothing **:** FREE
**2 :** not called for by the circumstances **:** UNWARRANTED ⟨*gratuitous* insolence⟩ ⟨a *gratuitous* assumption⟩
— **gra·tu·itous·ly** *adverb*
— **gra·tu·itous·ness** *noun*
**gra·tu·ity** \grə-'tü-ə-tē, -'tyü-\ *noun, plural* **-ities** (1540)
**:** something given voluntarily or beyond obligation usually for some service; *especially* **:** TIP
**grat·u·late** \'gra-chə-,lāt\ *transitive verb* [Latin *gratulatus*, past participle of *gratulari* — more at CONGRATULATE] (1584)
*archaic* **:** CONGRATULATE
— **grat·u·la·tion** \,gra-chə-'lā-shən\ *noun*
— **grat·u·la·to·ry** \'gra-chə-lə-,tōr-ē, -,tòr-\ *adjective*
**grau·pel** \'graù-pəl\ *noun* [German] (1889)
**:** granular snow pellets — called also *soft hail*
**Grau·stark** \'graù-,stärk, 'grò-\ *noun* [*Graustark*, imaginary country in the novel *Graustark* (1901) by George B. McCutcheon (died 1928) American novelist] (1941)
**:** an imaginary land of high romance; *also* **:** a highly romantic piece of writing
— **Grau·stark·ian** \graù-'stär-kē-ən, grò-\ *adjective*
**gra·va·men** \grə-'vā-mən\ *noun, plural* **-va·mens** *or* **-vam·i·na** \-'va-mə-nə\ [Late Latin, burden, from Latin *gravare* to burden, from *gravis*] (1647)
**:** the material or significant part of a grievance or complaint
¹**grave** \'grāv\ *transitive verb* **graved; grav·en** \'grā-vən\ *or* **graved; grav·ing** [Middle

English, from Old English *grafan;* akin to Old High German *graban* to dig, Old Church Slavonic po*greti* to bury] (before 12th century)
**1** *archaic* **:** DIG, EXCAVATE
**2 a :** to carve or shape with a chisel **:** SCULPTURE **b :** to carve or cut (as letters or figures) into a hard surface **:** ENGRAVE
**3 :** to impress or fix (as a thought) deeply
**²grave** *noun* [Middle English, from Old English *græf;* akin to Old High German *grab* grave, Old English *grafan* to dig] (before 12th century)
**1 :** an excavation for burial of a body; *broadly* **:** a burial place
**2 :** DEATH 1, 4
**³grave** *transitive verb* **graved; grav·ing** [Middle English *graven*] (15th century)
**:** to clean and pay with pitch ⟨*grave* a ship's bottom⟩
**⁴grave** \'grāv, *in sense 5 often* 'gräv\ *adjective* **grav·er; grav·est** [Middle French, from Latin *gravis* heavy, grave — more at GRIEVE] (1539)
**1 a** *obsolete* **:** AUTHORITATIVE, WEIGHTY **b :** meriting serious consideration **:** IMPORTANT ⟨*grave* problems⟩ **c :** likely to produce great harm or danger ⟨a *grave* mistake⟩ **d :** significantly serious **:** CONSIDERABLE, GREAT ⟨*grave* importance⟩
**2 :** having a serious and dignified quality or demeanor ⟨a *grave* and thoughtful look⟩
**3 :** drab in color **:** SOMBER
**4 :** low-pitched in sound
**5 a :** of an accent mark **:** having the form ` **b :** marked with a grave accent **c :** of the variety indicated by a grave accent
**synonym** see SERIOUS
— **grave·ly** *adverb*
— **grave·ness** *noun*
**⁵grave** \'grāv, 'gräv\ *noun* (1609)
**:** a grave accent ` used to show that a vowel is pronounced with a fall of pitch (as in ancient Greek), that a vowel has a certain quality (as *è* in French), that a final *e* is stressed and close and that a final *o* is stressed and low (as in Italian), that a syllable has a degree of stress between maximum and minimum (as in phonetic transcription), or that the *e* of the English ending *-ed* is to be pronounced (as in "this cursèd day")
**⁶gra·ve** \'grä-(ˌ)vā\ *adverb or adjective* [Italian, literally, grave, from Latin *gravis*] (1683)
**:** slowly and solemnly — used as a direction in music
**¹grav·el** \'gra-vəl\ *noun* [Middle English, from Old French *gravele,* diminutive of *grave, greve* pebbly ground, beach] (13th century)
**1** *obsolete* **:** SAND
**2 a :** loose rounded fragments of rock **b :** a stratum or deposit of gravel; *also* **:** a surface covered with gravel ⟨a *gravel* road⟩
**3 :** a deposit of small calculous concretions in the kidneys and urinary bladder
**²gravel** *transitive verb* **-eled** *or* **-elled; -el·ing** *or* **-el·ling** \'grav-liŋ, 'gra-və-\ (1543)
**1 :** to cover or spread with gravel
**2 a :** PERPLEX, CONFOUND **b :** IRRITATE, NETTLE
**³gravel** *adjective* (1939)
**:** GRAVELLY 2 — used of the human voice
**grav·el–blind** \'gra-vəl-ˌblīnd\ *adjective* [suggested by *sand-blind*] (1596)
**:** having very weak vision
**grave·less** \'grāv-ləs\ *adjective* (1606)
**1 :** not buried ⟨these *graveless* bones⟩
**2 :** not requiring graves **:** DEATHLESS ⟨the *graveless* home of the blessed⟩
**grav·el·ly** \'grav-lē, 'gra-və-\ *adjective* (14th century)
**1 :** of, containing, or covered with gravel
**2 :** having a rough or grating sound ⟨a *gravelly* voice⟩
**graven image** *noun* [*graven,* past participle of ¹*grave*] (14th century)
**:** an object of worship carved usually from wood or stone **:** IDOL

**grav·er** \'grā-vər\ *noun* [Middle English] (13th century)
**1 :** SCULPTOR, ENGRAVER
**2 :** any of various cutting or shaving tools used in graving or in hand metal-turning
**Graves' disease** \'grāvz-\ *noun* [Robert J. *Graves* (died 1853) Irish physician] (1868)
**:** a common form of hyperthyroidism characterized by goiter and often a slight protrusion of the eyeballs
**grave·side** \'grāv-ˌsīd\ *noun* (1838)
**:** the area beside a grave ⟨mourners at *graveside*⟩
**grave·stone** \'grāv-ˌstōn\ *noun* (14th century)
**:** a burial monument
**grave·yard** \-ˌyärd\ *noun* (1773)
**1 :** CEMETERY
**2 :** something resembling a graveyard ⟨an automobile *graveyard*⟩
**graveyard shift** *noun* (1908)
**:** a work shift beginning late at night (as 11 o'clock); *also* **:** the workers on such a shift
**gravi-** *combining form* [Middle French, from Latin, from *gravis*]
**:** weight ⟨*gravimetric*⟩
**grav·id** \'gra-vəd\ *adjective* [Latin *gravidus,* from *gravis* heavy] (1597)
**1 :** PREGNANT
**2 :** distended with or full of eggs
— **gra·vid·i·ty** \gra-'vi-də-tē\ *noun*
**grav·i·da** \'gra-və-də\ *noun, plural* **-i·das** *or* **-i·dae** \-və-ˌdē\ [Latin, from feminine of *gravidus*] (1926)
**:** a pregnant woman — often used with a number to indicate the number of pregnancies a woman has had ⟨a 4-*gravida*⟩
**gra·vim·e·ter** \gra-'vi-mə-tər, 'gra-və-ˌmē-\ *noun* [French *gravimètre,* from *gravi-* + *-mètre* -meter] (1932)
**:** a sensitive weighing instrument for measuring variations in the gravitational field of the earth or moon
**gravi·met·ric** \ˌgra-və-'me-trik\ *adjective* (1873)
**1 :** of or relating to measurement by weight
**2 :** of or relating to variations in the gravitational field determined by means of a gravimeter
— **gravi·met·ri·cal·ly** \-tri-k(ə-)lē\ *adverb*
**gra·vim·e·try** \gra-'vi-mə-trē\ *noun* (1858)
**:** the measurement of weight, a gravitational field, or density
**graving dock** *noun* (1840)
**:** DRY DOCK
**grav·i·tas** \'gra-və-ˌtäs, -ˌtas\ *noun* [Latin] (1924)
**:** high seriousness (as in a person's bearing or in the treatment of a subject)
**grav·i·tate** \'gra-və-ˌtāt\ *intransitive verb* **-tat·ed; -tat·ing** (1692)
**1 :** to move under the influence of gravitation
**2 a :** to move toward something **b :** to be drawn or attracted especially by natural inclination ⟨youngsters . . . *gravitate* toward a strong leader —Rose Friedman⟩
**grav·i·ta·tion** \ˌgra-və-'tā-shən\ *noun* (circa 1645)
**1 :** a force manifested by acceleration toward each other of two free material particles or bodies or of radiant-energy quanta **:** GRAVITY 3a(2)
**2 :** the action or process of gravitating
— **grav·i·ta·tion·al** \-shnəl, -shə-nᵊl\ *adjective*
— **grav·i·ta·tion·al·ly** *adverb*
— **grav·i·ta·tive** \'gra-və-ˌtā-tiv\ *adjective*
**gravitational lens** *noun* (1950)
**:** a massive celestial object (as a galaxy) that bends and focuses the light of another more distant object (as a quasar) by gravity and that is usually detected by the multiple images it forms of the second object
**gravitational wave** *noun* (1906)
**:** a hypothetical wave held to travel at the speed of light and to propagate the gravitational field — called also *gravity wave*

**grav·i·ton** \'gra-və-ˌtän\ *noun* [International Scientific Vocabulary *gravity* + ²*-on*] (1942)
**:** a hypothetical particle with zero charge and rest mass that is held to be the quantum of the gravitational field
**grav·i·ty** \'gra-və-tē\ *noun, plural* **-ties** *often attributive* [Middle French or Latin; Middle French *gravité,* from Latin *gravitat-, gravitas,* from *gravis*] (1509)
**1 a :** dignity or sobriety of bearing **b :** IMPORTANCE, SIGNIFICANCE; *especially* **:** SERIOUSNESS **c :** a serious situation or problem
**2 :** WEIGHT
**3 a (1) :** the gravitational attraction of the mass of the earth, the moon, or a planet for bodies at or near its surface **(2) :** a fundamental physical force that is responsible for interactions which occur because of mass between particles, between aggregations of matter (as stars and planets), and between particles (as photons) and aggregations of matter, that is $10^{39}$ times weaker than the strong force, and that extends over infinite distances but is dominant over macroscopic distances especially between aggregations of matter — called also *gravitation, gravitational force;* compare ELECTROMAGNETISM 2a, STRONG FORCE, WEAK FORCE **b :** ACCELERATION OF GRAVITY **c :** SPECIFIC GRAVITY
**grav·lax** *or* **grav·laks** \'gräv-ˌläks\ *noun* [Swedish *gravlax* or Norwegian *gravlaks,* from *grav* buried + Swedish *lax,* Norwegian *laks* salmon — more at LOX] (1977)
**:** salmon usually cured with salt, pepper, dill, and aquavit
**gra·vure** \grə-'vyùr, grā-\ *noun* [French, from *graver* to grave, of Germanic origin; akin to Old High German *graban* to dig, engrave — more at GRAVE] (1893)
**:** PHOTOGRAVURE
**gra·vy** \'grā-vē\ *noun, plural* **gravies** [Middle English *gravey,* from Middle French *gravé*] (14th century)
**1 :** a sauce made from the thickened and seasoned juices of cooked meat
**2 a :** something additional or unexpected that is pleasing or valuable ⟨with expenses now paid, future money is pure *gravy* —K. Crossen⟩ **b :** unearned or illicit gain **:** ⁵GRAFT
**gravy train** *noun* (circa 1927)
**:** a much exploited source of easy money; *also* **:** GRAVY 2a
**¹gray** \'grā\ *adjective* [Middle English, from Old English *grǣg;* akin to Old High German *grīs, grāo* gray] (before 12th century)
**1 a :** of the color gray **b :** tending toward gray ⟨blue-*gray* eyes⟩ **c :** dull in color
**2 :** having the hair gray **:** HOARY
**3 :** clothed in gray
**4 a :** lacking cheer or brightness in mood, outlook, style, or flavor; *also* **:** DISMAL, GLOOMY ⟨a *gray* day⟩ **b :** prosaically ordinary **:** DULL, UNINTERESTING
**5 :** having an intermediate and often vaguely defined position, condition, or character ⟨an ethically *gray* area⟩
— **gray·ly** *adverb*
— **gray·ness** *noun*
**²gray** *noun* (13th century)
**1 :** something (as an animal, garment, cloth, or spot) of a gray color
**2 :** any of a series of neutral colors ranging between black and white
**3 :** one who wears a gray uniform: as **a :** a soldier in the Confederate army during the American Civil War **b :** the Confederate army
**³gray** (14th century)
*transitive verb*
**:** to make gray
*intransitive verb*

**1 :** to become gray ⟨*graying* hair⟩
**2 :** AGE; *also* **:** to contain an increasing percentage of older people

**gray·beard** \'grā-ˌbird\ *noun* (circa 1580)
**:** an old man

**gray birch** *noun* (1851)
**1 :** a small birch (*Betula populifolia*) of northeastern North America that has many lateral branches, grayish white bark, triangular leaves, and soft weak wood and that occurs especially in old fields reverting to woodland
**2 :** YELLOW BIRCH

**gray eminence** *noun* [translation of French *Éminence grise*, nickname of Père Joseph (François Joseph du Tremblay) (died 1638) French monk and diplomat who was confidant of Cardinal Richelieu, styled *Éminence rouge* (red eminence); from the colors of their respective habits] (1941)
**:** a person who exercises power behind the scenes

**gray·fish** \'grā-ˌfish\ *noun* (1917)
**:** DOGFISH

**gray fox** *noun* (circa 1679)
**:** a fox (*Urocyon cinereoargenteus*) with coarse gray hair and white underparts that occurs from southern Canada to northern South America

**gray·ish** \'grā-ish\ *adjective* (1562)
**1 :** somewhat gray
**2** *of a color* **:** low in saturation

**gray·ling** \'grā-liŋ\ *noun, plural* **grayling** *also* **graylings** (15th century)
**:** any of several freshwater salmonoid fishes (genus *Thymallus*) valued as food and sport fishes

**gray market** *noun* (1946)
**:** a market employing irregular but not illegal methods; *especially* **:** a market that legally circumvents authorized channels of distribution to sell goods at prices lower than those intended by the manufacturer

**gray matter** *noun* (1840)
**1 :** neural tissue especially of the brain and spinal cord that contains nerve-cell bodies as well as nerve fibers and has a brownish gray color
**2 :** BRAINS, INTELLECT

**gray squirrel** *noun* (1674)
**:** a common light gray to black squirrel (*Sciurus carolinensis*) that is native to eastern North America and has been introduced into England

**gray·wacke** \'grā-ˌwak, -ˌwa-kə\ *noun* [partial translation of German *Grauwacke*] (1811)
**:** a coarse usually dark gray sandstone or fine-grained conglomerate composed of firmly cemented fragments (as of quartz or feldspar)

**gray whale** *noun* (1860)
**:** a large baleen whale (*Eschrichtius robustus*) of the northern Pacific having short jaws and no dorsal fin

**gray wolf** *noun* (1814)
**:** a large usually gray Holarctic wolf (*Canis lupus*) now restricted to northern North America and Asia — called also *timber wolf*

**¹graze** \'grāz\ *verb* **grazed; graz·ing** [Middle English *grasen*, from Old English *grasian*, from *græs* grass] (before 12th century)
*intransitive verb*
**1 :** to feed on growing herbage, attached algae, or phytoplankton
**2 :** to eat small amounts of various foods several times a day
*transitive verb*
**1 a :** to crop and eat in the field **b :** to feed on the herbage of
**2 a :** to put to graze ⟨*grazed* the cows on the meadow⟩ **b :** to put cattle to graze on
**3 :** to supply herbage for the grazing of
— **graze·able** *or* **graz·able** \'grā-zə-bəl\ *adjective*
— **graz·er** *noun*

**²graze** *noun* (1692)
**1 :** an act of grazing
**2 :** herbage for grazing

**³graze** *verb* **grazed; graz·ing** [perhaps from ¹*graze*] (1604)
*transitive verb*
**1 :** to touch lightly in passing
**2 :** ABRADE, SCRATCH ⟨*grazed* her knee when she fell⟩
*intransitive verb*
**:** to touch or rub against something in passing

**⁴graze** *noun* (1847)
**:** a scraping along a surface or an abrasion made by it; *especially* **:** a superficial abrasion of the skin

**gra·zier** \'grā-zhər\ *noun* (15th century)
**1 :** a person who grazes cattle; *broadly* **:** RANCHER
**2** *Australian* **:** a sheep raiser

**grazing** *noun* (1517)
**:** herbage or land for grazing

**¹grease** \'grēs\ *noun* [Middle English *grese*, from Old French *craisse, graisse*, from (assumed) Vulgar Latin *crassia*, from Latin *crassus* fat] (13th century)
**1 a :** rendered animal fat **b :** oily matter **c :** a thick lubricant
**2 :** wool as it comes from the sheep retaining the natural oils or fats
— **grease·less** \'grēs-ləs\ *adjective*
— **grease·proof** \'grēs-'prüf\ *adjective*
— **in the grease** *of wool or fur* **:** in the natural uncleaned condition

**²grease** \'grēs, 'grēz\ *transitive verb* **greased; greas·ing** (14th century)
**1 :** to smear or daub with grease
**2 :** to lubricate with grease
**3 :** to soil with grease
**4 :** to hasten the process or progress of; *also* **:** FACILITATE
— **grease the hand of** *or* **grease the palm of :** BRIBE

**grease·ball** \'grēs-ˌbȯl\ *noun* (circa 1922)
**:** a person of Hispanic or Mediterranean descent — usually used disparagingly

**grease monkey** *noun* (1928)
**:** MECHANIC

**grease·paint** \'grēs-ˌpānt\ *noun* (1886)
**1 :** a melted tallow or grease used in theater makeup
**2 :** theater makeup

**grease pencil** *noun* (1944)
**:** a pencil in which the marking substance is pigment and grease

**greaseproof paper** *noun* (1900)
*British* **:** a heavy stiff waxed paper — called also *greaseproof*

**greas·er** \'grē-zər, -sər\ *noun* [¹*grease*] (1641)
**1 :** one that greases
**2 :** a native or inhabitant of Latin America or a Mediterranean land; *especially* **:** MEXICAN — usually used disparagingly
**3 :** an aggressive swaggering young white male usually of working-class background

**grease·wood** \'grēs-ˌwu̇d\ *noun* (1838)
**:** a low stiff shrub (*Sarcobatus vermiculatus*) of the goosefoot family common in alkaline soils in the western U.S.; *also* **:** any of various related or similar shrubs

**greasy** \'grē-sē, -zē\ *adjective* **greas·i·er; -est** (1514)
**1 a :** smeared or soiled with grease ⟨*greasy* clothes⟩ **b :** oily in appearance, texture, or manner ⟨his *greasy* smile —Jack London⟩ **c :** SLIPPERY
**2 :** containing an unusual amount of grease ⟨*greasy* food⟩
— **greas·i·ly** \-sə-lē, -zə-\ *adverb*
— **greas·i·ness** \-sē-nəs, -zē-\ *noun*

**greasy spoon** *noun* (circa 1925)
**:** a dingy small cheap restaurant

**¹great** \'grāt, *Southern also* 'gre(ə)t\ *adjective* [Middle English *grete*, from Old English *grēat*; akin to Old High German *grōz* large] (before 12th century)
**1 a :** notably large in size **:** HUGE **b :** of a kind characterized by relative largeness — used in plant and animal names **c :** ELABORATE, AMPLE ⟨*great* detail⟩

**2 a :** large in number or measure **:** NUMEROUS ⟨*great* multitudes⟩ **b :** PREDOMINANT ⟨the *great* majority⟩
**3 :** remarkable in magnitude, degree, or effectiveness ⟨*great* bloodshed⟩
**4 :** full of emotion ⟨*great* with anger⟩
**5 a :** EMINENT, DISTINGUISHED ⟨a *great* poet⟩ **b :** chief or preeminent over others — often used in titles ⟨Lord *Great* Chamberlain⟩ **c :** ARISTOCRATIC, GRAND ⟨*great* ladies⟩
**6 :** long continued ⟨a *great* while⟩
**7 :** PRINCIPAL, MAIN ⟨a reception in the *great* hall⟩
**8 :** more remote in a family relationship by a single generation than a specified relative ⟨*great*-grandfather⟩
**9 :** markedly superior in character or quality; *especially* **:** NOBLE ⟨*great* of soul⟩
**10 a :** remarkably skilled ⟨*great* at tennis⟩ **b :** marked by enthusiasm **:** KEEN ⟨*great* on science fiction⟩
**11 —** used as a generalized term of approval ⟨had a *great* time⟩ ⟨it was just *great*⟩
— **great·ness** *noun*

**²great** *adverb* (13th century)
**:** in a great manner **:** SUCCESSFULLY, WELL ⟨things are going *great*⟩

**³great** *noun, plural* **great** *or* **greats** (13th century)
**:** an outstandingly superior or skillful person

**great ape** *noun* (1949)
**:** any of a family (Pongidae) of primates including the gorilla, orangutan, and chimpanzees — called also *pongid*

**great auk** *noun* (circa 1828)
**:** an extinct large flightless auk (*Pinguinus impennis*) formerly abundant along North Atlantic coasts

**great–aunt** *noun* (1656)
**:** GRANDAUNT

**Great Bear** *noun*
**:** URSA MAJOR

**great blue heron** *noun* (1835)
**:** a large slaty-blue American heron (*Ardea herodias*) with a crested head

**great circle** *noun* (1594)
**:** a circle formed on the surface of a sphere by the intersection of a plane that passes through the center of the sphere; *specifically* **:** such a circle on the surface of the earth an arc of which connecting two terrestrial points constitutes the shortest distance on the earth's surface between them

**great·coat** \'grāt-ˌkōt\ *noun* (circa 1685)
**:** a heavy overcoat

**Great Dane** *noun* (1774)
**:** any of a breed of tall massive powerful smooth-coated dogs

**great divide** *noun* [the *Great Divide*, North American watershed] (1868)
**:** a significant point of division; *especially* **:** DEATH

**great·en** \'grā-t°n\ *verb* **great·ened; great·en·ing** \'grā-t°n-iŋ\ (1614)
*transitive verb*
**:** to make greater
*intransitive verb*
**:** to become greater

**great·er** *adjective, often capitalized* [comparative of *great*] (1882)
**:** consisting of a central city together with adjacent areas that are naturally or administratively connected with it ⟨*Greater* London⟩

**greater yellowlegs** *noun plural but singular or plural in construction* (circa 1909)
**:** a common North American marsh and shorebird (*Tringa melanoleuca*) that is largely gray above and white below with black or dark gray flecks and yellow legs — compare LESSER YELLOWLEGS

**greatest common divisor** *noun* (circa 1924)
**:** the largest integer or the polynomial of highest degree that is an exact divisor of each of two or more integers or polynomials — called also *greatest common factor*

**great group** *noun* (1960)
: a group of soils that is characterized by common characteristics usually developed under the influence of environmental factors (as vegetation and climate) active over a considerable geographic range and that comprises one or more families of soil — called also *great soil group*

**great·heart·ed** \'grāt-,här-təd\ *adjective* (14th century)
**1** : characterized by bravery : COURAGEOUS
**2** : GENEROUS, MAGNANIMOUS
— **great·heart·ed·ly** *adverb*
— **great·heart·ed·ness** *noun*

**great horned owl** *noun* (1812)
: a large American owl (*Bubo virginianus*) with conspicuous ear tufts

**great laurel** *noun* (1784)
: a large-leaved evergreen rhododendron (*Rhododendron maximum*) of eastern North America with rosy bell-shaped flowers more or less speckled with green — called also *rosebay rhododendron*

**great·ly** \'grāt-lē\ *adverb* (13th century)
**1** : to a great extent or degree : very much ⟨contributed *greatly* to improved relations⟩ ⟨not *greatly* bothered⟩
**2** : in a great manner : NOBLY, MAGNANIMOUSLY ⟨a man may live *greatly* in the law —O. W. Holmes (died 1935)⟩

**Great Mogul** *noun* (1588)
: the sovereign of the empire founded in India by the Moguls in the 16th century

**great–nephew** *noun* (1581)
: GRANDNEPHEW

**great–niece** *noun* (1884)
: GRANDNIECE

**great octave** *noun* (circa 1854)
: the musical octave that begins on the second C below middle C — see PITCH illustration

**great power** *noun, often G&P capitalized* (circa 1890)
: one of the nations that figure most decisively in international affairs : SUPERPOWER

**Great Pyr·e·nees** \-'pir-ə-,nēz\ *noun, plural* **Great Pyrenees** (1938)
: any of a breed of large heavy-coated white dogs often used to guard livestock

**great room** *noun* (1700)
: a large room usually combining several functions (as of a dining room, living room, and family room)

**Great Russian** *noun* (1854)
: RUSSIAN 1b
— **Great Russian** *adjective*

Great Pyrenees

**great seal** *noun* (15th century)
: a large seal that constitutes an emblem of sovereignty and is used especially for the authentication of important documents

**great skua** *noun* (circa 1954)
: a large seabird (*Catharacta skua*) that is related to the jaeger, has dusky plumage and broad rounded wings, breeds chiefly along arctic and antarctic shores, and forages over most cold and temperate seas

**great–uncle** *noun* (1656)
: GRANDUNCLE

**great vowel shift** *noun, often G&V&S capitalized* (1909)
: a change in pronunciation of the long vowels of Middle English that began in the 15th century and continued into the 16th century in which the high vowels were diphthongized and the other vowels were raised

**great white shark** *noun* (circa 1931)
: a large mackerel shark (*Carcharodon carcharias*) of warm seas that is bluish when young but becomes whitish with age and is a man-eater — called also *white shark*; see SHARK illustration

**great year** *noun* (circa 1741)
: the period of about 25,800 years required for one complete cycle of the equinoxes around the ecliptic

**greave** \'grēv\ *noun* [Middle English *greve*, from Middle French] (14th century)
: armor for the leg below the knee

**grebe** \'grēb\ *noun* [French *grèbe*] (1766)
: any of a family (Podicipedidae) of swimming and diving birds closely related to the loons but having lobate toes — compare DABCHICK

**Gre·cian** \'grē-shən\ *adjective* [Middle English *greciane*, from Latin *Graecia* Greece] (15th century)
: GREEK
— **Grecian** *noun*
— **gre·cian·ize** \-shə-,nīz\ *transitive verb, often capitalized*

**Gre·cism** \'grē-,si-zəm\ *noun* (1570)
**1** : a Greek idiom
**2** : a quality or style imitative of Greek art or culture

**gre·cize** \-,sīz\ *transitive verb* **gre·cized; gre·ciz·ing** *often capitalized* (1692)
: to make Greek or Hellenistic in character

**Gre·co-** \'grē-kō, 'grē-\ *or* **Grae·co-** \'grē-kō\ *combining form* [Latin *Graeco-*, from *Graecus*]
**1** : Greece : Greeks ⟨*Greco*phile⟩
**2** : Greek and ⟨*Graeco*-Roman⟩

**¹gree** \'grē\ *noun* [Middle English, from Middle French *grē* step, degree, from Latin *gradus* — more at GRADE] (14th century)
*Scottish* : MASTERY, SUPERIORITY

**²gree** *verb* **greed; gree·ing** [Middle English *green*, short for *agreen*] (14th century)
*dialect* : AGREE

**greed** \'grēd\ *noun* [back-formation from *greedy*] (1609)
: excessive or reprehensible acquisitiveness : AVARICE

**greedy** \'grē-dē\ *adjective* **greed·i·er; -est** [Middle English *gredy*, from Old English *grǣdig*; akin to Old High German *grātac* greedy] (before 12th century)
**1** : having a strong desire for food or drink
**2** : marked by greed
**3** : EAGER, KEEN ⟨elated and *greedy* for the future —Frances G. Patton⟩
*synonym* see COVETOUS
— **greed·i·ly** \'grē-dᵊl-ē\ *adverb*
— **greed·i·ness** \'grē-dē-nəs\ *noun*

**¹Greek** \'grēk\ *noun* [Middle English *Greke*, from Old English *Grēca*, from Latin *Graecus*, from Greek *Graikos*] (before 12th century)
**1 a** : a native or inhabitant of ancient or modern Greece **b** : a person of Greek descent
**2 a** : the language used by the Greeks from prehistoric times to the present constituting a branch of Indo-European — see INDO-EUROPEAN LANGUAGES table **b** : ancient Greek as used from the time of the earliest records to the end of the 2d century A.D. — see INDO-EUROPEAN LANGUAGES table **c** *often not capitalized* [translation of Latin *Graecum* (in the medieval phrase *Graecum est; non potest legi* It is Greek; it cannot be read)] : something unintelligible ⟨it's *Greek* to me⟩
**3** : a member of a Greek-letter fraternity or sorority

**²Greek** *adjective* (14th century)
**1** : of, relating to, or characteristic of Greece, the Greeks, or Greek ⟨*Greek* architecture⟩
**2 a** : EASTERN ORTHODOX **b** : of or relating to an Eastern church using the Byzantine rite in Greek **c** : of or relating to the established Orthodox church of Greece

**Greek Catholic** *noun* (1909)
**1** : a member of an Eastern church
**2** : a member of an Eastern rite of the Roman Catholic Church

**Greek cross** *noun* (1725)
: a cross having an upright and a transverse shaft equal in length and intersecting at their middles — see CROSS illustration

**Greek fire** *noun* (circa 1823)
: an incendiary composition used in warfare by the Byzantine Greeks that is said to have burst into flame on wetting

**Greek·less** \'grēk-ləs\ *adjective* (1891)
: not proficient in Greek

**Greek Orthodox** *adjective* (circa 1900)
: EASTERN ORTHODOX; *specifically* : GREEK 2c

**Greek Revival** *noun* (1918)
**1** : a style of architecture in the first half of the 19th century marked by the use or imitation of Greek orders
**2** : a style of decoration (as of furniture) using or imitating the decorative motifs of ancient Greece

**¹green** \'grēn\ *adjective* [Middle English *grene*, from Old English *grēne*; akin to Old English *grōwan* to grow] (before 12th century)
**1** : of the color green
**2 a** : covered by green growth or foliage ⟨*green* fields⟩ **b** *of winter* : MILD, CLEMENT **c** : consisting of green plants and usually edible herbage ⟨a *green* salad⟩
**3** : pleasantly alluring
**4** : YOUTHFUL, VIGOROUS
**5** : not ripened or matured : IMMATURE ⟨*green* apples⟩ ⟨tender *green* grasses⟩
**6** : FRESH, NEW
**7 a** : marked by a pale, sickly, or nauseated appearance **b** : ENVIOUS 1 — used especially in the phrase *green with envy*
**8 a** : not fully processed or treated: as (1) : not aged ⟨*green* liquor⟩ (2) : not dressed or tanned ⟨*green* hides⟩ (3) : freshly sawed : UNSEASONED **b** : not in condition for a particular use
**9 a** : deficient in training, knowledge, or experience **b** : deficient in sophistication and savoir faire : NAIVE **c** : not fully qualified for or experienced in a particular function ⟨*green* horse⟩
**10 a** *often capitalized* : relating to or being an environmentalist political movement **b** : concerned with or supporting environmentalism
— **green·ish** \'grē-nish\ *adjective*
— **green·ish·ness** *noun*
— **green·ly** *adverb*
— **green·ness** \'grē(n)-nəs\ *noun*
— **green around the gills** : pale or sickly in appearance

**²green** (before 12th century)
*intransitive verb*
: to become green
*transitive verb*
**1** : to make green
**2** : REJUVENATE, REVITALIZE

**³green** *noun* (13th century)
**1** : a color whose hue is somewhat less yellow than that of growing fresh grass or of the emerald or is that of the part of the spectrum lying between blue and yellow
**2** : something of a green color
**3** : green vegetation: as **a** *plural* : leafy parts of plants for use as decoration **b** *plural* (1) : leafy herbs (as spinach, dandelions, Swiss chard) that are cooked as a vegetable : POTHERBS (2) : GREEN VEGETABLES
**4** : a grassy plain or plot: as **a** : a common or park in the center of a town or village **b** : PUTTING GREEN
**5** : MONEY; *especially* : GREENBACKS
**6** *often capitalized* : ENVIRONMENTALIST; *especially* : a member of an environmentalist political party
— **greeny** \'grē-nē\ *adjective*

**green alga** *noun* (1903)

---

\ə\ abut \ᵊ\ kitten \ər\ further \a\ ash \ā\ ace
\ä\ mop, mar \aú\ out \ch\ chin \e\ bet \ē\ easy
\g\ go \i\ hit \ī\ ice \j\ job \ŋ\ sing \ō\ go
\ȯ\ law \ȯi\ boy \th\ thin \t͟h\ the \ü\ loot \ú\ foot
\y\ yet \zh\ vision    *see also* Guide to Pronunciation

: any of a division (Chlorophyta) of green-colored algae that have chloroplasts and occur especially in freshwater

**green·back** \'grēn-,bak\ *noun* (1862)
: a legal-tender note issued by the U.S. government

**green·back·er** \-,ba-kər\ *noun* (1876)
**1** *capitalized* : a member of a post-Civil War American political party opposing reduction in the amount of paper money in circulation
**2** : one who advocates a paper currency backed only by the U.S. government
— **green·back·ism** \-,ki-zəm\ *noun*

**green bean** *noun* (1847)
: a kidney bean that is used as a snap bean when the pods are colored green

**green·belt** \'grēn-,belt\ *noun* (1932)
: a belt of parkways, parks, or farmlands that encircles a community

**Green Beret** *noun* [from the beret worn by Special Forces soldiers] (1962)
: a member of the U.S. Army Special Forces

**green·bri·er** \-,brī(-ə)r\ *noun* (circa 1785)
: any of a genus (*Smilax*) of woody or herbaceous vines of the lily family; *especially* : a prickly vine (*S. rotundifolia*) of the eastern U.S. with umbels of small greenish flowers

**green·bug** \-,bəg\ *noun* (1712)
: a green aphid (*Schizaphis graminum*) very destructive to small grains

**green card** *noun* [from the fact that it was formerly colored green] (1969)
: an identity card attesting the permanent resident status of an alien in the U.S.
— **green–carder** *noun*

**green corn** *noun* (1645)
: the young tender ears of Indian corn

**green dragon** *noun* (circa 1818)
: an American arum (*Arisaema dracontium*) with digitate leaves, slender green spathe, and elongated spadix

**green·ery** \'grēn-rē, 'grē-nər-ē\ *noun, plural* **-er·ies** (1797)
**1** : green foliage or plants
**2** : GREEN 3a

**green–eyed** \'grē-,nīd\ *adjective* (1596)
: JEALOUS

**green–eyed monster** *noun* (1604)
: JEALOUSY

**green·finch** \'grēn-,finch\ *noun* (15th century)
: a very common European finch (*Carduelis chloris*) having olive-green and yellow plumage

**green fingers** *noun plural* (1934)
: GREEN THUMB

**green flash** *noun* (1912)
: a momentary green appearance of the uppermost part of the sun's disk at sunrise or sunset that results from atmospheric refraction

**green·fly** \'grēn-,flī\ *noun* (circa 1750)
*British* : APHID; *especially* : GREEN PEACH APHID

**green·gage** \-,gāj\ *noun* [green + Sir William *Gage* (died 1820) English botanist] (1724)
: any of several rather small rounded greenish or greenish yellow cultivated plums

**green gland** *noun* (circa 1890)
: one of a pair of large green glands in some crustaceans (as crayfishes) that have an excretory function and open at the bases of the larger antennae

**green·gro·cer** \'grēn-,grō-sər, -shər\ *noun* (1723)
*chiefly British* : a retailer of fresh vegetables and fruit
— **green·gro·cery** \-,grō-sə-rē, -,grōsh-rē\ *noun*

**green·head** \'grēn-,hed\ *noun* (1837)
: any of several green-eyed horseflies (as *Tabanus nigrovittatus*)

**green·heart** \-,härt\ *noun* (1756)
: a tropical South American evergreen tree (*Ocotea rodiaei* synonym *Nectandra rodiaei*) of the laurel family with a hard greenish wood; *also* : its wood

**green·horn** \-,hórn\ *noun* [obsolete *greenhorn* (animal with young horns)] (1682)

**1** : an inexperienced or unsophisticated person
**2** : a newcomer (as to a country) unacquainted with local manners and customs

**¹green·house** \-,haús\ *noun* (1664)
**1** : a structure enclosed (as by glass) and used for the cultivation or protection of tender plants
**2** : a clear plastic shell (as a canopy) covering a section of an airplane; *also* : a compartment (as for a bombardier) enclosed by such a shell

**²greenhouse** *adjective* (1969)
: of, relating to, or caused by the greenhouse effect 〈*greenhouse* warming〉 〈*greenhouse* gas〉

**greenhouse effect** *noun* (1937)
: warming of the surface and lower atmosphere of a planet (as the earth or Venus) that is caused by conversion of solar radiation into heat in a process involving selective transmission of short wave solar radiation by the atmosphere, its absorption by the planet's surface, and reradiation as infrared which is absorbed and partly reradiated back to the surface by atmospheric gases

**green·ing** \'grē-niŋ\ *noun* (1664)
: any of several green-skinned apples

**green·keep·er** \'grēn-,kē-pər\ *or* **greens·keep·er** \'grēnz-\ *noun* (circa 1730)
: a person responsible for the care and upkeep of a golf course

**green·let** \'grēn-lət\ *noun* (1831)
: VIREO

**green light** *noun* [from the green traffic light which signals permission to proceed] (1937)
: authority or permission to proceed

**green·ling** \'grēn-liŋ\ *noun* (circa 1898)
: any of several food fishes (family Hexagrammidae) of the rocky coasts of the northern Pacific; *especially* : a common food and sport fish (*Hexagrammos decagrammus*)

**green·mail** \'grēn-,mā(ə)l\ *noun* (1983)
: the practice of buying enough of a company's stock to threaten a hostile takeover and reselling it to the company at a price above market value; *also* : the money paid for such stock
— **greenmail** *transitive verb*
— **green·mail·er** \-,mā-lər\ *noun*

**green manure** *noun* (1842)
: an herbaceous crop (as clover) plowed under while green to enrich the soil
— **green–manure** *transitive verb*

**green mold** *noun* (1919)
: a green or green-spored mold (as of the genera *Penicillium* or *Aspergillus*)

**green monkey** *noun* (1840)
: a long-tailed monkey of any of several African races of a guenon (*Cercopithecus aethiops*) having greenish-appearing hair and often used in medical research

**gree·nock·ite** \'grē-nə-,kīt\ *noun* [Charles M. Cathcart, Lord *Greenock* (died 1859) English soldier] (1844)
: a mineral consisting of native cadmium sulfide occurring in yellow translucent hexagonal crystals or as an earthy incrustation

**green onion** *noun* (1847)
: a young onion pulled before the bulb has enlarged and used especially in salads

**green paper** *noun, often G&P capitalized* (1967)
*British* : a government document that proposes and invites discussion on approaches to a problem

**green peach aphid** *noun* (1922)
: a nearly cosmopolitan yellowish green aphid (*Myzus persicae*) that is frequently a vector of plant virus diseases

**green pepper** *noun* (1700)
: a sweet pepper before it turns red at maturity

**green revolution** *noun* (1968)
: the great increase in production of food grains (as rice and wheat) due to the introduction of high-yielding varieties, to the use of pesticides, and to better management techniques

**green·room** \'grēn-,rüm, -,rum\ *noun* (1701)

: a room in a theater or concert hall where performers can relax before or after appearances

**green·sand** \-,sand\ *noun* (1796)
: a sedimentary deposit that consists largely of dark greenish grains of glauconite often mingled with clay or sand

**greens fee** \'grēnz-\ *noun* (1909)
: a fee paid for the privilege of playing on a golf course — called also *green fee*

**green·shank** \'grēn-,shaŋk\ *noun* (1766)
: an Old World sandpiper (*Tringa nebularia*) with greenish legs and a slightly upturned bill

**green·sick·ness** \-,sik-nəs\ *noun* (1583)
: CHLOROSIS
— **green·sick** *adjective*

**green snake** *noun* (1709)
: either of two bright green harmless largely insectivorous North American colubrid snakes (*Opheodrys vernalis* and *O. aestivus*)

**green soap** *noun* (circa 1840)
: a soft soap made from vegetable oils and used especially in the treatment of skin diseases

**green·stick fracture** \'grēn-,stik-\ *noun* (circa 1885)
: a bone fracture in a young individual in which the bone is partly broken and partly bent

**green·stone** \'grēn-,stōn\ *noun* (circa 1784)
**1** : NEPHRITE
**2** : any of numerous usually altered dark green compact rocks (as diorite)

**green·stuff** \-,stəf\ *noun* (1851)
: green vegetation used as foodstuff

**green sunfish** *noun* (circa 1896)
: a sunfish (*Lepomis cyanellus*) of the Great Lakes region and southwestward to the Rio Grande that is largely greenish above with a blue spot on each scale

**green·sward** \-,swórd\ *noun* (1600)
: turf green with growing grass

**green tea** *noun* (1704)
: tea that is light in color from incomplete fermentation of the leaf before firing

**green thumb** *noun* (1943)
: an unusual ability to make plants grow
— **green–thumbed** \'grēn-'thəmd\ *adjective*

**green turtle** *noun* (1657)
: a large usually herbivorous sea turtle (*Chelonia mydas*) of warm waters with a smooth greenish or olive-colored shell

**green vegetable** *noun* (1826)
: a vegetable whose foliage or foliage-bearing stalks are the chief edible part

**green·way** \'grēn-,wā\ *noun* (1966)
: a corridor of undeveloped land in or near a city that is designed for recreational use

**Green·wich mean time** \'gri-nij, 'gre-, -nich\ *noun, often M&T capitalized* [*Greenwich*, England] (1938)
: the mean solar time of the meridian of Greenwich used as the prime basis of standard time throughout the world — called also *Greenwich time*

**green·wing** \'grēn-,wiŋ\ *noun* (circa 1889)
: GREEN-WINGED TEAL

**green–winged teal** \'grēn-,wiŋ(d)-\ *noun* (1792)
: a small dabbling duck (*Anas crecca*) the male of which has a chestnut head with a green eye patch and a metallic green area on the wing speculum

**green·wood** \'grēn-,wùd\ *noun* (14th century)
: a forest green with foliage

**¹greet** \'grēt\ *transitive verb* [Middle English *greten*, from Old English *grētan*; akin to Old English *grǣtan* to weep] (before 12th century)
**1** : to address with expression of kind wishes
: HAIL
**2 a** : to meet or react to in a specified manner 〈*greeted* him with boos〉 **b** : to occur as a response to 〈apathy *greeted* the plan〉
**3** : to appear to the perception of 〈a surprising sight *greeted* her eyes〉
— **greet·er** *noun*

**²greet** *intransitive verb* **grat** \'grat\; **grut·ten** \'grə-tⁿn\ [Middle English *greten,* from Old English *grǣtan;* akin to Old Norse *grāta* to weep] (before 12th century)
*Scottish* **:** WEEP, LAMENT

**greet·ing** *noun* (before 12th century)
**1 :** a salutation at meeting
**2 :** an expression of good wishes **:** REGARDS — usually used in plural (holiday *greetings*)

**greeting card** *noun* (1898)
**:** a piece of paper or thin paperboard having any of a variety of shapes and formats and bearing a greeting or message of sentiment

**greg·a·rine** \'gre-gə-ˌrīn\ *noun* [ultimately from Latin *gregarius*] (1867)
**:** any of a subclass (Gregarinia) of parasitic vermiform sporozoan protozoans that occur especially in insects and other invertebrates
— **gregarine** *adjective*

**gre·gar·i·ous** \gri-'gar-ē-əs, -'ger-\ *adjective* [Latin *gregarius* of a flock or herd, from *greg-, grex* flock, herd] (1668)
**1 a :** tending to associate with others of one's kind **:** SOCIAL **b :** marked by or indicating a liking for companionship **:** SOCIABLE **c :** of or relating to a social group
**2 a** *of a plant* **:** growing in a cluster or a colony **b :** living in contiguous nests but not forming a true colony — used especially of wasps and bees ◆
— **gre·gar·i·ous·ly** *adverb*
— **gre·gar·i·ous·ness** *noun*

**¹Gre·go·ri·an** \gri-'gōr-ē-ən, -'gȯr-\ *adjective* (1642)
**:** of or relating to Pope Gregory XIII or the Gregorian calendar

**²Gregorian** *adjective* (1653)
**1 :** of or relating to Pope Gregory I
**2 :** of, relating to, or having the characteristics of Gregorian chant

**³Gregorian** *adjective* [Saint *Gregory* the Illuminator (died 332), apostle of Armenia] (1955)
**:** of or relating to the Armenian national church

**Gregorian calendar** *noun* (circa 1771)
**:** a calendar in general use introduced in 1582 by Pope Gregory XIII as a revision of the Julian calendar, adopted in Great Britain and the American colonies in 1752, marked by the suppression of 10 days or after 1700 11 days, and having leap years in every year divisible by four with the restriction that centesimal years are leap years only when divisible by 400 — see MONTH table

**Gregorian chant** *noun* (1751)
**:** a monodic and rhythmically free liturgical chant of the Roman Catholic Church

**greige** \'grā(zh)\ *adjective* [French *grège* raw (of silk), from Italian *greggio*] (1926)
**:** being in an unbleached undyed state as taken from a loom — used of textiles

**grei·sen** \'grī-zⁿn\ *noun* [German] (1878)
**:** a crystalline rock consisting of quartz and mica that is common in Cornwall and Saxony

**grem·lin** \'grem-lən\ *noun* [origin unknown] (1941)
**:** a cause of error or equipment malfunction (as in aircraft) conceived of as a small mischievous gnome

**gre·nade** \grə-'nād\ *noun* [Middle French, pomegranate, from Late Latin *granata,* from Latin, feminine of *granatus* seedy, from *granum* grain — more at CORN] (1591)
**:** a small missile that contains an explosive or a chemical agent (as tear gas, a flame producer, or a smoke producer) and that is thrown by hand or projected (as by a rifle or special launcher)

**gren·a·dier** \ˌgren-ə-'dir\ *noun* [French, from *grenade* grenade] (1676)
**1 a :** a soldier who carries and throws grenades **b :** a member of a special regiment or corps formerly armed with grenades
**2 :** any of various deep-sea fishes (family Macruridae) that are related to the cods and

have an elongate tapering body and compressed pointed tail

**gren·a·dine** \ˌgre-nə-'dēn, 'gre-nə-ˌ\ *noun* [French, from *grenade* coarse silk fabric, pomegranate] (1852)
**1 :** an open-weave fabric of various fibers
**2 :** a moderate reddish orange
**3 :** a syrup flavored with pomegranates and used in mixed drinks

**Gren·del** \'gren-dᵊl\ *noun* [Old English]
**:** a monstrous man-eating descendant of Cain slain by Beowulf in the Old English poem *Beowulf*

**Gresh·am's law** \'gre-shəmz-\ *noun* [Sir Thomas *Gresham*] (1858)
**:** an observation in economics: when two coins are equal in debt-paying value but unequal in intrinsic value, the one having the lesser intrinsic value tends to remain in circulation and the other to be hoarded or exported as bullion; *broadly* **:** any process by which inferior products or practices drive out superior ones

**Gret·na Green** \ˌgret-nə-'gren\ *noun* [*Gretna Green,* village in Scotland] (1813)
**:** a place where many eloping couples are married

**Gre·vy's zebra** \(ˌ)grā-'vēz-\ *noun* [Jules *Grévy*] (1891)
**:** a zebra (*Equus grevyi*) of eastern Africa with narrow stripes and a white belly

**grew** *past of* GROW

**grew·some** *variant of* GRUESOME

**grey** *variant of* GRAY

**grey friar** *noun, often G&F capitalized* (14th century)
**:** a Franciscan friar

**grey·hound** \'grā-ˌhau̇nd\ *noun* [Middle English *grehound,* from Old English *grīghund,* from *grīg-* (akin to Old Norse *grey* bitch) + *hund* hound] (before 12th century)
**:** any of a breed of tall slender graceful smooth-coated dogs characterized by swiftness and keen sight and used for coursing game and racing; *also* **:** any of several related dogs

**greyhound**

**grey·lag** \-ˌlag\ *noun* [perhaps from *gray* + *lag* (last)] (circa 1713)
**:** the common gray wild goose (*Anser anser*) of Europe — called also *greylag goose*

**grib·ble** \'gri-bəl\ *noun* [perhaps alteration of ²*grub*] (1838)
**:** either of two small marine isopods (*Limnoria lignorum* and *L. tripunctata*) that destroy submerged timber

**grid** \'grid\ *noun* [back-formation from *gridiron*] (1839)
**1 :** GRATING
**2 a** (1) **:** a perforated or ridged metal plate used as a conductor in a storage battery (2) **:** an electrode consisting of a mesh or a spiral of fine wire in an electron tube (3) **:** a network of conductors for distribution of electric power; *also* **:** a network of radio or television stations **b :** a network of uniformly spaced horizontal and perpendicular lines (as for locating points on a map); *also* **:** something resembling such a network (a road *grid*) **c :** GRIDIRON 3; *broadly* **:** FOOTBALL
**3 :** the starting positions of cars on a racecourse
**4 :** a device in a photocomposer on which are located the characters to be exposed as the text is composed

**grid·der** \'gri-dər\ *noun* (1928)
**:** a football player

**grid·dle** \'gri-dᵊl\ *noun* [Middle English *gredil* gridiron, from Old North French, from Latin *craticulum,* diminutive of *cratis* wickerwork — more at HURDLE] (14th century)

**:** a flat metal surface or pan on which food is cooked by dry heat

**griddle cake** *noun* (1783)
**:** PANCAKE

**grid·iron** \'grid-ˌī(-ə)rn\ *noun* [Middle English *gredire*] (14th century)
**1 :** a grate for broiling food
**2 :** something consisting of or covered with a network
**3 :** a football field

**grid·lock** \-ˌläk\ *noun* (1980)
**1 :** a traffic jam in which a grid of intersecting streets is so completely congested that no vehicular movement is possible
**2 :** a situation resembling a gridlock
— **gridlock** *transitive verb*

**grief** \'grēf\ *noun* [Middle English *gref,* from Middle French, heavy, grave, from (assumed) Vulgar Latin *grevis,* alteration of Latin *gravis*] (15th century)
**1** *obsolete* **:** GRIEVANCE 3
**2 a :** deep and poignant distress caused by or as if by bereavement **b :** a cause of such suffering
**3 a :** an unfortunate outcome **:** DISASTER — used chiefly in the phrase *come to grief* **b :** MISHAP, MISADVENTURE **c :** TROUBLE, ANNOYANCE (enough *grief* for one day)
*synonym* see SORROW

**griev·ance** \'grē-vən(t)s\ *noun* (14th century)
**1** *obsolete* **:** SUFFERING, DISTRESS
**2 :** a cause of distress (as an unsatisfactory working condition) felt to afford reason for complaint or resistance
**3 :** the formal expression of a grievance **:** COMPLAINT
*synonym* see INJUSTICE

**grievance committee** *noun* (1927)
**:** a committee formed by a labor union or by employer and employees jointly to discuss and where possible to eliminate grievances

**griev·ant** \-vənt\ *noun* (1958)
**:** one who submits a grievance for arbitration

**grieve** \'grēv\ *verb* **grieved; griev·ing** [Middle English *greven,* from Old French *grever,* from Latin *gravare* to burden, from *gravis* heavy, grave; akin to Greek *barys* heavy, Sanskrit *guru*] (13th century)
*transitive verb*
**:** to cause to suffer **:** DISTRESS
*intransitive verb*
**:** to feel grief **:** SORROW
— **griev·er** *noun*

**griev·ous** \'grē-vəs\ *adjective* (13th century)
**1 :** causing or characterized by severe pain, suffering, or sorrow (a *grievous* wound) (a *grievous* loss)
**2 :** OPPRESSIVE, ONEROUS (*grievous* costs of war)
**3 :** SERIOUS, GRAVE (*grievous* fault)

---

◇ WORD HISTORY
**gregarious** *Gregarious,* which is not usually an unfavorable word, is the improbable linguistic cousin of *egregious,* which is now usually used of something conspicuously bad. Both have as their base *grex,* the Latin word for "herd" or "flock." Whereas *egregious* is etymologically "apart from the herd or flock," *gregarious* literally means "of or relating to a herd or flock." When *gregarious* first appeared in English in the 17th century, with the meaning "inclined to associate with others of one's kind," it was used of animals naturally living and breeding in groups. Not till the next century was the word applied to people with a marked fondness for companionship. See in addition EGREGIOUS.

---

\ə\ abut \ᵊ\ kitten \ər\ further \a\ ash \ā\ ace
\ä\ mop, mar \au̇\ out \ch\ chin \e\ bet \ē\ easy
\g\ go \i\ hit \ī\ ice \j\ job \ŋ\ sing \ō\ go
\ȯ\ law \ȯi\ boy \th\ thin \t͟h\ the \ü\ loot \u̇\ foot
\y\ yet \zh\ vision    *see also* Guide to Pronunciation

— **griev·ous·ly** *adverb*
— **griev·ous·ness** *noun*
**grif·fin** *or* **grif·fon** \'gri-fən\ *noun* [Middle English *griffon*, from Middle French *grifon*, from *grif*, from Latin *gryphus*, from Greek *gryp-*, *gryps*] (14th century)
: a mythical animal typically having the head, forepart, and wings of an eagle and the body, hind legs, and tail of a lion

**grif·fon** \'gri-fən\ *noun* [French, literally, griffin] (1882)
**1 :** BRUSSELS GRIFFON
**2 :** WIREHAIRED POINTING GRIFFON

**grift** \'grift\ *transitive verb* [*grift*, noun, perhaps alteration of *graft*] (1915)
*slang* : to obtain (money) illicitly (as in a confidence game)
— **grift** *noun, slang*
— **grift·er** *noun, slang*

**grig** \'grig\ *noun* [Middle English *grege*] (1566)
: a lively lighthearted usually small or young person

**gri·gri** *variant of* GRIS-GRIS
¹**grill** \'gril\ *transitive verb* (1668)
**1 :** to broil on a grill; *also* : to fry or toast on a griddle
**2 a :** to torment as if by broiling **b :** to question intensely ⟨the police *grilled* the suspect⟩
— **grill·er** *noun*
²**grill** *noun* [French *gril*, from Latin *craticulum* — more at GRIDDLE] (1685)
**1 :** a cooking utensil of parallel bars on which food is exposed to heat (as from charcoal or electricity)
**2 :** food that is broiled usually on a grill — compare MIXED GRILL
**3 :** a usually informal restaurant or dining room

**gril·lage** \'gri-lij\ *noun* [French, from *griller* to supply with grillwork, from *gril* ] (1776)
**1 :** a framework of timber or steel for support in marshy or treacherous soil
**2 :** a framework for supporting a load (as a column)

**grille** *or* **grill** \'gril\ *noun* [French *grille*, alteration of Old French *greille*, from Latin *craticula*, diminutive of *cratis* wickerwork — more at HURDLE] (1686)
**1 :** a grating forming a barrier or screen; *especially* : an ornamental one at the front end of an automobile
**2 :** an opening covered with a grille

**grill·room** \'gril-ˌrüm, -ˌrum\ *noun* (1883)
: GRILL 3
**grill·work** \'gril-ˌwərk\ *noun* (1896)
: work constituting or resembling a grille
**grilse** \'grils\ *noun, plural* **grilse** [Middle English *grills*] (15th century)
: a young Atlantic salmon returning to its native river to spawn for the first time after one winter at sea; *broadly* : any of various salmon at such a stage of development

**grim** \'grim\ *adjective* **grim·mer; grim·mest** [Middle English, from Old English *grimm;* akin to Old High German *grimm* fierce, Greek *chremetizein* to neigh] (before 12th century)
**1 :** fierce in disposition or action : SAVAGE
**2 a :** stern or forbidding in action or appearance ⟨a *grim* taskmaster⟩ **b :** SOMBER, GLOOMY
**3 :** ghastly, repellent, or sinister in character ⟨a *grim* tale⟩
**4 :** UNFLINCHING, UNYIELDING ⟨*grim* determination⟩
— **grim·ly** *adverb*
— **grim·ness** *noun*
**gri·mace** \'gri-məs, gri-'mās\ *noun* [French, from Middle French, alteration of *grimache*, of Germanic origin; akin to Old English *grīma* mask] (1651)

: a facial expression usually of disgust or disapproval
— **grimace** *intransitive verb*
— **gri·mac·er** *noun*
**gri·mal·kin** \gri-'mȯ(l)-kən, -'mal-\ *noun* [*gray* + *malkin*] (1630)
: a domestic cat; *especially* : an old female cat
**grime** \'grīm\ *noun* [Middle Dutch *grime* soot, mask; akin to Old English *grīma* mask] (14th century)
: soot, smut, or dirt adhering to or embedded in a surface; *broadly* : accumulated dirtiness and disorder
— **grime** *transitive verb*
**Grimm's law** \'grimz-\ *noun* [Jacob *Grimm*] (1838)
: a statement in historical linguistics: Proto-Indo-European voiceless stops became Proto-Germanic voiceless fricatives (as in Greek *pyr, treis, kardia* compared with English *fire, three, heart*), Proto-Indo-European voiced stops became Proto-Germanic voiceless stops (as in Latin *duo, genus* compared with English *two, kin*), and Proto-Indo-European voiced aspirated stops became Proto-Germanic voiced fricatives (as in Sanskrit *nābhi, madhya* "mid" compared with English *navel*, Old Norse *mithr* "mid")
**grim reaper** *noun, often G&R capitalized* (circa 1927)
: death especially when personified as a man or skeleton with a scythe
**grimy** \'grī-mē\ *adjective* **grim·i·er; -est** (1612)
: full of or covered with grime : DIRTY
— **grim·i·ness** *noun*
**grin** \'grin\ *intransitive verb* **grinned; grin·ning** [Middle English *grennen*, from Old English *grennian;* akin to Old High German *grennen* to snarl] (before 12th century)
: to draw back the lips so as to show the teeth especially in amusement or laughter; *broadly* : SMILE
— **grin** *noun*
— **grin·ner** *noun*
— **grin·ning·ly** \'gri-niŋ-lē\ *adverb*
**grinch** \'grinch\ *noun* [from the *Grinch*, character in the children's story *How the Grinch Stole Christmas* (1957) by Dr. Seuss] (1979)
: KILLJOY, SPOILSPORT
¹**grind** \'grīnd\ *verb* **ground** \'graünd\; **grind·ing** [Middle English, from Old English *grindan;* akin to Latin *frendere* to crush, grind] (before 12th century)
*transitive verb*
**1 :** to reduce to powder or small fragments by friction (as in a mill or with the teeth)
**2 :** to wear down, polish, or sharpen by friction ⟨*grind* an ax⟩
**3 a :** OPPRESS, HARASS **b :** to weaken or destroy gradually — usually used with *down* ⟨poverty *ground* her spirit down⟩
**4 a :** to press together with a rotating motion ⟨*grind* the teeth⟩ **b :** to rub or press harshly ⟨*ground* the cigarette out⟩
**5 :** to operate or produce by turning a crank ⟨*grind* a hand organ⟩
*intransitive verb*
**1 :** to perform the operation of grinding
**2 :** to become pulverized, polished, or sharpened by friction
**3 :** to move with difficulty or friction especially so as to make a grating noise ⟨gears *grinding*⟩
**4 :** DRUDGE; *especially* : to study hard ⟨*grind* for an exam⟩
**5 :** to rotate the hips in an erotic manner (as in a burlesque striptease)
— **grind·ing·ly** \'grīn-diŋ-lē\ *adverb*
²**grind** *noun* (13th century)
**1 a :** an act of grinding **b :** the sound of grinding
**2 a :** dreary, monotonous, or difficult labor, study, or routine **b :** one who works or studies excessively

**3 :** the result of grinding; *also* : material ground to a particular degree of fineness ⟨a drip *grind* of coffee⟩
**4 :** the act of rotating the hips in an erotic manner
**synonym** see WORK
**grind·er** \'grīn-dər\ *noun* (14th century)
**1 a :** MOLAR **b** *plural* : TEETH
**2 :** one that grinds
**3 :** a machine or device for grinding
**4 :** SUBMARINE 2
**grind house** *noun* (1927)
: an often shabby movie theater having continuous showings especially of pornographic or violent films
**grind out** *transitive verb* (1868)
: to produce in a mechanical way
**grind·stone** \'grīn-ˌstōn\ *noun* (13th century)
**1 :** MILLSTONE 1
**2 :** a flat circular stone of natural sandstone that revolves on an axle and is used for grinding, shaping, or smoothing
**grin·go** \'griŋ-(ˌ)gō\ *noun, plural* **gringos** [Spanish, alteration of *griego* Greek, stranger, from Latin *Graecus* Greek] (1849)
: a foreigner in Spain or Latin America especially when of English or American origin; *broadly* : a non-Hispanic person — often used disparagingly ◆
**gri·ot** \'grē-ˌō\ *noun* [French] (1906)
: any of a class of musician-entertainers of western Africa whose performances include tribal histories and genealogies
¹**grip** \'grip\ *transitive verb* **gripped; grip·ping** [Middle English *grippen*, from Old English *grippan;* akin to Old English *grīpan*] (before 12th century)
**1 :** to seize or hold firmly
**2 :** to hold the interest of strongly ⟨a story that *grips* the reader⟩
— **grip·per** *noun*
— **grip·ping·ly** \'gri-piŋ-lē\ *adverb*
²**grip** *noun* (before 12th century)
**1 a :** a strong or tenacious grasp **b :** strength in gripping **c :** manner or style of gripping
**2 a :** a firm tenacious hold typically giving control, mastery, or understanding **b :** mental grasp
**3 :** a part or device for gripping
**4 :** a part by which something is grasped; *especially* : HANDLE
**5 :** SUITCASE
**6 :** STAGEHAND
¹**gripe** \'grīp\ *verb* **griped; grip·ing** [Middle English, from Old English *grīpan;* akin to Old High German *grīfan* to grasp, Lithuanian *griebti*] (before 12th century)
*transitive verb*
**1** *archaic :* SEIZE, GRASP
**2 a :** AFFLICT, DISTRESS **b :** IRRITATE, VEX
**3 :** to cause pinching and spasmodic pain in the bowels of
*intransitive verb*
**1 :** to experience gripes

◇ WORD HISTORY
**gringo** In English the expression "it's all Greek to me" is nearly equivalent to "I haven't a clue as to what it means." Similarly, Spanish *hablar en griego* means literally "to speak Greek" and figuratively "to speak unintelligibly." In the 18th century, *gringo*, usually explained as an alteration of *griego*, appeared in Spanish with the same sense "unintelligible speech," and became common in Latin America in the meaning "foreigner." *Gringo* made its way into English because Mexicans used it freely to refer derogatorily to Anglo-Americans. There is no basis to the story that American soldiers during the Mexican War (1846–48) often sang Robert Burns's "Green Grow the Rashes, O!" and that "green grow" was misinterpreted as *gringo* by the Mexicans.

**2 :** to complain with grumbling
— **grip·er** noun

**²gripe** noun (13th century)
**1** archaic **:** CLUTCH, GRASP; broadly **:** CONTROL, MASTERY
**2 :** a pinching spasmodic intestinal pain — usually used in plural
**3 :** GRIEVANCE, COMPLAINT

**grip·man** \'grip-mən, -,man\ noun (1886)
**:** a cable car operator

**grippe** \'grip\ noun [French, literally, seizure] (1776)
**:** an acute febrile contagious virus disease; especially **:** INFLUENZA 1
— **grippy** \'gri-pē\ adjective

**grip·sack** \'grip-,sak\ noun (1877)
**:** SUITCASE

**gri·saille** \gri-'zī, -'zā(ə)l\ noun [French, from gris gray, from Middle French — more at GRIZZLE] (1848)
**:** decoration in tones of a single color and especially gray designed to produce a three-dimensional effect

**Gri·sel·da** \gri-'zel-də\ noun [Middle English, from Italian]
**:** a woman of humble origins in medieval legend who endures tests of wifely patience laid on her by her wellborn husband

**gris·e·o·ful·vin** \,gri-zē-ō-'ful-vən, ,gri-sē-, -'fəl-\ noun [New Latin griseofulvum, specific epithet of Penicillium griseofulvum, mold from which it is obtained] (1939)
**:** an antibiotic $C_{17}H_{17}ClO_6$ used systematically in treating superficial fungal infections

**gri·sette** \gri-'zet\ noun [French, from grisette, cheap unbleached cloth, from gris] (1723)
**1 :** a young French working-class woman
**2 :** a young woman combining part-time prostitution with some other occupation

**gris-gris** \'grē-(,)grē\ noun, plural **gris-gris** \-(,)grēz\ [French] (1698)
**:** an amulet or incantation used chiefly by people of black African ancestry

**gris·ly** \'griz-lē\ adjective **gris·li·er; -est** [Middle English, from Old English grislic, from gris- (akin to Old English āgrīsan to fear); akin to Old High German grīsenlīh terrible] (12th century)
**1 :** inspiring horror or intense fear ⟨houses that were dark and grisly under the blank, cold sky —D. H. Lawrence⟩
**2 :** inspiring disgust or distaste ⟨a grisly account of the fire⟩
**synonym** see GHASTLY
— **gris·li·ness** noun

**grist** \'grist\ noun [Middle English, from Old English grīst; akin to Old English grindan to grind] (before 12th century)
**1 a :** grain or a batch of grain for grinding **b :** the product obtained from a grist of grain including the flour or meal and the grain offals
**2 :** a required or usual amount
**3 :** matter of interest or value forming the basis of a story or analysis
**4 :** something turned to advantage or use — used especially in the phrase grist for one's mill

**gris·tle** \'gri-səl, -zəl\ noun [Middle English gristil, from Old English gristle; akin to Middle Low German gristel gristle] (before 12th century)
**:** CARTILAGE; broadly **:** tough cartilaginous, tendinous, or fibrous matter especially in table meats

**gris·tly** \'gri-sə-lē, 'gris-lē, 'griz-\ adjective **gris·tli·er; -est** (14th century)
**:** consisting of or containing gristle ⟨gristly steak⟩
— **gris·tli·ness** noun

**grist·mill** \'grist-,mil\ noun (1602)
**:** a mill for grinding grain

**¹grit** \'grit\ noun [Middle English grete, from Old English grēot; akin to Old High German grioz sand] (before 12th century)

**1 a :** SAND, GRAVEL **b :** a hard sharp granule (as of sand); also **:** material (as many abrasives) composed of such granules
**2 :** any of several sandstones
**3 a :** the structure of a stone that adapts it to grinding **b :** the size of abrasive particles usually expressed as their mesh
**4 :** firmness of mind or spirit **:** unyielding courage in the face of hardship or danger
**5** capitalized **:** a Liberal in Canadian politics

**²grit** verb **grit·ted; grit·ting** (1762)
intransitive verb
**:** to give forth a grating sound
transitive verb
**1 :** to cause (as one's teeth) to grind or grate
**2 :** to cover or spread with grit; especially **:** to smooth (as marble) with a coarse abrasive

**grith** \'grith\ noun [Middle English, from Old English, from Old Norse, security] (before 12th century)
**:** peace, security, or sanctuary imposed or guaranteed in early medieval England under various special conditions

**grits** \'grits\ noun plural but singular or plural in construction [perhaps partly from ¹grit, partly from dialect grit coarse meal, from Old English grytt; akin to Old English grēot] (1579)
**:** coarsely ground hulled grain; especially **:** ground hominy with the germ removed

**grit·ty** \'gri-tē\ adjective **grit·ti·er; -est** (1598)
**1 :** containing or resembling grit
**2 :** courageously persistent **:** PLUCKY
**3 :** having strong qualities of tough uncompromising realism ⟨a gritty novel⟩
— **grit·ti·ly** \'gri-t°l-ē\ adverb
— **grit·ti·ness** \'gri-tē-nəs\ noun

**¹griz·zle** \'gri-zəl\ noun [Middle English grisel, adjective, gray, from Middle French, from gris, of Germanic origin; akin to Old High German grīs gray] (1601)
**1** archaic **:** gray hair
**2 a :** a roan coat pattern or color **b :** a gray or roan animal

**²grizzle** verb **griz·zled; griz·zling** \'griz-liŋ, 'griz-ə-\ (1740)
transitive verb
**:** to make grayish
intransitive verb
**1 :** GRIPE, GRUMBLE
**2 :** to become grayish

**griz·zled** \'gri-zəld\ adjective (15th century)
**:** sprinkled or streaked with gray **:** GRAYING ⟨a grizzled beard⟩

**¹griz·zly** \'griz-lē\ adjective **griz·zli·er; -est** (1594)
**:** GRIZZLED

**²grizzly** variant of GRISLY

**grizzly bear** noun (1791)
**:** a very large brown bear (Ursus arctos horribilis) of the uplands of western North America — called also grizzly

**groan** \'grōn\ verb [Middle English gronen, from Old English grānian; akin to Old High German grīnan to growl] (before 12th century)
intransitive verb
**1 :** to utter a deep moan indicative of pain, grief, or annoyance
**2 :** to make a harsh sound (as of creaking) under sudden or prolonged strain
transitive verb
**:** to utter or express with groaning
— **groan** noun

**groan·er** \'grō-nər\ noun (1795)
**1 :** one that groans
**2 :** a stale or corny joke, observation, or story

**¹groat** \'grōt\ noun [Middle English grotes, plural, from Old English grotan, plural of grot; akin to Old English grēot grit] (12th century)
**1** usually plural but singular or plural in construction **:** hulled grain broken into fragments larger than grits
**2 :** a grain (as of oats) exclusive of the hull

**²groat** noun [Middle English groot, from Middle Dutch] (14th century)
**:** an old British coin worth four pennies

**gro·cer** \'grō-sər, -shər\ noun [Middle English, from Middle French grossier wholesaler, from gros coarse, wholesale — more at GROSS] (15th century)
**:** a dealer in staple foodstuffs, meats, produce, and dairy products and usually household supplies

**gro·cery** \'grōs-rē, 'grō-sə-; 'grōsh-rē\ noun, plural **-cer·ies** (15th century)
**1** plural **:** commodities sold by a grocer — usually singular in British usage
**2 :** a grocer's store

**grog** \'gräg\ noun [Old Grog, nickname of Edward Vernon (died 1757) English admiral responsible for diluting the sailors' rum] (1770)
**1 :** alcoholic liquor; especially **:** liquor (as rum) cut with water and now often served hot with lemon juice and sugar sometimes added
**2 :** refractory materials (as crushed pottery and firebricks) used in the manufacture of refractory products (as crucibles) to reduce shrinkage in drying and firing ◆

**grog·gy** \'grä-gē\ adjective **grog·gi·er; -est** [grog] (1832)
**:** weak and unsteady on the feet or in action
— **grog·gi·ly** \'grä-gə-lē\ adverb
— **grog·gi·ness** \'grä-gē-nəs\ noun

**gro·gram** \'grä-grəm, 'grō-\ noun [Middle French gros grain coarse texture] (1562)
**:** a coarse loosely woven fabric of silk, silk and mohair, or silk and wool — compare GROSGRAIN

**grog·shop** \'gräg-,shäp\ noun (1790)
chiefly British **:** a usually low-class barroom

**¹groin** \'groin\ noun [alteration of Middle English grynde, from Old English, abyss; akin to Old English grund ground] (circa 1532)
**1 :** the fold or depression marking the juncture of the lower abdomen and the inner part of the thigh; also **:** the region of this line
**2 a :** the projecting curved line along which two intersecting vaults meet **b :** a rib that covers this edge
**3 :** a rigid structure built out from a shore to protect the shore

groin 2a

\ə\ abut \ᵊ\ kitten \ər\ further \a\ ash \ā\ ace
\ä\ mop, mar \au̇\ out \ch\ chin \e\ bet \ē\ easy
\g\ go \i\ hit \ī\ ice \j\ job \ŋ\ sing \ō\ go
\o̊\ law \o̊i\ boy \th\ thin \t͟h\ the \ü\ loot \u̇\ foot
\y\ yet \zh\ vision    see also Guide to Pronunciation

from erosion, to trap sand, or to direct a current for scouring a channel

²**groin** *transitive verb* (circa 1816)
**:** to build or equip with groins

**grom·met** \'grä-mət, 'grə-\ *noun* [obsolete French *gormette* curb of a bridle] (1626)
**1 :** a flexible loop that serves as a fastening, support, or reinforcement
**2 :** an eyelet of firm material to strengthen or protect an opening or to insulate or protect something passed through it

**grom·well** \'gräm-,wel, -wəl\ *noun* [Middle English *gromil*, from Middle French] (14th century)
**:** any of a genus (*Lithospermum*) of plants of the borage family having polished white stony nutlets

¹**groom** \'grüm, 'grum\ *noun* [Middle English *grom*] (14th century)
**1** *archaic* **:** MAN, FELLOW
**2 a** (1) *archaic* **:** MANSERVANT (2) **:** one of several officers of the English royal household **b :** a person responsible for the feeding, exercising, and stabling of horses
**3 :** BRIDEGROOM

²**groom** (1809)
*transitive verb*
**1 :** to clean and condition (as a horse or dog)
**2 :** to make neat or attractive ⟨an impeccably *groomed* woman⟩
**3 :** to get into readiness for a specific objective **:** PREPARE ⟨was being *groomed* as a presidential candidate⟩
*intransitive verb*
**:** to groom oneself

**groom·er** \'grü-mər\ *noun* (circa 1890)
**:** one who grooms (as dogs)

**grooms·man** \'grümz-mən, 'grumz-\ *noun* (1698)
**:** a male friend who attends a bridegroom at his wedding

¹**groove** \'grüv\ *noun* [Middle English *groof*; akin to Old English *grafan* to dig — more at GRAVE] (1659)
**1 :** a long narrow channel or depression
**2 a :** a fixed routine **:** RUT **b :** a situation suited to one's abilities or interests **:** NICHE
**3 :** top form ⟨a great talker when he is in the *groove*⟩
**4 :** the middle of the strike zone in baseball where a pitch is most easily hit ⟨a fastball right in the *groove*⟩
**5 :** an enjoyable or exciting experience
**6 :** a pronounced enjoyable rhythm

²**groove** *verb* **grooved; groov·ing** (1686)
*transitive verb*
**1 a :** to make a groove in **b :** to join by a groove
**2 :** to perfect by repeated practice ⟨*grooved* her golf swing⟩
**3 :** to throw (a pitch) in the groove
*intransitive verb*
**1 :** to become joined or fitted by a groove
**2 :** to form a groove
**3 :** to enjoy oneself intensely
**4 :** to interact harmoniously ⟨contemporary minds and rock *groove* together —Benjamin DeMott⟩
**— groov·er** *noun*

**groovy** \'grü-vē\ *adjective* **groov·i·er; -est** (circa 1937)
**1 :** MARVELOUS, WONDERFUL, EXCELLENT ⟨felt that this poetry was . . . enjoyable, not to mention *groovy* —R. M. Muçcigrosso⟩
**2 :** HIP ⟨a younger and *groovier* audience —Robert MacKenzie⟩

**grope** \'grōp\ *verb* **groped; grop·ing** [Middle English, from Old English *grāpian;* akin to Old English *grīpan* to seize] (before 12th century)
*intransitive verb*
**1 :** to feel about blindly or uncertainly in search ⟨*grope* for the light switch⟩
**2 :** to look for something blindly or uncertainly ⟨*grope* for the right words⟩
**3 :** to feel one's way

*transitive verb*
**1 :** FEEL UP
**2 :** to find (as one's way) by groping
**— grope** *noun*
**— grop·er** *noun*

**gros·beak** \'grōs-,bēk\ *noun* [part translation of French *grosbec*, from *gros* thick + *bec* beak] (circa 1678)
**:** any of several finches of Europe or America having large stout conical bills

**gro·schen** \'grō-shən, 'grŏ-\ *noun, plural* **groschen** [German] (1946)
**— see** *schilling* at MONEY table

**gros·grain** \'grō-,grān\ *noun* [French *gros grain* coarse texture] (1869)
**:** a strong close-woven corded fabric usually of silk or rayon and often with cotton filler — compare GROGRAM

¹**gross** \'grōs\ *adjective* [Middle English, from Middle French *gros* thick, coarse, from Latin *grossus*] (14th century)
**1 a** *archaic* **:** immediately obvious **b** (1) **:** glaringly noticeable usually because of inexcusable badness or objectionableness ⟨*gross* error⟩ (2) **:** OUT-AND-OUT, UTTER ⟨*gross* injustice⟩ **c :** visible without the aid of a microscope
**2 a :** BIG, BULKY; *especially* **:** excessively fat **b :** growing or spreading with excessive luxuriance
**3 a :** of, relating to, or dealing with general aspects or broad distinctions **b :** consisting of an overall total exclusive of deductions ⟨*gross* income⟩ — compare NET
**4 :** made up of material or perceptible elements
**5** *archaic* **:** not fastidious in taste **:** UNDISCRIMINATING
**6 a :** coarse in nature or behavior **:** UNREFINED **b :** gravely deficient in civility or decency **:** crudely vulgar ⟨merely *gross*, a scatological rather than a pornographic impropriety —Aldous Huxley⟩ **c** *slang* **:** inspiring disgust or distaste ⟨that sandwich looks *gross*⟩
**7 :** deficient in knowledge **:** IGNORANT, UNTUTORED
*synonym* see COARSE, FLAGRANT
**— gross·ly** *adverb*
**— gross·ness** *noun*

²**gross** *noun* (1579)
**1** *obsolete* **:** AMOUNT, SUM
**2 :** overall total exclusive of deductions

³**gross** *transitive verb* (1884)
**:** to earn or bring in (an overall total) exclusive of deductions (as for taxes or expenses)
**— gross·er** *noun*

⁴**gross** *noun, plural* **gross** [Middle English *groce*, from Middle French *grosse*, from feminine of *gros*] (14th century)
**:** an aggregate of 12 dozen things ⟨a *gross* of pencils⟩

**gross anatomy** *noun* (1888)
**:** a branch of anatomy that deals with the macroscopic structure of tissues and organs

**gross national product** *noun* (1947)
**:** the total value of the goods and services produced by the residents of a nation during a specified period (as a year)

**gross–out** \'grō-,saut\ *noun, often attributive* (1973)
**:** something inspiring disgust or distaste

**gross out** *transitive verb* (1968)
**:** to offend, insult, or disgust by something gross

**gros·su·lar** \'gräs-yə-lər\ *noun* [New Latin *Grossularia*, genus name of the gooseberry] (1819)
**:** a variety of garnet that is most commonly green and consists of calcium aluminum silicate

**gros·su·la·rite** \-lə-,rīt\ *noun* [German *Grossularit*, from New Latin *Grossularia*] (circa 1847)
**:** GROSSULAR

**gro·szy** \'grŏ-shē\ *also* **grosz** *or* **grosze** \'grŏsh\ *noun, plural* **groszy** [Polish] (1916)
**— see** *zloty* at MONEY table

**grot** \'grät\ *noun* [Middle French *grotte*, from Italian *grotta*] (1506)
**:** GROTTO

¹**gro·tesque** \grō-'tesk\ *noun* [Middle French & Old Italian; Middle French, from Old Italian (*pittura*) *grottesca*, literally, cave painting, feminine of *grottesco* of a cave, from *grotta*] (1561)
**1 a :** a style of decorative art characterized by fanciful or fantastic human and animal forms often interwoven with foliage or similar figures that may distort the natural into absurdity, ugliness, or caricature **b :** a piece of work in this style
**2 :** one that is grotesque
**3 :** SANS SERIF ◆

²**grotesque** *adjective* (1603)
**:** of, relating to, or having the characteristics of the grotesque: as **a :** FANCIFUL, BIZARRE **b :** absurdly incongruous **c :** departing markedly from the natural, the expected, or the typical
*synonym* see FANTASTIC
**— gro·tesque·ly** *adverb*
**— gro·tesque·ness** *noun*

**gro·tes·que·rie** *also* **gro·tes·que·ry** \grō-'tes-kə-rē\ *noun, plural* **-ries** [*grotesque* + French *-erie* -ery] (circa 1666)
**1 :** something that is grotesque
**2 :** the quality or state of being grotesque **:** GROTESQUENESS

**grot·to** \'grä-(,)tō\ *noun, plural* **grottoes** *also* **grottos** [Italian *grotta, grotto*, from Latin *crypta* cavern, crypt] (1617)
**1 :** CAVE
**2 :** an artificial recess or structure made to resemble a natural cave

**grot·ty** \'grä-tē\ *adjective* **grot·ti·er; -est** [origin unknown] (1964)
*chiefly British* **:** wretchedly shabby **:** of poor quality

**grouch** \'grauch\ *noun* [probably alteration of *grutch* (grudge)] (circa 1895)
**1 a :** a fit of bad temper **b :** GRUDGE, COMPLAINT
**2 :** a habitually irritable or complaining person **:** GRUMBLER
**— grouch** *intransitive verb*

**grouchy** \'grau-chē\ *adjective* **grouch·i·er; -est** (circa 1895)
**:** given to grumbling **:** PEEVISH
**— grouch·i·ly** \-chə-lē\ *adverb*
**— grouch·i·ness** \-chē-nəs\ *noun*

¹**ground** \'graund\ *noun, often attributive* [Middle English, from Old English *grund;* akin to Old High German *grunt* ground] (before 12th century)

◇ WORD HISTORY
**grotesque** In the middle of the 15th century at Rome, when antiquarian interest in the city's cultural legacy was high, remnants of ancient Roman decorative painting were found in underground chambers of the Domus Aurea, the vast palace of the emperor Nero that had been largely demolished and covered over by newer structures. Inspired by these finds, Renaissance painters and sculptors created a style of decorative art with fantastic combinations of human and animal forms interwoven with strange fruits and flowers. Examples of the style were dubbed after their ancient inspiration *grottesche*, short for *pitture grottesche*, literally, "cave paintings." The adjective *grottesco*, which acquired the sense " having the characteristics of *grottesche*" was borrowed into French and English, with the English word eventually copying the French form. By about the middle of the 17th century *grotesque* in both languages had developed the more extended senses "bizarre" or "absurdly incongruous" that the word still has today.

**1 a :** the bottom of a body of water **b** *plural* (1) **:** SEDIMENT 1 (2) **:** ground coffee beans after brewing
**2 a :** a basis for belief, action, or argument ⟨*ground* for complaint⟩ — often used in plural **b** (1) **:** a fundamental logical condition (2) **:** a basic metaphysical cause
**3 a :** a surrounding area **:** BACKGROUND **b :** material that serves as a substratum
**4 a :** the surface of the earth **b :** an area used for a particular purpose ⟨parade *ground*⟩ ⟨fishing *grounds*⟩ **c** *plural* **:** the area around and belonging to a house or other building **d :** an area to be won or defended in or as if in battle **e :** an area of knowledge or special interest ⟨covered a lot of *ground* in his lecture⟩
**5 a :** SOIL, EARTH **b :** a special soil
**6 a :** an object that makes an electrical connection with the earth **b :** a large conducting body (as the earth) used as a common return for an electric circuit and as an arbitrary zero of potential **c :** electric connection with a ground
**7 :** a football offense utilizing primarily running plays
**— from the ground up 1 :** entirely new or afresh **2 :** from top to bottom **:** THOROUGHLY
**— into the ground :** beyond what is necessary or tolerable **:** to exhaustion ⟨labored an issue *into the ground* —*Newsweek*⟩
**— off the ground :** in or as if in flight **:** off to a good start ⟨the program never got *off the ground*⟩
**— on the ground :** at the scene of action
**— to ground 1 :** into a burrow ⟨the fox went *to ground*⟩ **2 :** into hiding ⟨might need to make a run for it and go *to ground* someplace —Edward Hoagland⟩
**²ground** (13th century)
*transitive verb*
**1 a :** to bring to or place on the ground **b :** to cause to run aground
**2 a :** to provide a reason or justification for ⟨our fears about technological change may be well *grounded* —L. K. Williams⟩ **b :** to furnish with a foundation of knowledge **:** BASE ⟨an understanding . . . that is *grounded* in fact —Michael Kimmelman⟩
**3 :** to connect electrically with a ground
**4 a :** to restrict to the ground ⟨*ground* a pilot⟩ **b :** to prohibit from taking part in some usual activities ⟨*grounded* her for a week⟩
**5 :** to throw (a football) intentionally to the ground to avoid being tackled for a loss
*intransitive verb*
**1 :** to have a ground or basis **:** RELY
**2 :** to run aground
**3 :** to hit a grounder
**³ground** *past and past participle of* GRIND
**ground ball** *noun* (1857)
**:** a batted baseball that bounds or rolls along the ground
**ground bass** *noun* (1699)
**:** a short bass passage continually repeated below constantly changing melody and harmony
**ground beetle** *noun* (1848)
**:** any of a large cosmopolitan family (Carabidae) of soil-inhabiting usually carnivorous often shiny black or metallic beetles commonly having fused elytra
**ground·break·er** \'graún(d)-ˌbrā-kər\ *noun* (1940)
**:** one that innovates **:** PIONEER
**ground·break·ing** \-ˌbrā-kiŋ\ *adjective* (1907)
**:** markedly innovative ⟨has written a *groundbreaking* work⟩
**ground·burst** \-ˌbərst\ *noun* (circa 1951)
**:** the detonation of a nuclear warhead at ground level
**ground–cher·ry** \'graún(d)-ˌcher-ē\ *noun* (1807)
**:** any of numerous chiefly New World plants (genus *Physalis*) of the nightshade family with pulpy fruits in papery husks; *also* **:** the fruit of the ground-cherry

**ground cloth** *noun* (1931)
**:** a waterproof sheet placed on the ground for protection (as of a sleeping bag) against soil moisture
**ground cover** *noun* (1900)
**1 :** the small plants on a forest floor except young trees
**2 a :** a planting of low plants (as ivy) that covers the ground in place of turf **b :** a plant adapted for use as ground cover
**ground crew** *noun* (1934)
**:** the mechanics and technicians who maintain and service an airplane
**ground–effect machine** *noun* [from the lift provided by compression of air between the vehicle and the ground] (1962)
**:** HOVERCRAFT
**ground·er** \'graún-dər\ *noun* (circa 1867)
**:** GROUND BALL
**ground·fish** \'graún(d)-ˌfish\ *noun* (1856)
**:** a bottom fish; *especially* **:** a marine fish (as a cod, haddock, pollack, or flounder) of commercial importance
**ground floor** *noun* (1601)
**1 :** the floor of a house most nearly on a level with the ground — compare FIRST FLOOR
**2 :** a favorable position or privileged opportunity usually obtained by early participants — used especially in the phrase *in on the ground floor*
**ground glass** *noun* (1848)
**:** glass with a light-diffusing surface produced by etching or abrading
**ground·hog** \'graún(d)-ˌhóg, -ˌhäg\ *noun* (1742)
**:** WOODCHUCK
**Groundhog Day** *noun* [from the legend that a groundhog emerging from its burrow returns to hibernate if it sees its shadow on this day] (1871)
**:** February 2 that traditionally indicates six more weeks of winter if sunny or an early spring if cloudy
**ground·ing** \'graún-diŋ\ *noun* (1644)
**:** training or instruction in the fundamentals of a field of knowledge
**ground ivy** *noun* (14th century)
**:** a trailing mint (*Glechoma hederacea*) with rounded leaves and blue-purple flowers
**ground·less** \'graún(d)-ləs\ *adjective* (1620)
**:** having no ground or foundation ⟨*groundless* fears⟩
**— ground·less·ly** *adverb*
**— ground·less·ness** *noun*
**ground·ling** \'graún(d)-liŋ\ *noun* (1602)
**1 a :** a spectator who stood in the pit of an Elizabethan theater **b :** a person of unsophisticated taste
**2 :** one that lives or works on or near the ground
**ground loop** *noun* (1928)
**:** a sharp uncontrollable turn made by an aircraft on the ground and usually caused by an unbalanced drag (as from a wingtip touching the ground)
**ground·mass** \'graún(d)-ˌmas\ *noun* (1879)
**:** the fine-grained or glassy base of a porphyry in which the larger distinct crystals are embedded
**ground meristem** *noun* (1938)
**:** the part of a primary apical meristem remaining after differentiation of protoderm and procambium
**ground·nut** \'graún(d)-ˌnət\ *noun* (1602)
**1 a :** any of several plants having edible tuberous roots; *especially* **:** a North American leguminous vine (*Apios americana*) with pinnate leaves and clusters of brownish purple fragrant flowers **b :** the root of a groundnut
**2** *chiefly British* **:** PEANUT
**ground·out** \'graún-ˌdaút\ *noun* (1965)
**:** a play in baseball in which a batter is put out after hitting a grounder to an infielder
**ground pine** *noun* (1551)
**1 :** a European bugle (*Ajuga chamaepitys*) with a resinous odor

**2 :** any of several club mosses (especially *Lycopodium clavatum* and *L. complanatum*) with long creeping stems and erect branches
**ground plan** *noun* (1731)
**1 :** a plan of a floor of a building as distinguished from an elevation
**2 :** a first or basic plan
**ground rent** *noun* (1667)
**:** the rent paid by a lessee for the use of land especially for building
**ground rule** *noun* (1890)
**1 :** a sports rule adopted to modify play on a particular field, court, or course
**2 :** a rule of procedure ⟨*ground rules* for selecting a superintendent —*American School Board Journal*⟩
**¹ground·sel** \'graún(d)-səl\ *noun* [Middle English *groundeswele*, from Old English *grundeswelge*, from *grund* ground + *swelgan* to swallow — more at SWALLOW] (before 12th century)
**:** any of various senecios (as the nearly cosmopolitan weed *Senecio vulgaris*)
**²groundsel** *noun* [Middle English *ground sille*, from *ground* + *sille* sill] (15th century)
**:** a foundation timber
**ground·sheet** \'graún(d)-ˌshēt\ *noun* (1907)
**:** GROUND CLOTH
**grounds·keep·er** \'graún(d)z-ˌkē-pər\ *noun* (1903)
**:** a person who cares for the grounds of a usually large property (as a sports field)
**ground sloth** *noun* (1860)
**:** any of various often huge extinct American edentates related to the recent sloths
**grounds·man** \'graún(d)z-mən\ *noun* (1886)
*chiefly British* **:** GROUNDSKEEPER
**ground speed** *noun* (1917)
**:** the speed (as of an airplane) with relation to the ground — compare AIRSPEED
**ground squirrel** *noun* (1688)
**:** any of various burrowing rodents (especially genus *Spermophilus*) of North America and Eurasia that are related to the squirrels and often live in colonies especially in open areas — called also *spermophile*
**ground state** *noun* (1926)
**:** the state of a physical system (as of an atomic nucleus or an atom) having the least energy of all the possible states — called also *ground level*
**ground stroke** *noun* (1895)
**:** a stroke made (as in tennis) by hitting a ball that has rebounded from the ground — compare VOLLEY
**ground substance** *noun* (1882)
**:** a more or less homogeneous matrix in which the specific differentiated elements of a system are suspended: **a :** the intercellular substance of tissues **b :** CYTOSOL
**ground·swell** \'graún(d)z-ˌswel\ *noun* (1818)
**1** *usually* **ground swell :** a broad deep undulation of the ocean caused by an often distant gale or seismic disturbance
**2 :** a rapid spontaneous growth (as of political opinion) ⟨a *groundswell* of support⟩
**ground·wa·ter** \-ˌwó-tər, -ˌwä-\ *noun* (circa 1889)
**:** water within the earth that supplies wells and springs
**ground wave** *noun* (1925)
**:** a radio wave that is propagated along the surface of the earth
**ground·wood** \'graúnd-ˌwúd\ *noun* [³*ground*] (1885)
**:** wood ground up and used to make pulp for paper
**ground·work** \'graúnd-ˌwərk\ *noun* (15th century)

\ə\ abut \ᵊ\ kitten \ər\ further \a\ ash \ā\ ace
\ä\ mop, mar \aú\ out \ch\ chin \e\ bet \ē\ easy
\g\ go \i\ hit \ī\ ice \j\ job \ŋ\ sing \ō\ go
\ó\ law \ói\ boy \th\ thin \th\ the \ü\ loot \ú\ foot
\y\ yet \zh\ vision    *see also* Guide to Pronunciation

: FOUNDATION, BASIS ⟨laid the *groundwork* for a new program⟩; *also* : preparation made beforehand ⟨the *groundwork* was done before the winter tour —Susan Reiter⟩

**ground zero** *noun* (1946)
**1** : the point directly above, below, or at which a nuclear explosion occurs
**2** : the center or origin of rapid, intense, or violent activity or change
**3** : the very beginning : SQUARE ONE

**¹group** \ˈgrüp\ *noun, often attributive* [French *groupe,* from Italian *gruppo,* of Germanic origin; akin to Old High German *kropf* craw — more at CROP] (1686)
**1** : two or more figures forming a complete unit in a composition
**2 a** : a number of individuals assembled together or having some unifying relationship **b** : an assemblage of objects regarded as a unit **c** (1) : a military unit consisting of a headquarters and attached battalions (2) : a unit of the U.S. Air Force higher than a squadron and lower than a wing
**3 a** : an assemblage of related organisms — often used to avoid taxonomic connotations when the kind or degree of relationship is not clearly defined **b** (1) : two or more atoms joined together or sometimes a single atom forming part of a molecule; *especially* : FUNCTIONAL GROUP ⟨a methyl *group*⟩ (2) : an assemblage of elements forming one of the vertical columns of the periodic table **c** : a stratigraphic division comprising rocks deposited during an era
**4** : a mathematical set that is closed under a binary associative operation, contains an identity element, and has an inverse for every element

**²group** (1718)
*transitive verb*
**1** : to combine in a group
**2** : to assign to a group : CLASSIFY
*intransitive verb*
**1** : to form a group
**2** : to belong to a group
**3** : to make groups of closely spaced hits on a target ⟨the gun *grouped* beautifully —R. C. Ruark⟩
— **group·able** \ˈgrü-pə-bəl\ *adjective*

**group captain** *noun* (1919)
: a commissioned officer in the British air force who ranks with a colonel in the army

**group dynamics** *noun plural but singular or plural in construction* (1939)
: the interacting forces within a small human group; *also* : the sociological study of these forces

**grou·per** \ˈgrü-pər\ *noun, plural* **groupers** *also* **grouper** [Portuguese *garoupa*] (1671)
: any of numerous fishes (family Serranidae and especially genera *Epinephelus* and *Mycteroperca*) that are typically large solitary bottom-dwelling fishes of warm seas

**group·ie** \ˈgrü-pē\ *noun* (1967)
**1** : a fan of a rock group who usually follows the group around on concert tours
**2** : an admirer of a celebrity who attends as many of his or her public appearances as possible
**3** : ENTHUSIAST, AFICIONADO ⟨a political *groupie*⟩ ⟨golf *groupies*⟩

**group·ing** \ˈgrü-piŋ\ *noun* (1748)
**1** : the act or process of combining in groups
**2** : a set of objects combined in a group ⟨a furniture *grouping*⟩

**group practice** *noun* (1942)
: medicine practiced by a group of associated physicians or dentists (as specialists in different fields) working as partners or as partners and employees

**group theory** *noun* (1898)
: a branch of mathematics concerned with finding all mathematical groups and determining their properties

**group therapy** *noun* (1943)

: therapy in the presence of a therapist in which several patients discuss and share their personal problems — called also *group psychotherapy*
— **group therapist** *noun*

**group·think** \ˈgrüp-ˌthiŋk\ *noun* [¹*group* + *-think* (as in *doublethink*)] (1952)
: a pattern of thought characterized by self-deception, forced manufacture of consent, and conformity to group values and ethics

**grou·pus·cule** \grü-ˈpəs-ˌkyül\ *noun* [French, from *groupe* group + *-uscule* (as in *corpuscule* corpuscle)] (1969)
: a small group of political activists

**¹grouse** \ˈgraůs\ *noun, plural* **grouse** *or* **grouses** [origin unknown] (1531)
: any of numerous chiefly ground-dwelling birds (family Tetraonidae) that are usually of reddish brown or other protective color and have feathered legs and that include many important game birds

**²grouse** *intransitive verb* **groused; grousing** [origin unknown] (1887)
: COMPLAIN, GRUMBLE
— **grous·er** *noun*

**³grouse** *noun* (1918)
: COMPLAINT

**¹grout** \ˈgraůt\ *noun* [Middle English, coarse meal, from Old English *grūt;* akin to Old English *grēot* grit] (1638)
**1 a** : thin mortar used for filling spaces (as the joints in masonry); *also* : any of various other materials (as a mixture of cement and water or chemicals that solidify) used for a similar purpose **b** : PLASTER
**2** : LEES

**²grout** *transitive verb* (1838)
**1** : to fill up or finish with grout
**2** : to fix in place by means of grout ⟨*grout* a bolt into a wall⟩
— **grout·er** *noun*

**grove** \ˈgrōv\ *noun* [Middle English, from Old English *grāf*] (before 12th century)
**1** : a small wood without underbrush ⟨a picnic *grove*⟩
**2** : a planting of fruit or nut trees

**grov·el** \ˈgrä-vəl, ˈgrə-\ *intransitive verb* **-eled** *or* **-elled; -el·ing** *or* **-el·ling** [back-formation from *groveling* prone, from *groveling,* adverb, from Middle English, from *gruf,* adverb, on the face (from Old Norse *ā grūfu*) + *-ling*] (1593)
**1** : to creep with the face to the ground : CRAWL
**2 a** : to lie or creep with the body prostrate in token of subservience or abasement **b** : to abase oneself
**3** : to give oneself over to what is base or unworthy : WALLOW ⟨*groveling* in self-pity⟩
— **grov·el·er** \-v°l-ər\ *noun*
— **grov·el·ing·ly** \-v°l-iŋ-lē\ *adverb*

**groves of academe** *often A capitalized* (1849)
: the academic world

**grow** \ˈgrō\ *verb* **grew** \ˈgrü\; **grown** \ˈgrōn\; **grow·ing** [Middle English, from Old English *grōwan;* akin to Old High German *gruowan* to grow] (before 12th century)
*intransitive verb*
**1 a** : to spring up and develop to maturity **b** : to be able to grow in some place or situation ⟨trees that *grow* in the tropics⟩ **c** : to assume some relation through or as if through a process of natural growth ⟨ferns *growing* from the rocks⟩
**2 a** : to increase in size by assimilation of material into the living organism or by accretion of material in a nonbiological process (as crystallization) **b** : INCREASE, EXPAND ⟨*grows* in wisdom⟩
**3** : to develop from a parent source ⟨the book *grew* out of a series of lectures⟩

**4 a** : to pass into a condition : BECOME ⟨*grew* pale⟩ **b** : to have an increasing influence ⟨habit *grows* on a person⟩ **c** : to become increasingly acceptable or attractive ⟨didn't like it at first, but it *grew* on him⟩
*transitive verb*
**1** : to cause to grow ⟨*grow* wheat⟩
**2** : DEVELOP 5
— **grow·er** \ˈgrō-(ə-)r\ *noun*
— **grow·ing·ly** \ˈgrō-iŋ-lē\ *adverb*

**growing pains** *noun plural* (1810)
**1** : pains in the legs of growing children having no demonstrable relation to growth
**2** : the stresses and strains attending a new project or development

**growing point** *noun* (1835)
: the undifferentiated end of a plant shoot from which additional shoot tissues differentiate

**¹growl** \ˈgraů(ə)l\ *verb* [Middle English *groulen, grollen*] (14th century)
*intransitive verb*
**1 a** : RUMBLE ⟨his stomach *growled*⟩ **b** : to utter a growl ⟨the dog *growled* at the stranger⟩
**2** : to complain angrily
*transitive verb*
: to utter with a growl : utter angrily

**²growl** *noun* (1727)
: a deep guttural inarticulate sound

**growl·er** \ˈgraů-lər\ *noun* (1753)
**1** : one that growls
**2** : a container (as a can or pitcher) for beer bought by the measure
**3** : a small iceberg

**growl·ing** \ˈgraů-liŋ\ *adjective* (1752)
: marked by a growl ⟨a low *growling* voice⟩ ⟨listened to the *growling* thunder⟩
— **growl·ing·ly** \-liŋ-lē\ *adverb*

**growly** \ˈgraů-lē\ *adjective* **growl·i·er; -est** (1920)
: resembling a growl ⟨a *growly* voice⟩
— **growl·i·ness** *noun*

**grown** \ˈgrōn\ *adjective* (1645)
**1** : fully grown : MATURE ⟨*grown* men and women⟩
**2** : covered or surrounded with vegetation ⟨land well *grown* with trees⟩
**3 a** : cultivated or produced in a specified way or locality — used in combination ⟨shade-*grown* tobacco⟩ **b** : overgrown with — used in combination ⟨a weed-*grown* patio⟩

**¹grown-up** \ˈgrōn-ˌnəp\ *adjective* (1633)
: not childish or immature : ADULT

**²grown-up** *noun* (1813)
: ADULT

**growth** \ˈgrōth\ *noun* (1557)
**1 a** (1) : a stage in the process of growing : SIZE (2) : full growth **b** : the process of growing **c** : progressive development : EVOLUTION **d** : INCREASE, EXPANSION ⟨the *growth* of the oil industry⟩
**2 a** : something that grows or has grown **b** : an abnormal proliferation of tissue (as a tumor) **c** : OUTGROWTH **d** : the result of growth : PRODUCT
**3** : a producing especially by growing ⟨fruits of his own *growth*⟩

**growth company** *noun* (1959)
: a company that grows at a greater rate than the economy as a whole and that usually directs a relatively high proportion of income back into the business

**growth factor** *noun* (1926)
: a substance (as a vitamin $B_{12}$ or an interleukin) that promotes growth and especially cellular growth

**growth hormone** *noun* (1924)
**1** : a vertebrate polypeptide hormone that is secreted by the anterior lobe of the pituitary gland and regulates growth — called also *somatotropin*
**2** : GROWTH REGULATOR

**growth regulator** *noun* (1936)
: any of various synthetic or naturally occurring plant substances (as an auxin or gibberellin) that regulate growth

**growth ring** *noun* (1907)

: a layer of wood (as an annual ring) produced during a single period of growth

**growthy** \'grō-thē\ *adjective* **growth·i·er; -est** (1884)
*of livestock* : exceptionally fast in growing and gaining weight
— **growth·i·ness** \-nəs\ *noun*

**grow up** *intransitive verb* (1535)
: to grow toward or arrive at full stature or physical or mental maturity ⟨*growing up* intellectually, socially, and physically⟩

**groyne** \'gróin\ *noun* [by alteration] (1582)
: GROIN 3

**¹grub** \'grəb\ *verb* **grubbed; grub·bing** [Middle English *grubben;* akin to Old English *grafan* to dig — more at GRAVE] (14th century)
*transitive verb*
**1** : to clear by digging up roots and stumps
**2** : to dig up by or as if by the roots
*intransitive verb*
**1 a** : to dig in the ground especially for something that is difficult to find or extract **b** : to search about ⟨*grubbed* in the countryside for food —*Lamp*⟩
**2** : TOIL, DRUDGE ⟨folks who *grub* for money —James Street⟩
— **grub·ber** *noun*

**²grub** *noun* [Middle English *grubbe*, from *grubben*] (15th century)
**1** : a soft thick wormlike larva of an insect
**2 a** : one who does menial work : DRUDGE **b** : a slovenly person
**3** : FOOD

**grub·by** \'grə-bē\ *adjective* **grub·bi·er; -est** (1725)
**1** : infested with fly maggots
**2 a** : DIRTY, GRIMY ⟨*grubby* hands⟩ **b** : SLOVENLY, SLOPPY
**3** : worthy of contempt : BASE ⟨*grubby* political motives⟩
— **grub·bi·ly** \'grə-bə-lē\ *adverb*
— **grub·bi·ness** \'grə-bē-nəs\ *noun*

**¹grub·stake** \'grəb-,stāk\ *noun* (1863)
**1** : supplies or funds furnished a mining prospector on promise of a share in his discoveries
**2** : material assistance (as a loan) provided for launching an enterprise or for a person in difficult circumstances

**²grubstake** *transitive verb* (1879)
: to provide with a grubstake
— **grub·stak·er** *noun*

**Grub Street** \'grəb-\ *noun* [*Grub Street*, London, formerly inhabited by literary hacks] (1630)
: the world or category of needy literary hacks

**¹grudge** \'grəj\ *transitive verb* **grudged; grudg·ing** [Middle English *grucchen, grudgen* to grumble, complain, from Middle French *groucier*, of Germanic origin; akin to Middle High German *grogezen* to howl] (14th century)
: to be unwilling to give or admit : give or allow reluctantly or resentfully ⟨didn't *grudge* the time⟩
— **grudg·er** *noun*

**²grudge** *noun* (15th century)
: a feeling of deep-seated resentment or ill will
*synonym* see MALICE

**grudg·ing** \'grə-jiŋ\ *adjective* (circa 1533)
**1** : UNWILLING, RELUCTANT
**2** : done, given, or allowed unwillingly, reluctantly, or sparingly ⟨*grudging* compliance⟩
— **grudg·ing·ly** \-jiŋ-lē\ *adverb*

**gru·el** \'grü-əl\ *noun* [Middle English *grewel,* from Middle French *gruel,* of Germanic origin; akin to Old English *grūt* grout] (14th century)
**1** : a thin porridge
**2** *chiefly British* : PUNISHMENT

**gru·el·ing** *or* **gru·el·ling** \'grü-ə-liŋ\ *adjective* [from present participle of obsolete *gruel* (to exhaust)] (1852)
: trying or taxing to the point of exhaustion : PUNISHING ⟨a *grueling* race⟩
— **gru·el·ing·ly** \-liŋ-lē\ *adverb*

**grue·some** \'grü-səm\ *adjective* [alteration of earlier *growsome,* from English dialect *grow, grue* to shiver, from Middle English *gruen,* probably from Middle Dutch *grūwen,* akin to Old High German *ingrūēn* to shiver] (1816)
: inspiring horror or repulsion : GRISLY
*synonym* see GHASTLY
— **grue·some·ly** *adverb*
— **grue·some·ness** *noun*

**¹gruff** \'grəf\ *adjective* [Dutch *grof;* akin to Old High German *grob* coarse, *hruf* scurf — more at DANDRUFF] (1706)
**1** : rough, brusque, or stern in manner, speech, or aspect ⟨a *gruff* reply⟩
**2** : being deep and harsh : HOARSE ⟨a *gruff* voice⟩
*synonym* see BLUFF
— **gruff·ly** *adverb*
— **gruff·ness** *noun*

**²gruff** *transitive verb* (1706)
: to utter in a gruff voice or manner

**grum·ble** \'grəm-bəl\ *verb* **grum·bled; grum·bling** \-b(ə-)liŋ\ [probably from Middle French *grommeler,* ultimately from Middle Dutch *grommen;* akin to Old High German *grimm* grim] (circa 1586)
*intransitive verb*
**1** : to mutter in discontent
**2** : GROWL, RUMBLE
*transitive verb*
: to express with grumbling
— **grumble** *noun*
— **grum·bler** \-b(ə-)lər\ *noun*
— **grum·bling·ly** \-b(ə-)liŋ-lē\ *adverb*
— **grum·bly** \-b(ə-)lē\ *adjective*

**grum·met** \'grə-mət\ *variant of* GROMMET

**¹grump** \'grəmp\ *noun* [obsolete English *grumps* (snubs, slights)] (1844)
**1** : a fit of ill humor or sulkiness — usually used in plural
**2** : a person given to complaining

**²grump** (1875)
*intransitive verb*
**1** : SULK
**2** : GRUMBLE, COMPLAIN
*transitive verb*
: to utter in a grumpy manner

**grumpy** \'grəm-pē\ *adjective* **grump·i·er; -est** (1778)
: moodily cross : SURLY
— **grump·i·ly** \-pə-lē\ *adverb*
— **grump·i·ness** \-pē-nəs\ *noun*

**grunge** \'grənj\ *noun* [back-formation from *grungy*] (1965)
**1** : one that is grungy
**2** : rock music incorporating elements of punk rock and heavy metal; *also* : the untidy working-class fashions typical of fans of grunge

**grun·gy** \'grən-jē\ *adjective* **grun·gi·er; -est** [origin unknown] (1965)
: shabby or dirty in character or condition

**grun·ion** \'grən-yən\ *noun* [probably from Spanish *gruñón* grunter] (1917)
: a silversides (*Leuresthes tenuis*) of the California coast notable for the regularity with which it comes inshore to spawn at nearly full moon

**¹grunt** \'grənt\ *verb* [Middle English *grunten,* from Old English *grunnettan,* frequentative of *grunian,* of imitative origin] (before 12th century)
*intransitive verb*
: to utter a grunt
*transitive verb*
: to utter with a grunt
— **grunt·er** *noun*

**²grunt** *noun* (1553)
**1 a** : the deep short sound characteristic of a hog **b** : a similar sound
**2** [from the noise it makes when taken from the water] : any of a family (Haemulidae synonym Pomadasyidae) of chiefly tropical marine bony fishes

**3** : a dessert made by dropping biscuit dough on top of boiling berries and steaming ⟨blueberry *grunt*⟩
**4** : a U.S. army or marine foot soldier especially in the Vietnam war
**5** : one who does routine unglamorous work — often used attributively ⟨*grunt* work⟩

**grunt 2**

**grun·tle** \'grən-t⁰l\ *transitive verb* **grun·tled; grun·tling** \'grənt-liŋ, 'grən-t⁰l-iŋ\ [back-formation from *disgruntle*] (1926)
: to put in a good humor ⟨were *gruntled* with a good meal and good conversation —W. P. Webb⟩

**grutch** \'grəch\ *transitive verb* [Middle English *grucchen*] (14th century)
*obsolete* : BEGRUDGE

**grutten** *past participle of* GREET

**Gru·yère** \grü-'yer, grē-\ *noun* [*Gruyère,* district in Switzerland] (1802)
**1** : a firm cheese with small holes and a nutty flavor that is of Swiss origin
**2** : a process cheese made from natural Gruyère

**gryph·on** *variant of* GRIFFIN

**G–string** \'jē-,striŋ\ *noun* [origin unknown] (1878)
: a strip of cloth passed between the legs and supported by a waist cord that is worn especially by striptease dancers

**G suit** *noun* [gravity *suit*] (1944)
: a suit designed to counteract the physiological effects of acceleration on an aviator or astronaut

**GT** \,jē-'tē\ *noun* [Italian *Gran Turismo*] (1966)
: GRAND TOURING CAR

**GTP** \,jē-(,)tē-'pē\ *noun* [guanosine *tri*phosphate] (1961)
: an energy-rich nucleotide analogous to ATP that is composed of guanine, ribose, and three phosphate groups and is necessary for peptide-bond formation during protein synthesis — called also *guanosine triphosphate*

**$G_2$ phase** \,jē-'tü-\ *noun* [growth] (1968)
: the period in the cell cycle from the completion of DNA replication to the beginning of cell division — compare $G_1$ PHASE, M PHASE, S PHASE

**gua·ca·mo·le** \,gwä-kə-'mō-lē\ *noun* [Mexican Spanish, from Nahuatl *āhuacamōlli,* from *āhuacatl* avocado + *mōlli* sauce] (1920)
: pureed or mashed avocado seasoned with condiments
*word history* see AVOCADO

**gua·cha·ro** \'gwä-chə-,rō\ *noun, plural* **-ros** *or* **-roes** [American Spanish *guácharo*] (1830)
: OILBIRD

**guai·ac** \'gwī-,ak, 'gī-\ *noun* [New Latin *Guaiacum*] (circa 1751)
: GUAIACUM 2

**guai·a·cum** \'gwī-ə-kəm, 'gī-\ *noun* [New Latin, from Spanish *guayaco,* from Taino *guayacan*] (1553)
**1** : any of a genus (*Guaiacum*) of the caltrop family of tropical American evergreen trees and shrubs having pinnate leaves, usually blue flowers, and capsular fruit
**2 a** : the hard greenish brown wood of a guaiacum (especially *Guaiacum officinale*) **b** : a resin with a faint balsamic odor that is obtained from the trunk of two guaiacums (*G. officinale* and *G. sanctum*) and often used as a clinical reagent

---

\ə\ **abut** \⁰\ **kitten** \ər\ **further** \a\ **ash** \ā\ **ace**
\ä\ **mop, mar** \au̇\ **out** \ch\ **chin** \e\ **bet** \ē\ **easy**
\g\ **go** \i\ **hit** \ī\ **ice** \j\ **job** \ŋ\ **sing** \ō\ **go**
\ȯ\ **law** \oi\ **boy** \th\ **thin** \ṯẖ\ **the** \ü\ **loot** \u̇\ **foot**
\y\ **yet** \zh\ **vision** *see also* Guide to Pronunciation

**guan** \'gwän\ *noun* [alteration of earlier *quam*, probably from Cuna (Chibchan language of Panama) *kwama*] (1743)
: any of various large tropical American lowland-forest birds (family Cracidae) that somewhat resemble turkeys

guan

**gua·na·co** \gwə-'nä-(,)kō\ *noun, plural* **-cos** *also* **-co** [Spanish, from Quechua *wanaku*] (1604)
: a South American mammal (*Lama guanicoe*) of dry open country that has a soft thick fawn-colored coat and is related to the camel but lacks a dorsal hump

**gua·neth·i·dine** \gwä-'ne-thə-,dēn\ *noun* [*guanidine* + *eth-*] (1959)
: a drug $C_{10}H_{22}N_4$ used especially as the sulfate in treating severe high blood pressure

**gua·ni·dine** \'gwä-nə-,dēn\ *noun* [International Scientific Vocabulary, from *guanine*] (circa 1864)
: a base $CH_5N_3$ derived from guanine, found especially in young tissues, and used in organic synthesis and as a parasympathetic stimulant in medicine especially as the hydrochloride salt

**gua·nine** \'gwä-,nēn\ *noun* [*guano* + *-ine*; from its being found especially in guano] (1850)
: a purine base $C_5H_5N_5O$ that codes genetic information in the polynucleotide chain of DNA or RNA — compare ADENINE, CYTOSINE, THYMINE, URACIL

**gua·no** \'gwä-(,)nō\ *noun* [Spanish, from Quechua *wanu* fertilizer, dung] (1604)
: a substance composed chiefly of the excrement of seafowl and used as a fertilizer; *also* : a similar substance (as bat excrement or cannery waste) especially when used for fertilizer

**gua·no·sine** \'gwä-nə-,sēn\ *noun* [*guan-* (as in *guanine*) + *ribose* + *-ine*] (1909)
: a nucleoside $C_{10}H_{13}N_5O_5$ composed of guanine and ribose

**guanosine triphosphate** *noun* (circa 1962)
: GTP

**guar** \'gwär\ *noun* [Hindi *guār*] (1882)
: a drought-tolerant legume (*Cyamopsis tetragonoloba*) cultivated in warm regions as a vegetable, for forage, and for its seeds which produce guar gum

**gua·ra·ni** \,gwär-ə-'nē\ *noun* [Spanish *guaraní*] (1797)
**1** *capitalized* **a** *plural* **guarani** *or* **guaranis** : a member of a Tupi-Guaranian people of Bolivia, Paraguay, and southern Brazil **b** : the language of the Guarani
**2** *plural* **guaranies** *also* **guaranis** — see MONEY table

**¹guar·an·tee** \,gar-ən-'tē, ,gär- *also* 'gar-ən-, *or* 'gär-ən-,\ *noun* [probably alteration of ¹*guaranty*] (1710)
**1** : GUARANTOR
**2** : GUARANTY 1
**3** : an assurance for the fulfillment of a condition: as **a** : an agreement by which one person undertakes to secure another in the possession or enjoyment of something **b** : an assurance of the quality of or of the length of use to be expected from a product offered for sale often with a promise of reimbursement
**4** : GUARANTY 4

**²guarantee** *transitive verb* **-teed; -tee·ing** (1791)
**1** : to undertake to answer for the debt, default, or miscarriage of
**2** : to engage for the existence, permanence, or nature of : undertake to do or secure ⟨*guarantee* the winning of three tricks⟩
**3** : to give security to
**4** : to assert confidently

**guar·an·tor** \,gar-ən-'tór, 'gar-ən-tər, ,gär-, 'gär-\ *noun* (circa 1828)
**1** : one that makes or gives a guaranty
**2** : one that guarantees

**¹guar·an·ty** \'gar-ən-,tē, 'gär-\ *noun, plural* **-ties** [Middle French *garantie*, from Old French, from *garantir* to guarantee, from *garant* warrant, of Germanic origin; akin to Old High German *werēnto* guarantor — more at WARRANT] (1592)
**1** : an undertaking to answer for the payment of a debt or the performance of a duty of another in case of the other's default or miscarriage
**2** : GUARANTEE 3
**3** : GUARANTOR
**4** : something given as security : PLEDGE
**5** : the protection of a right afforded by legal provision (as in a constitution)

**²guaranty** *transitive verb* **-tied; -ty·ing** (1753)
: GUARANTEE

**¹guard** \'gärd\ *noun* [Middle English *garde*, from Middle French, from Old French, from *garder* to guard, defend, of Germanic origin; akin to Old High German *wartēn* to watch, take care — more at WARD] (15th century)
**1** : one assigned to protect or oversee another: as **a** : a person or a body of persons on sentinel duty **b** *plural* : troops attached to the person of the sovereign **c** *British* : CONDUCTOR
**2 a** : a defensive state or attitude ⟨asked him out when his *guard* was down⟩ **b** : a defensive position (as in boxing)
**3 a** : the act or duty of protecting or defending **b** : the state of being protected : PROTECTION
**4** : a protective or safety device; *specifically* : a device for protecting a machine part or the operator of a machine
**5** *archaic* : PRECAUTION
**6 a** : a position or player next to the center in a football line **b** : a player stationed in the backcourt in basketball
— **off guard** : in an unprepared or unsuspecting state
— **on guard** : defensively watchful : ALERT

**²guard** (1500)
*transitive verb*
**1** : to protect an edge of with an ornamental border
**2 a** : to protect from danger especially by watchful attention : make secure ⟨police *guarding* our cities⟩ **b** : to stand at the entrance of as if on guard or as a barrier **c** : to tend to carefully : PRESERVE, PROTECT ⟨*guarded* their privacy⟩
**3** *archaic* : ESCORT
**4 a** : to watch over so as to prevent escape, disclosure, or indiscretion **b** : to attempt to prevent (an opponent) from playing effectively or scoring
*intransitive verb*
: to watch by way of caution or defense : stand guard
**synonym** see DEFEND
— **guard·er** *noun*

**¹guar·dant** \'gär-d°nt\ *adjective* [Middle French *gardant*, present participle of *garder* to guard, look at] (1572)
: having the head turned toward the spectator — used of a heraldic animal whose body is seen from the side ⟨a lion passant *guardant*⟩

**²guardant** *noun* (1591)
*obsolete* : GUARDIAN

**guard cell** *noun* (1875)
: one of the two crescent-shaped epidermal cells that border and open and close a plant stoma

**guard·ed** \'gär-dəd\ *adjective* (1709)
: CAUTIOUS, CIRCUMSPECT
— **guard·ed·ly** *adverb*
— **guard·ed·ness** *noun*

**guard hair** *noun* (1913)
: one of the long coarse hairs forming a protective coating over the undercoat of a mammal

**guard·house** \'gärd-,hau̇s\ *noun* (1592)
**1** : a building occupied by a guard or used as a headquarters by soldiers on guard duty
**2** : a military jail

**guard·ian** \'gär-dē-ən\ *noun* (15th century)
**1** : one that guards : CUSTODIAN
**2** : a superior of a Franciscan monastery
**3** : one who has the care of the person or property of another
— **guard·ian·ship** \-,ship\ *noun*

**guardian angel** *noun* (circa 1631)
: an angel believed to have special care of a particular individual; *broadly* : SAVIOR 1, PROTECTOR

**guard of honor** (1887)
: HONOR GUARD

**guard·rail** \'gär-,drāl\ *noun* (1860)
: a railing for guarding against danger or trespass; *especially* : a barrier (as of steel cables) placed along the edge of a highway at dangerous points

**guard·room** \'gär-,drüm, -,dru̇m\ *noun* (1762)
**1** : a room occupied by a military guard during its term of duty
**2** : a room where military prisoners are confined

**guards·man** \'gärdz-mən\ *noun* (1817)
: a member of a military body called *guard* or *guards*

**guar gum** *noun* (1950)
: a gum that consists of the ground endosperm of guar seeds and is used especially as a thickening agent and as a sizing material for paper and textiles

**Guar·ne·ri·us** \gwär-'nir-ē-əs, -'ner-\ *noun* [New Latin, from Italian *Guarneri*] (1866)
: a violin made by one of the Italian Guarneri family in the 17th and 18th centuries

**gua·va** \'gwä-və\ *noun* [Spanish *guaba*, *guayaba*, perhaps from Taino] (1604)
**1** : any of several tropical American shrubs or small trees (genus *Psidium*) of the myrtle family; *especially* : a shrubby tree (*P. guajava*) widely cultivated for its sweet acid yellow or pink fruit
**2** : the globose to pear-shaped fruit of a guava

**gua·ya·be·ra** \,gwī-ə-'bér-ə\ *noun* [American Spanish] (1947)
: a usually short-sleeved lightweight sport shirt designed to be worn untucked

**gua·yu·le** \gwī-'ü-lē, wī-\ *noun* [American Spanish, from Nahuatl *cuauholli* or *huauholli*] (1906)
: a much-branched composite shrub (*Parthenium argentatum*) of Mexico and the southwestern U.S. cultivated as a source of rubber

**gu·ber·na·to·ri·al** \gü-bə(r)-nə-'tōr-ē-əl, ,gyü-, ,gü-, -'tȯr-\ *adjective* [Latin *gubernator* governor, steersman, from *gubernare* to govern — more at GOVERN] (1734)
: of or relating to a governor

**guck** \'gək\ *noun* [perhaps alteration of *goo*] (1949)
: oozy sloppy dirt or debris; *broadly* : GOO, GUNK

**¹gud·geon** \'gə-jən\ *noun* [Middle English *gudyon*, from Middle French *goujon*] (15th century)
**1** : PIVOT 1, JOURNAL
**2** : a socket for a rudder pintle

**²gudgeon** *noun* [Middle English *gojune*, from Middle French *gouvion*, *gougon*, from Latin *gobion-*, *gobio*, alteration of *gobius* — more at GOBY] (15th century)
: a small European freshwater fish (*Gobio gobio*) related to the carps and often used for food or bait

**gudgeon pin** *noun* (1891)
: WRIST PIN

**Gud·run** \'gu̇d-,rün\ *noun* [Old Norse *Guthrūn*]
: the wife of Sigurd and later of Atli in Norse mythology

**guel·der rose** \'gel-də(r)-\ *noun* [*Guelderland*, *Gelderland*, Netherlands] (1597)

: a bush of a cultivated variety of the cranberry bush with large globose heads of sterile flowers

**Guelf** *or* **Guelph** \'gwelf\ *noun* [Italian *Guelfo*] (1579)
: a member of a papal and popular political party in medieval Italy that opposed the authority of the German emperors in Italy — compare GHIBELLINE

**gue·non** \'gwe-nən; gə-nōⁿ\ *noun* [French] (1838)
: any of various long-tailed chiefly arboreal African monkeys (genera *Cercopithecus* and *Erythrocebus*)

**guer·don** \'gər-dᵊn\ *noun* [Middle English, from Middle French, from Old French, of Germanic origin; akin to Old High German *widarlōn* reward] (14th century)
: REWARD, RECOMPENSE
— **guerdon** *transitive verb*

**gue·ri·don** \gä-rē-dōⁿ\ *noun* [French *guéridon*, from *Gueridon*, character in 17th century farces and popular songs] (1853)
: a small usually ornately carved and embellished stand or table

**guern·sey** \'gərn-zē\ *noun, plural* **guern·seys** *often capitalized* [*Guernsey*, Channel islands] (1834)
: any of a breed of fawn and white dairy cattle that are larger than the jersey and produce rich yellowish milk

**guernsey**

**¹guer·ril·la** *or* **gue·ril·la** \gə-'ri-lə, ge-, g(y)i-\ *noun* [Spanish *guerrilla*, from diminutive of *guerra* war, of Germanic origin; akin to Old High German *werra* strife — more at WAR] (1809)
: a person who engages in irregular warfare especially as a member of an independent unit carrying out harassment and sabotage ◆
**²guerrilla** *adjective* (1811)
: of, relating to, or characteristic of guerrillas especially in being aggressive, radical, or unconventional

**guerrilla theater** *noun* (1968)
: STREET THEATER

**¹guess** \'ges\ *verb* [Middle English *gessen*, probably of Scandinavian origin; akin to Old Norse *geta* to get, guess — more at GET] (14th century)
*transitive verb*
**1** : to form an opinion of from little or no evidence
**2** : BELIEVE, SUPPOSE ⟨I *guess* you're right⟩
**3** : to arrive at a correct conclusion about by conjecture, chance, or intuition ⟨*guess* the answer⟩
*intransitive verb*
: to make a guess
— **guess·able** \'ge-sə-bəl\ *adjective*
— **guess·er** *noun*
**²guess** *noun* (14th century)
: CONJECTURE, SURMISE

**guess·ti·mate** \'ges-tə-mət\ *noun* [blend of *guess* and *estimate*] (1923)
: an estimate usually made without adequate information
— **guess·ti·mate** \-ˌmāt\ *transitive verb*

**guess·work** \'ges-ˌwərk\ *noun* (1725)
: work performed or results obtained by guess
: CONJECTURE

**¹guest** \'gest\ *noun* [Middle English *gest*, from Old Norse *gestr;* akin to Old English *giest* guest, stranger, Latin *hostis* stranger, enemy] (13th century)
**1 a** : a person entertained in one's house **b** : a person to whom hospitality is extended **c** : a person who pays for the services of an establishment (as a hotel or restaurant)

**2** : an organism (as an insect) sharing the dwelling of another; *especially* : INQUILINE
**3** : a substance that is incorporated in a host substance
**4** : a usually prominent person not a regular member of a cast or organization who appears in a program or performance
**²guest** (14th century)
*transitive verb*
: to receive as a guest
*intransitive verb*
: to appear as a guest

**guest worker** *noun* (1967)
: a foreign laborer working temporarily in an industrialized usually European country

**guff** \'gəf\ *noun* [probably imitative] (1888)
: NONSENSE, HUMBUG

**guf·faw** \(ˌ)gə-'fȯ, 'gə-ˌfȯ\ *noun* [imitative] (1720)
: a loud or boisterous burst of laughter
— **guf·faw** \(ˌ)gə-'fȯ\ *intransitive verb*

**gug·gle** \'gə-gəl\ *intransitive verb* **gug·gled; gug·gling** \-g(ə-)liŋ\ [imitative] (1611)
: GURGLE
— **guggle** *noun*

**guid·able** \'gī-də-bəl\ *adjective* (1676)
: capable of being guided

**guid·ance** \'gī-dᵊn(t)s\ *noun* (1590)
**1** : the act or process of guiding
**2 a** : the direction provided by a guide **b** : advice on vocational or educational problems given to students
**3** : the process of controlling the course of a projectile by a built-in mechanism

**¹guide** \'gīd\ *noun* [Middle English, from Middle French, from Old Provençal *guida*, of Germanic origin; akin to Old English *wītan* to look after, *witan* to know — more at WIT] (14th century)
**1 a** : one that leads or directs another's way **b** : a person who exhibits and explains points of interest **c** : something that provides a person with guiding information **d** : SIGNPOST 1 **e** : a person who directs another's conduct or course of life
**2 a** : a device for steadying or directing the motion of something **b** : a ring or loop for holding the line of a fishing rod in position **c** : a sheet or a card with projecting tab for labeling inserted in a card index to facilitate reference
**3** : a member of a unit on whom the movements or alignments of a military command are regulated — used especially in commands ⟨*guide* right⟩
**²guide** *verb* **guid·ed; guid·ing** (14th century)
*transitive verb*
**1** : to act as a guide to : direct in a way or course
**2 a** : to direct, supervise, or influence usually to a particular end **b** : to superintend the training or instruction of
*intransitive verb*
: to act or work as a guide ☆
— **guid·er** *noun*

**guide·book** \'gīd-ˌbu̇k\ *noun* (1814)
: HANDBOOK 1; *especially* : a book of information for travelers

**guided missile** *noun* (1945)
: a missile whose course may be altered during flight (as by a target-seeking radar device)

**guide dog** *noun* (1932)
: a dog trained to lead the blind

**guide·line** \'gīd-ˌlīn\ *noun* (1785)
: a line by which one is guided: as **a** : a cord or rope to aid a passer over a difficult point or to permit retracing a course **b** : an indication or outline of policy or conduct

**guide·post** \-ˌpōst\ *noun* (1761)
**1** : INDICATION, SIGN
**2** : GUIDELINE b

**guide·way** \-ˌwā\ *noun* (1876)
: a channel or track for controlling the line of motion of something

**guide word** *noun* (circa 1928)

: either of the terms at the head of a page of an alphabetical reference work (as a dictionary) indicating the alphabetically first and last words on the page

**gui·don** \'gī-ˌdän, -dᵊn\ *noun* [Middle French, from *guide*] (1548)
**1** : a small flag; *especially* : one borne by a military unit as a unit marker
**2** : one who carries a guidon

**guid·will·ie** \gēd-'wi-lē, gid-\ *adjective* [Scots *guidwill* goodwill] (1788)
*Scottish* : CORDIAL, CHEERING

**guild** \'gild\ *noun* [Middle English *gilde*, from Old Norse *gildi* payment, guild; akin to Old English *gield* tribute, guild — more at GELD] (14th century)
: an association of people with similar interests or pursuits; *especially* : a medieval association of merchants or craftsmen
— **guild·ship** \'gil(d)-ˌship\ *noun*

**guil·der** \'gil-dər\ *noun* [Middle English *gylder, gyldren,* modification of Middle Dutch *gulden*] (15th century)
: GULDEN

**guild·hall** \'gild-ˌhȯl\ *noun* (14th century)
: a hall where a guild or corporation usually assembles

**guilds·man** \'gil(d)z-mən\ *noun* (1873)
**1** : a guild member
**2** : an advocate of guild socialism

**guild socialism** *noun* (1912)

---

☆ SYNONYMS
**Guide, lead, steer, pilot, engineer**
mean to direct in a course or show the way to be followed. GUIDE implies intimate knowledge of the way and of all its difficulties and dangers ⟨*guided* the scouts through the cave⟩. LEAD implies showing the way and often keeping those that follow under control and in order ⟨*led* his team to victory⟩. STEER implies an ability to keep to a chosen course and stresses the capacity of maneuvering correctly ⟨*steered* the ship through a narrow channel⟩. PILOT suggests guidance over a dangerous, intricate, or complicated course ⟨*piloted* the bill through the Senate⟩. ENGINEER implies guidance by one who finds ways to avoid or overcome difficulties in achieving an end or carrying out a plan ⟨*engineered* his son's election to the governorship⟩.

---

◇ WORD HISTORY
**guerrilla** In Spanish, the word *guerrilla*, a diminutive of *guerra* "war," was used from the early 16th century for a party of skirmishers who engaged the enemy in advance of the main force. After a popular uprising against Napoleonic rule in Spain broke out in 1808, *guerrilla* was applied to bands of Spanish partisans who harrassed French troops. The Duke of Wellington, commander of the British army in Spain, used the word in a dispatch, and it came to be adopted in Britain, though by a curious misunderstanding it was applied to a single partisan rather than to a band. The error may perhaps have been due to Wellington himself, though by 1812 the French borrowing *guérilla* was being used in a parallel way. *Guerrilla* also became an attributive adjective at an early date, appearing in a poem by Sir Walter Scott in 1811; the still common phrase *guerrilla warfare* was in use by at least the 1840s.

---

: an early 20th century English socialistic theory advocating state ownership of industry with control and management by guilds of workers

**guile** \'gī(ə)l\ *noun* [Middle English, from Old French, probably of Germanic origin; akin to Old English *wigle* divination — more at WITCH] (13th century)
**1** : deceitful cunning : DUPLICITY
**2** *obsolete* : STRATAGEM, TRICK
— **guile·ful** \-fəl\ *adjective*
— **guile·ful·ly** \-fə-lē\ *adverb*
— **guile·ful·ness** *noun*
**guile·less** \'gī(ə)l-ləs\ *adjective* (1728)
: INNOCENT, NAIVE
— **guile·less·ly** *adverb*
— **guile·less·ness** *noun*
**Guil·lain–Bar·ré syndrome** \,gē-,lan-bä-'rā-, ,gē-yaⁿ-\ *noun* [Georges *Guillain* (died 1961) French physician and Jean A. *Barré* (born 1880) French neurologist] (1940)
: a polyneuritis of unknown cause characterized especially by muscle weakness and paralysis
**guil·le·met** \,gē-(y)ə-'mā, ,gi-lə-'met\ *noun* [French, from diminutive of *Guillaume* William (perhaps a printer's name)] (circa 1905)
: either of the marks « or » used as quotation marks in French writing
**guil·le·mot** \'gi-lə-,mät\ *noun* [French, from Middle French, diminutive of *Guillaume* William] (1678)
**1** *British* : a common murre (*Uria aalge*)
**2** : any of a genus (*Cepphus*) of narrow-billed auks of northern seas
**guil·loche** \gi-'lōsh, gē-'(y)ōsh\ *noun* [French *guillochis*] (circa 1842)
**1** : an architectural ornament formed of two or more interlaced bands with openings containing round devices
**2** : a pattern (as on metalwork) made by interlacing curved lines
**guil·lo·tine** \'gi-lə-,tēn, ,gē-(y)ə-', ,gē-(y)ə-,\ *noun* [French, from Joseph *Guillotin* (died 1814) French physician] (1793)
**1** : a machine for beheading by means of a heavy blade that slides down in vertical guides
**2** : a shearing machine or instrument (as a paper cutter) that in action resembles a guillotine
**3** *chiefly British* : closure by the imposition of a predetermined time limit on the consideration of specific sections of a bill or portions of other legislative business ◆
— **guillotine** *transitive verb*
**guilt** \'gilt\ *noun* [Middle English, delinquency, guilt, from Old English *gylt* delinquency] (before 12th century)
**1** : the fact of having committed a breach of conduct especially violating law and involving a penalty; *broadly* : guilty conduct
**2 a** : the state of one who has committed an offense especially consciously **b** : feelings of culpability especially for imagined offenses or from a sense of inadequacy : SELF-REPROACH
**3** : a feeling of culpability for offenses
**guilt·less** \'gilt-ləs\ *adjective* (13th century)
: INNOCENT
— **guilt·less·ly** *adverb*
— **guilt·less·ness** *noun*
**guilty** \'gil-tē\ *adjective* **guilt·i·er; -est** (before 12th century)
**1** : justly chargeable with or responsible for a usually grave breach of conduct or a crime
**2** *obsolete* : justly liable to or deserving of a penalty
**3 a** : suggesting or involving guilt ⟨*guilty* looks⟩ **b** : aware of or suffering from guilt ⟨*guilty* consciences⟩
**synonym** see BLAMEWORTHY
— **guilt·i·ly** \-tə-lē\ *adverb*
— **guilt·i·ness** \-tē-nəs\ *noun*
**guimpe** \'gamp, 'gimp\ *noun* [French, from Old French *guimple*, of Germanic origin; akin to Old English *wimpel* wimple] (1850)
**1** : a blouse worn under a jumper or pinafore

**2** : a wide cloth used by some nuns to cover the neck and shoulders
**3** [by alteration] : ¹GIMP
**guin·ea** \'gi-nē\ *noun* [*Guinea*, Africa, supposed source of the gold from which it was made] (1664)
**1** : an English gold coin issued from 1663 to 1813 and fixed in 1717 at 21 shillings
**2** : a unit of value equal to one pound and one shilling
**guinea fowl** *noun* (1788)
: an African bird (*Numida meleagris*) related to the pheasants, raised for food in many parts of the world, and marked by a bare neck and head and slaty plumage speckled with white; *broadly* : any of several related birds

**guinea fowl**

**guinea grass** *noun* (1785)
: a tall African forage grass (*Panicum maximum*) introduced into tropical America and the southern U.S.
**guinea hen** *noun* (1599)
: a female guinea fowl; *broadly* : GUINEA FOWL
**guinea pepper** *noun* (1597)
: GRAINS OF PARADISE
**guinea pig** *noun* (1664)
**1** : a small stout-bodied short-eared tailless domesticated rodent (*Cavia porcellus*) often kept as a pet and widely used in biological research — called also *cavy*
**2** : a subject of research, experimentation, or testing
**guinea worm** *noun* (1699)
: a slender nematode worm (*Dracunculus medinensis*) of tropical regions parasitic in mammals including humans and having an adult female that infests subcutaneous tissues and may attain a length of several feet
**Guin·e·vere** \'gwi-nə-,vir, *British also* 'gi-\ *noun*
: the wife of King Arthur and mistress of Lancelot
**gui·pure** \gi-'pyür, -'pür\ *noun* [French] (1843)
: a heavy large-patterned decorative lace
**gui·ro** \'wē-(,)rō, 'gwir-(,)ō\ *noun* [American Spanish *güiro*, literally, calabash] (1898)
: a percussion instrument of Latin-American origin made of a serrated gourd and played by scraping a stick along its surface
**gui·sard** \'gī-zərd\ *noun* [obsolete Scots *gyze* to disguise, from Middle English *gyzen* to dress, from *guise*, *gyze* guise] (1626)
*chiefly Scottish* : MASKER, MUMMER
**guise** \'gīz\ *noun* [Middle English, from Old French, of Germanic origin; akin to Old High German *wīsa* manner — more at WISE] (13th century)
**1** : a form or style of dress : COSTUME
**2 a** *obsolete* : MANNER, FASHION **b** *archaic* : a customary way of speaking or behaving
**3 a** : external appearance : SEMBLANCE **b** : PRETEXT
**gui·tar** \gə-'tär, gi-, *especially Southern & Midland also* 'gi-,tär\ *noun* [French *guitare*, from Spanish *guitarra*, from Arabic *qītār*, from Greek *kithara* cithara] (1621)
: a flat-bodied stringed instrument with a long fretted neck and usually six strings plucked with a pick or with the fingers

**guitar: 1** electric, **2** acoustic

— **gui·tar·ist** \-ist\ *noun*
**gui·tar·fish** \-,fish\ *noun* (circa 1900)
: any of several viviparous rays (family Rhinobatidae) somewhat like a guitar in shape viewed from above
**Gu·ja·ra·ti** \,gü-jə-'rä-tē, ,gu̇-\ *noun* [Hindi *gujarātī*, from *Gujarāt* Gujarat] (1808)
**1** *or* **Gu·je·ra·ti** \*same*\ : the Indo-Aryan language of Gujarat and neighboring regions in northwestern India
**2** *or* **Guj·ra·ti** \gu̇j-'rä-, gu̇j-'rä-\ : a member of a people chiefly of Gujarat speaking the Gujarati language
**gul** \'gül\ *noun* [Persian] (1813)
*archaic* : ROSE 1
**gu·lag** \'gü-,läg\ *noun, often capitalized* [Russian, from *Glavnoe upravlenie ispravitel'no-trudovykh lagereĭ* chief administration of corrective labor camps] (1974)
: the penal system of the U.S.S.R. consisting of a network of labor camps; *also* : LABOR CAMP 1
**gu·lar** \'g(y)ü-lər\ *adjective* [Latin *gula* throat — more at GLUTTON] (1828)
: of, relating to, or situated on the throat
**gulch** \'gəlch\ *noun* [perhaps from English dialect *gulch* to gulp, from Middle English *gulchen*] (1832)
: a deep or precipitous cleft : RAVINE; *especially* : one occupied by a torrent
**gul·den** \'gül-dən, 'gu̇l-\ *noun, plural* **guldens** *or* **gulden** [Middle English (Scots), from Middle Dutch *gulden florijn* golden florin] (15th century)
— see MONEY table
**gules** \'gyü(ə)lz\ *noun, plural* **gules** [Middle English *goules*, from Middle French] (14th century)
: the heraldic color red
**¹gulf** \'gəlf\ *noun* [Middle English *goulf*, from Middle French *golfe*, from Italian *golfo*, from Late Latin *colpus*, from Greek *kolpos* bosom, gulf; akin to Old English *hwealf* vault, Old High German *walbo*] (15th century)
**1** : a part of an ocean or sea extending into the land
**2** : a deep chasm : ABYSS
**3** : WHIRLPOOL
**4** : a wide gap ⟨the *gulf* between generations⟩
**²gulf** *transitive verb* (1807)
: ENGULF
**gulf·weed** \'gəlf-,wēd\ *noun* [*Gulf* of Mexico] (1674)
: any of several sargassums; *especially* : a branching olive-brown seaweed (*Sargassum bacciferum*) of tropical American seas with numerous berrylike air vesicles

◇ WORD HISTORY
**guillotine**   Joseph-Ignace Guillotin (1738–1814) was a French physician and member of the National Assembly during the early months of the French Revolution. On October 10, 1789, in a proposed egalitarian revision of the penal code, Guillotin advocated that all death sentences be carried out by decapitation—a method formerly reserved to the nobility, common criminals usually being hung—and that the executioner's sword or ax be replaced for humane reasons by a machine. Various devices for beheading were already in existence, and one was perfected by a German mechanic named Schmitt, under the supervision of a French surgeon, Antoine Louis. The new machine, first used in 1792 and made famous during the Reign of Terror of 1793–94, was initially and appropriately called the *Louison* or *Louisette*. But *guillotine*, maliciously suggested by a journalist of royalist sympathies in 1790, was readily accepted, most likely in part because Guillotin was a better-known figure than Louis and was disliked by other politicians for his bluntness of speech.

**¹gull** \'gəl\ *noun* [Middle English, of Celtic origin; akin to Welsh *gwylan* gull] (15th century)
: any of numerous long-winged web-footed aquatic birds (subfamily Larinae of the family Laridae); *especially* : a usually gray and white bird (as of the genus *Larus*) differing from a tern in usually larger size, stouter build, thicker somewhat hooked bill, less pointed wings, and short unforked tail

**²gull** *transitive verb* [obsolete *gull* gullet, from Middle English *golle,* from Middle French *goule*] (circa 1550)
: to take advantage of (one who is foolish or unwary) : DECEIVE
**synonym** see DUPE

**³gull** *noun* (1594)
: a person who is easily deceived or cheated : DUPE

**Gul·lah** \'gə-lə\ *noun* (1822)
**1** : a member of a group of blacks inhabiting the sea islands and coastal districts of South Carolina, Georgia, and northeastern Florida
**2** : an English-based creole spoken by the Gullahs that is marked by vocabulary and grammatical elements from various African languages

**gul·let** \'gə-lət\ *noun* [Middle English *golet,* from Middle French *goulet,* diminutive of *goule* throat, from Latin *gula* — more at GLUTTON] (14th century)
**1** : ESOPHAGUS; *broadly* : THROAT
**2** : an invagination of the protoplasm in various protozoans (as a paramecium) that sometimes functions in the intake of food
**3** : the space between the tips of adjacent saw teeth

**gull·ible** *also* **gull·able** \'gə-lə-bəl\ *adjective* (1818)
: easily duped or cheated
— **gull·ibil·i·ty** \ˌgə-lə-'bi-lə-tē\ *noun*
— **gull·ibly** \'gə-lə-blē\ *adverb*

**Gul·li·ver** \'gə-lə-vər\ *noun*
: an Englishman in Jonathan Swift's satire *Gulliver's Travels* who makes voyages to the imaginary lands of the Lilliputians, Brobdingnagians, Laputans, and Houyhnhnms

**¹gul·ly** \'gù-lē, 'gə-\ *noun, plural* **gullies** [short for English dialect *gully knife*] (1582)
*dialect British* : a large knife

**²gul·ly** *also* **gul·ley** \'gə-lē\ *noun, plural* **gullies** [obsolete English *gully* (gullet)] (1637)
**1** : a trench which was originally worn in the earth by running water and through which water often runs after rains
**2** : a small valley or gulch

**³gul·ly** \'gə-lē\ *verb* **gul·lied; gul·ly·ing** (1754)
*transitive verb*
: to make gullies in
*intransitive verb*
: to undergo erosion : form gullies

**gully erosion** *noun* (1928)
: soil erosion produced by running water

**gu·los·i·ty** \g(y)ü-'lä-sə-tē\ *noun* [Middle English *gulosite,* from Late Latin *gulositas,* from Latin *gulosus* gluttonous, from *gula* gullet] (15th century)
: excessive appetite : GREEDINESS

**gulp** \'gəlp\ *verb* [Middle English, from a Middle Dutch or Middle Low German word akin to Dutch & Frisian *gulpen* to bubble forth, drink deep; akin to Old English *gielpan* to boast — more at YELP] (14th century)
*transitive verb*
**1** : to swallow hurriedly or greedily or in one swallow
**2** : to keep back as if by swallowing ⟨*gulp* down a sob⟩
**3** : to take in readily as if by swallowing ⟨*gulp* down knowledge⟩
*intransitive verb*
: to catch the breath as if in taking a long drink
— **gulp** *noun*
— **gulp·er** *noun*

**¹gum** \'gəm\ *noun* [Middle English *gome,* from Old English *gōma* palate; akin to Old High German *guomo* palate, and perhaps to Greek *chaos* abyss] (before 12th century)
: the tissue that surrounds the necks of teeth and covers the alveolar parts of the jaws; *broadly* : the alveolar portion of a jaw with its enveloping soft tissues

**²gum** *transitive verb* **gummed; gum·ming** (1777)
**1** : to enlarge gullets of (a saw)
**2** : to chew with the gums

**³gum** *noun* [Middle English *gomme,* from Middle French, from Latin *cummi, gummi,* from Greek *kommi,* from Egyptian *qmyt*] (14th century)
**1 a** : any of numerous colloidal polysaccharide substances of plant origin that are gelatinous when moist but harden on drying and are salts of complex organic acids — compare MUCILAGE 1 **b** : any of various plant exudates (as an oleoresin or gum resin)
**2** : a substance or deposit resembling a plant gum (as in sticky or adhesive quality)
**3 a** : a tree (as a black gum) that yields gum **b** *Australian* : EUCALYPTUS
**4** : the wood or lumber of a gum; *especially* : that of the sweet gum
**5** : CHEWING GUM

**⁴gum** *verb* **gummed; gum·ming** (1597)
*transitive verb*
: to clog, impede, or damage with or as if with gum ⟨*gum* up the works⟩
*intransitive verb*
**1** : to exude or form gum
**2** : to become gummy
— **gum·mer** *noun*

**gum arabic** *noun* (14th century)
: a water-soluble gum obtained from several acacias (especially *Acacia senegal*) and used especially in the manufacture of inks, adhesives, pharmaceuticals, and confections

**¹gum·bo** \'gəm-(ˌ)bō\ *noun, plural* **gumbos** [American French *gombo,* of Bantu origin; akin to Umbundu *ochinggômbo* okra] (1805)
**1** : a soup thickened with okra pods or filé and containing meat or seafoods and usually vegetables
**2** : OKRA 1
**3 a** : any of various fine-grained silty soils especially of the central U.S. that when wet become impervious and soapy or waxy and very sticky **b** : a heavy sticky mud
**4** : MIXTURE, MÉLANGE
— **gumbo** *adjective*

**²gumbo** *noun, often capitalized* [American French *gombo,* perhaps from Kongo *nkômbô* runaway slave] (1838)
: CREOLE 4a

**gum·boil** \'gəm-ˌbȯil\ *noun* (1753)
: an abscess in the gum

**gum·bo–lim·bo** \ˌgəm-bō-'lim-(ˌ)bō\ *noun* [origin unknown] (1837)
: a tree (*Bursera simaruba* of the family Burseraceae) of southern Florida and the American tropics that has a smooth coppery bark and supplies a reddish resin used locally in cements and varnishes

**gum boot** *noun* (1850)
: a rubber boot

**gum·drop** \'gəm-ˌdräp\ *noun* (1860)
: a sugar-coated candy made usually from corn syrup with gelatin or gum arabic

**gum·ma** \'gə-mə\ *noun, plural* **gummas** *also* **gum·ma·ta** \'gə-mə-tə\ [New Latin *gummat-, gumma,* from Late Latin, gum, alteration of Latin *gummi* gum] (circa 1722)
: a tumor of gummy or rubbery consistency that is characteristic of the tertiary stage of syphilis
— **gum·ma·tous** \-mə-təs\ *adjective*

**gum·mite** \'gə-ˌmīt\ *noun* (1868)
: a yellow to reddish brown mixture of hydrous oxides of uranium, thorium, and lead

**gum·mo·sis** \ˌgə-'mō-səs\ *noun* [New Latin] (1882)
: a pathological production of gummy exudate in a plant; *also* : a plant disease marked by gummosis

**gum·mous** \'gə-məs\ *adjective* (1669)
: resembling or composed of gum

**gum·my** \'gə-mē\ *adjective* **gum·mi·er; -est** (14th century)
**1** : VISCOUS, STICKY
**2 a** : consisting of or containing gum **b** : covered with gum
— **gum·mi·ness** *noun*

**gump·tion** \'gəm(p)-shən\ *noun* [origin unknown] (1719)
**1** *chiefly dialect* : COMMON SENSE, HORSE SENSE
**2** : ENTERPRISE, INITIATIVE ⟨lacked the *gumption* to try⟩

**gum resin** *noun* (1712)
: a product consisting essentially of a mixture of gum and resin usually obtained by making an incision in a plant and allowing the juice which exudes to solidify

**¹gum·shoe** \'gəm-ˌshü\ *noun* (1906)
: DETECTIVE

**²gumshoe** *intransitive verb* **gum·shoed; gum·shoe·ing** (1930)
: to engage in detective work

**gum tragacanth** *noun* (1573)
: TRAGACANTH

**gum tree** *noun* (1676)
: ³GUM 3

**gum turpentine** *noun* (1926)
: TURPENTINE 2a

**gum·wood** \'gəm-ˌwu̇d\ *noun* (1709)
: ³GUM 4

**¹gun** \'gən\ *noun* [Middle English *gonne, gunne*] (14th century)
**1 a** : a piece of ordnance usually with high muzzle velocity and comparatively flat trajectory **b** : a portable firearm (as a rifle or handgun) **c** : a device that throws a projectile
**2 a** : a discharge of a gun especially as a salute or signal **b** : a signal marking a beginning or ending
**3 a** : HUNTER **b** : GUNMAN
**4** : something suggesting a gun in shape or function
**5** : THROTTLE
— **gunned** \'gənd\ *adjective*
— **under the gun** : under pressure or attack

**²gun** *verb* **gunned; gun·ning** (1622)
*intransitive verb*
: to hunt with a gun
*transitive verb*
**1 a** : to fire on **b** : SHOOT ⟨*gunned* down by a hit man⟩
**2 a** : to open up the throttle of so as to increase speed ⟨*gun* the engine⟩ **b** : FIRE 3b ⟨*gunned* the ball to first base⟩
— **gun for** : to aim at or go after with determination or effort

**gun·boat** \'gən-ˌbōt\ *noun* (1777)
: an armed ship of shallow draft

**gunboat diplomacy** *noun* (1927)
: diplomacy backed by the use or threat of military force

**gun control** *noun* (1969)
: regulation of the selling, owning, and use of guns

**gun·cot·ton** \-ˌkä-tᵊn\ *noun* (1846)
: NITROCELLULOSE; *especially* : an explosive highly nitrated product used chiefly in smokeless powder

**gun·dog** \-ˌdȯg\ *noun* (1744)
: a dog trained to work with hunters by locating and retrieving game

**gun·fight** \-ˌfīt\ *noun* (1659)
: a hostile encounter in which antagonists fire upon each other
— **gun·fight·er** \-ˌfī-tər\ *noun*

**gun·fire** \-,fī(-ə)r\ *noun* (1801)
: the firing of guns
**gun·flint** \-,flint\ *noun* (1731)
: a small sharp flint fashioned to ignite the priming in a flintlock
**gung ho** \'gəŋ-'hō\ *adjective* [*Gung ho!*, motto (interpreted as meaning "work together") adopted by certain U.S. marines, from Chinese (Beijing) *gōnghé*, short for *Zhōngguó Gōngyè Hézuò Shè* Chinese Industrial Cooperative Society] (1942)
: extremely or overly zealous or enthusiastic ◆
**gun·ite** \'gə-,nīt\ *noun* (1914)
: a building material consisting of a mixture of cement, sand, and water that is sprayed onto a mold
**gunk** \'gəŋk\ *noun* [from *Gunk*, trademark for a cleaning solvent] (1943)
: filthy, sticky, or greasy matter
— **gunky** \'gəŋ-kē\ *adjective*
**gun lap** *noun* (circa 1949)
: the final lap of a race in track signaled by the firing of a gun as the leader begins the lap
**gun·man** \-mən\ *noun* (1624)
**1 :** a man armed with a gun; *especially* **:** a professional killer
**2 :** a man noted for speed or skill in handling a gun
**gun·met·al** \'gən-,me-t°l\ *noun* (1541)
**1 :** a metal used for guns; *specifically* **:** a bronze formerly much used as a material for cannon
**2 :** an alloy or metal treated to imitate nearly black tarnished copper-alloy gunmetal
**3 :** a bluish gray color
**gun moll** \-,mäl, -,mȯl\ *noun* [slang *gun* thief, rascal, by shortening & alteration from *gonoph, ganef* thief — more at GANEF] (circa 1908)
*slang* **:** MOLL 2b
**Gun·nar** \'gü,när, 'gü-, -nər\ *noun* [Old Norse *Gunnarr*]
: the king of the Nibelungs and husband of Brynhild in Norse mythology
**¹gun·nel** \'gə-n°l\ *noun variant of* GUNWALE
**²gunnel** *noun* [origin unknown] (1740)
: a small slimy elongate north Atlantic blenny (*Pholis gunnellus*); *broadly* **:** any fish of the family (Pholidae) to which the gunnel belongs
**gun·ner** \'gə-nər\ *noun* (14th century)
**1 :** a soldier or airman who operates or aims a gun
**2 :** one who hunts with a gun
**3 :** a warrant officer who supervises ordnance and ordnance stores
**gun·nery** \'gən-rē, 'gə-nə-\ *noun* (1605)
: the use of guns; *especially* **:** the science of the flight of projectiles and of the effective use of guns
**gunnery sergeant** *noun* (circa 1961)
: a noncommissioned officer in the marine corps ranking above a staff sergeant and below a master sergeant or first sergeant
**gun·ny·sack** \'gə-nē-,sak\ *noun* [*gunny* coarse fabric, of Indo-Aryan origin; akin to Hindi *gon sack*, Punjabi *gūṇī*] (1862)
: a sack made of a coarse heavy fabric (as burlap)
**gun·play** \'gən-,plā\ *noun* (1881)
: the shooting of small arms with intent to scare or kill
**gun·point** \-,pȯint\ *noun* (1951)
: the muzzle of a gun
— **at gunpoint :** under a threat of death by being shot
**gun·pow·der** \-,paù-dər\ *noun* (15th century)
: an explosive mixture of potassium nitrate, charcoal, and sulfur used in gunnery and blasting; *broadly* **:** any of various powders used in guns as propelling charges
**gun room** *noun* (1626)
: quarters on a British warship originally used by the gunner and his mates but now by midshipmen and junior officers
**gun·run·ner** \'gən-,rə-nər\ *noun* (1899)

: one that traffics in contraband arms and ammunition
— **gun·run·ning** \-,rə-niŋ\ *noun*
**gun·sel** \'gən(t)-səl\ *noun* [slang *gunsel* catamite, perhaps modification of Yiddish *gendzl* gosling] (1944)
*slang* **:** GUNMAN
**gun·ship** \'gən-,ship\ *noun* (1966)
: a helicopter or cargo aircraft armed with rockets and machine guns
**gun·shot** \'gən-,shät\ *noun* (15th century)
**1 :** shot or a projectile fired from a gun
**2 :** the range of a gun
**3 :** the firing of a gun
**gun–shy** \-,shī\ *adjective* (1884)
**1 :** afraid of loud noise (as that of a gun)
**2 :** markedly distrustful, afraid, or cautious
**gun·sling·er** \-,sliŋ-ər\ *noun* (1928)
: a person noted for speed and skill in handling and shooting a gun especially in the American West
**gun·sling·ing** \-,sliŋ-iŋ\ *noun* (circa 1944)
: the shooting of a gun especially in a gunfight
**gun·smith** \-,smith\ *noun* (1588)
: one who designs, makes, or repairs small firearms
— **gun·smith·ing** \-,smi-thiŋ\ *noun*
**Gun·ter's chain** \'gən-tərz-\ *noun* [Edmund *Gunter*] (circa 1679)
: a chain 66 feet (20.1 meters) long that is the unit of length for surveys of U.S. public lands
**Gun·ther** \'gùn-tər\ *noun* [German]
: a Burgundian king and husband of Brunhild in Germanic legend
**gun·wale** *also* **gun·nel** \'gə-n°l\ *noun* [Middle English *gonne-wale*, from *gonne* gun + ¹*wale*; from its former use as a support for guns] (15th century)
: the upper edge of a ship's or boat's side
— **to the gunwales :** as full as possible
**gup·py** \'gə-pē\ *noun, plural* **guppies** [R.J.L. Guppy (died 1916) Trinidadian naturalist] (1925)
: a small live-bearer (*Poecilia reticulata* of the family Poeciliidae) of Barbados, Trinidad, and Venezuela often kept as an aquarium fish

guppy: *1* female, *2* male

**gur·gle** \'gər-gəl\ *intransitive verb* **gur·gled; gur·gling** \-g(ə-)liŋ\ [probably imitative] (1713)
**1 :** to flow in a broken irregular current (the brook *gurgling* over the rocks)
**2 :** to make a sound like that of a gurgling liquid (the baby *gurgling* in his crib)
— **gurgle** *noun*
**Gur·kha** \'gùr-kə, 'gər-\ *noun* [*Ghurka*, member of a Rajput clan who dominated Nepal in the 18th century] (1811)
: a soldier from Nepal in the British or Indian army
**gur·nard** \'gər-nərd\ *noun, plural* **gurnard** *or* **gurnards** [Middle English, from Middle French *gornart*, irregular from *grognier* to grunt, from Latin *grunnire*, of imitative origin] (14th century)
: SEA ROBIN — compare FLYING GURNARD
**gur·ney** \'gər-nē\ *noun, plural* **gurneys** [probably from the name *Gurney*] (1939)
: a wheeled cot or stretcher
**gur·ry** \'gər-ē, 'gə-rē\ *noun* [origin unknown] (1850)
: fishing offal
**gu·ru** \'gùr-(,)ü *also* gə-'rü\ *noun, plural* **gurus** [Hindi *gurū*, from Sanskrit *guru*, *guru*, adjective, heavy, venerable — more at GRIEVE] (1613)
**1 :** a personal religious teacher and spiritual guide in Hinduism
**2 a :** a teacher and especially intellectual guide in matters of fundamental concern **b** **:** one who is an acknowledged leader or chief

proponent **c** **:** a person with knowledge or expertise **:** EXPERT
**¹gush** \'gəsh\ *verb* [Middle English *guschen*] (15th century)
*intransitive verb*
**1 :** to issue copiously or violently
**2 :** to emit a sudden copious flow
**3 :** to make an effusive display of affection or enthusiasm (an aunt *gushing* over the baby)
*transitive verb*
**1 :** to emit in a copious free flow
**2 :** to say or write effusively
— **gush·ing·ly** \'gə-shiŋ-lē\ *adverb*
**²gush** *noun* (circa 1682)
**1 a :** a sudden outpouring **b** **:** something emitted in a gushing forth
**2 :** an effusive display or outpouring
**gush·er** \'gə-shər\ *noun* (1864)
: one that gushes; *specifically* **:** an oil well with a copious natural flow
**gushy** \'gə-shē\ *adjective* **gush·i·er; -est** (1845)
: marked by effusive sentimentality
— **gush·i·ly** \'gə-shə-lē\ *adverb*
— **gush·i·ness** \'gə-shē-nəs\ *noun*
**gus·set** \'gə-sət\ *noun* [Middle English, piece of armor covering the joints in a suit of armor, from Middle French *gousset*] (circa 1570)
**1 :** a usually diamond-shaped or triangular insert in a seam (as of a sleeve, pocketbook, or shoe upper) to provide expansion or reinforcement
**2 :** a plate or bracket for strengthening an angle in framework (as in a building or bridge)
— **gusset** *transitive verb*
**gus·sy up** \'gə-sē-'əp\ *transitive verb* **gussied up; gus·sy·ing up** [origin unknown] (1952)
: DRESS UP, EMBELLISH
**¹gust** \'gəst\ *noun* [Middle English *guste*, from Latin *gustus*; akin to Latin *gustare* to taste — more at CHOOSE] (15th century)
**1** *obsolete* **a :** the sensation of taste **b** **:** INCLINATION, LIKING
**2 :** keen delight
**²gust** *noun* [probably from Old Norse *gustr*; akin to Old High German *gussa* flood, and perhaps to Old English *gēotan* to pour — more at FOUND] (1588)
**1 :** a sudden brief rush of wind
**2 :** a sudden outburst **:** SURGE (a *gust* of emotion)
— **gust·i·ly** \'gəs-tə-lē\ *adverb*

◇ WORD HISTORY

**gung ho** The Chinese Industrial Cooperative Society was organized in 1938 to develop light industry in areas of China not overrun by the Japanese, and was supported by both Communists and Chiang Kai-shek's Nationalists. The Chinese name of the society, *Zhōngguó Gōngyè Hézuò Shé*, was conventionally shortened to *Gōnghé*. A U.S. Marine Corps lieutenant colonel, Evans Carlson, while an observer with the Communists' 8th Route Army in 1937–38, became an admirer of their tactics. When Carlson formed the Marines' 2nd Raider Battalion at Camp Elliott, California, in February, 1942, he tried to instill the Communists' unity of purpose in his men. He told them that "Gung ho" was the motto of the Chinese Industrial Cooperatives (which Carlson seems to have associated with the Communists) and meant "work together." (In fact, though *gōng* may be translated "work" and *hé* "to join," *Gōnghé* is simply the shortened form of a name and not the Chinese equivalent of "to work together.") Carlson's training program soon lapsed, but *gung ho* spread beyond the 2nd Raider Battalion. At first alluding positively to Marine Corps esprit, it eventually took on the negative sense "excessively zealous" and spread from military to civilian use.

— **gust·i·ness** \-tē-nəs\ noun
— **gusty** \-tē\ adjective

³**gust** intransitive verb (1813)
: to blow in gusts ⟨winds gusting up to 40 mph⟩

**gus·ta·tion** \ˌgəs-'tā-shən\ noun [Latin gustation-, gustatio, from gustare] (1599)
: the act or sensation of tasting

**gus·ta·to·ry** \'gəs-tə-ˌtōr-ē, -ˌtor-\ adjective (1684)
: relating to or associated with eating or the sense of taste
— **gus·ta·to·ri·ly** \ˌgəs-tə-'tōr-ə-lē, -'tor-\ adverb

**gus·to** \'gəs-(ˌ)tō\ noun, plural **gustoes** [Italian, from Latin gustus, past participle] (1620)
**1 a** : an individual or special taste ⟨different gustoes⟩ **b** : enthusiastic and vigorous enjoyment or appreciation **c** : vitality marked by an abundance of vigor and enthusiasm
**2** archaic : artistic style

¹**gut** \'gət\ noun [Middle English, from Old English guttas, plural; probably akin to Old English gēotan to pour] (before 12th century)
**1 a** (1) : BOWELS, ENTRAILS — usually used in plural (2) : the basic visceral or emotional part of a person **b** : the alimentary canal or part of it (as the intestine or stomach) **c** : BELLY, ABDOMEN **d** : CATGUT
**2** plural : the inner essential parts ⟨the guts of a car⟩
**3** : a narrow passage; also : a narrow waterway or small creek
**4** : the sac of silk taken from a silkworm ready to spin its cocoon and drawn out into a thread for use as a snell
**5** plural : fortitude and stamina in coping with what alarms, repels, or discourages : COURAGE, PLUCK
**6** : GUT COURSE

²**gut** transitive verb **gut·ted; gut·ting** (14th century)
**1 a** : EVISCERATE **b** : to extract all the essential passages or portions from
**2 a** : to destroy the inside of ⟨fire gutted the building⟩ **b** : to destroy the essential power or effectiveness of ⟨inflation gutting the economy⟩
— **gut it out** : PERSEVERE

³**gut** adjective (1964)
**1** : arising from one's inmost self : VISCERAL ⟨a gut reaction⟩
**2** : having strong impact or immediate relevance ⟨gut issues⟩

**gut·buck·et** \'gət-ˌbə-kət\ noun (1929)
**1** : BARRELHOUSE 2
**2** : a homemade bass fiddle consisting of a stick attached to an inverted washtub and having a single string

**gut course** noun (1948)
: a course (as in college) that is easily passed

**gut·less** \'gət-ləs\ adjective (1900)
**1** : lacking courage : COWARDLY
**2** : lacking significance or vitality
— **gut·less·ness** noun

**gutsy** \'gət-sē\ adjective **guts·i·er; -est** (circa 1893)
**1** : marked by courage, pluck, or determination ⟨a gutsy little fighter⟩ ⟨a gutsy decision⟩
**2 a** : expressing or characterized by basic physical senses or passions ⟨gutsy macho talk⟩ ⟨gutsy country blues⟩ **b** : rough or plain in style : not bland or sophisticated ⟨a gutsy soup⟩
— **gut·si·ly** \-sə-lē\ adverb
— **guts·i·ness** noun

**gut·ta** \'gə-tə, 'gu̇-tə\ noun, plural **gut·tae** \'gə-ˌtē, 'gu̇-, -ˌtī\ [Latin, literally, drop] (1563)
: one of a series of ornaments in the Doric entablature that is usually in the form of a frustum of a cone

**gut·ta–per·cha** \ˌgə-tə-'pər-chə\ noun [Malay gĕtah-pĕrcha, from gĕtah sap, latex + pĕrcha scrap, rag] (1845)
: a tough plastic substance from the latex of several Malaysian trees (genera Payena and

Palaquium) of the sapodilla family that resembles rubber but contains more resin and is used especially as insulation and in dentistry

**gut·ta·tion** \ˌgə-'tā-shən\ noun [Latin gutta drop] (circa 1889)
: the exudation of liquid water from the uninjured surface of a plant leaf

¹**gut·ter** \'gə-tər\ noun [Middle English goter, from Middle French goutiere, from goute drop, from Latin gutta] (14th century)
**1 a** : a trough along the eaves to catch and carry off rainwater **b** : a low area (as at the edge of a street) to carry off surface water (as to a sewer) **c** : a trough or groove to catch and direct something ⟨the gutters of a bowling alley⟩
**2** : a white space formed by the adjoining inside margins of two facing pages (as of a book)
**3** : the lowest or most vulgar level or condition of human life

²**gutter** (14th century)
transitive verb
**1** : to cut or wear gutters in
**2** : to provide with a gutter
intransitive verb
**1 a** : to flow in rivulets **b** of a candle : to melt away through a channel out of the side of the cup hollowed out by the burning wick
**2** : to incline downward in a draft ⟨the candle flame guttering⟩

³**gutter** adjective (15th century)
: of, relating to, or characteristic of the gutter; especially : marked by extreme vulgarity, cheapness, or indecency ⟨gutter politics⟩

**gut·ter·ing** \-iŋ\ noun (1703)
**1** : material for gutters
**2** : GUTTER 1a

**gutter out** intransitive verb (1875)
**1** : to become gradually weaker and then go out ⟨the candle guttered out⟩
**2** : to end feebly or undramatically ⟨his screen career had slowly guttered out⟩

**gut·ter·snipe** \'gə-tər-ˌsnīp\ noun (circa 1869)
**1** : STREET ARAB
**2** : a person of the lowest moral or economic station
— **gut·ter·snip·ish** \-ˌsnī-pish\ adjective

**gut·tur·al** \'gə-tə-rəl, 'gə-trəl\ adjective [Middle French, probably from Medieval Latin gutturalis, from Latin guttur throat] (1594)
**1** : articulated in the throat ⟨guttural sounds⟩
**2** : VELAR
**3** : being or marked by utterance that is strange, unpleasant, or disagreeable
— **guttural** noun
— **gut·tur·al·ism** \'gə-tə-rə-ˌli-zəm, 'gə-trə-\ noun

**gut·ty** \'gə-tē\ adjective **gut·ti·er; -est** (1947)
**1** : GUTSY 1 ⟨a gutty quarterback⟩
**2** : having a vigorous challenging quality ⟨gutty realism⟩

**gut–wrench·ing** \'gət-ˌren-chiŋ\ adjective (1974)
: causing mental or emotional anguish

¹**guy** \'gī\ noun [probably from Dutch gei brail] (1623)
: a rope, chain, rod, or wire attached to something as a brace or guide — called also guyline

²**guy** transitive verb (1712)
: to steady or reinforce with a guy

³**guy** noun [Guy Fawkes] (1806)
**1** often capitalized : a grotesque effigy of Guy Fawkes traditionally displayed and burned in England on Guy Fawkes Day
**2** chiefly British : a person of grotesque appearance
**3 a** : MAN, FELLOW **b** : PERSON — used in plural to refer to the members of a group regardless of sex ⟨saw her and the rest of the guys⟩ ◆

⁴**guy** transitive verb (1854)
: to make fun of : RIDICULE

**Guy Fawkes Day** \'gī-'fȯks-\ noun (1825)
: November 5 observed in England in commemoration of the seizure of Guy Fawkes in 1605 for an attempt to blow up the houses of Parliament

**guy·ot** \'gē-(ˌ)ō\ noun [Arnold H. Guyot (died 1884) American geographer & geologist] (1946)
: a flat-topped seamount

**guz·zle** \'gə-zəl\ verb **guz·zled; guz·zling** \'gəz-liŋ, 'gə-zə-\ [origin unknown] (1583)
intransitive verb
: to drink especially liquor greedily, continually, or habitually
transitive verb
: to drink greedily or habitually ⟨guzzle beer⟩
— **guz·zler** \'gəz-lər, 'gə-zə-\ noun

**gwe·duc** \'gü-ē-ˌdək\ variant of GEODUCK

**gybe** \'jīb\ variant of JIBE

**gym** \'jim\ noun (circa 1871)
**1** : GYMNASIUM
**2** : PHYSICAL EDUCATION
**3** : a usually metal frame supporting an assortment of outdoor play equipment (as a swing, seesaw, and rings)

**gym·kha·na** \jim-'kä-nə, -'ka-\ noun [probably modification of Hindi gēdkhāna, literally, ball court] (1877)
: a meet featuring sports contests or athletic skills: as **a** : competitive games on horseback **b** : a timed contest for automobiles featuring a series of events designed to test driving skill

**gym·na·si·um** \sense 1 jim-'nā-zē-əm, -zhəm; sense 2 usually gim-'nä-zē-əm\ noun, plural **-na·si·ums** or **-na·sia** \-'nä-zē-ə, -'nä-zhə; -'nä-zē-ə\ [Latin, exercise ground, school, from Greek gymnasion, from gymnazein to exercise naked, from gymnos naked — more at NAKED] (1598)
**1 a** : a large room used for various indoor sports (as basketball or boxing) and usually equipped with gymnastic apparatus **b** : a building (as on a college campus) containing space and equipment for various indoor sports activities and usually including spectator accommodations, locker and shower rooms, offices, classrooms, and a swimming pool

◇ WORD HISTORY
**guy** On November 4, 1605, Guy Fawkes was arrested in London and later executed for having planted barrels of gunpowder in the cellars of the houses of Parliament as part of a conspiracy to blow up the buildings. The failure of this conspiracy, now known as the Gunpowder Plot, is still celebrated in England on the evening of November 5, Guy Fawkes Day, when bonfires are traditionally lit and fireworks set off. On the bonfires are burned effigies of Guy Fawkes made from old clothes stuffed with straw and rags. By the early part of the 19th century these effigies had come to be called guys. The use of this word was extended to other similar effigies and then to a person of grotesque appearance or dress. In the U.S., where Guy Fawkes' demise has apparently never been celebrated, the word guy has had an extraordinary career, passing in the course of the last two centuries from the meaning "person who is an object of derision or pity" to "man, fellow" to a gender-neutral "person." The last sense is heard particularly in the phrase you guys, first attested in 1896, which sometimes amounts to little more than a familiar plural form of the second-person pronoun.

\ə\ abut \ᵊ\ kitten \ər\ further \a\ ash \ā\ ace
\ä\ mop, mar \au̇\ out \ch\ chin \e\ bet \ē\ easy
\g\ go \i\ hit \ī\ ice \j\ job \ŋ\ sing \ō\ go
\ȯ\ law \ȯi\ boy \th\ thin \th\ the \ü\ loot \u̇\ foot
\y\ yet \zh\ vision see also Guide to Pronunciation

**2** [German, from Latin, *school*] **:** a European secondary school that prepares students for the university ◆

**gym·nast** \'jim-,nast, -nəst\ *noun* [Middle French *gymnaste*, from Greek *gymnastēs* trainer, from *gymnazein*] (1594)
**:** one trained in gymnastics

**¹gym·nas·tic** \jim-'nas-tik\ *adjective* (1574)
**:** of or relating to gymnastics **:** ATHLETIC
— **gym·nas·ti·cal·ly** \-ti-k(ə-)lē\ *adverb*

**²gymnastic** *noun* (1652)
**1** *plural but singular in construction* **a :** physical exercises designed to develop strength and coordination **b :** a competitive sport in which individuals perform optional and prescribed acrobatic feats mostly on special apparatus in order to demonstrate strength, balance, and body control
**2 :** an exercise in intellectual or artistic dexterity ⟨my earlier philosophic study had been an intellectual *gymnastic* —John Dewey⟩ ⟨mental *gymnastics*⟩
**3 :** a physical feat or contortion ⟨the *gymnastics* necessary for the killer to have swung from the fire escape —E. D. Radin⟩

**gym·nos·o·phist** \jim-'nä-sə-fist\ *noun* [Latin *gymnosophista*, from Greek *gymnosophistēs*, from *gymnos* + *sophistēs* wise man, sophist] (15th century)
**:** any of a sect of ascetics in ancient India who went naked and practiced meditation

**gym·no·sperm** \'jim-nə-,spərm\ *noun* [ultimately from Greek *gymnos* + *sperma* seed — more at SPERM] (circa 1838)
**:** any of a class (Gymnospermae) of woody vascular seed plants (as conifers) that produce naked seeds not enclosed in an ovary and that in some instances have motile spermatozoids
— **gym·no·sper·mous** \,jim-nə-'spər-məs\ *adjective*
— **gym·no·sper·my** \'jim-nə-,spər-mē\ *noun*

**gyn-** *or* **gyno-** *combining form* [Greek *gyn-*, from *gynē* woman — more at QUEEN]
**:** female reproductive organ **:** ovary ⟨*gyno*phore⟩

**gy·nae·col·o·gy** *chiefly British variant of* GYNECOLOGY

**gyn·an·dro·morph** \,gin-'an-drə-,mórf, ,jin-\ *noun* [International Scientific Vocabulary, from Greek *gynandros* + *-morph*] (circa 1890)
**:** an abnormal individual exhibiting characters of both sexes in various parts of the body **:** a sexual mosaic
— **gyn·an·dro·mor·phic** \(,)gin-,an-drə-'mòr-fik, (,)jin-\ *adjective*
— **gyn·an·dro·mor·phism** \-,fi-zəm\ *noun*
— **gyn·an·dro·mor·phy** \,gin-'an-drə-,mòr-fē, ,jin-\ *noun*

**gyn·an·drous** \gin-'an-drəs, ,jin-\ *adjective* [Greek *gynandros* of doubtful sex, from *gynē* woman + *andr-*, *anēr* man — more at ANDR-] (1807)
**:** having the androecium and gynoecium united in a column

**-gyne** *noun combining form* [Greek *gynē*]
**:** female reproductive organ ⟨tricho*gyne*⟩

**gynec-** *or* **gyneco-** *also* **gynaec-** *or* **gynaeco-** *combining form* [Greek *gynaik-*, *gynaiko-*, from *gynaik-*, *gynē* woman — more at QUEEN]
**:** woman ⟨*gyneco*logy⟩

**gy·ne·coc·ra·cy** \,gī-ni-'kä-krə-sē, ,ji-\ *noun*, *plural* **-cies** [Greek *gynaikokratia*, from *gynaik-* + *-kratia* -cracy] (1612)
**:** political supremacy of women
— **gy·ne·co·crat·ic** \,gī-ni-kō-'kra-tik, ,ji-\ *adjective*

**gy·ne·coid** \'gī-ni-,kóid, 'ji-\ *adjective* (1907)
**:** typical or characteristic of the human female ⟨*gynecoid* pelvis⟩

**gy·ne·col·o·gy** \,gī-nə-'kä-lə-jē, ,ji-\ *noun* [International Scientific Vocabulary] (circa 1847)

**:** a branch of medicine that deals with the diseases and routine physical care of the reproductive system of women
— **gy·ne·co·log·ic** \,gī-ni-kə-'lä-jik, ,ji-\ *or* **gy·ne·co·log·i·cal** \-ji-kəl\ *adjective*
— **gy·ne·col·o·gist** \,gī-nə-'kä-lə-jist, ,ji-\ *noun*

**gy·ne·co·mas·tia** \,gī-nə-kō-'mas-tē-ə\ *noun* [New Latin, from *gynec-* + Greek *mastos* breast + New Latin *-ia*] (1881)
**:** excessive development of the breast in the male

**gy·noe·ci·um** \ji-'nē-shē-əm, gī-, -sē-\ *noun*, *plural* **-cia** \-shē-ə, -sē-\ [New Latin, alteration of Latin *gynaeceum* women's apartments, from Greek *gynaikeion*, from *gynaik-*, *gynē*] (1832)
**:** the aggregate of carpels or pistils in a flower

**gy·no·gen·e·sis** \,gī-nə-'je-nə-səs\ *noun* [New Latin] (1925)
**:** development in which the embryo contains only maternal chromosomes due to activation of an egg by a sperm that degenerates without fusing with the egg nucleus
— **gy·no·ge·net·ic** \-jə-'ne-tik\ *adjective*

**gy·no·phore** \'gī-nə-,fōr, 'ji-, -,fòr\ *noun* (1821)
**:** a prolongation of the receptacle (as in a caper flower) with the gynoecium at its apex

**-gynous** *adjective combining form* [New Latin *-gynus*, from Greek *-gynos*, from *gynē* woman — more at QUEEN]
**1 :** of, relating to, or having (such or so many) wives ⟨mono*gynous*⟩
**2 :** situated (in a specified place) in relation to a female organ of a plant ⟨hypo*gynous*⟩

**-gyny** *noun combining form*
**1 :** existence of or condition of having (such or so many) wives ⟨poly*gyny*⟩
**2 :** condition of being situated (in a specified place) in relation to a female organ of a plant ⟨epi*gyny*⟩

**¹gyp** \'jip\ *noun* [probably short for *gypsy*] (1750)
**1** *British* **:** a college servant
**2 a :** CHEAT, SWINDLER **b :** FRAUD, SWINDLE

**²gyp** *verb* **gypped; gyp·ping** (1880)
**:** CHEAT

**gyp·se·ous** \'jip-sē-əs\ *adjective* (1661)
**:** resembling, containing, or consisting of gypsum ⟨*gypseous* clay loam⟩

**gyp·sif·er·ous** \jip-'si-f(ə-)rəs\ *adjective* (circa 1847)
**:** containing gypsum

**gyp·soph·i·la** \jip-'sä-fə-lə\ *noun* [New Latin, from Latin *gypsum* + New Latin *-phila* -phil] (1771)
**:** any of a large genus (*Gypsophila*) of Old World herbs of the pink family having small delicate usually paniculate flowers

**gyp·sum** \'jip-səm\ *noun* [Latin, from Greek *gypsos*] (14th century)
**1 :** a widely distributed mineral consisting of hydrous calcium sulfate that is used especially as a soil amendment and in making plaster of paris
**2 :** PLASTERBOARD

**gyp·sy** \'jip-sē\ *intransitive verb* **gyp·sied; gyp·sy·ing** (circa 1627)
**:** to live or roam like a Gypsy

**Gyp·sy** \'jip-sē\ *noun*, *plural* **Gypsies** [by shortening & alteration from *Egyptian*] (1537)
**1 :** a member of a traditionally itinerant people who originated in northern India and now live chiefly in south and southwest Asia, Europe, and North America
**2 :** ROMANY 2
**3** *not capitalized* **:** one that resembles a Gypsy; *especially* **:** WANDERER

**gypsy cab** *noun* (1964)
**:** a taxicab licensed only to answer calls; *especially* **:** such a cab that cruises in search of passengers

**gypsy moth** *noun* (1819)
**:** an Old World tussock moth (*Lymantria dispar*) that was introduced about 1869 into the

U.S. and has a grayish brown mottled hairy caterpillar which is a destructive defoliator of many trees

**gyr-** *or* **gyro-** *combining form* [probably from Middle French, from Latin, from Greek, from *gyros* rounded]
**1 :** ring **:** circle **:** spiral ⟨*gyro*magnetic⟩
**2 :** gyroscope ⟨*gyro*compass⟩

**gyr·ase** \'jī-,rās\ *noun* [*gyr-* + *-ase*] (1976)
**:** an enzyme that catalyzes the breaking and rejoining of bonds linking adjacent nucleotides in DNA to generate supercoiled DNA helices

**¹gy·rate** \'jī-,rāt\ *adjective* (1830)
**:** winding or coiled around **:** CONVOLUTED ⟨*gyrate* branches of a tree⟩

**²gyrate** *intransitive verb* **gy·rat·ed; gy·rat·ing** (1830)
**1 :** to revolve around a point or axis
**2 :** to oscillate with or as if with a circular or spiral motion
— **gy·ra·tor** \-,rā-tər\ *noun*
— **gy·ra·to·ry** \'jī-rə-,tōr-ē, -,tòr-\ *adjective*

**gy·ra·tion** \jī-'rā-shən\ *noun* (1615)
**1 :** an act or instance of gyrating
**2 :** something (as a coil of a shell) that is gyrate
— **gy·ra·tion·al** \-shnəl, -shə-n°l\ *adjective*

**¹gyre** \'jī(-ə)r\ *noun* [Latin *gyrus*, from Greek *gyros*] (1566)
**:** a circular or spiral motion or form; *especially* **:** a giant circular oceanic surface current
— **gy·ral** \'jī-rəl\ *adjective*

**²gyre** *intransitive verb* **gyred; gyr·ing** [Late Latin *gyrare*, from Latin *gyrus*] (1593)
**:** to move in a circle or spiral

**gy·rene** \jī-'rēn\ *noun* [probably alteration of *marine*] (1944)
*slang* **:** a U.S. marine

**gyr·fal·con** \'jər-,fal-kən, -,fòl- *also* -,fò-kən\ *noun* [Middle English *gerfaucun*, from Old French *girfaucon*, probably from *gir* vulture (from Old High German *gīr*) + *faucon* falcon] (14th century)
**:** an arctic falcon (*Falco rusticolus*) that occurs in several color forms and is the largest of all falcons

**gyrfalcon**

**¹gy·ro** \'jī-(,)rō\ *noun, plural* **gyros** (1910)
**1** : GYROCOMPASS
**2** : GYROSCOPE
**²gy·ro** \'yē-,rō, 'zhir-ō\ *noun, plural* **gyros**
[New Greek *gyros* turn, from Greek; from the rotation of the meat on a spit] (1971)
: a sandwich especially of lamb and beef, tomato, and onion on pita bread
**Gy·ro** \'jī-(,)rō\ *noun, plural* **Gyros** [*Gyro* International (association)] (1971)
: a member of a major international service club
**gy·ro·com·pass** \'jī-rō-,kəm-pəs *also* -,käm-\ *noun* (1910)
: a compass consisting of a continuously driven gyroscope whose spinning axis is confined to a horizontal plane so that the earth's rotation causes it to assume a position parallel to the earth's axis and thus point to the true north
**gy·ro·fre·quen·cy** \-,frē-kwən(t)-sē\ *noun* (1938)
: the frequency with which a charged particle (as an electron) executes spiral gyrations in moving obliquely across a magnetic field
**gyro horizon** *noun* (1938)
: ARTIFICIAL HORIZON

**gy·ro·mag·net·ic** \,jī-rō-mag-'ne-tik\ *adjective* (1922)
: of or relating to the magnetic properties of a rotating electrical particle
**gyromagnetic ratio** *noun* (1922)
: the ratio of the magnetic moment of a spinning charged particle to its angular momentum
**gy·ron** \'jī-rən\ *noun* [Middle French *giron* gore, of Germanic origin; akin to Old High German *gēra* wedge-shaped object, Old English *gār* spear — more at GORE] (1572)
: a heraldic charge of triangular form having one side at the edge of the field and the opposite angle usually at the fess point
**gy·ro·plane** \'jī-rə-,plān\ *noun* [International Scientific Vocabulary] (1907)
: an airplane balanced and supported by the aerodynamic forces acting on rapidly rotating horizontal or slightly inclined airfoils
**gy·ro·scope** \'jī-rə-,skōp, *British also* 'gī-\ *noun* [French] (1856)
: a wheel or disk mounted to spin rapidly about an axis and also free to rotate about one or both of two axes perpendicular to each other and to the axis of spin so that a rotation of one of the two mutually perpendicular axes results from application of torque to the other

when the wheel is spinning and so that the entire apparatus offers considerable opposition depending on the angular momentum to any torque that would change the direction of the axis of spin
— **gy·ro·scop·ic** \,jī-rə-'skä-pik\ *adjective*
— **gy·ro·scop·i·cal·ly** \-pi-k(ə-)lē\ *adverb*
**gy·ro·sta·bi·liz·er** \,jī-rō-'stā-bə-,lī-zər\ *noun* (1921)
: a stabilizing device (as for a ship or airplane) that consists of a continuously driven gyro spinning about a vertical axis and pivoted so that its axis of spin may be tipped fore-and-aft in the vertical plane and that serves to oppose sideways motion — called also *gy·ro·stat* \'jī-rə-,stat\
**gy·rus** \'jī-rəs\ *noun, plural* **gy·ri** \'jī-,rī\ [New Latin, from Latin, circle — more at GYRE] (circa 1842)
: a convoluted ridge (as a convolution of the brain) between anatomical grooves
**gyve** \'jīv, 'gīv\ *noun* [Middle English] (13th century)
: FETTER, SHACKLE
— **gyve** *transitive verb*

\ə\ abut \ᵊ\ kitten \ər\ further \a\ ash \ā\ ace
\ä\ mop, mar \au̇\ out \ch\ chin \e\ bet \ē\ easy
\g\ go \i\ hit \ī\ ice \j\ job \ŋ\ sing \ō\ go
\ȯ\ law \ȯi\ boy \th\ thin \th̲\ the \ü\ loot \u̇\ foot
\y\ yet \zh\ vision *see also* Guide to Pronunciation

# H

H *is the eighth letter of the English alphabet and of most alphabets closely related to that of English. It came through Latin via Etruscan from Greek, which took it from a Phoenician letter* hēth, *standing for a laryngeal aspirate (a consonant with the sound of a very forceful English* h). *In Greek it was called* eta *and was assigned to the long open* e *sound (as in English* café; *see* E) *except in the western alphabet, where it designated the rough breathing (that is, the sound of* h *in* helium). *This aspirated pronunciation passed through Etruscan and Latin to English. Small* h *evolved from a late Roman form of the capital in which the second upright line had been shortened to nearly the height of the horizontal cross-stroke. In a later Roman cursive script, the cross-stroke and shortened right vertical stroke were merged into a single downward-curving line.*

---

**h** \'äch\ *noun, plural* **h's** *or* **hs** \'ā-chəz\ *often capitalized, often attributive* (before 12th century)
**1 a :** the 8th letter of the English alphabet **b :** a graphic representation of this letter **c :** a speech counterpart of orthographic *h*
**2 :** a graphic device for reproducing the letter *h*
**3 :** one designated *h* especially as the 8th in order or class
**4 :** something shaped like the letter H
**ha** \'hä\ *interjection* [Middle English, from Old English] (before 12th century)
— used especially to express surprise or joy
**Ha·ba·cuc** \'ha-bə-ˌkək, hə-'ba-kək\ *noun* [Late Latin, from Hebrew *Ḥăbaqqūq*]
**:** HABAKKUK
**Ha·bak·kuk** \'ha-bə-ˌkək, hə-'ba-kək\ *noun* [Hebrew *Ḥăbaqqūq*]
**1 :** a Hebrew prophet of 7th century B.C. Judah who prophesied an imminent Chaldean invasion
**2 :** a prophetic book of canonical Jewish and Christian Scripture — see BIBLE table
**ha·ba·ne·ra** \ˌ(h)ä-bə-'ner-ə\ *noun* [Spanish (*danza*) *habanera*, literally, Havanan dance] (1878)
**1 :** a Cuban dance in slow duple time
**2 :** the music for the habanera
**hab·da·lah** \ˌhäv-də-'lä, häv-'dò-lə\ *noun, often capitalized* [Hebrew *habhdālāh* separation] (1733)
**:** a Jewish ceremony marking the close of a Sabbath or holy day
**ha·be·as cor·pus** \'hā-bē-əs-'kòr-pəs\ *noun* [Middle English, from Medieval Latin, literally, you should have the body (the opening words of the writ)] (15th century)
**1 :** any of several common-law writs issued to bring a party before a court or judge; *especially* **:** HABEAS CORPUS AD SUBJICIENDUM
**2 :** the right of a citizen to obtain a writ of habeas corpus as a protection against illegal imprisonment
**habeas corpus ad sub·ji·ci·en·dum** \-ˌad-səb-ˌyi-kē-'en-dəm\ *noun* [New Latin, literally, you should have the body for submitting] (1768)
**:** a writ for inquiring into the lawfulness of the restraint of a person who is imprisoned or detained in another's custody
**hab·er·dash·er** \'ha-bə(r)-ˌda-shər\ *noun* [Middle English *haberdassher*, from modification of Anglo-French *hapertas* petty merchandise] (14th century)
**1** *British* **:** a dealer in notions
**2 :** a dealer in men's clothing and accessories
**hab·er·dash·ery** \-ˌda-sh(ə-)rē\ *noun, plural* **-er·ies** (1593)
**1 :** goods sold by a haberdasher
**2 :** a haberdasher's shop

**ha·ber·geon** \'ha-bər-jən, hə-'bər-jē-ən, -jən\ *noun* [Middle English *haubergeoun*, from Middle French *haubergeon*, diminutive of *hauberc* hauberk] (14th century)
**1 :** a medieval jacket of mail shorter than a hauberk
**2 :** HAUBERK
**Ha·ber process** \'hä-bər-\ *noun* [Fritz *Haber* (died 1934) German chemist] (1916)
**:** a catalytic process for synthesizing ammonia from nitrogen and hydrogen
**hab·ile** \'ha-bəl, -ˌbīl\ *adjective* [French, from Latin *habilis* — more at ABLE] (15th century)
**:** having general skill **:** ABLE, SKILLFUL
**ha·bil·i·ment** \hə-'bi-lə-mənt\ *noun* [Middle French *habillement*, from *habiller* to dress, prepare, from Old French *abiller*, from *bille* log — more at BILLET] (15th century)
**1** *plural* **:** characteristic apparatus **:** FITTINGS ⟨the *habiliments* of civilization —W. P. Webb⟩
**2 a :** the dress characteristic of an occupation or occasion — usually used in plural **b :** CLOTHES — usually used in plural
**ha·bil·i·tate** \hə-'bi-lə-ˌtāt\ *verb* **-tat·ed; -tat·ing** [Late Latin *habilitatus*, past participle of *habilitare*, from Latin *habilitas* ability — more at ABILITY] (1604)
*transitive verb*
**1 :** to make fit or capable (as for functioning in society)
**2 :** CLOTHE, DRESS
*intransitive verb*
**:** to qualify oneself
— **ha·bil·i·ta·tion** \-ˌbi-lə-'tā-shən\ *noun*
**¹hab·it** \'ha-bət\ *noun* [Middle English, from Old French, from Latin *habitus* condition, character, from *habēre* to have, hold — more at GIVE] (13th century)
**1** *archaic* **:** CLOTHING
**2 a :** a costume characteristic of a calling, rank, or function ⟨a nun's *habit*⟩ **b :** a costume worn for horseback riding
**3 :** manner of conducting oneself **:** BEARING
**4 :** bodily appearance or makeup ⟨a man of fleshy *habit*⟩
**5 :** the prevailing disposition or character of a person's thoughts and feelings **:** mental makeup
**6 :** a settled tendency or usual manner of behavior
**7 a :** a behavior pattern acquired by frequent repetition or physiologic exposure that shows itself in regularity or increased facility of performance **b :** an acquired mode of behavior that has become nearly or completely involuntary **c :** ADDICTION
**8 :** characteristic mode of growth or occurrence ⟨a grass similar to Indian corn in *habit*⟩
**9** *of a crystal* **:** characteristic assemblage of forms at crystallization leading to a usual appearance ☆

**²habit** *transitive verb* (1594)
**:** CLOTHE, DRESS
**hab·it·able** \'ha-bə-tə-bəl *also* hə-'bi-tə-\ *adjective* (14th century)
**:** capable of being lived in **:** suitable for habitation
— **hab·it·abil·i·ty** \ˌha-bə-tə-'bi-lə-tē\ *noun*
— **hab·it·able·ness** \'ha-bə-tə-bəl-nes\ *noun*
— **hab·it·ably** \-blē\ *adverb*
**ha·bi·tant** *noun* (15th century)
**1** \'ha-bə-tənt\ **:** INHABITANT, RESIDENT
**2** \ˌ(h)a-bi-'täⁿ\ *also* **ha·bi·tan** \-'täⁿ\ **:** a settler or descendant of a settler of French origin working as a farmer in Canada
**hab·i·tat** \'ha-bə-ˌtat\ *noun* [Latin, it inhabits, from *habitare*] (1796)
**1 a :** the place or environment where a plant or animal naturally or normally lives and grows **b :** the typical place of residence of a person or a group **c :** a housing for a controlled physical environment in which people can live under surrounding inhospitable conditions (as under the sea)
**2 :** the place where something is commonly found
**hab·i·ta·tion** \ˌha-bə-'tā-shən\ *noun* [Middle English *habitacioun*, from Middle French *habitation*, from Latin *habitation-*, *habitatio*, from *habitare* to inhabit, frequentative of *habēre*] (14th century)
**1 :** the act of inhabiting **:** OCCUPANCY
**2 :** a dwelling place **:** RESIDENCE
**3 :** SETTLEMENT, COLONY
**hab·it-form·ing** \'ha-bət-ˌfòr-miŋ\ *adjective* (1913)
**:** inducing the formation of an addiction
**ha·bit·u·al** \hə-'bi-ch(ə-)wəl, ha-, -'bi-chəl\ *adjective* (1611)
**1 :** having the nature of a habit **:** being in accordance with habit **:** CUSTOMARY ⟨*habitual* smoking⟩
**2 :** doing, practicing, or acting in some manner by force of habit ⟨*habitual* drunkard⟩
**3 :** resorted to on a regular basis ⟨our *habitual* diet⟩
**4 :** inherent in an individual ⟨*habitual* grace⟩
*synonym* see USUAL
— **ha·bit·u·al·ly** *adverb*
— **ha·bit·u·al·ness** *noun*
**ha·bit·u·ate** \hə-'bi-chə-ˌwāt, ha-\ *verb* **-at·ed; -at·ing** (15th century)
*transitive verb*
**1 :** to make used to something **:** ACCUSTOM
**2 :** FREQUENT 1
*intransitive verb*
**1 :** to cause habituation
**2 :** to undergo habituation ⟨*habituate* to a stimulus⟩
**ha·bit·u·a·tion** \-ˌbi-chə-'wā-shən\ *noun* (15th century)
**1 :** the process of habituating **:** the state of being habituated

---

☆ **SYNONYMS**
**Habit, practice, usage, custom, wont** mean a way of acting fixed through repetition. HABIT implies a doing unconsciously and often compulsively ⟨had a *habit* of tapping his fingers⟩. PRACTICE suggests an act or method followed with regularity and usually through choice ⟨our *practice* is to honor all major credit cards⟩. USAGE suggests a customary action so generally followed that it has become a social norm ⟨western-style dress is now common *usage* in international business⟩. CUSTOM applies to a practice or usage so steadily associated with an individual or group as to have almost the force of unwritten law ⟨the *custom* of wearing black at funerals⟩. WONT usually applies to an habitual manner, method, or practice of an individual or group ⟨as was her *wont,* she slept until noon⟩.

**2 a** : tolerance to the effects of a drug acquired through continued use **b** : psychological dependence on a drug after a period of use — compare ADDICTION
**3** : decrease in responsiveness upon repeated exposure to a stimulus
**hab·i·tude** \'ha-bə-ˌtüd, ˌtyüd\ *noun* (14th century)
**1** *archaic* : native or essential character
**2** *obsolete* : habitual association
**3 a** : habitual disposition or mode of behavior or procedure **b** : CUSTOM
**ha·bi·tué** *also* **ha·bi·tue** \hə-'bi-chə-ˌwā, ha-, -ˌbi-chə-\ *noun* [French, from past participle of *habituer* to frequent, from Late Latin *habituare* to habituate, from Latin *habitus*] (1818)
**1** : one who may be regularly found in or at a particular place or kind of place ⟨café *habitués*⟩
**2** : DEVOTEE ⟨an *habitué* of science-fiction movies⟩
**hab·i·tus** \'ha-bə-təs\ *noun, plural* **habitus** \-təs, -ˌtüs\ [New Latin, from Latin] (1886)
: HABIT; *specifically* : body build and constitution especially as related to predisposition to disease
**ha·boob** \hə-'büb\ *noun* [Arabic *habūb* violent storm] (1897)
: a violent dust storm or sandstorm especially of Sudan
**Habs·burg** \'haps-, 'häps-\ *variant of* HAPSBURG
**ha·ček** \'hä-ˌchek\ *noun* [Czech *háček,* literally, little hook] (1953)
: a diacritic ˇ placed over a letter (as in č) to modify it : an inverted circumflex
**ha·cen·da·do** \ˌ(h)ä-sⁿ-'dä-ˌ(ˌ)dō\ *also* **ha·ci·en·da·do** \ˌhä-sē-en-\ *noun, plural* **-dos** [Spanish, from *hacienda*] (1840)
: the owner or proprietor of a hacienda
**¹ha·chure** \ha-'shúr\ *noun* [French, from *hacher* to chop up, hash] (1858)
: a short line used for shading and denoting surfaces in relief (as in map drawing) and drawn in the direction of slope
**²hachure** *transitive verb* **ha·chured; ha·chur·ing** (circa 1859)
: to shade with or show by hachures
**ha·ci·en·da** \ˌ(h)ä-sē-'en-də\ *noun* [Spanish, from Old Spanish *facienda,* from Latin, literally, things to be done, neuter plural of *faciendus,* gerundive of *facere* to do — more at DO] (circa 1772)
**1** : a large estate especially in a Spanish-speaking country : PLANTATION
**2** : the main dwelling of a hacienda
**¹hack** \'hak\ *verb* [Middle English *hakken,* from Old English *-haccian;* akin to Old High German *hacchōn* to hack, Old English *hōc* hook] (13th century)
*transitive verb*
**1 a** : to cut or sever with repeated irregular or unskillful blows **b** : to cut or shape by or as if by crude or ruthless strokes ⟨*hacking* out new election districts⟩ **c** : ANNOY, VEX — often used with *off*
**2** : to clear or make by or as if by cutting away vegetation ⟨*hacked* his way through the brush⟩
**3 a** : to manage successfully ⟨just couldn't *hack* the new job⟩ **b** : TOLERATE ⟨I can't *hack* all this noise⟩
*intransitive verb*
**1 a** : to make chopping strokes or blows ⟨*hacked* at the weeds⟩; *also* : to make cuts as if by chopping ⟨*hacking* away at the work force⟩
**b** : to play inexpert golf
**2** : to cough in a short dry manner
**3** : LOAF — usually used with *around*
**4 a** : to write computer programs for enjoyment **b** : to gain access to a computer illegally
**²hack** *noun* (14th century)
**1** : an implement for hacking
**2** : NICK, NOTCH
**3** : a short dry cough
**4** : a hacking stroke or blow

**5** : restriction to quarters as punishment for naval officers — usually used in the phrase *under hack*
**³hack** *noun* [short for *hackney*] (circa 1721)
**1 a** (1) : a horse let out for common hire (2) : a horse used in all kinds of work **b** : a horse worn out in service : JADE **c** : a light easy saddle horse; *especially* : a three-gaited saddle horse **d** : a ride on a horse
**2 a** : HACKNEY **b** (1) : TAXICAB (2) : CABDRIVER
**3 a** : a person who works solely for mercenary reasons : HIRELING ⟨party *hacks*⟩ **b** : a writer who works on order; *also* : a writer who aims solely for commercial success
**⁴hack** *adjective* (circa 1734)
**1** : working for hire especially with mediocre professional standards
**2** : performed by, suited to, or characteristic of a hack ⟨*hack* writing⟩
**3** : HACKNEYED, TRITE
**⁵hack** (circa 1888)
*intransitive verb*
**1** : to ride or drive at an ordinary pace or over the roads especially as distinguished from racing or hunting
**2** : to operate a taxicab
*transitive verb*
: to ride (a horse) at an ordinary pace
**⁶hack** *noun* [origin unknown] (circa 1914)
*slang* : a guard especially at a prison
**hack·a·more** \'ha-kə-ˌmōr, -ˌmȯr\ *noun* [by folk etymology from Spanish *jáquima* bridle] (1850)
: a bridle with a loop capable of being tightened about the nose in place of a bit or with a slip noose passed over the lower jaw
**hack·ber·ry** \'hak-ˌber-ē\ *noun* [alteration of *hagberry* (a cherry resembling the chokecherry)] (1779)
: any of a genus (*Celtis*) of trees and shrubs of the elm family with small often edible berries; *also* : its wood
**hack·er** \'ha-kər\ *noun* (14th century)
**1** : one that hacks
**2** : a person who is inexperienced or unskilled at a particular activity ⟨a tennis *hacker*⟩
**3** : an expert at programming and solving problems with a computer
**4** : a person who illegally gains access to and sometimes tampers with information in a computer system
**hack·ie** \'ha-kē\ *noun* (circa 1926)
: CABDRIVER
**¹hack·le** \'ha-kəl\ *noun* [Middle English *hakell;* akin to Old High German *hāko* hook — more at HOOK] (15th century)
**1 a** : one of the long narrow feathers on the neck or saddle of a bird **b** : the neck plumage of the domestic fowl
**2** : a comb or board with long metal teeth for dressing flax, hemp, or jute
**3** *plural* **a** : erectile hairs along the neck and back especially of a dog **b** : TEMPER, DANDER
**4 a** : an artificial fishing fly made chiefly of the filaments of a cock's neck feathers **b** : filaments of cock feather projecting from the head of an artificial fly
**²hackle** *transitive verb* **hack·led; hack·ling** \'ha-k(ə-)liŋ\ (1616)
: to comb out with a hackle
— **hack·ler** \-k(ə-)lər\ *noun*
**hack·ly** \'ha-k(ə-)lē\ *adjective* (1796)
: having the appearance of something hacked : JAGGED
**hack·man** \'hak-mən\ *noun* (1796)
: CABDRIVER
**hack·ma·tack** \'hak-mə-ˌtak\ *noun* [earlier *hakmantak,* probably from Western Abenaki (Algonquian language of New Hampshire and Vermont)] (1792)
: TAMARACK
**¹hack·ney** \'hak-nē\ *noun, plural* **hack·neys** [Middle English *hakeney*] (14th century)

**1 a** : a horse suitable for ordinary riding or driving **b** : a trotting horse used chiefly for driving **c** *often capitalized* : any of an English breed of rather compact usually chestnut, bay, or brown high-stepping horses
**2** *obsolete* : one that works for hire

hackney 1c

**3** : a carriage or automobile kept for hire
**²hackney** *adjective* (1589)
**1** : kept for public hire
**2** : HACKNEYED
**3** *archaic* : done or suitable for doing by a drudge
**³hackney** *transitive verb* **hack·neyed; hack·ney·ing** (1596)
**1 a** : to make common or frequent use of **b** : to make trite, vulgar, or commonplace
**2** *archaic* : to make sophisticated or jaded
**hackney coach** *noun* (1635)
: a coach kept for hire; *especially* : a four-wheeled carriage drawn by two horses and having seats for six persons
**hack·neyed** \'hak-nēd\ *adjective* (1749)
: lacking in freshness or originality
**synonym** see TRITE
**hack·saw** \'hak-ˌsȯ\ *noun* (1654)
: a fine-tooth saw with a blade under tension in a frame that is used for cutting hard materials (as metal)
**hack·work** \-ˌwərk\ *noun* (1851)
: literary, artistic, or professional work done on order usually according to formula and in conformity with commercial standards
**had** *past and past participle of* HAVE
**ha·dal** \'hā-dᵊl\ *adjective* [French, from *Hadès* Hades] (1959)
: of, relating to, or being the parts of the ocean below 6000 meters
**had·dock** \'ha-dək\ *noun, plural* **haddock** *also* **haddocks** [Middle English *haddok*] (14th century)
: an important food fish (*Melanogrammus aeglefinus*) that is usually smaller than the related cod and that occurs on both sides of the North Atlantic
**Ha·des** \'hā-ˌ(ˌ)dēz\ *noun* [Greek *Haidēs*]
**1** : PLUTO
**2** : the underground abode of the dead in Greek mythology
**3** : SHEOL
**4** *often not capitalized* : HELL
**ha·dith** \hə-'dēth\ *noun, plural* **hadith** *or* **hadiths** *often capitalized* [Arabic *ḥadīth,* literally, speech, report] (circa 1817)
**1** : a narrative record of the sayings or customs of Muhammad and his companions
**2** : the collective body of traditions relating to Muhammad and his companions
**hadj, hadji** *variant of* HAJJ, HAJJI
**Had·ley cell** \'had-lē-\ *noun* [George *Hadley* (died 1768) English scientific writer] (1969)
: a pattern of atmospheric circulation in which warm air rises near the equator, cools as it travels poleward at high altitude, sinks as cold air, and warms as it travels equatorward; *also* : a similar atmospheric circulation pattern on another planet (as Mars)
**hadn't** \'ha-dᵊnt, -dᵊn, *dialect also* 'ha-tᵊn(t) *or* 'hant\ (1695)
: had not
**had·ron** \'ha-ˌdrän\ *noun* [International Scientific Vocabulary *hadr-* thick, heavy (from Greek *hadros* thick) + ²-*on*] (1962)

---

\ə\ abut \ᵊ\ kitten \ər\ further \a\ ash \ā\ ace
\ä\ mop, mar \au̇\ out \ch\ chin \e\ bet \ē\ easy
\g\ go \i\ hit \ī\ ice \j\ job \ŋ\ sing \ō\ go
\ȯ\ law \ȯi\ boy \th\ thin \th\ the \ü\ loot \u̇\ foot
\y\ yet \zh\ vision    *see also* Guide to Pronunciation

: any of the subatomic particles that are made up of quarks and are subject to the strong force
— **ha·dron·ic** \ha-'drä-nik\ *adjective*

**had·ro·saur** \'ha-drə-ˌsȯr\ *noun* [New Latin *Hadrosaurus*, genus name, from Greek *hadros* thick, bulky + *sauros* lizard] (1877)
: any of a family (Hadrosauridae) of medium-sized bipedal herbivorous dinosaurs of the Upper Cretaceous with long flat snouts and an often crested skull

**hadst** \'hadst, hədst, *or* t *for* d\ *archaic past 2d singular of* HAVE

**hae** \'hā\ *chiefly Scottish variant of* HAVE

**haem** *chiefly British variant of* HEME

**haem-** *or* **haemo-** *chiefly British variant of* HEM-

**haema-** *chiefly British variant of* HEMA-

**haemat-** *or* **haemato-** *chiefly British variant of* HEMAT-

**hae·ma·tite** *British variant of* HEMATITE

**-haemia** *chiefly British variant of* -EMIA

**haet** \'hāt\ *noun* [contraction of Scots *hae it* (as in *Deil hae it!* Devil take it!)] (1603)
*chiefly Scottish* : a small quantity : WHIT, BIT

**haf·fet** \'ha-fət\ *noun* [Middle English (Scots) *halfheid*, from Middle English *half* half + *hed* head] (1513)
*Scottish* : CHEEK, TEMPLE

**haf·ni·um** \'haf-nē-əm\ *noun* [New Latin, from *Hafnia* (Copenhagen), Denmark] (1923)
: a metallic element that resembles zirconium in its chemical properties and occurs in zirconium minerals and that readily absorbs neutrons — see ELEMENT table

**¹haft** \'haft\ *noun* [Middle English, from Old English *hæft*; akin to Old English *hebban* to lift — more at HEAVE] (before 12th century)
: the handle of a weapon or tool

**²haft** *transitive verb* (15th century)
: to set in or furnish with a haft

**haf·ta·rah** *or* **haf·to·rah** \häf-'tȯr-ə, ˌhäf-tə-'rä\ *noun* [Hebrew *haphṭārāh* conclusion] (1723)
: one of the biblical selections from the Books of the Prophets read after the parashah in the Jewish synagogue service

**¹hag** \'hag\ *noun* [Middle English *hagge* demon, old woman] (14th century)
**1** : an ugly, slatternly, or evil-looking old woman
**2** *archaic* **a** : a female demon **b** : an evil or frightening spirit : HOBGOBLIN
**3** : WITCH
— **hag·gish** \'ha-gish\ *adjective*

**²hag** *noun* [Scots, break in a moor, from Old Norse *hǫgg* cut, cleft; akin to Old English *hēawan* to hew] (1662)
**1** *British* : QUAGMIRE, BOG
**2** *British* : a firm spot in a bog

**Ha·gar** \'hā-ˌgär, -gər\ *noun* [Hebrew *Hāghār*]
: a concubine of Abraham driven into the desert with her son Ishmael because of Sarah's jealousy according to the account in Genesis

**hag·fish** \'hag-ˌfish\ *noun* (1611)
: any of a family (Myxinidae) of marine cyclostomes that are related to the lampreys and in general resemble eels but have a round mouth surrounded by barbels and that feed upon other fishes and invertebrates by boring into their bodies

**Hag·ga·dah** \hə-'gä-də, hä-, -'gȯ-\ *noun*, *plural* **Hag·ga·doth** \-'gä-ˌdōt, -'gȯ-, -ˌdȯth\ [Hebrew *haggādhāh*] (1856)
**1** : ancient Jewish lore forming especially the nonlegal part of the Talmud
**2** : the prayer book containing the seder ritual
— **hag·ga·dic** \-'gä-dik, -'gȯ-\ *adjective*, often capitalized

**hag·ga·dist** \-'gä-dist, -'gȯ-\ *noun*, often capitalized (1886)
**1** : a haggadic writer
**2** : a student of the Haggadah
— **hag·ga·dis·tic** \ˌha-gə-'dis-tik, ˌhä-\ *adjective*, often capitalized

**Hag·gai** \'ha-gē-ˌī, 'ha-ˌgī\ *noun* [Hebrew *Ḥaggai*]

**1** : a Hebrew prophet who flourished about 500 B.C. and who advocated that the Temple in Jerusalem be rebuilt
**2** : a prophetic book of canonical Jewish and Christian Scriptures — see BIBLE table

**¹hag·gard** \'ha-gərd\ *adjective* [Middle French *hagard*] (1567)
**1** *of a hawk* : not tamed
**2 a** : wild in appearance **b** : having a worn or emaciated appearance : GAUNT ⟨*haggard* faces looked up sadly from out of the straw —W. M. Thackeray⟩
— **hag·gard·ly** *adverb*
— **hag·gard·ness** *noun*

**²haggard** *noun* (1567)
**1** : an adult hawk caught wild
**2** *obsolete* : an intractable person

**hag·gis** \'ha-gəs\ *noun* [Middle English *hagese*] (15th century)
: a traditionally Scottish dish that consists of the heart, liver, and lungs of a sheep or a calf minced with suet, onions, oatmeal, and seasonings boiled in the stomach of the animal

**¹hag·gle** \'ha-gəl\ *verb* **hag·gled; hag·gling** \-g(ə-)liŋ\ [frequentative of *hag* (to hew)] (1599)
*transitive verb*
**1** : to cut roughly or clumsily : HACK
**2** *archaic* : to annoy or exhaust with wrangling
*intransitive verb*
: BARGAIN, WRANGLE
— **hag·gler** \-g(ə-)lər\ *noun*

**²haggle** *noun* (1858)
: an act or instance of haggling

**hagi-** *or* **hagio-** *combining form* [Late Latin, from Greek, from *hagios*]
**1** : holy ⟨*hagioscope*⟩
**2** : saints ⟨*hagiography*⟩

**Ha·gi·og·ra·pha** \ˌha-gē-'ä-grə-fə, ˌhā-, -jē-\ *noun plural but singular or plural in construction* [Late Latin, from Late Greek, from *hagio-* + *graphein* to write — more at CARVE] (1583)
: the third part of the Jewish scriptures — see BIBLE table

**ha·gi·og·ra·pher** \-fər\ *noun* (1849)
: a writer of hagiography

**ha·gio·graph·ic** \ˌha-gē-ə-'gra-fik, ˌhā-, -jē-\ *also* **ha·gio·graph·i·cal** \-fi-kəl\ *adjective* (1819)
**1** : of or relating to hagiography
**2** : of or relating to the Hagiographa

**ha·gi·og·ra·phy** \-gē-'ä-grə-fē, -jē-\ *noun* (1821)
**1** : biography of saints or venerated persons
**2** : idealizing or idolizing biography

**ha·gi·ol·o·gy** \-gē-'ä-lə-jē, -jē-\ *noun* (1807)
**1** : literature dealing with venerated persons or writings
**2** : a list of venerated figures
— **ha·gi·o·log·ic** \-gē-ə-'lä-jik, -jē-\ *or* **ha·gi·o·log·i·cal** \-ji-kəl\ *adjective*

**ha·gio·scope** \'ha-gē-ə-ˌskōp, 'hā-jē-\ *noun* (circa 1840)
: an opening in the interior walls of a cruciform church so placed as to afford a view of the altar to those in the transept
— **ha·gio·scop·ic** \ˌha-gē-ə-'skä-pik, ˌhā-, -jē-\ *adjective*

**hag·ride** \'hag-ˌrīd\ *transitive verb* **-rode** \-ˌrōd\; **-rid·den** \-ˌri-dᵊn\ (1702)
: HARASS, TORMENT

**hah** *variant of* HA

**¹ha-ha** \(')hä-'hä\ *interjection* [Middle English, from Old English *ha ha*] (before 12th century)
— used to express amusement or derision

**²ha-ha** \'hä-ˌhä\ *noun* [French *haha*] (1749)
: SUNK FENCE

**hahn·ium** \'hä-nē-əm\ *noun* [New Latin, from Otto *Hahn*] (1970)
: UNNILPENTIUM

**Hai·da** \'hī-də\ *noun*, *plural* **Haida** *or* **Hai·das** (1841)

**1** : a member of an American Indian people of the Queen Charlotte islands, British Columbia, and Prince of Wales island, Alaska
**2** : the language of the Haida people

**haik** \'hīk\ *noun* [Arabic *ḥāʾik*] (1713)
: a voluminous piece of usually white cloth worn as an outer garment in northern Africa

**hai·ku** \'hī-(ˌ)kü\ *noun*, *plural* **haiku** [Japanese] (1902)
: an unrhymed verse form of Japanese origin having three lines containing usually 5, 7, and 5 syllables respectively; *also* : a poem in this form usually having a seasonal reference — compare TANKA

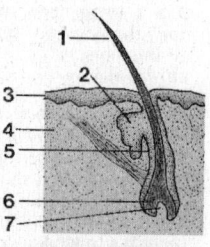

haik

**¹hail** \'hā(ə)l\ *noun* [Middle English, from Old English *hægl*; akin to Old High German *hagal* hail] (before 12th century)
**1** : precipitation in the form of small balls or lumps usually consisting of concentric layers of clear ice and compact snow
**2** : something that gives the effect of a shower of hail ⟨a *hail* of rifle fire⟩

**²hail** *intransitive verb* (before 12th century)
**1** : to precipitate hail ⟨it was *hailing* hard⟩
**2** : to pour down or strike like hail

**³hail** *interjection* [Middle English, from Old Norse *heill*, from *heill* healthy — more at WHOLE] (13th century)
**1** *archaic* — used as a salutation
**2** — used to express acclamation ⟨*hail* to the chief —Sir Walter Scott⟩

**⁴hail** (13th century)
*transitive verb*
**1 a** : SALUTE, GREET **b** : to greet with enthusiastic approval : ACCLAIM
**2** : to greet or summon by calling ⟨*hail* a taxi⟩
*intransitive verb*
: to call out; *especially* : to call a greeting to a passing ship
— **hail·er** \'hā-lər\ *noun*
— **hail from** : to be or have been native to or a resident of

**⁵hail** *noun* (1500)
**1** : an exclamation of greeting or acclamation
**2** : a calling to attract attention
**3** : hearing distance ⟨stayed within *hail*⟩

**hail-fel·low** \'hāl-ˌfe-(ˌ)lō\ *adjective* (1580)
: HAIL-FELLOW-WELL-MET
— **hail-fellow** *noun*

**hail-fel·low-well-met** \-lō-ˌwel-'met, -lə-ˌwel-\ *adjective* [from the archaic salutation "Hail, fellow! Well met!"] (1581)
: heartily informal : COMRADELY
— **hail-fellow-well-met** *noun*

**Hail Mary** *noun* [translation of Medieval Latin *Ave, Maria*, from the opening words] (15th century)
: a Roman Catholic prayer to the Virgin Mary that consists of salutations and a plea for her intercession

**hail·stone** \'hā(ə)l-ˌstōn\ *noun* (before 12th century)
: a pellet of hail

**hail·storm** \-ˌstȯrm\ *noun* (15th century)
: a storm accompanied by hail

**hair** \'har, 'her\ *noun*, *often attributive* [Middle English, from Old English *hær*; akin to Old High German *hār* hair] (before 12th century)
**1 a** : a slender threadlike outgrowth of the epidermis of an animal; *especially* : one of the usually pigmented filaments that form the characteristic coat of a mammal **b** : the hairy covering of

hair 1a: *1* shaft, *2* sebaceous gland, *3* epidermis, *4* dermis, *5* hair follicle, *6* bulb, *7* papilla

an animal or a body part; *especially* **:** the coating of hairs on a human head
**2 :** HAIRCLOTH
**3 a :** a minute distance or amount ⟨won by a *hair*⟩ **b :** a precise degree ⟨aligned to a *hair*⟩
**4** *obsolete* **:** NATURE, CHARACTER
**5 :** a filamentous structure that resembles hair ⟨leaf *hair*⟩
— **hair·less** *adjective*
— **hair·less·ness** *noun*
— **hair·like** \-ˌlīk\ *adjective*
**hair ball** *noun* (1712)
**:** a compact mass of hair formed in the stomach especially of a shedding animal (as a cat) that cleanses its coat by licking
¹**hair·breadth** \'har-ˌbretth, 'her-, -ˌbreth, -ˌbredth\ *or* **hairs·breadth** \'harz-, 'herz-\ *noun* (1561)
**:** a very small distance or margin
²**hairbreadth** *adjective* (1604)
**:** very narrow **:** CLOSE ⟨a *hairbreadth* escape⟩
**hair·brush** \'har-ˌbrəsh, 'her-\ *noun* (1599)
**:** a brush for the hair
**hair cell** *noun* (circa 1890)
**:** a cell with hairlike processes; *especially* **:** one of the sensory cells in the auditory epithelium of the organ of Corti
**hair·cloth** \'har-ˌklȯth, 'her-\ *noun* (1500)
**:** any of various stiff wiry fabrics especially of horsehair or camel hair used for upholstery or for stiffening in garments
**hair·cut** \-ˌkət\ *noun* (1899)
**:** the act, process, or result of cutting and shaping the hair
— **hair·cut·ter** \-ˌkə-tər\ *noun*
— **hair·cut·ting** \-ˌkə-tiŋ\ *noun*
**hair·do** \-ˌdü\ *noun, plural* **hairdos** (1932)
**:** a way of wearing the hair **:** COIFFURE
**hair·dress·er** \-ˌdre-sər\ *noun* (1770)
**1 :** one whose occupation is the dressing or cutting of hair
**2** *British* **:** BARBER
**hair·dress·ing** \-ˌdre-siŋ\ *noun* (1771)
**1 a :** the action or process of washing, cutting, curling, or arranging the hair **b :** the occupation of a hairdresser
**2 :** a preparation for grooming and styling the hair
**haired** \'hard, 'herd\ *adjective* (14th century)
**:** having hair especially of a specified kind — usually used in combination ⟨dark-*haired*⟩
**hair follicle** *noun* (1838)
**:** the tubular epithelial sheath that surrounds the lower part of the hair shaft and encloses at the bottom a vascular papilla supplying the growing basal part of the hair with nourishment
**hair·line** \-ˈlīn\ *noun* (1846)
**1 :** a very slender line: as **a :** a tiny line or crack on a surface ⟨a *hairline* bone fracture⟩ **b :** a fine line connecting thicker strokes in a printed letter
**2 :** HAIRBREADTH
**3 a :** a textile design consisting of lengthwise or crosswise lines usually one thread wide **b :** a fabric with such a design
**4 a :** the outline of scalp hair especially on the forehead **b :** the way the hair frames the face
— **hairline** *adjective*
**hair·piece** \-ˌpēs\ *noun* (1926)
**1 :** supplementary hair (as a switch) used in some feminine coiffures
**2 :** TOUPEE 2
¹**hair·pin** \-ˌpin\ *noun* (1779)
**1 :** a pin to hold the hair in place; *specifically* **:** a long U-shaped pin
**2 :** something shaped like a hairpin; *specifically* **:** a sharp U-shaped turn in a road
²**hairpin** *adjective* (1887)
**:** having the shape of a hairpin ⟨a *hairpin* turn⟩; *also* **:** having hairpin turns ⟨a steep *hairpin* road⟩
**hair·rais·er** \'har-ˌrā-zər, 'her-\ *noun* (1897)
**:** THRILLER
**hair·rais·ing** \-ˌrā-ziŋ\ *adjective* (1900)

**:** causing terror, excitement, or astonishment
— **hair-rais·ing·ly** \-ziŋ-lē\ *adverb*
**hair seal** *noun* (1865)
**:** any of a family (Phocidae) of seals having a coarse hairy coat, the hind limbs reduced to swimming flippers, and no external ears — called also *true seal*; compare EARED SEAL
**hair shirt** *noun* (14th century)
**1 :** a shirt made of rough animal hair worn next to the skin as a penance
**2 :** one that irritates like a hair shirt
**hair·split·ter** \'har-ˌspli-tər, 'her-\ *noun* (1849)
**:** one that makes excessively fine distinctions in reasoning **:** QUIBBLER
— **hair·split·ting** \-ˌspli-tiŋ\ *adjective or noun*
**hair·spring** \-ˌspriŋ\ *noun* (1830)
**:** a slender spiraled recoil spring that regulates the motion of the balance wheel of a timepiece
**hair·streak** \-ˌstrēk\ *noun* (1816)
**:** any of a subfamily (Theclinae of the family Lycaenidae) of small butterflies usually having striped markings on the underside of the wings and thin filamentous projections from the hind wings
**hair·style** \'har-ˌstīl, 'her-\ *noun* (1913)
**:** HAIRDO
**hair·styl·ing** \-ˌstī-liŋ\ *noun* (1936)
**:** the work of a hairstylist
**hair·styl·ist** \-ˌstī-list\ *noun* (1935)
**:** HAIRDRESSER; *especially* **:** one who does creative styling of coiffures
**hair-trigger** *adjective* (1834)
**1 :** immediately responsive to the slightest stimulus ⟨a *hair-trigger* temper⟩
**2 :** delicately adjusted or easily disrupted
**hair trigger** *noun* (1806)
**:** a gun trigger so adjusted as to permit the firearm to be fired by a very slight pressure
**hair·worm** \'har-ˌwərm, 'her-\ *noun* (1658)
**1 :** any of a phylum (Nematomorpha) of elongated worms that have separate sexes, are parasitic in arthropods as larvae, and are free-living in water as adults — called also *horse-hair worm*
**2 :** any of a genus (*Capillaria*) of nematode worms that include serious parasites of the alimentary tract of fowls and tissue and organ parasites of mammals
**hairy** \'har-ē, 'her-\ *adjective* **hair·i·er; -est** (14th century)
**1 a :** covered with hair or hairlike material **b :** having a downy fuzz on the stems and leaves
**2 :** made of or resembling hair
**3 a :** tending to cause nervous tension (as from danger) ⟨a *hairy* adventure⟩ **b :** difficult to deal with or comprehend ⟨a *hairy* math problem⟩
— **hair·i·ness** \'har-ē-nəs, 'her-\ *noun*
**hairy cell leukemia** *noun* (1979)
**:** a lymphocytic leukemia that is usually of B cell origin and is characterized by malignant cells with a ciliated appearance
**hairy-chest·ed** \-ˈches-təd\ *adjective* (circa 1937)
**:** characterized by especially exaggerated or stereotypical manliness
**hairy vetch** *noun* (1901)
**:** a Eurasian vetch (*Vicia villosa*) extensively cultivated as a cover and early forage crop
**hairy woodpecker** *noun* (circa 1728)
**:** a common North American woodpecker (*Picoides villosus*) closely resembling the downy woodpecker but larger with a longer bill
**Hai·tian** \'hā-shən *also* 'hā-tē-ən\ *noun* (1805)
**1 :** a native or inhabitant of Haiti
**2 :** HAITIAN CREOLE
— **Haitian** *adjective*
**Haitian Creole** *noun* (circa 1938)
**:** a French-based creole spoken by Haitians
**hajj** \'haj\ *noun* [Arabic *ḥajj*] (1673)
**:** the pilgrimage to Mecca prescribed as a religious duty for Muslims
**hajji** \'ha-jē\ *noun* [Arabic *ḥajjī*, from *ḥajj*] (1609)

**:** one who has made a pilgrimage to Mecca — often used as a title
**hake** \'hāk\ *noun* [Middle English] (14th century)
**:** any of several marine food fishes (as of the genera *Merluccius* and *Urophycis*) that are related to the common Atlantic cod
¹**ha·kim** \'hä-kəm\ *noun* [Arabic *ḥākim*] (1611)
**:** an administrator in a Muslim country
²**ha·kim** \hä-ˈkēm\ *noun* [Arabic *ḥakīm*, literally, wise one] (1638)
**:** a physician in a Muslim country
**hal-** *or* **halo-** *combining form* [French, from Greek, from *hals* — more at SALT]
**1 :** salt ⟨*halo*phyte⟩
**2** [International Scientific Vocabulary, from *halogen*] **:** halogen ⟨*hal*ide⟩
**ha·la·kah** *or* **ha·la·cha** \hä-ˈlä-kə, ˌhä-lə-ˈkä\ *noun, often capitalized* [Hebrew *halākhāh*, literally, way] (1856)
**:** the body of Jewish law supplementing the scriptural law and forming especially the legal part of the Talmud
— **ha·lak·ic** \hə-ˈlä-kik, hä-ˈlä-\ *adjective, often capitalized*
**ha·la·la** \hə-ˈlä-lə\ *noun, plural* **halala** *or* **halalas** [Arabic] (1970)
— see *riyal* at MONEY table
**ha·la·tion** \hā-ˈlä-shən\ *noun* [*halo* + *-ation*] (1859)
**1 :** the spreading of light beyond its proper boundaries in a developed photographic image
**2 :** a bright ring that sometimes surrounds a bright object on a television screen
**hal·berd** \'hal-bərd, 'hȯl-\ *also* **hal·bert** \-bərt\ *noun* [Middle English, from Middle French *hallebarde*, from Middle High German *helmbarte*, from *helm* handle (from Old High German *helmo*) + *barte* ax, from Old High German *barta;* akin to Old High German *bart* beard — more at HELM, BEARD] (15th century)
**:** a weapon especially of the 15th and 16th centuries consisting typically of a battle-ax and pike mounted on a handle about six feet long
¹**hal·cy·on** \'hal-sē-ən\ *noun* [Middle English *alceon*, from Latin *halcyon*, from Greek *alkyōn, halkyōn*] (14th century)
**1 :** a bird identified with the kingfisher and held in ancient legend to nest at sea about the time of the winter solstice and to calm the waves during incubation
**2 :** KINGFISHER ◆

---

◇ WORD HISTORY

**halcyon** According to Greek myth, Alkyone, the daughter of Aeolus, god of the winds, was so distraught on learning that her husband had been killed in a shipwreck that she threw herself into the sea and was changed into a kingfisher. Henceforth the bird was known to the Greeks as *alkyōn* or *halkyōn* (the latter by association with *hals*, meaning "sea"). Legend had it that the kingfisher built a floating nest on the sea every year before the winter solstice. For two weeks before and after the solstice Aeolus charmed the wind and the waves while the bird incubated its eggs, and *alkyonides hēmerai* (literally, "kingfisher days") became a proverbial expression for a time of peace and tranquility. The Romans borrowed the Greek word as *alcyon* or *halcyon*, and the Latin word found its way into Middle English as a poetic name for the kingfisher. Subsequently, *halcyon* has been used as an adjective meaning first "calm, tranquil" and later "happy" or "prosperous." It usually modifies *days* or another noun denoting a period of time.

---

\ə\ abut \ᵊ\ kitten \ər\ further \a\ ash \ā\ ace
\ä\ mop, mar \au̇\ out \ch\ chin \e\ bet \ē\ easy
\g\ go \i\ hit \ī\ ice \j\ job \ŋ\ sing \ō\ go
\ȯ\ law \ȯi\ boy \th\ thin \t͟h\ the \ü\ loot \u̇\ foot
\y\ yet \zh\ vision   *see also* Guide to Pronunciation

**²halcyon** *adjective* (1540)
**1 :** of or relating to the halcyon or its nesting period
**2 a :** CALM, PEACEFUL **b :** HAPPY, GOLDEN **c** : PROSPEROUS, AFFLUENT

**¹hale** \'hā(ə)l\ *adjective* [partly from Middle English (northern) *hale,* from Old English *hāl;* partly from Middle English *hail,* from Old Norse *heill* — more at WHOLE] (before 12th century)
: free from defect, disease, or infirmity : SOUND; *also* : retaining exceptional health and vigor 〈a *hale* and hearty old man〉
**synonym** see HEALTHY

**²hale** *transitive verb* **haled; hal·ing** [Middle English *halen,* from Old French *haler* — more at HAUL] (13th century)
**1 :** HAUL, PULL
**2 :** to compel to go

**ha·ler** \'hä-lər, -ˌler\ *noun, plural* **ha·le·ru** \'hä-lə-ˌrü\ [Czech *haléř,* genitive plural *haléřů*] (circa 1934)
— see *koruna* at MONEY table

**¹half** \'haf, 'håf\ *noun, plural* **halves** \'havz, 'håvz\ [Middle English, from Old English *healf;* akin to Old High German *halb* half] (before 12th century)
**1 a :** either of two equal parts into which a thing is divisible; *also* : a part of a thing approximately equal to the remainder — often used without *of* 〈*half* the distance〉 **b :** half an hour — used in designation of time
**2 :** one of a pair: as **a :** PARTNER **b :** SEMESTER, TERM **c :** either of the two equal periods that together make up the playing time of some games (as football); *also* : the midpoint in playing time 〈the score was tied at the *half*〉
**3 :** HALF-DOLLAR
**4 :** HALFBACK
— **by half :** by a great deal
— **by halves :** in part : HALFHEARTEDLY
— **half again as :** one-and-a-half times as 〈*half again as* many〉
— **in half :** into two equal or nearly equal parts

**²half** *adjective* (before 12th century)
**1 a :** being one of two equal parts 〈a *half* share〉 〈a *half* sheet of paper〉 **b** (1) **:** amounting to approximately half 〈a *half* mile〉 〈a *half* million〉 (2) **:** falling short of the full or complete thing : PARTIAL 〈*half* measures〉 〈a *half* smile〉
**2 :** extending over or covering only half 〈a *half* window〉 〈a *half* mask〉
— **half·ness** *noun*

**³half** *adverb* (12th century)
**1 a :** in an equal part or degree 〈the crowd was *half* jeering, *half* respectful〉 **b :** not completely : PARTIALLY 〈*half* persuaded〉
**2 :** by any means : AT ALL 〈her singing isn't *half* bad〉

**half-and-half** \ˌhaf-ᵊn-'haf, ˌhåf-ᵊn-'håf\ *noun* (1756)
: something that is approximately half one thing and half another: as **a :** a mixture of two malt beverages (as dark and light beer) **b :** a mixture of cream and whole milk
— **half-and-half** *adjective or adverb*

**half-assed** \'haf-'ast, 'håf-'åst\ *adjective* (circa 1932)
**1 :** lacking significance, adequacy, or completeness — often considered vulgar
**2 :** lacking intelligence, character, or effectiveness — often considered vulgar
— **half-assed** *adverb*

**half-back** \'haf-ˌbak, 'håf-\ *noun* (1882)
**1 :** one of the backs stationed near either flank in football
**2 :** a player stationed immediately behind the forward line (as in field hockey, soccer, or rugby)

**half-baked** \-'bākt\ *adjective* (1621)
**1 a :** lacking adequate planning or forethought 〈a *half-baked* scheme for getting rich〉 **b** : lacking in judgment, intelligence, or common sense

**2 :** imperfectly baked : UNDERDONE

**half-beak** \-ˌbēk\ *noun* (1880)
: any of various narrow-bodied fishes of warm waters that have an elongated lower jaw and are grouped with the flying fishes (family Exocoetidae) or placed in their own family (Hemiramphidae)

**half-blood** \-'bləd\ *or* **half-blood·ed** \-'blə-dəd\ *adjective* (1605)
: having half blood or being a half blood

**half blood** *noun* (1553)
**1 a :** the relation between persons having only one parent in common **b :** a person so related to another
**2 :** HALF-BREED
**3 :** GRADE 4

**half boot** *noun* (1787)
: a boot with a top reaching above the ankle and ending below the knee

**half-bound** \'haf-ˌbaund, 'håf-\ *adjective* (1775)
*of a book* : bound in material of two qualities with the material of better quality on the spine and corners
— **half binding** *noun*

**half-bred** \-ˌbred\ *adjective* (1701)
: having one purebred parent
— **half-bred** *noun*

**half-breed** \-ˌbrēd\ *noun* (1760)
: the offspring of parents of different races; *especially* : the offspring of an American Indian and a white person — often used disparagingly
— **half-breed** *adjective*

**half brother** *noun* (14th century)
: a brother related through one parent only

**half-caste** \'haf-ˌkast, 'håf-\ *noun* (1789)
: one of mixed racial descent : HALF-BREED
— **half-caste** *adjective*

**half cock** *noun* (1745)
**1 :** the position of the hammer of a firearm when about half retracted and held by the sear so that it cannot be operated by a pull on the trigger
**2** *chiefly British* **:** a state of inadequate preparation or mental confusion 〈go off at *half cock*〉

**half-cocked** \'haf-'käkt, 'håf-\ *adjective* (1809)
**1 :** being at half cock
**2 :** lacking adequate preparation or forethought 〈go off *half-cocked*〉

**half-court** \'haf-'kōrt, -'kort, 'håf-\ *noun* (1888)
: a dividing line that separates a playing court into equal halves (as in basketball); *also* : the area comprising each half

**half crown** *noun* (1542)
: a British coin worth two shillings and sixpence used as legal tender until 1970

**half dime** *noun* (1792)
: a silver 5-cent coin struck by the U.S. mint in 1792 and from 1794 to 1873

**half disme** *noun* (1792)
: a half dime struck in 1792

**half-dol·lar** \'haf-'dä-lər, 'håf-\ *noun* (1786)
**1 :** a coin representing one half of a dollar
**2 :** the sum of 50 cents

**half duplex** *noun* (1950)
: a mode of communication especially with a computer via telephone line in which information can be sent in only one direction at a time — compare DUPLEX

**half eagle** *noun* (1786)
: a 5-dollar gold piece issued by the U.S. from 1795 to 1916 and in 1929

**half-hardy** *adjective* (1824)
*of a plant* : able to withstand a moderately low temperature but injured by severe freezing and surviving the winter in cold climates only if carefully protected

**half-heart·ed** \'haf-'här-təd, 'håf-\ *adjective* (15th century)
: lacking heart, spirit, or interest
— **half-heart·ed·ly** *adverb*
— **half-heart·ed·ness** *noun*

**half hitch** *noun* (1769)
: a simple knot tied by passing the end of a line around an object, across the main part of the line, and then through the resulting loop — see KNOT illustration

**half hour** *noun* (15th century)
**1 :** thirty minutes
**2 :** the middle point of an hour
— **half-hour·ly** \'haf-'au̇(-ə)r-lē, 'håf-\ *adverb or adjective*

**half-knot** \'haf-ˌnät, 'håf-\ *noun* (1933)
: a knot intertwining the ends of two cords and used in tying other knots

**half-length** \'haf-'leŋ(k)th, 'håf-\ *noun* (1699)
: something (as a portrait) that is or represents only half the complete length

**half-life** \-ˌlīf\ *noun* (1907)
**1 :** the time required for half of something to undergo a process: as **a :** the time required for half of the atoms of a radioactive substance to become disintegrated **b :** the time required for half the amount of a substance (as a drug or radioactive tracer) in or introduced into a living system or ecosystem to be eliminated or disintegrated by natural processes
**2 :** a period of usefulness or popularity preceding decline or obsolescence 〈slang usually has a short *half-life*〉

**half-light** \-ˌlīt\ *noun* (1625)
: dim grayish light

**half line** *noun* (circa 1914)
: a straight line extending from a point indefinitely in one direction only

**¹half-mast** \-'mast\ *noun* (1627)
: a point some distance but not necessarily halfway down below the top of a mast or staff or the peak of a gaff

**²half-mast** *transitive verb* (1891)
: to cause to hang at half-mast 〈*half-mast* a flag〉

**half-moon** \'haf-ˌmün, 'håf-\ *noun* (15th century)
**1 :** the moon when half its disk appears illuminated
**2 :** something shaped like a crescent
**3 :** the lunule of a fingernail
— **half-moon** *adjective*

**half nelson** *noun* (1889)
: a wrestling hold in which one arm is thrust under the corresponding arm of an opponent and the hand placed on the back of the opponent's neck — compare FULL NELSON

**half note** *noun* (1597)
: a musical note with the time value of ½ of a whole note — see NOTE illustration

**half-pen·ny** \'hāp-nē, 'hā-pə-, US also 'haf-ˌpe-nē, -ˌpe-nē\ *noun* (13th century)
**1** *plural* **halfpence** \'hā-pən(t)s, US also 'haf-ˌpen(t)s, 'håf-\ *or* **halfpennies :** a former British coin representing one half of a penny
**2 :** the sum of half a penny
**3 :** a small amount
— **halfpenny** *adjective*

**¹half-pint** \'haf-ˌpīnt, 'håf-\ *noun* (1611)
**1 :** half a pint
**2 :** a short, small, or inconsequential person

**²half-pint** *adjective* (circa 1926)
: of less than average size : DIMINUTIVE

**half plane** *noun* (1891)
: the part of a plane on one side of an indefinitely extended straight line drawn in the plane

**half rest** *noun* (circa 1899)
: a musical rest corresponding in time value to a half note — see REST illustration

**half shell** *noun* (1860)
: either of the valves of a bivalve
— **on the half shell :** served in a half shell 〈oysters *on the half shell*〉

**half sister** *noun* (13th century)
: a sister related through one parent only

**half-slip** \'haf-ˌslip, 'håf-\ *noun* (circa 1948)
: a topless slip with an elasticized waistband

**half-sole** *transitive verb* (1795)
: to put half soles on

**half sole** *noun* (1865)
: a shoe sole extending from the shank forward
**half sovereign** *noun* (circa 1504)
: a British gold coin worth 10 shillings
**half–space** \'haf-ˌspās, 'háf-\ *noun* (1962)
: the part of three-dimensional euclidean space lying on one side of a plane
**half–staff** \-'staf\ *noun* (1708)
: HALF-MAST
**half step** *noun* (1904)
**1** : a walking step of 15 inches or in double time of 18 inches
**2** : a musical interval (as E-F or B-C) equivalent to one twelfth of an octave — called also *semitone*
**half–timber** *or* **half–tim·bered** \'haf-'tim-bərd, 'háf-\ *adjective* (circa 1876)
*of a building* : constructed of wood framing with spaces filled with masonry
— **half–tim·ber·ing** \-b(ə-)riŋ\ *noun*
**half–time** \-ˌtīm\ *noun* (1871)
: an intermission between halves of a game or contest (as in football or basketball)
**half–time** *adjective* (1961)
: involving or working half the standard hours
— **half–time** *adverb*
**half title** *noun* (1879)
: the title of a book appearing alone on a right-hand page immediately preceding the title page; *also* : the page itself
**half·tone** \'haf-ˌtōn, 'háf-\ *noun* (1651)
**1** : HALF STEP 2
**2 a** : any of the shades of gray between the darkest and the lightest parts of a photographic image **b** : a photoengraving made from an image photographed through a screen and then etched so that the details of the image are reproduced in dots
— **halftone** *adjective*
**half–track** \-ˌtrak\ *noun* (1935)
**1** : an endless chain-track drive system that propels a vehicle supported in front by a pair of wheels
**2** : a motor vehicle propelled by half-tracks; *specifically* : one lightly armored for military use
— **half–track** *or* **half–tracked** \-ˌtrakt\ *adjective*
**half–truth** \-ˌtrüth\ *noun* (1658)
**1** : a statement that is only partially true
**2** : a statement that mingles truth and falsehood with deliberate intent to deceive
**half volley** *noun* (1843)
: a stroke of a ball (as in tennis) at the instant it rebounds from the ground
— **half–volley** *verb*
**half·way** \'haf-ˌwā, 'háf-\ *adjective* (1694)
**1** : midway between two points
**2** : PARTIAL
— **halfway** *adverb*
**halfway house** *noun* (1694)
**1 a** : a place to stop midway on a journey **b** : a halfway place in a progression
**2** : a residence for formerly institutionalized individuals (as mental patients, drug addicts, or convicts) that is designed to facilitate their readjustment to private life
**half–wit** \'haf-ˌwit, 'háf-\ *noun* (1640)
: a foolish or imbecilic person
— **half–wit·ted** \-'wi-təd\ *adjective*
— **half–wit·ted·ness** *noun*
**half–world** \-ˌwərld\ *noun* (1870)
: DEMIMONDE
**hal·i·but** \'ha-lə-bət *also* 'hä-\ *noun, plural* **halibut** *also* **halibuts** [Middle English *halybutte,* from *haly,* holy *holy* + *butte* flatfish, from Middle Dutch or Middle Low German *but;* from its being eaten on holy days] (14th century)
: any of several marine flatfishes (especially *Hippoglossus hippoglossus* of the Atlantic and *H. stenolepis* of the Pacific) that are widely used for food and include some of the largest bony fishes
**ha·lide** \'ha-ˌlīd, 'hä-\ *noun* (1876)

: a binary compound of a halogen with a more electropositive element or radical
**hal·i·dom** \'ha-lə-dəm\ *or* **hal·i·dome** \-lə-ˌdōm\ *noun* [Middle English, from Old English *hāligdōm,* from *hālig* holy + *-dōm* -dom] (before 12th century)
*archaic* : something held sacred
**ha·lite** \'ha-ˌlīt, 'hä-\ *noun* (1868)
: ROCK SALT
**hal·i·to·sis** \ˌha-lə-'tō-səs\ *noun* [New Latin, from Latin *halitus* breath, from *halare* to breathe — more at EXHALE] (1874)
: a condition of having fetid breath
**hall** \'hȯl\ *noun* [Middle English *halle,* from Old English *heall;* akin to Latin *cella* small room, *celare* to conceal — more at HELL] (before 12th century)
**1 a** : the castle or house of a medieval king or noble **b** : the chief living room in such a structure
**2** : the manor house of a landed proprietor
**3** : a large usually imposing building for public or semipublic purposes
**4 a** (1) : a building used by a college or university for some special purpose (2) : DORMITORY **b** : a college or a division of a college at some universities **c** (1) : the common dining room of an English college (2) : a meal served there
**5 a** : the entrance room of a building : LOBBY **b** : a corridor or passage in a building
**6** : a large room for assembly : AUDITORIUM
**7** : a place used for public entertainment
**hal·lah** \'kä-lə, 'hä-\ *variant of* CHALLAH
**Hall effect** \'hȯl-\ *noun* [Edwin H. *Hall* (died 1938) American physicist] (circa 1889)
: a potential difference observed between the edges of a conducting strip carrying a longitudinal current when placed in a magnetic field perpendicular to the plane of the strip
**Hal·lel** \hä-'lā(ə)l\ *noun* [Hebrew *hallēl* praise] (1702)
: a selection comprising Psalms 113–118 chanted during Jewish feasts (as the Passover)
**¹hal·le·lu·jah** \ˌha-lə-'lü-yə\ *interjection* [Hebrew *hallĕlūyāh* praise (ye) the Lord] (1535)
— used to express praise, joy, or thanks
**²hallelujah** *noun* (1625)
: a shout or song of praise or thanksgiving
**hal·liard** *variant of* HALYARD
**¹hall·mark** \'hȯl-ˌmärk\ *noun* [Goldsmiths' *Hall,* London, England, where gold and silver articles were assayed and stamped] (1721)
**1 a** : an official mark stamped on gold and silver articles in England to attest their purity **b** : a mark or device placed or stamped on an article of trade to indicate origin, purity, or genuineness
**2** : a distinguishing characteristic, trait, or feature (the dramatic flourishes which are the *hallmark* of the trial lawyer —Marion K. Sanders)
**²hallmark** *transitive verb* (1773)
: to stamp with a hallmark
**hal·lo** \hə-'lō, ha-\ *or* **hal·loo** \-'lü\ *variant of* HOLLO
**Hall of Fame** (circa 1909)
**1** : a structure housing memorials to famous or illustrious individuals usually chosen by a group of electors
**2** : a group of individuals in a particular category (as a sport) who have been selected as particularly illustrious
— **Hall of Fam·er** \-'fā-mər\
**hal·low** \'ha-(ˌ)lō\ *transitive verb* [Middle English *halowen,* from Old English *hālgian,* from *hālig* holy — more at HOLY] (before 12th century)
**1** : to make holy or set apart for holy use
**2** : to respect greatly : VENERATE
*synonym* see DEVOTE
**hal·lowed** \'ha-(ˌ)lōd, 'ha-ləd, *in the Lord's Prayer often* 'ha-lə-wəd\ *adjective* (before 12th century)
**1** : HOLY, CONSECRATED
**2** : SACRED, REVERED (*hallowed* customs)

**Hal·low·een** *also* **Hal·low·e'en** \ˌha-lə-'wēn, ˌhä-\ *noun* [short for *All Hallow Even* (All Saints' Eve)] (circa 1700)
: October 31 observed especially with dressing up in disguise, trick-or-treating, and displaying jack-o'-lanterns during the evening ☐
**Hal·low·mas** \'ha-lō-ˌmas, 'ha-lə-, -məs\ *noun* [short for Middle English *Alholowmesse,* from Old English *ealra halgena mæsse,* literally, all saints' mass] (14th century)
: ALL SAINTS' DAY
**halls of ivy** [from the traditional training of ivy on the walls of older college buildings] (1965)
: UNIVERSITY, COLLEGE
**Hall·statt** *also* **Hall·stadt** \'hȯl-ˌstat; 'häl-ˌshtät, -ˌstät\ *adjective* [*Hallstatt,* Austria] (1899)
: of or relating to the earlier period of the Iron Age in Europe
**hal·lu·ci·nate** \hə-'lü-sᵊn-ˌāt\ *verb* **-nat·ed; -nat·ing** [Latin *hallucinatus,* past participle of *hallucinari, allucinari* to prate, dream, modification of Greek *alyein* to be distressed, to wander] (circa 1834)
*transitive verb*
**1** : to affect with visions or imaginary perceptions
**2** : to perceive or experience as an hallucination
*intransitive verb*
: to have hallucinations
— **hal·lu·ci·na·tor** \-ˌā-tər\ *noun*
**hal·lu·ci·na·tion** \hə-ˌlü-sᵊn-'ā-shən\ *noun* (1629)
**1 a** : perception of objects with no reality usually arising from disorder of the nervous system or in response to drugs (as LSD) **b** : the object so perceived
**2** : an unfounded or mistaken impression or notion : DELUSION
**hal·lu·ci·na·to·ry** \hə-'lü-sᵊn-ə-ˌtōr-ē, -ˌtȯr-\ *adjective* (1830)
**1** : tending to produce hallucination (*hallucinatory* drugs)
**2** : resembling, involving, or being an hallucination (*hallucinatory* dreams) (an *hallucinatory* figure)
**hal·lu·ci·no·gen** \hə-'lü-sᵊn-ə-jən\ *noun* [*hallucination* + *-o-* + *-gen*] (1954)
: a substance that induces hallucinations
— **hal·lu·ci·no·gen·ic** \-ˌlü-sᵊn-ə-'je-nik\ *adjective or noun*
**hal·lu·ci·no·sis** \hə-ˌlü-sᵊn-'ō-səs\ *noun* [New Latin] (1905)
: a pathological mental state characterized by hallucinations
**hal·lux** \'ha-ləks\ *noun, plural* **hal·lu·ces** \'ha-lə-ˌsēz, 'hal-yə-\ [New Latin, from Latin *hallus, hallux*] (1831)

---

☐ USAGE
**Halloween** Nothing sends chills down the spine of some English speakers like the pronunciation \ˌhä-lə-'wēn\. The first half of the word, it is argued, comes from the verb *hallow,* whose first syllable is pronounced \'ha-\. In earlier centuries, though, *hallow* had a second pronunciation rhyming with *swallow,* and so \ˌhä-lə-'wēn\ is a natural pronunciation of the name of the October holiday. The disputed variant is common throughout the United States but not in Great Britain. Those who insist that the pronunciation of *Halloween* should be the sum of its parts should consider their own pronunciations of the first vowels of *Christmas* and *Michaelmas.*

---

\ə\ abut  \ᵊ\ kitten  \ər\ further  \a\ ash  \ā\ ace
\ä\ mop, mar  \au̇\ out  \ch\ chin  \e\ bet  \ē\ easy
\g\ go  \i\ hit  \ī\ ice  \j\ job  \ŋ\ sing  \ō\ go
\ȯ\ law  \ȯi\ boy  \th\ thin  \th\ the  \ü\ loot  \u̇\ foot
\y\ yet  \zh\ vision  *see also* Guide to Pronunciation

: the innermost digit (as the big toe) of a hind or lower limb

**hall·way** \'hȯl-ˌwā\ *noun* (1876)
**1** : an entrance hall
**2** : CORRIDOR

**hal·ma** \'hal-mə\ *noun* [Greek *halma* leap, from *hallesthai* to leap — more at SALLY] (1889)
: a game played on a square board and having rules similar to those of Chinese checkers

**¹ha·lo** \'hā-(ˌ)lō\ *noun, plural* **halos** *or* **haloes** [Latin *halos*, from Greek *halōs* threshing floor, disk, halo] (1603)
**1** : a circle of light appearing to surround the sun or moon and resulting from refraction or reflection of light by ice particles in the atmosphere
**2** : something resembling a halo: as **a** : NIMBUS **b** : a region of space surrounding a galaxy that is sparsely populated with luminous objects (as globular clusters) but is believed to contain a great deal of dark matter **c** : a differentiated zone surrounding a central zone or object
**3** : the aura of glory, veneration, or sentiment surrounding an idealized person or thing

**²halo** *transitive verb* (1801)
: to form into or surround with a halo ⟨rainbows *haloed* the waterfalls —Michael Crawford⟩

**halo-** — see HAL-

**hal·o·car·bon** \'ha-lə-ˌkär-bən\ *noun* (1950)
: any of various compounds (as fluorocarbon) of carbon and one or more halogens

**hal·o·cline** \'ha-lə-ˌklīn\ *noun* (1960)
: a usually vertical gradient in salinity (as of the ocean)

**halo effect** *noun* (circa 1928)
: generalization from the perception of one outstanding personality trait to an overly favorable evaluation of the whole personality

**hal·o·gen** \'ha-lə-jən\ *noun* [Swedish, from *hal-* + *-gen*] (1842)
: any of the five elements fluorine, chlorine, bromine, iodine, and astatine that form part of group VII A of the periodic table and exist in the free state normally as diatomic molecules
— **ha·log·e·nous** \ha-'lä-jə-nəs\ *adjective*

**ha·lo·ge·nate** \ha-'lä-jə-ˌnāt, ha-'lä-jə-\ *transitive verb* **-nat·ed; -nat·ing** (1882)
: to treat or cause to combine with a halogen
— **ha·lo·ge·na·tion** \ˌha-lə-jə-'nā-shən, ha-ˌlä-jə-\ *noun*

**hal·o·ge·ton** \ˌha-lə-jə-'jē-ˌtän\ *noun* [New Latin, from *hal-* + Greek *geitōn* neighbor] (1943)
: a coarse annual herb (*Halogeton glomeratus*) of the goosefoot family that is a noxious weed in western American ranges

**hal·o·mor·phic** \ˌha-lə-'mȯr-fik\ *adjective* (circa 1938)
*of a soil* : developed in the presence of neutral or alkali salts or both

**hal·o·per·i·dol** \ˌha-lō-'per-ə-ˌdȯl, -ˌdōl\ *noun* [*hal-* + p*iperi*dine + *-ol*] (1960)
: a depressant $C_{21}H_{23}ClFNO_2$ of the central nervous system used especially as an antipsychotic drug

**hal·o·phile** \'ha-lə-ˌfīl\ *noun* [International Scientific Vocabulary] (1923)
: an organism that flourishes in a salty environment
— **hal·o·phil·ic** \ˌha-lə-'fi-lik\ *adjective*

**hal·o·phyte** \'ha-lə-ˌfīt\ *noun* [International Scientific Vocabulary] (circa 1886)
: a plant (as saltbush or sea lavender) that grows in salty soil and usually has a physiological resemblance to a true xerophyte
— **hal·o·phyt·ic** \ˌha-lə-'fi-tik\ *adjective*

**hal·o·thane** \'ha-lə-ˌthān\ *noun* [*halo-* + *ethane*] (1957)
: a nonexplosive inhalational anesthetic $C_2HBrClF_3$

**¹halt** \'hȯlt\ *adjective* [Middle English, from Old English *healt*; akin to Old High German *halz* lame] (before 12th century)
: LAME

**²halt** *intransitive verb* (before 12th century)

**1** : to walk or proceed lamely : LIMP
**2** : to stand in perplexity or doubt between alternate courses : WAVER
**3** : to display weakness or imperfection : FALTER

**³halt** *noun* [German, from Middle High German, from *halt*, imperative of *halten* to hold, from Old High German *haltan* — more at HOLD] (circa 1598)
: STOP

**⁴halt** (1656)
*intransitive verb*
**1** : to cease marching or journeying
**2** : DISCONTINUE, TERMINATE ⟨the project *halted* for lack of funds⟩
*transitive verb*
**1** : to bring to a stop ⟨the strike *halted* subways and buses⟩
**2** : to cause the discontinuance of : END

**¹hal·ter** \'hȯl-tər\ *noun* [Middle English, from Old English *hælftre*; akin to Old High German *halftra* halter, Old English *hielfe* helve] (before 12th century)
**1 a** : a rope or strap for leading or tying an animal **b** : a headstall usually with noseband and throatlatch to which a lead may be attached
**2** : a rope for hanging criminals : NOOSE; *also* : death by hanging
**3** : a woman's blouse that leaves the back, arms, and midriff bare and that is typically held in place by straps around the neck and across the back

halter 1b

**²halter** *transitive verb* **hal·tered; hal·ter·ing** \-t(ə-)riŋ\ (14th century)
**1 a** : to catch with or as if with a halter; *also* : to put a halter on **b** : HANG
**2** : to put restraint upon : HAMPER

**hal·ter·break** \'hȯl-tər-ˌbrāk\ *transitive verb* **-broke** \-ˌbrōk\; **-bro·ken** \-ˌbrō-kən\; **-break·ing** (1837)
: to break (as a colt) to a halter

**hal·tere** \'hȯl-ˌtir, 'hal-\ *noun, plural* **hal·teres** \'hȯl-ˌtirz, 'hal-; hȯl-'tir-ēz, hal-\ [New Latin *halter*, from Latin, jumping weight, from Greek *haltēr*, from *hallesthai* to leap — more at SALLY] (1823)
: one of a pair of club-shaped organs in a dipteran insect that are the modified second pair of wings and function as sensory flight stabilizers

**halt·ing** \'hȯl-tiŋ\ *adjective* (1585)
: marked by a lack of sureness or effectiveness ⟨spoke in a *halting* manner⟩
— **halt·ing·ly** \-tiŋ-lē\ *adverb*

**hal·vah** *or* **hal·va** \häl-'vä; 'häl-(ˌ)vä, -və\ *noun* [Yiddish *halva*, from Romanian, from Turkish *helva*, from Arabic *ḥalwā* sweetmeat] (1846)
: a flaky confection of crushed sesame seeds in a base of syrup (as of honey)

**halve** \'hav, 'hȧv\ *transitive verb* **halved; halv·ing** [Middle English, from *half* half] (13th century)
**1 a** : to divide into two equal parts **b** : to reduce to one half ⟨*halving* the present cost⟩ **c** : to share equally
**2** : to play (as a hole in golf) in the same number of strokes as one's opponent

**halv·ers** \'ha-vərz, 'hȧ-\ *noun plural* (1517)
: half shares : HALVES

**halves** *plural of* HALF

**hal·yard** \'hal-yərd\ *noun* [Middle English *halier*, from *halen* to pull — more at HALE] (14th century)
: a rope or tackle for hoisting and lowering something (as sails)

**¹ham** \'ham\ *noun* [Middle English *hamme*, from Old English *hamm*; akin to Old High German *hamma* ham, Greek *knēmē* shinbone, Old Irish *cnáim* bone] (before 12th century)

**1 a** : the hollow of the knee **b** : a buttock with its associated thigh — usually used in plural
**2** : a cut of meat consisting of a thigh; *especially* : one from a hog
**3** [short for *hamfatter*, from "The *Ham-fat* Man*," minstrel song] **a** : a showy performer; *especially* : an actor performing in an exaggerated theatrical style **b** : a licensed operator of an amateur radio station
**4** : a cushion used especially by tailors for pressing curved areas of garments
— **ham** *adjective*

**²ham** *verb* **hammed; ham·ming** (1933)
*transitive verb*
: to execute with exaggerated speech or gestures : OVERACT
*intransitive verb*
: to overplay a part

**Ham** \'ham\ *noun* [Hebrew]
: a son of Noah held to be the progenitor of the Egyptians, Nubians, and Canaanites

**hama·dry·ad** \ˌha-mə-'drī-əd, -ˌad\ *noun* [Latin *hamadryad-, hamadryas*, from Greek, from *hama* together with + *dryad-, dryas* dryad — more at SAME] (14th century)
**1** : WOOD NYMPH
**2** : KING COBRA

**hama·dry·as baboon** \ˌha-mə-'drī-əs-\ *noun* [New Latin *hamadryas*, from Latin] (circa 1890)
: a baboon (*Papio hamadryas*) that has a reddish pink muzzle and a large bare patch of pink skin on each buttock and that was venerated by the ancient Egyptians — called also *sacred baboon*

**ha·mal** *also* **ham·mal** \hə-'mäl\ *noun* [Arabic *ḥammāl* porter] (circa 1760)
: a porter in eastern countries (as Turkey)

**Ha·man** \'hā-mən\ *noun* [Hebrew *Hāmān*]
: an enemy of the Jews hanged according to the book of Esther for plotting their destruction

**ha·man·tasch** \'hä-mən-ˌtäsh, 'hȯ-, -ˌtȯsh\ *noun, plural* **-tasch·en** \-ˌtä-shən, -ˌtȯ-\ [Yiddish *homentash*, from *Homen* Haman + *tash* pocket, bag] (1927)
: a three-cornered pastry with a filling (as of poppy seeds or prunes) traditionally eaten during the Jewish holiday Purim

**ha·mar·tia** \ˌhä-ˌmär-'tē-ə\ *noun* [Greek, from *hamartanein* to miss the mark, err] (1927)
: TRAGIC FLAW

**ha·mate** \'hā-ˌmāt\ *noun* [Latin *hamatus* hooked, from *hamus* hook] (1924)
: a bone on the inner side of the second row of the carpus in mammals

**ham·burg·er** \'ham-ˌbər-gər\ *or* **ham·burg** \-ˌbərg\ *noun* [German *Hamburger* of Hamburg, Germany] (1884)
**1 a** : ground beef **b** : a patty of ground beef
**2** : a sandwich consisting of a patty of hamburger in a split round bun

**¹hame** \'hām\ *noun* [Middle English] (14th century)
: one of two curved supports attached to the collar of a draft horse to which the traces are fastened

**²hame** *Scottish variant of* HOME

**ham–fist·ed** \'ham-ˌfis-təd\ *adjective* (1928)
: HAM-HANDED

**ham–hand·ed** \-'han-dəd\ *adjective* (1918)
: lacking dexterity or grace : HEAVY-HANDED
— **ham–hand·ed·ly** \-lē\ *adverb*
— **ham–hand·ed·ness** \-dəd-nəs\ *noun*

**Ham·il·to·ni·an** \ˌha-məl-'tō-nē-ən\ *noun* [Sir William *Hamilton* (died 1865) Irish mathematician] (1933)
: a function that is used to describe a dynamic system (as the motion of a particle) in terms of components of momentum and coordinates of space and time and that is equal to the total energy of the system when time is not explicitly part of the function — compare LAGRANGIAN

**Ham·il·to·ni·an·ism** \-nē-ə-ˌni-zəm\ *noun* (1901)

: the political principles and ideas held by or associated with Alexander Hamilton that center around a belief in a strong central government, broad interpretation of the federal constitution, encouragement of an industrial and commercial economy, and a general distrust of the political capacity or wisdom of the common man

— **Hamiltonian** \-'tō-nē-ən\ *adjective*

**Ham·ite** \'ha-ˌmīt\ *noun* [*Ham*] (1854)
: a member of a Hamitic-speaking people

¹**Ham·it·ic** \ha-'mi-tik, hə-\ *adjective* (1844)
: of, relating to, or characteristic of the Hamites or one of the Hamitic languages

²**Hamitic** *noun* (circa 1890)
: HAMITIC LANGUAGES

**Hamitic languages** *noun plural* (circa 1890)
: any of various groupings of non-Semitic Afro-Asiatic languages (as Berber, Egyptian, and Cushitic) that were formerly thought to comprise a single branch of the Afro-Asiatic family

**Ham·i·to–Se·mit·ic** \ˌha-mə-(ˌ)tō-sə-'mi-tik, hə-'mi-tō-\ *adjective* (1901)
: of, relating to, or constituting the Afro-Asiatic languages

— **Hamito–Semitic** *noun*

**ham·let** \'ham-lət\ *noun* [Middle English, from Middle French *hamelet*, diminutive of *ham* village, of Germanic origin; akin to Old English *hām* village, home] (before 12th century)
: a small village

**Ham·let** \'ham-lət\ *noun*
: a legendary Danish prince and hero of Shakespeare's play *Hamlet*

¹**ham·mer** \'ha-mər\ *noun* [Middle English *hamer*, from Old English *hamor*; akin to Old High German *hamar* hammer, and perhaps to Old Church Slavonic *kamen-*, *kamy* stone, Greek *akmē* point, edge — more at EDGE] (before 12th century)
**1 a** : a hand tool consisting of a solid head set crosswise on a handle and used for pounding **b** : a power tool that often substitutes a metal block or a drill for the hammerhead
**2** : something that resembles a hammer in form or action: as **a** : a lever with a striking head for ringing a bell or striking a gong **b** (1) : an arm that strikes the cap in a percussion lock to ignite the propelling charge (2) : a part of the action of a modern gun that strikes the primer of the cartridge in firing or that strikes the firing pin to ignite the cartridge **c** : MALLEUS **d** : GAVEL **e** (1) : a padded mallet in a piano action for striking a string (2) : a hand mallet for playing on various percussion instruments (as a xylophone)
**3** : a metal sphere thrown for distance in the hammer throw
**4** : ACCELERATOR b

— **under the hammer** : for sale at auction

²**hammer** *verb* **ham·mered; ham·mer·ing** \'ha-mər-iŋ, 'ham-riŋ\ (14th century)
*intransitive verb*
**1** : to strike blows especially repeatedly with or as if with a hammer : POUND
**2** : to make repeated efforts; *especially* : to reiterate an opinion or attitude ⟨the lectures all *hammered* away at the same points⟩
*transitive verb*
**1 a** : to beat, drive, or shape with repeated blows of a hammer **b** : to fasten or build with a hammer
**2** : to strike or drive with a force suggesting a hammer blow or repeated blows ⟨*hammered* the ball over the fence⟩ ⟨tried to *hammer* me into submission⟩

— **ham·mer·er** \'ha-mər-ər\ *noun*

**hammer and sickle** *noun* (1921)
: an emblem consisting of a crossed hammer and sickle used especially as a symbol of Soviet Communism

**hammer and tongs** *adverb* (circa 1780)

: with great force, vigor, or violence ⟨went at it *hammer and tongs*⟩

— **hammer–and–tongs** *adjective*

**hammer dulcimer** *noun* (1953)
: DULCIMER 1 — called also *hammered dulcimer*

**hammered** *adjective* (1522)
: having surface indentations produced or appearing to have been produced by hammering ⟨*hammered* copper⟩

**ham·mer·head** \'ha-mər-ˌhed\ *noun* (1562)
**1** : the striking part of a hammer
**2** : BLOCKHEAD
**3** : any of a family (Sphyrnidae) of active voracious medium-sized sharks that have the eyes at the ends of lateral extensions of the flattened head — see SHARK illustration

**ham·mer·less** \-ləs\ *adjective* (1875)
: having the hammer concealed ⟨a *hammerless* revolver⟩

**ham·mer·lock** \-ˌläk\ *noun* (1897)
: a wrestling hold in which an opponent's arm is held bent behind his back; *broadly* : a strong hold

**hammer mill** *noun* (1610)
: a grinder or crusher in which materials are broken up by hammers

**hammer out** *transitive verb* (circa 1632)
: to produce or bring about as if by repeated blows ⟨*hammered out* an agreement⟩

**hammer throw** *noun* (1898)
: a field event in which a usually 16-pound metal sphere attached to a flexible handle is thrown for distance

**ham·mer·toe** \'ha-mər-ˌtō\ *noun* (circa 1885)
: a deformed claw-shaped toe and especially the second that results from permanent angular flexion between one or both phalangeal joints

¹**ham·mock** \'ha-mək\ *noun* [Spanish *hamaca*, from Taino] (1555)
: a swinging couch or bed usually made of netting or canvas and slung by cords from supports at each end

²**hammock** *noun* [origin unknown] (1555)
**1** : HUMMOCK
**2** : a fertile area in the southern U.S. and especially Florida that is usually higher than its surroundings and that is characterized by hardwood vegetation and deep humus-rich soil

**ham·my** \'ha-mē\ *adjective* **ham·mi·er; -est** (1929)
: marked by exaggerated and usually self-conscious theatricality

— **ham·mi·ly** \'ha-mə-lē\ *adverb*
— **ham·mi·ness** \'ha-mē-nəs\ *noun*

¹**ham·per** \'ham-pər\ *transitive verb* **ham·pered; ham·per·ing** \-p(ə-)riŋ\ [Middle English] (14th century)
**1 a** : to restrict the movement of by bonds or obstacles : IMPEDE **b** : to interfere with the operation of : DISRUPT
**2 a** : CURB, RESTRAIN **b** : to interfere with : ENCUMBER ☆

²**hamper** *noun* [Middle English *hampere*, alteration of *hanaper*, literally, case to hold goblets, from Middle French *hanapier*, from *hanap* goblet, of Germanic origin; akin to Old English *hnæpp* bowl] (14th century)
: a large basket usually with a cover for packing, storing, or transporting articles (as food or laundry)

**Hamp·shire** \'ham(p)-ˌshir, -shər\ *noun* [*Hampshire*, England] (1918)
**1** : any of a British breed of large hornless black-faced mutton-producing sheep — called also *Hampshire Down*
**2** : any of an American breed of black white-belted swine

**ham·ster** \'ham(p)-stər\ *noun* [German, from Old High German *hamustro*, of Slavic origin; akin to Old Russian *choměstorŭ* hamster, of Iranian origin; akin to Avestan *hamaēstar* oppressor] (1607)

: any of a subfamily (Cricetinae) of small Old World rodents having very large cheek pouches

¹**ham·string** \'ham-ˌstriŋ\ *noun* (1565)
**1 a** : either of two groups of tendons at the back of the human knee **b** : HAMSTRING MUSCLE
**2** : a large tendon above and behind the hock of a quadruped

²**hamstring** *transitive verb* **-strung** \-ˌstrəŋ\; **-string·ing** \-ˌstriŋ-iŋ\ (1641)
**1** : to make ineffective or powerless : CRIPPLE ⟨*hamstrung* by guilt⟩
**2** : to cripple by cutting the leg tendons

**hamstring muscle** *noun* (circa 1888)
: any of three muscles at the back of the thigh that function to flex and rotate the leg and extend the thigh

**ham·u·lus** \'ham-yə-ləs\ *noun, plural* **-u·li** \-ˌlī, -ˌlē\ [New Latin, from Latin, diminutive of *hamus* hook] (circa 1751)
: a hook or hooked process (as of a bone)

**ham·za** *or* **ham·zah** \'ham-zə, 'häm-\ *noun* [Arabic *hamzah*, literally, compression] (1938)
: the sign for a glottal stop in Arabic orthography usually represented in English by an apostrophe

**Han** \'hän\ *noun* [Chinese (Beijing) *Hàn*] (1736)
**1** : a Chinese dynasty dated 207 B.C.–A.D. 220 and marked by centralized control through an appointive bureaucracy, a revival of learning, and the penetration of Buddhism
**2** : the Chinese peoples especially as distinguished from non-Chinese (as Mongolian) elements in the population

¹**hand** \'hand\ *noun, often attributive* [Middle English, from Old English; akin to Old High German *hant* hand] (before 12th century)
**1 a** (1) : the terminal part of the vertebrate forelimb when modified (as in humans) as a grasping organ (2) : the forelimb segment (as the terminal section of a bird's wing) of a vertebrate higher than the fishes that corresponds to the hand irrespective of its form or functional specialization **b** : a part serving the function of or resembling a hand: as (1) : the hind foot of an ape (2) : the chela of a crustacean **c** : something resembling a hand: as (1) : an indicator or pointer on a dial ⟨the *hands* of a clock⟩ (2) : INDEX 5 (3) : a cluster of bananas developed from a single flower group (4) : a branched rootstock of ginger (5) : a bunch of large leaves (as of tobacco) tied together usually with another leaf
**2 a** : personal possession — usually used in plural ⟨the documents fell into the *hands* of

☆ **SYNONYMS**
**Hamper, trammel, clog, fetter, shackle, manacle** mean to hinder or impede in moving, progressing, or acting. HAMPER may imply the effect of any impeding or restraining influence ⟨*hampered* the investigation by refusing to cooperate⟩. TRAMMEL suggests entangling by or confining within a net ⟨rules that *trammel* the artist's creativity⟩. CLOG usually implies a slowing by something extraneous or encumbering ⟨a court system *clogged* by frivolous suits⟩. FETTER suggests a restraining so severe that freedom to move or progress is almost lost ⟨a nation *fettered* by an antiquated class system⟩. SHACKLE and MANACLE are stronger than FETTER and suggest total loss of freedom ⟨a mind *shackled* by stubborn prejudice⟩ ⟨a people *manacled* by tyranny⟩.

\ə\ abut \ᵊ\ kitten \ər\ further \a\ ash \ā\ ace
\ä\ mop, mar \au̇\ out \ch\ chin \e\ bet \ē\ easy
\g\ go \i\ hit \ī\ ice \j\ job \ŋ\ sing \ō\ go
\o̊\ law \o̊i\ boy \th\ thin \th̲\ the \ü\ loot \u̇\ foot
\y\ yet \zh\ vision *see also* Guide to Pronunciation

the enemy⟩ **b :** CONTROL, SUPERVISION — usually used in plural ⟨left the matter in her *hands*⟩
**3 a :** SIDE, DIRECTION ⟨men fighting on either *hand*⟩ **b :** one of two sides or aspects of an issue or argument ⟨on the one *hand* we can appeal for peace, and on the other, declare war⟩
**4 :** a pledge especially of betrothal or bestowal in marriage
**5 a :** style of penmanship : HANDWRITING ⟨wrote in a fancy *hand*⟩ **b :** SIGNATURE
**6 a :** SKILL, ABILITY ⟨tried her *hand* at sailing⟩ **b :** an instrumental part ⟨had a *hand* in the victory⟩
**7 :** a unit of measure equal to 4 inches (10.2 centimeters) used especially for the height of horses
**8 a :** assistance or aid especially involving physical effort ⟨lend a *hand*⟩ **b :** PARTICIPATION, INTEREST **c :** a round of applause
**9 a** (1) **:** a player in a card game or board game (2) **:** the cards or pieces held by a player **b :** a single round in a game **c :** the force or solidity of one's position (as in negotiations)
**10 a :** a person who performs or executes a particular work ⟨two portraits by the same *hand*⟩ **b** (1) **:** a person employed at manual labor or general tasks ⟨a ranch *hand*⟩ (2) **:** WORKER, EMPLOYEE ⟨employed over a hundred *hands*⟩ **c :** a member of a ship's crew ⟨all *hands* on deck⟩ **d :** a person skilled in a particular action or pursuit **e :** a specialist or veteran in a usually designated activity or region ⟨a China *hand*⟩
**11 a :** HANDIWORK, DOINGS **b :** style of execution : WORKMANSHIP ⟨the *hand* of a master⟩ **c :** the feel of or tactile reaction to something (as silk or leather)
**12 :** a punch made with a specified hand ⟨knocked him out with a good right *hand*⟩
— **at hand 1 :** near in time or place : within reach ⟨use whatever ingredients are *at hand*⟩ **2 :** currently receiving or deserving attention ⟨the business *at hand*⟩
— **at the hands of** *also* **at the hand of** **:** by or through the action of
— **by hand 1 :** with the hands or a hand-worked implement (as a tool or pen) rather than with a machine **2 :** from one individual directly to another ⟨deliver the document *by hand*⟩
— **in hand 1 :** in one's possession or control **2 :** in preparation **3 :** under consideration
— **on all hands** *or* **on every hand :** EVERYWHERE
— **on hand 1 :** in present possession or readily available **2 :** about to appear : PENDING **3 :** in attendance : PRESENT
— **on one's hands :** in one's possession or care ⟨too much time *on my hands*⟩
— **out of hand 1 :** without delay or deliberation; *also* **:** in a summary or peremptory manner **2 :** done with : FINISHED **3 :** out of control **4 :** with the hands ⟨fruit eaten *out of hand*⟩
— **to hand 1 :** into possession **2 :** within reach

**²hand** *adverb* (before 12th century)
**:** with the hands rather than by machine
**³hand** *transitive verb* (15th century)
**1 a** *obsolete* **:** to touch or manage with the hands; *also* **:** to deal with **b :** FURL
**2 :** to lead, guide, or assist with the hand ⟨*hand* a lady into a bus⟩
**3 a :** to give, pass, or transmit with the hand ⟨*hand* a letter to her⟩ **b :** to present or provide with ⟨*handed* him a surprise⟩
— **hand it to :** to give credit to : concede the excellence of
**hand and foot** *adverb* (before 12th century)
**:** TOTALLY, ASSIDUOUSLY
**hand ax** *noun* (13th century)
**1 :** a short-handled ax intended for use with one hand
**2 :** a prehistoric stone tool having one end pointed for cutting and the other end rounded for holding in the hand

**hand·bag** \'han(d)-ˌbag\ *noun* (1862)
**1 :** SUITCASE
**2 :** a bag held in the hand or hung from a shoulder strap and used for carrying small personal articles and money
**hand·ball** \-ˌbȯl\ *noun* (1886)
**1 :** a game played in a walled court or against a single wall or board by two or four players who use their hands to strike the ball
**2 :** a small rubber ball used in handball
**hand·bar·row** \-ˌbar-(ˌ)ō\ *noun* (15th century)
**:** a flat rectangular frame with handles at both ends that is carried by two persons
**hand·bas·ket** \-ˌbas-kət\ *noun* (15th century)
**:** a small portable basket — usually used in the phrase *to hell in a handbasket* denoting rapid and utter ruination
**hand·bell** \-ˌbel\ *noun* (before 12th century)
**:** a small bell with a handle; *especially* **:** one of a set tuned in a scale for musical performance
**hand·bill** \-ˌbil\ *noun* (1753)
**:** a small printed sheet to be distributed (as for advertising) by hand
**hand·blown** \-ˈblōn\ *adjective* (1925)
**:** made by glassblowing and molded by hand
**hand·book** \-ˌbu̇k\ *noun* (before 12th century)
**1 a :** a book capable of being conveniently carried as a ready reference : MANUAL **b :** a concise reference book covering a particular subject
**2 a :** a bookmaker's book of bets **b :** a place where bookmaking is carried on
**hand·breadth** \-ˌbretth, -ˌbreth, -ˌbredth\ *noun* (before 12th century)
**:** any of various units of length varying from about 2½ to 4 inches based on the breadth of a hand
**hand·car** \'han(d)-ˌkär\ *noun* (1850)
**:** a small four-wheeled railroad car propelled by a hand-operated mechanism or by a small motor
**hand·cart** \-ˌkärt\ *noun* (1640)
**:** a cart drawn or pushed by hand
**hand cheese** *noun* (1890)
**:** a soft cheese with a sharp pungent odor and flavor that was originally molded by hand
**hand·clasp** \'han(d)-ˌklasp\ *noun* (1583)
**:** HANDSHAKE
**¹hand·craft** \-ˌkraft\ *noun* (before 12th century)
**:** HANDICRAFT
**²handcraft** *transitive verb* (1947)
**:** to fashion by handicraft
**hand·crafts·man** \-ˌkraf(t)-smən\ *noun* (15th century)
**:** a person who is skilled in handicraft
— **hand·crafts·man·ship** \-ship\ *noun*
**¹hand·cuff** \-ˌkəf\ *noun* (1695)
**:** a metal fastening that can be locked around a wrist and is usually connected by a chain or bar with another such fastening — usually used in plural
**²handcuff** *transitive verb* (1720)
**1 :** to apply handcuffs to : MANACLE
**2 :** to hold in check : make ineffective or powerless
**hand down** *transitive verb* (1692)
**1 :** to transmit in succession (as from father to son)
**2 :** to make official formulation of and express (the opinion of a court)
**hand·ed** \'han-dəd\ *adjective* (15th century)
**1 :** having a hand or hands especially of a specified kind or number — usually used in combination ⟨a large-*handed* man⟩
**2 :** using a specified hand or number of hands — used in combination ⟨right-*handed*⟩ ⟨a one-*handed* catch⟩
**hand·ed·ness** \-nəs\ *noun* (1915)
**1 :** a tendency to use one hand rather than the other
**2 a :** the property of an object (as a molecule) of not being identical with its mirror image **b :** either of the two configurations of an object that may exist in forms which are nonidentical mirror images

**hand·fast** \'han(d)-ˌfast\ *noun* [Middle English, from Old English *handfæst*] (1611)
*archaic* **:** a contract or covenant especially of betrothal or marriage
**hand–feed** \'han(d)-ˈfēd\ *transitive verb* **-fed** \-ˈfed\; **-feed·ing** (1805)
**:** to feed (as animals) by hand
**hand·ful** \'han(d)-ˌfu̇l\ *noun*, *plural* **handfuls** \-ˌfu̇lz\ *also* **hands·ful** \'han(d)z-ˌfu̇l\ (before 12th century)
**1 :** as much or as many as the hand will grasp
**2 :** a small quantity or number
**3 :** as much as one can manage
**hand glass** *noun* (1882)
**:** a small mirror with a handle
**hand·grip** \'han(d)-ˌgrip\ *noun* (before 12th century)
**1 :** a grasping with the hand
**2 :** HANDLE
**3** *plural* **:** hand-to-hand combat
**hand·gun** \-ˌgən\ *noun* (15th century)
**:** a firearm (as a revolver or pistol) designed to be held and fired with one hand
**hand·held** \-ˌheld, -ˈheld\ *adjective* (1923)
**:** held in the hand; *especially* **:** designed to be operated while being held in the hand ⟨*hand-held* computers⟩
— **handheld** \-ˌheld\ *noun*
**hand·hold** \'hand-ˌhōld\ *noun* (1643)
**1 :** HOLD, GRIP
**2 :** something to hold on to (as in mountain climbing)
**hand–hold·ing** \-ˌhōl-diŋ\ *noun* (1967)
**:** solicitous attention, support, or instruction (as in the use of new technology)
**¹hand·i·cap** \'han-di-ˌkap, -dē-\ *noun* [obsolete English *handicap* (a game in which forfeit money was held in a cap), from *hand in cap*] (1754)
**1 a :** a race or contest in which an artificial advantage is given or disadvantage imposed on a contestant to equalize chances of winning **b :** an advantage given or disadvantage imposed usually in the form of points, strokes, weight to be carried, or distance from the target or goal
**2 a :** a disadvantage that makes achievement unusually difficult **b :** a physical disability ◆
**²handicap** *transitive verb* **-capped; -capping** (1852)
**1 a :** to give a handicap to **b :** to assess the relative winning chances of (contestants) or the likely winner of (a contest)
**2 :** to put at a disadvantage

◇ **WORD HISTORY**
**handicap** *Handicap*, from *hand in cap*, was an old form of barter. Two people who wished to make an exchange asked a third to act as umpire. All three put forfeit money in a cap, into which each of the two barterers inserted a hand. The umpire described the goods to be traded and set the additional amount the owner of the less valuable article should pay the other in order that the exchange might be fair. The barterers withdrew their hands from the cap empty to signify the refusal of the umpire's decision, or full to indicate acceptance. If the hands of both barterers were full, the exchange was made and the umpire pocketed the forfeit money. If both barterers came up empty-handed, there was no exchange but the umpire took the money. Otherwise, each barterer kept his own property, and the one who had accepted the umpire's decision took the forfeit money as well. Later, a horse race arranged in accordance with the rules of handicap was called a *handicap race*. The umpire decided how much extra weight the better horse should carry. The word was eventually extended to other contests, and also came to signify the advantage or disadvantage imposed.

**hand·i·capped** *adjective* (1915)
: having a physical or mental disability that substantially limits activity especially in relation to employment or education; *also* : of or reserved for handicapped persons ⟨*handicapped* parking spaces⟩

**hand·i·cap·per** \-ˌka-pər\ *noun* (1754)
**1** : a person who assigns handicaps
**2** : a person who predicts the winners in a race (as a horse race)
**3** : a person who competes with a (specified) handicap (as in golf) — usually used in combination ⟨a 5-*handicapper*⟩

**hand·i·craft** \'han-di-ˌkraft, -dē-\ *noun* [Middle English *handi-crafte*, alteration of *hand-craft*] (13th century)
**1 a** : manual skill **b** : an occupation requiring skill with the hands
**2** : the articles fashioned by those engaged in handicraft
— **hand·i·craft·er** \-ˌkraf-tər\ *noun*

**hand·i·crafts·man** \-ˌkraf(t)-smən\ *noun* (1551)
: a person who engages in a handicraft : ARTISAN

**Hand·ie-Talk·ie** \ˌhan-dē-'tò-kē\ *trademark*
— used for a small portable radio transmitter-receiver

**hand·i·ly** \'han-də-lē\ *adverb* (1719)
**1** : in a dexterous manner
**2** : EASILY ⟨defeated the other candidate *handily*⟩
**3** : conveniently nearby

**hand in** *transitive verb* (1837)
: SUBMIT 2 ⟨*hand in* your homework⟩

**hand in glove** *or* **hand and glove** *adverb* (1680)
: in extremely close relationship or agreement ⟨working *hand in glove* with the police⟩

**hand in hand** *adverb* (15th century)
**1** : with hands clasped (as in intimacy or affection)
**2** : in close association : TOGETHER

**hand·i·work** \'han-di-ˌwərk, -dē-\ *noun* [Middle English *handiwerk*, from Old English *handgeweorc*, from *hand* + *geweorc*, from *ge-* (collective prefix) + *weorc* work — more at CO-] (before 12th century)
**1 a** : work done by the hands **b** : work done personally
**2** : the product of handiwork

**hand·ker·chief** \'haŋ-kər-chəf, -(ˌ)chif, -ˌchēf\ *noun, plural* **-chiefs** *also* **-chieves** \-chəfs, -(ˌ)chifs, -ˌchēvz, -ˌchēfs, -chəvz, -(ˌ)chivz\ (1530)
**1** : a small usually square piece of cloth used for usually personal purposes (as blowing the nose) or as a clothing accessory
**2** : KERCHIEF 1

**¹han·dle** \'han-d°l\ *noun* [Middle English *handel*, from Old English *handle*; akin to Old English *hand*] (before 12th century)
**1** : a part that is designed especially to be grasped by the hand
**2** : something that resembles a handle
**3 a** : TITLE 8 **b** : NAME; *also* : NICKNAME
**4** : HAND 11c
**5** : the total amount of money bet on a race, game, or event
**6** : a means of understanding or controlling ⟨can't quite get a *handle* on things⟩
— **han·dled** \-d°ld\ *adjective*
— **han·dle·less** \-d°l-(l)əs\ *adjective*
— **off the handle** : into a state of sudden and violent anger — usually used with *fly*

**²handle** *verb* **han·dled; han·dling** \'han(d)-liŋ, 'han-d°l-iŋ\ (before 12th century)
*transitive verb*
**1 a** : to try or examine (as by touching, feeling, or moving) with the hand ⟨*handle* silk to judge its weight⟩ **b** : to manage with the hands ⟨*handle* a horse⟩
**2 a** : to deal with in writing or speaking or in the plastic arts **b** : to have overall responsibility for supervising or directing : MANAGE ⟨a

lawyer *handles* all my affairs⟩ **c** : to train and act as second for (a boxer) **d** : to put up with : STAND ⟨can't *handle* the heat⟩
**3** : to act on or perform a required function with regard to ⟨*handle* the day's mail⟩
**4** : to engage in the buying, selling, or distributing of (a commodity)
*intransitive verb*
: to act, behave, or feel in a certain way when handled or directed ⟨a car that *handles* well⟩
— **han·dle·able** \-d°l-ə-bəl\ *adjective*

**han·dle·bar** \'han-d°l-ˌbär\ *noun* (1891)
: a straight or bent bar with a handle at each end; *specifically* : one used to steer a bicycle or similar vehicle — usually used in plural

**handlebar mustache** *noun* (1933)
: a heavy mustache with long sections that curve upward at each end

**hand lens** *noun* (1930)
: a magnifying glass to be held in the hand

**han·dler** \'han(d)-lər, 'han-d°l-ər\ *noun* (14th century)
**1** : one that handles something
**2 a** : a person in immediate physical charge of an animal; *especially* : a person who exhibits dogs at shows or field trials **b** : a person who trains or acts as second for a boxer **c** : a manager of a political figure or campaign

**hand·less** \'han(d)-ləs\ *adjective* (15th century)
**1** : having no hands
**2** : inefficient in manual tasks : CLUMSY

**han·dling** \'han(d)-liŋ, 'han-d°l-iŋ\ *noun* (before 12th century)
**1 a** : the action of one that handles something **b** : a process by which something is handled in a commercial transaction; *especially* : the packaging and shipping of an object or material (as to a consumer)
**2** : the manner in which something is treated (as in a musical, literary, or art work)

**hand·list** \'han(d)-ˌlist\ *noun* (1859)
: a list (as of books) for purposes of reference or checking

**hand·made** \'han(d)-'mād\ *adjective* (1613)
: made by hand or by a hand process

**hand·maid·en** \-ˌmā-d°n\ *also* **hand·maid** \-ˌmād\ *noun* (13th century)
**1** : a personal maid or female servant
**2** : something whose essential function is to serve or assist ⟨criticism is not the enemy of art but rather its *handmaiden* —Gary Michael⟩

**hand–me–down** \'han(d)-mē-ˌdaún\ *adjective* (1827)
**1** : put in use by one person or group after being used, discarded, or handed down by another ⟨*hand-me-down* clothes⟩ ⟨*hand-me-down* anecdotes⟩
**2** : ready-made and usually cheap and shoddy
— **hand–me–down** *noun*

**hand off** (1949)
*transitive verb*
: to hand (a football) to a nearby teammate on a play
*intransitive verb*
: to hand off a football
— **hand·off** \'han-ˌdòf\ *noun*

**hand on** *transitive verb* (1865)
: HAND DOWN

**hand organ** *noun* (1796)
: a barrel organ operated by a hand crank

**hand·out** \'han-ˌdaút\ *noun* (1882)
**1** : a portion of food, clothing, or money given to or as if to a beggar
**2** : a folder or circular of information for free distribution
**3** : a prepared statement released to the news media

**hand out** *transitive verb* (1877)
**1 a** : to give without charge **b** : to give freely
**2** : ADMINISTER ⟨*handed out* a severe punishment⟩

**hand over** *transitive verb* (1816)
: to yield control of
— **hand·over** \'han-ˌdō-vər\ *noun*

**hand over fist** *adverb* (1825)

: quickly and in large amounts

**hand·pick** \'han(d)-'pik\ *transitive verb* (1831)
**1** : to pick by hand as opposed to a machine process
**2** : to select personally or for personal ends

**hand·press** \-ˌpres\ *noun* (1679)
: a hand-operated press

**hand·print** \-ˌprint\ *noun* (1886)
: an impression of a hand on a surface

**hand puppet** *noun* (1947)
: PUPPET 1a

**hand·rail** \'han(d)-ˌrāl\ *noun* (1793)
: a narrow rail for grasping with the hand as a support

**hand running** *adverb* (1828)
*dialect* : in unbroken succession

**hand·saw** \'han(d)-ˌsò\ *noun* (14th century)
: a saw designed to be used with one hand

**hands·breadth** \'han(d)z-ˌbredth, -ˌbretth\ *variant of* HANDBREADTH

**hands down** \'han(d)z-'daún\ *adverb* (1867)
**1** : without much effort : EASILY
**2** : without question
— **hands–down** \'han(d)z-ˌdaún\ *adjective*

**¹hand·sel** \'han(t)-səl\ *noun* [Middle English *hansell*] (14th century)
**1** : a gift made as a token of good wishes or luck especially at the beginning of a new year
**2** : something received first (as in a day of trading) and taken to be a token of good luck
**3 a** : a first installment : earnest money **b** : EARNEST, FORETASTE

**²handsel** *transitive verb* **-seled** *or* **-selled; -sel·ing** *or* **-sel·ling** \-s(ə-)liŋ\ (15th century)
**1** : to give a handsel to
**2** : to inaugurate with a token or gesture of luck or pleasure
**3** : to use or do for the first time

**hand·set** \'han(d)-ˌset\ *noun* (circa 1919)
: a combined telephone transmitter and receiver mounted on a handle

**hand·shake** \-ˌshāk\ *noun* (1873)
: a clasping of right hands by two people (as in greeting or farewell)

**hands–off** \'han(d)z-'òf\ *adjective* (1902)
: characterized by noninterference ⟨a *hands-off* policy toward the internal affairs of other nations⟩

**hand·some** \'han(t)-səm\ *adjective* **hand·som·er; -est** [Middle English *handsom* easy to manipulate] (1530)
**1** *chiefly dialect* : APPROPRIATE, SUITABLE
**2** : moderately large : SIZABLE ⟨a painting that commanded a *handsome* price⟩
**3** : marked by skill or cleverness : ADROIT
**4** : marked by graciousness or generosity : LIBERAL ⟨*handsome* contributions to charity⟩
**5** : having a pleasing and usually impressive or dignified appearance
*synonym* see BEAUTIFUL
— **hand·some·ly** *adverb*
— **hand·some·ness** *noun*

**hands–on** \'han(d)-'zòn, -'zän\ *adjective* (1969)
**1** : relating to, being, or providing direct practical experience in the operation or functioning of something ⟨*hands-on* training⟩; *also* : involving or allowing use of or touching with the hands ⟨a *hands-on* museum display⟩
**2** : characterized by active personal involvement ⟨a *hands-on* manager⟩

**hand·spike** \'han(d)-ˌspīk\ *noun* [by folk etymology from Dutch *handspaak*, from *hand* hand + *spaak* pole; akin to Old English *spāca* spoke] (1615)
: a bar used as a lever

**hand·spring** \-ˌspriŋ\ *noun* (1875)

: an acrobatic feat in which the body turns forward or backward in a full circle from a standing position and lands first on the hands and then on the feet

**hand·stand** \-,stand\ *noun* (1899)
: an act of supporting the body on the hands with the trunk and legs balanced in the air

**hand–to–hand** \'han-tə-'hand, -də-\ *adjective* (1836)
: involving physical contact or close enough range for physical contact ⟨*hand-to-hand* fighting⟩

**hand to hand** *adverb* (circa 1533)
: at very close range

**hand–to–mouth** \-'mauth\ *adjective* (1748)
: having or providing nothing to spare beyond basic necessities ⟨a *hand-to-mouth* existence⟩

**hand truck** *noun* (1920)
: a small hand-propelled truck; *especially* : TRUCK 3b

**hand up** *transitive verb* (1970)
*of a jury* : to deliver (an indictment) to a judge or higher judicial authority

**hand·wheel** \'han(d)-,(h)wēl\ *noun* (circa 1889)
: a wheel worked by hand

**hand·work** \'hand-,wərk\ *noun* (before 12th century)
: work done with the hands and not by machines : HANDIWORK
— **hand·work·er** \-,wər-kər\ *noun*

**hand·wo·ven** \-'wō-vən\ *adjective* (1880)
**1** : produced on a hand-operated loom
**2** : woven by hand ⟨*handwoven* baskets⟩

**hand·wring·ing** \-,riŋ-iŋ\ *noun* (1922)
: an overwrought expression of concern or guilt
— **hand·wring·er** *noun*

**hand·write** \-,rīt\ *transitive verb* **-wrote** \-,rōt\; **-writ·ten** \-,ri-t°n\; **-writ·ing** \-,rī-tiŋ\ [back-formation from *handwriting*] (circa 1853)
: to write by hand

**hand·writ·ing** \'hand-,rī-tiŋ\ *noun* (15th century)
**1** : writing done by hand; *especially* : the form of writing peculiar to a particular person
**2** : something written by hand
— **handwriting on the wall** : an omen of one's unpleasant fate

**hand·wrought** \'hand-'rȯt\ *adjective* (1876)
: fashioned by hand or chiefly by hand processes ⟨*handwrought* silver⟩

**han·dy** \'han-dē\ *adjective* **hand·i·er; -est** (1650)
**1 a** : conveniently near **b** : convenient for use **c** *of a ship* : easily handled
**2** : clever in using the hands especially in a variety of useful ways ⟨*handy* with a hammer as well as with a paintbrush⟩
— **hand·i·ness** *noun*

**handy·man** \-dē-,man\ *noun* (1872)
**1** : one who does odd jobs
**2** : one competent in a variety of small skills or inventive or ingenious in repair or maintenance work — called also *handyperson*

**¹hang** \'haŋ\ *verb* **hung** \'həŋ\ *also* **hanged** \'haŋd\; **hang·ing** \'haŋ-iŋ\ [partly from Middle English *hon*, from Old English *hōn*, transitive verb; partly from Middle English *hangen*, from Old English *hangian*, intransitive verb & transitive verb; both akin to Old High German *hāhan*, transitive verb, to hang, *hangēn*, intransitive verb — more at CUNCTATION] (before 12th century)
*transitive verb*
**1 a** : to fasten to some elevated point without support from below : SUSPEND **b** : to suspend by the neck until dead — often *hanged* in the past; often used as a mild oath ⟨I'll be *hanged*⟩ **c** : to fasten so as to allow free motion within given limits upon a point of suspension ⟨*hang* a door⟩ **d** : to adjust the hem of (a skirt) so as to hang evenly and at a proper height
**2** : to furnish with hanging decorations (as flags or bunting)

**3** : to hold or bear in a suspended or inclined manner ⟨*hung* his head in shame⟩
**4** : to apply to a wall ⟨*hang* wallpaper⟩
**5** : to display (pictures) in a gallery
**6** : to throw (as a curveball) so that it fails to break properly
**7** : to make (a turn) especially while driving ⟨*hang* a right⟩ ⟨*hung* a quick U-turn —Tom Clancy⟩
*intransitive verb*
**1 a** : to remain suspended or fastened to some point above without support from below : DANGLE **b** : to die by hanging — often *hanged* in the past ⟨he *hanged* for his crimes⟩
**2** : to remain poised or stationary in the air ⟨clouds *hanging* low overhead⟩
**3** : LINGER, PERSIST
**4** : to be imminent : IMPEND ⟨doom *hung* over the nation⟩
**5** : to fall or droop from a usually tense or taut position
**6** : DEPEND ⟨election *hangs* on one vote⟩
**7 a** (1) : to take hold for support : CLING ⟨she *hung* on his arm⟩ (2) : to keep persistent contact ⟨dogs *hung* to the trail⟩ **b** : to be burdensome or oppressive ⟨time *hangs* on his hands⟩
**8** : to be uncertain or in suspense ⟨the decision is still *hanging*⟩
**9** : to lean, incline, or jut over or downward
**10** : to be in a state of rapt attention ⟨*hung* on her every word⟩
**11** : to fit or fall from the figure in easy lines ⟨the coat *hangs* loosely⟩
**12** *of a thrown ball* : to fail to break or drop as intended ◻
— **hang·able** \'haŋ-ə-bəl\ *adjective*
— **hang fire 1** : to be slow in the explosion of a charge after its primer has been discharged **2** : DELAY, HESITATE **3** : to remain unsettled or unresolved
— **hang it up** : to cease an activity or effort
— **hang loose** : to remain calm or relaxed
— **hang one on 1** : to inflict a blow on **2** *slang* : to get very drunk
— **hang one's hat** : to situate oneself in (as a residence or place of employment)
— **hang tough** : to remain resolute in the face of adversity : HANG IN

**²hang** *noun* (circa 1797)
**1** : the manner in which a thing hangs
**2** : DECLIVITY, SLOPE; *also* : DROOP
**3** : facility with or an understanding of something ⟨can't get the *hang* of this⟩
**4** : a hesitation or slackening in motion or in a course
— **give a hang** *or* **care a hang** : to be the least bit concerned or worried

**hang about** *intransitive verb* (1849)
*British* : HANG AROUND

**¹han·gar** \'haŋ-ər, 'haŋ-gər\ *noun* [French] (1852)
: SHELTER, SHED; *especially* : a covered and usually enclosed area for housing and repairing aircraft

**²hangar** *transitive verb* (1943)
: to place or store in a hangar

**hang around** (1830)
*intransitive verb*
**1** : to pass time or stay aimlessly : loiter idly
**2** : to spend one's time in company
*transitive verb*
: to pass time or stay aimlessly in or at ⟨*hung around* the house all day⟩

**hang back** *intransitive verb* (1581)
**1** : to drag behind others
**2** : to be reluctant

**¹hang·dog** \'haŋ-,dȯg\ *adjective* (1677)
**1** : SAD, DEJECTED
**2** : SHEEPISH

**²hangdog** *noun* (1687)
: a despicable or miserable person

**hang·er** \'haŋ-ər\ *noun* (15th century)
**1** : one that hangs or causes to be hung or hanged

**2** : something that hangs, overhangs, or is suspended: as **a** : a decorative strip of cloth **b** : a small sword formerly used by seamen **c** *chiefly British* : a small wood on steeply sloping land
**3** : a device by which or to which something is hung or hangs: as **a** : a strap on a sword belt by which a sword or dagger can be suspended **b** : a loop by which a garment is hung up **c** : a device that fits inside or around a garment for hanging from a hook or rod

**hang·er–on** \-,ȯn, -,än\ *noun, plural* **hangers–on** (1542)
: one that hangs around a person, place, or institution especially for personal gain

**hang glider** *noun* (1930)
: a kitelike glider from which a harnessed rider hangs while gliding down from a cliff or hill
— **hang glid·ing** *noun*

hang glider

**hang in** *intransitive verb* (1966)
: to refuse to be discouraged or intimidated : show pluck ⟨*hang in* there⟩

**¹hang·ing** \'haŋ-iŋ\ *adjective* (12th century)
**1** : situated or lying on steeply sloping ground
**2 a** : jutting out : OVERHANGING ⟨a *hanging* rock⟩ **b** : supported only by the wall on one side ⟨a *hanging* staircase⟩
**3** *archaic* : downcast in appearance
**4** : adapted for sustaining a hanging object
**5** : deserving, likely to cause, or prone to inflict death by hanging

**²hanging** *noun* (14th century)
**1** : an execution by strangling or breaking the neck by a suspended noose
**2** : something hung: as **a** : CURTAIN **b** : a covering (as a tapestry) for a wall
**3** : a downward slope : DECLIVITY

**hanging indention** *noun* (1904)
: indention of all the lines of a paragraph except the first

**hang·man** \'haŋ-mən\ *noun* (14th century)
: one who hangs a condemned person; *also* : a public executioner

**hang·nail** \-,nāl\ *noun* [by folk etymology from *agnail* (inflammation about the nail), from Middle English, corn on the foot or toe, from Old English *angnægl*, from *ang-* (akin to *enge* tight, painful) + *nægl* nail — more at ANGER] (1678)
: a bit of skin hanging loose at the side or root of a fingernail ◆

**hang off** *intransitive verb* (1641)
: HANG BACK

**hang on** *intransitive verb* (circa 1719)
**1** : to keep hold : hold onto something
**2** : to persist tenaciously ⟨a cold that *hung on* all spring⟩
**3** : HOLD ON 2 ⟨*hang on* a second while I look it up⟩
— **hang on to** : to hold, grip, or keep tenaciously ⟨*hang on to* your money⟩

**hang·out** \'haŋ-,aut\ *noun* (circa 1893)

◻ USAGE
**hang** For both transitive and intransitive senses 1b the past and past participle *hung*, as well as *hanged*, is standard. *Hanged* is most appropriate for official executions ⟨he was to be *hanged*, cut down whilst still alive . . . and his bowels torn out —Louis Allen⟩ but *hung* is also used ⟨gave orders that she should be *hung* —Peter Quennell⟩. *Hung* is more appropriate for less formal hangings ⟨by morning I'll be *hung* in effigy —Ronald Reagan⟩.

: a favorite place for spending time; *also* : a place frequented for entertainment or for socializing
**hang out** (14th century)
*intransitive verb*
**1** : to protrude and droop
**2 a** *slang* : LIVE, RESIDE **b** : HANG AROUND
*transitive verb*
: to display outside as an announcement to the public — used chiefly in the phrase *hang out one's shingle*
**hang·over** \'haŋ-ˌō-vər\ *noun* (1894)
**1** : something (as a surviving custom) that remains from what is past
**2 a** : disagreeable physical effects following heavy consumption of alcohol or the use of drugs **b** : a letdown following great excitement or excess
**hang·tag** \'haŋ-ˌtag\ *noun* (1952)
: a tag attached to an article of merchandise giving information about its material and proper care
**hang time** *noun* (1976)
: the amount of time a kicked football remains in the air; *also* : the length of time a leaping athlete is in the air
**hang together** *intransitive verb* (1551)
**1** : to remain united : stand by one another
**2** : to have unity : form a consistent or coherent whole
**Hang·town fry** \'haŋ-ˌtaùn-\ *noun, often F capitalized* [*Hangtown,* nickname for Placerville, Calif.] (1949)
: an omelet or scrambled eggs containing oysters
**han·gul** \'hän-ˌgül\ *noun, often capitalized* [Korean *hangŭl*] (1946)
: the alphabetic script in which Korean is written
**hang–up** \'haŋ-ˌəp\ *noun* (1959)
: a source of mental or emotional difficulty; *broadly* : PROBLEM
**hang up** (12th century)
*transitive verb*
**1 a** : to place on a hook or hanger designed for the purpose ⟨*hang up* your coat⟩ **b** : to replace (a telephone receiver) on the cradle so that the connection is broken
**2** : to keep delayed, suspended, or held up
**3** : to cause to stick or snag immovably ⟨the ship was *hung up* on a sandbar⟩
*intransitive verb*
**1** : to break a telephone connection
**2** : to become stuck or snagged so as to be immovable
**ha·ni·wa** \'hä-nə-ˌwä\ *noun plural, often capitalized* [Japanese] (1931)
: large hollow baked clay sculptures placed on ancient Japanese burial mounds
**hank** \'haŋk\ *noun* [Middle English, of Scandinavian origin; akin to Old Norse *hǫnk* hank; akin to Old English *hangian* to hang] (14th century)
**1** : COIL, LOOP; *specifically* : a coiled or looped bundle (as of yarn or rope) usually containing a definite yardage
**2** : any of a series of rings or clips by which a jib or staysail is attached to a stay
**han·ker** \'haŋ-kər\ *intransitive verb* **han·kered; han·ker·ing** \-k(ə-)riŋ\ [probably from Flemish *hankeren,* frequentative of *hangen* to hang; akin to Old English *hangian*] (1642)
: to have a strong or persistent desire : YEARN — often used with *for* or *after*
**synonym** see LONG
— **han·ker·er** \-kər-ər\ *noun*
**han·kie** *or* **han·ky** \'haŋ-kē\ *noun, plural* **hankies** [*handkerchief* + *-ie*] (1895)
: HANDKERCHIEF
**han·ky–pan·ky** \ˌhaŋ-kē-'paŋ-kē\ *noun* [origin unknown] (1841)
**1** : questionable or underhanded activity
**2** : sexual dalliance
**¹Han·o·ve·ri·an** \ˌha-nə-'vir-ē-ən, -'ver-\ *adjective* [*Hanover,* Germany] (circa 1775)

**1** : of, relating to, or supporting the German ducal house of Hanover
**2** : of or relating to the British royal house that ruled from 1714 to 1901
**²Hanoverian** *noun* (1827)
: a member or supporter of the ducal or of the British royal Hanoverian house
**Han·sa** \'han(t)-sə, 'hän-(ˌ)zä\ *or* **Hanse** \'han(t)s, 'hän-zə\ *noun* [*Hansa* from Medieval Latin, from Middle Low German *hanse*; *Hanse* from Middle English *Hanze,* from Middle French *hanse,* from Middle Low German] (15th century)
**1** : a league originally constituted of merchants of various free German cities dealing abroad in the medieval period and later of the cities themselves and organized to secure greater safety and privileges in trading
**2** : a medieval merchant guild or trading association
— **Han·se·at·ic** \ˌhan(t)-sē-'a-tik\ *noun or adjective*
**Han·sard** \'han(t)-sərd, 'han-ˌsärd\ *noun* [Luke *Hansard*] (circa 1859)
: the official published report of debates in a Commonwealth parliament
**han·sel** *variant of* HANDSEL
**Han·sen's disease** \'han(t)-sənz-\ *noun* [Armauer *Hansen* (died 1912) Norwegian physician] (1938)
: LEPROSY
**han·som** \'han(t)-səm\ *noun* [Joseph A. *Hansom* (died 1882) English architect] (1847)
: a light 2-wheeled covered carriage with the driver's seat elevated behind — called also *hansom cab*
**hant** \'hant\ *dialect variant of* HAUNT
**Ha·nuk·kah** \'hä-nə-kə, 'kä-\ *noun* [Hebrew *ḥanukkāh* dedication] (1891)
: an 8-day Jewish holiday beginning on the 25th of Kislev and commemorating the rededication of the Temple of Jerusalem after its defilement by Antiochus of Syria
**hao** \'haù\ *noun, plural* **hao** [Vietnamese *hào*] (1948)
: a monetary unit of Vietnam equal to ¹/₁₀ dong
**hao·le** \'haù-lē, -(ˌ)lā\ *noun* [Hawaiian] (1834)
: one who is not descended from the aboriginal Polynesian inhabitants of Hawaii; *especially* : WHITE — sometimes used disparagingly
**¹hap** \'hap\ *noun* [Middle English, from Old Norse *happ* good luck; akin to Old English *gehæp* suitable, Old Church Slavonic *kobĭ* lot, fate] (13th century)
**1** : HAPPENING 1
**2** : CHANCE, FORTUNE
**²hap** *intransitive verb* **happed; hap·ping** (14th century)
: HAPPEN
**³hap** *transitive verb* **happed; hap·ping** [Middle English *happen*] (14th century)
*dialect* : CLOTHE, COVER
**⁴hap** *noun* (1724)
*dialect* : something (as a bed quilt or cloak) that serves as a covering or wrap
**ha·pa hao·le** \ˌhä-pə-'haù-lē, -(ˌ)lā\ *adjective* [Hawaiian, from *hapa* half (from English *half*) + *haole*] (1919)
: of part-white ancestry or origin; *especially* : of white and Hawaiian ancestry
**ha·pax le·go·me·non** \ˌha-ˌpaks-li-'gä-mə-ˌnän, ˌhä-ˌpäks-, -nən\ *noun, plural* **hapax le·go·me·na** \-nə\ [Greek, something said only once] (1882)
: a word or form occurring only once in a document or corpus
**ha·'pen·ny** \'hāp-nē, 'hā-pə-\ *noun* [by contraction] (circa 1550)

: HALFPENNY
**¹hap·haz·ard** \(ˌ)hap-'ha-zərd\ *noun* [¹*hap* + *hazard*] (1576)
: CHANCE
**²haphazard** *adjective* (1671)
: marked by lack of plan, order, or direction
**synonym** see RANDOM
— **hap·haz·ard** *adverb*
— **hap·haz·ard·ly** *adverb*
— **hap·haz·ard·ness** *noun*
— **hap·haz·ard·ry** \-zər-drē\ *noun*
**hapl-** *or* **haplo-** *combining form* [New Latin, from Greek, from *haploos,* from *ha-* one (akin to *homos* same) + *-ploos* multiplied by; akin to Latin *-plex* -fold — more at SAME, -FOLD]
**1** : single ⟨*haplology*⟩
**2** : haploid ⟨*haplont*⟩
**hap·less** \'ha-pləs\ *adjective* (14th century)
: having no luck : UNFORTUNATE
— **hap·less·ly** *adverb*
— **hap·less·ness** *noun*
**hap·loid** \'ha-ˌplóid\ *adjective* [International Scientific Vocabulary, from Greek *haploeidēs* single, from *haploos*] (1908)
: having the gametic number of chromosomes or half the number characteristic of somatic cells — compare DIPLOID
— **haploid** *noun*
— **hap·loi·dy** \-ˌplói-dē\ *noun*
**hap·lol·o·gy** \ha-'plä-lə-jē\ *noun* (1895)
: contraction of a word by omission of one or more similar sounds or syllables (as in *mineralogy* for \**mineralology* or \'prä-blē\ for *probably*)
**hap·lont** \'ha-ˌplänt\ *noun* [International Scientific Vocabulary] (1920)
: an organism (as some primitive algae) having a diploid zygote that undergoes meiosis to produce haploid cells — compare DIPLONT
— **hap·lon·tic** \ha-'plän-tik\ *adjective*
**hap·lo·type** \'ha-plō-ˌtīp\ *noun* (1969)
: a set of genes that determine different antigens but are closely enough linked to be inherited as a unit; *also* : the antigenic phenotype determined by a haplotype
**hap·ly** \'ha-plē\ *adverb* (14th century)
: by chance, luck, or accident
**hap·pen** \'ha-pən, -pᵊm\ *intransitive verb* **hap·pened; hap·pen·ing** \'hap-niŋ, 'ha-pə-\ [Middle English, from *hap*] (14th century)
**1** : to occur by chance — often used with *it* ⟨it so *happens* I'm going your way⟩
**2** : to come into being or occur as an event, process, or result ⟨mistakes will *happen*⟩ ⟨what good things *happened* to you?⟩

hansom

---

◇ WORD HISTORY

**hangnail** *Hangnail* is altered by folk etymology from *angnail* or *agnail,* which in its earliest sense did not mean what we now call a hangnail. In Old English *angnægl* was used to mean "corn on the foot," with the second element, *nægl,* referring not to a fingernail or toenail but rather to the nail we drive in with a hammer, the head of an iron nail being likened to a hard corn. By the 16th century the association of *-nail* with the body's nails led to a new sense, "a sore or inflammation around a fingernail or toenail." The first element *ang-* or *ag-,* which is related to an Old English adjective *enge,* meaning "tight, painful," had ceased to be interpretable since Old English. In the next century it was altered to *hang-,* and the dominant sense of both *hangnail* and *agnail* came to be "a bit of loose skin at the side or root of a fingernail."

---

\ə\ abut \ᵊ\ kitten \ər\ further \a\ ash \ā\ ace
\ä\ mop, mar \aù\ out \ch\ chin \e\ bet \ē\ easy
\g\ go \i\ hit \ī\ ice \j\ job \ŋ\ sing \ō\ go
\ó\ law \ói\ boy \th\ thin \th\ the \ü\ loot \ù\ foot
\y\ yet \zh\ vision *see also* Guide to Pronunciation

**3 :** to do, encounter, or attain something by or as if by chance ⟨*happened* to overhear the plotters⟩
**4 a :** to meet or discover something by chance ⟨*happened* upon a system that worked —Richard Corbin⟩ **b :** to come or go casually **:** make a chance appearance ⟨he *happened* into the room just then⟩
**5 :** to come especially by way of injury or harm ⟨I promise nothing will *happen* to you⟩

**hap·pen·chance** \'ha-pən-ˌchan(t)s, 'ha-pᵊm-\ *noun* (1876)
**:** HAPPENSTANCE

**hap·pen·ing** *noun* (1551)
**1 :** something that happens **:** OCCURRENCE
**2 :** an event or series of events designed to evoke a spontaneous reaction to sensory, emotional, or spiritual stimuli
**3 :** something (as an event) that is particularly interesting, entertaining, or important

**hap·pen·stance** \'ha-pən-ˌstan(t)s, 'ha-pᵊm-\ *noun* [*happen* + circum*stance*] (1897)
**:** a circumstance especially that is due to chance
**— hap·pen·stance** *adjective*

**hap·pi·ly** \'ha-pə-lē\ *adverb* (14th century)
**1 a :** in a fortunate manner **b :** as it fortunately happens ⟨*happily*, some boyhood pleasures don't change —P. A. Witteman⟩
**2** *archaic* **:** by chance
**3 :** in a happy manner or state ⟨lived *happily* ever after⟩
**4 :** in an adequate or fitting manner **:** SUCCESSFULLY

**hap·pi·ness** \'ha-pi-nəs\ *noun* (15th century)
**1** *obsolete* **:** good fortune **:** PROSPERITY
**2 a :** a state of well-being and contentment **:** JOY **b :** a pleasurable or satisfying experience
**3 :** FELICITY, APTNESS

**hap·py** \'ha-pē\ *adjective* **hap·pi·er; -est** [Middle English, from *hap*] (14th century)
**1 :** favored by luck or fortune **:** FORTUNATE
**2 :** notably fitting, effective, or well adapted **:** FELICITOUS ⟨a *happy* choice⟩
**3 a :** enjoying or characterized by well-being and contentment **:** JOYOUS **b :** expressing or suggestive of happiness **:** PLEASANT **c :** GLAD, PLEASED **d :** having or marked by an atmosphere of good fellowship **:** FRIENDLY
**4 a :** characterized by a dazed irresponsible state ⟨a punch-*happy* boxer⟩ **b :** impulsively or obsessively quick to use or do something ⟨trigger-*happy*⟩ **c :** enthusiastic about something to the point of obsession **:** OBSESSED ⟨education-conscious and statistic-*happy* —Helen Rowen⟩
**synonym** see LUCKY, FIT

**hap·py–go–lucky** \ˌha-pē-gō-'lə-kē\ *adjective* (1856)
**:** blithely unconcerned **:** CAREFREE

**happy hour** *noun* (1961)
**:** a period of time during which the price of drinks (as at a bar) is reduced or hors d'oeuvres are served free

**happy hunting ground** *noun* (1837)
**1 :** the paradise of some American Indian tribes to which the souls of warriors and hunters pass after death to spend a happy hereafter in hunting and feasting
**2 :** a choice or profitable area of activity or exploitation

**happy talk** *noun* (1973)
**:** informal talk among the participants in a television news broadcast; *also* **:** a broadcast format featuring such talk

**Haps·burg** \'haps-ˌbərg, 'häps-ˌbùrg\ *adjective* [*Habsburg*, Aargau, Switzerland] (circa 1895)
**:** of or relating to the German royal house to which belong the rulers of Austria from 1278 to 1918, the rulers of Spain from 1516 to 1700, and many of the Holy Roman emperors
**— Hapsburg** *noun*

**hap·ten** \'hap-ˌten\ *noun* [German, from Greek *haptein* to fasten] (1921)
**:** a small separable part of an antigen that reacts specifically with an antibody but is inca-

pable of stimulating antibody production except in combination with a carrier protein molecule
**— hap·ten·ic** \hap-'te-nik\ *adjective*

**hap·tic** \'hap-tik\ *adjective* [International Scientific Vocabulary, from Greek *haptesthai* to touch] (circa 1890)
**1 :** relating to or based on the sense of touch
**2 :** characterized by a predilection for the sense of touch ⟨a *haptic* person⟩

**hap·to·glo·bin** \'hap-tə-ˌglō-bən\ *noun* [International Scientific Vocabulary, from Greek *haptein* + International Scientific Vocabulary hem*oglobin*] (1941)
**:** any of several carbohydrate-containing serum alpha globulins that can combine with free hemoglobin in the plasma

**hara–kiri** \ˌhar-i-'kir-ē, -'kar-ē\ *noun* [Japanese *harakiri*, from *hara* belly + *kiri* cutting] (1840)
**1 :** ritual suicide by disembowelment practiced by the Japanese samurai or formerly decreed by a court in lieu of the death penalty
**2 :** SUICIDE 1b

**¹ha·rangue** \hə-'raŋ\ *noun* [Middle English *arang*, from Middle French *arenge*, from Old Italian *aringa*, from *aringare* to speak in public, from *aringo* public assembly, of Germanic origin; akin to Old High German *hring* ring] (15th century)
**1 :** a speech addressed to a public assembly
**2 :** a ranting speech or writing
**3 :** LECTURE

**²harangue** *verb* **ha·rangued; ha·rangu·ing** (1660)
*intransitive verb*
**:** to make a harangue **:** DECLAIM
*transitive verb*
**:** to address in a harangue ⟨*haranguing* me . . . on the folly of my ways —Jay Jacobs⟩
**— ha·rangu·er** *noun*

**ha·rass** \hə-'ras, 'har-əs\ *transitive verb* [French *harasser*, from Middle French, from *harer* to set a dog on, from Old French *hare*, interjection used to incite dogs, of Germanic origin; akin to Old High German *hier* here — more at HERE] (1617)
**1 a :** EXHAUST, FATIGUE **b :** to annoy persistently
**2 :** to worry and impede by repeated raids ⟨*harassed* the enemy⟩ ◼
**synonym** see WORRY
**— ha·rass·er** *noun*
**— ha·rass·ment** \-mənt\ *noun*

**¹har·bin·ger** \'här-bən-jər\ *noun* [Middle English *herbergere*, from Middle French, host, from *herberge* hostelry, of Germanic origin; akin to Old High German *heriberga*] (14th century)
**1** *archaic* **:** a person sent ahead to provide lodgings
**2 a :** one that pioneers in or initiates a major change **:** PRECURSOR **b :** one that presages or foreshadows what is to come ◆
**synonym** see FORERUNNER

**²harbinger** *transitive verb* (1646)
**:** to be a harbinger of **:** PRESAGE

**¹har·bor** \'här-bər\ *noun* [Middle English *herbere*, *herberwe*, from Old English *herebeorg* military quarters, from *here* army (akin to Old High German *heri*) + *beorg* refuge; akin to Old English *burg* fortified town — more at HARRY, BOROUGH] (12th century)
**1 :** a place of security and comfort **:** REFUGE
**2 :** a part of a body of water protected and deep enough to furnish anchorage; *especially* **:** one with port facilities
*word history* see HARBINGER
**— har·bor·ful** \-ˌfùl\ *noun*
**— har·bor·less** \-ləs\ *adjective*

**²harbor** *verb* **har·bored; har·bor·ing** \-b(ə-)riŋ\ (12th century)
*transitive verb*
**1 a :** to give shelter or refuge to **b :** to be the home or habitat of ⟨the ledges still *harbor* rattlesnakes⟩; *broadly* **:** CONTAIN 2

**2 :** to hold especially persistently in the mind **:** CHERISH ⟨*harbored* a grudge⟩
*intransitive verb*
**1 :** to take shelter in or as if in a harbor
**2 :** LIVE
**— har·bor·er** \-bər-ər\ *noun*

**har·bor·age** \-bə-rij\ *noun* (15th century)
**:** SHELTER, HARBOR

**har·bor·mas·ter** \'här-bər-ˌmas-tər\ *noun* (1769)
**:** an officer who executes the regulations respecting the use of a harbor

**harbor seal** *noun* (1766)
**:** a small seal (*Phoca vitulina*) that occurs along oceanic coasts of the northern hemisphere and often ascends rivers

**har·bor·side** \'här-bər-ˌsīd\ *adjective* (1924)
**:** located next to a harbor

**har·bour** *chiefly British variant of* HARBOR

**¹hard** \'härd\ *adjective* [Middle English, from Old English *heard*; akin to Old High German *hart* hard, Greek *kratos* strength] (before 12th century)
**1 a :** not easily penetrated **:** not easily yielding to pressure **b** *of cheese* **:** not capable of being spread **:** very firm
**2 a** *of liquor* (1) **:** having a harsh or acid taste (2) **:** strongly alcoholic **b :** characterized by the presence of salts (as of calcium or magnesium) that prevent lathering with soap ⟨*hard* water⟩
**3 a :** of or relating to radiation of relatively high penetrating power ⟨*hard* X rays⟩ **b :** having or producing relatively great photographic contrast ⟨a *hard* negative⟩
**4 a :** metallic as distinct from paper ⟨*hard* money⟩ **b** *of currency* **:** convertible into gold **c :** stable in value **:** usable as currency ⟨paid in *hard* cash⟩ **d** *of currency* **:** readily acceptable in international trade **e :** being high and firm ⟨*hard* prices⟩
**5 a :** firmly and closely twisted ⟨*hard* yarns⟩ **b :** having a smooth close napless finish ⟨a *hard* worsted⟩

**6 a** : physically fit ⟨in good *hard* condition⟩ **b** : resistant to stress (as disease) **c** : free of weakness or defects
**7 a** (1) : FIRM, DEFINITE ⟨reached a *hard* agreement⟩ (2) : not speculative or conjectural : FACTUAL ⟨*hard* evidence⟩ (3) : important or informative rather than sensational or entertaining ⟨*hard* news⟩ **b** : CLOSE, SEARCHING ⟨gave a *hard* look⟩ **c** : free from sentimentality or illusion : REALISTIC ⟨good *hard* sense⟩ **d** : lacking in responsiveness : OBDURATE, UNFEELING ⟨a *hard* heart⟩
**8 a** (1) : difficult to bear or endure ⟨*hard* luck⟩ ⟨*hard* times⟩ (2) : OPPRESSIVE, INEQUITABLE ⟨sales taxes are *hard* on the poor⟩ ⟨a *hard* restriction⟩ **b** (1) : lacking consideration, compassion, or gentleness : CALLOUS ⟨a *hard* greedy landlord⟩ (2) : INCORRIGIBLE, TOUGH ⟨a *hard* gang⟩ **c** (1) : harsh, severe, or offensive in tendency or effect ⟨said some *hard* things⟩ (2) : RESENTFUL ⟨*hard* feelings⟩ (3) : STRICT, UNRELENTING ⟨drives a *hard* bargain⟩ **d** : INCLEMENT ⟨*hard* winter⟩ **e** (1) : intense in force, manner, or degree ⟨*hard* blows⟩ (2) : demanding the exertion of energy : calling for stamina and endurance ⟨*hard* work⟩ (3) : performing or carrying on with great energy, intensity, or persistence ⟨a *hard* worker⟩ **f** : EXTREME 4a ⟨the *hard* political right⟩
**9 a** : characterized by sharp or harsh outline, rigid execution, and stiff drawing **b** : sharply defined : STARK ⟨*hard* shadows⟩ **c** : lacking in shading, delicacy, or resonance ⟨*hard* singing tones⟩ **d** : sounding as in *arcing* and *geese* respectively — used of *c* and *g* **e** : suggestive of toughness or insensitivity ⟨*hard* eyes⟩
**10 a** (1) : difficult to accomplish or resolve : TROUBLESOME ⟨*hard* problems⟩ ⟨the true story was *hard* to come by⟩ (2) : difficult to comprehend or explain ⟨a *hard* concept⟩ **b** : having difficulty in doing something ⟨*hard* of hearing⟩ **c** : difficult to magnetize or demagnetize
**11** : being at once addictive and gravely detrimental to health ⟨such *hard* drugs as heroin⟩
**12** : resistant to biodegradation ⟨*hard* detergents⟩ ⟨*hard* pesticides like DDT⟩
**13** : being, schooled in, or using the methods of the natural sciences and especially of the physical sciences ⟨a *hard* scientist⟩ ☆

**²hard** *adverb* (before 12th century)
**1 a** : with great or utmost effort or energy : STRENUOUSLY ⟨were *hard* at work⟩ ⟨the children played *hard*⟩ **b** : in a violent manner : FIERCELY **c** : to the full extent — usually used in nautical directions ⟨steer *hard* aport⟩ **d** : to an immoderate degree ⟨hitting the bottle *hard*⟩ **e** : in a searching, close, or concentrated manner ⟨stared *hard* at me⟩
**2 a** : in such a manner as to cause hardship, difficulty, or pain **b** : with rancor, bitterness, or grief ⟨took the defeat *hard*⟩
**3** : in a firm manner : TIGHTLY
**4** : to the point of hardness ⟨frozen *hard*⟩
**5** : close in time or space ⟨stands *hard* by the river⟩

**hard–and–fast** \ˌhär-dᵊn-ˈfast\ *adjective* (1867)
: not to be modified or evaded : STRICT ⟨a *hard-and-fast* rule⟩
**hard-ass** \ˈhär-ˌdas\ *noun* (1972)
: a tough, demanding, or uncompromising person — often considered vulgar
— **hard–assed** \ˌdast\ *adjective*
**hard-back** \ˈhärd-ˌbak\ *noun* (1952)
: a book bound in hard covers
**hard-ball** \ˌbȯl\ *noun* (circa 1883)
**1** : BASEBALL
**2** : forceful uncompromising methods employed to gain an end ⟨played political *hardball*⟩
**hard–bit-ten** \ˈbi-tᵊn\ *adjective* (1784)
**1** : inclined to bite hard
**2** : seasoned or steeled by difficult experience : TOUGH
**hard-board** \ˈhärd-ˌbȯrd, -ˌbȯrd\ *noun* (1925)

: a very dense fiberboard usually having one smooth face
**hard–boil** \ˈbȯi(ə)l\ *transitive verb* [back-formation from *hard-boiled*] (1895)
: to cook (an egg) in the shell until both white and yolk have solidified
**hard–boiled** \ˈbȯi(ə)ld\ *adjective* (1886)
**1 a** : devoid of sentimentality : TOUGH ⟨a *hard-boiled* drill sergeant⟩ **b** : of, relating to, or being a detective story featuring a tough unsentimental protagonist and a matter-of-fact attitude towards violence
**2** : HARDHEADED, PRACTICAL ⟨handle aid programs on a friendly but *hard-boiled* business basis —*N.Y. Times*⟩
**hard-boot** \ˌbüt\ *noun* (1922)
: an especially small-time horseman
**hard-bound** \ˌbaȯnd\ *adjective* (1926)
: HARDCOVER
**hard candy** *noun* (1925)
: a candy made of sugar and corn syrup boiled without crystallizing
**hard-case** \ˈhärd-ˈkās\ *adjective* (1896)
: HARD-BITTEN, TOUGH
**hard case** \ˌkās\ *noun* (1836)
: a tough or hardened person
**hard cheese** *noun* (1861)
*chiefly British* : tough luck — often used interjectionally
**hard cider** *noun* (1789)
: fermented apple juice
**hard clam** *noun* (1846)
: a clam with a thick hard shell; *specifically* : QUAHOG
**hard coal** *noun* (1846)
: ANTHRACITE
**hard–coat·ed** \ˈhärd-ˈkō-təd\ *adjective* (circa 1898)
*of a dog* : having a crisp harsh-textured coat
**hard copy** *noun* (1954)
: a copy of textual or graphic information (as from microfilm or computer storage) produced on paper in normal size
**hard–core** \ˈkōr, -ˈkȯr\ *adjective* (1940)
**1 a** : of, relating to, or being part of a hard core ⟨*hard-core* poverty⟩ ⟨the *hard-core* unemployed⟩ **b** : CONFIRMED, DIE-HARD ⟨*hard-core* rock fans⟩ ⟨a *hard-core* liberal⟩
**2** *of pornography* : containing explicit descriptions of sex acts or scenes of actual sex acts — compare SOFT-CORE
**3** : characterized by or being the purest or most basic form of something : FUNDAMENTAL ⟨a room gussied up in *hard-core* French provincial style —John Canaday⟩
**hard core** *noun* (1936)
**1** : a central or fundamental and usually enduring group or part: as **a** : a relatively small enduring core of society marked by apparent resistance to change or inability to escape a persistent wretched condition (as poverty or chronic unemployment) **b** : a militant or fiercely loyal faction
**2** *usually* **hard-core** \ˌkōr, -ˌkȯr\ *chiefly British* : hard material in pieces (as broken bricks or stone) used as a bottom (as in making roads and in foundations)
**hard·cov·er** \ˈhärd-ˈkə-vər\ *adjective* (1949)
**1** : having rigid boards on the sides covered in cloth or paper ⟨*hardcover* books⟩
**2** : of or relating to hardcover books ⟨*hardcover* sales⟩
— **hardcover** *noun*
**hard disk** *noun* (1978)
: a rigid metal disk that is sealed against dust and is used as a high-capacity storage device for a microcomputer
**hard drive** *noun* (1983)
: a disk drive containing one or more hard disks
**hard–edge** \ˈhärd-ˈej\ *adjective* (1961)
: of or relating to abstract painting characterized by geometric forms with clearly defined boundaries
**hard–edged** \ˌˈejd\ *adjective* (1954)

: having a tough, driving, or sharp quality ⟨*hard-edged* stories about life in the city⟩
**hard·en** \ˈhär-dᵊn\ *verb* **hard·ened; hard·en·ing** \ˈhärd-niŋ, ˈhär-dᵊn-iŋ\ (13th century)
*transitive verb*
**1** : to make hard or harder
**2** : to confirm in disposition, feelings, or action; *especially* : to make callous ⟨*hardened* his heart⟩
**3 a** : INURE, TOUGHEN ⟨*harden* troops⟩ **b** : to inure to unfavorable environmental conditions (as cold) — often used with *off* ⟨*harden* off plants⟩
**4** : to protect from blast, heat, or radiation (as by a thick barrier or placement underground)
*intransitive verb*
**1** : to become hard or harder
**2 a** : to become firm, stable, or settled **b** : to assume an appearance of harshness or severity ⟨her face *hardened* at the word⟩
**hard·en·er** \ˈhärd-nər, ˈhär-dᵊn-ər\ *noun* (1611)
: one that hardens; *especially* : a substance added (as to a paint or varnish) to harden the film
**hard·en·ing** *noun* (1953)
: SCLEROSIS ⟨*hardening* of the arteries⟩
**hard–fist·ed** \ˈhärd-ˈfis-təd\ *adjective* (circa 1656)
**1** : STINGY, CLOSEFISTED
**2** : HARDHANDED 2
**hard goods** *noun plural* (1934)
: DURABLES
**hard·hack** \ˈhärd-ˌhak\ *noun* (1814)
: a shrubby American spirea (*Spiraea tomentosa*) with dense terminal panicles of pink or occasionally white flowers and leaves having a hairy and yellow to rust-colored underside
**hard·hand·ed** \ˌ-ˈhan-dəd\ *adjective* (1590)
**1** : having hands made hard by labor
**2** : STRICT, OPPRESSIVE
— **hard·hand·ed·ness** *noun*
**hard hat** \*usually* -ˈhat *for 1 and* -ˌhat *for 2 & 3*\ *noun* (1926)
**1 a** : a protective hat made of rigid material (as metal or fiberglass) and worn especially by construction workers **b** : a construction worker
**2** : a conservative who is intolerant of opposing views
**hard·head** \ˈhärd-ˌhed\ *noun* (15th century)
**1 a** : a hardheaded person **b** : BLOCKHEAD
**2** *plural* **hardheads** *also* **hardhead** : any of several fishes especially with a spiny or bony head; *especially* : ATLANTIC CROAKER
**hard·head·ed** \ˌ-ˈhe-dəd\ *adjective* (1583)
**1** : STUBBORN, WILLFUL
**2** : concerned with or involving practical considerations : SOBER, REALISTIC ⟨some *hardheaded* advice⟩ ⟨a *hardheaded* observer of winds and tides⟩
— **hard·head·ed·ly** *adverb*
— **hard·head·ed·ness** *noun*
**hard–heart·ed** \ˈhär-təd\ *adjective* (13th century)
: lacking in sympathetic understanding : UNFEELING, PITILESS

---

☆ **SYNONYMS**
**Hard, difficult, arduous** mean demanding great exertion or effort. HARD implies the opposite of all that is easy ⟨farming is *hard* work⟩. DIFFICULT implies the presence of obstacles to be surmounted or puzzles to be resolved and suggests the need of skill, patience, or courage ⟨the *difficult* ascent of the main face of the mountain⟩. ARDUOUS stresses the need of laborious and persevering exertion ⟨the *arduous* task of rebuilding⟩.

---

— **hard–heart·ed·ly** *adverb*
— **hard–heart·ed·ness** *noun*
**hard–hit·ting** \-'hi·tiŋ\ *adjective* (1926)
: strikingly effective in force or result ⟨a *hard-hitting* exposé⟩ ⟨plain *hard-hitting* English⟩
**har·di·hood** \'här-dē-ˌhůd\ *noun* (1570)
**1 a** : resolute courage and fortitude **b** : resolute and self-assured audacity often carried to the point of impudent insolence
**2** : VIGOR, ROBUSTNESS
**synonym** see TEMERITY
**har·di·ment** \-mənt\ *noun* [Middle English, from Middle French, from Old French, from *hardi* bold, hardy] (14th century)
**1** *archaic* : HARDIHOOD
**2** *obsolete* : a bold deed
**har·ding·grass** \'här-diŋ-ˌgras\ *noun, often capitalized* [R. R. *Harding* (flourished about 1900) Australian botanist] (1917)
: a perennial grass (*Phalaris tuberosa* variety *stenoptera*) widely used as a forage grass
**hard knocks** *noun plural* (1913)
: rough unsparing treatment (as in use or in life) — often used in the phrase *school of hard knocks*
**hard labor** *noun* (1841)
: compulsory labor of imprisoned criminals as a part of the prison discipline
**hard–line** \'härd-'līn\ *adjective* (1962)
: advocating or involving a rigidly uncompromising course of action
— **hard–lin·er** \-'lī-nər\ *noun*
**hard lines** *noun plural* (1824)
*chiefly British* : hard luck — often used interjectionally
**hard·ly** \'härd-lē\ *adverb* (before 12th century)
**1** : with force : VIGOROUSLY
**2** : in a severe manner : HARSHLY
**3** : with difficulty : PAINFULLY
**4 a** — used to emphasize a minimal amount ⟨I *hardly* knew her⟩ ⟨almost never — *hardly* a scratch on it⟩ **b** — used to soften a negative ⟨you can't *hardly* tell who anyone is —G. B. Shaw⟩
**5** : certainly not ⟨that news is *hardly* surprising⟩ ▯
**hard maple** *noun* (1790)
: SUGAR MAPLE
**hard–mouthed** \'härd-'maůthd, -'maůtht\ *adjective* (1617)
**1** *of a horse* : not sensitive to the bit
**2** : OBSTINATE, STUBBORN
**hard·ness** \-nəs\ *noun* (before 12th century)
**1** : the quality or state of being hard
**2 a** : the cohesion of the particles on the surface of a mineral as determined by its capacity to scratch another or be itself scratched — compare MOHS' SCALE **b** : resistance of metal to indentation under a static load or to scratching
**hard·nose** \'härd-ˌnōz\ *noun* (circa 1960)
: a hard-nosed person
**hard–nosed** \'härd-'nōzd\ *adjective* (circa 1927)
**1** : being tough, stubborn, or uncompromising
**2** : HARDHEADED 2, TOUGH-MINDED
**hard–of–hear·ing** \ˌhär-də(v)-'hir-iŋ\ *adjective* (1564)
: of or relating to a defective but functional sense of hearing
**hard–on** \'här-ˌdȯn, -ˌdän\ *noun, plural* **hard–ons** (circa 1893)
: an erection of the penis — sometimes considered vulgar
**hard palate** *noun* (circa 1847)
: the bony anterior part of the palate forming the roof of the mouth
**hard·pan** \'härd-ˌpan\ *noun* (1817)
**1** : a cemented or compacted and often clayey layer in soil that is impenetrable by roots
**2** : a fundamental part : BEDROCK
**hard pine** *noun* (1884)
: a pine (as longleaf pine or pitch pine) that has hard wood and leaves usually in groups of two or three; *also* : the wood of a hard pine
**hard–pressed** \'härd-'prest\ *adjective* (1825)

: HARD PUT; *also* : being under financial strain
**hard put** *adjective* (1893)
: barely able : faced with difficulty or perplexity ⟨was *hard put* to find an explanation⟩
**hard rock** *noun* (1967)
: rock music marked by a heavy regular beat, high amplification, and usually frenzied performances
**hard rubber** *noun* (1860)
: a firm rubber or rubber product; *especially* : a normally black horny substance made by vulcanizing natural rubber with high percentages of sulfur
**hard sauce** *noun* (1880)
: a creamed mixture of butter and powdered sugar often with added cream and flavoring (as vanilla or rum)
**hard·scrab·ble** \'härd-ˌskra-bəl\ *adjective* (1804)
**1 a** : being or relating to a place of barren or barely arable soil ⟨a *hardscrabble* farm⟩ ⟨*hardscrabble* prairies⟩ **b** : getting a meager living from poor soil ⟨a *hardscrabble* farmer⟩
**2** : marked by poverty ⟨a *hardscrabble* cotton town⟩ ⟨a *hardscrabble* childhood⟩
**hard sell** *noun* (1952)
: aggressive high-pressure salesmanship — compare SOFT SELL
**hard–set** \'härd-'set\ *adjective* (1813)
: RIGID, FIXED
**hard–shell** \-ˌshel\ *or* **hard–shelled** \-ˌsheld\ *adjective* (1838)
**1** : FUNDAMENTAL 2b, FUNDAMENTALIST ⟨a *hard-shell* preacher⟩ ⟨*hard-shell* Baptists⟩; *also* : UNCOMPROMISING, HIDEBOUND ⟨a *hard-shell* conservative⟩
**hard–shell clam** *noun* (1799)
: QUAHOG — called also *hard-shelled clam*
**hard–shell crab** *noun* (1902)
: a crab that has not recently shed its shell — called also *hard-shelled crab*
**hard·ship** \'härd-ˌship\ *noun* (13th century)
**1** : PRIVATION, SUFFERING
**2** : something that causes or entails suffering or privation
**hard·stand** \-ˌstand\ *noun* (1944)
: a paved area for parking an airplane
**hard·stand·ing** \-ˌstan-diŋ\ *noun* (1944)
*chiefly British* : HARDSTAND; *also* : PARKING LOT
**hard stone** *noun* (1931)
: an opaque usually semiprecious stone that can be shaped or carved (as for jewelery or mosaics)
**hard·tack** \-ˌtak\ *noun, plural* **hardtack** *or* **hardtacks** (1836)
**1** : a saltless hard biscuit, bread, or cracker
**2** : any of several mountain mahoganies (especially *Cercocarpus betuloides*)
**hard–times token** *noun* (1922)
: any of the tokens issued during the controversy between the Jackson administration and the bank of the U.S.
**hard·top** \'härd-ˌtäp\ *noun* (1950)
: an automobile or a motorboat having a permanent rigid top; *also* : such an automobile styled to resemble a convertible
**hard up** *adjective* (1821)
**1** : short of money
**2** : poorly provided ⟨*hard up* for friends⟩
**hard·ware** \'härd-ˌwar, -ˌwer\ *noun* (circa 1515)
**1** : ware (as fittings, cutlery, tools, utensils, or parts of machines) made of metal
**2** : major items of equipment or their components used for a particular purpose (educational *hardware*) as **a** : military equipment **b** : the physical components (as electronic and electrical devices) of a vehicle (as a spacecraft) or an apparatus (as a computer)
**hardware cloth** *noun* (circa 1914)
: rugged galvanized screening
**hard wheat** *noun* (1812)
: a wheat with hard flinty kernels that are high in gluten and that yield a flour especially suitable for bread and macaroni

**hard–wired** \'härd-ˌwird\ *adjective* (1968)
: implemented in the form of permanent electronic circuits; *also* : having permanent electrical connections ⟨*hardwired* phone⟩
**hard–won** \-'wən\ *adjective* (circa 1843)
: gained by great effort
**¹hard·wood** \'härd-ˌwůd\ *noun* (1568)
**1** : the wood of an angiospermous tree as distinguished from that of a coniferous tree
**2** : a tree that yields hardwood
**²hardwood** *adjective* (circa 1817)
**1** : having or made of hardwood ⟨*hardwood* floors⟩
**2** : consisting of mature woody tissue ⟨*hardwood* cuttings⟩
**hard·work·ing** \'härd-'wər-kiŋ\ *adjective* (1774)
: INDUSTRIOUS
**har·dy** \'här-dē\ *adjective* **har·di·er; -est** [Middle English *hardi*, from Old French, from (assumed) Old French *hardir* to make hard, of Germanic origin; akin to Old English *heard* hard] (13th century)
**1** : BOLD, BRAVE
**2** : AUDACIOUS, BRAZEN
**3 a** : inured to fatigue or hardships : ROBUST **b** : capable of withstanding adverse conditions ⟨*hardy* outdoor furniture⟩ ⟨*hardy* plants⟩ ⟨*hardy* cattle⟩
— **har·di·ly** \'här-dᵊl-ē\ *adverb*
— **har·di·ness** \'här-dē-nəs\ *noun*
**Har·dy–Wein·berg law** \ˌhär-dē-'wīn-ˌbərg-\ *noun* [G. H. *Hardy* (died 1947) English mathematician and W. *Weinberg*, 20th century German scientist] (1950)
: a fundamental principle of population genetics: population gene frequencies and genotype frequencies remain constant from generation to generation if mating is random and if mutation, selection, immigration, and emigration do not occur — called also *Hardy-Weinberg principle*
**¹hare** \'har, 'her\ *noun, plural* **hare** *or* **hares** [Middle English, from Old English *hara*; akin to Old High German *haso* hare, Sanskrit *śaśa*, Old English *hasu* gray] (before 12th century)
: any of various swift long-eared lagomorph mammals (family Leporidae and especially genus *Lepus*) that are usually solitary or sometimes live in pairs and have the young open-eyed and furred at birth — compare RABBIT 1A
**²hare** *intransitive verb* **hared; har·ing** (1719)
: to go swiftly : ³TEAR
**hare and hounds** *noun* (circa 1845)
: a game in which some of the players leave a trail and others try to follow the trail to find and catch them
**hare·bell** \'har-ˌbel, 'her-\ *noun* (1765)
: a slender blue-flowered herb (*Campanula rotundifolia*) with linear leaves on the stem
**hare·brained** \-'brānd\ *adjective* (1534)
: FOOLISH 1, 2a
**Ha·re Krish·na** \ˌhär-ē-'krish-nə, ˌhar-\ *noun, plural* **Hare Krishna** *or* **Hare Krishnas**

☐ USAGE
**hardly** *Hardly* in sense 5 is used sometimes with *not* for emphasis (just another day at the office? Not *hardly*). In sense 4b with a negative verb (as *can't, wouldn't, didn't*) it does not make a double negative but softens the negative. In "you can't *hardly* find a red one," the sense is that you can find a red one, but only with difficulty; in "you can't find a red one," the sense is that red ones are simply not available. Use of *hardly* with a negative verb is a speech form; it is most commonly heard in Southern and Midland speech areas. In other speech areas and in all discursive prose, *hardly* is normally used with a positive (you can *hardly* find a red one).

[from *Hare Krishna*, phrase in a chant, from Hindi *hare Kṛṣṇa* O Krishna!] (1969)
**:** a member of a religious group dedicated to the worship of the Hindu god Krishna

**hare·lip** \'har-ˌlip, 'her-\ *noun* (1567)
**:** a congenital deformity characterized by a cleft upper lip resulting from failure of the embryonic parts of the lip to unite

**har·em** \'har-əm, 'her-\ *noun* [Arabic *ḥarīm*, literally, something forbidden & *ḥaram*, literally, sanctuary] (1623)
**1 a :** a usually secluded house or part of a house allotted to women in a Muslim household **b :** the wives, concubines, female relatives, and servants occupying a harem
**2 :** a group of women associated with one man
**3 :** a group of females associated with one male — used of polygamous animals

**harem pants** *noun* [from their oriental appearance] (1952)
**:** women's loose trousers that fit closely at the ankle

**har·i·cot** \'(h)ar-i-ˌkō\ *noun* [French] (1653)
**:** the ripe seed or the unripe pod of any of several beans (genus *Phaseolus* and especially *P. vulgaris*)

**ha·ri·jan** \ˌhär-i-'jän\ *noun, often capitalized* [Sanskrit *harijana* one belonging to the god Vishnu, from *Hari* Vishnu + *jana* person] (1931)
**:** a member of the outcaste group in India **:** UNTOUCHABLE

**hari-kari** \ˌhar-i-'kar-ē, -'kir-\ *variant of* HARA-KIRI

**hark** \'härk\ *intransitive verb* [Middle English *herkien;* akin to Old High German *hōrechen* to listen, Old English *hīeran* to hear] (14th century)
**:** to pay close attention **:** LISTEN

**hark back** *intransitive verb* (1829)
**1 :** to turn back to an earlier topic or circumstance
**2 :** to go back to something as an origin or source

**harken** *intransitive verb* (before 12th century)
**1 :** HEARKEN
**2 :** HARK BACK — usually used with *back*

**har·le·quin** \'här-li-k(w)ən\ *noun* [ultimately from Italian *arlecchino*, from Middle French *Helquin*, a demon] (1590)
**1 a** *capitalized* **:** a character in comedy and pantomime with a shaved head, masked face, variegated tights, and wooden sword **b :** BUFFOON
**2 a :** a variegated pattern (as of a textile) **b :** a combination of patches on a solid ground of contrasting color (as in the coats of some dogs)

**har·le·quin·ade** \ˌhär-li-k(w)ə-'nād\ *noun* (1790)
**:** a play or pantomime in which Harlequin has a leading role

**Harlequin**

**har·lot** \'här-lət\ *noun* [Middle English, from Old French *herlot* rogue] (15th century)
**:** PROSTITUTE

**har·lot·ry** \-lə-trē\ *noun, plural* **-ries** (14th century)
**1 :** sexual profligacy **:** PROSTITUTION
**2 :** an unprincipled or immoral woman ⟨he sups tonight with a *harlotry* —Shakespeare⟩

**¹harm** \'härm\ *noun* [Middle English, from Old English *hearm;* akin to Old High German *harm* injury, Old Church Slavonic *sramŭ* shame] (before 12th century)
**1 :** physical or mental damage **:** INJURY
**2 :** MISCHIEF, HURT

**²harm** *transitive verb* (before 12th century)
**:** to cause harm to
**synonym** *see* INJURE
— **harm·er** *noun*

**har·mat·tan** \ˌhär-mə-'tan, här-'ma-t°n\ *noun, often capitalized* [Twi *haramata*] (1671)

**:** a dust-laden wind on the Atlantic coast of Africa in some seasons

**harm·ful** \'härm-fəl\ *adjective* (14th century)
**:** of a kind likely to be damaging **:** INJURIOUS
— **harm·ful·ly** \-fə-lē\ *adverb*
— **harm·ful·ness** *noun*

**harm·less** \'härm-ləs\ *adjective* (14th century)
**1 :** free from harm, liability, or loss
**2 :** lacking capacity or intent to injure **:** INNOCUOUS
— **harm·less·ly** *adverb*
— **harm·less·ness** *noun*

**¹har·mon·ic** \här-'mä-nik\ *adjective* (1570)
**1 :** MUSICAL
**2 :** of or relating to musical harmony or a harmonic
**3 :** pleasing to the ear **:** HARMONIOUS
**4 :** of an integrated nature **:** CONGRUOUS
— **har·mon·i·cal·ly** \-ni-k(ə-)lē\ *adverb*

**²harmonic** *noun* (1777)
**1 a :** OVERTONE; *especially* **:** one whose vibration frequency is an integral multiple of that of the fundamental **b :** a flutelike tone produced on a stringed instrument by touching a vibrating string at a nodal point
**2 :** a component frequency of a complex wave (as of electromagnetic energy) that is an integral multiple of the fundamental frequency

**har·mon·i·ca** \här-'mä-ni-kə\ *noun* [Italian *armonica*, feminine of *armonico* harmonious] (1762)
**1 :** GLASS HARMONICA
**2 :** a small rectangular wind instrument with free reeds recessed in air slots from which tones are sounded by exhaling and inhaling
— **har·mon·i·cist** \-nə-sist\ *noun*

**harmonic analysis** *noun* (1867)
**:** the expression of a periodic function as a sum of sines and cosines and specifically by a Fourier series

**harmonic mean** *noun* (1856)
**:** the reciprocal of the arithmetic mean of the reciprocals of a finite set of numbers

**harmonic motion** *noun* (1867)
**:** a periodic motion (as of a sounding violin string or swinging pendulum) that has a single frequency or amplitude or a periodic motion that is composed of two or more such simple periodic motions

**harmonic progression** *noun* (1856)
**:** a sequence of numbers whose reciprocals form an arithmetic progression

**harmonic series** *noun* (1866)
**:** a series of the form

$$1 + \frac{1}{2^\alpha} + \frac{1}{3^\alpha} + \frac{1}{4^\alpha} \cdots$$

which diverges for $0 \leq \alpha \leq 1$ and converges for $\alpha > 1$

**har·mo·ni·ous** \här-'mō-nē-əs\ *adjective* (1530)
**1 :** musically concordant
**2 :** having the parts agreeably related **:** CONGRUOUS ⟨blended into a *harmonious* whole⟩
**3 :** marked by accord in sentiment or action
— **har·mo·ni·ous·ly** *adverb*
— **har·mo·ni·ous·ness** *noun*

**har·mo·nise** *British variant of* HARMONIZE

**har·mo·ni·um** \här-'mō-nē-əm\ *noun* [French, from Middle French *harmonie, armonie*] (1847)
**:** REED ORGAN

**har·mo·nize** \'här-mə-ˌnīz\ *verb* **-nized; -niz·ing** (15th century)
*intransitive verb*
**1 :** to play or sing in harmony
**2 :** to be in harmony
*transitive verb*
**1 :** to bring into consonance or accord
**2 :** to provide or accompany with harmony
— **har·mo·ni·za·tion** \ˌhär-mə-nə-'zā-shən\ *noun*
— **har·mo·niz·er** \'här-mə-ˌnī-zər\ *noun*

**har·mo·ny** \'här-mə-nē\ *noun, plural* **-nies** [Middle English *armony*, from Middle French *armonie*, from Latin *harmonia*, from Greek, joint, harmony, from *harmos* joint — more at ARM] (14th century)
**1** *archaic* **:** tuneful sound **:** MELODY
**2 a :** the combination of simultaneous musical notes in a chord **b :** the structure of music with respect to the composition and progression of chords **c :** the science of the structure, relation, and progression of chords
**3 a :** pleasing or congruent arrangement of parts ⟨a painting exhibiting *harmony* of color and line⟩ **b :** CORRESPONDENCE, ACCORD ⟨lives in *harmony* with her neighbors⟩ **c :** internal calm **:** TRANQUILLITY
**4 a :** an interweaving of different accounts into a single narrative **b :** a systematic arrangement of parallel literary passages (as of the Gospels) for the purpose of showing agreement or harmony

**harm's way** *noun* (circa 1661)
**:** a dangerous place or situation ⟨was placed in *harm's way*⟩ ⟨got them out of *harm's way*⟩

**¹har·ness** \'här-nəs\ *noun* [Middle English *herneis* baggage, gear, from Old French] (14th century)
**1 a :** the gear other than a yoke of a draft animal **b :** GEAR, EQUIPMENT; *especially* **:** military equipment for a horse or man
**2 a :** occupational surroundings or routine ⟨get back into *harness* after a vacation⟩ **b :** close association ⟨ability to work in *harness* with others —R. P. Brooks⟩
**3 a :** something that resembles a harness (as in holding or fastening something) ⟨a parachute *harness*⟩ **b :** prefabricated wiring with insulation and terminals ready to be attached
**4 :** a part of a loom which holds and controls the heddles

**²harness** *transitive verb* (14th century)
**1 a :** to put a harness on **b :** to attach by means of a harness
**2 :** to tie together **:** YOKE
**3 :** UTILIZE ⟨*harness* the computer's potential⟩

**harness horse** *noun* (1861)
**:** a horse for racing or working in harness

**harness racing** *noun* (1901)
**:** the sport of racing standardbred horses harnessed to 2-wheeled sulkies

**¹harp** \'härp\ *noun* [Middle English, from Old English *hearpe;* akin to Old High German *harpha* harp] (before 12th century)
**1 :** a plucked stringed instrument consisting of a resonator, an arched or angled neck that may be supported by a post, and strings of graded length that are perpendicular to the soundboard
**2 :** something that resembles a harp
**3 :** HARMONICA 2
— **harp·ist** \'här-pist\ *noun*

**harp 1**

**²harp** *intransitive verb* (before 12th century)
**1 :** to play on a harp
**2 :** to dwell on or recur to a subject tiresomely or monotonously — usually used with *on*

**harp·er** \'här-pər\ *noun* (before 12th century)
**1 :** a harp player
**2 :** one that harps

**har·poon** \här-'pün\ *noun* [probably from Dutch *harpoen*, from Old French *harpon* brooch, from *harper* to grapple] (1625)
**:** a barbed spear or javelin used especially in hunting large fish or whales
— **harpoon** *transitive verb*
— **har·poon·er** *noun*

**harp seal** *noun* [from the shape of its markings] (1766)
: a dark-faced seal (*Phoca groenlandicus*) of the North Atlantic that is a variable light gray with the male usually having a dark crescent on its back and sides

**harp·si·chord** \'härp-si-ˌkȯrd\ *noun* [modification of Italian *arpicordo*, from *arpa* harp + *corda* string] (1611)
: a stringed instrument resembling a grand piano but usually having two keyboards and two or more strings for each note and producing tones by the plucking of strings with plectra
— **harp·si·chord·ist** \-ˌkȯr-dist\ *noun*

**har·py** \'här-pē\ *noun, plural* **harpies** [Latin *Harpyia*, from Greek] (1513)
**1** *capitalized* : a foul malign creature in Greek mythology that is part woman and part bird
**2 a** : a predatory person : LEECH **b** : a shrewish woman

**harpy eagle** *noun* (1830)
: a large powerful crested eagle (*Harpia harpyja*) of Central and South America

**har·que·bus** \'här-kwi-(ˌ)bəs, -kə-bəs\ *noun* [Middle French *harquebuse, arquebuse,* modification of Middle Dutch *hakebusse,* from *hake* hook + *busse* tube, box, gun, from Late Latin *buxis* box] (1532)
: a matchlock gun invented in the 15th century which was portable but heavy and was usually fired from a support
— **har·que·bus·ier** \ˌhär-kwi-(ˌ)bə-'sir, -kə-bə-\ *noun*

**har·ri·dan** \'har-ə-dᵊn\ *noun* [perhaps modification of French *haridelle* old horse, gaunt woman] (circa 1700)
: SHREW 2

**har·ried** \'har-ēd\ *adjective* (circa 1915)
: beset by problems : HARASSED

**¹har·ri·er** \'har-ē-ər\ *noun* [irregular from ¹*hare*] (1542)
**1** : any of a breed of hunting dogs resembling a small foxhound and originally bred for hunting rabbits
**2** : a runner on a cross-country team

**²harrier** *noun* [alteration of *harrower,* from ¹*harrow*] (1556)
: any of a genus (*Circus*) of slender hawks having long angled wings and long legs and feeding chiefly on small mammals, reptiles, and insects

**³harrier** *noun* (1596)
: one that harries

**¹har·row** \'har-(ˌ)ō\ *transitive verb* [Middle English *harwen,* from Old English *hergian*] (before 12th century)
*archaic* : PILLAGE, PLUNDER

**²harrow** *noun* [Middle English *harwe,* probably of Scandinavian origin; akin to Old Norse *hervi* harrow] (14th century)
: a cultivating implement set with spikes, spring teeth, or disks and used primarily for pulverizing and smoothing the soil

**³harrow** *transitive verb* (14th century)
**1** : to cultivate with a harrow
**2** : TORMENT, VEX
— **har·row·er** \'har-ə-wər\ *noun*

**har·rumph** \hə-'rəm(p)f\ *intransitive verb* [imitative] (1942)
**1** : to clear the throat in a pompous way
**2** : to comment disapprovingly

**har·ry** \'har-ē\ *transitive verb* **har·ried; har·ry·ing** [Middle English *harien,* from Old English *hergian;* akin to Old High German *heriōn* to lay waste, *heri* army, Greek *koiranos* ruler] (before 12th century)
**1** : to make a pillaging or destructive raid on : ASSAULT
**2** : to force to move along by harassing ⟨*harrying* the terrified horses down out of the mountains —R. A. Sokolov⟩
**3** : to torment by or as if by constant attack
**synonym** see WORRY

**harsh** \'härsh\ *adjective* [Middle English *harsk,* of Scandinavian origin; akin to Norwegian *harsk* harsh] (14th century)

**1** : having a coarse uneven surface that is rough or unpleasant to the touch
**2 a** : causing a disagreeable or painful sensory reaction : IRRITATING **b** : physically discomforting : PAINFUL
**3** : unduly exacting : SEVERE
**4** : lacking in aesthetic appeal or refinement : CRUDE
**synonym** see ROUGH
— **harsh·ly** *adverb*
— **harsh·ness** *noun*

**harsh·en** \'här-shən\ *verb* **harsh·ened; harsh·en·ing** \-sh(ə-)niŋ\ (1824)
*transitive verb*
: to make (as a voice) harsh
*intransitive verb*
: to become harsh ⟨saw the grain of his skin *harshening* over face bones —Elizabeth Bowen⟩

**hart** \'härt\ *noun* [Middle English *hert,* from Old English *heort;* akin to Latin *cervus* hart, Greek *keras* horn — more at HORN] (before 12th century)
*chiefly British* : the male of the red deer especially when over five years old : STAG — compare HIND

**harte·beest** \'här-tə-ˌbēst\ *noun* [obsolete Afrikaans (now *hartbees*), from Dutch, from *hart* deer + *beest* beast] (1786)
: either of two large African antelopes (*Alcelaphus buselaphus* and *Sigmoceros lichtensteini*) with long faces and short annulate divergent horns; *also* : a smaller antelope (*Damaliscus hunteri* synonym *Beatragus hunteri*) of eastern Africa having a horizontal white line between the eyes

**harts·horn** \'härts-ˌhȯrn\ *noun* [from the earlier use of hart's horns as the chief source of ammonia] (1685)
: a preparation of ammonia used as smelling salts

**har·um–scar·um** \ˌhar-əm-'skar-əm, ˌher-əm-'sker-\ *adjective* [perhaps from archaic *hare* (to harass) + *scare*] (1751)
: RECKLESS, IRRESPONSIBLE
— **harum–scarum** *adverb*

**ha·rus·pex** \hə-'rəs-ˌpeks, 'har-əs-\ *noun, plural* **ha·rus·pi·ces** \hə-'rəs-pə-ˌsēz\ [Latin, from *haru-* (akin to *chordē* gut, cord) + *-spex,* from *specere* to look — more at YARN, SPY] (1584)
: a diviner in ancient Rome basing his predictions on inspection of the entrails of sacrificial animals

**ha·rus·pi·ca·tion** \hə-ˌrəs-pə-'kā-shən\ *noun* (1871)
*chiefly British* : an act or instance of foretelling something

**¹har·vest** \'här-vəst\ *noun, often attributive* [Middle English *hervest,* from Old English *hærfest;* akin to Latin *carpere* to pluck, gather, Greek *karpos* fruit] (before 12th century)
**1** : the season for gathering in agricultural crops
**2** : the act or process of gathering in a crop
**3 a** : a mature crop (as of grain or fruit) : YIELD **b** : the quantity of a natural product gathered in a single season ⟨deer *harvest*⟩ ⟨ice *harvest*⟩
**4** : an accumulated store or productive result ⟨a fantastic revenue *harvest* from lower tax rates —Peter Passell⟩

**²harvest** (15th century)
*transitive verb*
**1 a** : to gather in (a crop) : REAP **b** : to gather, catch, hunt, or kill (as salmon, oysters, or deer) for human use, sport, or population control **c** : to remove or extract (as living cells, tissues, or organs) from culture or a living or recently deceased body especially for transplanting
**2 a** : to accumulate a store of ⟨has now *harvested* this new generation's scholarly labors —M. J. Wiener⟩ **b** : to win by achievement ⟨the team *harvested* several awards⟩
*intransitive verb*
: to gather in a crop especially for food
— **har·vest·able** \-və-stə-bəl\ *adjective*
— **har·vest·er** *noun*

**harvest fly** *noun* (circa 1753)
: CICADA

**harvest home** *noun* (1596)
**1** : the gathering or the time of harvest
**2** : a feast at the close of harvest
**3** : a song sung by the reapers at the close of the harvest

**har·vest·man** \'här-vəs(t)-mən\ *noun* (1830)
: an arachnid (order Phalangida) that superficially resembles a true spider but has a small rounded body and very long slender legs — called also *daddy longlegs*

**harvest mite** *noun* (1873)
: CHIGGER 2

**harvest moon** *noun* (1706)
: the full moon nearest the time of the September equinox

**har·vest·time** \'här-vəs(t)-ˌtīm\ *noun* (14th century)
: the time during which an annual crop (as wheat) is harvested

**has** *present 3d singular of* HAVE

**has–been** \'haz-ˌbin, *chiefly British* -ˌbēn\ *noun* (1606)
: one that has passed the peak of effectiveness or popularity

**ha·sen·pfef·fer** \'hä-zᵊn-ˌ(p)fe-fər, 'hä-sᵊn-\ *noun* [German, from *Hase* hare + *Pfeffer* pepper] (1892)
: a highly seasoned stew made of marinated rabbit meat

**¹hash** \'hash\ *transitive verb* [French *hacher,* from Old French *hachier,* from *hache* battle-ax, of Germanic origin; akin to Old High German *hāppa* sickle; akin to Greek *koptein* to cut — more at CAPON] (1590)
**1 a** : to chop (as meat and potatoes) into small pieces **b** : CONFUSE, MUDDLE
**2** : to talk about : REVIEW — often used with *over* or *out*

**²hash** *noun* (circa 1663)
**1** : chopped food; *specifically* : chopped meat mixed with potatoes and browned
**2** : a restatement of something that is already known
**3 a** : HODGEPODGE, JUMBLE **b** : a confused muddle ⟨made a *hash* of the whole project⟩

**³hash** *noun* (1959)
: HASHISH

**hash browns** *noun plural* (1951)
: boiled potatoes that have been diced, mixed with chopped onions and shortening, and fried usually until they form a browned cake — called also *hash brown potatoes, hashed brown potatoes, hashed browns*

**Hash·em·ite** *or* **Hash·im·ite** \'ha-shə-ˌmīt\ *noun* [*Hashim,* great-grandfather of Muhammad] (1697)
: a member of an Arab family having common ancestry with Muhammad and founding dynasties in countries of the eastern Mediterranean

**hash house** *noun* (1869)
: an inexpensive eating place

**hash·ish** \'ha-ˌshēsh, ha-'shēsh\ *noun* [Arabic *hashīsh*] (1598)
: the concentrated resin from the flowering tops of the female hemp plant (*Cannabis sativa*) that is smoked, chewed, or drunk for its intoxicating effect — called also *charas;* compare BHANG, MARIJUANA

**hash mark** *noun* (1907)
**1** : SERVICE STRIPE
**2** : INBOUNDS LINE

**Ha·sid** \'ha-səd, 'kä-\ *noun, plural* **Ha·si·dim** \'ha-sə-dəm, kä-'sē-\ [Hebrew *ḥāsīdh* pious] (1812)
**1** : a member of a Jewish sect of the second century B.C. opposed to Hellenism and devoted to the strict observance of the ritual law

**2** *also* **Has·sid** **:** a member of a Jewish mystical sect founded in Poland about 1750 in opposition to rationalism and ritual laxity
— **Ha·sid·ic** *also* **Has·sid·ic** \ha-'si-dik, hä-, kä-\ *adjective*
**Ha·si·dism** \'ha-sə-ˌdi-zəm, 'hä-, 'kä-\ *noun* (1893)
**1 :** the practices and beliefs of the Hasidim
**2 :** the Hasidic movement
**Has·mo·nae·an** *or* **Has·mo·ne·an** \ˌhaz-mə-'nē-ən\ *noun* [Late Latin *Asmonaeus* Hasmon, ancestor of the Maccabees, from Greek *Asamōnaios*] (1620)
**:** a member of the Maccabees
— **Hasmonaean** *or* **Hasmonean** *adjective*
**hasn't** \'ha-zᵊnt, -zᵊn\ (1746)
**:** has not
**hasp** \'hasp\ *noun* [Middle English, alteration from Old English *hæpse;* akin to Middle High German *haspe* hasp] (before 12th century)
**:** any of several devices for fastening; *especially* **:** a fastener especially for a door or lid consisting of a hinged metal strap that fits over a staple and is secured by a pin or padlock
— **hasp** *transitive verb*

hasp

¹**has·sle** \'ha-səl\ *noun* (1945)
**1 :** a heated often protracted argument **:** WRANGLE
**2 :** a violent skirmish **:** FIGHT
**3 a :** a state of confusion **:** TURMOIL **b :** an annoying or troublesome concern
²**hassle** *verb* **has·sled; has·sling** \-s(ə-)liŋ\ [perhaps blend of *harass* and *hustle*] (1951)
*intransitive verb*
**:** ARGUE, FIGHT ⟨*hassled* with the umpire⟩
*transitive verb*
**:** to annoy persistently or acutely **:** HARASS ⟨he gets *hassled* in the street because he dresses funny —William Kloman⟩
**has·sock** \'ha-sək\ *noun* [Middle English, sedge, from Old English *hassuc*] (before 12th century)
**1 :** TUSSOCK
**2 a :** a cushion for kneeling ⟨a church *hassock*⟩ **b :** a padded cushion or low stool that serves as a seat or leg rest
**hast** \'hast, (h)əst\ *archaic present 2d singular of* HAVE
**has·tate** \'has-ˌtāt\ *adjective* [New Latin *hastatus,* from Latin *hasta* spear — more at YARD] (1788)
**1 :** triangular with sharp basal lobes spreading away from the base of the petiole ⟨*hastate* leaves⟩ — see LEAF illustration
**2 :** shaped like a spear or the head of a spear ⟨a *hastate* spot of a bird⟩
¹**haste** \'hāst\ *noun* [Middle English, from Middle French, of Germanic origin; akin to Old English *hǣst* violence] (14th century)
**1 :** rapidity of motion **:** SWIFTNESS
**2 :** rash or headlong action **:** PRECIPITATENESS ⟨the beauty of speed uncontaminated by *haste* —*Harper's*⟩
**3 :** undue eagerness to act ☆
²**haste** *verb* **hast·ed; hast·ing** (14th century)
*transitive verb*
*archaic* **:** to urge on **:** HASTEN
*intransitive verb*
**:** to move or act swiftly
**has·ten** \'hā-sᵊn\ *verb* **has·tened; has·ten·ing** \'hās-niŋ, 'hā-sᵊn-iŋ\ (1568)
*intransitive verb*
**:** to move or act quickly
*transitive verb*
**1 :** to urge on ⟨*hastened* her to the door —A. J. Cronin⟩
**2 :** ACCELERATE ⟨*hasten* the coming of a new order —D. W. Brogan⟩

— **has·ten·er** \'hās-nər, 'hā-sᵊn-ər\ *noun*
**hast·i·ly** \'hā-stə-lē\ *adverb* (14th century)
**:** in haste **:** HURRIEDLY
**hasty** \'hā-stē\ *adjective* **hast·i·er; -est** (14th century)
**1 a** *archaic* **:** rapid in action or movement **:** SPEEDY **b :** done or made in a hurry **c :** fast and typically superficial ⟨made a *hasty* examination of the wound⟩
**2 :** EAGER, IMPATIENT
**3 :** PRECIPITATE, RASH
**4 :** prone to anger **:** IRRITABLE
*synonym* see FAST
— **hast·i·ness** *noun*
**hasty pudding** *noun* (1599)
**1** *British* **:** a porridge of oatmeal or flour boiled in water
**2** *New England* **a :** cornmeal mush **b :** INDIAN PUDDING
¹**hat** \'hat\ *noun* [Middle English, from Old English *hæt;* akin to Old High German *huot* head covering — more at HOOD] (before 12th century)
**1 :** a covering for the head usually having a shaped crown and brim
**2 a :** a distinctive head covering worn as a symbol of office **b :** an office, position, or role assumed by or as if by the wearing of a special hat
— **hat·less** \-ləs\ *adjective*
²**hat** *verb* **hat·ted; hat·ting** (15th century)
*transitive verb*
**:** to furnish or provide with a hat
*intransitive verb*
**:** to make or supply hats
**hat·band** \'hat-ˌband\ *noun* (15th century)
**:** a band (as of fabric, leather, or cord) around the crown of a hat just above the brim
**hat·box** \-ˌbäks\ *noun* (1794)
**1 :** a box for holding or storing a hat
**2 :** a usually round piece of luggage designed especially for carrying hats
¹**hatch** \'hach\ *noun* [Middle English *hache,* from Old English *hæc;* akin to Middle Dutch *hecke* trapdoor] (before 12th century)
**1 :** a small door or opening (as in an airplane or spaceship) ⟨an escape *hatch*⟩
**2 a :** an opening in the deck of a ship or in the floor or roof of a building **b :** the covering for such an opening **c :** HATCHWAY **d :** COMPARTMENT
**3 :** FLOODGATE
²**hatch** *verb* [Middle English *hacchen;* akin to Middle High German *hecken* to mate] (13th century)
*intransitive verb*
**1 :** to produce young by incubation
**2 a :** to emerge from an egg, chrysalis, or pupa **b :** to give forth young or imagoes
**3 :** to incubate eggs **:** BROOD
*transitive verb*
**1 a :** to produce (young) from an egg by applying natural or artificial heat **b :** INCUBATE 1
**2 :** to bring into being **:** ORIGINATE; *especially* **:** to concoct in secret
— **hatch·abil·i·ty** \ˌha-chə-'bi-lə-tē\ *noun*
— **hatch·able** \'ha-chə-bəl\ *adjective*
— **hatch·er** *noun*
³**hatch** *noun* (1601)
**1 :** an act or instance of hatching
**2 :** a brood of hatched young
⁴**hatch** *transitive verb* [Middle English *hachen,* from Middle French *hacher* to inlay, chop up, from Old French *hachier* — more at HASH] (15th century)
**1 :** to inlay with narrow bands of distinguishable material ⟨a silver handle *hatched* with gold⟩
**2 :** to mark (as a drawing or engraving) with fine closely spaced lines
⁵**hatch** *noun* (1658)
**:** LINE; *especially* **:** one used to give the effect of shading
**hatch·back** \'hach-ˌbak\ *noun* (1970)

**:** an automobile the back of which consists of a hatch that opens upward; *also* **:** the back itself
**hat-check** \'hat-ˌchek\ *adjective* (1917)
**:** employed in checking hats and articles of outdoor clothing ⟨a *hatcheck* girl⟩
**hatch·ery** \'ha-chə-rē\ *noun, plural* **-er·ies** (1880)
**:** a place for hatching eggs (as of poultry or fish)
**hatch·et** \'ha-chət\ *noun* [Middle English *hachet,* from Middle French *hachette,* diminutive of *hache* battle-ax — more at HASH] (14th century)
**1 :** a short-handled ax often with a hammerhead to be used with one hand
**2 :** TOMAHAWK
**hatchet face** *noun* (circa 1666)
**:** a thin sharp face
— **hatch·et–faced** \'ha-chət-ˌfāst\ *adjective*
**hatchet job** *noun* (1944)
**:** a forceful or malicious verbal attack
**hatchet man** *noun* (1880)
**1 :** one hired for murder, coercion, or attack
**2 a :** a writer specializing in invective **b :** a person hired to perform underhanded or unscrupulous tasks (as ruin reputations)
**hatchet work** *noun* (1944)
**:** the work of a hatchet man
**hatch·ing** *noun* (1662)
**:** the engraving or drawing of fine lines in close proximity especially to give an effect of shading; *also* **:** the pattern so made
**hatch·ling** \'hach-liŋ\ *noun* (1899)
**:** a recently hatched animal
**hatch·ment** \'hach-mənt\ *noun* [perhaps alteration of *achievement*] (1548)
**:** a panel on which a coat of arms of a deceased person is temporarily displayed
**hatch·way** \'hach-ˌwā\ *noun* (1626)
**:** a passage giving access usually by a ladder or stairs to an enclosed space (as a cellar); *also* **:** HATCH 2a
¹**hate** \'hāt\ *noun, often attributive* [Middle English, from Old English *hete;* akin to Old High German *haz* hate, Greek *kēdos* care] (before 12th century)
**1 a :** intense hostility and aversion usually deriving from fear, anger, or sense of injury **b :** extreme dislike or antipathy **:** LOATHING ⟨had a great *hate* of hard work⟩
**2 :** an object of hatred ⟨a generation whose finest *hate* had been big business —F. L. Paxson⟩
²**hate** *verb* **hat·ed; hat·ing** (before 12th century)
*transitive verb*
**1 :** to feel extreme enmity toward ⟨*hates* his country's enemies⟩

---

☆ **SYNONYMS**
**Haste, hurry, speed, expedition, dispatch** mean quickness in movement or action. HASTE applies to personal action and implies urgency and precipitancy and often rashness ⟨marry in *haste*⟩. HURRY often has a strong suggestion of agitated bustle or confusion ⟨in the *hurry* of departure she forgot her toothbrush⟩. SPEED suggests swift efficiency in movement or action ⟨exercises to increase your reading *speed*⟩. EXPEDITION and DISPATCH both imply speed and efficiency in handling affairs but EXPEDITION stresses ease or efficiency of performance and DISPATCH stresses promptness in concluding matters ⟨the case came to trial with *expedition*⟩ ⟨paid bills with *dispatch*⟩.

---

**2** : to have a strong aversion to : find very distasteful 〈*hated* to have to meet strangers〉 〈*hate* hypocrisy〉
*intransitive verb*
: to express or feel extreme enmity or active hostility ☆
— **hat·er** *noun*
— **hate one's guts** : to hate someone with great intensity
**hate crime** *noun* (1989)
: any of various crimes (as assault or defacement of property) when motivated by hostility to the victim as a member of a group (as one based on color, creed, gender, or sexual orientation)
**hate·ful** \'hāt-fəl\ *adjective* (14th century)
**1** : full of hate : MALICIOUS
**2** : deserving of or arousing hate
— **hate·ful·ly** \-fə-lē\ *adverb*
— **hate·ful·ness** *noun*
**hath** \'hath, (h)əth\ *archaic present 3d singular of* HAVE
**hatha yo·ga** \'hə-tə-'yō-gə, 'hä-\ *noun* [Sanskrit *haṭha* force + *yoga* yoga] (1890)
: a system of physical exercises for the control and perfection of the body that constitutes one of the four chief Hindu disciplines
**hat in hand** *adverb* (1851)
: in an attitude of respectful humility 〈have to go *hat in hand* to apologize〉
**hat·mak·er** \'hat-ˌmā-kər\ *noun* (15th century)
: one who makes hats
**ha·tred** \'hā-trəd\ *noun* [Middle English, from *hate* + Old English *ræden* condition — more at KINDRED] (12th century)
**1** : HATE
**2** : prejudiced hostility or animosity 〈old racial prejudices and national *hatreds* —Peter Thomson〉
**hat·ter** \'ha-tər\ *noun* (14th century)
: one that makes, sells, or cleans and repairs hats
**hat trick** *noun* [probably from the former practice of rewarding the feat with the gift of a hat] (1877)
**1** : the retiring of three batsmen with three consecutive balls by a bowler in cricket
**2** : the scoring of three goals in one game (as of hockey or soccer) by a single player
**3** : a succession of three victories, successes, or related accomplishments 〈scored a *hat trick* when her three best steers corralled top honors —*People*〉
**hau·berk** \'hȯ-(ˌ)bərk\ *noun* [Middle English, from Old French *hauberc*, of Germanic origin; akin to Old English *healsbeorg* neck armor] (14th century)
: a tunic of chain mail worn as defensive armor from the 12th to the 14th century
**haugh** \'hȯ(k)\ *noun* [Middle English (Scots) *halch*, from Old English *healh* corner of land; akin to Old English *holh* hole] (before 12th century)
*Scottish* : a low-lying meadow by the side of a river
**haugh·ty** \'hȯ-tē, 'hä-\ *adjective*
**haugh·ti·er; -est** [obsolete *haught*, from Middle English *haute*, from Middle French *haut*, literally, high, from Latin *altus* — more at OLD] (15th century)
: blatantly and disdainfully proud
*synonym* see PROUD
— **haugh·ti·ly** \'hȯ-tᵊl-ē, 'hä-\ *adverb*
— **haugh·ti·ness** \'hȯ-tē-nəs, 'hä-\ *noun*
**¹haul** \'hȯl\ *verb* [Middle English *halen* to pull, from Old French *haler*, of Germanic origin; akin to Middle Dutch *halen* to pull; akin to Old English *geholian* to obtain] (13th century)
*transitive verb*
**1 a** : to exert traction on : DRAW 〈*haul* a wagon〉 **b** : to obtain or move by or as if by hauling 〈was *hauled* to parties night after night by his wife〉 **c** : to transport in a vehicle : CART

*1 hauberk*

**2** : to change the course of (a ship) especially so as to sail closer to the wind
**3** : to bring before an authority for interrogation or judgment : HALE 〈*haul* traffic violators into court〉
*intransitive verb*
**1** : to exert traction : PULL
**2** : to move along : PROCEED
**3** : to furnish transportation
**4** *of the wind* : SHIFT
— **haul ass** : to move quickly — often considered vulgar
**²haul** *noun* (1670)
**1 a** : the act or process of hauling : PULL **b** : a device for hauling
**2 a** : the result of an effort to obtain, collect, or win 〈the burglar's *haul*〉 **b** : the fish taken in a single draft of a net
**3 a** : transportation by hauling **b** : the length or course of a transportation route 〈a long *haul*〉 **c** : a quantity transported : LOAD
**haul·age** \'hȯ-lij\ *noun* (1826)
**1** : the act or process of hauling
**2** : a charge made for hauling
**haul·er** \'hȯ-lər\ *noun* (1674)
: one that hauls: as **a** : a commercial establishment or worker whose business is hauling **b** : an automotive vehicle for hauling goods or material
**haul·ier** \'hȯl-yər\ *British variant of* HAULER
**haulm** \'hȯm\ *noun* [Middle English *halm*, from Old English *healm*; akin to Old High German *halm* stem, Latin *culmus* stalk, Greek *kalamos* reed] (before 12th century)
: the stems or tops of crop plants (as peas or potatoes) especially after the crop has been gathered
**haul off** *intransitive verb* (1870)
: to get ready — used with *and* and a following verb describing a usually sudden and violent act 〈I *hauled off* and hit him〉
**haunch** \'hȯnch, 'hänch\ *noun* [Middle English *haunche*, from Old French *hanche*, of Germanic origin; akin to Middle Dutch *hanke* haunch] (13th century)
**1 a** : HIP 1a **b** : HINDQUARTER 2 — usually used in plural
**2** : HINDQUARTER 1
**3** : either side of an arch between the springing and the crown
— **on one's haunches** : in a squatting position
**¹haunt** \'hȯnt, 'hänt\ *verb* [Middle English, from Old French *hanter*, probably from Old Norse *heimta* to lead home, pull, claim, from *heimr* home] (14th century)
*transitive verb*
**1 a** : to visit often : FREQUENT **b** : to continually seek the company of
**2 a** : to have a disquieting or harmful effect on : TROUBLE 〈problems we ignore now will come back to *haunt* us〉 **b** : to recur constantly and spontaneously to 〈the tune *haunted* her〉 **c** : to reappear continually in 〈a sense of tension that *haunts* his writing〉
**3** : to visit or inhabit as a ghost
*intransitive verb*
**1** : to stay around or persist : LINGER
**2** : to appear habitually as a ghost
— **haunt·er** *noun*
— **haunt·ing·ly** \'hȯn-tiŋ-lē, 'hän-\ *adverb*
**²haunt** \'hȯnt, 'hänt, 2 is usually 'hänt\ *noun* (14th century)
**1** : a place habitually frequented
**2** *chiefly dialect* : GHOST
**Hau·sa** \'haù-sə, -zə\ *noun, plural* **Hausa** *or* **Hausas** (1853)
**1** : the Chadic language of the Hausa people widely used in western Africa as a trade language
**2** : a member of a black people of northern Nigeria and southern Niger
**haus·frau** \'haùs-ˌfraù\ *noun* [German, from *Haus* house + *Frau* woman, wife] (1798)
: HOUSEWIFE

**haus·tel·lum** \hȯ-'ste-ləm\ *noun, plural* **-la** \-lə\ [New Latin, diminutive of Latin *haustrum* scoop on a waterwheel, from *haurire* to drink, draw — more at EXHAUST] (1816)
: a proboscis (as of an insect) adapted to suck blood or juices of plants
**haus·to·ri·al** \hȯ-'stōr-ē-əl, -'stȯr-\ *adjective* (1894)
: of, relating to, or having a haustorium
**haus·to·ri·um** \-ē-əm\ *noun, plural* **-ria** \-ē-ə\ [New Latin, from Latin *haurire*] (1875)
: a food-absorbing outgrowth of a plant organ (as a hypha or stem)
**haut·bois** *or* **haut·boy** \'(h)ō-ˌbȯi\ *noun, plural* **hautbois** \-ˌbȯiz\ *or* **haut·boys** [Middle French *hautbois*, from *haut* high + *bois* wood] (1575)
: OBOE
**haute** \'ōt\ *also* **haut** \'ōt, 'ō\ *adjective* [French] (1787)
: FASHIONABLE, HIGH-CLASS 〈*haute* interior decorators〉 〈a store filled with *haute* kitsch〉
**haute cou·ture** \ˌōt-kü-'tùr\ *noun* [French, literally, high sewing] (1908)
: the houses or designers that create exclusive and often trend-setting fashions for women; *also* : the fashions created
**haute cui·sine** \-kwi-'zēn\ *noun* [French, literally, high cooking] (1928)
: artful or elaborate cuisine; *especially* : traditionally elaborate French cuisine
**haute école** \-ā-'kȯl, -'kəl\ *noun* [French, literally, high school] (1858)
: a highly stylized form of classical riding : advanced dressage
**hau·teur** \hȯ-'tər, (h)ō-\ *noun* [French, from *haut* high — more at HAUGHTY] (circa 1628)
: ARROGANCE, HAUGHTINESS
**haut monde** \ō-'mänd, ō-mōⁿd\ *also* **haute monde** \ōt-\ *noun* [French, literally, high world] (1864)
: high society
**Ha·vana** \hə-'va-nə\ *noun* [probably from Spanish *habano*, from *habano* of Havana, from La *Habana* (Havana), Cuba] (1826)
**1** : a cigar made from Cuban tobacco
**2** : a tobacco originally grown in Cuba
**Ha·var·ti** \hə-'vär-tē\ *noun* [*Havarti*, locale in Denmark] (1957)
: a semisoft Danish cheese having a porous texture and usually a mild flavor
**havdalah** *variant of* HABDALAH
**¹have** \'hav, (h)əv, v; *in* "have to" *meaning* "must" *usually* 'haf\ *verb* **had** \'had, (h)əd, d\; **hav·ing** \'ha-viŋ\; **has** \'haz, (h)əz, z, s; *in* "has to" *meaning* "must" *usually* 'has\ [Middle English, from Old English *habban*; akin to Old High German *habēn* to have, and perhaps to *hevan* to lift — more at HEAVE] (before 12th century)
*transitive verb*
**1 a** : to hold or maintain as a possession, privilege, or entitlement 〈they *have* a new car〉 〈I *have* my rights〉 **b** : to hold in one's use, service, regard, or at one's disposal 〈the group will *have* enough tickets for everyone〉 〈we don't *have* time to stay〉 **c** : to hold, include, or contain as a part or whole 〈the car *has* power brakes〉 〈April *has* 30 days〉

**2 :** to feel obligation in regard to — usually used with an infinitive with *to* ⟨we *have* things to do⟩ ⟨*have* a deadline to meet⟩
**3 :** to stand in a certain relationship to ⟨*has* three fine children⟩ ⟨we will *have* the wind at our backs⟩
**4 a :** to acquire or get possession of **:** OBTAIN ⟨these shoes are the best to be *had*⟩ **b :** RECEIVE ⟨*had* news⟩ **c :** ACCEPT; *specifically* **:** to accept in marriage **d :** to copulate with
**5 a :** to be marked or characterized by (a quality, attribute, or faculty) ⟨both *have* red hair⟩ ⟨*has* a way with words⟩ **b :** EXHIBIT, SHOW ⟨*had* the gall to refuse⟩ **c :** USE, EXERCISE ⟨*have* mercy on us⟩
**6 a :** to experience especially by submitting to, undergoing, or suffering ⟨I *have* a cold⟩ **b :** to make the effort to perform (an action) or engage in (an activity) ⟨*have* a look at that cut⟩ **c :** to entertain in the mind ⟨*have* an opinion⟩
**7 a :** to cause or command to do something — used with the infinitive without *to* ⟨*have* the children stay⟩ **b :** to cause to be in a certain place or state ⟨*has* people around at all times⟩
**8 :** ALLOW ⟨we'll *have* no more of that⟩
**9 :** to be competent in ⟨*has* only a little French⟩
**10 a :** to hold in a position of disadvantage or certain defeat ⟨we *have* him now⟩ **b :** to take advantage of **:** TRICK, FOOL ⟨been *had* by a partner⟩
**11 :** BEGET, BEAR ⟨*have* a baby⟩
**12 :** to partake of ⟨*have* dinner⟩ ⟨*have* a smoke⟩
**13 :** BRIBE, SUBORN ⟨can be *had* for a price⟩
*verbal auxiliary*
**1** — used with the past participle to form the present perfect, past perfect, or future perfect ⟨*has* gone home⟩ ⟨*had* already eaten⟩ ⟨will *have* finished dinner by then⟩
**2 :** to be compelled, obliged, or required — used with an infinitive with *to* or *to* alone ⟨we *had* to go⟩ ⟨do what you *have* to⟩ ⟨it *has* to be said⟩
— **had better** *or* **had best :** would be wise to
— **have at :** to go at or deal with **:** ATTACK
— **have coming :** to deserve or merit what one gets, benefits by, or suffers ⟨he *had* that coming⟩
— **have done :** FINISH, STOP
— **have done with :** to bring to an end **:** have no further concern with ⟨let us *have* done with name-calling⟩
— **have had it 1 :** to have had or have done all one is going to be allowed to **2 :** to have experienced, endured, or suffered all one can
— **have it :** ASSERT, CLAIM ⟨rumor *has it* that he was drunk⟩
— **have it in for :** to intend to do harm to
— **have it out :** to settle a matter of contention by discussion or a fight
— **have none of :** to refuse to have anything to do with
— **have one's eye on 1 a :** to look at **b :** to watch constantly and attentively **2 :** to have as an objective
— **have to do with 1 :** to deal with ⟨the story *has to do with* real people —Alice M. Jordan⟩ **2 :** to have a specified relationship with or effect on ⟨the size of the brain *has* nothing *to do with* intelligence —Ruth Benedict⟩

**²have** \'hav\ *noun* (1836)
**:** one that is well-endowed especially in material wealth

**have·lock** \'hav-ˌläk, -lək\ *noun* [Sir Henry *Havelock*] (1861)
**:** a covering attached to a cap to protect the neck from the sun or bad weather

**ha·ven** \'hā-vən\ *noun* [Middle English, from Old English *hæfen;* akin to Middle High German *habene* harbor] (before 12th century)
**1 :** HARBOR, PORT

**2 :** a place of safety **:** ASYLUM
**3 :** a place offering favorable opportunities or conditions ⟨a tourist's *haven*⟩
— **haven** *transitive verb*

**have-not** \'hav-ˌnät, -ˈnät\ *noun* (1836)
**:** one that is poor especially in material wealth

**haven't** \'ha-vənt, 'ha-bᵊm(t)\ (1777)
**:** have not

**have on** *transitive verb* (before 12th century)
**1 :** WEAR ⟨*has* on a new suit⟩
**2** *chiefly British* **:** to trick or deceive intentionally **:** PUT ON 5
**3 :** to have plans for ⟨what do you *have* on for tomorrow⟩

**ha·ver** \'hā-vər\ *intransitive verb* [origin unknown] (1866)
*chiefly British* **:** to hem and haw

**hav·er·sack** \'ha-vər-ˌsak\ *noun* [French *havresac,* from German *Habersack* bag for oats, from *Haber* oats + *Sack* bag] (1749)
**:** a bag similar to a knapsack but worn over one shoulder

**ha·ver·sian canal** \hə-ˈvər-zhən-\ *noun, often H capitalized* [Clopton *Havers* (died 1702) English physician & anatomist] (1842)
**:** any of the small canals through which the blood vessels ramify in bone

**haversian system** *noun, often H capitalized* (circa 1846)
**:** a haversian canal with the concentrically arranged laminae of bone that surround it

**¹hav·oc** \'ha-vək, -vik\ *noun* [Middle English *havok,* from Anglo-French, modification of Old French *havot* plunder] (15th century)
**1 :** wide and general destruction **:** DEVASTATION
**2 :** great confusion and disorder ⟨children can create *havoc* in a house⟩

**²havoc** *transitive verb* **hav·ocked; hav·ock·ing** (1577)
**:** to lay waste **:** DESTROY

**¹haw** \'hȯ\ *noun* [Middle English *hawe,* from Old English *haga* — more at HEDGE] (before 12th century)
**1 :** a hawthorn berry
**2 :** HAWTHORN

**²haw** *noun* [origin unknown] (15th century)
**:** NICTITATING MEMBRANE; *especially* **:** an inflamed nictitating membrane of a domesticated mammal

**³haw** *intransitive verb* [imitative] (1632)
**1 :** to utter the sound represented by *haw* ⟨hemmed and *hawed* before answering⟩
**2 :** EQUIVOCATE ⟨the administration hemmed and *hawed* over the students' demands⟩

**⁴haw** *interjection* (1679)
— often used to indicate a vocalized pause in speaking

**⁵haw** \'hȯ\ *verb* [origin unknown] (1777)
*verb imperative*
— used as a direction to turn to the left; compare GEE
*intransitive verb*
**:** to turn to the near or left side

**Hawaii–Aleutian time** *noun* (1983)
**:** the time of the 10th time zone west of Greenwich that includes the Hawaiian islands and the Aleutians west of the Fox group

**Ha·wai·ian** \hə-ˈwä-yən, -ˈwī-(y)ən, -ˈwȯ-yən\ *noun* (circa 1864)
**1 :** a native or resident of Hawaii; *especially* **:** one of Polynesian ancestry
**2 :** the Polynesian language of the Hawaiians
— **Hawaiian** *adjective*

**Hawaiian goose** *noun* (circa 1909)
**:** NENE

**Hawaiian guitar** *noun* (1928)
**:** a usually electric stringed instrument having a long fretted neck and six to eight steel strings that are plucked while being pressed with a movable steel bar for a glissando effect

**Hawaiian shirt** *noun* (1962)
**:** a usually short-sleeved sport shirt with a colorful pattern

**haw·finch** \'hȯ-ˌfinch\ *noun* [¹*haw*] (circa 1674)
**:** an Old World finch (*Coccothraustes coccothraustes*) with a large heavy bill and short thick neck and the male marked with black, white, and brown

**¹hawk** \'hȯk\ *noun* [Middle English *hauk,* from Old English *hafoc;* akin to Old High German *habuh* hawk, Russian *kobets* a falcon] (before 12th century)
**1 :** any of numerous diurnal birds of prey belonging to a suborder (Falcones of the order Falconiformes) and including all the smaller members of this group; *especially* **:** ACCIPITER — compare OWL
**2 :** a small board or metal sheet with a handle on the underside used to hold mortar
**3 :** one who takes a militant attitude and advocates immediate vigorous action; *especially* **:** a supporter of a war or warlike policy — compare DOVE
— **hawk·ish** \'hȯ-kish\ *adjective*
— **hawk·ish·ly** *adverb*
— **hawk·ish·ness** *noun*

**²hawk** (14th century)
*intransitive verb*
**1 :** to hunt birds by means of a trained hawk
**2 :** to soar and strike like a hawk
*transitive verb*
**:** to hunt on the wing like a hawk

**³hawk** *verb* [imitative] (1581)
*transitive verb*
**:** to raise by trying to clear the throat ⟨*hawk* up phlegm⟩
*intransitive verb*
**:** to utter a harsh guttural sound in or as if in hawking

**⁴hawk** *noun* (1604)
**:** an audible effort to force up phlegm from the throat

**⁵hawk** *transitive verb* [back-formation from ²*hawker*] (1713)
**:** to offer for sale by calling out in the street ⟨*hawking* newspapers⟩; *broadly* **:** SELL

**¹hawk·er** \'hȯ-kər\ *noun* [Middle English, from Old English *hafocere,* from *hafoc* ] (before 12th century)
**:** FALCONER

**²hawker** *noun* [by folk etymology from Low German *höker,* from Middle Low German *höker,* from *höken* to peddle] (1512)
**:** one that hawks wares

**Hawk·eye** \'hȯ-ˌkī\ *noun* (1823)
**:** a native or resident of Iowa — used as a nickname

**hawk·eyed** \'hȯ-ˌkīd\ *adjective* (circa 1818)
**:** having keen sight

**hawk·moth** \'hȯk-ˌmȯth\ *noun* (1785)
**:** any of a family (Sphingidae) of stout-bodied moths with a long proboscis, long narrow more or less pointed forewings, and small hind wings — called also *sphinx*

**hawks·bill** \'hȯks-ˌbil\ *noun* (1712)
**:** a small brown or brown and yellow sea turtle (*Eretmochelys imbricata*) of warm waters that has a carapace of overlapping plates — compare TORTOISESHELL 1

**hawksbill**

**hawk·shaw** \'hȯk-ˌshȯ\ *noun* [from *Hawkshaw,* detective in the play *The Ticket of Leave Man* (1863) by Tom Taylor] (1888)
**:** DETECTIVE

**hawk·weed** \'hȯk-ˌwēd\ *noun* (1562)

\ə\ abut \ᵊ\ kitten \ər\ further \a\ ash \ā\ ace \ä\ mop, mar \aȯ\ out \ch\ chin \e\ bet \ē\ easy \g\ go \i\ hit \ī\ ice \j\ job \ŋ\ sing \ō\ go \ȯ\ law \ȯi\ boy \th\ thin \th\ the \ü\ loot \ u̇\ foot \y\ yet \zh\ vision *see also* Guide to Pronunciation

: any of a genus (*Hieracium*) of composite plants usually having flower heads with red or orange rays — compare ORANGE HAWKWEED

**hawse** \'hȯz\ *noun* [alteration of Middle English *halse*, from Old Norse *hals* neck, hawse — more at COLLAR] (14th century)
**1 a :** the part of a ship's bow that contains the hawseholes **b :** HAWSEHOLE
**2 :** the distance between a ship's bow and her anchor

**hawse·hole** \-ˌhōl\ *noun* (1664)
: a hole in the bow of a ship through which a cable passes

**haw·ser** \'hȯ-zər\ *noun* [Middle English, from Anglo-French *hauceour*, from Middle French *haucier* to hoist, from (assumed) Vulgar Latin *altiare*, from Latin *altus* high — more at OLD] (13th century)
: a large rope for towing, mooring, or securing a ship

**haw·ser–laid** \'hȯ-zər-ˌlād\ *adjective* (1769)
: composed of three ropes laid together right-handed with each containing three strands twisted together

**haw·thorn** \'hȯ-ˌthȯrn\ *noun* [Middle English *hawethorn*, from Old English *hagathorn*, from *haga* hawthorn + *thorn* — more at HEDGE] (before 12th century)
: any of a genus (*Crataegus*) of spring-flowering spiny shrubs of the rose family with glossy and often lobed leaves, white or pink fragrant flowers, and small red fruits

**Haw·thorne effect** \'hȯ-ˌthȯrn-\ *noun* [from the *Hawthorne* Works of the Western Electric Co., Cicero, Ill., where its existence was established by experiment] (1962)
: the stimulation to output or accomplishment that results from the mere fact of being under observation; *also* : such an increase in output or accomplishment

**¹hay** \'hā\ *noun* [Middle English *hey*, from Old English *hīeg*; akin to Old High German *hewi* hay, Old English *hēawan* to hew] (before 12th century)
**1 :** herbage and especially grass mowed and cured for fodder
**2 :** REWARD
**3** *slang* : BED
**4 :** a small sum of money ⟨a saving of . . . $14 million is not *hay* —H. C. Schonberg⟩

**²hay** (1556)
*intransitive verb*
: to cut, cure, and store hay
*transitive verb*
: to feed with hay

**hay·cock** \'hā-ˌkäk\ *noun* (13th century)
: a somewhat rounded conical pile of hay

**hay fever** *noun* (1829)
: an acute allergic rhinitis and conjunctivitis; *especially* : POLLINOSIS

**hay·lage** \'hā-lij\ *noun* [*hay* + si*lage*] (circa 1958)
: a stored forage that is essentially a grass silage wilted to 35 to 50 percent moisture

**hay·loft** \'hā-ˌlȯft\ *noun* (1573)
: a loft especially for storing hay

**hay·mak·er** \-ˌmā-kər\ *noun* (1912)
: a powerful blow

**hay·mow** \-ˌmau̇\ *noun* (15th century)
: a mow especially of or for hay

**hay·rack** \-ˌrak\ *noun* (1825)
**1 :** a feeding rack that holds hay for livestock
**2 :** a frame mounted on the running gear of a wagon and used especially in hauling hay or straw; *also* : a wagon equipped with a hayrack

**hay·rick** \-ˌrik\ *noun* (15th century)
: a relatively large sometimes thatched outdoor pile of hay : HAYSTACK

**hay·ride** \-ˌrīd\ *noun* (1896)
: a pleasure ride usually at night by a group in a wagon, sleigh, or open truck partly filled with straw or hay

**hay–scent·ed fern** \'hā-ˌsen-təd-\ *noun* (1915)

: a common fern (*Dennstaedtia punctilobula*) of eastern North America with fragrant finely divided pale green fronds

**hay·seed** \'hā-ˌsēd\ *noun, plural* **hayseed** *or* **hayseeds** (1577)
**1 a :** seed shattered from hay **b :** clinging bits of straw or chaff from hay
**2** *plural* **hayseeds** : BUMPKIN, YOKEL

**hay·stack** \-ˌstak\ *noun* (15th century)
**1 :** a stack of hay
**2 :** a vertical standing wave in turbulent river waters

**hay·wire** \-ˌwīr\ *adverb or adjective* [from the use of baling wire for makeshift repairs] (1929)
**1 :** being out of order or having gone wrong ⟨the radio went *haywire*⟩
**2 :** emotionally or mentally upset or out of control : CRAZY ⟨is going *haywire* with grief⟩

**ha·zan** \kə-'zän, 'kä-z⁼n\ *noun, plural* **ha·za·nim** \kə-'zä-nəm\ [Late Hebrew *ḥazzān*] (1650)
**1 :** an official of a Jewish synagogue or community of the period when the Talmud was compiled
**2 :** CANTOR 2

**¹haz·ard** \'ha-zərd\ *noun* [Middle English, from Middle French *hasard*, from Arabic *az-zahr* the die] (14th century)
**1 :** a game of chance like craps played with two dice
**2 :** a source of danger
**3 a :** CHANCE, RISK **b :** a chance event : ACCIDENT
**4** *obsolete* : STAKE 3a
**5 :** a golf-course obstacle ◆
**— at hazard :** at stake

**²hazard** *transitive verb* (1530)
: VENTURE, RISK ⟨*hazard* a guess as to the outcome⟩

**haz·ard·ous** \'ha-zər-dəs\ *adjective* (1585)
**1 :** depending on hazard or chance
**2 :** involving or exposing one to risk (as of loss or harm) ⟨a *hazardous* occupation⟩ ⟨disposing of *hazardous* waste⟩
*synonym* see DANGEROUS
**— haz·ard·ous·ly** *adverb*
**— haz·ard·ous·ness** *noun*

**¹haze** \'hāz\ *noun* [probably back-formation from *hazy*] (1706)
**1 a :** fine dust, smoke, or light vapor causing lack of transparency of the air **b :** a cloudy appearance in a transparent liquid or solid; *also* : a dullness of finish (as on furniture)
**2 :** something suggesting atmospheric haze; *especially* : vagueness of mind or mental perception

**²haze** *verb* **hazed; haz·ing** (1801)
*transitive verb*
: to make hazy, dull, or cloudy
*intransitive verb*
: to become hazy or cloudy

**³haze** *transitive verb* **hazed; haz·ing** [origin unknown] (1840)
**1 a :** to harass by exacting unnecessary or disagreeable work **b :** to harass by banter, ridicule, or criticism
**2 :** to haze by way of initiation ⟨*haze* the fraternity pledges⟩
**3** *West* : to drive (as cattle or horses) from horseback
**— haz·er** *noun*

**¹ha·zel** \'hā-zəl\ *noun* [Middle English *hasel*, from Old English *hæsel*; akin to Old High German *hasal* hazel, Latin *corulus*] (before 12th century)
**1 :** any of a genus (*Corylus* and especially the American *C. americana* and the European *C. avellana*) of shrubs or small trees of the birch family bearing nuts enclosed in a leafy involucre
**2 :** a light brown to strong yellowish brown

**²hazel** *adjective* (14th century)
**1 :** consisting of hazels or of the wood of the hazel
**2 :** of the color hazel

**hazel hen** *noun* (1661)
: a European woodland grouse (*Bonasa bonasia*) related to the ruffed grouse — called also *hazel grouse*

**ha·zel·nut** \'hā-zəl-ˌnət\ *noun* (before 12th century)
: the nut of a hazel

**haz·ing** \'hā-ziŋ\ *noun* (circa 1855)
: the action of hazing; *especially* : an initiation process involving harassment

**hazy** \'hā-zē\ *adjective* **haz·i·er; -est** [origin unknown] (1625)
**1 :** obscured or made dim or cloudy by or as if by haze
**2 :** VAGUE, INDEFINITE ⟨has only a *hazy* recollection⟩; *also* : UNCERTAIN ⟨I'm *hazy* on that point⟩
**— haz·i·ly** \-zə-lē\ *adverb*
**— haz·i·ness** \-zē-nəs\ *noun*

**H–bomb** \'āch-ˌbäm\ *noun* (1950)
: HYDROGEN BOMB

**HDL** \ˌāch-(ˌ)dē-'el\ *noun* [*h*igh-*d*ensity *l*ipoprotein] (circa 1965)
: a cholesterol-poor protein-rich lipoprotein of blood plasma correlated with reduced risk of atherosclerosis — compare LDL

**¹he** \'hē, ē\ *pronoun* [Middle English, from Old English *hē*; akin to Old English *hēo* she, *hit* it, Old High German *hē* he, Latin *cis, citra* on this side, Greek *ekeinos* that person] (before 12th century)
**1 :** that male one who is neither speaker nor hearer ⟨*he* is my father⟩ — compare HIM, HIS, IT, SHE, THEY
**2** — used in a generic sense or when the sex of the person is unspecified ⟨*he* that hath ears to hear, let him hear —Matthew 11:15 (Authorized Version)⟩ ⟨one should do the best *he* can⟩ ▪

**²he** \'hē\ *noun* (before 12th century)
**1 :** a male person or animal
**2 :** one that is strongly masculine or has strong masculine appeal — usually used in combination ⟨that's what I call *he*-literature —Sinclair Lewis⟩

**³he** \'hā\ *noun* [Hebrew *hē'*] (1639)
: the 5th letter of the Hebrew alphabet — see ALPHABET table.

**¹head** \'hed\ *noun* [Middle English *hed*, from Old English *hēafod*; akin to Old High German *houbit* head, Latin *caput*] (before 12th century)
**1 :** the upper or anterior division of the animal body that contains the brain, the chief sense organs, and the mouth
**2 a :** the seat of the intellect : MIND ⟨two *heads* are better than one⟩ **b :** a person with respect to mental qualities ⟨let wiser *heads* prevail⟩ **c :** natural aptitude or talent ⟨a good *head* for figures⟩ **d :** mental or emotional control : POISE ⟨a level *head*⟩ **e :** HEADACHE
**3 :** the obverse of a coin — usually used in plural ⟨*heads*, I win⟩

---

◇ WORD HISTORY ·

**hazard** *Hazard* was once only a game played with dice. The French archbishop William of Tyre, writing his Latin history of the Crusades late in the 12th century, explained the origin of this hazard and its name (*hasard* in Old French). The game was invented, he said, to pass the time during the siege of a castle in Palestine called *Hazard* or *Azart*. Unfortunately for the credibility of William's theory, the name of the castle seems actually to have been '*Ain Zarba*, and the name of the game was certainly never that. The French word did not originate in the time of the Crusades, however, and most likely comes from post-classical Arabic *az-zahr* "the die (one of the dice)." Old French *hasard* was borrowed into Middle English, and within a few centuries what had been a venture on the outcome of a throw of the dice could be any venture or risk.

**4 a :** PERSON, INDIVIDUAL ⟨count *heads*⟩ **b** *plural* **head :** one of a number (as of domestic animals)
**5 a :** the end that is upper or higher or opposite the foot ⟨the *head* of the table⟩ ⟨*head* of a sail⟩ **b :** the source of a stream **c :** either end of something (as a drum) whose two ends need not be distinguished
**6 :** DIRECTOR, LEADER: as **a :** HEADMASTER **b :** one in charge of a division or department in an office or institution ⟨the *head* of the English department⟩
**7 a :** CAPITULUM 2 **b :** the foliaged part of a plant especially when consisting of a compact mass of leaves or close fructification
**8 a :** the leading element of a military column or a procession **b :** HEADWAY
**9 a :** the uppermost extremity or projecting part of an object **:** TOP **b :** the striking part of a weapon, tool, or implement **c :** the rounded proximal end of a long bone (as the humerus) **d :** the end of a muscle nearest the origin — compare ORIGIN **e :** the oval part of a printed musical note
**10 a :** a body of water kept in reserve at a height; *also* **:** the containing bank, dam, or wall **b :** a mass of water in motion
**11 a :** the difference in elevation between two points in a body of fluid **b :** the resulting pressure of the fluid at the lower point expressible as this height; *broadly* **:** pressure of a fluid
**12 a :** the bow and adjacent parts of a ship **b :** a ship's toilet; *broadly* **:** TOILET
**13 :** the approximate length of the head of a horse ⟨won by a *head*⟩
**14 :** the place of leadership, honor, or command ⟨at the *head* of her class⟩
**15 a** (1) **:** a word or series of words often in larger letters placed at the beginning of a passage or at the top of a page in order to introduce or categorize (2) **:** a separate part or topic **b :** a portion of a page or sheet that is above the first line of printing
**16 :** the foam or scum that rises on a fermenting or effervescing liquid (as beer)
**17 a :** the part of a boil, pimple, or abscess at which it is likely to break **b :** culminating point of action **:** CRISIS ⟨events came to a *head*⟩
**18 a :** a part or attachment of a machine or machine tool containing a device (as a cutter or drill); *also* **:** the part of an apparatus that performs the chief function or a particular function **b :** an electromagnet used as a transducer in magnetic recording for recording on, reading, or erasing a magnetic medium (as tape)
**19 :** an immediate constituent of a construction that can have the same grammatical function as the whole (as *man* in "an old man", "a very old man", or "the man in the street")
**20 a :** one who uses a drug **b :** DEVOTEE ⟨chili *heads*⟩
**21 :** FELLATIO, CUNNILINGUS — usually used with *give;* often considered vulgar
**— by the head :** drawing the greater depth of water forward
**— off one's head :** CRAZY, DISTRACTED
**— out of one's head :** DELIRIOUS
**— over one's head 1 :** beyond one's comprehension or competence ⟨the most awful intellectual detail, all of it *over my head* —E. B. White⟩ **2 :** so as to pass over one's superior standing or authority ⟨went *over my head* to complain⟩
²**head** *adjective* (before 12th century)
**1 :** of, relating to, or intended for the head
**2 :** PRINCIPAL, CHIEF ⟨*head* cook⟩
**3 :** situated at the head
**4 :** coming from in front ⟨*head* sea⟩
³**head** (14th century)
*transitive verb*
**1 :** BEHEAD
**2 a :** to put a head on **:** fit a head to ⟨*head* an arrow⟩ **b :** to form the head or top of ⟨tower *headed* by a spire⟩
**3 :** to act as leader or head to ⟨*head* a revolt⟩

**4 a :** to get in front of so as to hinder, stop, or turn back **b :** to take a lead over (as a racehorse) **:** SURPASS **c :** to pass (a stream) by going round above the source
**5 a :** to put something at the head of (as a list) **b :** to stand as the first or leading member of ⟨*heads* the list of heroes⟩
**6 :** to set the course of ⟨*head* a ship northward⟩
**7 :** to drive (as a soccer ball) with the head
*intransitive verb*
**1 :** to form a head ⟨this cabbage *heads* early⟩
**2 :** to point or proceed in a certain direction ⟨the fleet was *heading* out⟩
**3 :** to have a source **:** ORIGINATE
**head·ache** \'he-ˌdāk\ *noun* (before 12th century)
**1 :** pain in the head
**2 :** a vexatious or baffling situation or problem
**— head·achy** \-ˌdā-kē\ *adjective*
**head and shoulders** *adverb* (circa 1864)
**:** beyond comparison **:** by far ⟨*head and shoulders* above the competition⟩
**head·band** \'hed-ˌband\ *noun* (1535)
**1 :** a band worn on or around the head
**2 :** a narrow strip of cloth sewn or glued by hand to a book at the extreme ends of the backbone
**head·board** \-ˌbōrd, -ˌbȯrd\ *noun* (1730)
**:** a board forming the head (as of a bed)
**head·cheese** \-ˌchēz\ *noun* (1841)
**:** a jellied loaf or sausage made from edible parts of the head, feet, and sometimes the tongue and heart especially of a pig
**head cold** *noun* (1937)
**:** a common cold centered in the nasal passages and adjacent mucous tissues
**head·dress** \'hed-ˌdres\ *noun* (1703)
**:** an often elaborate covering for the head
**head·ed** \'he-dəd\ *adjective* (13th century)
**1 :** having a head or a heading
**2 :** having a head or heads of a specified kind or number — used in combination ⟨became light-*headed* from the fever⟩ ⟨a round*headed* screw⟩

**headdress**

**head·er** \'he-dər\ *noun* (15th century)
**1 :** one that removes heads; *especially* **:** a grain-harvesting machine that cuts off the grain heads and elevates them to a wagon
**2 a :** a brick or stone laid in a wall with its end toward the face of the wall **b :** a beam fitted at one side of an opening to support free ends of floor joists, studs, or rafters **c :** a horizontal structural or finish piece over an opening **:** LINTEL **d :** a conduit (as an exhaust pipe for a many-cylindered engine) into which a number of smaller conduits open **e :** a mounting plate through which electrical terminals pass from a sealed device (as a transistor)
**3 :** a fall or dive headfirst
**4 :** a shot or pass in soccer made by heading the ball
**5 :** HEAD 15a(1)
**head·first** \'hed-'fərst\ *adverb* (circa 1828)
**:** with the head foremost **:** HEADLONG ⟨dove *headfirst* into the waves⟩
**— headfirst** *adjective*
**head·fore·most** \-ˈfȯr-ˌmōst, -ˈfȯr-\ *adverb* (1697)
**:** HEADFIRST
**head·gate** \'hed-ˌgāt\ *noun* (1832)
**:** a gate for controlling the water flowing into a channel (as an irrigation ditch)
**head·gear** \-ˌgir\ *noun* (15th century)
**1 :** a covering or protective device for the head
**2 :** a harness for a horse's head
**head·hunt·er** \-ˌhən-tər\ *noun* (1853)
**1 :** one that engages in head-hunting
**2 :** a recruiter of personnel especially at the executive level

**head–hunt·ing** \-ˌhən-tiŋ\ *noun* (1853)
**1 :** the act or custom of seeking out, decapitating, and preserving the heads of enemies as trophies
**2 :** a seeking to deprive usually political enemies of position or influence
**head·ing** \'he-diŋ\ *noun* (1676)
**1 a :** something that forms or serves as a head; *especially* **:** an inscription, headline, or title standing at the top or beginning (as of a letter or chapter) **b :** the address and date at the beginning of a letter showing its place and time of origin
**2 :** the compass direction in which the longitudinal axis of a ship or aircraft points; *broadly* **:** DIRECTION
**3 :** DRIFT 6
**head·lamp** \-ˌlamp\ *noun* (1885)
**:** HEADLIGHT
**head·land** \'hed-lənd, -ˌland\ *noun* (before 12th century)
**1 :** unplowed land at the ends of furrows or near a fence

□ **USAGE**
**he** Since English has no third-person singular pronoun of common gender, the problem of how to refer to a singular noun antecedent that can apply to either sex—such as *person*—has no perfect solution. From the earliest days of the language two approaches have been generally adopted: the use of *he* and the use of *they.* By the 18th century, grammarians had begun to be troubled by the use of the plural pronoun to refer to a singular antecedent. Such use violated number agreement. On the other hand, the use of *he* violated gender agreement. Some writers avoided the problem by using two pronouns (the reader's heart (if *he* or *she* have any) —Henry Fielding). The grammarians then hit upon the idea that the masculine pronoun included the feminine, and the generic *he* was created. Grammarians and usage commentators of the next two centuries have in general insisted on the generic *he* and have disparaged both *he or she* and *they.* But in the later 20th century generic *he* has met greater resistance, and more writers have sought alternative solutions, no single one of which works well in all cases. The consistent use of *she* can readily seem laughable in sentences like "show me a person who isn't concerned about her weight and I'll show you a man." The alternation of masculine and feminine pronouns can produce sentences like "Have the patient lie down no matter how she feels. Have him do this even though she acts all right and insists you leave him alone." So *he or she* has come in for increased use, but the paired pronouns are hard to use consistently. Some writers have started off with *he or she* and failed to follow through, lapsing into *he* or *him* in subsequent sentences. Many handbooks suggest recasting sentences in the plural so that the plural pronouns can be used without violation of number agreement. But here the common disapproval of *they* can cause writers to produce sentences in which a plural noun antecedent is followed by *he or she.* Those for whom the old solution of using the plural pronoun, now quite widely adopted, will not work and those who dislike generic *he* will have to be especially alert in using *he or she* or another approach. See in addition ANYBODY, EVERYBODY, NOBODY, THEY.

**2 :** a point of usually high land jutting out into a body of water **:** PROMONTORY
**head·less** \-ləs\ *adjective* (before 12th century)
**1 a :** having no head **b :** having the head cut off **:** BEHEADED
**2 :** having no chief
**3 :** lacking good sense or prudence **:** FOOLISH
— **head·less·ness** *noun*
**head·light** \-,līt\ *noun* (1861)
**1 :** a light with a reflector and special lens mounted on the front of a vehicle to illuminate the road ahead; *also* **:** the beam cast by a headlight
**2 :** a light worn on the forehead (as of a miner or physician)
**¹head·line** \-,līn\ *noun* (1824)
**1 :** words set at the head of a passage or page to introduce or categorize
**2 a :** a head of a newspaper story or article usually printed in large type and giving the gist of the story or article that follows **b** *plural* **:** front-page news ⟨the scandal made *headlines*⟩
**²headline** *transitive verb* (1891)
**1 :** to provide with a headline
**2 :** to publicize highly
**3 :** to be engaged as a leading performer in (a show)
**head·lin·er** \'hed-,lī-nər\ *noun* (1896)
**1 :** the principal performer in a show **:** STAR; *broadly* **:** PERSONALITY 4b
**2 :** fabric covering the inside of the roof of an automobile
**head linesman** *noun* (circa 1949)
**:** a football linesman
**head·lock** \'hed-,läk\ *noun* (1905)
**:** a hold in which a wrestler encircles his opponent's head with one arm
**¹head·long** \-'lȯṅ\ *adverb* [Middle English *hedlong*, alteration of *hedling*, from *hed* head] (14th century)
**1 :** HEADFIRST
**2 :** without deliberation **:** RECKLESSLY
**3 :** without pause or delay
**²head·long** \-,lȯṅ\ *adjective* (circa 1550)
**1** *archaic* **:** STEEP, PRECIPITOUS
**2 :** lacking in calmness or restraint **:** PRECIPITATE ⟨a *headlong* torrent of emotion⟩
**3 :** plunging headforemost
**synonym** see PRECIPITATE
**head louse** *noun* (1547)
**:** one of a variety (*Pediculus humanus capitis*) of the common louse that lives on the human scalp
**head·man** *noun* (before 12th century)
**1 a** \'hed-'man\ **:** FOREMAN, OVERSEER **b** \-'man, -,man\ **:** a lesser chief of a primitive community
**2** \-mən\ **:** HEADSMAN
**head·mas·ter** \'hed-,mas-tər, -'mas-\ *noun* (1576)
**:** a man heading the staff of a private school **:** PRINCIPAL
— **head·mas·ter·ship** \-,ship\ *noun*
**head·mis·tress** \-,mis-trəs, -'mis-\ *noun* (1872)
**:** a woman heading the staff of a private school
**head·most** \'hed-,mōst\ *adjective* (1628)
**:** most advanced **:** LEADING
**head·note** \-,nōt\ *noun* (1855)
**1 :** a prefixed note of comment or explanation
**2 :** a note prefixed to the report of a decided legal case
**head off** *transitive verb* (1841)
**:** to turn back or turn aside **:** BLOCK, PREVENT ⟨*head* them *off* at the pass⟩ ⟨attempts to *head off* the imminent crisis⟩
**¹head–on** \'hed-'ȯn, -'än\ *adverb* (1840)
**1 :** with the head or front making the initial contact ⟨the cars collided *head-on*⟩
**2 :** in direct opposition, confrontation, or contradiction ⟨met the problem *head-on*⟩
**²head–on** *adjective* (1903)

**1 :** having the front facing in the direction of initial contact or line of sight ⟨a *head-on* collision⟩
**2 :** FRONTAL
**head over heels** *adverb* (1771)
**1 a :** in or as if in a somersault **:** HELTER-SKELTER **b :** UPSIDE DOWN
**2 :** very much **:** DEEPLY ⟨*head over heels* in love⟩
**head·phone** \'hed-,fōn\ *noun* (1914)
**:** an earphone held over the ear by a band worn on the head — usually used in plural
**head·piece** \-,pēs\ *noun* (1535)
**1 a :** a protective or defensive covering for the head **b :** an ornamental, ceremonial, or traditional covering for the head
**2 :** BRAINS, INTELLIGENCE
**3 :** an ornament especially at the beginning of a chapter
**head·pin** \-,pin\ *noun* (1927)
**:** a bowling pin that stands foremost in the arrangement of pins
**head·quar·ter** \'hed-,kwȯ(r)-tər, -,kȯr-, (')hed-'\ (1903)
*transitive verb*
**:** to place in headquarters
*intransitive verb*
**:** to make one's headquarters
**head·quar·ters** \-tərz\ *noun plural but singular or plural in construction* (1647)
**1 :** a place from which a commander performs the functions of command
**2 :** the administrative center of an enterprise
**head·rest** \-,rest\ *noun* (1853)
**1 :** a support for the head
**2 :** HEAD RESTRAINT
**head restraint** *noun* (1967)
**:** a resilient pad at the top of the back of an automobile seat especially for preventing whiplash injury
**head rhyme** *noun* (circa 1943)
**:** ALLITERATION
**head·room** \'hed-,rüm, -,rum\ *noun* (1851)
**:** vertical space in which to stand, sit, or move
**head·sail** \-,sāl, -səl\ *noun* (1627)
**:** a sail set forward of the foremast
**head·set** \-,set\ *noun* (1921)
**1 :** an attachment for holding an earphone and transmitter at one's head
**2 :** a pair of headphones
**head·ship** \-,ship\ *noun* (1582)
**:** the position, office, or dignity of a head
**head shop** *noun* (1968)
**:** a shop specializing in articles (as hashish pipes and roach clips) of interest to drug users
**head·shrink·er** \-,shriṅ-kər, *especially Southern* -,sriṅ-\ *noun* (1950)
**:** SHRINK 3
**heads·man** \'hedz-mən\ *noun* (1601)
**:** one that beheads **:** EXECUTIONER
**head·space** \'hed-,spās\ *noun* (1936)
**:** the volume above a liquid or solid in a closed container
**head·spring** \'hed-,spriṅ\ *noun* (14th century)
**:** FOUNTAINHEAD, SOURCE
**head·stall** \-,stȯl\ *noun* (14th century)
**:** a part of a bridle or halter that encircles the head
**head·stand** \-,stand\ *noun* (circa 1934)
**:** the gymnastic feat of standing on one's head usually with support from the hands
**head start** *noun* (1886)
**1 :** an advantage granted or achieved at the beginning of a race, a chase, or a competition ⟨a 10-minute *head start*⟩
**2 :** a favorable or promising beginning
**head·stock** \'hed-,stäk\ *noun* (1731)
**:** a bearing or pedestal for a revolving or moving part; *specifically* **:** a part of a lathe that holds the revolving spindle and its attachments
**head·stone** \-,stōn\ *noun* (1775)
**:** a memorial stone at the head of a grave
**head·stream** \-,strēm\ *noun* (14th century)
**:** a stream that is the source of a river
**head·strong** \-,strȯṅ\ *adjective* (14th century)

**1 :** not easily restrained **:** impatient of control, advice, or suggestions
**2 :** directed by ungovernable will ⟨violent *headstrong* actions⟩
**synonym** see UNRULY
**heads–up** \'hed-'zəp\ *adjective* (1947)
**:** ALERT, RESOURCEFUL ⟨*heads-up* football⟩
**heads up** *interjection* (circa 1941)
**—** used as a warning to look out for danger especially overhead or to clear a passageway
**head–to–head** *adverb or adjective* (circa 1728)
**:** in a direct confrontation or encounter usually between individuals
**head–wait·er** \'hed-'wā-tər\ *noun* (1805)
**:** the head of the dining-room staff of a restaurant or hotel
**head·wa·ter** \-,wȯ-tər, -,wä-\ *noun* (1802)
**:** the source of a stream — usually used in plural
**head·way** \-,wā\ *noun* (1748)
**1 a :** motion or rate of motion in a forward direction **b :** ADVANCE, PROGRESS
**2 :** headroom (as under an arch) sufficient to allow passage
**3 :** the time interval between two vehicles traveling in the same direction on the same route
**head·word** \'hed-,wərd\ *noun* (circa 1823)
**1 :** a word or term placed at the beginning (as of a chapter or an entry in an encyclopedia)
**2 :** HEAD 19
**head·work** \-,wərk\ *noun* (1837)
**:** mental labor; *especially* **:** clever thinking
**heady** \'he-dē\ *adjective* **head·i·er; -est** (14th century)
**1 a :** WILLFUL, RASH ⟨*heady* opinions⟩ **b :** VIOLENT, IMPETUOUS
**2 a :** tending to intoxicate or make giddy or elated ⟨*heady* wine⟩ ⟨being in such distinguished company was a *heady* experience⟩ **b :** GIDDY, EXHILARATED ⟨*heady* with his success⟩ **c :** RICH ⟨a *heady* sauce⟩ ⟨a *heady* variety⟩ **d :** IMPRESSIVE ⟨a man of *heady* accomplishments⟩
**3 a :** marked by or showing good judgment **:** SHREWD, INTELLIGENT **b :** intellectually stimulating or demanding
— **head·i·ly** \'he-dᵊl-ē\ *adverb*
— **head·i·ness** \'he-dē-nəs\ *noun*
**heal** \'hē(ə)l\ *verb* [Middle English *helen*, from Old English *hǣlan*; akin to Old High German *heilen* to heal, Old English *hāl* whole — more at WHOLE] (before 12th century)
*transitive verb*
**1 a :** to make sound or whole ⟨*heal* a wound⟩ **b :** to restore to health
**2 a :** to cause (an undesirable condition) to be overcome **:** MEND ⟨the troubles . . . had not been forgotten, but they had been *healed* —William Power⟩ **b :** to patch up (a breach or division) ⟨*heal* a breach between friends⟩
**3 :** to restore to original purity or integrity ⟨*healed* of sin⟩
*intransitive verb*
**:** to return to a sound state
**heal·er** \'hē-lər\ *noun* (12th century)
**1 :** one that heals
**2 :** a Christian Science practitioner
**health** \'helth *also* 'heltth\ *noun, often attributive* [Middle English *helthe*, from Old English *hǣlth*, from *hāl*] (before 12th century)
**1 a :** the condition of being sound in body, mind, or spirit; *especially* **:** freedom from physical disease or pain **b :** the general condition of the body ⟨in poor *health*⟩ ⟨enjoys good *health*⟩
**2 a :** flourishing condition **:** WELL-BEING ⟨defending the *health* of the beloved oceans —Peter Wilkinson⟩ **b :** general condition or state ⟨poor economic *health*⟩
**3 :** a toast to someone's health or prosperity
**health food** *noun* (1882)
**:** a food promoted as highly conducive to health

**health·ful** \'helth-fəl *also* 'heltth-\ *adjective* (14th century)
**1** : beneficial to health of body or mind
**2** : HEALTHY ⟨he felt incapable of looking into the girl's pretty, *healthful* face —Saul Bellow⟩
☆
*usage* see HEALTHY
— **health·ful·ness** *noun*
**health insurance** *noun* (1901)
: insurance against loss through illness of the insured; *especially* : insurance providing compensation for medical expenses
**health maintenance organization** *noun* (1973)
: HMO
**health spa** *noun* (1960)
: a commercial establishment (as a resort) providing facilities devoted to health and fitness
**healthy** \'hel-thē *also* 'helt-\ *adjective* **health·i·er; -est** (1552)
**1** : enjoying health and vigor of body, mind, or spirit : WELL
**2** : evincing health ⟨a *healthy* complexion⟩
**3** : conducive to health ⟨walk three miles every day . . . a beastly bore, but *healthy* —G. S. Patton⟩
**4 a** : PROSPEROUS, FLOURISHING **b** : not small or feeble : CONSIDERABLE ☆ ▪
— **health·i·ly** \-thə-lē\ *adverb*
— **health·i·ness** \-thē-nəs\ *noun*
¹**heap** \'hēp\ *noun* [Middle English *heep*, from Old English *hēap*; akin to Old High German *houf* heap] (before 12th century)
**1** : a collection of things thrown one on another : PILE
**2** : a great number or large quantity : LOT
²**heap** *transitive verb* (before 12th century)
**1 a** : to throw or lay in a heap : pile or collect in great quantity ⟨his sole object was to *heap* up riches⟩ **b** : to form or round into a heap ⟨*heaped* the dirt into a mound⟩ **c** : to form a heap on : load heavily ⟨*heap* the plates with food⟩
**2** : to accord or bestow lavishly or in large quantities ⟨*heaped* honors upon them⟩
**hear** \'hir\ *verb* **heard** \'hərd\; **hear·ing** \'hir-iŋ\ [Middle English *heren*, from Old English *hīeran*; akin to Old High German *hōren* to hear, and probably to Latin *cavēre* to be on guard, Greek *akouein* to hear] (before 12th century)
*transitive verb*
**1** : to perceive or apprehend by the ear
**2** : to gain knowledge of by hearing
**3 a** : to listen to with attention : HEED **b** : ATTEND ⟨*hear* mass⟩
**4 a** : to give a legal hearing to **b** : to take testimony from ⟨*hear* witnesses⟩
*intransitive verb*
**1** : to have the capacity of apprehending sound
**2 a** : to gain information : LEARN **b** : to receive communication ⟨*heard* from her recently⟩
**3** : to entertain the idea — used in the negative ⟨wouldn't *hear* of it⟩
**4** — often used in the expression *Hear! Hear!* to express approval (as during a speech)
— **hear·er** \'hir-ər\ *noun*
**hear·ing** *noun* (13th century)
**1 a** : the process, function, or power of perceiving sound; *specifically* : the special sense by which noises and tones are received as stimuli **b** : EARSHOT
**2 a** : opportunity to be heard, to present one's side of a case, or to be generally known or appreciated **b** (1) : a listening to arguments (2) : a preliminary examination in criminal procedure **c** : a session (as of a legislative committee) in which testimony is taken from witnesses
**3** *chiefly dialect* : a piece of news
**hearing aid** *noun* (1922)
: an electronic device usually worn by a person for amplifying sound before it reaches the receptor organs
**hearing dog** *noun* (1952)
: a dog trained to alert its deaf or hearing-

impaired owner to sounds (as of a doorbell, alarm, or telephone) — called also *hearing ear dog*
**hear·ken** \'här-kən\ *verb* **hear·kened; hear·ken·ing** \'härk-niŋ, 'här-kə-\ [Middle English *herknen*, from Old English *heorcnian*; akin to Old High German *hōrechen* to listen, Old English *hīeran* to hear] (before 12th century)
*intransitive verb*
**1** : LISTEN
**2** : to give respectful attention
*transitive verb*
*archaic* : to give heed to : HEAR
**hearken back** *intransitive verb* (1933)
: HARK BACK
**hear·say** \'hir-,sā\ *noun* (circa 1532)
: RUMOR
**hearsay evidence** *noun* (1753)
: evidence based not on a witness's personal knowledge but on another's statement not made under oath
¹**hearse** \'hərs\ *noun* [Middle English *herse*, from Middle French *herce* harrow, frame for holding candles, from Latin *hirpic-, hirpex* harrow] (14th century)
**1 a** : an elaborate framework erected over a coffin or tomb to which memorial verses or epitaphs are attached **b** : a triangular candelabrum for 15 candles used especially at Tenebrae
**2 a** *archaic* : COFFIN **b** *obsolete* : BIER 2
**3** : a vehicle for conveying the dead to the grave ◆
²**hearse** *transitive verb* **hearsed; hears·ing** (1592)
**1 a** *archaic* : to place on or in a hearse **b** : to convey in a hearse
**2** : BURY
¹**heart** \'härt\ *noun* [Middle English *hert*, from Old English *heorte*; akin to Old High German *herza* heart, Latin *cord-, cor*, Greek *kardia*] (before 12th century)
**1 a** : a hollow muscular organ of vertebrate animals that by its rhythmic contraction acts as a force pump maintaining the circulation of the blood **b** : a structure in an invertebrate animal functionally analogous to the vertebrate heart **c** : BREAST, BOSOM **d** : something resembling a heart in shape; *specifically* : a stylized representation of a heart
**2 a** : a playing card marked with a stylized figure of a red heart **b** *plural* : the suit comprising cards marked with hearts **c** *plural but singular or plural in construction* : a game in which the object is to avoid taking tricks containing hearts

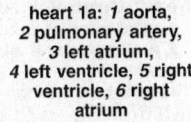

heart 1a: *1* aorta, *2* pulmonary artery, *3* left atrium, *4* left ventricle, *5* right ventricle, *6* right atrium

**3 a :** PERSONALITY, DISPOSITION ⟨a cold *heart*⟩ **b** *obsolete :* INTELLECT
**4 :** the emotional or moral as distinguished from the intellectual nature: as **a :** generous disposition : COMPASSION ⟨a leader with *heart*⟩ **b :** LOVE, AFFECTIONS ⟨won her *heart*⟩ **c :** COURAGE, ARDOR ⟨never lost *heart*⟩
**5 :** one's innermost character, feelings, or inclinations ⟨knew it in his *heart*⟩ ⟨a man after my own *heart*⟩
**6 a :** the central or innermost part : CENTER **b :** the essential or most vital part of something **c :** the younger central compact part of a leafy rosette (as a head of lettuce)
— **at heart :** in essence : BASICALLY, ESSENTIALLY
— **by heart :** by rote or from memory
— **to heart :** with deep concern
²**heart** *transitive verb* (before 12th century)
**1** *archaic :* HEARTEN
**2** *archaic :* to fix in the heart
**heart·ache** \'härt-ˌāk\ *noun* (1602)
**:** anguish of mind : SORROW
**heart attack** *noun* (1928)
**:** an acute episode of heart disease (as myocardial infarction) due to insufficient blood supply to the heart muscle especially when caused by a coronary thrombosis or a coronary occlusion
**heart·beat** \'härt-ˌbēt\ *noun* (1850)
**1 :** one complete pulsation of the heart
**2 :** the vital center or driving impulse
**heart block** *noun* (1903)
**:** incoordination of the heartbeat in which the atria and ventricles beat independently and which is marked by decreased cardiac output
**heart·break** \'härt-ˌbrāk\ *noun* (14th century)
**:** crushing grief
**heart·break·er** \-ˌbrā-kər\ *noun* (1863)
**:** one that causes heartbreak
**heart·break·ing** \-ˌbrā-kiŋ\ *adjective* (1591)
**1 a :** causing intense sorrow or distress **b :** extremely trying or difficult
**2 :** producing an intense emotional reaction or response ⟨*heartbreaking* beauty⟩
— **heart·break·ing·ly** \-kiŋ-lē\ *adverb*
**heart·bro·ken** \-ˌbrō-kən\ *adjective* (circa 1586)
**:** overcome by sorrow
**heart·burn** \-ˌbərn\ *noun* (1597)
**:** a burning discomfort behind the lower part of the sternum usually related to spasm of the lower end of the esophagus or of the upper part of the stomach
**heart·burn·ing** \-ˌbər-niŋ\ *noun* (1513)
**:** intense or rancorous jealousy or resentment
**heart disease** *noun* (1864)
**:** an abnormal organic condition of the heart or of the heart and circulation
**heart·ed** \'här-təd\ *adjective* (13th century)
**1 :** having a heart especially of a specified kind — usually used in combination ⟨a faint-*hearted* leader⟩ ⟨a light*hearted* wanderer⟩
**2 :** seated in the heart
**heart·en** \'här-tᵊn\ *transitive verb* **heart·ened; heart·en·ing** \'härt-niŋ, 'har-tᵊn-iŋ\ (1526)
**:** to give heart to : CHEER
*synonym* see ENCOURAGE
— **heart·en·ing·ly** \-niŋ-lē, -tᵊn-iŋ-\ *adverb*
**heart failure** *noun* (1894)
**1 :** a condition in which the heart is unable to pump blood at an adequate rate or in adequate volume
**2 :** cessation of heartbeat : DEATH
**heart·felt** \'härt-ˌfelt\ *adjective* (1734)
**:** deeply felt : EARNEST
*synonym* see SINCERE
**heart–free** \'härt-ˌfrē\ *adjective* (1748)
**:** not in love
**hearth** \'härth\ *noun* [Middle English *herth*, from Old English *heorth*; akin to Old High German *herd* hearth, and probably to Sanskrit *kūḍayāti* he scorches] (before 12th century)
**1 a :** a brick, stone, or cement area in front of

a fireplace **b :** the floor of a fireplace; *also* **:** FIREPLACE **c :** the lowest section of a furnace; *especially :* the section of a furnace on which the ore or metal is exposed to the flame or heat
**2 :** HOME
**3 :** a vital or creative center ⟨the central *hearth* of occidental civilization —A. L. Kroeber⟩
**hearth·stone** \-ˌstōn\ *noun* (14th century)
**1 :** stone forming a hearth
**2 :** HOME
**heart·i·ly** \'här-tᵊl-ē\ *adverb* (14th century)
**1 :** in a hearty manner
**2 a :** with all sincerity : WHOLEHEARTEDLY **b :** with zest or gusto
**3 :** WHOLLY, THOROUGHLY ⟨*heartily* sick of all this talk⟩
**heart·land** \'härt-ˌland\ *noun* (1904)
**:** a central area: as **a :** a central land area (as northern Eurasia) having strategic advantages **b :** a central geographical region especially of the U.S. in which mainstream or traditional values predominate
**heart·less** \-ləs\ *adjective* (14th century)
**1** *archaic :* SPIRITLESS
**2 :** lacking feeling : CRUEL
— **heart·less·ly** *adverb*
— **heart·less·ness** *noun*
**heart–lung machine** *noun* (1953)
**:** a mechanical pump that maintains circulation during heart surgery by shunting blood away from the heart, oxygenating it, and returning it to the body
**heart·rend·ing** \'härt-ˌren-diŋ\ *adjective* (1594)
**:** HEARTBREAKING 1a
— **heart·rend·ing·ly** \-diŋ-lē\ *adverb*
**hearts·ease** \'härts-ˌēz\ *noun* (15th century)
**1 :** peace of mind : TRANQUILLITY
**2 :** any of various violas; *especially :* JOHNNY-JUMP-UP
**heart·sick** \'härt-ˌsik\ *adjective* (1526)
**:** very despondent : DEPRESSED
— **heart·sick·ness** *noun*
**heart·some** \'hert-səm\ *adjective* (1596)
*chiefly Scottish :* giving spirit or vigor : ANIMATING, ENLIVENING
— **heart·some·ly** *adverb, chiefly Scottish*
**heart·sore** \'härt-ˌsōr, -ˌsȯr\ *adjective* (1591)
**:** HEARTSICK
**heart·string** \-ˌstriŋ\ *noun* (15th century)
**1** *obsolete :* a nerve once believed to sustain the heart
**2 :** the deepest emotions or affections ⟨pulled at his *heartstrings*⟩
**heart·throb** \-ˌthräb\ *noun* (1839)
**1 :** the throb of a heart
**2 a :** sentimental emotion : PASSION **b :** SWEETHEART
¹**heart–to–heart** \'härt-tə-'härt\ *adjective* (1867)
**:** SINCERE, FRANK ⟨a *heart-to-heart* talk⟩
²**heart–to–heart** *noun* (1910)
**:** a frank, serious, and often intimate conversation
**heart·warm·ing** \'härt-ˌwȯr-miŋ\ *adjective* (1899)
**:** inspiring sympathetic feeling : CHEERING
— **heart–warm·er** *noun*
**heart–whole** \-ˌhōl\ *adjective* (1600)
**1 :** HEART-FREE
**2 :** SINCERE, GENUINE
**heart·wood** \-ˌwu̇d\ *noun* (1810)
**:** the older harder nonliving central wood of trees that is usually darker, denser, less permeable, and more durable than the surrounding sapwood
**heart·worm** \-ˌwərm\ *noun* (1888)
**:** a filarial worm (*Dirofilaria immitis*) that is a parasite especially in the right heart of dogs and is transmitted by mosquitoes; *also :* infestation or disease caused by the heartworm
¹**hearty** \'här-tē\ *adjective* **heart·i·er; -est** (14th century)
**1 a :** giving unqualified support ⟨a *hearty* en-

dorsement⟩ **b :** enthusiastically or exuberantly cordial : JOVIAL **c :** expressed unrestrainedly
**2 a :** exhibiting vigorous good health **b** (1) **:** having a good appetite (2) **:** abundant, rich, or flavorful enough to satisfy the appetite
**3 :** VIGOROUS, VEHEMENT ⟨a *hearty* pull⟩
*synonym* see SINCERE
— **heart·i·ness** *noun*
²**hearty** *noun, plural* **heart·ies** (1803)
**:** a hearty fellow; *also :* SAILOR
¹**heat** \'hēt\ *verb* [Middle English *heten*, from Old English *hǣtan*; akin to Old English *hāt* hot] (before 12th century)
*intransitive verb*
**1 :** to become warm or hot
**2 :** to start to spoil from heat
*transitive verb*
**1 :** to make warm or hot
**2 :** EXCITE
— **heat·able** \'hē-tə-bəl\ *adjective*
²**heat** *noun* [Middle English *hete*, from Old English *hǣte, hǣtu*; akin to Old English *hāt* hot] (before 12th century)
**1 a** (1) **:** a condition of being hot : WARMTH (2) **:** a marked or notable degree of hotness **b :** pathological excessive bodily temperature **c :** a hot place or situation **d** (1) **:** a period of heat (2) **:** a single complete operation of heating; *also :* the quantity of material so heated **e** (1) **:** added energy that causes substances to rise in temperature, fuse, evaporate, expand, or undergo any of various other related changes, that flows to a body by contact with or radiation from bodies at higher temperatures, and that can be produced in a body (as by compression) (2) **:** the energy associated with the random motions of the molecules, atoms, or smaller structural units of which matter is composed **f :** appearance, condition, or color of a body as indicating its temperature
**2 a :** intensity of feeling or reaction : PASSION **b :** the height or stress of an action or condition ⟨in the *heat* of battle⟩ **c :** sexual excitement especially in a female mammal; *specifically :* ESTRUS
**3 :** a single continuous effort: as **a :** a single round of a contest (as a race) having two or more rounds for each contestant **b :** one of several preliminary contests held to eliminate less competent contenders
**4 :** pungency of flavor
**5 a** *slang* (1) **:** the intensification of law-enforcement activity or investigation (2) **:** POLICE **b :** PRESSURE, COERCION **c :** ABUSE, CRITICISM ⟨took a lot of *heat*⟩
**6 :** SMOKE 8
— **heat·less** \'hēt-ləs\ *adjective*
— **heat·proof** \-'prüf\ *adjective*
**heat cramps** *noun plural* (1938)
**:** a condition that is marked by sudden development of cramps in skeletal muscles and that results from prolonged work in high temperatures accompanied by profuse perspiration with loss of sodium chloride from the body
**heat·ed** \'hē-təd\ *adjective* (1886)
**:** marked by anger ⟨a *heated* argument⟩
— **heat·ed·ly** *adverb*
**heat engine** *noun* (circa 1895)
**:** a mechanism (as an internal-combustion engine) for converting heat energy into mechanical or electrical energy
**heat·er** \'hē-tər\ *noun* (15th century)
**1 :** one that heats; *especially :* a device that imparts heat or holds something to be heated
**2 :** FASTBALL
**heat exchanger** *noun* (1902)
**:** a device (as an automobile radiator) for transferring heat from one fluid to another without allowing them to mix
**heat exhaustion** *noun* (1939)
**:** a condition marked by weakness, nausea, dizziness, and profuse sweating that results from physical exertion in a hot environment — called also *heat prostration;* compare HEATSTROKE
**heath** \'hēth\ *noun* [Middle English *heth*, from

Old English *hǣth;* akin to Old High German *heida* heather, Old Welsh *coit* forest] (before 12th century)
**1 a :** a tract of wasteland **b :** an extensive area of rather level open uncultivated land usually with poor coarse soil, inferior drainage, and a surface rich in peat or peaty humus
**2 a :** any of a family (Ericaceae, the heath family) of shrubby dicotyledonous and often evergreen plants that thrive on open barren usually acid and ill-drained soil; *especially* **:** an evergreen subshrub of either of two genera (*Erica* and *Calluna*) with whorls of needlelike leaves and clusters of small flowers **b :** any of various plants that resemble true heaths
— **heath·less** \-ləs\ *adjective*
— **heath·like** \-,līk\ *adjective*
— **heathy** \'hē-thē\ *adjective*

**¹hea·then** \'hē-thən\ *adjective* [Middle English *hethen,* from Old English *hǣthen;* akin to Old High German *heidan* heathen, and probably to Old English *hǣth* heath] (before 12th century)
**1 :** of or relating to heathens, their religions, or their customs
**2 :** STRANGE, UNCIVILIZED
**²heathen** *noun, plural* **heathens** *or* **heathen** (before 12th century)
**1 :** an unconverted member of a people or nation that does not acknowledge the God of the Bible
**2 :** an uncivilized or irreligious person
— **hea·then·dom** \-dəm\ *noun*
— **hea·then·ism** \-thə-,ni-zəm\ *noun*
— **hea·then·ize** \-thə-,nīz\ *transitive verb*
**hea·then·ish** \'hē-thə-nish\ *adjective* (1593)
**:** resembling or characteristic of heathens **:** BARBAROUS
— **hea·then·ish·ly** *adverb*

**¹heath·er** \'he-thər\ *noun* [Middle English (northern) *hather*] (14th century)
**:** HEATH 2a; *especially* **:** a common Eurasian heath (*Calluna vulgaris*) of northern and alpine regions that has small crowded sessile leaves and racemes of tiny usually purplish pink flowers and is naturalized in the northeastern U.S.
**²heather** *adjective* (1615)
**:** HEATHERY
**heath·ery** \'he-thə-rē, 'he-thə-\ *adjective* (1535)
**1 :** of, relating to, or resembling heather
**2 :** having flecks of various colors ⟨a soft *heathery* tweed⟩
**heath hen** *noun* (1644)
**:** a now extinct grouse (*Tympanuchus cupido cupido*) of the northeastern U.S. — compare PRAIRIE CHICKEN
**heath·land** \'hēth-,land\ *noun* (1819)
**:** HEATH 1
**heat lightning** *noun* (1834)
**:** vivid and extensive flashes of electric light without thunder seen near the horizon especially at the close of a hot day and ascribed to far-off lightning reflected by high clouds
**heat prostration** *noun* (1938)
**:** HEAT EXHAUSTION
**heat pump** *noun* (1894)
**:** an apparatus for heating or cooling a building by transferring heat by mechanical means from or to a reservoir (as the ground, water, or air) outside the building
**heat rash** *noun* (1887)
**:** PRICKLY HEAT
**heat shield** *noun* (1962)
**:** a barrier of ablative material to protect a space capsule from heat on its entry into an atmosphere
**heat sink** *noun* (1936)
**:** a substance or device for the absorption or dissipation of unwanted heat (as from a process or an electronic device)
**heat·stroke** \'hēt-,strōk\ *noun* (1874)
**:** a condition marked especially by cessation of sweating, extremely high body temperature, and collapse that results from prolonged exposure to high temperature — compare HEAT EXHAUSTION
**heat–treat** \'hēt-,trēt\ *transitive verb* (1907)
**:** to subject to heat; *especially* **:** to treat (as metals) by heating and cooling in a way that will produce desired properties
— **heat treater** *noun*
— **heat treatment** *noun*
**heat wave** *noun* (1893)
**:** a period of unusually hot weather

**¹heave** \'hēv\ *verb* **heaved** *or* **hove** \'hōv\; **heav·ing** [Middle English *heven,* from Old English *hebban;* akin to Old High German *heffen* to lift, Latin *capere* to take] (before 12th century)
*transitive verb*
**1** *obsolete* **:** ELEVATE
**2 :** LIFT, RAISE
**3 :** THROW, CAST
**4 a :** to cause to swell or rise **b :** to displace (as a rock stratum) especially by a fault
**5 :** to utter with obvious effort or with a deep breath
**6 :** HAUL, DRAW
*intransitive verb*
**1 :** LABOR, STRUGGLE
**2 :** RETCH
**3 a :** to rise and fall rhythmically **b :** PANT
**4 a :** PULL, PUSH **b :** to move a ship in a specified direction or manner **c** *past usually* **hove :** to move in an indicated way — used of a ship
**5 :** to rise or become thrown or raised up
*synonym* see LIFT
— **heav·er** *noun*
— **heave to :** to bring a ship to a stop
**²heave** *noun* (circa 1571)
**1 a :** an effort to heave or raise **b :** HURL, CAST
**2 :** an upward motion **:** RISING; *especially* **:** a rhythmical rising
**3 :** horizontal displacement especially by the faulting of a rock
**4** *plural but singular or plural in construction* **:** chronic pulmonary emphysema of the horse resulting in difficult expiration, heaving of the flanks, and a persistent cough
**heave–ho** \'hēv-'hō\ *noun* [from *heave ho!,* interjection used when heaving on a rope] (1947)
**:** DISMISSAL ⟨gave him the old *heave-ho*⟩
**heav·en** \'he-vən\ *noun* [Middle English *heven,* from Old English *heofon;* akin to Old High German *himil* heaven] (before 12th century)
**1 :** the expanse of space that seems to be over the earth like a dome **:** FIRMAMENT — usually used in plural
**2 a** *often capitalized* **:** the dwelling place of the Deity and the joyful abode of the blessed dead **b :** a spiritual state of everlasting communion with God
**3** *capitalized* **:** GOD 1
**4 :** a place or condition of utmost happiness
**5** *Christian Science* **:** a state of thought in which sin is absent and the harmony of divine Mind is manifest
**heav·en·ly** \-lē\ *adjective* (before 12th century)
**1 :** of or relating to heaven or the heavens **:** CELESTIAL ⟨the *heavenly* choirs⟩ ⟨use a telescope to study the *heavenly* bodies⟩
**2 a :** suggesting the blessed state of heaven **:** BEATIFIC ⟨*heavenly* peace⟩ **b :** DELIGHTFUL
— **heav·en·li·ness** *noun*
**heav·en–sent** \-,sent\ *adjective* (circa 1649)
**:** PROVIDENTIAL
**heav·en·ward** \-wərd\ *adverb or adjective* (13th century)
**:** toward heaven
**heav·en·wards** \-wərdz\ *adverb* (1650)
**:** HEAVENWARD
**heavier–than–air** *adjective* (1903)
**:** of greater weight than the air displaced
**heavi·ly** \'he-və-lē\ *adverb* (before 12th century)
**1 :** to a great degree **:** SEVERELY
**2 :** slowly and laboriously **:** DULLY
**3** *archaic* **:** with sorrow **:** GRIEVOUSLY
**4 :** in a heavy manner
**Heav·i·side layer** \'he-vē-,sīd-\ *noun* [Oliver *Heaviside*] (1912)
**:** IONOSPHERE
**¹heavy** \'he-vē\ *adjective* **heavi·er; -est** [Middle English *hevy,* from Old English *hefig;* akin to Old High German *hebīc* heavy, Old English *hebban* to lift — more at HEAVE] (before 12th century)
**1 a :** having great weight; *also* **:** characterized by mass or weight ⟨how *heavy* is it?⟩ **b :** having a high specific gravity **:** having great weight in proportion to bulk **c (1)** *of an isotope* **:** having or being atoms of greater than normal mass for that element **(2)** *of a compound* **:** containing heavy isotopes
**2 :** hard to bear; *specifically* **:** GRIEVOUS, AFFLICTIVE ⟨a *heavy* sorrow⟩
**3 :** of weighty import **:** SERIOUS
**4 :** DEEP, PROFOUND
**5 a :** borne down by something oppressive **:** BURDENED **b :** PREGNANT; *especially* **:** approaching parturition
**6 a :** slow or dull from loss of vitality or resiliency **:** SLUGGISH **b :** lacking sparkle or vivacity **:** DRAB **c :** lacking mirth or gaiety **:** DOLEFUL **d :** characterized by declining prices
**7 :** dulled with weariness **:** DROWSY
**8 :** greater in quantity or quality than the average of its kind or class: as **a :** of unusually large size or amount ⟨a *heavy* turnout⟩ ⟨*heavy* traffic⟩ **b :** of great force ⟨*heavy* seas⟩ **c :** threatening to rain or snow **d (1) :** impeding motion **(2) :** full of clay and inclined to hold water **e :** coming as if from a depth **:** LOUD ⟨*heavy* breathing⟩ **f :** THICK, COARSE **g :** OPPRESSIVE ⟨*heavy* odor⟩ **h :** STEEP, ACUTE **i :** LABORIOUS, DIFFICULT ⟨*heavy* going⟩ **j :** IMMODERATE ⟨a *heavy* smoker⟩ **k :** more powerful than usual for its kind ⟨*heavy* cavalry⟩ ⟨*heavy* cruiser⟩ **l :** of large capacity or output
**9 a :** very rich and hard to digest ⟨*heavy* desserts⟩ **b :** not properly raised or leavened ⟨*heavy* bread⟩
**10 :** producing goods (as coal, steel, or chemicals) used in the production of other goods ⟨*heavy* industry⟩
**11 a :** having stress ⟨*heavy* rhythm⟩ — used especially of syllables in accentual verse **b :** being the strongest degree of stress in speech
**12 :** relating to theatrical parts of a grave or somber nature
**13 :** LONG 9 ⟨*heavy* on ideas⟩
**14 :** IMPORTANT, PROMINENT ⟨a *heavy* politician⟩ ☆
— **heavi·ness** *noun*
**²heavy** *adverb* (before 12th century)
**:** in a heavy manner **:** HEAVILY

☆ **SYNONYMS**
**Heavy, weighty, ponderous, cumbrous, cumbersome** mean having great weight. HEAVY implies that something has greater density or thickness than the average of its kind or class ⟨a *heavy* child for his age⟩. WEIGHTY suggests having actual and not just relative weight ⟨a load of *weighty* boxes⟩. PONDEROUS implies having great weight because of size and massiveness with resulting great inertia ⟨*ponderous* elephants in a circus parade⟩. CUMBROUS and CUMBERSOME imply heaviness and bulkiness that make for difficulty in grasping, moving, carrying, or manipulating ⟨wrestled with the *cumbrous* furniture⟩ ⟨early cameras were *cumbersome* and inconvenient⟩.

\ə\ abut \ᵊ\ kitten \ər\ further \a\ ash \ā\ ace
\ä\ mop, mar \au̇\ out \ch\ chin \e\ bet \ē\ easy
\g\ go \i\ hit \ī\ ice \j\ job \ŋ\ sing \ō\ go
\ȯ\ law \ȯi\ boy \th\ thin \ṯh\ the \ü\ loot \u̇\ foot
\y\ yet \zh\ vision *see also* Guide to Pronunciation

**³heavy** *noun, plural* **heav·ies** (1897)
**1 :** HEAVYWEIGHT 2
**2 a :** a theatrical role of a dignified or somber character; *also* **:** an actor playing such a role **b** **:** VILLAIN 4 **c :** someone or something influential, serious, or important

**heavy chain** *noun* (1964)
**:** either of the two larger of the four polypeptide chains comprising antibodies — compare LIGHT CHAIN

**heavy cream** *noun* (1930)
**:** a cream that is markedly thick; *especially* **:** cream that by law contains not less than 36 percent butterfat

**heavy–du·ty** \'he-vē-'dü-tē, -'dyü-\ *adjective* (1914)
**1 :** able or designed to withstand unusual strain
**2 :** INTENSIVE ⟨*heavy-duty* bargaining⟩

**heavy–foot·ed** \-'fu̇-təd\ *adjective* (1625)
**:** heavy and slow in movement

**heavy–hand·ed** \-'han-dəd\ *adjective* (1647)
**1 :** CLUMSY
**2 :** OPPRESSIVE, HARSH
— **heavy–hand·ed·ly** *adverb*
— **heavy–hand·ed·ness** *noun*

**heavy·heart·ed** \-'här-təd\ *adjective* (14th century)
**:** DESPONDENT, SADDENED
— **heavy·heart·ed·ly** *adverb*
— **heavy·heart·ed·ness** *noun*

**heavy hitter** *noun* (1976)
**:** BIG SHOT, HEAVY

**heavy hydrogen** *noun* (1933)
**:** DEUTERIUM

**heavy metal** *noun* (1974)
**:** energetic and highly amplified electronic rock music having a hard beat

**heavy·set** \,he-vē-'set\ *adjective* (1922)
**:** stocky and compact and sometimes tending to stoutness in build

**heavy water** *noun* (1933)
**1 :** the compound D₂O composed of deuterium and oxygen — called also *deuterium oxide*
**2 :** water enriched in deuterium

**heavy·weight** \'he-vē-,wāt\ *noun* (1857)
**1 :** one that is above average in weight
**2 :** one in the usually heaviest class of contestants: as **a :** a boxer in an unlimited weight division — compare LIGHT HEAVYWEIGHT **b :** a weight lifter weighing more than 198 pounds
**3 :** BIG SHOT, HEAVY

**heb·do·mad** \'heb-də-,mad\ *noun* [Latin *hebdomad-, hebdomas*, from Greek, from *hebdomos* seventh, from *hepta* seven — more at SEVEN] (1545)
**1 :** a group of seven
**2 :** a period of seven days **:** WEEK

**heb·dom·a·dal** \heb-'dä-mə-d°l\ *adjective* (1711)
**:** WEEKLY
— **heb·dom·a·dal·ly** \-d°l-ē\ *adverb*

**hebe** \'hēb\ *noun, often capitalized* [short for *Hebrew*] (1932)
**:** JEW — usually taken to be offensive

**He·be** \'hē-bē\ *noun* [Latin, from Greek *Hēbē*]
**:** the Greek goddess of youth and a cupbearer to the gods

**he·be·phre·nia** \,hē-bə-'frē-nē-ə, -'fre-nē-\ *noun* [New Latin, irregular from Greek *hēbētēs* young adult (from *hēbē* youth) + English *-phrenia*; from the childish behavior which is often found with it] (1883)
**:** a form of schizophrenia characterized especially by incoherence, delusions lacking an underlying theme, and affect that is flat, inappropriate, or silly
— **he·be·phre·nic** \-'fre-nik, -'frē-nik\ *adjective or noun*

**heb·e·tate** \'he-bə-,tāt\ *transitive verb* **-tat·ed; -tat·ing** [Latin *hebetatus*, past participle of *hebetare*, from *hebet-, hebes* dull] (1574)
**:** to make dull or obtuse
— **heb·e·ta·tion** \,he-bə-'tā-shən\ *noun*

**heb·e·tude** \'he-bə-,tüd, -,tyüd\ *noun* [Late Latin *hebetudo*, from *hebēre* to be dull; akin to Latin *hebes* dull] (circa 1621)

**:** LETHARGY, DULLNESS
— **heb·e·tu·di·nous** \,he-bə-'tü-d°n-əs, -'tyü-\ *adjective*

**He·bra·ic** \hi-'brā-ik\ *adjective* [Middle English *Ebrayke*, from Late Latin *Hebraicus*, from Greek *Hebraikos*, from *Hebraios*] (14th century)
**:** of, relating to, or characteristic of the Hebrews or their language or culture
— **He·bra·i·cal·ly** \-'brā-ə-k(ə-)lē\ *adverb*

**He·bra·ism** \'hē-(,)brā-,i-zəm\ *noun* (1570)
**1 :** a characteristic feature of Hebrew occurring in another language
**2 :** the thought, spirit, or practice characteristic of the Hebrews
**3 :** a moral theory or emphasis attributed to the Hebrews

**He·bra·ist** \-,brā-ist\ *noun* (circa 1755)
**:** a specialist in Hebrew and Hebraic studies

**He·bra·is·tic** \,hē-brā-'is-tik\ *adjective* (1690)
**1 :** marked by Hebraisms
**2 :** HEBRAIC

**he·bra·ize** \'hē-brā-,īz\ *verb* **-ized; -iz·ing** *often capitalized* (1645)
*intransitive verb*
**:** to use Hebraisms
*transitive verb*
**:** to make Hebraic in character or form
— **he·bra·iza·tion** \,hē-,brā-ə-'zā-shən\ *noun, often capitalized*

**He·brew** \'hē-(,)brü\ *noun* [Middle English *Ebreu*, from Old French, from Late Latin *Hebraeus*, from Latin, adjective, from Greek *Hebraios*, from Aramaic *'Ebrai*] (13th century)
**1 a :** the Semitic language of the ancient Hebrews **b :** any of various later forms of this language
**2 :** a member of or descendant from one of a group of northern Semitic peoples including the Israelites; *especially* **:** ISRAELITE
— **Hebrew** *adjective*

**He·brews** \'hē-(,)brüz\ *noun plural but singular in construction*
**:** a theological treatise addressed to early Christians and included as a book in the New Testament — see BIBLE table

**Hec·ate** \'he-kə-tē, 'he-kət\ *noun* [Latin, from Greek *Hekatē*]
**:** a Greek goddess associated especially with the underworld, night, and witchcraft

**hec·a·tomb** \'he-kə-,tōm\ *noun* [Latin *hecatombe*, from Greek *hekatombē*, from *hekaton* hundred + *-bē*; akin to Greek *bous* cow — more at HUNDRED, COW] (circa 1592)
**1 :** an ancient Greek and Roman sacrifice of 100 oxen or cattle
**2 :** the sacrifice or slaughter of many victims

**heck** \'hek\ *noun* [euphemism] (1887)
**:** HELL ⟨a *heck* of a lot of money⟩

**heck·le** \'he-kəl\ *transitive verb* **heck·led; heck·ling** \-k(ə-)liŋ\ [Middle English *hekelen* to dress flax, scratch, from *heckele* hackle; akin to Old High German *hāko* hook — more at HOOK] (circa 1825)
**:** to harass and try to disconcert with questions, challenges, or gibes **:** BADGER
*synonym* see BAIT
— **heck·ler** \-k(ə-)lər\ *noun*

**hect-** *or* **hecto-** *combining form* [French, irregular from Greek *hekaton*]
**:** hundred ⟨*hectare*⟩

**hect·are** \'hek-,tar, -,ter, -,tär\ *noun* [French, from *hect-* + *are* ²are] (1810)
— see METRIC SYSTEM table

**hec·tic** \'hek-tik\ *adjective* [Middle English *etyk*, from Middle French *etique*, from Late Latin *hecticus*, from Greek *hektikos* habitual, consumptive, from *echein* to have — more at SCHEME] (14th century)
**1 :** of, relating to, or being a fluctuating but persistent fever (as in tuberculosis)
**2 :** having a hectic fever
**3 :** RED, FLUSHED
**4 :** characterized by activity, excitement, or confusion ⟨the *hectic* days before Christmas⟩
— **hec·ti·cal·ly** \-ti-k(ə-)lē\ *adverb*

**hec·to·gram** \'hek-tə-,gram\ *noun* [French *hectogramme*, from *hect-* + *gramme* gram] (1810)
— see METRIC SYSTEM table

**hec·to·graph** \-,graf\ *noun* [German *Hektograph*, from *hekto-* hect- + *-graph* -graph] (1880)
**:** a machine for making copies of a writing or drawing produced on a gelatin surface
— **hectograph** *transitive verb*

**hec·to·li·ter** \'hek-tə-,lē-tər\ *noun* [French *hectolitre*, from *hect-* + *litre* liter] (1810)
— see METRIC SYSTEM table

**hec·to·me·ter** \'hek-tə-,mē-tər, hek-'tä-mə-tər\ *noun* [French *hectomètre*, from *hect-* + *mètre* meter] (1810)
— see METRIC SYSTEM table

**¹hec·tor** \'hek-tər\ *noun* [Latin, from Greek *Hektōr*]
**1** *capitalized* **:** a son of Priam, husband of Andromache, and Trojan champion slain by Achilles
**2 :** BULLY, BRAGGART ◆

**²hector** *verb* **hec·tored; hec·tor·ing** \-t(ə-)riŋ\ (1660)
*intransitive verb*
**:** to play the bully **:** SWAGGER
*transitive verb*
**:** to intimidate or harass by bluster or personal pressure
*synonym* see BAIT
— **hec·tor·ing·ly** \-t(ə-)riŋ-lē\ *adverb*

**Hec·u·ba** \'he-kyə-bə\ *noun* [Latin, from Greek *Hekabē*]
**:** the wife of Priam in Homer's *Iliad*

**he'd** \'hēd, ēd\ (circa 1600)
**:** he had **:** he would

**hed·dle** \'he-d°l\ *noun* [probably alteration of Middle English *helde*, from Old English *hefeld*; akin to Old Norse *hafald* heddle, Old English *hebban* to lift — more at HEAVE] (1513)
**:** one of the sets of parallel cords or wires that with their mounting compose the harness used to guide warp threads in a loom

**he·der** \'kā-dər, 'ke-\ *noun* [Yiddish *kheyder*, from Hebrew *hedher* room] (1882)
**:** an elementary Jewish school in which children are taught to read the Torah and other books in Hebrew

**¹hedge** \'hej\ *noun* [Middle English *hegge*, from Old English *hecg*; akin to Old English *haga* hedge, hawthorn] (before 12th century)
**1 a :** a fence or boundary formed by a dense row of shrubs or low trees **b :** BARRIER, LIMIT
**2 :** a means of protection or defense (as against financial loss)
**3 :** a calculatedly noncommittal or evasive statement

**²hedge** *verb* **hedged; hedg·ing** (14th century)

◇ WORD HISTORY

**hector** In Homer's account of the Trojan War, Hector, the great Trojan hero, is portrayed as the ideal warrior: fearless combatant, loving son and husband, steadfast friend. After his death at the hands of Achilles, he is buried with the highest honors. From the 14th century the name *Hector* has been used allusively in English literature for a valiant warrior. The word apparently acquired its pejorative sense in the latter half of the 17th century. At that time there appeared on the streets of London rowdy toughs who were known as *Hectors*. While they may have perceived themselves as gallant young blades, to the general populace they were blustering, swaggering bullies who brandished their swords, intimidated passersby, and engaged in vandalism. Thus *Hector* deteriorated into a synonym for a braggart and a bully. The conversion of *hector* into a verb soon followed.

*transitive verb*
**1 :** to enclose or protect with or as if with a hedge **:** ENCIRCLE
**2 :** to hem in or obstruct with or as if with a barrier **:** HINDER ⟨*hedged* about by special regulations and statutes —Sandi Rosenbloom⟩
**3 :** to protect oneself from losing or failing by a counterbalancing action ⟨*hedge* a bet⟩
*intransitive verb*
**1 :** to plant, form, or trim a hedge
**2 :** to evade the risk of commitment especially by leaving open a way of retreat **:** TRIM
**3 :** to protect oneself financially: as **a :** to buy or sell commodity futures as a protection against loss due to price fluctuation **b :** to minimize the risk of a bet
— **hedg·er** *noun*
— **hedg·ing·ly** \'he-jiŋ-lē\ *adverb*
³**hedge** *adjective* (14th century)
**1 :** of, relating to, or designed for a hedge
**2 :** born, living, or made near or as if near hedges **:** ROADSIDE
**3 :** INFERIOR 3
**hedge fund** *noun* (1967)
**:** an investing group usually in the form of a limited partnership that employs speculative techniques in the hope of obtaining large capital gains
**hedge·hog** \'hej-,hȯg, -,häg\ *noun* (15th century)

hedgehog 1a

**1 a :** any of a subfamily (Erinaceinae) of Old World nocturnal insectivores that have both hair and spines which they present outwardly by rolling themselves up when threatened **b :** any of several spiny mammals (as a porcupine)
**2 a :** a military defensive obstacle (as of barbed wire) **b :** a well-fortified military stronghold
**hedge·hop** \-,häp\ *intransitive verb* [back-formation from *hedgehopper*] (1926)
**:** to fly an airplane close to the ground and rise over obstacles as they appear
— **hedge·hop·per** *noun*
**hedge·pig** \-,pig\ *noun* (1605)
**:** HEDGEHOG
**hedge·row** \-,rō\ *noun* (before 12th century)
**:** a row of shrubs or trees enclosing or separating fields
**he·don·ic** \hi-'dä-nik\ *adjective* (1656)
**1 :** of, relating to, or characterized by pleasure
**2 :** of, relating to, or characterized by hedonism
— **he·don·i·cal·ly** \-ni-k(ə-)lē\ *adverb*
**he·do·nism** \'hē-d°n-,i-zəm\ *noun* [Greek *hēdonē* pleasure; akin to Greek *hēdys* sweet — more at SWEET] (1856)
**1 :** the doctrine that pleasure or happiness is the sole or chief good in life
**2 :** a way of life based on or suggesting the principles of hedonism
— **he·do·nist** \-d°n-ist\ *noun*
— **he·do·nis·tic** \,hē-d°n-'is-tik\ *adjective*
— **he·do·nis·ti·cal·ly** \-ti-k(ə-)lē\ *adverb*
**-he·dral** \'hē-drəl\ *adjective combining form* [New Latin *-hedron*]
**:** having (such) a surface or (such or so many) surfaces ⟨dihedral⟩
**-he·dron** \'hē-drən\ *noun combining form, plural* **-hedrons** or **-he·dra** \-drə\ [New Latin, from Greek *-edron*, from *hedra* seat — more at SIT]
**:** crystal or geometrical figure having a (specified) form or number of surfaces ⟨penta*hedron*⟩ ⟨trapezo*hedron*⟩
**hee·bie-jee·bies** \,hē-bē-'jē-bēz\ *noun plural* [coined by Billy DeBeck (died 1942) American cartoonist] (1923)
**:** JITTERS, CREEPS

¹**heed** \'hēd\ *verb* [Middle English, from Old English *hēdan;* akin to Old High German *huota* guard, Old English *hōd* hood] (before 12th century)
*intransitive verb*
**:** to pay attention
*transitive verb*
**:** to give consideration or attention to **:** MIND ⟨*heed* what he says⟩ ⟨*heed* the call⟩
²**heed** *noun* (14th century)
**:** ATTENTION, NOTICE
**heed·ful** \'hēd-fəl\ *adjective* (1548)
**:** taking heed **:** ATTENTIVE ⟨*heedful* of what they were doing⟩
— **heed·ful·ly** \-fə-lē\ *adverb*
— **heed·ful·ness** *noun*
**heed·less** \-ləs\ *adjective* (1579)
**:** not taking heed **:** INCONSIDERATE, THOUGHTLESS ⟨*heedless* follies of unbridled youth —John DeBruyn⟩
— **heed·less·ly** *adverb*
— **heed·less·ness** *noun*
**hee–haw** \'hē-,hȯ, -'hȯ\ *noun* [imitative] (1815)
**1 :** the bray of a donkey
**2 :** a loud rude laugh **:** GUFFAW
— **hee–haw** *intransitive verb*
¹**heel** \'hē(ə)l\ *noun* [Middle English, from Old English *hēla;* akin to Old Norse *hæll* heel, Old English *hōh* — more at HOCK] (before 12th century)
**1 a :** the back of the human foot below the ankle and behind the arch **b :** the part of the hind limb of other vertebrates that is homologous with the human heel
**2 :** an anatomical structure suggestive of the human heel; *especially* **:** the part of the palm of the hand nearest the wrist
**3 :** one of the crusty ends of a loaf of bread
**4 a :** the part (as of a shoe) that covers the human heel **b :** a solid attachment of a shoe or boot forming the back of the sole under the heel of the foot
**5 :** a rear, low, or bottom part: as **a :** the after end of a ship's keel or the lower end of a mast **b :** the base of a tuber or cutting of a plant used for propagation **c :** the base of a ladder
**6 :** a contemptible person
— **heel·less** \'hē(ə)l-ləs\ *adjective*
— **by the heels :** in a tight grip
— **down at heel** or **down at the heel :** in or into a run-down or shabby condition
— **on the heels of :** immediately following
— **to heel 1 :** close behind **2 :** into agreement or line
— **under heel :** under control or subjection
²**heel** (1605)
*transitive verb*
**1 a :** to furnish with a heel **b :** to supply especially with money
**2 a :** to exert pressure on, propel, or strike with the heel ⟨*heeled* her horse⟩ **b :** to urge (as a lagging animal) by following closely or by nipping at the heels ⟨dogs *heeling* cattle⟩
*intransitive verb*
**:** to move along at someone's heels
³**heel** *verb* [alteration of Middle English *heelden*, from Old English *hieldan;* akin to Old High German *hald* inclined, Lithuanian *šalis* side, region] (1575)
*intransitive verb*
**:** to lean to one side **:** TIP; *especially, of a boat or ship* **:** to lean temporarily (as from the action of wind or waves) — compare LIST
*transitive verb*
**:** to cause (a boat) to heel
⁴**heel** *noun* (1760)
**:** a tilt (as of a boat) to one side; *also* **:** the extent of such a tilt
**heel–and–toe** \,hē-lən-'tō\ *adjective* (1827)
**:** marked by a stride in which the heel of one foot touches the ground before the toe of the other foot leaves it ⟨*heel-and-toe* walking⟩
**heel·ball** \'hē(ə)l-,bȯl\ *noun* (1822)

**:** a composition of wax and lampblack used by shoemakers for polishing and by antiquarians for making rubbings of inscriptions
**heel·er** \'hē-lər\ *noun* (1665)
**1 a :** one that heels **b :** AUSTRALIAN CATTLE DOG
**2 a :** a henchman of a local political boss **b :** a worker for a local party organization; *especially* **:** WARD HEELER
**heel fly** *noun* (1878)
**:** CATTLE GRUB
**heel·piece** \'hē(ə)l-,pēs\ *noun* (1709)
**:** a piece designed for or forming the heel (as of a shoe)
**heel·tap** \-,tap\ *noun* (1780)
**:** a small quantity of alcoholic beverage remaining (as in a glass after drinking)
¹**heft** \'heft\ *noun* [from *heave*, after such pairs as *weave* : *weft*] (15th century)
**1 a :** WEIGHT, HEAVINESS **b :** IMPORTANCE, INFLUENCE
**2** *archaic* **:** the greater part of something **:** BULK
²**heft** *transitive verb* (1661)
**1 :** to heave up **:** HOIST
**2 :** to test the weight of by lifting ⟨*hefting* the rod . . . to get the feel of it —*Consumer Reports*⟩
**hefty** \'hef-tē\ *adjective* **heft·i·er; -est** (1867)
**1 :** quite heavy
**2 a :** marked by bigness, bulk, and usually strength ⟨a *hefty* football player⟩ **b :** POWERFUL, MIGHTY **c :** impressively large **:** SUBSTANTIAL ⟨*hefty* portions⟩
— **heft·i·ly** \-tə-lē\ *adverb*
— **heft·i·ness** \-tē-nəs\ *noun*
**he·gari** \hi-'gar-ē, -'gar-ə, -'ger-; 'hī-,gir\ *noun* [Arabic dialect (Sudan) *hegiri*] (1919)
**:** any of several Sudanese grain sorghums having chalky white seeds including one grown in the southwestern U.S.
¹**He·ge·li·an** \hā-'gā-lē-ən, hi-\ *adjective* (1838)
**:** of, relating to, or characteristic of Hegel, his philosophy, or his dialectic method
²**Hegelian** *noun* (1843)
**:** a follower of Hegel **:** an adherent of Hegelianism
**He·ge·li·an·ism** \-lē-ə-,ni-zəm\ *noun* (1846)
**:** the philosophy of Hegel that places ultimate reality in ideas rather than in things and that uses dialectic to comprehend an absolute idea behind phenomena
**he·ge·mo·ny** \hi-'je-mə-nē, -'ge-; 'he-jə-,mō-nē\ *noun* [Greek *hēgemonia*, from *hēgemōn* leader, from *hēgeisthai* to lead — more at SEEK] (1567)
**:** preponderant influence or authority over others **:** DOMINATION
— **heg·e·mon·ic** \,he-jə-'mä-nik, ,he-gə-\ *adjective*
**he·gi·ra** *also* **he·ji·ra** \hi-'jī-rə, 'he-jə-rə\ *noun* [the *Hegira*, flight of Muhammad from Mecca in A.D. 622, from Medieval Latin, from Arabic *hijrah*, literally, flight] (1753)
**:** a journey especially when undertaken to escape from a dangerous or undesirable situation **:** EXODUS
**Hei·del·berg man** \'hī-d°l-,bərg-, -,berg-\ *noun* [*Heidelberg*, Germany] (1920)
**:** an early Pleistocene man known from a massive fossilized jaw with distinctly human dentition and now classified with the pithecanthropines
**heif·er** \'he-fər\ *noun* [Middle English *hayfare*, from Old English *hēahfore*] (before 12th century)
**:** a young cow; *especially* **:** one that has not had a calf

**heigh–ho** \'hī-'hō, 'hā-\ *interjection* (circa 1553)

— used typically to express boredom, weariness, or sadness or sometimes as a cry of encouragement

**height** \'hīt, ÷'hītth\ *noun* [Middle English *heighthe*, from Old English *hīehthu;* akin to Old High German *hōhida* height, Old English *hēah* high] (before 12th century)
**1 a :** the highest part : SUMMIT **b :** highest or most advanced point : ZENITH ⟨at the *height* of his powers⟩
**2 a :** the distance from the bottom to the top of something standing upright **b :** the extent of elevation above a level
**3 :** the condition of being tall or high
**4 a :** an extent of land rising to a considerable degree above the surrounding country **b : a** high point or position
**5** *obsolete* : an advanced social rank ☆ ◆

**height·en** \'hīt-t°n\ *verb* **height·ened; height·en·ing** \'hīt-niŋ, 'hī-t°n-iŋ\ (1523)
*transitive verb*
**1 a :** to increase the amount or degree of : AUGMENT **b :** to make brighter or more intense : DEEPEN **c :** to bring out more strongly : point up **d :** to make more acute : SHARPEN
**2 a :** to raise high or higher : ELEVATE **b :** to raise above the ordinary or trite
**3** *obsolete* : ELATE
*intransitive verb*
**1** *archaic* : GROW, RISE
**2 a :** to become great or greater in amount, degree, or extent **b :** to become brighter or more intense

**height to paper** (1771)
: the height of printing type standardized at 0.9186 inch (2.333 centimeters) in English-speaking countries

**Heim·lich maneuver** \'hīm-lik-\ *noun* [Henry J. *Heimlich* (born 1920) American surgeon] (1974)
: the manual application of sudden upward pressure on the upper abdomen of a choking victim to force a foreign object from the windpipe

**hei·nie** \'hī-nē\ *noun* [alteration of ²*hinder*] (1940)
*slang* : BUTTOCKS

**hei·nous** \'hā-nəs\ *adjective* [Middle English, from Middle French *haineus*, from *haine* hate, from *hair* to hate, of Germanic origin; akin to Old High German *haz* hate — more at HATE] (14th century)
: hatefully or shockingly evil : ABOMINABLE
— **hei·nous·ly** *adverb*
— **hei·nous·ness** *noun*

**¹heir** \'ar, 'er\ *noun* [Middle English, from Old French, from Latin *hered-, heres;* akin to Greek *chēros* bereaved] (13th century)
**1 :** one who inherits or is entitled to inherit property
**2 :** one who inherits or is entitled to succeed to a hereditary rank, title, or office ⟨*heir* to the throne⟩
**3 :** one who receives or is entitled to receive some endowment or quality from a parent or predecessor
— **heir·less** \-ləs\ *adjective*
— **heir·ship** \-,ship\ *noun*

**²heir** *transitive verb* (14th century)
*chiefly dialect* : INHERIT

**heir apparent** *noun, plural* **heirs apparent** (14th century)
**1 :** an heir whose right to an inheritance is indefeasible in law if he survives the legal ancestor
**2 :** HEIR PRESUMPTIVE
**3 :** one whose succession especially to a position or role appears certain under existing circumstances

**heir at law** (1729)
: an heir in whom an intestate's real property is vested by operation of law

**heir·ess** \'ar-əs, 'er-\ *noun* (1607)

: a female heir; *especially* : a female heir to great wealth

**heir·loom** \'ar-,lüm, 'er-\ *noun* [Middle English *heirlome*, from *heir* + *lome* implement — more at LOOM] (15th century)
**1 :** a piece of property that descends to the heir as an inseparable part of an inheritance of real property
**2 :** something of special value handed on from one generation to another

**heir presumptive** *noun, plural* **heirs presumptive** (circa 1737)
: an heir whose legal right to an inheritance may be defeated (as by the birth of a nearer relative)

**Hei·sen·berg uncertainty principle** \'hī-z°n-,bərg-, -,bərk-\ *noun* [Werner *Heisenberg*] (1939)
: UNCERTAINTY PRINCIPLE — called also *Heisenberg's uncertainty principle*

**¹heist** \'hīst\ *transitive verb* [variant of ¹*hoist*] (1865)
**1** *chiefly dialect* : HOIST
**2** *slang* **a :** to commit armed robbery on **b :** STEAL 1a

**²heist** *noun* (1930)
*slang* : armed robbery : HOLDUP; *also* : THEFT

**Hel** \'hel\ *noun* [Old Norse]
: the Norse goddess of the dead and queen of the underworld

**hela cell** \'he-lə-\ *noun, often H&1stL capitalized* [*Henrietta Lacks* (died 1951) patient from whom the cells were taken] (1953)
: a cell of a continuously cultured strain isolated from a human uterine cervical carcinoma in 1951 and used in biomedical research especially to culture viruses

**held** *past and past participle of* HOLD

**hel·den·te·nor** \'hel-dən-,tā-,nȯr, -,nōr, -,te-nər\ *noun, often capitalized* [German, from *Held* hero + *Tenor* tenor] (circa 1903)
: a tenor with a powerful dramatic voice well suited to heroic (as Wagnerian) roles

**Helen of Troy** \,he-lə-nəv-'trói\
: the wife of Menelaus whose abduction by Paris brings about the Trojan War

**¹heli-** *or* **helio-** *combining form* [Latin, from Greek *hēli-, hēlio-*, from *hēlios* — more at SOLAR]
: sun ⟨*helio*centric⟩

**²heli-** *combining form* [by shortening]
: helicopter ⟨*heli*port⟩

**he·li·a·cal** \hi-'lī-ə-kəl\ *adjective* [Late Latin *heliacus*, from Greek *hēliakos*, from *hēlios*] (1545)
: relating to or near the sun — used especially of the last setting of a star before and its first rising after invisibility due to conjunction with the sun
— **he·li·a·cal·ly** \-k(ə-)lē\ *adverb*

**helic-** *or* **helico-** *combining form* [Greek *helik-, heliko-*, from *helik-, helix* spiral — more at HELIX]
: helix ⟨*helic*al⟩

**he·li·cal** \'he-li-kəl, 'hē-\ *adjective* (1591)
: of, relating to, or having the form of a helix; *broadly* : SPIRAL 1a
— **he·li·cal·ly** \-k(ə-)lē\ *adverb*

**he·li·coid** \'he-lə-,kȯid, 'hē-\ *or* **he·li·coi·dal** \,he-lə-'kȯi-d°l, ,hē-\ *adjective* (1704)
**1 :** forming or arranged in a spiral
**2 :** having the form of a flat coil or flattened spiral ⟨*helicoid* snail shell⟩

**he·li·con** \'he-lə-,kän, -i-kən\ *noun* [probably from Greek *helik-, helix* + English *-on* (as in *bombardon*); from its tube's forming a spiral encircling the player's body] (1875)
: a large circular tuba similar to a sousaphone but lacking an adjustable bell

**¹he·li·cop·ter** \'he-lə-,käp-tər, 'hē-\ *noun* [French *hélicoptère*, from Greek *heliko-* + *pteron* wing — more at FEATHER] (1887)
: an aircraft whose lift is derived from the aerodynamic forces acting on one or more powered rotors turning about substantially vertical axes

**²helicopter** (1952)
*intransitive verb*
: to travel by helicopter
*transitive verb*
: to transport by helicopter

**he·lio·cen·tric** \,hē-lē-ō-'sen-trik\ *adjective* (1685)
**1 :** referred to or measured from the sun's center or appearing as if seen from it
**2 :** having or relating to the sun as center — compare GEOCENTRIC

helicon

**he·lio·graph** \-,graf\ *noun* [International Scientific Vocabulary] (1877)
: an apparatus for telegraphing by means of the sun's rays flashed from a mirror
— **heliograph** *transitive verb*

**he·lio·graph·ic** \,hē-lē-ə-'gra-fik\ *adjective* (1706)
: measured on the sun's disk ⟨*heliographic* latitude⟩

**he·li·ol·a·try** \,hē-lē-'ä-lə-trē\ *noun* (circa 1828)
: sun worship
— **he·li·ol·a·trous** \-trəs\ *adjective*

**he·li·om·e·ter** \,hē-lē-'ä-mə-tər\ *noun* [French *héliomètre*, from *hélio-* ¹*heli-* + *-mètre* -meter] (1753)
: a visual telescope that has a divided objective designed for measuring the apparent diameter of the sun but also used for measuring angles between celestial bodies or between points on the moon
— **he·lio·met·ric** \,hē-lē-ō-'me-trik\ *adjective*
— **he·lio·met·ri·cal·ly** \-tri-k(ə-)lē\ *adverb*

**He·li·os** \'hē-lē-əs, -(,)ōs\ *noun* [Greek *Hēlios*]

---

☆ **SYNONYMS**
**Height, altitude, elevation** mean vertical distance either between the top and bottom of something or between a base and something above it. HEIGHT refers to something measured vertically whether high or low ⟨a wall two meters in *height*⟩. ALTITUDE and ELEVATION apply to height as measured by angular measurement or atmospheric pressure; ALTITUDE is preferable when referring to vertical distance above the surface of the earth or above sea level; ELEVATION is used especially in reference to vertical height on land ⟨fly at an *altitude* of 10,000 meters⟩ ⟨Denver is a city with a high *elevation*⟩.

---

◇ **WORD HISTORY**
**height** The word *height* stands in peculiar contrast to *width, breadth,* and *length* in having a final \t\ sound rather than \th\. Only a couple of centuries ago, however, there was a *highth* or *highth* that competed in popularity with *height* and was common enough in literary English to be used by Milton in *Paradise Lost*. The form with final *t* arose in northern dialects of Middle English while the *gh* sound in *heighth* was still pronounced, having approximately the sound of \k\ in the German name *Bach* or the Scots pronunciation of *loch*. But because few other English words ended in the consonant cluster \kth\, the second sound lost its fricative quality and became a simple \t\, remaining so even after the \k\ sound had been lost. In dialects of southern England the cluster was preserved until the \k\ sound was lost, but by the 19th century *heighth*, despite its correspondence to the other nouns of dimension, had been largely ousted by *height*.

: the god of the sun in Greek mythology —
compare SOL

**he·lio·stat** \'hē-lē-ə-ˌstat\ *noun* [New Latin
*heliostata,* from ¹*heli-* + Greek *-statēs* -stat]
(1747)
: an instrument consisting of a mirror mounted
on an axis moved by clockwork by which a
sunbeam is steadily reflected in one direction

**he·lio·trope** \'hē-lē-ə-ˌtrōp, 'hēl-yə-, *British
also* 'hel-yə-\ *noun* [Latin *heliotropium,* from
Greek *hēliotropion,* from *hēlio-* ¹*heli-* + *tropos*
turn; from its flowers' turning toward the sun
— more at TROPE] (circa 1626)
**1** : any of a genus
(*Heliotropium*) of
herbs or shrubs of
the borage family —
compare GARDEN HE-
LIOTROPE
**2** : BLOODSTONE
**3** : a variable color
averaging a moder-
ate to reddish purple

**he·li·ot·ro·pism**
\ˌhē-lē-'ä-trə-ˌpi-zəm\
*noun* (circa 1854)
: phototropism in
which sunlight is the
orienting stimulus
— **he·lio·tro·pic** \-lē-ə-'trō-pik, -'trä-\ *adjective*

**he·lio·zo·an** \ˌhē-lē-ə-'zō-ən\ *noun* [New Latin *Heliozoa,* from ¹*heli-* + *-zoa*] (circa 1889)
: any of a class (Heliozoa) of free-living holo-
zoic usually freshwater rhizopod protozoans
that reproduce by binary fission or budding

**he·li·pad** \'he-lə-ˌpad, 'hē-\ *noun* (1960)
: HELIPORT

**he·li·port** \-ˌpōrt, -ˌpȯrt\ *noun* (1948)
: a landing and takeoff place for a helicopter

**he·li·ski·ing** \-ˌskē-iŋ\ *noun* (1976)
: downhill skiing on remote mountains
reached by helicopter

**he·li·um** \'hē-lē-əm, 'hēl-yəm\ *noun* [New Latin, from Greek *hēlios*] (1872)
: a light colorless nonflammable gaseous element found especially in natural gases and
used chiefly for inflating airships and bal-
loons, for filling incandescent lamps, and for
cryogenic research — see ELEMENT table

**he·lix** \'hē-liks\ *noun, plural* **he·li·ces** \'he-
lə-,sēz, 'hē-\ *also* **he·lix·es** \'hē-lik-səz\ [Lat-
in, from Greek; akin to Greek *eilyein* to roll,
wrap — more at VOLUBLE] (1563)
**1** : something spiral in form: as **a** : an ornamental volute **b** : a coil formed by winding
wire around a uniform tube
**2** : the incurved rim of the external ear
**3** : a curve traced on a cylinder or cone by the
rotation of a point crossing its right sections at
a constant oblique angle; *broadly* : SPIRAL 1b

**hell** \'hel\ *noun* [Middle English, from Old English; akin to Old English *helan* to conceal,
Old High German *helan,* Latin *celare,* Greek
*kalyptein*] (before 12th century)
**1 a** (1) : a nether world in which the dead continue to exist : HADES (2) : the nether realm of
the devil and the demons in which the damned
suffer everlasting punishment — often used
in curses ⟨go to *hell*⟩ or as a generalized term
of abuse ⟨the *hell* with it⟩ **b** *Christian Science*
: ERROR 2b, SIN
**2 a** : a place or state of misery, torment, or
wickedness ⟨war is *hell* —W. T. Sherman⟩ **b**
: a place or state of turmoil or destruction ⟨all
*hell* broke loose⟩ **c** : a severe scolding ⟨got
*hell* for coming in late⟩ **d** : unrestrained fun or
sportiveness ⟨the kids were full of *hell*⟩ —
often used in the phrase *for the hell of it* especially to suggest action on impulse or without
a serious motive ⟨decided to go for the *hell* of
it⟩
**3** *archaic* : a tailor's receptacle
**4** — used as an interjection ⟨*hell,* I don't
know!⟩ or as an intensive ⟨hurts like *hell*⟩
⟨funny as *hell*⟩; often used in the phrase *hell of*

*a* ⟨it was one *hell* of a good fight⟩ or *hell out
of* ⟨scared the *hell* out of him⟩ or with *the* or *in*
⟨moved way the *hell* up north⟩ ⟨what in *hell* is
wrong, now?⟩
— **from hell** : being the worst or most
dreadful of its kind
— **hell on** : very hard on or destructive to
⟨the constant traveling is *hell on* your digestive system⟩
— **hell or high water** : difficulties of
whatever kind or size ⟨will stand by her convictions come *hell or high water*⟩
— **hell to pay** : dire consequences ⟨if he's
late there'll be *hell to pay*⟩

**he'll** \'hē(ə)l, 'hil, ēl, il\ (1588)
: he will : he shall

**hel·la·cious** \he-'lā-shəs\ *adjective* [*hell* +
*-acious* (as in *audacious*)] (1943)
**1** : exceptionally powerful or violent
**2** : remarkably good
**3** : extremely difficult
**4** : extraordinarily large
— **hel·la·cious·ly** *adverb*

**hell·ben·der** \'hel-ˌben-dər\ *noun* (1812)
: a large aquatic usual-
ly gray salamander
(*Cryptobranchus alle-
ganiensis*) of the Ohio
valley region

**hell–bent** \-ˌbent\ *adjective* (1835)
: stubbornly and often
recklessly determined
or intent ⟨hell-bent on
winning⟩
— **hell–bent** *ad-
verb*

**hell–broth** \-ˌbrȯth\
*noun* (1605)
: a brew for working black magic

hellbender

**hell·cat** \-ˌkat\ *noun* (circa 1605)
**1** : WITCH 2
**2** : a violently temperamental person; *especially* : an ill-tempered woman

**hel·le·bore** \'he-lə-ˌbōr, -ˌbȯr\ *noun* [Middle
English *elebre,* from Latin *elleborus, helleborus,* from Greek *helleboros*] (15th century)
**1** : any of a genus (*Helleborus*) of poisonous
herbs of the buttercup family having showy
flowers with petaloid sepals; *also* : the dried
rhizome or an extract or powder of this formerly used in medicine
**2** : a poisonous herb (genus *Veratrum*) of the
lily family; *also* : the dried rhizome of a hellebore (*Veratrum album* or *V. viride*) or a powder or extract of this containing alkaloids used
as a cardiac and respiratory depressant and as
an insecticide

**Hel·lene** \'he-ˌlēn\ *noun* [Greek *Hellēn*]
(1662)
: GREEK 1a

**¹Hel·len·ic** \he-'le-nik, hə-\ *adjective* (1644)
: of or relating to Greece, its people, or its language; *specifically* : of or relating to ancient
Greek history, culture, or art before the Hellenistic period

**²Hellenic** *noun* (1847)
: GREEK 2a

**Hel·le·nism** \'he-lə-ˌni-zəm\ *noun* (1609)
**1** : GRECISM 1
**2** : devotion to or imitation of ancient Greek
thought, customs, or styles
**3** : Greek civilization especially as modified
in the Hellenistic period by oriental influences
**4** : a body of humanistic and classical ideals
associated with ancient Greece and including
reason, the pursuit of knowledge and the arts,
moderation, civic responsibility, and bodily
development

**Hel·le·nist** \-nist\ *noun* (1613)
**1** : a person living in Hellenistic times who
was Greek in language, outlook, and way of
life but was not Greek in ancestry; *especially*
: a hellenized Jew
**2** : a specialist in the language or culture of
ancient Greece

**Hel·le·nis·tic** \ˌhe-lə-'nis-tik\ *adjective* (circa
1706)
**1** : of or relating to Greek history, culture, or
art after Alexander the Great
**2** : of or relating to the Hellenists
— **Hel·le·nis·ti·cal·ly** \-ti-k(ə-)lē\ *adverb*

**hel·le·nize** \'he-lə-ˌnīz\ *verb* **-nized; -niz-
ing** *often capitalized* (1613)
*intransitive verb*
: to become Greek or Hellenistic
*transitive verb*
: to make Greek or Hellenistic in form or culture
— **hel·le·ni·za·tion** \ˌhe-lə-nə-'zā-shən\
*noun, often capitalized*

**hell·er** \'he-lər\ *noun* (circa 1895)
: HELLION

**hel·leri** \'he-lə-ˌrī, -ˌ(ˌ)rē\ *noun, plural* **-ler·ies**
[New Latin (specific epithet of *Xiphophorus
helleri*), from C. *Heller,* 20th century tropical
fish collector] (1931)
**1** : SWORDTAIL
**2** : any of various brightly colored aquarium
fishes developed by hybridization of sword-
tails and platys

**hell·fire** \'hel-ˌfīr\ *noun* (before 12th century)
: the eternal fire of hell that tortures sinners
— **hellfire** *adjective*

**¹hell–for–leather** *adverb* (1889)
: in a hell-for-leather manner : at full speed
⟨rode *hell-for-leather* down the trail⟩

**²hell–for–leather** *adjective* (1920)
: marked by determined recklessness, great
speed, or lack of restraint ⟨a cocky, *hell-for-
leather* fighting man —H. H. Martin⟩

**hell·gram·mite** \'hel-grə-ˌmīt\ *noun* [origin
unknown] (1866)
: a carnivorous aquatic North American insect
larva that is the young form of a dobsonfly
(especially *Corydalis cornutus*) and is used for
fish bait

**hell·hole** \'hel-ˌhōl\ *noun* (1866)
: a place of extreme misery or squalor

**hell·hound** \-ˌhau̇nd\ *noun* (before 12th century)
**1** : a dog represented in mythology as a guardian of the underworld
**2** : a fiendish person

**hel·lion** \'hel-yən\ *noun* [probably alteration
(influenced by *hell*) of *hallion* (scamp)] (1787)
: a troublesome or mischievous person

**hell·ish** \'he-lish\ *adjective* (circa 1530)
: of, resembling, or befitting hell; *broadly*
: TERRIBLE
— **hell·ish·ly** *adverb*
— **hell·ish·ness** *noun*

**hel·lo** \hə-'lō, he-\ *noun, plural* **hellos** [alter-
ation of *hollo*] (1889)
: an expression or gesture of greeting — used
interjectionally in greeting, in answering the
telephone, or to express surprise

**hell–rais·er** \'hel-ˌrā-zər\ *noun* (1914)
: one given to wild, boisterous, or intemperate
behavior
— **hell–rais·ing** \-ˌrā-ziŋ\ *noun or adjective*

**¹helm** \'helm\ *noun* [Middle English, from Old
English] (before 12th century)
: HELMET 1

**²helm** *transitive verb* (before 12th century)
: to cover or furnish with a helmet

**³helm** *noun* [Middle English *helme,* from Old
English *helma;* akin to Old High German
*helmo* tiller] (before 12th century)
**1 a** : a lever or wheel controlling the rudder of
a ship for steering; *broadly* : the entire apparatus for steering a ship **b** : position of the helm
with respect to the amidships position ⟨turn
the *helm* hard alee⟩
**2** : a position of control : HEAD ⟨a new dean is
at the *helm* of the medical school⟩

---

\ə\ abut  \ᵊ\ kitten  \ər\ further  \a\ ash  \ā\ ace
\ä\ mop, mar  \au̇\ out  \ch\ chin  \e\ bet  \ē\ easy
\g\ go  \i\ hit  \ī\ ice  \j\ job  \ŋ\ sing  \ō\ go
\ȯ\ law  \ȯi\ boy  \th\ thin  \th\ the  \ü\ loot  \u̇\ foot
\y\ yet  \zh\ vision  *see also* Guide to Pronunciation

**⁴helm** *transitive verb* (1603)
: to direct with or as if with a helm : STEER

**hel·met** \'hel-mət\ *noun* [Middle French, diminutive of *helme* helmet, of Germanic origin; akin to Old English *helm* helmet, Old High German *helan* to conceal — more at HELL] (15th century)
**1** : a covering or enclosing headpiece of ancient or medieval armor — see ARMOR illustration
**2** : any of various protective head coverings usually made of a hard material to resist impact
**3** : something resembling a helmet
— **hel·met·ed** \-mə-təd\ *adjective*
— **hel·met·like** \-mət-,līk\ *adjective*

**hel·minth** \'hel-,min(t)th\ *noun* [Greek *helminth-, helmis*] (1852)
: a parasitic worm (as a tapeworm, liver fluke, ascarid, or leech); *especially* : an intestinal worm
— **hel·min·thic** \hel-'min(t)-thik\ *adjective*

**hel·min·thi·a·sis** \,hel-mən-'thī-ə-səs\ *noun, plural* **-a·ses** \-ə-,sēz\ [New Latin] (circa 1811)
: infestation with or disease caused by parasitic worms

**hel·min·thol·o·gy** \-'thä-lə-jē\ *noun* (1819)
: a branch of zoology concerned with helminths; *especially* : the study of parasitic worms

**helms·man** \'helmz-mən\ *noun* (1627)
: the person at the helm : STEERSMAN
— **helms·man·ship** \-,ship\ *noun*

**he·lo** \'hē-(,)lō\ *noun, plural* **helos** [by shortening & alteration] (1968)
: HELICOPTER

**hel·ot** \'he-lət\ *noun* [Latin *Helotes*, plural, from Greek *Heilōtes*] (1579)
**1** *capitalized* : a member of a class of serfs in ancient Sparta
**2** : SERF, SLAVE
— **hel·ot·ry** \'he-lə-trē\ *noun*

**hel·ot·ism** \'he-lə-,ti-zəm\ *noun* (circa 1900)
: the physiological relation existing in a lichen where a fungus appears to control an alga

**¹help** \'help; *Southern often* 'hep *also* 'heəp\ *verb* [Middle English, from Old English *helpan*; akin to Old High German *helfan* to help, and perhaps to Lithuanian *šelpti*] (before 12th century)
*transitive verb*
**1** : to give assistance or support to ⟨*help* a child with homework⟩
**2 a** : to make more pleasant or bearable : IMPROVE, RELIEVE ⟨bright curtains will *help* the room⟩ ⟨took an aspirin to *help* her headache⟩ **b** *archaic* : RESCUE, SAVE
**3 a** : to be of use to : BENEFIT **b** : to further the advancement of : PROMOTE
**4 a** : to change for the better **b** : to refrain from : AVOID **c** : to keep from occurring : PREVENT ⟨they couldn't *help* the accident⟩ **d** : to restrain (oneself) from doing something ⟨knew they shouldn't go but couldn't *help* themselves⟩
**5** : to serve with food or drink especially at a meal ⟨told the guests to *help* themselves⟩
**6** : to appropriate something for (oneself) ⟨*helped* himself to the car keys⟩
*intransitive verb*
**1** : give assistance or support — often used with *out*
**2** : to be of use or benefit
**synonym** see IMPROVE
— **so help me** : upon my word : believe it or not

**²help** *noun* (before 12th century)
**1** : AID, ASSISTANCE
**2** : a source of aid ⟨printed *helps* to the memory —C. S. Braden⟩
**3** : REMEDY, RELIEF ⟨there was no *help* for it⟩
**4 a** : one who serves or assists another (as in housework) : HELPER **b** : EMPLOYEE ⟨*help* wanted⟩ — often used collectively ⟨the hired *help*⟩

**help·er** *noun* (13th century)

: one that helps; *especially* : a relatively unskilled worker who assists a skilled worker usually by manual labor

**helper T cell** *noun* (1976)
: a T cell that participates in an immune response by recognizing a foreign antigen and secreting lymphokines to activate T cell and B cell proliferation, that usually carries CD4 molecular markers on its cell surface, and that is reduced to 20 percent or less of normal numbers in AIDS — called also *helper cell, T-helper cell*

**help·ful** \'help-fəl; *Southern often* 'hep- *also* 'heəp-\ *adjective* (14th century)
: of service or assistance : USEFUL
— **help·ful·ly** \-fə-lē\ *adverb*
— **help·ful·ness** *noun*

**help·ing** *noun* (1883)
: a portion of food : SERVING

**helping hand** *noun* (15th century)
: HAND 8a

**help·ing verb** *noun* (1711)
: an auxiliary verb

**help·less** \'help-ləs; *Southern often* 'hep-ləs *also* 'heəp-\ *adjective* (before 12th century)
**1** : lacking protection or support : DEFENSELESS
**2 a** : marked by an inability to act or react ⟨the crowd looked on in *helpless* horror —*Current Biography*⟩ **b** : not able to be controlled or restrained ⟨*helpless* laughter⟩
— **help·less·ly** *adverb*
— **help·less·ness** *noun*

**help·mate** \'help-,māt; *Southern often* 'hep- *also* 'heəp-\ *noun* [by folk etymology from *helpmeet*] (circa 1714)
: one who is a companion and helper; *especially* : WIFE

**help·meet** \-,mēt\ *noun* [²*help* + *meet*, adjective] (1673)
: HELPMATE

**¹hel·ter–skel·ter** \,hel-tər-'skel-tər\ *adverb* [perhaps from Middle English *skelten* to come, go] (1593)
**1** : in undue haste, confusion, or disorder ⟨ran *helter-skelter*, getting in each other's way —F. V. W. Mason⟩
**2** : in a haphazard manner

**²helter–skelter** *noun* (1713)
**1** : a disorderly confusion : TURMOIL
**2** *British* : a spiral slide around a tower at an amusement park

**³helter–skelter** *adjective* (1785)
**1** : confusedly hurried : PRECIPITATE
**2** : marked by a lack of order or plan : HAPHAZARD ⟨the *helter-skelter* arrangement of the papers, all mussed and frayed —Jean Stafford⟩

**helve** \'helv\ *noun* [Middle English, from Old English *hielfe*; probably akin to Old English *helma* helm] (before 12th century)
: a handle of a tool or weapon : HAFT

**Hel·ve·tii** \hel-'vē-shē-,ī\ *noun plural* [Latin] (1889)
: an early Celtic people in the area of western Switzerland at the time of Julius Caesar

**¹hem** \'hem\ *noun* [Middle English, from Old English; akin to Middle High German *hemmen* to hem in, Armenian *kamel* to press] (before 12th century)
**1** : a border of a cloth article doubled back and stitched down
**2** : RIM, MARGIN ⟨bright green *hem* of reeds about the ponds —R. M. Lockley⟩

**²hem** *verb* **hemmed; hem·ming** (14th century)
*transitive verb*
**1 a** : to finish with a hem **b** : BORDER, EDGE
**2** : to surround in a restrictive manner : CONFINE — usually used with *in* ⟨*hemmed* in by enemy troops⟩
*intransitive verb*
: to make a hem in sewing
— **hem·mer** *noun*

**³hem** \'hem\ *intransitive verb* **hemmed; hem·ming** (15th century)
**1** : to utter the sound represented by *hem* ⟨*hemmed* and hawed before answering⟩

**2** : EQUIVOCATE ⟨the administration *hemmed* and hawed over the students' demands⟩

**⁴hem** \*usually read as* 'hem\ *interjection* [imitative]
— often used to indicate a vocalized pause in speaking

**hem-** *or* **hemo-** *combining form* [Middle French *hemo-*, from Latin *haem-, haemo-*, from Greek *haim-, haimo-*, from *haima*]
: blood ⟨*hem*agglutination⟩ ⟨*hemo*flagellate⟩

**hema-** *combining form* [New Latin, from Greek *haima*]
: HEM- ⟨*hema*cytometer⟩

**he·ma·cy·tom·e·ter** \,hē-mə-sī-'tä-mə-tər\ *noun* (1877)
: an instrument for counting blood cells

**hem·ag·glu·ti·na·tion** \,hē-mə-,glü-t°n-'ā-shən\ *noun* (1907)
: agglutination of red blood cells
— **hem·ag·glu·ti·nate** \-'glü-t°n-,āt\ *transitive verb*

**hem·ag·glu·ti·nin** \-'glü-t°n-ən\ *noun* [International Scientific Vocabulary] (circa 1903)
: an agglutinin (as an antibody or viral capsid protein) that causes hemagglutination

**he–man** \'hē-,man\ *noun* (1832)
: a strong virile man

**hem·an·gi·o·ma** \,hē-,man-jē-'ō-mə\ *noun* [New Latin, from *hem-* + *angioma*] (circa 1890)
: a usually benign tumor made up of blood vessels that typically occurs as a purplish or reddish slightly elevated area of skin

**hemat-** *or* **hemato-** *combining form* [Latin *haemat-, haemato-*, from Greek *haimat-, haimato-*, from *haimat-, haima*]
: HEM- ⟨*hemato*genous⟩

**he·ma·tin** \'hē-mə-tən\ *noun* (1845)
: a brownish black or bluish black derivative $C_{34}H_{33}N_4O_5Fe$ of oxidized heme; *also* : any of several similar compounds

**he·ma·tin·ic** \,hē-mə-'ti-nik\ *noun* (1855)
: an agent that tends to stimulate blood cell formation or to increase the hemoglobin in the blood
— **hematinic** *adjective*

**he·ma·tite** \'hē-mə-,tīt\ *noun* (1540)
: a mineral constituting an important iron ore and occurring in crystals or in a red earthy form
— **he·ma·tit·ic** \,hē-mə-'ti-tik\ *adjective*

**he·mat·o·crit** \hi-'ma-tə-krət, -,krit\ *noun* [International Scientific Vocabulary *hemat-* + Greek *kritēs* judge, from *krinein* to judge — more at CERTAIN] (circa 1903)
**1** : an instrument for determining usually by centrifugation the relative amounts of plasma and corpuscles in blood
**2** : the ratio of the volume of packed red blood cells to the volume of whole blood as determined by a hematocrit

**he·ma·tog·e·nous** \,hē-mə-'tä-jə-nəs\ *adjective* (1886)
**1** : producing blood
**2** : involving, spread by, or arising in the blood ⟨*hematogenous* spread of infection⟩

**he·ma·to·log·ic** \,hē-mə-t°l-'ä-jik\ *also* **he·ma·to·log·i·cal** \-ji-kəl\ *adjective* (1854)
: of or relating to blood or to hematology

**he·ma·tol·o·gy** \,hē-mə-'tä-lə-jē\ *noun* (circa 1811)
: a medical science that deals with the blood and blood-forming organs
— **he·ma·tol·o·gist** \-jist\ *noun*

**he·ma·to·ma** \-'tō-mə\ *noun, plural* **-mas** *or* **-ma·ta** \-mə-tə\ [New Latin] (circa 1849)
: a mass of usually clotted blood that forms in a tissue, organ, or body space as a result of a broken blood vessel

**he·ma·toph·a·gous** \-'tä-fə-gəs\ *adjective* [International Scientific Vocabulary] (circa 1854)
: feeding on blood

**he·ma·to·poi·e·sis** \hi-,ma-tə-pói-'ē-səs, ,hē-mə-tō-\ *noun* [New Latin] (circa 1854)

**:** the formation of blood or of blood cells in the living body

— **he·ma·to·poi·et·ic** \-'e-tik\ *adjective*

**he·ma·to·por·phy·rin** \-'pòr-fə-rən\ *noun* [International Scientific Vocabulary] (1885)

**:** any of several isomeric porphyrins $C_{34}H_{38}O_6N_4$ that are hydrated derivatives of protoporphyrins; *especially* **:** the deep red crystalline pigment obtained by treating hematin or heme with acid

**he·ma·tox·y·lin** \,hē-mə-'täk-sə-lən\ *noun* [International Scientific Vocabulary, from New Latin *Haematoxylon*, genus of plants] (circa 1847)

**:** a crystalline phenolic compound $C_{16}H_{14}O_6$ found in logwood and used chiefly as a biological stain

**he·ma·tu·ria** \-'tùr-ē-ə, -'tyùr-\ *noun* [New Latin] (circa 1811)

**:** the presence of blood or blood cells in the urine

**heme** \'hēm\ *noun* [International Scientific Vocabulary, from *hematin*] (1925)

**:** the deep red iron-containing prosthetic group $C_{34}H_{32}N_4O_4Fe$ of hemoglobin and myoglobin

**hem·el·y·tron** \he-'me-lə-,trän\ *noun, plural* **-tra** \-trə\ [New Latin, from *hemi-* + *elytron*] (circa 1889)

**:** one of the basally thickened anterior wings of various insects (as true bugs)

**hem·ero·cal·lis** \,he-mə-rō-'ka-ləs\ *noun* [New Latin, from Greek *hēmerokalles*, from *hēmera* day + *kallos* beauty] (1625)

**:** DAYLILY

**hem·er·y·thrin** \hē-'mer-ə-thrən\ *noun* [*hem-* + *erythr-* + ¹*-in*] (1903)

**:** an iron-containing respiratory pigment in the blood of various invertebrates (as some annelids)

**hemi-** *prefix* [Middle English, from Latin, from Greek *hēmi-* — more at SEMI-]

**:** half ⟨*hemi*hedral⟩

**-hemia** — see -EMIA

**hemi·ac·e·tal** \,he-mē-'a-sə-,tal\ *noun* (1893)

**:** any of a class of compounds characterized by the grouping C(OH)(OR) where R is an alkyl group and usually formed as intermediates in the preparation of acetals from aldehydes or ketones

**he·mic** \'hē-mik\ *adjective* (1857)

**:** of, relating to, or produced by the blood or the circulation of blood ⟨a *hemic* murmur⟩

**hemi·cel·lu·lose** \,he-mi-'sel-yə-,lōs, -,lōz\ *noun* [International Scientific Vocabulary] (1891)

**:** any of various plant polysaccharides less complex than cellulose and easily hydrolyzable to simple sugars and other products

**hemi·chor·date** \-'kòr-dət, -'kòr-,dāt\ *noun* [New Latin *Hemichordata*, from *hemi-* + *Chordata* chordates] (1885)

**:** any of a phylum (Hemichordata) of wormlike marine animals (as an acorn worm) that have in the proboscis an outgrowth of the pharyngeal wall which superficially resembles the notochord of chordates

**hemi·cy·cle** \'he-mi-,sī-kəl\ *noun* [French *hémicycle*, from Latin *hemicyclium*, from Greek *hēmikyklion*, from *hēmi-* + *kyklos* circle — more at CYCLE] (15th century)

**:** a curved or semicircular structure or arrangement

**hemi·demi·semi·qua·ver** \,he-mi-,de-mi-'se-mi-,kwā-vər\ *noun* (1853)

**:** SIXTY-FOURTH NOTE

**hemi·he·dral** \,he-mi-'hē-drəl\ *adjective* [*hemi-* + *-hedron*] (1837)

*of a crystal* **:** having half the faces required by complete symmetry — compare HOLOHEDRAL, TETARTOHEDRAL

**hemi·hy·drate** \-'hī-,drāt\ *noun* (circa 1901)

**:** a hydrate (as plaster of paris) containing half a mole of water to one mole of the compound forming the hydrate

— **hemi·hy·drat·ed** \-,drā-təd\ *adjective*

**hemi·me·tab·o·lous** \,he-mi-mə-'ta-bə-ləs\ *adjective* (1870)

**:** characterized by incomplete metamorphosis ⟨*hemimetabolous* insects⟩ — compare HOLOMETABOLOUS

**hemi·mor·phic** \,he-mi-'mòr-fik\ *adjective* [International Scientific Vocabulary] (circa 1859)

*of a crystal* **:** having different crystalline forms at each end of a crystallographic axis

— **hemi·mor·phism** \-,fi-zəm\ *noun*

**he·min** \'hē-mən\ *noun* [International Scientific Vocabulary] (circa 1857)

**:** a red-brown to blue-black crystalline salt $C_{34}H_{32}N_4O_4FeCl$ derived from oxidized heme but usually obtained in a characteristic crystalline form from hemoglobin

**hemi·o·la** \,he-mē-'ō-lə\ *noun* [Late Latin *hemiolia*, from Greek *hēmiolia* ratio of one and a half to one, from *hēmi-* + *holos* whole — more at SAFE] (circa 1934)

**:** a musical rhythmic alteration in which six equal notes may be heard as two groups of three or three groups of two

**hemi·ple·gia** \,he-mi-'plē-j(ē-)ə\ *noun* [New Latin, from Middle Greek *hēmiplēgia* paralysis, from Greek *hēmi-* + *-plēgia* -plegia] (1600)

**:** total or partial paralysis of one side of the body that results from disease of or injury to the motor centers of the brain

— **hemi·ple·gic** \-jik\ *adjective or noun*

**he·mip·ter·an** \hi-'mip-tə-rən\ *noun* [ultimately from Greek *hēmi-* + *pteron* wing — more at FEATHER] (circa 1864)

**:** any of a large order (Hemiptera) of hemimetabolous insects (as the true bugs) that have hemelytra and mouthparts adapted to piercing and sucking

— **he·mip·ter·ous** \-rəs\ *adjective*

**hemi·sphere** \'he-mə-,sfir\ *noun* [Middle English *hemispere*, from Latin *hemisphaerium*, from Greek *hēmisphairion*, from *hēmi-* + *sphairion*, diminutive of *sphaira* sphere] (14th century)

**1 a :** a half of the celestial sphere divided into two halves by the horizon, the celestial equator, or the ecliptic **b :** half of a spherical or roughly spherical body (as a planet); *specifically* **:** the northern or southern half of the earth divided by the equator or the eastern or western half divided by a meridian **c :** the inhabitants of a terrestrial hemisphere

**2 :** REALM, PROVINCE

**3 :** one of two half spheres formed by a plane through the sphere's center

**4 :** a map or projection of a celestial or terrestrial hemisphere

**5 :** CEREBRAL HEMISPHERE

— **hemi·spher·ic** \,he-mə-'sfir-ik, -'sfer-\ *or* **hemi·spher·i·cal** \-'sfir-i-kəl, -'sfer-\ *adjective*

**hemi·stich** \'he-mi-,stik\ *noun* [Latin *hemistichium*, from Greek *hēmistichion*, from *hēmi-* + *stichos* line, verse; akin to Greek *steichein* to go — more at STAIR] (1575)

**:** half a poetic line of verse usually divided by a caesura

**hemi·zy·gous** \,he-mi-'zī-gəs\ *adjective* (circa 1921)

**:** having or characterized by one or more genes (as in a genetic deficiency or in an X chromosome paired with a Y chromosome) that have no allelic counterparts

**hem·line** \'hem-,līn\ *noun* (1923)

**:** the line formed by the lower edge of a dress, skirt, or coat

**hem·lock** \'hem-,läk\ *noun* [Middle English *hemlok*, from Old English *hemlic*] (before 12th century)

**1 a :** any of several poisonous herbs (as a poison hemlock or a water hemlock) of the carrot family having finely cut leaves and small white flowers **b :** a drug or lethal drink prepared from the poison hemlock (*Conium maculatum*)

**2 :** any of a genus (*Tsuga*) of evergreen coniferous trees of the pine family; *also* **:** the soft light splintery wood of a hemlock

**hemo-** — see HEM-

**he·mo·chro·ma·to·sis** \,hē-mə-,krō-mə-'tō-səs\ *noun* [New Latin, from *hem-* + *chromat-* + *-osis*] (1899)

**:** a metabolic disorder involving the deposition of iron-containing pigments in the tissues and characterized by bronzing of the skin, diabetes, and weakness

**he·mo·coel** \'hē-mə-,sēl\ *noun* (1839)

**:** a body cavity (as in arthropods or some mollusks) that contains blood or hemolymph and functions as part of the circulatory system

**he·mo·cy·a·nin** \,hē-mō-'sī-ə-nən\ *noun* [International Scientific Vocabulary *hem-* + *cyan-* + ¹*-in*] (1885)

**:** a colorless copper-containing respiratory pigment in the circulatory fluid of various arthropods and mollusks

**he·mo·cyte** \'hē-mə-,sīt\ *noun* [International Scientific Vocabulary] (circa 1903)

**:** a blood cell especially of an invertebrate animal

**he·mo·cy·tom·e·ter** \,hē-mə-sī-'tä-mə-tər\ *noun* [International Scientific Vocabulary] (1877)

**:** HEMACYTOMETER

**he·mo·di·al·y·sis** \,hē-mō-dī-'a-lə-səs\ *noun* (1947)

**:** the process of removing blood from an artery (as of a kidney patient), purifying it by dialysis, adding vital substances, and returning it to a vein

**he·mo·di·lu·tion** \-dī-'lü-shən, -də-\ *noun* (1939)

**:** decreased concentration of cells and solids in the blood resulting from gain of fluid

**he·mo·dy·nam·ic** \-dī-'na-mik, -də-\ *adjective* (1907)

**1 :** of, relating to, or involving hemodynamics **2 :** relating to or functioning in the mechanics of blood circulation

— **he·mo·dy·nam·i·cal·ly** \-mi-k(ə-)lē\ *adverb*

**he·mo·dy·nam·ics** \-miks\ *noun plural but singular or plural in construction* (circa 1857)

**1 :** a branch of physiology that deals with the circulation of the blood **2 :** the forces or mechanisms involved in circulation

**he·mo·fla·gel·late** \,hē-mō-'fla-jə-lət, -,lāt; -flə-'je-lət\ *noun* (1909)

**:** a flagellate (as a trypanosome) that is a blood parasite

**he·mo·glo·bin** \'hē-mə-,glō-bən\ *noun* [International Scientific Vocabulary, short for earlier *hematoglobulin*] (1869)

**1 :** an iron-containing respiratory pigment of vertebrate red blood cells that consists of a globin composed of four subunits each of which is linked to a heme molecule, that functions in oxygen transport to the tissues after conversion to oxygenated form in the gills or lungs, and that assists in carbon dioxide transport back to the gills or lungs after surrender of its oxygen **2 :** any of numerous iron-containing respiratory pigments of invertebrates and some plants (as yeasts)

**he·mo·glo·bin·op·a·thy** \,hē-mə-,glō-bə-'nä-pə-thē\ *noun, plural* **-thies** (1957)

**:** a blood disorder (as sickle-cell anemia) caused by a genetically determined change in the molecular structure of hemoglobin

**hemoglobin S** *noun* (1954)

**:** an abnormal hemoglobin that occurs in the red blood cells in sickle-cell anemia and sickle-cell trait

---

\ə\ abut \ᵊ\ kitten \ər\ further \a\ ash \ā\ ace
\ä\ mop, mar \au̇\ out \ch\ chin \e\ bet \ē\ easy
\g\ go \i\ hit \ī\ ice \j\ job \ŋ\ sing \ō\ go
\ò\ law \ȯi\ boy \th\ thin \t̲h̲\ the \ü\ loot \u̇\ foot
\y\ yet \zh\ vision   *see also* Guide to Pronunciation

**he·mo·glo·bin·uria** \,hē-mə-,glō-bə-'nùr-ē-ə, -'nyùr-\ *noun* [New Latin] (1866)
**:** the presence of free hemoglobin in the urine
— **he·mo·glo·bin·uric** \-'nùr-ik, -'nyùr-\ *adjective*

**he·mo·lymph** \'hē-mə-,lim(p)f\ *noun* (1885)
**:** the circulatory fluid of various invertebrate animals that is functionally comparable to the blood and lymph of vertebrates

**he·mo·ly·sin** \hē-mə-'lī-sᵊn\ *noun* [International Scientific Vocabulary] (1900)
**:** a substance that causes the dissolution of red blood cells

**he·mo·ly·sis** \hi-'mä-lə-səs, ,hē-mə-'lī-səs\ *noun* [New Latin] (1890)
**:** lysis of red blood cells with liberation of hemoglobin
— **he·mo·lyt·ic** \,hē-mə-'li-tik\ *adjective*

**hemolytic anemia** *noun* (1938)
**:** anemia caused by excessive destruction (as in chemical poisoning, infection, or sickle-cell anemia) of red blood cells

**hemolytic disease of the newborn** (1948)
**:** ERYTHROBLASTOSIS FETALIS

**he·mo·lyze** \'hē-mə-,līz\ *verb* **-lyzed; -lyz·ing** [irregular from *hemolysis*] (1902)
*transitive verb*
**:** to cause hemolysis of
*intransitive verb*
**:** to undergo hemolysis

**he·mo·phil·ia** \,hē-mə-'fi-lē-ə\ *noun* [New Latin] (1872)
**:** a sex-linked hereditary blood defect that occurs almost exclusively in males and is characterized by delayed clotting of the blood and consequent difficulty in controlling hemorrhage even after minor injuries

**¹he·mo·phil·i·ac** \-'fi-lē-,ak\ *adjective* (1896)
**:** of, resembling, or affected with hemophilia

**²hemophiliac** *noun* (1897)
**:** one affected with hemophilia — called also *bleeder*

**he·mo·phil·ic** \-'fi-lik\ *noun or adjective* (1864)
**:** HEMOPHILIAC

**he·mo·poi·e·sis** \,hē-mə-pòi-'ē-səs\ *noun* [New Latin] (circa 1900)
**:** HEMATOPOIESIS
— **he·mo·poi·et·ic** \-'e-tik\ *adjective*

**he·mo·pro·tein** \-'prō-,tēn, -'prō-tē-ən\ *noun* (1948)
**:** a conjugated protein (as hemoglobin or cytochrome) whose prosthetic group is a porphyrin combined with iron

**he·mop·ty·sis** \hi-'mäp-tə-səs\ *noun* [New Latin, from *hem-* + Greek *ptysis* act of spitting, from *ptyein* to spit — more at SPEW] (1646)
**:** expectoration of blood from some part of the respiratory tract

**¹hem·or·rhage** \'hem-rij, 'he-mə-\ *noun* [Latin *haemorrhagia,* from Greek *haimorrhagia,* from *haimo-* hem- + *-rrhagia*] (1671)
**:** a copious discharge of blood from the blood vessels
— **hem·or·rhag·ic** \,he-mə-'ra-jik\ *adjective*

**²hemorrhage** *verb* **-rhaged; -rhag·ing** (1928)
*intransitive verb*
**:** to undergo heavy or uncontrollable bleeding
*transitive verb*
**:** to lose rapidly and uncontrollably ⟨*hemorrhage* money⟩

**hemorrhagic fever** *noun* (1948)
**:** any of a diverse group of arthropod-borne virus diseases characterized by a sudden onset, fever, aching, bleeding in the internal organs, petechiae, and shock

**hem·or·rhoid** \'hem-,ròid, 'he-mə-\ *noun* [Middle English *emeroides,* plural, from Middle French *hemorrhoides,* from Latin *haemorrhoidae,* from Greek *haimorrhoides,* from *haimorrhoos* flowing with blood, from *haimo-*

*hem-* + *rhein* to flow — more at STREAM] (14th century)
**:** a mass of dilated veins in swollen tissue at the margin of the anus or nearby within the rectum — usually used in plural; called also *piles*

**¹hem·or·rhoid·al** \,hem-'ròi-dᵊl, ,he-mə-\ *noun* (15th century)
**:** a hemorrhoidal part (as an artery or vein)

**²hemorrhoidal** *adjective* (1651)
**1 :** of, relating to, or involving hemorrhoids
**2 :** RECTAL

**he·mo·sid·er·in** \,hē-mō-'si-də-rən\ *noun* [International Scientific Vocabulary *hem-* + *sider-* + ¹*-in*] (circa 1885)
**:** a yellowish brown granular pigment that is formed in some phagocytic cells by the breakdown of hemoglobin and is probably essentially a denatured form of ferritin

**he·mo·sta·sis** \,hē-mə-'stā-səs\ *noun* [New Latin, from Greek *haimostasis* styptic, from *haimo-* hem- + *-stasis*] (1843)
**:** arrest of bleeding

**he·mo·stat** \'hē-mə-,stat\ *noun* (circa 1900)
**:** HEMOSTATIC; *especially* **:** an instrument for compressing a bleeding vessel

**¹he·mo·stat·ic** \,hē-mə-'sta-tik\ *noun* (circa 1706)
**:** a hemostatic agent

**²hemostatic** *adjective* (1834)
**1 :** of or caused by hemostasis
**2 :** serving to check bleeding

**hemp** \'hemp\ *noun* [Middle English, from Old English *hænep;* akin to Old High German *hanaf* hemp, Greek *kannabis*] (before 12th century)
**1 a :** a tall widely cultivated Asian herb (*Cannabis sativa*) of the mulberry family with tough bast fiber used especially for cordage **b :** the fiber of hemp **c :** a psychoactive drug (as marijuana or hashish) from hemp
**2 :** a fiber (as jute) from a plant other than the true hemp; *also* **:** a plant yielding such fiber

**hemp·en** \'hem-pən\ *adjective* (14th century)
**:** composed of hemp

**hemp nettle** *noun* (1801)
**:** any of a genus (*Galeopsis*) of coarse Old World herbs of the mint family; *especially* **:** a bristly Eurasian herb (*G. tetrahit*) naturalized in the U.S. as a weed

**¹hem·stitch** \'hem-,stich\ *transitive verb* (1839)
**:** to decorate (as a border) with hemstitch
— **hem·stitch·er** *noun*

**²hemstitch** *noun* (1853)
**1 :** decorative needlework similar to drawnwork that is used especially on or next to the stitching line of hems
**2 :** a stitch used in hemstitching

**hen** \'hen\ *noun* [Middle English, from Old English *henn;* akin to Old English *hana* rooster — more at CHANT] (before 12th century)
**1 a :** a female chicken especially over a year old; *broadly* **:** a female bird **b :** the female of various mostly aquatic animals (as lobsters or fish)
**2 :** WOMAN; *especially* **:** a fussy middle-aged woman

**hen and chickens** *noun* (1884)
**:** any of several plants having offsets, runners, or flowers that send out shoots; *especially*
**:** HOUSELEEK

**hen·bane** \'hen-,bān\ *noun* (14th century)
**:** a poisonous fetid Old World herb (*Hyoscyamus niger*) of the nightshade family having sticky hairy dentate leaves and yellowish brown flowers and yielding hyoscyamine and scopolamine

**hen·bit** \'hen-,bit\ *noun* (1597)
**:** a Eurasian herb (*Lamium amplexicaule*) of the mint family that has scalloped reniform

leaves and purplish flowers and is naturalized in North America

**hence** \'hen(t)s\ *adverb* [Middle English *hennes, henne,* from Old English *heonan;* akin to Old High German *hinnan* away, Old English *hēr* here] (13th century)
**1 :** from this place **:** AWAY
**2 a** *archaic* **:** HENCEFORTH **b :** from this time
**3 :** because of a preceding fact or premise **:** THEREFORE
**4 :** from this source or origin
— **from hence** *archaic* **:** from this place **:** from this time

**hence·forth** \'hen(t)s-,fòrth, -,fòrth, hen(t)s-'\ *adverb* (14th century)
**:** from this point on

**hence·for·ward** \hen(t)s-'fòr-wərd\ *adverb* (14th century)
**:** HENCEFORTH

**hench·man** \'hench-mən\ *noun* [Middle English *henshman, hengestman* groom, from *hengest* stallion (from Old English) + *man;* akin to Old High German *hengist* gelding] (15th century)
**1** *obsolete* **:** a squire or page to a person of high rank
**2 a :** a trusted follower **:** a right-hand man **b :** a political follower whose support is chiefly for personal advantage **c :** a member of a gang

**hen·deca·syl·lab·ic** \(,)hen-,de-kə-sə-'la-bik\ *adjective* [Latin *hendecasyllabus,* from Greek *hendeka* eleven (from *hen-, heis* one + *deka* ten) + *syllabē* syllable — more at SAME, TEN] (circa 1751)
**:** consisting of 11 syllables or composed of verses of 11 syllables
— **hendecasyllabic** *noun*
— **hen·deca·syl·la·ble** \hen-'de-kə-,si-lə-bəl, (,)hen-,de-kə-'\ *noun*

**hen·di·a·dys** \hen-'dī-ə-dəs\ *noun* [Late Latin *hendiadys, hendiadyoin,* modification of Greek *hen dia dyoin,* literally, one through two] (circa 1577)
**:** the expression of an idea by the use of usually two independent words connected by *and* (as *nice and warm*) instead of the usual combination of independent word and its modifier (as *nicely warm*)

**hen·e·quen** \'he-ni-kən, ,he-ni-'ken\ *noun* [Spanish *henequén*] (1880)
**:** a strong yellowish or reddish hard fiber obtained from the leaves of a tropical American agave chiefly in Yucatán and used especially for binder twine; *also* **:** a plant (*Agave fourcroydes*) that yields henequen

**hen·house** \'hen-,haùs\ *noun* (circa 1513)
**:** a house or shelter for fowl

**Hen·le's loop** \'hen-lēz-\ *noun* (circa 1890)
**:** LOOP OF HENLE

**¹hen·na** \'he-nə\ *noun* [Arabic *ḥinnā'*] (1600)
**1 :** a reddish brown dye obtained from leaves of the henna plant and used especially on hair
**2 :** an Old World tropical shrub or small tree (*Lawsonia inermis*) of the loosestrife family with small opposite leaves and axillary panicles of fragrant white flowers

**²henna** *transitive verb* (1919)
**:** to dye (as hair) with henna

**hen·nery** \'he-nə-rē\ *noun, plural* **-ner·ies** (1850)
**:** a poultry farm; *also* **:** an enclosure for poultry

**heno·the·ism** \'he-nə-(,)thē-,i-zəm\ *noun* [German *Henotheismus,* from Greek *hen-, heis* one + *theos* god — more at SAME] (1860)
**:** the worship of one god without denying the existence of other gods
— **heno·the·ist** \-,thē-ist\ *noun*
— **heno·the·is·tic** \,he-nə-thē-'is-tik\ *adjective*

**hen party** *noun* (circa 1885)
**:** a party for women only

**hen·peck** \'hen-,pek\ *transitive verb* (1688)
**:** to subject (one's husband) to persistent nagging and domination

hemstitch

**hen·ry** \'hen-rē\ *noun, plural* **henrys** *or* **hen·ries** [Joseph *Henry*] (circa 1890)
: the practical meter-kilogram-second unit of inductance equal to the self-inductance of a circuit or the mutual inductance of two circuits in which the variation of one ampere per second results in an induced electromotive force of one volt

**hent** \'hent\ *transitive verb* [Middle English, from Old English *hentan* — more at HUNT] *archaic* (before 12th century)
: SEIZE

**hen track** *noun* (1907)
: an illegible or scarcely legible mark intended as handwriting — called also *hen scratch*

¹**hep** \'hep, 'həp, 'hət\ *interjection* [origin unknown] (1862)
— used to mark a marching cadence

²**hep** \'hep\ *adjective* [origin unknown] (1904)
: ⁴HIP

**hep·a·rin** \'he-pə-rən\ *noun* [International Scientific Vocabulary, from Greek *hēpar* liver] (1918)
: a mucopolysaccharide sulfuric acid ester that is found especially in liver, that prolongs the clotting time of blood, and that is used medically
— **hep·a·rin·ized** \-rə-ˌnīzd\ *adjective*

**hepat-** *or* **hepato-** *combining form* [Latin, from Greek *hēpat-, hēpato-*, from *hēpat-, hēp-ar*; akin to Latin *jecur* liver]
1 : liver ⟨*hepatectomy*⟩ ⟨*hepatotoxic*⟩
2 : hepatic and ⟨*hepatocellular*⟩

**hep·a·tec·to·my** \ˌhe-pə-'tek-tə-mē\ *noun, plural* **-mies** (circa 1890)
: excision of the liver or of part of the liver
— **hep·a·tec·to·mized** \-ˌmīzd\ *adjective*

¹**he·pat·ic** \hi-'pa-tik\ *adjective* [Latin *hepaticus*, from Greek *hēpatikos*, from *hēpat-, hēp-ar*] (1599)
: of, relating to, affecting, associated with, supplying, or draining the liver ⟨a *hepatic* complaint⟩ ⟨*hepatic* arteries⟩

²**hepatic** *noun* (1900)
: LIVERWORT

**he·pat·i·ca** \hi-'pa-ti-kə\ *noun* [New Latin, from Medieval Latin, liverwort, from Latin, feminine of *hepaticus*] (1578)
: any of a genus (*Hepatica*) of herbs of the buttercup family with lobed leaves and delicate flowers

**hep·a·ti·tis** \ˌhe-pə-'tī-təs\ *noun, plural* **-tit·i·des** \-'ti-tə-ˌdēz\ [New Latin] (circa 1751)
1 : inflammation of the liver
2 : a disease or condition (as hepatitis A or hepatitis B) marked by inflammation of the liver

**hepatitis A** *noun* (1972)
: an acute usually benign hepatitis caused by an RNA virus that does not persist in the blood serum and is transmitted especially in food and water contaminated with infected fecal matter — called also *infectious hepatitis*

**hepatitis B** *noun* (1972)
: a sometimes fatal hepatitis caused by a double-stranded DNA virus that tends to persist in the blood serum and is transmitted especially by contact with infected blood (as by transfusion) or blood products — called also *serum hepatitis*

**he·pa·to·cel·lu·lar** \ˌhe-pə-tō-'sel-yə-lər, hi-ˌpa-tə-'sel-\ *adjective* (1940)
: of or involving hepatocytes ⟨*hepatocellular* carcinoma⟩

**he·pa·to·cyte** \hi-'pa-tə-ˌsīt, 'he-pə-tə-\ *noun* (1965)
: an epithelial parenchymatous cell of the liver

**he·pa·to·ma** \ˌhe-pə-'tō-mə\ *noun, plural* **-mas** *or* **-ma·ta** \-mə-tə\ [New Latin] (circa 1923)
: a usually malignant tumor of the liver

**he·pa·to·meg·a·ly** \ˌhe-pə-tō-'me-gə-lē, hi-ˌpa-tə-'me-\ *noun, plural* **-lies** (circa 1901)
: enlargement of the liver

**he·pa·to·pan·cre·as** \-'paŋ-krē-əs, -'pan-\ *noun* (1884)
: a glandular structure (as of a crustacean) that combines the digestive functions of the vertebrate liver and pancreas

**hep·a·to·tox·ic** \-'täk-sik\ *adjective* (1926)
: relating to or causing injury to the liver ⟨*hepatotoxic* drugs⟩

**hep·a·to·tox·ic·i·ty** \-täk-'si-sə-tē\ *noun* (1952)
1 : a state of toxic damage to the liver
2 : a tendency or capacity to cause hepatotoxicity

**hep·cat** \'hep-ˌkat\ *noun* (1938)
: HIPSTER

**He·phaes·tus** \hi-'fes-təs, -'fēs-\ *noun* [Latin, from Greek *Hēphaistos*]
: the Greek god of fire and metalworking — compare VULCAN

**hepped up** *adjective* (1947)
: ENTHUSIASTIC

**Hep·ple·white** \'he-pəl-ˌhwīt, -ˌwīt\ *adjective* [George *Hepplewhite*] (1897)
: of, relating to, or imitating a style of furniture originating in late 18th century England

**hepta-** *or* **hept-** *combining form* [Greek, from *hepta* — more at SEVEN]
1 : seven ⟨*heptameter*⟩
2 : containing seven atoms, groups, or equivalents ⟨*heptane*⟩

**hep·ta·chlor** \'hep-tə-ˌklȯr, -ˌklór\ *noun* [*hepta-* + *chlorine*] (1949)
: a cyclodiene chlorinated hydrocarbon pesticide $C_{10}H_5Cl_7$ that causes liver disease in animals and is a suspected human carcinogen

**hep·tad** \'hep-ˌtad\ *noun* [Greek *heptad-, heptas*, from *hepta*] (1660)
: a group of seven

**hep·ta·gon** \'hep-tə-ˌgän\ *noun* [Greek *heptagōnos* heptagonal, from *hepta + gōnia* angle — more at -GON] (1570)
: a polygon of seven angles and seven sides
— **hep·tag·o·nal** \hep-'ta-gə-n°l\ *adjective*

heptagon

**hep·tam·e·ter** \hep-'ta-mə-tər\ *noun* (circa 1898)
: a line of verse consisting of seven metrical feet

**hep·tane** \'hep-ˌtān\ *noun* (1877)
: any of several isomeric alkanes $C_7H_{16}$; especially : the liquid normal isomer occurring in petroleum and used especially as a solvent and in determining octane numbers

**hep·tar·chy** \'hep-ˌtär-kē\ *noun* (1576)
: a hypothetical confederacy of seven Anglo-Saxon kingdoms of the 7th and 8th centuries

**Hep·ta·teuch** \'hep-tə-ˌtük, -ˌtyük\ *noun* [Late Latin *heptateuchos*, from Greek, from *hepta + teuchos* book — more at PENTATEUCH] (1678)
: the first seven books of the canonical Jewish and Christian Scriptures

**hep·tose** \'hep-ˌtōs, -ˌtōz\ *noun* (1890)
: any of various monosaccharides $C_7H_{14}O_7$ containing seven carbon atoms in a molecule

¹**her** \(h)ər, 'hər\ *adjective* [Middle English *hire*, from Old English *hiere*, genitive of *hēo* she — more at HE] (before 12th century)
: of or relating to her or herself especially as possessor, agent, or object of an action ⟨*her* house⟩ ⟨*her* research⟩ ⟨*her* rescue⟩ — compare ¹SHE

²**her** *pronoun* objective case of SHE

**He·ra** \'hir-ə, 'hē-rə, 'her-ə\ *noun* [Greek *Hēra, Hērē*]
: the sister and consort of Zeus — compare JUNO

**Her·a·cles** \'her-ə-ˌklēz\ *noun* [Greek *Hēraklēs*]
: HERCULES

¹**her·ald** \'her-əld\ *noun* [Middle English, from Middle French *hiraut*, from an (assumed) Germanic compound whose first component is akin to Old High German *heri* army, and whose second is akin to Old High German *waltan* to rule — more at HARRY, WIELD] (14th century)
1 a : an official at a tournament of arms with duties including the making of announcements and the marshaling of combatants b : an officer with the status of ambassador acting as official messenger between leaders especially in war c (1) : OFFICER OF ARMS (2) : an officer of arms ranking above a pursuivant and below a king of arms
2 : an official crier or messenger
3 a : one that precedes or foreshadows b : one that conveys news or proclaims : ANNOUNCER ⟨it was the lark, the *herald* of the morn —Shakespeare⟩ c : one who actively promotes or advocates : EXPONENT
**synonym** see FORERUNNER

²**herald** *transitive verb* (14th century)
1 : to give notice of : ANNOUNCE
2 a : to greet especially with enthusiasm : HAIL b : PUBLICIZE
3 : to signal the approach of : FORESHADOW

**he·ral·dic** \he-'ral-dik, hə-\ *adjective* (1772)
: of or relating to heralds or heraldry
— **he·ral·di·cal·ly** \-di-k(ə-)lē\ *adverb*

**her·ald·ry** \'her-əl-drē\ *noun, plural* **-ries** (1572)
1 : the practice of devising, blazoning, and granting armorial insignia and of tracing and recording genealogies
2 : an armorial ensign; *broadly* : INSIGNIA
3 : PAGEANTRY

**herb** \'ərb, *US also & British usually* 'hərb\ *noun, often attributive* [Middle English *herbe*, from Old French, from Latin *herba*] (14th century)
1 : a seed-producing annual, biennial, or perennial that does not develop persistent woody tissue but dies down at the end of a growing season
2 : a plant or plant part valued for its medicinal, savory, or aromatic qualities
3 *slang* : MARIJUANA 2
— **herb·like** \'(h)ər-ˌblīk\ *adjective*
— **herby** \'(h)ər-bē\ *adjective*

**her·ba·ceous** \ˌ(h)ər-'bā-shəs\ *adjective* (1646)
1 a : of, relating to, or having the characteristics of an herb b *of a stem* : having little or no woody tissue and persisting usually for a single growing season
2 : having the texture, color, or appearance of a leaf

**herb·age** \'(h)ər-bij\ *noun* (14th century)
1 : herbaceous vegetation (as grass) especially when used for grazing
2 : the succulent parts of herbaceous plants

¹**herb·al** \'(h)ər-bəl\ *noun* (1516)
1 : a book about plants especially with reference to their medicinal properties
2 *archaic* : HERBARIUM 1

²**herbal** *adjective* (1612)
: of, relating to, or made of herbs

**herb·al·ist** \'(h)ər-bə-list\ *noun* (1589)
1 : one who practices healing by the use of herbs
2 : one who collects or grows herbs

**her·bar·i·um** \ˌ(h)ər-'bar-ē-əm, -'ber-\ *noun, plural* **-ia** \-ē-ə\ (1776)
1 : a collection of dried plant specimens usually mounted and systematically arranged for reference
2 : a place that houses an herbarium

**herb doctor** *noun* (1828)
: HERBALIST 1

**herbed** \'(h)ərbd\ *adjective* (1950)
: seasoned with herbs

**her·bi·cide** \'(h)ər-bə-ˌsīd\ *noun* [Latin *herba* + International Scientific Vocabulary *-cide*] (1899)

**:** an agent used to destroy or inhibit plant growth

— **her·bi·cid·al** \,(h)ər-bə-'sī-d°l\ *adjective*
— **her·bi·cid·al·ly** \-d°l-ē\ *adverb*

**her·bi·vore** \'(h)ər-bə-,vŏr, -,vòr\ *noun* [New Latin *Herbivora,* group of mammals, from neuter plural of *herbivorus*] (1854)
**:** a plant-eating animal

**her·biv·o·rous** \,(h)ər-'biv-rəs, -'biv-ə-\ *adjective* [New Latin *herbivorus,* from Latin *herba* grass + *-vorus* -vorous] (1661)
**:** feeding on plants

— **her·biv·o·ry** \-'biv-ə-rē\ *noun*

**herb Rob·ert** \'(h)ərb-'rä-bərt\ *noun* [Medieval Latin *herba Roberti,* probably from *Robertus* (Saint Robert) (died 1067) French ecclesiastic] (13th century)
**:** a sticky low geranium (*Geranium robertianum*) with small reddish purple flowers

**Her·cu·le·an** \,hər-kyə-'lē-ən, ,hər-'kyü-lē-\ *adjective* (1593)
**1 :** of, relating to, or characteristic of Hercules
**2** *often not capitalized* **:** of extraordinary power, extent, intensity, or difficulty

**Her·cu·les** \'hər-kyə-,lēz\ *noun* [Latin, from Greek *Hēraklēs*]
**1 :** a mythical Greek hero renowned for his great strength and especially for performing 12 labors imposed on him by Hera
**2** [Latin (genitive *Herculis*)] **:** a northern constellation between Corona Borealis and Lyra

**Her·cu·les'–club** \'hər-kyə-,lēz-,kləb\ *noun* (1847)
**1 :** a small prickly eastern U.S. tree (*Aralia spinosa*) of the ginseng family — called also *angelica tree*
**2 :** a small prickly southern U.S. tree (*Zanthoxylum clava-herculis*) of the rue family

**¹herd** \'hərd\ *noun* [Middle English, from Old English *heord;* akin to Old High German *herta* herd, Middle Welsh *cordd* troop, Lithuanian *kerdžius* shepherd] (before 12th century)
**1 a :** a number of animals of one kind kept together under human control **b :** a congregation of gregarious wild animals
**2 a** (1) **:** a group of people usually having a common bond (2) **:** a large assemblage of like things **b :** the undistinguished masses **:** CROWD ⟨isolate the individual prophets from the *herd* —Norman Cousins⟩

— **herd·like** \-,līk\ *adjective*

**²herd** (13th century)
*transitive verb*
**1 a :** to gather, lead, or drive as if in a herd ⟨seventy-five boys and girls were *herded* by six or eight teachers —W. A. White⟩ **b :** to keep or move (animals) together
**2 :** to place in a group
*intransitive verb*
**1 :** to assemble or move in a herd
**2 :** to place oneself in a group **:** ASSOCIATE

**herd·er** \'hər-dər\ *noun* (1635)
**:** one that herds; *specifically* **:** HERDSMAN 1

**herds·man** \'hərdz-mən\ *noun* (1603)
**1 :** a manager, breeder, or tender of livestock
**2** *capitalized* **:** BOÖTES

**¹here** \'hir\ *adverb* [Middle English, from Old English *hēr;* akin to Old High German *hier* here, Old English *hē* he] (before 12th century)
**1 a :** in or at this place ⟨turn *here*⟩ — often used interjectionally especially in answering a roll call **b :** NOW ⟨*here* it's morning already⟩ **c :** in an arbitrary location ⟨a book *here,* a paper there⟩
**2 :** at or in this point, particular, or case ⟨*here* we agree⟩
**3 :** in the present life or state
**4 :** HITHER ⟨come *here*⟩
**5** — used interjectionally in rebuke or encouragement
— **here goes** — used interjectionally to express resolution or resignation especially at the beginning of a difficult or unpleasant undertaking

— **neither here nor there :** having no interest or relevance **:** of no consequence ⟨comfort is *neither here nor there* to a real sailor⟩

**²here** *adjective* (15th century)
**1** — used for emphasis especially after a demonstrative pronoun or after a noun modified by a demonstrative adjective ⟨this book *here*⟩
**2** *nonstandard* — used for emphasis after a demonstrative adjective but before the noun modified ⟨this *here* book⟩

**³here** *noun* (1605)
**:** this place

**here·abouts** \'hir-ə-,baùts\ *or* **here·about** \-,baùt\ *adverb* (13th century)
**:** in this vicinity

**¹here·af·ter** \hir-'af-tər\ *adverb* (before 12th century)
**1 :** after this in sequence or in time
**2 :** in some future time or state

**²hereafter** *noun, often capitalized* (1546)
**1 :** FUTURE
**2 :** an existence beyond earthly life

**³hereafter** *adjective* (1591)
*archaic* **:** FUTURE

**here and now** *noun* (1829)
**:** the present time — used with *the* ⟨man's obligation is in the *here and now* —W. H. Whyte⟩

**here and there** *adverb* (14th century)
**1 :** in one place and another
**2 :** from time to time

**here·away** \'hir-ə-,wā\ *or* **here·aways** \-,wāz\ *adverb* (14th century)
*dialect* **:** HEREABOUTS

**here·by** \hir-'bī, 'hir-,\ *adverb* (13th century)
**:** by this means

**her·e·dit·a·ment** \,her-ə-'di-tə-mənt\ *noun* [Medieval Latin *hereditamentum,* from Late Latin *hereditare* to inherit, from Latin *hered-, heres*] (15th century)
**:** heritable property

**he·red·i·tar·i·an** \hə-,re-də-'ter-ē-ən\ *noun* (1881)
**:** an advocate of the theory that individual differences in human beings can be accounted for primarily on the basis of genetics

— **hereditarian** *adjective*

**he·red·i·tary** \hə-'re-də-,ter-ē\ *adjective* [Latin *hereditarius,* from *hereditas*] (15th century)
**1 a :** genetically transmitted or transmittable from parent to offspring **b :** characteristic of or fostered by one's predecessors
**2 a :** received or passing by inheritance or required to pass by inheritance or by reason of birth **b :** having title or possession through inheritance or by reason of birth
**3 :** of a kind established by tradition ⟨*hereditary* enemies⟩
**4 :** of or relating to inheritance or heredity
*synonym* see INNATE

— **he·red·i·tar·i·ly** \-,re-də-'ter-ə-lē\ *adverb*

**he·red·i·ty** \hə-'re-də-tē\ *noun* [Middle French *heredité,* from Latin *hereditat-, hereditas,* from *hered-, heres* heir — more at HEIR] (circa 1540)
**1 a :** INHERITANCE **b :** TRADITION
**2 a :** the sum of the qualities and potentialities genetically derived from one's ancestors **b :** the transmission of such qualities from ancestor to descendant through the genes

**Her·e·ford** \'hər-fərd *sometimes* 'her-ə-\ *noun* [*Hereford* former county in England] (1805)
**:** any of a breed of hardy red-coated beef cattle of English origin with white faces and markings

**here·in** \hir-'in\ *adverb* (before 12th century)
**:** in this

**here·in·above** \(,)hir-,in-ə-'bəv\ *adverb* (circa 1812)
**:** at a prior point in this writing or document

**here·in·af·ter** \,hir-ə-'naf-tər\ *adverb* (1590)
**:** in the following part of this writing or document

**here·in·be·fore** \(,)hir-,in-bi-'fŏr, -'fòr\ *adverb* (1687)

**:** in the preceding part of this writing or document

**here·in·be·low** \-bi-'lō\ *adverb* (1946)
**:** at a subsequent point in this writing or document

**here·of** \hir-'əv, -'äv\ *adverb* (before 12th century)
**:** of this

**here·on** \-'òn, -'än\ *adverb* (12th century)
**:** on this

**He·re·ro** \hə-'rer-(,)ō, 'her-ə-,rō\ *noun, plural* **Herero** *or* **Hereros** (1880)
**:** a member of a Bantu people of central Namibia

**he·re·si·arch** \hə-'rē-zē-,ärk, 'her-ə-sē-\ *noun* [Late Latin *haeresiarcha,* from Late Greek *hairesiarchēs,* from *hairesis* + Greek *-archēs* -arch] (1624)
**:** an originator or chief advocate of a heresy

**her·e·sy** \'her-ə-sē\ *noun, plural* **-sies** [Middle English *heresie,* from Old French, from Late Latin *haeresis,* from Late Greek *hairesis,* from Greek, action of taking, choice, sect, from *hairein* to take] (13th century)
**1 a :** adherence to a religious opinion contrary to church dogma **b :** denial of a revealed truth by a baptized member of the Roman Catholic Church **c :** an opinion or doctrine contrary to church dogma
**2 a :** dissent or deviation from a dominant theory, opinion, or practice **b :** an opinion, doctrine, or practice contrary to the truth or to generally accepted beliefs or standards

**her·e·tic** \'her-ə-,tik\ *noun* (14th century)
**1 :** a dissenter from established church dogma; *especially* **:** a baptized member of the Roman Catholic Church who disavows a revealed truth
**2 :** one who dissents from an accepted belief or doctrine **:** NONCONFORMIST

**he·ret·i·cal** \hə-'re-ti-kəl\ *also* **he·re·tic** \'her-ə-,tik\ *adjective* (15th century)
**1 :** of, relating to, or characterized by heresy
**2 :** of, relating to, or characterized by departure from accepted beliefs or standards **:** UNORTHODOX

— **he·ret·i·cal·ly** \hə-'re-ti-k(ə-)lē\ *adverb*

**here·to** \hir-'tü\ *adverb* (12th century)
**:** to this writing or document

**here·to·fore** \'hir-tə-,fŏr, -,fòr, ,hir-tə-'\ *adverb* (13th century)
**:** up to this time **:** HITHERTO

**here·un·der** \hir-'ən-dər\ *adverb* (15th century)
**:** under or in accordance with this writing or document

**here·un·to** \hir-'ən-(,)tü, ,hir-(,)ən-'tü\ *adverb* (1509)
**:** to this

**here·up·on** \'hir-ə-,pòn, -,pän, ,hir-ə-'\ *adverb* (12th century)
**:** on this **:** immediately after this

**here·with** \hir-'with, -'with\ *adverb* (before 12th century)
**1 :** with this communication **:** enclosed in this
**2 :** HEREBY

**He·rez** \hə-'rez\ *or* **He·riz** \-'riz\ *noun* [*Herez, Heriz,* town in Iran] (circa 1922)
**:** a Persian rug characterized by a large central geometric medallion and by angular floral designs

**her·i·ot** \'her-ē-ət\ *noun* [Middle English, from Old English *heregeatwe,* plural, military equipment, from *here* army (akin to Old High German *heri* army) + *geatwe* equipment — more at HARRY] (before 12th century)
**:** a feudal duty or tribute due under English law to a lord on the death of a tenant

**her·i·ta·bil·i·ty** \,her-ə-tə-'bi-lə-tē\ *noun* (1832)
**1 :** the quality or state of being heritable
**2 :** the proportion of observed variation in a particular trait (as intelligence) that can be attributed to inherited genetic factors in contrast to environmental ones

**her·i·ta·ble** \'her-ə-tə-bəl\ *adjective* (14th century)
**1** : capable of being inherited or of passing by inheritance
**2** : HEREDITARY

**her·i·tage** \'her-ə-tij\ *noun* [Middle English, from Middle French, from *heriter* to inherit, from Late Latin *hereditare*, from Latin *hered-, heres* heir — more at HEIR] (13th century)
**1** : property that descends to an heir
**2 a** : something transmitted by or acquired from a predecessor : LEGACY, INHERITANCE **b** : TRADITION
**3** : something possessed as a result of one's natural situation or birth : BIRTHRIGHT ⟨the nation's *heritage* of tolerance⟩

**her·i·tor** \'her-ə-tər\ *noun* (15th century)
: one that inherits : INHERITOR

**herky–jerky** \'hər-kē-'jər-kē\ *adjective* [reduplication of *jerky*] (1957)
: characterized by sudden, irregular, or unpredictable movement or style

**herm** \'hərm\ *noun* [Latin *hermes*, from Greek *hermēs* statue of Hermes, herm, from *Hermēs*] (circa 1580)
: a statue in the form of a square stone pillar surmounted by a bust or head especially of Hermes

**her·ma** \'hər-mə\ *noun, plural* **her·mae** \-,mē, -,mī\ *or* **her·mai** \-,mī\ (1638)
: HERM

**her·maph·ro·dite** \(,)hər-'ma-frə-,dīt\ *noun* [Middle English *hermofrodite*, from Latin *hermaphroditus*, from Greek *hermaphroditos*, from *Hermaphroditos*] (14th century)
**1** : an animal or plant having both male and female reproductive organs
**2** : something that is a combination of diverse elements
— **hermaphrodite** *adjective*
— **her·maph·ro·dit·ic** \(,)hər-,ma-frə-'di-tik\ *adjective*
— **her·maph·ro·dit·ism** \-'ma-frə-,dī-,ti-zəm\ *noun*

**Her·maph·ro·di·tus** \(,)hər-,ma-frə-'dī-təs\ *noun* [Latin, from Greek *Hermaphroditos*, from *Hermēs* + *Aphroditē* Aphrodite]
: a son of Hermes and Aphrodite who becomes joined in one body with a nymph while bathing

**her·ma·typ·ic** \,hər-mə-'ti-pik\ *adjective* [Greek *herma* prop, reef + *typtein* to strike, coin + English *-ic* — more at TYPE] (1950)
: building reefs ⟨*hermatypic* corals⟩

**her·me·neu·ti·cal** \,hər-mə-'nü-ti-kəl, -'nyü-\ *or* **her·me·neu·tic** \-tik\ *adjective* [Greek *hermēneutikos*, from *hermēneuein* to interpret, from *hermēneus* interpreter] (1678)
: of or relating to hermeneutics : INTERPRETATIVE
— **her·me·neu·ti·cal·ly** \-ti-k(ə-)lē\ *adverb*

**her·me·neu·tics** \-tiks\ *noun plural but singular or plural in construction* (1737)
: the study of the methodological principles of interpretation (as of the Bible)

**Her·mes** \'hər-(,)mēz\ *noun* [Latin, from Greek *Hermēs*]
: a Greek god of commerce, eloquence, invention, travel, and theft who serves as herald and messenger of the other gods — compare MERCURY

**Hermes Tris·me·gis·tus** \-,tris-mə-'jis-təs\ *noun* [Medieval Latin, from Greek *Hermēs trismegistos*, literally, Hermes thrice greatest]
: a legendary author of works embodying magical, astrological, and alchemical doctrines

**her·met·ic** \(,)hər-'me-tik\ *also* **her·met·i·cal** \-ti-kəl\ *adjective* [New Latin *hermeticus*, from *Hermet-, Hermes Trismegistus*] (1605)
**1** *often capitalized* **a** : of or relating to the Gnostic writings or teachings arising in the first three centuries A.D. and attributed to Hermes Trismegistus **b** : relating to or characterized by occultism or abstruseness : RECONDITE

**2** [from the belief that Hermes Trismegistus invented a magic seal to keep vessels airtight]
**a** : AIRTIGHT ⟨*hermetic* seal⟩ **b** : impervious to external influence ⟨trapped inside the *hermetic* military machine —Jack Newfield⟩ **c** : RECLUSE, SOLITARY ⟨leads a *hermetic* life⟩ ◆
— **her·met·i·cal·ly** \-ti-k(ə-)lē\ *adverb*

**her·met·i·cism** \-'me-tə-,si-zəm\ *noun, often capitalized* (1897)
: HERMETISM

**her·me·tism** \'hər-mə-,ti-zəm\ *noun, often capitalized* (1897)
**1 a** : a system of ideas based on hermetic teachings **b** : adherence to or practice of hermetic doctrine
**2** : the practice of being hermetically mysterious ⟨it is not . . . willful *hermetism*, if the message of their art is veiled and indirect —R. J. Goldwater⟩
— **her·me·tist** \-mə-tist\ *noun*

**her·mit** \'hər-mət\ *noun* [Middle English *eremite*, from Old French, from Late Latin *eremita*, from Late Greek *erēmitēs*, from Greek, adjective, living in the desert, from *erēmia* desert, from *erēmos* desolate] (12th century)
**1 a** : one that retires from society and lives in solitude especially for religious reasons : RECLUSE **b** *obsolete* : BEADSMAN
**2** : a spiced molasses cookie
— **her·mit·ism** \'hər-mə-,ti-zəm\ *noun*

**her·mit·age** \'hər-mə-tij\ *noun* (14th century)
**1 a** : the habitation of a hermit **b** : a secluded residence or private retreat : HIDEAWAY **c** : MONASTERY
**2** : the life or condition of a hermit

**Her·mi·tage** \'(h)er-mi-'täzh\ *noun* [Tain-l'*Ermitage*, commune in France] (1680)
: a red or white Rhone valley wine

**hermit crab** *noun* (1735)
: any of numerous chiefly marine decapod crustaceans (especially families Diogenidae, Paguridae, and Parapaguridae) having soft asymmetrical abdomens and occupying the empty shells of gastropods

**hermit crab**

**Her·mi·tian matrix** \er-'mē-shən-, ,hər-'mi-shən-\ *noun* [Charles *Hermite* (died 1901) French mathematician] (1935)
: a square matrix having the property that each pair of elements in the *i*th row and *j*th column and in the *j*th row and *i*th column are conjugate complex numbers

**hern** \'hern, 'hərn\ *dialect variant of* HERON

**her·nia** \'hər-nē-ə\ *noun, plural* **-ni·as** *or* **-ni·ae** \-nē-,ē, -nē-,ī\ [Latin — more at YARN] (14th century)
: a protrusion of an organ or part through connective tissue or through a wall of the cavity in which it is normally enclosed — called also *rupture*
— **her·ni·al** \-nē-əl\ *adjective*

**her·ni·ate** \'hər-nē-,āt\ *intransitive verb* **-at·ed; -at·ing** (circa 1922)
: to protrude through an abnormal body opening : RUPTURE
— **her·ni·a·tion** \,hər-nē-'ā-shən\ *noun*

**he·ro** \'hir-(,)ō, 'hē-(,)rō\ *noun, plural* **heroes** [Latin *heros*, from Greek *hērōs*] (14th century)
**1 a** : a mythological or legendary figure often of divine descent endowed with great strength or ability **b** : an illustrious warrior **c** : a man admired for his achievements and noble qualities **d** : one that shows great courage
**2 a** : the principal male character in a literary or dramatic work **b** : the central figure in an event, period, or movement
**3** *plural usually* **heros** : SUBMARINE 2
**4** : an object of extreme admiration and devotion : IDOL

**Hero** *noun* [Latin, from Greek *Hērō*]

: a legendary priestess of Aphrodite loved by Leander

**¹he·ro·ic** \hi-'rō-ik *also* her-'ō- *or* hē-'rō-\ *also* **he·ro·i·cal** \-i-kəl\ *adjective* (1549)
**1** : of, relating to, or resembling heroes especially of antiquity
**2 a** : exhibiting or marked by courage and daring **b** : supremely noble or self-sacrificing
**3 a** : of impressive size, power, extent, or effect : POTENT ⟨*heroic* doses⟩ ⟨a *heroic* voice⟩ **b** (1) : of great intensity : EXTREME, DRASTIC ⟨*heroic* effort⟩ (2) : of a kind that is likely only to be undertaken to save a life ⟨*heroic* surgery⟩
**4** : of, relating to, or constituting drama written during the Restoration in heroic couplets and concerned with a conflict between love and honor
— **he·ro·i·cal·ly** \-i-k(ə-)lē\ *adverb*

**²heroic** *noun* (1596)
**1** : a heroic verse or poem
**2** *plural* **a** : flamboyantly heroic language or action **b** : heroic action or behavior **c** : determined effort especially in the face of difficulty

**heroic couplet** *noun* (1889)
: a rhyming couplet in iambic pentameter

**he·roi·com·ic** \hi-,rō-i-'kä-mik\ *or* **he·roi·com·i·cal** \-'kä-mi-kəl\ *adjective* [French *héroïcomique*, from *héroïque* heroic + *comique* comic] (1756)
: comic by being ludicrously noble, bold, or elevated

**heroic poem** *noun* (1693)
: an epic or a poem in epic style

**heroic stanza** *noun* (circa 1922)
: a rhymed quatrain in heroic verse with a rhyme scheme of *abab* — called also *heroic quatrain*

**heroic verse** *noun* (1586)
**1** : dactylic hexameter especially of epic verse of classical times — called also *heroic meter*
**2** : the iambic pentameter used especially in English epic poetry during the 17th and 18th centuries — called also *heroic line, heroic meter*

**her·o·in** \'her-ə-wən\ *noun* [from *Heroin*, a trademark] (1898)
: a strongly physiologically addictive narcotic $C_{21}H_{23}NO_5$ that is made by acetylation of but is more potent than morphine and that is prohibited for medical use in the U.S. but is used illicitly for its euphoric effects
— **her·o·in·ism** \-wə-,ni-zəm\ *noun*

◇ **WORD HISTORY**
**hermetic** Thoth was an ancient Egyptian god of wisdom whose cult in the Nile valley endured for millennia. The Greeks who settled in Egypt after its conquest by Alexander the Great and created a blend of Egyptian and Hellenistic culture identified their god Hermes with Thoth, who was then renamed in Greek *Hermēs Trismegistos* "thrice-greatest Hermes," a rough translation of one of Thoth's Egyptian titles. Thoth-Hermes was the reputed author of a set of treatises, the *Hermetica*, containing revelation on mystical subjects as well as astrological and alchemical speculation, nearly all of which was Greek rather than Egyptian in origin. In medieval alchemical tradition Hermes Trismegistus, as his name was latinized, was the inventor of a seal that kept vessels airtight. From this tradition come the most common meanings of *hermetic* in English, "airtight" and by extension "impervious to external influence."

**her·o·ine** \'her-ə-wən, 'hir-\ *noun* [Latin *heroina*, from Greek *hērōïnē*, feminine of *hērōs*] (1609)
**1 a :** a mythological or legendary woman having the qualities of a hero **b :** a woman admired and emulated for her achievements and qualities
**2 a :** the principal female character in a literary or dramatic work **b :** the central female figure in an event or period
**her·o·ism** \'her-ə-,wi-zəm *also* 'hir-\ *noun* (1717)
**1 :** heroic conduct especially as exhibited in fulfilling a high purpose or attaining a noble end
**2 :** the qualities of a hero
**he·ro·ize** \'hē-(,)rō-,īz, 'hir-(,)ō-; 'her-ə-,wīz\ *transitive verb* **-ized; -iz·ing** (1738)
**:** to make heroic
**her·on** \'her-ən\ *noun, plural* **herons** *also* **heron** [Middle English *heiroun*, from Middle French *hairon*, of Germanic origin; akin to Old High German *heigaro* heron] (14th century)
**:** any of various long-necked wading birds (family Ardeidae) with a long tapering bill, large wings, and soft plumage
**her·on·ry** \-ən-rē\ *noun, plural* **-ries** (1616)
**:** a heron rookery
**hero–worship** *transitive verb* (1884)
**:** to feel or express hero worship for
**— hero–worshiper** *noun*
**hero worship** *noun* (1774)
**1 :** veneration of a hero
**2 :** foolish or excessive adulation for an individual
**her·pes** \'hər-(,)pēz\ *noun* [Latin, from Greek *herpēs*, from *herpein* to creep — more at SERPENT] (14th century)
**:** any of several inflammatory virus diseases of the skin characterized by clusters of vesicles; *especially* **:** HERPES SIMPLEX
**— her·pet·ic** \(,)hər-'pe-tik\ *adjective*
**her·pes sim·plex** \-'sim-,pleks\ *noun* [New Latin, literally, simple herpes] (1907)
**:** either of two virus diseases marked in one case by groups of watery blisters on the skin or mucous membranes (as of the mouth and lips) above the waist and in the other by such blisters on the genitals
**her·pes·vi·rus** \-'vī-rəs\ *noun* (1925)
**:** any of a group of DNA-containing viruses that replicate in cell nuclei and produce herpes
**herpes zos·ter** \-'zäs-tər\ *noun* [New Latin, literally, girdle herpes] (1807)
**:** an acute viral inflammation of the sensory ganglia of spinal and cranial nerves associated with a vesicular eruption and neuralgic pains and caused by reactivation of the poxvirus causing chicken pox — called also *shingles*
**her·pe·tol·o·gy** \,hər-pə-'tä-lə-jē\ *noun* [Greek *herpeton* quadruped, reptile, from neuter of *herpetos* crawling, from *herpein*] (1824)
**:** a branch of zoology dealing with reptiles and amphibians
**— her·pe·to·log·i·cal** \-tə-'lä-ji-kəl\ *adjective*
**— her·pe·tol·o·gist** \,hər-pə-'tä-lə-jist\ *noun*
**Herr** \(,)her\ *noun, plural* **Her·ren** \,her-ən, (,)hern\ [German] (1653)
**—** used among German-speaking people as a title equivalent to *Mr.*
**her·ren·volk** \'her-ən-,fōk, -,fōlk\ *noun, often capitalized* [German] (1940)
**:** MASTER RACE
**her·ring** \'her-iŋ\ *noun, plural* **herring** *or* **herrings** [Middle English *hering*, from Old English *hæring;* akin to Old High German *hārinc* herring] (before 12th century)
**1 :** either of two clupeid food fishes (genus *Clupeus*): **a :** one (*C. harengus*) that is abundant in the temperate and colder parts of the North Atlantic and that in the adult state is preserved by smoking or salting and in the young state is extensively canned and sold as

sardines **b :** one (*C. pallasi* synonym *C. h. pallasi*) of the North Pacific harvested especially for its roe
**2 :** CLUPEID
**¹her·ring·bone** \'her-iŋ-,bōn\ *noun, often attributive* (1659)
**1 :** a pattern made up of rows of parallel lines which in any two adjacent rows slope in opposite directions
**2 a :** a twilled fabric with a herringbone pattern; *also* **:** a suit made of this fabric **b :** a herringbone arrangement (as of materials or parts)

**herringbone 1**

**3 :** a method in skiing of ascending a slope by herringboning
**²herringbone** (1787)
*transitive verb*
**1 :** to produce a herringbone pattern on
**2 :** to arrange in a herringbone pattern
*intransitive verb*
**1 :** to produce a herringbone pattern
**2 :** to ascend a slope by toeing out on skis and placing the weight on the inner side
**herring gull** *noun* (1857)
**:** a common large gull (*Larus argentatus*) of the northern hemisphere that as an adult is largely white with a gray mantle, dark wing tips, pink feet, and yellow bill
**hers** \'hərz\ *pronoun, singular or plural in construction*
**:** that which belongs to her — used without a following noun as a pronoun equivalent in meaning to the adjective *her*
**her·self** \(h)ər-'self, *Southern also* -'sef\ *pronoun* (before 12th century)
**1 :** that identical female one — compare ¹SHE: used reflexively, for emphasis, in absolute constructions, or in place of *her* especially when joined to another object (she considers *herself* lucky) (she *herself* did it) (*herself* an orphan, she understood the situation) (accepted the award for her colleagues and *herself*)
**2 :** her normal, healthy, or sane condition or self
**3** *chiefly Irish & Scottish* **:** a woman of consequence; *especially* **:** the mistress of the house
**her·sto·ry** \'hər-st(ə-)rē\ *noun, plural* **-ries** [blend of *her* and *history*] (1971)
**:** HISTORY; *specifically* **:** history considered or presented from a feminist viewpoint or with special attention to the experience of women
**hertz** \'hərts, 'herts\ *noun, plural* **hertz** [Heinrich R. *Hertz*] (circa 1928)
**:** a unit of frequency equal to one cycle per second — abbreviation *Hz*
**he's** \'hēz, ēz\ (1588)
**:** he is : he has
**he/she** \'hē-'shē; hē-ər-; 'hē-'slash-\ *pronoun* (1974)
**:** he or she — used in writing as a pronoun of common gender
**Hesh·van** \'kesh-vən\ *noun* [Hebrew *Ḥeshwān*] (circa 1769)
**:** the 2d month of the civil year or the 8th month of the ecclesiastical year in the Jewish calendar — see MONTH table
**hes·i·tance** \'he-zə-tən(t)s\ *noun* (1601)
**:** HESITANCY
**hes·i·tan·cy** \-tən(t)-sē\ *noun, plural* **-cies** (1617)
**1 :** the quality or state of being hesitant: as **a :** INDECISION **b :** RELUCTANCE (took that drastic step only with the greatest *hesitancy*)
**2 :** HESITATION 1
**hes·i·tant** \'he-zə-tənt\ *adjective* (1647)
**:** tending to hesitate
**synonym** see DISINCLINED
**— hes·i·tant·ly** *adverb*
**hes·i·tate** \'he-zə-,tāt\ *verb* **-tat·ed; -tat·ing** [Latin *haesitatus*, past participle of *haesitare* to stick fast, hesitate, frequentative of *haerēre* to stick] (circa 1623)

*intransitive verb*
**1 :** to hold back in doubt or indecision
**2 :** to delay momentarily : PAUSE
**3 :** STAMMER
*transitive verb*
**:** to hold back from in doubt or uncertainty (wouldn't *hesitate* to commit herself) ☆
**— hes·i·tat·er** *noun*
**— hes·i·tat·ing·ly** \-,tā-tiŋ-lē\ *adverb*
**hes·i·ta·tion** \,he-zə-'tā-shən\ *noun* (14th century)
**1 :** an act or instance of hesitating
**2 :** a pausing or faltering in speech
**Hes·pe·ri·an** \he-'spir-ē-ən\ *adjective* [Latin *Hesperia*, the west, from Greek, from feminine of *hesperios* of the evening, western, from *hesperos* evening — more at WEST] (15th century)
**:** WESTERN, OCCIDENTAL
**Hes·per·i·des** \he-'sper-ə-,dēz\ *noun plural* [Latin, from Greek]
**1 :** the nymphs in classical mythology who guard with the aid of a dragon a garden in which golden apples grow
**2 :** a legendary garden at the western extremity of the world producing golden apples
**hes·per·i·din** \he-'sper-ə-d'n\ *noun* [New Latin *hesperidium* orange, from Latin *Hesperides*] (1838)
**:** a crystalline glycoside $C_{28}H_{34}O_{15}$ found in most citrus fruits and especially in orange peel
**hes·per·id·i·um** \,hes-pə-'ri-dē-əm\ *noun, plural* **-id·ia** \-dē-ə\ [New Latin] (circa 1866)
**:** a berry (as an orange or lime) having a leathery rind
**Hes·per·us** \'hes-p(ə-)rəs\ *noun* [Middle English, from Latin, from Greek *Hesperos*] (14th century)
**:** EVENING STAR 1
**hes·sian** \'he-shən\ *noun* (1729)
**1** *capitalized* **a :** a native of Hesse **b :** a German mercenary serving in the British forces during the American Revolution; *broadly* **:** a mercenary soldier
**2** *chiefly British* **:** BURLAP
**Hessian boot** *noun* (1809)
**:** a high boot that extends to just below the knee and is commonly ornamented with a tassel and that was introduced into England by the Hessians early in the 19th century
**Hessian fly** *noun* (1786)
**:** a small dipteran fly (*Mayetiola destructor*) that is destructive to wheat in the U.S.
**hess·ite** \'he-,sīt\ *noun* [German *Hessit*, from Henry *Hess* (died 1850) Swiss chemist] (1849)
**:** a mineral consisting of a lead-gray sectile silver telluride
**hes·so·nite** \'he-s³n-,īt\ *variant of* ESSONITE
**hest** \'hest\ *noun* [Middle English *hest, hes*, from Old English *hǣs;* akin to Old English *hātan* to command — more at HIGHT] (before 12th century)
*archaic* **:** COMMAND, PRECEPT
**Hes·tia** \'hes-tē-ə; 'hes-chə, 'hesh-\ *noun* [Greek]
**:** the Greek goddess of the hearth and chief goddess of domestic activity — compare VESTA

☆ **SYNONYMS**
**Hesitate, waver, vacillate, falter**
mean to show irresolution or uncertainty. HESITATE implies a pause before deciding or acting or choosing (*hesitated* before answering the question). WAVER implies hesitation after seeming to decide and so connotes weakness or a retreat (*wavered* in his support of the rebels). VACILLATE implies prolonged hesitation from inability to reach a firm decision (*vacillated* until events were out of control). FALTER implies a wavering or stumbling and often connotes nervousness, lack of courage, or outright fear (never once *faltered* during her testimony).

**he·tae·ra** \hi-'tir-ə\ *or* **he·tai·ra** \-'tī-rə\ *noun, plural* **he·tae·rae** \-'tir-(,)ē\ *or* **he·taeras** *or* **hetairas** *or* **he·tai·rai** \-'tī-,rī\ [Greek *hetaira*, literally, companion, feminine of *hetairos*] (1820)
**1 :** one of a class of highly cultivated courtesans in ancient Greece
**2 :** DEMIMONDAINE

**heter-** *or* **hetero-** *combining form* [Middle French or Late Latin; Middle French, from Late Latin, from Greek, from *heteros;* akin to Greek *heis* one — more at SAME]
**1 :** other than usual **:** other **:** different ⟨*heterophyllous*⟩
**2 :** containing atoms of different kinds ⟨*heterocyclic*⟩

**het·ero** \'he-tə-,rō\ *noun, plural* **-er·os** (1933)
**:** HETEROSEXUAL
— **hetero** *adjective*

**het·ero·at·om** \'he-tə-rō-,a-təm\ *noun* (1900)
**:** an atom other than carbon in the ring of a heterocyclic compound

**het·ero·aux·in** \,he-tə-rō-'ök-sən\ *noun* (1935)
**:** INDOLEACETIC ACID

**het·ero·cer·cal** \-'sər-kəl\ *adjective* (1838)
**1** *of a fish tail fin* **:** having the upper lobe larger than the lower with the vertebral column extending into the upper lobe
**2 :** having or relating to a heterocercal tail fin

**het·ero·chro·ma·tin** \-'krō-mə-tən\ *noun* [German] (1932)
**:** densely staining chromatin that appears as nodules in or along chromosomes and contains relatively few genes
— **het·ero·chro·mat·ic** \-krə-'ma-tik\ *adjective*

**¹het·ero·clite** \'he-tə-rə-,klīt\ *noun* (1580)
**1 :** a word irregular in inflection; *especially* **:** a noun irregular in declension
**2 :** one that deviates from common rules or forms

**²heteroclite** *adjective* [Middle French or Late Latin; Middle French, from Late Latin *heteroclitus*, from Greek *heteroklitos*, from *heter-* + *klinein* to lean, inflect — more at LEAN] (1598)
**:** deviating from common forms or rules

**het·ero·cy·clic** \,he-tə-rō-'sī-klik, -'si-\ *adjective* [International Scientific Vocabulary] (1899)
**:** relating to, characterized by, or being a ring composed of atoms of more than one kind
— **het·ero·cy·cle** \'he-tə-rō-,sī-kəl\ *noun*
— **heterocyclic** *noun*

**het·ero·cyst** \'he-tə-rō-,sist\ *noun* (1872)
**:** a large transparent thick-walled cell that is found in the filaments of some blue-green algae and is the site of nitrogen fixation
— **het·ero·cys·tous** \,he-tə-rō-'sis-təs\ *adjective*

**het·ero·dox** \'he-tə-rə-,däks, 'he-trə-\ *adjective* [Late Latin *heterodoxus*, from Greek *heterodoxos*, from *heter-* + *doxa* opinion — more at DOXOLOGY] (circa 1650)
**1 :** contrary to or different from an acknowledged standard, a traditional form, or an established religion **:** UNORTHODOX, UNCONVENTIONAL ⟨a *heterodox* book⟩ ⟨*heterodox* ideas⟩
**2 :** holding unorthodox opinions or doctrines

**het·ero·doxy** \-,däk-sē\ *noun, plural* **-dox·ies** (1659)
**1 :** the quality or state of being heterodox
**2 :** a heterodox opinion or doctrine

**het·ero·du·plex** \,he-tə-rō-'dü-,pleks, -'dyü-\ *noun* (1962)
**:** a nucleic-acid molecule composed of two chains with each derived from a different parent molecule
— **heteroduplex** *adjective*

**¹het·ero·dyne** \'he-tə-rə-,dīn, 'he-trə-\ *adjective* [*heter-* + *-dyne*, modification of Greek *dynamis* power — more at DYNAMIC] (1908)
**:** of or relating to the production of an electrical beat between two radio frequencies of which one usually is that of a received signal

carrying current and the other that of an uninterrupted current introduced into the apparatus; *also* **:** of or relating to the production of a beat between two optical frequencies

**²heterodyne** *transitive verb* **-dyned; -dyn·ing** (1923)
**:** to combine (as a radio frequency) with a different frequency so that a beat is produced

**het·er·oe·cious** \,he-tə-'rē-shəs\ *adjective* [*heter-* + Greek *oikia* house — more at VICINITY] (1882)
**:** passing through the different stages in the life cycle on alternate and often unrelated hosts ⟨*heteroecious* insects⟩
— **het·er·oe·cism** \-'rē-,si-zəm\ *noun*

**het·ero·ga·mete** \,he-tə-rō-'ga-,mēt *also* -gə-'mēt\ *noun* [International Scientific Vocabulary] (1897)
**:** either of a pair of gametes that differ in form, size, or behavior and occur typically as large nonmotile oogametes and small motile sperms

**het·ero·ga·met·ic** \-gə-'me-tik\ *adjective* (1910)
**:** forming two kinds of gametes of which one produces male offspring and the other female offspring ⟨the human male is *heterogametic*⟩
— **het·ero·gam·e·ty** \-'gam-ə-tē\ *noun*

**het·er·og·a·mous** \,he-tə-'rä-gə-məs\ *adjective* (1839)
**:** having or characterized by fusion of unlike gametes — compare ANISOGAMOUS, ISOGAMOUS

**het·er·og·a·my** \-mē\ *noun* (circa 1894)
**1 :** sexual reproduction involving fusion of unlike gametes often differing in size, structure, and physiology
**2 :** the condition of reproducing by heterogamy

**het·ero·ge·ne·ity** \,he-tə-rō-jə-'nē-ə-tē, ,he-trō-\ *noun* (1641)
**:** the quality or state of being heterogeneous

**het·ero·ge·neous** \,he-tə-rə-'jē-nē-əs, ,he-trə-, -nyəs\ *adjective* [Medieval Latin *heterogeneus*, from Greek *heterogenēs*, from *heter-* + *genos* kind — more at KIN] (1630)
**:** consisting of dissimilar or diverse ingredients or constituents **:** MIXED
— **het·ero·ge·neous·ly** *adverb*
— **het·ero·ge·neous·ness** *noun*

**het·er·og·e·nous** \,he-tə-'rä-jə-nəs\ *adjective* (1695)
**:** HETEROGENEOUS

**het·er·og·e·ny** \-nē\ *noun* (1838)
**:** a heterogenous collection or group

**het·er·og·o·ny** \,he-tə-'rä-gə-nē\ *noun* (circa 1887)
**1 :** ALTERNATION OF GENERATIONS; *especially* **:** alternation of a dioecious with a parthenogenetic generation
**2 :** ALLOMETRY
— **het·ero·gon·ic** \,he-tə-rə-'gä-nik\ *adjective*

**het·ero·graft** \'he-tə-rō-,graft\ *noun* (1923)
**:** a graft of tissue taken from a donor of one species and grafted into a recipient of another species — called also *xenograft*; compare HOMOGRAFT

**het·ero·kary·on** \,he-tə-rō-'kar-ē-,än, -ən\ *noun* [New Latin, from *heter-* + *karyon*, *caryon* nucleus, from Greek *karyon* nut, kernel] (1941)
**:** a cell (as in the mycelium of a fungus) that contains two or more genetically unlike nuclei

**het·ero·kary·o·sis** \,he-tə-rō-,kar-ē-'ō-səs\ *noun* [New Latin] (1916)
**:** the condition of having cells that are heterokaryons
— **het·ero·kary·ot·ic** \-ē-'ä-tik\ *adjective*

**het·er·ol·o·gous** \-'rä-lə-gəs\ *adjective* [*heter-* + *-logous* (as in *homologous*)] (1893)
**:** derived from a different species ⟨*heterologous* DNAs⟩ ⟨*heterologous* transplants⟩
— **het·er·ol·o·gous·ly** *adverb*

**het·ero·ly·sis** \,he-tə-'rä-lə-səs, -ə-rə-'lī-səs\ *noun* [New Latin] (1938)

**:** decomposition of a compound into two oppositely charged particles or ions
— **het·ero·lyt·ic** \-ə-rə-'li-tik\ *adjective*

**het·ero·mor·phic** \'he-tə-rə-'mòr-fik\ *adjective* [International Scientific Vocabulary] (circa 1859)
**1 :** deviating from the usual form
**2 :** exhibiting diversity of form or forms ⟨*heteromorphic* pairs of chromosomes⟩
— **het·ero·mor·phism** \-,fi-zəm\ *noun*

**het·er·on·o·mous** \,he-tə-'rä-nə-məs\ *adjective* (circa 1871)
**:** subject to external controls and impositions

**het·er·on·o·my** \-mē\ *noun* [*heter-* + *-nomy* (as in *autonomy*)] (1798)
**:** subjection to something else; *especially* **:** a lack of moral freedom or self-determination

**het·ero·nym** \'he-tə-rə-,nim\ *noun* (circa 1889)
**:** one of two or more homographs (as a *bass* voice and *bass*, a fish) that differ in pronunciation and meaning

**het·ero·phile** \'he-tə-rə-,fīl\ *or* **het·ero·phil** \-,fil\ *adjective* (circa 1920)
**:** relating to or being any of a group of antigens in organisms of different species that induce the formation of antibodies that will cross-react with the other antigens of the group; *also* **:** being or relating to any of these antibodies

**het·er·oph·o·ny** \,he-tə-'rä-fə-nē\ *noun, plural* **-nies** [Greek *heterophōnia* diversity of note, from *heter-* + *-phōnia* -phony] (1919)
**:** independent variation on a single melody by two or more voices

**het·ero·phyl·lous** \,he-tə-rō-'fi-ləs\ *adjective* (circa 1828)
**:** having the foliage leaves of more than one form on the same plant or stem
— **het·ero·phyl·ly** \-fi-lē\ *noun*

**het·ero·ploid** \'he-tə-rə-,plòid\ *adjective* [International Scientific Vocabulary] (1926)
**:** having a chromosome number that deviates from and is not an integral multiple of the number characteristic of a given species
— **heteroploid** *noun*
— **het·ero·ploi·dy** \-,plòi-dē\ *noun*

**het·er·op·ter·ous** \,he-tə-'räp-tə-rəs\ *adjective* [ultimately from Greek *heter-* + *pteron* wing — more at FEATHER] (1895)
**:** of or relating to an insect order or suborder (Heteroptera) comprising the true bugs

**¹het·ero·sex·u·al** \,he-tə-rō-'sek-sh(ə-)wəl, -'sek-shəl\ *adjective* [International Scientific Vocabulary] (1892)
**1 a :** of, relating to, or characterized by a tendency to direct sexual desire toward the opposite sex **b :** of, relating to, or involving sexual intercourse between individuals of opposite sex
**2 :** of or relating to different sexes
— **het·ero·sex·u·al·i·ty** \-,sek-shə-'wa-lə-tē\ *noun*
— **het·ero·sex·u·al·ly** \-'sek-sh(ə-)wə-lē, -'sek-shə-lē\ *adverb*

**²heterosexual** *noun* (1920)
**:** a heterosexual person

**het·er·o·sis** \,he-tə-'rō-səs\ *noun* [New Latin] (1914)
**:** the marked vigor or capacity for growth often exhibited by crossbred animals or plants — called also *hybrid vigor*
— **het·er·ot·ic** \-'rä-tik\ *adjective*

**het·ero·spo·ry** \'he-tə-rə-,spōr-ē, -,spòr-; ,he-tə-'räs-pə-rē\ *noun* (1898)
**:** the production of microspores and megaspores (as in seed plants and some ferns)
— **het·ero·spo·rous** \,he-tə-rə-'spōr-əs, -'spòr-; -'räs-pə-rəs\ *adjective*

---

\ə\ abut \ᵊ\ kitten \ər\ further \a\ ash \ā\ ace \ä\ mop, mar \aù\ out \ch\ chin \e\ bet \ē\ easy \g\ go \i\ hit \ī\ ice \j\ job \ŋ\ sing \ō\ go \ò\ law \òi\ boy \th\ thin \th\ the \ü\ loot \ù\ foot \y\ yet \zh\ vision *see also* Guide to Pronunciation

**het·ero·thal·lic** \,he-tə-rō-'tha-lik\ *adjective* [heter- + thallus + -ic] (1904)
**1 :** having two or more morphologically similar haploid phases or types of which individuals from the same type are mutually sterile but individuals from different types are cross-fertile ⟨*heterothallic* fungi⟩ ⟨*heterothallic* spores⟩
**2 :** DIOECIOUS
— **het·ero·thal·lism** \-'tha-,li-zəm\ *noun*
**het·ero·top·ic** \-rə-'tä-pik\ *adjective* [heter- + Greek *topos* place] (1878)
**:** occurring in an abnormal place ⟨*heterotopic* bone formation⟩ ⟨*heterotopic* liver transplantation⟩
**het·ero·troph** \'he-tə-rə-,trōf, -,träf\ *noun* (circa 1900)
**:** a heterotrophic individual
**het·ero·tro·phic** \,he-tə-rə-'trō-fik\ *adjective* (1893)
**:** requiring complex organic compounds of nitrogen and carbon for metabolic synthesis
— **het·ero·tro·phi·cal·ly** \-fi-k(ə-)lē\ *adverb*
— **het·ero·tro·phy** \,he-tə-'rä-trə-fē, 'he-tə-rə-,trō-\ *noun*
**het·ero·typ·ic** \,he-tə-rō-'ti-pik\ *adjective* (1889)
**:** different in kind, arrangement, or form
**het·ero·zy·go·sis** \-(,)zī-'gō-səs\ *noun* [New Latin] (1902)
**:** HETEROZYGOSITY
**het·ero·zy·gos·i·ty** \-'gä-sə-tē\ *noun* (1912)
**:** the state of being heterozygous
**het·ero·zy·gote** \-'zī-,gōt\ *noun* (1902)
**:** a heterozygous individual
**het·ero·zy·gous** \-gəs\ *adjective* (1902)
**:** having the two alleles at corresponding loci on homologous chromosomes different for one or more loci
**heth** \'kät, 'käth, 'ket, 'keth\ *noun* [Hebrew *ḥēth*] (1823)
**:** the 8th letter of the Hebrew alphabet — see ALPHABET table
**het·man** \'het-mən\ *noun, plural* **hetmans** [Ukrainian *het'man*] (1710)
**:** a cossack leader
**het up** \'het-'əp\ *adjective* [het, dialect past of *heat*] (1909)
**:** highly excited : UPSET
**heu·land·ite** \'hyü-lən-,dīt\ *noun* [Henry *Heuland*, 19th century English mineral collector] (1822)
**:** a zeolite consisting of a hydrous aluminosilicate of sodium and calcium
**¹heu·ris·tic** \hyu-'ris-tik\ *adjective* [German *heuristisch*, from New Latin *heuristicus*, from Greek *heuriskein* to discover; akin to Old Irish fo-*fúair* he found] (1821)
**:** involving or serving as an aid to learning, discovery, or problem-solving by experimental and especially trial-and-error methods ⟨*heuristic* techniques⟩ ⟨a *heuristic* assumption⟩; *also*
**:** of or relating to exploratory problem-solving techniques that utilize self-educating techniques (as the evaluation of feedback) to improve performance ⟨a *heuristic* computer program⟩
— **heu·ris·ti·cal·ly** \-ti-k(ə-)lē\ *adverb*
**²heuristic** *noun* (1860)
**1 :** the study or practice of heuristic procedure
**2 :** heuristic argument
**3 :** a heuristic method or procedure
**hew** \'hyü\ *verb* **hewed** *or* **hewn** \'hyün\; **hew·ing** [Middle English, from Old English *hēawan*; akin to Old High German *houwan* to hew, Lithuanian *kauti* to forge, Latin *cudere* to beat] (before 12th century)
*transitive verb*
**1 :** to cut with blows of a heavy cutting instrument
**2 :** to fell by blows of an ax ⟨*hew* a tree⟩
**3 :** to give form or shape to with or as if with heavy cutting blows ⟨*hewed* their farms from the wilderness —J. T. Shotwell⟩
*intransitive verb*

**1 :** to make cutting blows
**2 :** CONFORM, ADHERE — often used in the phrase *hew to the line* ⟨no pressure . . . on newspapers to *hew* to the official line —*N.Y. Times Magazine*⟩
— **hew·er** *noun*
**¹hex** \'heks\ *verb* [Pennsylvania German *hexe*, from German *hexen*, from *Hexe* witch, from Old High German *hagzissa*; akin to Middle English *hagge* hag] (1830)
*intransitive verb*
**:** to practice witchcraft
*transitive verb*
**1 :** to put a hex on
**2 :** to affect as if by an evil spell : JINX ⟨giving in to an unscientific fear of *hexing* the whole project —Daniel Lang⟩
— **hex·er** *noun*
**²hex** *noun* (1856)
**1 :** a person who practices witchcraft : WITCH
**2 :** SPELL, JINX
**³hex** *adjective* (1924)
**:** HEXAGONAL ⟨a bolt with a *hex* head⟩
**⁴hex** *adjective or noun* (1970)
**:** HEXADECIMAL
**hexa-** *or* **hex-** *combining form* [Greek, from *hex* six — more at SIX]
**1 :** six ⟨*hexa*ploid⟩
**2 :** containing six atoms, groups, or equivalents ⟨*hexa*ne⟩
**hexa·chlo·ro·eth·ane** \,hek-sə-,klōr-ō-'e-,thän, -,klór-\ *or* **hexa·chlor·eth·ane** \-,klōr-'e-, -,klór-\ *noun* [International Scientific Vocabulary] (1898)
**:** a toxic crystalline compound $C_2Cl_6$ used especially in smoke bombs and in the control of liver flukes in ruminants
**hexa·chlo·ro·phene** \-'klōr-ə-,fēn, -'klór-\ *noun* [hexa- + chlor- + phenol] (1948)
**:** a powdered phenolic bacteria-inhibiting agent $C_{13}Cl_6H_6O_2$
**hexa·chord** \'hek-sə-,kórd\ *noun* [hexa- + Greek *chordē* string — more at YARN] (1730)
**:** a diatonic series of six tones having a semitone between the third and fourth tones
**hexa·dec·i·mal** \,hek-sə-'des-məl, -'de-sə-\ *adjective* (1954)
**:** of, relating to, or being a number system with a base of 16
— **hexadecimal** *noun*
**hexa·gon** \'hek-sə-,gän\ *noun* [Greek *hexagōnon*, neuter of *hexagōnos* hexagonal, from hexa- + *gōnia* angle — more at -GON] (1570)
**:** a polygon of six angles and six sides
**hex·ag·o·nal** \hek-'sa-gə-nᵊl\ *adjective* (1571)
**1 :** having six angles and six sides
**2 :** having a hexagon as section or base
**3 :** relating to or being a crystal system characterized by three equal lateral axes intersecting at angles of 60 degrees and a vertical axis of variable length at right angles
— **hex·ag·o·nal·ly** \-nᵊl-ē\ *adverb*
**hexa·gram** \'hek-sə-,gram\ *noun* [International Scientific Vocabulary] (1871)
**:** a plane figure that has the shape of a 6-pointed star, that consists of two intersecting congruent equilateral triangles having the same point as center and their sides parallel, and that can be formed by constructing external equilateral triangles on the sides of a regular hexagon — compare SOLOMON'S SEAL 2

hexagram

**hexa·he·dron** \,hek-sə-'hē-drən\ *noun, plural* **-drons** *also* **-dra** \-drə\ [Late Latin, from Greek *hexaedron*, from neuter of *hexaedros* of six surfaces, from hexa- + *hedra* seat — more at SIT] (1571)
**:** a polyhedron of six faces (as a cube)
**hexa·hy·drate** \-'hī-,drāt\ *noun* (1908)
**:** a chemical compound with six molecules of water
**hex·am·e·ter** \hek-'sa-mə-tər\ *noun* [Latin, from Greek *hexametron*, from neuter of *hex-*

*ametros* having six measures, from hexa- + *metron* measure — more at MEASURE] (1546)
**:** a line of verse consisting of six metrical feet
**hexa·me·tho·ni·um** \,hek-sə-mə-'thō-nē-əm\ *noun* [hexa- + meth- + -onium] (1949)
**:** either of two compounds $C_{12}H_{30}Br_2N_2$ or $C_{12}H_{30}Cl_2N_2$ used as ganglionic blocking agents in the treatment of hypertension
**hexa·meth·y·lene·tet·ra·mine** \,hek-sə-'me-thə-,lēn-'te-trə-,mēn\ *noun* [International Scientific Vocabulary hexa- + methylene + tetra- + amine] (1888)
**:** a crystalline compound $C_6H_{12}N_4$ used especially as an accelerator in vulcanizing rubber and as a urinary antiseptic — compare METHENAMINE
**hex·ane** \'hek-,sān\ *noun* [International Scientific Vocabulary] (1877)
**:** any of several isomeric volatile liquid alkanes $C_6H_{14}$ found in petroleum
**hex·a·no·ic acid** \,hek-sə-'nō-ik-\ *noun* [International Scientific Vocabulary hexane + -oic] (1926)
**:** CAPROIC ACID
**hexa·ploid** \'hek-sə-,plóid\ *adjective* [International Scientific Vocabulary] (1912)
**:** having or being six times the monoploid chromosome number
— **hexaploid** *noun*
— **hexa·ploi·dy** \-,plói-dē\ *noun*
**¹hexa·pod** \'hek-sə-,päd\ *noun* [Greek *hexapod-, hexapous* having six feet, from hexa- + *pod-, pous* foot — more at FOOT] (1668)
**:** INSECT 1b
**²hexapod** *adjective* (circa 1847)
**1 :** six-footed
**2 :** of or relating to insects
**Hexa·teuch** \'hek-sə-,tük, -,tyük\ *noun* [hexa- + Greek *teuchos* book — more at PENTATEUCH] (1878)
**:** the first six books of the Bible
**hex·e·rei** \,hek-sə-'rī\ *noun* [Pennsylvania German, from German, from *Hexe* witch] (1898)
**:** WITCHCRAFT
**hexo·bar·bi·tal** \,hek-sə-'bär-bə-,tól\ *noun* [hexo- (from hexa-) + barbital] (1941)
**:** a barbiturate $C_{12}H_{16}N_2O_3$ used as a sedative and hypnotic and in the form of its soluble sodium salt as an intravenous anesthetic of short duration
**hexo·ki·nase** \,hek-sə-'kī-,nās, -,nāz\ *noun* [hexose + kinase] (1930)
**:** any of a group of enzymes that accelerate the phosphorylation of hexoses (as in the formation of glucose-6-phosphate from glucose and ATP) in carbohydrate metabolism
**hex·os·a·min·i·dase** \,hek-,sä-sə-'mi-nə-,dās, -,dāz\ *noun* [hexose + amino + -ide + -ase] (1969)
**:** either of two hydrolytic enzymes that catalyze the splitting off of a hexose from a ganglioside and are deficient in some metabolic diseases (as a variant of Tay-Sachs disease)
**hex·o·san** \'hek-sə-,san\ *noun* (1894)
**:** a polysaccharide yielding only hexoses on hydrolysis
**hex·ose** \'hek-,sōs, -,sōz\ *noun* [International Scientific Vocabulary] (1892)
**:** a monosaccharide (as glucose) containing six carbon atoms in the molecule
**hex·yl** \'hek-səl\ *noun* [International Scientific Vocabulary] (1869)
**:** an alkyl radical $C_6H_{13}-$ derived from a hexane
**hex·yl·res·or·cin·ol** \,hek-səl-rə-'zór-s°n-,ól, -,ōl\ *noun* (1924)
**:** a crystalline phenol $C_{12}H_{18}O_2$ used as an antiseptic and anthelmintic
**hey** \'hā\ *interjection* [Middle English] (13th century)
— used especially to call attention or to express interrogation, surprise, or exultation
**¹hey·day** \'hā-,dā\ *interjection* [irregular from *hey*] (1672)
*archaic* — used to express elation or wonder
**²heyday** *noun* (1590)

**1** *archaic* : high spirits
**2** : the period of one's greatest strength, vigor, or prosperity

**hey presto** \(')hā-'pres-(,)tō\ *interjection* (1731)
*British* : suddenly as if by magic

**Hez·e·ki·ah** \,he-zə-'kī-ə\ *noun* [Hebrew *Ḥizqīyāh*]
: a king of Judah under whom the kingdom underwent a ruinous Assyrian invasion at the end of the 8th century B.C.

**hi** \'hī(-ē)\ *interjection* [Middle English *hy*] (15th century)
— used especially as a greeting

**hi·a·tal** \hī-'ā-t°l\ *adjective* (1909)
: of, relating to, or involving a hiatus

**hiatal hernia** *noun* (circa 1944)
: a hernia in which an anatomical part (as the stomach) protrudes through the esophageal hiatus of the diaphragm — called also *hiatus hernia*

**hi·a·tus** \hī-'ā-təs\ *noun* [Latin, from *hiare* to yawn — more at YAWN] (1563)
**1 a** : a break in or as if in a material object : GAP ⟨the *hiatus* between the theory and the practice of the party —J. G. Colton⟩ **b** : a gap or passage in an anatomical part or organ
**2 a** : an interruption in time or continuity : BREAK **b** : the occurrence of two vowel sounds without pause or intervening consonantal sound

**Hi·a·wa·tha** \hī-ə-'wȯ-thə, ,hē-ə-, -'wä-\ *noun*
: the Indian hero of Longfellow's poem *The Song of Hiawatha*

**hi·ba·chi** \hi-'bä-chē\ *noun* [Japanese] (1863)
: a charcoal brazier

**hi·ber·nac·u·lum** \,hī-bər-'na-kyə-ləm\ *noun*, *plural* **-la** \-lə\ [New Latin, from Latin, winter residence, from *hibernare*] (1789)
: a shelter occupied during the winter by a dormant animal (as an insect or reptile)

**hi·ber·nal** \hī-'bər-n°l\ *adjective* (1646)
: of, relating to, or occurring in winter

**hi·ber·nate** \'hī-bər-,nāt\ *intransitive verb* **-nat·ed; -nat·ing** [Latin *hibernatus*, past participle of *hibernare* to pass the winter, from *hibernus* of winter; akin to Latin *hiems* winter, Greek *cheimōn*] (circa 1802)
**1** : to pass the winter in a torpid or resting state
**2** : to be or become inactive or dormant
— **hi·ber·na·tion** \,hī-bər-'nā-shən\ *noun*
— **hi·ber·na·tor** \'hī-bər-,nā-tər\ *noun*

**¹Hi·ber·ni·an** \hī-'bər-nē-ən\ *adjective* [Latin *Hibernia* Ireland] (1632)
: of, relating to, or characteristic of Ireland or the Irish

**²Hibernian** *noun* (1709)
: a native or inhabitant of Ireland

**Hi·ber·no-** *combining form* [Latin *Hibernia*]
**1** : Irish and ⟨*Hiberno*-British⟩
**2** : Irish ⟨*Hiberno*-English⟩

**Hiberno–English** *noun* (1985)
: the English language spoken in Ireland

**hi·bis·cus** \hī-'bis-kəs, hə-\ *noun* [New Latin, from Latin, marshmallow] (1706)
: any of a large genus (*Hibiscus*) of herbs, shrubs, or small trees of the mallow family with large showy flowers and usually dentate leaves

**¹hic·cup** *also* **hic·cough** \'hi-(,)kəp\ *noun* [imitative] (circa 1580)
**1** : a spasmodic inhalation with closure of the glottis accompanied by a peculiar sound
**2** : an attack of hiccuping — usually used in plural but singular or plural in construction

**²hiccup** *also* **hiccough** *intransitive verb* **hic·cuped** *also* **hic·cupped; hic·cup·ing** *also* **hic·cup·ping** (circa 1580)
: to make a hiccup; *also* : to be affected with hiccups

**hic ja·cet** \'hik-'jā-sət, 'hēk-'yä-kət\ *noun* [Latin, literally, here lies] (1654)
: EPITAPH

**¹hick** \'hik\ *noun* [*Hick*, nickname for *Richard*] (circa 1690)

: an unsophisticated provincial person
— **hick·ish** \'hi-kish\ *adjective*

**²hick** *adjective* (1920)
: UNSOPHISTICATED, PROVINCIAL ⟨a *hick* town⟩

**¹hick·ey** \'hi-kē\ *noun*, *plural* **hickeys** [origin unknown] (1913)
: DEVICE, GADGET

**²hickey** *noun*, *plural* **hickeys** [origin unknown] (circa 1915)
**1 a** : PIMPLE **b** : a temporary red mark on the skin (as one produced by biting and sucking)
**2** *plural also* **hick·ies** : a small imperfection in printing

**hick·o·ry** \'hi-k(ə-)rē\ *noun*, *plural* **-ries** [short for obsolete *pokahickory*, from Virginia Algonquian *pawcohiccora* food prepared from pounded nuts] (1670)
**1 a** : any of a genus (*Carya*) of North American hardwood trees of the walnut family that often have sweet edible nuts **b** : the usually tough wood of a hickory
**2** : a switch or cane (as of hickory wood) used especially for punishing a child
— **hickory** *adjective*

**hid** \'hid\ *adjective* (12th century)
: HIDDEN

**hi·dal·go** \hi-'dal-(,)gō, ē-'thäl-\ *noun*, *plural* **-gos** *often capitalized* [Spanish, from Old Spanish *fijo dalgo*, literally, son of something] (1594)
: a member of the lower nobility of Spain

**Hi·dat·sa** \hi-'dät-sə\ *noun*, *plural* **Hidatsa** *also* **Hidatsas** (1873)
**1** : a member of an American Indian people of the Missouri River valley in North Dakota
**2** : the Siouan language of the Hidatsa

**hid·den** \'hi-d°n\ *adjective* (13th century)
**1** : being out of sight or not readily apparent : CONCEALED
**2** : OBSCURE, UNEXPLAINED, UNDISCLOSED
— **hid·den·ness** \-nəs\ *noun*

**hidden agenda** *noun* (1971)
: an ulterior motive

**hid·den·ite** \'hi-d°n-,īt\ *noun* [William E. *Hidden* (died 1918) American mineralogist] (1881)
: a transparent yellow to green spodumene valued as a gem

**hidden tax** *noun* (1936)
**1** : a tax that is ultimately paid by someone other than the person on whom it is levied
**2** : an economic inequity that reduces one's real income or buying power

**¹hide** \'hīd\ *noun* [Middle English, from Old English *hīgid*, *hīd*] (before 12th century)
: any of various old English units of land area; *especially* : a unit of 120 acres

**²hide** *verb* **hid** \'hid\; **hid·den** \'hi-d°n\ *or* **hid; hid·ing** \'hī-diŋ\ [Middle English *hiden*, from Old English *hȳdan*; akin to Greek *keuthein* to conceal] (before 12th century)
*transitive verb*
**1 a** : to put out of sight : SECRETE **b** : to conceal for shelter or protection : SHIELD
**2** : to keep secret
**3** : to screen from or as if from view : OBSCURE
**4** : to turn (the eyes or face) away in shame or anger
*intransitive verb*
**1** : to remain out of sight — often used with *out*
**2** : to seek protection or evade responsibility
☆
— **hid·er** \'hī-dər\ *noun*

**³hide** *noun* (14th century)
*chiefly British* : BLIND 2

**⁴hide** *noun* [Middle English, from Old English *hȳd*; akin to Old High German *hūt* hide, Latin *cutis* skin, Greek *kytos* hollow vessel] (before 12th century)
**1** : the skin of an animal whether raw or dressed — used especially of large heavy skins
**2** : the life or physical well-being of a person ⟨betrayed his friend to save his own *hide*⟩

— **hide or hair** *or* **hide nor hair** : a vestige or trace of someone or something ⟨a wife he hadn't seen *hide or hair* of in over 20 years —H. L. Davis⟩

**⁵hide** *transitive verb* **hid·ed; hid·ing** (circa 1825)
: to give a beating to : FLOG

**hide–and–seek** \,hī-d°n-'sēk\ *noun* (circa 1727)
: a children's game in which one player does not look while others hide and then goes to find them

**hide·away** \'hī-də-,wā\ *noun* (1926)
: RETREAT, HIDEOUT

**hide·bound** \'hīd-,baȯnd\ *adjective* (1559)
**1** *of a domestic animal* : having a dry skin lacking in pliancy and adhering closely to the underlying flesh
**2** : having an inflexible or ultraconservative character

**hid·eous** \'hi-dē-əs\ *adjective* [alteration of Middle English *hidous*, from Middle French, from *hisde*, *hide* terror] (14th century)
**1** : offensive to the senses and especially to sight : exceedingly ugly
**2** : morally offensive : SHOCKING
— **hid·eos·ity** \,hi-dē-'ä-sə-tē\ *noun*
— **hid·eous·ly** *adverb*
— **hid·eous·ness** *noun*

**hide·out** \'hī-,daȯt\ *noun* (1904)
: a place of refuge, retreat, or concealment

**hid·ey-hole** *or* **hidy–hole** \'hī-dē-,hōl\ *noun* [alteration of earlier *hiding-hole*] (1817)
: HIDEAWAY

**hie** \'hī\ *verb* **hied; hy·ing** *or* **hie·ing** [Middle English, from Old English *hīgian* to strive, hasten] (12th century)
*intransitive verb*
: to go quickly : HASTEN
*transitive verb*
: to cause (oneself) to go quickly

**hi·er·arch** \'hī-(ə-),rärk\ *noun* [Middle English *ierarchis*, plural, from Middle French or Medieval Latin; Middle French *hierarche*, from Medieval Latin *hierarcha*, from Greek *hierarchēs*, from *hieros* sacred + *-archēs* -arch] (15th century)
**1** : a religious leader in a position of authority
**2** : a person high in a hierarchy
— **hi·er·ar·chal** \,hī-(ə-)'rär-kəl\ *adjective*

**hi·er·ar·chi·cal** \,hī-(ə-)'rär-ki-kəl *also* hir-'är-\ *or* **hi·er·ar·chic** \-kik\ *adjective* (1561)
: of, relating to, or arranged in a hierarchy
— **hi·er·ar·chi·cal·ly** \-ki-k(ə-)lē\ *adverb*

**hi·er·ar·chize** \'hī-(ə-),rär-,kīz\ *transitive verb* **-chized; -chiz·ing** (1884)
: to arrange in a hierarchy

**hi·er·ar·chy** \'hī-(ə-),rär-kē *also* 'hi(-ə)r-,är-\ *noun*, *plural* **-chies** (14th century)
**1** : a division of angels
**2 a** : a ruling body of clergy organized into orders or ranks each subordinate to the one above it; *especially* : the bishops of a province

---

☆ SYNONYMS
**Hide, conceal, screen, secrete, bury** mean to withhold or withdraw from sight. HIDE may or may not suggest intent ⟨*hide* in the closet⟩ ⟨a house *hidden* in the woods⟩. CONCEAL usually does imply intent and often specifically implies a refusal to divulge ⟨*concealed* the weapon⟩. SCREEN implies an interposing of something that prevents discovery ⟨a house *screened* by trees⟩. SECRETE suggests a depositing in a place unknown to others ⟨*secreted* the amulet inside his shirt⟩. BURY implies covering up so as to hide completely ⟨*buried* the treasure⟩.

---

\ə\ abut  \°\ kitten  \ər\ further  \a\ ash  \ā\ ace
\ä\ mop, mar  \aȯ\ out  \ch\ chin  \e\ bet  \ē\ easy
\g\ go  \i\ hit  \ī\ ice  \j\ job  \ŋ\ sing  \ō\ go
\ȯ\ law  \ȯi\ boy  \th\ thin  \th\ the  \ü\ loot  \ȯ\ foot
\y\ yet  \zh\ vision     *see also* Guide to Pronunciation

or nation **b :** church government by a hierarchy

**3 :** a body of persons in authority

**4 :** the classification of a group of people according to ability or to economic, social, or professional standing; *also* **:** the group so classified

**5 :** a graded or ranked series ⟨Christian *hierarchy* of values⟩ ⟨a machine's *hierarchy* of responses⟩

**hi·er·at·ic** \ˌhī-(ə-)'ra-tik\ *adjective* [Latin *hieraticus* sacerdotal, from Greek *hieratikos*, from *hierasthai* to perform priestly functions, from *hieros* sacred; probably akin to Sanskrit *iṣara* vigorous] (1669)

**1 :** constituting or belonging to a cursive form of ancient Egyptian writing simpler than the hieroglyphic

**2 :** SACERDOTAL

**3 :** highly stylized or formal ⟨*hieratic* poses⟩
— **hi·er·at·i·cal·ly** \-ti-k(ə-)lē\ *adverb*

**hi·ero·dule** \'hī-(ə-)rō-ˌdü(ə)l, hī-'er-ə-, -ˌdyü(ə)l\ *noun* [Late Latin *hierodulus*, from Greek *hierodoulos*, from *hieron* temple + *doulos* slave] (1835)

**:** a slave or prostitute in the service of a temple (as in ancient Greece)

**hi·ero·glyph** \'hī-(ə-)rə-ˌglif\ *noun* [French *hiéroglyphe*, from Middle French, back-formation from *hieroglyphique*] (1598)

**1 :** a character used in a system of hieroglyphic writing

**2 :** something that resembles a hieroglyph

**¹hi·ero·glyph·ic** \ˌhī-(ə-)rə-'gli-fik\ *also* **hi·ero·glyph·i·cal** \-fi-kəl\ *adjective* [Middle French *hieroglyphique*, from Late Latin *hieroglyphicus*, from Greek *hieroglyphikos*, from *hieros* + *glyphein* to carve — more at CLEAVE] (1585)

**1 :** written in, constituting, or belonging to a system of writing mainly in pictorial characters

**2 :** inscribed with hieroglyphic

**3 :** resembling hieroglyphic in difficulty of decipherment
— **hi·ero·glyph·i·cal·ly** \-fi-k(ə-)lē\ *adverb*

**²hieroglyphic** *noun* (1586)

**1 :** HIEROGLYPH

**2 :** a system of hieroglyphic writing; *specifically* **:** the picture script

hieroglyphic 2

of the ancient Egyptian priesthood — often used in plural but singular or plural in construction

**3 :** something that resembles a hieroglyph especially in difficulty of decipherment

**hi·ero·phant** \'hī-(ə-)rə-ˌfant, hī-'er-ə-fənt\ *noun* [Late Latin *hierophanta*, from Greek *hierophantēs*, from *hieros* + *phainein* to show — more at FANCY] (1677)

**1 :** a priest in ancient Greece; *specifically* **:** the chief priest of the Eleusinian mysteries

**2 a :** EXPOSITOR **b :** ADVOCATE
— **hi·ero·phan·tic** \ˌhī-(ə-)rə-'fan-tik, (ˌ)hī-ˌer-ə-\ *adjective*

**hi·fa·lu·tin** *variant of* HIGHFALUTIN

**hi-fi** \'hī-'fī\ *noun* (1950)

**1 :** HIGH FIDELITY

**2 :** equipment for reproduction of sound with high fidelity

**hig·gle** \'hi-gəl\ *intransitive verb* **hig·gled**; **hig·gling** \-g(ə-)liŋ\ [probably alteration of *haggle*] (1633)

**:** HAGGLE
— **hig·gler** \-g(ə-)lər\ *noun*

**hig·gle·dy–pig·gle·dy** \ˌhi-gəl-dē-'pi-gəl-dē\ *adverb* [origin unknown] (circa 1598)

**:** in a confused, disordered, or random manner ⟨tiny hovels piled *higgledy-piggledy* against each other —Edward Behr⟩
— **higgledy–piggledy** *adjective*

**¹high** \'hī\ *adjective* [Middle English, from Old English *hēah*; akin to Old High German *hōh* high, Lithuanian *kaukaras* hill] (before 12th century)

**1 a :** having large extension upward **:** taller than average, usual, or expected ⟨a *high* wall⟩ **b :** having a specified elevation **:** TALL ⟨six feet *high*⟩ — often used in combinations ⟨sky-*high*⟩ ⟨waist-*high*⟩

**2 a** (1) **:** advanced toward the acme or culmination ⟨*high* summer⟩ (2) **:** advanced toward the most active or culminating period ⟨on the Riviera during *high* season⟩ (3) **:** constituting the late, most fully developed, or most creative stage or period ⟨*high* Gothic⟩ (4) **:** advanced in complexity, development, or elaboration ⟨the *higher* apes⟩ ⟨*higher* mathematics⟩ **b :** verging on lateness — usually used in the phrase *high time* **c :** long past **:** REMOTE ⟨*high* antiquity⟩

**3 :** elevated in pitch ⟨a *high* note⟩

**4 :** relatively far from the equator ⟨*high* latitude⟩

**5 :** rich in quality **:** LUXURIOUS ⟨*high* living⟩

**6 :** slightly tainted ⟨*high* game⟩; *also* **:** MALODOROUS ⟨smelled rather *high*⟩

**7 :** exalted in character **:** NOBLE ⟨*high* purposes⟩

**8 :** of greater degree, amount, cost, value, or content than average, usual, or expected ⟨*high* prices⟩ ⟨food *high* in iron⟩ ⟨the *high* bid⟩

**9 :** of relatively great importance: as **a :** foremost in rank, dignity, or standing ⟨*high* officials⟩ **b :** SERIOUS, GRAVE ⟨*high* crimes⟩ **c :** observed with the utmost solemnity ⟨*high* religious observances⟩ **d :** CRITICAL, CLIMACTIC ⟨the *high* point of the novel⟩ **e :** intellectually or artistically of the first order ⟨*high* culture⟩ **f :** marked by sublime, heroic, or stirring events or subject matter ⟨*high* tragedy⟩ ⟨*high* adventure⟩

**10 :** FORCIBLE, STRONG ⟨*high* winds⟩

**11 :** stressing matters of doctrine and ceremony; *specifically* **:** HIGH CHURCH

**12 a :** filled with or expressing great joy or excitement ⟨*high* spirits⟩ **b :** INTOXICATED; *also* **:** excited or stupefied by or as if by a drug

**13 :** articulated with some part of the tongue close to the palate ⟨a *high* vowel⟩ ☆
— **high on :** enthusiastically in favor or support of

**²high** *adverb* (before 12th century)

**1 :** at or to a high place, altitude, level, or degree ⟨climbed *higher*⟩ ⟨passions ran *high*⟩

**2 :** WELL, LUXURIOUSLY — often used in the phrases *high off the hog* and *high on the hog*

**³high** *noun* (13th century)

**1 :** an elevated place or region: as **a :** HILL, KNOLL **b :** the space overhead **:** SKY — usually used with *on* **c :** HEAVEN — usually used with *on*

**2 :** a region of high barometric pressure — called also *anticyclone*

**3 a :** a high point or level **:** HEIGHT ⟨sales reached a new *high*⟩ **b :** the transmission gear of a vehicle (as an automobile) giving the highest speed of travel

**4 a :** an excited, euphoric, or stupefied state produced by or as if by a drug **b :** a state of elation or high spirits

**high altar** *noun* (before 12th century)

**:** the principal altar in a church

**high analysis** *adjective* (1949)

*of a fertilizer* **:** containing more than 20 percent of total plant nutrients

**high and dry** *adjective* (1822)

**1 :** being out of reach of the current or tide or out of the water

**2 :** being in a helpless or abandoned position

**high and low** *adverb* (14th century)

**:** EVERYWHERE

**high–and–mighty** *adjective* (1654)

**:** characterized by arrogance **:** IMPERIOUS

**¹high·ball** \'hī-ˌból\ *noun* (1897)

**1 :** a railroad signal for a train to proceed at full speed

**2 :** an iced drink containing liquor (as whiskey) and water or a carbonated beverage and served in a tall glass

**²highball** *intransitive verb* (1912)

**:** to go at full or high speed ⟨a *highballing* express train⟩

**high beam** *noun* (1939)

**:** the long-range focus of a vehicle headlight

**high-bind·er** \'hī-ˌbīn-dər\ *noun* [the *Highbinders*, gang of ruffians in New York City (about 1806)] (1876)

**1 :** a professional killer operating in the Chinese quarter of an American city

**2 :** a corrupt politician

**high blood pressure** *noun* (1916)

**:** HYPERTENSION

**high·born** \'hī-'bórn\ *adjective* (13th century)

**:** of noble birth

**high·boy** \-ˌbói\ *noun* (1891)

**:** a tall chest of drawers with a legged base

**high·bred** \-'bred\ *adjective* (1674)

**:** coming from superior stock

**high·brow** \-ˌbraú\ *noun* (circa 1903)

**:** a person who possesses or has pretensions to superior learning or culture
— **highbrow** *adjective*
— **high·browed** \-ˌbraúd\ *adjective*
— **high·brow·ism** \-ˌbraú-ˌi-zəm\ *noun*

highboy

**high·bush** \-'búsh\ *adjective* (1805)

**:** forming a notably tall or erect bush; *also* **:** borne on a highbush plant

**highbush blueberry** *noun* (1913)

**:** a variable moisture-loving North American shrub (*Vaccinium corymbosum*) that is the source of most cultivated blueberries; *also* **:** its fruit

**high chair** *noun* (1848)

**:** a child's chair with long legs, a footrest, and usually a feeding tray

**High Church** *adjective* (1687)

**:** favoring especially in Anglican worship the sacerdotal, liturgical, ceremonial, and traditional elements in worship

**High Churchman** *noun* (1687)

**:** an Anglican who adheres to High Church elements in worship

**high–class** \'hī-'klas\ *adjective* (1864)

**:** of superior quality or status

**high comedy** *noun* (1895)

**:** comedy employing subtle characterizations and witty dialogue — compare LOW COMEDY

**high command** *noun* (1917)

**1 :** the supreme headquarters of a military force

**2 :** the highest leaders in an organization

**high commissioner** *noun* (1881)

**:** a principal or a high-ranking commissioner; *especially* **:** an ambassadorial representative of the government of one country stationed in another

**high–con·cept** \'hī-'kän-ˌsept\ *adjective* (1985)

☆ **SYNONYMS**

**High, tall, lofty** mean above the average in height. HIGH implies marked extension upward and is applied chiefly to things which rise from a base or foundation or are placed at a conspicuous height above a lower level ⟨a *high* hill⟩ ⟨a *high* ceiling⟩. TALL applies to what grows or rises high by comparison with others of its kind and usually implies relative narrowness ⟨a *tall* thin man⟩. LOFTY suggests great or imposing altitude ⟨*lofty* mountain peaks⟩.

: having or exploiting elements (as fast action, glamour, or suspense) that appeal to a wide audience ⟨*high-concept* movies⟩

**high–count** \'hī-'kaủnt\ *adjective* (1926)
: having a large number of warp and weft yarns to the square inch ⟨*high-count* percale sheeting⟩

**high court** *noun* (14th century)
: SUPREME COURT

**high–density lipoprotein** *noun* (1960)
: HDL

**high–end** \'hī-'end\ *adjective* (1980)
: UPSCALE ⟨*high-end* boutiques⟩

**high–energy** *adjective* (1934)
**1 a** : having such speed and kinetic energy as to exhibit relativistic departure from classical laws of motion — used especially of elementary particles whose velocity has been imparted by an accelerator **b** : of or relating to high-energy particles ⟨a *high-energy* reaction⟩
**2** : yielding a relatively large amount of energy when undergoing hydrolysis ⟨*high-energy* phosphate bonds in ATP⟩

**high–energy physics** *noun* (1964)
: PARTICLE PHYSICS

**higher criticism** *noun* (1836)
: study of biblical writings to determine their literary history and the purpose and meaning of the authors — compare LOWER CRITICISM
— **higher critic** *noun*

**higher education** *noun* (1866)
: education beyond the secondary level; *especially* : education provided by a college or university

**higher law** *noun* (1844)
: a principle of divine or moral law that is considered to be superior to constitutions and enacted legislation

**higher learning** *noun* (1926)
: education, learning, or scholarship on the collegiate or university level

**high·er–up** \,hī-ə-'rəp, 'hī-ə-,\ *noun* (1911)
: a superior officer or official

**high explosive** *noun* (1877)
: an explosive (as TNT) that generates gas with extreme rapidity and has a shattering effect

**high·fa·lu·tin** \,hī-fə-'lü-t°n\ *adjective* [perhaps from ²*high* + alteration of *fluting*, present participle of *flute*] (1839)
**1** : PRETENTIOUS
**2** : expressed in or marked by the use of high-flown bombastic language : POMPOUS

**high fashion** *noun* (1945)
**1** : HIGH STYLE
**2** : HAUTE COUTURE

**high fidelity** *noun* (1934)
: the reproduction of an effect (as sound or an image) with a high degree of faithfulness to the original
— **high–fidelity** *adjective*

**high five** *noun* (1981)
: a slapping of upraised right hands by two people (as in celebration)
— **high–five** *verb*

**high·fli·er** *or* **high·fly·er** \'hī-,flī-(-ə)r\ *noun* (circa 1961)
**1** : a stock whose price rises much more rapidly than the market average
**2** : a company whose stock is a highflier
**3** : an ambitiously competitive person with high aspirations

**high–flown** \'hī-'flōn\ *adjective* (1647)
**1** : exceedingly or excessively high or favorable
**2** : having an excessively embellished or inflated character : PRETENTIOUS ⟨inflated rhetoric and *high-flown* vocabulary —James Yaffe⟩

**high–fly·ing** \-'flī-iŋ\ *adjective* (1581)
**1** : marked by extravagance, pretension, or excessive ambition
**2** : rising to considerable height

**high frequency** *noun* (1892)
: a radio frequency between very high frequency and medium frequency — see RADIO FREQUENCY table

**high gear** *noun* (1896)
**1** : HIGH 3b
**2** : a state of intense or maximum activity — usually used with *in*

**High German** *noun* (1673)
**1** : German as natively used in southern and central Germany
**2** : GERMAN 3b

**high–grade** *adjective* (1878)
**1** : of superior grade or quality ⟨*high-grade* bonds⟩
**2** : being near the upper or most favorable extreme of a specified range

**high ground** *noun* (1944)
: a position of advantage or preeminence

**high–hand·ed** \-'han-dəd\ *adjective* (1631)
: having or showing no regard for the rights, concerns, or feelings of others : ARBITRARY, OVERBEARING
— **high–hand·ed·ly** *adverb*
— **high–hand·ed·ness** *noun*

**high–hat** \'hī-'hat\ *adjective* (1924)
: SUPERCILIOUS, SNOBBISH
— **high–hat** *transitive verb*

**high hat** *noun* (1889)
**1** : ¹BEAVER 2
**2** *or* **hi–hat** : a pair of cymbals operated by a foot pedal

**high heels** *noun plural* (1671)
: shoes with high heels

**High Holiday** *noun* (1946)
: either of two important Jewish holidays: **a** : ROSH HASHANAH **b** : YOM KIPPUR

**high horse** *noun* (1721)
: an arrogant and unyielding mood or attitude

**high·jack** \'hī-,jak\ *variant of* HIJACK

**high jinks** *noun plural* (1825)
: boisterous or rambunctious carryings-on : carefree antics or horseplay

**high jump** *noun* (1895)
: a jump for height over a horizontal bar in a track-and-field contest
— **high jumper** *noun*

**¹high·land** \'hī-lənd\ *noun* (before 12th century)
: elevated or mountainous land

**²highland** *adjective* (15th century)
**1** : of or relating to a highland
**2** *capitalized* : of or relating to the Highlands of Scotland

**high·land·er** \-lən-dər\ *noun* (1610)
**1** : an inhabitant of a highland
**2** *capitalized* : an inhabitant of the Highlands of Scotland

**Highland fling** *noun* (1804)
: a lively Scottish folk dance

**high–lev·el** \'hī-'le-vəl\ *adjective* (1876)
**1** : occurring, done, or placed at a high level
**2** : being of high importance or rank ⟨*high-level* diplomats⟩
**3** : of, relating to, or being a computer programming language (as BASIC or Pascal) which is similar to a natural language (as English) and in which each statement is translated by a compiler usually into several machine language instructions

**¹high·light** \'hī-,līt\ *noun* (circa 1889)
**1** : the lightest spot or area (as in a painting) : any of several spots in a modeled drawing or painting that receives the greatest amount of illumination
**2** : something (as an event or detail) that is of major significance or special interest

**²highlight** *transitive verb* **-light·ed; -light·ing** (1927)
**1** : to throw a strong light on
**2 a** : to center attention on **b** : to constitute a highlight of

**high–low–jack** \,hī-,lō-'jak\ *noun* (1818)
: an all-fours game in which scores are made by winning the highest trump, the lowest trump, the jack of trumps, and either the ten of trumps or the most points

**high·ly** \'hī-lē\ *adverb* (before 12th century)
**1** : in or to a high place, level, or rank
**2** : in or to a high degree or amount

**3** : with approval : FAVORABLY

**high mass** *noun, often H&M capitalized* (12th century)
: a mass marked by the singing of prescribed parts by the celebrant and the choir or congregation

**high–mind·ed** \'hī-'mīn-dəd\ *adjective* (1556)
: marked by elevated principles and feelings; *also* : PRETENTIOUS ⟨too *high-minded* to read any fiction —Alfred Kazin⟩
— **high–mind·ed·ly** *adverb*
— **high–mind·ed·ness** *noun*

**high–muck–a–muck** \,hī-'mə-ki-,mək\ *or* **high–muck·e·ty–muck** \,hī-'mə-kə-tē-,mək\ *noun* [by folk etymology from Chinook Jargon *hayo makamak* plenty to eat] (1856)
: an important and often arrogant person ◆

**high·ness** \'hī-nəs\ *noun* (before 12th century)
**1** : the quality or state of being high
**2** — used as a title for a person of exalted rank (as a king or prince)

**high noon** *noun* (1523)
**1** : precisely noon
**2** : the most advanced, flourishing, or creative stage or period ⟨the *high noon* of her career⟩

**high–octane** *adjective* (1932)
**1** : having a high octane number and hence good antiknock properties ⟨*high-octane* gasoline⟩
**2** : HIGH-POWERED

**high–pitched** \'hī-'picht\ *adjective* (1748)
**1** : having a high pitch ⟨a *high-pitched* voice⟩
**2** : marked by or exhibiting strong feeling : AGITATED ⟨a *high-pitched*, almost frantic campaign —Geoffrey Rice⟩

**high place** *noun* (14th century)
: a temple or altar used by the ancient Semites and built usually on a hill or elevation

**high polymer** *noun* (1942)
: a substance (as polystyrene) consisting of molecules that are large multiples of units of low molecular weight

**high–pow·ered** \'hī-'paủ(-ə)rd\ *also* **high–pow·er** \-'paủ(-ə)r\ *adjective* (1893)
**1** : having great drive, energy, or capacity : DYNAMIC ⟨a *high-powered* executive⟩

---

◇ WORD HISTORY

**high–muck–a–muck** Chinook Jargon was a pidgin spoken in the Pacific Northwest during the 19th century. Its vocabulary was drawn largely from lower Chinook, once spoken at the mouth of the Columbia River, and Nootka, spoken by an Indian people living on western Vancouver Island. A small number of words from Chinook Jargon have found their way into American and Canadian English, of which the most curious is the phrase *hayo makamak*, literally "plenty of food," both elements of which are Nootka in origin (*ḥayo*, literally "ten" and *ma·ho·maq*- "eat"). Somehow this phrase was transplanted from the Northwest to central California, where it surfaced in 1856 as a colloquialism meaning not "plenty of food," but "big shot." Presumably the first syllable was transformed by folk-etymology into *high*, though how *makamak* came to be interpreted as "person" is unclear. Indians of local importance in Northwest Coast cultures would give potlatches at which *hayo makamak* would be distributed, but there is no evidence that the phrase was transferred from food to person in Chinook Jargon. At any rate, once established, further variants of *high-muck-a-muck* have proliferated, such as *high-muckety-muck*, *high-monkey-monk*, and—by a second round of folk-etymology—*high mogul*.

---

\ə\ abut \°\ kitten \ər\ further \a\ ash \ā\ ace
\ä\ mop, mar \aủ\ out \ch\ chin \e\ bet \ē\ easy
\g\ go \i\ hit \ī\ ice \j\ job \ŋ\ sing \ō\ go
\ȯ\ law \ȯi\ boy \th\ thin \th\ the \ü\ loot \ủ\ foot
\y\ yet \zh\ vision *see also* Guide to Pronunciation

**2 :** having or conferring great influence ⟨a *high-powered* job⟩

**¹high–pressure** *adjective* (1824)
**1 a :** having or involving a high or comparatively high pressure especially greatly exceeding that of the atmosphere **b :** having a high barometric pressure
**2 a :** using or involving aggressive and insistent sales techniques **b :** imposing or involving severe strain or tension ⟨*high-pressure* occupations⟩

**²high–pressure** *transitive verb* (1926)
**:** to sell or influence by high-pressure tactics

**high priest** *noun* (14th century)
**1 :** a chief priest especially of the ancient Jewish Levitical priesthood traditionally traced from Aaron
**2 :** a priest of the Melchizedek priesthood in the Mormon Church
**3 :** the head of a movement or chief exponent of a doctrine or an art
**— high priesthood** *noun*

**high priestess** *noun* (1645)
**:** a chief priestess

**high relief** *noun* (circa 1828)
**:** sculptural relief in which at least half of the circumference of the modeled form projects

**high–rise** \'hī-'rīz\ *adjective* (1954)
**1 :** being multistory and equipped with elevators ⟨*high-rise* apartments⟩
**2 :** of, relating to, or characterized by high-rise buildings
**— high–rise** \'hī-,\ *noun*

**high road** *noun* (1709)
**1 :** HIGHWAY
**2 :** the easiest course
**3 :** an ethical course

**high roller** *noun* (1881)
**1 :** a person who spends freely in luxurious living
**2 :** a person who gambles recklessly or for high stakes
**— high–rolling** *adjective*

**¹high school** *noun* (1824)
**:** a school especially in the U.S. usually including grades 9–12 or 10–12
**— high school·er** \-'skü-lər\ *noun*

**²high school** *noun* [translation of French *haute école*] (1884)
**:** a system of advanced exercises in horsemanship

**high sea** *noun* (before 12th century)
**:** the open part of a sea or ocean especially outside territorial waters — usually used in plural

**high sign** *noun* (1902)
**:** a gesture used as a signal (as of approval or warning) — usually used in the phrase *give the high sign*

**high–sound·ing** \'hī-'saùn-diŋ\ *adjective* (1784)
**:** POMPOUS, IMPOSING

**high–speed** \'hī-'spēd\ *adjective* (1873)
**1 :** operated or adapted for operation at high speed
**2 :** relating to the production of short-exposure photographs of rapidly moving objects or events of short duration

**high–spir·it·ed** \-'spir-ə-təd\ *adjective* (circa 1631)
**:** characterized by a bold or energetic spirit
**— high–spir·it·ed·ly** *adverb*
**— high–spir·it·ed·ness** *noun*

**high–spot** \'hī-,spät\ *noun* (1910)
**:** HIGHLIGHT 2

**high–stick·ing** \-,sti-kiŋ\ *noun* (1947)
**:** the act of carrying the blade of the stick at an illegal height in ice hockey

**high street** *noun* (before 12th century)
*British* **:** a main or principal street

**high–strung** \'hī-'strəŋ\ *adjective* (1748)
**:** having an extremely nervous or sensitive temperament

**high style** *noun* (1939)
**:** the newest style in fashion or design usually adopted by a limited number of people

**hight** \'hīt\ *adjective* [Middle English, past participle (earlier past) of *hoten* to command, call, be called, from Old English *hātan;* akin to Old High German *heizzan* to command, call] (15th century)
*archaic* **:** being called **:** NAMED

**high table** *noun* (1711)
**:** an elevated table in the dining room of a British college for use by the master and fellows and distinguished guests

**high·tail** \'hī-,tāl\ *intransitive verb* (1925)
**:** to move at full speed or rapidly often in making a retreat — usually used with *it*

**high tea** *noun* (1831)
**:** a fairly substantial late afternoon or early evening meal at which tea is served

**high tech** \-'tek\ *noun* (1973)
**1 :** HIGH TECHNOLOGY
**2 :** a style of interior design featuring industrial products, materials, or designs
**— high–tech** *adjective*

**high technology** *noun* (1968)
**:** scientific technology involving the production or use of advanced or sophisticated devices especially in the fields of electronics and computers

**high–tension** *adjective* (1905)
**:** having or using a high voltage

**high–test** *adjective* (1923)
**:** meeting a high standard; *also* **:** HIGH-OCTANE

**high tide** *noun* (1745)
**1 :** the tide when the water is at its greatest elevation
**2 :** culminating point **:** CLIMAX

**high–toned** \'hī-'tōnd\ *adjective* (1807)
**1 :** high in social, moral, or intellectual quality
**2 :** PRETENTIOUS, POMPOUS

**high–top** \'hī-,täp\ *adjective* (1966)
**:** extending up over the ankle ⟨*high-top* sneakers⟩
**— high–tops** *noun plural*

**high treason** *noun* (15th century)
**:** TREASON 2

**high–volt·age** \'hī-'vōl-tij\ *adjective* (1948)
**:** marked by great energy **:** ELECTRIC, DYNAMIC ⟨a *high-voltage* performance⟩

**high–water** *adjective* (1856)
**:** unusually short ⟨*high-water* pants⟩

**high water** *noun* (15th century)
**:** a high stage of the water in a river or lake; *also* **:** HIGH TIDE

**high–water mark** *noun* (1814)
**:** highest point **:** PEAK

**high·way** \'hī-,wā\ *noun* (before 12th century)
**:** a public way; *especially* **:** a main direct road

**high·way·man** \-mən\ *noun* (1649)
**:** a person who robs travelers on a road

**highway robbery** *noun* (1778)
**1 :** robbery committed on or near a public highway usually against travelers
**2 :** excessive profit or advantage derived from a business transaction

**high–wire** \'hī-,wī(-ə)r\ *adjective* (1956)
**1 :** involving great risk ⟨a financial *high-wire* act⟩
**2 :** DARING ⟨*high-wire* prose⟩

**high–wrought** \'hī-'rȯt\ *adjective* (1604)
**:** extremely agitated

**high yellow** *noun* (1923)
**:** a black person of light complexion — called also *high yal·ler* \-'ya-lər\; often taken to be offensive

**hi–hat** *variant of* HIGH HAT 2

**hi·jack** \'hī-,jak\ *transitive verb* [origin unknown] (1923)
**1 a :** to steal by stopping a vehicle on the highway **b :** to commandeer (a flying airplane) especially by coercing the pilot at gunpoint **c :** to stop and steal from (a vehicle in transit) **d :** KIDNAP
**2 a :** to steal or rob as if by hijacking **b :** to subject to extortion or swindling
**— hijack** *noun*
**— hi·jack·er** *noun*

**hi·jinks** \'hī-,jiŋks\ *variant of* HIGH JINKS

**¹hike** \'hīk\ *verb* **hiked; hik·ing** [perhaps akin to ¹*hitch*] (1804)
*intransitive verb*
**1 a :** to go on a hike **b :** to travel by any means
**2 :** to rise up; *especially* **:** to work upward out of place ⟨skirt had *hiked* up in back⟩
*transitive verb*
**1 a :** to move, pull, or raise with a sudden motion ⟨*hiked* himself onto the top bunk⟩ **b :** SNAP 6b **c :** to raise in amount sharply or suddenly ⟨*hike* rents⟩
**2 :** to take on a hike
**— hik·er** *noun*

**²hike** *noun* (1865)
**1 :** a long walk especially for pleasure or exercise
**2 :** an increase especially in quantity or amount ⟨a new wage *hike*⟩
**3 :** SNAP 11

**hi·lar** \'hī-lər\ *adjective* (circa 1859)
**:** of, relating to, or located near a hilum

**hi·lar·i·ous** \hi-'lar-ē-əs, hī-, -'ler-\ *adjective* [irregular from Latin *hilarus, hilaris* cheerful, from Greek *hilaros*] (circa 1840)
**:** marked by or affording hilarity
**— hi·lar·i·ous·ly** *adverb*
**— hi·lar·i·ous·ness** *noun*

**hi·lar·i·ty** \-ə-tē\ *noun* (15th century)
**:** high spirits that may be carried to the point of boisterous conviviality or merriment

**Hil·bert space** \'hil-bərt-\ *noun* [David *Hilbert*] (1939)
**:** a vector space for which a scalar product is defined and in which every Cauchy sequence composed of elements in the space converges to a limit in the space

**hil·ding** \'hil-diŋ\ *noun* [*hilding*, adjective (base)] (1592)
*archaic* **:** a base contemptible person

**¹hill** \'hil\ *noun* [Middle English, from Old English *hyll;* akin to Latin *collis* hill, *culmen* top] (before 12th century)
**1 :** a usually rounded natural elevation of land lower than a mountain
**2 :** an artificial heap or mound (as of earth)
**3 :** several seeds or plants planted in a group rather than a row
**4 :** SLOPE, INCLINE

**²hill** *transitive verb* (1581)
**1 :** to form into a heap
**2 :** to draw earth around the roots or base of
**— hill·er** *noun*

**hill·bil·ly** \'hil-,bi-lē\ *noun, plural* **-lies** [¹*hill* + *Billy,* nickname for *William*] (1900)
**:** a person from a backwoods area

**hillbilly music** *noun* (1943)
**:** COUNTRY MUSIC

**hill climb** *noun* (1905)
**:** a road race for automobiles or motorcycles in which competitors are individually timed up a hill

**hill·crest** \'hil-,krest\ *noun* (circa 1898)
**:** the top line of a hill

**hill mynah** *noun* (circa 1890)
**:** a largely black Asian mynah (*Gracula religiosa*) often tamed and taught to pronounce words

**hill·ock** \'hi-lək\ *noun* (14th century)
**:** a small hill
**— hill·ocky** \-lə-kē\ *adjective*

**Hill reaction** \'hil-\ *noun* [Robert *Hill* (died 1991) British biochemist] (1950)
**:** the light-dependent transfer of electrons by chloroplasts in photosynthesis that results in the cleavage of water molecules and liberation of oxygen

**hill·side** \-,sīd\ *noun* (14th century)
**:** a part of a hill between the top and the foot

**hill·top** \'hil-,täp\ *noun* (15th century)
**:** the highest part of a hill

**hilly** \'hi-lē\ *adjective* **hill·i·er; -est** (14th century)
**:** abounding in hills

**hilt** \'hilt\ *noun* [Middle English, from Old English; akin to Old High German *helza* hilt] (before 12th century)
**:** a handle especially of a sword or dagger
— **to the hilt :** to the very limit **:** COMPLETELY

**hi·lum** \'hī-ləm\ *noun, plural* **hi·la** \-lə\ [New Latin, from Latin, trifle] (circa 1753)
**1 :** a scar on a seed (as a bean) marking the point of attachment of the ovule
**2 :** a notch in or opening from a bodily part suggesting the hilum of a bean

**him** \im, 'him\ *pronoun objective case of* HE

**Hi·ma·la·yan** \ˌhi-mə-'lā-ən, hi-'mäl-yən, -'mä-lē-ən\ *noun* [*Himalaya* Mountains] (1949)
**:** any of a breed of domestic cats developed by crossing the Persian and the Siamese and having the stocky build and long thick coat of the former and the blue eyes and coat patterns of the latter

**Himalayan**

**hi·mat·i·on** \hi-'ma-tē-ˌän, -ən\ *noun* [Greek, diminutive of *heimat-, heima* garment; akin to Greek *hennynai* to clothe — more at WEAR] (1850)
**:** a rectangular cloth draped over the left shoulder and about the body and worn as a garment in ancient Greece

**him/her** \'him-'hər, 'hi-mər-, 'him-'slash-\ *pronoun objective case of* HE/SHE

**him·self** \(h)im-'self, *Southern also* -'sef\ *pronoun* (before 12th century)
**1 a :** that identical male one — compare [i]HE; used reflexively, for emphasis, in absolute constructions, and in place of *him* especially when joined to another object ⟨considers *himself* lucky⟩ ⟨he *himself* did it⟩ ⟨*himself* unhappy, he understood the situation⟩ ⟨a gift to his wife and *himself*⟩ **b :** used reflexively when the sex of the antecedent is unspecified ⟨everyone must fend for *himself*⟩
**2 :** his normal, healthy, or sane condition or self
**3** *chiefly Irish & Scottish :* a man of consequence; *especially :* the master of the house

**hin** \'hin\ *noun* [Hebrew *hīn*, from Egyptian *hnw*] (14th century)
**:** an ancient Hebrew unit of liquid measure equal to about 1.5 gallons (5.7 liters)

**Hi·na·ya·na** \ˌhi-nə-'yä-nə, ˌhē-\ *noun* [Sanskrit *hīnayāna* lesser vehicle] (1868)
**:** THERAVADA
— **Hi·na·ya·nist** \-'yä-nist\ *noun*
— **Hi·na·ya·nis·tic** \-yä-'nis-tik\ *adjective*

**[1]hind** \'hīnd\ *noun, plural* **hinds** *also* **hind** [Middle English, from Old English; akin to Old High German *hinta* hind, Greek *kemas* young deer] (before 12th century)
**1 :** the female of the red deer — compare HART
**2 :** any of various spotted groupers (especially genus *Epinephelus*)

**[2]hind** *noun* [Middle English *hine* servant, farmhand, from Old English *hīna*, genitive of *hīwan*, plural, members of a household; akin to Old High German *hīwo* spouse, Latin *civis* fellow citizen, and probably to Old Irish *cóim* dear, Lithuanian *šeima* family] (1520)
**1 :** a British farm assistant
**2** *archaic :* RUSTIC

**[3]hind** *adjective* [Middle English, probably back-formation from Old English *hinder*, adverb, behind; akin to Old High German *hintar*, preposition, behind] (14th century)
**:** of or forming the part that follows or is behind **:** REAR

**hind·brain** \'hīn(d)-ˌbrān\ *noun* (1888)

**1 :** the posterior of the three primary divisions of the developing vertebrate brain or the corresponding part of the adult brain that includes the cerebellum, the medulla oblongata, and in mammals the pons and that controls autonomic functions and equilibrium — called also *rhombencephalon*; compare METENCEPHALON, MYELENCEPHALON
**2 :** the posterior segment of the brain of an invertebrate

**[1]hin·der** \'hin-dər\ *verb* **hin·dered; hin·der·ing** \-d(ə-)riŋ\ [Middle English *hindren*, from Old English *hindrian*; akin to Old English *hinder* behind] (before 12th century)
*transitive verb*
**1 :** to make slow or difficult the progress of **:** HAMPER
**2 :** to hold back **:** CHECK
*intransitive verb*
**:** to delay, impede, or prevent action ☆
— **hin·der·er** \-dər-ər\ *noun*

**[2]hind·er** \'hīn-dər\ *adjective* [Middle English, from Old English *hinder*, adverb] (13th century)
**:** situated behind or in the rear **:** POSTERIOR

**hind-gut** \'hīn(d)-ˌgət\ *noun* (1878)
**:** the posterior part of the alimentary canal

**Hin·di** \'hin-(ˌ)dē\ *noun* [Hindi *hindī*, from *Hind* India, from Persian] (1801)
**1 :** a literary and official language of northern India
**2 :** a complex of Indo-Aryan languages and dialects of northern India for which Hindi is the usual literary language
— **Hindi** *adjective*

**hind·most** \'hīn(d)-ˌmōst\ *adjective* (14th century)
**:** farthest to the rear **:** LAST

**hind·quar·ter** \-ˌkwó(r)-tər, -ˌkó(r)-\ *noun* (1881)
**1 :** one side of the back half of the carcass of a quadruped including a leg and usually one or more ribs
**2** *plural :* the hind pair of legs of a quadruped; *broadly :* all the structures of a quadruped that lie posterior to the attachment of the hind legs to the trunk

**hin·drance** \'hin-drən(t)s\ *noun* (1526)
**1 :** the state of being hindered
**2 :** IMPEDIMENT
**3 :** the action of hindering

**hind·sight** \'hīn(d)-ˌsīt\ *noun* (1866)
**:** perception of the nature of an event after it has happened

**[1]Hin·du** *also* **Hin·doo** \'hin-(ˌ)dü\ *noun* [Persian *Hindū* inhabitant of India, from *Hind* India] (1662)
**1 :** an adherent of Hinduism
**2 :** a native or inhabitant of India

**[2]Hindu** *also* **Hindoo** *adjective* (1698)
**:** of, relating to, or characteristic of the Hindus or Hinduism

**Hindu–Arabic** *adjective* (1925)
**:** relating to, being, or composed of Arabic numerals ⟨*Hindu-Arabic* numeration system⟩

**Hindu calendar** *noun* (circa 1909)
**:** a lunar calendar usually dating from 3101 B.C. and used especially in India

**Hin·du·ism** \'hin-(ˌ)dü-ˌi-zəm\ *noun* (1809)
**:** the dominant religion of India that emphasizes dharma with its resulting ritual and social observances and often mystical contemplation and ascetic practices

**[1]Hin·du·stani** *also* **Hin·do·stani** \ˌhin-dù-'sta-nē, -'stä-nē\ *noun* [Hindi *Hindūstānī*, from Persian *Hindūstān* India] (1808)
**:** a group of Indo-Aryan dialects of northern India of which literary Hindi and Urdu are considered diverse written forms

**[2]Hindustani** *also* **Hindostani** *adjective* (1800)
**:** of or relating to Hindustan or its people or Hindustani

**hind wing** *noun* (1899)
**:** either of the posterior wings of a 4-winged insect

**[1]hinge** \'hinj\ *noun* [Middle English *heng;* akin to Middle Dutch *henge* hook, Old English *hangian* to hang] (14th century)
**1 a :** a jointed or flexible device on which a door, lid, or other swinging part turns **b :** a flexible ligamentous joint **c :** a small piece of thin gummed paper used in fastening a postage stamp in an album
**2 :** a determining factor **:** TURNING POINT

**[2]hinge** *verb* **hinged; hing·ing** (1719)
*intransitive verb*
**:** to be contingent on a single consideration or point — used with *on* or *upon*
*transitive verb*
**:** to attach by or furnish with hinges

**hinge joint** *noun* (1802)
**:** a joint between bones (as at the elbow) that permits motion in only one plane

**hin·ny** \'hi-nē\ *noun, plural* **hinnies** [Latin *hinnus*, from Greek *innos*] (1688)
**:** a hybrid between a stallion and a female donkey — compare MULE

**[1]hint** \'hint\ *noun* [probably alteration of obsolete *hent* act of seizing, from *hent* verb] (1604)
**1** *archaic :* OPPORTUNITY, TURN
**2 a :** a statement conveying by implication what it is preferred not to say explicitly **b :** an indirect or summary suggestion ⟨helpful *hints*⟩
**3 :** a slight indication of the existence, approach, or nature of something **:** CLUE
**4 :** a very small amount **:** SUGGESTION

**[2]hint** (1648)
*transitive verb*
**:** to convey indirectly and by allusion rather than explicitly ⟨a suspicion that she scarcely dared to *hint*⟩
*intransitive verb*
**:** to give a hint — usually used with *at*
**synonym** see SUGGEST
— **hint·er** *noun*

**hin·ter·land** \'hin-tər-ˌland, -lənd\ *noun* [German, from *hinter* hinder + *Land*] (1890)
**1 :** a region lying inland from a coast
**2 a :** a region remote from urban areas **b :** a region lying beyond major metropolitan or cultural centers

**[1]hip** \'hip\ *noun* [Middle English *hipe*, from Old English *hēope;* akin to Old High German *hiafo* hip] (before 12th century)
**:** ROSE HIP

**[2]hip** *noun* [Middle English, from Old English *hype;* akin to Old High German *huf* hip] (before 12th century)
**1 a :** the laterally projecting region of each side of the lower or posterior part of the mammalian trunk formed by the lateral parts of the pelvis and upper part of the femur together with the fleshy parts covering them **b :** HIP JOINT
**2 :** the external angle formed by the meeting of two sloping sides of a roof that have their wall plates running in different directions

\ə\ abut \ə\ kitten \ər\ further \a\ ash \ā\ ace
\ä\ mop, mar \aú\ out \ch\ chin \e\ bet \ē\ easy
\g\ go \i\ hit \ī\ ice \j\ job \ŋ\ sing \ō\ go
\ó\ law \ói\ boy \th\ thin \th\ the \ü\ loot \ú\ foot
\y\ yet \zh\ vision *see also* Guide to Pronunciation

**³hip** *interjection* [origin unknown] (1827)
— used in a cheer ⟨*hip hip* hooray⟩
**⁴hip** *adjective* **hip·per; hip·pest** [alteration of ²*hep*] (1904)
: characterized by a keen informed awareness of or involvement in the newest developments or styles
**⁵hip** *transitive verb* **hipped; hip·ping** (circa 1932)
: to make aware : TELL, INFORM
**⁶hip** *noun* (1952)
: HIPNESS
**hip and thigh** *adverb* (1560)
: in a fierce or ruthless manner : UNSPARINGLY
**hip·bone** \'hip-'bōn, -,bōn\ *noun* (12th century)
: INNOMINATE BONE
**hip boot** *noun* (1893)
: a waterproof boot reaching to the hips
**hip–hop** \'hip-,häp\ *noun, often attributive* [perhaps from ⁴*hip* + ¹*hop*] (1983)
: a subculture especially of inner-city youths whose amusements include rap music, graffiti, and break dancing; *also* : an element or art form prevalent within this subculture
**hip joint** *noun* (1794)
: the articulation between the femur and the innominate bone
**hip·line** \'hip-,līn\ *noun* (1907)
**1** : an arbitrary line encircling the fullest part of the hips
**2** : body circumference at the hips
**hip·ness** \'hip-nəs\ *noun* (1946)
: the quality or state of being hip
**¹hipped** \'hipt\ *adjective* (1508)
**1** : having hips especially of a specified kind — often used in combination ⟨a broad-*hipped* person⟩
**2** : constructed with hips ⟨a *hipped* roof⟩
**²hipped** *adjective* [*hip* (hypochondria)] (circa 1710)
: DEPRESSED
**³hipped** *adjective* [⁵*hip*] (1920)
: extremely absorbed or interested ⟨*hipped* on astrology⟩
**hip·pie** *or* **hip·py** \'hi-pē\ *noun, plural* **hip·pies** [⁴*hip* + -*ie*] (1965)
: a usually young person who rejects the mores of established society (as by dressing unconventionally or favoring communal living) and advocates a nonviolent ethic; *broadly* : a long-haired unconventionally dressed young person
— **hip·pie·dom** \-pē-dəm\ *noun*
— **hip·pie·ness** *or* **hip·pi·ness** \-pē-nəs\ *noun*
**hip·po** \'hi-(,)pō\ *noun, plural* **hippos** (1872)
: HIPPOPOTAMUS
**hip·po·cam·pus** \,hi-pə-'kam-pəs\ *noun, plural* **-pi** \-,pī, -,(,)pē\ [New Latin, from Greek *hippokampos* sea horse, from *hippos* horse + *kampos* sea monster — more at EQUINE] (1706)
: a curved elongated ridge that extends over the floor of the descending horn of each lateral ventricle of the brain and consists of gray matter covered on the ventricular surface with white matter
— **hip·po·cam·pal** \-pəl\ *adjective*
**hip·po·cras** \'hi-pə-,kras\ *noun* [Middle English *ypocras*, from *Ypocras* Hippocrates, to whom its invention was ascribed] (14th century)
: a mulled wine popular in medieval Europe
**Hip·po·crat·ic** \,hi-pə-'kra-tik\ *adjective* (circa 1620)
: of or relating to Hippocrates or to the school of medicine that took his name
**Hippocratic oath** *noun* (1747)
: an oath embodying a code of medical ethics usually taken by those about to begin medical practice
**Hip·po·crene** \'hi-pə-,krēn, ,hi-pə-'krē-nē\ *noun* [Latin, from Greek *Hippokrēnē*] (1605)

: a fountain on Mount Helicon sacred to the Muses and believed to be a source of poetic inspiration
**hip·po·drome** \'hi-pə-,drōm\ *noun* [Middle French, from Latin *hippodromos*, from Greek, from *hippos* + *dromos* racecourse — more at DROMEDARY] (1585)
**1** : an oval stadium for horse and chariot races in ancient Greece
**2** : an arena for equestrian performances
**hip·po·griff** \-,grif\ *noun* [French *hippogriffe*, from Italian *ippogrifo*, from *ippo-* (from Greek *hippos* horse) + *grifo* griffin, from Latin *gryphus*] (circa 1656)
: a legendary animal having the foreparts of a griffin and the body of a horse
**Hip·pol·y·ta** \hi-'pä-lə-tə\ *noun* [Latin, from Greek *Hippolytē*]
: a queen of the Amazons given in marriage to Theseus by Hercules
**Hip·pol·y·tus** \-ə-təs\ *noun* [Latin, from Greek *Hippolytos*]
: a son of Theseus falsely accused of amorous advances by his stepmother and killed by his father through the agency of Poseidon
**Hip·pom·e·nes** \hi-'pä-mə-nēz\ *noun* [Latin, from Greek *Hippomenēs*]
: the successful suitor of Atalanta in Greek mythology
**hip·po·pot·a·mus** \,hi-pə-'pä-tə-məs\ *noun, plural* **-mus·es** *or* **-mi** \-,mī, -,(,)mē\ [Latin, from Greek *hippopotamos*, alteration of *hippos potamios*, literally, riverine horse] (1563)
: a very large herbivorous 4-toed chiefly aquatic artiodactyl mammal (*Hippopotamus amphibius*) of sub-Saharan Africa with an extremely large head and mouth, bare and very thick grayish skin, and short legs; *also* : a smaller closely related mammal (*Choeropsis liberiensis*) of western Africa ◆

hippopotamus

**hip·py** \'hi-pē\ *adjective* (1919)
: having large hips
**hip roof** *noun* (circa 1741)
: a roof having sloping ends and sloping sides — see ROOF illustration
**hip–shoot·ing** \'hip-,shü-tiŋ\ *noun* (1951)
: action or reaction that is quick and often reckless
— **hip shooter** *noun*
**hip·ster** \'hip-stər\ *noun* [⁴*hip*] (circa 1941)
: a person who is unusually aware of and interested in new and unconventional patterns (as in jazz or the use of stimulants)
**hip·ster·ism** \-stə-,ri-zəm\ *noun* (1958)
**1** : HIPNESS
**2** : the way of life characteristic of hipsters
**hi·ra·ga·na** \,hir-ə-'gä-nə\ *noun* [Japanese, from *hira-* ordinary + *kana* syllabary] (1859)
: the cursive script that is one of two sets of symbols of Japanese syllabic writing — compare KATAKANA
**¹hire** \'hī-(ə)r\ *noun* [Middle English, from Old English *hȳr*; akin to Old Saxon *hūria* hire] (before 12th century)
**1 a** : payment for the temporary use of something **b** : payment for labor or personal services : WAGES
**2 a** : the act or an instance of hiring **b** : the state of being hired : EMPLOYMENT
**3** *British* : RENTAL — often used attributively
**4** : one who is hired ⟨starting wage for the new *hires*⟩
— **for hire** *also* **on hire** : available for use or service in return for payment
**²hire** *verb* **hired; hir·ing** (before 12th century)
*transitive verb*
**1 a** : to engage the personal services of for a set sum ⟨*hire* a crew⟩ **b** : to engage the temporary use of for a fixed sum ⟨*hire* a hall⟩

**2** : to grant the personal services of or temporary use of for a fixed sum ⟨*hire* themselves out⟩
**3** : to get done for pay ⟨*hire* the mowing done⟩
*intransitive verb*
: to take employment ⟨*hire* out as a guide during the tourist season⟩ ☆
— **hir·er** *noun*
**hired gun** *noun* (1971)
: an expert hired to do a specific job; *especially* : HIRELING — often used disparagingly
**hire·ling** \'hī(-ə)r-liŋ\ *noun* (before 12th century)
: a person who serves for hire especially for purely mercenary motives
**hire purchase** *noun* (1895)
*chiefly British* : purchase on the installment plan
**hiring hall** *noun* (1934)
: a union-operated placement office where registered applicants are referred in rotation to jobs
**hir·sute** \'hər-,süt, 'hir-, ,hər-', hir-'\ *adjective* [Latin *hirsutus*; akin to Latin *horrēre* to bristle — more at HORROR] (1621)
: HAIRY 1; *especially* : covered with coarse stiff hairs ⟨*hirsute* leaf⟩
— **hir·sute·ness** *noun*
**hir·sut·ism** \'hər-sə-,ti-zəm, 'hir-\ *noun* (1927)
: excessive growth of hair of normal or abnormal distribution
**hi·ru·din** \hi-'rü-d⁼n, 'hir-(y)ə-\ *noun* [from *Hirudin*, a trademark] (1905)
: an anticoagulant extracted from the buccal glands of a leech
**¹his** \(h)iz, ,hiz\ *adjective* [Middle English, from Old English, genitive of *hē* he] (before 12th century)
: of or relating to him or himself especially as possessor, agent, or object of an action ⟨*his* house⟩ ⟨*his* writings⟩ ⟨*his* confirmation⟩ — compare ¹HE

---

☆ **SYNONYMS**
**Hire, let, lease, rent, charter** mean to engage or grant for use at a price. HIRE and LET, strictly speaking, are complementary terms, HIRE implying the act of engaging or taking for use and LET the granting of use ⟨we *hired* a car for the summer⟩ ⟨decided to *let* the cottage to a young couple⟩. LEASE strictly implies a letting under the terms of a contract but is often applied to hiring on a lease ⟨the diplomat *leased* an apartment for a year⟩. RENT stresses the payment of money for the full use of property and may imply either hiring or letting ⟨instead of buying a house, they decided to *rent*⟩ ⟨will not *rent* to families with children⟩. CHARTER applies to the hiring or letting of a vehicle usually for exclusive use ⟨*charter* a bus to go to the game⟩.

---

◇ **WORD HISTORY**
**hippopotamus** The bulky African mammal that spends its daytime hours submerged up to its eyes in a river owes its English name to the ancient Greeks. The historian Herodotus referred to this animal, which he may have seen in Egypt, as *ho hippos ho potamios* "the riverine horse." This epithet was reduced by later Greek writers to *hippopotamos* (which by normal rules of Greek compounding should mean "horse river"). Despite its name, the hippopotamus, which may weigh up to five tons, is more closely related to hogs than horses. Greek *hippos* "horse" was also applied to a species of marine fish that bore even less resemblance to a horse than a hippopotamus does—paralleling to some degree English *sea horse* (which resembles a horse) and *redhorse* (which does not).

**²his** \'hiz\ *pronoun, singular or plural in construction* (before 12th century)
**:** that which belongs to him — used without a following noun as a pronoun equivalent in meaning to the adjective *his*

**his/her** \'hiz-ˌhər, 'hi-zər-'hər, 'hiz-'slash-\ *adjective* (1952)
**:** his or her — used in writing as an adjective of common gender

**His·pan·ic** \hi-'spa-nik\ *adjective* [Latin *hispanicus,* from *Hispania* Iberian Peninsula, Spain] (circa 1889)
**:** of, relating to, or being a person of Latin American descent living in the U.S.; *especially* **:** one of Cuban, Mexican, or Puerto Rican origin
— **Hispanic** *noun*
— **His·pan·i·cism** \-'spa-nə-ˌsi-zəm\ *noun*
— **His·pan·i·cist** \-sist\ *noun*
— **His·pan·i·cize** \-ˌsīz\ *transitive verb*

**his·pa·ni·dad** \ˌis-ˌpa-ni-'thä(th)\ *noun* (1941)
**:** HISPANISM 1

**his·pa·nism** \'his-pə-ˌni-zəm\ *noun, often capitalized* (1940)
**1 :** a movement to reassert the cultural unity of Spain and Latin America
**2 :** a characteristic feature of Spanish occurring in another language

**His·pa·nist** \-nist\ *noun* (1786)
**:** a scholar specially informed in Spanish or Portuguese language, literature, linguistics, or civilization

**His·pa·no** \hi-'spa-(ˌ)nō, 'his-pə-ˌnō\ *noun,* *plural* **-nos** [American Spanish *hispano,* probably short for *hispanoamericano,* literally, Spanish-American] (1946)
**:** a native or resident of the southwestern U.S. descended from Spaniards settled there before annexation; *also* **:** MEXICAN 1

**his·pid** \'his-pəd\ *adjective* [Latin *hispidus;* akin to Latin *horrēre*] (1646)
**:** rough or covered with bristles, stiff hairs, or minute spines ⟨*hispid* leaf⟩

**hiss** \'his\ *verb* [Middle English, of imitative origin] (14th century)
*intransitive verb*
**:** to make a sharp sibilant sound ⟨the crowd *hissed* in disapproval⟩ ⟨*hissing* steam⟩
*transitive verb*
**1 :** to express disapproval of by hissing
**2 :** to utter or whisper angrily or threateningly and with a hiss
— **hiss** *noun*
— **hiss·er** *noun*

**his·self** \(h)i-'self, -'sef\ *pronoun* (12th century)
*chiefly dialect* **:** HIMSELF 1

**hissy** \'hi-sē\ *noun* [perhaps by shortening & alteration from *hysterical*] (circa 1934)
*chiefly Southern & southern Midland* **:** TANTRUM — called also *hissy fit*

**¹hist** \s *often prolonged and usually with* p *preceding and* t *following; often read as* 'hist\ *interjection* [origin unknown] (1592)
— used to attract attention

**²hist** \'hīst\ *dialect variant of* HOIST

**hist-** *or* **histo-** *combining form* [French, from Greek *histos* mast, loom beam, web, from *histanai* to cause to stand — more at STAND]
**:** tissue ⟨*histo*physiology⟩

**his·ta·mi·nase** \hi-'sta-mə-ˌnās, 'his-tə-mə-, -ˌnāz\ *noun* [International Scientific Vocabulary] (1930)
**:** a widely occurring flavoprotein enzyme that oxidizes histamine and various diamines

**his·ta·mine** \'his-tə-ˌmēn, -mən\ *noun* [International Scientific Vocabulary *hist-* + *amine*] (circa 1913)
**:** a compound $C_5H_9N_3$ especially of mammalian tissues that causes dilatation of capillaries, contraction of smooth muscle, and stimulation of gastric acid secretion, that is released during allergic reactions, and that is formed by decarboxylation of histidine

**his·ta·min·er·gic** \ˌhis-tə-mə-'nər-jik\ *adjective* [International Scientific Vocabulary] (1936)
*of autonomic nerve fibers* **:** liberating or activated by histamine ⟨*histaminergic* receptors⟩

**his·ti·dine** \'his-tə-ˌdēn\ *noun* [International Scientific Vocabulary *hist-* + *-idine*] (1896)
**:** a crystalline essential amino acid $C_6H_9N_3O_2$ formed by the hydrolysis of most proteins

**his·tio·cyte** \'his-tē-ə-ˌsīt\ *noun* [Greek *histion* web (diminutive of *histos*) + International Scientific Vocabulary *-cyte*] (1924)
**:** a nonmotile macrophage of extravascular tissues and especially connective tissue
— **his·tio·cyt·ic** \ˌhis-tē-ə-'si-tik\ *adjective*

**his·to·chem·is·try** \ˌhis-tō-'ke-mə-strē\ *noun* [International Scientific Vocabulary] (circa 1860)
**:** a science that combines the techniques of biochemistry and histology in the study of the chemical constitution of cells and tissues
— **his·to·chem·i·cal** \-'ke-mi-kəl\ *adjective*
— **his·to·chem·i·cal·ly** \-k(ə-)lē\ *adverb*

**his·to·com·pat·i·bil·i·ty** \'his-(ˌ)tō-kəm-ˌpa-tə-'bi-lə-tē\ *noun* (1948)
**:** a state of mutual tolerance that allows some tissues to be grafted effectively to others

**his·to·gen·e·sis** \ˌhis-tə-'je-nə-səs\ *noun* [New Latin] (circa 1854)
**:** the formation and differentiation of tissues
— **his·to·ge·net·ic** \-jə-'ne-tik\ *adjective*

**his·to·gram** \'his-tə-ˌgram\ *noun* [Greek *histos* mast, web + English *-gram*] (1891)
**:** a representation of a frequency distribution by means of rectangles whose widths represent class intervals and whose areas are proportional to the corresponding frequencies

**his·tol·o·gy** \his-'tä-lə-jē\ *noun, plural* **-gies** [French *histologie,* from *hist-* + *-logie* -logy] (circa 1847)
**1 :** a branch of anatomy that deals with the minute structure of animal and plant tissues as discernible with the microscope
**2 :** a treatise on histology
**3 :** tissue structure or organization
— **his·to·log·i·cal** \ˌhis-tə-'lä-ji-kəl\ *or* **his·to·log·ic** \-'lä-jik\ *adjective*
— **his·to·log·i·cal·ly** \-ji-k(ə-)lē\ *adverb*
— **his·tol·o·gist** \his-'tä-lə-jist\ *noun*

**his·tol·y·sis** \his-'tä-lə-səs\ *noun* [New Latin] (circa 1857)
**:** the breakdown of bodily tissues

**his·tone** \'his-ˌtōn\ *noun* [German *Histon*] (1885)
**:** any of various simple water-soluble proteins that are rich in the basic amino acids lysine and arginine and are complexed with DNA in the nucleosomes of eukaryotic chromatin

**his·to·pa·thol·o·gy** \ˌhis-tō-pə-'thä-lə-jē, -pa-\ *noun* [International Scientific Vocabulary] (1896)
**1 :** a branch of pathology concerned with the tissue changes characteristic of disease
**2 :** the tissue changes that affect a part or accompany a disease
— **his·to·path·o·log·ic** \-ˌpa-thə-'lä-jik\ *or* **his·to·path·o·log·i·cal** \-ji-kəl\ *adjective*
— **his·to·path·o·log·i·cal·ly** \-ji-k(ə-)lē\ *adverb*
— **his·to·pa·thol·o·gist** \-pə-'thä-lə-jist, -pa-\ *noun*

**his·to·phys·i·ol·o·gy** \-ˌfi-zē-'ä-lə-jē\ *noun* (circa 1886)
**1 :** a branch of physiology concerned with the function and activities of tissues
**2 :** structural and functional tissue organization
— **his·to·phys·i·o·log·i·cal** \-ē-ə-'lä-ji-kəl\ *or* **his·to·phys·i·o·log·ic** \-jik\ *adjective*

**his·to·plas·mo·sis** \ˌhis-tə-plaz-'mō-səs\ *noun* [New Latin, from *Histoplasma,* genus of fungi] (1907)

**:** a respiratory disease with symptoms like those of influenza that is caused by a fungus (*Histoplasma capsulatum*) and is marked by benign involvement of lymph nodes of the trachea and bronchi or by severe progressive generalized involvement of the lymph nodes and the reticuloendothelial system

**his·to·ri·an** \hi-'stōr-ē-ən, -'stòr-, -'stär-\ *noun* (15th century)
**1 :** a student or writer of history; *especially* **:** one that produces a scholarly synthesis
**2 :** a writer or compiler of a chronicle

**his·tor·ic** \hi-'stòr-ik, -'stär-\ *adjective* (1607)
**:** HISTORICAL: as **a :** famous or important in history ⟨*historic* battlefields⟩ **b :** having great and lasting importance ⟨an *historic* occasion⟩ **c :** known or established in the past ⟨*historic* interest rates⟩ **d :** dating from or preserved from a past time or culture ⟨*historic* buildings⟩ ⟨*historic* artifacts⟩

**his·tor·i·cal** \-i-kəl\ *adjective* (15th century)
**1 a :** of, relating to, or having the character of history **b :** based on history **c :** used in the past and reproduced in historical presentations
**2 :** famous in history **:** HISTORIC a
**3 a :** SECONDARY 1c **b :** DIACHRONIC ⟨*historical* grammar⟩
— **his·tor·i·cal·ness** \-i-kəl-nəs\ *noun*
— **his·tor·i·cal·ly** \-i-k(ə-)lē\ *adverb* (1550)
**1 :** in accordance with or with respect to history ⟨an *historically* accurate account⟩
**2 :** in the past ⟨*historically,* stagnant cities seldom have recovered —Jane Jacobs⟩

**historical materialism** *noun* (1925)
**:** the Marxist theory of history and society that holds that ideas and social institutions develop only as the superstructure of a material economic base — compare DIALECTICAL MATERIALISM

**historical present** *noun* (1867)
**:** the present tense used in relating past events

**his·tor·i·cism** \hi-'stòr-ə-ˌsi-zəm, -'stär-\ *noun* (1895)
**:** a theory, doctrine, or style that emphasizes the importance of history: as **a :** a theory in which history is seen as a standard of value or as a determinant of events **b :** a style (as in architecture) characterized by the use of traditional forms and elements
— **his·tor·i·cist** \-sist\ *adjective or noun*

**his·to·ric·i·ty** \ˌhis-tə-'ri-sə-tē\ *noun* (1880)
**:** historical actuality

**his·tor·i·cize** \hi-'stòr-ə-ˌsīz, -'stär-\ *verb* **-cized; -ciz·ing** (1846)
*transitive verb*
**:** to make historical
*intransitive verb*
**:** to use historical material

**his·to·ri·og·ra·pher** \hi-ˌstōr-ē-'ä-grə-fər, -ˌstòr-\ *noun* [Middle French *historiographeur,* from Late Latin *historiographus,* from Greek *historiographos,* from *historia* + *graphein* to write — more at CARVE] (15th century)
**:** HISTORIAN

**his·to·ri·og·ra·phy** \-fē\ *noun* (1569)
**1 a :** the writing of history; *especially* **:** the writing of history based on the critical examination of sources, the selection of particulars from the authentic materials, and the synthesis of particulars into a narrative that will stand the test of critical methods **b :** the principles, theory, and history of historical writing ⟨a course in *historiography*⟩
**2 :** the product of historical writing **:** a body of historical literature
— **his·to·rio·graph·i·cal** \-ē-ə-'gra-fi-kəl\ *also* **his·to·rio·graph·ic** \-fik\ *adjective*
— **his·to·rio·graph·i·cal·ly** \-ē-ə-'gra-fi-k(ə-)lē\ *adverb*

\ə\ abut \ᵊ\ kitten \ər\ further \a\ ash \ā\ ace \ä\ mop, mar \au̇\ out \ch\ chin \e\ bet \ē\ easy \g\ go \i\ hit \ī\ ice \j\ job \ŋ\ sing \ō\ go \ȯ\ law \ȯi\ boy \th\ thin \th\ the \ü\ loot \u̇\ foot \y\ yet \zh\ vision    *see also* Guide to Pronunciation

**his·to·ry** \'his-t(ə‚)rē\ *noun, plural* **-ries** [Latin *historia*, from Greek, inquiry, history, from *histōr, istōr* knowing, learned; akin to Greek *eidenai* to know — more at WIT] (14th century)
**1 :** TALE, STORY
**2 a :** a chronological record of significant events (as affecting a nation or institution) often including an explanation of their causes **b :** a treatise presenting systematically related natural phenomena **c :** an account of a patient's medical background **d :** an established record ⟨a prisoner with a *history* of violence⟩
**3 :** a branch of knowledge that records and explains past events ⟨medieval *history*⟩
**4 a :** events that form the subject matter of a history **b :** events of the past **c :** one that is finished or done for ⟨the winning streak was *history*⟩ ⟨you're *history*⟩ **d :** previous treatment, handling, or experience (as of a metal)

**his·tri·on·ic** \‚his-trē-'ä-nik\ *adjective* [Late Latin *histrionicus*, from Latin *histrion-, histrio* actor] (1648)
**1 :** deliberately affected : THEATRICAL
**2 :** of or relating to actors, acting, or the theater
**synonym** *see* DRAMATIC
— **his·tri·on·i·cal·ly** \-ni-k(ə-)lē\ *adverb*

**his·tri·on·ics** \-niks\ *noun plural but singular or plural in construction* (1864)
**1 :** theatrical performances
**2 :** deliberate display of emotion for effect

**¹hit** \'hit\ *verb* **hit; hit·ting** [Middle English, from Old English *hittan*, from Old Norse *hitta* to meet with, hit] (before 12th century)
*transitive verb*
**1 a :** to reach with or as if with a blow **b :** to come in contact with ⟨the ball *hit* the window⟩
**2 a :** to cause to come into contact **b :** to deliver (as a blow) by action **c :** to apply forcefully or suddenly ⟨*hit* the brakes⟩
**3 :** to affect especially detrimentally ⟨farmers *hit* by drought⟩
**4 :** to make a request of ⟨*hit* his friend for 10 dollars⟩ — often used with *up*
**5 :** to discover or meet especially by chance
**6 a :** to accord with : SUIT **b :** REACH, ATTAIN ⟨prices *hit* a new high⟩ **c :** to arrive or appear at, in, or on ⟨*hit* town⟩ ⟨the best time to *hit* the stores⟩ **d** *of fish* : to bite at or on **e :** to reflect accurately ⟨*hit* the right note⟩ **f :** to reach or strike (as a target) especially for a score in a game or contest ⟨couldn't seem to *hit* the basket⟩ **g :** BAT 2b
**7 :** to indulge in excessively ⟨*hit* the bottle⟩
*intransitive verb*
**1 a :** to strike a blow **b :** to arrive with a forceful effect like that of a blow ⟨the storm *hit*⟩
**2 a :** to come into contact with something **b :** ATTACK **c** *of a fish* : STRIKE 11b **d :** BAT 1
**3 :** to succeed in attaining or coming up with something — often used with *on* or *upon* ⟨*hit* on a solution⟩
**4** *obsolete* : to be in agreement : SUIT
**5** *of an internal-combustion engine* : to fire the charge in the cylinders
— **hit·ter** *noun*
— **hit it big :** to achieve great success
— **hit it off :** to get along well : become friends ⟨they *hit it off* immediately⟩
— **hit on :** to make especially sexual overtures to
— **hit one's stride :** to reach one's best speed or highest potential
— **hit the books :** to study especially with intensity
— **hit the fan :** to have a major usually undesirable impact
— **hit the hay** *or* **hit the sack :** to go to bed
— **hit the high points** *or* **hit the high spots :** to touch on or at the most important points or places
— **hit the jackpot :** to become notably and unexpectedly successful

— **hit the nail on the head :** to be exactly right
— **hit the road :** LEAVE, TRAVEL; *also* : to set out
— **hit the roof** *or* **hit the ceiling :** to give vent to a burst of anger or angry protest
— **hit the spot :** to give complete or special satisfaction — used especially of food or drink

**²hit** *noun* (15th century)
**1 :** an act or instance of hitting or being hit ⟨more *hits* than misses⟩ ⟨took a financial *hit*⟩
**2 a :** a stroke of luck **b :** a great success
**3 :** a telling or critical remark
**4 :** BASE HIT
**5 :** a quantity of a narcotic drug ingested at one time
**6 :** a premeditated murder committed especially by a member of a crime syndicate
— **hit·less** \'hit-ləs\ *adjective*

**hit–and–miss** \‚hi-t°n-'mis\ *adjective* (1897)
**:** sometimes successful and sometimes not
**:** not reliably good or successful

**¹hit–and–run** \-'rən\ *adjective* (1899)
**1 :** being or relating to a hit-and-run in baseball
**2 :** being or involving a motor-vehicle driver who does not stop after being involved in an accident
**3 :** involving or intended for quick specific action or results

**²hit–and–run** *noun* (1904)
**:** a baseball play calling for a runner on first to begin running as a pitch is delivered and for the batter to attempt to hit the pitch

**³hit–and–run** *intransitive verb* (1966)
**:** to execute a hit-and-run play in baseball

**¹hitch** \'hich\ *verb* [Middle English *hytchen*] (14th century)
*transitive verb*
**1 :** to move by jerks or with a tug
**2 a :** to catch or fasten by or as if by a hook or knot ⟨*hitched* his horse to the fence post⟩ **b** (1) **:** to connect (a vehicle or implement) with a source of motive power ⟨*hitch* a rake to a tractor⟩ (2) **:** to attach (a source of motive power) to a vehicle or instrument ⟨*hitch* the horses to the wagon⟩ **c :** to join in marriage ⟨got *hitched*⟩
**3 :** HITCHHIKE
*intransitive verb*
**1 :** to move with halts and jerks : HOBBLE
**2 a :** to become entangled, made fast, or linked **b :** to become joined in marriage
**3 :** HITCHHIKE
— **hitch·er** *noun*

**²hitch** *noun* (1664)
**1 :** LIMP
**2 :** a sudden movement or pull : JERK ⟨gave his trousers a *hitch*⟩
**3 a :** a sudden halt : STOPPAGE **b :** a usually unforeseen difficulty or obstacle ⟨the plan went off without a *hitch*⟩
**4 :** the act or fact of catching hold
**5 :** a connection between a vehicle or implement and a detachable source of power (as a tractor or horse)
**6 :** a delimited period especially of military service
**7 :** any of various knots used to form a temporary noose in a line or to secure a line temporarily to an object
**8 :** LIFT 5b

**hitch·hike** \'hich-‚hīk\ (1926)
*intransitive verb*
**1 :** to travel by securing free rides from passing vehicles
**2 :** to be carried or transported by chance or unintentionally ⟨destructive insects *hitchhiking* on ships⟩
*transitive verb*
**:** to solicit and obtain (a free ride) especially in a passing vehicle
— **hitch·hik·er** *noun*

**hitch up** *intransitive verb* (1817)
**:** to hitch a draft animal or team to a vehicle

**hi–tech** *variant of* HIGH-TECH

**¹hith·er** \'hi-thər\ *adverb* [Middle English *hider, hither*, from Old English *hider*; akin to Gothic *hidre* hither, Latin *citra* on this side — more at HE] (before 12th century)
**:** to this place

**²hither** *adjective* (14th century)
**:** being on the near or adjacent side

**hith·er·most** \-‚mōst\ *adjective* (1563)
**:** nearest on this side

**hith·er·to** \-‚tü, ‚hi-thər-'tü\ *adverb* (13th century)
**:** up to this or that time

**hith·er·ward** \'hi-thə(r)-wərd\ *adverb* (before 12th century)
**:** HITHER

**Hit·ler·ism** \'hit-lə-‚ri-zəm\ *noun* (1930)
**:** the principles and policies associated with Hitler
— **Hit·ler·ite** \-‚rīt\ *noun or adjective*

**hit list** *noun* (1972)
**:** a list of persons or programs to be opposed or eliminated; *broadly* : a list of those targeted for special attention or treatment

**hit man** *noun* (1968)
**1 :** a professional assassin who works for a crime syndicate
**2 :** HATCHET MAN

**hit–or–miss** \‚hit-ər-'mis\ *adjective* (1848)
**:** marked by a lack of care, forethought, system, or plan; *also* : HIT-AND-MISS

**hit or miss** *adverb* (1606)
**:** in a hit-or-miss manner : HAPHAZARDLY

**hit parade** *noun* (1929)
**:** a group or listing of the most popular or noteworthy items of a particular kind (as popular songs)

**Hit·tite** \'hi-‚tīt\ *noun* [Hebrew *Ḥittī*, from Hittite *ḥatti*] (1608)
**1 :** a member of a conquering people in Asia Minor and Syria with an empire in the 2d millennium B.C.
**2 :** the extinct Indo-European language of the Hittites — see INDO-EUROPEAN LANGUAGES table
— **Hittite** *adjective*

**HIV** \‚āch-‚ī-'vē\ *noun* (1986)
**:** any of a group of retroviruses and especially HIV-1 that infect and destroy helper T cells of the immune system causing the marked reduction in their numbers that is diagnostic of AIDS — called also *AIDS virus, human immunodeficiency virus*

**¹hive** \'hīv\ *noun* [Middle English, from Old English *hȳf*; perhaps akin to Old Norse *hūfr* ship's hull, Latin *cūpa* tub, Sanskrit *kūpa* cave] (before 12th century)
**1 :** a container for housing honeybees
**2 :** a colony of bees
**3 :** a place swarming with activity
— **hive·less** \-ləs\ *adjective*

**²hive** *verb* **hived; hiv·ing** (14th century)
*intransitive verb*
**1** *of bees* : to enter and take possession of a hive
**2 :** to reside in close association
*transitive verb*
**1 :** to collect into a hive
**2 :** to store up in or as if in a hive

**hive off** (circa 1856)
*intransitive verb*
*chiefly British* : to break away from or as if from a group : become separate
*transitive verb*
*chiefly British* : to make separate: as **a :** to remove from a group ⟨*hive off* the youngest campers into another room⟩ **b :** to assign (as assets or responsibilities) to another **c :** SPIN OFF

**hives** \'hīvz\ *noun plural but singular or plural in construction* [origin unknown] (circa 1500)
**:** URTICARIA

**HIV–1** \-'wən\ *noun* (1986)
**:** a retrovirus that is the most common HIV

**hiz·zon·er** \,hi-'zä-nər\ *noun, often capitalized* [alteration of *his honor*] (circa 1924)
— used as a title for a man holding the office of mayor

**HLA** \,āch-(,)el-'ā\ *noun* [*human leukocyte antigen*] (1968)
**1** : the major histocompatibility complex in humans
**2** : a genetic locus, gene, or antigen of HLA — often used with one or more letters to designate a locus or with letters and a number to designate an allele at the locus or the antigen corresponding to the locus and allele

**HMO** \,āch-(,)em-'ō\ *noun* (1972)
: an organization that provides comprehensive health care to voluntarily enrolled individuals and families in a particular geographic area by member physicians with limited referral to outside specialists and that is financed by fixed periodic payments determined in advance — called also *health maintenance organization*

**ho** \'hō\ *interjection* [Middle English] (15th century)
— used especially to attract attention to something specified ⟨land *ho*⟩

**hoa·gie** *also* **hoa·gy** \'hō-gē\ *noun, plural* **hoagies** [origin unknown] (1955)
: SUBMARINE 2

**¹hoar** \'hōr, 'hȯr\ *adjective* [Middle English *hor*, from Old English *hār*; akin to Old High German *hēr* hoary] (before 12th century)
: HOARY

**²hoar** *noun* [Middle English *hor* hoariness, from *hor*, adjective] (1567)
: FROST 1c

**¹hoard** \'hōrd, 'hȯrd\ *noun* [Middle English *hord*, from Old English; akin to Gothic *huzd* treasure, Old English *hȳdan* to hide] (before 12th century)
: a supply or fund stored up and often hidden away

**²hoard** (before 12th century)
*transitive verb*
**1** : to lay up a hoard of
**2** : to keep (as one's thoughts) to oneself
*intransitive verb*
: to lay up a hoard
— **hoard·er** *noun*

**hoard·ing** \'hōr-diŋ, 'hȯr-\ *noun* [*hourd, hoard* (hoarding)] (circa 1823)
**1** : a temporary board fence put about a building being erected or repaired — called also *hoard*
**2** *British* : BILLBOARD

**hoar·frost** \'hōr-,frȯst, 'hȯr-\ *noun* (14th century)
: FROST 1c

**hoarse** \'hōrs, 'hȯrs\ *adjective* **hoars·er; hoars·est** [Middle English *hos, hors*, probably from (assumed) Old Norse *hārs*; akin to Old English *hās* hoarse, Old High German *heis*] (before 12th century)
**1** : rough or harsh in sound : GRATING ⟨a *hoarse* voice⟩
**2** : having a hoarse voice ⟨shouted himself *hoarse*⟩
— **hoarse·ly** *adverb*
— **hoarse·ness** *noun*

**hoars·en** \'hōr-sᵊn, 'hȯr-\ *verb* **hoars·ened; hoars·en·ing** \'hōrs-niŋ, 'hȯrs-, 'hōr-sə-, 'hȯr-\ (1748)
*transitive verb*
: to make hoarse
*intransitive verb*
: to become hoarse

**hoary** \'hōr-ē, 'hȯr-\ *adjective* **hoar·i·er; -est** (1530)
**1** : gray or white with or as if with age
**2** : extremely old : ANCIENT ⟨*hoary* legends⟩
— **hoar·i·ness** *noun*

**hoa·tzin** \wä(t)-'sēn\ *noun* [Nahuatl *huāctzin* the laughing falcon (*Herpetotheres cachinnans*)] (1661)
: a crested large South American bird (*Opisthocomos hoazin* synonym *O. hoatzin*) with

blue facial skin, red eyes, brown plumage marked with white above, and claws on the first and second digits of the wing when young

hoatzin

**¹hoax** \'hōks\ *transitive verb* [probably contraction of *hocus*] (circa 1796)
: to trick into believing or accepting as genuine something false and often preposterous
*synonym* see DUPE
— **hoax·er** *noun*

**²hoax** *noun* (1808)
**1** : an act intended to trick or dupe : IMPOSTURE
**2** : something accepted or established by fraud or fabrication

**¹hob** \'häb\ *noun* [Middle English *hobbe*, from *Hobbe*, nickname for Robert] (15th century)
**1** *dialect English* : HOBGOBLIN, ELF
**2** : MISCHIEF, TROUBLE — used with *play* and *raise* ⟨always raising *hob*⟩

**²hob** *noun* [origin unknown] (1511)
**1** : a projection at the back or side of a fireplace on which something may be kept warm
**2** : a cutting tool used for cutting the teeth of worm wheels or gears

**³hob** *transitive verb* **hobbed; hob·bing** (1799)
**1** : to cut with a hob
**2** : to furnish with hobnails

**Hobbes·ian** \'häb-zē-ən\ *adjective* (1776)
: of or relating to the English philosopher Thomas Hobbes or Hobbism

**Hob·bism** \'hä-,bi-zəm\ *noun* (1691)
: the philosophical system of Thomas Hobbes; *especially* : the Hobbesian theory that people have a fundamental right to self-preservation and to pursue selfish aims but will relinquish these rights to an absolute monarch in the interest of common safety and happiness
— **Hob·bist** \'hä-bist\ *noun or adjective*

**hob·bit** \'hä-bət\ *noun* [coined by J.R.R. Tolkien] (1937)
: a member of a fictitious peaceful and genial race of small humanlike creatures that dwell underground

**¹hob·ble** \'hä-bəl\ *verb* **hob·bled; hob·bling** \-b(ə-)liŋ\ [Middle English *hoblen;* akin to Middle Dutch *hobbelen* to turn, roll] (14th century)
*intransitive verb*
: to move along unsteadily or with difficulty; *especially* : to limp along
*transitive verb*
**1** : to cause to limp : make lame : CRIPPLE
**2** [probably alteration of *hopple* (to hobble)] **a** : to fasten together the legs of (as a horse) to prevent straying : FETTER **b** : to place under handicap : HAMPER, IMPEDE
— **hob·bler** \-b(ə-)lər\ *noun*

**²hobble** *noun* (1726)
**1** : a hobbling movement
**2** *archaic* : an awkward situation
**3** : something used to hobble an animal

**hob·ble·bush** \'hä-bəl-,bůsh\ *noun* (circa 1818)
: a white-flowered shrubby viburnum (*Viburnum alnifolium*) of northeastern North America having serrate rounded leaves and red berries

**hob·ble·de·hoy** \'hä-bəl-di-,hȯi\ *noun* [origin unknown] (1540)
: an awkward gawky youth

**hobble skirt** *noun* (1911)
: a skirt constricted at the bottom

**¹hob·by** \'hä-bē\ *noun, plural* **hobbies** [Middle English *hoby*, from Middle French *hobé*] (15th century)
: a small Old World falcon (*Falco subbuteo*) formerly trained to catch small birds (as larks)

**²hobby** *noun, plural* **hobbies** [short for *hobbyhorse*] (1816)
: a pursuit outside one's regular occupation engaged in especially for relaxation

— **hob·by·ist** \-bē-ist\ *noun*

**hob·by·horse** \'hä-bē-,hȯrs\ *noun* [*hobby* (small light horse)] (1557)
**1 a** : a figure of a horse fastened about the waist in the morris dance **b** : a dancer wearing this figure
**2** *obsolete* : BUFFOON
**3 a** : a stick having an imitation horse's head at one end that a child pretends to ride **b** : ROCKING HORSE **c** : a toy horse suspended by springs from a frame
**4 a** : a topic to which one constantly reverts **b** : ²HOBBY

**hob·gob·lin** \'häb-,gäb-lən\ *noun* (1530)
**1** : a mischievous goblin
**2** : BOGEY 2, BUGABOO

**hob·nail** \-,nāl\ *noun* [²*hob*] (1592)
: a short large-headed nail for studding shoe soles
— **hob·nailed** \-,nāld\ *adjective*

**hob·nob** \-,näb\ *intransitive verb* **hob·nobbed; hob·nob·bing** [from the obsolete phrase *drink hobnob* (to drink alternately to one another)] (1763)
**1** *archaic* : to drink sociably
**2** : to associate familiarly ◆
— **hob·nob·ber** *noun*

**¹ho·bo** \'hō-(,)bō\ *noun, plural* **hoboes** *also* **hobos** [origin unknown] (1889)
**1** : a migratory worker
**2** : a homeless and usually penniless person who wanders from place to place

**²hobo** *intransitive verb* (1906)
: to live or travel in the manner of a hobo

**Hob·son's choice** \'häb-sənz-\ *noun* [Thomas *Hobson* (died 1631) English liveryman, who required every customer to take the horse nearest the door] (1649)
: an apparently free choice when there is no real alternative

**¹hock** \'häk\ *noun* [Middle English *hoch, hough*, from Old English *hōh* heel; akin to Old Norse *hāsin* hock] (1540)
**1 a** : the tarsal joint or region in the hind limb of a digitigrade quadruped (as the horse) corresponding to the human ankle but elevated and bending backward — see HORSE illustration **b** : a joint of a fowl's leg that corresponds to the hock of a quadruped

◇ **WORD HISTORY**
**hobnob** *Hobnob*, which first appears in Shakespeare in this form, meant in various contexts "one way or another," "hit or miss," or "give and take." This linguistic Siamese twin appears originally to have been a phrase, because from its earliest appearance as *habbe or nhabbe* in 1542, *hob* is commonly separated from *nob* by an intervening word, as *hob or nob, hob a nob,* or *hob and nob*. The form *habnab*, attested earlier and probably older than *hobnob*, may descend from a joining of early Middle English *habbe*, a subjunctive form of *haven* "to have" and *nabbe*, the negative form of *habbe* (from Old English *nabban*, a contraction of *ne* "not" and *habban* "to have"). The original meaning of *habbe (or) nabbe* would thus have been "may he have or may he not have." In the 18th century, people drinking to each other's health began to use *hob and nob* and its variants—first with the verb *drink* and then as a verb itself—to suggest alternation, first one person and then another lifting a glass. To *hob-and-nob* or to *hobnob* with someone began in the 19th century to refer to simple social intercourse, with no implication of drinking.

**2 :** a small cut of meat from either the front or hind leg just above the foot ⟨ham *hocks*⟩

**²hock** *noun, often capitalized* [modification of German *Hochheimer*, from *Hochheim*, Germany] (circa 1625)

*chiefly British* **:** RHINE WINE 1

**³hock** *transitive verb* (1878)

**:** PAWN

**— hock·er** *noun*

**⁴hock** *noun* [Dutch *hok* pen, prison] (1883)

**1 a :** ²PAWN 2 ⟨got his watch out of *hock*⟩ **b :** DEBT 3 ⟨in *hock* to the bank⟩

**2 :** PRISON

**hock·ey** \'hä-kē\ *noun* [perhaps from Middle French *hoquet* shepherd's crook, diminutive of *hoc* hook, of Germanic origin; akin to Old English *hōc* hook] (1527)

**1 :** FIELD HOCKEY

**2 :** ICE HOCKEY

**hock·shop** \'häk-,shäp\ *noun* (1871)

**:** PAWNSHOP

**ho·cus** \'hō-kəs\ *transitive verb* **ho·cussed** *or* **ho·cused; ho·cus·sing** *or* **ho·cus·ing** [obsolete *hocus*, noun, short for *hocus-pocus*] (1675)

**1 :** to perpetrate a trick or hoax on **:** DECEIVE

**2 :** to befuddle often with drugged liquor; *also* **:** DOPE, DRUG ⟨*hocussed* the favorite before the race⟩

**¹ho·cus-po·cus** \,hō-kəs-'pō-kəs\ *noun* [probably from *hocus pocus*, imitation Latin phrase used by jugglers] (1647)

**1 :** SLEIGHT OF HAND

**2 :** nonsense or sham used especially to cloak deception

**²hocus-pocus** *transitive verb* **-cussed** *or* **-cused; -cus·sing** *or* **-cus·ing** (1774)

**:** to play tricks on

**hod** \'häd\ *noun* [probably from Middle Dutch *hodde*; akin to Middle High German *hotte* cradle] (1573)

**1 :** a tray or trough that has a pole handle and that is borne on the shoulder for carrying loads (as of mortar or brick)

**2 :** a coal scuttle

**hod carrier** *noun* (1771)

**:** a laborer employed in carrying supplies to bricklayers, stonemasons, cement finishers, or plasterers on the job

**hodge·podge** \'häj-,päj\ *noun* [alteration of *hotchpotch*] (15th century)

**:** a heterogeneous mixture **:** JUMBLE

**Hodg·kin's disease** \'häj-kinz-\ *noun* [Thomas *Hodgkin* (died 1866) English physician] (1865)

**:** a neoplastic disease that is characterized by progressive enlargement of lymph nodes, spleen, and liver and by progressive anemia

**ho·do·scope** \'hä-də-,skōp, 'hō-\ *noun* [Greek *hodos* road, path + English *-scope*] (circa 1933)

**:** an instrument for tracing the paths of ionizing particles by means of ion counters in close array

**¹hoe** \'hō\ *noun* [Middle English *howe*, from Middle French *houe*, of Germanic origin; akin to Old High German *houwa* mattock, *houwan* to hew — more at HEW] (14th century)

**1 :** any of various implements for tilling, mixing, or raking; *especially* **:** an implement with a thin flat blade on a long handle used especially for cultivating, weeding, or loosening the earth around plants

**2 :** BACKHOE

**²hoe** *verb* **hoed; hoe·ing** (15th century)

*intransitive verb*

**:** to use a hoe **:** work with a hoe

*transitive verb*

**1 :** to weed, cultivate, or thin (a crop) with a hoe

**2 :** to remove (weeds) by hoeing

**3 :** to dress or cultivate (land) by hoeing

**— ho·er** \'hō-(-ə)r\ *noun*

**hoe·cake** \'hō-,kāk\ *noun* (1745)

**:** a small cake made of cornmeal

**hoe·down** \-,daůn\ *noun* (1841)

**1 :** SQUARE DANCE

**2 :** a gathering featuring hoedowns

**¹hog** \'hóg, 'häg\ *noun, plural* **hogs** *also* **hog** [Middle English *hogge*, from Old English *hogg*] (14th century)

**1 :** a domestic swine especially when weighing more than 120 pounds; *broadly* **:** any of various wild and domestic swine

**2** *usually* **hogg** *British* **:** a young unshorn sheep; *also* **:** wool from such a sheep

**3 a :** a selfish, gluttonous, or filthy person **b :** one that uses something to excess ⟨old cars that are gas *hogs*⟩

**²hog** *verb* **hogged; hog·ging** (1769)

*transitive verb*

**1 :** to cut (a horse's mane) short **:** ROACH

**2 :** to cause to arch

**3 :** to take in excess of one's due ⟨*hog* the credit⟩

**4 :** to tear up or shred (as waste wood) into bits by machine

*intransitive verb*

**:** to become curved upward in the middle — used of a ship's bottom or keel

**ho·gan** \'hō-,gän\ *noun* [Navajo *hooghan*] (1871)

**:** a Navajo Indian dwelling usually made of logs and mud with a door traditionally facing east

**hogan**

**hog·back** \'hóg-,bak, 'häg-\ *noun* (1840)

**:** a ridge of land formed by the outcropping edges of tilted strata; *broadly* **:** a ridge with a sharp summit and steeply sloping sides

**hog cholera** *noun* (1859)

**:** a highly infectious often fatal virus disease of swine characterized by fever, loss of appetite, weakness, erythematous lesions especially in light-skinned animals, and severe leukopenia

**hog·fish** \'hóg-,fish, 'häg-\ *noun* (1734)

**:** a large West Indian and Florida wrasse (*Lachnolaimus maximus*) often used for food

**hog·get** \'hä-gət, 'hó-\ *noun* [Middle English, from ¹*hog* + *-et*] (15th century)

*chiefly British* **:** HOG 2

**hog·gish** \'hó-gish, 'hä-\ *adjective* (15th century)

**:** grossly selfish, gluttonous, or filthy

**— hog·gish·ly** *adverb*

**— hog·gish·ness** *noun*

**hog heaven** *noun* (1945)

**:** an extremely satisfying state or situation

**Hog·ma·nay** \,häg-mə-'nā, 'häg-mə-,\ *noun* [origin unknown] (circa 1680)

**1** *Scottish* **:** the eve of New Year's Day

**2** *Scottish* **:** a gift solicited or given at Hogmanay

**hog-nose snake** \'hóg-,nōz-, 'häg-\ *noun* (1736)

**:** any of a genus (*Heterodon*) of rather small harmless stout-bodied North American colubrid snakes with keeled scales and an upturned snout that seldom bite but hiss wildly and often play dead when disturbed — called also *hog-nosed snake, puff adder*

**hog score** *noun* [*hog* (curling stone that fails to reach the score)] (1685)

**:** a line which is marked across a curling rink seven yards from the tee and beyond which a stone must pass or be removed from the ice — called also *hog line*

**hogs·head** \'hógz-,hed, 'hägz-\ *noun* (14th century)

**1 :** a large cask or barrel

**2 :** any of various units of capacity; *especially* **:** a U.S. unit equal to 63 gallons (238 liters)

**hog sucker** *noun* (1877)

**:** a North American sucker (*Hypentelium nigricans*) that is brassy olive marked with brown and is sometimes used for food

**hog-tie** \'hóg-,tī, 'häg-\ *transitive verb* (1894)

**1 :** to tie together the feet of

**2 :** to make helpless

**hog·wash** \-,wósh, -,wäsh\ *noun* (15th century)

**1 :** SWILL 2a, SLOP

**2 :** NONSENSE, BALDERDASH

**hog-wild** \-'wī(ə)ld\ *adjective* (1904)

**:** lacking in restraint of judgment or temper ⟨*hog-wild* enthusiasm⟩ ⟨would go *hog-wild* if unconfined by constitutional limitations —Leo Egan⟩

**¹Ho·hen·stau·fen** \'hō-ən-,shtaů-fən, -,staů-\ *noun* (circa 1895)

**:** a member of the Hohenstaufen family; *especially* **:** a Hohenstaufen monarch

**²Hohenstaufen** *adjective* (1921)

**:** of or relating to a princely German family that reigned over the Holy Roman Empire from 1138–1254 and over Sicily from 1194–1266

**¹Ho·hen·zol·lern** \,hō-ən-'zä-lərn, -'zó-\ *noun* (circa 1895)

**:** a member of the Hohenzollern family; *especially* **:** a Hohenzollern monarch

**²Hohenzollern** *adjective* (1924)

**:** of or relating to a princely German family that reigned in Prussia from 1701–1918 and in Germany from 1871–1918

**Ho·ho·kam** \,hō-hō-'käm\ *noun, plural* **Hohokam** [O'odham (Uto-Aztecan language of southern Arizona) *huhugam*, literally, those who have gone] (1884)

**:** a member of a prehistoric desert culture of the southwestern U.S. centering in the Gila Valley of Arizona and characterized especially by irrigated agriculture

**— Hohokam** *adjective*

**ho-hum** \'hō-'həm\ *adjective* (1969)

**1 :** ROUTINE, DULL ⟨a *ho-hum* existence⟩

**2 :** BORED, INDIFFERENT ⟨a *ho-hum* reaction⟩

**ho hum** *interjection* [imitative] (1924)

**—** used to express weariness, boredom, or disdain

**hoick** \'hóik\ *transitive verb* [probably alteration of ¹*hike*] (1898)

**:** to move or pull abruptly **:** YANK ⟨was *hoicked* out of my job —Vincent Sheean⟩

**hoi pol·loi** \,hói-pə-'lói\ *noun plural* [Greek, the many] (1837)

**:** the general populace **:** MASSES ▨

**hoise** \'hóiz\ *transitive verb* **hoised** *or* **hoist** \'hóist\; **hois·ing** \'hói-ziŋ\ [alteration of *hysse* to hoist, perhaps from Low German *hissen*] (1509)

**:** HOIST

**— hoist with one's own petard** **:** victimized or hurt by one's own scheme

**¹hoist** \'hóist, *chiefly dialect* 'hīst\ *verb* [alteration of *hoise*] (15th century)

*transitive verb*

**1 :** LIFT, RAISE; *especially* **:** to raise into position by or as if by means of tackle

**2 :** DRINK 1 ⟨*hoist* a few beers⟩

*hod 1*

*intransitive verb*
: to become hoisted : RISE
**synonym** see LIFT
— **hoist·er** *noun*
²**hoist** *noun* (1654)
**1** : an act of hoisting : LIFT
**2** : an apparatus for hoisting
**3** : the height of a flag when viewed flying
¹**hoi·ty-toi·ty** \ˌhȯi-tē-ˈtȯi-tē, ˌhī-tē-ˈtī-tē\ *noun* [rhyming compound from English dialect *hoit* to play the fool] (1668)
: thoughtless giddy behavior
²**hoity–toity** *adjective* (1690)
**1** : thoughtlessly silly or frivolous : FLIGHTY
**2** : marked by an air of assumed importance : HIGHFALUTIN
**hoke** \ˈhōk\ *transitive verb* **hoked; hok·ing** [*hokum*] (1925)
: to give an impressive but false value or quality to : FAKE — usually used with *up* ⟨used parts of B-grade movies to *hoke* up a film —Robert Sherrill⟩
**hok·ey** \ˈhō-kē\ *adjective* **hok·i·er; -est** (1927)
**1** : ¹CORNY 3 ⟨the usual *hokey* melodrama⟩
**2** : obviously contrived : PHONY ⟨the plots are tricky but not *hokey* —Cleveland Amory⟩
— **hok·ey·ness** *or* **hok·i·ness** \ˈhō-kē-nəs\ *noun*
— **hok·i·ly** \ˈhō-kə-lē\ *adverb*
**ho·key-po·key** \ˌhō-kē-ˈpō-kē\ *noun* (circa 1878)
**1** : HOCUS-POCUS 2
**2** : ice cream sold by street vendors
**hok·ku** \ˈhȯ-(ˌ)kü\ *noun, plural* **hokku** [Japanese] (1898)
: HAIKU
**ho·kum** \ˈhō-kəm\ *noun* [probably blend of *hocus-pocus* and *bunkum*] (1917)
**1** : a device used (as by showmen) to evoke a desired audience response
**2** : pretentious nonsense : BUNKUM
**hol-** *or* **holo-** *combining form* [Middle English, from Old French, from Latin, from Greek, from *holos* whole — more at SAFE]
**1** : complete : total ⟨*holohedral*⟩
**2** : completely : totally ⟨*holandric*⟩
**hol·an·dric** \hō-ˈlan-drik, hä-\ *adjective* [International Scientific Vocabulary, from *hol-* + *andr-* + *-ic*] (1930)
: transmitted by a gene in the nonhomologous portion of the Y chromosome
**Hol·arc·tic** \hō-ˈlärk-tik, hä-, -ˈlär-tik\ *adjective* (1883)
: of, relating to, or being the biogeographic region including the northern parts of the Old and the New Worlds and comprising the Nearctic and Palearctic regions or subregions
¹**hold** \ˈhōld\ *verb* **held** \ˈheld\; **hold·ing** [Middle English, from Old English *healdan*; akin to Old High German *haltan* to hold, and perhaps to Latin *celer* rapid, Greek *klonos* agitation] (before 12th century)
*transitive verb*
**1 a** : to have possession or ownership of or have at one's disposal ⟨*holds* property worth millions⟩ ⟨the bank *holds* the title to the car⟩ **b** : to have as a privilege or position of responsibility ⟨*hold* a professorship⟩ **c** : to have as a mark of distinction ⟨*holds* the record for the 100-yard dash⟩ ⟨*holds* a PhD⟩
**2** : to keep under restraint ⟨*hold* price increases to a minimum⟩: as **a** : to prevent free expression of ⟨*hold* your temper⟩ **b** : to prevent from some action ⟨ordered the troops to *hold* fire⟩ ⟨the only restraining motive which may *hold* the hand of a tyrant —Thomas Jefferson⟩ **c** : to keep back from use ⟨ask them to *hold* a room for us⟩ ⟨I'll have a hot dog, and *hold* the mustard⟩ **d** : to delay temporarily the handling of ⟨please *hold* all my calls⟩
**3** : to make liable or accountable or bound to an obligation ⟨I'll *hold* you to your promise⟩
**4 a** : to have or maintain in the grasp ⟨*hold* my hand⟩ ⟨this is how you *hold* the racket⟩;

also : AIM, POINT ⟨*held* a gun on them⟩ **b** : to support in a particular position or keep from falling or moving ⟨*hold* me up so I can see⟩ ⟨*hold* the ladder steady⟩ ⟨a clamp *holds* the whole thing together⟩ ⟨*hold* your head up⟩ **c** : to bear the pressure of : SUPPORT ⟨can the roof *hold* all of that weight⟩
**5** : to prevent from leaving or getting away ⟨*hold* the train⟩: as **a** : to avoid emitting or letting out ⟨how long can you *hold* your breath⟩ **b** : to restrain as or as if a captive ⟨the suspect was *held* without bail⟩ ⟨*held* them at gunpoint⟩; *also* : to have strong appeal to ⟨the book *held* my interest throughout⟩
**6 a** : to enclose and keep in a container or within bounds : CONTAIN ⟨the jug *holds* one gallon⟩ ⟨this corral will not *hold* all of the horses⟩ **b** : to be able to consume easily or without undue effect ⟨can't *hold* any more pie⟩; *especially* : to be able to drink (alcoholic beverages) without becoming noticeably drunk ⟨can't *hold* your liquor⟩ **c** : ACCOMMODATE ⟨the restaurant *holds* 400 diners⟩ **d** : to have as a principal or essential feature or attribute ⟨the book *holds* a number of surprises⟩; *also* : to have in store ⟨no one knows what the future *holds*⟩
**7 a** : to have in the mind or express as a judgment, opinion, or belief ⟨I *hold* the view that this is wrong⟩ ⟨*hold* a grudge⟩ ⟨*holding* that it is nobody's business but his —Jack Olsen⟩ — often used with *against* ⟨in America they *hold* everything you say against you —Paul McCartney⟩ **b** : to think of in a particular way : REGARD ⟨were *held* in high esteem⟩
**8 a** : to assemble for and carry on the activity of ⟨*held* a convention⟩ **b** : to cause to be carried on : CONDUCT ⟨will *hold* a seminar⟩ **c** : to produce or sponsor especially as a public exhibition ⟨will *hold* an art show⟩
**9 a** : to maintain occupation, control, or defense of ⟨the troops *held* the ridge⟩; *also* : to resist the offensive efforts or advance of ⟨*held* the opposing team to just two points⟩ **b** : to maintain (a certain condition, situation, or course of action) without change ⟨*hold* a course due east⟩
**10** : to cover (a part of the body) especially for protection ⟨had to *hold* their ears because of the cold⟩
*intransitive verb*
**1 a** : to maintain position : refuse to give ground ⟨the defensive line is *holding*⟩ **b** : to continue in the same way or to the same degree : LAST ⟨hopes the weather will *hold*⟩ — often used with *up*
**2** : to derive right or title — often used with *of* or *from*
**3** : to be or remain valid : APPLY ⟨the rule *holds* in most cases⟩ — often used in the phrase *hold true*
**4** : to maintain a grasp on something : remain fastened to something ⟨the anchor *held* in the rough sea⟩
**5** : to go ahead as one has been going ⟨*held* south for several miles⟩
**6** : to bear or carry oneself ⟨asked him to *hold* still⟩
**7** : to forbear an intended or threatened action : HALT, PAUSE — often used as a command
**8** : to stop counting during a countdown
**9** *slang* : to have illicit drug material in one's possession
**synonym** see CONTAIN
— **hold a candle to** : to qualify for comparison with
— **hold court** : to be the center of attention among friends or admirers
— **hold forth** : to speak at length : EXPATIATE
— **hold hands** : to engage one's hand with another's especially as an expression of affection
— **hold one's horses** : to slow down or stop for a moment — usually used in the imperative

— **hold one's own** : to do well in the face of difficulty or opposition
— **hold one's tongue** : to keep silent
— **hold sway** : to have a dominant influence : RULE
— **hold the bag 1** : to be left empty-handed **2** : to bear alone a responsibility that should have been shared by others
— **hold the fort 1** : to maintain a firm position **2** : to take care of usual affairs ⟨is *holding the fort* until the manager returns⟩
— **hold the line** : to maintain the current position or situation ⟨*hold the line* on prices⟩
— **hold to** : to give firm assent to : adhere to strongly ⟨*holds to* his promise⟩
— **hold to account** : to hold responsible
— **hold water** : to stand up under criticism or analysis
— **hold with** : to agree with or approve of
²**hold** *noun* (14th century)
**1** : STRONGHOLD 1
**2 a** : CONFINEMENT, CUSTODY **b** : PRISON
**3 a** (1) : the act or the manner of holding or grasping : GRIP ⟨released his *hold* on the handle⟩ (2) : a manner of grasping an opponent in wrestling **b** : a nonphysical bond that attaches, restrains, or constrains or by which something is affected, controlled, or dominated ⟨has lost its *hold* on the broad public —Oscar Cargill⟩ : full comprehension ⟨get *hold* of exactly what is happening —J. P. Lyford⟩ **d** : full or immediate control : POSSESSION ⟨get *hold* of yourself⟩ ⟨wants to get *hold* of a road map⟩ **e** : TOUCH 14 — used with *of* ⟨tried to get *hold* of me⟩
**4** : something that may be grasped as a support
**5 a** : FERMATA **b** : the time between the onset and the release of a vocal articulation
**6** : a sudden motionless posture at the end of a dance
**7 a** : an order or indication that something is to be reserved or delayed **b** : a delay in a countdown (as in launching a spacecraft)
— **on hold 1** : into a state of interruption during a telephone call when one party switches to another line without totally disconnecting the other party **2** : into a state or period of indefinite suspension ⟨put our plans *on hold*⟩
³**hold** *noun* [alteration of *hole*] (1591)
**1** : the interior of a ship below decks; *especially* : the cargo deck of a ship
**2** : the cargo compartment of a plane
**hold·all** \ˈhōl-ˌdȯl\ *noun* (1851)
*chiefly British* : an often cloth traveling case or bag
**hold–back** \ˈhōl(d)-ˌbak\ *noun* (1581)
**1** : something that retains or restrains
**2 a** : the act of holding back **b** : something held back
**hold back** (1535)
*transitive verb*
**1** : to hinder the progress or achievement of : RESTRAIN
**2** : to refrain from revealing or parting with
*intransitive verb*
**1** : to keep oneself in check
**2** : to refrain from revealing or parting with something
**hold–down** \ˈhōl-ˌdau̇n\ *noun* (1888)
**1** : something used to fasten an object in place
**2 a** : an act of holding down **b** : LIMIT ⟨agreed to wage-rate *hold-downs*⟩
**hold down** *transitive verb* (1533)
**1** : to keep within limits ⟨*hold* the noise *down*⟩
**2** : to assume the responsibility for ⟨*holding down* two jobs⟩
**hold·en** \ˈhōl-dən\ *archaic past participle of* HOLD
**hold·er** \ˈhōl-dər\ *noun* (14th century)

**1 :** a person that holds: as **a** (1) **:** OWNER (2) **:** TENANT **b :** a person in possession of and legally entitled to receive payment of a bill, note, or check
**2 :** a device that holds ⟨cigarette *holder*⟩
**holder in due course** (1882)
**:** one other than the original recipient who holds a legally effective negotiable instrument (as a promissory note) and who has a right to collect from and no responsibility toward the issuer
**hold·fast** \'hōl(d)-ˌfast\ *noun* (1566)
**1 :** something to which something else may be firmly secured
**2 a :** a part by which a plant clings to a flat surface **b :** an organ by which a parasitic animal attaches itself to its host
¹**hold·ing** \'hōl-diŋ\ *noun* (15th century)
**1 a :** land held especially by a vassal or tenant **b :** property (as land or securities) owned — usually used in plural
**2 :** a ruling of a court especially on an issue of law raised in a case — compare DICTUM
**3 :** something that holds
²**holding** *adjective* (1568)
**1 :** having the effect of holding back or delaying something ⟨the [war] represented a *holding* action against the spread of world Communism —Sidney Offit⟩
**2 :** intended for usually temporary storage or retention ⟨a *holding* tank⟩
**holding company** *noun* (1906)
**:** a company whose primary business is holding a controlling interest in the securities of other companies — compare INVESTMENT COMPANY
**holding pattern** *noun* (circa 1952)
**1 :** the usually oval course flown (as over an airport) by aircraft awaiting clearance especially to land
**2 :** a state of waiting or suspended activity or progress
**hold off** (15th century)
*transitive verb*
**1 :** to block from an objective **:** DELAY
**2 :** to defer action on **:** POSTPONE
**3 :** to fight to a standoff **:** WITHSTAND
*intransitive verb*
**:** to defer or temporarily stop doing something
**hold on** *intransitive verb* (13th century)
**1 a :** to maintain a condition or position **:** PERSIST **b :** to maintain a grasp on something **:** HANG ON
**2 :** to await something (as a telephone connection) desired or requested; *broadly* **:** WAIT
**— hold on to :** to maintain possession of or adherence to
**hold·out** \'hōl-ˌdaut\ *noun* (1945)
**:** one that holds out (as in negotiations); *also* **:** an instance of holding out
**hold out** (1585)
*intransitive verb*
**1 :** to remain unsubdued or operative **:** continue to cope or function
**2 :** to refuse to go along with others in a concerted action or to come to an agreement ⟨*holding out* for a shorter workweek⟩
*transitive verb*
**1 :** to present as something realizable **:** PROFFER
**2 :** to represent to be
**— hold out on :** to withhold something (as information) from
**hold·over** \'hōl-ˌdō-vər\ *noun* (1893)
**:** one that is held over
**hold over** (1647)
*intransitive verb*
**:** to continue (as in office) for a prolonged period
*transitive verb*
**1 a :** POSTPONE, DEFER **b :** to retain in a condition or position from an earlier period
**2 :** to prolong the engagement of ⟨the film was *held over* another week⟩
**hold·up** \'hōl-ˌdəp\ *noun* (1837)
**1 :** DELAY

**2 :** a robbery carried out at gunpoint
**hold up** (1851)
*transitive verb*
**1 :** to rob at gunpoint
**2 :** DELAY, IMPEDE
**3 :** to call attention to **:** single out ⟨his work was *held up* to ridicule⟩ ⟨*hold* this *up* as perfection —*Times Literary Supplement*⟩
*intransitive verb*
**:** to continue in the same condition without failing or losing effectiveness or force ⟨you seem to be *holding up* under the strain⟩
¹**hole** \'hōl\ *noun* [Middle English, from Old English *hol* (from neuter of *hol*, adjective, hollow) & *holh*; akin to Old High German *hol*, adjective, hollow; perhaps akin to Old English *helan* to conceal — more at HELL] (before 12th century)
**1 a :** an opening through something **:** PERFORATION ⟨have a *hole* in my coat⟩ **b :** an area where something is missing **:** GAP: as (1) **:** a serious discrepancy **:** FLAW, WEAKNESS ⟨there are *holes* in your logic⟩ (2) **:** an opening in a defensive formation; *especially* **:** the area of a baseball field between the positions of shortstop and third baseman (3) **:** a defect in a crystal (as of a semiconductor) that is due to an electron's having left its normal position in one of the crystal bonds and that is equivalent in many respects to a positively charged particle
**2 :** a hollowed-out place: as **a :** a cave, pit, or well in the ground **b :** BURROW **c :** an unusually deep place in a body of water
**3 :** a wretched or dreary place
**4 a :** a shallow cylindrical hole in the putting green of a golf course into which the ball is played **b :** a part of the golf course from tee to putting green ⟨just beginning play on the third *hole*⟩; *also* **:** the play on such a hole as a unit of scoring ⟨won the *hole* by two strokes⟩
**5 a :** an awkward position or circumstance **:** FIX ⟨got the rebels out of a *hole* at the battle —Kenneth Roberts⟩ **b :** a position of owing or losing money ⟨$10 million in the *hole*⟩ ⟨raising money to get out of the *hole*⟩
**— in the hole 1 :** having a score below zero **2 :** at a disadvantage
²**hole** *verb* **holed; hol·ing** (before 12th century)
*transitive verb*
**1 :** to make a hole in
**2 :** to drive or hit into a hole
*intransitive verb*
**:** to make a hole in something
**hole–and–corner** *adjective* (1835)
**1 :** being or carried on in a place away from public view **:** CLANDESTINE
**2 :** INSIGNIFICANT
**hole card** *noun* (1908)
**:** a card in stud poker that is properly dealt facedown and that the holder need not expose before the showdown
**hole in one** (1925)
**:** ACE 4
**hole–in–the–wall** *noun, plural* **holes–in–the–wall** (1856)
**:** a small and often unpretentious out-of-the-way place (as a restaurant)
**hole out** *intransitive verb* (1857)
**:** to play one's ball into the hole in golf
**hole up** (1875)
*intransitive verb*
**:** to take refuge or shelter in or as if in a hole or cave
*transitive verb*
**:** to place in or as if in a refuge or hiding place
**hol·ey** \'hō-lē\ *adjective* (13th century)
**:** having holes
¹**hol·i·day** \'hä-lə-ˌdā, *British usually* 'hä-lə-dē\ *noun* [Middle English, from Old English *hāligdæg*, from *hālig* holy + *dæg* day] (before 12th century)
**1 :** HOLY DAY

**2 :** a day on which one is exempt from work; *specifically* **:** a day marked by a general suspension of work in commemoration of an event
**3** *chiefly British* **:** a period of relaxation **:** VACATION — often used in the phrase *on holiday*; often used in plural
²**holiday** *intransitive verb* (1869)
**:** to take or spend a holiday especially in travel or at a resort
**— hol·i·day·er** *noun*
**hol·i·day·mak·er** \'hä-lə-dē-ˌmā-kər, 'hä-lə-ˌdā-\ *noun* (1836)
*chiefly British* **:** VACATIONER
**hol·i·days** \-lə-ˌdāz, *British usually* -lə-ˌdēz\ *adverb* (circa 1961)
**:** on holidays repeatedly **:** on any holiday
**ho·li·er–than–thou** \ˌhō-lē-ər-thən-'thau\ *adjective* (1859)
**:** marked by an air of superior piety or morality
¹**ho·li·ness** \'hō-lē-nəs\ *noun* (before 12th century)
**1 :** the quality or state of being holy — used as a title for various high religious dignitaries ⟨his *holiness* the pope⟩
**2 :** SANCTIFICATION 2
²**holiness** *adjective, often capitalized* (1888)
**:** emphasizing the doctrine of the second blessing; *specifically* **:** of or relating to a perfectionist movement arising in U.S. Protestantism in the late 19th century
**ho·lism** \'hō-ˌli-zəm\ *noun* [*hol-* + *-ism*] (1926)
**1 :** a theory that the universe and especially living nature is correctly seen in terms of interacting wholes (as of living organisms) that are more than the mere sum of elementary particles
**2 :** a holistic study or method of treatment
**— hol·ist** \'hō-list\ *noun*
**ho·lis·tic** \hō-'lis-tik\ *adjective* (1926)
**1 :** of or relating to holism
**2 :** relating to or concerned with wholes or with complete systems rather than with the analysis of, treatment of, or dissection into parts ⟨*holistic* medicine attempts to treat both the mind and the body⟩ ⟨*holistic* ecology views man and the environment as a single system⟩
**— ho·lis·ti·cal·ly** \-ti-k(ə-)lē\ *adverb*
**hol·land** \'hä-lənd\ *noun, often capitalized* [Middle English *holand*, from *Holand*, county in the Netherlands, from Middle Dutch *Holland*] (14th century)
**:** a cotton or linen fabric in plain weave usually heavily sized or glazed and used for window shades, bookbinding, and clothing
**hol·lan·daise** \ˌhä-lən-'dāz\ *noun* [French *sauce hollandaise*, literally, Dutch sauce] (1907)
**:** a rich sauce made basically of butter, egg yolks, and lemon juice or vinegar
**Hol·lands** \'hä-lən(d)z\ *noun* [Dutch *hollandsch*, from *hollandsch genever* Dutch gin] (1788)
**:** gin made in the Netherlands — called also *Holland gin*
¹**hol·ler** \'hä-lər\ *verb* **hol·lered; hol·ler·ing** \'häl-riŋ, 'hä-lə-\ [alteration of *hollo*] (1699)
*intransitive verb*
**1 :** to cry out (as to attract attention or in pain) **:** SHOUT
**2 :** GRIPE, COMPLAIN
*transitive verb*
**:** to call out (a word or phrase)
²**holler** *noun* (1825)
**1 :** SHOUT, CRY
**2 :** COMPLAINT
**3 :** a freely improvised work song of black Americans ⟨field *hollers*⟩
³**holler** *chiefly dialect variant of* HOLLOW
**Hol·ler·ith card** \'hä-lə-rith-\ *noun* [Herman *Hollerith* (died 1929) American engineer] (1946)
**:** PUNCHED CARD

**Hollerith code** *noun* (1962)
: a system for encoding alphanumeric information on punched cards

**¹hol·lo** *also* **hol·loa** \'hä-(‚)lō\ *or* **hol·la** \'hä-lə\ (14th century)
*intransitive verb*
: to cry hollo : HOLLER
*transitive verb*
**1** : to call or cry hollo to
**2** : to utter loudly : HOLLER

**²hollo** *also* **holloa** *or* **holla** *noun, plural* **hollos** *also* **holloas** *or* **hollas** (15th century)
: an exclamation or call of hollo

**³hol·lo** \hä-'lō, hə-; 'hä-(‚)\ *also* **hol·loa** \hä-'lō, hə-\ *or* **hol·la** \hə-'lä, 'hä-(‚)\ *interjection* [origin unknown] (1588)
**1** — used to attract attention (as when a fox is spied during a fox hunt)
**2** — used as a call of encouragement or jubilation

**¹hollow** *noun* (before 12th century)
**1** : an unfilled space : CAVITY, HOLE
**2** : a depressed or low part of a surface; *especially* : a small valley or basin

**²hol·low** \'hä-(‚)lō\ *adjective* **hol·low·er** \'hä-lə-wər\; **hol·low·est** \-lə-wəst\ [Middle English *holw, holh*, from *holh* hole, den, from Old English *holh* hole, hollow — more at HOLE] (13th century)
**1** : having an indentation or inward curve : CONCAVE, SUNKEN
**2** : having a cavity within ⟨*hollow* tree⟩
**3** : lacking in real value, sincerity, or substance : FALSE, MEANINGLESS ⟨*hollow* promises⟩ ⟨a victory over a weakling is *hollow* and without triumph —Ernest Beaglehole⟩
**4** : reverberating like a sound made in or by beating on a large empty enclosure : MUFFLED
**synonym** see VAIN
— **hol·low·ly** \'hä-lō-lē, -lə-lē\ *adverb*
— **hol·low·ness** *noun*

**³hollow** (15th century)
*transitive verb*
**1** : to make hollow
**2** : to form by a hollowing action — usually used with *out* ⟨rain barrels *hollowed* out from trees —Robert Shaplen⟩
*intransitive verb*
: to become hollow

**⁴hollow** *adverb* (1601)
**1** : so as to have a hollow sound
**2** : COMPLETELY, THOROUGHLY ⟨an ongoing story that has the old cowboy-and-Indians genre beat *hollow* —Barbara Bannon⟩ — often used with *all*

**hol·low·ware** *or* **hol·lo·ware** \'hä-(‚)lō-‚war, -‚wer\ *noun* (1682)
: vessels (as bowls, cups, or vases) usually of pottery, glass, or metal that have a significant depth and volume — compare FLATWARE

**hol·ly** \'hä-lē\ *noun, plural* **hollies** [Middle English *holin, holly*, from Old English *holen*; akin to Old High German *hulis* holly, Middle Irish *cuilenn*] (before 12th century)
**1** : any of a genus (*Ilex* of the family Aquifoliaceae, the holly family) of trees and shrubs; *especially* : either of two (*I. opaca* of the eastern U.S. and *I. aquifolium* of Eurasia) with spiny-margined evergreen leaves and usually red berries often used for Christmas decorations
**2** : the foliage or branches of the holly

**hol·ly·hock** \'hä-lē-‚häk, -‚hòk\ *noun* [Middle English *holihoc* marshmallow, from *holi* holy + *hoc* mallow, from Old English] (1548)
: a tall widely cultivated perennial Chinese herb (*Alcea rosea* synonym *Althaea rosea*) of the mallow family with large coarse rounded leaves and tall spikes of showy flowers

**hollyhock**

**¹Hol·ly·wood** \'hä-lē-‚wùd\ *noun* [*Hollywood*, district of Los Angeles, Calif.] (1923)
: the American motion-picture industry
— **Hol·ly·wood·ish** \-‚wù-dish\ *adjective*

**²Hollywood** *adjective* (1935)
: of or characteristic of people in the American motion-picture industry ⟨*Hollywood* lifestyle⟩

**Hollywood bed** *noun* (1947)
: a mattress on a box spring supported by low legs and often having an upholstered headboard

**holm** \'hō(l)m\ *noun* [Middle English, from Old English, from Old Norse *hōlmr*; akin to Old English *hyll* hill] (before 12th century)
*British* : a small inland or inshore island; *also* : BOTTOMS

**Holmes·ian** \'hōm-zē-ən *also* 'hōlm-\ *adjective* [Sherlock *Holmes*, detective in stories by Sir Arthur Conan Doyle] (1929)
: of, characteristic of, or suggestive of the detective Sherlock Holmes

**hol·mi·um** \'hō(l)-mē-əm\ *noun* [New Latin, from *Holmia* Stockholm, Sweden] (1879)
: a metallic element of the rare-earth group that occurs with yttrium and forms highly magnetic compounds — see ELEMENT table

**holm oak** *noun* (1597)
: a southern European evergreen oak (*Quercus ilex*)

**holo-** — see HOL-

**ho·lo·blas·tic** \‚hō-lə-'blas-tik, ‚hä-\ *adjective* [International Scientific Vocabulary] (1872)
: characterized by cleavage planes that divide the whole egg into distinct and separate though coherent blastomeres — compare MEROBLASTIC

**ho·lo·caust** \'hō-lə-‚kost, 'hä- *also* -‚käst *or* 'hò-lə-‚kòst\ *noun* [Middle English, from Old French *holocauste*, from Late Latin *holocaustum*, from Greek *holokauston*, from neuter of *holokaustos* burnt whole, from *hol-* + *kaustos* burnt, from *kaiein* to burn — more at CAUSTIC] (13th century)
**1** : a sacrifice consumed by fire
**2** : a thorough destruction involving extensive loss of life especially through fire ⟨a nuclear *holocaust*⟩
**3 a** *often capitalized* : the mass slaughter of European civilians and especially Jews by the Nazis during World War II — usually used with *the* **b** : a mass slaughter of people; *especially* : GENOCIDE ◆

**Ho·lo·cene** \'hō-lə-‚sēn, 'hä-\ *adjective* [International Scientific Vocabulary] (1897)
: of, relating to, or being the present or post-Pleistocene geologic epoch — see GEOLOGIC TIME table
— **Holocene** *noun*

**ho·lo·crine** \-krən, -‚krīn, -‚krēn\ *adjective* [International Scientific Vocabulary *hol-* + Greek *krinein* to separate — more at CERTAIN] (circa 1905)
: producing or being a secretion resulting from lysis of secretory cells ⟨*holocrine* gland⟩

**ho·lo·en·zyme** \‚hō-lō-'en-‚zīm\ *noun* [International Scientific Vocabulary] (1943)
: a catalytically active enzyme consisting of an apoenzyme combined with its cofactor

**Ho·lo·fer·nes** \‚hä-lə-'fər-(‚)nēz, ‚hō-\ *noun* [Late Latin, from Greek *Holophernēs*]
: a general of Nebuchadnezzar's who led an Assyrian army against Israel and was beheaded in his sleep by Judith

**ho·lo·gram** \'hō-lə-‚gram, 'hä-\ *noun* (1949)
: a three-dimensional image reproduced from a pattern of interference produced by a split coherent beam of radiation (as a laser); *also* : the pattern of interference itself

**ho·lo·graph** \'hō-lə-‚graf, 'hä-\ *noun* [Late Latin *holographus*, from Late Greek *holographos*, from Greek *hol-* + *graphein* to write — more at CARVE] (circa 1623)
: a document wholly in the handwriting of its author; *also* : the handwriting itself ⟨a letter in the president's *holograph*⟩
— **holograph** *or* **ho·lo·graph·ic** \‚hō-lə-'gra-fik, ‚hä-\ *adjective*

**ho·log·ra·phy** \hō-'lä-grə-fē\ *noun* (1964)
: the art or process of making or using a hologram
— **ho·lo·graph** \'hō-lə-‚graf, 'hä-\ *transitive verb*
— **ho·log·ra·pher** \hō-'lä-grə-fər\ *noun*
— **ho·lo·graph·ic** \‚hō-lə-'gra-fik, ‚hä-\ *adjective*
— **ho·lo·graph·i·cal·ly** \-fi-k(ə-)lē\ *adverb*

**ho·lo·he·dral** \‚hō-lə-'hē-drəl, ‚hä-\ *adjective* (1837)
*of a crystal* : having all the faces required by complete symmetry — compare HEMIHEDRAL, TETARTOHEDRAL

**ho·lo·me·tab·o·lous** \‚hō-lō-mə-'ta-bə-ləs, ‚hä-\ *adjective* (1870)
: characterized by complete metamorphosis ⟨*holometabolous* insects⟩ — compare HEMIMETABOLOUS
— **ho·lo·me·tab·o·lism** \-‚li-zəm\ *noun*

**ho·lo·phras·tic** \‚hō-lə-'fras-tik, ‚hä-\ *adjective* [International Scientific Vocabulary *hol-* + -*phrastic* (from Greek *phrazein* to point out, declare)] (1860)
: expressing a complex of ideas in a single word or in a fixed phrase

**ho·lo·phyt·ic** \-'fi-tik\ *adjective* (1885)
: obtaining food after the manner of a green plant by photosynthetic activity

**ho·lo·thu·ri·an** \-'thúr-ē-ən, -'thyúr-\ *noun* [ultimately from Greek *holothourion* water polyp] (circa 1842)
: SEA CUCUMBER
— **holothurian** *adjective*

**ho·lo·type** \'hō-lə-‚tīp, 'hä-\ *noun* (1897)
**1** : the single specimen designated by an author as the type of a species or lesser taxon at the time of establishing the group
**2** : the type of a species or lesser taxon designated at a date later than that of establishing a group or by another person than the author of the taxon
— **ho·lo·typ·ic** \‚hō-lə-'ti-pik, ‚hä-\ *adjective*

**ho·lo·zo·ic** \‚hō-lə-'zō-ik, ‚hä-\ *adjective* (1885)
: characterized by food procurement after the manner of most animals by the ingestion of

◇ **WORD HISTORY**
**holocaust** The ancient Greek word *holokauston* meant literally "something completely burnt up." In the Septuagint, the Greek translation of Jewish scripture dating from the early centuries B.C., it renders the Hebrew word *kālil* "sacrifice consumed wholly on the altar." Borrowed from Greek through Latin, the English word *holocaust* by the 18th century had begun to lose as its primary sense "burnt offering" and to refer more generally to a destructive fire or any massive catastrophe, without implying sacrifice. It was the "catastrophe" sense of *holocaust* that Jewish historians writing in English adopted in the late 1950's when they used the word as a proper noun to refer to a single event, the Nazi slaughter of European Jews during World War II, in part to render Modern Hebrew *hurban* (literally, "destruction") or *shoa* (literally, "disaster, catastrophe"). *Holocaust* has in recent decades been applied to the mass murder of civilians at other times in history, and on occasion is virtually synonymous with *genocide*.

complex organic matter **:** HETEROTROPHIC ⟨*ho-lozoic* nutrition⟩

**holp** \'hō(l)p\ *chiefly dialect past of* HELP

**hol·pen** \'hō(l)-pən\ *chiefly dialect past participle of* HELP

**hols** \'hälz\ *noun plural* [short for *holidays*] (1905)
*British* **:** VACATION 2

**Hol·stein** \'hōl-ˌstēn, -ˌstīn\ *noun* [short for *Holstein-Friesian*] (1865)
**:** any of a breed of large usually black-and-white dairy cattle originally from northern Holland and Friesland that produce large quantities of comparatively low-fat milk

**Hol·stein–Frie·sian** \-'frē-zhən\ *noun* [*Holstein*, Germany, its later locality + *Friesian* (variant of *Frisian*)] (1889)
**:** HOLSTEIN

**hol·ster** \'hōl-stər\ *noun* [Dutch; akin to Old English *heolstor* cover, *helan* to conceal — more at HELL] (1663)
**:** a leather or fabric case for carrying a firearm on the person (as on the hip or chest), on a saddle, or in a vehicle

**holt** \'hōlt\ *noun* [Middle English, from Old English; akin to Old High German *holz* wood, Greek *klados* twig] (before 12th century)
*archaic* **:** a small woods **:** COPPICE

**ho·lus-bo·lus** \ˌhō-ləs-'bō-ləs\ *adverb* [probably reduplication of *bolus*] (1857)
**:** all at once

**ho·ly** \'hō-lē\ *adjective* **ho·li·er; -est** [Middle English, from Old English *hālig;* akin to Old English *hāl* whole — more at WHOLE] (before 12th century)
**1 :** exalted or worthy of complete devotion as one perfect in goodness and righteousness
**2 :** DIVINE ⟨for the Lord our God is *holy* —Psalms 99:9 (Authorized Version)⟩
**3 :** devoted entirely to the deity or the work of the deity ⟨a *holy* temple⟩ ⟨*holy* prophets⟩
**4 a :** having a divine quality ⟨*holy* love⟩ **b :** venerated as or as if sacred ⟨*holy* scripture⟩ ⟨a *holy* relic⟩ ⟨lampooning the *holy* conventions of playwriting —William Zinsser⟩
**5 —** used as an intensive ⟨this is a *holy* mess⟩ ⟨he was a *holy* terror when he drank —Thomas Wolfe⟩; often used in combination as a mild oath ⟨*holy* smoke⟩
**— ho·li·ly** \-lə-lē\ *adverb*

**holy city** *noun* (14th century)
**:** a city that is the center of religious worship and traditions

**Holy Communion** *noun* (1548)
**:** COMMUNION 2a

**holy day** *noun* (before 12th century)
**:** a day set aside for special religious observance

**holy day of obligation** (1909)
**:** a feast on which Roman Catholics are duty-bound to attend mass

**Holy Father** *noun* (15th century)
**:** POPE 1

**Holy Ghost** *noun* (before 12th century)
**:** the third person of the Trinity **:** HOLY SPIRIT

**Holy Grail** *noun* (1590)
**:** GRAIL

**Holy Joe** \'hō-lē-'jō\ *noun* (circa 1874)
*slang* **:** PARSON, CHAPLAIN

**Holy Office** *noun* (circa 1741)
**:** a congregation of the curia charged with protecting faith and morals

**holy of holies** [translation of Late Latin *sanctum sanctorum*, translation of Hebrew *qōdhesh haq-qŏdhāshīm*] (1641)
**:** the innermost and most sacred chamber of the Jewish tabernacle and temple

**holy oil** *noun* (14th century)
**:** olive oil blessed by a bishop for use in a sacrament or sacramental

**holy order** *noun, often H&O capitalized* (14th century)
**1 a :** MAJOR ORDER — usually used in plural **b :** one of the orders of the ministry in the Anglican or Episcopal church

**2 :** the rite or sacrament of ordination — usually used in plural

**Holy Roller** *noun* (1842)
**:** a member of one of the Protestant sects whose worship meetings are characterized by spontaneous expressions of emotional excitement — often taken to be offensive

**Holy Roman Empire** *noun* (1728)
**:** an empire consisting primarily of a loose confederation of German and Italian territories under the suzerainty of an emperor and existing from the 9th or 10th century to 1806

**Holy Saturday** *noun* (14th century)
**:** the Saturday before Easter

**Holy See** *noun* (1765)
**:** the see of the pope

**Holy Spirit** *noun* (14th century)
**:** the third person of the Christian Trinity

**ho·ly·stone** \'hō-lē-ˌstōn\ *noun* (circa 1823)
**:** a soft sandstone used to scrub a ship's decks
**— holystone** *transitive verb*

**Holy Synod** *noun* (1768)
**:** the governing body of a national Eastern church

**Holy Thursday** *noun* (13th century)
**1 :** ASCENSION DAY
**2 :** MAUNDY THURSDAY

**holy war** *noun* (1691)
**:** a war waged by religious partisans to propagate or defend their faith

**holy water** *noun* (before 12th century)
**:** water blessed by a priest and used as a purifying sacramental

**Holy Week** *noun* (1710)
**:** the week before Easter during which the last days of Christ's life are commemorated

**holy writ** *noun, often H&W capitalized* (before 12th century)
**1 :** BIBLE 1
**2 :** a writing or utterance having unquestionable authority ⟨its financial precepts were not necessarily *Holy Writ* —Herbert Stein⟩

**Holy Year** *noun* (1900)
**:** a Roman Catholic jubilee year

**hom-** *or* **homo-** *combining form* [Latin, from Greek, from *homos* — more at SAME]
**1 :** one and the same **:** similar **:** alike ⟨*homo*graph⟩ ⟨*homo*sporous⟩
**2 :** homosexual ⟨*homo*phobia⟩

**hom·age** \'ä-mij, 'hä-\ *noun* [Middle English, from Old French *hommage*, from *homme* man, vassal, from Latin *homin-, homo* human being; akin to Old English *guma* human being, Latin *humus* earth — more at HUMBLE] (14th century)
**1 a :** a feudal ceremony by which a man acknowledges himself the vassal of a lord **b :** the relationship between a feudal lord and his vassal **c :** an act done or payment made in meeting the obligations of vassalage
**2 a :** expression of high regard **:** RESPECT — often used with *pay* **b :** something that shows respect or attests to the worth or influence of another **:** TRIBUTE ⟨his long life filled with international *homages* to his unique musical talent —*People*⟩
**synonym** see HONOR
**usage** see HUMOR

**hom·ag·er** \'ä-mi-jər, 'hä-\ *noun* (15th century)
**:** VASSAL

**hom·bre** \'äm-brā, 'əm-, 'ōm-, -ˌbrē\ *noun* [Spanish, man, from Latin *homin-, homo*] (1846)
**:** GUY, FELLOW

**hom·burg** \'häm-ˌbərg\ *noun* [*Bad Homburg*, Germany] (1894)
**:** a man's felt hat with a stiff curled brim and a high crown creased lengthwise

**¹home** \'hōm\ *noun* [Middle English *hom*, from Old English *hām* village, home;

homburg

akin to Old High German *heim* home] (before 12th century)
**1 a :** one's place of residence **:** DOMICILE **b :** HOUSE
**2 :** the social unit formed by a family living together
**3 a :** a familiar or usual setting **:** congenial environment; *also* **:** the focus of one's domestic attention ⟨*home* is where the heart is⟩ **b :** HABITAT
**4 a :** a place of origin ⟨salmon returning to their *home* to spawn⟩; *also* **:** one's own country ⟨having troubles at *home* and abroad⟩ **b :** HEADQUARTERS 2 ⟨*home* of the dance company⟩
**5 :** an establishment providing residence and care for people with special needs ⟨*homes* for the elderly⟩ ⟨a *home* for unwed mothers⟩
**6 :** the objective in various games; *especially* **:** HOME PLATE
**— at home 1 :** relaxed and comfortable **:** at ease ⟨felt completely *at home* on the stage⟩ **2 :** in harmony with the surroundings **3 :** on familiar ground **:** KNOWLEDGEABLE ⟨teachers *at home* in their subject fields⟩

**²home** *adverb* (before 12th century)
**1 :** to, from, or at one's home ⟨go *home*⟩ ⟨left *home* at the age of 12⟩
**2 a :** to a final, closed, or ultimate position ⟨drive a nail *home*⟩ **b :** to or at an ultimate objective (as a goal or finish line)
**3 :** to a vital sensitive core ⟨the truth struck *home*⟩
**— home free :** out of jeopardy **:** in a comfortable position with respect to some objective

**³home** *adjective* (1552)
**1 :** of, relating to, or being a home, place of origin, or base of operations ⟨*home* office⟩ ⟨checkers in position on their *home* squares⟩
**2 :** prepared, done, or designed for use in a home ⟨*home* remedies⟩ ⟨*home* cooking⟩ ⟨a *home* videotape system⟩
**3 :** operating or occurring in a home area ⟨the *home* team⟩ ⟨*home* games⟩

**⁴home** *verb* **homed; hom·ing** (1765)
*intransitive verb*
**1 :** to go or return home
**2** *of an animal* **:** to return accurately to one's home or natal area from a distance
**3 :** to proceed to or toward a source of radiated energy used as a guide ⟨missiles *home* in on radar⟩
**4 :** to proceed or direct attention toward an objective ⟨science is *homing* in on the mysterious human process —Sam Glucksberg⟩
*transitive verb*
**:** to send to or provide with a home

**home·body** \'hōm-ˌbä-dē\ *noun* (1821)
**:** one whose life centers in the home

**¹home·bound** \'hōm-ˌbaund\ *adjective* [*home* + *¹bound*] (circa 1625)
**:** going homeward **:** bound for home ⟨*homebound* travelers⟩

**²homebound** *adjective* [*home* + *⁵bound*] (1882)
**:** confined to the home

**home·boy** \'hōm-ˌboi\ *noun* (1927)
**1 :** a boy or man from one's neighborhood, hometown, or region
**2 :** a fellow member of a youth gang

**home·bred** \'hōm-'bred\ *adjective* (1587)
**:** produced at home **:** INDIGENOUS

**home brew** *noun* (1853)
**:** an alcoholic beverage (as beer) made at home

**home·built** \'hōm-'bilt\ *adjective* (1676)
**:** HOMEMADE 1

**home·com·ing** \'hōm-ˌkə-miŋ\ *noun* (14th century)
**1 :** a return home
**2 :** the return of a group of people usually on a special occasion to a place formerly frequented or regarded as home; *especially* **:** an annual celebration for alumni at a college or university

**home computer** *noun* (1976)

: a small inexpensive microcomputer

**home economics** *noun plural but singular or plural in construction* (1899)
: the theory and practice of homemaking — called also *home ec* \-'ek\
— **home economist** *noun*

**home fries** *noun plural* (1951)
: potatoes that have usually been parboiled, sliced, and then fried — called also *home fried potatoes*

**home front** *noun* (1919)
: the sphere of civilian activity in war

**home-grown** \'hōm-'grōn\ *adjective* (1827)
**1** : grown or produced at home or in a particular local area ⟨*homegrown* vegetables⟩ ⟨*homegrown* films⟩
**2** : native to or characteristic of a particular area ⟨the festival will feature *homegrown* artists⟩

**home-land** \-,land *also* -lənd\ *noun* (1670)
**1** : native land : FATHERLAND
**2** : a state or area set aside to be a state for a people of a particular national, cultural, or racial origin; *especially* : BANTUSTAN

**home-less** \-ləs\ *adjective* (1615)
: having no home or permanent place of residence
— **home-less-ness** *noun*

**home-like** \'hōm-,līk\ *adjective* (1817)
: characteristic of a home

**home-ly** \'hōm-lē\ *adjective* **home-li-er; -est** (14th century)
**1** : suggestive or characteristic of a home
**2** : being something familiar with which one is at home ⟨satisfy themselves with houses, furniture, books and clothes that were worn and *homely* and friendly to the touch —Brendan Gill⟩
**3 a** : unaffectedly natural : SIMPLE **b** : not elaborate or complex ⟨*homely* virtues⟩
**4** : plain or unattractive in appearance
— **home-li-ness** *noun*

**home-made** \'hō(m)-'mād\ *adjective* (circa 1659)
**1** : made in the home, on the premises, or by one's own efforts
**2** : of domestic manufacture

**home-mak-er** \'hōm-,mā-kər\ *noun* (1876)
: one who manages a household especially as a wife and mother
— **home-mak-ing** \-kiŋ\ *noun or adjective*

**homeo-** *or* **homoeo-** *or* **homoeo-** *also* **homoio-** *combining form* [Latin & Greek; Latin *homoeo-*, from Greek *homoi-*, *homoio-*, from *homoios*, from *homos* same — more at SAME]
**1** : like : similar ⟨*homeostasis*⟩ ⟨*homeothermic*⟩
**2** : homeotic ⟨*homeobox*⟩

**ho-meo-box** \'hō-mē-ə-,bäks\ *noun* (1984)
: a short usually highly conserved DNA sequence in various eukaryotic genes (as many homeotic genes) that codes for a peptide which may be a DNA-binding protein

**ho-meo-mor-phism** \,hō-mē-ə-'mor-,fi-zəm\ *noun* [International Scientific Vocabulary] (1854)
: a function that is a one-to-one mapping between sets such that both the function and its inverse are continuous and that in topology exists for geometric figures which can be transformed one into the other by an elastic deformation
— **ho-meo-mor-phic** \-'mor-fik\ *adjective*

**ho-meo-path-ic** \,hō-mē-ə-'pa-thik\ *adjective* (1830)
**1** : of or relating to homeopathy
**2** : of a diluted or insipid nature ⟨a *homeopathic* abolitionist —W. A. White⟩
— **ho-meo-path-i-cal-ly** \-thi-k(ə-)lē\ *adverb*

**ho-me-op-a-thy** \,hō-mē-'ä-pə-thē, ,hä-\ *noun* [German *Homöopathie*, from *homöo-* homeo- + -*pathie* -pathy] (1826)
: a system of medical practice that treats a disease especially by the administration of minute doses of a remedy that would in

healthy persons produce symptoms similar to those of the disease
— **ho-meo-path** \'hō-mē-ə-,path\ *noun*

**ho-meo-sta-sis** \,hō-mē-ō-'stā-səs\ *noun* [New Latin] (1926)
: a relatively stable state of equilibrium or a tendency toward such a state between the different but interdependent elements or groups of elements of an organism, population, or group
— **ho-meo-stat-ic** \-'sta-tik\ *adjective*

**ho-meo-ther-mic** \-'thər-mik\ *adjective* (1870)
: WARM-BLOODED 1
— **ho-meo-therm** \'hō-mē-ō-,thərm\ *noun*
— **ho-meo-ther-my** \-,thər-mē\ *noun*

**ho-me-o-tic** \,hō-mē-'ä-tik, -hä-\ *adjective* [from *homeosis, homoeosis* a shift in structural development, from Greek *homoiōsis* assimilation, resemblance, from *homoioun* to make like, from *homoios*] (circa 1903)
: relating to or being a gene producing a usually major shift in structural development

**home plate** *noun* (1875)
: a 5-sided rubber slab at one corner of a baseball diamond at which a batter stands when batting and which must be touched by a base runner in order to score

**home-port** \'hōm-,pōrt, -,port\ *transitive verb* (1957)
: to provide with or assign to a home port

**home port** *noun* (circa 1891)
: the port from which a ship hails or from which it is documented

¹**ho-mer** \'hō-mər\ *noun* [Hebrew *ḥōmer*] (1535)
: an ancient Hebrew unit of capacity equal to about 10½ or later 11½ bushels or 100 gallons (378 liters)

²**hom-er** \'hō-mər\ *noun* [¹*home*] (1868)
**1** : HOME RUN
**2** : HOMING PIGEON

³**hom-er** *intransitive verb* (1940)
: to hit a home run

**home range** *noun* (1884)
: the area to which an animal usually confines its daily activities

**Ho-mer-ic** \hō-'mer-ik\ *adjective* (circa 1771)
**1** : of, relating to, or characteristic of the Greek poet Homer, his age, or his writings
**2** : of epic proportions : HEROIC ⟨*Homeric* feats of reporting —Stanley Walker⟩
— **Ho-mer-i-cal-ly** \-i-k(ə-)lē\ *adverb*

**home-room** \'hōm-,rüm, -,rum\ *noun* (1915)
: a classroom where pupils report especially at the beginning of each school day

**home rule** *noun* (1860)
: self-government or limited autonomy in internal affairs by a dependent political unit (as a territory or municipality)

**home run** *noun* (1856)
: a hit in baseball that enables the batter to make a complete circuit of the bases and score a run

**home-school** \'hōm-,skül\ (1986)
*intransitive verb*
: to teach school subjects to one's children at home
*transitive verb*
: to teach (one's children) at home
— **home-school-er** \-,skü-lər\ *noun*

**home screen** *noun* (1968)
: TELEVISION 2

**home-sick** \'hōm-,sik\ *adjective* (1756)
: longing for home and family while absent from them
— **home-sick-ness** *noun*

**home-site** \-,sīt\ *noun* (1911)
: a location of or suitable for a home

¹**home-spun** \-,spən\ *adjective* (1591)
**1 a** : spun or made at home **b** : made of homespun
**2** : SIMPLE, HOMELY ⟨*homespun* philosophy⟩

²**homespun** *noun* (1607)
: a loosely woven usually woolen or linen fabric originally made from homespun yarn

**home stand** *noun* (1965)
: a series of baseball games played at a team's home field

**home-stay** \'hōm-,stā\ *noun* (1956)
: a period during which a visitor in a foreign country lives with a local family

¹**home-stead** \'hōm-,sted, -stid\ *noun* (before 12th century)
**1 a** : the home and adjoining land occupied by a family **b** : an ancestral home **c** : HOUSE
**2** : a tract of land acquired from U.S. public lands by filing a record and living on and cultivating the tract

²**home-stead** \-,sted\ (1872)
*transitive verb*
: to acquire or occupy as a homestead
*intransitive verb*
: to acquire or settle on land under a homestead law
— **home-stead-er** \-,ste-dər\ *noun*

**homestead law** *noun* (1850)
**1** : a law exempting a homestead from attachment or sale under execution for general debts
**2** : any of several legislative acts authorizing the sale of public lands in homesteads

**home-stretch** \'hōm-'strech\ *noun* (1841)
**1** : the part of a racecourse between the last turn and the winning post
**2** : a final stage (as of a project)

**home-town** \-'taun\ *noun, often attributive* (1912)
: the city or town where one was born or grew up; *also* : the place of one's principal residence

**home truth** *noun* (1711)
**1** : an unpleasant fact that jars the sensibilities
**2** : a statement of undisputed fact

¹**home-ward** \'hōm-wərd\ *or* **home-wards** \-wərdz\ *adverb* (before 12th century)
: toward home ⟨look *homeward*, angel —John Milton⟩

²**homeward** *adjective* (1566)
: being or going in the direction of home

**home-work** \'hōm-,wərk\ *noun* (circa 1683)
**1** : piecework done at home for pay
**2** : an assignment given to a student to be completed outside the regular class period
**3** : preparatory reading or research (as for a discussion or a debate)

**hom-ey** \'hō-mē\ *adjective* **hom-i-er; -est** (1856)
: HOMELIKE ⟨a restaurant with a *homey* atmosphere⟩
— **hom-ey-ness** *or* **hom-i-ness** *noun*

**ho-mi-cid-al** \,hä-mə-'sī-d²l, ,hō-\ *adjective* (1725)
: of, relating to, or tending toward homicide
— **ho-mi-cid-al-ly** \-d²l-ē\ *adverb*

**ho-mi-cide** \'hä-mə-,sīd, 'hō-\ *noun* [in sense 1, from Middle English, from Middle French, from Latin *homicida*, from *homo* human being + -*cida* -cide; in sense 2, from Middle English, from Middle French, from Latin *homicidium*, from *homo* + -*cidium* -cide] (14th century)
**1** : a person who kills another
**2** : a killing of one human being by another

**hom-i-let-ic** \,hä-mə-'le-tik\ *or* **hom-i-let-i-cal** \-ti-kəl\ *adjective* [Late Latin *homileticus*, from Greek *homilētikos* of conversation, from *homilein*] (1644)
**1** : of, relating to, or resembling a homily
**2** : of or relating to homiletics; *also* : PREACHY

**hom-i-let-ics** \-tiks\ *noun plural but singular in construction* (1830)
: the art of preaching

**hom-i-ly** \'hä-mə-lē\ *noun, plural* **-lies** [Middle English *omelie*, from Middle French, from Late Latin *homilia*, from Late Greek, from Greek, conversation, discourse, from *homilein* to consort with, address, from *homilos* crowd,

assembly; akin to Greek *homos* same — more at SAME] (14th century)
**1 :** a usually short sermon
**2 :** a lecture or discourse on or of a moral theme
**3 :** an inspirational catchphrase; *also* **:** PLATITUDE

**homing pigeon** *noun* (1886)
**:** a racing pigeon trained to return home
**hom·i·nid** \'hä-mə-nəd, -,nid\ *noun* [New Latin *Hominidae*, from *Homin-, Homo* + *-idae*] (circa 1889)
**:** any of a family (Hominidae) of erect bipedal primate mammals comprising recent humans together with extinct ancestral and related forms
— **hominid** *adjective*
**hom·i·ni·za·tion** \,hä-mə-nə-'zā-shən\ *noun* [Latin *homin-, homo* + English *-ization*] (1952)
**:** the evolutionary development of human characteristics that differentiate hominids from their primate ancestors
**hom·i·noid** \'hä-mə-,nȯid\ *noun* [New Latin *Hominoidea*, from *Homin-, Homo* + *-oidea*, suffix of higher taxa, from Latin *-oïdes* [2]*-oid*] (1949)
**:** any of a superfamily (Hominoidea) of primates including recent hominids, gibbons, and pongids together with extinct ancestral and related forms (as of the genera *Proconsul* and *Dryopithecus*)
— **hominoid** *adjective*
**hom·i·ny** \'hä-mə-nē\ *noun* [Virginia Algonquian *-homen*, literally, that treated (in the way specified)] (1629)
**:** kernels of corn that have been soaked in a caustic solution (as of lye) and then washed to remove the hulls
**hominy grits** *noun plural but singular or plural in construction* (1879)
**:** GRITS
[1]**ho·mo** \'hō-(,)mō\ *noun, plural* **homos** [New Latin *Homin-, Homo*, from Latin, human being — more at HOMAGE] (1596)
**:** any of a genus (*Homo*) of primate mammals that includes modern humans (*H. sapiens*) and several extinct related species
[2]**homo** *noun, plural* **homos** [by shortening] (1929)
**:** HOMOSEXUAL — often used disparagingly
**homo-** — see HOM-
**ho·mo·cer·cal** \,hō-mə-'sər-kəl, ,hä-\ *adjective* (1838)
**1** *of a fish tail fin* **:** having the upper and lower lobes approximately symmetrical and the vertebral column ending at or near the middle of the base
**2 :** having or relating to a homocercal tail fin
**homoe-** — see HOMEO-
**ho·mo·erot·ic** \,hō-mō-i-'rä-tik\ *adjective* (1916)
**:** HOMOSEXUAL
— **ho·mo·erot·i·cism** \-'rä-tə-,si-zəm\ *noun*
**ho·mo·ga·met·ic** \,hō-mō-gə-'me-tik, ,hä-\ *adjective* (1910)
**:** forming gametes which all have the same type of sex chromosome
**ho·mog·a·my** \hō-'mä-gə-mē\ *noun* [German *Homogamie*, from *hom-* + *-gamie* -gamy] (1897)
**:** the mating of like with like
— **ho·mog·a·mous** \-məs\ *adjective*
**ho·mog·e·nate** \hō-'mä-jə-,nāt, hə-\ *noun* (1941)
**:** a product of homogenizing
**ho·mo·ge·ne·i·ty** \,hō-mə-jə-'nē-ə-tē, -'nā- *also* ÷-'nī-; *especially British* ,hä-\ *noun* (1625)
**1 :** the quality or state of being homogeneous
**2 :** the state of having identical distribution functions or values ⟨*homogeneity* of variances⟩
**ho·mo·ge·neous** \-'jē-nē-əs, -nyəs\ *adjective* [Medieval Latin *homogeneus, homogenus,*

from Greek *homogenēs,* from *hom-* + *genos* kind — more at KIN] (1641)
**1 :** of the same or a similar kind or nature
**2 :** of uniform structure or composition throughout ⟨a culturally *homogeneous* neighborhood⟩
**3 :** having the property that if each variable is replaced by a constant times that variable the constant can be factored out **:** having each term of the same degree if all variables are considered ⟨a *homogeneous* equation⟩
— **ho·mo·ge·neous·ly** *adverb*
— **ho·mo·ge·neous·ness** *noun*
**ho·mog·e·ni·sa·tion, ho·mog·e·nise**
*British variant of* HOMOGENIZATION, HOMOGENIZE
**ho·mog·e·ni·za·tion** \hō-,mä-jə-nə-'zā-shən, hə-\ *noun* (1908)
**1 :** the act or process of homogenizing
**2 :** the quality or state of being homogenized
**ho·mog·e·nize** \hō-'mä-jə-,nīz, hə-\ *verb* **-nized; -niz·ing** (1886)
*transitive verb*
**1 a :** to blend (diverse elements) into a uniform mixture **b :** to make homogeneous
**2 a :** to reduce to small particles of uniform size and distribute evenly usually in a liquid **b :** to reduce the particles of so that they are uniformly small and evenly distributed; *specifically* **:** to break up the fat globules of (milk) into very fine particles
*intransitive verb*
**:** to become homogenized
— **ho·mog·e·niz·er** *noun*
**ho·mog·e·nous** \-nəs\ *adjective* (1919)
**1 :** HOMOPLASTIC 2
**2 :** HOMOGENEOUS
**ho·mo·graft** \'hō-mə-,graft, 'hä-\ *noun* (1923)
**:** a graft of tissue taken from a donor of the same species as the recipient — compare HETEROGRAFT
**ho·mo·graph** \'hä-mə-,graf, 'hō-\ *noun* (1873)
**:** one of two or more words spelled alike but different in meaning or derivation or pronunciation (as the *bow* of a ship, a *bow* and arrow)
— **ho·mo·graph·ic** \,hä-mə-'gra-fik, ,hō-\ *adjective*
**homoio-** — see HOMEO-
**ho·moio·therm, ho·moio·ther·mic** *variant of* HOMEOTHERM, HOMEOTHERMIC
**ho·moi·ou·si·an** \,hō-,mȯi-'ü-zē-ən, hä-, -'ü-sē-\ *noun* [Late Greek *homoiousios* of like substance, from Greek *homoi-* homeo- + *ousia* essence, substance, from *ont-, ōn,* present participle of *einai* to be — more at IS] (1732)
**:** an adherent of an ecclesiastical party of the 4th century holding that the Son is essentially like the Father but not of the same substance
**ho·mol·o·gate** \hō-'mä-lə-,gāt, hə-\ *transitive verb* **-gat·ed; -gat·ing** [Medieval Latin *homologatus,* past participle of *homologare* to agree, from Greek *homologein,* from *homologos*] (1593)
**:** SANCTION, ALLOW; *especially* **:** to approve or confirm officially
— **ho·mol·o·ga·tion** \-,mä-lə-'gā-shən\ *noun*
**ho·mo·log·i·cal** \,hō-mə-'lä-ji-kəl, ,hä-\ *adjective* (circa 1847)
**1 :** HOMOLOGOUS
**2 :** of or relating to topological homology theory ⟨*homological* algebra⟩
— **ho·mo·log·i·cal·ly** \-ji-k(ə-)lē\ *adverb*
**ho·mol·o·gize** \hō-'mä-lə-,jīz, hə-\ *transitive verb* **-gized; -giz·ing** (1811)
**1 :** to make homologous
**2 :** to demonstrate the homology of
— **ho·mol·o·giz·er** *noun*
**ho·mol·o·gous** \hō-'mä-lə-gəs, hə-\ *adjective* [Greek *homologos* agreeing, from *hom-* + *legein* to say — more at LEGEND] (1660)
**1 a :** having the same relative position, value, or structure: as (1) **:** exhibiting biological homology (2) **:** having the same or allelic genes with genetic loci usually arranged in the same

order ⟨*homologous* chromosomes⟩ **b :** belonging to or consisting of a chemical series whose successive members have a regular difference in composition especially of one methylene group
**2 :** derived from or developed in response to organisms of the same species
**ho·mo·logue** *or* **ho·mo·log** \'hō-mə-,lȯg, 'hä-, -,läg\ *noun* (1848)
**:** something (as a chemical compound or a chromosome) homologous
**ho·mol·o·gy** \hō-'mä-lə-jē, hə-\ *noun, plural* **-gies** (circa 1656)
**1 :** a similarity often attributable to common origin
**2 a :** likeness in structure between parts of different organisms due to evolutionary differentiation from the same or a corresponding part of a remote ancestor — compare ANALOGY **b :** correspondence in structure between different parts of the same individual
**3 :** similarity of nucleotide or amino-acid sequence in nucleic acids, peptides, or proteins
**4 :** a branch of the theory of topology concerned with partitioning space into geometric components (as points, lines, and triangles) and with the study of the number and interrelationships of these components especially by the use of group theory — called also *homology theory*; compare COHOMOLOGY
**ho·mo·lyt·ic** \,hō-mə-'li-tik, ,hä-\ *adjective* (1941)
*of a chemical compound* **:** decomposing into two uncharged atoms or radicals
— **ho·mol·y·sis** \hō-'mä-lə-səs\ *noun*
**ho·mo·mor·phism** \,hō-mə-'mȯr-,fi-zəm, ,hä-\ *noun* [International Scientific Vocabulary] (1935)
**:** a mapping of a mathematical set (as a group, ring, or vector space) into or onto another set or itself in such a way that the result obtained by applying the operations to elements of the first set is mapped onto the result obtained by applying the corresponding operations to their respective images in the second set
— **ho·mo·mor·phic** \-fik\ *adjective*
**ho·mo·nu·cle·ar** \,hō-mə-'nü-klē-ər, ,hä-, -'nyü-, ÷-kyə-lər\ *adjective* (1930)
**:** of or relating to a molecule composed of identical nuclei
**hom·onym** \'hä-mə-,nim, 'hō-\ *noun* [Latin *homonymum,* from Greek *homōnymon,* from neuter of *homōnymos*] (1697)
**1 a :** HOMOPHONE **b :** HOMOGRAPH **c :** one of two or more words spelled and pronounced alike but different in meaning (as the noun *quail* and the verb *quail*)
**2 :** NAMESAKE
**3 :** a taxonomic designation rejected as invalid because the identical term has been used to designate another group of the same rank — compare SYNONYM
— **hom·onym·ic** \,hä-mə-'ni-mik, ,hō-\ *adjective*
**hom·on·y·mous** \hō-'mä-nə-məs\ *adjective* [Latin *homonymus* having the same name, from Greek *homōnymos,* from *hom-* + *onyma, onoma* name — more at NAME] (1621)
**1 :** AMBIGUOUS
**2 :** having the same designation
**3 :** of, relating to, or being homonyms **:** HOMONYMIC
— **hom·on·y·mous·ly** *adverb*
**hom·on·y·my** \-mē\ *noun* (1597)
**:** the quality or state of being homonymous
**ho·mo·ou·si·an** \,hō-,mō-'ü-zē-ən, hä-, -'ü-sē-\ *noun* [Late Greek *homoousios* of the same substance, from Greek *hom-* + *ousia* substance — more at HOMOIOUSIAN] (1565)
**:** an adherent of an ecclesiastical party of the 4th century holding to the doctrine of the Nicene Creed that the Son is of the same substance with the Father
**ho·mo·phile** \'hō-mə-,fīl\ *adjective* [hom- + [2]*-phil*] (1960)
**:** GAY 4b

**ho·mo·phobe** \-ˌfōb\ *noun* (1975)
: a person characterized by homophobia
**ho·mo·pho·bia** \ˌhō-mə-ˈfō-bē-ə\ *noun* (1969)
: irrational fear of, aversion to, or discrimination against homosexuality or homosexuals
— **ho·mo·pho·bic** \-ˈfō-bik\ *adjective*
**ho·mo·phone** \ˈhä-mə-ˌfōn, ˈhō-\ *noun* [International Scientific Vocabulary] (1843)
**1** : one of two or more words pronounced alike but different in meaning or derivation or spelling (as the words *to, too,* and *two*)
**2** : a character or group of characters pronounced the same as another character or group
— **ho·moph·o·nous** \hō-ˈmä-fə-nəs\ *adjective*
**ho·mo·phon·ic** \ˌhä-mə-ˈfä-nik, ˌhō-, -ˈfō-\ *adjective* [Greek *homophōnos* being in unison, from *hom-* + *phōnē* sound — more at BAN] (circa 1879)
**1** : CHORDAL
**2** : of or relating to homophones
— **ho·moph·o·ny** \hō-ˈmä-fə-nē\ *noun*
**ho·mo·plas·tic** \ˌhō-mə-ˈplas-tik, ˌhä-\ *adjective* (1870)
**1** : of or relating to homoplasy
**2** : of, relating to, or derived from another individual of the same species ⟨*homoplastic* grafts⟩
**ho·mo·pla·sy** \ˈhō-mə-ˌplā-sē, ˈhä-, -ˌpla-; hō-ˈmä-plə-sē\ *noun* (1870)
: correspondence between parts or organs acquired as the result of parallel evolution or convergence
**ho·mo·po·lar** \ˌhō-mə-ˈpō-lər, ˌhä-\ *adjective* (1896)
**1** *of a motor or generator* : using or producing direct current without the use of commutators
**2** : of or relating to a union of atoms of like polarity : NONIONIC
**ho·mo·pol·y·mer** \-ˈpä-lə-mər\ *noun* (1946)
: a polymer (as polyethylene) consisting of identical monomer units
— **ho·mo·pol·y·mer·ic** \-ˌpä-lə-ˈmer-ik\ *adjective*
**ho·mop·ter·an** \hō-ˈmäp-tə-rən\ *noun* [ultimately from Greek *hom-* + *pteron* wing — more at FEATHER] (circa 1842)
: any of a large order or suborder (Homoptera) of insects (as cicadas, aphids, and scale insects) that have sucking mouthparts
— **homopteran** *adjective*
— **ho·mop·ter·ous** \-rəs\ *adjective*
**homos** *plural of* HOMO
**Ho·mo sa·pi·ens** \ˌhō-(ˌ)mō-ˈsā-pē-ˌenz, -ˌenz, *especially British* -ˈsa-pē-ənz\ *noun* [New Latin, species name, from *Homo,* genus name + *sapiens,* specific epithet, from Latin, wise, intelligent — more at HOMO, SAPIENT] (1802)
: HUMANKIND
**ho·mo·sce·das·tic·i·ty** \ˌhō-mō-si-ˌdas-ˈti-sə-tē, ˌhä-\ *noun* [*hom-* + Greek *skedastikos* able to disperse, from *skedannynai* to disperse] (1905)
: the property of having equal statistical variances
— **ho·mo·sce·das·tic** \-ˈdas-tik\ *adjective*
**¹ho·mo·sex·u·al** \ˌhō-mə-ˈsek-sh(ə-)wəl, -ˈsek-shəl\ *adjective* (1892)
**1** : of, relating to, or characterized by a tendency to direct sexual desire toward another of the same sex
**2** : of, relating to, or involving sexual intercourse between persons of the same sex
— **ho·mo·sex·u·al·ly** *adverb*
**²homosexual** *noun* (1902)
: a homosexual person and especially a male
**ho·mo·sex·u·al·i·ty** \ˌhō-mə-ˌsek-shə-ˈwa-lə-tē\ *noun* (1892)
**1** : the quality or state of being homosexual
**2** : erotic activity with another of the same sex
**ho·mo·spo·rous** \ˌhō-mə-ˈspōr-əs, ˌhä-, -ˈspór-; hō-ˈmäs-pə-rəs\ *adjective* (1887)
: producing asexual spores of one kind only

**ho·mo·spo·ry** \ˈhō-mə-ˌspōr-ē, ˈhä-, -ˌspór-; hō-ˈmäs-pə-rē\ *noun* (1903)
: the production by various plants (as the club mosses and horsetails) of asexual spores of only one kind
**ho·mo·thal·lic** \ˌhō-mō-ˈtha-lik\ *adjective* [*hom-* + Greek *thallein* to sprout, grow — more at THALLUS] (1904)
**1** : having a haploid phase that produces two kinds of gametes capable of fusing to form a zygote — used especially of algae and fungi
**2** : MONOECIOUS
— **ho·mo·thal·lism** \-ˈtha-ˌli-zəm\ *noun*
**ho·mo·trans·plant** \ˌhō-mō-ˈtran(t)s-ˌplant, ˌhä-\ *noun* (1927)
: HOMOGRAFT
— **ho·mo·trans·plan·ta·tion** \-ˌtran(t)s-ˌplan-ˈtā-shən\ *noun*
**ho·mo·zy·go·sis** \ˌhō-mə-zi-ˈgō-səs, ˌhä-\ *noun* [New Latin] (1905)
: HOMOZYGOSITY
**ho·mo·zy·gos·i·ty** \-ˈgä-sə-tē\ *noun* (1916)
: the state of being homozygous
**ho·mo·zy·gote** \-ˈzī-ˌgōt\ *noun* [International Scientific Vocabulary] (1902)
: a homozygous individual
**ho·mo·zy·gous** \-ˈzī-gəs\ *adjective* (1902)
: having the two genes at corresponding loci on homologous chromosomes identical for one or more loci
— **ho·mo·zy·gous·ly** *adverb*
**ho·mun·cu·lus** \hō-ˈmən-kyə-ləs\ *noun, plural* **-li** \-ˌlī, -ˌlē\ [Latin, diminutive of *homin-, homo* human being — more at HOMAGE] (1656)
**1** : a little man : MANIKIN
**2** : a miniature adult that in the theory of preformation is held to inhabit the germ cell and to produce a mature individual merely by an increase in size
**homy** *variant of* HOMEY
**hon** \ˈhən\ *noun* (circa 1906)
: HONEY 2a
**hon·cho** \ˈhän-(ˌ)chō\ *noun, plural* **honchos** [Japanese *hanchō* squad leader, from *han* squad + *chō* head, chief] (1947)
: BOSS, BIG SHOT; *also* : HOTSHOT ◆
**¹hone** \ˈhōn\ *noun* [Middle English, from Old English *hān* stone; akin to Old Norse *hein* whetstone, Latin *cot-, cos,* Sanskrit *śiśāti* he whets] (14th century)
: WHETSTONE
**²hone** *transitive verb* **honed; hon·ing** (1826)
**1** : to sharpen or smooth with a whetstone
**2** : to make more acute, intense, or effective : WHET ⟨helped her *hone* her comic timing —Patricia Bosworth⟩
— **hon·er** *noun*
**³hone** *intransitive verb* **honed; hon·ing** [Middle French *hoigner* to grumble] (1600)
**1** *dialect* : YEARN — often used with *for* or *after*
**2** *dialect* : GRUMBLE, MOAN
**hone in** *intransitive verb* [alteration of *home in*] (1965)
: to move toward or focus attention on an objective ⟨looking back for the ball *honing in* —George Plimpton⟩ ⟨a missile *honing in* on its target —Bob Greene⟩ ⟨*hones in* on the plights and victories of the common man —Lisa Russell⟩ ■
**¹hon·est** \ˈä-nəst\ *adjective* [Middle English, from Middle French *honeste,* from Latin *honestus* honorable, from *honos, honor* honor] (14th century)
**1 a** : free from fraud or deception : LEGITIMATE, TRUTHFUL ⟨an *honest* plea⟩ **b** : GENUINE, REAL ⟨making *honest* stops at stop signs —*Christian Science Monitor*⟩ **c** : HUMBLE, PLAIN ⟨good *honest* food⟩
**2 a** : REPUTABLE, RESPECTABLE ⟨*honest* decent people⟩ **b** *chiefly British* : GOOD, WORTHY
**3** : CREDITABLE, PRAISEWORTHY ⟨an *honest* day's work⟩

**4 a** : marked by integrity **b** : marked by free, forthright, and sincere expression : FRANK ⟨an *honest* appraisal⟩ **c** : INNOCENT, SIMPLE
*synonym* see UPRIGHT
**²honest** *adverb* (1596)
**1** : in an honest manner : HONESTLY ⟨I have ever found thee *honest* true —Shakespeare⟩
**2** : with all sincerity ⟨I didn't do it, *honest*⟩
**honest broker** *noun* (circa 1884)
: a neutral mediator
**hon·est·ly** \ˈä-nəst-lē\ *adverb* (14th century)
**1** : in an honest manner: as **a** : without cheating ⟨counted the ballots *honestly*⟩ **b** : REALLY, GENUINELY ⟨was *honestly* scared⟩ **c** : without frills ⟨food *honestly* prepared⟩
**2** : to be honest : to tell the truth ⟨*honestly,* I don't know⟩
**hon·es·ty** \ˈä-nəs-tē\ *noun, plural* **-ties** (14th century)
**1** *obsolete* : CHASTITY
**2 a** : fairness and straightforwardness of conduct **b** : adherence to the facts : SINCERITY
**3** : any of a genus (*Lunaria*) of European herbs of the mustard family with toothed leaves and flat disk-shaped siliques ☆

---

☆ SYNONYMS

**Honesty, honor, integrity, probity**
mean uprightness of character or action. HONESTY implies a refusal to lie, steal, or deceive in any way. HONOR suggests an active or anxious regard for the standards of one's profession, calling, or position. INTEGRITY implies trustworthiness and incorruptibility to a degree that one is incapable of being false to a trust, responsibility, or pledge. PROBITY implies tried and proven honesty or integrity.

---

□ USAGE

**hone in** The few commentators who have noticed *hone in* consider it to be a mistake for *home in*. It may have arisen from *home in* by the weakening of the \m\ sound to \n\ or may perhaps simply be due to the influence of *hone*. Even though it seems to have established itself in American English (and its mention in a British usage book suggests it is used in British English too), your use of it especially in writing is likely to be called a mistake. *Home in* or in figurative use *zero in* is an easy alternative.

---

◇ WORD HISTORY

**honcho** *Honcho* is a relic of the large U.S. presence in Japan during the years following World War II, when the Japanese word *hanchō* "leader of the squad, section, or group" entered English. We are uncertain of the exact route by which this word found its way into American military argot in the mid-1950s, though it is known that the Japanese applied *hanchō* to British or Australian officers in charge of work parties in prisoner-of-war camps. Judging by the scarcity of print evidence, *honcho* was not well established in general colloquial English before the 1960s. By that time it had become part of American political jargon—an area where it continues to flourish in the 1990s. *Honcho* has occasionally been used as a verb meaning "to supervise," and in 1993 the cartoonist Garry Trudeau produced the derivative *honchette* to describe a female big shot—surely a sign of the naturalization of *honcho* in English.

---

\ə\ abut \ə⁾\ kitten \ər\ further \a\ ash \ā\ ace
\ä\ mop, mar \aù\ out \ch\ chin \e\ bet \ē\ easy
\g\ go \i\ hit \ī\ ice \j\ job \ŋ\ sing \ō\ go
\ò\ law \òi\ boy \th\ thin \t͟h\ the \ü\ loot \ù\ foot
\y\ yet \zh\ vision *see also* Guide to Pronunciation

**¹hon·ey** \'hə-nē\ *noun, plural* **honeys** [Middle English *hony*, from Old English *hunig;* akin to Old High German *honag* honey, Latin *canicae* bran] (before 12th century)
**1 a :** a sweet viscid material elaborated out of the nectar of flowers in the honey sac of various bees **b :** a sweet fluid resembling honey that is collected or elaborated by various insects
**2 a :** a loved one **:** SWEETHEART, DEAR **b :** a superlative example
**3 :** the quality or state of being sweet **:** SWEETNESS
**²honey** *verb* **hon·eyed** *also* **hon·ied** \'hə-nēd\; **hon·ey·ing** (14th century)
*transitive verb*
**1 :** to sweeten with or as if with honey
**2 :** to speak ingratiatingly to **:** FLATTER
*intransitive verb*
**:** to use blandishments or cajolery
**³honey** *adjective* (14th century)
**1 :** of, relating to, or resembling honey
**2 :** much loved **:** DEAR
**hon·ey·bee** \'hə-nē-ˌbē\ *noun* (15th century)
**:** a honey-producing bee (*Apis* and related genera); *especially* **:** a European bee (*A. mellifera*) introduced worldwide and kept in hives for the honey it produces

honeybees, left to right: worker, queen, drone

**¹hon·ey·comb** \-ˌkōm\ *noun* (before 12th century)
**1 :** a mass of hexagonal wax cells built by honeybees in their nest to contain their brood and stores of honey
**2 :** something that resembles a honeycomb in structure or appearance; *especially* **:** a strong lightweight cellular structural material
**²honeycomb** (1774)
*transitive verb*
**1 a :** to cause to be full of cavities like a honeycomb **b :** to make into a checkered pattern **:** FRET
**2 a :** to penetrate into every part **:** FILL **b :** SUBVERT, WEAKEN
*intransitive verb*
**:** to become pitted, checked, or cellular
**hon·ey·creep·er** \'hə-nē-ˌkrē-pər\ *noun* (1872)
**1 :** any of numerous small bright-colored oscine birds (especially genera *Cyanerpes* and *Chlorophanes* of the family Coerebidae) of tropical America
**2 :** any of a family (Drepanididae) of oscine birds that are found only in Hawaii
**hon·ey·dew** \-ˌdü, -ˌdyü\ *noun* (1577)
**:** a saccharine deposit secreted on the leaves of plants usually by aphids or scale insects or sometimes by a fungus
**honeydew melon** *noun* (1916)
**:** a pale smooth-skinned winter melon with sweet greenish flesh
**hon·ey·eat·er** \-ˌē-tər\ *noun* (1822)
**:** any of a family (Meliphagidae) of oscine birds chiefly of the South Pacific that have a long protrusible tongue adapted for extracting nectar and small insects from flowers
**hon·ey·guide** \-ˌgīd\ *noun* (1777)
**:** any of a family (Indicatoridae) of small plainly colored nonpasserine birds that inhabit Africa, the Himalayas, and the East Indies and that include some which lead people or animals to the nests of bees

**honey locust** *noun* (1743)
**:** a tall usually spiny North American leguminous tree (*Gleditsia triacanthos*) with very hard wood and long twisted pods containing a sweet edible pulp and seeds that resemble beans
**hon·ey·moon** \'hə-nē-ˌmün\ *noun* [from the idea that the first month of marriage is the sweetest] (1546)
**1 :** a period of harmony immediately following marriage
**2 :** a period of unusual harmony especially following the establishment of a new relationship
**3 :** a trip or vacation taken by a newly married couple
— **honeymoon** *intransitive verb*
— **hon·ey·moon·er** *noun*
**honey sac** *noun* (circa 1909)
**:** a distension of the esophagus of a bee in which honey is elaborated — called also *honey stomach*
**hon·ey·suck·le** \'hə-nē-ˌsə-kəl\ *noun* [Middle English *honysoukel* clover, alteration of *honysouke,* from Old English *hunisūce,* from *hunig* honey + *sūcan* to suck] (1548)
**:** any of a genus (*Lonicera* of the family Caprifoliaceae, the honeysuckle family) of shrubs with opposite leaves and often showy flowers rich in nectar; *broadly* **:** any of various plants (as a columbine or azalea) with tubular flowers rich in nectar

honeysuckle

**hong** \'häŋ, 'hȯŋ\ *noun* [Chinese (Guangdong) *hòhng,* literally, row] (1726)
**:** a commercial establishment or house of foreign trade in China
**¹honk** \'häŋk, 'hȯŋk\ *verb* [imitative] (circa 1835)
*intransitive verb*
**1 :** to make the characteristic cry of a goose
**2 :** to make a sound resembling the cry of a goose
*transitive verb*
**:** to cause (as a horn) to honk
— **honk·er** *noun*
**²honk** *noun* (1854)
**:** the characteristic cry of a goose; *also* **:** a similar sound
**hon·ky** *or* **hon·kie** *also* **hon·key** \'hȯŋ-kē, 'häŋ-\ *noun, plural* **honkies** *also* **honkeys** [probably alteration of *Hunky*] (1967)
**:** a white person — usually used disparagingly
**¹honk·y–tonk** \'häŋ-kē-ˌtäŋk, 'hȯŋ-kē-ˌtȯŋk\ *noun* [origin unknown] (circa 1909)
**1 :** a usually tawdry nightclub or dance hall; *especially* **:** one that features country music
**2 :** a district marked by places of cheap entertainment
**²honky–tonk** *adjective* (circa 1920)
**1 :** of, used in, or being a form of ragtime piano playing performed typically on an upright piano
**2 :** marked by or characteristic of honky-tonks
**¹hon·or** \'ä-nər\ *noun* [Middle English, from Old French *honor,* from Latin *honos, honor*] (13th century)
**1 a :** good name or public esteem **:** REPUTATION **b :** a showing of usually merited respect **:** RECOGNITION ⟨pay *honor* to our founder⟩
**2 :** PRIVILEGE
**3 :** a person of superior standing — now used especially as a title for a holder of high office ⟨if Your *Honor* please⟩
**4 :** one whose worth brings respect or fame **:** CREDIT ⟨an *honor* to the profession⟩
**5 :** the center point of the upper half of an armorial escutcheon

**6 :** an evidence or symbol of distinction: as **a :** an exalted title or rank **b** (1) **:** BADGE, DECORATION (2) **:** a ceremonial rite or observance ⟨buried with full military *honors*⟩ **c :** an award in a contest or field of competition **d** *archaic* **:** a gesture of deference **:** BOW **e** *plural* (1) **:** an academic distinction conferred on a superior student (2) **:** a course of study for superior students supplementing or replacing a regular course
**7 :** CHASTITY, PURITY ⟨fought fiercely for her *honor* and her life —Barton Black⟩
**8 a :** a keen sense of ethical conduct **:** INTEGRITY **b :** one's word given as a guarantee of performance
**9** *plural* **:** social courtesies or civilities extended by a host ⟨did the *honors* at the table⟩
**10 a** (1) **:** an ace, king, queen, jack, or ten especially of the trump suit in bridge (2) **:** the scoring value of honors held in bridge — usually used in plural **b :** the privilege of playing first from the tee in golf ☆
**²honor** *transitive verb* **hon·ored; hon·or·ing** \'ä-nə-riŋ, 'än-riŋ\ (13th century)
**1 a :** to regard or treat with honor or respect **b :** to confer honor on
**2 a :** to live up to or fulfill the terms of ⟨*honor* a commitment⟩ **b :** to accept as payment ⟨*honor* a credit card⟩
**3 :** to salute with a bow in square dancing
— **hon·or·ee** \ˌä-nə-'rē\ *noun*
— **hon·or·er** \'ä-nər-ər\ *noun*
**hon·or·able** \'ä-nər-(ə-)bəl, 'än-rə-\ *adjective* (14th century)
**1 :** deserving of honor
**2 a :** of great renown **:** ILLUSTRIOUS **b :** entitled to honor — used as a title for the children of certain British noblemen and for various government officials
**3 :** performed or accompanied with marks of honor or respect
**4 a :** attesting to creditable conduct **b :** consistent with an untarnished reputation ⟨an *honorable* withdrawal⟩
**5 :** characterized by integrity **:** guided by a high sense of honor and duty
*synonym* see UPRIGHT
— **hon·or·abil·i·ty** \ˌän-rə-'bi-lə-tē, ˌä-nə-\ *noun*
— **hon·or·able·ness** \'än-rə-bəl-nəs, 'ä-nə-\ *noun*
— **hon·or·ably** \-blē\ *adverb*
**honorable mention** *noun* (1866)
**:** a distinction conferred (as in a contest or exhibition) on works or persons of exceptional merit but not deserving of top honors
**hon·o·rar·i·um** \ˌä-nə-'rer-ē-əm\ *noun, plural* **-ia** \-ē-ə\ *also* **-i·ums** [Latin, from neuter of *honorarius*] (1658)
**:** a payment for a service (as making a speech) on which custom or propriety forbids a price to be set
**hon·or·ary** \'ä-nə-ˌrer-ē\ *adjective* [Latin *honorarius,* from *honor*] (1614)
**1 a :** having or conferring distinction **b :** COMMEMORATIVE
**2 :** dependent on honor for fulfillment

☆ **SYNONYMS**
**Honor, homage, reverence, deference** mean respect and esteem shown to another. HONOR may apply to the recognition of one's right to great respect or to any expression of such recognition ⟨the nomination is an *honor*⟩. HOMAGE adds the implication of accompanying praise ⟨paying *homage* to Shakespeare⟩. REVERENCE implies profound respect mingled with love, devotion, or awe ⟨great *reverence* for my father⟩. DEFERENCE implies a yielding or submitting to another's judgment or preference out of respect or reverence ⟨showed no *deference* to their elders⟩. See in addition HONESTY.

**3 a :** conferred or elected in recognition of achievement or service without the usual prerequisites or obligations ⟨an *honorary* degree⟩ ⟨an *honorary* member⟩ **b :** UNPAID, VOLUNTARY ⟨an *honorary* chairman⟩
— **hon·or·ari·ly** \ˌä-nə-ˈrer-ə-lē\ *adverb*
— **honorary** *noun*
**honor guard** *noun* (1925)
**:** a guard assigned to a ceremonial duty (as to accompany a casket at a military funeral)
**hon·or·if·ic** \ˌä-nə-ˈri-fik\ *adjective* (1650)
**1 :** conferring or conveying honor ⟨*honorific* titles⟩
**2 :** belonging to or constituting a class of grammatical forms used in speaking to or about a social superior
— **honorific** *noun*
— **hon·or·if·i·cal·ly** \-fi-k(ə-)lē\ *adverb*
**honor roll** *noun* (1909)
**:** a roster of names of persons deserving honor; *especially* **:** a list of students achieving academic distinction
**honor society** *noun* (1927)
**:** a society for the recognition of scholarly achievement especially of undergraduates
**honor system** *noun* (1904)
**:** a system (as at a college or prison) whereby persons are trusted to abide by the regulations (as for a code of conduct) without supervision or surveillance
**hon·our, hon·our·able** *chiefly British variant of* HONOR, HONORABLE
**¹hooch** \ˈhüch\ *noun* [short for *hoochinoo*, a distilled liquor made by the Hoochinoo (Hutsnuwu) Indians, a Tlingit tribe] (1897)
*slang* **:** alcoholic liquor especially when inferior or illicitly made or obtained ◆
**²hooch** *or* **hootch** \ˈhüch\ *noun* [modification of Japanese *uchi* house] (1960)
*slang* **:** a usually thatched hut; *broadly* **:** DWELLING
**¹hood** \ˈhu̇d\ *noun* [Middle English, from Old English *hōd;* akin to Old High German *huot* head covering, *huota* guard] (before 12th century)
**1 a** (1) **:** a flexible covering for the head and neck (2) **:** a protective covering for the head and face **b :** a covering for a hawk's head and eyes **c :** a covering for a horse's head; *also* **:** BLINDER
**2 a :** an ornamental scarf worn over an academic gown that indicates by its color the wearer's college or university **b :** a color marking or crest on the head of an animal or an expansion of the head that suggests a hood
**3 a :** something resembling a hood in form or use **b :** a cover for parts of mechanisms; *specifically* **:** the movable metal covering over the engine of an automobile **c** *chiefly British* **:** a top cover over the passenger section of a vehicle usually designed to be folded back **d :** an enclosure or canopy provided with a draft for carrying off disagreeable or noxious fumes, sprays, smokes, or dusts **e :** a covering for an opening (as a companion hatch) on a boat
— **hood** *transitive verb*
— **hood·like** \-ˌlīk\ *adjective*
**²hood** \ˈhu̇d, ˈhüd\ *noun* (1930)
**:** HOODLUM
— **hoody** \ˈhu̇-dē, ˈhü-\ *adjective*
**³hood** \ˈhu̇d\ *noun* [by shortening] (1967)
**:** NEIGHBORHOOD 4
**-hood** \ˌhu̇d\ *noun suffix* [Middle English *-hod,* from Old English *-hād;* akin to Old High German *-heit* state, Gothic *haidus* way, manner]
**1 :** state **:** condition **:** quality **:** character ⟨widower*hood*⟩ ⟨hardi*hood*⟩
**2 :** time **:** period ⟨child*hood*⟩
**3 :** instance of a (specified) state or quality ⟨false*hood*⟩
**4 :** individuals sharing a (specified) state or character ⟨brother*hood*⟩
**hood·ed** \ˈhu̇-dəd\ *adjective* (15th century)
**1 :** having a hood
**2 :** shaped like a hood ⟨*hooded* spathes⟩

**3 a :** having the head conspicuously different in color from the rest of the body ⟨*hooded* bird⟩ **b :** having a crest on the head that suggests a hood ⟨*hooded* seals⟩ **c :** having the skin at each side of the neck capable of expansion by movements of the ribs ⟨*hooded* cobra⟩
**4 :** half-closed ⟨*hooded* eyes⟩
— **hood·ed·ness** *noun*
**hood·lum** \ˈhüd-ləm, ˈhu̇d-\ *noun* [perhaps from German dialect (Swabia) *hudelum* disorderly] (1871)
**1 :** THUG; *especially* **:** one who commits acts of violence
**2 :** a young ruffian
— **hood·lum·ish** \-lə-mish\ *adjective*
— **hood·lum·ism** \-ˌmi-zəm\ *noun*
**hood·man–blind** \ˌhu̇d-mən-ˈblīnd\ *noun* (1565)
*archaic* **:** BLINDMAN'S BUFF
**¹hoo·doo** \ˈhü-(ˌ)dü\ *noun, plural* **hoodoos** [of African origin; akin to Hausa *hu³'du³'ba¹* to arouse resentment] (1875)
**1 :** a body of practices of sympathetic magic traditional especially among blacks in the southern U.S.
**2 :** a natural column of rock in western North America often in fantastic form
**3 :** something that brings bad luck
— **hoo·doo·ism** \-ˌi-zəm\ *noun*
**²hoodoo** *transitive verb* (1886)
**:** to cast a spell on; *broadly* **:** to be a source of misfortune to
**hood·wink** \ˈhu̇d-ˌwiŋk\ *transitive verb* [¹hood + wink] (1562)
**1** *archaic* **:** BLINDFOLD
**2** *obsolete* **:** HIDE
**3 :** to deceive by false appearance **:** DUPE
— **hood·wink·er** *noun*
**hoo·ey** \ˈhü-ē\ *noun* [origin unknown] (1924)
**:** NONSENSE
**¹hoof** \ˈhu̇f, ˈhüf\ *noun, plural* **hooves** \ˈhüvz, ˈhu̇vz\ *also* **hoofs** [Middle English, from Old English *hōf;* akin to Old High German *huof* hoof, Sanskrit *śapha*] (before 12th century)
**1 :** a curved covering of horn that protects the front of or encloses the ends of the digits of an ungulate mammal and that corresponds to a nail or claw
**2 :** a hoofed foot especially of a horse
— **on the hoof** of *a meat animal* **:** before butchering **:** LIVING ⟨90¢ a pound *on the hoof*⟩
**²hoof** (1641)
*transitive verb*
**1 :** WALK ⟨*hoofed* it to the lecture hall⟩
**2 :** KICK, TRAMPLE
*intransitive verb*
**:** to move on the feet; *especially* **:** DANCE
**hoof–and–mouth disease** *noun* (1884)
**:** FOOT-AND-MOUTH DISEASE
**hoof·beat** \ˈhu̇f-ˌbēt, ˈhüf-\ *noun* (1847)
**:** the sound of a hoof striking a hard surface (as the ground)
**hoofed** \ˈhu̇ft, ˈhüft, ˈhüvd, ˈhu̇vd\ *or* **hooved** \ˈhüvd, ˈhu̇vd\ *adjective* (1513)
**:** furnished with hooves **:** UNGULATE
**hoof·er** \ˈhu̇-fər, ˈhü-\ *noun* (circa 1918)
**:** a professional dancer
**hoof·print** \ˈhu̇f-ˌprint, ˈhüf-\ *noun* (1804)
**:** an impression or hollow made by a hoof
**hoo–ha** \ˈhü-ˌhä\ *noun* [probably from Yiddish *hu-ha* uproar, exclamation of surprise] (1931)
**:** UPROAR
**¹hook** \ˈhu̇k\ *noun* [Middle English, from Old English *hōc;* akin to Middle Dutch *hoec* fishhook, corner, Lithuanian *kengė* hook] (before 12th century)

**1 a :** a curved or bent device for catching, holding, or pulling **b :** something intended to attract and ensnare
**2 :** something curved or bent like a hook; *especially, plural* **:** FINGERS
**3 :** a flight or course of a ball that deviates from straight in a direction opposite to the dominant hand of the player propelling it; *also* **:** a ball following such a course — compare SLICE
**4 :** a short blow delivered with a circular motion by a boxer while the elbow remains bent and rigid
**5 :** HOOK SHOT
**6 :** BUTTONHOOK
**7 :** quick or summary removal — used with *get* or *give* ⟨the pitcher got the *hook* after giving up three runs⟩
**8 :** a device especially in music or writing that catches the attention
**9 :** a selling point or marketing scheme
— **by hook or by crook :** by any means
— **off the hook 1 :** out of trouble **2 :** free of responsibility or accountability
— **on one's own hook :** by oneself **:** INDEPENDENTLY
**²hook** (13th century)
*transitive verb*
**1 :** to form into a hook **:** CROOK
**2 a :** to seize or make fast by or as if by a hook **b :** to connect by or as if by a hook — often used with *up*
**3 :** STEAL, PILFER
**4 :** to make (as a rug) by drawing loops of yarn, thread, or cloth through a coarse fabric with a hook
**5 :** to hit or throw (a ball) so that a hook results
*intransitive verb*
**1 :** to form a hook **:** CURVE
**2 :** to become hooked
**3 :** to work as a prostitute
**hoo·kah** \ˈhu̇-kə, ˈhü-\ *noun* [Arabic *ḥuqqah* bottle of a water pipe] (1763)
**:** WATER PIPE 2
**hook and eye** *noun* (circa 1626)

hoof 2: 1, 2, 3, 4 parts of wall (1 toe, 2 side walls, 3 quarters, 4 buttresses), 5 bulbs, 6 sole, 7 white line, 8 frog

◇ WORD HISTORY

**hooch** The Tlingit Indians of the Alaskan panhandle, like indigenous peoples elsewhere in the world confronted with drastic cultural disruption, suffered from epidemic alcoholism in the 19th century. After Alaska was purchased from Russia in 1867, contact with U.S. troops, as well as an influx of American merchants ready to sell whiskey, greatly exacerbated the Indian drinking problem, to the point that the importation of distilled spirits into Alaska was banned in 1870. The Tlingit resourcefully responded by distilling their own liquor. Some Anglo-American, whose identity remains uncertain, introduced the Indians to a crude style of pot still, with mash made from potatoes, berries, and a crucial imported ingredient, molasses. The foul-tasting outcome was called by whites *hoochinoo* or *hoochenoo,* after the Hoochinoo or Hutsnuwu, a Tlingit tribe of Admiralty, Chichagof, and Baranof Islands. (The Tlingit name of the tribe, *xucnu·wú,* means literally "grizzly bear fort.") It is not clear that the Hutsnuwu drank or made more alcohol than their neighbors, but nonetheless *hoochinoo* became a common word for "illicit liquor" in Alaska, western Canada, and the western U.S. In the 1890s it was clipped to *hooch,* which in the Prohibition Era spread throughout American English.

\ə\ **abut** \ᵊ\ **kitten** \ər\ **further** \a\ **ash** \ā\ **ace** \ä\ **mop, mar** \au̇\ **out** \ch\ **chin** \e\ **bet** \ē\ **easy** \g\ **go** \i\ **hit** \ī\ **ice** \j\ **job** \ŋ\ **sing** \ō\ **go** \ȯ\ **law** \ȯi\ **boy** \th\ **thin** \t̲h̲\ **the** \ü\ **loot** \u̇\ **foot** \y\ **yet** \zh\ **vision** *see also* Guide to Pronunciation

: a 2-part fastening device (as on a garment or a door) consisting of a metal hook that catches over a bar or into a loop

**hook and ladder truck** *noun* (1865)
: a piece of mobile fire apparatus carrying ladders and usually other fire-fighting and rescue equipment — called also *hook and ladder, ladder truck*

**hook check** *noun* (circa 1939)
: an act or instance of attempting to knock the puck away from an opponent in ice hockey by hooking it with the stick

**hooked** \'hu̇kt, *1 is also* 'hu̇-kəd\ *adjective* (before 12th century)
**1** : having the form of a hook
**2** : provided with a hook
**3** : made by hooking ⟨a *hooked* rug⟩
**4 a** : addicted to narcotics **b** : fascinated by or devoted to something ⟨*hooked* on skiing⟩

**¹hook·er** \'hu̇-kər\ *noun* (1567)
**1** : one that hooks
**2** : DRINK ⟨a *hooker* of Scotch⟩
**3** : PROSTITUTE

**²hooker** *noun* [Dutch *hoeker*, alteration of Middle Dutch *hoecboot*, from *hoec* fishhook + *boot* boat] (1801)
: a one-masted fishing boat used on the English and Irish coasts; *also* : a small clumsy boat

**Hooke's law** \'hu̇ks-\ *noun* [Robert *Hooke*] (1853)
: a statement in physics: the stress within an elastic solid is proportional to the strain responsible for it

**hook·let** \'hu̇k-lət\ *noun* (circa 1839)
: a small hook

**hook, line and sinker** *adverb* [from analogy with a well-hooked fish] (1838)
: without hesitation or reservation : COMPLETE-LY ⟨fell for the story *hook, line and sinker*⟩

**hook shot** *noun* (circa 1932)
: a shot in basketball made usually while standing sideways to the basket by swinging the ball up in an arc with the far hand

**hook·up** \'hu̇k-ˌəp\ *noun* (1903)
**1** : a state of cooperation or alliance
**2** : an assemblage (as of circuits) used for a specific purpose (as radio transmission); *also* : the plan of such an assemblage
**3** : an arrangement of mechanical parts; *also* : CONNECTION ⟨a campsite with electric, water, and sewer *hookups*⟩

**hook up** *intransitive verb* (1925)
: to become associated especially in a working or social relationship

**hook·worm** \'hu̇k-ˌwərm\ *noun* (1902)
**1** : any of several parasitic nematode worms (family Ancylostomatidae) that have strong buccal hooks or plates for attaching to the host's intestinal lining and that include serious bloodsucking pests
**2** : ANCYLOSTOMIASIS

**hooky** *or* **hook·ey** \'hu̇-kē\ *noun, plural* **hook·ies** *or* **hookeys** [probably from slang *hook, hook it* (to make off)] (circa 1848)
: TRUANT — used chiefly in the phrase *play hooky*

**hoo·li·gan** \'hü-li-gən\ *noun* [perhaps from Patrick *Hooligan* (flourished 1898) Irish hoodlum in Southwark, London] (1898)
: RUFFIAN, HOODLUM
— **hoo·li·gan·ism** \-gə-ˌni-zəm\ *noun*

**¹hoop** \'hüp *also* 'hu̇p\ *noun, often attributive* [Middle English, from Old English *hōp*; akin to Middle Dutch *hoep* ring, hoop] (12th century)
**1** : a circular strip used especially for holding together the staves of containers or as a plaything
**2 a** : a circular figure or object : RING **b** : the rim of a basketball goal; *broadly* : the entire goal
**3** : a circle or series of circles of flexible material used to expand a woman's skirt
**4** : BASKETBALL — usually used in plural
— **hoop·like** \-ˌlīk\ *adjective*

**²hoop** *transitive verb* (15th century)
: to bind or fasten with or as if with a hoop
— **hoop·er** *noun*

**hoop·la** \'hü-ˌplä, 'hu̇-\ *noun* [French *houp-là*, interjection] (1877)
: excited commotion : TO-DO; *also* : BALLYHOO

**hoo·poe** \'hü-(ˌ)pü, -(ˌ)pō\ *noun* [alteration of obsolete *hoop*, from Middle French *huppe*, from Latin *upupa*, of imitative origin] (1668)
: a crested Old World nonpasserine bird (*Upupa epops* of the family Upupidae) having a slender decurved bill and barred black-and-white wings and tail

**hoop·skirt** \'hüp-'skərt *also* 'hu̇p-\ *noun* (1857)
: a skirt stiffened with or as if with hoops

**hoo·rah** \hu̇-'rä, -'rȯ\, **hoo·ray** \-'rā\ *variant of* HURRAH

**hoose·gow** \'hüs-ˌgau̇\ *noun* [Spanish *juzgado* panel of judges, courtroom, from past participle of *juzgar* to judge, from Latin *judicare* — more at JUDGE] (1909)
: JAIL

**Hoo·sier** \'hü-zhər\ *noun* [perhaps alteration of English dialect *hoozer* anything large of its kind] (1826)
: a native or resident of Indiana — used as a nickname
— **Hoosier** *adjective*

**¹hoot** \'hüt\ *verb* [Middle English *houten*, of imitative origin] (13th century)
*intransitive verb*
**1** : to shout or laugh usually derisively
**2** : to make the natural throat noise of an owl or a similar cry
**3** : to make a loud clamorous mechanical sound
*transitive verb*
**1** : to assail or drive out by hooting ⟨*hooted* down the speaker⟩
**2** : to express or utter with hoots ⟨*hooted* their disapproval⟩
— **hoot·er** *noun*

**²hoot** *noun* (15th century)
**1** : a sound of hooting; *especially* : the cry of an owl
**2** : a minimum amount or degree : the least bit ⟨don't give a *hoot*⟩
**3** : something or someone amusing ⟨the play is a real *hoot*⟩
— **hooty** \'hü-tē\ *adjective*

**³hoot** \'hüt\ *or* **hoots** \'hüts\ *interjection* [origin unknown] (1540)
*chiefly Scottish* — used to express impatience, dissatisfaction, or objection

**hoo·te·nan·ny** \'hü-tᵊn-ˌa-nē\ *noun, plural* **-nies** [origin unknown] (1925)
**1** *chiefly dialect* : GADGET
**2** : a gathering at which folksingers entertain often with the audience joining in

**Hoo·ver·ville** \'hü-vər-ˌvil\ *noun* [Herbert *Hoover* + *-ville*] (1933)
: a shantytown of temporary dwellings during the depression years in the U.S.; *broadly* : any similar area of temporary dwellings

**¹hop** \'häp\ *verb* **hopped; hop·ping** [Middle English *hoppen*, from Old English *hoppian*; probably akin to Old English *hype* hip] (before 12th century)
*intransitive verb*
**1** : to move by a quick springy leap or in a series of leaps; *also* : to move as if by hopping ⟨*hop* in the car⟩
**2** : to make a quick trip especially by air
*transitive verb*
**1** : to jump over ⟨*hop* a fence⟩
**2** : to ride on ⟨*hopped* a flight⟩; *also* : to ride surreptitiously and without authorization ⟨*hop* a freight train⟩

**²hop** *noun* (1508)
**1 a** : a short brisk leap especially on one leg **b** : BOUNCE, REBOUND ⟨shortstop scooped it up on the first *hop*⟩
**2** : DANCE 3
**3 a** : a flight in an aircraft **b** : a short trip

**³hop** *noun* [Middle English *hoppe*, from Middle Dutch; akin to Old High German *hopfo* hop] (15th century)
**1** *plural* : the ripe dried pistillate catkins of a hop used especially to impart a bitter flavor to malt liquors
**2** : a twining vine (*Humulus lupulus*) of the mulberry family with 3-lobed or 5-lobed leaves and inconspicuous flowers of which the pistillate ones are in glandular cone-shaped catkins

**⁴hop** *transitive verb* **hopped; hop·ping** (1572)
: to impregnate with hops

**¹hope** \'hōp\ *verb* **hoped; hop·ing** [Middle English, from Old English *hopian*; akin to Middle High German *hoffen* to hope] (before 12th century)
*intransitive verb*
**1** : to cherish a desire with anticipation ⟨*hopes* for a promotion⟩
**2** *archaic* : TRUST
*transitive verb*
**1** : to desire with expectation of obtainment
**2** : to expect with confidence : TRUST
**synonym** see EXPECT
— **hop·er** *noun*
— **hope against hope** : to hope without any basis for expecting fulfillment

**²hope** *noun* (before 12th century)
**1** *archaic* : TRUST, RELIANCE
**2 a** : desire accompanied by expectation of or belief in fulfillment ⟨came in *hopes* of seeing you⟩; *also* : expectation of fulfillment or success ⟨no *hope* of a cure⟩ **b** : someone or something on which hopes are centered ⟨our only *hope* for victory⟩ **c** : something hoped for

**hope chest** *noun* (1911)
: a young woman's accumulation of clothes and domestic furnishings (as silver and linen) kept in anticipation of her marriage; *also* : a chest for such an accumulation

**¹hope·ful** \'hōp-fəl\ *adjective* (1568)
**1** : having qualities which inspire hope ⟨*hopeful* signs of economic recovery⟩
**2** : full of hope : inclined to hope
— **hope·ful·ness** *noun*

**²hopeful** *noun* (1720)
: ASPIRANT ⟨Olympic *hopefuls*⟩

**hope·ful·ly** \'hōp-fə-lē\ *adverb* (circa 1639)
**1** : in a hopeful manner
**2** : it is hoped : I hope : we hope ■

**hope·less** \'hō-pləs\ *adjective* (1534)
**1 a** : having no expectation of good or success : DESPAIRING **b** : not susceptible to remedy or cure **c** : incapable of redemption or improvement
**2 a** : giving no ground for hope : DESPERATE **b** : incapable of solution, management, or accomplishment : IMPOSSIBLE
**synonym** see DESPONDENT
— **hope·less·ness** *noun*

**hope·less·ly** \-lē\ *adverb* (1616)

---

□ USAGE

**hopefully**   In the early 1960s the second sense of *hopefully*, which had been in sporadic use since around 1932, underwent a surge of popular use. A surge of popular criticism followed in reaction, but the criticism took no account of the grammar of adverbs. *Hopefully* in its second sense is a member of a class of adverbs known as disjuncts. Disjuncts serve as a means by which the author or speaker can comment directly to the reader or hearer usually on the content of the sentence to which they are attached. Many other adverbs (as *interestingly, frankly, clearly, luckily, unfortunately*) are similarly used; most are so ordinary as to excite no comment or interest whatsoever. The second sense of *hopefully* is entirely standard.

: in a hopeless manner — used especially as an intensifier ⟨the formerly despised and *hopelessly* middle-class game of golf —Ejner Jensen⟩

**hop·head** \'häp-,hed\ *noun* (1911)
*slang* : a drug addict

**hop hornbeam** *noun* (1785)
: a chiefly eastern U.S. tree (*Ostrya virginiana*) of the birch family with fruiting clusters resembling hops

**Ho·pi** \'hō-(,)pē\ *noun, plural* **Hopi** *or* **Hopis** [Hopi *hópi*, literally, good, peaceful] (1877)
**1** : a member of an American Indian people of northeastern Arizona
**2** : the Uto-Aztecan language of the Hopi people

**hop·lite** \'häp-,līt\ *noun* [Greek *hoplitēs*, from *hoplon* tool, weapon, from *hepein* to care for, work at — more at SEPULCHRE] (circa 1741)
: a heavily armed infantry soldier of ancient Greece

**hop-o'-my-thumb** \,hä-pə-mə-'thəm\ *noun* [earlier *hop on my thumb*, imperative issued to one supposedly small enough to be held in the hand] (1530)
: a very small person

**hopped-up** \'häpt-'əp, -,əp\ *adjective* (circa 1924)
**1 a** : being under the influence of a narcotic **b** : full of enthusiasm or excitement; *also* : overly excited **c** : more exciting or attractive than normal or usual
**2** : having more than usual power : being souped up

**hop·per** \'hä-pər\ *noun* (13th century)
**1 a** : one that hops **b** : a leaping insect; *specifically* : an immature hopping form of an insect (as a grasshopper or locust)
**2** [from the shaking motion of hoppers used to feed grain into a mill] **a** : a usually funnel-shaped receptacle for delivering material (as grain or coal); *also* : any of various other receptacles for the temporary storage of material **b** : a freight car with a floor sloping to one or more hinged doors for discharging bulk materials — called also *hopper car* **c** : a box in which a bill to be considered by a legislative body is dropped **d** : a tank holding liquid and having a device for releasing its contents through a pipe

**¹hop·ping** \'hä-piŋ\ *adverb* (1675)
: EXTREMELY, VIOLENTLY — used in the phrase *hopping mad*

**²hopping** *adjective* (1785)
**1** : intensely active : BUSY ⟨they kept us *hopping*⟩
**2** : extremely angry

**³hopping** *noun* (1879)
: a going from one place to another of the same kind — usually used in combination ⟨gallery-*hopping*⟩

**hopping John** \,hä-pən-'jän, -piŋ-\ *or* **hoppin' John** \,hä-pən-\ *noun, often H capitalized* (1838)
: a dish made essentially of cowpeas, rice, and salt pork or bacon

**hop·py** \'hä-pē\ *adjective* **hop·pi·er; -est** (circa 1889)
: having the taste or aroma of hops — used especially of ale or beer

**hop·sack** \'häp-,sak\ *also* **hop·sack·ing** \-,sa-kiŋ\ *noun* [Middle English *hopsak* sack for hops, from *hoppe* ³hop + *sak* sack] (1888)
: a rough-surfaced loosely woven clothing fabric

**¹hop·scotch** \'häp-,skäch\ *noun* [¹*hop* + *scotch* (line)] (1801)
: a child's game in which a player tosses an object (as a stone) into areas of a figure outlined on the ground and hops through the figure and back to regain the object

**²hopscotch** *intransitive verb* (1918)
: to move as if by hopping ⟨*hopscotched* across Europe⟩

**hop, skip, and jump** *noun* (1760)
: a short distance

**hop, step, and jump** *noun* (circa 1719)
: TRIPLE JUMP

**ho·ra** *also* **ho·rah** \'hōr-ə, 'hȯr-ə\ *noun* [New Hebrew *hōrāh*, from Romanian *horă*] (1878)
: a circle dance of Romania and Israel

**Ho·rae** \'hōr-,ē, 'hȯr-, -,ī\ *noun plural* [Latin, from Greek *Hōrai*]
: the Greek goddesses of the seasons

**ho·ra·ry** \'hōr-ər-ē, 'hȯr-, 'här-\ *adjective* [Medieval Latin *horarius*, from Latin *hora* hour — more at HOUR] (1632)
: of or relating to an hour; *also* : HOURLY

**Ho·ra·tio Al·ger** \hə-'rā-shō-'al-jər\ *adjective* (1925)
: of, relating to, or resembling the fiction of Horatio Alger in which success is achieved through self-reliance and hard work

**Ho·ra·tius** \hə-'rā-sh(ē-)əs\ *noun* [Latin]
: a hero in Roman legend noted for his defense of a bridge over the Tiber against the Etruscans

**horde** \'hōrd, 'hȯrd\ *noun* [Middle French, German, & Polish; Middle French & German, from Polish *horda*, from Ukrainian dialect *gorda*, alteration of Ukrainian *orda*, from Old Russian, from Turkic *orda, ordu* khan's residence] (1555)
**1 a** : a political subdivision of central Asian nomads **b** : a people or tribe of nomadic life
**2** : a teeming crowd or throng : SWARM ◆
*synonym* see CROWD

**hore·hound** \'hōr-,haůnd, 'hȯr-\ *noun* [Middle English *horhoune*, from Old English *hārhūne*, from *hār* hoary + *hūne* horehound — more at HOAR] (before 12th century)
**1 a** : a bitter mint (*Marrubium vulgare*) with downy leaves **b** : an extract or confection made from this plant
**2** : any of several mints resembling the horehound

**ho·ri·zon** \hə-'rī-z°n\ *noun* [Middle English *orizon*, from Late Latin *horizont-, horizon*, from Greek *horizont-, horizōn*, from present participle of *horizein* to bound, define, from *horos* boundary; perhaps akin to Latin *urvum* curved part of a plow] (14th century)
**1 a** : the apparent junction of earth and sky **b** : the great circle on the celestial sphere formed by the intersection of a plane tangent to the earth's surface at an observer's position with the celestial sphere **c** : range of perception or experience **d** : something that might be attained ⟨new *horizons*⟩
**2 a** : the geological deposit of a particular time usually identified by distinctive fossils **b** : any of the reasonably distinct layers of soil or its underlying material in a vertical section of land **c** : a cultural area or level of development indicated by separated groups of artifacts
— **ho·ri·zon·al** \-'rī-z°n-əl\ *adjective*

**ho·ri·zon·less** \-ləs\ *adjective* (circa 1839)
**1 a** : having no horizon **b** : ENDLESS 1
**2** : HOPELESS

**hor·i·zon·tal** \,hȯr-ə-'zän-t°l, ,här-\ *adjective* (1555)
**1 a** : of, relating to, or situated near the horizon **b** : parallel to, in the plane of, or operating in a plane parallel to the horizon or to a base line : LEVEL ⟨*horizontal* distance⟩ ⟨*horizontal* engine⟩
**2** : relating to, directed toward, or consisting of individuals or entities of similar status or on the same level ⟨*horizontal* mergers⟩ ⟨*horizontal* hostility⟩
— **horizontal** *noun*
— **hor·i·zon·tal·i·ty** \-,zän-'ta-lə-tē\ *noun*
— **hor·i·zon·tal·ly** \-'zän-t°l-ē\ *adverb*

**horizontal bar** *noun* (1827)
**1** : a steel bar supported in a horizontal position approximately eight feet above the floor and used for swinging feats in gymnastics
**2** : an event in gymnastics competition in which the horizontal bar is used

**hor·mo·go·ni·um** \,hȯr-mə-'gō-nē-əm\ *noun, plural* **-nia** \-nē-ə\ [New Latin, from Greek *hormos* chain, necklace + New Latin *-gonium* — more at SERIES] (1880)
: a portion of a filament in many blue-green algae that becomes detached as a reproductive body

**hor·mon·al** \hȯr-'mō-n°l\ *adjective* (1926)
: of, relating to, or effected by hormones
— **hor·mon·al·ly** \-n°l-ē\ *adverb*

**hor·mone** \'hȯr-,mōn\ *noun* [Greek *hormōn*, present participle of *horman* to stir up, from *hormē* impulse, assault; akin to Greek *ornynai* to rouse — more at RISE] (1905)
**1** : a product of living cells that circulates in body fluids or sap and produces a specific effect on the activity of cells remote from its point of origin; *especially* : one exerting a stimulatory effect on a cellular activity
**2** : a synthetic substance that acts like a hormone
— **hor·mone-like** \-,līk\ *adjective*

**horn** \'hȯrn\ *noun* [Middle English, from Old English; akin to Old High German *horn*, Latin *cornu*, Greek *keras*] (before 12th century)
**1 a** : one of the usually bony processes that arise from the head of many ungulates and that are found in some extinct mammals and reptiles: as (1) : one of the permanent paired hollow sheaths of keratin usually present in both sexes of cattle and their relatives that function chiefly for defense and arise from a bony core anchored to the skull — see COW illustration (2) : ANTLER (3) : a permanent solid horn of keratin that is attached to the nasal bone of a rhinoceros (4) : one of a pair of permanent bone protuberances from the skull of a giraffe or okapi that are covered with hairy skin **b** : a part like an animal's horn attributed especially to the devil **c** : a natural projection or excrescence from an animal resembling or suggestive of a horn **d** (1) : the tough fibrous material consisting chiefly of keratin that covers or forms the horns of cattle and related animals, hooves, or other horny parts (as claws or nails) (2) : a manufactured product (as a plastic) resembling horn **e** : a hollow horn used to hold something

◇ WORD HISTORY
**horde** In a 1985 novel, a young boy is described as owning "a horde of teddy bears." That *horde* can now be linked with something as innocuous as teddy bears demonstrates how far the word has strayed from its original application to divisions of the Mongols and Turks, whose forays beyond Central Asia in the Middle Ages terrified the world. The source of *horde* is ultimately Turkic *ordu* or *ordō,* meaning "royal camp" or "royal residence" in the earliest inscriptions. The word was borrowed from Turkic into Mongolian as *ordu* and after the division of Genghis Khan's empire following his death was associated with the field armies and encampments, such as the Golden Horde, that governed each part of the empire. The Turkic and Mongolian word was borrowed into Old Russian as *orda,* and, with the addition of a murmured \h\ in some forms of Ukrainian, was borrowed into Polish as *horda* and hence into Western European languages. The indistinct European image of a Central Asian army as a nomadic swarm led to the eventual generalization of the word *horde* to mean a large number of almost anything—even teddy bears.

\ə\ abut  \ᵊ\ kitten  \ər\ further  \a\ ash  \ā\ ace
\ä\ mop, mar  \aů\ out  \ch\ chin  \e\ bet  \ē\ easy
\g\ go  \i\ hit  \ī\ ice  \j\ job  \ŋ\ sing  \ō\ go
\ȯ\ law  \ȯi\ boy  \th\ thin  \t͟h\ the  \ü\ loot  \ů\ foot
\y\ yet  \zh\ vision  *see also* Guide to Pronunciation

**2 :** something resembling or suggestive of a horn: as **a :** one of the curved ends of a crescent **b :** a sharp mountain peak **c :** a body of land or water shaped like a horn **d :** a beak-shaped part of an anvil **e :** a high pommel of a saddle **f :** CORNU
**3 a :** an animal's horn used as a wind instrument **b :** a brass wind instrument: as (1) **:** HUNTING HORN (2) **:** FRENCH HORN **c :** a wind instrument used in a jazz band; *especially* **:** TRUMPET **d :** a usually electrical device that makes a noise like that of a horn
**4 :** a source of strength
**5 :** one of the equally disadvantageous alternatives presented by a dilemma
**6** *slang* **:** TELEPHONE
— **horn** *adjective*
— **horned** \'hórnd *also* 'hòr-nəd\ *adjective*
— **horned·ness** \'hòr-nəd-nəs, 'hòrn(d)-nəs\ *noun*
— **horn·less** \'hòrn-ləs\ *adjective*
— **horn·less·ness** *noun*
— **horn·like** \-,līk\ *adjective*
**horn·beam** \'hòrn-,bēm\ *noun* (14th century) **:** any of a genus (*Carpinus*) of trees of the birch family having smooth gray bark and hard white wood
**horn·bill** \-,bil\ *noun* (1773) **:** any of a family (Bucerotidae) of large non-passerine Old World birds having enormous bills
**horn·blende** \-,blend\ *noun* [German] (1770) **:** a mineral that is the common dark variety of aluminous amphibole; *broadly* **:** AMPHIBOLE 2
— **horn·blend·ic** \hòrn-'blen-dik\ *adjective*
**horn·book** \'hòrn-,bůk\ *noun* (circa 1595)
**1 :** a child's primer consisting of a sheet of parchment or paper protected by a sheet of transparent horn
**2 :** a rudimentary treatise
**horned lizard** *noun* (1806)
**:** HORNED TOAD
**horned owl** *noun* (14th century) **:** any of various owls having conspicuous tufts of feathers on the head
**horned pout** *noun* (1837) **:** a bullhead (genus *Ameiurus*); *especially* **:** a common bullhead (*A. nebulosus*) of the eastern U.S. that has been introduced into streams of the Pacific coast
**horned toad** \'hòrnd-; 'hòr-nəd-, -nət-\ *noun* (1806) **:** any of several small harmless insectivorous lizards (genus *Phrynosoma*) of the western U.S. and Mexico having hornlike spines
**horned viper** *noun* (1767)
**:** CERASTES
**hor·net** \'hòr-nət\ *noun* [Middle English *hernet*, from Old English *hyrnet*; akin to Old High German *hornaz* hornet, Latin *crabro*] (before 12th century) **:** any of the larger social wasps (family Vespidae) — compare YELLOW JACKET
**hornet's nest** *noun* (circa 1740)
**1 :** a troublesome or hazardous situation
**2 :** an angry reaction ⟨must have known that his frank comments . . . would stir up a *hornet's nest* —*U.S. Investor*⟩
**horn·fels** \'hòrn-,felz\ *noun* [German, from *Horn* horn + *Fels* cliff, rock] (1854) **:** a fine-grained silicate rock produced by metamorphism especially of slate
**horn fly** *noun* (1708) **:** a small black European fly (*Haematobia irritans*) that has been introduced into North America where it is a blood-sucking pest of cattle
**horn in** *intransitive verb* (1911) **:** to participate without invitation or consent **:** INTRUDE
**horn·ist** \'hòr-nist\ *noun* (1836) **:** one who plays a French horn
**horn–mad** \'hòrn-'mad\ *adjective* (1579) **:** furiously enraged
**horn of plenty** (circa 1586)
**:** CORNUCOPIA

**horn·pipe** \'hòrn-,pīp\ *noun* (15th century)
**1 :** a single-reed wind instrument consisting of a wooden or bone pipe with finger holes, a bell, and mouthpiece usually of horn
**2 :** a lively folk dance of the British Isles originally accompanied by hornpipe playing
**horn-rims** \-,rimz\ *noun plural* (1927) **:** glasses with horn rims
**horn·stone** \'hòrn-,stōn\ *noun* (1728) **:** a mineral that is a variety of quartz much like flint but more brittle
**horn·swog·gle** \-,swä-gəl\ *transitive verb* **-swog·gled; -swog·gling** \-g(ə-)liŋ\ [origin unknown] (circa 1829) *slang* **:** BAMBOOZLE, HOAX
**horn·tail** \-,tāl\ *noun* (1884) **:** any of various hymenopterous insects (family Siricidae) related to the typical sawflies but having larvae that burrow in woody plants and on the females a stout hornlike ovipositor for depositing the egg
**horn·worm** \-,wərm\ *noun* (1676) **:** a hawkmoth caterpillar having a hornlike tail process — compare TOMATO HORNWORM
**horn·wort** \-,wərt, -,wòrt\ *noun* (circa 1805) **:** any of a genus (*Ceratophyllum*) of rootless thin-stemmed aquatic herbs that have flowers with a sepaloid perianth and a single carpel
**horny** \'hòr-nē\ *adjective* **horn·i·er; -est** (14th century)
**1 a :** of or made of horn **b :** HARD, CALLOUS ⟨*horny*-handed⟩ **c :** compact and homogeneous with a dull luster — used of a mineral
**2 :** having horns
**3** [*horn* erect penis + -[1]*y*] **a :** desiring sexual gratification **b :** excited sexually
— **horn·i·ness** *noun*
**hor·o·loge** \'hòr-ə-,lōj, 'här-\ *noun* [Middle English, from Middle French, from Latin *horologium*, from Greek *hōrologion*, from *hōra* hour + *legein* to gather — more at YEAR, LEGEND] (14th century) **:** a timekeeping device
**hor·o·log·i·cal** \,hòr-ə-'lä-ji-kəl\ *adjective* (15th century) **:** of or relating to a horologe or horology
**ho·rol·o·gist** \hə-'rä-lə-jist\ *noun* (1798)
**1 :** a person skilled in the practice or theory of horology
**2 :** a maker of clocks or watches
**ho·rol·o·gy** \-jē\ *noun* [Greek *hōra* + English *-logy*] (1819)
**1 :** the science of measuring time
**2 :** the art of making instruments for indicating time
**horo·scope** \'hòr-ə-,skōp, 'här-\ *noun* [Middle English *oruscope*, from Middle French *horoscope*, from Latin *horoscopus*, from Greek *hōroskopos*, from *hōra* + *skopos* watcher; akin to Greek *skopein* to look at — more at SPY] (14th century)
**1 :** a diagram of the relative positions of planets and signs of the zodiac at a specific time (as at one's birth) for use by astrologers in inferring individual character and personality traits and in foretelling events of a person's life
**2 :** an astrological forecast
**hor·ren·dous** \hò-'ren-dəs, hä-, hə-\ *adjective* [Latin *horrendus*, from gerundive of *horrēre*] (1659) **:** perfectly horrid **:** DREADFUL ⟨the tax rate was *horrendous*⟩
— **hor·ren·dous·ly** *adverb*
**hor·rent** \'hòr-ənt, 'här-\ *adjective* [Latin *horrent-, horrens*, present participle of *horrēre*] (1667)
**1** *archaic* **:** covered with bristling points **:** BRISTLED
**2** *archaic* **:** standing up like bristles **:** BRISTLING
**hor·ri·ble** \'hòr-ə-bəl, 'här-\ *adjective* [Middle English *orrible, horrible*, from Middle French, from Latin *horribilis*, from *horrēre*] (14th century)
**1 :** marked by or conducive to horror

**2 :** extremely unpleasant or disagreeable
— **horrible** *noun*
— **hor·ri·ble·ness** *noun*
— **hor·ri·bly** \-blē\ *adverb*
**hor·rid** \'hòr-əd, 'här-\ *adjective* [Latin *horridus*, from *horrēre*] (1590)
**1** *archaic* **:** ROUGH, BRISTLING
**2 :** innately offensive or repulsive: **a :** inspiring horror **:** SHOCKING **b :** inspiring disgust or loathing **:** NASTY
— **hor·rid·ly** *adverb*
— **hor·rid·ness** *noun*
**hor·rif·ic** \hò-'ri-fik, hä-\ *adjective* (1653) **:** having the power to horrify ⟨a *horrific* account of the tragedy⟩
— **hor·rif·i·cal·ly** \-fi-k(ə-)lē\ *adverb*
**hor·ri·fy** \'hòr-ə-,fī, 'här-\ *transitive verb* **-fied; -fy·ing** (1791)
**1 :** to cause to feel horror
**2 :** to fill with distaste **:** SHOCK
*synonym* see DISMAY
— **hor·ri·fy·ing·ly** \-,fī-iŋ-lē\ *adverb*
[1]**hor·ror** \'hòr-ər, 'här-\ *noun* [Middle English *horrour*, from Middle French *horror*, from Latin, action of bristling, from *horrēre* to bristle, shiver; akin to Sanskrit *harṣate* he is excited] (14th century)
**1 a :** painful and intense fear, dread, or dismay ⟨astonishment giving place to *horror* on the faces of the people about me —H. G. Wells⟩ **b :** intense aversion or repugnance
**2 a :** the quality of inspiring horror **:** repulsive, horrible, or dismal quality or character ⟨contemplating the *horror* of their lives —Liam O'Flaherty⟩ **b :** something that inspires horror
**3** *plural* **:** a state of extreme depression or apprehension
[2]**horror** *adjective* (1797) **:** calculated to inspire feelings of dread or horror **:** BLOODCURDLING ⟨a *horror* story⟩
**hor·ror–struck** \-,strək\ *adjective* (1814) **:** struck with horror ⟨stood *horror-struck* as they watched . . . their own city destroyed —*Nashville Tennessean*⟩
**hors de com·bat** \,òr-də-kōⁿ-'bä\ *adverb or adjective* [French] (1757) **:** out of combat **:** DISABLED
**hors d'oeuvre** \òr-'dərv\ *noun, plural* **hors d'oeuvres** *also* **hors d'oeuvre** \-'dərv(z)\ [French *hors-d'œuvre*, literally, outside of the work] (1714) **:** any of various savory foods usually served as appetizers
[1]**horse** \'hòrs\ *noun, plural* **hors·es** *also* **horse** [Middle English *hors*, from Old English; akin to Old High German *hros* horse] (before 12th century)

horse 1a(1): *1* forehead, *2* forelock, *3* poll, *4* mane, *5* withers, *6* back, *7* flank, *8* loin, *9* haunch, *10* croup, *11* point of hip, *12* tail, *13* hock, *14* cannon, *15* gaskin, *16* thigh, *17* stifle, *18* barrel, *19* chestnut, *20* fetlock, *21* pastern, *22* hoof, *23* coronet, *24* knee, *25* forearm, *26* chest, *27* shoulder, *28* neck, *29* throatlatch, *30* cheek

**1 a** (1) : a large solid-hoofed herbivorous mammal (*Equus caballus,* family Equidae, the horse family) domesticated since a prehistoric period and used as a beast of burden, a draft animal, or for riding (2) : RACEHORSE ⟨play the *horses*⟩ **b** : a male horse; *especially* : STALLION **c** : a recent or extinct animal (as a zebra, ass, or onager) of the horse family
**2 a** : JACKSTAY **b** : a frame usually with legs used for supporting something (as planks or staging) **c** (1) : POMMEL HORSE (2) : VAULTING HORSE
**3** *horse plural* : CAVALRY
**4** : a mass of the same geological character as the wall rock occurring within a vein
**5** : HORSEPOWER
**6** *slang* : HEROIN
**7** : an athlete whose performance is consistently strong and reliable ⟨a team with the *horses* to win the pennant⟩
— **horse·less** \'hȯr-sləs\ *adjective*
— **horse·like** \'hȯrs-,līk\ *adjective*
— **from the horse's mouth** : from the original source

²**horse** *verb* **horsed; hors·ing** (before 12th century)
*transitive verb*
**1** : to provide with a horse
**2** : to move by brute force
*intransitive verb*
*of a mare* : to be in heat

³**horse** *adjective* (15th century)
**1 a** : of or relating to a horse **b** : hauled or powered by a horse ⟨a *horse* barge⟩
**2** : large or coarse of its kind
**3** : mounted on horses ⟨*horse* guards⟩

**horse–and–buggy** *adjective* (circa 1926)
**1** : of or relating to the era before the advent of certain socially revolutionizing inventions (as the automobile)
**2** : clinging to outdated attitudes or ideas : OLD-FASHIONED

**horse around** *intransitive verb* (circa 1928)
: to engage in horseplay ⟨*horse around* together, joking and laughing and pushing each other —D. K. Shipler⟩; *also* : FOOL AROUND 1

¹**horse·back** \'hȯrs-,bak\ *noun* (14th century)
: the back of a horse

²**horseback** *adverb* (1727)
: on horseback

³**horseback** *adjective* (1879)
: given without thorough consideration ⟨a *horseback* opinion⟩

**horse·bean** \'hȯrs-,bēn\ *noun* (1684)
**1** : BROAD BEAN
**2** : JERUSALEM THORN

**horse·car** \-,kär\ *noun* (1833)
**1** : a streetcar drawn by horses
**2** : a car fitted for transporting horses

**horse chestnut** *noun* (1597)
**1** : a large Asian tree (*Aesculus hippocastanum* of the family Hippocastanaceae, the horse-chestnut family) that has palmate leaves and erect conical clusters of showy flowers and is widely cultivated as an ornamental and shade tree and naturalized as an escape; *also* : BUCKEYE
**2** : the large glossy brown seed of a horse chestnut

**horse coper** *noun* (1614)
*British* : COPER

**horse·feath·ers** \'hȯrs-,fe-thərz\ *noun plural* (1928)
*slang* : NONSENSE, BALDERDASH

**horse·flesh** \-,flesh\ *noun* (15th century)
: horses considered especially with reference to riding, driving, or racing

**horse·fly** \-,flī\ *noun* (14th century)
: any of a family (Tabanidae) of swift usually large two-winged flies with bloodsucking females

**horse gentian** *noun* (1837)
: FEVERWORT

**horse·hair** \'hȯrs-,har, -,her\ *noun* (14th century)

**1** : the hair of a horse especially from the mane or tail
**2** : cloth made from horsehair

**horsehair worm** *noun* (circa 1753)
: HAIRWORM 1 — called also *horsehair snake*

**horse·hide** \'hȯrs-,hīd\ *noun* (14th century)
**1** : the dressed or raw hide of a horse
**2** : the ball used in the game of baseball

**horse latitudes** *noun plural* (1777)
: either of two belts or regions in the neighborhood of 30° N and 30° S latitude characterized by high pressure, calms, and light variable winds

**horse·laugh** \'hȯrs-,laf, -,láf\ *noun* (1713)
: a loud boisterous laugh : GUFFAW

**horseless carriage** *noun* (1895)
: AUTOMOBILE

**horse mackerel** *noun* (circa 1705)
**1** : any of various large carangid food fishes; *especially* : JACK MACKEREL
**2** : BLUEFIN TUNA

**horse·man** \'hȯr-smən\ *noun* (14th century)
**1** : a rider or driver of horses; *especially* : one whose skill is exceptional
**2** : a person skilled in caring for or managing horses
**3** : a person who breeds or raises horses
— **horse·man·ship** \-,ship\ *noun*

**horse·mint** \'hȯrs-,mint\ *noun* (before 12th century)
: any of various coarse mints; *especially* : MONARDA

**horse nettle** *noun* (circa 1818)
: a coarse prickly weed (*Solanum carolinense*) of the nightshade family with bright yellow fruit resembling berries

**horse opera** *noun* (1927)
: WESTERN 2

**horse·play** \'hȯrs-,plā\ *noun* (1589)
: rough or boisterous play

**horse·play·er** \-ər\ *noun* (1947)
: one who habitually bets on horse races

**horse·pow·er** \'hȯrs-,paù(-ə)r\ *noun* (1806)
**1** : the power that a horse exerts in pulling
**2** : a unit of power equal in the U.S. to 746 watts and nearly equivalent to the English gravitational unit of the same name that equals 550 foot-pounds of work per second
**3** : effective power ⟨intellectual *horsepower*⟩ ⟨computing *horsepower*⟩

**horse race** *noun* (1954)
: a close contest (as in politics)

**horse·rad·ish** \'hȯrs-,ra-dish, -,re-\ *noun* (1597)
**1** : a tall coarse white-flowered herb (*Armoracia lapathifolia*) of the mustard family
**2** : a condiment made from ground-up horseradish root

**horse's ass** \'hȯr-səz-\ *noun* (circa 1942)
: a stupid or incompetent person : BLOCKHEAD — often considered vulgar

**horse sense** *noun* (1832)
: COMMON SENSE

**horse·shit** \'hȯrs-,shit, 'hȯrsh-\ *noun* (1946)
: NONSENSE, BUNK — usually considered vulgar

**horse·shoe** \'hȯrs-,shü, 'hȯrsh-\ *noun* (14th century)
**1** : a usually U-shaped band of iron fitted and nailed to the rim of a horse's hoof to protect it
**2** : something (as a valley) shaped like a horseshoe
**3** *plural* : a game like quoits played with horseshoes or with horseshoe-shaped pieces of metal
— **horseshoe** *transitive verb*
— **horse·sho·er** \-,shü-ər\ *noun*

**horseshoe arch** *noun* (circa 1816)
: an arch having an intrados that widens above the springing before narrowing to a rounded or pointed crown — see ARCH illustration

**horseshoe crab** *noun* (1797)
: any of several closely related marine arthropods (order Xiphosura and class Merostomata) with a broad crescentic cephalothorax — called also *king crab*

**horse show** *noun* (1856)
: an exhibition of horses that usually includes competition in riding, driving, and jumping

**horse·tail** \'hȯrs-,tāl\ *noun* (15th century)
: EQUISETUM

**horse trade** *noun* (1846)
: negotiation accompanied by shrewd bargaining and reciprocal concessions ⟨a political *horse trade*⟩
— **horse–trade** *intransitive verb*
— **horse trader** *noun*

**horse·weed** \'hȯrs-,wēd\ *noun* (1790)
**1** : a common North American fleabane (*Conyza canadensis* synonym *Erigeron canadensis*) with linear leaves and small discoid heads of yellowish flowers
**2** : a coarse annual ragweed (*Ambrosia trifida*)

**horse·whip** \'hȯrs-,wip, 'hȯrs-,hwip\ *transitive verb* (1768)
: to flog with or as if with a whip made to be used on a horse
— **horse·whip·per** *noun*

**horse·wom·an** \'hȯrs-,wùm-ən\ *noun* (circa 1578)
**1** : a woman rider or driver of horses; *especially* : one whose skill is exceptional
**2** : a woman skilled in caring for or managing horses
**3** : a woman who breeds or raises horses

**hors·ey** *or* **horsy** \'hȯr-sē\ *adjective* **hors·i·er; -est** (1591)
**1** : of, relating to, or resembling a horse
**2** : having to do with horses or horse racing
**3** : characteristic of the manners, dress, or tastes of horsemen or horsewomen
— **hors·i·ly** \-sə-lē\ *adverb*
— **hors·i·ness** \-sē-nəs\ *noun*

**horst** \'hȯrst\ *noun* [German, literally, thicket] (1893)
: a block of the earth's crust separated by faults from adjacent relatively depressed blocks

**hor·ta·tive** \'hȯr-tə-tiv\ *adjective* [Late Latin *hortativus*, from Latin *hortatus*, past participle of *hortari* to urge — more at YEARN] (1623)
: giving exhortation : ADVISORY
— **hor·ta·tive·ly** *adverb*

**hor·ta·to·ry** \'hȯr-tə-,tōr-ē, -,tȯr-\ *adjective* (1586)
: HORTATIVE, EXHORTATORY

**hor·ti·cul·ture** \'hȯr-tə-,kəl-chər\ *noun* [Latin *hortus* garden + English *-i-* + *culture* — more at YARD] (1678)
: the science and art of growing fruits, vegetables, flowers, or ornamental plants
— **hor·ti·cul·tur·al** \,hȯr-tə-'kəl-chə-rəl\ *adjective*
— **hor·ti·cul·tur·al·ly** \-rə-lē\ *adverb*
— **hor·ti·cul·tur·ist** \-rist\ *noun*

**Ho·rus** \'hōr-əs, 'hȯr-\ *noun* [Late Latin, from Greek *Hōros,* from Egyptian *Ḥr*]
: the Egyptian god of light and the son of Osiris and Isis

**ho·san·na** *also* **ho·san·nah** \hō-'za-nə *also* -'zä-\ *interjection* [Middle English *osanna,* from Old English, from Late Latin, from Greek *hōsanna,* from Hebrew *hōshī'āh-nnā* pray, save (us)!] (before 12th century)
— used as a cry of acclamation and adoration
— **hosanna** *noun*

**HO scale** \(')ā-'chō-\ *noun* [*half* + *O* (*gauge*)] (1939)
: a scale of 3.5 millimeters to one foot used especially for model toys (as automobiles or trains)

¹**hose** \'hōz\ *noun, plural* **hose** *or* **hos·es** [Middle English, from Old English *hosa* stocking, husk; akin to Old High German *hosa* leg covering] (before 12th century)

\ə\ abut \ᵊ\ kitten \ər\ further \a\ ash \ā\ ace
\ä\ mop, mar \aù\ out \ch\ chin \e\ bet \ē\ easy
\g\ go \i\ hit \ī\ ice \j\ job \ŋ\ sing \ō\ go
\ȯ\ law \ȯi\ boy \th\ thin \ṯh\ the \ü\ loot \ù\ foot
\y\ yet \zh\ vision *see also* Guide to Pronunciation

**1** *plural* **hose a** (1) : a cloth leg covering that sometimes covers the foot (2) : STOCKING, SOCK **b** (1) : a close-fitting garment covering the legs and waist that is usually attached to a doublet by points (2) : short breeches reaching to the knee **2** : a flexible tube for conveying fluids (as from a faucet or hydrant)

**²hose** *transitive verb* **hosed; hos·ing** (1889) **1** : to spray, water, or wash with a hose — often used with *down* ⟨*hose* down a stable floor⟩ **2** *slang* **a** : to deprive of something due or expected : TRICK, CHEAT **b** : to shoot with automatic weapons fire

**Ho·sea** \hō-'zā-ə, -'zē-\ *noun* [Hebrew *Hōshēa'*] **1** : a Hebrew prophet of the 8th century B.C. **2** : a prophetic book of canonical Jewish and Christian Scripture — see BIBLE table

**ho·sel** \'hō-zəl\ *noun* [diminutive of ¹*hose*] (1899) : a socket in the head of a golf club into which the shaft is inserted

**hose·pipe** \'hōz-,pīp\ *noun* (1835) *chiefly British* : HOSE 2

**ho·siery** \'hōzh-rē, 'hōz-; 'hō-zhə-rē, -zə-\ *noun* (1796) **1** : HOSE 1a **2** *chiefly British* : KNITWEAR

**hos·pice** \'häs-pəs\ *noun* [French, from Latin *hospitium*, from *hospit-, hospes* host — more at HOST] (1818) **1** : a lodging for travelers, young persons, or the underprivileged especially when maintained by a religious order **2** : a facility or program designed to provide a caring environment for supplying the physical and emotional needs of the terminally ill

**hos·pi·ta·ble** \hä-'spi-tə-bəl, 'häs-(,)pi-\ *adjective* (circa 1570) **1 a** : given to generous and cordial reception of guests **b** : promising or suggesting generous and cordial welcome **c** : offering a pleasant or sustaining environment **2** : readily receptive : OPEN ⟨*hospitable* to new ideas⟩ — **hos·pi·ta·bly** \-blē\ *adverb*

**hos·pi·tal** \'häs-(,)pi-t²l\ *noun, often attributive* [Middle English, from Middle French, from Medieval Latin *hospitale* hospice, guest house, from neuter of Latin *hospitalis* of a guest, from *hospit-, hospes*] (14th century) **1** : a charitable institution for the needy, aged, infirm, or young **2** : an institution where the sick or injured are given medical or surgical care — usually used in British English without an article after a preposition **3** : a repair shop for specified small objects ⟨clock *hospital*⟩

**hos·pi·tal·ise** *British variant of* HOSPITALIZE

**hos·pi·tal·i·ty** \,häs-pə-'ta-lə-tē\ *noun, plural* **-ties** (14th century) : hospitable treatment, reception, or disposition

**hospitality suite** *noun* (1963) : a room or suite especially in a hotel set aside as a place for socializing especially for business purposes

**hos·pi·tal·ize** \'häs-,pi-t²l-,īz\ *transitive verb* **-ized; -iz·ing** (circa 1899) : to place in a hospital as a patient — **hos·pi·tal·iza·tion** \,häs-,pi-t²l-ə-'zā-shən\ *noun*

**Hos·pi·tal·ler** *or* **Hos·pi·tal·er** \-t²l-ər\ *noun* [Middle English *hospitalier*, from Middle French, from Medieval Latin *hospitalarius*, from Late Latin *hospitale*] (14th century) : a member of a religious military order established in Jerusalem in the 12th century

**¹host** \'hōst\ *noun* [Middle English, from Old French, from Late Latin *hostis*, from Latin, stranger, enemy — more at GUEST] (14th century)

**1** : ARMY **2** : a very large number : MULTITUDE

**²host** *intransitive verb* (15th century) : to assemble in a host usually for a hostile purpose

**³host** *noun* [Middle English *hoste* host, guest, from Old French, from Latin *hospit-, hospes*, probably from *hostis*] (14th century) **1 a** : one that receives or entertains guests socially, commercially, or officially **b** : one that provides facilities for an event or function ⟨our college served as *host* for the basketball tournament⟩ **2 a** : a living animal or plant affording subsistence or lodgment to a parasite **b** : the larger, stronger, or dominant member of a commensal or symbiotic pair **c** : an individual into which a tissue, part, or embryo is transplanted from another **3** : a mineral or rock that is older than the minerals or rocks in it; *also* : a substance that contains a usually small amount of another substance incorporated in its structure **4** : a radio or television emcee **5** : a computer that controls communications in a network that administers a database

**⁴host** *transitive verb* (15th century) **1** : to serve as host to, at, or for ⟨*host* friends⟩ ⟨*host* a dinner⟩ **2** : EMCEE ⟨*hosted* a series of TV programs⟩

**⁵host** *noun, often capitalized* [Middle English *hoste, oste*, from Middle French *hoiste*, from Late Latin & Latin; Late Latin *hostia* Eucharist, from Latin, sacrifice] (14th century) : the eucharistic bread

**hos·ta** \'hō-stə, 'hä-\ *noun* [New Latin, from Nicolaus *Host* (died 1834) Austrian botanist] (1828) : PLANTAIN LILY

**hos·tage** \'häs-tij\ *noun* [Middle English, from Old French, from *hoste*] (13th century) **1 a** : a person held by one party in a conflict as a pledge that promises will be kept or terms met by the other party **b** : a person taken by force to secure the taker's demands **2** : one that is involuntarily controlled by an outside influence

**¹hos·tel** \'häs-t²l\ *noun* [Middle English, from Old French, from Medieval Latin *hospitale* hospice] (14th century) **1** : INN **2 a** *chiefly British* : a supervised institutional residence **b** : a supervised lodging for usually young travelers — called also *youth hostel*

**²hostel** *intransitive verb* **-teled** *or* **-telled; -tel·ing** *or* **-tel·ling** (14th century) : to stay at hostels overnight in the course of traveling

**hos·tel·er** *or* **hos·tel·ler** \'häs-tə-lər\ *noun* (14th century) **1** : one that lodges guests or strangers **2** : a traveler who stops at hostels overnight

**hos·tel·ry** \'häs-t²l-rē\ *noun, plural* **-ries** (14th century) : INN, HOTEL

**¹host·ess** \'hōs-təs\ *noun* (14th century) **1** : a woman who entertains socially **2 a** : a woman in charge of a public dining room who seats diners **b** : a female employee on a public conveyance (as an airplane) who manages the provisioning of food and attends passengers **c** : a woman who acts as a dancing partner or companion to male patrons in a dance hall or bar

**²hostess** (1927) *intransitive verb* : to act as hostess *transitive verb* : to serve as hostess to

**hos·tile** \'häs-t²l, -,tīl\ *adjective* [Middle French or Latin; Middle French, from Latin *hostilis*, from *hostis*] (1580) **1 a** : of or relating to an enemy ⟨*hostile* fire⟩ **b** : marked by malevolence ⟨a *hostile* act⟩ **c** : openly opposed or resisting ⟨*hostile* critic⟩

⟨*hostile* to new ideas⟩ **d** : not hospitable ⟨a *hostile* environment⟩ **2 a** : of or relating to the opposing party in a legal controversy ⟨a *hostile* witness⟩ **b** : adverse to the interests of a property owner or corporation management ⟨a *hostile* takeover⟩ — **hostile** *noun* — **hos·tile·ly** \-t²l-(l)ē, -,tīl-lē\ *adverb*

**hos·til·i·ty** \hä-'sti-lə-tē\ *noun, plural* **-ties** (15th century) **1 a** : deep-seated usually mutual ill will **b** (1) : hostile action (2) *plural* : overt acts of warfare : WAR **2** : conflict, opposition, or resistance in thought or principle *synonym* see ENMITY

**hos·tler** \'häs-lər, 'äs-\ *noun* [Middle English, innkeeper, hostler, from *hostel*] (14th century) **1** : one who takes care of horses or mules **2** : one who moves locomotives in and out of a roundhouse; *also* : one who services locomotives

**host·ly** \'hōst-lē\ *adjective* (1893) : of or appropriate to a host

**¹hot** \'hät\ *adjective* **hot·ter; hot·test** [Middle English, from Old English *hāt*; akin to Old High German *heiz* hot, Lithuanian *kaisti* to get hot] (before 12th century) **1 a** : having a relatively high temperature **b** : capable of giving a sensation of heat or of burning, searing, or scalding **c** : having heat in a degree exceeding normal body heat **2 a** : VIOLENT, STORMY ⟨a *hot* temper⟩ ⟨a *hot* battle⟩; *also* : ANGRY ⟨got *hot* about the remark⟩ **b** : sexually excited or receptive; *also* : SEXY **c** : EAGER, ZEALOUS ⟨*hot* for reform⟩ **d** *of jazz* : emotionally exciting and marked by strong rhythms and free melodic improvisations **3** : having or causing the sensation of an uncomfortable degree of body heat ⟨*hot* and tired⟩ ⟨it's *hot* in here⟩ **4 a** : newly made : FRESH ⟨a *hot* scent⟩ ⟨*hot* off the press⟩ **b** : close to something sought ⟨*hot* on the trail⟩ **5 a** : suggestive of heat or of burning or glowing objects ⟨*hot* colors⟩ **b** : PUNGENT, PEPPERY **6 a** : of intense and immediate interest ⟨some *hot* gossip⟩ **b** : unusually lucky or favorable ⟨on a *hot* streak⟩ **c** : temporarily capable of unusual performance (as in a sport) **d** : currently popular or in demand ⟨a *hot* commodity⟩ **e** : very good ⟨a *hot* idea⟩ ⟨not feeling too *hot*⟩ **f** : ABSURD, UNBELIEVABLE ⟨wants to fight the champ? that's a *hot* one⟩ **7 a** : electrically energized especially with high voltage **b** : RADIOACTIVE; *also* : dealing with radioactive material **c** *of an atom or molecule* : being in an excited state **8 a** : recently and illegally obtained ⟨*hot* jewels⟩ **b** : wanted by the police; *also* : unsafe for a fugitive **9** : FAST ⟨a *hot* new fighter plane⟩ ⟨a *hot* lap around the track⟩ — **hot·ness** *noun* — **hot·tish** \'hä-tish\ *adjective* — **hot under the collar** : extremely exasperated or angry

**²hot** *adverb* (before 12th century) **1** : HOTLY **2** : FAST, QUICKLY

**³hot** *noun* (13th century) **1** : HEAT 1d(1) ⟨the *hot* of the day⟩ **2** : one that is hot (as a hot meal or a horse just after a workout) **3** *plural* : strong sexual desire — used with *the*

**⁴hot** *transitive verb* **hot·ted; hot·ting** (1561) *chiefly Southern, southern Midland, & British* : HEAT, WARM — usually used with *up*

**hot air** *noun* (1873) : empty talk

**hot·bed** \'hät-,bed\ *noun* (1626)

**1 :** a bed of soil enclosed in glass, heated especially by fermenting manure, and used for forcing or for raising seedlings
**2 :** an environment that favors rapid growth or development ⟨a *hotbed* of activity⟩
**hot-blood** \-,bləd\ *noun* (1798)
**1 :** one that is hot-blooded; *especially* **:** one having strong passions or a quick temper
**2 :** THOROUGHBRED 1
**hot-blood-ed** \-'blə-dəd\ *adjective* (1598)
**1 :** easily excited **:** PASSIONATE
**2** *of a horse* **:** having Arab or Thoroughbred ancestors
— **hot–blood-ed-ness** *noun*
**hot-box** \-,bäks\ *noun* (1848)
**:** a journal bearing (as of a railroad car) overheated by friction
**hot button** *noun* (1975)
**:** an emotional and usually controversial issue or concern that triggers immediate intense reaction
— **hot–button** *adjective*
**hot-cake** \-,kāk\ *noun* (1683)
**:** PANCAKE
— **like hotcakes :** at a rapid rate ⟨selling like *hotcakes*⟩
**hotch** \'häch\ *intransitive verb* [Middle English, probably from Middle French *hocher* to shake, from Old French *hochier*] (15th century)
**1** *Scottish* **:** WIGGLE, FIDGET
**2** *chiefly Scottish* **:** SWARM
**hotch-pot** \'häch-,pät\ *noun* [Anglo-French *hochepot*, from Old French, *hotchpotch*] (1552)
**:** the combining of properties into a common lot to ensure equality of division among heirs
**hotch-potch** \'häch-,päch\ *noun* [Middle English *hochepot*, from Middle French, from Old French, from *hochier* to shake + *pot*] (1583)
**1 a :** a thick soup or stew of vegetables, potatoes, and usually meat **b :** HODGEPODGE
**2 :** HOTCHPOT
**hot comb** *noun* (1970)
**:** a metal comb usually electrically heated for straightening or styling the hair
— **hot–comb** *transitive verb*
**hot corner** *noun* (1903)
**:** the fielding position of the third baseman in baseball
**hot-dog** \'hät-,dog\ *intransitive verb* [²*hot dog*] (1962)
**:** to perform in a conspicuous or often ostentatious manner; *especially* **:** to perform fancy stunts and maneuvers (as while surfing or skiing)
— **hot-dog-ger** \-,do-gər\ *noun*
**¹hot dog** \'hät-,dog\ *noun* (circa 1900)
**1 :** FRANKFURTER; *especially* **:** a frankfurter heated and served in a long split roll
**2** [perhaps from ²*hot dog*] **:** one that hotdogs; *also* **:** SHOW-OFF
**²hot dog** \'hät-'dog\ *interjection* (circa 1906)
— used to express approval or gratification
**ho-tel** \hō-'tel, 'hō-,\ *noun* [French *hôtel*, from Old French *hostel* hostel] (1765)
**:** an establishment that provides lodging and usually meals, entertainment, and various personal services for the public **:** INN
— **ho-tel-dom** \-dəm\ *noun*
**Hotel** (1952)
— a communications code word for the letter *h*
**ho-te-lier** \hō-'tel-yər; ,ō-t°l-'yā, ,ō-\ *noun* [French *hôtelier*, from Old French *hostelier*, from *hostel*] (1905)
**:** a proprietor or manager of a hotel
**ho-tel-man** \hō-'tel-,man, -mən\ *noun* (1920)
**:** one who is engaged in the hotel business especially in a supervisory or managerial capacity
**hot flash** *noun* (1910)
**:** a sudden brief flushing and sensation of heat caused by dilation of skin capillaries usually associated with menopausal endocrine imbalance — called also *hot flush*

**¹hot-foot** \'hät-,fut\ *adverb* (14th century)
**:** in haste
**²hotfoot** *intransitive verb* (1896)
**:** to go hotfoot **:** HURRY — usually used with *it*
**³hotfoot** *noun, plural* **hotfoots** (1934)
**:** a practical joke in which a match is surreptitiously inserted between the upper and the sole of a victim's shoe and lighted
**hot-head** \'hät-,hed\ *noun* (1660)
**:** a hotheaded person
**hot-head-ed** \-'he-dəd\ *adjective* (1641)
**:** FIERY, IMPETUOUS
— **hot-head-ed-ly** *adverb*
— **hot-head-ed-ness** *noun*
**¹hot-house** \-,haus\ *noun* (1511)
**1** *obsolete* **:** BORDELLO
**2 :** a greenhouse maintained at a high temperature especially for the culture of tropical plants
**3 :** HOTBED 2
**²hothouse** *adjective* (1838)
**1 :** grown in a hothouse
**2 :** suggestive of growth and development in a hothouse ⟨a *hothouse* existence⟩; *also* **:** suggesting a hothouse ⟨a *hothouse* atmosphere⟩
**hot line** *noun* (1955)
**1 :** a direct telephone line in constant operational readiness so as to facilitate immediate communication
**2 :** a usually toll-free telephone service available to the public for some specific purpose ⟨a consumer *hot line*⟩
**hot-ly** \'hät-lē\ *adverb* (15th century)
**:** in a hot manner ⟨a *hotly* contested series⟩
**hot–melt** \'hät-,melt\ *noun* (1939)
**:** a fast-drying nonvolatile adhesive applied hot in the molten state
**hot metal** *noun* (1960)
**:** composition in which the type is cast from molten metal
**hot money** *noun* (1936)
**:** investment funds intended for the highest short-term rate of return
**hot pepper** *noun* (1945)
**:** any of various small and usually thin-walled capsicum fruits of marked pungency; *also* **:** a plant bearing hot peppers
**hot plate** *noun* (1845)
**1 :** a heated iron plate for cooking
**2 :** a simple portable appliance for heating or for cooking in limited spaces
**hot pot** *noun* (1851)
**1 :** a stew of meat and vegetables
**2 :** FIREPOT 2
**hot potato** *noun* (1846)
**:** a controversial question or issue that involves unpleasant or dangerous consequences for anyone dealing with it
**hot pursuit** *noun* (circa 1922)
**:** close continuous pursuit of a fleeing suspected lawbreaker or hostile military force especially across territorial lines
**hot rod** *noun* (1945)
**:** an automobile rebuilt or modified for high speed and fast acceleration
— **hot–rod** \'hät-'räd\ *verb*
— **hot–rod-der** \'hät-,rä-dər\ *noun*
**hot seat** *noun* (1925)
**1** *slang* **:** ELECTRIC CHAIR
**2 :** a position of uneasiness, embarrassment, or anxiety
**hot-shot** \'hät-,shät\ *noun, often attributive* (circa 1925)
**1 :** a fast freight
**2 :** a person who is conspicuously talented or successful
**hot spot** *noun* (1929)
**1 :** a place of more than usual interest, activity, or action
**2 :** a place in the upper mantle of the earth at which hot magma from the lower mantle upwells to melt through the crust usually in the interior of a tectonic plate to form a volcanic feature; *also* **:** a place in the crust overlying a hot spot

**hot spring** *noun* (1669)
**:** a spring whose water issues at a temperature higher than that of its surroundings
**hot stuff** *noun* (1889)
**:** someone or something unusually good
**Hot-ten-tot** \'hä-t°n-,tät\ *noun* [Afrikaans] (1677)
**1 :** a member of any of a group of Khoisan-speaking pastoral peoples of southern Africa
**2 :** the group of Khoisan languages spoken by the Hottentots
**hot ticket** *noun* (1972)
**:** someone or something very popular **:** RAGE
**hot tub** *noun* (1975)
**:** a large usually wooden tub of hot water in which bathers soak and usually socialize
**hot up** (1878)
*intransitive verb*
*chiefly British* **:** to increase in intensity, pace, or excitement ⟨air raids began to *hot up* about the beginning of February —George Orwell⟩
*transitive verb*
*chiefly British* **:** to make livelier, speedier, or more intense
**hot war** *noun* (1947)
**:** a conflict involving actual fighting — compare COLD WAR
**hot water** *noun* (1537)
**:** TROUBLE 4, DIFFICULTY ⟨was in *hot water* with the authorities⟩
**hot–wire** \'hät-,wī-(ə)r\ *transitive verb* (1954)
**:** to start (as an automobile) by short-circuiting the ignition system
**¹hound** \'haund\ *noun* [Middle English, from Old English *hund;* akin to Old High German *hunt* dog, Latin *canis*, Greek *kyōn*] (before 12th century)
**1 a :** DOG **b :** a dog of any of various hunting breeds typically having large drooping ears and a deep voice and following their prey by scent
**2 :** a mean or despicable person
**3 :** DOGFISH
**4 :** a person who pursues like a hound; *especially* **:** one who avidly seeks or collects something ⟨autograph *hounds*⟩
**²hound** *transitive verb* (1528)
**1 :** to pursue with or as if with hounds
**2 :** to drive or affect by persistent harassing
*synonym* SEE BAIT
— **hound-er** *noun*
**hounds** \'haun(d)z\ *noun plural* [Middle English *houne*, from Old Norse *hūnn* knob at the top of a masthead] (15th century)
**:** the framing at the masthead of a ship that supports the heel of the topmast and the upper parts of the lower rigging
**hound's-tongue** \'haun(d)z-,təŋ\ *noun* (before 12th century)
**:** any of various coarse plants (genus *Cynoglossum*, especially *C. officinale*) of the borage family having tongue-shaped leaves and reddish flowers
**hounds-tooth check** *or* **hound's-tooth check** \'haun(d)z-,tüth-\ *noun* (1937)
**:** a usually small broken-check textile pattern
**hour** \'au(-ə)r\ *noun* [Middle English, from Old French *heure*, from Late Latin & Latin; Late Latin *hora* canonical hour, from Latin, hour of the day, from Greek *hōra* — more at YEAR] (13th century)
**1 :** a time or office for daily liturgical devotion; *especially* **:** CANONICAL HOUR
**2 :** the 24th part of a day **:** 60 minutes

**houndstooth check**

**3 a :** the time of day reckoned in two 12-hour periods **b** *plural* **:** the time reckoned in one 24-hour period from midnight to midnight using a 4-digit number of which the first two digits indicate the hour and the last two digits indicate the minute ⟨in the military 4:30 p.m. is called 1630 *hours*⟩
**4 a :** a customary or particular time ⟨lunch *hour*⟩ ⟨in our *hour* of need⟩ **b** *plural* **:** time of going to bed ⟨keeps late *hours*⟩; *also* **:** time of working ⟨banker's *hours*⟩
**5 :** an angular unit of right ascension equal to 15 degrees measured along the celestial equator
**6 :** the work done or distance traveled at normal rate in an hour ⟨the city was two *hours* away⟩
**7 a :** a class session **b :** CREDIT HOUR, SEMESTER HOUR
— **after hours :** after the regular quitting or closing time
**hour angle** *noun* (circa 1837)
**:** the angle between the celestial meridian of an observer and the hour circle of a celestial object measured westward from the meridian
**hour circle** *noun* (1690)
**:** a circle on the celestial sphere that passes through both celestial poles
¹**hour·glass** \'au̇(-ə)r-ˌglas\ *noun* (circa 1515)
**:** an instrument for measuring time consisting of a glass vessel having two compartments from the uppermost of which a quantity of sand, water, or mercury runs in an hour into the lower one
²**hourglass** *adjective* (circa 1834)
**:** shaped like an hourglass ⟨an *hourglass* figure⟩

**hourglass**

**hour hand** *noun* (1669)
**:** the short hand that marks the hours on the face of a watch or clock
**hou·ri** \'hu̇r-ē, 'hü-rē\ *noun* [French, from Persian *hūri*, from Arabic *hūrīyah*] (1737)
**1 :** one of the beautiful maidens that in Muslim belief live with the blessed in paradise
**2 :** a voluptuously beautiful young woman
**hour–long** \'au̇(-ə)r-ˌlȯŋ\ *adjective* (1803)
**:** lasting an hour
¹**hour·ly** \'au̇(-ə)r-lē\ *adverb* (15th century)
**:** at or during every hour; *also* **:** FREQUENTLY, CONTINUALLY
²**hourly** *adjective* (circa 1530)
**1 a :** occurring hour by hour ⟨*hourly* bus service⟩ **b :** FREQUENT, CONTINUAL ⟨in *hourly* expectation of the rain's stopping⟩
**2 :** computed in terms of an hour ⟨an *hourly* wage⟩
**3 :** paid by the hour ⟨*hourly* workers⟩
¹**house** \'hau̇s\ *noun, plural* **hous·es** \'hau̇-zəz *also* -səz\ *often attributive* [Middle English *hous*, from Old English *hūs*; akin to Old High German *hūs* house] (before 12th century)
**1 :** a building that serves as living quarters for one or a few families **:** HOME
**2 a** (1) **:** a shelter or refuge (as a nest or den) of a wild animal (2) **:** a natural covering (as a test or shell) that encloses and protects an animal or a colony of zooids **b :** a building in which something is housed ⟨a carriage *house*⟩
**3 a :** one of the 12 equal sectors in which the celestial sphere is divided in astrology **b :** a zodiacal sign that is the seat of a planet's greatest influence
**4 a :** HOUSEHOLD **b :** a family including ancestors, descendants, and kindred ⟨the *house* of Tudor⟩
**5 a :** a residence for a religious community or for students **b :** the community or students in residence
**6 a :** a legislative, deliberative, or consultative assembly; *especially* **:** one constituting a divi-

sion of a bicameral body **b :** the building or chamber where such an assembly meets **c :** a quorum of such an assembly
**7 a :** a place of business or entertainment **b** (1) **:** a business organization ⟨a publishing *house*⟩ (2) **:** a gambling establishment **c :** the audience in a theater or concert hall ⟨a full *house* on opening night⟩
**8 :** the circular area 12 feet in diameter surrounding the tee and within which a curling stone must rest in order to count
**9 :** a type of dance music mixed by a disc jockey that features overdubbing with a heavy repetitive drumbeat and repeated electronic melody lines
— **house·ful** \'hau̇s-ˌfu̇l\ *noun*
— **house·less** \'hau̇-sləs\ *adjective*
— **house·less·ness** *noun*
— **on the house :** without charge **:** FREE
²**house** \'hau̇z\ *verb* **housed; hous·ing** (before 12th century)
*transitive verb*
**1 a :** to provide with living quarters or shelter
**b :** to store in a house
**2 :** to encase, enclose, or shelter as if by putting in a house
**3 :** to serve as shelter for **:** CONTAIN
*intransitive verb*
**:** to take shelter **:** LODGE
**house arrest** *noun* (1936)
**:** confinement often under guard to one's house or quarters instead of in prison
**house·boat** \'hau̇s-ˌbōt\ *noun* (1790)
**:** a boat fitted for use as a dwelling; *especially* **:** a pleasure craft with a broad beam, a usually shallow draft, and a large superstructure resembling a house
— **house·boat·er** \-ˌbō-tər\ *noun*
**house·bound** \'hau̇s-ˌbau̇nd\ *adjective* (1878)
**:** confined to the house
**house·boy** \-ˌbȯi\ *noun* (circa 1898)
**:** HOUSEMAN
**house·break** \-ˌbrāk\ *transitive verb* **-broke** \-ˌbrōk\; **-bro·ken** \-ˌbrō-kən\; **-break·ing** [back-formation from *housebroken*] (1944)
**1 :** to make housebroken
**2 a :** to teach acceptable social manners to **b :** TAME, SUBDUE
**house·break·ing** \'hau̇s-ˌbrā-kiŋ\ *noun* (1617)
**:** an act of breaking open and entering the dwelling house of another with a felonious purpose
— **house·break·er** \-ˌbrā-kər\ *noun*
**house·bro·ken** \-ˌbrō-kən\ *adjective* (1900)
**1 :** trained to excretory habits acceptable in indoor living — used of a household pet
**2 :** made tractable or polite
**house call** *noun* (1960)
**:** a visit (as by a doctor or a repair person) to a home to provide a requested service
**house·carl** \-ˌkär(-ə)l\ *noun* [Old English *hūscarl*, from Old Norse *hūskarl*, from *hūs* house + *karl* man; akin to Old English *ceorl* churl] (before 12th century)
**:** a member of the bodyguard of a Danish or early English king or noble
**house cat** *noun* (1607)
**:** CAT 1a
**house·clean** \'hau̇s-ˌklēn\ *verb* [back-formation from *housecleaning*] (1863)
*intransitive verb*
**1 :** to clean a house and its furniture
**2 :** to get rid of unwanted or undesirable items or people
*transitive verb*
**1 :** to clean the surfaces and furnishings of
**2 :** to improve or reform by ridding of undesirable people or practices
— **house·clean·ing** *noun*
**house·coat** \'hau̇s-ˌkōt\ *noun* (1913)
**:** a woman's often long-skirted informal garment for wear around the house
**house cricket** *noun* (1774)
**:** a widely distributed cricket (*Acheta domesticus*) usually living in or about dwellings

**house detective** *noun* (1898)
**:** a person who is employed (as by a hotel) to prevent disorderly or improper conduct of patrons
**house·dress** \'hau̇s-ˌdres\ *noun* (1897)
**:** a dress with simple lines that is suitable for housework and is made usually of a washable fabric
**house·fa·ther** \-ˌfä-thər, -ˌfȧ-\ *noun* (1901)
**:** a man in charge of a dormitory, hall, or hostel
**house finch** *noun* (1869)
**:** a small finch (*Carpodacus mexicanus*) that has a male with a red head, breast, and rump and that is native to Mexico and the western U.S. and has been introduced in the eastern U.S.
**house·fly** \'hau̇s-ˌflī\ *noun* (15th century)
**:** a cosmopolitan dipteran fly (*Musca domestica*) that is often about human habitations and may act as a mechanical vector of diseases (as typhoid fever); *also* **:** any of various flies of similar appearance or habitat
**house·front** \-ˌfrənt\ *noun* (1838)
**:** the facade of a house
**house girl** *noun* (1835)
**:** HOUSEMAID
**house·guest** \'hau̇s-ˌgest\ *noun* (1917)
**:** GUEST 1a
¹**house·hold** \'hau̇s-ˌhōld, 'hau̇-ˌsōld\ *noun* (14th century)
**:** those who dwell under the same roof and compose a family; *also* **:** a social unit comprised of those living together in the same dwelling
²**household** *adjective* (14th century)
**1 :** of or relating to a household **:** DOMESTIC ⟨cooking and other *household* arts⟩
**2 :** FAMILIAR, COMMON ⟨a *household* name⟩
**house·hold·er** \'hau̇s-ˌhōl-dər, 'hau̇-ˌsōl-\ *noun* (14th century)
**:** a person who occupies a house or tenement alone or as the head of a household
**household troops** *noun plural* (1711)
**:** troops appointed to attend and guard a sovereign or the residence of a sovereign
**house·hus·band** \'hau̇s-ˌhəz-bənd\ *noun* (1955)
**:** a husband who does housekeeping usually while his wife earns the family income
**house·keep** \'hau̇s-ˌkēp\ *intransitive verb* **-kept** \-ˌkept\; **-keep·ing** [back-formation from *housekeeper*] (1842)
**:** to perform the routine duties (as cooking and cleaning) of managing a house
**house·keep·er** \-ˌkē-pər\ *noun* (1607)
**1 :** a woman employed to keep house
**2 :** HOUSEWIFE 1
**house·keep·ing** \-piŋ\ *noun* (1550)
**1 :** the management of a house and home affairs
**2 :** the care and management of property and the provision of equipment and services (as for an industrial organization)
**3 :** the routine tasks that must be done in order for a system to function or to function efficiently
¹**hou·sel** \'hau̇-zəl\ *noun* [Middle English, from Old English *hūsel* sacrifice, Eucharist; akin to Gothic *hunsl* sacrifice] (before 12th century)
*archaic* **:** the Eucharist or the act of administering or receiving it
²**housel** *transitive verb* (before 12th century)
*archaic* **:** to administer communion to
**house·leek** \'hau̇s-ˌlēk\ *noun* (14th century)
**:** a pink-flowered thick-leaved European plant (*Sempervivum tectorum*) of the orpine family that tends to form clusters of rosettes and is often grown in rock gardens; *broadly* **:** SEMPERVIVUM
**house·lights** \'hau̇s-ˌlīts\ *noun plural* (1920)
**:** the lights that illuminate the auditorium of a theater
**house·maid** \'hau̇s-ˌmād\ *noun* (circa 1694)
**:** a female servant employed to do housework

**housemaid's knee** *noun* [so called from its occurrence among women who work a great deal on their knees] (1831)
**:** a swelling over the knee due to an enlargement of the bursa in the front of the patella

**house·man** \'haùs-mən, -ˌman\ *noun* (1920)
**:** a person who performs general work about a house or hotel

**house·mas·ter** \-ˌmas-tər\ *noun* (1884)
**:** a master in charge of a house in a boy's boarding school

**house·mate** \'haùs-ˌmāt\ *noun* (circa 1810)
**:** a person who lives in the same house with another

**house·moth·er** \'haùs-ˌmə-thər\ *noun* (1882)
**:** a woman acting as hostess, chaperon, and often housekeeper in a group residence

**house mouse** *noun* (1835)
**:** a common nearly cosmopolitan grayish-brown mouse (*Mus musculus*) that usually lives and breeds about buildings, may act as a vector of diseases, and is an important laboratory animal

**house of assembly** (1653)
**:** a legislative body or the lower house of a legislature (as in various British colonies, protectorates, and countries of the Commonwealth)

**House of Burgesses** (1658)
**:** the colonial representative assembly of Virginia

**house of cards** (1903)
**:** a structure, situation, or institution that is insubstantial, shaky, or in constant danger of collapse

**House of Commons** (1621)
**:** the lower house of the British and Canadian parliaments

**house of correction** (circa 1576)
**:** an institution where persons who have committed a minor offense and are considered capable of reformation are confined

**house of delegates** (1783)
**:** HOUSE 6a; *especially* **:** the lower house of the state legislature in Maryland, Virginia, and West Virginia

**House of Lords** (1818)
**:** the upper house of the British Parliament composed of the lords temporal and spiritual

**house of representatives** (1716)
**:** the lower house of a legislative body (as the U.S. Congress)

**house of studies** (1929)
**:** an educational institution serving scholars of a religious order — called also *house of study*

**house organ** *noun* (1907)
**:** a periodical distributed by a business concern among its employees, sales personnel, or customers

**house·paint·er** \'haùs-ˌpān-tər\ *noun* (1689)
**:** one whose business or occupation is painting houses

**house·par·ent** \-ˌpar-ənt, -ˌper-\ *noun*
**:** an adult in charge of a dormitory, hall, hostel, or group residence

**house party** *noun* (1876)
**:** a party lasting over one or more nights at a residence (as a home or fraternity house)

**house·per·son** \'haùs-ˌpər-sᵊn\ *noun* (1974)
**:** a person who does housekeeping

**house·plant** \'haùs-ˌplant\ *noun* (1871)
**:** a plant grown or kept indoors

**house-proud** \'haùs-ˌpraùd\ *adjective* (1849)
*chiefly British* **:** proud of one's house or housekeeping

**hous·er** \'haù-zər\ *noun* (1940)
**:** one that promotes or administers housing projects

**house–rais·ing** \'haùs-ˌrā-ziŋ\ *noun* (1704)
**:** the joint erection of a house or its framework by a gathering of neighbors

**house·room** \-ˌrüm, -ˌrùm\ *noun* (1582)
**:** space for accommodation in or as if in a house ⟨given *houseroom* by a family all too eager to have a celebrity in their midst —Walter Kerr⟩

**house rule** *noun* (1947)
**:** a rule (as in a game) that applies only among a certain group or in a certain place

**house seat** *noun* (1948)
**:** a theater seat reserved by the management for a special guest

**house sitter** *noun* (1971)
**:** a person who occupies a dwelling to provide security and maintenance while the tenant is away
— **house–sit** \'haù(s)-ˌsit\ *intransitive verb*
— **house–sit·ting** \-ˌsi-tiŋ\ *noun*

**house sparrow** *noun* (1674)
**:** a sparrow (*Passer domesticus*) native to Eurasia that has been introduced worldwide and is found especially in urban and agricultural areas — called also *English sparrow*

**house–to–house** \ˌhaùs-tə-'haùs\ *adjective* (1859)
**:** going or done by going from one building to the next ⟨*house-to-house* fighting⟩

**house·top** \'haùs-ˌtäp\ *noun* (1526)
**:** ROOF; *especially* **:** the level surface of a flat roof
— **from the housetops :** for all to hear **:** OPENLY ⟨shouting their grievances *from the housetops*⟩

**house trailer** *noun* (1937)
**:** MOBILE HOME

**house–train** \'haùs-ˌtrān\ *transitive verb* (1924)
*chiefly British* **:** HOUSEBREAK

**house·wares** \'haùs-ˌwarz, -ˌwerz\ *noun plural* (1921)
**:** furnishings for a house; *especially* **:** small articles of household equipment (as cooking utensils or small appliances)

**house·warm·ing** \'haùs-ˌwor-miŋ\ *noun* (1577)
**:** a party to celebrate the taking possession of a house or premises

**house·wife** \'haùs-ˌwīf; *especially 2 & in early poetry* 'hə-zəf *or* -səf\ *noun, plural* **house·wives** \'haùs-ˌwīvz *also* 'haùz-ˌwīvz; 'hə-zəfs, -zəvz, -səfs, -səvz\ (13th century)
**1 :** a married woman in charge of a household
**2 :** a pocket-size container for small articles (as thread)
— **house·wife·li·ness** \-lē-nəs\ *noun*
— **house·wife·ly** \-lē\ *adjective*
— **house·wif·ery** \-ˌwī-f(ə-)rē; *British* -ˌ(ˌ)wi-f(ə-)rē *also* 'hə-zə-frē\ *noun*
— **house·wif·ey** \'haùs-ˌwī-fē\ *adjective*

**house·work** \'haùs-ˌwərk\ *noun* (1841)
**:** the work of housekeeping

**¹hous·ing** \'haù-ziŋ\ *noun* (14th century)
**1 a :** SHELTER, LODGING **b :** dwellings provided for people
**2 a :** a niche for a sculpture **b :** the space taken out of a structural member (as a timber) to admit the insertion of part of another
**3 :** something that covers or protects: as **a :** a case or enclosure (as for a mechanical part or an instrument) **b :** a casing (as an enclosed bearing) in which a shaft revolves **c :** a support (as a frame) for mechanical parts

**²housing** *noun* [Middle English, from *house* housing (from Middle French *houce,* of Germanic origin) + *-ing;* akin to Middle High German *hulft* covering] (15th century)
**:** CAPARISON 1

**housing development** *noun* (1951)
**:** a group of individual dwellings or apartment houses typically of similar design that are usually built and sold or leased by one management

**housing estate** *noun* (1920)
*British* **:** HOUSING DEVELOPMENT

**housing project** *noun* (circa 1937)
**:** a publicly supported and administered housing development planned usually for low-income families

**Hou·yhn·hnm** \'hwi-nəm, hü-'i-nəm\ *noun*
**:** a member of a race of horses endowed with reason in Swift's *Gulliver's Travels*

**hove** *past and past participle of* HEAVE

**hov·el** \'hə-vəl, 'hä-\ *noun* [Middle English] (15th century)
**1 :** an open shed or shelter
**2 :** TABERNACLE
**3 :** a small, wretched, and often dirty house **:** HUT

**hov·er** \'hə-vər, 'hä-\ *intransitive verb* **hov·ered; hov·er·ing** \-v(ə-)riŋ\ [Middle English *hoveren,* frequentative of *hoven* to hover] (15th century)
**1 a :** to hang fluttering in the air or on the wing **b :** to remain suspended over a place or object
**2 a :** to move to and fro near a place **:** fluctuate around a given point ⟨unemployment *hovered* around 10%⟩ **b :** to be in a state of uncertainty, irresolution, or suspense
— **hover** *noun*
— **hov·er·er** \-vər-ər\ *noun*

**hov·er·craft** \-vər-ˌkraft\ *noun* (1959)
**:** a vehicle that is supported above the surface of land or water by a cushion of air produced by downwardly directed fans

**¹how** \'haù\ *adverb* [Middle English, from Old English *hū;* akin to Old High German *hwuo* how, Old English *hwā* who — more at WHO] (before 12th century)
**1 a :** in what manner or way **b :** for what reason **:** WHY **c :** with what meaning **:** to what effect **d :** by what name or title ⟨*how* art thou called —Shakespeare⟩
**2 :** to what degree or extent
**3 :** in what state or condition ⟨*how* are you⟩
**4 :** at what price ⟨*how* a score of ewes now —Shakespeare⟩ ▫
— **how about :** what do you say to or think of ⟨*how about* it, are you going?⟩
— **how come :** how does it happen that **:** WHY

**²how** *conjunction* (before 12th century)
**1 a :** the way or manner in which ⟨remember *how* they fought⟩; *also* **:** the state or condition in which **b :** THAT ⟨told them *how* he had a situation —Charles Dickens⟩
**2 :** HOWEVER, AS ⟨a reader can shift his attention *how* he likes —William Empson⟩

**³how** \'haù\ *noun* (1533)
**1 :** a question about manner or method
**2 :** MANNER, METHOD

**¹how·be·it** \haù-'bē-ət\ *conjunction* (14th century)
**:** ALTHOUGH

**²howbeit** *adverb* (15th century)
**:** NEVERTHELESS

□ **USAGE**
**how** *How come* is a familiar phrase of obscure origin that first came to attention as an Americanism in the 19th century. It seems to scare writers on usage: most of them treat it as a highly informal or even slangy speech form and warn against its use in writing. But it is precisely in writing that the phrase surprises us—it is gaining improved status in print. It now appears commonly in the general prose of good writers ⟨if the car was going that fast, *how come* it wasn't more seriously damaged? —Calvin Trillin⟩ ⟨*how come* I never hear those sounds in the daytime? —Andy Rooney⟩ ⟨that's *how come* she knows about food —Harold Brodkey⟩ ⟨*The Tempest* begins with exactly the same *dramatis personae* as the *Mabinogi*. . . . *How come?* —Robert Graves⟩. This sort of use began about the end of World War II. The phrase is still not used in highly elevated prose.

\ə\ abut \ᵊ\ kitten \ər\ further \a\ ash \ā\ ace
\ä\ mop, mar \aù\ out \ch\ chin \e\ bet \ē\ easy
\g\ go \i\ hit \ī\ ice \j\ job \ŋ\ sing \ō\ go
\o\ law \oi\ boy \th\ thin \t͟h\ the \ü\ loot \ù\ foot
\y\ yet \zh\ vision *see also* Guide to Pronunciation

**how·dah** \'haù-də\ *noun* [Hindi *hauda,* from Arabic *hawdaj*] (1774)
: a seat or covered pavilion on the back of an elephant or camel

**how·dy** \'haù-dē\ *interjection* [alteration of *how do ye*] (1712)
— used to express greeting
— **howdy** *verb*

**howe** \'haù, 'hō\ *noun* [Middle English (northern) *holl* hollow place, from Old English *hol,* from *hol,* adjective, hollow — more at HOLE] (before 12th century)
*Scottish* : HOLLOW, VALLEY

**¹how·ev·er** \haù-'e-vər\ *conjunction* (14th century)
1 : in whatever manner or way that ⟨will help *however* I can⟩
2 *archaic* : ALTHOUGH

**²however** *adverb* (14th century)
1 a : in whatever manner or way ⟨shall serve you, sir, truly, *however* else —Shakespeare⟩ b : to whatever degree or extent ⟨has done this for *however* many thousands of years — Emma Hawkridge⟩
2 : in spite of that : on the other hand ⟨still seems possible, *however,* that conditions will improve⟩ ⟨would like to go; *however,* I think I'd better not⟩
3 : how in the world ⟨*however* did you manage to do it⟩

**howff** *or* **howf** \'haùf, 'hōf\ *noun* [Dutch *hof* enclosure; akin to Old English *hof* enclosure, and perhaps to *hufil* hill] (1711)
*Scottish* : HAUNT, RESORT

**how·it·zer** \'haù-ət-sər\ *noun* [Dutch *houwitser,* ultimately from Czech *houfnice* ballista] (1695)
: a short cannon used to fire projectiles at medium muzzle velocities and with relatively high trajectories

**howl** \'haù(ə)l\ *verb* [Middle English *houlen;* akin to Middle High German *hiulen* to howl] (14th century)
*intransitive verb*
1 : to emit a loud sustained doleful sound characteristic of members of the dog family
2 : to cry out loudly and without restraint under strong impulse (as pain, grief, or amusement)
3 : to go on a spree or rampage
*transitive verb*
1 : to utter with unrestrained outcry
2 : to drown out or cause to fail by adverse outcry — used especially with *down* ⟨howled down the speaker⟩
— **howl** *noun*

**howl·er** \'haù-lər\ *noun* (1800)
1 a : one that howls b : HOWLER MONKEY
2 : a humorous and ridiculous blunder

**howler monkey** *noun* (1932)
: any of a genus (*Alouatta*) of South and Central American monkeys that have a long prehensile tail and enlargement of the hyoid and laryngeal apparatus enabling them to make loud howling noises

**howler monkey**

**howl·ing** \'haù-liŋ\ *adjective* (1599)
1 : producing or marked by a sound resembling a sustained howl ⟨a *howling* storm⟩
2 : DESOLATE, WILD ⟨a *howling* wilderness⟩
3 : very great : PRONOUNCED ⟨a *howling* success⟩
— **howl·ing·ly** *adverb*

**how·so·ev·er** \,haù-sə-'we-vər\ *adverb* (14th century)
1 : in whatever manner
2 : to whatever degree or extent

**¹how–to** \'haù-'tü\ *adjective* (1926)
: giving practical instruction and advice (as on a craft) ⟨*how-to* books on all sorts of hobbies —Harry Milt⟩

**²how–to** *noun* (1954)
: a practical method or instruction ⟨the *how-tos* of balancing a checkbook⟩

**¹hoy** \'hòi\ *interjection* [Middle English] (14th century)
— used in attracting attention or in driving animals

**²hoy** *noun* [Middle English, from Middle Dutch *hoei*] (15th century)
1 : a small usually sloop-rigged coasting ship
2 : a heavy barge for bulky cargo

**hoya** \'hòi-(y)ə\ *noun* [New Latin, from Thomas *Hoy* (died 1821) English gardener] (1851)
: any of a genus (*Hoya*) of climbing Asian and Australian evergreen shrubs of the milkweed family

**hoy·den** \'hòi-d°n\ *noun* [perhaps from obsolete Dutch *heiden* country lout, from Middle Dutch, heathen; akin to Old English *hæthen* heathen] (1676)
: a girl or woman of saucy, boisterous, or carefree behavior
— **hoy·den·ish** \-ish\ *adjective*

**hoyle** \'hòi(ə)l\ *noun, often capitalized* [Edmond *Hoyle* (died 1769) English writer on games] (1906)
: an encyclopedia of the rules of indoor games and especially card games

**Hsia** \shē-'ä\ *noun* [Chinese (Beijing) *Xià*] (circa 1909)
: the legendary first dynasty of Chinese history traditionally dated from about 2200–1766 B.C.

**HTLV** \,āch-(,)tē-(,)el-'vē\ *noun* [human *T*-cell lymphotropic *virus*] (1980)
: any of several retroviruses — often used with a number or Roman numeral to indicate type

**HTLV–III** \-(,)vē-'thrē\ *noun* (1984)
: HIV-1

**hua·ra·che** \wə-'rä-chē, hə-\ *noun* [Mexican Spanish, from Tarascan *kʷaṛáči*] (1892)
: a low-heeled sandal having an upper made of interwoven leather strips

**hub** \'həb\ *noun* [probably alteration of ²*hob*] (1649)
1 : the central part of a circular object (as a wheel or propeller)
2 a : a center of activity : FOCAL POINT b : an airport or city through which an airline routes most of its traffic
3 : a steel punch from which a working die for a coin or medal is made

**hub–and–spoke** *adjective* (1980)
: being or relating to a system of routing air traffic in which a major airport serves as a central point for coordinating flights to and from other airports

**Hub·bard squash** \'hə-bərd-\ *noun* [probably from the name *Hubbard*] (1868)
: any of various often large variably green winter squashes — called also *Hubbard*

**hub·ble–bub·ble** \'hə-bəl-,bə-bəl\ *noun* [reduplication of *bubble*] (1634)
1 : WATER PIPE 2
2 : a flurry of sound or activity : COMMOTION

**hub·bub** \'hə-,bəb\ *noun* [perhaps of Irish origin; akin to Scottish Gaelic *ub ub,* interjection of contempt] (1555)
1 : NOISE, UPROAR
2 : CONFUSION, TURMOIL

**hub·by** \'hə-bē\ *noun, plural* **hubbies** [by alteration] (1688)
: HUSBAND

**hub·cap** \'həb-,kap\ *noun* (1903)
: a removable usually metal cap over the end of an axle; *especially* : one used on the wheel of a motor vehicle

**hu·bris** \'hyü-brəs\ *noun* [Greek *hybris*] (1884)
: exaggerated pride or self-confidence

— **hu·bris·tic** \hyü-'bris-tik\ *adjective*

**huck** \'hək\ *noun* (1851)
: HUCKABACK

**huck·a·back** \'hə-kə-,bak\ *noun* [origin unknown] (1690)
: an absorbent durable fabric of cotton, linen, or both used chiefly for towels

**huck·le·ber·ry** \'hə-kəl-,ber-ē\ *noun* [perhaps alteration of *hurtleberry* (huckleberry)] (1670)
1 : any of a genus (*Gaylussacia*) of American shrubs of the heath family; *also* : the edible dark blue to black usually acid berry (especially of *G. baccata*) with 10 nutlets
2 : BLUEBERRY

**¹huck·ster** \'hək-stər\ *noun* [Middle English *hukster,* from Middle Dutch *hokester,* from *hoeken* to peddle] (13th century)
1 : HAWKER, PEDDLER
2 : one who produces promotional material for commercial clients especially for radio or television
— **huck·ster·ism** \-stə-,ri-zəm\ *noun*

**²huckster** *verb* **huck·stered; huck·ster·ing** \-st(ə-)riŋ\ (1592)
*intransitive verb*
: HAGGLE
*transitive verb*
1 : to deal in or bargain over
2 : to promote by showmanship

**¹hud·dle** \'hə-d°l\ *verb* **hud·dled; hud·dling** \'həd-liŋ, 'hə-d°l-iŋ\ [probably from or akin to Middle English *hoderen* to huddle] (1579)
*transitive verb*
1 *British* : to arrange carelessly or hurriedly
2 a : to crowd together b : to draw (oneself) together : CROUCH
3 : to wrap closely in (as clothes)
*intransitive verb*
1 a : to gather in a close-packed group b : to curl up : CROUCH
2 a : to hold a consultation b : to gather in a huddle in football
— **hud·dler** \'həd-lər, 'hə-d°l-ər\ *noun*

**²huddle** *noun* (1586)
1 : a close-packed group : BUNCH ⟨*huddles* of children⟩ ⟨a *huddle* of cottages⟩
2 a : MEETING, CONFERENCE ⟨secret *huddles* were held by five leading Republicans —*Newsweek*⟩ b : a brief gathering of football players away from the line of scrimmage to receive instructions (as from the quarterback) for the next down

**Hu·di·bras·tic** \,hyü-də-'bras-tik\ *adjective* [irregular from *Hudibras,* satirical poem by Samuel Butler (died 1680)] (1712)
1 : written in humorous octosyllabic couplets
2 : MOCK-HEROIC
— **Hudibrastic** *noun*

**hue** \'hyü\ *noun* [Middle English *hewe,* from Old English *hīw;* akin to Old Norse *hȳ* plant down, Gothic *hiwi* form] (before 12th century)
1 : COMPLEXION, ASPECT ⟨political parties of every *hue* —Louis Wasserman⟩
2 a : COLOR b : gradation of color c : the attribute of colors that permits them to be classed as red, yellow, green, blue, or an intermediate between any contiguous pair of these colors — compare BRIGHTNESS 2, LIGHTNESS 2, SATURATION 4

**hue and cry** *noun* [*hue* (outcry)] (15th century)
1 a : a loud outcry formerly used in the pursuit of one who is suspected of a crime b : the pursuit of a suspect or a written proclamation for the capture of a suspect
2 : a clamor of alarm or protest
3 : HUBBUB

**hued** \'hyüd\ *adjective* (before 12th century)
: COLORED — usually used in combination ⟨green-*hued*⟩

**¹huff** \'həf\ *verb* [imitative] (1583)
*intransitive verb*
1 : to emit puffs (as of breath or steam)

**2 a :** to make empty threats : BLUSTER **b :** to react or behave indignantly ⟨*huffed* off in anger⟩
*transitive verb*
**1 :** to puff up : INFLATE
**2** *archaic* **:** to treat with contempt : BULLY
**3 :** to make angry
**4 :** to utter with indignation or scorn
²**huff** *noun* (1599)
**:** a usually peevish and transitory spell of anger or resentment ⟨quit in a *huff*⟩
*synonym* see OFFENSE
**huff·ish** \'hə-fish\ *adjective* (circa 1755)
**:** ARROGANT, SULKY
**huffy** \'hə-fē\ *adjective* **huff·i·er; -est** (1677)
**1 :** HAUGHTY, ARROGANT
**2 a :** roused to indignation : IRRITATED **b :** easily offended : TOUCHY
— **huff·i·ly** \'hə-fə-lē\ *adverb*
— **huff·i·ness** \-fē-nəs\ *noun*
**hug** \'həg\ *transitive verb* **hugged; hug·ging** [perhaps of Scandinavian origin; akin to Old Norse *hugga* to soothe] (1567)
**1 :** to press tightly especially in the arms
**2 a :** CONGRATULATE **b :** to hold fast : CHERISH ⟨*hugged* his miseries like a sulky child —John Buchan⟩
**3 :** to stay close to ⟨the road *hugs* the river⟩
— **hug** *noun*
— **hug·ga·ble** \'hə-gə-bəl\ *adjective*
**huge** \'hyüj, 'yüj\ *adjective* **hug·er; hug·est** [Middle English, from Old French *ahuge*] (12th century)
**:** very large or extensive: as **a :** of great size or area **b :** great in scale or degree ⟨a *huge* deficit⟩ **c :** great in scope or character ⟨a man of *huge* talent⟩
*synonym* see ENORMOUS
— **huge·ly** *adverb*
— **huge·ness** *noun*
**huge·ous** \'hyü-jəs, 'yü-\ *adjective* (1519)
**:** HUGE
— **huge·ous·ly** *adverb*
¹**hug·ger–mug·ger** \'hə-gər-,mə-gər\ *noun* [origin unknown] (1529)
**1 :** SECRECY
**2 :** CONFUSION, MUDDLE
²**hugger–mugger** *adjective* (1692)
**1 :** SECRET
**2 :** of a confused or disorderly nature : JUMBLED
— **hugger–mugger** *adverb*
**hug–me–tight** \'həg-mē-,tīt\ *noun* (1860)
**:** a woman's short usually knitted sleeveless close-fitting jacket
**Hu·gue·not** \'hyü-gə-,nät\ *noun* [Middle French, alteration of Middle French dialect *eyguenot*, adherent of a Swiss political movement, from German dialect *Eidgnosse* confederate] (1565)
**:** a member of the French Reformed communion especially of the 16th and 17th centuries
— **Hu·gue·not·ic** \,hyü-gə-'nä-tik\ *adjective*
— **Hu·gue·not·ism** \'hyü-gə-nä-,ti-zəm\ *noun*
**huh** \*a grunt articulated as a syllabic* m *or* n *with a voiceless onset, or as the syllable* 'hə *or* 'hən, *often ending in a glottal stop, and uttered with a range of intonations; often read as* 'hə\ *interjection* [imitative of a grunt] (1608)
— used to express surprise, disbelief, or confusion, or as an inquiry inviting affirmative reply
**Hui·chol** \wē-'chōl\ *noun, plural* **Huichol** *or* **Hui·cho·les** [Mexican Spanish] (1900)
**1 :** a member of an American Indian people of the mountains between Zacatecas and Nayarit, Mexico
**2 :** the Uto-Aztecan language of the Huichol people
— **Huichol** *adjective*
**hui·sa·che** \wē-'sä-chē\ *noun* [Mexican Spanish, from Nahuatl *huixachi*, from *huitzli* thorn + *ixachi* a great amount, many] (1838)

**:** a widely cultivated thorny shrubby acacia (*Acacia farnesiana*) of the southern U.S. and tropical America
**hu·la** \'hü-lə\ *also* **hu·la–hu·la** \,hü-lə-'hü-lə\ *noun* [Hawaiian] (1825)
**:** a sinuous Polynesian dance characterized by rhythmic movement of the hips and mimetic gestures with the hands and often accompanied by chants and rhythmic drumming
**hula hoop** *noun* (1958)
**:** a plastic hoop that is twirled around the body
¹**hulk** \'həlk\ *noun* [Middle English *hulke*, from Old English *hulc*, probably from Medieval Latin *holcas*, from Greek *holkas*, from *helkein* to pull — more at SULCUS] (before 12th century)
**1 a :** a heavy clumsy ship **b** (1) **:** the body of an old ship unfit for service (2) **:** a ship used as a prison — usually used in plural ⟨every prisoner sent to the *hulks* —Kenneth Roberts⟩ **c :** an abandoned wreck or shell (as of a building or automobile)
**2 :** one that is bulky or unwieldy ⟨a big *hulk* of a man⟩
²**hulk** *intransitive verb* (circa 1825)
**1** *dialect English* **:** to move ponderously
**2 :** to appear impressively large or massive : LOOM
**hulk·ing** \'həl-kiŋ\ *adjective* (1698)
**:** PONDEROUS, MASSIVE
¹**hull** \'həl\ *noun* [Middle English, from Old English *hulu*; akin to Old High German *hala* hull, Old English *helan* to conceal — more at HELL] (before 12th century)
**1 a :** the outer covering of a fruit or seed **b :** the persistent calyx or involucre that subtends some fruits
**2 a :** the frame or body of a ship or boat exclusive of masts, yards, sails, and rigging **b :** the main body of a usually large or heavy craft or vehicle (as an airship or tank)
**3 :** COVERING, CASING
— **hull–less** \'həl-ləs\ *adjective*
²**hull** *transitive verb* (14th century)
**:** to remove the hulls of : SHUCK
— **hull·er** *noun*
**hul·la·ba·loo** \'hə-lə-bə-,lü\ *noun, plural* **-loos** [perhaps from *hallo* + Scots *balloo*, interjection used to hush children] (1762)
**:** DIN; *also* **:** UPROAR
**hull down** *adverb or adjective* (1775)
*of a ship* **:** at such a distance that only the superstructure is visible
**hulled corn** *noun* (1788)
**:** whole grain corn from which the hulls have been removed by soaking or boiling in lye water
**hul·lo** \(,)hə-'lō\ *chiefly British variant of* HELLO
¹**hum** \'həm\ *verb* **hummed; hum·ming** [Middle English *hummen;* akin to Middle High German *hummen* to hum, Middle Dutch *hommel* bumblebee] (14th century)
*intransitive verb*
**1 a :** to utter a sound like that of the speech sound \m\ prolonged **b :** to make the natural noise of an insect in motion or a similar sound **:** DRONE **c :** to give forth a low continuous blend of sound
**2 a :** to be busily active ⟨the museum *hummed* with visitors⟩ **b :** to run smoothly ⟨the business started to *hum*⟩
*transitive verb*
**1 :** to sing with the lips closed and without articulation
**2 :** to affect or express by humming ⟨*hummed* his displeasure⟩
— **hum** *noun*
— **hum·ma·ble** \'hə-mə-bəl\ *adjective*
²**hum** *chiefly British variant of* HEM
¹**hu·man** \'hyü-mən, 'yü-\ *adjective* [Middle English *humain*, from Middle French, from Latin *humanus;* akin to Latin *homo* human being — more at HOMAGE] (14th century)
**1 :** of, relating to, or characteristic of humans
**2 :** consisting of humans

**3 a :** having human form or attributes **b :** susceptible to or representative of the sympathies and frailties of human nature ⟨such an inconsistency is very *human* —P. E. More⟩
*usage* see HUMOR
— **hu·man·ness** \-mən-nəs\ *noun*
²**human** *noun* (circa 1533)
**:** a bipedal primate mammal (*Homo sapiens*) **:** MAN; *broadly* **:** any living or extinct member of the family (Hominidae) to which the primate belongs
— **hu·man·like** \-mən-,līk\ *adjective*
**human being** *noun* (1800)
**:** HUMAN
**hu·mane** \hyü-'mān, yü-\ *adjective* [Middle English *humain*] (circa 1500)
**1 :** marked by compassion, sympathy, or consideration for humans or animals
**2 :** characterized by or tending to broad humanistic culture : HUMANISTIC ⟨*humane* studies⟩
— **hu·mane·ly** *adverb*
— **hu·mane·ness** \-'mān-nəs\ *noun*
**human ecology** *noun* (1907)
**1 :** a branch of sociology dealing especially with the spatial and temporal interrelationships between humans and their economic, social, and political organization
**2 :** the ecology of human communities and populations especially as concerned with preservation of environmental quality (as of air or water) through proper application of conservation and civil engineering practices
**human engineering** *noun* (1920)
**1 :** management of humans and their affairs especially in industry
**2 :** ERGONOMICS
**human immunodeficiency virus** *noun* (1986)
**:** HIV
**hu·man·ism** \'hyü-mə-,ni-zəm, 'yü-\ *noun* (1832)
**1 a :** devotion to the humanities : literary culture **b :** the revival of classical letters, individualistic and critical spirit, and emphasis on secular concerns characteristic of the Renaissance
**2 :** HUMANITARIANISM
**3 :** a doctrine, attitude, or way of life centered on human interests or values; *especially* **:** a philosophy that usually rejects supernaturalism and stresses an individual's dignity and worth and capacity for self-realization through reason
— **hu·man·ist** \-nist\ *noun or adjective*
— **hu·man·is·tic** \,hyü-mə-'nis-tik, ,yü-\ *adjective*
— **hu·man·is·ti·cal·ly** \-ti-k(ə-)lē\ *adverb*
**hu·man·i·tar·i·an** \hyü-,ma-nə-'ter-ē-ən, yü-\ *noun* (1844)
**:** a person promoting human welfare and social reform : PHILANTHROPIST
— **humanitarian** *adjective*
— **hu·man·i·tar·i·an·ism** \-ē-ə-,ni-zəm\ *noun*
**hu·man·i·ty** \hyü-'ma-nə-tē, yü-\ *noun, plural* **-ties** (14th century)
**1 :** the quality or state of being humane
**2 a :** the quality or state of being human **b** *plural* **:** human attributes or qualities ⟨his work has the ripeness of the 18th century, and its rough *humanities* —Pamela H. Johnson⟩
**3** *plural* **:** the branches of learning (as philosophy or languages) that investigate human constructs and concerns as opposed to natural processes (as in physics or chemistry)
**4 :** MANKIND 1
**hu·man·ize** \'hyü-mə-,nīz, 'yü-\ *transitive verb* **-ized; -iz·ing** (1603)

**1 a :** to represent as human **:** attribute human qualities to **b :** to adapt to human nature or use **2 :** to make humane
— **hu·man·iza·tion** \,hyü-mə-nə-'zā-shən, ,yü-\ *noun*
— **hu·man·iz·er** *noun*
**hu·man·kind** \'hyü-mən-ˌkīnd, 'yü-\ *noun singular but singular or plural in construction* (circa 1645)
**:** the human race
**hu·man·ly** \'hyü-mən-lē, 'yü-\ *adverb* (15th century)
**1 a :** with regard to human needs and emotions ⟨provide *humanly* for those who are not needed in the economy —E. F. Bacon⟩ **b :** with regard to or in keeping with human proneness to error or weakness ⟨*humanly* inaccurate⟩
**2 a :** from a human viewpoint ⟨*humanly* speaking, the process works . . . like this —Elizabeth Janeway⟩ **b :** within the range of human capacity ⟨did everything *humanly* possible⟩ **c :** by humans ⟨*humanly* made⟩
**human nature** *noun* (1668)
**:** the nature of humans; *especially* **:** the fundamental dispositions and traits of humans
**hu·man·oid** \'hyü-mə-ˌnȯid, 'yü-\ *adjective* (1918)
**:** having human form or characteristics ⟨*humanoid* dentition⟩ ⟨*humanoid* robots⟩
— **humanoid** *noun*
**human relations** *noun plural but usually singular in construction* (1946)
**1 :** a study of human problems arising from organizational and interpersonal relations (as in industry)
**2 :** a course, study, or program designed to develop better interpersonal and intergroup adjustments
**human resources** *noun plural* (1975)
**:** PERSONNEL 1a, 2 ⟨director of *human resources*⟩
**human rights** *noun plural* (1791)
**:** rights (as freedom from unlawful imprisonment, torture, and execution) regarded as belonging fundamentally to all persons
**hu·mate** \'hyü-ˌmāt, 'yü-\ *noun* (1844)
**:** a salt or ester of a humic acid
¹**hum·ble** \'həm-bəl *also chiefly Southern* 'əm-\ *adjective* **hum·bler** \-b(ə-)lər\; **humblest** \-b(ə-)ləst\ [Middle English, from Old French, from Latin *humilis* low, humble, from *humus* earth; akin to Greek *chthōn* earth, *chamai* on the ground] (13th century)
**1 :** not proud or haughty **:** not arrogant or assertive
**2 :** reflecting, expressing, or offered in a spirit of deference or submission ⟨a *humble* apology⟩
**3 a :** ranking low in a hierarchy or scale **:** INSIGNIFICANT, UNPRETENTIOUS **b :** not costly or luxurious ⟨a *humble* contraption⟩
*usage* see HUMOR
— **hum·ble·ness** \-bəl-nəs\ *noun*
— **hum·bly** \-blē\ *adverb*
²**humble** *transitive verb* **hum·bled; humbling** \-b(ə-)liŋ\ (14th century)
**1 :** to make humble in spirit or manner
**2 :** to destroy the power, independence, or prestige of
— **hum·bler** \-b(ə-)lər\ *noun*
— **hum·bling·ly** \-b(ə-)liŋ-lē\ *adverb*
**hum·ble–bee** \'həm-bəl-ˌbē\ *noun* [Middle English *humbylbee*, from *humbyl-* (akin to Middle Dutch *hommel* bumblebee) + *bee* — more at HUM] (15th century)
**:** BUMBLEBEE
**humble pie** *noun* (1830)
**:** a figurative serving of humiliation usually in the form of a forced submission, apology, or retraction — often used in the phrase *eat humble pie* ◆
¹**hum·bug** \'həm-ˌbəg\ *noun* [origin unknown] (1751)

**1 a :** something designed to deceive and mislead **b :** a willfully false, deceptive, or insincere person
**2 :** an attitude or spirit of pretense and deception
**3 :** NONSENSE, DRIVEL
**4** *British* **:** a hard usually mint-flavored candy
*synonym* see IMPOSTURE
— **hum·bug·gery** \-,bə-g(ə-)rē\ *noun*
²**humbug** *verb* **hum·bugged; hum·bugging** (1751)
*transitive verb*
**:** DECEIVE, HOAX
*intransitive verb*
**:** to engage in a hoax or deception
**hum·ding·er** \'həm-'diŋ-ər\ *noun* [probably alteration of *hummer*] (circa 1904)
**:** a striking or extraordinary person or thing
**hum·drum** \'həm-ˌdrəm\ *adjective* [reduplication of *hum*] (1553)
**:** MONOTONOUS, DULL
— **humdrum** *noun*
**hu·mec·tant** \hyü-'mek-tənt\ *noun* [Latin *humectant-, humectans,* present participle of *humectare* to moisten, from *humectus* moist, from *humēre* to be moist — more at HUMOR] (circa 1857)
**:** a substance that promotes retention of moisture
— **humectant** *adjective*
**hu·mer·al** \'hyü-mə-rəl\ *adjective* (1615)
**1 :** of, relating to, or situated in the region of the humerus or shoulder
**2 :** of, relating to, or being a body part analogous to the humerus or shoulder
— **humeral** *noun*
**humeral veil** *noun* (1853)
**:** an oblong vestment worn around the shoulders and over the hands by a priest holding a sacred vessel
**hu·mer·us** \'hyü-mə-rəs\ *noun, plural* **humeri** \-ˌrī, -ˌrē\ [Middle English, from Latin *humerus, umerus* upper arm, shoulder; akin to Gothic *ams* shoulder, Greek *ōmos*] (15th century)
**:** the long bone of the upper arm or forelimb extending from the shoulder to the elbow
**hu·mic** \'hyü-mik, 'yü-\ *adjective* (1844)
**:** of, relating to, or derived at least in part from humus
**humic acid** *noun* (1844)
**:** any of various organic acids obtained from humus
**hu·mid** \'hyü-məd, 'yü-\ *adjective* [French or Latin; French *humide,* from Latin *humidus,* from *humēre*] (15th century)
**:** containing or characterized by perceptible moisture especially to the point of being oppressive
*synonym* see WET
— **hu·mid·ly** *adverb*
**hu·mid·i·fi·er** \hyü-'mid-ə-ˌfī(-ə)r, yü-\ *noun* (1884)
**:** a device for supplying or maintaining humidity
**hu·mid·i·fy** \-ˌfī\ *transitive verb* **-fied; -fying** (1885)
**:** to make humid
— **hu·mid·i·fi·ca·tion** \-ˌmi-də-fə-'kāshən\ *noun*
**hu·mid·i·stat** \hyü-'mi-də-ˌstat, yü-\ *noun* (circa 1904)
**:** an instrument for regulating or maintaining the degree of humidity
**hu·mid·i·ty** \hyü-'mi-də-tē, yü-\ *noun, plural* **-ties** (15th century)
**:** a moderate degree of wetness especially of the atmosphere — compare RELATIVE HUMIDITY
**hu·mi·dor** \'hyü-mə-ˌdȯr, 'yü-\ *noun* [*humid* + *-or* (as in *cuspidor*)] (1903)
**:** a case or enclosure (as for storing cigars) in which the air is kept properly humidified
**hu·mi·fi·ca·tion** \,hyü-mə-fə-'kā-shən, ,yü-\ *noun* (1897)
**:** formation of or conversion into humus

**hu·mi·fied** \'hyü-mə-ˌfīd, 'yü-\ *adjective* (1906)
**:** converted into humus
**hu·mil·i·ate** \hyü-'mi-lē-ˌāt, 'yü-\ *transitive verb* **-at·ed; -at·ing** [Late Latin *humiliatus,* past participle of *humiliare,* from Latin *humilis* low — more at HUMBLE] (circa 1534)
**:** to reduce to a lower position in one's own eyes or others' eyes **:** MORTIFY
— **hu·mil·i·a·tion** \-ˌmi-lē-'ā-shən\ *noun*
**hu·mil·i·at·ing** \hyü-'mi-lē-ˌā-tiŋ, 'yü-\ *adjective* (1757)
**:** extremely destructive to one's self-respect or dignity **:** HUMBLING
— **hu·mil·i·at·ing·ly** \-tiŋ-lē\ *adverb*
**hu·mil·i·ty** \hyü-'mi-lə-tē, yü-\ *noun* (14th century)
**:** the quality or state of being humble
**hum·mer** \'hə-mər\ *noun* (1605)
**1 :** one that hums
**2 :** HUMMINGBIRD
**3 :** HUMDINGER
**4 :** FASTBALL
**hum·ming·bird** \'hə-miŋ-ˌbərd\ *noun* (1637)
**:** any of a family (Trochilidae) of tiny brightly colored nonpasserine New World birds related to the swifts and like them having narrow wings with long primaries, a slender bill, and a very extensile tongue
**hum·mock** \'hə-mək\ *noun* [alteration of ²*hammock*] (1555)
**1 :** a rounded knoll or hillock
**2 :** a ridge of ice
**3 :** ²HAMMOCK 2
— **hummock** *verb*
— **hum·mocky** \-mə-kē\ *adjective*
**hum·mus** \'hə-məs, 'hu̇-\ *noun* [Arabic *ḥummuṣ* chickpeas] (1950)
**:** a paste of pureed chickpeas usually mixed with sesame oil or sesame paste and eaten as a dip or sandwich spread
**hu·mon·gous** \hyü-'məŋ-gəs, yü-, -'mäŋ-\ *also* **hu·mun·gous** \-'məŋ-gəs\ *adjective* [perhaps alteration of *huge + monstrous*] (circa 1967)
**:** extremely large **:** HUGE
¹**hu·mor** \'hyü-mər, 'yü-\ *noun* [Middle English *humour,* from Middle French *humeur,* from Medieval Latin & Latin; Medieval Latin *humor,* from Latin *humor, umor* moisture; akin to Old Norse *vǫkr* damp, Latin *humēre* to be moist, and perhaps to Greek *hygros* wet] (14th century)

⬦ WORD HISTORY
**humble pie** The phrase *humble pie* appears to be a simple culinary metaphor for humility, though beneath its surface is a pun on an actual but now seldom-eaten dish. *Umble pie* is a pastry stuffed and baked with *umbles,* the edible viscera of an animal, typically a game animal such as a deer. The word *umbles* is altered from earlier *numbles* (the initial *n* apparently being dropped due to the proximity of the following nasal consonant). *Numbles* was a Middle English borrowing from Old French *nombles,* ultimately descended from Latin *lumbuli,* diminutive of *lumbi* (singular *lumbus*) "loins." (The word *loin* itself is from a French descendant of another derivative of *lumbus;* related words going back directly to Latin are *lumbar* and *lumbago.*) The loss of initial \h\ in British regional speech would have contributed to the association of *umble pie* with the adjective *humble,* though, curiously, the metaphorical *humble pie* is first noted in East Anglia, an area where the \h\ has not traditionally been dropped, and the spelling *humble pie* in reference to the literal pastry already appears in the 17th century—suggesting that the form with \h\ may have originated through something other than punning.

**1 a :** a normal functioning bodily semifluid or fluid (as the blood or lymph) **b :** a secretion (as a hormone) that is an excitant of activity **2 a** *in medieval physiology* **:** a fluid or juice of an animal or plant; *specifically* : one of the four fluids entering into the constitution of the body and determining by their relative proportions a person's health and temperament **b :** characteristic or habitual disposition or bent **:** TEMPERAMENT ⟨of cheerful *humor*⟩ **c :** an often temporary state of mind imposed especially by circumstances ⟨was in no *humor* to listen⟩ **d :** a sudden, unpredictable, or unreasoning inclination **:** WHIM ⟨the uncertain *humors* of nature⟩ **3 a :** that quality which appeals to a sense of the ludicrous or absurdly incongruous **b :** the mental faculty of discovering, expressing, or appreciating the ludicrous or absurdly incongruous **c :** something that is or is designed to be comical or amusing □ ◆
*synonym* see WIT
**— out of humor :** out of sorts
²**humor** *transitive verb* **hu·mored; hu·mor·ing** \'hyüm-riŋ, 'yüm-, 'hyü-mə-, 'yü-\ (1588)
**1 :** to soothe or content by indulgence
**2 :** to adapt oneself to
*synonym* see INDULGE
**hu·mor·al** \'hyü-mə-rəl, 'yü-\ *adjective* (15th century)
**1 :** of, relating to, proceeding from, or involving a bodily humor (as a hormone)
**2 :** relating to or being the part of immunity or the immune response that involves antibodies secreted by B cells and circulating in bodily fluids
**hu·mor·esque** \,hyü-mə-'resk, ,yü-\ *noun* [German *Humoreske*, from *Humor*, from Medieval Latin] (1889)
**:** a typically whimsical or fanciful musical composition
**hu·mor·ist** \'hyü-mə-rist, 'yü-\ *noun* (1589)
**1** *archaic* **:** a person subject to whims
**2 :** a person specializing in or noted for humor
**hu·mor·is·tic** \,hyü-mə-'ris-tik, ,yü-\ *adjective* (1818)
**:** HUMOROUS
**hu·mor·less** \'hyü-mər-ləs\ *adjective* (circa 1847)
**1 :** lacking a sense of humor
**2 :** lacking humorous characteristics
**— hu·mor·less·ly** \-lē\ *adverb*
**— hu·mor·less·ness** *noun*
**hu·mor·ous** \'hyüm-rəs, 'yüm-, 'hyü-mə-, 'yü-\ *adjective* (15th century)
**1** *obsolete* **:** HUMID
**2 a :** full of or characterized by humor **:** JOCULAR **b :** indicating or expressive of a sense of humor
*synonym* see WITTY
**— hu·mor·ous·ly** *adverb*
**— hu·mor·ous·ness** *noun*
**hu·mour** *chiefly British variant of* HUMOR
¹**hump** \'həmp\ *noun* [akin to Middle Low German *hump* bump] (1709)
**1 :** a rounded protuberance: as **a :** HUMPBACK 1 **b :** a fleshy protuberance on the back of an animal (as a camel, bison, or whale) **c** (1) **:** MOUND, HUMMOCK (2) **:** MOUNTAIN, RANGE ⟨the Himalayan *hump*⟩
**2** *British* **:** a fit of depression or sulking
**3 :** a difficult, trying, or critical phase or obstacle — often used in the phrase *over the hump*
**— humped** *adjective*
²**hump** (1835)
*transitive verb*
**1 :** to copulate with — often considered vulgar
**2 :** to exert (oneself) vigorously
**3 :** to make humpbacked **:** HUNCH
**4** *chiefly British* **:** to put or carry on the back **:** LUG; *also* **:** TRANSPORT
*intransitive verb*
**1 :** to exert oneself **:** HUSTLE
**2 :** to move swiftly **:** RACE

**hump·back** \-,bak, *for* 1 *also* -'bak\ *noun* (1697)
**1 :** a humped or crooked back; *also* **:** KYPHOSIS
**2 :** HUNCHBACK 1
**3 :** HUMPBACK WHALE
**4 :** PINK SALMON
**hump·backed** \-'bakt\ *adjective* (1681)
**1 :** having a humped back
**2 :** convexly curved ⟨a *humpbacked* bridge⟩
**humpback whale** *noun* (1725)
**:** a large baleen whale (*Megaptera novaeangliae*) that is black above and white below and has very long flippers, and fleshy tubercles along the snout

**humpback whale**

¹**humph** \'həm(p)f\ (1814)
*intransitive verb*
**:** to utter a humph
*transitive verb*
**:** to utter (as a remark) in a tone suggestive of a humph
²**humph** \a snort articulated as a syllabic m or n with a voiceless onset and ending in a nasal h or a glottal stop; often read as 'həm(p)f\ *interjection* [imitative of a grunt] (1815)
**—** used to express doubt or contempt
**hump·ty–dump·ty** \,həm(p)-tē-'dəm(p)-tē\ *noun, plural* **-dumpties** *often H&D capitalized* [*Humpty-Dumpty*, egg-shaped nursery rhyme character who fell from a wall and broke into bits] (1883)
**:** something that once broken is impossible or almost impossible to put back together
**humpy** \'həm-pē\ *adjective* **hump·i·er; -est** (1708)
**1 :** full of humps
**2 :** covered with humps
**hu·mus** \'hyü-məs, 'yü-\ *noun* [New Latin, from Latin, earth — more at HUMBLE] (1796)
**:** a brown or black complex variable material resulting from partial decomposition of plant or animal matter and forming the organic portion of soil
**hum·vee** \,həm-'vē, 'həm-,\ *noun* [from HMMWV (*H*igh *M*obility *M*ultipurpose *W*heeled *V*ehicle)] (1982) *often capitalized*
**:** a diesel-powered multipurpose U.S. military vehicle that replaced the jeep
**Hun** \'hən\ *noun* [Middle English, from Old English *Hunas*, plural, from Late Latin *Hunni*, plural] (before 12th century)
**1 :** a member of a nomadic central Asian people gaining control of a large part of central and eastern Europe under Attila about A.D. 450
**2** *often not capitalized* **:** a person who is wantonly destructive **:** VANDAL **b :** GERMAN; *especially* **:** a German soldier — usually used disparagingly
**Hu·nan** \'hü-'nän\ *or* **Hu·na·nese** \,hü-nə-'nēz, -'nēs\ *adjective* [*Hunan*, China] (1970)
**:** of, relating to, or being a hot and spicy style of Chinese cooking
¹**hunch** \'hənch\ *verb* [origin unknown] (1581)
*transitive verb*
**1 :** JOSTLE, SHOVE
**2 :** to thrust or bend over into a humped or crooked position
*intransitive verb*
**1 :** to thrust oneself forward
**2 a :** to assume a bent or crooked posture **b :** to draw oneself into a ball **:** curl up **c :** HUDDLE, SQUAT
²**hunch** *noun* (1630)
**1 :** an act or instance of hunching **:** PUSH
**2 a :** a thick piece **:** LUMP **b :** HUMP
**3 :** a strong intuitive feeling concerning especially a future event or result
**hunch·back** \'hənch-,bak\ *noun* (1712)
**1 :** a person with a humpback
**2 :** HUMPBACK 1
**— hunch·backed** \-'bakt\ *adjective*

**hun·dred** \'hən-drəd, -dərd\ *noun, plural* **hundreds** *or* **hundred** [Middle English, from Old English, from *hund* hundred + *-red* (akin to Gothic *rathjo* account, number); akin to Latin *centum* hundred, Greek he*katon*, Old English *tien* ten — more at TEN, REASON] (before 12th century)
**1** — see NUMBER table
**2** *hundreds plural* **a :** the numbers 100 to 999 **b :** a great number ⟨*hundreds* of times⟩
**3 :** a 100-dollar bill
**4 :** a subdivision of some English and American counties
**— hundred** *adj*
**— hun·dred·fold** \-,fōld\ *adjective or adverb*
**— hun·dredth** \-drədth, -dratth\ *adjective or noun*
**hun·dred–per·cent·er** \-pər-'sen-tər\ *noun* [*hundred-percent* (*American*)] (1921)
**:** a thoroughgoing nationalist
**— hun·dred–per·cent·ism** \-'sen-,ti-zəm\ *noun*
**hundreds place** *noun* (1937)
**:** the place three to the left of the decimal point in a number expressed in the Arabic system of notation
**hun·dred·weight** \'hən-drəd-,wāt, -dərd-,wāt\ *noun, plural* **hundredweight** *or* **hundredweights** (1577)

◇ WORD HISTORY

**humor** A theory of physiology first articulated by the ancient Greeks and popular throughout the Middle Ages and Renaissance held that the composition of the human body included four fluids: yellow bile or choler, black bile or melancholy, blood, and phlegm. The proper proportion of these fluids determined both the physical and mental well-being of an individual. In Middle English these fluids were referred to as *humours*, ultimately from Latin *umor*, meaning "moisture" or "bodily fluid." If in a natural combination, a *humour* was *goode* and stimulated health and good spirits, but if unnatural or corrupted, a *humour* was *ille* and led to sickness and ill spirits. In the course of the 16th and 17th centuries, *good humour* and *ill humour* lost their original physiological senses and began to refer strictly to mental states, whether fixed disposition or passing mood, and we continue to use *humor* in this way. The use of *humors* to mean "whims" led to other common modern applications of *humor*, for a person's faculty for appreciating the ludicrous (as in *sense of humor*) and correspondingly, the quality that appeals to this faculty (as in *to see the humor in a situation*).

\ə\ abut \ᵊ\ kitten \ər\ further \a\ ash \ā\ ace \ä\ mop, mar \aů\ out \ch\ chin \e\ bet \ē\ easy \g\ go \i\ hit \ī\ ice \j\ job \ŋ\ sing \ō\ go \ȯ\ law \ȯi\ boy \th\ thin \th\ the \ü\ loot \ů\ foot \y\ yet \zh\ vision *see also* Guide to Pronunciation

**1** : a unit of weight equal to 100 pounds — called also *short hundredweight*; see WEIGHT table
**2** *British* : a unit of weight equal to 112 pounds — called also *long hundredweight*

¹**hung** *past and past participle of* HANG

²**hung** *adjective* (1848)
: unable to reach a decision or verdict ⟨a *hung* jury⟩; *also, British* : not having a political party with an overall majority ⟨a *hung* parliament⟩

**Hun·gar·i·an** \,həŋ-'ger-ē-ən, -'gar-\ *noun* (1553)
**1 a** : a native or inhabitant of Hungary : MAGYAR **b** : a person of Hungarian descent
**2** : the Finno-Ugric language of the Hungarians
— **Hungarian** *adjective*

¹**hun·ger** \'həŋ-gər\ *noun* [Middle English, from Old English *hungor*; akin to Old High German *hungar* hunger, Lithuanian *kanka* torture] (before 12th century)
**1 a** : a craving or urgent need for food or a specific nutrient **b** : an uneasy sensation occasioned by the lack of food **c** : a weakened condition brought about by prolonged lack of food
**2** : a strong desire : CRAVING
— **from hunger** : very bad or inept ⟨the jokes were *from hunger* —Mordecai Richler⟩

²**hunger** *verb* **hun·gered; hun·ger·ing** \-g(ə-)riŋ\ (before 12th century)
*intransitive verb*
**1** : to feel or suffer hunger
**2** : to have an eager desire
*transitive verb*
: to make hungry
**synonym** see LONG

**hunger strike** *noun* (1889)
: refusal (as by a prisoner) to eat enough to sustain life
— **hunger striker** *noun*

**hung·over** \'həŋ-'ō-vər\ *adjective* (1941)
: suffering from a hangover

**hun·gry** \'həŋ-grē\ *adjective* **hun·gri·er; -est** [Middle English, from Old English *hungrig*; akin to Old English *hungor*] (before 12th century)
**1 a** : feeling hunger **b** : characterized by or characteristic of hunger or appetite
**2 a** : EAGER, AVID ⟨*hungry* for affection⟩ **b** : strongly motivated (as by ambition)
**3** : not rich or fertile : BARREN
— **hun·gri·ly** \-grə-lē\ *adverb*
— **hun·gri·ness** \-grē-nəs\ *noun*

**hung up** *adjective* (1948)
**1** : delayed or detained for a time
**2** : anxiously nervous
**3** : being much involved with: as **a** : being infatuated **b** : ENTHUSIASTIC **c** : PREOCCUPIED

**hunk** \'həŋk\ *noun* [Flemish *hunke*] (circa 1813)
**1** : a large lump, piece, or portion ⟨a *hunk* of bread⟩
**2** : an attractive well-built man

**hun·ker** \'həŋ-kər\ *intransitive verb* **hun·kered; hun·ker·ing** \-k(ə-)riŋ\ [perhaps of Scandinavian origin; akin to Old Norse *hūka* to squat; akin to Middle Low German *hōken* to squat, peddle — more at HAWKER] (1720)
**1** : CROUCH, SQUAT — usually used with *down*
**2** : to settle in or dig in for a sustained period — used with *down* ⟨*hunker* down for a good long wait —*New Yorker*⟩

**hun·kers** \'həŋ-kərz\ *noun plural* (1756)
: HAUNCHES

**hunks** \'həŋ(k)s\ *noun plural but singular in construction* [origin unknown] (1602)
: a surly ill-natured person; *especially* : MISER

**hunky** \'həŋ-kē\ *adjective* **hunk·i·er; -est** (1911)
: muscular and usually attractive ⟨*hunky* men⟩

**Hun·ky** *also* **Hun·kie** \'həŋ-kē\ *noun, plural* **Hunkies** [alteration of *Hungarian*] (circa 1896)

: a person of central or east European birth or descent — usually used disparagingly

**hun·ky-do·ry** \,həŋ-kē-'dōr-ē, -'dȯr-\ *adjective* [obsolete English dialect *hunk* (home base) + *-dory* (origin unknown)] (1866)
: quite satisfactory : FINE

**Hun·nish** \'hə-nish\ *adjective* (1820)
: relating to or resembling the Huns

¹**hunt** \'hənt\ *verb* [Middle English, from Old English *huntian*; akin to Old English *hentan* to seize] (before 12th century)
*transitive verb*
**1 a** : to pursue for food or in sport ⟨*hunt* buffalo⟩ **b** : to manage in the search for game ⟨*hunts* a pack of dogs⟩
**2 a** : to pursue with intent to capture ⟨*hunted* the escapees⟩ **b** : to search out : SEEK
**3** : to drive or chase especially by harrying ⟨members . . . were *hunted* from their homes —J. T. Adams⟩
**4** : to traverse in search of prey ⟨*hunts* the woods⟩
*intransitive verb*
**1** : to take part in a hunt
**2** : to attempt to find something
**3** : to oscillate alternately to each side (as of a neutral point) or to run alternately faster and slower — used especially of a device or machine

²**hunt** *noun* (14th century)
**1** : the act, the practice, or an instance of hunting
**2** : a group of mounted hunters and their hunting dogs

**hunt–and–peck** \,hənt-ᵊn-'pek\ *noun* (1939)
: a method of typing in which one looks at the keyboard and types using usually the forefingers

**hunt·er** \'hən-tər\ *noun* (13th century)
**1 a** : a person who hunts game **b** : a dog used or trained for hunting **c** : a horse used or adapted for use in hunting with hounds; *especially* : a fast strong horse trained for cross-country work and jumping
**2** : one that searches for something
**3** : a pocket watch with a hinged protective cover

**hunt·er–gath·er·er** \'hən-tər-'ga-thər-ər\ *noun* (1977)
: a member of a culture in which food is obtained by hunting, fishing, and foraging rather than by agriculture or animal husbandry

**hunter green** *noun* (circa 1930)
: a dark yellowish green

**hunt·ing** *noun* (before 12th century)
**1** : the act of one that hunts; *specifically* : the pursuit of game
**2** : the process of hunting
**3 a** : a periodic variation in speed of a synchronous electrical machine **b** : a self-induced and undesirable oscillation of a variable above and below the desired value in an automatic control system **c** : a continuous attempt by an automatically controlled system to find a desired equilibrium condition

**hunting horn** *noun* (1694)
: a signal horn used in the chase; *specifically* : a coiled circular horn with a flared bell and a cup-shaped mouthpiece

**Hun·ting·ton's chorea** \'hən-tiŋ-tənz-\ *noun* [George *Huntington* (died 1916) American physician] (1889)
: hereditary chorea usually developing in adult life and progressing to dementia — called also *Huntington's disease*

**hunt·ress** \'hən-trəs\ *noun* (14th century)
: a woman who hunts game; *also* : a female animal that hunts prey

**hunts·man** \'hən(t)-smən\ *noun* (1567)
**1** : HUNTER 1a
**2** : a person who manages a hunt and looks after the hounds

**hup** \'həp, 'hət\ *interjection* [probably alteration of ¹*hep*] (1951)
— used to mark a marching cadence

**hur·dies** \'hər-dēz\ *noun plural* [origin unknown] (14th century)
*dialect British* : RUMP

¹**hur·dle** \'hər-dᵊl\ *noun* [Middle English *hurdel*, from Old English *hyrdel*; akin to Old High German *hurt* hurdle, Latin *cratis* wickerwork, hurdle] (before 12th century)
**1 a** : a portable panel usually of wattled withes and stakes used especially for enclosing land or livestock **b** : a frame or sled formerly used in England for dragging traitors to execution

hurdle 2a

**2 a** : an artificial barrier over which racers must leap **b** *plural* : any of various track events in which a series of hurdles must be surmounted
**3** : BARRIER, OBSTACLE

²**hurdle** *transitive verb* **hur·dled; hur·dling** \'hərd-liŋ, 'hər-dᵊl-iŋ\ (1896)
**1** : to leap over especially while running (as in a sporting competition)
**2** : OVERCOME, SURMOUNT
— **hur·dler** \'hərd-lər, 'hər-dᵊl-ər\ *noun*

**hur·dy-gur·dy** \,hər-dē-'gər-dē, 'hər-dē-,\ *noun, plural* **-gurdies** [probably imitative] (1749)
**1** : a stringed instrument in which sound is produced by the friction of a rosined wheel turned by a crank against the strings and the pitches are varied by keys
**2** : any of various mechanical musical instruments (as the barrel organ)

**hurl** \'hər(-ə)l\ *verb* **hurled; hurl·ing** \'hər-liŋ\ [Middle English] (13th century)
*intransitive verb*
**1** : RUSH, HURTLE
**2** : PITCH 5a, b
*transitive verb*
**1** : to send or thrust with great vigor ⟨the forces that were to be *hurled* against the Turks —N. T. Gilroy⟩
**2** : to throw down with violence
**3 a** : to throw forcefully : FLING ⟨*hurled* the manuscript into the fire⟩ ⟨*hurled* myself over the fence⟩ **b** : PITCH 2a
**4** : to utter with vehemence ⟨*hurled* insults at the police⟩
**synonym** see THROW
— **hurl** *noun*
— **hurl·er** \'hər-lər\ *noun*

hurdy-gurdy 1

**hurl·ing** \'hər-liŋ\ *noun* (circa 1600)
: an Irish game resembling field hockey played between two teams of 15 players each

**hur·ly** \'hər-lē\ *noun* [probably short for *hurly-burly*] (1594)
: UPROAR, TUMULT

**hur·ly–bur·ly** \,hər-lē-'bər-lē\ *noun* [probably alteration & reduplication of *hurling*, gerund of *hurl*] (1539)
: UPROAR, TUMULT
— **hurly–burly** *adjective*

**Hu·ron** \'hyu̇r-ən, -,än\ *noun, plural* **Hurons** *or* **Huron** [French, literally, boor] (1658)
: a member of a confederacy of American Indian peoples formerly occupying the country between Georgian Bay and Lake Ontario

¹**hur·rah** \hu̇-'rȯ, -'rä, 'hu̇-,\ *noun* (1686)
**1 a** : EXCITEMENT, FANFARE **b** : CHEER 7
**2** : FUSS

²**hur·rah** \hu̇-'rȯ, -'rä\ *also* **hur·ray** \hu̇-'rā\ *interjection* [perhaps from German *hurra*] (1716)
— used to express joy, approbation, or encouragement

**Hur·ri·an** \\'hùr-ē-ən\ *noun* (1911)
**1** : a member of an ancient non-Semitic people of northern Mesopotamia, Syria, and eastern Asia Minor about 1500 B.C.
**2** : the language of the Hurrian people

**¹hur·ri·cane** \\'hər-ə-ˌkān, -i-kən, 'hə-rə-, 'hə-ri-\ *noun* [Spanish *huracán*, from Taino *hurakán*] (1555)
**1** : a tropical cyclone with winds of 74 miles (118 kilometers) per hour or greater that occurs especially in the western Atlantic, that is usually accompanied by rain, thunder, and lightning, and that sometimes moves into temperate latitudes — see BEAUFORT SCALE table
**2** : something resembling a hurricane especially in its turmoil

**²hurricane** *adjective* (1894)
: having or being a glass chimney providing protection from wind ⟨a *hurricane* lamp⟩

**hur·ried** \\'hər-ēd, 'hə-rēd\ *adjective* (1667)
**1** : going or working at speed
**2** : done in a hurry : HASTY
— **hur·ried·ly** \\'hər-əd-lē, 'hə-rəd-\ *adverb*
— **hur·ried·ness** \\'hər-ēd-nəs, 'hə-rēd-\ *noun*

**¹hur·ry** \\'hər-ē, 'hə-rē\ *verb* **hur·ried; hur·ry·ing** [perhaps from Middle English *horyen*] (1592)
*transitive verb*
**1 a** : to carry or cause to go with haste ⟨*hurry* them to the hospital⟩ **b** : to impel to rash or precipitate action
**2 a** : to impel to greater speed : PROD ⟨used spurs to *hurry* the horse⟩ **b** : EXPEDITE **c** : to perform with undue haste ⟨*hurry* a minuet⟩
*intransitive verb*
: to move or act with haste ⟨please *hurry* up⟩
— **hur·ri·er** *noun*

**²hurry** *noun* (1600)
**1** : disturbed or disorderly activity : COMMOTION
**2 a** : agitated and often bustling or disorderly haste **b** : a state of eagerness or urgency : RUSH
**synonym** see HASTE
— **in a hurry** : without delay : as rapidly as possible ⟨the police got there *in a hurry*⟩

**hur·ry-scur·ry** *or* **hur·ry–skur·ry** \\ˌhər-ē-'skər-ē, ˌhə-rē-'skə-rē\ *noun* [reduplication of ²*hurry*] (1754)
: a confused rush : TURMOIL
— **hurry-scurry** *adjective or adverb*

**hur·ry-up** \\'hər-ē-ˌəp, 'hə-rē-\ *adjective* (1902)
: speeded up : completed in a hurry ⟨a *hurry-up* dinner⟩

**¹hurt** \\'hərt\ *verb* **hurt; hurt·ing** [Middle English, probably from Old French *hurter* to collide with, probably of Germanic origin; akin to Old Norse *hrútr* male sheep] (13th century)
*transitive verb*
**1 a** : to inflict with physical pain : WOUND **b** : to do substantial or material harm to : DAMAGE ⟨the dry summer has *hurt* the land⟩
**2 a** : to cause emotional pain or anguish to : OFFEND **b** : to be detrimental to : HAMPER ⟨charges of graft *hurt* my chances of being elected⟩
*intransitive verb*
**1 a** : to suffer pain or grief **b** : to be in need — usually used with *for* ⟨*hurting* for money⟩
**2** : to cause damage or distress ⟨hit where it *hurts*⟩
**synonym** see INJURE
— **hurt** *adjective*
— **hurt·er** *noun*

**²hurt** *noun* (13th century)
**1** : a cause of injury or damage : BLOW
**2 a** : a bodily injury or wound **b** : mental distress or anguish : SUFFERING
**3** : WRONG, HARM

**hurt·ful** \\'hərt-fəl\ *adjective* (1526)
: causing injury, detriment, or suffering : DAMAGING
— **hurt·ful·ly** \-fə-lē\ *adverb*
— **hurt·ful·ness** *noun*

**hur·tle** \\'hərt-ᵊl\ *verb* **hur·tled; hur·tling** \\'hərt-liŋ, 'hər-tᵊl-iŋ\ [Middle English *hurtlen* to collide, frequentative of *hurten* to cause to strike, hurt] (14th century)
*intransitive verb*
: to move rapidly or forcefully
*transitive verb*
: HURL, FLING
— **hurtle** *noun*

**hurt·less** \\'hərt-ləs\ *adjective* (1549)
: causing no pain or injury : HARMLESS

**¹hus·band** \\'həz-bənd\ *noun* [Middle English *husbonde*, from Old English *hūsbonda* master of a house, from Old Norse *hūsbóndi*, from *hūs* house + *bōndi* householder; akin to Old Norse *būa* to inhabit; akin to Old English *būan* to dwell — more at BOWER] (13th century)
**1** : a male partner in a marriage
**2** *British* : MANAGER, STEWARD
**3** : a frugal manager
— **hus·band·ly** *adjective*

**²husband** *transitive verb* (15th century)
**1 a** : to manage prudently and economically **b** : to use sparingly : CONSERVE
**2** *archaic* : to find a husband for : MATE
— **hus·band·er** *noun*

**hus·band·man** \\'həz-bən(d)-mən\ *noun* (14th century)
**1** : one that plows and cultivates land : FARMER
**2** : a specialist in a branch of farm husbandry

**hus·band·ry** \\'həz-bən-drē\ *noun* (14th century)
**1** *archaic* : the care of a household
**2** : the control or judicious use of resources : CONSERVATION
**3 a** : the cultivation or production of plants and animals : AGRICULTURE **b** : the scientific control and management of a branch of farming and especially of domestic animals

**¹hush** \\'həsh\ *verb* [back-formation from *husht* (hushed), from Middle English *hussht*, from *huissht*, interjection used to enjoin silence] (1546)
*transitive verb*
**1** : CALM, QUIET ⟨*hushed* the children as they entered the library⟩
**2** : to put at rest : MOLLIFY
**3** : to keep from public knowledge : SUPPRESS ⟨*hush* the story up⟩
*intransitive verb*
: to become quiet

**²hush** *adjective* (1602)
**1** *archaic* : SILENT, STILL
**2** : intended to prevent the dissemination of certain information ⟨*hush* money⟩

**³hush** *noun* (1689)
: a silence or calm especially following noise : QUIET

**hush–hush** \\'həsh-ˌhəsh\ *adjective* (1916)
: SECRET, CONFIDENTIAL

**hush puppy** *noun* [from its occasional use as food for dogs] (circa 1918)
*chiefly Southern & southern Midland* : cornmeal dough shaped into small balls and fried in deep fat — usually used in plural

**¹husk** \\'həsk\ *noun* [Middle English] (14th century)
**1 a** : a usually dry or membranous outer covering (as a pod or hull or one composed of bracts) of various seeds and fruits; *also* : one of the constituent parts **b** : a carob pod
**2 a** : an outer layer : SHELL **b** : an emptied shell : REMNANT **c** : a supporting framework

**²husk** *transitive verb* (1562)
: to strip the husk from
— **husk·er** *noun*

**husk·ing** *noun* (1692)
: CORNHUSKING — called also *husking bee*

**husk–tomato** *noun* (1895)
: GROUND-CHERRY

**¹hus·ky** \\'həs-kē\ *adjective* **husk·i·er; -est** (1552)
: resembling, containing, or full of husks

**²hus·ky** \\'həs-kē\ *adjective* **husk·i·er; -est** [probably from *husk* (huskiness), from obsolete *husk* (to have a dry cough)] (circa 1722)
: hoarse with or as if with emotion
— **hus·ki·ly** \-kə-lē\ *adverb*
— **hus·ki·ness** \-kē-nəs\ *noun*

**³hus·ky** *noun, plural* **huskies** [shortening of *Huskemaw, Uskemaw* Eskimo, from Cree *aškime·w*; akin to Montagnais (Algonquian language of eastern Canada) *aiachkime8* Micmac, Eskimo — more at ESKIMO] (1852)
**1** : a heavy-coated working dog of the New World arctic region
**2** : SIBERIAN HUSKY

**⁴hus·ky** *noun, plural* **huskies** (1864)
: one that is husky

**⁵hus·ky** *adjective* **hus·ki·er; -est** [probably from ¹*husk*] (1869)
**1** : BURLY, ROBUST
**2** : LARGE

**hus·sar** \\(ˌ)hə-'zär, -'sär\ *noun* [Hungarian *huszár* hussar, (obsolete) highway robber, from Serbo-Croatian *husar* pirate, from Medieval Latin *cursarius* — more at CORSAIR] (1532)
: a member of any of various European units originally modeled on the Hungarian light cavalry of the 15th century

**Huss·ite** \\'hə-ˌsīt, 'hù-\ *noun* [New Latin *Hussita*, from John *Huss*] (1532)
: a member of the Bohemian religious and nationalist movement originating with John Huss
— **Hussite** *adjective*
— **Huss·it·ism** \-ˌsī-ˌti-zəm\ *noun*

**hus·sy** \\'hə-sē, -zē\ *noun, plural* **hussies** [alteration of Middle English *huswif* housewife, from *hus* house + *wif* wife, woman] (1505)
**1** : a lewd or brazen woman
**2** : a saucy or mischievous girl

**hus·tings** \\'həs-tiŋz\ *noun plural but singular or plural in construction* [Middle English, from Old English *hūsting*, from Old Norse *hūsthing*, from *hūs* house + *thing* assembly] (before 12th century)
**1 a** : a local court formerly held in various English municipalities and still held infrequently in London **b** : a local court in some cities in Virginia
**2 a** : a raised platform used until 1872 for the nomination of candidates for the British Parliament and for election speeches **b** : an election platform : STUMP **c** : the proceedings or locale of an election campaign ◆

◇ WORD HISTORY
**hustings** Hustings, now the haunt of politicians, were originally assemblies. Late Old English *hūsting*, the ancestor of modern *husting*, was a loan from Old Norse *hūsthing*, a compound of *hūs* "house" and *thing* "assembly"; the modifying *hūs* presumably signified that the assembly took place in a building rather than outdoors. After the Norman Conquest the *husting*, originally a sort of royal council, became a court hearing civil cases, especially one in London that met at the Guildhall, London's original seat of municipal government. *Hustings* was also apparently applied to a dais at one end of the Guildhall's Gothic meeting room, where the Court of Hustings met and where the lord mayor, sheriffs, and other officials were elected. At this point the history of *hustings* becomes murky, but it appears that about 1700, at a time when English electoral politics were taking something like their modern form, *hustings* was applied to any platform where a parliamentary seat was contested. In Hanoverian England this was typically a substantial structure erected in a large open space, where nomination speeches were made and the results of polling announced. Today in both Britain and the U.S. the hustings are usually the figurative rather than literal site of electioneering.

\ə\ abut \ᵊ\ kitten \ər\ further \a\ ash \ā\ ace
\ä\ mop, mar \aù\ out \ch\ chin \e\ bet \ē\ easy
\g\ go \i\ hit \ī\ ice \j\ job \ŋ\ sing \ō\ go
\ò\ law \òi\ boy \th\ thin \ṯh\ the \ü\ loot \ù\ foot
\y\ yet \zh\ vision *see also* Guide to Pronunciation

**hus·tle** \'hə-səl\ *verb* **hus·tled; hus·tling** \'hə-s(ə-)liŋ\ [Dutch *husselen* to shake, from Middle Dutch *hutselen*, frequentative of *hutsen*] (1751)
*transitive verb*
**1 a :** JOSTLE, SHOVE **b :** to convey forcibly or hurriedly **c :** to urge forward precipitately
**2 a :** to obtain by energetic activity ⟨*hustle* up new customers⟩ **b :** to sell something to or obtain something from by energetic and especially underhanded activity ⟨*hustling* the suckers⟩ **c :** to sell or promote energetically and aggressively ⟨*hustling* a new product⟩ **d :** to lure less skillful players into competing against oneself at (a gambling game) ⟨*hustle* pool⟩
*intransitive verb*
**1 :** SHOVE, PRESS
**2 :** HASTEN, HURRY
**3 a :** to make strenuous efforts to obtain especially money or business **b :** to obtain money by fraud or deception **c :** to engage in prostitution
**4 :** to play a game or sport in an alert aggressive manner
— **hustle** *noun*
— **hus·tler** \'hə-slər\ *noun*
**¹hut** \'hət\ *noun* [Middle French *hutte*, of Germanic origin; akin to Old High German *hutta* hut; probably akin to Old English *hȳd* skin, hide] (1658)
**1 :** an often small and temporary dwelling of simple construction **:** SHACK
**2 :** a simple shelter from the elements
— **hut** *verb*
**²hut** \'hət, 'həp\ *interjection* [probably alteration of ¹*hep*] (1948)
— used to mark a marching cadence
**hutch** \'həch\ *noun* [Middle English *huche*, from Old French] (13th century)
**1 a :** a chest or compartment for storage **b :** a cupboard usually surmounted by open shelves
**2 :** a pen or coop for an animal
**3 :** SHACK, SHANTY
**hut·ment** \'hət-mənt\ *noun* (1889)
**1 :** a collection of huts **:** ENCAMPMENT
**2 :** HUT
**Hut·ter·ite** \'hə-tə-,rīt, 'hü-\ *noun* [Jakob *Hutter* (died 1536) Moravian Anabaptist] (1910)
**:** a member of a Mennonite sect of northwestern U.S. and Canada living communally and holding property in common
— **Hut·te·ri·an** \,hə-'tir-ē-ən, hü-\ *adjective*
**Hu·tu** \'hü-(,)tü\ *noun, plural* **Hutu** or **Hutus** (1952)
**:** a member of a Bantu-speaking people of Rwanda and Burundi
**hutz·pah** or **hutz·pa** *variant of* CHUTZPAH
**huz·zah** or **huz·za** \(,)hə-'zä\ *noun* [origin unknown] (1573)
**:** an expression or shout of acclaim — often used interjectionally to express joy or approbation
**hy·a·cinth** \'hī-ə-(,)sin(t)th, -sən(t)th\ *noun* [Latin *hyacinthus*, a precious stone, a flowering plant, from Greek *hyakinthos*] (1553)
**1 a :** a precious stone of the ancients sometimes held to be the sapphire **b :** a gem zircon or essonite
**2 a :** a plant of the ancients held to be a lily, iris, larkspur, or gladiolus **b :** a bulbous herb (*Hyacinthus orientalis*) of the lily family that is native to the Mediterranean region but is widely grown for its dense spikes of fragrant flowers — compare GRAPE HYACINTH, WATER HYACINTH
**3 :** a light violet to moderate purple
— **hy·a·cin·thine** \,hī-ə-'sin(t)-thən\ *adjective*
**Hy·a·cin·thus** \,hī-ə-'sin(t)-thəs\ *noun* [Latin, from Greek *Hyakinthos*]

hyacinth
2b

**:** a youth loved and accidentally killed by Apollo who memorializes him with a hyacinth growing from the youth's blood
**Hy·a·des** \'hī-ə-,dēz\ *noun plural* [Latin, from Greek] (14th century)
**:** a V-shaped cluster of stars in the head of the constellation Taurus held by the ancients to indicate rainy weather when they rise with the sun
**hy·ae·na** *variant of* HYENA
**hyal-** or **hyalo-** *combining form* [Late Latin, glass, from Greek, from *hyalos*]
**:** glass **:** glassy ⟨*hyaline* (*hyaluronic* acid)
**¹hy·a·line** \'hī-ə-lən, -,līn\ *adjective* [Late Latin *hyalinus*, from Greek *hyalinos*, from *hyalos*] (circa 1661)
**:** transparent or nearly so and usually homogeneous
**²hy·a·line** \'hī-ə-lən, -,līn, *in sense 2* -lən or -,lēn\ *noun* (1667)
**1 :** something (as the clear atmosphere) that is transparent
**2** or **hy·a·lin** \-lən\ **:** any of several translucent nitrogenous substances related to chitin, found especially around cells, and readily stained by eosin
**hyaline cartilage** *noun* (1855)
**:** translucent bluish white cartilage with the cells embedded in an apparently homogeneous matrix present in joints and respiratory passages and forming most of the fetal skeleton
**hy·a·lite** \'hī-ə-,līt\ *noun* [German *Hyalit*, from Greek *hyalos*] (1794)
**:** a colorless opal that is clear as glass or sometimes translucent or whitish
**hy·a·loid** \-,lȯid\ *adjective* [Greek *hyaloeidēs*, from *hyalos*] (1835)
**:** GLASSY, TRANSPARENT
**hy·a·lo·plasm** \hī-'a-lə-,pla-zəm, 'hī-ə-lō-\ *noun* [probably from German *Hyaloplasma*, from *hyal-* + *-plasma* -plasm] (1886)
**:** CYTOSOL
**hy·al·uron·ic acid** \,hī-yü-'rä-nik-, ,hī-əl-yü-\ *noun* [International Scientific Vocabulary] (1934)
**:** a viscous mucopolysaccharide acid that occurs especially in the vitreous humor, the umbilical cord, and synovial fluid and as a cementing substance in the subcutaneous tissue
**hy·al·uron·i·dase** \-'rä-nə-,dās, -,dāz\ *noun* [International Scientific Vocabulary, from *hyaluronic* (*acid*) + *-idase* (as in *glucosidase*)] (1940)
**:** a mucolytic enzyme that facilitates the spread of fluids through tissues by lowering the viscosity of hyaluronic acid
**hy·brid** \'hī-brəd\ *noun* [Latin *hybrida*] (1601)
**1 :** an offspring of two animals or plants of different races, breeds, varieties, species, or genera
**2 :** a person whose background is a blend of two diverse cultures or traditions
**3 a :** something heterogeneous in origin or composition **:** COMPOSITE ⟨artificial *hybrids* of DNA and RNA⟩ ⟨a *hybrid* of medieval and Renaissance styles⟩ **b :** something (as a power plant, vehicle, or electronic circuit) that has two different types of components performing essentially the same function
— **hybrid** *adjective*
— **hy·brid·ism** \-brə-,di-zəm\ *noun*
— **hy·brid·i·ty** \hī-'bri-də-tē\ *noun*
**hybrid computer** *noun* (1968)
**:** a computer system consisting of a combination of analog and digital computer systems
**hy·brid·ize** \'hī-brə-,dīz\ *verb* **-ized; -iz·ing** (1845)
*transitive verb*
**:** to cause to produce hybrids **:** INTERBREED
*intransitive verb*
**:** to produce hybrids
— **hy·brid·iza·tion** \,hī-brə-də-'zā-shən\ *noun*
— **hy·brid·iz·er** *noun*
**hy·brid·oma** \,hī-brə-'dō-mə\ *noun* (1978)

**:** a hybrid cell produced by the fusion of an antibody-producing lymphocyte with a tumor cell and used to culture continuously a specific monoclonal antibody
**hybrid tea rose** *noun* (1926)
**:** any of numerous moderately hardy cultivated hybrid bush roses grown especially for their strongly recurrent bloom of large usually scentless flowers — called also *hybrid tea*
**hybrid vigor** *noun* (1918)
**:** HETEROSIS
**hy·bris** \'hī-brəs, 'hē-\ *variant of* HUBRIS
**hy·da·thode** \'hī-də-,thōd\ *noun* [International Scientific Vocabulary, from Greek *hydat-*, *hydōr* water + *hodos* road] (1895)
**:** a specialized pore on the leaves of higher plants that functions in the exudation of water
**hy·da·tid** \'hī-də-təd, -,tid\ *noun* [Greek *hydatid-*, *hydatis* watery cyst, from *hydat-*, *hydōr*] (1683)
**:** the larval cyst of a tapeworm (genus *Echinococcus*) occurring as a fluid-filled sac containing daughter cysts in which scolices develop
**hydr-** or **hydro-** *combining form* [Middle English *ydr-*, *ydro-*, from Old French, from Latin *hydr-*, *hydro-*, from Greek, from *hydōr* — more at WATER]
**1 a :** water ⟨*hydrous*⟩ ⟨*hydroelectric*⟩ **b :** liquid ⟨*hydrokinetic*⟩
**2 :** hydrogen **:** containing or combined with hydrogen ⟨*hydrocarbon*⟩ ⟨*hydroxyl*⟩
**3 :** hydroid ⟨*hydromedusa*⟩
**Hy·dra** \'hī-drə\ *noun* [Middle English *Ydra*, from Latin *Hydra*, from Greek]
**1 :** a many-headed serpent or monster in Greek mythology that was slain by Hercules and each head of which when cut off was replaced by two others
**2** *not capitalized* **:** a multifarious evil not to be overcome by a single effort
**3** [Latin (genitive *Hydrae*), from Greek] **:** a southern constellation of great length that lies south of Cancer, Sextans, Corvus, and Virgo and is represented on old maps by a serpent
**4** *not capitalized* [New Latin, from Latin, *Hydra*] **:** any of numerous small tubular freshwater hydrozoan polyps (*Hydra* and related genera) having at one end a mouth surrounded by tentacles
**hy·dra–head·ed** \,hī-drə-'he-dəd\ *adjective* (1599)
**:** having many centers or branches ⟨a *hydra-headed* organization⟩
**hy·dral·azine** \hī-'dra-lə-,zēn\ *noun* [*hydr-* + *phthal*ic (acid) + *azine*] (1952)
**:** a vasodilator $C_8H_8N_4$ used in the treatment of hypertension
**hy·dran·gea** \hī-'drān-jə\ *noun* [New Latin, from *hydr-* + Greek *angeion* vessel — more at ANGI-] (circa 1753)
**:** any of a genus (*Hydrangea*) of shrubs and one woody vine of the saxifrage family with opposite leaves and showy clusters of usually sterile white or tinted flowers
**hy·drant** \'hī-drənt\ *noun* (1806)
**1 :** a discharge pipe with a valve and spout at which water may be drawn from a water main (as for fighting fires) — called also *fireplug*
**2 :** FAUCET
**hy·dranth** \'hī-,dran(t)th\ *noun* [International Scientific Vocabulary *hydr-* + Greek *anthos* flower — more at ANTHOLOGY] (1874)
**:** one of the nutritive zooids of a hydroid colony
**hy·drase** \'hī-drās, -,drāz\ *noun* (1943)
**:** an enzyme that promotes the addition or removal of water to or from its substrate
**¹hy·drate** \'hī-,drāt\ *noun* (1802)
**:** a compound formed by the union of water with some other substance
**²hydrate** *verb* **hy·drat·ed; hy·drat·ing** (1850)
*transitive verb*
**:** to cause to take up or combine with water or the elements of water

*intransitive verb*
: to become a hydrate
— **hy·dra·tion** \hī-'drā-shən\ *noun*
— **hy·dra·tor** \'hī-,drā-tər\ *noun*
**hy·drau·lic** \hī-'drȯ-lik\ *adjective* [Latin *hydraulicus,* from Greek *hydraulikos,* from *hydraulis* hydraulic organ, from *hydr-* + *aulos* reed instrument — more at ALVEOLUS] (1661)
**1** : operated, moved, or effected by means of water
**2 a** : of or relating to hydraulics ⟨*hydraulic* engineer⟩ **b** : of or relating to water or other liquid in motion ⟨*hydraulic* erosion⟩
**3** : operated by the resistance offered or the pressure transmitted when a quantity of liquid (as water or oil) is forced through a comparatively small orifice or through a tube ⟨*hydraulic* brakes⟩
**4** : hardening or setting under water ⟨*hydraulic* cement⟩
— **hy·drau·li·cal·ly** \-li-k(ə-)lē\ *adverb*
**hy·drau·lics** \hī-'drȯ-liks\ *noun plural but singular in construction* (1671)
: a branch of science that deals with practical applications (as the transmission of energy or the effects of flow) of liquid (as water) in motion
**hy·dra·zide** \'hī-drə-,zīd\ *noun* (1888)
: any of a class of compounds resulting from the replacement of hydrogen by an acid group in hydrazine or in one of its derivatives
**hy·dra·zine** \'hī-drə-,zēn\ *noun* [International Scientific Vocabulary] (1887)
: a colorless fuming corrosive strongly reducing liquid base $N_2H_4$ used especially in fuels for rocket and jet engines; *also* : an organic base derived from this compound
**hy·dra·zo·ic acid** \,hī-drə-'zō-ik-\ *noun* [*hydr-* + *azo-* + ¹-*ic*] (1894)
: a colorless volatile poisonous explosive liquid $HN_3$ that has a foul odor and yields explosive salts of heavy metals
**hy·dric** \'hī-drik\ *adjective* (1926)
: characterized by, relating to, or requiring an abundance of moisture ⟨a *hydric* habitat⟩ ⟨a *hydric* plant⟩ — compare MESIC, XERIC
**-hydric** *adjective suffix*
: containing acid hydrogen ⟨mono*hydric*⟩
**hy·dride** \'hī-,drīd\ *noun* (1869)
: a compound of hydrogen with a more electropositive element or group
**hy·dri·od·ic acid** \,hī-drē-'ä-dik-\ *noun* [International Scientific Vocabulary] (1819)
: an aqueous solution of hydrogen iodide HI that is a strong acid resembling hydrochloric acid chemically and that is also a strong reducing agent
¹**hy·dro** \'hī-(,)drō\ *noun, plural* **hydros** [short for *hydropathic establishment*] (1882) *British* : an establishment offering hydropathic treatment (as for weight loss) : HEALTH SPA
²**hydro** *noun, often attributive* [short for *hydropower*] (1916)
: hydroelectric power
**hy·dro·bi·ol·o·gy** \,hī-drō-bī-'ä-lə-jē\ *noun* (1926)
: the biology of bodies or units of water; *especially* : LIMNOLOGY
— **hy·dro·bi·o·log·i·cal** \-,bī-ə-'lä-ji-kəl\ *adjective*
— **hy·dro·bi·ol·o·gist** \-bī-'ä-lə-jist\ *noun*
**hy·dro·bro·mic acid** \,hī-drə-'brō-mik-\ *noun* [International Scientific Vocabulary] (1836)
: an aqueous solution of hydrogen bromide HBr that is a strong acid resembling hydrochloric acid chemically, that is a weak reducing agent, and that is used especially for making bromides
**hy·dro·car·bon** \'hī-drō-,kär-bən\ *noun* (1826)
: an organic compound (as acetylene or butane) containing only carbon and hydrogen and often occurring in petroleum, natural gas, coal, and bitumens

**hy·dro·cele** \'hī-drə-,sēl\ *noun* [Latin, from Greek *hydrokēlē,* from *hydr-* + *kēlē* tumor — more at -CELE] (1597)
: an accumulation of serous fluid in a sacculated cavity (as the scrotum)
**hy·dro·ce·phal·ic** \,hī-drō-sə-'fa-lik\ *adjective* (1815)
: relating to, characterized by, or affected with hydrocephalus
— **hydrocephalic** *noun*
**hy·dro·ceph·a·lus** \-'se-fə-ləs\ *also* **hy·dro·ceph·a·ly** \-lē\ *noun* [New Latin *hydrocephalus,* from Late Latin *hydrocephalic,* adjective, from Greek *hydrokephalos,* from *hydr-* + *kephalē* head — more at CEPHALIC] (1670)
: an abnormal increase in the amount of cerebrospinal fluid within the cranial cavity that is accompanied by expansion of the cerebral ventricles, enlargement of the skull and especially the forehead, and atrophy of the brain
**hy·dro·chlo·ric acid** \,hī-drə-'klȯr-ik-, -'klȯr-\ *noun* [International Scientific Vocabulary] (circa 1828)
: an aqueous solution of hydrogen chloride HCl that is a strong corrosive irritating acid, is normally present in dilute form in gastric juice, and is widely used in industry and in the laboratory
**hy·dro·chlo·ride** \-'klȯr-,īd, -'klȯr-\ *noun* (1826)
: a chemical complex composed of an organic base (as an alkaloid) in association with hydrogen chloride
**hy·dro·chlo·ro·thi·a·zide** \-,klȯr-ə-'thī-ə-,zīd, -,klȯr-\ *noun* [*hydr-* + *chlor-* + *thia*zide + *-ide*] (1958)
: a diuretic and antihypertensive drug $C_7H_8ClN_3O_4S_2$
**hy·dro·col·loid** \,hī-drə-'kä-,lȯid\ *noun* (1916)
: a substance that yields a gel with water
— **hy·dro·col·loi·dal** \-kə-'lȯi-dᵊl, -kä-\ *adjective*
**hy·dro·cor·ti·sone** \-'kȯr-tə-,sōn, -,zōn\ *noun* (1951)
: a glucocorticoid $C_{21}H_{30}O_5$ of the adrenal cortex that is a derivative of cortisone and is used in the treatment of rheumatoid arthritis — called also *cortisol*
**hy·dro·crack·ing** \'hī-drə-,kra-kiŋ\ *noun* (1940)
: the cracking of hydrocarbons in the presence of hydrogen
— **hy·dro·crack** \-,krak\ *transitive verb*
— **hy·dro·crack·er** *noun*
**hy·dro·cy·an·ic acid** \,hī-drō-sī-'a-nik-\ *noun* [International Scientific Vocabulary] (1819)
: an aqueous solution of hydrogen cyanide HCN that is a poisonous weak acid and is used chiefly in fumigating and in organic synthesis
**hy·dro·dy·nam·ic** \-dī-'na-mik\ *also* **hy·dro·dy·nam·i·cal** \-mi-kəl\ *adjective* [New Latin *hydrodynamicus,* from *hydr-* + *dynamicus* dynamic] (circa 1828)
: of, relating to, or involving principles of hydrodynamics
— **hy·dro·dy·nam·i·cal·ly** \-mi-k(ə-)lē\ *adverb*
**hy·dro·dy·nam·ics** \-miks\ *noun plural but singular in construction* (1779)
: a branch of physics that deals with the motion of fluids and the forces acting on solid bodies immersed in fluids and in motion relative to them — compare HYDROSTATICS
— **hy·dro·dy·nam·i·cist** \-'na-mə-sist\ *noun*
**hy·dro·elec·tric** \,hī-drō-i-'lek-trik\ *adjective* [International Scientific Vocabulary] (1884)
: of or relating to production of electricity by waterpower ⟨constructed a *hydroelectric* power plant at the dam site⟩
— **hy·dro·elec·tri·cal·ly** \-tri-k(ə-)lē\ *adverb*

— **hy·dro·elec·tric·i·ty** \-,lek-'tri-sə-tē, -'tris-tē\ *noun*
**hy·dro·flu·or·ic acid** \,hī-drō-'flȯr-ik, -'flur-\ *noun* [International Scientific Vocabulary] (circa 1872)
: an aqueous solution of hydrogen fluoride HF that is a weak poisonous acid, that resembles hydrochloric acid chemically but attacks silica and silicates, and that is used especially in finishing and etching glass
**hy·dro·foil** \'hī-drə-,fȯil\ *noun* (1919)

**hydrofoil 2**

**1** : a body similar to an airfoil but designed for action in or on water
**2** : a motorboat that has metal plates or fins attached by struts fore and aft for lifting the hull clear of the water as speed is attained
**hy·dro·gen** \'hī-drə-jən, -dər-\ *noun* [French *hydrogène,* from *hydr-* + *-gène* -gen; from the fact that water is generated by its combustion] (1791)
: a nonmetallic element that is the simplest and lightest of the elements, is normally a colorless odorless highly flammable diatomic gas, and is used especially in synthesis — compare DEUTERIUM, TRITIUM; see ELEMENT table
— **hy·drog·e·nous** \hī-'drä-jə-nəs\ *adjective*
**hy·drog·e·nase** \hī-'drä-jə-,nās, -,nāz\ *noun* (1900)
: an enzyme of various microorganisms that promotes the formation and utilization of gaseous hydrogen
**hy·dro·ge·nate** \hī-'drä-jə-,nāt, 'hī-drə-\ *transitive verb* -**nat·ed; -nat·ing** (1809)
: to combine or treat with or expose to hydrogen; *especially* : to add hydrogen to the molecule of (an unsaturated organic compound)
— **hy·dro·ge·na·tion** \hī-,drä-jə-'nā-shən, ,hī-drə-\ *noun*
**hydrogen bomb** *noun* (1947)
: a bomb whose violent explosive power is due to the sudden release of atomic energy resulting from the fusion of light nuclei (as of hydrogen atoms) at very high temperature and pressure to form helium nuclei
**hydrogen bond** *noun* (1923)
: an electrostatic attraction between a hydrogen atom in one polar molecule (as of water) and a small electronegative atom (as of oxygen, nitrogen, or fluorine) in usually another molecule of the same or a different polar substance
— **hydrogen bonding** *noun*
**hydrogen bromide** *noun* (1885)
: a colorless irritating gas HBr that fumes in moist air and yields hydrobromic acid when dissolved in water
**hydrogen chloride** *noun* (1869)
: a colorless pungent poisonous gas HCl that fumes in moist air and yields hydrochloric acid when dissolved in water
**hydrogen cyanide** *noun* (1882)
**1** : a poisonous usually gaseous compound HCN that has the odor of bitter almonds
**2** : HYDROCYANIC ACID
**hydrogen fluoride** *noun* (1885)
: a colorless corrosive fuming usually gaseous compound HF that yields hydrofluoric acid when dissolved in water
**hydrogen iodide** *noun* (1885)
: an acrid colorless gas HI that fumes in moist air and yields hydriodic acid when dissolved in water

---

\ə\ abut \ᵊ\ kitten \ər\ further \a\ ash \ā\ ace
\ä\ mop, mar \au̇\ out \ch\ chin \e\ bet \ē\ easy
\g\ go \i\ hit \ī\ ice \j\ job \ŋ\ sing \ō\ go
\ȯ\ law \ȯi\ boy \th\ thin \t͟h\ the \ü\ loot \u̇\ foot
\y\ yet \zh\ vision *see also* Guide to Pronunciation

**hydrogen ion** *noun* (1896)
**1 :** the cation H⁺ of acids consisting of a hydrogen atom whose electron has been transferred to the anion of the acid
**2 :** HYDRONIUM
**hydrogen peroxide** *noun* (1872)
**:** an unstable compound $H_2O_2$ used especially as an oxidizing and bleaching agent, an antiseptic, and a propellant
**hydrogen sulfide** *noun* (1873)
**:** a flammable poisonous gas $H_2S$ that has an odor suggestive of rotten eggs and is found especially in many mineral waters and in putrefying matter
**hy·dro·graph·ic** \ˌhī-drə-'gra-fik\ *adjective* [French *hydrographique,* from Middle French, from *hydr-* + *-graphique* -graphic] (1665)
**1 :** of or relating to the characteristic features (as flow or depth) of bodies of water
**2 :** relating to the charting of bodies of water
— **hy·drog·ra·pher** \hī-'drä-grə-fər\ *noun*
— **hy·drog·ra·phy** \-grə-fē\ *noun*
**¹hy·droid** \'hī-ˌdròid\ *adjective* [ultimately from New Latin *Hydra*] (circa 1864)
**:** of or relating to a hydrozoan; *especially* **:** resembling a typical hydra
**²hydroid** (1865)
**:** HYDROZOAN; *especially* **:** a hydrozoan polyp as distinguished from a medusa
**hy·dro·ki·net·ic** \ˌhī-drō-kə-'ne-tik, -ˌ(ˌ)kī-\ *adjective* (1876)
**:** of or relating to the motions of fluids or the forces which produce or affect such motions — compare HYDROSTATIC
**hy·dro·lase** \'hī-drə-ˌlās, -ˌlāz\ *noun* [International Scientific Vocabulary, from New Latin *hydrolysis* + International Scientific Vocabulary *-ase*] (1910)
**:** a hydrolytic enzyme
**hydrologic cycle** *noun* (1936)
**:** the sequence of conditions through which water passes from vapor in the atmosphere through precipitation upon land or water surfaces and ultimately back into the atmosphere as a result of evaporation and transpiration — called also *hydrological cycle*
**hy·drol·o·gy** \hī-'drä-lə-jē\ *noun* [New Latin *hydrologia,* from Latin *hydr-* + *-logia* -logy] (1762)
**:** a science dealing with the properties, distribution, and circulation of water on and below the earth's surface and in the atmosphere
— **hy·dro·log·ic** \ˌhī-drə-'lä-jik\ *or* **hy·dro·log·i·cal** \-ji-kəl\ *adjective*
— **hy·dro·log·i·cal·ly** \-ji-k(ə-)lē\ *adverb*
— **hy·drol·o·gist** \hī-'drä-lə-jist\ *noun*
**hy·dro·ly·sate** \hī-'drä-lə-ˌsāt\ *also* **hy·dro·ly·zate** \-ˌzāt\ *noun* (1915)
**:** a product of hydrolysis
**hy·dro·ly·sis** \hī-'drä-lə-səs\ *noun* [New Latin] (1880)
**:** a chemical process of decomposition involving the splitting of a bond and the addition of the hydrogen cation and the hydroxide anion of water
— **hy·dro·lyt·ic** \ˌhī-drə-'li-tik\ *adjective*
— **hy·dro·lyt·i·cal·ly** \-ti-k(ə-)lē\ *adverb*
**hy·dro·lyze** \'hī-drə-ˌlīz\ *verb* **-lyzed; -lyz·ing** [International Scientific Vocabulary, from New Latin *hydrolysis*] (1880)
*transitive verb*
**:** to subject to hydrolysis
*intransitive verb*
**:** to undergo hydrolysis
— **hy·dro·lyz·able** \-ˌlī-zə-bəl\ *adjective*
**hy·dro·mag·net·ic** \ˌhī-drō-mag-'ne-tik\ *adjective* (1943)
**:** MAGNETOHYDRODYNAMIC
**hy·dro·man·cy** \'hī-drə-ˌman(t)-sē\ *noun* [Middle English *ydromancie,* from Middle French, from Latin *hydromantia,* from *hydr-* + *-mantia* -mancy] (14th century)
**:** divination by the appearance or motion of liquids (as water)
**hy·dro·me·chan·i·cal** \ˌhī-drō-mi-'ka-ni-kəl\ *adjective* (1825)

**:** relating to a branch of mechanics that deals with the equilibrium and motion of fluids and of solid bodies immersed in them
— **hy·dro·me·chan·ics** \-'ka-niks\ *noun plural but singular in construction*
**hy·dro·me·du·sa** \ˌhī-drō-mi-'dü-sə, -'dyü-, -zə\ *noun, plural* **-sae** \-ˌsē, -ˌzē\ [New Latin] (circa 1889)
**:** a medusa (as of the orders Anthomedusae and Leptomedusae) produced as a bud from a hydroid
**hy·dro·met·al·lur·gy** \ˌhī-drō-'me-tᵊl-ˌər-jē\ *noun* [International Scientific Vocabulary] (circa 1859)
**:** the treatment of ores by wet processes (as leaching)
— **hy·dro·met·al·lur·gi·cal** \-ˌme-tᵊl-'ər-ji-kəl\ *adjective*
— **hy·dro·met·al·lur·gist** \-'me-tᵊl-ˌər-jist\ *noun*
**hy·dro·me·te·or** \ˌhī-drō-'mē-tē-ər, -tē-ˌor\ *noun* [International Scientific Vocabulary] (1857)
**:** a product (as fog, rain, or hail) formed by the condensation of atmospheric water vapor
**hy·dro·me·te·o·rol·o·gy** \-ˌmē-tē-ə-'rä-lə-jē\ *noun* (circa 1859)
**:** a branch of meteorology that deals with water in the atmosphere especially as precipitation
— **hy·dro·me·te·o·ro·log·i·cal** \-tē-ˌór-ə-'lä-ji-kəl, -ˌär-ə-, -ə-rə-\ *adjective*
— **hy·dro·me·te·o·rol·o·gist** \-tē-ə-'rä-lə-jist\ *noun*
**hy·drom·e·ter** \hī-'drä-mə-tər\ *noun* (1675)
**:** an instrument for determining the specific gravity of a liquid (as battery acid or an alcohol solution) and hence its strength
— **hy·dro·met·ric** \ˌhī-drə-'me-trik\ *adjective*
**hy·dro·mor·phic** \ˌhī-drə-'mór-fik\ *adjective* (1938)
*of a soil* **:** developed in the presence of an excess of moisture which tends to suppress aerobic factors in soil-building
**hy·dron·ic** \hī-'drä-nik\ *adjective* [*hydr-* + *-onic* (as in *electronic*)] (1946)
**:** of, relating to, or being a system of heating or cooling that involves transfer of heat by a circulating fluid (as water or vapor) in a closed system of pipes
— **hy·dron·i·cal·ly** \-ni-k(ə-)lē\ *adverb*
**hy·dro·ni·um** \hī-'drō-nē-əm\ *noun* [International Scientific Vocabulary *hydr-* + *-onium*] (1908)
**:** a hydrated hydrogen ion $H_3O^+$
**hy·drop·a·thy** \hī-'drä-pə-thē\ *noun* [International Scientific Vocabulary] (1843)
**:** the empirical use of water in the treatment of disease — compare HYDROTHERAPY
— **hy·dro·path·ic** \ˌhī-drə-'pa-thik\ *adjective*
**hy·dro·per·ox·ide** \ˌhī-drō-pə-'räk-ˌsīd\ *noun* (1937)
**:** a compound containing an $O_2H$ group
**hy·dro·phane** \'hī-drə-ˌfān\ *noun* (1784)
**:** a semitranslucent opal that becomes translucent or transparent on immersion in water
**hy·dro·phil·ic** \ˌhī-drə-'fi-lik\ *adjective* [New Latin *hydrophilus,* from Greek *hydr-* + *-philos* -philous] (1916)
**:** of, relating to, or having a strong affinity for water ⟨hydrophilic proteins⟩
— **hy·dro·phi·lic·i·ty** \ˌhī-drə-fi-'li-sə-tē\ *noun*
**hy·dro·pho·bia** \ˌhī-drə-'fō-bē-ə\ *noun* [Late Latin, from Greek, from *hydr-* + *-phobia* -phobia] (1547)
**1 :** RABIES
**2 :** a morbid dread of water
**hy·dro·pho·bic** \-'fō-bik\ *adjective* (1807)
**1 :** of, relating to, or suffering from hydrophobia
**2 :** lacking affinity for water
— **hy·dro·pho·bic·i·ty** \-fō-'bi-sə-tē\ *noun*
**hy·dro·phone** \'hī-drə-ˌfōn\ *noun* (1860)

**:** an instrument for listening to sound transmitted through water
**hy·dro·phyte** \-ˌfīt\ *noun* [International Scientific Vocabulary] (1832)
**1 :** a perennial vascular aquatic plant having its overwintering buds under water
**2 :** a plant growing in water or in soil too waterlogged for most plants to survive
— **hy·dro·phyt·ic** \ˌhī-drə-'fi-tik\ *adjective*
**¹hy·dro·plane** \'hī-drə-ˌplān\ *noun* (1904)
**1 :** a powerboat designed for racing that skims the surface of the water
**2 :** SEAPLANE
**²hydroplane** *intransitive verb* (1962)
**:** to skim on water; *especially, of a vehicle* **:** to skid on a wet surface (as pavement) because a film of water on the surface causes the tires to lose contact with it
**hy·dro·pon·ics** \ˌhī-drə-'pä-niks\ *noun plural but singular in construction* [*hydr-* + *-ponics* (as in *geoponics* agriculture)] (1937)
**:** the growing of plants in nutrient solutions with or without an inert medium to provide mechanical support
— **hy·dro·pon·ic** \-nik\ *adjective*
— **hy·dro·pon·i·cal·ly** \-ni-k(ə-)lē\ *adverb*
**hy·dro·pow·er** \'hī-drə-ˌpaù-(-ə)r\ *noun* (1933)
**:** hydroelectric power
**hy·dro·qui·none** \ˌhī-drō-kwi-'nōn, -'kwi-ˌnōn\ *noun* [International Scientific Vocabulary] (circa 1872)
**:** a white crystalline strongly reducing phenol $C_6H_6O_2$ used especially as a photographic developer and as an antioxidant and stabilizer
**hy·dro·sere** \'hī-drə-ˌsir\ *noun* (1920)
**:** an ecological sere originating in an aquatic habitat
**hy·dro·sol** \'hī-drə-ˌsäl, -ˌsòl\ *noun* [*hydr-* + *-sol* (from *solution*)] (1864)
**:** a sol in which the liquid is water
— **hy·dro·sol·ic** \ˌhī-drə-'säl-ik\ *adjective*
**hy·dro·space** \-ˌspās\ *noun* (1963)
**:** the regions beneath the surface of the ocean
**hy·dro·sphere** \-ˌsfir\ *noun* [International Scientific Vocabulary] (1887)
**:** the aqueous vapor of the atmosphere; *broadly* **:** the aqueous envelope of the earth including bodies of water and aqueous vapor in the atmosphere
— **hy·dro·spher·ic** \ˌhī-drə-'sfir-ik, -'sfer-\ *adjective*
**hy·dro·stat·ic** \ˌhī-drə-'sta-tik\ *adjective* [probably from New Latin *hydrostaticus,* from *hydr-* + *staticus* static] (1666)
**:** of or relating to fluids at rest or to the pressures they exert or transmit — compare HYDROKINETIC
— **hy·dro·stat·i·cal·ly** \-ti-k(ə-)lē\ *adverb*
**hy·dro·stat·ics** \-tiks\ *noun plural but singular in construction* (1660)
**:** a branch of physics that deals with the characteristics of fluids at rest and especially with the pressure in a fluid or exerted by a fluid on an immersed body — compare HYDRODYNAMICS
**hy·dro·ther·a·py** \ˌhī-drə-'ther-ə-pē\ *noun* [International Scientific Vocabulary] (1876)
**:** the use of water especially externally in the treatment of disease or disability
**hy·dro·ther·mal** \ˌhī-drə-'thər-məl\ *adjective* [International Scientific Vocabulary] (1849)
**:** of or relating to hot water — used especially of the formation of minerals by hot solutions rising from a cooling magma
— **hy·dro·ther·mal·ly** \-mə-lē\ *adverb*
**hy·dro·tho·rax** \-'thōr-ˌaks, -'thòr-\ *noun* [New Latin] (1793)
**:** an excess of serous fluid in the pleural cavity; *especially* **:** an effusion resulting from failing circulation (as in heart disease or from lung infection)
**hy·drot·ro·pism** \hī-'drä-trə-ˌpi-zəm\ *noun* [International Scientific Vocabulary] (circa 1882)
**:** a tropism (as in plant roots) in which water or water vapor is the orienting factor

— **hy·dro·tro·pic** \,hī-drə-'trō-pik, -'trä-\ *adjective*

**hy·drous** \'hī-drəs\ *adjective* (1826)
: containing water usually in chemical association (as in hydrates)

**hy·drox·ide** \hī-'dräk-,sīd\ *noun* [International Scientific Vocabulary] (1851)
**1** : the univalent anion OH⁻ consisting of one atom of hydrogen and one of oxygen — called also *hydroxide ion*
**2** : an ionic compound of hydroxide with an element or group

**hy·droxy** \hī-'dräk-sē\ *adjective* [International Scientific Vocabulary, from *hydroxyl*] (1812)
: being or containing hydroxyl; *especially* : containing hydroxyl especially in place of hydrogen — usually used in combination ⟨*hydroxy*acetic acid⟩

**hy·droxy·ap·a·tite** \hī-,dräk-sē-'a-pə-,tīt\ *or* **hy·drox·yl·ap·a·tite** \-sə-'la-pə-,tīt\ *noun* (1912)
: a complex phosphate of calcium $Ca_5(PO_4)_3OH$ that occurs as a mineral and is the chief structural element of vertebrate bone

**hy·droxy·bu·tyr·ic acid** \hī-,dräk-sē-byü-'tir-ik-\ *noun* (1879)
: a hydroxy derivative $C_4H_8O_3$ of butyric acid that is excreted in increased quantities in the urine in diabetes

**hy·drox·yl** \hī-'dräk-səl\ *noun* [*hydr-* + *ox-* + *-yl*] (1869)
**1** : the chemical group or ion OH that consists of one atom of hydrogen and one of oxygen and is neutral or positively charged
**2** : HYDROXIDE 1
— **hy·drox·yl·ic** \,hī-,dräk-'si-lik\ *adjective*

**hy·drox·yl·amine** \hī-'dräk-sə-lə-,mēn, ,hī-,dräk-'si-lə-,mēn\ *noun* [International Scientific Vocabulary] (1869)
: a colorless odorless nitrogenous base $NH_3O$ that resembles ammonia in its reactions but is less basic and that is used especially as a reducing agent

**hy·drox·y·lase** \hī-'dräk-sə-,lās, -,lāz\ *noun* (1953)
: any of a group of enzymes that catalyze oxidation reactions in which one of the two atoms of molecular oxygen is incorporated into the substrate and the other is used to oxidize NADH or NADPH

**hy·drox·yl·ate** \hī-'dräk-sə-,lāt\ *transitive verb* **-at·ed; -at·ing** (circa 1909)
: to introduce hydroxyl into
— **hy·drox·yl·ation** \-,dräk-sə-'lā-shən\ *noun*

**hy·droxy·pro·line** \hī-,dräk-sē-'prō-,lēn\ *noun* (1905)
: an amino acid $C_5H_9NO_3$ that occurs naturally as a constituent of collagen

**hy·droxy·tryp·ta·mine** \-'trip-tə-,mēn\ *noun* (1949)
: SEROTONIN

**hy·droxy·urea** \-yù-'rē-ə\ *noun* (1949)
: a compound $CH_4N_2O_2$ used to treat some forms of leukemia

**hy·droxy·zine** \hī-'dräk-sə-,zēn\ *noun* [*hydroxy-* + piperazine] (1956)
: a compound $C_{21}H_{27}ClN_2O_2$ used as an antihistaminic and tranquilizer

**hy·dro·zo·an** \,hī-drə-'zō-ən\ *noun* [ultimately from Greek *hydr-* + *zōion* animal — more at ZO-] (1877)
: any of a class (Hydrozoa) of coelenterates that includes simple and compound polyps and jellyfishes having no stomodeum or gastric tentacles
— **hydrozoan** *adjective*

**hy·e·na** \hī-'ē-nə\ *noun, plural* **hyenas** *also* **hyena** [Middle English *hyene*, from Latin *hyaena*, from Greek *hyaina*, from *hys* hog — more at sow] (14th century)
: any of several large strong nocturnal carnivorous Old World mammals (family Hyaenidae) that usually feed as scavengers
— **hy·e·nic** \-'ē-nik, -'e-nik\ *adjective*

**Hy·ge·ia** \hī-'jē-ə\ *noun* [Latin, from Greek *Hygieia*]
: the goddess of health in Greek mythology

**hy·giene** \'hī-,jēn *also* hī-'\ *noun* [French *hygiène* & New Latin *hygieina*, from Greek, neuter plural of *hygieinos* healthful, from *hygiēs* healthy; akin to Sanskrit *su* well and to Latin *vivus* living — more at QUICK] (1671)
**1** : a science of the establishment and maintenance of health
**2** : conditions or practices (as of cleanliness) conducive to health
— **hy·gien·ic** \,hī-'jē-nik, -'je- *also* -jē-'e-nik\ *adjective*
— **hy·gien·i·cal·ly** \-ni-k(ə-)lē\ *adverb*
— **hy·gien·ist** \hī-'jē-nist, 'hī-,jē-, hī-'je-\ *noun*

**hy·gien·ics** \,hī-'jē-niks, -'je- *also* -jē-'e-niks\ *noun plural but singular in construction* (1855)
: HYGIENE 1

**hygr-** *also* **hygro-** *combining form* [Greek, from *hygros* wet — more at HUMOR]
: humidity : moisture ⟨*hygro*phyte⟩

**hy·gro·graph** \'hī-grə-,graf\ *noun* [International Scientific Vocabulary] (circa 1864)
: an instrument for recording automatically variations in atmospheric humidity

**hy·grom·e·ter** \hī-'grä-mə-tər\ *noun* [probably from French *hygromètre*, from *hygr-* + *-mètre* -meter] (1670)
: any of several instruments for measuring the humidity of the atmosphere
— **hy·gro·met·ric** \,hī-grə-'me-trik\ *adjective*

**hy·groph·i·lous** \hī-'grä-fə-ləs\ *adjective* (1863)
: living or growing in moist places

**hy·gro·phyte** \'hī-grə-,fīt\ *noun* [International Scientific Vocabulary] (1903)
: HYDROPHYTE
— **hy·gro·phyt·ic** \,hī-grə-'fi-tik\ *adjective*

**hy·gro·scop·ic** \,hī-grə-'skä-pik\ *adjective* [*hygroscope*, an instrument showing changes in humidity + *¹-ic;* from the use of such materials in the hygroscope] (1790)
**1** : readily taking up and retaining moisture
**2** : taken up and retained under some conditions of humidity and temperature ⟨*hygroscopic* water in clay⟩
— **hy·gro·scop·ic·i·ty** \-(,)skä-'pi-sə-tē\ *noun*

**hying** *present participle of* HIE

**Hyk·sos** \'hik-,säs, -,sōs\ *adjective* [Greek *Hyksōs*, dynasty ruling Egypt, perhaps from Egyptian *ḥq* ruler + *ḥśt* foreign land] (1602)
: of or relating to a Semite dynasty that ruled Egypt from about the 18th to the 16th century B.C.

**hy·la** \'hī-lə\ *noun* [New Latin, from Latin *Hylas*, a companion of Hercules] (1842)
: any of a genus (*Hyla*) of tree frogs

**hy·lo·zo·ism** \,hī-lə-'zō-,i-zəm\ *noun* [Greek *hylē* matter, literally, wood + *zōos* alive, living; akin to Greek *zōē* life — more at QUICK] (1678)
: a doctrine held especially by early Greek philosophers that all matter has life
— **hy·lo·zo·ist** \-'zō-ist\ *noun*
— **hy·lo·zo·is·tic** \-zō-'is-tik\ *adjective*

**hy·men** \'hī-mən\ *noun* [Late Latin, from Greek *hymēn* membrane] (1615)
: a fold of mucous membrane partly closing the orifice of the vagina
— **hy·men·al** \-mə-n°l\ *adjective*

**Hymen** *noun* [Latin, from Greek *Hymēn*]
: the Greek god of marriage

**¹hy·me·ne·al** \,hī-mə-'nē-əl\ *adjective* [Latin *hymenaeus* wedding song, wedding, from Greek *hymenaios*, from *Hymēn*] (1602)
: NUPTIAL
— **hy·me·ne·al·ly** \-'nē-ə-lē\ *adverb*

**²hymeneal** *noun* (1655)
**1** *plural, archaic* : NUPTIALS
**2** *archaic* : a wedding hymn

**hy·me·ni·um** \,hī-'mē-nē-əm\ *noun, plural* **-nia** \-nē-ə\ *or* **-niums** [New Latin, from Greek *hymēn*] (1830)
: a spore-bearing layer in fungi consisting of a group of asci or basidia often interspersed with sterile structures

**hy·me·nop·ter·an** \,hī-mə-'näp-tə-rən\ *noun* [New Latin *Hymenoptera*, from Greek, neuter plural of *hymenopteros* membrane-winged, from *hymēn* + *pteron* wing — more at FEATHER] (circa 1842)
: any of an order (Hymenoptera) of highly specialized insects with complete metamorphosis that include the bees, wasps, ants, ichneumon flies, sawflies, gall wasps, and related forms, often associate in large colonies with complex social organization, and have usually four membranous wings and the abdomen generally borne on a slender pedicel
— **hymenopteran** *adjective*
— **hy·me·nop·ter·ous** \-rəs\ *adjective*

**hy·me·nop·ter·on** \-tə-,rän, -rən\ *noun, plural* **-tera** \-rə\ *also* **-terons** [New Latin, from Greek, neuter of *hymenopteros*] (1877)
: HYMENOPTERAN

**¹hymn** \'him\ *noun* [Middle English *ymne*, from Old English *ymen*, from Latin *hymnus* song of praise, from Greek *hymnos*] (before 12th century)
**1 a** : a song of praise to God **b** : a metrical composition adapted for singing in a religious service
**2** : a song of praise or joy
**3** : something resembling a hymn : PAEAN

**²hymn** *verb* **hymned** \'himd\; **hymn·ing** \'hi-miŋ\ (1667)
*transitive verb*
: to praise or worship in or as if in hymns
*intransitive verb*
: to sing a hymn

**hym·nal** \'him-nəl\ *noun* [Middle English *hymnale*, from Medieval Latin, from Latin *hymnus*] (15th century)
: a collection of church hymns

**hym·na·ry** \'him-nə-rē\ *noun, plural* **-ries** (1888)
: HYMNAL

**hymn·book** \'him-,bùk\ *noun* (before 12th century)
: HYMNAL

**hym·no·dy** \'him-nə-dē\ *noun* [Late Latin *hymnodia*, from Greek *hymnōidia*, from *hymnos* + *aeidein* to sing — more at ODE] (1711)
**1** : hymn singing
**2** : hymn writing
**3** : the hymns of a time, place, or church

**hym·nol·o·gy** \him-'nä-lə-jē\ *noun* [Greek *hymnologia* singing of hymns, from *hymnos* + *-logia* -logy] (circa 1638)
**1** : HYMNODY
**2** : the study of hymns

**hy·oid** \'hī-,oid\ *adjective* [New Latin *hyoides* hyoid bone] (1842)
: of or relating to the hyoid bone

**hyoid bone** *noun* [New Latin *hyoides*, from Greek *hyoeidēs* shaped like the letter upsilon (Y, υ), being the hyoid bone, from *y, hy* upsilon] (circa 1811)
: a bone or complex of bones situated at the base of the tongue and supporting the tongue and its muscles

**hy·o·scine** \'hī-ə-,sēn\ *noun* [International Scientific Vocabulary *hyoscyamine + -ine*] (1872)
: SCOPOLAMINE; *especially* : the levorotatory form of scopolamine

**hy·o·scy·a·mine** \,hī-ə-'sī-ə-,mēn\ *noun* [German *Hyoscyamin*, from New Latin *Hyoscyamus*, genus of herbs, from Latin, henbane, from Greek *hyoskyamos*, literally, swine's

bean, from *hyos* (genitive of *hys* swine) + *kyamos* bean — more at SOW] (1858)
**:** a poisonous crystalline alkaloid $C_{17}H_{23}NO_3$ of which atropine is a racemic mixture; *especially* **:** its levorotatory form found especially in the plants belladonna and henbane and used similarly to atropine

**hyp-** — see HYPO-

**hyp·abys·sal** \,hi-pə-'bi-səl, ,hī-\ *adjective* [International Scientific Vocabulary] (1895)
**:** of or relating to a fine-grained igneous rock usually formed at a moderate distance below the surface
— **hyp·abys·sal·ly** \-sə-lē\ *adverb*

**hy·pae·thral** \hī-'pē-thrəl\ *adjective* [Latin *hypaethrus* exposed to the open air, from Greek *hypaithros,* from *hypo-* + *aithēr* ether, air — more at ETHER] (1794)
**1 :** having a roofless central space ⟨*hypaethral* temple⟩
**2 :** open to the sky

**hy·pal·la·ge** \hī-'pa-lə-jē, hi-\ *noun* [Latin, from Greek *hypallagē,* literally, interchange, from *hypallassein* to interchange, from *hypo-* + *allassein* to change, from *allos* other — more at ELSE] (1586)
**:** an interchange of two elements in a phrase or sentence from a more logical to a less logical relationship (as in "a mind is a terrible thing to waste" for "to waste a mind is a terrible thing")

**hy·pan·thi·um** \hī-'pan(t)-thē-əm\ *noun, plural* **-thia** \-thē-ə\ [New Latin, from *hypo-* + *anth-* + *-ium*] (circa 1855)
**:** an enlargement of the floral receptacle bearing on its rim the stamens, petals, and sepals and often enlarging and surrounding the fruits (as in the rose hip)

**¹hype** \'hīp\ *noun* [by shortening & alteration] (1924)
**1** *slang* **:** a narcotics addict
**2** *slang* **:** HYPODERMIC

**²hype** *transitive verb* **hyped; hyping** (1938)
**1 :** STIMULATE, ENLIVEN — usually used with *up*
**2 :** INCREASE
— **hyped–up** \'hīp-'dəp\ *adjective*

**³hype** *transitive verb* **hyped; hyp·ing** [origin unknown] (circa 1931)
**1 :** PUT ON, DECEIVE
**2 :** to promote or publicize extravagantly

**⁴hype** *noun* (1955)
**1 :** DECEPTION, PUT-ON
**2 :** PUBLICITY; *especially* **:** promotional publicity of an extravagant or contrived kind

**hy·per** \'hī-pər\ *adjective* [short for *hyperactive*] (1971)
**1 :** HIGH-STRUNG, EXCITABLE; *also* **:** highly excited
**2 :** extremely active

**hyper-** *prefix* [Middle English *iper-,* from Latin *hyper-,* from Greek, from *hyper* — more at OVER]
**1 :** above **:** beyond **:** SUPER- ⟨*hyper*market⟩
**2 a :** excessively ⟨*hyper*sensitive⟩ **b :** excessive ⟨*hyper*emia⟩
**3 :** that is or exists in a space of more than three dimensions ⟨*hyper*space⟩

hy·per·acu·ity
hy·per·acute
hy·per·aes·thet·ic
hy·per·ag·gres·sive
hy·per·alert
hy·per·arid
hy·per·arous·al
hy·per·aware
hy·per·aware·ness
hy·per·ca·tab·o·lism
hy·per·cau·tious
hy·per·charged
hy·per·civ·i·lized
hy·per·co·ag·u·la·bil·i·ty
hy·per·co·ag·u·la·ble
hy·per·com·pet·i·tive
hy·per·con·cen·tra·tion
hy·per·con·scious
hy·per·con·scious·ness
hy·per·de·vel·op·ment
hy·per·ef·fi·cient
hy·per·emo·tion·al
hy·per·emo·tion·al·i·ty
hy·per·en·dem·ic
hy·per·en·er·get·ic
hy·per·ex·cit·abil·i·ty
hy·per·ex·cit·able
hy·per·ex·cit·ed
hy·per·ex·cite·ment

hy·per·ex·cre·tion
hy·per·fas·tid·i·ous
hy·per·func·tion
hy·per·func·tion·al
hy·per·func·tion·ing
hy·per·im·mune
hy·per·im·mu·ni·za·tion
hy·per·im·mu·nize
hy·per·in·flat·ed
hy·per·in·ner·va·tion
hy·per·in·tel·lec·tu·al
hy·per·in·tel·li·gent
hy·per·in·tense
hy·per·in·vo·lu·tion
hy·per·ma·nia
hy·per·man·ic
hy·per·mas·cu·line
hy·per·met·a·bol·ic
hy·per·me·tab·o·lism
hy·per·mo·bil·i·ty
hy·per·mod·ern
hy·per·mod·ern·ist
hy·per·mu·ta·bil·i·ty
hy·per·mu·ta·ble
hy·per·na·tion·al·is·tic
hy·per·phys·i·cal
hy·per·pig·men·ta·tion
hy·per·pig·ment·ed

hy·per·pro·duc·er
hy·per·pro·duc·tion
hy·per·pure
hy·per·ra·tio·nal
hy·per·ra·tio·nal·i·ty
hy·per·re·ac·tive
hy·per·re·ac·tiv·i·ty
hy·per·re·ac·tor
hy·per·re·spon·sive
hy·per·ro·man·tic
hy·per·sa·line
hy·per·sa·lin·i·ty
hy·per·sal·i·va·tion
hy·per·se·cre·tion
hy·per·sen·si·ti·za·tion
hy·per·sen·si·tize
hy·per·som·no·lence
hy·per·stat·ic
hy·per·stim·u·late
hy·per·stim·u·la·tion
hy·per·sus·cep·ti·bil·i·ty
hy·per·sus·cep·ti·ble
hy·per·tense
hy·per·typ·i·cal
hy·per·vig·i·lance
hy·per·vig·i·lant
hy·per·vir·u·lent
hy·per·vis·cos·i·ty

**hy·per·acid·i·ty** \,hī-pər-ə-'si-də-tē\ *noun* (circa 1890)
**:** the condition of containing more than the normal amount of acid
— **hy·per·ac·id** \hī-pər-'a-səd\ *adjective*

**hy·per·ac·tive** \,hī-pər-'ak-tiv\ *adjective* (1867)
**:** affected with or exhibiting hyperactivity; *broadly* **:** more active than is usual or desirable
— **hyperactive** *noun*

**hy·per·ac·tiv·i·ty** \-,ak-'ti-və-tē\ *noun* (1888)
**:** the state or condition of being excessively or pathologically active; *especially* **:** ATTENTION DEFICIT DISORDER

**hy·per·aes·the·sia** *variant of* HYPERESTHESIA

**hy·per·al·i·men·ta·tion** \,hī-pər-,a-lə-mən-'tā-shən\ *noun* (1967)
**:** the administration of nutrients by intravenous feeding especially to patients who cannot ingest food through the alimentary tract

**hy·per·bar·ic** \,hī-pər-'bar-ik\ *adjective* [*hyper-* + *bar-* + ¹*-ic*] (1962)
**:** of, relating to, or utilizing greater than normal pressure (as of oxygen) ⟨*hyperbaric* chamber⟩ ⟨*hyperbaric* medicine⟩
— **hy·per·bar·i·cal·ly** \-i-k(ə-)lē\ *adverb*

**hy·per·bo·la** \hī-'pər-bə-lə\ *noun, plural* **-las** *or* **-lae** \-(,)lē\ [New Latin, from Greek *hyperbolē*] (1668)
**:** a plane curve generated by a point so moving that the difference of the distances from two fixed points is a constant **:** a curve formed by the intersection of a double right circular cone with a plane that cuts both halves of the cone

**hy·per·bo·le** \hī-'pər-bə-(,)lē\ *noun* [Latin, from Greek *hyperbolē* excess, hyperbole, hyperbola, from *hyperballein* to exceed, from *hyper-* + *ballein* to throw — more at DEVIL] (15th century)
**:** extravagant exaggeration (as "mile-high ice-cream cones")
— **hy·per·bo·list** \-list\ *noun*

hyperbola: *AB, CD* axes; *F, F'* foci; *xy, zw* asymptotes; *h, h', h'', h'''* hyperbola

**¹hy·per·bol·ic** \,hī-pər-'bä-lik\ *also* **hy·per·bol·i·cal** \-li-kəl\ *adjective* (15th century)
**:** of, relating to, or marked by hyperbole
— **hy·per·bol·i·cal·ly** \-li-k(ə-)lē\ *adverb*

**²hyperbolic** *adjective* (1646)
**1 :** of, relating to, or being analogous to a hyperbola
**2 :** of, relating to, or being a space in which more than one line parallel to a given line passes through a point ⟨*hyperbolic* geometry⟩

**hyperbolic function** *noun* (circa 1890)
**:** any of a set of six functions analogous to the trigonometric functions but related to the hyperbola in a way similar to that in which the trigonometric functions are related to a circle

**hyperbolic paraboloid** *noun* (1842)
**:** a saddle-shaped quadric surface whose sections by planes parallel to one coordinate plane are hyperbolas while those sections by planes parallel to the other two are parabolas if proper orientation of the coordinate axes is assumed

**hy·per·bo·lize** \hī-'pər-bə-,līz\ *verb* **-lized; -liz·ing** (1599)
*intransitive verb*
**:** to indulge in hyperbole
*transitive verb*
**:** to exaggerate to a hyperbolic degree

**hy·per·bo·loid** \-,lȯid\ *noun* (1743)
**:** a quadric surface whose sections by planes parallel to one coordinate plane are ellipses while those sections by planes parallel to the other two are hyperbolas if proper orientation of the axes is assumed
— **hy·per·bo·loi·dal** \(,)hī-,pər-bə-'lȯi-d°l\ *adjective*

**¹hy·per·bo·re·an** \,hī-pər-'bȯr-ē-ən, -'bȯr-; -(,)pər-bə-'rē-ən\ *noun* [Latin *Hyperborei* (plural), from Greek *Hyperboreoi,* from *hyper-* + *Boreas*] (15th century)
**1** *often capitalized* **:** a member of a people held by the ancient Greeks to live beyond the north wind in a region of perpetual sunshine
**2 :** an inhabitant of a cool northern climate

**²hyperborean** *adjective* (1591)
**1 :** of or relating to an extreme northern region **:** FROZEN
**2 :** of or relating to any of the arctic peoples

**hy·per·cal·ce·mia** \,hī-pər-,kal-'sē-mē-ə\ *noun* [New Latin] (1925)
**:** an excess of calcium in the blood
— **hy·per·cal·ce·mic** \-'sē-mik\ *adjective*

**hy·per·cap·nia** \-'kap-nē-ə\ *noun* [New Latin, from *hyper-* + Greek *kapnos* smoke; probably akin to Lithuanian *Kvapas* breath] (1908)
**:** the presence of excessive amounts of carbon dioxide in the blood
— **hy·per·cap·nic** \-nik\ *adjective*

**hy·per·cat·a·lex·is** \-,ka-tə-'lek-səs\ *noun, plural* **-lex·es** \-'lek-,sēz\ [New Latin] (circa 1890)
**:** the occurrence of an additional syllable after the final complete foot or dipody in a line of verse
— **hy·per·cat·a·lec·tic** \-'lek-tik\ *adjective*

**hy·per·charge** \'hī-pər-,chärj\ *noun* [short for *hyperonic charge,* from *hyperon*] (1956)
**:** a quantum characteristic of a group of subatomic particles governed by the strong force that is related to strangeness and is represented by a number equal to twice the average value of the electric charge of the group

**hy·per·cho·les·ter·ol·emia** \,hī-pər-kə-,les-tə-rə-'lē-mē-ə\ *noun* [New Latin] (circa 1894)
**:** the presence of excess cholesterol in the blood
— **hy·per·cho·les·ter·ol·emic** \-mik\ *adjective*

**hy·per·com·plex** \,hī-pər-'käm-,pleks\ *adjective* (circa 1889)
**:** of, relating to, or being the most general form of number that extends the complex number to an expression of the same type (as a quaternion) involving a finite number of units or components in which addition is by

components and multiplication does not have all of the properties of real or complex numbers

**hy·per·cor·rect** \ˌhī-pər-kə-'rekt\ *adjective* (1922)
: of, relating to, or characterized by the production of a nonstandard linguistic form or construction on the basis of a false analogy (as "badly" in "my eyes have gone badly" and "widely" in "open widely")
— **hy·per·cor·rec·tion** \-'rek-shən\ *noun*
— **hy·per·cor·rect·ly** \-'rek-(t)lē\ *adverb*
— **hy·per·cor·rect·ness** \-'rek(t)-nəs\ *noun*

**hy·per·crit·ic** \ˌhī-pər-'kri-tik\ *noun* [New Latin *hypercriticus*, from *hyper-* + Latin *criticus* critic] (1633)
: a carping or unduly censorious critic
— **hy·per·crit·i·cism** \-'kri-tə-ˌsi-zəm\ *noun*

**hy·per·crit·i·cal** \-'kri-ti-kəl\ *adjective* (1605)
: meticulously or excessively critical
**synonym** see CRITICAL
— **hy·per·crit·i·cal·ly** \-k(ə-)lē\ *adverb*

**hy·per·cube** \'hī-pər-ˌkyüb\ *noun* (1909)
**1** : a geometric figure (as a tesseract) in Euclidean space of *n* dimensions that is analogous to a cube in three dimensions
**2** : a computer architecture in which each processor is connected to *n* others based on analogy to a hypercube of *n* dimensions

**hy·per·emia** \ˌhī-pər-'ē-mē-ə\ *noun* [New Latin] (circa 1839)
: excess of blood in a body part : CONGESTION
— **hy·per·emic** \-mik\ *adjective*

**hy·per·es·the·sia** \ˌhī-pər-es-'thē-zh(ē-)ə\ *noun* [New Latin, from *hyper-* + *-esthesia* (as in *anesthesia*)] (circa 1852)
: unusual or pathological sensitivity of the skin or of a particular sense
— **hy·per·es·thet·ic** \-'the-tik\ *adjective*

**hy·per·eu·tec·tic** \ˌhī-pər-yü-'tek-tik\ *adjective* (1902)
: HYPEREUTECTOID

**hy·per·eu·tec·toid** \-ˌtȯid\ *adjective* (1908)
: containing the minor component in excess of that contained in the eutectoid

**hy·per·ex·tend** \ˌhī-pər-ik-'stend\ *transitive verb* (1883)
: to extend so that the angle between bones of a joint is greater than normal ⟨a *hyperextended* elbow⟩
— **hy·per·ex·ten·sion** \-'sten(t)-shən\ *noun*

**hy·per·fine** \'hī-pər-ˌfīn\ *adjective* (1926)
: being or relating to a fine-structure multiplet occurring in an atomic spectrum that is due to interaction between electrons and nuclear spin

**hy·per·fo·cal distance** \ˌhī-pər-'fō-kəl-\ *noun* [International Scientific Vocabulary] (1905)
: the nearest distance upon which a photographic lens may be focused to produce satisfactory definition at infinity

**hy·per·ga·my** \hī-'pər-gə-mē\ *noun, plural* **-mies** (1883)
: marriage into an equal or higher caste or social group

**hy·per·geo·met·ric distribution** \ˌhī-pər-ˌjē-ə-'me-trik-\ *noun* (1950)
: a probability function that gives the probability of obtaining exactly *x* elements of one kind and *n* − *x* elements of another if *n* elements are chosen at random without replacement from a finite population containing *N* elements of which *M* are of the first kind and *N* − *M* are of the second kind and has the form

$$f(x) = \frac{\binom{M}{x}\binom{N-M}{n-x}}{\binom{N}{n}} \text{ where } \binom{M}{x} = \frac{M!}{x!(M-x)!}$$

**hy·per·gly·ce·mia** \ˌhī-pər-glī-'sē-mē-ə\ *noun* [New Latin] (1894)

: excess of sugar in the blood
— **hy·per·gly·ce·mic** \-mik\ *adjective*

**hy·per·gol·ic** \ˌhī-pər-'gä-lik\ *adjective* [German *Hypergol* a hypergolic fuel, probably from *hyper-* + *erg-* + *-ol* (hydrocarbon)] (1947)
**1** : igniting upon contact of components without external aid (as a spark)
**2** : of, relating to, or using hypergolic fuel
— **hy·per·gol·i·cal·ly** \-li-k(ə-)lē\ *adverb*

**hy·per·hi·dro·sis** \ˌhī-pər-hī-'drō-səs\ *noun* [New Latin *hidrosis* perspiration, from Greek *hidrōsis*, from *hidroun* to sweat, from *hidrōs* sweat — more at SWEAT] (circa 1860)
: generalized or local excessive sweating

**hy·per·in·fla·tion** \ˌhī-pər-in-'flā-shən\ *noun* (1930)
: inflation growing at a very high rate in a very short time; *also* : a period of hyperinflation
— **hy·per·in·fla·tion·ary** \-shə-ˌnər-ē\ *adjective*

**hy·per·in·su·lin·ism** \ˌhī-pə-'rin(t)-s(ə-)lə-ˌni-zəm\ *noun* [International Scientific Vocabulary] (1924)
: the presence of excess insulin in the body resulting in hypoglycemia

**Hy·pe·ri·on** \hī-'pir-ē-ən\ *noun* [Latin, from Greek *Hyperiōn*]
: a Titan and the father of Aurora, Selene, and Helios

**hy·per·ir·ri·ta·bil·i·ty** \ˌhī-pər-ˌir-ə-tə-'bi-lə-tē\ *noun* (1913)
: abnormally great or uninhibited response to stimuli
— **hy·per·ir·ri·ta·ble** \-'ir-ə-tə-bəl\ *adjective*

**hy·per·ker·a·to·sis** \ˌhī-pər-ˌker-ə-'tō-səs\ *noun, plural* **-to·ses** \-'tō-ˌsēz\ [New Latin] (1841)
: hypertrophy of the corneous layer of the skin
— **hy·per·ker·a·tot·ic** \-'tä-tik\ *adjective*

**hy·per·ki·ne·sia** \-kə-'nē-zh(ē-)ə, -kī-\ *noun* [New Latin, from *hyperkinesis*] (circa 1848)
: HYPERKINESIS

**hy·per·ki·ne·sis** \-'nē-səs\ *noun* [New Latin] (circa 1855)
**1** : abnormally increased and sometimes uncontrollable activity or muscular movements
**2** : a condition especially of childhood characterized by hyperactivity

**hy·per·ki·net·ic** \-'ne-tik\ *adjective* (1888)
: of, relating to, or affected with hyperkinesis or hyperactivity ⟨the *hyperkinetic* child⟩; *also* : characterized by fast-paced or frenetic activity

**hy·per·li·pe·mia** \ˌhī-pər-lī-'pē-mē-ə\ *noun* [New Latin] (circa 1894)
: the presence of excess fat or lipids in the blood
— **hy·per·li·pe·mic** \-mik\ *adjective*

**hy·per·lip·id·emia** \-ˌli-pə-'dē-mē-ə\ *noun* [New Latin] (1961)
: HYPERLIPEMIA

**hy·per·mar·ket** \'hī-pər-ˌmär-kət\ *noun* (1970)
: a very large store that carries products found in a supermarket as well as merchandise commonly found in department stores

**hy·per·me·ter** \hī-'pər-mə-tər\ *noun* [Late Latin *hypermetrus* hypercatalectic, from Greek *hypermetros* beyond measure, beyond the meter, from *hyper-* + *metron* measure, meter] (circa 1656)
**1** : a verse marked by hypercatalexis
**2** : a period comprising more than two or three cola
— **hy·per·met·ric** \hī-pər-'me-trik\ *or* **hy·per·met·ri·cal** \-tri-kəl\ *adjective*

**hy·per·me·tro·pia** \ˌhī-pər-mi-'trō-pē-ə\ *noun* [New Latin, from Greek *hypermetros* + New Latin *-opia*] (1868)
: HYPEROPIA
— **hy·per·me·tro·pic** \-'trō-pik, -'trä-\ *adjective*

**hy·perm·ne·sia** \ˌhī-(ˌ)pərm-'nē-zh(ē-)ə\ *noun* [New Latin, from *hyper-* + *-mnesia* (as in *amnesia*)] (1882)
: abnormally vivid or complete memory or recall of the past
— **hy·perm·ne·sic** \-'nē-zik, -sik\ *adjective*

**hy·per·on** \'hī-pə-ˌrän\ *noun* [probably from *hyper-* + *²-on*] (1953)
: a fundamental particle of the baryon group that is greater in mass than a proton or neutron

**hy·per·opia** \ˌhī-pə-'rō-pē-ə\ *noun* [New Latin] (1884)
: a condition in which visual images come to a focus behind the retina of the eye and vision is better for distant than for near objects — called also *farsightedness*
— **hy·per·opic** \-'rō-pik, -'rä-\ *adjective*

**hy·per·os·to·sis** \ˌhī-pər-ˌäs-'tō-səs\ *noun, plural* **-to·ses** \-'tō-ˌsēz\ [New Latin] (circa 1836)
: excessive growth or thickening of bone tissue
— **hy·per·os·tot·ic** \-'tä-tik\ *adjective*

**hy·per·par·a·site** \ˌhī-pər-'par-ə-ˌsīt\ *noun* (circa 1889)
: a parasite that is parasitic upon another parasite
— **hy·per·par·a·sit·ic** \-ˌpar-ə-'si-tik\ *adjective*
— **hy·per·par·a·sit·ism** \-'par-ə-ˌsī-ˌti-zəm, -'par-ə-sə-\ *noun*

**hy·per·para·thy·roid·ism** \-ˌpar-ə-'thī-ˌrȯi-ˌdi-zəm\ *noun* (1917)
: the presence of excess parathyroid hormone in the body resulting in disturbance of calcium metabolism with increase in serum calcium and decrease in inorganic phosphorus, loss of calcium from bone, and renal damage with frequent kidney-stone formation

**hy·per·pha·gia** \-'fā-j(ē-)ə\ *noun* [New Latin] (1941)
: abnormally increased appetite for consumption of food frequently associated with injury to the hypothalamus
— **hy·per·phag·ic** \-'fa-jik\ *adjective*

**hy·per·pi·tu·ita·rism** \-pə-'tü-ə-tə-ˌri-zəm, -'tü-ə-ˌtri-, -'tyü-\ *noun* [International Scientific Vocabulary] (1909)
: excessive production of growth hormones by the pituitary gland
— **hy·per·pi·tu·itary** \-'tü-ə-ˌter-ē, -'tyü-\ *adjective*

**hy·per·plane** \'hī-pər-ˌplān\ *noun* (1903)
: a figure in hyperspace corresponding to a plane in ordinary space

**hy·per·pla·sia** \ˌhī-pər-'plā-zh(ē-)ə\ *noun* [New Latin] (1861)
: an abnormal or unusual increase in the elements composing a part (as cells composing a tissue)
— **hy·per·plas·tic** \-'plas-tik\ *adjective*

**hy·per·ploid** \'hī-pər-ˌplȯid\ *adjective* [International Scientific Vocabulary] (1930)
: having a chromosome number slightly greater than an exact multiple of the monoploid number
— **hyperploid** *noun*
— **hy·per·ploi·dy** \-ˌplȯi-dē\ *noun*

**hy·per·pnea** \ˌhī-pər-'nē-ə, -ˌpərp-'nē-\ *noun* [New Latin] (circa 1860)
: abnormally rapid or deep breathing
— **hy·per·pne·ic** \-'nē-ik\ *adjective*

**hy·per·po·lar·ize** \ˌhī-pər-'pō-lə-ˌrīz\ (1950) *transitive verb*
: to produce an increase in potential difference across (a biological membrane) ⟨a *hyperpolarized* nerve cell⟩

*intransitive verb*
**:** to undergo or produce an increase in potential difference across something
— **hy·per·po·lar·iza·tion** \-ˌpō-lə-rə-'zā-shən\ *noun*

**hy·per·py·rex·ia** \-pī-'rek-sē-ə\ *noun* [New Latin] (1875)
**:** exceptionally high fever (as in a particular disease)

**hy·per·re·al·ism** \ˌhī-pər-'rē-ə-ˌli-zəm, -'ri-ə-\ *noun* (1937)
**:** realism in painting characterized by depiction of real life in an unusual or striking manner — compare PHOTO-REALISM
— **hy·per·re·al·ist** \-list\ *adjective*
— **hy·per·re·al·is·tic** \-ˌrē-ə-'lis-tik, -ˌri-\ *adjective*

**hy·per·sen·si·tive** \ˌhī-pər-'sen(t)-s(ə-)tiv\ *adjective* (1871)
**1 :** excessively or abnormally sensitive
**2 :** abnormally susceptible physiologically to a specific agent (as a drug or antigen)
— **hy·per·sen·si·tive·ness** *noun*
— **hy·per·sen·si·tiv·i·ty** \-ˌsen(t)-sə-'ti-və-tē\ *noun*

**hy·per·sex·u·al** \-'sek-sh(ə-)wəl, -'sek-shəl\ *adjective* (1942)
**:** exhibiting unusual or excessive concern with or indulgence in sexual activity
— **hy·per·sex·u·al·i·ty** \-ˌsek-shə-'wa-lə-tē\ *noun*

**hy·per·son·ic** \-'sä-nik\ *adjective* [International Scientific Vocabulary] (1946)
**1 :** of or relating to speed five or more times that of sound in air — compare SONIC
**2 :** moving, capable of moving, or utilizing air currents that move at hypersonic speed ⟨*hypersonic* wind tunnel⟩
— **hy·per·son·i·cal·ly** \-ni-k(ə-)lē\ *adverb*

**hy·per·space** \'hī-pər-ˌspās\ *noun* (1867)
**1 :** space of more than three dimensions
**2 :** a fictional space held to support extraordinary events (as travel faster than the speed of light)

**hy·per·sthene** \'hī-pərs-ˌthēn\ *noun* [French *hypersthène*, from Greek *hyper-* + *sthenos* strength] (circa 1808)
**:** an orthorhombic grayish or greenish black or dark brown pyroxene
— **hy·per·sthe·nic** \ˌhī-pərs-'the-nik, -'thē-\ *adjective*

**hy·per·sur·face** \'hī-pər-ˌsər-fəs\ *noun* (circa 1909)
**:** a figure that is the analogue in hyperspace of a surface in three-dimensional space

**hy·per·ten·sion** \ˌhī-pər-'ten(t)-shən\ *noun* [International Scientific Vocabulary] (1893)
**:** abnormally high blood pressure and especially arterial blood pressure; *also* **:** the systemic condition accompanying high blood pressure
— **hy·per·ten·sive** \ˌhī-pər-'ten(t)-siv\ *adjective or noun*

**hy·per·text** \'hī-pər-ˌtekst\ *noun* (1986)
**:** a database format in which information related to that on a display can be accessed directly from the display

**hy·per·ther·mia** \ˌhī-pər-'thər-mē-ə\ *noun* [New Latin, from *hyper-* + *therm-* + *-ia*] (1887)
**:** exceptionally high fever especially when induced artificially for therapeutic purposes
— **hy·per·ther·mic** \-mik\ *adjective*

**hy·per·thy·roid** \-'thī-ˌroid\ *adjective* [back-formation from *hyperthyroidism*] (1916)
**:** of, relating to, or affected with hyperthyroidism

**hy·per·thy·roid·ism** \-ˌroi-di-zəm\ *noun* [International Scientific Vocabulary] (circa 1900)
**:** excessive functional activity of the thyroid gland; *also* **:** the resulting condition marked especially by increased metabolic rate, enlargement of the thyroid gland, rapid heart rate, and high blood pressure

**hy·per·to·nia** \ˌhī-pər-'tō-nē-ə\ *noun* (circa 1842)
**:** HYPERTONICITY

**hy·per·ton·ic** \-'tä-nik\ *adjective* [International Scientific Vocabulary] (1855)
**1 :** exhibiting excessive tone or tension ⟨a *hypertonic* baby⟩ ⟨a *hypertonic* bladder⟩
**2 :** having a higher osmotic pressure than a surrounding medium or a fluid under comparison

**hy·per·to·nic·i·ty** \-tə-'ni-sə-tē\ *noun* (1886)
**:** the quality or state of being hypertonic

**¹hy·per·tro·phy** \hī-'pər-trə-fē\ *noun, plural* **-phies** [probably from New Latin *hypertrophia*, from *hyper-* + *-trophia* -trophy] (1834)
**1 :** excessive development of an organ or part; *specifically* **:** increase in bulk (as by thickening of muscle fibers) without multiplication of parts
**2 :** exaggerated growth or complexity
— **hy·per·tro·phic** \ˌhī-pər-'trō-fik\ *adjective*

**²hypertrophy** *intransitive verb* **-phied; -phy·ing** (1883)
**:** to undergo hypertrophy

**hy·per·ur·ban·ism** \ˌhī-pər-'ər-bə-ˌni-zəm\ *noun* (1925)
**:** use of hypercorrect forms in language; *also* **:** such a form

**hy·per·uri·ce·mia** \ˌhī-pər-ˌyu̇r-ə-'sē-mē-ə\ *noun* [New Latin] (circa 1894)
**:** excess uric acid in the blood

**hy·per·ve·loc·i·ty** \-və-'lä-sə-tē, -'läs-tē\ *noun* (1949)
**:** a high or relatively high velocity; *especially* **:** one greater than 10,000 feet (3048 meters) per second

**hy·per·ven·ti·late** \ˌhī-pər-'ven-t²l-ˌāt\ *intransitive verb* (1931)
**:** to breathe rapidly and deeply **:** undergo hyperventilation

**hy·per·ven·ti·la·tion** \-ˌven-t²l-'ā-shən\ *noun* (1928)
**:** excessive rate and depth of respiration leading to abnormal loss of carbon dioxide from the blood

**hy·per·vi·ta·min·osis** \-ˌvī-tə-mə-'nō-səs\ *noun, plural* **-oses** \-'nō-ˌsēz\ [New Latin] (1928)
**:** an abnormal state resulting from excessive intake of one or more vitamins

**hy·pha** \'hī-fə\ *noun, plural* **hy·phae** \-(ˌ)fē\ [New Latin, from Greek *hyphē* web; akin to Greek *hyphos* web — more at WEAVE] (1866)
**:** one of the threads that make up the mycelium of a fungus, increase by apical growth, and are coenocytic or transversely septate
— **hy·phal** \-fəl\ *adjective*

**¹hy·phen** \'hī-fən\ *noun* [Late Latin & Greek; Late Latin, from Greek, from *hyph' hen* under one, from *hypo* under + *hen*, neuter of *heis* one — more at UP, SAME] (circa 1620)
**:** a punctuation mark - used especially to divide or to compound words, word elements, or numbers
— **hy·phen·less** \-ləs\ *adjective*

**²hyphen** *transitive verb* (1814)
**:** HYPHENATE

**¹hy·phen·ate** \'hī-fə-ˌnāt\ *transitive verb* **-at·ed; -at·ing** (circa 1889)
**:** to connect (as two words) or divide (as a word at the end of a line of print) with a hyphen
— **hy·phen·ation** \ˌhī-fə-'nā-shən\ *noun*

**²hyphenate** *noun* [from the hyphens in the titles of such people, as *producer-director*] (1974)
**:** a person who performs more than one function (as on a filmmaking project)

**hyphenated** *adjective* [from the use of hyphenated words (as German-American) to designate foreign-born citizens of the U.S.] (circa 1893)
**:** of, relating to, or being an individual or unit of mixed or diverse background or composition ⟨*hyphenated* Americans⟩

**hypn-** *or* **hypno-** *combining form* [French, from Late Latin, from Greek, from *hypnos* — more at SOMNOLENT]

**1 :** sleep ⟨*hypno*pompic⟩
**2 :** hypnotism ⟨*hypno*therapy⟩

**hyp·na·go·gic** *also* **hyp·no·go·gic** \ˌhip-nə-'gä-jik, -'gō-\ *adjective* [French *hypnagogique*, from Greek *hypn-* + *-agōgos* leading, inducing, from *agein* to lead — more at AGENT] (1886)
**:** of, relating to, or associated with the drowsiness preceding sleep

**hyp·noid** \'hip-ˌnȯid\ *or* **hyp·noi·dal** \hip-'nȯi-d²l\ *adjective* (1898)
**:** of or relating to sleep or hypnosis

**hyp·no·pom·pic** \ˌhip-nə-'päm-pik\ *adjective* [*hypn-* + Greek *pompē* act of sending — more at POMP] (circa 1901)
**:** associated with the semiconsciousness preceding waking ⟨*hypnopompic* illusions⟩

**Hyp·nos** \'hip-nəs, -ˌnōs\ *noun* [Greek]
**:** the Greek god of sleep

**hyp·no·sis** \hip-'nō-səs\ *noun, plural* **-no·ses** \-ˌsēz\ [New Latin] (1876)
**1 :** a state that resembles sleep but is induced by a person whose suggestions are readily accepted by the subject
**2 :** any of various conditions that resemble sleep
**3 :** HYPNOTISM 1

**hyp·no·ther·a·py** \ˌhip-nō-'ther-ə-pē\ *noun* (1897)
**1 :** the treatment of disease by hypnotism
**2 :** psychotherapy that facilitates suggestion, reeducation, or analysis by means of hypnosis
— **hyp·no·ther·a·pist** \-pist\ *noun*

**¹hyp·not·ic** \hip-'nä-tik\ *adjective* [French or Late Latin; French *hypnotique*, from Late Latin *hypnoticus*, from Greek *hypnōtikos*, from *hypnoun* to put to sleep, from *hypnos*] (1625)
**1 :** tending to produce sleep **:** SOPORIFIC
**2 a :** of or relating to hypnosis or hypnotism **b :** readily holding the attention ⟨a *hypnotic* personality⟩ ⟨a simple *hypnotic* beat⟩
— **hyp·not·i·cal·ly** \-ti-k(ə-)lē\ *adverb*

**²hypnotic** *noun* (1681)
**1 :** a sleep-inducing agent **:** SOPORIFIC
**2 :** one that is or can be hypnotized

**hyp·no·tism** \'hip-nə-ˌti-zəm\ *noun* (1842)
**1 :** the study or act of inducing hypnosis — compare MESMERISM
**2 :** HYPNOSIS 1
— **hyp·no·tist** \-tist\ *noun*

**hyp·no·tize** \-ˌtīz\ *transitive verb* **-tized; -tiz·ing** (1843)
**1 :** to induce hypnosis in
**2 :** to dazzle or overcome by or as if by suggestion ⟨a voice that *hypnotizes* its hearers⟩ ⟨drivers *hypnotized* by speed⟩
— **hyp·no·tiz·abil·i·ty** \ˌhip-nə-ˌtī-zə-'bi-lə-tē\ *noun*
— **hyp·no·tiz·able** \'hip-nə-ˌtī-zə-bəl\ *adjective*

**¹hy·po** \'hī-(ˌ)pō\ *noun, plural* **hypos** (1711)
**:** HYPOCHONDRIA

**²hypo** *noun, plural* **hypos** [short for *hyposulfite* thiosulfate] (1855)
**:** SODIUM THIOSULFATE

**³hypo** *noun, plural* **hypos** (1925)
**1 :** HYPODERMIC SYRINGE
**2 :** HYPODERMIC INJECTION
**3 :** STIMULUS

**⁴hypo** *transitive verb* (1942)
**:** STIMULATE ⟨do everything possible to *hypo* the economy —Clem Morgello⟩

**hypo-** *or* **hyp-** *prefix* [Middle English *ypo-*, from Old French, from Late Latin *hypo-*, *hyp-*, from Greek, from *hypo* — more at UP]
**1 :** under **:** beneath **:** down ⟨*hypo*blast⟩ ⟨*hypo*dermic⟩
**2 :** less than normal or normally ⟨*hyp*esthesia⟩ ⟨*hypo*tension⟩
**3 :** in a lower state of oxidation **:** in a low and usually the lowest position in a series of compounds ⟨*hypo*chlorous acid⟩ ⟨*hypo*xanthine⟩

**hy·po·al·ler·gen·ic** \ˌhī-pō-ˌa-lər-'je-nik\ *adjective* (1940)

: having little likelihood of causing an allergic response ⟨*hypoallergenic* cosmetics⟩ ⟨*hypoallergenic* foods⟩

**hy·po·blast** \'hī-pə-,blast\ *noun* (1875)
: the endoderm of an embryo

**hy·po·cal·ce·mia** \,hī-pō-,kal-'sē-mē-ə\ *noun* [New Latin] (1925)
: a deficiency of calcium in the blood
— **hy·po·cal·ce·mic** \-mik\ *adjective*

**hy·po·caust** \'hī-pə-,köst\ *noun* [Latin *hypocaustum*, from Greek *hypokauston*, from *hypokaiein* to light a fire under, from *hypo-* + *kaiein* to burn] (1678)
: an ancient Roman central heating system with underground furnace and tile flues to distribute the heat

**hy·po·cen·ter** \'hī-pə-,sen-tər\ *noun* (1905)
**1** : the focus of an earthquake — compare EPICENTER 1
**2** : the point on the earth's surface directly below the center of a nuclear bomb explosion
— **hy·po·cen·tral** \,hī-pə-'sen-trəl\ *adjective*

**hy·po·chlo·rite** \,hī-pə-'klōr-,īt, -'klor-\ *noun* (circa 1849)
: a salt or ester of hypochlorous acid

**hy·po·chlo·rous acid** \,hī-pə-'klōr-əs-, -'klor-\ *noun* [International Scientific Vocabulary] (1841)
: an unstable strongly oxidizing but weak acid HClO obtained in solution along with hydrochloric acid by reaction of chlorine with water and used especially in the form of salts as an oxidizing agent, bleaching agent, disinfectant, and chlorinating agent

**hy·po·chon·dria** \,hī-pə-'kän-drē-ə\ *noun* [New Latin, from Late Latin, plural, upper abdomen (formerly regarded as the seat of hypochondria), from Greek, literally, the parts under the cartilage (of the breastbone), from *hypo-* + *chondros* cartilage] (1668)
: extreme depression of mind or spirits often centered on imaginary physical ailments; *specifically* : HYPOCHONDRIASIS ◆

**¹hy·po·chon·dri·ac** \-drē-,ak\ *adjective* [French *hypochondriaque*, from Greek *hypochondriakos*, from *hypochondria*] (1599)
**1** : HYPOCHONDRIACAL
**2** : of, relating to, or being the two regions of the abdomen lying on either side of the epigastric region and above the lumbar regions

**²hypochondriac** *noun* (1639)
: one affected by hypochondria

**hy·po·chon·dri·a·cal** \-kən-'drī-ə-kəl, -,kän-\ *adjective* (1621)
: affected or produced by hypochondria
— **hy·po·chon·dri·a·cal·ly** \-k(ə-)lē\ *adverb*

**hy·po·chon·dri·a·sis** \-'drī-ə-səs\ *noun, plural* **-a·ses** \-,sēz\ [New Latin] (1766)
: morbid concern about one's health especially when accompanied by delusions of physical disease

**hy·po·chro·mic anemia** \,hī-pə-'krō-mik-\ *noun* (1934)
: an anemia marked by deficient hemoglobin and usually microcytic red blood cells

**hy·po·co·rism** \hī-'pä-kə-,ri-zəm\, \,hī-pə-'kōr-,i-, -'kor-\ *noun* [Late Latin *hypocorisma*, from Greek *hypokorisma*, from *hypokorizesthai* to call by pet names, from *hypo-* + *korizesthai* to caress, from *koros* boy, *korē* girl] (1850)
**1** : a pet name
**2** : the use of pet names
— **hy·po·co·ris·tic** \,hī-pə-kə-'ris-tik\ *or* **hy·po·co·ris·ti·cal** \-ti-kəl\ *adjective*
— **hy·po·co·ris·ti·cal·ly** \-ti-k(ə-)lē\ *adverb*

**hy·po·cot·yl** \'hī-pə-,kä-t°l\ *noun* [International Scientific Vocabulary *hypo-* + *coty*ledon] (1880)
: the part of the axis of a plant embryo or seedling below the cotyledon — see PLUMULE illustration

**hy·poc·ri·sy** \hi-'pä-krə-sē\ *also* hī-\ *noun, plural* **-sies** [Middle English *ypocrisie*, from Old French, from Late Latin *hypocrisis*, from Greek *hypokrisis* act of playing a part on the stage, hypocrisy, from *hypokrinesthai* to answer, act on the stage, from *hypo-* + *krinein* to decide — more at CERTAIN] (13th century)
**1** : a feigning to be what one is not or to believe what one does not; *especially* : the false assumption of an appearance of virtue or religion
**2** : an act or instance of hypocrisy

**hyp·o·crite** \'hi-pə-,krit\ *noun* [Middle English *ypocrite*, from Old French, from Late Latin *hypocrita*, from Greek *hypokritēs* actor, hypocrite, from *hypokrinesthai*] (13th century)
: a person who puts on a false appearance of virtue or religion
— **hypocrite** *adjective*

**hyp·o·crit·i·cal** \,hi-pə-'kri-ti-kəl\ *adjective* (1561)
: characterized by hypocrisy; *also* : being a hypocrite
— **hyp·o·crit·i·cal·ly** \-k(ə-)lē\ *adverb*

**hy·po·cy·cloid** \,hī-pō-'sī-,klóid\ *noun* (1843)
: a curve traced by a point on the circumference of a circle rolling internally on the circumference of a fixed circle

**hy·po·der·mal** \,hī-pə-'dər-məl\ *adjective* (1854)
**1** : of or relating to a hypodermis
**2** : lying beneath an outer skin or epidermis

**¹hy·po·der·mic** \-mik\ *adjective* [International Scientific Vocabulary] (1863)
**1** : adapted for use in or administered by injection beneath the skin
**2** : of or relating to the parts beneath the skin
**3** : resembling a hypodermic injection in effect : STIMULATING
— **hy·po·der·mi·cal·ly** \-mi-k(ə-)lē\ *adverb*

**²hypodermic** *noun* (circa 1889)
**1** : HYPODERMIC INJECTION
**2** : HYPODERMIC SYRINGE

**hypodermic injection** *noun* (1868)
: an injection made into the subcutaneous tissues

**hypodermic needle** *noun* (circa 1909)
**1** : NEEDLE 1c(1)
**2** : a hypodermic syringe complete with needle

**hypodermic syringe** *noun* (1893)
: a small syringe used with a hollow needle for injection of material into or beneath the skin

**hy·po·der·mis** \,hī-pə-'dər-məs\ *noun* [New Latin] (circa 1866)
**1** : the tissue immediately beneath the epidermis of a plant especially when modified to serve as a supporting and protecting layer
**2** : the cellular layer that underlies and secretes the chitinous cuticle (as of an arthropod)
**3** : SUPERFICIAL FASCIA

**hy·po·dip·loid** \,hī-pō-'di-,plóid\ *adjective* (1962)
: having slightly fewer than the diploid number of chromosomes
— **hy·po·dip·loi·dy** \-,plói-dē\ *noun*

**hy·po·eu·tec·toid** \,hī-pō-yu̇-'tek-,tóid\ *adjective* (1911)
: containing less of the minor component than is contained in the eutectoid

**hy·po·gas·tric** \,hī-pə-'gas-trik\ *adjective* [French *hypogastrique*, from *hypogastre* hypogastric region, from Greek *hypogastrion*, from *hypo-* + *gastr-, gastēr* belly — more at GASTRIC] (1656)
: of or relating to the lower median region of the abdomen

**hy·po·ge·al** \,hī-pə-'jē-əl\ *or* **hy·po·ge·an** \-'jē-ən\ *or* **hy·po·ge·ous** \-'jē-əs\ *adjective* [Late Latin *hypogeus* subterranean, from Greek *hypogaios*, from *hypo-* + *gaia* earth] (1686)
**1** : growing or living below the surface of the ground
**2** *of a cotyledon* : remaining below the ground while the epicotyl elongates

**hy·po·gene** \'hī-pə-,jēn\ *adjective* [*hypo-* + Greek *-genēs* born, produced — more at -GEN] (1831)
: formed, crystallized, or lying at depths below the earth's surface : PLUTONIC — used of various rocks

**hy·po·ge·um** \,hī-pə-'jē-əm\ *noun, plural* **-gea** \-'jē-ə\ [Latin, from Greek *hypogaion*, from neuter of *hypogaios*] (1706)
: the subterranean part of an ancient building; *also* : an ancient underground burial chamber

**hy·po·glos·sal** \,hī-pə-'glä-səl\ *adjective* (1831)
: of or relating to the hypoglossal nerves

**hypoglossal nerve** *noun* (1848)
: either of the 12th and final pair of cranial nerves which are motor nerves arising from the medulla oblongata and supplying muscles of the tongue in higher vertebrates — called also *hypoglossal*

**hy·po·gly·ce·mia** \,hī-pō-glī-'sē-mē-ə\ *noun* [New Latin] (circa 1894)
: abnormal decrease of sugar in the blood
— **hy·po·gly·ce·mic** \-mik\ *adjective or noun*

**hy·pog·y·nous** \hī-'pä-jə-nəs\ *adjective* (1821)
**1** *of a floral organ* : inserted upon the receptacle or axis below the gynoecium and free from it
**2** : having hypogynous floral organs
— **hy·pog·y·ny** \-nē\ *noun*

**hy·po·ka·le·mia** \,hī-pō-,kā-'lē-mē-ə\ *noun* [New Latin, from *hypo-* + *kalium* potassium (from *kali* alkali, from Arabic *qily* saltwort) + *-emia*] (1949)
: a deficiency of potassium in the blood
— **hy·po·ka·le·mic** \-mik\ *adjective*

**hy·po·lim·ni·on** \,hī-pō-'lim-nē-,än, -nē-ən\ *noun, plural* **-nia** \-nē-ə\ [New Latin, from *hypo-* + Greek *limnion*, diminutive of *limnē* lake — more at LIMNETIC] (1928)
: the part of a lake below the thermocline made up of water that is stagnant and of essentially uniform temperature except during the period of overturn

---

◇ WORD HISTORY

**hypochondria** A hypochondriac's ailment is deemed to be mental rather than physical, but etymologically *hypochondria* has nothing to do with the head. The ancient Greek noun *chondros* meant "cartilage," and the adjective *hypochondrios* meant "located under the cartilage of the breastbone and ribs." Formed from this adjective was the plural noun *hypochondria*, designating the area of the abdomen below the rib cartilage and above the navel. In Greek medical doctrine the spleen and kidneys, located in this part of the abdomen, secreted black bile, or melancholy, an excess of which caused low spirits, and the ancient physician Galen characterized depression as *hypochondriakon nosēma* "the ailment of the upper abdominal organs." The English adjective *hypochondriac*, borrowed from Greek through French, was used in the 17th century to mean "suffering from depression," and later in the century the noun *hypochondria* came into use, either as a Latinism created by removing the final letter from *hypochondriac*, or by construing the Greek and Latin neuter plural noun *hypochondria* as feminine singular. The narrowing of *hypochondria* to morbid concern about one's health—in more formal medical terminology *hypochondriasis*—dates from the late 18th and 19th centuries.

---

\ə\ abut \ᵊ\ kitten \ər\ further \a\ ash \ā\ ace \ä\ mop, mar \au̇\ out \ch\ chin \e\ bet \ē\ easy \g\ go \i\ hit \ī\ ice \j\ job \ŋ\ sing \ō\ go \ȯ\ law \ȯi\ boy \th\ thin \th\ the \ü\ loot \u̇\ foot \y\ yet \zh\ vision *see also* Guide to Pronunciation

**hy·po·mag·ne·se·mia** \ˌhī-pə-ˌmag-nə-ˈsē-mē-ə\ *noun* [New Latin, from *hypo-* + *magnesium* + *-emia*] (1933)
: deficiency of magnesium in the blood especially of cattle

**hy·po·ma·nia** \ˌhī-pə-ˈmā-nē-ə, -nyə\ *noun* [New Latin] (1882)
: a mild mania especially when part of a manic-depressive cycle
— **hy·po·man·ic** \-ˈma-nik\ *adjective*

**hy·po·morph** \ˈhī-pə-ˌmȯrf\ *noun* (1926)
: a mutant gene having a similar but weaker effect than the corresponding wild-type gene
— **hy·po·mor·phic** \ˌhī-pə-ˈmȯr-fik\ *adjective*

**hy·po·para·thy·roid·ism** \ˈhī-pō-ˌpar-ə-ˈthī-ˌrȯi-ˌdi-zəm\ *noun* (1910)
: deficiency of parathyroid hormone in the body; *also* : the resultant abnormal state marked by low serum calcium and a tendency to chronic tetany

**hy·po·phar·ynx** \-ˈfar-iŋ(k)s, -ˈfer-\ *noun* [New Latin] (1826)
**1** : an appendage or thickened fold on the floor of the mouth of many insects that resembles a tongue
**2** : the laryngeal part of the pharynx extending from the hyoid bone to the lower margin of the cricoid cartilage

**hy·po·phy·se·al** *also* **hy·po·phy·si·al** \(ˌ)hī-ˌpä-fə-ˈsē-əl, ˌhī-pə-, -ˈzē-; ˌhī-pə-ˈfi-zē-əl\ *adjective* [irregular from New Latin *hypophysis*] (1882)
: of or relating to the hypophysis

**hy·poph·y·sec·to·mize** \(ˌ)hī-ˌpä-fə-ˈsek-tə-ˌmīz\ *transitive verb* **-mized; -miz·ing** (1910)
: to remove the pituitary gland from

**hy·poph·y·sec·to·my** \-mē\ *noun, plural* **-mies** (1909)
: surgical removal of the pituitary gland

**hy·poph·y·sis** \hī-ˈpä-fə-səs\ *noun, plural* **-y·ses** \-ˌsēz\ [New Latin, from Greek, attachment underneath, from *hypophyein* to grow beneath, from *hypo-* + *phyein* to grow, produce — more at BE] (1825)
: PITUITARY GLAND

**hy·po·pi·tu·ita·rism** \ˌhī-pō-pə-ˈtü-ə-tə-ˌri-zəm, -ˈtü-ə-ˌtri-, -ˈtyü-\ *noun* [International Scientific Vocabulary] (1909)
: deficient production of growth hormones by the pituitary gland
— **hy·po·pi·tu·itary** \-ˈtü-ə-ˌter-ē, -ˈtyü-\ *adjective*

**hy·po·pla·sia** \-ˈplā-zh(ē-)ə\ *noun* [New Latin] (1889)
: a condition of arrested development in which an organ or part remains below the normal size or in an immature state
— **hy·po·plas·tic** \-ˈplas-tik\ *adjective*

**hy·po·ploid** \ˈhī-pə-ˌplȯid\ *adjective* (1930)
: having a chromosome number slightly less than an exact multiple of the monoploid number
— **hypoploid** *noun*

**hy·po·sen·si·ti·za·tion** \ˌhī-pō-ˌsen(t)-sə-tə-ˈzā-shən, -ˌsen(t)-stə-ˈzā-\ *noun* (1922)
: the state or process of being reduced in sensitivity especially to an allergen : DESENSITIZATION
— **hy·po·sen·si·tize** \-ˈsen(t)-sə-ˌtīz\ *transitive verb*

**hy·po·spa·di·as** \ˌhī-pə-ˈspā-dē-əs\ *noun* [New Latin, from Greek, man with hypospadias, from *hypo-* + *-spadias*, from *-spad-, -spas* something torn, from *span* to tear, pluck off] (circa 1855)
: an abnormality of the penis in which the urethra opens on the undersurface

**hy·pos·ta·sis** \hī-ˈpäs-tə-səs\ *noun, plural* **-ta·ses** \-ˌsēz\ [Late Latin, substance, sediment, from Greek, support, foundation, substance, sediment, from *hyphistasthai* to stand under, support, from *hypo-* + *histasthai* to be standing — more at STAND] (1590)

**1 a** : something that settles at the bottom of a fluid **b** : the settling of blood in the dependent parts of an organ or body
**2** : PERSON 3
**3 a** : the substance or essential nature of an individual **b** : something that is hypostatized
**4** [New Latin, from Late Latin] : failure of a gene to produce its usual effect when coupled with another gene that is epistatic toward it
— **hy·po·stat·ic** \ˌhī-pə-ˈsta-tik\ *adjective*
— **hy·po·stat·i·cal·ly** \-ti-k(ə-)lē\ *adverb*

**hy·pos·ta·tize** \hī-ˈpäs-tə-ˌtīz\ *transitive verb* **-tized; -tiz·ing** [Greek *hypostatos* substantially existing, from *hyphistasthai*] (1829)
: to attribute real identity to (a concept)
— **hy·pos·ta·ti·za·tion** \-ˌpäs-tə-tə-ˈzā-shən\ *noun*

**hy·po·stome** \ˈhī-pə-ˌstōm\ *noun* [International Scientific Vocabulary *hypo-* + *-stome* (from Greek *stoma* mouth) — more at STOMACH] (circa 1862)
: any of several structures associated with the mouth: as **a** : the manubrium of a hydrozoan **b** : a rodlike organ that arises at the base of the beak in various mites and ticks

**hy·po·style** \ˈhī-pə-ˌstīl\ *adjective* [Greek *hypostylos*, from *hypo-* + *stylos* pillar — more at STEER] (1831)
: having the roof resting on rows of columns
— **hypostyle** *noun*

**hy·po·tac·tic** \ˌhī-pə-ˈtak-tik\ *adjective* [Greek *hypotaktikos*, from *hypotassein*] (1896)
: of or relating to hypotaxis

**hy·po·tax·is** \-ˈtak-səs\ *noun* [New Latin, from Greek, subjection, from *hypotassein* to arrange under, from *hypo-* + *tassein* to arrange] (1883)
: syntactic subordination (as by a conjunction)

**hy·po·ten·sion** \ˌhī-pō-ˈten(t)-shən\ *noun* [International Scientific Vocabulary] (1893)
: abnormally low blood pressure

**¹hy·po·ten·sive** \ˌhī-pō-ˈten(t)-siv\ *adjective* (1904)
**1** : characterized by or due to hypotension
**2** : causing low blood pressure or a lowering of blood pressure ⟨*hypotensive* drugs⟩

**²hypotensive** *noun* (1941)
: a person with hypotension

**hy·pot·e·nuse** \hī-ˈpä-t°n-ˌüs, -ˌyüz\ *also* **hy·poth·e·nuse** \-ˈpä-thən-\ *noun* [Latin *hypotenusa*, from Greek *hypoteinousa*, from feminine of *hypoteinōn*, present participle of *hypoteinein* to subtend, from *hypo-* + *teinein* to stretch — more at THIN] (1594)
**1** : the side of a right-angled triangle that is opposite the right angle
**2** : the length of a hypotenuse

**hy·po·tha·lam·ic** \ˌhī-pō-thə-ˈla-mik\ *adjective* (1899)
: of or relating to the hypothalamus

*ac* hypotenuse

**hy·po·thal·a·mus** \-ˈtha-lə-məs\ *noun* [New Latin] (1896)
: a basal part of the diencephalon that lies beneath the thalamus on each side, forms the floor of the third ventricle, and includes vital autonomic regulatory centers

**¹hy·poth·e·cate** \hī-ˈpä-thə-ˌkāt, hī-\ *transitive verb* **-cat·ed; -cat·ing** [Medieval Latin *hypothecare* to pledge, from Late Latin *hypotheca* pledge, from Greek *hypothēkē*, from *hypotithenai* to put under, deposit as a pledge] (1681)
: to pledge as security without delivery of title or possession
— **hy·poth·e·ca·tion** \-ˌpä-thə-ˈkā-shən\ *noun*
— **hy·poth·e·ca·tor** \-ˈpä-thə-ˌkā-tər\ *noun*

**²hy·poth·e·cate** \hī-ˈpä-thə-ˌkāt\ *transitive verb* **-cat·ed; -cat·ing** [Greek *hypothēkē* suggestion, from *hypotithenai*] (1906)
: HYPOTHESIZE

**hy·po·ther·mal** \ˌhī-pō-ˈthər-məl\ *adjective* (1944)

: of or relating to a hydrothermal metalliferous ore vein deposited at high temperature

**hy·po·ther·mia** \-ˈthər-mē-ə\ *noun* [New Latin] (circa 1886)
: subnormal temperature of the body
— **hy·po·ther·mic** \-mik\ *adjective*

**hy·poth·e·sis** \hī-ˈpä-thə-səs\ *noun, plural* **-e·ses** \-ˌsēz\ [Greek, from *hypotithenai* to put under, suppose, from *hypo-* + *tithenai* to put — more at DO] (circa 1656)
**1 a** : an assumption or concession made for the sake of argument **b** : an interpretation of a practical situation or condition taken as the ground for action
**2** : a tentative assumption made in order to draw out and test its logical or empirical consequences
**3** : the antecedent clause of a conditional statement ☆

**hy·poth·e·size** \-ˌsīz\ *verb* **-sized; -siz·ing** (1738)
*intransitive verb*
: to make a hypothesis
*transitive verb*
: to adopt as a hypothesis

**hy·po·thet·i·cal** \ˌhī-pə-ˈthe-ti-kəl\ *adjective* (1588)
: being or involving a hypothesis : CONJECTURAL ⟨*hypothetical* arguments⟩ ⟨a *hypothetical* situation⟩
— **hy·po·thet·i·cal·ly** \-ti-k(ə-)lē\ *adverb*

**hy·po·thet·i·co–de·duc·tive** \ˌhī-pə-ˈthe-ti-ˌkō-di-ˈdək-tiv\ *adjective* (1912)
: relating to, being, or making use of the method of proposing hypotheses and testing their acceptability or falsity by determining whether their logical consequences are consistent with observed data

**hy·po·thy·roid** \ˌhī-pō-ˈthī-ˌrȯid\ *adjective* (1909)
: of, relating to, or affected with hypothyroidism

**hy·po·thy·roid·ism** \-ˌrȯi-ˌdi-zəm\ *noun* [International Scientific Vocabulary] (1905)
: deficient activity of the thyroid gland; *also* : a resultant bodily condition characterized by lowered metabolic rate and general loss of vigor

**hy·po·to·nia** \ˌhī-pə-ˈtō-nē-ə, -pō-\ *noun* [New Latin] (circa 1886)
: the state of having hypotonic muscle tone

**hy·po·ton·ic** \ˌhī-pə-ˈtä-nik\ *adjective* [International Scientific Vocabulary] (1895)
**1** : having deficient tone or tension ⟨*hypotonic* children⟩
**2** : having a lower osmotic pressure than a surrounding medium or a fluid under comparison ⟨*hypotonic* organisms⟩
— **hy·po·to·nic·i·ty** \-tə-ˈni-sə-tē\ *noun*

**hy·po·xan·thine** \ˌhī-pō-ˈzan-ˌthēn\ *noun* [International Scientific Vocabulary] (circa 1857)
: a purine base $C_5H_4N_4O$ found in plant and animal tissues that yields xanthine on oxidation

**hyp·ox·emia** \ˌhi-ˌpäk-ˈsē-mē-ə, ˌhī-\ *noun* [New Latin] (circa 1886)
: deficient oxygenation of the blood
— **hyp·ox·emic** \-mik\ *adjective*

**hyp·ox·ia** \hi-ˈpäk-sē-ə, hī-\ *noun* [New Latin] (1941)

☆ **SYNONYMS**
**Hypothesis, theory, law** mean a formula derived by inference from scientific data that explains a principle operating in nature. HYPOTHESIS implies insufficient evidence to provide more than a tentative explanation ⟨a *hypothesis* explaining the extinction of the dinosaurs⟩. THEORY implies a greater range of evidence and greater likelihood of truth ⟨the *theory* of evolution⟩. LAW implies a statement of order and relation in nature that has been found to be invariable under the same conditions ⟨the *law* of gravitation⟩.

: a deficiency of oxygen reaching the tissues of the body
— **hyp·ox·ic** \-sik\ *adjective*
**hyp·som·e·ter** \hip-'sä-mə-tər\ *noun* [International Scientific Vocabulary, from Greek *hypsos* height (akin to Old English *ūp* up) + International Scientific Vocabulary *-meter* — more at UP] (1927)
: any of various instruments for determining the height of trees by triangulation
**hyp·so·met·ric** \,hip-sə-'me-trik\ *adjective* [Greek *hypsos*] (1845)
: of, relating to, or indicating elevation (as on a map) ⟨*hypsometric* curve⟩
**hy·rax** \'hī-,raks\ *noun, plural* **hy·rax·es** \-,rak-səz\ *also* **hy·ra·ces** \-rə-,sēz\ [Greek *hyrak-, hyrax* shrew] (1832)
: any of a family (Procaviidae) of small ungulate mammals of Africa and the Middle East characterized by thickset body with short legs and ears and rudimentary tail, feet with soft pads and broad nails, and teeth of which the molars resemble those of the rhinoceros and the incisors those of rodents — called also *coney, dassie*

hyrax

**hy·son** \'hī-sᵊn\ *noun* [Chinese (Guangdong) *héichēun*, literally, bright spring] (1740)
: a Chinese green tea made from thinly rolled and twisted leaves
**hys·sop** \'hi-səp\ *noun* [Middle English *ysop*, from Old English *ysope*, from Latin *hyssopus*, from Greek *hyssōpos*, of Semitic origin; akin to Hebrew *ēzōbh* hyssop] (before 12th century)
**1** : a plant used in purificatory sprinkling rites by the ancient Hebrews
**2** : a European mint (*Hyssopus officinalis*) that has highly aromatic and pungent leaves and is sometimes used as a potherb

**hyster-** *or* **hystero-** *combining form* [French or Latin; French *hystér-*, from Latin *hyster-*, from Greek, from *hystera*]
: womb ⟨*hystero*ectomy⟩
**hys·ter·ec·to·my** \,his-tə-'rek-tə-mē\ *noun, plural* **-mies** (circa 1886)
: surgical removal of the uterus
— **hys·ter·ec·to·mized** \-tə-,mīzd\ *adjective*
**hys·ter·e·sis** \,his-tə-'rē-səs\ *noun, plural* **-e·ses** \-,sēz\ [New Latin, from Greek *hysterēsis* shortcoming, from *hysterein* to be late, fall short, from *hysteros* later — more at OUT] (1881)
: a retardation of an effect when the forces acting upon a body are changed (as if from viscosity or internal friction); *especially* : a lagging in the values of resulting magnetization in a magnetic material (as iron) due to a changing magnetizing force
— **hys·ter·et·ic** \-'re-tik\ *adjective*
**hys·te·ria** \his-'ter-ē-ə, -'tir-\ *noun* [New Latin, from English *hysteric*, adjective, from Latin *hystericus*, from Greek *hysterikos*, from *hystera* womb; from the Greek notion that hysteria was peculiar to women and caused by disturbances of the uterus] (1801)
**1** : a psychoneurosis marked by emotional excitability and disturbances of the psychic, sensory, vasomotor, and visceral functions
**2** : behavior exhibiting overwhelming or unmanageable fear or emotional excess ⟨political *hysteria*⟩ ◆
— **hys·ter·ic** \-'ter-ik\ *noun*
— **hys·ter·i·cal** \-'ter-i-kəl\ *also* **hysteric** *adjective*
— **hys·ter·i·cal·ly** \-i-k(ə-)lē\ *adverb*
**hys·ter·ics** \-'ter-iks\ *noun plural but singular or plural in construction* (1721)
: a fit of uncontrollable laughter or crying
**hys·ter·oid** \'his-tə-,rȯid\ *adjective* (circa 1855)
: resembling or tending toward hysteria
**hys·ter·on prot·er·on** \,his-tə-,rän-'prä-tə-,rän, -tə-rən-'prä-tə-rən, -'prȯ-\ *noun* [Late Lat-

in, from Greek, literally, (the) later earlier, (the) latter first] (1565)
: a figure of speech consisting of the reversal of a natural or rational order (as in "then came the thunder and the lightning")
**hys·ter·ot·o·my** \,his-tə-'rä-tə-mē\ *noun, plural* **-mies** [New Latin *hysterotomia*, from *hyster-* + *-tomia* -tomy] (1801)
: surgical incision of the uterus; *especially*
: CESAREAN SECTION

◇ WORD HISTORY

**hysteria**    Since the earliest days of civilization physicians have attempted to treat psychological disorders that manifest themselves physically, through tics and tremors, seizures, and a variety of other symptoms, including what sufferers experience as numbness and partial paralysis. Following ancient Egyptian medical lore, Greek physicians from Hippocrates to Galen believed that these ailments were unique to women and resulted from disturbances in the uterus. The collective labeling of such symptoms in Greek as *hysterika pathē* "sufferings of the womb," rendered in Latin as *hysterica passio,* gave rise to the term *hysteria* in English around the end of the 18th century, with counterparts in other European languages, such as French *hystérie* and German *Hysterie.* The boundaries of what constitutes hysteria, its diverse expression in different cultures, and the difficulties in separating it from genuine neurological disease are all issues that still preoccupy psychiatrists. The word itself has gradually been slipping from the usage of medical professionals. Most of the phenomena traditionally called *hysteria* are now put under the rubric *conversion reaction,* based on Freud's German term *Konversionshysterie,* which embodies his hypothesis that psychic anxiety is "converted" into bodily expression.

# I

I *is the ninth letter of the English alphabet and of most alphabets closely related to it. The character can be traced back through Latin, Etruscan and Greek* (iota) *to Phoenician* yōdh, *and probably ultimately to Egyptian. In Phoenician* i *represented a fricative (a consonant pronounced with air friction) articulated like the* y *in English* yet, *but it also had the value of a vowel in certain positions, and only the vowel pronunciation was taken over by the Greeks. In Latin and Old English,* i *had both vowel and consonant* y *sounds. Several hundred years later,* i *was used in English to spell both the vowel sound and the consonant sound* j *(as in modern* jewel*). By the 17th century, English used the* J *letter form (see* ᴊ*) exclusively for the consonant, and* I *exclusively for the vowel. Small* i *developed through a reduction in the size of the capital letter and the addition of an accent mark (later a dot) above the vertical stroke to distinguish it from adjacent letters (as* m, n, *and* u*) having identically formed strokes.*

---

**i** \'ī\ *noun, plural* **i's** *or* **is** \'īz\ *often capitalized, often attributive* (before 12th century)
**1 a** : the 9th letter of the English alphabet **b** : a graphic representation of this letter **c** : a speech counterpart of orthographic *i*
**2** : ᴏɴᴇ — see ɴᴜᴍʙᴇʀ table
**3** : a graphic device for reproducing the letter *i*
**4** : one designated *i* especially as the 9th in order or class
**5** : something shaped like the letter I
**6** : a unit vector parallel to the x-axis
**7** [abbreviation for *incomplete*] **a** : a grade rating a student's work as incomplete **b** : one graded or rated with an I
**8** : ɪ ꜰᴏʀᴍᴀᴛɪᴏɴ

**¹I** \'ī, ə\ *pronoun* [Middle English, from Old English *ic;* akin to Old High German *ih* I, Latin *ego,* Greek *egō*] (before 12th century)
: the one who is speaking or writing ⟨*I* feel fine⟩ — compare ᴍᴇ, ᴍɪɴᴇ, ᴍʏ, ᴡᴇ
**usage** see ᴍᴇ

**²I** \'ī\ *noun, plural* **I's** *or* **Is** \'īz\ (1539)
: someone aware of possessing a personal individuality : sᴇʟꜰ

**-i-** [Middle English, from Old French, from Latin, thematic vowel of most nouns and adjectives in combination]
— used as a connective vowel to join word elements especially of Latin origin ⟨matr*i*lineal⟩ ⟨rat*i*cide⟩

**¹-ia** *noun suffix* [New Latin, from Latin & Greek, suffix forming feminine nouns]
**1** : pathological condition ⟨hyster*ia*⟩
**2** : genus of plants or animals ⟨Fuchs*ia*⟩
**3** : territory : world : society ⟨suburb*ia*⟩

**²-ia** *noun plural suffix* [New Latin, from Latin (neuter plural of *-ius,* adjective ending) & Greek, neuter plural of *-ios,* adjective ending]
**1** : higher taxon (as class or order) consisting of (such plants or animals) ⟨Saur*ia*⟩
**2** : things derived from or relating to (something specified) ⟨milita*ria*⟩

**³-ia** *plural of* -ɪᴜᴍ

**Ia·go** \ē-'ä-(ˌ)gō\ *noun*
: the villain of Shakespeare's tragedy *Othello*

**-ial** *adjective suffix* [Middle English, from Middle French, from Latin *-ialis,* from *-i-* + *-alis* -al]
: ¹-ᴀʟ ⟨manor*ial*⟩

**iamb** \'ī-ˌam(b)\ *or* **iam·bus** \ī-'am-bəs\ *noun, plural* **iambs** \'ī-ˌamz\ *or* **iam·bus·es** [Latin *iambus,* from Greek *iambos*] (1586)
: a metrical foot consisting of one short syllable followed by one long syllable or of one unstressed syllable followed by one stressed syllable (as in *above*)
— **iam·bic** \ī-'am-bik\ *adjective or noun*

**-ian** — see -ᴀɴ

---

**-iana** — see -ᴀɴᴀ

**-iasis** *noun suffix, plural* **-iases** [New Latin, from Latin, from Greek, suffix of action, from denominative verbs in *-ian, -iazein*]
: disease having characteristics of or produced by (something specified) ⟨onchocerc*iasis*⟩ ⟨ancylostom*iasis*⟩

**-iatric** *also* **-iatrical** *adjective combining form* [New Latin *-iatria*]
: of or relating to (such) medical treatment or healing ⟨pedi*atric*⟩

**-iatrics** *noun plural combining form but singular or plural in construction*
: medical treatment ⟨pedi*atrics*⟩

**iat·ro·gen·ic** \(ˌ)ī-ˌa-trə-'je-nik\ *adjective* [Greek *iatros* physician + English *-genic*] (1924)
: induced inadvertently by a physician or surgeon or by medical treatment or diagnostic procedures ⟨an *iatrogenic* rash⟩
— **iat·ro·gen·i·cal·ly** \-'je-ni-k(ə-)lē\ *adverb*

**-iatry** *noun combining form* [French *-iatrie,* from New Latin *-iatria,* from Greek *iatreia* art of healing, from *iatros* healer, from *iasthai* to heal]
: medical treatment : healing ⟨pod*iatry*⟩

**I band** \'ī-\ *noun* (1948)
: an isotropic band of a striated muscle fiber

**I beam** *noun* (circa 1889)
: an iron or steel beam that is I-shaped in cross section

**¹Ibe·ri·an** \ī-'bir-ē-ən\ *noun* [*Iberia,* ancient region of the Caucasus] (1601)
: a member of one or more peoples anciently inhabiting the Caucasus in Asia between the Black and Caspian seas
— **Iberian** *adjective*

**²Iberian** *noun* [*Iberia,* peninsula in Europe] (1611)
**1 a** : a member of one or more peoples anciently inhabiting parts of the peninsula comprising Spain and Portugal **b** : a native or inhabitant of Spain or Portugal or the Basque region
**2** : one or more of the languages of the ancient Iberians
— **Iberian** *adjective*

**ibex** \'ī-ˌbeks\ *noun, plural* **ibex** *or* **ibex·es** [Latin] (1607)
: any of several wild goats (genus *Capra,* especially *C. ibex*) living chiefly in high mountain areas of the Old World and having large recurved horns transversely ridged in front

**ibi·dem** \'i-bə-ˌdem; i-'bī-dəm, -'bē-\ *adverb* [Latin] (circa 1771)
: in the same place

**-ibility** — see -ᴀʙɪʟɪᴛʏ

---

**ibis** \'ī-bəs\ *noun, plural* **ibis** *or* **ibis·es** [Middle English, from Latin, from Greek, from Egyptian *hb*] (14th century)
: any of various wading birds (family Threskiornithidae) related to the herons but distinguished by a long slender downwardly curved bill

ibis

**Ibi·zan hound** \i-'bē-zən-\ *noun* [*Ibiza* Island] (1960)
: any of a breed of slender agile medium-sized hunting dogs developed in the Balearic Islands with a short and smooth or a wirehaired coat

**-ible** — see -ᴀʙʟᴇ

**Ibo** \'ē-(ˌ)bō\ *noun, plural* **Ibo** *or* **Ibos** (1732)
**1** : a member of a people of the area around the lower Niger in Africa
**2** : the language of the Ibo people

Ibizan hound

**Ib·sen·ism** \'ib-sə-ˌni-zəm, 'ip-\ *noun* (1890)
**1** : dramatic invention or construction characteristic of Ibsen
**2** : championship of Ibsen's plays and ideas
— **Ib·sen·ite** \-ˌnīt\ *noun or adjective*

**ibu·pro·fen** \ˌī-byü-'prō-fən *also* ī-'byü-prə-fən\ *noun* [*is-* + *bu*tyl + *pro*pionic acid + *-fen* (alteration of *phenyl*)] (1969)
: a nonsteroidal anti-inflammatory drug $C_{13}H_{18}O_2$ used to relieve pain and fever

**¹IC** \ˌī-'sē\ *noun* (1947)
: ɪᴍᴍᴇᴅɪᴀᴛᴇ ᴄᴏɴꜱᴛɪᴛᴜᴇɴᴛ

**²IC** *noun* (1966)
: ɪɴᴛᴇɢʀᴀᴛᴇᴅ ᴄɪʀᴄᴜɪᴛ

**¹-ic** *adjective suffix* [Middle English, from Old French & Latin; Old French *-ique,* from Latin *-icus* — more at -ʏ]
**1** : having the character or form of : being ⟨panoram*ic*⟩ : consisting of ⟨run*ic*⟩
**2 a** : of or relating to ⟨alderman*ic*⟩ **b** : related to, derived from, or containing ⟨alcohol*ic*⟩
**3** : in the manner of : like that of : characteristic of ⟨Byron*ic*⟩
**4** : associated or dealing with ⟨Ved*ic*⟩ : utilizing ⟨electron*ic*⟩
**5** : characterized by : exhibiting ⟨nostalg*ic*⟩ : affected with ⟨allerg*ic*⟩
**6** : caused by ⟨amoeb*ic*⟩
**7** : tending to produce ⟨analges*ic*⟩
**8** : having a valence relatively higher than in compounds or ions named with an adjective ending in *-ous* ⟨ferr*ic* iron⟩

**²-ic** *noun suffix*
: one having the character or nature of : one belonging to or associated with : one exhibiting or affected by : one that produces

**-ical** *adjective suffix* [Middle English, from Late Latin *-icalis* (as in *clericalis* clerical, *radicalis* radical)]
: -ɪᴄ ⟨symmetr*ical*⟩ ⟨geolog*ical*⟩ — sometimes differing from *-ic* in that adjectives formed with *-ical* have a wider or more transferred semantic range than corresponding adjectives in *-ic*

**Ic·a·rus** \'i-kə-rəs\ *noun* [Latin, from Greek *Ikaros*]
: the son of Daedalus who to escape imprisonment flies by means of artificial wings but falls into the sea and drowns when the wax of his wings melts as he flies too near the sun

**ICBM** \ˌī-ˌsē-(ˌ)bē-'em\ *noun, plural* **ICBM's** *or* **ICBMs** \-'emz\ (1955)
: an intercontinental ballistic missile

**¹ice** \'īs\ *noun, often attributive* [Middle English *is*, from Old English *īs;* akin to Old High German *īs* ice, Avestan *isu-* icy] (before 12th century)
**1 a :** frozen water **b :** a sheet or stretch of ice
**2 :** a substance resembling ice; *especially* **:** the solid state of a substance usually found as a gas or liquid ⟨ammonia *ice* in the rings of Saturn⟩
**3 :** a state of coldness (as from formality or reserve)
**4 a :** a frozen dessert containing a flavoring (as fruit juice); *especially* **:** one containing no milk or cream **b** *British* **:** a serving of ice cream
**5** *slang* **:** DIAMONDS; *broadly* **:** JEWELRY
**6 :** an undercover premium paid to a theater employee for choice theater tickets
— **ice·less** \'ī-sləs\ *adjective*
— **on ice 1 :** with every likelihood of being won or accomplished **2 :** in reserve or safekeeping
**²ice** *verb* **iced; ic·ing** (15th century)
*transitive verb*
**1 a :** to coat with or convert into ice **b :** to chill with ice **c :** to supply with ice
**2 :** to cover with or as if with icing
**3 :** to put on ice
**4 :** SECURE 1b ⟨made two free throws . . . to *ice* the win —Jack McCallum⟩
**5 :** to shoot (an ice hockey puck) the length of the rink and beyond the opponents' goal line
**6** *slang* **:** KILL 1a
*intransitive verb*
**1 :** to become ice-cold
**2 a :** to become covered with ice — often used with *up* or *over* **b :** to have ice form inside ⟨the carburetor *iced* up⟩
**ice age** *noun* (1873)
**1 :** a time of widespread glaciation
**2** *I&A capitalized* **:** the Pleistocene glacial epoch
**ice ax** *noun* (1820)
**:** a combination pick and adze with a spiked handle that is used in mountain climbing
**ice bag** *noun* (1883)
**:** a waterproof bag to hold ice for local application of cold to the body
**ice·berg** \'īs-,bərg\ *noun* [probably part translation of Danish or Norwegian *isberg*, from *is* ice + *berg* mountain] (1820)
**1 :** a large floating mass of ice detached from a glacier
**2 :** an emotionally cold person
**3 :** ICEBERG LETTUCE

ice ax

**iceberg lettuce** *noun* (1893)
**:** any of various crisp light green lettuces that when mature have the leaves arranged in a compact head
**ice·blink** \-,bliŋk\ *noun* (1817)
**:** a glare in the sky over an ice field
**ice·boat** \-,bōt\ *noun* (circa 1819)
**:** a skeleton boat or frame on runners propelled on ice usually by sails
**ice·boat·ing** \-,bō-tiŋ\ *noun* (1885)
**:** the sport of sailing in iceboats
— **ice·boat·er** \-,bō-tər\ *noun*
**ice·bound** \-,baùnd\ *adjective* (1641)
**:** surrounded, obstructed, or covered by ice
**ice·box** \-,bäks\ *noun* (1846)
**:** REFRIGERATOR
**ice·break·er** \-,brā-kər\ *noun* (1875)
**1 :** a ship equipped to make and maintain a channel through ice
**2 :** something that breaks the ice on a project or occasion; *especially* **:** MIXER 1c
**ice cap** *noun* (circa 1860)
**1 :** an ice bag shaped to the head
**2 :** a cover of perennial ice and snow; *specifically* **:** a glacier forming on an extensive area of relatively level land and flowing outward from its center

**ice–cold** \'īs-'kōld\ *adjective* (before 12th century)
**:** extremely cold
**ice–cream** *adjective* (1890)
**:** of a color similar to that of vanilla ice cream
**ice cream** \'īs-'krēm, 'īs-,\ *noun* (1744)
**:** a sweet flavored frozen food containing cream or butterfat and usually eggs
**ice–cream chair** *noun* [from its use in ice cream parlors] (1949)
**:** a small armless chair with a circular seat for use at a table (as at a café)
**ice–cream cone** *noun* (1909)
**:** a thin crisp edible cone for holding ice cream; *also* **:** one filled with ice cream
**ice dancing** *noun* (1925)
**:** a sport in which ice-skating pairs perform to music routines similar to ballroom dances
**ice·fall** \'īs-,föl\ *noun* (1817)
**1 :** a frozen waterfall
**2 :** the mass of usually jagged blocks into which a glacier may break when it moves down a steep declivity
**ice field** *noun* (1694)
**1 :** an extensive sheet of sea ice
**2 :** ICE CAP 2
**ice floe** *noun* (1819)
**:** a usually large flat free mass of floating sea ice
**ice fog** *noun* (1856)
**:** a fog composed of ice particles
**ice hockey** *noun* (1883)
**:** a game played on an ice rink by two teams of six players on skates whose object is to drive a puck into the opponents' goal with a hockey stick
**ice·house** \'īs-,haùs, 'ī-,saùs\ *noun* (1687)
**:** a building in which ice is made or stored
**¹Ice·lan·dic** \ī-'slan-dik\ *adjective* (1674)
**:** of, relating to, or characteristic of Iceland, the Icelanders, or Icelandic
**²Icelandic** *noun* (circa 1824)
**:** the North Germanic language of Iceland
**Ice·land moss** \'ī-slən(d)-, -,slan(d)-\ *noun* (1805)
**:** a lichen (*Cetraria islandica*) of mountainous and arctic regions sometimes used in medicine or as food
**Iceland poppy** *noun* (1884)
**:** a poppy (*Papaver nudicaule*) of holarctic regions often cultivated for its usually single showy flowers
**Iceland spar** *noun* (1771)
**:** a doubly refracting transparent calcite
**ice·man** \'īs-,man\ *noun* (1833)
**1 :** one who sells or delivers ice
**2 :** a man skilled in traveling on ice
**ice milk** *noun* (1947)
**:** a sweetened frozen food made of skim milk
**Ice·ni** \ī-'sē-,nī\ *noun plural* [Latin] (circa 1891)
**:** an ancient British people that under their queen Boudicca revolted against the Romans in A.D. 60
— **Ice·ni·an** \-'sē-nē-ən\ *or* **Ice·nic** \-'sē-nik, -'se-\ *adjective*
**ice–out** \'īs-,aút\ *noun* (1951)
**:** the disappearance of ice from the surface of a body of water (as a lake) as a result of thawing
**ice pack** *noun* (1853)
**:** an expanse of pack ice
**ice pick** *noun* (circa 1877)
**:** a hand tool ending in a spike for chipping ice
**ice plant** *noun* (1753)
**:** an Old World annual herb (*Mesembryanthemum crystallinum*) of the carpetweed family that has fleshy foliage covered with glistening papillate dots or vesicles and is widely naturalized in warm regions; *broadly* **:** FIG MARIGOLD
**ice point** *noun* (1903)
**:** the freezing point of water of 0° Celsius or 273.15 Kelvin at standard atmospheric pressure
**ice sheet** *noun* (1873)

**:** ICE CAP 2
**ice show** *noun* (1948)
**:** an entertainment consisting of various exhibitions by ice-skaters usually with musical accompaniment
**ice–skate** \'ī(s)-,skāt\ *intransitive verb* (circa 1948)
**:** to skate on ice
— **ice–skat·er** \-,skā-tər\ *noun*
**ice skate** *noun* (1897)
**:** a shoe with a metal runner attached for ice-skating
**ice storm** *noun* (1876)
**:** a storm in which falling rain freezes on contact
**ice water** *noun* (1722)
**:** chilled or iced water especially served as a beverage
**ich·neu·mon** \ik-'nü-mən, -'nyü-\ *noun* [Middle English, from Latin, from Greek *ichneumōn,* literally, tracker, from *ichneuein* to track, from *ichnos* footprint] (15th century)
**1 :** a mongoose (*Herpestes ichneumon*) of Africa, southern Europe, and southwestern Asia
**2 :** ICHNEUMON FLY
**ichneumon fly** *noun* (1713)
**:** any of a large superfamily (Ichneumonoidea) of hymenopterous insects whose larvae are usually internal parasites of other insect larvae and especially of caterpillars
**ichor** \'ī-,kȯr, -kər\ *noun* [Greek *ichōr*] (15th century)
**1 :** a thin watery or blood-tinged discharge
**2 :** an ethereal fluid taking the place of blood in the veins of the ancient Greek gods
— **ichor·ous** \-kə-rəs\ *adjective*
**ichthy-** *or* **ichthyo-** *combining form* [Latin, from Greek, from *ichthys;* akin to Armenian *jukn* fish, Lithuanian *žuvis*]
**:** fish ⟨*ichthyology*⟩
**ich·thyo·fau·na** \,ik-thē-ō-'fö-nə, -'fä-\ *noun* [New Latin] (1883)
**:** the fish life of a region
— **ich·thyo·fau·nal** \-'fö-nᵊl, -'fä-\ *adjective*
**ich·thy·ol·o·gy** \,ik-thē-'ä-lə-jē\ *noun* (1646)
**:** a branch of zoology that deals with fishes
— **ich·thy·o·log·i·cal** \-thē-ə-'lä-ji-kəl\ *adjective*
— **ich·thy·o·log·i·cal·ly** \-k(ə-)lē\ *adverb*
— **ich·thy·ol·o·gist** \-thē-'ä-lə-jist\ *noun*
**ich·thy·oph·a·gous** \,ik-thē-'ä-fə-gəs\ *adjective* [Greek *ichthyophagos,* from *ichthy-* + *-phagos* -phagous] (circa 1828)
**:** eating or subsisting on fish
**ich·thy·o·saur** \'ik-thē-ə-,sȯr\ *noun* [ultimately from Greek *ichthy-* + *sauros* lizard] (1830)
**:** any of an order (Ichthyosauria) of extinct marine reptiles of the Mesozoic specialized for aquatic life by a streamlined body with a long snout, limbs reduced to small fins for steering, and a large lunate caudal fin
— **ich·thyo·sau·ri·an** \,ik-thē-ə-'sȯr-ē-ən\ *adjective or noun*
**-ician** *noun suffix* [Middle English, from Old French *-icien,* from Latin *-ica* (as in *rhetorica* rhetoric) + Old French *-ien* -ian]
**:** specialist **:** practitioner ⟨beauti*cian*⟩
**ici·cle** \'ī-,si-kəl\ *noun* [Middle English *isikel,* from *is* ice + *ikel* icicle, from Old English *gicel;* akin to Old High German *ihilla* icicle, Middle Irish *aig* ice] (14th century)
**1 :** a pendent mass of ice formed by the freezing of dripping water
**2 :** an emotionally cold person

**3 :** a long narrow strip (as of foil) used to decorate a Christmas tree ◆

**¹ic·ing** \'ī-siŋ\ *noun* (1769)
**1 :** a sweet flavored usually creamy mixture used to coat baked goods (as cupcakes) — called also *frosting*
**2 :** something that adds to the interest, value, or appeal of an item or event — often used in the phrase *icing on the cake*

**²icing** *noun* (1948)
**:** an act by an ice-hockey player of shooting a puck from within the defensive zone or defensive half of the rink beyond the opponents' goal line but not into the goal

**ick·er** \'i-kər\ *noun* [(assumed) Middle English (Scots dialect), from Old English ēar, eher — more at EAR] (1513)
*Scottish* **:** a head of grain

**icky** \'i-kē\ *adjective* **ick·i·er; -est** [perhaps baby talk alteration of *sticky*] (1929)
**:** offensive to the senses or sensibilities **:** DISTASTEFUL ⟨put off by her *icky* triteness —Renata Adler⟩
— **ick·i·ness** \-nəs\ *noun*

**icon** \'ī-,kän\ *noun* [Latin, from Greek *eikōn*, from *eikenai* to resemble] (1572)
**1 :** a usually pictorial representation **:** IMAGE
**2** [Late Greek *eikōn*, from Greek] **:** a conventional religious image typically painted on a small wooden panel and used in the devotions of Eastern Christians
**3 :** an object of uncritical devotion **:** IDOL
**4 :** EMBLEM, SYMBOL ⟨the house became an *icon* of 1860's residential architecture —Paul Goldberger⟩
**5 a :** a sign (as a word or graphic symbol) whose form suggests its meaning **b :** a graphic symbol on a computer display screen that suggests the purpose of an available function
— **icon·ic** \ī-'kä-nik\ *adjective*
— **icon·i·cal·ly** \-ni-k(ə-)lē\ *adverb*

**icon-** *or* **icono-** *combining form* [Greek *eikon-, eikono-*, from *eikon-, eikōn*]
**:** image ⟨*icono*latry⟩

**ico·nic·i·ty** \,ī-kə-'ni-sə-tē\ *noun* (1946)
**:** correspondence between form and meaning ⟨the *iconicity* of the Roman numeral III⟩

**icon·o·clasm** \ī-'kä-nə-,kla-zəm\ *noun* (1797)
**:** the doctrine, practice, or attitude of an iconoclast

**icon·o·clast** \-,klast\ *noun* [Medieval Latin *iconoclastes*, from Middle Greek *eikonoklastēs*, literally, image destroyer, from Greek *eikono-* + *klan* to break — more at CLAST] (1641)
**1 :** one who destroys religious images or opposes their veneration
**2 :** one who attacks settled beliefs or institutions
— **icon·o·clas·tic** \(,)ī-,kä-nə-'klas-tik\ *adjective*
— **icon·o·clas·ti·cal·ly** \-ti-k(ə-)lē\ *adverb*

**ico·nog·ra·pher** \,ī-kə-'nä-grə-fər\ *noun* (1888)
**1 :** a maker of figures or drawings especially of a conventional type
**2 :** a student of iconography

**icon·o·graph·ic** \(,)ī-,kä-nə-'gra-fik\ *or* **icon·o·graph·i·cal** \-fi-kəl\ *adjective* (circa 1855)
**1 :** of or relating to iconography
**2 :** representing something by pictures or diagrams
— **icon·o·graph·i·cal·ly** \-fi-k(ə-)lē\ *adverb*

**ico·nog·ra·phy** \,ī-kə-'nä-grə-fē\ *noun, plural* **-phies** [Medieval Latin *iconographia*, from Greek *eikonographia* sketch, description, from *eikonographein* to describe, from *eikon-* + *graphein* to write — more at CARVE] (1678)
**1 :** pictorial material relating to or illustrating a subject
**2 :** the traditional or conventional images or symbols associated with a subject and especially a religious or legendary subject

**3 :** the imagery or symbolism of a work of art, an artist, or a body of art
**4 :** ICONOLOGY

**ico·nol·a·try** \-'nä-lə-trē\ *noun* (1624)
**:** the worship of images or icons

**ico·nol·o·gy** \-'nä-lə-jē\ *noun* [French *iconologie*, from *icono-* icon- + *-logie* -logy] (circa 1736)
**:** the study of icons or artistic symbolism
— **icon·o·log·i·cal** \(,)ī-,kä-n°l-'ä-ji-kəl\ *adjective*

**icon·o·scope** \ī-'kä-nə-,skōp\ *noun* [from *Iconoscope*, a trademark] (1932)
**:** a camera tube containing an electron gun and a photoemissive mosaic screen of which each cell produces a charge proportional to the varying light intensity of the image focused on the screen

**ico·nos·ta·sis** \,ī-kə-'näs-tə-səs, (,)ī-'kä-nə-,stä-səs\ *noun, plural* **-ta·ses** \-,sēz\ [modification of Middle Greek *eikonostasion*, from Late Greek, shrine, from Greek *eikono-* + *-stasion* (from *histanai* to stand) — more at STAND] (1833)
**:** a screen or partition with doors and tiers of icons that separates the bema from the nave in Eastern churches

**ico·sa·he·dral** \(,)ī-,kō-sə-'hē-drəl, -,kä-\ *adjective* (circa 1828)
**:** of or having the form of an icosahedron

**ico·sa·he·dron** \-drən\ *noun, plural* **-drons** *or* **-dra** \-drə\ [Greek *eikosaedron*, from *eikosi* twenty + *-edron* -hedron — more at VIGESIMAL] (1570)
**:** a polyhedron having 20 faces

**-ics** *noun plural suffix but singular or plural in construction* [¹-ic + ²-s; translation of Greek *-ika*, from neuter plural of *-ikos* -ic]
**1 :** study **:** knowledge **:** skill **:** practice ⟨linguist*ics*⟩ ⟨electron*ics*⟩
**2 :** characteristic actions or activities ⟨acrobat*ics*⟩
**3 :** characteristic qualities, operations, or phenomena ⟨mechan*ics*⟩

**ic·ter·ic** \ik-'ter-ik\ *adjective* (circa 1600)
**:** of, relating to, or affected with jaundice

**ic·ter·us** \'ik-tə-rəs\ *noun* [New Latin, from Greek *ikteros*] (circa 1706)
**:** JAUNDICE

**ic·tus** \'ik-təs\ *noun* [Latin, literally, blow, from *icere* to strike] (1752)
**:** the recurring stress or beat in a rhythmic or metrical series of sounds

**icy** \'ī-sē\ *adjective* **ic·i·er; -est** (before 12th century)
**1 a :** covered with, abounding in, or consisting of ice **b :** intensely cold
**2 :** characterized by coldness **:** FRIGID ⟨an *icy* stare⟩; *also* **:** STEELY ⟨*icy* nerves⟩
— **ic·i·ly** \-sə-lē\ *adverb*
— **ic·i·ness** \-sē-nəs\ *noun*

**id** \'id\ *noun* [New Latin, from Latin, it] (1924)
**:** the one of the three divisions of the psyche in psychoanalytic theory that is completely unconscious and is the source of psychic energy derived from instinctual needs and drives — compare EGO, SUPEREGO

**¹-id** *noun suffix* [in sense 1, from Latin *-ides*, masculine patronymic suffix, from Greek *-idēs*; in sense 2, from Italian *-ide*, from Latin *-id-, -is*, feminine patronymic suffix, from Greek]
**1 :** one belonging to a (specified) dynastic line ⟨Abbas*id*⟩
**2 :** meteor associated with or radiating from a (specified) constellation or comet ⟨Perse*id*⟩

**²-id** *noun suffix* [probably from Latin *-id-, -is*, feminine patronymic suffix, from Greek]
**:** body **:** particle ⟨chromat*id*⟩

**I'd** \'īd\ (circa 1592)
**:** I would **:** I had **:** I should

**-idae** *noun plural suffix* [New Latin, from Latin, from Greek *-idai*, plural of *-idēs*]
**:** members of the family of — in names of zoological families ⟨Fel*idae*⟩

**Ida·ho** \'ī-də-,hō\ *noun, plural* **Idahos** *or* **Idahoes** (1934)
**:** an elongated baking potato grown especially in the state of Idaho

**ID card** \'ī-'dē-\ *noun* (circa 1945)
**:** a card bearing identifying data (as age or organizational membership) about the individual whose name appears thereon — called also *identification card, identity card*

**-ide** *also* **-id** *noun suffix* [German & French; German *-id*, from French *-ide* (as in *oxide*)]
**1 :** binary chemical compound — added to the contracted name of the nonmetallic or more electronegative element ⟨hydrogen sulf*ide*⟩ or group ⟨cyan*ide*⟩
**2 :** chemical compound derived from or related to another (usually specified) compound ⟨anhydr*ide*⟩ ⟨glucos*ide*⟩

**idea** \ī-'dē-ə *also* 'ī-(,)dē-ə *or* 'ī-dē\ *noun* [Middle English, from Latin, from Greek, from *idein* to see — more at WIT] (14th century)
**1 a :** a transcendent entity that is a real pattern of which existing things are imperfect representations **b :** a standard of perfection **:** IDEAL **c :** a plan for action **:** DESIGN
**2** *archaic* **:** a visible representation of a conception **:** a replica of a pattern
**3 a** *obsolete* **:** an image recalled by memory **b :** an indefinite or unformed conception **c :** an entity (as a thought, concept, sensation, or image) actually or potentially present to consciousness
**4 :** a formulated thought or opinion
**5 :** whatever is known or supposed about something ⟨a child's *idea* of time⟩
**6 :** the central meaning or chief end of a particular action or situation
**7** *Christian Science* **:** an image in Mind ☆

---

☆ **SYNONYMS**
**Idea, concept, conception, thought, notion, impression** mean what exists in the mind as a representation (as of something comprehended) or as a formulation (as of a plan). IDEA may apply to a mental image or formulation of something seen or known or imagined, to a pure abstraction, or to something assumed or vaguely sensed ⟨innovative *ideas*⟩ ⟨my *idea* of paradise⟩. CONCEPT may apply to the idea formed by consideration of instances of a species or genus or, more broadly, to any idea of what a thing ought to be ⟨a society with no *concept* of private property⟩. CONCEPTION is often interchangeable with CONCEPT; it may stress the process of imagining or formulating rather than the result ⟨our changing *conception* of what constitutes art⟩. THOUGHT is likely to suggest the result of reflecting, reasoning, or meditating rather than of imagining ⟨commit your *thoughts* to paper⟩. NOTION suggests an idea not much resolved by analysis or reflection and may suggest the capricious or accidental ⟨you have the oddest *notions*⟩. IMPRESSION applies to an idea or notion resulting immediately from some stimulation of the senses ⟨the first *impression* is of soaring height⟩.

---

◇ **WORD HISTORY**
**icicle** The Old English noun *gicel* is found as early as the first half of the 8th century translating Latin *stiria* "icicle." *Gicel* became Middle English *ikyl* or *ikel* and later Modern English *ickle*, which was still in use around the middle of this century in Derbyshire and Yorkshire. The word for *ice* in Old English was *is*, and in a manuscript of about the year 1000 we find *stiria* translated with seeming redundancy as *ises gicel*, that is, "icicle of ice." Some three hundred years later in Middle English appeared the compound that we know today as *icicle*, which means precisely what *ises gicel* meant a thousand years ago.

— **idea·less** \ī-'dē-ə-ləs\ *adjective*

¹**ide·al** \ī-'dē(-ə)l, 'ī-\ *adjective* [Middle English *ydeall*, from Late Latin *idealis*, from Latin *idea*] (15th century)
**1** : existing as an archetypal idea
**2 a** : existing as a mental image or in fancy or imagination only; *broadly* : lacking practicality **b** : relating to or constituting mental images, ideas, or conceptions
**3 a** : of, relating to, or embodying an ideal **b** : conforming exactly to an ideal, law, or standard : PERFECT ⟨an *ideal* gas⟩ — compare REAL 2b(3)
**4** : of or relating to philosophical idealism

²**ideal** *noun* (15th century)
**1** : a standard of perfection, beauty, or excellence
**2** : one regarded as exemplifying an ideal and often taken as a model for imitation
**3** : an ultimate object or aim of endeavor : GOAL
**4** : a subset of a mathematical ring that is closed under addition and subtraction and contains the products of any given element of the subset with each element of the ring
synonym see MODEL
— **ide·al·less** \ī-'dē(-ə)l-ləs\ *adjective*

**ide·al·ise** *British variant of* IDEALIZE

**ide·al·ism** \ī-'dē-(ə-)ˌliz-əm, 'ī-(ˌ)dē-\ *noun* (1796)
**1 a** (1) : a theory that ultimate reality lies in a realm transcending phenomena (2) : a theory that the essential nature of reality lies in consciousness or reason **b** (1) : a theory that only the perceptible is real (2) : a theory that only mental states or entities are knowable
**2 a** : the practice of forming ideals or living under their influence **b** : something that is idealized
**3** : literary or artistic theory or practice that affirms the preeminent value of imagination as compared with faithful copying of nature — compare REALISM

¹**ide·al·ist** \-(ə-)list\ *noun* (1701)
**1 a** : an adherent of a philosophical theory of idealism **b** : an artist or author who advocates or practices idealism in art or writing
**2** : one guided by ideals; *especially* : one that places ideals before practical considerations

²**idealist** *adjective* (1875)
: IDEALISTIC

**ide·al·is·tic** \(ˌ)ī-dē-(ə-)'lis-tik, ˌī-dē-\ *adjective* (1829)
: of or relating to idealists or idealism
— **ide·al·is·ti·cal·ly** \-ti-k(ə-)lē\ *adverb*

**ide·al·i·ty** \ˌī-dē-'a-lə-tē\ *noun, plural* **-ties** (1817)
**1 a** : the quality or state of being ideal **b** : existence only in idea
**2** : something imaginary or idealized

**ide·al·ize** \ī-'dē-(ə-)ˌlīz\ *verb* **-ized; -iz·ing** (1786)
*intransitive verb*
**1** : to form ideals
**2** : to work idealistically
*transitive verb*
**1 a** : to give an ideal form or value to **b** : to attribute ideal characteristics to
**2** : to treat idealistically
— **ide·al·i·za·tion** \-ˌdē-(ə-)lə-'zā-shən\ *noun*
— **ide·al·iz·er** \-'dē-(ə-)ˌlī-zər\ *noun*

**ide·al·ly** \ī-'dē-ə-lē, -'dē(-ə)-lē\ *adverb* (1598)
**1** : in idea or imagination : MENTALLY
**2** : in relation to an exemplar
**3 a** : conformably to or in respect to an ideal : PERFECTLY **b** : for best results ⟨*ideally*, the counselor should vary his techniques for each applicant —T. M. Martinez⟩ **c** : in accordance with an ideal or typical standard : CLASSICALLY

**ideal point** *noun* (1879)
: a point added to the plane or to space to eliminate special cases; *specifically* : the point at infinity added in projective geometry as the assumed intersection of two parallel lines

**ide·ate** \'ī-dē-ˌāt\ *verb* **-at·ed; -at·ing** (1610)

*transitive verb*
: to form an idea or conception of
*intransitive verb*
: to form an idea

**ide·a·tion** \ˌī-dē-'ā-shən\ *noun* (1818)
: the forming of ideas (as of things not present to the senses)

**ide·a·tion·al** \-shnəl, -shə-nᵊl\ *adjective* (1853)
: of, relating to, or produced by ideation; *broadly* : of or relating to ideas
— **ide·a·tion·al·ly** *adverb*

**idée fixe** \(ˌ)ē-ˌdā-'fēks\ *noun, plural* **idées fixes** \*same*\ [French, literally, fixed idea] (1836)
: an idea that dominates one's mind especially for a prolonged period : OBSESSION

**idem** \'ī-ˌdem, 'ē-, 'i-\ *pronoun* [Middle English, from Latin, same — more at IDENTITY] (14th century)
: something previously mentioned : SAME

**idem·po·tent** \'ī-dəm-ˌpō-t²nt\ *adjective* [Latin *idem* same + *potent-, potens* having power — more at POTENT] (1870)
: relating to or being a mathematical quantity which when applied to itself under a given binary operation (as multiplication) equals itself; *also* : relating to or being an operation under which a mathematical quantity is idempotent
— **idempotent** *noun*

**iden·tic** \ī-'den-tik, ə-\ *adjective* (1649)
: IDENTICAL: as **a** : constituting a diplomatic action or expression in which two or more governments follow precisely the same course or employ an identical form **b** : constituting an action or expression in which a government follows precisely the same course or employs identical forms with reference to two or more other governments

**iden·ti·cal** \ī-'den-ti-kəl, ə-\ *adjective* [probably from Medieval Latin *identicus*, from Late Latin *identitas*] (1599)
**1** : being the same : SELFSAME ⟨the *identical* place we stopped before⟩
**2** : having such close resemblance as to be essentially the same ⟨*identical* hats⟩ — often used with *to* or *with*
**3 a** : having the same cause or origin ⟨*identical* infections⟩ **b** : MONOZYGOTIC
synonym see SAME
— **iden·ti·cal·ly** \-k(ə-)lē\ *adverb*
— **iden·ti·cal·ness** \-kəl-nəs\ *noun*

**iden·ti·fi·ca·tion** \ī-ˌden-tə-fə-'kā-shən, ə-\ *noun* (1644)
**1 a** : an act of identifying : the state of being identified **b** : evidence of identity
**2 a** : psychological orientation of the self in regard to something (as a person or group) with a resulting feeling of close emotional association **b** : a largely unconscious process whereby an individual models thoughts, feelings, and actions after those attributed to an object that has been incorporated as a mental image

**identification card** *noun* (1908)
: ID CARD

**iden·ti·fi·er** \ī-'den-tə-ˌfī(-ə)r, ə-\ *noun* (1889)
: one that identifies

**iden·ti·fy** \ī-'den-tə-ˌfī, ə-\ *verb* **-fied; -fy·ing** (1644)
*transitive verb*
**1 a** : to cause to be or become identical **b** : to conceive as united (as in spirit, outlook, or principle) ⟨groups that are *identified* with conservation⟩
**2 a** : to establish the identity of **b** : to determine the taxonomic position of (a biological specimen)
*intransitive verb*
**1** : to be or become the same
**2** : to practice psychological identification ⟨*identify* with the hero of a novel⟩
— **iden·ti·fi·able** \-ˌden-tə-'fī-ə-bəl\ *adjective*
— **iden·ti·fi·ably** \-blē\ *adverb*

**iden·ti·ty** \ī-'den-tə-tē, ə-, -'de-nə-\ *noun, plural* **-ties** [Middle French *identité*, from Late Latin *identitat-, identitas*, probably from Latin *identidem* repeatedly, contraction of *idem et idem*, literally, same and same] (1570)
**1 a** : sameness of essential or generic character in different instances **b** : sameness in all that constitutes the objective reality of a thing : ONENESS
**2 a** : the distinguishing character or personality of an individual : INDIVIDUALITY **b** : the relation established by psychological identification
**3** : the condition of being the same with something described or asserted ⟨establish the *identity* of stolen goods⟩
**4** : an equation that is satisfied for all values of the symbols
**5** : IDENTITY ELEMENT

**identity card** *noun* (1900)
: ID CARD

**identity crisis** *noun* (1954)
**1** : personal psychosocial conflict especially in adolescence that involves confusion about one's social role and often a sense of loss of continuity to one's personality
**2** : a state of confusion in an institution or organization regarding its nature or direction

**identity element** *noun* (1902)
: an element (as 0 in the set of all integers under addition or 1 in the set of positive integers under multiplication) that leaves any element of the set to which it belongs unchanged when combined with it by a specified operation

**identity matrix** *noun* (circa 1929)
: a square matrix that has numeral 1's along the principal diagonal and 0's elsewhere

**ideo-** *combining form* [French *idéo-*, from Greek *idea*]
: idea ⟨*ideo*gram⟩

**ideo·gram** \'i-dē-ə-ˌgram, 'ī-\ *noun* (circa 1840)
**1** : a picture or symbol used in a system of writing to represent a thing or an idea but not a particular word or phrase for it; *especially* : one that represents not the object pictured but some thing or idea that the object pictured is supposed to suggest
**2** : LOGOGRAM
— **ideo·gram·ic** *or* **ideo·gram·mic** \ˌi-dē-ə-'gra-mik, ˌī-\ *adjective*
— **ideo·gram·mat·ic** \-dē-ō-grə-'ma-tik\ *adjective*

**ideo·graph** \'i-dē-ə-ˌgraf, 'ī-\ *noun* (1835)
: IDEOGRAM
— **ideo·graph·ic** \ˌi-dē-ə-'gra-fik, ˌī-\ *adjective*
— **ideo·graph·i·cal·ly** \-fi-k(ə-)lē\ *adverb*

**ide·og·ra·phy** \ˌi-dē-'ä-grə-fē, ˌī-\ *noun* (1836)
**1** : the use of ideograms
**2** : the representation of ideas by graphic symbols

**ideo·log·i·cal** \ˌī-dē-ə-'lä-ji-kəl, ˌi-\ *also* **ideo·log·ic** \-'lä-jik\ *adjective* (1797)
**1** : relating to or concerned with ideas
**2** : of, relating to, or based on ideology
— **ideo·log·i·cal·ly** \-'lä-ji-k(ə-)lē\ *adverb*

**ide·ol·o·gize** \ˌī-dē-'ä-lə-ˌjīz, ˌi-\ *transitive verb* **-gized; -giz·ing** (1860)
: to give an ideological character or interpretation to; *especially* : to change or interpret in relation to a sociopolitical ideology often seen as biased or limited

**ideo·logue** *also* **idea·logue** \'ī-dē-ə-ˌlóg, -ˌläg\ *noun* [French *idéologue*, back-formation from *idéologie*] (1815)
**1** : an impractical idealist : THEORIST
**2** : an often blindly partisan advocate or adherent of a particular ideology

\ə\ abut \ᵊ\ kitten \ər\ **further** \a\ ash \ā\ ace \ä\ mop, mar \aù\ out \ch\ chin \e\ bet \ē\ easy \g\ go \i\ hit \ī\ ice \j\ job \ŋ\ sing \ō\ go \ò\ law \ói\ boy \th\ thin \t͟h\ the \ü\ loot \ù\ foot \y\ yet \zh\ vision    *see also* Guide to Pronunciation

**ide·ol·o·gy** \ˌī-dē-'ä-lə-jē, ˌi-\ *also* **ide·al·o·gy** \-'ä-lə-jē, -'a-\ *noun, plural* **-gies** [French *idéologie,* from *idéo-* ideo- + *-logie* -logy] (1813)
**1 :** visionary theorizing
**2 a :** a systematic body of concepts especially about human life or culture **b :** a manner or the content of thinking characteristic of an individual, group, or culture **c :** the integrated assertions, theories and aims that constitute a sociopolitical program
— **ide·ol·o·gist** \-jist\ *noun*
**ideo·mo·tor** \ˌī-dē-ə-'mō-tər, ˌi-\ *adjective* [International Scientific Vocabulary] (1867)
**:** not reflex but motivated by an idea ⟨*ideomotor* muscular activity⟩
**ides** \'īdz\ *noun plural but singular or plural in construction* [Middle English, from Middle French, from Latin *idus*] (14th century)
**:** the 15th day of March, May, July, or October or the 13th day of any other month in the ancient Roman calendar; *broadly* **:** this day and the seven days preceding it
**-idin** *or* **-idine** *noun suffix* [International Scientific Vocabulary *-ide* + *-in, -ine*]
**:** chemical compound related in origin or structure to another compound ⟨tolu*idine*⟩ ⟨guan*idine*⟩
**idio-** *combining form* [Greek, from *idios* — more at IDIOT]
**:** one's own **:** personal **:** separate **:** distinct ⟨*idio*blast⟩
**id·i·o·blast** \'i-dē-ə-ˌblast\ *noun* [International Scientific Vocabulary] (1822)
**:** a plant cell (as a sclereid) that differs markedly from neighboring cells
— **id·io·blas·tic** \ˌi-dē-ə-'blas-tik\ *adjective*
**id·i·o·cy** \'i-dē-ə-sē\ *noun, plural* **-cies** (circa 1529)
**1 :** extreme mental retardation commonly due to incomplete or abnormal development of the brain
**2 :** something notably stupid or foolish
**id·i·o·graph·ic** \ˌi-dē-ə-'gra-fik\ *adjective* [International Scientific Vocabulary] (circa 1890)
**:** relating to or dealing with something concrete, individual, or unique
**id·i·o·lect** \'i-dē-ə-ˌlekt\ *noun* [idio- + -lect (as in *dialect*)] (1948)
**:** the language or speech pattern of one individual at a particular period of life
— **id·io·lec·tal** \ˌi-dē-ə-'lek-t³l\ *adjective*
**id·i·om** \'i-dē-əm\ *noun* [Middle French & Late Latin; Middle French *idiome,* from Late Latin *idioma* individual peculiarity of language, from Greek *idiōmat-, idiōma,* from *idiousthai* to appropriate, from *idios*] (1588)
**1 a :** the language peculiar to a people or to a district, community, or class **:** DIALECT **b :** the syntactical, grammatical, or structural form peculiar to a language
**2 :** an expression in the usage of a language that is peculiar to itself either grammatically (as *no, it wasn't me*) or in having a meaning that cannot be derived from the conjoined meanings of its elements (as *Monday week* for "the Monday a week after next Monday")
**3 :** a style or form of artistic expression that is characteristic of an individual, a period or movement, or a medium or instrument ⟨the modern jazz *idiom*⟩; *broadly* **:** MANNER, STYLE ⟨a new culinary *idiom*⟩
**id·i·o·mat·ic** \ˌi-dē-ə-'ma-tik\ *adjective* (1712)
**1 :** of, relating to, or conforming to idiom
**2 :** peculiar to a particular group, individual, or style
— **id·i·o·mat·i·cal·ly** \-ti-k(ə-)lē\ *adverb*
— **id·i·o·mat·ic·ness** \-tik-nəs\ *noun*
**id·i·o·mor·phic** \ˌi-dē-ə-'mȯr-fik\ *adjective* [Greek *idiomorphos,* from *idio-* + *-morphos* -morphous] (1887)
**:** having the proper form or shape — used of minerals whose crystalline growth has not been interfered with
**id·i·o·path·ic** \ˌi-dē-ə-'pa-thik\ *adjective* (1669)

**1 :** arising spontaneously or from an obscure or unknown cause **:** PRIMARY
**2 :** peculiar to the individual
— **id·i·o·path·i·cal·ly** \-'pa-thi-k(ə-)lē\ *adverb*
**id·i·o·syn·cra·sy** \ˌi-dē-ə-'siŋ-krə-sē\ *noun, plural* **-sies** [Greek *idiosynkrasia,* from *idio-* + *synkerannynai* to blend, from *syn-* + *kerannynai* to mingle, mix — more at CRATER] (1604)
**1 a :** a peculiarity of constitution or temperament **:** an individualizing characteristic or quality **b :** individual hypersensitiveness (as to a drug or food)
**2 :** characteristic peculiarity (as of temperament); *broadly* **:** ECCENTRICITY
— **id·i·o·syn·crat·ic** \ˌi-dē-ō-(ˌ)sin-'kra-tik\ *adjective*
— **id·i·o·syn·crat·i·cal·ly** \-'kra-ti-k(ə-)lē\ *adverb*
**id·i·ot** \'i-dē-ət\ *noun* [Middle English, from Latin *idiota* ignorant person, from Greek *idiōtēs* one in a private station, layman, ignorant person, from *idios* one's own, private; akin to Latin *suus* one's own — more at SUICIDE] (14th century)
**1 :** a person affected with idiocy; *especially* **:** a feebleminded person having a mental age not exceeding three years and requiring complete custodial care
**2 :** a foolish or stupid person ◆
— **idiot** *adjective*
**idiot box** *noun* (circa 1955)
**:** TELEVISION
**id·i·ot·ic** \ˌi-dē-'ä-tik\ *also* **id·i·ot·i·cal** \-'ä-ti-kəl\ *adjective* (1713)
**1 :** characterized by idiocy
**2 :** showing complete lack of thought or common sense **:** FOOLISH
— **id·i·ot·i·cal·ly** \-ti-k(ə-)lē\ *adverb*
**¹id·i·o·tism** \'i-dē-ə-ˌti-zəm\ *noun* [Middle French *idiotisme,* from Latin *idiotismus* common speech, from Greek *idiōtismos,* from *idiōtēs*] (1588)
**1** *obsolete* **:** IDIOM 1
**2 :** IDIOM 2
**²id·i·ot·ism** \'i-dē-ə-(ˌ)ti-zəm\ *noun* [idiot + -ism] (circa 1611)
*archaic* **:** IDIOCY 2
**idiot light** *noun* (1966)
**:** a colored light on an instrument panel (as of an automobile) designed to give a warning (as of low oil pressure)
**idiot sa·vant** \'ē-ˌdyō-sä-'vä^n, *or same as* IDIOT *and* SAVANT *for respective singular and plural forms*\ *noun, plural* **idiots savants** \-ˌdyō-sä-'vä^n(z)\ *or* **idiot savants** \-'vä^n(z)\ [French, literally, learned idiot] (1927)
**1 :** a mentally defective person who exhibits exceptional skill or brilliance in some limited field
**2 :** a person who is highly knowledgeable about one subject but knows little about anything else
**-idium** *noun suffix, plural* **-idiums** *or* **-idia** [New Latin, from Greek *-idion,* diminutive suffix]
**:** small one ⟨antherid*ium*⟩
**¹idle** \'ī-d³l\ *adjective* **idler** \'īd-lər, 'ī-d³l-ər\; **idlest** \'īd-ləst, 'ī-d³l-əst\ [Middle English *idel,* from Old English *īdel;* akin to Old High German *ītal* worthless] (before 12th century)
**1 :** lacking worth or basis **:** VAIN ⟨*idle* chatter⟩ ⟨*idle* pleasure⟩
**2 :** not occupied or employed: as **a :** having no employment **:** INACTIVE ⟨*idle* workers⟩ **b :** not turned to normal or appropriate use ⟨*idle* funds⟩ ⟨*idle* farmland⟩ **c :** not scheduled to compete ⟨the team will be *idle* tomorrow⟩
**3 a :** SHIFTLESS, LAZY **b :** having no evident lawful means of support
*synonym* see VAIN, INACTIVE
— **idle·ness** \'ī-d³l-nəs\ *noun*
— **idly** \'īd-lē, 'ī-d³l-ē\ *adverb*
**²idle** *verb* **idled; idling** \'īd-liŋ, 'ī-d³l-iŋ\ (1592)

*intransitive verb*
**1 a :** to spend time in idleness **b :** to move idly
**2 :** to run at low power and often disconnected usually so that power is not used for useful work ⟨the engine is *idling*⟩
*transitive verb*
**1 :** to pass in idleness
**2 :** to make idle ⟨workers *idled* by a strike⟩
**3 :** to cause to idle
— **idler** \'īd-lər, 'ī-d³l-ər\ *noun*
**idler pulley** *noun* (circa 1890)
**:** a guide or tightening pulley for a belt or chain
**idler wheel** *noun* (1805)
**1 :** a wheel, gear, or roller used to transfer motion or to guide or support something
**2 :** IDLER PULLEY

**idler wheel 1**

**idlesse** \'īd-ləs, īd-'les\ *noun* [Middle English, from *idle* + *-esse* (as in *richesse* wealth) — more at RICHES] (15th century)
**:** the quality or state of being idle **:** IDLENESS
**ido·crase** \'ī-də-ˌkrās, 'i-, -ˌkrāz\ *noun* [French, from Greek *eidos* form + *krasis* mixture, from *kerannynai* to mix — more at CRATER] (1804)
**:** a mineral that is a complex silicate of calcium, magnesium, iron, and aluminum
**idol** \'ī-d³l\ [Middle English, from Old French *idole,* from Late Latin *idolum,* from Greek *eidōlon* image, idol; akin to Greek *eidos* form — more at IDYLL] (13th century)
**1 :** a representation or symbol of an object of worship; *broadly* **:** a false god
**2 a :** a likeness of something **b** *obsolete* **:** PRETENDER, IMPOSTOR
**3 :** a form or appearance visible but without substance ⟨an enchanted phantom, a lifeless *idol* —P. B. Shelley⟩
**4 :** an object of extreme devotion ⟨a movie *idol*⟩; *also* **:** IDEAL 2
**5 :** a false conception **:** FALLACY
**idol·a·ter** *or* **idol·a·tor** \ī-'dä-lə-tər\ *noun* [Middle English, from Middle French *idolatrer,* from Late Latin *idololatres,* from Greek *eidōlolatrēs,* from *eidōlon* + *-latrēs* -later] (14th century)
**1 :** a worshiper of idols
**2 :** a person that admires intensely and often blindly one that is not usually a subject of worship
**idol·a·trous** \ī-'dä-lə-trəs\ *adjective* (1543)
**1 :** of or relating to idolatry
**2 :** having the character of idolatry ⟨the religion of *idolatrous* nationalism —Aldous Huxley⟩
**3 :** given to idolatry
— **idol·a·trous·ly** *adverb*

— **idol·a·trous·ness** *noun*

**idol·a·try** \-trē\ *noun, plural* **-tries** (13th century)
**1** : the worship of a physical object as a god
**2** : immoderate attachment or devotion to something

**idol·ize** \'ī-d°l-,īz\ *verb* **-ized; -iz·ing** (1598)
*transitive verb*
: to worship as a god; *broadly* : to love or admire to excess ⟨the common people whom he so *idolized* —*Times Literary Supplement*⟩
*intransitive verb*
: to practice idolatry
— **idol·i·za·tion** \,ī-d°l-ə-'zā-shən\ *noun*
— **idol·iz·er** \'ī-d°l-,ī-zər\ *noun*

**idyll** *also* **idyl** \'ī-d°l, *British usually* 'i-(,)dil\ *noun* [Latin *idyllium*, from Greek *eidyllion*, from diminutive of *eidos* form; akin to Greek *idein* to see — more at WIT] (1586)
**1 a** : a simple descriptive work in poetry or prose that deals with rustic life or pastoral scenes or suggests a mood of peace and contentment **b** : a narrative poem (as Tennyson's *Idylls of the King*) treating an epic, romantic, or tragic theme
**2 a** : a lighthearted carefree episode that is a fit subject for an idyll **b** : a romantic interlude

**idyl·lic** \ī-'di-lik, *chiefly British* i-\ *adjective* (1856)
**1** : of, relating to, or being an idyll
**2** : pleasing or picturesque in natural simplicity
— **idyl·li·cal·ly** \-'di-li-k(ə-)lē\ *adverb*

**-ie** *also* **-y** *noun suffix* [Middle English]
**1** : little one : dear little one ⟨bird*ie*⟩ ⟨sonny⟩
**2** : one belonging to : one having to do with ⟨town*ie*⟩ : one who is ⟨preem*ie*⟩
**3** : one of (such) a kind or quality ⟨cut*ie*⟩ ⟨tough*ie*⟩

**-ier** — see -ER

**¹if** \'if, əf\ *conjunction* [Middle English, from Old English *gif;* akin to Old High German *ibu* if] (before 12th century)
**1 a** : in the event that **b** : allowing that **c** : on the assumption that **d** : on condition that
**2** : WHETHER ⟨asked *if* the mail had come⟩ ⟨I doubt *if* I'll pass the course⟩
**3** — used as a function word to introduce an exclamation expressing a wish ⟨*if* it would only rain⟩
**4** : even though ⟨an interesting *if* untenable argument⟩
— **if anything** : on the contrary even : perhaps even ⟨*if anything,* you ought to apologize⟩

**²if** \'if\ *noun* (1513)
**1** : CONDITION, STIPULATION ⟨the question . . . depends on too many *ifs* to allow an answer —*Encounter*⟩
**2** : SUPPOSITION

**-iferous** *adjective combining form* [Middle English, from Latin *-ifer,* from *-i-* + *-fer* -ferous]
: -FEROUS

**iff** \'if-°n(d)-'ōn-lē-,if; 'if, *sometimes read with a prolonged* f\ *conjunction* [alteration of ¹*if*] (1955)
: if and only if ⟨two figures are congruent *iff* one can be placed over the other so that they coincide⟩

**if·fy** \'i-fē\ *adjective* [¹*if*] (1937)
: abounding in contingencies or unknown qualities or conditions : UNCERTAIN ⟨an *iffy* proposition⟩
— **if·fi·ness** *noun*

**-ification** *noun suffix* [Middle English *-ificacioun,* from Middle French & Latin; Middle French *-ification,* from Latin *-ification-, -ificatio,* from *-i-* + *-ficatio* -fication]
: -FICATION ⟨desert*ification*⟩

**-iform** *adjective combining form* [Middle French & Latin; Middle French *-iforme,* from Latin *-iformis,* from *-i-* + *-formis* -form]
: -FORM ⟨patell*iform*⟩

**I formation** *noun* (1951)
: an offensive football formation in which the running backs line up in a line directly behind the quarterback — compare T FORMATION

**-ify** *verb suffix* [Middle English *-ifien,* from Old French *-ifier,* from Latin *-ificare,* from *-i-* + *-ficare* -fy]
: -FY

**IgA** \,ī-(,)jē-'ā\ *noun* [immunoglobulin] (1969)
: a class of immunoglobulins found in external bodily secretions (as saliva, tears, and sweat)

**Ig·bo** \'ig-(,)bō\ *variant of* IBO

**IgE** \,ī-(,)jē-'ē\ *noun* (1969)
: a class of immunoglobulins that function especially in allergic reactions

**IgG** \-'jē\ *noun* (1969)
: a class of immunoglobulins that includes the most common antibodies circulating in the blood

**ig·loo** \'i-(,)glü\ *noun, plural* **igloos** [Inuit *iglu* house] (1856)
**1** : an Eskimo house usually made of sod, wood, or stone when permanent or of blocks of snow or ice in the shape of a dome when built for temporary purposes
**2** : a building or structure shaped like a dome

igloo 1

**IgM** \,ī-(,)jē-'em\ *noun* (1969)
: a class of immunoglobulins that includes antibodies that appear early in the immune response

**ig·ne·ous** \'ig-nē-əs\ *adjective* [Latin *igneus,* from *ignis* fire; akin to Sanskrit *agni* fire] (1664)
**1** : of, relating to, or resembling fire : FIERY
**2 a** : relating to, resulting from, or suggestive of the intrusion or extrusion of magma or volcanic activity **b** : formed by solidification of magma ⟨*igneous* rock⟩

**ig·nes·cent** \ig-'ne-s°nt\ *adjective* [Latin *ignescent-, ignescens,* present participle of *ignescere* to catch fire, from *ignis*] (circa 1828)
: VOLATILE

**ig·nim·brite** \'ig-nəm-,brīt\ *noun* [German *Ignimbrit,* from Latin *ignis* + *imbr-* (from *imber* rain) + German *-it* ¹-ite — more at IMBRICATE] (1932)
: a hard rock formed by solidification of chiefly fine deposits of volcanic ash

**ig·nis fat·u·us** \'ig-nəs-'fa-chə-wəs, -'fach-wəs\ *noun, plural* **ig·nes fat·ui** \-,nēz-'fa-chə-,wī\ [Medieval Latin, literally, foolish fire] (circa 1563)
**1** : a light that sometimes appears in the night over marshy ground and is often attributable to the combustion of gas from decomposed organic matter
**2** : a deceptive goal or hope

**ig·nite** \ig-'nīt\ *verb* **ig·nit·ed; ig·nit·ing** [Latin *ignitus,* past participle of *ignire* to ignite, from *ignis*] (1666)
*transitive verb*
**1** : to subject to fire or intense heat; *especially* : to render luminous by heat
**2 a** : to set afire; *also* : KINDLE **b** : to cause (a fuel) to burn
**3** : to heat up : EXCITE ⟨oppression that *ignited* the hatred of the people⟩
*intransitive verb*
**1** : to catch fire
**2** : to begin to glow
— **ig·nit·abil·i·ty** \ig-,nī-tə-'bi-lə-tē\ *noun*
— **ig·nit·able** *also* **ig·nit·ible** \-'nī-tə-bəl\ *adjective*
— **ig·nit·er** *also* **ig·ni·tor** \-'nī-tər\ *noun*

**ig·ni·tion** \ig-'ni-shən\ *noun* (1612)
**1** : the act or action of igniting: as **a** : the starting of a fire **b** : the heating of a plasma to a temperature high enough to sustain nuclear fusion
**2** : the process or means (as an electric spark) of igniting a fuel mixture

**ig·ni·tron** \ig-'nī-,trän\ *noun* [Latin *ignis* fire + English *-tron*] (1933)
: a mercury-containing rectifier tube in which the arc is struck again at the beginning of each cycle by a special electrode separately energized by an auxiliary circuit

**ig·no·ble** \ig-'nō-bəl\ *adjective* [Middle English, from Middle French, from Latin *ignobilis,* from *in-* + Old Latin *gnobilis* noble] (15th century)
**1** : of low birth or common origin : PLEBEIAN
**2** : characterized by baseness, lowness, or meanness
*synonym* see MEAN
— **ig·no·bil·i·ty** \,ig-nō-'bi-lə-tē\ *noun*
— **ig·no·ble·ness** \ig-'nō-bəl-nəs\ *noun*
— **ig·no·bly** \-blē *also* -bə-lē\ *adverb*

**ig·no·min·i·ous** \,ig-nə-'mi-nē-əs\ *adjective* (15th century)
**1** : marked with or characterized by disgrace or shame : DISHONORABLE
**2** : deserving of shame or infamy : DESPICABLE
**3** : HUMILIATING, DEGRADING ⟨suffered an *ignominious* defeat⟩
— **ig·no·min·i·ous·ly** *adverb*
— **ig·no·min·i·ous·ness** *noun*

**ig·no·mi·ny** \'ig-nə-,mi-nē, -mə-nē *also* ig-'nä-mə-nē\ *noun, plural* **-nies** [Middle French or Latin; Middle French *ignominie,* from Latin *ignominia,* from *ig-* (as in *ignorare* to be ignorant of, ignore) + *nomin-, nomen* name, repute — more at NAME] (1540)
**1** : deep personal humiliation and disgrace
**2** : disgraceful or dishonorable conduct, quality, or action
*synonym* see DISGRACE

**ig·no·ra·mus** \,ig-nə-'rā-məs *also* -'ra-\ *noun, plural* **-mus·es** *also* **-mi** \-mē\ [*Ignoramus,* ignorant lawyer in *Ignoramus* (1615), play by George Ruggle, from Latin, literally, we are ignorant of (it) (circa 1616)
: an utterly ignorant person : DUNCE ◆

**ig·no·rance** \'ig-n(ə-)rən(t)s\ *noun* (13th century)
: the state or fact of being ignorant

**ig·no·rant** \'ig-n(ə-)rənt\ *adjective* (14th century)
**1 a** : destitute of knowledge or education ⟨an *ignorant* society⟩; *also* : lacking knowledge or comprehension of the thing specified ⟨parents

*ignorant* of modern mathematics⟩ **b** : resulting from or showing lack of knowledge or intelligence ⟨*ignorant* errors⟩
**2** : UNAWARE, UNINFORMED ☆
— **ig·no·rant·ly** *adverb*
— **ig·no·rant·ness** *noun*
**ig·no·ra·tio elen·chi** \ˌig-nə-ˈrä-tē-ˌō-i-ˈleⁿ-ˌkē\ *noun* [Latin, literally, ignorance of proof] (1588)
: a fallacy in logic of supposing a point proved or disproved by an argument proving or disproving something not at issue
**ig·nore** \ig-ˈnōr, -ˈnȯr\ *transitive verb* **ig-nored; ig·nor·ing** [obsolete *ignore* to be ignorant of, from French *ignorer*, from Latin *ignorare*, from *ignarus* ignorant, unknown, from *in-* + *gnoscere, noscere* to know — more at KNOW] (1801)
**1** : to refuse to take notice of
**2** : to reject (a bill of indictment) as ungrounded
**synonym** see NEGLECT
— **ig·nor·able** \-ˈnȯr-ə-bəl, -ˈnȯr-\ *adjective*
— **ig·nor·er** *noun*
**Igo·rot** \ˌē-gə-ˈrōt\ *noun, plural* **Igorot** *or* **Igorots** (1821)
**1** : a member of any of several related peoples of northwestern Luzon, Philippines
**2** : any of the Austronesian languages of the Igorot
**Igraine** \i-ˈgrān\ *noun*
: the wife of Uther and mother of King Arthur
**igua·na** \i-ˈgwä-nə\ *noun* [Spanish, from Arawak & Carib *iwana*] (1555)
: any of various large herbivorous typically dark-colored tropical American lizards (family Iguanidae) that have a serrated dorsal crest and are important as human food in their native habitat; *broadly* : any of various large lizards

**iguana**

**iguan·odon** \i-ˈgwä-nə-ˌdän\ *noun* [New Latin *Iguanodont-, Iguanodon*, from Spanish *iguana* + Greek *odōn* tooth, from *odont-, odous* — more at TOOTH] (1830)
: any of a genus (*Iguanodon*) of very large herbivorous dinosaurs of the early Cretaceous
**IHS** \ˈī-ˌäch-ˈes\ [Late Latin, part transliteration of Greek IHΣ, abbreviation for IHΣOYΣ *Iēsous* Jesus]
— used as a Christian symbol and monogram for *Jesus*
**ikat** \ˈē-ˌkät\ *noun* [Malay, tying] (1927)
: a fabric in which the yarns have been tie-dyed before weaving
**ike·ba·na** \ˌi-kā-ˈbä-nə, ˌi-ki-, ˌē-\ *noun* [Japanese, from *ikeru* to keep alive, arrange + *hana* flower] (1901)
: the Japanese art of flower arranging that emphasizes form and balance
**ikon** *variant of* ICON
**il-** — see IN-
**ilang-ilang** *variant of* YLANG-YLANG
**¹-ile** *adjective suffix* [Middle English, from Middle French, from Latin *-ilis*]
: tending to or capable of ⟨contrac*tile*⟩
**²-ile** *noun suffix* [*-ile* (as in quar*tile*, noun)]
: segment of a (specified) size in a frequency distribution ⟨dec*ile*⟩
**il·e·i·tis** \ˌi-lē-ˈī-təs\ *noun* [New Latin] (circa 1855)
: inflammation of the ileum
**il·e·um** \ˈi-lē-əm\ *noun, plural* **il·ea** \-lē-ə\ [New Latin, alteration of Latin *ilia*, plural, groin, viscera] (1682)
: the last division of the small intestine extending between the jejunum and large intestine
— **il·e·al** \-lē-əl\ *adjective*
**il·e·us** \ˈi-lē-əs\ *noun* [Latin, from Greek *eileos*, from *eilyein* to roll — more at VOLUBLE] (1693)

: mechanical or functional obstruction of the bowel
**ilex** \ˈī-ˌleks\ *noun* [Middle English, from Latin] (14th century)
**1** : HOLM OAK
**2** : HOLLY 1
**il·i·ac** \ˈi-lē-ˌak\ *also* **il·i·al** \ˈi-lē-əl\ *adjective* [Late Latin *iliacus*, from Latin *ilium*] (1541)
: of, relating to, or located near the ilium
**Il·i·ad** \ˈi-lē-əd, -ˌad\ *noun* [*Iliad*, ancient Greek epic poem attributed to Homer, from Latin *Iliad-, Ilias*, from Greek, from *Ilion* Troy] (1603)
**1 a** : a series of miseries or disastrous events
**b** : a series of exploits regarded as suitable for an epic
**2** : a long narrative; *especially* : an epic in the Homeric tradition
— **Il·i·ad·ic** \ˌi-lē-ˈa-dik\ *adjective*
**il·i·um** \ˈi-lē-əm\ *noun, plural* **il·ia** \-lē-ə\ [New Latin, alteration of Latin *ilia*] (1706)
: the dorsal, upper, and largest one of the three bones composing either lateral half of the pelvis
**¹ilk** \ˈilk\ *pronoun* [Middle English, from Old English *ilca*, from a prehistoric compound whose constituents are akin respectively to Gothic *is* he (akin to Latin *is* he, that) and Old English *gelīc* like — more at ITERATE, LIKE] (before 12th century)
*chiefly Scottish* : SAME — used with *that* especially in the names of landed families
**²ilk** *noun* (1790)
: SORT, KIND ⟨the rejection of these books or others of like *ilk* —Kathleen Molz⟩
**³ilk** *pronoun* [Middle English, adjective & pronoun, from Old English *ylc, ælc* — more at EACH] (before 12th century)
*chiefly Scottish* : EACH
**il·ka** \ˈil-kə\ *adjective* [Middle English, from *ilk* + *a* (indefinite article)] (13th century)
*chiefly Scottish* : EACH, EVERY
**¹ill** \ˈil\ *adjective* **worse** \ˈwərs\; **worst** \ˈwərst\ [Middle English, from Old Norse *illr*] (12th century)
**1 a** *chiefly Scottish* : IMMORAL, VICIOUS **b** : resulting from, accompanied by, or indicative of an evil or malevolent intention ⟨*ill* deeds⟩ **c** : attributing evil or an objectionable quality ⟨held an *ill* opinion of his neighbors⟩
**2 a** : causing suffering or distress ⟨*ill* weather⟩ **b** *comparative also* **ill·er** (1) : not normal or sound ⟨*ill* health⟩ (2) : not in good health; *also* : NAUSEATED
**3 a** : not suited to circumstances or not to one's advantage : UNLUCKY ⟨an *ill* omen⟩ **b** : involving difficulty : HARD ⟨an *ill* man to please⟩
**4 a** : not meeting an accepted standard ⟨*ill* manners⟩ **b** *archaic* : notably unskillful or inefficient
**5** : UNFRIENDLY, HOSTILE ⟨*ill* feeling⟩
**²ill** *adverb* **worse; worst** (13th century)
**1 a** : with displeasure or hostility **b** : in a harsh manner **c** : so as to reflect unfavorably ⟨spoke *ill* of the neighbors⟩
**2** : in a reprehensible manner
**3** : HARDLY, SCARCELY ⟨can *ill* afford such extravagances⟩
**4 a** : in an unfortunate manner : BADLY, UNLUCKILY ⟨*ill* fares the land . . . where wealth accumulates, and men decay —Oliver Goldsmith⟩ **b** : in a faulty, inefficient, insufficient, or unpleasant manner — often used in combination ⟨the methods used may be *ill*-adapted to the aims in view —R. M. Hutchins⟩
**³ill** *noun* (13th century)
**1** : the reverse of good : EVIL
**2 a** : MISFORTUNE, DISTRESS **b** (1) : AILMENT, SICKNESS (2) : something that disturbs or afflicts : TROUBLE ⟨economic and social *ills*⟩
**3** : something that reflects unfavorably ⟨spoke no *ill* of him⟩
**I'll** \ˈī(ə)l\ (1567)
: I will : I shall

**ill-ad·vised** \ˌi-ləd-ˈvīzd\ *adjective* (circa 1592)
: resulting from or showing lack of wise and sufficient counsel or deliberation ⟨an *ill*-advised decision⟩
— **ill-ad·vis·ed·ly** \-ˈvī-zəd-lē\ *adverb*
**ill at ease** *adjective* (14th century)
: not feeling easy : UNCOMFORTABLE
**il·la·tion** \i-ˈlā-shən\ *noun* [Late Latin *illation-, illatio*, from Latin, action of bringing in, from *inferre* (past participle *illatus*) to bring in, from *in-* + *ferre* to carry — more at TOLERATE, BEAR] (1533)
**1** : the action of inferring : INFERENCE
**2** : a conclusion inferred
**¹il·la·tive** \ˈi-lə-tiv, i-ˈlā-\ *adjective* (1591)
**1** : a word (as *therefore*) or phrase (as *as a consequence*) introducing an inference
**2** : ILLATION 2
**²illative** *adjective* (1611)
: INFERENTIAL
— **il·la·tive·ly** *adverb*
**il·laud·able** \(ˌ)i(l)-ˈlȯ-də-bəl\ *adjective* [Latin *illaudabilis*, from *in-* + *laudabilis* laudable] (1589)
: deserving no praise
— **il·laud·ably** \-blē\ *adverb*
**ill-be·ing** \ˈil-ˈbē-iŋ\ *noun* (1840)
: a condition of being deficient in health, happiness, or prosperity
**ill-bod·ing** \-ˈbō-diŋ\ *adjective* (1591)
: boding evil : INAUSPICIOUS
**ill-bred** \-ˈbred\ *adjective* (1604)
: badly brought up or showing bad upbringing : IMPOLITE
**¹il·le·gal** \(ˌ)i(l)-ˈlē-gəl\ *adjective* [Middle French or Medieval Latin; Middle French *illegal*, from Medieval Latin *illegalis*, from Latin *in-* + *legalis* legal] (1538)
: not according to or authorized by law : UNLAWFUL, ILLICIT; *also* : not sanctioned by official rules (as of a game)
— **il·le·gal·i·ty** \ˌi-li-ˈga-lə-tē\ *noun*
— **il·le·gal·ly** \(ˌ)i(l)-ˈlē-gə-lē\ *adverb*
**²illegal** *noun* (1939)
: an illegal immigrant
**il·le·gal·ize** \(ˌ)i(l)-ˈlē-gə-ˌlīz\ *transitive verb* (circa 1818)
: to make or declare illegal
— **il·le·gal·i·za·tion** \-ˌlē-gə-lə-ˈzā-shən\ *noun*
**il·leg·i·ble** \(ˌ)i(l)-ˈle-jə-bəl\ *adjective* (1640)
: not legible : UNDECIPHERABLE ⟨*illegible* writing⟩
— **il·leg·i·bil·i·ty** \-ˌle-jə-ˈbi-lə-tē\ *noun*
— **il·leg·i·bly** \-ˈle-jə-blē\ *adverb*
**il·le·git·i·ma·cy** \ˌi-li-ˈji-tə-mə-sē\ *noun* (1680)
**1** : the quality or state of being illegitimate
**2** : BASTARDY 2
**il·le·git·i·mate** \-ˈji-tə-mət\ *adjective* (1536)
**1** : not recognized as lawful offspring; *specifically* : born of parents not married to each other
**2** : not rightly deduced or inferred : ILLOGICAL

---

☆ **SYNONYMS**
**Ignorant, illiterate, unlettered, untutored, unlearned** mean not having knowledge. IGNORANT may imply a general condition or it may apply to lack of knowledge or awareness of a particular thing ⟨an *ignorant* fool⟩ ⟨*ignorant* of nuclear physics⟩. ILLITERATE applies to either an absolute or a relative inability to read and write ⟨much of the population is still *illiterate*⟩. UNLETTERED implies ignorance of the knowledge gained by reading ⟨an allusion meaningless to the *unlettered*⟩. UNTUTORED may imply lack of schooling in the arts and ways of civilization ⟨strange monuments built by an *untutored* people⟩. UNLEARNED suggests ignorance of advanced subjects ⟨poetry not for academics but for the *unlearned* masses⟩.

**3** : departing from the regular : ERRATIC
**4 a** : not sanctioned by law : ILLEGAL **b** : not authorized by good usage **c** *of a taxon* : published but not in accordance with the rules of the relevant international code
— **il·le·git·i·mate·ly** *adverb*

**ill-fat·ed** \'il-'fā-təd\ *adjective* (1710)
**1** : having or destined to a hapless fate : UNFORTUNATE ⟨an *ill-fated* expedition⟩
**2** : that causes or marks the beginning of misfortune

**ill-fa·vored** \-'fā-vərd\ *adjective* (circa 1530)
**1** : unattractive in physical appearance; *especially* : having an ugly face
**2** : OFFENSIVE, OBJECTIONABLE

**ill-got·ten** \-'gä-t°n\ *adjective* (1552)
: acquired by illicit or improper means ⟨*ill-gotten* gains⟩

**ill-hu·mored** \'il-'hyü-mərd, -'yü-\ *adjective* (1687)
: SURLY, IRRITABLE
— **ill-hu·mored·ly** *adverb*

**il·lib·er·al** \(,)i(l)-'li-b(ə-)rəl\ *adjective* [Middle French or Latin; Middle French, from Latin *illiberalis* ignoble, stingy, from Latin *in-* + *liberalis* liberal] (1535)
: not liberal: as **a** *archaic* (1) : lacking a liberal education (2) : lacking culture and refinement **b** : not requiring the background of a liberal arts education ⟨*illiberal* occupations⟩ **c** *archaic* : not generous : STINGY **d** : not broadminded : BIGOTED **e** : opposed to liberalism
— **il·lib·er·al·i·ty** \-,li-bə-'ra-lə-tē\ *noun*
— **il·lib·er·al·ly** \-'li-b(ə-)rə-lē\ *adverb*
— **il·lib·er·al·ness** \-b(ə-)rəl-nəs\ *noun*

**il·lib·er·al·ism** \-b(ə-)rə-,li-zəm\ *noun* (1839)
: opposition to or lack of liberalism

**il·lic·it** \(,)i(l)-'li-sət\ *adjective* [Latin *illicitus*, from *in-* + *licitus* lawful — more at LICIT] (1506)
: not permitted : UNLAWFUL
— **il·lic·it·ly** *adverb*

**il·lim·it·able** \(,)i(l)-'li-mə-tə-bəl\ *adjective* (1596)
: incapable of being limited or bounded : MEASURELESS ⟨the *illimitable* reaches of space and time⟩
— **il·lim·it·abil·i·ty** \-,li-mə-tə-'bi-lə-tē\ *noun*
— **il·lim·it·able·ness** \-'li-mə-tə-bəl-nəs\ *noun*
— **il·lim·it·ably** \-blē\ *adverb*

**Il·li·nois** \,i-lə-'nöi *also* -'nöiz\ *noun, plural* **Illinois** [French, of Algonquian origin] (1703)
**1** *plural* : a confederacy of American Indian peoples of Illinois, Iowa, and Wisconsin
**2** : a member of any of the Illinois peoples

**il·liq·uid** \(,)i(l)-'lik-wəd\ *adjective* (1913)
**1** : not being cash or readily convertible into cash ⟨*illiquid* holdings⟩
**2** : deficient in liquid assets ⟨an *illiquid* bank⟩
— **il·li·quid·i·ty** \-,li-'kwi-də-tē\ *noun*

**il·lite** \'i-,līt\ *noun* [*Illinois*, state of U.S. + ¹-*ite*] (1937)
: any of a group of clay minerals having essentially the crystal structure of muscovite
— **il·lit·ic** \i-'li-tik\ *adjective*

**il·lit·er·a·cy** \(,)i(l)-'li-t(ə-)rə-sē\ *noun, plural* **-cies** (1660)
**1** : the quality or state of being illiterate; *especially* : inability to read or write
**2** : a mistake or crudity (as in speaking) typical of one who is illiterate

**il·lit·er·ate** \(,)i(l)-'li-t(ə-)rət\ *adjective* [Middle English, from Latin *illiteratus*, from *in-* + *litteratus* literate] (15th century)
**1** : having little or no education; *especially* : unable to read or write
**2 a** : showing or marked by a lack of familiarity with language and literature **b** : violating approved patterns of speaking or writing
**3** : showing or marked by a lack of acquaintance with the fundamentals of a particular field of knowledge
**synonym** see IGNORANT
— **illiterate** *noun*

— **il·lit·er·ate·ly** *adverb*
— **il·lit·er·ate·ness** *noun*

**ill-man·nered** \'il-'ma-nərd\ *adjective* (15th century)
: having bad manners : RUDE

**ill-na·tured** \-'nā-chərd\ *adjective* (1605)
**1** : MALEVOLENT, SPITEFUL
**2** : having a bad disposition : CROSS, SURLY
— **ill-na·tured·ly** *adverb*

**ill·ness** \'il-nəs\ *noun* (circa 1500)
**1** *obsolete* **a** : WICKEDNESS **b** : UNPLEASANTNESS
**2 a** : an unhealthy condition of body or mind **b** : SICKNESS 2

**il·lo·cu·tion·ary** \,i-lə-'kyü-shə-,ner-ē, ,i(l)-lō-\ *adjective* [²*in-* + *locution*] (1955)
: relating to or being the communicative effect (as commanding or requesting) of an utterance ⟨"There's a snake under you" may have the *illocutionary* force of a warning⟩

**il·log·ic** \(,)i(l)-'lä-jik\ *noun* [back-formation from *illogical*] (1856)
: the quality or state of being illogical : ILLOGICALITY

**il·log·i·cal** \-ji-kəl\ *adjective* (1588)
**1** : not observing the principles of logic
**2** : devoid of logic : SENSELESS
— **il·log·i·cal·i·ty** \-,lä-jə-'ka-lə-tē\ *noun*
— **il·log·i·cal·ly** \-'lä-ji-k(ə-)lē\ *adverb*
— **il·log·i·cal·ness** \-kəl-nəs\ *noun*

**ill-sort·ed** \'il-'sör-təd\ *adjective* (1691)
**1** : not well matched ⟨he and his wife were an *ill-sorted* pair —Lord Byron⟩
**2** *Scottish* : much displeased

**ill-starred** \-'stärd\ *adjective* (1604)
: ILL-FATED, UNLUCKY ⟨an *ill-starred* venture⟩

**ill-tem·pered** \-'tem-pərd\ *adjective* (1601)
: ILL-NATURED, QUARRELSOME
— **ill-tem·pered·ly** \-lē\ *adverb*

**ill-treat** \-'trēt\ *transitive verb* (1689)
: to treat cruelly or improperly : MALTREAT
— **ill-treat·ment** \-mənt\ *noun*

**il·lume** \i-'lüm\ *transitive verb* **il·lumed; il·lum·ing** (1602)
: ILLUMINATE

**il·lu·mi·nance** \i-'lü-mə-nən(t)s\ *noun* (circa 1938)
: ILLUMINATION 2

**il·lu·mi·nant** \-nənt\ *noun* (1644)
: an illuminating device or substance

¹**il·lu·mi·nate** \i-'lü-mə-nət\ *adjective* (15th century)
**1** *archaic* : brightened with light
**2** *archaic* : intellectually or spiritually enlightened

²**il·lu·mi·nate** \-,nāt\ *transitive verb* **-nat·ed; -nat·ing** [Middle English, from Latin *illuminatus*, past participle of *illuminare*, from *in-* + *luminare* to light up, from *lumin-, lumen* light — more at LUMINARY] (15th century)
**1 a** : to enlighten spiritually or intellectually **b** (1) : to supply or brighten with light (2) : to make luminous or shining **c** *archaic* : to set alight **d** : to subject to radiation
**2** : to make clear : ELUCIDATE
**3** : to make illustrious or resplendent
**4** : to decorate (as a manuscript) with gold or silver or brilliant colors or with often elaborate designs or miniature pictures
— **il·lu·mi·nat·ing·ly** \-,nā-tiŋ-lē\ *adverb*
— **il·lu·mi·na·tor** \-,nā-tər\ *noun*

³**il·lu·mi·nate** \-nət\ *noun* (1600)
*archaic* : one having or claiming unusual enlightenment

**il·lu·mi·na·ti** \i-,lü-mə-'nä-tē\ *noun plural* [Italian & New Latin; Italian, from New Latin, from Latin, plural of *illuminatus*] (1599)
**1** *capitalized* : any of various groups claiming special religious enlightenment
**2** : persons who are or who claim to be unusually enlightened

**il·lu·mi·na·tion** \i-,lü-mə-'nā-shən\ *noun* (14th century)

**1** : the action of illuminating or state of being illuminated: as **a** : spiritual or intellectual enlightenment **b** (1) : a lighting up (2) : decorative lighting or lighting effects **c** : decoration by the art of illuminating
**2** : the luminous flux per unit area on an intercepting surface at any given point
**3** : one of the decorative features used in the art of illuminating or in decorative lighting

**il·lu·mi·na·tive** \i-'lü-mə-,nā-tiv\ *adjective* (1644)
: of, relating to, or producing illumination : ILLUMINATING

**il·lu·mine** \i-'lü-mən\ *transitive verb* **-mined; -min·ing** (14th century)
: ILLUMINATE
— **il·lu·min·able** \-mə-nə-bəl\ *adjective*

**il·lu·mi·nism** \-mə-,ni-zəm\ *noun* (1798)
**1** : belief in or claim to a personal enlightenment not accessible to mankind in general
**2** *capitalized* : beliefs or claims viewed as forming doctrine or principles of Illuminati
— **il·lu·mi·nist** \-nist\ *noun*

**ill-us·age** \'il-'yü-sij, -zij\ *noun* (1593)
: harsh, unkind, or abusive treatment

**ill-use** \-'yüz\ *transitive verb* (1841)
: to use badly : MALTREAT, ABUSE

**il·lu·sion** \i-'lü-zhən\ *noun* [Middle English, from Middle French, from Late Latin *illusion-, illusio*, from Latin, action of mocking, from *illudere* to mock at, from *in-* + *ludere* to play, mock — more at LUDICROUS] (14th century)
**1 a** *obsolete* : the action of deceiving **b** (1) : the state or fact of being intellectually deceived or misled : MISAPPREHENSION (2) : an instance of such deception

illusion 2a(1): *a* and *b* are equal in length

**2 a** (1) : a misleading image presented to the vision (2) : something that deceives or misleads intellectually **b** (1) : perception of something objectively existing in such a way as to cause misinterpretation of its actual nature (2) : HALLUCINATION 1 (3) : a pattern capable of reversible perspective
**3** : a fine plain transparent bobbinet or tulle usually made of silk and used for veils, trimmings, and dresses
— **il·lu·sion·al** \-'lüzh-nəl, -'lü-zhə-n°l\ *adjective*

**il·lu·sion·ary** \i-'lü-zhə-,ner-ē\ *adjective* (1886)
: ILLUSORY

**il·lu·sion·ism** \i-'lü-zhə-,ni-zəm\ *noun* (1911)
: the use of artistic techniques (as perspective or shading) to create the illusion of reality especially in a work of art

**il·lu·sion·ist** \i-'lüzh-nist, -'lü-zhə-\ *noun* (1850)
: one who produces illusory effects: as **a** : one (as an artist) whose work is marked by illusionism **b** : a sleight-of-hand performer or a magician
— **il·lu·sion·is·tic** \-,lü-zhə-'nis-tik\ *adjective*
— **il·lu·sion·is·ti·cal·ly** \-ti-k(ə-)lē\ *adverb*

**il·lu·sive** \i-'lü-siv, -ziv\ *adjective* (1606)
: ILLUSORY
— **il·lu·sive·ly** *adverb*
— **il·lu·sive·ness** *noun*

**il·lu·so·ry** \i-'lüs-rē, -'lüz-; -'lü-sə-, -zə-\ *adjective* (circa 1631)

: based on or producing illusion : DECEPTIVE ⟨*illusory* hopes⟩
**synonym** see APPARENT
— **il·lu·so·ri·ly** \-rə-lē\ *adverb*
— **il·lu·so·ri·ness** \-rē-nəs\ *noun*
**il·lus·trate** \'i-ləs-ˌtrāt *also* i-'ləs-\ *verb* **-trat·ed; -trat·ing** [Latin *illustratus*, past participle of *illustrare*, from *in-* + *lustrare* to purify, make bright — more at LUSTER] (1526)
*transitive verb*
**1** *obsolete* **a :** ENLIGHTEN **b :** to light up
**2 a** *archaic* **:** to make illustrious **b** *obsolete* (1) **:** to make bright (2) **:** ADORN
**3 a :** to make clear **:** CLARIFY **b :** to make clear by giving or by serving as an example or instance **c :** to provide with visual features intended to explain or decorate ⟨*illustrate* a book⟩
**4 :** to show clearly **:** DEMONSTRATE
*intransitive verb*
**:** to give an example or instance
— **il·lus·tra·tor** \'i-ləs-ˌtrā-tər *also* i-'ləs-\ *noun*
**il·lus·tra·tion** \ˌi-ləs-'trā-shən *also* i-ˌləs-\ *noun* (14th century)
**1 a :** the action of illustrating **:** the condition of being illustrated **b** *archaic* **:** the action of making illustrious or honored or distinguished
**2 :** something that serves to illustrate: as **a :** an example or instance that helps make something clear **b :** a picture or diagram that helps make something clear or attractive
**synonym** see INSTANCE
— **il·lus·tra·tion·al** \-shnəl, -shə-nᵊl\ *adjective*
**il·lus·tra·tive** \i-'ləs-trə-tiv *also* 'i-lə-ˌstrā-\ *adjective* (1643)
**:** serving, tending, or designed to illustrate ⟨*illustrative* examples⟩
— **il·lus·tra·tive·ly** *adverb*
**il·lus·tri·ous** \i-'ləs-trē-əs\ *adjective* [Latin *illustris*, probably from *illustrare*] (1588)
**1 :** notably or brilliantly outstanding because of dignity or achievements or actions **:** EMINENT
**2** *archaic* **a :** shining brightly with light **b :** clearly evident
**synonym** see FAMOUS
— **il·lus·tri·ous·ly** *adverb*
— **il·lus·tri·ous·ness** *noun*
**il·lu·vi·al** \i-'lü-vē-əl\ *adjective* (1924)
**:** of, relating to, or marked by illuviation or illuviated materials or areas
**il·lu·vi·a·tion** \i-ˌlü-vē-'ā-shən\ *noun* [²*in-* + *-luviation* (as in *eluviation*)] (1928)
**:** accumulation of dissolved or suspended soil materials in one area or horizon as a result of eluviation from another
— **il·lu·vi·at·ed** \i-'lü-vē-ˌā-təd\ *adjective*
**ill will** *noun* (14th century)
**:** unfriendly feeling
**synonym** see MALICE
**ill-wish·er** \'il-ˌwi-shər, -'wi-\ *noun* (1607)
**:** one that wishes ill to another
**il·ly** \'i(l)-lē\ *adverb* (15th century)
**:** not wisely or well **:** BADLY, ILL ⟨his *illy* concealed pride —Della Lutes⟩
**Il·lyr·i·an** \i-'lir-ē-ən\ *noun* (1584)
**1 :** a native or inhabitant of ancient Illyria
**2 :** the poorly attested Indo-European languages of the Illyrians — see INDO-EUROPEAN LANGUAGES table
— **Illyrian** *adjective*
**il·men·ite** \'il-mə-ˌnīt\ *noun* [German *Ilmenit*, from *Ilmen* range, Ural Mts., Russia] (circa 1827)
**:** a usually massive iron-black mineral composed of iron, titanium, and oxygen that is a titanium ore
**Ilo·ca·no** *or* **Ilo·ka·no** \ˌē-lə-'kä-(ˌ)nō, ˌi-\ *noun, plural* **Ilocano** *or* **Ilocanos** *or* **Ilokano** *or* **Ilokanos** (1898)
**1 :** a member of a major people of northern Luzon in the Philippines
**2 :** the Austronesian language of the Ilocano people

**im-** — see IN-
**I'm** \'īm\ (circa 1594)
**:** I am
¹**im·age** \'i-mij\ *noun* [Middle English, from Old French, short for *imagene*, from Latin *imagin-, imago*; perhaps akin to Latin *imitari* to imitate] (13th century)
**1 :** a reproduction or imitation of the form of a person or thing; *especially* **:** an imitation in solid form **:** STATUE
**2 a :** the optical counterpart of an object produced by an optical device (as a lens or mirror) or an electronic device **b :** a likeness of an object produced on a photographic material
**3 a :** exact likeness **:** SEMBLANCE ⟨God created man in his own *image* —Genesis 1:27 (Revised Standard Version)⟩ **b :** a person strikingly like another person ⟨she is the *image* of her mother⟩
**4 a :** a tangible or visible representation **:** INCARNATION ⟨the *image* of filial devotion⟩ **b** *archaic* **:** an illusory form **:** APPARITION
**5 a** (1) **:** a mental picture of something not actually present **:** IMPRESSION (2) **:** a mental conception held in common by members of a group and symbolic of a basic attitude and orientation ⟨a disorderly courtroom can seriously tarnish a community's *image* of justice —Herbert Brownell⟩ **b :** IDEA, CONCEPT
**6 :** a vivid or graphic representation or description
**7 :** FIGURE OF SPEECH
**8 :** a popular conception (as of a person, institution, or nation) projected especially through the mass media ⟨promoting a corporate *image* of brotherly love and concern —R. C. Buck⟩
**9 :** a set of values given by a mathematical function (as a homomorphism) that corresponds to a particular subset of the domain
²**image** *transitive verb* **im·aged; im·ag·ing** (14th century)
**1 :** to call up a mental picture of **:** IMAGINE
**2 :** to describe or portray in language especially in a vivid manner
**3 a :** to create a representation of; *also* **:** to form an image of **b :** to represent symbolically
**4 a :** REFLECT, MIRROR **b :** to make appear **:** PROJECT
— **im·ag·er** \'i-mi-jər\ *noun*
**image orthicon** *noun* (1945)
**:** a highly sensitive television image tube
**im·ag·ery** \'i-mij-rē, -mi-jə-\ *noun, plural* **-er·ies** (14th century)
**1 a :** the product of image makers **:** IMAGES; *also* **:** the art of making images **b :** pictures produced by an imaging system
**2 :** figurative language
**3 :** mental images; *especially* **:** the products of imagination
**image tube** *noun* (1936)
**:** an electron tube in which incident electromagnetic radiation (as light or infrared) produces a visible image on its fluorescent screen duplicating the original pattern of radiation — called also **image converter**
**imag·in·able** \i-'maj-nə-bəl, -'ma-jə-\ *adjective* (14th century)
**:** capable of being imagined **:** CONCEIVABLE
— **imag·in·able·ness** *noun*
— **imag·in·ably** \-blē\ *adverb*
¹**imag·i·nal** \i-'ma-jə-nᵊl\ *adjective* [*imagine* + ¹*-al*] (1647)
**:** of or relating to imagination, images, or imagery
²**ima·gi·nal** \i-'ma-jə-nᵊl, -'mā-; -'mä-gə-\ *adjective* [New Latin *imagin-, imago*] (1877)
**:** of or relating to the insect imago
**imag·i·nary** \i-'ma-jə-ˌner-ē\ *adjective* (14th century)
**1 a :** existing only in imagination **:** lacking factual reality **b :** formed or characterized imaginatively or arbitrarily ⟨his canvases, chiefly *imaginary*, somber landscapes —*Current Biography*⟩ ☆
**2 :** containing or relating to the imaginary unit ⟨*imaginary* roots⟩ ☆

— **imag·i·nari·ly** \i-ˌma-jə-'ner-ə-lē\ *adverb*
— **imag·i·nari·ness** \-'ma-jə-ˌner-ē-nəs\ *noun*
**imaginary number** *noun* (circa 1911)
**:** a complex number (as 2 + 3*i*) in which the coefficient of the imaginary unit is not zero — called also *imaginary;* compare PURE IMAGINARY
**imaginary part** *noun* (circa 1929)
**:** the part of a complex number (as 3*i* in 2 + 3*i*) that has the imaginary unit as a factor
**imaginary unit** *noun* (circa 1911)
**:** the positive square root of minus 1 denoted by *i* or + $\sqrt{-1}$
**imag·i·na·tion** \i-ˌma-jə-'nā-shən\ *noun* [Middle English, from Middle French, from Latin *imagination-, imaginatio*, from *imaginari*] (14th century)
**1 :** the act or power of forming a mental image of something not present to the senses or never before wholly perceived in reality
**2 a :** creative ability **b :** ability to confront and deal with a problem **:** RESOURCEFULNESS **c :** the thinking or active mind **:** INTEREST ⟨stories that fired the *imagination*⟩
**3 a :** a creation of the mind; *especially* **:** an idealized or poetic creation **b :** fanciful or empty assumption
**imag·i·na·tive** \i-'maj-nə-tiv; -'ma-jə-ˌnā-, -nə-\ *adjective* (14th century)
**1 a :** of, relating to, or characterized by imagination **b :** devoid of truth **:** FALSE
**2 :** given to imagining **:** having a lively imagination
**3 :** of or relating to images; *especially* **:** showing a command of imagery
— **imag·i·na·tive·ly** *adverb*
— **imag·i·na·tive·ness** *noun*
**imag·ine** \i-'ma-jən\ *verb* **imag·ined; imag·in·ing** \-'maj-niŋ, -'ma-jə-\ [Middle English, from Middle French *imaginer*, from Latin *imaginari*, from *imagin-, imago* image] (14th century)
*transitive verb*
**1 :** to form a mental image of (something not present)
**2** *archaic* **:** PLAN, SCHEME
**3 :** SUPPOSE, GUESS ⟨I *imagine* it will rain⟩
**4 :** to form a notion of without sufficient basis **:** FANCY ⟨*imagines* himself to be a charming conversationalist⟩
*intransitive verb*
**1 :** to use the imagination
**2 :** BELIEVE 3
**synonym** see THINK
**im·ag·ing** \'i-mi-jiŋ\ *noun* (1967)
**:** the action or process of producing an image especially by means other than visible light ⟨acoustic *imaging*⟩ — compare MAGNETIC RESONANCE IMAGING
**im·ag·ism** \'i-mi-ˌji-zəm\ *noun, often capitalized* (1912)

---

☆ **SYNONYMS**
**Imaginary, fanciful, visionary, fantastic, chimerical, quixotic** mean unreal or unbelievable. IMAGINARY applies to something which is fictitious and purely the product of one's imagination ⟨an *imaginary* desert isle⟩. FANCIFUL suggests the free play of the imagination ⟨a teller of *fanciful* stories⟩. VISIONARY stresses impracticality or incapability of realization ⟨*visionary* schemes⟩. FANTASTIC implies incredibility or strangeness beyond belief ⟨a *fantastic* world inhabited by monsters⟩. CHIMERICAL combines the implication of VISIONARY and FANTASTIC ⟨*chimerical* dreams of future progress⟩. QUIXOTIC implies a devotion to romantic or chivalrous ideals unrestrained by ordinary prudence and common sense ⟨a *quixotic* crusade⟩.

: a 20th century movement in poetry advocating free verse and the expression of ideas and emotions through clear precise images

— **im·ag·ist** \-mi-jist\ *noun or adjective, often capitalized*

— **im·ag·is·tic** \ˌi-mi-'jis-tik\ *adjective*

— **im·ag·is·ti·cal·ly** \-ti-k(ə-)lē\ *adverb*

**ima·go** \i-'mä-(ˌ)gō, -'mä-\ *noun, plural* **ima·goes** *or* **ima·gi·nes** \-'mä-gə-ˌnēz, -'mä-; -'mä-jə-, -'ma-\ [New Latin, from Latin, image] (circa 1797)

**1** : an insect in its final, adult, sexually mature, and typically winged state

**2** : an idealized mental image of another person or the self

*word history* see LARVA

**imam** \i-'mäm, ē-', -'mam\ *noun, often capitalized* [Arabic *imām*] (1613)

**1** : the prayer leader of a mosque

**2** : a Muslim leader of the line of Ali held by Shiites to be the divinely appointed, sinless, infallible successors of Muhammad

**3** : any of various rulers that claim descent from Muhammad and exercise spiritual and temporal leadership over a Muslim region

**imam·ate** \-'mä-ˌmät, -'ma-\ *noun, often capitalized* (circa 1741)

**1** : the office of an imam

**2** : the region or country ruled by an imam

**ima·ret** \i-'mär-ət\ *noun* [Turkish] (1613)

: an inn or hospice in Turkey

**Ima·ri** \i-'mär-ē\ *noun* [*Imari,* Japan] (1875)

: a multicolored Japanese porcelain usually characterized by elaborate floral designs

— **Imari** *adjective*

**im·bal·ance** \(ˌ)im-'ba-lən(t)s\ *noun* (circa 1890)

: lack of balance : the state of being out of equilibrium or out of proportion ⟨a vitamin *imbalance*⟩ ⟨racial *imbalance* in schools⟩

— **im·bal·anced** \-lən(t)st\ *adjective*

**im·be·cile** \'im-bə-səl, -ˌsil\ *noun* [French *imbécile,* noun, from adjective, weak, weak-minded, from Latin *imbecillus*] (1802)

**1** : a mentally deficient person; *especially* : a feebleminded person having a mental age of three to seven years and requiring supervision in the performance of routine daily tasks of self-care

**2** : FOOL, IDIOT

— **imbecile** *or* **im·be·cil·ic** \ˌim-bə-'si-lik\ *adjective*

**im·be·cil·i·ty** \ˌim-bə-'si-lə-tē\ *noun, plural* **-ties** (1533)

**1** : the quality or state of being imbecile or an imbecile

**2 a** : utter foolishness; *also* : FUTILITY **b** : something that is foolish or nonsensical

**im·bed** *variant of* EMBED

**im·bibe** \im-'bīb\ *verb* **im·bibed; im·bib·ing** [in sense 1, from Middle English *enbiben,* from Middle French *embiber,* from Latin *imbibere* to drink in, conceive, from *in-* + *bibere* to drink; in other senses, from Latin *imbibere* — more at POTABLE] (14th century)

*transitive verb*

**1** *archaic* : SOAK, STEEP

**2 a** : to receive into the mind and retain ⟨*imbibe* moral principles⟩ **b** : to assimilate or take into solution

**3 a** : DRINK **b** : to take in or up ⟨a sponge *imbibes* moisture⟩

*intransitive verb*

**1** : DRINK 2

**2 a** : to take in liquid **b** : to absorb or assimilate moisture, gas, light, or heat

— **im·bib·er** *noun*

**im·bi·bi·tion** \ˌim-bə-'bi-shən\ *noun* (15th century)

: the act or action of imbibing; *especially* : the taking up of fluid by a colloidal system resulting in swelling

— **im·bi·bi·tion·al** \-'bish-nəl, -'bi-shə-nᵊl\ *adjective*

**im·bit·ter** *variant of* EMBITTER

**im·bo·som** *variant of* EMBOSOM

---

**¹im·bri·cate** \'im-bri-kət\ *adjective* [Late Latin *imbricatus,* past participle of *imbricare* to cover with pantiles, from Latin *imbric-, imbrex* pantile, from *imbr-, imber* rain; akin to Greek *ombros* rain] (circa 1610)

: lying lapped over each other in regular order ⟨*imbricate* scales⟩

**²im·bri·cate** \'im-brə-ˌkāt\ *transitive verb* **-cat·ed; -cat·ing** (1784)

: OVERLAP; *especially* : to overlap like roof tiles

**im·bri·ca·tion** \ˌim-brə-'kā-shən\ *noun* (1713)

**1** : an overlapping of edges (as of tiles or scales)

**2** : a decoration or pattern showing imbrication

**imbrication**

**im·bro·glio** \im-'brōl-(ˌ)yō\ *noun, plural* **-glios** [Italian, from *imbrogliare* to entangle, from Middle French *embrouiller* — more at EMBROIL] (1750)

**1** : a confused mass

**2 a** : an intricate or complicated situation (as in a drama or novel) **b** : an acutely painful or embarrassing misunderstanding **c** : a violently confused or bitterly complicated altercation : EMBROILMENT

**im·brown** *variant of* EMBROWN

**im·brue** \im-'brü\ *transitive verb* **im·brued; im·bru·ing** [Middle English *enbrewen,* probably from Middle French *abrevrer, embevrer* to soak, drench, ultimately from Latin *bibere* to drink — more at POTABLE] (15th century)

: STAIN

**im·brute** \im-'brüt\ *verb* **im·brut·ed; im·brut·ing** (1634)

*intransitive verb*

: to sink to the level of a brute

*transitive verb*

: to degrade to the level of a brute

**im·bue** \-'byü\ *transitive verb* **im·bued; im·bu·ing** [Latin *imbuere*] (1555)

**1** : to permeate or influence as if by dyeing ⟨the spirit that *imbues* the new constitution⟩

**2** : to tinge or dye deeply

*synonym* see INFUSE

**im·id·az·ole** \ˌi-mə-'da-ˌzōl\ *noun* [International Scientific Vocabulary] (1892)

: a white crystalline heterocyclic base $C_3H_4N_2$ that is an antimetabolite related to histidine; *broadly* : any of various derivatives of this

**im·ide** \'i-ˌmīd\ *noun* [International Scientific Vocabulary, alteration of *amide*] (1857)

: a compound containing the NH group that is derived from ammonia by replacement of two hydrogen atoms by a metal or an equivalent of acid groups — compare AMIDE

— **im·id·ic** \i-'mi-dik\ *adjective*

**im·i·do** \'i-mə-ˌdō\ *adjective* (1881)

: relating to or containing the NH group or its substituted form NR united to one or two acid groups

**im·ine** \'i-ˌmēn\ *noun* [International Scientific Vocabulary, alteration of *amine*] (1883)

: a compound containing the NH group or its substituted form NR that is derived from ammonia by replacement of two hydrogen atoms by a hydrocarbon group or other nonacid organic group

**im·i·no** \'i-mə-ˌnō\ *adjective* (1903)

: relating to or containing the NH group or its substituted form NR united to a group other than an acid group

**imip·ra·mine** \i-'mi-prə-ˌmēn\ *noun* [*imide* + *propyl* + *amine*] (1958)

: a tricyclic antidepressant drug $C_{19}H_{24}N_2$

**im·i·ta·ble** \'i-mə-tə-bəl\ *adjective* (1550)

: capable or worthy of being imitated or copied

**im·i·tate** \'i-mə-ˌtāt\ *transitive verb* **-tat·ed; -tat·ing** [Latin *imitatus,* past participle of *imitari* — more at IMAGE] (1534)

**1** : to follow as a pattern, model, or example

**2** : to be or appear like : RESEMBLE

**3** : to produce a copy of : REPRODUCE

---

**4** : MIMIC, COUNTERFEIT ⟨can *imitate* his father's booming voice⟩

*synonym* see COPY

— **im·i·ta·tor** \-ˌtā-tər\ *noun*

**¹im·i·ta·tion** \ˌi-mə-'tā-shən\ *noun* (14th century)

**1** : an act or instance of imitating

**2** : something produced as a copy : COUNTERFEIT

**3** : a literary work designed to reproduce the style of another author

**4** : the repetition by one voice of a melody, phrase, or motive stated earlier in the composition by a different voice

**5** : the quality of an object in possessing some of the nature or attributes of a transcendent idea

**6** : the assumption of behavior observed in other individuals

**²imitation** *adjective* (1840)

: resembling something else that is usually genuine and of better quality : not real ⟨*imitation* leather⟩

**im·i·ta·tive** \'i-mə-ˌtā-tiv, *especially British* -tə-tiv\ *adjective* (1584)

**1 a** : marked by imitation ⟨acting is an *imitative* art⟩ **b** : reproducing or representing a natural sound : ONOMATOPOEIC ⟨"hiss" is an *imitative* word⟩ **c** : exhibiting mimicry

**2** : inclined to imitate

**3** : imitating something superior : COUNTERFEIT

— **im·i·ta·tive·ly** *adverb*

— **im·i·ta·tive·ness** *noun*

**im·mac·u·la·cy** \i-'ma-kyə-lə-sē\ *noun* (1799)

: the quality or state of being immaculate

**im·mac·u·late** \i-'ma-kyə-lət\ *adjective* [Middle English *immaculat,* from Latin *immaculatus,* from *in-* + *maculatus* stained — more at MACULATE] (15th century)

**1** : having no stain or blemish : PURE

**2** : containing no flaw or error

**3 a** : spotlessly clean **b** : having no colored spots or marks ⟨petals *immaculate*⟩

— **im·mac·u·late·ly** *adverb*

**Immaculate Conception** *noun* (1687)

**1** : the conception of the Virgin Mary in which as decreed in Roman Catholic dogma her soul was preserved free from original sin by divine grace

**2** : December 8 observed as a Roman Catholic feast in commemoration of the Immaculate Conception

**im·mane** \i-'mān\ *adjective* [Latin *immanis,* from *in-* + *manus* good — more at MATURE] (1602)

*archaic* : HUGE; *also* : monstrous in character

**im·ma·nence** \'i-mə-nən(t)s\ *noun* (1816)

: the quality or state of being immanent : INHERENCE

**im·ma·nen·cy** \-nən(t)-sē\ *noun* (1659)

: IMMANENCE

**im·ma·nent** \-nənt\ *adjective* [Late Latin *immanent-, immanens,* present participle of *immanēre* to remain in place, from Latin *in-* + *manēre* to remain — more at MANSION] (1535)

: remaining or operating within a domain of reality or realm of discourse : INHERENT; *specifically* : having existence or effect only within the mind or consciousness — compare TRANSCENDENT

— **im·ma·nent·ly** *adverb*

**im·ma·nent·ism** \-nən-ˌti-zəm\ *noun* (1907)

: any of several theories according to which God or an abstract mind or spirit pervades the world

— **im·ma·nent·ist** \-nən-tist, -ˌnen-\ *noun or adjective*

---

\ə\ abut \ᵊ\ kitten \ər\ further \a\ ash \ā\ ace \ä\ mop, mar \au̇\ out \ch\ chin \e\ bet \ē\ easy \g\ go \i\ hit \ī\ ice \j\ job \ŋ\ sing \ō\ go \ȯ\ law \ȯi\ boy \th\ thin \t͟h\ the \ü\ loot \u̇\ foot \y\ yet \zh\ vision *see also* Guide to Pronunciation

— **im·ma·nent·is·tic** \ˌi-mə-nən-'tis-tik\ *adjective*

**Im·man·u·el** \i-'man-yə-wəl, -yəl\ *noun* [Middle English *Emanuel*, from Late Latin *Emmanuel*, from Greek *Emmanouēl*, from Hebrew *'immānū'ēl*, literally, with us is God] (15th century)
: MESSIAH 1

**im·ma·te·ri·al** \ˌi-mə-'tir-ē-əl\ *adjective* [Middle English *immateriel*, from Middle French, from Late Latin *immaterialis*, from Latin *in-* + Late Latin *materialis* material] (14th century)
**1** : not consisting of matter : INCORPOREAL
**2** : of no substantial consequence : UNIMPORTANT

**im·ma·te·ri·al·ism** \-ē-ə-ˌli-zəm\ *noun* (1713)
: a philosophical theory that material things have no reality except as mental perceptions
— **im·ma·te·ri·al·ist** \-list\ *noun*

**im·ma·te·ri·al·i·ty** \ˌi-mə-ˌtir-ē-'a-lə-tē\ *noun, plural* **-ties** (1570)
**1** : the quality or state of being immaterial
**2** : something immaterial

**im·ma·te·ri·al·ize** \-'tir-ē-ə-ˌlīz\ *transitive verb* (1661)
: to make immaterial or incorporeal

**im·ma·ture** \ˌi-mə-'tur, -'tyur, -'chur\ *adjective* [Latin *immaturus*, from *in-* + *maturus* mature] (1548)
**1** *archaic* : PREMATURE
**2 a** : lacking complete growth, differentiation, or development ⟨a thin *immature* soil⟩ **b** : having the potential capacity to attain a definitive form or state : CRUDE, UNFINISHED ⟨a vigorous but *immature* school of art⟩ **c** : exhibiting less than an expected degree of maturity ⟨emotionally *immature* adults⟩
— **immature** *noun*
— **im·ma·ture·ly** *adverb*
— **im·ma·tu·ri·ty** \-'tur-ə-tē, -'tyur-, -'chur-\ *noun*

**im·mea·sur·able** \(ˌ)i(m)-'mezh-rə-bəl, -'māzh-; -'me-zhə-rə-, -'mā-, -zhər-bəl\ *adjective* (14th century)
: incapable of being measured; *broadly* : indefinitely extensive
— **im·mea·sur·able·ness** *noun*
— **im·mea·sur·ably** \-blē\ *adverb*

**im·me·di·a·cy** \i-'mē-dē-ə-sē, *British often* -'mē-jə-sē\ *noun, plural* **-cies** (1605)
**1** : the quality or state of being immediate
**2** : something that is immediate — usually used in plural

**im·me·di·ate** \i-'mē-dē-ət, *British often* -'mē-jit\ *adjective* [Middle English, from Late Latin *immediatus*, from Latin *in-* + Late Latin *mediatus* intermediate — more at MEDIATE] (15th century)
**1 a** : acting or being without the intervention of another object, cause, or agency : DIRECT ⟨the *immediate* cause of death⟩ **b** : present to the mind independently of other states or factors ⟨*immediate* awareness⟩ **c** : involving or derived from a single premise ⟨an *immediate* inference⟩
**2** : being next in line or relation ⟨the *immediate* family⟩
**3 a** : existing without intervening space or substance ⟨brought into *immediate* contact⟩ **b** : being near at hand ⟨the *immediate* neighborhood⟩
**4 a** : occurring, acting, or accomplished without loss or interval of time : INSTANT ⟨an *immediate* need⟩ **b** (1) : near to or related to the present ⟨the *immediate* past⟩ (2) : of or relating to the here and now : CURRENT ⟨too busy with *immediate* concerns to worry about the future⟩
**5** : directly touching or concerning a person or thing ⟨the child's *immediate* world is the classroom⟩

**immediate constituent** *noun* (1933)
: any of the meaningful constituents directly forming a larger linguistic construction (as a phrase or sentence)

**¹im·me·di·ate·ly** \i-'mē-dē-ət-lē *also* -'mē-dit-, *British often* -'mē-jət-\ *adverb* (15th century)
**1** : in direct connection or relation : DIRECTLY ⟨the parties *immediately* involved in the case⟩ ⟨the house *immediately* beyond this one⟩
**2** : without interval of time : STRAIGHTWAY

**²immediately** *conjunction* (1839)
*chiefly British* : AS SOON AS

**im·me·di·ate·ness** *noun* (1633)
: IMMEDIACY 1

**im·med·i·ca·ble** \(ˌ)i(m)-'me-di-kə-bəl\ *adjective* [Latin *immedicabilis*, from *in-* + *medicabilis* medicable] (1533)
: INCURABLE ⟨wounds *immedicable* —John Milton⟩
— **im·med·i·ca·bly** \-blē\ *adverb*

**Im·mel·mann** \'i-məl-mən\ *noun* [Max *Immelmann*] (1917)
: a maneuver in which an airplane reverses direction by executing half of a loop upwards followed by half of a roll — called also *Immelmann turn*

**im·me·mo·ri·al** \ˌi-mə-'mōr-ē-əl, -'mȯr-\ *adjective* [probably from French *immémorial*, from Middle French, from Medieval Latin *immemorialis* lacking memory, from Latin *in-* + *memorialis* memorial] (1602)
: extending or existing since beyond the reach of memory, record, or tradition ⟨existing from time *immemorial*⟩
— **im·me·mo·ri·al·ly** \-ē-ə-lē\ *adverb*

**im·mense** \i-'men(t)s\ *adjective* [Middle English, from Middle French, from Latin *immensus* immeasurable, from *in-* + *mensus*, past participle of *metiri* to measure — more at MEASURE] (15th century)
**1** : marked by greatness especially in size or degree; *especially* : transcending ordinary means of measurement ⟨the *immense* and boundless universe⟩
**2** : supremely good : EXCELLENT
*synonym* see ENORMOUS
— **im·mense·ly** *adverb*
— **im·mense·ness** *noun*

**im·men·si·ty** \i-'men(t)-sə-tē\ *noun, plural* **-ties** (15th century)
**1** : the quality or state of being immense
**2** : something immense

**im·men·su·ra·ble** \(ˌ)i(m)-'men(t)s-rə-bəl, -'men(t)sh-; -'men(t)-sə-, -shə-\ *adjective* [Middle English, from Late Latin *immensurabilis*, from Latin *in-* + Late Latin *mensurabilis* measurable — more at MENSURABLE] (15th century)
: IMMEASURABLE

**im·merge** \i-'mərj\ *intransitive verb* **im·merged; im·merg·ing** [Latin *immergere*] (1706)
: to plunge into or immerse oneself in something

**im·merse** \i-'mərs\ *transitive verb* **im·mersed; im·mers·ing** [Middle English, from Latin *immersus*, past participle of *immergere*, from *in-* + *mergere* to merge] (15th century)
**1** : to plunge into something that surrounds or covers; *especially* : to plunge or dip into a fluid
**2** : ENGROSS, ABSORB ⟨completely *immersed* in his work⟩
**3** : to baptize by immersion

**im·mers·ible** \i-'mər-sə-bəl\ *adjective* (circa 1846)
: capable of being totally submerged in water without damage to the heating element ⟨an *immersible* electric frying pan⟩

**im·mer·sion** \i-'mər-zhən, -shən\ *noun* (15th century)
: an act of immersing : a state of being immersed; *specifically* : baptism by complete submersion of the person in water

**immersion heater** *noun* (1914)
: a usually electric unit that heats the liquid in which it is immersed

**im·mesh** \i-'mesh\ *variant of* ENMESH

**im·me·thod·i·cal** \ˌi-mə-'thä-di-kəl\ *adjective* (1605)
: not methodical
— **im·me·thod·i·cal·ly** \-k(ə-)lē\ *adverb*

**im·mi·grant** \'i-mi-grənt\ *noun* (1789)
: one that immigrates: as **a** : a person who comes to a country to take up permanent residence **b** : a plant or animal that becomes established in an area where it was previously unknown
— **immigrant** *adjective*

**im·mi·grate** \'i-mə-ˌgrāt\ *verb* **-grat·ed; -grat·ing** [Latin *immigratus*, past participle of *immigrare* to remove, go in, from *in-* + *migrare* to migrate] (circa 1623)
*intransitive verb*
: to enter and usually become established; *especially* : to come into a country of which one is not a native for permanent residence
*transitive verb*
: to bring in or send as immigrants
— **im·mi·gra·tion** \ˌi-mə-'grā-shən\ *noun*
— **im·mi·gra·tion·al** \-shnəl, -shə-nᵊl\ *adjective*

**im·mi·nence** \'i-mə-nən(t)s\ *noun* (1606)
**1** : something imminent; *especially* : impending evil or danger
**2** : the quality or state of being imminent

**im·mi·nen·cy** \-nən-sē\ *noun* (1665)
: IMMINENCE 2

**im·mi·nent** \'i-mə-nənt\ *adjective* [Latin *imminent-, imminens*, present participle of *imminēre* to project, threaten, from *in-* + *-minēre* (akin to Latin *mont-, mons* mountain) — more at MOUNT] (1528)
: ready to take place; *especially* : hanging threateningly over one's head ⟨was in *imminent* danger of being run over⟩
— **im·mi·nent·ly** *adverb*

**im·min·gle** \i-'miŋ-gəl\ *verb* (1606)
: BLEND, INTERMINGLE

**im·mis·ci·ble** \(ˌ)i(m)-'mi-sə-bəl\ *adjective* (1671)
: incapable of mixing or attaining homogeneity
— **im·mis·ci·bil·i·ty** \-ˌmi-sə-'bi-lə-tē\ *noun*

**im·mit·i·ga·ble** \(ˌ)i(m)-'mi-ti-gə-bəl\ *adjective* [Late Latin *immitigabilis*, from Latin *in-* + *mitigare* to mitigate] (1576)
: not capable of being mitigated
— **im·mit·i·ga·bly** \-blē\ *adverb*

**im·mit·tance** \(ˌ)i(m)-'mi-tᵊn(t)s\ *noun* [*impedance* + *admittance*] (circa 1948)
: electrical admittance or impedance

**im·mix** \i-'miks\ *transitive verb* [back-formation from *immixed* mixed in, from Middle English *immixte*, from Latin *immixtus*, past participle of *immiscēre*, from *in-* + *miscēre* to mix — more at MIX] (15th century)
: to mix intimately : COMMINGLE
— **im·mix·ture** \-'miks-chər\ *noun*

**im·mo·bile** \(ˌ)i(m)-'mō-bəl, -ˌbīl *also* -ˌbēl\ *adjective* [Middle English *in-mobill*, from Latin *immobilis*, from *in-* + *mobilis* mobile] (14th century)
**1** : incapable of being moved : FIXED
**2** : not moving : MOTIONLESS ⟨keep the patient *immobile*⟩
— **im·mo·bil·i·ty** \ˌi-(ˌ)mō-'bi-lə-tē\ *noun*

**im·mo·bi·lism** \i-'mō-bə-ˌli-zəm\ *noun* (1949)
: a policy of extreme conservatism and opposition to change

**im·mo·bi·lize** \i-'mō-bə-ˌlīz\ *transitive verb* (1871)
: to make immobile: as **a** : to prevent freedom of movement or effective use of ⟨the planes were *immobilized* by bad weather⟩ **b** : to reduce or eliminate motion of (the body or a part) by mechanical means or by strict bed rest **c** : to withhold (money or capital) from circulation
— **im·mo·bi·li·za·tion** \-ˌmō-bə-lə-'zā-shən\ *noun*
— **im·mo·bi·liz·er** \-'mō-bə-ˌlī-zər\ *noun*

**im·mod·er·a·cy** \(ˌ)i(m)-'mä-d(ə-)rə-sē\ *noun* (1682)
: lack of moderation

**im·mod·er·ate** \-d(ə-)rət\ *adjective* [Middle English *immoderat*, from Latin *immoderatus*, from *in-* + *moderatus*, past participle of *moderare* to moderate] (14th century)
: exceeding just, usual, or suitable bounds ⟨*immoderate* pride⟩ ⟨an *immoderate* appetite⟩
**synonym** see EXCESSIVE
— **im·mod·er·ate·ly** *adverb*
— **im·mod·er·ate·ness** *noun*
— **im·mod·er·a·tion** \(ˌ)i-ˌmä-də-'rā-shən\ *noun*

**im·mod·est** \(ˌ)i(m)-'mä-dəst\ *adjective* [Latin *immodestus*, from *in-* + *modestus* modest] (circa 1570)
: not modest; *specifically* : not conforming to the sexual mores of a particular time or place
— **im·mod·est·ly** *adverb*
— **im·mod·es·ty** \-də-stē\ *noun*

**im·mo·late** \'i-mə-ˌlāt\ *transitive verb* **-lat·ed; -lat·ing** [Latin *immolatus*, past participle of *immolare*, from *in-* + *mola* spelt grits; from the custom of sprinkling victims with sacrificial meal; akin to Latin *molere* to grind — more at MEAL] (1548)
**1** : to offer in sacrifice; *especially* : to kill as a sacrificial victim
**2** : to kill or destroy often by fire
— **im·mo·la·tor** \-ˌlā-tər\ *noun*

**im·mo·la·tion** \ˌi-mə-'lā-shən\ *noun* (15th century)
**1** : the act of immolating : the state of being immolated
**2** : something that is immolated

**im·mor·al** \(ˌ)i(m)-'mȯr-əl, -'mär-\ *adjective* (1660)
: not moral; *broadly* : conflicting with generally or traditionally held moral principles
— **im·mor·al·ly** \-ə-lē\ *adverb*

**im·mor·al·ist** \-ə-list\ *noun* (1697)
: an advocate of immorality
— **im·mor·al·ism** \-ˌli-zəm\ *noun*

**im·mo·ral·i·ty** \ˌi-(ˌ)mȯ-'ra-lə-tē, ˌi-mə-\ *noun* (circa 1566)
**1** : the quality or state of being immoral; *especially* : UNCHASTITY
**2** : an immoral act or practice

**¹im·mor·tal** \(ˌ)i-'mȯr-t³l\ *adjective* [Middle English, from Latin *immortalis*, from *in-* + *mortalis* mortal] (14th century)
**1** : exempt from death ⟨the *immortal* gods⟩
**2** : exempt from oblivion : IMPERISHABLE ⟨*immortal* fame⟩
**3** : connected with or relating to immortality
— **im·mor·tal·ly** \-t³l-ē\ *adverb*

**²immortal** *noun* (1684)
**1 a** : one exempt from death **b** *plural, often capitalized* : the gods of the Greek and Roman pantheon
**2 a** : a person whose fame is lasting **b** *capitalized* : any of the 40 members of the Académie Française

**im·mor·tal·ise** *British variant of* IMMORTALIZE

**im·mor·tal·i·ty** \ˌi-mȯr-'ta-lə-tē\ *noun* (14th century)
: the quality or state of being immortal: **a** : unending existence **b** : lasting fame

**im·mor·tal·ize** \i-'mȯr-t³l-ˌīz\ *transitive verb* **-ized; -iz·ing** (circa 1566)
: to make immortal
— **im·mor·tal·i·za·tion** \-ˌmȯr-t³l-ə-'zā-shən\ *noun*
— **im·mor·tal·iz·er** \-'mȯr-t³l-ˌī-zər\ *noun*

**im·mor·telle** \ˌi-mȯr-'tel\ *noun* [French, from feminine of *immortel* immortal, from Latin *immortalis*] (1832)
: EVERLASTING 3

**im·mo·tile** \(ˌ)i(m)-'mō-t³l, -ˌtīl\ *adjective* (1872)
: lacking motility

**¹im·mov·able** \(ˌ)i(m)-'mü-və-bəl\ *adjective* (14th century)
**1** : incapable of being moved; *broadly* : not moving or not intended to be moved
**2 a** : STEADFAST, UNYIELDING **b** : not capable of being moved emotionally
— **im·mov·abil·i·ty** \-ˌmü-və-'bi-lə-tē\ *noun*
— **im·mov·able·ness** \-'mü-və-bəl-nəs\ *noun*
— **im·mov·ably** \-blē\ *adverb*

**²immovable** *noun* (1588)
**1** : one that cannot be moved
**2** *plural* : real property as opposed to movable property

**im·mune** \i-'myün\ *adjective* [Middle English, from Latin *immunis*, from *in-* + *munia* services, obligations; akin to Latin *munus* service — more at MEAN] (15th century)
**1 a** : FREE, EXEMPT ⟨*immune* from further taxation⟩ **b** : marked by protection ⟨some criminal leaders are *immune* from arrest⟩
**2** : not susceptible or responsive ⟨*immune* to all pleas⟩; *especially* : having a high degree of resistance to a disease ⟨*immune* to diphtheria⟩
**3 a** : having or producing antibodies or lymphocytes capable of reacting with a specific antigen ⟨an *immune* serum⟩ **b** : produced by, involved in, or concerned with immunity or an immune response ⟨*immune* agglutinins⟩ ⟨*immune* globulins⟩
— **immune** *noun*

**immune response** *noun* (1953)
: a bodily response to an antigen that occurs when lymphocytes identify the antigenic molecule as foreign and induce the formation of antibodies and lymphocytes capable of reacting with it and rendering it harmless — called also *immune reaction*

**immune system** *noun* (circa 1919)
: the bodily system that protects the body from foreign substances, cells, and tissues by producing the immune response and that includes especially the thymus, spleen, lymph nodes, special deposits of lymphoid tissue (as in the gastrointestinal tract and bone marrow), lymphocytes including the B cells and T cells, and antibodies

**im·mu·ni·ty** \i-'myü-nə-tē\ *noun, plural* **-ties** (14th century)
: the quality or state of being immune; *especially* : a condition of being able to resist a particular disease especially through preventing development of a pathogenic microorganism or by counteracting the effects of its products

**im·mu·nize** \'i-myə-ˌnīz\ *transitive verb* **-nized; -niz·ing** (1892)
: to make immune
— **im·mu·ni·za·tion** \ˌi-myə-nə-'zā-shən *also* ˌi-ˌmyü-nə-\ *noun*

**immuno-** *combining form* [International Scientific Vocabulary, from *immune*]
**1** : physiological immunity ⟨*immuno*logy⟩
**2** : immunologic ⟨*immuno*chemistry⟩ : immunologically ⟨*immuno*competent⟩ : immunology and ⟨*immuno*genetics⟩

**im·mu·no·as·say** \ˌi-myə-nō-'a-ˌsā, i-ˌmyü-nō-, -a-'sā\ *noun* (1959)
: the identification of a substance (as a protein) based on its capacity to act as an antigen
— **im·mu·no·as·say·able** \-a-'sā-ə-bəl\ *adjective*

**im·mu·no·blot** \'i-myə-nə-ˌblät, i-'myü-(ˌ)nō-\ *noun* (1982)
: a blot in which a radioactively labeled antibody is used as the molecular probe
— **im·mu·no·blot·ting** \-ˌblä-tiŋ\ *noun*

**im·mu·no·chem·is·try** \ˌi-myə-nō-'ke-mə-strē, i-ˌmyü-nō-\ *noun* [International Scientific Vocabulary] (1907)
: a branch of chemistry that deals with the chemical aspects of immunology
— **im·mu·no·chem·i·cal** \-'ke-mi-kəl\ *adjective*
— **im·mu·no·chem·i·cal·ly** \-k(ə-)lē\ *adverb*
— **im·mu·no·chem·ist** \-'ke-mist\ *noun*

**im·mu·no·com·pe·tence** \-'käm-pə-tən(t)s\ *noun* (1967)
: the capacity for a normal immune response
— **im·mu·no·com·pe·tent** \-tənt\ *adjective*

**im·mu·no·com·pro·mised** \-'käm-prə-ˌmīzd\ *adjective* (1979)
: having the immune system impaired or weakened (as by drugs or illness) ⟨*immuno*compromised patients⟩

**im·mu·no·cy·to·chem·is·try** \-ˌsī-tō-'ke-mə-strē\ *noun* (1960)
: the application of biochemistry to cellular immunology
— **im·mu·no·cy·to·chem·i·cal** \-'kə-mi-kəl\ *adjective*
— **im·mu·no·cy·to·chem·i·cal·ly** \-'ke-mi-k(ə-)lē\ *adverb*

**im·mu·no·de·fi·cien·cy** \-di-'fi-shən(t)-sē\ *noun* (1969)
: inability to produce a normal complement of antibodies or immunologically sensitized T cells especially in response to specific antigens
— **im·mu·no·de·fi·cient** \-shənt\ *adjective*

**im·mu·no·di·ag·no·sis** \-ˌdī-ig-'nō-səs, -əg-\ *noun* (1972)
: diagnosis (as of cancer) by immunological methods
— **im·mu·no·di·ag·nos·tic** \-'näs-tik\ *adjective*

**im·mu·no·dif·fu·sion** \-di-'fyü-zhən\ *noun* (1959)
: any of several techniques for obtaining a precipitate between an antibody and its specific antigen by suspending one in a gel and letting the other migrate through it from a well or by letting both antibody and antigen migrate through the gel from separate wells to form an area of precipitation

**im·mu·no·elec·tro·pho·re·sis** \-ə-ˌlek-trə-fə-'rē-səs\ *noun, plural* **-re·ses** \-ˌsēz\ (1958)
: electrophoretic separation of proteins followed by identification by the formation of precipitates through specific immunologic reactions
— **im·mu·no·elec·tro·pho·ret·ic** \-'re-tik\ *adjective*
— **im·mu·no·elec·tro·pho·ret·i·cal·ly** \-ti-k(ə-)lē\ *adverb*

**im·mu·no·flu·o·res·cence** \-ˌ(ˌ)flȯ-'re-s³n(t)s, -ˌ(ˌ)flō-, -ˌflu̇-(ə-)\ *noun* (1960)
: the labeling of antibodies or antigens with fluorescent dyes especially for the purpose of demonstrating the presence of a particular antigen or antibody in a tissue preparation or smear
— **im·mu·no·flu·o·res·cent** \-s³nt\ *adjective*

**im·mu·no·gen** \i-'myü-nə-jən, -ˌjen\ *noun* [from *Immunogen*, a trademark] (1959)
: an antigen that produces an immune response

**im·mu·no·ge·net·ics** \ˌi-myə-nō-jə-'ne-tiks, i-ˌmyü-nō-\ *noun plural but singular in construction* (1936)
: a branch of immunology concerned with the interrelations of heredity, disease, and the immune system and its components (as antibodies)
— **im·mu·no·ge·net·ic** \-tik\ *adjective*
— **im·mu·no·ge·net·i·cal·ly** \-ti-k(ə-)lē\ *adverb*
— **im·mu·no·ge·net·i·cist** \-jə-'ne-tə-sist\ *noun*

**im·mu·no·gen·ic** \ˌi-myə-nō-'je-nik, i-ˌmyü-nō-\ *adjective* (circa 1923)
: relating to or producing an immune response ⟨*immunogenic* substances⟩

\ə\ abut \³\ kitten \ər\ further \a\ ash \ā\ ace \ä\ mop, mar \au̇\ out \ch\ chin \e\ bet \ē\ easy \g\ go \i\ hit \ī\ ice \j\ job \ŋ\ sing \ō\ go \ȯ\ law \ȯi\ boy \th\ thin \t͟h\ the \ü\ loot \u̇\ foot \y\ yet \zh\ vision *see also* Guide to Pronunciation

— **im·mu·no·gen·e·sis** \-'je-nə-səs\ *noun*
— **im·mu·no·ge·nic·i·ty** \-jə-'ni-sə-tē\ *noun*

**im·mu·no·glob·u·lin** \-'glä-byə-lən\ *noun* (1953)
**:** ANTIBODY

**im·mu·no·he·ma·tol·o·gy** \-,hē-mə-'tä-lə-jē\ *noun* (1950)
**:** a branch of immunology that deals with the immunologic properties of blood
— **im·mu·no·he·ma·to·log·ic** \-,hē-mə-t°l-'ä-jik\ *or* **im·mu·no·he·ma·to·log·i·cal** \-'ä-ji-kəl\ *adjective*
— **im·mu·no·he·ma·tol·o·gist** \-,hē-mə-'tä-lə-jist\ *noun*

**im·mu·no·his·to·chem·i·cal** \-,his-tō-'ke-mi-kəl\ *adjective* (1960)
**:** of or relating to the application of histochemical and immunologic methods to chemical analysis of living cells and tissues
— **im·mu·no·his·to·chem·is·try** \-'ke-mə-strē\ *noun*

**im·mu·nol·o·gy** \,i-myə-'nä-lə-jē\ *noun* [International Scientific Vocabulary] (1910)
**:** a science that deals with the immune system and the cell-mediated and humoral aspects of immunity and immune responses
— **im·mu·no·log·ic** \-nə-'lä-jik\ *or* **im·mu·no·log·i·cal** \-'lä-ji-kəl\ *adjective*
— **im·mu·no·log·i·cal·ly** \-ji-k(ə-)lē\ *adverb*
— **im·mu·nol·o·gist** \,i-myə-'nä-lə-jist\ *noun*

**im·mu·no·mod·u·la·tor** \,i-myə-nō-'mä-jə-,lā-tər, i-,myü-nō-\ *noun* (1977)
**:** a substance that affects the functioning of the immune system
— **im·mu·no·mod·u·la·to·ry** \-'mä-jə-lə-,tōr-ē, -,tōr-\ *adjective*

**im·mu·no·pa·thol·o·gy** \-pə-'thä-lə-jē, -pa-\ *noun* (1959)
**:** a branch of medicine that deals with immune responses associated with disease
— **im·mu·no·path·o·log·ic** \-,pa-thə-'lä-jik\ *or* **im·mu·no·path·o·log·i·cal** \-ji-kəl\ *adjective*
— **im·mu·no·pa·thol·o·gist** \-pə-'thä-lə-jist, -pa-\ *noun*

**im·mu·no·pre·cip·i·ta·tion** \-pri-,si-pə-'tā-shən\ *noun* (1966)
**:** precipitation of a complex of an antibody and its specific antigen
— **im·mu·no·pre·cip·i·tate** \-'si-pə-tət, -pə-,tāt\ *noun*
— **im·mu·no·pre·cip·i·tate** \-pə-,tāt\ *transitive verb*

**im·mu·no·re·ac·tive** \-rē-'ak-tiv\ *adjective* (1966)
**:** reacting to particular antigens or haptens ⟨*immunoreactive* lymphocytes⟩
— **im·mu·no·re·ac·tiv·i·ty** \-(,)rē-,ak-'ti-və-tē\ *noun*

**im·mu·no·reg·u·la·to·ry** \-'re-gyə-lə-,tōr-ē, -,tōr-\ *adjective* (1971)
**:** of or relating to the regulation of the immune system ⟨*immunoregulatory* T cells⟩
— **im·mu·no·reg·u·la·tion** \-,re-gyə-'lā-shən, -gə-\ *noun*

**im·mu·no·sor·bent** \-'sòr-bənt\ *adjective* (1966)
**:** relating to or using a substrate consisting of a specific antibody or antigen chemically combined with an insoluble substance (as cellulose) to selectively remove the corresponding specific antigen or antibody from solution
— **immunosorbent** *noun*

**im·mu·no·sup·pres·sion** \-sə-'pre-shən\ *noun* (1963)
**:** suppression (as by drugs) of natural immune responses
— **im·mu·no·sup·press** \-sə-'pres\ *transitive verb*
— **im·mu·no·sup·pres·sant** \-'pre-s°nt\ *noun or adjective*
— **im·mu·no·sup·pres·sive** \-'pre-siv\ *adjective*

**im·mu·no·ther·a·py** \-'ther-ə-pē\ *noun* [International Scientific Vocabulary] (circa 1911)
**:** treatment of or prophylaxis against disease by attempting to produce active or passive immunity
— **im·mu·no·ther·a·peu·tic** \-,ther-ə-'pyü-tik\ *adjective*

**im·mure** \i-'myùr\ *transitive verb* **im·mured; im·mur·ing** [Medieval Latin *immurare*, from Latin *in-* + *murus* wall — more at MUNITION] (1583)
**1 a :** to enclose within or as if within walls **b :** IMPRISON
**2 :** to build into a wall; *especially* **:** to entomb in a wall
— **im·mure·ment** \-'myùr-mənt\ *noun*

**im·mu·ta·ble** \(,)i(m)-'myü-tə-bəl\ *adjective* [Middle English, from Latin *immutabilis*, from *in-* + *mutabilis* mutable] (15th century)
**:** not capable of or susceptible to change
— **im·mu·ta·bil·i·ty** \-,myü-tə-'bi-lə-tē\ *noun*
— **im·mu·ta·ble·ness** \-'myü-tə-bəl-nəs\ *noun*
— **im·mu·ta·bly** \-blē\ *adverb*

**¹imp** \'imp\ *noun* [Middle English *impe*, from Old English *impa*, from *impian* to imp] (before 12th century)
**1** *obsolete* **:** SHOOT, BUD; *also* **:** GRAFT
**2 a :** a small demon **:** FIEND **b :** a mischievous child **:** URCHIN ◆

**²imp** *transitive verb* [Middle English, from Old English *impian* to graft, from (assumed) Vulgar Latin *imputare*, from Late Latin *impotus* grafted shoot, from Greek *emphytos* implanted, from *emphyein* to implant, from *em-* ²*en-* + *phyein* to bring forth — more at BE] (15th century)
**1 :** to graft or repair (a wing, tail, or feather) with a feather to improve a falcon's flying capacity
**2 :** to equip with wings

**¹im·pact** \im-'pakt\ *verb* [Latin *impactus*, past participle of *impingere* to push against — more at IMPINGE] (1601)
*transitive verb*
**1 a :** to fix firmly by or as if by packing or wedging **b :** to press together
**2 a :** to have an impact on **:** impinge on **b :** to strike forcefully; *also* **:** to cause to strike forcefully
*intransitive verb*
**1 :** to have an impact
**2 :** to impinge or make contact especially forcefully
— **im·pac·tive** \im-'pak-tiv\ *adjective*
— **im·pac·tor** *also* **im·pact·er** \-tər\ *noun*

**²im·pact** \'im-,pakt\ *noun* (1781)
**1 a :** an impinging or striking especially of one body against another **b :** a forceful contact, collision, or onset; *also* **:** the impetus communicated to or as if in a collision
**2 :** the force of impression of one thing on another **:** a significant or major effect ⟨the *impact* of science on our society⟩ ⟨an environmental *impact* study⟩

**impact crater** *noun* (1895)
**:** CRATER 1b

**im·pact·ed** \im-'pak-təd\ *adjective* (circa 1616)
**1 a :** packed or wedged in **b :** deeply entrenched **:** not easily changed or removed
**2** *of a tooth* **:** wedged between the jawbone and another tooth
**3 :** of, relating to, or being an area (as a school district) providing tax-supported services to a population having a large proportion of federal employees and especially those living or working on tax-exempt federal property ⟨aid to education in *impacted* areas⟩

**im·pac·tion** \im-'pak-shən\ *noun* (1739)
**:** the act of becoming or the state of being impacted; *especially* **:** lodgment of something (as feces) in a body passage or cavity

**impact printer** *noun* (1968)

**:** a printing device in which a printing element directly strikes a surface (as in a typewriter)

**im·paint** \im-'pānt\ *transitive verb* (1596)
*obsolete* **:** PAINT, DEPICT

**im·pair** \im-'par, -'per\ *transitive verb* [Middle English *empeiren*, from Middle French *empeirer*, from (assumed) Vulgar Latin *impejorare*, from Latin *in-* + Late Latin *pejorare* to make worse — more at PEJORATIVE] (14th century)
**:** to damage or make worse by or as if by diminishing in some material respect ⟨his health was *impaired* by overwork⟩ ⟨the strike seriously *impaired* community services⟩
*synonym* see INJURE
— **im·pair·er** *noun*
— **im·pair·ment** \-mənt\ *noun*

**im·paired** \-'pard, -'perd\ *adjective* (1605)
**:** being in a less than perfect or whole condition: as **a :** handicapped or functionally defective — often used in combination ⟨hearing-*impaired*⟩ **b** *chiefly Canadian* **:** DRUNK ⟨driving while *impaired*⟩

**im·pa·la** \im-'pa-lə, -'pä-\ *noun, plural* **impa·las** *or* **impala** [Zulu] (1875)
**:** a large brownish African antelope (*Aepyceros melampus*) that in the male has slender lyrate horns

impala

**im·pale** \im-'pā(ə)l\ *transitive verb* **im·paled; im·pal·ing** [Middle French & Medieval Latin; Middle French *empaler*, from Medieval Latin *impalare*, from Latin *in-* + *palus* stake — more at POLE] (1605)
**1 :** to join (coats of arms) on a heraldic shield divided vertically by a pale
**2 a :** to pierce with or as if with something pointed; *especially* **:** to torture or kill by fixing on a sharp stake **b :** to fix in an inescapable or helpless position
— **im·pale·ment** \-mənt\ *noun*
— **im·pal·er** \-'pā-lər\ *noun*

**im·pal·pa·ble** \(,)im-'pal-pə-bəl\ *adjective* (1509)
**1 a :** incapable of being felt by touch **:** INTANGIBLE ⟨the *impalpable* aura of power that emanated from him —Osbert Sitwell⟩ **b :** so finely divided that no grains or grit can be felt ⟨rock worn to an *impalpable* powder⟩
**2 :** not readily discerned by the mind
— **im·pal·pa·bil·i·ty** \-,pal-pə-'bi-lə-tē\ *noun*
— **im·pal·pa·bly** \-'pal-pə-blē\ *adverb*

**im·pan·el** \im-'pa-n°l\ *transitive verb* (15th century)
**:** to enroll in or on a panel ⟨*impanel* a jury⟩

◇ **WORD HISTORY**
**imp** *Imp*, which now usually refers to either a small demon or a mischievous child, has its origin in the unlikely field of horticulture. Old English *impa* or *impe* meant "graft" or "young shoot of a plant" and was a derivative of the verb *impian* "to graft." By later Middle English *impe* could mean metaphorically "offspring" or "child," a sense that survived at least into the 19th century. The frequency of phrases such as *imp of the devil* (i.e., "offspring of the devil") and *imp of hell* led to the use of *imp* without qualification to denote a demon, the evil parentage of the offspring being understood. By the 18th century the demonic sense had, as had the words *demon* and *devil* themselves, given rise to a less forceful usage: *imp* could be applied to nothing more than a naughty child.

**im·par·a·dise** \im-'par-ə-ˌdīs, -ˌdīz\ *transitive verb* **-dised; -dis·ing** (1592)
: ENRAPTURE
**im·par·i·ty** \(ˌ)im-'par-ə-tē\ *noun, plural* **-ties** [Late Latin *imparitas*, from Latin *impar* unequal, from *in-* + *par* equal] (1563)
: INEQUALITY, DISPARITY
**im·part** \im-'pärt\ *transitive verb* [Middle French & Latin; Middle French *impartir*, from Latin *impartire*, from *in-* + *partire* to divide, part] (15th century)
**1** : to give, convey, or grant from or as if from a store 〈her experience *imparted* authority to her words〉 〈the flavor *imparted* by herbs〉
**2** : to communicate the knowledge of : DISCLOSE 〈*imparted* my scheme to no one〉
— **im·par·ta·tion** \ˌim-ˌpär-'tā-shən\ *noun*
— **im·part·ment** \im-'pärt-mənt\ *noun*
**im·par·tial** \(ˌ)im-'pär-shəl\ *adjective* (1587)
: not partial or biased : treating or affecting all equally
**synonym** see FAIR
— **im·par·tial·i·ty** \-ˌpär-shē-'a-lə-tē, -ˌpär-'sha-\ *noun*
— **im·par·tial·ly** \-'pär-sh(ə-)lē\ *adverb*
**im·par·ti·ble** \(ˌ)im-'pär-tə-bəl\ *adjective* [Late Latin *impartibilis*, from Latin *in-* + Late Latin *partibilis* divisible, from Latin *partire*] (14th century)
: not partible : not subject to partition
— **im·par·ti·bly** \-blē\ *adverb*
**im·pass·able** \(ˌ)im-'pa-sə-bəl\ *adjective* (1568)
: incapable of being passed, traveled, crossed, or surmounted
— **im·pass·abil·i·ty** \-ˌpa-sə-'bi-lə-tē\ *noun*
— **im·pass·able·ness** \-'pa-sə-bəl-nəs\ *noun*
— **im·pass·ably** \-blē\ *adverb*
**im·passe** \'im-ˌpas, im-'\ *noun* [French, from *in-* + *passer* to pass] (1851)
**1 a** : a predicament affording no obvious escape **b** : DEADLOCK
**2** : an impassable road or way : CUL-DE-SAC
**im·pas·si·ble** \(ˌ)im-'pa-sə-bəl\ *adjective* [Middle English, from Middle French or Late Latin; Middle French, from Late Latin *impassibilis*, from Latin *in-* + Late Latin *passibilis* passible] (14th century)
**1 a** : incapable of suffering or of experiencing pain **b** : inaccessible to injury
**2** : incapable of feeling : IMPASSIVE
— **im·pas·si·bil·i·ty** \-ˌpa-sə-'bi-lə-tē\ *noun*
— **im·pas·si·bly** \-'pa-sə-blē\ *adverb*
**im·pas·sion** \im-'pa-shən\ *transitive verb* **im·pas·sioned; im·pas·sion·ing** \-sh(ə-)niŋ\ [probably from Italian *impassionare*, from *in-* (from Latin) + *passione* passion, from Late Latin *passion-, passio*] (1591)
: to arouse the feelings or passions of
**impassioned** *adjective* (1603)
: filled with passion or zeal : showing great warmth or intensity of feeling ☆
**im·pas·sive** \(ˌ)im-'pa-siv\ *adjective* (1605)
**1 a** *archaic* : unsusceptible to pain **b** : unsusceptible to physical feeling : INSENSIBLE **c** : unsusceptible to or destitute of emotion : APATHETIC
**2** : giving no sign of feeling or emotion : EXPRESSIONLESS ☆
— **im·pas·sive·ly** *adverb*
— **im·pas·sive·ness** *noun*
— **im·pas·siv·i·ty** \ˌim-ˌpa-'si-və-tē\ *noun*
**im·paste** \im-'pāst\ *transitive verb* [Italian *impastare*, from *in-* (from Latin) + *pasta* paste, from Late Latin] (1576)
*obsolete* : to make into a paste or crust
**im·pas·to** \im-'pas-(ˌ)tō, -'päs-\ *noun, plural* **-tos** [Italian, from *impastare*] (1784)
**1** : the thick application of a pigment to a canvas or panel in painting; *also* : the body of pigment so applied
**2** : raised decoration on ceramic ware usually of slip or enamel

**im·pa·toed** \-(ˌ)tōd\ *adjective*
**im·pa·tience** \(ˌ)im-'pā-shən(t)s\ *noun* (13th century)
: the quality or state of being impatient
**im·pa·tiens** \im-'pā-shənz, -shən(t)s\ *noun* [New Latin, from Latin, impatient] (1885)
: any of a widely distributed genus (*Impatiens*, family Balsaminaceae) of annual herbs with irregular spurred or saccate flowers and dehiscent capsules — compare TOUCH-ME-NOT
**im·pa·tient** \im-'pā-shənt\ *adjective* [Middle English *impacient*, from Middle French, from Latin *impatient-, impatiens*, from *in-* + *patient-, patiens* patient] (14th century)
**1 a** : not patient : restless or short of temper especially under irritation, delay, or opposition **b** : INTOLERANT 〈*impatient* of delay〉
**2** : prompted or marked by impatience 〈an *impatient* reply〉
**3** : eagerly desirous : ANXIOUS 〈*impatient* to get home〉
— **im·pa·tient·ly** *adverb*
**im·pawn** \im-'pón, -'pän\ *transitive verb* (1596)
*archaic* : to put in pawn : PLEDGE
¹**im·peach** \im-'pēch\ *transitive verb* [Middle English *empechen*, from Middle French *empeechier* to hinder, from Late Latin *impedicare* to fetter, from Latin *in-* + *pedica* fetter, from *ped-, pes* foot — more at FOOT] (14th century)
**1 a** : to bring an accusation against **b** : to charge with a crime or misdemeanor; *specifically* : to charge (a public official) before a competent tribunal with misconduct in office
**2** : to cast doubt on; *especially* : to challenge the credibility or validity of 〈*impeach* the testimony of a witness〉
**3** : to remove from office especially for misconduct ▢
— **im·peach·able** \-'pē-chə-bəl\ *adjective*
— **im·peach·ment** \-'pēch-mənt\ *noun*
²**impeach** *noun* (1590)
*obsolete* : CHARGE, IMPEACHMENT
**im·pearl** \im-'pər(-ə)l\ *transitive verb* [probably from Middle French *emperler*, from *en-* + *perle* pearl] (15th century)
: to form into pearls; *also* : to form of or adorn with pearls
**im·pec·ca·ble** \(ˌ)im-'pek-ə-bəl\ *adjective* [Latin *impeccabilis*, from *in-* + *peccare* to sin] (1531)
**1** : not capable of sinning or liable to sin
**2** : free from fault or blame : FLAWLESS 〈spoke *impeccable* French〉
— **im·pec·ca·bil·i·ty** \-ˌpe-kə-'bi-lə-tē\ *noun*
— **im·pec·ca·bly** \-'pe-kə-blē\ *adverb*
**im·pe·cu·nious** \ˌim-pi-'kyü-nyəs, -nē-əs\ *adjective* [¹*in-* + obsolete English *pecunious* rich, from Middle English, from Latin *pecuniosus*, from *pecunia* money — more at FEE] (1596)
: having very little or no money usually habitually : PENNILESS
— **im·pe·cu·ni·os·i·ty** \-ˌkyü-nē-'ä-sə-tē\ *noun*
— **im·pe·cu·nious·ly** *adverb*
— **im·pe·cu·nious·ness** *noun*
**im·ped·ance** \im-'pē-d°n(t)s\ *noun* (1886)
: something that impedes : HINDRANCE: as **a** : the apparent opposition in an electrical circuit to the flow of an alternating current that is analogous to the actual electrical resistance to a direct current and that is the ratio of effective electromotive force to the effective current **b** : the ratio of the pressure to the volume displacement at a given surface in a sound-transmitting medium
**im·pede** \im-'pēd\ *transitive verb* **im·ped·ed; im·ped·ing** [Latin *impedire*, from *in-* + *ped-, pes* foot — more at FOOT] (1605)
: to interfere with or slow the progress of
**synonym** see HINDER
— **im·ped·er** *noun*
**im·ped·i·ment** \im-'pe-də-mənt\ *noun* (14th century)

**1** : something that impedes; *especially* : an organic obstruction to speech
**2** : a bar or hindrance (as lack of sufficient age) to a lawful marriage
**im·ped·i·men·ta** \(ˌ)im-ˌpe-də-'men-tə\ *noun plural* [Latin, plural of *impedimentum* impediment, from *impedire*] (1600)
**1** : APPURTENANCES, EQUIPMENT
**2** : things that impede
**im·pel** \im-'pel\ *transitive verb* **im·pelled; im·pel·ling** [Latin *impellere*, from *in-* + *pellere* to drive — more at FELT] (15th century)
**1** : to urge or drive forward or on by or as if by the exertion of strong moral pressure : FORCE
**2** : to impart motion to : PROPEL
**synonym** see MOVE

---

☆ SYNONYMS
**Impassioned, passionate, ardent, fervent, fervid, perfervid** mean showing intense feeling. IMPASSIONED implies warmth and intensity without violence and suggests fluent verbal expression 〈an *impassioned* plea for justice〉. PASSIONATE implies great vehemence and often violence and wasteful diffusion of emotion 〈a *passionate* denunciation〉. ARDENT implies an intense degree of zeal, devotion, or enthusiasm 〈an *ardent* supporter of human rights〉. FERVENT stresses sincerity and steadiness of emotional warmth or zeal 〈*fervent* good wishes〉. FERVID suggests warmly and spontaneously and often feverishly expressed emotion 〈*fervid* love letters〉. PERFERVID implies the expression of exaggerated or overwrought feelings 〈*perfervid* expressions of patriotism〉.

**Impassive, stoic, phlegmatic, apathetic, stolid** mean unresponsive to something that might normally excite interest or emotion. IMPASSIVE stresses the absence of any external sign of emotion in action or facial expression 〈met the news with an *impassive* look〉. STOIC implies an apparent indifference to pleasure or especially to pain often as a matter of principle or self-discipline 〈was resolutely *stoic* even in adversity〉. PHLEGMATIC implies a temperament or constitution hard to arouse 〈a *phlegmatic* man unmoved by tears〉. APATHETIC may imply a puzzling or deplorable indifference or inertness 〈charitable appeals met an *apathetic* response〉. STOLID implies an habitual absence of interest, responsiveness, or curiosity 〈*stolid* workers wedded to routine〉.

---

▢ USAGE
**impeach** Back in 1970 a newspaperman took an informal poll of people who worked for the paper and discovered that 10 out of 13 believed *impeach* meant "to remove from office" rather than "to charge with misconduct in office." This is a meaning many people know—our evidence goes back to before World War I—but seldom seen in print. (It is sense 3 here.) But the strong presence of this meaning in people's minds can make many uses of *impeach* ambiguous 〈(who, by the way, was later *impeached* for corruption!) —Julian Huxley〉. Was he removed or merely charged with corruption? A writer must reckon on with the sense "remove from office" when writing for the general public and take care to make the context clear.

\ə\ abut \ᵊ\ kitten \ər\ further \a\ ash \ā\ ace \ä\ mop, mar \aú\ out \ch\ chin \e\ bet \ē\ easy \g\ go \i\ hit \ī\ ice \j\ job \ŋ\ sing \ō\ go \ó\ law \ói\ boy \th\ thin \t͟h\ the \ü\ loot \ú\ foot \y\ yet \zh\ vision *see also* Guide to Pronunciation

**im·pel·ler** also **im·pel·lor** \im-'pe-lər\ noun (1685)
**1** : one that impels
**2** : ROTOR; also : a blade of a rotor

**im·pend** \im-'pend\ intransitive verb [Latin *impendēre*, from *in-* + *pendēre* to hang — more at PENDANT] (1599)
**1 a** : to hover threateningly : MENACE **b** : to be about to occur
**2** archaic : to hang suspended

**im·pen·dent** \im-'pen-dənt\ adjective (1590)
: being near at hand : APPROACHING

**im·pen·e·tra·bil·i·ty** \(,)im-,pe-nə-trə-'bi-lə-tē\ noun (1665)
**1** : the inability of two portions of matter to occupy the same space at the same time
**2** : the quality or state of being impenetrable

**im·pen·e·tra·ble** \(,)im-'pe-nə-trə-bəl\ adjective [Middle English *impenetrabel*, from Middle French *impenetrable*, from Latin *impenetrabilis*, from *in-* + *penetrabilis* penetrable] (15th century)
**1 a** : incapable of being penetrated or pierced **b** : inaccessible to knowledge, reason, or sympathy : IMPERVIOUS
**2** : incapable of being comprehended : INSCRUTABLE
— **im·pen·e·tra·bly** \-blē\ adverb

**im·pen·i·tence** \(,)im-'pe-nə-tən(t)s\ noun (1624)
archaic : the quality or state of being impenitent

**im·pen·i·tent** \-tənt\ adjective [Middle English, from Late Latin *impaenitent-, impaenitens*, from Latin *in-* + *paenitent-, paenitens* penitent] (15th century)
: not penitent
— **im·pen·i·tent·ly** adverb

**¹im·per·a·tive** \im-'per-ə-tiv\ adjective [Middle English *imperatyf*, from Late Latin *imperativus*, from Latin *imperatus*, past participle of *imperare* to command — more at EMPEROR] (15th century)
**1 a** : of, relating to, or constituting the grammatical mood that expresses the will to influence the behavior of another **b** : expressive of a command, entreaty, or exhortation **c** : having power to restrain, control, and direct
**2** : not to be avoided or evaded : NECESSARY ⟨an *imperative* duty⟩
synonym see MASTERFUL
— **im·per·a·tive·ly** adverb
— **im·per·a·tive·ness** noun

**²imperative** noun (1530)
**1** : the imperative mood or a verb form or verbal phrase expressing it
**2** : something that is imperative: as **a** : COMMAND, ORDER **b** : RULE, GUIDE **c** : an obligatory act or duty **d** : an imperative judgment or proposition

**im·pe·ra·tor** \,im-pə-'rä-tər, -,tòr\ noun [Latin — more at EMPEROR] (circa 1580)
: a commander in chief or emperor of the ancient Romans
— **im·per·a·to·ri·al** \(,)im-,per-ə-'tōr-ē-əl, -'tòr-\ adjective

**im·per·ceiv·able** \,im-pər-'sē-və-bəl\ adjective (circa 1617)
archaic : IMPERCEPTIBLE

**im·per·cep·ti·ble** \,im-pər-'sep-tə-bəl\ adjective [Middle French, from Medieval Latin *imperceptibilis*, from Latin *in-* + Late Latin *perceptibilis* perceptible] (15th century)
: not perceptible by a sense or by the mind : extremely slight, gradual, or subtle
— **im·per·cep·ti·bly** \-'sep-tə-blē\ adverb

**im·per·cep·tive** \,im-pər-'sep-tiv\ adjective (1661)
: not perceptive
— **im·per·cep·tive·ness** noun

**im·per·cip·i·ence** \-'si-pē-ən(t)s\ noun (1891)
: the quality or state of being imperceptive
— **im·per·cip·i·ent** \-ənt\ adjective

**¹im·per·fect** \(,)im-'pər-fikt\ adjective [alteration of Middle English *imperfit*, from Middle French *imparfait*, from Latin *imperfectus*, from *in-* + *perfectus* perfect] (1570)
**1** : not perfect: as **a** : DEFECTIVE **b** of a flower : having stamens or pistils but not both **c** : lacking or not involving sexual reproduction ⟨the *imperfect* stage of a fungus⟩
**2** : of, relating to, or constituting a verb tense used to designate a continuing state or an incomplete action especially in the past
**3** : not enforceable at law
— **im·per·fect·ly** \-fik(t)-lē\ adverb
— **im·per·fect·ness** \-fik(t)-nəs\ noun

**²imperfect** noun (1871)
: an imperfect tense; also : the verb form expressing it

**imperfect fungus** noun (circa 1895)
: any of various fungi (order Fungi Imperfecti synonym Deuteromycetes) of which only the conidial stage is known

**im·per·fec·tion** \,im-pər-'fek-shən\ noun (14th century)
: the quality or state of being imperfect; also : FAULT, BLEMISH

**im·per·fec·tive** \,im-pər-'fek-tiv\ adjective (1887)
of a verb form or aspect : expressing action as incomplete or without reference to completion or as reiterated — compare PERFECTIVE
— **imperfective** noun

**im·per·fo·rate** \(,)im-'pər-f(ə-)rət, -fə-,rāt\ adjective (1673)
**1** : having no opening or aperture; specifically : lacking the usual or normal opening
**2** of a stamp or a sheet of stamps : lacking perforations or roulettes

**¹im·pe·ri·al** \im-'pir-ē-əl\ adjective [Middle English, from Middle French, from Late Latin *imperialis*, from Latin *imperium* command, empire] (14th century)
**1 a** : of, relating to, befitting, or suggestive of an empire or an emperor **b** (1) : of or relating to the United Kingdom as distinguished from the constituent parts (2) : of or relating to the Commonwealth and British Empire
**2 a** : SOVEREIGN **b** : REGAL, IMPERIOUS
**3** : of superior or unusual size or excellence
**4** : belonging to the official British series of weights and measures — see WEIGHT table
— **im·pe·ri·al·ly** \-ə-lē\ adverb

**²imperial** noun (circa 1524)
**1** capitalized : an adherent or soldier of the Holy Roman emperor
**2** : EMPEROR
**3** [French *impériale*; from the beard worn by Napoléon III] : a pointed beard growing below the lower lip
**4** : something of unusual size or excellence

**im·pe·ri·al·ism** \im-'pir-ē-ə-,li-zəm\ noun (1851)
**1** : imperial government, authority, or system
**2** : the policy, practice, or advocacy of extending the power and dominion of a nation especially by direct territorial acquisitions or by gaining indirect control over the political or economic life of other areas; broadly : the extension or imposition of power, authority, or influence ⟨union *imperialism*⟩
— **im·pe·ri·al·ist** \-list\ noun or adjective
— **im·pe·ri·al·is·tic** \-,pir-ē-ə-'lis-tik\ adjective
— **im·pe·ri·al·is·ti·cal·ly** \-ti-k(ə-)lē\ adverb

**imperial moth** noun (circa 1904)
: a large American saturniid moth (*Eacles imperialis*) marked with yellow and lilac or purplish brown

**im·per·il** \im-'per-əl\ transitive verb **-iled** or **-illed; -il·ing** or **-il·ling** (15th century)
: to bring into peril : ENDANGER

imperial moth

— **im·per·il·ment** \-mənt\ noun

**im·pe·ri·ous** \im-'pir-ē-əs\ adjective [Latin *imperiosus*, from *imperium*] (1540)
**1** : befitting or characteristic of one of eminent rank or attainments : COMMANDING, DOMINANT ⟨an *imperious* manner⟩ **b** : marked by arrogant assurance : DOMINEERING
**2** : intensely compelling : URGENT ⟨the *imperious* problems of the new age —J. F. Kennedy⟩
synonym see MASTERFUL
— **im·pe·ri·ous·ly** adverb
— **im·pe·ri·ous·ness** noun

**im·per·ish·able** \(,)im-'per-i-shə-bəl\ adjective (1648)
**1** : not perishable or subject to decay
**2** : enduring or occurring forever ⟨*imperishable* fame⟩
— **im·per·ish·abil·i·ty** \-,per-i-shə-'bi-lə-tē\ noun
— **imperishable** noun
— **im·per·ish·able·ness** \-'per-i-shə-bəl-nəs\ noun
— **im·per·ish·ably** \-blē\ adverb

**im·pe·ri·um** \im-'pir-ē-əm\ noun [Latin — more at EMPIRE] (1651)
**1 a** : supreme power or absolute dominion : CONTROL **b** : EMPIRE
**2** : the right to command or to employ the force of the state : SOVEREIGNTY

**im·per·ma·nence** \(,)im-'pərm-nən(t)s, -'pər-mə-\ noun (1796)
: the quality or state of being impermanent

**im·per·ma·nen·cy** \-nən(t)-sē\ noun (1648)
: IMPERMANENCE

**im·per·ma·nent** \-nənt\ adjective (1653)
: not permanent : TRANSIENT
— **im·per·ma·nent·ly** adverb

**im·per·me·able** \(,)im-'pər-mē-ə-bəl\ adjective [Late Latin *impermeabilis*, from Latin *in-* + Late Latin *permeabilis* permeable] (1697)
: not permitting passage (as of a fluid) through its substance; broadly : IMPERVIOUS
— **im·per·me·abil·i·ty** \-,pər-mē-ə-'bi-lə-tē\ noun

**im·per·mis·si·ble** \,im-pər-'mi-sə-bəl\ adjective (1858)
: not permissible
— **im·per·mis·si·bil·i·ty** \-,mi-sə-'bi-lə-tē\ noun
— **im·per·mis·si·bly** \-'mi-sə-blē\ adverb

**im·per·son·al** \(,)im-'pərs-nəl, -'pər-s°n-əl\ adjective [Middle English, from Late Latin *impersonalis*, from Latin *in-* + Late Latin *personalis* personal] (15th century)
**1 a** : denoting the verbal action of an unspecified agent and hence used with no expressed subject (as *methinks*) or with a merely formal subject (as *rained* in *it rained*) **b** of a pronoun : INDEFINITE
**2 a** : having no personal reference or connection ⟨*impersonal* criticism⟩ **b** : not engaging the human personality or emotions ⟨the machine as compared with the hand tool is an *impersonal* agency —John Dewey⟩ **c** : not existing as a person : not having human qualities or characteristics
— **im·per·son·al·i·ty** \-,pər-s°n-'a-lə-tē\ noun
— **im·per·son·al·ly** \-'pərs-nə-lē, -'pər-s°n-ə-lē\ adverb

**im·per·son·al·ize** \(,)im-'pərs-nə-,līz, -'pər-s°n-ə-\ transitive verb (circa 1899)
: to make impersonal
— **im·per·son·al·i·za·tion** \-,pərs-nə-lə-'zā-shən, -,pər-s°n-ə-\ noun

**im·per·son·ate** \im-'pər-s°n-,āt\ transitive verb **-at·ed; -at·ing** (1715)
: to assume or act the character of : PERSONATE
— **im·per·son·a·tion** \-,pər-s°n-'ā-shən\ noun
— **im·per·son·a·tor** \-'pər-s°n-,ā-tər\ noun

**im·per·ti·nence** \(,)im-'pər-t°n-ən(t)s, -'pərt-nən(t)s\ noun (1603)
**1** : the quality or state of being impertinent: as **a** : IRRELEVANCE, INAPPROPRIATENESS **b** : INCIVILITY, INSOLENCE

**2** : an instance of impertinence

**im·per·ti·nen·cy** \-ən(t)-sē, -nən(t)-\ *noun, plural* **-cies** (1589)
: IMPERTINENCE

**im·per·ti·nent** \(ˌ)im-ˈpər-tᵊn-ənt, -ˈpərt-nənt\ *adjective* [Middle English, from Middle French, from Late Latin *impertinent-, impertinens,* from Latin *in-* + *pertinent-, pertinens,* present participle of *pertinēre* to pertain] (14th century)
**1** : not pertinent : IRRELEVANT
**2 a** : not restrained within due or proper bounds especially of propriety or good taste ⟨*impertinent* curiosity⟩ **b** : given to or characterized by insolent rudeness ⟨an *impertinent* answer⟩ ☆
— **im·per·ti·nent·ly** *adverb*

**im·per·turb·able** \ˌim-pər-ˈtər-bə-bəl\ *adjective* [Middle English, from Late Latin *imperturbabilis,* from Latin *in-* + *perturbare* to perturb] (15th century)
: marked by extreme calm, impassivity, and steadiness : SERENE
**synonym** see COOL
— **im·per·turb·abil·i·ty** \-ˌtər-bə-ˈbi-lə-tē\ *noun*
— **im·per·turb·ably** \-ˈtər-bə-blē\ *adverb*

**im·per·vi·ous** \(ˌ)im-ˈpər-vē-əs\ *adjective* [Latin *impervius,* from *in-* + *pervius* pervious] (1650)
**1 a** : not allowing entrance or passage : IMPENETRABLE ⟨a coat *impervious* to rain⟩ **b** : not capable of being damaged or harmed ⟨a carpet *impervious* to rough treatment⟩
**2** : not capable of being affected or disturbed ⟨*impervious* to criticism⟩
— **im·per·vi·ous·ly** *adverb*
— **im·per·vi·ous·ness** *noun*

**im·pe·tig·i·nous** \ˌim-pə-ˈti-jə-nəs\ *adjective* (1620)
: of, relating to, or resembling impetigo ⟨*impetiginous* lesions⟩

**im·pe·ti·go** \ˌim-pə-ˈtē-(ˌ)gō, -ˈtī-\ *noun* [Latin, from *impetere* to attack — more at IMPETUS] (14th century)
: an acute contagious staphylococcal or streptococcal skin disease characterized by vesicles, pustules, and yellowish crusts

**im·pe·trate** \ˈim-pə-ˌtrāt\ *transitive verb* **-trat·ed; -trat·ing** [Latin *impetratus,* past participle of *impetrare,* from *in-* + *patrare* to accomplish — more at PERPETRATE] (circa 1534)
**1** : to obtain by request or entreaty
**2** : to ask for : ENTREAT
— **im·pe·tra·tion** \ˌim-pə-ˈtrā-shən\ *noun*

**im·pet·u·os·i·ty** \im-ˌpe-chə-ˈwä-sə-tē\ *noun, plural* **-ties** (15th century)
**1** : the quality or state of being impetuous
**2** : an impetuous action or impulse

**im·pet·u·ous** \im-ˈpech-wəs, -ˈpe-chə-\ *adjective* [Middle English, from Middle French *impetueux,* from Late Latin *impetuosus,* from Latin *impetus*] (14th century)
**1** : marked by impulsive vehemence or passion ⟨an *impetuous* temperament⟩
**2** : marked by force and violence of movement or action ⟨an *impetuous* wind⟩
**synonym** see PRECIPITATE
— **im·pet·u·ous·ly** *adverb*
— **im·pet·u·ous·ness** *noun*

**im·pe·tus** \ˈim-pə-təs\ *noun* [Latin, assault, impetus, from *impetere* to attack, from *in-* + *petere* to go to, seek — more at FEATHER] (1641)
**1 a** (1) : a driving force : IMPULSE (2) : INCENTIVE, STIMULUS **b** : stimulation or encouragement resulting in increased activity
**2** : the property possessed by a moving body in virtue of its mass and its motion — used of bodies moving suddenly or violently to indicate the origin and intensity of the motion

**im·pi·e·ty** \(ˌ)im-ˈpī-ə-tē\ *noun, plural* **-ties** (14th century)
**1** : the quality or state of being impious : IRREVERENCE
**2** : an impious act

**im·pinge** \im-ˈpinj\ *intransitive verb* **impinged; im·ping·ing** [Latin *impingere,* from *in-* + *pangere* to fasten, drive in — more at PACT] (1605)
**1** : to strike or dash especially with a sharp collision ⟨I heard the rain *impinge* upon the earth —James Joyce⟩
**2** : to have an effect : make an impression ⟨waiting for the germ of a new idea to *impinge* upon my mind —Phyllis Bentley⟩
**3** : ENCROACH, INFRINGE ⟨*impinge* on other people's rights⟩
— **im·pinge·ment** \-ˈpinj-mənt\ *noun*

**im·pi·ous** \ˈim-pē-əs, (ˌ)im-ˈpī-\ *adjective* [Latin *impius,* from *in-* + *pius* pious] (1542)
: not pious : lacking in reverence or proper respect (as for God or one's parents) : IRREVERENT
— **im·pi·ous·ly** *adverb*

**imp·ish** \ˈim-pish\ *adjective* (1652)
: of, relating to, or befitting an imp; *especially* : MISCHIEVOUS
— **imp·ish·ly** *adverb*
— **imp·ish·ness** *noun*

**im·pla·ca·ble** \(ˌ)im-ˈpla-kə-bəl, -ˈplā-\ *adjective* [Middle French or Latin; Middle French, from Latin *implacabilis,* from *in-* + *placabilis* placable] (15th century)
: not placable : not capable of being appeased, significantly changed, or mitigated ⟨an *implacable* enemy⟩
— **im·pla·ca·bil·i·ty** \-ˌpla-kə-ˈbi-lə-tē, -ˌplā-\ *noun*
— **im·pla·ca·bly** \-ˈpla-kə-blē, -ˈplā-\ *adverb*

**¹im·plant** \im-ˈplant\ *transitive verb* (15th century)
**1 a** : to fix or set securely or deeply ⟨a ruby *implanted* in the idol's forehead⟩ **b** : to set permanently in the consciousness or habit patterns : INCULCATE
**2** : to insert in a living site (as for growth, slow release, or formation of an organic union) ⟨subcutaneously *implanted* hormone pellets⟩ ☆
— **im·plant·able** \-ˈplan-tə-bəl\ *adjective*
— **im·plant·er** \im-ˈplan-tər\ *noun*

**²im·plant** \ˈim-ˌplant\ *noun* (1890)
: something (as a graft or pellet) implanted in tissue

**im·plan·ta·tion** \ˌim-ˌplan-ˈtā-shən\ *noun* (1578)
**1 a** : the act or process of implanting something **b** : the state resulting from being implanted
**2** *in placental mammals* : the process of attachment of the embryo to the maternal uterine wall

**im·plau·si·ble** \(ˌ)im-ˈplȯ-zə-bəl\ *adjective* (circa 1677)
: not plausible : provoking disbelief
— **im·plau·si·bil·i·ty** \-ˌplȯ-zə-ˈbi-lə-tē\ *noun*
— **im·plau·si·bly** \-ˈplȯ-zə-blē\ *adverb*

**im·plead** \im-ˈplēd\ *transitive verb* [Middle English *empleden,* from Middle French *emplaider,* from Old French *emplaidier,* from *en-* + *plaidier* to plead] (14th century)
: to sue or prosecute at law

**¹im·ple·ment** \ˈim-plə-mənt\ *noun* [Middle English, from Late Latin *implementum* action of filling up, from Latin *implēre* to fill up, from *in-* + *plēre* to fill — more at FULL] (15th century)
**1** : an article serving to equip ⟨the *implements* of religious worship⟩
**2** : a device used in the performance of a task
**3** : one that serves as an instrument or tool ⟨the partnership agreement does not seem to be a very potent *implement* —H. B. Hoffman⟩ ☆

**²im·ple·ment** \-ˌment\ *transitive verb* (1806)
**1** : CARRY OUT, ACCOMPLISH; *especially* : to give practical effect to and ensure of actual fulfillment by concrete measures
**2** : to provide instruments or means of expression for

**— im·ple·men·ta·tion** \ˌim-plə-mən-ˈtā-shən, -ˌmen-\ *noun*

**— im·ple·men·ter** *or* **im·ple·men·tor** \ˈim-plə-ˌmən-tər\ *noun*

**im·pli·cate** \ˈim-plə-ˌkāt\ *transitive verb* **-cat·ed; -cat·ing** [Middle English, to convey by implication, from Medieval Latin *implicatus,* past participle of *implicare,* from Latin, to entwine, involve — more at EMPLOY] (15th century)
**1** : to involve as a consequence, corollary, or natural inference : IMPLY
**2** *archaic* : to fold or twist together : ENTWINE
**3 a** : to bring into intimate or incriminating connection **b** : to involve in the nature or operation of something

**im·pli·ca·tion** \ˌim-plə-ˈkā-shən\ *noun* (15th century)
**1 a** : the act of implicating : the state of being implicated **b** : close connection; *especially* : an incriminating involvement

---

**2 a :** the act of implying **:** the state of being implied **b** (1) **:** a logical relation between two propositions that fails to hold only if the first is true and the second is false (2) **:** a logical relationship between two propositions in which if the first is true the second is true (3) **:** a statement exhibiting a relation of implication **3 :** something implied: as **a :** SUGGESTION **b :** a possible significance ⟨the book has political *implications*⟩
— **im·pli·ca·tive** \'im-plə-ˌkā-tiv, im-'pli-kə-\ *adjective*
— **im·pli·ca·tive·ly** *adverb*
— **im·pli·ca·tive·ness** *noun*

**im·plic·it** \im-'pli-sət\ *adjective* [Latin *implicitus*, past participle of *implicare*] (1599) **1 a :** capable of being understood from something else though unexpressed **:** IMPLIED ⟨an *implicit* assumption⟩ **b :** involved in the nature or essence of something though not revealed, expressed, or developed **:** POTENTIAL ⟨a sculptor may see different figures *implicit* in a block of stone —John Dewey⟩ **c** *of a mathematical function* **:** defined by an expression in which the dependent variable and the one or more independent variables are not separated on opposite sides of an equation — compare EXPLICIT 4 **2 :** being without doubt or reserve **:** UNQUESTIONING
— **im·plic·it·ly** *adverb*
— **im·plic·it·ness** *noun*

**implicit differentiation** *noun* (circa 1889) **:** the process of finding the derivative of a dependent variable in an implicit function by differentiating each term separately, by expressing the derivative of the dependent variable as a symbol, and by solving the resulting expression for the symbol

**im·plode** \im-'plōd\ *verb* **im·plod·ed; im·plod·ing** [²*in-* + *-plode* (as in *explode*)] (1881) *intransitive verb* **1 a :** to burst inward ⟨a blow causing a vacuum tube to *implode*⟩ **b :** to undergo violent compression ⟨massive stars which *implode*⟩ **2 :** to collapse inward as if from external pressure; *also* **:** to become greatly reduced as if from collapsing *transitive verb* **:** to cause to implode

**im·plore** \im-'plōr, -'plȯr\ *transitive verb* **im·plored; im·plor·ing** [Middle French or Latin; Middle French *implorer*, from Latin *implorare*, from *in-* + *plorare* to cry out] (circa 1540) **1 :** to call upon in supplication **:** BESEECH **2 :** to call or pray for earnestly **:** ENTREAT
**synonym** see BEG
— **im·plor·ing·ly** *adverb*

**im·plo·sion** \im-'plō-zhən\ *noun* [²*in-* + *-plosion* (as in *explosion*)] (1877) **1 :** the inrush of air in forming a suction stop **2 :** the action of imploding **3 :** the act or action of bringing to or as if to a center; *also* **:** INTEGRATION ⟨this *implosion* of cultures makes realistic for the first time the age-old vision of a world culture —Kenneth Keniston⟩
— **im·plo·sive** \-'plō-siv, -ziv\ *adjective or noun*

**im·ply** \im-'plī\ *transitive verb* **im·plied; im·ply·ing** [Middle English *emplien*, from Middle French *emplier*, from Latin *implicare*] (14th century) **1** *obsolete* **:** ENFOLD, ENTWINE **2 :** to involve or indicate by inference, association, or necessary consequence rather than by direct statement ⟨rights *imply* obligations⟩ **3 :** to contain potentially **4 :** to express indirectly ⟨his silence *implied* consent⟩
**synonym** see SUGGEST
**usage** see INFER

**im·po·lite** \ˌim-pə-'līt\ *adjective* [Latin *impolitus*, from *in-* + *politus* polite] (1739)

**:** not polite **:** RUDE
— **im·po·lite·ly** *adverb*
— **im·po·lite·ness** *noun*

**im·pol·i·tic** \(ˌ)im-'pä-lə-ˌtik\ *adjective* (circa 1600) **:** not politic **:** RASH
— **im·po·lit·i·cal** \-pə-'li-ti-kəl\ *adjective*
— **im·po·lit·i·cal·ly** \-'li-ti-k(ə-)lē\ *adverb*
— **im·pol·i·tic·ly** \-'pä-lə-ˌti-klē\ *adverb*

**im·pon·der·a·ble** \(ˌ)im-'pän-d(ə-)rə-bəl\ *adjective* [Medieval Latin *imponderabilis*, from Latin *in-* + Late Latin *ponderabilis* ponderable] (1794) **:** not ponderable **:** incapable of being weighed or evaluated with exactness
— **im·pon·der·a·bil·i·ty** \-ˌpän-d(ə-)rə-'bi-lə-tē\ *noun*
— **imponderable** *noun*
— **im·pon·der·a·bly** \-'pän-d(ə-)rə-blē\ *adverb*

**im·pone** \im-'pōn\ *transitive verb* **im·poned; im·pon·ing** [Latin *imponere* to put upon, from *in-* + *ponere* to put — more at POSITION] (circa 1623) *obsolete* **:** WAGER, BET

**¹im·port** \im-'pōrt, -'pȯrt, 'im-,\ *verb* [Middle English, from Latin *importare* to bring into, from *in-* + *portare* to carry — more at FARE] (15th century) *transitive verb* **1 a :** to bear or convey as meaning or portent **:** SIGNIFY **b** *archaic* **:** EXPRESS, STATE **c :** IMPLY **2 :** to bring from a foreign or external source; *especially* **:** to bring (as merchandise) into a place or country from another country **3** *archaic* **:** to be of importance to **:** CONCERN *intransitive verb* **:** to be of consequence **:** MATTER
— **im·port·able** \im-'pōr-tə-bəl, -'pȯr-, 'im-,\ *adjective*
— **im·port·er** *noun*

**²im·port** \'im-ˌpōrt, -ˌpȯrt\ *noun* (circa 1568) **1 :** IMPORTANCE; *especially* **:** relative importance ⟨it is hard to determine the *import* of this decision⟩ **2 :** PURPORT, SIGNIFICATION **3 :** something that is imported **4 :** IMPORTATION

**im·por·tance** \im-'pȯr-tᵊn(t)s, *especially* Southern & New England -tən(t)s, -dən(t)s\ *noun* (1508) **1 a :** the quality or state of being important **:** CONSEQUENCE **b :** an important aspect or bearing **:** SIGNIFICANCE **2** *obsolete* **:** IMPORT, MEANING **3** *obsolete* **:** IMPORTUNITY **4** *obsolete* **:** a weighty matter ☆

**im·por·tan·cy** \-tᵊn(t)-sē, -tən(t)-, -dən(t)-\ *noun* (1540) *archaic* **:** IMPORTANCE

**im·por·tant** \im-'pȯr-tᵊnt, *especially Southern & New England* -tənt, -dənt\ *adjective* [Middle English *importante*, from Medieval Latin *important-, importans*, present participle of *importare* to signify, from Latin, to bring into] (15th century) **1 :** marked by or indicative of significant worth or consequence **:** valuable in content or relationship **2** *obsolete* **:** IMPORTUNATE, URGENT **3 :** giving evidence of a feeling of self-importance
**usage** see IMPORTANTLY

**im·por·tant·ly** \-lē\ *adverb* (1647) **1 :** in an important way ⟨contributed *importantly* to the language of the field —Ernst Mayr⟩ ⟨cleared his throat *importantly* and waited —E. K. Gann⟩ ⟨the real story is *importantly* different —Alexander Woollcott⟩ **2 :** it is important that ⟨more *importantly* he stands a chance of having his publication barred —H. L. Mencken⟩ ☐

**im·por·ta·tion** \ˌim-ˌpȯr-'tā-shən, -ˌpȯr-, -pər-\ *noun* (1601) **1 :** the act or practice of importing **2 :** something imported

**imported cabbageworm** *noun* (1892) **:** a small cosmopolitan white butterfly (*Pieris rapae*) or its larva which is a pest of cruciferous plants and especially cabbage

**imported fire ant** *noun* (circa 1949) **:** either of two mound-building South American fire ants (*Solenopsis richteri* and *S. invicta*) introduced into the southeastern U.S. that are agricultural pests and can produce stings requiring medical attention

**im·por·tu·nate** \im-'pȯr-chə-nət, -tyu̇-nət\ *adjective* (1529) **1 :** troublesomely urgent **:** overly persistent in request or demand **2 :** TROUBLESOME
— **im·por·tu·nate·ly** *adverb*
— **im·por·tu·nate·ness** *noun*

**¹im·por·tune** \ˌim-pər-'tün, -'tyün; im-'pȯr-ˌ, -chən\ *adjective* [Middle English, from Middle French & Latin; Middle French *importun*, from Latin *importunus*, from *in-* + *-portunus* (as in *opportunus* fit) — more at OPPORTUNE] (15th century) **:** IMPORTUNATE
— **im·por·tune·ly** *adverb*

**²importune** *verb* **-tuned; -tun·ing** (1530) *transitive verb* **1 a :** to press or urge with troublesome persistence **b** *archaic* **:** to request or beg for urgently **2 :** ANNOY, TROUBLE *intransitive verb* **:** to beg, urge, or solicit persistently or troublesomely
**synonym** see BEG
— **im·por·tun·er** *noun*

**im·por·tu·ni·ty** \ˌim-pər-'tü-nə-tē, -'tyü-\ *noun, plural* **-ties** (15th century) **1 :** the quality or state of being importunate **2 :** an importunate request or demand

---

☆ **SYNONYMS**
**Importance, consequence, moment, weight, significance** mean a quality or aspect having great worth or significance. IMPORTANCE implies a value judgment of the superior worth or influence of something or someone ⟨a region with no cities of *importance*⟩. CONSEQUENCE generally implies importance because of probable or possible effects ⟨the style you choose is of little *consequence*⟩. MOMENT implies conspicuous or self-evident consequence ⟨a decision of great *moment*⟩. WEIGHT implies a judgment of the immediate relative importance of something ⟨the argument carried no *weight* with the judge⟩. SIGNIFICANCE implies a quality or character that should mark a thing as important but that is not self-evident and may or may not be recognized ⟨the treaty's *significance*⟩.

---

☐ **USAGE**
**importantly** A number of commentators have objected to *importantly* as a sentence modifier (sense 2) and have recommended *important* instead. Actually both the adverb and the adjective are in reputable standard use in this function. *Important* is always used with *more* or *most* ⟨had bronze weapons and composite bows; more *important*, they utilized the horse and war chariot —Harry A. Gailey, Jr.⟩ ⟨second and most *important*, the book contains no important woman character —F. Scott Fitzgerald⟩. *Importantly* is somewhat more flexible in not requiring *more* or *most* ⟨sticks and, just as *importantly*, unsticks easily —Phoebe Hawkins⟩ ⟨*importantly*, the leaven in the mixture is quality —George O'Brien⟩.

**im·pose** \im-'pōz\ *verb* **im·posed; im·pos·ing** [Middle French *imposer*, from Latin *imponere*, literally, to put upon (perfect indicative *imposui*), from *in-* + *ponere* to put — more at POSITION] (1581)
*transitive verb*
**1 a :** to establish or apply by authority ⟨*impose* a tax⟩ ⟨*impose* new restrictions⟩ ⟨*impose* penalties⟩ **b :** to establish or bring about as if by force ⟨those limits *imposed* by our own inadequacies —C. H. Plimpton⟩
**2 a :** PLACE, SET **b :** to arrange (as pages) in the proper order for printing
**3 :** PASS OFF ⟨*impose* fake antiques on the public⟩
**4 :** to force into the company or on the attention of another ⟨*impose* oneself on others⟩
*intransitive verb*
**:** to take unwarranted advantage of something ⟨*imposed* on his good nature⟩
— **im·pos·er** *noun*
**im·pos·ing** \im-'pō-ziŋ\ *adjective* (1786)
**:** impressive in size, bearing, dignity, or grandeur
**synonym** see GRAND
— **im·pos·ing·ly** \-ziŋ-lē\ *adverb*
**im·po·si·tion** \,im-pə-'zi-shən\ *noun* (14th century)
**1 :** something imposed: as **a :** LEVY, TAX **b :** an excessive or uncalled-for requirement or burden
**2 :** the act of imposing
**3 :** DECEPTION
**4 :** the order of arrangement of imposed pages
**im·pos·si·bil·i·ty** \(,)im-,pä-sə-'bi-lə-tē\ *noun* (14th century)
**1 :** the quality or state of being impossible
**2 :** something impossible
**im·pos·si·ble** \(,)im-'pä-sə-bəl\ *adjective* [Middle English, from Middle French & Latin; Middle French, from Latin *impossibilis*, from *in-* + *possibilis* possible] (14th century)
**1 a :** incapable of being or of occurring **b :** felt to be incapable of being done, attained, or fulfilled **:** insuperably difficult
**2 a :** extremely undesirable **:** UNACCEPTABLE **b :** extremely awkward or difficult to deal with
— **im·pos·si·ble·ness** *noun*
**im·pos·si·bly** \-blē\ *adverb* (circa 1580)
**1 :** not possibly
**2 :** to an improbable degree **:** UNBELIEVABLY ⟨an *impossibly* green lawn⟩
**¹im·post** \'im-,pōst\ *noun* [Middle French, from Medieval Latin *impositum*, from Latin, neuter of *impositus*, past participle of *imponere*] (1568)
**:** something imposed or levied **:** TAX
**²impost** *noun* [French *imposte*, ultimately from Latin *impositus*] (1664)
**:** a block, capital, or molding from which an arch springs — see ARCH illustration
**im·pos·tor** *or* **im·pos·ter** \im-'päs-tər\ *noun* [Late Latin *impostor*, from Latin *imponere*] (1624)
**:** one that assumes false identity or title for the purpose of deception
**im·pos·tume** \im-'päs-,chüm\ *or* **im·pos·thume** \-,thüm, -,thyüm\ *noun* [Middle English *emposteme*, ultimately from Greek *apostēma*, from *aphistanai* to remove, from *apo-* + *histanai* to cause to stand — more at STAND] (14th century)
*archaic* **:** ABSCESS
**im·pos·ture** \im-'päs-chər\ *noun* [Late Latin *impostura*, from Latin *impositus, impostus*, past participle of *imponere*] (1537)
**1 :** the act or practice of deceiving by means of an assumed character or name
**2 :** an instance of imposture ☆
**im·po·tence** \'im-pə-tən(t)s\ *noun* (15th century)
**:** the quality or state of being impotent
**im·po·ten·cy** \-tən(t)-sē\ *noun* (15th century)
**:** IMPOTENCE
**im·po·tent** \'im-pə-tənt\ *adjective* [Middle English, from Middle French & Latin; Middle

French, from Latin *impotent-, impotens*, from *in-* + *potent-, potens* potent] (14th century)
**1 a :** not potent **:** lacking in power, strength, or vigor **:** HELPLESS **b :** unable to copulate; *broadly* **:** STERILE — usually used of males
**2** *obsolete* **:** incapable of self-restraint **:** UNGOVERNABLE
— **impotent** *noun*
— **im·po·tent·ly** *adverb*
**im·pound** \im-'paůnd\ *transitive verb* (15th century)
**1 a :** to shut up in or as if in a pound **:** CONFINE
**b :** to seize and hold in the custody of the law
**c :** to take possession of ⟨she was dismissed and her manuscript *impounded* —Jonathan Weiner⟩
**2 :** to collect and confine (water) in or as if in a reservoir
**im·pound·ment** \-'paůn(d)-mənt\ *noun* (circa 1665)
**1 :** the act of impounding **:** the state of being impounded
**2 :** a body of water formed by impounding
**im·pov·er·ish** \im-'päv-rish, -'pä-və-\ *transitive verb* [Middle English *enpoverisen*, from Middle French *empoviss-*, stem of *empovrir*, from *en-* + *povre* poor — more at POOR] (15th century)
**1 :** to make poor
**2 :** to deprive of strength, richness, or fertility by depleting or draining of something essential
**synonym** see DEPLETE
— **im·pov·er·ish·er** *noun*
— **im·pov·er·ish·ment** \-mənt\ *noun*
**impoverished** *adjective* (1950)
*of a fauna or flora* **:** represented by few species or individuals
**im·prac·ti·ca·ble** \(,)im-'prak-ti-kə-bəl\ *adjective* (1653)
**1 :** IMPASSABLE ⟨an *impracticable* road⟩
**2 :** not practicable **:** incapable of being performed or accomplished by the means employed or at command
— **im·prac·ti·ca·bil·i·ty** \-,prak-ti-kə-'bi-lə-tē\ *noun*
— **im·prac·ti·ca·bly** \-'prak-ti-kə-blē\ *adverb*
**im·prac·ti·cal** \(,)im-'prak-ti-kəl\ *adjective* (1865)
**:** not practical: as **a :** not wise to put into or keep in practice or effect **b :** incapable of dealing sensibly or prudently with practical matters **c :** IMPRACTICABLE **d :** IDEALISTIC
— **im·prac·ti·cal·i·ty** \-,prak-ti-'ka-lə-tē\ *noun*
— **im·prac·ti·cal·ly** \-'prak-ti-k(ə-)lē\ *adverb*
**im·pre·cate** \'im-pri-,kāt\ *verb* **-cat·ed; -cat·ing** [Latin *imprecatus*, past participle of *imprecari*, from *in-* + *precari* to pray — more at PRAY] (1613)
*transitive verb*
**:** to invoke evil on **:** CURSE
*intransitive verb*
**:** to utter curses
**im·pre·ca·tion** \,im-pri-'kā-shən\ *noun* (15th century)
**1 :** CURSE
**2 :** the act of imprecating
— **im·pre·ca·to·ry** \'im-pri-kə-,tōr-ē, im-'pre-kə-, -,tòr-\ *adjective*
**im·pre·cise** \,im-pri-'sīs\ *adjective* (1805)
**:** not precise **:** INEXACT, VAGUE
— **im·pre·cise·ly** *adverb*
— **im·pre·cise·ness** *noun*
— **im·pre·ci·sion** \-'si-zhən\ *noun*
**im·preg·na·ble** \im-'preg-nə-bəl\ *adjective* [Middle English *imprenable*, from Middle French, from *in-* + *prenable* vulnerable to capture, from *prendre* to take — more at PRIZE] (15th century)
**1 :** incapable of being taken by assault **:** UNCONQUERABLE
**2 :** UNASSAILABLE; *also* **:** IMPENETRABLE

— **im·preg·na·bil·i·ty** \(,)im-,preg-nə-'bi-lə-tē\ *noun*
— **im·preg·na·ble·ness** \im-'preg-nə-bəl-nəs\ *noun*
— **im·preg·na·bly** \-blē\ *adverb*
**im·preg·nant** \im-'preg-nənt\ *noun* (1926)
**:** a substance used for impregnating another substance
**¹im·preg·nate** \im-'preg-,nāt, 'im-,\ *transitive verb* **-nat·ed; -nat·ing** [Late Latin *impraegnatus*, past participle of *impraegnare*, from Latin *in-* + *praegnas* pregnant] (1605)
**1 a :** to cause to be filled, imbued, permeated, or saturated **b :** to permeate thoroughly
**2 :** to make pregnant **:** FERTILIZE
**synonym** see SOAK
— **im·preg·na·tion** \(,)im-,preg-'nā-shən\ *noun*
— **im·preg·na·tor** \im-'preg-,nā-tər, 'im-,\ *noun*
**²im·preg·nate** \im-'preg-nət\ *adjective* (1646)
**:** being filled or saturated
**im·pre·sa** \im-'prā-zə, -sə\ *noun* [Italian, literally, undertaking] (1588)
**:** a device with a motto used in the 16th and 17th centuries; *broadly* **:** EMBLEM
**im·pre·sa·rio** \,im-prə-'sär-ē-,ō, -'sar-, -'zär-\ *noun, plural* **-ri·os** [Italian, from *impresa* undertaking, from *imprendere* to undertake, from (assumed) Vulgar Latin *imprehendere* — more at EMPRISE] (1746)
**1 :** the promoter, manager, or conductor of an opera or concert company
**2 :** a person who puts on or sponsors an entertainment (as a television show or sports event)
**3 :** MANAGER, DIRECTOR
**¹im·press** \im-'pres\ *verb* [Middle English, from Latin *impressus*, past participle of *imprimere*, from *in-* + *premere* to press — more at PRESS] (14th century)
*transitive verb*
**1 a :** to apply with pressure so as to imprint **b :** to produce (as a mark) by pressure **c :** to mark by or as if by pressure or stamping
**2 a :** to produce a vivid impression of **b :** to affect especially forcibly or deeply **:** INFLUENCE
**3 :** TRANSFER, TRANSMIT
*intransitive verb*
**:** to produce an impression
**synonym** see AFFECT
— **im·press·ibil·i·ty** \-,pre-sə-'bi-lə-tē\ *noun*
— **im·press·ible** \-'pre-sə-bəl\ *adjective*
**²im·press** \'im-,pres *also* im-'\ *noun* (1590)

---

☆ **SYNONYMS**
**Imposture, fraud, sham, fake, humbug, counterfeit** mean a thing made to seem other than it is. IMPOSTURE applies to any situation in which a spurious object or performance is passed off as genuine ⟨their claim of environmental concern is an *imposture*⟩. FRAUD usually implies a deliberate perversion of the truth ⟨the diary was exposed as a *fraud*⟩. SHAM applies to fraudulent imitation of a real thing or action ⟨condemned the election as a *sham*⟩. FAKE implies an imitation of or substitution for the genuine but does not necessarily imply dishonesty ⟨these jewels are *fakes;* the real ones are in the vault⟩. HUMBUG suggests elaborate pretense usually so flagrant as to be transparent ⟨creating publicity by foisting *humbugs* on a gullible public⟩. COUNTERFEIT applies especially to the close imitation of something valuable ⟨20-dollar bills that were *counterfeits*⟩.

---

\ə\ abut \ᵊ\ kitten \ər\ further \a\ ash \ā\ ace
\ä\ mop, mar \aů\ out \ch\ chin \e\ bet \ē\ easy
\g\ go \i\ hit \ī\ ice \j\ job \ŋ\ sing \ō\ go
\ò\ law \òi\ boy \th\ thin \t͟h\ the \ü\ loot \ů\ foot
\y\ yet \zh\ vision *see also* Guide to Pronunciation

**1 :** a characteristic or distinctive mark **:** STAMP ⟨the *impress* of a fresh and vital intelligence is stamped . . . in his work —Lytton Strachey⟩ **2 :** IMPRESSION, EFFECT ⟨have an *impress* on history⟩ **3 :** the act of impressing **4 a :** a mark made by pressure **:** IMPRINT **b :** an image of something formed by or as if by pressure; *especially* **:** SEAL **c :** a product of pressure or influence

³**im·press** \im-'pres\ *transitive verb* [²*in-* + ³*press*] (1596) **1 :** to levy or take by force for public service; *especially* **:** to force into naval service **2 a :** to procure or enlist by forcible persuasion **b :** FORCE ⟨*impressed* him into a white coat for the Christmas festivities —Nancy Hale⟩

⁴**im·press** \'im-ˌpres *also* im-'\ *noun* (1602) **:** IMPRESSMENT

**im·pres·sion** \im-'pre-shən\ *noun* (14th century) **1 a :** a characteristic, trait, or feature resulting from some influence ⟨the *impression* on behavior produced by the social milieu⟩ **b :** an effect of alteration or improvement ⟨the settlement left little *impression* on the wilderness⟩ **c :** a telling image impressed on the senses or the mind **2 :** the effect produced by impressing: as **a :** a stamp, form, or figure resulting from physical contact **b :** an imprint of the teeth and adjacent portions of the jaw for use in dentistry **c :** an especially marked and often favorable influence or effect on feeling, sense, or mind **3 :** the act of impressing: as **a :** an affecting by stamping or pressing **b :** a communicating of a mold, trait, or character by an external force or influence **4 a :** the amount of pressure with which an inked printing surface deposits its ink on the paper **b :** one instance of the meeting of a printing surface and the material being printed; *also* **:** a single print or copy so made **c :** all the copies (as of a book) printed in one continuous operation from a single makeready **5 :** an often indistinct or imprecise notion or remembrance **6 :** the first coat of color in painting **b :** a coat of paint for ornament or preservation **7 :** an imitation or representation of salient features in an artistic or theatrical medium; *especially* **:** an imitation in caricature of a noted personality as a form of theatrical entertainment

**synonym** see IDEA

**im·pres·sion·able** \im-'pre-sh(ə-)nə-bəl\ *adjective* (1836) **:** capable of being easily impressed
— **im·pres·sion·abil·i·ty** \-ˌpre-sh(ə-)nə-'bi-lə-tē\ *noun*

**im·pres·sion·ism** \im-'pre-shə-ˌni-zəm\ *noun* (1882) **1** *often capitalized* **:** a theory or practice in painting especially among French painters of about 1870 of depicting the natural appearances of objects by means of dabs or strokes of primary unmixed colors in order to simulate actual reflected light **2 a :** the depiction (as in literature) of scene, emotion, or character by details intended to achieve a vividness or effectiveness more by evoking subjective and sensory impressions than by recreating an objective reality **b :** a style of musical composition designed to create subtle moods and impressions

**im·pres·sion·ist** \im-'pre-sh(ə-)nist\ *noun* (1876) **1** *often capitalized* **:** one (as a painter) who practices or adheres to the theories of impressionism **2 :** an entertainer who does impressions

**im·pres·sion·is·tic** \(ˌ)im-ˌpre-shə-'nis-tik\ *adjective* (1886)

**1** *or* **im·pres·sion·ist** \im-'pre-sh(ə-)nist\ *often capitalized* **:** of, relating to, or constituting impressionism **2 :** based on or involving impression as distinct from expertise or fact ⟨intuitions and *impressionistic* anecdotal accounts —Sidney Hook⟩
— **im·pres·sion·is·ti·cal·ly** \(ˌ)im-ˌpre-shə-'nis-ti-k(ə-)lē\ *adverb*

**im·pres·sive** \im-'pre-siv\ *adjective* (1598) **:** making or tending to make a marked impression **:** having the power to excite attention, awe, or admiration

**synonym** see MOVING
— **im·pres·sive·ly** *adverb*
— **im·pres·sive·ness** *noun*

**im·press·ment** \im-'pres-mənt\ *noun* (1787) **:** the act of seizing for public use or of impressing into public service

**im·pres·sure** \im-'pre-shər\ *noun* (1600) *archaic* **:** a mark made by pressure **:** IMPRESSION

**im·prest** \'im-ˌprest\ *noun* [obsolete *imprest* to lend, probably from Italian *imprestare*] (1568) **:** a loan or advance of money

**im·pri·ma·tur** \ˌim-prə-'mä-ˌtùr, im-'pri-mə-ˌtùr, -ˌtyùr\ *noun* [New Latin, let it be printed, from *imprimere* to print, from Latin, to imprint, impress — more at IMPRESS] (1640) **1 a :** a license to print or publish especially by Roman Catholic episcopal authority **b :** approval of a publication under circumstances of official censorship **2 a :** SANCTION, APPROVAL **b :** IMPRINT **c :** a mark of approval or distinction

**im·pri·mis** \im-'prī-məs, -'prē-\ *adverb* [Middle English *imprimis*, from Latin *in primis* among the first (things)] (15th century) **:** in the first place — used to introduce a list of items or considerations

¹**im·print** \im-'print, 'im-ˌ\ (14th century) *transitive verb* **1 :** to mark by or as if by pressure **:** IMPRESS **2 a :** to fix indelibly or permanently (as on the memory) **b :** to subject to or induce by imprinting ⟨an *imprinted* preference⟩ *intransitive verb* **:** to undergo imprinting
— **im·print·er** \-'prin-tər, -ˌprin-\ *noun*

²**im·print** \'im-ˌprint\ *noun* [Middle English *enpreent*, from Middle French *empreinte*, from feminine of *empreint*, past participle of *empreindre* to imprint, from Latin *imprimere*] (15th century) **:** something imprinted or printed: as **a :** a mark or depression made by pressure ⟨the fossil *imprint* of a dinosaur's foot⟩ **b :** an identifying name (as of a publisher) placed conspicuously on a product; *also* **:** the name under which a publisher issues books **c :** an indelible distinguishing effect or influence

**im·print·ing** \'im-ˌprin-tiŋ, im-'\ *noun* (1937) **:** a rapid learning process that takes place early in the life of a social animal (as a greylag goose) and establishes a behavior pattern (as recognition of and attraction to its own kind or a substitute)

**im·pris·on** \im-'pri-zᵊn\ *transitive verb* [Middle English, from Old French *emprisoner*, from *en-* + *prison* prison] (14th century) **:** to put in or as if in prison **:** CONFINE
— **im·pris·on·ment** \-mənt\ *noun*

**im·prob·a·ble** \(ˌ)im-'prä-bə-bəl, -'präb-bəl\ *adjective* [Middle French or Latin; Middle French, from Latin *improbabilis*, from *in-* + *probabilis* probable] (1598) **:** unlikely to be true or to occur; *also* **:** unlikely but real or true
— **im·prob·a·bil·i·ty** \-ˌprä-bə-'bi-lə-tē\ *noun*
— **im·prob·a·bly** \-'prä-bə-blē, -'präb-blē\ *adverb*

¹**im·promp·tu** \im-'präm(p)-(ˌ)tü, -(ˌ)tyü\ *noun* [French, from *impromptu* extemporaneously, from Latin *in promptu* in readiness] (1683)

**1 :** something that is impromptu **2 :** a musical composition suggesting improvisation

²**impromptu** *adjective* (1764) **1 :** made, done, or formed on or as if on the spur of the moment **:** IMPROVISED **2 :** composed or uttered without previous preparation **:** EXTEMPORANEOUS
— **impromptu** *adverb*

**im·prop·er** \(ˌ)im-'prä-pər\ *adjective* [Middle English, from Middle French *impropre*, from Latin *improprius*, from *in-* + *proprius* proper] (15th century) **:** not proper: as **a :** not in accord with fact, truth, or right procedure **:** INCORRECT ⟨*improper* inference⟩ **b :** not regularly or normally formed or not properly so called **c :** not suited to the circumstances, design, or end ⟨*improper* medicine⟩ **d :** not in accord with propriety, modesty, good manners, or good taste

**synonym** see INDECOROUS
— **im·prop·er·ly** *adverb*
— **im·prop·er·ness** *noun*

**improper fraction** *noun* (1542) **:** a fraction whose numerator is equal to, larger than, or of equal or higher degree than the denominator

**improper integral** *noun* (circa 1942) **:** a definite integral whose region of integration is unbounded or includes a point at which the integrand is undefined or tends to infinity

**im·pro·pri·e·ty** \ˌim-p(r)ə-'prī-ə-tē\ *noun, plural* **-ties** [French or Late Latin; French *impropriété*, from Late Latin *improprietat-*, *improprietas*, from Latin *improprius*] (1607) **1 :** an improper or indecorous act or remark; *especially* **:** an unacceptable use of a word or of language **2 :** the quality or state of being improper

**im·prove** \im-'prüv\ *verb* **im·proved; im·prov·ing** [Anglo-French *emprouer* to invest profitably, from Old French *en-* + *prou* advantage, from Late Latin *prode* — more at PROUD] (circa 1529) *transitive verb* **1** *archaic* **:** EMPLOY, USE **2 a :** to enhance in value or quality **:** make better **b :** to increase the value of (land or property) by making it more useful for humans (as by cultivation or the erection of buildings) **c :** to grade and drain (a road) and apply surfacing material other than pavement **3 :** to use to good purpose *intransitive verb* **1 :** to advance or make progress in what is desirable **2 :** to make useful additions or amendments ☆
— **im·prov·abil·i·ty** \(ˌ)im-ˌprü-və-'bi-lə-tē\ *noun*
— **im·prov·able** \-'prü-və-bəl\ *adjective*
— **im·prov·er** *noun*

**im·prove·ment** \im-'prüv-mənt\ *noun* (circa 1550) **1 :** the act or process of improving **2 a :** the state of being improved; *especially* **:** enhanced value or excellence **b :** an instance of such improvement **:** something that enhances value or excellence

---

☆ SYNONYMS
**Improve, better, help, ameliorate** mean to make more acceptable or to bring nearer a standard. IMPROVE and BETTER are general and interchangeable and apply to what can be made better whether it is good or bad ⟨measures to further *improve* the quality of medical care⟩ ⟨immigrants hoping to *better* their lot⟩. HELP implies a bettering that still leaves room for improvement ⟨a coat of paint would *help* that house⟩. AMELIORATE implies making more tolerable or acceptable conditions that are hard to endure ⟨tried to *ameliorate* the lives of people in the tenements⟩.

**im·prov·i·dence** \(,)im-'prä-və-dən(t)s, -,den(t)s\ *noun* (15th century)
: the quality or state of being improvident

**im·prov·i·dent** \-dənt, -,dent\ *adjective* [Late Latin *improvident-, improvidens,* from Latin *in-* + *provident-, providens* provident] (1624)
: not provident : not foreseeing and providing for the future
— **im·prov·i·dent·ly** *adverb*

**im·pro·vi·sa·tion** \(,)im-,prä-və-'zā-shən, ,im-prə-və- *also* ,im-prə-(,)vī-\ *noun* (1786)
**1** : the act or art of improvising
**2** : something (as a musical or dramatic composition) improvised
— **im·pro·vi·sa·tion·al** \-shnəl, -shə-n°l\ *adjective*
— **im·pro·vi·sa·tion·al·ly** *adverb*

**im·prov·i·sa·tor** \im-'prä-və-,zā-tər\ *noun* (1795)
: one that improvises
— **im·pro·vi·sa·to·ri·al** \(,)im-,prä-və-zə-'tōr-ē-əl, -'tor-\ *adjective*
— **im·pro·vi·sa·to·ry** \im-'prä-və-zə-,tōr-ē, ,im-prə-,vī-zə-, -,tòr-\ *adjective*

**im·pro·vi·sa·to·re** \(,)im-,prä-və-zə-'tōr-ē, ,im-prə-,vē-zə-, -'tòr-\ *noun, plural* **-to·ri** \-'tōr-ē, -'tór-\ *or* **-tores** [Italian *improvvisatore,* from *improvvisare*] (1765)
: one that improvises (as verse) usually extemporaneously

**im·pro·vise** \'im-prə-,vīz *also* ,im-prə-'\ *verb* **-vised; -vis·ing** [French *improviser,* from Italian *improvvisare,* from *improvviso* sudden, from Latin *improvisus,* literally, unforeseen, from *in-* + *provisus,* past participle of *providēre* to see ahead — more at PROVIDE] (1826)
*transitive verb*
**1** : to compose, recite, play, or sing extemporaneously
**2** : to make, invent, or arrange offhand
**3** : to fabricate out of what is conveniently on hand
*intransitive verb*
: to improvise something
— **im·pro·vis·er** *or* **im·pro·vi·sor** \-,vī-zər, -'vī-\ *noun*

**im·pru·dence** \(,)im-'prü-d°n(t)s\ *noun* (15th century)
**1** : the quality or state of being imprudent
**2** : an imprudent act

**im·pru·dent** \-d°nt\ *adjective* [Middle English, from Latin *imprudent-, imprudens,* from *in-* + *prudent-, prudens* prudent] (14th century)
: not prudent : lacking discretion
— **im·pru·dent·ly** *adverb*

**im·pu·dence** \'im-pyə-dən(t)s\ *noun* (14th century)
: the quality or state of being impudent

**im·pu·dent** \-dənt\ *adjective* [Middle English, from Latin *impudent-, impudens,* from *in-* + *pudent-, pudens,* present participle of *pudēre* to feel shame] (14th century)
**1** *obsolete* : lacking modesty
**2** : marked by contemptuous or cocky boldness or disregard of others : INSOLENT
— **im·pu·dent·ly** *adverb*

**im·pu·dic·i·ty** \,im-pyü-'di-sə-tē\ *noun* [Middle French *impudicité,* from Latin *impudicus* immodest, from *in-* + *pudicus* modest, from *pudēre*] (1528)
: lack of modesty : SHAMELESSNESS

**im·pugn** \im-'pyün\ *transitive verb* [Middle English, to assail, from Middle French *impugner,* from Latin *inpugnare,* from *in-* + *pugnare* to fight — more at PUNGENT] (14th century)
**1** : to assail by words or arguments : oppose or attack as false or lacking integrity
**2** *obsolete* **a** : ASSAIL **b** : RESIST
— **im·pugn·able** \-'pyü-nə-bəl\ *adjective*
— **im·pugn·er** \-nər\ *noun*

**im·puis·sance** \(,)im-'pwi-s°n(t)s, (,)im-'pyü-ə-sən(t)s; ,im-pyü-'i-s°n(t)s\ *noun* [Middle En-

glish, from Middle French, from *in-* + *puissance* puissance, power] (15th century)
: WEAKNESS, POWERLESSNESS

**im·puis·sant** \-s°nt, -sənt\ *adjective* [French] (1629)
: WEAK, POWERLESS

**¹im·pulse** \'im-,pəls, im-'\ *transitive verb* **im·pulsed; im·puls·ing** (1611)
: to give an impulse to

**²im·pulse** \'im-,pəls\ *noun* [Latin *impulsus,* from *impellere* to impel] (1647)
**1 a** : INSPIRATION, MOTIVATION **b** : a force so communicated as to produce motion suddenly **c** : INCENTIVE
**2 a** : the act of driving onward with sudden force : IMPULSION **b** : motion produced by such an impulsion : IMPETUS **c** : a wave of excitation transmitted through tissues and especially nerve fibers and muscles that results in physiological activity or inhibition
**3 a** : a sudden spontaneous inclination or incitement to some usually unpremeditated action **b** : a propensity or natural tendency usually other than rational
**4 a** : the product of the average value of a force and the time during which it acts : the change in momentum produced by the force **b** : PULSE 4a
**synonym** see MOTIVE

**im·pul·sion** \im-'pəl-shən\ *noun* (15th century)
**1 a** : the act of impelling : the state of being impelled **b** : an impelling force **c** : an onward tendency derived from an impulsion
**2** : IMPULSE 3a
**3** : COMPULSION 2

**im·pul·sive** \im-'pəl-siv\ *adjective* (15th century)
**1** : having the power of or actually driving or impelling
**2** : actuated by or prone to act on impulse
**3** : acting momentarily
**synonym** see SPONTANEOUS
— **im·pul·sive·ly** *adverb*
— **im·pul·sive·ness** *noun*
— **im·pul·siv·i·ty** \-,pəl-'si-və-tē\ *noun*

**im·pu·ni·ty** \im-'pyü-nə-tē\ *noun* [Middle French or Latin; Middle French *impunité,* from Latin *impunitat-, impunitas,* from *impune* without punishment, from *in-* + *poena* punishment — more at PAIN] (1532)
: exemption or freedom from punishment, harm, or loss

**im·pure** \(,)im-'pyür\ *adjective* [Middle English, from Middle French & Latin; Middle French, from Latin *impurus,* from *in-* + *purus* pure] (15th century)
: not pure: as **a** : LEWD, UNCHASTE **b** : containing something unclean : FOUL ⟨*impure* water⟩ **c** : ritually unclean **d** : mixed or impregnated with an extraneous and usually unwanted substance ⟨an *impure* chemical⟩
— **im·pure·ly** *adverb*
— **im·pure·ness** *noun*

**im·pu·ri·ty** \(,)im-'pyür-ə-tē\ *noun, plural* **-ties** (15th century)
**1** : something that is impure or makes something else impure
**2** : the quality or state of being impure

**im·pu·ta·tion** \,im-pyə-'tā-shən\ *noun* (1581)
**1** : the act of imputing: as **a** : ATTRIBUTION, ASCRIPTION **b** : ACCUSATION **c** : INSINUATION
**2** : something imputed
— **im·pu·ta·tive** \im-'pyü-tə-tiv\ *adjective*
— **im·pu·ta·tive·ly** *adverb*

**im·pute** \im-'pyüt\ *transitive verb* **im·put·ed; im·put·ing** [Middle English *inputen,* from Latin *imputare,* from *in-* + *putare* to consider] (14th century)
**1** : to lay the responsibility or blame for often falsely or unjustly
**2** : to credit to a person or a cause : ATTRIBUTE ⟨our vices as well as our virtues have been *imputed* to bodily derangement —B. N. Cardozo⟩
**synonym** see ASCRIBE

**im·put·abil·i·ty** \-,pyü-tə-'bi-lə-tē\ *noun*
**im·put·able** \-'pyü-tə-bəl\ *adjective*

**¹in** \'in, ən, °n\ *preposition* [Middle English, from Old English; akin to Old High German *in* in, Latin *in,* Greek *en*] (before 12th century)
**1 a** : used as a function word to indicate inclusion, location, or position within limits ⟨*in* the lake⟩ ⟨wounded *in* the leg⟩ ⟨*in* the summer⟩ **b** : INTO 1 ⟨went *in* the house⟩
**2** — used as a function word to indicate means, medium, or instrumentality ⟨written *in* pencil⟩ ⟨bound *in* leather⟩
**3 a** — used as a function word to indicate limitation, qualification, or circumstance ⟨alike *in* some respects⟩ ⟨left *in* a hurry⟩ **b** : INTO 2a ⟨broke *in* pieces⟩
**4** — used as a function word to indicate purpose ⟨said *in* reply⟩
**5** — used as a function word to indicate the larger member of a ratio ⟨one *in* six is eligible⟩

**²in** \'in\ *adverb* (before 12th century)
**1 a** : to or toward the inside especially of a house or other building ⟨come *in*⟩ (2) : to or toward some destination or particular place ⟨flew *in* on the first plane⟩ (3) : at close quarters : NEAR ⟨play close *in*⟩ **b** : so as to incorporate ⟨mix *in* the flour⟩ — often used in combination ⟨built-*in* bookcases⟩ **c** : to or at an appropriate place ⟨fit a piece *in*⟩
**2 a** : within a particular place; *especially* : within the customary place of residence or business ⟨the doctor is *in*⟩ **b** : in the position of participant, insider, or officeholder — often used with *on* ⟨*in* on the joke⟩ **c** (1) : on good terms (2) : in a specified relation ⟨*in* bad with the boss⟩ (3) : in a position of assured or definitive success **d** : in vogue or season **e** ⟨*of* an oil well⟩ : in production **f** : in one's presence, possession, or control ⟨after the crops are *in*⟩ **g** : from a condition of indistinguishability to one of clarity ⟨fade *in*⟩
— **in for** : certain to experience ⟨*in for* a rude awakening⟩

**³in** \'in\ *adjective* (1599)
**1 a** : that is located inside or within ⟨the *in* part⟩ **b** : that is in position, operation, or power ⟨the *in* party⟩ **c** : INSIDE 2
**2** : that is directed or bound inward : INCOMING ⟨the *in* train⟩
**3 a** : extremely fashionable ⟨the *in* thing to do⟩ **b** : keenly aware of and responsive to what is new and smart ⟨the *in* crowd⟩

**⁴in** \'in\ *noun* (1764)
**1** : one who is in office or power or on the inside ⟨a matter of *ins* versus outs⟩
**2** : INFLUENCE, PULL ⟨enjoyed some sort of *in* with the commandant —Henriette Roosenburg⟩

**¹in-** *or* **il-** *or* **im-** *or* **ir-** *prefix* [Middle English, from Middle French, from Latin; akin to Old English *un-*]
: not : NON-, UN- — usually *il-* before *l* ⟨*illogical⟩, *im-* before *b, m,* or *p* ⟨*imbalance⟩ ⟨*immoral⟩ ⟨*impractical⟩, *ir-* before *r* ⟨*irreducible⟩, and *in-* before other sounds ⟨*inconclusive⟩

**²in-** *or* **il-** *or* **im-** *or* **ir-** *prefix* [Middle English, from Middle French, from Latin, from *in* in, into]
**1** : in : within : into : toward : on — usually *il-* before *l* ⟨*illuviation⟩, *im-* before *b, m,* or *p* ⟨*immingle⟩, *ir-* before *r* ⟨*irradiance⟩, and *in-* before other sounds ⟨*infiltrate⟩
**2** : ¹EN- ⟨*imbrute⟩ ⟨*imperil⟩ ⟨*inspirit⟩

**¹-in** *noun suffix* [French *-ine,* from Latin *-ina,* feminine of *-inus* of or belonging to — more at -EN]
**1 a** : neutral chemical compound ⟨insul*in*⟩ **b** : enzyme ⟨pancreat*in*⟩ **c** : antibiotic ⟨penicill*in*⟩
**2** : ²-INE 1a, b ⟨epinephr*in*⟩

\ə\ abut \°\ kitten \ər\ further \a\ ash \ā\ ace \ä\ mop, mar \au̇\ out \ch\ chin \e\ bet \ē\ easy \g\ go \i\ hit \ī\ ice \j\ job \ŋ\ sing \ō\ go \ȯ\ law \ȯi\ boy \th\ thin \th\ the \ü\ loot \u̇\ foot \y\ yet \zh\ vision *see also* Guide to Pronunciation

**3** : pharmaceutical product ⟨niac*in*⟩

**²-in** *combining form* [sit-*in*]
: organized public protest by means of or in favor of : demonstration ⟨teach-*in*⟩ ⟨love-*in*⟩

**in·abil·i·ty** \ˌi-nə-'bi-lə-tē\ *noun* [Middle English *inabilite*, from Middle French *inhabilité*, from *in-* + *habilité* ability] (15th century)
: lack of sufficient power, resources, or capacity ⟨his *inability* to do math⟩

**in ab·sen·tia** \ˌin-ab-'sen(t)-sh(ē-)ə\ *adverb* [Latin] (1886)
: in absence ⟨gave him the award *in absentia*⟩

**in·ac·ces·si·ble** \ˌi-nik-'se-sə-bəl, ˌ(ˌ)i-ˌnak-\ *adjective* [Middle English, from Middle French or Late Latin; Middle French, from Late Latin *inaccessibilis*, from Latin *in-* + Late Latin *accessibilis* accessible] (15th century)
: not accessible
— **in·ac·ces·si·bil·i·ty** \-ˌse-sə-'bi-lə-tē\ *noun*
— **in·ac·ces·si·bly** \-'se-sə-blē\ *adverb*

**in·ac·cu·ra·cy** \(ˌ)i-'na-kyə-rə-sē, -k(ə-)rə-sē\ *noun, plural* **-cies** (circa 1755)
**1** : the quality or state of being inaccurate
**2** : MISTAKE, ERROR

**in·ac·cu·rate** \-'a-kyə-rət, -k(ə-)rət\ *adjective* (1738)
: not accurate : FAULTY
— **in·ac·cu·rate·ly** \-kyə-rət-lē, -k(ə-)rət-, -kyərt-\ *adverb*

**in·ac·tion** \(ˌ)i-'nak-shən\ *noun* (1707)
: lack of action or activity : IDLENESS

**in·ac·ti·vate** \(ˌ)i-'nak-tə-ˌvāt\ *transitive verb* (1906)
: to make inactive
— **in·ac·ti·va·tion** \-ˌnak-tə-'vā-shən\ *noun*

**in·ac·tive** \(ˌ)i-'nak-tiv\ *adjective* (1664)
: not active: as **a** (1) : SEDENTARY (2) : INDOLENT, SLUGGISH **b** (1) : being out of use (2) : relating to or being members of the armed forces who are not performing or available for military duties (3) *of a disease* : QUIESCENT **c** (1) : chemically inert (2) : optically neutral in polarized light **d** : biologically inert especially because of the loss of some quality (as infectivity or antigenicity) ☆
— **in·ac·tive·ly** *adverb*
— **in·ac·tiv·i·ty** \-ˌnak-'ti-və-tē\ *noun*

**in·ad·e·qua·cy** \(ˌ)i-'na-di-kwə-sē\ *noun, plural* **-cies** (1787)
**1** : the quality or state of being inadequate
**2** : INSUFFICIENCY, DEFICIENCY

**in·ad·e·quate** \-kwət\ *adjective* (1671)
: not adequate : INSUFFICIENT; *also* : not capable
— **in·ad·e·quate·ly** *adverb*
— **in·ad·e·quate·ness** *noun*

**in·ad·mis·si·ble** \ˌi-nəd-'mi-sə-bəl\ *adjective* (1776)
: not admissible
— **in·ad·mis·si·bil·i·ty** \-ˌmi-sə-'bi-lə-tē\ *noun*
— **in·ad·mis·si·bly** \-'mi-sə-blē\ *adverb*

**in·ad·ver·tence** \ˌi-nəd-'vər-t³n(t)s\ *noun* [Middle English, from Medieval Latin *inadvertentia*, from Latin *in-* + *advertent-, advertens*, present participle of *advertere* to advert] (15th century)
**1** : the fact or action of being inadvertent
**2** : a result of inattention : OVERSIGHT

**in·ad·ver·ten·cy** \-t³n(t)-sē\ *noun, plural* **-cies** (1592)
: INADVERTENCE

**in·ad·ver·tent** \-t³nt\ *adjective* [back-formation from *inadvertence*] (1653)
**1** : not focusing the mind on a matter : INATTENTIVE
**2** : UNINTENTIONAL
— **in·ad·ver·tent·ly** *adverb*

**in·ad·vis·able** \ˌi-nəd-'vī-zə-bəl\ *adjective* (1870)
: not advisable
— **in·ad·vis·abil·i·ty** \-ˌvī-zə-'bi-lə-tē\ *noun*

**-inae** *noun plural suffix* [New Latin *-īnae*, from Latin, feminine plural of *-īnus*]
: members of the subfamily of — in all names of zoological subfamilies in recent classifications ⟨Fel*inae*⟩

**in·alien·able** \(ˌ)i-'nāl-yə-nə-bəl, -'nā-lē-ə-nə-\ *adjective* [probably from French *inaliénable*, from *in-* + *aliénable* alienable] (circa 1645)
: incapable of being alienated, surrendered, or transferred ⟨*inalienable* rights⟩
— **in·alien·abil·i·ty** \-ˌnāl-yə-nə-'bi-lə-tē, -ˌnā-lē-ə-nə-\ *noun*
— **in·alien·ably** \-'nāl-yə-nə-blē, -'nā-lē-ə-nə-\ *adverb*

**in·al·ter·able** \(ˌ)i-'nȯl-t(ə-)rə-bəl\ *adjective* (1541)
: not alterable : UNALTERABLE
— **in·al·ter·abil·i·ty** \-ˌnȯl-t(ə-)rə-'bi-lə-tē\ *noun*
— **in·al·ter·able·ness** \-'nȯl-t(ə-)rə-bəl-nəs\ *noun*
— **in·al·ter·ably** \-blē\ *adverb*

**in·amo·ra·ta** \i-ˌna-mə-'rä-tə\ *noun* [Italian *innamorata*, from feminine of *innamorato*, past participle of *innamorare* to inspire with love, from *in-* (from Latin) + *amore* love, from Latin *amor* — more at AMOROUS] (1651)
: a woman with whom one is in love or has intimate relations

**in–and–in** \ˌin-ən(d)-'in\ *adverb or adjective* (1765)
: in repeated generations of the same or closely related stock ⟨families . . . of one blood through mating or marrying *in-and-in* —F. H. Giddings⟩ ⟨*in-and-in* breeding⟩

**¹inane** \i-'nān\ *adjective* **inan·er; -est** [Latin *inanis*] (1662)
**1** : EMPTY, INSUBSTANTIAL
**2** : lacking significance, meaning, or point : SILLY
**synonym** see INSIPID
— **inane·ly** *adverb*
— **inane·ness** \-'nān-nəs\ *noun*

**²inane** *noun* (1677)
: void or empty space ⟨a voyage into the limitless *inane* —V. G. Childe⟩

**in·an·i·mate** \(ˌ)i-'na-nə-mət\ *adjective* [Middle English, from Late Latin *inanimatus*, from Latin *in-* + *animatus*, past participle of *animare* to animate] (15th century)
**1** : not animate: **a** : not endowed with life or spirit **b** : lacking consciousness or power of motion
**2** : not animated or lively : DULL
— **in·an·i·mate·ly** *adverb*
— **in·an·i·mate·ness** *noun*

**in·a·ni·tion** \ˌi-nə-'ni-shən\ *noun* (14th century)
: the quality or state of being empty: **a** : the loss of vitality that results from lack of food and water **b** : the absence or loss of social, moral, or intellectual vitality or vigor

**inan·i·ty** \i-'na-nə-tē\ *noun, plural* **-ties** (1603)
**1** : the quality or state of being inane: as **a** : lack of substance : EMPTINESS **b** : vapid, pointless, or fatuous character : SHALLOWNESS
**2** : something that is inane

**in·ap·par·ent** \ˌi-nə-'par-ənt, -'per-\ *adjective* (1626)
: not apparent
— **in·ap·par·ent·ly** *adverb*

**in·ap·peas·able** \ˌi-nə-'pē-zə-bəl\ *adjective* (1803)
: UNAPPEASABLE

**in·ap·pe·tence** \(ˌ)i-'na-pə-tən(t)s\ *noun* (circa 1691)
: loss or lack of appetite

**in·ap·pli·ca·ble** \(ˌ)i-'na-pli-kə-bəl *also* ˌi-nə-'pli-kə-\ *adjective* (1656)
: not applicable : IRRELEVANT
— **in·ap·pli·ca·bil·i·ty** \-ˌna-pli-kə-'bi-lə-tē *also* ˌi-nə-ˌpli-kə-\ *noun*
— **in·ap·pli·ca·bly** \(ˌ)i-'na-pli-kə-blē *also* ˌi-nə-'pli-kə-\ *adverb*

**in·ap·po·site** \(ˌ)i-'na-pə-zət\ *adjective* (1661)
: not apposite
— **in·ap·po·site·ly** *adverb*
— **in·ap·po·site·ness** *noun*

**in·ap·pre·cia·ble** \ˌi-nə-'prē-shə-bəl, -'pri-sh(ē-)ə-bəl\ *adjective* [probably from French *inappréciable*, from Middle French *inappreciable*, from *in-* + *appreciable*] (1802)
: too small to be perceived
— **in·ap·pre·cia·bly** \-blē\ *adverb*

**in·ap·pre·cia·tive** \ˌi-nə-'prē-shə-tiv, -'pri- *also* -'prē-shē-ˌā-\ *adjective* (1869)
: not appreciative
— **in·ap·pre·cia·tive·ly** *adverb*
— **in·ap·pre·cia·tive·ness** *noun*

**in·ap·proach·able** \ˌi-nə-'prō-chə-bəl\ *adjective* (circa 1828)
: not approachable : INACCESSIBLE

**in·ap·pro·pri·ate** \ˌi-nə-'prō-prē-ət\ *adjective* (1804)
: not appropriate : UNSUITABLE
— **in·ap·pro·pri·ate·ly** *adverb*
— **in·ap·pro·pri·ate·ness** *noun*

**in·apt** \(ˌ)i-'napt\ *adjective* (circa 1670)
: not apt: **a** : not suitable **b** : INEPT
— **in·apt·ly** \-'nap(t)-lē\ *adverb*
— **in·apt·ness** \-nəs\ *noun*

**in·ap·ti·tude** \(ˌ)i-'nap-tə-ˌtüd, -ˌtyüd\ *noun* (1620)
: lack of aptitude

**in·ar·gu·able** \(ˌ)i-'när-gyə-wə-bəl\ *adjective* (circa 1875)
: not arguable
— **in·ar·gu·ably** \-blē\ *adverb*

**in·ar·tic·u·la·cy** \ˌi-(ˌ)när-'ti-kyə-lə-sē\ *noun* (1921)
: the quality or state of being inarticulate

**¹in·ar·tic·u·late** \-kyə-lət\ *adjective* [Late Latin *inarticulatus*, from Latin *in-* + *articulatus*, past participle of *articulare* to utter distinctly — more at ARTICULATE] (1603)
**1 a** *of a sound* : uttered or formed without the definite articulations of intelligible speech **b** (1) : incapable of speech especially under stress of emotion : MUTE (2) : incapable of being expressed by speech ⟨*inarticulate* fear⟩ (3) : not voiced or expressed : UNSPOKEN ⟨society functions on many *inarticulate* premises⟩
**2** : incapable of giving coherent, clear, or effective expression to one's ideas or feelings
**3** [New Latin *inarticulatus*, from Latin *in-* + New Latin *articulatus* articulate] : relating to, characteristic of, or being an inarticulate or its shell
— **in·ar·tic·u·late·ly** *adverb*
— **in·ar·tic·u·late·ness** *noun*

**²inarticulate** *noun* (1952)
: any of a class (Inarticulata) of brachiopods lacking a hinge connecting the two shell valves

**in·ar·tis·tic** \ˌi-när-'tis-tik\ *adjective* (1859)
**1** : not conforming to the principles of art

---

☆ **SYNONYMS**
**Inactive, idle, inert, passive, supine**
mean not engaged in work or activity. INACTIVE applies to anyone or anything not in action or in operation or at work ⟨on *inactive* status as an astronaut⟩ ⟨*inactive* accounts⟩. IDLE applies to persons that are not busy or occupied or to their powers or their implements ⟨workers were *idle* in the fields⟩. INERT as applied to things implies powerlessness to move or to affect other things; as applied to persons it suggests an inherent or habitual indisposition to activity ⟨*inert* ingredients in drugs⟩ ⟨an *inert* citizenry⟩. PASSIVE implies immobility or lack of normally expected response to an external force or influence and often suggests deliberate submissiveness or self-control ⟨*passive* resistance⟩. SUPINE applies only to persons and commonly implies abjectness or indolence ⟨a *supine* willingness to play the fool⟩.

**2 :** not appreciative of art
— **in·ar·tis·ti·cal·ly** \-ti-k(ə-)lē\ adverb
**in·as·much as** \,i-nəz-'mə-chəz, -'mäch-,əz\ conjunction (14th century)
**1 :** in the degree that **:** INSOFAR AS
**2 :** in view of the fact that **:** SINCE
**in·at·ten·tion** \,i-nə-'ten(t)-shən\ noun (circa 1670)
**:** failure to pay attention
**in·at·ten·tive** \-'ten-tiv\ adjective (1692)
**:** not attentive
— **in·at·ten·tive·ly** adverb
— **in·at·ten·tive·ness** noun
**in·au·di·ble** \(,)i-'nȯ-də-bəl\ adjective [Late Latin inaudibilis, from Latin in- + Late Latin audibilis audible] (1601)
**:** not audible
— **in·au·di·bil·i·ty** \(,)i-,nȯ-də-'bi-lə-tē\ noun
— **in·au·di·bly** \(,)i-'nȯ-də-blē\ adverb
**¹in·au·gu·ral** \i-'nȯ-gyə-rəl, -g(ə-)rəl\ adjective (1689)
**1 :** of or relating to an inauguration
**2 :** marking a beginning **:** first in a projected series
**²inaugural** noun (1832)
**1 :** an inaugural address
**2 :** INAUGURATION
**in·au·gu·rate** \i-'nȯ-gyə-,rāt, -gə-,rāt\ transitive verb **-rat·ed; -rat·ing** [Latin inauguratus, past participle of inaugurare, literally, to practice augury, from in- + augurare to augur; from the rites connected with augury] (1606)
**1 :** to induct into an office with suitable ceremonies
**2 a :** to dedicate ceremoniously **:** observe formally the beginning of **b :** to bring about the beginning of
**synonym** see BEGIN
— **in·au·gu·ra·tor** \-,rā-tər\ noun
**in·au·gu·ra·tion** \-,nȯ-gyə-'rā-shən, -gə-\ noun (1569)
**:** an act of inaugurating; especially **:** a ceremonial induction into office
**Inauguration Day** noun (1829)
**:** January 20 following a presidential election on which the president of the U.S. is inaugurated
**in·aus·pi·cious** \,i-,nȯ-'spi-shəs\ adjective (1592)
**:** not auspicious
— **in·aus·pi·cious·ly** adverb
— **in·aus·pi·cious·ness** noun
**in·au·then·tic** \,i-,nȯ-'then-tik\ adjective (1860)
**:** not authentic
— **in·au·then·tic·i·ty** \,i-,nȯ-,then-'ti-sə-tē, -thən-\ noun
**in–be·tween** \,in-bi-'twēn\ adjective or noun (1815)
**:** INTERMEDIATE
**in between** adverb or preposition (1892)
**:** BETWEEN
**¹in·board** \'in-,bȯrd, -,bȯrd\ adverb (1830)
**1 :** inside the line of a ship's bulwarks or hull
**2 :** toward the center line of a vehicle or craft (as a ship or aircraft)
**²inboard** adjective (1847)
**1 :** located inboard ⟨an inboard engine⟩ ⟨an inboard spoiler⟩
**2** of a boat **:** having an inboard engine
**³inboard** noun (1950)
**:** a boat with an inboard motor
**in·born** \'in-'bȯrn\ adjective (1513)
**1 :** present from or as if from birth
**2 :** HEREDITARY, INHERITED
**synonym** see INNATE
**in·bound** \'in-'baůnd\ adjective (1894)
**:** inward bound
**in·bounds** \'in-'baůn(d)z\ adjective (1968)
**:** involving putting a basketball in play by passing it onto the court from out of bounds
**inbounds line** noun (circa 1961)
**:** either of two broken lines running the length of a football field at right angles to the yard lines

**in·breathe** \'in-,brēṯẖ\ transitive verb (14th century)
**:** to breathe (something) in **:** INHALE
**in·bred** \'in-'bred\ adjective (circa 1592)
**1 :** rooted and ingrained in one's nature as deeply as if implanted by heredity ⟨an inbred love of freedom⟩
**2** [from past participle of inbreed] **:** subjected to or produced by inbreeding
**synonym** see INNATE
— **in·bred** \'in-,bred\ noun
**in·breed** \'in-,brēd\ verb **-bred** \-'bred\; **-breed·ing** (1599)
transitive verb
**:** to subject to inbreeding
intransitive verb
**:** to engage in inbreeding
**in·breed·ing** \'in-,brē-diŋ\ noun (circa 1842)
**1 :** the interbreeding of closely related individuals especially to preserve and fix desirable characters of and to eliminate unfavorable characters from a stock
**2 :** confinement to a narrow range or a local or limited field of choice
**in·built** \'in-'bilt\ adjective (1923)
chiefly British **:** BUILT-IN
**In·ca** \'iŋ-kə\ noun [Spanish, from Quechua inka ruler of the Inca empire] (1594)
**1 a :** a member of the Quechuan peoples of Peru maintaining an empire until the Spanish conquest **b :** a king or noble of the Inca empire
**2 :** a member of any people under Inca influence
— **In·ca·ic** \in-'kā-ik\ adjective
— **In·can** \'iŋ-kən\ adjective
**in·cal·cu·la·ble** \(,)in-'kal-kyə-lə-bəl\ adjective (1795)
**:** not capable of being calculated: as **a :** very great **b :** not predictable **:** UNCERTAIN
— **in·cal·cu·la·bil·i·ty** \-,kal-kyə-lə-'bi-lə-tē\ noun
— **in·cal·cu·la·bly** \-'kal-kyə-lə-blē\ adverb
**in·ca·les·cence** \,in-kə-'le-s°n(t)s, ,iŋ-\ noun [Latin incalescere to become warm, from in- + calescere to become warm, inchoative of calēre to be warm — more at LEE] (1646)
**:** a growing warm or ardent
— **in·ca·les·cent** \-s°nt\ adjective
**in camera** adverb [New Latin, literally, in a chamber] (1882)
**:** in private **:** SECRETLY
**in·can·desce** \,in-kən-'des also -(,)kan-\ intransitive verb **-desced; -desc·ing** [Latin incandescere] (1874)
**:** to be or become incandescent
**in·can·des·cence** \,in-kən-'de-s°n(t)s also -(,)kan-\ noun (1656)
**:** the quality or state of being incandescent; especially **:** emission by a hot body of radiation that makes it visible
**in·can·des·cent** \-s°nt\ adjective [probably from French, from Latin incandescent-, incandescens, present participle of incandescere to become hot, from in- + candescere to become hot, from candēre to glow — more at CANDID] (1794)
**1 a :** white, glowing, or luminous with intense heat **b :** strikingly bright, radiant, or clear **c :** marked by brilliance especially of expression ⟨incandescent wit⟩ **d :** characterized by glowing zeal **:** ARDENT ⟨incandescent affection⟩
**2 a :** of, relating to, or being light produced by incandescence **b :** producing light by incandescence
— **in·can·des·cent·ly** adverb
**incandescent lamp** noun (1881)
**:** an electric lamp in which a filament gives off light when heated to incandescence by an electric current — called also incandescent, incandescent bulb, incandescent lightbulb, lightbulb
**in·cant** \in-'kant\ intransitive verb [Latin incantare] (1945)
**:** RECITE, UTTER

**in·can·ta·tion** \,in-,kan-'tā-shən\ noun [Middle English incantacioun, from Middle French incantation, from Late Latin incantation-, incantatio, from Latin incantare to enchant — more at ENCHANT] (14th century)
**:** a use of spells or verbal charms spoken or sung as a part of a ritual of magic; also **:** a written or recited formula of words designed to produce a particular effect
— **in·can·ta·tion·al** \-shnəl, -shə-n°l\ adjective
— **in·can·ta·to·ry** \in-'kan-tə-,tōr-ē, -,tȯr-\ adjective

**incandescent lamp:** *1* bulb containing gas, *2* filament, *3* connecting and supporting wires, *4* exhaust tube, *5* screw base, *6* base contact

**in·ca·pa·ble** \(,)in-'kā-pə-bəl\ adjective [Middle French, from in- + capable capable] (1594)
**1 :** lacking capacity, ability, or qualification for the purpose or end in view: as **a** archaic **:** not able to take in, hold, or keep **b** archaic **:** not receptive **c :** not being in a state or of a kind to admit **:** INSUSCEPTIBLE **d :** not able or fit for the doing or performance **:** INCOMPETENT
**2 :** lacking legal qualification or power (as by reason of mental incompetence) **:** DISQUALIFIED
— **in·ca·pa·bil·i·ty** \-,kā-pə-'bi-lə-tē\ noun
— **in·ca·pa·ble·ness** \-'kā-pə-bəl-nəs\ noun
— **in·ca·pa·bly** \-blē\ adverb
**in·ca·pac·i·tate** \,in-kə-'pa-sə-,tāt\ transitive verb **-tat·ed; -tat·ing** (1657)
**1 :** to make legally incapable or ineligible
**2 :** to deprive of capacity or natural power **:** DISABLE
— **in·ca·pac·i·ta·tion** \-,pa-sə-'tā-shən\ noun
**in·ca·pac·i·ty** \,in-kə-'pa-sə-tē, -'pas-tē\ noun, plural **-ties** [French incapacité, from Middle French, from in- + capacité capacity] (1611)
**:** the quality or state of being incapable; especially **:** lack of physical or intellectual power or of natural or legal qualifications
**in·car·cer·ate** \in-'kär-sə-,rāt\ transitive verb **-at·ed; -at·ing** [Latin incarceratus, past participle of incarcerare, from in- + carcer prison] (1560)
**1 :** to put in prison
**2 :** to subject to confinement
— **in·car·cer·a·tion** \(,)in-,kär-sə-'rā-shən\ noun
**in·car·di·na·tion** \(,)in-,kär-d°n-'ā-shən\ noun [Late Latin incardination-, incardinatio, from incardinare to ordain as chief priest, from Latin in- ²in- + Late Latin cardinalis principal — more at CARDINAL] (1897)
**:** the formal acceptance by a diocese of a clergyman from another diocese
**¹in·car·na·dine** \in-'kär-nə-,dīn, -,dēn, -dən\ adjective [Middle French incarnadin, from Old Italian incarnadino, from incarnato flesh-colored, from Late Latin incarnatus] (1591)
**1 :** having the pinkish color of flesh
**2 :** RED; especially **:** BLOODRED
**²incarnadine** transitive verb **-dined; -din·ing** (1605)
**:** to make incarnadine **:** REDDEN
**¹in·car·nate** \in-'kär-nət, -,nāt\ adjective [Middle English incarnat, from Late Latin incarnatus, past participle of incarnare to incarnate, from Latin in- + carn-, caro flesh — more at CARNAL] (14th century)

**1 a** : invested with bodily and especially human nature and form **b** : made manifest or comprehensible : EMBODIED ⟨a fiend *incarnate*⟩ **2** : INCARNADINE ⟨*incarnate* clover⟩

²**in·car·nate** \in-'kär-ˌnāt, 'in-ˌ\ *transitive verb* **-nat·ed; -nat·ing** (1533)
: to make incarnate: as **a** : to give bodily form and substance to **b** (1) : to give a concrete or actual form to : ACTUALIZE (2) : to constitute an embodiment or type of ⟨no one culture *incarnates* every important human value —Denis Goulet⟩

**in·car·na·tion** \ˌin-(ˌ)kär-'nā-shən\ *noun* (14th century)
**1 a** (1) : the embodiment of a deity or spirit in some earthly form (2) *capitalized* : the union of divinity with humanity in Jesus Christ **b** : a concrete or actual form of a quality or concept; *especially* : a person showing a trait or typical character to a marked degree ⟨she is the *incarnation* of goodness⟩ **2** : the act of incarnating : the state of being incarnate **3** : a particular physical form or state : VERSION ⟨in another *incarnation* he might be a first vice-president —Walter Teller⟩ ⟨TV and movie *incarnations* of the story⟩

**in·case** *variant of* ENCASE

**in case** *conjunction* (14th century)
**1** : IF ⟨*in case* we are surprised, keep by me —Washington Irving⟩ **2** : as a precaution against the event that ⟨carries a gun *in case* he is attacked⟩

**in·cau·tion** \(ˌ)in-'kȯ-shən\ *noun* (circa 1720)
: lack of caution : HEEDLESSNESS

**in·cau·tious** \-shəs\ *adjective* (circa 1703)
: lacking in caution : CARELESS
— **in·cau·tious·ly** *adverb*
— **in·cau·tious·ness** *noun*

**in·cen·di·a·rism** \in-'sen-dē-ə-ˌri-zəm\ *noun* (circa 1710)
: incendiary action or behavior

¹**in·cen·di·ary** \in-'sen-dē-ˌer-ē; -'sen-də-rē, -dyə-\ *noun, plural* **-ar·ies** [Middle English, from Latin *incendiarius*, from *incendium* conflagration, from *incendere*] (15th century)
**1 a** : a person who deliberately sets fire to a building or other property **b** : an incendiary agent (as a bomb) **2** : a person who excites factions, quarrels, or sedition : AGITATOR

²**incendiary** *adjective* (15th century)
**1** : of, relating to, or involving a deliberate burning of property **2** : tending to excite or inflame : INFLAMMATORY ⟨*incendiary* speeches⟩ **3 a** : igniting combustible materials spontaneously **b** : of, relating to, or being a weapon (as a bomb) designed to start fires

¹**in·cense** \'in-ˌsen(t)s\ *noun* [Middle English *encens*, from Old French, from Late Latin *incensum*, from Latin, neuter of *incensus*, past participle of *incendere* to set on fire, from *in- + -cendere* to burn; akin to Latin *candēre* to glow — more at CANDID] (13th century)
**1** : material used to produce a fragrant odor when burned **2** : the perfume exhaled from some spices and gums when burned; *broadly* : a pleasing scent **3** : pleasing attention : FLATTERY

²**incense** *transitive verb* **in·censed; in·cens·ing** (13th century)
**1** : to apply or offer incense to **2** : to perfume with incense

³**in·cense** \in-'sen(t)s\ *transitive verb* **in·censed; in·cens·ing** [Middle English *encensen*, from Middle French *incenser*, from Latin *incensus*] (15th century)
**1** *archaic* : to cause (a passion or emotion) to become aroused **2** : to arouse the extreme anger or indignation of

**in·cen·ter** \'in-ˌsen-tər\ *noun* [inscribe + ¹*center*] (circa 1890)

: the single point in which the three bisectors of the interior angles of a triangle intersect and which is the center of the inscribed circle

**in·cen·tive** \in-'sen-tiv\ *noun* [Middle English, from Late Latin *incentivum*, from neuter of *incentivus* stimulating, from Latin, setting the tune, from *incentus*, past participle of *incinere* to set the tune, from *in- + canere* to sing — more at CHANT] (15th century)
: something that incites or has a tendency to incite to determination or action
*synonym* see MOTIVE
— **incentive** *adjective*

**in·cep·tion** \in-'sep-shən\ *noun* [Middle English *incepcion*, from Latin *inception-*, *inceptio*, from *incipere* to begin, from *in- + capere* to take] (15th century)
: an act, process, or instance of beginning : COMMENCEMENT
*synonym* see ORIGIN

¹**in·cep·tive** \in-'sep-tiv\ *noun* (1612)
: an inchoative verb

²**inceptive** *adjective* (1656)
**1** : INCHOATIVE 2 **2** : of or relating to a beginning
— **in·cep·tive·ly** *adverb*

**in·cer·ti·tude** \(ˌ)in-'sər-tə-ˌtüd, -ˌtyüd\ *noun* [Middle English, from Middle French, from Late Latin *incertitudo*, from Latin *in- + Late Latin *certitudo* certitude] (15th century)
: UNCERTAINTY: **a** : absence of assurance or confidence : DOUBT **b** : the quality or state of being unstable or insecure

**in·ces·san·cy** \(ˌ)in-'se-s⁵n(t)-sē\ *noun* (1615)
: the quality or state of being incessant

**in·ces·sant** \(ˌ)in-'se-s⁵nt\ *adjective* [Middle English *incessaunt*, from Late Latin *incessant-*, *incessans*, from Latin *in- + cessant-*, *cessans*, present participle of *cessare* to delay — more at CEASE] (15th century)
: continuing or following without interruption : UNCEASING
*synonym* see CONTINUAL
— **in·ces·sant·ly** *adverb*

**in·cest** \'in-ˌsest\ *noun* [Middle English, from Latin *incestus* sexual impurity, from *incestus* impure, from *in- + castus* pure — more at CASTE] (13th century)
: sexual intercourse between persons so closely related that they are forbidden by law to marry; *also* : the statutory crime of such a relationship

**in·ces·tu·ous** \in-'ses-chə-wəs, -'sesh-\ *adjective* (1532)
**1** : constituting or involving incest **2** : guilty of incest
— **in·ces·tu·ous·ly** *adverb*
— **in·ces·tu·ous·ness** *noun*

¹**inch** \'inch\ *noun* [Middle English, from Old English *ynce*, from Latin *uncia* — more at OUNCE] (before 12th century)
**1** : a unit of length equal to ¹⁄₃₆ yard — see WEIGHT table **2** : a small amount, distance, or degree ⟨is like cutting a dog's tail off by *inches* —Milton Friedman⟩ **3** *plural* : STATURE, HEIGHT **4 a** : a fall (as of rain or snow) sufficient to cover a surface or to fill a gauge to the depth of one inch **b** : a degree of atmospheric or other pressure sufficient to balance the weight of a column of liquid (as mercury) one inch high in a barometer or manometer
— **every inch** : to the utmost degree ⟨looks *every inch* a winner⟩
— **within an inch of** : almost to the point of

²**inch** (1599)
*intransitive verb*
: to move by small degrees : progress slowly ⟨the long line of people *inching* up the stairs⟩
*transitive verb*
: to cause to move slowly ⟨sooner or later they begin *inching* prices back up —*Forbes*⟩

³**inch** *noun* [Middle English (Scots dialect), from Scottish Gaelic *innis*] (15th century)
*chiefly Scottish* : ISLAND

**inched** \'incht\ *adjective* (1605)
: measuring a specified number of inches

**-inch·er** \'in-chər\ *noun combining form*
: one that has a dimension of a specified number of inches ⟨a four-*incher*⟩

**inch·meal** \'inch-ˌmēl, -'mē(ə)l\ *adverb* [¹*inch* + *-meal* (as in *piecemeal*)] (1530)
: LITTLE BY LITTLE. GRADUALLY

**in·cho·ate** \in-'kō-ət, 'in-kə-ˌwāt\ *adjective* [Latin *inchoatus*, past participle of *inchoare* to start work on, perhaps from *in- + cohum* part of a yoke to which the beam of a plow is fitted] (1534)
: being only partly in existence or operation; *especially* : imperfectly formed or formulated : FORMLESS ⟨misty, *inchoate* suspicions that all is not well with the nation —J. M. Perry⟩
— **in·cho·ate·ly** *adverb*
— **in·cho·ate·ness** *noun*

**in·cho·a·tive** \in-'kō-ə-tiv\ *adjective* (circa 1631)
**1** : INITIAL, FORMATIVE ⟨the *inchoative* stages⟩ **2** : denoting the beginning of an action, state, or occurrence — used of verbs
— **inchoative** *noun*
— **in·cho·a·tive·ly** *adverb*

**inch·worm** \'inch-ˌwərm\ *noun* (circa 1861)
: LOOPER 1

**in·ci·dence** \'in(t)-sə-dən(t)s, -ˌden(t)s\ *noun* (1626)
**1 a** : ANGLE OF INCIDENCE **b** : the arrival of something (as a projectile or a ray of light) at a surface **2 a** : an act or the fact or manner of falling upon or affecting : OCCURRENCE **b** : rate of occurrence or influence ⟨a high *incidence* of crime⟩

¹**in·ci·dent** \'in(t)-sə-dənt, -ˌdent\ *noun* [Middle English, from Middle French, from Medieval Latin *incident-*, *incidens*, from Latin, present participle of *incidere* to fall into, from *in- + cadere* to fall — more at CHANCE] (15th century)
**1** : something dependent on or subordinate to something else of greater or principal importance **2 a** : an occurrence of an action or situation that is a separate unit of experience : HAPPENING **b** : an accompanying minor occurrence or condition : CONCOMITANT **3** : an action likely to lead to grave consequences especially in diplomatic matters ⟨a serious border *incident*⟩
*synonym* see OCCURRENCE

²**incident** *adjective* (15th century)
**1** : occurring or likely to occur especially as a minor consequence or accompaniment ⟨the confusion *incident* to moving day⟩ **2** : dependent on or relating to another thing in law **3** : falling or striking on something ⟨*incident* light rays⟩

¹**in·ci·den·tal** \ˌin(t)-sə-'den-t⁵l\ *adjective* (1616)
**1** : being likely to ensue as a chance or minor consequence ⟨social obligations *incidental* to the job⟩ **2** : occurring merely by chance or without intention or calculation

²**incidental** *noun* (1707)
**1** *plural* : minor items (as of expense) that are not particularized **2** : something that is incidental

**in·ci·den·tal·ly** \-'den-t⁵l-ē, *especially for* 2 -'dent-lē\ *adverb* (1665)
**1** : in an incidental manner : not intentionally ⟨the arrant nonsense of some of his statements is *incidentally* hilarious —John Lahr⟩ **2** : by way of interjection or digression : by the way ⟨fortunate in having a good teacher . . . —still living, *incidentally* —John Fischer⟩

**incidental music** *noun* (1864)
: descriptive music played during a play to project a mood or to accompany stage action

**in·cin·er·ate** \in-'si-nə-ˌrāt\ *transitive verb* **-at·ed; -at·ing** [Medieval Latin *incineratus*, past participle of *incinerare*, from Latin *in-* + *ciner-, cinis* ashes; akin to Greek *konis* dust, ashes] (1555)
: to cause to burn to ashes
— **in·cin·er·a·tion** \-ˌsi-nə-'rā-shən\ *noun*

**in·cin·er·a·tor** \in-'si-nə-ˌrā-tər\ *noun* (1883)
: one that incinerates; *especially* : a furnace or a container for incinerating waste materials

**in·cip·i·ence** \in-'si-pē-ən(t)s\ *noun* (circa 1864)
: INCIPIENCY

**in·cip·i·en·cy** \-ən(t)-sē\ *noun* (1817)
: the state or fact of being incipient : BEGINNING

**in·cip·i·ent** \-ənt\ *adjective* [Latin *incipient-, incipiens*, present participle of *incipere* to begin — more at INCEPTION] (1669)
: beginning to come into being or to become apparent ⟨an *incipient* solar system⟩ ⟨evidence of *incipient* racial tension⟩
— **in·cip·i·ent·ly** *adverb*

**in·ci·pit** \'in(t)-sə-pət, 'iŋ-kə-ˌpit; in-'si-pət, -'ki-\ *noun* [Latin, it begins, from *incipere*] (1897)
: the first part : BEGINNING; *specifically* : the opening words of a text of a medieval manuscript or early printed book

**in·ci·sal** \in-'sī-zəl, -səl\ *adjective* (1903)
: relating to, involving, or being the cutting edge or surface of a tooth (as an incisor)

**in·cise** \in-'sīz, -'sīs\ *transitive verb* **in·cised; in·cis·ing** [Middle French or Latin; Middle French *inciser*, from Latin *incisus*, past participle of *incidere*, from *in-* + *caedere* to cut] (1567)
**1** : to cut into
**2 a** : to carve figures, letters, or devices into : ENGRAVE **b** : to carve (as an inscription) into a surface

**incised** *adjective* (15th century)
**1** : cut in : ENGRAVED; *especially* : decorated with incised figures
**2** : having a margin that is deeply and sharply notched ⟨an *incised* leaf⟩

**in·ci·sion** \in-'si-zhən\ *noun* (14th century)
**1 a** : CUT, GASH; *specifically* : a wound made especially in surgery by incising the body **b** : a marginal notch (as in a leaf)
**2** : an act of incising something
**3** : the quality or state of being incisive

**in·ci·sive** \in-'sī-siv\ *adjective* (circa 1850)
: impressively direct and decisive (as in manner or presentation)
— **in·ci·sive·ly** *adverb*
— **in·ci·sive·ness** *noun*

**in·ci·sor** \in-'sī-zər\ *noun* (1666)
: a front tooth typically adapted for cutting; *especially* : one of the cutting teeth in mammals located between the canines when canines are present — see TOOTH illustration

**in·ci·ta·tion** \ˌin-ˌsī-'tā-shən, ˌin(t)-sə-\ *noun* (15th century)
**1** : an act of inciting : STIMULATION
**2** : something that incites to action : INCENTIVE

**in·cite** \in-'sīt\ *transitive verb* **in·cit·ed; in·cit·ing** [Middle French *inciter*, from Latin *incitare*, from *in-* + *citare* to put in motion — more at CITE] (15th century)
: to move to action : stir up : spur on : urge on ☆
— **in·cit·ant** \-'sī-tᵊnt\ *noun*
— **in·cite·ment** \-'sīt-mənt\ *noun*
— **in·cit·er** *noun*

**in·ci·vil·i·ty** \ˌin(t)-sə-'vi-lə-tē\ *noun* [Middle French *incivilité*, from Late Latin *incivilitat-, incivilitas*, from *incivilis*, from Latin *in-* + *civilis* civil] (1584)
**1** : the quality or state of being uncivil
**2** : a rude or discourteous act

**in·clem·en·cy** \(ˌ)in-'kle-mən(t)-sē\ *noun* (1559)

: the quality or state of being inclement

**in·clem·ent** \(ˌ)in-'kle-mənt, 'in-klə-\ *adjective* [Latin *inclement-, inclemens*, from *in-* + *clement-, clemens* clement] (1621)
: lacking mildness: as **a** *archaic* : severe in temper or action : UNMERCIFUL **b** : physically severe : STORMY ⟨*inclement* weather⟩
— **in·clem·ent·ly** *adverb*

**in·clin·able** \in-'klī-nə-bəl\ *adjective* (15th century)
: having a tendency or inclination; *also* : disposed to favor or think well of

**in·cli·na·tion** \ˌin-klə-'nā-shən, ˌiŋ-\ *noun* (14th century)
**1 a** *obsolete* : natural disposition : CHARACTER **b** : a particular disposition of mind or character : PROPENSITY; *especially* : LIKING ⟨had little *inclination* for housekeeping⟩
**2** : an act or the action of bending or inclining: as **a** : BOW, NOD **b** : a tilting of something
**3 a** : a deviation from the true vertical or horizontal : SLANT; *also* : the degree of such deviation **b** : an inclined surface : SLOPE **c** (1) : the angle determined by two lines or planes (2) : the angle made by a line with the x-axis measured counterclockwise from the positive direction of that axis
**4** : a tendency to a particular aspect, state, character, or action ⟨the clutch has an *inclination* to slip⟩
— **in·cli·na·tion·al** \-shnəl, -shə-nᵊl\ *adjective*

¹**in·cline** \in-'klīn\ *verb* **in·clined; in·clin·ing** [Middle English, from Middle French *incliner*, from Latin *inclinare*, from *in-* + *clinare* to lean — more at LEAN] (14th century)
*intransitive verb*
**1** : to bend the head or body forward : BOW
**2** : to lean, tend, or become drawn toward an opinion or course of conduct
**3** : to deviate from a line, direction, or course; *specifically* : to deviate from the vertical or horizontal
*transitive verb*
**1** : to cause to stoop or bow : BEND
**2** : to have influence on : PERSUADE ⟨his love of books *inclined* him toward a literary career⟩
**3** : to give a bend or slant to ☆
— **in·clin·er** *noun*

²**in·cline** \'in-ˌklīn\ *noun* (1846)
: an inclined plane : GRADE, SLOPE

**in·clined** \in-'klīnd, 2 *also* 'in-ˌ\ *adjective* (14th century)
**1** : having inclination, disposition, or tendency
**2 a** : having a leaning or slope **b** : making an angle with a line or plane

**inclined plane** *noun* (1710)
: a plane surface that makes an oblique angle with the plane of the horizon

**in·clin·ing** \in-'klī-niŋ\ *noun* (14th century)
**1** : INCLINATION
**2** *archaic* : PARTY, FOLLOWING

**in·cli·nom·e·ter** \ˌin-klə-'nä-mə-tər, ˌiŋ-; ˌin-ˌklī-\ *noun* (1852)
: an instrument for indicating the inclination to the horizontal of an axis (as of an airplane)

**in·clip** \in-'klip\ *transitive verb* (1608)
*archaic* : CLASP, ENCLOSE

**inclose, inclosure** *variant of* ENCLOSE, ENCLOSURE

**in·clude** \in-'klüd\ *transitive verb* **in·clud·ed; in·clud·ing** [Middle English, from Latin *includere*, from *in-* + *claudere* to close — more at CLOSE] (15th century)
**1** : to shut up : ENCLOSE
**2** : to take in or comprise as a part of a whole
**3** : to contain between or within ⟨two sides and the *included* angle⟩ ☆
— **in·clud·able** *or* **in·clud·ible** \-'klü-də-bəl\ *adjective*

**in·clu·sion** \in-'klü-zhən\ *noun* [Latin *inclusion-, inclusio*, from *includere*] (1600)
**1** : the act of including : the state of being included
**2** : something that is included: as **a** : a gaseous, liquid, or solid foreign body enclosed in

a mass (as of a mineral) **b** : a passive usually temporary product of cell activity (as a starch grain) within the cytoplasm or nucleus
**3** : a relation between two classes that exists when all members of the first are also members of the second — compare MEMBERSHIP 3

**inclusion body** *noun* (circa 1919)
: an inclusion, abnormal structure, or foreign cell within a cell; *specifically* : an intracellular body that is characteristic of some virus diseases and that is the site of virus multiplication

**in·clu·sive** \in-'klü-siv, -ziv\ *adjective* (15th century)
**1** : comprehending stated limits or extremes ⟨from Monday to Friday *inclusive*⟩
**2 a** : broad in orientation or scope **b** : covering or intended to cover all items, costs, or services
— **in·clu·sive·ly** *adverb*
— **in·clu·sive·ness** *noun*

**inclusive disjunction** *noun* (1942)
: a complex sentence in logic that is true when either or both of its constituent propositions are true — see TRUTH TABLE table

**inclusive of** *preposition* (1709)
: including or taking into account ⟨the cost of building *inclusive of* materials⟩

**in·co·erc·ible** \ˌin-kō-'ər-sə-bəl\ *adjective* (1710)

---

☆ **SYNONYMS**
**Incite, instigate, abet, foment** mean to spur to action. INCITE stresses a stirring up and urging on, and may or may not imply initiating ⟨*inciting* a riot⟩. INSTIGATE definitely implies responsibility for initiating another's action and often connotes underhandedness or evil intention ⟨*instigated* a conspiracy⟩. ABET implies both assisting and encouraging ⟨aiding and *abetting* the enemy⟩. FOMENT implies persistence in goading ⟨*fomenting* rebellion⟩.

**Incline, bias, dispose, predispose** mean to influence one to have or take an attitude toward something. INCLINE implies a tendency to favor one of two or more actions or conclusions ⟨I *incline* to agree⟩. BIAS suggests a settled and predictable leaning in one direction and connotes unfair prejudice ⟨the experience *biased* him against foreigners⟩. DISPOSE suggests an affecting of one's mood or temper so as to incline one toward something ⟨her nature *disposes* her to trust others⟩. PREDISPOSE implies the operation of a disposing influence well in advance of the opportunity to manifest itself ⟨does fictional violence *predispose* them to accept real violence?⟩.

**Include, comprehend, embrace, involve** mean to contain within as part of the whole. INCLUDE suggests the containment of something as a constituent, component, or subordinate part of a larger whole ⟨the price of dinner *includes* dessert⟩. COMPREHEND implies that something comes within the scope of a statement or definition ⟨his system *comprehends* all history⟩. EMBRACE implies a gathering of separate items within a whole ⟨her faith *embraces* both Christian and non-Christian beliefs⟩. INVOLVE suggests inclusion by virtue of the nature of the whole, whether by being its natural or inevitable consequence ⟨the new job *involves* a lot of detail⟩.

---

\ə\ abut \ᵊ\ kitten \ər\ further \a\ ash \ā\ ace
\ä\ mop, mar \au\ out \ch\ chin \e\ bet \ē\ easy
\g\ go \i\ hit \ī\ ice \j\ job \ŋ\ sing \ō\ go
\ȯ\ law \ȯi\ boy \th\ thin \th\ the \ü\ loot \u̇\ foot
\y\ yet \zh\ vision *see also* Guide to Pronunciation

**:** incapable of being controlled, checked, or confined

**in·cog·i·tant** \in-ˈkä-jə-tənt\ *adjective* [Latin *incogitant-, incogitans,* from *in-* + *cogitant-, cogitans,* present participle of *cogitare* to cogitate] (1628)
**:** THOUGHTLESS, INCONSIDERATE

**in·cog·ni·ta** \in-ˈkäg-ˈnē-tə *also* in-ˈkäg-nə-tə\ *adverb or adjective* [Italian, feminine of *incognito*] (1638)
**:** INCOGNITO — used only of a woman
— **incognita** *noun*

**¹in·cog·ni·to** \in-ˌkäg-ˈnē-(ˌ)tō *also* in-ˈkäg-nə-ˌtō\ *adverb or adjective* [Italian, from Latin *incognitus* unknown, from *in-* + *cognitus,* past participle of *cognoscere* to know — more at COGNITION] (1635)
**:** with one's identity concealed

**²incognito** *noun, plural* **-tos** (1638)
**1 :** one appearing or living incognito
**2 :** the state or assumed identity of one living or traveling incognito or incognita

**in·cog·ni·zant** \(ˌ)in-ˈkäg-nə-zənt\ *adjective* (1837)
**:** lacking awareness or consciousness
— **in·cog·ni·zance** \-zən(t)s\ *noun*

**in·co·her·ence** \ˌin-kō-ˈhir-ən(t)s, -ˈher-\ *noun* (1611)
**1 :** the quality or state of being incoherent
**2 :** something that is incoherent

**in·co·her·ent** \-ənt\ *adjective* (1626)
**1 :** lacking coherence: as **a :** lacking cohesion **:** LOOSE **b :** lacking orderly continuity, arrangement, or relevance **:** INCONSISTENT
**2 :** lacking clarity or intelligibility **:** INCOMPREHENSIBLE
— **in·co·her·ent·ly** *adverb*

**in·com·bus·ti·ble** \ˌin-kəm-ˈbəs-tə-bəl\ *adjective* [Middle English, probably from Middle French, from *in-* + *combustible* combustible] (15th century)
**:** not combustible **:** incapable of being burned
— **in·com·bus·ti·bil·i·ty** \-ˌbəs-tə-ˈbi-lə-tē\ *noun*
— **incombustible** *noun*

**in·come** \ˈin-ˌkəm *also* ˈin-kəm *or* ˈiŋ-kəm\ *noun* (14th century)
**1 :** a coming in **:** ENTRANCE; INFLUX ⟨fluctuations in the nutrient *income* of a body of water⟩
**2 :** a gain or recurrent benefit usually measured in money that derives from capital or labor; *also* **:** the amount of such gain received in a period of time ⟨has an *income* of $20,000 a year⟩

**income account** *noun* (1869)
**:** a financial statement of a business showing the details of revenues, costs, expenses, losses, and profits for a given period — called also *income statement*

**income bond** *noun* (circa 1864)
**:** a bond that pays interest at a rate based on the issuer's earnings

**income tax** *noun* (1799)
**:** a tax on the net income of an individual or a business

**¹in·com·ing** \ˈin-ˌkə-miŋ\ *noun* (14th century)
**1 :** the act of coming in **:** ARRIVAL
**2 :** INCOME — usually used in plural

**²incoming** *adjective* (1753)
**1 :** coming in **:** ARRIVING ⟨an *incoming* ship⟩ ⟨*incoming* mail⟩
**2 :** taking a new place or position especially as part of a succession ⟨the *incoming* president⟩
**3 :** just starting or beginning ⟨the *incoming* year⟩

**in·com·men·su·ra·ble** \ˌin-kə-ˈmen(t)s-rə-bəl, -ˈmen(t)sh-; -ˈmen(t)-sə-, -shə-\ *adjective* (1570)
**:** not commensurable; *broadly* **:** lacking a basis of comparison in respect to a quality normally subject to comparison
— **in·com·men·su·ra·bil·i·ty** \-ˌmen(t)s-rə-ˈbi-lə-tē, -ˌmen(t)sh-; -ˌmen(t)-sə-, -shə-\ *noun*
— **incommensurable** *noun*

**— in·com·men·su·ra·bly** \-ˈmen(t)s-rə-blē, -ˈmen(t)sh-; -ˈmen(t)-sə-, -shə-\ *adverb*

**in·com·men·su·rate** \-ˈmen(t)s-rət, -ˈmen(t)sh-; -ˈmen(t)-sə-, -shə-\ *adjective* (1650)
**:** not commensurate: as **a :** INCOMMENSURABLE **b :** INADEQUATE **c :** DISPROPORTIONATE

**in·com·mode** \ˌin-kə-ˈmōd\ *transitive verb* **-mod·ed; -mod·ing** [Middle French *incommoder,* from Latin *incommodare,* from *incommodus* inconvenient, from *in-* + *commodus* convenient — more at COMMODE] (1598)
**:** to give inconvenience or distress to **:** DISTURB

**in·com·mo·di·ous** \ˌin-kə-ˈmō-dē-əs\ *adjective* (1551)
**:** not commodious **:** INCONVENIENT
— **in·com·mo·di·ous·ly** *adverb*
— **in·com·mo·di·ous·ness** *noun*

**in·com·mod·i·ty** \-ˈmä-də-tē\ *noun* (15th century)
**:** a source of inconvenience **:** DISADVANTAGE

**in·com·mu·ni·ca·ble** \ˌin-kə-ˈmyü-ni-kə-bəl\ *adjective* [Middle French or Late Latin; Middle French, from Late Latin *incommunicabilis,* from Latin *in-* + Late Latin *communicabilis* communicable] (1568)
**:** not communicable: as **a :** incapable of being communicated or imparted **b :** UNCOMMUNICATIVE
— **in·com·mu·ni·ca·bil·i·ty** \-ˌmyü-ni-kə-ˈbi-lə-tē\ *noun*
— **in·com·mu·ni·ca·bly** \-ˈmyü-ni-kə-blē\ *adverb*

**in·com·mu·ni·ca·do** \-ˌmyü-nə-ˈkä-(ˌ)dō\ *adverb or adjective* [Spanish *incomunicado,* from past participle of *incomunicar* to deprive of communication, from *in-* (from Latin) + *comunicar* to communicate, from Latin *communicare*] (1844)
**:** without means of communication; *also* **:** in solitary confinement

**in·com·mu·ni·ca·tive** \-ˈmyü-nə-ˌkā-tiv, -ni-kə-tiv\ *adjective* (1670)
**:** UNCOMMUNICATIVE

**in·com·mut·able** \ˌin-kə-ˈmyü-tə-bəl\ *adjective* [Middle English, from Latin *incommutabilis,* from *in-* + *commutabilis* commutable] (15th century)
**:** not commutable: as **a :** not interchangeable **b :** UNCHANGEABLE
— **in·com·mut·ably** \-blē\ *adverb*

**in·com·pa·ra·ble** \(ˌ)in-ˈkäm-p(ə-)rə-bəl, ÷ˌin-kəm-ˈpar-ə-\ *adjective* [Middle English, from Middle French, from Latin *incomparabilis,* from *in-* + *comparabilis* comparable] (15th century)
**1 :** eminent beyond comparison **:** MATCHLESS
**2 :** not suitable for comparison
— **in·com·pa·ra·bil·i·ty** \(ˌ)in-ˌkäm-p(ə-)rə-ˈbi-lə-tē, ÷ˌin-kəm-ˌpar-ə-\ *noun*
— **in·com·pa·ra·bly** \(ˌ)in-ˈkäm-p(ə-)rə-blē, ÷ˌin-kəm-ˈpar-ə-\ *adverb*

**in·com·pat·i·bil·i·ty** \ˌin-kəm-ˌpa-tə-ˈbi-lə-tē\ *noun, plural* **-ties** (1611)
**1 a :** the quality or state of being incompatible **b :** lack of interfertility between two plants
**2** *plural* **:** mutually antagonistic things or qualities

**in·com·pat·i·ble** \ˌin-kəm-ˈpa-tə-bəl\ *adjective* [Middle English, from Middle French & Medieval Latin; Middle French, from Medieval Latin *incompatibilis,* from Latin *in-* + Medieval Latin *compatibilis* compatible] (15th century)
**1 :** incapable of being held by one person at one time — used of offices that make conflicting demands on the holder
**2 :** not compatible: as **a :** incapable of association or harmonious coexistence ⟨*incompatible* colors⟩ **b :** unsuitable for use together because of undesirable chemical or physiological effects ⟨*incompatible* drugs⟩ **c :** not both true ⟨*incompatible* propositions⟩ **d :** incapable of blending into a stable homogeneous mixture
— **incompatible** *noun*
— **in·com·pat·i·bly** \-blē\ *adverb*

**in·com·pe·tence** \(ˌ)in-ˈkäm-pə-tən(t)s\ *noun* (1663)
**:** the state or fact of being incompetent

**in·com·pe·ten·cy** \-tən(t)-sē\ *noun* (1611)
**:** INCOMPETENCE

**in·com·pe·tent** \(ˌ)in-ˈkäm-pə-tənt\ *adjective* [Middle French *incompétent,* from *in-* + *compétent* competent] (1597)
**1 :** not legally qualified
**2 :** inadequate to or unsuitable for a particular purpose
**3 a :** lacking the qualities needed for effective action **b :** unable to function properly ⟨*incompetent* heart valves⟩
— **incompetent** *noun*
— **in·com·pe·tent·ly** *adverb*

**in·com·plete** \ˌin-kəm-ˈplēt\ *adjective* [Middle English *incompleet,* from Late Latin *incompletus,* from Latin *in-* + *completus* complete] (14th century)
**1 :** not complete **:** UNFINISHED: as **a :** lacking a part; *especially* **:** lacking one or more sets of floral organs **b** *of insect metamorphosis* **:** characterized by the absence of a pupal stage between the immature stages and the adult of an insect in which the young usually resemble the adult — compare COMPLETE 5
**2** *of a football pass* **:** not legally caught
— **in·com·plete·ly** *adverb*
— **in·com·plete·ness** *noun*

**in·com·pli·ant** \ˌin-kəm-ˈplī-ənt\ *adjective* (1647)
**:** not compliant or pliable

**in·com·pre·hen·si·ble** \(ˌ)in-ˌkäm-pri-ˈhen(t)-sə-bəl\ *adjective* [Middle English, from Latin *incomprehensibilis,* from *in-* + *comprehensibilis* comprehensible] (14th century)
**1** *archaic* **:** having or subject to no limits
**2 :** impossible to comprehend **:** UNINTELLIGIBLE
— **in·com·pre·hen·si·bil·i·ty** \-ˌhen(t)-sə-ˈbi-lə-tē\ *noun*
— **in·com·pre·hen·si·ble·ness** *noun*
— **in·com·pre·hen·si·bly** \-ˈhen(t)-sə-blē\ *adverb*

**in·com·pre·hen·sion** \-ˈhen(t)-shən\ *noun* (1605)
**:** lack of comprehension or understanding

**in·com·press·ible** \ˌin-kəm-ˈpre-sə-bəl\ *adjective* (circa 1736)
**:** incapable of or resistant to compression

**in·com·put·able** \ˌin-kəm-ˈpyü-tə-bəl\ *adjective* (1606)
**:** not computable **:** very great
— **in·com·put·ably** \-blē\ *adverb*

**in·con·ceiv·able** \ˌin-kən-ˈsē-və-bəl\ *adjective* (circa 1631)
**:** not conceivable: as **a :** impossible to comprehend **b :** UNBELIEVABLE
— **in·con·ceiv·abil·i·ty** \-ˌsē-və-ˈbi-lə-tē\ *noun*
— **in·con·ceiv·able·ness** \-ˈsē-və-bəl-nəs\ *noun*
— **in·con·ceiv·ably** \-blē\ *adverb*

**in·con·cin·ni·ty** \ˌin-kən-ˈsi-nə-tē\ *noun* [Latin *inconcinnitas,* from *in-* + *concinnitas* concinnity] (circa 1616)
**:** lack of suitability or congruity **:** INELEGANCE

**in·con·clu·sive** \ˌin-kən-ˈklü-siv, -ziv\ *adjective* (1707)
**:** leading to no conclusion or definite result
— **in·con·clu·sive·ly** *adverb*
— **in·con·clu·sive·ness** *noun*

**in·con·dite** \in-ˈkän-dət, -ˌdīt\ *adjective* [Latin *inconditus,* from *in-* + *conditus,* past participle of *condere* to put together, from *com-* + *-dere* to put — more at DO] (1539)
**:** badly put together **:** CRUDE

**in·con·for·mi·ty** \ˌin-kən-ˈfȯr-mə-tē\ *noun* (1594)
**:** NONCONFORMITY

**in·con·gru·ence** \ˌin-kən-ˈgrü-ən(t)s, (ˌ)in-ˈkäŋ-grə-wən(t)s\ *noun* (1610)
**:** INCONGRUITY

**in·con·gru·ent** \-ənt, -wənt\ *adjective* [Middle English, from Latin *incongruent-, incongruens*, from *in-* + *congruent-, congruens* congruent] (15th century)
: not congruent ⟨*incongruent* triangles⟩
— **in·con·gru·ent·ly** *adverb*

**in·con·gru·i·ty** \ˌin-kən-ˈgrü-ə-tē, -ˌkän-\ *noun, plural* **-ties** (circa 1532)
**1** : the quality or state of being incongruous
**2** : something that is incongruous

**in·con·gru·ous** \(ˌ)in-ˈkäŋ-grə-wəs\ *adjective* [Late Latin *incongruus*, from Latin *in-* + *congruus* congruous] (1611)
: lacking congruity: as **a** : not harmonious : INCOMPATIBLE ⟨*incongruous* colors⟩ **b** : not conforming : DISAGREEING ⟨conduct *incongruous* with principle⟩ **c** : inconsistent within itself ⟨an *incongruous* story⟩ **d** : lacking propriety : UNSUITABLE ⟨*incongruous* manners⟩
— **in·con·gru·ous·ly** *adverb*
— **in·con·gru·ous·ness** *noun*

**in·con·scient** \(ˌ)in-ˈkän(t)-shənt\ *adjective* [probably from French, from *in-* + *conscient* mindful, from Latin *conscient-, consciens*, present participle of *conscire* to be conscious — more at CONSCIENCE] (1885)
: UNCONSCIOUS, MINDLESS

**in·con·sec·u·tive** \ˌin-kən-ˈse-kyə-tiv, -kə-tiv\ *adjective* (1831)
: not consecutive

**in·con·se·quence** \(ˌ)in-ˈkän(t)-sə-ˌkwen(t)s, -si-kwən(t)s\ *noun* (1588)
: the quality or state of being inconsequent

**in·con·se·quent** \-ˌkwent, -kwənt\ *adjective* [Late Latin *inconsequent-, inconsequens*, from Latin *in-* + *consequent-, consequens* consequent] (1579)
**1 a** : lacking reasonable sequence : ILLOGICAL **b** : INCONSECUTIVE
**2** : INCONSEQUENTIAL 2
**3** : IRRELEVANT
— **in·con·se·quent·ly** *adverb*

**in·con·se·quen·tial** \(ˌ)in-ˌkän(t)-sə-ˈkwen(t)-shəl\ *adjective* (1621)
**1 a** : ILLOGICAL **b** : IRRELEVANT
**2** : of no significance : UNIMPORTANT
— **in·con·se·quen·ti·al·i·ty** \-ˌkwen(t)-shē-ˈa-lə-tē\ *noun*
— **in·con·se·quen·tial·ly** \-ˈkwen(t)-shlē, -ˈkwen(t)-shə-\ *adverb*

**in·con·sid·er·able** \ˌin-kən-ˈsi-dər-(ə-)bəl, -ˈsi-drə-bəl\ *adjective* [French, from *in-* + *considerable* considerable, from Medieval Latin *considerabilis*] (1637)
: not considerable : TRIVIAL
— **in·con·sid·er·able·ness** *noun*
— **in·con·sid·er·ably** \-blē\ *adverb*

**in·con·sid·er·ate** \ˌin-kən-ˈsi-d(ə-)rət\ *adjective* [Middle English *inconsyderatt*, from Latin *inconsideratus*, from *in-* + *consideratus* considerate] (15th century)
**1 a** : HEEDLESS, THOUGHTLESS **b** : careless of the rights or feelings of others
**2** : not adequately considered : ILL-ADVISED
— **in·con·sid·er·ate·ly** *adverb*
— **in·con·sid·er·ate·ness** *noun*
— **in·con·sid·er·ation** \-ˌsi-də-ˈrā-shən\ *noun*

**in·con·sis·tence** \ˌin-kən-ˈsis-tən(t)s\ *noun* (1643)
: INCONSISTENCY

**in·con·sis·ten·cy** \ˌin-kən-ˈsis-tən-sē\ *noun* (1647)
**1** : an instance of being inconsistent
**2** : the quality or state of being inconsistent

**in·con·sis·tent** \-tənt\ *adjective* (1646)
: lacking consistency: as **a** : not compatible with another fact or claim ⟨*inconsistent* statements⟩ **b** : containing incompatible elements ⟨an *inconsistent* argument⟩ **c** : incoherent or illogical in thought or actions : CHANGEABLE **d** : not satisfiable by the same set of values for the unknowns ⟨*inconsistent* equations⟩ ⟨*inconsistent* inequalities⟩
— **in·con·sis·tent·ly** *adverb*

**in·con·sol·able** \ˌin-kən-ˈsō-lə-bəl\ *adjective* [Latin *inconsolabilis*, from *in-* + *consolabilis* consolable] (1596)
: incapable of being consoled : DISCONSOLATE
— **in·con·sol·able·ness** *noun*
— **in·con·sol·ably** \-blē\ *adverb*

**in·con·so·nance** \(ˌ)in-ˈkän(t)-s(ə-)nən(t)s\ *noun* (circa 1811)
: lack of consonance or harmony : DISAGREEMENT

**in·con·so·nant** \-s(ə-)nənt\ *adjective* (1658)
: not consonant : DISCORDANT

**in·con·spic·u·ous** \ˌin-kən-ˈspi-kyə-wəs\ *adjective* [Latin *inconspicuus*, from *in-* + *conspicuus* conspicuous] (1648)
: not readily noticeable
— **in·con·spic·u·ous·ly** *adverb*
— **in·con·spic·u·ous·ness** *noun*

**in·con·stan·cy** \(ˌ)in-ˈkän(t)-stən(t)-sē\ *noun* (1526)
: the quality or state of being inconstant

**in·con·stant** \-stənt\ *adjective* [Middle English, from Middle French, from Latin *inconstant-, inconstans*, from *in-* + *constant-, constans* constant] (15th century)
: likely to change frequently without apparent or cogent reason ☆
— **in·con·stant·ly** *adverb*

**in·con·sum·able** \ˌin-kən-ˈsü-mə-bəl\ *adjective* (1646)
: not capable of being consumed
— **in·con·sum·ably** \-blē\ *adverb*

**in·con·test·able** \ˌin-kən-ˈtes-tə-bəl\ *adjective* [French, from *in-* + *contestable*, from *contester* to contest] (1673)
: not contestable : INDISPUTABLE
— **in·con·test·abil·i·ty** \-ˌtes-tə-ˈbi-lə-tē\ *noun*
— **in·con·test·ably** \-ˈtes-tə-blē\ *adverb*

**in·con·ti·nence** \(ˌ)in-ˈkän-t³n-ən(t)s\ *noun* (14th century)
: the quality or state of being incontinent: as **a** : failure to restrain sexual appetite : UNCHASTITY **b** : inability of the body to control the evacuative functions

**in·con·ti·nen·cy** \-ən(t)-sē\ *noun* (15th century)
: INCONTINENCE

**¹in·con·ti·nent** \(ˌ)in-ˈkän-t³n-ənt\ *adjective* [Middle English, from Middle French or Latin; Middle French *incontinent*, from Latin *incontinent-, incontinens*, from *in-* + *continent-, continens* continent] (14th century)
: not continent: as **a** (1) : lacking self-restraint (2) : not being under control **b** : unable to retain a bodily discharge (as urine) voluntarily

**²incontinent** *adverb* [Middle English, from Middle French, from Late Latin *in continenti*] (15th century)
: ¹INCONTINENTLY

**¹in·con·ti·nent·ly** *adverb* (15th century)
: without delay : IMMEDIATELY

**²incontinently** *adverb* (circa 1552)
: in an incontinent or unrestrained manner: as **a** : without moral restraint : LEWDLY **b** : without due or reasonable consideration

**in·con·trol·la·ble** \ˌin-kən-ˈtrō-lə-bəl\ *adjective* (1599)
: UNCONTROLLABLE

**in·con·tro·vert·ible** \(ˌ)in-ˌkän-trə-ˈvər-tə-bəl\ *adjective* (1646)
: not open to question : INDISPUTABLE ⟨*incontrovertible* evidence⟩
— **in·con·tro·vert·ibly** \-blē\ *adverb*

**¹in·con·ve·nience** \ˌin-kən-ˈvē-nyən(t)s\ *noun* [Middle English, harm, damage, from Late Latin *inconvenientia*, from Latin *inconvenient-, inconveniens*] (1547)
**1** : something that is inconvenient
**2** : the quality or state of being inconvenient

**²inconvenience** *transitive verb* **-nienced; -nienc·ing** (circa 1656)
: to subject to inconvenience : put to trouble

**in·con·ve·nien·cy** \ˌin-kən-ˈvē-nyən(t)-sē\ *noun, plural* **-cies** (circa 1552)
: INCONVENIENCE

**in·con·ve·nient** \ˌin-kən-ˈvē-nyənt\ *adjective* [Middle English, from Middle French, from Latin *inconvenient-, inconveniens*, from *in-* + *convenient-, conveniens* convenient] (1651)
: not convenient especially in giving trouble or annoyance : INOPPORTUNE
— **in·con·ve·nient·ly** *adverb*

**in·con·vert·ible** \-ˈvər-tə-bəl\ *adjective* [probably from Late Latin *inconvertibilis*, from Latin *in-* + *convertibilis* convertible] (1646)
: not convertible: as **a** *of paper money* : not exchangeable for coin **b** *of a currency* : not exchangeable for a foreign currency
— **in·con·vert·ibil·i·ty** \-ˌvər-tə-ˈbi-lə-tē\ *noun*
— **in·con·vert·ibly** \-ˈvər-tə-blē\ *adverb*

**in·con·vin·ci·ble** \ˌin-kən-ˈvin(t)-sə-bəl\ *adjective* (1674)
: incapable of being convinced

**in·co·or·di·na·tion** \-(ˌ)kō-ˌȯr-d³n-ˈā-shən\ *noun* (1876)
: lack of coordination especially of muscular movements resulting from loss of voluntary control

**¹in·cor·po·rate** \in-ˈkȯr-pə-ˌrāt\ *verb* **-rat·ed; -rat·ing** [Middle English, from Late Latin *incorporatus*, past participle of *incorporare*, from Latin *in-* + *corpor-, corpus* body — more at MIDRIFF] (14th century)
*transitive verb*
**1 a** : to unite or work into something already existent so as to form an indistinguishable whole **b** : to blend or combine thoroughly
**2 a** : to form into a legal corporation **b** : to admit to membership in a corporate body
**3** : to give material form to : EMBODY
*intransitive verb*
**1** : to unite in or as one body
**2** : to form or become a corporation
— **in·cor·po·ra·ble** \-p(ə-)rə-bəl\ *adjective*
— **in·cor·po·ra·tion** \-ˌkȯr-pə-ˈrā-shən\ *noun*
— **in·cor·po·ra·tive** \-ˈkȯr-pə-ˌrā-tiv, -p(ə-)rə-tiv\ *adjective*
— **in·cor·po·ra·tor** \-pə-ˌrā-tər\ *noun*

**²in·cor·po·rate** \in-ˈkȯr-p(ə-)rət\ *adjective* (14th century)
: INCORPORATED

**in·cor·po·rat·ed** \-pə-ˌrā-təd\ *adjective* (1599)
**1** : united in one body
**2** : formed into a legal corporation

**in·cor·po·re·al** \ˌin-(ˌ)kȯr-ˈpōr-ē-əl, -ˈpȯr-\ *adjective* [Middle English *incorporealle*, from Latin *incorporeus*, from *in-* + *corporeus* corporeal] (15th century)

---

☆ **SYNONYMS**
**Inconstant, fickle, capricious, mercurial, unstable** mean lacking firmness or steadiness (as in purpose or devotion). INCONSTANT implies an incapacity for steadiness and an inherent tendency to change ⟨an *inconstant* friend⟩. FICKLE suggests unreliability because of perverse changeability and incapacity for steadfastness ⟨performers discover how *fickle* fans can be⟩. CAPRICIOUS suggests motivation by sudden whim or fancy and stresses unpredictability ⟨an utterly *capricious* critic⟩. MERCURIAL implies a rapid changeability in mood ⟨made anxious by her boss's *mercurial* temperament⟩. UNSTABLE implies an incapacity for remaining in a fixed position or steady course and applies especially to a lack of emotional balance ⟨too *unstable* to hold a job⟩.

---

**1 :** not corporeal **:** having no material body or form
**2 :** of, relating to, or constituting a right that is based on property (as bonds or patents) which has no intrinsic value
— **in·cor·po·re·al·ly** \-ə-lē\ *adverb*
**in·cor·po·re·ity** \(ˌ)in-ˌkȯr-pə-'rē-ə-tē\ *noun* (1601)
**:** the quality or state of being incorporeal **:** IMMATERIALITY

**in·cor·rect** \ˌin-kə-'rekt\ *adjective* [Middle English, from Middle French or Latin; Middle French, from Latin *incorrectus*, from *in-* + *correctus* correct] (15th century)
**1** *obsolete* **:** not corrected or chastened
**2 a :** INACCURATE, FAULTY **b :** not true **:** WRONG
**3 :** UNBECOMING, IMPROPER
— **in·cor·rect·ly** \-'rek(t)-lē\ *adverb*
— **in·cor·rect·ness** \-nəs\ *noun*
**in·cor·ri·gi·ble** \(ˌ)in-'kȯr-ə-jə-bəl, -'kär-\ *adjective* [Middle English, from Late Latin *incorrigibilis*, from Latin *in-* + *corrigere* to correct — more at CORRECT] (14th century)
**:** incapable of being corrected or amended: as
**a** (1) **:** not reformable **:** DEPRAVED (2) **:** DELINQUENT **b :** not manageable **:** UNRULY **c :** UNALTERABLE, INVETERATE
— **in·cor·ri·gi·bil·i·ty** \-ˌkȯr-ə-jə-'bi-lə-tē, -ˌkär-\ *noun*
— **incorrigible** *noun*
— **in·cor·ri·gi·ble·ness** \-'kȯr-ə-jə-bəl-nəs, -'kär-\ *noun*
— **in·cor·ri·gi·bly** \-blē\ *adverb*
**in·cor·rupt** \ˌin-kə-'rəpt\ *also* **in·cor·rupt·ed** \-'rəp-təd\ *adjective* [Middle English, from Latin *incorruptus*, from *in-* + *corruptus* corrupt] (14th century)
**:** free from corruption: as **a** *obsolete* **:** not affected with decay **b :** not defiled or depraved **:** UPRIGHT **c :** free from error
— **in·cor·rupt·ly** \-'rəp(t)-lē\ *adverb*
— **in·cor·rupt·ness** \-nəs\ *noun*
**in·cor·rupt·ible** \ˌin-kə-'rəp-tə-bəl\ *adjective* (14th century)
**:** incapable of corruption: as **a :** not subject to decay or dissolution **b :** incapable of being bribed or morally corrupted
— **in·cor·rupt·ibil·i·ty** \-ˌrəp-tə-'bi-lə-tē\ *noun*
— **incorruptible** *noun*
— **in·cor·rupt·ibly** \-'rəp-tə-blē\ *adverb*
**in·cor·rup·tion** \ˌin-kə-'rəp-shən\ *noun* (14th century)
*archaic* **:** the quality or state of being free from physical decay
**¹in·crease** \in-'krēs, 'in-ˌ\ *verb* **in·creased; in·creas·ing** [Middle English *encresen*, from Middle French *encreistre*, from Latin *increscere*, from *in-* + *crescere* to grow — more at CRESCENT] (14th century)
*intransitive verb*
**1 :** to become progressively greater (as in size, amount, number, or intensity)
**2 :** to multiply by the production of young
*transitive verb*
**1 :** to make greater **:** AUGMENT
**2** *obsolete* **:** ENRICH ☆
— **in·creas·able** \-'krē-sə-bəl, -ˌkrē-\ *adjective*
— **in·creas·er** *noun*
**²in·crease** \'in-ˌkrēs, in-'\ *noun* (14th century)
**1 :** the act or process of increasing: as **a :** addition or enlargement in size, extent, or quantity **b** *obsolete* **:** PROPAGATION
**2 :** something that is added to an original stock or amount by augmentation or growth (as offspring, produce, profit)
**in·creas·ing·ly** \in-'krē-siŋ-lē, 'in-ˌkrē-\ *adverb* (14th century)
**:** to an increasing degree
**in·cre·ate** \ˌin-krē-'āt, in-'krē-ət\ *adjective* [Middle English *increat*, from Late Latin *increatus*, from Latin *in-* + *creatus*, past participle of *creare* to create] (15th century)
**:** UNCREATED

**in·cred·i·ble** \(ˌ)in-'kre-də-bəl\ *adjective* [Middle English, from Latin *incredibilis*, from *in-* + *credibilis* credible] (15th century)
**:** too extraordinary and improbable to be believed; *also* **:** hard to believe
— **in·cred·i·bil·i·ty** \-ˌkre-də-'bi-lə-tē\ *noun*
— **in·cred·i·ble·ness** \-'kre-də-bəl-nəs\ *noun*
— **in·cred·i·bly** \-blē\ *adverb* (circa 1500)
**1 :** in an incredible manner
**2 :** EXTREMELY ⟨*incredibly* difficult⟩
**in·cre·du·li·ty** \ˌin-kri-'dü-lə-tē, -'dyü-\ *noun* (15th century)
**:** the quality or state of being incredulous **:** DISBELIEF
**in·cred·u·lous** \(ˌ)in-'kre-jə-ləs, -dyə-ləs\ *adjective* [Latin *incredulus*, from *in-* + *credulus* credulous] (1579)
**1 :** unwilling to admit or accept what is offered as true **:** not credulous **:** SKEPTICAL
**2 :** INCREDIBLE
**3 :** expressing incredulity ◼
— **in·cred·u·lous·ly** *adverb*
**in·cre·ment** \'iŋ-krə-mənt, 'in-\ *noun* [Middle English, from Latin *incrementum*, from *increscere* to increase] (15th century)
**1 :** the action or process of increasing especially in quantity or value **:** ENLARGEMENT
**2 a :** something gained or added **b :** one of a series of regular consecutive additions **c :** a minute increase in quantity
**3 :** the amount or degree by which something changes; *especially* **:** the amount of positive or negative change in the value of one or more of a set of variables
— **in·cre·men·tal** \ˌiŋ-krə-'men-t°l, ˌin-\ *adjective*
— **in·cre·men·tal·ly** \-t°l-ē\ *adverb*
**in·cre·men·tal·ism** \ˌiŋ-krə-'men-t°l-ˌi-zəm\ *noun* (1966)
**:** a policy or advocacy of a policy of political or social change by degrees **:** GRADUALISM
— **in·cre·men·tal·ist** \-t°l-ist\ *noun*
**incremental repetition** *noun* (1918)
**:** repetition in each stanza (as of a ballad) of part of the preceding stanza usually with a slight change in wording for dramatic effect
**in·cres·cent** \in-'kre-s°nt\ *adjective* [Latin *increscent-, increscens*, present participle of *increscere*] (circa 1658)
**:** becoming gradually greater **:** WAXING ⟨the *increscent* moon⟩
**in·crim·i·nate** \in-'kri-mə-ˌnāt\ *transitive verb* **-nat·ed; -nat·ing** [Late Latin *incriminatus*, past participle of *incriminare*, from Latin *in-* + *crimin-, crimen* crime] (circa 1736)
**:** to charge with or show evidence or proof of involvement in a crime or fault
— **in·crim·i·na·tion** \-ˌkri-mə-'nā-shən\ *noun*
— **in·crim·i·na·to·ry** \-'krim-nə-ˌtȯr-ē, -'kri-mə-, -ˌtȯr-\ *adjective*
**incrust** *variant of* ENCRUST
**in·crus·ta·tion** \ˌin-ˌkrəs-'tā-shən\ *noun* [Latin *incrustation-, incrustatio*, from *incrustare* to encrust] (1644)
**1 a :** a crust or hard coating **b :** a growth or accumulation (as of habits, opinions, or customs) resembling a crust
**2 :** the act of encrusting **:** the state of being encrusted
**3 a :** OVERLAY **a b :** INLAY
**in·cu·bate** \'iŋ-kyə-ˌbāt, 'in-\ *verb* **-bat·ed; -bat·ing** [Latin *incubatus*, past participle of *incubare*, from *in-* + *cubare* to lie] (circa 1721)
*transitive verb*
**1 :** to sit on (eggs) so as to hatch by the warmth of the body; *also* **:** to maintain (as an embryo or a chemically active system) under conditions favorable for hatching, development, or reaction
**2 :** to cause (as an idea) to develop
*intransitive verb*
**1 :** to sit on eggs

**2 :** to undergo incubation
— **in·cu·ba·tive** \-ˌbā-tiv\ *adjective*
— **in·cu·ba·to·ry** \-kyə-bə-ˌtȯr-ē, -ˌbā-tə-rē\ *adjective*
**in·cu·ba·tion** \ˌiŋ-kyə-'bā-shən, ˌin-\ *noun* (1646)
**1 :** the act or process of incubating
**2 :** INCUBATION PERIOD
**incubation period** *noun* (1879)
**:** the period between the infection of an individual by a pathogen and the manifestation of the disease it causes
**in·cu·ba·tor** \'iŋ-kyə-ˌbā-tər, 'in-\ *noun* (1857)
**:** one that incubates: as **a :** an apparatus by which eggs are hatched artificially **b :** an apparatus with a chamber used to provide controlled environmental conditions especially for the cultivation of microorganisms or the care and protection of premature or sick babies
**in·cu·bus** \'iŋ-kyə-bəs, 'in-\ *noun, plural* **-bi** \-ˌbī, -ˌbē\ *also* **-bus·es** [Middle English, from Late Latin, from Latin *incubare*] (13th century)
**1 :** an evil spirit that lies on persons in their sleep; *especially* **:** one that has sexual intercourse with women while they are sleeping — compare SUCCUBUS
**2 :** NIGHTMARE 2
**3 :** one that oppresses or burdens like a nightmare
**in·cul·cate** \in-'kəl-ˌkāt, 'in-(ˌ)\ *transitive verb* **-cat·ed; -cat·ing** [Latin *inculcatus*, past participle of *inculcare*, literally, to tread on, from *in-* + *calcare* to trample, from *calc-, calx* heel] (1550)
**:** to teach and impress by frequent repetitions or admonitions
**synonym** see IMPLANT
— **in·cul·ca·tion** \ˌin-(ˌ)kəl-'kā-shən\ *noun*
— **in·cul·ca·tor** \in-'kəl-ˌkā-tər, 'in-(ˌ)\ *noun*
**in·cul·pa·ble** \(ˌ)in-'kəl-pə-bəl\ *adjective* (15th century)
**:** free from guilt **:** BLAMELESS
**in·cul·pate** \in-'kəl-ˌpāt, 'in-(ˌ)\ *transitive verb* **-pat·ed; -pat·ing** [Late Latin *inculpatus*, from Latin *in-* + *culpatus*, past participle of *culpare* to blame, from *culpa* guilt] (1799)
**:** INCRIMINATE
— **in·cul·pa·tion** \ˌin-(ˌ)kəl-'pā-shən\ *noun*
— **in·cul·pa·to·ry** \in-'kəl-pə-ˌtȯr-ē, -ˌtȯr-\ *adjective*
**in·cult** \in-'kəlt\ *adjective* [Latin *incultus*, from *in-* + *cultus*, past participle of *colere* to cultivate — more at WHEEL] (1599)

---

☆ **SYNONYMS**
**Increase, enlarge, augment, multiply** mean to make or become greater. INCREASE used intransitively implies progressive growth in size, amount, or intensity ⟨his waistline *increased* with age⟩; used transitively it may imply simple not necessarily progressive addition ⟨*increased* her landholdings⟩. ENLARGE implies expansion or extension that makes greater in size or capacity ⟨*enlarged* the kitchen⟩. AUGMENT implies addition to what is already well grown or well developed ⟨the inheritance *augmented* his fortune⟩. MULTIPLY implies increase in number by natural generation or by indefinite repetition of a process ⟨with each attempt the problems *multiplied*⟩.

---

▢ **USAGE**
**incredulous** Sense 2 has been revived in this century after a couple of centuries of disuse. Although it is a sense with good literary precedent—among others Shakespeare used it—many people think it is a result of confusion with *incredible*, which is still the usual word in this sense.

: COARSE, UNCULTURED

**in·cum·ben·cy** \in-'kəm-bən(t)-sē\ *noun, plural* **-cies** (circa 1608)
**1** : something that is incumbent : DUTY
**2** : the quality or state of being incumbent
**3** : the sphere of action or period of office of an incumbent

¹**in·cum·bent** \in-'kəm-bənt\ *noun* [Middle English, from Latin *incumbent-, incumbens,* present participle of *incumbere* to lie down on, from *in-* + *-cumbere* to lie down; akin to *cubare* to lie] (15th century)
**1** : the holder of an office or ecclesiastical benefice
**2** : OCCUPANT

²**incumbent** *adjective* (1567)
**1** : imposed as a duty : OBLIGATORY
**2** : having the status of an incumbent; *especially* : occupying a specified office
**3** : lying or resting on something else
**4** : bent over so as to rest on or touch an underlying surface

**incumber** *variant of* ENCUMBER

**in·cu·na·ble** \in-'kyü-nə-bəl\ *noun* [French, from New Latin *incunabulum*] (1886)
: INCUNABULUM

**in·cu·nab·u·lum** \,in-kyə-'naᵇbyə-ləm, ,iŋ-\ *noun, plural* **-la** \-lə\ [New Latin, from Latin *incunabula,* plural, bands holding the baby in a cradle, from *in-* + *cunae* cradle] (circa 1859)
**1** : a book printed before 1501
**2** : a work of art or of industry of an early period

**in·cur** \in-'kər\ *transitive verb* **in·curred; in·cur·ring** [Middle English *incurren,* from Latin *incurrere,* literally, to run into, from *in-* + *currere* to run — more at CAR] (15th century)
: to become liable or subject to : bring down upon oneself ⟨*incur* expenses⟩

**in·cur·able** \(,)in-'kyùr-ə-bəl\ *adjective* [Middle English, from Middle French or Late Latin; Middle French, from Late Latin *incurabilis,* from Latin *in-* + *curabilis* curable] (14th century)
: not curable ⟨an *incurable* disease⟩; *broadly* : not likely to be changed or corrected ⟨*incurable* optimism⟩
— **incurable** *noun*
— **in·cur·ably** \-blē\ *adverb*

**in·cu·ri·ous** \(,)in-'kyùr-ē-əs\ *adjective* [Latin *incuriosus,* from *in-* + *curiosus* curious] (circa 1618)
: lacking a normal or usual curiosity : UNINTERESTED ⟨a blank *incurious* stare⟩
*synonym* see INDIFFERENT
— **in·cu·ri·os·i·ty** \-,kyùr-ē-'ä-sə-tē\ *noun*
— **in·cu·ri·ous·ly** \-'kyùr-ē-əs-lē\ *adverb*
— **in·cu·ri·ous·ness** *noun*

**in·cur·rence** \in-'kər-ən(t)s, -'kə-rən(t)s\ *noun* (circa 1656)
: the act or process of incurring

**in·cur·rent** \-ənt, -rənt\ *adjective* [Latin *incurrent-, incurrens,* present participle of *incurrere*] (circa 1856)
: giving passage to a current that flows inward

**in·cur·sion** \in-'kər-zhən\ *noun* [Middle English, from Middle French or Latin; Middle French, from Latin *incursion-, incursio,* from *incurrere*] (15th century)
**1** : a hostile entrance into a territory : RAID
**2** : an entering in or into (as an activity or undertaking) ⟨his only *incursion* into the arts⟩

**in·cur·vate** \'in-,kər-,vāt, (,)in-'kər-\ *transitive verb* **-vat·ed; -vat·ing** (1578)
: to cause to curve inward : BEND
— **in·cur·vate** \'in-,kər-,vāt, (,)in-'kər-vət\ *adjective*
— **in·cur·va·tion** \,in-,kər-'vā-shən\ *noun*
— **in·cur·va·ture** \(,)in-'kər-və-,chùr, -chər, -,tyùr, -,tür\ *noun*

**in·curve** \(,)in-'kərv, 'in-,\ *transitive verb* [Latin *incurvare,* from *in-* + *curvare* to curve, from *curvus* curved — more at CURVE] (1610)
: to bend so as to curve inward

**in·cus** \'iŋ-kəs\ *noun, plural* **in·cu·des** \iŋ-'kyü-(,)dēz, 'iŋ-kyə-,dēz\ [New Latin, from Latin, anvil, from *incudere*] (1669)
: the middle bone of a chain of three small bones in the ear of a mammal — called also *anvil*; see EAR illustration

**in·cuse** \in-'kyüz, -'kyüs\ *adjective* [Latin *incusus,* past participle of *incudere* to stamp, strike, from *in-* + *cudere* to beat — more at HEW] (1818)
: formed by stamping or punching in — used chiefly of old coins or features of their design

**Ind** \'ind, 'īnd\ *noun* (13th century)
**1** *archaic* : India
**2** *obsolete* : Indies

**ind-** *or* **indo-** *combining form* [International Scientific Vocabulary, from Latin *indicum* — more at INDIGO]
**1** : indigo ⟨*indoxyl*⟩
**2** : resembling indigo (as in color) ⟨*indophenol*⟩

**in·da·ba** \in-'dä-bə\ *noun* [Zulu *indaba* affair] (1827)
*chiefly South African* : CONFERENCE, PARLEY

**in·da·gate** \'in-də-,gāt\ *transitive verb* **-gat·ed; -gat·ing** [Latin *indagatus,* past participle of *indagare,* from *indago* ring of hunters encircling game, act of searching, from Old Latin *indu* in + Latin *agere* to drive — more at END-, AGENT] (circa 1623)
: to search into : INVESTIGATE
— **in·da·ga·tion** \,in-də-'gā-shən\ *noun*
— **in·da·ga·tor** \'in-də-,gā-tər\ *noun*

**in·debt·ed** \in-'de-təd\ *adjective* [Middle English *indetted,* from Old French *endeté,* past participle of *endeter* to involve in debt, from *en-* + *dete* debt] (13th century)
**1** : owing gratitude or recognition to another : BEHOLDEN
**2** : owing money

**in·debt·ed·ness** *noun* (1647)
**1** : the condition of being indebted
**2** : something (as an amount of money) that is owed

**in·de·cen·cy** \(,)in-'dē-s°n(t)-sē\ *noun* (1589)
**1** : the quality or state of being indecent
**2** : something (as a word or action) that is indecent

**in·de·cent** \-s°nt\ *adjective* [Middle French or Latin; Middle French *indécent,* from Latin *indecent-, indecens,* from *in-* + *decent-, decens* decent] (circa 1587)
: not decent; *especially* : grossly unseemly or offensive to manners or morals
— **in·de·cent·ly** *adverb*

**indecent assault** *noun* (1861)
: an immoral act or series of acts exclusive of rape committed against another person without consent

**indecent exposure** *noun* (1851)
: intentional exposure of part of one's body (as the genitals) in a place where such exposure is likely to be an offense against the generally accepted standards of decency

**in·de·ci·pher·able** \,in-di-'sī-f(ə-)rə-bəl\ *adjective* (1802)
: incapable of being deciphered

**in·de·ci·sion** \,in-di-'si-zhən\ *noun* [French *indécision,* from *indécis* undecided, from Late Latin *indecisus,* from Latin *in-* + *decisus,* past participle of *decidere* to decide] (circa 1763)
: a wavering between two or more possible courses of action : IRRESOLUTION

**in·de·ci·sive** \,in-di-'sī-siv\ *adjective* (1726)
**1** : not decisive : INCONCLUSIVE
**2** : marked by or prone to indecision : IRRESOLUTE
**3** : not clearly marked out : INDEFINITE
— **in·de·ci·sive·ly** *adverb*
— **in·de·ci·sive·ness** *noun*

**in·de·clin·able** \,in-di-'klī-nə-bəl\ *adjective* [Middle English, from Middle French, from Late Latin *indeclinabilis,* from Latin *in-* + Late Latin *declinabilis* capable of being inflected, from Latin *declinare* to inflect — more at DECLINE] (14th century)

: having no grammatical inflections

**in·de·com·pos·able** \,in-,dē-kəm-'pō-zə-bəl\ *adjective* (1807)
: not capable of being separated into component parts or elements

**in·de·co·rous** \(,)in-'de-k(ə-)rəs; ,in-di-'kōr-əs, -'kór-\ *adjective* [Latin *indecorus,* from *in-* + *decorus* decorous] (1682)
: not decorous : conflicting with accepted standards of good conduct or good taste ☆
— **in·de·co·rous·ly** *adverb*
— **in·de·co·rous·ness** *noun*

**in·de·co·rum** \,in-di-'kōr-əm, -'kór-\ *noun* [Latin, neuter of *indecorus*] (1575)
**1** : something that is indecorous
**2** : lack of decorum : IMPROPRIETY

**in·deed** \in-'dēd\ *adverb* (14th century)
**1** : without any question : TRULY, UNDENIABLY — often used interjectionally to express irony or disbelief or surprise
**2** : in reality
**3** : all things considered : as a matter of fact

**in·de·fat·i·ga·ble** \,in-di-'fa-ti-gə-bəl\ *adjective* [Middle French, from Latin *indefatigabilis,* from *in-* + *defatigare* to fatigue, from *de-* + *fatigare* to fatigue] (1611)
: incapable of being fatigued : UNTIRING
— **in·de·fat·i·ga·bil·i·ty** \-,fa-ti-gə-'bi-lə-tē\ *noun*
— **in·de·fat·i·ga·ble·ness** \-'fa-ti-gə-bəl-nəs\ *noun*
— **in·de·fat·i·ga·bly** \-blē\ *adverb*

**in·de·fea·si·ble** \-'fē-zə-bəl\ *adjective* (1548)
: not capable of being annulled or voided or undone ⟨an *indefeasible* right⟩
— **in·de·fea·si·bil·i·ty** \-,fē-zə-'bi-lə-tē\ *noun*
— **in·de·fea·si·bly** \-'fē-zə-blē\ *adverb*

**in·de·fec·ti·ble** \-'fek-tə-bəl\ *adjective* (1659)
**1** : not subject to failure or decay : LASTING
**2** : free of faults : FLAWLESS
— **in·de·fec·ti·bil·i·ty** \-,fek-tə-'bi-lə-tē\ *noun*
— **in·de·fec·ti·bly** \-'fek-tə-blē\ *adverb*

**in·de·fen·si·ble** \-'fen(t)-sə-bəl\ *adjective* (1529)
**1 a** : incapable of being maintained as right or valid : UNTENABLE **b** : incapable of being justified or excused : INEXCUSABLE
**2** : incapable of being protected against physical attack
— **in·de·fen·si·bil·i·ty** \-,fen(t)-sə-'bi-lə-tē\ *noun*
— **in·de·fen·si·bly** \-'fen(t)-sə-blē\ *adverb*

**in·de·fin·able** \-'fī-nə-bəl\ *adjective* (1810)
: incapable of being precisely described or analyzed

---

☆ **SYNONYMS**
**Indecorous, improper, unseemly, unbecoming, indelicate** mean not conforming to what is accepted as right, fitting, or in good taste. INDECOROUS suggests a violation of accepted standards of good manners ⟨*indecorous* behavior⟩. IMPROPER applies to a broader range of transgressions of rules not only of social behavior but of ethical practice or logical procedure or prescribed method ⟨*improper* use of campaign contributions⟩. UNSEEMLY adds a suggestion of special inappropriateness to a situation or an offensiveness to good taste ⟨remarried with *unseemly* haste⟩. UNBECOMING suggests behavior or language that does not suit one's character or status ⟨conduct *unbecoming* to an officer⟩. INDELICATE implies a lack of modesty or of tact or of refined perception of feeling ⟨*indelicate* expressions for bodily functions⟩.

---

\ə\ abut \ᵊ\ kitten \ər\ further \a\ ash \ā\ ace
\ä\ mop, mar \aù\ out \ch\ chin \e\ bet \ē\ easy
\g\ go \i\ hit \ī\ ice \j\ job \ŋ\ sing \ō\ go
\ò\ law \òi\ boy \th\ thin \t͟h\ the \ü\ loot \ù\ foot
\y\ yet \zh\ vision *see also* Guide to Pronunciation

— **in·de·fin·abil·i·ty** \-,fī-nə-'bi-lə-tē\ *noun*
— **indefinable** *noun*
— **in·de·fin·able·ness** \-'fī-nə-bəl-nəs\ *noun*
— **in·de·fin·ably** \-blē\ *adverb*
**in·def·i·nite** \(,)in-'def-nət, -'de-fə-\ *adjective* [Latin *indefinitus,* from *in-* + *definitus* definite] (1530)
**:** not definite: as **a :** typically designating an unidentified, generic, or unfamiliar person or thing ⟨the *indefinite* articles *a* and *an*⟩ ⟨*indefinite* pronouns⟩ **b :** not precise **c :** VAGUE **c :** having no exact limits **d** *of floral organs* **:** numerous and difficult to ascertain in number
— **indefinite** *noun*
— **in·def·i·nite·ly** *adverb*
— **in·def·i·nite·ness** *noun*
**indefinite integral** *noun* (circa 1877)
**:** any function whose derivative is a given function
**in·de·his·cent** \,in-di-'his-ᵊnt\ *adjective* (1832)
**:** remaining closed at maturity ⟨*indehiscent* fruits⟩
— **in·de·his·cence** \-sᵊn(t)s\ *noun*
**in·del·i·ble** \in-'de-lə-bəl\ *adjective* [Middle English *indelyble,* from Medieval Latin *indelibilis,* alteration of Latin *indelebilis,* from *in-* + *delēre* to delete] (15th century)
**1 a :** that cannot be removed, washed away, or erased **b :** making marks that cannot easily be removed ⟨an *indelible* pencil⟩
**2 a :** LASTING ⟨*indelible* memories⟩ **b :** UNFORGETTABLE, MEMORABLE ⟨an *indelible* performance⟩
— **in·del·i·bil·i·ty** \(,)in-,de-lə-'bi-lə-tē\ *noun*
— **in·del·i·bly** \in-'de-lə-blē\ *adverb*
**in·del·i·ca·cy** \(,)in-'de-li-kə-sē\ *noun* (1712)
**1 :** the quality or state of being indelicate
**2 :** something that is indelicate
**in·del·i·cate** \-li-kət\ *adjective* (1742)
**:** not delicate: **a** (1) **:** lacking in or offending against propriety **:** IMPROPER (2) **:** verging on the indecent **:** COARSE **b :** marked by a lack of feeling for the sensibilities of others **:** TACTLESS
**synonym** see INDECOROUS
— **in·del·i·cate·ly** *adverb*
— **in·del·i·cate·ness** *noun*
**in·dem·ni·fi·ca·tion** \in-,dem-nə-fə-'kā-shən\ *noun* (1732)
**1 a :** the action of indemnifying **b :** the condition of being indemnified
**2 :** INDEMNITY 2b
**in·dem·ni·fy** \in-'dem-nə-,fī\ *transitive verb* **-fied; -fy·ing** [Latin *indemnis* unharmed, from *in-* + *damnum* damage] (circa 1611)
**1 :** to secure against hurt, loss, or damage
**2 :** to make compensation to for incurred hurt, loss, or damage
**synonym** see PAY
— **in·dem·ni·fi·er** \-,fī-(ə)r\ *noun*
**in·dem·ni·ty** \in-'dem-nə-tē\ *noun, plural* **-ties** (15th century)
**1 a :** security against hurt, loss, or damage **b :** exemption from incurred penalties or liabilities
**2 a :** INDEMNIFICATION 1 **b :** something that indemnifies
**in·de·mon·stra·ble** \,in-di-'män(t)-strə-bəl, (,)in-'dem-ən-strə-\ *adjective* (1570)
**:** incapable of being demonstrated **:** not subject to proof
— **in·de·mon·stra·bly** \-blē\ *adverb*
¹**in·dent** \in-'dent\ *verb* [Middle English, from Middle French *endenter,* from Old French, from *en-* + *dent* tooth, from Latin *dent-, dens* — more at TOOTH] (14th century)
*transitive verb*
**1 a :** to divide (a document) so as to produce sections with irregular edges that can be matched for authentication **b :** to draw up (as a deed) in two or more exactly corresponding copies
**2 :** to notch the edge of **:** make jagged
**3 :** INDENTURE

**4 :** to set (as a line of a paragraph) in from the margin
**5** *chiefly British* **:** to order by an indent
*intransitive verb*
**1** *obsolete* **:** to make a formal or express agreement
**2 :** to form an indentation
**3** *chiefly British* **:** to make out an indent for something
— **in·dent·er** *noun*
— **indent on 1** *chiefly British* **:** to make a requisition on **2** *chiefly British* **:** to draw on
²**in·dent** \in-'dent, 'in-,\ *noun* (15th century)
**1 a :** INDENTURE 1 **b :** a certificate issued by the U.S. at the close of the American Revolution for the principal or interest on the public debt
**2** *chiefly British* **a :** an official requisition **b :** a purchase order for goods especially when sent from a foreign country
**3 :** INDENTION
³**in·dent** \in-'dent\ *transitive verb* [Middle English *endenten,* from *en-* + *denten* to dent] (15th century)
**1 :** to force inward so as to form a depression
**2 :** to form a dent in
— **in·dent·er** *noun*
⁴**in·dent** \in-'dent, 'in-,\ *noun* (1596)
**:** INDENTATION
**in·den·ta·tion** \,in-,den-'tā-shən\ *noun* (circa 1728)
**1 a :** an angular cut in an edge **:** NOTCH **b :** a recess in a surface
**2 :** the action of indenting **:** the condition of being indented
**3 :** DENT
**4 :** INDENTION 2b
**in·den·tion** \in-'den(t)-shən\ *noun* (1763)
**1** *archaic* **:** INDENTATION 1
**2 a :** the action of indenting **:** the condition of being indented **b :** the blank space produced by indenting
¹**in·den·ture** \in-'den(t)-shər\ *noun* [Middle English *endenture,* from Middle French, from *endenter*] (14th century)
**1 a** (1) **:** a document or a section of a document that is indented (2) **:** a formal or official document usually executed in two or more copies (3) **:** a contract binding one person to work for another for a given period of time — usually used in plural **b :** a formal certificate (as an inventory or voucher) prepared for purposes of control **c :** a document stating the terms under which a security (as a bond) is issued
**2 :** INDENTATION 1
**3** [³*indent*] **:** DENT
²**indenture** *transitive verb* **in·den·tured; in·den·tur·ing** \-'den(t)-shriŋ, -'den(t)-shə-riŋ\ (1676)
**:** to bind (as an apprentice) by or as if by indentures
**indentured servant** *noun* (1723)
**:** a person who signs and is bound by indentures to work for another for a specified time especially in return for payment of travel expenses and maintenance
**in·de·pen·dence** \,in-də-'pen-dən(t)s\ *noun* (1640)
**1 :** the quality or state of being independent
**2** *archaic* **:** COMPETENCE 1
**Independence Day** *noun* (1791)
**:** a civil holiday for the celebration of the anniversary of the beginnings of national independence; *specifically* **:** July 4 observed as a legal holiday in the U.S. in commemoration of the adoption of the Declaration of Independence in 1776
**in·de·pen·den·cy** \,in-də-'pen-dən(t)-sē\ *noun* (circa 1611)
**1 :** INDEPENDENCE 1
**2** *capitalized* **:** the Independent polity or movement
**3 :** an independent political unit
¹**in·de·pen·dent** \,in-də-'pen-dənt\ *adjective* (1611)

**1 :** not dependent: as **a** (1) **:** not subject to control by others **:** SELF-GOVERNING (2) **:** not affiliated with a larger controlling unit **b** (1) **:** not requiring or relying on something else **:** not contingent ⟨an *independent* conclusion⟩ (2) **:** not looking to others for one's opinions or for guidance in conduct (3) **:** not bound by or committed to a political party **c** (1) **:** not requiring or relying on others (as for care or livelihood) ⟨*independent* of her parents⟩ (2) **:** being enough to free one from the necessity of working for a living ⟨a man of *independent* means⟩ **d :** showing a desire for freedom ⟨an *independent* manner⟩ **e** (1) **:** not determined by or capable of being deduced or derived from or expressed in terms of members (as axioms or equations) of the set under consideration; *especially* **:** having linear independence ⟨an *independent* set of vectors⟩ (2) **:** having the property that the joint probability (as of events or samples) or the joint probability density function (as of random variables) equals the product of the probabilities or probability density functions of separate occurrence
**2** *capitalized* **:** of or relating to the Independents
**3 a :** MAIN 5 ⟨an *independent* clause⟩ **b :** neither deducible from nor incompatible with another statement ⟨*independent* postulates⟩
**synonym** see FREE
— **in·de·pen·dent·ly** *adverb*
²**independent** *noun* (1644)
**1** *capitalized* **:** a sectarian of an English religious movement for congregational autonomy originating in the late 16th century, giving rise to Congregationalists, Baptists, and Friends, and forming one of the major political groupings of the period of Cromwell
**2 :** one that is independent; *especially, often capitalized* **:** one that is not bound by or definitively committed to a political party
**independent assortment** *noun* (circa 1948)
**:** formation of random combinations of chromosomes in meiosis and of genes on different pairs of homologous chromosomes by the passage according to the laws of probability of one of each diploid pair of homologous chromosomes into each gamete independently of each other pair
**independent variable** *noun* (1852)
**:** a mathematical variable whose value is specified first and determines the value of one or more other values in an expression or function
**in–depth** \(')in-'depth\ *adjective* (1965)
**:** COMPREHENSIVE, THOROUGH ⟨an *in-depth* study⟩
**in·de·scrib·able** \,in-di-'skrī-bə-bəl\ *adjective* (1794)
**1 :** that cannot be described ⟨an *indescribable* sensation⟩
**2 :** surpassing description ⟨*indescribable* joy⟩
— **in·de·scrib·able·ness** *noun*
— **in·de·scrib·ably** \-blē\ *adverb*
**in·de·struc·ti·ble** \,in-di-'strək-tə-bəl\ *adjective* [probably from Late Latin *indestructibilis,* from Latin *in-* + *destructus,* past participle of *destruere* to tear down — more at DESTROY] (1667)
**:** incapable of being destroyed, ruined, or rendered ineffective
— **in·de·struc·ti·bil·i·ty** \-,strək-tə-'bi-lə-tē\ *noun*
— **in·de·struc·ti·ble·ness** \-'strək-tə-bəl-nəs\ *noun*
— **in·de·struc·ti·bly** \-blē\ *adverb*
**in·de·ter·min·able** \,in-di-'tərm-nə-bəl, -'tər-mə-\ *adjective* (15th century)
**1 :** incapable of being definitely decided or settled
**2 :** incapable of being definitely fixed or ascertained
— **in·de·ter·min·ably** \-blē\ *adverb*
**in·de·ter·mi·na·cy** \-nə-sē\ *noun* (1649)

: the quality or state of being indeterminate

**indeterminacy principle** *noun* (circa 1928)
: UNCERTAINTY PRINCIPLE

**in·de·ter·mi·nate** \,in-di-'tərm-nət, -'tər-mə-\ *adjective* [Middle English *indeterminat*, from Late Latin *indeterminatus*, from Latin *in-* + *determinatus*, past participle of *determinare* to determine] (14th century)
**1 a** : not definitely or precisely determined or fixed : VAGUE **b** : not known in advance **c** : not leading to a definite end or result
**2** : having an infinite number of solutions ⟨a system of *indeterminate* equations⟩
**3** : being one of the seven undefined mathematical expressions

$$\frac{0}{0}, \frac{\infty}{\infty}, \infty \cdot 0, 1^{\infty}, 0^{0}, \infty^{0}, \infty - \infty$$

**4** : characterized by sequential flowering from the lateral or basal buds to the central or uppermost buds; *also* : characterized by growth in which the main stem continues to elongate indefinitely without being limited by a terminal inflorescence — compare DETERMINATE 4
— **in·de·ter·mi·nate·ly** *adverb*
— **in·de·ter·mi·nate·ness** *noun*
— **in·de·ter·mi·na·tion** \-,tər-mə-'nā-shən\ *noun*

**in·de·ter·min·ism** \-'tər-mə-,ni-zəm\ *noun* (1874)
**1 a** : a theory that the will is free and that deliberate choice and actions are not determined by or predictable from antecedent causes **b** : a theory that holds that not every event has a cause
**2** : the quality or state of being indeterminate; *especially* : UNPREDICTABILITY
— **in·de·ter·min·ist** \-'tərm-nist, -'tər-mə-\ *noun*
— **in·de·ter·min·is·tic** \-,tər-mə-'nis-tik\ *adjective*

**¹in·dex** \'in-,deks\ *noun, plural* **in·dex·es** *or* **in·di·ces** \-də-,sēz\ [Latin *indic-, index*, from *indicare* to indicate] (1571)
**1 a** : a device (as the pointer on a scale or the gnomon of a sundial) that serves to indicate a value or quantity **b** : something (as a physical feature or a mode of expression) that leads one to a particular fact or conclusion : INDICATION
**2** : a list (as of bibliographical information or citations to a body of literature) arranged usually in alphabetical order of some specified datum (as author, subject, or keyword): as **a** : a list of items (as topics or names) treated in a printed work that gives for each item the page number where it may be found **b** : THUMB INDEX **c** : a bibliographical analysis of groups of publications that is usually published periodically
**3** : a list of restricted or prohibited material; *specifically, capitalized* : a list of books the reading of which is prohibited or restricted for Roman Catholics by the church authorities
**4** *plural usually* **indices** : a number or symbol or expression (as an exponent) associated with another to indicate a mathematical operation to be performed or to indicate use or position in an arrangement
**5** : a character ☞ used to direct attention to a note or paragraph — called also *fist*
**6 a** : a number (as a ratio) derived from a series of observations and used as an indicator or measure; *specifically* : INDEX NUMBER **b** : the ratio of one dimension of a thing (as an anatomical structure) to another dimension

**²index** (1720)
*transitive verb*
**1 a** : to provide with an index **b** : to list in an index ⟨all persons and places mentioned are carefully *indexed*⟩
**2** : to serve as an index of
**3** : to regulate (as wages, prices, or interest rates) by indexation

*intransitive verb*
: to index something
— **in·dex·er** *noun*

**in·dex·ation** \,in-dek-'sā-shən\ *noun* (1960)
: a system of economic control in which certain variables (as wages and interest) are tied to a cost-of-living index so that both rise or fall at the same rate and the detrimental effect of inflation is theoretically eliminated

**index finger** *noun* (1849)
: FOREFINGER

**index fossil** *noun* (1900)
: a fossil usually with a narrow time range and wide spatial distribution that is used in the identification of related geologic formations

**¹in·dex·i·cal** \(,)in-'dek-si-kəl\ *adjective* (circa 1828)
**1** : of or relating to an index
**2 a** : varying in reference with the individual speaker ⟨the *indexical* words *I, here, now*⟩ **b** : associated with or identifying an individual speaker ⟨*indexical* features of speech⟩

**²indexical** *noun* (1971)
: an indexical word, sign, or feature

**indexing** *noun* (1957)
: INDEXATION

**index number** *noun* (circa 1896)
: a number used to indicate change in magnitude (as of cost or price) as compared with the magnitude at some specified time usually taken as 100

**index of refraction** (1829)
: the ratio of the speed of radiation (as light) in one medium (as a vacuum) to that in another medium

**indi-** — see IND-

**In·dia** \'in-dē-ə\ (circa 1952)
— a communications code word for the letter *i*

**india ink** *noun, often 1st I capitalized* (1665)
**1** : a solid black pigment (as specially prepared lampblack) used in drawing and lettering
**2** : a fluid ink consisting usually of a fine suspension of india ink in a liquid

**In·dia·man** \'in-dē-ə-mən\ *noun* (1709)
: a merchant ship formerly used in trade with India; *especially* : a large sailing ship used in this trade

**In·di·an** \'in-dē-ən, *dialect* -jən *or* -din\ *noun* (14th century)
**1 a** : a native or inhabitant of India or of the East Indies **b** : a person of Indian descent
**2 a** [from the belief held by Columbus that the lands he discovered were part of Asia] : AMERICAN INDIAN **b** : one of the native languages of American Indians
— **Indian** *adjective*
— **In·di·an·ness** *noun*

**Indian agent** *noun* (1807)
: an official representative of the U.S. federal government to American Indian tribes especially on reservations

**Indian club** *noun* (1857)
: a usually wooden club shaped like a large bottle or tenpin that is swung for gymnastic exercise

**Indian corn** *noun* (1617)
**1** : a tall widely cultivated American cereal grass (*Zea mays*) bearing seeds on elongated ears
**2** : the ears of Indian corn; *also* : its edible seeds

**Indian elephant** *noun* (1607)
: ELEPHANT 1b

**Indian file** *noun* (1758)
: SINGLE FILE

**Indian giver** *noun* (circa 1848)
: a person who gives something to another and then takes it back or expects an equivalent in return
— **Indian giving** *noun*

**Indian hemp** *noun* (1619)
**1** : an American dogbane (*Apocynum cannabinum*) with milky juice, tough fibrous bark, and an emetic and cathartic root

**2** : HEMP 1

**In·di·an·ism** \'in-dē-ə-,ni-zəm\ *noun* (1651)
**1** : the qualities or culture distinctive of American Indians
**2** : policy designed to further the interests or culture of American Indians
— **In·di·an·ist** \-nist\ *adjective or noun*

**In·di·an·ize** \'in-dē-ə-,nīz\ *transitive verb* **-ized; -izing** (1702)
**1** : to cause to acquire or conform to the characteristics, culture, or usage of American Indians or of India
**2** : to bring (as a region) under the cultural or political influence or control of India
— **In·di·an·i·za·tion** \,in-dē-ə-(,)nī-'zā-shən\ *noun*

**Indian licorice** *noun* (circa 1890)
: ROSARY PEA 1

**Indian meal** *noun* (1609)
: CORNMEAL

**Indian paintbrush** *noun* (circa 1892)
**1** : any of a genus (*Castilleja*) of herbaceous plants of the snapdragon family that have brightly colored bracts — called also *painted cup*
**2** : ORANGE HAWKWEED

**Indian paintbrush**

**Indian pipe** *noun* (circa 1818)
: a waxy white saprophytic herb (*Monotropa uniflora* of the family Monotropaceae, the Indian-pipe family) of Asia and North America having leaves reduced to scales

**Indian pudding** *noun* (1722)
: a baked pudding made chiefly of cornmeal, milk, and molasses

**Indian red** *noun* (circa 1753)
**1** : any of various usually dark red pigments consisting chiefly of iron oxide
**2** : a strong or moderate reddish brown

**Indian sign** *noun* (1910)
: HEX, SPELL

**Indian summer** *noun* (1778)

**Indian pipe**

**1** : a period of warm or mild weather in late autumn or early winter
**2** : a happy or flourishing period occurring toward the end of something ⟨life in the *Indian summer* of Czarist Russia —John Davenport⟩

**Indian tobacco** *noun* (circa 1618)
**1** : an American wild lobelia (*Lobelia inflata*) with small blue or white flowers
**2** : a wild tobacco (*Nicotiana bigelovii*) found in dry valleys from southern California to southern Oregon

**In·di·an–wres·tle** \'in-dē-ən-,re-səl, -,ra-\ *intransitive verb* [back-formation from *Indian wrestling*] (1938)
: to engage in Indian wrestling

**Indian wrestling** *noun* (1913)
**1** : wrestling in which two people lie side by side on their backs in reversed position locking their near arms and raising and locking the corresponding legs and attempt to force each other's leg down and turn the other wrestler facedown
**2** : wrestling in which two people stand face to face gripping usually their right hands and setting the outsides of the corresponding feet together and attempt to force each other off balance
**3** : ARM WRESTLING

**India paper** *noun* (1768)

---

\ə\ abut \ᵊ\ kitten \ər\ further \a\ ash \ā\ ace
\ä\ mop, mar \aů\ out \ch\ chin \e\ bet \ē\ easy
\g\ go \i\ hit \ī\ ice \j\ job \ŋ\ sing \ō\ go
\ȯ\ law \ȯi\ boy \th\ thin \t̲h̲\ the \ü\ loot \ů\ foot
\y\ yet \zh\ vision     *see also* Guide to Pronunciation

**1** : a thin absorbent paper used especially for proving inked intaglio surfaces (as steel engravings) **2** : a thin tough opaque printing paper

**india rubber** *noun, often I capitalized* (1790) : ¹RUBBER 2a

**In·dic** \'in-dik\ *adjective* (1877) **1** : of or relating to the subcontinent of India : INDIAN **2** : of, relating to, or constituting the Indo-Aryan branch of the Indo-European languages — **Indic** *noun*

**in·di·can** \'in-də-ˌkan\ *noun* [Latin *indicum* indigo — more at INDIGO] (1859) **1** : an indigo-forming substance $C_8H_7NO_4S$ found as a salt in urine and other animal fluids; *also* : its potassium salt $C_8H_6KNO_4S$ **2** : a glucoside $C_{14}H_{17}NO_6$ occurring especially in the indigo plant and being a source of natural indigo

**in·di·cant** \'in-di-kənt\ *noun* (1623) : something that serves to indicate

**in·di·cate** \'in-də-ˌkāt\ *transitive verb* **-cat·ed; -cat·ing** [Latin *indicatus*, past participle of *indicare*, from *in-* + *dicare* to proclaim, dedicate — more at DICTION] (circa 1609) **1 a** : to point out or point to **b** : to be a sign, symptom, or index of ⟨the high fever *indicates* a serious condition⟩ **c** : to demonstrate or suggest the necessity or advisability of ⟨*indicated* the need for a new school⟩ **2** : to state or express briefly ⟨*indicated* a desire to cooperate⟩

**in·di·ca·tion** \ˌin-də-'kā-shən\ *noun* (15th century) **1 a** : something that serves to indicate **b** : something that is indicated as advisable or necessary **2** : the action of indicating — **in·di·ca·tion·al** \-shnəl, -shə-nᵊl\ *adjective*

¹**in·dic·a·tive** \in-'di-kə-tiv\ *adjective* (15th century) **1** : of, relating to, or constituting a verb form or set of verb forms that represents the denoted act or state as an objective fact ⟨the *indicative* mood⟩ **2** : serving to indicate ⟨actions *indicative* of fear⟩ — **in·dic·a·tive·ly** *adverb*

²**indicative** *noun* (1530) **1** : the indicative mood of a language **2** : a form in the indicative mood

**in·di·ca·tor** \'in-də-ˌkā-tər\ *noun* (1666) **1** : one that indicates: as **a** : an index hand (as on a dial) : POINTER **b** (1) : GAUGE 2b, DIAL 4a (2) : an instrument for automatically making a diagram that indicates the pressure in and volume of the working fluid of an engine throughout the cycle **2 a** : a substance (as litmus) used to show visually (as by change of color) the condition of a solution with respect to the presence of a particular material (as a free acid or alkali) **b** : TRACER 4b **3** : an organism or ecological community so strictly associated with particular environmental conditions that its presence is indicative of the existence of these conditions **4** : any of a group of statistical values (as level of employment) that taken together give an indication of the health of the economy — **in·dic·a·to·ry** \in-'di-kə-ˌtōr-ē, -ˌtor-\ *adjective*

**indices** *plural of* INDEX

**in·di·cia** \in-'di-sh(ē-)ə\ *noun plural* [Latin, plural of *indicium* sign, from *indicare*] (circa 1626) **1** : distinctive marks : INDICATIONS **2** : postal markings often imprinted on mail or on labels to be affixed to mail

**in·dict** \in-'dīt\ *transitive verb* [alteration of earlier *indite*, from Middle English *inditen*, from Anglo-French *enditer*, from Old French, to write down — more at INDITE] (circa 1626)

**1** : to charge with a fault or offense : CRITICIZE, ACCUSE **2** : to charge with a crime by the finding or presentment of a jury (as a grand jury) in due form of law — **in·dict·er** *or* **in·dict·or** \-'dī-tər\ *noun*

**in·dict·able** \-'dī-tə-bəl\ *adjective* (circa 1706) **1** : subject to being indicted : liable to indictment **2** : making one liable to indictment ⟨an *indictable* offense⟩

**in·dic·tion** \in-'dik-shən\ *noun* [Middle English *indiccioun*, from Late Latin *indiction-, indictio*, from Latin, proclamation, from *indicere* to proclaim, from *in-* + *dicere* to say — more at DICTION] (14th century) : a 15-year cycle used as a chronological unit in several ancient and medieval systems

**in·dict·ment** \in-'dīt-mənt\ *noun* (14th century) **1 a** : the action or the legal process of indicting **b** : the state of being indicted **2** : a formal written statement framed by a prosecuting authority and found by a jury (as a grand jury) charging a person with an offense **3** : an expression of strong disapproval ⟨an *indictment* of contemporary morality⟩

**in·die** \'in-dē\ *noun* [by shortening & alteration from *independent*] (1928) : something (as an unaffiliated record or motion-picture production company) independent — **indie** *adjective*

**in·dif·fer·ence** \in-'di-fərn(t)s, -f(ə-)rən(t)s\ *noun* (15th century) **1** : the quality, state, or fact of being indifferent **2 a** *archaic* : lack of difference or distinction between two or more things **b** : absence of compulsion to or toward one thing or another

**in·dif·fer·en·cy** \-fərn(t)-sē, -f(ə-)rən(t)-sē\ *noun* (15th century) *archaic* : INDIFFERENCE

**in·dif·fer·ent** \in-'di-fərnt, -f(ə-)rənt\ *adjective* [Middle English, from Middle French or Latin; Middle French, regarded as neither good nor bad, from Latin *indifferent-, indifferens*, from *in-* + *different-, differens*, present participle of *differre* to be different — more at DIFFER] (14th century) **1** : marked by impartiality : UNBIASED **2 a** : that does not matter one way or the other **b** : of no importance or value one way or the other **3 a** : marked by no special liking for or dislike of something ⟨*indifferent* about which task he was given⟩ **b** : marked by a lack of interest, enthusiasm, or concern for something : APATHETIC ⟨*indifferent* to suffering and poverty⟩ **4** : being neither excessive nor inadequate : MODERATE ⟨hills of *indifferent* size⟩ **5 a** : being neither good nor bad : MEDIOCRE ⟨does *indifferent* work⟩ **b** : being neither right nor wrong **6** : characterized by lack of active quality : NEUTRAL **7 a** : not differentiated **b** : capable of development in more than one direction; *especially* : not yet embryologically determined ☆ — **in·dif·fer·ent·ly** *adverb*

**in·dif·fer·ent·ism** \-fərn-ˌti-zəm, -f(ə-)rən-\ *noun* (1827) : INDIFFERENCE; *specifically* : belief that all religions are equally valid — **in·dif·fer·ent·ist** \-fərn-tist, -f(ə-)rən-\ *noun*

**in·di·gence** \'in-di-jən(t)s\ *noun* (14th century) : a level of poverty in which real hardship and deprivation are suffered and comforts of life are wholly lacking **synonym** see POVERTY

**in·di·gene** \'in-də-ˌjēn\ *also* **in·di·gen** \-di-jən, -də-ˌjen\ *noun* [Latin *indigena*] (1598) : NATIVE

**in·dig·e·nize** \in-'di-jə-ˌnīz\ *transitive verb* **-nized; -niz·ing** (1951) : to cause to have indigenous characteristics — **in·dig·e·ni·za·tion** \-ˌdi-jə-nə-'zā-shən, -ˌnī-'\ *noun*

**in·dig·e·nous** \in-'di-jə-nəs\ *adjective* [Late Latin *indigenus*, from Latin *indigena*, noun, native, from Old Latin *indu, endo*, within + Latin *gignere* to beget — more at END-, KIN] (1646) **1** : having originated in and being produced, growing, living, or occurring naturally in a particular region or environment **2** : INNATE, INBORN **synonym** see NATIVE — **in·dig·e·nous·ly** *adverb* — **in·dig·e·nous·ness** *noun*

**in·di·gent** \'in-di-jənt\ *adjective* [Middle English, from Middle French, from Latin *indigent-, indigens*, present participle of *indigēre* to need, from Old Latin *indu* + Latin *egēre* to need; perhaps akin to Old High German *ekrōdi* thin] (15th century) **1** : suffering from indigence : IMPOVERISHED **2 a** *archaic* : DEFICIENT **b** *archaic* : totally lacking in something specified — **indigent** *noun*

**in·di·gest·ed** \ˌin-(ˌ)dī-'jes-təd, -də-\ *adjective* (1587) : not carefully thought out or arranged : FORMLESS

**in·di·gest·ible** \-'jes-tə-bəl\ *adjective* [Middle English, from Late Latin *indigestibilis*, from Latin *in-* + Late Latin *digestibilis* digestible] (15th century) : not digestible : not easily digested — **in·di·gest·ibil·i·ty** \-ˌjes-tə-'bi-lə-tē\ *noun* — **indigestible** *noun*

**in·di·ges·tion** \-'jes-chən, -'jesh-\ *noun* (14th century) **1** : inability to digest or difficulty in digesting something **2** : a case or attack of indigestion

**in·dign** \in-'dīn\ *adjective* [Middle English *indigne*, from Middle French, from Latin *indignus*] (14th century) **1** *archaic* : UNWORTHY, UNDESERVING **2** *obsolete* : UNBECOMING, DISGRACEFUL

**in·dig·nant** \in-'dig-nənt\ *adjective* [Latin *indignant-, indignans*, present participle of *indignari* to be indignant, from *indignus* unworthy, from *in-* + *dignus* worthy — more at DECENT] (1590) : filled with or marked by indignation ⟨became *indignant* at the accusation⟩ — **in·dig·nant·ly** *adverb*

**in·dig·na·tion** \ˌin-dig-'nā-shən\ *noun* (14th century)

---

☆ **SYNONYMS**
**Indifferent, unconcerned, incurious, aloof, detached, disinterested** mean not showing or feeling interest. INDIFFERENT implies neutrality of attitude from lack of inclination, preference, or prejudice ⟨*indifferent* to the dictates of fashion⟩. UNCONCERNED suggests a lack of sensitivity or regard for others' needs or troubles ⟨*unconcerned* about the homeless⟩. INCURIOUS implies an inability to take a normal interest due to dullness of mind or to self-centeredness ⟨*incurious* about the world⟩. ALOOF suggests a cool reserve arising from a sense of superiority or disdain for inferiors or from shyness ⟨*aloof* from his coworkers⟩. DETACHED implies an objective attitude achieved through absence of prejudice or selfishness ⟨observed family gatherings with *detached* amusement⟩. DISINTERESTED implies a circumstantial freedom from concern for personal or especially financial advantage that enables one to judge or advise without bias ⟨judged by a panel of *disinterested* observers⟩.

: anger aroused by something unjust, unworthy, or mean
**synonym** see ANGER

**in·dig·ni·ty** \in-'dig-nə-tē\ *noun, plural* **-ties** [Latin *indignitat-, indignitas,* from *indignus*] (1584)
**1 a :** an act that offends against a person's dignity or self-respect : INSULT **b :** humiliating treatment
**2** *obsolete* **:** lack or loss of dignity or honor

**in·di·go** \'in-di-ˌgō\ *noun, plural* **-gos** or **-goes** [Italian dialect, from Latin *indicum,* from Greek *indikon,* from neuter of *indikos* Indic, from *Indos* India] (1555)
**1 a :** a blue vat dye obtained from plants (as indigo plants) **b :** the principal coloring matter $C_{16}H_{10}N_2O_2$ of natural indigo usually synthesized as a blue powder with a coppery luster
**2 :** INDIGO PLANT
**3 :** a deep reddish blue

**indigo bunting** *noun* (1783)
: a common small American finch (*Passerina cyanea*) of which the male is largely indigo-blue in spring and summer

**indigo plant** *noun* (1757)
: a plant that yields indigo; *especially* **:** any of a genus (*Indigofera*) of leguminous herbs

**indigo snake** *noun* (circa 1885)
: a large blue-black or brownish colubrid snake (*Drymarchon corais*) of the southeastern U.S. and Texas to Argentina — called also *gopher snake*

**in·di·go·tin** \in-'di-gə-tən, ˌin-di-'gō-t°n\ *noun* [French *indigotine,* irregular from *indigo* indigo] (1838)
: INDIGO 1b

**in·di·rect** \ˌin-də-'rekt, -(ˌ)dī-\ *adjective* [Middle English, from Medieval Latin *indirectus,* from Latin *in-* + *directus* direct — more at DRESS] (14th century)
: not direct : as **a** (1) : deviating from a direct line or course : ROUNDABOUT (2) : not going straight to the point ⟨an *indirect* accusation⟩ (3) : being or involving proof of a proposition or theorem by demonstration that its negation leads to an absurdity or contradiction **b :** not straightforward and open : DECEITFUL **c :** not directly aimed at or achieved ⟨*indirect* consequences⟩ **d :** stating what a real or supposed original speaker said with changes in wording that conform the statement grammatically to the sentence in which it is included ⟨*indirect* discourse⟩ ⟨an *indirect* question⟩ **e :** not effected by the action of the people or the electorate ⟨*indirect* government representation⟩
— **in·di·rect·ly** \-'rek(t)-lē\ *adverb*
— **in·di·rect·ness** \-nəs\ *noun*

**indirect cost** *noun* (circa 1909)
: a cost that is not identifiable with a specific product, function, or activity

**indirect evidence** *noun* (1824)
: evidence that establishes immediately collateral facts from which the main fact may be inferred : CIRCUMSTANTIAL EVIDENCE

**in·di·rec·tion** \ˌin-də-'rek-shən, -(ˌ)dī-\ *noun* (1590)
**1 a :** indirect action or procedure **b :** lack of direction : AIMLESSNESS
**2 a :** lack of straightforwardness and openness : DECEITFULNESS **b :** something (as an act or statement) marked by lack of straightforwardness ⟨hated diplomatic *indirections* —*Review of Reviews*⟩

**indirect lighting** *noun* (1922)
: lighting in which the light emitted by a source is diffusely reflected (as by the ceiling)

**indirect object** *noun* (1879)
: a grammatical object representing the secondary goal of the action of its verb (as *her* in "I gave her the book")

**in·dis·cern·ible** \ˌin-di-'sər-nə-bəl, -'zər-\ *adjective* (1635)
: incapable of being discerned : not recognizable as distinct

**in·dis·ci·plin·able** \(ˌ)in-ˌdi-sə-'pli-nə-bəl; -'di-sə-plə-\ *adjective* (1600)

: not subject to or capable of being disciplined

**in·dis·ci·pline** \(ˌ)in-'di-sə-plən\ *noun* (1783)
: lack of discipline
— **in·dis·ci·plined** \-plənd, -(ˌ)plīnd\ *adjective*

**in·dis·cov·er·able** \ˌin-dis-'kəv-rə-bəl, -'kə-və-\ *adjective* (1640)
: not discoverable

**in·dis·creet** \ˌin-di-'skrēt\ *adjective* [Middle English *indiscrete,* from Middle French & Late Latin; Middle French *indiscret,* from Late Latin *indiscretus,* from Latin, indistinguishable, from *in-* + *discretus,* past participle of *discernere* to separate — more at DISCERN] (15th century)
: not discreet : IMPRUDENT
— **in·dis·creet·ly** *adverb*
— **in·dis·creet·ness** *noun*

**in·dis·cre·tion** \ˌin-dis-'kre-shən\ *noun* (14th century)
**1 :** lack of discretion : IMPRUDENCE ⟨dietary *indiscretion*⟩
**2 a :** something (as an act or remark) marked by lack of discretion **b :** an act at variance with the accepted morality of a society ⟨resigned because of financial *indiscretions*⟩

**in·dis·crim·i·nate** \ˌin-dis-'krim-nət, -'kri-mə-\ *adjective* (circa 1598)
**1 a :** not marked by careful distinction : deficient in discrimination and discernment ⟨*indiscriminate* reading habits⟩ ⟨*indiscriminate* mass destruction⟩ **b :** HAPHAZARD, RANDOM ⟨*indiscriminate* application of a law⟩
**2 a :** PROMISCUOUS, UNRESTRAINED ⟨*indiscriminate* sexual behavior⟩ **b :** HETEROGENEOUS, MOTLEY ⟨an *indiscriminate* collection⟩
— **in·dis·crim·i·nate·ly** *adverb*
— **in·dis·crim·i·nate·ness** *noun*

**in·dis·crim·i·nat·ing** \-'kri-mə-ˌnā-tiŋ\ *adjective* (circa 1767)
: not discriminating
— **in·dis·crim·i·nat·ing·ly** \-tiŋ-lē\ *adverb*

**in·dis·crim·i·na·tion** \-ˌkri-mə-'nā-shən\ *noun* (1649)
: lack of discrimination

**in·dis·pens·able** \ˌin-di-'spen(t)-sə-bəl\ *adjective* (1653)
**1 :** not subject to being set aside or neglected ⟨an *indispensable* obligation⟩
**2 :** absolutely necessary : ESSENTIAL ⟨an *indispensable* member of the staff⟩
— **in·dis·pens·abil·i·ty** \-ˌspen(t)-sə-'bi-lə-tē\ *noun*
— **indispensable** *noun*
— **in·dis·pens·able·ness** \-'spen(t)-sə-bəl-nəs\ *noun*
— **in·dis·pens·ably** \-blē\ *adverb*

**in·dis·pose** \ˌin-di-'spōz\ *transitive verb* **-posed; -pos·ing** [probably back-formation from *indisposed*] (1657)
**1 a :** to make unfit : DISQUALIFY **b :** to make averse : DISINCLINE
**2** *archaic* **:** to cause to be in poor physical health

**in·dis·posed** \-'spōzd\ *adjective* (15th century)
**1 :** slightly ill
**2 :** AVERSE

**in·dis·po·si·tion** \(ˌ)in-ˌdis-pə-'zi-shən\ *noun* (15th century)
: the condition of being indisposed: **a :** DISINCLINATION **b :** a usually slight illness

**in·dis·put·able** \ˌin-di-'spyü-tə-bəl, (ˌ)in-'dis-pyə-\ *adjective* [Late Latin *indisputabilis,* from Latin *in-* + *disputabilis* disputable] (1551)
: not disputable : UNQUESTIONABLE ⟨*indisputable* proof⟩
— **in·dis·put·able·ness** *noun*
— **in·dis·put·ably** \-blē\ *adverb*

**in·dis·so·cia·ble** \ˌin-di-'sō-sh(ē-)ə-bəl, -sē-ə-\ *adjective* (1855)
: not dissociated : INSEPARABLE
— **in·dis·so·cia·bly** \-blē\ *adverb*

**in·dis·sol·u·ble** \ˌin-di-'säl-yə-bəl\ *adjective* (1542)

: not dissoluble; *especially* **:** incapable of being annulled, undone, or broken : PERMANENT ⟨an *indissoluble* contract⟩
— **in·dis·sol·u·bil·i·ty** \-ˌsäl-yə-'bi-lə-tē\ *noun*
— **in·dis·sol·u·ble·ness** \-'säl-yə-bəl-nəs\ *noun*
— **in·dis·sol·u·bly** \-blē\ *adverb*

**in·dis·tinct** \ˌin-di-'stiŋ(k)t\ *adjective* [Latin *indistinctus,* from *in-* + *distinctus* distinct] (1526)
: not distinct: as **a :** not sharply outlined or separable : BLURRED ⟨*indistinct* figures in the fog⟩ **b :** FAINT, DIM ⟨an *indistinct* light in the distance⟩ **c :** not clearly recognizable or understandable : UNCERTAIN
— **in·dis·tinct·ly** \-'stiŋ(k)t-lē, -'stiŋ-klē\ *adverb*
— **in·dis·tinct·ness** \-'stiŋ(k)t-nəs, -'stiŋk-nəs\ *noun*

**in·dis·tinc·tive** \-'stiŋ(k)-tiv\ *adjective* (1846)
: lacking distinctive qualities

**in·dis·tin·guish·able** \ˌin-di-'stiŋ-gwi-shə-bəl, -'stiŋ-wi-\ *adjective* (1606)
: not distinguishable: as **a :** indeterminate in shape or structure **b :** not clearly recognizable or understandable **c :** lacking identifying or individualizing qualities
— **in·dis·tin·guish·abil·i·ty** \-ˌstiŋ-gwi-shə-'bi-lə-tē, -ˌstiŋ-wi-\ *noun*
— **in·dis·tin·guish·able·ness** \-'stiŋ-gwi-shə-bəl-nəs, -'stiŋ-wi-\ *noun*
— **in·dis·tin·guish·ably** \-blē\ *adverb*

**in·dite** \in-'dīt\ *transitive verb* **in·dit·ed; in·dit·ing** [Middle English *enditen,* from Old French *enditer* to write down, proclaim, from (assumed) Vulgar Latin *indictare* to proclaim, frequentative of Latin *indicere* to proclaim, from *in-* + *dicere* to say — more at DICTION] (14th century)
**1 a :** MAKE UP, COMPOSE ⟨*indite* a poem⟩ **b :** to give literary or formal expression to **c :** to put down in writing ⟨*indite* a message⟩
**2** *obsolete* **:** DICTATE
— **in·dit·er** *noun*

**in·di·um** \'in-dē-əm\ *noun* [International Scientific Vocabulary *ind-* + New Latin *-ium*] (1864)
: a malleable fusible silvery metallic element that is chiefly trivalent, occurs especially in sphalerite ores, and is used as a plating for bearings, in alloys having a low melting point, and in the making of transistors — see ELEMENT table

**indium antimonide** *noun* (1957)
: a synthetic compound InSb of indium and antimony that is a semiconducting and photosensitive material and is used especially in infrared photodetectors

**¹in·di·vid·u·al** \ˌin-də-'vij-wəl, -'vi-jə-wəl, -'vi-jəl\ *adjective* [Medieval Latin *individualis,* from Latin *individuus* indivisible, from *in-* + *dividuus* divided, from *dividere* to divide] (15th century)
**1** *obsolete* **:** INSEPARABLE
**2 a :** of, relating to, or distinctively associated with an individual ⟨an *individual* effort⟩ **b :** being an individual or existing as an indivisible whole **c :** intended for one person ⟨an *individual* serving⟩
**3 :** existing as a distinct entity : SEPARATE
**4 :** having marked individuality ⟨an *individual* style⟩
**synonym** see SPECIAL, CHARACTERISTIC
— **in·di·vid·u·al·ly** *adverb*

**²individual** *noun* (1605)
**1 a :** a particular being or thing as distinguished from a class, species, or collection: as

\ə\ abut \ᵊ\ kitten \ər\ further \a\ ash \ā\ ace
\ä\ mop, mar \au̇\ out \ch\ chin \e\ bet \ē\ easy
\g\ go \i\ hit \ī\ ice \j\ job \ŋ\ sing \ō\ go
\ȯ\ law \ȯi\ boy \th\ thin \t͟h\ the \ü\ loot \u̇\ foot
\y\ yet \zh\ vision *see also* Guide to Pronunciation

(1) **:** a single human being as contrasted with a social group or institution ⟨a teacher who works with *individuals*⟩ (2) **:** a single organism as distinguished from a group **b :** a particular person ⟨are you the *individual* I spoke with on the telephone?⟩
**2 :** an indivisible entity
**3 :** the reference of a name or variable of the lowest logical type in a calculus
**in·di·vid·u·al·ise** *British variant of* INDIVIDUALIZE
**in·di·vid·u·al·ism** \,in-də-'vij-wə-,li-zəm, -'vi-jə-wə-, -'vi-jə-,li-\ *noun* (1827)
**1 a** (1) **:** a doctrine that the interests of the individual are or ought to be ethically paramount; *also* **:** conduct guided by such a doctrine (2) **:** the conception that all values, rights, and duties originate in individuals **b :** a theory maintaining the political and economic independence of the individual and stressing individual initiative, action, and interests; *also* **:** conduct or practice guided by such a theory
**2 a :** INDIVIDUALITY **b :** an individual peculiarity **:** IDIOSYNCRASY
**in·di·vid·u·al·ist** \-list\ *noun* (1840)
**1 :** one that pursues a markedly independent course in thought or action
**2 :** one that advocates or practices individualism
— **individualist** *or* **in·di·vid·u·al·is·tic** \-,vij-wə-'lis-tik, -,vi-jə-wə-, -,vi-jə-'lis-\ *adjective*
— **in·di·vid·u·al·is·ti·cal·ly** \-'lis-ti-k(ə-)lē\ *adverb*
**in·di·vid·u·al·i·ty** \-,vi-jə-'wa-lə-tē\ *noun, plural* **-ties** (1614)
**1 a :** total character peculiar to and distinguishing an individual from others **b :** PERSONALITY
**2** *archaic* **:** the quality or state of being indivisible
**3 :** separate or distinct existence
**4 :** INDIVIDUAL, PERSON
**in·di·vid·u·al·ize** \-'vij-wə-,līz, -'vi-jə-wə-, -'vi-jə-,līz\ *transitive verb* **-ized; -iz·ing** (1637)
**1 :** to make individual in character
**2 :** to treat or notice individually **:** PARTICULARIZE
**3 :** to adapt to the needs or special circumstances of an individual ⟨*individualize* teaching according to student ability⟩
— **in·di·vid·u·al·i·za·tion** \-,vij-wə-lə-'zā-shən, -,vi-jə-wə-, -,vi-jə-lə-\ *noun*
**individual medley** *noun* (circa 1949)
**:** a swimming race in which each contestant swims each part of the course with a different stroke
**individual retirement account** *noun* (1974)
**:** IRA
**in·di·vid·u·ate** \,in-də-'vi-jə-,wāt\ *transitive verb* **-at·ed; -at·ing** (1614)
**1 :** to give individuality to
**2 :** to form into a distinct entity
**in·di·vid·u·a·tion** \-,vi-jə-'wā-shən\ *noun* (1628)
**1 :** the act or process of individuating: as **a** (1) **:** the development of the individual from the universal (2) **:** the determination of the individual in the general **b :** the process by which individuals in society become differentiated from one another **c :** regional differentiation along a primary embryonic axis
**2 :** the state of being individuated; *specifically* **:** INDIVIDUALITY
**in·di·vis·i·ble** \,in-də-'vi-zə-bəl\ *adjective* [Middle English, from Late Latin *indivisibilis*, from Latin *in-* + Late Latin *divisibilis* divisible] (14th century)
**:** not divisible
— **in·di·vis·i·bil·i·ty** \-,vi-zə-'bi-lə-tē\ *noun*
— **indivisible** *noun*
— **in·di·vis·i·bly** \-'vi-zə-blē\ *adverb*
**indo-** — see IND-

**Indo-** *combining form* [Greek, from *Indos* India]
**1 :** India or the East Indies ⟨*Indo*-Pakistani⟩
**2 :** Indo-European ⟨*Indo*-Hittite⟩
**In·do-Ar·y·an** \,in-dō-'ar-ē-ən, -'er-; -'är-yən\ *noun* (1881)
**1 :** a member of one of the peoples of the Indian subcontinent speaking an Indo-European language
**2 :** one of the early Indo-European invaders of southern Asia
**3 :** a branch of the Indo-European language family that includes Hindi, Bengali, Punjabi, and other languages spoken primarily in India, Pakistan, Bangladesh, and Sri Lanka — see INDO-EUROPEAN LANGUAGES table
— **Indo-Aryan** *adjective*
**In·do-Chi·nese** \-,chī-'nēz, -'nēs\ *noun* (circa 1934)
**1 :** a native or inhabitant of Indochina
**2 :** SINO-TIBETAN
— **Indo-Chinese** *adjective*
**in·doc·ile** \(,)in-'dä-səl *also* -,sīl, *especially British* -'dō-,sīl\ *adjective* [Middle French, from Latin *indocilis*, from *in-* + *docilis* docile] (1603)
**:** unwilling or indisposed to be taught or disciplined **:** INTRACTABLE
— **in·do·cil·i·ty** \,in-dä-'si-lə-tē, -dō-\ *noun*
**in·doc·tri·nate** \in-'däk-trə-,nāt\ *transitive verb* **-nat·ed; -nat·ing** [probably from Middle English *endoctrinen*, from Middle French *endoctriner*, from Old French, from *en-* + *doctrine* doctrine] (1626)
**1 :** to instruct especially in fundamentals or rudiments **:** TEACH
**2 :** to imbue with a usually partisan or sectarian opinion, point of view, or principle
— **in·doc·tri·na·tion** \(,)in-,däk-trə-'nā-shən\ *noun*
— **in·doc·tri·na·tor** \in-'däk-trə-,nā-tər\ *noun*
**¹In·do-Eu·ro·pe·an** \,in-dō-,yur-ə-'pē-ən\ *adjective* (1814)
**:** of, relating to, or constituting the Indo-European languages
**²Indo-European** *noun* (1864)
**1 :** INDO-EUROPEAN LANGUAGES
**2 a :** an unrecorded prehistoric language from which the Indo-European languages are descended **b :** a member of the people speaking this language
**In·do-Eu·ro·pe·an·ist** \-,yur-ə-'pē-ə-nist\ *noun* (1926)
**:** a specialist in Indo-European linguistics
**Indo-European languages** *noun plural* (1864)
**:** a family of languages comprising those spoken in most of Europe and in the parts of the world colonized by Europeans since 1500 and also in Persia, the subcontinent of India, and some other parts of Asia
**In·do-Ger·man·ic** \,in-dō-jər-'ma-nik\ *adjective* (1835)
**:** INDO-EUROPEAN
— **Indo-Germanic** *noun*
**In·do-Hit·tite** \-'hi-,tīt\ *noun* (1930)
**1 :** a hypothetical parent language of Indo-European and Anatolian
**2 :** a language family including Indo-European and Anatolian
— **Indo-Hittite** *adjective*
**In·do-Ira·ni·an** \-ir-'ā-nē-ən\ *adjective* (1876)
**:** of, relating to, or constituting a subfamily of the Indo-European languages that consists of the Indo-Aryan and the Iranian branches — see INDO-EUROPEAN LANGUAGES table
— **Indo-Iranian** *noun*
**in·dole** \'in-,dōl\ *noun* [International Scientific Vocabulary *ind-* + *-ole*] (1869)
**:** a crystalline compound $C_8H_7N$ that is a decomposition product of proteins containing tryptophan, that can be made synthetically, and that is used in perfumes; *also* **:** a derivative of indole

**in·dole·ace·tic acid** \,in-(,)dō-lə-'sē-tik-\ *noun* (1937)
**:** a crystalline plant hormone $C_{10}H_9NO_2$ that is a naturally occurring auxin promoting growth and rooting of plants — called also *heteroauxin*
**in·dole·bu·tyr·ic acid** \,in-(,)dōl-byü-'tir-ik-\ *noun* (1936)
**:** a crystalline acid $C_{12}H_{13}NO_2$ similar to indoleacetic acid in its effects on plants
**in·do·lence** \'in-də-lən(t)s\ *noun* (1710)
**:** inclination to laziness **:** SLOTH
**in·do·lent** \-lənt\ *adjective* [Late Latin *indolent-, indolens* insensitive to pain, from Latin *in-* + *dolent-, dolens*, present participle of *dolēre* to feel pain] (1663)
**1 a :** causing little or no pain **b :** slow to develop or heal
**2 a :** averse to activity, effort, or movement **:** habitually lazy **b :** conducing to or encouraging laziness ⟨*indolent* heat⟩ **c :** exhibiting indolence ⟨an *indolent* sigh⟩
**synonym** see LAZY
— **in·do·lent·ly** *adverb*
**In·dol·o·gy** \(,)in-'dä-lə-jē\ *noun* (1888)
**:** the study of India and its people
— **In·dol·o·gist** \-jist\ *noun*
**in·do·meth·a·cin** \,in-dō-'me-thə-sən\ *noun* [*indole* + *meth-* + *a*cetic acid + ¹*-in*] (1963)
**:** a nonsteroidal drug $C_{19}H_{16}ClNO_4$ with anti-inflammatory, analgesic, and antipyretic properties used especially in treating arthritis
**in·dom·i·ta·ble** \in-'dä-mə-tə-bəl\ *adjective* [Late Latin *indomitabilis*, from Latin *in-* + *domitare* to tame — more at DAUNT] (1830)
**:** incapable of being subdued **:** UNCONQUERABLE ⟨*indomitable* courage⟩
— **in·dom·i·ta·bil·i·ty** \(,)in-,dä-mə-tə-'bi-lə-tē\ *noun*
— **in·dom·i·ta·ble·ness** \in-'dä-mə-tə-bəl-nəs\ *noun*
— **in·dom·i·ta·bly** \-blē\ *adverb*
**In·do·ne·sian** \,in-də-'nē-zhən, -shən\ *noun* (1850)
**1 :** a native or inhabitant of the Malay Archipelago
**2 a :** a native or inhabitant of the Republic of Indonesia **b :** the language based on Malay that is the national language of the Republic of Indonesia
— **Indonesian** *adjective*
**in·door** \'in-,dōr, -'dôr\ *adjective* (1711)
**1 :** of or relating to the interior of a building
**2 :** living, located, or carried on within a building ⟨an *indoor* sport⟩
**in·doors** \'in-'dōrz, (,)in-, -'dôrz\ *adverb* (1832)
**:** in or into a building
**in·do·phe·nol** \,in-dō-'fē-,nōl, -,nòl, ,in-(,)dō-fi-'\ *noun* [International Scientific Vocabulary] (circa 1881)
**:** any of various blue or green dyes
**in·dorse, in·dorse·ment** *variant of* ENDORSE, ENDORSEMENT
**in·dox·yl** \in-'däk-səl\ *noun* [International Scientific Vocabulary *ind-* + hydr*oxyl*] (circa 1886)
**:** a crystalline compound $C_8H_7NO$ found in plants and animals or synthesized as a step in indigo manufacture
**in·draft** \'in-,draft, -,dràft\ *noun* (1594)
**1 :** an inward flow or current (as of air or water)
**2 :** a drawing or pulling in
**in·drawn** \'in-,dròn\ *adjective* (1751)
**1 :** ALOOF, RESERVED
**2 :** drawn in
**in·dri** \'in-drē\ *noun, plural* **indris** [French, from Malagasy *indry* look!] (1839)
**:** a large black-and-white Madagascan lemur (*Indri indri*) that is about two feet long with a rudimentary tail
**in·du·bi·ta·ble** \(,)in-'dü-bə-tə-bəl, -'dyü-\ *adjective* [Middle English *indubitabyll*, from Latin *indubitabilis*, from *in-* + *dubitabilis* dubitable] (15th century)

# INDO-EUROPEAN LANGUAGES

| BRANCH | GROUP | LANGUAGES AND MAJOR DIALECTS[1] | | | PROVENIENCE |
|--------|-------|-------|-------|-------|-------------|
| | | ANCIENT | MEDIEVAL | MODERN | |
| | Anatolian | *Hittite, Lydian, Lycian* *Luwian, Palaic* *Hieroglyphic Luwian* | | | ancient Asia Minor |
| INDO-IRANIAN | Kafiri (Nuristani) | | | languages of eastern Afghanistan | Afghanistan |
| INDO-IRANIAN | Indo-Aryan — Sanskritic | *Sanskrit, Pali* *Prakrits* | *Prakrits* | | India |
| INDO-IRANIAN | Indo-Aryan | | | Shina, Khowar | Upper Indus valley |
| INDO-IRANIAN | Indo-Aryan | | | Kashmiri | Kashmir |
| INDO-IRANIAN | Indo-Aryan | | | Lahnda | western Punjab |
| INDO-IRANIAN | Indo-Aryan | | | Sindhi | Sind |
| INDO-IRANIAN | Indo-Aryan | | | Panjabi | Punjab |
| INDO-IRANIAN | Indo-Aryan | | | Rajasthani | Rajasthan |
| INDO-IRANIAN | Indo-Aryan | | | Gujarati | Gujarat |
| INDO-IRANIAN | Indo-Aryan | | | Marathi | western India |
| INDO-IRANIAN | Indo-Aryan | | | Konkani | western India |
| INDO-IRANIAN | Indo-Aryan | | | Oriya | Orissa |
| INDO-IRANIAN | Indo-Aryan | | | Bengali | Bangladesh, West Bengal |
| INDO-IRANIAN | Indo-Aryan | | | Assamese | Assam |
| INDO-IRANIAN | Indo-Aryan | | | Bhojpuri | Bihar, Uttar Pradesh |
| INDO-IRANIAN | Indo-Aryan | | | Hindi | northern India |
| INDO-IRANIAN | Indo-Aryan | | | Urdu | Pakistan, India |
| INDO-IRANIAN | Indo-Aryan | | | Nepali | Nepal |
| INDO-IRANIAN | Indo-Aryan | | | Sinhalese | Sri Lanka |
| INDO-IRANIAN | Indo-Aryan | | | Romany | uncertain |
| INDO-IRANIAN | Iranian — West | *Old Persian* | *Pahlavi* Persian | | Persia |
| INDO-IRANIAN | Iranian — West | | | Persian | Iran |
| INDO-IRANIAN | Iranian — West | | | Kurdish | Iran, Iraq, Turkey |
| INDO-IRANIAN | Iranian — West | | | Baluchi | Pakistan |
| INDO-IRANIAN | Iranian — West | | | Tajiki | Tajikistan |
| INDO-IRANIAN | Iranian — East | Avestan | | | ancient Persia |
| INDO-IRANIAN | Iranian — East | | *Sogdian, Khotanese* | | central Asia |
| INDO-IRANIAN | Iranian — East | | | Pashto | Afghanistan, Pakistan |
| INDO-IRANIAN | Iranian — East | | | Ossetic | Caucasus |
| | Armenian | | Armenian | Armenian | Asia Minor, Caucasus |
| | Greek or Hellenic | Greek | Greek | Greek | Greece, the eastern Mediterranean |
| BALTO-SLAVIC | Baltic | | *Old Prussian* | | East Prussia |
| BALTO-SLAVIC | Baltic | | | Lithuanian | Lithuania |
| BALTO-SLAVIC | Baltic | | | Latvian | Latvia |
| BALTO-SLAVIC | Slavic — South | | Old Church Slavonic | | |
| BALTO-SLAVIC | Slavic — South | | | Slovene | Slovenia |
| BALTO-SLAVIC | Slavic — South | | | Serbo-Croatian | Croatia, Bosnia and Herzegovina, Serbia, Montenegro |
| BALTO-SLAVIC | Slavic — South | | | Macedonian | Macedonia |
| BALTO-SLAVIC | Slavic — South | | | Bulgarian | Bulgaria |
| BALTO-SLAVIC | Slavic — West | | | Czech, Slovak | Czechoslovakia |
| BALTO-SLAVIC | Slavic — West | | | Polish, Kashubian | Poland |
| BALTO-SLAVIC | Slavic — West | | | Wendish, *Polabian* | Germany |
| BALTO-SLAVIC | Slavic — East | | *Old Russian* | Russian | Russia |
| BALTO-SLAVIC | Slavic — East | | | Ukrainian | Ukraine |
| BALTO-SLAVIC | Slavic — East | | | Belorussian | Belarus |
| | Albanian | | | Albanian | Albania, Serbia, Macedonia |
| | Scantily recorded and of uncertain affinities within Indo-European | *Ligurian, Messapian,* *Illyrian, Thracian,* *Phrygian* | | | ancient Italy; Balkans; Asia Minor |
| | Tocharian | | *Tocharian A* *Tocharian B* | | central Asia |
| GERMANIC | East | | *Gothic* | | eastern Europe |
| GERMANIC | North | | *Old Norse* | | |
| GERMANIC | North | | | Icelandic | Iceland |
| GERMANIC | North | | | Faeroese | Faeroe Islands |
| GERMANIC | North | | | Norwegian | Norway |
| GERMANIC | North | | | Swedish | Sweden |
| GERMANIC | North | | | Danish | Denmark |
| GERMANIC | West | | *Old High German* *Middle High German* | German | Germany, Switzerland, Austria |
| GERMANIC | West | | | Yiddish | Germany, eastern Europe |
| GERMANIC | West | | *Old Saxon* *Middle Low German* *Middle Dutch* | Low German | northern Germany |
| GERMANIC | West | | | Dutch | Netherlands |
| GERMANIC | West | | | Afrikaans | South Africa |
| GERMANIC | West | | | Flemish | Belgium |
| GERMANIC | West | | *Old Frisian* | Frisian | Netherlands, Germany |
| GERMANIC | West | | *Old English* *Middle English* | English | England |
| ITALIC | | *Venetic, Oscan, Umbrian,* *Faliscan* Latin | | | ancient Italy |
| ITALIC | | | | Portuguese | Portugal |
| ITALIC | | | | Spanish | Spain |
| ITALIC | | | | Judeo-Spanish | Mediterranean lands |
| ITALIC | | | | Catalan | Spain (Catalonia) |
| ITALIC | | | *Old Provençal* | Provençal | southern France |
| ITALIC | | | *Old French* *Middle French* | French | France, Belgium, Switzerland |
| ITALIC | | | | Italian | Italy, Switzerland |
| ITALIC | | | | Rhaeto-Romance | Switzerland, Italy |
| ITALIC | | | | Sardinian | Sardinia |
| ITALIC | | | | *Dalmation* | Adriatic coast |
| ITALIC | | | | Romanian | Romania, Balkans |
| CELTIC | Continental | *Gaulish* | | | Gaul |
| CELTIC | Goidelic | | *Old Irish* *Middle Irish* | Irish | Ireland |
| CELTIC | Goidelic | | | Scottish Gaelic | Scotland |
| CELTIC | Goidelic | | | *Manx* | Isle of Man |
| CELTIC | Brythonic | | *Old Welsh* *Middle Welsh* | Welsh | Wales |
| CELTIC | Brythonic | | *Old Cornish* | *Cornish* | Cornwall |
| CELTIC | Brythonic | | *Old Breton* | Breton | Brittany |

[1]Italics denote dead languages. Languages listed in roman type in the ancient or medieval column survive only in some special use, as in literary composition or liturgy.

: too evident to be doubted : UNQUESTIONABLE
— **in·du·bi·ta·bil·i·ty** \-ˌdü-bə-tə-'bi-lə-tē, -ˌdyü-\ *noun*
— **in·du·bi·ta·ble·ness** \-'dü-bə-tə-bəl-nəs, -'dyü-\ *noun*
— **in·du·bi·ta·bly** \-blē\ *adverb*
**in·duce** \in-'düs, -'dyüs\ *transitive verb* **in·duced; in·duc·ing** [Middle English, from Latin *inducere*, from *in-* + *ducere* to lead — more at TOW] (14th century)
**1 a :** to move by persuasion or influence **b :** to call forth or bring about by influence or stimulation
**2 a :** EFFECT, CAUSE **b :** to cause the formation of **c :** to produce (as an electric current) by induction
**3 :** to determine by induction; *specifically* : to infer from particulars
**in·duce·ment** \in-'düs-mənt, -'dyüs-\ *noun* (1594)
**1 :** a motive or consideration that leads one to action or to additional or more effective actions
**2 :** the act or process of inducing
**3 :** matter presented by way of introduction or background to explain the principal allegations of a legal cause, plea, or defense
*synonym* see MOTIVE
**in·duc·er** \-'dü-sər, -'dyü-\ *noun* (1554)
: one that induces; *especially* : a substance that is capable of activating a structural gene by combining with and inactivating a genetic repressor
**in·duc·ible** \in-'dü-sə-bəl, -'dyü-\ *adjective* (circa 1677)
: capable of being induced; *especially* : formed by a cell in response to the presence of its substrate ⟨*inducible* enzymes⟩ — compare CONSTITUTIVE
— **in·duc·ibil·i·ty** \-ˌdü-sə-'bi-lə-tē, -ˌdyü-\ *noun*
**in·duct** \in-'dəkt\ *transitive verb* [Middle English, from Medieval Latin *inductus*, past participle of *inducere*, from Latin] (14th century)
**1 :** to put in formal possession (as of a benefice or office) : INSTALL ⟨was *inducted* as president of the college⟩
**2 a :** to admit as a member ⟨*inducted* into a scholastic society⟩ **b :** INTRODUCE, INITIATE **c :** to enroll for military training or service (as under a selective service act)
**3 :** LEAD, CONDUCT
**in·duc·tance** \in-'dək-tən(t)s\ *noun* (1886)
**1 a :** a property of an electric circuit by which an electromotive force is induced in it by a variation of current either in the circuit itself or in a neighboring circuit **b :** the measure of this property that is equal to the ratio of the induced electromotive force to the rate of change of the inducing current
**2 :** a circuit or a device possessing inductance
**in·duct·ee** \(ˌ)in-ˌdək-'tē, in-'dək-ˌ\ *noun* (1940)
: one who is inducted
**in·duc·tion** \in-'dək-shən\ *noun* (14th century)
**1 a :** the act or process of inducting (as into office) **b :** an initial experience : INITIATION **c :** the formality by which a civilian is inducted into military service
**2 a** (1) **:** inference of a generalized conclusion from particular instances — compare DEDUCTION 2a (2) **:** a conclusion arrived at by induction **b :** mathematical demonstration of the validity of a law concerning all the positive integers by proving that it holds for the integer 1 and that if it holds for all the integers preceding a given integer it must hold for the next following integer
**3 :** a preface, prologue, or introductory scene especially of an early English play
**4 a :** the act of bringing forward or adducing (as facts or particulars) **b :** the act of causing or bringing on or about **c :** the process by which an electrical conductor becomes electrified when near a charged body, by which a magnetizable body becomes magnetized when

in a magnetic field or in the magnetic flux set up by a magnetomotive force, or by which an electromotive force is produced in a circuit by varying the magnetic field linked with the circuit **d :** the inspiration of the fuel-air charge from the carburetor into the combustion chamber of an internal-combustion engine **e :** the sum of the processes by which the fate of embryonic cells is determined and morphogenetic differentiation brought about
**induction coil** *noun* (1837)
: an apparatus for obtaining intermittent high voltage consisting of a primary coil through which the direct current flows, an interrupter, and a secondary coil of a larger number of turns in which the high voltage is induced
**induction heating** *noun* (1919)
: heating of material by means of an electric current that is caused to flow through the material or its container by electromagnetic induction
**induction motor** *noun* (1897)
: an alternating-current motor in which torque is produced by the reaction between a varying magnetic field generated in the stator and the current induced in the coils of the rotor
**in·duc·tive** \in-'dək-tiv\ *adjective* (15th century)
**1 :** leading on : INDUCING
**2 :** of, relating to, or employing mathematical or logical induction ⟨*inductive* reasoning⟩
**3 :** of or relating to inductance or electrical induction
**4 :** INTRODUCTORY
**5 :** involving the action of an embryological inductor : tending to produce induction
— **in·duc·tive·ly** *adverb*
**in·duc·tor** \in-'dək-tər\ *noun* (1652)
**1 :** one that inducts
**2 a :** a part of an electrical apparatus that acts upon another or is itself acted upon by induction **b :** REACTOR 2
**3 :** ORGANIZER 2
**in·due** *variant of* ENDUE
**in·dulge** \in-'dəlj\ *verb* **in·dulged; in·dulg·ing** [Latin *indulgēre* to be complaisant] (circa 1623)
*transitive verb*
**1 a :** to give free rein to **b :** to take unrestrained pleasure in : GRATIFY
**2 a :** to yield to the desire of : HUMOR **b :** to treat with excessive leniency, generosity, or consideration
*intransitive verb*
: to indulge oneself ☆
— **in·dulg·er** *noun*
**in·dul·gence** \in-'dəl-jən(t)s\ *noun* (14th century)
**1 :** remission of part or all of the temporal and especially purgatorial punishment that according to Roman Catholicism is due for sins whose eternal punishment has been remitted and whose guilt has been pardoned (as through the sacrament of reconciliation)
**2 :** the act of indulging : the state of being indulgent
**3 a :** an indulgent act **b :** an extension of time for payment or performance granted as a favor
**4 a :** the act of indulging in something; *especially* : SELF-INDULGENCE **b :** something indulged in ⟨walk off gastronomic *indulgences* —Barbara L. Michaels⟩
**in·dul·gent** \in-'dəl-jənt\ *adjective* [Latin *indulgent-, indulgens*, present participle of *indulgēre*] (1509)
: indulging or characterized by indulgence; *especially* : LENIENT
— **in·dul·gent·ly** *adverb*
**in·dult** \'in-ˌdəlt, in-'\ *noun* [Middle English (Scots), from Medieval Latin *indultum*, from Late Latin, grant, from Latin, neuter of *indultus*, past participle of *indulgēre*] (15th century)
: a special often temporary dispensation granted in the Roman Catholic Church

¹**in·du·rate** \'in-də-rət, -dyə-; in-'dùr-ət, -'dyùr-\ *adjective* (14th century)
: physically or morally hardened
²**in·du·rate** \'in-də-ˌrāt, -dyə-\ *verb* **-rat·ed; -rat·ing** [Latin *induratus*, past participle of *indurare*, from *in-* + *durare* to harden, from *durus* hard — more at DURING] (1538)
*transitive verb*
**1 :** to make unfeeling, stubborn, or obdurate
**2 :** to make hardy : INURE
**3 :** to make hard ⟨great heat *indurates* clay⟩
**4 :** to establish firmly : CONFIRM
*intransitive verb*
**1 :** to grow hard : HARDEN
**2 :** to become established
**in·du·rat·ed** \-ˌrā-təd\ *adjective* (1604)
: having become firm or hard especially by increase of fibrous elements ⟨*indurated* tissue⟩
**in·du·ra·tion** \ˌin-də-'rā-shən, -dyə-\ *noun* (14th century)
: the process of or condition produced by growing hard; *specifically* : sclerosis especially when associated with inflammation
— **in·du·ra·tive** \'in-də-ˌrā-tiv, -dyə-; in-'dür-ə-, -'dyùr-\ *adjective*
**in·du·si·um** \in-'dü-zē-əm, -'dyü-, -zhē-\ *noun, plural* **-sia** \-zē-ə, -zhē-\ [New Latin, from Latin, tunic] (1807)
: an investing outgrowth or membrane: as **a** : an outgrowth of a fern frond that invests the sori **b** : the annulus of a fungus especially when large and full
¹**in·dus·tri·al** \in-'dəs-trē-əl\ *adjective* (15th century)
**1 :** of or relating to industry
**2 :** derived from human industry ⟨*industrial* wealth⟩
**3 :** engaged in industry ⟨the *industrial* classes⟩
**4 :** used in or developed for use in industry ⟨*industrial* diamonds⟩; *also* : HEAVY-DUTY ⟨an *industrial* zipper⟩
**5 :** characterized by highly developed industries ⟨an *industrial* nation⟩
— **in·dus·tri·al·ly** \-trē-ə-lē\ *adverb*
²**industrial** *noun* (1865)
**1 a :** one that is employed in industry **b :** a company engaged in industrial production or service
**2 :** a stock or bond issued by an industrial corporation or enterprise
**industrial action** *noun* (circa 1931)
*British* : JOB ACTION
**industrial archaeology** *noun* (1951)
: the study of the buildings, machinery, and equipment of the industrial revolution
— **industrial archaeologist** *noun*
**industrial arts** *noun plural but singular in construction* (circa 1925)
: a subject taught in elementary and secondary schools that aims at developing manual skill and familiarity with tools and machines
**industrial engineering** *noun* (circa 1924)

☆ SYNONYMS
**Indulge, pamper, humor, spoil, baby, mollycoddle** mean to show undue favor to a person's desires and feelings. INDULGE implies excessive compliance and weakness in gratifying another's or one's own desires ⟨*indulged* myself with food at the slightest excuse⟩. PAMPER implies inordinate gratification of desire for luxury and comfort with consequent enervating effect ⟨*pampered* by the amenities of modern living⟩. HUMOR stresses a yielding to a person's moods or whims ⟨*humored* him by letting him tell the story⟩. SPOIL stresses the injurious effects on character by indulging or pampering ⟨foolish parents *spoil* their children⟩. BABY suggests excessive care, attention, or solicitude ⟨*babying* students by grading too easily⟩. MOLLYCODDLE suggests an excessive degree of care and attention to another's health or welfare ⟨refused to *mollycoddle* her malingering son⟩.

: engineering that deals with the design, improvement, and installation of integrated systems (as of people, materials, and energy) in industry
— **industrial engineer** *noun*

**in·dus·tri·al·ise** *British variant of* INDUSTRIALIZE

**in·dus·tri·al·ism** \in-'dəs-trē-ə-,li-zəm\ *noun* (1831)
: social organization in which industries and especially large-scale industries are dominant

**in·dus·tri·al·ist** \-list\ *noun* (1864)
: one owning or engaged in the management of an industry : MANUFACTURER

**in·dus·tri·al·ize** \in-'dəs-trē-ə-,līz\ *verb* **-ized; -iz·ing** (1882)
*transitive verb*
: to make industrial ⟨*industrialize* an agricultural region⟩
*intransitive verb*
: to become industrial
— **in·dus·tri·al·i·za·tion** \-,dəs-trē-ə-lə-'zā-shən\ *noun*

**industrial melanism** *noun* (1943)
: genetically determined melanism as a population phenomenon especially in moths in which the proportion of dark individuals tends to increase due to differential predation especially by birds which more easily find and eat lighter-colored individuals in habitats darkened by industrial pollution

**industrial psychology** *noun* (1917)
: the application of the findings and methods of experimental, clinical, and social psychology to industrial concerns
— **industrial psychologist** *noun*

**industrial relations** *noun plural* (1904)
: the dealings or relationships of a usually large business or industrial enterprise with its own workers, with labor in general, with governmental agencies, or with the public

**industrial revolution** *noun* (1848)
: a rapid major change in an economy (as in England in the late 18th century) marked by the general introduction of power-driven machinery or by an important change in the prevailing types and methods of use of such machines

**industrial school** *noun* (1853)
: a school specializing in the teaching of industrial arts; *specifically* : one for juvenile delinquents

**industrial sociology** *noun* (1948)
: sociological analysis directed at institutions and social relationships within and largely controlled or affected by industry

**in·dus·tri·al–strength** \in-'dəs-trē-əl-'stren(k)th, -'stren(t)th\ *adjective* (1976)
: of industrial quality; *also* : marked by more than usual power or durability ⟨*industrial-strength* boots⟩ ⟨an *industrial-strength* voice⟩

**industrial union** *noun* (1902)
: a labor union open to workers in an industry irrespective of their occupation or craft — compare CRAFT UNION

**in·dus·tri·ous** \in-'dəs-trē-əs\ *adjective* (15th century)
**1** *obsolete* : SKILLFUL, INGENIOUS
**2** : persistently active : ZEALOUS
**3** : constantly, regularly, or habitually occupied : DILIGENT
*synonym see* BUSY
— **in·dus·tri·ous·ly** *adverb*
— **in·dus·tri·ous·ness** *noun*

**in·dus·try** \'in-(,)dəs-trē\ *noun, plural* **-tries** [Middle English *industrie* skill, employment involving skill, from Middle French, from Latin *industria* diligence, from *industrius* diligent, from Old Latin *indostruus*, perhaps from *indu* in + *-struus* (akin to Latin *struere* to build) — more at END-, STREW] (15th century)
**1** : diligence in an employment or pursuit; *especially* : steady or habitual effort
**2 a** : systematic labor especially for some useful purpose or the creation of something of

value **b** : a department or branch of a craft, art, business, or manufacture; *especially* : one that employs a large personnel and capital especially in manufacturing **c** : a distinct group of productive or profit-making enterprises ⟨the banking *industry*⟩ **d** : manufacturing activity as a whole ⟨the nation's *industry*⟩
**3** : work devoted to the study of a particular subject or author ⟨the Shakespeare *industry*⟩
*synonym see* BUSINESS

**in·dwell** \in-'dwel, 'in-,\ (14th century)
*intransitive verb*
: to exist as an inner activating spirit, force, or principle
*transitive verb*
: to exist within as an activating spirit, force, or principle
— **in·dwell·er** *noun*

**in·dwell·ing** \'in-,dwe-liŋ\ *adjective* (1646)
**1** : being an inner activating or guiding force
**2** : left within a bodily organ or passage especially to promote drainage — used of an implanted tube (as a catheter)

**¹-ine** *adjective suffix*
**1** [Middle English *-in, -ine,* from Middle French & Latin; Middle French *-in,* from Latin *-īnus* — more at -EN] : of or relating to ⟨estuar*ine*⟩
**2** [Middle English *-in, -ine,* from Middle French & Latin; Middle French *-in,* from Latin *-īnus,* from Greek *-inos* — more at -EN] : made of : like ⟨opal*ine*⟩

**²-ine** *noun suffix* [Middle English *-ine, -in,* from Middle French & Latin; Middle French *-ine,* from Latin *-īna,* from feminine of *-īnus,* adjective suffix]
**1** : chemical substance: as **a** : halogen element ⟨chlor*ine*⟩ **b** : basic or base-containing carbon compound that contains nitrogen ⟨quin*ine*⟩ ⟨cyst*ine*⟩ **c** : mixture of compounds (as of hydrocarbons) ⟨gasol*ine*⟩ **d** : hydride ⟨ars*ine*⟩
**2** : -IN 1a
**3** : commercial product or material ⟨glass*ine*⟩

**in·ebri·ant** \i-'nē-brē-ənt\ *noun* (1819)
: INTOXICANT

**¹in·ebri·ate** \i-'nē-brē-,āt\ *transitive verb* **-at·ed; -at·ing** [Latin *inebriatus,* past participle of *inebriare,* from *in-* + *ebriare* to intoxicate, from *ebrius* drunk] (15th century)
**1** : to exhilarate or stupefy as if by liquor
**2** : to make drunk : INTOXICATE
— **in·ebri·a·tion** \-,nē-brē-'ā-shən\ *noun*

**²in·ebri·ate** \i-'nē-brē-ət, -,āt\ *adjective* (15th century)
**1** : affected by alcohol : DRUNK
**2** : addicted to excessive drinking

**³in·ebri·ate** \-ət\ *noun* (circa 1796)
: one who is drunk; *especially* : DRUNKARD

**in·ebri·at·ed** \-brē-,ā-təd\ *adjective* (1609)
: exhilarated or confused by or as if by alcohol : INTOXICATED

**in·ebri·ety** \,i-ni-'brī-ə-tē\ *noun* [probably blend of *inebriation* and *ebriety* drunkenness] (1801)
: the state of being inebriated : DRUNKENNESS

**in·ed·i·ble** \(,)i-'ne-də-bəl\ *adjective* (circa 1834)
: not fit to be eaten

**in·ed·u·ca·ble** \(,)i-'ne-jə-kə-bəl\ *adjective* (1884)
: incapable of being educated
— **in·ed·u·ca·bil·i·ty** \-,ne-jə-kə-'bi-lə-tē\ *noun*

**in·ef·fa·ble** \(,)i-'ne-fə-bəl\ *adjective* [Middle English, from Middle French, from Latin *ineffabilis,* from *in-* + *effabilis* capable of being expressed, from *effari* to speak out, from *ex-* + *fari* to speak — more at BAN] (14th century)
**1 a** : incapable of being expressed in words : INDESCRIBABLE ⟨*ineffable* joy⟩ **b** : UNSPEAKABLE ⟨*ineffable* disgust⟩
**2** : not to be uttered : TABOO ⟨the *ineffable* name of Jehovah⟩
— **in·ef·fa·bil·i·ty** \-,ne-fə-'bi-lə-tē\ *noun*
— **in·ef·fa·ble·ness** \-'ne-fə-bəl-nəs\ *noun*
— **in·ef·fa·bly** \-blē\ *adverb*

**in·ef·face·able** \,i-nə-'fā-sə-bəl\ *adjective* [probably from French *ineffaçable,* from Middle French, from *in-* + *effaçable* effaceable] (1804)
: not effaceable : INERADICABLE
— **in·ef·face·abil·i·ty** \-,fā-sə-'bi-lə-tē\ *noun*
— **in·ef·face·ably** \-'fā-sə-blē\ *adverb*

**in·ef·fec·tive** \,i-nə-'fek-tiv\ *adjective* (1649)
**1** : not producing an intended effect : INEFFECTUAL ⟨*ineffective* lighting⟩
**2** : not capable of performing efficiently or as expected : INCAPABLE ⟨an *ineffective* executive⟩
— **in·ef·fec·tive·ly** *adverb*
— **in·ef·fec·tive·ness** *noun*

**in·ef·fec·tu·al** \,i-nə-'fek-chə(-wə)l, -'feksh-wəl\ *adjective* (15th century)
**1** : not producing the proper or intended effect : FUTILE
**2** : INEFFECTIVE 2
— **in·ef·fec·tu·al·i·ty** \-,fek-chə-'wa-lə-tē\ *noun*
— **in·ef·fec·tu·al·ly** \-'fek-chə(-wə)-lē, -'fek-shwə-\ *adverb*
— **in·ef·fec·tu·al·ness** *noun*

**in·ef·fi·ca·cious** \(,)i-,ne-fə-'kā-shəs\ *adjective* (1658)
: lacking the power to produce a desired effect : INEFFECTIVE
— **in·ef·fi·ca·cious·ly** *adverb*
— **in·ef·fi·ca·cious·ness** *noun*

**in·ef·fi·ca·cy** \(,)i-'ne-fi-kə-sē\ *noun* [Late Latin *inefficacia,* from Latin *inefficac-, inefficax* inefficacious, from *in-* + *efficac-, efficax* efficacious] (circa 1615)
: lack of power to produce a desired effect

**in·ef·fi·cien·cy** \,i-nə-'fi-shən(t)-sē\ *noun, plural* **-cies** (1749)
**1** : the quality or state of being inefficient
**2** : something that is inefficient

**in·ef·fi·cient** \-'fi-shənt\ *adjective* (1750)
: not efficient: as **a** : not producing the effect intended or desired **b** : wasteful of time or energy ⟨*inefficient* operating procedures⟩ **c** : INCAPABLE, INCOMPETENT ⟨an *inefficient* worker⟩
— **inefficient** *noun*
— **in·ef·fi·cient·ly** *adverb*

**in·egal·i·tar·i·an** \,i-ni-,ga-lə-'ter-ē-ən\ *adjective* (1940)
: marked by disparity in social and economic standing

**in·elas·tic** \,i-nə-'las-tik\ *adjective* (1748)
: not elastic: as **a** : slow to react or respond to changing conditions **b** : INFLEXIBLE, UNYIELDING
— **in·elas·tic·i·ty** \,i-ni-,las-'ti-s(ə-)tē, (,)i-,nē-,las-\ *noun*

**inelastic collision** *noun* (1937)
: a collision in which part of the kinetic energy of the colliding particles changes into another form of energy (as radiation)

**inelastic scattering** *noun* (1938)
: a scattering of particles as the result of inelastic collision in which the total kinetic energy of the colliding particles changes

**in·el·e·gance** \(,)i-'ne-li-gən(t)s\ *noun* (1726)
: lack of elegance

**in·el·e·gant** \-gənt\ *adjective* [Middle French, from Latin *inelegant-, inelegans,* from *in-* + *elegant-, elegans* elegant] (circa 1570)
: lacking in refinement, grace, or good taste
— **in·el·e·gant·ly** *adverb*

**in·el·i·gi·ble** \(,)i-'ne-lə-jə-bəl\ *adjective* [French *inéligible,* from *in-* + *éligible* eligible] (1770)
: not eligible: as **a** : not qualified for an office or position **b** : not permitted under football rules to catch a forward pass
— **in·el·i·gi·bil·i·ty** \-,ne-lə-jə-'bi-lə-tē\ *noun*

\ə\ abut \ᵊ\ kitten \ər\ further \a\ ash \ā\ ace
\ä\ mop, mar \aú\ out \ch\ chin \e\ bet \ē\ easy
\g\ go \i\ hit \ī\ ice \j\ job \ŋ\ sing \ō\ go
\ò\ law \òi\ boy \th\ thin \th\ the \ü\ loot \ú\ foot
\y\ yet \zh\ vision     *see also* Guide to Pronunciation

— **ineligible** *noun*

**in·el·o·quent** \(ˌ)i-ˈne-lə-kwənt\ *adjective* (circa 1530)
: not eloquent
— **in·el·o·quent·ly** *adverb*

**in·eluc·ta·ble** \ˌi-ni-ˈlək-tə-bəl\ *adjective* [Latin *ineluctabilis*, from *in-* + *eluctari* to struggle clear of, from *ex-* + *luctari* to struggle, wrestle; akin to Latin *luxus* dislocated — more at LOCK] (circa 1623)
: not to be avoided, changed, or resisted : INEVITABLE
— **in·eluc·ta·bil·i·ty** \-ˌlək-tə-ˈbi-lə-tē\ *noun*
— **in·eluc·ta·bly** \-ˈlək-tə-blē\ *adverb*

**in·elud·ible** \ˌi-ni-ˈlü-də-bəl\ *adjective* (1662)
: INESCAPABLE

**in·enar·ra·ble** \ˌi-ni-ˈnar-ə-bəl\ *adjective* [Middle English, from Middle French, from Latin *inenarrabilis*, from *in-* + *enarrare* to explain in detail, from *e-* + *narrare* to narrate] (15th century)
: incapable of being narrated : INDESCRIBABLE

**in·ept** \i-ˈnept\ *adjective* [Middle French *inepte*, from Latin *ineptus*, from *in-* + *aptus* apt] (1542)
**1** : lacking in fitness or aptitude : UNFIT
**2** : lacking sense or reason : FOOLISH
**3** : not suitable to the time, place, or occasion
: inappropriate often to an absurd degree
**4** : generally incompetent : BUNGLING
***synonym*** see AWKWARD
— **in·ept·ly** \-ˈnep(t)-lē\ *adverb*
— **in·ept·ness** \-nəs\ *noun*

**in·ep·ti·tude** \(ˌ)i-ˈnep-tə-ˌtüd, -ˌtyüd\ *noun* [Latin *ineptitudo*, from *ineptus*] (1615)
: the quality or state of being inept; *especially* : INCOMPETENCE

**in·equal·i·ty** \ˌi-ni-ˈkwä-lə-tē\ *noun* [Middle English *inequalite*, from Middle French *inequalité*, from Latin *inaequalitat-, inaequalitas*, from *inaequalis* unequal, from *in-* + *aequalis* equal] (15th century)
**1** : the quality of being unequal or uneven: as **a** : lack of evenness **b** : social disparity **c** : disparity of distribution or opportunity **d** : the condition of being variable : CHANGEABLENESS
**2** : an instance of being unequal
**3** : a formal statement of inequality between two quantities usually separated by a sign of inequality (as <, >, or ≠ signifying respectively *is less than, is greater than*, or *is not equal to*)

**in·eq·ui·ta·ble** \(ˌ)i-ˈne-kwə-tə-bəl\ *adjective* (1667)
: not equitable : UNFAIR
— **in·eq·ui·ta·bly** \-blē\ *adverb*

**in·eq·ui·ty** \(ˌ)i-ˈne-kwə-tē\ *noun* (1556)
**1** : INJUSTICE, UNFAIRNESS
**2** : an instance of injustice or unfairness

**in·equi·valve** \(ˌ)i-ˈnē-kwə-ˌvalv\ *also* **in·equi·valved** \-ˌvalvd\ *adjective* (1776)
: having the valves unequal in size and form — used of a bivalve mollusk or shell

**in·erad·i·ca·ble** \ˌi-ni-ˈra-di-kə-bəl\ *adjective* (1818)
: incapable of being eradicated
— **in·erad·i·ca·bil·i·ty** \-ˌra-di-kə-ˈbi-lə-tē\ *noun*
— **in·erad·i·ca·bly** \-ˈra-di-kə-blē\ *adverb*

**in·er·ran·cy** \(ˌ)i-ˈner-ən(t)-sē\ *noun* (circa 1834)
: exemption from error : INFALLIBILITY 〈the question of biblical *inerrancy*〉

**in·er·rant** \-ənt\ *adjective* [Latin *inerrant-, inerrans*, from *in-* + *errant-, errans*, present participle of *errare* to err] (1837)
: free from error

**in·ert** \i-ˈnərt\ *adjective* [Latin *inert-, iners* unskilled, idle, from *in-* + *art-, ars* skill — more at ARM] (1647)
**1** : lacking the power to move
**2** : very slow to move or act : SLUGGISH
**3** : deficient in active properties; *especially* : lacking a usual or anticipated chemical or biological action
***synonym*** see INACTIVE
— **inert** *noun*
— **in·ert·ly** *adverb*
— **in·ert·ness** *noun*

**inert gas** *noun* (1898)
: NOBLE GAS

**in·er·tia** \i-ˈnər-shə, -shē-ə\ *noun* [New Latin, from Latin, lack of skill, from *inert-, iners*] (1713)
**1 a** : a property of matter by which it remains at rest or in uniform motion in the same straight line unless acted upon by some external force **b** : an analogous property of other physical quantities (as electricity)
**2** : indisposition to motion, exertion, or change : INERTNESS
— **in·er·tial** \-shəl\ *adjective*
— **in·er·tial·ly** \-ˈnər-sh(ə-)lē\ *adverb*

**inertial guidance** *noun* (circa 1948)
: guidance (as of an aircraft or spacecraft) by means of self-contained automatically controlling devices that respond to inertial forces — called also *inertial navigation*

**in·es·cap·able** \ˌi-nə-ˈskā-pə-bəl\ *adjective* (1792)
: incapable of being avoided, ignored, or denied : INEVITABLE
— **in·es·cap·ably** \-blē\ *adverb*

**in·es·sen·tial** \ˌi-nə-ˈsen(t)-shəl\ *adjective* (1677)
**1** : having no essence
**2** : not essential : UNESSENTIAL
— **inessential** *noun*

**in·es·ti·ma·ble** \(ˌ)i-ˈnes-tə-mə-bəl\ *adjective* [Middle English, from Middle French, from Latin *inaestimabilis*, from *in-* + *aestimabilis* estimable] (14th century)
**1** : incapable of being estimated or computed 〈storms caused *inestimable* damage〉
**2** : too valuable or excellent to be measured or appreciated 〈has performed an *inestimable* service for his country〉
— **in·es·ti·ma·bly** \-blē\ *adverb*

**in·ev·i·ta·ble** \i-ˈne-və-tə-bəl\ *adjective* [Middle English, from Latin *inevitabilis*, from *in-* + *evitabilis* evitable] (14th century)
: incapable of being avoided or evaded
— **in·ev·i·ta·bil·i·ty** \-ˌne-və-tə-ˈbi-lə-tē\ *noun*
— **in·ev·i·ta·ble·ness** \-ˈne-və-tə-bəl-nəs\ *noun*

**in·ev·i·ta·bly** \-blē\ *adverb* (15th century)
**1** : in an inevitable way
**2** : as is to be expected 〈*inevitably*, it rained〉

**in·ex·act** \ˌi-nig-ˈzakt\ *adjective* [French, from *in-* + *exact* exact] (circa 1828)
**1** : not precisely correct or true : INACCURATE 〈an *inexact* translation〉
**2** : not rigorous and careful 〈an *inexact* thinker〉
— **in·ex·act·ly** \-ˈzak(t)-lē\ *adverb*
— **in·ex·act·ness** \-nəs\ *noun*

**in·ex·ac·ti·tude** \(ˌ)i-ˌnig-ˈzak-tə-ˌtüd, -ˌtyüd\ *noun* [French, from *inexact*] (1782)
**1** : lack of exactitude or precision
**2** : an instance of inexactness

**in ex·cel·sis** \ˌin-ik-ˈsel-səs *also* -ˈchel-\ *adverb* [Late Latin, on high] (1602)
: in the highest degree

**in·ex·cus·able** \ˌi-nik-ˈskyü-zə-bəl\ *adjective* [Middle English, from Latin *inexcusabilis*, from *in-* + *excusabilis* excusable] (15th century)
: being without excuse or justification
— **in·ex·cus·able·ness** *noun*
— **in·ex·cus·ably** \-blē\ *adverb*

**in·ex·haust·ible** \ˌi-nig-ˈzȯ-stə-bəl\ *adjective* (1601)
: not exhaustible: as **a** : incapable of being used up 〈*inexhaustible* riches〉 **b** : incapable of being wearied or worn out 〈an *inexhaustible* hiker〉
— **in·ex·haust·ibil·i·ty** \-ˌzȯ-stə-ˈbi-lə-tē\ *noun*
— **in·ex·haust·ible·ness** \-ˈzȯ-stə-bəl-nəs\ *noun*
— **in·ex·haust·ibly** \-blē\ *adverb*

**in·ex·is·tence** \ˌi-nig-ˈzis-tən(t)s\ *noun* (circa 1623)
: absence of existence : NONEXISTENCE

**in·ex·is·tent** \-tənt\ *adjective* [Late Latin *inexsistent-, inexsistens*, from Latin *in-* + *exsistent-, exsistens*, present participle of *exsistere* to exist] (1646)
: not having existence : NONEXISTENT

**in·ex·o·ra·ble** \(ˌ)i-ˈneks-rə-bəl, -ˈnek-sə-, -ˈneg-zə-rə-\ *adjective* [Latin *inexorabilis*, from *in-* + *exorabilis* pliant, from *exorare* to prevail upon, from *ex-* + *orare* to speak — more at ORATION] (1553)
: not to be persuaded or moved by entreaty : RELENTLESS
— **in·ex·o·ra·bil·i·ty** \(ˌ)i-ˌneks-rə-ˈbi-lə-tē, -ˌnek-sə-, -ˌneg-zə-\ *noun*
— **in·ex·o·ra·ble·ness** \-ˈneks-rə-bəl-nəs, -ˈnek-sə-, -ˈneg-zə-\ *noun*
— **in·ex·o·ra·bly** \-blē\ *adverb*

**in·ex·pe·di·ence** \ˌi-nik-ˈspē-dē-ən(t)s\ *noun* (1608)
: INEXPEDIENCY

**in·ex·pe·di·en·cy** \-ən(t)-sē\ *noun* (1641)
: the quality or fact of being inexpedient

**in·ex·pe·di·ent** \-ənt\ *adjective* (1608)
: not expedient : INADVISABLE
— **in·ex·pe·di·ent·ly** *adverb*

**in·ex·pen·sive** \ˌi-nik-ˈspen(t)-siv\ *adjective* (circa 1846)
: reasonable in price : CHEAP
— **in·ex·pen·sive·ly** *adverb*
— **in·ex·pen·sive·ness** *noun*

**in·ex·pe·ri·ence** \ˌi-nik-ˈspir-ē-ən(t)s\ *noun* [Middle French, from Late Latin *inexperientia*, from Latin *in-* + *experientia* experience] (1598)
**1** : lack of practical experience
**2** : lack of knowledge of the ways of the world
— **in·ex·pe·ri·enced** \-ən(t)st\ *adjective*

**in·ex·pert** \(ˌ)i-ˈnek-ˌspərt, ˌi-nik-ˈ\ *adjective* [Middle English, from Middle French, from Latin *inexpertus*, from *in-* + *expertus* expert] (15th century)
: not expert : UNSKILLED
— **in·ex·pert** \-ˈnek-ˌspərt\ *noun*
— **in·ex·pert·ly** \-ˈnek-ˌspərt-lē, ˌi-nik-ˈ\ *adverb*
— **in·ex·pert·ness** *noun*

**in·ex·pi·a·ble** \(ˌ)i-ˈnek-spē-ə-bəl\ *adjective* [Middle English *inexpyable*, from Latin *inexpiabilis*, from *in-* + *expiare* to expiate] (15th century)
**1** : not capable of being atoned for
**2** *obsolete* : IMPLACABLE, UNAPPEASABLE
— **in·ex·pi·a·bly** \-blē\ *adverb*

**in·ex·plain·able** \ˌi-nik-ˈsplā-nə-bəl\ *adjective* (circa 1923)
: INEXPLICABLE

**in·ex·pli·ca·ble** \ˌi-nik-ˈspli-kə-bəl, (ˌ)i-ˈnek-(ˌ)spli-\ *adjective* [Middle English, from Middle French, from Latin *inexplicabilis*, from *in-* + *explicabilis* explicable] (15th century)
: incapable of being explained, interpreted, or accounted for
— **in·ex·pli·ca·bil·i·ty** \ˌi-nik-ˌspli-kə-ˈbi-lə-tē, (ˌ)i-ˌnek-(ˌ)spli-\ *noun*
— **in·ex·pli·ca·ble·ness** \ˌi-nik-ˈspli-kə-bəl-nəs, (ˌ)i-ˈnek-(ˌ)spli-\ *noun*
— **in·ex·pli·ca·bly** \-blē\ *adverb*

**in·ex·plic·it** \ˌi-nik-ˈspli-sət\ *adjective* (circa 1812)
: not explicit

**in·ex·press·ible** \-ˈspre-sə-bəl\ *adjective* (1625)
: not capable of being expressed : INDESCRIBABLE
— **in·ex·press·ibil·i·ty** \-ˌspre-sə-ˈbi-lə-tē\ *noun*

— **in·ex·press·ible·ness** \-'spre-sə-bəl-nəs\ *noun*

— **in·ex·press·ibly** \-blē\ *adverb*

**in·ex·pres·sive** \-'spre-siv\ *adjective* (1652)

**1** *archaic* : INEXPRESSIBLE

**2** : lacking expression or meaning ⟨an *inexpressive* face⟩

— **in·ex·pres·sive·ly** *adverb*

— **in·ex·pres·sive·ness** *noun*

**in·ex·pug·na·ble** \,i-nik-'spəg-nə-bəl, -'spyü-nə-\ *adjective* [Middle English *in-expugnabull*, from Middle French, from Latin *inexpugnabilis*, from *in-* + *expugnare* to take by storm, from *ex-* + *pugnare* to fight — more at PUNGENT] (15th century)

**1** : incapable of being subdued or overthrown : IMPREGNABLE ⟨an *inexpugnable* position⟩

**2** : STABLE, FIXED ⟨*inexpugnable* hatred⟩

— **in·ex·pug·na·ble·ness** *noun*

— **in·ex·pug·na·bly** \-blē\ *adverb*

**in·ex·pung·ible** \,i-nik-'spən-jə-bəl\ *adjective* [*in-* + *expunge*] (1888)

: incapable of being obliterated

**in ex·ten·so** \,in-ik-'sten(t)-(,)sō\ *adverb* [Medieval Latin] (1826)

: at full length ⟨the passage was quoted *in extenso*⟩

**in·ex·tin·guish·able** \,i-nik-'stiŋ-gwi-shə-bəl, -'stiŋ-wi-\ *adjective* (15th century)

: not extinguishable : UNQUENCHABLE ⟨an *inextinguishable* flame⟩ ⟨an *inextinguishable* longing⟩

— **in·ex·tin·guish·ably** \-blē\ *adverb*

**in ex·tre·mis** \,in-ik-'strē-məs, -'strā-\ *adverb* [Latin] (circa 1530)

: in extreme circumstances; *especially* : at the point of death

**in·ex·tri·ca·ble** \,i-nik-'stri-kə-bəl, (,)i-'nek-(,)stri-\ *adjective* [Middle English, from Middle French or Latin; Middle French, from Latin *inextricabilis*, from *in-* + *extricabilis* extricable] (15th century)

**1** : forming a maze or tangle from which it is impossible to get free

**2 a** : incapable of being disentangled or untied ⟨an *inextricable* knot⟩ **b** : not capable of being solved

— **in·ex·tri·ca·bil·i·ty** \,i-nik-,stri-kə-'bi-lə-tē, (,)i-,nek-(,)stri-\ *noun*

— **in·ex·tri·ca·bly** \,i-nik-'stri-kə-blē, (,)i-'nek-(,)stri-\ *adverb*

**in·fal·li·ble** \(,)in-'fa-lə-bəl\ *adjective* [Middle English, from Medieval Latin *infallibilis*, from Latin *in-* + Late Latin *fallibilis* fallible] (15th century)

**1** : incapable of error : UNERRING ⟨an *infallible* memory⟩

**2** : not liable to mislead, deceive, or disappoint : CERTAIN ⟨an *infallible* remedy⟩

**3** : incapable of error in defining doctrines touching faith or morals

— **in·fal·li·bil·i·ty** \-,fa-lə-'bi-lə-tē\ *noun*

— **in·fal·li·bly** \-'fa-lə-blē\ *adverb*

**in·fall·ing** \'in-,fȯ-liŋ\ *adjective* (1964)

: moving under the influence of gravity toward a celestial object (as a black hole)

— **in·fall** \-,fȯl\ *noun*

**in·fa·mous** \'in-fə-məs\ *adjective* [Middle English, from Latin *infamis*, from *in-* + *fama* fame] (14th century)

**1** : having a reputation of the worst kind

**2** : causing or bringing infamy : DISGRACEFUL

**3** : convicted of an offense bringing infamy

— **in·fa·mous·ly** *adverb*

**in·fa·my** \-mē\ *noun, plural* **-mies** (15th century)

**1** : evil reputation brought about by something grossly criminal, shocking, or brutal

**2 a** : an extreme and publicly known criminal or evil act **b** : the state of being infamous

**synonym** see DISGRACE

**in·fan·cy** \'in-fən(t)-sē\ *noun, plural* **-cies** (14th century)

**1** : early childhood

**2** : a beginning or early period of existence

**3** : the legal status of an infant

¹**in·fant** \'in-fənt\ *noun* [Middle English *enfaunt*, from Middle French *enfant*, from Latin *infant-, infans*, from *infant-, infans*, adjective, incapable of speech, young, from *in-* + *fant-, fans*, present participle of *fari* to speak — more at BAN] (14th century)

**1** : a child in the first period of life

**2** : a person who is not of full age : MINOR ◊

²**infant** *adjective* (circa 1586)

**1** : intended for young children

**2** : being in an early stage of development

**3** : of, relating to, or being in infancy

**in·fan·ta** \in-'fan-tə, -'fän-\ *noun* [Spanish & Portuguese, feminine of *infante*] (1593)

: a daughter of a Spanish or Portuguese monarch

**in·fan·te** \in-'fan-tē, -'fän-(,)tā\ *noun* [Spanish & Portuguese, literally, infant, from Latin *infant-, infans*] (1555)

: a younger son of a Spanish or Portuguese monarch

**in·fan·ti·cide** \in-'fan-tə-,sīd\ *noun* [Late Latin *infanticidium*, from Latin *infant-, infans* + *-i-* + *-cidium* -cide] (circa 1656)

**1** : the killing of an infant

**2** [Late Latin *infanticida*, from Latin *infant-, infans* + *-i-* + *-cida* -cide] : one who kills an infant

— **in·fan·ti·ci·dal** \-,fan-tə-'sī-d°l\ *adjective*

**in·fan·tile** \'in-fən-,tīl, -t°l, -,tēl, -(,)til\ *adjective* (1696)

**1** : of or relating to infants or infancy

**2** : suitable to or characteristic of an infant; *especially* : very immature

— **in·fan·til·i·ty** \,in-fən-'ti-lə-tē\ *noun*

**infantile paralysis** *noun* (1843)

: POLIOMYELITIS

**in·fan·til·ism** \'in-fən-,tī-,li-zəm, -tə-,li-; in-'fan-t°l-,i-\ *noun* (1895)

**1** : retention of childish physical, mental, or emotional qualities in adult life; *especially* : failure to attain sexual maturity

**2** : an act or expression that indicates lack of maturity

**in·fan·til·ize** \'in-fən-,tī-,līz, -fən-t°l-,īz; in-'fan-t°l-,īz\ *transitive verb* **-ized; -iz·ing** (1943)

**1** : to make or keep infantile

**2** : to treat as if infantile

— **in·fan·til·i·za·tion** \,in-fən-,tī-lə-'zā-shən, -fən-t°l-ə-; in-,fan-t°l-ə-\ *noun*

**in·fan·tine** \'in-fən-,tīn, -,tēn\ *adjective* (1603)

: INFANTILE, CHILDISH

**in·fan·try** \'in-fən-trē\ *noun, plural* **-tries** [Middle French & Old Italian; Middle French *infanterie*, from Old Italian *infanteria*, from *infante* boy, foot soldier, from Latin *infant-, infans*] (1579)

**1 a** : soldiers trained, armed, and equipped to fight on foot **b** : a branch of an army composed of these soldiers

**2** : an infantry regiment or division ◊

**in·fan·try·man** \-trē-mən\ *noun* (1883)

: an infantry soldier

**infant school** *noun* (1824)

*British* : a school for children aged five to seven or eight

**in·farct** \'in-,färkt, in-'\ *noun* [Latin *infarctus*, past participle of *infarcire* to stuff, from *in-* + *farcire* to stuff] (1873)

: an area of necrosis in a tissue or organ resulting from obstruction of the local circulation by a thrombus or embolus

— **in·farct·ed** \in-'färk-təd\ *adjective*

— **in·farc·tion** \in-'färk-shən\ *noun*

**in·fare** \'in-,far, -,fer\ *noun* [Middle English, entrance, from Old English *infær*, from *in* + *fær* way, from *faran* to go — more at FARE] (1595)

*chiefly dialect* : a reception for a newly married couple

¹**in·fat·u·ate** \in-'fa-chə-wət\ *adjective* (15th century)

: being in an infatuated state or condition

²**in·fat·u·ate** \-,wāt\ *transitive verb* **-at·ed; -at·ing** [Latin *infatuatus*, past participle of *infatuare*, from *in-* + *fatuus* fatuous] (1533)

**1** : to cause to be foolish : deprive of sound judgment

**2** : to inspire with a foolish or extravagant love or admiration

— **in·fat·u·a·tion** \-,fa-chə-'wā-shən\ *noun*

**in·fau·na** \'in-,fȯ-nə, -,fä-\ *noun* [New Latin, from ²*in-* + *fauna*] (1914)

: benthic fauna living in the substrate and especially in a soft sea bottom — compare EPIFAUNA

— **in·fau·nal** \-,fȯ-n°l, -,fä-\ *adjective*

**in·fea·si·ble** \(,)in-'fē-zə-bəl\ *adjective* (1533)

: not feasible : IMPRACTICABLE

— **in·fea·si·bil·i·ty** \-,fē-zə-'bi-lə-tē\ *noun*

**in·fect** \in-'fekt\ *transitive verb* [Middle English, from Latin *infectus*, past participle of *inficere*, from *in-* + *facere* to make, do — more at DO] (14th century)

**1** : to contaminate with a disease-producing substance or agent (as bacteria)

**2 a** : to communicate a pathogen or a disease to **b** *of a pathogenic organism* : to invade (an individual or organ) usually by penetration **c** *of a computer virus* : to become transmitted and copied to (as a computer)

---

◊ **WORD HISTORY**

**infant**   To the frustrated parent of a sick, bawling infant incapable of saying just where it hurts, the etymology of *infant* must seem especially apt. In Latin the adjective *infans* literally meant "not speaking, incapable of speech." The noun *infans* designated a very young child who had not yet learned to talk. Later, however, the scope of *infans* was broadened to include any child, no matter how talkative. When the word was adopted into the Romance languages, the broader usage was carried over also. Like French, from which it had directly borrowed the word, English originally used *infant* for any child. Over time, English reverted to the earlier Latin sense, restricting *infant* to a child still young enough to be called a baby.

**infantry**   In the 20th century U.S. Army, the infantry's training film epithet is "queen of battle," and the combat infantryman's badge is a coveted mark of honor, though colloquialisms such as *dogface* and *grunt* express another viewpoint about the status of the ordinary foot soldier. The history of the word *infantry*, moreover, reveals a rather lowly origin for this branch of arms. The Italian word *fante*, descended from Latin *infans* "infant, child," originally meant "child," later "youth, boy," and then "servant." In the early 14th century, *fante* also took on the sense "foot soldier." In the High Middle Ages he was typically a lowly figure, who was often no more than a servant in a horseman's retinue and of little value on the battlefield. But in the 15th and 16th centuries the situation changed, as foot soldiers equipped first with longbows and crossbows and then with pikes and matchlock guns achieved dominance over mounted troops in cumbersome armor. The *fanteria*, that is, the *fanti* or foot soldiers collectively, became a significant branch of arms, and the Italian word, in the more Latinate form *infanteria*, was borrowed into French as *infanterie* in the 1500s and later in the same century into English as *infantry*.

---

\ə\ abut \ə\ kitten \ər\ further \a\ ash \ā\ ace
\ä\ mop, mar \au̇\ out \ch\ chin \e\ bet \ē\ easy
\g\ go \i\ hit \ī\ ice \j\ job \ŋ\ sing \ō\ go
\ȯ\ law \ȯi\ boy \th\ thin \th\ the \ü\ loot \u̇\ foot
\y\ yet \zh\ vision   *see also* Guide to Pronunciation

**3 a :** CONTAMINATE, CORRUPT ⟨the inflated writing that *infects* such stories⟩ **b :** to work upon or seize upon so as to induce sympathy, belief, or support ⟨trying to *infect* their salespeople with their enthusiasm⟩
— **in·fec·tor** \-'fek-tər\ *noun*
**in·fec·tion** \in-'fek-shən\ *noun* (14th century)
**1 :** the act or result of affecting injuriously
**2 :** an infective agent or material contaminated with an infective agent
**3 a :** the state produced by the establishment of an infective agent in or on a suitable host **b :** a disease resulting from infection
**4 :** an act or process of infecting; *also* **:** the establishment of a pathogen in its host after invasion
**5 :** the communication of emotions or qualities through example or contact
**in·fec·tious** \-shəs\ *adjective* (1542)
**1 a :** capable of causing infection **b :** communicable by infection — compare CONTAGIOUS
**2 :** that corrupts or contaminates
**3 :** spreading or capable of spreading rapidly to others ⟨their enthusiasm was *infectious*⟩ ⟨an *infectious* grin⟩
— **in·fec·tious·ly** *adverb*
— **in·fec·tious·ness** *noun*
**infectious hepatitis** *noun* (circa 1941)
**:** HEPATITIS A
**infectious mononucleosis** *noun* (1920)
**:** an acute infectious disease associated with Epstein-Barr virus and characterized by fever, swelling of lymph nodes, and lymphocytosis
**in·fec·tive** \in-'fek-tiv\ *adjective* (14th century)
**1 :** producing or capable of producing infection
**2 :** affecting others **:** INFECTIOUS
— **in·fec·tiv·i·ty** \(,)in-,fek-'ti-və-tē\ *noun*
**in·fe·lic·i·tous** \,in-fi-'li-sə-təs\ *adjective* (1835)
**:** not appropriate in application or expression
— **in·fe·lic·i·tous·ly** *adverb*
**in·fe·lic·i·ty** \-sə-tē\ *noun, plural* **-ties** [Middle English *infelicite* unhappiness, from Latin *infelicitas,* from *infelic-, infelix* unhappy, from *in-* + *felic-, felix* fruitful — more at FEMININE] (1617)
**1 :** the quality or state of being infelicitous
**2 :** something that is infelicitous
**in·fer** \in-'fər\ *verb* **in·ferred; in·fer·ring** [Middle French or Latin; Middle French *inferer,* from Latin *inferre,* literally, to carry or bring into, from *in-* + *ferre* to carry — more at BEAR] (1528)
*transitive verb*
**1 :** to derive as a conclusion from facts or premises ⟨we see smoke and *infer* fire —L. A. White⟩ — compare IMPLY
**2 :** GUESS, SURMISE ⟨your letter . . . allows me to *infer* that you are as well as ever —O. W. Holmes (died 1935)⟩
**3 a :** to involve as a normal outcome of thought **b :** to point out **:** INDICATE ⟨this doth *infer* the zeal I had to see him —Shakespeare⟩
**4 :** SUGGEST, HINT ⟨another survey . . . *infers* that two-thirds of all present computer installations are not paying for themselves —H. R. Chellman⟩
*intransitive verb*
**:** to draw inferences ⟨men . . . have observed, *inferred,* and reasoned . . . to all kinds of results —John Dewey⟩ ☆ ▪
— **in·fer·able** *also* **in·fer·ri·ble** \in-'fər-ə-bəl\ *adjective*
— **in·fer·rer** \-'fər-ər\ *noun*
**in·fer·ence** \'in-f(ə-)rən(t)s, -fərn(t)s\ *noun* (1594)
**1 :** the act or process of inferring: as **a :** the act of passing from one proposition, statement, or judgment considered as true to another whose truth is believed to follow from that of the former **b :** the act of passing from statistical sample data to generalizations (as of the value of population parameters) usually with calculated degrees of certainty

**2 :** something that is inferred; *especially* **:** a proposition arrived at by inference
**3 :** the premises and conclusion of a process of inferring
**in·fer·en·tial** \,in-fə-'ren(t)-shəl\ *adjective* [Medieval Latin *inferentia,* from Latin *inferent-, inferens,* present participle of *inferre*] (1657)
**1 :** relating to, involving, or resembling inference
**2 :** deduced or deducible by inference
**in·fer·en·tial·ly** \-'ren(t)-sh(ə-)lē\ *adverb* (1691)
**:** by way of inference **:** through inference
**in·fe·ri·or** \in-'fir-ē-ər\ *adjective* [Middle English, from Latin, comparative of *inferus* lower — more at UNDER] (15th century)
**1 :** situated lower down **:** LOWER
**2 a :** of low or lower degree or rank **b :** of poor quality **:** MEDIOCRE
**3 :** of little or less importance, value, or merit ⟨always felt *inferior* to his older brother⟩
**4 a :** situated below another and especially another similar superior part of an upright body **b :** situated in a relatively low posterior or ventral position in a quadrupedal body **c** (1) **:** situated below another plant part or organ (2) **:** ABAXIAL
**5 :** relating to or being a subscript
— **inferior** *noun*
— **in·fe·ri·or·i·ty** \(,)in-,fir-ē-'ór-ə-tē, -'är-\ *noun*
— **in·fe·ri·or·ly** \in-'fir-ē-ər-lē\ *adverb*
**inferior conjunction** *noun* (1833)
**:** a conjunction of an inferior planet with the sun in which the planet is aligned between the earth and the sun
**inferiority complex** *noun* (1922)
**1 :** an acute sense of personal inferiority often resulting either in timidity or through overcompensation in exaggerated aggressiveness
**2 :** a collective sense of cultural, regional, or national inferiority
**inferior planet** *noun* (1658)
**:** either of the planets Mercury and Venus whose orbits lie within that of the earth
**in·fer·nal** \in-'fər-nᵊl\ *adjective* [Middle English, from Middle French, from Late Latin *infernalis,* from *infernus* hell, from Latin, lower, from *inferus*] (14th century)
**1 :** of or relating to a nether world of the dead
**2 a :** of or relating to hell **b :** HELLISH, DIABOLICAL
**3 :** DAMNABLE ⟨an *infernal* nuisance⟩
— **in·fer·nal·ly** \-nᵊl-ē\ *adverb*
**infernal machine** *noun* (1810)
**:** a machine or apparatus maliciously designed to explode and destroy life or property; *especially* **:** a concealed or disguised bomb
**in·fer·no** \in-'fər-(,)nō\ *noun, plural* **-nos** [Italian, hell, from Late Latin *infernus*] (1834)
**:** a place or a state that resembles or suggests hell ⟨the *inferno* of war⟩; *also* **:** intense heat ⟨the roaring *inferno* of the blast furnace⟩
**in·fer·tile** \(')in-'fər-tᵊl\ *adjective* [Middle French, from Late Latin *infertilis,* from Latin *in-* + *fertilis* fertile] (1597)
**:** not fertile or productive ⟨*infertile* eggs⟩ ⟨*infertile* fields⟩
— **in·fer·til·i·ty** \,in-(,)fər-'ti-lə-tē\ *noun*
**in·fest** \in-'fest\ *transitive verb* [French *infester,* from Latin *infestare,* from *infestus* hostile] (1602)
**1 :** to spread or swarm in or over in a troublesome manner ⟨a slum *infested* with crime⟩ ⟨shark-*infested* waters⟩
**2 :** to live in or on as a parasite
— **in·fes·tant** \-'fes-tənt\ *noun*
— **in·fes·ta·tion** \,in-,fes-'tā-shən\ *noun*
— **in·fest·er** \in-'fes-tər\ *noun*
**in·fi·del** \'in-fə-dᵊl, -fə-,del\ *noun* [Middle English *infidele,* from Middle French, from Late Latin *infidelis* unbelieving, from Latin, unfaithful, from *in-* + *fidelis* faithful — more at FIDELITY] (15th century)

**1 :** one who is not a Christian or who opposes Christianity
**2 a :** an unbeliever with respect to a particular religion **b :** one who acknowledges no religious belief
**3 :** a disbeliever in something specified or understood
— **infidel** *adjective*
**in·fi·del·i·ty** \,in-fə-'de-lə-tē, -(,)fī-\ *noun, plural* **-ties** (15th century)
**1 :** lack of belief in a religion
**2 a :** unfaithfulness to a moral obligation **:** DISLOYALTY **b :** marital unfaithfulness or an instance of it
**in·field** \'in-,fēld\ *noun* (1606)
**1 :** a field near a farmhouse
**2 a :** the area of a baseball field enclosed by the three bases and home plate **b :** the defensive positions comprising first base, second base, shortstop, and third base; *also* **:** the players who play these positions
**3 :** the area enclosed by a racetrack or running track
**in·field·er** \-,fēl-dər\ *noun* (1867)
**:** a baseball player who plays in the infield
**infield hit** *noun* (1912)
**:** a base hit on a ball that does not leave the infield
**infield out** *noun* (1926)
**:** a ground ball on which the batter is put out by an infielder
**in·fight·ing** \'in-,fī-tiŋ\ *noun* (1816)

---

☆ **SYNONYMS**
**Infer, deduce, conclude, judge, gather** mean to arrive at a mental conclusion. IN-FER implies arriving at a conclusion by reasoning from evidence; if the evidence is slight, the term comes close to *surmise* ⟨from that remark, I *inferred* that they knew each other⟩. DEDUCE often adds to INFER the special implication of drawing a particular inference from a generalization ⟨denied we could *deduce* anything important from human mortality⟩. CONCLUDE implies arriving at a necessary inference at the end of a chain of reasoning ⟨*concluded* that only the accused could be guilty⟩. JUDGE stresses a weighing of the evidence on which a conclusion is based ⟨*judge* people by their actions⟩. GATH-ER suggests an intuitive forming of a conclusion from implications ⟨*gathered* their desire to be alone without a word⟩.

---

□ **USAGE**
**infer** Sir Thomas More is the first writer known to have used both *infer* and *imply* in their approved senses (1528). He is also the first to have used *infer* in a sense close in meaning to *imply* (1533). Both of these uses of *infer* coexisted without comment until some time around the end of World War I. Since then, senses 3 and 4 of *infer* have been frequently condemned as an undesirable blurring of a useful distinction. The actual blurring has been done by the commentators. Sense 3, descended from More's use of 1533, does not occur with a personal subject. When objections arose, they were to a use with a personal subject (now sense 4). Since dictionaries did not recognize this use specifically, the objectors assumed that sense 3 was the one they found illogical, even though it had been in respectable use for four centuries. The actual usage condemned was a spoken one never used in logical discourse. At present sense 4 is found in print chiefly in letters to the editor and other informal prose, not in serious intellectual writing. The controversy over sense 4 has apparently reduced the frequency of use of sense 3.

**1 :** fighting or boxing at close quarters
**2 :** rough-and-tumble fighting
**3 :** prolonged and often bitter dissension or rivalry among members of a group or organization ⟨bureaucratic *infighting*⟩
— **in·fight** \'in-,fīt\ *intransitive verb*
— **in·fight·er** \-,fī-tər\ *noun*

**in·fil·trate** \in-'fil-,trāt, 'in-(,)\ *verb* **-trat·ed; -trat·ing** (1758)
*transitive verb*
**1 :** to cause (as a liquid) to permeate something by penetrating its pores or interstices
**2 :** to pass into or through (a substance) by filtering or permeating
**3 :** to pass (troops) singly or in small groups through gaps in the enemy line
**4 :** to enter or become established in gradually or unobtrusively usually for subversive purposes ⟨the intelligence staff had been *infiltrated* by spies⟩
*intransitive verb*
**:** to enter, permeate, or pass through a substance or area by filtering or by insinuating gradually
— **infiltrate** *noun*
— **in·fil·tra·tion** \,in-(,)fil-'trā-shən\ *noun*
— **in·fil·tra·tive** \'in-(,)fil-,trā-tiv, in-'fil-trə-\ *adjective*
— **in·fil·tra·tor** \in-'fil-,trā-tər, 'in-(,)\ *noun*

**¹in·fi·nite** \'in-fə-nət\ *adjective* [Middle English *infinit*, from Middle French or Latin; Middle French, from Latin *infinitus*, from *in-* + *finitus* finite] (14th century)
**1 :** extending indefinitely **:** ENDLESS ⟨*infinite* space⟩
**2 :** immeasurably or inconceivably great or extensive **:** INEXHAUSTIBLE ⟨*infinite* patience⟩
**3 :** subject to no limitation or external determination
**4 a :** extending beyond, lying beyond, or being greater than any preassigned finite value however large ⟨*infinite* number of positive numbers⟩ **b :** extending to infinity ⟨*infinite* plane surface⟩ **c :** characterized by an infinite number of elements or terms ⟨an *infinite* set⟩ ⟨an *infinite* series⟩
— **in·fi·nite·ly** *adverb*
— **in·fi·nite·ness** *noun*

**²infinite** *noun* (1535)
**:** something that is infinite (as in extent, duration, or number)

**¹in·fin·i·tes·i·mal** \(,)in-,fi-nə-'te-sə-məl, -zə-məl\ *noun* [New Latin *infinitesimus* infinite in rank, from Latin *infinitus*] (1706)
**:** an infinitesimal quantity or variable

**²infinitesimal** *adjective* (1710)
**1 :** taking on values arbitrarily close to but greater than zero
**2 :** immeasurably or incalculably small
— **in·fin·i·tes·i·mal·ly** \-mə-lē\ *adverb*

**infinitesimal calculus** *noun* (1801)
**:** CALCULUS 1b

**in·fin·i·ti·val** \(,)in-,fi-nə-'tī-vəl\ *adjective* (1869)
**:** relating to the infinitive

**¹in·fin·i·tive** \in-'fi-nə-tiv\ *adjective* [Middle English *infinityf*, from Late Latin *infinitivus*, from Latin *infinitus*] (15th century)
**:** formed with the infinitive
— **in·fin·i·tive·ly** *adverb*

**²infinitive** *noun* (1530)
**:** a verb form normally identical in English with the first person singular that performs some functions of a noun and at the same time displays some characteristics of a verb and that is used with *to* (as in "I asked him *to go*") except with auxiliary and various other verbs (as in "no one saw him *leave*")

**in·fin·i·tude** \in-'fi-nə-,tüd, -,tyüd\ *noun* (1641)
**1 :** the quality or state of being infinite **:** INFINITENESS
**2 :** something that is infinite especially in extent
**3 :** an infinite number or quantity

**in·fin·i·ty** \in-'fi-nə-tē\ *noun, plural* **-ties** (14th century)

---

**1 a :** the quality of being infinite **b :** unlimited extent of time, space, or quantity **:** BOUNDLESSNESS
**2 :** an indefinitely great number or amount ⟨an *infinity* of stars⟩
**3 a :** the limit of the value of a function or variable when it tends to become numerically larger than any preassigned finite number **b :** a part of a geometric magnitude that lies beyond any part whose distance from a given reference position is finite ⟨do parallel lines ever meet if they extend to *infinity*⟩ **c :** a transfinite number (as aleph-null)
**4 :** a distance so great that the rays of light from a point source at that distance may be regarded as parallel

**in·firm** \in-'fərm\ *adjective* [Middle English, from Latin *infirmus*, from *in-* + *firmus* firm] (14th century)
**1 :** of poor or deteriorated vitality; *especially* **:** feeble from age
**2 :** weak of mind, will, or character **:** IRRESOLUTE, VACILLATING
**3 :** not solid or stable **:** INSECURE
*synonym* see WEAK
— **in·firm·ly** *adverb*

**in·fir·ma·ry** \in-'fərm-rē, -'fər-mə-\ *noun, plural* **-ries** (15th century)
**:** a place where the infirm or sick are lodged for care and treatment

**in·fir·mi·ty** \in-'fər-mə-tē\ *noun, plural* **-ties** (14th century)
**1 a :** the quality or state of being infirm **b :** the condition of being feeble **:** FRAILTY
**2 :** DISEASE, MALADY
**3 :** a personal failing **:** FOIBLE ⟨one of the besetting *infirmities* of living creatures is egotism —A. J. Toynbee⟩

**¹in·fix** \'in-,fiks, in-'\ *transitive verb* [Latin *infixus*, past participle of *infigere*, from *in-* + *figere* to fasten — more at FIX] (1502)
**1 :** to fasten or fix by piercing or thrusting in
**2 :** to impress firmly in the consciousness or disposition
**3 :** to insert (as a sound or letter) as an infix
*synonym* see IMPLANT
— **in·fix·a·tion** \,in-(,)fik-'sā-shən\ *noun*

**²in·fix** \'in-,fiks\ *noun* (1881)
**:** a derivational or inflectional affix appearing in the body of a word (as Sanskrit *-n-* in *vindami* "I know" as contrasted with *vid* "to know")

**³in·fix** \*same as* ²\ *adjective* (1971)
**:** characterized by placement of a binary operator between the operands ⟨*a + b* is expressed in *infix* notation⟩ — compare POSTFIX, PREFIX

**in fla·gran·te de·lic·to** \,in-flə-,grän-tē-di-'lik-(,)tō, -,gran-\ *adverb* (1772)
**:** FLAGRANTE DELICTO

**in·flame** \in-'flām\ *verb* **in·flamed; in·flaming** [Middle English *enflamen*, from Middle French *enflamer*, from Latin *inflammare*, from *in-* + *flamma* flame] (14th century)
*transitive verb*
**1 a :** to excite to excessive or uncontrollable action or feeling **b :** to make more heated or violent **:** INTENSIFY ⟨insults served only to *inflame* the feud⟩
**2 :** to set on fire **:** KINDLE
**3 :** to cause to redden or grow hot from anger or excitement
**4 :** to cause inflammation in (bodily tissue)
*intransitive verb*
**1 :** to burst into flame
**2 :** to become excited or angered
**3 :** to become affected with inflammation
— **in·flam·er** *noun*

**in·flam·ma·ble** \in-'fla-mə-bəl\ *adjective* [French, from Medieval Latin *inflammabilis*, from Latin *inflammare*] (1605)
**1 :** FLAMMABLE
**2 :** easily inflamed, excited, or angered **:** IRASCIBLE
— **in·flam·ma·bil·i·ty** \-,fla-mə-'bi-lə-tē\ *noun*
— **inflammable** *noun*

---

— **in·flam·ma·ble·ness** \-'fla-mə-bəl-nəs\ *noun*
— **in·flam·ma·bly** \-blē\ *adverb*

**in·flam·ma·tion** \,in-flə-'mā-shən\ *noun* (15th century)
**1 :** a local response to cellular injury that is marked by capillary dilatation, leukocytic infiltration, redness, heat, and pain and that serves as a mechanism initiating the elimination of noxious agents and of damaged tissue
**2 :** the act of inflaming **:** the state of being inflamed

**in·flam·ma·to·ry** \in-'fla-mə-,tōr-ē, -,tȯr-\ *adjective* (circa 1711)
**1 :** tending to excite anger, disorder, or tumult **:** SEDITIOUS
**2 :** tending to inflame or excite the senses
**3 :** accompanied by or tending to cause inflammation
— **in·flam·ma·to·ri·ly** \-,fla-mə-'tōr-ə-lē, -'tȯr-\ *adverb*

**in·flat·able** \in-'flā-tə-bəl\ *adjective* (1878)
**:** capable of being inflated ⟨an *inflatable* boat⟩
— **inflatable** *noun*

**in·flate** \in-'flāt\ *verb* **in·flat·ed; in·flat·ing** [Middle English, from Latin *inflatus*, past participle of *inflare*, from *in-* + *flare* to blow — more at BLOW] (15th century)
*transitive verb*
**1 :** to swell or distend with air or gas
**2 :** to puff up **:** ELATE
**3 :** to expand or increase abnormally or imprudently
*intransitive verb*
**:** to become inflated
*synonym* see EXPAND
— **in·fla·tor** *or* **in·flat·er** \-'flā-tər\ *noun*

**inflated** *adjective* (1652)
**1 :** elaborated or heightened by artificial or empty means ⟨an *inflated* style of writing⟩
**2 :** distended with air or gas
**3 :** expanded to an abnormal or unjustifiable volume or level ⟨*inflated* prices⟩
**4 :** being hollow and enlarged or distended

**in·fla·tion** \in-'flā-shən\ *noun* (14th century)
**1 :** an act of inflating **:** a state of being inflated: as **a :** DISTENSION **b :** a hypothetical extremely brief period of very rapid expansion of the universe immediately following the big bang **c :** empty pretentiousness **:** POMPOSITY
**2 :** an increase in the volume of money and credit relative to available goods and services resulting in a continuing rise in the general price level

**in·fla·tion·ary** \-shə-,ner-ē\ *adjective* (1920)
**:** of, characterized by, or productive of inflation

**inflationary spiral** *noun* (1931)
**:** a continuous rise in prices that is sustained by the tendency of wage increases and cost increases to react on each other

**in·fla·tion·ism** \in-'flā-shə-,ni-zəm\ *noun* (1919)
**:** the policy of economic inflation
— **in·fla·tion·ist** \-sh(ə-)nist\ *noun or adjective*

**in·flect** \in-'flekt\ *verb* [Middle English, from Latin *inflectere*, from *in-* + *flectere* to bend] (15th century)
*transitive verb*
**1 :** to turn from a direct line or course **:** CURVE
**2 :** to vary (a word) by inflection **:** DECLINE, CONJUGATE
**3 :** to change or vary the pitch of (as the voice)
*intransitive verb*
**:** to become modified by inflection
— **in·flect·able** \-'flek-tə-bəl\ *adjective*
— **in·flec·tive** \-'flek-tiv\ *adjective*

---

**in·flec·tion** \in-'flek-shən\ noun (1531)
**1** : the act or result of curving or bending : BEND
**2** : change in pitch or loudness of the voice
**3 a** : the change of form that words undergo to mark such distinctions as those of case, gender, number, tense, person, mood, or voice **b** : a form, suffix, or element involved in such variation **c** : ACCIDENCE
**4 a** : change in curvature of an arc or curve from concave to convex or conversely **b** : IN-FLECTION POINT

**in·flec·tion·al** \-shnəl, -shə-n°l\ adjective (1832)
: of, relating to, or characterized by inflection ⟨an inflectional suffix⟩
— **in·flec·tion·al·ly** adverb

**inflection point** noun (circa 1721)
: a point on a curve that separates an arc concave upward from one concave downward and vice versa

**in·flexed** \'in-,flekst\ adjective [Latin inflexus, past participle of inflectere] (1661)
: bent or turned abruptly inward or downward or toward the axis ⟨inflexed petals⟩

**in·flex·i·ble** \(,)in-'flek-sə-bəl\ adjective [Middle English, from Latin inflexibilis, from in- + flexibilis flexible] (14th century)
**1** : rigidly firm in will or purpose : UNYIELDING
**2** : not readily bent : lacking or deficient in suppleness
**3** : incapable of change : UNALTERABLE ☆
— **in·flex·i·bil·i·ty** \-,flek-sə-'bi-lə-tē\ noun
— **in·flex·i·ble·ness** \-'flek-sə-bəl-nəs\ noun
— **in·flex·i·bly** \-blē\ adverb

**in·flex·ion** chiefly British variant of INFLECTION

**in·flict** \in-'flikt\ transitive verb [Latin inflictus, past participle of infligere, from in- + fligere to strike — more at PROFLIGATE] (1566)
**1** : AFFLICT
**2 a** : to give by or as if by striking ⟨inflict pain⟩ **b** : to cause (something unpleasant) to be endured ⟨inflict my annual message upon the church —Mark Twain⟩
— **in·flict·er** or **in·flic·tor** \-'flik-tər\ noun
— **in·flic·tive** \-tiv\ adjective

**in·flic·tion** \in-'flik-shən\ noun (1534)
**1** : the act of inflicting
**2** : something (as punishment or suffering) that is inflicted

**in·flight** \'in-'flīt\ (,)in-\ adjective (1944)
: made, carried out, or provided for use or enjoyment while in flight ⟨in-flight movies⟩

**in·flo·res·cence** \,in-flə-'re-s°n(t)s\ noun [New Latin inflorescentia, from Late Latin inflorescent-, inflorescens, present participle of inflorescere to begin to bloom, from Latin in- + florescere to begin to bloom — more at FLORESCENCE] (1760)
**1 a** (1) : the mode of development and arrangement of flowers on an axis (2) : a floral axis with its appendages; also : a flower cluster **b** : a cluster of reproductive organs in a moss usually subtended by a bract

inflorescence 1a(1): *1* raceme, *2* corymb, *3* umbel, *4* compound umbel, *5* capitulum, *6* spike, *7* compound spike, *8* panicle, *9* cyme

**2** : the budding and unfolding of blossoms : FLOWERING

**in·flow** \'in-,flō\ noun (1839)
: a flowing in ⟨the inflow of air⟩ ⟨an inflow of funds⟩

**¹in·flu·ence** \'in-,flü-ən(t)s, especially Southern in-'\ noun [Middle English, from Middle French, from Medieval Latin influentia, from Latin influent-, influens, present participle of influere to flow in, from in- + fluere to flow — more at FLUID] (14th century)
**1 a** : an ethereal fluid held to flow from the stars and to affect the actions of humans **b** : an emanation of occult power held to derive from stars
**2** : an emanation of spiritual or moral force
**3 a** : the act or power of producing an effect without apparent exertion of force or direct exercise of command **b** : corrupt interference with authority for personal gain
**4** : the power or capacity of causing an effect in indirect or intangible ways : SWAY
**5** : one that exerts influence ☆
— **under the influence** : affected by alcohol : DRUNK ⟨was arrested for driving under the influence⟩

**²influence** transitive verb **-enced; -enc·ing** (1658)
**1** : to affect or alter by indirect or intangible means : SWAY
**2** : to have an effect on the condition or development of : MODIFY
**synonym** see AFFECT
— **in·flu·ence·able** \-ən(t)-sə-bəl\ adjective

**¹in·flu·ent** \'in-,flü-ənt, in-'\ adjective (15th century)
: flowing in

**²influent** noun (1859)
**1** : something that flows in: as **a** : a tributary stream **b** : fluid input into a reservoir or process
**2** : a factor (as a particular animal) modifying the balance and stability of an ecological community

**¹in·flu·en·tial** \,in-(,)flü-'en(t)-shəl\ adjective (1570)
: exerting or possessing influence
— **in·flu·en·tial·ly** \-'en(t)-sh(ə-)lē\ adverb

**²influential** noun (1831)
: one who has great influence

**in·flu·en·za** \,in-(,)flü-'en-zə\ noun [Italian, literally, influence, from Medieval Latin influentia; from the belief that epidemics were due to the influence of the stars] (1743)
**1** : an acute highly contagious virus disease caused by various strains of a myxovirus (family Orthomyxoviridae) and characterized by sudden onset, fever, prostration, severe aches and pains, and progressive inflammation of the respiratory mucous membrane; broadly : a human respiratory infection of undetermined cause
**2** : any of numerous febrile usually virus diseases of domestic animals marked by respiratory symptoms, inflammation of mucous membranes, and often systemic involvement ◆
— **in·flu·en·zal** \-zəl\ adjective

**in·flux** \'in-,fləks\ noun [Medieval Latin influxus, from Latin influere] (1626)
: a coming in ⟨an influx of tourists⟩

**in·fo** \'in-(,)fō\ noun (1913)
: INFORMATION

**in·fold** \in-'fōld\ (15th century)
transitive verb
: ENFOLD, ENVELOP
intransitive verb
: to fold inward or toward one another

**in·fo·mer·cial** \'in-(,)fō-,mər-shəl, -fə-\ noun [information + ²commercial] (1981)
: a television program that is an extended advertisement often including a discussion or demonstration

**in·form** \in-'form\ verb [Middle English, from Middle French enformer, from Latin informare, from in- + forma form] (14th century)
transitive verb
**1** obsolete : to give material form to
**2 a** : to give character or essence to ⟨the principles which inform modern teaching⟩ **b** : to be the characteristic quality of : ANIMATE ⟨the compassion that informs her work⟩
**3** obsolete : GUIDE, DIRECT
**4** obsolete : to make known
**5** : to communicate knowledge to ⟨inform a prisoner of his rights⟩
intransitive verb
**1** : to impart information or knowledge
**2** : to give information (as of another's wrongdoing) to an authority ☆

---

☆ SYNONYMS

**Inflexible, obdurate, adamant** mean unwilling to alter a predetermined course or purpose. INFLEXIBLE implies rigid adherence or even slavish conformity to principle ⟨inflexible in their demands⟩. OBDURATE stresses hardness of heart and insensitivity to appeals for mercy or the influence of divine grace ⟨obdurate in his refusal to grant clemency⟩. ADAMANT implies utter immovability in the face of all temptation or entreaty ⟨adamant that the work should continue⟩. See in addition STIFF.

**Influence, authority, prestige, weight, credit** mean power exerted over the minds or behavior of others. INFLUENCE may apply to a force exercised and received consciously or unconsciously ⟨used her influence to get the bill passed⟩. AUTHORITY implies the power of winning devotion or allegiance or of compelling acceptance and belief ⟨his opinions lacked authority⟩. PRESTIGE implies the ascendancy given by conspicuous excellence or reputation for superiority ⟨the prestige of the newspaper⟩. WEIGHT implies measurable or decisive influence in determining acts or choices ⟨their wishes obviously carried much weight⟩. CREDIT suggests influence that arises from the confidence of others ⟨his credit with the press⟩.

---

◇ WORD HISTORY

**influenza** The Italian word *influenza* was, like English *influence*, originally an astrological term. The effect that the stars and planets were assumed to have on humans was ascribed in a sometimes literal, sometimes metaphorical way to the "inflow" of some ethereal liquid from the heavens. Also like the English word, *influenza* came to denote any sort of effect produced without seeming exertion by its source, but the Italian word in the Middle Ages was also applied more narrowly to outbreaks of disease supposedly brought about by unusual conjunctions of the planets. In the 17th and 18th centuries, the scope of *influenza* narrowed still further, to refer specifically to the infectious disease we now call by this name. The word first appeared in English through reports of an influenza outbreak in Italy during the winter of 1743, and it reappeared in reports of the major European epidemics of 1761–62 and 1802–03, when the disease also reached Britain. In 1933, after the great influenza pandemic of 1918–19 had killed half a million people in the U.S., American and British researchers identified the myxovirus that causes the disease.

**in·for·mal** \(ˌ)in-ˈfȯr-məl\ *adjective* (1585)
**1 :** marked by the absence of formality or ceremony ⟨an *informal* meeting⟩ ⟨an *informal* group⟩
**2 :** characteristic of or appropriate to ordinary, casual, or familiar use ⟨*informal* English⟩ ⟨*informal* clothes⟩
— **in·for·mal·i·ty** \-(ˌ)fȯr-ˈma-lə-tē, -fər-\ *noun*
— **in·for·mal·ly** \-ˈfȯr-mə-lē\ *adverb*
**in·for·mant** \in-ˈfȯr-mənt\ *noun* (1693)
**:** a person who gives information: as **a :** IN-FORMER **b :** one who supplies cultural or linguistic data in response to interrogation by an investigator
**in for·ma pau·pe·ris** \ˌin-ˌfȯr-mə-ˈpȯ-pə-rəs, -ˈpau̇-\ *adjective or adverb* [Latin, in the form of a pauper] (1592)
**:** as a poor person
**in·for·mat·ics** \ˌin-fər-ˈma-tiks\ *noun plural but singular in construction* [International Scientific Vocabulary *informa*tion + *-ics*] (circa 1967)
*chiefly British* **:** INFORMATION SCIENCE
**in·for·ma·tion** \ˌin-fər-ˈmā-shən\ *noun* (14th century)
**1 :** the communication or reception of knowledge or intelligence
**2 a** (1) **:** knowledge obtained from investigation, study, or instruction (2) **:** INTELLIGENCE, NEWS (3) **:** FACTS, DATA **b :** the attribute inherent in and communicated by one of two or more alternative sequences or arrangements of something (as nucleotides in DNA or binary digits in a computer program) that produce specific effects **c** (1) **:** a signal or character (as in a communication system or computer) representing data (2) **:** something (as a message, experimental data, or a picture) which justifies change in a construct (as a plan or theory) that represents physical or mental experience or another construct **d :** a quantitative measure of the content of information; *specifically* **:** a numerical quantity that measures the uncertainty in the outcome of an experiment to be performed
**3 :** the act of informing against a person
**4 :** a formal accusation of a crime made by a prosecuting officer as distinguished from an indictment presented by a grand jury
— **in·for·ma·tion·al** \-shnəl, -shə-nᵊl\ *adjective*
— **in·for·ma·tion·al·ly** *adverb*
**information retrieval** *noun* (1950)
**:** the techniques of storing and recovering and often disseminating recorded data especially through the use of a computerized system
**information science** *noun* (1960)
**:** the collection, classification, storage, retrieval, and dissemination of recorded knowledge treated both as a pure and as an applied science
**information theory** *noun* (1950)
**:** a theory that deals statistically with information, with the measurement of its content in terms of its distinguishing essential characteristics or by the number of alternatives from which it makes a choice possible, and with the efficiency of processes of communication between humans and machines
**in·for·ma·tive** \in-ˈfȯr-mə-tiv\ *adjective* (1655)
**:** imparting knowledge **:** INSTRUCTIVE
— **in·for·ma·tive·ly** *adverb*
— **in·for·ma·tive·ness** *noun*
**in·for·ma·to·ry** \-mə-ˌtȯr-ē, -ˌtȯr-\ *adjective* (circa 1879)
**:** conveying information
— **in·for·ma·to·ri·ly** \in-ˌfȯr-mə-ˈtȯr-ə-lē, -ˈtȯr-\ *adverb*
**in·formed** \in-ˈfȯrmd\ *adjective* (15th century)
**1 a :** having information ⟨*informed* sources⟩ ⟨*informed* observers⟩ **b :** based on possession of information ⟨an *informed* opinion⟩

**2 :** EDUCATED, KNOWLEDGEABLE ⟨what the *informed* person should know⟩
— **in·formed·ly** \-ˈfȯrmd-lē, -ˈfȯr-məd-lē\ *adverb*
**informed consent** *noun* (circa 1967)
**:** consent to surgery by a patient or to participation in a medical experiment by a subject after achieving an understanding of what is involved
**in·form·er** \in-ˈfȯr-mər\ *noun* (14th century)
**1 :** one that imparts knowledge or news
**2 :** one that informs against another; *specifically* **:** one who makes a practice especially for a financial reward of informing against others for violations of penal laws
**in·fo·tain·ment** \ˌin-(ˌ)fō-ˈtān-mənt\ *noun* [*info*rmation + enter*tainment*] (1982)
**:** a television program that presents information (as news) in a manner intended to be entertaining
**in·fra** \ˈin-frə *also* -ˌfrä\ *adverb* [Latin] (circa 1740)
**:** later in this writing **:** BELOW ⟨for additional examples see *infra*⟩
**infra-** *prefix* [Latin *infra* — more at UNDER]
**1 :** below ⟨*infra*human⟩ ⟨*infra*sonic⟩
**2 :** within ⟨*infra*specific⟩
**3 :** below in a scale or series ⟨*infra*red⟩
**in·frac·tion** \in-ˈfrak-shən\ *noun* [Middle English, from Medieval Latin *infraction-, infractio*, from Latin, subduing, from *infringere* to break — more at INFRINGE] (15th century)
**:** the act of infringing **:** VIOLATION
— **in·fract** \in-ˈfrakt\ *transitive verb*
**in·fra dig** \ˈin-frə-ˈdig, -(ˌ)frä-\ *adjective* [short for Latin *infra dignitatem*] (1824)
**:** being beneath one's dignity **:** UNDIGNIFIED ⟨while his work . . . was financially profitable, it was just a bit *infra dig* —John McCarten⟩
**in·fra·hu·man** \ˌin-frə-ˈhyü-mən, -(ˌ)frä-, -ˈyü-\ *adjective* (1847)
**:** less or lower than human ⟨*infrahuman* primates⟩
— **infrahuman** *noun*
**in·fran·gi·ble** \(ˌ)in-ˈfran-jə-bəl\ *adjective* [Middle French, from Late Latin *infrangibilis*, from Latin *in-* + *frangere* to break — more at BREAK] (1597)
**1 :** not capable of being broken or separated into parts
**2 :** not to be infringed or violated
— **in·fran·gi·bil·i·ty** \-ˌfran-jə-ˈbi-lə-tē\ *noun*
— **in·fran·gi·bly** \-ˈfran-jə-blē\ *adverb*
**in·fra·red** \ˌin-frə-ˈred, -(ˌ)frä-, -fə-\ *adjective* (1881)
**1 :** situated outside the visible spectrum at its red end — used of radiation having a wavelength between about 700 nanometers and 1 millimeter
**2 :** relating to, producing, or employing infrared radiation ⟨*infrared* therapy⟩
**3 :** sensitive to infrared radiation ⟨*infrared* photographic film⟩
— **infrared** *noun*
**in·fra·son·ic** \ˌin-frə-ˈsä-nik, -(ˌ)frä-\ *adjective* (1927)
**1 :** having or relating to a frequency below the audibility range of the human ear
**2 :** utilizing or produced by infrasonic waves or vibrations
**in·fra·spe·cif·ic** \-spi-ˈsi-fik\ *adjective* (1939)
**:** included within a species ⟨*infraspecific* variability⟩
**in·fra·struc·ture** \ˈin-frə-ˌstrək-chər, -(ˌ)frä-\ *noun* (1927)
**1 :** the underlying foundation or basic framework (as of a system or organization)
**2 :** the permanent installations required for military purposes
**3 :** the system of public works of a country, state, or region; *also* **:** the resources (as personnel, buildings, or equipment) required for an activity

**in·fre·quence** \(ˌ)in-ˈfrē-kwən(t)s\ *noun* (1644)
**:** INFREQUENCY
**in·fre·quen·cy** \-kwən(t)-sē\ *noun* (1677)
**:** rarity of occurrence
**in·fre·quent** \(ˌ)in-ˈfrē-kwənt\ *adjective* [Latin *infrequent-, infrequens*, from *in-* + *frequent-, frequens* frequent] (1531)
**1 :** seldom happening or occurring **:** RARE
**2 :** placed or occurring at wide intervals in space or time ⟨a slope scattered with *infrequent* pines⟩ ⟨*infrequent* visits⟩ ☆
— **in·fre·quent·ly** *adverb*
**in·fringe** \in-ˈfrinj\ *verb* **in·fringed; in·fring·ing** [Medieval Latin *infringere*, from Latin, to break, crush, from *in-* + *frangere* to break — more at BREAK] (1533)
*transitive verb*
**1 :** to encroach upon in a way that violates law or the rights of another ⟨*infringe* a patent⟩
**2** *obsolete* **:** DEFEAT, FRUSTRATE
*intransitive verb*
**:** ENCROACH — used with *on* or *upon* ⟨*infringe* on our rights⟩
**synonym** see TRESPASS
— **in·fring·er** *noun*
**in·fringe·ment** \in-ˈfrinj-mənt\ *noun* (1628)
**1 :** the act of infringing **:** VIOLATION
**2 :** an encroachment or trespass on a right or privilege
**in·fun·dib·u·lar** \ˌin-(ˌ)fən-ˈdi-byə-lər\ *adjective* (1795)
**1 :** INFUNDIBULIFORM
**2 :** of, relating to, or having an infundibulum
**in·fun·dib·u·li·form** \-lə-ˌfȯrm\ *adjective* [New Latin *infundibulum* + English *-iform*] (1752)
**:** having the form of a funnel or cone
**in·fun·dib·u·lum** \ˌin-(ˌ)fən-ˈdi-byə-ləm\ *noun, plural* **-la** \-lə\ [New Latin, from Latin, funnel — more at FUNNEL] (1543)
**:** any of various funnel-shaped organs or parts: as **a :** the hollow conical process of gray matter by which the pituitary gland is continuous with the brain **b :** the calyx of a kidney **c :** the abdominal opening of a fallopian tube
**¹in·fu·ri·ate** \in-ˈfyu̇r-ē-ˌāt\ *transitive verb* **-at·ed; -at·ing** [Medieval Latin *infuriatus*,

---

☆ **SYNONYMS**
**Inform, acquaint, apprise, notify** mean to make one aware of something. INFORM implies the imparting of knowledge especially of facts or occurrences ⟨*informed* us of the crisis⟩. ACQUAINT lays stress on introducing to or familiarizing with ⟨*acquaint* yourself with the keyboard⟩. APPRISE implies communicating something of special interest or importance ⟨keep us *apprised* of the situation⟩. NOTIFY implies sending notice of something requiring attention or demanding action ⟨*notified* the witness when to appear⟩.

**Infrequent, uncommon, scarce, rare, sporadic** mean not common or abundant. INFREQUENT implies occurrence at wide intervals in space or time ⟨*infrequent* family visits⟩. UNCOMMON suggests a frequency below normal expectation ⟨smallpox is now *uncommon* in many countries⟩. SCARCE implies falling short of a standard or required abundance ⟨jobs were *scarce* during the Depression⟩. RARE suggests extreme scarcity or infrequency and often implies consequent high value ⟨*rare* first editions⟩. SPORADIC implies occurrence in scattered instances or isolated outbursts ⟨*sporadic* cases of influenza⟩.

---

\ə\ abut \ᵊ\ kitten \ər\ further \a\ ash \ā\ ace
\ä\ mop, mar \au̇\ out \ch\ chin \e\ bet \ē\ easy
\g\ go \i\ hit \ī\ ice \j\ job \ŋ\ sing \ō\ go
\ȯ\ law \ȯi\ boy \th\ thin \t͟h\ the \ü\ loot \u̇\ foot
\y\ yet \zh\ vision    *see also* Guide to Pronunciation

past participle of *infuriare*, from Latin *in-* + *furia* fury] (1667)
**:** to make furious
— **in·fu·ri·at·ing·ly** \-ˌā-tiŋ-lē\ *adverb*
— **in·fu·ri·a·tion** \-ˌfyŭr-ē-ˈā-shən\ *noun*
²**in·fu·ri·ate** \in-ˈfyŭr-ē-ət\ *adjective* (1667)
**:** furiously angry
**in·fuse** \in-ˈfyüz\ *transitive verb* **in·fused;** **in·fus·ing** [Middle English, to pour in, from Middle French & Latin; Middle French *infuser*, from Latin *infusus*, past participle of *infundere* to pour in, from *in-* + *fundere* to pour — more at FOUND] (1526)
**1 a :** to cause to be permeated with something (as a principle or quality) that alters usually for the better ⟨*infuse* the team with confidence⟩ **b :** INTRODUCE, INSINUATE ⟨a new spirit was *infused* into American art —*American Guide Series: New York*⟩
**2 :** INSPIRE, ANIMATE ⟨the sense of purpose that *infuses* scientific research⟩
**3 :** to steep in liquid (as water) without boiling so as to extract the soluble constituents or principles ☆
— **in·fus·er** *noun*
**in·fus·ible** \(ˌ)in-ˈfyü-zə-bəl\ *adjective* (1555)
**:** incapable of being fused **:** very difficult to fuse
— **in·fus·ibil·i·ty** \-ˌfyü-zə-ˈbi-lə-tē\ *noun*
— **in·fus·ible·ness** \-ˈfyü-zə-bəl-nəs\ *noun*
**in·fu·sion** \in-ˈfyü-zhən\ *noun* (15th century)
**1 :** the act or process of infusing
**2 :** a product obtained by infusing
**3 :** the continuous slow introduction of a solution especially into a vein
**in·fu·so·ri·al earth** \ˌin-fyü-ˈzōr-ē-əl-, -ˈsōr-, -ˈzȯr-, -ˈsȯr-\ *noun* (1882)
**:** KIESELGUHR
**in·fu·so·ri·an** \-ē-ən\ *noun* [ultimately from Latin *infusus*] (1859)
**:** any of a heterogeneous group of minute organisms found especially in decomposing infusions of organic matter; *especially* **:** a ciliated protozoan
— **infusorian** *adjective*
¹**-ing** \iŋ *also* ēŋ; *in some dialects & in other dialects informally* in, ən *also* ēn; *after certain consonants* ᵊn, ᵊm, ᵊŋ\ *noun suffix* [Middle English, from Old English *-ung, -ing*, suffix forming nouns from verbs; akin to Old High German *-ung*, suffix forming nouns from verbs]
**1 :** action or process ⟨runn*ing*⟩ ⟨sleep*ing*⟩ **:** instance of an action or process ⟨a meet*ing*⟩
**2 a :** product or result of an action or process ⟨an engrav*ing*⟩ — often in plural ⟨earn*ings*⟩ **b :** something used in an action or process ⟨a bed cover*ing*⟩ ⟨the lin*ing* of a coat⟩
**3 :** action or process connected with (a specified thing) ⟨boat*ing*⟩
**4 :** something connected with, consisting of, or used in making (a specified thing) ⟨scaffold*ing*⟩ ⟨shirt*ing*⟩
**5 :** something related to (a specified concept) ⟨off*ing*⟩
²**-ing** *noun suffix* [Middle English, from Old English *-ing, -ung;* akin to Old High German *-ing* one of a (specified) kind]
**:** one of a (specified) kind ⟨sweet*ing*⟩
³**-ing** *verb suffix or adjective suffix* [Middle English, probably from ¹*-ing*]
— used to form the present participle ⟨sail*ing*⟩ and sometimes to form an adjective resembling a present participle but not derived from a verb ⟨swashbuckl*ing*⟩ ■
**in·gath·er** \ˈin-ˌga-ᵺər, -ˌge-\ (1557)
*transitive verb*
**:** to gather in
*intransitive verb*
**:** ASSEMBLE
— **in·gath·er·ing** \-ˌgaᵺ-riŋ, -ˌgeᵺ-; -ˌgaᵺə-, -ˌge-\ *noun*
**in·ge·nious** \in-ˈjēn-yəs\ *adjective* [Middle English *ingenyous*, from Middle French *in-*

*genieux*, from Latin *ingeniosus*, from *ingenium* natural capacity — more at ENGINE] (15th century)
**1** *obsolete* **:** showing or calling for intelligence, aptitude, or discernment
**2 :** marked by especial aptitude at discovering, inventing, or contriving
**3 :** marked by originality, resourcefulness, and cleverness in conception or execution ⟨an *ingenious* contraption⟩
**synonym** *see* CLEVER
— **in·ge·nious·ly** *adverb*
— **in·ge·nious·ness** *noun*
**in·ge·nue** *or* **in·gé·nue** \ˈan-jə-ˌnü, ˈän-; ˈaⁿ-zhə-, ˈäⁿ-\ *noun* [French *ingénue*, feminine of *ingénu* ingenuous, from Latin *ingenuus*] (1848)
**1 :** a naive girl or young woman
**2 :** the stage role of an ingenue; *also* **:** an actress playing such a role
**in·ge·nu·i·ty** \ˌin-jə-ˈnü-ə-tē, -ˈnyü-\ *noun, plural* **-ties** (circa 1592)
**1** *obsolete* **:** CANDOR, INGENUOUSNESS
**2 a :** skill or cleverness in devising or combining **:** INVENTIVENESS **b :** cleverness or aptness of design or contrivance
**3 :** an ingenious device or contrivance
¹**in·gen·u·ous** \in-ˈjen-yə-wəs\ *adjective* [by alteration] (1588)
*obsolete* **:** INGENIOUS
²**ingenuous** *adjective* [Latin *ingenuus* native, free born, from *in-* + *gignere* to beget — more at KIN] (1588)
**1** *obsolete* **:** NOBLE, HONORABLE
**2 a :** showing innocent or childlike simplicity and candidness **b :** lacking craft or subtlety
**synonym** *see* NATURAL
— **in·gen·u·ous·ly** *adverb*
— **in·gen·u·ous·ness** *noun*
**in·gest** \in-ˈjest\ *transitive verb* [Latin *ingestus*, past participle of *ingerere* to carry in, from *in-* + *gerere* to bear] (1620)
**:** to take in for or as if for digestion
— **in·gest·ible** \-ˈjes-tə-bəl\ *adjective*
— **in·ges·tion** \-ˈjes-chən, -ˈjesh-\ *noun*
— **in·ges·tive** \-ˈjes-tiv\ *adjective*
**in·ges·ta** \in-ˈjes-tə\ *noun plural* [New Latin, from Latin, neuter plural of *ingestus*] (1727)
**:** material taken into the body by way of the digestive tract
**in·gle** \ˈiŋ-gəl, ˈiŋ-əl\ *noun* [Scottish Gaelic *aingeal*] (1508)
**1 :** a fire in a fireplace
**2 :** FIREPLACE
**3 :** CORNER, ANGLE
**in·gle·nook** \-ˌnŭk\ *noun* (1772)
**:** a nook by a large open fireplace; *also* **:** a bench or settle occupying this nook
**in·glo·ri·ous** \(ˌ)in-ˈglōr-ē-əs, -ˈglȯr-\ *adjective* [Latin *inglorius*, from *in-* + *gloria* glory] (1573)
**1 :** SHAMEFUL, IGNOMINIOUS
**2 :** not glorious **:** lacking fame or honor
— **in·glo·ri·ous·ly** *adverb*
— **in·glo·ri·ous·ness** *noun*
**in·got** \ˈiŋ-gət\ *noun* [Middle English, perhaps modification of Middle French *lingot* ingot of metal, incorrectly divided as *l'ingot*, as if from *le* the, from Latin *ille* that] (14th century)
**1 :** a mold in which metal is cast
**2 :** a mass of metal cast into a convenient shape for storage or transportation to be later processed
**ingot iron** *noun* (1877)
**:** iron containing only small proportions of impurities (as less than 0.05 percent carbon)
¹**in·grain** \(ˌ)in-ˈgrān\ *transitive verb* (circa 1641)
**:** to work indelibly into the natural texture or mental or moral constitution
**synonym** *see* INFUSE
²**in·grain** \ˈin-ˌgrān\ *adjective* (1766)
**1 a :** made of fiber that is dyed before being spun into yarn **b :** made of yarn that is dyed before being woven or knitted
**2 :** thoroughly worked in **:** INNATE
³**in·grain** \ˈin-ˌgrān\ *noun* (circa 1890)

**:** innate quality or character
**in·grained** \ˈin-ˌgrānd, (ˌ)in-ˈ\ *adjective* (1599)
**1 :** worked into the grain or fiber
**2 :** forming a part of the essence or inmost being **:** DEEP-SEATED ⟨*ingrained* prejudice⟩
— **in·grained·ly** \ˈin-ˌgrā-nəd-lē, ˈin-ˌgrānd-lē, (ˌ)in-ˈ\ *adverb*
**in·grate** \ˈin-ˌgrāt\ *noun* [Latin *ingratus* ungrateful, from *in-* + *gratus* grateful, — more at GRACE] (1622)
**:** an ungrateful person
**in·gra·ti·ate** \in-ˈgrā-shē-ˌāt\ *transitive verb* **-at·ed; -at·ing** [²*in-* + Latin *gratia* grace] (1622)
**:** to gain favor or favorable acceptance for by deliberate effort — usually used with *with* ⟨*ingratiate* themselves with the community leaders —William Attwood⟩
— **in·gra·ti·a·tion** \-ˌgrā-shē-ˈā-shən\ *noun*
— **in·gra·tia·to·ry** \-ˈgrā-sh(ē-)ə-ˌtōr-ē, -ˌtȯr-\ *adjective*
**ingratiating** *adjective* (1655)
**1 :** capable of winning favor **:** PLEASING ⟨an *ingratiating* smile⟩
**2 :** intended or adopted in order to gain favor **:** FLATTERING
— **in·gra·ti·at·ing·ly** \-ˈgrā-shē-ˌā-tiŋ-lē\ *adverb*
**in·grat·i·tude** \(ˌ)in-ˈgra-tə-ˌtüd, -ˌtyüd\ *noun* [Middle English, from Middle French, from Medieval Latin *ingratitudo*, from Latin *in-* + Late Latin *gratitudo* gratitude] (14th century)
**:** forgetfulness of or poor return for kindness received **:** UNGRATEFULNESS

---

☆ **SYNONYMS**
**Infuse, suffuse, imbue, ingrain, inoculate, leaven** mean to introduce one thing into another so as to affect it throughout. IN-FUSE implies a pouring in of something that gives new life or significance ⟨new members *infused* enthusiasm into the club⟩. SUFFUSE implies a spreading through of something that gives an unusual color or quality ⟨a room *suffused* with light⟩. IMBUE implies the introduction of a quality that fills and permeates the whole being ⟨*imbue* students with intellectual curiosity⟩. INGRAIN, used only in the passive or past participle, suggests the deep implanting of a quality or trait ⟨clung to *ingrained* habits⟩. INOCULATE implies an imbuing or implanting with a germinal idea and often suggests surreptitiousness or subtlety ⟨an electorate *inoculated* with dangerous ideas⟩. LEAVEN implies introducing something that enlivens, tempers, or markedly alters the total quality ⟨a serious play *leavened* with comic moments⟩.

---

☐ **USAGE**
**-ing** Though the pronunciation of *-ing* with the consonant \n\, misleadingly referred to as "dropping the *g*," is often deprecated, this pronunciation is frequently heard. It is not known for certain why the Middle English present participle ending *-ende* was replaced by *-ing*. Analogy with the earlier noun suffix *-ing* probably had something to do with it. In early Modern English, present participles were regularly formed with *-ing* pronounced \iŋ\ (as can still be heard in a few dialects) and later \iŋ\. Evidence also shows that some speakers used \in\ and by the 18th century this pronunciation became widespread. Though teachers (with some success) campaigned against it, \in\ remained a feature of the speech of many of the best speakers in Britain and the U.S. well into this century. It has by now lost its respectability, at least when attention is drawn to it, but throughout the U.S. it persists largely unnoticed and in some dialects it predominates over \iŋ\.

**in·gre·di·ent** \in-'grē-dē-ənt\ noun [Middle English, from Latin ingredient-, ingrediens, present participle of ingredi to go into, from in- + gradi to go — more at GRADE] (15th century)
: something that enters into a compound or is a component part of any combination or mixture : CONSTITUENT
synonym see ELEMENT
— **ingredient** adjective

**in·gress** \'in-,gres\ noun [Middle English, from Latin ingressus, from ingredi] (15th century)
**1** : the act of entering : ENTRANCE
**2** : the power or liberty of entrance or access
— **in·gres·sion** \in-'gre-shən\ noun

**in·gres·sive** \in-'gre-siv\ adjective (1649)
**1** : of, relating to, or involving ingress; especially : produced by ingress of air into the vocal tract ⟨ingressive sounds⟩
**2** : INCHOATIVE 2
— **ingressive** noun
— **in·gres·sive·ness** noun

**in–group** \'in-,grüp\ noun (1907)
**1** : a group with which one feels a sense of solidarity or community of interests — compare OUT-GROUP
**2** : CLIQUE

**in·grow·ing** \'in-,grō-iŋ\ adjective (1869)
: growing or tending inward

**in·grown** \-,grōn\ adjective (1670)
**1** : grown in; specifically : having the free tip or edge embedded in the flesh ⟨an ingrown toenail⟩
**2** : having the direction of growth or activity or interest inward rather than outward : WITHDRAWN
— **in·grown·ness** \(,)in-'grōn-nəs\ noun

**in·growth** \'in-,grōth\ noun (1870)
**1** : a growing inward (as to fill a void)
**2** : something that grows in or into a space

**in·gui·nal** \'iŋ-gwə-n°l\ adjective [Middle English inguynale, from Latin inguinalis, from inguin-, inguen groin — more at ADEN-] (15th century)
: of, relating to, or situated in the region of the groin or in either of the lowest lateral regions of the abdomen ⟨inguinal hernia⟩

**in·gur·gi·tate** \in-'gər-jə-,tāt\ transitive verb **-tat·ed; -tat·ing** [Latin ingurgitatus, past participle of ingurgitare, from in- + gurgit-, gurges whirlpool — more at VORACIOUS] (circa 1570)
: to swallow greedily or in large quantities : GUZZLE
— **in·gur·gi·ta·tion** \(,)in-,gər-jə-'tā-shən\ noun

**in·hab·it** \in-'ha-bət\ verb [Middle English enhabiten, from Middle French & Latin; Middle French enhabiter, from Latin inhabitare, from in- + habitare to dwell, frequentative of habēre to have — more at GIVE] (14th century)
transitive verb
**1** : to occupy as a place of settled residence or habitat : live in ⟨inhabit a small house⟩
**2** : to be present in or occupy in any manner or form ⟨the human beings who inhabit this tale —Al Newman⟩
intransitive verb
archaic : to have residence in a place : DWELL
— **in·hab·it·able** \-bə-tə-bəl\ adjective
— **in·hab·it·er** noun

**in·hab·i·tan·cy** \in-'ha-bə-tən(t)-sē\ noun (1681)
: INHABITATION

**in·hab·i·tant** \in-'ha-bə-tənt\ noun (15th century)
: one that occupies a particular place regularly, routinely, or for a period of time ⟨inhabitants of large cities⟩ ⟨the tapeworm is an inhabitant of the intestine⟩

**in·hab·i·ta·tion** \in-,ha-bə-'tā-shən\ noun (15th century)
: the act of inhabiting : the state of being inhabited

**inhabited** adjective (15th century)
: having inhabitants

**in·hal·ant** \in-'hā-lənt\ noun (circa 1834)
: something (as an allergen or medication) that is inhaled
— **inhalant** adjective

**in·ha·la·tion** \,in-hə-'lā-shən, ,i-n°l-'ā-\ noun (circa 1623)
**1** : the act or an instance of inhaling
**2** : material (as medication) to be taken in by inhaling
— **in·ha·la·tion·al** \-shnəl, -shə-n°l\ adjective

**in·ha·la·tor** \'in-hə-,lā-tər, 'i-n°l-,ā-\ noun (1925)
: a device providing a mixture of oxygen and carbon dioxide for breathing that is used especially in conjunction with artificial respiration

**in·hale** \in-'hā(ə)l\ verb **in·haled; in·hal·ing** [in- + exhale] (1725)
transitive verb
**1** : to draw in by breathing
**2** : to take in eagerly or greedily ⟨inhaled about four meals at once —Ring Lardner⟩
intransitive verb
: to breathe in
— **in·hale** \in-', -'in-\ noun

**in·hal·er** \in-'hā-lər\ noun (1778)
**1** : a device by means of which medicinal material is inhaled
**2** : one that inhales

**in·har·mon·ic** \,in-(,)här-'mä-nik\ adjective (circa 1828)
: not harmonic

**in·har·mo·ni·ous** \-'mō-nē-əs\ adjective (1711)
**1** : not harmonious : DISCORDANT
**2** : not fitting or congenial : CONFLICTING
— **in·har·mo·ni·ous·ly** adverb
— **in·har·mo·ni·ous·ness** noun

**in·har·mo·ny** \(,)in-'här-mə-nē\ noun (1799)
: DISCORD

**in·here** \in-'hir\ intransitive verb **in·hered; in·her·ing** [Latin inhaerēre, from in- + haerēre to adhere] (15th century)
: to be inherent

**in·her·ence** \in-'hir-ən(t)s, -'her-\ noun (1577)
: the quality, state, or fact of inhering

**in·her·ent** \-ənt\ adjective [Latin inhaerent-, inhaerens, present participle of inhaerēre] (1581)
: involved in the constitution or essential character of something : belonging by nature or habit : INTRINSIC
— **in·her·ent·ly** adverb

**in·her·it** \in-'her-ət\ verb [Middle English enheriten to make one an heir, inherit, from Middle French enheriter to make one an heir, from Late Latin inhereditare, from Latin in- + hereditas inheritance — more at HEREDITY] (14th century)
transitive verb
**1** : to come into possession of or receive especially as a right or divine portion ⟨and every one who has left houses or brothers or sisters . . . for my name's sake, will receive a hundredfold, and inherit eternal life —Matthew 19:29 (Revised Standard Version)⟩
**2 a** : to receive from an ancestor as a right or title descendible by law at the ancestor's death **b** : to receive as a devise or legacy
**3** : to receive from ancestors by genetic transmission ⟨inherit a strong constitution⟩
**4** : to have in turn or receive as if from an ancestor ⟨inherited the problem from his predecessor⟩
intransitive verb
: to take or hold a possession or rights by inheritance
— **in·her·i·tor** \-ə-tər\ noun
— **in·her·i·tress** \-ə-trəs\ or **in·her·i·trix** \-ə-(,)triks\ noun

**in·her·it·able** \in-'her-ə-tə-bəl\ adjective (15th century)
**1** : capable of being inherited : TRANSMISSIBLE
**2** : capable of taking by inheritance

**— in·her·it·abil·i·ty** \-,her-ə-tə-'bi-lə-tē\ noun
**— in·her·it·able·ness** \-'her-ə-tə-bəl-nəs\ noun

**in·her·i·tance** \in-'her-ə-tən(t)s\ noun (14th century)
**1 a** : the act of inheriting property **b** : the reception of genetic qualities by transmission from parent to offspring **c** : the acquisition of a possession, condition, or trait from past generations
**2** : something that is or may be inherited
**3 a** : TRADITION **b** : a valuable possession that is a common heritage from nature
**4** obsolete : POSSESSION

**inheritance tax** noun (1841)
**1** : an excise in the form of a percentage of the value of the property received that is levied on the privilege of an heir to inherit property
**2** : DEATH TAX; especially : ESTATE TAX

**in·hib·in** \in-'hi-bən\ noun [Latin inhibēre to inhibit + English 1-in] (1932)
: a human hormone that is secreted by Sertoli cells in the male and granulosa cells in the female and that inhibits the secretion of follicle-stimulating hormone

**in·hib·it** \in-'hi-bət\ verb [Middle English, from Latin inhibitus, past participle of inhibēre, from in- 2in- + habēre to have — more at HABIT] (15th century)
transitive verb
**1** : to prohibit from doing something
**2 a** : to hold in check : RESTRAIN **b** : to discourage from free or spontaneous activity especially through the operation of inner psychological impediments or of social controls
intransitive verb
: to cause inhibition
synonym see FORBID
**— in·hib·i·tive** \-bə-tiv\ adjective
**— in·hib·i·to·ry** \-bə-,tōr-ē, -,tȯr-\ adjective

**in·hi·bi·tion** \,in-hə-'bi-shən, ,i-nə-\ noun (14th century)
**1 a** : the act of inhibiting : the state of being inhibited **b** : something that forbids, debars, or restricts
**2** : an inner impediment to free activity, expression, or functioning: as **a** : a psychic activity imposing restraint upon another activity **b** : a restraining of the function of a bodily organ or an agent (as an enzyme)

**in·hib·i·tor** \in-'hi-bə-tər\ noun (circa 1611)
: one that inhibits; especially : an agent that slows or interferes with a chemical action

**in·hold·ing** \'in-,hōl-diŋ\ noun (1947)
: privately owned land inside the boundary of a national park

**in·ho·mo·ge·ne·i·ty** \(,)in-,hō-mə-jə-'nē-ə-tē, -'nā- also ÷-'nī-; especially British -,hä-mə-\ noun, plural **-ties** (1899)
**1** : the condition of not being homogeneous
**2** : a part that is not homogeneous with the larger uniform mass in which it occurs; especially : a localized collection of matter in the universe
**— in·ho·mo·ge·neous** \-'jē-nē-əs, -nyəs\ adjective

**in·hos·pi·ta·ble** \,in-(,)hä-'spi-tə-bəl, (,)in-'häs-(,)pi-\ adjective (circa 1570)
**1** : not showing hospitality : not friendly or receptive
**2** : providing no shelter or sustenance
**— in·hos·pi·ta·ble·ness** noun
**— in·hos·pi·ta·bly** \-blē\ adverb

**in·hos·pi·tal·i·ty** \(,)in-,häs-pə-'ta-lə-tē\ noun (circa 1576)
: the quality or state of being inhospitable

**in–house** \'in-,haús, -'haús\ adjective (circa 1956)

: existing, originating, or carried on within a group or organization or its facilities : not outside ⟨an *in-house* publication⟩ ⟨a company's *in-house* staff⟩
— **in·house** *adverb*
**in·hu·man** \(ˌ)in-'hyü-mən, -'yü-\ *adjective* [Middle English *inhumayne*, from Middle French & Latin; Middle French *inhumain*, from Latin *inhumanus*, from *in-* + *humanus* human] (15th century)
**1 a :** lacking pity, kindness, or mercy : SAVAGE ⟨an *inhuman* tyrant⟩ **b :** COLD, IMPERSONAL ⟨his usual quiet, almost *inhuman* courtesy —F. Tennyson Jesse⟩ **c :** not worthy of or conforming to the needs of human beings ⟨*inhuman* living conditions⟩
**2 :** of or suggesting a nonhuman class of beings
— **in·hu·man·ly** *adverb*
— **in·hu·man·ness** \-mən-nəs\ *noun*
**in·hu·mane** \ˌin-(ˌ)hyü-'mān, -(ˌ)yü-\ *adjective* [Middle French *inhumain* & Latin *inhumanus*] (1599)
: not humane : INHUMAN 1
— **in·hu·mane·ly** *adverb*
**in·hu·man·i·ty** \-'ma-nə-tē\ *noun, plural* **-ties** (15th century)
**1 a :** the quality or state of being cruel or barbarous **b :** a cruel or barbarous act
**2 :** absence of warmth or geniality : IMPERSONALITY
**in·hume** \in-'hyüm\ *transitive verb* **in·humed; in·hum·ing** [probably from French *inhumer*, from Medieval Latin *inhumare*, from Latin *in-* + *humus* earth — more at HUMBLE] (1604)
: BURY, INTER
— **in·hu·ma·tion** \ˌin-hyü-'mā-shən\ *noun*
**in·im·i·cal** \i-'ni-mi-kəl\ *adjective* [Late Latin *inimicalis*, from Latin *inimicus* enemy — more at ENEMY] (1573)
**1 :** being adverse often by reason of hostility or malevolence
**2 a :** having the disposition of an enemy : HOSTILE **b :** reflecting or indicating hostility : UNFRIENDLY
— **in·im·i·cal·ly** \-mi-k(ə-)lē\ *adverb*
**in·im·i·ta·ble** \(ˌ)i-'ni-mə-tə-bəl\ *adjective* [Middle English, from Middle French or Latin; Middle French, from Latin *inimitabilis*, from *in-* + *imitabilis* imitable] (15th century)
: not capable of being imitated : MATCHLESS
— **in·im·i·ta·ble·ness** *noun*
— **in·im·i·ta·bly** \-blē\ *adverb*
**in·i·on** \'i-nē-ˌän, -ən\ *noun* [New Latin, from Greek, back of the head, diminutive of *in-, is* sinew, tendon] (circa 1811)
: the external occipital protuberance of the skull
**in·iq·ui·tous** \i-'ni-kwə-təs\ *adjective* (1726)
: characterized by iniquity
**synonym** see VICIOUS
— **in·iq·ui·tous·ly** *adverb*
— **in·iq·ui·tous·ness** *noun*
**in·iq·ui·ty** \-kwə-tē\ *noun, plural* **-ties** [Middle English *iniquite*, from Middle French *iniquité*, from Latin *iniquitat-, iniquitas*, from *iniquus* uneven, from *in-* + *aequus* equal] (14th century)
**1 :** gross injustice : WICKEDNESS
**2 :** a wicked act or thing : SIN
**¹ini·tial** \i-'ni-shəl\ *adjective* [Middle French & Latin; Middle French, from Latin *initialis*, from *initium* beginning, from *inire* to go into, from *in-* + *ire* to go — more at ISSUE] (1526)
**1 :** of or relating to the beginning : INCIPIENT
**2 :** placed at the beginning : FIRST
— **ini·tial·ly** \i-'ni-sh(ə-)lē\ *adverb*
— **ini·tial·ness** \i-'ni-shəl-nəs\ *noun*
**²initial** *noun* (1627)
**1 a :** the first letter of a name **b** *plural* : the first letter of each word in a full name ⟨found that their *initials* were identical⟩
**2 :** a large letter beginning a text or a division or paragraph

**3 :** ANLAGE, PRECURSOR; *specifically* **:** a meristematic cell
**³initial** *transitive verb* **ini·tialed** *or* **ini·tialled; ini·tial·ing** *or* **ini·tial·ling** \i-'nish(ə-)liŋ\ (circa 1864)
**1 :** to affix an initial to
**2 :** to authenticate or give preliminary approval to by affixing the initials of an authorizing representative
**ini·tial·ism** \i-'ni-shə-ˌli-zəm\ *noun* (1899)
: an acronym formed from initial letters
**ini·tial·ize** \-ˌlīz\ *transitive verb* **-ized; -iz·ing** (1957)
: to set (as a computer program counter) to a starting position, value, or configuration
— **ini·tial·i·za·tion** \i-ˌni-sh(ə-)lə-'zā-shən\ *noun*
**initial rhyme** *noun* (1838)
: ALLITERATION
**initial side** *noun* (1957)
: a stationary straight line that contains a point about which another straight line is rotated to form an angle — compare TERMINAL SIDE
**¹ini·ti·ate** \i-'ni-shē-ˌāt\ *transitive verb* **-at·ed; -at·ing** [Late Latin *initiatus*, past participle of *initiare*, from Latin, to induct, from *initium*] (circa 1573)
**1 :** to cause or facilitate the beginning of : set going ⟨*initiate* a program of reform⟩ ⟨enzymes that *initiate* fermentation⟩
**2 :** to induct into membership by or as if by special rites
**3 :** to instruct in the rudiments or principles of something : INTRODUCE
**synonym** see BEGIN
— **ini·ti·a·tor** \-ˌā-tər\ *noun*
**²ini·ti·ate** \i-'ni-shē(-ē-)ət\ *adjective* (1605)
**1** *obsolete* : relating to an initiate
**2 a :** initiated or properly admitted (as to membership or an office) **b :** instructed in some secret knowledge
**³ini·ti·ate** \i-'ni-shē(-ē-)ət\ *noun* (1811)
**1 :** a person who is undergoing or has undergone an initiation
**2 :** a person who is instructed or adept in some special field
**ini·ti·a·tion** \i-ˌni-shē-'ā-shən\ *noun* (1583)
**1 a :** the act or an instance of initiating **b :** the process of being initiated **c :** the rites, ceremonies, ordeals, or instructions with which one is made a member of a sect or society or is invested with a particular function or status
**2 :** the condition of being initiated into some experience or sphere of activity : KNOWLEDGEABLENESS
**¹ini·tia·tive** \i-'ni-shə-tiv *also* -shē-ə-tiv\ *adjective* (1795)
: of or relating to initiation : INTRODUCTORY, PRELIMINARY
**²initiative** *noun* (1793)
**1 :** an introductory step ⟨took the *initiative* in attempting to settle the issue⟩
**2 :** energy or aptitude displayed in initiation of action : ENTERPRISE ⟨showed great *initiative*⟩
**3 a :** the right to initiate legislative action **b :** a procedure enabling a specified number of voters by petition to propose a law and secure its submission to the electorate or to the legislature for approval — compare REFERENDUM 1
— **on one's own initiative :** at one's own discretion : independently of outside influence or control
**ini·tia·to·ry** \i-'ni-sh(ē-)ə-ˌtōr-ē, -ˌtȯr-\ *adjective* (circa 1615)
**1 :** constituting a beginning
**2 :** tending or serving to initiate
**in·ject** \in-'jekt\ *transitive verb* [Latin *injectus*, past participle of *inicere*, from *in-* + *jacere* to throw — more at JET] (1601)
**1 a :** to introduce into something forcefully ⟨*inject* fuel into an engine⟩ **b :** to force a fluid into (as for medical purposes)
**2 :** to introduce as an element or factor in or into some situation or subject ⟨condemning

any attempt to *inject* religious bigotry into the campaign —*Current Biography*⟩
— **in·ject·able** \-'jek-tə-bəl\ *adjective or noun*
— **in·jec·tor** \-'jek-tər\ *noun*
**in·jec·tant** \-'jek-tənt\ *noun* (1950)
: a substance that is injected into something
**in·jec·tion** \in-'jek-shən\ *noun* (15th century)
**1 a :** an act or instance of injecting **b :** the placing of an artificial satellite or a spacecraft into an orbit or on a trajectory; *also* **:** the time or place at which injection occurs
**2 :** something (as a medication) that is injected
**3 :** a mathematical function that is a one-to-one mapping — compare BIJECTION, SURJECTION
**injection molding** *noun* (1932)
: a method of forming articles (as of plastic) by heating the molding material until it can flow and injecting it into a mold
— **injection–molded** *adjective*
**in·jec·tive** \in-'jek-tiv\ *adjective* (1952)
: being a one-to-one mathematical function
**in–joke** \'in-ˌjōk, -'jōk\ *noun* (1964)
: a joke for or about a select group of people
**in·ju·di·cious** \ˌin-jü-'di-shəs\ *adjective* (1649)
: not judicious : INDISCREET, UNWISE
— **in·ju·di·cious·ly** *adverb*
— **in·ju·di·cious·ness** *noun*
**in·junc·tion** \in-'jəŋ(k)-shən\ *noun* [Middle English *injunccion*, from Middle French & Late Latin; Middle French *injonction*, from Late Latin *injunction-, injunctio*, from Latin *injungere* to enjoin — more at ENJOIN] (15th century)
**1 :** the act or an instance of enjoining : ORDER, ADMONITION
**2 :** a writ granted by a court of equity whereby one is required to do or to refrain from doing a specified act
— **in·junc·tive** \-'jəŋ(k)-tiv\ *adjective*
**in·jure** \'in-jər\ *transitive verb* **in·jured; in·jur·ing** \'inj-riŋ, 'in-jə-\ [Middle English *enjuren*, from Middle French *enjurier*, from Late Latin *injuriare*, from Latin *injuria* injury] (15th century)
**1 a :** to do an injustice to : WRONG **b :** to harm, impair, or tarnish the standing of **c :** to give pain to ⟨*injure* a person's pride⟩
**2 a :** to inflict bodily hurt on **b :** to impair the soundness of **c :** to inflict material damage or loss on ☆
— **in·jur·er** \'in-jər-ər\ *noun*
**in·ju·ri·ous** \in-'jur-ē-əs\ *adjective* (15th century)
**1 :** inflicting or tending to inflict injury : DETRIMENTAL ⟨*injurious* to health⟩
**2 :** ABUSIVE, DEFAMATORY ⟨speak not *injurious* words —George Washington⟩
— **in·ju·ri·ous·ly** *adverb*
— **in·ju·ri·ous·ness** *noun*

---

☆ **SYNONYMS**
**Injure, harm, hurt, damage, impair, mar** mean to affect injuriously. INJURE implies the inflicting of anything detrimental to one's looks, comfort, health, or success ⟨badly *injured* in an accident⟩. HARM often stresses the inflicting of pain, suffering, or loss ⟨careful not to *harm* the animals⟩. HURT implies inflicting a wound to the body or to the feelings ⟨*hurt* by their callous remarks⟩. DAMAGE suggests injury that lowers value or impairs usefulness ⟨a table *damaged* in shipping⟩. IMPAIR suggests a making less complete or efficient by deterioration or diminution ⟨years of smoking had *impaired* his health⟩. MAR applies to injury that spoils perfection (as of a surface) or causes disfigurement ⟨the text is *marred* by many typos⟩.

**in·ju·ry** \'inj-rē, 'in-jə-\ *noun, plural* **-ries** [Middle English *injurie*, from Latin *injuria*, from *injurus* injurious, from *in-* + *jur-, jus* right — more at JUST] (14th century) **1 a** : an act that damages or hurts : WRONG **b** : violation of another's rights for which the law allows an action to recover damages **2** : hurt, damage, or loss sustained
**synonym** see INJUSTICE

**in·jus·tice** \(ˌ)in-'jəs-təs\ *noun* [Middle English, from Middle French, from Latin *injustitia*, from *injustus* unjust, from *in-* + *justus* just] (14th century) **1** : absence of justice : violation of right or of the rights of another : UNFAIRNESS **2** : an unjust act : WRONG ☆

**¹ink** \'iŋk\ *noun, often attributive* [Middle English *enke*, from Old French, from Late Latin *encaustum*, from neuter of Latin *encaustus* burned in, from Greek *enkaustos*, verbal of *enkaiein* to burn in — more at ENCAUSTIC] (13th century) **1** : a colored usually liquid material for writing and printing **2** : the black protective secretion of a cephalopod **3** *slang* : PUBLICITY 2d
— **ink·i·ness** \'iŋ-kē-nəs\ *noun*
— **inky** \'iŋ-kē\ *adjective*

**²ink** *transitive verb* (1562) **1** : to put ink on ⟨*ink* a pen⟩; *also* : to draw or write on in ink **2 a** : SIGN 2a ⟨*inked* a new contract⟩ **b** : SIGN 4

**ink·ber·ry** \'iŋk-ˌber-ē\ *noun* [from the use of the berries for making ink] (1765) **1 a** : a holly (*Ilex glabra*) of eastern North America with evergreen oblong leathery leaves and small usually black berries **b** : POKEWEED **2** : the fruit of an inkberry

**ink·blot test** \'iŋk-ˌblät-\ *noun* (1928) : any of several psychological tests (as a Rorschach test) based on the interpretation of irregular figures (as blots of ink)

**¹ink·horn** \'iŋk-ˌhȯrn\ *noun* (14th century) : a small portable bottle (as of horn) for holding ink

**²inkhorn** *adjective* (1543) : ostentatiously learned : PEDANTIC ⟨*inkhorn* terms⟩

**in–kind** \'in-ˈkīnd\ *adjective* (1973) : consisting of something (as goods or commodities) other than money ⟨*in-kind* relief for the poor⟩

**ink–jet** \'iŋk-ˈjet\ *adjective* (1976) : of, relating to, or being a dot matrix printer in which electrically charged droplets of ink are projected onto the paper

**in·kle** \'iŋ-kəl\ *noun* [origin unknown] (1541) : a colored linen tape or braid woven on a very narrow loom and used for trimming; *also* : the thread used

**in·kling** \'iŋ-kliŋ\ *noun* [Middle English *yngkiling* whisper, mention, probably from *inclen* to hint at; akin to Old English *inca* suspicion] (1513) **1** : a slight indication or suggestion : HINT, CLUE ⟨there was no path—no *inkling* even of a track —*New Yorker*⟩ **2** : a slight knowledge or vague notion ⟨had not the faintest *inkling* of what it was all about —H. W. Carter⟩

**ink·stand** \'iŋk-ˌstand\ *noun* (1773) : INKWELL; *also* : a stand with fittings for holding ink and pens

**ink·stone** \'iŋk-ˌstōn\ *noun* (circa 1889) : a stone used in Chinese art and calligraphy on which dry ink and water are mixed

**ink·well** \'iŋk-ˌwel\ *noun* (circa 1875) : a container (as in a desk) for ink

**inky cap** *noun* (1923) : a mushroom (genus *Coprinus*, especially *C. atramentarius*) whose pileus deliquesces into an inky fluid after the spores have matured — called also *ink cap*

**in·laid** \'in-ˈlād\ *adjective* (1598) **1 a** : set into a surface in a decorative design

⟨tables with *inlaid* marble⟩ **b** : decorated with a design or material set into a surface ⟨a table with an *inlaid* top⟩ **2** *of linoleum* : having a design that goes all the way through to the backing

**¹in·land** \'in-ˌland, -lənd\ *adjective* (1546) **1** *chiefly British* : not foreign : DOMESTIC **2** : of or relating to the interior of a country

**²inland** *noun* (1573) : the interior part of a country

**³inland** *adverb* (1600) : into or toward the interior

**in·land·er** \'in-ˌlan-dər, -lən-\ *noun* (1610) : one who lives inland

**in·law** \'in-ˌlȯ\ *noun* [mother-*in-law*, etc.] (1894) : a relative by marriage

**¹in·lay** \(ˌ)in-'lā, 'in-ˌ\ *transitive verb* **in·laid** \-'lād, -ˌlād\; **in·lay·ing** (1596) **1 a** : to set into a surface or ground material **b** : to adorn with insertions **c** : to insert (as a color plate) into a mat or other reinforcement **2** : to rub, beat, or fuse (as wire) into an incision in metal, wood, or stone
— **in·lay·er** *noun*

**²in·lay** \'in-ˌlā\ *noun* (1667) **1** : inlaid work or a decorative inlaid pattern **2** : a tooth filling shaped to fit a cavity and then cemented into place

**in·let** \'in-ˌlet, -lət\ *noun* [from its letting water in] (circa 1576) **1 a** : a bay or recess in the shore of a sea, lake, or river; *also* : CREEK **b** : a narrow water passage between peninsulas or through a barrier island leading to a bay or lagoon **2** : a way of entering; *especially* : an opening for intake

**in·li·er** \'in-ˌlī-(ə)r\ *noun* [³*in* + out*lier*] (circa 1859) **1** : a mass of rock whose outcrop is surrounded by rock of younger age **2** : a distinct area or formation completely surrounded by another; *also* : ENCLAVE

**in–line** \'in-'līn, ˌin-\ *adjective or adverb* (1929) : having the parts or units arranged in a straight line; *also* : being so arranged

**in–line engine** \(ˌ)in-'līn-, 'in-ˌ\ *noun* (1929) : an internal combustion engine in which the cylinders are arranged in one or more straight lines

**in–line skate** *noun* (1989) : a roller skate whose four wheels are set in-line for greater speed and maneuverability
— **in–line skating** *noun*

**¹in lo·co pa·ren·tis** \in-ˌlō-kō-pə-'ren-təs\ *adverb* [Latin] (1828) : in the place of a parent

**²in loco parentis** *noun* (1968) : regulation or supervision by an administrative body (as at a university) acting in loco parentis

**in·ly** \'in-lē\ *adverb* (before 12th century) **1** : INWARDLY **2** : in a manner suggesting great depth of knowledge or understanding : THOROUGHLY

**in·mate** \'in-ˌmāt\ *noun* (1589) : any of a group occupying a single place of residence; *especially* : a person confined (as in a prison or hospital)

**in me·di·as res** \in-'me-dē-əs-'räs, -'mē-dē-əs-'rēz\ *adverb* [Latin, literally, into the midst of things] (1786) : in or into the middle of a narrative or plot

**in me·mo·ri·am** \ˌin-mə-'mȯr-ē-əm, -'mȯr-\ *preposition* [Latin] (1850) : in memory of — used especially in epitaphs

**in–mi·grant** \'in-ˌmī-grənt\ *noun* (1942) : one that in-migrates

**in–mi·grate** \'in-ˌmī-ˌgrāt\ *intransitive verb* (1942)

*inky cap*

: to move into or come to live in a region or community especially as part of a large-scale and continuing movement of population — compare OUT-MIGRATE
— **in–mi·gra·tion** \ˌin-mī-'grā-shən\ *noun*

**in·most** \'in-ˌmōst\ *adjective* [Middle English, from Old English *innemest*, superlative of *inne*, adverb, in, within, from *in*, adverb] (before 12th century) : deepest within : farthest from the outside

**¹inn** \'in\ *noun* [Middle English, from Old English; akin to Old Norse *inni* dwelling, inn, Old English *in*, adverb] (before 12th century) **1 a** : an establishment for the lodging and entertaining of travelers **b** : TAVERN **2** : a residence formerly provided for British students in London and especially for students of law

**²inn** *intransitive verb* (14th century) : to put up at an inn

**in·nards** \'i-nərdz\ *noun plural* [alteration of *inwards*] (circa 1825) **1** : the internal organs of a human being or animal; *especially* : VISCERA **2** : the internal parts especially of a structure or mechanism

**in·nate** \i-'nāt, 'i-ˌ\ *adjective* [Middle English *innat*, from Latin *innatus*, past participle of *innasci* to be born in, from *in-* + *nasci* to be born — more at NATION] (15th century) **1** : existing in, belonging to, or determined by factors present in an individual from birth : NATIVE, INBORN ⟨*innate* behavior⟩ **2** : belonging to the essential nature of something : INHERENT **3** : originating in or derived from the mind or the constitution of the intellect rather than from experience ☆
— **in·nate·ly** *adverb*
— **in·nate·ness** *noun*

---

☆ **SYNONYMS**
**Injustice, injury, wrong, grievance** mean an act that inflicts undeserved hurt. IN-JUSTICE applies to any act that involves unfairness to another or violation of his rights ⟨the *injustices* suffered by the lower classes⟩. INJURY applies in law specifically to an injustice for which one may sue to recover compensation ⟨libel constitutes a legal *injury*⟩. WRONG applies also in law to any act punishable according to the criminal code; it may apply more generally to any flagrant injustice ⟨determined to right society's *wrongs*⟩. GRIEVANCE applies to any circumstance or condition that constitutes an injustice to the sufferer and gives just ground for complaint ⟨investigating employee *grievances*⟩.

**Innate, inborn, inbred, congenital, hereditary** mean not acquired after birth. INNATE applies to qualities or characteristics that are part of one's inner essential nature ⟨an *innate* sense of fair play⟩. INBORN suggests a quality or tendency either actually present at birth or so marked and deep-seated as to seem so ⟨her *inborn* love of nature⟩. INBRED suggests something either acquired from parents by heredity or so deeply rooted and ingrained as to seem acquired in that way ⟨*inbred* political loyalties⟩. CONGENITAL and HEREDITARY refer to what is acquired before or at birth, the former to things acquired during fetal development and the latter to things transmitted from one's ancestors ⟨a *congenital* heart murmur⟩ ⟨eye color is *hereditary*⟩.

---

\ə\ abut \ˀ\ kitten \ər\ further \a\ ash \ā\ ace \ä\ mop, mar \au̇\ out \ch\ chin \e\ bet \ē\ easy \g\ go \i\ hit \ī\ ice \j\ job \ŋ\ sing \ō\ go \ȯ\ law \ȯi\ boy \th\ thin \th̲\ the \ü\ loot \u̇\ foot \y\ yet \zh\ vision *see also* Guide to Pronunciation

**in·ner** \'i-nər\ *adjective* [Middle English, from Old English *innera*, comparative of *inne* within] (before 12th century) **1 a :** situated farther in ⟨the inner bark⟩ **b :** being near a center especially of influence ⟨the *inner* circles of political power⟩ **2 :** of or relating to the mind or spirit ⟨the *inner* life⟩ **— inner** *noun* **— in·ner·ly** *adverb*

**inner city** *noun* (1961) **:** the usually older, poorer, and more densely populated central section of a city **— inner–city** *adjective*

**in·ner–di·rect·ed** \'i-nər-də-'rek-təd, -(,)dī-\ *adjective* (1950) **:** directed in thought and action by one's own scale of values as opposed to external norms

**inner ear** *noun* (circa 1923) **:** the essential organ of hearing and equilibrium that is located in the temporal bone, is innervated by the auditory nerve, and includes the vestibule, the semicircular canals, and the cochlea

**inner light** *noun, often I&L capitalized* (1856) **:** a divine presence held (as in Quaker doctrine) to enlighten and guide the soul

**1in·ner·most** \'i-nər-,mōst\ *adjective* (14th century) **:** farthest inward **:** INMOST

**2innermost** *noun* (14th century) **:** the inmost part

**inner planet** *noun* (1951) **:** any of the planets Mercury, Venus, Earth, and Mars whose orbits are within the asteroid belt

**inner product** *noun* (circa 1911) **:** SCALAR PRODUCT

**in·ner·sole** \'i-nər-,sōl\ *noun* (circa 1892) **:** INSOLE

**inner space** *noun* (1958) **1 :** space at or near the earth's surface and especially under the sea **2 :** one's inner self

**in·ner·spring** \'i-nər-'spriŋ\ *adjective* (1928) **:** having coil springs inside a padded casing ⟨*innerspring* mattress⟩

**inner tube** *noun* (1895) **:** an airtight rubber tube inside a pneumatic tire to hold air under pressure

**in·ner·vate** \i-'nər-,vāt, 'i-(,)nər-\ *transitive verb* **-vat·ed; -vat·ing** (1870) **:** to supply with nerves **— in·ner·va·tion** \,i-(,)nər-'vā-shən, i-,nər-\ *noun*

**in·ning** \'i-niŋ\ *noun* [2in + 1-ing] (1735) **1 a** *plural but singular or plural in construction* **:** a division of a cricket match **b :** a division of a baseball game consisting of a turn at bat for each team; *also* **:** a baseball team's turn at bat ending with the third out **c :** a player's turn (as in horseshoes, pool, or croquet) **2 :** a chance or opportunity for action or accomplishment — usually used in plural but singular or plural in construction ⟨that momentous *innings* which was to project him into world politics —*Times Literary Supplement*⟩

**inn·keep·er** \'in-,kē-pər\ *noun* (15th century) **1 :** a proprietor of an inn **2 :** HOTELMAN

**in·no·cence** \'i-nə-sən(t)s\ *noun* (14th century) **1 a :** freedom from guilt or sin through being unacquainted with evil **:** BLAMELESSNESS **b :** CHASTITY **c :** freedom from legal guilt of a particular crime or offense **d** (1) **:** freedom from guile or cunning **:** SIMPLICITY (2) **:** lack of worldly experience or sophistication **e :** lack of knowledge **:** IGNORANCE ⟨written in entire *innocence* of the Italian language —E. R. Bentley⟩ **2 :** one that is innocent **3 :** BLUET

**in·no·cen·cy** \-sən(t)-sē\ *noun, plural* **-cies** (14th century) **:** INNOCENCE; *also* **:** an innocent action or quality

**in·no·cent** \'i-nə-sənt\ *adjective* [Middle English, from Middle French, from Latin *inno-cent-, innocens*, from *in-* + *nocent-, nocens* wicked, from present participle of *nocēre* to harm — more at NOXIOUS] (14th century) **1 a :** free from guilt or sin especially through lack of knowledge of evil **:** BLAMELESS ⟨an *innocent* child⟩ **b :** harmless in effect or intention ⟨searching for a hidden motive in even the most *innocent* conversation —Leonard Wibberley⟩; *also* **:** CANDID ⟨gave me an *innocent* gaze⟩ **c :** free from legal guilt or fault; *also* **:** LAWFUL ⟨a wholly *innocent* transaction⟩ **2 a :** lacking or reflecting a lack of sophistication, guile, or self-consciousness **:** ARTLESS, INGENUOUS **b :** IGNORANT ⟨almost entirely *innocent* of Latin —C. L. Wrenn⟩; *also* **:** UNAWARE ⟨perfectly *innocent* of the confusion he had created —B. R. Haydon⟩ **3 :** lacking or deprived of something ⟨her face *innocent* of cosmetics —Marcia Davenport⟩ **— innocent** *noun* **— in·no·cent·ly** *adverb*

**in·noc·u·ous** \i-'nä-kyə-wəs\ *adjective* [Latin *innocuus*, from *in-* + *nocēre*] (1598) **1 :** producing no injury **:** HARMLESS **2 :** not likely to give offense or to arouse strong feelings or hostility **:** INOFFENSIVE, INSIPID **— in·noc·u·ous·ly** *adverb* **— in·noc·u·ous·ness** *noun*

**in·nom·i·nate** \i-'nä-mə-nət\ *adjective* [Late Latin *innominatus*, from Latin *in-* + *nomina-tus*, past participle of *nominare* to nominate] (1638) **:** having no name **:** UNNAMED; *also* **:** ANONYMOUS

**innominate artery** *noun* (1870) **:** BRACHIOCEPHALIC ARTERY

**innominate bone** *noun* (1866) **:** the large flaring bone that constitutes a lateral half of the pelvis in mammals and is composed of the ilium, ischium, and pubis which are fused into one bone in the adult

**innominate vein** *noun* (1876) **:** BRACHIOCEPHALIC VEIN

**in·no·vate** \'i-nə-,vāt\ *verb* **-vat·ed; -vat·ing** [Latin *innovatus*, past participle of *inno-vare*, from *in-* + *novus* new — more at NEW] (1548) *transitive verb* **1 :** to introduce as or as if new **2** *archaic* **:** to effect a change in ⟨the dictates of my father were . . . not to be altered, *inno-vated*, or even discussed —Sir Walter Scott⟩ *intransitive verb* **:** to make changes **:** do something in a new way **— in·no·va·tor** \-,vā-tər\ *noun* **— in·no·va·to·ry** \'i-nə-və-,tōr-ē, -,tòr-; 'i-nə-,vā-tə-rē\ *adjective*

**in·no·va·tion** \,i-nə-'vā-shən\ *noun* (15th century) **1 :** the introduction of something new **2 :** a new idea, method, or device **:** NOVELTY **— in·no·va·tion·al** \-shnəl, -shə-n³l\ *adjective*

**in·no·va·tive** \'i-nə-,vā-tiv\ *adjective* (1608) **:** characterized by, tending to, or introducing innovations **— in·no·va·tive·ly** *adverb* **— in·no·va·tive·ness** *noun*

**Inns of Court** (15th century) **1 :** the four sets of buildings in London belonging to four societies of students and practitioners of the law **2 :** the four societies that alone admit to practice at the English bar

**in·nu·en·do** \,in-yə-'wen-(,)dō\ *noun, plural* **-dos** *or* **-does** [Latin, by hinting, from *innu-ere* to hint, from *in-* + *nuere* to nod — more at NUMEN] (1678) **1 a :** an oblique allusion **:** HINT, INSINUATION; *especially* **:** a veiled or equivocal reflection on character or reputation **b :** the use of such allusions ⟨resorting to *innuendo*⟩ **2 :** a parenthetical explanation introduced into the text of a legal document ◆

**In·nu·it** *variant of* INUIT

**in·nu·mer·a·ble** \i-'nüm-rə-bəl, -'nyüm-; -'n(y)ü-mə-\ *adjective* [Middle English, from Latin *innumerabilis*, from *in-* + *numerabilis* numerable] (14th century) **:** too many to be numbered **:** COUNTLESS; *also* **:** very many **— in·nu·mer·a·bly** \-blē\ *adverb*

**in·nu·mer·ate** \-rət\ *adjective* (1959) **:** marked by an ignorance of mathematics and the scientific approach **— in·nu·mer·a·cy** \-rə-sē\ *noun* **— innumerate** *noun*

**in·nu·mer·ous** \-rəs\ *adjective* [Latin *innu-merus*, from *in-* + *numerus* number] (1531) **:** INNUMERABLE

**in·ob·ser·vance** \,i-nəb-'zər-vən(t)s\ *noun* [French & Latin; French, from Latin *inobser-vantia*, from *in-* + *observantia* observance] (1611) **1 :** lack of attention **:** HEEDLESSNESS **2 :** failure to fulfill **:** NONOBSERVANCE **— in·ob·ser·vant** \-vənt\ *adjective*

**in·oc·u·lant** \i-'nä-kyə-lənt\ *noun* (1898) **:** INOCULUM

**in·oc·u·late** \i-'nä-kyə-,lāt\ *transitive verb* **-lat·ed; -lat·ing** [Middle English, to insert a bud in a plant, from Latin *inoculatus*, past participle of *inoculare*, from *in-* + *oculus* eye, bud — more at EYE] (1721) **1 a :** to introduce a microorganism into ⟨*inoc-ulate* mice with anthrax⟩ ⟨beans inoculated with nitrogen-fixing bacteria⟩ **b :** to introduce (as a microorganism) into a suitable situation for growth **c :** to introduce immunologically active material (as an antibody or antigen) into especially in order to treat or prevent a disease ⟨*inoculate* children against diphtheria⟩ **2 :** to introduce something into the mind of **3 :** to protect as if by inoculation ◆

---

◇ WORD HISTORY

**innuendo** The verb *innuere* in classical Latin meant "to nod, beckon, or make a sign to" a person, and in Medieval Latin more generally "to hint" or "to insinuate." The ablative case of the gerund was *innuendo*, which meant literally "by hinting." In medieval legal documents *innuendo* introduced inserted remarks, meaning in effect "to wit " or "that is to say," and the word was adopted with the same function into English legal usage. By the late 17th century *innuendo* was used as a noun referring to the insertion itself, and more broadly to any indirect suggestion or veiled allusion. The notion of the invidious possibilities of such a remark came to predominate so that today *innuendo* typically refers to an insinuation that is at best catty, at worst defamatory.

**inoculate** In both Latin and English, the word for "eye" (*oculus* in Latin) has been used metaphorically to denote something that looks like or is suggestive of a person's organ of sight. The circular markings on a peacock's tail and the undeveloped buds on a potato are common examples of this use of *eye*. In horticulture, as the Romans learned, the *oculus* or bud from one plant can be grafted onto another plant for propagation. The Latin verb *inoculare* was derived from *oculus* to refer to this procedure. On the basis of the past participle, *inoculatus*, this verb was borrowed into English in the 15th century with the same meaning. In the 18th century medical researchers discovered that introducing a small amount of an infective agent into a person made that person immune to a normal attack of the disease. By analogy with the implanting of a bud, the inserting of an infective agent into the body was also referred to by the verb *inoculate*.

**synonym** see INFUSE
— **in·oc·u·la·tive** \-ˌlā-tiv\ *adjective*
— **in·oc·u·la·tor** \-ˌlā-tər\ *noun*
**in·oc·u·la·tion** \i-ˌnä-kyə-'lā-shən\ *noun* (1714)
**1 :** the act or process or an instance of inoculating; *especially* **:** the introduction of a pathogen or antigen into a living organism to stimulate the production of antibodies
**2 :** INOCULUM
**in·oc·u·lum** \i-'nä-kyə-ləm\ *noun, plural* **-la** \-lə\ [New Latin, from Latin *inoculare*] (1902)
**:** material used for inoculation
**in·of·fen·sive** \ˌi-nə-'fen(t)-siv\ *adjective* (1646)
**1 :** causing no harm or injury
**2 a :** giving no provocation **:** PEACEABLE **b** **:** not objectionable to the senses
— **in·of·fen·sive·ly** *adverb*
— **in·of·fen·sive·ness** *noun*
**in·op·er·a·ble** \(ˌ)i-'nä-p(ə-)rə-bəl\ *adjective* [probably from French *inopérable*] (1886)
**1 :** not treatable or remediable by surgery ⟨*inoperable* cancer⟩
**2 :** INOPERATIVE
**in·op·er·a·tive** \-'nä-p(ə-)rə-tiv, -'nä-pə-ˌrā-\ *adjective* (circa 1631)
**:** not operative: as **a :** not functioning ⟨an *inoperative* clock⟩ **b :** having no effect or force ⟨an *inoperative* law⟩
— **in·op·er·a·tive·ness** *noun*
**in·oper·cu·late** \ˌi-nō-'pər-kyə-lət\ *adjective* (circa 1836)
**:** having no operculum
— **inoperculate** *noun*
**in·op·por·tune** \(ˌ)i-ˌnä-pər-'tün, -'tyün\ *adjective* [Latin *inopportunus*, from *in-* + *opportunus* opportune] (circa 1507)
**:** INCONVENIENT, UNSEASONABLE
— **in·op·por·tune·ly** *adverb*
— **in·op·por·tune·ness** \-'t(y)ün-nəs\ *noun*
**in order that** *conjunction* (1711)
**:** THAT 2a(1)
**in·or·di·nate** \i-'nȯr-d°n-ət, -'nȯrd-nət\ *adjective* [Middle English *inordinat*, from Latin *inordinatus*, from *in-* + *ordinatus*, past participle of *ordinare* to arrange — more at ORDAIN] (14th century)
**1** *archaic* **:** DISORDERLY, UNREGULATED
**2 :** exceeding reasonable limits **:** IMMODERATE
**synonym** see EXCESSIVE
— **in·or·di·nate·ly** *adverb*
— **in·or·di·nate·ness** *noun*
**in·or·gan·ic** \ˌi-(ˌ)nȯr-'ga-nik\ *adjective* (1794)
**1 a (1) :** being or composed of matter other than plant or animal **:** MINERAL **(2) :** forming or belonging to the inanimate world **b :** of, relating to, or dealt with by a branch of chemistry concerned with substances not usually classed as organic
**2 :** not arising from natural growth **:** ARTIFICIAL; *also* **:** lacking structure, character, or vitality ⟨dull *inorganic* things, without individuality or prestige —John Buchan⟩
— **in·or·gan·i·cal·ly** \-ni-k(ə-)lē\ *adverb*
**in·os·cu·late** \i-'näs-kyə-ˌlāt\ *verb* **-lat·ed; -lat·ing** [²*in-* + *osculate*] (1671)
**:** JOIN, UNITE
— **in·os·cu·la·tion** \(ˌ)i-ˌnäs-kyə-'lā-shən\ *noun*
**ino·si·tol** \i-'nō-sə-ˌtȯl, ī-'nō-, -ˌtōl\ *noun* [International Scientific Vocabulary, from *inosite* inositol, from Greek *in-, is* sinew + International Scientific Vocabulary ²-*ose* + ¹-*ite*] (1891)
**:** any of several crystalline stereoisomeric cyclic alcohols $C_6H_{12}O_6$; *especially* **:** MYOINOSITOL
**ino·tro·pic** \ˌē-nə-'trō-pik, ˌī-nə-, -'trä-\ *adjective* [International Scientific Vocabulary *ino-* (from Greek *in-, is* sinew) + -*tropic*] (1903)
**:** relating to or influencing the force of muscular contractions
**in·pa·tient** \'in-ˌpā-shənt\ *noun* (1760)

**:** a hospital patient who receives lodging and food as well as treatment — compare OUTPATIENT
**in per·so·nam** \ˌin-pər-'sō-ˌnam, -ˌnäm\ *adverb or adjective* [Late Latin, against a person] (circa 1860)
**:** against a person for the purpose of imposing a liability or obligation — used especially of legal actions, judgments, or jurisdiction; compare IN REM
**in pet·to** \in-'pe-(ˌ)tō\ *adverb or adjective* [Italian, literally, in the breast] (circa 1674)
**1 :** in private **:** SECRETLY
**2 :** in miniature
**in·pour·ing** \'in-ˌpȯr-iŋ, -ˌpȯr-\ *noun* (1721)
**:** INRUSH
**in–print** \'in-'print\ *adjective* (1950)
**:** being in print
**in–pro·cess** \(ˌ)in-'prä-ˌses, -'prō-, -ˌsəs\ *adjective* (1925)
**:** of, relating to, or being goods in manufacture as distinguished from raw materials or from finished products
**in pro·pria per·so·na** \in-'prō-prē-ə-pər-'sō-nə\ *adverb* [Medieval Latin] (1654)
**:** in one's own person or character **:** PERSONALLY; *especially* **:** without the assistance of an attorney
¹**in·put** \'in-ˌpu̇t\ *noun* (1753)
**1 :** something that is put in: as **a :** an amount put in ⟨increased *input* of fertilizer increases crop yield⟩ **b :** power or energy put into a machine or system for storage, conversion in kind, or conversion of characteristics usually with the intent of sizable recovery in the form of output **c :** a component of production (as land, labor, or raw materials) **d :** information fed into a data processing system or computer **e :** ADVICE, OPINION, COMMENT
**2 :** the means by which or the point at which an input (as of energy, material, or data) is made
**3 :** the act or process of putting in
²**input** *transitive verb* **in·put·ted** *or* **input; in·put·ting** (1946)
**:** to enter (as data) into a computer or data processing system
**in·quest** \'in-ˌkwest\ *noun* [Middle English, from Old French *enqueste*, from (assumed) Vulgar Latin *inquaesta*, feminine of *inquaestus*, past participle of *inquaerere* to inquire] (13th century)
**1 a :** a judicial or official inquiry or examination especially before a jury ⟨a coroner's *inquest*⟩ **b :** a body of people (as a jury) assembled to hold such an inquiry **c :** the finding of the jury upon such inquiry or the document recording it
**2 :** INQUIRY, INVESTIGATION
**in·qui·etude** \(ˌ)in-'kwī-ə-ˌtüd, -ˌtyüd\ *noun* [Middle English, from Middle French or Late Latin; Middle French, from Late Latin *inquietudo*, from Latin *inquietus* disturbed, from *in-* + *quietus* quiet] (15th century)
**:** disturbed state **:** DISQUIETUDE
**in·qui·line** \'in-kwə-ˌlīn, 'iŋ-, -lən\ *noun* [Latin *inquilinus* tenant, lodger, from *in-* + *colere* to cultivate, dwell — more at WHEEL] (1879)
**:** an animal that lives habitually in the nest or abode of some other species
**in·quire** \in-'kwīr\ *verb* **in·quired; in·quir·ing** [Middle English *enquiren*, from Old French *enquerre*, from (assumed) Vulgar Latin *inquaerere*, alteration of Latin *inquirere*, from *in-* + *quaerere* to seek] (13th century)
*transitive verb*
**1 :** to ask about ⟨some kindred spirit shall *inquire* thy fate —Thomas Gray⟩
**2 :** to search into **:** INVESTIGATE
*intransitive verb*
**1 :** to put a question **:** seek for information by questioning ⟨*inquired* about the horses⟩
**2 :** to make investigation or inquiry — often used with *into*
**synonym** see ASK
— **in·quir·er** *noun*

— **in·quir·ing·ly** \-'kwī-riŋ-lē\ *adverb*
— **inquire after :** to ask about the health of
**in·qui·ry** \in-'kwīr-ē, 'in-ˌ; 'in-kwə-rē, 'iŋ-; 'in-ˌkwir-ē\ *noun, plural* **-ries** (15th century)
**1 :** examination into facts or principles **:** RESEARCH
**2 :** a request for information
**3 :** a systematic investigation often of a matter of public interest
**in·qui·si·tion** \ˌin-kwə-'zi-shən, ˌiŋ-\ *noun* [Middle English *inquisicioun*, from Middle French *inquisition*, from Latin *inquisition-, inquisitio*, from *inquirere*] (14th century)
**1 :** the act of inquiring **:** EXAMINATION
**2 :** a judicial or official inquiry or examination usually before a jury; *also* **:** the finding of the jury
**3 a** *capitalized* **:** a former Roman Catholic tribunal for the discovery and punishment of heresy **b :** an investigation conducted with little regard for individual rights **c :** a severe questioning
— **in·qui·si·tion·al** \-'zi-sh(ə-)n°l\ *adjective*
**in·quis·i·tive** \in-'kwi-zə-tiv\ *adjective* (14th century)
**1 :** given to examination or investigation
**2 :** inclined to ask questions; *especially* **:** inordinately or improperly curious about the affairs of others
**synonym** see CURIOUS
— **in·quis·i·tive·ly** *adverb*
— **in·quis·i·tive·ness** *noun*
**in·quis·i·tor** \in-'kwi-zə-tər\ *noun* (1504)
**:** one who inquires or makes inquisition; *especially* **:** one who is unduly harsh, severe, or hostile in making an inquiry
— **in·quis·i·to·ri·al** \-ˌkwi-zə-'tōr-ē-əl, -'tȯr-\ *adjective*
— **in·quis·i·to·ri·al·ly** \-ē-ə-lē\ *adverb*
**in re** \in-'rā, -'rē\ *preposition* [Latin] (1877)
**:** in the matter of **:** CONCERNING, RE — often used in the title or name of a law case
**in rem** \in-'rem\ *adverb or adjective* [Late Latin] (circa 1860)
**:** against a thing (as a right, status, or property) — used especially of legal actions, judgments, or jurisdiction; compare IN PERSONAM
**in–residence** *adjective* (1845)
**:** being officially associated with an organization in a specified capacity — usually used in combination ⟨writer-*in-residence* at the university⟩
**in·ro** \'in-(ˌ)rō\ *noun, plural* **inro** [Japanese *inrō*] (1617)
**:** a small compartmented and usually ornamented container hung from an obi to hold small objects (as medicines and perfumes)
**in·road** \'in-ˌrōd\ *noun* (1548)
**1 :** a sudden hostile incursion **:** RAID
**2 :** an advance or penetration often at the expense of someone or something — usually used in plural
**in·rush** \'in-ˌrəsh\ *noun* (1817)
**:** a crowding or flooding in
**in·sa·lu·bri·ous** \ˌin-sə-'lü-brē-əs\ *adjective* [Latin *insalubris*, from *in-* + *salubris* healthful — more at SAFE] (1615)
**:** not conducive to health **:** UNWHOLESOME ⟨an *insalubrious* climate⟩
— **in·sa·lu·bri·ty** \-brə-tē\ *noun*
**ins and outs** \ˌin-zən(d)-'au̇ts\ *noun plural* (circa 1670)
**1 :** characteristic peculiarities or technicalities
**2 :** RAMIFICATIONS
**in·sane** \(ˌ)in-'sān\ *adjective* [Latin *insanus*, from *in-* + *sanus* sane] (circa 1550)
**1 :** mentally disordered **:** exhibiting insanity
**2 :** used by, typical of, or intended for insane persons ⟨an *insane* asylum⟩

\ə\ abut \°\ kitten \ər\ further \a\ ash \ā\ ace
\ä\ mop, mar \au̇\ out \ch\ chin \e\ bet \ē\ easy
\g\ go \i\ hit \ī\ ice \j\ job \ŋ\ sing \ō\ go
\ȯ\ law \ȯi\ boy \th\ thin \th\ the \ü\ loot \u̇\ foot
\y\ yet \zh\ vision *see also* Guide to Pronunciation

**3 :** ABSORD ⟨an *insane* scheme for making money⟩
— **in·sane·ly** *adverb*
— **in·sane·ness** \-'sān-nəs\ *noun*
**in·san·i·tary** \(ˌ)in-'sa-nə-ˌter-ē\ *adjective* (1874)
**:** unclean enough to endanger health **:** CONTAMINATED
— **in·san·i·ta·tion** \in-ˌsa-nə-'tā-shən\ *noun*
**in·san·i·ty** \in-'sa-nə-tē\ *noun, plural* **-ties** (1590)
**1 a :** a deranged state of the mind usually occurring as a specific disorder (as schizophrenia) and usually excluding such states as mental retardation, psychoneurosis, and various character disorders **b :** a mental disorder
**2 :** such unsoundness of mind or lack of understanding as prevents one from having the mental capacity required by law to enter into a particular relationship, status, or transaction or as removes one from criminal or civil responsibility
**3 a :** extreme folly or unreasonableness **b :** something utterly foolish or unreasonable
**in·sa·tia·ble** \(ˌ)in-'sā-shə-bəl\ *adjective* [Middle English *insaciable*, from Middle French, from Latin *insatiabilis*, from *in-* + *satiare* to satisfy — more at SATIATE] (15th century)
**:** incapable of being satisfied **:** QUENCHLESS ⟨had an *insatiable* desire for wealth⟩
— **in·sa·tia·bil·i·ty** \(ˌ)in-ˌsā-shə-'bi-lə-tē\ *noun*
— **in·sa·tia·ble·ness** \(ˌ)in-'sā-shə-bəl-nəs\ *noun*
— **in·sa·tia·bly** \-blē\ *adverb*
**in·sa·tiate** \(ˌ)in-'sā-sh(ē-)ət\ *adjective* (15th century)
**:** INSATIABLE
— **in·sa·tiate·ly** *adverb*
— **in·sa·tiate·ness** *noun*
**in·scribe** \in-'skrīb\ *transitive verb* [Middle English, from Latin *inscribere*, from *in-* + *scribere* to write — more at SCRIBE] (15th century)
**1 a :** to write, engrave, or print as a lasting record **b :** to enter on a list **:** ENROLL
**2 a :** to write, engrave, or print characters upon **b :** to autograph or address (a book) as a gift
**3 :** to dedicate to someone
**4 :** to draw within a figure so as to touch in as many places as possible ⟨a regular polygon *inscribed* in a circle⟩
**5** *British* **:** to register the name of the holder of (a security)
— **in·scrib·er** *noun*
**in·scrip·tion** \in-'skrip-shən\ *noun* [Middle English *inscripcioun*, from Latin *inscription-, inscriptio*, from *inscribere*] (14th century)
**1 a :** something that is inscribed; *also* **:** SUPERSCRIPTION **b :** EPIGRAPH **2 c :** the wording on a coin, medal, seal, or currency note
**2 :** the dedication of a book or work of art
**3 a :** the act of inscribing **b :** the entering of a name on or as if on a list **:** ENROLLMENT
**4** *British* **a :** the act of inscribing securities **b** *plural* **:** inscribed securities
— **in·scrip·tion·al** \-shnəl, -shə-nᵊl\ *adjective*
**in·scrip·tive** \in-'skrip-tiv\ *adjective* (1740)
**:** relating to or constituting an inscription
— **in·scrip·tive·ly** *adverb*
**in·scroll** \in-'skrōl\ *transitive verb* (1596)
*archaic* **:** to write on a scroll **:** RECORD
**in·scru·ta·ble** \in-'skrü-tə-bəl\ *adjective* [Middle English, from Late Latin *inscrutabilis*, from Latin *in-* + *scrutari* to search — more at SCRUTINY] (15th century)
**:** not readily investigated, interpreted, or understood **:** MYSTERIOUS
— **in·scru·ta·bil·i·ty** \-ˌskrü-tə-'bi-lə-tē\ *noun*
— **in·scru·ta·ble·ness** \-'skrü-tə-bəl-nəs\ *noun*

— **in·scru·ta·bly** \-blē\ *adverb*
**in·sculp** \in-'skəlp\ *transitive verb* [Middle English, from Latin *insculpere*, from *in-* + *scalpere* to scratch, carve — more at SHELF] (15th century)
*archaic* **:** ENGRAVE, SCULPTURE
**in·seam** \'in-ˌsēm\ *noun* (1886)
**:** the seam on the inside of the leg of a pair of pants; *also* **:** the length of this seam
**in·sect** \'in-ˌsekt\ *noun* [Latin *insectum*, from neuter of *insectus*, past participle of *insecare* to cut into, from *in-* + *secare* to cut — more at SAW] (1601)
**1 a :** any of numerous small invertebrate animals (as spiders or centipedes) that are more or less obviously segmented **b :** any of a class (Insecta) of arthropods (as bugs or bees) with well-defined head, thorax, and abdomen, only three pairs of legs, and typically one or two pairs of wings
**2 :** a trivial or contemptible person ♦
— **insect** *adjective*

insect 1b: *1* labial palpus, *2* maxillary palpus, *3* simple eye, *4* antenna, *5* compound eye, *6* prothorax, *7* tympanum, *8* wing, *9* ovipositor, *10* spiracles, *11* abdomen, *12* metathorax, *13* mesothorax

**in·sec·ta·ry** \'in-ˌsek-tə-rē, in-'\ *noun, plural* **-ries** (1888)
**:** a place for the keeping or rearing of living insects
**in·sec·ti·cid·al** \(ˌ)in-ˌsek-tə-'sī-dᵊl\ *adjective* (1857)
**1 :** destroying or controlling insects
**2 :** of or relating to an insecticide
— **in·sec·ti·cid·al·ly** \-dᵊl-ē\ *adverb*
**in·sec·ti·cide** \in-'sek-tə-ˌsīd\ *noun* [International Scientific Vocabulary] (1865)
**:** an agent that destroys insects
**in·sec·tile** \(ˌ)in-'sek-tᵊl, -ˌtīl, -(ˌ)til\ *adjective* (circa 1626)
**:** being or suggestive of an insect
**in·sec·ti·vore** \in-'sek-tə-ˌvōr, -ˌvòr\ *noun* [New Latin *Insectivora*, from Latin *insectum* + *-vorus -vorous*] (1840)
**1 :** any of an order (Insectivora) of mammals comprising forms (as moles, shrews, and hedgehogs) that are mostly small, insectivorous, and nocturnal
**2 :** an insectivorous plant or animal
**in·sec·tiv·o·rous** \ˌin-ˌsek-'tiv-rəs, -'ti-və-\ *adjective* (1661)
**:** depending on insects as food
**in·se·cure** \ˌin-si-'kyùr\ *adjective* [Medieval Latin *insecurus*, from Latin *in-* + *securus* secure] (1649)
**1 :** not confident or sure **:** UNCERTAIN ⟨feeling somewhat *insecure* of his reception⟩
**2 :** not adequately guarded or sustained **:** UNSAFE ⟨an *insecure* investment⟩
**3 :** not firmly fastened or fixed **:** SHAKY ⟨the hinge is loose and *insecure*⟩
**4 a :** not highly stable or well-adjusted ⟨an *insecure* marriage⟩ **b :** deficient in assurance **:** beset by fear and anxiety ⟨always felt *insecure* in a group of strangers⟩
— **in·se·cure·ly** *adverb*
— **in·se·cure·ness** *noun*
— **in·se·cu·ri·ty** \-'kyùr-ə-tē\ *noun*
**in·sel·berg** \'in(t)-səl-ˌbərg, 'in-zəl-, -ˌberg\ *noun, plural* **-bergs** *also* **-ber·ge** \-ˌbər-gə, -ˌber-\ [German, from *Insel* island + *Berg* mountain] (1913)

**:** an isolated mountain
**in·sem·i·nate** \in-'se-mə-ˌnāt\ *transitive verb* **-nat·ed; -nat·ing** [Latin *inseminatus*, past participle of *inseminare*, from *in-* + *semin-, semen* seed — more at SEMEN] (circa 1623)
**1 :** SOW
**2 :** to introduce semen into the genital tract of (a female)
*synonym* see IMPLANT
— **in·sem·i·na·tion** \-ˌse-mə-'nā-shən\ *noun*
**in·sem·i·na·tor** \-'se-mə-ˌnā-tər\ *noun* (1944)
**:** one that inseminates cattle artificially
**in·sen·sate** \(ˌ)in-'sen-ˌsāt, -sət\ *adjective* [Late Latin *insensatus*, from Latin *in-* + Late Latin *sensatus* having sense, from Latin *sensus* sense] (15th century)
**1 :** lacking sense or understanding; *also* **:** FOOLISH
**2 :** lacking animate awareness or sensation
**3 :** lacking humane feeling **:** BRUTAL
— **in·sen·sate·ly** *adverb*
**in·sen·si·ble** \(ˌ)in-'sen(t)-sə-bəl\ *adjective* [Middle English, from Middle French & Latin; Middle French, from Latin *insensibilis*, from *in-* + *sensibilis* sensible] (14th century)
**1 :** IMPERCEPTIBLE ⟨dampened by an *insensible* dew⟩; *broadly* **:** SLIGHT, GRADUAL ⟨*insensible* motion⟩
**2 :** incapable or bereft of feeling or sensation: as **a :** not endowed with life or spirit **:** INSENTIENT ⟨*insensible* earth⟩ **b :** UNCONSCIOUS ⟨knocked *insensible* by a sudden blow⟩ **c :** lacking sensory perception or ability to react ⟨*insensible* to pain⟩
**3 a :** lacking emotional response **:** APATHETIC, INDIFFERENT ⟨*insensible* to fear⟩ **b :** UNAWARE ⟨*insensible* of their danger⟩
**4** *archaic* **:** STUPID, SENSELESS
**5 :** not intelligible **:** MEANINGLESS
**6 :** lacking delicacy or refinement
— **in·sen·si·bil·i·ty** \(ˌ)in-ˌsen(t)-sə-'bi-lə-tē\ *noun*
— **in·sen·si·ble·ness** \(ˌ)in-'sen(t)-sə-bəl-nəs\ *noun*
— **in·sen·si·bly** \-blē\ *adverb*
**in·sen·si·tive** \(ˌ)in-'sen(t)-s(ə-)tiv\ *adjective* (1834)
**1 a :** not responsive or susceptible ⟨*insensitive* to the demands of the public⟩ **b :** lacking feeling or tact ⟨so *insensitive* as to laugh at someone in pain⟩
**2 :** not physically or chemically sensitive
— **in·sen·si·tive·ly** *adverb*
— **in·sen·si·tive·ness** *noun*
— **in·sen·si·tiv·i·ty** \(ˌ)in-ˌsen(t)-sə-'ti-və-tē\ *noun*
**in·sen·tient** \(ˌ)in-'sen(t)-sh(ē-)ənt\ *adjective* (1764)
**:** lacking perception, consciousness, or animation
— **in·sen·tience** \-sh(ē-)ən(t)s\ *noun*
**in·sep·a·ra·ble** \(ˌ)in-'se-p(ə-)rə-bəl\ *adjective* [Middle English, from Latin *inseparabilis*, from *in-* + *separabilis* separable] (14th century)

: incapable of being separated or disjoined
— **in·sep·a·ra·bil·i·ty** \(ˌ)in-ˌse-p(ə-)rə-'bi-lə-tē\ *noun*
— **inseparable** *noun*
— **in·sep·a·ra·ble·ness** \(ˌ)in-'se-p(ə-)rə-bəl-nəs\ *noun*
— **in·sep·a·ra·bly** \-blē\ *adverb*
¹**in·sert** \in-'sərt\ *verb* [Latin *insertus,* past participle of *inserere,* from *in-* + *serere* to join — more at SERIES] (1529)
*transitive verb*
**1** : to put or thrust in ⟨*insert* the key in the lock⟩ ⟨*insert* a spacecraft into orbit⟩
**2** : to put or introduce into the body of something : INTERPOLATE ⟨*insert* a change in a manuscript⟩
**3** : to set in and make fast; *especially* : to insert by sewing between two cut edges
**4** : to place into action (as in a game) ⟨*insert* a new pitcher⟩
*intransitive verb*
*of a muscle* : to be in attachment to the part to be moved
**synonym** see INTRODUCE
— **in·sert·er** *noun*
²**in·sert** \'in-ˌsərt\ *noun* (circa 1889)
: something that is inserted or is for insertion; *especially* : written or printed material inserted (as between the leaves of a book)
**in·ser·tion** \in-'sər-shən\ *noun* (1539)
**1** : something that is inserted: as **a** : the part of a muscle that inserts **b** : the mode or place of attachment of an organ or part **c** : embroidery or needlework inserted as ornament between two pieces of fabric **d** : a section of genetic material that is inserted into an existing gene sequence
**2 a** : the act or process of inserting **b** : the mutational process producing a genetic insertion
— **in·ser·tion·al** \-shnəl, -shə-nᵊl\ *adjective*
**in·ser·vice** \'in-ˌsər-vəs\ *adjective* (1928)
**1** : going on or continuing while one is fully employed ⟨*in-service* teacher education workshops⟩
**2** : of, relating to, or being one that is fully employed ⟨*in-service* police officers⟩
¹**in·set** \'in-ˌset\ *noun* (1559)
**1 a** : a place where something flows in : CHANNEL **b** : a setting or flowing in
**2** : something that is inset: as **a** : a small graphic representation (as a map or picture) set within a larger one **b** : a piece of cloth set into a garment (as for decoration) **c** : a part or section of a utensil that fits into an outer part
²**in·set** \'in-ˌset, in-'\ *transitive verb* **inset** *or* **in·set·ted; in·set·ting** (1658)
**1** : SET IN; *especially* : to insert within something else in such a way as to be visible
**2** : to provide with an inset
¹**in·shore** \'in-ˌshōr, -'shòr\ *adjective* (1701)
**1** : situated, living, or carried on near shore
**2** : moving toward shore ⟨an *inshore* current⟩
²**inshore** *adverb* (1748)
: to or toward shore ⟨boats driven *inshore* by the storm⟩
¹**in·side** \(ˌ)in-'sīd, 'in-ˌ\ *noun* (14th century)
**1 a** : an interior or internal part or place : the part within **b** : inward nature, thoughts, or feeling **c** : VISCERA, ENTRAILS — usually used in plural
**2** : an inner side or surface
**3 a** : a position of power, trust, or familiarity ⟨only someone on the *inside* could have told⟩ **b** : confidential information ⟨has the *inside* on what happened at the convention⟩
**4** : the area nearest a specified or implied point of reference: as **a** : the side of home plate nearest the batter **b** : the middle portion of a playing area **c** : the area near or underneath the basket in basketball
²**inside** *adverb* (15th century)
**1** : on the inner side
**2** : in or into the interior
**3** : to or on the inside
**4** : in prison
³**inside** *adjective* (1611)

**1** : of, relating to, or being on or near the inside ⟨an *inside* pitch⟩
**2 a** : relating or known to a select group ⟨*inside* information⟩ **b** : BEHIND-THE-SCENES
⁴**inside** *preposition* (1791)
**1 a** : in or into or as if in or into the interior of
**b** : on the inner side of
**2** : WITHIN ⟨*inside* an hour⟩
**inside address** *noun* (circa 1941)
: ADDRESS 5c
**inside of** *preposition* (1839)
: INSIDE
**inside out** *adverb* (circa 1600)
**1** : in such a manner that the inner surface becomes the outer ⟨turned the shirt *inside out*⟩
**2** : to a thorough degree ⟨knows the subject *inside out*⟩
**3** : in or into a state of disarray often involving drastic reorganization ⟨turned the business *inside out*⟩
**in·sid·er** \(ˌ)in-'sī-dər, 'in-ˌ\ *noun* (1848)
: a person recognized or accepted as a member of a group, category, or organization: as **a** : a person who is in a position of power or has access to confidential information **b** : one (as an officer or director) who is in a position to have special knowledge of the affairs of or to influence the decisions of a company
**insider trading** *noun* (1966)
: the illegal use of insider information for profit in financial trading
**inside track** *noun* (1857)
: an advantageous competitive position ⟨the owner's son has the *inside track* for the job⟩
**in·sid·i·ous** \in-'si-dē-əs\ *adjective* [Latin *insidiosus,* from *insidiae* ambush, from *insidēre* to sit in, sit on, from *in-* + *sedēre* to sit — more at SIT] (1545)
**1 a** : awaiting a chance to entrap : TREACHEROUS **b** : harmful but enticing : SEDUCTIVE ⟨*insidious* drugs⟩
**2 a** : having a gradual and cumulative effect : SUBTLE ⟨the *insidious* pressures of modern life⟩ **b** *of a disease* : developing so gradually as to be well established before becoming apparent
— **in·sid·i·ous·ly** *adverb*
— **in·sid·i·ous·ness** *noun*
**in·sight** \'in-ˌsīt\ *noun* (13th century)
**1** : the power or act of seeing into a situation : PENETRATION
**2** : the act or result of apprehending the inner nature of things or of seeing intuitively
**synonym** see DISCERNMENT
**in·sight·ful** \'in-ˌsīt-fəl, in-'\ *adjective* (1907)
: exhibiting or characterized by insight
— **in·sight·ful·ly** *adverb*
**in·sig·nia** \in-'sig-nē-ə\ *or* **in·sig·ne** \-(ˌ)nē\ *noun, plural* **-nia** *or* **-ni·as** [Latin *insignia,* plural of *insigne* mark, badge, from neuter of *insignis* marked, distinguished, from *in-* + *signum* mark — more at SIGN] (1648)
**1** : a badge of authority or honor
**2** : a distinguishing mark or sign
**in·sig·nif·i·cance** \ˌin(t)-sig-'ni-fi-kən(t)s\ *noun* (1699)
: the quality or state of being insignificant
**in·sig·nif·i·can·cy** \-kən(t)-sē\ *noun, plural* **-cies** (1651)
**1** : INSIGNIFICANCE
**2** : an insignificant thing or person
**in·sig·nif·i·cant** \-kənt\ *adjective* (1651)
: not significant: as **a** : lacking meaning or import : INCONSEQUENTIAL **b** : not worth considering : UNIMPORTANT **c** : lacking weight, position, or influence : CONTEMPTIBLE **d** : small in size, quantity, or number
— **in·sig·nif·i·cant·ly** *adverb*
**in·sin·cere** \ˌin-sin-'sir, -sən-\ *adjective* [Latin *insincerus,* from *in-* + *sincerus* sincere] (1634)
: not sincere : HYPOCRITICAL
— **in·sin·cere·ly** *adverb*
— **in·sin·cer·i·ty** \-'ser-ə-tē *also* -'sir-\ *noun*
**in·sin·u·ate** \in-'sin-yə-ˌwāt\ *verb* **-at·ed; -at·ing** [Latin *insinuatus,* past participle of

*insinuare,* from *in-* + *sinuare* to bend, curve, from *sinus* curve] (1529)
*transitive verb*
**1 a** : to introduce (as an idea) gradually or in a subtle, indirect, or covert way ⟨*insinuate* doubts into a trusting mind⟩ **b** : to impart or communicate with artful or oblique reference
**2** : to introduce (as oneself) by stealthy, smooth, or artful means
*intransitive verb*
**1** *archaic* : to enter gently, slowly, or imperceptibly : CREEP
**2** *archaic* : to ingratiate oneself
**synonym** see INTRODUCE, SUGGEST
— **in·sin·u·a·tive** \-ˌwā-tiv\ *adjective*
— **in·sin·u·a·tor** \-ˌwā-tər\ *noun*
**insinuating** *adjective* (1591)
**1** : winning favor and confidence by imperceptible degrees : INGRATIATING
**2** : tending gradually to cause doubt, distrust, or change of outlook often in a slyly subtle manner ⟨*insinuating* remarks⟩
— **in·sin·u·at·ing·ly** *adverb*
**in·sin·u·a·tion** \(ˌ)in-ˌsin-yə-'wā-shən\ *noun* (1526)
**1** : the act or process of insinuating
**2** : something that is insinuated; *especially* : a sly, subtle, and usually derogatory utterance
**in·sip·id** \in-'si-pəd\ *adjective* [French & Late Latin; French *insipide,* from Late Latin *insipidus,* from Latin *in-* + *sapidus* savory, from *sapere* to taste — more at SAGE] (1609)
**1** : lacking taste or savor : TASTELESS
**2** : lacking in qualities that interest, stimulate, or challenge : DULL, FLAT ☆
— **in·si·pid·i·ty** \ˌin-sə-'pi-də-tē\ *noun*
— **in·sip·id·ly** \in-'si-pəd-lē\ *adverb*
**in·sist** \in-'sist\ *verb* [Middle French or Latin; Middle French *insister,* from Latin *insistere* to stand upon, persist, from *in-* + *sistere* to take a stand; akin to Latin *stare* to stand — more at STAND] (1586)
*intransitive verb*
**1** : to be emphatic, firm, or resolute about something intended, demanded, or required ⟨they *insist* on going⟩
**2** *archaic* : PERSIST
*transitive verb*
: to maintain in a persistent or positive manner ⟨*insisted* that the story was true⟩
**in·sis·tence** \in-'sis-tən(t)s\ *noun* (15th century)
**1** : the act or an instance of insisting
**2** : the quality or state of being insistent : URGENCY
**in·sis·ten·cy** \-tən(t)-sē\ *noun, plural* **-cies** (1859)
: INSISTENCE

---

☆ **SYNONYMS**
**Insipid, vapid, flat, jejune, banal, inane** mean devoid of qualities that make for spirit and character. INSIPID implies a lack of sufficient taste or savor to please or interest ⟨an *insipid* romance with platitudes on every page⟩. VAPID suggests a lack of liveliness, force, or spirit ⟨an exciting story given a *vapid* treatment⟩. FLAT applies to things that have lost their sparkle or zest ⟨although well-regarded in its day, the novel now seems *flat*⟩. JEJUNE suggests a lack of rewarding or satisfying substance ⟨a *jejune* and gassy speech⟩. BANAL stresses the complete absence of freshness, novelty, or immediacy ⟨a *banal* tale of unrequited love⟩. INANE implies a lack of any significant or convincing quality ⟨an *inane* interpretation of the play⟩.

---

\ə\ abut \ᵊ\ kitten \ər\ further \a\ ash \ā\ ace
\ä\ mop, mar \aù\ out \ch\ chin \e\ bet \ē\ easy
\g\ go \i\ hit \ī\ ice \j\ job \ŋ\ sing \ō\ go
\ò\ law \òi\ boy \th\ thin \tẖ\ the \ü\ loot \ù\ foot
\y\ yet \zh\ vision *see also* Guide to Pronunciation

**in·sis·tent** \in-'sis-tənt\ *adjective* [Latin *insistent-, insistens,* present participle of *insistere*] (1868)
**1 :** disposed to insist **:** PERSISTENT
**2 :** compelling attention ⟨the *insistent* pounding of the waves⟩
— **in·sis·tent·ly** *adverb*

**in si·tu** \(,)in-'sī-(,)tü, -'si-, -(,)tyü *also* -'sē-, -(,)chü\ *adverb or adjective* [Latin, in position] (1740)
**:** in the natural or original position or place

**in·so·bri·ety** \,in-sə-'brī-ə-tē, -sō-\ *noun* (circa 1611)
**:** lack of sobriety or moderation; *especially* **:** intemperance in drinking

**in·so·cia·ble** \(,)in-'sō-shə-bəl\ *adjective* [Latin *insociabilis,* from *in-* + *sociabilis* sociable] (1588)
**:** not sociable
— **in·so·cia·bil·i·ty** \-(,)sō-shə-'bi-lə-tē\ *noun*
— **in·so·cia·bly** \-'sō-shə-blē\ *adverb*

**in·so·far** \,in-sə-'fär\ *adverb* (1596)
**:** to such extent or degree

**insofar as** *conjunction* (15th century)
**:** to the extent or degree that

**in·so·la·tion** \,in-(,)sō-'lā-shən\ *noun* [French or Latin; French, from Latin *insolation-, insolatio,* from *insolare* to expose to the sun, from *in-* + *sol* sun — more at SOLAR] (1617)
**1 :** exposure to the sun's rays
**2 :** SUNSTROKE
**3 a :** solar radiation that has been received **b :** the rate of delivery of direct solar radiation per unit of horizontal surface; *broadly* **:** that relating to total solar radiation

**in·sole** \'in-,sōl\ *noun* (circa 1861)
**1 :** an inside sole of a shoe
**2 :** a loose thin strip placed inside a shoe for warmth or comfort

**in·so·lence** \'in(t)-s(ə-)lən(t)s\ *noun* (14th century)
**1 :** the quality or state of being insolent
**2 :** an instance of insolent conduct or treatment

**in·so·lent** \-s(ə-)lənt\ *adjective* [Middle English, from Latin *insolent-, insolens* unaccustomed, overbearing, from *in-* + *solens,* present participle of *solēre* to be accustomed; perhaps akin to Latin *sodalis* comrade — more at SIB] (14th century)
**1 :** insultingly contemptuous in speech or conduct **:** OVERBEARING
**2 :** exhibiting boldness or effrontery **:** IMPUDENT
*synonym* see PROUD
— **insolent** *noun*
— **in·so·lent·ly** *adverb*

**in·sol·u·bi·lize** \(,)in-'säl-yə-bə-,līz\ *transitive verb* (1897)
**:** to make insoluble
— **in·sol·u·bi·li·za·tion** \-,säl-yə-bə-lə-'zā-shən\ *noun*

**in·sol·u·ble** \(,)in-'säl-yə-bəl\ *adjective* [Middle English *insolible,* from Latin *insolubilis,* from *in-* + *solvere* to free, dissolve — more at SOLVE] (14th century)
**:** not soluble: as **a** *archaic* **:** INDISSOLUBLE **b :** having or admitting of no solution or explanation **c :** incapable of being dissolved in a liquid; *also* **:** soluble only with difficulty or to a slight degree
— **in·sol·u·bil·i·ty** \-,säl-yə-'bi-lə-tē\ *noun*
— **insoluble** *noun*
— **in·sol·u·ble·ness** \-'säl-yə-bəl-nəs\ *noun*
— **in·sol·u·bly** \-blē\ *adverb*

**in·solv·able** \(,)in-'säl-və-bəl, -'sȯl-\ *adjective* (1693)
**:** admitting no solution ⟨an apparently *insolvable* problem⟩
— **in·solv·ably** \-blē\ *adverb*

**in·sol·vent** \(,)in-'säl-vənt, -'sȯl-\ *adjective* (1591)
**1 a (1) :** unable to pay debts as they fall due in the usual course of business **(2) :** having liabilities in excess of a reasonable market value of assets held **b :** insufficient to pay all debts ⟨an *insolvent* estate⟩ **c :** not up to a normal standard or complement **:** IMPOVERISHED
**2 :** relating to or for the relief of insolvents
— **in·sol·ven·cy** \-vən(t)-sē\ *noun*
— **insolvent** *noun*

**in·som·nia** \in-'säm-nē-ə\ *noun* [Latin, from *insomnis* sleepless, from *in-* + *somnus* sleep — more at SOMNOLENT] (circa 1623)
**:** prolonged and usually abnormal inability to obtain adequate sleep
— **in·som·ni·ac** \-nē-,ak\ *adjective or noun*

**in·so·much as** \,in(t)-sō-'məch-\ *conjunction* (14th century)
**:** INASMUCH AS

**insomuch that** *conjunction* (14th century)
**:** so 1

**in·sou·ci·ance** \in-'sü-sē-ən(t)s, aⁿ-süs-yäⁿs\ *noun* [French, from *in-* + *soucier* to trouble, disturb, from Latin *sollicitare* — more at SOLICIT] (1799)
**:** lighthearted unconcern **:** NONCHALANCE
— **in·sou·ci·ant** \in-'sü-sē-ənt, aⁿ-süs-yäⁿ\ *adjective*
— **in·sou·ci·ant·ly** \in-'sü-sē-ənt-lē\ *adverb*

**in·soul** *variant of* ENSOUL

**in·span** \in-'span, 'in-,\ *verb* [Afrikaans, from Dutch *inspannen*] (circa 1827)
*chiefly South African* **:** YOKE, HARNESS

**in·spect** \in-'spekt\ *verb* [Latin *inspectus,* past participle of *inspicere,* from *in-* + *specere* to look — more at SPY] (circa 1623)
*transitive verb*
**1 :** to view closely in critical appraisal **:** look over
**2 :** to examine officially ⟨*inspects* the barracks every Friday⟩
*intransitive verb*
**:** to make an inspection
*synonym* see SCRUTINIZE
— **in·spec·tive** \-'spek-tiv\ *adjective*

**in·spec·tion** \in-'spek-shən\ *noun* (14th century)
**1 a :** the act of inspecting **b :** recognition of a familiar pattern leading to immediate solution of a mathematical problem ⟨solve an equation by *inspection*⟩
**2 :** a checking or testing of an individual against established standards

**inspection arms** *noun* [from the command *inspection arms!*] (circa 1884)
**:** a position in the manual of arms in which the rifle is held at port arms with the chamber open for inspection; *also* **:** a command to assume this position

**in·spec·tor** \in-'spek-tər\ *noun* (1602)
**1 :** a person employed to inspect something
**2 a :** a police officer who is in charge of usually several precincts and ranks below a superintendent or deputy superintendent **b :** a person appointed to oversee a polling place
— **in·spec·tor·ship** \-,ship\ *noun*

**in·spec·tor·ate** \in-'spek-t(ə-)rət\ *noun* (1762)
**1 :** the office, position, work, or district of an inspector
**2 :** a body of inspectors

**inspector general** *noun* (1702)
**:** a person who heads an inspectorate or a system of inspection (as of an army)

**in·sphere** *variant of* ENSPHERE

**in·spi·ra·tion** \,in(t)-spə-'rā-shən, -(,)spi-\ *noun* (14th century)
**1 a :** a divine influence or action on a person believed to qualify him or her to receive and communicate sacred revelation **b :** the action or power of moving the intellect or emotions **c :** the act of influencing or suggesting opinions
**2 :** the act of drawing in; *specifically* **:** the drawing of air into the lungs

**3 a :** the quality or state of being inspired **b :** something that is inspired ⟨a scheme that was pure *inspiration*⟩
**4 :** an inspiring agent or influence
— **in·spi·ra·tion·al** \-shnəl, -shə-nᵊl\ *adjective*
— **in·spi·ra·tion·al·ly** *adverb*

**in·spi·ra·tor** \'in(t)-spə-,rā-tər, -(,)spi-\ *noun* (1624)
**:** one that inspires ⟨teachers who are *inspirators* of the young⟩

**in·spi·ra·to·ry** \in-'spī-rə-,tȯr-ē, 'in(t)-sp(ə-)rə-, -,tȯr-\ *adjective* (1773)
**:** of, relating to, used for, or associated with inspiration

**in·spire** \in-'spīr\ *verb* **in·spired; in·spir·ing** [Middle English, from Middle French & Latin; Middle French *inspirer,* from Latin *inspirare,* from *in-* + *spirare* to breathe] (14th century)
*transitive verb*
**1 a :** to influence, move, or guide by divine or supernatural inspiration **b :** to exert an animating, enlivening, or exalting influence on ⟨was particularly *inspired* by the Romanticists⟩ **c :** to spur on **:** IMPEL, MOTIVATE ⟨threats don't necessarily *inspire* people to work⟩ **d :** AFFECT ⟨seeing the old room again *inspired* him with nostalgia⟩
**2 a** *archaic* **:** to breathe or blow into or upon **b** *archaic* **:** to infuse (as life) by breathing
**3 a :** to communicate to an agent supernaturally **b :** to draw forth or bring out ⟨thoughts *inspired* by a visit to the cathedral⟩
**4 :** INHALE 1
**5 a :** BRING ABOUT, OCCASION ⟨the book was *inspired* by his travels in the Far East⟩ **b :** INCITE
**6 :** to spread (rumor) by indirect means or through the agency of another
*intransitive verb*
**:** INHALE
— **in·spir·er** *noun*

**inspired** *adjective* (15th century)
**:** outstanding or brilliant in a way or to a degree suggestive of divine inspiration ⟨gave an *inspired* performance⟩

**inspiring** *adjective* (1717)
**:** having an animating or exalting effect

**in·spir·it** \in-'spir-ət\ *transitive verb* (15th century)
**:** to fill with spirit
*synonym* see ENCOURAGE
— **in·spir·it·ing·ly** \-ə-tiŋ-lē\ *adverb*

**in·spis·sate** \in-'spi-,sāt, 'in(t)-spə-,sāt\ *transitive verb* **-sat·ed; -sat·ing** [Late Latin *inspissatus,* past participle of *inspissare,* from Latin *in-* + *spissus* slow, dense; akin to Greek *spidnos* compact, Lithuanian *spisti* to form a swarm] (1626)
**:** to make thick or thicker
— **in·spis·sa·tion** \,in(t)-spə-'sā-shən, (,)in-,spi-'sā-\ *noun*
— **in·spis·sa·tor** \in-'spi-,sā-tər, 'in(t)-spə-,sā-\ *noun*

**in·spis·sat·ed** \in-'spi-,sā-təd, 'in(t)-spə-,sā-\ *adjective* (1603)
**:** thickened in consistency; *broadly* **:** made or having become thick, heavy, or intense

**in·sta·bil·i·ty** \,in(t)-stə-'bi-lə-tē\ *noun* (15th century)
**:** the quality or state of being unstable; *especially* **:** lack of emotional or mental stability

**in·sta·ble** \(,)in-'stā-bəl\ *adjective* [Middle French or Latin; Middle French, from Latin *instabilis,* from *in-* + *stabilis* stable] (15th century)
**:** UNSTABLE

**in·stall** *also* **in·stal** \in-'stȯl\ *transitive verb* **in·stalled; in·stall·ing** [Middle English, from Middle French *installer,* from Medieval Latin *installare,* from Latin *in-* + Medieval Latin *stallum* stall, from Old High German *stal*] (15th century)

**1 a :** to place in an office or dignity by seating in a stall or official seat **b :** to induct into an office, rank, or order ⟨*installed* the new president⟩
**2 :** to establish in an indicated place, condition, or status ⟨*installing* herself in front of the fireplace⟩
**3 :** to set up for use or service ⟨had an exhaust fan *installed* in the kitchen⟩
— **in·stall·er** *noun*
**in·stal·la·tion** \,in(t)-stə-'lā-shən\ *noun* (15th century)
**1 :** the act of installing **:** the state of being installed
**2 :** something that is installed for use
**3 :** a military camp, fort, or base
¹**in·stall·ment** *also* **in·stal·ment** \in-'stȯl-mənt\ *noun* (1589)
**:** INSTALLATION 1
²**installment** *also* **instalment** *noun* [alteration of earlier *estallment* payment by installment, derivative of Old French *estaler* to place, fix, from *estal* place, of Germanic origin; akin to Old High German *stal* place, stall] (1776)
**1 :** one of the parts into which a debt is divided when payment is made at intervals
**2 a :** one of several parts (as of a publication) presented at intervals **b :** one part of a serial story
— **installment** *adjective*
**installment plan** *noun* (1876)
**:** a system of paying for goods by installments
¹**in·stance** \'in(t)-stən(t)s\ *noun* (14th century)
**1 a** *archaic* **:** urgent or earnest solicitation **b :** INSTIGATION, REQUEST ⟨am writing to you at the *instance* of my client⟩ **c** *obsolete* **:** an impelling cause or motive
**2 a** *archaic* **:** EXCEPTION **b :** an individual illustrative of a category or brought forward in support or disproof of a generalization **c** *obsolete* **:** TOKEN, SIGN
**3 :** the institution and prosecution of a lawsuit **:** SUIT
**4 :** a step, stage, or situation viewed as part of a process or series of events ⟨prefers, in this *instance*, to remain anonymous —*Times Literary Supplement*⟩ ☆
— **for in·stance** \fə-'rin(t)-stən()s, 'frin(t)-\ **:** as an instance or example ⟨older people like my grandmother, *for instance*⟩
²**instance** *transitive verb* **in·stanced; in·stanc·ing** (1601)
**1 :** to illustrate or demonstrate by an instance
**2 :** to mention as a case or example **:** CITE
**in·stan·cy** \'in(t)-stən(t)-sē\ *noun, plural* **-cies** (1515)
**1 :** URGENCY, INSISTENCE
**2 :** nearness of approach **:** IMMINENCE
**3 :** immediacy of occurrence or action **:** INSTANTANEOUSNESS
¹**in·stant** \'in(t)-stənt\ *noun* [Middle English, from Medieval Latin *instant-, instans*, from *instant-, instans*, adjective, instant, from Latin] (14th century)
**1 :** an infinitesimal space of time; *especially* **:** a point in time separating two states ⟨at the *instant* of death⟩
**2 :** the present or current month
²**instant** *adjective* [Middle English, from Middle French or Latin; Middle French, from Latin *instant-, instans*, from present participle of *instare* to stand upon, urge, from *in-* + *stare* to stand — more at STAND] (15th century)
**1 :** IMPORTUNATE, URGENT
**2 a :** PRESENT, CURRENT ⟨previous felonies not related to the *instant* crime⟩ **b :** of or occurring in the present month
**3 :** IMMEDIATE, DIRECT ⟨the play was an *instant* success⟩
**4 a** (1) **:** premixed or precooked for easy final preparation ⟨*instant* pudding⟩ (2) **:** appearing in or as if in ready-to-use form ⟨*instant* culture⟩ **b :** immediately soluble in water ⟨*instant* coffee⟩

**5 :** produced or occurring with or as if with extreme rapidity and ease
— **in·stant·ness** *noun*
**in·stan·ta·neous** \,in(t)-stən-'tā-nē-əs, -nyəs\ *adjective* [Medieval Latin *instantaneus*, from *instant-, instans*, noun] (1651)
**1 :** done, occurring, or acting without any perceptible duration of time ⟨death was *instantaneous*⟩
**2 :** done without any delay being purposely introduced ⟨took *instantaneous* action to correct the abuse⟩
**3 :** occurring or present at a particular instant ⟨*instantaneous* velocity⟩
— **in·stan·ta·ne·ity** \,in-,stan-tᵊn-'ē-ə-tē, ,in(t)-stən-tə-'nē-\ *noun*
— **in·stan·ta·neous·ly** \,in(t)-stən-'tā-nē-əs-lē, -nyəs-lē\ *adverb*
— **in·stan·ta·neous·ness** *noun*
**in·stan·ter** \in-'stan-tər\ *adverb* [Medieval Latin, from *instant-, instans*] (1688)
**:** at once
**in·stan·ti·ate** \in-'stan(t)-shē-,āt\ *transitive verb* **-at·ed; -at·ing** (1949)
**:** to represent (an abstraction) by a concrete instance ⟨heroes *instantiate* ideals —W. J. Bennett⟩
— **in·stan·ti·a·tion** \-,stan(t)-shē-'ā-shən\ *noun*
¹**in·stant·ly** \'in(t)-stənt-lē\ *adverb* (15th century)
**1 :** with importunity **:** URGENTLY
**2 :** without the least delay **:** IMMEDIATELY
²**instantly** *conjunction* (1793)
**:** as soon as ⟨he ran across the grass *instantly* he perceived his mother —W. M. Thackeray⟩
**instant replay** *noun* (1966)
**:** a videotape recording of an action (as a play in football) that can be played back (as in slow motion) immediately after the action has been completed; *also* **:** the playing of such a recording
**in·star** \'in-,stär\ *noun* [New Latin, from Latin, equivalent] (1895)
**:** a stage in the life of an arthropod (as an insect) between two successive molts; *also* **:** an individual in a specified instar
**in·state** \in-'stāt\ *transitive verb* (1603)
**1** *obsolete* **a :** INVEST, ENDOW **b :** BESTOW, CONFER
**2 :** to set or establish in a rank or office **:** INSTALL
**in sta·tu quo** \in-,stā-(,)tü-'kwō, -,sta-; -,sta-(,)chü-\ *adverb* [New Latin, literally, in the state in which] (1602)
**:** in the former or same state
**in·stau·ra·tion** \,in-,stȯ-'rā-shən, ,in(t)-stə-\ *noun* [Latin *instauration-, instauratio*, from *instaurare* to renew, restore — more at STORE] (circa 1603)
**1 :** restoration after decay, lapse, or dilapidation
**2 :** an act of instituting or establishing something
**in·stead** \in-'sted\ *adverb* (1667)
**1 :** as a substitute or equivalent ⟨was going to write but called *instead*⟩
**2 :** as an alternative to something expressed or implied **:** RATHER ⟨longed *instead* for a quiet country life⟩
**in·stead of** \in-'ste-də(v), -'sti-\ *preposition* [Middle English *in sted of*] (13th century)
**:** in place of **:** as a substitute for or alternative to
**in·step** \'in-,step\ *noun* (15th century)
**1 :** the arched middle portion of the human foot in front of the ankle joint; *especially* **:** its upper surface
**2 :** the part of a shoe or stocking that fits over the instep

**instep 1**

**in·sti·gate** \'in(t)-stə-,gāt\ *transitive verb* **-gat·ed; -gat·ing** [Latin *instigatus*, past participle of *instigare* — more at STICK] (1542)
**:** to goad or urge forward **:** PROVOKE
*synonym* see INCITE
— **in·sti·ga·tion** \,in(t)-stə-'gā-shən\ *noun*
— **in·sti·ga·tive** \'in(t)-stə-,gā-tiv\ *adjective*
— **in·sti·ga·tor** \-,gā-tər\ *noun*
**in·still** *also* **in·stil** \in-'stil\ *transitive verb* **in·stilled; in·still·ing** [Middle English, from Middle French & Latin; Middle French *instiller*, from Latin *instillare*, from *in-* + *stillare* to drip, from *stilla* drop] (15th century)
**1 :** to cause to enter drop by drop ⟨*instill* medication into the infected eye⟩
**2 :** to impart gradually ⟨*instilling* a love of learning in children⟩
*synonym* see IMPLANT
— **in·stil·la·tion** \,in(t)-stə-'lā-shən, -(,)sti-\ *noun*
— **in·still·er** \in-'sti-lər\ *noun*
— **in·still·ment** \-mənt\ *noun*
¹**in·stinct** \'in-,stiŋ(k)t\ *noun* [Middle English, from Latin *instinctus* impulse, from *instinguere* to incite; akin to Latin *instigare* to instigate] (15th century)
**1 :** a natural or inherent aptitude, impulse, or capacity ⟨had an *instinct* for the right word⟩
**2 a :** a largely inheritable and unalterable tendency of an organism to make a complex and specific response to environmental stimuli without involving reason **b :** behavior that is mediated by reactions below the conscious level
— **in·stinc·tu·al** \in-'stiŋ(k)-chə-wəl, -chəl, -shwəl\ *adjective*
— **in·stinc·tu·al·ly** *adverb*
²**in·stinct** \in-'stiŋ(k)t, 'in-,\ *adjective* (1667)
**1** *obsolete* **:** impelled by an inner or animating or exciting agency
**2 :** profoundly imbued **:** INFUSED ⟨my mood, *instinct* with romance —S. J. Perelman⟩
**in·stinc·tive** \in-'stiŋ(k)-tiv\ *adjective* (15th century)
**1 :** of, relating to, or being instinct
**2 :** prompted by natural instinct or propensity **:** arising spontaneously ⟨an *instinctive* fear of innovation —V. L. Parrington⟩
*synonym* see SPONTANEOUS
— **in·stinc·tive·ly** *adverb*
¹**in·sti·tute** \'in(t)-stə-,tüt, -,tyüt\ *transitive verb* **-tut·ed; -tut·ing** [Middle English, from

\ə\ abut  \ᵊ\ kitten  \ər\ further  \a\ ash  \ā\ ace
\ä\ mop, mar  \au̇\ out  \ch\ chin  \e\ bet  \ē\ easy
\g\ go  \i\ hit  \ī\ ice  \j\ job  \ŋ\ sing  \ō\ go
\ȯ\ law  \ȯi\ boy  \th\ thin  \t͟h\ the  \ü\ loot  \u̇\ foot
\y\ yet  \zh\ vision  *see also* Guide to Pronunciation

Latin *institutus*, past participle of *instituere*, from *in-* + *statuere* to set up — more at STATUTE] (14th century)
**1 :** to establish in a position or office
**2 a :** to originate and get established : ORGANIZE ⟨*instituted* reading clinics⟩ **b :** to set going : INAUGURATE ⟨*instituting* an investigation of the charges⟩
— **in·sti·tut·er** *or* **in·sti·tu·tor** \-ˌtü-tər, -ˌtyü-\ *noun*

²**institute** *noun* (1546)
**:** something that is instituted: as **a** (1) **:** an elementary principle recognized as authoritative (2) *plural* **:** a collection of such principles and precepts; *especially* **:** a legal compendium **b :** an organization for the promotion of a cause **:** ASSOCIATION ⟨a research *institute*⟩ ⟨an *institute* for the blind⟩ **c :** an educational institution and especially one devoted to technical fields **d :** a usually brief intensive course of instruction on selected topics relating to a particular field ⟨an urban studies *institute*⟩

**in·sti·tu·tion** \ˌin(t)-stə-ˈtü-shən, -ˈtyü-\ *noun* (14th century)
**1 :** an act of instituting : ESTABLISHMENT
**2 a :** a significant practice, relationship, or organization in a society or culture ⟨the *institution* of marriage⟩; *also* **:** something or someone firmly associated with a place or thing ⟨she has become an *institution* in the theater⟩ **b :** an established organization or corporation (as a college or university) especially of a public character; *also* **:** ASYLUM 4
— **in·sti·tu·tion·al** \-shnəl, -shə-nᵊl\ *adjective*
— **in·sti·tu·tion·al·ly** *adverb*

**in·sti·tu·tion·al·ise** *British variant of* INSTITUTIONALIZE

**in·sti·tu·tion·al·ism** \-shnə-ˌli-zəm, -shə-nᵊl-ˌi-zəm\ *noun* (1862)
**1 :** emphasis on organization (as in religion) at the expense of other factors
**2 :** public institutional care of handicapped, delinquent, or dependent persons
**3 :** an economic school of thought that emphasizes the role of social institutions in influencing economic behavior
— **in·sti·tu·tion·al·ist** \-shnə-list, -shə-nᵊl-ist\ *noun*

**in·sti·tu·tion·al·ize** \-shnə-ˌlīz, -shə-nᵊl-ˌīz\ *transitive verb* **-ized; -iz·ing** (1865)
**1 :** to make into an institution : give character of an institution to ⟨*institutionalized* housing⟩; *especially* **:** to incorporate into a structured and often highly formalized system ⟨*institutionalized* values⟩
**2 :** to put in the care of an institution ⟨*institutionalize* alcoholics⟩
— **in·sti·tu·tion·al·i·za·tion** \-ˌtü-shnə-lə-ˈzā-shən, -shə-nᵊl-ə-ˈzā-\ *noun*

**in–store** \ˈin-ˈstȯr, -ˈstȯr\ *adjective* (1961)
**:** relating to or being an operation or activity located or taking place inside a store ⟨*in-store* consumer survey⟩

**in·struct** \in-ˈstrəkt\ *transitive verb* [Middle English, from Latin *instructus*, past participle of *instruere*, from *in-* + *struere* to build — more at STRUCTURE] (15th century)
**1 :** to give knowledge to : TEACH, TRAIN
**2 :** to provide with authoritative information or advice ⟨the judge *instructed* the jury⟩
**3 :** to give an order or command to : DIRECT
**synonym** *see* TEACH, COMMAND

**in·struc·tion** \in-ˈstrək-shən\ *noun* (15th century)
**1 a :** PRECEPT ⟨prevailing cultural *instructions*⟩ **b :** a direction calling for compliance : ORDER — usually used in plural ⟨had *instructions* not to admit strangers⟩ **c** *plural* **:** an outline or manual of technical procedure : DIRECTIONS **d :** a code that tells a computer to perform a particular operation
**2 :** the action, practice, or profession of teaching
— **in·struc·tion·al** \-shnəl, -shə-nᵊl\ *adjective*

**in·struc·tive** \in-ˈstrək-tiv\ *adjective* (1611)
**:** carrying a lesson : ENLIGHTENING
— **in·struc·tive·ly** *adverb*
— **in·struc·tive·ness** *noun*
**in·struc·tor** \in-ˈstrək-tər\ *noun* (15th century)
**:** one that instructs : TEACHER; *especially* **:** a college teacher below professorial rank
— **in·struc·tor·ship** \-ˌship\ *noun*
**in·struc·tress** \-ˈstrək-trəs\ *noun* (1630)
**:** a woman who is an instructor

¹**in·stru·ment** \ˈin(t)-strə-mənt\ *noun* [Middle English, from Latin *instrumentum*, from *instruere* to arrange, instruct] (14th century)
**1 :** a device used to produce music
**2 a :** a means whereby something is achieved, performed, or furthered **b :** one used by another as a means or aid : DUPE, TOOL
**3 :** IMPLEMENT; *especially* **:** one designed for precision work
**4 :** a formal legal document (as a deed, bond, or agreement)
**5 a :** a measuring device for determining the present value of a quantity under observation **b :** an electrical or mechanical device used in navigating an airplane; *especially* **:** such a device used as the sole means of navigating
**synonym** *see* IMPLEMENT
²**in·stru·ment** \-ˌment\ *transitive verb* (1752)
**1 :** to address a legal instrument to
**2 :** to score for musical performance : ORCHESTRATE
**3 :** to equip with instruments especially for measuring and recording data ⟨an *instrumented* spacecraft⟩
**in·stru·men·tal** \ˌin(t)-strə-ˈmen-tᵊl\ *adjective* (14th century)
**1 a :** serving as a means, agent, or tool ⟨was *instrumental* in organizing the strike⟩ **b :** of, relating to, or done with an instrument or tool
**2 :** relating to, composed for, or performed on a musical instrument
**3 :** of, relating to, or being a grammatical case or form expressing means or agency
**4 :** of or relating to instrumentalism
**5 :** OPERANT 3 ⟨*instrumental* learning⟩ ⟨*instrumental* conditioning⟩
— **instrumental** *noun*
— **in·stru·men·tal·ly** \-tᵊl-ē\ *adverb*
**in·stru·men·tal·ism** \-i-zəm\ *noun* (1909)
**:** a doctrine that ideas are instruments of action and that their usefulness determines their truth
**in·stru·men·tal·ist** \-ist\ *noun* (1823)
**1 :** a player on a musical instrument
**2 :** an exponent of instrumentalism
— **instrumentalist** *adjective*
**in·stru·men·tal·i·ty** \ˌin(t)-strə-mən-ˈta-lə-tē, -ˌmen-\ *noun, plural* **-ties** (1651)
**1 :** the quality or state of being instrumental
**2 :** MEANS, AGENCY
**in·stru·men·ta·tion** \ˌin(t)-strə-mən-ˈtā-shən, -ˌmen-\ *noun* (1845)
**1 :** the arrangement or composition of music for instruments especially for a band or orchestra
**2 :** the use or application of instruments (as for observation, measurement, or control)
**3 :** instruments for a particular purpose; *also* **:** a selection or arrangement of instruments
**instrument flying** *noun* (1928)
**:** navigation of an airplane by instruments only
**instrument landing** *noun* (1938)
**:** a landing made with limited visibility by means of instruments and by ground radio direction
**instrument panel** *noun* (1922)
**:** a panel on which instruments are mounted; *especially* **:** DASHBOARD 2
**in·sub·or·di·nate** \ˌin(t)-sə-ˈbȯr-dᵊn-ət, -ˈbȯrd-nət\ *adjective* (circa 1828)
**:** disobedient to authority
— **insubordinate** *noun*
— **in·sub·or·di·nate·ly** *adverb*
— **in·sub·or·di·na·tion** \-ˌbȯr-dᵊn-ˈā-shən\ *noun*

**in·sub·stan·tial** \ˌin(t)-səb-ˈstan(t)-shəl\ *adjective* [probably from French *insubstantiel*, from Late Latin *insubstantialis*, from Latin *in-* + Late Latin *substantialis* substantial] (1607)
**:** not substantial: as **a :** lacking substance or material nature **b :** lacking firmness or solidity **:** FLIMSY
— **in·sub·stan·ti·al·i·ty** \-ˌstan(t)-shē-ˈa-lə-tē\ *noun*
**in·suf·fer·able** \(ˌ)in-ˈsə-f(ə-)rə-bəl\ *adjective* (15th century)
**:** not to be endured : INTOLERABLE ⟨an *insufferable* bore⟩
— **in·suf·fer·able·ness** *noun*
— **in·suf·fer·ably** \-blē\ *adverb*
**in·suf·fi·cien·cy** \ˌin(t)-sə-ˈfi-shən(t)-sē\ *noun, plural* **-cies** (1526)
**1 :** the quality or state of being insufficient: as **a :** lack of mental or moral fitness : INCOMPETENCE ⟨the *insufficiency* of this person for public office⟩ **b :** lack of adequate supply ⟨*insufficiency* of provisions⟩ **c :** lack of physical power or capacity; *specifically* **:** inability of an organ or body part to function normally
**2 :** something that is insufficient or falls short of expectations
**in·suf·fi·cient** \ˌin(t)-sə-ˈfi-shənt\ *adjective* [Middle English, from Middle French, from Late Latin *insufficient-, insufficiens*, from Latin *in-* + *sufficient-, sufficiens* sufficient] (14th century)
**:** not sufficient : INADEQUATE; *especially* **:** lacking adequate power, capacity, or competence
— **in·suf·fi·cient·ly** *adverb*
**in·suf·fla·tion** \ˌin(t)-sə-ˈflā-shən, in-ˌsə-ˈflā-\ *noun* [Middle English *insufflacion*, from Middle French *insufflation*, from Late Latin *insufflation-, insufflatio*, from *insufflare* to blow upon, from Latin *in-* + *sufflare* to inflate, from *sub-* + *flare* to blow — more at BLOW] (15th century)
**:** an act or the action of blowing on, into, or in: as **a :** a Christian ceremonial rite of exorcism performed by breathing on a person **b :** the act of blowing something (as a gas, powder, or vapor) into a body cavity
— **in·suf·flate** \ˈin(t)-sə-ˌflāt, in-ˈsə-ˌflāt\ *transitive verb*
— **in·suf·fla·tor** \-ˌflā-tər\ *noun*
**in·su·lant** \ˈin(t)-sə-lənt\ *noun* (circa 1929)
*chiefly British* **:** INSULATION 2
**in·su·lar** \ˈin(t)-sü-lər, -syü-, ˈin-shə-lər\ *adjective* [Late Latin *insularis*, from Latin *insula* island] (1611)
**1 a :** of, relating to, or constituting an island **b :** dwelling or situated on an island ⟨*insular* residents⟩
**2 :** characteristic of an isolated people; *especially* **:** being, having, or reflecting a narrow provincial viewpoint
**3 :** of or relating to an island of cells or tissue
— **in·su·lar·ism** \-lə-ˌri-zəm\ *noun*
— **in·su·lar·i·ty** \ˌin(t)-sü-ˈlar-ə-tē, -syü-, ˌin-shə-ˈlar-\ *noun*
— **in·su·lar·ly** \ˈin(t)-sü-lər-lē, -syü-, ˈin-shə-\ *adverb*
**in·su·late** \ˈin(t)-sə-ˌlāt\ *transitive verb* **-lat·ed; -lat·ing** [Latin *insula*] (circa 1741)
**:** to place in a detached situation : ISOLATE; *especially* **:** to separate from conducting bodies by means of nonconductors so as to prevent transfer of electricity, heat, or sound
**in·su·la·tion** \ˌin(t)-sə-ˈlā-shən\ *noun* (1798)
**1 a :** the action of insulating **b :** the state of being insulated
**2 :** material used in insulating
**in·su·la·tor** \ˈin(t)-sə-ˌlā-tər\ *noun* (1801)
**:** one that insulates: as **a :** a material that is a poor conductor (as of electricity or heat) — compare SEMICONDUCTOR **b :** a device made of an electrical insulating material and used for separating or supporting conductors
**in·su·lin** \ˈin(t)-s(ə-)lən\ *noun* [New Latin *insula* islet (of Langerhans), from Latin, island] (1914)

: a protein pancreatic hormone secreted by the islets of Langerhans that is essential especially for the metabolism of carbohydrates and is used in the treatment and control of diabetes mellitus

**insulin shock** *noun* (1925)
: hypoglycemia associated with the presence of excessive insulin in the system and characterized by progressive development of coma

**¹in·sult** \in-ˈsəlt\ *verb* [Middle French or Latin; Middle French *insulter*, from Latin *insultare*, literally, to spring upon, from *in-* + *saltare* to leap — more at SALTATION] (1540)
*intransitive verb*
*archaic* : to behave with pride or arrogance : VAUNT
*transitive verb*
: to treat with insolence, indignity, or contempt : AFFRONT; *also* : to affect offensively or damagingly ⟨doggerel that *insults* the reader's intelligence⟩
**synonym** see OFFEND
— **in·sult·er** *noun*
— **in·sult·ing·ly** \in-ˈsəl-tiŋ-lē\ *adverb*
**²in·sult** \ˈin-ˌsəlt\ *noun* (1671)
**1** : a gross indignity
**2** : injury to the body or one of its parts; *also* : something that causes or has a potential for causing such insult ⟨pollution and other environmental *insults*⟩
**in·su·per·a·ble** \(ˌ)in-ˈsü-p(ə-)rə-bəl\ *adjective* [Middle English, from Middle French & Latin; Middle French, from Latin *insuperabilis*, from *in-* + *superare* to surmount, from *super* over — more at OVER] (14th century)
: incapable of being surmounted, overcome, passed over, or solved ⟨*insuperable* difficulties⟩
— **in·su·per·a·bly** \-blē\ *adverb*
**in·sup·port·able** \ˌin(t)-sə-ˈpōr-tə-bəl, -ˈpȯr-\ *adjective* [Middle French or Late Latin; Middle French, from Late Latin *insupportabilis*, from Latin *in-* + *supportare* to support] (circa 1530)
: not supportable: **a** : more than can be endured ⟨*insupportable* pain⟩ **b** : impossible to justify ⟨*insupportable* charges⟩
— **in·sup·port·ably** \-blē\ *adverb*
**in·sup·press·ible** \ˌin(t)-sə-ˈpre-sə-bəl\ *adjective* (1610)
: IRREPRESSIBLE
**in·sur·able** \in-ˈshu̇r-ə-bəl\ *adjective* (1810)
: that may be insured
— **in·sur·abil·i·ty** \-ˌshu̇r-ə-ˈbi-lə-tē\ *noun*
**¹in·sur·ance** \in-ˈshu̇r-ən(t)s also ˈin-ˌ\ *noun* (1651)
**1 a** : the business of insuring persons or property **b** : coverage by contract whereby one party undertakes to indemnify or guarantee another against loss by a specified contingency or peril **c** : the sum for which something is insured
**2** : a means of guaranteeing protection or safety ⟨the contract is your *insurance* against price changes⟩
**²insurance** *adjective* (1954)
: being a score that adds to a team's lead and makes it impossible for the opposing team to tie the game with its next score ⟨*insurance* run⟩
**in·sure** \in-ˈshu̇r\ *verb* **in·sured; in·sur·ing** [Middle English, to assure, probably alteration of *assuren*] (1635)
*transitive verb*
**1** : to provide or obtain insurance on or for
**2** : to make certain especially by taking necessary measures and precautions
*intransitive verb*
: to contract to give or take insurance
**synonym** see ENSURE
**insured** *noun* (1681)
: a person whose life or property is insured
**in·sur·er** \in-ˈshu̇r-ər\ *noun* (1654)
: one that insures; *specifically* : an insurance underwriter
**in·sur·gence** \in-ˈsər-jən(t)s\ *noun* (1847)

: an act or the action of being insurgent : INSURRECTION
**in·sur·gen·cy** \-jən(t)-sē\ *noun, plural* **-cies** (1803)
**1** : the quality or state of being insurgent; *specifically* : a condition of revolt against a government that is less than an organized revolution and that is not recognized as belligerency
**2** : INSURGENCE
**¹in·sur·gent** \-jənt\ *noun* [Latin *insurgent-, insurgens*, present participle of *insurgere* to rise up, from *in-* + *surgere* to rise — more at SURGE] (1765)
**1** : a person who revolts against civil authority or an established government; *especially* : a rebel not recognized as a belligerent
**2** : one who acts contrary to the policies and decisions of one's own political party
**²insurgent** *adjective* (1814)
: rising in opposition to civil authority or established leadership : REBELLIOUS
— **in·sur·gent·ly** *adverb*
**in·sur·mount·able** \ˌin(t)-sər-ˈmau̇n-tə-bəl\ *adjective* (1690)
: incapable of being surmounted : INSUPERABLE ⟨*insurmountable* problems⟩
— **in·sur·mount·ably** \-blē\ *adverb*
**in·sur·rec·tion** \ˌin(t)-sə-ˈrek-shən\ *noun* [Middle English, from Middle French, from Late Latin *insurrection-, insurrectio*, from *insurgere*] (15th century)
: an act or instance of revolting against civil authority or an established government
**synonym** see REBELLION
— **in·sur·rec·tion·al** \-shnəl, -shə-nᵊl\ *adjective*
— **in·sur·rec·tion·ary** \-shə-ˌner-ē\ *adjective or noun*
— **in·sur·rec·tion·ist** \-sh(ə-)nist\ *noun*
**in·sus·cep·ti·ble** \ˌin(t)-sə-ˈsep-tə-bəl\ *adjective* (1603)
: not susceptible ⟨*insusceptible* to flattery⟩
— **in·sus·cep·ti·bil·i·ty** \-ˌsep-tə-ˈbi-lə-tē\ *noun*
— **in·sus·cep·ti·bly** \ˌin(t)-sə-ˈsep-tə-blē\ *adverb*
**in·tact** \in-ˈtakt\ *adjective* [Middle English *intacte*, from Latin *intactus*, from *in-* + *tactus*, past participle of *tangere* to touch — more at TANGENT] (15th century)
**1** : untouched especially by anything that harms or diminishes : ENTIRE, UNINJURED
**2** *of a living body or its parts* : having no relevant component removed or destroyed: **a** : physically virginal **b** : not castrated
**synonym** see PERFECT
— **in·tact·ness** \-ˈtak(t)-nəs\ *noun*
**in·ta·glio** \in-ˈtal-(ˌ)yō, -ˈtäl-; -ˈta-glē-ˌō, -ˈtä-\ *noun, plural* **-glios** [Italian, from *intagliare* to engrave, cut, from Medieval Latin *intaliare*, from Latin *in-* + Late Latin *taliare* to cut — more at TAILOR] (1644)
**1 a** : an engraving or incised figure in stone or other hard material depressed below the surface so that an impression from the design yields an image in relief **b** : the art or process of executing intaglios **c** : printing (as in die stamping and gravure) done from a plate in which the image is sunk below the surface
**2** : something (as a gem) carved in intaglio
**in·take** \ˈin-ˌtāk\ *noun* (15th century)
**1** : an opening through which fluid enters an enclosure
**2 a** : a taking in **b** (1) : the amount taken in (2) : something (as energy) taken in : INPUT
**¹in·tan·gi·ble** \(ˌ)in-ˈtan-jə-bəl\ *adjective* [French or Medieval Latin; French, from Medieval Latin *intangibilis*, from Latin *in-* + Late Latin *tangibilis* tangible] (1640)
: not tangible : IMPALPABLE

**intaglio 1a**

— **in·tan·gi·bil·i·ty** \-ˌtan-jə-ˈbi-lə-tē\ *noun*
— **in·tan·gi·ble·ness** \-ˈtan-jə-bəl-nəs\ *noun*
— **in·tan·gi·bly** \-blē\ *adverb*
**²intangible** *noun* (1914)
: something intangible; *specifically* : an asset (as goodwill) that is not corporeal
**in·tar·sia** \in-ˈtär-sē-ə\ *noun* [German, modification of Italian *intarsio*] (1867)
**1** : a mosaic usually of wood fitted into a support; *also* : the art or process of making such a mosaic
**2** : a colored design knitted on both sides of a fabric (as in a sweater)
**in·te·ger** \ˈin-ti-jər\ *noun* [Latin, adjective, whole, entire — more at ENTIRE] (1571)
**1** : any of the natural numbers, the negatives of these numbers, or zero
**2** : a complete entity
**in·te·gra·ble** \ˈin-ti-grə-bəl\ *adjective* (circa 1741)
: capable of being integrated ⟨*integrable* functions⟩
— **in·te·gra·bil·i·ty** \ˌin-ti-grə-ˈbi-lə-tē\ *noun*
**¹in·te·gral** \ˈin-ti-grəl (*usually so in mathematics*); in-ˈte-grəl also -ˈtē- also ÷ˈin-trə-gəl\ *adjective* (1551)
**1 a** : essential to completeness : CONSTITUENT ⟨an *integral* part of the curriculum⟩ **b** (1) : being, containing, or relating to one or more mathematical integers (2) : relating to or concerned with mathematical integrals or integration **c** : formed as a unit with another part ⟨a seat with *integral* headrest⟩
**2** : composed of integral parts
**3** : lacking nothing essential : ENTIRE
— **in·te·gral·i·ty** \ˌin-tə-ˈgra-lə-tē\ *noun*
— **in·te·gral·ly** \ˈin-ti-grə-lē; in-ˈte-grə- also -ˈtē-\ *adverb*
**²integral** *noun* (circa 1741)
: the result of a mathematical integration — compare DEFINITE INTEGRAL, INDEFINITE INTEGRAL
**integral calculus** *noun* (circa 1741)
: a branch of mathematics concerned with the theory and applications (as in the determination of lengths, areas, and volumes and in the solution of differential equations) of integrals and integration
**integral domain** *noun* (1937)
: a mathematical ring in which multiplication is commutative, which has a multiplicative identity element, and which contains no pair of nonzero elements whose product is zero ⟨the integers under the operations of addition and multiplication form an *integral domain*⟩
**in·te·grand** \ˈin-tə-ˌgrand\ *noun* [Latin *integrandus*, gerundive of *integrare*] (1897)
: a mathematical expression to be integrated
**in·te·grate** \ˈin-tə-ˌgrāt\ *verb* **-grat·ed; -grat·ing** [Latin *integratus*, past participle of *integrare*, from *integr-, integer*] (1638)
*transitive verb*
**1** : to form, coordinate, or blend into a functioning or unified whole : UNITE
**2** : to find the integral of (as a function or equation)
**3 a** : to unite with something else **b** : to incorporate into a larger unit
**4 a** : to end the segregation of and bring into equal membership in society or an organization **b** : DESEGREGATE ⟨*integrate* school districts⟩
*intransitive verb*
: to become integrated
**integrated** *adjective* (1922)
**1** : marked by the unified control of all aspects of industrial production from raw materials

\ə\ abut \ᵊ\ kitten \ər\ further \a\ ash \ā\ ace \ä\ mop, mar \au̇\ out \ch\ chin \e\ bet \ē\ easy \g\ go \i\ hit \ī\ ice \j\ job \ŋ\ sing \ō\ go \ȯ\ law \ȯi\ boy \th\ thin \th\ the \ü\ loot \u̇\ foot \y\ yet \zh\ vision *see also* Guide to Pronunciation through distribution of finished products ⟨*integrated* companies⟩ ⟨*integrated* production⟩ **2 :** characterized by integration and especially racial integration ⟨an *integrated* society⟩ ⟨*integrated* schools⟩

**integrated circuit** *noun* (1962)
**:** a tiny complex of electronic components and their connections that is produced in or on a small slice of material (as silicon)
— **integrated circuitry** *noun*

**in·te·gra·tion** \,in-tə-'grā-shən\ *noun* (1620)
**1 :** the act or process or an instance of integrating: as **a :** incorporation as equals into society or an organization of individuals of different groups (as races) **b :** coordination of mental processes into a normal effective personality or with the individual's environment
**2 a :** the operation of finding a function whose differential is known **b :** the operation of solving a differential equation

**in·te·gra·tion·ist** \-sh(ə-)nist\ *noun* (1951)
**:** a person who believes in, advocates, or practices social integration
— **integrationist** *adjective*

**in·te·gra·tive** \'in-tə-,grā-tiv\ *adjective* (1862)
**:** serving to integrate or favoring integration **:** directed toward integration

**in·te·gra·tor** \-,grā-tər\ *noun* (1876)·
**:** one that integrates; *especially* **:** a device or computer unit that totalizes variable quantities in a manner comparable to mathematical integration

**in·teg·ri·ty** \in-'te-grə-tē\ *noun* [Middle English *integrite*, from Middle French & Latin; Middle French *intégrité*, from Latin *integritat-, integritas*, from *integr-, integer* entire] (14th century)
**1 :** firm adherence to a code of especially moral or artistic values **:** INCORRUPTIBILITY
**2 :** an unimpaired condition **:** SOUNDNESS
**3 :** the quality or state of being complete or undivided **:** COMPLETENESS
*synonym* see HONESTY

**in·teg·u·ment** \in-'te-gyə-mənt\ *noun* [Latin *integumentum*, from *integere* to cover, from *in-* + *tegere* to cover — more at THATCH] (circa 1611)
**:** something that covers or encloses; *especially* **:** an enveloping layer (as a skin, membrane, or husk) of an organism or one of its parts
— **in·teg·u·men·ta·ry** \-'men-t(ə-)rē\ *adjective*

**in·tel·lect** \'in-tᵊl-,ekt\ *noun* [Middle English, from Middle French or Latin; Middle French, from Latin *intellectus*, from *intellegere* to understand — more at INTELLIGENT] (14th century)
**1 a :** the power of knowing as distinguished from the power to feel and to will **:** the capacity for knowledge **b :** the capacity for rational or intelligent thought especially when highly developed
**2 :** a person with great intellectual powers

**in·tel·lec·tion** \,in-tᵊl-'ek-shən\ *noun* (1579)
**1 :** an act of the intellect **:** THOUGHT
**2 :** exercise of the intellect **:** REASONING

**in·tel·lec·tive** \-'ek-tiv\ *adjective* (15th century)
**:** having, relating to, or belonging to the intellect **:** RATIONAL
— **in·tel·lec·tive·ly** *adverb*

¹**in·tel·lec·tu·al** \,in-tᵊl-'ek-chə-wəl, -chəl, -shwəl\ *adjective* (14th century)
**1 a :** of or relating to the intellect or its use **b :** developed or chiefly guided by the intellect rather than by emotion or experience **:** RATIONAL **c :** requiring use of the intellect
**2 a :** given to study, reflection, and speculation **b :** engaged in activity requiring the creative use of the intellect
— **in·tel·lec·tu·al·i·ty** \-,ek-chə-'wa-lə-tē\ *noun*
— **in·tel·lec·tu·al·ly** \-'ek-chə-wə-lē, -chə-lē, -shwə-lē\ *adverb*
— **in·tel·lec·tu·al·ness** \-'ek-chə-wəl-nəs, -chəl-, -shwəl-\ *noun*

²**intellectual** *noun* (1615)
**1** *plural, archaic* **:** intellectual powers
**2 :** an intellectual person

**in·tel·lec·tu·al·ism** \,in-tᵊl-'ek-chə-wə-,li-zəm, -chə-,li-, -shwə,li-\ *noun* (1838)
**:** devotion to the exercise of intellect or to intellectual pursuits
— **in·tel·lec·tu·al·ist** \-list\ *noun or adjective*
— **in·tel·lec·tu·al·is·tic** \-,ek-chə-wə-'lis-tik, -chə-'lis-, -shwə-'lis-\ *adjective*

**in·tel·lec·tu·al·ize** \,in-tᵊl-'ek-chə-wə-,līz, -chə-,līz, -shwə-,līz\ *transitive verb* **-ized; -iz·ing** (circa 1819)
**:** to give rational form or content to
— **in·tel·lec·tu·al·i·za·tion** \-,ek-chə-wə-lə-'zā-shən, -chə-lə-, -shwə-lə-\ *noun*
— **in·tel·lec·tu·al·iz·er** \-'ek-chə-wə-,lī-zər, -chə-,lī-, -shwə-,lī-\ *noun*

**in·tel·li·gence** \in-'te-lə-jən(t)s\ *noun* [Middle English, from Middle French, from Latin *intelligentia*, from *intelligent-, intelligens* intelligent] (14th century)
**1 a** (1) **:** the ability to learn or understand or to deal with new or trying situations **:** REASON; *also* **:** the skilled use of reason (2) **:** the ability to apply knowledge to manipulate one's environment or to think abstractly as measured by objective criteria (as tests) **b** *Christian Science* **:** the basic eternal quality of divine Mind **c :** mental acuteness **:** SHREWDNESS
**2 a :** an intelligent entity; *especially* **:** ANGEL **b :** intelligent minds or mind ⟨cosmic *intelligence*⟩
**3 :** the act of understanding **:** COMPREHENSION
**4 a :** INFORMATION, NEWS **b :** information concerning an enemy or possible enemy or an area; *also* **:** an agency engaged in obtaining such information
**5 :** the ability to perform computer functions

**intelligence quotient** *noun* (1916)
**:** a number used to express the apparent relative intelligence of a person that is the ratio multiplied by 100 of the mental age as reported on a standardized test to the chronological age

**in·tel·li·genc·er** \in-'te-lə-jən(t)-sər; -'te-lə-,jen(t)-, -,te-lə-\ *noun* (1581)
**1 :** a secret agent **:** SPY
**2 :** a bringer of news **:** REPORTER

**intelligence test** *noun* (1914)
**:** a test designed to determine the relative mental capacity of a person

**in·tel·li·gent** \in-'te-lə-jənt\ *adjective* [Latin *intelligent-, intelligens*, present participle of *intelligere, intellegere* to understand, from *inter-* + *legere* to gather, select — more at LEGEND] (1509)
**1 a :** having or indicating a high or satisfactory degree of intelligence and mental capacity **b :** revealing or reflecting good judgment or sound thought **:** SKILLFUL
**2 a :** possessing intelligence **b :** guided or directed by intellect **:** RATIONAL
**3 a :** guided or controlled by a computer; *especially* **:** using a built-in microprocessor for automatic operation, for processing of data, or for achieving greater versatility — compare DUMB 7 **b :** able to produce printed material from digital signals ⟨an *intelligent* copier⟩ ☆
— **in·tel·li·gen·tial** \-,te-lə-'jen(t)-shəl\ *adjective*
— **in·tel·li·gent·ly** \-'te-lə-jənt-lē\ *adverb*

**in·tel·li·gent·sia** \in-,te-lə-'jen(t)-sē-ə, -'gen(t)-\ *noun* [Russian *intelligentsiya*, from Latin *intelligentia* intelligence] (1907)
**:** intellectuals who form an artistic, social, or political vanguard or elite

**in·tel·li·gi·ble** \in-'te-lə-jə-bəl\ *adjective* [Middle English, from Latin *intelligibilis*, from *intelligere*] (14th century)
**1 :** apprehensible by the intellect only
**2 :** capable of being understood or comprehended
— **in·tel·li·gi·bil·i·ty** \-,te-lə-jə-'bi-lə-tē\ *noun*

— **in·tel·li·gi·ble·ness** \-'te-lə-jə-bəl-nəs\ *noun*
— **in·tel·li·gi·bly** \-blē\ *adverb*

**in·tem·per·ance** \(,)in-'tem-p(ə-)rən(t)s\ *noun* (15th century)
**:** lack of moderation; *especially* **:** habitual or excessive drinking of intoxicants

**in·tem·per·ate** \-p(ə-)rət\ *adjective* [Middle English *intemperat*, from Latin *intemperatus*, from *in-* + *temperatus*, past participle of *temperare* to temper] (14th century)
**:** not temperate ⟨*intemperate* criticism⟩; *especially* **:** given to excessive use of intoxicating liquors
— **in·tem·per·ate·ly** *adverb*
— **in·tem·per·ate·ness** *noun*

**in·tend** \in-'tend\ *verb* [Middle English *entenden, intenden*, from Middle French *entendre* to purpose, from Latin *intendere* to stretch out, direct, aim at, from *in-* + *tendere* to stretch — more at THIN] (14th century)
*transitive verb*
**1 :** to direct the mind on
**2** *archaic* **:** to proceed on (a course)
**3 a :** SIGNIFY, MEAN **b :** to refer to
**4 a :** to have in mind as a purpose or goal **:** PLAN **b :** to design for a specified use or future
*intransitive verb*
*archaic* **:** SET OUT, START
— **in·tend·er** *noun*

**in·ten·dance** \in-'ten-dən(t)s\ *noun* (1739)
**1 :** MANAGEMENT, SUPERINTENDENCE
**2 :** an administrative department

**in·ten·dant** \-dənt\ *noun* [French, from Middle French, from Latin *intendent-, intendens*, present participle of *intendere* to intend, attend] (1652)
**:** an administrative official (as a governor) especially under the French, Spanish, or Portuguese monarchies

¹**intended** *adjective* (15th century)
**1 :** expected to be such in the future ⟨an *intended* career⟩ ⟨his *intended* bride⟩
**2 :** INTENTIONAL
— **in·tend·ed·ly** *adverb*

²**intended** *noun* (1767)
**:** the person to whom another is engaged

**intending** *adjective* (1788)
**:** PROSPECTIVE, ASPIRING ⟨an *intending* teacher⟩

**in·tend·ment** \in-'ten(d)-mənt\ *noun* (14th century)
**:** the true meaning or intention especially of a law

**in·ten·er·ate** \in-'te-nə-,rāt\ *transitive verb* **-at·ed; -at·ing** [²*in-* + Latin *tener* soft, tender — more at TENDER] (1595)
**:** to make tender **:** SOFTEN
— **in·ten·er·a·tion** \-,te-nə-'rā-shən\ *noun*

**in·tense** \in-'ten(t)s\ *adjective* [Middle English, from Middle French, from Latin *intensus*, from past participle of *intendere* to stretch out] (15th century)
**1 a :** existing in an extreme degree ⟨the excitement was *intense*⟩ ⟨*intense* pain⟩ **b :** having or showing a characteristic in extreme degree ⟨*intense* colors⟩

☆ SYNONYMS
**Intelligent, clever, alert, quick-witted** mean mentally keen or quick. INTELLIGENT stresses success in coping with new situations and solving problems ⟨an *intelligent* person could assemble it fast⟩. CLEVER implies native ability or aptness and sometimes suggests a lack of more substantial qualities ⟨*clever* with words⟩. ALERT stresses quickness in perceiving and understanding ⟨*alert* to new technology⟩. QUICK-WITTED implies promptness in finding answers in debate or in devising expedients in moments of danger or challenge ⟨no match for his *quick-witted* opponent⟩.

**2 :** marked by or expressive of great zeal, energy, determination, or concentration ⟨*intense* effort⟩
**3 a :** exhibiting strong feeling or earnestness of purpose ⟨an *intense* student⟩ **b :** deeply felt
— **in·tense·ly** *adverb*
— **in·tense·ness** *noun*
**in·ten·si·fi·er** \in-'ten(t)-sə-ˌfī(-ə)r\ *noun* (1835)
: one that intensifies; *especially* : INTENSIVE
**in·ten·si·fy** \in-'ten(t)-sə-ˌfī\ *verb* **-fied; -fy·ing** (1817)
*transitive verb*
**1 :** to make intense or more intensive : STRENGTHEN
**2 a :** to increase the density and contrast of (a photographic image) by chemical treatment **b** : to make more acute : SHARPEN
*intransitive verb*
: to become intense or more intensive : grow stronger or more acute
— **in·ten·si·fi·ca·tion** \-ˌten(t)s-fə-'kā-shən, -ˌten(t)-sə-\ *noun*
**in·ten·sion** \in-'ten(t)-shən\ *noun* (1604)
**1 :** INTENSITY
**2 :** CONNOTATION 3
— **in·ten·sion·al** \-'tench-nəl, -'ten(t)-shə-n²l\ *adjective*
— **in·ten·sion·al·i·ty** \-ˌten(t)-shə-'na-lə-tē\ *noun*
— **in·ten·sion·al·ly** \-'tench-nə-lē, -'ten(t)-shə-n²l-ē\ *adverb*
**in·ten·si·ty** \in-'ten(t)-sə-tē\ *noun, plural* **-ties** (1665)
**1 :** the quality or state of being intense; *especially* : extreme degree of strength, force, energy, or feeling
**2 :** the magnitude of a quantity (as force or energy) per unit (as of area, charge, mass, or time)
**3 :** SATURATION 4a
¹**in·ten·sive** \in-'ten(t)-siv\ *adjective* (15th century)
: of, relating to, or marked by intensity or intensification: as **a :** highly concentrated ⟨*intensive* study⟩ **b :** tending to strengthen or increase; *especially* : tending to give force or emphasis ⟨*intensive* adverb⟩ **c :** constituting or relating to a method designed to increase productivity by the expenditure of more capital and labor rather than by increase in scope ⟨*intensive* farming⟩
— **in·ten·sive·ly** *adverb*
— **in·ten·sive·ness** *noun*
²**intensive** *noun* (1813)
: an intensive linguistic element
**intensive care** *noun* (1963)
: special medical equipment and services for taking care of seriously ill patients ⟨heart patients in *intensive care*⟩ ⟨an *intensive care* unit⟩
¹**in·tent** \in-'tent\ *noun* [Middle English *entent*, from Old French, from Late Latin *intentus*, from Latin, act of stretching out, from *intendere*] (13th century)
**1 a :** the act or fact of intending : PURPOSE; *especially* : the design or purpose to commit a wrongful or criminal act ⟨admitted wounding him with *intent*⟩ **b :** the state of mind with which an act is done : VOLITION
**2 :** a usually clearly formulated or planned intention : AIM
**3 a :** MEANING, SIGNIFICANCE **b :** CONNOTATION 3
*synonym* see INTENTION
²**intent** *adjective* [Latin *intentus*, from past participle of *intendere*] (14th century)
**1 :** directed with strained or eager attention : CONCENTRATED
**2 :** having the mind, attention, or will concentrated on something or some end or purpose ⟨*intent* on their work⟩
— **in·tent·ly** *adverb*
— **in·tent·ness** *noun*
**in·ten·tion** \in-'ten(t)-shən\ *noun* (14th century)

**1 :** a determination to act in a certain way : RESOLVE
**2 :** IMPORT, SIGNIFICANCE
**3 a :** what one intends to do or bring about **b** : the object for which a prayer, mass, or pious act is offered
**4 :** a process or manner of healing of incised wounds
**5 :** CONCEPT; *especially* : a concept considered as the product of attention directed to an object of knowledge
**6** *plural* : purpose with respect to marriage ☆
**in·ten·tion·al** \in-'tench-nəl, -'ten(t)-shə-n²l\ *adjective* (circa 1727)
**1 :** done by intention or design : INTENDED ⟨*intentional* damage⟩
**2 a :** of or relating to epistemological intention **b :** having external reference
*synonym* see VOLUNTARY
— **in·ten·tion·al·i·ty** \-ˌten(t)-shə-'na-lə-tē\ *noun*
— **in·ten·tion·al·ly** \in-'tench-nə-lē, -'ten(t)-shə-n²l-ē\ *adverb*
**in·ter** \in-'tər\ *transitive verb* **in·terred; in·ter·ring** [Middle English *enteren*, from Middle French *enterrer*, from (assumed) Vulgar Latin *interrare*, from *in-* + Latin *terra* earth — more at TERRACE] (14th century)
: to deposit (a dead body) in the earth or in a tomb
**inter-** *prefix* [Middle English *inter-, enter-*, from Middle French & Latin; Middle French *inter-, entre-*, from Latin *inter-*, from *inter*; akin to Old High German *untar* among, Greek *enteron* intestine, Old English *in* in]
**1 :** between : among : in the midst ⟨*inter*crop⟩ ⟨*inter*penetrate⟩ ⟨*inter*stellar⟩
**2 :** reciprocal ⟨*inter*relation⟩ : reciprocally ⟨*inter*marry⟩
**3 :** located between ⟨*inter*face⟩
**4 :** carried on between ⟨*inter*national⟩
**5 :** occurring between ⟨*inter*borough⟩ : intervening ⟨*inter*glacial⟩
**6 :** shared by, involving, or derived from two or more ⟨*inter*faith⟩
**7 :** between the limits of : within ⟨*inter*tropical⟩
**8 :** existing between ⟨*inter*communal⟩ ⟨*inter*company⟩

in·ter·Af·ri·can
in·ter·agen·cy
in·ter·al·le·lic
in·ter·Amer·i·can
in·ter·an·i·ma·tion
in·ter·an·nu·al
in·ter·as·so·ci·a·tion
in·ter·atom·ic
in·ter·avail·abil·i·ty
in·ter·bank
in·ter·ba·sin
in·ter·bed
in·ter·be·hav·ior
in·ter·be·hav·ior·al
in·ter·bor·ough
in·ter·branch
in·ter·cal·i·bra·tion
in·ter·cam·pus
in·ter·caste
in·ter·cell
in·ter·cel·lu·lar
in·ter·chain
in·ter·chan·nel
in·ter·chro·mo·som·al
in·ter·church
in·ter·city
in·ter·clan
in·ter·class
in·ter·club
in·ter·clus·ter
in·ter·coast·al
in·ter·co·lo·nial
in·ter·com·mu·nal
in·ter·com·mu·ni·ty
in·ter·com·pa·ny

in·ter·com·pare
in·ter·com·par·i·son
in·ter·com·pre·hen·si·bil·i·ty
in·ter·cor·po·rate
in·ter·cor·re·late
in·ter·cor·re·la·tion
in·ter·cor·ti·cal
in·ter·coun·try
in·ter·coun·ty
in·ter·cou·ple
in·ter·cra·ter
in·ter·crys·tal·line
in·ter·cul·tur·al
in·ter·cul·tur·al·ly
in·ter·cul·ture
in·ter·deal·er
in·ter·de·nom·i·na·tion·al
in·ter·de·part·men·tal
in·ter·de·part·men·tal·ly
in·ter·de·pend
in·ter·de·pen·dence
in·ter·de·pen·den·cy
in·ter·de·pen·dent
in·ter·de·pen·dent·ly
in·ter·di·a·lec·tal
in·ter·dis·trict
in·ter·di·vi·sion·al
in·ter·do·min·ion
in·ter·elec·trode
in·ter·elec·tron
in·ter·elec·tron·ic
in·ter·ep·i·dem·ic
in·ter·eth·nic

in·ter·fac·ul·ty
in·ter·fa·mil·ial
in·ter·fam·i·ly
in·ter·fi·ber
in·ter·firm
in·ter·flow
in·ter·flu·vi·al
in·ter·fold
in·ter·fra·ter·ni·ty
in·ter·gang
in·ter·gen·er·a·tion
in·ter·gen·er·a·tion·al
in·ter·ge·ner·ic
in·ter·graft
in·ter·gran·u·lar
in·ter·group
in·ter·hemi·spher·ic
in·ter·in·di·vid·u·al
in·ter·in·dus·try
in·ter·in·flu·ence
in·ter·in·sti·tu·tion·al
in·ter·in·volve
in·ter·ion·ic
in·ter·is·land
in·ter·ju·ris·dic·tion·al
in·ter·la·cus·trine
in·ter·lam·i·nar
in·ter·lay
in·ter·lay·er
in·ter·lend
in·ter·li·brary
in·ter·lin·er
in·ter·lob·u·lar
in·ter·lo·cal
in·ter·male
in·ter·mar·gin·al
in·ter·mem·brane
in·ter·men·stru·al
in·ter·min·is·te·ri·al
in·ter·mi·tot·ic
in·ter·mo·lec·u·lar
in·ter·mo·lec·u·lar·ly
in·ter·moun·tain
in·ter·nu·cle·ar
in·ter·nu·cle·on
in·ter·nu·cle·on·ic
in·ter·nu·cle·o·tide
in·ter·ob·serv·er

in·ter·ocean
in·ter·oce·an·ic
in·ter·of·fice
in·ter·op·er·a·tive
in·ter·or·bit·al
in·ter·or·gan
in·ter·or·ga·ni·za·tion·al
in·ter·pan·dem·ic
in·ter·par·ish
in·ter·pa·ro·chi·al
in·ter·par·ox·ys·mal
in·ter·par·ti·cle
in·ter·par·ty
in·ter·per·cep·tu·al
in·ter·per·me·ate
in·ter·pha·lan·ge·al
in·ter·plan·e·tary
in·ter·plu·vi·al
in·ter·point
in·ter·pop·u·la·tion
in·ter·pop·u·la·tion·al
in·ter·pro·fes·sion·al
in·ter·pro·vin·cial
in·ter·psy·chic
in·ter·re·gion·al
in·ter·re·li·gious
in·ter·re·nal
in·ter·row
in·ter·school
in·ter·sec·tion·al
in·ter·seg·ment
in·ter·seg·men·tal
in·ter·sen·so·ry
in·ter·so·ci·etal
in·ter·so·ci·ety
in·ter·stage
in·ter·sta·tion
in·ter·stim·u·la·tion
in·ter·stim·u·lus
in·ter·strain
in·ter·strand
in·ter·strat·i·fi·ca·tion
in·ter·strat·i·fy
in·ter·sub·sti·tut·abil·i·ty
in·ter·sub·sti·tut·able
in·ter·sys·tem
in·ter·term

\ə\ abut \ᵊ\ kitten \ər\ further \a\ ash \ā\ ace \ä\ mop, mar \au̇\ out \ch\ chin \e\ bet \ē\ easy \g\ go \i\ hit \ī\ ice \j\ job \ŋ\ sing \ō\ go \ȯ\ law \ȯi\ boy \th\ thin \t͟h\ the \ü\ loot \u̇\ foot \y\ yet \zh\ vision *see also* Guide to Pronunciation

in·ter·ter·mi·nal
in·ter·ter·ri·to·ri·al
in·ter·trans·lat·able
in·ter·tri·al
in·ter·trib·al
in·ter·troop
in·ter·union
in·ter·unit
in·ter·uni·ver·si·ty
in·ter·ur·ban
in·ter·val·ley

in·ter·ven·tric·u·lar
in·ter·ver·te·bral
in·ter·vil·lage
in·ter·vis·i·bil·i·ty
in·ter·vis·i·ble
in·ter·vis·i·ta·tion
in·ter·war
in·ter·work
in·ter·work·ing
in·ter·zon·al
in·ter·zone

**in·ter·a·bang** *variant of* INTERROBANG

**in·ter·act** \,in-tə-'rakt\ *intransitive verb* (1839)
: to act upon one another

**in·ter·ac·tant** \-'rak-tənt\ *noun* (1949)
: one that interacts

**in·ter·ac·tion** \,in-tə-'rak-shən\ *noun* (1832)
: mutual or reciprocal action or influence
— **in·ter·ac·tion·al** \-shnəl, -shə-nəl\ *adjective*

**in·ter·ac·tive** \-'rak-tiv\ *adjective* (1832)
**1 :** mutually or reciprocally active
**2 :** of, relating to, or being a two-way electronic communication system (as a telephone, cable television, or a computer) that involves a user's orders (as for information or merchandise) or responses (as to a poll)
— **in·ter·ac·tive·ly** *adverb*

**in·ter alia** \,in-tər-'ā-lē-ə, -'ä-\ *adverb* [Latin] (1665)
: among other things

**in·ter ali·os** \-lē-,ōs\ *adverb* [Latin] (circa 1670)
: among other persons

**in·ter·al·lied** \,in-tər-'a-,līd, -ə-'līd\ *adjective* (1917)
: relating to, composed of, or involving allies

**in·ter·breed** \,in-tər-'brēd\ *verb* **-bred** \-'bred\; **-breed·ing** (1859)
*intransitive verb*
: to breed together: as **a :** CROSSBREED **b :** to breed within a closed population
*transitive verb*
: to cause to breed together

**in·ter·ca·la·ry** \in-'tər-kə-,ler-ē, ,in-tər-'ka-lə-rē\ *adjective* [Latin *intercalarius,* from *intercalare*] (1614)
**1 a :** inserted in a calendar ⟨an *intercalary* day⟩ **b** *of a year* **:** containing an intercalary period (as a day or month)
**2 :** inserted between other things or parts : INTERPOLATED

**in·ter·ca·late** \in-'tər-kə-,lāt\ *transitive verb* **-lat·ed; -lat·ing** [Latin *intercalatus,* past participle of *intercalare,* from *inter-* + *calare* to proclaim, call — more at LOW] (1603)
**1 :** to insert (as a day) in a calendar
**2 :** to insert between or among existing elements or layers
**synonym** see INTRODUCE
— **in·ter·ca·la·tion** \-,tər-kə-'lā-shən\ *noun*

**in·ter·cede** \,in-tər-'sēd\ *intransitive verb* **-ced·ed; -ced·ing** [Latin *intercedere,* from *inter-* + *cedere* to go] (1597)
: to intervene between parties with a view to reconciling differences : MEDIATE
**synonym** see INTERPOSE
— **in·ter·ced·er** *noun*

**in·ter·cen·sal** \,in-tər-'sen(t)-səl\ *adjective* (1887)
: occurring between censuses ⟨*intercensal* estimates⟩ ⟨*intercensal* period⟩

**¹in·ter·cept** \,in-tər-'sept\ *transitive verb* [Middle English, from Latin *interceptus,* past participle of *intercipere,* from *inter-* + *capere* to take, seize — more at HEAVE] (15th century)
**1** *obsolete* **:** PREVENT, HINDER
**2 a :** to stop, seize, or interrupt in progress or course or before arrival **b :** to receive (a communication or signal directed elsewhere) usually secretly
**3** *obsolete* **:** to interrupt communication or connection with

**4 :** to include (part of a curve, surface, or solid) between two points, curves, or surfaces ⟨the part of a circumference *intercepted* between two radii⟩
**5 a :** to gain possession of (an opponent's pass) **b :** to intercept a pass thrown by (an opponent)

**²in·ter·cept** \'in-tər-,sept\ *noun* (1821)
**1 :** the distance from the origin to a point where a graph crosses a coordinate axis
**2 :** INTERCEPTION; *especially* **:** the interception of a missile by an interceptor or of a target by a missile
**3 :** a message, code, or signal that is intercepted (as by monitoring radio communications)

**in·ter·cep·tion** \,in-tər-'sep-shən\ *noun* (15th century)
**1 a :** the action of intercepting **b :** the state of being intercepted
**2 :** something that is intercepted; *especially* **:** an intercepted forward pass

**in·ter·cep·tor** *also* **in·ter·cept·er** \,in-tər-'sep-tər\ *noun* (1598)
: one that intercepts; *specifically* **:** a light high-speed fast-climbing fighter plane or missile designed for defense against raiding bombers or missiles

**in·ter·ces·sion** \,in-tər-'se-shən\ *noun* [Middle English, from Middle French or Latin; Middle French, from Latin *intercession-, intercessio,* from *intercedere*] (15th century)
**1 :** the act of interceding
**2 :** prayer, petition, or entreaty in favor of another
— **in·ter·ces·sion·al** \-'sesh-nəl, -'se-shə-nəl\ *adjective*
— **in·ter·ces·sor** \-'se-sər\ *noun*
— **in·ter·ces·so·ry** \-'ses-rē, -'se-sə-rē\ *adjective*

**¹in·ter·change** \,in-tər-'chānj\ *verb* [Middle English *entrechaungen,* from Middle French *entrechangier,* from Old French, from *entre-* inter- + *changier* to change] (14th century)
*transitive verb*
**1 :** to put each of (two things) in the place of the other
**2 :** EXCHANGE
*intransitive verb*
: to change places mutually
— **in·ter·chang·er** *noun*

**²in·ter·change** \'in-tər-,chānj\ *noun* (15th century)
**1 :** the act, process, or an instance of interchanging : EXCHANGE
**2 :** a junction of two or more highways by a system of separate levels that permit traffic to pass from one to another without the crossing of traffic streams

**in·ter·change·able** \,in-tər-'chān-jə-bəl\ *adjective* (14th century)
: capable of being interchanged; *especially* **:** permitting mutual substitution ⟨*interchangeable* parts⟩
— **in·ter·change·abil·i·ty** \-,chān-jə-'bi-lə-tē\ *noun*
— **in·ter·change·able·ness** \-'chān-jə-bəl-nəs\ *noun*
— **in·ter·change·ably** \-blē\ *adverb*

**in·ter·col·le·giate** \,in-tər-kə-'lē-jət, -jē-ət\ *adjective* (circa 1874)
: existing, carried on, or participating in activities between colleges ⟨*intercollegiate* athletics⟩

**in·ter·co·lum·ni·a·tion** \,in-tər-kə-,ləm-nē-'ā-shən\ *noun* [Latin *intercolumnium* space between two columns, from *inter-* + *columna* column] (1624)
**1 :** the clear space between the columns of a series
**2 :** the system of spacing of the columns of a colonnade

**in·ter·com** \'in-tər-,käm\ *noun* [short for *intercommunication system*] (1940)
: a two-way communication system with a microphone and loudspeaker at each station for localized use

**in·ter·com·mu·ni·cate** \,in-tər-kə-'myü-nə-,kāt\ *intransitive verb* (1586)
**1 :** to exchange communication with one another
**2 :** to afford passage from one to another
— **in·ter·com·mu·ni·ca·tion** \-,myü-nə-'kā-shən\ *noun*

**intercommunication system** *noun* (1911)
: INTERCOM

**in·ter·com·mu·nion** \,in-tər-kə-'myü-nyən\ *noun* (1921)
: interdenominational participation in communion

**in·ter·con·nect** \,in-tər-kə-'nekt\ (1865)
*transitive verb*
: to connect with one another
*intransitive verb*
: to be or become mutually connected
— **in·ter·con·nec·tion** \-'nek-shən\ *noun*

**interconnected** *adjective* (1865)
**1 :** mutually joined or related ⟨*interconnected* highways⟩ ⟨*interconnected* political issues⟩
**2 :** having internal connections between the parts or elements
— **in·ter·con·nec·ted·ness** *noun*

**in·ter·con·ti·nen·tal** \,in-tər-,kän-t°n-'en-t°l\ *adjective* (circa 1855)
**1 :** extending among continents or carried on between continents
**2 :** capable of traveling between continents ⟨*intercontinental* ballistic missile⟩

**in·ter·con·ver·sion** \,in-tər-kən-'vər-zhən, -shən\ *noun* (1865)
: mutual conversion ⟨*interconversion* of chemical compounds⟩
— **in·ter·con·vert** \-'vərt\ *transitive verb*
— **in·ter·con·vert·ibil·i·ty** \-,vər-tə-'bi-lə-tē\ *noun*
— **in·ter·con·vert·ible** \-'vər-tə-bəl\ *adjective*

**in·ter·cool·er** \,in-tər-'kü-lər\ *noun* (1899)
: a device for cooling a fluid (as air) between successive heat-generating processes

**in·ter·cos·tal** \,in-tər-'käs-t°l\ *adjective* [New Latin *intercostalis,* from Latin *inter-* + *costa* rib — more at COAST] (1597)
: situated or extending between the ribs ⟨*intercostal* spaces⟩ ⟨*intercostal* muscles⟩
— **intercostal** *noun*

**in·ter·course** \'in-tər-,kōrs, -,kȯrs\ *noun* [Middle English *intercurse,* probably from Middle French *entrecours,* from Medieval Latin *intercursus,* from Latin, act of running between, from *intercurrere* to run between, from *inter-* + *currere* to run — more at CAR] (15th century)
**1 :** connection or dealings between persons or groups
**2 :** exchange especially of thoughts or feelings : COMMUNION
**3 :** physical sexual contact between individuals that involves the genitalia of at least one person ⟨heterosexual *intercourse*⟩ ⟨anal *intercourse*⟩ ⟨oral *intercourse*⟩; *especially* **:** SEXUAL INTERCOURSE 1

**in·ter·crop** \,in-tər-'kräp, 'in-tər-,\ (1898)
*transitive verb*
: to grow a crop in between (another)
*intransitive verb*
: to grow two or more crops simultaneously (as in alternate rows) on the same plot
— **in·ter·crop** \'in-tər-,kräp\ *noun*

**¹in·ter·cross** \,in-tər-'krȯs\ *verb* (1711)
: CROSS

**²in·ter·cross** \'in-tər-,krȯs\ *noun* (1859)
: an instance or a product of crossbreeding

**in·ter·cur·rent** \,in-tər-'kər-ənt, -'kə-rənt\ *adjective* [Latin *intercurrent-, intercurrens,* present participle of *intercurrere*] (1611)
: occurring during and modifying the course of another disease ⟨an *intercurrent* infection⟩

**in·ter·cut** \,in-tər-'kət\ (1938)
*transitive verb*
**1 :** to insert (a contrasting camera shot) into a take by cutting

**2 :** to insert a contrasting camera shot into (a take) by cutting
*intransitive verb*
**:** to alternate contrasting camera shots by cutting

**in·ter·den·tal** \ˌin-tər-'den-t<sup>ə</sup>l\ *adjective* (circa 1874)
**1 :** situated or intended for use between the teeth
**2 :** formed with the tip of the tongue between the upper and lower front teeth
— **in·ter·den·tal·ly** \-t<sup>ə</sup>l-ē\ *adverb*

**¹in·ter·dict** \'in-tər-ˌdikt\ *noun* [Middle English, alteration of *entredit*, from Old French, from Latin *interdictum* prohibition, from neuter of *interdictus*, past participle of *interdicere* to interpose, forbid, from *inter-* + *dicere* to say — more at DICTION] (15th century)
**1 :** a Roman Catholic ecclesiastical censure withdrawing most sacraments and Christian burial from a person or district
**2 :** a prohibitory decree : PROHIBITION

**²in·ter·dict** \ˌin-tər-'dikt\ *transitive verb* (15th century)
**1 :** to lay under or prohibit by an interdict
**2 :** to forbid in a usually formal or authoritative manner
**3 :** to destroy, damage, or cut off (as an enemy line of supply) by firepower to stop or hamper an enemy
*synonym* see FORBID
— **in·ter·dic·tion** \-'dik-shən\ *noun*
— **in·ter·dic·tive** \-'dik-tiv\ *adjective*
— **in·ter·dic·tor** \-tər\ *noun*
— **in·ter·dic·to·ry** \-t(ə-)rē\ *adjective*

**in·ter·dif·fu·sion** \-di-'fyü-zhən\ *noun* (circa 1872)
**:** the process of diffusing and mixing freely so as to approach a homogeneous mixture
— **in·ter·dif·fuse** \-'fyüz\ *intransitive verb*

**in·ter·dig·i·tate** \-'di-jə-ˌtāt\ *intransitive verb*
**-tat·ed; -tat·ing** [*inter-* + Latin *digitus* finger — more at TOE] (circa 1849)
**:** to become interlocked like the fingers of folded hands
— **in·ter·dig·i·ta·tion** \-ˌdi-jə-'tā-shən\ *noun*

**in·ter·dis·ci·plin·ary** \-'di-sə-plə-ˌner-ē\ *adjective* (1926)
**:** involving two or more academic, scientific, or artistic disciplines

**¹in·ter·est** \'in-t(ə-)rəst; 'in-tə-ˌrest, -ˌtrest; 'in-tərst\ *noun* [Middle English, probably alteration of earlier *interesse*, from Anglo-French & Medieval Latin; Anglo-French, from Medieval Latin, from Latin, to be between, make a difference, concern, from *inter-* + *esse* to be — more at IS] (15th century)
**1 a** (1) **:** right, title, or legal share in something (2) **:** participation in advantage and responsibility **b :** BUSINESS, COMPANY
**2 a :** a charge for borrowed money generally a percentage of the amount borrowed **b :** an excess above what is due or expected ⟨returned the insults with *interest*⟩
**3 :** ADVANTAGE, BENEFIT; *also* **:** SELF-INTEREST
**4 :** SPECIAL INTEREST
**5 a :** a feeling that accompanies or causes special attention to an object or class of objects **:** CONCERN **b :** something that arouses such attention **c :** a quality in a thing arousing interest

**²interest** *transitive verb* (1608)
**1 :** to induce or persuade to participate or engage
**2 :** to engage the attention or arouse the interest of

**in·ter·est·ed** *adjective* (1602)
**1 :** having the attention engaged ⟨*interested* listeners⟩
**2 :** being affected or involved ⟨*interested* parties⟩
— **in·ter·est·ed·ly** *adverb*
**interest group** *noun* (1908)

**:** a group of persons having a common identifying interest that often provides a basis for action

**in·ter·est·ing** \'in-t(ə-)rəs-tiŋ; 'in-tə-ˌres-, 'in-ˌtres-; 'in-tərs-\ *adjective* (1768)
**:** holding the attention **:** arousing interest
— **in·ter·est·ing·ness** *noun*

**in·ter·est·ing·ly** \-lē\ *adverb* (1811)
**1 :** in an interesting manner
**2 :** as a matter of interest

**¹in·ter·face** \'in-tər-ˌfās\ *noun* (1882)
**1 :** a surface forming a common boundary of two bodies, spaces, or phases ⟨an oil-water *interface*⟩
**2 a :** the place at which independent and often unrelated systems meet and act on or communicate with each other ⟨the man-machine *interface*⟩ **b :** the means by which interaction or communication is achieved at an interface
— **in·ter·fa·cial** \ˌin-tər-'fā-shəl\ *adjective*

**²interface** (1962)
*transitive verb*
**1 :** to connect by means of an interface ⟨*interface* a machine with a computer⟩
**2 :** to serve as an interface for
*intransitive verb*
**1 :** to become interfaced
**2 :** to interact or coordinate harmoniously

**in·ter·fac·ing** \-ˌfā-siŋ\ *noun* (1942)
**:** fabric sewn between the facing and the outside of a garment (as in a collar or cuff) for stiffening and shape retention

**in·ter·faith** \ˌin-tər-'fāth\ *adjective* (1932)
**:** involving persons of different religious faiths

**in·ter·fere** \ˌin-tə(r)-'fir\ *intransitive verb*
**-fered; -fer·ing** [Middle English *enterferen*, from Middle French (*s'*)*entreferir* to strike one another, from Old French, from *entre-* inter- + *ferir* to strike, from Latin *ferire* — more at BORE] (15th century)
**1 :** to interpose in a way that hinders or impedes **:** come into collision or be in opposition
**2 :** to strike one foot against the opposite foot or ankle in walking or running — used especially of horses
**3 :** to enter into or take a part in the concerns of others
**4 :** to act reciprocally so as to augment, diminish, or otherwise affect one another — used of waves
*synonym* see INTERPOSE
— **in·ter·fer·er** *noun*

**in·ter·fer·ence** \-'fir-ən(t)s\ *noun* (1783)
**1 a :** the act or process of interfering **b :** something that interferes **:** OBSTRUCTION
**2 :** the mutual effect on meeting of two wave trains (as of light or sound) that constitutes alternating areas of increased and decreased amplitude (as light and dark lines or louder and softer sound)
**3 a :** the legal blocking of an opponent in football to make way for the ballcarrier **b :** the illegal hindering of an opponent in sports
**4 :** partial or complete inhibition or sometimes facilitation of other genetic crossovers in the vicinity of a chromosomal locus where a preceding crossover has occurred
**5 a :** confusion of a received radio signal due to the presence of noise (as atmospherics) or signals from two or more transmitters on a single frequency **b :** something that produces such confusion
**6 :** the disturbing effect of new learning on the performance of previously learned behavior with which it is inconsistent
— **in·ter·fer·en·tial** \-fə-'ren(t)-shəl, -ˌfir-'en(t)-\ *adjective*

**in·ter·fer·o·gram** \ˌin-tə(r)-'fir-ə-ˌgram\ *noun* (1921)
**:** a photographic record made by an apparatus for recording optical interference phenomena

**in·ter·fer·om·e·ter** \ˌin-tə(r)-fə-'rä-mə-tər, -ˌfi-'rä-\ *noun* [International Scientific Vocabulary] (1897)

**:** an instrument that utilizes the interference of waves (as of light) for precise determinations (as of distance or wavelength)
— **in·ter·fer·o·met·ric** \-ˌfir-ə-'me-trik\ *adjective*
— **in·ter·fer·o·met·ri·cal·ly** \-tri-k(ə-)lē\ *adverb*
— **in·ter·fer·om·e·try** \-fə-'rä-mə-trē, -ˌfi-ˌrä-\ *noun*

**in·ter·fer·on** \ˌin-tə(r)-'fir-ˌän\ *noun* [*interfere* + *²-on*] (1957)
**:** any of a group of heat-stable soluble basic antiviral glycoproteins of low molecular weight that are produced usually by cells exposed to the action of a virus, sometimes to the action of another intracellular parasite (as a bacterium), or experimentally to the action of some chemicals

**in·ter·fer·tile** \ˌin-tər-'fər-t<sup>ə</sup>l\ *adjective* (1899)
**:** capable of interbreeding
— **in·ter·fer·til·i·ty** \-(ˌ)fər-'ti-lə-tē\ *noun*

**in·ter·file** \ˌin-tər-'fī(ə)l\ *transitive verb* (1950)
**:** to arrange in or add to a file **:** FILE

**in·ter·fluve** \'in-tər-ˌflüv\ *noun* [*inter-* + Latin *fluvius* river — more at FLUVIAL] (1895)
**:** the area between adjacent streams flowing in the same direction

**in·ter·fuse** \ˌin-tər-'fyüz\ *verb* [Latin *interfusus*, past participle of *interfundere* to pour between, from *inter-* + *fundere* to pour — more at FOUND] (1593)
*transitive verb*
**1 :** to combine by fusing **:** BLEND
**2 :** to add as if by fusing **:** INFUSE
*intransitive verb*
**:** BLEND, FUSE
— **in·ter·fu·sion** \-'fyü-zhən\ *noun*

**in·ter·ga·lac·tic** \ˌin-tər-gə-'lak-tik\ *adjective* (1928)
**1 :** situated in or relating to the spaces between galaxies
**2 :** of, relating to, or occurring in outer space ⟨*intergalactic* battles⟩

**in·ter·gla·cial** \-'glā-shəl\ *noun* (1867)
**:** a warm period between glacial epochs
— **interglacial** *adjective*

**in·ter·gov·ern·men·tal** \-ˌgə-vər(n)-'men-t<sup>ə</sup>l\ *adjective* (1927)
**:** existing or occurring between two or more governments or levels of government

**in·ter·gra·da·tion** \-grā-'dā-shən, -grə-\ *noun* (1874)
**:** the condition of an individual or population that intergrades
— **in·ter·gra·da·tion·al** \-shnəl, -shə-n<sup>ə</sup>l\ *adjective*

**¹in·ter·grade** \ˌin-tər-'grād\ *intransitive verb* (1874)
**:** to merge gradually one with another through a continuous series of intermediate forms

**²in·ter·grade** \'in-tər-ˌgrād\ *noun* (1888)
**:** an intermediate form

**in·ter·growth** \'in-tər-ˌgrōth\ *noun* (1844)
**:** a growing between or together; *also* **:** the product of such growth

**¹in·ter·im** \'in-tə-rəm\ *noun* [Latin, adverb, meanwhile, from *inter* between — more at INTER-] (circa 1580)
**:** an intervening time **:** INTERVAL

**²interim** *adjective* (1604)
**:** done, made, appointed, or occurring for an interim

**¹in·te·ri·or** \in-'tir-ē-ər\ *adjective* [Middle French & Latin; Middle French, from Latin, comparative of (assumed) Old Latin *interus* inward, on the inside; akin to Latin *inter*] (15th century)
**1 :** lying, occurring, or functioning within the limiting boundaries **:** INNER ⟨an *interior* point of a triangle⟩

\ə\ abut \<sup>ə</sup>\ kitten \ər\ further \a\ ash \ā\ ace
\ä\ mop, mar \aů\ out \ch\ chin \e\ bet \ē\ easy
\g\ go \i\ hit \ī\ ice \j\ job \ŋ\ sing \ō\ go
\ȯ\ law \ȯi\ boy \th\ thin \t̲h̲\ the \ü\ loot \ů\ foot
\y\ yet \zh\ vision *see also* Guide to Pronunciation

**2 :** belonging to mental or spiritual life ⟨a simple *interior* piety⟩
**3 :** belonging to the inner constitution or concealed nature of something ⟨*interior* meaning of a poem⟩
**4 :** lying away or remote from the border or shore
— **in·te·ri·or·ly** \in-'tir-ē-ər-lē\ *adverb*
**²interior** *noun* (1596)
**1 :** the inner or spiritual nature **:** CHARACTER
**2 :** the interior part (as of a country or island)
**3 :** the internal or inner part of a thing **:** INSIDE
**4 :** the internal affairs of a state or nation
**5 :** a representation (as in a play or movie) of the interior of a building
**interior angle** *noun* (1756)
**1 :** the inner of the two angles formed where two sides of a polygon come together
**2 :** any of the four angles formed in the area between a pair of parallel lines when a third line cuts them

*agh, bgh, ghd, ghc*
**interior angle 2**

**interior decoration** *noun* (1807)
**:** INTERIOR DESIGN
**interior decorator** *noun* (1867)
**:** INTERIOR DESIGNER, DECORATOR
**interior design** *noun* (1927)
**:** the art or practice of planning and supervising the design and execution of architectural interiors and their furnishings
**interior designer** *noun* (1938)
**:** one who specializes in interior design
**in·te·ri·or·ise** *British variant of* INTERIORIZE
**in·te·ri·or·i·ty** \(,)in-,tir-ē-'òr-ə-tē, -'är-\ *noun* (1701)
**:** interior quality or character; *also* **:** inner life or substance ⟨characters that lack *interiority*⟩
**in·te·ri·or·ize** \in-'tir-ē-ə-,rīz\ *transitive verb* **-ized; -iz·ing** (1906)
**:** to make interior; *especially* **:** to make a part of one's own inner being or mental structure
— **in·te·ri·or·i·za·tion** \-,tir-ē-ə-rə-'zā-shən\ *noun*
**interior monologue** *noun* (1922)
**:** a usually extended representation in monologue of a fictional character's thought and feeling
**in·ter·ject** \,in-tər-'jekt\ *transitive verb* [Latin *interjectus,* past participle of *intericere,* from *inter-* + *jacere* to throw — more at JET] (1588)
**:** to throw in between or among other things **:** INTERPOLATE ⟨*interject* a remark⟩
**synonym** see INTRODUCE
— **in·ter·jec·tor** \-'jek-tər\ *noun*
— **in·ter·jec·to·ry** \-t(ə-)rē\ *adjective*
**in·ter·jec·tion** \,int-ər-'jek-shən\ *noun* (15th century)
**1 a :** the act of uttering exclamations **:** EJACULATION **b :** the act of putting in between **:** INTERPOSITION
**2 :** an ejaculatory utterance usually lacking grammatical connection: as **a :** a word or phrase used in exclamation (as *Heavens! Dear me!*) **b :** a cry or inarticulate utterance (as *Alas! ouch! phooey! ugh!*) expressing an emotion
**3 :** something that is interjected or that interrupts
**in·ter·jec·tion·al** \-shnəl, -shə-nᵊl\ *adjective* (1761)
**1 :** of, relating to, or constituting an interjection **:** EJACULATORY
**2 :** thrown in between other words **:** PARENTHETICAL
— **in·ter·jec·tion·al·ly** *adverb*
**in·ter·lace** \,in-tər-'lās\ *verb* [Middle English *entrelacen,* from Middle French *entrelacer,* from Old French *entrelacier,* from *entre-* inter- + *lacier* to lace] (14th century)
*transitive verb*

**1 :** to unite by or as if by lacing together **:** INTERWEAVE
**2 :** to vary by alternation or intermixture **:** INTERSPERSE ⟨narrative *interlaced* with anecdotes⟩
*intransitive verb*
**:** to cross one another as if woven together **:** INTERTWINE
— **in·ter·lace·ment** \-mənt\ *noun*
**in·ter·lard** \,in-tər-'lärd\ *transitive verb* [Middle French *entrelarder,* from Old French, from *entre-* + *larder* to lard, from *lard,* noun] (circa 1587)
**:** to vary by intermixture **:** INTERSPERSE, INTERLACE
**in·ter·leave** \,in-tər-'lēv\ *transitive verb* **-leaved; -leav·ing** (1668)
**:** to arrange in or as if in alternate layers
**in·ter·leu·kin** \,in-tər-'lü-kən\ *noun* [*inter-* + *leuk-* + ¹-*in*] (1979)
**:** any of several compounds of low molecular weight that are produced by lymphocytes, macrophages, and monocytes and that function especially in regulation of the immune system and especially cell-mediated immunity
**in·ter·leu·kin-1** \-'wən\ *noun* (1979)
**:** an interleukin produced especially by monocytes and macrophages that regulates immune responses by activating lymphocytes and mediates other biological processes (as the onset of fever) usually associated with infection and inflammation
**in·ter·leu·kin-2** \-'tü\ *noun* (1979)
**:** an interleukin produced by antigen-stimulated helper T cells in the presence of interleukin-1 that induces proliferation of immune cells (as T cells and B cells) and is used experimentally especially in treating certain cancers
**¹in·ter·line** \,in-tər-'līn\ *transitive verb* [Middle English *enterlinen,* from Medieval Latin *interlineare,* from Latin *inter-* + *linea* line] (15th century)
**:** to insert between lines already written or printed
— **in·ter·lin·e·a·tion** \-,li-nē-'ā-shən\ *noun*
**²interline** *transitive verb* [Middle English, from *inter-* + *linen* to line] (15th century)
**:** to provide (a garment) with an interlining
**³interline** *adjective* (1897)
**:** relating to, involving, or carried by two or more transportation lines
**¹in·ter·lin·ear** \,in-tər-'li-nē-ər\ *adjective* [Middle English *interliniare,* from Medieval Latin *interlinearis,* from Latin *inter-* + *linea* line] (15th century)
**1 :** inserted between lines already written or printed
**2 :** written or printed in different languages or texts in alternate lines
— **in·ter·lin·ear·ly** *adverb*
**²interlinear** *noun* (1850)
**:** a book having interlinear matter; *especially* **:** a book in a foreign language with interlinear translation
**in·ter·lin·ing** \'in-tər-,lī-niŋ\ *noun* (1881)
**:** a lining (as of a coat) sewn between the ordinary lining and the outside fabric
**in·ter·link** \,in-tər-'liŋk\ *transitive verb* (1587)
**:** to link together
— **in·ter·link** \'in-tər-,liŋk\ *noun*
**¹in·ter·lock** \,in-tər-'läk\ (1632)
*intransitive verb*
**:** to become locked together or interconnected
*transitive verb*
**1 :** to lock together **:** UNITE
**2 :** to connect so that the motion or operation of any part is constrained by another
**²in·ter·lock** \'in-tər-,läk\ *noun* (1874)
**1 :** the quality, state, sense, or an instance of being interlocked
**2 :** an arrangement in which the operation of one part or mechanism automatically brings about or prevents the operation of another ⟨a safety *interlock*⟩

**3 a :** a stretchable fabric made on a circular knitting machine and consisting of two ribbed fabrics joined by interlocking **b :** a garment made of interlock
**in·ter·loc·u·tor** \,in-tər-'lä-kyə-tər\ *noun* [Latin *interloqui* to speak between, issue an interlocutory decree, from *inter-* + *loqui* to speak] (1514)
**1 :** one who takes part in dialogue or conversation
**2 :** a man in the middle of the line in a minstrel show who questions the end men and acts as leader
**in·ter·loc·u·to·ry** \-kyə-,tōr-ē, -,tòr-\ *adjective* (15th century)
**:** pronounced during the progress of a legal action and having only provisional force ⟨*interlocutory* decree⟩
**in·ter·lope** \,in-tər-'lōp, 'in-tər-,\ *intransitive verb* **-loped; -lop·ing** [probably back-formation from *interloper,* from *inter-* + *-loper* (akin to Middle Dutch *lopen* to run, Old English *hlēapan* to leap) — more at LEAP] (1615)
**1 :** to encroach on the rights (as in trade) of others
**2 :** INTRUDE, INTERFERE
**in·ter·lop·er** \'in-tər-,lō-pər, ,in-tər-'\ *noun* (circa 1590)
**:** one that interlopes: as **a :** an illegal or unlicensed trader **b :** one that intrudes in a place or sphere of activity
**in·ter·lude** \'in-tər-,lüd\ *noun* [Middle English *enterlude,* from Medieval Latin *interludium,* from Latin *inter-* + *ludus* play — more at LUDICROUS] (14th century)
**1 :** a usually short simple play or dramatic entertainment
**2 :** an intervening or interruptive period, space, or event **:** INTERVAL
**3 :** a musical composition inserted between the parts of a longer composition, a drama, or a religious service
**in·ter·lu·nar** \,in-tər-'lü-nər\ *also* **in·ter·lu·na·ry** \-nə-rē\ *adjective* [probably from Middle French *interlunaire,* from Latin *interlunium* interlunar period, from *inter-* + *luna* moon — more at LUNAR] (1598)
**:** relating to the interval between old and new moon when the moon is invisible
**in·ter·mar·riage** \,in-tər-'mar-ij\ *noun* (1579)
**1 :** ENDOGAMY
**2 :** marriage between members of different groups
**in·ter·mar·ry** \-'mar-ē\ *intransitive verb* (1574)
**1 a :** to marry each other **b :** to marry within a group
**2 :** to become connected by intermarriage
**in·ter·med·dle** \,in-tər-'me-dᵊl\ *intransitive verb* [Middle English *entermedlen,* from Middle French *entremedler,* from Old French *entremedler,* from *entre-* inter- + *medler* to mix — more at MEDDLE] (15th century)
**:** to meddle impertinently and officiously and usually so as to interfere
— **in·ter·med·dler** \-'med-lər, -'me-dᵊl-ər\ *noun*
**in·ter·me·di·a·cy** \,in-tər-'mē-dē-ə-sē\ *noun* (1713)
**1 :** the act or action of intermediating
**2 :** the quality or state of being intermediate
**¹in·ter·me·di·ary** \,in-tər-'mē-dē-,er-ē\ *adjective* (1788)
**1 :** INTERMEDIATE
**2 :** acting as a mediator ⟨an *intermediary* agent⟩ ⟨an *intermediary* particle⟩
**²intermediary** *noun, plural* **-ar·ies** (1791)
**1 a :** MEDIATOR, GO-BETWEEN **b :** MEDIUM, MEANS
**2 :** an intermediate form, product, or stage
**¹in·ter·me·di·ate** \,in-tər-'mē-dē-ət\ *adjective* [Medieval Latin *intermediatus,* from Latin *intermedius,* from *inter-* + *medius* mid, middle — more at MID] (15th century)

**1 :** being or occurring at the middle place, stage, or degree or between extremes **2 :** of or relating to an intermediate school ⟨an *intermediate* curriculum⟩
— **in·ter·me·di·ate·ly** *adverb*
— **in·ter·me·di·ate·ness** *noun*
²**intermediate** *noun* (1650)
**1 :** one that is intermediate
**2 :** MEDIATOR, GO-BETWEEN
**3 a :** a chemical compound synthesized from simpler compounds and usually intended to be used in later syntheses of more complex products **b :** a usually short-lived chemical species formed in a reaction as an intermediate step between the starting material and the final product
**4 :** an automobile larger than a compact but smaller than a full-sized automobile
³**in·ter·me·di·ate** \-dē-,āt\ *intransitive verb* [Medieval Latin *intermediatus*, past participle of *intermediare*, from Latin *inter-* + Late Latin *mediare* to mediate] (1610)
**1 :** INTERVENE, INTERPOSE
**2 :** to act as an intermediate
**intermediate host** *noun* (1878)
**1 :** a host which is normally used by a parasite in the course of its life cycle and in which it may multiply asexually but not sexually — compare DEFINITIVE HOST
**2 a :** RESERVOIR **3 b :** VECTOR
**intermediate school** *noun* (1842)
**1 :** JUNIOR HIGH SCHOOL
**2 :** a school usually comprising grades 4 to 6
**intermediate vector boson** *noun* (1968)
**:** any of three particles that mediate the weak force — called also *intermediate boson*; compare W PARTICLE, Z PARTICLE
**in·ter·me·di·a·tion** \,in-tər-,mē-dē-'ā-shən\ *noun* (1602)
**:** the act of coming between **:** INTERVENTION, MEDIATION
**in·ter·me·din** \,in-tər-'mē-d°n\ *noun* (1932)
**:** MELANOCYTE-STIMULATING HORMONE
**in·ter·ment** \in-'tər-mənt\ *noun* (14th century)
**:** the act or ceremony of interring
**in·ter·mesh** \in-tər-'mesh\ (circa 1903)
*intransitive verb*
**:** INTERLOCK
*transitive verb*
**:** to mesh together **:** INTERLOCK
**in·ter·me·tal·lic** \,in-tər-mə-'ta-lik\ *adjective* (1900)
**:** composed of two or more metals or of a metal and a nonmetal; *especially* **:** being an alloy having a characteristic crystal structure and usually a definite composition ⟨*intermetallic* compound⟩
— **intermetallic** *noun*
**in·ter·mez·zo** \,in-tər-'met-(,)sō, -'med-(,)zō\ *noun, plural* **-zi** \-(,)sē, -(,)zē\ *or* **-zos** [Italian, ultimately from Latin *intermedius* intermediate] (1771)
**1 :** a short light entr'acte
**2 a :** a movement coming between the major sections of an extended musical work (as an opera) **b :** a short independent instrumental composition
**3 :** a usually brief interlude or diversion
**in·ter·mi·na·ble** \(,)in-'tərm-nə-bəl, -'tər-mə-\ *adjective* [Middle English, from Late Latin *interminabilis*, from Latin *in-* + *terminare* to terminate] (15th century)
**:** having or seeming to have no end; *especially* **:** wearisomely protracted ⟨an *interminable* sermon⟩
— **in·ter·mi·na·ble·ness** *noun*
— **in·ter·mi·na·bly** \-blē\ *adverb*
**in·ter·min·gle** \,in-tər-'miŋ-gəl\ *verb* (15th century)
**:** INTERMIX
**in·ter·mis·sion** \,in-tər-'mi-shən\ *noun* [Middle English *intermyssyown*, from Latin *intermission-, intermissio*, from *intermittere*] (15th century)
**1 :** the act of intermitting **:** the state of being intermitted

**2 :** an interval between the parts of an entertainment (as the acts of a play)
— **in·ter·mis·sion·less** *adjective*
**in·ter·mit** \-'mit\ *verb* **-mit·ted; -mit·ting** [Latin *intermittere*, from *inter-* + *mittere* to send] (circa 1542)
*transitive verb*
**:** to cause to cease for a time or at intervals **:** DISCONTINUE
*intransitive verb*
**:** to be intermittent
— **in·ter·mit·ter** *noun*
**in·ter·mit·tence** \-'mi-tən(t)s\ *noun* (1796)
**:** the quality or state of being intermittent
**in·ter·mit·ten·cy** \-'mi-tən(t)-sē\ *noun* (1662)
**:** INTERMITTENCE
**in·ter·mit·tent** \-'mi-t°nt\ *adjective* [Latin *intermittent-, intermittens*, present participle of *intermittere*] (1601)
**:** coming and going at intervals **:** not continuous ⟨*intermittent* rain⟩; *also* **:** OCCASIONAL ⟨*intermittent* trips abroad⟩
— **in·ter·mit·tent·ly** *adverb*
**in·ter·mix** \,in-tər-'miks\ *verb* [back-formation from obsolete *intermixt* intermingled, from Latin *intermixtus*, past participle of *intermiscēre* to intermix, from *inter-* + *miscēre* to mix — more at MIX] (1542)
*transitive verb*
**:** to mix together
*intransitive verb*
**:** to become mixed together
— **in·ter·mix·ture** \-'miks-chər\ *noun*
**in·ter·mod·al** \-'mō-dəl\ *adjective* (1963)
**1 :** being or involving transportation by more than one form of carrier during a single journey
**2 :** used for intermodal transport
**in·ter·mod·u·la·tion** \-,mä-jə-'lā-shən\ *noun* [International Scientific Vocabulary] (1931)
**:** the production in an electrical device of currents having frequencies equal to the sums and differences of frequencies supplied to the device or of their harmonics
**in·ter·mon·tane** \,in-tər-'män-,tān *or* in-ter-mont \'in-tər-,mänt\ *adjective* [Latin *mont-, mons* mount] (1807)
**:** situated between mountains ⟨an *intermontane* basin⟩
¹**in·tern** *or* **in·terne** \in-'tərn, 'in-,\ *adjective* [Middle French *interne*, from Latin *internus*] (circa 1500)
*archaic* **:** INTERNAL
²**in·tern** \'in-,tərn, in-'\ *transitive verb* (1866)
**:** to confine or impound especially during a war ⟨*intern* enemy aliens⟩
— **in·tern·ee** \(,)in-,tər-'nē\ *noun*
— **in·tern·ment** \in-'tərn-mənt, 'in-,\ *noun*
³**in·tern** *also* **in·terne** \'in-,tərn\ *noun* [French *interne*, from *interne*, adjective] (circa 1879)
**:** an advanced student or graduate usually in a professional field (as medicine or teaching) gaining supervised practical experience (as in a hospital or classroom)
— **in·tern·ship** \-,ship\ *noun*
⁴**in·tern** \'in-,tərn\ *intransitive verb* (circa 1928)
**:** to act as an intern
**in·ter·nal** \in-'tər-n°l, 'in-,\ *adjective* [Middle English *internalle*, from Latin *internus*; akin to Latin *inter* between] (15th century)
**1 :** existing or situated within the limits or surface of something: as **a** (1) **:** situated near the inside of the body (2) **:** situated on the side toward the median plane of the body **b :** of, relating to, or occurring within the confines of an organized structure (as a club, company, or state) ⟨*internal* affairs⟩
**2 :** relating or belonging to or existing within the mind
**3 :** INTRINSIC, INHERENT ⟨*internal* evidence of forgery in a document⟩
**4 :** present or arising within an organism or one of its parts ⟨*internal* stimulus⟩

**5 :** applied or intended for application through the stomach by being swallowed ⟨an *internal* remedy⟩
— **in·ter·nal·i·ty** \,in-tər-'na-lə-tē\ *noun*
— **in·ter·nal·ly** \in-'tər-n°l-ē\ *adverb*
**internal combustion engine** *noun* (1884)
**:** a heat engine in which the combustion that generates the heat takes place inside the engine proper instead of in a furnace
**in·ter·nal·ise** *British variant of* INTERNALIZE
**in·ter·nal·ize** \in-'tər-n°l-,īz\ *transitive verb* **-ized; -iz·ing** (1884)
**:** to give a subjective character to; *specifically* **:** to incorporate (as values or patterns of culture) within the self as conscious or subconscious guiding principles through learning or socialization
— **in·ter·nal·i·za·tion** \-,tər-n°l-ə-'zā-shən\ *noun*
**internal medicine** *noun* (circa 1904)
**:** a branch of medicine that deals with the diagnosis and treatment of diseases not requiring surgery
**internal respiration** *noun* (circa 1890)
**:** an exchange of gases between the cells of the body and the blood by way of the fluid bathing the cells — compare EXTERNAL RESPIRATION
**internal rhyme** *noun* (1903)
**:** rhyme between a word within a line and another either at the end of the same line or within another line
**internal secretion** *noun* (1895)
**:** HORMONE
¹**in·ter·na·tion·al** \,in-tər-'nash-nəl, -'na-shə-n°l\ *adjective* (1780)
**1 :** of, relating to, or affecting two or more nations ⟨*international* trade⟩
**2 :** of, relating to, or constituting a group or association having members in two or more nations ⟨*international* movement⟩
**3 :** active, known, or reaching beyond national boundaries ⟨an *international* reputation⟩
— **in·ter·na·tion·al·i·ty** \-,na-shə-'na-lə-tē\ *noun*
— **in·ter·na·tion·al·ly** \-'nash-nə-lē, -'na-shə-n°l-ē\ *adverb*
²**international** *noun* (1870)
**:** one that is international; *especially* **:** an organization of international scope
**international date line** *noun* (circa 1909)
**:** an arbitrary line approximately along the 180th meridian designated as the place where each calendar day begins
**in·ter·na·tion·al·ise** *British variant of* INTERNATIONALIZE
**in·ter·na·tion·al·ism** \-'nash-nə-,li-zəm, -'na-shə-n°l-,i-zəm\ *noun* (1851)
**1 :** international character, principles, interests, or outlook
**2 a :** a policy of cooperation among nations **b :** an attitude or belief favoring such a policy
— **in·ter·na·tion·al·ist** \-list, -ist\ *noun or adjective*
**in·ter·na·tion·al·ize** \,in-tər-'nash-nə-,līz, -'na-shə-n°l-,īz\ *transitive verb* (circa 1864)
**:** to make international; *also* **:** to place under international control ⟨a proposal to *internationalize* the city⟩
— **in·ter·na·tion·al·i·za·tion** \-,nash-nə-lə-'zā-shən, -,na-shə-n°l-ə-\ *noun*
**international law** *noun* (circa 1828)
**:** a body of rules that control or affect the rights of nations in their relations with each other
**International Phonetic Alphabet** *noun* (1898)
**:** IPA
**international pitch** *noun* (1904)

---

\ə\ abut  \°\ kitten  \ər\ further  \a\ ash  \ā\ ace
\ä\ mop, mar  \au̇\ out  \ch\ chin  \e\ bet  \ē\ easy
\g\ go  \i\ hit  \ī\ ice  \j\ job  \ŋ\ sing  \ō\ go
\ȯ\ law  \ȯi\ boy  \th\ thin  \th\ the  \ü\ loot  \u̇\ foot
\y\ yet  \zh\ vision  *see also* Guide to Pronunciation

: a tuning standard of 440 vibrations per second for A above middle C

**international relations** *noun plural but singular in construction* (1951)
: a branch of political science concerned with relations between nations and primarily with foreign policies

**International Scientific Vocabulary** *noun* (circa 1959)
: a part of the vocabulary of the sciences and other specialized studies that consists of words or other linguistic forms current in two or more languages and differing from New Latin in being adapted to the structure of the individual languages in which they appear

**International Style** *noun* (1932)
**1** : a style in European art of the 14th and early 15th centuries marked by sinuous line, rich color, and decorative surface detail
**2** : a style in architecture developed in the 1920s that uses modern materials (as steel, glass, and reinforced concrete), expresses structure directly, and eliminates nonstructural ornament

**International System of Units** *noun* (1961)
: a system of units based on the metric system and developed and refined by international convention especially for scientific work

**international unit** *noun* (1922)
: a quantity of a biologic (as a vitamin) that produces a particular biological effect agreed upon as an international standard

**in·ter·ne·cine** \,in-tər-'ne-,sēn, -'nē-s°n, -'nē-,sīn, -nə-'sēn; in-'tər-nə-,sēn\ *adjective* [Latin *internecinus*, from *internecare* to destroy, kill, from *inter-* + *necare* to kill, from *nec-*, *nex* violent death — more at NOXIOUS] (1663)
**1** : marked by slaughter : DEADLY; *especially* : mutually destructive
**2** : of, relating to, or involving conflict within a group ⟨bitter *internecine* feuds⟩ ◆

**in·ter·neu·ron** \,in-tər-'nür-,än, -'nyür-\ *noun* (1939)
: an internuncial neuron
— **in·ter·neu·ro·nal** \-'nür-ə-n°l, -'nyür-; -nù-'rō-, -nyü-'\ *adjective*

**in·ter·nist** \'in-,tər-nist\ *noun* (1904)
: a specialist in internal medicine

**in·ter·node** \'in-tər-,nōd\ *noun* [Latin *internodium*, from *inter-* + *nodus* knot] (1667)
: an interval or part between two nodes (as of a stem)
— **in·ter·nod·al** \,in-tər-'nō-d°l\ *adjective*

**in·ter·nun·ci·al** \,in-tər-'nən(t)-sē-əl, -'nùn(t)-\ *adjective* (1845)
**1** : of or relating to an internuncio
**2** : serving to link sensory and motor neurons

**in·ter·nun·cio** \,in-tər-'nən(t)-sē-,ō, -'nùn(t)-\ *noun* [Italian *internunzio*, from Latin *internuntius*, *internuncius*, from *inter-* + *nuntius*, *nuncius* messenger] (1641)
**1** : a messenger between two parties : GO-BETWEEN
**2** : a papal legate of lower rank than a nuncio

**in·ter·o·cep·tive** \,in-tə-rō-'sep-tiv\ *adjective* [*interior* + *-o-* + *-ceptive* (as in *receptive*)] (circa 1921)
: of, relating to, or being stimuli arising within the body and especially in the viscera

**in·ter·o·cep·tor** \-'tər\ *noun* (1906)
: a sensory receptor excited by interoceptive stimuli

**in·ter·op·er·a·bil·i·ty** \,in-tə-,rä-p(ə-)rə-'bi-lə-tē\ *noun* (1977)
: ability of a system (as a weapons system) to use the parts or equipment of another system
— **in·ter·op·er·a·ble** \-'rä-p(ə-)rə-bəl\ *adjective*

**in·ter·pel·late** \,in-tər-'pe-,lāt, -pə-'lāt\ *transitive verb* **-lat·ed; -lat·ing** [Latin *interpellatus*, past participle of *interpellare* to interrupt, from *inter-* + *-pellare* (from *pellere* to drive) — more at FELT] (1874)
: to question (as a foreign minister) formally concerning an official action or policy or personal conduct
— **in·ter·pel·la·tion** \-pə-'lā-shən\ *noun*
— **in·ter·pel·la·tor** \-'pe-,lā-tər, -pə-'lā-\ *noun*

**in·ter·pen·e·trate** \,in-tər-'pe-nə-,trāt\ (circa 1810)
*intransitive verb*
: to penetrate mutually
*transitive verb*
: to penetrate between, within, or throughout : PERMEATE
— **in·ter·pen·e·tra·tion** \-,pe-nə-'trā-shən\ *noun*

**in·ter·per·son·al** \-'pərs-nəl, -'pər-s°n-əl\ *adjective* (1842)
: being, relating to, or involving relations between persons
— **in·ter·per·son·al·ly** *adverb*

**in·ter·phase** \'in-tər-,fāz\ *noun* (1913)
: the interval between the end of one mitotic or meiotic division and the beginning of another

**in·ter·plant** \,in-tər-'plant\ *transitive verb* (1911)
: to plant a crop between (plants of another kind); *also* : to set out young trees among (existing growth)

**in·ter·play** \'in-tər-,plā\ *noun* (1862)
: INTERACTION ⟨the *interplay* of opposing forces⟩
— **in·ter·play** \,in-tər-', 'in-tər-,\ *intransitive verb*

**in·ter·plead** \,in-tər-'plēd\ *intransitive verb* [Anglo-French *enterpleder*, from *enter-* + *pleder* to plead, from Old French *plaidier* — more at PLEAD] (1567)
: to go to trial with each other in order to determine a right on which the action of a third party depends

**¹in·ter·plead·er** \-'plē-dər\ *noun* [Anglo-French *enterpleder*, from *enterpleder*, verb] (1567)
: a proceeding to enable a person to compel parties making the same claim against him to litigate the matter between themselves

**²interpleader** *noun* (circa 1846)
: one that interpleads

**in·ter·po·late** \in-'tər-pə-,lāt\ *verb* **-lat·ed; -lat·ing** [Latin *interpolatus*, past participle of *interpolare* to refurbish, alter, interpolate, from *inter-* + *-polare* (from *polire* to polish)] (1612)
*transitive verb*
**1** : to alter or corrupt (as a text) by inserting new or foreign matter **b** : to insert (words) into a text or into a conversation
**2** : to insert between other things or parts : INTERCALATE
**3** : to estimate values of (a function) between two known values
*intransitive verb*
: to make insertions (as of estimated values)
**synonym** see INTRODUCE
— **in·ter·po·la·tion** \-,tər-pə-'lā-shən\ *noun*
— **in·ter·po·la·tive** \-'tər-pə-,lā-tiv\ *adjective*
— **in·ter·po·la·tor** \-,lā-tər\ *noun*

**in·ter·pose** \,in-tər-'pōz\ *verb* **-posed; -pos·ing** [Middle French *interposer*, from Latin *interponere* (perfect indicative *interposui*), from *inter-* + *ponere* to put — more at POSITION] (1582)
*transitive verb*
**1 a** : to place in an intervening position **b** : to put (oneself) between : INTRUDE
**2** : to put forth by way of interference or intervention
**3** : to introduce or throw in between the parts of a conversation or argument
*intransitive verb*
**1** : to be or come between
**2** : to step in between parties at variance : INTERVENE

**3** : INTERRUPT ☆
— **in·ter·pos·er** *noun*

**in·ter·po·si·tion** \-pə-'zi-shən\ *noun* (14th century)
**1 a** : the act of interposing **b** : the action of a state whereby its sovereignty is placed between its citizens and the federal government
**2** : something interposed

**in·ter·pret** \in-'tər-prət, -pət\ *verb* [Middle English, from Middle French & Latin; Middle French *interpreter*, from Latin *interpretari*, from *interpret-*, *interpres* agent, negotiator, interpreter] (14th century)
*transitive verb*
**1** : to explain or tell the meaning of : present in understandable terms
**2** : to conceive in the light of individual belief, judgment, or circumstance : CONSTRUE
**3** : to represent by means of art : bring to realization by performance or direction ⟨*interprets* a role⟩
*intransitive verb*
: to act as an interpreter between speakers of different languages
**synonym** see EXPLAIN
— **in·ter·pret·abil·i·ty** \-,tər-prə-tə-'bi-lə-tē, -pə-tə-\ *noun*
— **in·ter·pret·able** \-'tər-prə-tə-bəl, -pə-tə-\ *adjective*

**in·ter·pre·ta·tion** \in-,tər-prə-'tā-shən, -pə-\ *noun* (14th century)
**1** : the act or the result of interpreting : EXPLANATION
**2** : a particular adaptation or version of a work, method, or style
**3** : a teaching technique that combines factual with stimulating explanatory information ⟨natural history *interpretation* program⟩

---

☆ SYNONYMS
**Interpose, interfere, intervene, mediate, intercede** mean to come or go between. INTERPOSE often implies no more than this ⟨*interposed* herself between him and the door⟩. INTERFERE implies hindering ⟨noise *interfered* with my concentration⟩. INTERVENE may imply an occurring in space or time between two things or a stepping in to stop a conflict ⟨quarreled until the manager *intervened*⟩. MEDIATE implies intervening between hostile factions ⟨*mediated* between the parties⟩. INTERCEDE implies acting in behalf of an offender in begging mercy or forgiveness ⟨*interceded* on our behalf⟩. See in addition INTRODUCE.

---

◇ WORD HISTORY
**internecine** In Latin the verb *necare* meant "to kill" and the verb *internecare* "to kill without exception, massacre." In this instance the familiar Latin prefix *inter-* did not mean "between" but served to signify the completion of an action. The derivative adjective *internecinus* thus had the meaning of "fought to the death, devastating." In 1755, when Samuel Johnson published his great dictionary, it became clear that he had apparently interpreted the *inter-* of *internecine* as meaning "between" and so had defined the word as "endeavouring mutual destruction." In 1828, when Noah Webster defined *internecine*, he gave only the original sense of "deadly, destructive"; the Johnsonian sense of "mutually destructive" was not added until later revisions. Ironically, the invented Johnsonian sense won favor among the learned and superseded the original meaning entirely. In the 20th century the meaning of *internecine* was extended to include bitter—but bloodless—conflict within a group, and this has become the dominant sense.

— **in·ter·pre·ta·tion·al** \-shnəl, -shə-nᵊl\ *adjective*
— **in·ter·pre·ta·tive** \in-'tər-prə-ˌtā-tiv *also* -prə-tə-tiv\ *adjective*
— **in·ter·pre·ta·tive·ly** *adverb*
— **in·ter·pre·tive** \-'tər-prə-tiv, -pə-\ *adjective*
— **in·ter·pre·tive·ly** *adverb*

**in·ter·pret·er** \in-'tər-prə-tər, -pə-\ *noun* (14th century)
**1** : one that interprets: as **a** : one who translates orally for parties conversing in different languages **b** : one who explains or expounds
**2 a** : a machine that prints on punched cards the symbols recorded in them by perforations **b** : a computer program that translates an instruction into machine language and executes it before going to the next instruction

**in·ter·prox·i·mal** \ˌin-tər-'präk-sə-məl\ *adjective* (1897)
: situated or used in the areas between adjoining teeth ⟨*interproximal* space⟩

**in·ter·pu·pil·lary** \ˌin-tər-'pyü-pə-ˌler-ē\ *adjective* (circa 1904)
: extending between the pupils of the eyes; *also* : extending between the centers of a pair of spectacle lenses ⟨*interpupillary* distance⟩

**in·ter·ra·cial** \-'rā-shəl\ *adjective* (1888)
: of, involving, or designed for members of different races
— **in·ter·ra·cial·ly** \-shə-lē\ *adverb*

**interred** *past and past participle of* INTER

**in·ter·reg·num** \ˌin-tə-'reg-nəm\ *noun, plural* **-nums** *or* **-na** \-nə\ [Latin, from *inter-* + *regnum* reign — more at REIGN] (1590)
**1** : the time during which a throne is vacant between two successive reigns or regimes
**2** : a period during which the normal functions of government or control are suspended
**3** : a lapse or pause in a continuous series

**in·ter·re·late** \ˌin-tə(r)-ri-'lāt\ (1888)
*transitive verb*
: to bring into mutual relation
*intransitive verb*
: to have mutual relationship
— **in·ter·re·la·tion** \-'lā-shən\ *noun*
— **in·ter·re·la·tion·ship** \-ˌship\ *noun*

**in·ter·re·lat·ed** \-'lā-təd\ *adjective* (1827)
: having a mutual or reciprocal relation
— **in·ter·re·lat·ed·ly** *adverb*
— **in·ter·re·lat·ed·ness** *noun*

**interring** *present participle of* INTER

**in·ter·ro·bang** \in-'ter-ə-ˌbaŋ\ *noun* [*interrogation* (point) + *bang* (printers' slang for *exclamation point*)] (1967)
: a punctuation mark ‽ designed for use especially at the end of an exclamatory rhetorical question

**in·ter·ro·gate** \in-'ter-ə-ˌgāt\ *transitive verb* **-gat·ed; -gat·ing** [Latin *interrogatus*, past participle of *interrogare*, from *inter-* + *rogare* to ask — more at RIGHT] (15th century)
**1** : to question formally and systematically
**2** : to give or send out a signal to (as a transponder or computer) for triggering an appropriate response
**synonym** see ASK
— **in·ter·ro·ga·tee** \-ˌter-ə-(ˌ)gā-'tē\ *noun*
— **in·ter·ro·ga·tion** \-ˌter-ə-'gā-shən\ *noun*
— **in·ter·ro·ga·tion·al** \-shnəl, -shə-nᵊl\ *adjective*

**interrogation point** *noun* (circa 1864)
: QUESTION MARK

**¹in·ter·rog·a·tive** \ˌin-tə-'rä-gə-tiv\ *adjective* (15th century)
**1 a** : used in a question **b** : having the form or force of a question
**2** : INQUISITIVE, QUESTIONING
— **in·ter·rog·a·tive·ly** *adverb*

**²interrogative** *noun* (1522)
**1** : a word (as *who, what, which*) or a particle (as Latin *-ne*) used in asking questions
**2** : QUESTION 1a

**in·ter·ro·ga·tor** \in-'ter-ə-ˌgā-tər\ *noun* (1751)
**1** : one that interrogates

**2** : a radio transmitter and receiver for sending out a signal that triggers a transponder and for receiving and displaying the reply

**¹in·ter·rog·a·to·ry** \ˌin-tə-'rä-gə-ˌtōr-ē, -ˌtòr-\ *noun, plural* **-ries** (1533)
: a formal question or inquiry; *especially* : a written question required to be answered under direction of a court

**²interrogatory** *adjective* (1576)
: INTERROGATIVE

**in·ter·ro·gee** \in-ˌter-ə-'gē\ *noun* (1919)
: one who is interrogated

**¹in·ter·rupt** \ˌin-tə-'rəpt\ *verb* [Middle English, from Latin *interruptus*, past participle of *interrumpere*, from *inter-* + *rumpere* to break — more at REAVE] (15th century)
*transitive verb*
**1** : to stop or hinder by breaking in
**2** : to break the uniformity or continuity of
*intransitive verb*
: to break in upon an action; *especially* : to break in with questions or remarks while another is speaking
— **in·ter·rupt·ible** \-'rəp-tə-bəl\ *adjective*
— **in·ter·rup·tion** \-'rəp-shən\ *noun*
— **in·ter·rup·tive** \-'rəp-tiv\ *adverb*

**²in·ter·rupt** \in-tə-'rəpt, 'in-tə-ˌ\ *noun* (1957)
: a feature of a computer that permits the execution of a program to be interrupted in order to perform a special set of operations; *also* : the interruption itself

**in·ter·rupt·er** *also* **in·ter·rup·tor** \ˌin-tə-'rəp-tər\ *noun* (circa 1512)
: one that interrupts; *especially* : a device for interrupting an electric current usually automatically

**in·ter·scho·las·tic** \ˌin-tər-skə-'las-tik\ *adjective* (1879)
: existing or carried on between schools ⟨*interscholastic* athletics⟩

**in·ter se** \ˌin-tər-'sā, -'sē\ *adverb or adjective* [Latin] (1845)
: among or between themselves

**in·ter·sect** \ˌin-tər-'sekt\ *verb* [Latin *intersectus*, past participle of *intersecare*, from *inter-* + *secare* to cut — more at SAW] (1615)
*transitive verb*
: to pierce or divide by passing through or across : CROSS
*intransitive verb*
**1** : to meet and cross at a point
**2** : to share a common area : OVERLAP

**in·ter·sec·tion** \ˌin-tər-'sek-shən, *especially in sense 2* 'in-tər-ˌ\ *noun* (1559)
**1** : the act or process of intersecting
**2** : a place or area where two or more things (as streets) intersect
**3 a** : the set of elements common to two or more sets; *especially* : the set of points common to two geometric configurations **b** : the operation of finding the intersection of two or more sets

*a* **intersection 3a**

**in·ter·ser·vice** \ˌin-tər-'sər-vəs\ *adjective* (1946)
: existing between or relating to two or more of the armed services ⟨*interservice* rivalry⟩

**in·ter·ses·sion** \'in-tər-ˌse-shən\ *noun* (1932)
: a period between two academic sessions or terms sometimes utilized for brief concentrated courses

**in·ter·sex** \'in-tər-ˌseks\ *noun* [International Scientific Vocabulary] (1910)
: an intersexual individual

**in·ter·sex·u·al** \ˌin-tər-'sek-shə-wəl, -shwəl, -shəl\ *adjective* [International Scientific Vocabulary] (circa 1866)
**1** : existing between sexes ⟨*intersexual* hostility⟩
**2** : intermediate in sexual characters between a typical male and a typical female
— **in·ter·sex·u·al·i·ty** \-ˌsek-shə-'wa-lə-tē\ *noun*

— **in·ter·sex·u·al·ly** \-'sek-shə-wə-lē, -shwə-lē, -shə-lē\ *adverb*

**¹in·ter·space** \'in-tər-ˌspās\ *noun* (15th century)
: an intervening space : INTERVAL

**²in·ter·space** \ˌin-tər-'spās\ *transitive verb* (1685)
: to occupy or fill the space between

**in·ter·spe·cif·ic** \ˌin-tər-spi-'si-fik\ *also* **in·ter·spe·cies** \-'spē-(ˌ)shēz, -(ˌ)sēz\ *adjective* (1889)
: existing, occurring, or arising between species ⟨*interspecific* hybrid⟩

**in·ter·sperse** \ˌin-tər-'spərs\ *transitive verb* **-spersed; -spers·ing** [Latin *interspersus* interspersed, from *inter-* + *sparsus*, past participle of *spargere* to scatter — more at SPARK] (1566)
**1** : to place something at intervals in or among
**2** : to insert at intervals among other things ⟨*interspersing* drawings throughout the text⟩
— **in·ter·sper·sion** \-'spər-zhən, -shən\ *noun*

**in·ter·sta·di·al** \ˌin-tər-'stā-dē-əl\ *noun* [International Scientific Vocabulary *inter-* + New Latin *stadium* stage, phase, from Latin — more at STADIUM] (1914)
: a subdivision within a glacial stage marking a temporary retreat of the ice

**¹in·ter·state** \ˌin-tər-'stāt\ *adjective* (1844)
: of, connecting, or existing between two or more states especially of the U.S. ⟨*interstate* commerce⟩

**²in·ter·state** \'in-tər-ˌstāt\ *noun* (1968)
: any of a system of expressways connecting most major U.S. cities — called also *interstate highway*

**in·ter·stel·lar** \-'ste-lər\ *adjective* (1626)
: located, taking place, or traveling among the stars especially of the Milky Way galaxy

**in·ter·ster·ile** \-'ster-əl, *chiefly British* -ˌīl\ *adjective* (1916)
: incapable of producing offspring by interbreeding
— **in·ter·ste·ril·i·ty** \-stə-'ri-lə-tē\ *noun*

**in·ter·stice** \in-'tər-stəs\ *noun, plural* **-stic·es** \-stə-ˌsēz, -stə-səz\ [Middle English, from Latin *interstitium*, from *inter-* + *-stit-, -stes* standing (as in *superstes* standing over) — more at SUPERSTITION] (15th century)
**1 a** : a space that intervenes between things; *especially* : one between closely spaced things **b** : a gap or break in something generally continuous ⟨the *interstices* of society⟩ ⟨passages of genuine literary merit in the *interstices* of the ludicrous . . . plots —Joyce Carol Oates⟩
**2** : a short space of time between events

**in·ter·sti·tial** \ˌin-tər-'sti-shəl\ *adjective* (1646)
**1** : relating to or situated in the interstices
**2 a** : situated within but not restricted to or characteristic of a particular organ or tissue — used especially of fibrous tissue **b** : affecting the interstitial tissues of an organ or part
**3** : relating or relating to a crystalline compound in which usually small atoms or ions of a nonmetal occupy holes between the larger metal atoms or ions in the crystal lattice
— **in·ter·sti·tial·ly** \-shə-lē\ *adverb*

**in·ter·sub·jec·tive** \ˌin-tər-səb-'jek-tiv\ *adjective* (1899)
**1** : involving or occurring between separate conscious minds ⟨*intersubjective* communication⟩
**2** : accessible to or capable of being established for two or more subjects : OBJECTIVE
— **in·ter·sub·jec·tive·ly** *adverb*
— **in·ter·sub·jec·tiv·i·ty** \-(ˌ)səb-ˌjek-'ti-və-tē\ *noun*

**in·ter·tes·ta·men·tal** \-ˌtes-tə-ˈmen-t⁰l\ *adjective* (1929)
**:** of, relating to, or forming the period of two centuries between the composition of the last book of the Old Testament and the first book of the New Testament
**in·ter·tid·al** \-ˈtī-d⁰l\ *adjective* (1883)
**:** of, relating to, or being the part of the littoral zone above low-tide mark
— **in·ter·tid·al·ly** \-d⁰l-ē\ *adverb*
**in·ter·tie** \ˈin-tər-ˌtī\ *noun* (1951)
**:** an interconnection permitting passage of current between two or more electric utility systems
**in·ter·till** \ˌin-tər-ˈtil\ *transitive verb* (1912)
**:** to cultivate between the rows of (a crop)
— **in·ter·till·age** \-ˈti-lij\ *noun*
**in·ter·trop·i·cal** \-ˈträ-pi-kəl\ *adjective* (1794)
**1 :** situated between or within the tropics
**2 :** relating to regions within the tropics
**:** TROPICAL
**in·ter·twine** \-ˈtwīn\ (1641)
*transitive verb*
**:** to unite by twining one with another
*intransitive verb*
**:** to twine about one another; *also* **:** to become mutually involved
— **in·ter·twine·ment** \-mənt\ *noun*
**in·ter·twist** \-ˈtwist\ *verb* (circa 1659)
**:** INTERTWINE
— **in·ter·twist** \ˈin-tər-ˌtwist\ *noun*
**in·ter·val** \ˈin-tər-vəl\ *noun* [Middle English *intervalle*, from Middle French, from Latin *intervallum* space between ramparts, interval, from *inter-* + *vallum* rampart — more at WALL] (14th century)
**1 a :** a space of time between events or states **b** *British* **:** INTERMISSION
**2 a :** a space between objects, units, points, or states **b :** difference in pitch between tones
**3 :** a set of real numbers between two numbers either including or excluding one or both of them
**4 :** one of a series of fast-paced runs interspersed with jogging for training (as of a runner)
— **in·ter·val·lic** \ˌin-tər-ˈva-lik\ *adjective*
**in·ter·vale** \ˈin-tər-vəl, -ˌvāl\ *noun* [obsolete *intervale* interval] (1647)
*chiefly New England* **:** BOTTOMLAND
**in·ter·val·om·e·ter** \ˌin-tər-və-ˈlä-mə-tər\ *noun* (1933)
**:** a device that operates a control (as for a camera shutter) at regular intervals
**in·ter·vene** \ˌin-tər-ˈvēn\ *intransitive verb* **-vened; -ven·ing** [Latin *intervenire* to come between, from *inter-* + *venire* to come — more at COME] (1587)
**1 :** to occur, fall, or come between points of time or events
**2 :** to enter or appear as an irrelevant or extraneous feature or circumstance
**3 :** to come in or between by way of hindrance or modification 〈*intervene* to stop a fight〉
**4 :** to occur or lie between two things
**5 a :** to become a third party to a legal proceeding begun by others for the protection of an alleged interest **b :** to interfere usually by force or threat of force in another nation's internal affairs especially to compel or prevent an action or to maintain or alter a condition
*synonym* see INTERPOSE
— **in·ter·ven·tion** \-ˈven(t)-shən\ *noun*
**in·ter·ve·nor** \-ˈvē-nər, -ˌnȯr\ *or* **in·ter·ven·er** \-ˈvē-nər\ *noun* (1621)
**:** one who intervenes; *especially* **:** one who intervenes as a third party in a legal proceeding
**in·ter·ven·tion·ism** \-ˈven(t)-shə-ˌni-zəm\ *noun* (1923)
**:** the theory or practice of intervening; *specifically* **:** governmental interference in economic affairs at home or in political affairs of another country
— **in·ter·ven·tion·ist** \-ˈvench-nist, -ˈven(t)-shə-nist\ *noun or adjective*

**in·ter·ver·te·bral disk** \ˌin-tər-ˈvər-tə-brəl-, -(ˌ)vər-ˈtē-\ *noun* (circa 1860)
**:** any of the tough elastic disks that are interposed between the centra of adjoining vertebrae and that consist of an outer fibrous ring enclosing an inner pulpy nucleus
**in·ter·view** \ˈin-tər-ˌvyü\ *noun* [Middle French *entrevue*, from (s')*entrevoir* to see one another, meet, from *entre-* inter- + *voir* to see — more at VIEW] (1514)
**1 :** a formal consultation usually to evaluate qualifications (as of a prospective student or employee)
**2 a :** a meeting at which information is obtained (as by a reporter, television commentator, or pollster) from a person **b :** a report or reproduction of information so obtained
**3 :** INTERVIEWEE
— **interview** *verb*
— **in·ter·view·er** *noun*
**in·ter·view·ee** \ˌin-tər-(ˌ)vyü-ˈē\ *noun* (1884)
**:** one who is interviewed
**in·ter vi·vos** \ˈin-tər-ˈvē-ˌvōs, -ˈvī-\ *adverb or adjective* [Late Latin] (1837)
**:** between living persons 〈transaction *inter vivos*〉; *especially* **:** from one living person to another 〈*inter vivos* gifts〉 〈property transferred *inter vivos*〉
**in·ter·vo·cal·ic** \ˌin-tər-vō-ˈka-lik\ *adjective* (1887)
**:** immediately preceded and immediately followed by a vowel
— **in·ter·vo·cal·i·cal·ly** \-li-k(ə-)lē\ *adverb*
**in·ter·weave** \ˌin-tər-ˈwēv\ *verb* **-wove** \-ˈwōv\ *also* **-weaved; -wo·ven** \-ˈwō-vən\ *also* **-weaved; -weav·ing** (1598)
*transitive verb*
**1 :** to weave together
**2 :** to mix or blend together 〈*interweaving* his own insights . . . with letters and memoirs —Phoebe Adams〉
*intransitive verb*
**:** INTERTWINE, INTERMINGLE
— **in·ter·weave** \ˈin-tər-ˌwēv\ *noun*
— **in·ter·wo·ven** \ˌin-tər-ˈwō-vən\ *adjective*
**in·tes·ta·cy** \in-ˈtes-tə-sē\ *noun* (1767)
**:** the quality or state of being or dying intestate
**¹in·tes·tate** \in-ˈtes-ˌtāt, -tət\ *adjective* [Middle English, from Latin *intestatus*, from *in-* + *testatus* testate] (14th century)
**1 :** having made no valid will 〈died *intestate*〉
**2 :** not disposed of by will 〈an *intestate* estate〉
**²intestate** *noun* (1658)
**:** one who dies intestate
**in·tes·ti·nal** \in-ˈtes-tə-n⁰l, -ˈtes(t)-nəl, -ˈtes-ⁿn-əl, *British often* ˌin-(ˌ)tes-ˈtī-n⁰l\ *adjective* (15th century)
**1 :** affecting or occurring in the intestine; *also* **:** living in the intestine
**2 :** of, relating to, or being the intestine
— **in·tes·ti·nal·ly** *adverb*
**intestinal fortitude** *noun* [euphemism for *guts*] (circa 1937)
**:** COURAGE, STAMINA
**¹in·tes·tine** \in-ˈtes-tən\ *adjective* [Middle English, from Middle French or Latin; Middle French *intestin*, from Latin *intestinus*, from *intus* within — more at ENT-] (15th century)
**:** INTERNAL; *specifically* **:** of or relating to the internal affairs of a state or country 〈*intestine* war〉
**²intestine** *noun* [Middle English, from Middle French *intestin*, from Latin *intestinum*, from neuter of *intestinus*] (15th century)

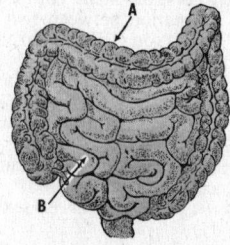

**intestine:** *A* large intestine, *B* small intestine

**:** the tubular part of the alimentary canal that extends from the stomach to the anus
**in·ti** \ˈin-tē\ *noun* [Quechua, sun] (1985)
**:** the basic monetary unit of Peru from 1985 to 1990
**in·ti·ma** \ˈin-tə-mə\ *noun, plural* **-mae** \-ˌmē, -ˌmī\ *or* **-mas** [New Latin, from Latin, feminine of *intimus*] (1873)
**:** the innermost coat of an organ (as a blood vessel) consisting usually of an endothelial layer backed by connective tissue and elastic tissue
— **in·ti·mal** \-məl\ *adjective*
**in·ti·ma·cy** \ˈin-tə-mə-sē\ *noun, plural* **-cies** (1641)
**1 :** the state of being intimate **:** FAMILIARITY
**2 :** something of a personal or private nature
**¹in·ti·mate** \ˈin-tə-ˌmāt\ *transitive verb* **-mat·ed; -mat·ing** [Late Latin *intimatus*, past participle of *intimare* to put in, announce, from Latin *intimus* innermost, superlative of (assumed) Old Latin *interus* inward — more at INTERIOR] (1522)
**1 :** to make known especially publicly or formally **:** ANNOUNCE
**2 :** to communicate delicately and indirectly **:** HINT
*synonym* see SUGGEST
— **in·ti·mat·er** *noun*
— **in·ti·ma·tion** \ˌin-tə-ˈmā-shən\ *noun*
**²in·ti·mate** \ˈin-tə-mət\ *adjective* [alteration of obsolete *intime*, from Latin *intimus*] (1632)
**1 a :** INTRINSIC, ESSENTIAL **b :** belonging to or characterizing one's deepest nature
**2 :** marked by very close association, contact, or familiarity 〈*intimate* knowledge of the law〉
**3 a :** marked by a warm friendship developing through long association **b :** suggesting informal warmth or privacy 〈*intimate* clubs〉
**4 :** of a very personal or private nature
— **in·ti·mate·ly** *adverb*
— **in·ti·mate·ness** *noun*
**³in·ti·mate** \ˈin-tə-mət\ *noun* (1659)
**:** an intimate friend or confidant
**in·tim·i·date** \in-ˈti-mə-ˌdāt\ *transitive verb* **-dat·ed; -dat·ing** [Medieval Latin *intimidatus*, past participle of *intimidare*, from Latin *in-* + *timidus* timid] (1646)
**:** to make timid or fearful **:** FRIGHTEN; *especially* **:** to compel or deter by or as if by threats ☆
— **in·tim·i·dat·ing·ly** \-ˌdā-tiŋ-lē\ *adverb*
— **in·tim·i·da·tion** \-ˌti-mə-ˈdā-shən\ *noun*
— **in·tim·i·da·tor** \-ˈti-mə-ˌdā-tər\ *noun*
**in·tim·i·da·to·ry** \-ˈti-mə-də-ˌtōr-ē, -ˌtȯr-\ *adjective* (circa 1846)
**:** tending to intimidate
**in·tinc·tion** \in-ˈtiŋ(k)-shən\ *noun* [Late Latin *intinction-, intinctio* baptism, from Latin *intingere* to dip in, from *in-* + *tingere* to dip, moisten — more at TINGE] (1872)
**:** the administration of the sacrament of Communion by dipping the bread in the wine and giving both together to the communicant

---

☆ **SYNONYMS**
**Intimidate, cow, bulldoze, bully, browbeat** mean to frighten into submission. INTIMIDATE implies inducing fear or a sense of inferiority into another 〈*intimidated* by so many other bright freshmen〉. COW implies reduction to a state where the spirit is broken or all courage is lost 〈not at all *cowed* by the odds against making it in show business〉. BULLDOZE implies an intimidating or an overcoming of resistance usually by urgings, demands, or threats 〈*bulldozed* the city council into approving the plan〉. BULLY implies intimidation through threats, insults, or aggressive behavior 〈*bullied* into giving up their lunch money〉. BROWBEAT implies a cowing through arrogant, scornful, contemptuous, or insolent treatment 〈*browbeat* the witness into a contradiction〉.

**in·tine** \'in-ˌtēn\ *noun* [probably from German, from Latin *intus* within + New Latin *in-* fibrous tissue, from Greek *in-, is* tendon] (1835) : the inner mostly cellulose wall of a spore (as a pollen grain)

**in·tit·ule** \in-'ti-(ˌ)chü(ə)l\ *transitive verb* **-uled; -ul·ing** [Middle French *intituler,* from Late Latin *intitulare,* from Latin *in-* + *titulus* title] (15th century) *British* : to furnish (as a legislative act) with a title or designation

**in·to** \'in-(ˌ)tü, -tə\ *preposition* [Middle English, from Old English *intō,* from ²*in* + *tō* to] (before 12th century) **1** — used as a function word to indicate entry, introduction, insertion, superposition, or inclusion ⟨came *into* the house⟩ ⟨enter *into* an alliance⟩ **2 a** : to the state, condition, or form of ⟨got *into* trouble⟩ **b** : to the occupation, action, or possession of ⟨go *into* farming⟩ **c** : involved with or interested in ⟨*into* hard drugs⟩ ⟨*into* Latin epigrammatists⟩ **3** — used as a function word to indicate a period of time or an extent of space part of which is passed or occupied ⟨far *into* the night⟩ **4** : in the direction of ⟨looking *into* the sun⟩ **5** : to a position of contact with : AGAINST ⟨ran *into* a wall⟩ **6** — used as a function word to indicate the dividend in division ⟨dividing 3 *into* 6 gives 2⟩

**in·tol·er·a·ble** \(ˌ)in-'täl-rə-bəl, -'tä-lə-rə-, -'tä-lər-bəl\ *adjective* [Middle English, from Latin *intolerabilis,* from *in-* + *tolerabilis* tolerable] (15th century) **1** : not tolerable : UNBEARABLE ⟨*intolerable* pain⟩ **2** : EXCESSIVE — **in·tol·er·a·bil·i·ty** \-ˌtäl-rə-'bi-lə-tē, -ˌtä-lə-rə-, -ˌtä-lər-\ *noun* — **in·tol·er·a·ble·ness** \-'täl-rə-bəl-nəs, -'tä-lə-rə-, -'tä-lər-bəl-\ *noun* — **in·tol·er·a·bly** \-blē\ *adverb*

**in·tol·er·ance** \(ˌ)in-'täl-rən(t)s, -'tä-lə-\ *noun* (1765) : the quality or state of being intolerant; *especially* : exceptional sensitivity (as to a drug)

**in·tol·er·ant** \-rənt\ *adjective* (circa 1735) **1** : unable or unwilling to endure ⟨a plant *intolerant* of direct sunlight⟩ ⟨*intolerant* of criticism⟩ **2 a** : unwilling to grant equal freedom of expression especially in religious matters **b** : unwilling to grant or share social, political, or professional rights : BIGOTED — **in·tol·er·ant·ly** *adverb* — **in·tol·er·ant·ness** *noun*

**in·to·nate** \'in-tə-ˌnāt, -(ˌ)tō-\ *transitive verb* **-nat·ed; -nat·ing** (1795) : INTONE, UTTER

**in·to·na·tion** \ˌin-tə-'nā-shən, -(ˌ)tō-\ *noun* (1620) **1** : the act of intoning and especially of chanting **2** : something that is intoned; *specifically* : the opening tones of a Gregorian chant **3** : the ability to play or sing notes in tune **4** : manner of utterance; *specifically* : the rise and fall in pitch of the voice in speech — **in·to·na·tion·al** \-shnəl, -shə-nᵊl\ *adjective*

**in·tone** \in-'tōn\ *verb* **in·toned; in·ton·ing** [Middle English *entonen,* from Middle French *entoner,* from Medieval Latin *intonare,* from Latin *in-* + *tonus* tone] (15th century) *transitive verb* : to utter in musical or prolonged tones : recite in singing tones or in a monotone *intransitive verb* : to utter something in singing tones or in monotone — **in·ton·er** *noun*

**in to·to** \in-'tō-(ˌ)tō\ *adverb* [Latin, on the whole] (1796) : TOTALLY, ENTIRELY

**in·tox·i·cant** \in-'täk-si-kənt\ *noun* (1863) : something that intoxicates; *especially* : an alcoholic drink — **intoxicant** *adjective*

¹**in·tox·i·cate** \-si-kət\ *adjective* (15th century) *archaic* : INTOXICATED

²**in·tox·i·cate** \-sə-ˌkāt\ *transitive verb* **-cat·ed; -cat·ing** [Middle English, from Medieval Latin *intoxicatus,* past participle of *intoxicare,* from Latin *in-* + *toxicum* poison — more at TOXIC] (15th century) **1** : POISON **2 a** : to excite or stupefy by alcohol or a drug especially to the point where physical and mental control is markedly diminished **b** : to excite or elate to the point of enthusiasm or frenzy

**in·tox·i·cat·ed** \-sə-ˌkā-təd\ *adjective* (1576) : affected by or as if by alcohol : DRUNK — **in·tox·i·cat·ed·ly** \-ˌkā-təd-lē\ *adverb*

**in·tox·i·ca·tion** \in-ˌtäk-sə-'kā-shən\ *noun* (15th century) **1** : an abnormal state that is essentially a poisoning ⟨intestinal *intoxication*⟩ **2 a** : the condition of being drunk : INEBRIATION **b** : a strong excitement or elation

**in·tra-** \'in-trə, -(ˌ)trä\ *prefix* [Late Latin, from Latin *intra,* from (assumed) Old Latin *interus,* adjective, inward — more at INTERIOR] **1 a** : within ⟨*intra*galactic⟩ **b** : during ⟨*intra*-day⟩ **c** : between layers of ⟨*intra*dermal⟩ **2** : INTRO- ⟨an *intra*muscular injection⟩

**in·tra–ar·te·ri·al** \-är-'tir-ē-əl\ *adjective* (1897) : situated or occurring within, administered into, or involving entry by way of an artery — **in·tra–ar·te·ri·al·ly** \-ē-ə-lē\ *adverb*

**in·tra–ar·tic·u·lar** \-är-'ti-kyə-lər\ *adjective* (circa 1888) : situated within, occurring within, or administered by entry into a joint

**in·tra·car·di·ac** \-'kär-dē-ˌak\ *also* **in·tra·car·di·al** \-dē-əl\ *adjective* (1876) : situated or occurring within or introduced or involving entry into the heart ⟨*intracardiac* surgery⟩ ⟨an *intracardiac* catheter⟩ — **in·tra·car·di·al·ly** \-dē-ə-lē\ *adverb*

**in·tra·cel·lu·lar** \-'sel-yə-lər\ *adjective* (1876) : existing, occurring, or functioning within a cell ⟨*intracellular* parasites⟩ — **in·tra·cel·lu·lar·ly** *adverb*

**in·tra·ce·re·bral** \-sə-'rē-brəl, -'ser-ə-\ *adjective* (1881) : situated in, introduced into, or made into the cerebrum ⟨*intracerebral* injections⟩ ⟨*intracerebral* bleeding⟩ — **in·tra·ce·re·bral·ly** \-brə-lē\ *adverb*

**in·tra·com·pa·ny** \-'kəmp-nē, -'kəm-pə-\ *adjective* (1926) : occurring within or taking place between branches or employees of a company ⟨*intracompany* income⟩

**in·tra·cra·ni·al** \-'krā-nē-əl\ *adjective* (circa 1849) : existing or occurring within the cranium; *also* : affecting or involving intracranial structures — **in·tra·cra·ni·al·ly** \-nē-ə-lē\ *adverb*

**in·trac·ta·ble** \(ˌ)in-'trak-tə-bəl\ *adjective* [Latin *intractabilis,* from *in-* + *tractabilis* tractable] (1531) **1** : not easily governed, managed, or directed : OBSTINATE **2** : not easily manipulated or wrought ⟨*intractable* metal⟩ **3** : not easily relieved or cured ⟨*intractable* pain⟩ **synonym** SEE UNRULY — **in·trac·ta·bil·i·ty** \(ˌ)in-ˌtrak-tə-'bi-lə-tē\ *noun* — **in·trac·ta·bly** \-blē\ *adverb*

**in·tra·cu·ta·ne·ous** \ˌin-trə-kyù-'tā-nē-əs, -(ˌ)trä-\ *adjective* (1885) : INTRADERMAL — **in·tra·cu·ta·ne·ous·ly** *adverb*

**in·tra·day** \'in-trə-ˌdā, -(ˌ)trä-\ *adjective* (1950) : occurring in the course of a single day ⟨the market showed wide *intraday* fluctuations⟩

**in·tra·der·mal** \ˌin-trə-'dər-məl, -(ˌ)trä-\ *adjective* (circa 1900) : situated, occurring, or done within or between the layers of the skin; *also* : administered by entering the skin ⟨*intradermal* injections⟩ — **in·tra·der·mal·ly** \-mə-lē\ *adverb*

**intradermal test** *noun* (1916) : a test for immunity or hypersensitivity made by injecting a minute amount of diluted antigen into the skin

**in·tra·dos** \'in-trə-ˌdäs, -ˌdō; in-'trä-ˌdäs\ *noun, plural* **-dos** \-ˌdōz, -ˌdäs\ *or* **-dos·es** \-ˌdä-səz\ [French, from Latin *intra* within + French *dos* back — more at DOSSIER] (1772) : the interior curve of an arch — see ARCH illustration

**in·tra·ga·lac·tic** \ˌin-trə-gə-'lak-tik, -(ˌ)trä-\ *adjective* (1964) : situated or occurring within the confines of a single galaxy

**in·tra·gen·ic** \-'je-nik\ *adjective* (1937) : being or occurring within a gene ⟨*intragenic* recombination⟩ ⟨*intragenic* mutation⟩

**in·tra·mo·lec·u·lar** \-mə-'le-kyə-lər\ *adjective* [International Scientific Vocabulary] (1884) : existing or acting within the molecule; *also* : formed by reaction between different parts of the same molecule — **in·tra·mo·lec·u·lar·ly** *adverb*

**in·tra·mu·ral** \-'myùr-əl\ *adjective* (1846) **1 a** : being or occurring within the limits usually of a community, organization, or institution **b** : competed only within the student body ⟨*intramural* sports⟩ **2** : situated or occurring within the substance of the walls of an organ — **in·tra·mu·ral·ly** \-ə-lē\ *adverb*

**in·tra·mus·cu·lar** \-'məs-kyə-lər\ *adjective* [International Scientific Vocabulary] (1874) : situated in, occurring in, or administered by entering a muscle — **in·tra·mus·cu·lar·ly** *adverb*

**in·tra·na·sal** \-'nā-zəl\ *adjective* (1886) : lying within or administered by way of the nasal structures — **in·tra·na·sal·ly** \-'nāz-lē, -'nā-zə-\ *adverb*

**in·tran·si·geance** \in-'tran(t)-sə-jən(t)s, -'tran-zə-\ *noun* [French] (1899) : INTRANSIGENCE — **in·tran·si·geant** \-jənt\ *adjective or noun* — **in·tran·si·geant·ly** *adverb*

**in·tran·si·gence** \-jən(t)s\ *noun* (1882) : the quality or state of being intransigent

**in·tran·si·gent** \-jənt\ *adjective* [Spanish *intransigente,* from *in-* + *transigente,* present participle of *transigir* to compromise, from Latin *transigere* to come to an agreement — more at TRANSACT] (circa 1879) **1 a** : refusing to compromise or to abandon an extreme position or attitude : UNCOMPROMISING **b** : IRRECONCILABLE **2** : characteristic of an intransigent person — **intransigent** *noun* — **in·tran·si·gent·ly** *adverb*

**in·tran·si·tive** \(ˌ)in-'tran(t)-sə-tiv, -'tran-zə-; -'tran(t)s-tiv\ *adjective* [Late Latin *intransitivus,* from Latin *in-* + Late Latin *transitivus* transitive] (1612) : not transitive; *especially* : characterized by not having or containing a direct object ⟨an *intransitive* verb⟩ — **in·tran·si·tive·ly** *adverb*

— **in·tran·si·tive·ness** *noun*

— **in·tran·si·tiv·i·ty** \(,)in-,tran(t)-sə-'ti-və-tē, -,tran-zə-\ *noun*

**in·tra·oc·u·lar** \,in-trə-'ä-kyə-lər, -,(,)trä-\ *adjective* [International Scientific Vocabulary] (1826)
**:** implanted in, occurring in, or administered by entering the eyeball

— **in·tra·oc·u·lar·ly** *adverb*

**in·tra·per·i·to·ne·al** \,in-trə-,per-ə-t°n-'ē-əl\ *adjective* (circa 1836)
**:** existing within or administered by entering the peritoneum

— **in·tra·per·i·to·ne·al·ly** \-'ē-ə-lē\ *adverb*

**in·tra·per·son·al** \-'pərs-nəl, -'pər-s°n-əl\ *adjective* (1909)
**:** occurring within the individual mind or self ⟨*intrapersonal* concerns of the aged⟩

**in·tra·plate** \'in-trə-,plāt, -,(,)trä-\ *adjective* (1973)
**:** relating to or occurring within the interior of a tectonic plate ⟨an *intraplate* earthquake⟩

**in·tra·pop·u·la·tion** \'in-trə-,pä-pyə-'lā-shən, -,(,)trä-\ *adjective* (1959)
**:** occurring within or taking place between members of a population

**in·tra·pre·neur** \,in-trə-prə-'nər, -'nůr, -'nyůr\ *noun* [*intra-* + *entrepreneur*] (1982)
**:** a corporate executive who develops new enterprises within the corporation

— **in·tra·pre·neur·ial** \-'nər-ē-əl, -'n(y)ůr-\ *adjective*

**in·tra·psy·chic** \,in-trə-'sī-kik, -,(,)trä-\ *adjective* (1917)
**:** being or occurring within the psyche, mind, or personality

— **in·tra·psy·chi·cal·ly** \-ki-k(ə-)lē\ *adverb*

**in·tra·spe·cies** \-'spē-(,)shēz, -,(,)sēz\ *adjective* (1927)
**:** INTRASPECIFIC

**in·tra·spe·cif·ic** \-spi-'si-fik\ *adjective* (1919)
**:** occurring within a species or involving members of one species

**in·tra·state** \-'stāt\ *adjective* (1903)
**:** existing or occurring within a state

**in·tra·the·cal** \-'thē-kəl\ *adjective* (1887)
**:** introduced into or occurring in the space under the arachnoid membrane of the brain or spinal cord

— **in·tra·the·cal·ly** \-k(ə-)lē\ *adverb*

**in·tra·tho·rac·ic** \-thə-'ra-sik\ *adjective* [International Scientific Vocabulary] (1862)
**:** situated or occurring within the thorax ⟨*intrathoracic* pressure⟩

— **in·tra·tho·rac·i·cal·ly** *adverb*

**in·tra·uter·ine** \-'yü-tə-rən, -,rīn\ *adjective* [International Scientific Vocabulary] (circa 1836)
**:** situated, used, or occurring within the uterus; *also* **:** involving the part of development that takes place in the uterus

**intrauterine device** *noun* (1964)
**:** a device inserted and left in the uterus to prevent effective conception — called also *intrauterine contraceptive device, IUD*

**in·tra·vas·cu·lar** \,in-trə-'vas-kyə-lər, -,(,)trä-\ *adjective* (1876)
**:** situated in, occurring in, or administered by entry into a blood vessel ⟨*intravascular* thrombosis⟩ ⟨an *intravascular* injection⟩

— **in·tra·vas·cu·lar·ly** *adverb*

**in·tra·ve·nous** \,in-trə-'vē-nəs\ *adjective* [International Scientific Vocabulary] (circa 1849)
**:** situated, performed, or occurring within or entering by way of a vein; *also* **:** used in intravenous procedures

— **in·tra·ve·nous·ly** *adverb*

**in·tra·ven·tric·u·lar** \,in-trə-ven-'tri-kyə-lər, -,(,)trä\ *adjective* (1882)
**:** situated within, occurring within, or administered into a ventricle

— **in·tra·ven·tric·u·lar·ly** *adverb*

**in·tra·vi·tal** \-'vī-t°l\ *adjective* [International Scientific Vocabulary] (circa 1890)
**1 :** performed upon or found in a living subject
**2 :** having or utilizing the property of staining cells without killing them — compare SUPRAVITAL

— **in·tra·vi·tal·ly** \-t°l-ē\ *adverb*

**in·tra·vi·tam** \-'vī-,tam, -'wē-,täm\ *adjective* [New Latin *intra vitam* during life] (1881)
**:** INTRAVITAL

**in·tra·zon·al** \,in-trə-'zō-n°l, -,(,)trä-\ *adjective* (1927)
**:** of, relating to, or being a soil or a major soil group marked by relatively well-developed characteristics that are determined primarily by essentially local factors (as the parent material) rather than climate and vegetation — compare AZONAL, ZONAL

**intreat** *archaic variant of* ENTREAT

**intrench** *variant of* ENTRENCH

**in·trep·id** \in-'tre-pəd\ *adjective* [Latin *intrepidus*, from *in-* + *trepidus* alarmed — more at TREPIDATION] (1697)
**:** characterized by resolute fearlessness, fortitude, and endurance

— **in·tre·pid·i·ty** \,in-trə-'pi-də-tē\ *noun*
— **in·trep·id·ly** \in-'tre-pəd-lē\ *adverb*
— **in·trep·id·ness** *noun*

**in·tri·ca·cy** \'in-tri-kə-sē\ *noun, plural* **-cies** (1602)
**1 :** the quality or state of being intricate
**2 :** something intricate ⟨the *intricacies* of a plot⟩

**in·tri·cate** \'in-tri-kət\ *adjective* [Middle English, from Latin *intricatus*, past participle of *intricare* to entangle, from *in-* + *tricae* trifles, complications] (15th century)
**1 :** having many complexly interrelating parts or elements **:** COMPLICATED
**2 :** difficult to resolve or analyze
*synonym* see COMPLEX

— **in·tri·cate·ly** *adverb*
— **in·tri·cate·ness** *noun*

**in·tri·gant** *or* **in·tri·guant** \,in-trē-'gänt, ,an-, -'gä\ *noun* [French *intrigant*, from Italian *intrigante*, present participle of *intrigare*] (1781)
**:** one that intrigues

**¹in·trigue** \in-'trēg\ *verb* **in·trigued; in·trigu·ing** [French *intriguer*, from Italian *intrigare*, from Latin *intricare*] (1612)
*transitive verb*
**1 :** CHEAT, TRICK
**2 :** to accomplish by intrigue ⟨*intrigued* myself into the club⟩
**3** *obsolete* **:** ENTANGLE
**4 :** to arouse the interest, desire, or curiosity of ⟨*intrigued* by the tale⟩
*intransitive verb*
**:** to carry on an intrigue; *especially* **:** PLOT, SCHEME

— **in·trigu·er** *noun*

**²in·trigue** \'in-,trēg, in-'\ *noun* (1647)
**1 a :** a secret scheme **:** MACHINATION **b :** the practice of engaging in intrigues
**2 :** a clandestine love affair
*synonym* see PLOT

**in·trigu·ing** \in-'trē-giŋ\ *adjective* (1909)
**:** engaging the interest to a marked degree **:** FASCINATING

— **in·trigu·ing·ly** \-giŋ-lē\ *adverb*

**in·trin·sic** \in-'trin-zik, -'trin(t)-sik\ *adjective* [Middle French *intrinsèque* internal, from Late Latin *intrinsecus*, from Latin, adverb, inwardly; akin to Latin *intra* within — more at INTRA-] (1642)
**1 a :** belonging to the essential nature or constitution of a thing ⟨the *intrinsic* worth of a gem⟩ ⟨the *intrinsic* brightness of a star⟩ **b :** being or relating to a semiconductor in which the concentration of charge carriers is characteristic of the material itself instead of the content of any impurities it contains
**2 a :** originating or due to causes within a body, organ, or part ⟨an *intrinsic* metabolic disease⟩ **b :** originating and included wholly within an organ or part ⟨*intrinsic* muscles⟩ — compare EXTRINSIC 1b

— **in·trin·si·cal·ly** \-zi-k(ə-)lē, -si-\ *adverb*

**in·trin·si·cal** \-zi-kəl, -si-\ *adjective* (circa 1548)
*archaic* **:** INTRINSIC

**intrinsic factor** *noun* (1930)
**:** a substance produced by normal gastrointestinal mucosa that facilitates absorption of vitamin B$_{12}$

**in·tro** \'in-(,)trō\ *noun, plural* **intros** (circa 1899)
**:** INTRODUCTION

**intro-** *prefix* [Middle English, from Middle French, from Latin, from *intro* inside, to the inside, from (assumed) Old Latin *interus*, adjective, inward]
**1 :** in **:** into ⟨*intro*jection⟩
**2 :** inward **:** within ⟨*intro*vert⟩ — compare EXTRO-

**in·tro·duce** \,in-trə-'düs, -'dyüs\ *transitive verb* **-duced; -duc·ing** [Middle English, from Latin *introducere*, from *intro-* + *ducere* to lead — more at TOW] (15th century)
**1 :** to lead or bring in especially for the first time
**2 a :** to bring into play **b :** to bring into practice or use **:** INSTITUTE
**3 :** to lead to or make known by a formal act, announcement, or recommendation: as **a :** to cause to be acquainted **b :** to present formally at court or into society **c :** to present or announce formally or officially or by an official reading **d :** to make preliminary explanatory or laudatory remarks about **e :** to bring (as an actor or singer) before the public for the first time
**4 :** PLACE, INSERT
**5 :** to bring to a knowledge of something ☆

— **in·tro·duc·er** *noun*

**in·tro·duc·tion** \,in-trə-'dək-shən\ *noun* [Middle English *introduccioun* act of introducing, from Middle French *introduction*, from Latin *introduction-, introductio*, from *introducere*] (14th century)
**1 :** something that introduces: as **a** (1) **:** a part of a book or treatise preliminary to the main portion (2) **:** a preliminary treatise or course of study **b :** a short introductory musical passage
**2 :** the act or process of introducing **:** the state of being introduced
**3 :** a putting in **:** INSERTION
**4 :** something introduced; *specifically* **:** a new or exotic plant or animal

**in·tro·duc·to·ry** \,in-trə-'dək-t(ə-)rē\ *adjective* (1605)
**:** of, relating to, or being a first step that sets something going or in proper perspective ⟨an *introductory* course in calculus⟩

---

☆ **SYNONYMS**
**Introduce, insert, insinuate, interpolate, intercalate, interpose, interject** mean to put between or among others. INTRODUCE is a general term for bringing or placing a thing or person into a group or body already in existence (*introduced* a new topic into the conversation). INSERT implies putting into a fixed or open space between or among (*inserted* a clause in the contract). INSINUATE implies introducing gradually or by gentle pressure (*insinuated* himself into the group). INTERPOLATE applies to the inserting of something extraneous or spurious (*interpolated* her own comments into the report). INTERCALATE suggests an intrusive inserting of something in an existing series or sequence (new chapters *intercalated* with the old). INTERPOSE suggests inserting an obstruction or cause of delay (*interpose* barriers to communication). INTERJECT implies an abrupt or forced introduction (*interjected* a question).

— **in·tro·duc·to·ri·ly** \-t(ə-)rə-lē\ *adverb*

**in·tro·gres·sion** \,in-trə-'gre-shən\ *noun* [*intro-* + *-gression* (as in *regression*)] (1938) : the entry or introduction of a gene from one gene complex into another

— **in·tro·gres·sant** \-'gre-sᵊnt\ *adjective or noun*

— **in·tro·gres·sive** \-'gre-siv\ *adjective*

**in·troit** \'in-,tròit, -,trō-ət, in-'\ *noun* [Middle English, from Middle French *introite*, from Medieval Latin *introitus*, from Latin, entrance, from *introire* to go in, from *intro-* + *ire* to go — more at ISSUE] (15th century) **1** *often capitalized* : the first part of the traditional proper of the Mass consisting of an antiphon, verse from a psalm, and the Gloria Patri **2** : a piece of music sung or played at the beginning of a worship service

**in·tro·ject** \,in-trə-'jekt\ *transitive verb* [back-formation from *introjection*, from International Scientific Vocabulary *intro-* + *projection*] (1925) : to incorporate (attitudes or ideas) into one's personality unconsciously

— **in·tro·jec·tion** \-'jek-shən\ *noun*

**in·tro·mis·sion** \,in-trə-'mi-shən\ *noun* [French, from Middle French, from Medieval Latin *intromission-, intromissio*, from Latin *intromittere*] (1601) : the act or process of intromitting; *especially* : the insertion or period of insertion of the penis in the vagina in copulation

**in·tro·mit** \-'mit\ *transitive verb* **-mit·ted; -mit·ting** [Latin *intromittere*, from *intro-* + *mittere* to send] (circa 1588) : to send or put in : INSERT

— **in·tro·mit·tent** \-'mi-tᵊnt\ *adjective*

— **in·tro·mit·ter** \-tər\ *noun*

**in·tron** \'in-,trän\ *noun* [*inter*vening sequence + ²-*on*] (1978) : a polynucleotide sequence in a nucleic acid that does not code information for protein synthesis and is removed before translation of messenger RNA — compare EXON

**in·trorse** \'in-,tròrs\ *adjective* [Latin *introrsus*, adverb, inward, from *intro-* + *versus* toward, from past participle of *vertere* to turn — more at WORTH] (1842) : facing inward or toward the axis of growth ⟨an *introrse* anther⟩

**in·tro·spec·tion** \,in-trə-'spek-shən\ *noun* [Latin *introspectus*, past participle of *introspicere* to look inside, from *intro-* + *specere* to look — more at SPY] (circa 1677) : a reflective looking inward : an examination of one's own thoughts and feelings

— **in·tro·spect** \-'spekt\ *verb*

— **in·tro·spec·tion·al** \-'spek-shnəl, -shə-nᵊl\ *adjective*

— **in·tro·spec·tive** \-'spek-tiv\ *adjective*

— **in·tro·spec·tive·ly** \-'spek-tiv-lē\ *adverb*

— **in·tro·spec·tive·ness** *noun*

**in·tro·spec·tion·ism** \-shə-,ni-zəm\ *noun* (1922) : a doctrine that psychology must be based essentially on data derived from introspection — compare BEHAVIORISM

— **in·tro·spec·tion·ist** \-sh(ə-)nist\ *or* **in·tro·spec·tion·is·tic** \-,spek-shə-'nis-tik\ *adjective*

— **introspectionist** *noun*

**in·tro·ver·sion** \,in-trə-'vər-zhən, -shən\ *noun* [*intro-* + *-version* (as in *diversion*)] (1654) **1** : the act of introverting : the state of being introverted **2** : the state or tendency toward being wholly or predominantly concerned with and interested in one's own mental life

— **in·tro·ver·sive** \-'vər-siv, -ziv\ *adjective*

— **in·tro·ver·sive·ly** *adverb*

¹**in·tro·vert** \'in-trə-,vərt\ *transitive verb* [*intro-* + *-vert* (as in *divert*)] (1669) : to turn inward or in upon itself: as **a** : to concentrate or direct upon oneself **b** : to produce psychological introversion in

²**introvert** *noun* (1883)

**1** : something (as the retractile proboscis of some worms) that is or can be drawn in especially by invagination **2** : one whose personality is characterized by introversion; *broadly* : a reserved or shy person

**in·trude** \in-'trüd\ *verb* **in·trud·ed; in·trud·ing** [Middle English, from Latin *intrudere* to thrust in, from *in-* + *trudere* to thrust — more at THREAT] (15th century) *intransitive verb* **1** : to thrust oneself in without invitation, permission, or welcome **2** : to enter as a geological intrusion *transitive verb* **1** : to thrust or force in or upon someone or something especially without permission, welcome, or fitness **2** : to cause to enter as if by force

— **in·trud·er** *noun*

**in·tru·sion** \in-'trü-zhən\ *noun* [Middle English, from Middle French, from Medieval Latin *intrusion-, intrusio*, from Latin *intrudere*] (15th century) **1** : the act of intruding or the state of being intruded; *especially* : the act of wrongfully entering upon, seizing, or taking possession of the property of another **2** : the forcible entry of molten rock or magma into or between other rock formations; *also* : the intruded magma

**in·tru·sive** \in-'trü-siv, -ziv\ *adjective* (15th century) **1 a** : characterized by intrusion **b** : intruding where one is not welcome or invited **2 a** : projecting inward ⟨an *intrusive* arm of the sea⟩ **b** (1) *of a rock* : having been forced while in a plastic state into cavities or between layers (2) : PLUTONIC **3** : having nothing that corresponds to a sound or letter in orthography or etymon ⟨*intrusive* \t\ in \'mints\ for *mince*⟩

**synonym** see IMPERTINENT

— **intrusive** *noun*

— **in·tru·sive·ly** *adverb*

— **in·tru·sive·ness** *noun*

**intrust** *variant of* ENTRUST

**in·tu·ba·tion** \,in-,tü-'bā-shən, -(,)tyü-, -tə-\ *noun* (1887) : the introduction of a tube into a hollow organ (as the trachea)

— **in·tu·bate** \'in-(,)tü-,bāt, -(,)tyü-, -tə-\ *transitive verb*

**in·tu·it** \in-'tü-ət, -'tyü-\ *transitive verb* (1855) : to apprehend by intuition

— **in·tu·it·able** \-ə-tə-bəl\ *adjective*

**in·tu·i·tion** \,in-tü-'wi-shən, -tyü-\ *noun* [Middle English *intuycyon*, from Late Latin *intuition-, intuitio* act of contemplating, from Latin *intueri* to look at, contemplate, from *in-* + *tueri* to look at] (15th century) **1** : quick and ready insight **2 a** : immediate apprehension or cognition **b** : knowledge or conviction gained by intuition **c** : the power or faculty of attaining to direct knowledge or cognition without evident rational thought and inference

— **in·tu·i·tion·al** \-'wish-nəl, -'wi-shə-nᵊl\ *adjective*

**in·tu·i·tion·ism** \,in-tü-'wi-shə-,ni-zəm\ *noun* (1847) **1 a** : a doctrine that objects of perception are intuitively known to be real **b** : a doctrine that there are basic truths intuitively known **2** : a doctrine that right or wrong or fundamental principles about what is right and wrong can be intuited **3** : a philosophical thesis that human beings have a direct intuitive understanding of mathematics and that rejects the principle that every mathematical statement must be true or false

— **in·tu·i·tion·ist** \-sh(ə-)nist\ *adjective or noun*

**in·tu·i·tive** \in-'tü-ə-tiv, -'tyü-\ *adjective* (1621)

**1 a** : known or perceived by intuition : directly apprehended ⟨had an *intuitive* awareness of his sister's feelings⟩ **b** : knowable by intuition **2** : knowing or perceiving by intuition **3** : possessing or given to intuition or insight ⟨an *intuitive* mind⟩

— **in·tu·i·tive·ly** *adverb*

— **in·tu·i·tive·ness** *noun*

**in·tu·mes·cence** \,in-tü-'me-sᵊn(t)s, -tyü-\ *noun* [French, from Latin *intumescere* to swell up, from *in-* + *tumescere* to swell — more at TUMESCENCE] (circa 1656) : a swollen or enlarged part of a plant or animal; *also* : the process of swelling up or enlarging

**in·tu·mes·cent** \-sᵊnt\ *adjective* (1953) *of paint* : swelling and charring when exposed to flame

**in·tus·sus·cept** \,in-tə-sə-'sept\ *verb* [back-formation from *intussusception*] (1802) *transitive verb* : to take in by or cause to undergo intussusception; *especially* : INVAGINATE *intransitive verb* : to undergo intussusception

**in·tus·sus·cep·tion** \-'sep-shən\ *noun* [Latin *intus* within + *susception-, susceptio* action of undertaking, from *suscipere* to take up — more at SUSCEPTIBLE] (1707) : a drawing in of something from without: as **a** : INVAGINATION; *especially* : the slipping of a length of intestine into an adjacent portion usually producing obstruction **b** : the assimilation of new material and its dispersal among preexistent matter

— **in·tus·sus·cep·tive** \-'sep-tiv\ *adjective*

**In·u·it** \'i-nü-wət, -nyü-\ *noun* [Inuit *inuit*, plural of *inuk* person] (1765) **1** *plural* **Inuit** *or* **Inuits a** (1) : the Eskimo people of North America and Greenland (2) : the Eskimo people of Canada **b** : a member of such people **2 a** : ESKIMO 2 **b** : the group of Eskimo dialects spoken from northwestern Canada to Greenland

**Inuk·ti·tut** \i-'nük-tə-,tüt\ *noun* (1974) : the group of Eskimo dialects spoken by the Inuit of central and eastern arctic Canada

**in·u·lin** \'in-yə-lən\ *noun* [probably from German *Inulin*, from Latin *inula* elecampane] (1813) : a tasteless white polysaccharide found especially dissolved in the sap of the roots and rhizomes of composite plants

**in·unc·tion** \i-'nəŋ(k)-shən\ *noun* [Middle English, from Latin *inunction-, inunctio*, from *inunguere* to anoint — more at ANOINT] (15th century) : an act of applying oil or ointment : ANOINTING

**in·un·date** \'i-(,)nən-,dāt\ *transitive verb* **-dat·ed; -dat·ing** [Latin *inundatus*, past participle of *inundare*, from *in-* + *unda* wave — more at WATER] (1590) **1** : to cover with a flood : OVERFLOW **2** : OVERWHELM

— **in·un·da·tion** \,i-(,)nən-'dā-shən\ *noun*

— **in·un·da·tor** \'i-(,)nən-,dā-tər\ *noun*

— **in·un·da·to·ry** \i-'nən-də-,tōr-ē, -,tòr-\ *adjective*

**In·u·pi·at** \i-'nü-pē-,ät, -'nyü-\ *also* **In·u·pi·aq** \-,äk\ *noun* [Inupiat *inᵘupiaq*, plural *inᵘupiat*, literally, real person] (1967) **1** *plural* **Inupiat** *or* **Inupiats** *also* **Inupiaq** *or* **Inupiaqs** : a member of the Eskimo people of northern Alaska **2** : the language of the Inupiat people

**in·ure** \i-'nùr, -'nyùr\ *verb* **in·ured; in·ur·ing** [Middle English *enuren*, from *en-* + *ure*, noun,

use, custom, from Middle French *uevre* work, practice, from Latin *opera* work — more at OPERA] (15th century)
*transitive verb*
**:** to accustom to accept something undesirable
*intransitive verb*
**:** to become of advantage
— **in·ure·ment** \-mənt\ *noun*
**in·urn** \i-'nərn\ *transitive verb* (1602)
**1 :** ENTOMB
**2 :** to place (as cremated remains) in an urn
**in utero** \in-'yü-tə-ˌrō\ *adverb or adjective* [Latin] (1713)
**:** in the uterus **:** before birth ⟨a disease acquired *in utero*⟩ ⟨an *in utero* diagnosis⟩
**in·utile** \(ˌ)in-'yü-t°l, -ˌtīl\ *adjective* [Middle English, from Middle French, from Latin *inutilis*, from *in-* + *utilis* useful — more at UTILITY] (15th century)
**:** USELESS, UNUSABLE
— **in·util·i·ty** \ˌin-yü-'ti-lə-tē\ *noun*
**in vac·uo** \in-'va-kyə-ˌwō\ *adverb* [New Latin] (1660)
**:** in a vacuum
**in·vade** \in-'vād\ *transitive verb* **in·vad·ed; in·vad·ing** [Middle English, from Latin *invadere*, from *in-* + *vadere* to go — more at WADE] (15th century)
**1 :** to enter for conquest or plunder
**2 :** to encroach upon **:** INFRINGE
**3 a :** to spread over or into as if invading **:** PERMEATE ⟨doubts *invade* his mind⟩ **b :** to affect injuriously and progressively ⟨gangrene *invades* healthy tissue⟩
*synonym* see TRESPASS
— **in·vad·er** *noun*
**in·vag·i·nate** \in-'va-jə-ˌnāt\ *verb* **-nat·ed; -nat·ing** [Medieval Latin *invaginatus*, past participle of *invaginare*, from Latin *in-* + *vagina* sheath] (circa 1656)
*transitive verb*
**1 :** ENCLOSE, SHEATHE
**2 :** to fold in so that an outer becomes an inner surface
*intransitive verb*
**:** to undergo invagination
**in·vag·i·na·tion** \-ˌva-jə-'nā-shən\ *noun* (circa 1658)
**1 :** an act or process of invaginating; *especially* **:** the formation of a gastrula by an infolding of part of the wall of the blastula
**2 :** an invaginated part
**¹in·val·id** \(ˌ)in-'va-ləd\ *adjective* [Latin *invalidus* weak, from *in-* + *validus* strong — more at VALID] (1542)
**:** not valid: **a :** being without foundation or force in fact, truth, or law **b :** logically inconsequent
— **in·val·id·ly** \-lē\ *adverb*
**²in·va·lid** \'in-və-ləd, *British usually* -ˌlēd\ *adjective* [Latin & French; French *invalide*, from Latin *invalidus*] (1642)
**1 :** suffering from disease or disability **:** SICKLY
**2 :** of, relating to, or suited to one that is sick
**³invalid** \*same as* ²\ *noun* (1709)
**:** one that is sickly or disabled
**⁴in·va·lid** \'in-və-ləd, -ˌlid, *British usually* -ˌlēd or ˌin-və-'lēd\ *transitive verb* (1787)
**1 :** to remove from active duty by reason of sickness or disability
**2 :** to make sickly or disabled
**in·val·i·date** \(ˌ)in-'va-lə-ˌdāt\ *transitive verb* (1649)
**:** to make invalid; *especially* **:** to weaken or destroy the cogency of
*synonym* see NULLIFY
— **in·val·i·da·tion** \-ˌva-lə-'dā-shən\ *noun*
— **in·val·i·da·tor** \in-'va-lə-ˌdā-tər\ *noun*
**in·va·lid·ism** \'in-və-lə-ˌdi-zəm\ *noun* (1794)
**:** a chronic condition of being an invalid
**in·val·id·i·ty** \ˌin-və-'li-də-tē, -va-\ *noun, plural* **-ties** (circa 1550)
**1 :** lack of validity or cogency
**2 :** incapacitating bodily disability; *also* **:** INVALIDISM

**in·valu·able** \(ˌ)in-'val-yə-bəl, -yə-wə-bəl\ *adjective* [¹*in-* + *value*, verb + *-able*] (1576)
**:** valuable beyond estimation **:** PRICELESS
— **in·valu·able·ness** *noun*
— **in·valu·ably** \-blē\ *adverb*
**in·var** \'in-ˌvär\ *noun, often capitalized* [from *Invar*, a trademark] (1902)
**:** an iron-nickel alloy that expands little on heating
**in·vari·able** \(ˌ)in-'ver-ē-ə-bəl, -'var-\ *adjective* (15th century)
**:** not changing or capable of change **:** CONSTANT
— **in·vari·abil·i·ty** \-ˌver-ē-ə-'bi-lə-tē, -ˌvar-\ *noun*
— **invariable** *noun*
— **in·vari·ably** \-blē\ *adverb*
**in·vari·ance** \(ˌ)in-'ver-ē-ən(t)s, -'var-\ *noun* (1878)
**:** the quality or state of being invariant
**in·vari·ant** \-ənt\ *adjective* (1874)
**:** CONSTANT, UNCHANGING; *specifically* **:** unchanged by specified mathematical or physical operations or transformations ⟨*invariant* factor⟩
— **invariant** *noun*
**in·va·sion** \in-'vā-zhən\ *noun* [Middle English *invasioune*, from Middle French *invasion*, from Late Latin *invasion-, invasio,* from Latin *invadere* to invade] (15th century)
**1 :** an act of invading; *especially* **:** incursion of an army for conquest or plunder
**2 :** the incoming or spread of something usually hurtful
**in·va·sive** \-siv, -ziv\ *adjective* (1598)
**1 :** of, relating to, or characterized by military aggression
**2 :** tending to spread; *especially* **:** tending to invade healthy tissue ⟨*invasive* cancer cells⟩
**3 :** tending to infringe
**4 :** involving entry into the living body (as by incision or by insertion of an instrument) ⟨*invasive* diagnostic techniques⟩
— **in·va·sive·ness** *noun*
**¹in·vec·tive** \in-'vek-tiv\ *adjective* [Middle English *invectif*, from Middle French, from Latin *invectivus*, from *invectus*, past participle of *invehere*] (15th century)
**:** of, relating to, or characterized by insult or abuse
— **in·vec·tive·ly** *adverb*
— **in·vec·tive·ness** *noun*
**²invective** *noun* (1523)
**1 :** an abusive expression or speech
**2 :** insulting or abusive language **:** VITUPERATION
*synonym* see ABUSE
**in·veigh** \in-'vā\ *intransitive verb* [Latin *invehi* to attack, inveigh, passive of *invehere* to carry in, from *in-* + *vehere* to carry — more at WAY] (1529)
**:** to protest or complain bitterly or vehemently **:** RAIL
— **in·veigh·er** *noun*
**in·vei·gle** \in-'vā-gəl *sometimes* -'vē-\ *transitive verb* **in·vei·gled; in·vei·gling** \-g(ə-)liŋ\ [modification of Middle French *aveugler* to blind, hoodwink, from Old French *avogler*, from *avogle* blind, from Medieval Latin *ab oculis*, literally, lacking eyes] (1539)
**1 :** to win over by wiles **:** ENTICE
**2 :** to acquire by ingenuity or flattery ◆
*synonym* see LURE
— **in·vei·gle·ment** \-gəl-mənt\ *noun*
— **in·vei·gler** \-g(ə-)lər\ *noun*
**in·vent** \in-'vent\ *transitive verb* [Middle English, from Latin *inventus*, past participle of *invenire* to come upon, find, from *in-* + *venire* to come — more at COME] (15th century)
**1** *archaic* **:** FIND, DISCOVER
**2 :** to devise by thinking **:** FABRICATE
**3 :** to produce (as something useful) for the first time through the use of the imagination or of ingenious thinking and experiment
— **in·ven·tor** \-'ven-tər\ *noun*
— **in·ven·tress** \-'ven-trəs\ *noun*

**in·ven·tion** \in-'ven(t)-shən\ *noun* (14th century)
**1 :** DISCOVERY, FINDING
**2 :** productive imagination **:** INVENTIVENESS
**3 a :** something invented: as (1) **:** a product of the imagination; *especially* **:** a false conception (2) **:** a device, contrivance, or process originated after study and experiment **b :** a short keyboard composition featuring two or three part counterpoint
**4 :** the act or process of inventing
**in·ven·tive** \in-'ven-tiv\ *adjective* (15th century)
**1 :** adept or prolific at producing inventions **:** CREATIVE
**2 :** characterized by invention
— **in·ven·tive·ly** *adverb*
— **in·ven·tive·ness** *noun*
**¹in·ven·to·ry** \'in-vən-ˌtōr-ē, -ˌtor-\ *noun, plural* **-ries** (1523)
**1 a :** an itemized list of current assets: as (1) **:** a catalog of the property of an individual or estate (2) **:** a list of goods on hand **b :** a survey of natural resources **c :** a list of traits, preferences, attitudes, interests, or abilities used to evaluate personal characteristics or skills
**2 :** the quantity of goods or materials on hand **:** STOCK
**3 :** the act or process of taking an inventory
— **in·ven·to·ri·al** \ˌin-vən-'tōr-ē-əl\ *adjective*
— **in·ven·to·ri·al·ly** \-ē-ə-lē\ *adverb*
**²inventory** *transitive verb* **-ried; -ry·ing** (1602)
**:** to make an inventory of **:** CATALOG
**in·ver·ness** \ˌin-vər-'nes\ *noun* [*Inverness*, Scotland] (1863)
**:** a loose belted coat having a cape with a close-fitting round collar
**¹in·verse** \(ˌ)in-'vərs, 'in-ˌ\ *adjective* [Latin *inversus*, from past participle of *invertere*] (15th century)
**1 :** opposite in order, nature, or effect
**2 :** being an inverse function ⟨*inverse* sine⟩
**²inverse** *noun* (circa 1681)
**1 :** something of a contrary nature or quality **:** OPPOSITE, REVERSE
**2 :** a proposition or theorem formed by contradicting both the subject and predicate or both the hypothesis and conclusion

inverness

of a given proposition or theorem ⟨the *inverse* of "if *A* then *B*" is "if not-*A* then not-*B*"⟩ — compare CONTRAPOSITIVE
**3 a :** INVERSE FUNCTION; *also* **:** an operation (as subtraction) that undoes the effect of another operation **b :** a set element that is related to another element in such a way that the result of applying a given binary operation to them is an identity element of the set
**inverse function** *noun* (1816)
**:** a function that is derived from a given function by interchanging the two variables — compare LOGARITHMIC FUNCTION
**in·verse·ly** \'in-ˌvərs-lē, (ˌ)in-'\ *adverb* (1660)
**1 :** in an inverse order or manner
**2 :** in the manner of inverse variation ⟨varies *inversely*⟩
**inversely proportional** *adjective* (circa 1890)
**:** related by inverse variation — compare DIRECTLY PROPORTIONAL
**inverse square law** *noun* (1921)
**:** a statement in physics: a given physical quantity (as illumination) varies with the distance from the source inversely as the square of the distance
**inverse variation** *noun* (1936)
**1 :** mathematical relationship between two variables which can be expressed by an equation in which the product of two variables is equal to a constant
**2 :** an equation or function expressing inverse variation — compare DIRECT VARIATION
**in·ver·sion** \in-'vər-zhən, -shən\ *noun* (1586)
**1 :** a reversal of position, order, form, or relationship: as **a** (1) **:** a change in normal word order; *especially* **:** the placement of a verb before its subject (2) **:** the process or result of changing or reversing the relative positions of the notes of a musical interval, chord, or phrase **b :** the condition of being turned inward or inside out **c :** a breaking off of a chromosome section and its subsequent reattachment in inverted position; *also* **:** a chromosomal section that has undergone this process
**2 :** the act or process of inverting
**3 a :** a change in the order of the terms of a mathematical proportion effected by inverting each ratio **b :** the operation of forming the inverse of a magnitude, a function, an operation, or an element
**4 a :** the conversion of dextrorotatory sucrose into a levorotatory mixture of glucose and fructose **b :** a change from one stereochemical figuration at a chiral center in a usually organic molecule to the opposite configuration that is brought about by a reaction in which a substitution of one group is made for a different group
**5 :** HOMOSEXUALITY
**6 :** an increase of temperature with height through a layer of air
**in·ver·sive** \-'vər-siv, -ziv\ *adjective* (1875)
**:** marked by inversion
**¹in·vert** \in-'vərt\ *transitive verb* [Latin *invertere*, from *in-* + *vertere* to turn — more at WORTH] (1533)
**1 a :** to reverse in position, order, or relationship **b :** to subject to inversion
**2 a :** to turn inside out or upside down **b :** to turn inward
**3 :** to find the mathematical reciprocal of ⟨to divide using fractions, *invert* the divisor and multiply⟩
**synonym** see REVERSE
**²in·vert** \'in-ˌvərt\ *noun* (1838)
**:** one characterized by inversion; *especially* **:** HOMOSEXUAL
**in·ver·tase** \in-'vər-ˌtās, -ˌtāz; 'in-vər-ˌ\ *noun* [International Scientific Vocabulary] (1887)
**:** an enzyme that catalyzes the hydrolysis of sucrose
**in·ver·te·brate** \(ˌ)in-'vər-tə-brət, -ˌbrāt\ *adjective* [New Latin *invertebratus*, from Latin *in-* + New Latin *vertebratus* vertebrate] (1838)

**1 :** lacking a spinal column; *also* **:** of or relating to invertebrate animals
**2 :** lacking in strength or vitality **:** WEAK
**— invertebrate** *noun*
**inverted comma** *noun* (1789)
*chiefly British* **:** QUOTATION MARK
**in·vert·er** \in-'vər-tər\ *noun* (1611)
**1 :** one that inverts
**2 :** a device for converting direct current into alternating current
**in·vert·ible** \in-'vər-tə-bəl\ *adjective* (1881)
**:** capable of being inverted or subjected to inversion ⟨an *invertible* matrix⟩
**invert sugar** *noun* (1880)
**:** a mixture of dextrose and levulose found in fruits or produced artificially by the inversion of sucrose
**¹in·vest** \in-'vest\ *transitive verb* [Latin *investire* to clothe, surround, from *in-* + *vestis* garment — more at WEAR] (circa 1534)
**1** [Medieval Latin *investire*, from Latin, to clothe] **a :** to array in the symbols of office or honor **b :** to furnish with power or authority **c :** to grant someone control or authority over **:** VEST
**2 :** to cover completely **:** ENVELOP
**3 :** CLOTHE, ADORN
**4** [Middle French *investir*, from Old Italian *investire*, from Latin, to surround] **:** to surround with troops or ships so as to prevent escape or entry
**5 :** to endow with a quality **:** INFUSE
**²invest** *verb* [Italian *investire* to clothe, invest money, from Latin, to clothe] (1613)
*transitive verb*
**1 :** to commit (money) in order to earn a financial return
**2 :** to make use of for future benefits or advantages
*intransitive verb*
**:** to make an investment
**— in·vest·able** \-'ves-tə-bəl\ *adjective*
**— in·ves·tor** \-tər\ *noun*
**in·ves·ti·gate** \in-'ves-tə-ˌgāt\ *verb* **-gat·ed; -gat·ing** [Latin *investigatus*, past participle of *investigare* to track, investigate, from *in-* + *vestigium* footprint, track] (circa 1510)
*transitive verb*
**:** to observe or study by close examination and systematic inquiry
*intransitive verb*
**:** to make a systematic examination; *especially* **:** to conduct an official inquiry
**— in·ves·ti·ga·tion** \-ˌves-tə-'gā-shən\ *noun*
**— in·ves·ti·ga·tion·al** \-shnəl, -shə-nᵊl\ *adjective*
**— in·ves·ti·ga·tive** \-'ves-tə-ˌgā-tiv\ *adjective*
**— in·ves·ti·ga·tor** \-ˌgā-tər\ *noun*
**— in·ves·ti·ga·to·ry** \-'ves-ti-gə-ˌtōr-ē, -ˌtȯr-\ *adjective*
**in·ves·ti·ture** \in-'ves-tə-ˌchu̇r, -chər, -ˌtyu̇r, -ˌtu̇r\ *noun* [Middle English, from Medieval Latin *investitura*, from *investitus*, past participle of *investire*] (14th century)
**1 :** the act of establishing in office or ratifying
**2 :** something that covers or adorns
**¹in·vest·ment** \in-'ves(t)-mənt\ *noun* [¹*invest*] (1597)
**1 a** *archaic* **:** VESTMENT **b :** an outer layer **:** ENVELOPE
**2 :** INVESTITURE 1
**3 :** BLOCKADE, SIEGE
**²investment** *noun* [²*invest*] (1615)
**:** the outlay of money usually for income or profit **:** capital outlay; *also* **:** the sum invested or the property purchased
**investment company** *noun* (circa 1917)
**:** a company whose primary business is holding securities of other companies purely for investment purposes — compare HOLDING COMPANY
**in·vet·er·a·cy** \in-'ve-t(ə-)rə-sē\ *noun* [*inveterate* + *-cy*] (circa 1719)

**:** the quality or state of being obstinate or persistent **:** TENACITY
**in·vet·er·ate** \in-'ve-t(ə-)rət\ *adjective* [Middle English, from Latin *inveteratus*, from past participle of *inveterare* to age (transitive verb), from *in-* + *veter-, vetus* old — more at WETHER] (14th century)
**1 :** firmly established by long persistence ⟨the *inveterate* tendency to overlook the obvious⟩
**2 :** confirmed in a habit **:** HABITUAL ⟨an *inveterate* liar⟩ ☆
**— in·vet·er·ate·ly** *adverb*
**in·vi·a·ble** \(ˌ)in-'vī-ə-bəl\ *adjective* [International Scientific Vocabulary] (1918)
**:** incapable of surviving especially because of a deleterious genetic constitution
**— in·vi·a·bil·i·ty** \-ˌvī-ə-'bi-lə-tē\ *noun*
**in·vid·i·ous** \in-'vi-dē-əs\ *adjective* [Latin *invidiosus* envious, invidious, from *invidia* envy — more at ENVY] (1606)
**1 :** tending to cause discontent, animosity, or envy ⟨the *invidious* task of arbitration⟩
**2 :** ENVIOUS
**3 a :** of an unpleasant or objectionable nature **:** OBNOXIOUS ⟨*invidious* remarks⟩ **b :** of a kind to cause harm or resentment ⟨an *invidious* comparison⟩
**synonym** see REPUGNANT
**— in·vid·i·ous·ly** *adverb*
**— in·vid·i·ous·ness** *noun*
**in·vig·i·late** \in-'vi-jə-ˌlāt\ *verb* **-lat·ed; -lat·ing** [Latin *invigilatus*, past participle of *invigilare* to stay awake, be watchful, from *in-* + *vigilare* to stay awake — more at VIGILANT] (1553)
*intransitive verb*
**:** to keep watch; *especially, British* **:** to supervise students at an examination
*transitive verb*
**:** SUPERVISE, MONITOR
**— in·vig·i·la·tion** \-ˌvi-jə-'lā-shən\ *noun*
**— in·vig·i·la·tor** \-'vi-jə-ˌlā-tər\ *noun*
**in·vig·o·rate** \in-'vi-gə-ˌrāt\ *transitive verb* **-rat·ed; -rat·ing** [probably from *in-* + *vigor*] (1646)
**:** to give life and energy to **:** ANIMATE; *also* **:** STIMULATE 1
**— in·vig·o·rat·ing·ly** \-ˌrā-tiŋ-lē\ *adverb*
**— in·vig·o·ra·tion** \-ˌvi-gə-'rā-shən\ *noun*
**— in·vig·o·ra·tor** \-'vi-gə-ˌrā-tər\ *noun*
**in·vin·ci·ble** \(ˌ)in-'vin(t)-sə-bəl\ *adjective* [Middle English, from Middle French, from Late Latin *invincibilis*, from Latin *in-* + *vincere* to conquer — more at VICTOR] (15th century)
**:** incapable of being conquered, overcome, or subdued
**— in·vin·ci·bil·i·ty** \-ˌvin(t)-sə-'bi-lə-tē\ *noun*
**— in·vin·ci·ble·ness** \-'vin(t)-sə-bəl-nəs\ *noun*
**— in·vin·ci·bly** \-blē\ *adverb*

---

☆ **SYNONYMS**
**Inveterate, confirmed, chronic** mean firmly established. INVETERATE applies to a habit, attitude or feeling of such long existence as to be practically ineradicable or unalterable ⟨an *inveterate* smoker⟩. CONFIRMED implies a growing stronger and firmer with time so as to resist change or reform ⟨a *confirmed* bachelor⟩. CHRONIC suggests something that is persistent or endlessly recurrent and troublesome ⟨a *chronic* complainer⟩.

---

\ə\ abut \ᵊ\ kitten \ər\ further \a\ ash \ā\ ace
\ä\ mop, mar \au̇\ out \ch\ chin \e\ bet \ē\ easy
\g\ go \i\ hit \ī\ ice \j\ job \ŋ\ sing \ō\ go
\ȯ\ law \ȯi\ boy \th\ thin \th̲\ the \ü\ loot \u̇\ foot
\y\ yet \zh\ vision *see also* Guide to Pronunciation

**in·vi·o·la·ble** \(,)in-'vī-ə-lə-bəl\ *adjective* [Middle English, from Middle French or Latin; Middle French, from Latin *inviolabilis*, from *in-* + *violare* to violate] (15th century) **1** : secure from violation or profanation **2** : secure from assault or trespass : UNASSAILABLE
— **in·vi·o·la·bil·i·ty** \-,vī-ə-lə-'bi-lə-tē\ *noun*
— **in·vi·o·la·ble·ness** \-'vī-ə-lə-bəl-nəs\ *noun*
— **in·vi·o·la·bly** \-blē\ *adverb*

**in·vi·o·la·cy** \(,)in-'vī-ə-lə-sē\ *noun* (circa 1846) : the quality or state of being inviolate

**in·vi·o·late** \-'vī-ə-lət\ *adjective* (15th century) : not violated or profaned; *especially* : PURE
— **in·vi·o·late·ly** *adverb*
— **in·vi·o·late·ness** *noun*

**in·vis·cid** \(,)in-'vi-səd\ *adjective* (circa 1889) **1** : having zero viscosity **2** : of or relating to an inviscid fluid ⟨*inviscid* flow⟩

**in·vis·i·ble** \(,)in-'vi-zə-bəl\ *adjective* [Middle English, from Middle French, from Latin *invisibilis*, from *in-* + *visibilis* visible] (14th century) **1 a** : incapable by nature of being seen **b** : inaccessible to view : HIDDEN **2** : IMPERCEPTIBLE, INCONSPICUOUS **3 a** : not appearing in published financial statements **b** : not reflected in statistics
— **in·vis·i·bil·i·ty** \-,vi-zə-'bi-lə-tē\ *noun*
— **invisible** *noun*
— **in·vis·i·ble·ness** \-'vi-zə-bəl-nəs\ *noun*
— **in·vis·i·bly** \-blē\ *adverb*

**in·vi·ta·tion** \,in-və-'tā-shən\ *noun* (15th century) **1 a** : the act of inviting **b** : an often formal request to be present or participate **2** : INCENTIVE, INDUCEMENT

**in·vi·ta·tion·al** \-shnəl, -shə-nᵊl\ *adjective* (1922) **1** : prepared or entered in response to a request ⟨an *invitational* article⟩ **2** : limited to invited participants ⟨an *invitational* tournament⟩
— **invitational** *noun*

**¹in·vi·ta·to·ry** \in-'vī-tə-,tōr-ē, -,tȯr-\ *adjective* (14th century) : containing an invitation

**²invitatory** *noun, plural* **-ries** (14th century) : an invitatory psalm or antiphon

**¹in·vite** \in-'vīt\ *transitive verb* **in·vit·ed; in·vit·ing** [Middle French or Latin; Middle French *inviter*, from Latin *invitare*] (1533) **1 a** : to offer an incentive or inducement to : ENTICE **b** : to increase the likelihood of **2 a** : to request the presence or participation of **b** : to request formally **c** : to urge politely : WELCOME
— **in·vit·er** *noun*

**²in·vite** \'in-,vīt\ *noun* (1659) : INVITATION ]

**in·vi·tee** \,in-və-'tē, -,vī-\ *noun* (1803) : an invited person

**inviting** \in-'vī-tiŋ\ *adjective* (1604) : ATTRACTIVE, TEMPTING
— **in·vit·ing·ly** \-tiŋ-lē\ *adverb*

**in vi·tro** \in-'vē-(,)trō, -'vi-\ *adverb or adjective* [New Latin, literally, in glass] (circa 1894) : outside the living body and in an artificial environment

**in vi·vo** \in-'vē-(,)vō\ *adverb or adjective* [New Latin, literally, in the living] (1901) : in the living body of a plant or animal

**in·vo·cate** \'in-və-,kāt\ *transitive verb* (1526) *archaic* : INVOKE

**in·vo·ca·tion** \,in-və-'kā-shən\ *noun* [Middle English *invocacioun*, from Middle French *invocation*, from Latin *invocation-, invocatio*, from *invocare*] (14th century) **1 a** : the act or process of petitioning for help or support; *specifically, often capitalized* : a prayer of entreaty (as at the beginning of a service of worship) **b** : a calling upon for authority or justification **2** : a formula for conjuring : INCANTATION **3** : an act of legal or moral implementation : ENFORCEMENT
— **in·vo·ca·tion·al** \-shnəl, -shə-nᵊl\ *adjective*
— **in·voc·a·to·ry** \in-'vä-kə-,tōr-ē, -,tȯr-\ *adjective*

**¹in·voice** \'in-,vȯis\ *noun* [modification of Middle French *envois*, plural of *envoi* message — more at ENVOI] (1560) **1** : an itemized list of goods shipped usually specifying the price and the terms of sale : BILL **2** : a consignment of merchandise

**²invoice** *transitive verb* **in·voiced; in·voic·ing** (1698) : to send an invoice for or to

**in·voke** \in-'vōk\ *transitive verb* **in·voked; in·vok·ing** [Middle English, from Middle French *invoquer*, from Latin *invocare*, from *in-* + *vocare* to call, from *voc-, vox* voice — more at VOICE] (15th century) **1 a** : to petition for help or support **b** : to appeal to or cite as authority **2** : to call forth by incantation : CONJURE **3** : to make an earnest request for : SOLICIT **4** : to put into effect or operation : IMPLEMENT **5** : BRING ABOUT, CAUSE
— **in·vok·er** *noun*

**in·vo·lu·cre** \'in-və-,lü-kər\ *noun* [French, from New Latin *involucrum*] (1794) : one or more whorls of bracts situated below and close to a flower, flower cluster, or fruit
— **in·vo·lu·cral** \,in-və-'lü-krəl\ *adjective*
— **in·vo·lu·crate** \-krət, -,krāt\ *adjective*

**in·vo·lu·crum** \,in-və-'lü-krəm\ *noun, plural* **-cra** \-krə\ [New Latin, sheath, involucre, from Latin, wrapper, from *involvere* to wrap] (circa 1677) : a surrounding envelope or sheath

**in·vol·un·tary** \(,)in-'vä-lən-,ter-ē\ *adjective* [Middle English *involuntari*, from Late Latin *involuntarius*, from Latin *in-* + *voluntarius* voluntary] (15th century) **1** : done contrary to or without choice **2** : COMPULSORY **3** : not subject to control of the will : REFLEX
— **in·vol·un·tari·ly** \-,vä-lən-'ter-ə-lē\ *adverb*
— **in·vol·un·tari·ness** \-'vä-lən-,ter-ē-nəs\ *noun*

**involuntary manslaughter** *noun* (circa 1879) : manslaughter resulting from the failure to perform a legal duty expressly required to safeguard human life, from the commission of an unlawful act not constituting a felony, or from the commission of a lawful act in a negligent or improper manner

**involuntary muscle** *noun* (1840) : muscle governing reflex functions and not under direct voluntary control; *especially* : SMOOTH MUSCLE

**¹in·vo·lute** \'in-və-,lüt\ *adjective* [Latin *involutus* concealed, from past participle of *involvere*] (1661) **1 a** : curled spirally **b** (1) : curled or curved inward (2) : having the edges rolled over the upper surface toward the midrib ⟨an *involute* leaf⟩ **c** : having the form of an involute ⟨a gear with *involute* teeth⟩ **2** : INVOLVED, INTRICATE

**²involute** *noun* (circa 1796) : a curve traced by a point on a thread kept taut as it is unwound from another curve ⟨*involute* of a circle⟩

**³in·vo·lute** \,in-və-'lüt\ *intransitive verb* **-lut·ed; -lut·ing** (1816) **1** : to become involute **2 a** : to return to a former condition **b** : to become cleared up : DISAPPEAR

**in·vo·lu·tion** \,in-və-'lü-shən\ *noun* [Latin *involution-, involutio*, from *involvere*] (circa 1611) **1 a** (1) : the act or an instance of enfolding or entangling : INVOLVEMENT (2) : an involved grammatical construction usually characterized by the insertion of clauses between the subject and predicate **b** : COMPLEXITY, INTRICACY **2** : EXPONENTIATION **3 a** : an inward curvature or penetration **b** : the formation of a gastrula by ingrowth of cells formed at the dorsal lip **4** : a shrinking or return to a former size **5** : the regressive alterations of a body or its parts characteristic of the aging process; *specifically* : decline marked by a decrease of bodily vigor and in women by menopause
— **in·vo·lu·tion·al** \-shnəl, -shə-nᵊl\ *adjective*

**in·volve** \in-'välv, -'vȯlv *also* -'väv *or* -'vȯv\ *transitive verb* **in·volved; in·volv·ing** [Middle English, to roll up, wrap, from Latin *involvere*, from *in-* + *volvere* to roll — more at VOLUBLE] (14th century) **1** *archaic* : to enfold or envelop so as to encumber **2 a** : to engage as a participant ⟨workers *involved* in building a house⟩ **b** : to oblige to take part ⟨right of Congress to *involve* the nation in war⟩ **c** : to occupy (as oneself) absorbingly; *especially* : to commit (as oneself) emotionally ⟨was *involved* with a married man⟩ **3** : to surround as if with a wrapping : ENVELOP **4 a** *archaic* : to wind, coil, or wreathe about **b** : to relate closely : CONNECT **5 a** : to have within or as part of itself : INCLUDE **b** : to require as a necessary accompaniment : ENTAIL **c** : to have an effect on *synonym* see INCLUDE
— **in·volve·ment** \-'välv-mənt, -'vȯlv-\ *noun*
— **in·volv·er** *noun*

**in·volved** \-'välvd, -'vȯlvd *also* -'vävd *or* -'vȯvd\ *adjective* (15th century) **1** : INVOLUTE, TWISTED **2 a** : marked by extreme and often needless or excessive complexity **b** : difficult to deal with because of complexity or disorder **3** : being affected or implicated *synonym* see COMPLEX
— **in·volv·ed·ly** \-'väl-vəd-lē, -'vȯl- *also* -'vä-vəd- *or* -'vȯ-\ *adverb*

**in·vul·ner·a·ble** \(,)in-'vəl-n(ə-)rə-bəl, -nər-bəl\ *adjective* [Latin *invulnerabilis*, from *in-* + *vulnerare* to wound — more at VULNERABLE] (1595) **1** : incapable of being wounded, injured, or harmed **2** : immune to or proof against attack : IMPREGNABLE
— **in·vul·ner·a·bil·i·ty** \-,vəl-n(ə-)rə-'bi-lə-tē\ *noun*
— **in·vul·ner·a·ble·ness** \-'vəl-n(ə-)rə-bəl-nəs, -nər-bəl-\ *noun*
— **in·vul·ner·a·bly** \-blē\ *adverb*

**¹in·ward** \'in-wərd\ *adjective* [Middle English, from Old English *inweard* (akin to Old High German *inwert*), from *in* + *-weard* ward] (before 12th century) **1** : situated on the inside : INNER **2 a** : of or relating to the mind or spirit ⟨*inward* peace⟩ **b** : absorbed in one's own mental or spiritual life : INTROSPECTIVE **3** : marked by close acquaintance : FAMILIAR **4** : directed toward the interior

**²inward** *or* **in·wards** \-wərdz\ *adverb* (before 12th century)

**involute** *a, p, p, p, p* traced by any point *p* of the thread *t* unwinding from curve *c*

**1 :** toward the inside, center, or interior
**2 :** toward the inner being
³**inward** *noun* (before 12th century)
**1 :** something that is inward
**2 in·wards** \'in-ərdz, -wərdz\ *plural* **:** IN-
NARDS
**Inward Light** *noun* (1706)
**:** INNER LIGHT
**in·ward·ly** \'in-wərd-lē\ *adverb* (before 12th
century)
**1 :** in the innermost being **:** MENTALLY, SPIRITU-
ALLY
**2 a :** beneath the surface **:** INTERNALLY ⟨bled
*inwardly*⟩ **b :** to oneself **:** PRIVATELY ⟨cursed
*inwardly*⟩
**in·ward·ness** *noun* (14th century)
**1 :** internal quality or substance
**2 :** close acquaintance **:** FAMILIARITY
**3 :** fundamental nature **:** ESSENCE
**4 :** absorption in one's own mental or spiritual
life
**in·weave** \(,)in-'wēv\ *transitive verb* **-wove**
\-'wōv\ *also* **-weaved; -wo·ven** \-'wō-vən\
*also* **-weaved; -weav·ing** (15th century)
**:** INTERWEAVE, INTERLACE
**in·wrought** \(,)in-'ròt, 'in-\ *adjective* (1637)
**1 :** having decoration worked in **:** ORNAMENT-
ED; *especially* **:** decorated with embroidery
**2 :** worked in especially as decoration
**in–your–face** *adjective* (1982)
**:** characterized by or being bold and often arrogant aggressiveness ⟨*in-your-face* basket-
ball⟩
**Io** \'ī-(,)ō\ *noun* [Latin, from Greek *Iō*]
**:** a maiden loved by Zeus and changed by him
into a heifer so that she might escape the jealous rage of Hera
**iod-** *or* **iodo-** *combining form* [French *iode*]
**:** iodine ⟨*iodize*⟩ ⟨*iodo*form⟩
**io·date** \'ī-ə-,dāt, -dət\ *noun* [French, from
*iode*] (1826)
**:** a salt of iodic acid
**iod·ic acid** \ī-'ä-dik-\ *noun* [French *iodique*,
from *iode*] (1826)
**:** a crystalline oxidizing solid HIO₃ formed by
oxidation of iodine
**io·dide** \'ī-ə-,dīd\ *noun* [International Scientific
Vocabulary] (1822)
**:** a salt of hydriodic acid; *also* **:** the univalent
anion I⁻ of such a salt
**io·din·ate** \'ī-ə-də-,nāt\ *transitive verb* **-at-
ed; -at·ing** (1908)
**:** to treat or cause to combine with iodine or a
compound of iodine
— **io·din·ation** \,ī-ə-də-'nā-shən\ *noun*
**io·dine** \'ī-ə-,dīn, -d°n, -,dēn\ *noun, often attributive* [French *iode*, from Greek *ioeidēs* violet colored, from *ion* violet] (1814)
**1 :** a nonmetallic halogen element obtained
usually as heavy shining blackish gray crystals
and used especially in medicine, photography,
and analysis — see ELEMENT table
**2 :** a tincture of iodine used especially as a
topical antiseptic
**io·dise** *British variant of* IODIZE
**io·dize** \'ī-ə-,dīz\ *transitive verb* **io·dized; io-
diz·ing** (1841)
**:** to treat with iodine or an iodide ⟨*iodized* salt⟩
**io·do·form** \ī-'ō-də-,fòrm, -'ä-\ *noun* [Interna-
tional Scientific Vocabulary *iod-* + *-form* (as
in *chloroform*)] (1838)
**:** a yellow crystalline volatile compound CHI₃
with a penetrating persistent odor that is used
as an antiseptic dressing
**io·do·phor** \-,fòr\ *noun* [*iod-* + Greek *-phoros*
carrier — more at -PHORE] (1952)
**:** a complex of iodine and a surface-active
agent that releases iodine gradually and serves
as a disinfectant
**io·dop·sin** \,ī-ə-'däp-sən\ *noun* [*iod-* (from
Greek *ioeidēs* violet colored) + Greek *opsis*
sight, vision + English *-in* — more at OPTIC]
(1938)
**:** a photosensitive violet pigment in the retinal
cones that is similar to rhodopsin but more la-

bile, is formed from vitamin A, and is important in daylight vision
**io moth** \'ī-(,)ō-\ *noun* [Latin *Io*] (1870)
**:** a chiefly North American saturniid moth
(*Automeris io*) having a large circular eyelike
spot on the upper surface of each hind wing
and a larva with stinging spines
**ion** \'ī-ən, 'ī-,än\ *noun* [Greek, neuter of *iōn*,
present participle of *ienai* to go — more at IS-
SUE] (circa 1834)
**1 :** an atom or group of atoms that carries a
positive or negative electric charge as a result
of having lost or gained one or more electrons
**2 :** a charged subatomic particle (as a free
electron)
**-ion** *noun suffix* [Middle English *-ioun, -ion*,
from Old French *-ion*, from Latin *-ion-, -io*]
**1 a :** act or process ⟨valida*tion*⟩ **b :** result of an
act or process ⟨regula*tion*⟩
**2 :** state or condition ⟨hydra*tion*⟩
**ion engine** *noun* (1958)
**:** a reaction engine deriving thrust from the
ejection of a stream of ionized particles
**ion exchange** *noun* (1923)
**:** a reversible interchange of one kind of ion
present on an insoluble solid with another of
like charge present in a solution surrounding
the solid with the reaction being used especially for softening or demineralizing water, the
purification of chemicals, or the separation of
substances
— **ion exchanger** *noun*
**ion exchange resin** *noun* (1943)
**:** an insoluble material of high molecular
weight that contains groups which can be exchanged with ions in a solution with which it
is in contact
**Io·ni·an** \ī-'ō-nē-ən\ *noun* [*Ionia*, Asia Minor]
(1550)
**1 :** a member of any of the Greek peoples who
settled on the islands of the Aegean Sea and
the western shore of Asia Minor toward the
end of the second millennium B.C.
**2 :** a native or inhabitant of Ionia
— **Ionian** *adjective*
**ion·ic** \ī-'ä-nik\ *adjective* [International Scientific Vocabulary] (1890)
**1 :** of, relating to, existing as, or characterized
by ions ⟨*ionic* gases⟩ ⟨the *ionic* charge⟩
**2 :** based on or functioning by means of ions
⟨*ionic* conduction⟩ ⟨an *ionic* lattice⟩
— **ion·ic·i·ty** \,ī-ə-'ni-sə-tē\ *noun*
¹**Ion·ic** \ī-'ä-nik\ *adjective* [Latin & Middle
French; Middle French *ionique*, from Latin
*ionicus*, from Greek *iōnikos*, from *Iōnia* Ionia]
(1585)
**1 :** of or relating to the ancient Greek architectural order distinguished especially by fluted
columns on bases and scroll volutes in its capitals — see ORDER illustration
**2 :** of or relating to Ionia or the Ionians
²**Ionic** *noun* (1668)
**:** a dialect of ancient Greek spoken especially
in Ionia and the Cyclades
**ionic bond** *noun* (1939)
**:** a chemical bond formed between oppositely
charged species because of their mutual electrostatic attraction
**ion·ise** *British variant of* IONIZE
**io·ni·um** \ī-'ō-nē-əm\ *noun* [*ion*; from its ionizing action] (1907)
**:** a natural radioactive isotope of thorium having a mass number of 230
**ionization chamber** *noun* (1904)
**:** a partially evacuated tube provided with
electrodes so that its conductivity due to the
ionization of the residual gas reveals the presence of ionizing radiation
**ion·ize** \'ī-ə-,nīz\ *verb* **ion·ized; ion·iz·ing**
[International Scientific Vocabulary] (1898)
*transitive verb*
**:** to convert wholly or partly into ions
*intransitive verb*
**:** to become ionized
— **ion·iz·able** \-,nī-zə-bəl\ *adjective*
— **ion·i·za·tion** \,ī-ə-nə-'zā-shən\ *noun*

— **ion·iz·er** \'ī-ə-,nī-zər\ *noun*
**ion·o·phore** \ī-'ä-nə-,fòr, -,fòr\ *noun* (circa
1955)
**:** a compound that facilitates transmission of
an ion (as of calcium) across a lipid barrier (as
in a cell membrane) by combining with the
ion or by increasing the permeability of the
barrier to it
**ion·o·sphere** \ī-'ä-nə-,sfir\ *noun* (1926)
**:** the part of the earth's atmosphere in which
ionization of atmospheric gases affects the
propagation of radio waves, which extends
from about 30 miles (50 kilometers) to the ex-
osphere, which is divided into regions of one
or more layers whose altitudes and degrees of
ionization vary with time of day, season, and
solar cycle, and which is contiguous with the
upper portion of the mesosphere and the thermosphere; *also* **:** a comparable region of
charged particles surrounding another celestial
body (as Venus)
— **ion·o·spher·ic** \,ī-,ä-nə-'sfir-ik, -'sfer-\
*adjective*
— **ion·o·spher·i·cal·ly** \-i-k(ə-)lē\ *adverb*
**ion·to·pho·re·sis** \(,)ī-,än-tə-fə-'rē-səs\ *noun,
plural* **-re·ses** \-,sēz\ [New Latin, from *ionto-*
ion (from Greek *iont-, iōn*, present participle
of *ienai*) + *-phoresis*] (1909)
**:** the introduction of an ionized substance (as a
drug) through intact skin by the application of
a direct electric current
— **ion·to·pho·ret·ic** \-'re-tik\ *adjective*
— **ion·to·pho·ret·i·cal·ly** \-ti-k(ə-)lē\ *adverb*
**io·ta** \ī-'ō-tə\ *noun* [Latin, from Greek *iōta*, of
Semitic origin; akin to Hebrew *yōdh* yod]
(1607)
**1 :** the 9th letter of the Greek alphabet — see
ALPHABET table
**2 :** an infinitesimal amount **:** JOT
**IOU** \,ī-(,)ō-'yü\ *noun* [from the pronunciation
of *I owe you*] (1795)
**1 :** a paper that has on it the letters IOU, a
stated sum, and a signature and that is given as
an acknowledgment of debt
**2 :** DEBT, OBLIGATION
**-ious** *adjective suffix* [Middle English, partly
from Old French *-ious, -ieux*, from Latin
*-iosus*, from *-i-*, penultimate vowel of some
noun stems + *-osus* -ous; partly from Latin
*-ius*, adjective suffix]
**:** -OUS ⟨edac*ious*⟩
**IPA** \,ī-(,)pē-'ā\ *noun* [*International Phonetic
Alphabet*] (1933)
**:** an alphabet designed to represent each human speech sound with a unique symbol
**ip·e·cac** \'i-pi-,kak\ *or* **ipe·ca·cu·a·nha** \,i-
pi-,ka-kyə-'wä-nə, -nyə\ *noun* [Portuguese *ipecacuanha*, from Tupi *ipekaaguéne*] (1682)
**1 :** the dried rhizome and roots of either of
two tropical American plants (*Cephaelis
acuminata* and *C. ipecacuanha*) of the madder
family used especially as a source of emetine;
*also* **:** either of these plants
**2 :** an emetic and expectorant drug that contains emetine and is prepared from ipecac especially as a syrup for use in treating accidental poisoning
**Iph·i·ge·nia** \,i-fə-jə-'nī-ə\ *noun* [Latin, from
Greek *Iphigeneia*]
**:** a daughter of Agamemnon nearly sacrificed
by him to Artemis but saved by her and made
a priestess
**ipro·ni·a·zid** \,ī-prə-'nī-ə-zəd\ *noun* [blend of
*isoniazid* and *propyl*] (1952)
**:** a derivative C₉H₁₃N₃O of isoniazid that is
used as a monoamine oxidase inhibitor and
was formerly used in treating tuberculosis
**ip·se dix·it** \'ip-sē-'dik-sət\ *noun* [Latin, he
himself said it] (15th century)

| | | |
|---|---|---|
| \ə\ abut | \ᵊ\ kitten | \ər\ **further** \a\ ash \ā\ ace |
| \ä\ mop, mar | \aú\ out | \ch\ chin \e\ bet \ē\ easy |
| \g\ go | \i\ hit | \ī\ ice \j\ job \ŋ\ sing \ō\ go |
| \ò\ law | \òi\ boy | \th\ thin \th\ the \ü\ loot \ú\ foot |
| \y\ yet | \zh\ vision | *see also* Guide to Pronunciation |

: an assertion made but not proved : DICTUM

**ip·si·lat·er·al** \,ip-si-'la-t(ə-)rəl\ *adjective* [International Scientific Vocabulary, from Latin *ipse* self, himself + *later-, latus* side] (1907)
: situated or appearing on or affecting the same side of the body
— **ip·si·lat·er·al·ly** \-t(ə-)rə-lē\ *adverb*

**ip·sis·si·ma ver·ba** \ip-'si-sə-mə-'vər-bə\ *noun plural* [New Latin, literally, the selfsame words] (1807)
: the exact language used by someone quoted

**ip·so fac·to** \'ip-(,)sō-'fak-(,)tō\ *adverb* [New Latin, literally, by the fact itself] (1548)
: by that very fact or act : as an inevitable result

**IQ** \,ī-'kyü\ *noun* (1920)
: INTELLIGENCE QUOTIENT

**ir-** — see IN-

**IRA** \,ī-(,)är-'ā; 'ī-rə\ *noun, plural* **IRAs** [*individual retirement account*] (1974)
: a savings account in which a person may deposit up to a stipulated amount each year with the deposits deductible from taxable income and both deposits and interest taxable after the person's retirement

**Ira·ni·an** \i-'rä-nē-ən, -'ra-, -'rä-; ī-'\ *noun* (1789)
**1** : a native or inhabitant of Iran
**2** : a branch of the Indo-European family of languages that includes Persian — see INDO-EUROPEAN LANGUAGES table
— **Iranian** *adjective*

**iras·ci·ble** \i-'ra-sə-bəl\ *adjective* [Middle French, from Late Latin *irascibilis,* from Latin *irasci* to become angry, be angry, from *ira*] (circa 1530)
: marked by hot temper and easily provoked anger
— **iras·ci·bil·i·ty** \-,ra-sə-'bi-lə-tē\ *noun*
— **iras·ci·ble·ness** \i-'ra-sə-bəl-nəs\ *noun*
— **iras·ci·bly** \-blē\ *adverb*

**irate** \ī-'rāt, 'ī-,, i-'rāt\ *adjective* (1838)
**1** : roused to ire ⟨an *irate* taxpayer⟩
**2** : arising from anger ⟨*irate* words⟩
— **irate·ly** *adverb*
— **irate·ness** *noun*

**ire** \'īr\ *noun* [Middle English, from Middle French, from Latin *ira;* perhaps akin to Greek *oistros* gadfly, frenzy] (14th century)
: intense and usually openly displayed anger
**synonym** see ANGER
— **ire** *transitive verb*
— **ire·ful** \-fəl\ *adjective*

**ire·nic** \ī-'re-nik, -'rē-\ *adjective* [Greek *eirēnikos,* from *eirēnē* peace] (circa 1864)
: favoring, conducive to, or operating toward peace, moderation, or conciliation
— **ire·ni·cal·ly** \-'re-ni-k(ə-)lē, -'rē-\ *adverb*

**irid-** *or* **irido-** *combining form*
**1** [Latin *irid-, iris*] : rainbow ⟨*irid*escent⟩
**2** [New Latin *irid-, iris*] : iris of the eye ⟨*irid*ology⟩

**ir·i·des·cence** \,ir-ə-'de-s⁰n(t)s\ *noun* (1804)
**1** : a lustrous rainbowlike play of color caused by differential refraction of light waves (as from an oil slick, soap bubble, or fish scales) that tends to change as the angle of view changes
**2** : a lustrous or attractive quality or effect ⟨the agglomeration of power which . . . gives them a certain *iridescence* of glamor and superiority —Margaret Landon⟩

**ir·i·des·cent** \-s⁰nt\ *adjective* (1791)
: having or exhibiting iridescence
— **ir·i·des·cent·ly** *adverb*

**irid·ic** \i-'ri-dik, ī-'ri-dik\ *adjective* (circa 1890)
: of or relating to the iris of the eye

**irid·i·um** \i-'ri-dē-əm\ *noun* [New Latin, from Latin *irid-, iris;* from the colors produced by its dissolving in hydrochloric acid] (1804)
: a silver-white hard brittle very heavy metallic element — see ELEMENT table

**ir·i·dol·o·gy** \,ī-rə-'dä-lə-jē\ *noun, plural* **-gies** (circa 1923)
: the study of the iris of the eye for indications of bodily health and disease

— **ir·i·dol·o·gist** \-jist\ *noun*

**ir·id·os·mine** \,ir-ə-'däz-,mēn\ *noun* [German, from New Latin *iridium + osmium*] (1827)
: a mineral that is a native iridium osmium alloy usually containing some rhodium and platinum

¹**iris** \'ī-rəs\ *noun, plural* **iris·es** *or* **iri·des** \'ī-rə-,dēz, 'ir-ə-\ [Middle English, from Latin *irid-, iris* rainbow, iris plant, from Greek, rainbow, iris plant, iris of the eye — more at WIRE] (15th century)
**1** : RAINBOW
**2** [New Latin *irid-, iris,* from Greek] **a** : the opaque contractile diaphragm perforated by the pupil and forming the colored portion of the eye — see EYE illustration **b** : IRIS DIAPHRAGM; *also* : a similar device with a circular opening that can be varied in size
**3** *or plural* **iris** [New Latin *Irid-, Iris,* genus name, from Latin] : any of a large genus (*Iris* of the family Iridaceae, the iris family) of perennial herbaceous plants with linear usually basal leaves and large showy flowers

²**iris** *transitive verb* (1816)
: to make iridescent

**Iris** \'ī-rəs\ *noun* [Latin, from Greek]
: the Greek goddess of the rainbow and a messenger of the gods

**iris diaphragm** *noun* (1867)
: an adjustable diaphragm of thin opaque plates that can be turned by a ring so as to change the diameter of a central opening usually to regulate the aperture of a lens

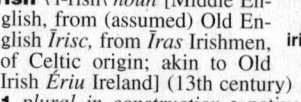
iris diaphragm

**Irish** \'ī-rish\ *noun* [Middle English, from (assumed) Old English *Īrisc,* from *Īras* Irishmen, of Celtic origin; akin to Old Irish *Ériu* Ireland] (13th century)
**1** *plural in construction* : natives or inhabitants of Ireland or their descendants especially when of Celtic speech or culture
**2 a** : the Celtic language of Ireland especially as used since the later medieval period **b** : English spoken by the Irish
**3** : IRISH WHISKEY
— **Irish** *adjective*

**Irish bull** *noun* (1802)
: an incongruous statement (as "it was hereditary in his family to have no children")

**Irish coffee** *noun* (1950)
: hot sugared coffee and Irish whiskey topped with whipped cream

**Irish confetti** *noun* (1922)
: a rock or brick used as a missile

**Irish Gaelic** *noun* (1891)
: IRISH 2a

**Irish·ism** \'ī-ri-,shi-zəm\ *noun* (1734)
**1** : a word, phrase, or expression characteristic of the Irish
**2** : IRISH BULL

**Irish·ly** \'ī-rish-lē\ *adverb* (1571)
: in a manner characteristic of the Irish

**Irish mail** *noun* (1908)
: a 3- or 4-wheeled toy vehicle activated by a hand lever

**Irish·man** \'ī-rish-mən\ *noun* (13th century)
**1** : a native or inhabitant of Ireland
**2** : one that is of Irish descent

**Irish moss** *noun* (1845)
**1** : the dried and bleached plants of a red alga (especially *Chondrus crispus*) used as an agent for thickening or emulsifying or as a demulcent
**2** : a red alga that is a source of Irish moss — called also *carrageen*

**Irish·ness** \'ī-rish-nəs\ *noun* (1804)
: the fact or quality of being Irish

**Irish potato** *noun* (1664)
: POTATO 2b

**Irish·ry** \'ī-rish-rē\ *noun, plural* **-ries** (14th century)
**1** : IRISH 1
**2 a** : Irish quality or character **b** : an Irish peculiarity or trait

**Irish setter** *noun* (1866)
: any of a breed of bird dogs generally comparable to English setters but with a mahogany-red coat

**Irish stew** *noun* (1814)
: a stew having as its principal ingredients meat (as lamb), potatoes, and onions in a thick gravy

**Irish terrier** *noun* (1857)
: any of a breed of active medium-sized terriers developed in Ireland and characterized by a dense close usually reddish wiry coat

**Irish water spaniel** *noun* (1885)
: any of a breed of large retrievers characterized by a topknot, a heavy curly coat which is dark liver in color, and a short-haired tail

**Irish whiskey** *noun* (1798)
: whiskey made in Ireland chiefly of barley

**Irish wolfhound** *noun* (1880)
: any of a breed of very tall heavily built hounds having a rough wiry coat

Irish wolfhound

**Irish·wom·an** \'ī-rish-,wu̇-mən\ *noun* (15th century)
: a woman born in Ireland or of Irish descent

**iri·tis** \ī-'rī-təs\ *noun* [New Latin, irregular from *iris*] (1818)
: inflammation of the iris of the eye

¹**irk** \'ərk\ *transitive verb* [Middle English] (15th century)
: to make weary, irritated, or bored
**synonym** see ANNOY

²**irk** *noun* (circa 1570)
**1** : the fact of being annoying
**2** : a source of annoyance

**irk·some** \'ərk-səm\ *adjective* (15th century)
: tending to irk : TEDIOUS ⟨an *irksome* task⟩
— **irk·some·ly** *adverb*
— **irk·some·ness** *noun*

**iro·ko** \ə-'rō-(,)kō\ *noun* [Yoruba *ìrokò*] (1890)
: a large tropical western African tree (*Chlorophora excelsa*) of the mulberry family having strong streaky insect-resistant wood which is often used as a teak substitute; *also* : this wood

¹**iron** \'ī(-ə)rn\ *noun* [Middle English, from Old English *īsern, īren;* akin to Old High German *īsarn* iron] (before 12th century)
**1** : a heavy malleable ductile magnetic silver-white metallic element that readily rusts in moist air, occurs native in meteorites and combined in most igneous rocks, is the most used of metals, and is vital to biological processes — see ELEMENT table
**2** : something made of iron: as **a** *plural* : shackles for the hands or legs **b** : a heated metal implement used for branding or cauterizing **c** : a household device usually with a flat metal base that is heated to smooth, finish, or press (as cloth) **d** : STIRRUP — usually used in plural **e** : any of a series of numbered golf clubs having relatively thin metal heads — compare WOOD
**3** : great strength, hardness, or determination
**usage** see ASK
— **iron in the fire 1** : a matter requiring close attention **2** : a prospective course of action

²**iron** *adjective* (before 12th century)
**1** : of, relating to, or made of iron
**2** : resembling iron
**3 a** : strong and healthy : ROBUST **b** : INFLEXIBLE, UNRELENTING ⟨*iron* determination⟩ **c** : holding or binding fast ⟨an *iron* grip⟩
— **iron·ness** \'ī(-ə)rn-nəs\ *noun*

³**iron** (15th century)
*transitive verb*
**1** : to furnish or cover with iron

**2** : to shackle with irons
**3 a** : to smooth with or as if with a heated iron ⟨*iron* a shirt⟩ **b** : to remove (as wrinkles) by ironing
*intransitive verb*
: to smooth or press cloth or clothing with a heated iron

**Iron Age** *noun* (1879)
: the period of human culture characterized by the smelting of iron and its use in industry beginning somewhat before 1000 B.C. in western Asia and Egypt

**iron·bark** \ˈī(-ə)rn-ˌbärk\ *noun* (1799)
: any of several Australian eucalypti having hard gray bark and heavy hard durable wood used especially in heavy construction; *also* : this wood

**iron·bound** \-ˈbaůnd\ *adjective* (14th century)
: bound with or as if with iron: as **a** : HARSH, RUGGED ⟨*ironbound* coast⟩ **b** : STERN, RIGOROUS ⟨*ironbound* traditions⟩

¹**iron·clad** \-ˈklad\ *adjective* (circa 1847)
**1** : sheathed in iron armor — used especially of naval vessels
**2** : so firm or secure as to be unbreakable: as **a** : BINDING ⟨an *ironclad* oath⟩ **b** : having no obvious weakness ⟨an *ironclad* case against the defendant⟩

²**iron·clad** \-ˌklad\ *noun* (1862)
: an armored naval vessel especially of the mid to late nineteenth century

**iron curtain** *noun* (1819)
**1** : an impenetrable barrier ⟨the *iron curtain* between the ego and the unconscious —C. J. Rolo⟩
**2** : a political, military, and ideological barrier that cuts off and isolates an area; *specifically, often capitalized* : one isolating an area under Soviet control

**iron·er** \ˈī(-ə)r-nər\ *noun* (1773)
: one that irons; *specifically* : MANGLE

**iron·fisted** \ˈī(-ə)rn-ˈfis-təd\ *adjective* (1599)
**1** : STINGY, MISERLY
**2** : being both harsh and ruthless ⟨*ironfisted* methods⟩

**iron gray** *noun* (before 12th century)
: a slightly greenish dark gray

**iron hand** *noun* (1703)
: stern or rigorous control ⟨ruled with an *iron hand*⟩
— **iron·hand·ed** \ˈī(-ə)rn-ˈhan-dəd\ *adjective*

**iron·heart·ed** \ˈī(-ə)rn-ˈhär-təd\ *adjective* (1600)
: CRUEL, HARD-HEARTED

**iron horse** *noun* (1840)
: LOCOMOTIVE 1; *especially* : a steam locomotive

**iron·ic** \ī-ˈrä-nik *also* i-ˈrä-\ *or* **iron·i·cal** \-ni-kəl\ *adjective* (1576)
**1** : relating to, containing, or constituting irony
**2** : given to irony
*synonym* see SARCASTIC
— **iron·i·cal·ness** \-ni-kəl-nəs\ *noun*

**iron·i·cal·ly** \-ni-k(ə-)lē\ *adverb* (1576)
**1** : in an ironic manner
**2** : it is ironic, curious, or surprising

**iron·ing** \ˈī(-ə)r-niŋ\ *noun* (circa 1710)
**1** : the action or process of smoothing or pressing with or as if with a heated iron
**2** : clothes ironed or to be ironed

**ironing board** *noun* (1843)
: a flat padded cloth-covered surface on which clothes are ironed

**iro·nist** \ˈī-rə-nist\ *noun* (1727)
: one who uses irony especially in the development of a literary work or theme

**iro·nize** \-ˌnīz\ *verb* **-nized; -niz·ing** (1602)
*transitive verb*
: to make ironic in appearance or effect
*intransitive verb*
: to use irony : speak or behave ironically

**iron lung** *noun* (1932)
: a device for artificial respiration in which rhythmic alternations in the air pressure in a chamber surrounding a patient's chest force air into and out of the lungs

**iron maiden** *noun* (circa 1895)
: a supposed medieval torture device consisting of a hollow iron statue or coffin in the shape of a woman that is lined with spikes which impale the enclosed victim

**iron man** *noun* (1914)
: a man of unusual physical endurance

**iron·mas·ter** \ˈī(-ə)rn-ˌmas-tər\ *noun* (1674)
: a manufacturer of iron

**iron·mon·ger** \-ˌməŋ-gər, -ˌmäŋ-\ *noun* (14th century)
*British* : a dealer in iron and hardware

**iron·mon·gery** \-g(ə-)rē\ *noun* (1711)
: something made of metal; *especially, British* : HARDWARE 1

**iron out** *transitive verb* (1870)
**1** : to make smooth or flat by or as if by pressing
**2** : to resolve or work out a solution to ⟨*ironed out* their differences⟩

**iron oxide** *noun* (1885)
: any of several oxides of iron: as **a** : FERRIC OXIDE **b** : FERROUS OXIDE

**iron pyrites** *noun* (circa 1817)
: PYRITE — called also *iron pyrite*

**iron ration** *noun* (1876)
: an emergency ration

**iron·side** \-ˌsīd\ *noun* (13th century)
: a man of great strength or bravery

**iron·stone** \ˈī(-ə)rn-ˌstōn\ *noun* (1522)
**1** : a hard sedimentary rock rich in iron; *especially* : a siderite in a coal region
**2** : IRONSTONE CHINA

**ironstone china** *noun* (1825)
: a hard heavy durable white pottery developed in England early in the 19th century

**iron sulfide** *noun* (1885)
: any of several sulfides of iron

**iron·ware** \ˈī(-ə)rn-ˌwar, -ˌwer\ *noun* (15th century)
: articles made of iron

**iron·weed** \-ˌwēd\ *noun* (1819)
: any of several mostly weedy American composite plants (genus *Vernonia*) usually having alternate leaves and perfect red, purple, or white tubular flowers in terminal cymose heads

**iron·wood** \-ˌwůd\ *noun* (1657)
**1** : any of numerous trees and shrubs (as a hornbeam or hop hornbeam) with exceptionally tough or hard wood
**2** : the wood of an ironwood

**iron·work** \-ˌwərk\ *noun* (15th century)
**1** : work in iron; *also* : something made of iron
**2** *plural but singular or plural in construction* : a mill or building where iron or steel is smelted or heavy iron or steel products are made
— **iron·work·er** \-ˌwər-kər\ *noun*

**iro·ny** \ˈī-rə-nē *also* ˈī(-ə)r-nē\ *noun, plural* **-nies** [Latin *ironia*, from Greek *eirōnia*, from *eirōn* dissembler] (1502)
**1** : a pretense of ignorance and of willingness to learn from another assumed in order to make the other's false conceptions conspicuous by adroit questioning — called also *Socratic irony*
**2 a** : the use of words to express something other than and especially the opposite of the literal meaning **b** : a usually humorous or sardonic literary style or form characterized by irony **c** : an ironic expression or utterance
**3 a** (1) : incongruity between the actual result of a sequence of events and the normal or expected result (2) : an event or result marked by such incongruity **b** : incongruity between a situation developed in a drama and the accompanying words or actions that is understood by the audience but not by the characters in the play — called also *dramatic irony, tragic irony*
*synonym* see WIT

**Iro·quoi·an** \ˌir-ə-ˈkwȯi-ən\ *noun* (1697)

**1** : a member of any of the peoples constituting the Iroquois
**2** : an American Indian language family of eastern North America including Cayuga, Cherokee, Mohawk, Onondaga, Oneida, Seneca, and Tuscarora
— **Iroquoian** *adjective*

**Ir·o·quois** \ˈir-ə-ˌkwȯi *also* -ˌkwä\ *noun, plural* **Iroquois** \-ˌkwȯi(z), -ˌkwä(z)\ [French, probably of Algonquian origin] (1666)
**1** *plural* : an American Indian confederacy originally of New York consisting of the Cayuga, Mohawk, Oneida, Onondaga, and Seneca and later including the Tuscarora
**2** : a member of any of the Iroquois peoples

**ir·ra·di·ance** \i-ˈrā-dē-ən(t)s\ *noun* (1667)
**1** : RADIANCE 1
**2** : the density of radiation incident on a given surface usually expressed in watts per square centimeter or square meter

**ir·ra·di·ate** \i-ˈrā-dē-ˌāt\ *verb* **-at·ed; -at·ing** [Latin *irradiatus*, past participle of *irradiare*, from *in-* + *radius* ray] (1603)
*transitive verb*
**1 a** : to cast rays of light upon : ILLUMINATE **b** : to enlighten intellectually or spiritually **c** : to affect or treat by radiant energy (as heat); *specifically* : to treat by exposure to radiation
**2** : to emit like rays of light : RADIATE ⟨*irradiating* strength and comfort⟩
*intransitive verb*
*archaic* : to emit rays : SHINE
— **ir·ra·di·a·tive** \-ˌā-tiv\ *adjective*
— **ir·ra·di·a·tor** \-ˌā-tər\ *noun*

**ir·ra·di·a·tion** \i-ˌrā-dē-ˈā-shən\ *noun* (1901)
**1** : exposure to radiation (as X rays or alpha particles)
**2** : application of radiation (as X rays or ultraviolet light) especially for therapeutic purposes

**ir·rad·i·ca·ble** \i-ˈra-di-kə-bəl, ˌi(r)-\ *adjective* [Medieval Latin *irradicabilis*, from Latin *in-* + *radic-, radix* root — more at ROOT] (1728)
: impossible to eradicate : DEEP-ROOTED
— **ir·rad·i·ca·bly** \-blē\ *adverb*

¹**ir·ra·tio·nal** \i-ˈra-sh(ə-)nəl, ˌi(r)-\ *adjective* [Middle English, from Latin *irrationalis*, from *in-* + *rationalis* rational] (14th century)
: not rational: as **a** (1) : not endowed with reason or understanding (2) : lacking usual or normal mental clarity or coherence **b** : not governed by or according to reason ⟨*irrational* fears⟩ **c** *Greek & Latin prosody* (1) *of a syllable* : having a quantity other than that required by the meter (2) *of a foot* : containing such a syllable **d** (1) : being an irrational number ⟨an *irrational* root of an equation⟩ (2) : having a numerical value that is an irrational number ⟨a length that is *irrational*⟩
— **ir·ra·tio·nal·i·ty** \-ˌra-shə-ˈna-lə-tē\ *noun*
— **ir·ra·tio·nal·ly** \-ˈra-sh(ə-)nə-lē\ *adverb*

²**irrational** *noun* (1646)
**1** : an irrational being
**2** : IRRATIONAL NUMBER

**ir·ra·tio·nal·ism** \i-ˈra-sh(ə-)nə-ˌli-zəm\ *noun* (1811)
**1** : a system emphasizing intuition, instinct, feeling, or faith rather than reason or holding that the universe is governed by irrational forces
**2** : the quality or state of being irrational
— **ir·ra·tio·nal·ist** \-list\ *noun or adjective*
— **ir·ra·tio·nal·is·tic** \-ˌra-sh(ə-)nə-ˈlis-tik\ *adjective*

**irrational number** *noun* (1551)
: a number that can be expressed as an infinite decimal with no set of consecutive digits repeating itself indefinitely and that cannot be expressed as the quotient of two integers

**ir·re·al** \i-'rē(-ə)l, ˌi(r)-, -'ri(-ə)l\ *adjective* (1944)
: not real

**ir·re·al·i·ty** \ˌir-ē-'a-lə-tē\ *noun* (1803)
: UNREALITY

**ir·re·claim·able** \ˌir-i-'klā-mə-bəl\ *adjective* (1662)
: incapable of being reclaimed
— **ir·re·claim·ably** \-blē\ *adverb*

¹**ir·rec·on·cil·able** \i-ˌre-kən-'sī-lə-bəl, -'re-kən-ˌ, ˌi(r)-\ *adjective* (1599)
: impossible to reconcile
— **ir·rec·on·cil·abil·i·ty** \-ˌre-kən-ˌsī-lə-'bi-lə-tē\ *noun*
— **ir·rec·on·cil·able·ness** \-ˌre-kən-'sī-lə-bəl-nəs, -'re-kən-ˌ\ *noun*
— **ir·rec·on·cil·ably** \-blē\ *adverb*

²**irreconcilable** *noun* (1748)
: one that is irreconcilable; *especially* : a member of a group (as a political party) opposing compromise or collaboration

**ir·re·cov·er·able** \ˌir-i-'kəv-rə-bəl, -'kə-və-\ *adjective* (15th century)
: not capable of being recovered or rectified : IRREPARABLE
— **ir·re·cov·er·able·ness** *noun*
— **ir·re·cov·er·ably** \-blē\ *adverb*

**ir·re·cus·a·ble** \ˌir-i-'kyü-zə-bəl\ *adjective* [Late Latin *irrecusabilis*, from Latin *in-* + *recusare* to reject, refuse — more at RECUSANT] (1776)
: not subject to exception or rejection
— **ir·re·cus·a·bly** \-blē\ *adverb*

**ir·re·deem·able** \ˌir-i-'dē-mə-bəl\ *adjective* (1609)
**1** : not redeemable: as **a** : not terminable by payment of the principal 〈*irredeemable* bond〉 **b** : INCONVERTIBLE a
**2** : being beyond remedy : HOPELESS 〈*irredeemable* mistakes〉
— **ir·re·deem·ably** \-blē\ *adverb*

**ir·re·den·ta** \ˌir-i-'den-tə\ *noun* [Italian *Italia irredenta*, literally, unredeemed Italy, Italian-speaking territory not incorporated in Italy] (1914)
: a territory historically or ethnically related to one political unit but under the political control of another

**ir·re·den·tism** \-'den-ˌti-zəm\ *noun* (1883)
: a political principle or policy directed toward the incorporation of irredentas within the boundaries of their historically or ethnically related political unit
— **ir·re·den·tist** \-'den-tist\ *noun or adjective*

**ir·re·duc·ible** \ˌir-i-'dü-sə-bəl, -'dyü-\ *adjective* (1633)
: impossible to transform into or restore to a desired or simpler condition 〈an *irreducible* matrix〉; *specifically* : incapable of being factored into polynomials of lower degree with coefficients in some given field (as the rational numbers) or integral domain (as the integers) 〈an *irreducible* equation〉
— **ir·re·duc·ibil·i·ty** \-ˌdü-sə-'bi-lə-tē, -ˌdyü-\ *noun*
— **ir·re·duc·ibly** \-'dü-sə-blē, -'dyü-\ *adverb*

**ir·re·flex·ive** \ˌir-i-'flek-siv\ *adjective* (circa 1890)
: being a relation for which the reflexive property does not hold for any element of a given set

**ir·re·form·able** \ˌir-i-'fȯr-mə-bəl\ *adjective* (1609)
**1** : incapable of being reformed : INCORRIGIBLE
**2** : not subject to revision or alteration 〈*irreformable* dogma〉
— **ir·re·form·abil·i·ty** \-ˌfȯr-mə-'bi-lə-tē\ *noun*

**ir·re·fra·ga·ble** \i-'re-frə-gə-bəl, ˌi(r)-; ˌir-i-'fra-gə-\ *adjective* [Late Latin *irrefragabilis*, from Latin *in-* + *refragari* to oppose, from *re-* + *-fragari* (as in *suffragari* to vote for); akin to Latin *suffragium* suffrage] (1533)

**1** : impossible to refute 〈*irrefragable* arguments〉
**2** : impossible to break or alter 〈*irrefragable* rules〉
— **ir·re·fra·ga·bil·i·ty** \i-ˌre-frə-gə-'bi-lə-tē, ˌi(r)-; ˌir-i-ˌfra-gə-\ *noun*
— **ir·ref·ra·ga·bly** \i-'re-frə-gə-blē, ˌi(r)-; ˌir-i-'fra-gə-\ *adverb*

**ir·re·fut·able** \ˌir-i-'fyü-tə-bəl; i-'re-fyə-tə-, ˌi(r)-\ *adjective* [Late Latin *irrefutabilis*, from Latin *in-* + *refutare* to refute] (1620)
: impossible to refute : INCONTROVERTIBLE 〈*irrefutable* proof〉
— **ir·re·fut·abil·i·ty** \ˌir-i-ˌfyü-tə-'bi-lə-tē; i-ˌre-fyə-tə-, ˌi(r)-\ *noun*
— **ir·re·fut·ably** \ˌir-i-'fyü-tə-blē; i-'re-fyə-tə-, ˌi(r)-\ *adverb*

**ir·re·gard·less** \ˌir-i-'gärd-ləs\ *adverb* [probably blend of *irrespective* and *regardless*] (circa 1912)
*nonstandard* : REGARDLESS □

¹**ir·reg·u·lar** \i-'re-gyə-lər, ˌi(r)-\ *adjective* [Middle English *irreguler*, from Middle French, from Late Latin *irregularis* not in accordance with rule, from Latin *in-* + *regularis* regular] (14th century)
**1 a** : not being or acting in accord with laws, rules, or established custom 〈*irregular* conduct〉 **b** : not conforming to the usual pattern of inflection 〈*irregular* verbs〉; *specifically* : STRONG 16 **c** : not following a usual or prescribed procedure; *especially, British* : celebrated without either proclamation of the banns or publication of intention to marry 〈*irregular* marriage〉
**2** : not belonging to or a part of a regular organized group; *specifically* : not belonging to a regular army but raised for a special purpose 〈*irregular* troops〉
**3 a** : lacking perfect symmetry or evenness 〈an *irregular* coastline〉 **b** : ZYGOMORPHIC 〈*irregular* flowers〉
**4** : lacking continuity or regularity especially of occurrence or activity 〈*irregular* employment〉 ☆
— **ir·reg·u·lar·ly** *adverb*

²**irregular** *noun* (15th century)
: one that is irregular: as **a** : a soldier who is not a member of a regular military force **b** *plural* : merchandise that has minor defects or that falls next below the manufacturer's standard for firsts

**ir·reg·u·lar·i·ty** \i-ˌre-gyə-'la-rə-tē, ˌi(r)-\ *noun, plural* **-ties** [Middle English *irregularite*, from Middle French *irregularité*, from Medieval Latin *irregularitat-, irregularitas*, from Late Latin *irregularis*] (14th century)
**1** : something that is irregular (as improper or dishonest conduct) 〈alleged *irregularities* in the city government〉
**2** : the quality or state of being irregular
**3** : CONSTIPATION

**ir·rel·a·tive** \-'re-lə-tiv\ *adjective* (1640)
: not relative: **a** : not related **b** : IRRELEVANT
— **ir·rel·a·tive·ly** *adverb*

**ir·rel·e·vance** \-'re-lə-vən(t)s\ *noun* (1847)
**1** : the quality or state of being irrelevant
**2** : something irrelevant

**ir·rel·e·van·cy** \-vən(t)-sē\ *noun, plural* **-cies** (1592)
: IRRELEVANCE

**ir·rel·e·vant** \-vənt\ *adjective* (1786)
: not relevant : INAPPLICABLE 〈that statement is *irrelevant* to your argument〉
— **ir·rel·e·vant·ly** *adverb*

**ir·re·li·gion** \ˌir-i-'li-jən\ *noun* [Middle French or Late Latin; Middle French, from Late Latin *irreligion-, irreligio*, from Latin *in-* + *religion-, religio* religion] (1598)
: the quality or state of being irreligious
— **ir·re·li·gion·ist** \-'lij-nist, -'li-jə-\ *noun*

**ir·re·li·gious** \-'li-jəs\ *adjective* (15th century)
**1** : neglectful of religion : lacking religious emotions, doctrines, or practices 〈so *irreligious* that they exploit popular religion for professional purposes —G. B. Shaw〉

**2** : indicating lack of religion
— **ir·re·li·gious·ly** *adverb*

**ir·re·me·able** \i-'rē-mē-ə-bəl, ˌi(r)-\ *adjective* [Latin *irremeabilis*, from *in-* + *remeare* to go back, from *re-* + *meare* to go — more at PERMEATE] (1569)
: offering no possibility of return

**ir·re·me·di·able** \ˌir-i-'mē-dē-ə-bəl\ *adjective* [Middle English, from Latin *irremediabilis*, from *in-* + *remediabilis* remediable] (15th century)
: not remediable; *specifically* : INCURABLE
— **ir·re·me·di·able·ness** *noun*
— **ir·re·me·di·a·bly** \-blē\ *adverb*

**ir·re·mov·able** \-'mü-və-bəl\ *adjective* (1598)
: not removable
— **ir·re·mov·abil·i·ty** \-ˌmü-və-'bi-lə-tē\ *noun*
— **ir·re·mov·ably** \-'mü-və-blē\ *adverb*

**ir·rep·a·ra·ble** \i-'re-p(ə-)rə-bəl, ˌi(r)- *also* ÷ˌir-(r)ə-'par-ə-bəl\ *adjective* [Middle English, from Middle French, from Latin *irreparabilis*, from *in-* + *reparabilis* reparable] (15th century)
: not reparable : IRREMEDIABLE 〈*irreparable* damage〉
— **ir·rep·a·ra·ble·ness** *noun*
— **ir·rep·a·ra·bly** \-blē\ *adverb*

**ir·re·peal·able** \ˌir-i-'pē-lə-bəl\ *adjective* (1633)
: not repealable
— **ir·re·peal·abil·i·ty** \-ˌpē-lə-'bi-lə-tē\ *noun*

**ir·re·place·able** \-'plā-sə-bəl\ *adjective* (1807)
: not replaceable
— **ir·re·place·abil·i·ty** \-ˌplā-sə-'bi-lə-tē\ *noun*
— **ir·re·place·able·ness** \-'plā-sə-bəl-nəs\ *noun*
— **ir·re·place·ably** \-blē\ *adverb*

**ir·re·press·ible** \-'pre-sə-bəl\ *adjective* (1811)
: impossible to repress, restrain, or control 〈*irrepressible* curiosity〉
— **ir·re·press·ibil·i·ty** \-ˌpre-sə-'bi-lə-tē\ *noun*
— **ir·re·press·ibly** \-'pre-sə-blē\ *adverb*

**ir·re·proach·able** \-'prō-chə-bəl\ *adjective* (1634)

---

☆ **SYNONYMS**
**Irregular, anomalous, unnatural** mean not conforming to rule, law, or custom. IRREGULAR implies not conforming to a law or regulation imposed for the sake of uniformity in method, practice, or conduct 〈concerned about his *irregular* behavior〉. ANOMALOUS implies not conforming to what might be expected because of the class or type to which it belongs or the laws that govern its existence 〈her drive made her an *anomalous* figure in a sleepy organization〉. UNNATURAL suggests what is contrary to nature or to principles or standards felt to be essential to the well-being of civilized society 〈prisoners treated with *unnatural* cruelty〉.

---

□ **USAGE**
**irregardless** *Irregardless* originated in dialectal American speech in the early 20th century. Its fairly widespread use in speech called it to the attention of usage commentators as early as 1927. The most frequently repeated remark about it is that "there is no such word." There is such a word, however. It is still used primarily in speech, although it can be found from time to time in edited prose. Its reputation has not risen over the years, and it is still a long way from general acceptance. Use *regardless* instead.

: not reproachable : BLAMELESS, IMPECCABLE ⟨*irreproachable* conduct⟩
— **ir·re·proach·abil·i·ty** \-ˌprō-chə-'bi-lə-tē\ *noun*
— **ir·re·proach·able·ness** \-'prō-chə-bəl-nəs\ *noun*
— **ir·re·proach·ably** \-blē\ *adverb*
**ir·re·pro·duc·ible** \i-ˌrē-prə-'dü-sə-bəl, ˌi(r)-, -'dyü-\ *adjective* (1868)
: not reproducible
— **ir·re·pro·duc·ibil·i·ty** \-dü-sə-'bi-lə-tē, -ˌdyü-\ *noun*
**ir·re·sist·ible** \ˌir-i-'zis-tə-bəl\ *adjective* (1597)
: impossible to resist ⟨an *irresistible* attraction⟩
— **ir·re·sist·ibil·i·ty** \-ˌzis-tə-'bi-lə-tē\ *noun*
— **ir·re·sist·ible·ness** \-'zis-tə-bəl-nəs\ *noun*
— **ir·re·sist·ibly** \-blē\ *adverb*
**ir·re·sol·u·ble** \-'zäl-yə-bəl\ *adjective* [Latin *irresolubilis,* from *in-* + *resolvere* to resolve] (1666)
**1** *archaic* : INDISSOLUBLE
**2** : having or admitting of no solution or explanation
**ir·res·o·lute** \i-'re-zə-ˌlüt, ˌi(r)-, -lət\ *adjective* (1579)
: uncertain how to act or proceed : VACILLATING
— **ir·res·o·lute·ly** \-ˌlüt-lē, -lət-; -ˌre-zə-'lüt-\ *adverb*
— **ir·res·o·lute·ness** \-ˌlüt-nəs, -lət-, -'lüt-\ *noun*
— **ir·res·o·lu·tion** \-ˌre-zə-'lü-shən\ *noun*
**ir·re·solv·able** \ˌir-i-'zäl-və-bəl, -'zól-\ *adjective* (1660)
: incapable of being resolved; *also* : not analyzable
**ir·re·spec·tive of** \ˌir-i-'spek-tiv-\ *preposition* (1839)
: REGARDLESS OF ⟨free public schools open to all *irrespective of* race, color, or creed —J. B. Conant⟩
¹**ir·re·spon·si·ble** \ˌir-i-'spän(t)-sə-bəl\ *adjective* (1648)
: not responsible: as **a** : not answerable to higher authority ⟨an *irresponsible* dictatorship⟩ **b** : said or done with no sense of responsibility ⟨*irresponsible* accusations⟩ **c** : lacking a sense of responsibility **d** : unable especially mentally or financially to bear responsibility
— **ir·re·spon·si·bil·i·ty** \ˌir-i-ˌspän(t)-sə-'bi-lə-tē\ *noun*
— **ir·re·spon·si·ble·ness** \ˌir-i-'spän(t)-sə-bəl-nəs\ *noun*
— **ir·re·spon·si·bly** \-blē\ *adverb*
²**irresponsible** *noun* (1894)
: one that is irresponsible
**ir·re·spon·sive** \ˌir-i-'spän(t)-siv\ *adjective* (circa 1846)
: not responsive; *especially* : not able, ready, or inclined to respond
— **ir·re·spon·sive·ness** *noun*
**ir·re·triev·able** \ˌir-i-'trē-və-bəl\ *adjective* (1702)
: not retrievable : impossible to regain or recover
— **ir·re·triev·abil·i·ty** \-ˌtrē-və-'bi-lə-tē\ *noun*
— **ir·re·triev·ably** \ˌir-i-'trē-və-blē\ *adverb*
**ir·rev·er·ence** \i-'rev-rəns, ˌi(r)-, -'re-və-; -'re-vərn(t)s\ *noun* (14th century)
**1** : lack of reverence
**2** : an irreverent act or utterance
**ir·rev·er·ent** \-rənt; -vərnt\ *adjective* [Middle English, from Latin *irreverent-, irreverens,* from *in-* + *reverent-, reverens* reverent] (15th century)
: lacking proper respect or seriousness; *also* : SATIRIC
— **ir·rev·er·ent·ly** *adverb*
**ir·re·vers·ible** \ˌir-i-'vər-sə-bəl\ *adjective* (1630)
: not reversible

— **ir·re·vers·ibil·i·ty** \-ˌvər-sə-'bi-lə-tē\ *noun*
— **ir·re·vers·ibly** \-'vər-sə-blē\ *adverb*
**ir·rev·o·ca·ble** \i-'re-və-kə-bəl, ˌi(r)- *sometimes* ˌir-(r)ə-'vō-kə-\ *adjective* [Middle English, from Latin *irrevocabilis,* from *in-* + *revocabilis* revocable] (14th century)
: not possible to revoke : UNALTERABLE ⟨an *irrevocable* decision⟩
— **ir·rev·o·ca·bil·i·ty** \-ˌre-və-kə-'bi-lə-tē, ˌir-(r)ə-ˌvō-kə-\ *noun*
— **ir·rev·o·ca·ble·ness** \-'re-və-kə-bəl-nəs, ˌir-(r)ə-'vō-kə-\ *noun*
— **ir·rev·o·ca·bly** \-blē\ *adverb*
**ir·ri·den·ta** *variant of* IRREDENTA
**ir·ri·gate** \'ir-ə-ˌgāt\ *verb* **-gat·ed; -gat·ing** [Latin *irrigatus,* past participle of *irrigare,* from *in-* + *rigare* to water; perhaps akin to Old High German *regan* rain — more at RAIN] (1615)
*transitive verb*
**1** : WET, MOISTEN: as **a** : to supply (as land) with water by artificial means **b** : to flush (a body part) with a stream of liquid (as in removing a foreign body or medicating)
**2** : to refresh as if by watering
*intransitive verb*
: to practice irrigation
— **ir·ri·ga·tion** \ˌir-ə-'gā-shən\ *noun*
— **ir·ri·ga·tor** \'ir-ə-ˌgā-tər\ *noun*
**ir·ri·ta·bil·i·ty** \ˌir-ə-tə-'bi-lə-tē\ *noun, plural* **-ties** (1755)
**1** : the property of protoplasm and of living organisms that permits them to react to stimuli
**2** : the quality or state of being irritable: as **a** : quick excitability to annoyance, impatience, or anger : PETULANCE **b** : abnormal or excessive excitability of an organ or part of the body
**ir·ri·ta·ble** \'ir-ə-tə-bəl\ *adjective* (1662)
: capable of being irritated: as **a** : easily exasperated or excited **b** : responsive to stimuli
— **ir·ri·ta·ble·ness** *noun*
— **ir·ri·ta·bly** \-blē\ *adverb*
¹**ir·ri·tant** \'ir-ə-tənt\ *adjective* (1636)
: causing irritation; *specifically* : tending to produce physical irritation
²**irritant** *noun* (1802)
: something that irritates or excites
**ir·ri·tate** \'ir-ə-ˌtāt\ *verb* **-tat·ed; -tat·ing** [Latin *irritatus,* past participle of *irritare*] (1598)
*transitive verb*
**1** : to provoke impatience, anger, or displeasure in : ANNOY
**2** : to induce irritability in or of
*intransitive verb*
: to cause or induce displeasure or irritation ☆
— **ir·ri·tat·ing·ly** \-ˌtā-tiŋ-lē\ *adverb*
**irritated** *adjective* (1595)
: subjected to irritation; *especially* : roughened, reddened, or inflamed by an irritant ⟨*irritated* eyes⟩
**ir·ri·ta·tion** \ˌir-ə-'tā-shən\ *noun* (15th century)
**1 a** : the act of irritating **b** : something that irritates **c** : the state of being irritated
**2** : a condition of irritability, soreness, roughness, or inflammation of a bodily part
**ir·ri·ta·tive** \'ir-ə-ˌtā-tiv\ *adjective* (1644)
**1** : serving to excite : IRRITATING
**2** : accompanied with or produced by irritation ⟨*irritative* coughing⟩
**ir·ro·ta·tion·al** \ˌir-(r)ō-'tā-shnəl, -shə-nºl\ *adjective* (1875)
**1** : not rotating or involving rotation ⟨an *irrotational* electric field⟩
**2** : free of vortices ⟨*irrotational* flow⟩
**ir·rupt** \i-'rəpt\ *intransitive verb* [Latin *irruptus,* past participle of *irrumpere,* from *in-* + *rumpere* to break — more at REAVE] (1886)
**1** : to rush in forcibly or violently
**2** *of a natural population* : to undergo a sudden upsurge in numbers especially when natural ecological balances and checks are disturbed
**3** : ERUPT 1c ⟨the crowd *irrupted* in a fervor of patriotism —*Time*⟩

— **ir·rup·tion** \-'rəp-shən\ *noun*
**ir·rup·tive** \-'rəp-tiv\ *adjective* (1593)
: irrupting or tending to irrupt
— **ir·rup·tive·ly** *adverb*
**is** [Middle English, from Old English; akin to Old High German *ist* is (from *sīn* to be), Latin *est* (from *esse* to be), Greek *esti* (from *einai* to be)] *present 3d singular of* BE, *dialect present 1st & 2d singular of* BE, *substandard present plural of* BE
**is-** *or* **iso-** *combining form* [Late Latin, from Greek, from *isos* equal]
**1** : equal : homogeneous : uniform ⟨*isentropic*⟩
**2** : isomeric ⟨*isocyanate*⟩
**3** : for or from different individuals of the same species ⟨*isoagglutinin*⟩
**Isaac** \'ī-zik, -zək\ *noun* [Late Latin, from Hebrew *Yiṣḥāq*]
: the son of Abraham and father of Jacob according to the account in Genesis
**Isa·iah** \ī-'zā-ə, *chiefly British* -'zī-\ *noun* [Hebrew *Yĕsha'ăyāhū*]
**1** : a major Hebrew prophet in Judah about 740 to 701 B.C.
**2** : a prophetic book of canonical Jewish and Christian Scripture — see BIBLE table
**Isa·ias** \-əs\ *noun* [Late Latin, from Greek *Ēsaias,* from Hebrew *Yĕsha'ăyāhū*]
: ISAIAH
**is·al·lo·bar** \(ˌ)ī-'sa-lə-ˌbär\ *noun* [International Scientific Vocabulary *is-* + *all-* + *-bar* (as in *isobar*)] (1909)
: an imaginary line or a line on a chart connecting the places of equal change of atmospheric pressure within a specified time
— **is·al·lo·bar·ic** \ˌī-ˌsa-lə-'bär-ik, -'bar-\ *adjective*
**is·chae·mia** *chiefly British variant of* ISCHEMIA
**is·che·mia** \is-'kē-mē-ə\ *noun* [New Latin *ischaemia,* from *ischaemus* styptic, from Greek *ischaimos,* from *ischein* to restrain (akin to Greek *echein* to hold) + *haima* blood — more at SCHEME] (circa 1860)
: localized tissue anemia due to obstruction of the inflow of arterial blood
— **is·che·mic** \-mik\ *adjective*
**is·chi·um** \'is-kē-əm\ *noun, plural* **is·chia** \-ə\ [Latin, hip joint, from Greek *ischion*] (1646)
: the dorsal and posterior of the three principal bones composing either half of the pelvis
— **is·chi·al** \-əl\ *adjective*
**-ise** *verb suffix, chiefly British*
: -IZE

---

☆ **SYNONYMS**
**Irritate, exasperate, nettle, provoke, rile, peeve** mean to excite a feeling of anger or annoyance. IRRITATE implies an often gradual arousing of angry feelings that may range from mere impatience to rage ⟨constant nagging that *irritated* me greatly⟩. EXASPERATE suggests galling annoyance and the arousing of extreme impatience ⟨his *exasperating* habit of putting off needed decisions⟩. NETTLE suggests a sharp but passing annoyance or stinging ⟨your pompous attitude *nettled* several people⟩. PROVOKE implies an arousing of strong annoyance that may excite to action ⟨remarks made solely to *provoke* her⟩. RILE implies inducing an angry or resentful agitation ⟨the new work schedules *riled* the employees⟩. PEEVE suggests arousing fretful often petty or querulous irritation ⟨a toddler *peeved* at being refused a cookie⟩.

---

\ə\ abut \ᵊ\ kitten \ər\ further \a\ ash \ā\ ace \ä\ mop, mar \aú\ out \ch\ chin \e\ bet \ē\ easy \g\ go \i\ hit \ī\ ice \j\ job \ŋ\ sing \ō\ go \ó\ law \ói\ boy \th\ thin \t͟h\ the \ü\ loot \ú\ foot \y\ yet \zh\ vision *see also* Guide to Pronunciation

**is·en·tro·pic** \ˌī-sᵊn-'trō-pik, -'trä-\ adjective (1873)
: of or relating to equal or constant entropy; especially : taking place without change of entropy
— **is·en·tro·pi·cal·ly** \-'trō-pi-k(ə-)lē, -'trä-\ adverb

**Iseult** \is-'ült, iz-\ noun [Old French Isolt, Iseut]
: ISOLDE

**-ish** adjective suffix [Middle English, from Old English -isc; akin to Old High German -isc, -ish, Greek -iskos, diminutive suffix]
1 : of, relating to, or being — chiefly in adjectives indicating nationality or ethnic group ⟨Finnish⟩
2 a : characteristic of ⟨boyish⟩ ⟨Pollyannaish⟩ b : inclined or liable to ⟨bookish⟩ ⟨qualmish⟩
3 a : having a touch or trace of ⟨purplish⟩ : somewhat ⟨darkish⟩ b : having the approximate age of ⟨fortyish⟩

**Ish·ma·el** \'ish-(ˌ)mā-əl, -mē-\ noun [Hebrew Yishmā'ēl]
1 : the outcast son of Abraham and Hagar according to the account in Genesis
2 : a social outcast

**Ish·ma·el·ite** \-ə-ˌlīt\ noun (14th century)
1 : a descendant of Ishmael
2 : ISHMAEL 2
— **Ish·ma·el·it·ish** \-ˌlī-tish\ adjective
— **Ish·ma·el·it·ism** \-ˌlī-ti-zəm\ noun

**isin·glass** \'ī-zᵊn-ˌglas, 'ī-ziŋ-\ noun [probably by folk etymology from obsolete Dutch huizenblas, from Middle Dutch huusblase, from huus sturgeon + blase bladder] (1545)
1 : a semitransparent whitish very pure gelatin prepared from the air bladders of fishes (as sturgeons) and used especially as a clarifying agent and in jellies and glue
2 : MICA

**Isis** \'ī-səs\ noun [Latin Isid-, Isis, from Greek, from Egyptian 'st]
: an Egyptian nature goddess and wife and sister of Osiris

**Is·lam** \is-'läm, iz-, -'lam, 'is-ˌ, 'iz-ˌ\ noun [Arabic islām submission (to the will of God)] (1817)
1 : the religious faith of Muslims including belief in Allah as the sole deity and in Muhammad as his prophet
2 a : the civilization erected upon Islamic faith b : the group of modern nations in which Islam is the dominant religion
— **Is·lam·ic** \is-'lä-mik, iz-, -'la-\ adjective
— **Is·lam·ics** \-miks\ noun plural but singular or plural in construction

**Islamic calendar** noun (1974)
: a lunar calendar reckoned from the Hegira in A.D. 622 and organized in cycles of 30 years
— see MONTH table

**Islamic era** noun (1975)
: the era used in Muslim countries for numbering Islamic calendar years since the Hegira

**Is·lam·ism** \is-'lä-ˌmi-zəm, iz-, -'la-; 'iz-lə-\ noun (1747)
: the faith, doctrine, or cause of Islam
— **Is·lam·ist** \-mist\ noun

**Is·lam·ize** \'iz-lə-ˌmīz; is-'lä-ˌmīz, iz-, -'la-\ transitive verb **-ized; -iz·ing** (circa 1846)
: to make Islamic; especially : to convert to Islam
— **Is·lam·i·za·tion** \ˌiz-lə-mə-'zā-shən; is-ˌlä-mə-, iz-, -ˌla-\ noun

**¹is·land** \'ī-lənd\ noun [alteration (influenced by Old French isle) of earlier iland, from Middle English, from Old English igland (akin to Old Norse eyland), from ig island (akin to Old English ēa river, Latin aqua water) + land land] (before 12th century)
1 : a tract of land surrounded by water and smaller than a continent
2 : something resembling an island especially in its isolated or surrounded position: as a : a usually raised area within a thoroughfare, parking lot, or driveway used especially to separate or direct traffic b : a superstructure on the deck of a ship (as an aircraft carrier) c : a kitchen counter that is approachable from all sides
3 : an isolated group or area; especially : an isolated ethnological group

**²island** transitive verb (1661)
1 a : to make into or as if into an island b : to dot with or as if with islands
2 : ISOLATE

**is·land·er** \'ī-lən-dər\ noun (circa 1550)
: a native or inhabitant of an island

**is·land–hop** \'ī-lənd-ˌhäp\ intransitive verb (1944)
: to travel from island to island in a chain

**island universe** noun (1867)
: a galaxy other than the Milky Way

**¹isle** \'ī(ə)l\ noun [Middle English, from Old French, from Latin insula] (13th century)
: ISLAND; especially : ISLET

**²isle** transitive verb **isled; isl·ing** (circa 1576)
1 : to make an isle of
2 : to place on or as if on an isle

**is·let** \'ī-lət\ noun (1538)
: a little island

**islet of Lang·er·hans** \-'läŋ-ər-ˌhänz, -ˌhän(t)s\ [Paul Langerhans (died 1888) German physician] (1896)
: any of the groups of small slightly granular endocrine cells that form anastomosing trabeculae among the tubules and alveoli of the pancreas and secrete insulin and glucagon — called also islet

**ism** \'i-zəm\ noun [-ism] (1680)
: a distinctive doctrine, cause, or theory

**-ism** noun suffix [Middle English -isme, from Middle French & Latin; Middle French, partly from Latin -isma (from Greek) & partly from Latin -ismus, from Greek -ismos; Greek -isma & -ismos, from verbs in -izein -ize]
1 a : act : practice : process ⟨criticism⟩ ⟨plagiarism⟩ b : manner of action or behavior characteristic of a (specified) person or thing ⟨animalism⟩ c : prejudice or discrimination on the basis of a (specified) attribute ⟨racism⟩ ⟨sexism⟩
2 a : state : condition : property ⟨barbarianism⟩ b : abnormal state or condition resulting from excess of a (specified) thing ⟨alcoholism⟩ or marked by resemblance to (such) a person or thing ⟨mongolism⟩
3 a : doctrine : theory : cult ⟨Buddhism⟩ b : adherence to a system or a class of principles ⟨stoicism⟩
4 : characteristic or peculiar feature or trait ⟨colloquialism⟩

**isn't** \'i-zᵊnt, -ᵊn, dialect also 'i-dᵊn(t) or 'in(t)\ (1710)
: is not

**iso-** — see IS-

**iso·ag·glu·ti·nin** \ˌī-(ˌ)sō-ə-'glü-tᵊn-ən\ noun (circa 1903)
: an agglutinin from one individual that is specific for a cell type (as of red blood cells) possessed by some individuals of the same species

**iso·al·lox·a·zine** \-ə-'läk-sə-ˌzēn\ noun [is- + allantoic + oxalic + azine] (1936)
: a yellow solid $C_{10}H_6N_4O_2$ that is the precursor of various flavins (as riboflavin)

**iso·an·ti·body** \-'an-ti-ˌbä-dē\ noun (1919)
: ALLOANTIBODY

**iso·an·ti·gen** \-'an-ti-jən\ noun [International Scientific Vocabulary] (1936)
: ALLOANTIGEN
— **iso·an·ti·gen·ic** \ˌī-(ˌ)sō-ˌan-ti-'je-nik\ adjective

**iso·bar** \'ī-sə-ˌbär\ noun [International Scientific Vocabulary is- + -bar (from Greek baros weight); akin to Greek barys heavy — more at GRIEVE] (circa 1864)
1 : an imaginary line or a line on a map or chart connecting or marking places on the surface of the earth where the height of the barometer reduced to sea level is the same either at a given time or for a certain period
2 : one of two or more atoms or elements having the same atomic weights or mass numbers but different atomic numbers

**iso·bar·ic** \ˌī-sə-'bär-ik, -'bar-\ adjective [International Scientific Vocabulary] (1878)
1 : of or relating to an isobar
2 : characterized by constant or equal pressure ⟨an isobaric process⟩

**iso·bu·tane** \ˌī-sō-'byü-ˌtān\ noun [International Scientific Vocabulary] (1876)
: a gaseous branched-chain hydrocarbon $(CH_3)_3CH$ isomeric with normal butane that is used especially as a fuel

**iso·bu·tyl·ene** \-'byü-tᵊl-ˌēn\ noun [International Scientific Vocabulary] (1872)
: a gaseous butylene $C_4H_8$ used especially in making butyl rubber and gasoline components

**iso·ca·lo·ric** \-kə-'lór-ik, -'lōr-, -'lär-; -'ka-lə-rik\ adjective (1922)
: having similar caloric values ⟨isocaloric diets⟩

**iso·car·box·az·id** \-ˌkär-'bäk-sə-zəd\ noun [is- + carb- + ox- + hydrazide] (1959)
: an antidepressant drug $C_{12}H_{13}N_3O_2$

**iso·chro·mo·some** \ˌī-sə-'krō-mə-ˌsōm, -ˌzōm\ noun (1939)
: a chromosome produced by transverse splitting of the centromere so that both arms are derived from the dyad on one side of the centromere of the parental chromosome and each arm has identical genes arranged in the same order counting away from the centromere

**iso·chron** \'ī-sə-ˌkrän\ or **iso·chrone** \-ˌkrōn\ noun [International Scientific Vocabulary is- + -chron (from Greek chronos time)] (1881)
: an imaginary line or a line on a chart connecting points at which an event occurs simultaneously or which represents the same time or time difference

**iso·chro·nal** \ī-'sä-krə-nᵊl, ˌī-sə-'krō-\ adjective [Greek isochronos, from is- + chronos time] (1680)
: uniform in time : having equal duration : recurring at regular intervals
— **iso·chro·nal·ly** \-nᵊl-ē\ adverb
— **iso·chro·nism** \ī-'sä-krə-ˌni-zəm, ˌī-sə-'krō-\ noun

**iso·chro·nous** \ī-'sä-krə-nəs, ˌī-sə-'krō-\ adjective [Greek isochronos] (1706)
: ISOCHRONAL
— **iso·chro·nous·ly** adverb

**iso·cit·ric acid** \ˌī-sə-'si-trik-\ noun (1869)
: a crystalline isomer of citric acid that occurs especially as an intermediate stage in the Krebs cycle

**iso·cy·a·nate** \ˌī-sō-'sī-ə-ˌnāt, -nət\ noun [International Scientific Vocabulary] (1872)
: an ester of isomeric cyanic acid used especially in plastics and adhesives

**iso·cy·clic** \-'sī-klik, -'si-\ adjective [International Scientific Vocabulary] (1900)
: having or being a ring composed of atoms of only one element; especially : CARBOCYCLIC

**iso·di·a·met·ric** \-ˌdī-ə-'me-trik\ adjective [International Scientific Vocabulary] (circa 1879)
: having equal diameters

**iso·dose** \'ī-sə-ˌdōs\ adjective [International Scientific Vocabulary] (1922)
: of or relating to points or zones in a medium that receive equal doses of radiation

**iso·elec·tric** \ˌī-sō-i-'lek-trik\ adjective [International Scientific Vocabulary] (1877)
1 : having or representing zero difference of electric potential
2 : being the pH at which the electrolyte will not migrate in an electrical field ⟨the isoelectric point of a protein⟩

**isoelectric focusing** noun (1971)
: an electrophoretic technique for separating proteins by causing them to migrate under the

influence of an electric field through a medium (as a gel) having a pH gradient to locations with pH values corresponding to their isoelectric points

**iso·elec·tron·ic** \ˌī-i-ˌlek-'trä-nik\ *adjective* [International Scientific Vocabulary] (1926)
: having the same number of electrons or valence electrons
— **iso·elec·tron·i·cal·ly** \-ni-k(ə-)lē\ *adverb*

**iso·en·zyme** \-'en-ˌzīm\ *noun* (1960)
: any of two or more chemically distinct but functionally similar enzymes
— **iso·en·zy·mat·ic** \-ˌen-zə-'ma-tik, -zī-\ *adjective*
— **iso·en·zy·mic** \-en-'zī-mik\ *adjective*

**iso·ga·mete** \-'ga-ˌmēt *also* -gə-'mēt\ *noun* [International Scientific Vocabulary] (1891)
: a gamete indistinguishable in form or size or behavior from another gamete with which it can unite to form a zygote
— **iso·ga·met·ic** \-gə-'me-tik\ *adjective*

**isog·a·mous** \ī-'sä-gə-məs\ *adjective* [probably from (assumed) New Latin *isogamus*, from *is-* + *-gamus* -gamous] (1887)
: having or involving isogametes — compare HETEROGAMOUS
— **isog·a·my** \-mē\ *noun*

**iso·ge·ne·ic** \ˌī-sō-jə-'nē-ik, -'nā-\ *adjective* [alteration of *isogenic*] (1963)
: SYNGENEIC ⟨an *isogeneic* graft⟩

**iso·gen·ic** \-'je-nik\ *adjective* [*is-* + *gene* + ¹*-ic*] (circa 1931)
: characterized by essentially identical genes ⟨identical twins are *isogenic*⟩

**iso·gloss** \'ī-sə-ˌgläs, -ˌglós\ *noun* [International Scientific Vocabulary *is-* + Greek *glóssa* language — more at GLOSS] (1925)
**1** : a boundary line between places or regions that differ in a particular linguistic feature
**2** : a line on a map representing an isogloss
— **iso·gloss·al** \ˌī-sə-'glä-səl, -'glò-\ *adjective*
— **iso·gloss·ic** \-'glä-sik, -'glò-\ *adjective*

**iso·gon·ic** \ˌī-sə-'gä-nik\ *adjective* [*isogony*, from *is-* + *-gony*] (1924)
: exhibiting equivalent relative growth of parts such that size relations remain constant
— **isog·o·ny** \ī-'sä-gə-nē\ *noun*

**isogonic line** *noun* (circa 1859)
: an imaginary line or a line on a map joining points on the earth's surface at which the magnetic declination is the same — called also *isogonal*

**iso·graft** \'ī-sə-ˌgraft\ *noun* (1958)
: a homograft between genetically identical or nearly identical individuals
— **isograft** *transitive verb*

**iso·gram** \'ī-sə-ˌgram\ *noun* (1889)
: ISOLINE

**iso·hy·et** \ˌī-sō-'hī-ət\ *noun* [International Scientific Vocabulary *is-* + Greek *hyetos* rain, from *hyein* to rain; probably akin to Tocharian B *swese* rain] (1899)
: a line on a map or chart connecting areas of equal rainfall
— **iso·hy·et·al** \-ə-təl\ *adjective*

**iso·la·ble** \'ī-sə-lə-bəl *also* 'i-\ *also* **iso·lat·able** \ˌī-sə-'lā-tə-bəl *also* ˌi-\ *adjective* (circa 1855)
: capable of being isolated

¹**iso·late** \'ī-sə-ˌlāt *also* 'i-\ *transitive verb* **-lat·ed; -lat·ing** [back-formation from *isolated* set apart, from French *isolé*, from Italian *isolato*, from *isola* island, from Latin *insula*] (1807)
**1** : to set apart from others; *also* : QUARANTINE
**2** : to select from among others; *especially* : to separate from another substance so as to obtain pure or in a free state
**3** : INSULATE
— **iso·la·tor** \-ˌlā-tər\ *noun*

²**iso·late** \-lət, -ˌlāt\ *adjective* (1819)
: being alone : SOLITARY, ISOLATED

³**iso·late** \-lət, -ˌlāt\ *noun* (1890)
**1** : a product of isolating : an individual, population, or kind obtained by or resulting from selection or separation
**2** : an individual socially withdrawn or removed from society

**isolated** *adjective* (1763)
**1** : occurring alone or once : UNIQUE
**2** : SPORADIC

**iso·la·tion** \ˌī-sə-'lā-shən *also* ˌi-\ *noun* (1833)
: the action of isolating : the condition of being isolated
**synonym** see SOLITUDE

**iso·la·tion·ism** \-shə-ˌni-zəm\ *noun* (1922)
: a policy of national isolation by abstention from alliances and other international political and economic relations
— **iso·la·tion·ist** \-sh(ə-)nist\ *noun or adjective*

**Isol·de** \i-'zōl-də, -'sōl-\ *noun* [German, from Old French *Isolt, Iseut*]
**1** : an Irish princess married to King Mark of Cornwall and loved by Tristram
**2** : the daughter of the King of Brittany and wife of Tristram

**iso·leu·cine** \ˌī-sō-'lü-ˌsēn\ *noun* [International Scientific Vocabulary] (1903)
: a crystalline essential amino acid $C_6H_{13}NO_2$ isomeric with leucine

**iso·line** \'ī-(ˌ)sō-ˌlīn\ *noun* (1944)
: a line on a map or chart along which there is a constant value (as of temperature or rainfall)

**iso·mer** \'ī-sə-mər\ *noun* [International Scientific Vocabulary, back-formation from *isomeric*] (1866)
**1** : one of two or more compounds, radicals, or ions that contain the same number of atoms of the same elements but differ in structural arrangement and properties
**2** : a nuclide isomeric with one or more others

**isom·er·ase** \ī-'sä-mə-ˌrās, -ˌrāz\ *noun* (1927)
: an enzyme that catalyzes the conversion of its substrate to an isomeric form

**iso·mer·ic** \ˌī-sə-'mer-ik\ *adjective* [German *isomerisch*, from Greek *isomerēs* equally divided, from *is-* + *meros* part — more at MERIT] (1838)
: of, relating to, or exhibiting isomerism

**isom·er·ism** \ī-'sä-mə-ˌri-zəm\ *noun* (1839)
**1** : the relationship of two or more chemical species that are isomers
**2** : the relation of two or more nuclides with the same mass numbers and atomic numbers but different energy states and rates of radioactive decay

**isom·er·ize** \ī-'sä-mə-ˌrīz\ *verb* **-ized; -iz·ing** (1891)
*intransitive verb*
: to become changed into an isomeric form
*transitive verb*
: to cause to isomerize
— **isom·er·i·za·tion** \-ˌsä-mə-rə-'zā-shən\ *noun*

**iso·met·ric** \ˌī-sə-'me-trik\ *adjective* (circa 1855)
**1** : of, relating to, or characterized by equality of measure; *especially* : relating to or being a crystallographic system characterized by three equal axes at right angles
**2** : of, relating to, involving, or being muscular contraction (as in isometrics) against resistance, without significant shortening of muscle fibers, and with marked increase in muscle tone — compare ISOTONIC
— **iso·met·ri·cal·ly** \-tri-k(ə-)lē\ *adverb*

**isometric line** *noun* (circa 1911)
**1** : a line representing changes of pressure or temperature under conditions of constant volume
**2** : a line (as a contour line) drawn on a map and indicating a true constant value throughout its extent

**iso·met·rics** \ˌī-sə-'me-triks\ *noun plural but singular or plural in construction* (1962)
: exercise or a system of exercises in which opposing muscles are so contracted that there

is little shortening but great increase in tone of muscle fibers involved

**isom·e·try** \ī-'sä-mə-trē\ *noun, plural* **-tries** (1941)
: a mapping of a metric space onto another or onto itself so that the distance between any two points in the original space is the same as the distance between their images in the second space ⟨rotation and translation are *isometries* of the plane⟩

**iso·mor·phic** \ˌī-sə-'mòr-fik\ *adjective* (1862)
**1 a** : being of identical or similar form, shape, or structure ⟨*isomorphic* crystals⟩ **b** : having sporophytic and gametophytic generations alike in size and shape
**2** : related by an isomorphism ⟨*isomorphic* mathematical rings⟩
— **iso·mor·phi·cal·ly** \-fi-k(ə-)lē\ *adverb*

**iso·mor·phism** \ˌī-sə-'mòr-ˌfi-zəm\ *noun* [International Scientific Vocabulary] (circa 1828)
**1** : the quality or state of being isomorphic: as
**a** : similarity in organisms of different ancestry resulting from convergence **b** : similarity of crystalline form between chemical compounds
**2** : a one-to-one correspondence between two mathematical sets; *especially* : a homomorphism that is one-to-one — compare ENDOMORPHISM

**iso·mor·phous** \ˌī-sə-'mòr-fəs\ *adjective* (circa 1828)
: ISOMORPHIC 1a
— **iso·morph** \'ī-sə-ˌmòrf\ *noun*

**iso·ni·a·zid** \ˌī-sə-'nī-ə-zəd\ *noun* [*is-* + nicotinic acid + hydr*azide*] (1952)
: a crystalline compound $C_6H_7N_3O$ used in treating tuberculosis

**iso·oc·tane** \ˌī-sō-'äk-ˌtān\ *noun* [International Scientific Vocabulary] (1909)
: an octane of branched-chain structure or a mixture of such octanes; *especially* : a flammable liquid octane used in determining the octane number of fuels

**iso·pach** \'ī-sə-ˌpak\ *noun* [*is-* + *-pach* (from Greek *pachys* thick) — more at PACHYDERM] (circa 1935)
: an isoline that connects points of equal thickness of a geological stratum formation or group of formations

**iso·phote** \'ī-sə-ˌfōt\ *noun* [International Scientific Vocabulary *is-* + *-phote* (from Greek *phōt-, phōs* light) — more at FANCY] (circa 1909)
: a curve on a chart joining points of equal light intensity from a given source
— **iso·phot·al** \ˌī-sə-'fō-təl\ *adjective*

**iso·pi·es·tic** \ˌī-sō-pē-'es-tik, -pī-\ *adjective* [*is-* + Greek *piestos*, verbal of *piezein* to press — more at PIEZO-] (1873)
: of, relating to, or marked by equal pressure

**iso·pleth** \'ī-sə-ˌpleth\ *noun* [International Scientific Vocabulary *is-* + Greek *plēthos* quantity; akin to Greek *plēthein* to be full — more at FULL] (1908)
**1** : an isoline on a graph showing the occurrence or frequency of a phenomenon as a function of two variables
**2** : a line on a map connecting points at which a given variable has a specified constant value
— **iso·pleth·ic** \ˌī-sə-'ple-thik\ *adjective*

**iso·pod** \'ī-sə-ˌpäd\ *noun* [ultimately from Greek *is-* + *pod-, pous* foot — more at FOOT] (circa 1835)
: any of a large order (Isopoda) of small sessile-eyed crustaceans with the body composed of seven free thoracic segments each bearing a pair of similar legs
— **isopod** *adjective*

**iso·pren·a·line** \ˌī-sə-'pre-nᵊl-ən\ *noun* [probably from *iso*propyl + ad*renaline*] (1951)

: ISOPROTERENOL

**iso·prene** \'ī-sə-ˌprēn\ noun [probably from is- + propyl + -ene] (1860)
: a flammable liquid unsaturated hydrocarbon $C_5H_8$ used especially in synthetic rubber

**iso·pren·oid** \ˌī-sə-'prē-ˌnȯid\ adjective (1940)
: relating to, containing, or being a branched-chain grouping characteristic of isoprene

**iso·pro·pyl** \ˌī-sə-'prō-pəl\ noun, often attributive [International Scientific Vocabulary] (1866)
: the alkyl radical isomeric with normal propyl — often used in combination

**isopropyl alcohol** noun (1872)
: a volatile flammable alcohol $C_3H_8O$ used especially as a solvent and rubbing alcohol

**iso·pro·ter·e·nol** \ˌī-sə-prō-'ter-ə-ˌnȯl, -ˌnōl\ noun [isopropyl + arterenol norepinephrine, from Arterenol, a trademark] (1957)
: a drug $C_{11}H_{17}NO_3$ used in the treatment of asthma

**iso·pyc·nic** \ˌī-sō-'pik-nik\ adjective [is- + Greek pyknos dense] (circa 1890)
1 : of, relating to, or marked by equal or constant density
2 : being or produced by a technique (as centrifugation) in which the components of a mixture are separated on the basis of differences in density

**isos·ce·les** \ī-'säs-ˌlēz, -'sä-sə-\ adjective [Late Latin isosceles having two equal sides, from Greek isoskelēs, from is- + skelos leg; perhaps akin to Old English sceol wry] (1551)
1 of a triangle : having two equal sides — see TRIANGLE illustration
2 of a trapezoid : having the two nonparallel sides equal

**is·os·mot·ic** \ˌī-säz-'mä-tik, -ˌsäs-\ adjective [International Scientific Vocabulary] (1895)
: of, relating to, or exhibiting equal osmotic pressure ⟨isosmotic solutions⟩
— **is·os·mot·i·cal·ly** \-'mä-ti-k(ə-)lē\ adverb

**iso·spin** \'ī-sə-ˌspin\ noun (1961)
: a quantum characteristic of a group of closely related subatomic particles (as a proton and a neutron) handled mathematically like ordinary spin with the possible orientations in a hypothetical space specifying the number of particles of differing electric charge comprising the group — called also isotopic spin

**isos·ta·sy** \ī-'säs-tə-sē\ noun [International Scientific Vocabulary is- + Greek -stasia condition of standing, from histanai to cause to stand — more at STAND] (1889)
1 : general equilibrium in the earth's crust maintained by a yielding flow of rock material beneath the surface under gravitative stress
2 : the quality or state of being subjected to equal pressure from every side
— **iso·stat·ic** \ˌī-sə-'sta-tik\ adjective
— **iso·stat·i·cal·ly** \-'sta-ti-k(ə-)lē\ adverb

**iso·tach** \'ī-sə-ˌtak\ noun [International Scientific Vocabulary is- + -tach (from Greek tachys quick)] (1947)
: a line on a map or chart connecting points of equal wind speed

**iso·tac·tic** \ˌī-sə-'tak-tik\ adjective (1955)
: having or relating to a stereochemical regularity of structure in the repeating units of a polymer — compare ATACTIC

**iso·therm** \'ī-sə-ˌthərm\ noun [French isotherme, adjective] (1859)
1 : a line on a map or chart of the earth's surface connecting points having the same temperature at a given time or the same mean temperature for a given period
2 : a line on a chart representing changes of volume or pressure under conditions of constant temperature

**iso·ther·mal** \ˌī-sə-'thər-məl\ adjective [French isotherme, from is- + -therme (from Greek thermos hot) — more at THERM] (1826)
1 : of, relating to, or marked by equality of temperature

2 : of, relating to, or marked by changes of volume or pressure under conditions of constant temperature
— **iso·ther·mal·ly** \-mə-lē\ adverb

**iso·ton·ic** \ˌī-sə-'tä-nik\ adjective [International Scientific Vocabulary] (1891)
1 : of, relating to, or being muscular contraction in the absence of significant resistance, with marked shortening of muscle fibers, and without great increase in muscle tone — compare ISOMETRIC
2 : ISOSMOTIC — used of solutions
— **iso·ton·i·cal·ly** \-ni-k(ə-)lē\ adverb
— **iso·to·nic·i·ty** \-tō-'ni-sə-tē\ noun

**iso·tope** \'ī-sə-ˌtōp\ noun [is- + Greek topos place] (1913)
1 : any of two or more species of atoms of a chemical element with the same atomic number and nearly identical chemical behavior but with differing atomic mass or mass number and different physical properties
2 : NUCLIDE
— **iso·to·pic** \ˌī-sə-'tä-pik, -'tō-\ adjective
— **iso·to·pi·cal·ly** \-'tä-pi-k(ə-)lē, -'tō-\ adverb

**isotopic spin** noun (1937)
: ISOSPIN

**iso·tro·pic** \ˌī-sə-'trō-pik, -'trä-\ adjective [International Scientific Vocabulary] (circa 1860)
: exhibiting properties (as velocity of light transmission) with the same values when measured along axes in all directions ⟨an isotropic crystal⟩
— **isot·ro·py** \ī-'sä-trə-pē\ noun

**iso·zyme** \'ī-sə-ˌzīm\ noun (1959)
: ISOENZYME
— **iso·zy·mic** \ˌī-sə-'zī-mik\ adjective

**Is·ra·el** \'iz-rē-əl, -(ˌ)rā- also 'is- or 'iz-rəl\ noun [Middle English, from Old English, from Late Latin, from Greek Israēl, from Hebrew Yiśrāʾēl]
1 : JACOB 2
2 : the Jewish people
3 : a people chosen by God
— **Israel** adjective

**¹Is·rae·li** \iz-'rā-lē also ˌiz-rə-'ā-lē\ adjective [New Hebrew yiśrĕʾēlī, from Hebrew, Israelite, noun & adjective, from Yiśrāʾēl] (1948)
: of or relating to the people or the republic of Israel

**²Israeli** noun, plural **Israelis** also **Israeli** (1948)
: a native or inhabitant of the republic of Israel

**¹Is·ra·el·ite** \'iz-r(ē-)ə-ˌlīt\ noun [Middle English, from Late Latin Israelita, from Greek Israēlitēs, from Israēl] (14th century)
: a descendant of the Hebrew patriarch Jacob; specifically : a native or inhabitant of the ancient northern kingdom of Israel

**²Israelite** adjective (1851)
: of or relating to Israel or to the Israelites

**Is·sa·char** \'i-sə-ˌkär\ noun [Late Latin, from Greek, from Hebrew Yiśśākhār]
: a son of Jacob and the traditional eponymous ancestor of one of the tribes of Israel

**is·sei** \(ˌ)ē-'sā, 'ē-ˌsā\ noun, plural **issei** often capitalized [Japanese, literally, first generation] (1937)
: a Japanese immigrant especially to the U.S.

**is·su·able** \'i-shü-ə-bəl\ adjective (circa 1570)
1 : open to contest, debate, or litigation
2 : authorized for issue ⟨bonds issuable under the merger terms⟩
3 : possible as a result or consequence
— **is·su·ably** \-blē\ adverb

**is·su·ance** \'i-shə-wən(t)s\ noun (1863)
: ISSUE 2, 9a

**is·su·ant** \-wənt\ adjective (1610)
1 of a heraldic animal : rising with only the upper part visible
2 archaic : coming forth : EMERGING

**¹is·sue** \'i-(ˌ)shü, chiefly Southern 'i-shə, chiefly British 'is-(ˌ)yü\ noun [Middle English, exit, proceeds, from Middle French, from Old French, from issir to come out, go out, from Latin exire to go out, from ex- + ire to go;

akin to Gothic iddja he went, Greek ienai to go, Sanskrit eti he goes] (14th century)
1 plural : proceeds from a source of revenue (as an estate)
2 : the action of going, coming, or flowing out : EGRESS, EMERGENCE
3 : a means or place of going out : EXIT, OUTLET
4 : OFFSPRING, PROGENY ⟨died without issue⟩
5 a : a final outcome that usually constitutes a solution (as of a problem) or resolution (as of a difficulty) b obsolete : a final conclusion or decision about something arrived at after consideration c archaic : TERMINATION, END ⟨hope that his enterprise would have a prosperous issue —T. B. Macaulay⟩
6 a : a matter that is in dispute between two or more parties b : the point at which an unsettled matter is ready for a decision ⟨brought the matter to an issue⟩
7 : a discharge (as of blood) from the body
8 a : something coming forth from a specified source ⟨issues of a disordered imagination⟩ b obsolete : DEED
9 a : the act of publishing or officially giving out or making available ⟨the next issue of commemorative stamps⟩ ⟨issue of supplies by the quartermaster⟩ b : the thing or the whole quantity of things given out at one time ⟨read the latest issue⟩
— **is·sue·less** \'i-shü-ləs\ adjective
— **at issue** 1 : in a state of controversy : in disagreement 2 also **in issue** : under discussion or in dispute

**²issue** verb **is·sued; is·su·ing** (14th century)
intransitive verb
1 a : to go, come, or flow out b : to come forth : EMERGE c : to come to an issue of law or fact in pleading
2 : ACCRUE ⟨profits issuing from the sale of the stock⟩
3 : to descend from a specified parent or ancestor
4 : to be a consequence or final outcome : EMANATE, RESULT
5 : to appear or become available through being officially put forth or distributed
6 : EVENTUATE, TERMINATE
transitive verb
1 : to cause to come forth : DISCHARGE, EMIT
2 a : to put forth or distribute usually officially ⟨government issued a new airmail stamp⟩ ⟨issue orders⟩ b : to send out for sale or circulation : PUBLISH c British : PROVIDE 2b, SUPPLY
synonym see SPRING
— **is·su·er** noun

**¹-ist** noun suffix [Middle English -iste, from Old French & Latin; Old French -iste, from Latin -ista, -istes, from Greek -istēs, from verbs in -izein -ize]
1 a : one that performs a (specified) action ⟨cyclist⟩ : one that makes or produces a (specified) thing ⟨novelist⟩ b : one that plays a (specified) musical instrument ⟨harpist⟩ c : one that operates a (specified) mechanical instrument or contrivance ⟨automobilist⟩
2 : one that specializes in a (specified) art or science or skill ⟨geologist⟩ ⟨ventriloquist⟩
3 : one that adheres to or advocates a (specified) doctrine or system or code of behavior ⟨socialist⟩ ⟨royalist⟩ ⟨hedonist⟩ or that of a (specified) individual ⟨Calvinist⟩ ⟨Darwinist⟩

**²-ist** adjective suffix
: of, relating to, or characteristic of ⟨elitist⟩

**¹isth·mi·an** \'is-mē-ən\ noun (1601)
1 : a native or inhabitant of an isthmus
2 capitalized : a native or inhabitant of the Isthmus of Panama

**²isthmian** adjective (1603)
: of, relating to, or situated in or near an isthmus: as a often capitalized : of or relating to the Isthmus of Corinth in Greece or the games

held there in ancient times **b** *often capitalized* **:** of or relating to the Isthmus of Panama connecting the North American and South American continents

**isth·mic** \'is-mik\ *adjective* (1585)
**:** of or relating to an anatomical isthmus

**isth·mus** \'is-məs\ *noun* [Latin, from Greek *isthmos*] (1555)
**1 :** a narrow strip of land connecting two larger land areas
**2 :** a narrow anatomical part or passage connecting two larger structures or cavities

**is·tle** \'ist-lē\ *noun* [American Spanish *ixtle*, from Nahuatl *īchtli*] (1883)
**:** a strong fiber (as for cordage or basketwork) from various tropical American plants (as of the genus *Agave*)

**¹it** \'it, ət\ *pronoun* [Middle English, from Old English *hit* — more at HE] (before 12th century)
**1 :** that one — used as subject or direct object or indirect object of a verb or object of a preposition usually in reference to a lifeless thing ⟨took a quick look at the house and noticed *it* was very old⟩, a plant ⟨there is a rosebush near the fence and *it* is now blooming⟩, a person or animal whose sex is unknown or disregarded ⟨don't know who *it* is⟩, a group of individuals or things, or an abstract entity ⟨beauty is everywhere and *it* is a source of joy⟩; compare HE, ITS, SHE, THEY
**2** — used as subject of an impersonal verb that expresses a condition or action without reference to an agent ⟨*it* is raining⟩
**3 a** — used as anticipatory subject or object of a verb ⟨*it* is necessary to repeat the whole thing⟩; often used to shift emphasis to a part of a statement other than the subject ⟨*it* was in this city that the treaty was signed⟩ **b** — used with many verbs as a direct object with little or no meaning ⟨footed *it* back to camp⟩
**4** — used to refer to an explicit or implicit state of affairs or circumstances ⟨how is *it* going⟩
**5 :** a crucial or climactic point ⟨this is *it*⟩

**²it** \'it\ *noun* (1842)
**:** the player in a game who performs the principal action of the game (as trying to find others in hide-and-seek)

**it·a·con·ic acid** \,i-tə-'kä-nik-\ *noun* [International Scientific Vocabulary, anagram of *aconitic acid*, $C_3H_3(COOH)_3$, from *aconite*] (circa 1872)
**:** a crystalline dicarboxylic acid $C_5H_6O_4$ obtained usually by fermentation of sugars with molds (genus *Aspergillus*) and used as a monomer for polymers and polyesters

**¹Ital·ian** \ə-'tal-yən, i- *also* ,ī-\ *noun* (14th century)
**1 a :** a native or inhabitant of Italy **b :** a person of Italian descent
**2 :** the Romance language of the Italians

**²Italian** *adjective* (15th century)
**:** of, relating to, or characteristic of Italy, the Italians, or Italian

**ital·ian·ate** \-yə-,nāt\ *transitive verb* **-at·ed; -at·ing** *often capitalized* (1553)
**:** ITALIANIZE

**Ital·ian·ate** \-nət, -,nāt\ *adjective* (1572)
**:** Italian in quality or characteristics

**Italian dressing** *noun* (circa 1902)
**:** a salad dressing flavored especially with garlic and oregano

**Italian grey·hound** *noun* (1743)
**:** any of a breed of toy dogs resembling the standard greyhound in miniature

**ital·ian·ise** *often capitalized, British variant of* ITALIANIZE

**Italian greyhound**

**Ital·ian·ism** \ə-'tal-yə-,ni-zəm, i- *also* ,ī-\ *noun* (1594)
**1 a :** a quality characteristic of Italy or the Italian people **b :** a characteristic feature of Italian occurring in another language
**2 a :** specialized interest in or emulation of Italian qualities or achievements **b :** promotion or love of Italian policies or ideals

**ital·ian·ize** \ə-'tal-yə-,nīz, i- *also* ,ī-\ *verb* **-ized; -iz·ing** *often capitalized* (circa 1611)
*intransitive verb*
**:** to act Italian; *specifically* **:** to follow the style or technique of recognized Italian painters
*transitive verb*
**:** to make Italian (as in appearance or behavior)
— **Ital·ian·i·za·tion** \-,tal-yə-nə-'zā-shən\ *noun*

**Italian sandwich** *noun* (circa 1953)
**:** SUBMARINE 2

**Italian sonnet** *noun* (1879)
**:** a sonnet consisting of an octave rhyming *abba abba* and a sestet rhyming in any of various patterns (as *cde cde* or *cdc dcd*) — called also *Petrarchan sonnet*

**¹ital·ic** \ə-'ta-lik, i-, ī-\ *adjective* (1612)
**1 a :** of or relating to a type style with characters that slant upward to the right (as in "*these words are italic*") — compare ROMAN **b :** of or relating to a style of slanted cursive handwriting developed in the 15th and 16th centuries
**2** *capitalized* **:** of or relating to ancient Italy, its peoples, or their Indo-European languages

**²italic** *noun* (1676)
**1 :** an italic character or type
**2** *capitalized* **:** a branch of the Indo-European language family that includes Latin, Oscan, and Umbrian — see INDO-EUROPEAN LANGUAGES table

**ital·i·cise** *British variant of* ITALICIZE

**ital·i·cize** \ə-'ta-lə-,sīz, i-, ī-\ *transitive verb* **-cized; -ciz·ing** (1795)
**1 :** to print in italics or underscore with a single line
**2 :** EMPHASIZE ⟨the microphone *italicizes* every curdled top note —P. G. Davis⟩
— **ital·i·ci·za·tion** \-,ta-lə-sə-'zā-shən\ *noun*

**Ita·lo-** \i-'ta-lō *also* 'i-t°l-ō\ *combining form*
**1 :** Italian ⟨*Italo*phile⟩
**2 :** Italian and ⟨*Italo*-Austrian⟩

**Ita·lo·phile** \i-'ta-lə-,fīl\ *adjective* (circa 1902)
**:** friendly to or favoring what is Italian
— **Italophile** *noun*

**¹itch** \'ich\ *verb* [Middle English *icchen*, from Old English *giccan*; akin to Old High German *jucchen* to itch] (before 12th century)
*intransitive verb*
**1 a :** to have an itch ⟨her arm *itched*⟩ **b :** to produce an itchy sensation ⟨long underwear that *itches*⟩
**2 :** to have a restless desire or hankering for something ⟨were *itching* to go outside⟩
*transitive verb*
**1 :** to cause to itch
**2 :** VEX, IRRITATE

**²itch** *noun* (before 12th century)
**1 a :** an uneasy irritating sensation in the upper surface of the skin usually held to result from mild stimulation of pain receptors **b :** a skin disorder accompanied by such a sensation; *especially* **:** a contagious eruption caused by a mite (*Sarcoptes scabiei*) that burrows in the skin and causes intense itching
**2 a :** a restless usually constant often compulsive desire ⟨an *itch* to travel⟩ **b :** LUST, PRURIENCE
— **itch·i·ness** \'i-chē-nəs\ *noun*
— **itchy** \'i-chē\ *adjective*

**it'd** \'i-təd, ,id\ (1859)
**:** it had **:** it would

**¹-ite** *noun suffix* [Middle English, from Old French & Latin; Old French, from Latin *-ita, -ites*, from Greek *-itēs*]
**1 a :** native **:** resident ⟨Brooklyn*ite*⟩ **b :** descendant ⟨Ephraim*ite*⟩ **c :** adherent **:** follower ⟨Jacob*ite*⟩ ⟨Pusey*ite*⟩

**2 a** (1) **:** product ⟨metabol*ite*⟩ (2) **:** commercially manufactured product ⟨ebon*ite*⟩ **b :** -ITOL ⟨mann*ite*⟩
**3** [New Latin *-ites*, from Latin] **:** fossil ⟨ammon*ite*⟩
**4 :** mineral ⟨erythr*ite*⟩ **:** rock ⟨anorthos*ite*⟩
**5** [French, from Latin *-ita, -ites*] **:** segment or constituent part of a body or of a bodily part ⟨som*ite*⟩ ⟨dendr*ite*⟩

**²-ite** *noun suffix* [French, alteration of *-ate* -ate, from New Latin *-atum*]
**:** salt or ester of an acid with a name ending in *-ous* ⟨nitr*ite*⟩

**¹item** \'ī-,tem, 'ī-təm\ *adverb* [Middle English, from Latin, from *ita* thus] (14th century)
**:** and in addition **:** ALSO — used to introduce each article in a list or enumeration

**²item** \'ī-təm\ *noun* (1571)
**1** *obsolete* **:** WARNING, HINT
**2 :** a distinct part in an enumeration, account, or series **:** ARTICLE
**3 :** an object of attention, concern, or interest
**4 :** a separate piece of news or information
**5 :** a couple in a romantic or sexual relationship ☆

**³item** \'ī-təm\ *transitive verb* (1601)
**1** *archaic* **:** COMPUTE, RECKON
**2** *archaic* **:** to set down the particular details of

**item·ise** *British variant of* ITEMIZE

**item·i·za·tion** \,ī-tə-mə-'zā-shən\ *noun* (1894)
**:** the act of itemizing; *also* **:** an itemized list

**item·ize** \'ī-tə-,mīz\ *transitive verb* **-ized; -iz·ing** (1857)
**:** to set down in detail or by particulars **:** LIST ⟨*itemized* all expenses⟩

**it·er·ance** \'i-tə-rən(t)s\ *noun* (1604)
**:** REPETITION

**it·er·ant** \-rənt\ *adjective* (1626)
**:** marked by repetition, reiteration, or recurrence ⟨*iterant* echoes⟩

**it·er·ate** \'i-tə-,rāt\ *transitive verb* **-at·ed; -at·ing** [Latin *iteratus*, past participle of *iterare*, from *iterum* again; akin to Latin *is* he, that, *ita* thus, Sanskrit *itara* the other, *iti* thus] (1533)
**:** to say or do again or again and again **:** REITERATE

**it·er·a·tion** \,i-tə-'rā-shən\ *noun* (15th century)
**1 :** the action or a process of iterating or repeating: as **a :** a procedure in which repetition of a sequence of operations yields results successively closer to a desired result **b :** the repetition of a sequence of computer instructions a specified number of times or until a condition is met — compare RECURSION
**2 :** one execution of a sequence of operations or instructions in an iteration

**it·er·a·tive** \'i-tə-,rā-tiv, -rə-\ *adjective* (15th century)
**:** involving repetition: as **a :** expressing repetition of a verbal action **b :** relating to or being iteration of an operation or procedure
— **it·er·a·tive·ly** *adverb*

---

☆ **SYNONYMS**
**Item, detail, particular** mean one of the distinct parts of a whole. ITEM applies to each thing specified separately in a list or in a group of things that might be listed or enumerated ⟨every *item* on the list⟩. DETAIL applies to one of the small component parts of a larger whole such as a task, building, painting, narration, or process ⟨leave the *details* to others⟩. PARTICULAR stresses the smallness, singleness, and especially the concreteness of a detail or item ⟨a description that included few *particulars*⟩.

---

**ithy·phal·lic** \ˌi-thi-'fa-lik\ *adjective* [Late Latin *ithyphallicus,* from Greek *ithyphallikos,* from *ithyphallos* erect phallus, from *ithys* straight + *phallos* phallus] (1795)
**1 :** of or relating to the phallus carried in procession in ancient festivals of Bacchus
**2 a :** having an erect penis — usually used of figures in an art representation **b :** OBSCENE, LEWD
**itin·er·an·cy** \ī-'ti-nə-rən(t)-sē\ *noun* (1789)
**1 :** a system (as in the Methodist Church) of rotating ministers who itinerate
**2 a :** the act of itinerating **b :** the state of being itinerant
**itin·er·ant** \-rənt\ *adjective* [Late Latin *itinerant-, itinerans,* present participle of *itinerari* to journey, from Latin *itiner-, iter* journey, way; akin to Hittite *itar* way, Latin *ire* to go — more at ISSUE] (circa 1576)
**:** traveling from place to place; *especially* **:** covering a circuit ⟨*itinerant* preacher⟩
— **itinerant** *noun*
— **itin·er·ant·ly** *adverb*
**itin·er·ary** \ī-'ti-nə-ˌrer-ē, ə-, *chiefly British* ÷-'ti-nə-rē\ *noun, plural* **-ar·ies** (15th century)
**1 :** the route of a journey or tour or the proposed outline of one
**2 :** a travel diary
**3 :** a traveler's guidebook
— **itinerary** *adjective*
**itin·er·ate** \ī-'ti-nə-ˌrāt, ə-\ *intransitive verb* **-at·ed; -at·ing** (1775)
**:** to travel a preaching or judicial circuit
— **itin·er·a·tion** \-ˌti-nə-'rā-shən\ *noun*
**-itious** *adjective suffix* [Latin *-icius, -itius*]
**:** of, relating to, or having the characteristics of ⟨excrement*itious*⟩
**-itis** *noun suffix, plural* **-itises** *also* **-itides** *or* **-ites** [New Latin, from Latin & Greek; Latin, from Greek, from feminine of *-itēs* -ite]
**1 :** disease or inflammation ⟨bronch*itis*⟩
**2** *plural usually* **-itises :** condition likened to a disease — chiefly in nonce formations ⟨tele·vision*itis*⟩
**it·ll** \'i-t°l\ (1824)
**:** it will **:** it shall
**-itol** *noun suffix* [International Scientific Vocabulary ¹*-ite* + ¹*-ol*]
**:** polyhydroxy alcohol usually related to a sugar ⟨mann*itol*⟩
**its** \'its, əts\ *adjective* (1598)
**:** of or relating to it or itself especially as possessor, agent, or object of an action ⟨going to *its* kennel⟩ ⟨a child proud of *its* first drawings⟩ ⟨*its* final enactment into law⟩
**it's** \'its, əts\ (circa 1555)
**:** it is **:** it has
**it·self** \it-'self, ət-, *Southern also* -'sef\ *pronoun* (before 12th century)
**1 :** that identical one — compare IT 1; used reflexively ⟨watched the cat giving *itself* a bath⟩, for emphasis ⟨the letter *itself* was missing⟩, or in absolute constructions ⟨*itself* a splendid specimen of classic art, it has been exhibited throughout the world⟩
**2 :** its normal, healthy, or sane condition
— **in itself :** in its own nature **:** INTRINSICALLY ⟨was not *in itself* bad⟩
**it·ty-bit·ty** \ˌi-tē-'bi-tē\ *or* **it·sy-bit·sy** \ˌit-sē-'bit-sē\ *adjective* [probably from baby talk for *little bit*] (1938)
**:** extremely small **:** TINY
**-ity** *noun suffix, plural* **-ities** [Middle English *-ite,* from Old French or Latin; Old French *-ité,* from Latin *-itat-, -itas,* from *-i-* (stem vowel of adjectives) + *-tat-, -tas* -ity; akin to Greek *-tēt-, -tēs* -ity]
**:** quality **:** state **:** degree ⟨alkalin*ity*⟩ ⟨theatrical*ity*⟩
**IUD** \ˌī-(ˌ)yü-'dē\ *noun* (1965)
**:** INTRAUTERINE DEVICE
**-ium** *noun suffix*
**1** [New Latin, from Latin, ending of some neuter nouns] **a :** a chemical element ⟨sod*ium*⟩ **b :** cation ⟨tetrazol*ium*⟩

**2** *plural* **-iums** *or* **-ia** [New Latin, from Latin, from Greek *-ion*] **:** small one **:** mass — especially in botanical terms ⟨pollin*ium*⟩
**IV** \ˌī-'vē\ *noun, plural* **IVs** [intravenous] (circa 1955)
**:** an apparatus used to administer an intravenous injection or feeding; *also* **:** such an injection or feeding
**-ive** *adjective suffix* [Middle English *-if, -ive,* from Middle French & Latin; Middle French *-if,* from Latin *-ivus*]
**:** that performs or tends toward an (indicated) action ⟨amus*ive*⟩
**I've** \'īv\ (1586)
**:** I have
**iver·mec·tin** \ˌī-vər-'mek-tən\ *noun* [perhaps from d*i-* + New Latin a*vermitilis* (specific epithet of *Streptomyces avermitilis,* bacterium from which it is derived) + English *-ect-* (of unknown origin) + ¹*-in*] (1981)
**:** a drug mixture of two structurally similar semisynthetic lactones that is used in veterinary medicine as an anthelmintic, acaricide, and insecticide and in human medicine to treat onchocerciasis
**ivied** \'ī-vēd\ *adjective* (circa 1771)
**1 :** overgrown with ivy
**2 :** ACADEMIC
**ivo·ry** \'īv-rē, 'ī-və-rē\ *noun, plural* **-ries** [Middle English *ivorie,* from Old French *ivoire,* from Latin *eboreus* of ivory, from *ebor-, ebur* ivory, from Egyptian *ʾb, ʾbw* elephant, ivory] (13th century)
**1 a :** the hard creamy-white modified dentine that composes the tusks of a tusked mammal (as an elephant, walrus, or narwhal) **b :** a tusk that yields ivory
**2 :** a variable color averaging a pale yellow
**3** *slang* **:** TOOTH
**4 :** something (as a piano key) made of ivory or of a similar substance
— **ivory** *adjective*
**ivo·ry-bill** \-ˌbil\ *noun* (1787)
**:** IVORY-BILLED WOODPECKER
**ivo·ry–billed woodpecker** \-'bild-\ *noun* (1811)
**:** a very large black-and-white woodpecker (*Campephilus principalis*) of the southeastern U.S. and Cuba that has a showy red crest in the male and is presumed extinct in the U.S.
**ivory black** *noun* (1634)
**:** a fine black pigment made by calcining ivory
**ivory nut** *noun* (circa 1847)
**:** the nutlike seed of a South American palm (*Phytelephas macrocarpa*) containing a very hard endosperm used for carving and turning — compare VEGETABLE IVORY

ivory-billed
woodpecker

**ivory tower** *noun* [translation of French *tour d'ivoire*] (1911)
**1 :** an impractical often escapist attitude marked by aloof lack of concern with or interest in practical matters or urgent problems
**2 :** a secluded place that affords the means of treating practical issues with an impractical often escapist attitude; *especially* **:** a place of learning
— **ivory–tower** *adjective*
— **ivo·ry–tow·er·ish** \-'taủ-(ə-)rish\ *adjective*
**ivo·ry–tow·ered** \-'taủ-(-ə)rd\ *adjective* (1937)
**:** divorced from reality and practical matters ⟨an *ivory-towered* recluse⟩
**¹ivy** \'ī-vē\ *noun, plural* **ivies** [Middle English, from Old English *ïfig;* akin to Old High German *ebah* ivy] (before 12th century)
**1 :** a widely cultivated ornamental climbing or prostrate or sometimes shrubby chiefly Eurasian vine (*Hedera helix*) of the ginseng fami-

ly with evergreen leaves, small yellowish flowers, and black berries
**2 :** POISON IVY
**3** *often capitalized* **:** an Ivy League college

**²ivy** *adjective* [from the prevalence of ivy-covered buildings on the campuses of older U.S. colleges] (1933)
**1 :** ACADEMIC
**2 :** IVY LEAGUE

ivy 1

**Ivy League** *adjective* (1939)
**1 :** of, relating to, or characteristic of a group of long-established eastern U.S. colleges widely regarded as high in scholastic and social prestige
**2 :** of, relating to, or characteristic of the students of Ivy League colleges
**Ivy Leaguer** *noun* (1943)
**:** a student at or a graduate of an Ivy League college
**iwis** \ē-'wis, ī-\ *adverb* [Middle English, from Old English *gewis* certain; akin to Old High German *giwisso* certainly, Old English *witan* to know — more at WIT] (12th century) *archaic* **:** SURELY
**Ix·i·on** \ik-'sī-ən\ *noun* [Latin, from Greek *Ix·iōn*]
**:** a Thessalian king bound by Zeus to a burning wheel in Tartarus for attempting to seduce Hera
**ix·o·did** \'ik-sə-ˌdid, ik-'sō-dəd\ *adjective* [ultimately from Greek *ixōdēs* sticky, from *ixos* birdlime] (circa 1909)
**:** of, relating to, or being a typical tick (family Ixodidae)
— **ixodid** *noun*
**Iyar** \'ē-ˌyär\ *noun* [Hebrew *Iyyār*] (1737)
**:** the 8th month of the civil year or the 2d month of the ecclesiastical year in the Jewish calendar — see MONTH table
**-i·za·tion** \ə-'zā-shən *also* (ˌ)ī-'zā-\ *noun suffix*
**:** action, process, or result of making ⟨social·*ization*⟩
**-ize** *verb suffix* [Middle English *-isen,* from Old French *-iser,* from Late Latin *-izare,* from Greek *-izein*]
**1 a (1) :** cause to be or conform to or resemble ⟨system*ize*⟩ ⟨American*ize*⟩ **:** cause to be formed into ⟨union*ize*⟩ **(2) :** subject to a (specified) action ⟨plagiar*ize*⟩ **(3) :** impregnate or treat or combine with ⟨alumin*ize*⟩ **b :** treat like ⟨idol*ize*⟩ **c :** treat according to the method of ⟨bowdler*ize*⟩
**2 a :** become **:** become like ⟨crystall*ize*⟩ **b :** be productive in or of ⟨hypothes*ize*⟩ **:** engage in a (specified) activity ⟨philosoph*ize*⟩ **c :** adopt or spread the manner of activity or the teaching of ⟨Platon*ize*⟩ ∎
**iz·zard** \'i-zərd\ *noun* [alteration of earlier *ezod, ezed,* probably from Middle French *et zede* and Z] (circa 1726)
*chiefly dialect* **:** the letter *z*

**J**

J *is the tenth letter of the English alphabet. In Latin i was used for either a vowel sound or for a consonant sound like the y in English yet. The letter form j was developed as a lengthened form of i during the Middle Ages and was used in certain positions, such as at the beginning of a word as an equivalent for the shorter form. In those positions it had exactly the same value as i. Because the initial i was usually consonantal, the j that so often took its place gradually became differentiated from i in sound as well as form. It was not, however, until the 17th century that the distinction of j as a consonant and i as a vowel was fully established and the capital form J introduced. In English, what is now the regular sound of j, as in jet, dates from the 11th century. It came with the Normans from the continent, where it was the consonant sound of i and j in French.*

---

**j** \'jā\ *noun, plural* **j's** *or* **js** \'jāz\ *often capitalized, often attributive* (15th century)
**1 a :** the 10th letter of the English alphabet **b :** a speech counterpart of orthographic *j*
**2 a :** a graphic device for reproducing the letter *j* **b :** a unit vector parallel to the y-axis
**3 :** one designated *j* especially as the 10th in order or class
**4 :** something shaped like the letter J
**¹jab** \'jab\ *verb* **jabbed; jab·bing** [alteration of *job* to strike] (1827)
*transitive verb*
**1 a :** to pierce with or as if with a sharp object **:** STAB **b :** to poke quickly or abruptly **:** THRUST
**2 :** to strike with a short straight blow
*intransitive verb*
**1 :** to make quick or abrupt thrusts with a sharp object
**2 :** to strike a person with a short straight blow
**²jab** *noun* (1872)
**:** an act of jabbing; *especially* **:** a short straight boxing punch delivered with the leading hand
**¹jab·ber** \'ja-bər\ *verb* **jab·bered; jab·ber·ing** \'ja-b(ə-)riŋ\ [Middle English *jaberen*, of imitative origin] (15th century)
*intransitive verb*
**:** to talk rapidly, indistinctly, or unintelligibly
*transitive verb*
**:** to speak rapidly or indistinctly
— **jab·ber·er** \'ja-bər-ər\ *noun*
**²jabber** *noun* (1727)
**:** GIBBERISH, CHATTER
**jab·ber·wocky** \'ja-bər-,wä-kē\ *noun* [*Jabberwocky*, nonsense poem by Lewis Carroll] (1908)
**:** meaningless speech or writing ◆
**jab·i·ru** \,zha-bə-'rü\ *noun* [Portuguese, from Tupi & Guarani *jabirú*] (1774)
**:** any of several large tropical storks
**jab·o·ran·di** \,zha-bə-,ran-'dē, -'ran-dē\ *noun* [Portuguese, from Tupi *yaborandí*] (circa 1875)
**:** the dried leaves of two South American shrubs (*Pilocarpus jaborandi* and *P. microphyllus*) of the rue family that are a source of pilocarpine
**ja·bot** \zha-'bō, 'ja-,bō\ *noun* [French] (1823)
**1 :** a fall of lace or cloth attached to the front of a neckband and worn especially by men in the 18th century
**2 :** a pleated frill of cloth or lace attached down the center front of a woman's blouse or dress
**ja·bo·ti·ca·ba** \zhə-,bü-ti-'kä-bə\ *noun* [Portuguese, from Tupi] (1824)
**:** a Brazilian tree (*Myrciaria cauliflora*) of the myrtle family cultivated in warm regions for its edible usually purplish fruit

jabot 1

**ja·cal** \hə-'käl\ *noun, plural* **ja·ca·les** \-'kä-(,)lās\ *also* **ja·cals** [Mexican Spanish, from Nahuatl *xahcalli*] (1838)
**:** a hut in Mexico and southwestern U.S. with a thatched roof and walls made of upright poles or sticks covered and chinked with mud or clay
**jac·a·mar** \'zha-kə-,mär\ *noun* [French, from Tupi *jacamá-ciri*] (1825)
**:** any of a family (Galbulidae) of usually iridescent green or bronze insectivorous birds of Central and South American tropical forests
**ja·ca·na** \jə-'kä-nə, ,zha-sə°n-'a°\ *noun* [Portuguese *jaçaná*, from Tupi & Guarani] (circa 1753)
**:** any of a family (Jacanidae) of long-legged and long-toed tropical wading birds that frequent coastal freshwater marshes and ponds
**jac·a·ran·da** \,ja-kə-'ran-də\ *noun* [New Latin, from Portuguese *jacarandá* a tree of this genus, from Tupi] (circa 1753)
**:** any of a genus (*Jacaranda*) of pinnate-leaved tropical American trees of the trumpet-creeper family with showy usually blue flowers in panicles
**ja·cinth** \'jā-sə°n(t)th, 'ja-\ *noun* [Middle English *iacinct*, from Old French *jacinthe*, from Latin *hyacinthus*, a flowering plant, a gem] (13th century)
**1 :** HYACINTH
**2 :** a gem more nearly orange in color than a hyacinth
**¹jack** \'jak\ *noun* [Middle English *Jacke*, familiar term of address to a social inferior, nickname for *Johan* John] (1548)
**1 a :** MAN — usually used as an intensive in such phrases as *every man jack* **b** *often capitalized* **:** SAILOR **c** (1) **:** SERVANT, LABORER (2) **:** LUMBERJACK
**2 :** any of various usually mechanical devices: as **a :** a device for turning a spit **b :** a usually portable mechanism or device for exerting pressure or lifting a heavy body a short distance
**3 :** something that supports or holds in position: as **a :** an iron bar at a topgallant masthead to support a royal mast and spread the royal shrouds **b :** a wooden brace fastened behind a scenic unit in a stage set to prop it up
**4 a :** any of several fishes; *especially* **:** any of various carangids **b :** a male donkey **c :** JACK-RABBIT **d :** any of several birds (as a jackdaw)
**5 a :** a small white target ball in lawn bowling **b :** a small national flag flown by a ship **c** (1) *plural but singular in construction* **:** a game played with a set of small objects that are tossed, caught, and moved in various figures (2) **:** a small 6-pointed metal object used in the game of jacks
**6 a :** a playing card carrying the figure of a soldier or servant and ranking usually below the queen **b :** JACKPOT 1a(2)
**7** *slang* **:** MONEY

**8 :** a female fitting in an electric circuit used with a plug to make a connection with another circuit
**9 a :** APPLEJACK **b :** BRANDY
**10 :** JACKKNIFE 2
**11 :** MONTEREY JACK
**²jack** (circa 1841)
*intransitive verb*
**:** to hunt or fish at night with a jacklight
*transitive verb*
**1 :** to hunt or fish for at night with a jacklight
**2 a :** to move or lift by or as if by a jack **b :** to raise the level of — usually used with *up* 〈*jack* up the price〉 **c :** to take to task
— **jack·er** *noun*
**jack·al** \'ja-kəl *also* -,kól\ *noun* [Turkish *çakal*, from Persian *shagāl*, of Indo-Aryan origin; akin to Sanskrit *sṛgāla* jackal] (1603)
**1 :** any of several small omnivorous canids (as *Canis aureus*) of Africa and Asia having large ears, long legs, and bushy tails
**2 a :** a person who performs routine or menial tasks for another **b :** a person who serves or collaborates with another especially in the commission of base acts
**Jack–a–Lent** \'ja-kə-,lent\ *noun* [¹*jack* + *a* (of) + *Lent*] (1598)
**1 :** a small stuffed puppet set up to be pelted for fun in Lent
**2 :** a simple or insignificant person
**jack·a·napes** \'ja-kə-,nāps\ *noun* [Middle English *Jack Napis*, nickname for William de la Pole (died 1450) duke of Suffolk] (1526)
**1 :** MONKEY, APE
**2 a :** an impudent or conceited fellow **b :** a saucy or mischievous child
**jack·ass** \'jak-,as\ *noun* (1727)
**1 :** DONKEY; *especially* **:** a male donkey
**2 :** a stupid person **:** FOOL
**jack·ass·ery** \'jak-,a-sə-rē, -,as-rē\ *noun, plural* **-er·ies** (1833)
**:** foolish action or behavior
**jack bean** *noun* (1885)
**:** a bushy annual tropical American legume (genus *Canavalia*); *especially* **:** a plant (*C. ensiformis*) grown especially for forage
**jack·boot** \'jak-,büt\ *noun* (1686)
**1 :** a heavy military boot made of glossy black leather extending above the knee and worn especially during the 17th and 18th centuries
**2 :** the spirit or policy of militarism or totalitarianism
**3 :** a laceless military boot reaching to the calf
**jack·boot·ed** \-,bü-təd\ *adjective* (1846)
**1 :** wearing jackboots
**2 :** ruthlessly and violently oppressive 〈*jackbooted* force〉

---

◇ WORD HISTORY

**jabberwocky** Lewis Carroll's poem "Jabberwocky," published in *Through the Looking-Glass*, the second of his Alice-in-Wonderland books, is a wonderful example of nonsense verse. In the opening lines "Twas brillig and the slithy toves/Did gyre and gimble in the wabe," the words appear to be English, and we can tell which are nouns, adjectives, and verbs, but as evocative as they are they mean nothing. Lewis Carroll simply created them for the purposes of the poem. The word *jabberwocky*, a mock derivative of *jabberwock*, the fantastic monster in the poem, has become a generic term for words (or sometimes acts) that seem as though they should make sense but do not. In one bound *jabberwocky* has leapt from nonsense to metalanguage (language we use to talk about language).

---

\ə\ **abut**   \ə'\ **kitten**   \ər\ **further**   \a\ **ash**   \ā\ **ace**
\ä\ **mop, mar**   \aú\ **out**   \ch\ **chin**   \e\ **bet**   \ē\ **easy**
\g\ **go**   \i\ **hit**   \ī\ **ice**   \j\ **job**   \ŋ\ **sing**   \ō\ **go**
\ó\ **law**   \ói\ **boy**   \th\ **thin**   \th\ **the**   \ü\ **loot**   \ú\ **foot**
\y\ **yet**   \zh\ **vision**   *see also* Guide to Pronunciation

**jack cheese** *noun, often J capitalized* [alteration of David *Jacks,* 19th century California landowner] (1912)
**:** MONTEREY JACK

**jack crevalle** *noun* (1948)
**:** a carangid fish (*Caranx hippos*) that is an important food fish along the west coast of Florida

**jack·daw** \'jak-,dò\ *noun* (1543)
**1 :** a common black and gray bird (*Corvus monedula*) of Eurasia and northern Africa that is related to but smaller than the common crow
**2 :** GRACKLE 1

¹**jack·et** \'ja-kət\ *noun* [Middle English *jaket,* from Middle French *jaquet,* diminutive of *jaque* short jacket, from *jacque* peasant, from the name *Jacques* James] (15th century)
**1 a :** a garment for the upper body usually having a front opening, collar, lapels, sleeves, and pockets **b :** something worn or fastened around the body but not for use as clothing
**2 a** (1) **:** the natural covering of an animal (2) **:** the fur or wool of a mammal **b :** the skin of a potato
**3 :** an outer covering or casing: as **a** (1) **:** a thermally nonconducting cover (2) **:** a covering that encloses an intermediate space through which an temperature-controlling fluid circulates (3) **:** a tough cold-worked metal casing that forms the outer shell of a built-up bullet **b** (1) **:** a wrapper or open envelope for a document (2) **:** an envelope for enclosing registered mail during delivery from one post office to another **c** (1) **:** a detachable protective cover for a book (2) **:** a paper or paperboard envelope for a phonograph record
**— jack·et·less** \-ləs\ *adjective*

²**jacket** *transitive verb* (1856)
**:** to put a jacket on **:** enclose in or with a jacket

**Jack Frost** *noun* (1826)
**:** frost or frosty weather personified

**jack·fruit** \'jak-,früt\ *noun* [Portuguese *jaca* jackfruit, from Malayalam *cakka*] (1830)
**:** a large tropical Asian tree (*Artocarpus heterophyllus*) related to the breadfruit that yields a fine-grained yellow wood and immense fruits which contain an edible pulp and nutritious seeds; *also* **:** its fruit

**jack·ham·mer** \'jak-,ha-mər\ *noun* (1916)
**1 :** a pneumatically operated percussive rock-drilling tool usually held in the hands
**2 :** a device in which a tool (as a chisel for breaking up pavements) is driven percussively by compressed air
**— jackhammer** *verb*

**jack–in–the–box** \'ja-kən-thə-,bäks\ *noun, plural* **jack–in–the–box·es** *or* **jacks–in–the–box** (1702)
**:** a toy consisting of a small box out of which a figure (as of a clown's head) springs when the lid is raised

**jack–in–the–pul·pit** \,ja-kən-thə-'púl-,pit, -pət *also* -'pəl-\ *noun, plural* **jack–in–the–pulpits** *or* **jacks–in–the–pulpit** (1837)
**:** an American spring-flowering woodland herb (*Arisaema triphyllum* synonym *A. atrorubens*) of the arum family having an upright club-shaped spadix arched over by a green and purple spathe

¹**jack·knife** \'jak-,nīf\ *noun* (1711)
**1 :** a large strong pocket-knife
**2 :** a dive executed headfirst in which the diver bends from the waist and touches the ankles while holding the knees unbent and then straightens out

jack-in-the-pulpit

²**jackknife** (1806) *transitive verb*
**1 :** to cut with a jackknife

**2 :** to cause to double up like a jackknife
*intransitive verb*
**1 :** to double up like a jackknife
**2 :** to turn and form an angle of 90 degrees or less with each other — used especially of a tractor-trailer combination

**jack·leg** \'jak-,leg, -,lāg\ *adjective* [¹*jack* + -*leg* (as in *blackleg*)] (1850)
**1 a :** lacking skill or training **:** AMATEUR ⟨a *jackleg* carpenter⟩ **b :** characterized by unscrupulousness, dishonesty, or lack of professional standards ⟨a *jackleg* lawyer⟩
**2 :** designed as a temporary expedient **:** MAKESHIFT
**— jackleg** *noun*

**jack·light** \-,līt\ *noun* (circa 1841)
**:** a light used especially in hunting or fishing at night

**jack mackerel** *noun* (1882)
**:** a California carangid food fish (*Trachurus symmetricus*) that is iridescent green or bluish above and silvery below

**jack–of–all–trades** \,ja-kə-,vòl-'trādz\ *noun, plural* **jacks–of–all–trades** (1618)
**:** a person who can do passable work at various tasks **:** a handy versatile person

**jack off** *verb* [probably alteration of *jerk off*] (1959)
**:** MASTURBATE — usually considered vulgar

**jack–o'–lan·tern** \'ja-kə-,lan-tərn\ *noun* (1750)
**1 :** IGNIS FATUUS
**2 :** a lantern made of a pumpkin cut to look like a human face
**3 :** a large orangish gill fungus (*Omphalotus olearius* synonym *Clitocybe illudens*) that is poisonous and luminescent

**jack pine** *noun* (1883)
**:** a slender pine (*Pinus banksiana*) of northern North America that has two stout needles in each fascicle and wood used especially for pulpwood

**jack plane** *noun* (circa 1816)
**:** a medium-sized general-purpose plane used in carpentry and joinery

**jack·pot** \'jak-,pät\ *noun* (1881)
**1 a** (1) **:** a hand or game of draw poker in which a pair of jacks or better is required to open (2) **:** a large pot (as in poker) formed by the accumulation of stakes from previous play **b** (1) **:** a combination on a slot machine that wins a top prize or all the coins available for paying out (2) **:** the sum so won **c :** a large fund of money or other reward formed by the accumulation of unwon prizes
**2 :** an impressive often unexpected success or reward
**3** *chiefly West* **:** a tight spot **:** JAM

**jack·rab·bit** \-,ra-bət\ *noun* [¹*jack* (jackass) + *rabbit*; from its long ears] (1863)
**:** any of several large hares (genus *Lepus*) of western North America having very long ears and long hind legs

**Jack Russell terrier** \'jak-'rə-səl-\ *noun* [*Jack* (John) *Russell* (died 1883) English clergyman & dog breeder] (1961)
**:** any of a breed of small terriers having a usually white coat with brown, black, or tricolor markings — called also *Jack Russell*

**jack salmon** *noun* (1871)
**1 :** WALLEYE 3
**2 :** GRILSE

**jack·screw** \'jak-,skrü\ *noun* (1769)
**:** SCREW JACK

**jack·smelt** \-,smelt\ *noun* (1949)
**:** a large silversides (*Atherinopsis californiensis*) of the Pacific coast of North America that is the chief commercial smelt of the California markets

**Jack·son Day** \'jak-sən-\ *noun* [Andrew *Jackson;* from his defense of New Orleans] (1885)
**:** January 8 celebrated as a legal holiday in Louisiana to commemorate the successful defense of New Orleans in 1815

**jack stand** *noun* (1968)

**:** a stand whose height may be adjusted and fixed by a pin and which is used to support an automobile that has been raised by a jack

**jack·stay** \-,stā\ *noun* (circa 1840)
**1 :** an iron rod, wooden bar, or wire rope along a yard of a ship to which the sails are fastened
**2 :** a support of wood, iron, or rope running up a mast on which the parrel of a yard travels

**jack·straw** \-,strò\ *noun* (1801)
**1** *plural but singular in construction* **:** a game in which a set of straws or thin strips is let fall in a heap with each player in turn trying to remove one at a time without disturbing the rest
**2 :** one of the pieces used in the game jackstraws

**jack–tar** \-'tär\ *noun, often capitalized* (1781)
**:** SAILOR

**jack–up** \'jak-,əp\ *noun* (1965)
**:** a drilling rig used in offshore drilling whose drilling platform is a barge from which legs are lowered to the bottom when over the drill site and which is raised above the water and supported on the legs to conduct drilling operations

**Ja·cob** \'jā-kəb\ *noun* [Late Latin, from Greek *Iacōb,* from Hebrew *Ya'ăqōbh*]
**1 :** a son of Isaac and Rebekah, the twin brother of Esau, and heir of God's promise of blessing to Abraham
**2 :** the ancient Hebrew nation

**Jac·o·be·an** \,ja-kə-'bē-ən\ *adjective* [New Latin *Jacobaeus,* from *Jacobus* James] (1844)
**:** of, relating to, or characteristic of James I of England or his age
**— Jacobean** *noun*

**jacobean lily** *noun, often J capitalized* [Late Latin *Jacobus* (Saint James)] (circa 1774)
**:** a Mexican bulbous herb (*Sprekelia formosissima*) of the amaryllis family cultivated for its bright red solitary flower

**Ja·co·bi·an** \jə-'kō-bē-ən, yä-\ *noun* [K. G. J. *Jacobi* (died 1851) German mathematician] (1881)
**:** a determinant defined for a finite number of functions of the same number of variables in which each row consists of the first partial derivatives of the same function with respect to each of the variables

**Jac·o·bin** \'ja-kə-bən\ *noun* [Middle English, from Middle French, from Medieval Latin *Jacobinus,* from Late Latin *Jacobus* (Saint James); from the location of the first Dominican convent in the street of Saint James, Paris] (14th century)
**1 :** DOMINICAN
**2** [French, from *Jacobin* Dominican; from the group's founding in the Dominican convent in Paris] **:** a member of an extremist or radical political group; *especially* **:** a member of such a group advocating egalitarian democracy and engaging in terrorist activities during the French Revolution of 1789
**— Jac·o·bin·ic** \,ja-kə-'bi-nik\ *or* **Jac·o·bin·i·cal** \-ni-kəl\ *adjective*
**— Jac·o·bin·ism** \'ja-kə-bə-,ni-zəm\ *noun*

¹**Jac·o·bite** \'ja-kə-,bīt\ *noun* [Middle English, from Medieval Latin *Jacobita,* from *Jacobus* Baradaeus (Jacob Baradai) (died 578) Syrian monk] (15th century)
**:** a member of any of various Monophysite Eastern churches; *especially* **:** a member of the Monophysite Syrian church

²**Jacobite** *noun* [*Jacobus* (James II)] (1689)
**:** a partisan of James II of England or of the Stuarts after the revolution of 1688
**— Jac·o·bit·i·cal** \,ja-kə-'bi-ti-kəl\ *adjective*
**— Jac·o·bit·ism** \'ja-kə-,bī-,ti-zəm\ *noun*

**Ja·cob's ladder** \'jā-kəbz-\ *noun* [from the ladder seen in a dream by Jacob in Genesis 28:12] (1733)
**1 :** any of a genus (*Polemonium*) of herbs of the phlox family that have pinnate leaves, an herbaceous calyx, a bell-shaped corolla with stamens with their filaments bent downward,

and a several-seeded capsule; *especially* **:** a perennial (*P. caeruleum*) of European origin with bright blue or occasionally white flowers **2 :** a marine ladder of rope or chain with wooden or iron rungs

**Ja·cob·son's organ** \'jā-kəb-sənz-\ *noun* [Ludvig L. *Jacobson* (died 1843) Danish anatomist] (1885)
**:** either of a pair of small pits that are situated one on either side of the nasal septum (as in higher vertebrates) or in the buccal cavity and that are rudimentary in humans but developed in reptiles, amphibians, and some mammals as chemoreceptors

**Ja·co·bus** \jə-'kō-bəs\ *noun* [*Jacobus* (James I), during whose reign unites were coined] (1612)
**:** UNITE

**jac·o·net** \'ja-kə-,net\ *noun* [modification of Urdu *jagannāthī*] (1769)
**:** a lightweight cotton cloth used for clothing and bandages

**jac·quard** \'ja-,kärd\ *noun, often capitalized, often attributive* [Joseph *Jacquard*] (1841)
**1 a :** the control mechanism of a Jacquard loom **:** JACQUARD LOOM
**2 :** a fabric of intricate variegated weave or pattern

**Jacquard loom** *noun* (1851)
**:** a loom designed to weave fabrics of intricate design whose control mechanism makes use of cards with holes punched in them

**jac·que·rie** \,zhä-kə-'rē, ,zha-\ *noun, often capitalized* [Middle French, from the French peasant revolt in 1358, from *jacque* peasant — more at JACKET] (1523)
**:** a peasants' revolt

**jac·ti·ta·tion** \,jak-tə-'tā-shən\ *noun* [Late Latin *jactitation-*, *jactitatio*, from *jactitare*, frequentative of Latin *jactare* to throw — more at JET] (1665)
**:** a tossing to and fro or jerking and twitching of the body

**Ja·cuz·zi** \jə-'kü-zē\ *trademark*
— used for a whirlpool bath and a recreational bathing tub or pool

**¹jade** \'jād\ *noun* [Middle English] (14th century)
**1 :** a broken-down, vicious, or worthless horse
**2 a :** a disreputable woman **b :** a flirtatious girl

**²jade** *verb* **jad·ed; jad·ing** (1598)
*transitive verb*
**1 a :** to wear out by overwork or abuse **b :** to tire or dull through repetition or excess
**2** *obsolete* **:** to make ridiculous
*intransitive verb*
**:** to become weary or dulled
**synonym** *see* TIRE

**³jade** *noun* [French, from obsolete Spanish (*piedra de la*) *ijada*, literally, loin stone, ultimately from Latin *ilia*, plural, flanks; from the belief that jade cures renal colic] (1657)
**1 :** either of two tough compact typically green gemstones that take a high polish: **a :** JADEITE **b :** NEPHRITE
**2 :** a sculpture or artifact of jade
**3 :** JADE GREEN ◆

**jaded** *adjective* (1600)
**1 :** fatigued by overwork **:** EXHAUSTED
**2 :** dulled by experience or by surfeit
— **jad·ed·ly** *adverb*
— **jad·ed·ness** *noun*

**jade green** *noun* (1892)
**:** a light bluish green

**jade·ite** \'jā-,dīt\ *noun* [French] (1865)
**:** a monoclinic mineral that is a silicate of sodium and aluminum and is a jade
— **ja·dit·ic** \jā-'di-tik\ *adjective*

**jade plant** *noun* (1944)
**:** any of several succulent plants (genus *Crassula*) of the orpine family cultivated as foliage plants

**jae·ger** \'yā-gər\ *noun* [German *Jäger*] (1809)

**1 a :** HUNTER, HUNTSMAN **b :** one attending a person of rank or wealth and wearing hunter's costume
**2 :** any of several large dark-colored birds (genus *Stercorarius* of the family Stercorariidae) of northern seas that are strong fliers and that tend to harass weaker birds until they drop or disgorge their prey

**¹jag** \'jag\ *verb* **jagged; jag·ging** [Middle English *jaggen*] (15th century)
*transitive verb*
**1** *chiefly dialect* **:** PRICK, STAB
**2 :** to cut indentations into; *also* **:** to form teeth on (a saw) by cutting indentations
*intransitive verb*
**1 :** PRICK, THRUST
**2 :** to move in jerks
— **jag·ger** *noun*

**²jag** *noun* (1578)
**:** a sharp projecting part **:** BARB

**³jag** *noun* [origin unknown] (1597)
**1 :** a small load
**2 a :** a state or feeling of exhilaration or intoxication usually induced by liquor **b :** SPREE ⟨a crying *jag*⟩

**jag·ged** \'ja-gəd\ *adjective* (1577)
**1 :** having a sharply uneven edge or surface
**2 :** having a harsh, rough, or irregular quality
— **jag·ged·ly** *adverb*
— **jag·ged·ness** *noun*

**jag·gery** \'ja-gə-rē\ *noun* [Portuguese *jágara*, probably from Malayalam *chakkara* sugar] (1598)
**:** an unrefined brown sugar made from palm sap

**jag·gy** \'ja-gē\ *adjective* (1717)
**:** JAGGED, NOTCHED

**jag·uar** \'ja-,gwär, -gyə-,wär, -gwər, *especially British* 'ja-gyə-wər\ *noun* [Spanish *yaguar* & Portuguese *jaguar*, from Guarani *yaguara* & Tupi *jaguara*] (1604)
**:** a large cat (*Panthera onca* synonym *Felis onca*) chiefly of Central and South America that is larger and stockier than the leopard and is brownish yellow or buff with black spots

jaguar

**jag·ua·run·di** \,zha-gwə-'rən-dē\ *also* **jag·ua·ron·di** \-rän-\ *noun* [American Spanish, from Guarani *yaguarundi*] (circa 1885)
**:** a slender long-tailed short-legged black, gray, or reddish wildcat (*Felis yagouaroundi*) chiefly of Central and South America

**Jah** \'jä\ *noun* [Hebrew *Yāh*] (1975)
**:** the Supreme Being of Rastafarianism

**Jah·veh** \'yä-(,)vā\ *variant of* YAHWEH

**jai alai** \'hī-,lī, ,hī-ə-'lī\ *noun* [Spanish, from Basque, from *jai* festival + *alai* merry] (1903)
**:** a court game somewhat like handball played usually by two or four players with a ball and a long curved wicker basket strapped to the wrist

**¹jail** \'jā(ə)l\ *noun* [Middle English *jaiole*, from Old French, from Late Latin *caveola*, diminutive of Latin *cavea* cage — more at CAGE] (13th century)
**1 :** a place of confinement for persons held in lawful custody; *specifically* **:** such a place under the jurisdiction of a local government (as a county) for the confinement of persons awaiting trial or those convicted of minor crimes — compare PRISON
**2 :** confinement in a jail

**²jail** *transitive verb* (1604)
**:** to confine in or as if in a jail

**jail·bait** \'jā(ə)l-,bāt\ *noun* (1930)
**:** a girl under the age of consent with whom sexual intercourse is unlawful and constitutes statutory rape

**jail·bird** \-,bərd\ *noun* (1603)

**:** a person confined in jail; *specifically* **:** an habitual criminal

**jail·break** \-,brāk\ *noun* (1910)
**:** a forcible escape from jail

**jail·er** *or* **jail·or** \'jā-lər\ *noun* (13th century)
**1 :** a keeper of a jail
**2 :** one that restricts another's liberty as if by imprisonment

**jail·house** \'jā(ə)l-,haus\ *noun* (1812)
**:** JAIL 1

**jailhouse lawyer** *noun* (1969)
**:** a prison inmate self-taught in the law who tries to gain release through legal maneuvers or who advises fellow inmates on their legal problems

**Jain** \'jīn\ *or* **Jai·na** \'jī-nə\ *noun* [Hindi *Jain*, from Sanskrit *Jaina*] (1805)
**:** an adherent of Jainism

**Jain·ism** \'jī-,ni-zəm\ *noun* (1858)
**:** a religion of India originating in the 6th century B.C. and teaching liberation of the soul by right knowledge, right faith, and right conduct

**jake** \'jāk\ *adjective* [origin unknown] (1914)
*slang* **:** ALL RIGHT, FINE

**jake leg** \'jāk-,leg, -,lāg\ *noun* [*jake* grain alcohol flavored with an alcoholic extract of ginger] (1932)
**:** a paralysis caused by drinking improperly distilled or contaminated liquor

**jakes** \'jāks\ *noun plural but singular or plural in construction* [perhaps from French *Jacques* James] (1538)
**:** PRIVY 1

**jal·ap** \'ja-ləp, 'jä-\ *noun* [French & Spanish; French *jalap*, from Spanish *jalapa*, from *Jalapa*, Mexico] (1644)
**1 a :** the dried tuberous root of a Mexican plant (*Ipomoea purga* synonym *Exogonium purga*) of the morning-glory family; *also* **:** a powdered purgative drug prepared from it that contains resinous glycosides **b :** the root or derived drug of plants related to the one supplying jalap
**2 :** a plant yielding jalap

**ja·la·pe·ño** *also* **ja·la·pe·no** \,hä-lə-'pā-(,)nyō, ,ha-, -'pā-(,)nō, -'pē-(,)nō\ *noun, plural* **-ños** *also* **-nos** [Mexican Spanish, from *jalapeño*, adjective, of Jalapa] (1939)
**:** a small plump dark green Mexican hot pepper — called also *jalapeño pepper*

**ja·lopy** \jə-'lä-pē\ *noun, plural* **ja·lop·ies** [origin unknown] (1928)
**:** a dilapidated old vehicle (as an automobile)

**jal·ou·sie** \'ja-lə-sē\ *noun* [French, literally, jealousy, from Old French *jelous* jealous] (1766)

**1 :** a blind with adjustable horizontal slats for admitting light and air while excluding direct sun and rain
**2 :** a window made of adjustable glass louvers that control ventilation

**¹jam** \'jam\ *verb* **jammed; jam·ming** [origin unknown] (1706)
*intransitive verb*
**1 a :** to become blocked or wedged **b :** to become unworkable through the jamming of a movable part
**2 :** to force one's way into a restricted space
**3 :** to take part in a jam session
*transitive verb*
**1 a :** to press into a close or tight position ⟨*jam* his hat on⟩ **b** (1) **:** to cause to become wedged so as to be unworkable ⟨*jam* the typewriter keys⟩ (2) **:** to make unworkable by jamming **c :** to block passage of **:** OBSTRUCT **d :** to fill often to excess **:** PACK ⟨the crowd *jammed* the theater⟩
**2 :** to push forcibly; *especially* **:** to apply (brakes) suddenly and forcibly — used with *on*
**3 :** CRUSH, BRUISE
**4 a :** to make unintelligible by sending out interfering signals or messages **b :** to make (as a radar apparatus) ineffective by jamming signals or by causing reflection of radar waves
**5 :** to pitch inside to (a batter)
**— jam·mer** \'ja-mər\ *noun*

**²jam** *noun* (1805)
**1 a :** an act or instance of jamming **b :** a crowded mass that impedes or blocks ⟨a traffic *jam*⟩
**2 a :** the quality or state of being jammed **b :** the pressure or congestion of a crowd **:** CRUSH
**3 :** a difficult state of affairs **:** FIX ⟨got into a *jam*⟩
**4 :** JAM SESSION
**5 :** DUNK SHOT

**³jam** *noun* [probably from ¹*jam*] (circa 1736)
**:** a food made by boiling fruit and sugar to a thick consistency
**— jam·my** \'ja-mē\ *adjective*

**Jamaica rum** *noun* (circa 1900)
**:** a heavy-bodied rum made by slow fermentation and marked by a pungent bouquet

**jamb** \'jam\ *noun* [Middle English *jambe*, from Middle French, literally, leg, from Late Latin *gamba* — more at GAMBIT] (14th century)
**1 :** an upright piece or surface forming the side of an opening (as for a door, window, or fireplace)
**2 :** a projecting columnar part or mass

**jam·ba·laya** \ˌjäm-bə-'lī-ə\ *noun* [Louisiana French, from Provençal *jambalaia*] (1872)
**1 :** rice cooked usually with ham, sausage, chicken, shrimp, or oysters and seasoned with herbs
**2 :** a mixture of diverse elements ⟨curious *jambalayas* of competing elements —Neil Hickey⟩

**jam·beau** \'jam-(ˌ)bō\ *noun, plural* **jam·beaux** \-(ˌ)bōz\ [Middle English, from (assumed) Anglo-French, from Middle French *jambe*] (14th century)
**:** a piece of medieval armor for the leg below the knee — see ARMOR illustration

**jam·bo·ree** \ˌjam-bə-'rē\ *noun* [origin unknown] (1864)
**1 :** a noisy or unrestrained carouse
**2 a :** a large festive gathering **b :** a national or international camping assembly of Boy Scouts
**3 :** a long mixed program of entertainment

**James** \'jāmz\ *noun* [Middle English, from Middle French, from (assumed) Vulgar Latin *Jacomus*, alteration of Late Latin *Jacobus, Jacob* Jacob]
**1 :** an apostle, son of Zebedee, and brother of the apostle John according to the Gospel accounts
**2 :** an apostle and son of Alphaeus according to the Gospel accounts — called also *James the Less*

**3 :** a brother of Jesus traditionally held to be the author of the New Testament Epistle of James
**4 :** a moral lecture addressed to early Christians and included as a book in the New Testament — see BIBLE table

**jam·mies** \'ja-mēz\ *noun plural* [by shortening & alteration] (1973)
**:** PAJAMAS 2

**jam–pack** \'jam-'pak\ *transitive verb* (1924)
**:** to pack tightly or to excess

**Jams** \'jamz\ *trademark*
— used for knee-length loose-fitting swim trunks

**jam session** *noun* [²*jam*] (1933)
**:** an often impromptu performance by a group especially of jazz musicians that is characterized by improvisation

**Jam·shid** *or* **Jam·shyd** \jam-'shēd\ *noun* [Persian *Jamshīd*]
**:** an early legendary king of Persia who reigned for 700 years

**jam–up** \'jam-ˌəp\ *noun* (1941)
**:** JAM 1

**Jane Doe** \'jān-'dō\ *noun* (1936)
**:** a female party to legal proceedings whose true name is unknown

**Jane·ite** \'jā-ˌnīt\ *noun* (1896)
**:** an enthusiastic admirer of Jane Austen's writings

**¹jan·gle** \'jaŋ-gəl\ *verb* **jan·gled; jan·gling** \-g(ə-)liŋ\ [Middle English, from Middle French *jangler*, of Germanic origin; akin to Middle Dutch *jangelen* to grumble] (14th century)
*intransitive verb*
**1 :** to talk idly
**2 :** to quarrel verbally
**3 :** to make a harsh or discordant often ringing sound ⟨keys *jangling* in my pocket⟩
*transitive verb*
**1 :** to utter or sound in a discordant, babbling, or chattering way
**2 a :** to cause to sound harshly or inharmoniously **b :** to excite to tense irritation ⟨*jangled* nerves⟩
**— jan·gler** \-g(ə-)lər\ *noun*

**²jangle** *noun* (14th century)
**1 :** idle talk
**2 :** noisy quarreling
**3 :** a discordant often ringing sound **:** DISCORD

**jan·gly** \'jaŋ-g(ə-)lē\ *adjective* (1892)
**:** marked by jangling **:** having a jangling quality ⟨*jangly* earrings⟩ ⟨*jangly* guitar music⟩

**jan·is·sary** *or* **jan·i·zary** \'ja-nə-ˌser-ē, -ˌzer-\ *noun, plural* **-sar·ies** *or* **-zar·ies** [Italian *gianizzero*, from Turkish *yeniçeri*, from *yeni* new + *çeri* soldier] (1529)
**1** *often capitalized* **:** a soldier of an elite corps of Turkish troops organized in the 14th century and abolished in 1826
**2 :** a member of a group of loyal or subservient troops, officials, or supporters

**jan·i·tor** \'ja-nə-tər\ *noun* [Latin, from *janus* arch, gate] (1629)
**1 :** DOORKEEPER
**2 :** one who keeps the premises of a building (as an apartment or office) clean, tends the heating system, and makes minor repairs
**— jan·i·to·ri·al** \ˌja-nə-'tōr-ē-əl, -'tor-\ *adjective*

**Jan·sen·ism** \'jan(t)-sə-ˌni-zəm\ *noun* [French *jansénisme*, from Cornelis *Jansen*] (circa 1656)
**1 :** a system of doctrine based on moral determinism, defended by various reformist factions among 17th and 18th century western European Roman Catholic clergy, religious, and scholars, and condemned as heretical by papal authority
**2 :** a puritanical attitude (as toward sex)
**— Jan·sen·ist** \-nist\ *noun*
**— Jan·sen·is·tic** \ˌjan(t)-sə-'nis-tik\ *adjective*

**Jan·u·ary** \'jan-yə-ˌwer-ē\ *noun, plural* **-ar·ies** *or* **-ar·ys** [Middle English *Januarie*, from Latin *Januarius*, 1st month of the ancient Roman year, from *Janus*] (14th century)
**:** the 1st month of the Gregorian calendar

**Ja·nus** \'jā-nəs\ *noun* [Latin]
**:** a Roman god that is identified with doors, gates, and all beginnings and that is represented artistically with two opposite faces

**Janus–faced** \-ˌfāst\ *adjective* (1682)
**:** having two contrasting aspects; *especially* **:** DUPLICITOUS, TWO-FACED

**Janus green** *noun* [probably from *Janus*, a trademark] (1898)
**:** a basic azine dye used especially as a biological stain (as for mitochondria)

**Jap** \'jap\ *noun or adjective* (1886)
**:** JAPANESE — usually used disparagingly

**JAP** \'jap\ *noun* (circa 1973)
**:** JEWISH AMERICAN PRINCESS — usually used disparagingly

**¹ja·pan** \jə-'pan\ *adjective* (1673)
**:** of, relating to, or originating in Japan **:** of a kind or style characteristic of Japanese workmanship

**²japan** *noun* (1688)
**1 a :** any of several varnishes yielding a hard brilliant finish **b :** a hard dark coating containing asphalt and a drier that is used especially on metal and fixed by heating — called also *japan black*
**2 :** work (as lacquer ware) finished and decorated in the Japanese manner

**³japan** *transitive verb* **ja·panned; ja·pan·ning** (1688)
**1 :** to cover with or as if with a coat of japan
**2 :** to give a high gloss to
**— ja·pan·ner** *noun*

**Jap·a·nese** \ˌja-pə-'nēz, -'nēs\ *noun, plural* **Japanese** (1604)
**1 a :** a native or inhabitant of Japan **b :** a person of Japanese descent
**2 :** the language of the Japanese
**— Japanese** *adjective*

**Japanese an·drom·e·da** \-ˌan-'drä-mə-də\ *noun* [New Latin *Andromeda*, genus of plants, from Latin *Andromeda*, Ethiopian princess, from Greek *Andromedē*] (1948)
**:** a shrubby evergreen Asian heath (*Pieris japonica*) with glossy leaves and drooping clusters of usually whitish flowers

**Japanese beetle** *noun* (1900)
**:** a small metallic green and brown scarab beetle (*Popillia japonica*) that has been introduced into America from Japan and as a grub feeds on the roots of grasses and decaying vegetation and as an adult eats foliage and fruits

**Japanese cedar** *noun* (circa 1880)
**:** a large evergreen tree (*Cryptomeria japonica*) grown especially in China and Japan for its valuable soft wood

**Japanese iris** *noun* (1883)
**:** any of various beardless garden irises (especially *Iris kaempferi*) with very large showy flowers

**Japanese lacquer** *noun* (1876)
**:** LACQUER 1b

**Japanese maple** *noun* (1898)
**:** a maple (*Acer palmatum*) of Japan, China, and Korea with purple flowers and usually deeply parted leaves that is widely cultivated as a shrub or small tree

**Japanese millet** *noun* (1900)
**:** a coarse annual grass (*Echinochloa frumentacea*) cultivated especially in Asia for its edible seeds

**Japanese plum** *noun* (1893)
**:** a tree (*Prunus salicina*) native to China and cultivated in Japan that bears Japanese plums; *also* **:** the large usually yellow to light red fruit of a Japanese plum

**Japanese quail** *noun* (1963)
: a quail (*Coturnix japonica* synonym *C. coturnix japonica*) from China and Japan that is often used in laboratory research

**Japanese quince** *noun* (1900)
: a hardy Chinese ornamental shrub (*Chaenomeles speciosa* synonym *C. lagenaria*) of the rose family with scarlet, pink, or white flowers

**Japanese spurge** *noun* (1924)
: a low Japanese herb or subshrub (*Pachysandra terminalis*) of the box family often used as a ground cover

**Jap·a·nize** \'ja-pə-ˌnīz\ *transitive verb* **-nized; -niz·ing** (1890)
**1** : to make Japanese
**2** : to bring (as an area or industry) under the influence of Japan
— **Jap·a·ni·za·tion** \ˌja-pə-nə-'zā-shən\ *noun*

**Japan wax** *noun* (1859)
: a yellowish fat obtained from the berries of several sumacs (as *Rhus verniciflua* and *R. succedanea*) and used chiefly in polishes

**¹jape** \'jāp\ *verb* **japed; jap·ing** [Middle English] (14th century)
*intransitive verb*
: to say or do something jokingly or mockingly
*transitive verb*
: to make mocking fun of
— **jap·er** \'jā-pər\ *noun*
— **jap·ery** \'jā-p(ə-)rē\ *noun*

**²jape** *noun* (14th century)
: something designed to arouse amusement or laughter: as **a** : an amusing literary or dramatic production **b** : GIBE

**Ja·pheth** \'jā-fəth\ *noun* [Latin *Japheth* or Greek *Iapheth*, from Hebrew *Yepheth*]
: a son of Noah held to be the progenitor of the Medes and Greeks

**ja·po·nais·e·rie** \zhä-ˌpō-ne-zə-'rē, -nez-'rē\ *noun, often capitalized* [French, from *japonais* Japanese] (1896)
: a style in art reflecting Japanese qualities or motifs; *also* : an object or decoration in this style

**ja·pon·i·ca** \jə-'pä-ni-kə\ *noun* [New Latin, from feminine of *Japonicus* Japanese, from *Japonia* Japan] (1819)
: JAPANESE QUINCE

**¹jar** \'jär\ *verb* **jarred; jar·ring** [probably of imitative origin] (1526)
*intransitive verb*
**1 a** : to make a harsh or discordant sound **b** : to have a harshly disagreeable or disconcerting effect **c** : to be out of harmony; *specifically* : BICKER
**2** : to undergo severe vibration
*transitive verb*
: to cause to jar: as **a** : to affect disagreeably : UNSETTLE **b** : to make unstable : SHAKE
— **jar·ring·ly** \'jär-iŋ-lē\ *adverb*

**²jar** *noun* (1537)
**1 a** : a state or manifestation of discord or conflict **b** : a harsh grating sound
**2 a** : a sudden or unexpected shake **b** : an unsettling shock **c** : an unpleasant break or conflict in rhythm, flow, or transition

**³jar** *noun* [Middle French *jarre*, from Old Provençal *jarra*, from Arabic *jarrah* earthen water vessel] (1592)
**1** : a widemouthed container made typically of earthenware or glass
**2** : as much as a jar will hold
— **jar·ful** \-ˌful\ *noun*

**⁴jar** *noun* [alteration of earlier *char* turn, from Middle English — more at CHARE] (1674)
*archaic* : the position of being ajar — usually used in the phrase *on the jar*

**jar·di·niere** *or* **jar·di·nière** \ˌjär-dᵊn-'ir, ˌzhär-dᵊn-'yer, -'er\ *noun* [French *jardinière*, literally, female gardener] (1841)
**1 a** : an ornamental stand for plants or flowers **b** : a large usually ceramic flowerpot holder
**2** : a garnish for meat consisting of several cooked vegetables cut into pieces

**¹jar·gon** \'jär-gən, -ˌgän\ *noun* [Middle English, from Middle French] (14th century)
**1 a** : confused unintelligible language **b** : a strange, outlandish, or barbarous language or dialect **c** : a hybrid language or dialect simplified in vocabulary and grammar and used for communication between peoples of different speech
**2** : the technical terminology or characteristic idiom of a special activity or group
**3** : obscure and often pretentious language marked by circumlocutions and long words
— **jar·gon·ish** \-gə-nish\ *adjective*
— **jar·gon·is·tic** \ˌjär-gə-'nis-tik\ *adjective*

**²jargon** *intransitive verb* (14th century)
**1** : TWITTER, WARBLE
**2** : JARGONIZE

**jar·gon·ize** \'jär-gə-ˌnīz\ *verb* **-ized; -iz·ing** (1803)
*intransitive verb*
: to speak or write jargon
*transitive verb*
**1** : to express in jargon
**2** : to make into jargon

**jar·goon** \jär-'gün\ *or* **jar·gon** \-'gän\ *noun* [French *jargon* — more at ZIRCON] (1769)
: a colorless, pale yellow, or smoky zircon

**jar·head** \'jär-ˌhed\ *noun* (circa 1960)
*slang* : MARINE 2

**jarl** \'yär(-ə)l\ *noun* [Old Norse — more at EARL]
: a Scandinavian noble ranking immediately below the king

**jar·rah** \'jar-ə\ *noun* [Nyungar (Australian aboriginal language of southwest Western Australia) *jarily*] (circa 1866)
: a eucalyptus (*Eucalyptus marginata*) of western Australia with rough bark and alternate leaves; *also* : its wood

**jas·mine** \'jaz-mən\ *noun* [French *jasmin*, from Arabic *yāsamīn*, from Persian] (1562)
**1 a** : any of numerous often climbing shrubs (genus *Jasminum*) of the olive family that usually have extremely fragrant flowers; *especially* : a tall-climbing semievergreen Asian shrub (*J. officinale*) with fragrant white flowers from which oil is extracted for use in perfumes **b** : any of numerous plants having sweet-scented flowers; *especially* : YELLOW JESSAMINE
**2** : a light yellow

jasmine 1a

**Ja·son** \'jā-sᵊn\ *noun* [Latin *Iason*, from Greek *Iasōn*]
: a legendary Greek hero distinguished for his successful quest of the Golden Fleece

**jas·per** \'jas-pər\ *noun* [Middle English *jaspre*, from Middle French, from Latin *jaspis*, from Greek *iaspis*, of Semitic origin; akin to Hebrew *yāshĕpheh* jasper] (14th century)
**1** : an opaque cryptocrystalline quartz of any of several colors; *especially* : green chalcedony
**2** : colored stoneware with raised white decoration
**3** : a blackish green
— **jas·pery** \-pə-rē\ *adjective*

**jas·per·ware** \'jas-pər-ˌwar, -wer\ *noun* (1863)
: JASPER 2

**jas·sid** \'ja-səd\ *noun* [ultimately from Greek *Iasos*, town in Asia Minor] (1892)
: any of numerous small leafhoppers that include many economically significant pests of cultivated plants; *broadly* : LEAFHOPPER

**Jat** \'jät\ *noun* [Hindi *Jāṭ*] (1622)
: a member of an Indo-Aryan people of the Punjab and Uttar Pradesh

**jaunce** \'jön(t)s, 'jän(t)s\ *intransitive verb* [origin unknown] (1593)
*archaic* : PRANCE

**jaun·dice** \'jön-dəs, 'jän-\ *noun* [Middle English *jaundis*, from Middle French *jaunisse*, from *jaune* yellow, from Latin *galbinus* greenish yellow] (14th century)
**1** : yellowish pigmentation of the skin, tissues, and body fluids caused by the deposition of bile pigments
**2** : a disease or abnormal condition characterized by jaundice
**3** : a state or attitude characterized by satiety, distaste, or hostility

**jaun·diced** \-dəst\ *adjective* (1640)
**1** : affected with or as if with jaundice
**2** : exhibiting or influenced by envy, distaste, or hostility ⟨a *jaundiced* eye⟩

**¹jaunt** \'jönt, 'jänt\ *intransitive verb* [origin unknown] (1575)
**1** *archaic* : to trudge about
**2** : to make a usually short journey for pleasure

**²jaunt** *noun* (1592)
**1** *archaic* : a tiring trip
**2** : an excursion undertaken especially for pleasure

**jaunting car** *noun* (1801)
: a light 2-wheeled open horse-drawn vehicle used especially in Ireland with lengthwise seats placed face-to-face or back to back

**jaun·ty** \'jön-tē, 'jän-\ *adjective* **jaun·ti·er; -est** [modification of French *gentil*] (1662)
**1** *archaic* **a** : GENTEEL **b** : STYLISH
**2** : sprightly in manner or appearance : LIVELY
— **jaun·ti·ly** \'jön-tᵊl-ē, 'jän-\ *adverb*
— **jaun·ti·ness** \'jön-tē-nəs, 'jän-\ *noun*

**ja·va** \'ja-və, 'jä-, -vē\ *noun, often capitalized* [*Java*, island of Indonesia] (1850)
: COFFEE

**Java man** \'jä-və-, 'ja-\ *noun* (1911)
: a Pleistocene hominid known from fragmentary skeletons found in Trinil and Djetis, Java and now classified with the pithecanthropines

**Ja·va·nese** \ˌja-və-'nēz, ˌjä-, -'nēs\ *noun, plural* **Javanese** [*Java* + *-nese* (as in *Japanese*)] (1704)
**1** : a member of an Indonesian people inhabiting the island of Java
**2** : an Austronesian language of the Javanese people
— **Javanese** *adjective*

**jav·e·lin** \'jav-lən, 'ja-və-\ *noun* [Middle English *chafeveleyn*, from Middle French *javeline*, alteration of *javelot*, of Celtic origin; akin to Old Irish *gabul* forked stick] (15th century)
**1** : a light spear thrown as a weapon of war or in hunting
**2** : a slender usually metal shaft at least 260 centimeters long that is thrown for distance in a field event

**ja·ve·li·na** \ˌhä-və-'lē-nə\ *noun* [American Spanish *jabalina*, from Spanish, feminine of *jabalí* wild boar, from Arabic *jabalīy*] (1822)
: PECCARY

**Ja·velle water** \zha-'vel, zhə-\ *noun* [*Javel*, former village in France] (1890)
: an aqueous solution of sodium hypochlorite used as a disinfectant or a bleaching agent

**¹jaw** \'jö\ *noun* [Middle English] (14th century)
**1 a** : either of two complex cartilaginous or bony structures in most vertebrates that border the mouth, support the soft parts enclosing it, usually bear teeth on their oral margin, and are an upper that is more or less firmly fused with the skull and a lower that is hinged, movable, and articulated with the temporal bone of either side **b** : the parts constituting the walls of the mouth and serving to open and close it —

usually used in plural **c** : any of various organs of invertebrates that perform the function of the vertebrate jaws
**2** : something resembling the jaw of an animal: as **a** : one of the sides of a narrow pass or channel **b** : either of two or more opposable parts that open and close for holding or crushing something between them
**3 a** : a space lying between or as if between open jaws ⟨escaped from out of the *jaws* of the whale⟩ **b** : a position or situation in which one is threatened ⟨rode into the *jaws* of danger⟩
**4** : a friendly chat
²**jaw** (1748)
*intransitive verb*
: to talk especially abusively, indignantly, or long-windedly
*transitive verb*
: to talk to in a scolding or boring manner
**jaw·bone** \'jȯ-ˌbōn\ *noun* (15th century)
: JAW 1a; *especially* : MANDIBLE
**jaw·bon·ing** \-ˌbō-niŋ\ *noun* (1969)
: the use of public appeals (as by a president) to influence the actions especially of business and labor leaders; *broadly* : the use of spoken persuasion
— **jaw·bone** \-ˌbōn\ *transitive verb*
**jaw·break·er** \-ˌbrā-kər\ *noun* (1839)
**1** : a word difficult to pronounce
**2** : a round hard candy
**jawed** \'jȯd\ *adjective* (circa 1529)
: having jaws ⟨*jawed* fishes⟩ — usually used in combination ⟨square-*jawed*⟩ ⟨a 3-*jawed* chuck⟩
**jaw·less fish** \'jȯ-ləs-\ *noun* (circa 1941)
: any of the taxonomic group (Agnatha) of primitive vertebrates without jaws including cyclostomes and extinct related forms — compare BONY FISH, CARTILAGINOUS FISH
**jaw·line** \'jȯ-ˌlīn\ *noun* (1924)
: the outline of the lower jaw
¹**jay** \'jā\ *noun* [Middle English, from Middle French *jai*, from Late Latin *gaius*] (14th century)
**1 a** : a predominantly fawn-colored Old World bird (*Garrulus glandarius*) of the crow family with a black-and-white crest and wings marked with black, white, and blue **b** : any of various usually crested and largely blue chiefly New World birds that are related to the common Old World jay and have roving habits and harsh voices
**2 a** : an impertinent chatterer **b** : DANDY 1 **c** : GREENHORN
**3** : a moderate blue
²**jay** *noun* (circa 1889)
**1** : the letter *j*
**2** : JOINT 4
**jay·bird** \'jā-ˌbərd\ *noun* (1661)
: ¹JAY 1, 2
**Jay·cee** \ˌjā-'sē\ *noun* [from the initials of *Junior Citizens,* former name of the organization] (1938)
: a member of a major national and international civic organization
**jay·gee** \'jā-'jē\ *noun* [junior grade] (1943)
: LIEUTENANT JUNIOR GRADE
**jay·hawk·er** \'jā-ˌhȯ-kər\ *noun* (1858)
**1 a** *often capitalized* : a member of a band of antislavery guerrillas in Kansas and Missouri before and during the Civil War **b** : BANDIT
**2** *capitalized* : a native or resident of Kansas — used as a nickname
**jay·vee** \ˌjā-'vē\ *noun* [junior *v*arsity] (1937)
**1** : JUNIOR VARSITY
**2** : a member of a junior varsity team
**jay·walk** \'jā-ˌwȯk\ *intransitive verb* (1919)
: to cross a street carelessly or in an illegal manner so as to be endangered by traffic
— **jay·walk·er** *noun*
¹**jazz** \'jaz\ *noun, often attributive* [origin unknown] (1913)
**1 a** : American music developed especially from ragtime and blues and characterized by propulsive syncopated rhythms, polyphonic

ensemble playing, varying degrees of improvisation, and often deliberate distortions of pitch and timbre **b** : popular dance music influenced by jazz and played in a loud rhythmic manner
**2** : empty talk : HUMBUG ⟨spouted all the scientific *jazz* —Pete Martin⟩
**3** : similar but unspecified things : STUFF ⟨that wind, and the waves, and all that *jazz* —John Updike⟩
— **jazz·like** \-ˌlīk\ *adjective*
²**jazz** (1917)
*transitive verb*
**1 a** : ENLIVEN — usually used with *up* **b** : ACCELERATE
**2** : to play in the manner of jazz
*intransitive verb*
**1** : to go here and there : GAD
**2** : to dance to or play jazz
**jazz·man** \'jaz-ˌman, -mən\ *noun* (1926)
: a jazz musician
**jazz–rock** \-'räk\ *noun* (1968)
: a blend of jazz and rock music
**jazzy** \'ja-zē\ *adjective* **jazz·i·er; -est** (1919)
**1** : having the characteristics of jazz
**2** : marked by unrestraint, animation, or flashiness
— **jazz·i·ly** \'ja-zə-lē\ *adverb*
— **jazz·i·ness** \'ja-zē-nəs\ *noun*
**J–bar lift** \'jā-ˌbär-\ *noun* (1954)
: a ski lift having a series of J-shaped bars each of which pulls one skier
**jeal·ous** \'je-ləs\ *adjective* [Middle English *jelous,* from Old French, from (assumed) Vulgar Latin *zelosus,* from Late Latin *zelus* zeal — more at ZEAL] (13th century)
**1 a** : intolerant of rivalry or unfaithfulness **b** : disposed to suspect rivalry or unfaithfulness
**2** : hostile toward a rival or one believed to enjoy an advantage
**3** : vigilant in guarding a possession ⟨new colonies were *jealous* of their new independence —Scott Buchanan⟩
— **jeal·ous·ly** *adverb*
— **jeal·ous·ness** *noun*
**jeal·ou·sy** \'je-lə-sē\ *noun, plural* **-sies** (13th century)
**1** : a jealous disposition, attitude, or feeling
**2** : zealous vigilance
**jean** \'jēn\ *noun* [short for *jean fustian,* from Middle English *Gene* Genoa, Italy + *fustian*] (1577)
**1** : a durable twilled cotton cloth used especially for sportswear and work clothes
**2** : pants that are usually close-fitting and made especially of jean or denim — usually used in plural
¹**jeep** \'jēp\ *noun* [probably from *g. p.* (abbreviation of *general purpose*)] (1940)
: a small general-purpose motor vehicle with 80-inch wheelbase, ¼-ton capacity, and four-wheel drive used by the U.S. army in World War II; *also* : a similar but larger and more powerful U.S. army vehicle ◆
²**jeep** *intransitive verb* (1942)
: to travel by jeep
**Jeep** *trademark*
— used for a civilian automotive vehicle
**jee·pers** \'jē-pərz\ *also* **jee·pers cree·pers** \-'krē-pərz\ *interjection* [*jeepers,* euphemism for *Jesus; jeepers creepers,* euphemism for *Jesus Christ*] (1927)
— used as a mild oath
**jeep·ney** \'jēp-nē\ *noun* [*jeep* + *jit*ney] (circa 1949)
: a Philippine jitney bus converted from a jeep
¹**jeer** \'jir\ *verb* [origin unknown] (1561)
*intransitive verb*
: to speak or cry out with derision or mockery
*transitive verb*
: to deride with jeers : TAUNT
**synonym** see SCOFF
— **jeer·er** *noun*
— **jeer·ing·ly** \-iŋ-lē\ *adverb*

²**jeer** *noun* (1625)
: a jeering remark or sound : TAUNT
**jeez** \'jēz\ *interjection* [euphemism for *Jesus*] (1923)
— used as a mild oath or introductory expletive (as to express surprise)
**je·fe** \'hā-(ˌ)fā, 'he-; 'he-fē\ *noun* [Spanish, from French *chef,* from Middle French *chief* — more at CHIEF] (1903)
: CHIEF, LEADER
**Jef·fer·son Da·vis's Birthday** \'je-fər-sən-'dā-və-səz-\ *noun* (1929)
: the first Monday in June observed as a legal holiday in many Southern states
**Jef·fer·son Day** \'je-fər-sən-\ *noun* (1936)
: April 13 observed as a holiday in Alabama in commemoration of Thomas Jefferson's birthday
**Jef·frey pine** \'je-frē-\ *noun* [John *Jeffrey* (died 1854) Scottish botanical explorer] (1858)
: a pine (*Pinus jeffreyi*) of the western U.S. having long needles in groups of three
**je·had** *variant of* JIHAD
**Je·hosh·a·phat** \ji-'hä-sə-ˌfat, -shə-\ *noun* [Hebrew *Yĕhōshāphāth*]
: a king of Judah who brought Judah into an alliance with the northern kingdom of Israel in the 9th century B.C.
**Je·ho·vah** \ji-'hō-və\ *noun* [New Latin, reading (as *Yĕhōwāh*) of Hebrew *yhwh* Yahweh with the vowel points of *ʾadhōnāy* my lord] (1530)
: GOD 1
**Jehovah's Witness** *noun* (1932)
: a member of a group that witness by distributing literature and by personal evangelism to beliefs in the theocratic reign of God, the sinfulness of organized religions and governments, and an imminent millennium
**je·hu** \'jē-(ˌ)hyü, -(ˌ)hü\ *noun* [Hebrew *Yēhū*]
**1** *capitalized* : a king of Israel in the 9th century B.C. who according to the account in II Kings had Jezebel killed in accordance with Elijah's prophecy
**2** : a driver of a coach or cab
**je·ju·nal** \ji-'jü-nᵊl\ *adjective* (circa 1887)
: of or relating to the jejunum
**je·june** \ji-'jün\ *adjective* [Latin *jejunus* empty of food, hungry, meager] (1646)
**1** : lacking nutritive value ⟨*jejune* diets⟩
**2** : devoid of significance or interest : DULL ⟨*jejune* lectures⟩

---

◇ WORD HISTORY

**jeep** A common etymology of *jeep* claims that the word was vocalized from *g.p.* (general purpose), stenciled on military vehicles. Whatever merit this hypothesis has, *jeep* in its early days saw a wide range of applications. Perhaps the progenitor of all of them was a character named Eugene the Jeep that first appeared in March 1936 in Elzie C. Segar's comic strip *Thimble Theater,* featuring Popeye. In a short story of 1938, *jeep* means "nerd," a direction that seems to have been continued by the sense "trainee," U.S. Army slang during World War II. In 1936 *jeep* was applied to an oil company's recording device, and in 1940 to an agricultural tractor converted to military use. In the same year, a wire-service article defined *jeep* as Army vernacular for "any very small plane, helicopter, or gadget." To the Air Corps, *jeep* was a small trainer, and to the Navy an escort carrier. The now familiar use of *jeep* for a 1/4-ton military vehicle was first noted in February 1941, but in the early years of the war, some soldiers applied *jeep* to a now forgotten 3/4-ton command car, while the 1/4-ton vehicle was known as a *peep.*

**3 :** JUVENILE, PUERILE ⟨*jejune* reflections on life and art⟩ ■ ◆
**synonym** see INSIPID
— **je·june·ly** *adverb*
— **je·june·ness** \-'jün-nəs\ *noun*
**je·ju·num** \ji-'jü-nəm\ *noun* [Middle English, from Medieval Latin, from neuter of Latin *jejunus*] (14th century)
**:** the section of the small intestine that comprises the first two fifths beyond the duodenum and that is larger, thicker-walled, and more vascular and has more circular folds than the ileum
**Je·kyll and Hyde** \'je-kə-lən-'hīd *also* 'jē- *or* 'jā-\ *noun* [Dr. *Jekyll* & Mr. *Hyde*, representing the two-sided personality of the protagonist in *The Strange Case of Dr. Jekyll and Mr. Hyde* (1886) by R. L. Stevenson] (circa 1922)
**:** one having a two-sided personality one side of which is good and the other evil
**jell** \'jel\ *verb* [back-formation from *jelly*] (1869)
*intransitive verb*
**1 :** to come to the consistency of jelly **:** CONGEAL, SET
**2 :** to take shape and achieve distinctness **:** become cohesive
*transitive verb*
**:** to cause to jell
**jellied gasoline** *noun* (1944)
**:** NAPALM
**Jell–O** \'je-(,)lō\ *trademark*
— used for a gelatin dessert usually with the flavor and color of fruit
**¹jel·ly** \'je-lē\ *noun, plural* **jellies** [Middle English *gelly*, from Middle French *gelee*, from feminine of *gelé*, past participle of *geler* to freeze, congeal, from Latin *gelare* — more at COLD] (14th century)
**1 :** a soft somewhat elastic food product made usually with gelatin or pectin; *especially* **:** a fruit product made by boiling sugar and the juice of fruit
**2 :** a substance resembling jelly in consistency
**3 :** a state of fear or irresolution
**4 :** a shapeless structureless mass **:** PULP
— **jel·ly·like** \-,līk\ *adjective*
**²jelly** *verb* **jel·lied; jel·ly·ing** (1590)
*intransitive verb*
**1 :** JELL
**2 :** to make jelly
*transitive verb*
**:** to bring to the consistency of jelly
**jelly bean** *noun* (1905)
**:** a sugar-glazed bean-shaped candy
**jel·ly·fish** \'je-lē-,fish\ *noun* (1841)
**1 a :** a free-swimming marine coelenterate that is the sexually reproducing form of a hydrozoan or scyphozoan and has a nearly transparent saucer-shaped body and extensile marginal tentacles studded with stinging cells **b :** SIPHONOPHORE **c :** CTENOPHORE
**2 :** a person lacking backbone or firmness
**jelly roll** *noun* (1895)
**:** a thin sheet of sponge cake spread with jelly and rolled up
**jel·u·tong** \'je-lə-,tȯŋ\ *noun* [Malay *jělutong*] (circa 1836)
**1 :** any of several trees (genus *Dyera*) of the dogbane family
**2 :** the resinous rubbery latex of a jelutong (especially *Dyera costulata*) used especially as a chicle substitute
**jem·my** \'je-mē\ *noun, plural* **jemmies** [from the name *Jemmy*] (circa 1811)
*British* **:** JIMMY
**je ne sais quoi** \zhə-nə-,sā-'kwä\ *noun* [French, literally, I know not what] (circa 1656)
**:** something that cannot be adequately described or expressed
**jen·net** \'he-nā, 'je-nət\ *noun* [Middle English *genett*, from Middle French *genet*, from Catalan, Zenete (member of a Berber people), horse] (15th century)
**1 :** a small Spanish horse

**2 a :** a female donkey **b :** HINNY
**jen·ny** \'je-nē\ *noun, plural* **jennies** [from the name *Jenny*] (1600)
**1 a :** a female bird ⟨*jenny* wren⟩ **b :** a female donkey
**2 :** SPINNING JENNY
**je·on** \(,)jā-'ȯn\ *noun, plural* **jeon** [Korean *chŏn*] (circa 1969)
**:** the chon of South Korea
**jeop·ard** \'je-pərd\ *transitive verb* [Middle English, back-formation from *jeopardie*] (14th century)
**:** JEOPARDIZE
**jeop·ar·dise** *British variant of* JEOPARDIZE
**jeop·ar·dize** \'je-pər-,dīz\ *transitive verb* **-dized; -diz·ing** (1582)
**:** to expose to danger or risk **:** IMPERIL
**jeop·ar·dy** \'je-pər-dē\ *noun* [Middle English *jeopardie*, from Anglo-French *juparti*, from Old French *jeu parti* alternative, literally, divided game] (14th century)
**1 :** exposure to or imminence of death, loss, or injury **:** DANGER
**2 :** the danger that an accused person is subjected to when on trial for a criminal offense ◆
**je·quir·i·ty bean** \jə-'kwir-ə-tē-\ *noun* [French *jékwirity*] (circa 1889)
**1 :** the poisonous scarlet and black seed of the rosary pea often used for beads
**2 :** ROSARY PEA 1
**jer·boa** \jər-'bō-ə, jer-\ *noun* [New Latin, from Arabic *yarbū'*] (1662)
**:** any of several social nocturnal Old World jumping rodents (family Dipodidae) with long hind legs and long tail
**jer·e·mi·ad** \,jer-ə-'mī-əd, -,ad\ *noun* [French *jérémiade*, from *Jérémie* Jeremiah, from Late Latin *Jeremias*] (1780)
**:** a prolonged lamentation or complaint; *also* **:** a cautionary or angry harangue ◆
**Jer·e·mi·ah** \-'mī-ə\ *noun* [Late Latin *Jeremias*, from Greek *Hieremias*, from Hebrew *Yirměyāh*]
**1 :** a major Hebrew prophet of the 6th and 7th centuries B.C.
**2 :** one who is pessimistic about the present and foresees a calamitous future
**3 :** a prophetic book of canonical Jewish and Christian Scripture — see BIBLE table
**Jer·e·mi·as** \-'mī-əs\ *noun* [Late Latin]
**:** JEREMIAH
**¹jerk** \'jərk\ *noun* [probably alteration of *yerk*] (1575)
**1 :** a single quick motion of short duration
**2 a :** jolting, bouncing, or thrusting motions **b :** a tendency to produce spasmodic motions
**3 a :** an involuntary spasmodic muscular movement due to reflex action **b** *plural* **:** involuntary twitchings due to nervous excitement
**4 :** an annoyingly stupid or foolish person
**5 :** the pushing of a weight from shoulder height to a position overhead in weight lifting
**²jerk** (1589)
*transitive verb*
**1 :** to give a quick suddenly arrested push, pull, or twist to
**2 :** to propel or move with or as if with a quick suddenly arrested motion
**3 :** to mix and serve (as sodas) behind a soda fountain
*intransitive verb*
**1 :** to make a sudden spasmodic motion
**2 :** to move in short abrupt motions or with frequent jolts
— **jerk·er** *noun*
**³jerk** *transitive verb* [back-formation from ¹*jerky*] (1707)
**:** to preserve (meat) in long sun-dried slices
**jerk around** *transitive verb* (1941)
**:** to treat badly especially by being underhanded or inconsistent

**jer·kin** \'jər-kən\ *noun* [origin unknown] (1519)
: a close-fitting hip-length usually sleeveless jacket

**jerk off** *verb* (circa 1904)
: MASTURBATE — usually considered vulgar

**jerk·wa·ter** \'jərk-ˌwȯ-tər, -ˌwä-\ *adjective* [from *jerkwater* rural train] (1888)
**1** : remote and unimportant ⟨*jerkwater* towns⟩
**2** : TRIVIAL

**¹jer·ky** \'jər-kē\ *noun* [Spanish *charqui*, from Quechua *ch'arki*] (1850)
: jerked meat

**²jerky** \'jər-kē\ *adjective* **jerk·i·er; -est** (1858)
**1 a** : moving along with or marked by fits and starts **b** : characterized by abrupt transitions
**2** : INANE, FOOLISH
— **jerk·i·ly** \-kə-lē\ *adverb*
— **jerk·i·ness** \-kē-nəs\ *noun*

**jer·o·bo·am** \ˌjer-ə-'bō-əm\ *noun* [*Jeroboam* I (died about 912 B.C.) king of the northern kingdom of Israel] (1816)
: an oversize wine bottle holding about three liters

**jer·ri·can** *or* **jerry can** \'jer-ē-ˌkan\ *noun* [*Jerry* + *can*; from its German design] (1943)
: a narrow flat-sided liquid container holding five gallons (about 19 liters)

**Jer·ry** \'jer-ē\ *noun, plural* **Jerries** [by shortening & alteration] (1898)
*chiefly British* : GERMAN

**jer·ry–build** \'jer-ē-ˌbild\ *transitive verb* **-built** \-ˌbilt\; **-build·ing** [back-formation from *jerry-built*] (1885)
: to build cheaply and flimsily
— **jer·ry–build·er** *noun*

**jer·ry–built** *adjective* [origin unknown] (1869)
**1** : built cheaply and unsubstantially
**2** : carelessly or hastily put together

**jer·sey** \'jər-zē\ *noun, plural* **jerseys** [*Jersey*, one of the Channel Islands] (1587)
**1** : a plain weft-knitted fabric made of wool, cotton, nylon, rayon, or silk and used especially for clothing
**2** : any of various close-fitting usually circular-knitted garments especially for the upper body
**3** *often capitalized* : any of a breed of small short-horned predominantly yellowish brown or fawn dairy cattle noted for their rich milk

**Jersey pine** *noun* (1743)
: VIRGINIA PINE

**Je·ru·sa·lem artichoke** \jə-'rü-s(ə-)ləm-, -'rüz-ləm-, -'rü-zə-\ *noun* [*Jerusalem* by folk etymology from Italian *girasole* girasole] (1641)
: a perennial American sunflower (*Helianthus tuberosus*) widely cultivated for its tubers that are used as a vegetable and as a livestock feed

**Jerusalem cherry** *noun* [*Jerusalem*, Palestine] (1788)
: either of two plants (*Solanum pseudocapsicum* and *S. capsicastrum*) of the nightshade family cultivated as ornamental houseplants for their orange to red berries

**Jerusalem cricket** *noun* (1947)
: a large-headed burrowing nocturnal orthopteran insect (*Stenopelmatus fuscus*) of the southwestern U.S.

**Jerusalem thorn** *noun* (1866)
: a tropical American leguminous

**Jerusalem cricket**

spiny shrub or shrubby tree (*Parkinsonia aculeata*) with pinnate leaves and showy racemose yellow flowers that is widely cultivated

**jess** \'jes\ *noun* [Middle English *ges*, from Middle French *gies*, from plural of *jet* throw, from *jeter* to throw — more at JET] (14th century)
: a short strap secured on the leg of a hawk and usually provided with a ring for attaching a leash
— **jessed** \'jest\ *adjective*

**jes·sa·mine** \'jes-mən, 'je-sə-\ *variant of* JASMINE

**Jes·se** \'je-sē\ *noun* [Hebrew *Yishay*]
: the father of David, king of Israel, according to the account in I Samuel

**jest** \'jest\ *noun* [Middle English *geste* - idle tale, story in verse, from Old French, from Latin *gesta* deeds, from neuter plural of *gestus*, past participle of *gerere* to bear, wage] (circa 1548)
**1** : an utterance (as a jeer or quip) intended to be taken as mockery or humor
**2 a** : PRANK **b** : a ludicrous circumstance or incident
**3 a** : a frivolous mood or manner ⟨spoken in *jest*⟩ **b** : gaiety and merriment
**4** : LAUGHINGSTOCK
**synonym** see FUN
— **jest** *verb*

**jest·er** \'jes-tər\ *noun* (14th century)
**1** : FOOL 2a
**2** : one given to jests

**Je·su·it** \'je-zü-ət, -zhü- *also* -zyü-\ *noun* [New Latin *Jesuita*, from Late Latin *Jesus*] (1559)
**1** : a member of the Roman Catholic Society of Jesus founded by Saint Ignatius Loyola in 1534 and devoted to missionary and educational work
**2** : one given to intrigue or equivocation
— **je·su·it·ic** \ˌje-zü-'(w)i-tik, -zhü-, -zyü-\ *or* **je·su·it·i·cal** \-ti-kəl\ *adjective, often capitalized*
— **je·su·it·i·cal·ly** \-ti-k(ə-)lē\ *adverb, often capitalized*
— **je·su·it·ism** \'je-zü-ə-ˌti-zəm, -zhü-, -zyü-\ *or* **je·su·it·ry** \-ə-trē\ *noun, often capitalized*

**Je·sus** \'jē-zəs, -zəz *also* -ˌzəs *and* -ˌzəz\ *noun* [Late Latin, from Greek *Iēsous*, from Hebrew *Yēshūa'*]
**1** : the Jewish religious teacher whose life, death, and resurrection as reported by the Evangelists are the basis of the Christian message of salvation — called also *Jesus Christ*
**2** *Christian Science* : the highest human corporeal concept of the divine idea rebuking and destroying error and bringing to light man's immortality

**¹jet** \'jet\ *noun* [Middle English, from Middle French *jaiet*, from Latin *gagates*, from Greek *gagatēs*, from *Gagas*, town and river in Asia Minor] (14th century)
**1** : a compact velvet-black coal that takes a good polish and is often used for jewelry
**2** : an intense black

**²jet** *adjective* (1716)
: of the color jet

**³jet** *verb* **jet·ted; jet·ting** [French *jeter*, literally, to throw, from Middle French, from Latin *jactare* to throw, frequentative of *jacere* to throw; akin to Greek *hienai* to send] (1692)
*intransitive verb*
: to spout forth : GUSH
*transitive verb*
: to emit in a stream : SPOUT

**⁴jet** *noun* (circa 1696)
**1 a** (1) : a usually forceful stream of fluid (as water or gas) discharged from a narrow opening or a nozzle (2) : a narrow stream of material (as plasma) emanating or appearing to emanate from a celestial object (as a radio galaxy) **b** : a nozzle for a jet of fluid
**2** : something issuing as if in a jet ⟨talk poured from her in a brilliant *jet* —*Time*⟩
**3 a** : JET ENGINE **b** : an airplane powered by one or more jet engines
**4** : a long narrow current of high-speed winds (as a jet stream)
— **jet·like** \-ˌlīk\ *adjective*

**⁵jet** *intransitive verb* **jet·ted; jet·ting** (1949)
**1** : to travel by jet airplane

**2** : to move or progress by or as if by jet propulsion

**jet–bead** \'jet-ˌbēd\ *noun* (circa 1930)
: a shrub (*Rhodotypos scandens*) that has black shining fruit and is used as an ornamental

**jet–black** \-'blak\ *adjective* (15th century)
: black as jet

**je·té** \zhə-'tā\ *noun* [French, from past participle of *jeter*] (1830)
: a springing jump in ballet made from one foot to the other in any direction

**jet engine** *noun* (1943)
: an engine that produces motion as a result of the rearward discharge of a jet of fluid; *specifically* : an airplane engine that uses atmospheric oxygen to burn fuel and produces a rearward discharge of heated air and exhaust gases — see AIRPLANE illustration

**jet lag** *noun* (1969)
: a condition that is characterized by various psychological and physiological effects (as fatigue and irritability), occurs following long flight through several time zones, and probably results from disruption of circadian rhythms in the human body
— **jet–lagged** \'jet-ˌlagd\ *adjective*

**jet·lin·er** \'jet-ˌlī-nər\ *noun* (1949)
: a jet-propelled airliner

**jet·port** \'jet-ˌpȯrt, -ˌpȯrt\ *noun* (1961)
: an airport designed to handle jet airplanes

**jet–pro·pelled** \'jet-prə-'peld\ *adjective* (1877)
**1** : moving by jet propulsion
**2** : suggestive of the speed and force of a jet airplane

**jet propulsion** *noun* (1867)
: propulsion of a body produced by the forwardly directed forces of the reaction resulting from the rearward discharge of a jet of fluid; *especially* : propulsion of an airplane by jet engines

**jet·sam** \'jet-səm\ *noun* [alteration of *jettison*] (1570)
**1** : the part of a ship, its equipment, or its cargo that is cast overboard to lighten the load in time of distress and that sinks or is washed ashore
**2** : FLOTSAM 2

**jet set** *noun* (1951)
: an international social group of wealthy individuals who frequent fashionable resorts
— **jet–set·ter** \-ˌse-tər\ *noun*
— **jet–set·ting** \-ˌse-tiŋ\ *adjective*

**jet stream** *noun* (1947)
: a long narrow meandering current of high-speed winds near the tropopause blowing from a generally westerly direction and often exceeding a speed of 250 miles (402 kilometers) per hour

**¹jet·ti·son** \'je-tə-sən, -zən\ *noun* [Middle English *jetteson*, from Anglo-French *getteson*, from Old French *getaison* action of throwing, from Latin *jactation-, jactatio*, from *jactare* — more at JET] (15th century)
: a voluntary sacrifice of cargo to lighten a ship's load in time of distress

**²jettison** *transitive verb* (1848)
**1** : to make jettison of
**2** : to get rid of as superfluous or encumbering : DISCARD
**3** : to drop from an airplane or spacecraft in flight
— **jet·ti·son·able** \-sə-nə-bəl, -zə-\ *adjective*

**¹jet·ty** \'je-tē\ *noun, plural* **jetties** [Middle English *jette*, from Middle French *jetee*, from feminine of *jeté*, past participle of *jeter* to throw — more at JET] (15th century)
**1 a** : a structure extended into a sea, lake, or river to influence the current or tide or to protect a harbor **b** : a protecting frame of a pier
**2** : a landing wharf

**²jetty** *intransitive verb* **jet·tied; jet·ty·ing** (1598)
: PROJECT, JUT

**³jetty** *adjective* (1586)
: black as jet

**jeu d'es·prit** \zhœ-des-prē\ *noun, plural* **jeux d'esprit** \*same*\ [French, literally, play of the mind] (1712)
: a witty comment or composition

**jeu·nesse do·rée** \zhœ-nes-dò-rā\ *noun* [French, gilded youth] (1836)
: young people of wealth and fashion

**Jew** \'jü\ *noun* [Middle English, from Old French *gyu*, from Latin *Judaeus*, from Greek *Ioudaios*, from Hebrew *Yĕhūdhī*, from *Yĕhūdhāh* Judah, Jewish kingdom] (13th century)
**1 a** : a member of the tribe of Judah **b** : ISRA-ELITE
**2** : a member of a nation existing in Palestine from the 6th century B.C. to the 1st century A.D.
**3** : a person belonging to a continuation through descent or conversion of the ancient Jewish people
**4** : one whose religion is Judaism

**¹jew·el** \'jü-əl, 'jül *also* 'jú(-ə)l\ *noun, often attributive* [Middle English *juel*, from Old French, probably diminutive of *jeu* game, play, from Latin *jocus* game, joke — more at JOKE] (13th century)
**1** : an ornament of precious metal often set with stones or decorated with enamel and worn as an accessory of dress
**2** : one that is highly esteemed
**3** : a precious stone : GEM
**4** : a bearing for a pivot (as in a watch) made of crystal, glass, or a gem
— **jew·el·like** \-,līk\ *adjective*

**²jewel** *transitive verb* **-eled** *or* **-elled; -el·ing** *or* **-el·ling** (1601)
**1** : to adorn or equip with jewels
**2** : to give beauty to as if with jewels : EMBELLISH

**jewel box** *noun* (1831)
**1** : a small box or case designed to hold jewelry
**2** : something small and exquisite
**3** : a clear plastic case for a compact disc

**jew·el·er** *or* **jew·el·ler** \'jü-ə-lər, 'jü-lər *also* 'jú(-ə)-lər\ *noun* (14th century)
**1** : one who makes or repairs jewelry
**2** : one who deals in jewelry, precious stones, watches, and usually silverware and china

**jew·el·lery** *chiefly British variant of* JEWELRY

**jew·el·ry** \'jü-əl-rē, 'jül-rē, 'jú(-ə)l-rē\ *noun* (14th century)
: JEWELS; *especially* : objects of precious metal often set with gems and worn for personal adornment

**jew·el·weed** \-,wēd\ *noun* (1818)
: TOUCH-ME-NOT

**Jew·ess** \'jü-əs\ *noun* (14th century)
: a Jewish girl or woman — sometimes taken to be offensive

**jew·fish** \'jü-,fish\ *noun* (1679)
: any of various large groupers (especially *Epinephelus itajara*) that are usually dusky green, brown, or blackish, thickheaded, and rough-scaled

**Jew·ish** \'jü-ish\ *adjective* (circa 1546)
: of, relating to, or characteristic of the Jews; *also* : being a Jew
— **Jew·ish·ly** *adverb*
— **Jew·ish·ness** *noun*

**Jewish American Princess** *noun* (1979)
: a stereotypical well-to-do or spoiled American Jewish girl or woman — called also *Jewish Princess*; often used disparagingly

**Jewish calendar** *noun* (circa 1888)
: a calendar in use among Jewish peoples that is reckoned from the year 3761 B.C. and dates in its present form from about A.D. 360 — see MONTH table

**Jew·ry** \'jú(-ə)r-ē, 'jü-rē\ *noun* (14th century)
**1** *plural* **Jewries** : a community of Jews
**2** : the Jewish people

## JEWISH YEARS 5754–5773

| JEWISH YEAR | | A.D. |
|---|---|---|
| 5754 | begins | September 16, 1993 |
| 5755 | begins | September 6, 1994 |
| 5756 | begins | September 25, 1995 |
| 5757 | begins | September 14, 1996 |
| 5758 | begins | October 2, 1997 |
| 5759 | begins | September 21, 1998 |
| 5760 | begins | September 11, 1999 |
| 5761 | begins | September 30, 2000 |
| 5762 | begins | September 18, 2001 |
| 5763 | begins | September 7, 2002 |
| 5764 | begins | September 27, 2003 |
| 5765 | begins | September 16, 2004 |
| 5766 | begins | October 4, 2005 |
| 5767 | begins | September 23, 2006 |
| 5768 | begins | September 13, 2007 |
| 5769 | begins | September 30, 2008 |
| 5770 | begins | September 19, 2009 |
| 5771 | begins | September 9, 2010 |
| 5772 | begins | September 29, 2011 |
| 5773 | begins | September 17, 2012 |

**Jew's harp** *or* **Jews' harp** \'jüz-,härp, 'jüs-\ *noun* (1595)
: a small lyre-shaped instrument that when held between the teeth gives tones from a metal tongue struck by the finger

**Jew's harp**

**Jez·e·bel** \'je-zə-,bel\ *noun* [Hebrew *Izebhel*]
**1** : the Phoenician wife of Ahab who according to the account in I and II Kings pressed the cult of Baal on the Israelite kingdom but was finally killed in accordance with Elijah's prophecy
**2** *often not capitalized* : an impudent, shameless, or morally unrestrained woman

**JHVH** *variant of* YHWH

**jiao** \jē-'aù\ *noun* [Chinese (Beijing) *jiǎo*] (1949)
: a monetary unit of the People's Republic of China equal to ¹/₁₀ yuan

**¹jib** \'jib\ *noun* [origin unknown] (1661)
: a triangular sail set on a stay extending usually from the head of the foremast to the bowsprit or the jibboom; *also* : the small triangular headsail on a sloop — see SAIL illustration

**²jib** *noun* [probably by shortening & alteration from *gibbet*] (1764)
**1** : the projecting arm of a crane
**2** : a derrick boom

**³jib** *intransitive verb* **jibbed; jib·bing** [probably from *jib* to shift from one side of a ship to the other, perhaps from ¹*jib*] (1811)
: to refuse to proceed further : BALK
— **jib·ber** *noun*

**jib·boom** \'ji(b)-'büm\ *noun* [¹*jib* + *boom*] (1748)
: a spar that forms an extension of the bowsprit

**¹jibe** \'jīb\ *variant of* GIBE

**²jibe** *verb* **jibed; jib·ing** [perhaps modification of Dutch *gijben*] (1693)
*intransitive verb*
**1** : to shift suddenly and forcibly from one side to the other — used of a fore-and-aft sail
**2** : to change a vessel's course when sailing with the wind so that as the stern passes through the eye of the wind the boom swings to the opposite side
*transitive verb*
: to cause to jibe

**³jibe** *intransitive verb* **jibed; jib·ing** [origin unknown] (1813)
: to be in accord : AGREE

**ji·ca·ma** \'hē-kə-mə\ *noun* [Mexican Spanish *jícama*, from Nahuatl *xīcamatl*] (circa 1909)
: an edible starchy tuberous root of a leguminous tropical American vine (*Pachyrhizus erosus*)

**Ji·ca·ril·la** \,hē-kə-'rē-yə\ *noun, plural* **Jicarilla** *or* **Jicarillas** [American Spanish *apaches de la xicarilla*, literally, gourd-cup Apaches, from *Cerro de la Xicarilla*, literally, gourd-cup peak, unidentified mountain in Jicarilla territory] (1850)
**1** : a member of an Apache people originally of southeastern Colorado, northern New Mexico, and adjacent areas and now living chiefly in northern New Mexico
**2** : the language of the Jicarilla people

**jiff** \'jif\ *noun* (1797)
: JIFFY

**jif·fy** \'ji-fē\ *noun, plural* **jiffies** [origin unknown] (1779)
: MOMENT, INSTANT ⟨ready in a *jiffy*⟩

**¹jig** \'jig\ *noun* [perhaps from Middle French *giguer* to frolic, from *gigue* fiddle, of Germanic origin; akin to Old High German *gīga* fiddle; akin to Old Norse *geiga* to turn aside] (circa 1560)
**1 a** : any of several lively springy dances in triple rhythm **b** : music to which a jig may be danced
**2** : TRICK, GAME — used chiefly in the phrase *the jig is up*
**3 a** : any of several fishing devices that are jerked up and down or drawn through the water **b** : a device used to maintain mechanically the correct positional relationship between a piece of work and the tool or between parts of work during assembly **c** : a device in which crushed ore is concentrated or coal is cleaned by agitating in water
— **in jig time** : in a short time : QUICKLY

**²jig** *verb* **jigged; jig·ging** (1604)
*intransitive verb*
**1 a** : to move with rapid jerky motions **b** : to dance a jig
**2** : to fish with a jig
*transitive verb*
**1** : to dance in the rapid lively manner of a jig
**2 a** : to give a rapid jerky motion to **b** : to separate (a mineral or ore from waste) with a jig
**3** : to catch (a fish) with a jig
**4** : to machine by means of a jig-controlled tool operation

**³jig** *noun* [short for *jigaboo* black person] (1927)
: BLACK 4 — usually taken to be offensive

**¹jig·ger** \'ji-gər\ *noun* (1675)
**1** : one that jigs or operates a jig
**2** : any of several sails
**3** : JIG 3a
**4 a** (1) : a mechanical device usually with a jerky reciprocating motion (2) : a mold or a machine incorporating a revolving mold on which ceramic items (as plates) are formed **b** : GADGET, DOODAD
**5** : a measure used in mixing drinks that usually holds 1 to 2 ounces (30 to 60 milliliters)

**²jigger** *noun* [perhaps from Wolof *jiga* insect] (1781)
: CHIGGER

**³jigger** *verb* [frequentative of ²*jig*] (1867)
*intransitive verb*
: to jerk up and down
*transitive verb*
: to alter or rearrange especially by manipulating ⟨*jigger* an election district⟩

**jig·gery-pok·ery** \'ji-gər-ē-'pō-kər-ē\ *noun* [probably alteration of Scots *joukery-pawkery*, from *jouk* to dodge, cheat + *pawk* trick, wile] (circa 1892)
: underhanded manipulation or dealings : TRICKERY

**jig·gle** \'ji-gəl\ *verb* **jig·gled; jig·gling** \-g(ə-)liŋ\ [frequentative of ²*jig*] (1836)
*transitive verb*
**:** to cause to move with quick little jerks or oscillating motions
*intransitive verb*
**:** to move from or as if from being jiggled
— **jiggle** *noun*
— **jig·gly** \-g(ə-)lē\ *adjective*

¹**jig·saw** \'jig-,sȯ\ *noun* (1873)
**1 :** a machine saw with a narrow vertically reciprocating blade for cutting curved and irregular lines or ornamental patterns in openwork
**2 :** SCROLL SAW 1
**3 :** JIGSAW PUZZLE

²**jigsaw** *transitive verb* (1873)
**1 :** to cut or form by or as if by a jigsaw
**2 :** to arrange or place in an intricate or interlocking way

³**jigsaw** *adjective* (1884)
**:** suggesting a jigsaw puzzle or its separate pieces

**jigsaw puzzle** *noun* (1919)
**:** a puzzle consisting of small irregularly cut pieces that are to be fitted together to form a picture; *also* **:** something suggesting a jigsaw puzzle

**ji·had** \ji-'häd, *chiefly British* -'had\ *noun* [Arabic *jihād*] (1869)
**1 :** a holy war waged on behalf of Islam as a religious duty
**2 :** a crusade for a principle or belief

**jil·lion** \'jil-yən\ *noun* [*j* + *-illion* (as in *million*)] (circa 1942)
**:** an indeterminately large number
— **jillion** *adjective*

¹**jilt** \'jilt\ *transitive verb* (1673)
**:** to drop (a lover) capriciously or unfeelingly
— **jilt·er** *noun*

²**jilt** *noun* [alteration of *jillet* flirtatious girl] (circa 1674)
**:** one who jilts a lover

**jim crow** \'jim-'krō\ *noun, often J&C capitalized* [*Jim Crow*, stereotype black man in a 19th century song-and-dance act] (1838)
**1 :** BLACK 4 — usually taken to be offensive
**2 :** ethnic discrimination especially against blacks by legal enforcement or traditional sanctions
— **jim crow** *adjective, often J&C capitalized*
— **jim crow·ism** \-,i-zəm\ *noun, often J&C capitalized*

**jim–dan·dy** \'jim-'dan-dē\ *noun* [from the name *Jim*] (1887)
**:** something excellent of its kind

**jim·jams** \'jim-,jamz\ *noun plural* [perhaps alteration of *delirium tremens*] (1852)
**:** JITTERS

**jim·mies** \'ji-mēz\ *noun plural* [origin unknown] (circa 1947)
**:** tiny rod-shaped bits of usually chocolate-flavored candy often sprinkled on ice cream

¹**jim·my** \'ji-mē\ *noun, plural* **jimmies** [from the name *Jimmy*] (1848)
**:** a short crowbar

²**jimmy** *transitive verb* **jim·mied; jim·my·ing** (1893)
**:** to force open with or as if with a jimmy ⟨the burglar *jimmied* a window⟩

**jim·son·weed** \'jim(p)-sən-,wēd\ *noun, often capitalized* [*Jamestown*, Va.] (1832)
**:** a poisonous tall coarse annual weed (*Datura stramonium*) of the nightshade family with rank-smelling foliage and large white or violet trumpet-shaped flowers succeeded by globose prickly fruits

¹**jin·gle** \'jiŋ-gəl\ *verb* **jin·gled; jin·gling** \-g(ə-)liŋ\ [Middle English *ginglen*, of imitative origin] (14th century)
*intransitive verb*
**1 :** to make a light clinking or tinkling sound
**2 :** to rhyme or sound in a catchy repetitious manner
*transitive verb*
**:** to cause to jingle

— **jin·gler** \-g(ə-)lər\ *noun*

²**jingle** *noun* (1599)
**1 a :** a light clinking or tinkling sound **b :** a catchy repetition of sounds in a poem
**2 a :** something that jingles **b :** a short verse or song marked by catchy repetition
— **jin·gly** \-g(ə-)lē\ *adjective*

¹**jin·go** \'jiŋ-(,)gō\ *interjection* [probably euphemism for *Jesus*] (1694)
— used as a mild oath usually in the phrase *by jingo*

²**jingo** *noun, plural* **jingoes** [from the fact that the phrase *by jingo* appeared in the refrain of a chauvinistic song] (1878)
**:** one characterized by jingoism
— **jin·go·ish** \-ish\ *adjective*

**jin·go·ism** \'jiŋ-(,)gō-,i-zəm\ *noun* (1878)
**:** extreme chauvinism or nationalism marked especially by a belligerent foreign policy ◆
— **jin·go·ist** \-ist\ *noun or adjective*
— **jin·go·is·tic** \,jiŋ-gō-'is-tik\ *adjective*
— **jin·go·is·ti·cal·ly** \-ti-k(ə-)lē\ *adverb*

¹**jink** \'jiŋk\ *intransitive verb* [origin unknown] (1785)
**:** to move quickly or unexpectedly with sudden turns and shifts (as in dodging)

²**jink** *noun* (1786)
**1 :** a quick evasive turn **:** SLIP
**2** *plural* **:** PRANKS, FROLICS; *especially* **:** HIGH JINKS

**jin·ni** \'jē-nē, 'ji-, jə-'nē\ *or* **jinn** \'jin\ *noun, plural* **jinn** *or* **jinns** [Arabic *jinnī* demon] (1684)
**1 :** one of a class of spirits that according to Muslim demonology inhabit the earth, assume various forms, and exercise supernatural power
**2 :** GENIE 2

**jin·rick·sha** *or* **jin·rik·i·sha** \jin-'rik-,shȯ\ *noun* [Japanese] (1874)
**:** RICKSHA

¹**jinx** \'jiŋ(k)s\ *noun* [perhaps alteration of *jynx* wryneck; from the use of wrynecks in witchcraft] (1911)
**:** one that brings bad luck; *also* **:** the state or spell of bad luck brought on by a jinx

²**jinx** *transitive verb* (1917)
**:** to foredoom to failure or misfortune **:** bring bad luck to

**ji·pi·ja·pa** \,hē-pē-'hä-pə\ *noun* [Spanish, from *Jipijapa*, Ecuador] (1858)
**1 :** a Central and South American plant (*Carludovica palmata* of the family Cyclanthaceae) resembling a palm
**2 :** PANAMA

**jit·ney** \'jit-nē\ *noun, plural* **jitneys** [origin unknown] (1903)
**1** *slang* **:** NICKEL 2a(1)
**2** [from the original 5 cent fare] **:** BUS 1a; *especially* **:** a small bus that carries passengers over a regular route on a flexible schedule

¹**jit·ter** \'ji-tər\ *noun* [origin unknown] (1929)
**1** *plural* **:** a sense of panic or extreme nervousness ⟨had a bad case of the *jitters* before his performance⟩
**2 :** the state of mind or the movement of one that jitters
**3 :** irregular random movement (as of a pointer or an image on a television screen); *also* **:** vibratory motion

²**jitter** *intransitive verb* (1931)
**1 :** to be nervous or act in a nervous way
**2 :** to make continuous fast repetitive movements

¹**jit·ter·bug** \'ji-tər-,bəg\ *noun* (1938)
**1 :** a jazz variation of the two-step in which couples swing, balance, and twirl in standardized patterns and often with vigorous acrobatics
**2 :** one who dances the jitterbug

²**jitterbug** *intransitive verb* (1939)
**1 :** to dance the jitterbug
**2 :** to move around or back and forth with quick often jerky movements especially to confuse or disconcert an opponent in sports

**jit·tery** \'ji-tə-rē\ *adjective* (1931)

**1 :** suffering from the jitters
**2 :** marked by jittering movements
— **jit·ter·i·ness** \-nəs\ *noun*

**jiu·jit·su, jiu·jut·su** *variant of* JUJITSU

¹**jive** \'jīv\ *noun* [origin unknown] (1928)
**1 :** swing music or the dancing performed to it
**2 a :** glib, deceptive, or foolish talk **b :** the jargon of hipsters **c :** a special jargon of difficult or slang terms
— **jivey** \'jī-vē\ *adjective*

²**jive** *verb* **jived; jiv·ing** (1928)
*transitive verb*
**1 :** TEASE 3, CAJOLE
**2 :** SWING 5
*intransitive verb*
**1 :** KID
**2 :** to dance to or play jive

³**jive** *adjective* (1953)
*slang* **:** PHONY

**jo** \'jō\ *noun, plural* **joes** [alteration of *joy*] (circa 1529)
*chiefly Scottish* **:** SWEETHEART, DEAR

¹**job** \'jäb\ *noun* [perhaps from obsolete English *job* lump] (circa 1627)
**1 a :** a piece of work; *especially* **:** a small miscellaneous piece of work undertaken on order at a stated rate **b :** the object or material on which work is being done **c :** something produced by or as if by work ⟨do a better *job* next time⟩ **d :** an example of a usually specified type **:** ITEM ⟨this *job* is round-necked and sleeveless —Lois Long⟩
**2 a :** something done for private advantage ⟨suspected the whole incident was a put-up *job*⟩ **b :** a criminal enterprise; *specifically* **:** ROBBERY **c :** a damaging or destructive bit of work ⟨did a *job* on him⟩
**3 a** (1) **:** something that has to be done **:** TASK (2) **:** an undertaking requiring unusual exertion ⟨it was a real *job* to talk over that noise⟩ **b :** a specific duty, role, or function ⟨a regular remunerative position **d** *chiefly British* **:** state of affairs — used with *bad* or *good* ⟨it was a good *job* you didn't hit the old man —E. L. Thomas⟩
*synonym* see TASK
— **on the job :** at work

²**job** *verb* **jobbed; job·bing** (1694)
*intransitive verb*
**1 :** to do odd or occasional pieces of work for hire
**2 :** to carry on public business for private gain
**3 :** to carry on the business of a middleman or wholesaler
*transitive verb*

---

◇ WORD HISTORY

**jingoism** The word *jingoism* grew out of an issue that bedeviled 19th century European diplomats, the Eastern Question. As the Ottoman Empire, "the sick man of Europe," gradually collapsed, the other major European powers came into constant conflict on when and how to carve it up among themselves. Britain's policy was to support Turkey in order to prevent any other single power from overwhelming it, and pursuit of this aim led to war with Russia in 1854–55 and a near-war in 1878, when Russian troops, in support of their Slavic coreligionists fighting Ottoman rule in the Balkans, reached the outskirts of Constantinople. With the dispatch of the British fleet to Constantinople, anti-Russian sentiment mounted and the words of a music-hall song expressed the patriotic fervor of some Britons: "We don't want to fight, yet by jingo if we do, we've got the ships, we've got the men, we've got the money too." The song made *jingo* a catchword for a militant patriot. War never came, and the Eastern Question was temporarily settled by an international conference in Berlin, but *jingoism* has remained in English as a byword for excessive patriotism.

**1 :** to buy and sell (as stock) for profit **:** SPEC-ULATE
**2 :** to hire or let by the job or for a period of service
**3 :** to get, deal with, or effect by jobbery
**4 :** to do or cause to be done by separate portions or lots **:** SUBCONTRACT
**5 :** to penalize or deprive unfairly

**³job** *adjective* (1710)
**1** *British* **:** that is for hire for a given service or period
**2 :** used in, engaged in, or done as job work ⟨a *job* shop⟩
**3 :** of or relating to a job or to employment ⟨a guarantee of *job* security⟩

**Job** \'jōb\ *noun* [Latin, from Greek *Iōb*, from Hebrew *Iyyōbh*]
**1 :** the hero of the book of Job who endures afflictions with fortitude and faith
**2 :** a narrative and poetic book of canonical Jewish and Christian Scripture — see BIBLE table

**job action** *noun* (circa 1968)
**:** a temporary action (as a slowdown) by workers as a protest and means of forcing compliance with demands

**job·ber** \'jä-bər\ *noun* (1670)
**:** one that jobs: as **a** (1) **:** WHOLESALER; *specifically* **:** a wholesaler who operates on a small scale or who sells only to retailers and institutions (2) **:** STOCKJOBBER **a b :** a person who works by the job

**job·bery** \'jä-b(ə-)rē\ *noun* (1832)
**:** the act or practice of jobbing; *especially* **:** corruption in public office

**job·hold·er** \'jäb-ˌhōl-dər\ *noun* (1904)
**:** a person having a regular job

**job–hop·ping** \-ˌhä-piŋ\ *noun* (circa 1952)
**:** the practice of moving from job to job
— **job–hop·per** \-ˌhä-pər\ *noun*

**job·less** \'jäb-ləs\ *adjective* (1919)
**1 :** having no job
**2 :** of or relating to those having no job
— **job·less·ness** *noun*

**job lot** *noun* (1851)
**1 :** a miscellaneous collection of goods for sale as a lot usually to a retailer
**2 :** a miscellaneous and usually inferior collection or group

**Job's comforter** \'jōbz-\ *noun* [from the tone of the speeches made to Job by his friends] (1738)
**:** a person who discourages or depresses while seemingly giving comfort and consolation

**Job's tears** *noun plural* (1597)
**1 :** hard pearly white seeds often used as beads
**2** *singular in construction* **:** an Asian grass (*Coix lacryma-jobi*) whose seeds are Job's tears

**Jo·cas·ta** \jō-'kas-tə\ *noun* [Latin, from Greek *Iokastē*]
**:** a queen of Thebes who marries Oedipus not knowing that he is her son

**¹jock** \'jäk\ *noun* (1826)
**1 :** JOCKEY
**2 :** DISC JOCKEY

**²jock** *noun* [*jockstrap*] (1922)
**1 :** ATHLETIC SUPPORTER
**2 :** ATHLETE; *especially* **:** a college athlete

**¹jock·ey** \'jä-kē\ *noun, plural* **jockeys** [*Jockey*, Scots nickname for *John*] (1670)
**1 :** a person who rides or drives a horse especially as a professional in a race
**2 :** a person who operates or works with a specified vehicle, device, or object **:** OPERATOR ⟨an accountant, a pencil *jockey* — with almost no association with the out-of-doors —James Selder⟩

**²jockey** *verb* **jock·eyed; jock·ey·ing** (1708)
*transitive verb*
**1 :** to deal shrewdly or fraudulently with

**2 a :** to ride or drive (a horse) as a jockey **b :** DRIVE, OPERATE
**3 a :** to maneuver or manipulate by adroit or devious means ⟨was *jockeyed* out of the job⟩ **b :** to change the position of by a series of movements ⟨*jockey* a truck into position⟩
*intransitive verb*
**1 :** to act as a jockey
**2 :** to maneuver for advantage — often used in the phrase *jockey for position*

**jockey club** *noun* (1775)
**:** an association for the promotion and regulation of horse racing

**jock itch** *noun* [²*jock*] (1950)
**:** ringworm of the crotch **:** TINEA CRURIS

**jock·strap** \'jäk-ˌstrap\ *noun* [English slang *jock* penis + English *strap*] (1886)
**:** ATHLETIC SUPPORTER

**jo·cose** \jō-'kōs, jə-\ *adjective* [Latin *jocosus*, from *jocus* joke] (1673)
**1 :** given to joking **:** MERRY
**2 :** characterized by joking **:** HUMOROUS
**synonym** see WITTY
— **jo·cose·ly** *adverb*
— **jo·cose·ness** *noun*
— **jo·cos·i·ty** \jō-'kä-sə-tē, jə-\ *noun*

**joc·u·lar** \'jä-kyə-lər\ *adjective* [Latin *jocularis*, from *joculus*, diminutive of *jocus*] (1626)
**1 :** given to jesting **:** habitually jolly or jocund
**2 :** characterized by jesting **:** PLAYFUL
**synonym** see WITTY
— **joc·u·lar·i·ty** \ˌjä-kyə-'lar-ə-tē\ *noun*
— **joc·u·lar·ly** \'jä-kyə-lər-lē\ *adverb*

**jo·cund** \'jä-kənd *also* 'jō-(ˌ)kənd\ *adjective* [Middle English, from Late Latin *jocundus*, alteration of Latin *jucundus*, from *juvare* to help] (14th century)
**:** marked by or suggestive of high spirits and lively mirthfulness ⟨a poet could not but be gay, in such a *jocund* company —William Wordsworth⟩
**synonym** see MERRY
— **jo·cun·di·ty** \jō-'kən-də-tē, jä-\ *noun*
— **jo·cund·ly** \'jä-kənd-lē, 'jō-(ˌ)\ *adverb*

**jodh·pur** \'jäd-(ˌ)pər\ *noun* [*Jodhpur*, India] (1899)
**1** *plural* **:** riding breeches cut full through the hips and close-fitting from knee to ankle
**2 :** an ankle-high boot fastened with a strap that is buckled at the side — called also *jodhpur boot*

**joe** \'jō\ *noun, often capitalized* [from *Joe*, nickname for *Joseph*] (1846)
**:** FELLOW, GUY ⟨an average *joe*⟩

**Jo·el** \'jō-(ə)l\ *noun* [Latin, from Greek *Iōēl*, from Hebrew *Yō'ēl*]
**1 :** the traditionally assumed author of the book of Joel
**2 :** a narrative and apocalyptic book of canonical Jewish and Christian Scripture — see BIBLE table

**joe–pye weed** \'jō-ˌpī-\ *noun* [origin unknown] (circa 1818)
**:** any of several tall American perennial composite herbs (especially *Eupatorium maculatum* and *E. purpureum*) with whorled leaves and corymbose heads of typically purple tubular flowers

**jo·ey** \'jō-ē\ *noun* [origin unknown] (1839)
*Australian* **:** a baby animal; *especially* **:** a baby kangaroo

**¹jog** \'jäg, 'jog\ *verb* **jogged; jog·ging** [probably alteration of *shog*] (1548)
*transitive verb*
**1 :** to give a slight shake or push to **:** NUDGE
**2 :** to rouse to alertness ⟨*jogged* his memory⟩
**3 :** to cause (as a horse) to go at a jog
**4 :** to align the edges of (piled sheets of paper) by hitting or shaking against a flat surface
*intransitive verb*
**1 :** to move up and down or about with a short heavy motion ⟨his . . . holster *jogging* against his hip —Thomas Williams⟩
**2 a :** to run or ride at a slow trot **b :** to go at a slow, leisurely, or monotonous pace **:** TRUDGE

**²jog** *noun* (1635)
**1 :** a slight shake **:** PUSH
**2 a :** a movement, pace, or instance of jogging (as for exercise) **b :** a horse's slow measured trot

**³jog** *noun* [probably alteration of ²*jag*] (1715)
**1 a :** a projecting or retreating part (as of a line or surface) **b :** the space in the angle of a jog
**2 :** a brief abrupt change in direction

**⁴jog** *intransitive verb* **jogged; jog·ging** (1953)
**:** to make a jog ⟨the road *jogs* to the right⟩

**jog·ger** \'jä-gər, 'jo-\ *noun* (circa 1700)
**1 :** one that jogs
**2 :** a device for jogging piled sheets of paper

**jog·gle** \'jä-gəl\ *verb* **jog·gled; jog·gling** \-g(ə-)liŋ\ [frequentative of ¹*jog*] (1513)
*transitive verb*
**:** to shake slightly
*intransitive verb*
**:** to move shakily or jerkily
— **jog·gler** \-g(ə-)lər\ *noun*

**²joggle** *noun* (circa 1727)
**:** ²JOG 2a

**³joggle** *noun* [diminutive of ³*jog*] (1793)
**1 :** a notch or tooth in a joining surface (as of a piece of building material) to prevent slipping
**2 :** a dowel for joining two adjacent blocks of masonry

**⁴joggle** *transitive verb* **jog·gled; jog·gling** \'jä-g(ə-)liŋ\ (1820)
**:** to join by means of a joggle so as to prevent sliding apart

**jog trot** *noun* (1796)
**1 :** ²JOG 2b
**2 :** a routine habit or course of action

**Jo·han·nine** \jō-'ha-ˌnīn, -nən\ *adjective* [Late Latin *Johannes* John] (1861)
**:** of, relating to, or characteristic of the apostle John or the New Testament books ascribed to him

**Jo·han·nis·berg Riesling** \yō-'hä-nəs-ˌberg-\ *noun* [*Johannisberg*, village in Germany] (1976)
**:** a Riesling produced in the U.S. (as in California)

**john** \'jän\ *noun* [from the name *John*] (1856)
**1 :** TOILET
**2 :** a prostitute's client

**John** \'jän\ *noun* [Late Latin *Johannes*, from Greek *Iōannēs*, from Hebrew *Yōhānān*]
**1 :** a Jewish prophet who according to Gospel accounts foretold Jesus's messianic ministry and baptized him — called also *John the Baptist*
**2 :** an apostle who according to various Christian traditions wrote the fourth Gospel, the three Johannine Epistles, and the Book of Revelation
**3 :** the fourth Gospel in the New Testament — see BIBLE table
**4 :** any of three short didactic letters addressed to early Christians and included in the New Testament — see BIBLE table

**John Barleycorn** *noun* (circa 1620)
**:** alcoholic liquor personified

**john·boat** \'jän-ˌbōt\ *noun* [from the name *John*] (1905)
**:** a narrow flat-bottomed square-ended boat usually propelled by a pole or paddle and used on inland waterways

**John Bull** \-'bůl\ *noun* [*John Bull*, character typifying the English nation in *The History of John Bull* (1712) by John Arbuthnot] (1778)
**1 :** the English nation personified **:** the English people
**2 :** a typical Englishman
— **John Bull·ish** \-'bů-lish\ *adjective*

Job's tears 2

\ə\ abut \ᵊ\ kitten \ər\ further \a\ ash \ā\ ace
\ä\ mop, mar \aů\ out \ch\ chin \e\ bet \ē\ easy
\g\ go \i\ hit \ī\ ice \j\ job \ŋ\ sing \ō\ go
\o\ law \oi\ boy \th\ thin \th\ the \ü\ loot \ů\ foot
\y\ yet \zh\ vision *see also* Guide to Pronunciation

— **John Bull·ish·ness** *noun*
— **John Bull·ism** \-ˌli-zəm\ *noun*
**John Doe** \-ˈdō\ *noun* (1768)
**1 :** a party to legal proceedings whose true name is unknown
**2 :** an average man
**John Do·ry** \-ˈdōr-ē, -ˈdȯr-\ *noun, plural* **John Dories** [earlier *dory,* from Middle English *dorre,* from Middle French *doree,* literally, gilded one] (1754)
**:** a common yellow to olive food fish (*Zeus faber*) of Europe and Africa with an oval compressed body, long dorsal spines, and a dark spot on each side; *also* **:** a closely related and possibly identical fish (*Z. capensis*) widely distributed in southern seas
**Joh·ne's disease** \ˈyō-nəz-\ *noun* [Heinrich A. *Johne* (died 1910) German bacteriologist] (1907)
**:** a chronic often fatal contagious enteritis of ruminants and especially of cattle that is caused by a bacterium (*Mycobacterium paratuberculosis*) and is characterized by persistent diarrhea and gradual emaciation
**John Han·cock** \ˈjän-ˌhan-ˌkäk\ *noun* [*John Hancock;* from the prominence of his signature on the Declaration of Independence] (1903)
**:** an autograph signature
**John Hen·ry** \-ˈhen-rē\ *noun* [from the name *John Henry,* from confusion with *John Hancock*] (1914)
**:** an autograph signature
**John Mark** *noun*
**:** MARK 1a
**john·ny** \ˈjä-nē\ *noun, plural* **johnnies** [from the name *Johnny*] (1673)
**1** *often capitalized* **:** FELLOW, GUY
**2 :** a short-sleeved collarless gown that is open in the back and is worn by persons (as hospital patients) undergoing medical examination or treatment
**john·ny·cake** \ˈjä-nē-ˌkāk\ *noun* [probably from the name *Johnny*] (1739)
**:** a bread made with cornmeal
**John·ny–come–late·ly** \ˈjä-nē-(ˌ)kəm-ˈlāt-lē\ *noun, plural* **Johnny–come–latelies** *or* **Johnnies–come–lately** (1839)
**1 :** a late or recent arrival **:** NEWCOMER
**2 :** UPSTART (established families tend to hold themselves above the *Johnny-come-latelies* —William Zeckendorf (died 1976))
**John·ny–jump–up** \ˌjä-nē-ˈjəmp-ˌəp\ *noun* (1842)
**1 :** a common and long-cultivated European viola (*Viola tricolor*) which has short-spurred flowers usually blue or purple mixed with white and yellow and from which most of the garden pansies are derived; *broadly* **:** any of various small-flowered cultivated pansies
**2 :** any of various American violets
**John·ny–on–the–spot** \ˈjä-nē-ˌȯn-thə-ˈspät, -ˌän-\ *noun* (1896)
**:** a person who is on hand and ready to perform a service or respond to an emergency
**Johnny Reb** \-ˈreb\ *noun* [from the name *Johnny* + *reb* rebel] (1865)
**:** a Confederate soldier
**John·son·ese** \ˌjän(t)-sə-ˈnēz, -ˈnēs\ *noun* [Samuel *Johnson*] (1843)
**:** a literary style characterized by balanced phraseology and Latinate diction
**john·son·grass** \ˈjän(t)-sən-ˌgras\ *noun, often capitalized* [William *Johnston* (died 1859) American agriculturist] (1884)
**:** a tall perennial sorghum (*Sorghum halepense*) originally of the Mediterranean region that is widely used for forage in warm areas and often becomes naturalized
**joie de vi·vre** \ˌzhwä-də-ˈvēvrʳ\ *noun* [French, literally, joy of living] (1889)
**:** keen or buoyant enjoyment of life
**¹join** \ˈjȯin\ *verb* [Middle English, from Old French *joindre,* from Latin *jungere* — more at YOKE] (13th century)
*transitive verb*

**1 a :** to put or bring together so as to form a unit (*join* two blocks of wood with glue) **b :** to connect (as points) by a line **c :** ADJOIN
**2 :** to put or bring into close association or relationship (*joined* in marriage)
**3 :** to engage in (battle)
**4 a :** to come into the company of (*joined* us for lunch) **b :** to associate oneself with (*joined* the church)
*intransitive verb*
**1 a :** to come together so as to be connected (nouns *join* to form compounds) **b :** ADJOIN (the two estates *join*)
**2 :** to come into close association or relationship: as **a :** to form an alliance **b :** to become a member of a group **c :** to take part in a collective activity (*join* in singing) ☆
— **join·able** \ˈjȯi-nə-bəl\ *adjective*
**²join** *noun* (1825)
**1 :** JOINT
**2 :** UNION 2d
**join·der** \ˈjȯin-dər\ *noun* [French *joindre* to join, from Old French] (1601)
**1 :** CONJUNCTION 1
**2 a** (1) **:** a joining of parties as plaintiffs or defendants in a suit (2) **:** a joining of causes of action or defense **b :** acceptance of an issue tendered
**join·er** \ˈjȯi-nər\ *noun* (14th century)
**:** one that joins: as **a :** a person whose occupation is to construct articles by joining pieces of wood **b :** a gregarious or civic-minded person who joins many organizations
**join·ery** \ˈjȯi-nə-rē, ˈjȯin-rē\ *noun* (1678)
**1 :** the art or trade of a joiner
**2 :** work done by a joiner
**join·ing** \ˈjȯi-niŋ\ *noun* (14th century)
**1 :** the act or an instance of joining one thing to another **:** JUNCTURE
**2 a :** the place or manner of being joined together **b :** something that joins two things together
**¹joint** \ˈjȯint\ *noun* [Middle English *jointe,* from Old French, from *joindre*] (13th century)
**1 a** (1) **:** the point of contact between elements of an animal skeleton with the parts that surround and support it (2) **:** NODE 5b **b :** a part or space included between two articulations, knots, or nodes **c :** a large piece of meat for roasting
**2 a :** a place where two things or parts are joined **b :** a space between the adjacent surfaces of two bodies joined and held together (as by cement or mortar) **c :** a fracture or crack in rock not accompanied by dislocation **d :** the flexing part of a cover along either backbone edge of a book **e :** the junction of two or more members of a framed structure **f :** a union formed by two abutting rails in a track including the elements (as bars and bolts) necessary to hold the abutting rails together **g :** an area at which two ends, surfaces, or edges are attached
**3 a :** a shabby or disreputable place of entertainment **b :** PLACE, ESTABLISHMENT **c** *slang* **:** PRISON 2
**4 :** a marijuana cigarette
— **joint·ed** \ˈjȯin-təd\ *adjective*
— **joint·ed·ly** *adverb*
— **joint·ed·ness** *noun*
— **out of joint 1 a** *of a bone* **:** having the head slipped from its socket **b :** at variance **2 a :** DISORDERED 2a **b :** being out of humor **:** DISSATISFIED
**²joint** *adjective* [Middle English, from Middle French, from past participle of *joindre,* from Old French] (14th century)
**1 :** UNITED, COMBINED (the *joint* influences of culture and climate)
**2 :** common to two or more: as **a** (1) **:** involving the united activity of two or more (a *joint* effort) (2) **:** constituting an activity, operation, or organization in which elements of more than one armed service participate (*joint* maneuvers) (3) **:** constituting an action or expression of two or more governments (*joint* peace

talks) **b :** shared by or affecting two or more (a *joint* fine)
**3 :** united, joined, or sharing with another (as in a right or status) (*joint* heirs)
**4 :** being a function of or involving two or more variables and especially random variables
— **joint·ly** *adverb*
**³joint** *verb* [¹*joint*] (1530)
*transitive verb*
**1 :** to separate the joints of (as meat)
**2 a :** to unite by a joint **:** fit together **b :** to provide with a joint **:** ARTICULATE **c :** to prepare (as a board) for joining by planing the edge
*intransitive verb*
**1 :** to fit as if by joints (the stones *joint* neatly)
**2 :** to form joints as a stage in growth — used especially of small grains
**Joint Chiefs of Staff** (1946)
**:** a military advisory group composed of the chiefs of staff of the army and air force, the chief of naval operations, and sometimes the commandant of the marine corps
**joint·er** \ˈjȯin-tər\ *noun* (1678)
**:** one that joints; *especially* **:** any of various tools used in making joints
**joint grass** *noun* (1835)
**:** a coarse creeping grass (*Paspalum distichum*) with jointed stems that is used for fodder and for erosion control
**joint resolution** *noun* (1838)
**:** a resolution passed by both houses of a legislative body that has the force of law when signed by or passed over the veto of the executive
**join·tress** \ˈjȯin-trəs\ *noun* (1602)
**:** a woman having a legal jointure
**joint–stock company** *noun* (1776)
**:** a company or association consisting of individuals organized to conduct a business for gain and having a joint stock of capital represented by shares owned individually by the members and transferable without the consent of the group
**join·ture** \ˈjȯin-chər\ *noun* (14th century)
**1 a :** an act of joining **:** the state of being joined **b :** JOINT
**2 a :** an estate settled on a wife to be taken by her in lieu of dower **b :** a settlement on the wife of a freehold estate for her lifetime
**joint–worm** \ˈjȯint-ˌwərm\ *noun* (1851)
**:** the larva of any of several small chalcid wasps (genus *Harmolita*) that attacks the stems of grain and causes swellings like galls at or just above the first joint
**joist** \ˈjȯist\ *noun* [Middle English *joiste,* from Middle French *giste,* from (assumed) Vulgar

---

☆ **SYNONYMS**
**Join, combine, unite, connect, link, associate, relate** mean to bring or come together into some manner of union. JOIN implies a bringing into contact or conjunction of any degree of closeness (*joined* forces in an effort to win). COMBINE implies some merging or mingling with corresponding loss of identity of each unit (*combined* jazz and rock to create a new music). UNITE implies somewhat greater loss of separate identity (the colonies *united* to form a republic). CONNECT suggests a loose or external attachment with little or no loss of identity (a mutual defense treaty *connected* the two nations). LINK may imply strong connection or inseparability of elements still retaining identity (a name forever *linked* with liberty). ASSOCIATE stresses the mere fact of frequent occurrence or existence together in space or in logical relation (opera is popularly *associated* with high society). RELATE suggests the existence of a real or presumed logical connection (*related* what he observed to what he already knew).

Latin *jacitum,* from Latin *jacēre* to lie — more at ADJACENT] (15th century)
: any of the small timbers or metal beams ranged parallel from wall to wall in a structure to support a floor or ceiling

**jo·jo·ba** \hə-'hō-bə\ *noun* [Mexican Spanish] (1923)
: a shrub or small tree (*Simmondsia chinensis* synonym *S. californica*) of the box family of southwestern North America with edible seeds that yield a valuable liquid wax

¹**joke** \'jōk\ *noun* [Latin *jocus;* perhaps akin to Old High German *gehan* to say, Sanskrit *yācati* he asks] (1670)
**1 a :** something said or done to provoke laughter; *especially* **:** a brief oral narrative with a climactic humorous twist **b** (1) **:** the humorous or ridiculous element in something (2) **:** an instance of jesting **:** KIDDING ⟨can't take a *joke*⟩ **c :** PRACTICAL JOKE **d :** LAUGHINGSTOCK
**2 :** something not to be taken seriously **:** a trifling matter ⟨consider his skiing a *joke* —Harold Callender⟩ — often used in negative construction ⟨it is no *joke* to be lost in the desert⟩

²**joke** *verb* **joked; jok·ing** (1670)
*intransitive verb*
: to make jokes **:** JEST
*transitive verb*
: to make the object of a joke **:** KID
— **jok·ing·ly** \'jō-kiŋ-lē\ *adverb*

**jok·er** \'jō-kər\ *noun* (1729)
**1 a :** a person given to joking **:** WAG **b :** FELLOW, GUY; *especially* **:** an insignificant, obnoxious, or incompetent person ⟨a shame to let a *joker* like this win —Harold Robbins⟩
**2 :** a playing card added to a pack as a wild card or as the highest-ranking card
**3 a** (1) **:** an ambiguous or apparently immaterial clause inserted in a legislative bill to make it inoperative or uncertain in some respect (2) **:** an unsuspected, misleading, or misunderstood clause, phrase, or word in a document that nullifies or greatly alters it **b :** something (as an expedient or stratagem) held in reserve to gain an end or escape from a predicament **c :** an unsuspected or not readily apparent fact, factor, or condition that thwarts or nullifies a seeming advantage

**jok·ey** *also* **joky** \'jō-kē\ *adjective* **jok·i·er; -est** (circa 1825)
**1 :** given to joking
**2 :** HUMOROUS, COMICAL
**3 :** amusingly ridiculous **:** LAUGHABLE
— **jok·i·ly** \-kə-lē\ *adverb*
— **jok·i·ness** \-kē-nəs\ *noun*

**jol·li·fi·ca·tion** \ˌjä-li-fə-'kā-shən\ *noun* (1809)
: FESTIVITY, MERRYMAKING

**jol·li·ty** \'jä-lə-tē\ *noun, plural* **-ties** (14th century)
**1 :** the quality or state of being jolly **:** MERRIMENT
**2** *British* **:** a festive gathering

¹**jol·ly** \'jä-lē\ *adjective* **jol·li·er; -est** [Middle English *joli,* from Old French] (14th century)
**1 a** (1) **:** full of high spirits **:** JOYOUS (2) **:** given to conviviality **:** JOVIAL **b :** expressing, suggesting, or inspiring gaiety **:** CHEERFUL
**2 :** extremely pleasant or agreeable **:** SPLENDID
**synonym** *see* MERRY

²**jolly** *adverb* (1549)
: VERY ⟨would . . . do as they were *jolly* well told —John Stockbridge⟩

³**jolly** *verb* **jol·lied; jol·ly·ing** (1610)
*intransitive verb*
: to engage in good-natured banter
*transitive verb*
: to put or try to put in good humor especially to gain an end

⁴**jolly** *noun, plural* **jollies** (1905)
**1** *chiefly British* **:** a good time **:** JOLLIFICATION

**2** *plural* **:** KICKS ⟨get their *jollies* by reenacting famous murders —H. F. Waters⟩

**jol·ly boat** \'jä-lē-\ *noun* [origin unknown] (circa 1741)
: a ship's boat of medium size used for general-purpose work

**Jol·ly Rog·er** \'jä-lē-'rä-jər\ *noun* [probably from ¹*jolly* + the name *Roger*] (circa 1785)
: a black flag with a white skull and crossbones formerly used by pirates as their ensign

¹**jolt** \'jōlt\ *verb* [probably blend of obsolete *joll* to strike and *jot* to bump] (1596)
*transitive verb*
**1 :** to cause to move with a sudden jerky motion
**2 :** to give a knock or blow to; *specifically* **:** to jar with a quick or hard blow
**3 a :** to disturb the composure of ⟨crudely *jolted* out of that mood —Virginia Woolf⟩ **b :** to interfere with roughly, abruptly, and disconcertingly ⟨determination to pursue his own course was *jolted* badly —F. L. Paxson⟩
*intransitive verb*
: to move with a sudden jerky motion
— **jolt·er** *noun*

²**jolt** *noun* (1599)
**1 :** an abrupt sharp jerky blow or movement
**2 a** (1) **:** a sudden feeling of shock, surprise, or disappointment (2) **:** an event or development causing such a feeling ⟨the defeat was quite a *jolt*⟩ **b :** a serious check or reverse ⟨a severe financial *jolt*⟩
**3 :** a small potent or bracing portion ⟨a *jolt* of horseradish⟩
— **jolty** \'jōl-tē\ *adjective*

**jolt–wag·on** \'jōlt-ˌwa-gən\ *noun* (1886)
*Midland* **:** a farm wagon

**Jo·nah** \'jō-nə, *3 is also* -nər\ *noun* [Hebrew *Yōnāh*]
**1 :** an Israelite prophet who according to the account in the book of Johah resisted a divine call to preach repentance to the people of Nineveh, was swallowed and vomited by a great fish, and eventually carried out his mission
**2 :** a narrative book of canonical Jewish and Christian Scripture — see BIBLE table
**3 :** one believed to bring bad luck

**Jo·nas** \'jō-nəs\ *noun* [Late Latin, from Hebrew *Yōnāh*]
: JONAH

**Jon·a·than** \'jä-nə-thən\ *noun* [Hebrew *Yōnāthān*]
**1 :** a son of Saul and friend of David according to the account in I Samuel
**2 :** AMERICAN; *especially* **:** a New Englander
**3 :** any of a variety of red-skinned apple

**jon·gleur** \zhōⁿ-'glər\ *noun* [French, from Old French *jogleour* — more at JUGGLER] (1779)
: an itinerant medieval entertainer proficient in juggling, acrobatics, music, and recitation

**jon·quil** \'jän-kwəl, 'jäŋ-\ *noun* [French *jonquille,* from Spanish *junquillo,* diminutive of *junco* reed, from Latin *juncus*] (1629)
: a Mediterranean perennial bulbous herb (*Narcissus jonquilla*) of the amaryllis family with long linear leaves that is widely cultivated for its yellow or white fragrant short-tubed clustered flowers — compare DAFFODIL

**Jor·dan almond** \'jòr-dᵊn-\ *noun* [Middle English *jardin almande,* from Middle French *jardin* garden + Middle English *almande* almond] (1615)
: a large Spanish almond especially when salted or coated with sugar of various colors

**Jor·dan curve** \zhòr-'däⁿ-, 'jòr-dᵊn-\ *noun* [Camille *Jordan* (died 1922) French mathematician] (1900)
: SIMPLE CLOSED CURVE

**Jordan curve theorem** *noun* (1947)
: a fundamental theorem of topology: every simple closed curve divides the plane into two regions for which it is the common boundary

**jo·rum** \'jōr-əm, 'jòr-\ *noun* [perhaps from *Joram* in the Bible who "brought with him vessels of silver" (2 Samuel 8:10—Authorized Version)] (1730)

: a large drinking vessel or its contents

**jo·seph** \'jō-zəf *also* -səf\ *noun* [Latin, from Greek *Iōsēph,* from Hebrew *Yōsēph*]
**1** *capitalized* **a :** a son of Jacob who according to the account in Genesis rose to high political office in Egypt after being sold into slavery by his brothers **b :** the husband of Mary the mother of Jesus according to the Gospel accounts
**2 :** a long cloak worn especially by women in the 18th century

**Jo·seph·ite** \-zə-ˌfīt, -sə-\ *noun* (1890)
: a member of Saint Joseph's Society of the Sacred Heart founded in 1871 in Baltimore, Md. and devoted to missionary work among black Americans

**Joseph of Ar·i·ma·thea** \-ˌar-ə-mə-'thē-ə\
: a rich councillor of the Sanhedrin who according to the Gospel accounts placed the body of Jesus in his own tomb and according to medieval legend took the Holy Grail to England

**Jo·seph·son junction** \'jō-zəf-sən- *also* -səf-sən-\ *noun* [Brian D. *Josephson*] (1965)
: an electronic fast-switching device that consists of two layers of superconducting metal separated by a thin layer of insulator through which low current flows but increased current causes the insulator to block the flow

¹**josh** \'jäsh\ *verb* [origin unknown] (1852)
*transitive verb*
: to tease good-naturedly **:** KID
*intransitive verb*
: to engage in banter **:** JOKE
— **josh·er** *noun*

²**josh** *noun* (1878)
: a good-humored joke **:** JEST

**Josh·ua** \'jä-sh(ə-)wə\ *noun* [Hebrew *Yĕhōshūaʻ*]
**1 :** the divinely commissioned successor of Moses and military leader of the Israelites during the conquest of Canaan according to the account in the book of Joshua
**2 :** a mainly narrative book of canonical Jewish and Christian Scripture — see BIBLE table

**Joshua tree** *noun* (1884)
: a tall branched arborescent yucca (*Yucca brevifolia*) of the southwestern U.S. that has clustered greenish white flowers

Joshua tree

**joss** \'jäs, 'jòs\ *noun* [Chinese Pidgin English, from Portuguese *deus* god, from Latin — more at DEITY] (1711)
: a Chinese idol or cult image

**joss house** *noun* (1771)
: a Chinese temple or shrine

**joss stick** *noun* (1845)
: a slender stick of incense burned in front of a joss

¹**jos·tle** \'jä-səl\ *verb* **jos·tled; jos·tling** \-s(ə-)liŋ\ [alteration of *justle,* frequentative of ¹*joust*] (1546)
*intransitive verb*
**1 a :** to come in contact or into collision **b :** to make one's way by pushing and shoving **c :** to exist in close proximity
**2 :** to vie in gaining an objective **:** CONTEND
*transitive verb*
**1 a :** to come in contact or into collision with **b :** to force by pushing **:** ELBOW **c :** to stir up **:** AGITATE **d :** to exist in close proximity with
**2 :** to vie with in attaining an objective

²**jostle** *noun* (1611)
**1 :** a jostling encounter or experience

**2 :** the state of being crowded or jostled together

**Jos·ue** \'jä-shü-(,)ē\ *noun* [Late Latin, from Hebrew *Yĕhōshūa'*]
**:** JOSHUA

**¹jot** \'jät\ *noun* [Latin *iota, jota* iota] (1500)
**:** the least bit : IOTA ◆

**²jot** *transitive verb* **jot·ted; jot·ting** (1721)
**:** to write briefly or hurriedly **:** set down in the form of a note ⟨*jot* this down⟩

**jotting** *noun* (1814)
**:** a brief note : MEMORANDUM

**Jo·tun** *also* **Jo·tunn** \'yō-t°n, -,tùn\ *noun* [Old Norse *jǫtunn*]
**:** a member of a race of giants in Norse mythology

**Jo·tun·heim** *also* **Jo·tunn·heim** \-,hīm, -,hām\ *noun* [Old Norse *Jǫtunheimar*]
**:** the home of the Jotuns in Norse mythology

**jou·al** \zhù-'al, -'äl, -'àl\ *noun* [Canadian French, rendering of a nonstandard pronunciation of French *cheval* horse] (1962)
**:** spoken Canadian French; *especially* **:** the local forms of the spoken French of Quebec that differ the most from prescribed forms

**joule** \'jü(ə)l *also* ÷'jaù(ə)l\ *noun* [James P. *Joule*] (1882)
**:** a unit of work or energy equal to the work done by a force of one newton acting through a distance of one meter

**¹jounce** \'jaùn(t)s\ *verb* **jounced; jounc·ing** [Middle English] (15th century)
*intransitive verb*
**:** to move in an up-and-down manner : BOUNCE
*transitive verb*
**:** to cause to jounce

**²jounce** *noun* (circa 1787)
**:** JOLT

**jouncy** \'jaùn(t)-sē\ *adjective* **jounc·i·er; -est** (1943)
**:** marked by a jouncing motion or effect

**jour·nal** \'jər-n°l\ *noun* [Middle English, service book containing the day hours, from Middle French, from *journal*, adjective, daily, from Latin *diurnalis*, from *diurnus* of the day, from *dies* day — more at DEITY] (15th century)
**1 a :** a record of current transactions; *especially* **:** a book of original entry in double-entry bookkeeping **b :** an account of day-to-day events **c :** a record of experiences, ideas, or reflections kept regularly for private use **d :** a record of transactions kept by a deliberative or legislative body **e :** LOG 3, 4
**2 a :** a daily newspaper **b :** a periodical dealing especially with matters of current interest
**3 :** the part of a rotating shaft, axle, roll, or spindle that turns in a bearing

**journal box** *noun* (circa 1859)
**:** a metal housing to support and protect a journal bearing

**jour·nal·ese** \,jər-n°l-'ēz, -'ēs\ *noun* (1882)
**:** a style of writing held to be characteristic of newspapers

**jour·nal·ism** \'jər-n°l-,i-zəm\ *noun* (1833)
**1 a :** the collection and editing of news for presentation through the media **b :** the public press **c :** an academic study concerned with the collection and editing of news or the management of a news medium
**2 a :** writing designed for publication in a newspaper or magazine **b :** writing characterized by a direct presentation of facts or description of events without an attempt at interpretation **c :** writing designed to appeal to current popular taste or public interest

**jour·nal·ist** \-n°l-ist\ *noun* (1693)
**1 a :** a person engaged in journalism; *especially* **:** a writer or editor for a news medium **b** **:** a writer who aims at a mass audience
**2 :** a person who keeps a journal

**jour·nal·is·tic** \,jər-n°l-'is-tik\ *adjective* (1829)
**:** of, relating to, or characteristic of journalism or journalists
**— jour·nal·is·ti·cal·ly** \-ti-k(ə-)lē\ *adverb*

**jour·nal·ize** \'jər-n°l-,īz\ *verb* **-ized; -iz·ing** (1766)
*transitive verb*
**:** to record in a journal
*intransitive verb*
**1 :** to keep a journal in accounting
**2 :** to keep a personal journal
**— jour·nal·iz·er** *noun*

**¹jour·ney** \'jər-nē\ *noun, plural* **journeys** [Middle English, from Old French *journee* day's journey, from *jour* day, from Late Latin *diurnum*, from Latin, neuter of *diurnus*] (13th century)
**1 :** travel or passage from one place to another **:** TRIP
**2** *chiefly dialect* **:** a day's travel
**3 :** something suggesting travel or passage from one place to another ⟨the *journey* from youth to maturity⟩ ⟨a *journey* through time⟩

**²journey** *verb* **jour·neyed; jour·ney·ing** (14th century)
*intransitive verb*
**:** to go on a journey **:** TRAVEL
*transitive verb*
**:** to travel over or through
**— jour·ney·er** *noun*

**jour·ney·man** \-mən\ *noun* [Middle English, from *journey* journey, a day's labor + *man*] (15th century)
**1 :** a worker who has learned a trade and works for another person usually by the day
**2 :** an experienced reliable worker or performer especially as distinguished from one who is brilliant or colorful ⟨a good *journeyman* trumpeter *—New Yorker*⟩ ⟨a *journeyman* outfielder⟩

**jour·ney·work** \-,wərk\ *noun* (1601)
**1 :** work done by a journeyman
**2 :** HACKWORK

**¹joust** \'jaùst *sometimes* 'jəst *or* 'jüst\ *intransitive verb* [Middle English, from Middle French *juster* to unite, joust, from (assumed) Vulgar Latin *juxtare*, from Latin *juxta* near; akin to Latin *jungere* to join — more at YOKE] (14th century)
**1 a :** to fight on horseback as a knight or man-at-arms **b :** to engage in combat with lances on horseback
**2 :** to engage in personal combat or competition
**— joust·er** *noun*

**²joust** *noun* (14th century)
**1 a :** a combat on horseback between two knights with lances especially as part of a tournament **b** *plural* **:** TOURNAMENT
**2 :** a personal combat or competition **:** STRUGGLE

**Jove** \'jōv\ *noun* [Latin *Jov-, Juppiter*]
**:** JUPITER — often used interjectionally to express surprise or agreement especially in the phrase *by Jove*

**jo·vial** \'jō-vē-əl, -vyəl\ *adjective* (1592)
**1** *capitalized* **:** of or relating to Jove
**2 :** markedly good-humored especially as evidenced by jollity and conviviality
**synonym** see MERRY
**— jo·vi·al·i·ty** \,jō-vē-'a-lə-tē\ *noun*
**— jo·vial·ly** \'jō-vē-ə-lē, -vyə-\ *adverb*

**Jo·vi·an** \'jō-vē-ən\ *adjective* (1530)
**:** of, relating to, or characteristic of the god or planet Jupiter

**jow** \'jaù\ *noun* [Middle English *jollen* to knock] (1515)
*chiefly Scottish* **:** STROKE, TOLL

**jo·war** \jə-'wär\ *noun* [Hindi *joār, juwār*, from Sanskrit *yavākāra* barley-shaped, from *yava* barley + *karoti* he makes] (1800)
**:** DURRA

**¹jowl** \'jaù(ə)l *sometimes* 'jōl\ *noun* [alteration of Middle English *choll*] (15th century)
**:** a cut of fish consisting of the head and usually adjacent parts

**²jowl** *noun* [alteration of Middle English *cholle*, probably from Old English *ceole* throat — more at GLUTTON] (1591)

**:** usually slack flesh (as a dewlap, wattle, or the pendulous part of a double chin) associated with the cheeks, lower jaw, or throat

**³jowl** *noun* [alteration of Middle English *chavel*, from Old English *ceafl*; akin to Middle High German *kivel* jaw, Avestan *zafar-* mouth] (1598)
**1 a :** JAW; *especially* **:** MANDIBLE **b :** one of the lateral halves of the mandible
**2 a :** CHEEK 1 **b :** the cheek meat of a hog ⟨a dinner of boiled *jowls*⟩

**jowly** \'jaù-lē *sometimes* 'jō-\ *adjective* **jowl·i·er; -est** (circa 1873)
**:** having marked jowls **:** having full or saggy flesh about the lower cheeks and jaw area ⟨elderly man with a disillusioned *jowly* face —John Dos Passos⟩

**¹joy** \'jòi\ *noun* [Middle English, from Old French *joie*, from Latin *gaudia*, plural of *gaudium*, from *gaudēre* to rejoice; probably akin to Greek *gēthein* to rejoice] (13th century)
**1 a :** the emotion evoked by well-being, success, or good fortune or by the prospect of possessing what one desires **:** DELIGHT **b :** the expression or exhibition of such emotion **:** GAIETY
**2 :** a state of happiness or felicity **:** BLISS
**3 :** a source or cause of delight
**— joy·less** \-ləs\ *adjective*
**— joy·less·ly** *adverb*
**— joy·less·ness** *noun*

**²joy** (14th century)
*intransitive verb*
**:** to experience great pleasure or delight **:** REJOICE
*transitive verb*
**1** *archaic* **:** GLADDEN
**2** *archaic* **:** ENJOY

**joy·ance** \'jòi-ən(t)s\ *noun* (circa 1586)
*archaic* **:** DELIGHT, ENJOYMENT

**joy·ful** \'jòi-fəl\ *adjective* (13th century)
**:** experiencing, causing, or showing joy **:** HAPPY
**— joy·ful·ly** \-fə-lē\ *adverb*
**— joy·ful·ness** *noun*

**joy·ous** \'jòi-əs\ *adjective* (14th century)
**:** JOYFUL
**— joy·ous·ly** *adverb*
**— joy·ous·ness** *noun*

**joy·pop** \'jòi-,päp\ *intransitive verb* (1953)
**:** to use habit-forming drugs occasionally or irregularly without becoming addicted
**— joy·pop·per** *noun*

**joy·ride** \'jòi-,rīd\ *noun* (1909)
**1 :** a ride taken for pleasure (as in a car or aircraft); *especially* **:** an automobile ride marked by reckless driving (as in a stolen car)
**2 :** conduct or action resembling a joyride especially in disregard of cost or consequences
**— joyride** *intransitive verb*
**— joy·rid·er** \-,rī-dər\ *noun*
**— joy·rid·ing** *noun*

◇ WORD HISTORY
**jot** "Till heaven and earth pass, one jot or one tittle shall in no wise pass from the law, till all be fulfilled." These are the words, in the King James Version, of Christ's assurance (Matthew 5:18) that He had not "come to destroy the law or the prophets." Not the smallest letter, not even a single stroke of a letter, we are told, will be lost. The word *jot* first appeared in English in William Tyndale's translation of Matthew's Gospel, in 1526. Tyndale simply put in an anglicized form the Latin word *jota* (or *iota*), itself simply a transliteration of the Greek name of the ninth letter in the Greek alphabet. The Gospel writer may have had in mind *yōdh*, the smallest letter in the Hebrew alphabet. The transfer across language boundaries was easily made because the Greek equivalent, *iōta*, was also the smallest letter in its alphabet. A *jot* is now simply "a very small part."

**joy·stick** \-,stik\ *noun* [perhaps from English slang *joystick* penis] (1910)
**1** : a lever in an airplane that operates the elevators by a fore-and-aft motion and the ailerons by a side-to-side motion
**2** : a control for any of various devices (as a computer display) that resembles an airplane's joystick especially in being capable of motion in two or more directions

**J/psi particle** \,jā-'sī-, -'psī-\ *noun* (1977)
: an unstable neutral fundamental particle of the meson group that has a mass about 6000 times the mass of an electron — called also *J particle, psi particle*

**ju·ba** \'jü-bə\ *noun* [origin unknown] (1834)
: a dance of Southern plantation blacks accompanied by complexly rhythmic hand clapping and slapping of the knees and thighs

**Ju·bal** \'jü-bəl\ *noun* [Hebrew *Yūbhāl*]
: a descendant of Cain who according to the account in Genesis is the father of those who play the harp and organ

**ju·bi·lance** \'jü-bə-lən(t)s\ *noun* (1864)
: JUBILATION 1

**ju·bi·lant** \'jü-bə-lənt\ *adjective* (1667)
: EXULTANT
— **ju·bi·lant·ly** *adverb*

**ju·bi·lar·i·an** \,jü-bə-'ler-ē-ən, -'lar-\ *noun* (1782)
: one celebrating a jubilee

**ju·bi·late** \'jü-bə-,lāt\ *intransitive verb* **-lat·ed; -lat·ing** [Latin *jubilatus*, past participle of *jubilare;* akin to Middle High German *jū* (exclamation of joy), Greek *iygē* shout] (circa 1641)
: REJOICE

**Ju·bi·la·te** \,yü-bə-'lä-,tā, ,jü-\ *noun* [Latin, 2d person plural imperative of *jubilare*] (1549)
**1 a** : the 100th Psalm in the Authorized Version **b** *not capitalized* : a joyous song or outburst
**2** : the third Sunday after Easter

**ju·bi·la·tion** \,jü-bə-'lā-shən\ *noun* (14th century)
**1** : an act of rejoicing : the state of being jubilant
**2** : an expression of great joy

**¹ju·bi·lee** \'jü-bə-(,)lē, ,jü-bə-'lē\ *noun* [Middle English, from Middle French & Late Latin; Middle French *jubilé*, from Late Latin *jubilaeus*, modification of Late Greek *iōbēlaios*, from Hebrew *yōbhēl* ram's horn, jubilee] (14th century)
**1** *often capitalized* : a year of emancipation and restoration provided by ancient Hebrew law to be kept every 50 years by the emancipation of Hebrew slaves, restoration of alienated lands to their former owners, and omission of all cultivation of the land
**2 a** : a special anniversary; *especially* : a 50th anniversary **b** : a celebration of such an anniversary
**3 a** : a period of time proclaimed by the Roman Catholic pope ordinarily every 25 years as a time of special solemnity **b** : a special plenary indulgence granted during a year of jubilee to Roman Catholics who perform certain specified works of repentance and piety
**4 a** : JUBILATION **b** : a season of celebration
**5** : an Afro-American religious song usually referring to a time of future happiness ♦

**²jubilee** *adjective, often capitalized* (1951)
: FLAMBÉ ⟨cherries *jubilee*⟩

**Ju·dah** \'jü-də\ *noun* [Hebrew *Yĕhūdhāh*]
: a son of Jacob and the traditional eponymous ancestor of one of the tribes of Israel

**Ju·da·ic** \jü-'dā-ik\ *also* **Ju·da·i·cal** \-'dā-ə-kəl\ *adjective* [Middle English *Judeical*, from Latin *judaicus*, from Greek *ioudaikos*, from *Ioudaios* Jew — more at JEW] (15th century)
: of, relating to, or characteristic of Jews or Judaism

**Ju·da·i·ca** \-'dā-ə-kə\ *noun plural* [Latin, neuter plural of *Judaicus*] (1923)
: literary or historical materials relating to Jews or Judaism

**Ju·da·ism** \'jü-də-,i-zəm, 'jü-dē-, 'jü-(,)dā-, *British also* 'jü-,di-zəm\ *noun* (14th century)
**1** : a religion developed among the ancient Hebrews and characterized by belief in one transcendent God who has revealed himself to Abraham, Moses, and the Hebrew prophets and by a religious life in accordance with Scriptures and rabbinic traditions
**2** : conformity to Jewish rites, ceremonies, and practices
**3** : the cultural, social, and religious beliefs and practices of the Jews
**4** : the whole body of Jews : the Jewish people

**Ju·da·ist** \'jü-də-ist, 'jü-dē-, jü-'dā-\ *noun* (circa 1846)
: one that believes in or practices Judaism
— **Ju·da·is·tic** \,jü-də-'is-tik, ,jü-dē-, ,jü-(,)dā-\ *adjective*

**Ju·da·ize** \'jü-də-,īz, 'jü-dē-, 'jü-(,)dā-\ *verb* **-ized; -iz·ing** (1582)
*intransitive verb*
: to adopt the customs, beliefs, or character of a Jew
*transitive verb*
: to make Jewish
— **Ju·da·i·za·tion** \,jü-də-ə-'zā-shən, ,jü-dē-ə-, ,jü-(,)dā-ə-\ *noun*
— **Ju·da·iz·er** \'jü-də-,īz-ər, 'jü-dē-, 'jü-(,)dā-\ *noun*

**Ju·das** \'jü-dəs\ *noun* [Late Latin, from Greek *Ioudas*, from Hebrew *Yĕhūdhāh*]
**1 a** : the apostle who in the Gospel accounts betrayed Jesus **b** : a son of James and one of the twelve apostles
**2** : TRAITOR; *especially* : one who betrays under the guise of friendship
**3** *not capitalized* : PEEPHOLE — called also *judas hole, judas window*

**Judas Is·car·i·ot** \-is-'kar-ē-ət\ *noun* [Late Latin *Judas Iscariotes*, from Greek *Ioudas Iskariōtēs*]
: JUDAS 1a

**Judas tree** *noun* [from the belief that Judas Iscariot hanged himself from a tree of this kind] (1668)
: any of a genus (*Cercis*) of leguminous trees and shrubs (as a redbud) often cultivated for their showy flowers; *especially* : a Eurasian tree (*C. siliquastrum*) with purplish rosy flowers

**¹jud·der** \'jə-dər\ *intransitive verb* [probably alteration of *shudder*] (1931)
*chiefly British* : to vibrate with intensity ⟨the engine stalled and kept *juddering* —Roy Spicer⟩

**²judder** *noun* (1935)
*chiefly British* : the action or sound of juddering

**Jude** \'jüd\ *noun* [Late Latin *Judas*]
**1** : the author of the New Testament Epistle of Jude
**2** : a short hortatory epistle addressed to early Christians and included as a book in the New Testament — see BIBLE table

**Ju·deo–Chris·tian** \jü-,dā-ō-'kris-chən, -'krish- *also* ,jü-dē-ō- *or* jü-,dē-ō-\ *adjective* [Latin *Judaeus* Jew — more at JEW] (1899)
: having historical roots in both Judaism and Christianity

**Ju·deo–Span·ish** \-'spa-nish\ *noun* (1851)
: the Romance language of Sephardic Jews especially in the Balkans and Asia Minor

**¹judge** \'jəj\ *verb* **judged; judg·ing** [Middle English *juggen*, from Old French *jugier*, from Latin *judicare*, from *judic-, judex* judge, from *jus* right, law + *dicere* to decide, say — more at JUST, DICTION] (13th century)
*transitive verb*
**1** : to form an opinion about through careful weighing of evidence and testing of premises
**2** : to sit in judgment on : TRY
**3** : to determine or pronounce after inquiry and deliberation
**4** : GOVERN, RULE — used of a Hebrew tribal leader

**5** : to form an estimate or evaluation of; *especially* : to form a negative opinion about ⟨shouldn't *judge* him because of his accent⟩
**6** : to hold as an opinion : GUESS, THINK ⟨I *judge* she knew what she was doing⟩
*intransitive verb*
**1** : to form an opinion
**2** : to decide as a judge
**synonym** see INFER
— **judg·er** *noun*

**²judge** *noun* [Middle English *juge*, from Middle French, from Latin *judex*] (14th century)
: one who judges: as **a** : a public official authorized to decide questions brought before a court **b** *often capitalized* : a tribal hero exercising leadership among the Hebrews after the death of Joshua **c** : one appointed to decide in a contest or competition : UMPIRE **d** : one who gives an authoritative opinion : CRITIC
— **judge·ship** \-,ship\ *noun*

**judge advocate** *noun* (1748)
**1** : an officer assigned to the judge advocate general's corps or department
**2** : a staff officer serving as legal adviser to a military commander

**judge advocate general** *noun* (1862)
: the senior legal officer and chief legal adviser in the army, air force, or navy

**Judg·es** \'jə-jəz\ *noun*
: a narrative and historical book of Jewish and Christian Scripture — see BIBLE table

**judg·mat·ic** \,jəj-'ma-tik\ *or* **judg·mat·i·cal** \-ti-kəl\ *adjective* [probably irregular from *judgment*] (1826)
: JUDICIOUS
— **judg·mat·i·cal·ly** \-ti-k(ə-)lē\ *adverb*

**judg·ment** *or* **judge·ment** \'jəj-mənt\ *noun* (13th century)
**1 a** : a formal utterance of an authoritative opinion **b** : an opinion so pronounced
**2 a** : a formal decision given by a court **b** (1) : an obligation (as a debt) created by the decree of a court (2) : a certificate evidencing such a decree
**3 a** *capitalized* : the final judging of mankind by God **b** : a divine sentence or decision; *specifically* : a calamity held to be sent by God
**4 a** : the process of forming an opinion or evaluation by discerning and comparing **b** : an opinion or estimate so formed
**5 a** : the capacity for judging : DISCERNMENT **b** : the exercise of this capacity
**6** : a proposition stating something believed or asserted
**synonym** see SENSE

---

◇ WORD HISTORY

**jubilee** Ancient Hebrew law established every 50th year as a year of emancipation and restoration. All Hebrew slaves were freed; lands were restored to their former owners; fields were left uncultivated. This year took its name, *yōbhēl*, from the ram's horn trumpets sounded to proclaim its advent. Since neither the Greeks nor the Romans held comparable celebrations, when the Hebrew scriptures were translated into Greek and later into Latin, the Hebrew name for this joyful time was retained. The Greeks simply put *yōbhēl* into Greek form as *iōbēlaios*. Under the influence of the Latin verb *jubilare*, which meant "to let out joyful shouts," *iōbēlaios* became *jubilaeus* in Late Latin. Since its introduction into English, in John Wycliffe's translation of the Bible, *jubilee* has broadened in meaning considerably. It is now used for any 50th anniversary and even for other special anniversaries.

---

\ə\ abut \ᵊ\ kitten \ər\ further \a\ ash \ā\ ace
\ä\ mop, mar \au̇\ out \ch\ chin \e\ bet \ē\ easy
\g\ go \i\ hit \ī\ ice \j\ job \ŋ\ sing \ō\ go
\ȯ\ law \ȯi\ boy \th\ thin \th\ the \ü\ loot \u̇\ foot
\y\ yet \zh\ vision *see also* Guide to Pronunciation

**judg·men·tal** \ˌjəj-'men-t³l\ *adjective* (1909)
**1** : of, relating to, or involving judgment
**2** : characterized by a tendency to judge harshly
— **judg·men·tal·ly** \-ē\
**judgment day** *noun* (1591)
**1** *J&D capitalized* : the day of God's judgment of mankind at the end of the world according to various theologies
**2** : a day of final judgment
**ju·di·ca·to·ry** \'jü-di-kə-ˌtōr-ē, -ˌtȯr-\ *noun, plural* **-ries** (circa 1575)
**1** : JUDICIARY 1a
**2** : JUDICATURE 2
**ju·di·ca·ture** \'jü-di-kə-ˌchu̇r, -chər, -ˌtyu̇r, -ˌtu̇r\ *noun* [Middle French, from Medieval Latin *judicatura,* from Latin *judicatus,* past participle of *judicare*] (circa 1530)
**1** : the action of judging : the administration of justice
**2** : a court of justice
**3** : JUDICIARY 1
**ju·di·cial** \ju̇-'di-shəl\ *adjective* [Middle English, from Latin *judicialis,* from *judicium* judgment, from *judex*] (14th century)
**1 a** : of or relating to a judgment, the function of judging, the administration of justice, or the judiciary ⟨*judicial* processes⟩ **b** : belonging to the branch of government that is charged with trying all cases that involve the government and with the administration of justice within its jurisdiction — compare EXECUTIVE, LEGISLATIVE
**2** : ordered or enforced by a court ⟨*judicial* decisions⟩
**3** : of, characterized by, or expressing judgment : CRITICAL 1b
**4** : arising from a judgment of God
**5** : belonging or appropriate to a judge or the judiciary
— **ju·di·cial·ly** \-'di-sh(ə-)lē\ *adverb*
**judicial review** *noun* (circa 1924)
**1** : REVIEW 5
**2** : a constitutional doctrine that gives to a court system the power to annul legislative or executive acts which the judges declare to be unconstitutional
**ju·di·cia·ry** \ju̇-'di-shē-ˌer-ē, -'di-shə-rē\ *noun* [*judiciary,* adjective, from Latin *judiciarius* judicial, from *judicium*] (1787)
**1 a** : a system of courts of law **b** : the judges of these courts
**2** : a branch of government in which judicial power is vested
— **judiciary** *adjective*
**ju·di·cious** \ju̇-'di-shəs\ *adjective* (1598)
: having, exercising, or characterized by sound judgment : DISCREET
**synonym** see WISE
— **ju·di·cious·ly** *adverb*
— **ju·di·cious·ness** *noun*
**Ju·dith** \'jü-dəth\ *noun* [Late Latin, from Greek *Ioudith,* from Hebrew *Yĕhūdhīth*]
**1** : the Jewish heroine who saves the city of Bethulia in the book of Judith
**2** : a book of Scripture included in the Roman Catholic canon of the Old Testament and in the Protestant Apocrypha — see BIBLE table
**ju·do** \'jü-(ˌ)dō\ *noun* [Japanese *jūdō,* from *jū* weakness, gentleness + *dō* art] (1889)
: a sport developed from jujitsu that emphasizes the use of quick movement and leverage to throw an opponent
— **judo·ist** \-ˌō-ist\ *noun*
**¹jug** \'jəg\ *noun* [perhaps from *Jug,* nickname for *Joan*] (1538)
**1 a** *chiefly British* : a small pitcher **b** (1) : a large deep usually earthenware or glass container with a narrow mouth and a handle (2) : the contents of such a container : JUGFUL
**2** : JAIL, PRISON
**²jug** *transitive verb* **jugged; jug·ging** (1747)
**1** : to stew (as a hare) in an earthenware vessel
**2** : JAIL, IMPRISON
**ju·gate** \'jü-ˌgāt, -gət\ *adjective* [New Latin *jugum* yoke] (circa 1887)

**1** : having parts arranged in pairs : PAIRED
**2** : having a jugum
**jug band** *noun* (circa 1933)
: a band that uses primitive or improvised instruments (as jugs, washboards, and kazoos) to play blues, jazz, and folk music
**jug·ful** \'jəg-ˌfu̇l\ *noun* (1831)
**1** : as much as a jug will hold
**2** : a great deal — used in the phrase *not by a jugful*
**jug·ger·naut** \'jə-gər-ˌnȯt, -ˌnät\ *noun* [Hindi *Jagannāth,* literally, lord of the world, title of Vishnu] (1841)
**1** *chiefly British* : a large heavy truck
**2** : a massive inexorable force, campaign, movement, or object that crushes whatever is in its path ⟨an advertising *juggernaut*⟩ ⟨a political *juggernaut*⟩ ◆
**¹jug·gle** \'jə-gəl\ *verb* **jug·gled; jug·gling** \-g(ə-)liŋ\ [Middle English *jogelen,* from Middle French *jogler* to joke, from Latin *joculari,* from *joculus,* diminutive of *jocus* joke] (15th century)
*intransitive verb*
**1** : to perform the tricks of a juggler
**2** : to engage in manipulation especially in order to achieve a desired end
*transitive verb*
**1 a** : to practice deceit or trickery on : BEGUILE
**b** : to manipulate or rearrange especially in order to achieve a desired end ⟨*juggle* an account to hide a loss⟩
**2 a** : to toss in the manner of a juggler **b** : to hold or balance precariously
**3** : to handle or deal with usually several things (as obligations) at one time so as to satisfy often competing requirements ⟨*juggle* the responsibilities of family life and full-time job —Jane S. Gould⟩
**²juggle** *noun* (1664)
: an act or instance of juggling: **a** : a trick of magic **b** : a show of manual dexterity **c** : an act of manipulation especially to achieve a desired end
**jug·gler** \'jə-g(ə-)lər\ *noun* [Middle English *jogelour,* from Old English *geogelere* jester, from Old French *jogleour,* from Latin *joculator,* from *joculari*] (14th century)
**1 a** : one who performs tricks or acts of magic or deftness **b** : one skilled in keeping several objects in motion in the air at the same time by alternately tossing and catching them
**2** : one who manipulates especially in order to achieve a desired end
**jug·glery** \'jə-glə-rē\ *noun* (14th century)
**1** : the art or practice of a juggler
**2** : manipulation or trickery especially to achieve a desired end
**¹jug·u·lar** \'jə-gyə-lər *also* 'jü- *also* -g(ə-)lər\ *adjective* [Late Latin *jugularis,* from Latin *jugulum* collarbone, throat, from *jugum* yoke] (1597)
**1** : of or relating to the throat or neck
**2** : of or relating to the jugular vein
**²jugular** *noun* (1615)
**1** : JUGULAR VEIN
**2** : the most vital or vulnerable part of something ⟨showed an instinct for the *jugular* in competition⟩
**jugular vein** *noun* (1597)
: any of several veins of each side of the neck that return blood from the head
**ju·gum** \'jü-gəm\ *noun, plural* **ju·ga** \-gə\ *or* **jugums** [New Latin, from Latin, yoke — more at YOKE] (1893)
: the most posterior and basal region of an insect's wing modified in some lepidopterans into a lobe that couples the fore and hind wings during flight
**jug wine** *noun* (1972)
: table wine sold in large bottles
**¹juice** \'jüs\ *noun* [Middle English *jus,* from Old French, broth, juice, from Latin; akin to Old Norse *ostr* cheese, Greek *zymē* leaven, Sanskrit *yūṣa* broth] (14th century)

**1** : the extractable fluid contents of cells or tissues
**2 a** *plural* : the natural fluids of an animal body **b** : the liquid or moisture contained in something
**3 a** : the inherent quality of a thing : ESSENCE
**b** : STRENGTH, VIGOR, VITALITY
**4** : a medium (as electricity or gasoline) that supplies power
**5** *slang* : LIQUOR
**6** *slang* : exorbitant interest exacted of a borrower under the threat of violence
**7** *slang* : INFLUENCE, CLOUT
**8** : a motivating, inspiring, or enabling force or factor ⟨creative *juices*⟩
— **juice·less** \'jüs-ləs\ *adjective*
**²juice** *transitive verb* **juiced; juic·ing** (1603)
**1** : to add juice to
**2** : to extract the juice of
**juiced** \'jüst\ *adjective* (1592)
**1** : containing juice — usually used in combination ⟨precious-*juiced* flowers —Shakespeare⟩
**2** *slang* : DRUNK 1a
**juice·head** \'jüs-ˌhed\ *noun* (1955)
*slang* : ALCOHOLIC
**juic·er** \'jü-sər\ *noun* (1938)
**1** : an appliance for extracting juice from fruit or vegetables
**2** *slang* : a heavy or habitual drinker
**juice up** *transitive verb* (1955)
: to give life, energy, or spirit to
**juicy** \'jü-sē\ *adjective* **juic·i·er; -est** (15th century)
**1** : having much juice : SUCCULENT
**2** : rewarding or profitable especially financially : FAT ⟨*juicy* contract⟩ ⟨a *juicy* dramatic role⟩
**3 a** : rich in interest : COLORFUL ⟨*juicy* details⟩ **b** : SENSATIONAL, RACY ⟨a *juicy* scandal⟩ **c** : full of vitality : LUSTY
— **juic·i·ly** \-sə-lē\ *adverb*
— **juic·i·ness** \-sē-nəs\ *noun*
**ju·jit·su** *or* **ju·jut·su** \jü-'jit-(ˌ)sü\ *noun* [Japanese *jūjutsu,* from *jū* weakness, gentleness + *jutsu* art, skill] (1875)
: an art of weaponless fighting employing holds, throws, and paralyzing blows to subdue or disable an opponent
**ju·ju** \'jü-(ˌ)jü\ *noun* [of West African origin; akin to Hausa *jùju* fetish] (1894)
**1** : a fetish, charm, or amulet of West African peoples
**2** : the magic attributed to or associated with jujus

---

◇ WORD HISTORY
**juggernaut** *Jagannātha* (meaning "world-lord" in Sanskrit) is a form of the Hindu deity Krishna worshipped mainly in northeastern India. The god's chief annual festival involves a procession in which his image is mounted on an enormous wooden chariot, about 35 feet square and 45 feet high, which is wheeled from his temple at Puri, in the state of Orissa, to his nearby country house. Accounts by western travelers dating back to the Middle Ages claimed that some of Jagannātha's devotees would allow themselves to be crushed beneath the wheels of the chariot in sacrifice to their god. British officials in the 19th century determined that these reports were greatly exaggerated; occasionally people with painful illnesses or suicidal tendencies would throw themselves in front of the chariot, but most deaths during the celebration resulted accidentally, through the crush of thousands of pilgrims striving to touch the god's vehicle. Despite the spuriousness of the belief, the English form *juggernaut* began to be used in the 19th century to denote a massive, inexorable force or object that crushes everything in its path.

**ju·jube** \'jü-,jüb, *especially for 2* 'jü-jù-,bē\ *noun* [Middle English, from Medieval Latin *jujuba*, alteration of Latin *zizyphum*, from Greek *zizyphon*] (14th century) **1 a :** an edible drupaceous fruit of any of several trees (genus *Ziziphus*) of the buckthorn family; *especially* **:** one of an Asian tree (*Z. jujuba*) **b :** a tree producing this fruit **2 :** a fruit-flavored gumdrop or lozenge

**juke** \'jük\ *verb* **juked; juk·ing** [probably alteration of English dialect *jouk* to cheat, deceive] (1967) *transitive verb* **:** to fake out of position (as in football) *intransitive verb* **:** to juke someone

**juke·box** \'jük-,bäks\ *noun* [*juke* brothel, akin to Gullah *juke* disorderly, of West African origin; akin to Bambara *dzugu* wicked] (1939) **:** a coin-operated phonograph or compact-disc player that automatically plays recordings selected from its list

**juke joint** *noun* (1937) **:** a small inexpensive establishment for eating, drinking, or dancing to the music of a jukebox

**ju·lep** \'jü-ləp\ *noun* [Middle English, from Middle French, from Arabic *julāb*, from Persian *gulāb*, from *gul* rose + *āb* water] (14th century) **1 :** a drink consisting of sweet syrup, flavoring, and water **2 :** a drink consisting of a liquor (as bourbon or brandy) and sugar poured over crushed ice and garnished with mint

**Ju·lian calendar** \'jül-yən-\ *noun* [Latin *julianus*, from Gaius *Julius* Caesar] (circa 1771) **:** a calendar introduced in Rome in 46 B.C. establishing the 12-month year of 365 days with each fourth year having 366 days and the months each having 31 or 30 days except for February which has 28 or in leap years 29 days — compare GREGORIAN CALENDAR

**¹ju·li·enne** \,jü-lē-'en, ,zhü-\ *noun* [French, short for *potage à la julienne*, probably from *Julienne* woman's name] (1841) **1 :** a consommé containing julienned vegetables **2 a :** food (as meat or vegetables) that has been julienned **b :** a preparation or garnish of julienned food ⟨a *julienne* of leeks⟩ — **julienne** *adjective*

**²julienne** *transitive verb* **-enned; -en·ning** (circa 1930) **:** to slice into thin strips the size of matchsticks ⟨wash and *julienne* the carrots⟩

**Ju·liet** \'jül-yət, ,jü-lē-'et, 'jü-lē-,\ *noun* **:** the heroine of Shakespeare's tragedy *Romeo and Juliet* who dies for love of Romeo

**Ju·li·ett** \,jü-lē-'et\ [probably irregular from *Juliet*] (1952) — a communications códe word for the letter *j*

**Ju·ly** \jù-'lī\ *noun* [Middle English *Julie*, from Old English *Julius*, from Latin, from Gaius *Julius* Caesar] (13th century) **:** the 7th month of the Gregorian calendar

**Ju·ma·da** \jù-'ma-də\ *noun* [Arabic *Jumāda*] (1771) **:** either of two months of the Islamic year: **a :** the 5th month **b :** the 6th month — see MONTH table

**¹jum·ble** \'jəm-bəl\ *verb* **jum·bled; jum·bling** \-b(ə-)liŋ\ [perhaps imitative] (circa 1529) *intransitive verb* **:** to move in a confused or disordered manner *transitive verb* **:** to mix into a confused or disordered mass — often used with *up*

**²jumble** *noun* (1661) **1 a :** a mass of things mingled together without order or plan **:** HODGEPODGE **b :** a state of confusion **2** *British* **:** articles for a rummage sale

**³jumble** *noun* [origin unknown] (1615)

**:** a small thin usually ring-shaped sugared cookie or cake

**jumble sale** *noun* (1898) *British* **:** RUMMAGE SALE

**jum·bo** \'jəm-(,)bō\ *noun, plural* **jumbos** [*Jumbo*, a huge elephant exhibited by P. T. Barnum] (1883) **:** a very large specimen of its kind — **jumbo** *adjective*

**¹jump** \'jəmp\ *verb* [probably akin to Low German *gumpen* to jump] (1530) *intransitive verb* **1 a :** to spring into the air **:** LEAP; *especially* **:** to spring free from the ground or other base by the muscular action of feet and legs **b :** to move suddenly or involuntarily **:** START **c :** to move over a position occupied by an opponent's piece in a board game often thereby capturing the piece **d :** to undergo a vertical or lateral displacement owing to improper alignment of the film on a projector mechanism **e :** to start out or forward **:** BEGIN — usually used with *off* ⟨*jump* off to a big lead⟩ **f :** to move energetically **:** HUSTLE **g :** to go from one sequence of instructions in a computer program to another ⟨*jump* to a subroutine⟩ **2 :** COINCIDE, AGREE **3 a :** to move haphazardly or irregularly **:** shift abruptly ⟨*jumped* from job to job⟩ **b :** to change or abandon employment especially in violation of contract **c :** to rise suddenly in rank or status **d :** to undergo a sudden sharp change in value ⟨prices *jumped*⟩ **e :** to make a jump in bridge **f :** to make a hurried judgment ⟨*jump* to conclusions⟩ **g :** to show eagerness ⟨*jumped* at the chance⟩ **h :** to enter hastily ⟨*jump* on the bandwagon⟩ **4 :** to make a sudden physical or verbal attack ⟨*jumped* on him for his criticism⟩ **5 :** to bustle with activity ⟨the bar was *jumping* with young people⟩ *transitive verb* **1 a :** to leap over ⟨*jump* a hurdle⟩ **b :** to move over (a piece) in a board game **c :** to act, move, or begin before (as a signal) ⟨*jump* the green light⟩ **d :** to leap aboard ⟨*jump* a freight⟩ **2** *obsolete* **:** RISK, HAZARD **3 a :** to escape from **:** AVOID **b :** to leave hastily or in violation of contract ⟨*jump* town without paying their bills —Hamilton Basso⟩ **c :** to depart from (a normal course) ⟨*jump* the track⟩ **4 a :** to make a sudden physical or verbal attack on **b :** to occupy illegally ⟨*jump* a mining claim⟩ **5 a** (1) **:** to cause to leap (2) **:** to cause (game) to break cover **b :** START, FLUSH **b :** to elevate in rank or status **c :** to raise (a bridge partner's bid) by more than one rank **d :** to increase suddenly and sharply — **jump bail :** to abscond after being released from prison on bail — **jump ship 1 :** to leave the company of a ship without authority **2 :** to desert a cause or party especially abruptly **:** DEFECT — **jump the gun 1 :** to start in a race before the starting signal **2 :** to act, move, or begin something before the proper time — **jump the queue** *British* **:** to advance directly to or as if to the head of a line

**²jump** *adverb* (1539) *obsolete* **:** EXACTLY, PAT

**³jump** *noun* (circa 1552) **1 a** (1) **:** an act of jumping **:** LEAP (2) **:** any of several sports competitions featuring a leap, spring, or bound (3) **:** a space cleared or covered by a leap (4) **:** an obstacle to be jumped over or from **b :** a sudden involuntary movement **:** START **c :** a move made in a board game by jumping **d :** a transfer from one sequence of instructions in a computer program to a different sequence ⟨conditional *jump*⟩ **2** *obsolete* **:** VENTURE **3 a** (1) **:** a sharp sudden increase (2) **:** a bid in bridge of more tricks than are necessary to overcall the preceding bid — compare SHIFT

**b :** an abrupt change or transition **c** (1) **:** a quick short journey (2) **:** one in a series of moves from one place to another **4 :** an advantage at the start ⟨desirous of getting the *jump* on the competition —Elmer Davis⟩

**jump ball** *noun* (1924) **:** a method of putting a basketball into play by tossing it into the air between two opponents who jump up and attempt to tap the ball to a teammate

**jump boot** *noun* (1942) **:** a boot worn especially by paratroopers

**jump cut** *noun* (1948) **:** a sudden often jarring cut from one shot or scene to another without intervening devices (as fade-outs or dissolves); *broadly* **:** an abrupt transition (as in a narrative) — **jump-cut** \'jəmp-,kət\ *verb*

**¹jump·er** \'jəm-pər\ *noun* (1611) **1 :** a person who jumps **2 a :** any of various devices operating with a jumping motion **b :** any of several sleds **c :** a short wire used to close a break or cut out part of a circuit **3 :** any of several jumping animals; *especially* **:** a saddle horse trained to jump obstacles **4 :** JUMP SHOT

**²jum·per** \'jəm-pər\ *noun* [probably from English dialect *jump* jumper] (1853) **1 :** a loose blouse or jacket worn by workmen **2 :** a sleeveless one-piece dress worn usually with a blouse **3 :** a child's coverall — usually used in plural **4** *chiefly British* **:** SWEATER 2

**jumper cables** *noun plural* (circa 1926) **:** a pair of heavy-duty electrical cables with alligator clamps used to make a connection for jump-starting a vehicle

**jump hook** *noun* (1982) **:** a hook shot in which the player jumps before releasing the ball

**jumping bean** *noun* (circa 1889) **:** a seed of any of several Mexican shrubs (genera *Sebastiania* and *Sapium*) of the spurge family that tumbles about because of the movements of the larva of a small moth (*Carpocapsa saltitans*) inside it

**jumping jack** *noun* (1883) **1 :** a toy figure of a man jointed and made to jump or dance by means of strings or a sliding stick **2 :** a conditioning exercise performed from a standing position by jumping to a position with legs spread and hands touching overhead and then to the original position — called also *side-straddle hop*

**jumping mouse** *noun* (1826) **:** any of several small hibernating North American rodents (family Zapodidae) with long hind legs and tail and no cheek pouches

**jumping-off place** \,jəm-piŋ-'öf-\ *noun* (1826) **1 :** a remote or isolated place **2 :** a place or point from which an enterprise, investigation, or discussion is launched — called also *jumping-off point*

**jumping plant louse** *noun* (circa 1901) **:** any of numerous plant lice (family Psyllidae) with the femurs thickened and adapted for leaping

**jumping spider** *noun* (1813) **:** any of a family (Salticidae) of small spiders that stalk and leap upon their prey

**jump jet** *noun* (1964) **:** a military jet aircraft with vertical takeoff and landing capability

**jump-off** \'jəm-,pöf\ *noun* (1917) **1 :** the start of a race or an attack

\ə\ abut \°\ kitten \ər\ further \a\ ash \ā\ ace
\ä\ mop, mar \aú\ out \ch\ chin \e\ bet \ē\ easy
\g\ go \i\ hit \ī\ ice \j\ job \ŋ\ sing \ō\ go
\ò\ law \òi\ boy \th\ thin \th\ the \ü\ loot \ù\ foot
\y\ yet \zh\ vision *see also* Guide to Pronunciation

**2** : a jumping competition to break a tie at the end of regular competition (as in a horse show)

**jump pass** *noun* (circa 1948)
: a pass made by a player (as in football or basketball) while jumping

**jump rope** *noun* (1834)
: a rope used for exercises and children's games that involve jumping over the usually twirling rope each time it reaches its lowest point; *also* : a game played with a jump rope

**jump seat** *noun* (circa 1864)
**1** : a movable carriage seat
**2** : a folding seat between the front and rear seats of a passenger automobile

**jump shot** *noun* (1948)
: a shot in basketball made by jumping into the air and releasing the ball with one or both hands at the peak of the jump

**jump–start** \'jəmp-ˌstärt\ *transitive verb* (1973)
**1** : to start (an engine or vehicle) by temporary connection to an external power source (as another vehicle's battery)
**2 a** : to get off to a speedy start ⟨advertising can *jump-start* a political campaign⟩ **b** : to impart fresh or renewed energy to : ENERGIZE ⟨a plan to *jump-start* the stagnant economy⟩
— **jump start** *noun*

**jump·suit** \'jəmp-ˌsüt\ *noun* (1944)
**1** : a coverall worn by parachutists for jumping
**2** : a one-piece garment consisting of a blouse or shirt with attached trousers or shorts

**jumpy** \'jəm-pē\ *adjective* **jump·i·er; -est** (1869)
**1** : characterized by jumps or sudden variations
**2** : NERVOUS, JITTERY
— **jump·i·ness** *noun*

**jun** \'jən\ *noun, plural* **jun** [Korean *chŏn*] (1966)
: the chon of North Korea

**jun·co** \'jəŋ-(ˌ)kō\ *noun, plural* **juncos** *or* **juncoes** [New Latin, from Spanish, reed — more at JONQUIL] (1887)
: any of a genus (*Junco*) of small widely distributed American finches usually having a pink bill, ashy gray head and back, and conspicuous white lateral tail feathers

**junc·tion** \'jəŋ(k)-shən\ *noun* [Latin *junction-, junctio*, from *jungere* to join — more at YOKE] (1711)
**1** : an act of joining : the state of being joined
**2 a** : a place or point of meeting **b** : an intersection of roads especially where one terminates **c** : a point (as in a thermocouple) at which dissimilar metals make contact **d** : an interface in a semiconductor device between regions with different electrical characteristics
**3** : something that joins
— **junc·tion·al** \-shnəl, -shə-n°l\ *adjective*

**junc·tur·al** \'jəŋ(k)-chə-rəl, 'jəŋ(k)-shrəl\ *adjective* (1942)
: of or relating to phonetic juncture

**junc·ture** \'jəŋ(k)-chər\ *noun* (14th century)
**1 a** : JOINT, CONNECTION **b** : the manner of transition or mode of relationship between two consecutive sounds in speech
**2** : an instance of joining : UNION, JUNCTION
**3** : a point of time; *especially* : one made critical by a concurrence of circumstances ☆

**June** \'jün\ *noun* [Middle English, from Middle French & Latin; Middle French *Juin*, from Latin *Junius*] (14th century)
: the 6th month of the Gregorian calendar

**June·ber·ry** \'jün-ˌber-ē\ *noun* (circa 1810)
: SERVICEBERRY

**june bug** *noun, often J capitalized* (1829)
: any of numerous rather large leaf-eating scarab beetles (subfamily Melolonthinae) that fly chiefly in late spring and have larvae that are white grubs which live in soil and feed chiefly on the roots of grasses and other plants
— called also *june beetle*

**Jung·ian** \'yüŋ-ē-ən\ *adjective* (circa 1930)

: of, relating to, or characteristic of C. G. Jung or his psychological doctrines
— **Jungian** *noun*

**jun·gle** \'jəŋ-gəl\ *noun, often attributive* [Hindi *jaṅgal* forest, from Sanskrit *jaṅgala* desert region] (1776)
**1 a** : an impenetrable thicket or tangled mass of tropical vegetation **b** : a tract overgrown with thickets or masses of vegetation
**2** : a hobo camp
**3 a** (1) : a confused or disordered mass of objects : JUMBLE (2) : something that baffles or frustrates by its tangled or complex character : MAZE ⟨the *jungle* of housing laws —Bernard Taper⟩ **b** : a place of ruthless struggle for survival ⟨the city is a *jungle* where no one is safe after dark —Stuart Chase⟩
— **jun·gle·like** \-gə(l)-ˌlīk\ *adjective*
— **jun·gly** \-g(ə-)lē\ *adjective*

**jun·gled** \-gəld\ *adjective* (1842)
: abounding in jungle ⟨a *jungled* island⟩

**jungle fowl** *noun* (circa 1825)
: any of several Asian wild birds (genus *Gallus*) related to the pheasants; *especially* : a bird (*G. gallus*) of southeastern Asia from which domestic fowls have probably descended

**jungle gym** *noun* [from *Junglegym*, a trademark] (1923)
: a structure of vertical and horizontal bars for use by children at play

**¹ju·nior** \'jün-yər\ *adjective* [Latin, comparative of *juvenis* young — more at YOUNG] (13th century)
**1 a** : less advanced in age : YOUNGER — used chiefly to distinguish a son with the same given name as his father **b** (1) : YOUTHFUL (2) : designed for young people and especially adolescents **c** : of more recent date and therefore inferior or subordinate ⟨a *junior* lien⟩
**2 a** : lower in standing or rank ⟨*junior* partners⟩ **b** : duplicating or suggesting on a smaller scale something typically large or powerful ⟨a *junior* gale⟩
**3** : of or relating to juniors or the class of juniors at an educational institution ⟨the *junior* prom⟩

**²junior** *noun* [Latin, noun & adjective] (1526)
**1 a** (1) : a person who is younger than another ⟨a man six years my *junior*⟩ (2) : a male child : SON (3) : a young person **b** : a clothing size for women and girls with slight figures
**2 a** : a person holding a lower position in a hierarchy of ranks **b** : a student in the next-to-the-last year before graduating from an educational institution
**3** *capitalized* : a member of a program of the Girl Scouts for girls in the third through sixth grades in school

**ju·nior·ate** \'jün-yə-ˌrāt, -rət\ *noun* (1845)
**1** : a course of high school or college study for candidates for the priesthood, brotherhood, or sisterhood; *specifically* : one preparatory to the course in philosophy
**2** : a seminary for juniorate training

**junior college** *noun* (1899)
: an educational institution that offers two years of studies corresponding to those in the first two years of a four-year college and that often offers technical, vocational, and liberal studies to the adults of a community

**junior high school** *noun* (1909)
: a school usually including grades 7 to 9 — called also *junior high*

**Junior Leaguer** *noun* (1938)
: a member of a league of young women organized for volunteer service to civic and social organizations

**junior miss** *noun* (1927)
**1** : an adolescent girl
**2** : JUNIOR 1b

**junior varsity** *noun* (1949)
: a team composed of members lacking the experience or qualification required for the varsity

**ju·ni·per** \'jü-nə-pər\ *noun* [Middle English *junipere*, from Latin *juniperus*] (14th century)
**1** : any of numerous shrubs or trees (genus *Juniperus*) of the cypress family with leaves resembling needles or scales and female cones usually resembling berries
**2** : any of several coniferous trees resembling true junipers

**juniper oil** *noun* (circa 1889)
: an acrid essential oil obtained from the fruit of a common juniper (*Juniperus communis*) and used especially in gin and liqueurs

**juniper tar** *noun* (circa 1930)
: a tarry liquid used locally in treating skin diseases and obtained by distillation from the wood of a Eurasian juniper (*Juniperus oxycedrus*) — called also *cade oil, juniper tar oil*

**¹junk** \'jəŋk\ *noun* [Middle English *jonke*] (14th century)
**1** : pieces of old cable or cordage used especially to make gaskets, mats, swabs, or oakum
**2 a** (1) : old iron, glass, paper, or other waste that may be used again in some form (2) : secondhand, worn, or discarded articles (3) : CLUTTER 1b **b** : something of poor quality : TRASH **c** : something of little meaning, worth, or significance
**3** *slang* : NARCOTICS; *especially* : HEROIN
**4** : JUNK BOND
**5** : baseball pitches other than fastballs (as curveballs or change-ups)
— **junky** \'jəŋ-kē\ *adjective*

**²junk** *transitive verb* (1916)
: to get rid of as worthless : SCRAP
**synonym** see DISCARD

**³junk** *noun* [Portuguese *junco*, from Javanese *joṇ*] (1613)
: any of various ships of Chinese waters with bluff lines, a high poop and overhanging stem, little or no keel, high pole masts, and a deep rudder

junk

**junk art** *noun* (1962)
: three-dimensional art made from discarded material (as metal, mortar, glass, or wood)
— **junk artist** *noun*

**junk bond** *noun* (1976)
: a high-risk bond that offers a high yield and is often issued to finance a takeover of a company

**junk·er** \'jəŋ-kər\ *noun* [¹junk + ²-er] (1944)
: something (as an automobile) of such age and condition as to be ready for scrapping

**Jun·ker** \'yuṅ-kər\ noun [German, from Old High German junchērro, literally, young lord] (1554)
: a member of the Prussian landed aristocracy
— **Jun·ker·dom** \-kər-dəm\ noun
— **Jun·ker·ism** \-kə-ˌri-zəm\ noun

**¹jun·ket** \'jən-kət\ noun [Middle English ioncate, ultimately from (assumed) Vulgar Latin juncata, from Latin juncus rush] (15th century)
**1** : a dessert of sweetened flavored milk set with rennet
**2 a** : a festive social affair **b** : TRIP, JOURNEY; especially : a trip made by an official at public expense ◆

**²junket** intransitive verb (1555)
**1** : FEAST, BANQUET
**2** : to go on a junket
— **jun·ke·teer** \ˌjən-kə-'tir\ or **jun·ket·er** \'jən-kə-tər\ noun

**junk food** noun (1971)
**1** : food that is high in calories but low in nutritional content
**2** : something that is appealing or enjoyable but of little or no real value ⟨the ultimate in junk food for young minds —Cleveland Amory⟩

**junk·ie** also **junky** \'jən-kē\ noun, plural **junk·ies** (1923)
**1** slang **a** : a narcotics peddler or addict **b** : a person who derives inordinate pleasure from or who is dependent on something ⟨sugar junkie⟩ ⟨television news junkie⟩
**2** : a junk dealer

**junk mail** noun (1954)
: third-class mail (as advertising circulars) that is often addressed to "occupant" or "resident"

**junk sculpture** noun (1965)
: JUNK ART

**junk·yard** \'jəŋk-ˌyärd\ noun (1880)
: a yard used to store sometimes resalable junk

**Ju·no** \'jü-(ˌ)nō\ noun
: the wife of Jupiter, queen of heaven, and goddess of light, birth, women, and marriage — compare HERA

**Ju·no·esque** \ˌjü-(ˌ)nō-'esk\ adjective (1888)
: marked by stately beauty

**jun·ta** \'hu̇n-tə, 'jən-, 'hən-\ noun [Spanish, from feminine of junto joined, from Latin junctus, past participle of jungere to join — more at YOKE] (1622)
**1** : a council or committee for political or governmental purposes; especially : a group of persons controlling a government especially after a revolutionary seizure of power
**2** : JUNTO

**jun·to** \'jən-(ˌ)tō\ noun, plural **juntos** [probably alteration of junta] (1623)
: a group of persons joined for a common purpose

**Ju·pi·ter** \'jü-pə-tər\ noun [Latin]
**1** : the chief Roman god, husband of Juno, god of light, of the sky and weather, and of the state and its welfare and its laws — compare ZEUS
**2** : the largest of the planets and fifth in order from the sun — see PLANET table

**ju·ral** \'ju̇r-əl\ adjective [Latin jur-, jus law] (1635)
**1** : of or relating to law
**2** : of or relating to rights or obligations
— **ju·ral·ly** \-ə-lē\ adverb

**Ju·ras·sic** \ju̇-'ra-sik\ adjective [French jurassique, from Jura mountain range] (1831)
: of, relating to, or being the period of the Mesozoic era between the Triassic and the Cretaceous or the corresponding system of rocks marked by the presence of dinosaurs and the first appearance of birds — see GEOLOGIC TIME table
— **Jurassic** noun

**ju·rat** \'ju̇r-ˌat\ noun [short for Latin juratum (est) it has been sworn, 3d singular perfect passive of jurare to swear — more at JURY] (1796)
: a certificate added to an affidavit stating when, before whom, and where it was made

**ju·rel** \hu̇-'rel\ noun [Spanish] (1772)
: any of several food fishes (family Carangidae) of warm seas

**ju·rid·i·cal** \ju̇-'ri-di-kəl\ also **ju·rid·ic** \-dik\ adjective [Latin juridicus, from jur-, jus + dicere to say — more at DICTION] (1502)
**1** : of or relating to the administration of justice or the office of a judge
**2** : of or relating to law or jurisprudence : LEGAL
— **ju·rid·i·cal·ly** \-di-k(ə-)lē\ adverb

**ju·ris·con·sult** \ˌju̇r-əs-'kän-ˌsəlt, -kən-'\ noun [Latin jurisconsultus, from juris (genitive of jus) + consultus, past participle of consulere to consult] (1605)
: JURIST; especially : one learned in international and public law

**ju·ris·dic·tion** \ˌju̇r-əs-'dik-shən\ noun [Middle English jurisdiccioun, from Middle French & Latin; Middle French juridiction, from Latin jurisdiction-, jurisdictio, from juris + diction-, dictio act of saying — more at DICTION] (14th century)
**1** : the power, right, or authority to interpret and apply the law
**2 a** : the authority of a sovereign power to govern or legislate **b** : the power or right to exercise authority : CONTROL
**3** : the limits or territory within which authority may be exercised
synonym see POWER
— **ju·ris·dic·tion·al** \-shnəl, -shə-nᵊl\ adjective
— **ju·ris·dic·tion·al·ly** adverb

**Ju·ris Doctor** \'ju̇r-əs-\ noun [Latin, doctor of law] (1969)
: a degree equivalent to bachelor of laws

**ju·ris·pru·dence** \ˌju̇r-əs-'prü-dᵊn(t)s\ noun (circa 1656)
**1 a** : a system or body of law **b** : the course of court decisions
**2** : the science or philosophy of law
**3** : a department of law ⟨medical jurisprudence⟩
— **ju·ris·pru·den·tial** \-prü-'den(t)-shəl\ adjective
— **ju·ris·pru·den·tial·ly** \-'den(t)-sh(ə-)lē\ adverb

**ju·ris·pru·dent** \-'prü-dᵊnt\ noun [Late Latin jurisprudent-, jurisprudens, from Latin juris + prudent-, prudens skilled, prudent] (1628)
: JURIST

**ju·rist** \'ju̇r-ist\ noun [Middle French juriste, from Medieval Latin jurista, from Latin jur-, jus] (15th century)
: one having a thorough knowledge of law; especially : JUDGE

**ju·ris·tic** \ju̇-'ris-tik\ adjective (1831)
**1** : of or relating to a jurist or jurisprudence
**2** : of, relating to, or recognized in law
— **ju·ris·ti·cal·ly** \-ti-k(ə-)lē\ adverb

**ju·ror** \'ju̇r-ər, 'ju̇r-ˌȯr\ noun (14th century)
**1 a** : a member of a jury **b** : a person summoned to serve on a jury
**2** : a person who takes an oath (as of allegiance)

**¹ju·ry** \'ju̇r-ē\ noun, plural **juries** [Middle English jure, from Anglo-French juree, from Old French jurer to swear, from Latin jurare, from jur-, jus] (15th century)
**1** : a body of persons sworn to give a verdict on some matter submitted to them; especially : a body of persons legally selected and sworn to inquire into any matter of fact and to give their verdict according to the evidence
**2** : a committee for judging and awarding prizes at a contest or exhibition
**3** : one (as the public or test results) that will decide — used especially in the phrase the jury is still out

**²jury** adjective [origin unknown] (1616)
: improvised for temporary use especially in an emergency : MAKESHIFT ⟨a jury mast⟩ ⟨a jury rig⟩

**³jury** transitive verb **jur·ied; jury·ing** (1947)
: to select material as appropriate for exhibition in (as an art show) — used chiefly as a participle ⟨a juried show⟩

**ju·ry–rig** \'ju̇r-ē-ˌrig, -'rig\ transitive verb [²jury] (1788)
: to erect, construct, or arrange in a makeshift fashion

**jus gen·ti·um** \'yüs-'gen-tē-əm\ noun [Latin, law of nations] (1548)
: INTERNATIONAL LAW

**jus san·gui·nis** \-'säṅ-gwə-nəs\ noun [Latin, right of blood] (1902)
: a rule that a child's citizenship is determined by its parents' citizenship

**jus·sive** \'jə-siv\ noun [Latin jussus, past participle of jubēre to order; akin to Greek hysmínē battle] (1846)
: a word, form, case, or mood expressing command
— **jussive** adjective

**jus so·li** \'yüs-'sō-ˌlē\ noun [Latin, right of the soil] (1902)
: a rule that the citizenship of a child is determined by the place of its birth

**¹just** \'jəst, 'jüst\ variant of JOUST

**²just** \'jəst\ adjective [Middle English, from Middle French & Latin; Middle French juste, from Latin justus, from jus right, law; akin to Sanskrit yos welfare] (14th century)
**1 a** : having a basis in or conforming to fact or reason : REASONABLE ⟨a just but not a generous decision⟩ **b** archaic : faithful to an original **c** : conforming to a standard of correctness : PROPER ⟨just proportions⟩
**2 a** (1) : acting or being in conformity with what is morally upright or good : RIGHTEOUS ⟨a just war⟩ (2) : being what is merited : DESERVED ⟨a just punishment⟩ **b** : legally correct : LAWFUL ⟨just title to an estate⟩
synonym see FAIR, UPRIGHT
— **just·ly** adverb
— **just·ness** \'jəs(t)-nəs\ noun

**³just** \'jəst, 'jist, 'jest also without t\ adverb (15th century)
**1 a** : EXACTLY, PRECISELY ⟨just right⟩ **b** : very recently ⟨the bell just rang⟩
**2 a** : by a very small margin : BARELY ⟨just too late⟩ **b** : IMMEDIATELY, DIRECTLY ⟨just west of here⟩

◇ WORD HISTORY
**junket** Juncus is the Latin word for "rush." The stems of that marsh plant have long been the source of plaiting for mats and baskets. French inherited juncus as jonc, and derivatives of jonc in the medieval French of Normandy came to denote rush baskets, as well as soft, unripened cheeses made in such baskets. One such derivative is presumed to be the source of Middle English ioncate (with the suffix perhaps influenced by Medieval Latin juncata), a name for a sweetened dish of curds and cream; in the form junket this word is still applied to desserts made from sweetened milk or cream. Back in the 16th century, however, we find that junket embarked on a long semantic journey away from desserts. Its meaning was extended from any sweet dish to a feast or banquet that presumably featured such dishes, and then to any banquet, a usage that lasted at least into the 19th century. In the U.S. junket became a picnic or pleasure trip, and by the later 19th century the word had entered the political vocabulary as a derogatory expression for a politician's trip at taxpayers' expense.

\ə\ abut \ᵊ\ kitten \ər\ further \a\ ash \ā\ ace
\ä\ mop, mar \au̇\ out \ch\ chin \e\ bet \ē\ easy
\g\ go \i\ hit \ī\ ice \j\ job \ŋ\ sing \ō\ go
\ȯ\ law \ȯi\ boy \th\ thin \th\ the \ü\ loot \u̇\ foot
\y\ yet \zh\ vision see also Guide to Pronunciation

**3 a :** ONLY, SIMPLY ⟨*just* last year⟩ ⟨*just* be yourself⟩ **b :** QUITE, VERY ⟨*just* wonderful⟩
**4 :** PERHAPS, POSSIBLY ⟨it *just* might work⟩
— **just about :** ALMOST ⟨the work is *just about* done⟩
**just–folks** \'jəs(t)-'fōks\ *adjective* (1952)
**:** marked by the absence of formality or sophistication **:** UNPRETENTIOUS ⟨her *just-folks* manner⟩
**jus·tice** \'jəs-təs\ *noun* [Middle English, from Old English & Old French; Old English *justice*, from Old French *justice*, from Latin *justitia*, from *justus*] (12th century)
**1 a :** the maintenance or administration of what is just especially by the impartial adjustment of conflicting claims or the assignment of merited rewards or punishments **b :** JUDGE **c :** the administration of law; *especially* **:** the establishment or determination of rights according to the rules of law or equity
**2 a :** the quality of being just, impartial, or fair **b** (1) **:** the principle or ideal of just dealing or right action (2) **:** conformity to this principle or ideal **:** RIGHTEOUSNESS **c :** the quality of conforming to law
**3 :** conformity to truth, fact, or reason **:** CORRECTNESS
**justice of the peace** (15th century)
**:** a local magistrate empowered chiefly to administer summary justice in minor cases, to commit for trial, and to administer oaths and perform marriages
**jus·ti·cia·ble** \,jə-'sti-sh(ē-)ə-bəl\ *adjective* (15th century)
**1 :** liable to trial in a court of justice ⟨a *justiciable* offense⟩
**2 :** capable of being decided by legal principles or by a court of justice
— **jus·ti·cia·bil·i·ty** \,jə-,sti-sh(ē-)ə-'bi-lə-tē\ *noun*
**jus·ti·ci·ar** \,jə-'sti-shē-ər, -,är\ *noun* [Middle English, from Medieval Latin *justitiarius*, from Latin *justitia*] (circa 1580)
**:** the chief political and judicial officer of the Norman and later kings of England until the 13th century
**jus·ti·fi·able** \'jəs-tə-,fī-ə-bəl\ *adjective* (1561)
**:** capable of being justified **:** EXCUSABLE ⟨*justifiable* family pride —*Current Biography*⟩
— **jus·ti·fi·abil·i·ty** \,jəs-tə-,fī-ə-'bi-lə-tē\ *noun*
— **jus·ti·fi·ably** \'jəs-tə-,fī-ə-blē\ *adverb*
**jus·ti·fi·ca·tion** \,jəs-tə-fə-'kā-shən\ *noun* (14th century)
**1 :** the act, process, or state of being justified by God
**2 a :** the act or an instance of justifying **:** VINDICATION **b :** something that justifies
**3 :** the process or result of justifying lines of text
**jus·ti·fi·ca·tive** \'jəs-tə-fə-,kā-tiv\ *adjective* (1611)
**:** JUSTIFICATORY
**jus·ti·fi·ca·to·ry** \,jəs-'ti-fi-kə-,tōr-ē, -,tòr-; 'jəs-tə-fə-,kā-tə-rē\ *adjective* (1579)

**:** tending or serving to justify **:** VINDICATORY
**jus·ti·fy** \'jəs-tə-,fī\ *verb* **-fied; -fy·ing** [Middle English *justifien*, from Middle French or Late Latin; Middle French *justifier*, from Late Latin *justificare*, from Latin *justus*] (14th century)
*transitive verb*
**1 a :** to prove or show to be just, right, or reasonable **b** (1) **:** to show to have had a sufficient legal reason (2) **:** to qualify (oneself) as a surety by taking oath to the ownership of sufficient property
**2 a** *archaic* **:** to administer justice to **b** *archaic* **:** ABSOLVE **c :** to judge, regard, or treat as righteous and worthy of salvation
**3 a :** to space (as lines of text) so that the lines come out even at the margin **b :** to make even by justifying ⟨*justified* margins⟩
*intransitive verb*
**1 a :** to show a sufficient lawful reason for an act done **b :** to qualify as bail or surety
**2 :** to justify lines of text
*synonym* see MAINTAIN
— **jus·ti·fi·er** \-,fī(-ə)r\ *noun*
**just-in-time** *noun, often attributive* (1981)
**:** a manufacturing strategy wherein parts are produced or delivered only as needed
**¹jut** \'jət\ *verb* **jut·ted; jut·ting** [perhaps short for ²*jutty*] (circa 1573)
*intransitive verb*
**:** to extend out, up, or forward **:** PROJECT ⟨mountains *jutting* into the sky⟩ ⟨a *jutting* jaw⟩
*transitive verb*
**:** to cause to project
**²jut** *noun* (1786)
**:** something that juts **:** PROJECTION
**jute** \'jüt\ *noun* [Bengali *jhuṭo*] (1746)
**:** the glossy fiber of either of two East Indian plants (*Corchorus olitorius* and *C. capsularis*) of the linden family used chiefly for sacking, burlap, and twine; *also* **:** a plant producing jute
**Jute** \'jüt\ *noun* [Middle English, from Medieval Latin *Jutae* Jutes, of Germanic origin; akin to Old English *Eotenas* Jutes] (14th century)
**:** a member of a Germanic people invading England from the Continent and settling in Kent in the 5th century
— **Jut·ish** \'jü-tish\ *adjective*
**¹jut·ty** \'jə-tē\ *noun, plural* **jutties** [Middle English] (15th century)
**1** *archaic* **:** JETTY
**2 :** a projecting part of a building
**²jutty** *transitive verb* **jut·tied; jut·ty·ing** (1599)
*obsolete* **:** to project beyond
**ju·ve·nes·cence** \,jü-və-'ne-s°n(t)s\ *noun* (1800)
**:** the state of being youthful or of growing young
— **ju·ve·nes·cent** \-s°nt\ *adjective*
**¹ju·ve·nile** \'jü-və-,nīl, -n°l\ *adjective* [French or Latin; French *juvénile*, from Latin *juvenilis*, from *juvenis* young person — more at YOUNG] (1625)

**1 a :** physiologically immature or undeveloped **:** YOUNG **b :** derived from sources within the earth and coming to the surface for the first time — used especially of water and gas
**2 :** of, relating to, characteristic of, or suitable for children or young people ⟨*juvenile* books⟩
**3 :** reflecting psychological or intellectual immaturity **:** CHILDISH
**²juvenile** *noun* (1733)
**1 a :** a young person **:** YOUTH **b :** a book for children or young people
**2 :** a young individual resembling an adult of its kind except in size and reproductive activity: as **a :** a fledged bird not yet in adult plumage **b :** a 2-year-old racehorse
**3 :** an actor or actress who plays youthful parts
**juvenile court** *noun* (1899)
**:** a court that has special jurisdiction over delinquent and dependent children usually up to the age of 18
**juvenile delinquency** *noun* (1816)
**1 :** conduct by a juvenile characterized by antisocial behavior that is beyond parental control and therefore subject to legal action
**2 :** a violation of the law committed by a juvenile and not punishable by death or life imprisonment
— **juvenile delinquent** *noun*
**juvenile hormone** *noun* (1940)
**:** an insect hormone that is secreted by the corpora allata, inhibits maturation to the imago, and plays a role in reproduction
**juvenile officer** *noun* (1954)
**:** a police officer charged with the detection, prosecution, and care of juvenile delinquents
**ju·ve·nil·ia** \,jü-və-'ni-lē-ə\ *noun plural* [Latin, neuter plural of *juvenilis*] (1622)
**1 :** compositions produced in the artist's or author's youth
**2 :** artistic or literary compositions suited to or designed for the young
**ju·ve·nil·i·ty** \,jü-və-'ni-lə-tē\ *noun, plural* **-ties** (circa 1623)
**1 :** the quality or state of being juvenile **:** YOUTHFULNESS
**2 a :** immaturity of thought or conduct **b :** an instance of being juvenile
**jux·ta·pose** \'jək-stə-,pōz\ *transitive verb* **-posed; -pos·ing** [probably back-formation from *juxtaposition*] (1851)
**:** to place side by side ⟨*juxtapose* unexpected combinations of colors, shapes and ideas —J. F. T. Bugental⟩
**juxtaposed** *adjective* (1855)
**:** placed side by side **:** being in juxtaposition
*synonym* see ADJACENT
**jux·ta·po·si·tion** \,jək-stə-pə-'zi-shən\ *noun* [Latin *juxta* near + English *position* — more at JOUST] (1654)
**:** the act or an instance of placing two or more things side by side; *also* **:** the state of being so placed
— **jux·ta·po·si·tion·al** \-'zish-nəl, -'zi-shə-n°l\ *adjective*

# K

K *is the eleventh letter of the English alphabet. It came through Latin, via Etruscan, from Greek, where it was called* kappa; *Greek took it from the Phoenician* kaph. *In all these languages* k *represented practically the same sound as in English, but in Latin, the Romance languages, and Old English it was largely replaced by* c. *Eventually, however, the phonetic ambiguity of that letter, which stood for both the* g *and* k *sounds in Latin and presented other problems of interpretation in Romance and Old English, led to the revival of the old letter for the sound* k. *This is true in English especially before* e *and* i *(as in* kine, *plural for* cow), *before* n *(as in* knife, *from Old English* cnīf), *and more recently in loan words from many sources (such as* kugel *from German,* karaoke *from Japanese, and* Koran *from Arabic). In many words (for example,* knead, knight, *and* know) k *has become silent before* n, *though once it was pronounced. It is frequent also after short vowels in the combination* ck, *which is pronounced like simple* k, *as in* black. *The small form of* k *developed through a downsizing of the capital form.*

**k** \'kā\ *noun, plural* **k's** *or* **ks** \'kāz\ *often capitalized, often attributive* (before 12th century)
**1 a** : the 11th letter of the English alphabet **b** : a graphic representation of this letter **c** : a speech counterpart of orthographic *k*
**2** : a graphic device for reproducing the letter *k*
**3** : one designated *k* especially as the 11th in order or class
**4** : something shaped like the letter K
**5** : a unit vector parallel to the z-axis
**6** [*kilo-*] : THOUSAND ⟨a salary of $24*K*⟩
**7** [*kilo-*] : a unit of computer storage capacity equal to 1024 bytes ⟨a computer memory of 64*K*⟩
**8** *capitalized* : STRIKEOUT

**Kaa·ba** \'kä-bə\ *noun* [Arabic *ka'bah*, literally, cubic building] (1734)
: a small stone building in the court of the Great Mosque at Mecca that contains a sacred black stone and is the goal of Islamic pilgrimage and the point toward which Muslims turn in praying

**ka·ba·la** *or* **kab·ba·la** *or* **kab·ba·lah** *variant of* CABALA

**ka·bob** \kə-'bäb *also* 'kā-,\ *noun* [Persian, Hindi, Arabic & Turkish; Persian & Hindi *kabāb*, from Arabic, from Turkish *kebap*] (1673)
: cubes of meat (as lamb or beef) marinated and cooked with vegetables (as onions, tomatoes, and green peppers) usually on a skewer

**Ka·bu·ki** \kə-'bü-kē, 'kä-bù-(,)kē\ *noun* [Japanese] (1899)
: traditional Japanese popular drama with singing and dancing performed in a highly stylized manner

**Ka·byle** \kə-'bī(ə)l\ *noun* [Arabic *qabā'il*, plural of *qabīlah* tribe] (1738)
**1** : a member of a Berber people living in the mountainous coastal area east of Algiers
**2** : the Berber language of the Kabyles

**ka·chi·na** \kə-'chē-nə\ *noun* [Hopi *qacína*] (1888)
**1** : one of the deified ancestral spirits believed among the Hopi and other Pueblo Indians to visit the pueblos at intervals
**2** : one of the elaborately masked kachina impersonators that dance at agricultural ceremonies
**3** : a doll representing a kachina

**kad·dish** \'kä-dish\ *noun, often capitalized* [Aramaic *qaddīsh* holy] (1613)
: a Jewish prayer recited in the daily ritual of the synagogue and by mourners at public services after the death of a close relative

**kaf·fee·klatsch** \'kò-fē-,klach, 'kä-fē-, -,kläch, -,klòch\ *noun, often capitalized* [German, from *Kaffee* coffee + *Klatsch* gossip] (1888)
: an informal social gathering for coffee and conversation

**Kaf·fir** *or* **Kaf·ir** \'ka-fər\ *noun* [Arabic *kāfir* infidel] (1778)
**1** *archaic* : a member of a group of southern African Bantu-speaking peoples
**2** *often not capitalized, chiefly South African* : a black African — usually used disparagingly

**kaf·fi·yeh** \kə-'fē-ə\ *noun* [Arabic *kūfīyah, kaffīyah*, from al-*Kufah* Al Kufa, town in Iraq] (circa 1817)
: an Arab headdress consisting of a square of cloth folded to form a triangle and held on by a cord

**kaf·ir** \'ka-fər\ *noun* (circa 1785)
: a grain sorghum (*Sorghum caffrorum*) with stout short-jointed somewhat juicy stalks and erect heads

**Kaf·ir** \'ka-fər\ *noun* [Arabic *kāfir*] (1759)
: a member of a group of peoples of the Hindu Kush in northeastern Afghanistan

**Kaf·iri** \'ka-fə-rē\ *noun* (1901)
: the group of languages spoken by the Kafirs that constitutes a distinct branch of Indo-Iranian — see INDO-EUROPEAN LANGUAGES table

**Kaf·ka·esque** \,käf-kə-'esk, ,kaf-\ *adjective* (1946)
: of, relating to, or suggestive of Franz Kafka or his writings; *especially* : having a nightmarishly complex, bizarre, or illogical quality ⟨*Kafkaesque* bureaucratic delays⟩

**kaf·tan** *variant of* CAFTAN

**ka·hu·na** \kə-'hü-nə\ *noun* [Hawaiian] (1886)
: a Hawaiian witch doctor

**kai·nite** \'kī-,nīt, 'kā-\ *also* **kai·nit** \kī-'nēt\ *noun* [German *Kainit*, from Greek *kainos* new — more at RECENT] (1868)
: a natural salt KMg(SO₄)Cl·3H₂O consisting of a hydrous sulfate and chloride of magnesium and potassium that is used as a fertilizer and as a source of potassium and magnesium compounds

**kai·ser** \'kī-zər\ *noun* [Middle English, from Old Norse *keisari*; akin to Old High German *keisur* emperor; both from a prehistoric Germanic word borrowed from Latin *Caesar*, cognomen of the Emperor Augustus] (13th century)
: EMPEROR; *especially* : the ruler of Germany from 1871 to 1918 ◆

— **kai·ser·dom** \-zər-dəm\ *noun*
— **kai·ser·ism** \-zə-,ri-zəm\ *noun*
**kai·se·rin** \'kī-zə-rən\ *noun* [German, feminine of *Kaiser*] (circa 1888)
: the wife of a kaiser
**kaiser roll** *noun* (circa 1898)
: a crusty roll often used for sandwiches
**ka·ka** \'kä-kə\ *noun* [Maori] (circa 1774)
: an olive brown New Zealand parrot (*Nestor meridionalis*) with gray and red markings
**ka·ka·po** \,kä-kə-'pō\ *noun, plural* **-pos** [Maori] (1843)
: a large chiefly nocturnal burrowing New Zealand parrot (*Strigops habroptilus*) that has green and brown barred plumage and well-developed wings with little power of flight
**ka·ke·mo·no** \,kä-ki-'mō-(,)nō\ *noun, plural* **-nos** [Japanese] (1890)
: a vertical Japanese ornamental pictorial or calligraphic scroll
**ka·ki·e·mon** \,kä-kē-'ā-,män\ *noun, often capitalized* [Sakaida *Kakiemon* (flourished 1650) Japanese potter] (1890)
: a Japanese porcelain decorated with enamel
**ka·la–azar** \,kä-lə-ə-'zär, ,ka-\ *noun* [Hindi *kālā-āzār* black disease, from Hindi *kālā* black + Persian *āzār* disease] (1882)
: a severe infectious disease chiefly of tropical areas that is marked by fever, progressive anemia, leukopenia, and enlargement of the spleen and liver and caused by a flagellate (*Leishmania donovani*) transmitted by the bite of sand flies
**ka·lan·choe** \,ka-lən-'kō-ē *also* kə-'laŋ-kə-(,)wē *or* 'ka-lən-,chō\ *noun* [New Latin] (1830)
: any of a genus (*Kalanchoe*) of chiefly African tropical succulent herbs or shrubs of the orpine family often cultivated as ornamentals — compare BRYOPHYLLUM
**kale** \'kā(ə)l\ *noun* [Scots, from Middle English (northern) *cal*, from Old English *cāl* — more at COLE] (14th century)
**1 a** : COLE **b** : a hardy cabbage (*Brassica oleracea acephala*) with curled often finely incised leaves that do not form a dense head
**2** *slang* : MONEY

\ə\ abut \ᵊ\ kitten \ər\ further \a\ ash \ā\ ace
\ä\ mop, mar \aù\ out \ch\ chin \e\ bet \ē\ easy
\g\ go \i\ hit \ī\ ice \j\ job \ŋ\ sing \ō\ go
\ò\ law \òi\ boy \th\ thin \t͟h\ the \ü\ loot \ù\ foot
\y\ yet \zh\ vision *see also* Guide to Pronunciation

**ka·lei·do·scope** \kə-'lī-də-,skōp\ *noun* [Greek *kalos* beautiful + *eidos* form + English *-scope* — more at IDYLL] (1817)
**1** : an instrument containing loose bits of colored material (as glass or plastic) between two flat plates and two plane mirrors so placed that changes of position of the bits of material are reflected in an endless variety of patterns
**2** : something resembling a kaleidoscope: as **a** : a variegated changing pattern or scene ⟨the lake a *kaleidoscope* of changing colors — Robert Gibbings⟩ **b** : a succession of changing phases or actions ⟨a . . . *kaleidoscope* of shifting values, information, fashions —Frank McLaughlin⟩
— **ka·lei·do·scop·ic** \-,lī-də-'skä-pik\ *adjective*
— **ka·lei·do·scop·i·cal·ly** \-pi-k(ə-)lē\ *adverb*
**ka·lends** *variant of* CALENDS
**kal·li·din** \'ka-lə-dən\ *noun* [German, from *Kalli*krein + Peptid peptide + *-in*] (1950)
: either of two vasodilator kinins formed from blood plasma globulin by the action of kallikrein: **a** : BRADYKININ **b** : one with a terminal lysine amino-acid residue added to bradykinin
**kal·li·kre·in** \,ka-lə-'krē-ən, kə-'li-krē-ən\ *noun* [German, from Greek *kallikreas* sweetbread, pancreas, from *kalli-* beautiful (from *kallos* beauty) + *kreas* flesh — more at RAW] (1930)
: a hypotensive protease that liberates kinins from blood plasma proteins and is used therapeutically for vasodilation
**Kal·muck** *or* **Kal·muk** \'kal-,mək, kal-'\ *or* **Kal·myk** \kal-'mik\ *noun* [Russian *kalmyk*, from Volga Tatar *kalmık*] (1613)
**1** : a member of a Buddhist Mongol people originally of Dzungaria living mainly northwest of the Caspian Sea in Russia
**2** : the Mongolian language of the Kalmucks
**Ka·ma** \'kä-mə\ *noun* [Sanskrit *Kāma*, from *kāma* love]
: the Hindu god of love
**ka·ma·ai·na** \,kä-mə-'ī-nə\ *noun* [Hawaiian *kama'āina*, from *kama* child + *'āina* land] (1903)
: one who has lived in Hawaii for a long time
**kame** \'kām\ *noun* [Scots, kame, comb, from Middle English (northern) *camb* comb, from Old English] (1795)
: a short ridge, hill, or mound of stratified drift deposited by glacial meltwater
**Ka·me·ha·me·ha Day** \kə-,mā-ə-'mā-(,)hä-\ *noun* (1925)
: June 11 observed as a holiday in Hawaii in commemoration of the birthday of Kamehameha I
**¹ka·mi·ka·ze** \,kä-mi-'kä-zē\ *noun* [Japanese, literally, divine wind] (1945)
**1** : a member of a Japanese air attack corps in World War II assigned to make a suicidal crash on a target (as a ship)
**2** : an airplane containing explosives to be flown in a suicide crash on a target ◆
**²kamikaze** *adjective* (1945)
**1** : of, relating to, being, or resembling a kamikaze
**2** : having or showing reckless disregard for safety or personal welfare
**kam·pong** \'käm-,pȯŋ, 'kam-\ *noun* [Malay] (1844)
: a hamlet or village in a Malay-speaking country
**ka·na** \'kä-nə\ *noun, plural* **kana** *often attributive* [Japanese] (1727)
: a Japanese system of syllabic writing having characters that can be used exclusively for writing foreign words or in combination with kanji (as for indicating pronunciations or grammatical inflections); *also* : a single character belonging to the kana system — compare HIRAGANA, KATAKANA
**Ka·nak** \kə-'näk, -'nak\ *noun* [French *canaque*, probably from English *Kanaka* South Sea islander, from Hawaiian, person] (1910)

: a native Melanesian inhabitant of New Caledonia
**kana·my·cin** \,ka-nə-'mī-sᵊn\ *noun* [New Latin *kanamyceticus*, specific epithet of *Streptomyces kanamyceticus*] (1957)
: a broad-spectrum antibiotic from a Japanese soil streptomyces (*Streptomyces kanamyceticus*)
**Kan·a·rese** \,ka-nə-'rēz, -'rēs\ *noun, plural* **Kanarese** [*Kanara*, India] (1847)
**1** : KANNADA
**2** : a member of a Kannada-speaking people of Karnataka, southern India
**kan·ban** \'kän-,bän\ *noun, often attributive* [Japanese, sign, placard; from the cards used on assembly lines to signal that parts are needed] (1982)
: JUST-IN-TIME
**kan·ga·roo** \,kaŋ-gə-'rü\ *noun, plural* **-roos** [Guugu Yimidhirr (Australian aboriginal language of northern Queensland) *gaṉurru*] (1770)
: any of various herbivorous leaping marsupial mammals (family Macropodidae) of Australia, New Guinea, and adjacent islands with a small head, large ears, long powerful hind legs, a long thick tail used as a support and in balancing, and rather small forelegs not used in progression ◆

kangaroo

**kangaroo court** *noun* (1853)
**1** : a mock court in which the principles of law and justice are disregarded or perverted
**2** : a court characterized by irresponsible, unauthorized, or irregular status or procedures
**3** : judgment or punishment given outside of legal procedure
**kangaroo rat** *noun* (1867)
: any of a genus (*Dipodomys*) of pouched nocturnal burrowing rodents of arid parts of the western U.S. and Mexico

kangaroo rat

**kan·ji** \'kän-(,)jē\ *noun, plural* **kanji** *often attributive* [Japanese] (1920)
: a Japanese system of writing that utilizes characters borrowed or adapted from Chinese writing; *also* : a single character belonging to the kanji system — compare KANA
**Kan·na·da** \'kä-nə-də *also* 'ka-\ *noun* [Kannada *kannaḍa*] (1856)
: the major Dravidian language of Karnataka, southern India
**kan·te·le** \'kän-tə-lə\ *noun* [Finnish] (circa 1903)
: a traditional Finnish zither originally having five strings but now having as many as thirty
**ka·o·lin** \'kā-ə-lən\ *noun* [French *kaolin*, from *Gaoling* hill in China] (circa 1741)
: a fine usually white clay that is used in ceramics and refractories, as a filler or extender, and in medicine especially as an adsorbent in the treatment of diarrhea
**ka·o·lin·ite** \-lə-,nīt\ *noun* (1867)
: a mineral consisting of a hydrous silicate of aluminum that constitutes the principal mineral in kaolin
— **ka·o·lin·it·ic** \,kā-ə-lə-'ni-tik\ *adjective*
**ka·on** \'kā-,än\ *noun* [International Scientific Vocabulary *ka* kay (from *K-meson*, its earlier name) + ²*-on*] (1958)
: an unstable meson that occurs in both charged and neutral forms and is about 970 times more massive than an electron
**ka·pell·mei·ster** \kə-'pel-,mī-stər, kä-\ *noun, often capitalized* [German, from *Kapelle* choir + *Meister* master] (1838)
: the director of a choir or orchestra

**kaph** \'käf, 'kȯf\ *noun* [Hebrew, literally, palm of the hand] (circa 1823)
: the 11th letter of the Hebrew alphabet — see ALPHABET table
**ka·pok** \'kā-,päk\ *noun* [Malay] (circa 1750)
: a mass of silky fibers that clothe the seeds of the ceiba tree and are used especially as a filling for mattresses, life preservers, and sleeping bags and as insulation
**Ka·po·si's sarcoma** \'ka-pə-sēz- *also* -shēz-, kə-'pō-sēz\ *noun* [Moritz *Kaposi* (died 1902) Hungarian dermatologist] (1916)
: a neoplastic disease associated especially with AIDS, affecting especially the skin and mucous membranes, and characterized usually by the formation of pink to reddish-brown or bluish plaques, macules, papules, or nodules
**kap·pa** \'ka-pə\ *noun* [Middle English, from Greek, of Semitic origin; akin to Hebrew *kaph*] (15th century)
: the 10th letter of the Greek alphabet — see ALPHABET table
**ka·put** *also* **ka·putt** \kə-'pút, kä-, -'püt\ *adjective* [German *kaputt*, from French *capot* not having made a trick at piquet] (1895)
**1** : utterly finished, defeated, or destroyed

◇ **WORD HISTORY**

**kamikaze**    In 1274 and 1281 Kublai Khan, the Mongol emperor of China, sent out great fleets to conquer Japan. Providential storms dispersed the fleets on both occasions and by saving the country reinforced the Japanese belief that the Shinto gods would forever protect Japan from invasion. The storms became known in Japanese history as *kamikaze*, literally, "divine wind." In the fall of 1944, as Japanese military fortunes in World War II declined dramatically, pilots were recruited who were willing to give up their lives for their country by crashing specially prepared planes—in effect flying bombs—into American ships. These pilots were members of several units called collectively *Kamikaze Tokubetsu Kōgekitai* (or *Tokkōtai*) ("Kamikaze Special Attack Force") after the storms that had saved Japan some seven centuries earlier. The kamikaze's drastic methods made a greater impression on Americans than did his patriotic goal. *Kamikaze*, originally borrowed into English as a name for the suicidal pilot, is now an adjective meaning "suicidal" or "reckless of personal safety or welfare."

**kangaroo**    *Kangaroo* is the oldest and probably the best-known word borrowed from an Australian Aboriginal language, though for many years its origin was in doubt. During a voyage along the Australian coast in 1770, the English explorer James Cook was forced to beach and repair his ship near the Endeavor River in northern Queensland. Cook's party recorded a number of words from the native Australians in a language now called Guugu Yimidhirr. Among these words was one pronounced /gaṉurru/, recorded as *kangaroo*, and under this name the Australian marsupial became known when Cook returned to Europe. Controversy began when in 1820 a British naval officer revisited the Endeavor River area but failed to elicit the word again. This led to the notion that Cook's party had been mistaken, and that *kangaroo*, if it was a native Australian word, must have meant something quite different from "kangaroo." Not until 1972 was the mystery cleared up, when the linguist John Haviland began the first thorough study of Guugu Yimidhirr. He again elicited the word, more than 200 years after Cook's expedition, as the name for a large, dark kangaroo, probably the male of the species *Macropus giganteus*.

**2 :** unable to function **: USELESS** ⟨my battery went *kaput* —Henry James Jr.⟩
**3 :** hopelessly outmoded ◆
**kar·a·bi·ner** *variant of* CARABINER
**Kara·ism** \'kar-ə-ˌi-zəm\ *noun* [Late Hebrew *qĕrāīm* Karaites, from Hebrew *qārā* to read] (circa 1883)
**:** a Jewish doctrine originating in Baghdad in the 8th century that rejects rabbinism and talmudism and bases its tenets on Scripture alone
— **Kara·ite** \-,īt\ *noun*
**kar·a·kul** \'kar-ə-kəl\ *noun* [*Karakul,* village in Uzbekistan] (1853)

**1** *often capitalized*
**:** any of a breed of hardy fat-tailed sheep from Uzbekistan with a narrow body and coarse wiry fur
**2 :** the tightly curled glossy coat of the newborn lamb of a karakul valued as fur

karakul 1

**kar·a·o·ke** \,kar-ē-'ō-kē, kə-'rō-kē, ,kä-rä-'ō-(,)kä\ *noun* [Japanese, from *kara* empty + *ōke,* short for *ōkesutora* orchestra] (1982)
**:** a device that plays instrumental accompaniments for a selection of songs to which the user sings along and that records the user's singing with the music
**kar·at** \'kar-ət\ *noun* [Middle English, probably from Middle French *carat,* from Medieval Latin *carratus* unit of weight for precious stones — more at CARAT] (15th century)
**:** a unit of fineness for gold equal to 1/24 part of pure gold in an alloy
**ka·ra·te** \kə-'rä-tē\ *noun* [Japanese, from *kara* empty + *te* hand] (1955)
**:** an Oriental art of self-defense in which an attacker is disabled by crippling kicks and punches
— **ka·ra·te·ist** \-tē-ist\ *noun*
**ka·ra·ya gum** \kə-'rī-ə-\ *noun* [Hindi *karāyal* resin] (1916)
**:** any of several vegetable gums similar to tragacanth and often used as substitutes for it that are obtained from tropical Asian trees (genera *Sterculia* of the family Sterculiaceae and *Cochlospermum* of the family Bixaceae); *especially* **:** one derived from an Indian tree (*S. urens*)
**Ka·re·lian** \kə-'rē-lē-ən, -'rēl-yən\ *noun* (1855)
**1 :** a native or inhabitant of Karelia
**2 :** the Finno-Ugric language of the Karelians
— **Karelian** *adjective*
**Ka·ren** \kə-'ren\ *noun, plural* **Karen** *or* **Ka·rens** (1833)
**1 :** a member of a group of peoples of eastern and southern Myanmar
**2 a :** a group of languages spoken by the Karen peoples **b :** a language of this group
**kar·ma** \'kär-mə *also* 'kər-\ *noun* [Sanskrit *karma* fate, work] (1827)
**1** *often capitalized* **:** the force generated by a person's actions held in Hinduism and Buddhism to perpetuate transmigration and in its ethical consequences to determine the nature of the person's next existence
**2 :** VIBRATION 4
— **kar·mic** \-mik\ *adjective*
**ka·roo** *or* **kar·roo** \kə-'rü\ *noun, plural* **ka·roos** *or* **karroos** [Afrikaans *karo*] (1789)
**:** a dry tableland of southern Africa
**ka·ross** \kə-'räs\ *noun* [Afrikaans *karos*] (1785)
**:** a simple garment or rug of skins used especially by native tribesmen of southern Africa
**karst** \'kärst\ *noun* [German] (1902)
**:** an irregular limestone region with sinks, underground streams, and caverns
— **karst·ic** \'kär-stik\ *adjective*
**kart** \'kärt\ *noun* [probably from *GoKart,* a trademark] (1959)

**:** a miniature motorcar used especially in racing
— **kart·ing** *noun*
**kary-** *or* **karyo-** *also* **cary-** *or* **caryo-** *combining form* [New Latin, from Greek *karyon* nut — more at CAREEN]
**1 :** nucleus of a cell ⟨*karyo*kinesis⟩
**2 :** nut : kernel ⟨*cary*opsis⟩
**kar·y·og·a·my** \,kar-ē-'ä-gə-mē\ *noun, plural* **-mies** (1891)
**:** the fusion of cell nuclei (as in fertilization)
**kar·yo·ki·ne·sis** \,kar-ē-ō-kə-'nē-səs, -kī-\ *noun* [New Latin] (1882)
**1 :** the nuclear phenomena characteristic of mitosis
**2 :** the whole process of mitosis
— **kar·yo·ki·net·ic** \-'ne-tik\ *adjective*
**kar·y·ol·o·gy** \,kar-ē-'ä-lə-jē\ *noun* [International Scientific Vocabulary] (1895)
**1 :** the minute cytological characteristics of the cell nucleus especially with regard to the chromosomes
**2 :** a branch of cytology concerned with the karyology of cell nuclei
— **kar·y·o·log·i·cal** \-ē-ə-'lä-ji-kəl\ *also* **kar·y·o·log·ic** \-jik\ *adjective*
**kar·yo·lymph** \'kar-ē-ō-,lim(p)f\ *noun* [International Scientific Vocabulary] (1899)
**: NUCLEAR SAP**
**kar·yo·some** \'kar-ē-ə-,sōm\ *noun* [International Scientific Vocabulary] (1889)
**:** a mass of chromatin in a cell nucleus that resembles a nucleolus
**¹kar·yo·type** \'kar-ē-ə-,tīp\ *noun* [International Scientific Vocabulary] (1929)
**:** the chromosomal characteristics of a cell; *also* **:** the chromosomes themselves or a representation of them
— **kar·yo·typ·ic** \,kar-ē-ə-'ti-pik\ *adjective*
— **kar·yo·typ·i·cal·ly** \-pi-k(ə-)lē\ *adverb*
**²karyotype** *transitive verb*
**:** to determine the karyotype of
**Kas·bah** *variant of* CASBAH
**ka·sha** \'kä-shə, 'ka-\ *noun* [Russian] (1808)
**1 :** a porridge made usually from buckwheat groats
**2 :** kasha grain before cooking
**Ka·shan** \kə-'shän\ *noun* [*Kashan,* Iran] (1920)
**:** an Oriental rug with floral motifs in soft colors
**Kash·mir** *variant of* CASHMERE
**Kash·miri** \kash-'mir-ē, kazh-\ *noun, plural* **Kashmiris** *or* **Kashmiri** (1880)
**1 :** an Indo-Aryan language spoken in Kashmir
**2 :** a native or inhabitant of Kashmir
**kash·ruth** *or* **kash·rut** \kä-'shrüt, -'shrüth\ *noun* [Hebrew *kashrūth,* literally, fitness] (1907)
**1 :** the Jewish dietary laws
**2 :** the state of being kosher
**Ka·shu·bi·an** \kə-'shü-bē-ən\ *noun* [*Kashube* a member of a Slavic people] (1919)
**:** a Slavic language spoken in the vicinity of Gdansk
**kat** *variant of* KHAT
**ka·ta** \'kä-(,)tä\ *noun, plural* **kata** *or* **katas** [Japanese, literally, model, pattern] (1945)
**:** a set combination of positions and movements (as in karate) performed as an exercise
**kat·a·bat·ic** \,ka-tə-'ba-tik\ *adjective* [Greek *katabatos* descending, verbal of *katabainein* to go down, from *kata-* cata- + *bainein* to go — more at COME] (1918)
**:** relating to or being a wind produced by the flow of cold dense air down a slope (as of a mountain or glacier) in an area subject to radiational cooling
**ka·ta·ka·na** \,kä-tə-'kä-nə\ *noun* [Japanese, from *kata* part + *kana* kana] (1727)
**:** the form of Japanese syllabic writing used especially for scientific terms, official documents, and words adopted from other languages — compare HIRAGANA
**ka·tchi·na** *or* **ka·tci·na** *variant of* KACHINA

**Ka·tha·re·vu·sa** \,kä-thə-'re-və-,sä\ *noun* [New Greek *kathareuousa,* from Greek, feminine of *kathareuōn,* present participle of *kathareuein* to be pure, from *katharos* pure] (1936)
**:** modern Greek conforming to classic Greek usage
**ka·thar·sis** *variant of* CATHARSIS
**ka·ty·did** \'kā-tē-,did\ *noun* [imitative] (1784)
**:** any of several large green American long-horned grasshoppers usually having stridulating organs on the forewings of the males that produce a loud shrill sound
**kat·zen·jam·mer** \'kat-sən-,ja-mər\ *noun* [German, from *Katze* cat + *Jammer* distress] (1849)
**1 :** HANGOVER
**2 :** DISTRESS 2
**3 :** a discordant clamor
**kau·ri** \'kaù(-ə)r-ē\ *noun* [Maori *kawri*] (1823)
**1 :** any of various trees (genus *Agathis*) of the araucaria family; *especially* **:** a tall timber tree (*A. australis*) of New Zealand having fine white straight-grained wood
**2 :** a light-colored to brown resin from the kauri tree found as a fossil in the ground or collected from living trees and used especially in varnishes and linoleum — called also *kauri gum, kauri resin*
**ka·va** \'kä-və\ *noun* [Tongan & Marquesan, literally, bitter] (1810)
**1 :** an Australasian shrubby pepper (*Piper methysticum*) from whose crushed root an intoxicating beverage is made
**2 :** the beverage made from kava
**kay** \'kā\ *noun* (14th century)
**:** the letter *k*
**Kay** \'kā\ *noun*
**:** a boastful overbearing knight of the Round Table who is foster brother and seneschal of King Arthur
**kay·ak** \'kī-,ak\ *noun* [Inuit *qayaq*] (1757)
**1 :** an Eskimo canoe made of a frame covered with skins except for a small opening in the center and propelled by a double-bladed paddle
**2 :** a portable boat styled like an Eskimo kayak
— **kay·ak·er** \-,a-kər\ *noun*
— **kay·ak·ing** \-kiŋ\ *noun*
**¹kayo** \(,)kā-'ō, 'kā-(,)ō\ *noun* [pronunciation of *KO,* abbreviation] (1920)
**: KNOCKOUT**
**²kayo** *transitive verb* **kay·oed; kayo·ing** (1923)
**:** KNOCK OUT
**Ka·zak** \kə-'zak, -'zäk\ *noun* [*Kazak* (Kazakh), town in Azerbaijan] (1900)
**:** an Oriental rug in bold colors with geometric designs or stylized plant and animal forms

\ə\ **abut** \ᵊ\ **kitten** \ər\ **further** \a\ **ash** \ā\ **ace**
\ä\ **mop, mar** \aù\ **out** \ch\ **chin** \e\ **bet** \ē\ **easy**
\g\ **go** \i\ **hit** \ī\ **ice** \j\ **job** \ŋ\ **sing** \ō\ **go**
\ò\ **law** \òi\ **boy** \th\ **thin** \t͟h\ **the** \ü\ **loot** \ù\ **foot**
\y\ **yet** \zh\ **vision** *see also* Guide to Pronunciation

**Ka·zakh** \kə-'zak, -'zäk\ *noun* [Russian *kazakh*, from Kazakh *kazak*] (1832)
**1** : a member of a Turkic people of Kazakhstan and other countries of central Asia
**2** : the language of the Kazakhs

**ka·zoo** \kə-'zü\ *noun, plural* **kazoos** [imitative] (1884)
: an instrument that imparts a buzzing quality to the human voice and that usually consists of a small metal or plastic tube with a side hole covered by a thin membrane

**K-band** \'kā-\ *noun* (circa 1948)
: a segment of the radio spectrum that lies between 10.9 GHz and 36.0 GHz and spans the upper superhigh-frequency and lower extremely-high-frequency bands and that is used especially for police radars, satellite communication, and astronomical observation

**kea** \'kē-ə\ *noun* [Maori] (1862)
: a large mostly dull green New Zealand parrot (*Nestor notabilis*) that is normally insectivorous but sometimes destroys sheep by slashing the back to feed on the kidney fat

**ke·bab** *or* **ke·bob** *variant of* KABOB

**keb·buck** *or* **keb·bock** \'ke-bək\ *noun* [Middle English (Scots dialect) *cabok*, from Scottish Gaelic *ceapag*] (15th century)
*dialect British* : a whole wheel or ball of cheese

**¹kedge** \'kej\ *transitive verb* **kedged; kedging** [Middle English *caggen*] (1627)
: to move (a ship) by means of a line attached to a kedge dropped at the distance and in the direction desired

**²kedge** *noun* (circa 1769)
: a small anchor used especially in kedging

**ked·ge·ree** \'ke-jə-rē\ *noun* [Hindi *khicaṛī*, from Sanskrit *khiccā*] (1662)
**1** : an Indian dish of seasoned rice, beans, lentils, and sometimes smoked fish
**2** : cooked or smoked fish, rice, hard-boiled eggs, and seasoning heated in cream

**¹keek** \'kēk\ *intransitive verb* [Middle English *kiken*] (14th century)
*chiefly Scottish* : PEEP, LOOK

**²keek** *noun* (1721)
*chiefly Scottish* : PEEP, LOOK

**¹keel** \'kē(ə)l\ *verb* [Middle English *kelen*, from Old English *cēlan*, from *cōl* cool] (before 12th century)
*chiefly dialect* : COOL

**²keel** *noun* [Middle English *kele*, from Middle Dutch *kiel*; akin to Old English *cēol* ship] (14th century)
: a flat-bottomed barge used especially on the Tyne to carry coal

**³keel** *noun* [Middle English *kele*, from Old Norse *kjǫlr*; akin to Old English *ceole* throat, beak of a ship — more at GLUTTON] (14th century)
**1 a** : the chief structural member of a boat or ship that extends longitudinally along the center of its bottom and that often projects from the bottom; *also* : this projection **b** : SHIP
**2** : a projection suggesting a keel; *especially* : CARINA
— **keeled** \'kē(ə)ld\ *adjective*
— **keel·less** \'kē(ə)l-ləs\ *adjective*

**⁴keel** *intransitive verb* (1832)
**1** : to fall in or as if in a faint — usually used with *over*
**2** : to heel or lean precariously

**⁵keel** *noun* [Middle English (Scots dialect) *keyle*] (15th century)
*chiefly dialect* : RED OCHER

**keel·boat** \'kē(ə)l-ˌbōt\ *noun* (1695)
: a shallow covered keeled riverboat that is usually rowed, poled, or towed and that is used for freight

**keel·haul** \-ˌhȯl\ *transitive verb* [Dutch *kielhalen*, from *kiel* keel + *halen* to haul] (1666)
**1** : to haul under the keel of a ship as punishment or torture
**2** : to rebuke severely

**keel·son** \'kel-sən, 'kē(ə)l-\ *noun* [Middle English *kelswayn*, probably of Scandinavian origin; akin to Swedish *kölsvin* keelson] (1598)
: a longitudinal structure running above and fastened to the keel of a ship in order to stiffen and strengthen its framework

**¹keen** \'kēn\ *adjective* [Middle English *kene* brave, sharp, from Old English *cēne* brave; akin to Old High German *kuoni* brave] (13th century)
**1 a** : having a fine edge or point : SHARP ⟨a *keen* sword⟩ **b** : affecting one as if by cutting ⟨*keen* sarcasm⟩ **c** : pungent to the sense ⟨a *keen* scent⟩
**2 a** (1) : showing a quick and ardent responsiveness : ENTHUSIASTIC ⟨a *keen* swimmer⟩ (2) : EAGER ⟨was *keen* to begin⟩ **b** *of emotion or feeling* : INTENSE ⟨the *keen* delight in the chase —F. W. Maitland⟩
**3 a** : intellectually alert : having or characteristic of a quick penetrating mind ⟨a *keen* student⟩ ⟨a *keen* awareness of the problem⟩; *also* : shrewdly astute ⟨*keen* bargainers⟩ **b** : sharply contested ⟨*keen* debate⟩ **c** : extremely sensitive in perception ⟨*keen* eyes⟩
**4** : WONDERFUL, EXCELLENT
*synonym* see SHARP, EAGER
— **keen·ly** *adverb*
— **keen·ness** \'kēn-nəs\ *noun*

**²keen** *noun* (1830)
: a lamentation for the dead uttered in a loud wailing voice or sometimes in a wordless cry

**³keen** *verb* [Irish *caoinim* I lament] (1845)
*intransitive verb*
**1 a** : to lament with a keen **b** : to make a sound suggestive of a keen
**2** : to lament, mourn, or complain loudly
*transitive verb*
: to utter by keening
— **keen·er** *noun*

**¹keep** \'kēp\ *verb* **kept** \'kept\; **keep·ing** [Middle English *kepen*, from Old English *cēpan*; perhaps akin to Old High German *chapfen* to look] (before 12th century)
*transitive verb*
**1** : to take notice of by appropriate conduct : FULFILL: as **a** : to be faithful to ⟨*keep* a promise⟩ **b** : to act fittingly in relation to ⟨*keep* the Sabbath⟩ **c** : to conform to in habits or conduct ⟨*keep* late hours⟩ **d** : to stay in accord with (a beat) ⟨*keep* time⟩
**2** : PRESERVE, MAINTAIN: as **a** : to watch over and defend ⟨*keep* us from harm⟩ **b** (1) : to take care of : TEND ⟨*keep* a garden⟩ (2) : SUPPORT (3) : to maintain in a good, fitting, or orderly condition — usually used with *up* **c** : to continue to maintain ⟨*keep* watch⟩ **d** (1) : to cause to remain in a given place, situation, or condition ⟨*keep* him waiting⟩ (2) : to preserve (food) in an unspoiled condition **e** : to have or maintain in one's service or at one's disposal ⟨*keep* a mistress⟩ — often used with *on* ⟨*kept* the cook on⟩; *also* : to lodge or feed for pay ⟨*keep* boarders⟩ **f** (1) : to maintain a record in ⟨*keep* a diary⟩ (2) : to enter in a book ⟨*keep* records⟩ **g** : to have customarily in stock for sale
**3 a** : to restrain from departure or removal : DETAIN ⟨*keep* children in after school⟩ **b** : HOLD BACK, RESTRAIN ⟨*keep* them from going⟩ ⟨*kept* him back with difficulty⟩ **c** : SAVE, RESERVE ⟨*keep* some for later⟩ ⟨*kept* some out for a friend⟩ **d** : to refrain from revealing ⟨*keep* a secret⟩
**4 a** : to retain in one's possession or power ⟨*kept* the money we found⟩ **b** : to refrain from granting, giving, or allowing ⟨*kept* the news back⟩ **c** : to have in control ⟨*keep* your temper⟩
**5** : to confine oneself to ⟨*keep* my room⟩
**6 a** : to stay or continue in ⟨*keep* the path⟩ ⟨*keep* your seat⟩ **b** : to stay or remain on or in usually against opposition : HOLD ⟨*kept* her ground⟩
**7** : CONDUCT, MANAGE ⟨*keep* a tearoom⟩
*intransitive verb*
**1** *chiefly British* : LIVE, LODGE

**2 a** : to maintain a course, direction, or progress ⟨*keep* to the right⟩ **b** : to continue usually without interruption ⟨*keep* talking⟩ ⟨*keep* quiet⟩ ⟨*keep* on smiling⟩ **c** : to persist in a practice ⟨*kept* bothering them⟩ ⟨*kept* on smoking in spite of warnings⟩
**3** : STAY, REMAIN ⟨*keep* out of the way⟩ ⟨*keep* off the grass⟩: as **a** : to stay even — usually used with *up* ⟨*keep* up with the Joneses⟩ **b** : to remain in good condition ⟨meat will *keep* in the freezer⟩ **c** : to remain secret ⟨the secret would *keep*⟩ **d** : to call for no immediate action ⟨the matter will *keep* until morning⟩
**4** : ABSTAIN, REFRAIN ⟨can't *keep* from talking⟩
**5** : to be in session ⟨school will *keep* through the winter —W. M. Thayer⟩
**6** *of a quarterback* : to retain possession of a football especially after faking a handoff ☆☆
— **keep an eye on** : WATCH
— **keep at** : to persist in doing or concerning oneself with
— **keep company** : to go together as frequent companions or in courtship
— **keep house** : to manage a household
— **keep one's distance** *or* **keep at a distance** : to stay aloof : maintain a reserved attitude
— **keep one's eyes open** *or* **keep one's eyes peeled** : to be on the alert : be watchful
— **keep one's hand in** : to keep in practice
— **keep pace** : to stay even; *also* : KEEP UP
— **keep step** : to keep in step
— **keep to 1 a** : to stay in **b** : to limit oneself to **2** : to abide by
— **keep to oneself 1** : to keep secret ⟨*kept* the facts *to myself*⟩ **2** : to remain solitary or apart from other people

**²keep** *noun* (1579)
**1 a** *archaic* : CUSTODY, CHARGE **b** : MAINTENANCE
**2** : one that keeps or protects: as **a** : FORTRESS, CASTLE; *specifically* : the strongest and securest part of a medieval castle **b** : one whose job is to keep or tend **c** : PRISON, JAIL
**3** : the means or provisions by which one is kept ⟨earned his *keep*⟩
**4** : KEEPER 4

---

☆ **SYNONYMS**
**Keep, observe, celebrate, commemorate** mean to notice or honor a day, occasion, or deed. KEEP stresses the idea of not neglecting or violating ⟨*kept* the Sabbath by refraining from work⟩. OBSERVE suggests marking the occasion by ceremonious performance ⟨not all holidays are *observed* nationally⟩. CELEBRATE suggests acknowledging an occasion by festivity ⟨traditionally *celebrates* Thanksgiving with a huge dinner⟩. COMMEMORATE suggests that an occasion is marked by observances that remind one of the origin and significance of the day ⟨*commemorate* Memorial Day with the laying of wreaths⟩.

**Keep, retain, detain, withhold, reserve** mean to hold in one's possession or under one's control. KEEP may suggest a holding securely in one's possession, custody, or control ⟨*keep* this while I'm gone⟩. RETAIN implies continued keeping, especially against threatened seizure or forced loss ⟨managed to *retain* their dignity even in poverty⟩. DETAIN suggests a delay in letting go ⟨*detained* them for questioning⟩. WITHHOLD implies restraint in letting go or a refusal to let go ⟨*withheld* information from the authorities⟩. RESERVE suggests a keeping in store for future use ⟨*reserve* some of your energy for the last mile⟩.

**— for keeps 1 a :** with the provision that one keep what one has won (played marbles *for keeps*) **b :** with deadly seriousness **2 :** for an indefinitely long time **:** PERMANENTLY **3 :** with the result of ending the matter

**keep back** *intransitive verb* (1837)
**:** to refrain from approaching or advancing near something (police asked the spectators to *keep back*)

**keep down** *transitive verb* (1581)
**1 :** to keep in control (*keep* expenses *down*)
**2 :** to prevent from growing, advancing, or succeeding

**keep·er** \'kē-pər\ *noun* (14th century)
**1 :** one that keeps: as **a :** PROTECTOR **b :** GAMEKEEPER **c :** WARDEN **d :** CUSTODIAN **e** *chiefly British* **:** CURATOR
**2 :** any of various devices for keeping something in position
**3 a :** one fit or suitable for keeping; *especially* **:** a fish large enough to be legally caught and kept **b :** a domestic animal considered with respect to how easy it is to care for (an easy *keeper*)
**4 :** an offensive football play in which the quarterback runs with the ball

**keep·ing** \'kē-piŋ\ *noun* (14th century)
**1 :** the act of one that keeps: as **a :** CUSTODY, MAINTENANCE **b :** OBSERVANCE **c :** a reserving or preserving for future use
**2 a :** the means by which something is kept **:** SUPPORT, PROVISION **b :** the state of being kept or the condition in which something is kept (the house is in good *keeping*)
**3 :** CONFORMITY (in *keeping* with good taste) (out of *keeping* with the decor)

**keep·sake** \'kēp-ˌsāk\ *noun* [¹*keep* + *-sake* (as in *namesake*)] (1790)
**:** something kept or given to be kept as a memento

**keep up** (15th century)
*transitive verb*
**:** to persist or persevere in (*kept up* the good work); *also* **:** MAINTAIN, SUSTAIN (*keep* standards *up*)
*intransitive verb*
**1 :** to keep adequately informed or up-to-date (*keep up* on international affairs)
**2 :** to continue without interruption (rain *kept up* all night)
**3 :** to maintain contact or relations with (*keep up* with old friends)

**kees·hond** \'kās-ˌhȯnt\ *noun, plural* **kees·hon·den** \-ˌhȯn-dən\ [Dutch, probably from *Kees*, nickname for *Cornelis* Cornelius + *hond* dog, from Middle Dutch; akin to Old English *hund* hound] (1926)
**:** any of a Dutch breed of compact medium-sized dogs that have a dense heavy grayish coat and a foxy head

**kef** \'kēf, 'kef, 'kāf\ *noun* [Arabic *kayf* pleasure] (1808)
**1 :** a state of dreamy tranquillity
**2 :** a smoking material (as marijuana) that produces kef

**kef·fi·yeh** *variant of* KAFFIYEH

**ke·fir** \ke-'fir; 'kē-fər, 'ke-\ *noun* [Russian] (1884)
**:** a beverage of fermented cow's milk

**keg** \'keg, *dialect* 'kag, 'käg\ *noun* [Middle English *kag*, of Scandinavian origin; akin to Old Norse *kaggi* keg] (circa 1632)
**1 :** a small cask or barrel having a capacity of 30 gallons (136.4 liters) or less
**2 :** the contents of a keg

**keg·ler** \'ke-glər, 'kā-\ *noun* [German, from *kegeln* to bowl, from *Kegel* bowling pin, from Old High German *kegil* stake, peg] (1932)
**:** ¹BOWLER

**keg·ling** \'ke-gliŋ, 'kā-\ *noun* (1938)
**:** BOWLING

**keis·ter** \'kēs-tər, 'kīs-\ *or* **kees·ter** \'kēs-\ *noun* [English slang *keister* satchel] (1931)
*slang* **:** BUTTOCKS

**ke·lim** *variant of* KILIM

**kel·ly green** \'ke-lē-\ *noun, often K capitalized* [from the common Irish name *Kelly*; from the association of Ireland with the color green] (circa 1935)
**:** a strong yellowish green

**ke·loid** \'kē-ˌlȯid\ *noun* [French *kéloïde*, from Greek *chēlē* claw] (1854)
**:** a thick scar resulting from excessive growth of fibrous tissue
**— keloid** *adjective*
**— ke·loi·dal** \kē-'lȯi-dᵊl\ *adjective*

**kelp** \'kelp\ *noun* [Middle English *culp*] (14th century)
**1 a :** any of various large brown seaweeds (order Laminariales) **b :** a mass of large seaweeds
**2 :** the ashes of seaweed used especially as a source of iodine

**kelp bass** *noun* (circa 1936)
**:** a mottled sea bass (*Paralabrax clathratus*) that occurs along the Pacific coast of the U.S. and is an important sport fish

**¹kel·pie** \'kel-pē\ *noun* [perhaps from Scottish Gaelic *cailpeach, colpach* heifer, colt] (1747)
**:** a water sprite of Scottish folklore that delights in or brings about the drowning of wayfarers

**²kelpie** *noun* [*Kelpie*, name of a dog of this breed] (1903)
**:** any of a breed of energetic working dogs developed in Australia from British sheepdogs

**Kelt** \'kelt\, **Kelt·ic** \'kel-tik\ *variant of* CELT, CELTIC

**kel·vin** \'kel-vən\ *noun* (1968)
**:** the base unit of temperature in the International System of Units that is equal to 1/273.16 of the Kelvin scale temperature of the triple point of water

**Kelvin** *adjective* [William Thomson, Lord *Kelvin*] (1908)
**:** relating to, conforming to, or having a thermometric scale on which the unit of measurement equals the Celsius degree and according to which absolute zero is 0 K, the equivalent of $-273.15°C$

**kemp** \'kemp\ *noun* [Middle English *kempe* coarse hair, probably of Scandinavian origin; akin to Old Norse *kampr* mustache; akin to Old English *cenep* mustache] (1641)
**:** a coarse fiber especially of wool that is usually short, wavy, and white, has little affinity for dye, and is used in mixed wools

**Kemp's ridley** \'kemps-\ *noun* [Richard M. *Kemp* (flourished 1873) American amateur naturalist] (1979)
**:** RIDLEY a

**kempt** \'kem(p)t\ *adjective* [back-formation from *unkempt*] (1929)
**:** neatly kept **:** TRIM

**¹ken** \'ken\ *verb* **kenned; ken·ning** [Middle English *kennen*, from Old English *cennan* to make known & Old Norse *kenna* to perceive; both akin to Old English *can* know — more at CAN] (13th century)
*transitive verb*
**1** *archaic* **:** SEE
**2** *chiefly dialect* **:** RECOGNIZE
**3** *chiefly Scottish* **:** KNOW
*intransitive verb*
*chiefly Scottish* **:** KNOW

**²ken** *noun* (1590)
**1 a :** the range of vision **b :** SIGHT, VIEW ('tis double death to drown in *ken* of shore —Shakespeare)
**2 :** the range of perception, understanding, or knowledge (abstract words that are beyond the *ken* of young children —Lois M. Rettie)

**ke·naf** \kə-'naf\ *noun* [Persian] (1891)
**:** an African hibiscus (*Hibiscus cannabinus*) widely cultivated for its fiber; *also* **:** the fiber used especially for cordage

**Ken·dal green** \'ken-dᵊl-\ *noun* [*Kendal*, England] (1514)
**:** a green woolen cloth resembling homespun or tweed

**ken·do** \'ken-(ˌ)dō\ *noun* [Japanese *kendō*, from *ken* sword + *dō* art] (1921)
**:** a Japanese sport of fencing with bamboo swords

**¹ken·nel** \'ke-nᵊl\ *noun* [Middle English *kenel*, ultimately from (assumed) Vulgar Latin *canile*, from Latin *canis* dog — more at HOUND] (14th century)
**1 a :** a shelter for a dog or cat **b :** an establishment for the breeding or boarding of dogs or cats
**2 :** a pack of dogs

**²kennel** *verb* **-neled** *or* **-nelled; -nel·ing** *or* **-nel·ling** (1552)
*intransitive verb*
**:** to take shelter in or as if in a kennel
*transitive verb*
**:** to put or keep in or as if in a kennel

**³kennel** *noun* [alteration of *cannel* gutter] (15th century)
**:** a gutter in a street

**¹ken·ning** \'ke-niŋ\ *noun* [Middle English, sight, view, from gerund of *kennen*] (1786)
*chiefly Scottish* **:** a perceptible but small amount

**²kenning** *noun* [Old Norse, from *kenna*] (1883)
**:** a metaphorical compound word or phrase (as *swan-road* for *ocean*) used especially in Old English and Old Norse poetry

**ke·no** \'kē-(ˌ)nō\ *noun* [French *quine*, set of five winning numbers in a lottery + English *-o* (as in *lotto*)] (1814)
**:** a game resembling bingo

**ken·speck·le** \'ken-ˌspe-kəl\ *adjective* [probably of Scandinavian origin; akin to Norwegian *kjennspak* quick to recognize] (1616)
*chiefly Scottish* **:** CONSPICUOUS

**kent·ledge** \'kent-lij\ *noun* [origin unknown] (1607)
**:** pig iron or scrap metal used as ballast

**Ken·tucky bluegrass** \kən-'tə-kē-\ *noun* [*Kentucky*, state of U.S.] (1849)
**:** a valuable Old World pasture and meadow grass (*Poa pratensis*) naturalized in America — called also *bluegrass*

**Kentucky coffee tree** *noun* (1785)
**:** a tall North American leguminous tree (*Gymnocladus dioica*) with bipinnate leaves and large woody brown pods whose seeds have been used as a substitute for coffee

**Kentucky rifle** *noun* (1832)
**:** a muzzle-loading long-barreled flintlock rifle developed in the 18th century in Pennsylvania and used extensively on the American frontier

**Ke·ogh plan** \'kē-(ˌ)ō-\ *noun* [Eugene James *Keogh* (died 1989) American politician] (1974)
**:** an individual retirement account for the self-employed

**ke·pi** \'kā-pē, 'ke-\ *also* **ké·pi** \'kā-\ *noun* [French *képi*, from German dialect (Switzerland) *käppi* cap] (1861)
**:** a military cap with a round flat top sloping toward the front and a visor

**kept** *past and past participle of* KEEP

**kerat-** *or* **kerato-** *combining form* [International Scientific Vocabulary, from Greek *kerato-, keras* horn — more at HORN]
**:** cornea (*keratitis*)

**ker·a·tin** \'ker-ə-tᵊn\ *noun* [International Scientific Vocabulary] (circa 1849)
**:** any of various sulfur-containing fibrous proteins that form the chemical basis of horny epidermal tissues (as hair and nails)
**— ke·ra·ti·nous** \kə-'ra-tᵊn-əs\ *adjective*

**ke·ra·ti·ni·za·tion** \ˌker-ə-tə-nə-'zā-shən, kə-ˌra-tᵊn-ə-\ *noun* (circa 1887)
**:** conversion into keratin or keratinous tissue
**— ke·ra·ti·nize** \'ker-ə-tə-ˌnīz, kə-'ra-tᵊn-ˌīz\ *verb*

**ke·ra·ti·no·phil·ic** \ˌker-ə-tə-nə-'fi-lik, kə-ˌra-tᵊn-ə-\ *adjective* (1946)

**:** exhibiting affinity for keratin (as in hair, skin, feathers, or horns) — used chiefly of fungi capable of growing on such materials

**ker·a·ti·tis** \,ker-ə-'tī-təs\ *noun, plural* **-tit·i·des** \-'ti-tə-,dēz\ [New Latin] (1858)
**:** inflammation of the cornea of the eye

**ker·a·to·con·junc·ti·vi·tis** \'ker-ə-tō-kən-,jəŋ(k)-tə-'vī-təs\ *noun* [New Latin] (1887)
**:** combined inflammation of the cornea and conjunctiva

**ker·a·to·plas·ty** \'ker-ə-tō-,plas-tē\ *noun, plural* **-ties** (circa 1857)
**:** plastic surgery on the cornea; *especially* **:** corneal grafting

**ker·a·to·sis** \,ker-ə-'tō-səs\ *noun, plural* **-to·ses** \-,sēz\ [New Latin] (1885)
**:** an area of skin marked by overgrowth of horny tissue
— **ker·a·tot·ic** \-'tä-tik\ *adjective*

**kerb** \'kərb\ *noun* (1805)
*British* **:** CURB 5

**ker·chief** \'kər-chəf, -,chēf\ *noun, plural* **ker·chiefs** \-chəfs, -,chēfs\ *also* **ker·chieves** \-,chēvz\ [Middle English *courchef*, from Old French *cuevrechief*, from *covrir* to cover + *chief* head — more at CHIEF] (13th century)
**1 :** a square of cloth used as a head covering or worn as a scarf around the neck
**2 :** HANDKERCHIEF 1
— **ker·chiefed** \-chəft, -,chēft\ *adjective*

**kerf** \'kərf\ *noun* [Middle English, action of cutting, from Old English *cyrf*; akin to Old English *ceorfan* to carve — more at CARVE] (1523)
**1 :** a slit or notch made by a saw or cutting torch
**2 :** the width of cut made by a saw or cutting torch

**ker·fuf·fle** \kər-'fə-fəl\ *noun* [alteration of *carfuffle*, from Scots *car-* (probably from Scottish Gaelic *cearr* wrong, awkward) + *fuffle* to become disheveled] (1946)
*chiefly British* **:** DISTURBANCE, FUSS

**Ker·man** \kər-'män, ker-\ *variant of* KIRMAN

**ker·mes** \'kər-(,)mēz\ *noun* [French *kermès*, from Arabic *qirmiz*] (1603)
**:** the dried bodies of the females of various scale insects (genus *Kermes*) that are found on a Mediterranean oak (*Quercus coccifera*) and constitute a red dyestuff; *also* **:** the dye

**ker·mis** \'kər-məs\ *or* **ker·mess** \-məs, -,mes\ *or* **ker·messe** \-məs, -,mes\ *noun* [Dutch *kermis*, from Middle Dutch *kercmisse*, from *kerc, kerke* church + *misse* mass, church festival] (1577)
**1 :** an outdoor festival of the Low Countries
**2 :** a fair held usually for charitable purposes

**¹kern** *or* **kerne** \'kərn, 'kern\ *noun* [Middle English *kerne*, from Middle Irish *cethern* band of soldiers] (15th century)
**1 :** a light-armed foot soldier of medieval Ireland or Scotland
**2 :** YOKEL

**²kern** \'kərn\ *noun* [French *carne* corner, from French dialect, from Latin *cardin-, cardo* hinge] (1683)
**:** a part of a typeset letter that projects beyond its side bearings

**ker·nel** \'kər-nᵊl\ *noun* [Middle English, from Old English *cyrnel*, diminutive of *corn*] (before 12th century)
**1** *chiefly dialect* **:** a fruit seed
**2 :** the inner softer part of a seed, fruit stone, or nut
**3 :** a whole seed of a cereal ⟨a *kernel* of corn⟩
**4 :** a central or essential part **:** GERM ⟨like many stereotypes . . . this one too contains some *kernels* of truth —S. M. Lyman⟩
**5 :** a subset of the elements of one set (as a group) that a function (as a homomorphism) maps onto an identity element of another set

**kern·ite** \'kər-,nīt\ *noun* [*Kern* Co., Calif.] (1927)
**:** a mineral that consists of a hydrous borate of sodium and is an important source of borax

**ker·o·gen** \'ker-ə-jən\ *noun* [Greek *kēros* wax + English *-gen* — more at CERUMEN] (1906)
**:** bituminous material occurring in shale and yielding oil when heated

**ker·o·sene** *or* **ker·o·sine** \'ker-ə-,sēn, ,ker-ə-', 'kar-, ,kar-\ *noun* [Greek *kēros* + English *-ene* (as in *camphene*)] (1854)
**:** a flammable hydrocarbon oil usually obtained by distillation of petroleum and used for a fuel and as a solvent and thinner

**ker·ria** \'ker-ē-ə\ *noun* [New Latin, from William *Kerr* (died 1814) English gardener] (1823)
**:** a shrub (*Kerria japonica*) of the rose family that is native to China and Japan and has solitary yellow and often double flowers

**ker·ry** \'ker-ē\ *noun, plural* **kerries** *often capitalized* [County *Kerry*, Ireland] (1829)
**:** any of an Irish breed of small hardy black dairy cattle

**Kerry blue terrier** *noun* (1922)
**:** any of an Irish breed of medium-sized terriers with a long squarish head, deep chest, and silky bluish coat

**ker·sey** \'kər-zē\ *noun, plural* **kerseys** [Middle English, from *Kersey*, England] (14th century)
**1 a :** a coarse ribbed woolen cloth for hose and work clothes **b :** a heavy wool or wool and cotton fabric used especially for uniforms and coats
**2 :** a garment of kersey

**ker·sey·mere** \'kər-zē-,mir\ *noun* [alteration of *cassimere*] (1798)
**:** a fine woolen fabric with a close nap made in fancy twill weaves

**ke·ryg·ma** \kə-'rig-mə\ *noun* [Greek *kērygma*, from *kēryssein* to proclaim, from *kēryx* herald — more at CADUCEUS] (1889)
**:** the apostolic proclamation of salvation through Jesus Christ
— **ker·yg·mat·ic** \,ker-ig-'ma-tik\ *adjective*

**kes·trel** \'kes-trəl\ *noun* [Middle English *castrel*, from Middle French *crecerelle*, from *crecelle* rattle; from its cry] (15th century)
**:** any of various small chiefly Old World falcons (genus *Falco*) that usually hover in the air while searching for prey: as **a :** a common Eurasian falcon (*F. tinnunculus*) **b :** an American falcon (*F. sparverius*) having a reddish brown back and tail and bluish gray wings

**ket-** *or* **keto-** *combining form* [International Scientific Vocabulary]
**:** ketone ⟨*ketosis*⟩

**ketch** \'kech\ *noun* [alteration of *catch*, from Middle English *cache*] (circa 1649)
**:** a fore-and-aft rigged vessel similar to a yawl but with a larger mizzen and with the mizzenmast stepped farther forward

**ketch·up** \'ke-chəp, 'ka-\ *noun* [Malay *kĕchap* fish sauce] (circa 1690)
**:** a seasoned pureed condiment usually made from tomatoes

ketch

**ke·tene** \'kē-,tēn\ *noun* [International Scientific Vocabulary] (1907)
**:** a colorless poisonous gas $C_2H_2O$ of penetrating odor used especially as an acetylating agent; *also* **:** any of various derivatives of this compound

**ke·to** \'kē-(,)tō\ *adjective* [ket-] (1891)
**:** of or relating to a ketone; *also* **:** containing a ketone group

**ke·to·gen·e·sis** \,kē-tō-'je-nə-səs\ *noun* [New Latin] (1915)
**:** the production of ketone bodies (as in diabetes)
— **ke·to·gen·ic** \-'je-nik\ *adjective*

**ke·to·glu·tar·ic acid** \-glü-'tar-ik-\ *noun* (1908)
**:** either of two crystalline keto derivatives $C_5H_6O_5$ of glutaric acid; *especially* **:** the alpha keto isomer formed in various metabolic processes (as the Krebs cycle)

**ke·tone** \'kē-,tōn\ *noun* [German *Keton*, alteration of *Aceton* acetone] (1851)
**:** an organic compound (as acetone) with a carbonyl group attached to two carbon atoms
— **ke·ton·ic** \kē-'tä-nik\ *adjective*

**ketone body** *noun* (1915)
**:** any of the three compounds acetoacetic acid, acetone, and beta-hydroxybutyric acid which are normal intermediates in lipid metabolism and accumulate in the blood and urine in abnormal amounts in conditions of impaired metabolism (as diabetes mellitus)

**ke·tose** \'kē-,tōs, -,tōz\ *noun* [International Scientific Vocabulary] (1902)
**:** a sugar (as fructose) containing one ketone group per molecule

**ke·to·sis** \kē-'tō-səs\ *noun* [New Latin] (1917)
**:** an abnormal increase of ketone bodies in the body
— **ke·tot·ic** \-'tä-tik\ *adjective*

**ke·to·ste·roid** \,kē-tō-'stir-,óid *also* -'ster-\ *noun* [International Scientific Vocabulary] (1939)
**:** a steroid (as cortisone or estrone) containing a ketone group

**ket·tle** \'ke-tᵊl\ *noun* [Middle English *ketel*, from Old Norse *ketill* (akin to Old English *cietel* kettle), both from a prehistoric Germanic word borrowed from Latin *catillus*, diminutive of *catinus* bowl] (13th century)
**1 :** a metallic vessel usually used for boiling liquids; *especially* **:** TEAKETTLE
**2 :** KETTLEDRUM
**3 a :** POTHOLE 1b **b :** a steep-sided hollow without surface drainage especially in a deposit of glacial drift

**ket·tle·drum** \-,drəm\ *noun* (1602)
**:** a percussion instrument that consists of a hollow brass, copper, or fiberglass hemisphere with a calfskin or plastic head whose tension can be changed to vary the pitch

kettledrum

**kettle of fish** (1742)
**1 :** a bad state of affairs **:** MESS
**2 :** something to be considered or reckoned with **:** MATTER ⟨books and discs . . . were two very different *kettles of fish* —Roland Gelatt⟩

**Kew·pie** \'kyü-pē\ *trademark*
— used for a small chubby doll with a topknot of hair

**¹key** \'kē\ *noun* [Middle English, from Old English *cæg*; akin to Old Frisian *kēi* key] (before 12th century)
**1 a :** a usually metal instrument by which the bolt of a lock is turned **b :** any of various devices having the form or function of such a key
**2 a :** a means of gaining or preventing entrance, possession, or control **b :** an instrumental or deciding factor
**3 a :** something that gives an explanation or identification or provides a solution ⟨the *key* to a riddle⟩ **b :** a list of words or phrases giving an explanation of symbols or abbreviations **c :** an aid to interpretation or identification **:** CLUE **d :** an arrangement of the salient characters of a group of plants or animals or of taxa designed to facilitate identification **e :** a map legend
**4 a** (1) **:** COTTER PIN (2) **:** COTTER **b :** a keystone in an arch **c :** a small piece of wood or metal used as a wedge or for preventing motion between parts

**5 a :** one of the levers of a keyboard musical instrument that actuates the mechanism and produces the tones **b :** a lever that controls a vent in the side of a woodwind instrument or a valve in a brass instrument **c :** a part to be depressed by a finger that serves as one unit of a keyboard
**6 :** SAMARA
**7 :** a system of tones and harmonies generated from a hierarchical scale of seven tones based on a tonic ⟨the *key* of G major⟩
**8 a :** characteristic style or tone **b :** the tone or pitch of a voice **c :** the predominant tone of a photograph with respect to its lightness or darkness
**9 :** a decoration or charm resembling a key
**10 :** a small switch for opening or closing an electric circuit ⟨a telegraph *key*⟩
**11 :** the set of instructions governing the encipherment and decipherment of messages
**12 :** a free-throw area in basketball
— **keyed** \'kēd\ *adjective*
— **key·less** \'kē-ləs\ *adjective*
²**key** (14th century)
*transitive verb*
**1 :** to lock with or as if with a key **:** FASTEN: as
**a :** to secure (as a pulley on a shaft) by a key
**b :** to finish off (an arch) by inserting a keystone
**2 :** to regulate the musical pitch of
**3 :** to bring into harmony or conformity **:** make appropriate **:** ATTUNE ⟨remarks *keyed* to a situation⟩
**4 :** to identify (a biological specimen) by a key
**5 :** to provide with identifying or explanatory cross-references ⟨instructions *keyed* to accompanying drawings —John Gartner⟩
**6 :** to make nervous, tense, or excited — usually used with *up* ⟨was *keyed* up over her impending operation⟩
**7 :** KEYBOARD — often used with *in*
*intransitive verb*
**1 :** to use a key
**2 :** to observe the position or movement of an opposing player in football in order to anticipate the play — usually used with *on*
**3 :** KEYBOARD
³**key** *adjective* (1913)
**:** IMPORTANT, FUNDAMENTAL ⟨*key* issues⟩
⁴**key** *noun* [Spanish *cayo*, from Taino] (1697)
**:** a low island or reef; *specifically* **:** any of the coral islets off the southern coast of Florida
⁵**key** *noun* [by shortening & alteration from *kilo*] (1968)
*slang* **:** a kilogram especially of marijuana or heroin
¹**key·board** \'kē-,bōrd, -,bȯrd\ *noun* (1819)
**1 :** a bank of keys on a musical instrument (as a piano) that usually consists of seven white and five raised black keys to the octave
**2 :** an assemblage of systematically arranged keys by which a machine or device is operated
**3 :** a board on which keys for locks are hung
²**keyboard** (1961)
*transitive verb*
**:** to capture or set (as data or text) by means of a keyboard
*intransitive verb*
**:** to operate a machine (as for typesetting) by means of a keyboard
— **key·board·er** *noun*
**key·board·ist** \'kē-,bȯr-dist, -,bȯr-\ *noun* (1973)
**:** a person who plays a keyboard musical instrument
**key·but·ton** \'kē-,bə-t°n\ *noun* (circa 1920)
**:** KEY 5c
**key club** *noun* [from the key to the premises provided to each member] (1962)
**:** an informal private club serving liquor and providing entertainment
**key deer** *noun, often K capitalized* (1950)
**:** a very small rare white-tailed deer (*Odocoileus virginianus clavium*) native to the Florida Keys

**key grip** \,kē-\ *noun* (1979)
**:** the technician in charge of moving and setting up camera tracks and scenery in a motion-picture or television production
¹**key·hole** \'kē-,hōl\ *noun* (circa 1592)
**1 :** a hole for receiving a key
**2 :** KEY 12
²**keyhole** *adjective* (1937)
**1 :** revealingly intimate ⟨a *keyhole* report⟩
**2 :** intent on revealing intimate details ⟨*keyhole* columnists⟩
**keyhole saw** *noun* (1777)
**:** a narrow pointed fine-toothed handsaw used for cutting curves of short radius
**key light** *noun* (circa 1937)
**:** the main light illuminating a photographic subject
**key lime** *noun, often K capitalized* (1929)
**:** a lime grown especially in the Florida Keys and adjacent areas
**key lime pie** *noun, often K capitalized* (1954)
**:** a usually meringue-topped lime-custard pie traditionally made from key limes
**Keynes·ian·ism** \'kān-zē-ə-,ni-zəm\ *noun* (1946)
**:** the economic theories and programs ascribed to John M. Keynes and his followers; *specifically* **:** the advocacy of monetary and fiscal programs by government to increase employment and spending
— **Keynes·ian** \'kān-zē-ən\ *noun or adjective*
¹**key·note** \'kē-,nōt\ *noun* (1776)
**1 :** the first and harmonically fundamental tone of a scale
**2 :** the fundamental or central fact, idea, or mood ⟨sadness is the *keynote* of this little collection —*Books Abroad*⟩
²**keynote** *transitive verb* (1914)
**1 :** to set the keynote of
**2 :** to deliver the keynote address at
— **key·not·er** *noun*
**keynote address** *noun* (circa 1908)
**:** an address designed to present the issues of primary interest to an assembly (as a political convention) and often to arouse unity and enthusiasm — called also *keynote speech*
**keynote speaker** *noun* (1950)
**:** one who delivers a keynote address
**key·pad** \'kē-,pad\ *noun* (1975)
**:** a small often handheld keyboard
¹**key·punch** \'kē-,pənch\ *noun* (1918)
**:** a machine with a keyboard used to cut holes or notches in punched cards
²**keypunch** *transitive verb* (1959)
**:** to enter (data) on punched cards with a keypunch
— **key·punch·er** *noun*
**key signature** *noun* (1875)
**:** the sharps or flats placed after a clef in music to indicate the key
**key·stone** \'kē-,stōn\ *noun* (circa 1637)
**1 :** the wedge-shaped piece at the crown of an arch that locks the other pieces in place — see ARCH illustration
**2 :** something on which associated things depend for support ⟨determination, a *keystone* of the puritan ethic —L. S. Lewis⟩
¹**key·stroke** \-,strōk\ *noun* (circa 1910)
**:** the act or an instance of depressing a key on a keyboard
²**keystroke** *transitive verb* (1966)
**:** KEYBOARD
**key·way** \-,wā\ *noun* (circa 1864)
**1 :** a groove or channel for a key
**2 :** the aperture for the key in a lock having a flat metal key
**key word** *noun* (1859)
**:** a word that is a key: as **a :** a word exemplifying the meaning or value of a letter or symbol **b** *usually* **key·word** \-,wərd\ **:** a significant word from a title or document used as an index to content
**khad·dar** \'kä-dər\ *or* **kha·di** \'kä-dē\ *noun* [Hindi *khādar, khādī*] (circa 1885)
**:** homespun cotton cloth of India

**kha·ki** \'ka-kē, 'kä-, *Canadian often* 'kär-\ *noun* [Hindi *khākī* dust-colored, from *khāk* dust, from Persian] (1857)
**1 :** a light yellowish brown
**2 a :** a khaki-colored cloth made usually of cotton or wool and used especially for military uniforms **b :** a garment of this cloth; *especially* **:** a military uniform — usually used in plural ◆
— **khaki** *adjective*
**Khal·kha** \'kal-kə, 'kȧl-kə\ *noun* (1873)
**1 :** a member of a Mongol people of Outer Mongolia
**2 :** the language of the Khalkha people used as the official language of the Mongolian People's Republic
**kham·sin** \kam-'sēn\ *noun* [Arabic *rīḥ al-khamsīn* the wind of the fifty (days between Easter and Pentecost)] (1685)
**:** a hot southerly Egyptian wind
¹**khan** \'kän *also* 'kan\ *noun* [Middle English *caan*, from Middle French, of Turkic origin; akin to Turkish *han* prince] (15th century)
**1 :** a medieval sovereign of China and ruler over the Turkish, Tatar, and Mongol tribes
**2 :** a local chieftain or man of rank in some countries of central Asia
²**khan** *noun* [Arabic *khān*] (1614)
**:** a caravansary or rest house in some Asian countries
**khan·ate** \'kä-,nāt *also* 'ka-\ *noun* (1799)
**:** the state or jurisdiction of a khan
**khap·ra beetle** \'ka-prə-, 'kä-\ *noun* [Hindi *khaprā*, literally, destroyer] (1928)
**:** a dermestid beetle (*Trogoderma granarium*) that is native to the Indian subcontinent and is now a serious pest of stored grain in most parts of the world
**khat** \'kät\ *noun* [Arabic *qāt*] (1858)
**:** a shrub (*Catha edulis*) cultivated in the Middle East and Africa for its leaves and buds that are the source of an habituating stimulant when chewed or used as a tea
**khe·dive** \kə-'dēv\ *noun* [French *khédive*, from Turkish *hidiv*] (1867)
**:** a ruler of Egypt from 1867 to 1914 governing as a viceroy of the sultan of Turkey
— **khe·div·ial** \-'dē-vē-əl\ *or* **khe·div·al** \-'dē-vəl\ *adjective*

---

◇ WORD HISTORY

**khaki** *Khaki*, like *bungalow*, *cot*, and *shampoo*, is a by-product of British rule in India, though for the average user of English these words have lost all association with the Raj. The Hindi word *khākī* "dust-colored, brown" was applied to the color of a uniform cloth used by units of Britain's Indian Army in the mid-19th century. Dull brown field uniforms were most likely originally adopted for their ease of maintenance on dirty trails, though as the range of a rifle increased and battlefield tactics changed in the later 19th century, it was doubtless realized that drab clothing was valuable as camouflage. By the time of the South African War (1899–1902), all colonial units of the British Army were dressed in the color, and *khaki* became linked with support for the army and a militaristic foreign policy. (The vote of 1900, when patriotic Britons returned to Parliament the same Conservatives who had started the war with the Boers, went down in history as the "Khaki Election.") Contemporary retailers in the U.S., however, to judge by their advertising, associate khaki clothing with fashionable casualness and a summery look rather than with military uniforms or British India.

---

\ə\ abut \ᵊ\ kitten \ər\ further \a\ ash \ā\ ace
\ä\ mop, mar \aú\ out \ch\ chin \e\ bet \ē\ easy
\g\ go \i\ hit \ī\ ice \j\ job \ŋ\ sing \ō\ go
\ȯ\ law \ȯi\ boy \th\ thin \th\ the \ü\ loot \ú\ foot
\y\ yet \zh\ vision *see also* Guide to Pronunciation

**Khmer** \kə-'mer\ *noun, plural* **Khmer** *or* **Khmers** (1876)
**1 :** a member of an aboriginal people of Cambodia
**2 :** the Mon-Khmer language of the Khmer people that is the official language of Cambodia
— **Khmer** *adjective*
**Khoi·khoi** \'kói-,kói\ *noun, plural* **Khoikhoi** (1791)
**:** HOTTENTOT
**Khoi·san** \'kói-,sän, -'sän\ *noun* [*Khoí*khoi + *San*] (1930)
**1 :** a group of African peoples speaking Khoisan languages
**2 :** a family of African languages comprising principally Hottentot and the Bushman languages
**khoum** \'küm, 'kum\ *noun* [modification of Arabic *khums*, literally, one fifth] (1973)
— see *ouguiya* at MONEY table
**Kho·war** \'kō-,wär\ *noun* (1882)
**:** an Indo-Aryan language of northwest Pakistan
**ki·ang** \kē-'äŋ\ *noun* [Tibetan *rkyaṅ*] (1869)
**:** an Asian wild ass *(Equus hemionus kiang* synonym *E. kiang)* usually with reddish back and sides and white underparts, muzzle, and legs
**kiaugh** \'kyák\ *noun* [origin unknown] (1786) *Scottish* **:** TROUBLE, ANXIETY
**kib·be** *or* **kib·beh** *or* **kib·bi** \'ki-bē\ *noun* [Arabic *kubbah*] (1937)
**:** a Near Eastern dish of ground lamb and bulgur that is eaten cooked or raw
¹**kib·ble** \'ki-bəl\ *transitive verb* **kib·bled; kib·bling** \-b(ə-)liŋ\ [origin unknown] (circa 1790)
**:** to grind coarsely *(kibbled* dog biscuit) *(kibbled* grain)
²**kibble** *noun* (1942)
**:** coarsely ground meal or grain (as for animal feed)
**kib·butz** \ki-'buts, -'büts\ *noun, plural* **kib·but·zim** \-,but-'sēm, -,büt-\ [New Hebrew *qibbūṣ*] (1944)
**:** a communal farm or settlement in Israel
**kib·butz·nik** \-'but-snik, -'büt-\ *noun* [Yiddish *kibutsnik*, from *kibuts* kibbutz (from New Hebrew *qibbūṣ*) + *-nik*, agent suffix] (1947)
**:** a member of a kibbutz
**kibe** \'kīb\ *noun* [Middle English] (14th century)
**:** an ulcerated chilblain especially on the heel
**ki·bitz** *also* **kib·bitz** \'ki-bəts, kə-'bits\ *verb* [Yiddish *kibetsn*] (1927)
*intransitive verb*
**:** to act as a kibitzer
*transitive verb*
**:** to observe as a kibitzer; *especially* **:** to be a kibitzer at *(kibitz* a card game)
**ki·bitz·er** *also* **kib·bitz·er** \'ki-bət-sər, kə-'bit-\ *noun* (1922)
**:** one who looks on and often offers unwanted advice or comment especially at a card game; *broadly* **:** one who offers opinions
**ki·bosh** \'kī-,bäsh, kī-'; ki-'bäsh\ *noun* [origin unknown] (1836)
**:** something that serves as a check or stop (put the *kibosh* on that) ◆
— **kibosh** *transitive verb*
¹**kick** \'kik\ *verb* [Middle English *kiken*] (14th century)
*intransitive verb*
**1 a :** to strike out with the foot or feet **b :** to make a kick in football
**2 a :** to show opposition **:** RESIST, REBEL **b :** to protest strenuously or urgently **:** express grave discontent; *broadly* **:** COMPLAIN
**3 :** to function with vitality and energy (alive and *kicking)*
**4** *of a firearm* **:** to recoil when fired
**5 :** to go from one place to another as circumstance or whim dictates
**6 :** to run at a faster speed during the last part of a race

*transitive verb*
**1 a :** to strike, thrust, or hit with the foot **b :** to strike suddenly and forcefully as if with the foot **c :** to remove from a position or status *(kicked* him off the team)
**2 :** to score by kicking a ball
**3 :** to heap reproaches upon (oneself) *(kicked* themselves for not going)
**4 :** to free oneself of (as a drug habit)
— **kick·able** \'ki-kə-bəl\ *adjective*
— **kick ass :** to kick butt — often considered vulgar
— **kick butt :** to use forceful or coercive measures in order to achieve a purpose; *also* **:** to succeed or win overwhelmingly
— **kick over the traces :** to cast off restraint, authority, or control
— **kick the bucket :** DIE
— **kick up one's heels 1 :** to show sudden delight **2 :** to have a lively time
— **kick upstairs :** to promote to a higher but less desirable position
²**kick** *noun* (1530)
**1 a :** a blow or sudden forceful thrust with the foot; *specifically* **:** a sudden propelling of a ball with the foot **b :** the power to kick **c :** a rhythmic motion of the legs used in swimming **d :** a burst of speed in racing
**2 :** a sudden forceful jolt or thrust suggesting a kick; *especially* **:** the recoil of a gun
**3 :** POCKET, WALLET
**4 a :** a feeling or expression of opposition or objection (a *kick* against the administration) **b :** the grounds for objection
**5 a :** an effect suggestive of a kick (chili with a *kick)* **b :** a stimulating or pleasurable effect or experience **c :** pursuit of an absorbing or obsessive new interest (a skiing *kick)*
**6 :** a sudden and striking surprise, revelation, or turn of events
**kick around** (1839)
*intransitive verb*
**1 :** to wander or pass time aimlessly
**2 :** to lie about mostly unnoticed or forgotten
*transitive verb*
**1 :** to treat in an inconsiderate or high-handed fashion
**2 :** to consider, examine, or discuss from various angles
**kick–ass** \'kik-,as\ *adjective* (1970)
**:** strikingly tough, aggressive, or uncompromising — often considered vulgar
**kick·back** \'kik-,bak\ *noun* (1920)
**1 :** a sharp violent reaction
**2 :** a return of a part of a sum received often because of confidential agreement or coercion (every city contract had been let with a ten percent *kickback* to city officials —D. K. Shipler)
**kick·board** \-,bórd, -,bórd\ *noun* (1949)
**:** a buoyant rectangular board held by a swimmer while developing kicking techniques
**kick·box·ing** \-,bäk-siŋ\ *noun* (1971)
**:** boxing in which boxers are permitted to kick with bare feet as in karate
— **kick·box·er** \-sər\ *noun*
**kick·er** *noun* (circa 1580)
**1 :** one that kicks or kicks something
**2 :** KICK 6
**kick in** (1908)
*transitive verb*
**:** CONTRIBUTE
*intransitive verb*
**1** *slang* **:** DIE
**2 :** to make a contribution
**kick·off** \'kik-,óf\ *noun* (1857)
**1 :** a kick that puts the ball into play in a football or soccer game
**2 :** COMMENCEMENT 1 (the campaign *kickoff)*
**kick off** (1857)
*intransitive verb*
**1 :** to start or resume play in football by a placekick
**2 :** to begin proceedings
**3** *slang* **:** DIE

*transitive verb*
**:** to mark the beginning of
**kick out** *transitive verb* (1697)
**:** to dismiss or eject forcefully or summarily
**kick over** (1951)
*intransitive verb*
**:** to begin to fire — used of an internal combustion engine
*transitive verb*
**:** TURN OVER 1b
**kick pleat** *noun* (1926)
**:** a short inverted pleat (as at the bottom of a skirt) used to give breadth
**kick·shaw** \'kik-,shó\ *noun* [by folk etymology from French *quelque chose* something] (1597)
**1 :** a fancy dish **:** DELICACY
**2 :** TRINKET, GEWGAW
**kick·stand** \'kik-,stand\ *noun* [from its being put in position by a kick] (1947)
**:** a swiveling metal bar or rod for holding up a 2-wheeled vehicle (as a bicycle) when not in use
**kick turn** *noun* (1910)
**:** a standing half turn in skiing made by swinging one ski high with a jerk and planting it in the desired direction and then lifting the other ski into a parallel position
**kick·up** \'kik-,əp\ *noun* (circa 1793)
**:** a noisy quarrel **:** ROW
**kick up** (1756)
*transitive verb*
**1 :** to stir up **:** PROVOKE *(kick up* a fuss)
**2 :** to cause to rise upward (clouds of dust *kicked up* by passing cars)
*intransitive verb*
**:** to give evidence of disorder
**kicky** \'ki-kē\ *adjective* (1966)
**:** providing a kick or thrill **:** EXCITING; *also* **:** excitingly fashionable
¹**kid** \'kid\ *noun* [Middle English *kide*, of Scandinavian origin; akin to Old Norse *kith* kid] (13th century)
**1 a :** a young goat **b :** a young individual of various animals related to the goat
**2 a :** the flesh, fur, or skin of a kid **b :** something made of kid
**3 :** a young person; *especially* **:** CHILD — often used as a generalized reference to one especially younger or less experienced (the *kid* on the pro golf tour) (poor *kid)*
— **kid·dish** \'ki-dish\ *adjective*
²**kid** *intransitive verb* **kid·ded; kid·ding** (15th century)

◇ WORD HISTORY
**kibosh** The word *kibosh* is first recorded in 1836 in an early sketch by Charles Dickens (spelled *kye-bosk*, with a perhaps erroneous final *k*). Nine years later *kye-bosh* resurfaces in a dictionary of British underworld argot defined as "eighteen pence"; the connection between this and the more familiar "check" or "stop" sense is unclear. For over a century this peculiar colloquialism has taxed the ingenuity of etymologists, with minimal results: beyond the fact that it was prominent enough in lower-class London speech to attract Dickens's attention in the 1830s we know nothing for certain. Claims were once made that the word was Yiddish, though no remotely plausible Yiddish source has ever been produced. Another hypothesis is that its source is Irish *caidhp bháis,* literally, "coif (or cap) of death," variously explained as headgear a judge put on when pronouncing a death sentence, or—somewhat more plausibly—as a covering pulled over the face of a dead person when a coffin was closed. But evidence for any metaphorical use of this phrase in Irish appears to be lacking, and *kibosh* is not recorded in English as spoken in Ireland until decades after Dickens must have heard it in London.

: to bring forth young — used of a goat or an antelope

**³kid** *verb* **kid·ded; kid·ding** [probably from ¹*kid*] (1902)
*transitive verb*
**1 :** to deceive as a joke ⟨it's the truth; I wouldn't *kid* you⟩
**2 :** to make fun of
*intransitive verb*
: to engage in good-humored fooling or horseplay — often used with *around*
— **kid·der** *noun*
— **kid·ding·ly** \'ki-diŋ-lē\ *adverb*

**Kid·der·min·ster** \'ki-dər-ˌmin(t)-stər\ *noun* [*Kidderminster*, England] (1836)
: an ingrain carpet — called also *Kidderminster carpet*

**kid·die** *or* **kid·dy** \'ki-dē\ *noun, plural* **kid·dies** *often attributive* [¹*kid*] (1889)
: a small child

**kid·dush** \'ki-dəsh, -dish; ki-'düsh\ *noun* [Late Hebrew *qiddūsh* sanctification] (1753)
: a ceremonial blessing pronounced over wine or bread in a Jewish home or synagogue on a holy day (as the Sabbath)

**kid–glove** \'kid-ˌgləv\ *adjective* (1888)
: marked by extreme care or deference ⟨*kid-glove* treatment⟩

**kid glove** *noun* (1832)
: a dress glove made of kid leather
— **kid–gloved** \'kid-ˌgləvd\ *adjective*
— **with kid gloves** : with special consideration

**kid leather** *noun* (1687)
**1 :** a soft pliable leather made from kidskin
**2 :** a glove leather made from lambskin or goatskin

**kid·nap** \'kid-ˌnap\ *transitive verb* **-napped** *or* **-naped** \-ˌnapt\; **-nap·ping** *or* **-nap·ing** [probably back-formation from *kidnapper*, from *kid* + obsolete *napper* thief] (1682)
: to seize and detain or carry away by unlawful force or fraud and often with a demand for ransom
— **kid·nap·pee** *or* **kid·nap·ee** \ˌkid-ˌna-'pē\ *noun*
— **kid·nap·per** *or* **kid·nap·er** *noun*

**kid·ney** \'kid-nē\ *noun, plural* **kidneys** [Middle English] (14th century)
**1 a :** one of a pair of vertebrate organs situated in the body cavity near the spinal column that excrete waste products of metabolism, in humans are bean-shaped organs about 4½ inches (11½ centimeters) long lying behind the peritoneum in a mass of fatty tissue, and consist chiefly of nephrons by which urine is secreted, collected, and discharged into a main cavity whence it is conveyed by the ureter to the bladder **b :** any of various excretory organs of invertebrate animals
**2 :** the kidney of an animal eaten as food
**3 :** sort or kind especially with regard to temperament ⟨a nice helpful guy, of a different *kidney* entirely from the . . . Secret Police —Paula Lecler⟩

**kidney bean** *noun* (1548)
**1 :** an edible and nutritious seed of any cultivated bean of the common species (*Phaseolus vulgaris*); *especially* **:** a large dark red bean seed
**2 :** a plant bearing kidney beans

**kidney stone** *noun* (1946)
: a calculus in the kidney

**kid·skin** \'kid-ˌskin\ *noun* (14th century)
: the skin of a young or sometimes a mature goat; *also* **:** KID LEATHER

**kid stuff** *noun* (1929)
**1 :** something befitting or appropriate only to children
**2 :** something extremely simple or easy

**kiel·ba·sa** \kēl-'bä-sə, kil- *also* ki-'bä-sə\ *noun, plural* **-basas** *also* **-ba·sy** \-'bä-sē\ [Polish *kiełbasa*] (circa 1939)
: a smoked sausage of Polish origin

**kie·sel·guhr** \'kē-zəl-ˌgu̇r\ *noun* [German *Kieselgur*] (1875)

: loose or porous diatomite

**kie·ser·ite** \'kē-zə-ˌrīt\ *noun* [German *Kieserit*, from Dietrich *Kieser* (died 1862) German physician] (1862)
: a mineral that is a white hydrous magnesium sulfate

**kif** \'kif, 'kēf\ *variant of* KEF

**kike** \'kīk\ *noun* [origin unknown] (1904)
: JEW — usually taken to be offensive

**Ki·ku·yu** \kē-'kü-(ˌ)yü\ *noun, plural* **Kikuyu** *or* **Kikuyus** (1894)
**1 :** a member of a Bantu-speaking people of Kenya
**2 :** the Bantu language of the Kikuyu people

**kil·der·kin** \'kil-dər-kən\ *noun* [Middle English, from Middle Dutch *kindekijn*, from Medieval Latin *quintale* quintal] (14th century)
**1 :** an English unit of capacity equal to ½ barrel
**2 :** CASK

**ki·lim** \kē-'lēm\ *noun* [Turkish, from Persian *kilīm*] (1881)
: a pileless handwoven reversible rug or covering made in Turkey, Kurdistan, the Caucasus, Iran, and western Turkestan

**¹kill** \'kil\ *verb* [Middle English, perhaps from (assumed) Old English *cyllan;* akin to Old English *cwellan* to kill — more at QUELL] (14th century)
*transitive verb*
**1 a :** to deprive of life **b** (1) **:** to slaughter (as a hog) for food (2) **:** to convert a food animal into (a kind of meat) by slaughtering
**2 a :** to put an end to ⟨*kill* competition⟩ **b :** DEFEAT, VETO ⟨*killed* the amendment⟩ **c :** to mark for omission; *also* **:** DELETE
**3 a :** to destroy the vital or essential quality of ⟨*killed* the pain with drugs⟩ **b :** to cause to stop ⟨*kill* the motor⟩ **c :** to check the flow of current through
**4 :** to make a markedly favorable impression on ⟨she *killed* the audience⟩
**5 :** to get through uneventfully ⟨*kill* time⟩; *also* **:** to get through (the time of a penalty) without being scored on ⟨*kill* a penalty⟩
**6 a :** to cause extreme pain to **b :** to tire almost to the point of collapse
**7 :** to hit (a shot) so hard in various games that a return is impossible
**8 :** to consume (as a drink) totally
*intransitive verb*
**1 :** to deprive one of life
**2 :** to make a markedly favorable impression ⟨was dressed to *kill*⟩ ☆

**²kill** *noun* (1814)
**1 :** an act or instance of killing
**2 :** something killed: as **a** (1) **:** an animal shot in a hunt (2) **:** animals killed in a hunt, season, or particular period of time **b :** an enemy unit (as an airplane or ship) destroyed by military action **c :** a return shot in any of various games (as badminton, handball, or table tennis) that is too hard for an opponent to handle

**³kill** *noun, often capitalized* [Dutch *kil*] (1669)
: CHANNEL, CREEK — used chiefly in place names in Delaware, Pennsylvania, and New York

**kill·deer** \'kil-ˌdir\ *noun, plural* **killdeers** *or* **killdeer** [imitative] (1731)
: an American plover (*Charadrius vociferus*) characterized by two black breast bands and a plaintive penetrating cry

**¹kill·er** \'ki-lər\ *noun* (15th century)
**1 :** one that kills
**2 :** KILLER WHALE
**3 a :** one that has a forceful, violent, or striking impact **b :** one that is extremely difficult to deal with

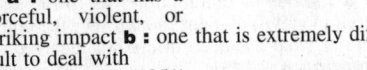
**killdeer**

**²killer** *adjective* (1951)
**1 :** strikingly impressive or effective ⟨a *killer* smile⟩ ⟨a *killer* résumé⟩

**2 :** extremely difficult to deal with ⟨a *killer* fastball⟩; *also* **:** causing death or devastation ⟨a *killer* tornado⟩

**killer bee** *noun* (1976)
: AFRICANIZED BEE

**killer cell** *noun* (1972)
: a T cell that functions in cell-mediated immunity by destroying a cell (as a tumor cell) having a specific antigenic molecule on its surface — called also *killer T cell*

**killer instinct** *noun* (1931)
: an aggressive tenacious urge for domination in a struggle to attain a set goal

**killer whale** *noun* (1884)
: a small gregarious whale (*Orcinus orca*) that is black with a white ventral side and white oval-shaped patches behind the eyes and attains a length of 20 to 30 feet (6.1 to 9.1 meters) — called also *orca*

**kil·li·fish** \'ki-li-ˌfish\ *noun* [*killie* killifish (perhaps from ³*kill* + *fish*) (1836)
**1 :** any of a family (Cyprinodontidae) of numerous small oviparous fishes much used as bait and in mosquito control
**2 :** any of a family (Poeciliidae) of livebearers

**¹kill·ing** \'ki-liŋ\ *noun* (15th century)
**1 :** the act of one that kills
**2 :** KILL 2a
**3 :** a sudden notable gain or profit

**²killing** *adjective* (15th century)
**1 :** that kills or relates to killing
**2 :** highly amusing
**3 :** extremely difficult to deal with ⟨the suspense is *killing*⟩; *also* **:** calling for great strength, stamina, or endurance ⟨a *killing* schedule⟩
— **kill·ing·ly** \-lē\ *adverb*

**kill-joy** \'kil-ˌjȯi\ *noun* (1776)
: one who spoils the pleasure of others

**kill off** *transitive verb* (1607)
: to destroy in large numbers or totally

**kiln** \'kiln, 'kil\ *noun* [Middle English *kilne*, from Old English *cyln*, from Latin *culina* kitchen, from *coquere* to cook — more at COOK] (before 12th century)
: an oven, furnace, or heated enclosure used for processing a substance by burning, firing, or drying
— **kiln** *transitive verb*

**ki·lo** \'kē-(ˌ)lō *also* 'ki-\ *noun, plural* **kilos** (1870)
: KILOGRAM

**Kilo** (1952)
— a communications code word for the letter *k*

**kilo-** *combining form* [French, modification of Greek *chilioi*]
: thousand ⟨*kiloton*⟩

---

**☆ SYNONYMS**

**Kill, slay, murder, assassinate, dispatch, execute** mean to deprive of life. KILL merely states the fact of death caused by an agency in any manner ⟨*killed* in an accident⟩ ⟨frost *killed* the plants⟩. SLAY is a chiefly literary term implying deliberateness and violence but not necessarily motive ⟨*slew* thousands of the Philistines⟩. MURDER specifically implies stealth and motive and premeditation and therefore full moral responsibility ⟨convicted of *murdering* a rival⟩. ASSASSINATE applies to deliberate killing openly or secretly often for political motives ⟨terrorists *assassinated* the Senator⟩. DISPATCH stresses quickness and directness in putting to death ⟨*dispatched* the sentry with one bullet⟩. EXECUTE stresses putting to death as a legal penalty ⟨*executed* by lethal gas⟩.

---

\ə\ abut \ᵊ\ kitten \ər\ **further** \a\ ash \ā\ **ace**
\ä\ mop, mar \au̇\ **out** \ch\ **chin** \e\ **bet** \ē\ **easy**
\g\ **go** \i\ **hit** \ī\ **ice** \j\ **job** \ŋ\ **sing** \ō\ **go**
\ȯ\ **law** \ȯi\ **boy** \th\ **thin** \t͟h\ **the** \ü\ **loot** \u̇\ **foot**
\y\ **yet** \zh\ **vision** *see also* Guide to Pronunciation

**ki·lo·bar** \'kē-lə-ˌbär, 'ki-lə-\ *noun* [International Scientific Vocabulary] (1926)
: a unit of pressure equal to 1000 bars

**ki·lo·base** \-ˌbās\ *noun* (1975)
: a unit of measure of the length of a nucleic-acid chain that equals one thousand base pairs

**ki·lo·bit** \-ˌbit\ *noun* [International Scientific Vocabulary] (1961)
**1** : 1000 bits
**2** : 1024 bits

**ki·lo·byte** \-ˌbīt\ *noun* [from the fact that 1024 ($2^{10}$) is the power of 2 closest to 1000] (1970)
: 1024 bytes

**ki·lo·cal·o·rie** \-ˌka-lə-rē, -ˈkal-rē\ *noun* [International Scientific Vocabulary] (1894)
: CALORIE 1b

**kilo·cy·cle** \'ki-lə-ˌsī-kəl\ *noun* [International Scientific Vocabulary] (1921)
: 1000 cycles; *especially* : KILOHERTZ

**ki·lo·gauss** \'kē-lə-ˌgau̇s, 'ki-lə-\ *noun* [International Scientific Vocabulary] (1895)
: 1000 gauss

**ki·lo·gram** \-ˌgram\ *noun* [French *kilogramme*, from *kilo-* + *gramme* gram] (1797)
**1** : the base unit of mass in the International System of Units that is equal to the mass of a prototype agreed upon by international convention and that is nearly equal to the mass of 1000 cubic centimeters of water at the temperature of its maximum density — see METRIC SYSTEM table
**2** : a unit of force equal to the weight of a kilogram mass under a gravitational attraction equal to that of the earth

**kilogram–meter** *noun* (1886)
: the meter-kilogram-second gravitational unit of work and energy equal to the work done by a kilogram force acting through a distance of one meter in the direction of the force : about 7.235 foot-pounds

**ki·lo·hertz** \'ki-lə-ˌhərts, 'kē-lə-, -ˌherts\ *noun* [International Scientific Vocabulary] (1929)
: 1000 hertz

**ki·lo·joule** \-ˌjü(ə)l\ *noun* [International Scientific Vocabulary] (circa 1889)
: 1000 joules

**kilo·li·ter** \'ki-lə-ˌlē-tər\ *noun* [French *kilolitre*, from *kilo-* + *litre* liter] (1810)
— see METRIC SYSTEM table

**ki·lo·me·ter** \÷kə-'lä-mə-tər, ÷ki-; 'ki-lə-ˌmē-tər\ *noun* [French *kilomètre*, from *kilo-* + *mètre* meter] (1810)
— see METRIC SYSTEM table ▯

**ki·lo·par·sec** \'ki-lə-ˌpär-ˌsek, 'kē-lə-\ *noun* (1922)
: 1000 parsecs

**ki·lo·pas·cal** \ˌki-lə-ˌpas-'kal\ *noun* (1978)
: 1000 pascals

**ki·lo·rad** \'ki-lə-ˌrad\ *noun* [International Scientific Vocabulary] (1965)
: 1000 rads

**ki·lo·ton** \-ˌtən *also* -ˌtän\ *noun* (1950)
**1** : 1000 tons
**2** : an explosive force equivalent to that of 1000 tons of TNT

**ki·lo·volt** \-ˌvōlt\ *noun* [International Scientific Vocabulary] (circa 1898)
: a unit of potential difference equal to 1000 volts

**kilo·watt** \'ki-lə-ˌwät\ *noun* [International Scientific Vocabulary] (1884)
: 1000 watts

**kilowatt–hour** *noun* (1892)
: a unit of work or energy equal to that expended by one kilowatt in one hour or to 3.6 million joules

**¹kilt** \'kilt\ *verb* [Middle English, of Scandinavian origin; akin to Old Norse *kjalta* lap, fold of a gathered skirt] (14th century)
*transitive verb*
**1** *chiefly dialect* : to tuck up (as a skirt)
**2** : to equip with a kilt
*intransitive verb*
: to move nimbly

**²kilt** *noun* (circa 1730)
**1** : a knee-length pleated skirt usually of tartan worn by men in Scotland and by Scottish regiments in the British armies
**2** : a garment that resembles a Scottish kilt

**kil·ter** \'kil-tər\ *noun* [origin unknown] (1628)
: proper or usual state or condition : ORDER ⟨out of *kilter*⟩

**kilt·ie** \'kil-tē\ *noun* (1842)
**1** *or* **kilty** : one who wears a kilt
**2** : a shoe with a long slashed tongue that folds over the instep; *also* : such a tongue

**kim·ber·lite** \'kim-bər-ˌlīt\ *noun* [*Kimberley*, South Africa + ¹*-ite*] (1887)
: an agglomerate biotite-peridotite that occurs in pipes especially in southern Africa and that often contains diamonds

**Kim·bun·du** \kim-'bùn-(ˌ)dü\ *noun* (circa 1895)
: a Bantu language of northern Angola

**kim·chi** *also* **kim·chee** \'kim-chē\ *noun* [Korean *kimch'i*] (1898)
: a vegetable pickle seasoned with garlic, red pepper, and ginger that is the national dish of Korea

**ki·mo·no** \kə-'mō-(ˌ)nō, -nə\ *noun, plural* **-nos** [Japanese, clothes, from *ki* wearing + *mono* thing] (1886)
**1** : a long robe with wide sleeves traditionally worn with a broad sash as an outer garment by the Japanese
**2** : a loose dressing gown or jacket
— **ki·mo·noed** \-(ˌ)nōd, -nəd\ *adjective*

**¹kin** \'kin\ *noun* [Middle English, from Old English *cynn*; akin to Old High German *chunni* race, Latin *genus* birth, race, kind, Greek *genos*, Latin *gignere* to beget, Greek *gignesthai* to be born] (before 12th century)
**1** : a group of persons of common ancestry : CLAN
**2 a** : one's relatives : KINDRED **b** : KINSMAN ⟨he wasn't any *kin* to you —Jean Stafford⟩
**3** *archaic* : KINSHIP

**²kin** *adjective* (1597)
: KINDRED, RELATED

**-kin** \kən\ *also* **-kins** \kənz\ *noun suffix* [Middle English, from Middle Dutch *-kin*; akin to Old High German *-chīn*, diminutive suffix]
: little ⟨cat*kin*⟩ ⟨baby*kins*⟩

**ki·na** \'kē-nə\ *noun* [New Guinea Pidgin, literally, a kind of shell] (1975)
— see MONEY table

**ki·nase** \'kī-ˌnās, -ˌnāz\ *noun* [International Scientific Vocabulary, from *kinetic*] (1947)
: an enzyme that catalyzes the transfer of phosphate groups from a high-energy phosphate-containing molecule (as ATP) to a substrate

**¹kind** \'kīnd\ *noun* [Middle English *kinde*, from Old English *cynd*; akin to Old English *cynn* kin] (before 12th century)
**1 a** *archaic* : NATURE **b** *archaic* : FAMILY, LINEAGE
**2** *archaic* : MANNER
**3** : fundamental nature or quality : ESSENCE
**4 a** : a group united by common traits or interests : CATEGORY **b** : a specific or recognized variety ⟨what *kind* of car do you drive⟩ **c** : a doubtful or barely admissible member of a category ⟨a *kind* of gray⟩
**5 a** : goods or commodities as distinguished from money ⟨payment in *kind*⟩ **b** : the equivalent of what has been offered or received
***synonym*** see TYPE
— **all kinds of 1** : MANY ⟨likes *all kinds of* sports⟩ **2** : plenty of ⟨has *all kinds of* time⟩

**²kind** *adjective* (14th century)
**1** *chiefly dialect* : AFFECTIONATE, LOVING
**2 a** : of a sympathetic or helpful nature **b** : of a forbearing nature : GENTLE **c** : arising from or characterized by sympathy or forbearance ⟨a *kind* act⟩
**3** : of a kind to give pleasure or relief

**kin·der·gar·ten** \'kin-də(r)-ˌgär-t°n, -d°n\ *noun* [German, from *Kinder* children + *Garten* garden] (1852)
: a school or class for children usually from four to six years old

**kin·der·gart·ner** \-ˌgärt-nər, -ˌgärd-\ *also* **kin·der·gar·ten·er** \-ˌgär-t°n-ər, -d°n-\ *noun* (1889)
**1** : a teacher at a kindergarten
**2** : a child attending or of an age to attend kindergarten

**kind-heart·ed** \ˌkīnd-'här-təd\ *adjective* (1535)
: marked by a sympathetic nature
— **kind-heart·ed·ly** *adverb*
— **kind-heart·ed·ness** *noun*

**¹kin·dle** \'kin-d°l\ *verb* **kin·dled; kin·dling** \'kin(d)-liŋ, 'kin-d°l-iŋ\ [Middle English, probably modification of Old Norse *kynda*; akin to Old High German *cuntesal* fire] (13th century)
*transitive verb*
**1** : to start (a fire) burning : LIGHT
**2 a** : to stir up : AROUSE ⟨*kindle* interest⟩ **b** : to bring into being : START
**3** : to cause to glow : ILLUMINATE
*intransitive verb*
**1** : to catch fire
**2 a** : to flare up **b** : to become animated
**3** : to become illuminated
— **kin·dler** \'kin(d)-lər, 'kin-d°l-ər\ *noun*

**²kindle** *verb* **kin·dled; kin·dling** [Middle English, from *kindle* young animal, probably from *kinde,* noun, kind] (13th century)
*transitive verb*
: BEAR — used especially of a rabbit
*intransitive verb*
: to bring forth young — used especially of a rabbit

**kind·less** \'kīn(d)-ləs\ *adjective* (13th century)
**1** *obsolete* : INHUMAN
**2** : DISAGREEABLE, UNCONGENIAL
— **kind·less·ly** *adverb*

**kind·li·ness** \'kīn(d)-lē-nəs\ *noun* (15th century)
**1** : the quality or state of being kindly
**2** : a kindly deed

**kin·dling** \'kin(d)-liŋ, 'kin-lən\ *noun* (1513)
: easily combustible material for starting a fire

**¹kind·ly** \'kīn(d)-lē\ *adjective* **kind·li·er; -est** [Middle English, from Old English *cyndelīc*, from *cynd*] (before 12th century)
**1 a** *obsolete* : NATURAL **b** *archaic* : LAWFUL
**2** : of an agreeable or beneficial nature : PLEASANT ⟨*kindly* climate⟩

kimono 1

**3 :** of a sympathetic or generous nature
**²kindly** *adverb* (before 12th century)
**1 a :** in the normal way **:** NATURALLY ⟨old wounds which had healed *kindly* —*American Mercury*⟩ **b :** READILY ⟨did not take *kindly* to suggestions⟩
**2 a :** in a kind manner **:** SYMPATHETICALLY **b :** as a gesture of goodwill ⟨would take it *kindly* if you would put in a good word⟩ **c :** in a gracious manner **:** COURTEOUSLY ⟨they *kindly* invited us along⟩ **d :** as a matter of courtesy **:** PLEASE ⟨would you *kindly* order me a cab⟩
**3** *chiefly Southern* **:** SOMEWHAT, KIND OF ⟨it's *kindly* embarrassing —Walter Davis⟩
**kind·ness** \'kīn(d)-nəs\ *noun* (13th century)
**1 :** a kind deed **:** FAVOR
**2 a :** the quality or state of being kind **b** *archaic* **:** AFFECTION
**kind of** *adverb* (1775)
**1 :** to a moderate degree **:** SOMEWHAT ⟨it's *kind of* late to begin⟩
**2 :** in a way that approximates **:** MORE OR LESS ⟨*kind of* sneaked up on us⟩
**¹kin·dred** \'kin-drəd\ *noun* [Middle English, from *kin* + Old English *rǣden* condition, from *rǣdan* to advise, read] (12th century)
**1 a :** a group of related individuals **b :** one's relatives
**2 :** family relationship **:** KINSHIP
**²kindred** *adjective* (14th century)
**1 :** of a similar nature or character **:** LIKE
**2 :** of the same ancestry
**kine** \'kīn\ *archaic plural of* COW
**kin·e·ma** \'ki-nə-mə\ *British variant of* CINEMA
**kin·e·mat·ics** \ˌki-nə-'ma-tiks *also* ˌkī-\ *noun plural but singular in construction* [French *cinématique,* from Greek *kinēmat-, kinēma* motion, from *kinein* to move] (1840)
**:** a branch of dynamics that deals with aspects of motion apart from considerations of mass and force
**— ki·ne·mat·ic** \-tik\ *or* **ki·ne·mat·i·cal** \-ti-kəl\ *adjective*
**— ki·ne·mat·i·cal·ly** \-ti-k(ə-)lē\ *adverb*
**¹ki·ne·scope** \'ki-nə-ˌskōp *also* ˌkī-\ *noun* [from *Kinescope,* a trademark] (1930)
**1 :** PICTURE TUBE
**2 :** a motion picture made from an image on a picture tube
**²kinescope** *transitive verb* **-scoped; -scop·ing** (1949)
**:** to make a kinescope of
**ki·ne·sics** \kə-'nē-siks, kī-, -ziks\ *noun plural but singular in construction* [Greek *kinēsis* motion + English *-ics*] (1952)
**:** a systematic study of the relationship between nonlinguistic body motions (as blushes, shrugs, or eye movement) and communication
**ki·ne·si·ol·o·gy** \kə-ˌnē-sē-'ä-lə-jē, kī-, -zē-\ *noun* [Greek *kinēsis*] (1894)
**:** the study of the principles of mechanics and anatomy in relation to human movement
**ki·ne·sis** \kə-'nē-səs, kī-\ *noun, plural* **ki·ne·ses** \-ˌsēz\ [New Latin, from Greek *kinēsis*] (1905)
**:** a movement that lacks directional orientation and depends upon the intensity of stimulation
**-kinesis** *noun combining form, plural* **-kineses** [New Latin, from Greek *kinēsis,* from *kinein* to move; akin to Latin *ciēre* to move]
**1 :** division ⟨karyo*kinesis*⟩
**2 :** production of motion ⟨tele*kinesis*⟩
**kin·es·the·sia** \ˌki-nəs-'thē-zh(ē-)ə, ˌkī-\ *or* **kin·es·the·sis** \-'thē-səs\ *noun, plural* **-the·sias** *or* **-the·ses** \-ˌsēz\ [New Latin, from Greek *kinein* + *aisthēsis* perception — more at ANESTHESIA] (1880)
**:** a sense mediated by end organs located in muscles, tendons, and joints and stimulated by bodily movements and tensions; *also* **:** sensory experience derived from this sense
**— kin·es·thet·ic** \-'the-tik\ *adjective*
**— kin·es·thet·i·cal·ly** \-ti-k(ə-)lē\ *adverb*

**kinet-** *or* **kineto-** *combining form* [Greek *ki-nētos* moving]
**:** movement **:** motion ⟨*kineto*some⟩
**ki·net·ic** \kə-'ne-tik *also* kī-\ *adjective* [Greek *kinētikos,* from *kinētos,* from *kinein*] (1864)
**1 :** of or relating to the motion of material bodies and the forces and energy associated therewith
**2 a :** ACTIVE, LIVELY **b :** DYNAMIC, ENERGIZING
**3 :** of or relating to kinetic art
**— ki·net·i·cal·ly** \-ti-k(ə-)lē\ *adverb*
**kinetic art** *noun* (1961)
**:** art (as sculpture or assemblage) having mechanical parts which can be set in motion
**— kinetic artist** *noun*
**kinetic energy** *noun* (1870)
**:** energy associated with motion
**ki·net·i·cist** \kə-'ne-tə-sist *also* kī-\ *noun* (1960)
**1 :** a specialist in kinetics
**2 :** a person who works in kinetic art **:** KINETIC ARTIST
**ki·net·ics** \kə-'ne-tiks *also* kī-\ *noun plural but singular or plural in construction* (circa 1859)
**1 a :** a branch of science that deals with the effects of forces upon the motions of material bodies or with changes in a physical or chemical system **b :** the rate of change in such a system
**2 :** the mechanism by which a physical or chemical change is effected
**kinetic theory** *noun* (1864)
**:** either of two theories in physics based on the fact that the minute particles of a substance are in vigorous motion: **a :** a theory that the particles of a gas move in straight lines with high average velocity, continually encounter one another and thus change their individual velocities and directions, and cause pressure by their impact against the walls of a container — called also *kinetic theory of gases* **b :** a theory that the temperature of a substance increases with an increase in either the average kinetic energy of the particles or the average potential energy of separation (as in fusion) of the particles or in both when heat is added — called also *kinetic theory of heat*
**ki·ne·tin** \'kī-nə-tən\ *noun* (1955)
**:** a cytokinin $C_{10}H_9N_5O$ that increases mitosis and callus formation
**ki·net·o·chore** \kə-'ne-tə-ˌkōr, kī-, -ˌkȯr\ *noun* [kinet- + Greek *chōros* place] (1934)
**:** CENTROMERE
**ki·net·o·plast** \kə-'ne-tə-ˌplast, kī-\ *noun* [International Scientific Vocabulary] (1925)
**:** an extranuclear cell organelle within a mitochondrion especially of trypanosomes that contains DNA
**ki·net·o·scope** \kə-'ne-tə-ˌskōp, kī-\ *noun* [from *Kinetoscope,* a trademark] (1894)
**:** a device for viewing through a magnifying lens a sequence of pictures on an endless band of film moved continuously over a light source and a rapidly rotating shutter that creates an illusion of motion
**ki·net·o·some** \-ˌsōm\ *noun* (1912)
**:** BASAL BODY
**kin·folk** \'kin-ˌfōk\ *or* **kinfolks** *noun plural* (1873)
**:** RELATIVES
**king** \'kiŋ\ *noun* [Middle English, from Old English *cyning;* akin to Old High German *kuning* king, Old English *cynn* kin] (before 12th century)
**1 a :** a male monarch of a major territorial unit; *especially* **:** one whose position is hereditary and who rules for life **b :** a paramount chief
**2** *capitalized* **:** GOD, CHRIST
**3 :** one that holds a preeminent position; *especially* **:** a chief among competitors
**4 :** the principal piece of each color in chess having the power to move ordinarily one square in

any direction and to capture opposing pieces but being obliged never to enter or remain in check
**5 :** a playing card marked with a stylized figure of a king
**6 :** a checker that has been crowned
**king·bird** \-ˌbərd\ *noun* (1778)
**:** any of various American tyrant flycatchers (genus *Tyrannus*)
**king·bolt** \-ˌbōlt\ *noun* (1825)
**:** a vertical bolt by which the forward axle and wheels of a vehicle or the trucks of a railroad car are connected with the other parts
**King Charles spaniel** \-'chär(-ə)lz-\ *noun* [*Charles* II of England] (1833)
**:** an English toy spaniel having a black and tan coat
**king cobra** *noun* (1894)
**:** a large cobra (*Ophiophagus hannah* synonym *Naja hannah*) of southeastern Asia and the Philippines that may attain a length of 18 feet (5.5 meters)

**king crab** *noun* (1698)
**1 :** HORSESHOE CRAB

king cobra

**2 :** any of several very large crabs; *especially* **:** one (*Paralithodes camtschaticus*) of the North Pacific caught commercially for food
**king·craft** \'kiŋ-ˌkraft\ *noun* (1643)
**:** the art of governing as a king
**king·cup** \-ˌkəp\ *noun* (1538)
**:** any of several plants of the buttercup family; *especially* **:** MARSH MARIGOLD
**king·dom** \'kiŋ-dəm\ *noun* (before 12th century)
**1** *archaic* **:** KINGSHIP
**2 :** a politically organized community or major territorial unit having a monarchical form of government headed by a king or queen
**3** *often capitalized* **a :** the eternal kingship of God **b :** the realm in which God's will is fulfilled
**4 a :** a realm or region in which something is dominant **b :** an area or sphere in which one holds a preeminent position
**5 a :** one of the three primary divisions into which natural objects are commonly classified — compare ANIMAL KINGDOM, MINERAL KINGDOM, PLANT KINGDOM **b :** a major category (as Plantae or Protista) in biological taxonomy that ranks above the phylum and is the highest and most encompassing group
**kingdom come** *noun* [from the phrase "Thy kingdom come" (Matthew 6:10)] (1785)
**:** the next world **:** HEAVEN
**king·fish** \'kiŋ-ˌfish\ *noun* (1750)
**1 :** any of several marine croakers (family Sciaenidae) **a :** any of three fishes (*Menticirrhus americanus, M. littoralis,* and *M. saxatilis*) of shallow coastal waters of the Atlantic Ocean **b :** a small silvery food and sport fish (*Genyonemus lineatus*) of inshore waters especially of California — called also *white croaker*
**2 :** KING MACKEREL
**3 :** an undisputed master in an area or group
**king·fish·er** \-ˌfi-shər\ *noun* (15th century)
**:** any of numerous nonpasserine birds (family Alcedinidae) that are usually crested and brightcolored with a short tail and a long stout sharp bill
**King James Version** \-'jāmz-\ *noun* [*James* I of England] (circa 1889)
**:** AUTHORIZED VERSION
**king·let** \'kiŋ-lət\ *noun* (1603)

**1 :** a weak or petty king
**2 :** any of several small birds (genus *Regulus*) that are related to the gnatcatchers
**king·ly** \'kiŋ-lē\ *adjective* **king·li·er; -est** (14th century)
**1 :** having royal rank
**2 :** of, relating to, or befitting a king
**3 :** MONARCHICAL
— **king·li·ness** *noun*
— **kingly** *adverb*
**king mackerel** *noun* (circa 1930)
**:** a mackerel (*Scomberomorus cavalla*) that is noted especially as a fighting sport fish
**king·mak·er** \'kiŋ-ˌmā-kər\ *noun* (1599)
**:** one having great influence over the choice of candidates for political office
**king of arms** (15th century)
**:** an officer of arms of the highest rank
**king penguin** *noun* (1885)
**:** a large penguin (*Aptenodytes patagonica*) chiefly of subantarctic regions
**king·pin** \'kiŋ-ˌpin\ *noun* (1801)
**1 :** any of several bowling pins: as **a :** HEADPIN **b :** the pin that stands in the middle of a triangular arrangement of bowling pins
**2 :** the chief person in a group or undertaking
**3 a :** KINGBOLT **b :** a pin connecting the two parts of a knuckle joint (as in an automobile steering linkage)
**king post** *noun* (1776)
**:** a vertical member connecting the apex of a triangular truss (as of a roof) with the base
**Kings** \'kiŋz\ *noun plural but singular in construction*
**1 :** either of two narrative and historical books of canonical Jewish and Christian Scripture — see BIBLE table
**2 :** any of four narrative and historical books in the former Roman Catholic canon of the Old Testament
**king salmon** *noun* (1881)
**:** CHINOOK SALMON
**King's Bench** *noun* (14th century)
**:** a division in the English superior courts system that hears civil and criminal cases
**King's Counsel** *noun* (1689)
**:** a barrister selected to serve as counsel to the British crown
**King's English** *noun* (1553)
**:** standard, pure, or correct English speech or usage
**king's evil** *noun, often K&E capitalized* [from the former belief that it could be healed by a king's touch] (14th century)
**:** SCROFULA
**king·ship** \'kiŋ-ˌship\ *noun* (14th century)
**1 :** the position, office, or dignity of a king
**2 :** the personality of a king
**3 :** government by a king
**king·side** \-ˌsīd\ *noun* (1941)
**:** the side of a chessboard containing the file on which the king sits at the beginning of the game
**king–size** \-ˌsīz\ *or* **king–sized** \-ˌsīzd\ *adjective* (1942)
**1 :** longer than the regular or standard size ⟨a *king-size* cigarette⟩
**2 :** unusually large
**3 a :** having dimensions of approximately 76 inches by 80 inches (about 1.9 by 2.0 meters) — used of a bed; compare FULL-SIZE, QUEEN-SIZE, TWIN-SIZE **b :** of a size that fits a king-size bed ⟨*king-size* sheets⟩
**king snake** *noun* (1709)
**:** any of numerous brightly marked colubrid snakes (genus *Lampropeltis*) chiefly of North and Central America
**king's ransom** *noun* (circa 1590)
**:** a very large sum
**king·wood** \-ˌwùd\ *noun* (circa 1851)
**:** the wood of any of several tropical American leguminous trees (especially genus *Dalbergia*); *especially* **:** the wood of a Brazilian tree (*D. cearensis*) used especially for furniture

**ki·nin** \'kī-nən\ *noun* [Greek *kinein* to move, stimulate + English ¹-*in* — more at -KINESIS] (1954)
**1 :** any of various polypeptide hormones that are formed locally in the tissues and cause dilation of blood vessels and contraction of smooth muscle
**2 :** CYTOKININ
**¹kink** \'kiŋk\ *noun* [Dutch; akin to Middle Low German *kinke* kink] (1678)
**1 :** a short tight twist or curl caused by a doubling or winding of something upon itself
**2 a :** a mental or physical peculiarity **:** ECCENTRICITY, QUIRK **b :** WHIM
**3 :** a clever unusual way of doing something
**4 :** a cramp in some part of the body
**5 :** an imperfection likely to cause difficulties in the operation of something
**²kink** (1697)
*intransitive verb*
**:** to form a kink
*transitive verb*
**:** to make a kink in
**kin·ka·jou** \'kiŋ-kə-ˌjü\ *noun* [French, alteration of *quincajou* wolverine, of Algonquian origin; akin to Ojibwa *kwiˀnkwaˀaˑˀke* wolverine] (1796)
**:** a nocturnal arboreal omnivorous mammal (*Potos flavus*) found from Mexico to South America that is related to the raccoon and has a long prehensile tail, large eyes, and yellowish brown fur
**kinky** \'kiŋ-kē\ *adjective* **kink·i·er; -est** (1844)
**1 :** closely twisted or curled
**2 :** relating to, having, or appealing to unconventional tastes especially in sex; *also* **:** sexually deviant
**3 :** OUTLANDISH, FAR-OUT
— **kink·i·ly** \'kiŋ-kə-lē\ *adverb*
— **kink·i·ness** \'kiŋ-kē-nəs\ *noun*
**kin·ni·kin·nick** \ˌki-ni-kə-'nik, 'ki-ni-kə-ˌ\ *noun* [of Algonquian origin; akin to Massachuset *kinukkinuk* mixture] (1799)
**:** a mixture of dried leaves and bark and sometimes tobacco smoked by the Indians and pioneers especially in the Ohio valley; *also* **:** a plant (as a sumac or dogwood) used in it
**-kins** — see -KIN
**kins·folk** \'kinz-ˌfōk\ *noun plural* (15th century)
**:** RELATIVES
**kin·ship** \'kin-ˌship\ *noun* (1833)
**:** the quality or state of being kin **:** RELATIONSHIP
**kins·man** \'kinz-mən\ *noun* (12th century)
**:** RELATIVE; *specifically* **:** a male relative
**kins·wom·an** \-ˌwù-mən\ *noun* (14th century)
**:** a female relative
**ki·osk** \'kē-ˌäsk\ *noun* [Turkish *köşk*, from Persian *kūshk* portico] (1625)
**1 :** an open summerhouse or pavilion
**2 :** a small structure with one or more open sides that is used to vend merchandise (as newspapers) or services (as film developing)
**Ki·o·wa** \'kī-ə-ˌwò, -ˌwä, -ˌwā\ *noun, plural* **Kiowa** *or* **Kiowas** (1808)
**1 :** a member of an American Indian people of what are now Colorado, Kansas, New Mexico, Oklahoma, and Texas
**2 :** the language of the Kiowa people
**¹kip** \'kip\ *noun* [obsolete Dutch; akin to Middle Low German *kip* bundle of hides] (circa 1525)
**:** a bundle of undressed hides of young or small animals; *also* **:** one of the hides
**²kip** *noun* [perhaps from Danish *kippe* cheap tavern] (1879)
**1 :** BED ⟨ready for the *kip* after this screwball day —K. M. Dodson⟩
**2** *chiefly British* **:** SLEEP, NAP ⟨roused the . . . family from their *kip* —Sylvia Margolis⟩
**³kip** *intransitive verb* **kipped; kip·ping** (circa 1889)
*British* **:** SLEEP — sometimes used with *down* ⟨*kip* down on a spare bed —Alice Glenday⟩

**⁴kip** *noun* [*kilo-* + *pound*] (1914)
**:** a unit of weight equal to 1000 pounds (4448 newtons) used to express deadweight load
**⁵kip** \'kip, 'gip\ *noun, plural* **kip** *or* **kips** [Lao *kìːp*, literally, ingot] (1955)
— see MONEY table
**¹kip·per** \'ki-pər\ *noun* [Middle English *kypre*, from Old English *cypera*; akin to Old English *coper* copper] (before 12th century)
**1 :** a male salmon or sea trout during or after the spawning season
**2 :** a kippered herring or salmon
**²kipper** *transitive verb* **kip·pered; kip·per·ing** \-p(ə-)riŋ\ (1773)
**:** to cure (split dressed fish) by salting and smoking
— **kip·per·er** \-pər-ər\ *noun*
**Kir·ghiz** \kir-'gēz\ *noun, plural* **Kirghiz** *or* **Kir·ghiz·es** [Kirghiz *kı̆rɣ́ı̆z*] (1600)
**1 :** a member of a Turkic people of Kyrgyzstan and adjacent areas of central Asia
**2 :** the language of the Kirghiz
**kirk** \'kirk, 'kərk\ *noun* [Middle English (northern dialect), from Old Norse *kirkja*, from Old English *cirice* — more at CHURCH] (12th century)
**1** *chiefly Scottish* **:** CHURCH
**2** *capitalized* **:** the national church of Scotland as distinguished from the Church of England or the Episcopal Church in Scotland
**Kir·li·an photography** \'kir-lē-ən-\ *noun* [Semyon D. & Valentina K. *Kirlian* (flourished 1939) Soviet inventors] (1972)
**:** a process in which an image is obtained by application of a high-frequency electric field to an object so that it radiates a characteristic pattern of luminescence that is recorded on photographic film
— **Kirlian photograph** *noun*
**Kir·man** \kər-'män, kir-\ *noun* [*Kirman*, province in Iran] (1876)
**:** a Persian carpet or rug characterized by elaborate fluid designs and soft colors
**kir·mess** \'kər-məs\ *variant of* KERMIS
**kirsch** \'kirsh\ *noun* [German, short for *Kirschwasser*, from *Kirsche* cherry + *Wasser* water] (1869)
**:** a dry colorless brandy distilled from the fermented juice of the black morello cherry
**Kirt·land's warbler** \'kərt-lən(d)z-\ *noun* [Jared P. *Kirtland* (died 1877) American naturalist] (1858)
**:** a rare warbler (*Dendroica kirtlandii*) of northeastern North America that breeds in Michigan and winters in the Bahamas
**kir·tle** \'kər-tᵊl\ *noun* [Middle English *kirtel*, from Old English *cyrtel*, from (assumed) Old English *curt* short, from Latin *curtus* shortened — more at SHEAR] (before 12th century)
**1 :** a tunic or coat worn by men especially in the Middle Ages
**2 :** a long gown or dress worn by women
**kish·ke** *also* **kish·ka** \'kish-kə\ *noun* [Yiddish *kishke* gut, sausage, of Slavic origin; akin to Polish *kiszka* gut, sausage] (circa 1936)
**:** beef or fowl casing stuffed (as with meat, flour, and spices) and cooked
**Kis·lev** \'kis-ləf\ *noun* [Hebrew *Kislēw*] (14th century)
**:** the 3d month of the civil year or the 9th month of the ecclesiastical year in the Jewish calendar — see MONTH table
**kis·met** \'kiz-ˌmet, -mət\ *noun, often capitalized* [Turkish, from Arabic *qismah* portion, lot] (1834)
**:** FATE 1, 2a
**¹kiss** \'kis\ *verb* [Middle English, from Old English *cyssan*; akin to Old High German *kussen* to kiss] (before 12th century)
*transitive verb*
**1 :** to touch with the lips especially as a mark of affection or greeting

**2 :** to touch gently or lightly ⟨wind gently *kissing* the trees⟩
*intransitive verb*
**1 :** to salute or caress one another with the lips
**2 :** to come in gentle contact
— **kiss·able** \'ki-sə-bəl\ *adjective*
— **kiss ass :** to act obsequiously especially to gain favor — usually considered vulgar
— **kiss good–bye 1 :** LEAVE **2 :** to resign oneself to the loss of
**²kiss** *noun* (before 12th century)
**1 :** a caress with the lips
**2 :** a gentle touch or contact
**3 a :** a small drop cookie made of meringue **b :** a bite-size piece of candy often wrapped in paper or foil
**4 :** an expression of affection ⟨sent him *kisses* in her letter⟩
**kiss–and–tell** \'kis-ᵊn(d)-'tel\ *adjective* (1949)
**:** telling details of private matters ⟨*kiss-and-tell* autobiographies⟩
**kiss·er** \'ki-sər\ *noun* (1537)
**1 :** one that kisses
**2** *slang* **a :** MOUTH **b :** FACE
**kissing bug** *noun* (1899)
**:** CONENOSE
**kissing cousin** *noun* (1941)
**1 :** a person and especially a relative whom one knows well enough to kiss more or less formally upon meeting
**2 :** one that is closely related in kind to something else
**kissing disease** *noun* [from the belief that it is frequently transmitted by kissing] (1962)
**:** INFECTIOUS MONONUCLEOSIS
**kiss of death** [from the kiss with which Judas betrayed Jesus (Mark 14:44–46)] (1943)
**:** something (as an act or association) ultimately causing ruin
**kiss off** *transitive verb* (circa 1935)
**:** to dismiss lightly ⟨*kisses* the other performers *off* as mere amateurs⟩
— **kiss-off** \'ki-ˌsòf\ *noun*
**kiss of life** (1961)
*chiefly British* **:** artificial respiration by the mouth-to-mouth method
**kiss of peace** (circa 1898)
**:** a ceremonial kiss, embrace, or handclasp used in Christian liturgies and especially the Eucharist as a sign of fraternal unity
**kist** \'kist\ *noun* [Middle English *kiste,* from Old Norse *kista,* ultimately from Latin *cista* — more at CHEST] (14th century)
*chiefly Scottish & South African* **:** CHEST 1b
**¹kit** \'kit\ *noun* [Middle English] (14th century)
**1** *dialect British* **:** a wooden tub
**2 a** (1) **:** a collection of articles usually for personal use ⟨a travel *kit*⟩ (2) **:** a set of tools or implements ⟨a carpenter's *kit*⟩ (3) **:** a set of parts to be assembled or worked up ⟨model-airplane *kit*⟩ (4) **:** a packaged collection of related material ⟨convention *kit*⟩ (5) *chiefly British* **:** GEAR ⟨run over to my billet and get some overnight *kit* —Lionel Shapiro⟩ **b :** a container for any of such sets or collections
**3 :** a group of persons or things — usually used in the phrase *the whole kit and caboodle*
**²kit** *transitive verb* **kit·ted; kit·ting** (1919)
*chiefly British* **:** EQUIP. OUTFIT — often used with *up* or *out*
**³kit** *noun* [origin unknown] (1519)
**:** a small narrow violin
**⁴kit** *noun* (1562)
**1 :** KITTEN
**2 :** a young or undersized fur-bearing animal; *also* **:** its pelt
**kit bag** *noun* [¹*kit*] (1893)
**1 :** KNAPSACK
**2 :** a suitcase usually with sides that fasten at the top or open to the full width of the bag
**kitch·en** \'ki-chən\ *noun* [Middle English *kichene,* from Old English *cycene,* from Late Latin *coquina,* from Latin *coquere* to cook — more at COOK] (before 12th century)
**1 :** a place (as a room) with cooking facilities

**2 :** the personnel that prepares, cooks, and serves food
**3 :** CUISINE
**kitchen cabinet** *noun* (1832)
**1 :** an informal group of advisers to one in a position of power (as the head of a government)
**2 :** a cupboard with drawers and shelves for use in a kitchen
**kitch·en·ette** \ˌki-chə-'net\ *noun* (1903)
**:** a small kitchen or an alcove containing cooking facilities
**kitchen garden** *noun* (1580)
**:** a garden in which plants (as vegetables or herbs) for use in the kitchen are cultivated
**kitchen midden** *noun* (1863)
**:** a refuse heap; *specifically* **:** a mound marking the site of a primitive human habitation
**kitchen police** *noun* (circa 1917)
**1 :** KP
**2 :** the work of KPs
**kitch·en–sink** \-'siŋk\ *adjective* (1941)
**1** *chiefly British* **:** portraying or emphasizing the squalid aspects of modern life ⟨the *kitchen-sink* realism of contemporary British drama —Current Biography⟩
**2 :** being or made up of a hodgepodge of disparate elements or ingredients
**kitch·en·ware** \-ˌwar, -ˌwer\ *noun* (1722)
**:** utensils and appliances for use in a kitchen
**¹kite** \'kīt\ *noun* [Middle English, from Old English *cȳta;* akin to Middle High German *kūze* owl] (before 12th century)
**1 :** any of various usually small hawks (family Accipitridae) with long narrow wings and often a notched or forked tail
**2 :** a person who preys on others
**3 :** a light frame covered usually with paper or cloth, often provided with a balancing tail, and designed to be flown in the air at the end of a long string
**4 :** a check drawn against uncollected funds in a bank account or fraudulently raised before cashing
**5 :** a light sail used in a light breeze usually in addition to the regular working sails; *especially* **:** SPINNAKER
— **kite·like** *adjective*
**²kite** *verb* **kit·ed; kit·ing** (1839)
*transitive verb*
**1 :** to use (a bad check) to get credit or money
**2 :** to cause to soar ⟨*kited* the prices they charged wealthy clients⟩
*intransitive verb*
**1 a :** to go in a rapid, carefree, or flighty manner **b :** to rise rapidly **:** SOAR ⟨the prices of necessities continue to *kite*⟩
**2 :** to get money or credit by a kite
**kit fox** *noun* [⁴*kit*] (1805)
**1 a :** SWIFT FOX **b :** a fox (*Vulpes macrotis*) of the southwestern U.S. and Mexico with exceptionally large ears and a black tip on the tail
**2 :** the fur or pelt of a kit fox
**kith** \'kith\ *noun* [Middle English, from Old English *cȳthth;* akin to *cūth* known — more at UNCOUTH] (before 12th century)
**:** familiar friends, neighbors, or relatives ⟨*kith* and kin⟩
**kith·a·ra** \'ki-thə-rə\ *noun* [Middle English *cithara,* from Latin, from Greek *kithara*] (14th century)
**:** an ancient Greek stringed instrument similar to but larger than the lyre and having a box-shaped resonator
**kithe** \'kīth\ *verb* **kithed; kith·ing** [Middle English, from Old English *cȳthan,* from *cūth*] (before 12th century)
*transitive verb*
*chiefly Scottish* **:** to make known
*intransitive verb*
*chiefly Scottish* **:** to become known
**kitsch** \'kich\ *noun* [German, kitsch, trash] (1925)
**:** something that appeals to popular or lowbrow taste and is often of poor quality
— **kitsch** *adjective*

— **kitschy** \'ki-chē\ *adjective*
**¹kit·ten** \'ki-tᵊn\ *noun* [Middle English *kitoun,* from (assumed) Old North French *caton,* diminutive of *cat,* from Late Latin *cattus*] (14th century)
**:** a young cat; *also* **:** an immature individual of various other small mammals
**²kitten** *intransitive verb* **kit·tened; kit·ten·ing** \'kit-niŋ, 'ki-tᵊn-iŋ\ (15th century)
**:** to give birth to kittens
**kit·ten·ish** \'kit-nish, 'ki-tᵊn-ish\ *adjective* (1754)
**:** resembling a kitten; *especially* **:** coyly playful
— **kit·ten·ish·ly** *adverb*
— **kit·ten·ish·ness** *noun*
**kit·ti·wake** \'ki-tē-ˌwāk\ *noun* [imitative] (1661)
**:** either of two cliff-nesting gulls (*Rissa tridactyla* and *R. brevirostris*) that winter on the open ocean
**¹kit·tle** \'ki-tᵊl\ *transitive verb* **kit·tled; kit·tling** \'kit-liŋ, 'ki-tᵊl-iŋ\ [Middle English (northern dialect) *kytyllen*] (before 12th century)
**1** *chiefly Scottish* **:** TICKLE
**2** *chiefly Scottish* **:** PERPLEX
**²kittle** *adjective* (1568)
*chiefly Scottish* **:** TICKLISH 2, TOUCHY
**¹kit·ty** \'ki-tē\ *noun, plural* **kitties** (1719)
**:** CAT 1a; *especially* **:** KITTEN
**²kitty** *noun, plural* **kitties** [¹*kit*] (circa 1887)
**1 :** a fund in a poker game made up of contributions from each pot
**2 :** a sum of money or collection of goods often made up of small contributions **:** POOL
**kit·ty–cor·ner** *or* **kit·ty–cor·nered** *variant of* CATERCORNER
**ki·va** \'kē-və\ *noun* [Hopi *kíva*] (1871)
**:** a Pueblo Indian ceremonial structure that is usually round and partly underground
**Ki·wa·ni·an** \kə-'wä-nē-ən\ *noun* [*Kiwanis (Club)*] (1921)
**:** a member of a major national and international service club
**ki·wi** \'kē-(ˌ)wē\ *noun* [Maori] (1835)
**1 :** any of a small genus (*Apteryx*) of flightless New Zealand birds with rudimentary wings, stout legs, a long bill, and grayish brown hairlike plumage
**2** *capitalized* **:** a native or resident of New Zealand — used as a nickname
**3 :** KIWIFRUIT

kiwi 1

**ki·wi·fruit** \-ˌfrüt\ *noun* (1966)
**:** the fruit of a Chinese gooseberry
**Klam·ath weed** \'kla-məth-\ *noun* [*Klamath (River)*] (1922)
**:** a European yellow-flowered perennial Saint-John's-wort (*Hypericum perforatum*) that is naturalized in North America especially in rangelands
**Klan** \'klan\ *noun* [(*Ku Klux) Klan*] (1867)
**:** an organization of Ku Kluxers; *also* **:** a subordinate unit of such an organization
— **Klan·ism** \-ˌi-zəm\ *noun*
— **Klans·man** \'klanz-mən\ *noun*
**klatch** *or* **klatsch** \'klach, 'kläch\ *noun* [German *Klatsch* gossip] (1941)
**:** a gathering characterized usually by informal conversation
**klav·ern** \'kla-vərn\ *noun, often capitalized* [blend of *Klan* and *cavern*] (circa 1924)
**:** a local unit of the Klan

**Klax·on** \'klak-sən\ *trademark*
— used for an electrically operated horn or warning signal

**kleb·si·el·la** \,kleb-zē-'e-lə\ *noun* [New Latin, from Edwin *Klebs* (died 1913) German pathologist] (1928)
: any of a genus (*Klebsiella*) of nonmotile gram-negative frequently encapsulated bacterial rods

**Klee·nex** \'klē-,neks\ *trademark*
— used for a cleansing tissue

**Klein bottle** \'klīn-\ *noun* [Felix *Klein* (died 1925) German mathematician] (1941)
: a one-sided surface that is formed by passing the narrow end of a tapered tube through the side of the tube and flaring this end out to join the other end

**klepht** \'kleft\ *noun, often capitalized* [New Greek *klephtēs*, literally, robber, from Greek *kleptēs*, from *kleptein*] (1820)
: a Greek belonging to any of several independent guerrilla communities formed after the Turkish conquest of Greece
— **kleph·tic** \'klef-tik\ *adjective, often capitalized*

**klepto-** *combining form* [Greek, from *kleptein* to steal; akin to Gothic *hlifan* to steal, Latin *clepere*]
: stealing : theft ⟨*klepto*mania⟩

**klep·to·ma·nia** \,klep-tə-'mā-nē-ə, -nyə\ *noun* [New Latin] (1830)
: a persistent neurotic impulse to steal especially without economic motive

**klep·to·ma·ni·ac** \-nē-,ak\ *noun* (1861)
: a person evidencing kleptomania

**klez·mer** \'klez-mər\ *noun, plural* **klez·mo·rim** \(,)klez-'mór-əm\ [Yiddish, from Hebrew *kĕlēy zemer* musical instruments] (1949)
**1** : a Jewish instrumentalist especially of traditional eastern European music
**2** : the music played by klezmorim

**klieg light** *or* **kleig light** \'klēg-\ *noun* [John H. *Kliegl* (died 1959) & Anton T. *Kliegl* (died 1919) German-born American lighting experts] (1919)
: a carbon arc lamp used especially in making motion pictures

**Kline·fel·ter's syndrome** \'klīn-,fel-tərz-\ *noun* [Harry F. *Klinefelter* (born 1912) American physician] (1950)
: an abnormal condition in a male characterized by usually two X and one Y chromosomes, infertility, and smallness of the testicles

**klis·ter** \'klis-tər\ *noun* [Norwegian, literally, paste, from Middle Low German *klīster*] (1936)
: a soft wax used on skis

**kloof** \'klüf\ *noun* [Afrikaans] (1731)
*South African* : a deep glen : RAVINE

**kludge** \'klüj\ *or* **kluge** \'klüj, 'klü-jē\ *noun* [origin unknown] (1962)
: a system and especially a computer system made up of poorly matched components

**klutz** \'kləts\ *noun* [Yiddish *klots*, literally, wooden beam, from Middle High German *kloz* lumpy mass — more at CLOUT] (1960)
: a clumsy person
— **klutz·i·ness** \'klət-sē-nəs\ *noun*
— **klutzy** \'klət-sē\ *adjective*

**kly·stron** \'klī-,strän\ *noun* [from *Klystron*, a trademark] (1939)
: an electron tube in which bunching of electrons is produced by electric fields and which is used for the generation and amplification of ultrahigh-frequency current

**K–me·son** \'kā-\ *noun* (1951)
: KAON

**knack** \'nak\ *noun* [Middle English *knak*] (14th century)
**1 a** : a clever trick or stratagem **b** : a clever way of doing something
**2** : a special ready capacity that is hard to analyze or teach

**3** *archaic* : an ingenious device; *broadly* : TOY, KNICKKNACK
**synonym** see GIFT

**knack·er** \'na-kər\ *noun* [probably from English dialect, saddlemaker] (1812)
**1** *British* : a buyer of worn-out domestic animals or their carcasses for use especially as animal food or fertilizer
**2** *British* : a buyer of old structures for their constituent materials

**knack·ered** \'na-kərd\ *adjective* [English slang *knacker* to kill, tire, perhaps from *knacker*, noun] (1886)
*British* : TIRED, EXHAUSTED

**knack·wurst** *variant of* KNOCKWURST

**¹knap** \'nap\ *noun* [Middle English, from Old English *cnæp*; akin to Old English *cnotta* knot] (before 12th century)
**1** *chiefly dialect* : a crest of a hill : SUMMIT
**2** *chiefly dialect* : a small hill

**²knap** *transitive verb* **knapped; knap·ping** [Middle English *knappen*, of imitative origin] (15th century)
**1** *dialect British* : ²RAP 1
**2** : to break with a quick blow; *especially* : to shape (as flints) by breaking off pieces
**3** *dialect British* : SNAP, CROP
**4** *dialect British* : CHATTER
— **knap·per** *noun*

**knap·sack** \'nap-,sak\ *noun* [Low German *knappsack* or Dutch *knapzak*, from Low German & Dutch *knappen* to make a snapping noise, eat + Low German *sack* or Dutch *zak* sack] (1603)
: a bag (as of canvas or nylon) strapped on the back and used for carrying supplies or personal belongings
— **knap·sacked** \-,sakt\ *adjective*

**knap·weed** \-,wēd\ *noun* [Middle English *knopwed*, from *knop* knop + *wed* weed] (15th century)
: any of various weedy centaureas; *especially* : a widely naturalized European perennial (*Centaurea nigra*) with tough wiry stems and knobby heads of purple flowers

**knave** \'nāv\ *noun* [Middle English, from Old English *cnafa*; akin to Old High German *knabo* boy] (before 12th century)
**1** *archaic* **a** : a boy servant **b** : a male servant **c** : a man of humble birth or position
**2** : a tricky deceitful fellow
**3** : JACK 6a

**knav·ery** \'nā-və-rē, 'nāv-rē\ *noun, plural* **-er·ies** (1528)
**1 a** : RASCALITY **b** : a roguish or mischievous act
**2** *obsolete* : roguish mischief

**knav·ish** \'nā-vish\ *adjective* (14th century)
: of, relating to, or characteristic of a knave; *especially* : DISHONEST
— **knav·ish·ly** *adverb*

**knead** \'nēd\ *transitive verb* [Middle English *kneden*, from Old English *cnedan*; akin to Old High German *knetan* to knead] (before 12th century)
**1 a** : to work and press into a mass with or as if with the hands ⟨*kneading* dough⟩ **b** : to manipulate or massage with a kneading motion ⟨*kneaded* sore neck muscles⟩
**2** : to form or shape by or as if by kneading
— **knead·a·ble** \'nē-də-bəl\ *adjective*
— **knead·er** *noun*

**¹knee** \'nē\ *noun, often attributive* [Middle English, from Old English *cnēow*; akin to Old High German *kneo* knee, Latin *genu*, Greek *gony*] (before 12th century)
**1 a** : a joint in the middle part of the human leg that is the articulation between the femur, tibia, and patella; *also* : the part of the leg that includes this joint **b** (1) : the joint in the hind leg of a four-footed vertebrate that corresponds to the human knee (2) : the carpal joint of the foreleg of a four-footed vertebrate **c** : the tarsal joint of a bird **d** : the joint between the femur and tibia of an insect

**2** : something resembling the human knee: as **a** : a piece of timber naturally or artificially bent for use in supporting structures coming together at an angle (as the deck beams of a ship) **b** : a rounded or conical process rising from the roots of various swamp-growing trees ⟨cypress *knee*⟩
**3** : the part of a garment covering the knee
**4** : a blow with the bent knee
— **kneed** \'nēd\ *adjective*
— **to one's knees** : into a state of submission or defeat

**²knee** *transitive verb* **kneed; knee·ing** (before 12th century)
**1** *archaic* : to bend the knee to
**2** : to strike with the knee

**knee breeches** *noun plural* (1833)
: BREECH 1a

**knee·cap** \'nē-,kap\ *noun* (1869)
: PATELLA

**knee·cap·ping** \'nē-,ka-piŋ\ *noun* (1974)
: the terrorist act or practice of maiming a person's knees (as by gunshot)
— **kneecap** *transitive verb*

**knee–deep** \-'dēp\ *adjective* (15th century)
**1 a** : sunk to the knees ⟨*knee-deep* in mud⟩ **b** : deeply engaged or occupied ⟨*knee-deep* in work⟩
**2** : KNEE-HIGH

**knee–high** \-'hī\ *adjective* (1743)
: rising or reaching upward to the knees ⟨*knee-high* stockings⟩
— **knee–high** \-,hī\ *noun*

**knee–hole** \-,hōl\ *noun* (1893)
: an open space (as under a desk) for the knees

**knee–jerk** \'nē-,jərk, -'jərk\ *adjective* (1951)
: readily predictable : AUTOMATIC ⟨*knee-jerk* reactions⟩; *also* : reacting in a readily predictable way ⟨*knee-jerk* liberals⟩

**knee jerk** *noun* (1876)
: an involuntary forward kick produced by a light blow on the tendon below the patella

**kneel** \'nē(ə)l\ *intransitive verb* **knelt** \'nelt\ *or* **kneeled; kneel·ing** [Middle English *knelen*, from Old English *cnēowlian*; akin to Old English *cnēow* knee] (before 12th century)
: to bend the knee : fall or rest on the knees

**kneel·er** \'nē-lər\ *noun* (14th century)
**1** : one that kneels
**2** : something (as a cushion or board) to kneel on

**knee·pan** \'nē-,pan\ *noun* (15th century)
: PATELLA

**knee–slap·per** \-,sla-pər\ *noun* (1966)
: an extremely funny joke, line, or story

**knee·sock** \-,säk\ *noun* (1964)
: a knee-high sock

**¹knell** \'nel\ *verb* [Middle English, from Old English *cnyllan*; akin to Middle High German *erknellen* to toll] (before 12th century)
*transitive verb*
: to summon or announce by or as if by a knell
*intransitive verb*
**1** : to ring especially for a death, funeral, or disaster : TOLL
**2** : to sound in an ominous manner or with an ominous effect

**²knell** *noun* (before 12th century)
**1** : a stroke or sound of a bell especially when rung slowly (as for a death, funeral, or disaster)
**2** : an indication of the end or the failure of something ⟨sounded the death *knell* for our hopes⟩

**knew** *past of* KNOW

**knick·er·bock·er** \'ni-kə(r)-,bä-kər\ *noun* [Diedrich *Knickerbocker*, fictitious author of *History of New York* (1809) by Washington Irving] (1848)
**1** *capitalized* : a descendant of the early Dutch settlers of New York; *broadly* : a native or resident of the city or state of New York — used as a nickname

**2** *plural* : KNICKERS ◆

**knick·ers** \'ni-kərz\ *noun, plural* [short for *knickerbockers*] (1881)
**1** : loose-fitting short pants gathered at the knee
**2** *chiefly British* : UNDERPANTS
**word history** see KNICKERBOCKER

**knick·knack** \'nik-,nak\ *noun* [reduplication of *knack*] (1682)
: a small trivial article usually intended for ornament

**¹knife** \'nīf\ *noun, plural* **knives** \'nīvz\ *often attributive* [Middle English *knif*, from Old English *cnīf*, perhaps from Old Norse *knīf*from; akin to Middle Low German *knīf* knife] (before 12th century)
**1 a** : a cutting instrument consisting of a sharp blade fastened to a handle **b** : a weapon resembling a knife
**2** : a sharp cutting blade or tool in a machine
**3** : SURGERY 4 — usually used in the phrase *under the knife*
— **knife-like** \'nīf-,līk\ *adjective*

**²knife** *verb* **knifed; knif·ing** (1865)
*transitive verb*
**1** : to use a knife on; *specifically* : to stab, slash, or wound with a knife
**2** : to cut, mark, or spread with a knife
**3** : to try to defeat by underhanded means
**4** : to move like a knife in ⟨birds *knifing* the autumn sky⟩
*intransitive verb*
: to cut a way with or as if with a knife blade ⟨the cruiser *knifed* through the heavy seas⟩

**knife–edge** \'nīf-,ej\ *noun* (1818)
**1** : a sharp wedge of steel or other hard material used as a fulcrum for a lever beam in a precision instrument
**2** : a sharp narrow knifelike edge

**knife–point** \-,point\ *noun* (circa 1911)
: the point of a knife
— **at knifepoint** : under a threat of being knifed

**¹knight** \'nīt\ *noun* [Middle English, from Old English *cniht* man-at-arms, boy, servant; akin to Old High German *kneht* youth, military follower] (before 12th century)
**1 a** (1) : a mounted man-at-arms serving a feudal superior; *especially* : a man ceremonially inducted into special military rank usually after completing service as page and squire (2) : a man honored by a sovereign for merit and in Great Britain ranking below a baronet (3) : a person of antiquity equal to a knight in rank **b** : a man devoted to the service of a lady as her attendant or champion **c** : a member of an order or society
**2** : either of two pieces of the same color in a set of chessmen having the power to make an L-shaped move of two squares in one row and one square in a perpendicular row over squares that may be occupied

**²knight** *transitive verb* (13th century)
: to make a knight of

**knight–er·rant** \'nīt-'er-ənt\ *noun, plural* **knights–errant** (14th century)
: a knight traveling in search of adventures in which to exhibit military skill, prowess, and generosity

**knight–er·rant·ry** \-'er-ən-trē\ *noun, plural* **knight–errantries** (1654)
**1** : the practice or actions of a knight-errant
**2** : quixotic conduct

**knight–hood** \'nīt-,hud\ *noun* (13th century)
**1** : the rank, dignity, or profession of a knight
**2** : the qualities befitting a knight : CHIVALRY
**3** : knights as a class or body

**knight·ly** \'nīt-lē\ *adjective* (14th century)
**1** : of, relating to, or characteristic of a knight
**2** : made up of knights
— **knight·li·ness** *noun*
— **knightly** *adverb*

**Knight of Co·lum·bus** \-kə-'ləm-bəs\ *noun, plural* **Knights of Columbus** [Christopher Columbus] (1882)

: a member of a benevolent and fraternal society of Roman Catholic men

**Knight of Pyth·i·as** \-'pi-thē-əs\ *noun, plural* **Knights of Pythias** (1869)
: a member of a secret benevolent and fraternal order

**Knight of the Mac·ca·bees** \-'ma-kə-,bēz\ *noun, plural* **Knights of the Maccabees** (1922)
: a member of a secret benevolent society

**Knight Templar** *noun, plural* **Knights Templars** *or* **Knights Templar** (1610)
**1** : TEMPLAR 1
**2** : a member of an order of Freemasonry conferring three orders in the York rite

**knish** \kə-'nish\ *noun* [Yiddish, from Polish *knysz*] (1916)
: a small round or square of dough stuffed with a filling (as potato) and baked or fried

**¹knit** \'nit\ *verb* **knit** *or* **knit·ted; knit·ting** [Middle English *knitten*, from Old English *cnyttan*; akin to Old English *cnotta* knot] (before 12th century)
*transitive verb*
**1** *chiefly dialect* : to tie together
**2 a** : to link firmly or closely ⟨*knitted* my hands⟩ **b** : to cause to grow together ⟨time and rest will *knit* a fractured bone⟩ **c** : to contract into wrinkles ⟨*knitted* her brow⟩
**3** : to form by interlacing yarn or thread in a series of connected loops with needles
*intransitive verb*
**1** : to make knitted fabrics or objects
**2 a** : to become compact **b** : to grow together
**c** : to become drawn together
— **knit·ter** *noun*

**²knit** *noun* (1596)
: KNIT STITCH; *also* : a knit fabric

**knit stitch** *noun* (circa 1885)
: a basic knitting stitch usually made with the yarn at the back of the work by inserting the right needle into the front part of a loop on the left needle from the left side, catching the yarn with the point of the right needle, and bringing it through the first loop to form a new loop — compare PURL STITCH

**knit·ting** *noun* (15th century)
**1** : the action or method of one that knits
**2** : work done or being done by one that knits

**knit·wear** \'nit-,war, -,wer\ *noun* (1926)
: knitted clothing

**knob** \'näb\ *noun* [Middle English *knobbe*; akin to Middle Low German *knubbe* knob] (before 12th century)
**1 a** : a rounded protuberance : LUMP **b** : a small rounded ornament or handle
**2** : a rounded usually isolated hill or mountain
— **knobbed** \'näbd\ *adjective*
— **knob·by** \'nä-bē\ *adjective*

**knob·bly** \'nä-b(ə-)lē\ *adjective* (1859)
: having very small knobs ⟨a *knobbly* mattress⟩

**knob·ker·rie** \'näb-,ker-ē\ *noun* [Afrikaans *knopkierie*, from *knop* knob + *kierie* club] (1844)
: a short wooden club with a knob at one end used as a missile or in close attack especially by Zulus of southern Africa

**¹knock** \'näk\ *verb* [Middle English *knoken*, from Old English *cnocian*; akin to Middle High German *knochen* to press] (before 12th century)
*intransitive verb*
**1** : to strike something with a sharp blow
**2** : to collide with something
**3 a** : BUSTLE ⟨heard them *knocking* around in the kitchen⟩ **b** : WANDER ⟨*knocked* about Europe all summer⟩
**4 a** : to make a pounding noise **b** : to have engine knock
**5** : to find fault
*transitive verb*
**1 a** (1) : to strike sharply (2) : to drive, force, or make by or as if by so striking **b** : to set forcibly in motion with a blow
**2** : to cause to collide
**3** : to find fault with ⟨never *knocks* a friend⟩

— **knock cold** : KNOCK OUT 2a(1)
— **knock dead** : to move strongly especially to admiration or applause ⟨a comedian who really *knocks* them *dead*⟩
— **knock for a loop 1 a** : OVERCOME ⟨*knocked* my opponent *for a loop*⟩ **b** : DEMOLISH ⟨*knocked* our idea *for a loop*⟩ **2** : DUMBFOUND, AMAZE ⟨the news *knocked* them *for a loop*⟩
— **knock one's socks off** : to overwhelm or amaze one ⟨a performance that will *knock your socks off*⟩
— **knock together** : to make or assemble especially hurriedly or in a makeshift way ⟨*knocked together* my own bookcase⟩

**²knock** *noun* (14th century)
**1 a** : a sharp blow : RAP, HIT ⟨a loud *knock* on the door⟩ **b** (1) : a severe misfortune or hardship (2) : SETBACK, REVERSAL
**2 a** : a pounding noise **b** : a sharp repetitive metallic noise caused by abnormal ignition in an automobile engine
**3** : a harsh and often petty criticism ⟨likes praise but can't stand the *knocks*⟩

**knock·about** \'nä-kə-,baut\ *adjective* (1880)
**1** : suitable for rough use ⟨*knockabout* clothing⟩
**2 a** : being noisy and rough : BOISTEROUS ⟨*knockabout* games⟩ **b** : characterized by boisterous antics and often extravagant burlesque ⟨*knockabout* comedy⟩
**3** *of a sailing vessel* : having a simplified rig marked by absence of bowsprit and topmast ⟨a *knockabout* sloop⟩
— **knockabout** *noun*

**knock back** *transitive verb* (circa 1931)
: DRINK, SWALLOW; *specifically* : to toss down (an alcoholic beverage)

**¹knock·down** \'näk-,daun\ *adjective* (1690)
**1** : having such force as to strike down or overwhelm ⟨a bewildering assortment of *knockdown* arguments —J. W. Krutch⟩
**2** : that can easily be assembled or disassembled ⟨a *knockdown* table⟩
**3** *chiefly British* : extremely low : REDUCED ⟨*knockdown* prices⟩

**²knockdown** *noun* (1809)
**1** : the action of knocking down

◇ **WORD HISTORY**

**knickerbocker**   In 1809 Washington Irving published *A History of New York*, a supposed work of the fictitious historian Diedrich Knickerbocker, as a genial satire of the early Dutch settlers of the New Netherlands. Irving most likely chose the name *Knickerbocker* for his fictional alter ego in humorous allusion to his friend Herman Knickerbocker, who was of Dutch descent. *Knickerbocker's History of New York* (as the work came to be known) had such an enduring popularity that by the middle of the 19th century New Yorkers of Dutch descent had taken to calling themselves "genuine Knickerbockers." *Knickerbocker* then went on to become a nickname for any native or resident of New York city or state. The use of *knickerbockers* as a term for knee breeches stems from an edition of Irving's work published in the 1850s with illustrations by English caricaturist George Cruikshank. Cruikshank depicted Diedrich Knickerbocker and his fellow Dutch burghers as wearing loose-fitting breeches gathered just below the knee. A coincidental revival of the fashion for knee breeches at that time prompted the adoption of *knickerbockers* for the garment. The shortened form *knickers* soon followed.

\ə\ abut \ᵊ\ kitten \ər\ further \a\ ash \ā\ ace
\ä\ mop, mar \au\ out \ch\ chin \e\ bet \ē\ easy
\g\ go \i\ hit \ī\ ice \j\ job \ŋ\ sing \ō\ go
\o\ law \oi\ boy \th\ thin \th\ the \ü\ loot \u\ foot
\y\ yet \zh\ vision   *see also* Guide to Pronunciation

**2 :** something (as a blow) that strikes down or overwhelms
**3 :** something (as a piece of furniture) that can be easily assembled or disassembled

**knock down** \'--daůn\ *transitive verb* (15th century)
**1 :** to strike to the ground with or as if with a sharp blow **:** FELL
**2 :** to dispose of (an item) to a bidder at an auction sale
**3 :** to take apart **:** DISASSEMBLE
**4 :** to receive as income or salary **:** EARN ⟨positions where they were able to *knock down* good money —*Infantry Journal*⟩
**5 :** REDUCE

**knock–down–drag–out** *or* **knock–down–and–drag–out** *adjective* (1834)
**:** marked by extreme violence or bitterness and by the showing of no mercy ⟨*knock-down-drag-out* political debates⟩
— **knock–down–drag–out** *noun*

**knock·er** \'nä-kər\ *noun* (14th century)
**1 :** one that knocks: as **a :** a metal ring, bar, or hammer hinged to a door for use in knocking **b :** a persistently pessimistic critic
**2 :** BREAST — usually used in plural; often considered vulgar

**knock-knee** \'näk-'nē, -'nē\ *noun* (1879)
**:** a condition in which the legs curve inward at the knees
— **knock–kneed** \-'nēd\ *adjective*

**knock·off** \'näk-,óf\ *noun* (1966)
**:** a copy that sells for less than the original; *broadly* **:** a copy or imitation of someone or something popular

**knock off** (1649)
*intransitive verb*
**:** to stop doing something
*transitive verb*
**1 :** to do hurriedly or routinely ⟨*knocked off* one painting after another⟩
**2 :** DISCONTINUE, STOP ⟨*knocked off* work at five⟩
**3 :** DEDUCT ⟨*knocked off* a little to make the price more attractive⟩
**4 a :** KILL ⟨*knocked off* two men . . . on mercenary grounds —Lewis Baker⟩ **b :** OVERCOME, DEFEAT ⟨*knocked off* each center of rebellion⟩
**5 :** ROB ⟨*knocked off* a couple of banks⟩
**6 :** to make a knockoff of **:** COPY, IMITATE ⟨*knocks off* popular dress designs⟩

**knock·out** \'näk-,aůt\ *noun* (1887)
**1 a :** the act of knocking out **:** the condition of being knocked out **b** (1) **:** the termination of a boxing match when one boxer has been knocked down and is unable to rise and resume boxing within a specified time (2) **:** TECHNICAL KNOCKOUT **c :** a blow that knocks out an opponent
**2 :** something sensationally striking, appealing, or attractive
— **knockout** *adjective*

**knock out** *transitive verb* (1856)
**1 :** to produce roughly or hastily
**2 a** (1) **:** to defeat (a boxing opponent) by a knockout (2) **:** to make unconscious ⟨the drug *knocked* him *out*⟩ **b :** to make inoperative or useless ⟨electricity was *knocked out* by the storm⟩ **c :** to get rid of **:** ELIMINATE ⟨*knocked out* illegal gambling⟩
**3 :** to tire out **:** EXHAUST ⟨*knocked* themselves *out* with work⟩
**4 :** to cause (an opposing pitcher) to be removed from a baseball game by a batting rally

**knockout drops** *noun plural* (1895)
**:** drops of a solution of a drug (as chloral hydrate) put into a drink to produce unconsciousness or stupefaction

**knock over** *transitive verb* (circa 1814)
**1 a** (1) **:** to strike to the ground **:** FELL (2) **:** OVERWHELM ⟨was *knocked over* by the news⟩ **b :** ELIMINATE ⟨*knocked over* every difficulty⟩
**2 a :** STEAL; *especially* **:** HIJACK ⟨*knocks over* a truckload of merchandise —J. B. Martin⟩ **b :** ROB ⟨*knocking over* a bank⟩

**knock up** *transitive verb* (1663)

**1** *British* **:** ROUSE, SUMMON
**2 :** to make pregnant — sometimes considered vulgar

**knock·wurst** \'näk-(,)wərst *also* -,vu̇(r)st, *sometimes* -,vu̇sht\ *noun* [German *Knackwurst*, from *knacken* to crackle (of imitative origin) + *Wurst* wurst] (circa 1929)
**:** a short thick heavily seasoned sausage

**¹knoll** \'nōl\ *noun* [Middle English *knol*, from Old English *cnoll*; akin to Old Norse *knollr* mountaintop] (before 12th century)
**:** a small round hill **:** MOUND

**²knoll** *verb* [Middle English, probably alteration of *knellen* to knell] (15th century)
*archaic* **:** KNELL

**knop** \'näp\ *noun* [Middle English, from Old English *-cnoppa* knob] (before 12th century)
**:** a usually ornamental knob
— **knopped** \'näpt\ *adjective*

**¹knot** \'nät\ *noun* [Middle English, from Old English *cnotta;* akin to Old High German *knoto* knot] (before 12th century)
**1 a :** an interlacement of the parts of one or more flexible bodies forming a lump or knob **b :** the lump or knob so formed **c :** a tight constriction or the sense of constriction ⟨my stomach was all in *knots*⟩
**2 :** something hard to solve **:** PROBLEM ⟨a matter full of legal *knots*⟩
**3 :** a bond of union; *especially* **:** the marriage bond
**4 a :** a protuberant lump or swelling in tissue ⟨a *knot* in a gland⟩ **b :** the base of a woody branch enclosed in the stem from which it arises; *also* **:** its section in lumber
**5 :** a cluster of persons or things **:** GROUP
**6 :** an ornamental bow of ribbon **:** COCKADE
**7 a :** a division of the log's line serving to measure a ship's speed **b** (1) **:** one nautical mile per hour (2) **:** one nautical mile — not used technically ◼

**²knot** *verb* **knot·ted; knot·ting** (1547)
*transitive verb*
**1 :** to tie in or with a knot **:** form knots in
**2 :** to unite closely or intricately **:** ENTANGLE
**3 :** TIE 4b ⟨*knotted* the score⟩
*intransitive verb*
**:** to form knots
— **knot·ter** *noun*

**³knot** *noun, plural* **knots** *or* **knot** [Middle English *knott*] (15th century)
**:** either of two sandpipers (*Calidris canutus* and *C. tenuirostris*) that breed in the Arctic and winter in temperate or warm parts of the New and Old World

**knot garden** *noun* (1519)
**:** an elaborately designed garden especially of flowers or herbs

**knot·grass** \'nät-,gras\ *noun* (1538)
**1 :** a cosmopolitan weed (*Polygonum aviculare*) of the buckwheat family with jointed

stems, prominent sheathing stipules, and minute flowers; *broadly* **:** any of several congeneric plants
**2 :** any of several grasses with markedly jointed stems; *especially* **:** JOINT GRASS

**knot·hole** \-,hōl\ *noun* (1726)
**:** a hole in a board or tree trunk where a knot or branch has come out

**knot·ted** \'nä-təd\ *adjective* (12th century)
**1 :** tied in or with a knot
**2 :** full of knots **:** GNARLED
**3 :** KNOTTY
**4 :** ornamented with knots or knobs

**knot·ty** \'nä-tē\ *adjective* **knot·ti·er; -est** (13th century)
**:** marked by or full of knots; *especially* **:** so full of difficulties and complications as to be likely to defy solution ⟨a *knotty* problem⟩
**synonym** see COMPLEX
— **knot·ti·ness** *noun*

**knotty pine** *noun* (circa 1898)
**:** pine wood that has a decorative distribution of knots and is used especially for interior finish

**knot·weed** \'nät-,wēd\ *noun* (1884)
**:** any of several herbs (genus *Polygonum*) of the buckwheat family with leaves and bracts jointed and having a very short petiole; *broadly* **:** POLYGONUM

**knout** \'naůt, *sometimes* 'nüt\ *noun* [Russian *knut*, of Scandinavian origin; akin to Old Norse *knūtr* knot; akin to Old English *cnotta*] (1716)
**:** a whip used for flogging
— **knout** *transitive verb*

**¹know** \'nō\ *verb* **knew** \'nü *also* 'nyü\; **known** \'nōn\; **know·ing** [Middle English, from Old English *cnāwan;* akin to Old High German *bichnāan* to recognize, Latin *gnoscere, noscere* to come to know, Greek *gignōskein*] (before 12th century)
*transitive verb*
**1 a** (1) **:** to perceive directly **:** have direct cognition of (2) **:** to have understanding of (importance of *knowing* oneself) (3) **:** to recognize the nature of **:** DISCERN **b** (1) **:** to recognize as being the same as something previously known (2) **:** to be acquainted or familiar with (3) **:** to have experience of
**2 a :** to be aware of the truth or factuality of **:** be convinced or certain of **b :** to have a practical understanding of ⟨*knows* how to write⟩
**3** *archaic* **:** to have sexual intercourse with
*intransitive verb*
**1 :** to have knowledge
**2 :** to be or become cognizant — sometimes used interjectionally with *you* especially as a filler in informal speech
— **know·able** \'nō-ə-bəl\ *adjective*
— **know·er** \'nō(-ə)r\ *noun*
— **know from :** to have knowledge of ⟨didn't *know from* sibling rivalry —Penny Marshall⟩

**²know** *noun* (1592)

---

□ USAGE

**knot**    It is a favorite notion of those who claim a knowledge of things nautical that the knot is a unit of speed only. One who chances to say or write *knots per hour* or *knots an hour* will be quickly corrected. And in truth it is a bit of a jump in meaning from a ship's speed measured by the number of knots tied at fixed intervals in a line run out in a half minute to a nautical mile. But this is no recent jump—it took place in the 18th century, and the earliest attestations are from a couple of famous English sailing men, including this one (the strong tide, though even here it ran five *knots* an hour —Captain James Cook). So criticism of *knots an hour* can elicit the polite reply that what was good enough for Captain Cook is good enough for a mere modern landlubber.

---

knot 1b: **1** Blackwall hitch, **2** carrick bend, **3** clove hitch, **4** cat's-paw, **5** figure eight, **6** granny knot, **7** bowline, **8** overhand knot, **9** fisherman's bend, **10** half hitch, **11** square knot, **12** slip knot, **13** stevedore knot, **14** true lover's knot, **15** surgeon's knot, **16** Turk's head, **17** sheet bend, **18** timber hitch, **19** seizing, **20** rolling hitch, **21** sheepshank

: KNOWLEDGE
— **in the know** : in possession of exclusive knowledge or information; *broadly* : WELL-INFORMED
**know-all** \\'nō-,ól\\ *noun* (circa 1864)
*chiefly British* : KNOW-IT-ALL
**know-how** \\'nō-,haú\\ *noun* (1838)
: knowledge of how to do something smoothly and efficiently : EXPERTISE
¹**know-ing** \\'nō-iŋ\\ *noun* (14th century)
: ACQUAINTANCE, COGNIZANCE
²**knowing** *adjective* (14th century)
**1** : having or reflecting knowledge, information, or intelligence
**2 a** : shrewdly and keenly alert : ASTUTE **b** : indicating possession of exclusive inside knowledge or information ⟨a *knowing* smile⟩
**3** : COGNITIVE
**4** : DELIBERATE ⟨*knowing* interference in the affairs of another⟩
— **know-ing-ly** *adverb*
— **know-ing-ness** *noun*
**know-it-all** \\'nō-ət-,ól\\ *noun* (1895)
: one who claims to know everything; *also* : one who disdains advice
— **know-it-all** *adjective*
**knowl-edge** \\'nä-lij\\ *noun* [Middle English *knowlege*, from *knowlechen* to acknowledge, irregular from *knowen*] (14th century)
**1** *obsolete* : COGNIZANCE
**2 a** (1) : the fact or condition of knowing something with familiarity gained through experience or association (2) : acquaintance with or understanding of a science, art, or technique **b** (1) : the fact or condition of being aware of something (2) : the range of one's information or understanding ⟨answered to the best of my *knowledge*⟩ **c** : the circumstance or condition of apprehending truth or fact through reasoning : COGNITION **d** : the fact or condition of having information or of being learned ⟨a man of unusual *knowledge*⟩
**3** *archaic* : SEXUAL INTERCOURSE
**4 a** : the sum of what is known : the body of truth, information, and principles acquired by mankind **b** *archaic* : a branch of learning ☆
**knowl-edge-able** \\'nä-lij-ə-bəl\\ *adjective* (1829)
: having or exhibiting knowledge or intelligence
— **knowl-edge-abil-i-ty** \\,nä-li-jə-'bi-lə-tē\\ *noun*
— **knowl-edge-able-ness** *noun*
— **knowl-edge-ably** \\-blē\\ *adverb*
**knowledge engineering** *noun* (1980)
: a branch of artificial intelligence that emphasizes the development and use of expert systems
— **knowledge engineer** *noun*
**known** \\'nōn\\ *adjective* (13th century)
: familiar : generally recognized ⟨a *known* authority on art⟩
**know-noth-ing** \\'nō-,nə-thiŋ\\ *noun* (1827)
**1 a** : IGNORAMUS **b** : AGNOSTIC
**2** *K&N capitalized* : a member of a 19th century secret American political organization hostile to the political influence of recent immigrants and Roman Catholics
**know-noth-ing-ism** \\-thiŋ-,i-zəm\\ *noun* (1854)
**1** *K&N capitalized* : the principles and policies of the Know-Nothings
**2** : the condition of knowing nothing or desiring to know nothing or the conviction that nothing can be known with certainty especially in religion or morality
**3** *often K&N capitalized* : a mid-twentieth century political attitude characterized by anti-intellectualism, exaggerated patriotism, and fear of foreign subversive influences
**knub-by** *variant of* NUBBY
¹**knuck-le** \\'nə-kəl\\ *noun* [Middle English *knokel*; akin to Middle High German *knöchel* knuckle] (14th century)
**1 a** : the rounded prominence formed by the ends of the two adjacent bones at a joint —

used especially of those at the joints of the fingers **b** : the joint of a knuckle
**2** : a cut of meat consisting of the tarsal or carpal joint with the adjoining flesh
**3** : something resembling a knuckle: as **a** (1) : one of the joining parts of a hinge through which a pin or rivet passes (2) : KNUCKLE JOINT **b** : the meeting of two surfaces at a sharp angle (as in a roof) **c** : a pivotal point
**4** *plural* : a set of metal finger rings or guards attached to a transverse piece and worn over the front of the doubled fist for use as a weapon — called also *brass knuckles*
— **knuck-led** *adjective*
²**knuckle** *verb* **knuck-led**; **knuck-ling** \\'nə-k(ə-)liŋ\\ (1740)
*intransitive verb*
: to place the knuckles on the ground in shooting a marble
*transitive verb*
: to press or rub with the knuckles
**knuck-le-ball** \\'nə-kəl-,ból\\ *noun* (1910)
: a baseball pitch in which the ball is gripped with the knuckles or the tips of the fingers pressed against the top and thrown with little speed or spin
— **knuck-le-ball-er** \\-,bó-lər\\ *noun*
**knuck-le-bone** \\'nək-əl-,bōn\\ *noun* (1577)
**1** : a bone (as a metatarsus or metacarpus of a sheep) used in games and formerly in divination
**2** *plural but singular in construction* : a game played with knucklebones or jacks
**knuckle down** *intransitive verb* (circa 1864)
: to apply oneself earnestly
**knuck-le-dust-er** \\'nə-kəl-,dəs-tər\\ *noun* (1858)
: KNUCKLE 4
**knuck-le-head** \\-,hed\\ *noun* (1942)
: DUMBBELL 2
— **knuck-le-head-ed** \\-,hed-əd\\ *adjective*
**knuckle joint** *noun* (circa 1864)
: a hinge joint in which a projection with an eye on one piece enters a jaw between two corresponding projections with eyes on another piece and is retained by a pin or rivet

knuckle joint

**knuck-ler** \\'nə-k(ə-)lər\\ *noun* (1928)
: KNUCKLEBALL
**knuckle under** *intransitive verb* (1869)
: GIVE IN, SUBMIT
**knur** \\'nər\\ *noun* [Middle English *knorre*; akin to Middle High German *knorre* burl] (14th century)
: a hard excrescence (as on a tree trunk)
: GNARL
**knurl** \\'nərl\\ *noun* [probably blend of *knur* and *gnarl*] (1608)
**1** : a small protuberance, excrescence, or knob
**2** : one of a series of small ridges or beads on a metal surface to aid in gripping
— **knurled** \\'nər(-ə)ld\\ *adjective*
— **knurly** \\'nər-lē\\ *adjective*
¹**KO** \\(,)kā-'ō, 'kā-(,)ō\\ *noun* [*knock out*] (1911)
: KNOCKOUT
²**KO** *transitive verb* **KO'd** \\kā-'ōd, 'kā-(,)ōd\\; **KO'ing** \\-'ō-iŋ, -(,)ō-\\ (1926)
: to knock out (as in boxing)
**koa** \\'kō-ə\\ *noun* [Hawaiian] (1850)
**1** : a Hawaiian timber tree (*Acacia koa*) with crescent-shaped leaves and white flowers borne in small round heads
**2** : the fine-grained red wood of the koa used especially for furniture
**ko-ala** \\kə-'wä-lə, kō-'ä-\\ *noun* [Dharuk (Australian aboriginal language of the Port Jackson area) *gulawaŋ*] (1803)
: an Australian arboreal marsupial (*Phascolarctos cinereus*) that has a broad head, large hairy ears, dense gray fur, and sharp claws and feeds on eucalyptus leaves — called also *koala bear*

**ko-an** \\'kō-,än\\ *noun* [Japanese *kōan*, from *kō* public + *an* proposition] (1945)
: a paradox to be meditated upon that is used to train Zen Buddhist monks to abandon ultimate dependence on reason and to force them into gaining sudden intuitive enlightenment
**ko-bo** \\'kō-(,)bō\\ *noun, plural* **kobo** [alteration of ¹*copper*] (1972)
— see *naira* at MONEY table

koala

**ko-bold** \\'kō-,bóld\\ *noun* [German — more at COBALT] (1830)
**1** : a gnome that in German folklore inhabits underground places
**2** : an often mischievous domestic spirit of German folklore
**Ko-di-ak bear** \\'kō-dē-,ak-\\ *noun* [*Kodiak* Island, Alaska] (1899)
: a large brown bear of the southern coast of Alaska and adjacent islands
**kohl** \\'kōl\\ *noun* [Arabic *kuḥl*] (1799)
: a preparation used especially in Arabia and Egypt to darken the edges of the eyelids
**kohl-ra-bi** \\kōl-'rä-bē *also* -'ra-\\ *noun, plural* -**bies** [German, from Italian *cavolo rapa*, from *cavolo* cabbage + *rapa* turnip] (1807)
: any of a race of cabbages (*Brassica oleracea gongylodes*) having a greatly enlarged, fleshy, turnip-shaped edible stem
**koi** \\'kói\\ *noun, plural* **koi** [Japanese] (1727)
: a carp (*Cyprinus carpio*) bred especially in Japan for large size and a variety of colors and often stocked in ornamental ponds
**koi-ne** *also* **koi-né** \\kói-'nā, 'kói-,; kē-'nē\\ *noun* [Greek *koinē*, from feminine of *koinos* common] (1909)
**1** *capitalized* : the Greek language commonly spoken and written in eastern Mediterranean countries in the Hellenistic and Roman periods
**2** : a dialect or language of a region that has become the common or standard language of a larger area
**ko-kan-ee** \\kō-'ka-nē\\ *noun* [perhaps from Shuswap (Salishan language of British Columbia) *kəknǽxʷ*] (1875)
: a small landlocked sockeye salmon — called also *kokanee salmon*
**kok-sa-ghyz** *or* **kok-sa-gyz** \\,kōk-sə-'gēz, ,käk-, -'giz\\ *noun* [Russian *kok-sagyz*] (1932)

☆ **SYNONYMS**
**Knowledge, learning, erudition, scholarship** mean what is or can be known by an individual or by mankind. KNOWLEDGE applies to facts or ideas acquired by study, investigation, observation, or experience ⟨rich in the *knowledge* of human nature⟩. LEARNING applies to knowledge acquired especially through formal, often advanced, schooling ⟨a book that demonstrates vast *learning*⟩. ERUDITION strongly implies the acquiring of profound, recondite, or bookish learning ⟨an *erudition* unusual even in a scholar⟩. SCHOLARSHIP implies the possession of learning characteristic of the advanced scholar in a specialized field of study or investigation ⟨a work of first-rate literary *scholarship*⟩.

\\ə\\ abut \\ə̇\\ kitten \\ər\\ further \\a\\ ash \\ā\\ ace
\\ä\\ mop, mar \\aú\\ out \\ch\\ chin \\e\\ bet \\ē\\ easy
\\g\\ go \\i\\ hit \\ī\\ ice \\j\\ job \\ŋ\\ sing \\ō\\ go
\\ó\\ law \\ói\\ boy \\th\\ thin \\t͟h\\ the \\ü\\ loot \\ú\\ foot
\\y\\ yet \\zh\\ vision *see also* Guide to Pronunciation

: a perennial Asian dandelion (*Taraxacum kok-saghyz*) cultivated for its fleshy roots that have a high rubber content

**ko·la** *variant of* COLA

**ko·la nut** \'kō-lə-\ *noun* [*kola*, perhaps modification of Malinke *kolo* kola nut] (1868)
: the bitter caffeine-containing chestnut-sized seed of a kola tree used especially as a masticatory and in beverages

**kola tree** *noun* (1937)
: an African tree (genus *Cola*, especially *C. nitida* and *C. acuminata* of the family Sterculiaceae) cultivated in various tropical areas for its kola nuts

**ko·lin·sky** \kə-'lin(t)-skē\ *noun, plural* **-skies** [origin unknown] (1851)
**1** : any of several Asian minks (especially *Mustela siberica*)
**2** : the fur or pelt of a kolinsky

**kol·khoz** \käl-'kòz, -'kòs\ *noun, plural* **kol·kho·zy** \-'kò-zē\ *or* **kol·khoz·es** \-'kò-zəz\ [Russian, from *kollektivnoe khozyaĭstvo* collective farm] (1921)
: a collective farm of the U.S.S.R.

**kol·khoz·nik** \käl-'kòz-nik\ *noun, plural* **-ni·ki** \-'ni-kē\ *or* **-niks** [Russian, from *kolkhoz* + *-nik*, agent suffix] (1944)
: a member of a kolkhoz

**Kol Ni·dre** \kōl-'ni-(,)drā, kòl-, -drə; -ni-'drä\ *noun* [Aramaic *kol nidhrē* all the vows; from the opening phrase of the prayer] (1881)
: a formula for the annulment of private vows chanted in the synagogue on the eve of Yom Kippur

**ko·lo** \'kō-(,)lō\ *noun, plural* **kolos** [Serbo-Croatian, literally, circle, wheel; akin to Greek *kyklos* circle — more at WHEEL] (1910)
: a central European folk dance in which dancers form a circle and progress slowly to right or left while one or more dancers perform elaborate steps in the center

**ko·mat·ik** \kō-'ma-tik\ *noun* [Inuit *qamutik*] (circa 1824)
: an Eskimo sledge with wooden runners and crossbars lashed with rawhide

**Ko·mo·do dragon** \kə-'mō-dō-\ *noun* [*Komodo* Island, Indonesia] (1927)
: an Indonesian monitor lizard (*Varanus komodoensis*) that is the largest of all known lizards and may attain a length of 10 feet (3 meters)

**ko·mon·dor** \'kä-mən-,dòr, 'kō-\ *noun, plural* **-dors** *or* **-dor·ok** \-,dòr-ək\ [Hungarian] (1931)
: any of a breed of large powerful shaggy-coated white dogs of Hungarian origin that are used to guard sheep

**Kom·so·mol** \'käm-sə-,mól, -,mōl\ *noun* [Russian, from *Kommunisticheskiĭ Soyuz Molodezhi* Communist Union of Youth] (1925)
: a Russian Communist youth organization

**Kon·go** \'käŋ-(,)gō\ *noun, plural* **Kongo** *or* **Kongos** (circa 1902)
**1** : a member of a Bantu people of the lower Congo river
**2** : the Bantu language of the Kongo people

**Kon·ka·ni** \'käŋ-kə-(,)nē\ *noun* [Marathi *Koṅkaṇī*] (1873)
: an Indo-Aryan language of the west coast of India

**koo·doo** *variant of* KUDU

**kook** \'kük\ *noun* [by shortening & alteration from *cuckoo*] (1960)
: one whose ideas or actions are eccentric, fantastic, or insane : SCREWBALL

**kook·a·bur·ra** \'kù-kə-,bər-ə, -,bə-rə\ *noun* [Wiradhuri (Australian aboriginal language of central New South Wales) *gugubarra*] (1834)
: a brownish kingfisher (*Dacelo novaeguineae* synonym *D. gigas*) of Australia that is about the size of a crow and has a call resembling loud laughter — called also *laughing jackass*

**kooky** *also* **kook·ie** \'kü-kē\ *adjective* **kook·i·er; -est** (1959)
: having the characteristics of a kook : CRAZY, OFFBEAT
— **kook·i·ness** *noun*

**ko·peck** *or* **ko·pek** \'kō-,pek\ *noun* [Russian *kopeĭka*] (1698)
— see *ruble* at MONEY table

**koph** *variant of* QOPH

**kop·je** *or* **kop·pie** \'kä-pē\ *noun* [Afrikaans *koppie*] (1848)
: a small hill especially on the African veld

**kor** *variant of* COR

**Ko·ran** \kə-'ran, -'rän; 'kòr-,an, 'kòr-\ *noun* [Arabic *qurʾān*] (circa 1615)
: the book composed of sacred writings accepted by Muslims as revelations made to Muhammad by Allah through the angel Gabriel
— **Ko·ran·ic** \kə-'ra-nik\ *adjective*

**Ko·rat** \kō-'rät, kó-\ *noun* [*Korat* province, Thailand] (1967)
: any of a breed of shorthaired domestic cats originating in Thailand and having a heart-shaped face, a silver-blue coat, and green eyes

**ko·re** \'kò-(,)rā, 'kó-\ *noun, plural* **ko·rai** \-,rī, -(,)rā\ [Greek *korē* girl; akin to Greek *koros* boy — more at CRESCENT] (1920)
: an ancient Greek statue of a clothed young woman standing with feet together

**Ko·re·an** \kə-'rē-ən, (,)kō-\ *noun, especially Southern* (1600)
**1** : a native or inhabitant of Korea
**2** : the language of the Korean people
— **Korean** *adjective*

**ko·ru·na** \'kòr-ə-,nä, 'kär-\ *noun, plural* **ko·ru·ny** \-ə-nē\ *or* **korunas** *or* **ko·run** \'kòr-ən, 'kär-\ [Czech, literally, crown, from Latin *corona* — more at CROWN] (1930)
— see MONEY table

**¹ko·sher** \'kō-shər\ *adjective* [Yiddish, from Hebrew *kāshēr* fit, proper] (1851)
**1 a** : sanctioned by Jewish law; *especially* : ritually fit for use ⟨*kosher* meat⟩ **b** : selling or serving food ritually fit according to Jewish law ⟨a *kosher* restaurant⟩
**2** : being proper, acceptable, or satisfactory ⟨found things going on that were not *kosher* —Homer Bigart⟩

**²kosher** *transitive verb* **ko·shered; ko·sher·ing** \-sh(ə-)riŋ\ (1871)
: to make kosher

**³kosher** *noun* (1886)
: the observance of kosher practices — used in the phrase *keep kosher*

**ko·to** \'kō-(,)tō\ *noun* [Japanese] (1795)
: a long Japanese zither having 13 silk strings

**kou·miss** \kü-'mis, 'kü-məs\ *noun* [Russian *kumys*, of Turkic origin; akin to Turkish *kımız* koumiss] (1598)
: a beverage of fermented mare's milk made originally by the nomadic peoples of central Asia

**kou·prey** \'kü-,prā\ *noun* [Khmer *ko:prey*] (1940)
: a short-haired ox (*Bos sauveli*) of forests of Cambodia, Thailand, and Vietnam having a large dewlap

**kou·ros** \'kü-,ròs\ *noun, plural* **kou·roi** \-(,)ròi\ [Greek *kouros, koros* boy — more at CRESCENT] (1920)
: an ancient Greek statue of a nude male youth standing with the left leg forward and arms at the sides

**¹kow·tow** \(,)kaù-'taù, 'kaù-,\ *noun* [Chinese (Beijing) *kòutóu*, from *kòu* to knock + *tóu* head] (1804)
: an act of kowtowing

**²kowtow** *intransitive verb* (1826)
**1** : to show obsequious deference : FAWN
**2** : to kneel and touch the forehead to the ground in token of homage, worship, or deep respect

**KP** \,kā-'pē\ *noun* [*k*itchen *p*olice] (1918)
**1** : an enlisted man detailed to assist the cooks in a military mess
**2** : the work of KPs

**¹kraal** \'król, 'kräl\ *noun* [Afrikaans, from Portuguese *curral* pen for cattle, enclosure, from (assumed) Vulgar Latin *currale* enclosure for vehicles — more at CORRAL] (1731)

**1 a** : a village of southern African natives **b** : the native village community
**2** : an enclosure for animals especially in southern Africa

**²kraal** *transitive verb* (1827)
: to pen in a kraal

**kraft** \'kräft, 'kraft\ *noun, often attributive* [German, literally, strength, from Old High German — more at CRAFT] (1906)
: a strong paper or paperboard made from wood pulp produced from wood chips boiled in an alkaline solution containing sodium sulfate

**krait** \'krīt\ *noun* [Hindi *karait*] (1874)
: any of a genus (*Bungarus*) of brightly banded extremely venomous nocturnal elapid snakes of Pakistan, India, southeastern Asia, and adjacent islands

**kra·ken** \'krä-kən\ *noun* [Norwegian dialect] (1755)
: a fabulous Scandinavian sea monster

**kra·ter** \'krä-tər, krä-'ter\ *noun* [Greek *kratēr* — more at CRATER] (circa 1736)
: a jar or vase of classical antiquity having a large round body and a wide mouth and used for mixing wine and water

**K ration** \'kā-\ *noun* [A. B. *Keys* (born 1904) American physiologist] (circa 1940)
: a lightweight packaged ration of emergency foods developed for the U.S. armed forces in World War II

**kraut** \'kraùt\ *noun* [German, cabbage, from Old High German *krūt*] (1855)
**1** : SAUERKRAUT
**2** *often capitalized* : GERMAN — usually used disparagingly

**Krebs cycle** \'krebz-\ *noun* [H. A. *Krebs*] (1941)
: a sequence of reactions in the living organism in which oxidation of acetic acid or acetyl equivalent provides energy for storage in phosphate bonds (as in ATP) — called also *citric acid cycle, tricarboxylic acid cycle*

**krem·lin** \'krem-lən\ *noun* [obsolete German *Kremelien* the citadel of Moscow, ultimately from Old Russian *kremlĭ*] (1662)
**1** : the citadel of a Russian city
**2** *capitalized* [the *Kremlin*, citadel of Moscow and seat of government of Russia and formerly of the U.S.S.R.] : the Russian government

**krem·lin·ol·o·gy** \,krem-lə-'nä-lə-jē\ *noun, often capitalized* (1958)
: the study of the policies and practices of the Soviet government
— **krem·lin·ol·o·gist** \-jist\ *noun, often capitalized*

**krep·lach** \'krep-lək, -,läk\ *noun* [Yiddish *kreplekh*, plural of *krepl* filled dumpling] (circa 1892)
: square or triangular dumplings filled with ground meat or cheese, boiled or fried, and usually served in soup

**kreu·zer** \'kròit-sər\ *noun* [German, from *Kreuz* cross; from its markings] (1547)
: a small coin formerly used in Austria and Germany

**krill** \'kril\ *noun* [Norwegian *kril* fry of fish] (1907)
: planktonic crustaceans and larvae (order Euphausiacea) that constitute the principal food of baleen whales

**krim·mer** \'kri-mər\ *noun* [German, from *Krim* Crimea] (1834)
: a gray fur made from the pelts of young lambs of the Crimean Peninsula region

**Krio** \'krē-ō\ *noun* [Krio, speaker of Krio, Krio language, perhaps from Yoruba *Kiriyó* Christian, ultimately from Portuguese *crioulo* Creole] (1955)
: an English-based creole spoken in Sierra Leone

**kris** \'krēs\ *noun* [Malay *kĕris*] (circa 1580)
: a Malay or Indonesian dagger with a ridged serpentine blade

**Krish·na** \'krish-nə, 'krēsh-\ *noun* [Sanskrit *Kṛṣṇa*] (1864)

: a deity or deified hero of later Hinduism worshiped as an incarnation of Vishnu

**Krish·na·ism** \-ˌi-zəm\ *noun* (1885)
: a widespread form of Hindu religion characterized by the worship of Krishna

**Kriss Krin·gle** \'kris-'kriŋ-gəl\ *noun* [modification of German *Christkindl* Christ child, Christmas gift, diminutive of *Christkind* Christ child] (1830)
: SANTA CLAUS

¹**kro·na** \'krō-nə\ *noun, plural* **kro·nor** \-ˌnȯr, -nər\ [Swedish, literally, crown] (1875)
— see MONEY table

²**kro·na** \'krō-nə\ *noun, plural* **kro·nur** \-nər\ [Icelandic *krōna*, literally, crown] (1886)
— see MONEY table

¹**kro·ne** \'krō-nə\ *noun, plural* **kro·ner** \-nər\ [Danish, literally, crown] (1885)
— see MONEY table

²**kro·ne** \'krō-nə\ *noun, plural* **kro·nen** \-nən\ [German, literally, crown] (1895)
**1** : the basic monetary unit of Austria from 1892 to 1925
**2** : a coin representing one krone

**Kro·neck·er delta** \'krō-ˌne-kər\ *noun* [Leopold *Kronecker* (died 1891) German mathematician] (1926)
: a function of two variables that is 1 when the variables have the same value and is 0 when they have different values

**Kru·ger·rand** \'krü-gə(r)-ˌrand, -ˌränd, -ˌränt\ *noun* [S.J.P. *Kruger* + *rand*] (1967)
: a one-ounce gold coin of the Republic of South Africa

**krumm·holz** \'krùm-ˌhōlts\ *noun, plural* **krummholz** [German, from *krumm* crooked + *Holz* wood] (1903)
: stunted forest characteristic of timberline

**krumm·horn** *also* **krum·horn** \'krəm-ˌhȯrn\ *noun* [German *Krummhorn*, from *krumm* curved + *Horn* horn] (circa 1696)
: a Renaissance double-reed woodwind instrument consisting of a curved boxwood tube and having a pierced cap covering the reed

**kryp·ton** \'krip-ˌtän\ *noun* [Greek, neuter of *kryptos* hidden — more at CRYPT] (1898)
: a colorless relatively inert gaseous element found in air at about one part per million and used especially in electric lamps — see ELEMENT table

**Ksha·tri·ya** \'ksha-trē-ə, 'cha-\ *noun* [Sanskrit *kṣatriya*, from *kṣatra* dominion — more at CHECK] (1794)
: a Hindu of an upper caste traditionally assigned to governing and military occupations

**Ku·che·an** \kü-'chē-ən\ *noun* [*Kuche, Kucha,* Sinkiang, China] (circa 1934)
: TOCHARIAN B

**ku·chen** \'kü-kən, -kən\ *noun, plural* **kuchen** [German, cake, from Old High German *kuocho* — more at CAKE] (1854)
: any of various coffee cakes made from sweet yeast dough

**ku·do** \'kü-(ˌ)dō, 'kyü-\ *noun, plural* **kudos** [back-formation from *kudos* (taken as a plural)] (1926)
**1** : AWARD, HONOR ⟨a score of honorary degrees and . . . other *kudos* —*Time*⟩
**2** : COMPLIMENT, PRAISE ⟨to all three should go some kind of special *kudo* for refusing to succumb —Al Hine⟩ ◼

**ku·dos** \'kü-ˌdäs, 'kyü-, -ˌdōs\ *noun* [Greek *kydos*] (1831)
**1** : fame and renown resulting from an act or achievement : PRESTIGE
**2** : praise given for achievement

**ku·du** \'kü-(ˌ)dü\ *noun, plural* **kudu** *or* **kudus** [Afrikaans *koedoe*] (1777)
: a large grayish brown African antelope (*Tragelaphus strepsiceros*) with large annulated spirally twisted horns; *also* : a related antelope (*T. imberbis*)

**kud·zu** \'kùd-(ˌ)zü, 'kəd-\ *noun* [Japanese *kuzu*] (1876)
: an Asian leguminous vine (*Pueraria lobata* synonym *P. thunbergiana*) that is used for for-

age and erosion control and that is often a serious weed in the southeastern U.S.

**ku·gel** \'kü-gəl\ *noun* [Yiddish *kugl,* from Middle High German *kugel* ball — more at CUDGEL] (1846)
: a baked pudding (as of potatoes or noodles) usually served as a side dish

**Ku Klux·er** \'kü-'klək-sər *also* 'kyü- *or* 'klü-\ *noun* (1880)
: a member of the Ku Klux Klan

— **Ku Klux·ism** \-'kləkˌsi-zəm\ *noun*

**Ku Klux Klan** \'kü-'kləks-'klan *also* 'kyü- *or* 'klü-\ *noun* (1867)
**1** : a post-Civil War secret society advocating white supremacy
**2** : a 20th century secret fraternal group held to confine its membership to American-born white Christians

**ku·lak** \'kü-ˌlak, -ˌläk, kü-'\ *noun* [Russian, literally, fist] (1877)
**1** : a prosperous or wealthy peasant farmer in 19th century Russia
**2** : a farmer characterized by Communists as having excessive wealth

**kul·tur** \kùl-'tùr\ *noun, often capitalized* [German, from Latin *cultura* culture] (1914)
**1** : CULTURE 5
**2** : culture emphasizing practical efficiency and individual subordination to the state
**3** : German culture held to be superior especially by militant Nazi and Hohenzollern expansionists

**Kul·tur·kampf** \-ˌkäm(p)f\ *noun* [German, from *Kultur* + *Kampf* conflict] (1879)
: conflict between civil government and religious authorities especially over control of education and church appointments

**ku·miss** *variant of* KOUMISS

**küm·mel** \'ki-məl\ *noun* [German, literally, caraway seed, from Old High German *kumīn* cumin] (1864)
: a colorless liqueur flavored principally with caraway seeds

**kum·quat** \'kəm-ˌkwät\ *noun* [Chinese (Guangdong) *gām-gwāt,* from *gām* gold + *gwāt* citrus fruit] (1699)
: any of several small yellow to orange citrus fruits with sweet spongy rind and somewhat acid pulp that are used chiefly for preserves; *also* : a tree or shrub (genus *Fortunella*) of the rue family that bears kumquats

**kun·da·li·ni** \ˌkùn-də-'lē-nē, ˌkən-\ *noun, often capitalized* [Sanskrit *kuṇḍalinī,* from feminine of *kuṇḍalin* circular, coiled, from *kuṇḍala* ring] (1905)
: the yogic life force that is held to lie coiled at the base of the spine until it is aroused and sent to the head to trigger enlightenment

**Kung** \'kùŋ, 'küŋ; *in* !*Kung the initial sound is a type of click*\ *noun, plural* **Kung** (1926)
**1** : a member of a people of southern Africa — usually preceded in writing by !
**2** : the Khoisan language of the !Kung people — usually preceded in writing by !

**kung fu** \ˌkəŋ-'fü, ˌkùŋ-\ *noun* [Chinese (Beijing) *gōngfu* skill, art] (1966)
: any of various Chinese arts of self-defense like karate

**kunz·ite** \'kùn(t)-ˌsīt\ *noun* [G. F. *Kunz* (died 1932) American gem expert] (1903)
: a spodumene that occurs in pinkish lilac crystals and is used as a gem

**Kurd** \'kùrd, 'kərd\ *noun* (1595)
: a member of a pastoral and agricultural people who inhabit a plateau region in adjoining parts of Turkey, Iran, Iraq, Syria, Armenia, and Azerbaijan

— **Kurd·ish** \'kùr-dish, 'kər-\ *adjective*

kudu

**Kurdish** *noun* (1813)
: the Iranian language of the Kurds

**Kur·di·stan** \ˌkùr-də-'stan, ˌkər-\ *noun* [*Kurdistan,* Asia] (1904)
: an Oriental rug woven by the Kurds and noted for fine colors

**kur·gan** \kùr-'gän, -'gan\ *noun* [Russian, of Turkic origin; akin to Turkish *kurgan* fortress, castle] (1889)
: a burial mound of eastern Europe or Siberia

**kur·ra·jong** \'kər-ə-ˌjòŋ, 'kə-rə-, -ˌjäŋ\ *noun* [Dharuk (Australian aboriginal language of the Port Jackson area) *garajuŋ*] (1823)
: any of several Australian trees or shrubs (family Sterculiaceae) having strong bast fiber used by Australian aborigines; *especially* : a widely planted shelter and forage tree (*Brachychiton populneum*)

**kur·to·sis** \(ˌ)kər-'tō-səs\ *noun* [Greek *kyrtōsis* convexity, from *kyrtos* convex — more at CURVE] (1905)
: the peakedness or flatness of the graph of a frequency distribution especially with respect to the concentration of values near the mean as compared with the normal distribution

**ku·ru** \'kùr-(ˌ)ü\ *noun* [Fore (language of eastern highland Papua New Guinea)] (1957)
: a rare progressive fatal encephalopathy that is caused by a slow virus, resembles Creutzfeldt-Jakob disease, and occurs among tribesmen in eastern New Guinea

**ku·rus** \kə-'rüsh\ *noun, plural* **kurus** [Turkish *kuruş*] (1882)
— see *lira* at MONEY table

**Ku·te·nai** \'kü-t°n-ˌā, -ˌē\ *noun, plural* **Kutenai** *or* **Kutenais** (1801)
**1** : a member of an American Indian people of the Rocky Mountains in both the U.S. and Canada
**2** : the language of the Kutenai people

**kvass** \'kväs, 'kfäs\ *noun* [Russian *kvas*] (circa 1553)
: a slightly alcoholic beverage of eastern Europe made from fermented mixed cereals and often flavored

¹**kvetch** \'kvech, 'kfech\ *intransitive verb* [Yiddish *kvetshn,* literally, to squeeze, pinch, from Middle High German *quetschen*] (circa 1952)
: to complain habitually : GRIPE

²**kvetch** *noun* (1964)
**1** : an habitual complainer
**2** : COMPLAINT 1
— **kvetchy** \'kve-chē, 'kfe-\ *adjective*

**Kwa** \'kwä\ *noun* (1857)
: a branch of the Niger-Congo language family that is spoken along the African coast and its hinterland from the Ivory Coast to southwestern Nigeria

**kwa·cha** \'kwä-chə\ *noun, plural* **kwacha** [Bemba or Chichewa (Bantu language of Malawi), literally, it dawns] (1966)

---

□ USAGE

**kudo** Some commentators hold that since *kudos* is a singular word it cannot be used as a plural and that the word *kudo* is impossible. But *kudo* does exist; it is simply one of the most recent words created by back-formation from another word misunderstood as a plural. *Kudos* was introduced into English in the 19th century; it was used in contexts where a reader unfamiliar with Greek could not be sure whether it was singular or plural. By the 1920s it began to appear as a plural, and about 25 years later *kudo* began to appear. It may have begun as a misunderstanding, but then so did *cherry* and *pea*.

---

— see MONEY table

**Kwa·ki·utl** \ˌkwä-kē-'yü-t°l, ˌkwä-'kyü-\ *noun, plural* **Kwakiutl** (1848)
**1** **:** a member of an American Indian people of the Canadian Pacific coast
**2** **:** the language of the Kwakiutl people

**kwan·za** \'kwän-zə\ *noun, plural* **kwanzas** *or* **kwanza** [*Kwanza* (Cuanza), river in Angola] (1978)
— see MONEY table

**Kwan·za** *or* **Kwan·zaa** \'kwän-zə\ *noun* [Swahili *kwanza* first] (1972)
**:** an African-American festival held in late December

**kwash·i·or·kor** \ˌkwä-shē-'òr-kər, -òr-'kòr\ *noun* [Ga (Kwa language of coastal Ghana) *kwàsìɔkɔ́* influence a child is said to be under when a second child comes] (1935)
**:** severe malnutrition in infants and children that is caused by a diet high in carbohydrate and low in protein

**KWIC** \'kwik\ *noun* [*keyword in context*] (1959)
**:** a computer-generated index alphabetized on a keyword that appears within a brief context

**ky·ack** \'kī-ˌak\ *noun* [origin unknown] (1901)
**:** a packsack to be swung on either side of a packsaddle

**ky·a·nite** \'kī-ə-ˌnīt\ *noun* [German *Zyanit,* from Greek *kyanos* dark blue enamel, lapis lazuli] (1794)
**:** an aluminum silicate $Al_2SiO_5$ that occurs usually in blue thin-bladed triclinic crystals and crystalline aggregates and is sometimes used as a gemstone

**kyat** \'chät\ *noun* [Burmese *cʸat*] (1952)
— see MONEY table

**ky·bosh** *chiefly British variant of* KIBOSH

**ky·mo·gram** \'kī-mə-ˌgram\ *noun* [International Scientific Vocabulary] (1923)
**:** a record made by a kymograph

**ky·mo·graph** \-ˌgraf\ *noun* [Greek *kyma* wave + International Scientific Vocabulary *-graph* — more at CYME] (1872)
**:** a device which graphically records motion or pressure (as of blood)

— **ky·mo·graph·ic** \ˌkī-mə-'gra-fik\ *adjective*
— **ky·mog·ra·phy** \kī-'mä-grə-fē\ *noun*

**Kym·ric** *variant of* CYMRIC

**ky·pho·sis** \kī-'fō-səs\ *noun* [New Latin, from Greek *kyphōsis,* from *kyphos* humpbacked] (1847)
**:** abnormal backward curvature of the spine
— **ky·phot·ic** \-'fä-tik\ *adjective*

**ky·rie** \'kir-ē-ˌā\ *noun, often capitalized* [Middle English, from Medieval Latin, from Late Latin *kyrie eleison,* transliteration of Greek *kyrie eleēson* Lord, have mercy] (14th century)
**:** a short liturgical prayer that begins with or consists of the words "Lord, have mercy"

**ky·rie elei·son** \ˌkir-ē-ˌā-ə-'lā-(ə-)ˌsän, -(ə-)sən *also* 'kir-ē-ə-'lā-\ *noun, often K&E capitalized* (13th century)
**:** KYRIE

**kyte** \'kīt\ *noun* [probably from Low German *küt* bowel] (circa 1540)
*chiefly Scottish* **:** BELLY 1, 2

**kythe** *variant of* KITHE

**L** *is the twelfth letter of the English alphabet. It came to Latin from Etruscan, and there from Greek, where it was called* lambda; *Greek, in turn, took its letter from Phoenician* lāmadh. *Throughout these migrations* L *has not varied greatly either in form or in value. In English it normally represents a lateral continuant, a sound produced by the free flow of air through the sides of the mouth when the center of the tongue touches the palate.* L *is also described as a liquid consonant, that is, one produced without air friction and capable of being prolonged like a vowel. In unaccented syllables the sound often forms a syllable by itself without a vowel sound, as in* medal, little. *It is silent in some words, especially after* a *or* o *and before* k, m, *or* f, *as in* talk, yolk, calm, *and* half. *The small* l *came into being when scribes replaced the horizontal stroke at the foot of the capital letter with a curved hook.*

---

**l** \ˈel\ *noun, plural* **l's** *or* **ls** \ˈelz\ *often capitalized, often attributive* (before 12th century)
**1 a :** the 12th letter of the English alphabet **b :** a graphic representation of this letter **c :** a speech counterpart of orthographic *l*
**2 :** fifty — see NUMBER table
**3 :** a graphic device for reproducing the letter *l*
**4 :** one designated *l* especially as the 12th in order or class
**5 :** something shaped like the letter L; *specifically :* ²ELL 1
**6 :** ²EL

**l-** *prefix* [International Scientific Vocabulary, from *lev-*]
**1** \ˌlē-(ˌ)vō, ˌel, ˈel\ **:** levorotatory ⟨*l*-tartaric acid⟩
**2** \ˌel, ˈel\ **:** having a similar configuration at a selected carbon atom to the configuration of levorotatory glyceraldehyde — usually printed as a small capital ⟨L-fructose⟩

¹**la** \ˈlȯ, ˈlä\ *interjection* [Middle English (northern dialect), from Old English *lā*] (before 12th century)
*chiefly dialect* — used for emphasis or expressing surprise

²**la** \ˈlä\ *noun* [Middle English, from Medieval Latin, from the syllable sung to this note in a medieval hymn to Saint John the Baptist] (14th century)
**:** the 6th tone of the diatonic scale in solmization

**laa·ger** \ˈlä-gər\ *noun* [obsolete Afrikaans *lager* (now *laer*), from German *Lager*, from Old High German *legar* couch — more at LAIR] (1850)
**1** *South African* **:** CAMP; *especially* **:** an encampment protected by a circle of wagons or armored vehicles
**2 :** a defensive position, policy, or attitude
— **laager** *intransitive verb*

**laa·ri** \ˈlä-(ˌ)rē\ *noun, plural* **laari** [probably from Divehi (Indo-Aryan language of the Maldive Islands), from Persian *lārī* piece of silver wire used as currency] (1983)
— see *rufiyaa* at MONEY table

**lab** \ˈlab\ *noun* (circa 1895)
**:** LABORATORY

**Lab** \ˈlab\ *noun* (1957)
**:** LABRADOR RETRIEVER

**la·ba·no·ta·tion** \ˌlä-bə-nō-ˈtā-shən, ˌlā-; lə-ˌbä-(ˌ)nō-\ *noun* [Rudolf *Laban* (died 1958) Hungarian dance theorist + English *notation*] (1952)
**:** a method of recording bodily movement (as in dance) on a staff by means of symbols (as of direction) that can be aligned with musical accompaniment

**lab·a·rum** \ˈla-bə-rəm\ *noun* [Late Latin] (1606)
**:** an imperial standard of the later Roman emperors resembling the vexillum; *especially* **:** the standard bearing the Chi-Rho adopted by Constantine after his conversion to Christianity

**lab·da·num** \ˈlab-də-nəm\ *noun* [Medieval Latin *lapdanum*] (14th century)
**:** a soft dark fragrant bitter oleoresin derived from various rockroses (genus *Cistus*) and used in making perfumes

¹**la·bel** \ˈlā-bəl\ *noun* [Middle English, from Middle French] (14th century)
**1** *archaic* **:** BAND, FILLET; *specifically* **:** one attached to a document to hold an appended seal
**2 :** a heraldic charge that consists of a narrow horizontal band with usually three pendants
**3 a :** a slip (as of paper or cloth) inscribed and affixed to something for identification or description **b :** written or printed matter accompanying an article to furnish identification or other information **c :** a descriptive or identifying word or phrase: as (1) **:** EPITHET (2) **:** a word or phrase used with a dictionary definition to provide additional information **d :** a usually radioactive isotope used in labeling
**4 :** an adhesive stamp (as for postage or revenue)
**5 a** (1) **:** a brand of commercial recordings issued under a usually trademarked name (2) **:** a recording so issued (3) **:** a company issuing such recordings **b :** the brand name of a retail store selling clothing, a clothing manufacturer, or a fashion designer

²**label** *transitive verb* **la·beled** *or* **la·belled**; **la·bel·ing** *or* **la·bel·ling** \ˈlā-b(ə-)liŋ\ (1601)
**1 a :** to affix a label to **b :** to describe or designate with or as if with a label
**2 a :** to distinguish (an element or atom) by using an isotope distinctive in some manner (as in mass or radioactivity) **b :** to distinguish (as a compound or cell) by introducing a traceable constituent (as a dye or labeled atom)
— **la·bel·able** \ˈlā-bə-lə-bəl\ *adjective*
— **la·bel·er** \ˈlā-b(ə-)lər\ *noun*

**la·bel·lum** \lə-ˈbe-ləm\ *noun, plural* **la·bel·la** \-lə\ [New Latin, from Latin, diminutive of *labrum* lip — more at LIP] (1830)
**1 :** the median and usually most morphologically distinct member of the corolla of an orchid
**2 :** a terminal part of the labium or labrum of various insects

**labia** *plural of* LABIUM

¹**la·bi·al** \ˈlā-bē-əl\ *adjective* [Medieval Latin *labialis*, from Latin *labium* lip] (1594)
**1 :** uttered with the participation of one or both lips ⟨the *labial* sounds \f\, \p\, and \ü\⟩
**2 :** of, relating to, or situated near the lips or labia
— **la·bi·al·ly** \-ə-lē\ *adverb*

²**labial** *noun* (1668)
**:** a labial consonant

**la·bi·al·ize** \ˈlā-bē-ə-ˌlīz\ *transitive verb* **-ized; -iz·ing** (1867)
**:** to make labial ⟨ROUND 1b(2)⟩
— **la·bi·al·i·za·tion** \ˌlā-bē-ə-lə-ˈzā-shən, -byə-lə-\ *noun*

**la·bia ma·jo·ra** \ˈlā-bē-ə-mə-ˈjōr-ə, -ˈjȯr-\ *noun plural* [New Latin, literally, larger lips] (1838)
**:** the outer fatty folds of the vulva bounding the vestibule

**labia mi·no·ra** \-mə-ˈnȯr-ə, -ˈnȯr-\ *noun plural* [New Latin, literally, smaller lips] (1838)
**:** the inner highly vascular largely connective-tissue folds of the vulva bounding the vestibule

¹**la·bi·ate** \ˈlā-bē-ət, -bē-ˌāt\ *adjective* [New Latin *labiatus*, from Latin *labium*] (1706)
**1 :** having the limb of a tubular corolla or calyx divided into two unequal parts projecting one over the other like two lips ⟨mints and the snapdragon are *labiate*⟩
**2 :** of or relating to the mint family

²**labiate** *noun* (1845)
**:** a plant of the mint family

**la·bile** \ˈlā-ˌbīl, -bəl\ *adjective* [French, from Middle French, prone to err, from Late Latin *labilis*, from Latin *labi* to slip — more at SLEEP] (1603)
**1 :** readily or continually undergoing chemical, physical, or biological change or breakdown **:** UNSTABLE ⟨a *labile* mineral⟩
**2 :** readily open to change
— **la·bil·i·ty** \lā-ˈbi-lə-tē\ *noun*

**labio-** *combining form* [Latin *labium*]
**:** labial and ⟨*labio*dental⟩

**la·bio·den·tal** \ˌlā-bē-ō-ˈden-t°l\ *adjective* (1669)
**:** uttered with the participation of the lip and teeth ⟨the *labiodental* sounds \f\ and \v\⟩
— **labiodental** *noun*

**la·bio·ve·lar** \-ˈvē-lər\ *adjective* [International Scientific Vocabulary] (1894)
**:** both labial and velar ⟨the *labiovelar* sound \w\⟩
— **labiovelar** *noun*

**la·bi·um** \ˈlā-bē-əm\ *noun, plural* **la·bia** \-ə\ [New Latin, from Latin, lip — more at LIP] (1634)
**1 :** any of the folds at the margin of the vulva — compare LABIA MAJORA, LABIA MINORA
**2 :** the lower lip of a labiate corolla
**3 a :** a lower mouthpart of an insect that is formed by the second pair of maxillae united in the middle line **b :** a liplike part of various invertebrates

¹**la·bor** \ˈlā-bər\ *noun* [Middle English, from Middle French, from Latin *labor*; perhaps akin to Latin *labare* to totter, *labi* to slip — more at SLEEP] (14th century)
**1 a :** expenditure of physical or mental effort especially when difficult or compulsory **b** (1) **:** human activity that provides the goods or services in an economy (2) **:** the services performed by workers for wages as distinguished from those rendered by entrepreneurs for profits **c :** the physical activities involved in giving birth; *also* **:** the period of such labor
**2 :** an act or process requiring labor **:** TASK
**3 :** a product of labor
**4 a :** an economic group comprising those who do manual labor or work for wages **b** (1) **:** workers employed in an establishment (2) **:** workers available for employment **c :** the organizations or officials representing groups of workers
**5** *usually* **Labour :** the Labour party of the United Kingdom or of another nation of the Commonwealth
*synonym* see WORK

\ə\ abut \ᵊ\ kitten \ər\ further \a\ ash \ā\ ace \ä\ mop, mar \aú\ out \ch\ chin \e\ bet \ē\ easy \g\ go \i\ hit \ī\ ice \j\ job \ŋ\ sing \ō\ go \ȯ\ law \ȯi\ boy \th\ thin \th\ the \ü\ loot \ú\ foot \y\ yet \zh\ vision *see also* Guide to Pronunciation

**²labor** *verb* **la·bored; la·bor·ing** \-b(ə-)riŋ\ (14th century)
*intransitive verb*
**1** : to exert one's powers of body or mind especially with painful or strenuous effort : WORK
**2** : to move with great effort ⟨the truck *labored* up the hill⟩
**3** : to be in the labor of giving birth
**4** : to suffer from some disadvantage or distress ⟨*labor* under a delusion⟩
**5** *of a ship* : to pitch or roll heavily
*transitive verb*
**1** *archaic* **a** : to spend labor on or produce by labor **b** : to strive to effect or achieve
**2** : to treat or work out in often laborious detail ⟨*labor* the obvious⟩
**3** : DISTRESS, BURDEN
**4** : to cause to labor
**³labor** *adjective* (1640)
**1** : of or relating to labor
**2** *capitalized* : of, relating to, or constituting a political party held to represent the interests of workers or made up largely of organized labor groups
**lab·o·ra·to·ry** \'la-b(ə-)rə-ˌtōr-ē, -ˌtȯr- *sometimes* 'la-bə(r)-, *or* lə-'bȯr-ə-, *British usually* lə-'bär-ə-t(ə-)rē\ *noun, plural* **-ries** *often attributive* [Medieval Latin *laboratorium*, from Latin *laborare* to labor, from *labor*] (1605)
**1 a** : a place equipped for experimental study in a science or for testing and analysis; *broadly* : a place providing opportunity for experimentation, observation, or practice in a field of study **b** : a place like a laboratory for testing, experimentation, or practice ⟨the *laboratory* of the mind⟩
**2** : an academic period set aside for laboratory work
**labor camp** *noun* (1900)
**1** : a penal colony where forced labor is performed
**2** : a camp for migratory laborers
**Labor Day** *noun* (1886)
: a day set aside for special recognition of working people: as **a** : the first Monday in September observed in the U.S. and Canada as a legal holiday **b** : May 1 in many countries
**la·bored** \'lā-bərd\ *adjective* (1608)
: produced or performed with labor ⟨*labored* breathing⟩; *also* : lacking ease of expression ⟨a *labored* speech⟩
**la·bor·er** \-bər-ər\ *noun* (14th century)
: one that labors; *specifically* : a person who does unskilled physical work for wages
**labor force** *noun* (1911)
: WORK FORCE
**la·bor–in·ten·sive** \'lā-bər-in-ˌten(t)-siv\ *adjective* (1953)
: having high labor costs per unit of output; *especially* : requiring greater expenditure on labor than in capital
**la·bo·ri·ous** \lə-'bōr-ē-əs, -'bȯr-\ *adjective* (14th century)
**1** : devoted to labor : INDUSTRIOUS
**2** : involving or characterized by hard or toilsome effort : LABORED
— **la·bo·ri·ous·ly** *adverb*
— **la·bo·ri·ous·ness** *noun*
**la·bor·ite** \'lā-bə-ˌrīt\ *noun* (1889)
**1** : a member of a group favoring the interests of labor
**2** *capitalized* **a** : a member of a political party devoted chiefly to the interests of labor **b** *usually* **La·bour·ite** : a member of the British Labour party
**la·bor-sav·ing** \'lā-bər-ˌsā-viŋ\ *adjective* (circa 1779)
: adapted to replace or decrease human and especially manual labor
**labor union** *noun* (1866)
: an organization of workers formed for the purpose of advancing its members' interests in respect to wages, benefits, and working conditions
**la·bour** *chiefly British variant of* LABOR

**lab·ra·dor·ite** \'la-brə-ˌdȯr-ˌīt\ *noun* [*Labrador* Peninsula, Canada] (1814)
: a triclinic feldspar showing a play of several colors
**Lab·ra·dor retriever** \'la-brə-ˌdȯr-\ *noun* [*Labrador*, Newfoundland] (1910)
: any of a breed of compact, strongly built retrievers largely developed in England from stock originating in Newfoundland and having a short dense black, yellow, or chocolate coat — called also *Lab, Labrador*
**Labrador tea** *noun* (1767)
: a low-growing ericaceous evergreen shrub (*Ledum groenlandicum*) chiefly of northern North America with white or creamy bell-shaped flowers and leaves sometimes used in making tea; *also* : a related Rocky Mountain shrub (*L. glandulosum*)
**la·bret** \'lā-brət\ *noun* [Latin *labrum*] (1857)
: an ornament worn in a perforation of the lip
**la·brum** \'lā-brəm\ *noun* [New Latin, from Latin, lip, edge — more at LIP] (1826)
: an upper or anterior mouthpart of an arthropod consisting of a single median piece in front of or above the mandibles
**la·bur·num** \lə-'bər-nəm\ *noun* [New Latin, from Latin] (1567)
: any of a small genus (*Laburnum* and especially *L. anagyroides*) of poisonous leguminous shrubs and trees of Eurasia with pendulous racemes of bright yellow flowers
**lab·y·rinth** \'la-bə-ˌrin(t)th, -rən(t)th\ *noun* [Middle English *laborintus*, from Latin *labyrinthus*, from Greek *labyrinthos*] (14th century)
**1 a** : a place constructed of or full of intricate passageways and blind alleys **b** : a maze (as in a garden) formed by paths separated by high hedges
**2** : something extremely complex or tortuous in structure, arrangement, or character : INTRICACY, PERPLEXITY ⟨a *labyrinth* of swamps and channels⟩ ⟨guided them through the *labyrinths* of city life —Paul Blanshard⟩
**3** : a tortuous anatomical structure; *especially* : the internal ear or its bony or membranous part
**lab·y·rin·thi·an** \ˌla-bə-'rin(t)-thē-ən\ *adjective* (1588)
: LABYRINTHINE
**lab·y·rin·thine** \-'rin(t)-thən; -'rin-ˌthīn, -ˌthēn\ *adjective* (1632)
**1** : of, relating to, or resembling a labyrinth : INTRICATE, INVOLVED
**2** : of, relating to, affecting, or originating in the internal ear ⟨*labyrinthine* lesions⟩
**lab·y·rin·tho·dont** \-'rin(t)-thə-ˌdänt\ *noun* [New Latin *Labyrinthodontia*, from Greek *labyrinthos* + *odont-, odous* tooth — more at TOOTH] (circa 1852)
: any of a superorder (Labyrinthodontia) of extinct amphibians of the Late Paleozoic and Early Mesozoic typically having bodies resembling salamanders or crocodiles and considered to be the earliest tetrapod vertebrates
— **labyrinthodont** *adjective*
**lac** \'lak\ *noun* [Persian *lak* & Hindi *lākh*, from Sanskrit *lākṣā*] (1598)
: a resinous substance secreted by a scale insect (*Laccifer lacca*) and used chiefly in the form of shellac
**lac·co·lith** \'la-kə-ˌlith\ *noun* [Greek *lakkos* pond, reservoir + English *-lith* — more at LAKE] (1879)
: a mass of igneous rock that is intruded between sedimentary beds and produces a domical bulging of the overlying strata
— **lac·co·lith·ic** \ˌla-kə-'li-thik\ *adjective*
**¹lace** \'lās\ *verb* **laced; lac·ing** [Middle English, from Old French *lacier*, from Latin *laqueare* to ensnare, from *laqueus*] (13th century)
*transitive verb*
**1** : to draw together the edges of by or as if by a lace passed through eyelets

**2** : to draw or pass (as a lace) through something (as eyelets)
**3** : to confine or compress by tightening laces of a garment
**4 a** : to adorn with or as if with lace **b** : to mark with streaks of color
**5** : BEAT, LASH
**6 a** : to add a dash of liquor to **b** : to add to something to impart pungency, savor, or zest ⟨a sauce *laced* with garlic⟩ ⟨conversation *laced* with sarcasm⟩ **c** : to adulterate with a substance ⟨*laced* a guard's coffee with a sedative⟩
*intransitive verb*
: to admit of being tied or fastened with a lace
— **lac·er** *noun*
**²lace** *noun* [Middle English, from Middle French *laz*, from Latin *laqueus* snare] (14th century)
**1** : a cord or string used for drawing together two edges (as of a garment or a shoe)
**2** : an ornamental braid for trimming coats or uniforms
**3** : an openwork usually figured fabric made of thread or yarn and used for trimmings, household coverings, and entire garments
— **laced** \'lāst\ *adjective*
— **lace·less** \'lās-ləs\ *adjective*
— **lace·like** \'lās-ˌlīk\ *adjective*
**lace–curtain** *adjective* (1934)
: copying middle-class attributes : aspiring to middle-class standing
**¹lac·er·ate** \'la-sə-ˌrāt\ *transitive verb* **-at·ed; -at·ing** [Middle English, from Latin *laceratus*, past participle of *lacerare* to tear; akin to Greek *lakis* tear] (15th century)
**1** : to tear or rend roughly
**2** : to cause sharp mental or emotional pain to : DISTRESS
— **lac·er·a·tive** \-ˌrā-tiv\ *adjective*
**²lac·er·ate** \-rət, -ˌrāt\ *or* **lac·er·at·ed** \-ˌrā-təd\ *adjective* (1542)
**1 a** : torn jaggedly : MANGLED **b** : extremely harrowed or distracted
**2** : having the edges deeply and irregularly cut ⟨a *lacerate* petal⟩
**lac·er·a·tion** \ˌla-sə-'rā-shən\ *noun* (1597)
**1** : the act of lacerating
**2** : a torn and ragged wound
**lace·wing** \'lās-ˌwiŋ\ *noun* (1854)
: any of various neuropterous insects (as genera *Chrysopa* and *Hemerobius*) having delicate lace-like wing venation, usually long antennae, and often brilliant eyes — called also *lacewing fly*

lacewing

**lace·work** \'lās-ˌwərk\ *noun* (1849)
: objects or patterns consisting of or resembling lace
**lac·ey** *variant of* LACY
**la·ches** \'la-chəz, 'lā-\ *noun, plural* **laches** [Middle English *lachesse*, from Middle French *laschesse*, from Old French *lasche* lax, ultimately from Latin *laxare* to loosen — more at LEASE] (14th century)
: negligence in the observance of duty or opportunity; *specifically* : undue delay in asserting a legal right or privilege
**lach·ry·mal** *or* **lac·ri·mal** \'la-krə-məl\ *adjective* [Middle French or Medieval Latin; Middle French *lacrymal*, from Medieval Latin *lacrimalis*, from Latin *lacrima* tear, from Old Latin *dacrima*, probably from Greek *dakry* — more at TEAR] (15th century)
**1** *usually* **lacrimal** : of, relating to, or being glands that produce tears
**2** : of, relating to, or marked by tears
**lach·ry·mose** \-ˌmōs\ *adjective* [Latin *lacrimosus*, from *lacrima*] (circa 1727)
**1** : given to tears or weeping : TEARFUL
**2** : tending to cause tears : MOURNFUL

— **lach·ry·mose·ly** *adverb*
— **lach·ry·mos·i·ty** \ˌla-krə-'mä-sə-tē\ *noun*

**lac·ing** \'lā-siŋ\ *noun* (14th century)
**1** : the action of one that laces
**2** : something that laces : LACE
**3** : a contrasting marginal band of color (as on a feather)
**4 a** : a dash of liquor in a food or beverage **b** : a trace or sprinkling that adds spice or flavor
**5** : a decisive defeat

**la·cin·i·ate** \lə-'si-nē-ət, -ˌāt\ *adjective* [Latin *lacinia* flap; akin to Latin *lacerare*] (circa 1760)
: bordered with a fringe; *especially* : cut into deep irregular usually pointed lobes 〈*laciniate* petals〉
— **la·cin·i·a·tion** \-ˌsi-nē-'ā-shən\ *noun*

**¹lack** \'lak\ (13th century)
*intransitive verb*
**1** : to be deficient or missing 〈time is *lacking* for a full explanation〉
**2** : to be short or have need of something 〈he will not *lack* for advisers〉
*transitive verb*
: to stand in need of : suffer from the absence or deficiency of 〈*lack* the necessities of life〉

**²lack** *noun* [Middle English *lak*; akin to Middle Dutch *lak* lack, Old Norse *lakr* defective] (14th century)
**1** : the fact or state of being wanting or deficient
**2** : something that is lacking or is needed

**lack·a·dai·si·cal** \ˌla-kə-'dā-zi-kəl\ *adjective* [irregular from *lackaday* + *-ical*] (1768)
: lacking life, spirit, or zest : LANGUID
— **lack·a·dai·si·cal·ly** \-k(ə-)lē\ *adverb*

**lack·a·day** \'la-kə-ˌdā\ *interjection* [by alteration & shortening from *alack the day*] (1695) *archaic* — used to express regret or deprecation

**¹lack·ey** \'la-kē\ *noun, plural* **lackeys** [Middle French *laquais*] (1523)
**1 a** : FOOTMAN 2, SERVANT **b** : someone who does menial tasks or runs errands for another
**2** : a servile follower : TOADY

**²lackey** *verb* **lack·eyed; lack·ey·ing** (1568)
*intransitive verb*
*obsolete* : to act as a lackey : TOADY
*transitive verb*
: to wait upon or serve obsequiously

**lack·lus·ter** \'lak-ˌləs-tər\ *adjective* (1600)
: lacking in sheen, brilliance, or vitality : DULL, MEDIOCRE
— **lackluster** *noun*

**la·con·ic** \lə-'kä-nik\ *adjective* [Latin *laconicus* Spartan, from Greek *lakōnikos*; from the Spartan reputation for terseness of speech] (1589)
: using or involving the use of a minimum of words : concise to the point of seeming rude or mysterious
**synonym** see CONCISE
— **la·con·i·cal·ly** \-ni-k(ə-)lē\ *adverb*

**lac·o·nism** \'la-kə-ˌni-zəm\ *noun* (1570)
**1** : brevity or terseness of expression or style
**2** : a laconic expression

**¹lac·quer** \'la-kər\ *noun* [Portuguese *lacré* sealing wax, from *laca* lac, from Arabic *lakk*, from Persian *lak* — more at LAC] (1592)
**1 a** : a spirit varnish (as shellac) **b** : any of various durable natural varnishes; *especially* : a varnish obtained from an Asian sumac (*Rhus verniciflua*) — called also *Japanese lacquer*
**2** : any of various clear or colored synthetic organic coatings that typically dry to form a film by evaporation of the solvent; *especially* : a solution of a cellulose derivative (as nitrocellulose)

**²lacquer** *transitive verb* **lac·quered; lac·quer·ing** \-k(ə-)riŋ\ (1688)
**1** : to coat with or as if with lacquer
**2** : to give a smooth finish or appearance to : make glossy

— **lac·quer·er** \-kər-ər\ *noun*

**lac·quer·ware** \-ˌwar, -ˌwer\ *noun* (1697)
: a decorative article usually made of wood and coated with lacquer; *also* : such articles or ware collectively

**lac·quer·work** \-ˌwərk\ *noun* (circa 1901)
: LACQUERWARE

**lac·ri·ma·tion** \ˌla-krə-'mā-shən\ *noun* (1572)
: the secretion of tears especially when abnormal or excessive

**lac·ri·ma·tor** *or* **lach·ry·ma·tor** \'la-krəˌmā-tər\ *noun* [Latin *lacrimare* to weep, from *lacrima* tear — more at LACHRYMAL] (1918)
: a tear-producing substance (as tear gas)

**la·crosse** \lə-'krós\ *noun* [Canadian French *la crosse*, literally, the crosier] (1718)
: a goal game in which players use a long-handled stick that has a triangular head with a mesh pouch for catching, carrying, and throwing the ball

**lact-** *or* **lacti-** *or* **lacto-** *combining form* [French & Latin; French, from Latin, from *lact-, lac* — more at GALAXY]
**1** : milk 〈*lacto*globulin〉
**2 a** : lactic acid 〈*lact*ate〉 **b** : lactose 〈*lact*ase〉

**lact·al·bu·min** \ˌlak-ˌtal-'byü-mən\ *noun* [International Scientific Vocabulary] (circa 1857)
: an albumin that is obtained from whey and is similar to serum albumin

**lac·tase** \'lak-ˌtās, -ˌtāz\ *noun* [International Scientific Vocabulary] (1891)
: an enzyme that hydrolyzes beta-galactosides (as lactose) and occurs especially in the intestines of young mammals and in yeasts

**¹lac·tate** \'lak-ˌtāt\ *noun* (circa 1794)
: a salt or ester of lactic acid

**²lactate** *intransitive verb* **lac·tat·ed; lac·tat·ing** [Latin *lactatus*, past participle of *lactare*, from *lact-, lac*] (circa 1889)
: to secrete milk
— **lac·ta·tion** \lak-'tā-shən\ *noun*
— **lac·ta·tion·al** \-shnəl, -shə-n°l\ *adjective*

**¹lac·te·al** \'lak-tē-əl\ *adjective* [Latin *lacteus* of milk, from *lact-, lac*] (circa 1658)
**1** : relating to, consisting of, producing, or resembling milk
**2 a** : conveying or containing a milky fluid **b** : of or relating to the lacteals

**²lacteal** *noun* (1680)
: any of the lymphatic vessels arising from the villi of the small intestine and conveying chyle to the thoracic duct

**lac·tic** \'lak-tik\ *adjective* (1790)
**1 a** : of or relating to milk **b** : obtained from sour milk or whey
**2** : involving the production of lactic acid

**lactic acid** *noun* (1790)
: a hygroscopic organic acid $C_3H_6O_3$ present normally in tissue, produced in carbohydrate matter usually by bacterial fermentation, and used especially in food and medicine and in industry

**lac·tif·er·ous** \lak-'ti-f(ə-)rəs\ *adjective* [French or Late Latin; French *lactifère*, from Late Latin *lactifer*, from Latin *lact-, lac* + *-fer*] (circa 1674)
**1** : yielding a milky juice 〈*lactiferous* plants〉
**2** : secreting or conveying milk

**lac·to·ba·cil·lus** \ˌlak-tō-bə-'si-ləs\ *noun* [New Latin] (1924)
: any of a genus (*Lactobacillus*) of lactic-acid-forming bacteria

**lac·to·gen·ic** \ˌlak-tə-'je-nik\ *adjective* (1933)
: inducing lactation 〈*lactogenic* hormones〉

**lac·to·glob·u·lin** \-'glä-byə-lən\ *noun* (1885)
: a crystalline protein fraction that is obtained from the whey of milk

**lac·tone** \'lak-ˌtōn\ *noun* [International Scientific Vocabulary] (1880)
: any of various cyclic esters formed from hydroxy acids
— **lac·ton·ic** \lak-'tä-nik\ *adjective*

**lac·tose** \'lak-ˌtōs, -ˌtōz\ *noun* [International Scientific Vocabulary] (1858)
: a disaccharide sugar $C_{12}H_{22}O_{11}$ that is present in milk and yields glucose and galac-

tose upon hydrolysis and yields especially lactic acid upon fermentation

**la·cu·na** \lə-'kü-nə, -'kyü-\ *noun, plural* **la·cu·nae** \-'kyü-(ˌ)nē, -'kü-ˌnī\ *or* **la·cu·nas** \-'kü-nəz, -'kyü-\ [Latin, pool, pit, gap — more at LAGOON] (1652)
**1** : a blank space or a missing part : GAP
**2** : a small cavity, pit, or discontinuity in an anatomical structure
— **la·cu·nar** \-'kü-nər, -'kyü-\ *also* **la·cu·nate** \lə-'kü-nət, -'kyü-, -ˌnät; 'la-kyə-ˌnāt\ *adjective*

**la·cus·trine** \lə-'kəs-trən\ *adjective* [French or Italian *lacustre*, from Latin *lacus* lake] (1830)
: of, relating to, formed in, living in, or growing in lakes 〈*lacustrine* deposits〉 〈*lacustrine* faunas〉

**lacy** \'lā-sē\ *adjective* **lac·i·er; -est** (1804)
: resembling or consisting of lace

**lad** \'lad\ *noun* [Middle English *ladde*] (14th century)
**1** : a male person of any age between early boyhood and maturity : BOY, YOUTH
**2** : FELLOW, CHAP

**lad·a·num** \'la-d°n-əm, 'lad-nəm\ *variant of* LABDANUM

**lad·der** \'la-dər\ *noun, often attributive* [Middle English, from Old English *hlæder*; akin to Old High German *leitara* ladder, Old English *hlinian* to lean — more at LEAN] (before 12th century)
**1** : a structure for climbing up or down that consists essentially of two long sidepieces joined at intervals by crosspieces on which one may step
**2** : something that resembles or suggests a ladder in form or use; *especially* : RUN 11a
**3** : a series of usually ascending steps or stages : SCALE 〈climbing up the corporate *ladder*〉
— **lad·der·like** \-ˌlīk\ *adjective*

**lad·der–back** \-ˌbak\ *adjective* (1908)
*of furniture* : having a back consisting of two upright posts connected by horizontal slats

**ladder truck** *noun* (1889)
: HOOK AND LADDER TRUCK

**lad·die** \'la-dē\ *noun* (1546)
: a young lad

**lade** \'lād\ *verb* **lad·ed; lad·ed** *or* **lad·en** \'lā-d°n\; **lad·ing** [Middle English, from Old English *hladan*; akin to Old High German *hladan* to load, Old Church Slavonic *klasti* to place] (before 12th century)
*transitive verb*
**1 a** : to put a load or burden on or in : LOAD **b** : to put or place as a load especially for shipment : SHIP **c** : to load heavily or oppressively
**2** : DIP, LADLE
*intransitive verb*
**1** : to take on cargo : LOAD
**2** : to take up or convey a liquid by dipping

**¹lad·en** \'lā-d°n\ *transitive verb* **lad·ened; lad·en·ing** \'lād-niŋ, 'lā-d°n-iŋ\ (1514)
: LADE

**²laden** *adjective* (before 12th century)
: carrying a load or burden

**la·di·da** \ˌlä-dē-'dä\ *also* **la·de·da** *adjective* [perhaps alteration of *lardy-dardy* foppish] (1895)
: affectedly refined in manners or tastes : PRETENTIOUS, ELEGANT

**la·dies** \'lā-dēz\ *noun plural but singular or plural in construction*
*chiefly British* : LADIES' ROOM

**ladies' man** *also* **lady's man** *noun* (1784)
: a man who shows a marked fondness for the company of women or is especially attentive to women

**ladies' room** *noun* (1870)
: a room equipped with lavatories and toilets for the use of women

**ladies' tresses** *noun plural but singular or plural in construction* (1548)
: any of a widely distributed genus (*Spiranthes*) of terrestrial orchids with slender often twisted spikes of white irregular flowers

**La·din** \lə-'dēn\ *noun* [Rhaeto-Romance, from Latin *Latinum* Latin] (1877)
**1 a :** a Rhaeto-Romance dialect of Alto Adige in northern Italy **b :** the Rhaeto-Romance dialects of the Engadine Valley in Switzerland
**2 :** one speaking Ladin as a mother tongue

**lad·ing** \'lā-diŋ\ *noun* (1500)
**1 a :** LOADING 1 **b :** an act of bailing, dipping, or ladling
**2 :** CARGO, FREIGHT

**la·di·no** \lə-'dē-(ˌ)nō\ *noun, plural* **-nos** [Spanish, literally, Latin, from Latin *latinus*] (1877)
**1** *often capitalized* [American Spanish] **:** a westernized Spanish-speaking Latin American; *especially* **:** MESTIZO
**2** *capitalized* [Judeo-Spanish, from Old Spanish] **:** JUDEO-SPANISH

**la·di·no clover** \lə-'dī-(ˌ)nō-, -nə-\ *noun* [perhaps irregular from *Lodi*, Italy + Italian *-ino*, adjective suffix] (1924)
: a large nutritious rapidly growing clover that is a variety of white clover and is widely planted especially for forage — called also *ladino*

**¹la·dle** \'lā-dᵊl\ *noun* [Middle English *ladel*, from Old English *hlædel*, from *hladan*] (before 12th century)
**1 :** a deep-bowled long-handled spoon used especially for dipping up and conveying liquids
**2 :** something resembling a ladle in form or function

**²ladle** *transitive verb* **la·dled; la·dling** \'lād-liŋ, 'lā-dᵊl-iŋ\ (1525)
: to take up and convey in or as if in a ladle

**la dol·ce vi·ta** \(ˌ)lä-ˌdōl-(ˌ)chä-'vē-(ˌ)tä\ *variant of* DOLCE VITA

**la·dy** \'lā-dē\ *noun, plural* **ladies** *often attributive* [Middle English, from Old English *hlæfdige*, from *hlāf* bread + *-dige* (akin to *dæge* kneader of bread) — more at LOAF, DAIRY] (before 12th century)
**1 a :** a woman having proprietary rights or authority especially as a feudal superior **b :** a woman receiving the homage or devotion of a knight or lover
**2** *capitalized* **:** VIRGIN MARY — usually used with *Our*
**3 a :** a woman of superior social position **b :** a woman of refinement and gentle manners **c :** WOMAN, FEMALE — often used in a courteous reference ⟨show the *lady* to a seat⟩ or usually in the plural in address ⟨*ladies* and gentlemen⟩
**4 a :** WIFE **b :** GIRLFRIEND, MISTRESS
**5 a :** any of various titled women in Great Britain — used as the customary title of (1) a marchioness, countess, viscountess, or baroness or (2) the wife of a knight, baronet, member of the peerage, or one having the courtesy title of *lord* and used as a courtesy title for the daughter of a duke, marquess, or earl **b :** a female member of an order of knighthood — compare DAME ◆

**la·dy·bug** \'lā-dē-ˌbəg\ *noun* [Our *Lady*, the Virgin Mary] (1699)
: any of numerous small nearly hemispherical often brightly colored beetles (family Coccinellidae) of temperate and tropical regions that usually feed both as larvae and adults on other insects — called also *lady beetle, ladybird, ladybird beetle*

ladybug

**lady chapel** *noun, often L&C capitalized* (15th century)
: a chapel dedicated to the Virgin Mary

**Lady Day** *noun* (13th century)
: ANNUNCIATION 1

**la·dy·fin·ger** \'lā-dē-ˌfiŋ-gər\ *noun* (1820)
: a small finger-shaped sponge cake

**la·dy·fish** \-ˌfish\ *noun* (1712)
**1 :** BONEFISH 1
**2 :** a large silvery food and sport fish (*Elops saurus*) that resembles a herring but is related to the tarpon

**la·dy–in–wait·ing** \'lā-dē-in-'wā-tiŋ\ *noun, plural* **ladies–in–waiting** (1862)
: a lady of a queen's or a princess's household appointed to wait on her

**la·dy–kill·er** \'lā-dē-ˌki-lər\ *noun* (circa 1810)
: a man who is extremely attractive to women

**la·dy·kin** \'lā-dē-kən\ *noun* (1853)
: a little lady

**la·dy·like** \-ˌlīk\ *adjective* (1586)
**1 :** becoming or suitable to a lady
**2 :** resembling a lady in appearance or manners **:** WELL-BRED
**3 a :** feeling or showing too much concern about elegance or propriety ⟨*ladylike* embarrassment at not being the wife of a real doctor —Lewis Vogler⟩ **b :** lacking in strength, force, or virility

**la·dy·love** \'lā-dē-ˌləv, ˌlā-dē-'\ *noun* (1733)
: SWEETHEART, MISTRESS

**lady of the house** (1816)
: the chief female in a household

**Lady of the Lake** (15th century)
: VIVIAN

**la·dy·ship** \'lā-dē-ˌship\ *noun* (13th century)
: the condition of being a lady **:** rank of lady — used as a title for a woman having the rank of lady ⟨her *Ladyship* is not at home⟩ ⟨if your *Ladyship* please⟩

**lady's slipper** *noun* (1597)
: any of several North American temperate-zone orchids (as of the genus *Cypripedium*) having flowers whose shape suggests a slipper — called also *lady slipper*

**la·dy's–smock** \-ˌsmäk\ *noun* (1588)
: CUCKOOFLOWER 1

**lady's thumb** *noun* (1837)
: a widely distributed weedy annual herb (*Polygonum persicaria*) that has large lanceolate leaves often with a blackish blotch suggesting a thumbprint

**La·er·tes** \lā-'ər-tēz\ *noun* [Latin, from Greek *Laertēs*]
**1 :** the father of Odysseus in Greek mythology
**2 :** the son of Polonius and brother of Ophelia in Shakespeare's *Hamlet*

lady's slipper

**Lae·ta·re Sunday** \lā-'tär-ē-, -'tar-\ *noun* [Latin *laetare*, singular imperative of *laetari* to rejoice] (circa 1870)
: the fourth Sunday in Lent

**la·e·trile** \'lā-ə-(ˌ)tril, -trəl\ *noun, often capitalized* [*lae*vorotary (levorotary) + ni*trile*] (1953)
: a drug derived especially from apricot pits that contains amygdalin and has been used in the treatment of cancer although of unproved effectiveness

**¹lag** \'lag\ *noun* [probably of Scandinavian origin; akin to Norwegian dialect *lagga* to go slowly] (1514)
**1 :** one that lags or is last
**2 a :** the act or the condition of lagging **b :** comparative slowness or retardation **c** (1) **:** an amount of lagging or the time during which lagging continues (2) **:** a space of time especially between related events or phenomena **:** INTERVAL
**3 :** the action of lagging for opening shot (as in marbles or billiards)

**²lag** *verb* **lagged; lag·ging** (1530)
*intransitive verb*

**1 a :** to stay or fall behind **:** LINGER, LOITER **b :** to move, function, or develop with comparative slowness **c :** to become retarded in attaining maximum value
**2 :** to slacken or weaken gradually **:** FLAG
**3 :** to toss or roll a marble toward a line or a cue ball toward the head cushion to determine order of play
*transitive verb*
**1 :** to lag behind ⟨current that *lags* the voltage⟩
**2 :** to pitch or shoot (as a coin or marble) at a mark
**synonym** see DELAY
— **lag·ger** *noun*

**³lag** *adjective* (1552)
: LAST, HINDMOST

**⁴lag** *noun* [probably of Scandinavian origin; akin to Old Norse *lǫgg* rim of a barrel] (1672)
**1 :** a barrel stave
**2 :** a stave, slat, or strip (as of wood or asbestos) forming part of a covering for a cylindrical object

**⁵lag** *transitive verb* **lagged; lag·ging** (1870)
: to cover or provide with lags

**⁶lag** *transitive verb* **lagged; lag·ging** [origin unknown] (circa 1812)
**1** *slang chiefly British* **:** to transport or jail for crime
**2** *slang chiefly British* **:** ARREST

**⁷lag** *noun* (circa 1812)
**1** *slang chiefly British* **a :** a person transported for crime **b :** CONVICT **c :** an ex-convict
**2** *slang chiefly British* **:** a jail sentence **:** STRETCH

**lag·an** \'la-gən\ *also* **lag·end** \-gənd\ *noun* [Middle French *lagan* or Medieval Latin *laganum*) debris washed up from the sea] (1641)
: goods thrown into the sea with a buoy attached so that they may be found again

**Lag b'Omer** \'läg-'bō-mər, ˌläg-bə-'ō-\ *noun* [Hebrew, 33d in Omer] (circa 1904)
: a Jewish holiday falling on the 33d day of the Omer and commemorating the heroism of Bar Kokhba and Akiba ben Joseph

**la·ger** \'lä-gər\ *noun* [German *Lagerbier* beer made for storage, from *Lager* storehouse + *Bier* beer] (circa 1853)
: a light beer brewed by slow fermentation and matured under refrigeration

**¹lag·gard** \'la-gərd\ *adjective* (1702)
: lagging or tending to lag **:** DILATORY
— **lag·gard·ly** *adverb or adjective*
— **lag·gard·ness** *noun*

◇ WORD HISTORY
**lady** *Hlǣfdige*, the Old English ancestor of the word *lady*, contains as an initial element *hlāf* "bread, loaf," as does *hlāford*, the ancestor of *lord*. The second element of the compound, *-dige*, is akin to *dæge* "(female) bread maker," ultimately a derivative of *dāg* "dough"; the word *dæge* developed in Middle English into *deye* "dairymaid" (dairy and bread-making duties apparently overlapping), which survives in Modern English packed inside the word *dairy*. We might have expected a *hlæfdige* in Anglo-Saxon times to have been domestic help, but by a semantic shift that has never been adequately explained, this personage was not a servant but rather the female head of a medieval household and the counterpart of a lord. Although more exalted uses of *lady*, into which *hlæfdige* had developed by later Middle English, survive in traditional collocations such as *lady of the house* and *Our Lady* (the Virgin Mary), in Modern English the word has broadened in sense to "woman of superior social position" and "woman of refinement and gentle manners," becoming the counterpart of *gentleman* rather than *lord*. See in addition LORD.

**²laggard** *noun* (1808)
: one that lags or lingers

**lag·ging** \'la-giŋ\ *noun* (1794)
: a lag or material used for making lags: as **a**
: material for thermal insulation especially around a cylindrical object **b** : planking used especially for preventing cave-ins in earthwork or for supporting an arch during construction

**la·gniappe** \'lan-ˌyap, lan-'\ *noun* [American French, from American Spanish *la ñapa* the lagniappe] (1849)
: a small gift given a customer by a merchant at the time of a purchase; *broadly* : something given or obtained gratuitously or by way of good measure

**lago·morph** \'la-gə-ˌmórf\ *noun* [ultimately from Greek *lagōs* hare + *morphē* form] (1882)
: any of an order (Lagomorpha) of gnawing herbivorous mammals having two pairs of incisors in the upper jaw one behind the other and comprising the rabbits, hares, and pikas

**la·goon** \lə-'gün\ *noun* [French & Italian; French *lagune*, from Italian *laguna*, from Latin *lacuna* pit, pool, from *lacus* lake] (1673)
**1** : a shallow sound, channel, or pond near or communicating with a larger body of water
**2** : a shallow artificial pool or pond (as for the processing of sewage or storage of a liquid)
— **la·goon·al** \-'gü-nᵊl\ *adjective*

**La·grang·ian** \lə-'grän-jē-ən, -'grän-zhē-\ *noun* [Joseph-Louis *Lagrange*] (1938)
: a function that describes the state of a dynamic system in terms of position coordinates and their time derivatives and that is equal to the difference between the potential energy and kinetic energy — compare HAMILTONIAN

**la·har** \'lä-ˌhär\ *noun* [Javanese] (1929)
: a mudflow composed of volcanic debris and water

**lah–de–dah, lah–dee–dah, lah–di–dah**
*variant of* LA-DI-DA

**Lahn·da** \'län-də\ *noun* (1901)
: an Indo-Aryan language of eastern Pakistan

**la·ical** \'lā-ə-kəl\ *or* **la·ic** \'lā-ik\ *adjective* [Late Latin *laicus*, from Late Greek *laïkos*, from Greek, of the people, from *laos* people] (circa 1587)
: of or relating to the laity : SECULAR
— **laic** *noun*
— **la·ical·ly** \'lā-ə-k(ə-)lē\ *adverb*

**la·i·cism** \'lā-ə-ˌsi-zəm\ *noun* (circa 1909)
: a political system characterized by the exclusion of ecclesiastical control and influence

**la·i·cize** \'lā-ə-ˌsīz\ *transitive verb* **la·i·cized; la·i·ciz·ing** (1870)
**1** : to reduce to lay status
**2** : to put under the direction of or open to the laity
— **la·i·ci·za·tion** \ˌlā-ə-sə-'zā-shən\ *noun*

**laid** *past and past participle of* LAY

**laid–back** \'lād-'bak, ˌlād-\ *adjective* (1969)
: having a relaxed style or character ⟨*laid-back* music⟩
— **laid–back·ness** \-nəs\ *noun*

**laid paper** \'lād-\ *noun* (1839)
: paper watermarked with fine lines running across the grain — compare WOVE PAPER

**laigh** \'lāk\ *Scottish variant of* LOW

**lain** *past participle of* LIE

**¹lair** \'lar, 'ler\ *noun* [Middle English, from Old English *leger*; akin to Old High German *legar* bed, Old English *licgan* to lie — more at LIE] (before 12th century)
**1** *dialect British* : a resting or sleeping place : BED
**2 a** : the resting or living place of a wild animal : DEN **b** : a refuge or place for hiding

**²lair** *verb* [Scots *lair* mire] (circa 1560)
*transitive verb*
*chiefly Scottish* : to cause to sink in mire
*intransitive verb*
*chiefly Scottish* : WALLOW

**laird** \'lard, 'lerd\ *noun* [Middle English (northern dialect) *lord, lard* lord] (14th century)
*chiefly Scottish* : a landed proprietor
— **laird·ly** \-lē\ *adjective*

**lais·ser–faire** *chiefly British variant of* LAISSEZ-FAIRE

**lais·ser–pas·ser** *chiefly British variant of* LAISSEZ-PASSER

**lais·sez–faire** \ˌle-ˌsā-'far, ˌlā-, -ˌzā-, -'fer\ *noun* [French *laissez faire*, imperative of *laisser faire* to let (people) do (as they choose)] (1825)
**1** : a doctrine opposing governmental interference in economic affairs beyond the minimum necessary for the maintenance of peace and property rights
**2** : a philosophy or practice characterized by a usually deliberate abstention from direction or interference especially with individual freedom of choice and action
— **laissez–faire** *adjective*

**lais·sez–pas·ser** \-ˌpa-'sā\ *noun* [French, from *laissez passer* let (someone) pass] (1914)
: PERMIT, PASS

**lai·tance** \'lā-tᵊn(t)s\ *noun* [French, from *lait* milk, from Latin *lact-, lac* — more at GALAXY] (circa 1902)
: an accumulation of fine particles on the surface of fresh concrete due to an upward movement of water (as when excessive mixing water is used)

**la·ity** \'lā-ə-tē\ *noun* [⁵*lay*] (15th century)
**1** : the people of a religious faith as distinguished from its clergy
**2** : the mass of the people as distinguished from those of a particular profession or those specially skilled

**La·ius** \'lā-əs, 'lī-əs\ *noun* [Latin, from Greek *Laïos*]
: a king of Thebes slain by his son Oedipus in fulfillment of an oracle

**¹lake** \'lāk\ *noun, often attributive* [Middle English, from Old French *lac* lake, from Latin *lacus*; akin to Old English *lagu* sea, Greek *lakkos* pond] (12th century)
: a considerable inland body of standing water; *also* : a pool of other liquid (as lava, oil, or pitch)
— **lake·like** \-ˌlīk\ *adjective*

**²lake** *noun* [French *laque* lac, from Old Provençal *laca*, from Arabic *lakk* — more at LACQUER] (1598)
**1 a** : a purplish red pigment prepared from lac or cochineal **b** : any of numerous usually bright translucent organic pigments composed essentially of a soluble dye absorbed on or combined with an inorganic carrier
**2** : CARMINE 2
— **laky** \'lā-kē\ *adjective*

**³lake** *verb* **laked; lak·ing** (1903)
*transitive verb*
: to cause (blood) to undergo a physiological change in which the hemoglobin becomes dissolved in the plasma
*intransitive verb*
*of blood* : to undergo the process by which hemoglobin becomes dissolved in the plasma

**lake dwelling** *noun* (1863)
: a dwelling built on piles in a lake; *specifically* : one built in prehistoric times
— **lake dweller** *noun*

**lake·front** \'lāk-ˌfrənt\ *noun* (1880)
: an area fronting on a lake

**lake herring** *noun* (1842)
: a cisco (*Coregonus artedii*) found from Lake Memphremagog to Lake Superior and northward and important as a commercial food fish

**Lake·land terrier** \'lāk-lənd-, -ˌland-\ *noun* [*Lakeland*, England] (1928)
: any of an English breed of rather small harsh-coated terriers

**lak·er** \'lā-kər\ *noun* (1823)
: one associated with a lake; *especially* : a fish living in or taken from a lake

**lake·shore** \'lāk-ˌshōr, -ˌshór\ *noun* (1798)
: the shore of a lake; *also* : LAKEFRONT

**lake·side** \-ˌsīd\ *noun* (1560)
: LAKEFRONT

**lake trout** *noun* (1668)
: any of various trout and salmon found in lakes; *especially* : MACKINAW TROUT

**lakh** \'läk, 'lak\ *noun* [Hindi *lākh*] (1599)
**1** : one hundred thousand ⟨50 *lakhs* of rupees⟩
**2** : a great number
— **lakh** *adjective*

**La·ko·ta** \lə-'kō-tə\ *noun, plural* **Lakota** *also* **Lakotas** (1927)
**1** : a member of a western division of the Dakota peoples
**2** : a dialect of Dakota

**-lalia** *noun combining form* [New Latin, from Greek *lalia* chatter, from *lalein* to chat]
: speech disorder (of a specified type) ⟨echo*lalia*⟩

**lal·lan** \'la-lən\ *or* **lal·land** \-lən(d)\ *Scottish variant of* LOWLAND

**Lal·lans** \'la-lənz\ *noun* (1785)
: Scots as spoken and written in the lowlands of Scotland

**Lal·ly** \'la-lē\ *trademark*
— used for a concrete-filled cylindrical steel structural column

**lal·ly·gag** *variant of* LOLLYGAG

**¹lam** \'lam\ *verb* **lammed; lam·ming** [of Scandinavian origin; akin to Old Norse *lemja* to thrash; akin to Old English *lama* lame] (1595)
*transitive verb*
: to beat soundly : THRASH
*intransitive verb*
**1** : STRIKE, THRASH
**2** : to flee hastily : SCRAM

**²lam** *noun* (1897)
: sudden or hurried flight especially from the law ⟨on the *lam*⟩

**la·ma** \'lä-mə\ *noun* [Tibetan *blama*] (1654)
: a Lamaist monk

**La·ma·ism** \'lä-mə-ˌi-zəm\ *noun* (1817)
: the Mahayana Buddhism of Tibet and Mongolia marked by tantric and shamanistic ritual and a dominant monastic hierarchy headed by the Dalai Lama
— **La·ma·ist** \-mə-ist\ *noun or adjective*
— **La·ma·is·tic** \ˌlä-mə-'is-tik\ *adjective*

**La·marck·ism** \lə-'märk-ˌki-zəm\ *noun* [J.-B. de Monet de *Lamarck*] (1884)
: a theory of organic evolution asserting that environmental changes cause structural changes in animals and plants that are transmitted to offspring
— **La·marck·ian** \-kē-ən\ *adjective*

**la·ma·sery** \'lä-mə-ˌser-ē\ *noun, plural* **-ser·ies** [French *lamaserie*, from *lama* + Persian *sarāī* palace] (1849)
: a monastery of lamas

**La·maze** \lə-'mäz\ *adjective* [Fernand *Lamaze* (died 1957) French obstetrician] (1965)
: relating to or being a method of childbirth that involves psychological and physical preparation by the mother in order to suppress pain and facilitate delivery without drugs

**¹lamb** \'lam\ *noun* [Middle English, from Old English; akin to Old High German *lamb* lamb] (before 12th century)
**1 a** : a young sheep; *especially* : one that is less than one year old or without permanent teeth **b** : the young of various animals (as the smaller antelopes) other than sheep
**2 a** : a gentle or weak person **b** : DEAR, PET **c** : a person easily cheated or deceived especially in trading securities

---

\ə\ abut \ᵊ\ kitten \ər\ further \a\ ash \ā\ ace
\ä\ mop, mar \au̇\ out \ch\ chin \e\ bet \ē\ easy
\g\ go \i\ hit \ī\ ice \j\ job \ŋ\ sing \ō\ go
\ȯ\ law \ȯi\ boy \th\ thin \t̲h̲\ the \ü\ loot \u̇\ foot
\y\ yet \zh\ vision    *see also* Guide to Pronunciation

**3 a :** the flesh of a lamb used as food **b :** LAMBSKIN

— **lamb·like** \-ˌlīk\ *adjective*

— **lamby** \'la-mē\ *adjective*

²**lamb** (1611) *intransitive verb* **:** to bring forth a lamb

*transitive verb*

**1 :** to bring forth (a lamb)

**2 :** to tend (ewes) at lambing time

— **lamb·er** \'la-mər\ *noun*

**lam·baste** *or* **lam·bast** \(ˌ)lam-'bāst, -'bast; 'lam-ˌ\ *transitive verb* [probably from ¹*lam* + *baste*] (1637)

**1 :** to assault violently **:** BEAT, WHIP

**2 :** to attack verbally **:** CENSURE

**lamb·da** \'lam-də\ *noun* [Middle English, from Greek, of Semitic origin; akin to Hebrew *lāmedh* lamed] (15th century)

**1 :** the 11th letter of the Greek alphabet — see ALPHABET table

**2 :** an uncharged unstable elementary particle that has a mass 2183 times that of an electron and that decays typically into a nucleon and a pion

**lam·ben·cy** \'lam-bən(t)-sē\ *noun, plural* **-cies** (1817)

**:** the quality, state, or an instance of being lambent

**lam·bent** \'lam-bənt\ *adjective* [Latin *lambent-, lambens*, present participle of *lambere* to lick — more at LAP] (1647)

**1 :** playing lightly on or over a surface **:** FLICKERING

**2 :** softly bright or radiant

**3 :** marked by lightness or brilliance especially of expression

— **lam·bent·ly** *adverb*

**lam·bert** \'lam-bərt\ *noun* [Johann H. *Lambert* (died 1777) German physicist & philosopher] (1915)

**:** the centimeter-gram-second unit of brightness equal to the brightness of a perfectly diffusing surface that radiates or reflects one lumen per square centimeter

**lamb·kill** \'lam-ˌkil\ *noun* (1790)

**:** SHEEP LAUREL

**lam·bre·quin** \'lam-bər-kən, -bri-kən\ *noun* [French] (circa 1725)

**1 :** a scarf used to cover a knight's helmet

**2 :** a short decorative drapery for a shelf edge or for the top of a window casing **:** VALANCE

**Lam·brus·co** \lam-'brü-(ˌ)skō, -'brù-\ *noun* [Italian, from Latin *labruscum* fruit of the wild grape *Vitis labrusca*] (1943)

**:** a fruity and fizzy red Italian table wine

**lamb's ears** *noun plural but usually singular in construction* (1930)

**:** a widely cultivated perennial herb (*Stachys byzantina* synonym *S. olympica*) of the mint family that occurs in southwestern Asia and has leaves covered with densely matted hairs

**lamb·skin** \'lam-ˌskin\ *noun* (14th century)

**:** a lamb's skin or a small fine-grade sheepskin or the leather made from either; *specifically* **:** such a skin dressed with the wool on and used especially for winter clothing

**lamb's lettuce** *noun* (1597)

**:** CORN SALAD

**lamb's–quar·ter** \'lamz-ˌkwȯ(r)-tər, -ˌkȯ(r)-\ *noun* (1773)

lamb 3a: *A* wholesale cuts: *1* leg, *2* loin, *3* rack, *4* breast, *5* shank, *6* shoulder; *B* retail cuts: *a* leg, *b* sirloin chops and roast, *c* loin chops, rolled loin roast, *d* patties and chopped roast, *e* rib chops, crown roast, *f* riblets, stew, and stuffed or rolled breast, *g* shoulder roast, shoulder chops, *h* neck slices, *i* shanks, *j* blade chops, *k* arm chops

**1 :** a goosefoot (*Chenopodium album*) having glaucous foliage that is sometimes used as greens — usually used in plural but singular or plural in construction

**2 :** any of several oraches — usually used in plural but singular or plural in construction

¹**lame** \'lām\ *adjective* **lam·er; lam·est** [Middle English, from Old English *lama;* akin to Old High German *lam* lame, Lithuanian *limti* to break down] (before 12th century)

**1 a :** having a body part and especially a limb so disabled as to impair freedom of movement **b :** marked by stiffness and soreness ⟨a *lame* shoulder⟩

**2 :** lacking needful or desirable substance **:** WEAK, INEFFECTUAL ⟨a *lame* excuse⟩

**3** *slang* **:** not being in the know **:** SQUARE

— **lame·ly** *adverb*

— **lame·ness** *noun*

²**lame** *transitive verb* **lamed; lam·ing** (14th century)

**1 :** to make lame **:** CRIPPLE

**2 :** to make weak or ineffective **:** DISABLE

³**lame** *noun* (1959)

*slang* **:** a person who is not in the know **:** SQUARE

⁴**lame** \'lām, 'lam\ *noun* [Middle French, from Latin *lamina*] (1586)

**1 :** a thin plate especially of metal **:** LAMINA

**2** *plural* **:** small overlapping steel plates joined to slide on one another (as in medieval armor)

**la·mé** \lä-'mā, la-\ *noun* [French] (1922)

**:** a brocaded clothing fabric made from any of various fibers combined with tinsel filling threads

**lame·brain** \'lām-ˌbrān\ *noun* (1944)

**:** a dull-witted person **:** DOLT

— **lamebrain** *or* **lame·brained** \-'brānd\ *adjective*

**la·med** \'lä-ˌmed\ *noun* [Hebrew *lāmedh*, literally, ox goad] (1665)

**:** the 12th letter of the Hebrew alphabet — see ALPHABET table

**lame duck** *noun* (1761)

**1 :** one that is weak or that falls behind in ability or achievement; *especially, chiefly British* **:** an ailing company

**2 :** an elected official or group continuing to hold office during the period between the election and the inauguration of a successor

**3 :** one whose position or term of office will soon end

— **lame–duck** \'lām-ˌdək\ *adjective*

**lamell-** *or* **lamelli-** *combining form* [New Latin, from *lamella*]

**:** lamella ⟨*lamelliform*⟩

**la·mel·la** \lə-'me-lə\ *noun, plural* **la·mel·lae** \-'me-(ˌ)lē, -ˌlī\ *also* **lamellas** [New Latin, from Latin, diminutive of *lamina* thin plate] (1678)

**:** a thin flat scale, membrane, or layer: as **a :** one of the thin plates composing the gills of a bivalve mollusk **b :** a gill of a mushroom

**la·mel·lar** \lə-'me-lər\ *adjective* (1794)

**1 :** composed of or arranged in lamellae

**2 :** LAMELLIFORM

**la·mel·late** \lə-'me-lət, 'la-mə-ˌlāt\ *adjective* (1826)

**1 :** composed of or furnished with lamellae

**2 :** LAMELLIFORM

— **la·mel·late·ly** *adverb*

**la·mel·li·branch** \lə-'me-lə-ˌbraŋk\ *noun, plural* **-branchs** [New Latin *Lamellibranchia*, from *lamell-* + Latin *branchia* gill] (1855)

**:** any of a class (Lamellibranchia) of bivalve mollusks (as clams, oysters, and mussels) that have the body bilaterally symmetrical, compressed, and enclosed within the mantle and that build up a shell whose right and left parts are connected by a hinge over the animal's back

— **lamellibranch** *adjective*

**la·mel·li·corn** \lə-'me-lə-ˌkȯrn\ *adjective* [ultimately from New Latin *lamella* + Latin *cornu* horn — more at HORN] (circa 1842)

**:** of, relating to, or belonging to a superfamily (Scarabaeoidea synonym Lamellicornia) of beetles (as a scarab or stag beetle) characterized by 5-jointed tarsi and club-tipped antennae often angled like an elbow

— **lamellicorn** *noun*

**la·mel·li·form** \-ˌfȯrm\ *adjective* (1819)

**:** having the form of a thin plate

¹**la·ment** \lə-'ment\ *verb* [Middle English *lementen*, from Middle French & Latin; Middle French *lamenter*, from Latin *lamentari*, from *lamentum*, noun, lament] (15th century)

*intransitive verb*

**:** to mourn aloud **:** WAIL

*transitive verb*

**1 :** to express sorrow, mourning, or regret for often demonstratively **:** MOURN

**2 :** to regret strongly

*synonym* see DEPLORE

²**lament** *noun* (1591)

**1 :** a crying out in grief **:** WAILING

**2 :** DIRGE, ELEGY

**3 :** COMPLAINT

**la·men·ta·ble** \'la-mən-tə-bəl, ÷lə-'men-\ *adjective* (15th century)

**1 :** that is to be regretted or lamented **:** DEPLORABLE

**2 :** expressing grief **:** MOURNFUL

— **la·men·ta·ble·ness** *noun*

— **la·men·ta·bly** \-blē\ *adverb*

**lam·en·ta·tion** \ˌla-mən-'tā-shən\ *noun* (14th century)

**:** an act or instance of lamenting

**Lam·en·ta·tions** \-shənz\ *noun plural but singular in construction*

**:** a poetic book on the fall of Jerusalem in canonical Jewish and Christian Scripture — see BIBLE table

**la·ment·ed** \lə-'men-təd\ *adjective* (1611)

**:** mourned for

— **la·ment·ed·ly** *adverb*

**la·mia** \'lā-mē-ə\ *noun* [Middle English, from Latin, from Greek, devouring monster; akin to Greek *lamyros* gluttonous] (14th century)

**:** a female demon **:** VAMPIRE

**lamin-** *combining form*

**:** lamina ⟨*laminar*⟩

**lam·i·na** \'la-mə-nə\ *noun, plural* **-nae** \-ˌnē, -ˌnī\ *or* **-nas** [Latin] (circa 1656)

**1 :** a thin plate or scale **:** LAYER

**2 :** the expanded part of a foliage leaf

**3 :** one of the narrow thin parallel plates of soft vascular sensitive tissue that cover the flesh within the wall of a hoof

**lam·i·nal** \'la-mə-nᵊl\ *adjective* (1825)

**1 :** LAMINAR

**2 :** produced with the blade of the tongue (as \sh\, \zh\, \ch\, \j\, or \y\) — compare APICAL

**lamina pro·pria** \-'prō-prē-ə\ *noun, plural* **laminae pro·pri·ae** \-prē-ˌē, -ˌī\ [New Latin, literally, proper lamina] (1937)

**:** a highly vascular layer of connective tissue under the basement membrane lining a layer of epithelium

**lam·i·nar** \'la-mə-nər\ *adjective* (1811)

**:** arranged in, consisting of, or resembling laminae

**laminar flow** *noun* (1935)

**:** streamline flow in a fluid near a solid boundary — compare TURBULENT FLOW

**lam·i·nar·ia** \ˌla-mə-'ner-ē-ə, -'nar-\ *noun* [New Latin, from Latin *lamina*] (1848)

**:** any of a genus (*Laminaria*) of large chiefly perennial kelps with an unbranched cylindrical or flattened stipe and a smooth or convoluted blade; *broadly* **:** any of various related kelps (order Laminariales)

— **lam·i·nar·i·an** \-ē-ən\ *adjective or noun*

**lam·i·nar·in** \ˌlam-ə-'ner-ən, -'nar-\ *noun* [International Scientific Vocabulary *laminar-* (from New Latin *Laminaria*) + ¹-*in*] (circa 1931)

**:** a polysaccharide found in various brown algae that yields only glucose on hydrolysis

¹**lam·i·nate** \'la-mə-ˌnāt\ *verb* **-nat·ed; -nat·ing** (1665)

*transitive verb*
**1** : to roll or compress into a thin plate
**2** : to separate into laminae
**3 a** : to make (as a windshield) by uniting superposed layers of one or more materials **b** : to unite (layers of material) by an adhesive or other means
*intransitive verb*
: to divide into laminae
— **lam·i·na·tor** \-nā-tər\ *noun*
²**lam·i·nate** \-nət, -ˌnāt\ *adjective* (1668)
**1** : consisting of laminae
**2** : bearing or covered with laminae
³**lam·i·nate** \-nət, -ˌnāt\ *noun* (1939)
: a product made by laminating
**lam·i·nat·ed** \-ˌnā-təd\ *adjective* (1665)
**1** : LAMINATE 1
**2 a** : composed of layers of firmly united material **b** : made by bonding or impregnating superposed layers (as of paper, wood, or fabric) with resin and compressing under heat
**lam·i·na·tion** \ˌla-mə-ˈnā-shən\ *noun* (circa 1676)
**1** : the process of laminating
**2** : the state of being laminated
**3** : a laminated structure
**4** : LAMINA
**lam·i·ni·tis** \ˌla-mə-ˈnī-təs\ *noun* [New Latin] (1843)
: inflammation of the laminae especially in the hoof of a horse — called also *founder*
**Lam·mas** \ˈla-məs\ *noun* [Middle English *Lammasse*, from Old English *hlāfmæsse*, from *hlāf* loaf, bread + *mæsse* mass; from the fact that formerly loaves from the first ripe grain were consecrated on this day] (before 12th century)
**1** : August 1 originally celebrated in England as a harvest festival — called also *Lammas Day*
**2** : the time of the year around Lammas Day
**Lam·mas·tide** \-ˌtīd\ *noun* (14th century)
: LAMMAS 2
**lam·mer·gei·er** *or* **lam·mer·gey·er** \ˈla-mər-ˌgī-(ə)r\ *noun* [German *Lämmergeier*, from *Lämmer* lambs + *Geier* vulture] (1817)
: a large Old World vulture (*Gypaetus barbatus*) that occurs in mountain regions and in flight resembles a huge falcon
**lamp** \ˈlamp\ *noun* [Middle English, from Old French *lampe*, from Latin *lampas*, from Greek, from *lampein* to shine; akin to Hittite *lap-* to burn] (13th century)
**1 a** : any of various devices for producing light or sometimes heat: as (1) : a vessel with a wick for burning an inflammable liquid (as oil) to produce light (2) : a glass bulb or tube that emits light produced by electricity (as an incandescent lamp or fluorescent lamp) **b** : a decorative appliance housing a lamp that is usually covered by a shade
**2** : a celestial body
**3** : a source of intellectual or spiritual illumination
**4** : EYE 1a — usually used in plural
**lamp·black** \-ˌblak\ *noun* (1598)
: a finely powdered black soot deposited in incomplete combustion of carbonaceous materials and used chiefly as a pigment (as in paints, enamels, and printing inks)
**lamp·brush chromosome** \ˈlamp-ˌbrəsh-\ *noun* (1911)
: a greatly enlarged diplotene chromosome that has apparently filamentous granular loops extending from the chromomeres and is characteristic of some animal oocytes
**lamp·light** \ˈlamp-ˌlīt\ *noun* (14th century)
: the light of a lamp
**lamp·light·er** \-ˌlī-tər\ *noun* (1750)
: one that lights a lamp
¹**lam·poon** \lam-ˈpün\ *noun* [French *lampon*] (1645)
: SATIRE 1; *specifically* : a harsh satire usually directed against an individual
²**lampoon** *transitive verb* (circa 1657)
: to make the subject of a lampoon : RIDICULE
— **lam·poon·er** *noun*

— **lam·poon·ery** \-ˈpü-nə-rē, -ˈpün-rē\ *noun*
**lamp·post** \ˈlam(p)-ˌpōst\ *noun* (1790)
: a post supporting a usually outdoor lamp or lantern
**lam·prey** \ˈlam-prē, -ˌprā\ *noun, plural* **lampreys** [Middle English, from Old French *lampreie*, from Medieval Latin *lampreda*] (14th century)
: any of a family (Petromyzontidae) of eel-shaped freshwater or anadromous jawless fishes that include those cyclostomes having well-developed eyes and a large disk-shaped suctorial mouth armed with horny teeth — called also *lamprey eel*
**lamp·shell** \ˈlamp-ˌshel\ *noun* [from the resemblance of the shell and its protruding peduncle to an ancient oil lamp with the wick protruding] (1854)
: BRACHIOPOD
**lam·ster** \ˈlam(p)-stər\ *also* **lam·is·ter** \ˈla-mə-stər\ *noun* [²*lam* + *-ster*] (1904)
: a fugitive especially from the law
**LAN** \ˈlan, ˌel-(ˌ)ā-ˈen\ *noun* (1982)
: LOCAL AREA NETWORK
**la·nai** \lə-ˈnī, lä-\ *noun* [Hawaiian *lānai*] (1823)
: PORCH, VERANDA
**Lan·ca·shire** \ˈlaŋ-kə-ˌshir, -shər\ *noun* [*Lancashire*, England] (1896)
: a moist crumbly white English cheese that is used especially in cooking
**Lan·cas·tri·an** \lan-ˈkas-trē-ən, laŋ-\ *adjective* [John of Gaunt, duke of *Lancaster*] (1612)
: of or relating to the English royal house that ruled from 1399 to 1461
¹**lance** \ˈlan(t)s\ *noun* [Middle English, from Old French, from Latin *lancea*] (14th century)
**1** : a steel-tipped spear carried by mounted knights or light cavalry
**2** : any of various sharp objects suggestive of a lance: as **a** : LANCET **b** : a spear used for killing whales or fish
**3** : LANCER 1b
²**lance** *verb* **lanced; lanc·ing** [Middle English *launcen*, from Middle French *lancer*, from Late Latin *lanceare*, from Latin *lancea*] (14th century)
*transitive verb*
**1 a** : to pierce with or as if with a lance **b** : to open with or as if with a lancet ⟨*lance* a boil⟩
**2** : to throw forward : HURL
*intransitive verb*
: to move forward quickly
**lance corporal** *noun* [*lance* (as in obsolete *lancepesade* lance corporal, from Middle French *lancepessade*)] (1786)
: an enlisted man in the marine corps ranking above a private first class and below a corporal
**lance·let** \ˈlan(t)-slət\ *noun* (circa 1836)
: any of a subphylum (Cephalochordata) of small translucent marine primitive chordate animals that are fishlike in appearance and usually live partially buried on the ocean floor — called also *amphioxus*
**Lan·ce·lot** \ˈlan(t)-sə-ˌlät, ˈlän(t)-, -s(ə-)lət\ *noun*
: a knight of the Round Table and lover of Queen Guinevere
**lan·ce·o·late** \ˈlan(t)-sē-ə-ˌlāt\ *adjective* [Late Latin *lanceolatus*, from Latin *lanceola*, diminutive of *lancea*] (circa 1760)
: shaped like a lance head; *specifically* : tapering to a point at the apex and sometimes at the base ⟨*lanceolate* leaves⟩ ⟨*lanceolate* prisms⟩ — see LEAF illustration
**lanc·er** \ˈlan(t)-sər\ *noun* (1590)
**1 a** : one who carries a lance **b** : a member of a military unit formerly composed of light cavalry armed with lances
**2** *plural but singular in construction* **a** : a set of five quadrilles each in a different meter **b** : the music for such dances
**lan·cet** \ˈlan(t)-sət\ *noun* (15th century)
**1** : a sharp-pointed and commonly 2-edged

surgical instrument used to make small incisions
**2 a** : LANCET WINDOW **b** : LANCET ARCH
**lancet arch** *noun* (circa 1823)
: an acutely pointed arch — see ARCH illustration
**lan·cet·ed** \ˈlan(t)-sə-təd\ *adjective* (1855)
: having a lancet arch or lancet windows
**lancet window** *noun* (1781)
: a high narrow window with an acutely pointed head and without tracery
**lance·wood** \ˈlan(t)s-ˌwud\ *noun* (1697)
: a tough elastic wood used especially for shafts, fishing rods, and bows; *also* : a tree (especially *Oxandra lanceolata*) yielding this wood
**lan·ci·nat·ing** \ˈlan(t)-sə-ˌnā-tiŋ\ *adjective* [*lancinate* to pierce, from Latin *lancinatus*, past participle of *lancinare*; akin to Latin *lacerare* to rend — more at LACERATE] (1762)
: characterized by piercing or stabbing sensations ⟨*lancinating* pain⟩
¹**land** \ˈland\ *noun, often attributive* [Middle English, from Old English; akin to Old High German *lant* land, Middle Irish *lann*] (before 12th century)
**1 a** : the solid part of the surface of the earth; *also* : a corresponding part of a celestial body (as the moon) **b** : ground or soil of a specified situation, nature, or quality ⟨dry *land*⟩ **c** : the surface of the earth and its natural resources
**2** : a portion of the earth's solid surface distinguishable by boundaries or ownership ⟨bought *land* in the country⟩: as **a** : COUNTRY ⟨campaigned across the *land*⟩ **b** : a rural area characterized by farming or ranching; *also* : farming or ranching as a way of life ⟨wanted to move back to the *land*⟩
**3** : REALM, DOMAIN ⟨in the *land* of dreams⟩ — sometimes used in combination ⟨movie*land*⟩
**4** : the people of a country ⟨the *land* rose in rebellion⟩
**5** : an area of a partly machined surface that is left without machining
— **land·less** \ˈland-ləs\ *adjective*
— **land·less·ness** \-nəs\ *noun*
²**land** (13th century)
*transitive verb*
**1** : to set or put on shore from a ship : DISEMBARK
**2 a** : to set down after conveying **b** : to cause to reach or come to rest in a particular place ⟨never *landed* a punch⟩ **c** : to bring to a specified condition ⟨his carelessness *landed* him in trouble⟩ **d** : to bring (as an airplane) to a landing
**3 a** : to catch and bring in (as a fish) **b** : GAIN, SECURE ⟨*land* a job⟩
*intransitive verb*
**1 a** : to go ashore from a ship : DISEMBARK **b** *of a ship or boat* : to touch at a place on shore
**2 a** : to come to the end of a course or to a stage in a journey : ARRIVE ⟨took the wrong subway and *landed* on the other side of town⟩ **b** : to come to be in a condition or situation ⟨*landed* in jail⟩ **c** : to strike or meet a surface (as after a fall) ⟨*landed* on my head⟩ **d** : to alight on a surface
**lan·dau** \ˈlan-ˌdau, -ˌdo\ *noun* [*Landau*, Bavaria, Germany] (1743)
: a four-wheel carriage with a top divided into two sections that can be let down, thrown back, or removed and with a raised seat outside for the driver

landau

**lan·dau·let** \ˌlan-dᵊl-ˈet\ *noun* (1794)
: a small landau

**land bank** *noun* (1696)
: a bank that provides financing for land development and for farm mortgages

**land·ed** \ˈlan-dəd\ *adjective* (15th century)
**1 :** having an estate in land ⟨*landed* proprietors⟩
**2 :** consisting in or derived from land or real estate ⟨*landed* wealth⟩

**land·er** \ˈlan-dər\ *noun* (1859)
: one that lands; *especially* **:** a space vehicle that is designed to land on a celestial body (as the moon or a planet)

**land·fall** \ˈlan(d)-ˌfȯl\ *noun* (1627)
**1 :** a sighting or making of land after a voyage or flight
**2 :** the land first sighted on a voyage or flight

**land·fill** \-ˌfil\ *noun* (1942)
**1 :** a system of trash and garbage disposal in which the waste is buried between layers of earth to build up low-lying land — called also *sanitary landfill*
**2 :** an area built up by landfill

**land·form** \-ˌfȯrm\ *noun* (1893)
: a natural feature of a land surface

**land·grab** \-ˌgrab\ *noun* (1860)
: a usually swift acquisition of land often by fraud or force
— **land–grab·ber** \-ˌgra-bər\ *noun*

**land grant** *noun* (1862)
: a grant of land made by the government especially for roads, railroads, or agricultural colleges

**land·hold·er** \ˈland-ˌhōl-dər\ *noun* (15th century)
: a holder or owner of land

**land·hold·ing** \-ˌhōl-diŋ\ *noun* (circa 1890)
**1 :** the state or fact of holding or owning land
**2 :** property in land
— **landholding** *adjective*

**land·ing** *noun* (15th century)
**1 :** an act or process of one that lands; *especially* **:** a going or bringing to a surface (as land or shore) after a voyage or flight
**2 :** a place for discharging and taking on passengers and cargo
**3 :** a level part of a staircase (as at the end of a flight of stairs)

**landing craft** *noun* (1940)
: any of numerous naval craft designed for conveying troops and equipment from a transport to a beach in an amphibious assault

**landing field** *noun* (circa 1920)
: a field where aircraft may land and take off

**landing gear** *noun* (1911)
: the part that supports the weight of an airplane or spacecraft when in contact with the land or water

**landing strip** *noun* (1930)
: AIRSTRIP

**land·la·dy** \ˈland-ˌlā-dē\ *noun* (circa 1536)
: a woman who is a landlord

**land·line** \-ˌlīn\ *noun* (1865)
: a line of communication (as by telephone cable) on land

**land·locked** \-ˌläkt\ *adjective* (1622)
**1 :** enclosed or nearly enclosed by land ⟨a *landlocked* country⟩
**2 :** confined to fresh water by some barrier ⟨*landlocked* salmon⟩

**land·lord** \-ˌlȯrd\ *noun* (before 12th century)
**1 :** the owner of property (as land, houses, or apartments) that is leased or rented to another
**2 :** the master of an inn or lodging house **:** INNKEEPER

**land·lord·ism** \-ˌlȯr-di-zəm\ *noun* (1844)
: an economic system or practice by which ownership of land is vested in one who leases it to cultivators

**land·lub·ber** \-ˌlə-bər\ *noun* (circa 1700)
: LANDSMAN 2 ⟨clumsy *landlubbers* learning to sail⟩
— **land·lub·ber·li·ness** \-bər-lē-nəs\ *noun*
— **land·lub·ber·ly** \-bər-lē\ *adjective*
— **land·lub·bing** \-biŋ\ *adjective*

**land·mark** \-ˌmärk\ *noun* (before 12th century)
**1 :** an object (as a stone or tree) that marks the boundary of land
**2 a :** a conspicuous object on land that marks a locality **b :** an anatomical structure used as a point of orientation in locating other structures
**3 :** an event or development that marks a turning point or a stage
**4 :** a structure (as a building) of unusual historical and usually aesthetic interest; *especially* **:** one that is officially designated and set aside for preservation

**land·mass** \-ˌmas\ *noun* (1856)
: a large area of land ⟨continental *landmasses*⟩

**land mine** *noun* (1890)
**1 :** a mine placed on or just below the surface of the ground and designed to be exploded by the weight of vehicles or troops passing over it
**2 :** BOOBY TRAP 1

**land office** *noun* (1681)
: a government office in which entries upon and sales of public land are registered

**land-office business** *noun* (1839)
: extensive and rapid business ⟨money changers . . . did a *land-office business* on payday —F. J. Haskin⟩

**land·own·er** \ˈland-ˌō-nər\ *noun* (circa 1733)
: an owner of land
— **land·own·er·ship** \-ˌship\ *noun*
— **land·own·ing** \-ˌō-niŋ\ *adjective or noun*

**land·poor** \ˈlan(d)-ˌpu̇r\ *adjective* (1873)
: owning so much unprofitable or encumbered land as to lack funds to develop the land or pay the charges due on it

**Land·ra·ce** \ˈlän(d)-ˌrä-sə\ *noun* [Danish, from *land* + *race*] (1935)
: a swine of any of several breeds locally developed in northern Europe

**land reform** *noun* (1846)
: measures designed to effect a more equitable distribution of agricultural land especially by governmental action; *also* **:** the resulting redistribution

**¹land·scape** \ˈlan(d)-ˌskāp\ *noun, often attributive* [Dutch *landschap*, from *land* + *-schap* -ship] (1598)
**1 a :** a picture representing a view of natural inland scenery **b :** the art of depicting such scenery
**2 a :** the landforms of a region in the aggregate **b :** a portion of territory that can be viewed at one time from one place **c :** a particular area of activity **:** SCENE ⟨political *landscape*⟩
**3** *obsolete* **:** VISTA, PROSPECT ◆

**²landscape** *verb* **land·scaped; land·scap·ing** (1914)
*transitive verb*
: to modify or ornament (a natural landscape) by altering the plant cover
*intransitive verb*
: to engage in landscape gardening
— **land·scap·er** *noun*

**landscape architect** *noun* (1863)
: one who develops land for human use and enjoyment through effective placement of structures, vehicular and pedestrian ways, and plantings
— **landscape architecture** *noun*

**landscape gardener** *noun* (circa 1763)
: one who is engaged in the development and decorative planting of gardens and grounds
— **landscape gardening** *noun*

**land·scap·ist** \ˈlan(d)-ˌskā-pist\ *noun* (1843)
: a painter of landscapes

**¹land·slide** \ˈlan(d)-ˌslīd\ *noun* (1838)
**1 :** the usually rapid downward movement of a mass of rock, earth, or artificial fill on a slope; *also* **:** the mass that moves down
**2 a :** a great majority of votes for one side **b :** an overwhelming victory

**²landslide** *intransitive verb* **-slid** \-ˌslid\; **-slid·ing** \-ˌslī-diŋ\ (1926)
**1 :** to produce a landslide

**2 :** to win an election by a heavy majority

**land·slip** \-ˌslip\ *noun* (1679)
: LANDSLIDE 1

**Lands·mål** *or* **Lands·maal** \ˈlän(t)s-ˌmȯl\ *noun* [Norwegian, from *land* country + *mål* speech] (1886)
: NYNORSK

**lands·man** \ˈlan(d)z-mən\ *noun* (1598)
**1 :** a fellow countryman
**2 :** one who lives on the land; *especially* **:** one who knows little or nothing of the sea or seamanship

**land·ward** \ˈland-wərd\ *adverb or adjective* (15th century)
: to or toward the land

**land yacht** *noun* (1928)
: a 3-wheel wind-driven recreation vehicle consisting usually of a bare-frame structure and a single sail and used especially on areas of firmly packed sand

**¹lane** \ˈlān\ *noun* [Middle English, from Old English *lanu*; akin to Middle Dutch *lane* lane] (before 12th century)
**1 :** a narrow passageway between fences or hedges
**2 :** a relatively narrow way or track: as **a :** an ocean route used by or prescribed for ships **b :** a strip of roadway for a single line of vehicles **c :** AIR LANE **d :** any of several parallel courses on a track or swimming pool in which a competitor must stay during a race **e :** an unmarked lengthwise division of a playing area which defines the playing zone of a particular player **f :** a narrow hardwood surface having pins at one end and a shallow channel along each side that is used in bowling **g :** FREE THROW LANE

**²lane** *Scottish variant of* LONE

**lane·way** \ˈlān-ˌwā\ *noun* (1882)
*British* **:** LANE

**lang·bein·ite** \ˈlaŋ-ˌbī-ˌnīt\ *noun* [German *Langbeinit*, from A. *Langbein*, 19th century German chemist] (circa 1897)
: a mineral that is a double sulfate of potassium and magnesium used in the fertilizer industry

**lang·lauf** \ˈläŋ-ˌlau̇f\ *noun* [German, from *lang* long + *Lauf* race] (1927)
: cross-country running or racing on skis
— **lang·lauf·er** \-ˌlau̇-fər\ *noun*

**lang·ley** \ˈlaŋ-lē\ *noun, plural* **langleys** [Samuel P. *Langley*] (1947)
: a unit of solar radiation equivalent to one gram calorie per square centimeter of irradiated surface

**Lan·go·bard** \ˈlaŋ-gə-ˌbärd\ *noun* [Latin *Langobardus*] (1788)
: LOMBARD 1a
— **Lan·go·bar·dic** \ˌlaŋ-gə-ˈbär-dik\ *adjective*

**lan·gouste** \län-ˈgüst\ *noun* [French, grasshopper, lobster, from Old French *languste*,

from Old Provençal *langosta,* from (assumed) Vulgar Latin *lacusta,* alteration of Latin *locusta*] (1832)
**:** SPINY LOBSTER

**lan·gous·tine** \ˌlaŋ-gə-'stēn\ *also* **lan·gos·ti·no** \ˌlaŋ-gə-'stē-(ˌ)nō\ *noun, plural* **-tines** *also* **-ti·nos** [*langoustine,* from French, diminutive of *langouste; langostino,* from Spanish, diminutive of *langosta* spiny lobster, locust, from (assumed) Vulgar Latin *lacusta*] (1915)
**:** any of several small lobsters (genera *Nephropsis* and *Metanephrops* of the family Nephropidae) widely used for food

**¹lang syne** \(ˌ)laŋ-'zīn, -'sīn\ *adverb* [Middle English (Scots), from *lang* long + *syne* since] (15th century)
*chiefly Scottish* **:** at a distant time in the past

**²lang syne** *noun* (1694)
*chiefly Scottish* **:** times past ⟨should auld acquaintance be forgot, and days o' auld *lang syne* —Robert Burns⟩

**lan·guage** \'laŋ-gwij, -wij\ *noun* [Middle English, from Old French, from *langue* tongue, language, from Latin *lingua* — more at TONGUE] (14th century)
**1 a :** the words, their pronunciation, and the methods of combining them used and understood by a community **b** (1) **:** audible, articulate, meaningful sound as produced by the action of the vocal organs (2) **:** a systematic means of communicating ideas or feelings by the use of conventionalized signs, sounds, gestures, or marks having understood meanings (3) **:** the suggestion by objects, actions, or conditions of associated ideas or feelings ⟨*language* in their very gesture —Shakespeare⟩ (4) **:** the means by which animals communicate (5) **:** a formal system of signs and symbols (as FORTRAN or a calculus in logic) including rules for the formation and transformation of admissible expressions (6) **:** MACHINE LANGUAGE 1
**2 a :** form or manner of verbal expression; *specifically* **:** STYLE **b :** the vocabulary and phraseology belonging to an art or a department of knowledge **c :** PROFANITY
**3 :** the study of language especially as a school subject

**language arts** *noun plural* (1948)
**:** the subjects (as reading, spelling, literature, and composition) that aim at developing the student's comprehension and capacity for use of written and oral language

**langue** \läⁿg\ *noun* [French, literally, language] (1924)
**:** language viewed abstractly as a system of forms and conventions used for communication in a community; *also* **:** COMPETENCE 3 — compare PAROLE

**langue d'oc** \läŋ-'dȯk, läⁿg-dȯk\ *noun* [French, from Old French, literally, language of *oc;* from the Provençal use of the word *oc* for "yes"] (1703)
**:** PROVENÇAL 2

**langue d'oïl** \läŋ-'dȯi(ə)l, -'dȯi; läⁿg-dȯ-ēl, -dȯi\ *noun* [French, from Old French, literally, language of *oïl;* from the French use of the word *oïl* for "yes"] (1703)
**:** FRENCH 1

**lan·guet** \'laŋ-gwət, laŋ-'gwet\ *noun* [Middle English, from Middle French *languete,* diminutive of *langue*] (15th century)
**:** something resembling the tongue in form or function

**lan·guid** \'laŋ-gwəd\ *adjective* [Middle French *languide,* from Latin *languidus,* from *languēre* to languish — more at SLACK] (1597)
**1 :** drooping or flagging from or as if from exhaustion **:** WEAK
**2 :** sluggish in character or disposition **:** LISTLESS
**3 :** lacking force or quickness of movement **:** SLOW
— **lan·guid·ly** *adverb*
— **lan·guid·ness** *noun*

## HOME LANGUAGES WITH OVER FORTY MILLION SPEAKERS[1]

| LANGUAGE | MILLIONS |
| --- | --- |
| Mandarin Chinese | 865 |
| English | 334 |
| Spanish | 283 |
| Arabic | 197 |
| Bengali | 181 |
| Hindi and Urdu | 172 |
| Portuguese | 161 |
| Russian | 156 |
| Japanese | 125 |
| German | 104 |
| Wu Chinese | 94 |
| Panjabi | 76 |
| Javanese | 76 |
| Telugu | 72 |
| Cantonese | 70 |
| Korean | 70 |
| Marathi | 68 |
| Italian | 68 |
| Tamil | 65 |
| French | 65 |
| Vietnamese | 61 |
| Awadhi[2] | 61 |
| Bhojpuri | 58 |
| Southern Min Chinese[3] | 55 |
| Turkish | 52 |
| Ukrainian | 50 |
| Thai and Lao | 47 |
| Polish | 42 |
| Gujarati | 41 |
| Persian | 40 |

[1]Compiled by William W. Gage, using information supplied in *Ethnologue: Languages of the World,* 11th ed. (Dallas: Summer Institute of Linguistics, 1988). Home language used here means the language usually spoken at home.

[2]Indo-Aryan language of eastern and central Uttar Pradesh.

[3]Group of Chinese dialects especially of Xiamen, Shantou, and Taiwan.

**lan·guish** \'laŋ-gwish\ *intransitive verb* [Middle English, from Middle French *languiss-,* stem of *languir,* from (assumed) Vulgar Latin *languire,* from Latin *languēre*] (14th century)
**1 a :** to be or become feeble, weak, or enervated **b :** to be or live in a state of depression or decreasing vitality
**2 a :** to become dispirited **:** PINE ⟨*languishing* in prison⟩ **b :** to suffer neglect ⟨the bill *languished* in the Senate for eight months⟩
**3 :** to assume an expression of grief or emotion appealing for sympathy
— **lan·guish·er** *noun*
— **lan·guish·ing·ly** \-gwi-shiŋ-lē\ *adverb*
— **lan·guish·ment** \-gwish-mənt\ *noun*

**lan·guor** \'laŋ-gər *also* -ər\ *noun* [Middle English, from Middle French, from Latin, from *languēre*] (14th century)
**1 :** weakness or weariness of body or mind
**2 :** listless indolence or inertia
**synonym** see LETHARGY

**lan·guor·ous** \'laŋ-gə-rəs, -grəs *also* -ə-rəs\ *adjective* (15th century)
**1 :** producing or tending to produce languor ⟨a *languorous* climate⟩
**2 :** full of or characterized by languor
— **lan·guor·ous·ly** *adverb*

**lan·gur** \läŋ-'gu̇r\ *noun* [Hindi *lāgūr*] (1825)
**:** any of several slender long-tailed Asian monkeys (subfamily Colobinae)

**langur**

**lank** \'laŋk\ *adjective* [Middle English, from Old English *hlanc;* akin to Old

High German *hlanca* loin] (before 12th century)
**1 :** not well filled out **:** SLENDER, THIN ⟨*lank* cattle⟩
**2 :** insufficient in quantity, degree, or extent ⟨*lank* grass⟩
**3 :** hanging straight and limp without spring or curl ⟨*lank* hair⟩
**synonym** see LEAN
— **lank·ly** *adverb*
— **lank·ness** *noun*

**lanky** \'laŋ-kē\ *adjective* **lank·i·er; -est** (1818)
**:** ungracefully tall and thin
**synonym** see LEAN
— **lank·i·ly** \-kə-lē\ *adverb*
— **lank·i·ness** \-kē-nəs\ *noun*

**lan·ner** \'la-nər\ *noun* [Middle English *laner,* from Middle French *lanier*] (14th century)
**:** a falcon (*Falco biarmicus*) of southern Europe, southwestern Asia, and Africa; *specifically* **:** a female lanner

**lan·ner·et** \ˌla-nə-'ret\ *noun* (15th century)
**:** a male lanner

**lan·o·lin** \'la-nᵊl-ən\ *noun* [Latin *lana* wool + International Scientific Vocabulary ³-*ol* + ¹-*in*] (1885)
**:** wool grease especially when refined for use in ointments and cosmetics

**lan·ta·na** \lan-'tä-nə\ *noun* [New Latin, from Italian dialect, viburnum] (1791)
**:** any of a genus (*Lantana*) of tropical shrubs of the vervain family with showy heads of small bright flowers

**lan·tern** \'lan-tərn\ *noun, often attributive* [Middle English *lanterne,* from Old French, from Latin *lanterna,* from Greek *lamptēr,* from *lampein* to shine — more at LAMP] (13th century)
**1 :** a usually portable protective case for a light with transparent openings — compare CHINESE LANTERN
**2 a** *obsolete* **:** LIGHTHOUSE **b :** the chamber in a lighthouse containing the light **c :** a structure with glazed or open sides above an opening in a roof for light or ventilation **d :** a small tower or cupola or one stage of a cupola
**3 :** PROJECTOR 2b

**lantern fish** *noun* (circa 1753)
**:** any of a family (Myctophidae) of small deep-sea bony fishes that have a large mouth, large eyes, and usually numerous photophores

**lantern fly** *noun* (circa 1753)
**:** any of several large brightly marked homopterous insects (family Fulgoridae) having the front of the head prolonged into a hollow structure

**lantern jaw** *noun* (1711)
**:** an undershot jaw
— **lan·tern-jawed** \'lan-tərn-ˌjȯd\ *adjective*

**lantern pinion** *noun* (circa 1859)
**:** a gear pinion having cylindrical bars instead of teeth

**lan·tha·nide** \'lan(t)-thə-ˌnīd\ *noun* [International Scientific Vocabulary] (1926)
**:** any in a series of elements of increasing atomic numbers beginning with lanthanum (57) or cerium (58) and ending with lutetium (71) — see PERIODIC TABLE table

**lan·tha·num** \-nəm\ *noun* [New Latin, from Greek *lanthanein* to escape notice — more at LATENT] (1841)
**:** a white soft malleable metallic element that occurs in rare-earth minerals — see ELEMENT table

**lant·horn** \'lan-tərn\ *noun* (1587)
*chiefly British* **:** LANTERN

**la·nu·gi·nous** \lə-'nü-jə-nəs, -'nyü-\ *adjective* [Latin *lanuginosus,* from *lanugin-, lanugo*] (1575)

---

\ə\ abut \ᵊ\ kitten \ər\ further \a\ ash \ā\ ace \ä\ mop, mar \au̇\ out \ch\ chin \e\ bet \ē\ easy \g\ go \i\ hit \ī\ ice \j\ job \ŋ\ sing \ō\ go \ȯ\ law \ȯi\ boy \th\ thin \t̲h̲\ the \ü\ loot \u̇\ foot \y\ yet \zh\ vision    *see also* Guide to Pronunciation

: covered with down or fine soft hair : DOWNY

**la·nu·go** \lə-'nü-(ˌ)gō, -'nyü-\ *noun* [Latin, down, from *lana* wool — more at WOOL] (15th century)
: a dense cottony or downy growth; *specifically* : the soft woolly hair that covers the fetus of some mammals

**lan·yard** \'lan-yərd\ *noun* [Middle English *lanyer* thong, strap, from Middle French *laniere*] (1626)
**1** : a piece of rope or line for fastening something in a ship; *especially* : one of the pieces passing through deadeyes to extend shrouds or stays
**2 a** : a cord or strap to hold something (as a knife or a whistle) and usually worn around the neck **b** : a cord worn as a symbol of a military citation
**3** : a strong line used to activate a system (as in firing a cannon or sounding a whistle)

**Lao** \'laů\ *noun, plural* **Lao** *or* **Laos** \'laůz\ (1808)
**1** : a member of a Buddhist people living in Laos and adjacent parts of northeastern Thailand
**2** : the Thai language of the Lao people
— **Lao** *adjective*

**La·oc·o·ön** \lā-'ä-kə-ˌwän\ *noun* [Latin, from Greek *Laokoōn*]
: a Trojan priest killed with his sons by two sea serpents after warning the Trojans against the wooden horse

**La·od·i·ce·an** \lā-ˌä-də-'sē-ən, ˌlā-ō-də-\ *adjective* [from the reproach to the church of the Laodiceans in Revelation 3:15–16] (1633)
: lukewarm or indifferent in religion or politics
— **Laodicean** *noun*

**Lao·tian** \lā-'ō-shən, 'laů-shən\ *noun* [probably from French *laotien*, adjective & noun, from *Lao*] (1847)
: LAO
— **Laotian** *adjective*

**¹lap** \'lap\ *noun* [Middle English *lappe*, from Old English *læppa;* akin to Old High German *lappa* flap] (before 12th century)
**1 a** : a loose overlapping or hanging panel or flap especially of a garment **b** *archaic* : the skirt of a coat or dress
**2 a** : the clothing that lies on the knees, thighs, and lower part of the trunk when one sits **b** : the front part of the lower trunk and thighs of a seated person
**3** : responsible custody : CONTROL ⟨going to drop the whole thing in your *lap* —Hamilton Basso⟩
— **lap·ful** \'lap-ˌfůl\ *noun*
— **the lap of luxury** : an environment of great ease, comfort, and wealth ⟨was reared in *the lap of luxury*⟩

**²lap** *verb* **lapped; lap·ping** (14th century)
*transitive verb*
**1 a** : to fold over or around something : WIND
**b** : to envelop entirely : SWATHE
**2** : to fold over especially into layers
**3** : to hold protectively in or as if in the lap : CUDDLE
**4 a** : to place over and cover a part of : OVERLAP ⟨*lap* shingles on a roof⟩ **b** : to join (as two boards) by a lap joint
**5 a** : to dress, smooth, or polish (as a metal surface) to a high degree of refinement or accuracy **b** : to shape or fit by working two surfaces together with or without abrasives until a very close fit is produced
**6 a** : to overtake and thereby lead or increase the lead over (another contestant) by a full circuit of a racecourse **b** : to complete the circuit of (a racecourse)
*intransitive verb*
**1** : FOLD, WIND
**2 a** : to project beyond or spread over something **b** : to lie partly over or alongside of something or of one another : OVERLAP
**3** : to traverse a course
— **lap·per** *noun*

**³lap** *noun* (1800)

**1 a** : the amount by which one object overlaps or projects beyond another **b** : the part of an object that overlaps another
**2** : a smoothing and polishing tool usually consisting of a piece of wood, leather, felt, or soft metal in a special shape used with or without an embedded abrasive
**3** : a doubling or layering of a flexible substance (as fibers or paper)
**4 a** : the act or an instance of traversing a course (as a racing track or swimming pool); *also* : the distance covered **b** : one segment of a larger unit (as a journey) **c** : one complete turn (as of a rope around a drum)

**⁴lap** *verb* **lapped; lap·ping** [Middle English, from Old English *lapian;* akin to Old High German *laffan* to lick, Latin *lambere,* Greek *laphyssein* to devour] (before 12th century)
*intransitive verb*
**1** : to take in food or drink with the tongue
**2 a** : to make a gentle intermittent splashing sound **b** : to move in little waves : WASH
*transitive verb*
**1 a** : to take in (food or drink) with the tongue **b** : to take in or absorb eagerly or quickly — used with *up* ⟨the crowd *lapped* up every word he said⟩
**2** : to flow or splash against in little waves
— **lap·per** *noun*

**⁵lap** *noun* (14th century)
**1 a** : an act or instance of lapping **b** : the amount that can be carried to the mouth by one lick or scoop of the tongue
**2** : a thin or weak beverage or food
**3** : a gentle splashing sound

**laparo-** *combining form* [Greek *lapara* flank, from *laparos* slack]
: abdominal wall ⟨*laparo*tomy⟩

**lap·a·ro·scope** \'la-p(ə-)rə-ˌskōp\ *noun* [International Scientific Vocabulary] (circa 1923)
: a fiberoptic instrument inserted through an incision in the abdominal wall and used to examine visually the interior of the peritoneal cavity

**lap·a·ros·co·py** \ˌla-pə-'räs-kə-pē\ *noun, plural* **-pies** (1916)
**1** : visual examination of the abdomen by means of a laparoscope
**2** : an operation involving laparoscopy; *especially* : one for sterilization of the female or for removal of ova that involves use of a laparoscope to guide surgical procedures within the abdomen
— **lap·a·ro·scop·ic** \-rə-'skä-pik\ *adjective*
— **lap·a·ros·co·pist** \ˌla-pə-'räs-kə-pist\ *noun*

**lap·a·rot·o·my** \ˌla-pə-'rä-tə-mē\ *noun, plural* **-mies** (1878)
: surgical section of the abdominal wall

**lap belt** *noun* (1952)
: a seat belt that fastens across the lap

**lap·board** \'lap-ˌbōrd, -ˌbȯrd\ *noun* (1804)
: a board used on the lap as a table or desk

**lap·dog** \-ˌdȯg\ *noun* (1645)
**1** : a small dog that may be held in the lap
**2** : a servile dependent or follower

**la·pel** \lə-'pel\ *noun* [diminutive of ¹*lap*] (1789)
: the part of a garment that is turned back; *specifically* : the fold of the front of a coat that is usually a continuation of the collar
— **la·pelled** *or* **la·peled** *adjective*

**lap·i·dar·i·an** \ˌla-pə-'der-ē-ən\ *adjective* (1683)
: LAPIDARY 1

**¹lap·i·dary** \'la-pə-ˌder-ē\ *noun, plural* **-dar·ies** (14th century)
**1** : a cutter, polisher, or engraver of precious stones usually other than diamonds
**2** : the art of cutting gems

**²lapidary** *adjective* [Latin *lapidarius* of stone, from *lapid-, lapis* stone] (1724)
**1** : having the elegance and precision associated with inscriptions on monumental stone ⟨the *lapidary* phrasing . . . and subtle condensa-

tions of emotions . . . reward attentive reading —G. A. Cardwell⟩
**2 a** : sculptured in or engraved on stone **b** : of or relating to precious stones or the art of cutting them

**la·pil·lus** \lə-'pi-ləs\ *noun, plural* **-li** \-ˌlī, -(ˌ)lē\ [Latin, diminutive of *lapis*] (1747)
: a small stony or glassy fragment of lava ejected in a volcanic eruption

**lap·in** \'la-pən\ *noun* [French] (1905)
**1** : RABBIT; *specifically* : a castrated male rabbit
**2** : rabbit fur usually sheared and dyed

**la·pis la·zu·li** \ˌlap-əs-'la-zə-lē, -'la-zhə-\ *noun* [Middle English, from Medieval Latin, from Latin *lapis* + Medieval Latin *lazuli,* genitive of *lazulum* lapis lazuli, from Arabic *lāzaward* — more at AZURE] (15th century)
: a semiprecious stone that is usually rich azure blue and is essentially a complex silicate often with spangles of iron pyrites — called also *lapis*

**lap joint** *noun* (1823)
: a joint made by overlapping two ends or edges and fastening them together
— **lap–joint·ed** \'lap-ˌjȯin-təd\ *adjective*

**La·place transform** \lə-'pläs-, -'plas-\ [Pierre Simon, Marquis de *Laplace*] (1942)
: a transformation of a function $f(x)$ into the function

$$g(t) = \int_0^\infty e^{-xt} f(x)dx$$

that is useful especially in reducing the solution of an ordinary linear differential equation with constant coefficients to the solution of a polynomial equation

**Lapp** \'lap\ *noun* [Swedish] (1859)
**1** : a member of a people of northern Scandinavia, Finland, and the Kola Peninsula of northern Russia who are traditionally fishermen, nomadic herders of caribou, and hunters of sea mammals
**2** : any or all of the closely related Finno-Ugric languages of the Lapps
— **Lapp·ish** *adjective or noun*

**lap·pet** \'la-pət\ *noun* (1573)
**1** : a fold or flap on a garment or headdress
**2** : a flat overlapping or hanging piece

**lap robe** *noun* (circa 1866)
: a covering (as a blanket) for the legs, lap, and feet especially of a passenger in a car or carriage

**Lap·sang souchong** \'läp-ˌsäŋ-, 'lap-ˌsaŋ-\ *noun* [origin unknown] (circa 1878)
: a souchong tea having a pronounced smoky flavor and aroma

**¹lapse** \'laps\ *noun* [Latin *lapsus,* from *labi* to slip — more at SLEEP] (1526)
**1 a** : a slight error typically due to forgetfulness or inattention ⟨a *lapse* in table manners⟩ **b** : a temporary deviation or fall especially from a higher to a lower state ⟨a *lapse* from grace⟩
**2** : a becoming less : DECLINE
**3 a** (1) : the termination of a right or privilege through neglect to exercise it within some limit of time (2) : termination of coverage for nonpayment of premiums **b** : INTERRUPTION, DISCONTINUANCE ⟨returned to college after a *lapse* of several years⟩
**4** : an abandonment of religious faith : APOSTASY
**5** : a passage of time; *also* : INTERVAL
*synonym* SEE ERROR

**²lapse** *verb* **lapsed; laps·ing** (1611)
*intransitive verb*
**1 a** : to fall from an attained and usually high level (as of morals or manners) to one much lower; *also* : to depart from an accepted pattern or standard **b** : to sink or slip gradually : SUBSIDE ⟨*lapsed* into unconsciousness⟩
**2** : to go out of existence : CEASE ⟨after a few polite exchanges, the conversation *lapsed*⟩

**3 :** to pass from one proprietor to another or from an original owner by omission or negligence ⟨allowed the insurance policy to *lapse*⟩
**4 a :** to glide along **:** PASS ⟨time *lapses*⟩
*transitive verb*
**:** to let slip **:** FORFEIT ⟨all of those who have *lapsed* their membership —*AAUP Bulletin*⟩
— **laps·er** *noun*

**lapsed** *adjective* (1638)
*of a person* **:** having given up or allowed the lapse of a former position, relationship, or commitment ⟨a *lapsed* Catholic⟩

**lapse rate** *noun* (1918)
**:** the adiabatic rate of decrease of atmospheric temperature with increasing altitude

**lap·strake** \'lap-ˌstrāk\ *adjective* (1771)
**:** CLINKER-BUILT

**lap·top** \'lap-ˌtäp\ *adjective* (1984)
**:** of a size and design that makes operation and use on one's lap convenient ⟨a *laptop* personal computer⟩ — compare DESKTOP
— **laptop** *noun*

**La·pu·tan** \lə-'pyü-t°n\ *noun*
**:** an inhabitant of a flying island in Swift's *Gulliver's Travels* characterized by a neglect of useful occupations and a devotion to visionary projects
— **Laputan** *adjective*

**lap·wing** \'lap-ˌwin\ *noun* [Middle English, by folk etymology from Old English *hlēapewince*; akin to Old English *hlēapan* to leap and to Old English *wincian* to wink] (14th century)
**:** a crested Old World plover (*Vanellus vanellus*) noted for its slow irregular flapping flight and shrill wailing cry; *also* **:** any of several related plovers

**Lar** \'lär\ *noun, plural* **Lar·es** \'lar-(ˌ)ēz, 'ler-\ [Latin — more at LARVA]
**:** a tutelary god or spirit associated with Vesta and the Penates as a guardian of the household by the ancient Romans

**lar·board** \'lär-bərd\ *noun* [Middle English *ladeborde*] (14th century)
**:** ⁵PORT
**word history** see STARBOARD
— **larboard** *adjective*

**lar·ce·ner** \'lärs-nər, 'lär-s°n-ər\ *noun* (circa 1635)
**:** LARCENIST

**lar·ce·nist** \-nist, -s°n-ist\ *noun* (1803)
**:** a person who commits larceny

**lar·ce·nous** \-nəs, -s°n-əs\ *adjective* (1742)
**1 :** having the character of or constituting larceny
**2 :** committing larceny
— **lar·ce·nous·ly** *adverb*

**lar·ce·ny** \-nē, -s°n-ē\ *noun, plural* **-nies** [Middle English, from Middle French *larcin* theft, from Latin *latrocinium* robbery, from *latron-, latro* mercenary soldier, probably from (assumed) Greek *latrōn*, from Greek *latron* pay] (15th century)
**:** the unlawful taking of personal property with intent to deprive the rightful owner of it permanently

**larch** \'lärch\ *noun* [probably from German *Lärche*, from Middle High German *lerche*, from Latin *laric-, larix*] (1548)
**:** any of a genus (*Larix*) of trees of the pine family with short fascicled deciduous leaves; *also* **:** the wood of a larch

**¹lard** \'lärd\ *transitive verb* (14th century)
**1 a :** to dress (meat) for cooking by inserting or covering with something (as strips of fat) **b :** to cover or soil with grease
**2 :** to decorate or intersperse with something ⟨the book is *larded* with anecdotes⟩

larch

**3** *obsolete* **:** to make rich with or as if with fat
**²lard** *noun* [Middle English, from Middle French, from Latin *lardum, laridum;* perhaps akin to Greek *larinos* fat] (14th century)
**:** a soft white solid or semisolid fat obtained by rendering fatty tissue of the hog
— **lardy** \'lär-dē\ *adjective*

**lar·der** \'lär-dər\ *noun* [Middle English, from Middle French *lardier*, from *lard*] (14th century)
**1 :** a place where food is stored **:** PANTRY
**2 :** a supply of food

**lar·doon** \lär-'dün\ *or* **lar·don** \'lär-ˌdän\ *noun* [Middle English, from Middle French *lardon* piece of fat pork, from *lard*] (14th century)
**:** a strip (as of salt pork) with which meat is larded

**lares and penates** \*see* LAR, PENATES\ *noun plural* (1775)
**1 :** household gods
**2 :** personal or household effects

**¹large** \'lärj\ *adjective* **larg·er; larg·est** [Middle English, from Old French, from Latin *largus*] (12th century)
**1** *obsolete* **:** LAVISH
**2** *obsolete* **a :** AMPLE, ABUNDANT **b :** EXTENSIVE, BROAD
**3 :** having more than usual power, capacity, or scope **:** COMPREHENSIVE ⟨take the *large* view⟩ ⟨will take a *larger* role in the negotiations⟩
**4 a :** exceeding most other things of like kind especially in quantity or size **:** BIG **b :** dealing in great numbers or quantities ⟨a *large* and highly profitable business⟩
**5** *obsolete* **a** *of language or expression* **:** COARSE, VULGAR **b :** lax in conduct **:** LOOSE
**6** *of a wind* **:** FAVORABLE
**7 :** EXTRAVAGANT, BOASTFUL ⟨*large* talk⟩
— **large·ness** *noun*
— **larg·ish** \'lär-jish\ *adjective*

**²large** *adverb* (14th century)
**1** *obsolete* **:** in abundance **:** AMPLY, LIBERALLY
**2 :** with the wind abaft the beam

**³large** *noun* (14th century)
*obsolete* **:** LIBERALITY, GENEROSITY
— **at large 1 a :** free of restraint or confinement ⟨the escaped prisoner is still *at large*⟩ **b :** without a specific subject or assignment ⟨critic *at large*⟩ **2 :** at length **3 :** in a general way **4 :** as a whole ⟨society *at large*⟩ **5 :** as the political representative of or to a whole area rather than of one of its subdivisions — used in combination with a preceding noun ⟨a congressman-*at-large*⟩
— **in the large :** on a large scale **:** in general

**large calorie** *noun* (circa 1909)
**:** CALORIE 1b

**large·heart·ed** \ˌlärj-'här-təd\ *adjective* (1645)
**:** having a generous disposition **:** SYMPATHETIC
— **large·heart·ed·ness** *noun*

**large intestine** *noun* (1823)
**:** the more terminal division of the vertebrate intestine that is wider and shorter than the small intestine, typically divided into cecum, colon, and rectum, and concerned especially with the resorption of water and the formation of feces

**large·ly** \'lärj-lē\ *adverb* (13th century)
**:** in a large manner; *especially* **:** to a large extent **:** MOSTLY, PRIMARILY

**large·mind·ed** \ˌlärj-'mīn-dəd\ *adjective* (1725)
**:** generous or comprehensive in outlook, range, or capacity
— **large·mind·ed·ly** *adverb*
— **large·mind·ed·ness** *noun*

**large·mouth bass** \'lärj-ˌmaùth-\ *noun* (1941)
**:** a large black bass (*Micropterus salmoides*) that is blackish green above and lighter below and has the maxillary bones of the upper jaw extending behind the eyes — called also *largemouth, largemouth black bass*

**large-print** \-'print\ *adjective* (1968)

**:** being set in a large size of type (as 14 point or larger) especially for use by the partially sighted ⟨*large-print* books⟩

**larger–than–life** *adjective* (1950)
**:** of the sort legends are made of ⟨*larger-than-life* heroes⟩

**large–scale integration** *noun* (1966)
**:** the process of placing a large number of circuits on a small chip

**lar·gesse** *or* **lar·gess** \lär-'zhes, lär-'jes *also* 'lär-ˌjes\ *noun* [Middle English *largesse*, from Old French, from *large*] (13th century)
**1 :** liberal giving (as of money) to or as if to an inferior; *also* **:** something so given
**2 :** GENEROSITY

**¹lar·ghet·to** \lär-'ge-(ˌ)tō\ *noun, plural* **-tos** (circa 1724)
**:** a movement played larghetto

**²larghetto** *adverb or adjective* [Italian, somewhat slow, from *largo*] (circa 1801)
**:** slower than andante but not so slow as largo — used as a direction in music

**¹lar·go** \'lär-(ˌ)gō\ *adverb or adjective* [Italian, slow, broad, from Latin *largus* abundant] (1683)
**:** at a very slow tempo — used as a direction in music

**²largo** *noun, plural* **largos** (circa 1724)
**:** a largo movement

**lar·i·at** \'lar-ē-ət, 'ler-\ *noun* [American Spanish *la reata* the lasso, from Spanish *la* the (feminine of *el*, from Latin *ille* that) + American Spanish *reata* lasso, from Spanish *reatar* to tie again, from *re-* + *atar* to tie, from Latin *aptare* to fit — more at ADAPT] (1832)
**:** a long light rope (as of hemp or leather) used with a running noose to catch livestock or with or without the noose to tether grazing animals **:** LASSO

**¹lark** \'lärk\ *noun* [Middle English *laveroc, laverke*, from Old English *lāwerce*; akin to Old High German *lērihha* lark] (before 12th century)
**:** any of a family (Alaudidae) of chiefly Old World songbirds that are usually brownish in color; *especially* **:** SKYLARK — compare MEADOWLARK

**²lark** *noun* [³*lark*] (circa 1811)
**:** something done solely for fun or adventure ⟨ran for office on a *lark*⟩

**³lark** *intransitive verb* [probably alteration of *lake* to frolic] (1813)
**:** to engage in harmless fun or mischief — often used with *about*
— **lark·er** *noun*

**lark·spur** \'lärk-ˌspər\ *noun* (1578)
**1 :** DELPHINIUM
**2 :** any of the delphiniums that are annuals, have the upper two petals of the corolla united and the bottom two missing, are now often placed in a separate genus (*Consolida*), and include several widely cultivated forms

**larky** \'lär-kē\ *adjective* **lark·i·er; -est** (1841)
**1 :** given to or ready for larking **:** SPORTIVE
**2 :** resulting from a lark
— **lark·i·ness** \-nəs\ *noun*

**lar·ri·gan** \'lar-i-gən\ *noun* [origin unknown] (1886)
**:** an oil-tanned moccasin with a leg often reaching the knee

**lar·ri·kin** \'lar-i-kən\ *noun* [origin unknown] (1868)
*chiefly Australian* **:** HOODLUM, ROWDY
— **larrikin** *adjective*

**¹lar·rup** \'lar-əp\ *noun* [origin unknown] (circa 1820)
*dialect* **:** ⁵BLOW

**²larrup** (circa 1823)
*transitive verb*
**1** *dialect* **:** to flog soundly **:** WHIP

\ə\ abut \°\ kitten \ər\ further \a\ ash \ā\ ace
\ä\ mop, mar \aù\ out \ch\ chin \e\ bet \ē\ easy
\g\ go \i\ hit \ī\ ice \j\ job \ŋ\ sing \ō\ go
\ò\ law \òi\ boy \th\ thin \th\ the \ü\ loot \ù\ foot
\y\ yet \zh\ vision    *see also* Guide to Pronunciation

**2** *dialect* **:** to defeat decisively **:** TROUNCE
*intransitive verb*
*dialect* **:** to move indolently or clumsily
**la·rum** \'lär-əm, 'lar-\ *noun* [short for *alarum*] (15th century)
*archaic* **:** ALARM
**lar·va** \'lär-və\ *noun, plural* **lar·vae** \-(,)vē, -,vī\ *also* **larvas** [New Latin, from Latin, specter, mask; akin to Latin *lar* Lar] (1768)
**1 :** the immature, wingless, and often worm-like feeding form that hatches from the egg of many insects, alters chiefly in size while passing through several molts, and is finally transformed into a pupa or chrysalis from which the adult emerges
**2 :** the early form of an animal (as a frog or sea urchin) that at birth or hatching is fundamentally unlike its parent and must metamorphose before assuming the adult characters ◆
— **lar·val** \-vəl\ *adjective*
**lar·vi·cide** \'lär-və-,sīd\ *noun* (circa 1888)
**:** an agent for killing larval pests
— **lar·vi·cid·al** \,lär-və-'sī-d°l\ *adjective*
**laryng-** *or* **laryngo-** *combining form* [New Latin, from Greek, from *laryng-, larynx*]
**:** larynx ⟨*laryngitis*⟩
**¹la·ryn·geal** \lə-'rin-jəl *also* -jē-əl; ,lar-ən-'jē-əl\ *adjective* (1795)
**1 :** of, relating to, or used on the larynx
**2 :** produced by or with constriction of the larynx ⟨*laryngeal* articulation of sounds⟩
**²laryngeal** *noun* (circa 1902)
**1 :** an anatomical part (as a nerve or artery) that supplies or is associated with the larynx
**2 a :** a laryngeal sound **b :** any of a set of several conjectured phonemes reconstructed for Proto-Indo-European chiefly on indirect evidence
**lar·yn·gec·to·mee** \,lar-ən-,jek-tə-'mē\ *noun* (1956)
**:** a person who has undergone laryngectomy
**lar·yn·gec·to·my** \-'jek-tə-mē\ *noun, plural* **-mies** (circa 1888)
**:** surgical removal of all or part of the larynx
— **lar·yn·gec·to·mized** \-tə-,mīzd\ *adjective*
**lar·yn·gi·tis** \,lar-ən-'jī-təs\ *noun* [New Latin] (circa 1834)
**:** inflammation of the larynx
— **lar·yn·git·ic** \-'ji-tik\ *adjective*
**lar·yn·gol·o·gy** \,lar-ən-'gä-lə-jē\ *noun* [International Scientific Vocabulary] (circa 1842)
**:** a branch of medicine dealing with diseases of the larynx and nasopharynx
**la·ryn·go·scope** \lə-'rin-gə-,skōp, -'rin-jə-\ *noun* [International Scientific Vocabulary] (1860)
**:** an instrument for examining the interior of the larynx
— **lar·yn·gos·co·py** \,lar-ən-'gäs-kə-pē\ *noun*
**lar·ynx** \'lar-in(k)s\ *noun, plural* **la·ryn·ges** \lə-'rin-(,)jēz\ *or* **lar·ynx·es** [New Latin *laryng-, larynx,* from Greek] (1578)
**:** the modified upper part of the trachea of air-breathing vertebrates that in humans, most other mammals, and a few lower forms contains the vocal cords
**la·sa·gna** \lə-'zän-yə\ *noun* [Italian *lasagna,* from (assumed) Vulgar Latin *lasania* cooking pot, its contents, from Latin *lasanum* chamber pot, from Greek *lasanon*] (1846)
**1** *also* **la·sa·gne** \-yə\ **:** pasta in the form of broad often ruffled ribbons
**2 :** a baked dish consisting chiefly of layers of boiled lasagna, cheese, and a seasoned sauce of tomatoes and usually meat
**las·car** \'las-kər\ *noun* [Hindi *lashkar* army] (1615)
**:** an Indian sailor, army servant, or artilleryman
**las·civ·i·ous** \lə-'si-vē-əs\ *adjective* [Late Latin *lasciviosus,* from Latin *lascivia* wantonness, from *lascivus* wanton — more at LUST] (15th century)
**:** LEWD, LUSTFUL

— **las·civ·i·ous·ly** *adverb*
— **las·civ·i·ous·ness** *noun*
**lase** \'lāz\ *intransitive verb* **lased; las·ing** [back-formation from *laser*] (1962)
**:** to emit coherent light
**la·ser** \'lā-zər\ *noun, often attributive* [*l*ight *a*mplification by *s*timulated *e*mission of *r*adiation] (1960)
**:** a device that utilizes the natural oscillations of atoms or molecules between energy levels for generating coherent electromagnetic radiation usually in the ultraviolet, visible, or infrared regions of the spectrum
**laser disc** *noun* (1980)
**:** OPTICAL DISK; *especially* **:** one on which programs are recorded for playback on a television set
**laser printer** *noun* (1979)
**:** a high-resolution printer for computer output that xerographically prints an image formed by a laser
**¹lash** \'lash\ *verb* [Middle English] (14th century)
*intransitive verb*
**1 :** to move violently or suddenly **:** DASH
**2 :** to thrash or beat violently ⟨rain *lashed* at the windowpanes⟩
**3 :** to make a verbal attack or retort — usually used with *out*
*transitive verb*
**1 a :** to whip or fling about violently ⟨the big cat *lashed* its tail about threateningly⟩ **b :** to strike or beat with or as if with a whip ⟨waves *lashed* the shore⟩
**2 a :** to assail with stinging words **b :** DRIVE, WHIP ⟨*lashed* them to fury with his speech⟩
— **lash·er** *noun*
**²lash** *noun* (14th century)
**1 a** (1) **:** a stroke with or as if with a whip (2) **:** the flexible part of a whip; *also* **:** WHIP **b :** punishment by whipping
**2 :** a beating, whipping, or driving force
**3 :** a stinging rebuke
**4 :** EYELASH
**5 :** the clearance or play between adjacent movable mechanical parts
**³lash** *transitive verb* [Middle English *lasschyn* to lace, from Middle French *lacier* — more at LACE] (1624)
**:** to bind with or as if with a line
— **lash·er** *noun*
**lash·ing** *noun* (1669)
**:** something used for binding, wrapping, or fastening
**lash·ings** \'la-shiŋz, -shənz\ *also* **lash·ins** \-shənz\ *noun plural* [from gerund of ¹*lash*] (1829)
*chiefly British* **:** a great plenty **:** ABUNDANCE ⟨piles of bread and butter and *lashings* of tea —Molly Weir⟩
**lash–up** \'lash-,əp\ *noun* [³*lash*] (1898)
**1 :** something hastily put together or improvised
**2 :** OUTFIT 3
**L–as·par·a·gi·nase** \'el-as-'par-ə-jə-,nās, -,nāz\ *noun* (1962)
**:** an enzyme that breaks down the physiologically commoner form of asparagine, is obtained especially from bacteria, and is used especially to treat leukemia
**lass** \'las\ *noun* [Middle English *las*] (14th century)
**1 :** a young woman **:** GIRL
**2 :** SWEETHEART
**Las·sa fever** \'la-sə-\ *noun* [*Lassa,* village in Nigeria] (1970)
**:** a virus disease especially of Africa that is characterized by a high fever, headaches, mouth ulcers, muscle aches, small hemorrhages under the skin, heart and kidney failure, and a high mortality rate
**las·sie** \'la-sē\ *noun* (1725)
**:** LASS 1
**las·si·tude** \'la-sə-,tüd, -,tyüd\ *noun* [Middle French, from Latin *lassitudo,* from *lassus* wea-

ry; probably akin to Old English *læt* late — more at LATE] (15th century)
**1 :** a condition of weariness or debility **:** FATIGUE
**2 :** a condition of listlessness **:** LANGUOR
**synonym** see LETHARGY
**¹las·so** \'la-(,)sō, la-'sü\ *transitive verb* (1807)
**:** to capture with or as if with a lasso **:** ROPE
— **las·so·er** *noun*
**²lasso** *noun, plural* **lassos** *or* **lassoes** [Spanish *lazo,* from Latin *laqueus* snare] (1808)
**:** a rope or long thong of leather with a noose used especially for catching horses and cattle **:** LARIAT
**¹last** \'last\ *verb* [Middle English, from Old English *læstan* to last, follow; akin to Old English *last* footprint] (before 12th century)
*intransitive verb*
**1 :** to continue in time
**2 a :** to remain fresh or unimpaired **:** ENDURE **b :** to manage to continue (as in a course of action) **c :** to continue to live
*transitive verb*
**1 :** to continue in existence or action as long as or longer than — often used with *out* ⟨couldn't *last* out the training program⟩
**2 :** to be enough for the needs of ⟨the supplies will *last* them a week⟩
**synonym** see CONTINUE
**word history** see LEARN
— **last·er** *noun*
**²last** *noun* [Middle English, from Old English *læste,* from *last* footprint; akin to Old High German *leist* shoemaker's last, Latin *lira* furrow — more at LEARN] (before 12th century)
**:** a form (as of metal or plastic) which is shaped like the human foot and over which a shoe is shaped or repaired
**word history** see LEARN
**³last** *transitive verb* (circa 1859)
**:** to shape with a last
— **last·er** *noun*
**⁴last** *adverb* [Middle English, from Old English *latost,* superlative of *læt* late] (before 12th century)
**1 :** after all others **:** at the end ⟨came *last* and left first⟩
**2 :** most lately ⟨saw him *last* in Rome⟩
**3 :** in conclusion ⟨*last,* let's consider the social aspect⟩
**⁵last** *adjective* (13th century)
**1 a :** following all the rest ⟨he was the *last* one out⟩ **b :** being the only remaining ⟨our *last* dollar⟩
**2 a :** belonging to the final stage (as of life) ⟨his *last* hours on earth⟩ **b :** administered to the seriously sick or dying ⟨the *last* rites of the church⟩
**3 a :** next before the present **:** most recent ⟨*last* week⟩ ⟨his *last* book was a failure⟩ **b :** most up-to-date **:** LATEST ⟨it's the *last* thing in fashion⟩

◇ WORD HISTORY
**larva** The designations *larva, pupa,* and *imago* for the three post-egg stages of an insect's life cycle are usually credited to Carolus Linnaeus, the founder of modern biological taxonomy. Biologists of the 18th century saw the adult as the only genuine form of the insect, and hence called it the *imago,* the proper "image" or representation of the creature as it actually is. The preceding stages were considered somehow unreal, or at best misleading, and so were named with the Latin words *pupa* "doll" and *larva,* which in classical Latin was a sort of ghostlike demon or a mask representing a demon. Although to modern biology larval stages such as caterpillars are as real and taxonomically valid as adults, the traditional terminology remains with us.

**4 a :** lowest in rank or standing; *also* : WORST **b :** farthest from a specified quality, attitude, or likelihood 〈would be the *last* person to fall for flattery〉 **5 a :** CONCLUSIVE 〈there is no *last* answer to the problem〉 **b :** highest in degree : SUPREME, ULTIMATE **c :** DISTINCT, SEPARATE — used as an intensive 〈ate every *last* piece of food〉 ☆ **— last·ly** *adverb*

**⁶last** *noun* (13th century) : something that is last **— at last** *or* **at long last :** at the end of a period of time : FINALLY 〈*at last* you've come home〉

**last–ditch** \'las(t)-,dich, -'dich\ *adjective* (1937) **1 :** fought or conducted from the last ditch : waged with desperation or unyielding defiance 〈*last-ditch* resistance〉 **2 :** made as a final effort especially to avert disaster 〈a *last-ditch* attempt to raise the money〉

**last ditch** *noun* (circa 1715) : a place of final defense or resort

**last–gasp** \'las(t)-'gasp\ *adjective* (1921) : done or coming at the very end **— last gasp** *noun*

**last hurrah** *noun* [from *The Last Hurrah* (1956) by Edwin O'Connor (died 1968) American novelist] (1966) : a final often valedictory effort, production, or appearance 〈his unsuccessful Senate run was his *last hurrah* —R. W. Daly〉

**last–in first–out** *adjective* (1940) : of, relating to, or being a method of inventory accounting that values stock on hand according to costs at the time of acquisition and not according to the cost of replacement

**¹last·ing** *adjective* (12th century) : existing or continuing a long while : ENDURING ☆ **— last·ing·ly** \'las-tiŋ-lē\ *adverb* **— last·ing·ness** *noun*

**²lasting** *noun* (15th century) **1** *archaic* : long life **2 :** a sturdy cotton or worsted cloth used especially in shoes and luggage

**Last Judgment** *noun* (14th century) : the judgment of mankind before God at the end of the world

**last minute** *noun* (1920) : the moment just before some climactic, decisive, or disastrous event

**last name** *noun* (1897) : SURNAME 2

**last rites** *noun* (1922) : EXTREME UNCTION

**last straw** *noun* [from the fable of the last straw that broke the camel's back when added to its burden] (1848) : the last of a series (as of events or indignities) that brings one beyond the point of endurance

**Last Supper** *noun* (14th century) : the supper eaten by Jesus and his disciples on the night of his betrayal

**Last Things** *noun plural* [translation of Medieval Latin *Novissima*] (1522) : events (as the resurrection and divine judgment of all humankind) marking the end of the world : eschatological happenings

**last word** *noun* (1563) **1 :** the final remark in a verbal exchange **2 a :** the power of final decision **b :** a definitive statement or treatment 〈this study will surely be the *last word* on the subject for many years〉 **3 :** the most advanced, up-to-date, or fashionable exemplar of its kind 〈the *last word* in sports cars〉

**lat** \'lat\ *noun* [Latvian *lats*, from *Latvija* Latvia] (1923) — see MONEY table

**lat·a·kia** \,la-tə-'kē-ə\ *noun* [*Latakia*, seaport in Syria] (1833) : a highly aromatic Turkish smoking tobacco

**¹latch** \'lach\ *intransitive verb* [Middle English *lachen*, from Old English *læccan*; perhaps akin to Greek *lambanein* to take, seize] (13th century) **1 :** to lay hold with or as if with the hands or arms — used with *on* or *onto* **2 :** to associate oneself intimately and often artfully — used with *on* or *onto* 〈*latched* onto a rich widow〉

**²latch** *noun* (13th century) : any of various devices in which mating mechanical parts engage to fasten but usually not to lock something: **a :** a fastener (as for a door) consisting essentially of a pivoted bar that falls into a notch **b :** a fastener (as for a door) in which a spring slides a bolt into a hole; *also* : NIGHT LATCH

**³latch** *transitive verb* (15th century) : to make fast with or as if with a latch

**latch·et** \'la-chət\ *noun* [Middle English *lachet*, from Middle French, shoestring, from *laz* snare, from Latin *laqueus*] (15th century) : a narrow leather strap, thong, or lace that fastens a shoe or sandal on the foot

**latch·key** \'lach-,kē\ *noun* (1825) : a key to an outside and especially a front door

**latchkey child** *noun* (1944) : a young child of working parents who must spend part of the day unsupervised (as at home) — called also *latchkey kid*

**latch·string** \-,striŋ\ *noun* (1791) : a string on a latch that may be left hanging outside the door to permit the raising of the latch from the outside or drawn inside to prevent intrusion

**¹late** \'lāt\ *adjective* **lat·er; lat·est** [Middle English, late, slow, from Old English *læt*; akin to Old High German *laz* slow, Old English *lætan* to let] (before 12th century) **1 a** (1) : coming or remaining after the due, usual, or proper time 〈a *late* spring〉 (2) : of, relating to, or imposed because of tardiness **b** : of or relating to an advanced stage in point of time or development 〈the *late* Middle Ages〉; *especially* : far advanced toward the close of the day or night 〈*late* hours〉 **2 a :** living comparatively recently — used of persons 〈the *late* John Doe〉 and often with reference to a specific relationship or status 〈his *late* wife〉 **b :** being something or holding some position or relationship recently but not now 〈the *late* belligerents〉 **c :** made, appearing, or happening just previous to the present time especially as the most recent of a succession 〈our *late* quarrel〉 ■ **synonym** *see* DEAD **— late·ness** *noun*

**²late** *adverb* **lat·er; lat·est** (before 12th century) **1 a :** after the usual or proper time 〈got to work *late*〉 **b :** at or to an advanced point of time **2 :** not long ago : RECENTLY 〈a man *late* of Chicago〉 **— of late :** in the period shortly or immediately preceding : RECENTLY 〈has been sick *of late*〉

**late blight** *noun* (1900) : a disease of solanaceous plants (as the potato and tomato) that is caused by a fungus (*Phytophthora infestans*) and is characterized by decay of stems, leaves, and in the potato also of tubers

**late·com·er** \'lāt-,kə-mər\ *noun* (1892) : one that arrives late; *also* : a recent arrival

**lat·ed** \'lā-təd\ *adjective* (circa 1592) : BELATED

**¹la·teen** \lə-'tēn\ *adjective* [French (*voile*) *latine*, literally, Latin (Mediterranean) sail] (circa 1741) : being or relating to a rig used especially on the north coast of Africa and characterized by a triangular sail extended by a long spar slung to a low mast

**²lateen** *noun* (circa 1775) **1** *also* **la·teen·er** \-'tē-nər\ : a lateen-rigged ship **2 :** a lateen sail

**Late Greek** *noun* (circa 1889) : the Greek language as used in the 3d to 6th centuries

**Late Hebrew** *noun* (1951) : the Hebrew language used by writers from about the 2d century B.C. to the early Middle Ages

**Late Latin** *noun* (1888) : the Latin language used by writers in the 3d to 6th centuries

---

☆ **SYNONYMS**
**Last, final, terminal, eventual, ultimate** mean following all others (as in time, order, or importance). LAST applies to something that comes at the end of a series but does not always imply that the series is completed or stopped 〈*last* page of a book〉 〈*last* news we had of him〉. FINAL applies to that which definitely closes a series, process, or progress 〈*final* day of school〉. TERMINAL may indicate a limit of extension, growth, or development 〈*terminal* phase of a disease〉. EVENTUAL applies to something that is bound to follow sooner or later as the final effect of causes already operating 〈*eventual* defeat of the enemy〉. ULTIMATE implies the last degree or stage of a long process beyond which further progress or change is impossible 〈the *ultimate* collapse of the system〉.

**Lasting, permanent, durable, stable** mean enduring for so long as to seem fixed or established. LASTING implies a capacity to continue indefinitely 〈a book that left a *lasting* impression on me〉. PERMANENT adds usually the implication of being designed or planned to stand or continue indefinitely 〈*permanent* living arrangements〉. DURABLE implies power to resist destructive agencies 〈*durable* fabrics〉. STABLE implies lastingness because of resistance to being overturned or displaced 〈a *stable* government〉.

---

☐ **USAGE**
**late** The definition of sense 2a above contains the words "comparatively recently." One of the hardest things for the user of this sense of *late* to decide is how long the word applies. The commentators—mostly newspaper editors—who have given the subject some thought have reached no consensus; their advice runs from "within the preceding decade" to "half a century." This certainly gives you some latitude, and our evidence shows that writers have in general taken advantage of that latitude. Two strictures are placed on the use of *late* by various critics. The first is that *late* should not be used of famous people everyone knows are dead; a couple of instances will show how little this is observed 〈the *late* Henry Ford —*N.Y. Times*〉 〈the *late* President John F. Kennedy —*Current Biography*〉. The other is that *late* should not be used if the person was alive at the time referred to; this too is little observed 〈the Senate Select Intelligence Committee, then . . . headed by the *late* Senator Frank Church —David Burnham〉 〈my *late* sister Lucy at one time decided to be on the safe side —George Bernard Shaw〉.

---

\ə\ **abut** \ᵊ\ **kitten** \ər\ **further** \a\ **ash** \ā\ **ace** \ä\ **mop, mar** \aů\ **out** \ch\ **chin** \e\ **bet** \ē\ **easy** \g\ **go** \i\ **hit** \ī\ **ice** \j\ **job** \ŋ\ **sing** \ō\ **go** \ȯ\ **law** \ȯi\ **boy** \th\ **thin** \t̲h̲\ **the** \ü\ **loot** \ů\ **foot** \y\ **yet** \zh\ **vision** *see also* Guide to Pronunciation

**late·ly** \'lāt-lē\ adverb (15th century)
: of late : RECENTLY ⟨has been friendlier lately⟩
**lat·en** \'lā-tᵊn\ verb **lat·ened; lat·en·ing**
\'lāt-niŋ, 'lā-tᵊn-iŋ\ (1880)
intransitive verb
: to grow late
transitive verb
: to cause to grow late
**la·ten·cy** \'lā-tᵊn(t)-sē\ noun, plural **-cies**
(circa 1638)
**1** : the quality or state of being latent : DOR-MANCY
**2** : something latent
**3** : a stage of personality development that extends from about the age of five to the beginning of puberty and during which sexual urges often appear to lie dormant
**4** : LATENT PERIOD 2
**latency period** noun (1910)
**1** : LATENCY 3
**2** : LATENT PERIOD
**La Tène** \lä-'ten, -'tān\ adjective [La Tène, shallows of the Lake of Neuchâtel, Switzerland] (1901)
: of or relating to the later period of the Iron Age in Europe assumed to date from 500 B.C. to A.D. 1
**la·ten·si·fi·ca·tion** \lā-,ten(t)-sə-fə-'kā-shən, lə-\ noun [blend of ¹latent and intensification] (1940)
: intensification of a latent photographic image by chemical treatment or exposure to light of low intensity
**¹la·tent** \'lā-tᵊnt\ adjective [Middle English, from Latin latent-, latens, from present participle of latēre to lie hidden; akin to Greek lanthanein to escape notice] (15th century)
: present and capable of becoming though not now visible, obvious, or active ⟨a latent infection⟩ ☆
— **la·tent·ly** adverb
**²latent** noun (1923)
: a fingerprint (as at the scene of a crime) that is scarcely visible but can be developed for study
**latent heat** noun (circa 1757)
: heat given off or absorbed in a process (as fusion or vaporization) other than a change of temperature
**latent period** noun (1837)
**1** : the incubation period of a disease
**2** : the interval between stimulation and response
**latent root** noun (1883)
: an eigenvalue of a matrix
**lat·er** \'lā-tər\ adverb (13th century)
: at some time subsequent to a given time : SUBSEQUENTLY, AFTERWARD ⟨four months later⟩ ⟨they later regretted their decision⟩ — often used with on ⟨experience that will be useful later on⟩
**-later** noun combining form [Middle English -latrer, from Middle French -latre, from Late Latin -latres, from Greek -latrēs; akin to Greek latron pay]
: worshiper ⟨bibliolater⟩
**lat·er·ad** \'la-tə-,rad\ adverb [Latin later-, latus] (1814)
: toward the side
**¹lat·er·al** \'la-tə-rəl also 'la-trəl\ adjective [Middle English laterale, from Latin lateralis, from later-, latus side] (15th century)
**1** : of or relating to the side
**2** : situated on, directed toward, or coming from the side
**3** : extending from side to side ⟨lateral axis of an airplane⟩
**4** : produced with passage of breath around the side of a constriction formed with the tongue ⟨\l\ is lateral⟩
— **lat·er·al·ly** adverb
**²lateral** noun (1851)
**1** : a branch from the main part (as in an irrigation or electrical system)

**2** : a pass in football thrown parallel to the line of scrimmage or in a direction away from the opponent's goal
**3** : a lateral speech sound
**³lateral** intransitive verb (1944)
: to throw a lateral
**lateral bud** noun (circa 1892)
: a bud that develops in the axil between a petiole and a stem
**lat·er·al·i·za·tion** \,la-tə-rə-lə-'zā-shən, ,la-trə-\ noun (circa 1899)
: localization of function or activity (as of verbal processes in the brain) on one side of the body in preference to the other
— **lat·er·al·ize** \'la-tə-rə-,līz, 'la-trə-\ transitive verb
**lateral line** noun (1870)
: a canal along the side of a fish containing pores that open into tubes supplied with sense organs sensitive to low vibrations; also : one of these tubes or sense organs
**lat·er·ite** \'la-tə-,rīt\ noun [Latin later brick] (1807)
: a residual product of rock decay that is red in color and has a high content in the oxides of iron and hydroxide of aluminum
— **lat·er·it·ic** \,la-tə-'ri-tik\ adjective
**lat·er·i·za·tion** \,la-tə-rə-'zā-shən\ noun (circa 1882)
: the process of conversion of rock to laterite
**¹lat·est** \'lā-təst\ adjective (1588)
**1** archaic : LAST
**2** : most recent ⟨the latest news⟩ ⟨the latest style⟩
**²latest** noun (1884)
**1** : the latest acceptable time — usually used in the phrase at the latest
**2** : something that is the most recent or currently fashionable ⟨the latest in diving techniques⟩
**late·wood** \'lāt-,wu̇d\ noun (circa 1933)
: SUMMERWOOD
**la·tex** \'lā-,teks\ noun, plural **la·ti·ces** \'lā-tə-,sēz, 'la-\ or **la·tex·es** [New Latin latic-, latex, from Latin fluid] (1835)
**1** : a milky usually white fluid that is produced by cells of various seed plants (as of the milkweed, spurge, and poppy families) and is the source of rubber, gutta-percha, chicle, and balata
**2** : a water emulsion of a synthetic rubber or plastic obtained by polymerization and used especially in coatings (as paint) and adhesives
**lath** \'lath also 'lath\ noun, plural **laths** or **lath** [Middle English, from (assumed) Old English læthth-; akin to Old High German latta lath, Welsh llath yard] (13th century)
**1** : a thin narrow strip of wood nailed to rafters, joists, or studding as a groundwork for slates, tiles, or plaster
**2** : a building material in sheets used as a base for plaster
**3** : a quantity of laths
— **lath** transitive verb
**¹lathe** \'lāth\ noun [probably from Middle English lath supporting stand] (circa 1611)
: a machine in which work is rotated about a horizontal axis and shaped by a fixed tool
**²lathe** transitive verb **lathed; lath·ing** (circa 1903)
: to cut or shape with a lathe
**¹lath·er** \'la-thər\ noun [(assumed) Middle English, from Old English lēathor; akin to Latin lavere to wash — more at LYE] (before 12th century)
**1 a** : a foam or froth formed when a detergent (as soap) is agitated in water **b** : foam or froth from profuse sweating (as on a horse)
**2** : an agitated or overwrought state : DITHER
— **lath·ery** \-th(ə-)rē\ adjective
**²lather** verb **lath·ered; lath·er·ing** \-th(ə-)riŋ\ (before 12th century)
transitive verb
**1** : to spread lather over
**2** : to beat severely : FLOG

intransitive verb
: to form a lather or a froth like lather
— **lath·er·er** \-thər-ər\ noun
**lath·y·rism** \'la-thə-,ri-zəm\ noun [New Latin Lathyrus, from Greek lathyros, a type of pea] (circa 1888)
: a diseased condition of humans, domestic animals, and especially horses that results from poisoning by a substance found in some legumes (genus Lathyrus and especially L. sativus) and is characterized especially by spastic paralysis of the hind or lower limbs
**lath·y·rit·ic** \,la-thə-'ri-tik\ adjective (1960)
: of, relating to, affected with, or characteristic of lathyrism ⟨lathyritic rats⟩ ⟨lathyritic cartilage⟩
**latices** plural of LATEX
**la·tic·i·fer** \lā-'ti-sə-fər\ noun [International Scientific Vocabulary latici- (from New Latin latic-, latex) + -fer] (circa 1928)
: a plant cell or vessel that contains latex
**la·ti·fun·dio** \,lä-tə-'fün-dē-,ō\ noun, plural **-di·os** [Spanish, from Latin latifundium] (circa 1902)
: a latifundium in Spain or Latin America
**lat·i·fun·di·um** \,la-tə-'fən-dē-əm\ noun, plural **-dia** \-dē-ə\ [Latin, from latus wide + fundus piece of landed property, foundation, bottom — more at BOTTOM] (1630)
: a great landed estate with primitive agriculture and labor often in a state of partial servitude
**lat·i·go** \'la-ti-,gō\ noun, plural **-gos** also **-goes** [Spanish látigo] (1873)
chiefly West : a long strap on a saddletree of a western saddle to adjust the cinch
**¹Lat·in** \'la-tᵊn\ adjective [Middle English, from Old English, from Latin Latinus, from Latium, ancient country of Italy] (before 12th century)
**1 a** : of, relating to, or composed in Latin **b** : ROMANCE
**2** : of or relating to Latium or the Latins
**3** : of or relating to the part of the Catholic Church that until recently used a Latin rite and forms the patriarchate of the pope
**4** : of or relating to the peoples or countries using Romance languages; specifically : of or relating to the peoples or countries of Latin America
**²Latin** noun (before 12th century)
**1** : the Italic language of ancient Latium and of Rome and until modern times the dominant language of school, church, and state in western Europe — see INDO-EUROPEAN LANGUAGES table
**2** : a member of the people of ancient Latium
**3** : a Catholic of the Latin rite
**4** : a member of one of the Latin peoples; specifically : a native or inhabitant of Latin America
**5** : LATIN ALPHABET
**Latin alphabet** noun (1823)
: an alphabet that was used for writing Latin and that has been modified for writing many modern languages
**Latin Americanist** noun (1972)
: a specialist in Latin American civilization
**Lat·in·ate** \'la-tᵊn-,āt\ adjective (1904)

---

☆ **SYNONYMS**
**Latent, dormant, quiescent, potential** mean not now showing signs of activity or existence. LATENT applies to a power or quality that has not yet come forth but may emerge and develop ⟨a latent desire for success⟩. DORMANT suggests the inactivity of something (as a feeling or power) as though sleeping ⟨their passion has lain dormant⟩. QUIESCENT suggests a usually temporary cessation of activity ⟨the disease was quiescent⟩. POTENTIAL applies to what does not yet have existence or effect but is likely soon to have ⟨a potential disaster⟩.

: of, relating to, resembling, or derived from Latin

**Latin cross** *noun* (1797)
: a figure of a cross having a long upright shaft and a shorter crossbar traversing it above the middle — see CROSS illustration

**Lat·in·ism** \'la-t³n-ˌi-zəm\ *noun* (circa 1570)
**1** : a characteristic feature of Latin occurring in another language
**2** : Latin quality or character

**Lat·in·ist** \'la-t³n-ist, 'lat-nist\ *noun* (15th century)
: a specialist in the Latin language or Roman culture

**la·tin·i·ty** \la-'ti-nə-tē, lə-\ *noun, often capitalized* (1619)
**1** : a manner of speaking or writing Latin
**2** : LATINISM 2

**lat·in·ize** \'la-t³n-ˌīz\ *verb* **-ized; -iz·ing** *often capitalized* (1589)
*transitive verb*
**1 a** *obsolete* : to translate into Latin **b** : to give a Latin form to **c** : to introduce Latinisms into **d** : ROMANIZE 2
**2** : to make Latin or Italian in doctrine, ideas, or traits; *specifically* : to cause to resemble the Roman Catholic Church
*intransitive verb*
**1** : to use Latinisms
**2** : to exhibit the influence of the Romans or of the Roman Catholic Church
— **lat·in·i·za·tion** \ˌla-t³n-ə-'zā-shən, ˌlat-nə-\ *noun*

**La·ti·no** \lə-'tē-(ˌ)nō\ *noun, plural* **-nos** [American Spanish, probably short for *latinoamericano* Latin American] (1946)
**1** : a native or inhabitant of Latin America
**2** : a person of Latin-American origin living in the U.S.
— **Latino** *adjective*

**Latin square** *noun* (1890)
: a square array which contains *n* different elements with each element occurring *n* times but with no element occurring twice in the same column or row and which is used especially in the statistical design of experiments (as in agriculture)

**lat·ish** \'lā-tish\ *adjective* (1611)
: somewhat late

**lat·i·tude** \'la-tə-ˌtüd, -ˌtyüd\ *noun* [Middle English, from Latin *latitudin-, latitudo,* from *latus* wide; akin to Old Church Slavonic *postĭlati* to spread] (14th century)
**1** *archaic* : extent or distance from side to side
: WIDTH
**2** : angular distance from some specified circle or plane of reference: as **a** : angular distance north or south from the earth's equator measured through 90 degrees **b** : angular distance of a celestial body from the ecliptic **c** : a region or locality as marked by its latitude

latitude 2a: hemisphere marked with parallels of latitude

**3 a** *archaic* : SCOPE, RANGE **b** : the range of exposures within which a film or plate will produce a negative or positive of satisfactory quality
**4** : freedom of action or choice
— **lat·i·tu·di·nal** \ˌla-tə-'tüd-nəl, -'tyüd-; -'tü-d³n-əl, -'tyü-\ *adjective*
— **lat·i·tu·di·nal·ly** *adverb*

**lat·i·tu·di·nar·i·an** \ˌla-tə-ˌtüd-³n-'er-ē-ən, -ˌtyü-\ *noun* (1662)
: a person who is broad and liberal in standards of religious belief and conduct
— **latitudinarian** *adjective*
— **lat·i·tu·di·nar·i·an·ism** \-ē-ə-ˌni-zəm\ *noun*

**lat·ke** \'lät-kə\ *noun* [Yiddish, pancake, from Ukrainian *oladka*] (1927)
: POTATO PANCAKE

**lat·o·sol** \'la-tə-ˌsól\ *noun* [irregular from Latin *later* brick + English *-sol* (as in *podsol,* variant of *podzol*)] (1949)
: a leached red and yellow tropical soil
— **lat·o·sol·ic** \ˌla-tə-'só-lik\ *adjective*

**la·trine** \lə-'trēn\ *noun* [French, from Latin *latrina,* contraction of *lavatrina,* from *lavare* to wash — more at LYE] (1642)
**1** : a receptacle (as a pit in the earth) for use as a toilet
**2** : TOILET

**-latry** *noun combining form* [Middle English *-latrie,* from Old French, from Late Latin *-latria,* from Greek, from *latreia; akin to* Greek *latron* pay]
: worship ⟨helio*latry*⟩

**lat·te** \'lä-(ˌ)tā\ *noun* (1991)
: CAFFE LATTE

**lat·ten** \'la-t³n\ *noun* [Middle English *laton,* from Middle French] (14th century)
: a yellow alloy identical to or resembling brass typically hammered into thin sheets and formerly much used for church utensils

**lat·ter** \'la-tər\ *adjective* [Middle English, from Old English *lætra,* comparative of *læt* late] (before 12th century)
**1 a** : belonging to a subsequent time or period
: more recent ⟨the *latter* stages of growth⟩ **b** : of or relating to the end ⟨in their *latter* days⟩ **c** : RECENT, PRESENT ⟨affected by *latter* calamities⟩
**2** : of, relating to, or being the second of two groups or things or the last of several groups or things referred to ⟨of ham and beef the *latter* meat is cheaper today⟩ ⟨of ham and beef the *latter* is cheaper today⟩

**lat·ter–day** \'la-tər-ˌdā\ *adjective* (1850)
**1** : of present or recent times ⟨*latter-day* prophets⟩
**2** : of a later or subsequent time

**Latter–day Saint** *noun, often D capitalized* (1834)
: a member of any of several religious bodies tracing their origin to Joseph Smith in 1830 and accepting the Book of Mormon as divine revelation : MORMON

**lat·ter·ly** *adverb* (1734)
**1** : LATER
**2** : of late : RECENTLY

**lat·tice** \'la-təs\ *noun* [Middle English *latis,* from Middle French *lattis*] (14th century)
**1 a** : a framework or structure of crossed wood or metal strips **b** : a window, door, or gate having a lattice **c** : a network or design resembling a lattice
**2** : a regular geometrical arrangement of points or objects over an area or in space; *specifically* : the arrangement of atoms in a crystal
**3** : a mathematical set that has some elements ordered and that is such that for any two elements there exists a greatest element in the subset of all elements less than or equal to both and a least element in the subset of all elements greater than or equal to both
— **lattice** *transitive verb*
— **lat·ticed** \-tist\ *adjective*

**lattice girder** *noun* (1852)
: a girder with top and bottom flanges connected by a latticework web

**lat·tice·work** \'la-təs-ˌwərk\ *noun* (15th century)
: a lattice or work made of lattices

**la·tus rec·tum** \ˌla-təs-'rek-təm\ *noun* [New Latin, literally, straight side] (1702)
: a chord of a conic section (as an ellipse) that passes through a focus and is parallel to the directrix

**Lat·vi·an** \'lat-vē-ən\ *noun* (1924)
**1** : the Baltic language of the Latvian people
**2** : a native or inhabitant of Latvia
— **Latvian** *adjective*

**lau·an** \'lü-ˌän, lü-'; laú-'än\ *noun* [Tagalog *lawaan*] (1894)
: any of various Philippine timbers (as of the genera *Shorea* and *Parashorea*) that are light

yellow to reddish brown or brown and include some which enter commerce as Philippine mahogany

**¹laud** \'lód\ *noun* [Middle English *laudes* (plural), from Medieval Latin, from Latin, plural of *laud-, laus* praise] (14th century)
**1** *plural but singular or plural in construction, often capitalized* : an office of solemn praise to God forming with matins the first of the canonical hours
**2** : PRAISE, ACCLAIM

**²laud** *transitive verb* [Latin *laudare,* from *laud-, laus*] (14th century)
: PRAISE, EXTOL

**laud·able** \'ló-də-bəl\ *adjective* (15th century)
: worthy of praise : COMMENDABLE
— **laud·able·ness** \'ló-də-bəl-nəs\ *noun*
— **laud·ably** \-blē\ *adverb*

**lau·da·num** \'lód-nəm, 'ló-d³n-əm\ *noun* [New Latin] (circa 1603)
**1** : any of various formerly used preparations of opium
**2** : a tincture of opium

**lau·da·tion** \ló-'dā-shən\ *noun* (15th century)
: the act of praising : EULOGY

**lau·da·tive** \'ló-də-tiv\ *adjective* (15th century)
: LAUDATORY

**lau·da·to·ry** \'ló-də-ˌtōr-ē, -ˌtór-\ *adjective* (1555)
: of, relating to, or expressing praise

**¹laugh** \'laf, 'láf\ *verb* [Middle English, from Old English *hliehhan;* akin to Old High German *lachēn* to laugh] (before 12th century)
*intransitive verb*
**1 a** : to show mirth, joy, or scorn with a smile and chuckle or explosive sound **b** : to find amusement or pleasure in something ⟨*laughed* at his own clumsiness⟩ **c** : to become amused or derisive ⟨a very skeptical public *laughed* at our early efforts —Graenum Berger⟩
**2 a** : to produce the sound or appearance of laughter ⟨a *laughing* brook⟩ **b** : to be of a kind that inspires joy
*transitive verb*
**1** : to influence or move by laughter ⟨*laughed* the bad singer off the stage⟩
**2** : to utter with a laugh
— **laugh·ing·ly** \'la-fiŋ-lē, 'lä-\ *adverb*

**²laugh** *noun* (1690)
**1** : the act of laughing
**2 a** : a cause for derision or merriment : JOKE **b** : an expression of scorn or mockery : JEER
**3** *plural* : DIVERSION, SPORT ⟨play baseball just for *laughs*⟩

**laugh·able** \'la-fə-bəl, 'lä-\ *adjective* (1596)
: of a kind to provoke laughter or sometimes derision : amusingly ridiculous ☆
— **laugh·able·ness** *noun*
— **laugh·ably** \-blē\ *adverb*

**laugh·er** \'la-fər, 'lä-\ *noun* (15th century)
**1** : one that laughs

**2 :** something (as a game) that is easily won or handled
**laughing gas** *noun* (circa 1842)
**:** NITROUS OXIDE
**laughing gull** *noun* (1789)
**:** an American gull (*Larus atricilla*) having a black head in breeding plumage and black wing tips blending into the gray upper side of the wings
**laughing jackass** *noun* (1798)
**:** KOOKABURRA
**laughing matter** *noun* (circa 1583)
**:** something not to be taken seriously — usually used in the phrase *no laughing matter*
**laugh·ing·stock** \'la-fiŋ-,stäk, 'lä-\ *noun* (1533)
**:** an object of ridicule
**laugh off** *transitive verb* (1715)
**:** to minimize by treating as amusingly or absurdly trivial
**laugh·ter** \'laf-tər, 'läf-\ *noun* [Middle English, from Old English *hleahtor*; akin to Old English *hliehhan*] (before 12th century)
**1 :** a sound of or as if of laughing
**2** *archaic* **:** a cause of merriment
**laugh track** *noun* (1962)
**:** laughter to accompany dialogue or action (as of a television program)
**launce** \'lòn(t)s, 'län(t)s\ *noun* [probably from ¹*lance*] (1623)
**:** SAND LANCE
¹**launch** \'lònch, 'länch\ *verb* [Middle English, from Old North French *lancher*, from Late Latin *lanceare* to wield a lance — more at LANCE] (14th century)
*transitive verb*
**1 a :** to throw forward **:** HURL **b :** to release, catapult, or send off (a self-propelled object) ⟨*launch* a rocket⟩
**2 a :** to set (a boat or ship) afloat **b :** to give (a person) a start ⟨*launched* in a new career⟩ **c** (1) **:** to originate or set in motion **:** INITIATE, INTRODUCE (2) **:** to get off to a good start
*intransitive verb*
**1 a :** to spring forward **:** TAKE OFF **b :** to throw oneself energetically **:** PLUNGE
**2 a** *archaic* **:** to slide down the ways **b :** to make a start
²**launch** *noun* (1749)
**:** an act or instance of launching
³**launch** *noun* [Spanish or Portuguese; Spanish *lancha*, from Portuguese] (1697)
**1 :** a large boat that operates from a ship
**2 :** a small motorboat that is open or that has the forepart of the hull covered
**launch·er** \'lòn-chər, 'län-\ *noun* (1911)
**:** one that launches: as **a :** a device for firing grenades **b :** a device for launching a missile **c :** LAUNCH VEHICLE
**launching pad** *noun* (1951)
**1 :** LAUNCHPAD
**2 :** SPRINGBOARD 2
**launch·pad** \'lònch-,pad, 'länch-\ *noun* (1958)
**:** a nonflammable platform from which a rocket, launch vehicle, or guided missile can be launched
**launch vehicle** *noun* (circa 1960)
**:** a rocket used to launch a satellite or spacecraft
**launch window** *noun* (1962)
**:** WINDOW 8
¹**laun·der** \'lòn-dər, 'län-\ *verb* **laun·dered; laun·der·ing** \-d(ə-)riŋ\ [Middle English *launder*, noun] (1664)
*transitive verb*
**1 :** to wash (as clothes) in water
**2 :** to make ready for use by washing and ironing ⟨a freshly *laundered* shirt⟩
**3 :** to transfer (as illegally obtained money or investments) through an outside party to conceal the true source
*intransitive verb*
**:** to wash or wash and iron clothing or household linens
— **laun·der·er** \-dər-ər\ *noun*

²**launder** *noun* [Middle English, launderer, from Middle French *lavandier*, from Medieval Latin *lavandarius*, from Latin *lavandus*, gerundive of *lavare* to wash — more at LYE] (1667)
**:** TROUGH; *especially* **:** a box conduit conveying particulate material suspended in water in ore dressing
**laun·der·ette** \,lòn-də-'ret, ,län-\ *also* **laun·drette** \-'dret\ *noun* [from *Launderette*, a service mark] (circa 1948)
**:** a self-service laundry
**laun·dress** \'lòn-drəs, 'län-\ *noun* (1550)
**:** a woman who is a laundry worker
**Laun·dro·mat** \'lòn-drə-,mat, 'län-\ *service mark*
— used for a self-service laundry
**laun·dry** \'lòn-drē, 'län-\ *noun, plural* **laun·dries** (14th century)
**1 a :** a room for doing the family wash **b :** a commercial laundering establishment
**2 :** clothes or linens that have been or are to be laundered
**laundry list** *noun* (1958)
**:** a usually long list of items ⟨the *laundry list* of new consumer-protection bills —N. C. Miller⟩
**laun·dry·man** \-mən\ *noun* (1708)
**:** a man who is a laundry worker
**Laun·fal** \'lòn-fəl, 'län-\ *noun*
**:** a knight of the Round Table in late Arthurian legend
**lau·ra** \'läv-rə\ *noun* [Late Greek, from Greek, lane] (circa 1752)
**:** a monastery of an Eastern church
¹**lau·re·ate** \'lòr-ē-ət, 'lär-\ *noun* [Middle English, crowned with laurel as a distinction, from Latin *laureatus*, from *laurea* laurel wreath, from feminine of *laureus* of laurel, from *laurus*] (circa 1529)
**:** the recipient of honor or recognition for achievement in an art or science; *specifically* **:** POET LAUREATE
— **laureate** *adjective*
— **lau·re·ate·ship** \-,ship\ *noun*
²**lau·re·ate** \'lòr-ē-,āt, 'lär-\ *transitive verb* **-at·ed; -at·ing** (circa 1610)
**1 :** to crown with or as if with a laurel wreath for excellence or achievement
**2 :** to appoint to the office of poet laureate
— **lau·re·a·tion** \,lòr-ē-'ā-shən, ,lär-\ *noun*
¹**lau·rel** \'lòr-əl, 'lär-\ *noun* [Middle English *lorel*, from Old French *lorier*, from *lor* laurel, from Latin *laurus*] (14th century)
**1 :** any of a genus (*Laurus* of the family Lauraceae, the laurel family) of evergreen trees that have alternate entire leaves, small tetramerous flowers surrounded by bracts, and fruits that are ovoid berries; *specifically* **:** a tree (*L. nobilis*) of southern Europe with foliage used by the ancient Greeks to crown victors in the Pythian games

**laurel 1**

**2 :** a tree or shrub that resembles the true laurel; *especially* **:** MOUNTAIN LAUREL
**3 :** a crown of laurel **:** HONOR — usually used in plural
²**laurel** *transitive verb* **-reled** *or* **-relled; -rel·ing** *or* **-rel·ling** (1631)
**:** to deck or crown with laurel
**lau·ric acid** \'lòr-ik-, 'lär-\ *noun* [International Scientific Vocabulary, from Latin *laurus*] (1873)
**:** a crystalline fatty acid $C_{12}H_{24}O_2$ found especially in coconut oil and used in making soaps, esters, and lauryl alcohol
**lau·ryl alcohol** \'lòr-əl-, 'lär-\ *noun* (1922)

**:** a compound $C_{12}H_{26}O$; *also* **:** a liquid mixture of this and other alcohols used especially in making detergents
**la·va** \'lä-və, 'la-\ *noun* [Italian, ultimately from Latin *labes* fall; akin to Latin *labi* to slide — more at SLEEP] (1759)
**:** molten rock that issues from a volcano or from a fissure in the earth's surface; *also* **:** such rock that has cooled and hardened
— **la·va·like** \-,līk\ *adjective*
**la·va·bo** \lə-'vä-(,)bō\ *noun, plural* **-bos** [Latin, I shall wash, from *lavare*] (circa 1858)
**1** *often capitalized* **:** a ceremony at Mass in which the celebrant washes his hands after offering the oblations and says Psalm 25:6–12 (Douay Version)
**2 a :** a washbasin and a tank with a spigot that are fastened to a wall **b :** this combination used as a planter
**la·vage** \lə-'väzh, British usually 'la-vij\ *noun* [French, from Middle French, from *laver* to wash, from Latin *lavare*] (circa 1895)
**:** WASHING; *especially* **:** the therapeutic washing out of an organ
**la·va·la·va** \,lä-və-'lä-və\ *noun* [Samoan, clothing] (circa 1891)
**:** a rectangular cloth of cotton print worn like a kilt or skirt in Polynesia and especially in Samoa
**la·va·liere** *or* **la·val·liere** \,lä-və-'lir, ,la-\ *noun* [French *lavallière* necktie with a large knot] (1906)
**:** a pendant on a fine chain that is worn as a necklace
**la·va·lier microphone** \,lä-və-'lir-, ,la-\ *or* **lavaliere microphone** \*same*\ *noun* (circa 1962)
**:** a small microphone hung around the neck of the user
**la·va·tion** \lā-'vā-shən\ *noun* [Latin *lavation-, lavatio*, from *lavare*] (15th century)
**:** the act or an instance of washing or cleansing
**lav·a·to·ry** \'la-və-,tōr-ē, -,tòr-, British -və-t(ə-)rē\ *noun, plural* **-ries** [Middle English *lavatorie*, from Medieval Latin *lavatorium*, from Latin *lavare* to wash — more at LYE] (14th century)
**1 :** a vessel (as a basin) for washing; *especially* **:** a fixed bowl or basin with running water and drainpipe for washing
**2 :** a room with conveniences for washing and usually with one or more toilets
**3 :** TOILET 3b
— **lavatory** *adjective*
¹**lave** \'lāv\ *noun* [Middle English (northern dialect), from Old English *lāf*; akin to Old English *belīfan* to remain — more at LEAVE] (before 12th century)
*chiefly dialect* **:** something that is left **:** RESIDUE
²**lave** *verb* **laved; lav·ing** [Middle English, from Old English *lafian*, from Latin *lavare*] (before 12th century)
*transitive verb*
**1 a :** WASH, BATHE **b :** to flow along or against
**2 :** POUR
*intransitive verb*
*archaic* **:** to wash oneself **:** BATHE
¹**lav·en·der** \'la-vən-dər\ *noun* [Middle English *lavendre*, from Anglo-French, from Medieval Latin *lavandula*] (13th century)
**1 a :** a Mediterranean mint (*Lavandula angustifolia* synonym *L. officinalis*) widely cultivated for its narrow aromatic leaves and spikes of lilac-purple flowers which are dried and used in sachets **b :** any of several plants congeneric with true lavender and used similarly but often considered inferior
**2 :** a pale purple
²**lavender** *transitive verb* **lav·en·dered; lav·en·der·ing** \-d(ə-)riŋ\ (1820)
**:** to sprinkle or perfume with lavender
¹**la·ver** \'lā-vər\ *noun* [Middle English *lavour*, from Middle French *lavoir*, from Medieval Latin *lavatorium*] (1535)

: a large basin used for ceremonial ablutions in the ancient Jewish Tabernacle and Temple worship

**²la·ver** \'lā-vər, 'lä-\ *noun* [New Latin, from Latin, a water plant] (1611)
: any of several common red algae (genus *Porphyra*) with fronds used for stewing or pickling

**La·vin·ia** \lə-'vi-nē-ə\ *noun* [Latin]
: a daughter of King Latinus in Virgil's *Aeneid* who is betrothed to Turnus but marries Aeneas

**¹lav·ish** \'la-vish\ *adjective* [Middle English *lavas* abundance, from Middle French *lavasse* downpour of rain, from *laver* to wash — more at LAVAGE] (15th century)
**1** : expending or bestowing profusely : PRODIGAL
**2 a** : expended or produced in abundance **b** : marked by profusion or excess
*synonym* see PROFUSE
— **lav·ish·ly** *adverb*
— **lav·ish·ness** *noun*

**²lavish** *transitive verb* (1542)
: to expend or bestow with profusion : SQUANDER

**lav·rock** \'lāv-rək, 'lav-\ *or* **la·ver·ock** \'la-və-\ *noun* [Middle English *laverok,* from Old English *lāwerce*] (14th century)
*chiefly Scottish* : LARK

**¹law** \'lö\ *noun* [Middle English, from Old English *lagu,* of Scandinavian origin; akin to Old Norse *lǫg* law; akin to Old English *licgan* to lie — more at LIE] (before 12th century)
**1 a** (1) : a binding custom or practice of a community : a rule of conduct or action prescribed or formally recognized as binding or enforced by a controlling authority (2) : the whole body of such customs, practices, or rules (3) : COMMON LAW **b** (1) : the control brought about by the existence or enforcement of such law (2) : the action of laws considered as a means of redressing wrongs; *also* : LITIGATION (3) : the agency of or an agent of established law **c** : a rule or order that it is advisable or obligatory to observe **d** : something compatible with or enforceable by established law **e** : CONTROL, AUTHORITY
**2 a** *often capitalized* : the revelation of the will of God set forth in the Old Testament **b** *capitalized* : the first part of the Jewish scriptures : PENTATEUCH, TORAH — see BIBLE table
**3** : a rule of construction or procedure ⟨the *laws* of poetry⟩
**4** : the whole body of laws relating to one subject
**5 a** : the legal profession **b** : law as a department of knowledge : JURISPRUDENCE **c** : legal knowledge
**6 a** : a statement of an order or relation of phenomena that so far as is known is invariable under the given conditions **b** : a general relation proved or assumed to hold between mathematical or logical expressions ☆ ◆
— **at law** : under or within the provisions of the law ⟨enforceable *at law*⟩

**²law** (circa 1550)
*intransitive verb*
: LITIGATE
*transitive verb*
*chiefly dialect* : to sue or prosecute at law

**law-abid·ing** \'lö-ə-,bī-diŋ\ *adjective* (1834)
: abiding by or obedient to the law
— **law-abid·ing·ness** *noun*

**law·break·er** \'lö-,brā-kər\ *noun* (15th century)
: one who violates the law
— **law·break·ing** \-kiŋ\ *adjective or noun*

**law·ful** \'lö-fəl\ *adjective* (14th century)
**1 a** : being in harmony with the law ⟨a *lawful* judgment⟩ **b** : constituted, authorized, or established by law : RIGHTFUL ⟨*lawful* institutions⟩
**2** : LAW-ABIDING ⟨*lawful* citizens⟩ ☆
— **law·ful·ly** \-f(ə-)lē\ *adverb*
— **law·ful·ness** \-fəl-nəs\ *noun*

**law·giv·er** \'lö-,gi-vər\ *noun* (14th century)

**1** : one who gives a code of laws to a people
**2** : LEGISLATOR

**law·less** \'lö-ləs\ *adjective* (12th century)
**1** : not regulated by or based on law
**2 a** : not restrained or controlled by law : UNRULY **b** : ILLEGAL
— **law·less·ly** *adverb*
— **law·less·ness** *noun*

**law·mak·er** \'lö-,mā-kər\ *noun* (14th century)
: one that makes laws : LEGISLATOR
— **law·mak·ing** \-kiŋ\

**law·man** \'lö-mən\ *noun* (1944)
: a law-enforcement officer (as a sheriff or marshal)

**law merchant** *noun, plural* **laws merchant** (15th century)
: the legal rules formerly applied to cases arising in commercial transactions

**¹lawn** \'lön, 'län\ *noun* [Middle English *launde,* from Middle French *lande* heath, of Celtic origin; akin to Middle Irish *lann* land — more at LAND] (14th century)
**1** *archaic* : an open space between woods : GLADE
**2** : ground (as around a house or in a garden or park) that is covered with grass and is kept mowed
**3** : a relatively even layer of bacteria covering the surface of a culture medium
— **lawn** *or* **lawny** \'lö-nē, 'lä-\ *adjective*

**²lawn** *noun* [Middle English, from *Laon,* France] (15th century)
: a fine sheer linen or cotton fabric of plain weave that is thinner than cambric
— **lawny** *adjective*

**lawn bowling** *noun* (circa 1929)
: a bowling game played on a green with wooden balls which are rolled at a jack

**lawn mower** *noun* (1869)
: a machine for cutting grass on lawns

**lawn tennis** *noun* (1874)
: TENNIS 2

**law of averages** (circa 1929)
: the commonsense observation that probability influences everyday life so that over the long term the possible outcomes of a repeated event occur with specific frequencies

**law of definite proportions** (circa 1909)
: a statement in chemistry: every definite compound always contains the same elements in the same proportions by weight

**law of dominance** (1942)
: MENDEL'S LAW 3

**law of independent assortment** (1943)
: MENDEL'S LAW 2

**law of large numbers** (1911)
: a theorem in mathematical statistics: the probability that the absolute value of the difference between the mean of a population sample and the mean of the population from which it is drawn is greater than an arbitrarily small amount approaches zero as the size of the sample approaches infinity

**Law of Moses** (14th century)
: PENTATEUCH, TORAH

**law of nations** (circa 1548)
: INTERNATIONAL LAW

**law of parsimony** (1837)
: OCCAM'S RAZOR

**law of segregation** (circa 1909)
: MENDEL'S LAW 1

**law of war** (1947)
: the code that governs or one of the rules that govern the rights and duties of belligerents in international war

**law·ren·ci·um** \lö-'ren(t)-sē-əm\ *noun* [New Latin, from Ernest O. *Lawrence*] (1961)
: a short-lived radioactive element that is produced artificially from californium — see ELEMENT table

**law·suit** \'lö-,süt\ *noun* (1624)
: a suit in law : a case before a court

**law·yer** \'lö-yər, 'löi-ər\ *noun* (14th century)
: one whose profession is to conduct lawsuits for clients or to advise as to legal rights and obligations in other matters

— **law·yer·like** \-,līk\ *adjective*
— **law·yer·ly** \-lē\ *adjective*

**law·yer·ing** \'lö-yə-riŋ, 'löi-ə-\ *noun* (1676)
: the profession or work of a lawyer

---

☆ SYNONYMS

**Law, rule, regulation, precept, statute, ordinance, canon** mean a principle governing action or procedure. LAW implies imposition by a sovereign authority and the obligation of obedience on the part of all subject to that authority ⟨obey the *law*⟩. RULE applies to more restricted or specific situations ⟨the *rules* of the game⟩. REGULATION implies prescription by authority in order to control an organization or system ⟨*regulations* affecting nuclear power plants⟩. PRECEPT commonly suggests something advisory and not obligatory communicated typically through teaching ⟨the *precepts* of effective writing⟩. STATUTE implies a law enacted by a legislative body ⟨a *statute* requiring the use of seat belts⟩. ORDINANCE applies to an order governing some detail of procedure or conduct enforced by a limited authority such as a municipality ⟨a city *ordinance*⟩. CANON suggests in nonreligious use a principle or rule of behavior or procedure commonly accepted as a valid guide ⟨the *canons* of good taste⟩. See in addition HYPOTHESIS.

**Lawful, legal, legitimate, licit** mean being in accordance with law. LAWFUL may apply to conformity with law of any sort (as natural, divine, common, or canon) ⟨the *lawful* sovereign⟩. LEGAL applies to what is sanctioned by law or in conformity with the law, especially as it is written or administered by the courts ⟨*legal* residents of the state⟩. LEGITIMATE may apply to a legal right or status but also, in extended use, to a right or status supported by tradition, custom, or accepted standards ⟨a perfectly *legitimate* question about finances⟩. LICIT applies to a strict conformity to the provisions of the law and applies especially to what is regulated by law ⟨the *licit* use of the drug by hospitals⟩.

---

◇ WORD HISTORY

**law**   The word *law* is part of the English language's abundant heritage from medieval Scandinavia. It was borrowed into late Old English from an unrecorded Old Norse noun *lagu* (whose existence is inferred from the linguistically later Old Icelandic form *log*). *Lagu* is the plural of *lag* "something laid, layer, stratum." The image of the law as a sort of edifice built up of past decisions and decrees is fairly natural. Other languages have resorted to similar metaphors, using derivatives of verbs meaning "to put or place" or "to erect" in order to express the notion of a law. Hence, for example, we have Greek *thesmos* "law, ordinance" (from *tithenai* "to place"), Latin *statutum* "ordinance, statute" (from *statuere* "to set upright, erect"), and German *Gesetz* "law" (from *setzen* "to put, set"). Old English did not lack an earlier word for "law"; this was *æ* or *æw*, which also meant "custom"—appropriately enough, since law and custom in preliterate societies typically overlap. This word may be akin to Latin *jus* "what is sanctioned, law," the ultimate source of English *jury, perjury, injury,* and a host of other words.

---

\ə\ abut \ᵊ\ kitten \ər\ further \a\ ash \ā\ ace \ä\ mop, mar \aù\ out \ch\ chin \e\ bet \ē\ easy \g\ go \i\ hit \ī\ ice \j\ job \ŋ\ sing \ō\ go \ò\ law \òi\ boy \th\ thin \t̶h\ the \ü\ loot \ù\ foot \y\ yet \zh\ vision *see also* Guide to Pronunciation

**lax** \'laks\ *adjective* [Middle English, from Latin *laxus* loose — more at SLACK] (14th century)
**1 a** *of the bowels* : LOOSE, OPEN **b** : having loose bowels
**2** : deficient in firmness : not stringent ⟨*lax* control⟩ ⟨a *lax* foreman⟩
**3 a** : not tense, firm, or rigid : SLACK ⟨a *lax* rope⟩ **b** : having an open or loose texture **c** : having the constituents spread apart ⟨a *lax* flower cluster⟩
**4** : articulated with the muscles involved in a relatively relaxed state (as the vowel \i\ in contrast with the vowel \ē\)
**synonym** see NEGLIGENT
— **lax·a·tion** \lak-'sā-shən\ *noun*
— **lax·ly** \'laks-lē\ *adverb*
— **lax·ness** *noun*
¹**lax·a·tive** \'lak-sə-tiv\ *adjective* [Middle English *laxatif*, from Medieval Latin *laxativus*, from Latin *laxatus*, past participle of *laxare* to loosen, from *laxus*] (14th century)
: having a tendency to loosen or relax; *specifically* : relieving constipation
²**laxative** *noun* (14th century)
: a usually mild laxative drug
**lax·ity** \'lak-sə-tē\ *noun* (1528)
: the quality or state of being lax
¹**lay** \'lā\ *verb* **laid** \'lād\; **lay·ing** [Middle English *leyen*, from Old English *lecgan*; akin to Old English *licgan* to lie — more at LIE] (before 12th century)
*transitive verb*
**1** : to beat or strike down with force
**2 a** : to put or set down **b** : to place for rest or sleep; *especially* : BURY
**3** : to bring forth and deposit (an egg)
**4** : CALM, ALLAY ⟨*lay* the dust⟩
**5** : BET, WAGER
**6** : to press down giving a smooth and even surface
**7 a** : to dispose or spread over or on a surface ⟨*lay* track⟩ ⟨*lay* plaster⟩ **b** : to set in order or position ⟨*lay* a table for dinner⟩ ⟨*lay* brick⟩ **c** : to put (strands) in place and twist to form a rope, hawser, or cable; *also* : to make by so doing ⟨*lay* up rope⟩
**8 a** : to impose as a duty, burden, or punishment ⟨*lay* a tax⟩ **b** : to put as a burden of reproach ⟨*laid* the blame on her⟩ **c** : to advance as an accusation : IMPUTE ⟨the disaster was *laid* to faulty inspection⟩
**9** : to place (something immaterial) on something ⟨*lay* stress on grammar⟩
**10** : PREPARE, CONTRIVE ⟨a well-*laid* plan⟩
**11 a** : to bring against or into contact with something : APPLY ⟨*laid* the watch to his ear⟩ **b** : to prepare or position for action or operation ⟨*lay* a fire in the fireplace⟩; *also* : to adjust (a gun) to the proper direction and elevation
**12** : to bring to a specified condition ⟨*lay* waste the land⟩
**13 a** : ASSERT, ALLEGE ⟨*lay* claim to an estate⟩ **b** : to submit for examination and judgment ⟨*laid* her case before the commission⟩
**14** : to copulate with — sometimes considered vulgar
*intransitive verb*
**1** : to produce and deposit eggs
**2** *nonstandard* : ¹LIE
**3** : WAGER, BET
**4** *dialect* : PLAN, PREPARE
**5 a** : to apply oneself vigorously ⟨*laid* to his oars⟩ **b** : to proceed to a specified place or position on a ship ⟨*lay* aloft⟩ ■
— **lay on the table 1** : to remove (a parliamentary motion) from consideration indefinitely **2** *British* : to put (as legislation) on the agenda
²**lay** *noun* (1590)
**1** : COVERT, LAIR
**2** : something (as a layer) that lies or is laid
**3 a** : line of action : PLAN **b** : line of work : OCCUPATION

**4 a** : terms of sale or employment : PRICE **b** : share of profit (as on a whaling voyage) paid in lieu of wages
**5 a** : the amount of advance of any point in a rope strand for one turn **b** : the nature of a fiber rope as determined by the amount of twist, the angle of the strands, and the angle of the threads in the strands
**6** : the way in which a thing lies or is laid in relation to something else ⟨the *lay* of the land⟩
**7** : the state of one that lays eggs ⟨hens coming into *lay*⟩
**8 a** : a partner in sexual intercourse — usually considered vulgar **b** : SEXUAL INTERCOURSE — usually considered vulgar
³**lay** *past of* LIE
⁴**lay** *noun* [Middle English, from Old French *lai*] (13th century)
**1** : a simple narrative poem : BALLAD
**2** : MELODY, SONG
⁵**lay** *adjective* [Middle English, from Middle French *lai*, from Late Latin *laicus*, from Greek *laikos* of the people, from *laos* people] (15th century)
**1** : of or relating to the laity : not ecclesiastical
**2** : of or relating to members of a religious house occupied with domestic or manual work ⟨a *lay* brother⟩
**3** : not of a particular profession ⟨the *lay* public⟩; *also* : lacking extensive knowledge of a particular subject
**lay·about** \'lā-ə-ˌbaut\ *noun* (1932)
: a lazy shiftless person : IDLER
**lay–away** \'lā-ə-ˌwā\ *noun* (1944)
: a purchasing agreement by which a retailer agrees to hold merchandise secured by a deposit until the price is paid in full by the customer
**lay away** *transitive verb* (circa 1928)
: to put aside for future use or delivery
**lay–by** \'lā-ˌbī\ *noun* (1939)
**1** *British* : TURNOUT 4b
**2** : the final operation (as a last cultivating) in the growing of a field crop
**lay by** *transitive verb* (15th century)
**1** : to lay aside : DISCARD
**2** : to store for future use : SAVE
**3** : to cultivate (as corn) for the last time
**lay day** *noun* (1845)
**1** : one of the days allowed by the charter for loading or unloading a vessel
**2** : a day of delay in port
**lay down** (13th century)
*transitive verb*
**1** : to give up : SURRENDER ⟨*lay down* your arms⟩
**2 a** : ESTABLISH, PRESCRIBE ⟨*lay down* a scale for a map⟩ **b** : to assert or command dogmatically ⟨*lay down* the law⟩
**3** : STORE, PRESERVE
**4 a** : to direct toward a target ⟨*lay down* a barrage⟩ **b** : to hit along the ground ⟨*laid down* a sacrifice bunt⟩
*intransitive verb*
*nonstandard* : to lie down
¹**lay·er** \'lā-ər, 'le(-ə)r\ *noun* (13th century)
**1** : one that lays (as a worker who lays brick or a hen that lays eggs)
**2 a** : one thickness, course, or fold laid or lying over or under another **b** : STRATUM **c** : HORIZON 2
**3 a** : a branch or shoot of a plant that roots while still attached to the parent plant **b** : a plant developed by layering
— **lay·ered** \'lā-ərd, 'le(-ə)rd\ *adjective*
²**layer** (1832)
*transitive verb*
**1** : to propagate (a plant) by means of layers
**2 a** : to place as a layer **b** : to place a layer on top of **c** : to form or arrange in layers
*intransitive verb*
**1 a** : to separate into layers **b** : to form out of superimposed layers
**2** *of a plant* : to form roots where a stem comes in contact with the ground

**lay·er·age** \'lā-ə-rij, 'le-ə-\ *noun* (1902)
: the practice, art, or process of rooting plants by layering
**lay·ette** \lā-'et\ *noun* [French, from Middle French, diminutive of *laye* box, from Middle Dutch *lade;* akin to Old English *hladan* to load — more at LADE] (1839)
: a complete outfit of clothing and equipment for a newborn infant
**lay figure** *noun* [obsolete English *layman* lay figure, from Dutch *leeman*] (1795)
**1** : a jointed model of the human body used by artists to show the disposition of drapery
**2** : a person likened to a dummy or puppet
**lay in** *transitive verb* (1579)
: LAY BY, SAVE
**laying on of hands** (15th century)
: the act of laying hands on a person's head to confer a spiritual blessing (as in Christian ordination, confirmation, or faith healing)
**lay·man** \'lā-mən\ *noun* (15th century)
**1** : a person who is not a member of the clergy
**2** : a person who does not belong to a particular profession or who is not expert in some field
**lay·off** \'lā-ˌof\ *noun* (1889)
**1** : a period of inactivity or idleness
**2** : the act of laying off an employee or a workforce; *also* : SHUTDOWN
**lay off** (1748)
*transitive verb*
**1** : to mark or measure off
**2** : to cease to employ (a worker) often temporarily
**3** *of a bookie* : to place all or part of (an accepted bet) with another bookie to reduce the risk
**4 a** : to leave undisturbed **b** : AVOID, QUIT
*intransitive verb*
**1** : to stop doing or taking something
**2** : to leave one alone ⟨wish you'd just *lay off*⟩
**lay on** (1600)
*transitive verb*
**1 a** : to apply by or as if by spreading on a surface ⟨*laying* it *on* thick⟩ **b** : PROVIDE, ARRANGE ⟨food *laid on* in abundance⟩ **c** : HAND OUT ⟨*laid on* awards⟩
**2** *chiefly British* : HIRE
*intransitive verb*
: ATTACK, BEAT
**lay·out** \'lā-ˌaut\ *noun* (1852)
**1** : the plan or design or arrangement of something that is laid out: as **a** : DUMMY 5b **b** : final arrangement of matter to be reproduced especially by printing
**2** : the act or process of planning or laying out in detail

---

☐ USAGE
**lay**   LAY has been used intransitively in the sense of "lie" since the 14th century. The practice was unremarked until around 1770; attempts to correct it have been a fixture of schoolbooks ever since. Generations of teachers and critics have succeeded in taming most literary and learned writing, but intransitive *lay* persists in familiar speech and is a bit more common in general prose than one might suspect. Much of the problem lies in the confusing similarity of the principal parts of the two words. Another influence may be a folk belief that *lie* is for people and *lay* is for things. Some commentators are ready to abandon the distinction, suggesting that *lay* is on the rise socially. But if it does rise to respectability, it is sure to do so slowly: many people have invested effort in learning to keep *lie* and *lay* distinct. Remember that even though many people do use *lay* for *lie*, others will judge you unfavorably if you do. See in addition SET.

**3 a :** something that is laid out ⟨a model train *layout*⟩ **b :** land or structures or rooms used for a particular purpose ⟨a cattle-ranching *layout*⟩; *also* : PLACE **c :** a set or outfit especially of tools

**lay out** *transitive verb* (15th century)
**1 :** DISPLAY, EXHIBIT
**2 :** SPEND
**3 a :** to prepare (a corpse) for viewing **b :** to knock flat or unconscious
**4 :** to plan in detail ⟨*lay out* a campaign⟩
**5 :** ARRANGE, DESIGN
**6 :** to mark (work) for drilling, machining, or filing

**lay·over** \'lā-,ō-vər\ *noun* (1873)
**:** STOPOVER

**lay over** (1838)
*transitive verb*
**:** POSTPONE
*intransitive verb*
**:** to make a stopover

**lay·peo·ple** \'lā-,pē-pəl\ *noun plural* (15th century)
**:** LAYPERSONS

**lay·per·son** \-,pər-s°n\ *noun* (1972)
**:** a member of the laity

**lay reader** *noun* (1751)
**:** an Anglican or Roman Catholic layman authorized to conduct parts of the church services not requiring a clergyman

**lay to** (1796)
*intransitive verb*
**:** LIE TO
*transitive verb*
**:** to bring (a ship) into the wind and hold stationary

**lay·up** \'lā-,əp\ *noun* (1925)
**1 :** the action of laying up or the condition of being laid up
**2 :** a shot in basketball made from near the basket usually by playing the ball off the backboard

**lay up** *transitive verb* (14th century)
**1 :** to store up : LAY BY
**2 :** to disable or confine with illness or injury
**3 :** to take out of active service

**lay·wom·an** \'lā-,wu̇-mən\ *noun* (1529)
**:** a woman who is a member of the laity

**la·zar** \'la-zər, 'lā-\ *noun* [Middle English, from Medieval Latin *lazarus,* from Late Latin *Lazarus*] (14th century)
**:** a person afflicted with a repulsive disease; *specifically* : LEPER

**laz·a·ret·to** \,la-zə-'re-(,)tō\ *or* **laz·a·rette** \-'ret\ *also* **laz·a·rette** \-'ret\ *noun, plural* **-rettos** *or* **-rets** *also* **-rettes** [Italian *lazzaretto,* alteration of *Nazaretto,* quarantine station in Venice, from *Santa Maria di Nazareth,* church on the island where it was located] (1549)
**1** *usually* **lazaretto** : an institution (as a hospital) for those with contagious diseases
**2 :** a building or a ship used for detention in quarantine
**3** *usually* **lazaret** : a space in a ship between decks used as a storeroom

**La·za·rist** \'la-zə-rist, lə-'zär-ist\ *noun* [College of Saint *Lazare,* Paris, former home of the congregation] (1747)
**:** VINCENTIAN

**Laz·a·rus** \'laz-rəs, 'la-zə-\ *noun* [Late Latin, from Greek *Lazaros,* from Hebrew *El'āzār*]
**1 :** a brother of Mary and Martha raised by Jesus from the dead according to the account in John 11
**2 :** the diseased beggar in the parable of the rich man and the beggar found in Luke 16

**laze** \'lāz\ *verb* **lazed; laz·ing** [backformation from *lazy*] (circa 1592)
*intransitive verb*
**:** to act or lie lazily : IDLE
*transitive verb*
**:** to pass (time) in idleness or relaxation
**— laze** *noun*

**la·zu·lite** \'la-zyü-,līt, -zhə-\ *noun* [German *Lazulith,* from Medieval Latin *lazulum* lapis lazuli] (1807)
**:** an often crystalline azure-blue mineral that is a hydrous phosphate of aluminum, iron, and magnesium

**¹la·zy** \'lā-zē\ *adjective* **la·zi·er; -est** [perhaps from Middle Low German *lasich* feeble; akin to Middle High German er*leswen* to become weak] (1549)
**1 a :** disinclined to activity or exertion : not energetic or vigorous **b :** encouraging inactivity or indolence ⟨a *lazy* summer day⟩
**2 :** moving slowly : SLUGGISH
**3 :** DROOPY, LAX ⟨a rabbit with *lazy* ears⟩
**4 :** placed on its side ⟨*lazy* E livestock brand⟩
**5 :** not rigorous or strict ⟨*lazy* scholarship⟩ ☆
**— la·zi·ly** \-zə-lē\ *adverb*
**— la·zi·ness** \-zē-nəs\ *noun*
**— la·zy·ish** \-zē-ish\ *adjective*

**²lazy** *intransitive verb* **la·zied; la·zy·ing** (1612)
**:** to move or lie lazily : LAZE

**la·zy·bones** \'lā-zē-,bōnz\ *noun plural but singular or plural in construction* (1592)
**:** a lazy person

**lazy eye** *noun* (1939)
**:** AMBLYOPIA; *also* : an eye affected with amblyopia

**lazy Su·san** \-'sü-z°n\ *noun* (1917)
**:** a revolving tray used for serving food, condiments, or relishes

**lazy tongs** *noun plural* (1836)
**:** a series of jointed and pivoted bars capable of great extension used to pick up or handle something at a distance

lazy tongs

**LCD** \,el-(,)sē-'dē\ *noun* [*liquid crystal display*] (1973)
**:** a constantly operating display (as of the time in a digital watch) that consists of segments of a liquid crystal whose reflectivity varies according to the voltage applied to them

**LD₅₀** \,el-,dē-'fif-tē\ *noun* [*lethal dose*] (1942)
**:** the amount of a toxic agent (as a poison, virus, or radiation) that is sufficient to kill 50% of a population of animals usually within a certain time

**LDL** \,el-(,)dē-'el\ *noun* [*low-density lipoprotein*] (1976)
**:** a cholesterol-rich protein-poor lipoprotein of blood plasma correlated with increased risk of atherosclerosis — compare HDL

**L-do·pa** \'el-'dō-pə\ *noun* (1939)
**:** the levorotatory form of dopa that is obtained especially from broad beans or prepared synthetically, stimulates the production of dopamine in the brain, and is used in treating Parkinson's disease

**lea** *or* **ley** \'lē, 'lā\ *noun* [Middle English *leye,* from Old English *lēah;* akin to Old High German *lōh* thicket, Latin *lucus* grove, *lux* light — more at LIGHT] (before 12th century)
**1 :** GRASSLAND, PASTURE
**2** *usually* **ley** : arable land used temporarily for hay or grazing

**¹leach** \'lēch\ *variant of* LEECH

**²leach** *verb* [*leach* vessel through which water is passed to extract lye] (1796)
*transitive verb*
**1 :** to dissolve out by the action of a percolating liquid ⟨*leach* out alkali from ashes⟩
**2 :** to subject to the action of percolating liquid (as water) in order to separate the soluble components
**3 a :** to remove (nutritive or harmful elements) from soil by percolation **b :** to draw out or remove as if by percolation ⟨all meaning has been *leached* from my life⟩
*intransitive verb*
**:** to pass out or through by percolation
**— leach·abil·i·ty** \,lē-chə-'bi-lə-tē\ *noun*
**— leach·able** \'lē-chə-bəl\ *adjective*
**— leach·er** *noun*

**leach·ate** \'lē-,chāt\ *noun* (1934)
**:** a solution or product obtained by leaching

**¹lead** \'lēd\ *verb* **led** \'led\; **lead·ing** [Middle English *leden,* from Old English *lǣdan;* akin to Old High German *leiten* to lead, Old English *līthan* to go] (before 12th century)
*transitive verb*
**1 a :** to guide on a way especially by going in advance **b :** to direct on a course or in a direction **c :** to serve as a channel for ⟨a pipe *leads* water to the house⟩
**2 :** to go through : LIVE ⟨*lead* a quiet life⟩
**3 a** (1) **:** to direct the operations, activity, or performance of ⟨*lead* an orchestra⟩ (2) **:** to have charge of ⟨*lead* a campaign⟩ (3) **:** to suggest to (a witness) the answer desired by asking leading questions **b** (1) **:** to go at the head of ⟨*lead* a parade⟩ (2) **:** to be first in or among ⟨*lead* the league⟩ (3) **:** to have a margin over ⟨*led* his opponent⟩
**4 :** to bring to some conclusion or condition ⟨*led* to believe otherwise⟩
**5 :** to begin play with ⟨*lead* trumps⟩
**6 a :** to aim in front of (a moving object) ⟨*lead* a duck⟩ **b :** to pass a ball or puck just in front of (a moving teammate)
*intransitive verb*
**1 a :** to guide someone or something along a way **b :** to lie, run, or open in a specified place or direction ⟨path *leads* uphill⟩ **c :** to guide a dance partner through the steps of a dance
**2 a :** to be first **b** (1) **:** BEGIN, OPEN (2) **:** to play the first card of a trick, round, or game
**3 :** to tend toward or have a result ⟨study *leading* to a degree⟩
**4 :** to direct the first of a series of blows at an opponent in boxing ■
**synonym** see GUIDE
**— lead one down the garden path** *also* **lead one up the garden path**
**:** HOODWINK, DECEIVE

**²lead** *noun* (15th century)
**1 a** (1) **:** LEADERSHIP (2) **:** EXAMPLE, PRECEDENT **b** (1) **:** position at the front : VANGUARD (2) **:** INITIATIVE (3) **:** the act or privilege of leading in cards; *also* : the card or suit led **c :** a margin or measure of advantage or superiority or position in advance
**2 :** one that leads: as **a :** LODE 1 **b :** a channel of water especially through a field of ice **c :** INDICATION, CLUE **d :** a principal role in a dramatic production; *also* : one who plays such a role **e :** LEASH 1 **f** (1) **:** an introductory section of a news story (2) **:** a news story of chief importance

\ə\ abut \°\ kitten \ər\ further \a\ ash \ā\ ace
\ä\ mop, mar \aů\ out \ch\ chin \e\ bet \ē\ easy
\g\ go \i\ hit \ī\ ice \j\ job \ŋ\ sing \ō\ go
\ȯ\ law \ȯi\ boy \th\ thin \th\ the \ü\ loot \ů\ foot
\y\ yet \zh\ vision *see also* Guide to Pronunciation

**3 :** an insulated electrical conductor connected to an electrical device
**4 :** the course of a rope from end to end
**5 :** the amount of axial advance of a point accompanying a complete turn of a thread (as of a screw or worm)
**6 :** a position taken by a base runner off a base toward the next
**7 :** the first punch of a series or an exchange of punches in boxing
— **lead·less** \-ləs\ *adjective*

**³lead** *adjective* (1828)
**:** acting or serving as a lead or leader ⟨a *lead* article⟩

**⁴lead** \'led\ *noun, often attributive* [Middle English *leed*, from Old English *lēad*; akin to Middle High German *lōt* lead] (before 12th century)
**1 :** a heavy soft malleable ductile plastic but inelastic bluish white metallic element found mostly in combination and used especially in pipes, cable sheaths, batteries, solder, and shields against radioactivity — see ELEMENT table
**2 a :** a plummet for sounding at sea **b** *plural, British* **:** a usually flat lead roof **c** *plural* **:** lead framing for panes in windows **d :** a thin strip of metal used to separate lines of type in printing
**3 a :** a thin stick of marking substance in or for a pencil **b :** WHITE LEAD
**4 :** BULLETS, PROJECTILES
**5 :** TETRAETHYL LEAD
— **lead·less** \-ləs\ *adjective*

**⁵lead** \'led\ *transitive verb* (14th century)
**1 :** to cover, line, or weight with lead
**2 :** to fix (window glass) in position with leads
**3 :** to put space between the lines of (typeset matter)
**4 :** to treat or mix with lead or a lead compound ⟨*leaded* gasoline⟩

**lead acetate** *noun* (1885)
**:** an acetate of lead; *especially* **:** a poisonous soluble salt $PbC_4H_6O_4{\cdot}3H_2O$

**lead arsenate** *noun* (circa 1903)
**:** an arsenate of lead: as **a :** an acid salt $PbHAsO_4$ used especially as an insecticide **b :** a neutral salt $Pb_3(AsO_4)_2$ used especially as an insecticide

**lead azide** *noun* (1918)
**:** a crystalline explosive compound $Pb(N_3)_2$ used as a detonating agent

**lead carbonate** *noun* (1873)
**:** a carbonate of lead; *especially* **:** a poisonous basic salt $Pb_3(OH)_2(CO_3)_2$ used especially as a white pigment

**lead chromate** *noun* (circa 1885)
**:** a chromate of lead; *especially* **:** CHROME YELLOW

**lead dioxide** *noun* (1885)
**:** a poisonous compound $PbO_2$ used especially as an oxidizing agent and as an electrode in batteries

**lead·en** \'le-dᵊn\ *adjective* (before 12th century)
**1 a :** made of lead **b :** of the color of lead **:** dull gray
**2 a :** oppressively heavy **b :** SLUGGISH **c :** lacking spirit or animation
— **lead·en·ly** *adverb*
— **lead·en·ness** \-dᵊn-(n)əs\ *noun*

**lead·er** \'le-dər\ *noun* (14th century)
**1 :** something that leads: as **a :** a primary or terminal shoot of a plant **b :** TENDON, SINEW **c** *plural* **:** dots or hyphens (as in an index) used to lead the eye horizontally **:** ELLIPSIS 2 **d** *chiefly British* **:** a newspaper editorial **e** (1) **:** something for guiding fish into a trap (2) **:** a short length of material for attaching the end of a fishing line to a lure or hook **f :** LOSS LEADER **g :** something that ranks first **h :** a blank section at the beginning or end of a reel of film or recorded tape

**2 :** a person who leads: as **a :** GUIDE, CONDUCTOR **b** (1) **:** a person who directs a military force or unit (2) **:** a person who has commanding authority or influence **c** (1) **:** the principal officer of a British political party (2) **:** a party member chosen to manage party activities in a legislative body (3) **:** such a party member presiding over the whole legislative body when the party constitutes a majority **d** (1) **:** CONDUCTOR c (2) **:** a first or principal performer of a group
**3 :** a horse placed in advance of the other horses of a team
— **lead·er·less** \-ləs\ *adjective*

**leader of the opposition** (1771)
**:** the principal member of the opposition party in a British legislative body who is given the status of a salaried government official and an important role in organizing the business of the house

**lead·er·ship** \'le-dər-ˌship\ *noun* (1821)
**1 :** the office or position of a leader
**2 :** capacity to lead
**3 :** the act or an instance of leading
**4 :** LEADERS

**lead glass** *noun* (1856)
**:** glass containing a high proportion of lead oxide and having extraordinary clarity and brilliance

**lead–in** \'led-ˌin\ *noun* (1913)
**:** something that leads into something else ⟨a *lead-in* to the commercial⟩
— **lead–in** *adjective*

**lead·ing** \'le-diŋ\ *adjective* (1597)
**1 :** coming or ranking first **:** FOREMOST
**2 :** exercising leadership
**3 :** providing direction or guidance ⟨a *leading* question⟩
**4 :** given most prominent display ⟨the *leading* story⟩

**leading edge** \'le-diŋ-\ *noun* (1877)
**1 :** the foremost edge of an airfoil
**2 :** the forward part of something that moves or seems to move

**leading lady** *noun* (1874)
**:** an actress who plays the leading female role (as in a play or movie)

**leading man** *noun* (1827)
**:** an actor who plays the leading male role (as in a play or movie)

**leading tone** *noun* (circa 1889)
**:** the seventh tone of a diatonic scale — called also *leading note*

**lead line** \'led-\ *noun* (15th century)
**:** SOUNDING LINE

**lead·man** \'led-ˌman, -mən\ *noun* (1939)
**:** a worker in charge of other workers

**lead monoxide** *noun* (circa 1909)
**:** a yellow to brownish red poisonous compound $PbO$ used in rubber manufacture and glassmaking

**lead·off** \'led-ˌof\ *noun* (circa 1886)
**1 :** a beginning or leading action
**2 :** one that leads off
— **leadoff** *adjective*

**lead off** \'led-\ (1817)
*transitive verb*
**1 :** to make a start on **:** OPEN
**2 :** to bat first for a baseball team in (an inning)
*intransitive verb*
**:** BEGIN; *also* **:** to come on or perform first

**lead on** *transitive verb* (1598)
**:** to entice or induce to proceed in a course especially when unwise or mistaken

**lead oxide** *noun* (circa 1926)
**:** any of several oxides of lead; *especially* **:** LEAD MONOXIDE

**lead pencil** \'led-\ *noun* (1688)
**:** a pencil using graphite as the marking material

**lead–pipe** \'led-ˌpīp\ *adjective* (1898)
**:** CERTAIN, GUARANTEED ⟨a *lead-pipe* cinch⟩

**lead·plant** \'led-ˌplant\ *noun* (circa 1833)

**:** a leguminous shrub (*Amorpha canescens*) of the western U.S. that has hoary pinnate leaves and bears dull-colored racemose flowers

**lead poisoning** *noun* (circa 1842)
**:** chronic intoxication that is produced by the absorption of lead into the system and is characterized by severe colicky pains, a dark line along the gums, and local muscular paralysis

**lead·screw** \'led-ˌskrü\ *noun* (circa 1889)
**:** a threaded rod on which a mechanism travels and can be positioned precisely

**leads·man** \'ledz-mən\ *noun* (1857)
**:** a man who uses a sounding lead to determine depth of water

**lead sulfide** *noun* (circa 1898)
**:** an insoluble black compound $PbS$ that occurs naturally as galena and is used in photoconductive cells

**lead time** \'led-\ *noun* (1944)
**:** the time between the beginning of a process or project and the appearance of its results

**lead–up** \'led-ˌəp\ *noun* (1942)
**:** something that leads up to or prepares the way for something else

**lead up** \'led-\ *intransitive verb* (1861)
**1 :** to prepare the way
**2 :** to make a gradual or indirect approach to a topic

**lead·work** \'led-ˌwərk\ *noun* (1641)
**:** articles made of or work done in lead

**leady** \'le-dē\ *adjective* **lead·i·er; -est** (14th century)
**:** containing or resembling lead

**¹leaf** \'lēf\ *noun, plural* **leaves** \'lēvz\ *also* **leafs** \'lēfs\ *often attributive* [Middle English *leef*, from Old English *lēaf*; akin to Old High German *loub* leaf] (before 12th century)
**1 a** (1) **:** a lateral outgrowth from a plant stem that is typically a flattened expanded variably shaped greenish organ, constitutes a unit of the foliage, and functions primarily in food manufacture by photosynthesis (2) **:** a modified leaf primarily engaged in functions other than food manufacture **b** (1) **:** FOLIAGE ⟨trees in full *leaf*⟩ **:** the leaves of a plant as an article of commerce
**2 :** something suggestive of a leaf: as **a :** a part of a book or folded sheet containing a page on each side **b** (1) **:** a part (as of window shutters, folding doors, or gates) that slides or is hinged (2) **:** the movable parts of a table top **c** (1) **:** a thin sheet or plate of any substance **:** LAMINA (2) **:** metal (as gold or silver) in sheets usually thinner than foil (3) **:** one of the plates of a leaf spring
— **leaf·less** \'lēf-ləs\ *adjective*
— **leaf·like** \'lēf-ˌlīk\ *adjective*

**²leaf** (1611)
*intransitive verb*
**1 :** to shoot out or produce leaves
**2 :** to turn over pages ⟨*leaf* through a book⟩

forms of leaf 1a(1): *1* needle-shaped, *2* linear, *3* lanceolate, *4* elliptical, *5* ensiform, *6* oblong, *7* oblanceolate with acuminate tip, *8* ovate with acute tip, *9* obovate, *10* spatulate, *11* fiddle-shaped, *12* cuneate, *13* deltoid, *14* cordate, *15* reniform, *16* orbiculate, *17* runcinate, *18* lyrate, *19* peltate, *20* hastate, *21* sagittate, *22* odd-pinnate, *23* abruptly pinnate, *24* trifoliolate, *25*, *26* palmate

*transitive verb*
: to turn over the pages of
**leaf·age** \'lē-fij\ *noun* (1599)
**1** : FOLIAGE 2
**2** : the representation of leafage (as in architecture)
**leaf bud** *noun* (1664)
: a bud that develops into a leafy shoot and does not produce flowers
**leaf butterfly** *noun* (1882)
: any of a genus (*Kallima*) of nymphalid butterflies of southern Asia and the East Indies that mimic leaves
**leaf curl** *noun* (1899)
: a plant disease caused by a fungus (genus *Taphrina*) or virus and characterized by curling of leaves; *especially* : PEACH LEAF CURL
**leafed** \'lēft\ *adjective* (1552)
: LEAVED
**leaf fat** *noun* (circa 1725)
: the fat that lines the abdominal cavity and encloses the kidneys; *especially* : that of a hog used in the manufacture of lard
**leaf·hop·per** \'lēf-,hä-pər\ *noun* (1852)
: any of a family (Cicadellidae) of small leaping homopterous insects that suck the juices of plants
**leaf lard** *noun* (circa 1847)
: high-quality lard made from leaf fat
**¹leaf·let** \'lēf-lət\ *noun* (1787)
**1 a** : one of the divisions of a compound leaf **b** : a small or young foliage leaf
**2** : a leaflike organ or part
**3** : a usually folded printed sheet intended for free distribution
**²leaflet** *verb* **-let·ed** *or* **-let·ted; -let·ing** *or* **-let·ting** (1962)
*intransitive verb*
: to hand out leaflets
*transitive verb*
: to hand out leaflets to
— **leaf·le·teer** \,lēf-lə-'tir\ *noun*
**leaf miner** *noun* (1830)
: any of various small insects (as moths or dipteran flies) that in the larval stages burrow in and eat the parenchyma of leaves
**leaf mold** *noun* (1845)
**1** : a compost or layer composed chiefly of decayed vegetable matter
**2** : a mold or mildew that affects foliage
**leaf roll** *noun* (1916)
: a virus disease of the potato that is transmitted by aphids and is characterized by an upward rolling of the leaf margins, smaller tubers, and netlike necrotic areas in the phloem
**leaf roller** *noun* (1830)
: any of various lepidopterans whose larvae make a nest by rolling up plant leaves
**leaf rust** *noun* (1865)
: a rust disease of plants and especially of wheat that affects primarily the leaves
**leaf scar** *noun* (1835)
: the mark left on a stem after a leaf falls
**leaf scorch** *noun* (circa 1909)
: any of various plant diseases characterized by a burned or scorched appearance of the foliage
**leaf spot** *noun* (circa 1895)
: any of various plant diseases characterized by discolored often circular spots on the leaves
**leaf spring** *noun* (circa 1893)
: a spring made of superposed strips or leaves
**leaf·stalk** \'lēf-,stök\ *noun* (circa 1776)
: PETIOLE
**leaf trace** *noun* [³*trace*] (1875)
: a trace associated with a leaf
**leafy** \'lē-fē\ *adjective* **leaf·i·er; -est** (15th century)
**1 a** : furnished with or abounding in leaves ⟨*leafy* woodlands⟩ **b** : having broad-bladed leaves ⟨mosses, grasses, and *leafy* plants⟩ **c** : consisting chiefly of leaves ⟨*leafy* vegetables⟩
**2** : resembling a leaf; *specifically* : LAMINATE
**leafy liverwort** *noun* (1922)

: any of an order (Jungermanniales) of usually epiphytic liverworts with a leafy gametophyte that has one ventral and two dorsal rows of leaves on the stem
**leafy spurge** *noun* (circa 1889)
: a tall perennial European herb (*Euphorbia esula*) that is naturalized in the northern U.S. and Canada
**¹league** \'lēg\ *noun* [Middle English *leuge, lege*, from Late Latin *leuga*] (14th century)
**1** : any of various units of distance from about 2.4 to 4.6 statute miles (3.9 to 7.4 kilometers)
**2** : a square league
**²league** *noun* [Middle English (Scots) *ligg*, from Middle French *ligue*, from Old Italian *liga*, from *ligare* to bind, from Latin — more at LIGATURE] (15th century)
**1 a** : an association of nations or other political entities for a common purpose **b** (1) : an association of persons or groups united by common interests or goals (2) : a group of sports teams that regularly play one another **c** : an informal alliance
**2** : CLASS, CATEGORY
**³league** *verb* **leagued; leagu·ing** (1604)
*transitive verb*
: to unite in a league
*intransitive verb*
: to form a league
**¹lea·guer** \'lē-gər\ *noun* [Dutch *leger*; akin to Old High German *legar* bed — more at LAIR] (1577)
**1** : a military camp
**2** : SIEGE
**²leaguer** *transitive verb* (circa 1720)
*archaic* : BESIEGE, BELEAGUER
**³leagu·er** \'lē-gər\ *noun* [²*league*] (1591)
: a member of a league
**¹leak** \'lēk\ *verb* [Middle English *leken*, from Old Norse *leka*; akin to Old English *leccan* to moisten, Middle Irish *legaid* it melts] (14th century)
*intransitive verb*
**1 a** : to enter or escape through an opening usually by a fault or mistake ⟨fumes *leak* in⟩ **b** : to let a substance or light in or out through an opening
**2 a** : to become known despite efforts at concealment **b** : to be the source of an information leak
*transitive verb*
**1** : to permit to enter or escape through or as if through a leak
**2** : to give out (information) surreptitiously ⟨*leaked* the story to the press⟩
— **leak·er** \'lē-kər\ *noun*
**²leak** *noun* (15th century)
**1 a** : a crack or hole that usually by mistake admits or lets escape **b** : something that permits the admission or escape of something else usually with prejudicial effect
**2** : the act, process, or an instance of leaking
**3** : an act of urinating — used especially in the phrase *take a leak; sometimes considered vulgar*
— **leak·proof** \'lēk-,prüf\ *adjective*
**leak·age** \'lē-kij\ *noun* (15th century)
**1 a** : the act or process or an instance of leaking **b** : loss of electricity especially due to faulty insulation
**2** : something or the amount that leaks
**leaky** \'lē-kē\ *adjective* **leak·i·er; -est** (15th century)
: permitting fluid to leak in or out
— **leak·i·ly** \-kə-lē\ *adverb*
— **leak·i·ness** \-kē-nəs\ *noun*
**leal** \'lē(ə)l\ *adjective* [Middle English *leel*, from Middle French *leial, leel* — more at LOYAL] (14th century)
*chiefly Scottish* : LOYAL, TRUE
— **leal·ly** \'lē-ə(l)-lē, 'lēl-lē\ *adverb*
**¹lean** \'lēn\ *verb* **leaned** \'lēnd, *chiefly British* 'lent\; **lean·ing** [Middle English *lenen*, from Old English *hleonian*; akin to Old High German *hlinēn* to lean, Greek *klinein*, Latin *clinare*] (before 12th century)

*intransitive verb*
**1 a** : to incline, deviate, or bend from a vertical position **b** : to cast one's weight to one side for support
**2** : to rely for support or inspiration
**3** : to incline in opinion, taste, or desire
*transitive verb*
: to cause to lean : INCLINE
— **lean on** : to apply pressure to
**²lean** *noun* (1776)
: the act or an instance of leaning : INCLINATION
**³lean** *adjective* [Middle English *lene*, from Old English *hlǣne*] (before 12th century)
**1 a** : lacking or deficient in flesh **b** : containing little or no fat
**2** : lacking richness, sufficiency, or productiveness
**3** : deficient in an essential or important quality or ingredient: as **a** *of ore* : containing little valuable mineral **b** : low in combustible component — used especially of fuel mixtures
**4** : characterized by economy (as of style, expression, or operation) ☆
— **lean·ly** *adverb*
— **lean·ness** \'lēn-nəs\ *noun*
**⁴lean** *transitive verb* (before 12th century)
: to make lean
**⁵lean** *noun* (15th century)
: the part of meat that consists principally of lean muscle
**Le·an·der** \lē-'an-dər\ *noun* [Latin, from Greek *Leandros*]
: a youth in Greek mythology who swims the Hellespont nightly to visit Hero and who ultimately drowns in one of the crossings
**lean·ing** \'lē-niŋ\ *noun* (15th century)
: a definite but not decisive attraction or tendency — often used in plural ☆
**leant** \'lent\ *chiefly British past of* LEAN
**¹lean-to** \'lēn-,tü\ *noun, plural* **lean–tos** \-,tüz\ (15th century)

---

☆ SYNONYMS
**Lean, spare, lank, lanky, gaunt, rawboned, scrawny, skinny** mean thin because of an absence of excess flesh. LEAN stresses lack of fat and of curving contours ⟨a *lean* racehorse⟩. SPARE suggests leanness from abstemious living or constant exercise ⟨the gymnast's *spare* figure⟩. LANK implies tallness as well as leanness ⟨the *lank* legs of the heron⟩. LANKY suggests awkwardness and loose-jointedness as well as thinness ⟨a *lanky* youth, all arms and legs⟩. GAUNT implies marked thinness or emaciation as from overwork or suffering ⟨a prisoner's *gaunt* face⟩. RAWBONED suggests a large ungainly build without implying undernourishment ⟨a *rawboned* farmer⟩. SCRAWNY and SKINNY imply an extreme leanness that suggests deficient strength and vitality ⟨a *scrawny* chicken⟩ ⟨*skinny* street urchins⟩.

**Leaning, propensity, proclivity, penchant** mean a strong instinct or liking for something. LEANING suggests a liking or attraction not strong enough to be decisive or uncontrollable ⟨a student with artistic *leanings*⟩. PROPENSITY implies a deeply ingrained and usually irresistible inclination ⟨a *propensity* to offer advice⟩. PROCLIVITY suggests a strong natural proneness usually to something objectionable or evil ⟨a *proclivity* for violence⟩. PENCHANT implies a strongly marked taste in the person or an irresistible attraction in the object ⟨a *penchant* for taking risks⟩.

---

\ə\ abut \ᵊ\ kitten \ər\ further \a\ ash \ā\ ace
\ä\ mop, mar \aù\ out \ch\ chin \e\ bet \ē\ easy
\g\ go \i\ hit \ī\ ice \j\ job \ŋ\ sing \ō\ go
\ò\ law \òi\ boy \th\ thin \th\ the \ü\ loot \ù\ foot
\y\ yet \zh\ vision see also Guide to Pronunciation

**1 :** a wing or extension of a building having a lean-to roof
**2 :** a rough shed or shelter with a lean-to roof
**²lean-to** *adjective* (1649)
**:** having only one slope or pitch ⟨*lean-to* roof⟩ — see ROOF illustration

**¹leap** \'lēp\ *verb* **leaped** *or* **leapt** \'lēpt *also* 'lept\; **leap·ing** \'lē-piŋ\ [Middle English *lepen,* from Old English *hlēapan;* akin to Old High German *hlouffan* to run] (before 12th century)
*intransitive verb*
**1 :** to spring free from or as if from the ground **:** JUMP ⟨*leap* over a fence⟩ ⟨a fish *leaps* out of the water⟩
**2 a :** to pass abruptly from one state or topic to another **b :** to act precipitately ⟨*leaped* at the chance⟩
*transitive verb*
**:** to pass over by leaping
— **leap·er** \'lē-pər\ *noun*

**²leap** *noun* (before 12th century)
**1 a :** an act of leaping **:** SPRING, BOUND **b** (1) **:** a place leaped over or from (2) **:** the distance covered by a leap
**2 a :** a sudden passage or transition ⟨a great *leap* forward⟩ **b :** a choice made in an area of ultimate concern ⟨a *leap* of faith⟩
— **by leaps and bounds :** with extraordinary rapidity

**¹leap·frog** \'lēp-ˌfrȯg, -ˌfräg\ *noun* (1599)
**:** a game in which one player bends down and is vaulted over by another player
**²leapfrog** *verb* **leap·frogged; leap·frog·ging** (1872)
*intransitive verb*
**:** to leap or progress in or as if in leapfrog
*transitive verb*
**1 :** to go ahead of (each other) in turn; *specifically* **:** to advance (two military units) by keeping one unit in action while moving the other unit past it to a position farther in front
**2 :** to evade by or as if by a bypass

**leap second** *noun* (1971)
**:** an intercalary second added to Coordinated Universal Time to compensate for the slowing of the earth's rotation and keep Coordinated Universal Time in synchrony with solar time

**leap year** *noun* (14th century)
**1 :** a year in the Gregorian calendar containing 366 days with February 29 as the extra day
**2 :** an intercalary year in any calendar

**Lear** \'lir\ *noun*
**:** a legendary king of Britain and hero of Shakespeare's tragedy *King Lear*

**learn** \'lərn\ *verb* **learned** \'lərnd, 'lərnt\; **learn·ing** [Middle English *lernen,* from Old English *leornian;* akin to Old High German *lernēn* to learn, Old English *last* footprint, Latin *lira* furrow, track] (before 12th century)
*transitive verb*
**1 a** (1) **:** to gain knowledge or understanding of or skill in by study, instruction, or experience ⟨*learn* a trade⟩ (2) **:** MEMORIZE ⟨*learn* the lines of a play⟩ **b :** to come to be able ⟨*learn* to dance⟩ **c :** to come to realize ⟨*learned* that honesty paid⟩
**2 a** *nonstandard* **:** TEACH **b** *obsolete* **:** to inform of something
**3 :** to come to know **:** HEAR ⟨we just *learned* that he was ill⟩
*intransitive verb*
**:** to acquire knowledge or skill or a behavioral tendency ◼ ◆
**synonym** see DISCOVER
— **learn·able** \'lər-nə-bəl\ *adjective*
— **learn·er** *noun*

**learned** *adjective* (14th century)
**1** \'lər-nəd\ **:** characterized by or associated with learning **:** ERUDITE
**2** \'lərnd, 'lərnt\ **:** acquired by learning ⟨*learned* behavior⟩
— **learn·ed·ly** \'lər-nəd-lē\ *adverb*
— **learn·ed·ness** \-nəd-nəs\ *noun*

**learn·ing** *noun* (before 12th century)
**1 :** the act or experience of one that learns

**2 :** knowledge or skill acquired by instruction or study
**3 :** modification of a behavioral tendency by experience (as exposure to conditioning)
**synonym** see KNOWLEDGE

**learning curve** *noun* (1922)
**:** a curve plotting performance against practice; *especially* **:** one graphing decline in unit costs with cumulative output

**learning disabled** *adjective* (1973)
**:** having difficulty in learning a basic scholastic skill because of a disorder (as dyslexia or attention deficit disorder) that interferes with the learning process
— **learning disability** *noun*

**learnt** \'lərnt\ *chiefly British past and past participle of* LEARN

**leary** *variant of* LEERY

**¹lease** \'lēs\ *noun* [Middle English *les,* from Anglo-French, from *lesser*] (14th century)
**1 :** a contract by which one conveys real estate, equipment, or facilities for a specified term and for a specified rent; *also* **:** the act of such conveyance or the term for which it is made
**2 :** a piece of land or property that is leased
**3 :** a continuance or opportunity for continuance ⟨a new *lease* on life⟩

**²lease** *transitive verb* **leased; leas·ing** [Anglo-French *lesser,* from Old French *laissier* to let go, from Latin *laxare* to loosen, from *laxus* slack — more at SLACK] (circa 1570)
**1 :** to grant by lease
**2 :** to hold under a lease
**synonym** see HIRE
— **leas·able** \'lē-sə-bəl\ *adjective*

**lease·back** \'lēs-ˌbak\ *noun* (1947)
**:** the sale of property with the understanding that the seller can lease it from the new owner

**lease·hold** \'lēs-ˌhōld\ *noun* (1720)
**1 :** a tenure by lease
**2 :** property held by lease
— **lease·hold·er** *noun*

**leash** \'lēsh\ *noun* [Middle English *lees, leshe,* from Middle French *laisse,* from Old French *laissier*] (14th century)
**1 a :** a line for leading or restraining an animal **b :** something that restrains
**2 a :** a set of three animals (as greyhounds, foxes, bucks, or hares) **b :** a set of three
— **leash** *transitive verb*

**leash law** *noun* (1966)
**:** an ordinance requiring dogs to be restrained when not confined to their owner's property

**leas·ing** \'lē-siŋ, -ziŋ\ *noun* [Middle English *lesing,* from Old English *lēasung,* from *lēasian* to lie, from *lēas* false] (before 12th century)
*archaic* **:** the act of lying; *also* **:** LIE, FALSEHOOD

**¹least** \'lēst\ *adjective superlative of* ¹LITTLE [Middle English *leest,* from Old English *lǣst,* superlative of *lǣssa* less] (before 12th century)
**1 :** lowest in importance or position
**2 a :** smallest in size or degree **b :** being a member of a kind distinguished by diminutive size ⟨*least* bittern⟩ **c :** smallest possible **:** SLIGHTEST

**²least** *noun* (12th century)
**:** one that is least
— **at least 1 :** at the minimum **2 :** in any case

**³least** *adverb superlative of* ²LITTLE (13th century)
**:** in the smallest or lowest degree
— **least of all :** especially not ⟨no one, *least of all* the children, paid attention⟩

**least common denominator** *noun* (1875)
**:** the least common multiple of two or more denominators

**least common multiple** *noun* (1823)
**1 :** the smallest common multiple of two or more numbers
**2 :** the common multiple of lowest degree of two or more polynomials

**least squares** *noun plural* (1825)
**:** a method of fitting a curve to a set of points representing statistical data in such a way that the sum of the squares of the distances of the points from the curve is a minimum

**least·ways** \'lēst-ˌwāz\ *adverb* (14th century) *dialect* **:** at least

**least·wise** \-ˌwīz\ *adverb* (15th century)
**:** at least

**¹leath·er** \'le-thər\ *noun* [Middle English *lether,* from Old English *lether-;* akin to Old High German *leder* leather, Old Irish *lethar*] (13th century)
**1 :** animal skin dressed for use
**2 :** the flap of the ear of a dog — see DOG illustration
**3 :** something wholly or partly made of leather
— **leather** *adjective*
— **leath·er·like** \-ˌlīk\ *adjective*

**²leather** *transitive verb* **leath·ered; leath·er·ing** \'le-thə-riŋ, 'leth-riŋ\ (13th century)
**1 :** to cover with leather
**2 :** to beat with a strap **:** THRASH

**leath·er·back** \'le-thər-ˌbak\ *noun* (circa 1855)
**:** the largest existing sea turtle (*Dermochelys coriacea*) distinguished by its flexible carapace composed of a mosaic of small bones embedded in a thick leathery skin

**leatherback**

**leath·er·ette** \ˌle-thə-ˈret\ *noun, often attributive* [from *Leatherette,* a trademark] (circa 1879)
**:** simulated leather

**leath·er·leaf** \'le-thər-ˌlēf\ *noun* (circa 1818)

---

: a north temperate ericaceous bog shrub (*Chamaedaphne calyculata*) with evergreen coriaceous leaves and small white cylindrical flowers

**leath·ern** \'le-thərn\ *adjective* (before 12th century)
: made of, consisting of, or resembling leather

**leath·er·neck** \-thər-,nek\ *noun* [from the leather collar formerly part of the uniform] (circa 1914)
: a member of the U.S. Marine Corps

**leath·er·wood** \'le-thər-,wùd\ *noun* (1743)
**1** : a small tree (*Dirca palustris*) of the mezereon family with pliant stems and yellow flowers
**2** : a small tree (*Cyrilla racemiflora*) of the southeastern U.S. related to the titi

**leath·ery** \'le-thə-rē, 'leth-rē\ *adjective* (circa 1552)
: resembling leather in appearance or consistency

**¹leave** \'lēv\ *verb* **left** \'left\; **leav·ing** [Middle English *leven,* from Old English *lǣfan;* akin to Old High German ver*leiben* to leave, Old English be*līfan* to be left over, and perhaps to Lithuanian *lipti* to adhere, Greek *lipos* grease, fat] (before 12th century)
*transitive verb*
**1 a** (1) : BEQUEATH, DEVISE ⟨*left* a fortune to his son⟩ (2) : to have remaining after one's death ⟨*leaves* a widow and two children⟩ **b** : to cause to remain as a trace or aftereffect ⟨oil *leaves* a stain⟩ ⟨the wound *left* an ugly scar⟩ **2 a** : to cause or allow to be or remain in a specified condition ⟨*leave* the door open⟩ ⟨his manner *left* me cold⟩ **b** : to fail to include or take along ⟨*left* the notes at home⟩ ⟨the movie *leaves* a lot out⟩ **c** : to have as a remainder ⟨4 from 7 *leaves* 3⟩ **d** : to permit to be or remain subject to another's action or control ⟨just *leave* everything to me⟩ **e** : LET **f** : to cause or allow to be or remain available ⟨*leave* room for expansion⟩ ⟨wanted to *leave* himself an out⟩ **3 a** : to go away from : DEPART ⟨*leave* the room⟩ **b** : DESERT, ABANDON ⟨*left* his wife⟩ **c** : to terminate association with : withdraw from ⟨*left* school before graduation⟩ **4** : to put, deposit, or deliver before or in the process of departing ⟨someone *left* a package for you⟩
*intransitive verb*
: SET OUT, DEPART ∎
— **leav·er** *noun*
— **leave alone** : to refrain from bothering or using

**²leave** *noun* [Middle English *leve,* from Old English *lēaf;* akin to Middle High German *loube* permission, Old English al*ȳfan* to allow — more at BELIEVE] (before 12th century)
**1 a** : permission to do something **b** : authorized especially extended absence from duty or employment **2** : an act of leaving : DEPARTURE

**³leave** *intransitive verb* **leaved; leav·ing** [Middle English *leven,* from *leef* leaf] (14th century)
: LEAF

**leaved** *adjective* (13th century)
: having leaves — usually used in combination ⟨palmate-*leaved*⟩ ⟨a four-*leaved* clover⟩

**¹leav·en** \'le-vən\ *noun* [Middle English *levain,* from Middle French, from (assumed) Vulgar Latin *levamen,* from Latin *levare* to raise — more at LEVER] (14th century)
**1 a** : a substance (as yeast) used to produce fermentation in dough or a liquid; *especially* : SOURDOUGH **b** : a material (as baking powder) used to produce a gas that lightens dough or batter **2** : something that modifies or lightens

**²leaven** *transitive verb* **leav·ened; leav·en·ing** \'lev-niŋ, 'le-və-\ (15th century)
**1** : to raise (as bread) with a leaven

**2** : to mingle or permeate with some modifying, alleviating, or vivifying element
**synonym** see INFUSE

**leav·en·ing** *noun* (circa 1626)
: a leavening agent : LEAVEN

**leave of absence** (1771)
**1** : permission to be absent from duty or employment
**2** : LEAVE 1b

**leave off** *verb* (14th century)
: STOP, CEASE

**leaves** *plural of* LEAF

**leave–tak·ing** \'lēv-,tā-kiŋ\ *noun* (14th century)
: DEPARTURE, FAREWELL

**leav·ings** \'lē-viŋz\ *noun plural* (14th century)
: REMNANTS, RESIDUE

**le·bens·raum** \'lā-bənz-,raùm, -bən(t)s-\ *noun, often capitalized* [German, from *Leben* living, life + *Raum* space] (1905)
**1** : territory believed especially by Nazis to be necessary for national existence or economic self-sufficiency
**2** : space required for life, growth, or activity

**¹lech** \'lech\ *noun* (circa 1830)
**1** : LETCH, LUST
**2** : LECHER

**²lech** *intransitive verb* (1911)
: LUST

**lech·er** \'le-chər\ *noun* [Middle English *lechour,* from Old French *lecheor,* from *lechier* to lick, live in debauchery, of Germanic origin; akin to Old High German *leckōn* to lick — more at LICK] (13th century)
: a man who engages in lechery

**lech·er·ous** \'le-chə-rəs, 'lech-rəs\ *adjective* (14th century)
: given to or suggestive of lechery
— **lech·er·ous·ly** *adverb*
— **lech·er·ous·ness** *noun*

**lech·ery** \-rē\ *noun* (13th century)
: inordinate indulgence in sexual activity : LASCIVIOUSNESS

**le·chwe** \'lēch-wē\ *noun, plural* **lechwe** *or* **lechwes** [probably from Sesotho *lets'a*] (1857)
: an antelope (*Kobus leche*) that inhabits wetlands of southern Africa; *also* : a related antelope (*K. megaceros*) of the Nile Valley in Sudan and Ethiopia

**lec·i·thin** \'le-sə-thən\ *noun* [International Scientific Vocabulary, from Greek *lekithos* yolk of an egg] (1861)
: any of several waxy hygroscopic phospholipids that are widely distributed in animals and plants, form colloidal solutions in water, and have emulsifying, wetting, and antioxidant properties; *also* : a mixture of or substance rich in lecithins

**lec·i·thin·ase** \-thə-,nās, -,nāz\ *noun* (1910)
: PHOSPHOLIPASE

**lec·tern** \'lek-tərn\ *noun* [Middle English *lettorne,* from Middle French *letrun,* from Medieval Latin *lectorinum,* from Latin *lector* reader, from *legere* to read — more at LEGEND] (14th century)
: a stand used to support a book in a convenient position for a standing reader; *especially* : one from which scripture lessons are read in a church service
**usage** see PODIUM

**lec·tion** \'lek-shən\ *noun* [Late Latin *lection-, lectio,* from Latin, act of reading — more at LESSON] (1608)
**1** : a liturgical lesson for a particular day
**2** [New Latin *lection-, lectio,* from Latin] : a variant reading of a text

**lec·tion·ary** \'lek-shə-,ner-ē\ *noun, plural* **-ar·ies** (1780)
: a book or list of lections for the church year

**lec·tor** \'lek-tər, -,tòr\ *noun* [Middle English, from Late Latin, reader of the lessons in a church service, from Latin, reader, from *legere*] (14th century)
: one who assists at a worship service chiefly by reading a lesson

**lec·to·type** \'lek-tə-,tīp\ *noun* [Greek *lektos* chosen (from *legein* to gather, choose) + English *type* — more at LEGEND] (circa 1905)
: a specimen chosen as the type of a species or subspecies if the author of the name fails to designate a type

**¹lec·ture** \'lek-chər, -shər\ *noun* [Middle English, act of reading, from Late Latin *lectura,* from Latin *lectus,* past participle of *legere*] (15th century)
**1** : a discourse given before an audience or class especially for instruction
**2** : a formal reproof
— **lec·ture·ship** \-,ship\ *noun*

**²lecture** *verb* **lec·tured; lec·tur·ing** \'lek-chə-riŋ, 'lek-shriŋ\ (circa 1590)
*intransitive verb*
: to deliver a lecture or a course of lectures
*transitive verb*
**1** : to deliver a lecture to
**2** : to reprove formally
— **lec·tur·er** \-chər-ər, -shrər\ *noun*

**led** *past and past participle of* LEAD

**LED** \,el-(,)ē-'dē\ *noun* [*l*ight-*e*mitting *d*iode] (1968)
: a semiconductor diode that emits light when a voltage is applied to it and that is used in an electronic display (as for a digital watch)

**Le·da** \'lē-də\ *noun* [Latin, from Greek *Lēda*]
: the mother of Clytemnestra and Castor by her husband Tyndareus and of Helen and Pollux by Zeus who comes to her in the form of a swan

**le·der·ho·sen** \'lā-dər-,hō-z°n\ *noun plural* [German, from Middle High German *lederhose,* from *leder* leather + *hose* trousers] (1936)
: leather shorts often with suspenders worn especially in Bavaria

**ledge** \'lej\ *noun* [Middle English *legge* bar of a gate] (1535)
**1** : a raised or projecting edge or molding intended to protect or check ⟨a window *ledge*⟩
**2** : an underwater ridge or reef especially near the shore
**3 a** : a narrow flat surface or shelf; *especially* : one that projects from a wall of rock **b** : rock that is solid or continuous enough to form ledges : BEDROCK ⟨the field was full of *ledge*⟩
**4** : LODE, VEIN
— **ledgy** \'le-jē\ *adjective*

**led·ger** \'le-jər\ *noun* [Middle English *legger,* probably from *leyen, leggen* to lay] (1588)
**1** : a book containing accounts to which debits and credits are posted from books of original entry
**2** : a horizontal timber secured to the uprights of scaffolding to support the putlog

**ledger line** *noun* (1700)
: a short line added above or below a musical staff to extend its range

**¹lee** \'lē\ *noun* [Middle English, from Old English *hlēo;* perhaps akin to Old High German *lāo* lukewarm, Latin *calēre* to be warm] (before 12th century)
**1** : protecting shelter
**2** : the side (as of a ship) that is sheltered from the wind

**²lee** *adjective* (15th century)

□ USAGE
**leave** *Leave* (sense 2e) with the infinitive but without *to* (*leave* it be) is a mostly spoken idiom used in writing especially for humorous effect. It is not often criticized in British English, but American commentators, adhering to an opinion first expressed in 1881, still dislike it.

\ə\ **abut** \ə\ **kitten** \ər\ **further** \a\ **ash** \ā\ **ace**
\ä\ **mop, mar** \aù\ **out** \ch\ **chin** \e\ **bet** \ē\ **easy**
\g\ **go** \i\ **hit** \ī\ **ice** \j\ **job** \ŋ\ **sing** \ō\ **go**
\ò\ **law** \òi\ **boy** \th\ **thin** \th\ **the** \ü\ **loot** \ù\ **foot**
\y\ **yet** \zh\ **vision** *see also* Guide to Pronunciation

**1 :** of or relating to the side sheltered from the wind — compare WEATHER
**2 :** facing in the direction of motion of an overriding glacier — used especially of a hillside

**lee·board** \'lē-ˌbōrd, -ˌbȯrd\ *noun* (1691)
**:** either of the wood or metal planes attached outside the hull of a sailboat to prevent leeway

¹**leech** \'lēch\ *noun* [Middle English *leche*, from Old English *lǣce*; akin to Old High German *lāhhi* physician] (before 12th century)
**1** *archaic* **:** PHYSICIAN, SURGEON
**2** [from its former use by physicians for bleeding patients] **:** any of numerous carnivorous or bloodsucking usually freshwater annelid worms (class Hirudinea) that have typically a flattened lanceolate segmented body with a sucker at each end
**3 :** a hanger-on who seeks advantage or gain
**synonym** see PARASITE
— **leech·like** \-ˌlīk\ *adjective*

²**leech** (1828)
*transitive verb*
**1 :** to bleed by the use of leeches
**2 :** to drain the substance of **:** EXHAUST
*intransitive verb*
**:** to attach oneself to a person as a leech

³**leech** *noun* [Middle English *leche*, from Middle Low German *līk* boltrope — more at LIGATURE] (15th century)
**1 :** either vertical edge of a square sail
**2 :** the after edge of a fore-and-aft sail

**leek** \'lēk\ *noun* [Middle English, from Old English *lēac*; akin to Old High German *louh* leek] (before 12th century)
**:** a biennial garden herb (*Allium ampeloprasum porrum*) of the lily family grown for its mildly pungent succulent linear leaves and especially for its thick cylindrical stalk

¹**leer** \'lir\ *intransitive verb* [probably from obsolete *leer* cheek] (1530)
**:** to cast a sidelong glance; *especially* **:** to give a leer
— **leer·ing·ly** \-iŋ-lē\ *adverb*

**leek**

²**leer** *noun* (1598)
**:** a lascivious, knowing, or wanton look

**leery** \'lir-ē\ *adjective* (1718)
**:** SUSPICIOUS, WARY — often used with *of*

**lees** \'lēz\ *noun plural* [Middle English *lie*, from Middle French, from Medieval Latin *lia*] (14th century)
**:** the sediment of a liquor (as wine) during fermentation and aging **:** DREGS

**Lee's Birthday** \'lēz-\ *noun* [Robert E. *Lee*] (1910)
**:** January 19 or the third Monday in January observed as a legal holiday in many southern states

**lee shore** *noun* (circa 1580)
**:** a shore lying off a ship's leeward side and constituting a severe danger in storm

¹**lee·ward** \'lē-wərd, *especially nautical* 'lü-ərd\ *noun* (1549)
**:** the lee side

²**leeward** *adjective* (1666)
**:** being in or facing the direction toward which the wind is blowing; *also* **:** being the side opposite the windward

**lee·way** \'lē-ˌwā\ *noun* (1669)
**1 a :** off-course lateral movement of a ship when under way **b :** the angle between the heading and the track of an airplane
**2 :** an allowable margin of freedom or variation **:** TOLERANCE

¹**left** \'left\ *adjective* [Middle English, from Old English, weak; akin to Middle Low German *lucht* left; from the left hand's being the weaker in most individuals] (13th century)
**1 a :** of, relating to, situated on, or being the side of the body in which the heart is mostly

located **b :** located nearer to the left hand than to the right **c** (1) **:** located on the left of an observer facing in the same direction as the object specified ⟨stage *left*⟩ (2) **:** located on the left when facing downstream ⟨the *left* bank of a river⟩
**2** *often capitalized* **:** of, adhering to, or constituted by the left especially in politics
— **left** *adverb*

²**left** *noun* (13th century)
**1 a :** the left hand **b :** the location or direction of the left side **c :** the part on the left side
**2 a :** LEFT FIELD **b :** a blow struck with the left fist
**3** *often capitalized* **a :** the part of a legislative chamber located to the left of the presiding officer **b :** the members of a continental European legislative body occupying the left as a result of holding more radical political views than other members
**4** *capitalized* **a :** those professing views usually characterized by desire to reform or overthrow the established order especially in politics and usually advocating change in the name of the greater freedom or well-being of the common man **b :** a radical as distinguished from a conservative position

³**left** *past and past participle of* LEAVE

**left–bank** *adjective, often L&B capitalized* (1929)
**:** of, relating to, situated in, or characteristic of the bohemian district of Paris on the left bank of the Seine River

**left field** *noun* (1857)
**1 :** the position of the player defending left field
**2 :** the part of the baseball outfield to the left looking out from the plate
**3 :** a state or position far from the mainstream (as of prevailing opinion) ⟨they were really out in *left field* with that idea⟩ **:** a source of the unexpected or illogical ⟨that question came out of *left field*⟩
— **left fielder** *noun*

**left–hand** \'left-ˌhand, 'lef-ˌtand\ *adjective* (1598)
**1 :** situated on the left
**2 :** LEFT-HANDED

**left–hand·ed** \-'han-dəd, -'tan-\ *adjective* (14th century)
**1 :** using the left hand habitually or more easily than the right; *also* **:** swinging from left to right ⟨a *left-handed* batter⟩
**2 :** relating to, designed for, or done with the left hand
**3 :** MORGANATIC
**4 a :** CLUMSY, AWKWARD **b :** INSINCERE, BACKHANDED, DUBIOUS ⟨a *left-handed* compliment⟩
**5 a :** having a direction contrary to that of the hands of a watch viewed from in front **:** COUNTERCLOCKWISE **b :** having a spiral structure or form that ascends or advances to the left ⟨a *left-handed* rope⟩
— **left–handed** *adverb*
— **left–hand·ed·ly** *adverb*
— **left–hand·ed·ness** *noun*

**left–hand·er** \-'han-dər, -'tan-\ *noun* (1881)
**:** a left-handed person

**left·ish** \'lef-tish\ *adjective* (1934)
**:** showing leftist tendencies

**left·ism** \'lef-ˌti-zəm\ *noun* (1920)
**1 :** the principles and views of the Left; *also* **:** the movement embodying these principles
**2 :** advocacy of or adherence to the doctrines of the Left
— **left·ist** \-tist\ *noun or adjective*

¹**left·over** \'left-ˌō-vər\ *noun* (1891)
**1 :** something that remains unused or unconsumed; *especially* **:** leftover food served at a later meal — usually used in plural
**2 :** an anachronistic survival **:** VESTIGE

²**left·over** *adjective* (1897)
**:** not consumed or used ⟨*leftover* food⟩ ⟨*leftover* space⟩

**left shoulder arms** *noun* [from the command *left shoulder arms!*] (circa 1918)

**:** a position in the manual of arms in which the butt of the rifle is held in the left hand with the barrel resting on the left shoulder; *also* **:** a command to assume this position

**left·ward** \'left-wərd\ *adjective or adverb* (15th century)
**:** being toward or on the left

**left wing** *noun* (1884)
**1 :** the leftist division of a group (as a political party)
**2 :** LEFT 4a
— **left–wing** *adjective*
— **left–wing·er** \'left-'wiŋ-ər\ *noun*

**lefty** \'lef-tē\ *noun, plural* **left·ies** (1886)
**1 :** LEFT-HANDER
**2 :** an advocate of leftism
— **lefty** *adjective*

¹**leg** \'leg *also* 'lāg\ *noun* [Middle English, from Old Norse *leggr*] (14th century)
**1 :** a limb of an animal used especially for supporting the body and for walking: as **a** (1) **:** one of the paired vertebrate limbs that in bipeds extend from the top of the thigh to the foot (2) **:** the part of such a limb between the knee and foot **b :** the back half of a hindquarter of a meat animal **c :** one of the rather generalized segmental appendages of an arthropod used in walking and crawling
**2 a :** a pole or bar serving as a support or prop ⟨the *legs* of a tripod⟩ **b :** a branch of a forked or jointed object ⟨the *legs* of a compass⟩
**3 a :** the part of an article of clothing that covers the leg **b :** the part of the upper (as of a boot) that extends above the ankle
**4 :** OBEISANCE, BOW — used chiefly in the phrase *to make a leg*
**5 :** a side of a right triangle that is not the hypotenuse; *also* **:** a side of an isosceles triangle that is not the base
**6 a :** the course and distance sailed by a boat on a single tack **b :** a portion of a trip **:** STAGE **c :** one section of a relay race **d :** one of several events or games necessary to be won to decide a competition ⟨won the first two *legs* of horse racing's Triple Crown⟩
**7 :** a branch or part of an object or system
— **leg·less** \-ləs\ *adjective*
— **a leg to stand on :** SUPPORT; *especially* **:** a basis for one's position in a controversy
— **on one's last legs :** at or near the end of one's resources **:** on the verge of failure, exhaustion, or ruin

²**leg** *intransitive verb* **legged; leg·ging** (1601)
**:** to use the legs in walking; *especially* **:** RUN

**leg·a·cy** \'le-gə-sē\ *noun, plural* **-cies** [Middle English *legacie* office of a legate, bequest, from Middle French or Medieval Latin; Middle French, office of a legate, from Medieval Latin *legatia,* from Latin *legatus*] (15th century)
**1 :** a gift by will especially of money or other personal property **:** BEQUEST
**2 :** something transmitted by or received from an ancestor or predecessor or from the past ⟨the *legacy* of the ancient philosophers⟩

¹**le·gal** \'lē-gəl\ *adjective* [Middle French, from Latin *legalis,* from *leg-, lex* law] (circa 1500)
**1 :** of or relating to law
**2 a :** deriving authority from or founded on law **:** DE JURE **b :** having a formal status derived from law often without a basis in actual fact **:** TITULAR ⟨a corporation is a *legal* but not a real person⟩ **c :** established by law; *especially* **:** STATUTORY
**3 :** conforming to or permitted by law or established rules
**4 :** recognized or made effective by a court of law as distinguished from a court of equity
**5 :** of, relating to, or having the characteristics of the profession of law or of one of its members
**6 :** created by the constructions of the law ⟨a *legal* fiction⟩
**synonym** see LAWFUL
— **le·gal·ly** \-gə-lē\ *adverb*

²**legal** *noun* (1526)
: one that conforms to rules or the law

**legal age** *noun* (circa 1904)
: the age at which a person enters into full adult legal rights and responsibilities (as of making contracts or wills)

**legal aid** *noun* (1890)
: aid provided by an organization established especially to serve the legal needs of the poor

**legal eagle** *noun* (1942)
: LAWYER

**le·gal·ese** \ˌlē-gə-ˈlēz, -ˈlēs\ *noun* (1914)
: the specialized language of the legal profession 〈replaced *legalese* with plain talk —Steve Weinberg〉

**legal holiday** *noun* (1867)
: a holiday established by legal authority and marked by restrictions on work and transaction of official business

**le·gal·ise** *British variant of* LEGALIZE

**le·gal·ism** \ˈlē-gə-ˌli-zəm\ *noun* (1838)
**1** : strict, literal, or excessive conformity to the law or to a religious or moral code 〈the institutionalized *legalism* that restricts free choice〉
**2** : a legal term or rule

**le·gal·ist** \-list\ *noun* (1646)
**1** : an advocate or adherent of moral legalism
**2** : one that views things from a legal standpoint; *especially* : one that places primary emphasis on legal principles or on the formal structure of governmental institutions
— **le·gal·is·tic** \ˌlē-gə-ˈlis-tik\ *adjective*
— **le·gal·is·ti·cal·ly** \-ti-k(ə-)lē\ *adverb*

**le·gal·i·ty** \li-ˈga-lə-tē\ *noun, plural* **-ties** (15th century)
**1** : attachment to or observance of law
**2** : the quality or state of being legal : LAWFULNESS
**3** *plural* : obligations imposed by law

**le·gal·ize** \ˈlē-gə-ˌlīz\ *transitive verb* **-ized; -iz·ing** (circa 1716)
: to make legal; *especially* : to give legal validity or sanction to
— **le·gal·i·za·tion** \ˌlē-gə-lə-ˈzā-shən\ *noun*
— **le·gal·iz·er** \ˈlē-gə-ˌlī-zər\ *noun*

**legal pad** *noun* (1967)
: a writing tablet of ruled yellow paper that is usually 8.5 by 14 inches (22 by 36 centimeters)

**legal reserve** *noun* (circa 1902)
: the minimum amount of bank deposits or life insurance company assets required by law to be kept as reserves

**legal tender** *noun* (1739)
: money that is legally valid for the payment of debts and that must be accepted for that purpose when offered

¹**leg·ate** \ˈle-gət\ *noun* [Middle English, from Middle French & Latin; Middle French *legat*, from Latin *legatus* deputy, emissary, from past participle of *legare* to depute, send as emissary, bequeath, from *leg-, lex*] (12th century)
: a usually official emissary
— **leg·ate·ship** \-ˌship\ *noun*

²**le·gate** \li-ˈgāt\ *transitive verb* **le·gat·ed; le·gat·ing** [*legatus*, past participle of *legare* to bequeath] (15th century)
: BEQUEATH 1
— **le·ga·tor** \-ˈgā-tər\ *noun*

**leg·a·tee** \ˌle-gə-ˈtē\ *noun* (circa 1688)
: one to whom a legacy is bequeathed or a devise is given

**leg·a·tine** \ˈle-gə-ˌtēn, -ˌtīn\ *adjective* (1611)
: of, headed by, or enacted under the authority of a legate

**le·ga·tion** \li-ˈgā-shən\ *noun* (14th century)
**1** : the sending forth of a legate
**2** : a body of deputies sent on a mission; *specifically* : a diplomatic mission in a foreign country headed by a minister
**3** : the official residence and office of a diplomatic minister in a foreign country

¹**le·ga·to** \li-ˈgä-(ˌ)tō\ *adverb or adjective* [Italian, literally, tied] (circa 1811)

: in a manner that is smooth and connected (as between successive tones) — used especially as a direction in music

²**legato** *noun* (1885)
: a smooth and connected manner of performance (as of music); *also* : a passage of music so performed

**leg·end** \ˈle-jənd\ *noun* [Middle English *legende*, from Middle French & Medieval Latin; Middle French *legende*, from Medieval Latin *legenda*, from Latin, feminine of *legendus*, gerundive of *legere* to gather, select, read; akin to Greek *legein* to gather, say, *logos* speech, word, reason] (14th century)
**1 a** : a story coming down from the past; *especially* : one popularly regarded as historical although not verifiable **b** : a body of such stories 〈a place in the *legend* of the frontier〉 **c** : a popular myth of recent origin **d** : a person or thing that inspires legends **e** : the subject of a legend 〈its violence was *legend* even in its own time —William Broyles Jr.〉
**2 a** : an inscription or title on an object (as a coin) **b** : CAPTION 2b **c** : an explanatory list of the symbols on a map or chart ◆

**leg·end·ary** \ˈle-jən-ˌder-ē\ *adjective* (circa 1587)
**1** : of, relating to, or characteristic of legend or a legend
**2** : WELL-KNOWN, FAMOUS
*synonym* see FICTITIOUS
— **leg·en·dar·i·ly** \ˌle-jən-ˈder-ə-lē\ *adverb*

**leg·end·ry** \ˈle-jən-drē\ *noun* (1849)
: a body of legends

**leg·er** \ˈle-jər\ *variant of* LEDGER

**leg·er·de·main** \ˌle-jər-də-ˈmān\ *noun* [Middle English, from Middle French *leger de main* light of hand] (15th century)
**1** : SLEIGHT OF HAND
**2** : a display of skill or adroitness

**le·ger·i·ty** \lə-ˈjer-ə-tē, le-\ *noun* [Middle French *legereté*, from Old French, lightness, from *leger* light, from (assumed) Vulgar Latin *leviarius*, from Latin *levis* — more at LIGHT] (1561)
: alert facile quickness of mind or body

**leger line** *noun* (circa 1775)
: LEDGER LINE

**leges** *plural of* LEX

**leg·ged** \ˈle-gəd *also* ˈlā-, *British usually* ˈlegd\ *adjective* (15th century)
: having a leg or legs especially of a specified kind or number — often used in combination 〈a four-*legged* animal〉

**leg·ging** *or* **leg·gin** \ˈle-gən *also* ˈlā-, -gin\ *noun* (1751)
: a covering (as of leather or cloth) for the leg — usually used in plural; *also* : TIGHTS

**leg·gy** \ˈle-gē *also* ˈlā-\ *adjective* **leg·gi·er; -est** (1787)
**1** : having disproportionately long legs
**2** : having long and attractive legs
**3** : SPINDLY — used of a plant
— **leg·gi·ness** \-nəs\ *noun*

**leg-hold trap** \ˈleg-ˌhōld-\ *noun* (1973)
: a jawed usually steel trap that is used to hold a wild mammal and operates by springing closed and clamping onto the leg of the animal that steps on it

**leg·horn** \ˈleg-ˌhȯrn; ˈle-ˌgȯrn, -gərn\ *noun* [*Leghorn*, Italy] (1740)
**1 a** : a fine plaited straw made from an Italian wheat **b** : a hat of this straw
**2** : any of a Mediterranean breed of small hardy fowls noted for their large production of white eggs

**leg·i·ble** \ˈle-jə-bəl\ *adjective* [Middle English, from Late Latin *legibilis*, from Latin *legere* to read] (14th century)
**1** : capable of being read or deciphered : PLAIN
**2** : capable of being discovered or understood
— **leg·i·bil·i·ty** \ˌle-jə-ˈbi-lə-tē\ *noun*
— **leg·i·bly** \ˈle-jə-blē\ *adverb*

¹**le·gion** \ˈlē-jən\ *noun* [Middle English, from Old French, from Latin *legion-, legio*, from *legere* to gather — more at LEGEND] (13th century)
**1** : the principal unit of the Roman army comprising 3000 to 6000 foot soldiers with cavalry
**2** : a large military force; *especially* : ARMY 1a
**3** : a very large number : MULTITUDE
**4** : a national association of ex-servicemen

²**legion** *adjective* (1678)
: MANY, NUMEROUS 〈the problems are *legion*〉

¹**le·gion·ary** \ˈlē-jə-ˌner-ē\ *adjective* [Latin *legionarius*, from *legion-, legio*] (15th century)
: of, relating to, or constituting a legion

²**legionary** *noun, plural* **-ar·ies** (1598)
: LEGIONNAIRE

**le·gion·naire** \ˌlē-jə-ˈnar, -ˈner\ *noun* [French *légionnaire*, from Latin *legionarius*] (1818)
: a member of a legion

**Legionnaires' disease** \-ˈnarz-, -ˈnerz-\ *also* **Legionnaire's disease** *noun* [from its first recognized occurrence at an American Legion convention in 1976] (1976)
: a lobar pneumonia caused by a bacterium (*Legionella pneumophila*)

**Legion of Honor** (1827)
: a French order conferred as a reward for civil or military merit

**Legion of Merit** (1943)
: a U.S. military decoration awarded for exceptionally meritorious conduct in the performance of outstanding services

**leg·is·late** \ˈle-jəs-ˌlāt\ *verb* **-lat·ed; -lat·ing** [back-formation from *legislator*] (1805)
*intransitive verb*
: to perform the function of legislation; *specifically* : to make or enact laws
*transitive verb*
: to cause, create, provide, or bring about by or as if by legislation

**leg·is·la·tion** \ˌle-jəs-ˈlā-shən\ *noun* (circa 1655)
**1** : the action of legislating; *specifically* : the exercise of the power and function of making rules (as laws) that have the force of authority by virtue of their promulgation by an official organ of a state or other organization
**2** : the enactments of a legislator or a legislative body
**3** : a matter of business for or under consideration by a legislative body

¹**leg·is·la·tive** \ˈle-jəs-ˌlā-tiv, -lə-\ *adjective* (circa 1641)
**1 a** : having the power or performing the function of legislating **b** : belonging to the branch of government that is charged with

◇ WORD HISTORY
**legend** The literal meaning of the Latin verb *legere* was "to gather," but it acquired extended senses such as "to pick out (sights or sounds)," "to make one's way over" and finally "to read." In Medieval Latin *legenda*, the gerundive of *legere*, meaning literally "a thing to be read," was used in specific reference to the story of the life of a saint. One of the most popular books of the later Middle Ages was the *Legenda Aurea* ("Golden Legend") of Jacobus de Voragine, a collection of saints' lives that incorporated a generous measure of fanciful material along with fact. When the word was borrowed, via French, into Middle English as *legende*, it continued to be used with specific reference to a saint's story. By the 17th century, however, *legend* had come to be applied to any story handed down from earlier times that, like the traditional saints' lives, was at best unverifiable.

\ə\ abut \ᵊ\ kitten \ər\ further \a\ ash \ā\ ace
\ä\ mop, mar \au̇\ out \ch\ chin \e\ bet \ē\ easy
\g\ go \i\ hit \ī\ ice \j\ job \ŋ\ sing \ō\ go
\ȯ\ law \ȯi\ boy \th\ thin \th\ the \ü\ loot \u̇\ foot
\y\ yet \zh\ vision   *see also* Guide to Pronunciation

such powers as making laws, levying and collecting taxes, and making financial appropriations — compare EXECUTIVE, JUDICIAL
**2 a :** of or relating to a legislature ⟨*legislative* committees⟩ **b :** composed of members of a legislature ⟨*legislative* caucus⟩ **c :** created by a legislature especially as distinguished from an executive or judicial body **d :** designed to assist a legislature or its members ⟨a *legislative* research agency⟩
**3 :** of, concerned with, or created by legislation
— **leg·is·la·tive·ly** *adverb*
**²legislative** *noun* (1642)
**:** the body or department exercising the power and function of legislating : LEGISLATURE
**legislative assembly** *noun, often L&A capitalized* (1836)
**1 :** a bicameral legislature (as in an American state)
**2 :** the lower house of a bicameral legislature
**3 :** a unicameral legislature; *especially* **:** one in a Canadian province
**legislative council** *noun, often L&C capitalized* (1787)
**1 :** a permanent committee chosen from both houses that meets between sessions of a state legislature to study state problems and plan a legislative program
**2 :** a unicameral legislature (as in a British colony)
**3 :** the upper house of a British bicameral legislature
**leg·is·la·tor** \'le-jəs-ˌlā-tȯr, -ˌlā-tər *also* ˌle-jəs-'lā-ˌtȯr\ *noun* [Latin *legis lator*, literally, proposer of a law, from *legis* (genitive of *lex* law) + *lator* proposer, from *ferre* (past participle *latus*) to carry, propose — more at TOLERATE, BEAR] (1603)
**:** one that makes laws especially for a political unit; *especially* **:** a member of a legislative body
— **leg·is·la·to·ri·al** \ˌle-jəs-lə-'tȯr-ē-əl, -'tȯr-\ *adjective*
— **leg·is·la·tor·ship** \'le-jəs-ˌlā-tər-ˌship\ *noun*
**leg·is·la·ture** \'le-jəs-ˌlā-chər *also* ˌle-jəs-', *British often* 'le-jəs-lə-\ *noun* (circa 1676)
**:** a body of persons having the power to legislate; *specifically* **:** an organized body having the authority to make laws for a political unit
**le·gist** \'lē-jist\ *noun* [Middle English, from Middle French *legiste*, from Medieval Latin *legista*, from Latin *leg-, lex*] (15th century)
**:** a specialist in law; *especially* **:** one learned in Roman or civil law
**le·git** \li-'jit\ *adjective* (1908)
*slang* **:** LEGITIMATE
**le·git·i·ma·cy** \li-'ji-tə-mə-sē\ *noun* (1691)
**:** the quality or state of being legitimate
**¹le·git·i·mate** \li-'ji-tə-mət\ *adjective* [Middle English *legitimat*, from Medieval Latin *legitimatus*, past participle of *legitimare* to legitimate, from Latin *legitimus* legitimate, from *leg-, lex* law] (15th century)
**1 a :** lawfully begotten; *specifically* **:** born in wedlock **b :** having full filial rights and obligations by birth ⟨a *legitimate* child⟩
**2 :** being exactly as purposed **:** neither spurious nor false ⟨*legitimate* grievance⟩ ⟨a *legitimate* practitioner⟩
**3 a :** accordant with law or with established legal forms and requirements ⟨a *legitimate* government⟩ **b :** ruling by or based on the strict principle of hereditary right ⟨a *legitimate* king⟩
**4 :** conforming to recognized principles or accepted rules and standards ⟨*legitimate* advertising expenditure⟩ ⟨*legitimate* inference⟩
**5 :** relating to plays acted by professional actors but not including revues, burlesque, or some forms of musical comedy ⟨the *legitimate* theater⟩
**synonym** see LAWFUL
— **le·git·i·mate·ly** *adverb*

**²le·git·i·mate** \-ˌmāt\ *transitive verb* **-mat·ed; -mat·ing** (1531)
**:** to make legitimate: **a** (1) **:** to give legal status or authorization to (2) **:** to show or affirm to be justified **b :** to put (a bastard) in the state of a legitimate child before the law by legal means
— **le·git·i·ma·tion** \-ˌji-tə-'mā-shən\ *noun*
— **le·git·i·mat·or** \-'ji-tə-ˌmā-tər\ *noun*
**le·git·i·ma·tize** \li-'ji-tə-mə-ˌtīz\ *transitive verb* **-tized; -tiz·ing** (1791)
**:** LEGITIMATE
**le·git·i·mise** *British variant of* LEGITIMIZE
**le·git·i·mism** \li-'ji-tə-ˌmi-zəm\ *noun, often capitalized* (1877)
**:** adherence to the principles of political legitimacy or to a person claiming legitimacy
— **le·git·i·mist** \-mist\ *noun, often capitalized*
— **legitimist** *adjective*
**le·git·i·mize** \-ˌmīz\ *transitive verb* **-mized; -miz·ing** (1848)
**:** LEGITIMATE
— **le·git·i·mi·za·tion** \-ˌji-tə-mə-'zā-shən\ *noun*
— **le·git·i·miz·er** \-'ji-tə-ˌmī-zər\ *noun*
**leg·man** \'leg-ˌman *also* 'lāg-\ *noun* (1923)
**1 :** a reporter assigned usually to gather information
**2 :** an assistant who performs various subordinate tasks (as gathering information or running errands)
**leg-of-mut·ton** *or* **leg-o'-mut·ton** \ˌle-gə(v)-'mə-tᵊn *also* ˌlāg-\ *adjective* (1840)
**:** having the approximately triangular shape or outline of a leg of mutton ⟨*leg-of-mutton* sleeve⟩ ⟨*leg-of-mutton* sail⟩
**leg out** *transitive verb* (1965)
**:** to make (as a base hit) by fast running
**leg-pull** \'leg-ˌpu̇l *also* 'lāg-\ *noun* [from the phrase *to pull one's leg*] (1915)
**:** a humorous deception or hoax
**leg·room** \-ˌrüm, -ˌru̇m\ *noun* (1926)
**:** space in which to extend the legs while seated
**le·gume** \'le-ˌgyüm, li-'gyüm\ *noun* [French *légume*, from Latin *legumin-, legumen* leguminous plant, from *legere* to gather — more at LEGEND] (1676)
**1 a :** the fruit or seed of leguminous plants (as peas or beans) used for food **b :** a vegetable used for food
**2 :** any of a large family (Leguminosae synonym Fabaceae) of dicotyledonous herbs, shrubs, and trees having fruits that are legumes (sense 3) or loments, bearing nodules on the roots that contain nitrogen-fixing bacteria, and including important food and forage plants (as peas, beans, or clovers)
**3 :** a dry dehiscent one-celled fruit developed from a simple superior ovary and usually dehiscing into two valves with the seeds attached to the ventral suture **:** POD
**le·gu·mi·nous** \li-'gyü-mə-nəs, le-\ *adjective* (15th century)
**1 :** of, relating to, or consisting of plants that are legumes
**2 :** resembling a legume
**leg up** *noun* (1837)
**1 :** a helping hand **:** BOOST
**2 :** HEAD START
**leg warmer** *noun* (1974)
**:** a usually knitted covering for the leg
**leg·work** \'leg-ˌwərk *also* 'lāg-\ *noun* (1891)
**:** active physical work (as in gathering information) that forms the basis of more creative or mentally exacting work (as writing a book)
**le·hua** \lā-'hü-ə\ *noun* [Hawaiian] (1888)
**:** a common very showy chiefly Polynesian tree (*Metrosideros collinus*) of the myrtle family having bright red flowers and a hard wood; *also* **:** its flower
**¹lei** \'lā, 'lā-ˌē\ *noun* [Hawaiian] (1843)
**:** a wreath or necklace usually of flowers or leaves
**²lei** \'lā\ *plural of* LEU

**Leices·ter** \'les-tər\ *noun* [*Leicester*, county in England] (1798)
**1 :** an individual of either of two English breeds of white-faced long-wool sheep raised especially for mutton
**2 :** a hard usually orange-colored cheese similar to cheddar
**leish·man·ia** \lēsh-'ma-nē-ə\ *noun* [New Latin, from Sir W. B. *Leishman*, (died 1926) British medical officer] (1914)
**:** any of a genus (*Leishmania*) of flagellate protozoans that are parasitic in the tissues of vertebrates; *broadly* **:** an organism resembling the leishmanias that is included in the family (Trypanosomatidae) to which they belong
— **leish·man·ial** \-nē-əl\ *adjective*
**leish·man·i·a·sis** \ˌlēsh-mə-'nī-ə-səs\ *noun* [New Latin] (1912)
**:** infection with or disease caused by leishmanias
**leis·ter** \'lēs-tər\ *noun* [of Scandinavian origin; akin to Old Norse *ljōstr* leister] (circa 1534)
**:** a spear armed with three or more barbed prongs for catching fish
**lei·sure** \'lē-zhər, 'le-\ *noun* [Middle English *leiser*, from Middle French *leisir*, from *leisir* to be permitted, from Latin *licēre*] (14th century)
**1 :** freedom provided by the cessation of activities; *especially* **:** time free from work or duties
**2 :** EASE, LEISURELINESS
— **leisure** *adjective*
— **at leisure** *or* **at one's leisure :** in one's leisure time **:** at one's convenience ⟨read the book *at her leisure*⟩
**lei·sured** \-zhərd\ *adjective* (1631)
**:** having leisure **:** LEISURELY
**¹lei·sure·ly** \-zhər-lē\ *adverb* (15th century)
**:** without haste **:** DELIBERATELY
**²leisurely** *adjective* (1604)
**:** characterized by leisure **:** UNHURRIED
— **lei·sure·li·ness** *noun*
**leisure suit** *noun* (1975)
**:** a suit consisting of a shirt jacket and matching trousers for informal wear
**leit·mo·tiv** *or* **leit·mo·tif** \'līt-mō-ˌtēf\ *noun* [German *Leitmotiv*, from *leiten* to lead + *Motiv* motive] (circa 1876)
**1 :** an associated melodic phrase or figure that accompanies the reappearance of an idea, person, or situation especially in a Wagnerian music drama
**2 :** a dominant recurring theme
**¹lek** \'lek\ *noun* [Swedish, short for *lekställe* mating ground, from *lek* mating, sport + *ställe* place] (1871)
**:** an assembly area where animals (as the prairie chicken) carry on display and courtship behavior
**²lek** *noun, plural* **leks** *or* **le·ke** \'le-kə\ *also* **lek** *or* **le·ku** \'le-(ˌ)kü\ [Albanian] (1927)
— see MONEY table
**lek·var** \'lek-ˌvär\ *noun* [Hungarian *lekvár* jam] (circa 1958)
**:** a prune butter used as a pastry filling
**le·man** \'le-mən, 'lē-\ *noun* [Middle English *lefman, leman*, from *lef* lief] (13th century)
*archaic* **:** SWEETHEART, LOVER; *especially* **:** MISTRESS
**¹lem·ma** \'le-mə\ *noun, plural* **lemmas** *or* **lem·ma·ta** \-mə-tə\ [Latin, from Greek *lēmma* thing taken, assumption, from *lambanein* to take — more at LATCH] (1570)
**1 :** an auxiliary proposition used in the demonstration of another proposition
**2 :** the argument or theme of a composition prefixed as a title or introduction; *also* **:** the heading or theme of a comment or note on a text
**3 :** a glossed word or phrase
**²lemma** *noun* [Greek, husk, from *lepein* to peel — more at LEPER] (1906)
**:** the lower of the two bracts enclosing the flower in the spikelet of grasses

**lem·ming** \'le-miŋ\ *noun* [Norwegian] (1713)
: any of various small short-tailed furry-footed rodents (as genera *Lemmus* and *Dicrostonyx*) of circumpolar distribution that are notable for the recurrent mass migrations of a European form (*L. lemmus*) which often continue into the sea where vast numbers are drowned
— **lem·ming·like** \-ˌlīk\ *adjective*

**lem·nis·cate** \lem-'nis-kət\ *noun* [New Latin *lemniscata*, from feminine of Latin *lemniscatus* with hanging ribbons, from *lemniscus*] (circa 1781)
: a figure-eight shaped curve whose equation in polar coordinates is $\rho^2 = a^2 \cos 2\theta$ or $\rho^2 = a^2 \sin 2\theta$

**lem·nis·cus** \lem-'nis-kəs\ *noun, plural* **-nis·ci** \-'nis-ˌkī, -ˌkē; -'ni-ˌsī\ [New Latin, from Latin, ribbon, from Greek *lēmniskos*] (circa 1905)
: a band of fibers and especially nerve fibers
— **lem·nis·cal** \-kəl\ *adjective*

**¹lem·on** \'le-mən\ *noun* [Middle English *lymon*, from Middle French *limon*, from Medieval Latin *limon-, limo*, from Arabic *laymūn*] (15th century)
**1 a :** an acid fruit that is botanically a many-seeded pale yellow oblong berry and is produced by a small thorny tree (*Citrus limon*) **b :** a tree that bears lemons
**2 :** one (as an automobile) that is unsatisfactory or defective
— **lem·ony** \'le-mə-nē\ *adjective*

lemon 1: branch with fruit and flowers

**²lemon** *adjective* (1598)
**1 :** of the color lemon yellow
**2 a :** containing lemon **b :** having the flavor or scent of lemon

**lem·on·ade** \ˌle-mə-'nād\ *noun* (1604)
: a beverage of sweetened lemon juice mixed with water

**lemon balm** *noun* (circa 1888)
: a bushy perennial Old World mint (*Melissa officinalis*) often cultivated for its fragrant lemon-flavored leaves

**lem·on·grass** \'le-mən-ˌgras\ *noun* (1801)
: a grass (*Cymbopogon citratus*) of robust habit that grows in tropical regions, is used as an herb, and is the source of an essential oil with an odor of lemon or verbena

**lemon law** *noun* (1982)
: a law offering car buyers relief (as by repair, replacement, or refund) for defects detected during a specified period after purchase

**lemon shark** *noun* (1942)
: a medium-sized requiem shark (*Negaprion brevirostris*) of the warm Atlantic that is yellowish brown to gray above with yellow or greenish sides

**lemon sole** *noun* (1876)
: any of several flatfishes and especially flounders: as **a :** a bottom-dwelling flounder (*Microstomus kitt*) of the northeastern Atlantic that is an important food fish **b :** WINTER FLOUNDER

**lemon yellow** *noun* (1807)
: a brilliant greenish yellow color

**lem·pi·ra** \lem-'pir-ə\ *noun* [American Spanish, from *Lempira*, 16th century Indian chief] (circa 1934)
— see MONEY table

**le·mur** \'lē-mər\ *noun* [New Latin, from Latin *lemures*, plural, ghosts] (1795)
: any of various arboreal chiefly nocturnal mammals that were formerly widespread but are now largely confined to Madagascar, are related to the monkeys but are usually regarded as constituting a distinct superfamily (Lemuroidea), and usually have a muzzle like a fox, large eyes, very soft woolly fur, and a long furry tail ◆

**le·mu·res** \'le-mə-ˌrās, 'lem-yə-ˌrēz\ *noun plural* [Latin] (1555)
: spirits of the unburied dead exorcised from homes in early Roman religious rites

**lend** \'lend\ *verb* **lent** \'lent\; **lend·ing** [Middle English *lenen, lenden*, from Old English *lǣnan*, from *lǣn* loan — more at LOAN] (before 12th century)
*transitive verb*
**1 a :** to give for temporary use on condition that the same or its equivalent be returned **b :** to let out (money) for temporary use on condition of repayment with interest
**2 a :** to give the assistance or support of : AFFORD, FURNISH ⟨a dispassionate and scholarly manner which *lends* great force to his criticisms —*Times Literary Supplement*⟩ **b :** to adapt or apply (oneself) readily : ACCOMMODATE ⟨a topic that *lends* itself admirably to class discussion⟩
*intransitive verb*
: to make a loan
*usage* see LOAN
— **lend·able** \'len-də-bəl\ *adjective*
— **lend·er** *noun*

**lending library** *noun* (1708)
: a library from which materials are lent; especially : RENTAL LIBRARY

**lend–lease** \'lend-'lēs\ *noun* [U.S. *Lend-Lease Act* (1941)] (1941)
: the transfer of goods and services to an ally to aid in a common cause with payment made by a return of the original items or their use in the cause or by a similar transfer of other goods and services
— **lend–lease** *transitive verb*

**length** \'leŋ(k)th, 'len(t)th\ *noun, plural* **lengths** \'leŋ(k)ths, 'len(t)ths, 'leŋ(k)s\ [Middle English *lengthe*, from Old English *lengthu*, from *lang* long] (before 12th century)
**1 a :** the longer or longest dimension of an object **b :** a measured distance or dimension ⟨10 feet in *length*⟩ — see METRIC SYSTEM table, WEIGHT table **c :** the quality or state of being long
**2 a :** duration or extent in time **b :** relative duration or stress of a sound
**3 a :** distance or extent in space **b :** the length of something taken as a unit of measure ⟨his horse led by a *length*⟩
**4 :** the degree to which something (as a course of action or a line of thought) is carried — often used in plural ⟨went to great *lengths* to learn the truth⟩
**5 a :** a long expanse or stretch **b :** a piece constituting or usable as part of a whole or of a connected series : SECTION ⟨a *length* of pipe⟩
**6 :** a vertical dimension of an article of clothing
— **at length 1 :** FULLY, COMPREHENSIVELY **2 :** at last : FINALLY

**length·en** \'leŋ(k)-thən, 'len(t)-\ *verb* **lengthened; length·en·ing** \'leŋ(k)th-niŋ, 'leŋ(k)-; 'leŋ(k)-thə-, 'len(t)-\ (14th century)
*transitive verb*
: to make longer
*intransitive verb*
: to grow longer
*synonym* see EXTEND
— **length·en·er** \'leŋ(k)th-nər, 'len(t)th-; 'leŋ(k)-thə-, 'len(t)-\ *noun*

**length·ways** \'leŋ(k)th-ˌwāz, 'len(t)th-\ *adverb* (1599)
: LENGTHWISE

**length·wise** \-ˌwīz\ *adverb* (circa 1580)
: in the direction of the length : LONGITUDINALLY
— **lengthwise** *adjective*

**lengthy** \'leŋ(k)-thē, 'len(t)-\ *adjective* **length·i·er; -est** (1689)
**1 :** protracted excessively : OVERLONG
**2 :** EXTENDED, LONG
— **length·i·ly** \-thə-lē\ *adverb*
— **length·i·ness** \-thē-nəs\ *noun*

**le·nience** \'lē-nyən(t)s, -nē-ən(t)s\ *noun* (1796)
: LENIENCY

**le·nien·cy** \'lē-nē-ən(t)-sē, -nyən(t)-sē\ *noun, plural* **-cies** (1780)
**1 :** the quality or state of being lenient
**2 :** a lenient disposition or practice
*synonym* see MERCY

**le·nient** \'lē-nē-ənt, -nyənt\ *adjective* [Latin *lenient-, leniens*, present participle of *lenire* to soften, soothe, from *lenis* soft, mild; probably akin to Lithuanian *lėnas* tranquil — more at LET] (1652)
**1 :** exerting a soothing or easing influence : relieving pain or stress
**2 :** of mild and tolerant disposition; *especially* : INDULGENT
— **le·nient·ly** *adverb*

**Leni-Len·a·pe** or **Len·ni-Len·a·pe** \ˌle-nē-'le-nə-pē, -lə-'nä-pē\ *noun* [Delaware (Unami dialects) *lǝni-lǝnáp'e*] (circa 1782)
: DELAWARE 1

**Le·nin·ism** \'le-nə-ˌni-zəm\ *noun* (1918)
: the political, economic, and social principles and policies advocated by Lenin; *especially* : the theory and practice of communism developed by or associated with Lenin
— **Le·nin·ist** \-nist\ *noun or adjective*
— **Le·nin·ite** \-ˌnīt\ *noun or adjective*

**le·nis** \'lē-nəs, 'lā-\ *adjective* [New Latin, from Latin, mild, smooth] (circa 1897)
: produced with an articulation that is lax in relation to another speech sound ⟨\t\ in *gutter* is lenis, \t\ in *toe* is fortis⟩

**len·i·tion** \lə-'ni-shən\ *noun* [Latin *lenire*] (1912)
: the change from fortis to lenis articulation

**len·i·tive** \'le-nə-tiv\ *adjective* [Middle English *lenitif*, from Middle French, from Medieval Latin *lenitivus*, from Latin *lenitus*, past participle of *lenire*] (15th century)
: alleviating pain or harshness : SOOTHING
— **lenitive** *noun*
— **len·i·tive·ly** *adverb*

**len·i·ty** \'le-nə-tē\ *noun* (1548)
: the quality or state of being lenient : CLEMENCY

**le·no** \'lē-(ˌ)nō\ *noun* [perhaps from French *linon* linen fabric, lawn, from Middle French *lin* flax, linen, from Latin *linum* flax] (1821)

lemur

\ə\ abut \ᵊ\ kitten \ər\ further \a\ ash \ā\ ace
\ä\ mop, mar \au̇\ out \ch\ chin \e\ bet \ē\ easy
\g\ go \i\ hit \ī\ ice \j\ job \ŋ\ sing \ō\ go
\ȯ\ law \ȯi\ boy \th\ thin \t̶h\ the \ü\ loot \u̇\ foot
\y\ yet \zh\ vision *see also* Guide to Pronunciation

**1 :** an open weave in which pairs of warp yarns cross one another and thereby lock the filling yarn in position
**2 :** a fabric made with a leno weave

**¹lens** *also* **lense** \'lenz\ *noun* [New Latin *lent-, lens,* from Latin, lentil; from its shape] (1693)
**1 a :** a piece of transparent material (as glass) that has two opposite regular surfaces either both curved or one curved and the other plane and that is used either singly or combined in an optical instrument for forming an image by focusing rays of light **b :** a combination of two or more simple lenses **c :** a piece of glass or plastic used (as in safety goggles or sunglasses) to protect the eye
**2 :** a device for directing or focusing radiation other than light (as sound waves, radio microwaves, or electrons)
**3 :** something shaped like a double-convex optical lens ⟨*lens* of sandstone⟩
**4 :** a highly transparent biconvex lens-shaped or nearly spherical body in the eye that focuses light rays (as upon the retina) — see EYE illustration
**5 :** something that facilitates and influences perception, comprehension, or evaluation ⟨the author's own *lens* seems blurred by bias —Seymour Topping⟩
— **lensed** \'lenzd\ *adjective*
— **lens·less** \'lenz-ləs\ *adjective*
**²lens** *transitive verb* (1942)
**:** to make a motion picture of **:** FILM
**lens·man** \-mən, -,man\ *noun* (1938)
**:** PHOTOGRAPHER
**Lent** \'lent\ *noun* [Middle English *lente* springtime, Lent, from Old English *lencten;* akin to Old High German *lenzin* spring] (13th century)
**:** the 40 weekdays from Ash Wednesday to Easter observed by the Roman Catholic, Eastern, and some Protestant churches as a period of penitence and fasting
**len·ta·men·te** \,len-tə-'men-(,)tā\ *adverb or adjective* [Italian, from *lento* slow] (1724)
**:** LENTO
**len·tan·do** \len-'tän-(,)dō\ *adverb or adjective* [Italian] (circa 1847)
**:** becoming slower — used as a direction in music
**Lent·en** \'len-t²n\ *adjective* (before 12th century)
**:** of, relating to, or suitable for Lent; *especially* **:** MEAGER ⟨*Lenten* fare⟩
**len·tic** \'len-tik\ *adjective* [Latin *lentus* sluggish] (circa 1938)
**:** of, relating to, or living in still waters (as lakes, ponds, or swamps) — compare LOTIC
**len·ti·cel** \'len-tə-,sel\ *noun* [New Latin *lenticella,* diminutive of Latin *lent-, lens* lentil] (circa 1864)
**:** a loose aggregation of cells which penetrates the surface (as of a stem) of a woody plant and through which gases are exchanged between the atmosphere and the underlying tissues
**len·tic·u·lar** \len-'ti-kyə-lər\ *adjective* [Middle English, from Latin *lenticularis* lentil-shaped, from *lenticula* lentil] (15th century)
**1 :** having the shape of a double-convex lens
**2 :** of or relating to a lens
**3 :** provided with or utilizing lenticules ⟨a *lenticular* screen⟩
**len·ti·cule** \'len-tə-,kyü(ə)l\ *noun* [Latin *lenticula*] (1942)
**1 :** any of the minute lenses on the base side of a film used in stereoscopic or color photography
**2 :** any of the tiny corrugations or grooves molded or embossed into the surface of a projection screen
**len·til** \'len-t²l\ *noun* [Middle English, from Old French *lentille,* from Latin *lenticula,* diminutive of *lent-, lens*] (13th century)
**1 :** a widely cultivated Eurasian annual leguminous plant (*Lens culinaris*) with flattened edible seeds and leafy stalks used as fodder

**2 :** the seed of the lentil
**len·tis·si·mo** \len-'ti-sə-,mō\ *adverb or adjective* [Italian, superlative of *lento*] (circa 1903)
**:** at a very slow tempo — used as a direction in music
**len·ti·vi·rus** \,len-tə-'vī-rəs\ *noun* [New Latin, from Latin *lentus* slow + New Latin *virus*] (1982)
**:** any of a group of retroviruses that cause slowly progressive often fatal animal diseases
**len·to** \'len-(,)tō\ *adverb or adjective* [Italian, from *lento,* adjective, slow, from Latin *lentus* pliant, sluggish, slow — more at LITHE] (circa 1724)
**:** at a slow tempo — used especially as a direction in music
**Leo** \'lē-(,)ō\ *noun* [Latin (genitive *Leonis*), literally, lion — more at LION]
**1 :** a northern constellation east of Cancer
**2 a :** the 5th sign of the zodiac in astrology — see ZODIAC table **b :** one born under this sign
— **Le·o·nine** \'lē-ə-,nīn\ *adjective*
**le·one** \lē-'ōn\ *noun, plural* **leones** *or* **leone** [*Sierra Leone*] (1964)
— see MONEY table
**Le·o·nid** \'lē-ə-nid\ *noun, plural* **Leonids** *or* **Le·on·i·des** \lē-'ä-nə-,dēz\ [Latin *Leon-, Leo;* from their appearing to radiate from a point in Leo] (1876)
**:** any of the meteors in a meteor shower occurring every year about November 14
**le·o·nine** \'lē-ə-,nīn\ *adjective* [Middle English, from Latin *leoninus,* from *leon-, leo*] (14th century)
**:** of, relating to, suggestive of, or resembling a lion
**leop·ard** \'le-pərd\ *noun* [Middle English, from Old French *leupart,* from Late Latin *leopardus,* from Greek *leopardos,* from *leōn* lion + *pardos* leopard] (13th century)
**1 :** a large strong cat (*Panthera pardus*) of southern Asia and Africa that is adept at climbing and is usually tawny or buff with black spots arranged in rosettes — called *also panther*
**2 :** a heraldic representation of a lion passant guardant
— **leop·ard·ess** \-pər-dəs\ *noun*

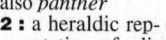
**leopard 1**

**leopard frog** *noun* (1839)
**:** a common North American frog (*Rana pipiens*) that is bright green or brown with large black white-margined blotches on the back; *also* **:** a similar frog (*R. sphenocephala*) of the southeastern U.S.
**leopard seal** *noun* (1893)
**:** a spotted slate gray seal (*Hydrurga leptonyx*) of the southern Atlantic to the southern Pacific that often feeds on other seals
**le·o·tard** \'lē-ə-,tärd\ *noun* [Jules *Léotard,* (died 1870) French aerial gymnast] (1886)
**:** a close-fitting one-piece garment worn especially by dancers, acrobats, and aerialists; *also* **:** TIGHTS — often used in plural
— **le·o·tard·ed** \-,tär-dəd\ *adjective*
**Lep·cha** \'lep-chə\ *noun, plural* **Lepcha** *or* **Lepchas** (1819)
**1 :** a member of a people of Sikkim, India
**2 :** the Tibeto-Burman language of the Lepcha people
**lep·er** \'le-pər\ *noun* [Middle English, from *lepre* leprosy, from Middle French, from Late Latin *lepra,* from Greek, from *lepein* to peel; perhaps akin to Lithuanian *lopas* piece, scrap] (14th century)
**1 :** a person affected with leprosy
**2 :** a person shunned for moral or social reasons

**lepid-** *or* **lepido-** *combining form* [New Latin, from Greek, from *lepid-, lepis* scale, from *lepein*]
**:** flake **:** scale ⟨*Lepidoptera*⟩
**le·pid·o·lite** \li-'pi-d²l-,īt\ *noun* [German *Lepidolith,* from *lepid-* + *-lith*] (circa 1796)
**:** a variable mineral that consists of a mica containing lithium and is used especially in glazes and enamels
**lep·i·dop·tera** \,le-pə-'däp-tə-rə\ *noun plural* (circa 1773)
**:** insects that are lepidopterans
**lep·i·dop·ter·an** \-rən\ *noun* [New Latin *Lepidoptera,* from *lepid-* + Greek *pteron* wing — more at FEATHER] (circa 1901)
**:** any of a large order (Lepidoptera) of insects comprising the butterflies, moths, and skippers that as adults have four broad or lanceolate wings usually covered with minute overlapping and often brightly colored scales and that as larvae are caterpillars
— **lepidopteran** *adjective*
— **lep·i·dop·ter·ous** \-tə-rəs\ *adjective*
**lep·i·dop·ter·ist** \-tə-rist\ *noun* (1826)
**:** a specialist in lepidopterology
**lep·i·dop·ter·ol·o·gy** \-,däp-tə-'rä-lə-jē\ *noun* (1898)
**:** a branch of entomology concerned with lepidopterans
— **lep·i·dop·ter·o·log·i·cal** \-tə-rə-'lä-ji-kəl\ *adjective*
— **lep·i·dop·ter·ol·o·gist** \-tə-'rä-lə-jist\ *noun*
**lep·i·dote** \'le-pə-,dōt\ *noun* [Greek *lepidōtos* scaly, from *lepid-, lepis*] (circa 1836)
**:** a rhododendron covered with scurf or scurfy scales
**lep·re·chaun** \'lep-rə-,kän, -,kȯn\ *noun* [Irish *leipreachán*] (1604)
**:** a mischievous elf of Irish folklore usually believed to reveal the hiding place of treasure if caught
— **lep·re·chaun·ish** \-,kä-nish, -,kȯ-\ *adjective*
**le·pro·ma·tous** \lə-'prä-mə-təs, -'prō-\ *adjective* [New Latin *lepromat-, leproma* leprous lesion, from Late Latin *lepra*] (1898)
**:** characterized by, exhibiting, or being leprosy with infective superficial granulomatous nodules
**lep·ro·sar·i·um** \,le-prə-'ser-ē-əm\ *noun, plural* **-iums** *or* **-ia** \-ē-ə\ [Medieval Latin, from Late Latin *leprosus*] (circa 1846)
**:** a hospital for leprosy patients
**lep·ro·sy** \'le-prə-sē\ *noun* [Middle English *lepruse,* from *leprous*] (15th century)
**1 :** a chronic disease caused by a bacillus (*Mycobacterium leprae*) and characterized by the formation of nodules or of macules that enlarge and spread accompanied with loss of sensation with eventual paralysis, wasting of muscle, and production of deformities and mutilations
**2 :** a morally or spiritually harmful influence
— **lep·rot·ic** \le-'prä-tik\ *adjective*
**lep·rous** \'le-prəs\ *adjective* [Middle English, from Late Latin *leprosus* leprous, from *lepra* leprosy — more at LEPER] (13th century)
**1 a :** infected with leprosy **b :** of, relating to, or resembling leprosy or a leper
**2 :** SCALY, SCURFY
— **lep·rous·ly** *adverb*
**-lepsy** *noun combining form* [Middle French *-lepsie,* from Late Latin *-lepsia,* from Greek *-lēpsis,* from *lambanein* to take, seize — more at LATCH]
**:** taking **:** seizure ⟨narco*lepsy*⟩
**lep·to·ceph·a·lus** \,lep-tə-'se-fə-ləs\ *noun, plural* **-li** \-,lī, -,lē\ [New Latin, from Greek *leptos* + *kephalē* head — more at CEPHALIC] (1769)
**:** a long thin small-headed transparent pelagic first larva of various eels
**¹lep·ton** \lep-'tän\ *noun, plural* **lep·ta** \-'tä\ [New Greek, from Greek, a small coin, from

neuter of *leptos* peeled, slender, small, from *lepein* to peel — more at LEPER] (circa 1741) — see *drachma* at MONEY table

**²lep·ton** \'lep-ˌtän\ *noun* [Greek *leptos* + English ²*-on*] (circa 1929)
: any of a family of particles (as electrons, muons, and neutrinos) that have spin quantum number ½ and that experience no strong forces
— **lep·ton·ic** \lep-'tä-nik\ *adjective*

**lep·to·some** \'lep-tə-ˌsōm\ *adjective* [German *Leptosom*, from Greek *leptos* + *sōma* body] (1931)
: ECTOMORPHIC
— **leptosome** *noun*

**lep·to·spire** \-ˌspīr\ *noun* [New Latin *Leptospira*, from Greek *leptos* + Latin *spira* coil — more at SPIRE] (1952)
: any of a genus (*Leptospira*) of slender aerobic spirochetes that are free-living or parasitic in mammals
— **lep·to·spir·al** \ˌlep-tə-'spī-rəl\ *adjective*

**lep·to·spi·ro·sis** \ˌlep-tə-spī-'rō-səs\ *noun*, *plural* **-ro·ses** \-ˌsēz\ [New Latin] (circa 1926)
: any of several diseases of humans and domestic animals that are caused by infection with leptospires

**lep·to·tene** \'lep-tə-ˌtēn\ *noun* [International Scientific Vocabulary] (1912)
: a stage of meiotic prophase immediately preceding synapsis in which the chromosomes appear as fine discrete threads
— **leptotene** *adjective*

**¹les·bi·an** \'lez-bē-ən\ *adjective, often capitalized* (1591)
**1** : of or relating to Lesbos
**2** [from the reputed homosexual band associated with Sappho of Lesbos] : of or relating to homosexuality between females

**²lesbian** *noun, often capitalized* (circa 1890)
: a female homosexual

**les·bi·an·ism** \'lez-bē-ə-ˌni-zəm\ *noun* (1870)
: female homosexuality

**lèse–ma·jes·té** *or* **lese maj·es·ty** \ˌläz-'ma-jə-stē, ˌlez-, ˌlēz-\ *noun* [Middle French *lese majesté*, from Latin *laesa majestas*, literally, injured majesty] (1536)
**1 a** : a crime (as treason) committed against a sovereign power **b** : an offense violating the dignity of a ruler as the representative of a sovereign power
**2** : a detraction from or affront to dignity or importance

**le·sion** \'lē-zhən\ *noun* [Middle English, from Middle French, from Latin *laesion-, laesio*, from *laedere* to injure] (15th century)
**1** : INJURY, HARM
**2** : an abnormal change in structure of an organ or part due to injury or disease; *especially* : one that is circumscribed and well defined
— **le·sioned** \-zhənd\ *adjective*

**les·pe·de·za** \ˌles-pə-'dē-zə\ *noun* [New Latin, irregular from V. M. de *Zespedes* (flourished 1785) Spanish governor of East Florida] (1891)
: any of a genus (*Lespedeza*) of herbaceous or shrubby leguminous plants including some widely used for forage, soil improvement, and especially hay

**¹less** \'les\ *adjective comparative of* ¹LITTLE [Middle English, partly from Old English *lǣs*, adverb & noun; partly from *lǣssa*, adjective; akin to Old Frisian *lēs* less] (before 12th century)
**1** : constituting a more limited number ⟨*less* than three⟩
**2** : of lower rank, degree, or importance ⟨no *less* a person than the president himself⟩
**3 a** : of reduced size, extent, or degree **b** : more limited in quantity ⟨in *less* time⟩ ∎

**²less** *adverb comparative of* ²LITTLE (before 12th century)
: to a lesser extent or degree
— **less and less** : to a progressively smaller size or extent

— **less than** : by no means : not at all ⟨*less than* honest in his replies⟩

**³less** *noun, plural* **less** (before 12th century)
**1** : a smaller portion or quantity
**2** : something of less importance

**⁴less** *preposition* (15th century)
: diminished by : MINUS

**-less** *adjective suffix* [Middle English *-les, -lesse*, from Old English *-lēas* devoid, false; akin to Old High German *lōs* loose, Old English *losian* to get lost — more at LOSE]
**1** : destitute of : not having ⟨wit*less*⟩ ⟨child*less*⟩
**2** : unable to be acted on or to act (in a specified way) ⟨daunt*less*⟩ ⟨fade*less*⟩

**les·see** \le-'sē\ *noun* [Middle English, from Anglo-French, from *lessé*, past participle of *lesser* to lease — more at LEASE] (15th century)
: one that holds real or personal property under a lease

**less·en** \'le-sᵊn\ *verb* **less·ened; less·en·ing** \'les-niŋ, 'le-sᵊn-iŋ\ (13th century)
*intransitive verb*
: to shrink in size, number, or degree : DECREASE
*transitive verb*
**1** : to reduce in size, extent, or degree
**2 a** *archaic* : to represent as of little value **b** : to lower in status or dignity : DEGRADE
*synonym* see DECREASE

**¹less·er** \'le-sər\ *adjective, comparative of* ¹LITTLE (13th century)
: of less size, quality, degree, or significance : of lower status

**²lesser** *adverb* (1539)
: LESS ⟨*lesser*-known⟩

**lesser celandine** *noun* (circa 1890)
: a yellow-flowered Eurasian perennial herb (*Ranunculus ficaria*) of the buttercup family naturalized in North America

**lesser cornstalk borer** *noun* (circa 1925)
: a pyralid moth (*Elasmopalpus lignosellus*) having slender greenish larvae that burrow in the stalk especially of Indian corn near ground level

**lesser peach tree borer** *noun* (circa 1924)
: a moth (*Synanthedon pictipes* family Aegeriidae) whose larva is a borer in the forks and crotches of stone-fruit trees and especially the peach

**lesser yellowlegs** *noun plural but singular or plural in construction* (circa 1903)
: a common American marsh and shore bird (*Tringa flavipes*) that closely resembles the greater yellowlegs in color and markings but is smaller with a shorter more slender bill

**¹les·son** \'le-sᵊn\ *noun* [Middle English, from Old French *leçon*, from Late Latin *lection-, lectio*, act of reading, from *legere* to read — more at LEGEND] (13th century)
**1** : a passage from sacred writings read in a service of worship
**2 a** : a piece of instruction **b** : a reading or exercise to be studied by a pupil **c** : a division of a course of instruction
**3 a** : something learned by study or experience ⟨his years of travel had taught him valuable *lessons*⟩ **b** : an instructive example ⟨the *lessons* of history⟩ **c** : REPRIMAND

**²lesson** *transitive verb* **les·soned; les·son·ing** \'le-sə-niŋ, 'les-niŋ\ (1555)
**1** : to give a lesson to : INSTRUCT
**2** : LECTURE, REBUKE

**les·sor** \'le-ˌsȯr, le-'sȯr\ *noun* [Middle English *lessour*, from Anglo-French, from *lesser* to lease] (14th century)
: one that conveys property by lease

**lest** \'lest\ *conjunction* [Middle English *les the, leste*, from Old English *thy lǣs the*, from *thy* (instrumental of *thæt* that) + *lǣs* + *the*, relative particle] (before 12th century)
: for fear that — used after an expression denoting fear or apprehension ⟨worried *lest* she should be late⟩ ⟨hesitant to speak out *lest* he be fired⟩

**¹let** \'let\ *transitive verb* **let·ted; letted** *or* **let; let·ting** [Middle English *letten*, from Old English *lettan* to delay, hinder; akin to Old High German *lezzen* to delay, hurt, Old English *lǣt* late] (before 12th century)
*archaic* : HINDER, PREVENT

**²let** *noun* (12th century)
**1** : something that impedes : OBSTRUCTION
**2** : a shot or point in racket games that does not count and must be replayed

**³let** *verb* **let; let·ting** [Middle English *leten*, from Old English *lǣtan*; akin to Old High German *lāzzan* to permit, and perhaps to Lithuanian *lėnas* tranquil] (before 12th century)
*transitive verb*
**1** : to cause to : MAKE ⟨*let* me know⟩
**2 a** : to offer or grant for rent or lease ⟨*let* rooms⟩ **b** : to assign especially after bids ⟨*let* a contract⟩
**3 a** : to give opportunity to or fail to prevent ⟨live and *let* live⟩ ⟨a break in the clouds *let* us see the summit⟩ ⟨*let* the opportunity slip⟩ **b** — used in the imperative to introduce a request or proposal ⟨*let* us pray⟩ **c** — used as an auxiliary to express a warning ⟨*let* him try⟩
**4** : to free from or as if from confinement ⟨*let* out a scream⟩ ⟨*let* blood⟩
**5** : to permit to enter, pass, or leave ⟨*let* them through⟩ ⟨*let* them off with a warning⟩
**6** : to make an adjustment to ⟨*let* out the waist⟩
*intransitive verb*
**1** : to become rented or leased
**2** : to become awarded to a contractor
*synonym* see HIRE
— **let alone** : to leave undisturbed; *also* : to leave to oneself
— **let fly** : to hurl an object
— **let go** : to dismiss from employment ⟨the firm *let* him *go* at the end of the month⟩
— **let it all hang out** : to reveal one's true feelings : act without dissimulation
— **let one have it** : to subject to vigorous assault
— **let rip 1** : to utter or release without restraint ⟨*let* 'er *rip*⟩ **2** : to do or utter something without restraint ⟨*let rip* at the press⟩
— **let the cat out of the bag** : to give away a secret

**-let** *noun suffix* [Middle English, from Middle French *-elet*, from *-el*, diminutive suffix (from Latin *-ellus*) + *-et*]
**1** : small one ⟨book*let*⟩
**2** : article worn on ⟨wrist*let*⟩

**let alone** *conjunction* (1812)
: to say nothing of : not to mention — used to add an example of narrower range by way

---

□ **USAGE**
**less** The traditional view is that *less* applies to matters of degree, value, or amount and modifies collective nouns, mass nouns, or nouns denoting an abstract whole while *fewer* applies to matters of number and modifies plural nouns. *Less* has been used to modify plural nouns since the days of King Alfred and the usage, though roundly decried, appears to be increasing. *Less* is more likely than *fewer* to modify plural nouns when distances, sums of money, and a few fixed phrases are involved ⟨*less* than 100 miles⟩ ⟨an investment of *less* than $2000⟩ ⟨in 25 words or *less*⟩ and as likely as *fewer* to modify periods of time ⟨in *less* (or *fewer*) than four hours⟩.

---

\ə\ **abut** \ᵊ\ **kitten** \ər\ **further** \a\ **ash** \ā\ **ace**
\ä\ **mop, mar** \aú\ **out** \ch\ **chin** \e\ **bet** \ē\ **easy**
\g\ **go** \i\ **hit** \ī\ **ice** \j\ **job** \ŋ\ **sing** \ō\ **go**
\ȯ\ **law** \ȯi\ **boy** \th\ **thin** \t͟h\ **the** \ü\ **loot** \ú\ **foot**
\y\ **yet** \zh\ **vision**    *see also* Guide to Pronunciation

of contrast especially in negative contexts ⟨believed that he would never walk again *let alone* play golf —*Sports Illustrated*⟩ ⟨great to read but bloody to speak, *let alone* sing —Robertson Davies⟩

**letch** \'lech\ *noun* [back-formation from *letcher*, alteration of *lecher*] (circa 1796)
: CRAVING; *specifically* : sexual desire

**let·down** \'let-ˌdau̇n\ *noun* (1768)
**1 a** : DISCOURAGEMENT, DISAPPOINTMENT **b** : a slackening of effort : RELAXATION
**2** : the descent of an aircraft or spacecraft to the point at which a landing approach is begun

**let down** *transitive verb* (12th century)
**1** : to allow to descend gradually
**2 a** : to fail to support ⟨felt her parents had *let* her *down*⟩ **b** : to fall short of the expectations of ⟨the plot *lets* you *down* at the end⟩

**¹le·thal** \'lē-thəl\ *adjective* [Latin *letalis, lethalis,* from *letum* death] (1604)
**1 a** : of, relating to, or causing death ⟨death by *lethal* injection⟩ **b** : capable of causing death ⟨*lethal* chemicals⟩
**2** : gravely damaging or destructive : DEVASTATING ⟨a *lethal* attack on his reputation⟩
**synonym** see DEADLY
— **le·thal·i·ty** \lē-'tha-lə-tē\ *noun*
— **le·thal·ly** \'lē-thə-lē\ *adverb*

**²lethal** *noun* (1917)
**1** : an abnormality of genetic origin causing the death of the organism possessing it
**2** : LETHAL GENE

**lethal gene** *noun* (1939)
: a gene that in some (as homozygous) conditions may prevent development or cause the death of an organism or its germ cells — called also *lethal factor, lethal mutant, lethal mutation*

**le·thar·gic** \lə-'thär-jik, le-\ *adjective* (14th century)
**1** : of, relating to, or characterized by lethargy : SLUGGISH
**2** : INDIFFERENT, APATHETIC
— **le·thar·gi·cal·ly** \-ji-k(ə-)lē\ *adverb*

**leth·ar·gy** \'le-thər-jē\ *noun* [Middle English *litargie,* from Medieval Latin *litargia,* from Late Latin *lethargia,* from Greek *lēthargia,* from *lēthargos* forgetful, lethargic, irregular from *lēthē*] (14th century)
**1** : abnormal drowsiness
**2** : the quality or state of being lazy, sluggish, or indifferent ☆

**le·the** \'lē-thē\ *noun* [Latin, from Greek *Lēthē,* from *lēthē* forgetfulness; akin to Greek *lanthanein* to escape notice, *lanthanesthai* to forget — more at LATENT]
**1** *capitalized* : a river in Hades whose waters cause drinkers to forget their past
**2** : OBLIVION, FORGETFULNESS
— **le·the·an** \'lē-thē-ən, li-'thē-\ *adjective, often capitalized*

**let on** *intransitive verb* (1725)
**1** : to make acknowledgment : ADMIT ⟨knows more than he *lets on*⟩
**2** : to reveal a secret ⟨nobody *let on* about the surprise party⟩
**3** : PRETEND ⟨*let on* to being a stranger⟩

**let out** *intransitive verb* (1888)
: to conclude a session or performance ⟨school *let out* in June⟩

**let's** \'lets, *in rapid speech* 'les\ (1573)
: let us

**Lett** \'let\ *noun* [German *Lette,* ultimately from Latvian *latvis*] (1589)
: LATVIAN 2

**¹let·ter** \'le-tər\ *noun* [Middle English, from Old French *lettre,* from Latin *littera* letter of the alphabet, *litterae,* plural, epistle, literature] (13th century)
**1** : a symbol usually written or printed representing a speech sound and constituting a unit of an alphabet
**2 a** : a direct or personal written or printed message addressed to a person or organization **b** : a written communication containing a grant — usually used in plural

**3** *plural but singular or plural in construction*
**a** : LITERATURE, BELLES LETTRES **b** : LEARNING
**4** : the strict or outward sense or significance ⟨the *letter* of the law⟩
**5 a** : a single piece of type **b** : a style of type
**6** : the initial of a school awarded to a student for achievement usually in athletics

**²letter** (1668)
*transitive verb*
**1** : to set down in letters : PRINT
**2** : to mark with letters
*intransitive verb*
: to win an athletic letter
— **let·ter·er** \-tər-ər\ *noun*

**³let·ter** \'le-tər\ *noun* (1552)
: one that rents or leases

**let·ter·boxed** \'le-tər-ˌbäkst\ *adjective* [perhaps from the resemblance of the picture on the TV screen or the bands above and below the picture to slots in a mailbox] (1989)
*of a video recording* : formatted so as to display the full rectangular frame of a wide-screen motion picture
— **let·ter·box·ing** \-ˌbäk-siŋ\ *noun*

**letter carrier** *noun* (circa 1552)
: a person who delivers mail

**let·tered** \'le-tərd\ *adjective* (14th century)
**1 a** : LEARNED, EDUCATED **b** : of, relating to, or characterized by learning : CULTURED
**2** : inscribed with or as if with letters

**let·ter·form** \'le-tər-ˌfȯrm\ *noun* (1908)
: the shape of a letter of an alphabet especially from the standpoint of design or development

**let·ter·head** \-ˌhed\ *noun* (circa 1887)
**1** : a sheet of stationery printed or engraved usually with the name and address of an organization
**2** : the heading at the top of a letterhead

**let·ter·ing** \'le-tə-riŋ\ *noun* (1811)
: letters used in an inscription

**let·ter·man** \'le-tər-mən\ *noun* (1926)
: an athlete who has earned a letter in a school sport

**letter missive** *noun, plural* **letters missive** [Middle English, from Middle French *lettre missive* letter intended to be sent] (15th century)
: a letter from a superior authority conveying a command, recommendation, permission, or invitation

**letter of credence** (14th century)
: a formal document attesting to the power of a diplomatic agent to act for the issuing government — called also *letters of credence*

**letter of credit** (1645)
**1** : a letter addressed by a banker to a correspondent certifying that a person named therein is entitled to draw on the writer's credit up to a certain sum
**2** : a letter addressed by a banker to a person to whom credit is given authorizing drafts on the issuing bank or on a bank in the person's country up to a certain sum and guaranteeing to accept the drafts if duly made

**letter of intent** (circa 1942)
: a written statement of the intention to enter into a formal agreement

**let·ter–per·fect** \'le-tər-'pər-fikt\ *adjective* (1845)
: correct to the smallest detail; *especially* : VERBATIM

**let·ter·press** \'le-tər-ˌpres\ *noun* (circa 1765)
**1** : the process of printing from an inked raised surface especially when the paper is impressed directly upon the surface
**2** *chiefly British* : text (as of a book) distinct from pictorial illustrations

**letters close** \-'klōs\ *noun plural* (1903)
: letters issued by a government or sovereign to a private person in a private matter

**letter sheet** *noun* (1851)
: a sheet of stationery that can be folded and sealed with the message inside to form its own envelope

**letters of administration** (15th century)

: a letter evidencing the right of an administrator to administer the goods or estate of a deceased person

**letters of marque** \-'märk\ (15th century)
: written authority granted to a private person by a government to seize the subjects of a foreign state or their goods; *specifically* : a license granted to a private person to fit out an armed ship to plunder the enemy

**let·ter·spac·ing** \'le-tər-ˌspā-siŋ\ *noun* (1917)
: insertion of space between the letters of a word

**letters patent** *noun plural* (14th century)
: a writing (as from a sovereign) that confers on a designated person a grant in a form open for public inspection

**¹Lett·ish** \'le-tish\ *adjective* (1831)
: of or relating to the Latvians or their language

**²Lettish** *noun* (1841)
: LATVIAN 1

**let·tre de ca·chet** \'le-trə-də-ˌka-'shā\ *noun, plural* **lettres de cachet** \-trə(z)-\ [French, literally, letter with a seal] (1718)
: a letter bearing an official seal and usually authorizing imprisonment without trial of a named person

**let·tuce** \'le-təs\ *noun* [Middle English *letuse,* from Middle French *laitues,* plural of *laitue,* from Latin *lactuca,* from *lact-, lac* milk; from its milky juice — more at GALAXY] (14th century)
: any of a genus (*Lactuca*) of composite plants; *especially* : a common garden vegetable (*L. sativa*) whose succulent leaves are used especially in salads ◆

**let·up** \'let-ˌəp\ *noun* (1837)
: a lessening of effort or intensity

**let up** *intransitive verb* (1787)
**1 a** : to diminish or slow down : SLACKEN **b** : CEASE, STOP
**2** : to become less severe — used with *on*

**leu** \'leu̇\ *noun, plural* **lei** \'lā\ [Romanian, literally, lion, from Latin *leo* — more at LION] (1879)
— see MONEY table

**leuc-** *or* **leuco-** *chiefly British variant of* LEUK-

---

☆ **SYNONYMS**
**Lethargy, languor, lassitude, stupor, torpor** mean physical or mental inertness. LETHARGY implies such drowsiness or aversion to activity as is induced by disease, injury, or drugs ⟨months of *lethargy* followed my accident⟩. LANGUOR suggests inertia induced by an enervating climate or illness or love ⟨*languor* induced by a tropical vacation⟩. LASSITUDE stresses listlessness or indifference resulting from fatigue or poor health ⟨a depression marked by *lassitude*⟩. STUPOR implies a deadening of the mind and senses by shock, narcotics, or intoxicants ⟨lapsed into an alcoholic *stupor*⟩. TORPOR implies a state of suspended animation as of hibernating animals but may suggest merely extreme sluggishness ⟨a once alert mind now in a *torpor*⟩.

---

◇ **WORD HISTORY**
**lettuce** Many types of lettuce have a milky white juice, and it is to this property that the vegetable owes its name. The earliest known Middle English form, *letuse,* is apparently borrowed from Old French *laitues,* the plural of *laitue.* The Old French word is descended in turn from *lactuca,* the Latin word that is still used as the scientific name for the vegetable. *Lactuca* is a derivative of *lac,* the Latin word for "milk."

**leu·cine** \'lü-ˌsēn\ *noun* [French, from *leuc-* leuk-] (1826)
: a white crystalline essential amino acid $C_6H_{13}NO_2$ obtained by the hydrolysis of most dietary proteins

**leu·cite** \'lü-ˌsīt\ *noun* [German *Leuzit*, from *leuz-* leuk-] (1799)
: a white or gray mineral consisting of a silicate of potassium and aluminum and occurring in igneous rocks
— **leu·cit·ic** \lü-'si-tik\ *adjective*

**leu·co·ci·din** \ˌlü-kō-'sī-d°n\ *noun* [International Scientific Vocabulary *leuc-* + *-cide* + [1]*-in*] (1894)
: a bacterial substance that destroys white blood cells

**leu·co·plast** \'lü-kə-ˌplast\ *noun* [International Scientific Vocabulary] (1886)
: a colorless plastid especially in the cytoplasm of interior plant tissues that is potentially capable of developing into a chloroplast

**leuk-** *or* **leuko-** *combining form* [New Latin *leuc-, leuco-,* from Greek *leuk-, leuko-,* from *leukos* — more at LIGHT]
1 : white : colorless : weakly colored ⟨*leuko*cyte⟩ ⟨*leuko*rrhea⟩
2 : leukocyte ⟨*leuk*emia⟩
3 : white matter of the brain ⟨*leuko*tomy⟩

**leu·kae·mia** *chiefly British variant of* LEUKEMIA

**leu·kae·mo·gen·e·sis** *chiefly British variant of* LEUKEMOGENESIS

**leu·ke·mia** \lü-'kē-mē-ə\ *noun* [New Latin] (circa 1855)
: an acute or chronic disease in humans and other warm-blooded animals characterized by an abnormal increase in the number of white blood cells in the tissues and often in the blood
— **leu·ke·mic** \-mik\ *adjective or noun*

**leu·ke·mo·gen·e·sis** \lü-ˌkē-mə-'je-nə-səs\ *noun* (1942)
: induction or production of leukemia
— **leu·ke·mo·gen·ic** \-'je-nik\ *adjective*

**leu·ke·moid** \-ˌmóid\ *adjective* (1926)
: resembling leukemia but not involving the same changes in the blood-forming organs

**leu·ko·cyte** \'lü-kə-ˌsīt\ *noun* [International Scientific Vocabulary] (1870)
: WHITE BLOOD CELL
— **leu·ko·cyt·ic** \ˌlü-kə-'si-tik\ *adjective*

**leu·ko·cy·to·sis** \ˌlü-kə-sī-'tō-səs, -kə-sə-\ *noun* [New Latin] (1866)
: an increase in the number of white blood cells in the circulating blood

**leu·ko·dys·tro·phy** \ˌlü-kō-'dis-trə-fē\ *noun, plural* **-phies** (1962)
: any of several genetically determined diseases characterized by degeneration of the white matter of the brain

**leu·ko·pe·nia** \ˌlü-kə-'pē-nē-ə\ *noun* [New Latin] (1898)
: a condition in which the number of white blood cells circulating in the blood is abnormally low
— **leu·ko·pe·nic** \-nik\ *adjective*

**leu·ko·pla·kia** \ˌlü-kō-'plā-kē-ə\ *noun* [New Latin, from *leuk-* + Greek *plak-, plax* flat surface — more at FLUKE] (circa 1888)
: an abnormal condition in which thickened white patches of epithelium occur on the mucous membranes (as of the mouth or vulva); *also* : a lesion or lesioned area of leukoplakia
— **leu·ko·pla·kic** \-'plā-kik\ *adjective*

**leu·ko·poi·e·sis** \-ˌpói-'ē-səs\ *noun* [New Latin] (circa 1913)
: the formation of white blood cells
— **leu·ko·poi·et·ic** \-'e-tik\ *adjective*

**leu·kor·rhea** \ˌlü-kə-'rē-ə\ *noun* [New Latin] (circa 1797)
: a whitish viscid discharge from the vagina resulting from inflammation or congestion of the mucous membrane
— **leu·kor·rhe·al** \-'rē-əl\ *adjective*

**leu·ko·sis** \lü-'kō-səs\ *noun, plural* **-ko·ses** \-ˌsēz\ [New Latin] (1922)

LEUKEMIA; *especially* : any of various leukemic diseases of poultry

**leu·kot·o·my** \lü-'kä-tə-mē\ *noun, plural* **-mies** (1937)
: LOBOTOMY

**leu·ko·tri·ene** \ˌlü-kō-'trī-ˌēn\ *noun* (1980)
: any of a group of eicosanoids that participate in allergic responses

**lev** \'lef\ *noun, plural* **le·va** \'le-və\ [Bulgarian, literally, lion] (circa 1900)
— see MONEY table

**lev-** *or* **levo-** *combining form* [French *lévo-,* from Latin *laevus* left; akin to Greek *laios* left]
1 : levorotatory ⟨*levulose*⟩
2 : to the left ⟨*levorotatory*⟩

**Le·val·loi·si·an** \ˌle-və-'lói-zē-ən, lə-ˌval-'wä-zē-\ *adjective* [*Levallois*-Perret, suburb of Paris, France] (1932)
: of or relating to a Middle Paleolithic culture characterized by a technique of manufacturing tools by striking flakes from a flint nodule

**le·vant** \lə-'vant\ *intransitive verb* [perhaps from Spanish *levantar* to break camp, ultimately from Latin *levare*] (1797)
*chiefly British* : to run away from a debt

**le·vant·er** \lə-'van-tər\ *noun* (1668)
1 *capitalized* : a native or inhabitant of the Levant
2 : a strong easterly Mediterranean wind

**Le·vant storax** \lə-'vant-\ *noun* (1937)
: STORAX 1a

**le·va·tor** \li-'vā-tər\ *noun, plural* **lev·a·to·res** \ˌle-və-'tōr-(ˌ)ēz\ *or* **le·va·tors** \li-'vā-tərz\ [New Latin, from Latin *levare* to raise — more at LEVER] (1615)
: a muscle that serves to raise a body part — compare DEPRESSOR

[1]**le·vee** \'le-vē\; lə-'vē, -'vā\ *noun* [French *lever,* from Middle French, act of arising, from (*se*) *lever* to rise] (1672)
1 : a reception held by a person of distinction on rising from bed
2 : an afternoon assembly at which the British sovereign or his or her representative receives only men
3 : a reception usually in honor of a particular person

[2]**lev·ee** \'le-vē\ *noun* [French *levée,* from Old French, act of raising, from *lever* to raise — more at LEVER] (circa 1720)
1 a : an embankment for preventing flooding b : a river landing place : PIER
2 : a continuous dike or ridge (as of earth) for confining the irrigation areas of land to be flooded

[3]**lev·ee** \'le-vē\ *transitive verb* **lev·eed; lev·ee·ing** (1832)
: to provide with a levee

[1]**lev·el** \'le-vəl\ *noun* [Middle English, plumb line, from Middle French *livel,* from (assumed) Vulgar Latin *libellum,* alteration of Latin *libella,* from diminutive of *libra* weight, balance] (14th century)
1 : a device for establishing a horizontal line or plane by means of a bubble in a liquid that shows adjustment to the horizontal by movement to the center of a slightly bowed glass tube
2 : a measurement of the difference of altitude of two points by means of a level
3 : horizontal condition; *especially* : equilibrium of a fluid marked by a horizontal surface of even altitude ⟨water seeks its own *level*⟩
4 a : an approximately horizontal line or surface taken as an index of altitude b : a practically horizontal surface or area (as of land)
5 : a position in a scale or rank ⟨funded at the national *level*⟩
6 a : a line or surface that cuts perpendicularly all plumb lines that it meets and hence would everywhere coincide with a surface of still water b : the plane of the horizon or a line in it
7 : a horizontal passage in a mine intended for regular working and transportation

8 : a concentration of a constituent especially of a body fluid (as blood)
9 : the magnitude of a quantity considered in relation to an arbitrary reference value; *broadly* : MAGNITUDE, INTENSITY ⟨a high *level* of hostility⟩
— **on the level** : BONA FIDE, HONEST

[2]**level** *verb* **-eled** *or* **-elled; -el·ing** *or* **-el·ling** \'le-və-liŋ, 'lev-liŋ\ (15th century)
*transitive verb*
1 : to make (a line or surface) horizontal : make flat or level ⟨*level* a field⟩ ⟨*level* off a house lot⟩
2 a : to bring to a horizontal aiming position b : AIM, DIRECT ⟨*leveled* a charge of fraud⟩
3 : to bring to a common level or plane : EQUALIZE ⟨love *levels* all ranks —W. S. Gilbert⟩
4 a : to lay level with or as if with the ground : RAZE b : to knock down ⟨*leveled* him with one punch⟩
5 : to make (as color) even or uniform
6 : to find the heights of different points in (a piece of land) especially with a surveyor's level
*intransitive verb*
1 : to attain or come to a level ⟨the plane *leveled* off at 10,000 feet⟩
2 : to aim a gun or other weapon horizontally
3 : to bring persons or things to a level
4 : to deal frankly and openly

[3]**level** *adjective* (15th century)
1 a : having no part higher than another : conforming to the curvature of the liquid parts of the earth's surface b : parallel with the plane of the horizon : HORIZONTAL
2 a : even or unvarying in height b : equal in advantage, progression, or standing c : proceeding monotonously or uneventfully d (1) : STEADY, UNWAVERING ⟨gave him a *level* look⟩ (2) : CALM, UNEXCITED ⟨spoke in *level* tones⟩
3 : REASONABLE, BALANCED ⟨arrive at a justly proportional and *level* judgment on this affair —Sir Winston Churchill⟩
4 : distributed evenly ⟨*level* stress⟩
5 : being a surface perpendicular to all lines of force in a field of force : EQUIPOTENTIAL
6 : suited to a particular rank or plane of ability or achievement ⟨top-*level* thinking⟩
7 : of or relating to the spreading out of a cost or charge in even payments over a period of time ☆
— **lev·el·ly** \'le-və(l)-lē\ *adverb*
— **lev·el·ness** \-vəl-nəs\ *noun*
— **level best** : very best

**level crossing** *noun* (circa 1841)
*British* : GRADE CROSSING

**lev·el·er** *or* **lev·el·ler** \'le-və-lər, 'lev-lər\ *noun* (1598)

☆ **SYNONYMS**
**Level, flat, plane, even, smooth** mean having a surface without bends, curves, or irregularities. LEVEL applies to a horizontal surface that lies on a line parallel with the horizon ⟨the vast prairies are nearly *level*⟩. FLAT applies to a surface devoid of noticeable curvatures, prominences, or depressions ⟨the work surface must be *flat*⟩. PLANE applies to any real or imaginary flat surface in which a straight line between any two points on it lies wholly within that surface ⟨the *plane* sides of a crystal⟩. EVEN applies to a surface that is noticeably flat or level or to a line that is observably straight ⟨trim the hedge so it is *even*⟩. SMOOTH applies especially to a polished surface free of irregularities ⟨a *smooth* skating rink⟩.

\ə\ **abut** \ᵊ\ **kitten** \ər\ **further** \a\ **ash** \ā\ **ace** \ä\ **mop, mar** \aú\ **out** \ch\ **chin** \e\ **bet** \ē\ **easy** \g\ **go** \i\ **hit** \ī\ **ice** \j\ **job** \ŋ\ **sing** \ō\ **go** \ó\ **law** \ói\ **boy** \th\ **thin** \t͟h\ **the** \ü\ **loot** \ú\ **foot** \y\ **yet** \zh\ **vision** *see also* Guide to Pronunciation

**1 :** one that levels
**2 a** *capitalized* **:** one of a group of radicals arising during the English Civil War and advocating equality before the law and religious toleration **b :** one favoring the removal of political, social, or economic inequalities **c :** something that tends to reduce or eliminate differences among individuals

**lev·el·head·ed** \ˌle-vəl-'he-dəd\ *adjective* (1879)
**:** having sound judgment **:** SENSIBLE
— **lev·el·head·ed·ness** *noun*

**leveling rod** *noun* (circa 1889)
**:** a graduated rod used in measuring the vertical distance between a point on the ground and the line of sight of a surveyor's level

**level off** *intransitive verb* (1919)
**:** to approach or reach a steady rate, volume, or amount **:** STABILIZE ⟨expect prices to *level off*⟩

**level of significance** (1925)
**:** the probability of rejecting the null hypothesis in a statistical test when it is true — called also *significance level*

**¹le·ver** \'le-vər, 'lē-\ *noun* [Middle English, from Middle French *levier*, from *lever* to raise, from Latin *levare*, from *levis* light in weight — more at LIGHT] (14th century)
**1 a :** a bar used for prying or dislodging something **b :** an inducing or compelling force **:** TOOL ⟨use food as a political *lever* —*Time*⟩
**2 a :** a rigid piece that transmits and modifies force or motion when forces are applied at two points and it turns about a third; *specifically* **:** a rigid bar used to exert a pressure or sustain a weight at one point of its length by the application of a force at a second and turning at a third on a fulcrum **b :** a projecting piece by which a mechanism is operated or adjusted

**²lever** *transitive verb* **le·vered; le·ver·ing** \'le-və-riŋ, 'lē-; 'lev-riŋ, 'lēv-\ (1876)
**1 :** to pry, raise, or move with or as if with a lever
**2 :** to operate (a device) in the manner of a lever

**¹le·ver·age** \'le-və-rij, 'lē-; 'lev-rij, 'lēv-\ *noun* (1830)
**1 :** the action of a lever or the mechanical advantage gained by it
**2 :** POWER, EFFECTIVENESS ⟨trying to gain more political *leverage*⟩
**3 :** the use of credit to enhance one's speculative capacity

**²leverage** *transitive verb* **-aged; -ag·ing** (1937)
**:** to provide (as a corporation) or supplement (as money) with leverage; *also* **:** to enhance as if by supplying with financial leverage

**lev·er·aged** \'le-və-rijd, 'lē-; 'lev-rijd, 'lēv-\ *adjective* (1953)
**1 :** having a high proportion of debt relative to equity
**2** *of the purchase of a company* **:** made with borrowed money that is secured by the assets of the company bought ⟨a *leveraged* buyout⟩

**lev·er·et** \'le-və-rət, 'lev-rət\ *noun* [Middle English, from (assumed) Middle French *levret*, from Middle French *levre* hare, from Latin *lepor-, lepus*] (15th century)
**:** a hare in its first year

**Le·vi** \'lē-,vī\ *noun* [Late Latin, from Hebrew *Lēwī*]
**:** a son of Jacob and the traditional eponymous ancestor of the priestly tribe of Levi

**levi·a·ble** \'le-vē-ə-bəl\ *adjective* (15th century)
**:** capable of being levied or levied upon

**le·vi·a·than** \li-'vī-ə-thən\ *noun* [Middle English, from Late Latin, from Hebrew *liwyāthān*]
**1 a** *often capitalized* **:** a sea monster defeated by Yahweh in various scriptural accounts **b :** a large sea animal
**2** *capitalized* **:** the political state; *especially* **:** a totalitarian state having a vast bureaucracy
**3 :** something large or formidable

— **leviathan** *adjective*

**levi·er** \'le-vē-ər\ *noun* (15th century)
**:** one that levies

**lev·i·gate** \'le-və-,gāt\ *transitive verb* **-gat·ed; -gat·ing** [Latin *levigatus*, past participle of *levigare* to make smooth, from *levis* smooth (akin to Greek *leios* smooth and perhaps to Latin *linere* to smear) + *-igare* (akin to *agere* to drive) — more at LIME, AGENT] (1612)
**1 :** POLISH, SMOOTH
**2 a :** to grind to a fine smooth powder while in moist condition **b :** to separate (fine powder) from coarser material by suspending in a liquid
— **lev·i·ga·tion** \ˌle-və-'gā-shən\ *noun*

**lev·in** \'le-vən\ *noun* [Middle English *levene*] (13th century)
*archaic* **:** LIGHTNING

**le·vi·rate** \'le-və-rət, 'lē-, -ˌrāt\ *noun* [Latin *levir* husband's brother; akin to Old English *tācor* husband's brother, Greek *daēr*] (1725)
**:** the sometimes compulsory marriage of a widow to a brother of her deceased husband
— **le·vi·rat·ic** \ˌle-və-'ra-tik, ˌlē-\ *adjective*

**Le·vi's** \'lē-ˌvīz\ *trademark*
— used especially for blue denim jeans

**lev·i·tate** \'le-və-ˌtāt\ *verb* **-tat·ed; -tat·ing** [*levity*] (1673)
*intransitive verb*
**:** to rise or float in the air especially in seeming defiance of gravitation
*transitive verb*
**:** to cause to levitate

**lev·i·ta·tion** \ˌle-və-'tā-shən\ *noun* (1668)
**:** the act or process of levitating; *especially* **:** the rising or lifting of a person or thing by means held to be supernatural
— **lev·i·ta·tion·al** \-shnəl, -shə-nᵊl\ *adjective*

**Le·vite** \'lē-ˌvīt\ *noun* (14th century)
**:** a member of the priestly Hebrew tribe of Levi; *specifically* **:** a Levite of non-Aaronic descent assigned to lesser ceremonial offices under the Levitical priests of the family of Aaron

**Le·vit·i·cal** \li-'vi-ti-kəl\ *adjective* [Late Latin *Leviticus*] (1535)
**:** of or relating to the Levites or to Leviticus

**Le·vit·i·cus** \-kəs\ *noun* [Late Latin, literally, of the Levites]
**:** the third book of canonical Jewish and Christian Scripture consisting mainly of priestly legislation — see BIBLE table

**lev·i·ty** \'le-və-tē\ *noun* [Latin *levitat-, levitas*, from *levis* light in weight — more at LIGHT] (1564)
**1 :** excessive or unseemly frivolity
**2 :** lack of steadiness **:** CHANGEABLENESS

**le·vo** \'lē-(ˌ)vō\ *adjective* (1938)
**:** LEVOROTATORY

**levo-** — see LEV-

**levo·do·pa** \ˌle-və-'dō-pə\ *noun* (1969)
**:** L-DOPA

**le·vo·ro·ta·to·ry** \-'rō-tə-ˌtōr-ē, -ˌtòr-\ *or* **le·vo·ro·ta·ry** \-'rō-tə-rē\ *adjective* (1873)
**:** turning toward the left or counterclockwise; *especially* **:** rotating the plane of polarization of light to the left — compare DEXTROROTATORY

**lev·u·lose** \'lev-yə-ˌlōs, -ˌlōz\ *noun* [International Scientific Vocabulary, irregular from *lev-* + *²-ose*] (1871)
**:** FRUCTOSE 2

**¹levy** \'le-vē\ *noun, plural* **lev·ies** [Middle English, from Old French *levee*, act of raising — more at LEVEE] (13th century)
**1 a :** the imposition or collection of an assessment **b :** an amount levied
**2 a :** the enlistment or conscription of men for military service **b :** troops raised by levy

**²levy** *verb* **lev·ied; levy·ing** (14th century)
*transitive verb*
**1 a :** to impose or collect by legal authority ⟨*levy* a tax⟩ **b :** to require by authority
**2 :** to enlist or conscript for military service
**3 :** to carry on (war) **:** WAGE

*intransitive verb*
**:** to seize property

**lewd** \'lüd\ *adjective* [Middle English *lewed* vulgar, from Old English *lǣwede* laical, ignorant] (14th century)
**1** *obsolete* **:** EVIL, WICKED
**2 a :** sexually unchaste or licentious **b :** OBSCENE, VULGAR
— **lewd·ly** *adverb*
— **lewd·ness** *noun*

**lew·is** \'lü-əs\ *noun* [probably from the name *Lewis*] (1743)
**:** an iron dovetailed tenon that is made in sections, can be fitted into a dovetail mortise, and is used in hoisting large stones

**Lew·is acid** \'lü-əs-\ *noun* [Gilbert N. *Lewis* (died 1946) American chemist] (1944)
**:** a substance that is capable of accepting an unshared pair of electrons from a base to form a covalent bond

**lew·is·ite** \'lü-ə-ˌsīt\ *noun* [Winford L. *Lewis* (died 1943) American chemist] (1919)
**:** a colorless or brown vesicant liquid $C_2H_2AsCl_3$ developed as a poison gas for war use

**lex** \'leks\ *noun, plural* **le·ges** \'lā-(ˌ)gās\ [Latin *leg-, lex*] (circa 1775)
**:** LAW

**lex·eme** \'lek-ˌsēm\ *noun* [Greek *lexis* word, speech + English *-eme*] (1940)
**:** a meaningful linguistic unit that is an item in the vocabulary of a language
— **lex·em·ic** \lek-'sē-mik\ *adjective*

**lex·i·cal** \'lek-si-kəl\ *adjective* (1836)
**1 :** of or relating to words or the vocabulary of a language as distinguished from its grammar and construction
**2 :** of or relating to a lexicon or to lexicography
— **lex·i·cal·i·ty** \ˌlek-sə-'ka-lə-tē\ *noun*
— **lex·i·cal·ly** \'lek-si-k(ə-)lē\ *adverb*

**lex·i·cal·i·sa·tion** *British variant of* LEXICALIZATION

**lex·i·cal·i·za·tion** \ˌlek-si-kə-lə-'zā-shən\ *noun* (1949)
**1 :** the realization of a meaning in a single word or morpheme rather than in a grammatical construction
**2 :** the treatment of a formerly freely composed, grammatically regular, and semantically transparent phrase or inflected form as a formally or semantically idiomatic expression
— **lex·i·cal·ize** \'lek-si-kə-ˌlīz\ *transitive verb*

**lexical meaning** *noun* (1933)
**:** the meaning of the base (as the word *play*) in a paradigm (as *plays, played, playing*) — compare GRAMMATICAL MEANING

**lex·i·cog·ra·pher** \ˌlek-sə-'kä-grə-fər\ *noun* [Late Greek *lexikographos*, from *lexikon* + Greek *-graphos* writer, from *graphein* to write] (1658)
**:** an author or editor of a dictionary

**lex·i·cog·ra·phy** \ˌlek-sə-'kä-grə-fē\ *noun* (1680)
**1 :** the editing or making of a dictionary
**2 :** the principles and practices of dictionary making
— **lex·i·co·graph·i·cal** \ˌlek-si-kō-'gra-fi-kəl\ *or* **lex·i·co·graph·ic** \-fik\ *adjective*
— **lex·i·co·graph·i·cal·ly** \-fi-k(ə-)lē\ *adverb*

**lex·i·col·o·gy** \ˌlek-sə-'kä-lə-jē\ *noun* [French *lexicologie*, from *lexico-* (from Late Greek *lexiko-*, from *lexikon*) + *-logie* -logy] (circa 1828)
**:** a branch of linguistics concerned with the signification and application of words
— **lex·i·col·o·gist** \-jist\ *noun*

**lex·i·con** \'lek-sə-ˌkän *also* -kən\ *noun, plural* **lex·i·ca** \-kə\ *or* **lexicons** [Late Greek *lexikon*, from neuter of *lexikos* of words, from Greek *lexis* word, speech, from *legein* to say — more at LEGEND] (1603)

**1** : a book containing an alphabetical arrangement of the words in a language and their definitions **:** DICTIONARY
**2 a** : the vocabulary of a language, an individual speaker or group of speakers, or a subject **b** : the total stock of morphemes in a language
**3** : REPERTOIRE, INVENTORY
**lex·is** \'lek-səs\ *noun, plural* **lex·es** \-,sēz\ [Greek, speech, word] (1960)
**:** LEXICON 2a
**ley** *variant of* LEA
**Ley·den jar** \'līd-ᵊn-\ *noun* [*Leiden, Leyden,* Netherlands] (1825)
**:** an electrical capacitor consisting of a glass jar coated inside and outside with metal foil and having the inner coating connected to a conducting rod passed through the insulating stopper
**L-form** \'el-,fȯrm\ *noun* [Lister Institute, London, where it was first isolated] (1948)
**:** a variant bacterium formed especially under stressful conditions and usually lacking a cell wall
**Lha·sa ap·so** \'lä-sə-'äp-(,)sō, 'la-sə-'ap-\ *noun, plural* **Lhasa apsos** *often* A *capitalized* [*Lhasa,* Tibet + Tibetan *apso*] (1935)
**:** any of a Tibetan breed of small dogs that have a dense coat of long hard straight hair, a heavy fall over the eyes, heavy whiskers and beard, and a well-feathered tail curled over the back — called also *Lhasa*

**Lhasa apso**

**li·a·bil·i·ty** \,lī-ə-'bi-lə-tē\ *noun, plural* **-ties** (circa 1809)
**1 a** : the quality or state of being liable **b** : PROBABILITY
**2** : something for which one is liable; *especially* : pecuniary obligation : DEBT — usually used in plural
**3** : one that acts as a disadvantage : DRAWBACK
**li·a·ble** \'lī-ə-bəl, *especially in sense 2 often* 'lī-bəl\ *adjective* [Middle English *lyable,* from (assumed) Anglo-French *liable,* from Old French *lier* to bind, from Latin *ligare* — more at LIGATURE] (15th century)
**1 a** : obligated according to law or equity : RESPONSIBLE **b** : subject to appropriation or attachment
**2 a** : being in a position to incur — used with *to* ⟨*liable* to a fine⟩ **b** : exposed or subject to some usually adverse contingency or action ⟨watch out or you're *liable* to fall⟩ ☆ ▪
**li·aise** \lē-'āz\ *intransitive verb* **li·aised; li·ais·ing** [back-formation from *liaison*] (1928) *chiefly British*
**1** : to establish liaison
**2** : to act as a liaison officer
**li·ai·son** \'lē-ə-,zän, lē-'ā-, ÷'lā-ə-\ *noun* [French, from Middle French, from *lier,* from Old French] (1759)
**1** : a binding or thickening agent used in cooking
**2 a** : a close bond or connection : INTERRELATIONSHIP **b** : an illicit sexual relationship : AFFAIR 3a
**3 a** : communication for establishing and maintaining mutual understanding and cooperation (as between parts of an armed force) **b** : one that establishes and maintains liaison
**4** : the pronunciation of an otherwise absent consonant sound at the end of the first of two consecutive words the second of which begins with a vowel sound and follows without pause
**li·a·na** \lē-'ä-nə, -'a-\ *also* **li·ane** \-'än, -'an\ *noun* [French *liane*] (1796)
**:** any of various usually woody vines especially of tropical rain forests that root in the ground
**li·ar** \'lī(-ə)r\ *noun* [Middle English, from Old English *lēogere,* from *lēogan* to lie — more at LIE] (before 12th century)

**:** one that tells lies
**Li·as** \'lī-əs\ *adjective* [*Lias,* division of the European Jurassic, from French, from English, a limestone rock] (1813)
*chiefly British* : LIASSIC
**Li·as·sic** \lī-'a-sik\ *adjective* [modification of French *liasique,* from *Lias*] (1833)
**:** of, relating to, or being a subdivision of the European Jurassic
**lib** \'lib\ *noun* (1970)
**:** LIBERATION 2
**li·ba·tion** \lī-'bā-shən\ *noun* [Latin *libation-, libatio,* from *libare* to pour as an offering; akin to Greek *leibein* to pour] (14th century)
**1 a** : an act of pouring a liquid as a sacrifice (as to a deity) **b** : a liquid (as wine) used in a libation
**2 a** : an act or instance of drinking often ceremoniously **b** : BEVERAGE; *especially* : a drink containing alcohol
**— li·ba·tion·ary** \-shə-,ner-ē\ *adjective*
**lib·ber** \'li-bər\ *noun* [*lib*] (1971)
**:** a person who supports a liberation movement especially for women — often used disparagingly
**li·bec·cio** \li-'be-chē-,ō, -'be-chō\ *or* **li·bec·chio** \-'be-kē-,ō\ *noun* [Italian *libeccio*] (1667)
**:** a southwest wind in Italy
**¹li·bel** \'lī-bəl\ *noun* [Middle English, written declaration, from Middle French, from Latin *libellus,* diminutive of *liber* book] (14th century)
**1 a** : a written statement in which a plaintiff in certain courts sets forth the cause of action or the relief sought **b** *archaic* : a handbill especially attacking or defaming someone
**2 a** : a written or oral defamatory statement or representation that conveys an unjustly unfavorable impression **b** (1) : a statement or representation published without just cause and tending to expose another to public contempt (2) : defamation of a person by written or representational means (3) : the publication of blasphemous, treasonable, seditious, or obscene writings or pictures (4) : the act, tort, or crime of publishing such a libel ◆
**²libel** *verb* **-beled** *or* **-belled; -bel·ing** *or* **-bel·ling** \-b(ə-)liŋ\ (1570)
*intransitive verb*
**:** to make libelous statements
*transitive verb*
**:** to make or publish a libel against
**— li·bel·er** \-b(ə-)lər\ *noun*
**— li·bel·ist** \-bə-list\ *noun*
**li·bel·ant** *or* **li·bel·lant** \'lī-bə-lənt\ *noun* (1726)
**:** one that institutes a suit by a libel
**li·bel·ee** *or* **li·bel·lee** \,lī-bə-'lē\ *noun* (circa 1856)
**:** one against whom a libel has been filed in a court
**li·bel·ous** *or* **li·bel·lous** \'lī-b(ə-)ləs\ *adjective* (1619)
**:** constituting or including a libel : DEFAMATORY ⟨a *libelous* statement⟩
**Li·be·ra** \'lē-bə-,rä, 'lē-brə\ *noun* [Latin, literally, deliver, imperative of *liberare* to liberate; from the first word of the responsory] (circa 1903)
**:** a Roman Catholic funeral responsory
**¹lib·er·al** \'li-b(ə-)rəl\ *adjective* [Middle English, from Middle French, from Latin *liberalis* suitable for a freeman, generous, from *liber* free; perhaps akin to Old English *lēodan* to grow, Greek *eleutheros* free] (14th century)
**1 a** : of, relating to, or based on the liberal arts ⟨*liberal* education⟩ **b** *archaic* : of or befitting a man of free birth
**2 a** : marked by generosity : OPENHANDED ⟨a *liberal* giver⟩ **b** : given or provided in a generous and openhanded way ⟨a *liberal* meal⟩ **c** : AMPLE, FULL

**3** *obsolete* : lacking moral restraint : LICENTIOUS
**4** : not literal or strict : LOOSE ⟨a *liberal* translation⟩
**5** : BROAD-MINDED; *especially* : not bound by authoritarianism, orthodoxy, or traditional forms
**6 a** : of, favoring, or based upon the principles of liberalism **b** *capitalized* : of or constituting a political party advocating or associated with the principles of political liberalism; *especially* : of or constituting a political party in the United Kingdom associated with ideals of individual especially economic freedom, greater individual participation in government, and

---

☆ **SYNONYMS**
**Liable, open, exposed, subject, prone, susceptible, sensitive** mean being by nature or through circumstances likely to experience something adverse. LIABLE implies a possibility or probability of incurring something because of position, nature, or particular situation ⟨*liable* to get lost⟩. OPEN stresses a lack of barriers preventing incurrence ⟨a claim *open* to question⟩. EXPOSED suggests lack of protection or powers of resistance against something actually present or threatening ⟨*exposed* to infection⟩. SUBJECT implies an openness for any reason to something that must be suffered or undergone ⟨all reports are *subject* to review⟩. PRONE stresses natural tendency or propensity to incur something ⟨*prone* to procrastination⟩. SUSCEPTIBLE implies conditions existing in one's nature or individual constitution that make incurrence probable ⟨very *susceptible* to flattery⟩. SENSITIVE implies a readiness to respond to or be influenced by forces or stimuli ⟨unduly *sensitive* to criticism⟩. See in addition RESPONSIBLE.

---

▢ **USAGE**
**liable** Both *liable* and *apt* when followed by an infinitive are used nearly interchangeably with *likely.* Although conflicting advice has been given over the years, most current commentators accept *apt* when so used. They generally recommend limiting *liable* to situations having an undesirable outcome, and our evidence shows that in edited writing it is more often so used than not.

---

◇ **WORD HISTORY**
**libel** The ancient Romans used the Latin noun *liber* to refer to the inner bark of a tree. Because this material was used to write on before the introduction of papyrus, *liber* came to be applied to a written document, especially a lengthy one; after papyrus became common, a *liber* was usually an entire papyrus scroll, hence a "book." *Libellus,* the diminutive of *liber,* was borrowed into French as *libelle,* which was in turn borrowed into 14th century English as *libel.* Both French and English originally used the word in the literal sense "little book," but in the 16th century, handbills and leaflets, being likened to little books, were also called libels in English. Because they were a popular means of spreading gossip and defamatory statements about famous people, the meaning of *libel* was extended to such defamatory statements as well as to the crime of writing them.

---

\ə\ abut \ᵊ\ kitten \ər\ further \a\ ash \ā\ ace
\ä\ mop, mar \aú\ out \ch\ chin \e\ bet \ē\ easy
\g\ go \i\ hit \ī\ ice \j\ job \ŋ\ sing \ō\ go
\ȯ\ law \ȯi\ boy \th\ thin \th\ the \ü\ loot \ú\ foot
\y\ yet \zh\ vision *see also* Guide to Pronunciation

constitutional, political, and administrative reforms designed to secure these objectives ☆
— **lib·er·al·ly** \-b(ə-)rə-lē\ *adverb*
— **lib·er·al·ness** *noun*

²**liberal** *noun* (1820)
: a person who is liberal: as **a** : one who is open-minded or not strict in the observance of orthodox, traditional, or established forms or ways **b** *capitalized* : a member or supporter of a liberal political party **c** : an advocate or adherent of liberalism especially in individual rights

**liberal arts** *noun plural* (14th century)
**1** : the medieval studies comprising the trivium and quadrivium
**2** : the studies (as language, philosophy, history, literature, abstract science) in a college or university intended to provide chiefly general knowledge and to develop the general intellectual capacities (as reason and judgment) as opposed to professional or vocational skills

**lib·er·al·ism** \'li-b(ə-)rə-ˌli-zəm\ *noun* (1819)
**1** : the quality or state of being liberal
**2 a** *often capitalized* : a movement in modern Protestantism emphasizing intellectual liberty and the spiritual and ethical content of Christianity **b** : a theory in economics emphasizing individual freedom from restraint and usually based on free competition, the self-regulating market, and the gold standard **c** : a political philosophy based on belief in progress, the essential goodness of the human race, and the autonomy of the individual and standing for the protection of political and civil liberties **d** *capitalized* : the principles and policies of a Liberal party
— **lib·er·al·ist** \-b(ə-)rə-list\ *noun or adjective*
— **lib·er·al·is·tic** \ˌli-b(ə-)rə-'lis-tik\ *adjective*

**lib·er·al·ise** *British variant of* LIBERALIZE

**lib·er·al·i·ty** \ˌli-bə-'ra-lə-tē\ *noun, plural* **-ties** (14th century)
: the quality or state of being liberal; *also* : an instance of this

**lib·er·al·ize** \'li-b(ə-)rə-ˌlīz\ *verb* **-ized; -iz·ing** (1774)
*transitive verb*
: to make liberal or more liberal
*intransitive verb*
: to become liberal or more liberal
— **lib·er·al·i·za·tion** \ˌli-b(ə-)rə-lə-'zā-shən\ *noun*
— **lib·er·al·iz·er** \'li-b(ə-)rə-ˌlī-zər\ *noun*

**lib·er·ate** \'li-bə-ˌrāt\ *transitive verb* **-at·ed; -at·ing** [Latin *liberatus,* past participle of *liberare,* from *liber*] (circa 1623)
**1** : to set at liberty : FREE; *specifically* : to free (as a country) from domination by a foreign power
**2** : to free from combination ⟨*liberate* the gas by adding acid⟩
**3** : to take or take over illegally or unjustly ⟨material *liberated* from a nearby construction site —Thorne Dreyer⟩
*synonym see* FREE
— **lib·er·a·tor** \-ˌā-tər\ *noun*

**liberated** *adjective* (1946)
: freed from or opposed to traditional social and sexual attitudes or roles ⟨a *liberated* woman⟩ ⟨a *liberated* marriage⟩

**lib·er·a·tion** \ˌli-bə-'rā-shən\ *noun* (15th century)
**1** : the act of liberating : the state of being liberated
**2** : a movement seeking equal rights and status for a group ⟨women's *liberation*⟩
— **lib·er·a·tion·ist** \-sh(ə-)nist\ *noun*

**liberation theology** *noun* (1972)
: a religious movement especially among Roman Catholic clergy in Latin America that combines political philosophy usually of a Marxist orientation with a theology of salvation as liberation from injustice
— **liberation theologian** *noun*

**lib·er·tar·i·an** \ˌli-bər-'ter-ē-ən\ *noun* (1789)
**1** : an advocate of the doctrine of free will
**2 a** : a person who upholds the principles of absolute and unrestricted liberty especially of thought and action **b** *capitalized* : a member of a political party advocating libertarian principles
— **libertarian** *adjective*
— **lib·er·tar·i·an·ism** \-ē-ə-ˌni-zəm\ *noun*

**lib·er·tin·age** \'li-bər-ˌtē-nij\ *noun* (1611)
: LIBERTINISM

**lib·er·tine** \'li-bər-ˌtēn\ *noun* [Middle English *libertyn* freedman, from Latin *libertinus,* from *libertinus,* adjective, of a freedman, from *libertus* freedman, from *liber*] (1577)
**1** : a freethinker especially in religious matters — usually used disparagingly
**2** : a person who is unrestrained by convention or morality; *specifically* : one leading a dissolute life
— **libertine** *adjective*

**lib·er·tin·ism** \'li-bər-ˌtē-ˌni-zəm, -tə-\ *noun* (1611)
: the quality or state of being libertine : the behavior of a libertine

**lib·er·ty** \'li-bər-tē\ *noun, plural* **-ties** [Middle English, from Middle French *liberté,* from Latin *libertat-, libertas,* from *liber* free — more at LIBERAL] (14th century)
**1** : the quality or state of being free: **a** : the power to do as one pleases **b** : freedom from physical restraint **c** : freedom from arbitrary or despotic control **d** : the positive enjoyment of various social, political, or economic rights and privileges **e** : the power of choice
**2 a** : a right or immunity enjoyed by prescription or by grant : PRIVILEGE **b** : permission especially to go freely within specified limits
**3** : an action going beyond normal limits: as **a** : a breach of etiquette or propriety : FAMILIARITY **b** : RISK, CHANCE ⟨took foolish *liberties* with his health⟩ **c** : a violation of rules or a deviation from standard practice **d** : a distortion of fact
**4** : a short authorized absence from naval duty usually for less than 48 hours
*synonym see* FREEDOM
— **at liberty 1** : FREE **2** : at leisure : UNOCCUPIED

**liberty cap** *noun* (1803)
: a close-fitting conical cap used as a symbol of liberty by the French revolutionists and in the U.S. before 1800

**liberty pole** *noun* (1770)
: a tall flagstaff surmounted by a liberty cap or the flag of a republic and set up as a symbol of liberty

**li·bid·i·nal** \lə-'bi-d°n-əl, -'bid-n°l\ *adjective* (1922)
: of or relating to the libido
— **li·bid·i·nal·ly** *adverb*

**li·bid·i·nous** \-d°n-əs, -'bid-nəs\ *adjective* [Middle English, from Middle French *libidineus,* from Latin *libidinosus,* from *libidin-, libido*] (15th century)
**1** : having or marked by lustful desires : LASCIVIOUS
**2** : LIBIDINAL
— **li·bid·i·nous·ly** *adverb*
— **li·bid·i·nous·ness** *noun*

**li·bi·do** \lə-'bē-(ˌ)dō *also* 'li-bə-ˌdō\ *noun, plural* **-dos** [New Latin *libidin-, libido,* from Latin, desire, lust, from *libēre* to please — more at LOVE] (1909)
**1** : emotional or psychic energy that in psychoanalytic theory is derived from primitive biological urges and that is usually goal-directed
**2** : sexual drive

**li·bra** \for 1 & 2a 'lē-brə, *sometimes* 'lī-brə, for 2b 'lē-brə *or* 'lēv-rə\ *noun* [Middle English, from Latin (genitive *Librae*), literally, scales, pound]
**1** *capitalized* **a** : a southern zodiacal constellation between Virgo and Scorpio represented

by a pair of scales **b** (1) : the 7th sign of the zodiac in astrology — see ZODIAC table (2) : one born under the sign of Libra
**2 a** *plural* **li·brae** \'lī-ˌbrē, 'lē-ˌbrī\ [Latin] : an ancient Roman unit of weight equal to 327.45 grams **b** [Spanish & Portuguese, from Latin] : any of various Spanish, Portuguese, Colombian, or Venezuelan units of weight

**Li·bran** \'lē-brən, 'lī-\ *noun* (1911)
: LIBRA 1b(2)

**li·brar·i·an** \lī-'brer-ē-ən\ *noun* (1703)
: a specialist in the care or management of a library
— **li·brar·i·an·ship** \-ˌship\ *noun*

**li·brary** \'lī-ˌbrer-ē; *British usually & US sometimes* -brər-ē; *US sometimes* -brē, ÷-ˌber-ē\ *noun, plural* **-brar·ies** [Middle English, from Medieval Latin *librarium,* from Latin, neuter of *librarius* of books, from *libr-, liber* inner bark, rind, book] (14th century)
**1 a** : a place in which literary, musical, artistic, or reference materials (as books, manuscripts, recordings, or films) are kept for use but not for sale **b** : a collection of such materials
**2 a** : a collection resembling or suggesting a library ⟨a *library* of computer programs⟩ ⟨wine *library*⟩ **b** : MORGUE 2
**3 a** : a series of related books issued by a publisher **b** : a collection of publications on the same subject
**4** : a collection of sequences of DNA and especially recombinant DNA that are maintained in a suitable cellular environment and that represent the genetic material of a particular organism or tissue ■

**library paste** *noun* (1953)
: a thick white adhesive made from starch

**library science** *noun* (circa 1904)
: the study or the principles and practices of library care and administration

**li·bra·tion** \lī-'brā-shən\ *noun* [Latin *libration-, libratio,* from *librare* to balance, from *libra* scales] (1669)
: an oscillation in the apparent aspect of a secondary body (as a planet or a satellite) as seen from the primary object around which it revolves
— **li·bra·tion·al** \-shnəl, -shə-n°l\ *adjective*
— **li·bra·to·ry** \'lī-brə-ˌtōr-ē, -ˌtȯr-\ *adjective*

---

☆ SYNONYMS
**Liberal, generous, bountiful, munificent** mean giving or given freely and unstintingly. LIBERAL suggests openhandedness in the giver and largeness in the thing or amount given ⟨a teacher *liberal* with her praise⟩. GENEROUS stresses warmhearted readiness to give more than size or importance of the gift ⟨a *generous* offer of help⟩. BOUNTIFUL suggests lavish, unremitting giving or providing ⟨children spoiled by *bountiful* presents⟩. MUNIFICENT suggests a scale of giving appropriate to lords or princes ⟨a *munificent* foundation grant⟩.

---

□ USAGE
**library** While the pronunciation \'lī-ˌbrer-ē\ is the most frequent variant in the U.S., the other variants are not uncommon. The contraction \'lī-brē\ and the dissimilated form \'lī-ˌbrer-ē\ result from the relative difficulty of repeating \r\ in successive syllables; our files contain citations for these variants from educated speakers, including college presidents and professors, as well as with somewhat greater frequency from less educated speakers.

**libration point** *noun* (1962)
: any of five positions in the plane of a celestial system consisting of one massive body orbiting another at which the gravitational influences of the two bodies are approximately equal

**li·bret·tist** \lə-'bre-tist\ *noun* (1862)
: the writer of a libretto

**li·bret·to** \lə-'bre-(,)tō\ *noun, plural* **-tos** *or* **-ti** \-(,)tē\ [Italian, diminutive of *libro* book, from Latin *libr-, liber*] (1742)
**1** : the text of a work (as an opera) for the musical theater
**2** : the book containing a libretto

**li·bri·form** \'lī-brə-,form\ *adjective* [Latin *libr-, liber* + International Scientific Vocabulary *-iform*] (1877)
: resembling phloem fibers

**Lib·ri·um** \'li-brē-əm\ *trademark*
— used for a preparation of chlordiazepoxide

**Lib·y·an** \'li-bē-ən\ *noun* (15th century)
**1** : a native or inhabitant of Libya
**2** : a language of ancient North Africa probably ancestral to Berber dialects
— **Libyan** *adjective*

**lice** *plural of* LOUSE

**¹li·cense** *or* **li·cence** \'lī-s°n(t)s\ *noun* [Middle English, from Middle French *licence*, from Latin *licentia*, from *licent-, licens*, present participle of *licēre* to be permitted] (14th century)
**1 a** : permission to act **b** : freedom of action
**2 a** : a permission granted by competent authority to engage in a business or occupation or in an activity otherwise unlawful **b** : a document, plate, or tag evidencing a license granted
**3 a** : freedom that allows or is used with irresponsibility **b** : disregard for standards of personal conduct : LICENTIOUSNESS
**4** : deviation from fact, form, or rule by an artist or writer for the sake of the effect gained
*synonym* see FREEDOM

**²license** *also* **licence** *transitive verb* **licensed; li·cens·ing** (15th century)
**1 a** : to issue a license to **b** : to permit or authorize especially by formal license
**2** : to give permission or consent to
— **li·cens·able** \-s°n(t)-sə-bəl\ *adjective*
— **li·cens·er** \-sər\ *or* **li·cen·sor** \-sər, ,lī-s°n-'sòr\ *noun*

**licensed practical nurse** *noun* (1951)
: a person who has undergone training and obtained a license (as from a state) conferring authorization to provide routine care for the sick

**li·cens·ee** \,lī-s°n(t)-'sē\ *noun* (circa 1864)
: one that is licensed

**license plate** *noun* (1926)
: a plate or tag (as of metal) attesting that a license has been secured and usually bearing a registration number

**li·cen·sure** \'lī-s°n-shər, -,shùr\ *noun* (circa 1846)
: the granting of licenses especially to practice a profession; *also* : the state of being licensed

**licente** *plural of* SENTE

**li·cen·ti·ate** \lī-'sen(t)-shē-ət, *especially in sense 2* li-\ *noun* [Medieval Latin *licentiatus*, from past participle of *licentiare* to allow, from Latin *licentia*] (1555)
**1** : one who has a license granted especially by a university to practice a profession
**2** : an academic degree ranking below that of doctor given by some European universities

**li·cen·tious** \lī-'sen(t)-shəs\ *adjective* [Latin *licentiosus*, from *licentia*] (1535)
**1** : lacking legal or moral restraints; *especially* : disregarding sexual restraints
**2** : marked by disregard for strict rules of correctness
— **li·cen·tious·ly** *adverb*
— **li·cen·tious·ness** *noun*

**li·chee** *variant of* LITCHI

**li·chen** \'lī-kən, *British also* 'li-chən\ *noun* [Latin, from Greek *leichēn, lichēn*, from *leichein* to lick] (circa 1657)

**1** : any of several skin diseases characterized by a papular eruption
**2** : any of numerous complex thallophytic plants made up of an alga and a fungus growing in symbiotic association on a solid surface (as a rock)
— **li·chened** \-kənd\ *adjective*
— **li·chen·ous** \-kə-nəs\ *adjective*

**li·chen·ol·o·gy** \,lī-kə-'nä-lə-jē\ *noun* [International Scientific Vocabulary] (1855)
: the study of lichens
— **li·chen·o·log·i·cal** \,lī-kə-nə-'lä-ji-kəl\ *adjective*
— **li·chen·ol·o·gist** \,lī-kə-'nä-lə-jist\ *noun*

**lich–gate** *variant of* LYCH-GATE

**licht** \'likt\ *Scottish variant of* LIGHT

**lic·it** \'li-sət\ *adjective* [Middle English, from Middle French *licite*, from Latin *licitus*, from past participle of *licēre* to be permitted — more at LICENSE] (15th century)
: conforming to the requirements of the law
: not forbidden by law : PERMISSIBLE
*synonym* see LAWFUL
— **lic·it·ly** *adverb*

**¹lick** \'lik\ *verb* [Middle English, from Old English *liccian*; akin to Old High German *leckōn* to lick, Latin *lingere*, Greek *leichein*] (before 12th century)
*transitive verb*
**1 a** (1) : to draw the tongue over ⟨*lick* a stamp⟩ (2) : to flicker over like a tongue **b** : to take into the mouth with the tongue : LAP
**2 a** : to strike repeatedly : THRASH **b** : to get the better of : OVERCOME, DEFEAT ⟨has *licked* every problem⟩
*intransitive verb*
**1** : to lap with or as if with the tongue
**2** : to dart like a tongue ⟨flames *licking* out of windows⟩
— **lick into shape** : to put into proper form or condition
— **lick one's wounds** : to recover from defeat or disappointment

**²lick** *noun* (1603)
**1 a** : an act or instance of licking **b** : a small amount : BIT ⟨couldn't swim a *lick*⟩ **c** : a hasty careless effort
**2 a** : a sharp hit : BLOW **b** : a directed effort : CRACK — usually used in plural; usually used in the phrase *get in one's licks*
**3 a** : a natural salt deposit (as a salt spring) that animals lick **b** : a block of often medicated saline preparation given to livestock to lick
**4** : a musical figure; *specifically* : an interpolated and usually improvised figure or flourish
**5** : a critical thrust : DIG, BARB
— **lick and a promise** : a perfunctory performance of a task

**lick·er·ish** \'li-k(ə-)rish\ *adjective* [alteration of *lickerous*, from Middle English *likerous*, from (assumed) Old North French *likerous*, from Old North French *leckeur* lecher] (14th century)
**1** : GREEDY, DESIROUS
**2** *obsolete* : tempting to the appetite
**3** : LECHEROUS
— **lick·er·ish·ly** *adverb*
— **lick·er·ish·ness** *noun*

**lick·e·ty–split** \,li-kə-tē-'split\ *adverb* [probably irregular from ¹*lick* + *split*] (circa 1859)
: at great speed

**lick·ing** *noun* (1756)
**1** : a sound thrashing : DRUBBING
**2** : DEFEAT

**lick·spit·tle** \'lik-,spi-t°l\ *noun* (1825)
: a fawning subordinate : TOADY

**lic·o·rice** \'li-k(ə-)rish, -k(ə-)rəs\ *noun* [Middle English *licorice*, from Old French, from Late Latin *liquiritia*, alteration of Latin *glycyrrhiza*, from Greek *glykyrrhiza*, from *glykys* sweet + *rhiza* root — more at DULCET, ROOT] (13th century)
**1 a** : the dried root of a European leguminous plant (*Glycyrrhiza glabra*) with pinnate leaves and spikes of blue flowers; *also* : an extract of this used especially in medicine, liquors, and

confectionery **b** : a candy flavored with licorice
**2** : a plant yielding licorice

**lic·tor** \'lik-tər\ *noun* [Middle English *littour*, from Latin *lictor*] (14th century)
: an ancient Roman officer who bore the fasces as the insignia of his office and whose duties included accompanying the chief magistrates in public appearances

**¹lid** \'lid\ *noun* [Middle English, from Old English *hlid*; akin to Old High German *hlit* cover, and probably to Old English *hlinian* to lean — more at LEAN] (before 12th century)
**1** : a movable cover for the opening of a hollow container (as a vessel or box)
**2** : EYELID
**3** : the operculum in mosses
**4** *slang* : HAT
**5** : something that confines, limits, or suppresses : CHECK, RESTRAINT
**6** : an ounce of marijuana

**²lid** *transitive verb* **lid·ded; lid·ding** (13th century)
: to cover or supply with a lid

**li·dar** \'lī-,där\ *noun* [*light* + *radar*] (1963)
: a device that is similar in operation to radar but emits pulsed laser light instead of microwaves

**lidded** *adjective* (before 12th century)
**1** : having or covered with a lid ⟨a *lidded* tureen⟩
**2** : having lids especially of a specified kind — usually used in combination ⟨heavy-*lidded* eyes⟩

**lid·less** \'lid-ləs\ *adjective* (14th century)
**1** : having no lid
**2** *archaic* : WATCHFUL

**li·do** \'lē-(,)dō\ *noun, plural* **lidos** [*Lido*, Italy] (1860)
: a fashionable beach resort

**li·do·caine** \'lī-də-,kān\ *noun* [acetani*lid* + *-o-* + *-caine*] (circa 1949)
: a crystalline compound $C_{14}H_{22}N_2O$ that is used in the form of its hydrochloride as a local anesthetic and as an antiarrhythmic agent

**¹lie** \'lī\ *intransitive verb* **lay** \'lā\; **lain** \'lān\; **ly·ing** \'lī-iŋ\ [Middle English, from Old English *licgan*; akin to Old High German *ligen* to lie, Latin *lectus* bed, Greek *lechos*] (before 12th century)
**1 a** : to be or to stay at rest in a horizontal position : be prostrate : REST, RECLINE ⟨*lie* motionless⟩ ⟨*lie* asleep⟩ **b** : to assume a horizontal position — often used with *down* **c** *archaic* : to reside temporarily : stay for the night : LODGE **d** : to have sexual intercourse — used with *with* **e** : to remain inactive (as in concealment) ⟨*lie* in wait⟩
**2** : to be in a helpless or defenseless state ⟨the town *lay* at the mercy of the invaders⟩
**3** *of an inanimate thing* : to be or remain in a flat or horizontal position upon a broad support ⟨books *lying* on the table⟩
**4** : to have direction : EXTEND ⟨the route *lay* to the west⟩
**5 a** : to occupy a certain relative place or position ⟨hills *lie* behind us⟩ **b** : to have a place in relation to something else ⟨the real reason *lies* deeper⟩ **c** : to have an effect through mere presence, weight, or relative position ⟨remorse *lay* heavily on him⟩ **d** : to be sustainable or admissible
**6** : to remain at anchor or becalmed
**7 a** : to have place : EXIST ⟨the choice *lay* between fighting or surrendering⟩ **b** : CONSIST, BELONG ⟨the success of the book *lies* in its direct style⟩ ⟨responsibility *lay* with the adults⟩
**8** : REMAIN; *especially* : to remain unused, unsought, or uncared for
*usage* see LAY

\ə\ abut \°\ kitten \ər\ further \a\ ash \ā\ ace \ä\ mop, mar \aù\ out \ch\ chin \e\ bet \ē\ easy \g\ go \i\ hit \ī\ ice \j\ job \ŋ\ sing \ō\ go \ò\ law \òi\ boy \th\ thin \th\ the \ü\ loot \ù\ foot \y\ yet \zh\ vision *see also* Guide to Pronunciation

— **li·er** \'lī(-ə)r\ *noun*

— **lie low 1 :** to lie prostrate, defeated, or disgraced **2 :** to stay in hiding **:** strive to avoid notice **3 :** to bide one's time **:** remain secretly ready for action

**²lie** *noun* (1697)
**1** *chiefly British* **:** LAY 6
**2 :** the position or situation in which something lies ⟨a golf ball in a difficult *lie*⟩
**3 :** the haunt of an animal (as a fish) **:** COVERT
**4** *British* **:** an act or instance of lying or resting

**³lie** *verb* **lied; ly·ing** \'lī-iŋ\ [Middle English, from Old English *lēogan;* akin to Old High German *liogan* to lie, Old Church Slavonic *lŭgati*] (before 12th century)
*intransitive verb*
**1 :** to make an untrue statement with intent to deceive
**2 :** to create a false or misleading impression
*transitive verb*
**:** to bring about by telling lies ⟨*lied* his way out of trouble⟩ ☆

**⁴lie** *noun* [Middle English *lige, lie,* from Old English *lyge;* akin to Old High German *lugī,* Old English *lēogan* to lie] (before 12th century)
**1 a :** an assertion of something known or believed by the speaker to be untrue with intent to deceive **b :** an untrue or inaccurate statement that may or may not be believed true by the speaker
**2 :** something that misleads or deceives
**3 :** a charge of lying

**lieb·frau·milch** \'lēp-,fraü-,milk, 'lēb-, -,milk, -,milsh\ *noun* [German, alteration of *Liebfrauenmilch,* from *Liebfrauenstift,* religious foundation in Worms, Germany + *Milch* milk] (1833)
**:** a fruity white Rhine wine

**lie by** *intransitive verb* (1613)
**:** to remain inactive **:** REST

**lied** \'lēt\ *noun, plural* **lie·der** \'lē-dər\ [German, song, from Old High German *liod*] (1852)
**:** a German art song especially of the 19th century

**Lie·der·kranz** \'lē-dər-,kran(t)s, -,krän(t)s\ *trademark*
— used for a pungent surface-ripened cheese

**lie detector** *noun* (1909)
**:** an instrument for detecting physiological evidence of the tension that accompanies lying

**lie down** *intransitive verb* (1888)
**1 :** to submit meekly or abjectly to defeat, disappointment, or insult ⟨won't take that criticism *lying down*⟩
**2 :** to fail to perform or to neglect one's part deliberately ⟨*lying down* on the job⟩

**¹lief** \'lēf, 'lēv\ *adjective* [Middle English *lief, lef,* from Old English *lēof;* akin to Old English *lufu* love] (before 12th century)
**1** *archaic* **:** DEAR, BELOVED
**2** *archaic* **:** WILLING, GLAD

**²lief** \'lēv, 'lēf\ *adverb* (13th century)
**:** SOON, GLADLY ⟨I'd as *lief* go as not⟩

**¹liege** \'lēj\ *adjective* [Middle English, from Old French, from Late Latin *laeticus,* from *laetus* serf, of Germanic origin; akin to Old Frisian *let* serf] (14th century)
**1 a :** having the right to feudal allegiance or service ⟨his *liege* lord⟩ **b :** obligated to render feudal allegiance and service
**2 :** FAITHFUL, LOYAL

**²liege** *noun* (14th century)
**1 a :** a vassal bound to feudal service and allegiance **b :** a loyal subject
**2 :** a feudal superior to whom allegiance and service are due

**liege man** *noun* (14th century)
**1 :** VASSAL
**2 :** a devoted follower

**lie-in** \'lī-,in\ *noun* (1963)
**:** an act of lying down (as in a public place) in organized protest or as a means of forcing compliance with demands

**lien** \'lēn, 'lē-ən\ *noun* [Middle French, tie, band, from Latin *ligamen,* from *ligare* to bind — more at LIGATURE] (1531)
**1 :** a charge upon real or personal property for the satisfaction of some debt or duty ordinarily arising by operation of law
**2 :** the security interest created by a mortgage

**lie off** *intransitive verb* (1573)
**1 :** to hold back in the early part of a race
**2 :** to keep a little away from the shore or another ship
**3 :** to cease work for a time

**lie over** *intransitive verb* (circa 1847)
**:** to await disposal or attention at a later time

**li·erne** \lē-'ərn, -'ern\ *noun* [French, from Middle French, probably from *lier* to bind, from Latin *ligare*] (1842)
**:** a rib in Gothic vaulting that passes from one intersection of the principal ribs to another

**lie to** *intransitive verb* (1711)
*of a ship* **:** to stay stationary with head to windward

**lieu** \'lü\ *noun* [Middle English *liue,* from Old French *lieu,* from Latin *locus* — more at STALL] (14th century)
*archaic* **:** PLACE, STEAD
— **in lieu :** INSTEAD
— **in lieu of :** in the place of **:** instead of

**lie up** *intransitive verb* (1699)
**1 :** to go into or remain in a dock
**2 :** to stay in bed or at rest

**lieu·ten·an·cy** \lü-'te-nən(t)-sē, *British* le(f)-'ten(t)-\ *noun* (15th century)
**:** the office, rank, or commission of a lieutenant

**lieu·ten·ant** \-'te-nənt\ *noun* [Middle English, from Middle French, from *lieu* + *tenant* holding, from *tenir* to hold, from Latin *tenēre* — more at THIN] (14th century)
**1 a :** an official empowered to act for a higher official **b :** an aide or representative of another in the performance of duty **:** ASSISTANT
**2 a** (1) **:** FIRST LIEUTENANT (2) **:** SECOND LIEUTENANT **b :** a commissioned officer in the navy or coast guard ranking above a lieutenant junior grade and below a lieutenant commander **c :** a fire or police department officer ranking below a captain

**lieutenant colonel** *noun* (1598)
**:** a commissioned officer in the army, air force, or marine corps ranking above a major and below a colonel

**lieutenant commander** *noun* (1839)
**:** a commissioned officer in the navy or coast guard ranking above a lieutenant and below a commander

**lieutenant general** *noun* (1589)
**:** a commissioned officer in the army, air force, or marine corps who ranks above a major general and whose insignia is three stars

**lieutenant governor** *noun* (1595)
**:** a deputy or subordinate governor: as **a :** an elected official serving as deputy to the governor of an American state **b :** the formal head of the government of a Canadian province appointed by the federal government as the representative of the crown

— **lieutenant governorship** *noun*

**lieutenant junior grade** *noun, plural* **lieutenants junior grade** (circa 1909)
**:** a commissioned officer in the navy or coast guard ranking above an ensign and below a lieutenant

**¹life** \'līf\ *noun, plural* **lives** \'līvz\ [Middle English *lif,* from Old English *līf;* akin to Old English *libban* to live — more at LIVE] (before 12th century)
**1 a :** the quality that distinguishes a vital and functional being from a dead body **b :** a principle or force that is considered to underlie the distinctive quality of animate beings — compare VITALISM 1 **c :** an organismic state characterized by capacity for metabolism, growth, reaction to stimuli, and reproduction
**2 a :** the sequence of physical and mental experiences that make up the existence of an in-

dividual **b :** one or more aspects of the process of living ⟨sex *life* of the frog⟩
**3 :** BIOGRAPHY 1
**4 :** spiritual existence transcending physical death
**5 a :** the period from birth to death **b :** a specific phase of earthly existence ⟨adult *life*⟩ **c :** the period from an event until death ⟨a judge appointed for *life*⟩ **d :** a sentence of imprisonment for the remainder of a convict's life
**6 :** a way or manner of living
**7 :** LIVELIHOOD
**8 :** a vital or living being; *specifically* **:** PERSON ⟨many *lives* were lost in the disaster⟩
**9 :** an animating and shaping force or principle
**10 :** SPIRIT, ANIMATION ⟨there was no *life* in her dancing⟩
**11 :** the form or pattern of something existing in reality ⟨painted from *life*⟩
**12 :** the period of duration, usefulness, or popularity of something ⟨the expected *life* of flashlight batteries⟩
**13 :** the period of existence (as of a subatomic particle) — compare HALF-LIFE
**14 :** a property (as resilience or elasticity) of an inanimate substance or object resembling the animate quality of a living being
**15 :** living beings (as of a particular kind or environment) ⟨forest *life*⟩
**16 a :** human activities **b :** animate activity and movement ⟨stirrings of *life*⟩ **c :** the activities of a given sphere, area, or time ⟨the political *life* of the country⟩
**17 :** one providing interest and vigor ⟨*life* of the party⟩
**18 :** an opportunity for continued viability ⟨gave the patient a new *life*⟩
**19** *capitalized, Christian Science* **:** GOD 1b
**20 :** something resembling animate life ⟨a grant saved the project's *life*⟩

**²life** *adjective* (13th century)
**1 :** of or relating to animate being
**2 :** LIFELONG ⟨a *life* member⟩
**3 :** using a living model ⟨a *life* class⟩
**4 :** of, relating to, or provided by life insurance ⟨a *life* policy⟩

**life–and–death** *also* **life–or–death** *adjective* (1822)
**:** involving or culminating in life or death **:** vitally important as if involving life or death

**life belt** *noun* (circa 1858)
**1** *chiefly British* **:** a life preserver in the form of a buoyant belt
**2 :** SAFETY BELT

**life·blood** \'līf-'bləd, -,bləd\ *noun* (1579)
**1 :** blood regarded as the seat of vitality
**2 :** a vital or life-giving force ⟨freedom of inquiry is the *lifeblood* of a university⟩

**life·boat** \-,bōt\ *noun* (1801)
**:** a sturdy buoyant boat (as one carried by a ship) for use in an emergency and especially in saving lives at sea

**life buoy** *noun* (1801)
**:** a ring-shaped life preserver

---

☆ **SYNONYMS**
**Lie, prevaricate, equivocate, palter, fib** mean to tell an untruth. LIE is the blunt term, imputing dishonesty ⟨*lied* about where he had been⟩. PREVARICATE softens the bluntness of LIE by implying quibbling or confusing the issue ⟨during the hearings the witness did his best to *prevaricate*⟩. EQUIVOCATE implies using words having more than one sense so as to seem to say one thing but intend another ⟨*equivocated* endlessly in an attempt to mislead her inquisitors⟩. PALTER implies making unreliable statements of fact or intention or insincere promises ⟨a swindler *paltering* with his investors⟩. FIB applies to a telling of a trivial untruth ⟨*fibbed* about the price of the new suit⟩.

**life-care** \'līf-ˌkar, -ˌker\ *adjective* (1980)
: of, relating to, or being a residential complex for elderly people that provides an apartment, personal and social services, and health care for life

**life cycle** *noun* (1873)
**1** : the series of stages in form and functional activity through which an organism passes between successive recurrences of a specified primary stage
**2** : LIFE HISTORY 2
**3** : a series of stages through which something (as an individual, culture, or manufactured product) passes during its lifetime

**life expectancy** *noun* (1935)
: the average life span of an individual

**life force** *noun* (1896)
: ÉLAN VITAL

**life-form** \'līf-ˌfȯrm, -ˌfȯrm\ *noun* (1899)
: the body form that characterizes a kind of organism (as a species) at maturity; *also* : a kind of organism

**life·ful** \'līf-fəl\ *adjective* (13th century)
*archaic* : full of or giving vitality

**life–giv·ing** \-ˌgi-viŋ\ *adjective* (1596)
: giving or having power to give life and spirit : INVIGORATING

**life·guard** \-ˌgärd\ *noun* (1896)
: a usually expert swimmer employed (as at a beach or a pool) to safeguard other swimmers
— **lifeguard** *intransitive verb*

**life history** *noun* (1870)
**1** : the history of an individual or thing
**2** : a history of the changes through which an organism passes in its development from the primary stage to its natural death

**life insurance** *noun* (1809)
: insurance providing for payment of a stipulated sum to a designated beneficiary upon death of the insured

**life jacket** *noun* (1883)
: a life preserver in the form of a buoyant vest

**life·less** \'līf-ləs\ *adjective* (before 12th century)
: having no life: **a** : DEAD **b** : INANIMATE **c** : lacking qualities expressive of life and vigor : INSIPID **d** : destitute of living beings
— **life·less·ly** *adverb*
— **life·less·ness** *noun*

**life·like** \'līf-ˌlīk\ *adjective* (14th century)
: accurately representing or imitating real life ⟨a *lifelike* portrait⟩
— **life·like·ness** *noun*

**life·line** \'līf-ˌlīn\ *noun* (1700)
**1** : a line (as a rope) used for saving or preserving life: as **a** : a line along the outer edge of the deck of a boat or ship **b** : a line used to keep contact with a person (as a diver or astronaut) in a dangerous or potentially dangerous situation
**2** : something regarded as indispensable for the maintaining or protection of life

**life list** *noun* (1960)
: a record kept of all birds sighted and identified by a birder

**life·long** \'līf-ˌlȯŋ\ *adjective* (1855)
**1** : lasting or continuing through life
**2** : LONG-STANDING

**life·man·ship** \'līf-mən-ˌship\ *noun* (1949)
: the skill or practice of achieving superiority or an appearance of superiority over others (as in conversation) by perplexing and demoralizing them

**life net** *noun* (circa 1904)
: a strong net or sheet (as of canvas) used (as by firefighters) to catch a person jumping from a burning building

**life of Ri·ley** *also* **life of Reil·ly** \-ˈrī-lē\ [from the name *Riley* or *Reilly*] (1923)
: a carefree comfortable way of living

**life peer** *noun* (1869)
: a British peer whose title is not hereditary
— **life peerage** *noun*

**life preserver** *noun* (1804)
**1** : a device (as a life jacket or life buoy) designed to save a person from drowning by providing buoyancy in water
**2** *chiefly British* : BLACKJACK 3

**lif·er** \'lī-fər\ *noun* (1827)
**1** : a person sentenced to imprisonment for life
**2** : a person who makes a career of one of the armed forces
**3** : a person who has made a lifelong commitment (as to a way of life)

**life raft** *noun* (1819)
: a raft usually made of wood or an inflatable material and designed for use by people forced into the water

**life ring** *noun* (circa 1909)
: LIFE BUOY

**life-sav·er** \'līf-ˌsā-vər\ *noun* (1887)
**1** : one trained to save lives of drowning persons
**2** : one that is at once timely and effective in time of distress or need

**¹life-sav·ing** \-ˌviŋ\ *adjective* (1858)
: designed for or used in saving lives ⟨*lifesaving* drugs⟩

**²lifesaving** *noun* (1919)
: the skill or practice of saving or protecting the lives especially of drowning persons

**life science** *noun* (1941)
: a branch of science (as biology, medicine, anthropology, or sociology) that deals with living organisms and life processes — usually used in plural
— **life scientist** *noun*

**life–size** \'līf-ˈsīz\ *or* **life–sized** \-ˈsīzd\ *adjective* (1841)
: of natural size : of the size of the original ⟨a *life-size* statue⟩

**life span** *noun* (1918)
**1** : the duration of existence of an individual
**2** : the average length of life of a kind of organism or of a material object especially in a particular environment or under specified circumstances

**life·style** \'līf-ˌstī(ə)l, -ˌstī(ə)l\ *noun* (1939)
: the typical way of life of an individual, group, or culture

**life–support** \-ˌsə-ˌpȯrt, -ˌpȯrt\ *adjective* (1965)
: providing support necessary to sustain life; *especially* : of or relating to a system providing such support ⟨*life-support* equipment⟩

**life support** *noun* (1975)
: medical life-support equipment ⟨the patient was placed on *life support*⟩

**life-support system** *noun* (1959)
: an artificial or natural system that provides all or some of the items (as oxygen, food, water, control of temperature and pressure, disposition of carbon dioxide and body wastes) necessary for maintaining life or health

**life table** *noun* (circa 1859)
: MORTALITY TABLE

**¹life·time** \'līf-ˌtīm\ *noun* (13th century)
**1 a** : the duration of the existence of a living being or a thing (as a star or a subatomic particle) **b** : LIFE 12
**2** : an amount accumulated or experienced in a lifetime ⟨a *lifetime* of regrets⟩

**²lifetime** *adjective* (1904)
**1** : LIFELONG
**2** : measured or achieved over the span of a career ⟨a baseball player's *lifetime* batting average⟩

**life vest** *noun* (1939)
: LIFE JACKET

**life·way** \-ˌwā\ *noun* (1948)
: LIFE 6

**life·work** \-ˈwərk\ *noun* (1871)
: the entire or principal work of one's lifetime; *also* : a work extending over a lifetime

**life zone** *noun* (1901)
: a region characterized by specific plants and animals

**¹lift** \'lift\ *noun* [Middle English, from Old English *lyft*] (before 12th century)
*chiefly Scottish* : HEAVENS, SKY

**²lift** *verb* [Middle English, from Old Norse *lypta;* akin to Old English *lyft* air — more at LOFT] (14th century)
*transitive verb*
**1 a** : to raise from a lower to a higher position : ELEVATE **b** : to raise in rank or condition **c** : to raise in rate or amount
**2** : to put an end to (a blockade or siege) by withdrawing or causing the withdrawal of investing forces
**3** : REVOKE, RESCIND ⟨*lift* an embargo⟩
**4 a** : STEAL ⟨had her purse *lifted*⟩ **b** : PLAGIARIZE **c** : to take out of normal setting ⟨*lift* a word out of context⟩
**5** : to take up (as a root crop or transplants) from the ground
**6** : to pay off (an obligation) ⟨*lift* a mortgage⟩
**7** : to move from one place to another (as by aircraft) : TRANSPORT
**8** : to take up (a fingerprint) from a surface
*intransitive verb*
**1 a** : ASCEND, RISE ⟨the rocket *lifted* off⟩ **b** : to appear elevated (as above surrounding objects)
**2** *of inclement weather* : to dissipate and clear
☆
— **lift·able** \'lif-tə-bəl\ *adjective*
— **lift·er** *noun*

**³lift** *noun* (14th century)
**1** : the amount that may be lifted at one time : LOAD
**2 a** : the action or an instance of lifting **b** : the action or an instance of rising **c** : elevated carriage (as of a body part) **d** : the lifting up (as of a dancer) usually by a partner
**3** : a device (as a handle or latch) for lifting
**4** : an act of stealing : THEFT
**5 a** : ASSISTANCE, HELP **b** : a ride especially along one's way
**6** : a layer in the heel of a shoe
**7** : a rise or advance in position or condition
**8** : a slight rise or elevation
**9** : the distance or extent to which something rises
**10** : an apparatus or machine used for hoisting: as **a** : a set of pumps used in a mine **b** *chiefly British* : ELEVATOR 1b **c** : an apparatus for raising an automobile (as for repair) **d** : SKI LIFT
**11 a** : an elevating influence **b** : an elevation of the spirit
**12 a** : the component of the total aerodynamic force acting on an airplane or airfoil that is perpendicular to the relative wind and that for an airplane constitutes the upward force that

---

☆ **SYNONYMS**
**Lift, raise, rear, elevate, hoist, heave, boost** mean to move from a lower to a higher place or position. LIFT usually implies exerting effort to overcome resistance of weight (*lift* the chair while I vacuum). RAISE carries a stronger implication of bringing up to the vertical or to a high position (scouts *raising* a flagpole). REAR may add an element of suddenness to RAISE (suddenly *reared* itself up on its hind legs). ELEVATE may replace LIFT or RAISE especially when exalting or enhancing is implied (*elevated* the taste of the public). HOIST implies lifting something heavy especially by mechanical means (*hoisted* the cargo on board). HEAVE implies lifting and throwing with great effort or strain (*heaved* the heavy crate inside). BOOST suggests assisting to climb or advance by a push (*boosted* his brother over the fence).

---

\ə\ abut \ə\ kitten \ər\ further \a\ ash \ā\ ace
\ä\ mop, mar \au̇\ out \ch\ chin \e\ bet \ē\ easy
\g\ go \i\ hit \ī\ ice \j\ job \ŋ\ sing \ō\ go
\ȯ\ law \ȯi\ boy \th\ thin \th\ the \ü\ loot \u̇\ foot
\y\ yet \zh\ vision　　*see also* Guide to Pronunciation

opposes the pull of gravity **b :** an updraft that can be used to increase altitude (as of a sailplane)

**13 :** an organized movement of people, equipment, or supplies by some form of transportation; *especially* : AIRLIFT

**lift·gate** \'lift-,gāt\ *noun* (1953)
**:** a rear panel (as on a station wagon) that opens upward

**lift·man** \-,man\ *noun* (1883)
*British* **:** an elevator operator

**lift·off** \'lif-,òf\ *noun* (circa 1956)
**:** a vertical takeoff by an aircraft or a rocket vehicle or missile

**lift truck** *noun* (1926)
**:** a small truck for lifting and transporting loads

**lig·a·ment** \'li-gə-mənt\ *noun* [Middle English, from Medieval Latin & Latin; Medieval Latin *ligamentum*, from Latin, band, tie, from *ligare*] (14th century)
**1 :** a tough band of tissue connecting the articular extremities of bones or supporting an organ in place
**2 :** a connecting or unifying bond ⟨the law of nations, the great *ligament* of mankind —Edmund Burke⟩
— **lig·a·men·tous** \-'men-təs\ *adjective*

**li·gand** \'li-gənd, 'lī-\ *noun* [Latin *ligandus*, gerundive of *ligare*] (1949)
**:** a group, ion, or molecule coordinated to a central atom or molecule in a complex

**li·gase** \'lī-,gās, -,gāz\ *noun* [International Scientific Vocabulary *lig-* (from Latin *ligare*) + *-ase*] (1961)
**:** SYNTHETASE

**li·gate** \'lī-,gāt, lī-'\ *transitive verb* **li·gat·ed; li·gat·ing** [Latin *ligatus*] (1599)
**:** to tie with a ligature

**li·ga·tion** \lī-'gā-shən\ *noun* (1597)
**1 :** an act of ligating
**2 :** something that binds : LIGATURE

**lig·a·ture** \'li-gə-,chùr, -chər, -,tùr, -,tyùr\ *noun* [Middle English, from Middle French, from Late Latin *ligatura*, from Latin *ligatus*, past participle of *ligare* to bind, tie; akin to Middle Low German *līk* band, boltrope, Albanian *lidh* I tie] (14th century)
**1 a :** something that is used to bind; *specifically* **:** a filament (as a thread) used in surgery
**b :** something that unites or connects : BOND
**2 :** the action of binding or tying
**3 :** a compound note in mensural notation indicating a group of musical notes to be sung to one syllable
**4 :** a printed or written character (as æ or ʄ) consisting of two or more letters or characters joined together

**¹light** \'līt\ *noun* [Middle English, from Old English *lēoht*; akin to Old High German *lioht* light, Latin *luc-, lux* light, *lucēre* to shine, Greek *leukos* white] (before 12th century)
**1 a :** something that makes vision possible **b :** the sensation aroused by stimulation of the visual receptors **c :** an electromagnetic radiation in the wavelength range including infrared, visible, ultraviolet, and X rays and traveling in a vacuum with a speed of about 186,281 miles (300,000 kilometers) per second; *specifically* **:** the part of this range that is visible to the human eye
**2 a :** DAYLIGHT **b :** DAWN
**3 :** a source of light: as **a :** a celestial body **b :** CANDLE **c :** an electric light
**4** *archaic* **:** SIGHT 4a
**5 a :** spiritual illumination **b :** INNER LIGHT **c :** ENLIGHTENMENT **d :** TRUTH
**6 a :** public knowledge ⟨facts brought to *light*⟩ **b :** a particular aspect or appearance presented to view ⟨saw the matter in a different *light*⟩
**7 :** a particular illumination
**8 :** something that enlightens or informs ⟨shed some *light* on the problem⟩
**9 :** a medium (as a window) through which light is admitted

**10** *plural* **:** a set of principles, standards, or opinions ⟨worship according to one's *lights* —Adrienne Koch⟩
**11 :** a noteworthy person in a particular place or field
**12 :** a particular expression of the eye
**13 a :** LIGHTHOUSE, BEACON **b :** TRAFFIC LIGHT
**14 :** the representation of light in art
**15 :** a flame for lighting something
— **in the light of 1 :** from the point of view of **2** *or* **in light of :** in view of

**²light** *adjective* (before 12th century)
**1 :** having light : BRIGHT ⟨a *light* airy room⟩
**2 a :** not dark, intense, or swarthy in color or coloring : PALE **b** *of colors* **:** medium in saturation and high in lightness ⟨*light* blue⟩
**3** *of coffee* **:** served with extra milk or cream

**³light** *verb* **lit** \'lit\ *or* **light·ed; light·ing** (before 12th century)
*intransitive verb*
**1 :** to become light : BRIGHTEN — usually used with *up* ⟨her face *lit* up⟩
**2 :** to take fire
**3 :** to ignite something (as a cigarette) — often used with *up*
*transitive verb*
**1 :** to set fire to
**2 a :** to conduct with a light : GUIDE **b :** ILLUMINATE ⟨rockets *light* up the sky⟩ **c :** ANIMATE, BRIGHTEN ⟨a smile *lit* up her face⟩

**⁴light** *adjective* [Middle English, from Old English *lēoht*; akin to Old High German *līhti* light, Latin *levis*, Greek *elachys* small] (before 12th century)
**1 a :** having little weight : not heavy **b :** designed to carry a comparatively small load ⟨a *light* truck⟩ **c :** having relatively little weight in proportion to bulk ⟨aluminum is a *light* metal⟩ **d :** containing less than the legal, standard, or usual weight ⟨a *light* coin⟩
**2 a :** of little importance : TRIVIAL **b :** not abundant ⟨*light* rain⟩ ⟨a *light* lunch⟩
**3 a :** easily disturbed ⟨a *light* sleeper⟩ **b :** exerting a minimum of force or pressure : GENTLE ⟨a *light* touch⟩ **c :** resulting from a very slight pressure : FAINT ⟨*light* print⟩
**4 a :** easily endurable ⟨a *light* illness⟩ **b :** requiring little effort ⟨*light* work⟩
**5 :** capable of moving swiftly or nimbly ⟨*light* on his feet⟩
**6 a :** FRIVOLOUS 1a ⟨*light* conduct⟩ **b :** lacking in stability : CHANGEABLE ⟨*light* opinions⟩ **c :** sexually promiscuous
**7 :** free from care : CHEERFUL
**8 :** less powerful but usually more mobile than usual for its kind ⟨*light* cavalry⟩
**9 a :** made with a lower calorie content or with less of some ingredient (as salt, fat, or alcohol) than usual ⟨*light* beer⟩ ⟨*light* salad dressing⟩ **b :** having a relatively mild flavor
**10 a :** easily digested ⟨a *light* soup⟩ **b :** well leavened ⟨a *light* crust⟩
**11 :** coarse and sandy or easily pulverized ⟨*light* soil⟩
**12 :** DIZZY, GIDDY ⟨felt *light* in the head⟩
**13 :** intended chiefly to entertain ⟨*light* verse⟩ ⟨*light* comedy⟩
**14 a :** carrying little or no cargo ⟨the ship returned *light*⟩ **b :** producing goods for direct consumption by the consumer ⟨*light* industry⟩
**15 :** not bearing a stress or accent ⟨a *light* syllable⟩
**16 :** having a clear soft quality ⟨a *light* voice⟩
**17 :** being in debt to the pot in a poker game ⟨three chips *light*⟩
**18 :** SHORT 5d ⟨*light* on experience⟩
*synonym* see EASY
— **light·ish** \'lī-tish\ *adjective*

**⁵light** *adverb* (before 12th century)
**1 :** LIGHTLY
**2 :** with little baggage ⟨travel *light*⟩

**⁶light** *intransitive verb* **lit** \'lit\ *or* **light·ed; light·ing** [Middle English, from Old English *līhtan*; akin to Old English *lēoht* light in weight] (before 12th century)
**1 :** DISMOUNT

**2 :** SETTLE, ALIGHT ⟨a bird *lit* on the lawn⟩
**3 :** to fall unexpectedly — usually used with *on* or *upon*
**4 :** to arrive by chance : HAPPEN — usually used with *on* or *upon* ⟨*lit* upon a solution⟩
— **light into :** to attack forcefully ⟨I *lit into* that food until I'd finished off the heel of the loaf —Helen Eustis⟩

**light adaptation** *noun* (1900)
**:** the process including contraction of the pupil and decrease in visual purple by which the eye adapts to conditions of increased illumination

**light–adapt·ed** \'līt-ə-,dap-təd\ *adjective* (1900)
**:** adjusted for vision in bright light : having undergone light adaptation

**light air** *noun* (circa 1881)
**:** wind having a speed of 1 to 3 miles (1.6 to 4.8 kilometers) per hour — see BEAUFORT SCALE table

**light bread** \'līt-,bred\ *noun* [²light] (1821)
*chiefly Southern & Midland* **:** bread in loaves made from white flour leavened with yeast

**light breeze** *noun* (circa 1881)
**:** wind having a speed of 4 to 7 miles (6.4 to 11 kilometers) per hour — see BEAUFORT SCALE table

**light–bulb** \'līt-,bəlb\ *noun* (1884)
**:** INCANDESCENT LAMP

**light chain** *noun* (1964)
**:** either of the two smaller of the four polypeptide chains comprising antibodies — compare HEAVY CHAIN

**light curve** *noun* (1890)
**:** a graph showing the variation in brightness of a celestial object (as a variable star) over a period of time

**light–emitting diode** *noun* (1970)
**:** LED

**¹light·en** \'līt-ᵊn\ *verb* **light·ened; light·en·ing** \'līt-niŋ, 'lī-t°n-iŋ\ [Middle English *lightenen*, from *light*] (14th century)
*transitive verb*
**1 :** to make light or clear : ILLUMINATE
**2** *archaic* **:** ENLIGHTEN
**3 :** to make (as a color) lighter
*intransitive verb*
**1 a** *archaic* **:** to shine brightly **b :** to grow lighter : BRIGHTEN
**2 :** to give out flashes of lightning
— **light·en·er** \'līt-nər, 'lī-t°n-ər\ *noun*

**²lighten** *verb* **light·ened; light·en·ing** \'līt-niŋ, 'lī-t°n-iŋ\ (14th century)
*transitive verb*
**1 a :** to relieve of a burden in whole or in part ⟨the news *lightened* his mind⟩ **b :** to reduce in weight or quantity : LESSEN ⟨*lighten* her duties⟩ **c :** to make less wearisome : ALLEVIATE ⟨*lighten* our sorrow⟩
**2 :** CHEER, GLADDEN
*intransitive verb*
**1 :** to become lighter or less burdensome
**2 :** to become more cheerful
*synonym* see RELIEVE
— **light·en·er** \'līt-nər, 'lī-t°n-ər\ *noun*

**lighten up** *intransitive verb* (circa 1968)
**:** to take things less seriously

**¹ligh·ter** \'lī-tər\ *noun* [Middle English, from (assumed) Middle Dutch *lichter*, from Middle Dutch *lichten* to unload; akin to Old English *lēoht* light in weight] (14th century)
**:** a large usually flat-bottomed barge used especially in unloading or loading ships

**²lighter** *transitive verb* (1840)
**:** to convey by a lighter

**³light·er** \'lī-tər\ *noun* (1553)
**1 :** one that lights or sets a fire
**2 :** a device for lighting a fire; *especially* **:** a mechanical or electrical device used for lighting cigarettes, cigars, or pipes

**ligh·ter·age** \'lī-tə-rij\ *noun* (15th century)
**1 :** the loading, unloading, or transportation of goods by means of a lighter
**2 :** a price paid for lightering

**lighter–than–air** *adjective* (1903)
**:** of less weight than the air displaced

**light·face** \'līt-ˌfās\ *noun* (circa 1871)
: a typeface having comparatively light thin lines; *also* : printing in lightface
— **light–faced** \-ˌfāst\ *adjective*

**light·fast** \-ˌfast\ *adjective* (1950)
: resistant to light and especially to sunlight; *especially* : colorfast to light
— **light–fast·ness** \-ˌfas(t)-nəs\ *noun*

**light–fin·gered** \-ˌfiŋ-gərd\ *adjective* (1547)
**1** : showing adroitness in stealing or a tendency to steal especially by picking pockets or shoplifting
**2** : having a light and dexterous touch : NIMBLE
— **light–fin·gered·ness** *noun*

**light–foot·ed** \-ˌfu̇-təd\ *also* **light–foot** \-ˌfu̇t\ *adjective* (15th century)
**1** : having a light and springy step
**2** : moving gracefully and nimbly

**light guide** *noun* (1951)
: an optical fiber used especially for telecommunication

**light–hand·ed** \'līt-ˌhan-dəd\ *adjective* (15th century)
: having a light or delicate touch : FACILE
— **light–hand·ed·ness** *noun*

**light–head·ed** \-ˌhe-dəd\ *adjective* (1537)
**1** : mentally disoriented : DIZZY
**2** : lacking in maturity or seriousness : FRIVOLOUS
— **light–head·ed·ly** *adverb*
— **light–head·ed·ness** *noun*

**light·heart·ed** \-ˌhär-təd\ *adjective* (15th century)
**1** : free from care, anxiety, or seriousness : GAY
**2** : cheerfully optimistic and hopeful : EASYGOING
— **light·heart·ed·ly** *adverb*
— **light·heart·ed·ness** *noun*

**light heavyweight** *noun* (1903)
: a boxer in a weight division having a maximum limit of 175 pounds for professionals and 178 pounds for amateurs — compare HEAVYWEIGHT, MIDDLEWEIGHT

**light·house** \'līt-ˌhau̇s\ *noun* (1622)
**1** : a structure (as a tower) with a powerful light that gives a continuous or intermittent signal to navigators
**2** : BEACON 3

**light housekeeping** *noun* (1904)
**1** : domestic work restricted to the less laborious duties
**2** : housekeeping in quarters with limited facilities for cooking

**light·ing** \'līt-iŋ\ *noun* (before 12th century)
**1 a** : ILLUMINATION **b** : IGNITION
**2** : an artificial supply of light or the apparatus providing it

**light·less** \'līt-ləs\ *adjective* (before 12th century)
**1** : receiving no light : DARK
**2** : giving no light

**light·ly** \'līt-lē\ *adverb* (before 12th century)
: in a light manner: as **a** : with little weight or force : GENTLY **b** : with indifference or carelessness : UNCONCERNEDLY ⟨the problem should not be passed over *lightly* —Shelly Halpern⟩ **c** : with little difficulty : EASILY **d** : GAILY, CHEERFULLY **e** : in an agile manner : NIMBLY, SWIFTLY **f** : in a small degree or amount ⟨*lightly* salted food⟩

**light meter** *noun* (1921)
: a small and often portable device for measuring illumination; *especially* : EXPOSURE METER

**light–mind·ed** \'līt-ˌmīn-dəd\ *adjective* (1611)
: lacking in seriousness : FRIVOLOUS
— **light–mind·ed·ly** *adverb*
— **light–mind·ed·ness** *noun*

**¹light·ness** \-nəs\ *noun* (before 12th century)
**1** : the quality or state of being illuminated : ILLUMINATION
**2** : the attribute of object colors by which the object appears to reflect or transmit more or less of the incident light — compare BRIGHTNESS 2, HUE 2c, SATURATION 4

**²lightness** *noun* (12th century)
**1** : the quality or state of being light especially in weight
**2** : lack of seriousness and stability of character often accompanied by casual heedlessness
**3 a** : the quality or state of being nimble **b** : an ease and gaiety of style or manner
**4** : a lack of weightiness or force : DELICACY

**¹light·ning** \'līt-niŋ\ *noun* [Middle English, from gerund of *lightenen* to lighten] (13th century)
**1** : the flashing of light produced by a discharge of atmospheric electricity; *also* : the discharge itself
**2** : a sudden stroke of fortune

**²lightning** *adjective* (1640)
: having or moving with or as if with the speed and suddenness of lightning ⟨a *lightning* assault⟩

**³lightning** *intransitive verb* **light·ninged; lightning** (1903)
: to discharge a flash of lightning

**lightning arrester** *noun* (1860)
: a device for protecting an electrical apparatus from damage by lightning

**lightning bug** *noun* (1778)
: FIREFLY

**lightning rod** *noun* (1789)
**1** : a grounded metallic rod set up on a structure (as a building) to protect it from lightning
**2** : one that serves to divert attack from another or as a frequent target of criticism

**light–o'–love** \ˌlīt-ə-ˈləv\ *also* **light–of–love** \-əv-'\ *noun, plural* **light–o'–loves** *also* **lights–of–love** (1589)
**1** : PROSTITUTE
**2** : LOVER, PARAMOUR

**light opera** *noun* (1882)
: OPERETTA

**light out** *intransitive verb* [⁶light] (1866)
**1** : to leave in a hurry ⟨*lit out* for home at once⟩
**2** : SET OFF

**light pen** *noun* (1958)
: a pen-shaped device for direct interaction with a computer through a cathode-ray tube display

**light pipe** *noun* (1950)
: an optical fiber or a solid transparent plastic rod for transmitting light lengthwise

**light·plane** \'līt-ˈplān\ *noun* (1923)
: a small and comparatively lightweight airplane; *especially* : a privately owned passenger airplane

**light pollution** *noun* (1971)
: artificial skylight (as from city lights) that interferes with astronomical observations

**light·proof** \'līt-ˌprüf\ *adjective* (1923)
: impenetrable by light

**light quantum** *noun* (1925)
: PHOTON; *especially* : one of luminous radiation

**light–rail** \'līt-ˌrā(ə)l\ *noun, often attributive* (1975)
: a means of urban railway transportation using trolley cars

**light reaction** *noun* (circa 1929)
: the phase of photosynthesis that requires the presence of light and that involves photophosphorylation

**lights** \'līts\ *noun plural* [Middle English *lightes*, from *light* light in weight] (12th century)
: the lungs especially of a slaughtered animal

**light·ship** \'līt-ˌship\ *noun* (1837)
: a ship equipped with a brilliant light and moored at a place dangerous to navigation

**light show** *noun* (1966)
: a kaleidoscopic display of colored lights, slides, and film loops

**¹light·some** \'līt-səm\ *adjective* (14th century)
**1** : free from care : LIGHTHEARTED
**2** : AIRY, NIMBLE
— **light·some·ly** *adverb*
— **light·some·ness** *noun*

**²lightsome** *adjective* (15th century)
**1** : well lighted : BRIGHT
**2** : giving light

**lights–out** \'līts-ˈau̇t\ *noun* (1868)
**1** : a command or signal for putting out lights
**2** : a prescribed bedtime for persons living under discipline

**light table** *noun* (circa 1948)
: a device that projects even light through a flat translucent surface over which films or tracings may be spread out and viewed

**light–tight** \'līt-ˌtīt\ *adjective* (1884)
: LIGHTPROOF

**light trap** *noun* (1906)
**1** : a device that allows movement of a sliding part or passage of a person (as into a darkroom) but excludes light
**2** : a device for collecting or destroying insects that consists of a bright light in association with a trapping or killing medium

**light water** *noun* (1933)
: WATER 1a — compare HEAVY WATER

**¹light·weight** \'līt-ˌwāt\ *noun* (1773)
**1** : one of less than average weight; *specifically* : a boxer in a weight division having a maximum limit of 135 pounds for professionals and 132 pounds for amateurs
**2** : one of little consequence or ability ⟨shows up its author as a *lightweight* —C. J. Rolo⟩

**²lightweight** *adjective* (1809)
**1** : lacking in earnestness, ability, or profundity : INCONSEQUENTIAL
**2** : having less than average weight
**3** : of, relating to, or characteristic of a lightweight ⟨the *lightweight* championship⟩

**light·wood** \'līt-ˌwu̇d, 'lī-təd\ *noun* (1685)
*chiefly Southern* : wood used for kindling; *especially* : coniferous wood abounding in pitch

**light–year** \'līt-ˌyir\ *noun* (1888)
**1** : a unit of length in astronomy equal to the distance that light travels in one year in a vacuum or about 5.88 trillion miles (9.46 trillion kilometers)
**2** : an extremely large measure of comparison (as of distance, time, or quality) ⟨seems like *light-years* ago⟩ ⟨has *light-years* more talent⟩ ⟨two minutes and yet *light-years* away from the crowded village —Suzanne Patterson⟩ ∎

**lign–** *or* **ligni–** *or* **ligno–** *combining form* [Latin *lign-, ligni-,* from *lignum*]
: wood ⟨*lignin*⟩ ⟨*lignocellulose*⟩

**lig·ne·ous** \'lig-nē-əs\ *adjective* [Latin *ligneus,* from *lignum* wood, probably from *legere* to gather — more at LEGEND] (1626)
: of or resembling wood

**lig·ni·fy** \'lig-nə-ˌfī\ *verb* **-fied; -fy·ing** [French *lignifier,* from Latin *lignum*] (circa 1828)
*transitive verb*
: to convert into wood or woody tissue

---

□ USAGE

**light–year** Although some commentators insist that *light-year* is a measure of distance only—literal or figurative—and not a measure of time, there is evidence that in general (though, not scientific) prose it is fairly commonly used for time ⟨cramming a . . . *light-year's* thought into three calendar months —Flann O'Brien⟩ ⟨events and circumstances that had seemed *light-years* gone —Brent Staples⟩ ⟨it seems more like a thousand days, and a *light-year* since Father died —James Clavell⟩ ⟨a thousand *light-years* ago, I thought —Dick Francis⟩. This extension of meaning should cause no surprise: how many people think of *year* as denoting distance?

---

*intransitive verb*
**:** to become wood or woody
— **lig·ni·fi·ca·tion** \ˌlig-nə-fə-ˈkā-shən\ *noun*

**lig·nin** \ˈlig-nən\ *noun* (1822)
**:** an amorphous polymer related to cellulose that provides rigidity and together with cellulose forms the woody cell walls of plants and the cementing material between them

**lig·nite** \ˈlig-ˌnīt\ *noun* [French, from Latin *lignum*] (circa 1808)
**:** a usually brownish black coal intermediate between peat and bituminous coal; *especially* **:** one in which the texture of the original wood is distinct — called also *brown coal*
— **lig·nit·ic** \lig-ˈni-tik\ *adjective*

**lig·no·cel·lu·lose** \ˌlig-nō-ˈsel-yə-ˌlōs, -ˌlōz\ *noun* [International Scientific Vocabulary] (1900)
**:** any of several closely related substances constituting the essential part of woody cell walls of plants and consisting of cellulose intimately associated with lignin
— **lig·no·cel·lu·los·ic** \-ˌsel-yə-ˈlō-sik, -zik\ *adjective*

**lig·no·sul·fo·nate** \-ˈsəl-fə-ˌnāt\ *noun* (1908)
**:** any of various compounds produced from the spent sulfite liquor in the pulping of softwood in papermaking and used especially for binders and dispersing agents

**lig·num vi·tae** \ˌlig-nəm-ˈvī-tē\ *noun, plural* **lignum vitaes** [New Latin, literally, wood of life] (1594)
**1 :** the very hard heavy wood of any of several tropical American guaiacums
**2 :** a tree yielding lignum vitae

**lig·u·la** \ˈli-gyə-lə\ *noun, plural* **-lae** \-ˌlē, -ˌlī\ *also* **-las** [New Latin] (circa 1760)
**1 :** LIGULE
**2 :** the distal lobed part of the labium of an insect

**lig·u·late** \ˈli-gyə-lət, -ˌlāt\ *adjective* (1760)
**1 :** furnished with ligules, ligulae, or ligulate corollas
**2** [Latin *ligula*] **:** shaped like a strap ⟨*ligulate* corolla of a ray flower⟩

**lig·ule** \ˈli-(ˌ)gyü(ə)l\ *noun* [New Latin *ligula*, from Latin, small tongue, strap, from *lingere* to lick — more at LICK] (circa 1847)
**:** a scalelike projection especially on a plant: as **a :** a thin appendage of a foliage leaf and especially of the sheath of a blade of grass **b :** a ligulate corolla of a ray floret in a composite head

**lig·ure** \ˈli-ˌgyùr, -gyər\ *noun* [Middle English *lygire*, from Late Latin *ligurius*, from Greek *ligyrion*] (13th century)
**:** a traditional precious stone that is probably the jacinth

**lik·able** *or* **like·able** \ˈlī-kə-bəl\ *adjective* (1730)
**:** having qualities that bring about a favorable regard **:** PLEASANT, AGREEABLE
— **lik·abil·i·ty** \ˌlī-kə-ˈbi-lə-tē\ *noun*
— **lik·able·ness** *noun*

**¹like** \ˈlīk\ *verb* **liked; lik·ing** [Middle English, from Old English *līcian*; akin to Old English *gelīc* alike] (before 12th century)
*transitive verb*
**1** *chiefly dialect* **:** to be suitable or agreeable to ⟨I like onions but they don't like me⟩
**2 a :** to feel attraction toward or take pleasure in **:** ENJOY ⟨*likes* baseball⟩ **b :** to feel toward **:** REGARD ⟨how would you *like* a change⟩
**3 :** to wish to have **:** WANT ⟨would *like* a drink⟩
**4 :** to do well in ⟨this plant *likes* dry soil⟩ ⟨my car does not *like* cold weather⟩
*intransitive verb*
**1** *dialect* **:** APPROVE
**2 :** to feel inclined **:** CHOOSE, PREFER ⟨leave any time you *like*⟩

**²like** *noun* (1851)
**1 :** LIKING, PREFERENCE
**2 :** something that one likes

**³like** *adjective* [Middle English, alteration of *ilich*, from Old English *gelīc* like, alike, from

*ge-*, associative prefix + *līc* body; akin to Old High German *gilīh* like, alike, Lithuanian *lygus* like — more at CO-] (13th century)
**1 a :** the same or nearly the same (as in appearance, character, or quantity) ⟨suits of *like* design⟩ — formerly used with *as, unto, of* ⟨it behoved him to be made *like* unto his brethren —Hebrews 2:17(Authorized Version)⟩ **b** *chiefly British* **:** closely resembling the subject or original ⟨the portrait is very *like*⟩
**2 :** LIKELY ⟨the importance of statistics as the one discipline *like* to give accuracy of mind —H. J. Laski⟩

**⁴like** *preposition* (13th century)
**1 a :** having the characteristics of **:** similar to ⟨his house is *like* a barn⟩ ⟨it's *like* when we were kids⟩ **b :** typical of ⟨was *like* him to do that⟩ **c :** comparable to **:** APPROXIMATING ⟨costs something *like* fifty cents⟩
**2 :** in the manner of **:** similarly to ⟨acts *like* a fool⟩
**3 :** as though there would be ⟨looks *like* rain⟩
**4 :** such as ⟨a subject *like* physics⟩
**5** — used to form intensive or ironic phrases ⟨fought *like* hell⟩ ⟨*like* fun he did⟩ ⟨laughed *like* anything⟩

**⁵like** *noun* (13th century)
**1 a :** one that is similar **:** COUNTERPART, EQUAL ⟨have . . . never seen the like before —Sir Winston Churchill⟩ **b :** KIND 4a ⟨put him and his *like* to some job —J. R. R. Tolkien⟩ — used with *the* and often followed by *of* and a substantive, or with a preceding possessive
**2 :** one of many that are similar to each other — used chiefly in proverbial expressions ⟨*like* breeds like⟩
— **and the like :** ET CETERA
— **the likes of 1 :** such people as **:** such things as ⟨reads *the likes of* Austen and Browning⟩ **2 :** such a one as and perhaps others similar to — often used with a singular object and usually with disparaging overtones ⟨have no use for *the likes of* you⟩

**⁶like** *adverb* (14th century)
**1** *archaic* **:** EQUALLY
**2 :** LIKELY, PROBABLY ⟨you'll try it, some day, *like* enough —Mark Twain⟩
**3 a :** to some extent **:** RATHER, ALTOGETHER ⟨saunter over nonchalantly *like* —Walter Karig⟩ **b** — used interjectionally in informal speech often to emphasize a word or phrase (as in "He was, *like*, gorgeous") or for an apologetic, vague, or unassertive effect (as in "I need to, like, borrow some money")
**4 :** NEARLY **:** APPROXIMATELY ⟨the actual interest is more *like* 18 percent⟩ — used interjectionally in informal speech with expressions of measurement ⟨it was, like, five feet long⟩ ⟨goes there every day, *like*⟩
— **as like as not** *or* **like as not :** PROBABLY

**⁷like** *conjunction* (14th century)
**1 a :** AS IF ⟨middle-aged men who looked *like* they might be out for their one night of the year —Norman Mailer⟩ **b** — used in intensive phrases ⟨drove *like* mad⟩ ⟨hurts *like* crazy⟩
**2 :** in the same way that **:** AS ⟨they raven down scenery *like* children do sweetmeats —John Keats⟩
**3 a :** in the way or manner that ⟨the violin sounds *like* an old masterpiece should⟩ ⟨did it *like* you told me⟩ **b** — used interjectionally in informal speech often with the verb *be* to introduce a quotation, paraphrase, or thought expressed by or imputed to the subject of the verb, or with *it's* to report a generally held opinion ⟨so I'm *like*, "Give me a break"⟩ ⟨it's *like*, "Who cares what he thinks?"⟩
**4 :** such as ⟨a bag *like* a doctor carries⟩ ⟨when your car has trouble — *like* when it won't start⟩ — used interjectionally in informal speech ⟨often stays up late, until *like* three in the morning⟩ ∎

**⁸like** *or* **liked** \ˈlīkt\ *verbal auxiliary* (15th century)

*chiefly dialect* **:** came near **:** was near ⟨so loud I *like* to fell out of bed —Helen Eustis⟩

**-like** *adjective combining form*
**:** resembling or characteristic of ⟨bell-*like*⟩ ⟨lady*like*⟩

**like·li·hood** \ˈlī-klē-ˌhùd\ *noun* (14th century)
**:** PROBABILITY ⟨a strong *likelihood* that he is correct —T. D. Anderson⟩

**¹like·ly** \ˈlī-klē\ *adjective* **like·li·er; -est** [Middle English, from Old Norse *glīkligr*, from *glīkr* like; akin to Old English *gelīc*] (14th century)
**1 :** having a high probability of occurring or being true **:** very probable ⟨rain is *likely* today⟩
**2 :** apparently qualified **:** SUITABLE ⟨a *likely* place⟩
**3 :** RELIABLE, CREDIBLE ⟨a *likely* enough story⟩
**4 :** PROMISING ⟨a *likely* candidate⟩
**5 :** ATTRACTIVE ⟨a *likely* child⟩

**²likely** *adverb* (14th century)
**:** in all probability **:** PROBABLY ⟨those who seek power will most *likely* wind up exercising it —Halton Arp⟩

**like–mind·ed** \ˈlīk-ˈmīn-dəd\ *adjective* (1526)
**:** having a like disposition or purpose **:** of the same mind or habit of thought
— **like–mind·ed·ly** *adverb*
— **like–mind·ed·ness** *noun*

**lik·en** \ˈlī-kən\ *transitive verb* **lik·ened; lik·en·ing** \ˈlī-kə-niŋ, ˈlīk-niŋ\ (14th century)
**:** COMPARE

**like·ness** \ˈlīk-nəs\ *noun* (before 12th century)
**1 :** COPY, PORTRAIT
**2 :** APPEARANCE, SEMBLANCE
**3 :** the quality or state of being like **:** RESEMBLANCE ☆

**like·wise** \ˈlīk-ˌwīz\ *adverb* (15th century)
**1 :** in like manner **:** SIMILARLY ⟨go and do *likewise*⟩

---

☆ SYNONYMS
**Likeness, similarity, resemblance, similitude, analogy** mean agreement or correspondence in details. LIKENESS implies a closer correspondence than SIMILARITY which often implies that things are merely somewhat alike ⟨a remarkable *likeness* to his late father⟩ ⟨some *similarity* between the two cases⟩. RESEMBLANCE implies similarity chiefly in appearance or external qualities ⟨statements that bear little *resemblance* to the truth⟩. SIMILITUDE applies chiefly to correspondence between abstractions ⟨two schools of social thought showing points of *similitude*⟩. ANALOGY implies likeness or parallelism in relations rather than in appearance or qualities ⟨pointed out *analogies* to past wars⟩.

---

□ USAGE
**like** *Like* has been used as a conjunction since the 14th century. In the 14th, 15th, and 16th centuries it was used in serious literature, but not often; in the 17th and 18th centuries it grew more frequent but less literary. It became markedly more frequent in literary use again in the 19th century. By mid-century it was coming under critical fire, but not from grammarians, oddly enough, who were wrangling over whether it could be called a preposition or not. There is no doubt that, after 600 years of use, conjunctive *like* is firmly established. It has been used by many prestigious literary figures of the past, though perhaps not in their most elevated works; in modern use it may be found in literature, journalism, and scholarly writing. While the present objection to it is perhaps more heated than rational, someone writing in a formal prose style may well prefer to use *as, as if, such as,* or an entirely different construction instead.

**2** : in addition

**3** : similarly so with me ⟨answered "*likewise*" to "Pleased to meet you"⟩

**lik·ing** \'lī-kiŋ\ *noun* (14th century)
: favorable regard ⟨FONDNESS, TASTE ⟨had a greater *liking* for law —E. M. Coulter⟩ ⟨took a *liking* to the newcomer⟩

**li·ku·ta** \li-'kü-tə\ *noun, plural* **ma·ku·ta** \mä-\ [of Bantu origin] (1967)
— see *zaire* at MONEY table

**li·lac** \'lī-,läk, -,lak, -lək\ *noun* [obsolete French (now *lilas*), from Arabic *līlak*, from Persian *nīlak* bluish, from *nīl* blue, from Sanskrit *nīla* dark blue] (1625)
**1 a** : a European shrub (*Syringa vulgaris*) of the olive family that is often an escape in North America and has cordate ovate leaves and large panicles of fragrant pink-purple or white flowers **b** : a tree or shrub congeneric with the lilac
**2** : a variable color averaging a moderate purple

**lil·an·ge·ni** \,li-lən-'ge-nē\ *noun, plural* **em·a·lan·ge·ni** \,e-mə-lən-'ge-nē\ [Swazi] (circa 1976)
— see MONEY table

**lil·ied** \'li-lēd\ *adjective* (1614)
**1** *archaic* : resembling a lily in fairness
**2** : full of or covered with lilies

**Lil·ith** \'li-ləth\ *noun* [Late Hebrew *līlīth*, from Hebrew, a female demon]
**1** : a female figure who in rabbinic legend is Adam's first wife, is supplanted by Eve, and becomes an evil spirit
**2** : a famous witch in medieval demonology

**Lil·li·put** \'li-li-(,)pət\ *noun*
: an island in Swift's *Gulliver's Travels* where the inhabitants are six inches tall

**lil·li·pu·tian** \,li-lə-'pyü-shən\ *adjective, often capitalized* (1726)
**1** : of, relating to, or characteristic of the Lilliputians or the island of Lilliput
**2 a** : SMALL, MINIATURE **b** : PETTY

**Lilliputian** *noun*
**1** : an inhabitant of Lilliput
**2** *often not capitalized* : one resembling a Lilliputian; *especially* : an undersized individual

**¹lilt** \'lilt\ *noun* (circa 1680)
**1** : a spirited and usually cheerful song or tune
**2** : a rhythmical swing, flow, or cadence
**3** : a springy buoyant movement

**²lilt** *verb* [Middle English *lulten* to sound an alarm] (1722)
*transitive verb*
: to sing or play in a lively cheerful manner
*intransitive verb*
**1** : to sing or speak rhythmically and with fluctuating pitch
**2** : to move in a lively springy manner

**lilt·ing** \'lil-tiŋ\ *adjective* (1800)
**1** : characterized by a rhythmical swing or cadence ⟨a *lilting* stride⟩
**2** : CHEERFUL, BUOYANT ⟨a *lilting* comedy⟩
— **lilt·ing·ly** \-lē\ *adverb*
— **lilt·ing·ness** *noun*

**¹lily** \'li-lē\ *noun, plural* **lil·ies** [Middle English *lilie*, from Old English, from Latin *lilium*] (before 12th century)
**1** : any of a genus (*Lilium* of the family Liliaceae, the lily family) of erect perennial leafy-stemmed bulbous herbs that are native to the northern hemisphere and are widely cultivated for their showy flowers; *broadly* : any of various plants of the lily family or of the related amaryllis or iris families
**2** : any of various plants with showy flowers: as **a** : a scarlet anemone (*Anemone coronaria*) of the Mediterranean region **b** : WATER LILY **c** : CALLA LILY
**3** : FLEUR-DE-LIS 2

**²lily** *adjective* (circa 1553)
: resembling a lily in fairness, purity, or fragility ⟨my lady's *lily* hand —John Keats⟩

**lily-liv·ered** \'li-lē-'li-vərd\ *adjective* (1605)
: lacking courage : COWARDLY ◆

**lily of the valley** (1563)
: a low perennial herb (*Convallaria majalis*) of the lily family that has usually two large oblong lanceolate leaves and a raceme of fragrant nodding bell-shaped white flowers

**lily pad** *noun* (1814)
: a floating leaf of a water lily

**¹lily-white** \'li-lē-'hwīt, -'wīt\ *adjective* (14th century)
**1** : white as a lily
**2** : characterized by or favoring the exclusion of blacks especially from politics
**3** : IRREPROACHABLE, PURE

**²lily-white** *noun* (circa 1903)
: a member of a lily-white political organization

**Li·ma** \'lē-mə\ (circa 1952)
— a communications code word for the letter *l*

**li·ma bean** \'lī-mə-\ *noun* [*Lima*, Peru] (1756)
**1 a** : a bushy or tall-growing tropical American bean (*Phaseolus limensis*) that is widely cultivated for its flat edible usually pale green or whitish seeds **b** : SIEVA BEAN
**2** : the seed of a lima bean

**li·ma·çon** \,lē-mə-'sōⁿ\ *noun* [French, literally, snail, from Old French, diminutive of *limaz* slug, snail, from Latin *limax;* akin to Russian *slimak* snail and probably to Old English *līm* birdlime — more at LIME] (1874)
: a curve that is the locus of a variable point on a line as the line revolves about a fixed point of intersection with a circle while the variable point is always a fixed distance along the line from its second and variable point of intersection with the circle

**¹limb** \'lim\ *noun* [Middle English *lim*, from Old English; akin to Old Norse *limr* limb and perhaps to Old English *lith* limb] (before 12th century)
**1 a** : one of the projecting paired appendages (as wings) of an animal body used especially for movement and grasping but sometimes modified into sensory or sexual organs **b** : a leg or arm of a human being
**2** : a large primary branch of a tree
**3** : an active member or agent
**4** : EXTENSION, BRANCH
**5** : a mischievous child
— **limb·less** \'lim-ləs\ *adjective*
— **limby** \'li-mē\ *adjective*
— **out on a limb** : in an exposed or dangerous position with little chance of retreat

**²limb** *transitive verb* (1674)
**1** : DISMEMBER
**2** : to cut off the limbs of (a felled tree)

**³limb** *noun* [Latin *limbus* border] (circa 1677)
**1** : the outer edge of the apparent disk of a celestial body
**2** : the expanded portion of an organ or structure; *especially* : the spreading upper portion of a gamopetalous corolla as distinguished from the lower tubular portion

**lim·ba** \'lim-bə\ *noun* [origin unknown] (1943)
**1** : a tall whitish-trunked West African tree (*Terminalia superba*) with straight-grained wood
**2** : the wood of a limba

**lim·beck** \'lim-,bek\ *noun* [Middle English *lembike*, from Medieval Latin *alembicum*] (14th century)
: ALEMBIC

**limbed** \'limd\ *adjective* (14th century)
: having limbs especially of a specified kind or number — usually used in combination ⟨strong-*limbed*⟩

**¹lim·ber** \'lim-bər\ *noun* [Middle English *lymour*] (15th century)
: a two-wheeled vehicle to which a gun or caisson may be attached

**²limber** *adjective* [origin unknown] (1565)
**1** : capable of being shaped : FLEXIBLE
**2** : having a supple and resilient quality (as of mind or body) : AGILE, NIMBLE
— **lim·ber·ly** *adverb*
— **lim·ber·ness** *noun*

**³limber** *verb* **lim·bered; lim·ber·ing** \-b(ə-)riŋ\ (1748)
*transitive verb*
: to cause to become limber ⟨*limber* up his fingers⟩
*intransitive verb*
: to become limber ⟨*limber* up by running⟩

**lim·bic** \'lim-bik\ *adjective* [New Latin *limbicus* of a border or margin, from Latin *limbus*] (1882)
: of, relating to, or being the limbic system of the brain

**limbic system** *noun* (1952)
: a group of subcortical structures (as the hypothalamus, the hippocampus, and the amygdala) of the brain that are concerned especially with emotion and motivation

**¹lim·bo** \'lim-(,)bō\ *noun, plural* **limbos** [Middle English, from Medieval Latin, ablative of *limbus* limbo, from Latin, border] (14th century)
**1** *often capitalized* : an abode of souls that are according to Roman Catholic theology barred from heaven because of not having received Christian baptism
**2 a** : a place or state of restraint or confinement **b** : a place or state of neglect or oblivion ⟨proposals kept in *limbo*⟩ **c** : an intermediate or transitional place or state **d** : a state of uncertainty

**²limbo** *noun, plural* **limbos** [English of Trinidad & Barbados; akin to Jamaican English *limba* to bend, from English ³*limber*] (circa 1950)
: a West Indian acrobatic dance originally for men that involves bending over backwards and passing under a horizontal pole lowered slightly for each successive pass

**Lim·burg·er** \'lim-,bər-gər\ *noun* [Flemish, one from Limburg, from *Limburg,* Belgium] (1817)
: a pungent semisoft surface-ripened cheese

**lim·bus** \'lim-bəs\ *noun* [Latin, border] (1877)
: the marginal region of the cornea of the eye by which it is continuous with the sclera

**¹lime** \'līm\ *noun* [Middle English, from Old English *līm;* akin to Old High German *līm* birdlime, Latin *limus* mud, slime, and perhaps to Latin *linere* to smear] (before 12th century)
**1** : BIRDLIME
**2 a** : a caustic highly infusible solid that consists of calcium oxide often together with magnesium oxide, that is obtained by calcining forms of calcium carbonate (as shells or limestone), and that is used in building (as in mortar and plaster) and in agriculture — called also *quicklime* **b** : a dry white powder consisting essentially of calcium hydroxide that is made by treating quicklime with water **c** : CALCIUM ⟨carbonate of *lime*⟩

◇ WORD HISTORY
**lily-livered** The basis of the word *lily-livered* lies in the former belief that a person's health and temperament are the product of a balance or imbalance of four bodily fluids, or humors: blood, phlegm, black bile, and yellow bile. It was thought that a deficiency of yellow bile or choler, the humor that governed anger, spirit, and courage, would leave a person's liver colorless or white. Someone with this deficiency, and so white-livered, would be spiritless and a coward. *Lily-livered* and *white-livered* have been used synonymously since the 16th century; but *lily-livered,* probably because of its alliteration, is now the more common expression. See in addition CHOLERA, HUMOR.

\ə\ abut \ᵊ\ kitten \ər\ further \a\ ash \ā\ ace
\ä\ mop, mar \au̇\ out \ch\ chin \e\ bet \ē\ easy
\g\ go \i\ hit \ī\ ice \j\ job \ŋ\ sing \ō\ go
\ȯ\ law \ȯi\ boy \th\ thin \t̷h\ the \ü\ loot \u̇\ foot
\y\ yet \zh\ vision *see also* Guide to Pronunciation

²**lime** *transitive verb* **limed; lim·ing** (13th century)
**1 :** to smear with a sticky substance (as birdlime)
**2 :** to entangle with or as if with birdlime
**3 :** to treat or cover with lime ⟨*lime* the lawn in the spring⟩

³**lime** *adjective* (15th century)
**:** of, relating to, or containing lime or limestone

⁴**lime** *noun* [alteration of Middle English *lind*, from Old English; akin to Old High German *linta* linden] (1625)
**:** LINDEN 1a

⁵**lime** *noun* [French, from Spanish *lima*, from Arabic *līma, līm*] (1638)
**1 :** the small globose yellowish green fruit of a lime with an acid juicy pulp used as a flavoring agent and as a source of vitamin C
**2 :** a spiny tropical citrus tree (*Citrus aurantifolia*) with elliptical oblong narrowly winged leaves

**lime·ade** \ˌlīm-'ād, 'lī-ˌmād\ *noun* (1892)
**:** a beverage of sweetened lime juice mixed with plain or carbonated water

**lime glass** *noun* (circa 1909)
**:** glass containing a substantial proportion of lime

**lime–juic·er** \'līm-ˌjü-sər\ *noun* [from the use of lime juice on British ships as a beverage to prevent scurvy] (1859)
**1** *slang* **:** ENGLISHMAN
**2** *slang* **a :** a British ship **b :** a British sailor

**lime·kiln** \-ˌkil, -ˌkiln\ *noun* (13th century)
**:** a kiln or furnace for reducing limestone or shells to lime by burning

¹**lime·light** \-ˌlīt\ *noun* (1826)
**1 a :** a stage lighting instrument producing illumination by means of an oxyhydrogen flame directed on a cylinder of lime and usually equipped with a lens to concentrate the light in a beam **b :** the white light produced by such an instrument **c** *British* **:** SPOTLIGHT
**2 :** the center of public attention

²**limelight** *transitive verb* (1909)
**:** to center attention on **:** SPOTLIGHT

**li·men** \'lī-mən\ *noun* [Latin *limin-, limen* transverse beam in a door frame, threshold; probably akin to Latin *limus* transverse] (1895)
**:** THRESHOLD 3a

**lim·er·ick** \'li-mə-rik, 'lim-rik\ *noun* [*Limerick*, Ireland] (1896)
**:** a light or humorous verse form of 5 chiefly anapestic verses of which lines 1, 2, and 5 are of 3 feet and lines 3 and 4 are of 2 feet with a rhyme scheme of *aabba*

**lime·stone** \'līm-ˌstōn\ *noun* (14th century)
**:** a rock that is formed chiefly by accumulation of organic remains (as shells or coral), consists mainly of calcium carbonate, is extensively used in building, and yields lime when burned

**lime–twig** \'līm-ˌtwig\ *noun* (15th century)
**1 :** a twig covered with birdlime to catch birds
**2 :** SNARE

**lime–wa·ter** \-ˌwȯ-tər, -ˌwä-\ *noun* (circa 1500)
**:** an alkaline water solution of calcium hydroxide used as an antacid

¹**lim·ey** \'lī-mē\ *noun, plural* **limeys** *often capitalized* [*lime*-juicer + ⁴-*y*] (1918)
**1** *slang* **:** a British sailor
**2** *slang* **:** ENGLISHMAN

²**limey** *variant of* LIMY

**lim·i·nal** \'li-mə-n°l\ *adjective* [Latin *limin-, limen* threshold] (1884)
**1 :** of or relating to a sensory threshold
**2 :** barely perceptible

¹**lim·it** \'li-mət\ *noun* [Middle English, from Middle French *limite*, from Latin *limit-, limes* boundary] (14th century)
**1 a :** something that bounds, restrains, or confines **b :** the utmost extent

**2 a :** a geographical or political boundary **b** *plural* **:** the place enclosed within a boundary **:** BOUNDS
**3 :** LIMITATION
**4 :** a determining feature or differentia in logic
**5 :** a prescribed maximum or minimum amount, quantity, or number: as **a :** the maximum quantity of game or fish that may be taken legally in a specified period **b :** a maximum established for a gambling bet, raise, or payoff
**6 a :** a number whose numerical difference from a mathematical function is arbitrarily small for all values of the independent variables that are sufficiently close to but not equal to given prescribed numbers or that are sufficiently large positively or negatively **b :** a number that for an infinite sequence of numbers is such that ultimately each of the remaining terms of the sequence differs from this number by less than any given positive amount
**7 :** something that is exasperating or intolerable
— **lim·it·less** \-ləs\ *adjective*
— **lim·it·less·ly** *adverb*
— **lim·it·less·ness** *noun*

²**limit** *transitive verb* (14th century)
**1 :** to assign certain limits to **:** PRESCRIBE ⟨reserved the right to *limit* use of the land⟩
**2 a :** to restrict the bounds or limits of ⟨the specialist can no longer *limit* himself to his specialty⟩ **b :** to curtail or reduce in quantity or extent ⟨we must *limit* the power of aggressors⟩ ☆
— **lim·it·able** \-mə-tə-bəl\ *adjective*
— **lim·it·er** *noun*

**lim·i·tary** \'li-mə-ˌter-ē\ *adjective* (1620)
**1** *archaic* **:** subject to limits
**2 a** *archaic* **:** of or relating to a boundary **b :** LIMITING, ENCLOSING

**lim·i·ta·tion** \ˌli-mə-'tā-shən\ *noun* (14th century)
**1 :** an act or instance of limiting
**2 :** the quality or state of being limited
**3 :** something that limits **:** RESTRAINT
**4 :** a certain period limited by statute after which actions, suits, or prosecutions cannot be brought in the courts
— **lim·i·ta·tion·al** \-shnəl, -shə-n°l\ *adjective*

**lim·i·ta·tive** \'li-mə-ˌtā-tiv\ *adjective* (1530)
**:** LIMITING, RESTRICTIVE

**lim·it·ed** *adjective* (1610)
**1 a :** confined within limits **:** RESTRICTED ⟨*limited* success⟩ **b** *of a train* **:** offering faster service especially by making a limited number of stops
**2 :** characterized by enforceable limitations prescribed (as by a constitution) upon the scope or exercise of powers ⟨a *limited* monarchy⟩
**3 :** lacking breadth and originality ⟨a bit *limited*; a bit thick in the head —Virginia Woolf⟩
— **lim·it·ed·ly** *adverb*
— **lim·it·ed·ness** *noun*

**limited–access** *adjective* (1944)
*of a road* **:** having access restricted to a relatively small number of points

**limited edition** *noun* (1903)
**:** an issue of something collectible (as books, prints, or medals) that is advertised to be limited to a relatively small number of copies

**limited liability** *noun* (1855)
**:** liability (as of a stockholder or shipowner) limited by statute or treaty

**limited partner** *noun* (1907)
**:** a partner in a venture who has no management authority and whose liability is restricted to the amount of his investment — compare GENERAL PARTNER
— **limited partnership** *noun*

**limited war** *noun* (1939)
**:** a war whose objective is less than the total defeat of the enemy

**lim·it·ing** *adjective* (1849)

**1 a :** functioning as a limit **:** RESTRICTIVE ⟨*limiting* value⟩ **b :** being an environmental factor (as a nutrient) that limits the population size of an organism
**2 :** serving to specify the application of the modified noun ⟨*this* in "this book" is a *limiting* word⟩
— **lim·it·ing·ly** *adverb*

**limit point** *noun* (1905)
**:** a point that is related to a set of points in such a way that every neighborhood of the point no matter how small contains another point belonging to the set — called also *point of accumulation*

**lim·i·trophe** \'li-mə-ˌtrōf, -ˌtrȯf\ *adjective* [French, from Late Latin *limitrophus* bordering upon, literally, providing subsistence for frontier troops, irregular from Latin *limit-, limes* boundary + Greek *trophos* feeder, from *trephein* to nourish] (1763)
**:** situated on a border or frontier **:** ADJACENT

**lim·mer** \'li-mər\ *noun* [Middle English (Scots)] (15th century)
**1** *chiefly Scottish* **:** SCOUNDREL
**2** *chiefly Scottish* **:** PROSTITUTE

**limn** \'lim\ *transitive verb* **limned; limn·ing** \'li-miŋ, 'lim-niŋ\ [Middle English *luminen, limnen* to illuminate (a manuscript), from Middle French *enluminer*, from Latin *illuminare* to illuminate] (1592)
**1 :** to draw or paint on a surface
**2 :** to outline in clear sharp detail **:** DELINEATE
**3 :** DESCRIBE
— **limn·er** \'li-mər, 'lim-nər\ *noun*

**lim·net·ic** \lim-'ne-tik\ *adjective* [International Scientific Vocabulary, from Greek *limnē* pool, marshy lake; perhaps akin to Latin *limus* mud — more at LIME] (1899)
**:** of, relating to, or inhabiting the open water of a body of fresh water ⟨*limnetic* environment⟩

**lim·nol·o·gy** \lim-'nä-lə-jē\ *noun* [Greek *limnē* + International Scientific Vocabulary -*logy*] (circa 1888)
**:** the scientific study of bodies of fresh water (as lakes)
— **lim·no·log·i·cal** \ˌlim-nə-'lä-ji-kəl\ *also*
**lim·no·log·ic** \-'lä-jik\ *adjective*
— **lim·nol·o·gist** \lim-'nä-lə-jist\ *noun*

**limo** \'li-(ˌ)mō\ *noun, plural* **lim·os** (1968)
**:** LIMOUSINE

**Li·moges** \li-'mōzh\ *noun* [*Limoges*, France] (1844)
**:** enamelware or porcelain made at Limoges

**lim·o·nene** \'li-mə-ˌnēn\ *noun* [International Scientific Vocabulary, from French *limon* lemon, from Middle French] (1845)
**:** a widely distributed terpene hydrocarbon $C_{10}H_{16}$ that occurs in essential oils (as of oranges or lemons) and has a lemon odor

**li·mo·nite** \'lī-mə-ˌnīt\ *noun* [German *Limonit*, from Greek *leimōn* wet meadow; akin to Greek *limnē* pool] (1823)
**:** a native hydrous ferric oxide of variable composition that is a major ore of iron
— **li·mo·nit·ic** \ˌlī-mə-'ni-tik\ *adjective*

---

☆ **SYNONYMS**
**Limit, restrict, circumscribe, confine**
mean to set bounds for. LIMIT implies setting a point or line (as in time, space, speed, or degree) beyond which something cannot or is not permitted to go ⟨visits are *limited* to 30 minutes⟩. RESTRICT suggests a narrowing or tightening or restraining within or as if within an encircling boundary ⟨laws intended to *restrict* the freedom of the press⟩. CIRCUMSCRIBE stresses a restriction on all sides and by clearly defined boundaries ⟨the work of the investigating committee was carefully *circumscribed*⟩. CONFINE suggests severe restraint and a resulting cramping, fettering, or hampering ⟨our freedom of choice was *confined* by finances⟩.

**Lim·ou·sin** \li-'mü-sin, 'li-mə-ˌzēn, lē-mü-'zaⁿ\ *noun* [*Limousin*, France] (1920)
: any of a French breed of medium-sized yellow-red cattle bred especially for meat

**lim·ou·sine** \'li-mə-ˌzēn, ˌli-mə-'\ *noun* [French, literally, cloak, from *Limousin*, France] (1902)
**1** : a large luxurious often chauffeur-driven sedan that sometimes has a glass partition separating the driver's seat from the passenger compartment
**2** : a large vehicle for transporting passengers to and from an airport

**limousine liberal** *noun* (1969)
: a wealthy political liberal

**¹limp** \'limp\ *intransitive verb* [probably from Middle English *lympen* to fall short; akin to Old English *limpan* to happen, *lemph*ealt lame] (circa 1570)
**1 a** : to walk lamely; *especially* : to walk favoring one leg **b** : to go unsteadily : FALTER
**2** : to proceed slowly or with difficulty ⟨the ship *limped* back to port⟩
— **limp·er** *noun*

**²limp** *noun* (1818)
: a limping movement or gait

**³limp** *adjective* [akin to ¹*limp*] (circa 1706)
**1 a** : lacking firm texture, substance, or structure ⟨*limp* curtains⟩ ⟨her hair hung *limp* about her shoulders⟩ **b** : not stiff or rigid ⟨a book in a *limp* binding⟩
**2 a** : WEARY, EXHAUSTED ⟨*limp* with fatigue⟩ **b** : lacking in strength, vigor, or firmness : SPIRITLESS
— **limp·ly** *adverb*
— **limp·ness** *noun*

**lim·pa** \'lim-pə\ *noun* [Swedish] (1948)
: rye bread made with molasses or brown sugar

**lim·pet** \'lim-pət\ *noun* [Middle English *lempet*, from Old English *lempedu*, from Medieval Latin *lampreda* lamprey] (before 12th century)
**1** : a marine gastropod mollusk (especially families Acmaeidae and Patellidae) that has a low conical shell broadly open beneath, browses over rocks or timbers in the littoral area, and clings very tightly when disturbed

**limpet 1**

**2** : one that clings tenaciously to someone or something
**3** : an explosive device designed to cling magnetically to a metallic surface (as the hull of a ship)

**lim·pid** \'lim-pəd\ *adjective* [French or Latin; French *limpide,* from Latin *limpidus,* perhaps from *lympha* water — more at LYMPH] (1613)
**1 a** : marked by transparency : PELLUCID ⟨*limpid* streams⟩ **b** : clear and simple in style ⟨*limpid* prose⟩
**2** : absolutely serene and untroubled
**synonym** see CLEAR
— **lim·pid·i·ty** \lim-'pi-də-tē\ *noun*
— **lim·pid·ly** \'lim-pəd-lē\ *adverb*
— **lim·pid·ness** *noun*

**limp·kin** \'lim(p)-kən\ *noun* [perhaps from ¹*limp*] (1871)
: a large brown wading bird (*Aramus guarauna*) of southern Georgia, Florida, and Central and South America that resembles a bittern but has a longer slightly curved bill, longer neck and legs, and white stripes on head and neck

**limp–wrist·ed** \'limp-ˌris-təd\ *adjective* (circa 1960)
**1** : EFFEMINATE
**2** : WEAK

**lim·u·lus** \'lim-yə-ləs\ *noun, plural* **-li** \-ˌlī, -ˌlē\ [New Latin, genus name, from Latin *limus* oblique, transverse — more at LIMEN] (1837)
: HORSESHOE CRAB

**limy** \'lī-mē\ *adjective* **lim·i·er; -est** (circa 1552)
**1** : smeared with or consisting of lime : VISCOUS
**2** : containing lime or limestone
**3** : resembling or having the qualities of lime

**lin·ac** \'li-ˌnak\ *noun* (1950)
: LINEAR ACCELERATOR

**lin·age** \'lī-nij\ *noun* (1884)
: the number of lines of printed or written matter

**lin·al·o·ol** \lə-'na-lə-ˌwȯl, lī-, -ˌwōl\ *noun* [International Scientific Vocabulary, from Mexican Spanish *lináloe,* tree yielding perfume, from Medieval Latin *lignum aloes,* literally, wood of the aloe] (1891)
: a fragrant liquid alcohol $C_{10}H_{18}O$ that occurs both free and in the form of esters in many essential oils and is used in perfumes, soaps, and flavoring materials

**linch·pin** \'linch-ˌpin\ *noun* [Middle English *lynspin,* from *lyns* linchpin (from Old English *lynis*) + *pin;* akin to Middle High German *luns* linchpin] (13th century)
**1** : a locking pin inserted crosswise (as through the end of an axle or shaft)
**2** : one that serves to hold together the elements of a complex ⟨the *linchpin* in the defense's case⟩

**Lin·coln** \'liŋ-kən\ *noun* [*Lincoln*shire, England] (1837)
: any of an English breed of long-wooled mutton-type sheep

**Lin·coln·i·ana** \(ˌ)liŋ-ˌkō-nē-'ä-nə, -'a-nə, -'ä-nə\ *noun plural* (1921)
: materials relating to Abraham Lincoln

**Lincoln's Birthday** \'liŋ-kənz-\ *noun* (1898)
**1** : February 12 observed as a legal holiday in many states of the U.S.
**2** : the first Monday in February observed as a legal holiday by some states of the U.S.

**lin·co·my·cin** \ˌliŋ-kə-'mī-sᵊn\ *noun* [New Latin *lincoln*ensis (specific epithet of *Streptomyces lincolnensis*) + English -*mycin*] (1963)
: an antibiotic obtained from an actinomycete (*Streptomyces lincolnensis*) and effective especially against gram-positive bacteria

**lin·dane** \'lin-ˌdān\ *noun* [T. van der *Lind*en, 20th century Dutch chemist] (circa 1949)
: an insecticide that consists chiefly of the gamma isomer of BHC and is biodegraded very slowly

**lin·den** \'lin-dən\ *noun* [Middle English, made of linden wood, from Old English, from *lind* linden tree; probably akin to Old English *līthe* gentle — more at LITHE] (1577)
**1** : any of a genus (*Tilia* of the family Tiliaceae, the linden family) of trees of temperate regions that are planted as shade trees and are distinguished by having cordate leaves and a winglike bract attached to the peduncle of the flower and fruit: as **a** : a European tree (*T. europaea*) much used for ornamental planting **b** : a tall forest tree (*T. americana*) chiefly of the central and eastern U.S. — called also *basswood, whitewood*

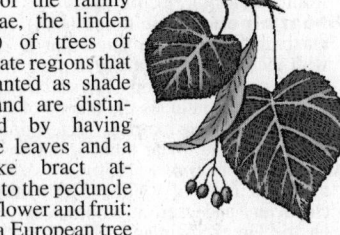
**linden 1: branch with bract and fruit**

**2** : the light fine-grained white wood of a linden; *especially* : BASSWOOD 2

**lin·dy** \'lin-dē\ *noun* [probably from *Lindy,* nickname of Charles A. Lindbergh] (1931)
: a jitterbug dance originating in Harlem and later developing many local variants

**¹line** \'līn\ *noun, often attributive* [Middle English; partly from Old French *ligne,* from Latin *linea,* from feminine of *lineus* made of flax, from *linum* flax; partly from Old English *līne;* akin to Old English *līn* flax — more at LINEN] (before 12th century)
**1 a** : THREAD, STRING, CORD, ROPE: as (1) : a comparatively strong slender cord (2) : CLOTHESLINE (3) : a rope used on shipboard **b** (1) : a device for catching fish consisting of a cord with hooks and other fishing gear (2) : scope for activity : ROPE **c** : a length of material used in measuring and leveling **d** : piping for conveying a fluid (as steam) **e** (1) : a wire or pair of wires connecting one telegraph or telephone station with another or a whole system of such wires; *also* : any circuit in an electronic communication system (2) : a telephone connection ⟨tried to get a *line*⟩; *also* : an individual telephone extension ⟨a call on *line* 2⟩ (3) : the principal circuits of an electric power system
**2 a** (1) : a horizontal row of written or printed characters; *also* : a blank row in lieu of such characters (2) : a unit in the rhythmic structure of verse formed by the grouping of a number of the smallest units of the rhythm (as metrical feet) (3) : an often numbered section of a computer program containing a single command or a small number of commands **b** : a short letter : NOTE **c** *plural* : a certificate of marriage **d** : the words making up a part in a drama — usually used in plural **e** : any of the successive horizontal rows of picture elements on the screen of a cathode-ray tube (as a television screen)
**3 a** : something (as a ridge or seam) that is distinct, elongated, and narrow **b** : a narrow crease (as on the face) : WRINKLE **c** : the course or direction of something in motion : ROUTE **d** (1) : a state of agreement or conformity : ACCORDANCE (2) : a state of order, control, or obedience ⟨you're getting out of *line*⟩ **e** : a boundary of an area ⟨the state *line*⟩ **f** : the track and roadbed of a railway **g** : an amount of cocaine that is arranged in a line to be inhaled through the nose
**4 a** : a course of conduct, action, or thought **b** : a field of activity or interest **c** : a glib often persuasive way of talking
**5 a** : LIMIT, RESTRAINT **b** *archaic* : position in life : LOT
**6 a** (1) : FAMILY, LINEAGE (2) : a strain produced and maintained especially by selective breeding or biological culture (3) : a chronological series **b** : dispositions made to cover extended military positions and presenting a front to the enemy — usually used in plural **c** : a military formation in which the different elements are abreast of each other **d** : naval ships arranged in a regular order **e** (1) : the combatant forces of an army distinguished from the staff corps and supply services (2) : the force of a regular navy **f** (1) : officers of the navy eligible for command at sea distinguished from officers of the staff (2) : officers of the army belonging to a combatant branch **g** : an arrangement or placement of persons or objects of one kind in an orderly series ⟨a *line* of trees⟩ ⟨stand on *line*⟩ ⟨waiting in *line*⟩; *also* : the persons or objects so positioned ⟨the *line* moved slowly at the bank⟩ **h** (1) : a group of public conveyances plying regularly under one management over a route (2) : a system of transportation together with its equipment, routes, and appurtenances; *also* : the company owning or operating it **i** : a succession of musical notes especially considered in melodic

\ə\ abut \ᵊ\ kitten \ər\ further \a\ ash \ā\ ace \ä\ mop, mar \au̇\ out \ch\ chin \e\ bet \ē\ easy \g\ go \i\ hit \ī\ ice \j\ job \ŋ\ sing \ō\ go \ȯ\ law \ȯi\ boy \th\ thin \th\ the \ü\ loot \u̇\ foot \y\ yet \zh\ vision *see also* Guide to Pronunciation

phrases **j** (1) **:** an arrangement of operations in manufacturing permitting sequential occurrence on various stages of production (2) **:** the personnel of an organization that are responsible for its stated objective **k** (1) **:** the 7 players including center, 2 guards, 2 tackles, and 2 ends who in offensive football play line up on or within one foot of the line of scrimmage (2) **:** the players who in defensive play line up within one yard of the line of scrimmage **7 :** a narrow elongated mark drawn or projected: as **a** (1) **:** a circle of latitude or longitude on a map (2) **:** EQUATOR **b :** a mark (as on a map) recording a boundary, division, or contour **c :** any of the horizontal parallel strokes on a music staff on or between which notes are placed — compare SPACE **d :** a mark (as by pencil) that forms part of the formal design of a picture distinguished from the shading or color **e :** a division on a bridge score dividing the score for bonuses from that for tricks **f** (1) **:** a demarcation of a limit with reference to which the playing of some game or sport is regulated — usually used in combination (2) **:** a marked or imaginary line across a playing area (as a football field) parallel to the end line (3) **:** LINE OF SCRIMMAGE **8 :** a straight or curved geometric element that is generated by a moving point and that has extension only along the path of the point **:** CURVE **9 a :** a defining outline **:** CONTOUR **b :** a general plan **:** MODEL — usually used in plural **10 a** *chiefly British* **:** PICA — used to indicate the size of large type **b :** the unit of fineness of halftones expressed as the number of screen lines to the linear inch **11 :** merchandise or services of the same general class for sale or regularly available **12 a :** a source of information **:** INSIGHT **b :** betting odds offered by a bookmaker especially on a sporting event **13 :** a complete game of 10 frames in bowling — called also *string* **14 :** LINE DRIVE — **liny** *also* **lin·ey** \'lī-nē\ *adjective* — **between the lines 1 :** by implication **:** in an indirect way **2 :** by way of inference — **down the line :** all the way **:** FULLY — **in line for :** due or in a position to receive — **on line :** in or into operation — **on the line 1 :** in complete commitment and at great risk ⟨puts his future *on the line* by backing that policy⟩ **2 :** on the border between two categories **3 :** IMMEDIATELY ⟨paid cash *on the line*⟩

**²line** *verb* **lined; lin·ing** (1530)
*transitive verb*
**1 :** to mark or cover with a line or lines ⟨*lined* paper⟩
**2 :** to depict with lines **:** DRAW
**3 :** to place or form a line along ⟨pedestrians *line* the walks⟩
**4 :** to form into a line or lines **:** ALIGN ⟨*line* up troops⟩
**5 :** to hit (as a baseball) hard and in a usually straight line
*intransitive verb*
**1 :** to hit a line drive in baseball
**2 :** to come into the correct relative position **:** ALIGN

**³line** *transitive verb* **lined; lin·ing** [Middle English, from *line* flax, from Old English *līn*] (14th century)
**1 :** to cover the inner surface of ⟨*line* a cloak with silk⟩
**2 :** to put something in the inside of **:** FILL
**3 :** to serve as the lining of ⟨tapestries *lined* the walls⟩
**4** *obsolete* **:** FORTIFY
— **line one's pockets :** to take money freely and especially dishonestly

**¹lin·e·age** \'li-nē-ij *also* 'li-nij\ *noun* (14th century)
**1 a :** descent in a line from a common progenitor **b :** DERIVATION
**2 :** a group of individuals tracing descent from a common ancestor; *especially* **:** such a group of persons whose common ancestor is regarded as its founder

**²line·age** \'lī-nij\ *variant of* LINAGE

**lin·e·al** \'li-nē-əl\ *adjective* (14th century)
**1 :** LINEAR
**2 :** composed of or arranged in lines
**3 a :** consisting of or being in a direct male or female line of ancestry — compare COLLATERAL 2 **b :** relating to or derived from ancestors **:** HEREDITARY **c :** descended in a direct line
**4 a :** belonging to one lineage ⟨*lineal* relatives⟩ **b :** of, relating to, or dealing with a lineage
— **lin·e·al·i·ty** \,li-nē-'a-lə-tē\ *noun*
— **lin·e·al·ly** \'li-nē-ə-lē\ *adverb*

**lin·e·a·ment** \'li-nē-ə-mənt\ *noun* [Middle English, from Latin *lineamentum,* from *lineare* to draw a line, from *linea*] (15th century)
**1 a :** an outline, feature, or contour of a body or figure and especially of a face — usually used in plural **b :** a linear topographic feature (as of the earth or a planet) that reveals a characteristic (as a fault or the subsurface structure)
**2 :** a distinguishing or characteristic feature — usually used in plural
— **lin·e·a·men·tal** \,li-nē-ə-'men-t°l\ *adjective*

**lin·e·ar** \'li-nē-ər\ *adjective* (circa 1656)
**1 a** (1) **:** of, relating to, resembling, or having a graph that is a line and especially a straight line **:** STRAIGHT (2) **:** involving a single dimension **b** (1) **:** of the first degree with respect to one or more variables (2) **:** of, relating to, based on, or being linear equations, linear differential equations, linear functions, linear transformations, or linear algebra **c** (1) **:** characterized by an emphasis on line ⟨*linear* art⟩ (2) **:** composed of simply drawn lines with little attempt at pictorial representation ⟨*linear* script⟩ **d :** consisting of a straight chain of atoms
**2 :** elongated with nearly parallel sides ⟨*linear* leaf⟩ — see LEAF illustration
**3 :** having or being a response or output that is directly proportional to the input
**4 :** of, relating to, or based or depending on sequential development ⟨*linear* thinking⟩ ⟨a *linear* narrative⟩
— **lin·e·ar·i·ty** \,li-nē-'ar-ə-tē\ *noun*
— **lin·e·ar·ly** \'li-nē-ər-lē\ *adverb*

**Linear A** \-'ā\ *noun* (1948)
**:** a linear form of writing used in Crete from the 18th to the 15th centuries B.C.

**linear accelerator** *noun* (1945)
**:** a device in which charged particles are accelerated in a straight line by successive impulses from a series of electric fields

**linear algebra** *noun* (circa 1884)
**:** a branch of mathematics that is concerned with mathematical structures closed under the operations of addition and scalar multiplication and that includes the theory of systems of linear equations, matrices, determinants, vector spaces, and linear transformations

**Linear B** \-'bē\ *noun* (1950)
**:** a linear form of writing employing syllabic characters and used at Knossos on Crete and on the Greek mainland from the 15th to the 12th centuries B.C. for documents in the Mycenaean language

**linear combination** *noun* (1960)
**:** a mathematical entity (as $4x + 5y + 6z$) which is composed of sums and differences of elements (as variables, matrices, or functions) especially when the coefficients are not all zero

**linear dependence** *noun* (1955)
**:** the property of one set (as of matrices or vectors) of having at least one linear combination of its elements equal to zero when the co-

efficients are taken from another given set and at least one of its coefficients is not equal to zero
— **linearly dependent** *adjective*

**linear equation** *noun* (1816)
**:** an equation of the first degree in any number of variables

**linear function** *noun* (circa 1889)
**1 :** a mathematical function in which the variables appear only in the first degree, are multiplied by constants, and are combined only by addition and subtraction
**2 :** LINEAR TRANSFORMATION

**linear independence** *noun* (1967)
**:** the property of a set (as of matrices or vectors) of having no linear combination of all its elements equal to zero when coefficients are taken from a given set unless the coefficient of each element is zero
— **linearly independent** *adjective*

**lin·e·ar·ise** *British variant of* LINEARIZE

**lin·e·ar·ize** \'li-nē-ə-,rīz\ *transitive verb* **-ized; -iz·ing** (1895)
**:** to give a linear form to; *also* **:** to project in linear form
— **lin·e·ar·i·za·tion** \,li-nē-ə-rə-'zā-shən\ *noun*

**linear measure** *noun* (circa 1890)
**1 :** a measure of length
**2 :** a system of measures of length

**linear motor** *noun* (1957)
**:** a motor that produces thrust in a straight line by direct induction rather than with the use of gears — called also *linear induction motor*

**linear perspective** *noun* (circa 1656)
**:** PERSPECTIVE 1a

**linear programming** *noun* (1949)
**:** a mathematical method of solving practical problems (as the allocation of resources) by means of linear functions where the variables involved are subject to constraints

**linear space** *noun* (circa 1889)
**:** VECTOR SPACE

**linear transformation** *noun* (circa 1889)
**1 :** a transformation in which the new variables are linear functions of the old variables
**2 :** a function that maps the vectors of one vector space onto the vectors of the same or another vector space with the same field of scalars in such a way that the image of the sum of two vectors equals the sum of their images and the image of the product of a scalar and a vector equals the product of the scalar and the image of the vector

**lin·e·a·tion** \,li-nē-'ā-shən\ *noun* [Middle English *lineacion* outline, from Latin *lineation-, lineatio,* from *lineare* to mark with lines, from *linea*] (14th century)
**1 a :** the action of marking with lines **:** DELINEATION **b :** OUTLINE
**2 :** an arrangement of lines

**line·back·er** \'līn-,ba-kər\ *noun* (1949)
**:** a defensive football player who lines up immediately behind the line of scrimmage to make tackles on running plays through the line or defend against short passes

**line·back·ing** \-,ba-kiŋ\ *noun* (1953)
**:** the action or art of playing linebacker

**line·breed·ing** \-,brē-diŋ\ *noun* (circa 1879)
**:** the interbreeding of individuals within a particular line of descent usually to perpetuate desirable characters
— **line·bred** \-,bred\ *adjective*

**line·cast·er** \-,kas-tər\ *noun* (1964)
**:** a machine that casts metal type in lines
— **line·cast·ing** \-,tiŋ\ *noun*

**line·cut** \'līn-,kət\ *noun* (circa 1909)
**:** a photoengraving of a line drawing

**line drawing** *noun* (1891)
**:** a drawing made in solid lines

**line drive** *noun* (1912)
**:** a batted baseball hit in a nearly straight line usually not far above the ground

**line engraving** *noun* (1802)
**:** an engraving cut by hand directly in the plate

**line graph** *noun* (circa 1924)
: a graph in which points representing values of a variable for suitable values of an independent variable are connected by a broken line

**line-haul** \'līn-,hȯl\ *noun* (circa 1923)
: the transporting of items or persons between terminals

**line item** *noun* (1962)
: an appropriation that is itemized on a separate line in a budget
— **line-item** \'līn-'ī-təm\ *adjective*

**line judge** *noun* (1970)
: a football linesman whose duties include keeping track of the official time for the game

**line-man** \'līn-mən\ *noun* (1876)
**1** : one who sets up or repairs electric wire communication or power lines — called also *linesman*
**2** : a player in the forward line of a team; *specifically* : a football player in the line

¹**lin-en** \'li-nən\ *adjective* [Middle English, from Old English *līnen*, from *līn* flax, from Latin *linum* flax; akin to Greek *linon* flax, thread] (before 12th century)
**1** : made of flax
**2** : made of or resembling linen

²**linen** *noun* (14th century)
**1 a** : cloth made of flax and noted for its strength, coolness, and luster **b** : thread or yarn spun from flax
**2** : clothing or household articles made of linen cloth or similar fabric
**3** : paper made from linen fibers or with a linen finish

**line of credit** (1917)
: the maximum credit allowed a buyer or borrower

**line of duty** (circa 1918)
: all that is authorized, required, or normally associated with some field of responsibility

**line officer** *noun* (1850)
: a commissioned officer assigned to the line of the army or navy — compare STAFF OFFICER

**line of force** (1873)
: a line in a field of force (as a magnetic or electric field) whose tangent at any point gives the direction of the field at that point

**line of scrimmage** (circa 1909)
: an imaginary line in football that is parallel to the goal lines and tangent to the nose of the ball laid on the ground and that marks the position of the ball at the start of each down

**line of sight** (1559)
**1** : a line from an observer's eye to a distant point
**2** : the straight path between a radio or television transmitting antenna and receiving antenna when unobstructed by the horizon

**line out** (1618)
*transitive verb*
**1** : to indicate with or as if with lines : OUTLINE ⟨*line out* a route⟩
**2** : to arrange in an extended line
**3** : BELT ⟨*line out* a song⟩
*intransitive verb*
**1** : to move rapidly ⟨*lined out* for home⟩
**2** : to make an out by hitting a baseball in a line drive that is caught

**line printer** *noun* (1955)
: a high-speed printing device (as for a computer) that prints each line as a unit rather than character by character

¹**lin-er** \'lī-nər\ *noun* (15th century)
**1** : one that makes, draws, or uses lines
**2 a** : a ship belonging to a regular line **b** : an airplane belonging to an airline
**3** : LINE DRIVE
**4** : something with which lines are made

²**liner** *noun* (1611)
**1** : one that lines or is used to line or back something
**2** : JACKET 3c(2)
— **lin-er-less** \-ləs\ *adjective*

**li-ner-board** \'lī-nər-,bȯrd, -,bȯrd\ *noun* (1948)

: a thin paperboard used for the flat facings of corrugated containerboard

**liner notes** *noun plural* (1955)
: comments or explanatory notes about a recording printed on the jacket or an insert

**line score** *noun* (1946)
: a score of a baseball game giving the runs, hits, and errors made by each team — compare BOX SCORE

**lines-man** \'līnz-mən\ *noun* (1883)
**1** : LINEMAN 1
**2** : an official who assists a referee in various games (as football or hockey) especially in determining if a ball, puck, or player is out-of-bounds or offside

**line squall** *noun* (1887)
: a squall or thunderstorm occurring along a cold front

**line storm** *noun* (1850)
: an equinoctial storm

**line-up** \'lī-,nəp\ *noun* (1889)
**1 a** : a list of players taking part in a game (as of baseball) **b** : the players on such a list
**2 a** : an alignment (as in entertainment or politics) of persons or things having a common purpose, distinction, or bond ⟨the show's star-studded *lineup*⟩ **b** : LINE 11 **c** : a television programming schedule
**3** : a line of persons arranged especially for inspection or for identification by police

**line up** (1864)
*intransitive verb*
**1** : to assume an orderly linear arrangement ⟨*line up* for inspection⟩
**2** : to align oneself ⟨he *lined up* with the liberals against the bill⟩
*transitive verb*
**1** : to put into alignment
**2** : to arrange for ⟨*line up* support for a candidate⟩

¹**ling** \'liŋ\ *noun* [Middle English; akin to Dutch *leng* ling, Old English *lang* long] (13th century)
**1** : any of various fishes (as a hake or burbot) of the cod family
**2** : LINGCOD

²**ling** *noun* [Middle English, from Old Norse *lyng*] (13th century)
: a heath plant; *especially* : a common Old World heather (*Calluna vulgaris*)

¹**-ling** *noun suffix* [Middle English, from Old English; akin to Old English *-ing*]
**1** : one connected with or having the quality of ⟨hire*ling*⟩
**2** : young, small, or inferior one ⟨duck*ling*⟩

²**-ling** *or* **-lings** *adverb suffix* [Middle English *-ling* (from Old English), *-linges* (from *-ling* + *-es* -s); akin to Old High German *-lingūn* -ling, Old English *lang* long]
: in (such) a direction or manner ⟨side*ling*⟩ ⟨flat*ling*⟩

**Lin-ga-la** \liŋ-'gä-lə\ *noun* (1922)
: a Bantu language widely used in trade and public affairs in the Congo River area

**lin-gam** \'liŋ-gəm\ *or* **lin-ga** \-gə\ *noun* [Sanskrit *liṅga* (nominative *liṅgam*), literally, characteristic] (1719)
: a stylized phallic symbol of the masculine cosmic principle and of the Hindu god Siva — compare YONI

**Lin-ga-yat** \liŋ-'gä-yət\ *noun* [Kannada *liṅgāyata*] (1901)
: a member of a Saiva sect of southern India marked by wearing of the lingam and characterized by denial of caste distinctions

**ling-cod** \'liŋ-,käd\ *noun* (1940)
: a large greenish-fleshed fish (*Ophiodon elongatus*) of the Pacific coast of North America that is an important food and sport fish and belongs to the same family as the greenlings

**lin-ger** \'liŋ-gər\ *verb* **lin-gered; lin-ger-ing** \-g(ə-)riŋ\ [Middle English (northern dialect) *lengeren* to dwell, frequentative of *lengen* to prolong, from Old English *lengan;* akin to Old English *lang* long] (14th century)

*intransitive verb*
**1** : to be slow in parting or in quitting something : TARRY
**2 a** : to remain alive although gradually dying **b** : to remain existent although often waning in strength, importance, or influence ⟨*lingering* doubts⟩
**3** : to be slow to act : PROCRASTINATE
**4** : to move slowly : SAUNTER
*transitive verb*
**1** *obsolete* : DELAY
**2** : to pass (as a period of time) slowly
— **lin-ger-er** \-gər-ər\ *noun*
— **lin-ger-ing-ly** \-g(ə-)riŋ-lē\ *adverb*

**lin-ge-rie** \,län-jə-'rā, ,län-zhə-, -'rē; 'lä<sup>n</sup>-zhə-(,)rē, 'län-zhə-, 'lä<sup>n</sup>-zhə-, -,rā\ *noun* [French, from Middle French, from *linge* linen, from Latin *lineus* made of linen — more at LINE] (1835)
**1** *archaic* : linen articles or garments
**2** : women's intimate apparel
— **lingerie** *adjective*

**lin-go** \'liŋ-(,)gō\ *noun, plural* **lingoes** [probably from Lingua Franca, language, tongue, from Provençal, from Latin *lingua* — more at TONGUE] (1660)
: strange or incomprehensible language or speech: as **a** : a foreign language **b** : the special vocabulary of a particular field of interest **c** : language characteristic of an individual

**ling-on-ber-ry** \'liŋ-ən-,ber-ē\ *noun* [Swedish *lingon* mountain cranberry; akin to Old Norse *lyng* ling] (1920)
: the fruit of the mountain cranberry; *also* : MOUNTAIN CRANBERRY

**lin-gua** \'liŋ-gwə\ *noun, plural* **lin-guae** \-,gwē, -,gwī\ [Latin — more at TONGUE] (circa 1826)
: a tongue or an organ resembling a tongue

**lin-gua fran-ca** \'liŋ-gwə-'fraŋ-kə\ *noun, plural* **lingua francas** *or* **lin-guae fran-cae** \-gwē-'fraŋ-(,)kē\ [Italian, literally, Frankish language] (1619)
**1** *often capitalized* : a common language consisting of Italian mixed with French, Spanish, Greek, and Arabic that was formerly spoken in Mediterranean ports
**2** : any of various languages used as common or commercial tongues among peoples of diverse speech
**3** : something resembling a common language

**lin-gual** \'liŋ-gwəl *also* 'liŋ-gyə-wəl\ *adjective* [Latin *lingua*] (1650)
**1 a** : of, relating to, or resembling the tongue **b** : lying near or next to the tongue; *especially* : relating to or being the surface of tooth next to the tongue **c** : produced by the tongue
**2** : LINGUISTIC
— **lin-gual-ly** *adverb*

**lin-gui-ne** *or* **lin-gui-ni** \liŋ-'gwē-nē\ *noun* [Italian, plural of *linguina*, diminutive of *lingua* tongue, from Latin] (circa 1948)
: narrow flat pasta

**lin-guist** \'liŋ-gwist\ *noun* [Latin *lingua* language, tongue] (1591)
**1** : a person accomplished in languages; *especially* : one who speaks several languages
**2** : a person who specializes in linguistics

**lin-guis-tic** \liŋ-'gwis-tik\ *also* **lin-guis-ti-cal** \-ti-kəl\ *adjective* (1846)
: of or relating to language or linguistics
— **lin-guis-ti-cal-ly** \-ti-k(ə-)lē\ *adverb*

**linguistic atlas** *noun* (1923)
: a publication containing a set of maps on which speech variations are recorded — called also *dialect atlas*

**linguistic form** *noun* (1921)
: a meaningful unit of speech (as a morpheme, word, or sentence) — called also *speech form*

**linguistic geography** *noun* (1926)
: local or regional variations of a language or dialect studied as a field of knowledge — called also *dialect geography*
— **linguistic geographer** *noun*

**lin·guis·ti·cian** \ˌliŋ-gwə-'sti-shən\ *noun* (1895)
: LINGUIST 2

**lin·guis·tics** \liŋ-'gwis-tiks\ *noun plural but singular in construction* (circa 1847)
: the study of human speech including the units, nature, structure, and modification of language

**lin·i·ment** \'li-nə-mənt\ *noun* [Middle English, from Late Latin *linimentum*, from Latin *linere* to smear — more at LIME] (15th century)
: a liquid or semiliquid preparation that is applied to the skin as an anodyne or a counterirritant

**lin·ing** \'lī-niŋ\ *noun* (14th century)
**1** : material that lines or that is used to line especially the inner surface of something (as a garment)
**2** : the act or process of providing something with a lining

**¹link** \'liŋk\ *noun* [Middle English, of Scandinavian origin; akin to Old Norse *hlekkr* chain; akin to Old English *hlanc* lank] (15th century)
**1** : a connecting structure: as **a** (1) : a single ring or division of a chain (2) : one of the standardized divisions of a surveyor's chain that is 7.92 inches (20.1 centimeters) long and serves as a measure of length **b** : CUFF LINK **c** : BOND 3c **d** : an intermediate rod or piece for transmitting force or motion; *especially* : a short connecting rod with a hole or pin at each end **e** : the fusible member of an electrical fuse
**2** : something analogous to a link of chain: as **a** : a segment of sausage in a chain **b** : a connecting element or factor ⟨found a *link* between smoking and cancer⟩ **c** : a unit in a communication system **d** : an identifier attached to an element (as an index term) in a system in order to indicate or permit connection with other similarly identified elements

**²link** (15th century)
*transitive verb*
: to couple or connect by or as if by a link
*intransitive verb*
: to become connected by or as if by a link
**synonym** see JOIN
— **link·er** *noun*

**³link** *noun* [perhaps modification of Medieval Latin *linchinus* candle, alteration of Latin *lychnus*, from Greek *lychnos;* akin to Greek *leukos* white — more at LIGHT] (1526)
: a torch formerly used to light a person's way through the streets

**⁴link** *intransitive verb* [origin unknown] (1715)
*Scottish* : to skip smartly along

**link·age** \'liŋ-kij\ *noun* (1874)
**1** : the manner or style of being united: as **a** : the manner in which atoms or radicals are linked in a molecule **b** : BOND 3c
**2** : the quality or state of being linked; *especially* : the relationship between genes on the same chromosome that causes them to be inherited together — compare MENDEL'S LAW 2
**3** : a system of links; *especially* : a system of links or bars which are jointed together and more or less constrained by having a link or links fixed and by means of which straight or nearly straight lines or other point paths may be traced
**4** : LINK 2b

**linkage group** *noun* (1921)
: a set of linked genes at different loci on the same chromosome

**link·boy** \'liŋk-ˌbȯi\ *noun* (1660)
: an attendant formerly employed to bear a light for a person on the streets at night

**linked** \'liŋ(k)t\ *adjective* (15th century)
**1** : marked by linkage and especially genetic linkage ⟨*linked* genes⟩
**2** : having or provided with links ⟨a *linked* list⟩

**linking verb** *noun* (1923)
: a word or expression (as a form of *be, become, feel,* or *seem*) that links a subject with its predicate

**link·man** \'liŋk-mən\ *noun* (1716)
**1** : LINKBOY
**2** *British* : a broadcasting moderator or anchorman

**links** \'liŋ(k)s\ *noun plural* [Middle English, from Old English *hlincas,* plural of *hlinc* ridge; akin to Old English *hlanc* lank] (15th century)
**1** *Scottish* : sand hills especially along the seashore
**2** : GOLF COURSE

**links·man** \'liŋ(k)s-mən\ *noun* (1937)
: one who plays golf

**link·up** \'liŋ-ˌkəp\ *noun* (1945)
**1** : establishment of contact : MEETING ⟨the *linkup* of two spacecraft⟩
**2 a** : something that serves as a linking device or factor **b** : a functional whole resulting from the linking up of separate elements ⟨an instructional TV *linkup*⟩

**linn** \'lin\ *noun* [Scottish Gaelic *linne* pool] (1513)
**1** *chiefly Scottish* : WATERFALL
**2** *chiefly Scottish* : PRECIPICE

**Lin·nae·an** *or* **Lin·ne·an** \lə-'nē-ən, -'nā-; 'li-nē-\ *adjective* [Carolus *Linnaeus*] (1753)
: of, relating to, or following the systematic methods of the Swedish botanist Linnaeus who established the system of binomial nomenclature

**lin·net** \'li-nət\ *noun* [Middle French *linette,* from *lin* flax, from Latin *linum;* from its feeding on flax seeds] (circa 1530)
: a common small brownish Old World finch (*Acanthis cannabina*) of which the male has red on the breast and crown during breeding season

**li·no** \'lī-(ˌ)nō\ *noun, plural* **linos** (1907)
*chiefly British* : LINOLEUM

**li·no·cut** \'lī-nō-ˌkət\ *noun* (1907)
: a print made from a design cut into a mounted piece of linoleum

**li·no·le·ate** \lə-'nō-lē-ˌāt\ *noun* (circa 1865)
: a salt or ester of linoleic acid

**lin·o·le·ic acid** \ˌli-nə-'lē-ik-, -'lā-\ *noun* [Greek *linon* flax + International Scientific Vocabulary *oleic (acid)*] (1857)
: a liquid unsaturated fatty acid $C_{18}H_{32}O_2$ found especially in semidrying oils (as peanut oil) and essential for the nutrition of some animals

**lin·o·le·nic acid** \-'lē-nik-, -'lā-\ *noun* [International Scientific Vocabulary, irregular from *linoleic*] (1887)
: a liquid unsaturated fatty acid $C_{18}H_{30}O_2$ found especially in drying oils (as linseed oil) and essential for the nutrition of some animals

**li·no·le·um** \lə-'nō-lē-əm, -'nōl-yəm\ *noun, often attributive* [Latin *linum* flax + *oleum* oil — more at OIL] (1878)
**1** : a floor covering made by laying on a burlap or canvas backing a mixture of solidified linseed oil with gums, cork dust or wood flour or both, and usually pigments
**2** : a material similar to linoleum

**Li·no·type** \'lī-nə-ˌtīp\ *trademark*
— used for a keyboard-operated typesetting machine that uses circulating matrices and produces each line of type in the form of a solid metal slug

**lin·sang** \'lin-ˌsaŋ\ *noun* [Javanese *lingsang*] (1821)
: either of two nocturnal chiefly forest-dwelling Asian mammals (*Prionodon pardicolor* and *P. linsang*) that resemble and are related to the mongooses, civets, and genets; *also* : a related mammal (*Poiana richardsoni*) of Africa

**lin·seed** \'lin-ˌsēd\ *noun* [Middle English, from Old English *līnsǣd,* from *līn* flax + *sǣd* seed — more at LINEN] (before 12th century)
: FLAXSEED

**linseed oil** *noun* (15th century)
: a yellowish drying oil obtained from flaxseed and used especially in paint, varnish, printing ink, and linoleum

**lin·sey–wool·sey** \ˌlin-zē-'wu̇l-zē\ *noun* [Middle English *lynsy wolsye*] (15th century)
: a coarse sturdy fabric of wool and linen or cotton

**lin·stock** \'lin-ˌstäk\ *noun* [Dutch *lontstok,* from *lont* match + *stok* stick] (1575)
: a staff having a pointed foot (as for sticking into the ground) and a forked tip and formerly used to hold a lighted match for firing cannon

**lint** \'lint\ *noun* [Middle English] (14th century)
**1 a** : a soft fleecy material made from linen usually by scraping **b** : fuzz consisting especially of fine ravelings and short fibers of yarn and fabric
**2** : a fibrous coat of thick convoluted hairs borne by cotton seeds that yields the cotton staple
— **linty** \'lin-tē\ *adjective*

**lin·tel** \'lin-t°l\ *noun* [Middle English, from Middle French, from Late Latin *limitaris* threshold, from Latin, constituting a boundary, from *limit-, limes* boundary] (14th century)
: a horizontal architectural member spanning and usually carrying the load above an opening

**lint·er** \'lin-tər\ *noun* (circa 1889)
**1** : a machine for removing linters
**2** *plural* : the fuzz of short fibers that adheres to cottonseed after ginning

**1 lintel**

**lint·white** \'lint-ˌhwīt, -ˌwīt\ *noun* [alteration of Middle English *lynkwhyt,* by folk etymology from Old English *līnetwige*] (1513)
: LINNET

**li·on** \'lī-ən\ *noun, plural* **lions** [Middle English, from Old French, from Latin *leon-, leo,* from Greek *leōn*] (12th century)
**1 a** *or plural* **lion** : a large heavily-built social cat (*Panthera leo* synonym *Leo leo*) of open or rocky areas chiefly of sub-Saharan Africa though once more widely distributed throughout Africa and southern Asia that has a tawny body with a tufted tail and a shaggy blackish or dark brown mane in the male **b** : any of several large wildcats; *especially* : COUGAR **c** *capitalized* : LEO
**2 a** : a person felt to resemble a lion (as in courage or ferocity) **b** : a person of outstanding interest or importance
**3** *capitalized* [*Lions (club)*] : a member of a major national and international service club
— **li·on·like** \-ˌlīk\ *adjective*

**li·on·ess** \'lī-ə-nəs\ *noun* (14th century)
: a female lion
*usage* see -ESS

**li·on·fish** \'lī-ən-ˌfish\ *noun* (circa 1907)
: any of several scorpion fishes (genus *Pterois*) of the Indian Ocean and the tropical Pacific that are brilliantly striped and barred with elongated fins and venomous dorsal spines

**li·on·heart·ed** \ˌlī-ən-ˌhär-təd\ *adjective* (1708)
: COURAGEOUS, BRAVE

**li·on·ise** *British variant of* LIONIZE

**li·on·ize** \'lī-ə-ˌnīz\ *transitive verb* **-ized; -izing** (1809)
**1** : to treat as an object of great interest or importance
**2** *British* : to show the sights of a place to
— **li·on·i·za·tion** \ˌlī-ə-nə-'zā-shən\ *noun*
— **li·on·iz·er** \'lī-ə-ˌnī-zər\ *noun*

**lion's share** *noun* (1790)
: the largest portion ⟨received the *lion's share* of the research money⟩

**¹lip** \'lip\ *noun* [Middle English, from Old English *lippa;* akin to Old High German *leffur* lip and probably to Latin *labium, labrum* lip] (before 12th century)

**1 :** either of two fleshy folds that surround the mouth in humans and many other vertebrates and are the organs of human speech; *also* **:** the red or pinkish margin of the human lip
**2** *slang* **:** BACK TALK
**3 a :** a fleshy edge or margin (as of a wound) **b :** LABIUM **c :** LABELLUM 1 **d :** a limb of a labiate corolla
**4 a :** the edge of a hollow vessel or cavity **b :** a projecting edge: as (1) **:** the beveled upper edge of the mouth of an organ flue pipe (2) **:** the sharp cutting edge on the end of a tool (as an auger) (3) **:** a short spout (as on a pitcher)
**5 :** EMBOUCHURE
— **lip·less** \-ləs\ *adjective*
— **lip·like** \-ˌlīk\ *adjective*
²**lip** *adjective* (1558)
**1 :** INSINCERE ⟨*lip* praise⟩
**2 :** produced with the participation of the lips **:** LABIAL ⟨*lip* consonants⟩
³**lip** *transitive verb* **lipped; lip·ping** (1604)
**1 :** to touch with the lips; *especially* **:** KISS
**2 :** UTTER
**3 :** to lap against **:** LICK
**4 :** to hit (a putt) so that the ball hits the edge of the cup but fails to drop in
**lip-** *or* **lipo-** *combining form* [New Latin, from Greek, from *lipos* — more at LEAVE]
**:** fat **:** fatty tissue **:** fatty ⟨*lip*oid⟩ ⟨*lipo*protein⟩
**li·pase** \ˈlī-ˌpās, -ˌpāz\ *noun* [International Scientific Vocabulary] (1897)
**:** an enzyme that hydrolyzes glycerides
**lip·id** \ˈli-pəd\ *also* **lip·ide** \-ˌpīd\ *noun* [International Scientific Vocabulary] (1912)
**:** any of various substances that are soluble in nonpolar organic solvents (as chloroform and ether), that with proteins and carbohydrates constitute the principal structural components of living cells, and that include fats, waxes, phosphatides, cerebrosides, and related and derived compounds
— **li·pid·ic** \li-ˈpi-dik\ *adjective*
**Lip·iz·zan** \ˌli-pət-ˈsän\ *or* **Lip·iz·zan·er** \-ˈsä-nər\ *also* **Lip·pi·zan** \-ˈsän\ *or* **Lip·pi·zan·er** \-ˈsä-nər\ *noun* [German *Lipizzaner, Lippizaner,* from *Lipizza, Lippiza,* former site of the Austrian Imperial Stud near Trieste, Italy] (1928)
**:** any of a breed of spirited horses developed from Spanish, Italian, Danish, and Arab stock that are usually born with a dark coat that lightens to white with age
**li·po·gen·e·sis** \ˌlī-pə-ˈje-nə-səs\ *noun* [New Latin] (1882)
**:** the formation of fatty acids from acetyl coenzyme A in the living body
**li·po·ic acid** \lī-ˈpō-ik-, li-\ *noun* [*lip-, lipo-*] (circa 1951)
**:** any of several microbial growth factors; *especially* **:** a crystalline compound $C_8H_{14}O_2S_2$ that is essential for the oxidation of alpha-keto acids (as pyruvic acid) in metabolism
¹**li·poid** \ˈlī-ˌpȯid, ˈli-\ *or* **li·poi·dal** \lī-ˈpȯi-d°l, li-\ *adjective* [International Scientific Vocabulary] (1876)
**:** resembling fat
²**lipoid** *noun* [International Scientific Vocabulary] (1906)
**:** LIPID
**li·pol·y·sis** \lī-ˈpä-lə-səs, li-\ *noun* [New Latin] (circa 1903)
**:** the hydrolysis of fat
— **li·po·lyt·ic** \ˌlī-pə-ˈli-tik, ˌli-\ *adjective*
**li·po·ma** \lī-ˈpō-mə, li-\ *noun, plural* **-mas** *or* **-ma·ta** \-mə-tə\ [New Latin] (1830)
**:** a tumor of fatty tissue
— **li·po·ma·tous** \-mə-təs\ *adjective*
**li·po·phil·ic** \ˌlī-pə-ˈfi-lik, ˌli-\ *adjective* (1939)
**:** having an affinity for lipids (as fats) ⟨a *lipo*philic metabolite⟩
**li·po·poly·sac·cha·ride** \ˌlī-pō-ˌpä-li-ˈsa-kə-ˌrīd, ˌli-\ *noun* (1950)
**:** a large molecule consisting of lipids and sugars joined by chemical bonds

**li·po·pro·tein** \-ˈprō-ˌtēn, -ˈprō-tē-ən\ *noun* (1909)
**:** a conjugated protein that is a complex of protein and lipid
**li·po·some** \ˈlī-pə-ˌsōm, ˈli-\ *noun* (1968)
**:** a vesicle composed of one or more concentric phospholipid bilayers and used medically especially to deliver a drug into the body
— **li·po·so·mal** \ˌlī-pə-ˈsō-məl, ˌli-\ *adjective*
**li·po·suc·tion** \ˈli-pə-ˌsək-shən, ˈlī-\ *noun* (1986)
**:** surgical removal of local fat deposits (as in the thighs) especially for cosmetic purposes
**li·po·tro·pic** \ˌlī-pō-ˈtrō-pik, ˌli-, -ˈträ-\ *adjective* [International Scientific Vocabulary] (1935)
**:** promoting the physiological utilization of fat ⟨*lipotropic* dietary factors⟩
**li·po·tro·pin** \-ˈtrō-pən\ *noun* (1964)
**:** either of two protein hormones of the pituitary gland that function in the mobilization of fat reserves
**lipped** \ˈlipt\ *adjective* (14th century)
**:** having a lip or lips especially of a specified kind or number — often used in combination ⟨tight-*lipped*⟩
**lip·pen** \ˈli-pən\ *verb* [Middle English *lipnien*] (12th century)
*intransitive verb*
*chiefly Scottish* **:** TRUST, RELY
*transitive verb*
*chiefly Scottish* **:** ENTRUST
**Lippes loop** \ˈli-pəs-, -ˌpēz-\ *noun* [Jack Lippes (born 1924) American physician] (1964)
**:** an S-shaped plastic intrauterine device
**lip·ping** \ˈli-piŋ\ *noun* (1894)
**1 :** outgrowth of bone in liplike form at a joint margin
**2 :** a piece of wood set in an archer's bow where a flaw has been cut out
**3 :** EMBOUCHURE 1
**lip·py** \ˈli-pē\ *adjective* **lip·pi·er; -est** (circa 1875)
**:** given to back talk
**lip-read** \ˈlip-ˌrēd\ *verb* **-read** \-ˌred\; **-read·ing** \-ˌrē-diŋ\ (1892)
*transitive verb*
**:** to understand by lipreading
*intransitive verb*
**:** to use lipreading
— **lip-read·er** \-ˌrē-dər\ *noun*
**lipreading** *noun* (1874)
**:** the interpreting of speech by watching the speaker's lip and facial movements without hearing the voice
**lip service** *noun* (1644)
**:** an avowal of advocacy, adherence, or allegiance expressed in words but not backed by deeds — usually used with *pay*
**lip·stick** \ˈlip-ˌstik\ *noun* (1880)
**:** a waxy solid usually colored cosmetic in stick form for the lips; *also* **:** a stick of such cosmetic with its case
— **lip·sticked** *adjective*
**lip-synch** *or* **lip-sync** \ˈlip-ˌsiŋk\ (circa 1961)
*transitive verb*
**:** to pretend to sing or say in synchronization with recorded sound
*intransitive verb*
**:** to lip-synch something
— **lip sync** *noun*
**li·quate** \ˈlī-ˌkwāt\ *transitive verb* **li·quat·ed; li·quat·ing** [Latin *liquatus,* past participle of *liquare* to make liquid; akin to Latin *liquēre*] (circa 1859)
**:** to cause (a more fusible substance) to separate out of a combination or mixture by the application of heat ⟨*liquate* metallic lead from its ore⟩
— **li·qua·tion** \lī-ˈkwā-shən\ *noun*
**liq·ue·fac·tion** \ˌli-kwə-ˈfak-shən\ *noun* [Middle English, from Late Latin *liquefaction-, liquefactio,* from Latin *liquefacere,* from

*liquēre* to be fluid + *facere* to make — more at DO] (15th century)
**1 :** the process of making or becoming liquid
**2 :** the state of being liquid
**liquefied petroleum gas** *noun* (1925)
**:** a compressed gas that consists of flammable hydrocarbons (as propane and butane) and is used especially as fuel or as raw material for chemical synthesis
**liq·ue·fy** *also* **liq·ui·fy** \ˈli-kwə-ˌfī\ *verb* **-fied; -fy·ing** [Middle English *liquefien,* from Middle French *liquefier,* from Latin *liquefacere*] (15th century)
*transitive verb*
**:** to reduce to a liquid state
*intransitive verb*
**:** to become liquid
— **liq·ue·fi·er** \-ˌfī(-ə)r\ *noun*
**li·ques·cent** \li-ˈkwe-s°nt\ *adjective* [Latin *liquescent-, liquescens,* present participle of *liquescere* to become fluid, inchoative of *liquēre*] (circa 1727)
**:** being or tending to become liquid **:** MELTING
**li·queur** \li-ˈkər, -ˈkür, -ˈkyür\ *noun* [French, from Old French *licour* liquid — more at LIQUOR] (1729)
**:** a usually sweetened alcoholic liquor (as brandy) flavored with fruit, spices, nuts, herbs, or seeds
¹**liq·uid** \ˈli-kwəd\ *adjective* [Middle English, from Middle French *liquide,* from Latin *liquidus,* from *liquēre* to be fluid; akin to Latin *lixa* water, lye, and perhaps to Old Irish *fliuch* damp] (14th century)
**1 :** flowing freely like water
**2 :** having the properties of a liquid **:** being neither solid nor gaseous
**3 a :** shining and clear ⟨large *liquid* eyes⟩ **b :** being musical and free of harshness in sound **c :** smooth and unconstrained in movement **d :** articulated without friction and capable of being prolonged like a vowel ⟨a *liquid* consonant⟩
**4 :** consisting of or capable of ready conversion into cash ⟨*liquid* assets⟩
— **li·quid·i·ty** \li-ˈkwi-də-tē\ *noun*
— **liq·uid·ly** \ˈli-kwəd-lē\ *adverb*
— **liq·uid·ness** *noun*
²**liquid** *noun* (1530)
**1 :** a liquid consonant
**2 :** a fluid (as water) that has no independent shape but has a definite volume and does not expand indefinitely and that is only slightly compressible
**liq·uid·am·bar** \ˌli-kwə-ˈdam-bər\ *noun* [New Latin, from Latin *liquidus* + Medieval Latin *ambar, ambra* amber] (circa 1577)
**1 :** any of a genus (*Liquidambar*) of trees of the witch-hazel family with monoecious flowers and a globose fruit of many woody carpels
**2 :** STORAX 1b
**liq·ui·date** \ˈli-kwə-ˌdāt\ *verb* **-dat·ed; -dat·ing** [Late Latin *liquidatus,* past participle of *liquidare* to melt, from Latin *liquidus*] (circa 1575)
*transitive verb*
**1 a** (1) **:** to determine by agreement or by litigation the precise amount of (indebtedness, damages, or accounts) (2) **:** to determine the liabilities and apportion assets toward discharging the indebtedness of **b :** to settle (a debt) by payment or other settlement
**2** *archaic* **:** to make clear
**3 :** to do away with
**4 :** to convert (assets) into cash
*intransitive verb*
**1 :** to liquidate debts, damages, or accounts
**2 :** to determine liabilities and apportion assets toward discharging indebtedness
— **liq·ui·da·tion** \ˌli-kwə-ˈdā-shən\ *noun*

**liq·ui·da·tor** \'li-kwə-,dā-tər\ *noun* (circa 1828)
: one that liquidates; *especially* : an individual appointed by law to liquidate assets

**liquid crystal** *noun* (1891)
: an organic liquid whose physical properties resemble those of a crystal in the formation of loosely ordered molecular arrays similar to a regular crystalline lattice and the anisotropic refraction of light

**liquid crystal display** *noun* (1968)
: LCD

**liq·uid·ize** \'li-kwə-,dīz\ *transitive verb* **-ized; -iz·ing** (1837)
: to cause to be liquid

**liquid measure** *noun* (circa 1855)
: a unit or series of units for measuring liquid capacity — see METRIC SYSTEM table, WEIGHT table

¹**li·quor** \'li-kər\ *noun* [Middle English *licour*, from Old French, from Latin *liquor*, from *liquēre*] (13th century)
: a liquid substance: as **a** : a usually distilled rather than fermented alcoholic beverage **b** : a watery solution of a drug **c** : BATH 2b(1)

²**liquor** *verb* **li·quored; li·quor·ing** \'li-k(ə-)riŋ\ (1502)
*transitive verb*
**1** : to dress (as leather) with oil or grease
**2** : to make drunk with alcoholic liquor — usually used with *up*
*intransitive verb*
: to drink alcoholic liquor especially to excess — usually used with *up*

**li·quo·rice** *chiefly British variant of* LICORICE

¹**li·ra** \'lir-ə, 'lē-rə\ *noun, plural* **li·re** \'lē-(,)rā\ *also* **liras** [Italian, from Latin *libra*, a unit of weight] (1617)
— see MONEY table

²**lira** *noun, plural* **liras** [Turkish, from Italian] (1871)
— see MONEY table

³**lira** *noun, plural* **li·roth** *or* **li·rot** \'lē-,rōt, -,rŏth\ [New Hebrew, from Italian] (circa 1946)
: the former Israeli pound

⁴**lira** *noun, plural* **li·ri** \'lē-(,)rē\ [Maltese, from Italian] (circa 1985)
— see MONEY table

**lir·i·pipe** \'lir-ə-,pīp\ *noun* [Medieval Latin *liripipium*] (1614)
: a pendent part of a tippet; *also* : TIPPET, SCARF

**lisente** *plural of* SENTE

**lisle** \'lī(ə)l\ *noun, often attributive* [*Lisle* Lille, France] (1851)
: a smooth tightly twisted thread usually made of long-staple cotton

¹**lisp** \'lisp\ *verb* [Middle English, from Old English *-wlyspian;* akin to Old High German *lispen* to lisp] (before 12th century)
*intransitive verb*
**1** : to pronounce the sibilants \s\ and \z\ imperfectly especially by turning them into \th\ and \t͟h\
**2** : to speak falteringly, childishly, or with a lisp
*transitive verb*
: to utter falteringly or with a lisp
— **lisp·er** *noun*

²**lisp** *noun* (circa 1625)
**1** : a speech defect or affectation characterized by lisping
**2** : a sound resembling a lisp

**LISP** \'lisp\ *noun* [*list* processing] (1959)
: a computer programming language that is designed for easy manipulation of data strings and is used extensively for work in artificial intelligence

**lis·some** *also* **lis·som** \'li-səm\ *adjective* [alteration of *lithesome*] (circa 1800)
**1 a** : easily flexed **b** : LITHE 2
**2** : NIMBLE
— **lis·some·ly** *adverb*
— **lis·some·ness** *noun*

¹**list** \'list\ *verb* [Middle English *lysten*, from Old English *lystan;* akin to Old English *lust* desire, lust] (before 12th century)
*transitive verb*
*archaic* : PLEASE, SUIT
*intransitive verb*
*archaic* : WISH, CHOOSE

²**list** *noun* [Middle English, probably from *lysten*] (13th century)
*archaic* : INCLINATION, CRAVING

³**list** *verb* [Middle English, from Old English *hlystan*, from *hlyst* hearing; akin to Old English *hlysnan* to listen] (before 12th century)
*intransitive verb*
*archaic* : LISTEN
*transitive verb*
*archaic* : to listen to : HEAR

⁴**list** *noun* [Middle English, from Old English *līste;* akin to Old High German *līsta* edge, Albanian *leth*] (before 12th century)
**1** : a band or strip of material: as **a** : LISTEL **b** : SELVAGE **c** : a narrow strip of wood cut from the edge of a board
**2** *plural but singular or plural in construction*
**a** : an arena for combat (as jousting) **b** : a field of competition or controversy
**3** *obsolete* : LIMIT, BOUNDARY
**4** : STRIPE

⁵**list** *transitive verb* (1635)
**1** : to cut away a narrow strip from the edge of
**2** : to prepare or plant (land) in ridges and furrows with a lister

⁶**list** *noun* [French *liste*, from Italian *lista*, of Germanic origin; akin to Old High German *līsta* edge] (1602)
**1 a** : a simple series of words or numerals (as the names of persons or objects) ⟨a guest *list*⟩ **b** : an official roster : ROLL
**2** : CATALOG, CHECKLIST
**3** : the total number to be considered or included ⟨a situation that heads their *list* of troubles⟩

⁷**list** (1614)
*transitive verb*
**1 a** : to make a list of : ENUMERATE **b** : to include on a list : REGISTER
**2** : to place (oneself) in a specified category ⟨*lists* himself as a political liberal⟩
**3** *archaic* : RECRUIT
*intransitive verb*
**1** *archaic* : ENLIST
**2** : to become entered in a catalog with a selling price ⟨a car that *lists* for $12,000⟩
— **list·ee** \li-'stē\ *noun*

⁸**list** *verb* [origin unknown] (1626)
*intransitive verb*
: to tilt to one side; *especially, of a boat or ship* : to tilt to one side in a state of equilibrium (as from an unbalanced load) — compare HEEL
*transitive verb*
: to cause to list

⁹**list** *noun* (1633)
: a deviation from the vertical : TILT; *also* : the extent of such a deviation

**lis·tel** \'lis-t°l, lis-'tel\ *noun* [French, from Italian *listello*, diminutive of *lista* fillet, roster] (1598)
: a narrow band in architecture : FILLET

¹**lis·ten** \'lis-°n\ *verb* **lis·tened; lis·ten·ing** \'lis-niŋ, 'li-s°n-iŋ\ [Middle English *listnen*, from Old English *hlysnan;* akin to Sanskrit *śroṣati* he hears, Old English *hlūd* loud] (before 12th century)
*transitive verb*
*archaic* : to give ear to : HEAR
*intransitive verb*
**1** : to pay attention to sound ⟨*listen* to music⟩
**2** : to hear something with thoughtful attention : give consideration ⟨*listen* to a plea⟩
**3** : to be alert to catch an expected sound ⟨*listen* for his step⟩
— **lis·ten·er** \'lis-nər, 'li-s°n-ər\ *noun*

²**listen** *noun* (1788)
: an act of listening

**lis·ten·able** \'lis-nə-bəl, 'li-s°n-ə-\ *adjective* (1942)
: agreeable to listen to

**lis·ten·er·ship** \'lis-nər-,ship, 'li-s°n-ər-\ *noun* (1943)
: the audience for a radio program or recording; *also* : the number or kind of that audience

**listen in** *intransitive verb* (1905)
**1** : to tune in to or monitor a broadcast
**2** : to listen to a conversation without participating in it; *especially* : EAVESDROP
— **lis·ten·er-in** \,lis-nər-'in, ,li-s°n-ər-\ *noun*

**listening post** *noun* (1942)
: a center for monitoring electronic communications (as of an enemy)

¹**list·er** \'lis-tər\ *noun* (1682)
: one that lists or catalogs

²**lister** *noun* [⁵*list*] (1887)
: a double-moldboard plow often equipped with a subsoiling attachment and used mainly where rainfall is limited

**lis·te·ri·o·sis** \lis-,tir-ē-'ō-səs\ *noun, plural* **-o·ses** \-,sēz\ [New Latin, from *Listeria*, from Joseph *Lister*] (1941)
: a serious commonly fatal encephalitic disease of a great variety of wild and domestic mammals and birds and occasionally humans that is caused by a bacterium (*Listeria monocytogenes*)

**list·ing** *noun* (1659)
**1** : an act or instance of making or including in a list
**2** : something that is listed

**list·less** \'list-ləs\ *adjective* [Middle English *listles*, from ²*list*] (15th century)
: characterized by lack of interest, energy, or spirit : LANGUID ⟨a *listless* melancholy attitude⟩
— **list·less·ly** *adverb*
— **list·less·ness** *noun*

**list price** *noun* (1871)
: the basic price of an item as published in a catalog, price list, or advertisement before any discounts are taken

¹**lit** \'lit\ *past and past participle of* LIGHT

²**lit** *noun* [by shortening] (1850)
: LITERATURE

³**lit** *adjective* [past participle of ³*light*] (1904)
: affected by alcohol : DRUNK

**lit·a·ny** \'li-t°n-ē, 'lit-nē\ *noun, plural* **-nies** [Middle English *letanie*, from Old French & Late Latin; Old French, from Late Latin *litania*, from Late Greek *litaneia*, from Greek, entreaty, from *litanos* suppliant] (13th century)
**1** : a prayer consisting of a series of invocations and supplications by the leader with alternate responses by the congregation
**2 a** : a resonant or repetitive chant ⟨a *litany* of cheering phrases —Herman Wouk⟩ **b** : a usually lengthy recitation or enumeration ⟨a familiar *litany* of complaints⟩

**li·tchi** \'lē-(,)chē, 'lī-\ *noun* [Chinese (Beijing) *lizhī*] (1588)
**1** : the oval fruit of a tree (*Litchi chinensis*) of the soapberry family having a hard scaly reddish outer covering and sweet whitish edible flesh that surrounds a single large seed — called also *litchi nut*
**2** : a tree bearing litchis

**lit crit** \'lit-,krit\ *noun* (1963)
: literary criticism

**lite** \'līt\ *variant of* ⁴LIGHT 9a

**-lite** *noun combining form* [French, alteration of *-lithe*, from Greek *lithos* stone]
: mineral ⟨rhodo*lite*⟩ : rock ⟨aero*lite*⟩ : fossil ⟨stromato*lite*⟩

**li·ter** \'lē-tər\ *noun* [French *litre*, from Medieval Latin *litra*, a measure, from Greek, a weight] (1797)
: a metric unit of capacity equal to one cubic decimeter — see METRIC SYSTEM table

**lit·er·a·cy** \'li-t(ə-)rə-sē\ *noun* (1883)
: the quality or state of being literate

¹**lit·er·al** \'li-t(ə-)rəl\ *adjective* [Middle English, from Middle French, from Medieval

Latin *litteralis,* from Latin, of a letter, from *littera* letter] (14th century)
**1 a :** according with the letter of the scriptures **b :** adhering to fact or to the ordinary construction or primary meaning of a term or expression **:** ACTUAL ⟨liberty in the *literal* sense is impossible —B. N. Cardozo⟩ **c :** free from exaggeration or embellishment ⟨the *literal* truth⟩ **d :** characterized by a concern mainly with facts ⟨a very *literal* man⟩
**2 :** of, relating to, or expressed in letters
**3 :** reproduced word for word **:** EXACT, VERBATIM ⟨a *literal* translation⟩
— **lit·er·al·i·ty** \ˌli-tə-'ra-lə-tē\ *noun*
— **lit·er·al·ness** \'li-t(ə-)rəl-nəs\ *noun*
**²literal** *noun* (1622)
**:** a small error usually of a single letter (as in writing)
**lit·er·al·ism** \'li-t(ə-)rə-ˌliz-əm\ *noun* (1644)
**1 :** adherence to the explicit substance of an idea or expression ⟨biblical *literalism*⟩
**2 :** fidelity to observable fact **:** REALISM
— **lit·er·al·ist** \-list\ *noun*
— **lit·er·al·is·tic** \ˌli-t(ə-)rə-'lis-tik\ *adjective*
**lit·er·al·ize** \'li-t(ə-)rə-ˌlīz\ *transitive verb* **-ized; -iz·ing** (1826)
**:** to make literal
— **lit·er·al·i·za·tion** \ˌli-t(ə-)rə-lə-'zā-shən\ *noun*
**lit·er·al·ly** \'li-tə-rə-lē, 'li-trə-lē, 'li-tər-lē\ *adverb* (1533)
**1 :** in a literal sense or manner **:** ACTUALLY ⟨took the remark *literally*⟩ ⟨was *literally* insane⟩
**2 :** in effect **:** VIRTUALLY ⟨will *literally* turn the world upside down to combat cruelty or injustice —Norman Cousins⟩ ▯
**lit·er·ary** \'li-tə-ˌrer-ē\ *adjective* (1749)
**1 a :** of, relating to, or having the characteristics of humane learning or literature **b :** BOOKISH 2 **c :** of or relating to books
**2 a :** WELL-READ **b :** of or relating to authors or scholars or to their professions
— **lit·er·ar·i·ly** \ˌli-tə-'rer-ə-lē\ *adverb*
— **lit·er·ar·i·ness** \'li-tə-ˌrer-ē-nəs\ *noun*
**literary executor** *noun* (1868)
**:** a person entrusted with the management of the papers and unpublished works of a deceased author
**¹lit·er·ate** \'li-tə-rət *also* 'li-trət\ *adjective* [Middle English *literat,* from Latin *litteratus* marked with letters, literate, from *litterae* letters, literature, from plural of *littera*] (15th century)
**1 a :** EDUCATED, CULTURED **b :** able to read and write
**2 a :** versed in literature or creative writing **:** LITERARY **b :** LUCID, POLISHED ⟨a *literate* essay⟩ **c :** having knowledge or competence ⟨computer-*literate*⟩ ⟨politically *literate*⟩
— **lit·er·ate·ly** *adverb*
— **lit·er·ate·ness** *noun*
**²literate** *noun* (circa 1550)
**1 :** an educated person
**2 :** a person who can read and write
**li·te·ra·ti** \ˌli-tə-'rä-(ˌ)tē\ *noun plural* [obsolete Italian *litterati,* from Latin, plural of *litteratus*] (1621)
**1 :** the educated class; *also* **:** INTELLIGENTSIA
**2 :** persons interested in literature or the arts
**lit·er·a·tim** \ˌli-tə-'rä-təm, -'rä-\ *adverb or adjective* [Medieval Latin, from Latin *littera*] (1643)
**:** letter for letter ⟨printed *literatim* from the manuscript —I. A. Gordon⟩
**lit·er·a·tion** \ˌli-tə-'rä-shən\ *noun* [Latin *littera* + English *-ation*] (circa 1889)
**:** the representation of sound or words by letters
**lit·er·a·tor** \'li-tə-ˌrā-tər, ˌli-tə-'rä-ˌtȯr\ *noun* (1791)
**:** LITTERATEUR
**lit·er·a·ture** \'li-tə-rə-ˌchu̇r, 'li-trə-ˌchu̇r, 'li-tə(r)-ˌchu̇r, -chər, -ˌtyu̇r, -ˌtu̇r\ *noun* [Middle

English, from Latin *litteratura* writing, grammar, learning, from *litteratus*] (14th century)
**1** *archaic* **:** literary culture
**2 :** the production of literary work especially as an occupation
**3 a** (1) **:** writings in prose or verse; *especially* **:** writings having excellence of form or expression and expressing ideas of permanent or universal interest (2) **:** an example of such writings ⟨what came out, though rarely *literature*, was always a roaring good story —*People*⟩ **b :** the body of written works produced in a particular language, country, or age **c :** the body of writings on a particular subject ⟨scientific *literature*⟩ **d :** printed matter (as leaflets or circulars) ⟨campaign *literature*⟩
**4 :** the aggregate of a usually specified type of musical compositions ⟨Brahms piano *literature*⟩
**lit·er·a·tus** \ˌli-tə-'rä-təs\ *noun* [New Latin, back-formation from English *literati* (taken as Latin)] (1704)
**:** a member of the literati
**lith-** *or* **litho-** *combining form* [Latin, from Greek, from *lithos*]
**:** stone ⟨*litho*logy⟩
**-lith** *noun combining form* [New Latin *-lithus* & French *-lithe,* from Greek *lithos*]
**1 :** structure or implement of stone ⟨mega*lith*⟩ ⟨*eolith*⟩
**2 :** calculus ⟨uro*lith*⟩
**3 :** -LITE ⟨lacco*lith*⟩
**li·tharge** \'li-ˌthärj, li-'\ *noun* [Middle English, from Middle French, from Latin *lithargyrus,* from Greek *lithargyros,* from *lithos* + *argyros* silver — more at ARGENT] (14th century)
**:** a fused lead monoxide; *broadly* **:** LEAD MONOXIDE
**lithe** \'līth, 'līth\ *adjective* [Middle English, from Old English *līthe* gentle; akin to Old High German *lindi* gentle, Latin *lentus* slow] (14th century)
**1 :** easily bent or flexed ⟨*lithe* steel⟩ ⟨a *lithe* vine⟩
**2 :** characterized by easy flexibility and grace ⟨a *lithe* dancer⟩ ⟨treading with a *lithe* silent step⟩; *also* **:** athletically slim ⟨the most *lithe* and graspable of waists —R. P. Warren⟩
— **lithe·ly** *adverb*
— **lithe·ness** *noun*
**lithe·some** \'līth-səm, 'līth-\ *adjective* (circa 1774)
**:** LISSOME
**li·thi·a·sis** \li-'thī-ə-səs\ *noun, plural* **-a·ses** \-ˌsēz\ [New Latin, from Greek, from *lithos*] (circa 1657)
**:** the formation of stony concretions in the body (as in the gallbladder)
**lith·ic** \'li-thik\ *adjective* [Greek *lithikos,* from *lithos*] (1797)
**1 :** STONY 1
**2 :** of, relating to, or being a stone tool
**-lithic** *adjective combining form* [*lithic*]
**:** relating to or characteristic of a (specified) stage in humankind's use of stone as a cultural tool ⟨Neo*lithic*⟩
**lith·i·fy** \'li-thə-ˌfī\ *verb* **-fied; -fy·ing** (1877)
*transitive verb*
**:** to change to stone **:** PETRIFY; *especially* **:** to convert (unconsolidated sediment) into solid rock
*intransitive verb*
**:** to become changed into stone
— **lith·i·fi·ca·tion** \ˌli-thə-fə-'kā-shən\ *noun*
**lith·i·um** \'li-thē-əm\ *noun* [New Latin, from *lithia* oxide of lithium, from Greek *lithos*] (1818)
**1 :** a soft silver-white element of the alkali metal group that is the lightest metal known and that is used in chemical synthesis and storage batteries — see ELEMENT table
**2 :** a salt of lithium (as lithium carbonate) used in psychiatric medicine

**lithium carbonate** *noun* (1873)
**:** a crystalline salt $Li_2CO_3$ used in the glass and ceramic industries and in medicine in the treatment of manic-depressive psychosis
**lithium fluoride** *noun* (1944)
**:** a crystalline salt LiF used especially in making prisms and ceramics and as a flux
**lithium ni·o·bate** \-'nī-ə-ˌbāt\ *noun* [*niobium* + ¹*-ate*] (1966)
**:** a crystalline material $LiNbO_3$ whose physical properties change in response to pressure or the presence of an electric field and which is used in fiber optics and as a synthetic gemstone
**litho** \'lī-(ˌ)thō\ *noun, plural* **lith·os** (circa 1889)
**1 :** LITHOGRAPH
**2 :** LITHOGRAPHY 1
**¹lith·o·graph** \'li-thə-ˌgraf\ *transitive verb* (1825)
**:** to produce, copy, or portray by lithography
— **li·thog·ra·pher** \li-'thä-grə-fər, 'li-thə-ˌgra-fər\ *noun*
**²lithograph** *noun* (1828)
**:** a print made by lithography
— **lith·o·graph·ic** \ˌli-thə-'gra-fik\ *adjective*
— **lith·o·graph·i·cal·ly** \-fi-k(ə-)lē\ *adverb*
**li·thog·ra·phy** \li-'thä-grə-fē\ *noun* [German *Lithographie,* from *lith-* + *-graphie* -graphy] (1813)
**1 :** the process of printing from a plane surface (as a smooth stone or metal plate) on which the image to be printed is ink-receptive and the blank area ink-repellent
**2 :** the process of producing patterns on semiconductor crystals for use as integrated circuits
**li·thol·o·gy** \li-'thä-lə-jē\ *noun, plural* **-gies** (1716)
**1 :** the study of rocks
**2 :** the character of a rock formation; *also* **:** a rock formation having a particular set of characteristics
— **lith·o·log·ic** \ˌli-thə-'lä-jik\ *or* **lith·o·log·i·cal** \-ji-kəl\ *adjective*
— **lith·o·log·i·cal·ly** \-ji-k(ə-)lē\ *adverb*
**lith·o·phane** \'li-thə-ˌfān\ *noun* [probably from German *Lithophan,* from Greek *lithos* + German *diaphan* diaphanous] (circa 1889)
**:** porcelain impressed with figures that are made distinct by transmitted light; *also* **:** an object of this material
**lith·o·phyte** \'li-thə-ˌfīt\ *noun* [French, from *lith-* + *-phyte*] (1774)
**:** a plant that grows on rock
**lith·o·pone** \'li-thə-ˌpōn\ *noun* [International Scientific Vocabulary *lith-* + Greek *ponos* work] (circa 1884)
**:** a white pigment consisting essentially of zinc sulfide and barium sulfate
**lith·o·sol** \'li-thə-ˌsäl, -ˌsȯl\ *noun* [*lith-* + Latin *solum* soil] (circa 1938)
**:** any of a group of shallow azonal soils consisting of imperfectly weathered rock fragments
**lith·o·sphere** \'li-thə-ˌsfir\ *noun* [International Scientific Vocabulary] (1887)

---

▯ USAGE
**literally** Since some people take sense 2 to be the opposite of sense 1, it has been frequently criticized as a misuse. Instead, the use is pure hyperbole intended to gain emphasis, but it often appears in contexts where no additional emphasis is necessary.

---

\ə\ **abut** \ᵊ\ **kitten** \ər\ **further** \a\ **ash** \ā\ **ace**
\ä\ **mop, mar** \au̇\ **out** \ch\ **chin** \e\ **bet** \ē\ **easy**
\g\ **go** \i\ **hit** \ī\ **ice** \j\ **job** \ŋ\ **sing** \ō\ **go**
\ȯ\ **law** \ȯi\ **boy** \th\ **thin** \t̲h̲\ **the** \ü\ **loot** \u̇\ **foot**
\y\ **yet** \zh\ **vision** *see also* Guide to Pronunciation

: the solid part of a celestial body (as the earth); *specifically* : the outer part of the solid earth composed of rock essentially like that exposed at the surface and usually considered to be about 50 miles (80 kilometers) in thickness
— **lith·o·spher·ic** \,li-thə-'sfir-ik, -'sfer-\ *adjective*

**li·thot·o·my** \li-'thä-tə-mē\ *noun, plural* **-mies** [Late Latin *lithotomia,* from Greek, from *lithotomein* to perform a lithotomy, from *lith-* + *temnein* to cut — more at TOME] (1721)
: surgical incision of the urinary bladder for removal of a stone

**lith·o·trip·sy** \'li-thə-,trip-sē\ *noun, plural* **-sies** [*lith-* + Greek *tripsis* a rubbing, from *tribein* to rub — more at THROW] (1834)
: the breaking of a stone (as by shock waves or crushing with a surgical instrument) in the urinary system into pieces small enough to be voided or washed out

**lith·o·trip·ter** *also* **lith·o·trip·tor** \'li-thə-,trip-tər\ *noun* [alteration of *lithontriptor,* from *lithontriptic* breaking up bladder stones, modification of Greek (*pharmaka tōn*) *lithōn thryptika* (drugs) capable of pulverizing stones] (1825)
: a device for performing lithotripsy; *especially* : a noninvasive device that pulverizes stones by focusing shock waves on a patient immersed in a water bath

**Lith·u·a·nian** \,li-thə-'wā-nē-ən, -nyən, *chiefly British* ,lith-yü-\ *noun* (1607)
**1** : a native or inhabitant of Lithuania
**2** : the Baltic language of the Lithuanian people
— **Lithuanian** *adjective*

**lit·i·gant** \'li-ti-gənt\ *noun* (1659)
: one engaged in a lawsuit
— **litigant** *adjective*

**lit·i·gate** \'li-tə-,gāt\ *verb* **-gat·ed; -gat·ing** [Latin *litigatus,* past participle of *litigare,* from *lit-, lis* lawsuit + *agere* to drive — more at AGENT] (1615)
*intransitive verb*
: to carry on a legal contest by judicial process
*transitive verb*
**1** *archaic* : DISPUTE
**2** : to contest in law
— **lit·i·ga·ble** \'li-ti-gə-bəl\ *adjective*
— **lit·i·ga·tion** \,li-tə-'gā-shən\ *noun*
— **lit·i·ga·tor** \'li-tə-,gā-tər\ *noun*

**li·ti·gious** \lə-'ti-jəs, li-\ *adjective* [Middle English, from Middle French *litigieux,* from Latin *litigiosus,* from *litigium* dispute, from *litigare*] (14th century)
**1 a** : DISPUTATIOUS, CONTENTIOUS **b** : prone to engage in lawsuits
**2** : subject to litigation
**3** : of, relating to, or marked by litigation
— **li·ti·gious·ly** *adverb*
— **li·ti·gious·ness** *noun*

**lit·mus** \'lit-məs\ *noun* [Middle English *litmose,* of Scandinavian origin; akin to Old Norse *litmosi* herbs used in dyeing, from *litr* color (akin to Old English *wlite* brightness) + *mosi* moss; akin to Old English *mōs* moss] (14th century)
**1** : a coloring matter from lichens that turns red in acid solutions and blue in alkaline solutions and is used as an acid-base indicator
**2** : the critical factor in a litmus test; *also* : LITMUS TEST

**litmus paper** *noun* (1803)
: unsized paper colored with litmus and used as an indicator

**litmus test** *noun* (1952)
: a test in which a single factor (as an attitude, event, or fact) is decisive

**li·to·tes** \'lī-tə-,tēz, 'li-, lī-'tō-,tēz\ *noun, plural* **litotes** [Greek *litotēs,* from *litos* simple, perhaps from *lit-, lis* linen cloth] (1589)
: understatement in which an affirmative is expressed by the negative of the contrary (as in "not a bad singer" or "not unhappy")

**li·tre** \'lē-tər\ *variant of* LITER
**lit·ten** \'li-t³n\ *adjective* [alteration of *lit,* past participle of *light*] (circa 1849)
*archaic* : being lighted

**¹lit·ter** \'li-tər\ *noun* [Middle English, from Middle French *litiere,* from *lit* bed, from Latin *lectus* — more at LIE] (14th century)
**1 a** : a covered and curtained couch provided with shafts and used for carrying a single passenger **b** : a device (as a stretcher) for carrying a sick or injured person
**2 a** (1) : material used as bedding

**litter 1a**

for animals (2) : material used to absorb the urine and feces of animals **b** : the uppermost slightly decayed layer of organic matter on the forest floor
**3** : the offspring at one birth of a multiparous animal
**4 a** : trash, wastepaper, or garbage lying scattered about ⟨trying to clean up the roadside *litter*⟩ **b** : an untidy accumulation of objects ⟨a shabby writing-desk covered with a *litter* of yellowish dusty documents —Joseph Conrad⟩
◆
— **lit·tery** \-tə-rē\ *adjective*

**²litter** (14th century)
*transitive verb*
**1** : BED 1a
**2** : to give birth to a litter of ⟨young⟩
**3 a** : to strew with scattered articles **b** : to scatter about in disorder **c** : to lie about in disorder ⟨their upside-down hats *littered* the top of the bar —Michael Chabon⟩ **d** : to mark with objects scattered at random ⟨a book *littered* with misprints⟩
*intransitive verb*
**1** : to give birth to a litter
**2** : to strew litter

**lit·te·rae hu·ma·ni·o·res** \'li-tə-,rī-hü-,mä-nē-'ōr-,ās, -'ōr-\ *noun plural* [Medieval Latin, literally, more humane letters] (1747)
: HUMANITIES

**lit·te·ra·teur** *or* **lit·té·ra·teur** \,li-tə-rə-'tər, ,li-trə-, -'tur\ *noun* [French *littérateur,* from Latin *litterator* critic, from *litterae* letters, literature] (1806)
: a literary person; *especially* : a professional writer

**lit·ter·bag** \'li-tər-,bag\ *noun* (1955)
: a bag used (as in an automobile) for temporary refuse disposal

**lit·ter·bug** \-,bəg\ *noun* (1947)
: one who litters a public area

**lit·ter·er** \'li-tər-ər\ *noun* (1928)
: LITTERBUG

**lit·ter·mate** \'li-tər-,māt\ *noun* (1921)
: one of the offspring in a litter in relation to the others

**¹lit·tle** \'li-t³l\ *adjective* **lit·tler** \'li-t³l-ər, 'lit-lər\ *or* **less** \'les\ *or* **less·er** \'le-sər\; **lit·tlest** \'li-t³l-əst, 'lit-ləst\ *or* **least** \'lēst\ [Middle English *littel,* from Old English *lȳtel;* akin to Old High German *luzzil* little] (before 12th century)
**1** : not big: as **a** : small in size or extent : TINY ⟨has *little* feet⟩ **b** : YOUNG ⟨was too *little* to remember⟩ **c** *of a plant or animal* : small in comparison with related forms — used in vernacular names **d** : small in number **e** : small in condition, distinction, or scope ⟨big business trampling on the *little* fellow⟩ **f** : NARROW, MEAN ⟨the pettiness of *little* minds⟩ **g** : pleasingly small ⟨a cute *little* thing⟩ **h** — used as an intensive ⟨why, you *little* devil!⟩
**2** : not much: as **a** : existing only in a small amount or to a slight degree ⟨has *little* money⟩

**b** : short in duration : BRIEF **c** : existing to an appreciable though not extensive degree or amount — used with *a* ⟨had a *little* money in the bank⟩
**3** : small in importance or interest : TRIVIAL
*synonym* see SMALL
— **lit·tle·ness** \'li-t³l-nəs\ *noun*

**²little** *adverb* **less** \'les\; **least** \'lēst\ (before 12th century)
**1 a** : in only a small quantity or degree : SLIGHTLY ⟨facts that were *little* known at the time⟩ **b** : not at all ⟨cared *little* for their neighbors⟩
**2** : RARELY, INFREQUENTLY

**³little** *noun* (before 12th century)
**1** : a small amount, quantity, or degree; *also* : practically nothing ⟨*little* has changed⟩
**2 a** : a short time **b** : a short distance
— **a little** : SOMEWHAT, RATHER ⟨found the play *a little* dull⟩
— **in little** : on a small scale; *especially* : in miniature

**Little Bear** *noun*
: URSA MINOR

**little bitty** *adjective* (1905)
: SMALL, TINY

**little bluestem** *noun* (circa 1898)
: a forage grass (*Schizachyrium scoparium* synonym *Andropogon scoparius*) of eastern and central North America

**little brown bat** *noun* (1842)
: a small widely distributed insectivorous North American bat (*Myotis lucifugus*) with brown fur

**little by little** *adverb* (15th century)
: by small degrees or amounts : GRADUALLY

**Little Dipper** *noun*
: the seven principal stars in Ursa Minor

**little finger** *noun* (before 12th century)
: the fourth and smallest finger of the hand counting the forefinger as the first

**little guy** *noun* (1863)
: LITTLE MAN

**Little Hours** *noun plural* (circa 1872)
: the offices of prime, terce, sext, and none forming part of the canonical hours

**little leaf** *noun* (1916)
: a plant disorder characterized by small and often chlorotic and distorted foliage: as **a** : a zinc-deficiency disease of deciduous woody plants (as grape, peach, and pecan) **b** : a destructive disease of unknown cause that affects southern pines and especially the shortleaf pine — called also *little-leaf disease*

**Little League** *noun* (1952)
: a commercially sponsored baseball league for boys and girls from 8 to 12 years old
— **Little Leaguer** *noun*

◇ WORD HISTORY
**litter** The diverse senses of the word *litter* all grew out of the basic notion "bed." In Old French *litiere,* a derivative of *lit* "bed," could refer to a sleeping place in a general way, but it was usually applied more narrowly either to a curtained portable couch or to straw spread on the ground as a sleeping place for animals. In borrowing the word, English retained both usages and added new ones. The "bedding for animals" sense was extended to the offspring of an animal such as a dog or cat that gives birth to a number of young at once. In a different direction, *litter* became not just straw for animal bedding but straw or similar material used for any purpose, and by the 18th century any odds and ends of rubbish lying scattered about, and hence a near-synonym for "trash" or "refuse." A much more recent development, presumably arising from euphemism, has extended *litter* to absorbent clay that a cat is trained to use not for sleeping or giving birth but for depositing its feces and urine.

**little magazine** *noun* (1900)
: a literary usually noncommercial magazine that features works especially of writers who are not well-known

**little man** *noun* (1933)
: the ordinary individual

**lit·tle·neck** \'li-t³l-,nek\ *noun* [Littleneck Bay, Long Island, N.Y.] (1883)
: a young quahog suitable to be eaten raw — called also *littleneck clam*

**Little Office** *noun* (circa 1872)
: an office in honor of the Virgin Mary like but shorter than the Divine Office

**little people** *noun plural* (circa 1731)
**1** : tiny imaginary beings (as fairies, elves, and leprechauns) of folklore
**2** : CHILDREN
**3** : MIDGETS
**4** : common people

**little slam** *noun* (circa 1897)
: the winning of all tricks except one in bridge

**little theater** *noun* (1812)
: a small theater for low-cost dramatic productions designed for a relatively limited audience

**little toe** *noun* (before 12th century)
: the outermost and smallest digit of the foot

**little woman** *noun* (1795)
: WIFE

**¹lit·to·ral** \'li-tə-rəl\ ;,li-tə-'ral, -'räl\ *adjective* [Latin *litoralis,* from *litor-, litus* seashore] (circa 1656)
: of, relating to, or situated or growing on or near a shore especially of the sea

**²littoral** *noun* (1828)
: a coastal region; *especially* : the shore zone between high and low watermarks

**lit up** *adjective* (circa 1914)
: DRUNK 1a

**li·tur·gi·cal** \lə-'tər-ji-kəl, li-\ *adjective* (1641)
**1** : of, relating to, or having the characteristics of liturgy
**2** : using or favoring the use of liturgy ⟨*liturgical* churches⟩
— **li·tur·gi·cal·ly** \-k(ə-)lē\ *adverb*

**li·tur·gics** \-jiks\ *noun plural but singular or plural in construction* (circa 1855)
: the practice or study of formal public worship

**li·tur·gi·ol·o·gist** \-,tər-jē-'ä-lə-jist\ *noun* (1866)
: LITURGIST 2

**li·tur·gi·ol·o·gy** \-jē\ *noun* (1863)
: LITURGICS

**lit·ur·gist** \'li-tər-jist\ *noun* (1649)
**1** : one who adheres to, compiles, or leads a liturgy
**2** : a specialist in liturgics

**lit·ur·gy** \'li-tər-jē\ *noun, plural* **-gies** [Late Latin *liturgia,* from Greek *leitourgia* public service, from Greek (Attic) *leïton* public building (from Greek *laos* — Attic *leōs* — people) + *-ourgia* -urgy] (1560)
**1** *often capitalized* : a eucharistic rite
**2** : a rite or body of rites prescribed for public worship
**3** : a customary repertoire of ideas, phrases, or observances

**liv·abil·i·ty** *also* **live·abil·i·ty** \,li-və-'bi-lə-tē\ *noun* (1914)
**1** : survival expectancy : VIABILITY — used especially of poultry and livestock
**2** : suitability for human living

**liv·able** *also* **live·able** \'li-və-bəl\ *adjective* (1814)
**1** : suitable for living in or with
**2** : ENDURABLE
— **liv·able·ness** *noun*

**¹live** \'liv\ *verb* **lived; liv·ing** [Middle English, from Old English *libban;* akin to Old High German *lebēn* to live] (before 12th century)
*intransitive verb*
**1** : to be alive : have the life of an animal or plant
**2** : to continue alive
**3** : to maintain oneself : SUBSIST

**4** : to occupy a home : DWELL ⟨*living* in a shabby room⟩ ⟨they had always *lived* in the country⟩
**5** : to attain eternal life ⟨though he die, yet shall he *live* —John 11:25 (Revised Standard Version)⟩
**6** : to conduct or pass one's life ⟨*lived* only for his work⟩
**7** : to remain in human memory or record ⟨the past *lives* in us all —W. R. Inge⟩
**8** : to have a life rich in experience
**9** : COHABIT
*transitive verb*
**1** : to pass through or spend the duration of ⟨*lived* their lives alone⟩
**2** : ACT OUT, PRACTICE — often used with *out* ⟨to *live* out their fantasies⟩
**3** : to exhibit vigor, gusto, or enthusiasm in ⟨*lived* life to the fullest⟩
— **live it up** : to live with gusto and usually fast and loose ⟨*lived it up* with wine and song —*Newsweek*⟩
— **live up to** : to act or be in accordance with ⟨had no intention of *living up to* his promise⟩

**²live** \'līv\ *adjective* [short for *alive*] (1542)
**1** : having life : LIVING
**2** : exerting force or containing energy: as **a** : AFIRE, GLOWING ⟨*live* coals⟩ **b** : connected to electric power **c** : charged with explosives and containing shot or a bullet ⟨*live* ammunition⟩; *also* : armed but not exploded ⟨a *live* bomb⟩ **d** : imparting or driven by power ⟨a *live* axle⟩ **e** : being in operation ⟨a *live* microphone⟩
**3** : abounding with life : VIVID
**4** : being in a pure native state
**5** : of bright vivid color
**6** : of continuing or current interest ⟨*live* issues⟩
**7 a** : not yet printed from or plated ⟨*live* type⟩ **b** : not yet typeset ⟨*live* copy⟩
**8 a** : of or involving a presentation (as a play or concert) in which both the performers and an audience are physically present ⟨a *live* record album⟩ ⟨a nightclub with *live* entertainment⟩ **b** : broadcast directly at the time of production ⟨a *live* radio program⟩
**9** : being in play ⟨a *live* ball⟩

**³live** \'līv\ *adverb* (1946)
: at the actual time of occurrence : during, from, or at a live production ⟨the programming originated *live* from New York City —*Current Biography*⟩

**live-bear·er** \'līv-,bar-ər, -,ber-\ *noun* (1934)
: a fish that brings forth living young rather than eggs; *especially* : any of a family (Poeciliidae) of numerous small surface-feeding fishes

**live-box** \-,bäks\ *noun* (1862)
: a box or pen suspended in water to keep aquatic animals alive

**-lived** \'līvd, 'livd\ *adjective combining form* [Middle English, from *lif* life]
: having a life of a specified kind or length ⟨long-*lived*⟩

**lived-in** \'liv-,din\ *adjective* (1873)
: of or suggesting long-term human habitation or use : COMFORTABLE

**live down** *transitive verb* (1842)
: to live so as to wipe out the memory or effects of ⟨made a mistake and couldn't *live* it *down*⟩

**live-for·ev·er** \'liv-fə-,re-vər\ *noun* (1597)
: SEDUM

**live-in** \'liv-,in\ *adjective* (1953)
**1** : living in one's place of employment ⟨a *live-in* maid⟩
**2** : involving or involved with cohabitation ⟨a *live-in* relationship⟩ ⟨a *live-in* partner⟩
— **live-in** *noun*

**live in** *intransitive verb* (1890)
: to live in one's place of employment : live in another's home

**live·li·hood** \'līv-lē-,hùd\ *noun* [alteration of Middle English *livelode* course of life, from

Old English *līflād,* from *līf* + *lād* course — more at LODE] (15th century)
**1** : means of support or subsistence
**2** *obsolete* : the quality or state of being lively

**live load** *noun* (1866)
: the load to which a structure is subjected in addition to its own weight

**live·long** \'liv-,lòn\ *adjective* [Middle English *lef·long,* from *lef* dear + *long* — more at LIEF] (15th century)
: WHOLE, ENTIRE ⟨the *livelong* day⟩

**live·ly** \'līv-lē\ *adjective* **live·li·er; -est** [Middle English, from Old English *līflīc,* from *līf* life] (before 12th century)
**1** *obsolete* : LIVING
**2** : briskly alert and energetic : VIGOROUS, ANIMATED ⟨a *lively* discussion⟩ ⟨*lively* children racing for home⟩
**3** : ACTIVE, INTENSE ⟨takes a *lively* interest in politics⟩
**4** : BRILLIANT, FRESH ⟨a *lively* wit⟩
**5** : imparting spirit or vivacity : STIMULATING ⟨many a peer of England brews *livelier* liquor than the Muse —A. E. Housman⟩
**6** : quick to rebound : RESILIENT
**7** : responding readily to the helm ⟨a *lively* boat⟩
**8** : full of life, movement, or incident ⟨*lively* streets at carnival time⟩ ☆
— **live·li·ly** \'līv-lə-lē\ *adverb*
— **live·li·ness** \'līv-lē-nəs\ *noun*
— **lively** *adverb*

**liv·en** \'lī-vən\ *verb* **liv·ened; liv·en·ing** \'lī-və-niŋ, 'līv-niŋ\ (1884)
*transitive verb*
: ENLIVEN — often used with *up* ⟨he . . . *livened* up the editorial page —*Current Biography*⟩
*intransitive verb*
: to become lively

**live oak** \'līv-\ *noun* (1610)
: any of several American evergreen oaks: as **a** : a medium-sized oak (*Quercus virginiana*) of southeastern North America often cultivated as a shelter and shade tree and noted for its extremely hard tough durable wood **b** : any of several oaks of the western U.S. with evergreen foliage and hard durable wood

**¹liv·er** \'li-vər\ *noun* [Middle English, from Old English *lifer;* akin to Old High German *lebra* liver] (before 12th century)
**1 a** : a large very vascular glandular organ of vertebrates that secretes bile and causes important changes in many of the substances contained in the blood (as by converting sugars into glycogen which it stores up until required and by forming urea) **b** : any of various large compound glands associated with the digestive tract of invertebrate animals and probably concerned with the secretion of digestive enzymes
**2** *archaic* : a determinant of the quality or temper of a man

---

☆ **SYNONYMS**
**Lively, animated, vivacious, sprightly, gay** mean keenly alive and spirited. LIVELY suggests briskness, alertness, or energy ⟨a *lively* debate on the issues⟩. ANIMATED applies to what is spirited and active ⟨an *animated* discussion of current events⟩. VIVACIOUS suggests an activeness of gesture and wit, often playful or alluring ⟨a *vivacious* party host⟩. SPRIGHTLY suggests lightness and spirited vigor of manner or wit ⟨a tuneful, *sprightly* musical⟩. GAY stresses complete freedom from care and overflowing spirits ⟨the *gay* spirit of Paris in the 1920s⟩.

---

\ə\ **abut** \³\ **kitten** \ər\ **further** \a\ **ash** \ā\ **ace**
\ä\ **mop, mar** \aù\ **out** \ch\ **chin** \e\ **bet** \ē\ **easy**
\g\ **go** \i\ **hit** \ī\ **ice** \j\ **job** \ŋ\ **sing** \ō\ **go**
\ò\ **law** \òi\ **boy** \th\ **thin** \t̲h̲\ **the** \ü\ **loot** \ù\ **foot**
\y\ **yet** \zh\ **vision** *see also* Guide to Pronunciation

**3** : the liver of an animal (as a calf or chicken) eaten as food
**4** : a grayish reddish brown — called also *liver brown, liver maroon*

**²liv·er** \'li-vər\ *noun* (14th century)
**1** : one that lives especially in a specified way ⟨a fast *liver*⟩
**2** : RESIDENT

**-livered** *adjective combining form*
: expressing vigor or courage considered suggestive of one with (such) a liver ⟨chicken*livered*⟩ ⟨lily-*livered*⟩

**liver fluke** *noun* (circa 1798)
: any of various trematode worms (as *Fasciola hepatica*) that invade the mammalian liver

**liv·er·ied** \'li-və-rēd, 'liv-rēd\ *adjective* (1634)
: wearing a livery ⟨a *liveried* chauffeur⟩

**liv·er·ish** \'li-və-rish, 'liv-rish\ *adjective* (1740)
**1** : resembling liver especially in color
**2 a** : suffering from liver disorder : BILIOUS **b** : PEEVISH, IRASCIBLE
**— liv·er·ish·ness** *noun*

**liver sausage** *noun* (1855)
: a sausage containing cooked ground liver and pork trimmings — called also *liver pudding*

**liver spots** *noun plural* (circa 1859)
: spots of dark pigmentation on the skin (as from exposure to sun) occurring especially among older people

**liv·er·wort** \'li-vər-,wərt, -,wòrt\ *noun* (before 12th century)
**1** : any of a class (Hepaticae) of bryophytic plants characterized by a thalloid gametophyte or sometimes an upright leafy gametophyte that resembles a moss
**2** : HEPATICA

**liv·er·wurst** \'li-və(r)-,wərst *also* -,vù(r)st; *sometimes* -,vùsht\ *noun* [part translation of German *Leberwurst*, from *Leber* liver + *Wurst* sausage] (1869)
: LIVER SAUSAGE

**¹liv·ery** \'li-və-rē, 'liv-rē\ *noun, plural* **-er·ies** [Middle English, from Middle French *livree*, literally, delivery, from *livrer* to deliver, from Latin *liberare* to free — more at LIBERATE] (14th century)
**1** *archaic* : the apportioning of provisions especially to servants : ALLOWANCE
**2 a** : the distinctive clothing or badge formerly worn by the retainers of a person of rank **b** : a servant's uniform **c** : distinctive dress : GARB **d** *chiefly British* : an identifying design (as on a vehicle) that designates ownership
**3** *archaic* **a** : one's retainers or retinue **b** : the members of a British livery company
**4** : the act of delivering legal possession of property
**5 a** : the feeding, stabling, and care of horses for pay **b** : LIVERY STABLE **c** : a concern offering vehicles (as boats) for rent

**²livery** *adjective* (1778)
**1** : resembling liver
**2** : suggesting liver disorder

**livery company** *noun* (1766)
: any of various London craft or trade associations that are descended from medieval guilds

**liv·ery·man** \'li-və-rē-mən, 'liv-rē-\ *noun* (1682)
**1** : a freeman of the City of London entitled to wear the livery of the company to which he belongs
**2** *archaic* : a liveried retainer
**3** : the keeper of a vehicle-rental service

**livery stable** *noun* (1705)
: a stable where horses and vehicles are kept for hire and where stabling is provided — called also *livery barn*

**lives** *plural of* LIFE

**live steam** *noun* (circa 1875)
: steam direct from a boiler and under full pressure

**live·stock** \'līv-,stäk\ *noun* (1742)
: animals kept or raised for use or pleasure; *especially* : farm animals kept for use and profit

**live·trap** \-,trap\ *transitive verb* (1944)
: to capture (an animal) in a live trap

**live trap** *noun* (circa 1875)
: a trap for catching an animal alive and uninjured

**live wire** *noun* (1903)
: an alert, active, or aggressive person

**liv·id** \'li-vəd\ *adjective* [French *livide*, from Latin *lividus*, from *livēre* to be blue; akin to Welsh *lliw* color and probably to Russian *sliva* plum] (1622)
**1** : discolored by bruising : BLACK-AND-BLUE ⟨the *livid* traces of the sharp scourges —Abraham Cowley⟩
**2** : ASHEN, PALLID ⟨this cross, thy *livid* face, thy pierced hands and feet —Walt Whitman⟩
**3** : REDDISH ⟨a fan of gladiolas blushed *livid* under the electric letters —Truman Capote⟩
**4** : very angry : ENRAGED ⟨was *livid* at his son's disobedience⟩
**— li·vid·i·ty** \li-'vi-də-tē\ *noun*
**— liv·id·ness** \'li-vəd-nəs\ *noun*

**¹liv·ing** \'li-viŋ\ *adjective* (before 12th century)
**1 a** : having life **b** : ACTIVE, FUNCTIONING ⟨*living* languages⟩
**2 a** : exhibiting the life or motion of nature : NATURAL ⟨the wilderness is a *living* museum . . . of natural history —*NEA Journal*⟩ **b** : ²LIVE 2a
**3 a** : full of life or vigor **b** : true to life : VIVID ⟨televised in *living* color⟩ **c** : suited for living ⟨the *living* area⟩
**4** : involving living persons
**5** : VERY — used as an intensive ⟨scared the *living* daylights out of me⟩
**— liv·ing·ness** *noun*

**²living** *noun* (14th century)
**1** : the condition of being alive
**2 a** : means of subsistence : LIVELIHOOD ⟨earning a *living*⟩ **b** *archaic* : ESTATE, PROPERTY **c** *British* : BENEFICE 1
**3** : conduct or manner of life ⟨the collegiate way of *living* —J. B. Conant⟩

**living death** *noun* (1671)
: life emptied of joys and satisfactions

**living fossil** *noun* (1922)
: an organism (as a horseshoe crab or a ginkgo tree) that has remained essentially unchanged from earlier geologic times and whose close relatives are usually extinct

**liv·ing·ly** \'li-viŋ-lē\ *adverb* (15th century)
: in a vital manner : REALISTICALLY

**living room** *noun* (1857)
**1** : a room in a residence used for the common social activities of the occupants
**2** : LEBENSRAUM — called also *living space*

**living standard** *noun* (1944)
: STANDARD OF LIVING

**living unit** *noun* (circa 1937)
: an apartment or house for use by one family

**living wage** *noun* (1888)
**1** : a subsistence wage
**2** : a wage sufficient to provide the necessities and comforts essential to an acceptable standard of living

**living will** *noun* (1972)
: a document in which the signer requests to be allowed to die rather than be kept alive by artificial means if disabled beyond a reasonable expectation of recovery

**livre** \lēvrᵉ\ *noun* [French, from Latin *libra*, a unit of weight] (1553)
**1** : an old French monetary unit equal to 20 sols
**2** : a coin representing one livre
**3** : the pound of Lebanon

**lix·iv·i·ate** \lik-'si-vē-,āt\ *transitive verb* **-at·ed; -at·ing** [Latin *lixivium* lye, from *lixivius* made of lye, from *lixa* lye — more at LIQUID] (1758)
: to extract a soluble constituent from (a solid mixture) by washing or percolation
**— lix·iv·i·a·tion** \(,)lik-si-vē-'ā-shən\ *noun*

**liz·ard** \'li-zərd\ *noun* [Middle English *liserd*, from Middle French *laisarde*, from Latin *lacerta*] (14th century)

**1** : any of a suborder (Lacertilia) of reptiles distinguished from the snakes by a fused inseparable lower jaw, a single temporal opening, two pairs of well differentiated functional limbs which may be lacking in burrowing forms, external ears, and eyes with movable lids; *broadly* : any relatively long-bodied reptile (as a crocodile or dinosaur) with legs and tapering tail
**2** : leather made from lizard skin

**lizard's tail** *noun* (circa 1753)
: a perennial herb (*Saururus cernuus* of the family Saururaceae) of North American wetlands having spikes of tiny white flowers

**'ll** \l, əl, ᵊl\ *verb* (1578)
: WILL ⟨you'*ll* be late⟩

**lla·ma** \'lä-mə, 'yä-mə\ *noun* [Spanish, from Quechua] (1600)

: any of a genus (*Lama*) of wild or domesticated South American ruminants related to the camels but smaller and without a hump; *especially* : the domesticated guanaco used especially in the Andes as a pack animal and a source of wool

**lla·no** \'lä-(,)nō, 'la-\ *noun, plural* **llanos** [Spanish, plain, from Latin *planum* — more at PLAIN] (1604)
: an open grassy plain in Spanish America or the southwestern U.S.

llama

**lo** \'lō\ *interjection* [Middle English, from Old English *lā*] (before 12th century)
— used to call attention or to express wonder or surprise ⟨*lo* these many years⟩

**loach** \'lōch\ *noun* [Middle English *loche*, from Middle French] (14th century)
: any of a family (Cobitidae) of small Old World freshwater fishes related to the carps

**¹load** \'lōd\ *noun* [Middle English *lod*, from Old English *lād* support, carrying — more at LODE] (12th century)
**1 a** : the quantity that can be carried at one time by a specified means; *especially* : a measured quantity of a commodity fixed for each type of carrier — often used in combination ⟨a boat*load* of tourists⟩ **b** : whatever is put on a person or pack animal to be carried : PACK **c** : whatever is put in a ship or vehicle or airplane for conveyance : CARGO; *especially* : a quantity of material assembled or packed as a shipping unit
**2 a** : a mass or weight supported by something ⟨branches bent low by their *load* of fruit⟩ **b** : the forces to which a structure is subjected due to superposed weight or to wind pressure on the vertical surfaces; *broadly* : the forces to which a given object is subjected
**3 a** : something that weighs down the mind or spirits ⟨took a *load* off her mind⟩ **b** : a burdensome or laborious responsibility ⟨always carried his share of the *load*⟩
**4** *slang* : an intoxicating amount of liquor drunk
**5** : a large quantity : LOT — usually used in plural
**6 a** : a charge for a firearm **b** : the quantity of material loaded into a device at one time
**7** : external resistance overcome by a machine or prime mover
**8 a** : power output (as of a power plant) or power consumption (as by a device) **b** : a device to which power is delivered
**9 a** (1) : the amount of work that a person carries or is expected to carry (2) : the amount of authorized work to be performed by a machine, a group, a department, or a factory **b** : the demand on the operating resources of a

system (as a telephone exchange or a refrigerating apparatus)
**10** *slang* **:** EYEFUL — used in the phrase *get a load of*
**11 :** an amount added (as to the price of a security or the net premium in insurance) to represent selling expense and profit to the distributor
**12 :** the decrease in capacity for survival of the average individual in a population due to the presence of deleterious genes in the gene pool 〈the mutational *load* is the genetic *load* caused by mutation〉

²**load** (15th century)
*transitive verb*
**1 a :** to put a load in or on 〈*load* a truck〉 **b :** to place in or on a means of conveyance 〈*load* freight〉
**2 a :** to encumber or oppress with something heavy, laborious, or disheartening **:** BURDEN 〈a company *loaded* down with debts〉 **b :** to place as a burden or obligation 〈*load* more work on him〉
**3 a :** to increase the weight of by adding something heavy **b :** to add a conditioning substance (as a mineral salt) to for body **c :** to weight or shape (dice) to fall unfairly **d :** to pack with one-sided or prejudicial influences **:** BIAS **e :** to charge with multiple meanings (as emotional associations or hidden implications) **f :** to weight (as a test) with factors influencing validity or outcome
**4 a :** to supply in abundance or excess **:** HEAP, PACK **b :** to put runners on (first, second, and third bases) in baseball
**5 a :** to put a load or charge in (a device or piece of equipment) 〈*load* a gun〉 **b :** to place or insert especially as a load in a device or piece of equipment 〈*load* film in a camera〉 〈*load* a program into a computer〉
**6 :** to alter (as an alcoholic drink) by adding an adulterant or drug
**7 a :** to add a load to (an insurance premium) **b :** to add a sum to after profits and expenses are accounted for 〈*loaded* prices〉
*intransitive verb*
**1 :** to receive a load
**2 :** to put a load on or in a carrier, device, or container; *especially* **:** to insert the charge or cartridge in the chamber of a firearm
**3 :** to go or go in as a load 〈sightseers *loading* onto a bus〉
— **load·er** *noun*
**load·ed** *adjective* (1886)
**1** *slang* **:** HIGH 12b
**2 :** having a large amount of money
**load factor** *noun* (1943)
**:** the percentage of available seats paid for and occupied in an aircraft
**load·ing** *noun* (15th century)
**1 :** a cargo, weight, or stress placed on something
**2 :** LOAD 11
**3 :** material used to load something **:** FILLER
**load line** *noun* (circa 1859)
**:** the line on a ship indicating the depth to which it sinks in the water when properly loaded — see PLIMSOLL MARK illustration
**load·mas·ter** \'lōd-,mas-tər\ *noun* (1961)
**:** a crew member of a transport aircraft who is in charge of the cargo
**load·star** *variant of* LODESTAR
**load·stone** *variant of* LODESTONE
¹**loaf** \'lōf\ *noun, plural* **loaves** \'lōvz\ [Middle English *lof,* from Old English *hlāf;* akin to Old High German *hleib* loaf] (before 12th century)
**1 :** a shaped or molded mass of bread
**2 :** a shaped or molded often symmetrical mass of food
**3** *slang British* **:** HEAD, MIND
²**loaf** *intransitive verb* [probably back-formation from *loafer*] (1835)
**:** to spend time in idleness

**loaf·er** \'lō-fər\ *noun* [perhaps short for *land-loafer,* from German *Landläufer* tramp, from *Land* + *Läufer* runner] (1830)
**:** one that loafs **:** IDLER
**Loafer** *trademark*
— used for a low step-in shoe
**loam** \'lōm, *chiefly Northern & Midland* 'lüm, *New England also* 'lüm\ *noun* [Middle English *lom,* from Old English *lām* clay, mud; akin to Old English *līm* lime] (12th century)
**1 a :** a mixture (as for plastering) composed chiefly of moistened clay **b :** a coarse molding sand used in founding
**2 :** SOIL; *specifically* **:** a soil consisting of a friable mixture of varying proportions of clay, silt, and sand
— **loamy** \'lō-mē, 'lü-, 'lü-\ *adjective*
¹**loan** \'lōn\ *noun* [Middle English *lon,* from Old Norse *lān;* akin to Old English *lǣn* loan, *lēon* to lend, Latin *linquere* to leave, Greek *leipein*] (12th century)
**1 a :** money lent at interest **b :** something lent usually for the borrower's temporary use
**2 a :** the grant of temporary use **b :** the temporary duty of a person transferred to another job for a limited time
**3 :** LOANWORD
²**loan** *transitive verb* (13th century)
**:** LEND
— **loan·able** \'lō-nə-bəl\ *adjective*
**lo and behold** *interjection* (1808)
— used to express wonder or surprise
**loan·er** \'lō-nər\ *noun* (1926)
**:** one (as a car or a watch) that is lent especially as a replacement for something being repaired
**loan·ing** \'lō-niŋ\ *noun* [Middle English *loning,* from *lone,* alteration of *lane*] (14th century)
**1** *dialect British* **:** LANE
**2** *dialect British* **:** a milking yard
**loan shark** *noun* (1905)
**:** one who lends money to individuals at exorbitant rates of interest
**loan–shark·ing** \-,shär-kiŋ\ *noun* (1914)
**:** the practice of lending money at exorbitant rates of interest
**loan translation** *noun* (circa 1933)
**:** a compound, derivative, or phrase that is introduced into a language through translation of the constituents of a term in another language (as *superman* from German *Übermensch*)
**loan·word** \'lōn-,wərd\ *noun* (1874)
**:** a word taken from another language and at least partly naturalized
**loath** \'lōth, 'lōth\ *also* **loathe** \'lōth, 'lōth\ *adjective* [Middle English *loth* loathsome, from Old English *lāth;* akin to Old High German *leid* loathsome, Old Irish *lius* loathing] (12th century)
**:** unwilling to do something contrary to one's ways of thinking **:** RELUCTANT
**synonym** see DISINCLINED
— **loath·ness** *noun*
**loathe** \'lōth\ *transitive verb* **loathed; loath·ing** [Middle English *lothen,* from Old English *lāthian* to dislike, be hateful, from *lāth*] (12th century)
**:** to dislike greatly and often with disgust or intolerance **:** DETEST
**synonym** see HATE
— **loath·er** *noun*
**loathing** *noun* (14th century)
**:** extreme disgust **:** DETESTATION
¹**loath·ly** \'lōth-lē, 'lōth-\ *adjective* (before 12th century)
**:** LOATHSOME, REPULSIVE
²**loath·ly** \'lōth-lē, 'lōth-\ *adverb* (15th century)
**:** not willingly **:** RELUCTANTLY
**loath·some** \'lōth-səm, 'lōth-\ *adjective* [Middle English *lothsum,* from *loth* evil, from Old English *lāth,* from *lāth,* adjective] (14th century)
**:** giving rise to loathing **:** DISGUSTING
— **loath·some·ly** *adverb*

— **loath·some·ness** *noun*
¹**lob** \'läb\ *noun* [probably of Low German origin; akin to Low German *lubbe* coarse person] (1508)
*dialect British* **:** a dull heavy person **:** LOUT
²**lob** *verb* **lobbed; lob·bing** [*lob* a loosely hanging object] (1599)
*transitive verb*
**1 :** to let hang heavily **:** DROOP
**2 :** to throw, hit, or propel easily or in a high arc
*intransitive verb*
**1 a :** to move slowly and heavily **b :** to move in an arc
**2 :** to hit a tennis ball easily in a high arc
³**lob** *noun* (1851)
**:** a soft high-arching shot, throw, or kick
**lob-** *or* **lobo-** *combining form* [*lobe*]
**:** lobe 〈*lobar*〉 〈*lobo*tomy〉
**lo·bar** \'lō-bər, -,bär\ *adjective* (circa 1856)
**:** of or relating to a lobe
**lo·bate** \'lō-,bāt\ *also* **lo·bat·ed** \-,bā-təd\ *adjective* [New Latin *lobatus,* from Late Latin *lobus*] (circa 1760)
**1 :** LOBED
**2 :** resembling a lobe
— **lo·ba·tion** \lō-'bā-shən\ *noun*
¹**lob·by** \'lä-bē\ *noun, plural* **lobbies** [Medieval Latin *lobium* gallery, of Germanic origin; akin to Old High German *louba* porch] (1593)
**1 :** a corridor or hall connected with a larger room or series of rooms and used as a passageway or waiting room: as **a :** an anteroom of a legislative chamber; *especially* **:** one of two anterooms of a British parliamentary chamber to which members go to vote during a division **b :** a large hall serving as a foyer (as of a hotel or theater)
**2 :** a group of persons engaged in lobbying especially as representatives of a particular interest group
²**lobby** *verb* **lob·bied; lob·by·ing** (1837)
*intransitive verb*
**:** to conduct activities aimed at influencing public officials and especially members of a legislative body on legislation
*transitive verb*
**1 :** to promote (as a project) or secure the passage of (as legislation) by influencing public officials
**2 :** to attempt to influence or sway (as a public official) toward a desired action
— **lob·by·er** *noun*
— **lob·by·ism** \-,i-zəm\ *noun*
— **lob·by·ist** \-ist\ *noun*
**lob·by·gow** \'lä-bē-,gaù\ *noun* [origin unknown] (1906)

□ USAGE
**loan** The verb *loan* is one of the words English settlers brought to America and continued to use after it had died out in Britain. Its use was soon noticed by British visitors and somewhat later by the New England literati, who considered it a bit provincial. It was flatly declared wrong in 1870 by a popular commentator, who based his objection on etymology. A later scholar showed that the commentator was ignorant of Old English and thus unsound in his objection, but by then it was too late, as the condemnation had been picked up by many other commentators. Although a surprising number of critics still voice objections, *loan* is entirely standard as a verb. You should note that it is used only literally; *lend* is the verb used for figurative expressions, such as "lending a hand" or "lending enchantment."

\ə\ abut  \ᵊ\ kitten  \ər\ further  \a\ ash  \ā\ ace
\ä\ mop, mar  \aú\ out  \ch\ chin  \e\ bet  \ē\ easy
\g\ go  \i\ hit  \ī\ ice  \j\ job  \ŋ\ sing  \ō\ go
\ò\ law  \òi\ boy  \th\ thin  \t̲h̲\ the  \ü\ loot  \ú\ foot
\y\ yet  \zh\ vision  *see also* Guide to Pronunciation

: an errand boy

**lobe** \'lōb\ *noun* [Middle French, from Late Latin *lobus,* from Greek *lobos*] (1541)
: a curved or rounded projection or division; *specifically* : a usually somewhat rounded projection or division of a bodily organ or part

**lo·bec·to·my** \lō-'bek-tə-mē\ *noun, plural* **-mies** [International Scientific Vocabulary] (circa 1911)
: surgical removal of a lobe of an organ (as a lung) or gland (as the thyroid)

**lobed** \'lōbd\ *adjective* (1787)
: having lobes ⟨palmately *lobed* leaves⟩

**lobe–fin** \'lōb-,fin\ *noun* (1941)
: CROSSOPTERYGIAN
— **lobe–finned** \-'find\ *adjective*

**lo·be·lia** \lō-'bēl-yə, -'bē-lē-ə\ *noun* [New Latin, from Matthias de *Lobel* (died 1616) Flemish botanist] (1739)
1 : any of a genus (*Lobelia* of the family Lobeliaceae, the lobelia family) of widely cultivated plants having terminal clusters of showy lipped flowers
2 : the leaves and tops of Indian tobacco

**lo·be·line** \lō-bə-,lēn\ *noun* [New Latin *Lobelia* + English ²-*ine*] (1852)
: a crystalline alkaloid $C_{22}H_{27}NO_2$ that is obtained from Indian tobacco and is used chiefly as a respiratory stimulant and as a smoking deterrent

**lob·lol·ly** \'läb-,lä-lē\ *noun, plural* **-lies** [probably from English dialect *lob* to boil + obsolete English dialect *lolly* broth] (1597)
1 *dialect* **a** : a thick gruel **b** : MIRE, MUDHOLE
2 *dialect* : LOUT
3 : LOBLOLLY PINE

**loblolly pine** *noun* (1760)
: a pine (*Pinus taeda*) of the southeastern U.S. with flaky bark, long needles in groups of three, and cones having spine-tipped scales; *also* : its coarse-grained wood

**lo·bo** \'lō-(,)bō\ *noun, plural* **lobos** [Spanish, wolf, from Latin *lupus* — more at WOLF] (1839)
: GRAY WOLF

**lo·bot·o·mise** *British variant of* LOBOTOMIZE

**lo·bot·o·mize** \lō-'bä-tə-,mīz\ *transitive verb* **-mized; -miz·ing** (1943)
1 : to perform a lobotomy on
2 : to deprive of sensitivity, intelligence, or vitality ⟨fear of prosecution was causing the press to *lobotomize* itself —Tony Eprile⟩

**lo·bot·o·my** \lō-'bä-tə-mē\ *noun, plural* **-mies** [International Scientific Vocabulary] (1936)
: surgical severance of nerve fibers connecting the frontal lobes to the thalamus for the relief of some mental disorders

**lob·scouse** \'läb-,skaůs\ *noun* [origin unknown] (1706)
: a sailor's dish of stewed or baked meat with vegetables and hardtack

**lob·ster** \'läb-stər\ *noun, often attributive* [Middle English, from Old English *loppestre,* from *loppe* spider] (before 12th century)
1 : any of a family (Nephropidae and especially *Homarus americanus*) of large edible marine decapod crustaceans that have stalked eyes, a pair of large claws, and a long abdomen and that include species from coasts on both sides of the North Atlantic and from the Cape of Good Hope
2 : SPINY LOBSTER
— **lob·ster·like** \-,līk\ *adjective*

**lob·ster·ing** \'läb-st(ə-)riŋ\ *noun* (1881)
: the activity or business of catching lobsters

**lob·ster·man** \-mən\ *noun* (1881)
: one whose business is lobstering

**lobster pot** *noun* (1764)
: an oblong case with slat sides and a funnel-shaped net used to trap lobsters — called also *lobster trap*

**lobster pot**

**lobster shift** *noun* (circa 1933)
: a work shift (as on a newspaper) that covers the late evening and early morning hours — called also *lobster trick*

**lobster ther·mi·dor** \-'thər-mə-,dȯr\ *noun* [*thermidor,* from French, from *Thermidor,* drama (1891) by Victorien Sardou] (1930)
: cooked lobster meat in a rich wine sauce stuffed into a lobster shell and browned

**lob·u·lar** \'lä-byə-lər\ *adjective* (1826)
: of, relating to, affecting, or resembling a lobule

**lob·u·lat·ed** \'lä-byə-,lā-təd\ *also* **lob·u·late** \-,lāt\ *adjective* (1783)
: made up of or having lobules ⟨the pancreas is a *lobulated* organ⟩
— **lob·u·la·tion** \,lä-byə-'lā-shən\ *noun*

**lob·ule** \'lä-(,)byü(ə)l\ *noun* (1682)
: a small lobe; *also* : a subdivision of a lobe

¹**lo·cal** \'lō-kəl\ *adjective* [Middle English *localle,* from Middle French *local,* from Late Latin *localis,* from Latin *locus* place — more at STALL] (15th century)
1 : characterized by or relating to position in space : having a definite spatial form or location
2 **a** : of, relating to, or characteristic of a particular place : not general or widespread **b** : of, relating to, or applicable to part of a whole
3 **a** : primarily serving the needs of a particular limited district **b** *of a public conveyance* : making all the stops on a route
4 : involving or affecting only a restricted part of the organism : TOPICAL
5 : of or relating to telephone communication within a specified area

²**local** *noun* (circa 1824)
: a local person or thing: as **a** : a local public conveyance (as a train or an elevator) **b** : a local or particular branch, lodge, or chapter of an organization (as a labor union) **c** *British* : a nearby or neighborhood pub

**local area network** *noun* (1981)
: a network of personal computers in a small area (as an office) that are linked by cable, can communicate directly with other devices in the network, and can share resources

**local color** *noun* (1884)
: the presentation of the features and peculiarities of a particular locality and its inhabitants in writing

**lo·cale** \lō-'kal\ *noun* [modification of French *local,* from *local,* adjective] (1772)
1 : a place or locality especially when viewed in relation to a particular event or characteristic
2 : SITE, SCENE ⟨the *locale* of a story⟩

**local government** *noun* (1844)
: the government of a specific local area constituting a subdivision of a major political unit (as a nation or state); *also* : the body of persons constituting such a government

**lo·cal·ise** *British variant of* LOCALIZE

**lo·cal·ism** \'lō-kə-,li-zəm\ *noun* (1823)
1 **a** : a local idiom **b** : a local peculiarity of speaking or acting
2 : affection or partiality for a particular place : SECTIONALISM

**lo·cal·ite** \'lō-kə-,līt\ *noun* (1951)
: a native or resident of the locality under consideration : LOCAL

**lo·cal·i·ty** \lō-'ka-lə-tē\ *noun, plural* **-ties** (1628)
1 : the fact or condition of having a location in space or time

2 : a particular place, situation, or location

**lo·cal·ize** \'lō-kə-,līz\ *verb* **-ized; -iz·ing** (1792)
*transitive verb*
1 : to make local : orient locally
2 : to assign to or keep within a definite locality
*intransitive verb*
: to accumulate in or be restricted to a specific or limited area ⟨an infection that *localizes* in the ear⟩
— **lo·cal·iz·abil·i·ty** \,lō-kə-,lī-zə-'bi-lə-tē\ *noun*
— **lo·cal·iz·able** \'lō-kə-,lī-zə-bəl\ *adjective*
— **lo·cal·i·za·tion** \,lō-kə-lə-'zā-shən\ *noun*

**lo·cal·ly** \'lō-k(ə-)lē\ *adverb* (15th century)
1 : with respect to a particular place or situation
2 : NEARBY
3 : in the region of origin

**local option** *noun* (1878)
: the power granted by a legislature to a political subdivision to determine by popular vote the local applicability of a law on a controversial issue (as the sale of liquor)

**local time** *noun* (1833)
: time based on the meridian through a particular place as contrasted with that of a time zone

**lo·cate** \'lō-,kāt, lō-'\ *verb* **lo·cat·ed; lo·cat·ing** [Latin *locatus,* past participle of *locare* to place, from *locus*] (1652)
*intransitive verb*
: to establish oneself or one's business : SETTLE
*transitive verb*
1 : to determine or indicate the place, site, or limits of
2 : to set or establish in a particular spot : STATION
3 : to seek out and determine the location of
4 : to find or fix the place of especially in a sequence : CLASSIFY
— **lo·cat·able** \-,kā-tə-bəl, -'kā-\ *adjective*

**lo·ca·tion** \lō-'kā-shən\ *noun* (1597)
1 **a** : a position or site occupied or available for occupancy or marked by some distinguishing feature : SITUATION **b** (1) : a tract of land designated for a purpose (2) *Australian* : FARM, STATION **c** : a place outside a motion-picture studio where a picture or part of it is filmed — usually used in the phrase *on location*
2 : the act or process of locating
— **lo·ca·tion·al** \-shnəl, -shə-nᵊl\ *adjective*
— **lo·ca·tion·al·ly** *adverb*

¹**loc·a·tive** \'lä-kə-tiv\ *noun* [Latin *locus* + English -*ative* (as in *vocative*)] (1804)
: the locative case; *also* : a word in that case

²**locative** *adjective* (1841)
: of or being a grammatical case that denotes place or the place where or wherein

**lo·ca·tor** *also* **lo·cat·er** \'lō-,kā-tər, lō-'\ *noun* (1784)
: one that locates something (as a mining claim or the course of a road)

**loch** \'läk, 'läḵ\ *noun* [Middle English (Scots) *louch,* from Scottish Gaelic *loch;* akin to Latin *lacus* lake — more at LAKE] (14th century)
1 *Scottish* : LAKE
2 *Scottish* : a bay or arm of the sea especially when nearly landlocked

**loch·an** \'lä-kən\ *noun* [Scottish Gaelic, diminutive of *loch*] (1670)
*Scottish* : a small lake

**loci** *plural of* LOCUS

¹**lock** \'läk\ *noun* [Middle English *lok,* from Old English *locc;* akin to Old High German *loc* lock, Greek *lygos* withe, Latin *luxus* dislocated] (before 12th century)
1 **a** : a tuft, tress, or ringlet of hair **b** *plural* : the hair of the head
2 : a cohering bunch (as of wool, cotton, or flax) : TUFT

**²lock** *noun* [Middle English *lok,* from Old English *loc;* akin to Old High German *loh* enclosure and perhaps to Old English *locc* lock of hair] (before 12th century)
**1 a :** a fastening (as for a door) operated by a key or a combination **b :** the mechanism for exploding the charge or cartridge of a firearm
**2 a :** an enclosure (as in a canal) with gates at each end used in raising or lowering boats as they pass from level to level **b :** AIR LOCK
**3 a :** a locking or fastening together **b :** an intricate mass of objects impeding each other (as in a traffic jam) **c :** a hold in wrestling secured on one part of the body; *broadly :* a controlling hold ⟨his paper . . . had a *lock* on a large part of the state —John Corry⟩
**4 :** one that is assured of success or favorable outcome

**³lock** (14th century)
*transitive verb*
**1 a :** to fasten the lock of **b :** to make fast with or as if with a lock ⟨*lock* up the house⟩
**2 a :** to fasten in or out or to make secure or inaccessible by or as if by means of locks ⟨*locked* himself away from the curious world⟩ ⟨*locked* her husband out⟩ **b :** to fix in a particular situation or method of operation ⟨a team firmly *locked* in last place⟩
**3 a :** to make fast, motionless, or inflexible especially by the interlacing or interlocking of parts ⟨*lock* wheels⟩ ⟨*lock* a knee⟩ **b :** to hold in a close embrace **c :** to grapple in combat; *also :* to bind closely ⟨administration and students were *locked* in conflict⟩
**4 :** to invest (capital) without assurance of easy convertibility into money
**5 :** to move or permit to pass (as a ship) by raising or lowering in a lock
*intransitive verb*
**1 a :** to become locked **b :** to be capable of being locked
**2 :** INTERLACE, INTERLOCK
**3 :** to go or pass by means of a lock (as in a canal)
— **lock·able** \ˈlä-kə-bəl\ *adjective*
— **lock horns :** to come into conflict
— **lock on** *also* **lock onto :** to sight and follow (a target) automatically using a sensor (as radar)

**lock·box** \ˈläk-ˌbäks\ *noun* (1872)
**:** a box (as a post-office box, strongbox, or safe-deposit box) that locks

**lock·down** \-ˌdaůn\ *noun* (1977)
**:** the confinement of prisoners to their cells for all or most of the day as a temporary security measure

**locked–in** \ˈläkt-ˈin\ *adjective* (1952)
**1 :** not subject to adjustment **:** FIXED ⟨*locked-in* interest rates⟩
**2 :** unable or unwilling to shift invested funds because of the tax effect of realizing capital gains

**lock·er** \ˈlä-kər\ *noun* (14th century)
**1 a :** a drawer, cupboard, or compartment that may be closed with a lock; *especially :* one for individual storage use **b :** a chest or compartment on shipboard for compact stowage of articles **c :** a refrigerated compartment or room for the storage of fresh or frozen foods ⟨a meat *locker*⟩
**2 :** one that locks

**lock·er–room** \ˈlä-kə(r)-ˌrüm\ *adjective* (1946)
**:** of, relating to, or suitable for use in a locker room; *especially :* of an earthy or sexual nature ⟨*locker-room* talk⟩

**locker room** *noun* (circa 1896)
**:** a room for changing clothes and for storing clothing and equipment in lockers; *especially :* one for use by sports players

**lock·et** \ˈlä-kət\ *noun* [Middle French *loquet* latch, from Middle Dutch *loke;* akin to Old English *loc*] (1679)
**:** a small case usually of precious metal that has space for a memento and that is worn typically suspended from a chain or necklace

**lock·jaw** \ˈläk-ˌjȯ\ *noun* (1803)
**:** an early symptom of tetanus characterized by spasm of the jaw muscles and inability to open the jaws; *also :* TETANUS

**lock·keep·er** \ˈläk-ˌkē-pər\ *noun* (1794)
**:** a person in charge of a lock (as on a canal)

**lock·nut** \-ˌnət\ *noun* (circa 1864)
**1 :** a nut screwed down hard on another to prevent it from slacking back
**2 :** a nut so constructed that it locks itself when screwed tight against another part

**lock·out** \ˈläk-ˌaůt\ *noun* (1854)
**:** the withholding of employment by an employer and the whole or partial closing of his business establishment in order to gain concessions from or resist demands of employees

**lock out** *transitive verb* (1868)
**:** to subject (a body of employees) to a lockout

**lock·ram** \ˈlä-krəm\ *noun* [Middle English *lokerham,* from *Locronan,* town in Brittany] (14th century)
**:** a coarse plain-woven linen formerly used in England

**lock·smith** \ˈläk-ˌsmith\ *noun* (13th century)
**:** a person who makes or repairs locks

**lock·smith·ing** \-ˌsmi-thiŋ\ *noun* (circa 1909)
**:** the work or business of a locksmith

**lock·step** \ˈläk-ˌstep\ *noun* (circa 1802)
**1 :** a mode of marching in step by a body of men going one after another as closely as possible
**2 :** a standard method or procedure that is mindlessly adhered to or that minimizes individuality
— **lockstep** *adjective*
— **in lockstep :** in perfect or rigid often mindless conformity or unison ⟨politicians marching *in lockstep* with the party line⟩

**lock·stitch** \ˈläk-ˌstich\ *noun* (circa 1859)
**:** a sewing machine stitch formed by the looping together of two threads one on each side of the material being sewn
— **lockstitch** *verb*

**lock, stock, and barrel** *adverb* [from the principal parts of a flintlock] (1842)
**:** WHOLLY, COMPLETELY ⟨the only thing which had not been sold *lock, stock, and barrel* with the . . . house was this piano —Marcia Davenport⟩

**lock·up** \ˈläk-ˌəp\ *noun* (1839)
**1 :** JAIL; *especially :* a local jail where persons are detained prior to court hearing
**2 :** an act of locking **:** the state of being locked

**¹lo·co** \ˈlō-(ˌ)kō\ *adverb or adjective* [Italian dialect, there, from Latin *in loco* in the place] (circa 1801)
**:** in the register as written — used as a direction in music

**²loco** *noun, plural* **locos** *or* **locoes** [Mexican Spanish, from Spanish, crazy] (1844)
**1 :** LOCOWEED
**2 :** LOCOISM

**³loco** *transitive verb* (1884)
**1 :** to poison with locoweed
**2 :** to make frenzied or crazy

**⁴loco** *adjective* [Spanish] (1887)
*slang :* mentally disordered **:** CRAZY, FRENZIED

**Lo·co·fo·co** \ˌlō-kə-ˈfō-(ˌ)kō\ *noun, plural* **-focos** [*locofoco,* a kind of friction match, probably from ¹*loco*motive + Italian *fuoco, foco* fire, from Latin *focus* hearth] (1835)
**1 :** a member of a radical group of New York Democrats organized in 1835 in opposition to the regular party organization
**2 :** DEMOCRAT 2

**lo·co·ism** \ˈlō-(ˌ)kō-ˌi-zəm\ *noun* (1900)
**:** a disease of horses, cattle, and sheep caused by chronic poisoning with locoweeds

**lo·co·mote** \ˈlō-kə-ˌmōt\ *intransitive verb* **-mot·ed; -mot·ing** [back-formation from *locomotion*] (1834)
**:** to move about

**lo·co·mo·tion** \ˌlō-kə-ˈmō-shən\ *noun* [Latin *locus* + English *motion*] (1646)
**1 :** an act or the power of moving from place to place

**2 :** TRAVEL ⟨interest in free *locomotion* and choice of occupation —Zechariah Chafee Jr.⟩

**¹lo·co·mo·tive** \ˌlō-kə-ˈmō-tiv\ *adjective* (1612)
**1 :** LOCOMOTORY
**2 :** of or relating to travel
**3 :** of, relating to, or being a machine that moves about by operation of its own mechanism

**²locomotive** *noun* (1829)
**1 :** a self-propelled vehicle that runs on rails and is used for moving railroad cars
**2 :** a school or college cheer characterized by a slow beginning and a progressive increase in speed

**lo·co·mo·tor** \ˌlō-kə-ˈmō-tər\ *adjective* (1870)
**1 :** of, relating to, or functioning in locomotion
**2 :** affecting or involving the locomotor organs

**locomotor ataxia** *noun* (1878)
**:** TABES DORSALIS

**lo·co·mo·to·ry** \ˌlō-kə-ˈmō-tə-rē\ *adjective* (circa 1836)
**1 :** LOCOMOTOR ⟨*locomotory* appendages⟩
**2 :** capable of moving independently from place to place ⟨*locomotory* animals⟩

**lo·co·weed** \ˈlō-(ˌ)kō-ˌwēd\ *noun* (1879)
**:** any of several leguminous plants (genera *Astragalus* and *Oxytropis*) of western North America that cause locoism in livestock

**loc·u·lar** \ˈlä-kyə-lər\ *adjective* (1784)
**:** having or composed of loculi — often used in combination ⟨uni*locular*⟩

**loc·ule** \ˈlä-(ˌ)kyü(ə)l\ *noun* [French, from Latin *loculus*] (circa 1888)
**:** LOCULUS; *especially :* any of the cells of a compound ovary of a plant
— **loc·uled** \-(ˌ)kyü(ə)ld\ *adjective*

**loc·u·li·ci·dal** \ˌlä-kyə-lə-ˈsī-dᵊl\ *adjective* [New Latin *loculus* + Latin *-cidere* to cut, from *caedere*] (circa 1819)
**:** dehiscing longitudinally so as to bisect each loculus ⟨*loculicidal* fruit⟩

**loc·u·lus** \ˈlä-kyə-ləs\ *noun, plural* **-li** \-ˌlī, -ˌlē\ [New Latin, from Latin, diminutive of *locus*] (1858)
**:** a small chamber or cavity especially in a plant or animal body

**lo·cum** \ˈlō-kəm\ *noun* (1901)
*chiefly British :* LOCUM TENENS

**locum te·nens** \-ˈtē-ˌnenz, -ˈte-, -nənz\ *noun, plural* **locum te·nen·tes** \-ti-ˈnen-ˌtēz\ [Medieval Latin, literally, (one) holding a place] (1641)
**:** one filling an office for a time or temporarily taking the place of another — used especially of a doctor or clergyman

**lo·cus** \ˈlō-kəs\ *noun, plural* **lo·ci** \ˈlō-ˌsī, -ˌkī, -ˌkē\ [Latin — more at STALL] (1715)
**1 a :** the place where something is situated or occurs **:** SITE, LOCATION ⟨was the culture of medicine in the beginning dispersed from a single focus or did it arise in several *loci*? —S. C. Harvey⟩ **b :** a center of activity, attention, or concentration ⟨in democracy the *locus* of power is in the people —H. G. Rickover⟩
**2 :** the set of all points whose location is determined by stated conditions
**3 :** the position in a chromosome of a particular gene or allele

**locus clas·si·cus** \-ˈkla-si-kəs\ *noun, plural* **loci clas·si·ci** \-ˈkla-sə-ˌsī, -ˌkī, -ˌkē\ [New Latin] (1853)
**1 :** a passage that has become a standard for the elucidation of a word or subject
**2 :** a classic case or example

**locus coe·ru·le·us** *also* **locus ce·ru·le·us** \-si-ˈrü-lē-əs\ *noun* [New Latin, literally, dark blue place] (circa 1889)

\ə\ abut \ᵊ\ kitten \ər\ further \a\ ash \ā\ ace \ä\ mop, mar \aů\ out \ch\ chin \e\ bet \ē\ easy \g\ go \i\ hit \ī\ ice \j\ job \ŋ\ sing \ō\ go \ȯ\ law \ȯi\ boy \th\ thin \t͟h\ the \ü\ loot \ů\ foot \y\ yet \zh\ vision *see also* Guide to Pronunciation

: a blue area of the brain stem with many norepinephrine-containing neurons

**lo·cust** \'lō-kəst\ *noun* [Middle English, from Latin *locusta*] (14th century)
**1** : SHORT-HORNED GRASSHOPPER; *especially* : a migratory grasshopper often traveling in vast swarms and stripping the areas passed of all vegetation
**2** : CICADA
**3 a** : any of various leguminous trees: as (1) : CAROB 1 (2) : BLACK LOCUST (3) : HONEY LOCUST **b** : the wood of a locust tree

**locust bean** *noun* (1847)
: CAROB

**lo·cu·tion** \lō-'kyü-shən\ *noun* [Middle English *locucioun*, from Latin *locution-, locutio*, from *loqui* to speak] (15th century)
**1** : a particular form of expression or a peculiarity of phrasing; *especially* : a word or expression characteristic of a region, group, or cultural level
**2** : style of discourse : PHRASEOLOGY

**lode** \'lōd\ *noun* [Middle English, from Old English *lād* course, support; akin to Old English *līthan* to go — more at LEAD] (before 12th century)
**1** *dialect English* : WATERWAY
**2** : an ore deposit
**3** : something that resembles a lode : an abundant store

**lo·den** \'lō-d°n\ *noun* [German, from Old High German *lodo* coarse cloth; akin to Old English *lotha* mantle] (1911)
**1** : a thick woolen cloth used for outer clothing
**2** : a variable color averaging a dull grayish green

**lode·star** \'lōd-ˌstär\ *noun* [Middle English *lode sterre*, from *lode* course, from Old English *lād*] (14th century)
**1** *archaic* : a star that leads or guides; *especially* : NORTH STAR
**2** : one that serves as an inspiration, model, or guide

**lode·stone** \-ˌstōn\ *noun* [obsolete *lode* course, from Middle English] (circa 1515)
**1** : magnetite possessing polarity
**2** : something that strongly attracts

**¹lodge** \'läj\ *verb* **lodged; lodg·ing** (13th century)
*transitive verb*
**1 a** (1) : to provide temporary quarters for (2) : to rent lodgings to **b** : to establish or settle in a place
**2** : to serve as a receptacle for : CONTAIN
**3** : to beat (as a crop) flat to the ground
**4** : to bring to an intended or a fixed position (as by throwing or thrusting)
**5** : to deposit for safeguard or preservation
**6** : to place or vest especially in a source, means, or agent
**7** : to lay (as a complaint) before a proper authority : FILE
*intransitive verb*
**1 a** : to occupy a place temporarily : SLEEP **b** (1) : to have a residence : DWELL (2) : to be a lodger
**2** : to come to a rest
**3** : to fall or lie down — used especially of hay or grain crops

**²lodge** *noun* [Middle English *loge*, from Old French, of Germanic origin; akin to Old High German *louba* porch] (13th century)
**1** *chiefly dialect* : a rude shelter or abode
**2 a** : a house set apart for residence in a particular season (as the hunting season) **b** : a resort hotel : INN
**3 a** : a house on an estate originally for the use of a gamekeeper, caretaker, or porter **b** : a shelter for an employee (as a gatekeeper)
**4** : a den or lair especially of gregarious animals
**5 a** : the meeting place of a branch of an organization and especially a fraternal organization **b** : the body of members of such a branch

**6 a** : WIGWAM **b** : a family of North American Indians

**lodge·pole pine** \'läj-ˌpōl-\ *noun* (1859)
: either of two pines of western North America with needles in pairs and short ovoid usually asymmetric cones: **a** : a scrubby chiefly coastal pine (*Pinus contorta*) with thick deeply furrowed bark and hard strong coarse-grained medium-light wood **b** : a tall straight pine (*P. contorta* variety *latifolia* synonym *P. murrayana*) with thin and little furrowed bark and soft weak fine-grained lightweight wood

**lodg·er** \'lä-jər\ *noun* (1596)
: ROOMER

**lodging** *noun* (14th century)
**1 a** : a place to live : DWELLING **b** : LODGMENT 3b
**2 a** (1) : sleeping accommodations ⟨found *lodging* in the barn⟩ (2) : a temporary place to stay ⟨a *lodging* for the night⟩ **b** : a room in the house of another used as a residence — usually used in plural
**3** : the act of lodging

**lodging house** *noun* (1766)
: ROOMING HOUSE

**lodg·ment** *or* **lodge·ment** \'läj-mənt\ *noun* (1598)
**1 a** : a lodging place : SHELTER **b** : ACCOMMODATIONS, LODGINGS ⟨found *lodgment* in the city⟩
**2 a** : the act, fact, or manner of lodging ⟨a hut for temporary *lodgment* of cattlemen⟩ **b** : a placing, depositing, or coming to rest
**3 a** : an accumulation or collection deposited in a place or remaining at rest **b** : a place of rest or deposit

**lod·i·cule** \'lä-di-ˌkyü(ə)l\ *noun* [Latin *lodicula*, diminutive of *lodic-, lodix* cover] (1864)
: one of usually two delicate membranous hyaline scales at the base of the ovary of a grass that by their swelling assist in anthesis

**loess** \'les, 'ləs, 'lō-əs, 'lərs\ *noun* [German *Löss*] (1833)
: an unstratified usually buff to yellowish brown loamy deposit found in North America, Europe, and Asia and believed to be chiefly deposited by the wind
— **loess·ial** \'le-sē-əl, 'lə-, lō-'e-, 'lər-\ *adjective*

**¹loft** \'lȯft\ *noun* [Middle English, from Old English, air, sky, from Old Norse *lopt;* akin to Old High German *luft* air] (13th century)
**1** : an upper room or floor : ATTIC
**2 a** : a gallery in a church or hall **b** : one of the upper floors of a warehouse or business building especially when not partitioned ⟨living in a converted *loft*⟩ **c** : HAYLOFT
**3 a** : the backward slant of the face of a golf-club head **b** : the act of lofting
**4** : the thickness of a fabric or insulating material (as goose down)
— **loft·like** \-ˌlīk\ *adjective*

**²loft** (1518)
*transitive verb*
**1** : to place, house, or store in a loft
**2** : to propel through the air or into space ⟨lofted a long hit to center⟩ ⟨instruments *lofted* by a powerful rocket⟩
**3** : to lay out a full-sized working drawing of the lines and contours of (as a ship's hull)
*intransitive verb*
**1** : to propel a ball high into the air
**2** : to rise high

**lofty** \'lȯf-tē\ *adjective* **loft·i·er; -est** (15th century)
**1 a** : elevated in character and spirit : NOBLE **b** : elevated in status : SUPERIOR
**2** : having a haughty overbearing manner : SUPERCILIOUS
**3 a** : rising to a great height : impressively high ⟨*lofty* mountains⟩ **b** : REMOTE, ESOTERIC
**synonym** see HIGH
— **loft·i·ly** \-tə-lē\ *adverb*
— **loft·i·ness** \-tē-nəs\ *noun*

**¹log** \'lȯg, 'läg\ *noun, often attributive* [Middle English *logge*, probably of Scandinavian ori-

gin; akin to Old Norse *lāg* fallen tree; akin to Old English *licgan* to lie — more at LIE] (14th century)
**1** : a usually bulky piece or length of unshaped timber; *especially* : a length of a tree trunk ready for sawing and over six feet (1.8 meters) long
**2** : an apparatus for measuring the rate of a ship's motion through the water that consists of a block fastened to a line and run out from a reel
**3 a** : the record of the rate of a ship's speed or of her daily progress; *also* : the full nautical record of a ship's voyage **b** : the full record of a flight by an aircraft
**4** : a record of performance, events, or day-to-day activities ⟨a computer *log*⟩

**²log** *verb* **logged; log·ging** (1699)
*transitive verb*
**1 a** : to cut (trees) for lumber **b** : to clear (land) of trees in lumbering — often used with *off*
**2** : to make a note or record of : enter details of or about in a log
**3 a** : to move (an indicated distance) or attain (an indicated speed) as noted in a log **b** (1) : to sail a ship or fly an airplane for (an indicated distance or period of time) (2) : to have (an indicated record) to one's credit : ACHIEVE
*intransitive verb*
: ³LUMBER 1

**³log** *noun, often attributive* [by shortening] (1631)
: LOGARITHM

**log-** *or* **logo-** *combining form* [Greek, from *logos* — more at LEGEND]
: word : thought : speech : discourse ⟨*logo*gram⟩ ⟨*logo*rrhea⟩

**-log** — see -LOGUE

**lo·gan·ber·ry** \'lō-gən-ˌber-ē\ *noun* [James H. Logan (died 1928) American lawyer + English *berry*] (1893)
: a red-fruited upright-growing dewberry regarded as a variety (*Rubus ursinus loganobaccus*) of a western dewberry or as a hybrid of a western dewberry and a red raspberry; *also* : its berry

**log·a·oe·dic** \ˌlä-gə-'ē-dik\ *adjective* [Late Latin *logaoedicus*, from Late Greek *logaoidikos*, from Greek *log-* + *aeidein* to sing; from the resemblance of such rhythm to prose — more at ODE] (1844)
: marked by the mixture of several meters; *specifically* : having a rhythm that uses both dactyls and trochees or anapests and iambs
— **logaoedic** *noun*

**log·a·rithm** \'lȯ-gə-ˌri-thəm, 'lä-\ *noun* [New Latin *logarithmus*, from *log-* + Greek *arithmos* number — more at ARITHMETIC] (circa 1616)
: the exponent that indicates the power to which a number is raised to produce a given number ⟨the *logarithm* of 100 to the base 10 is 2⟩
— **log·a·rith·mic** \ˌlȯ-gə-'rith-mik, ˌlä-\ *adjective*
— **log·a·rith·mi·cal·ly** \-mi-k(ə-)lē\ *adverb*

**logarithmic function** *noun* (1927)
: a function (as $y = \log_a x$ or $y = \ln x$) that is the inverse of an exponential function (as $y = a^x$ or $y = e^x$) so that the independent variable appears in a logarithm

**log·book** \'lȯg-ˌbu̇k, 'läg-\ *noun* (circa 1679)
: LOG 3, 4

**loge** \'lōzh\ *noun* [French, from Old French, a shelter — more at LODGE] (1749)
**1 a** : a small compartment : BOOTH **b** : a box in a theater
**2 a** : a small partitioned area **b** : a separate forward section of a theater mezzanine or balcony

**logged** \'lȯgd, 'lägd\ *adjective* (circa 1820)
**1** : HEAVY, SLUGGISH
**2** : sodden especially with water

**log·ger** \\'lȯ-gər, 'lä-\\ *noun* (1732)
: one engaged in logging

**log·ger·head** \\'lȯ-gər-,hed, 'lä-\\ *noun* [probably from English dialect *logger* block of wood + English *head*] (1588)
**1** *chiefly dialect* **a :** BLOCKHEAD **b :** HEAD; *especially* **:** a disproportionately large head
**2 a :** a very large carnivorous sea turtle (*Caretta caretta*) of subtropical and temperate waters **b :** ALLIGATOR SNAPPER
**3 :** an iron tool consisting of a long handle terminating in a ball or bulb that is heated and used to melt tar or to heat liquids
— **at loggerheads :** in or into a state of quarrelsome disagreement

**log·gets** *or* **log·gats** \\'lȯ-gəts, 'lä-\\ *noun plural but singular or plural in construction* [probably from ¹*log* + *-et*] (1581)
: a game formerly played in England in which participants throw pieces of wood at a stake

**log·gia** \\'lȯ-jē-ə, 'lȯ-(,)jä\\ *noun, plural* **log·gias** \\'lȯ-jē-əz, 'lȯ-(,)jäz\\ *also* **log·gie** \\'lȯ-(,)jä\\ [Italian, from Old French *loge* lodge] (1742)
: a roofed open gallery especially at an upper story overlooking an open court

**log·ic** \\'lä-jik\\ *noun* [Middle English *logik*, from Middle French *logique*, from Latin *logica*, from Greek *logikē*, from feminine of *logikos* of reason, from *logos* reason — more at LEGEND] (12th century)

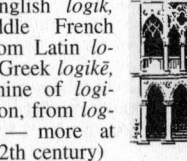

*1 loggia*

**1 a** (1) **:** a science that deals with the principles and criteria of validity of inference and demonstration **:** the science of the formal principles of reasoning (2) **:** a branch or variety of logic ⟨modal *logic*⟩ ⟨Boolean *logic*⟩ (3) **:** a branch of semiotic; *especially* **:** SYNTACTICS (4) **:** the formal principles of a branch of knowledge **b** (1) **:** a particular mode of reasoning viewed as valid or faulty (2) **:** RELEVANCE, PROPRIETY **c :** interrelation or sequence of facts or events when seen as inevitable or predictable **d :** the arrangement of circuit elements (as in a computer) needed for computation; *also* **:** the circuits themselves
**2 :** something that forces a decision apart from or in opposition to reason ⟨the *logic* of war⟩
— **lo·gi·cian** \\lō-'ji-shən\\ *noun*

**log·i·cal** \\'lä-ji-kəl\\ *adjective* (15th century)
**1 a** (1) **:** of, relating to, involving, or being in accordance with logic (2) **:** skilled in logic **b :** formally true or valid **:** ANALYTIC, DEDUCTIVE
**2 :** capable of reasoning or of using reason in an orderly cogent fashion ⟨a *logical* thinker⟩
— **log·i·cal·i·ty** \\,lä-jə-'ka-lə-tē\\ *noun*
— **log·i·cal·ly** \\'lä-ji-k(ə-)lē\\ *adverb*
— **log·i·cal·ness** \\-kəl-nəs\\ *noun*

**logical positivism** *noun* (1931)
: a 20th century philosophical movement that holds characteristically that all meaningful statements are either analytic or conclusively verifiable or at least confirmable by observation and experiment and that metaphysical theories are therefore strictly meaningless — called also *logical empiricism*
— **logical positivist** *noun*

**log in** *intransitive verb* (1962)
**:** LOG ON
— **log-in** \\'lȯg-,in, 'läg-\\ *noun*

**lo·gi·on** \\'lō-gē-,än\\ *noun, plural* **lo·gia** \\-gē-ə\\ *or* **logions** [Greek, diminutive of *logos*] (1875)
**:** SAYING; *especially* **:** a saying attributed to Jesus

¹**lo·gis·tic** \\lō-'jis-tik, lə-\\ *or* **lo·gis·ti·cal** \\-ti-kəl\\ *adjective* (1628)
**1 a :** of or relating to symbolic logic **b :** of or relating to the philosophical attempt to reduce mathematics to logic

**2 :** of or relating to logistics
**3** *logistic* **:** of, represented by, or relating to a logistic curve ⟨a *logistic* process⟩
— **lo·gis·ti·cal·ly** \\-ti-k(ə-)lē\\ *adverb*

²**logistic** *noun* (1905)
**:** SYMBOLIC LOGIC

**logistic curve** *noun* (circa 1903)
: an S-shaped curve that represents an exponential function and is used in mathematical models of growth processes

**lo·gis·ti·cian** \\,lō-jəs-'ti-shən\\ *noun* (1932)
: a specialist in logistics

**lo·gis·tics** \\lō-'jis-tiks, lə-\\ *noun plural but singular or plural in construction* [French *logistique* art of calculating, logistics, from Greek *logistikē* art of calculating, from feminine of *logistikos* of calculation, from *logizein* to calculate, from *logos* reason] (circa 1861)
**1 :** the aspect of military science dealing with the procurement, maintenance, and transportation of military matériel, facilities, and personnel
**2 :** the handling of the details of an operation

**log·jam** \\'lȯg-,jam, 'läg-\\ *noun* (1885)
**1 :** a jumble of logs jammed together in a watercourse
**2 a :** DEADLOCK, IMPASSE ⟨trying to break the *logjam* in negotiations⟩ **b :** BLOCKAGE

**log·nor·mal** \\,lȯg-'nȯr-məl, ,läg-\\ *adjective* (1945)
: relating to or being a normal distribution that is the distribution of the logarithm of a random variable; *also* **:** relating to or being such a random variable
— **log·nor·mal·i·ty** \\-nȯr-'ma-lə-tē\\ *noun*
— **log·nor·mal·ly** \\-'nȯr-mə-lē\\ *adverb*

**logo** \\'lō-(,)gō *also* 'lä-\\ *noun, plural* **log·os** \\-(,)gōz\\ (1937)
**1 :** LOGOTYPE
**2 :** an identifying statement **:** MOTTO

**Lo·go** \\'lō-(,)gō\\ *noun* [modification of Greek *logos* word] (1972)
: a computer programming language that employs simple English commands and is used especially for introducing school children to computers

**logo-** — see LOG-

**logo·gram** \\'lȯ-gə-,gram, 'lä-\\ *noun* (1840)
: a letter, symbol, or sign used to represent an entire word
— **logo·gram·mat·ic** \\,lȯ-gə-grə-'ma-tik, ,lä-\\ *adjective*

**logo·graph** \\'lȯ-gə-,graf, 'lä-\\ *noun* (circa 1888)
**:** LOGOGRAM

**logo·graph·ic** \\,lȯ-gə-'gra-fik, ,lä-\\ *adjective* (1801)
: of, relating to, or marked by the use of logographs **:** consisting of logographs
— **logo·graph·i·cal·ly** \\-fi-k(ə-)lē\\ *adverb*

**logo·griph** \\'lȯ-gə-,grif, 'lä-\\ *noun* [*log-* + Greek *griphos* reed basket, riddle — more at CRIB] (circa 1598)
: a word puzzle (as an anagram)

**lo·gom·a·chy** \\lō-'gä-mə-kē\\ *noun, plural* **-chies** [Greek *logomachia*, from *log-* + *machesthai* to fight] (1569)
**1 :** a dispute over or about words
**2 :** a controversy marked by verbiage

**log on** *intransitive verb* (1977)
: to establish communication and initiate interaction with a time-shared computer or network — often used with *to*
— **log-on** \\'lȯg-,ȯn, 'läg-,än\\ *noun*

**log·or·rhea** \\,lȯ-gə-'rē-ə, ,lä-\\ *noun* [New Latin] (circa 1892)
: excessive and often incoherent talkativeness or wordiness
— **log·or·rhe·ic** \\-'rē-ik\\ *adjective*

**Lo·gos** \\'lō-,gäs, -,gōs\\ *noun, plural* **Lo·goi** \\-,gȯi\\ [Greek, speech, word, reason — more at LEGEND] (1587)
**1 :** the divine wisdom manifest in the creation, government, and redemption of the world and often identified with the second person of the Trinity

**2 :** reason that in ancient Greek philosophy is the controlling principle in the universe

**logo·type** \\'lȯ-gə-,tīp, 'lä-\\ *noun* (circa 1816)
**1 :** a single piece of type or a single plate faced with a term (as the name of a newspaper or a trademark)
**2 :** an identifying symbol (as for advertising)

**log·roll** \\'lȯg-,rōl, 'läg-\\ *verb* [back-formation from *logrolling*] (1835)
*intransitive verb*
: to take part in logrolling
*transitive verb*
: to promote passage of by logrolling
— **log·roll·er** *noun*

**log·roll·ing** \\-,rō-liŋ\\ *noun* (1812)
**1** [from a former American custom of neighbors assisting one another in rolling logs into a pile for burning] **:** the exchanging of assistance or favors; *specifically* **:** the trading of votes by legislators to secure favorable action on projects of interest to each one
**2 :** the rolling of logs in water by treading; *also* **:** a sport in which contestants treading logs try to dislodge one another

**-logue** *or* **-log** *noun combining form* [Middle English *-logue*, from Old French, from Latin *-logus*, from Greek *-logos*, from *legein* to speak — more at LEGEND]
**1 :** discourse **:** talk ⟨duo*logue*⟩
**2 :** student **:** specialist ⟨sino*logue*⟩

**log·wood** \\'lȯg-,wùd, 'läg-\\ *noun* (1581)
**1 a :** a Mexican and West Indian leguminous tree (*Haematoxylon campechianum*) **b :** the very hard brown or brownish red heartwood of logwood
**2 :** a dye extracted from the heartwood of logwood — compare HEMATOXYLIN

**lo·gy** \\'lō-gē\\ *also* **log·gy** \\'lȯ-gē, 'lä-\\ *adjective* **lo·gi·er; -est** [perhaps from Dutch *log* heavy; akin to Middle Low German *luggich* lazy] (1847)
: marked by sluggishness and lack of vitality **:** GROGGY

**-logy** *noun combining form* [Middle English *-logie*, from Old French, from Latin *-logia*, from Greek, from *logos* word]
**1 :** oral or written expression ⟨phraseo*logy*⟩
**2 :** doctrine **:** theory **:** science ⟨ethno*logy*⟩

**Lo·hen·grin** \\'lō-ən-,grin\\ *noun* [German]
: a son of Parsifal and knight of the Holy Grail in Germanic legend

**loin** \\'lȯin\\ *noun* [Middle English *loyne*, from Middle French *loigne*, from (assumed) Vulgar Latin *lumbea*, from Latin *lumbus;* akin to Old English *lendenu* loins, Old Church Slavonic *lędvije*] (14th century)
**1 a :** the part of a human being or quadruped on each side of the spinal column between the hipbone and the false ribs **b :** a cut of meat comprising this part of one or both sides of a carcass with the adjoining half of the vertebrae included but without the flank
**2** *plural* **a :** the upper and lower abdominal regions and the region about the hips **b** (1) **:** the pubic region (2) **:** the generative organs

**loin·cloth** \\-,klȯth\\ *noun* (1859)
: a cloth worn about the loins often as the sole article of clothing in warm climates

**loi·ter** \\'lȯi-tər\\ *intransitive verb* [Middle English] (14th century)
**1 :** to delay an activity with aimless idle stops and pauses **:** DAWDLE
**2 a :** to remain in an area for no obvious reason **:** HANG AROUND **b :** to lag behind
*synonym* see DELAY
— **loiter** *noun*
— **loi·ter·er** \\-tər-ər\\ *noun*

**Lo·ki** \\'lō-kē\\ *noun* [Old Norse]
: a Norse god who contrives evil and mischief for his fellow gods

**Lo·li·ta** \lō-'lē-tə\ *noun* [from *Lolita,* character in the novel *Lolita* (1955) by Vladimir Nabokov] (1959)
: a precociously seductive girl

**¹loll** \'läl\ *verb* [Middle English] (14th century) *intransitive verb*
**1** : to hang loosely or laxly : DROOP
**2** : to act or move in a lax, lazy, or indolent manner : LOUNGE *transitive verb*
: to let droop or dangle
— **loll·er** \'lä-lər\ *noun*

**²loll** *noun* (1709)
*archaic* : the act of lolling : a relaxed posture

**Lol·lard** \'lä-lərd\ *noun* [Middle English, from Middle Dutch *lollaert,* from *lollen* to mutter] (14th century)
: one of the followers of Wycliffe who traveled in the 14th and 15th centuries as lay preachers throughout England and Scotland
— **Lol·lard·ism** \-lər-,di-zəm\ *noun*
— **Lol·lardy** \-lər-dē\ *noun*

**lol·li·pop** *or* **lol·ly·pop** \'lä-li-,päp\ *noun* [perhaps from English dialect *lolly* tongue + ²*pop*] (1784)
**1** : a lump of hard candy on the end of a stick
**2** *British* : a round stop sign on a pole used to stop traffic (as at a school crossing)

**lol·lop** \'lä-ləp\ *intransitive verb* [¹*loll* + -*op* (as in *gallop*)] (1745)
**1** *dialect English* : LOLL
**2** : to proceed with a bounding or bobbing motion

**lol·ly** \'lä-lē\ *noun, plural* **lollies** [short for *lollipop*] (1854)
**1** *British* : a piece of candy; *especially* : HARD CANDY
**2** *British* : MONEY

**lol·ly·gag** \'lä-lē-,gag\ *intransitive verb* **-gagged; -gag·ging** [origin unknown] (1868)
: FOOL AROUND 1 : DAWDLE

**Lom·bard** \'läm-,bärd, -bərd\ *noun* [Middle English *Lumbarde,* from Middle French *lombard,* from Old Italian *lombardo,* from Latin *Langobardus*] (14th century)
**1 a** : a member of a Germanic people that invaded Italy in A.D. 568, settled in the Po valley, and established a kingdom **b** : a native or inhabitant of Lombardy
**2** [from the prominence of Lombards as moneylenders] : BANKER, MONEYLENDER
— **Lom·bar·di·an** \läm-'bär-dē-ən\ *adjective*
— **Lom·bar·dic** \läm-'bär-dik\ *adjective*

**Lom·bar·dy poplar** \'läm-,bär-dē-, -bər-\ *noun* [*Lombardy,* Italy] (1766)
: a poplar of a staminate variety (*Populus nigra italica*) of a European poplar having a columnar shape and strongly ascending branches

**lo mein** \'lō-'mān, ,lō-\ *noun* [Chinese (Guangdong) *lòu-mihn* stirred noodles] (1970)
: a Chinese dish consisting of sliced vegetables, soft noodles, and usually meat or shrimp in bite-size pieces stir-fried in a seasoned sauce

**lo·ment** \'lō-,ment, -mənt\ *noun* [New Latin *lomentum,* from Latin, wash made from bean meal, from *lavere* to wash — more at LYE] (circa 1830)
: a dry indehiscent one-celled fruit that is produced from a single superior ovary and breaks transversely into numerous segments at maturity

**Lon·don broil** \'lən-dən-\ *noun* [*London,* England] (1946)
: a boneless cut of beef (as from the shoulder or flank) usually served sliced diagonally across the grain

**lone** \'lōn\ *adjective* [Middle English, short for *alone*] (14th century)
**1 a** : having no company : SOLITARY **b** : preferring solitude
**2** : ONLY, SOLE
**3** : situated by itself : ISOLATED
*synonym* see ALONE

— **lone·ness** \'lōn-nəs\ *noun*

**lone·li·ness** \'lōn-lē-nəs\ *noun* (circa 1586)
: the quality or state of being lonely

**lone·ly** \'lōn-lē\ *adjective* **lone·li·er; -est** (1607)
**1 a** : being without company : LONE **b** : cut off from others : SOLITARY
**2** : not frequented by human beings : DESOLATE
**3** : sad from being alone : LONESOME
**4** : producing a feeling of bleakness or desolation
*synonym* see ALONE
— **lone·li·ly** \-lə-lē\ *adverb*

**lonely hearts** *adjective* (1931)
: of or relating to lonely persons who are seeking companions or spouses

**lon·er** \'lō-nər\ *noun* (1947)
: one that avoids others; *especially* : INDIVIDUALIST

**lone ranger** *noun, often L&R capitalized* [*Lone Ranger,* hero of an American radio and television western] (1969)
: one who acts alone and without consultation or the approval of others; *broadly* : LONER

**¹lone·some** \'lōn(t)-səm\ *adjective* (1647)
**1 a** : sad or dejected as a result of lack of companionship or separation from others ⟨don't be *lonesome* while we are gone⟩ **b** : causing a feeling of loneliness ⟨the empty house seemed so *lonesome*⟩
**2 a** : REMOTE, UNFREQUENTED ⟨look down, look down that *lonesome* road —Gene Austin⟩ **b** : LONE
*synonym* see ALONE
— **lone·some·ly** *adverb*
— **lone·some·ness** *noun*

**²lonesome** *noun* (1899)
: SELF ⟨sat all by his *lonesome*⟩

**lone wolf** *noun* (1909)
: a person who prefers to work, act, or live alone

**¹long** \'lȯŋ\ *adjective* **lon·ger** \'lȯŋ-gər *also* -ər\; **lon·gest** \'lȯŋ-gəst *also* -əst\ [Middle English *long, lang,* from Old English; akin to Old High German *lang* long, Latin *longus*] (before 12th century)
**1 a** : extending for a considerable distance **b** : having greater length than usual **c** : having greater height than usual : TALL **d** : having a greater length than breadth : ELONGATED **e** : having a greater length than desirable or necessary **f** : FULL-LENGTH ⟨*long* pants⟩
**2 a** : having a specified length ⟨six feet *long*⟩ **b** : forming the chief linear dimension ⟨the *long* side of the room⟩
**3 a** : extending over a considerable time ⟨a *long* friendship⟩ **b** : having a specified duration ⟨two hours *long*⟩ **c** : prolonged beyond the usual time ⟨a *long* look⟩
**4 a** : containing many items in a series ⟨a *long* list⟩ **b** : having a specified number of units ⟨300 pages *long*⟩ **c** : consisting of a greater number or amount than usual : LARGE
**5 a** *of a speech sound* : having a relatively long duration **b** : being the member of a pair of similarly spelled vowel or vowel-containing sounds that is descended from a vowel long in duration ⟨*long* a in fate⟩ ⟨*long* i in sign⟩ **c** *of a syllable in prosody* (1) : of relatively extended duration (2) : bearing a stress or accent
**6** : having the capacity to reach, extend, or travel a considerable distance ⟨a *long* left jab⟩ ⟨tried to hit the *long* ball⟩
**7** : larger or longer than the standard ⟨a *long* count by the referee⟩
**8 a** : extending far into the future ⟨the thoughts of youth are *long, long* thoughts —H. W. Longfellow⟩ **b** : extending beyond what is known ⟨a *long* guess⟩ **c** : payable after a considerable period ⟨a *long* note⟩
**9** : possessing a high degree or a great deal of something specified : STRONG ⟨*long* on common sense⟩
**10 a** : of an unusual degree of difference between the amounts wagered on each side ⟨*long*

odds⟩ **b** : of or relating to the larger amount wagered ⟨take the *long* end of the bet⟩
**11** : subject to great odds
**12** : owning or accumulating securities or goods especially in anticipation of an advance in prices ⟨they are now *long* on wheat⟩ ⟨take a *long* position in steel⟩
— **long·ness** \'lȯŋ-nəs\ *noun*
— **before long** : in a short time : SOON
— **long in the tooth** : past one's best days : OLD
— **not long for** : having little time left to do or enjoy something

**²long** *adverb* (before 12th century)
**1** : for or during a long time ⟨*long* a popular hangout⟩
**2** : at or to a long distance : FAR ⟨*long*-traveled⟩
**3** : for the duration of a specified period
**4** : at a point of time far before or after a specified moment or event ⟨was excited *long* before the big day⟩
**5** : after or beyond a specified or implied time ⟨didn't stay *longer* than midnight⟩ ⟨said it was no *longer* possible⟩
**6** : for a considerable distance ⟨faded back and threw the ball *long*⟩
**7** : in or into a long position (as on a market)
— **so long** : GOOD-BYE

**³long** *noun* (before 12th century)
**1** : a long period of time
**2** : a long syllable
**3** : one taking a long position especially in a security or commodity market
**4 a** *plural* : long trousers **b** : a size in clothing for tall men
— **the long and short** *or* **the long and the short** : GIST

**⁴long** *intransitive verb* **longed; long·ing** \'lȯŋ-iŋ\ [Middle English, from Old English *langian;* akin to Old High German *langēn* to long, Old English *lang* long] (before 12th century)
: to feel a strong desire or craving especially for something not likely to be attained ⟨they *long* for peace but are driven to war⟩ ☆
— **long·er** \'lȯŋ-ər\ *noun*

**⁵long** *intransitive verb* [Middle English, from *along* (on) because (of)] (13th century)
*archaic* : to be suitable or fitting

**long–ago** \'lȯŋ-ə-'gō\ *adjective* (circa 1834)
: of or relating to the past ⟨*long-ago* leaders⟩

**long ago** *noun* (1851)
: the distant past

**lon·gan** \'lȯŋ-gən, -ən\ *noun* [Chinese (Beijing) *lóngyǎn,* literally, dragon's eye] (1732)
**1** : a pulpy fruit related to the litchi and produced by an Indian evergreen tree (*Euphoria longana*)
**2** : a tree that bears the longan

**lon·ga·nim·i·ty** \,lȯŋ-gə-'ni-mə-tē\ *noun* [Middle English *longanymyte,* from Late Latin *longanimitat-, longanimitas,* from *longanimis* patient, from Latin *longus* long + *animus* soul — more at ANIMATE] (15th century)

---

☆ **SYNONYMS**
**Long, yearn, hanker, pine, hunger, thirst** mean to have a strong desire for something. LONG implies a wishing with one's whole heart and often a striving to attain ⟨*longed* for some rest⟩. YEARN suggests an eager, restless, or painful longing ⟨*yearned* for a stage career⟩. HANKER suggests the uneasy promptings of unsatisfied appetite or desire ⟨always *hankering* for money⟩. PINE implies a languishing or a fruitless longing for what is impossible ⟨*pined* for a lost love⟩. HUNGER and THIRST imply an insistent or impatient craving or a compelling need ⟨*hungered* for a business of his own⟩ ⟨*thirsted* for absolute power⟩.

: a disposition to bear injuries patiently **:** FORBEARANCE

**long·boat** \'lòŋ-ˌbōt\ *noun* (15th century)
: a large oared boat usually carried by a merchant sailing ship

**long bone** *noun* (circa 1860)
: any of the elongated bones supporting a vertebrate limb and consisting of an essentially cylindrical shaft that contains marrow and ends in enlarged heads for articulation with other bones

**long·bow** \'lòŋ-ˌbō\ *noun* (14th century)
: a hand-drawn wooden bow held vertically and used especially by medieval English archers

**long·bow·man** \-mən\ *noun* (1925)
: an archer who uses a longbow

**long·case clock** \'lòŋ-ˌkās-\ *noun* (1892)
**:** GRANDFATHER CLOCK

**long–chain** *adjective* (1930)
: having a relatively long chain of atoms and especially carbon atoms in the molecule ⟨*long-chain* hydrocarbons⟩

**long–day** *adjective* (1920)
: responding to or relating to a long photoperiod — used especially of a plant; compare DAY-NEUTRAL, SHORT-DAY

**¹long–distance** *adjective* (1884)
**1 :** of or relating to telephone communication with a distant point
**2 a :** situated a long distance away **b :** going or covering a long distance ⟨*long-distance* roads⟩ ⟨a *long-distance* runner⟩ **c :** conducted or effective over long distance ⟨a *long-distance* courtship⟩ ⟨*long-distance* listening devices⟩

**²long–distance** *adverb* (circa 1961)
**1 :** by long-distance telephone
**2 :** over or from a long distance

**long distance** *noun* (1904)
**1 :** communication by long-distance telephone
**2 :** a telephone operator or exchange that gives long-distance connections

**long division** *noun* (1827)
: arithmetical division in which the several steps involved in the division are indicated in detail

**long–drawn–out** *or* **long–drawn** *adjective* (1646)
: extended to a great length

**lon·ge·ron** \'län-jə-ˌrän\ *noun* [French] (1912)
: a fore-and-aft framing member of an airplane fuselage

**lon·gev·i·ty** \län-'je-və-tē, lòn-\ *noun* [Late Latin *longaevitas*, from Latin *longaevus* long-lived, from *longus* long + *aevum* age — more at AYE] (1615)
**1 a :** a long duration of individual life **b :** length of life ⟨a study of *longevity*⟩
**2 :** long continuance **:** PERMANENCE, DURABILITY

**lon·ge·vous** \-'jē-vəs\ *adjective* (1680)
**:** LONG-LIVED

**long face** *noun* (1786)
: a facial expression of sadness or melancholy

**long green** *noun* (circa 1891)
*slang* **:** MONEY

**long·hair** \'lòŋ-ˌhar, -ˌher\ *noun* (1920)
**1 :** an impractical intellectual
**2 :** a person of artistic gifts or interests; *especially* **:** a lover of classical music
**3 :** a person with long hair; *especially* **:** HIPPIE
**4 :** a domestic cat having long outer fur
**— long·haired** \-'hard, -'herd\ *or* **long·hair** *adjective*

**long·hand** \-ˌhand\ *noun* (1666)
**:** HANDWRITING: **a :** characters or words written out fully by hand **b :** cursive writing

**long haul** *noun* (1936)
**1 :** a long distance
**2 :** a considerable period of time; *especially* **:** LONG RUN
**— long–haul** *adjective*

**long·head** \'lòŋ-ˌhed\ *noun* (1650)
: a dolichocephalic person

**long–head·ed** \-ˌhe-dəd\ *adjective* (circa 1700)
**1 :** having unusual foresight
**2 :** DOLICHOCEPHALIC
**— long·head·ed·ness** *noun*

**long–horn** \-ˌhòrn\ *noun* (1834)
**1 a :** any of the long-horned cattle of Spanish derivation formerly common in southwestern U.S. **b :** TEXAS LONGHORN 2
**2 :** a firm-textured usually mild cheese (as cheddar or Colby)

**long–horned beetle** \-ˌhòrn(d)-\ *noun* (1840)
: any of a family (Cerambycidae synonym Longicornia) of beetles usually distinguished by their very long antennae — called also *longhorn beetle*

**long–horned grasshopper** *noun* (1893)
: any of various grasshoppers (family Tettigoniidae) distinguished by their very long antennae

**long horse** *noun* (circa 1934)
**:** VAULTING HORSE

**long·house** \'lòŋ-ˌhaùs, -ˌhaùs\ *noun* (1643)
: a long communal dwelling of some North American Indians (as the Iroquois)

**long hundredweight** *noun* (circa 1934)
*British* **:** HUNDREDWEIGHT 2

**lon·gi·corn** \'län-jə-ˌkòrn\ *adjective* [ultimately from Latin *longus* long + *cornu* horn — more at HORN] (circa 1848)
**1 :** of, relating to, or being long-horned beetles
**2 :** having long antennae
**— longicorn** *noun*

**long·ing** \'lòŋ-iŋ\ *noun* (before 12th century)
: a strong desire especially for something unattainable **:** CRAVING
**— long·ing·ly** \-iŋ-lē\ *adverb*

**long·ish** \'lòŋ-ish\ *adjective* (1611)
: somewhat long **:** moderately long

**lon·gi·tude** \'län-jə-ˌtüd, -ˌtyüd, *British also* 'län-gə-\ *noun* [Middle English, from Latin *longitudin-, longitudo,* from *longus*] (14th century)
**1 a :** angular distance measured on a great circle of reference from the intersection of the adopted zero meridian with this reference circle to the similar intersection of the meridian passing through the object **b :** the arc or portion of the earth's equator intersected between the meridian of a given place and the prime meridian and expressed either in degrees or in time
**2** *archaic* **:** long duration

longitude 1a: hemisphere marked with meridians of longitude

**lon·gi·tu·di·nal** \ˌlän-jə-'tüd-nəl, -'tyüd-, -'t(y)ü-dᵊn-əl, *British also* ˌlän-gə-\ *adjective* (15th century)
**1 :** placed or running lengthwise
**2 :** of or relating to length or the lengthwise dimension
**3 :** involving the repeated observation or examination of a set of subjects over time with respect to one or more study variables
**— lon·gi·tu·di·nal·ly** *adverb*

**longitudinal wave** *noun* (circa 1931)
: a wave (as a sound wave) in which the particles of the medium vibrate in the direction of the line of advance of the wave

**long johns** \'lòŋ-ˌjänz\ *noun plural* (1943)
: long underwear

**long jump** *noun* (1882)
: a track-and-field event in which a jump for distance is made usually from a running start
**— long jumper** *noun*

**long–leaf pine** \'lòŋ-ˌlēf-\ *noun* (1796)
: a tall pine (*Pinus palustris*) of the southeastern U.S. with long needles in bundles of three and long cones that is a major timber tree; *also* : its tough coarse-grained reddish orange wood

**long–leaved pine** \-ˌlēv(d)-\ *noun* (1765)
**:** LONGLEAF PINE

**long·line** \'lòŋ-ˌlīn, -'līn\ *noun* (1876)
: a heavy fishing line that may be several miles long and that has baited hooks in series

**long–lin·er** \-ˌlī-nər\ *noun* (1909)
: one that fishes with a longline; *also* : a fishing vessel used in long-lining

**long–lin·ing** \-ˌlī-niŋ\ *noun* (1877)
: fishing with a longline

**long–lived** \'lòŋ-'livd *also* -'līvd\ *adjective* (14th century)
**1 :** having a long life **:** characterized by long life ⟨a *long-lived* family⟩
**2 :** lasting a long time **:** ENDURING ◼

**long meter** *noun* (1718)
: a quatrain in iambic tetrameter in which the second and fourth lines and often the first and third lines rhyme — called also *long measure*

**Lon·go·bard** \'lòŋ-gə-ˌbärd, 'läŋ-\ *noun, plural* **Longobards** *also* **Lon·go·bar·di** \ˌlòŋ-gə-'bär-ˌdī, ˌläŋ-, -dē\ [Middle English *Longobardes,* plural, from Latin *Langobardi, Longobardi*] (14th century)
**:** LOMBARD 1a
**— Lon·go·bar·dic** \ˌlòŋ-gə-'bär-dik, ˌläŋ-\ *adjective*

**long play** *noun* (1952)
: a long-playing record

**long–play·ing** \'lòŋ-'plā-iŋ\ *adjective* (1929)
: designed to be played at 33⅓ revolutions per minute — used of a microgroove record

**long–range** \-'rānj\ *adjective* (1854)
**1 :** relating to or fit for long distances ⟨*long-range* rockets⟩
**2 :** involving or taking into account a long period of time ⟨*long-range* planning⟩

**long run** *noun* (1627)
: a relatively long period of time — usually used in the phrase *in the long run*
**— long–run** \'lòŋ-'rən\ *adjective*

**long·shore·man** \'lòŋ-ˌshōr-mən, -ˌshòr-, ˌlòŋ-\ *noun* [*longshore,* short for *alongshore*] (1811)
: a person who loads and unloads ships at a seaport

**long·shor·ing** \'lòŋ-ˌshōr-iŋ, -ˌshòr-, ˌlòŋ-\ *noun* (1926)
: the act or occupation of working as a longshoreman

**long shot** \'lòŋ-ˌshät\ *noun* (1867)
**1 :** a venture involving great risk but promising a great reward if successful; *also* : a venture unlikely to succeed
**2 :** an entry (as in a horse race) given little chance of winning

\ə\ abut \ᵊ\ kitten \ər\ further \a\ ash \ā\ ace \ä\ mop, mar \aù\ out \ch\ chin \e\ bet \ē\ easy \g\ go \i\ hit \ī\ ice \j\ job \ŋ\ sing \ō\ go \ò\ law \òi\ boy \th\ thin \t͟h\ the \ü\ loot \ù\ foot \y\ yet \zh\ vision   *see also* Guide to Pronunciation

**3 :** a bet in which the chances of winning are slight but the possible winnings great
— **by a long shot :** by a great deal

**long·sight·ed** \-ˌsī-təd\ *adjective* (circa 1790)
**:** FARSIGHTED
— **long·sight·ed·ness** *noun*

**long since** *adverb* (14th century)
**1 :** long ago ⟨promises *long since* forgotten⟩
**2 :** for a long time ⟨has *long since* been a devoted friend⟩

**long·some** \ˈlȯŋ-səm\ *adjective* (before 12th century)
**:** tediously long
— **long·some·ly** *adverb*
— **long·some·ness** *noun*

**long·spur** \ˈlȯŋ-ˌspər\ *noun* (1831)
**:** any of several long-clawed finches (especially genus *Calcarius*) of the arctic regions and the Great Plains of North America

**long–stand·ing** \-ˈstan-diŋ\ *adjective* (1814)
**:** of long duration

**long–suf·fer·ing** \-ˌsə-f(ə-)riŋ, -ˈsə-\ *noun* (1526)
**:** long and patient endurance of offense
— **long–suffering** *adjective*
— **long–suf·fer·ing·ly** \-lē\ *adverb*

**long suit** *noun* (circa 1876)
**1 :** a holding of more than the average number of cards in a suit
**2 :** the activity or quality in which one excels

**long–term** \ˈlȯŋ-ˈtərm\ *adjective* (1904)
**1 :** occurring over or involving a relatively long period of time
**2 a :** of, relating to, or constituting a financial operation or obligation based on a considerable term and especially one of more than 10 years ⟨*long-term* bonds⟩ **b :** generated by assets held for longer than six months ⟨a *long-term* capital gain⟩

**long·time** \ˈlȯŋ-ˈtīm\ *adjective* (1584)
**:** having been so for a long time : LONG-STANDING ⟨a *longtime* friend⟩ ⟨a *longtime* friendship⟩

**Long Tom** \ˈlȯŋ-ˈtäm\ *noun* [from the name *Tom*] (1832)
**1 :** a large land gun having a long range
**2 :** a trough for washing gold-bearing earth

**long ton** *noun* (1829)
— see WEIGHT table

**lon·gueur** \lō<sup>n</sup>-ˈgœr\ *noun, plural* **longueurs** \-ˈgœr(z)\ [French, literally, length] (1791)
**:** a dull and tedious passage or section (as of a book)

**long view** *noun* (1912)
**:** an approach to a problem or situation that emphasizes long-range factors

**long–wind·ed** \ˌlȯŋ-ˈwin-dəd, ˈlȯŋ-ˌwin-\ *adjective* (1589)
**1 :** tediously long in speaking or writing
**2 :** not easily subject to loss of breath
— **long–wind·ed·ly** *adverb*
— **long–wind·ed·ness** *noun*

**¹loo** \ˈlü\ *noun* [short for obsolete English *lanterloo*, from French *lanturelu* twaddle] (1675)
**1 :** an old card game in which the winner of each trick or a majority of tricks takes a portion of the pool while losing players are obligated to contribute to the next pool
**2 :** money staked at loo

**²loo** *transitive verb* (1680)
**:** to obligate to contribute to a new pool at loo for failing to win a trick

**³loo** *noun* [origin unknown] (1940)
*chiefly British* **:** TOILET 3

**loo·by** \ˈlü-bē\ *noun, plural* **loobies** [Middle English *loby*] (14th century)
**:** an awkward clumsy fellow : LUBBER

**loo·fah** \ˈlü-fə\ *noun* [New Latin *luffa*, from Arabic *lūf*] (1887)
**1 :** any of a genus (*Luffa*) of Old World tropical plants of the gourd family with large fruits; *also* **:** its fruit
**2 :** a sponge consisting of the fibrous skeleton of the fruit of a loofah (especially *Luffa aegyptiaca*)

**¹look** \ˈlu̇k\ *verb* [Middle English, from Old

English *lōcian;* akin to Old Saxon *lōcōn* to look] (before 12th century)
*transitive verb*
**1 :** to make sure or take care (that something is done)
**2 :** to ascertain by the use of one's eyes
**3 a :** to exercise the power of vision upon **:** EXAMINE **b** *archaic* **:** to search for
**4 a :** EXPECT, ANTICIPATE ⟨we *look* to have a good year⟩ **b :** to have in mind as an end ⟨*looking* to win back some lost profits⟩
**5** *archaic* **:** to bring into a place or condition by the exercise of the power of vision
**6 :** to express by the eyes or facial expression
**7 :** to have an appearance that befits or accords with
*intransitive verb*
**1 a :** to exercise the power of vision : SEE **b** **:** to direct one's attention ⟨*look* upon the future with hope⟩ **c :** to direct the eyes
**2 :** to have the appearance or likelihood of being : SEEM ⟨it *looks* unlikely⟩ ⟨*looks* to be hard work⟩
**3 :** to have a specified outlook ⟨the house *looked* east⟩
**4 :** to gaze in wonder or surprise : STARE
**5 :** to show a tendency ⟨the evidence *looks* to acquittal⟩ ▪
*synonym* see EXPECT
— **look after :** to take care of
— **look at :** CONSIDER 1 ⟨*looking at* the possibility of relocating⟩
— **look down one's nose :** to view something with arrogance, disdain, or disapproval
— **look for :** to await with hope or anticipation
— **look forward :** to anticipate with pleasure or satisfaction ⟨*looking forward* to your visit⟩
— **look into :** EXPLORE 1a
— **look the other way :** to direct one's attention away from something unpleasant or troublesome
— **look to 1 :** to direct one's attention to ⟨*looking to* the future⟩ **2 :** to rely upon ⟨*looks to* reading for relaxation⟩

**²look** *noun* (13th century)
**1 a :** the act of looking **b :** GLANCE
**2 a :** the expression of the countenance **b :** physical appearance; *especially* **:** attractive physical appearance — usually used in plural **c :** a combination of design features giving a unified appearance ⟨a new *look* in design⟩
**3 :** the state or form in which something appears

**look–alike** \ˈlu̇-kə-ˌlīk\ *noun* (1947)
**:** one that looks like another : DOUBLE
— **look–alike** *adjective*

**look·down** \ˈlu̇k-ˌdau̇n\ *noun* (circa 1882)
**:** a silvery carangid fish (*Selene vomer*) chiefly of the Atlantic having a laterally compressed deep body and steeply sloping facial profile

**look down** *intransitive verb* (14th century)
**1 :** to be in a position that affords a downward view
**2 :** to regard with contempt : DESPISE — used with *on* or *upon*

**look·er** \ˈlu̇-kər\ *noun* (14th century)
**1 :** one that looks
**2 a :** one having an appearance of a specified kind **b :** one that has an attractive appearance : BEAUTY

**look·er–on** \ˌlu̇-kər-ˈȯn, -ˈän\ *noun, plural* **lookers–on** (1539)
**:** ONLOOKER

**look–in** \ˈlu̇k-ˌin\ *noun* (1870)
**1 :** a chance of success
**2 :** a quick pass in football to a receiver running diagonally toward the center of the field

**looking glass** *noun* (1562)
**:** MIRROR

**look·out** \ˈlu̇k-ˌau̇t\ *noun* (1699)
**1 :** one engaged in keeping watch : WATCHMAN
**2 :** an elevated place or structure affording a wide view for observation

**3 :** a careful looking or watching ⟨on the *lookout*⟩
**4 :** VIEW, OUTLOOK
**5 :** a matter of care or concern

**look out** *intransitive verb* (1602)
**:** to take care or concern oneself — used with *for* ⟨*looking out* for number one⟩

**look over** *transitive verb* (14th century)
**:** to inspect or examine especially in a cursory way

**look–see** \ˈlu̇k-ˈsē, -ˌsē\ *noun* (1883)
**:** a general survey : EVALUATION, INSPECTION

**look·up** \ˈlu̇k-ˌəp\ *noun* (1936)
**:** the process or an instance of looking something up; *especially* **:** the process of matching by computer the words of a text with material stored in memory

**look up** (14th century)
*intransitive verb*
**1 :** to cheer up ⟨*look up*—things are not all bad⟩
**2 :** to improve in prospects or conditions ⟨business is *looking up*⟩
*transitive verb*
**1 :** to search for in or as if in a reference work ⟨*look up* a phone number⟩
**2 :** to seek out especially for a brief visit

**¹loom** \ˈlüm\ *noun* [Middle English *lome* tool, loom, from Old English *gelōma* tool; akin to Middle Dutch *allame* tool] (15th century)
**:** a frame or machine for interlacing at right angles two or more sets of threads or yarns to form a cloth

**²loom** *intransitive verb* [origin unknown] (circa 1541)
**1 :** to come into sight in enlarged or distorted and indistinct form often as a result of atmospheric conditions
**2 a :** to appear in an impressively great or exaggerated form ⟨deficits *loomed* large⟩ **b :** to take shape as an impending occurrence

**³loom** *noun* (1836)
**:** the indistinct and exaggerated appearance of something seen on the horizon or through fog or darkness; *also* **:** a looming shadow or reflection

**¹loon** \ˈlün\ *noun* [Middle English *loun*] (15th century)
**1 :** LOUT, IDLER
**2** *chiefly Scottish* **:** BOY
**3 a :** a crazy person **b :** SIMPLETON

**²loon** *noun* [of Scandinavian origin; akin to Old Norse *lōmr* loon] (1634)

---

□ USAGE

**look**   Some people are offended or made uneasy by the construction in which *look* is followed by *to* and an infinitive. This construction, usually expressing expectation (*transitive verb* sense 4a), has been in use since the 17th century ⟨good morrow . . . I *look'd* to have found you with your headache and morning qualms —Thomas Shadwell⟩ ⟨is elderly now and . . . *looks* to be gathered to his fathers before the times get any worse —Rudyard Kipling⟩. In the 19th century the present participle began to turn up in this construction ⟨two lovers *looking* to be wed —A. E. Housman⟩. These uses carry the notion of purpose and are the beginning of sense 4b. This construction is very common at present ⟨had been *looking* to change jobs for several years —Curry Kirkpatrick⟩ ⟨*looking* to blaze her own trails as an actress —*Town & Country*⟩ ⟨a number of states are now *looking* to circumvent the national limit —Daniel Seligman⟩. The linking verb sense of *look* (*intransitive verb* sense 2) is commonly followed by *to be* ⟨sure *looked* to be the hero of this game —Rick Telander⟩ ⟨the baby *looks* to be about nine or ten months old —Léon Bing⟩. All of these constructions are standard.

: any of several large birds (genus *Gavia*) of Holarctic regions that feed on fish by diving and have their legs placed far back under the body for optimal locomotion underwater

**loo·ny** *also* **loo·ney** \'lü-nē\ *adjective* **loo·ni·er; -est** [by shortening & alteration from *lunatic*] (1872)
: CRAZY, FOOLISH
— **loo·ni·ness** *noun*
— **loony** *noun*

**loony bin** *noun* (1919)
: an insane asylum : MADHOUSE

**¹loop** \'lüp\ *noun* [Middle English *loupe*; perhaps akin to Middle Dutch *lupen* to watch, peer] (14th century)
*archaic* : LOOPHOLE 1a

**²loop** *noun* [Middle English *loupe*, of unknown origin] (14th century)
**1 a :** a curving or doubling of a line so as to form a closed or partly open curve within itself through which another line can be passed or into which a hook may be hooked **b :** such a fold of cord or ribbon serving as an ornament
**2 a :** something shaped like a loop **b :** a circular airplane maneuver executed in the vertical plane
**3 :** a ring or curved piece used to form a fastening, handle, or catch
**4 :** a closed electric circuit
**5 :** a piece of film or magnetic tape whose ends are spliced together so as to project or play back the same material continuously
**6 :** a series of instructions (as for a computer) that is repeated until a terminating condition is reached
**7 :** a sports league
**8 :** a select well-informed inner circle that is influential in decision making ⟨out of the policy *loop*⟩
— **for a loop :** into a state of amazement, confusion, or distress

**³loop** (1832)
*intransitive verb*
**1 :** to make or form a loop
**2 :** to execute a loop in an airplane
**3 :** to move in loops or in an arc
*transitive verb*
**1 a :** to make a loop in, on, or about **b :** to fasten with a loop
**2 :** to join (two courses of loops) in knitting
**3 :** to connect (electric conductors) so as to complete a loop
**4 :** to cause to move in an arc

**looped** \'lüpd\ *adjective* (1513)
**1 :** having, formed in, or characterized by loops ⟨*looped* fabrics⟩
**2 :** DRUNK 1a

**loop·er** \'lü-pər\ *noun* (1731)
**1 :** any of the usually rather small hairless caterpillars that are mostly larvae of moths (families Geometridae and Noctuidae) and move with a looping movement in which the anterior legs and the posterior prolegs are alternately made fast and released — called also *inchworm*
**2 :** one that loops

**¹loop·hole** \'lüp-ˌhōl\ *noun* [¹*loop*] (1591)
**1 a :** a small opening through which small arms may be fired **b :** a similar opening to admit light and air or to permit observation
**2 :** a means of escape; *especially* : an ambiguity or omission in the text through which the intent of a statute, contract, or obligation may be evaded

**²loophole** *transitive verb* (1664)
: to make loopholes in

**loop of Hen·le** \-'hen-lē\ [F. G. J. *Henle* (died 1885) German pathologist] (1890)
: a U-shaped part of the nephron of birds and mammals that lies between and is continuous with the proximal and distal convoluted tubules and that functions in water resorption

**loopy** \'lü-pē\ *adjective* **loop·i·er; -est** (1856)
**1 :** having or characterized by loops
**2 :** CRAZY, BIZARRE

**¹loose** \'lüs\ *adjective* **loos·er; loos·est** [Middle English *lous*, from Old Norse *lauss*; akin to Old High German *lōs* loose — more at -LESS] (13th century)
**1 a :** not rigidly fastened or securely attached **b (1) :** having worked partly free from attachments ⟨a *loose* tooth⟩ **(2) :** having relative freedom of movement **c :** produced freely and accompanied by raising of mucus ⟨a *loose* cough⟩ **d :** not tight-fitting
**2 a :** free from a state of confinement, restraint, or obligation ⟨a lion *loose* in the streets⟩ ⟨spend *loose* funds wisely⟩ **b :** not brought together in a bundle, container, or binding **c** *archaic* : DISCONNECTED, DETACHED
**3 :** not dense, close, or compact in structure or arrangement
**4 a :** lacking in restraint or power of restraint ⟨a *loose* tongue⟩ ⟨*loose* bowels⟩ **b :** lacking moral restraint : UNCHASTE
**5 a :** not tightly drawn or stretched : SLACK **b :** being flexible or relaxed ⟨stay *loose*⟩
**6 a :** lacking in precision, exactness, or care ⟨*loose* brushwork⟩ ⟨*loose* usage⟩ **b :** permitting freedom of interpretation
**7 :** not in the possession of either of two competing teams ⟨a *loose* ball⟩ ⟨a *loose* puck⟩
— **loose·ly** *adverb*
— **loose·ness** *noun*

**²loose** *verb* **loosed; loos·ing** (13th century)
*transitive verb*
**1 a :** to let loose : RELEASE **b :** to free from restraint
**2 :** to make loose : UNTIE ⟨*loose* a knot⟩
**3 :** to cast loose : DETACH
**4 :** to let fly : DISCHARGE
**5 :** to make less rigid, tight, or strict : RELAX
*intransitive verb*
: to let fly a missile (as an arrow) : FIRE

**³loose** *adverb* (15th century)
: in a loose manner : LOOSELY

**loose box** *noun* (1849)
*British* : BOX STALL

**loose cannon** *noun* (1981)
: a dangerously uncontrollable person or thing

**loose end** *noun* (1546)
**1 :** something left hanging loose
**2 :** a fragment of unfinished business — usually used in plural

**loose–joint·ed** \'lüs-'join-təd\ *adjective* (1859)
**1 :** having joints apparently not closely articulated
**2 :** characterized by unusually free movements
— **loose–joint·ed·ness** *noun*

**loose–leaf** \'lüs-'lēf\ *adjective* (1902)
**1 :** having leaves secured in book form in a cover whose backbone may be opened for adding, arranging, or removing leaves ⟨*loose-leaf* notebook⟩
**2 :** of, relating to, or used with a loose-leaf binding ⟨*loose-leaf* paper⟩

**loos·en** \'lü-sᵊn\ *verb* **loos·ened; loos·en·ing** \'lüs-niŋ, 'lü-sᵊn-iŋ\ (14th century)
*transitive verb*
**1 :** to release from restraint
**2 :** to make looser
**3 :** to relieve (the bowels) of constipation
**4 :** to cause or permit to become less strict — often used with *up*
*intransitive verb*
: to become loose or looser

**loosen up** *intransitive verb* (1938)
: to become less tense : RELAX

**loose sentence** *noun* (circa 1890)
: a sentence in which the principal clause comes first and subordinate modifiers or trailing elements follow

**loose smut** *noun* (1890)
: a smut disease of grains in which the entire head is transformed into a dusty mass of spores

**loose·strife** \'lü(s)-ˌstrīf\ *noun* [intended as translation of Greek *lysimacheios* loosestrife (as if from *lysis* act of loosing + *machesthai* to fight) — more at LYSIS] (1548)
**1 :** any of a genus (*Lysimachia*) of plants of the primrose family with leafy stems and usually yellow or white flowers
**2 :** any of a genus (*Lythrum*, family Lythraceae, the loosestrife family) of herbs having entire leaves and including some with showy spikes of purple flowers; *especially* : PURPLE LOOSESTRIFE

**loos·ey–goos·ey** \ˌlü-sē-'gü-sē\ *adjective* (1964)
: notably loose or relaxed : not tense

**¹loot** \'lüt\ *noun* [Hindi *lūt*; akin to Sanskrit *luṇtati* he plunders] (circa 1788)
**1 :** goods usually of considerable value taken in war : SPOILS
**2 :** something held to resemble goods of value seized in war: as **a :** something appropriated illegally often by force or violence **b :** illicit gains by public officials **c :** MONEY
**3 :** the action of looting
**synonym** see SPOIL

**²loot** (1845)
*transitive verb*
**1 a :** to plunder or sack in war **b :** to rob especially on a large scale and usually by violence or corruption
**2 :** to seize and carry away by force especially in war
*intransitive verb*
: to engage in robbing or plundering especially in war
— **loot·er** *noun*

**¹lop** \'läp\ *noun* [Middle English *loppe*] (14th century)
: material cut away from a tree; *especially* : parts discarded in lumbering

**²lop** *transitive verb* **lopped; lop·ping** (1519)
**1 a (1) :** to cut off branches or twigs from **(2) :** to sever from a woody plant **b (1)** *archaic* : to cut off the head or limbs of **(2) :** to cut from a person
**2 a :** to remove superfluous parts from **b :** to eliminate as unnecessary or undesirable — usually used with *off*
— **lop·per** *noun*

**³lop** *intransitive verb* **lopped; lop·ping** [perhaps imitative] (1578)
: to hang downward : DROOP

**¹lope** \'lōp\ *noun* [Middle English *loup*, *lope* leap, from Old Norse *hlaup*; akin to Old English *hlēapan* to leap — more at LEAP] (1809)
**1 :** an easy natural gait of a horse resembling a canter
**2 :** an easy usually bounding gait capable of being sustained for a long time

**²lope** *intransitive verb* **loped; lop·ing** (circa 1825)
: to move or ride at a lope
— **lop·er** *noun*

**lop–eared** \'läp-ˌird\ *adjective* (1687)
: having ears that droop

**loph·o·phore** \'lä-fə-ˌfōr, -ˌfȯr\ *noun* [Greek *lophos* crest + English *-phore*] (1850)
: a circular or horseshoe-shaped organ about the mouth especially of a brachiopod or bryozoan that bears tentacles and functions especially in food-getting

**lop–sid·ed** \'läp-ˌsī-dəd\ *adjective* (1711)
**1 :** leaning to one side
**2 :** lacking in balance, symmetry, or proportion : disproportionately heavy on one side ⟨a *lopsided* vote of 99–1⟩
— **lop·sid·ed·ly** *adverb*
— **lop·sid·ed·ness** *noun*

**lo·qua·cious** \lō-'kwā-shəs\ *adjective* [Latin *loquac-, loquax*, from *loqui* to speak] (1667)
**1 :** given to fluent or excessive talk : GARRULOUS
**2 :** full of excessive talk : WORDY
**synonym** see TALKATIVE

\ə\ abut \ᵊ\ kitten \ər\ further \a\ ash \ā\ ace
\ä\ mop, mar \au̇\ out \ch\ chin \e\ bet \ē\ easy
\g\ go \i\ hit \ī\ ice \j\ job \ŋ\ sing \ō\ go
\ȯ\ law \ȯi\ boy \th\ thin \t͟h\ the \ü\ loot \u̇\ foot
\y\ yet \zh\ vision *see also* Guide to Pronunciation

— **lo·qua·cious·ly** *adverb*

— **lo·qua·cious·ness** *noun*

**lo·quac·i·ty** \-'kwa-sə-tē\ *noun* (13th century)
: the quality or state of being very talkative

**lo·quat** \'lō-ˌkwät\ *noun* [Chinese (Guang-dong) *làuh-gwāt*] (1820)
: an Asian evergreen tree (*Eriobotrya japonica*) of the rose family often cultivated for its fruit; *also* : its small yellow edible fruit used especially for preserves

**lo·ran** \'lōr-ˌan, 'lȯr-\ *noun* [*long-range navigation*] (1932)
: a system of long-range navigation in which pulsed signals sent out by two pairs of radio stations are used to determine the geographical position of a ship or an airplane

**¹lord** \'lȯrd\ *noun* [Middle English *loverd, lord,* from Old English *hlāford,* from *hlāf* loaf + *weard* keeper — more at LOAF, WARD] (before 12th century)
1 : one having power and authority over others: **a** : a ruler by hereditary right or preeminence to whom service and obedience are due **b** : one of whom a fee or estate is held in feudal tenure **c** : an owner of land or other real property **d** *obsolete* : the male head of a household **e** : HUSBAND **f** : one that has achieved mastery or that exercises leadership or great power in some area ⟨a drug *lord*⟩
2 *capitalized* **a** : GOD 1 **b** : JESUS
3 : a man of rank or high position: as **a** : a feudal tenant whose right or title comes directly from the king **b** : a British nobleman: as (1) : BARON 2a (2) : an hereditary peer of the rank of marquess, earl, or viscount (3) : the son of a duke or a marquess or the eldest son of an earl (4) : a bishop of the Church of England **c** *plural, capitalized* : HOUSE OF LORDS
4 — used as a British title: as **a** — used as part of an official title ⟨*Lord* Advocate⟩ **b** — used informally in place of the full title for a marquess, earl, or viscount **c** — used for a baron **d** — used by courtesy before the name and surname of a younger son of a duke or a marquess
5 : a person chosen to preside over a festival

◆

**²lord** *intransitive verb* (14th century)
: to act like a lord; *especially* : to put on airs — usually used with *it* ⟨*lords* it over his friends⟩

**lord chancellor** *noun, plural* **lords chancellor** (15th century)
: a British officer of state who presides over the House of Lords in both its legislative and judicial capacities, serves as the head of the British judiciary, and is usually a leading member of the cabinet

**lord·ing** \'lȯr-diŋ\ *noun* (13th century)
1 *archaic* : LORD
2 *obsolete* : LORDLING

**lord·ling** \'lȯrd-liŋ\ *noun* (13th century)
: a little or insignificant lord

**lord·ly** \-lē\ *adjective* **lord·li·er; -est** (before 12th century)
1 **a** : of, relating to, or having the characteristics of a lord : DIGNIFIED **b** : GRAND, NOBLE
2 : exhibiting such pride and assurance as could only be felt as appropriate to one of the highest birth or rank
**synonym** see PROUD
— **lord·li·ness** *noun*
— **lordly** *adverb*

**lord of misrule** (15th century)
: a master of Christmas revels in England especially in the 15th and 16th centuries

**lor·do·sis** \lȯr-'dō-səs\ *noun* [New Latin, from Greek *lordōsis,* from *lordos* curving forward; akin to Old English be*lyrtan* to deceive] (1704)
1 : abnormal curvature of the spine forward
2 : a mating posture of some sexually receptive female mammals (as rats) in which the head and rump are raised and the back is arched downward
— **lor·dot·ic** \-'dä-tik\ *adjective*

**Lord Protector of the Commonwealth** (circa 1653)
: PROTECTOR 2b

**Lord's day** *noun, often D capitalized* (12th century)
: SUNDAY

**lord·ship** \'lȯrd-ˌship\ *noun* (before 12th century)
1 **a** : the rank or dignity of a lord — used as a title **b** : the authority or power of a lord : DOMINION
2 : the territory under the jurisdiction of a lord : SEIGNIORY

**Lord's Prayer** *noun* (circa 1549)
: the prayer with variant versions in Matthew and Luke that according to the Lucan account Christ taught his disciples

**Lord's Supper** *noun* (14th century)
: COMMUNION 2a

**Lord's table** *noun, often T capitalized* (1535)
: ALTAR 2

**Lordy** \'lȯr-dē\ *interjection* [¹*lord* (God) + ⁴-*y*] (1853)
— used to express surprise or strength of feeling

**¹lore** \'lōr, 'lȯr\ *noun* [Middle English, from Old English *lār;* akin to Old High German *lēra* doctrine, Old English *leornian* to learn] (before 12th century)
1 *archaic* : something that is taught : LESSON
2 : something that is learned: **a** : knowledge gained through study or experience **b** : traditional knowledge or belief
3 : a particular body of knowledge or tradition
**word history** see LEARN

**²lore** *noun* [New Latin *lorum,* from Latin, thong, rein; akin to Greek *eulēra* reins] (1828)
: the space between the eye and bill in a bird or the corresponding region in a reptile or fish
— **lo·re·al** \'lōr-ē-əl, 'lȯr-\ *adjective*

**Lo·re·lei** \'lōr-ə-ˌlī, 'lȯr-\ *noun* [German]
: a siren of Germanic legend whose singing lures Rhine River boatmen to destruction on a reef

**lor·gnette** \lȯrn-'yet\ *noun* [French, from *lorgner* to take a sidelong look at, from Middle French, from *lorgne* squinting] (1803)
: a pair of eyeglasses or opera glasses with a handle

**lor·gnon** \lȯrn-'yōⁿ\ *noun* [French, from *lorgner*] (1846)
: LORGNETTE

**lo·ri·ca** \lə-'rī-kə\ *noun, plural* **-cae** \-kē, -ˌsē\ [Latin] (circa 1706)
1 : a Roman cuirass of leather or metal
2 [New Latin, from Latin] : a hard protective case or shell (as of a rotifer)

**lor·i·keet** \'lȯr-ə-ˌkēt, 'lär-\ *noun* [*lory* + *-keet* (as in *parakeet*)] (1770)
: any of numerous small arboreal chiefly Australasian parrots (family Loriidae) that usually have long slender tongue papillae which form an organ resembling a brush

**lo·ris** \'lōr-əs, 'lȯr-\ *noun* [French, probably from obsolete Dutch *loeris* simpleton] (1774)
: any of several nocturnal slow-moving tailless arboreal primates (family Lorisidae): as **a** : a slim-bodied primate (*Loris tardigradus*) of southern India and Sri Lanka **b** : either of two larger related primates (*Nycticebus pygmaeus* or *N. coucang*) of southeastern Asia that are heavier limbed and slower moving

**loris a**

**lorn** \'lȯrn\ *adjective* [Middle English, from *loren,* past participle of *lesen* to lose, from Old English *lēosan* — more at LOSE] (14th century)
: DESOLATE, FORSAKEN

**Lor·raine cross** \lə-'rān-, lȯ-\ *noun* (1898)

: CROSS OF LORRAINE

**lor·ry** \'lȯr-ē, 'lär-\ *noun, plural* **lorries** [origin unknown] (1908)
*chiefly British* : MOTORTRUCK

**lo·ry** \'lȯr-ē, 'lȯr-\ *noun, plural* **lories** [Dutch, from Malay *nuri, luri*] (1682)
: any of numerous parrots (family Loriidae) of Australia, New Guinea, and adjacent islands related to the lorikeets and usually having the tongue papillose at the tip and the mandibles less toothed than in other parrots

**lose** \'lüz\ *verb* **lost** \'lȯst\; **los·ing** \'lü-ziŋ\ [Middle English, from Old English *losian* to perish, lose, from *los* destruction; akin to Old English *lēosan* to lose; akin to Old Norse *losa* to loosen, Latin *luere* to atone for, Greek *lyein* to loosen, dissolve, destroy] (before 12th century)
*transitive verb*
1 **a** : to bring to destruction — used chiefly in passive construction ⟨the ship was *lost* on the reef⟩ **b** : DAMN ⟨if he shall gain the whole world and *lose* his own soul —Matthew 16:26 (Authorized Version)⟩
2 : to miss from one's possession or from a customary or supposed place
3 : to suffer deprivation of : part with especially in an unforeseen or accidental manner
4 **a** : to suffer loss through the death or removal of or final separation from ⟨a person⟩ **b** : to fail to keep control of or allegiance of ⟨*lose* votes⟩ ⟨*lost* his temper⟩
5 **a** : to fail to use : let slip by : WASTE ⟨*lose* the tide⟩ **b** (1) : to fail to win, gain, or obtain ⟨*lose* a prize⟩ ⟨*lose* a contest⟩ (2) : to undergo defeat in ⟨*lost* every battle⟩ **c** : to fail to catch with the senses or the mind ⟨*lost* part of what she said⟩
6 : to cause the loss of ⟨one careless statement *lost* him the election⟩
7 : to fail to keep, sustain, or maintain ⟨*lost* my balance⟩
8 **a** : to cause to miss one's way or bearings ⟨*lost* himself in the maze of streets⟩ **b** : to make ⟨oneself⟩ withdrawn from immediate reality ⟨*lost* herself in daydreaming⟩
9 **a** : to wander or go astray from ⟨*lost* his way⟩ **b** : to draw away from : OUTSTRIP ⟨*lost* his pursuers⟩
10 : to fail to keep in sight or in mind
11 : to free oneself from : get rid of ⟨dieting to *lose* some weight⟩
*intransitive verb*
1 : to undergo deprivation of something of value
2 : to undergo defeat ⟨*lose* with good grace⟩
3 *of a timepiece* : to run slow
— **los·able** \'lü-zə-bəl\ *adjective*

— **los·able·ness** *noun*

— **lose ground :** to suffer loss or disadvantage **:** fail to advance or improve

— **lose one's heart :** to fall in love

**lo·sel** \'lō-zəl\ *noun* [Middle English, from *losen* (past participle of *lesen* to lose), alteration of *loren* — more at LORN] (14th century)
**:** a worthless person

**lose out** *intransitive verb* (circa 1858)
**:** to fail to win in competition **:** fail to receive an expected reward or gain

**los·er** \'lü-zər\ *noun* (1548)
**1 :** one that loses especially consistently
**2 :** one who is incompetent or unable to succeed; *also* **:** something doomed to fail or disappoint

**loss** \'lós\ *noun* [Middle English *los,* probably back-formation from *lost,* past participle of *losen* to lose] (13th century)
**1 :** DESTRUCTION, RUIN
**2 a :** the act of losing possession **b :** the harm or privation resulting from loss or separation **c :** an instance of losing
**3 :** a person or thing or an amount that is lost: as **a** *plural* **:** killed, wounded, or captured soldiers **b :** the power diminution of a circuit or circuit element corresponding to conversion of electrical energy into heat by resistance
**4 a :** failure to gain, win, obtain, or utilize **b :** an amount by which the cost of an article or service exceeds the selling price
**5 :** decrease in amount, magnitude, or degree
**6 :** the amount of an insured's financial detriment by death or damage that the insurer becomes liable for

— **at a loss :** UNCERTAIN, PUZZLED

— **for a loss :** into a state of distress

**loss leader** *noun* (1917)
**:** something (as merchandise) sold at a loss in order to draw customers

— **loss–leader** *adjective*

**loss ratio** *noun* (1926)
**:** the ratio between insurance losses incurred and premiums earned during a given period

**lossy** \'lò-sē\ *adjective* (1946)
**:** causing attenuation or dissipation of electrical energy ⟨a *lossy* transmission line⟩ ⟨a *lossy* dielectric⟩

**lost** \'lóst\ *adjective* [past participle of *lose*] (15th century)
**1 :** not made use of, won, or claimed
**2 a :** no longer possessed **b :** no longer known
**3 :** ruined or destroyed physically or morally **:** DESPERATE
**4 a :** taken away or beyond reach or attainment **:** DENIED ⟨regions *lost* to the faith⟩ **b :** INSENSIBLE, HARDENED ⟨*lost* to shame⟩
**5 a :** unable to find the way **b :** no longer visible **c :** lacking assurance or self-confidence **:** HELPLESS
**6 :** RAPT, ABSORBED ⟨*lost* in reverie⟩
**7 :** not appreciated or understood **:** WASTED ⟨their jokes were *lost* on me⟩

— **lost·ness** \'lòs(t)-nəs\ *noun*

**lost wax** *noun* (1909)
**:** a process used in metal casting that consists of making a wax model, coating it with a refractory to form a mold, heating until the wax melts and runs out of the mold, and then pouring metal into the vacant mold

**¹lot** \'lät\ *noun* [Middle English, from Old English *hlot;* akin to Old High German *hlōz*] (before 12th century)
**1 :** an object used as a counter in determining a question by chance
**2 a :** the use of lots as a means of deciding something **b :** the resulting choice
**3 a :** something that comes to one upon whom a lot has fallen **:** SHARE **b :** one's way of life or worldly fate **:** FORTUNE
**4 a :** a portion of land **b :** a measured parcel of land having fixed boundaries and designated on a plot or survey **c :** a motion-picture studio and its adjoining property

**5 a :** a number of units of an article, a single article, or a parcel of articles offered as one item (as in an auction sale) **b :** all the members of a present group, kind, or quantity —
**6 a :** a number of associated persons **:** SET **b :** KIND, SORT
**7 :** a considerable quantity or extent ⟨a *lot* of money⟩ ⟨*lots* of friends⟩ ☐

**synonym** see FATE

— **a lot 1 :** to a considerable degree or extent ⟨this is *a lot* nicer⟩ **2 :** OFTEN, FREQUENTLY ⟨runs *a lot* every day⟩ **3 :** LOTS

**²lot** *transitive verb* **lot·ted; lot·ting** (15th century)
**1 :** ALLOT, APPORTION
**2 :** to form or divide into lots

**Lot** \'lät\ *noun* [Hebrew *Lōṭ*]
**:** a nephew of Abraham who according to the account in Genesis escaped from the doomed city of Sodom with his wife who turned into a pillar of salt when she looked back

**lo·ta** *also* **lo·tah** \'lō-tə\ *noun* [Hindi *loṭā*] (1809)
**:** a small usually spherical water vessel of brass or copper used in India

**loth** \'lōth, 'lòth\ *variant of* LOATH

**lo·thar·io** \lō-'thar-ē-,ō, -'ther-, -'thär-\ *noun, plural* **-i·os** *often capitalized* [*Lotharic,* seducer in the play *The Fair Penitent* (1703) by Nicholas Rowe] (1756)
**:** a man whose chief interest is seducing women ◆

**lo·ti** \'lō-tē\ *noun, plural* **ma·lo·ti** \mə-'lō-tē\ [Sesotho] (1980)
— see MONEY table

**lo·tic** \'lō-tik\ *adjective* [Latin *lotus,* past participle of *lavere*] (1916)
**:** of, relating to, or living in actively moving water ⟨a *lotic* habitat⟩ — compare LENTIC

**lo·tion** \'lō-shən\ *noun* [Middle English *loscion,* from Latin *lotion-, lotio* act of washing, from *lavere* to wash — more at LYE] (14th century)
**:** a liquid preparation for cosmetic or external medicinal use

**lots** \'läts\ *adverb* [plural of ¹*lot*] (1891)
**:** MUCH ⟨feeling *lots* better⟩

**lotte** \'lät, 'lòt\ *noun* [French, from Middle French] (1977)
**:** MONKFISH

**lot·tery** \'lä-tə-rē *also* 'lä-trē\ *noun, plural* **-ter·ies** *often attributive* [Middle French *loterie,* from Middle Dutch, from *lot* lot; akin to Old English *hlot* lot] (1567)
**1 a :** a drawing of lots in which prizes are distributed to the winners among persons buying a chance **b :** a drawing of lots used to decide something
**2 :** an event or affair whose outcome is or seems to be determined by chance

**lot·to** \'lä-(,)tō\ *noun* [Italian, lottery, lotto, from French *lot* lot, of Germanic origin; akin to Old English *hlot* lot] (1778)
**:** a game of chance resembling bingo

**lo·tus** \'lō-təs\ *noun* [Latin & Greek; Latin *lotus,* from Greek *lōtos*] (circa 1541)
**1** *also* **lo·tos** \'lō-təs\
**:** a fruit eaten by the lotus-eaters and considered to cause indolence and dreamy contentment; *also* **:** a tree (as *Zizyphus lotus* of the buckthorn family) reputed to bear this fruit
**2 :** any of various water lilies including several represented in ancient Egyptian and Hindu art and religious symbolism
**3** [New Latin, from Latin] **a :** any of a genus (*Lotus*) of widely distributed upright leguminous herbs or subshrubs **b :** SWEET CLOVER

**lotus 2**

**lo·tus–eat·er** \-,ē-tər\ *noun* (1832)
**1 :** any of a people in Homer's *Odyssey* subsisting on the lotus and living in the dreamy indolence it induces
**2 :** an indolent person

**lo·tus·land** \-,land\ *noun* [from the Homeric land of lotus-eaters] (1842)
**1 :** a place inducing contentment especially through offering an idyllic living situation
**2 :** a state or an ideal marked by contentment often achieved through self-indulgence

**lotus position** *noun* [from the supposed resemblance of the position to a lotus blossom] (1953)
**:** a cross-legged sitting position used in yoga in which the right foot is on the left thigh and the left foot is on the right thigh

**louche** \'lüsh\ *adjective* [French, literally, cross-eyed, squint-eyed, from Latin *luscus* blind in one eye] (1819)
**:** not reputable or decent

**loud** \'laúd\ *adjective* [Middle English, from Old English *hlūd;* akin to Old High German *hlūt* loud, Latin in*clutus* famous, Greek *klytos,* Sanskrit *śṛnoti* he hears] (before 12th century)
**1 a :** marked by intensity or volume of sound **b :** producing a loud sound
**2 :** CLAMOROUS, NOISY

☐ USAGE

**lot** The phrases *a lot of* and *lots of* have been stigmatized as colloquial and unworthy of being used in writing since at least Ambrose Bierce did it in 1909. A surprising number of handbooks are still repeating his opinion even though the expressions are clearly well established and standard on all levels of usage except perhaps the most elevated. Literary use is common ⟨a *lot* of my old St. Louis chums will be out in the Spring —Mark Twain⟩ ⟨the Seurat paintings want a *lot* of seeing to appreciate —Arnold Bennett⟩ ⟨there were *lots* of people in Oxford like that —John Galsworthy⟩ ⟨I have sat around in bars with a *lot* of other ex-newspapermen —James Thurber⟩. Similarly the adverbial uses of *a lot* and *lots* are standard ⟨gave him something *a lot* more important —William Faulkner⟩ ⟨I hope you're *lots* better now —F. Scott Fitzgerald⟩. The spelling *alot* is rare in print and is generally considered a mistake, especially by editors and English teachers, who, along with computer spelling checkers, are evidently responsible for its rarity in print. It is by all accounts very common in spontaneously produced writing—notes, letters, drafts, memoranda, and the like. And it is well attested in the world of interactive computer networks, where no editors or spelling checkers are found.

◇ WORD HISTORY

**lothario** The word *lothario* derives from a character in a now seldom-performed tragedy, *The Fair Penitent* (1703) by Nicholas Rowe (1674–1718). In the play Lothario is a notorious seducer who is described as "haughty, gallant, and gay." He seduces Calista, an unfaithful wife and later the fair penitent of the title. Rowe's Lothario became a pattern for later characterizations in English literature, most notably Lovelace in Samuel Richardson's novel *Clarissa* (1747–48). Since the 18th century *lothario* has been used generically for a foppish, unscrupulous rake.

\ə\ **abut** \ᵊ\ **kitten** \ər\ **further** \a\ **ash** \ā\ **ace**
\ä\ **mop, mar** \aú\ **out** \ch\ **chin** \e\ **bet** \ē\ **easy**
\g\ **go** \i\ **hit** \ī\ **ice** \j\ **job** \ŋ\ **sing** \ō\ **go**
\ò\ **law** \òi\ **boy** \th\ **thin** \t̠h\ **the** \ü\ **loot** \ú\ **foot**
\y\ **yet** \zh\ **vision** *see also* Guide to Pronunciation

**3 :** obtrusive or offensive in appearance or smell **:** OBNOXIOUS ☆
— **loud** *adverb*
— **loud·ly** *adverb*

**loud·en** \'laủ-d°n\ *verb* **loud·ened; loud·en·ing** \'laủd-niŋ, 'laủ-d°n-iŋ\ (circa 1848)
*intransitive verb*
**:** to become loud
*transitive verb*
**:** to make loud

**loud–hail·er** \,laủd-'hā-lər\ *noun* (1941)
*chiefly British* **:** BULLHORN

**loud·mouth** \'laủd-,maủth\ *noun* (1914)
**:** a loudmouthed person

**loud·mouthed** \-,maủthd, -,maủtht\ *adjective* (1628)
**:** given to loud offensive talk

**loud·ness** *noun* (before 12th century)
**:** the attribute of a sound that determines the magnitude of the auditory sensation produced and that primarily depends on the amplitude of the sound wave involved

**loud·speak·er** \'laủd-,spē-kər\ *noun* (1920)
**:** a device that changes electrical signals into sounds loud enough to be heard at a distance

**Lou Geh·rig's disease** \,lü-'ger-igz-, -'gar-\ *noun* [*Lou Gehrig* (died 1941) American baseball player who suffered from the disease] (1958)
**:** AMYOTROPHIC LATERAL SCLEROSIS

**lough** \'läk, 'läẋ\ *noun* [Middle English, of Celtic origin; akin to Old Irish *loch* lake; akin to Latin *lacus* lake — more at LAKE] (14th century)
**1** *chiefly Irish* **:** LAKE
**2** *chiefly Irish* **:** a bay or inlet of the sea

**lou·is d'or** \,lü-ē-'dòr\ *noun, plural* **louis d'or** [French, from *Louis* XIII of France + *d'or* of gold] (1665)
**1 :** a French gold coin first struck in 1640 and issued up to the Revolution
**2 :** the French 20-franc gold piece issued after the Revolution

**Lou·is Qua·torze** \,lü-ē-kə-'tòrz\ *adjective* [French, Louis XIV] (1848)
**:** of, relating to, or characteristic of the architecture or furniture of the reign of Louis XIV of France

**Louis Quinze** \-'kaⁿz\ *adjective* [French, Louis XV] (1855)
**:** of, relating to, or characteristic of the architecture or furniture of the reign of Louis XV of France

**Louis Seize** \-'sāz, -'sez\ *adjective* [French, Louis XVI] (1882)
**:** of, relating to, or characteristic of the architecture or furniture of the reign of Louis XVI of France

**Louis Treize** \-'trāz, -'trez\ *adjective* [French, Louis XIII] (1883)
**:** of, relating to, or characteristic of the architecture or furniture of the reign of Louis XIII of France

**¹lounge** \'laủnj\ *verb* **lounged; loung·ing** [origin unknown] (1508)
*intransitive verb*
**:** to act or move idly or lazily **:** LOAF
*transitive verb*
**:** to pass (time) idly

**²lounge** *noun* (1775)
**1 :** a place for lounging: as **a :** a room in a private home or public building for leisure occupations **:** LIVING ROOM; *also* **:** LOBBY **b :** a room in a usually public building or vehicle often combining lounging, smoking, and toilet facilities
**2 :** a long couch

**lounge car** *noun* (1947)
**:** CLUB CAR

**lounge lizard** *noun* (1918)
**1 :** LADIES' MAN
**2 :** FOP
**3 :** a social parasite

**loung·er** \'laủn-jər\ *noun* (1508)
**1 :** one that lounges; *especially* **:** IDLER

**2 :** an article of clothing or furniture designed for comfort and leisure use

**lounge suit** *noun* (1901)
*chiefly British* **:** BUSINESS SUIT

**lounge·wear** \'laủnj-,war, -,wer\ *noun* (circa 1957)
**:** informal clothing usually designed to be worn at home

**loup** \'laủp, 'lōp\ *verb* [Middle English, from Old Norse *hlaupa*; akin to Old English *hlēapan* to leap — more at LEAP] (14th century)
*chiefly Scottish* **:** LEAP
— **loup** *noun*

**loupe** \'lüp\ *noun* [French] (circa 1775)
**:** a small magnifier used especially by jewelers and watchmakers

**loup–ga·rou** \,lü-gə-'rü\ *noun, plural* **loups–garous** \,lü-gə-'rü(z)\ [Middle French, from Old French *leu garoul*, from *leu* (from Latin *lupus*) wolf + *garoul* werewolf, of Germanic origin; akin to Old High German *werwolf* werewolf] (circa 1580)
**:** WEREWOLF

**lour** \'laủ(-ə)r\, **loury** \'laủ(ə)r-ē\ *variant of* LOWER, LOWERY

**¹louse** \'laủs\ *noun* [Middle English *lous*, from Old English *lūs*; akin to Old High German *lūs* louse, Welsh *llau* lice] (before 12th century)
**1** *plural* **lice** \'līs\ **a :** any of various small wingless usually flattened insects (orders Anoplura and Mallophaga) parasitic on warm-blooded animals **b :** a small usually sluggish arthropod that lives on other animals or on plants and sucks their blood or juices — usually used in combination ⟨plant *louse*⟩ **c :** any of several small arthropods that are not parasitic — usually used in combination ⟨book *louse*⟩ ⟨wood *louse*⟩
**2** *plural* **lous·es** \'laủ-səz\ **:** a contemptible person **:** HEEL

**²louse** \'laủs, 'laủz\ *transitive verb* **loused; lous·ing** (14th century)
**:** to pick lice from **:** DELOUSE

**louse up** (1934)
*transitive verb*
**:** FOUL UP, SNARL
*intransitive verb*
**:** to make a mess

**louse·wort** \'laủs-,wərt, -,wòrt\ *noun* (1597)
**:** any of a genus (*Pedicularis*) of herbs of the snapdragon family typically having pinnatifid leaves and bilabiate flowers in terminal spikes

**lousy** \'laủ-zē\ *adjective* **lous·i·er; -est** (14th century)
**1 :** infested with lice
**2 a :** totally repulsive **:** CONTEMPTIBLE **b :** miserably poor or inferior ⟨got *lousy* grades⟩ ⟨felt *lousy* after dinner⟩ **c :** amply supplied **:** REPLETE ⟨*lousy* with money⟩
**3** *of silk* **:** fuzzy and specked because of splitting of the fiber
— **lous·i·ly** \-zə-lē\ *adverb*
— **lous·i·ness** \-zē-nəs\ *noun*

**¹lout** \'laủt\ *intransitive verb* [Middle English, from Old English *lūtan*; akin to Old Norse *lūta* to bow down] (before 12th century)
**1 :** to bow in respect
**2 :** SUBMIT, YIELD

**²lout** *noun* [perhaps from Old Norse *lūtr* bent down, from *lūta*] (1542)
**:** an awkward brutish person

**³lout** *transitive verb* (circa 1530)
**:** to treat as a lout **:** SCORN

**lout·ish** \'laủ-tish\ *adjective* (1542)
**:** resembling or befitting a lout
*synonym* see BOORISH
— **lout·ish·ly** *adverb*
— **lout·ish·ness** *noun*

**lou·ver** *or* **lou·vre** \'lü-vər\ *noun* [Middle English *lover*, from Middle French *lovier*] (14th century)
**1 :** a roof lantern or turret often with slatted apertures for escape of smoke or admission of light in a medieval building
**2 a :** an opening provided with one or more slanted fixed or movable fins to allow flow of

air but to exclude rain or sun or to provide privacy **b :** a finned or vaned device for controlling a flow of air or the radiation of light **c :** a fin or shutter of a louver
— **lou·vered** *also* **lou·vred** \-vərd\ *adjective*

**lov·able** *also* **love·able** \'lə-və-bəl\ *adjective* (14th century)
**:** having qualities that attract affection
— **lov·abil·i·ty** \,lə-və-'bi-lə-tē\ *noun*
— **lov·able·ness** *noun*
— **lov·ably** \-blē\ *adverb*

**lov·age** \'lə-vij\ *noun* [Middle English *lovache*, from Anglo-French, from Late Latin *levisticum*, alteration of Latin *ligusticum*, from neuter of *ligusticus* Ligurian, from *Ligur-, Ligus*, noun, Ligurian] (14th century)
**:** any of several aromatic perennial herbs of the carrot family; *especially* **:** a European herb (*Levisticum officinale*) sometimes cultivated as a domestic remedy, flavoring agent, or potherb

**lov·a·stat·in** \'lō-və-,sta-tən, 'lə-, ,lō-və-', ,lə-\ *noun* [*lov-* (perhaps from *mevinolin*, an earlier name) + connective *-a-* + *stat* + ¹*-in*] (1987)
**:** a drug $C_{24}H_{36}O_8$ used to lower cholesterol levels in the blood

**lov·at** \'lə-vət\ *noun* [probably from T. A. Fraser, Lord *Lovat* (died 1875) Scottish nobleman who popularized muted tweeds] (1907)
**:** a predominantly dusty color mixture (as of green) in fabrics

**¹love** \'ləv\ *noun* [Middle English, from Old English *lufu*; akin to Old High German *luba* love, Old English *lēof* dear, Latin *lubēre, libēre* to please] (before 12th century)
**1 a** (1) **:** strong affection for another arising out of kinship or personal ties ⟨maternal *love* for a child⟩ (2) **:** attraction based on sexual desire **:** affection and tenderness felt by lovers (3) **:** affection based on admiration, benevolence, or common interests ⟨*love* for his old schoolmates⟩ **b :** an assurance of love ⟨give her my *love*⟩
**2 :** warm attachment, enthusiasm, or devotion ⟨*love* of the sea⟩
**3 a :** the object of attachment, devotion, or admiration ⟨baseball was his first *love*⟩ **b** (1) **:** a beloved person **:** DARLING — often used as a term of endearment (2) *British* — used as an informal term of address
**4 a :** unselfish loyal and benevolent concern for the good of another: as (1) **:** the fatherly concern of God for humankind (2) **:** brotherly concern for others **b :** a person's adoration of God
**5 :** a god or personification of love
**6 :** an amorous episode **:** LOVE AFFAIR
**7 :** the sexual embrace **:** COPULATION
**8 :** a score of zero (as in tennis)
**9** *capitalized, Christian Science* **:** GOD
— **at love :** holding one's opponent scoreless in tennis
— **in love :** inspired by affection

**²love** *verb* **loved; lov·ing** (before 12th century)
*transitive verb*
**1 :** to hold dear **:** CHERISH

**2 a :** to feel a lover's passion, devotion, or tenderness for **b** (1) **:** CARESS (2) **:** to fondle amorously (3) **:** to copulate with
**3 :** to like or desire actively **:** take pleasure in ⟨*loved* to play the violin⟩
**4 :** to thrive in ⟨the rose *loves* sunlight⟩
*intransitive verb*
**:** to feel affection or experience desire
**love affair** *noun* (1591)
**1 :** a romantic attachment or episode between lovers
**2 :** a lively enthusiasm ⟨America's *love affair* with baseball⟩
**love apple** *noun* [probably translation of French *pomme d'amour*] (1578)
**:** TOMATO
**love beads** *noun plural* (1968)
**:** beads worn as a symbol of love and peace
**love·bird** \'ləv-ˌbərd\ *noun* (1595)
**:** any of various small usually gray or green parrots (especially genus *Agapornis* of Africa) that show great affection for their mates
**love·bug** \-ˌbəg\ *noun* [from the fact that it is usually seen copulating] (circa 1966)
**:** a small black fly (*Plecia nearctica*) with a red thorax that swarms along highways in the Gulf states of the U.S.
**love child** *noun* (1805)
**:** an illegitimate child
**love feast** *noun* (1580)
**1 :** a meal eaten in common by a Christian congregation in token of brotherly love
**2 :** a gathering held to promote reconciliation and good feeling or show someone affectionate honor
**love grass** *noun* (1702)
**:** any of a genus (*Eragrostis*) of grasses that resemble the bluegrasses but have flattened spikelets and deciduous lemmas
**love handles** *noun plural* (1975)
**:** fatty bulges along the sides at the waist
**love–in** \'ləv-ˌin\ *noun* (1967)
**:** a gathering of people especially for the expression of their mutual love
**love–in–a–mist** \'ləv-ə-nə-ˌmist\ *noun* (circa 1760)
**:** a European and African annual herb (*Nigella damascena*) of the buttercup family having whitish flowers enveloped in numerous finely dissected bracts
**love knot** *noun* (14th century)
**:** a stylized knot sometimes used as an emblem of love
**love·less** \'ləv-ləs\ *adjective* (14th century)
**1 :** having no love
**2 :** not loved
— **love·less·ly** *adverb*
— **love·less·ness** *noun*
**love·lock** \-ˌläk\ *noun* (1592)
**:** a long lock of hair variously worn (as over the front of the shoulder) especially by men in the 17th and 18th centuries
**love·lorn** \-ˌlȯrn\ *adjective* (1634)
**:** bereft of love or of a lover
— **love·lorn·ness** \-ˌlȯrn-nəs\ *noun*
**¹love·ly** \'ləv-lē\ *adjective* **love·li·er; -est** (before 12th century)
**1** *obsolete* **:** LOVABLE
**2 :** delightful for beauty, harmony, or grace **:** ATTRACTIVE
**3 :** GRAND, SWELL
**4 :** eliciting love by moral or ideal worth
*synonym* see BEAUTIFUL
— **love·li·ly** \'ləv-lə-lē\ *adverb*
— **love·li·ness** \'ləv-lē-nəs\ *noun*
— **lovely** *adverb*
**²lovely** *noun, plural* **lovelies** (1652)
**1 :** a beautiful woman
**2 :** a lovely object
**love·mak·ing** \'ləv-ˌmā-kiŋ\ *noun* (15th century)
**1 :** COURTSHIP
**2 :** sexual activity; *especially* **:** COPULATION
**lov·er** \'lə-vər\ *noun* (13th century)
**1 a :** a person in love; *especially* **:** a man in

love with a woman **b** *plural* **:** two persons in love with each other
**2 :** an affectionate or benevolent friend
**3 :** DEVOTEE
**4 a :** PARAMOUR **b :** a person with whom one has sexual relations
**lov·er·ly** \-lē\ *adjective* (1875)
**:** resembling or befitting a lover
**love seat** *noun* (1904)
**:** a double chair, sofa, or settee for two persons
**love·sick** \'ləv-ˌsik\ *adjective* (15th century)
**1 :** languishing with love **:** YEARNING
**2 :** expressing a lover's longing
— **love·sick·ness** *noun*
**love·some** \-səm\ *adjective* (before 12th century)
**1 :** WINSOME, LOVELY
**2 :** AFFECTIONATE, AMOROUS
**lovey–dovey** \ˌlə-vē-'də-vē\ *adjective* (1886)
**:** expressing much love or sentimentality; *also* **:** MUSHY
— **lovey–dovey·ness** \-nəs\ *noun*
**lov·ing** \'lə-viŋ\ *adjective* (before 12th century)
**1 :** AFFECTIONATE
**2 :** PAINSTAKING
— **lov·ing·ly** \-viŋ-lē\ *adverb*
— **lov·ing·ness** *noun*
**loving cup** *noun* [from its former use in ceremonial drinking] (1812)
**1 :** a large ornamental drinking vessel with two or more handles
**2 :** a loving cup given as a token or trophy
**lov·ing–kind·ness** \ˌlə-viŋ-'kīn(d)-nəs\ *noun* (1535)
**:** tender and benevolent affection
**¹low** \'lō\ *intransitive verb* [Middle English *loowen*, from Old English *hlōwan*; akin to Old High German *hluoen* to moo, Latin *calare* to call, summon, Greek *kalein*] (before 12th century)
**:** MOO
**²low** *noun* (1549)
**:** the deep sustained sound characteristic especially of a cow
**³low** *adjective* **low·er** \'lō(-ə)r\; **low·est** \'lō-əst\ [Middle English *lah, low,* from Old Norse *lāgr*; akin to Middle High German *læge* low, flat; probably akin to Old English *licgan* to lie] (12th century)
**1 a :** having a small upward extension or elevation ⟨a *low* wall⟩ **b :** situated or passing little above a reference line, point, or plane ⟨*low* bridges⟩ **c** (1) **:** having a low-cut neckline (2) **:** not extending as high as the ankle ⟨*low* oxfords⟩
**2 a :** situated or passing below the normal level, surface, or base of measurement, or the mean elevation ⟨*low* ground⟩ **b :** marking a nadir or bottom ⟨the *low* point of his career⟩
**3 :** DEAD — used as a predicate adjective
**4 a :** not loud **:** SOFT **b :** FLAT 8a **c :** characterized by being toward the bottom of the range of pitch attainable (as by an instrument)
**5 a :** being near the equator ⟨*low* northern latitudes⟩ **b :** being near the horizon
**6 :** socially or economically humble in character or status ⟨*low* birth⟩
**7 a :** lacking strength, health, or vitality **:** WEAK, PROSTRATE ⟨very *low* with pneumonia⟩ **b :** lacking spirit or vivacity **:** DEPRESSED ⟨a *low* frame of mind⟩
**8 a :** of lesser degree, size, or amount than average or ordinary ⟨*low* energy⟩ **b** (1) **:** small in number or amount (2) **:** SUBSTANDARD, INADEQUATE ⟨a *low* level of employment⟩ ⟨a *low* income group⟩ (3) **:** CHEAP ⟨*low* prices⟩ (4) **:** SHORT, DEPLETED ⟨oil is in *low* supply⟩ **c :** of lesser position, rank, or order
**9 :** falling short of some standard: as **a :** lacking dignity or elevation ⟨a *low* style of writing⟩ **b :** morally reprehensible **:** BASE ⟨a *low* trick⟩ **c :** COARSE, VULGAR ⟨*low* language⟩
**10 a :** not advanced in complexity, development, or elaboration ⟨*low* organisms⟩ **b** *often capitalized* **:** LOW CHURCH

**11 :** UNFAVORABLE, DISPARAGING ⟨had a *low* opinion of him⟩
**12 :** designed for slow and usually the slowest speed ⟨*low* gear⟩
**13 :** articulated with a wide opening between the relatively flat tongue and the palate **:** OPEN ⟨\ä\ is a *low* vowel⟩
**14 :** intended to attract little attention ⟨kept a *low* profile⟩
*synonym* see BASE
— **low** *adverb*
— **low·ness** *noun*
**⁴low** *noun* (12th century)
**1 :** something that is low: as **a :** DEPTH **b :** a region of low barometric pressure
**2 :** the transmission gear of an automotive vehicle giving the lowest ratio of driveshaft to crankshaft speed
**⁵low** *or* **lowe** \'lō\ *noun* [Middle English, from Old Norse *logi, log;* akin to Old English *lēoht* light — more at LIGHT] (13th century)
*chiefly Scottish* **:** FLAME, BLAZE
**⁶low** *or* **lowe** *verb* **lowed; low·ing** (14th century)
*Scottish* **:** FLAME, BLAZE
**low·ball** \'lō-ˌbȯl\ *transitive verb* (circa 1961)
**:** to give (a customer) a deceptively low price or cost estimate
— **lowball** *noun*
**low beam** *noun* (circa 1952)
**:** the short-range focus of a vehicle headlight
**low blood pressure** *noun* (1924)
**:** HYPOTENSION
**low blow** *noun* (1952)
**:** an unprincipled attack ⟨gossip column that landed one *low blow* after another —James Fallows⟩
**low·born** \'lō-'bȯrn\ *adjective* (13th century)
**:** born in a low condition or rank
**low·boy** \-ˌbȯi\ *noun* (circa 1891)
**:** a chest or side table about three feet (one meter) high with drawers and usually with cabriole legs
**low·bred** \-'bred\ *adjective* (1757)
**:** RUDE, VULGAR
**low·brow** \-ˌbrau̇\ *noun* (1906)
**:** a person with little taste or intellectual interest
— **lowbrow** *adjective*

lowboy

**Low Church** *adjective* (1710)
**:** tending especially in Anglican worship to minimize emphasis on the priesthood, sacraments, and ceremonial in worship and often to emphasize evangelical principles
**Low Churchman** *noun* (1702)
**:** a person holding or advocating Low Church views
**low comedy** *noun* (1608)
**:** comedy employing burlesque, horseplay, or the representation of low life — compare HIGH COMEDY
**low country** *noun, often L&C capitalized* (15th century)
**:** a low-lying country or region; *especially* **:** the part of a southern state extending from the seacoast inland to the fall line
— **low–country** *adjective, often L&C capitalized*
**low–density lipoprotein** *noun* (1951)
**:** LDL
**low·down** \'lō-ˌdau̇n\ *noun* (1915)
**:** the inside facts **:** DOPE
**low–down** \'lō-(ˌ)dau̇n\ *adjective* (1850)
**1 :** CONTEMPTIBLE, BASE
**2 :** deeply emotional ⟨*low-down* blues⟩

\ə\ abut \ᵊ\ kitten \ər\ further \a\ ash \ā\ ace \ä\ mop, mar \au̇\ out \ch\ chin \e\ bet \ē\ easy \g\ go \i\ hit \ī\ ice \j\ job \ŋ\ sing \ō\ go \ȯ\ law \ȯi\ boy \th\ thin \t̲h̲\ the \ü\ loot \u̇\ foot \y\ yet \zh\ vision    *see also* Guide to Pronunciation

**low earth orbit** *noun* (1963)
: a usually circular orbit from about 90 to 600 miles (144 to 960 kilometers) above the earth

**low–end** \'lō-,end\ *adjective* (1926)
: of, relating to, or being the lowest priced merchandise in a manufacturer's line

¹**low·er** \'laŭ(-ə)r, 'lō(-ə)r\ *intransitive verb* [Middle English *louren*; akin to Middle High German *lūren* to lie in wait] (13th century)
**1** : to look sullen : FROWN
**2** : to be or become dark, gloomy, and threatening

²**lower** *noun* (14th century)
: FROWN

³**low·er** \'lō(-ə)r\ *adjective* [³low] (13th century)
**1** : relatively low in position, rank, or order
**2** : SOUTHERN ⟨*lower* New York State⟩
**3** : less advanced in the scale of evolutionary development
**4 a** : situated or held to be situated beneath the earth's surface **b** *capitalized* : being an earlier epoch or series of the period or series named ⟨*Lower* Cretaceous⟩ ⟨*Lower* Paleolithic⟩
**5** : constituting the popular and often the larger and more representative branch of a bicameral legislative body ⟨*lower* house⟩

⁴**low·er** \'lō(-ə)r\ *intransitive verb*
: to move down : DROP; *also* : DIMINISH
*transitive verb*
**1 a** : to let descend : LET DOWN **b** : to depress as to direction ⟨*lower* your aim⟩ **c** : to reduce the height of
**2 a** : to reduce in value, number, or amount **b** (1) : to bring down in quality or character : DEGRADE (2) : ABASE, HUMBLE **c** : to reduce the objective of

¹**low·er·case** \,lō(-ə)r-'kās\ *adjective* [from the compositor's practice of keeping such types in the lower of a pair of type cases] (1683)
*of a letter* : having as its typical form a f g or b n i rather than A F G or B N I
— **lowercase** *noun*

²**lowercase** *transitive verb* **-cased; -casing** (1908)
: to print or set in lowercase letters

**low·er–class** \,lō(-ə)r-'klas\ *adjective* (1892)
**1** : of, relating to, or characteristic of the lower class
**2** : being an inferior or low-ranking specimen of its kind

**lower class** *noun* (1772)
: a social class occupying a position below the middle class and having the lowest status in a society

**lower criticism** *noun* (circa 1889)
: criticism concerned with the recovery of original texts especially of Scripture through collation of extant manuscripts — compare HIGHER CRITICISM

**lower fungus** *noun* (1900)
: a fungus with hyphae absent or rudimentary and nonseptate

**low·er·ing** \'laŭ(-ə-)riŋ, 'lō-\ *adjective* (15th century)
: dark and threatening : GLOOMY

**low·er·most** \'lō(-ə)r-,mōst\ *adjective* (1547)
: LOWEST

**low·ery** \'laŭ(-ə-)rē, 'lō-\ *adjective* (15th century)
: GLOOMY, LOWERING

**lowest common denominator** *noun* (1924)
**1** : LEAST COMMON DENOMINATOR
**2** : something of small intellectual content designed to appeal to a lowbrow audience; *also* : such an audience

**lowest common multiple** *noun* (circa 1924)
: LEAST COMMON MULTIPLE

**lowest terms** *noun plural* (1806)
: the form of a fraction in which the numerator and denominator have no factor in common except 1 ⟨reduce a fraction to *lowest terms*⟩

**low frequency** *noun* (circa 1868)

: a radio frequency between medium frequency and very low frequency — see RADIO FREQUENCY table

**Low German** *noun* (1838)
**1** : the German dialects of northern Germany especially as used since the end of the medieval period : PLATTDEUTSCH
**2** : the West Germanic languages other than High German

**low–grade** \'lō-'grād\ *adjective* (1878)
**1** : of inferior grade or quality
**2** : being near that extreme of a specified range which is lowest, least intense, or least competent ⟨a *low-grade* fever⟩ ⟨a *low-grade* infection⟩

**low–key** \-'kē\ *also* **low–keyed** \-'kēd\ *adjective* (1907)
**1** : having or producing dark tones only with little contrast
**2** : of low intensity

¹**low·land** \'lō-lənd, -,land\ *noun* (15th century)
: low or level country

²**lowland** *adjective* (1508)
**1** *capitalized* : of or relating to the Lowlands of Scotland
**2** : of or relating to a lowland

**low·land·er** \-lən-dər, -,lan-\ *noun* (1692)
**1** *capitalized* : an inhabitant of the Lowlands of Scotland
**2** : a native or inhabitant of a lowland region

**Low Latin** *noun* (1872)
: postclassical Latin in its later stages

**low–lev·el** \'lō-'le-vəl\ *adjective* (1881)
**1** : occurring, done, or placed at a low level
**2** : being of low importance or rank

**low·life** \'lō-,līf\ *noun, plural* **low·lifes** \-,līfs\ *also* **low·lives** \-,līvz\ (1911)
**1** : a person of low social status
**2** : a person of low moral character
— **low–life** *adjective*

**low·light** \'lō-,līt\ *noun* (1941)
: a particularly bad or unpleasant event, detail, or part

**low·li·head** \'lō-lē-,hed\ *noun* [Middle English *lowliheed*, from *lowly* + *-hed* -hood; akin to Middle English *-hod* -hood] (15th century)
*archaic* : lowly state

¹**low·ly** \'lō-lē\ *adverb* (14th century)
**1** : in a humble or meek manner
**2** : in a low position, manner, or degree
**3** : not loudly

²**lowly** *adjective* **low·li·er; -est** (14th century)
**1** : humble in manner or spirit : free from self-assertive pride
**2** : not lofty or sublime : PROSAIC
**3** : ranking low in some hierarchy
**4** : of or relating to a low social or economic rank
**5** : low in the scale of biological or cultural evolution
— **low·li·ness** *noun*

**low–ly·ing** \'lō-'lī-iŋ\ *adjective* (1856)
**1** : rising relatively little above the base of measurement ⟨*low-lying* hills⟩
**2** : lying below the normal level, surface, or the base of measurement or mean elevation ⟨*low-lying* clouds⟩

**low mass** *noun, often L&M capitalized* (1568)
: a mass that is recited without singing by the celebrant, without a deacon, subdeacon, or choir assisting the celebrant, and without the use of incense

**low–mind·ed** \'lō-'mīn-dəd\ *adjective* (circa 1746)
: inclined to low or unworthy things
— **low–mind·ed·ly** *adverb*
— **low–mind·ed·ness** *noun*

**lown** \'laŭn, 'lün\ *adjective* [Middle English (Scots) *lowne*] (15th century)
*dialect* : CALM, QUIET

**low–pres·sure** \'lō-'pre-shər\ *adjective* (1827)
**1** : having, exerting, or operating under a relatively small pressure

**2** : EASYGOING

**low relief** *noun* (1711)
: BAS-RELIEF

**low–rent** \'lō-'rent\ *adjective* (1957)
: low in character, cost, or prestige ⟨*low-rent* thugs⟩ ⟨a *low-rent* movie⟩ ⟨a *low-rent* literary form⟩

**low–rise** \'lō-'rīz\ *adjective* (1957)
**1** : having few stories and not equipped with elevators ⟨a *low-rise* classroom building⟩
**2** : of, relating to, or characterized by low-rise buildings ⟨a *low-rise* housing development⟩

**low–slung** \'lō-,sləŋ\ *adjective* (1943)
: relatively low to the ground or floor ⟨a *low-slung* convertible⟩ ⟨a *low-slung* modern building⟩ ⟨a *low-slung* sofa⟩

**low–spir·it·ed** \'lō-'spir-ə-təd\ *adjective* (1693)
: DEJECTED, DEPRESSED
— **low–spir·it·ed·ly** *adverb*
— **low–spir·it·ed·ness** *noun*

**Low Sunday** *noun* (15th century)
: the Sunday following Easter

**low–tech** \'lō-'tek\ *adjective* (1981)
: technologically simple or unsophisticated ⟨*low-tech* industries⟩

**low tide** *noun* (1843)
: the farthest ebb of the tide

**low water** *noun* (15th century)
: a low stage of the water in a river or lake; *also* : LOW TIDE

¹**lox** \'läks\ *noun* [liquid oxygen] (1923)
: liquid oxygen

²**lox** *noun, plural* **lox** *or* **lox·es** [Yiddish *laks*, from Middle High German *lahs* salmon, from Old High German; akin to Old English *leax* salmon] (1941)
: smoked salmon

**lox·o·drome** \'läk-sə-,drōm\ *noun* [back-formation from *loxodromic* of a rhumb line, from French *loxodromique*, from Greek *loxos* oblique + *dromos* course — more at DROMEDARY] (1880)
: RHUMB LINE

**loy·al** \'lói(-ə)l\ *adjective* [Middle French, from Old French *leial, leel*, from Latin *legalis* legal] (1531)
**1** : unswerving in allegiance: as **a** : faithful in allegiance to one's lawful sovereign or government **b** : faithful to a private person to whom fidelity is due **c** : faithful to a cause, ideal, custom, institution, or product
**2** : showing loyalty
**3** *obsolete* : LAWFUL, LEGITIMATE
*synonym* see FAITHFUL
— **loy·al·ly** \'lói-ə-lē\ *adverb*

**loy·al·ist** \'lói-ə-list\ *noun* (1647)
: one who is or remains loyal especially to a political cause, party, government, or sovereign

**loy·al·ty** \'lói(-ə)l-tē\ *noun, plural* **-ties** [Middle English *loyaltee*, from Middle French *loialté*, from Old French *leialté*, from *leial*] (15th century)
: the quality or state or an instance of being loyal
*synonym* see FIDELITY

**loz·enge** \'lä-z°nj *also* -s°nj\ *noun* [Middle English *losenge*, from Middle French *losange*] (14th century)
**1** : a figure with four equal sides and two acute and two obtuse angles : DIAMOND
**2** : something shaped like a lozenge
**3** : a small often medicated candy

**LP** \,el-'pē\ *noun* [long-playing] (1948)
: a microgroove phonograph record designed to be played at 33⅓ revolutions per minute

**LPN** \,el-(,)pē-'en\ *noun* (1948)
: LICENSED PRACTICAL NURSE

**LSD** \,el-(,)es-'dē\ *noun* [German *Lysergsäure-Diäthylamid* lysergic acid diethylamide] (1950)
: an organic compound $C_{20}H_{25}N_3O$ that induces psychotic symptoms similar to those of schizophrenia — called also *lysergic acid diethylamide*

**lu·au** \'lü-ˌau̇\ *noun* [Hawaiian *lūʹau*] (1853)
: an Hawaiian feast
**Lu·ba·vitch·er** \'lü-bə-ˌvi-chər, lü-'bä-\ *noun* [Yiddish *lyubavitsher,* from *Lyubavitsh,* town in Belarus] (1954)
: a member of a Hasidic sect founded by Schneour Zalman of Lyady in the late 18th century
— **Lubavitcher** *adjective*
**lub·ber** \'lə-bər\ *noun* [Middle English *lobre, lobur*] (14th century)
**1** : a big clumsy fellow
**2** : a clumsy seaman
— **lub·ber·li·ness** \-lē-nəs\ *noun*
— **lub·ber·ly** \-lē\ *adjective or adverb*
**lubber line** *noun* (1889)
: a fixed line on the compass of a ship or airplane that is aligned with the longitudinal axis of the vehicle
**lubber's hole** *noun* (circa 1784)
: a hole in a square-rigger's top near the mast through which one may go farther aloft without going over the rim by the futtock shrouds
**lube** \'lüb\ *noun* [short for *lubricating oil*] (1926)
**1** : LUBRICANT
**2** : an application of a lubricant : LUBRICATION
**lu·bric** \'lü-brik\ *adjective* [Middle French *lubrique,* from Medieval Latin *lubricus*] (15th century)
*archaic* : LUBRICIOUS
— **lu·bri·cal** \-bri-kəl\ *adjective*
**lu·bri·cant** \'lü-bri-kənt\ *noun* (circa 1828)
**1** : a substance (as grease) capable of reducing friction, heat, and wear when introduced as a film between solid surfaces
**2** : something that lessens or prevents friction or difficulty
— **lubricant** *adjective*
**lu·bri·cate** \'lü-brə-ˌkāt\ *verb* **-cat·ed; -cat·ing** [Latin *lubricatus,* past participle of *lubricare,* from *lubricus* slippery — more at SLEEVE] (circa 1623)
*transitive verb*
**1** : to make smooth or slippery
**2** : to apply a lubricant to
*intransitive verb*
: to act as a lubricant
— **lu·bri·ca·tion** \ˌlü-brə-'kā-shən\ *noun*
— **lu·bri·ca·tive** \'lü-brə-ˌkā-tiv\ *adjective*
— **lu·bri·ca·tor** \-ˌkā-tər\ *noun*
**lu·bri·cious** \lü-'bri-shəs\ *or* **lu·bri·cous** \'lü-bri-kəs\ *adjective* [Medieval Latin *lubricus,* from Latin, slippery, easily led astray] (1535)
**1** : marked by wantonness : LECHEROUS; *also* : SALACIOUS
**2** [Latin *lubricus*] : having a smooth or slippery quality ⟨a *lubricious* skin⟩
— **lu·bri·cious·ly** *adverb*
**lu·bric·i·ty** \lü-'bri-sə-tē\ *noun, plural* **-ties** (15th century)
: the property or state of being lubricious; *also* : the capacity for reducing friction
**Lu·can** \'lü-kən\ *adjective* [Late Latin *lucanus,* from *Lucas* Luke, from Greek *Loukas*] (1890)
: of or relating to Luke or the Gospel ascribed to him
**lu·carne** \lü-'kärn\ *noun* [French] (circa 1825)
: DORMER
**Lu·ca·yo** \lü-'kī-(ˌ)ō\ *also* **Lu·ca·yan** \-'kī-ən\ *noun* (1929)
: a member of an Arawakan people of the Bahamas
**lu·cen·cy** \'lü-s°n(t)-sē\ *noun* (1656)
: the quality or state of being lucent
**lu·cent** \'lü-s°nt\ *adjective* [Middle English, from Latin *lucent-, lucens,* present participle of *lucēre* to shine — more at LIGHT] (15th century)
**1** : glowing with light : LUMINOUS
**2** : marked by clarity or translucence : CLEAR
— **lu·cent·ly** *adverb*
**lu·cern** *noun* [probably modification of German *lüchsern* of a lynx, from *Luchs* lynx] (circa 1533)
*obsolete* : LYNX
**lu·cerne** *also* **lu·cern** \lü-'sərn\ *noun* [French *luzerne,* from Provençal *luserno*] (1626)
*chiefly British* : ALFALFA
**lu·cid** \'lü-səd\ *adjective* [Latin *lucidus,* from *lucēre*] (1591)
**1 a** : suffused with light : LUMINOUS **b** : TRANSLUCENT
**2** : having full use of one's faculties : SANE
**3** : clear to the understanding : INTELLIGIBLE
**synonym** see CLEAR
— **lu·cid·ly** *adverb*
— **lu·cid·ness** *noun*
**lu·cid·i·ty** \lü-'si-də-tē\ *noun* (1851)
**1** : clearness of thought or style
**2** : a presumed capacity to perceive the truth directly and instantaneously : CLAIRVOYANCE
**Lu·ci·fer** \'lü-sə-fər\ *noun* [Middle English, the morning star, a fallen rebel archangel, the Devil, from Old English, from Latin, the morning star, from *lucifer* light-bearing, from *luc-, lux* light + *-fer* -ferous — more at LIGHT] (before 12th century)
**1** — used as a name of the devil
**2** : the planet Venus when appearing as the morning star
**3** *not capitalized* : a friction match having as active substances antimony sulfide and potassium chlorate
— **Lu·ci·fe·ri·an** \ˌlü-sə-'fir-ē-ən\ *adjective*
**lu·cif·er·ase** \lü-'si-fə-ˌrās, -ˌrāz\ *noun* [International Scientific Vocabulary, from *luciferin*] (1888)
: an enzyme that catalyzes the oxidation of luciferin
**lu·cif·er·in** \-f(ə-)rən\ *noun* [International Scientific Vocabulary, from Latin *lucifer* light-bearing] (1888)
: any of various organic substances in luminescent organisms (as fireflies) that upon oxidation produce a virtually heatless light
**lu·cif·er·ous** \lü-'si-f(ə-)rəs\ *adjective* [Latin *lucifer*] (1648)
: bringing light or insight : ILLUMINATING
**Lu·ci·na** \lü-'sī-nə\ *noun* [Latin, Roman goddess of childbirth] (1658)
*archaic* : MIDWIFE
**Lu·cite** \'lü-ˌsīt\ *trademark*
— used for an acrylic resin or plastic consisting essentially of polymerized methyl methacrylate
**¹luck** \'lək\ *noun* [Middle English *lucke,* from Middle Dutch *luc;* akin to Middle High German *gelücke* luck] (15th century)
**1 a** : a force that brings good fortune or adversity **b** : the events or circumstances that operate for or against an individual
**2** : favoring chance; *also* : SUCCESS
— **luck·less** \-ləs\ *adjective*
**²luck** *intransitive verb* (circa 1584)
**1** : to prosper or succeed especially through chance or good fortune — usually used with *out*
**2** : to come upon something desirable by chance — usually used with *out, on, onto,* or *into*
**luck·i·ly** \'lə-kə-lē\ *adverb* (1530)
**1** : in a lucky manner
**2** : FORTUNATELY 2 ⟨*luckily,* we were on time⟩
*usage* see HOPEFULLY
**lucky** \'lə-kē\ *adjective* **luck·i·er; -est** (15th century)
**1** : having good luck
**2** : happening by chance : FORTUITOUS
**3** : producing or resulting in good by chance : FAVORABLE
**4** : seeming to bring good luck ⟨a *lucky* rabbit's foot⟩ ☆
— **luck·i·ness** \'lə-kē-nəs\ *noun*
**lucky dip** *noun* (1925)
*British* : GRAB BAG
**lu·cra·tive** \'lü-krə-tiv\ *adjective* [Middle English *lucratif,* from Middle French, from Latin *lucrativus,* from *lucratus,* past participle of *lucrari* to gain, from *lucrum*] (15th century)
: producing wealth : PROFITABLE
— **lu·cra·tive·ly** *adverb*
— **lu·cra·tive·ness** *noun*
**lu·cre** \'lü-kər\ *noun* [Middle English, from Latin *lucrum;* probably akin to Old English *lēan* reward, Old High German *lōn,* Greek *apolauein* to enjoy] (14th century)
: monetary gain : PROFIT; *also* : MONEY
**lu·cu·bra·tion** \ˌlü-kyə-'brā-shən, ˌlü-kə-\ *noun* [Latin *lucubration-, lucubratio* study by night, work produced at night, from *lucubrare* to work by lamplight; akin to Latin *luc-, lux*] (1595)
: laborious or intensive study; *also* : the product of such study — usually used in plural
**lu·cu·lent** \'lü-kyə-lənt\ *adjective* [Latin *luculentus,* from *luc-, lux* light] (circa 1548)
: clear in thought or expression : LUCID
— **lu·cu·lent·ly** *adverb*
**Lu·cul·lan** \lü-'kə-lən\ *also* **Lu·cul·li·an** \-'kə-lē-ən\ *adjective* [Latin *lucullanus* of Licinius *Lucullus;* from his reputation for luxurious banquets] (1861)
: LAVISH, LUXURIOUS ⟨a *Lucullan* feast⟩
**Lud·dite** \'lə-ˌdīt\ *noun* [perhaps from Ned *Ludd,* 18th century Leicestershire workman who destroyed machinery] (1811)
: one of a group of early 19th century English workmen destroying laborsaving machinery as a protest; *broadly* : one who is opposed to especially technological change ◆

---

☆ SYNONYMS
**Lucky, fortunate, happy, providential** mean meeting with unforeseen success. LUCKY stresses the agency of chance in bringing about a favorable result ⟨won because of a *lucky* bounce⟩. FORTUNATE suggests being rewarded beyond one's deserts ⟨*fortunate* in my investments⟩. HAPPY combines the implications of LUCKY and FORTUNATE with stress on being blessed ⟨a series of *happy* accidents⟩. PROVIDENTIAL more definitely implies the help or intervention of a higher power ⟨a *providential* change in the weather⟩.

---

◇ WORD HISTORY
**Luddite** Since *Luddite* first appeared in the fall of 1811, it has never gone out of use as a label for those opposed to new technology and its consequences. But introduction of labor-saving machinery was only one of the origins of the rampages in the Midlands and North of England that gave rise to the word. The initial attacks by discontented stocking and lace makers in Nottinghamshire, when the possibly fictitious Ned Ludd's name first appears in anonymous letters as the movement's leader, were directed against stocking-making frames of a type dating back to Elizabethan times. The first Luddites' raids were a labor protest at a time when trade unions were proscribed by law and sabotage of machinery, whether old or new, was an available form of collective action. Moreover, the disturbances took place against a background of crop failures and economic depression caused by Britain's blockade of continental Europe during the Napoleonic Wars. Concerning the origin of the name Ned Ludd, nothing is known for certain. Tradition holds that Ned Ludd (or Ludlam) was a Leicestershire knitter who out of anger at his employer destroyed his knitting frame, and that subsequently his name was proverbially connected with frame-breaking.

---

\ə\ abut \ə°\ kitten \ər\ further \a\ ash \ā\ ace
\ä\ mop, mar \au̇\ out \ch\ chin \e\ bet \ē\ easy
\g\ go \i\ hit \ī\ ice \j\ job \ŋ\ sing \ō\ go
\o̅\ law \o̅i\ boy \th\ thin \t͟h\ the \ü\ loot \u̇\ foot
\y\ yet \zh\ vision *see also* Guide to Pronunciation

— **Luddite** *adjective*

**lu·dic** \'lü-dik\ *adjective* [French *ludique,* from Latin *ludus*] (1940)
: of, relating to, or characterized by play : PLAYFUL ⟨*ludic* behavior⟩ ⟨a *ludic* novel⟩

**lu·di·crous** \'lü-də-krəs\ *adjective* [Latin *ludicrus,* from *ludus* play, sport; perhaps akin to Greek *loidoros* abusive] (1782)
**1** : amusing or laughable through obvious absurdity, incongruity, exaggeration, or eccentricity
**2** : meriting derisive laughter or scorn as absurdly inept, false, or foolish
**synonym** see LAUGHABLE
— **lu·di·crous·ly** *adverb*
— **lu·di·crous·ness** *noun*

**lu·es** \'lü-(,)ēz\ *noun, plural* **lues** [New Latin, from Latin, plague; akin to Greek *lyein* to loosen, destroy — more at LOSE] (1634)
: SYPHILIS
— **lu·et·ic** \lü-'e-tik\ *adjective*

**¹luff** \'ləf\ *noun* [Middle English, weather side of a ship, luff, from Middle French *lof* weather side of ship] (14th century)
**1** : the act of sailing a ship nearer the wind
**2** : the forward edge of a fore-and-aft sail

**²luff** *intransitive verb* (14th century)
: to turn the head of a ship toward the wind

**luf·fa** *variant of* LOOFAH

**luft·mensch** \'lúft-,men(t)sh\ *noun, plural* **luft·mensch·en** \-,men(t)-shən\ [Yiddish *luftmentsh,* from *luft* air + *mentsh* human being] (1907)
: an impractical contemplative person having no definite business or income

**¹lug** \'ləg\ *verb* **lugged; lug·ging** [Middle English *luggen* to pull by the hair or ear, drag, probably of Scandinavian origin; akin to Norwegian *lugga* to pull by the hair] (14th century)
*transitive verb*
**1** : DRAG, PULL
**2** : to carry laboriously
**3** : to introduce in a forced manner ⟨*lugs* my name into the argument⟩
*intransitive verb*
**1** : to pull with effort : TUG
**2** : to move heavily or by jerks ⟨the car *lugs* on hills⟩
**3** *of a racehorse* : to swerve from the course toward or away from the inside rail

**²lug** *noun* (1616)
**1** *archaic* **a** : an act of lugging **b** : something that is lugged **c** : a shipping container for produce
**2** : LUGSAIL
**3** *plural* : superior airs or affectations ⟨put on *lugs*⟩
**4** *slang* : an exaction of money — used in the phrase *put the lug on*

**³lug** *noun* [Middle English (Scots) *lugge,* perhaps from Middle English *luggen*] (15th century)
**1** : something (as a handle) that projects like an ear: as **a** : a leather loop on a harness saddle through which the shaft passes **b** : a metal fitting to which electrical wires are soldered or connected
**2** *chiefly British* : EAR
**3** : a ridge (as on the bottom of a shoe) to increase traction
**4** : a nut used to secure a wheel on an automotive vehicle — called also *lug nut*
**5** : BLOCKHEAD, LOUT

**Lu·gan·da** \lü-'gän-də, -'gan-\ *noun* (1889)
: the Bantu language of the Ganda people

**luge** \'lüzh\ *noun* [French] (1905)
: a small sled that is ridden in a supine position and used especially in competition; *also* : the competition itself
— **luge** *intransitive verb*
— **lug·er** \'lü-zhər\ *noun*

**lug·gage** \'lə-gij\ *noun* (1596)
: something that is lugged; *especially* : suitcases for a traveler's belongings : BAGGAGE

**lug·ger** \'lə-gər\ *noun* [*lugsail*] (1757)
: a small fishing or coasting boat that carries one or more lugsails

**lug·sail** \'ləg-,sāl, -səl\ *noun* [perhaps from *³lug*] (1677)
: a 4-sided sail bent to an obliquely hanging yard that is hoisted and lowered with the sail

lugger

**lu·gu·bri·ous** \lú-'gü-brē-əs *also* -'gyü-\ *adjective* [Latin *lugubris,* from *lugēre* to mourn; akin to Greek *lygros* mournful] (1601)
**1** : MOURNFUL; *especially* : exaggeratedly or affectedly mournful ⟨dark, dramatic and *lugubrious* brooding —V. S. Pritchett⟩
**2** : DISMAL ⟨a *lugubrious* landscape⟩
— **lu·gu·bri·ous·ly** *adverb*
— **lu·gu·bri·ous·ness** *noun*

**lug·worm** \'ləg-,wərm\ *noun* [origin unknown] (1802)
: any of a genus (*Arenicola*) of marine polychaete worms that have a row of tufted gills along each side of the back and are used for bait

**Luk·an** \'lü-kən\ *variant of* LUCAN

**Luke** \'lük\ *noun* [Latin *Lucas,* from Greek *Loukas*]
**1** : a Gentile physician and companion of the apostle Paul traditionally identified as the author of the third Gospel in the New Testament and of the book of Acts
**2** : the third Gospel in the New Testament — see BIBLE table

**luke·warm** \'lük-'wórm\ *adjective* [Middle English, from *luke* lukewarm + *warm;* probably akin to Old High German *lāo* lukewarm — more at LEE] (14th century)
**1** : moderately warm : TEPID
**2** : lacking conviction : HALFHEARTED
— **luke·warm·ly** *adverb*
— **luke·warm·ness** *noun*

**¹lull** \'ləl\ *transitive verb* [Middle English; probably of imitative origin] (14th century)
**1** : to cause to sleep or rest : SOOTHE
**2** : to cause to relax vigilance

**²lull** *noun* (1719)
**1** *archaic* : something that lulls; *especially* : LULLABY
**2** : a temporary pause or decline in activity ⟨the early morning *lull* in urban noise⟩: as **a** : a temporary calm before or during a storm **b** : a temporary drop in business activity

**¹lul·la·by** \'lə-lə-,bī\ *noun, plural* **-bies** [obsolete English *lulla,* interjection used to lull a child (from Middle English) + *bye,* interjection used to lull a child, from Middle English *by*] (1588)
: a soothing refrain; *specifically* : a song to quiet children or lull them to sleep

**²lullaby** *transitive verb* **-bied; -by·ing** (1592)
: to quiet with or as if with a lullaby

**lu·lu** \'lü-(,)lü\ *noun* [probably from *Lulu,* nickname from *Louise*] (1886)
*slang* : one that is remarkable or wonderful

**lum** \'ləm\ *noun* [origin unknown] (circa 1628)
*chiefly Scottish* : CHIMNEY

**lum·ba·go** \,ləm-'bā-(,)gō\ *noun* [Latin, from *lumbus*] (circa 1693)
: usually painful muscular rheumatism involving the lumbar region

**lum·bar** \'ləm-bər, -,bär\ *adjective* [New Latin *lumbaris,* from Latin *lumbus* loin — more at LOIN] (circa 1656)
: of, relating to, or constituting the loins or the vertebrae between the thoracic vertebrae and sacrum ⟨*lumbar* region⟩

**¹lum·ber** \'ləm-bər\ *intransitive verb* **lum·bered; lum·ber·ing** \-b(ə-)riŋ\ [Middle English *lomeren*] (14th century)
**1** : to move ponderously
**2** : RUMBLE

**²lumber** *noun* [perhaps from *Lombard;* from the use of pawnshops as storehouses of disused property] (1552)
**1** : surplus or disused articles (as furniture) that are stored away
**2 a** : timber or logs especially when dressed for use **b** : any of various structural materials prepared in a form similar to lumber
— **lumber** *adjective*

**³lumber** *verb* **lum·bered; lum·ber·ing** \-b(ə-)riŋ\ (1642)
*transitive verb*
**1** : to clutter with or as if with lumber : ENCUMBER
**2** : to heap together in disorder
**3** : to log and saw the timber of
*intransitive verb*
**1** : to cut logs for lumber
**2** : to saw logs into lumber for the market
— **lum·ber·er** \-bər-ər\ *noun*

**lum·ber·jack** \'ləm-bər-,jak\ *noun* (1831)
: LOGGER

**lum·ber·man** \-mən\ *noun* (circa 1817)
: a person who is engaged in or oversees the business of cutting, processing, and marketing lumber

**lumber room** *noun* (1741)
: STOREROOM 1

**lum·ber·yard** \-,yärd\ *noun* (1786)
: a yard where a stock of lumber is kept for sale

**lum·bo·sa·cral** \,ləm-bō-'sa-krəl, -'sā-\ *adjective* (1840)
: relating to the lumbar and sacral regions or parts

**lu·men** \'lü-mən\ *noun, plural* **lumens** *also* **lu·mi·na** \-mə-nə\ [New Latin *lumin-, lumen,* from Latin, light, air shaft, opening] (1873)
**1** : the cavity of a tubular organ ⟨the *lumen* of a blood vessel⟩
**2** : the bore of a tube (as of a hollow needle or catheter)
**3** : a unit of luminous flux equal to the light emitted in a unit solid angle by a uniform point source of one candle intensity
— **lu·mi·nal** *also* **lu·men·al** \-mə-nᵊl\ *adjective*

**lumin-** *or* **lumini-** *combining form* [Middle English *lumin-,* from Latin *lumin-, lumen*]
: light ⟨*lumini*ferous⟩

**lu·mi·naire** \,lü-mə-'nar, -'ner\ *noun* [French, lamp, lighting] (1921)
: a complete lighting unit

**lu·mi·nance** \'lü-mə-nən(t)s\ *noun* (1880)
**1** : the quality or state of being luminous
**2** : the luminous intensity of a surface in a given direction per unit of projected area

**lu·mi·nar·ia** \,lü-mə-'ner-ē-ə\ *noun, plural* **-nar·i·as** [Spanish, decorative light, from Late Latin] (1949)
: a traditional Mexican Christmas lantern originally consisting of a candle set in sand inside a paper bag

**lu·mi·nary** \'lü-mə-,ner-ē\ *noun, plural* **-nar·ies** [Middle English *luminarye,* from Middle French & Late Latin; Middle French *luminaire* lamp, from Late Latin *luminaria,* plural of *luminare* lamp, heavenly body, from Latin, window, from *lumin-, lumen* light; akin to Latin *lucēre* to shine — more at LIGHT] (15th century)
**1** : a person of prominence or brilliant achievement
**2** : a body that gives light; *especially* : one of the celestial bodies
— **luminary** *adjective*

**lu·mi·nesce** \,lü-mə-'nes\ *intransitive verb* **-nesced; -nesc·ing** [back-formation from *luminescent*] (1896)
: to exhibit luminescence

**lu·mi·nes·cence** \-'ne-s°n(t)s\ *noun* (1889)
: the low-temperature emission of light (as by a chemical or physiological process); *also*
: light produced by luminescence
— **lu·mi·nes·cent** \-s°nt\ *adjective*
**lu·mi·nif·er·ous** \,lü-mə-'ni-f(ə-)rəs\ *adjective* (1801)
: transmitting, producing, or yielding light
**lu·mi·nism** \'lü-mə-,ni-zəm\ *noun, often capitalized* (circa 1974)
: a theory or practice of realist landscape and seascape painting developed in the U.S. in the mid 19th century and concerned with the study and depiction of effects of light and atmosphere
— **lu·mi·nist** \-nist\ *noun, often capitalized*
**lu·mi·nos·i·ty** \,lü-mə-'nä-sə-tē\ *noun, plural* **-ties** (1634)
**1 a :** the quality or state of being luminous **b :** something luminous
**2 a :** the relative quantity of light **b :** relative brightness of something
**3 :** the relative quantity of radiation emitted by a celestial source (as a star)
**lu·mi·nous** \'lü-mə-nəs\ *adjective* [Middle English, from Latin *luminosus*, from *lumin-, lumen*] (15th century)
**1 a :** emitting or reflecting usually steady, suffused, or glowing light **b :** of or relating to light or to luminous flux
**2 :** bathed in or exposed to steady light ⟨*luminous* with sunlight⟩
**3 :** CLEAR, ENLIGHTENING
**synonym** see BRIGHT
— **lu·mi·nous·ly** *adverb*
— **lu·mi·nous·ness** *noun*
**luminous energy** *noun* (circa 1931)
: energy transferred in the form of visible radiation
**luminous flux** *noun* (1925)
: radiant flux in the visible-wavelength range usually expressed in lumens instead of watts
**luminous paint** *noun* (circa 1889)
: a paint containing a phosphor (as zinc sulfide activated with copper) and so able to glow in the dark
**lum·mox** \'lə-məks, -miks\ *noun* [origin unknown] (circa 1825)
: a clumsy person
**¹lump** \'ləmp\ *noun* [Middle English] (14th century)
**1 :** a piece or mass of indefinite size and shape
**2 a :** AGGREGATE, TOTALITY ⟨taken in the *lump*⟩ **b :** MAJORITY
**3 :** PROTUBERANCE; *especially* **:** an abnormal swelling
**4 :** a person who is heavy and awkward; *also* **:** one who is stupid or dull
**5** *plural* **a :** BEATINGS, BRUISES ⟨had taken a lot of *lumps* growing up in the city⟩ **b :** DEFEAT, LOSS ⟨can cheerfully take his *lumps* on losers, because the payout is big on the winners —Martin Mayer⟩
— **lump in one's throat :** a constriction of the throat caused by emotion
**²lump** (1624)
*transitive verb*
**1 :** to group indiscriminately
**2 :** to make into lumps; *also* **:** to make lumps on or in
**3 :** to move noisily and clumsily
*intransitive verb*
**1 :** to become formed into lumps
**2 :** to move oneself noisily and clumsily
**³lump** *adjective* (circa 1700)
: not divided into parts ⟨*lump* sum⟩
**⁴lump** *transitive verb* [origin unknown] (1791)
: to put up with ⟨like it or *lump* it⟩
**lump·ec·to·my** \,ləm-'pek-tə-mē\ *noun, plural* **-mies** (1972)
: excision of a breast tumor with a limited amount of associated tissue
**¹lum·pen** \'lùm-pən, 'ləm-\ *adjective* [German *Lumpenproletariat* degraded section of the proletariat, from *Lump* contemptible person (from *Lumpen* rags) + *Proletariat*] (1936)
: of or relating to dispossessed and uprooted individuals cut off from the economic and social class with which they might normally be identified ⟨*lumpen* proletariat⟩ ⟨*lumpen* intellectuals⟩
**²lumpen** *noun, plural* **lumpen** *also* **lumpens** (1941)
: a member of the crude and uneducated lowest class of society
**lump·er** \'ləm-pər\ *noun* (circa 1785)
**1 :** a laborer employed to handle freight or cargo
**2 :** one who classifies organisms into large often variable taxonomic groups based on major characters — compare SPLITTER
**lump·fish** \'ləmp-,fish\ *noun* [obsolete English *lump* lumpfish (probably from Dutch *lomp* blenny, loach) + English *fish*] (circa 1620)
: a northern Atlantic usually greenish fish (*Cyclopterus lumpus* of the family Cyclopteridae) having rows of nodules on the body and eggs used as a caviar
**lump·ish** \'ləm-pish\ *adjective* (1528)
**1 :** DULL, SLUGGISH
**2** *obsolete* **:** low in spirits
**3 :** HEAVY, AWKWARD
**4 :** LUMPY 1a
**5 :** tediously slow or dull **:** BORING; *also* **:** LUMPY 3
— **lump·ish·ly** *adverb*
— **lump·ish·ness** *noun*
**lumpy** \'ləm-pē\ *adjective* **lump·i·er; -est** (1707)
**1 a :** filled or covered with lumps **b :** characterized by choppy waves
**2 :** having a heavy clumsy appearance
**3 :** uneven and often crude in style
— **lump·i·ly** \-pə-lē\ *adverb*
— **lump·i·ness** \-pē-nəs\ *noun*
**lumpy jaw** *noun* (1890)
: ACTINOMYCOSIS; *especially* **:** actinomycosis of the head in cattle
**lu·na·cy** \'lü-nə-sē\ *noun, plural* **-cies** [*lunatic*] (1541)
**1 :** any of various forms of insanity: as **a :** intermittent insanity once believed to be related to phases of the moon **b :** insanity amounting to lack of capacity or of responsibility in the eyes of the law
**2 :** wild foolishness **:** extravagant folly
**3 :** a foolish act
**lu·na moth** \'lü-nə-\ *noun* [New Latin *luna* (specific epithet of *Actias luna*), from Latin, moon] (1869)
: a large mostly pale green American saturniid moth (*Actias luna*) with long tails on the hind wings

luna moth

**lu·nar** \'lü-nər *also* -,när\ *adjective* [Middle English, from Latin *lunaris*, from *luna* moon; akin to Latin *lucēre* to shine — more at LIGHT] (15th century)
**1 :** CRESCENT, LUNATE
**2 a :** of or relating to the moon **b :** designed for use on the moon ⟨*lunar* vehicles⟩
**3 :** measured by the moon's revolution ⟨*lunar* month⟩
**lunar caustic** *noun* [obsolete *luna* silver, from Medieval Latin, from Latin, moon] (1771)
: silver nitrate especially when fused and molded into sticks for use as a caustic
**lunar eclipse** *noun* (circa 1737)
: an eclipse in which the moon near the full phase passes partially or wholly through the umbra of the earth's shadow — see ECLIPSE illustration
**lunar module** *noun* (1967)
: a space vehicle module designed to carry astronauts from the command module to the surface of the moon and back — called also *lunar excursion module*; abbreviation LEM

**lu·nate** \'lü-,nāt\ *adjective* [Latin *lunatus*, past participle of *lunare* to bend in a crescent, from *luna*] (circa 1777)
: shaped like a crescent
**lu·na·tic** \'lü-nə-,tik\ *adjective* [Middle English *lunatik*, from Old French or Late Latin; Old French *lunatique*, from Late Latin *lunaticus*, from Latin *luna*; from the belief that lunacy fluctuated with the phases of the moon] (14th century)
**1 a :** affected with lunacy **:** INSANE **b :** designed for the care of insane persons ⟨*lunatic* asylum⟩
**2 :** wildly foolish ◆
— **lunatic** *noun*
**lunatic fringe** *noun* (1913)
: the members of a usually political or social movement espousing extreme, eccentric, or fanatical views
**lu·na·tion** \lü-'nā-shən\ *noun* [Middle English *lunacioun*, from Medieval Latin *lunation-, lunatio*, from Latin *luna*] (14th century)
: the period of time averaging 29 days, 12 hours, 44 minutes, and 2.8 seconds elapsing between two successive new moons
**¹lunch** \'lənch\ *noun* [probably short for *luncheon*] (1812)
**1 :** a usually light meal; *especially* **:** one taken in the middle of the day
**2 :** the food prepared for a lunch
— **out to lunch** *slang* **:** out of touch with reality
**²lunch** (1823)
*intransitive verb*
: to eat lunch
*transitive verb*
: to treat to lunch
— **lunch·er** *noun*
**lunch counter** *noun* (1869)
**1 :** a long counter at which lunches are sold
**2 :** LUNCHEONETTE
**lun·cheon** \'lən-chən\ *noun* [perhaps alteration of *nuncheon* light snack] (circa 1652)
: LUNCH; *especially* **:** a formal usually midday meal as part of a meeting or for entertaining a guest
**lun·cheon·ette** \,lən-chə-'net\ *noun* (1924)
: a small restaurant serving light lunches

---

◇ WORD HISTORY

**lunatic** The word *lunatic* is based ultimately on an old folk-medical belief, that human behavior is affected by the phases of the moon. The full moon, in particular, was once thought to trigger phenomena as diverse as epilepsy and schizophrenia. Greek authors of late antiquity and the early Middle Ages used the adjectives *selēnoblēktos* or *selēnoplēktos*, literally, "moonstruck," to describe people influenced by the moon. (The word *moonstruck* is itself probably a loan translation of these words, introduced into English in the 17th century.) The Late Latin adjective *lunaticus*, a derivative of Latin *luna* "moon" (with the suffix of *fanaticus* "fanatic"), was coined to express the same notion. *Lunaticus* was borrowed into Old French as *lunatique* and from there into Middle English as *lunatik*. One peculiarity of *lunatic* that is due to its early appearance in English is its stress, which falls on the first syllable. All other English words ending in *-atic* are stressed on the *a*. Some words that were once stressed on the first syllable such as *phlegmatic* and *schismatic* have, in the last two centuries, joined the common pattern, so that *lunatic* now remains alone.

---

\ə\ abut \°\ kitten \ər\ further \a\ ash \ā\ ace
\ä\ mop, mar \aù\ out \ch\ chin \e\ bet \ē\ easy
\g\ go \i\ hit \ī\ ice \j\ job \ŋ\ sing \ō\ go
\ò\ law \òi\ boy \th\ thin \th\ the \ü\ loot \ù\ foot
\y\ yet \zh\ vision *see also* Guide to Pronunciation

**lunch·room** \'lənch-,rüm, -,rùm\ *noun* (1830)
**1** : LUNCHEONETTE
**2** : a room (as in a school) where lunches supplied on the premises or brought from home may be eaten

**lunch·time** \-,tīm\ *noun* (1859)
: the time at which lunch is usually eaten
: NOON

**lune** \'lün\ *noun* [Latin *luna* moon — more at LUNAR] (circa 1704)
: the part of a plane surface bounded by two intersecting arcs or of a spherical surface bounded by two great circles

**lunes** \'lünz\ *noun plural* [French, plural of *lune* crazy whim, from Middle French, moon, crazy whim, from Latin *luna*] (1602)
: fits of lunacy

**lu·nette** \lü-'net\ *noun* [French, from Old French *lunete* small object shaped like the moon, from *lune* moon] (circa 1673)
**1** : something that has the shape of a crescent or half-moon: as **a** : an opening in a vault especially for a window **b** : the surface at the upper part of a wall that is partly surrounded by a vault which the wall intersects and that is often filled by windows or by mural painting **c** : a low crescentic mound (as of sand) formed by the wind
**2** : the figure or shape of a crescent moon

**lung** \'lən\ *noun* [Middle English *lunge*, from Old English *lungen;* akin to Old High German *lungun* lung, *līhti* light in weight — more at LIGHT] (before 12th century)
**1 a** : one of the usually paired compound saccular thoracic organs that constitute the basic respiratory organ of air-breathing vertebrates **b** : any of various respiratory organs of invertebrates
**2 a** : a device enabling individuals abandoning a submarine to rise to the surface **b** : a mechanical device for regularly introducing fresh air into and withdrawing stale air from the lung : RESPIRATOR
   **— lung·ful** \-,fùl\ *noun*

**¹lunge** \'lənj\ *noun* [modification of French *allonge* extension, reach, from Old French *alonge*, from *alongier* to lengthen, from (assumed) Vulgar Latin *allongare*, from Latin *ad-* + Late Latin *longare*, from Latin *longus* long] (1748)
**1** : a quick thrust or jab (as of a sword) usually made by leaning or striding forward
**2** : a sudden forward rush or reach ⟨made a *lunge* to catch the ball⟩

**²lunge** *verb* **lunged; lung·ing** (1821)
*intransitive verb*
: to make a lunge : move with or as if with a lunge
*transitive verb*
: to thrust or propel (as a blow) in a lunge

**lunged** \'lənd\ *adjective* (1693)
**1** : having lungs : PULMONATE
**2** : having a lung or lungs of a specified kind or number — used in combination ⟨one-*lunged*⟩

**¹lung·er** \'lən-jər\ *noun* (1842)
: one that lunges

**²lung·er** \'lən-ər\ *noun* (1893)
: a person suffering from a chronic disease of the lungs; *especially* : one who is tubercular

**lung·fish** \'lən-,fish\ *noun* (1883)
: any of a subclass (Dipneusti) of bony fishes that breathe by a modified swim bladder as well as gills

**lung·worm** \-,wərm\ *noun* (1882)
: any of various nematodes that infest the lungs and air passages of mammals

**lung·wort** \-,wərt, -,wórt\ *noun* (before 12th century)
: any of several plants (as a mullein) formerly used in the treatment of respiratory disorders; *especially* : a European herb (*Pulmonaria officinalis*) of the borage family with hispid leaves and usually bluish flowers

**lu·ni·so·lar** \,lü-ni-'sō-lər *also* -,lär\ *adjective* [Latin *luna* moon + English *-i-* + *solar*] (1691)

: relating or attributed to the moon and the sun
**lun·ker** \'lən-kər\ *noun* [origin unknown] (1912)
: something large of its kind — used especially of a game fish

**lunk·head** \'ləŋk-,hed\ *noun* [probably alteration of *lump* + *head*] (1852)
: a stupid person : DOLT
   **— lunk·head·ed** \-,he-dəd\ *adjective*

**lu·nule** \'lü-(,)nyü\ *noun* [New Latin *lunula*, from Latin, crescent-shaped ornament, from diminutive of *luna* moon] (1828)
: a crescent-shaped body part or marking (as the whitish mark at the base of a fingernail)

**lu·ny** \'lü-nē\ *variant of* LOONY

**lu·pa·nar** \lü-'pä-nər, -'pä-\ *noun* [Latin, from *lupa* prostitute, literally, she-wolf, feminine of *lupus*] (1864)
: BROTHEL

**Lu·per·ca·lia** \,lü-pər-'kā-lē-ə, -'käl-yə\ *noun* [Latin, plural, from *Lupercus*, god of flocks] (1600)
: an ancient Roman festival celebrated February 15 to ensure fertility for the people, fields, and flocks
   **— Lu·per·ca·lian** \-'kā-lē-ən, -'käl-yən\ *adjective*

**¹lu·pine** *also* **lu·pin** \'lü-pən\ *noun* [Middle English, from Latin *lupinus, lupinum*, from *lupinus*, adjective] (14th century)
: any of a genus (*Lupinus*) of leguminous herbs including some poisonous forms and others cultivated for their long showy racemes of usually blue, purple, white, or yellow flowers or for green manure, fodder, or their edible seeds; *also* : an edible lupine seed

**²lu·pine** \-,pīn\ *adjective* [Latin *lupinus*, from *lupus* wolf — more at WOLF] (1660)
: WOLFISH

**lu·pus** \'lü-pəs\ *noun* [Middle English, from Medieval Latin, from Latin, wolf] (14th century)
: any of several diseases characterized by skin lesions; *especially* : SYSTEMIC LUPUS ERYTHEMATOSUS

**lupus er·y·the·ma·to·sus** \-,er-ə-,thē-mə-'tō-səs\ *noun* [New Latin, literally, erythematous lupus] (1860)
: a disorder characterized by skin inflammation; *especially* : SYSTEMIC LUPUS ERYTHEMATOSUS

**¹lurch** \'lərch\ *verb* [Middle English *lorchen*, probably alteration of *lurken* to lurk] (15th century)
*intransitive verb*
*dialect chiefly English* : to loiter about a place furtively : PROWL
*transitive verb*
**1** *obsolete* : STEAL
**2** *archaic* : CHEAT

**²lurch** *noun* [Middle French *lourche*, adjective, defeated by a lurch, deceived] (1598)
: a decisive defeat in which an opponent wins a game by more than double the defeated player's score especially in cribbage
   **— in the lurch** : in a vulnerable and unsupported position

**³lurch** *transitive verb* (circa 1651)
**1** *archaic* : to leave in the lurch
**2** : to defeat by a lurch (as in cribbage)

**⁴lurch** *noun* [origin unknown] (1819)
**1** : a sudden roll of a ship to one side
**2** : a jerking or swaying movement; *also* : STAGGER 3

**⁵lurch** *intransitive verb* (circa 1828)
: to roll or tip abruptly : PITCH; *also* : STAGGER

**lurch·er** \'lər-chər\ *noun* [¹*lurch*] (1528)
**1** *archaic* : a petty thief : PILFERER
**2** *British* : a crossbred dog; *especially* : one that resembles a greyhound
**3** *archaic* : one who lurks; *also* : SPY

**lur·dane** \'lər-d°n\ *noun* [Middle English *lurdan*, from Middle French *lourdin* dullard, from *lourd* dull, stupid, from Latin *luridus* lurid] (14th century)

*archaic* : a lazy stupid person
   **— lurdane** *adjective*

**¹lure** \'lùr\ *noun* [Middle English, from Middle French *loire*, of Germanic origin; akin to Middle High German *luoder* bait; perhaps akin to Old English *lathian* to invite, Old High German *ladōn*] (14th century)
**1** : an object usually of leather or feathers attached to a long cord and used by a falconer to recall or exercise a hawk
**2 a** : an inducement to pleasure or gain : ENTICEMENT **b** : APPEAL, ATTRACTION
**3** : a decoy for attracting animals to capture: as **a** : artificial bait used for catching fish **b** : an often luminous structure on the head of pediculate fishes that is used to attract prey

**²lure** *transitive verb* **lured; lur·ing** (14th century)
**1** : to recall or exercise (a hawk) by means of a lure
**2** : to draw with a hint of pleasure or gain : attract actively and strongly ☆

**Lur·ex** \'lùr-eks\ *trademark*
   — used for metallic yarn or thread

**lu·rid** \'lùr-əd\ *adjective* [Latin *luridus* pale yellow, sallow] (circa 1656)
**1 a** : wan and ghastly pale in appearance **b** : of any of several light or medium grayish colors ranging in hue from yellow to orange
**2** : shining with the red glow of fire seen through smoke or cloud
**3 a** : causing horror or revulsion : GRUESOME **b** : MELODRAMATIC, SENSATIONAL; *also* : SHOCKING ⟨paperbacks in the usual *lurid* covers —T. R. Fyvel⟩
   **synonym** see GHASTLY
   **— lu·rid·ly** *adverb*
   **— lu·rid·ness** *noun*

**lurk** \'lərk\ *intransitive verb* [Middle English; akin to Middle High German *lūren* to lie in wait — more at LOWER] (14th century)
**1 a** : to lie in wait in a place of concealment especially for an evil purpose **b** : to move furtively or inconspicuously **c** : to persist in staying
**2 a** : to be concealed but capable of being discovered; *specifically* : to constitute a latent threat **b** : to lie hidden ☆
   **— lurk·er** *noun*

---

☆ **SYNONYMS**
**Lure, entice, inveigle, decoy, tempt, seduce** mean to lead astray from one's true course. LURE implies a drawing into danger, evil, or difficulty through attracting and deceiving ⟨*lured* naive investors with get-rich-quick schemes⟩. ENTICE suggests drawing by artful or adroit means ⟨advertising designed to *entice* new customers⟩. INVEIGLE implies enticing by cajoling or flattering ⟨fund-raisers *inveigling* wealthy alumni⟩. DECOY implies a luring into entrapment by artifice ⟨attempting to *decoy* the enemy into an ambush⟩. TEMPT implies the presenting of an attraction so strong that it overcomes the restraints of conscience or better judgment ⟨*tempted* by the offer of money⟩. SEDUCE implies a leading astray by persuasion or false promises ⟨*seduced* by assurances of assistance⟩.

**Lurk, skulk, slink, sneak** mean to behave so as to escape attention. LURK implies a lying in wait in a place of concealment and often suggests an evil intent ⟨suspicious men *lurking* in alleyways⟩. SKULK suggests more strongly cowardice or fear or sinister intent ⟨something *skulking* in the shadows⟩. SLINK implies moving stealthily often merely to escape attention ⟨*slunk* around the corner⟩. SNEAK may add an implication of entering or leaving a place or evading a difficulty by furtive, indirect, or underhanded methods ⟨*sneaked* out early⟩.

**lus·cious** \'lə-shəs\ *adjective* [Middle English *lucius*, perhaps alteration of *licius*, short for *delicious*] (15th century)
**1 a** : having a delicious taste or smell : SWEET **b** *archaic* : excessively sweet : CLOYING **2** : sexually attractive : SEDUCTIVE, SEXY **3 a** : richly luxurious or appealing to the senses **b** : excessively ornate
— **lus·cious·ly** *adverb*
— **lus·cious·ness** *noun*

¹**lush** \'ləsh\ *adjective* [Middle English *lusch* soft, tender] (1610)
**1 a** : growing vigorously especially with luxuriant foliage ⟨*lush* grass⟩ **b** : lavishly productive: as (1) : FERTILE (2) : THRIVING (3) : characterized by abundance : PLENTIFUL (4) : PROSPEROUS, PROFITABLE **2 a** : SAVORY, DELICIOUS **b** : appealing to the senses ⟨the *lush* sounds of the orchestra⟩ **c** : OPULENT, SUMPTUOUS
*synonym* see PROFUSE
— **lush·ly** *adverb*
— **lush·ness** *noun*

²**lush** *noun* [origin unknown] (circa 1790)
**1** *slang* : intoxicating liquor : DRINK **2** : an habitual heavy drinker : DRUNKARD

³**lush** *verb* (circa 1811)
*slang* : DRINK

**Lu·so-** \'lü-(,)sō\ *combining form* [Portuguese, from *lusitano* Portuguese, from Latin *Lusitanus* of Lusitania (ancient region corresponding approximately to modern Portugal)]
: Portuguese and ⟨*Luso*-Brazilian⟩

¹**lust** \'ləst\ *noun* [Middle English, from Old English; akin to Old High German *lust* pleasure and perhaps to Latin *lascivus* wanton] (before 12th century)
**1** *obsolete* **a** : PLEASURE, DELIGHT **b** : personal inclination : WISH **2** : usually intense or unbridled sexual desire : LASCIVIOUSNESS **3 a** : an intense longing : CRAVING **b** : ENTHUSIASM, EAGERNESS

²**lust** *intransitive verb* (12th century)
: to have an intense desire or need : CRAVE; *specifically* : to have a sexual urge

¹**lus·ter** *or* **lus·tre** \'ləs-tər\ *noun* [Middle English *lustre*, from Latin *lustrum*] (14th century)
: a period of five years : LUSTRUM 2

²**luster** *or* **lustre** *noun* [Middle French *lustre*, from Old Italian *lustro*, from *lustrare* to brighten, from Latin, to purify ceremonially, from *lustrum*] (circa 1522)
**1** : a glow of reflected light : SHEEN; *specifically* : the appearance of the surface of a mineral dependent upon its reflecting qualities **2 a** : a glow of light from within : LUMINOSITY **b** : an inner beauty : RADIANCE **3** : a superficial attractiveness or appearance of excellence **4 a** : a glass pendant used especially to ornament a candlestick or chandelier **b** : a decorative object (as a chandelier) hung with glass pendants **5** *chiefly British* : a fabric with cotton warp and a filling of wool, mohair, or alpaca **6** : LUSTERWARE
— **lus·ter·less** \-tər-ləs\ *adjective*

³**luster** *or* **lustre** *verb* **lus·tered** *or* **lus·tred**; **lus·ter·ing** *or* **lus·tring** \-t(ə-)riŋ\ (1582)
*intransitive verb*
: to have luster : GLEAM
*transitive verb*
**1** : to give luster or distinction to **2** : to coat or treat with a substance that imparts luster

**lus·ter·ware** \'ləs-tər-,war, -,wer\ *noun* (1825)
: pottery with an iridescent metallic sheen in the glaze

**lust·ful** \'ləst-fəl\ *adjective* (14th century)
: excited by lust : LECHEROUS
— **lust·ful·ly** \-fə-lē\ *adverb*
— **lust·ful·ness** *noun*

**lust·i·hood** \'ləs-tē-,hu̇d\ *noun* (1599)
**1** : vigor of body or spirit : ROBUSTNESS **2** : sexual inclination or capacity

**lus·tral** \'ləs-trəl\ *adjective* [Latin *lustralis*, from *lustrum*] (1533)
: PURIFICATORY

**lus·trate** \'ləs-,trāt\ *transitive verb* **lus·trat·ed; lus·trat·ing** [Latin *lustratus*, past participle of *lustrare*] (1653)
: to purify ceremonially
— **lus·tra·tion** \,ləs-'trā-shən\ *noun*

¹**lus·tring** \'ləs-triŋ\ *noun* [modification of Italian *lustrino*] (1697)
*archaic* : LUTESTRING

²**lus·tring** \'ləs-t(ə-)riŋ\ *noun* [*lustring*, gerund of ³*luster*] (circa 1889)
: a finishing process (as calendering) for giving a gloss to yarns and cloth

**lus·trous** \'ləs-trəs\ *adjective* (1601)
**1** : reflecting light evenly and efficiently without glitter or sparkle ⟨a *lustrous* satin⟩ ⟨the *lustrous* glow of an opal⟩ **2** : radiant in character or reputation : ILLUSTRIOUS
*synonym* see BRIGHT
— **lus·trous·ly** *adverb*
— **lus·trous·ness** *noun*

**lus·trum** \'ləs-trəm\ *noun, plural* **lustrums** *or* **lus·tra** \-trə\ [Latin] (1590)
**1** : a period of five years **2 a** : a purification of the whole Roman people made in ancient times after the census every five years **b** : the Roman census

**lusty** \'ləs-tē\ *adjective* **lust·i·er; -est** (13th century)
**1** *archaic* : MERRY, JOYOUS **2** : LUSTFUL ⟨*lusty* passion⟩ **3 a** : full of strength and vitality : HEALTHY, VIGOROUS ⟨a young, *lusty*, growing country —Helen Harris⟩ **b** : HEARTY, ROBUST ⟨a *lusty* beef stew⟩ **c** : ENTHUSIASTIC, ROUSING ⟨a *lusty* rendition of the song⟩
*synonym* see VIGOROUS
— **lust·i·ly** \-tə-lē\ *adverb*
— **lust·i·ness** \-tē-nəs\ *noun*

¹**lute** \'lüt\ *noun* [Middle English, from Middle French *lut*, from Old Provençal *laut*, from Arabic *al-'ūd*, literally, the wood] (13th century)
: a stringed instrument having a large pear-shaped body, a vaulted back, a fretted fingerboard, and a head with tuning pegs which is often angled backward from the neck

²**lute** *transitive verb* **lut·ed; lut·ing** [Middle English, from Latin *lutare*, from *lutum* mud — more at POLLUTE] (14th century)
: to seal or cover (as a joint or surface) with lute

³**lute** *noun* (15th century)
: a substance (as cement or clay) for packing a joint or coating a porous surface to make it impervious to gas or liquid

**lute-** *or* **luteo-** *combining form* [New Latin (*corpus*) *luteum*]
: corpus luteum ⟨*lute*al⟩

**lu·te·al** \'lü-tē-əl\ *adjective* (1920)
: of, relating to, characterized by, or involving the corpus luteum ⟨the *luteal* phase of the menstrual cycle⟩

**lute·fisk** \'lüt-,fisk, 'lü-tə-\ *noun* [Norwegian, from *lute* to wash in lye solution + *fisk* fish] (1924)
: dried codfish that has been soaked in a water and lye solution before cooking

**lu·tein** \'lü-tē-ən, 'lü-,tēn\ *noun* (1869)
: an orange xanthophyll $C_{40}H_{56}O_2$ occurring in plants, animal fat, egg yolk, and the corpus luteum

**lu·tein·i·za·tion** \,lü-tē-ə-nə-'zā-shən, ,lü-tē-nə-\ *noun* (1929)
: the process of forming corpora lutea
— **lu·tein·ize** \'lü-tē-ə-,nīz, 'lü-,tē-,nīz\ *verb*

**luteinizing hormone** *noun* (1931)
: a hormone from the anterior lobe of the pituitary gland that in the female stimulates especially the development of corpora lutea and in the male the development of interstitial tissue in the testis

**luteinizing hormone–releasing hormone** *noun* (1970)
: a hormone secreted by the hypothalamus that stimulates the pituitary gland to release gonadotropins (as luteinizing hormone and follicle-stimulating hormone) — called also *luteinizing hormone-releasing factor*

**lu·te·nist** *or* **lu·ta·nist** \'lüt-°n-ist, 'lüt-nist\ *noun* [Medieval Latin *lutanista*, from *lutana* lute, probably from Middle French *lut* lute] (1600)
: a lute player

**lu·teo·tro·pic** \,lü-tē-ə-'trō-pik, -'trä-\ *or* **lu·teo·tro·phic** \-'trō-fik, -'trä-\ *adjective* (1941)
: acting on the corpora lutea

**luteotropic hormone** *or* **luteotrophic hormone** *noun* (1949)
: PROLACTIN

**lu·teo·tro·pin** \,lü-tē-ə-'trō-pən\ *or* **lu·teo·tro·phin** \-fən\ *noun* (1941)
: PROLACTIN

**lu·te·ous** \'lü-tē-əs\ *adjective* [Latin *luteus* yellow, from *lutum*, a plant (*Reseda luteola*) used for dyeing yellow] (1657)
: yellow tinged with green or brown

**lute·string** \'lüt-(,)striŋ\ *noun* [by folk etymology from Italian *lustrino* glossy fabric, from *lustro* luster] (1661)
: a plain glossy silk formerly much used for women's dresses and ribbons

**lu·te·tium** *also* **lu·te·cium** \lü-'tē-sh(ē-)əm\ *noun* [New Latin, from Latin *Lutetia*, ancient name of Paris] (1907)
: a metallic element of the rare-earth group — see ELEMENT table

¹**Lu·ther·an** \'lü-th(ə-)rən\ *noun* (1521)
: a member of a Lutheran church

²**Lutheran** *adjective* (1530)
**1** : of or relating to religious doctrines (as justification by faith alone) developed by Martin Luther or his followers **2** : of or relating to the Protestant churches adhering to Lutheran doctrines, liturgy, and polity
— **Lu·ther·an·ism** \-rə-,ni-zəm\ *noun*

**lu·thi·er** \'lü-tē-ər, -thē-ər\ *noun* [French, from *luth* lute (from Middle French *lut*)] (1879)
: one who makes stringed musical instruments (as violins or guitars)

**lutz** \'ləts\ *noun* [probably irregular from Gustave *Lussi* (born 1898) Swiss figure skater] (1938)
: a figure-skating jump from the outer edge of one skate with a full turn in the air and a return to the outer edge of the other skate

**Lu·wi·an** \'lü-ē-ən\ *noun* [*Luwi*, an ancient people of the southern coast of Asia Minor] (1924)
: an Anatolian language of the Indo-European language family — see INDO-EUROPEAN LANGUAGES table
— **Luwian** *adjective*

**lux** \'ləks\ *noun, plural* **lux** *or* **lux·es** [Latin, light — more at LIGHT] (1889)
: a unit of illumination equal to the direct illumination on a surface that is everywhere one meter from a uniform point source of one candle intensity or equal to one lumen per square meter

**lux·a·tion** \,lək-'sā-shən\ *noun* [Late Latin *luxation-, luxatio*, from Latin *luxare* to dislocate, from *luxus* dislocated — more at LOCK] (1552)

lute

\ə\ abut \ᵊ\ kitten \ər\ further \a\ ash \ā\ ace \ä\ mop, mar \au̇\ out \ch\ chin \e\ bet \ē\ easy \g\ go \i\ hit \ī\ ice \j\ job \ŋ\ sing \ō\ go \ȯ\ law \ȯi\ boy \th\ thin \t̲h̲\ the \ü\ loot \u̇\ foot \y\ yet \zh\ vision *see also* Guide to Pronunciation

: dislocation of an anatomical part (as a bone at a joint or the lens of the eye)

**luxe** \'lüks, 'ləks, 'lüks\ *noun* [French, from Latin *luxus* — more at LUXURY] (1558)
: LUXURY
— **luxe** *adjective*

**lux·u·ri·ance** \(ˌ)ləg-'zhür-ē-ən(t)s, (ˌ)lək-'shür-\ *noun* (circa 1746)
: the quality or state of being luxuriant

**lux·u·ri·ant** \-ē-ənt\ *adjective* (circa 1540)
**1 a** : yielding abundantly : FERTILE, FRUITFUL **b** : characterized by abundant growth : LUSH
**2** : abundantly and often extravagantly rich and varied : PROLIFIC
**3** : characterized by luxury : LUXURIOUS
*synonym* see PROFUSE
— **lux·u·ri·ant·ly** *adverb*

**lux·u·ri·ate** \-ē-ˌāt\ *intransitive verb* **-at·ed; -at·ing** [Latin *luxuriatus,* past participle of *luxuriare,* from *luxuria*] (1621)
**1 a** : to grow profusely : THRIVE **b** : to develop extensively
**2** : to indulge oneself luxuriously : REVEL

**lux·u·ri·ous** \(ˌ)ləg-'zhür-ē-əs, (ˌ)lək-'shür-\ *adjective* (14th century)
**1** : LECHEROUS
**2** : marked by or given to self-indulgence ⟨*luxurious* tastes⟩ ⟨*luxurious* feeling⟩
**3** : of, relating to, or marked by luxury ⟨*luxurious* accommodations⟩
**4** : of the finest and richest kind ⟨*luxurious* cashmeres⟩ ⟨a *luxurious* chocolate sauce⟩
*synonym* see SENSUOUS
— **lux·u·ri·ous·ly** *adverb*
— **lux·u·ri·ous·ness** *noun*

**lux·u·ry** \'lək-sh(ə-)rē, -zh(ə-)rē\ *noun, plural* **-ries** [Middle English *luxurie,* from Middle French, from Latin *luxuria* rankness, luxury, excess; akin to Latin *luxus* luxury, excess] (14th century)
**1** *archaic* : LECHERY, LUST
**2** : a condition of abundance or great ease and comfort : sumptuous environment ⟨lived in *luxury*⟩
**3 a** : something adding to pleasure or comfort but not absolutely necessary **b** : an indulgence in something that provides pleasure, satisfaction, or ease ⟨had the *luxury* of rejecting a handful of job offers . . . before accepting a choice assignment —Terri Minsky⟩
— **luxury** *adjective*

**lwei** \lə-'wā\ *noun, plural* **lwei** *also* **lweis** [probably from *Lwei* (Lué), name of several rivers in Angola] (circa 1979)
— see **kwanza** at MONEY table

**ly-** *or* **lyo-** *combining form* [International Scientific Vocabulary, from Greek *lyein* to loosen, dissolve — more at LOSE]
**1** : degrading : reduction ⟨*ly*ase⟩
**2** : dispersed state : dispersion ⟨*lyo*philic⟩

**¹-ly** \lē; *in some dialects, especially British, Southern, New England, often* li *but not shown at individual entries*\ *adjective suffix* [Middle English, from Old English *-līc, -lic;* akin to Old High German *-līh, -lic,* Old English *līc* body — more at LIKE]
**1** : like in appearance, manner, or nature : having the characteristics of ⟨queen*ly*⟩ ⟨father*ly*⟩
**2** : characterized by regular recurrence in (specified) units of time : every ⟨hour*ly*⟩

**²-ly** *adverb suffix* [Middle English, from Old English *-līce, -lice,* from *-līc,* adjective suffix]
**1 a** : in a (specified) manner ⟨slow*ly*⟩ **b** : at a (specified) time interval ⟨annual*ly*⟩
**2** : from a (specified) point of view ⟨eschatologica*ly*⟩
**3** : with respect to ⟨part*ly*⟩
**4** : to a (specified) degree ⟨relative*ly*⟩
**5** : in a (specified) place in a series ⟨second*ly*⟩

**ly·am–hound** \'lī-əm-ˌhau̇nd\ *or* **lyme–hound** \'līm-ˌhau̇nd\ *noun* [obsolete *lyam* leash] (1527)
*archaic* : BLOODHOUND

**ly·art** \'lī-ərt\ *adjective* [Middle English, from Middle French *liart*] (14th century)

*chiefly Scottish* : streaked with gray : GRAY

**ly·ase** \'lī-ˌās, -ˌāz\ *noun* (1965)
: an enzyme (as a decarboxylase) that forms double bonds by removing groups from a substrate other than by hydrolysis or that adds groups to double bonds

**ly·can·thro·py** \lī-'kan(t)-thrə-pē\ *noun* [New Latin *lycanthropia,* from Greek *lykanthrōpia,* from *lykanthrōpos* werewolf, from *lykos* wolf + *anthrōpos* human being — more at WOLF] (1594)
**1** : a delusion that one has become a wolf
**2** : the assumption of the form and characteristics of a wolf held to be possible by witchcraft or magic

**ly·cée** \lē-'sā\ *noun* [French, from Middle French, lyceum, from Latin *Lyceum*] (1865)
: a French public secondary school that prepares students for the university

**ly·ce·um** \lī-'sē-əm, 'lī-sē-\ *noun* [Latin *Lyceum,* gymnasium near Athens where Aristotle taught, from Greek *Lykeion,* from neuter of *lykeios,* epithet of Apollo] (1786)
**1** : a hall for public lectures or discussions
**2** : an association providing public lectures, concerts, and entertainments
**3** : LYCÉE

**ly·chee** *variant of* LITCHI

**lych–gate** \'lich-ˌgāt\ *noun* [Middle English *lycheyate,* from *lich* body, corpse (from Old English *līc*) + *gate, yate* gate] (15th century)
: a roofed gate in a churchyard under which a bier rests during the initial part of the burial service

**lych·nis** \'lik-nəs\ *noun* [New Latin, from Latin, a red flower, from Greek; akin to Greek *lychnos* lamp, Latin *lux* light — more at LIGHT] (1601)
: any of a genus (*Lychnis*) of herbs of the pink family with terminal cymes of showy mostly red or white flowers having 5 or rarely 4 styles

**Ly·cian** \'li-sh(ē-)ən\ *noun* (1598)
**1** : a native or inhabitant of Lycia
**2** : an Anatolian language of the Indo-European language family — see INDO-EUROPEAN LANGUAGES table
— **Lycian** *adjective*

**ly·co·pene** \'lī-kə-ˌpēn\ *noun* [International Scientific Vocabulary *lycop-* (from New Latin *Lycopersicon,* genus of herbs) + *-ene*] (circa 1929)
: a carotenoid pigment $C_{40}H_{56}$ that is the red coloring matter of the tomato

**ly·co·pod** \'lī-kə-ˌpäd\ *noun* [New Latin *Lycopodium*] (1861)
: LYCOPODIUM 1; *broadly* : CLUB MOSS

**ly·co·po·di·um** \ˌlī-kə-'pō-dē-əm\ *noun* [New Latin, from Greek *lykos* wolf + *podion,* diminutive of *pod-, pous* foot — more at FOOT] (circa 1706)
**1** : any of a large genus (*Lycopodium*) of erect or creeping club mosses with reduced or scale-like evergreen leaves
**2** : a fine yellowish flammable powder composed of lycopodium spores and used especially in pharmacy

**Ly·cra** \'lī-krə\ *trademark*
— used for a spandex synthetic fiber

**lydd·ite** \'li-ˌdīt\ *noun* [*Lydd,* England] (1888)
: a high explosive composed chiefly of picric acid

**Lyd·i·an** \'li-dē-ən\ *noun* (15th century)
**1** : a native or inhabitant of Lydia
**2** : an Anatolian language of the Indo-European language family — see INDO-EUROPEAN LANGUAGES table
— **Lydian** *adjective*

**lye** \'lī\ *noun* [Middle English, from Old English *lēag;* akin to Old High German *louga* lye, Latin *lavare, lavere* to wash, Greek *louein*] (before 12th century)
**1** : a strong alkaline liquor rich in potassium carbonate leached from wood ashes and used especially in making soap and washing; *broadly*

: a strong alkaline solution (as of sodium hydroxide or potassium hydroxide)
**2** : a solid caustic (as sodium hydroxide)

**ly·gus bug** \'lī-gəs-\ *noun* [New Latin *Lygus*] (1940)
: any of various small sucking bugs (genus *Lygus*) including some pests of cultivated plants

**¹ly·ing** \'lī-iŋ\ *present participle of* LIE

**²lying** *adjective* [Middle English *leghynge,* present participle of *lien* to lie] (14th century)
: marked by or containing falsehoods : FALSE ⟨a *lying* account of the accident⟩

**ly·ing–in** \ˌlī-iŋ-'in\ *noun, plural* **lyings–in** *or* **lying–ins** (15th century)
: the state attending and consequent to childbirth : CONFINEMENT

**Lyme disease** \'līm-\ *noun* [*Lyme,* Connecticut, where it was first reported] (1980)
: an acute inflammatory disease that is caused by a spirochete (*Borrelia burgdorferi*) transmitted by ticks (genus *Ixodes* and especially *I. dammini*), that is often characterized initially by a spreading red annular skin lesion at the site of the infection, fever, and chills, and that may result in joint pain, arthritis, and cardiac and neurological disorders

**lymph** \'lim(p)f\ *noun* [Latin *lympha,* water goddess, water, perhaps modification of Greek *nymphē* nymph — more at NUPTIAL] (circa 1673)
**1** *archaic* : the sap of plants
**2** [New Latin *lympha,* from Latin, water] : a pale coagulable fluid that bathes the tissues, passes into lymphatic channels and ducts, is discharged into the blood by way of the thoracic duct, and consists of a liquid portion resembling blood plasma and containing white blood cells but normally no red blood cells

**lymph-** *or* **lympho-** *combining form* [New Latin *lympha*]
: lymph : lymphatic tissue ⟨*lympho*granuloma⟩

**lymph·ad·e·ni·tis** \ˌlim-ˌfa-d°n-'ī-təs\ *noun* [New Latin, from *lymphaden* lymph gland, from *lymph-* + Greek *adēn* gland — more at ADEN-] (1860)
: inflammation of lymph nodes

**lymph·ad·e·nop·a·thy** \ˌlim-ˌfa-d°n-'ä-pə-thē\ *noun, plural* **-thies** (1920)
: abnormal enlargement of the lymph nodes

**lymph·an·gi·og·ra·phy** \ˌlim-ˌfan-jē-'ä-grə-fē\ *noun* (circa 1941)
: X-ray depiction of lymph vessels and nodes after use of a radiopaque material — called also *lymphography*
— **lymph·an·gio·gram** \(ˌ)lim-'fan-jē-ə-ˌgram\ *noun*
— **lymph·an·gio·graph·ic** \ˌlim-ˌfan-jē-ə-'gra-fik\ *adjective*

**¹lym·phat·ic** \lim-'fa-tik\ *adjective* (1649)
**1 a** : of, relating to, or produced by lymph, lymphoid tissue, or lymphocytes **b** : conveying lymph
**2** : lacking physical or mental energy : SLUGGISH
— **lym·phat·i·cal·ly** \-ti-k(ə-)lē\ *adverb*

**²lymphatic** *noun* (1667)
: a vessel that contains or conveys lymph — called also *lymph vessel*

**lymph gland** *noun* (circa 1858)
: LYMPH NODE

**lymph node** *noun* (1892)
: any of the rounded masses of lymphoid tissue that are surrounded by a capsule of connective tissue, are distributed along the lymphatic vessels, and contain numerous lymphocytes which filter the flow of lymph

**lym·pho·blast** \'lim(p)-fə-ˌblast\ *noun* [International Scientific Vocabulary] (circa 1909)
: a lymphocyte that has enlarged following stimulation by an antigen, has the capacity to recognize the stimulating antigen, and is undergoing proliferation and differentiation either to an effector state in which it functions to eliminate the antigen or to a memory state in which it functions to recognize the future reappearance of the antigen

— **lym·pho·blas·tic** \ˌlim(p)-fə-'blas-tik\ adjective

**lym·pho·cyte** \'lim(p)-fə-ˌsīt\ noun [International Scientific Vocabulary] (1890)
: any of the colorless weakly motile cells originating from stem cells and differentiating in lymphoid tissue (as of the thymus or bone marrow) that are the typical cellular elements of lymph, include the cellular mediators of immunity, and constitute 20 to 30 percent of the leukocytes of normal human blood — compare B CELL, T CELL

— **lym·pho·cyt·ic** \ˌlim(p)-fə-'si-tik\ adjective

**lymphocytic cho·rio·men·in·gi·tis** \-ˌkȯr-ē-ō-ˌme-nən-'jī-təs\ noun [New Latin choriomeningitis cerebral meningitis, from chorio- of a membrane resembling the chorion] (1934)
: an acute virus disease that is characterized by fever, nausea and vomiting, headache, stiff neck, and slow pulse, is marked by the presence of numerous lymphocytes in the cerebrospinal fluid, and is transmitted especially by rodents and bloodsucking insects

**lym·pho·cy·to·sis** \ˌlim(p)-fə-ˌsī-'tō-səs, -fə-sə-\ noun [New Latin, from International Scientific Vocabulary lymphocyte] (1896)
: an increase in the number of lymphocytes in the blood usually associated with chronic infections or inflammations

**lym·pho·gran·u·lo·ma** \'lim(p)-fō-ˌgran-yə-'lō-mə\ noun, plural **-mas** or **-ma·ta** \-mə-tə\ [New Latin] (1924)
: LYMPHOGRANULOMA VENEREUM

**lymphogranuloma in·gui·na·le** \-ˌiŋ-gwə-'nä-lē, -'na-, -'nā-\ noun [New Latin, inguinal lymphogranuloma] (1932)
: LYMPHOGRANULOMA VENEREUM

**lym·pho·gran·u·lo·ma·to·sis** \-ˌlō-mə-'tō-səs\ noun, plural **-to·ses** \-ˌsēz\ [New Latin lymphogranulomat-, lymphogranuloma + -osis] (1911)
: the development of benign or malignant nodular swellings of lymph nodes in various parts of the body; also : a condition characterized by these

**lymphogranuloma ve·ne·re·um** \-və-'nir-ē-əm\ noun [New Latin, venereal lymphogranuloma] (1938)
: a contagious venereal disease caused by various strains of a chlamydia (Chlamydia trachomatis) and marked by swelling and ulceration of lymphatic tissue in the iliac and inguinal regions

**lym·phog·ra·phy** \lim-'fä-grə-fē\ noun (circa 1935)
: LYMPHANGIOGRAPHY

— **lym·pho·gram** \'lim(p)-fə-ˌgram\ noun

— **lym·pho·graph·ic** \ˌlim-fə-'gra-fik\ adjective

**lym·phoid** \'lim-ˌfȯid\ adjective (1867)
**1** : of, relating to, or being tissue (as of the lymph nodes or thymus) containing lymphocytes
**2** : of, relating to, or resembling lymph

**lym·pho·kine** \'lim(p)-fə-ˌkīn\ noun [lymph- + -kine, from Greek kinein to move about — more at -KINESIS] (1969)
: any of various substances (as interleukin-2) of low molecular weight that are not immunoglobulins, are secreted by T cells in response to stimulation by antigens, and have a role (as the activation of macrophages or the enhancement or inhibition of antibody production) in cell-mediated immunity

**lym·pho·ma** \lim-'fō-mə\ noun, plural **-mas** or **-ma·ta** \-mə-tə\ [New Latin] (1873)
: a tumor of lymphoid tissue

— **lym·pho·ma·tous** \-mə-təs\ adjective

**lym·pho·ma·to·sis** \(ˌ)lim-ˌfō-mə-'tō-səs\ noun, plural **-to·ses** \-ˌsēz\ [New Latin lymphomat-, lymphoma + -osis] (circa 1900)
: the presence of multiple lymphomas in the body

**lym·pho·sar·co·ma** \ˌlim(p)-fə-sär-'kō-mə\ noun, plural **-mas** or **-ma·ta** \-mə-tə\ [New Latin] (1874)
: a malignant lymphoma that tends to metastasize freely especially along the regional lymphatic drainage

**lynch** \'linch\ transitive verb [lynch law] (1836)
: to put to death (as by hanging) by mob action without legal sanction ◆

— **lynch·er** noun

**lynch law** noun [William Lynch (died 1820) American vigilante] (1811)
: the punishment of presumed crimes or offenses usually by death without due process of law

**lynch·pin** variant of LINCHPIN

**lynx** \'liŋ(k)s\ noun, plural **lynx** or **lynx·es** [Middle English, from Latin, from Greek; akin to Old English lox lynx and probably to Greek leukos white — more at LIGHT] (14th century)
: any of several wildcats (genus Lynx) with relatively long legs, a short stubby tail, mottled coat, and often tufted ears: as **a** : a lynx (L. lynx) of northern Europe and Asia **b** : BOBCAT **c** : a North American lynx (L. canadensis) distinguished from the bobcat by its larger size, longer tufted ears, and wholly black tail tip — called also Canadian lynx

**lynx–eyed** \'liŋ(k)s-ˌīd\ adjective (1597)
: SHARP-SIGHTED

**lyo-** — see LY-

**ly·on·naise** \ˌlī-ə-'nāz\ adjective [French (à la) lyonnaise in the manner of Lyons, France] (1846)
: prepared with onions ⟨lyonnaise potatoes⟩

**Ly·on·nesse** \ˌlī-ə-'nes\ noun
: a country that according to Arthurian legend was contiguous to Cornwall before sinking beneath the sea

**lyo·phile** \'lī-ə-ˌfīl\ adjective [International Scientific Vocabulary] (1934)
**1** : of or relating to freeze-drying
**2** or **lyo·philed** \-ˌfīld\ : obtained by freeze-drying

**lyo·phil·ic** \ˌlī-ə-'fi-lik\ adjective (1911)
: marked by strong affinity between a dispersed phase and the liquid in which it is dispersed ⟨a lyophilic colloid⟩

**ly·oph·i·lise** British variant of LYOPHILIZE

**ly·oph·i·lize** \lī-'ä-fə-ˌlīz\ transitive verb **-lized; -liz·ing** (1938)
: FREEZE-DRY

— **ly·oph·i·li·za·tion** \-ˌä-fə-lə-'zā-shən\ noun

— **ly·oph·i·liz·er** \-'ä-fə-ˌlī-zər\ noun

**lyo·pho·bic** \ˌlī-ə-'fō-bik\ adjective (1911)
: marked by lack of strong affinity between a dispersed phase and the liquid in which it is dispersed ⟨a lyophobic colloid⟩

**Ly·ra** \'lī-rə\ noun [Latin (genitive Lyrae), literally, lyre]
: a northern constellation representing the lyre of Orpheus or Mercury and containing Vega

**ly·rate** \'lī-ˌrāt\ adjective (circa 1760)
: having or suggesting the shape of a lyre ⟨the lyrate horns of the impala⟩

**lyre** \'līr\ noun [Middle English lire, from Old French, from Latin lyra, from Greek] (13th century)
**1** : a stringed instrument of the harp class used by the ancient Greeks especially to accompany song and recitation
**2** capitalized : LYRA

**lyre·bird** \-ˌbərd\ noun (1834)
: either of two Australian passerine birds (genus Menura) distinguished in the male by very long tail feathers displayed in the shape of a lyre during courtship

lyre 1

¹**lyr·ic** \'lir-ik\ noun (1581)
**1** : a lyric composition; specifically : a lyric poem
**2** : the words of a song — often used in plural

²**lyric** adjective [Middle French or Latin; Middle French lyrique, from Latin lyricus, from Greek lyrikos, from lyra] (1589)
**1 a** : suitable for singing to the lyre or for being set to music and sung **b** : of, relating to, or being drama set to music; especially : OPERATIC ⟨lyric stage⟩
**2** : expressing direct usually intense personal emotion especially in a manner suggestive of song ⟨lyric poetry⟩ **b** : EXUBERANT, RHAPSODIC
**3** of an opera singer : having a light voice and a melodic style — compare DRAMATIC

**lyr·i·cal** \'lir-i-kəl\ adjective (1581)
: LYRIC

— **lyr·i·cal·ly** \-i-k(ə-)lē\ adverb

— **lyr·i·cal·ness** \-kəl-nəs\ noun

**lyr·i·cism** \'lir-ə-ˌsi-zəm\ noun (1760)
**1** : the quality or state of being lyric : SONGFULNESS
**2 a** : an intense personal quality expressive of feeling or emotion in an art (as poetry or music) **b** : EXUBERANCE ⟨the sort of author who inspires lyricism or invective, not judicious interpretation —Time⟩

**lyr·i·cist** \-sist\ noun (1881)
: a writer of lyrics

**lyr·ism** \'lir-ˌi-zəm\ noun (1859)
: LYRICISM

**lyr·ist** noun (circa 1656)
**1** \'līr-ist\ : a player on the lyre
**2** \'lir-ist\ : LYRICIST

**lys-** or **lysi-** or **lyso-** combining form [New Latin, from Greek lys-, lysi- loosening, from lysis]
: lysis ⟨lysin⟩

**ly·sate** \'lī-ˌsāt\ noun (1922)
: a product of lysis

**lyse** \'līs, 'līz\ verb **lysed; lys·ing** [back-formation from New Latin lysis] (1924)
transitive verb
: to cause to undergo lysis
intransitive verb
: to undergo lysis

**-lyse** chiefly British variant of -LYZE

**Ly·sen·ko·ism** \lə-'seŋ-kō-ˌi-zəm\ noun [Trofim Lysenko] (1948)
: a biological doctrine asserting the fundamental influence of somatic and environmental factors on heredity in contradiction of orthodox genetics

lyrebird

◇ WORD HISTORY

**lynch** Despite the claims made on behalf of numerous other Lynches, the weight of evidence for the eponymous word lynch falls on the side of Captain William Lynch (1742–1820). Lynch served with the Virginia militia and presided over a self-created tribunal that was organized to rid Pittsylvania County of a band of troublesome ruffians that had eluded the civil authorities. On 22 September 1780, Lynch and others entered into a compact stating their goals, reasons, and methods. Captain Lynch and his vigilantes became known as "lynch-men," and by 1782 their judicial code had become known as lynch's law and subsequently lynch law. By 1836 lynch law had given rise to the verb lynch in its modern meaning.

\ə\ abut  \ᵊ\ kitten  \ər\ further  \a\ ash  \ā\ ace
\ä\ mop, mar  \au̇\ out  \ch\ chin  \e\ bet  \ē\ easy
\g\ go  \i\ hit  \ī\ ice  \j\ job  \ŋ\ sing  \ō\ go
\ȯ\ law  \ȯi\ boy  \th\ thin  \t͟h\ the  \ü\ loot  \u̇\ foot
\y\ yet  \zh\ vision  see also Guide to Pronunciation

**ly·ser·gic acid** \lə-'sər-jik-, (ˌ)lī-\ *noun* [*lys-* + *ergot*] (1934)
**:** a crystalline acid $C_{16}H_{16}N_2O_2$ from ergotic alkaloids; *also* **:** LSD
**lysergic acid di·eth·yl·am·ide** \-ˌdī-ˌe-thə-'la-ˌmīd\ *noun* (1944)
**:** LSD
**ly·sim·e·ter** \lī-'si-mə-tər\ *noun* (1879)
**:** a device for measuring the percolation of water through soils and for determining the soluble constituents removed in the drainage
— **ly·si·met·ric** \ˌlī-sə-'me-trik\ *adjective*
**ly·sin** \'lī-sⁿ\ *noun* (1900)
**:** a substance (as an antibody) capable of causing lysis
**ly·sine** \'lī-ˌsēn\ *noun* (1892)
**:** a crystalline essential amino acid $C_6H_{14}N_2O_2$ obtained from the hydrolysis of various proteins
**ly·sis** \'lī-səs\ *noun, plural* **ly·ses** \-ˌsēz\ [New Latin, from Greek, act of loosening, dissolution, remission of fever, from *lyein* to loosen · — more at LOSE] (1543)
**1 :** the gradual decline of a disease process (as fever)
**2 :** a process of disintegration or dissolution (as of cells)

**-lysis** *noun combining form, plural* **-lyses** [New Latin, from Latin & Greek; Latin, loosening, from Greek, from *lysis*]
**1 :** decomposition ⟨electro*lysis*⟩
**2 :** disintegration **:** breaking down ⟨auto*lysis*⟩
**ly·so·gen** \'lī-sə-jən\ *noun* (circa 1934)
**:** a lysogenic bacterium or bacterial strain
**ly·so·gen·ic** \ˌlī-sə-'je-nik\ *adjective* [from the capacity of the prophage to lyse other bacteria] (1899)
**1 :** harboring a prophage as hereditary material ⟨*lysogenic* bacteria⟩
**2 :** TEMPERATE 3 ⟨*lysogenic* viruses⟩
— **ly·so·ge·nic·i·ty** \-jə-'ni-sə-tē\ *noun*
**ly·sog·e·nise** *British variant of* LYSOGENIZE
**ly·sog·e·nize** \lī-'sä-jə-ˌnīz\ *transitive verb*
**-nized; -niz·ing** (1953)
**:** to render lysogenic
— **ly·sog·e·ni·za·tion** \-ˌsä-jə-nə-'zā-shən\ *noun*
**ly·sog·e·ny** \lī-'sä-jə-nē\ *noun* (1956)
**:** the state of being lysogenic
**ly·so·lec·i·thin**    \ˌlī-sə-'le-sə-thən\    *noun* (1923)
**:** a hydrolytic substance formed by the enzymatic hydrolysis (as by some snake venoms) of a lecithin

**ly·so·some** \'lī-sə-ˌsōm\ *noun* [International Scientific Vocabulary *lys-* + ³*-some*] (1955)
**:** a saclike cellular organelle that contains various hydrolytic enzymes — see CELL illustration
— **ly·so·som·al** \ˌlī-sə-'sō-məl\ *adjective*
**ly·so·zyme** \'lī-sə-ˌzīm\ *noun* (1922)
**:** a basic bacteriolytic protein that hydrolyzes peptidoglycan and is present in egg white and in human tears and saliva
**-lyte** *noun combining form* [Greek *lytos* that may be untied, soluble, from *lyein*]
**:** substance capable of undergoing (such) decomposition ⟨electro*lyte*⟩
**lyt·ic** \'li-tik\ *adjective* [Greek *lytikos* able to loose, from *lyein*] (1889)
**:** of or relating to lysis or a lysin; *also* **:** productive of or effecting lysis (as of cells)
— **lyt·i·cal·ly** \-ti-k(ə-)lē\ *adverb*
**-lytic** *adjective suffix* [Greek *lytikos*]
**:** of, relating to, or effecting (such) decomposition ⟨hydro*lytic*⟩
**-lyze** *verb combining form* **-lyzed; -lyzing** [International Scientific Vocabulary, probably irregular from New Latin *-lysis*]
**:** produce or undergo lytic disintegration or dissolution ⟨electro*lyze*⟩

# M

M *is the thirteenth letter of the English alphabet. It comes through the Latin, via Etruscan, from the Greek* mu, *which took it from the Phoenician* mêm. *Its sound is that of a bilabial continuant, a sound formed by stopping the oral passage of air at the lips and allowing it to continue through the nose, giving the sound a nasal resonance. (For this reason* M *is also classified as a nasal consonant).* M *is silent only when initial before* n *in several words from Greek, as* mnemonic. *In related languages, English* m *corresponds to German* m, *Latin* m *or* n, *Greek* m *or* n, *and Sanskrit* m, *as in English* mouse, *German* Maus, *Latin* mus, *Greek* mys, *Sanskrit* mus; *and English* come, *German* kommen, *Latin* venire, *Greek* bainein, *Sanskrit* gamati *(goes). Small* m *developed by a rounding of the sharp angles and a reduction in size of the capital form of the letter.*

---

**m** \\'em\\ *noun, plural* **m's** *or* **ms** \\'emz\\ *often capitalized, often attributive* (before 12th century)
**1 a :** the 13th letter of the English alphabet **b :** a graphic representation of this letter **c : a** speech counterpart of orthographic *m*
**2 :** one thousand — see NUMBER table
**3 :** a graphic device for reproducing the letter *m*
**4 :** one designated *m* especially as the 13th in order or class
**5 :** something shaped like the letter M
**6 a :** EM 2 **b :** PICA 2

**'m** \\m\\ *verb* (circa 1594)
**:** AM ⟨I'*m* going⟩

**ma** \\'mä, 'mȯ\\ *noun* [short for *mama*] (1829)
**:** MOTHER

**ma'am** \\'mam, *after* "yes" *often* əm\\ *noun* (1668)
**:** MADAM

**ma–and–pa** \\,mä-ən-'pä, ,mȯ-ən-'pȯ\\ *adjective* (1965)
**:** MOM-AND-POP

**Mab** \\'mab\\ *noun*
**:** a queen of fairies in English literature

**mabe pearl** \\'mäb-\\ *noun* [origin unknown] (1952)
**:** a cultured pearl essentially hemispherical in form — called also *mabe*

**mac** \\'mak\\ *noun* (1901)
*British* **:** MACKINTOSH

**Mac** \\'mak\\ *noun* [*Mac-, Mc-*, patronymic prefix in Scottish and Irish surnames] (circa 1937)
**:** FELLOW — used informally to address a man whose name is not known

**ma·ca·bre** \\mə-'käb; -'kä-brə, -bər; -'käbrᵊ\\ *adjective* [French, from (*danse*) *macabre* dance of death, from Middle French (*danse de*) *Macabré*] (1889)
**1 :** having death as a subject **:** comprising or including a personalized representation of death
**2 :** dwelling on the gruesome
**3 :** tending to produce horror in a beholder
**synonym** see GHASTLY

**mac·ad·am** \\mə-'ka-dəm\\ *noun* [John L. *McAdam* (died 1836) British engineer] (1824)
**:** macadamized roadway or pavement especially with a bituminous binder ◆

**mac·a·da·mia nut** \\,ma-kə-'dā-mē-ə-\\ *noun* [New Latin *Macadamia*, from John *Macadam* (died 1865) Australian chemist] (1929)
**:** a hard-shelled nut somewhat resembling a filbert and produced by an Australian evergreen tree (*Macadamia integrifolia*) of the protea family that is cultivated extensively in Hawaii — called also *macadamia*

**mac·ad·am·ize** \\mə-'ka-də-,mīz\\ *transitive verb* **-ized; -iz·ing** (1826)
**:** to construct or finish (a road) by compacting into a solid mass a layer of small broken stone on a convex well-drained roadbed and using a binder (as cement or asphalt) for the mass

**ma·caque** \\mə-'kak, -'käk\\ *noun* [French, from Portuguese *macaco*] (1757)
**:** any of a genus (*Macaca*) of chiefly Asian monkeys typically having a sturdy build and including some short-tailed or tailless forms; *especially* **:** RHESUS MONKEY

**mac·a·ro·ni** \\,ma-kə-'rō-nē\\ *noun* [Italian *maccheroni*, plural of *maccherone*, from Italian dialect *maccarone* dumpling, macaroni] (1599)
**1 :** pasta made from semolina and shaped in the form of slender tubes
**2** *plural* **macaronis** *or* **macaronies a :** a member of a class of traveled young Englishmen of the late 18th and early 19th centuries who affected foreign ways **b :** an affected young man **:** FOP

**mac·a·ron·ic** \\-'rä-nik\\ *adjective* [New Latin *macaronicus*, from Italian dialect *maccarone* macaroni] (1638)
**1 :** characterized by a mixture of vernacular words with Latin words or with non-Latin words having Latin endings
**2 :** characterized by a mixture of two languages
**— macaronic** *noun*

**mac·a·roon** \\,ma-kə-'rün\\ *noun* [French *macaron*, from Italian dialect *maccarone*] (circa 1611)
**:** a small cookie composed chiefly of egg whites, sugar, and ground almonds or coconut

**ma·caw** \\mə-'kȯ\\ *noun* [Portuguese *macau*] (1668)
**:** any of numerous parrots (especially genus *Ara*) of South and Central America including some of the largest and showiest of parrots

**Mac·beth** \\mək-'beth, mak-\\ *noun*
**:** a Scottish general who is the protagonist of Shakespeare's tragedy *Macbeth*

macaw

**Mac·ca·bees** \\'ma-kə-(,)bēz\\ *noun plural* [Greek *Makkabaioi*, from plural of *Makkabaios*, surname of Judas Maccabaeus 2d century B.C. Jewish patriot] (1702)
**1 :** a priestly family leading a Jewish revolt begun in 168 B.C. against Hellenism and Syrian rule and reigning over Palestine from 142 B.C. to 63 B.C.
**2** *singular in construction* **:** either of two narrative and historical books included in the Roman Catholic canon of the Old Testament and in the Protestant Apocrypha — see BIBLE table
**— Mac·ca·be·an** \\,ma-kə-'bē-ən\\ *adjective*

**¹mace** \\'mās\\ *noun* [Middle English, from Middle French *macis*, from Latin *macir*, an East Indian spice, from Greek *makir*] (13th century)
**:** an aromatic spice consisting of the dried external fibrous covering of a nutmeg

**²mace** *noun* [Middle English, from Old French, from (assumed) Vulgar Latin *mattia*; akin to Latin *mateola* mallet] (14th century)
**1 a :** a heavy often spiked staff or club used especially in the Middle Ages for breaking armor **b :** a club used as a weapon
**2 a :** an ornamental staff borne as a symbol of authority before a public official or a legislative body **b :** one who carries a mace

**³mace** *transitive verb* **maced; mac·ing** (1968)
**:** to attack with the liquid Mace

**Mace** \\'mās\\ *trademark*
— used for a temporarily disabling liquid usually used as a spray

**ma·cé·doine** \\,ma-sə-'dwän\\ *noun* [French, from *Macédoine* Macedonia; perhaps from the mixture of ethnic groups in Macedonia] (1820)
**1 :** a confused mixture **:** MEDLEY
**2 :** a mixture of fruits or vegetables served as a salad or cocktail or in a jellied dessert or used in a sauce or as a garnish

**Mac·e·do·nian** \\,ma-sə-'dō-nyən, -nē-ən\\ *noun* (1582)
**1 :** a native or inhabitant of Macedonia
**2 :** the Slavic language of modern Macedonia
**3 :** the language of ancient Macedonia of uncertain affinity but generally assumed to be Indo-European

**mac·er·ate** \\'ma-sə-,rāt\\ *verb* **-at·ed; -at·ing** [Latin *maceratus*, past participle of *macerare* to soften, steep] (1547)
*transitive verb*
**1 :** to cause to waste away by or as if by excessive fasting
**2 :** to cause to become soft or separated into constituent elements by or as if by steeping in fluid; *broadly* **:** STEEP, SOAK
*intransitive verb*
**:** to soften and wear away especially as a result of being wetted or steeped
**— mac·er·a·tion** \\,ma-sə-'rā-shən\\ *noun*
**— mac·er·a·tor** \\'ma-sə-,rā-tər\\ *noun*

---

◇ **WORD HISTORY**
**macadam**    *Macadam* is named after the Scottish engineer John Loudon McAdam (1756–1836). Concerned about the poor condition of Scotland's roads at the end of the 18th century, McAdam studied the problem for a decade and a half. He concluded that roads constructed of small, similarly sized fragments of stone could withstand years of heavy traffic. Upon his appointment as surveyor-general of roads in Bristol in 1815, he began to put his theories into practice. By 1823 the superiority of his paving process was generally recognized, and four years later he was named surveyor-general of roads for Great Britain and was even offered a knighthood. His name evolved into a lowercase, generic noun, the spelling eventually undergoing alteration to produce a more conventional-looking word. McAdam's name also survives, albeit rather covertly, in *tarmac*, shortened from *tarmacadam*, which designates a road surfacing that incorporates a tar binder.

---

**Mach** \'mäk\ *noun* [Mach number] (1946)
**:** a usually high speed expressed by a Mach number ⟨an airplane flying at *Mach* 2⟩
**Mach·a·bees** \'ma-kə-(,)bēz\ *noun plural but singular in construction* [Middle English, from Late Latin *Machabaei*, modification of Greek *Makkabaioi*] (14th century)
**:** MACCABEES
**mâche** \'mäsh\ *noun* [French, perhaps alteration of French dialect *pomache*, from (assumed) Vulgar Latin *pomasca*, from Latin *pomum* fruit] (1961)
**:** CORN SALAD
**ma·chete** \mə-'she-tē, -'che-; -'shet\ *noun* [Spanish] (1598)
**:** a large heavy knife used for cutting sugarcane and underbrush and as a weapon
**Ma·chi·a·vel·lian** \,ma-kē-ə-'ve-lē-ən, -'vel-yən\ *adjective* [Niccolo *Machiavelli*] (1579)
**1 :** of or relating to Machiavelli or Machiavellianism
**2 :** suggesting the principles of conduct laid down by Machiavelli; *specifically* **:** marked by cunning, duplicity, or bad faith
— **Machiavellian** *noun*
**Ma·chi·a·vel·lian·ism** \-'ve-lē-ə-,ni-zəm, -'vel-yə-,ni-zəm\ *noun* (1626)
**:** the political theory of Machiavelli; *especially* **:** the view that politics is amoral and that any means however unscrupulous can justifiably be used in achieving political power
**ma·chic·o·la·tion** \mə-,chi-kə-'lā-shən\ *noun* [Medieval Latin *machicolare* to furnish with machicolations, from Middle French *machicoller*, from *machicoleis* machicolation, from *macher* to crush + *col* neck, from Latin *collum* — more at COLLAR] (1788)
**1 a :** an opening between the corbels of a projecting parapet or in the floor of a gallery or roof of a portal for discharging missiles upon assailants below — see BATTLEMENT illustration **b :** a gallery or parapet containing such openings
**2 :** construction imitating medieval machicolation
— **ma·chic·o·lat·ed** \mə-'chi-kə-,lā-təd\ *adjective*
**mach·i·nate** \'ma-kə-,nāt, 'ma-shə-\ *verb* **-nat·ed; -nat·ing** [Latin *machinatus*, past participle of *machinari*, from *machina* machine, contrivance] (1600)
*intransitive verb*
**:** to plan or plot especially to do harm
*transitive verb*
**:** to scheme or contrive to bring about **:** PLOT
— **mach·i·na·tor** \-,nā-tər\ *noun*
**mach·i·na·tion** \,ma-kə-'nā-shən, ,ma-shə-\ *noun* (15th century)
**1 :** an act of machinating
**2 :** a scheming or crafty action or artful design intended to accomplish some usually evil end ⟨backstage *machinations* and power plays that have dominated the film industry —Peter Bogdanovich⟩
*synonym* see PLOT
**¹ma·chine** \mə-'shēn\ *noun, often attributive* [Middle French, from Latin *machina*, from Greek *mēchanē* (Doric dialect *machana*), from *mēchos* means, expedient — more at MAY] (circa 1545)
**1 a** *archaic* **:** a constructed thing whether material or immaterial **b :** CONVEYANCE, VEHICLE; *especially* **:** AUTOMOBILE **c** *archaic* **:** a military engine **d :** any of various apparatuses formerly used to produce stage effects **e** (1) **:** an assemblage of parts that transmit forces, motion, and energy one to another in a predetermined manner (2) **:** an instrument (as a lever) designed to transmit or modify the application of power, force, or motion **f :** a mechanically, electrically, or electronically operated device for performing a task ⟨a calculating *machine*⟩ ⟨a card-sorting *machine*⟩ **g :** a coin-operated device ⟨a cigarette *machine*⟩ **h :** MACHINERY — used with *the* or in plural

**2 a :** a living organism or one of its functional systems **b :** a person or organization that resembles a machine (as in being methodical, tireless, or unemotional) **c** (1) **:** a combination of persons acting together for a common end along with the agencies they use (2) **:** a highly organized political group under the leadership of a boss or small clique
**3 :** a literary device or contrivance introduced for dramatic effect
**²machine** *transitive verb* **ma·chined; ma·chin·ing** (circa 1864)
**:** to process by or as if by machine; *especially* **:** to reduce or finish by or as if by turning, shaping, planing, or milling by machine-operated tools
— **ma·chin·abil·i·ty** *also* **ma·chine·abil·i·ty** \-,shē-nə-'bi-lə-tē\ *noun*
— **ma·chin·able** *also* **ma·chine·able** \-'shē-nə-bəl\ *adjective*
**ma·chine–gun** \mə-'shēn-,gən\ *adjective* (1906)
**:** characterized by rapidity and sharpness **:** RAPID-FIRE ⟨a comic's *machine-gun* delivery⟩
**machine gun** *noun* (1870)
**:** a gun for sustained rapid fire that uses bullets; *broadly* **:** an automatic weapon
— **machine–gun** *verb*
— **machine gun·ner** *noun*
**machine language** *noun* (1949)
**1 :** the set of symbolic instruction codes usually in binary form that is used to represent operations and data in a machine (as a computer)
**2 :** ASSEMBLY LANGUAGE
**ma·chine·like** \mə-'shēn-,līk\ *adjective* (circa 1712)
**:** resembling a machine especially in regularity of action or stereotyped uniformity of product
**machine pistol** *noun* (1940)
**:** a usually small submachine gun
**machine–readable** *adjective* (1961)
**:** directly usable by a computer ⟨*machine-readable* text⟩
**ma·chin·ery** \mə-'shē-nə-rē, -'shēn-rē\ *noun, plural* **-er·ies** (1687)
**1 a :** machines in general or as a functioning unit **b :** the working parts of a machine
**2 :** the means or system by which something is kept in action or a desired result is obtained ⟨the *machinery* of government⟩ ⟨genetic *machinery* of cells⟩
**machine shop** *noun* (1827)
**:** a workshop in which work is machined to size and assembled
**machine tool** *noun* (1861)
**:** a machine designed for shaping solid work
**ma·chin·ist** \mə-'shē-nist\ *noun* (circa 1706)
**1 a :** a worker who fabricates, assembles, or repairs machinery **b :** a craftsman skilled in the use of machine tools **c :** one who operates a machine
**2** *archaic* **:** a person in charge of the mechanical aspects of a theatrical production
**3 :** a warrant officer who supervises machinery and engine operation
**ma·chis·mo** \mä-'chēz-(,)mō, mə-, -'kēz-, -'kiz-, -'chiz-\ *noun* [Spanish, from *macho*] (1948)
**1 :** a strong sense of masculine pride **:** an exaggerated masculinity
**2 :** an exaggerated or exhilarating sense of power or strength
**Mach number** \'mäk-\ *noun* [Ernst *Mach* (died 1916) Austrian physicist] (1937)
**:** a number representing the ratio of the speed of a body (as an aircraft) to the speed of sound in a surrounding medium (as air)
**¹ma·cho** \'mä-(,)chō\ *adjective* [Spanish, literally, male, from Latin *masculus* — more at MASCULINE] (1928)
**:** characterized by machismo **:** aggressively virile
**²macho** *noun, plural* **machos** (1951)
**1 :** one who exhibits machismo
**2 :** MACHISMO
**mack** *variant of* MAC

**mack·er·el** \'ma-k(ə-)rəl\ *noun, plural* **mackerel** *or* **mackerels** [Middle English *makerel*, from Middle French] (14th century)
**1 :** a scombroid bony fish (*Scomber scombrus*) of the North Atlantic that is green above with dark blue bars and silvery below and is one of the most important food fishes
**2 :** any of a family (Scombridae) of fishes including the common mackerel; *especially* **:** a comparatively small member of this group as distinguished from a bonito or tuna

mackerel 1

**mackerel shark** *noun* (1819)
**:** any of a family (Lamnidae) of large pelagic sharks including the great white shark and mako sharks; *especially* **:** PORBEAGLE
**mackerel sky** *noun* (1669)
**:** a sky covered with rows of altocumulus or cirrocumulus clouds resembling the patterns on a mackerel's back
**mack·i·naw** \'ma-kə-,nȯ\ *noun* [*Mackinaw* (Mackinac), trading post at site of Mackinaw City, Michigan] (1836)
**1 :** a heavy woolen blanket formerly distributed by the U.S. government to the Indians
**2 a :** a heavy cloth of wool or wool and other fibers often with a plaid design and usually heavily napped and felted **b :** a short coat of mackinaw or similar heavy fabric
**Mackinaw trout** *noun* (1840)
**:** a large dark North American char (*Salvelinus namaycush*) that is an important commercial food fish in northern lakes
**mack·in·tosh** *also* **mac·in·tosh** \'ma-kən-,täsh\ *noun* [Charles *Macintosh* (died 1843) Scottish chemist & inventor] (1836)
**1** *chiefly British* **:** RAINCOAT
**2 :** a lightweight waterproof fabric originally of rubberized cotton
**Mac·lau·rin's series** \mə-'klȯr-ən(z)-\ *noun* [Colin *Maclaurin* (died 1746) Scottish mathematician] (circa 1909)
**:** a Taylor's series of the form

$$f(x) = f(0) + \frac{f'(0)}{1!}x + \frac{f''(0)}{2!}x^2 + \dots + \frac{f^{[n]}(0)}{n!}x^n + \dots$$

in which the expansion is about the reference point zero — called also *Maclaurin series*
**ma·cle** \'ma-kəl\ *noun* [French, wide-meshed net, lozenge voided, macle, from Old French *mesh*, lozenge voided, of Germanic origin; akin to Old High German *masca* mesh — more at MESH] (1801)
**1 :** a twin crystal
**2 :** a flat often triangular diamond that is usually a twin crystal
— **ma·cled** \'ma-kəld\ *adjective*
**ma·con** *also* **mâ·con** \ma-'kōⁿ\ *noun, often capitalized* [French *mâcon*, from *Mâcon*, France] (1863)
**:** a dry red or white wine produced in the area around Mâcon, France
**Mac·Pher·son strut** \mək-'fir-sᵊn-, -'fər-\ *noun* [Earle S. *MacPherson* (died 1960) American engineer] (1975)
**:** a component of an automobile suspension consisting of a shock absorber mounted within a coil spring
**macr-** *or* **macro-** *combining form* [French & Latin, from Greek *makr-, makro-* long, from *makros* — more at MEAGER]
**1 :** long ⟨*macrobiotic*⟩
**2 :** large ⟨*macromolecule*⟩
**mac·ra·mé** *also* **mac·ra·me** \'ma-krə-,mā\ *noun* [French or Italian; French *macramé*,

from Italian *macramè*, from Turkish *makrama* napkin, towel, from Arabic *miqramah* coverlet] (1869)
**:** a coarse lace or fringe made by knotting threads or cords in a geometrical pattern; *also*
**:** the art of tying knots in patterns

**¹mac·ro** \'ma-(,)krō\ *adjective* [*macr-*] (1923)
**1 :** being large, thick, or exceptionally prominent
**2 a :** of, involving, or intended for use with relatively large quantities or on a large scale **b** **:** of or relating to macroeconomics
**3 :** GROSS 1c

**²macro** *noun, plural* **macros** [short for *macroinstruction*] (1959)
**:** a single computer instruction that stands for a sequence of operations

**mac·ro·ag·gre·gate** \,ma-krō-'a-gri-gət\ *noun* (1926)
**:** a relatively large particle (as of soil or a protein)
— **mac·ro·ag·gre·gat·ed** \-,gā-təd\ *adjective*

**mac·ro·bi·ot·ic** \-bī-'ä-tik, -bē-\ *adjective* (1965)
**:** of, relating to, or being an extremely restricted diet (as one containing chiefly whole grains) that is held by its advocates to promote health and well-being although it may actually be deficient in essential nutrients (as fats)

**mac·ro·cosm** \'ma-krə-,kä-zəm\ *noun* [French *macrocosme*, from Medieval Latin *macrocosmos*, from Latin *macr-* + Greek *kosmos* order, universe] (1600)
**1 :** the great world **:** UNIVERSE
**2 :** a complex that is a large-scale reproduction of one of its constituents
— **mac·ro·cos·mic** \,ma-krə-'käz-mik\ *adjective*
— **mac·ro·cos·mi·cal·ly** \-mi-k(ə-)lē\ *adverb*

**mac·ro·cy·clic** \,ma-krō-'si-klik, -'sī-\ *adjective* (1936)
**:** containing or being a chemical ring that consists usually of 15 or more atoms

**mac·ro·cyte** \'ma-krə-,sīt\ *noun* [International Scientific Vocabulary] (circa 1889)
**:** an exceptionally large red blood cell occurring chiefly in anemias
— **mac·ro·cyt·ic** \,ma-krə-'si-tik\ *adjective*

**mac·ro·cy·to·sis** \,ma-krə-sī-'tō-səs, -krə-sə-\ *noun, plural* **-to·ses** \-,sēz\ [New Latin] (circa 1893)
**:** the occurrence of macrocytes in the blood

**mac·ro·eco·nom·ics** \'ma-krō-,e-kə-'nä-miks, -,ē-kə-\ *noun plural but usually singular in construction* (1948)
**:** a study of economics in terms of whole systems especially with reference to general levels of output and income and to the interrelations among sectors of the economy — compare MICROECONOMICS
— **mac·ro·eco·nom·ic** \-mik\ *adjective*

**mac·ro·evo·lu·tion** \'ma-krō-,e-və-'lü-shən *also* -,ē-və-\ *noun* (1939)
**:** evolution that results in relatively large and complex changes (as in species formation)
— **mac·ro·evo·lu·tion·ary** \-shə-,ner-ē\ *adjective*

**mac·ro·fos·sil** \'ma-krō-,fä-səl\ *noun* (1937)
**:** a fossil large enough to be observed by direct inspection

**mac·ro·ga·mete** \,ma-krō-'ga-,mēt *also* -gə-'mēt\ *noun* [International Scientific Vocabulary] (1899)
**:** the larger and usually female gamete of a heterogamous organism

**mac·ro·glob·u·lin** \-'glä-byə-lən\ *noun* [International Scientific Vocabulary] (1952)
**:** a highly polymerized globulin (as IgM) of high molecular weight

**mac·ro·glob·u·li·ne·mia** \-,glä-byə-lə-'nē-mē-ə\ *noun* [New Latin] (1949)
**:** a disorder characterized by increased blood serum viscosity and the presence of macroglobulins in the serum

**— mac·ro·glob·u·li·ne·mic** \-mik\ *adjective*

**mac·ro·in·struc·tion** \,ma-krō-in-'strək-shən\ *noun* (1959)
**:** MACRO

**macro lens** *noun* [*macr-*, from the fact that the focal length is greater than normal] (1961)
**:** a camera lens designed to focus at very short distances with up to life-size magnification of the image

**mac·ro·lep·i·dop·tera** \'ma-krō-,le-pə-'däp-tə-rə\ *noun plural* [New Latin] (1882)
**:** lepidoptera (as butterflies, skippers, saturniids, noctuids, and geometrids) that include most of the large forms and none of the minute ones

**mac·ro·mere** \'ma-krə-,mir\ *noun* (1877)
**:** a large blastomere — see BLASTULA illustration

**mac·ro·mol·e·cule** \,ma-krō-'mä-li-,kyü(ə)l\ *noun* [International Scientific Vocabulary] (circa 1929)
**:** a very large molecule (as of a protein or rubber)
— **mac·ro·mo·lec·u·lar** \-mə-'le-kyə-lər\ *adjective*

**ma·cron** \'mā-,krän, 'ma-, -krən\ *noun* [Greek *makron*, neuter of *makros* long] (1851)
**:** a mark ‾ placed over a vowel to indicate that the vowel is long or placed over a syllable or used alone to indicate a stressed or long syllable in a metrical foot

**mac·ro·nu·cle·us** \,ma-krō-'nü-klē-əs, -'nyü-\ *noun* [New Latin] (1892)
**:** a relatively large densely staining nucleus of most ciliate protozoans that is derived from micronuclei and controls various nonreproductive functions
— **mac·ro·nu·cle·ar** \,mak-rō-'nü-klē-ər, -'nyü-, ÷-kyə-lər\ *adjective*

**mac·ro·nu·tri·ent** \-'nü-trē-ənt, -'nyü-\ *noun* (1942)
**:** a chemical element (as nitrogen, phosphorus, or potassium) of which relatively large quantities are essential to the growth and health of a plant

**mac·ro·phage** \'ma-krə-,fāj\ *noun* [International Scientific Vocabulary] (1890)
**:** a phagocytic tissue cell of the reticuloendothelial system that may be fixed or freely motile, is derived from a monocyte, and functions in the protection of the body against infection and noxious substances — called also *histiocyte*
— **mac·ro·phag·ic** \,ma-krə-'fa-jik\ *adjective*

**mac·ro·pho·tog·ra·phy** \,ma-krō-fə-'tä-grə-fē\ *noun* (1889)
**:** the making of photographs in which the object is either unmagnified or slightly magnified up to a limit often of about 10 diameters
— **mac·ro·pho·to·graph** \-'fō-tə-,graf\ *noun*

**mac·ro·phyte** \'ma-krə-,fīt\ *noun* (circa 1909)
**:** a member of the macroscopic plant life especially of a body of water
— **mac·ro·phyt·ic** \,ma-krə-'fi-tik\ *adjective*

**mac·rop·ter·ous** \ma-'kräp-tə-rəs\ *adjective* [Greek *makropteros*, from *makr-* + *pteron* wing — more at FEATHER] (circa 1836)
**:** having long or large wings

**mac·ro·scale** \'ma-krō-,skāl\ *noun* (1931)
**:** a large often macroscopic scale

**mac·ro·scop·ic** \,ma-krō-'skä-pik\ *adjective* [International Scientific Vocabulary *macr-* + *-scopic* (as in *microscopic*)] (1872)
**1 :** large enough to be observed by the naked eye
**2 :** considered in terms of large units or elements
— **mac·ro·scop·i·cal·ly** \-pi-k(ə-)lē\ *adverb*

**mac·ro·struc·ture** \'ma-krō-,strək-chər\ *noun* (circa 1899)

**:** the structure (as of metal, a body part, or the soil) revealed by visual examination with little or no magnification
— **mac·ro·struc·tur·al** \,ma-krō-'strək-chə-rəl, -'strək-shə-rəl\ *adjective*

**mac·u·la** \'ma-kyə-lə\ *noun, plural* **-lae** \-,lē, -,lī\ *also* **-las** [Middle English, from Latin] (14th century)
**1 :** SPOT, BLOTCH; *especially* **:** MACULE
**2 :** an anatomical structure (as the macula lutea) having the form of a spot differentiated from surrounding tissues
— **mac·u·lar** \-lər\ *adjective*

**macula lu·tea** \-'lü-tē-ə\ *noun, plural* **mac·ulae lu·te·ae** \-tē-,ē, -tē-,ī\ [New Latin, literally, yellow spot] (1848)
**:** a small yellowish area lying slightly lateral to the center of the retina that constitutes the region of maximum visual acuity — called also *yellow spot*

**mac·u·late** \'ma-kyə-,lāt\ *or* **mac·u·lat·ed** \-,lā-təd\ *adjective* [Latin *maculatus*, past participle of *maculare* to stain, from *macula*] (15th century)
**1 :** marked with spots **:** BLOTCHED
**2 :** IMPURE, BESMIRCHED

**mac·u·la·tion** \,ma-kyə-'lā-shən\ *noun* (15th century)
**1** *archaic* **:** the state of being spotted
**2 a :** a blemish in the form of a discrete spot ⟨acne scars and *maculations*⟩ **b :** the arrangement of spots and markings on an animal or plant

**mac·ule** \'ma-(,)kyü(ə)l\ *noun* [French, from Latin *macula*] (1863)
**:** a patch of skin that is altered in color but usually not elevated and that is a characteristic feature of various diseases (as smallpox)

**ma·cum·ba** \mə-'küm-bə\ *noun* [Brazilian Portuguese] (1939)
**:** a polytheistic religion of African origin involving syncretistic elements and practiced mainly by Brazilian blacks in urban areas

**¹mad** \'mad\ *adjective* **mad·der; mad·dest** [Middle English *medd, madd*, from Old English *gemǣd*, past participle of (assumed) *gemǣdan* to madden, from *gemād* silly, mad; akin to Old High German *gimeit* foolish, crazy] (before 12th century)
**1 :** disordered in mind **:** INSANE
**2 a :** completely unrestrained by reason and judgment ⟨driven *mad* by the pain⟩ **b :** incapable of being explained or accounted for ⟨a *mad* decision⟩
**3 :** carried away by intense anger **:** FURIOUS ⟨*mad* at myself⟩ ⟨*mad* about the delay⟩
**4 :** carried away by enthusiasm or desire ⟨*mad* about horses⟩ ⟨*mad* for the boy next door⟩
**5 :** affected with rabies **:** RABID
**6 :** marked by wild gaiety and merriment **:** HILARIOUS
**7 :** intensely excited **:** FRANTIC ⟨*mad* with jealousy⟩
**8 :** marked by intense and often chaotic activity **:** WILD ⟨a *mad* scramble⟩
— **mad·dish** \'ma-dish\ *adjective*

**²mad** *verb* **mad·ded; mad·ding** (14th century)
**:** MADDEN

**³mad** *noun* (1834)
**1 :** a fit or mood of bad temper
**2 :** ANGER, FURY

**Mad·a·gas·car periwinkle** \,ma-də-'gas-kər-\ *noun* [*Madagascar*, Africa] (1821)
**:** ¹PERIWINKLE 1b

**mad·am** \'ma-dəm\ *noun, plural* **madams** [Middle English, from Middle French *ma dame*, literally, my lady] (14th century)

**1** *plural* **mes·dames** \mā-'däm, -'dam\ **:** LA-DY — used without a name as a form of respectful or polite address to a woman
**2 :** MISTRESS 1 — used as a title formerly with the given name but now with the surname or especially with a designation of rank or office ⟨*Madam* Chairman⟩ ⟨*Madam* President⟩
**3 :** the female head of a house of prostitution
**4 :** the female head of a household **:** WIFE
**ma·dame** \mə-'dam, ma-'\, *before a surname also* 'ma-dəm\ *noun* [French, from Old French *ma dame*] (1674)
**1** *plural* **mes·dames** \mā-'däm, -'dam\ — used as a title equivalent to *Mrs.* for a married woman not of English-speaking nationality
**2** *plural* **madames :** MADAM 3
**mad–brained** \'mad-'brānd\ *adjective* (1562) **:** RASH, HOTHEADED
**mad·cap** \'mad-,kap\ *adjective* (1588) **:** marked by capriciousness, recklessness, or foolishness
— **madcap** *noun*
**mad·den** \'ma-d°n\ *verb* **mad·dened; mad·den·ing** \'mad-niŋ, 'ma-d°n-iŋ\ (1735)
*intransitive verb*
**:** to become or act as if mad
*transitive verb*
**1 :** to drive mad **:** CRAZE
**2 :** to make intensely angry **:** ENRAGE
**maddening** *adjective* (1822)
**1 :** tending to craze
**2 a :** tending to infuriate **b :** tending to vex **:** IRRITATING
— **mad·den·ing·ly** \-lē\ *adverb*
**mad·der** \'ma-dər\ *noun* [Middle English, from Old English *mædere;* akin to Old High German *matara* madder] (before 12th century)
**1 :** a Eurasian herb (*Rubia tinctorum* of the family Rubiaceae, the madder family) with whorled leaves and small yellowish panicled flowers succeeded by berries; *broadly* **:** any of several related herbs (genus *Rubia*)
**2 a :** the root of the Eurasian madder used formerly in dyeing; *also* **:** an alizarin dye prepared from it **b :** a moderate to strong red
**mad·ding** \'ma-diŋ\ *adjective* (1579)
**:** acting in a frenzied manner ⟨the *madding* crowd⟩
**made** \'mād\ *adjective* [Middle English, from past participle of *maken* to make] (14th century)
**1 a :** FICTITIOUS, INVENTED ⟨a *made* excuse⟩ **b :** artificially produced **c :** put together of various ingredients ⟨a *made* dish⟩
**2 :** assured of success ⟨a *made* man⟩ — usually used in the phrase *have it made*
**Ma·dei·ra** \mə-'dir-ə, -'der-\ *noun* [Portuguese, from *Madeira* Islands] (1596)
**:** an amber-colored fortified wine from Madeira; *also* **:** a similar wine made elsewhere
**mad·e·leine** \'ma-d°l-ən, ,ma-d°l-'än\ *noun* [French, perhaps from *Madeleine* Paumier, 19th century French pastry cook] (1845)
**1 :** a small rich shell-shaped cake
**2 :** one that evokes a memory
**ma·de·moi·selle** \,mad-mwə-'zel, ,ma-də-, -mə-'zel, *sometimes* mam-'zel\ *noun, plural* **ma·de·moi·selles** \-'zelz\ *or* **mes·de·moi·selles** \,mād-mwə-'zel, ,mā-də-, -mə-'zel\ [Middle English *madamoiselle*, from Middle French, from Old French *ma damoisele*, literally, my (young) lady] (15th century)
**1 :** an unmarried French girl or woman — used as a title equivalent to *Miss* for an unmarried woman not of English-speaking nationality
**2 :** a French governess
**3 :** SILVER PERCH a
**made–to–order** *adjective* (circa 1908)
**1 :** produced to supply a special or an individual demand **:** CUSTOM-MADE
**2 :** ideally suited (as to a particular purpose) ⟨a ground ball *made-to-order* for a double play⟩
**made–up** \'mā-'dəp\ *adjective* (1607)
**1 :** fancifully conceived or falsely devised

**2 :** fully manufactured
**3 :** marked by the use of makeup
**mad·house** \'mad-,haús\ *noun* (1687)
**1 :** a place where insane persons are detained and treated
**2 :** a place of uproar or confusion
**Mad·i·son Avenue** \'ma-də-sən-\ *noun* [*Madison Avenue*, New York City, former center of the American advertising business] (1952)
**:** the American advertising industry
**mad·ly** \'mad-lē\ *adverb* (13th century)
**1 :** in a mad manner
**2 :** to an extreme or excessive degree ⟨*madly* in love⟩
**mad·man** \'mad-,man, -mən\ *noun* (14th century)
**:** a man who is or acts as if insane
**mad money** *noun* (1922)
**:** money that a woman carries to pay her fare home in case a date ends in a quarrel; *also* **:** money set aside for an emergency or personal use
**mad·ness** \'mad-nəs\ *noun* (14th century)
**1 :** the quality or state of being mad: as **a :** RAGE **b :** INSANITY **c :** extreme folly **d :** ECSTASY, ENTHUSIASM
**2 :** any of several ailments of animals marked by frenzied behavior; *specifically* **:** RABIES
**Ma·don·na** \mə-'dä-nə\ *noun* [Italian, from Old Italian *ma donna*, literally, my lady] (1584)
**1** *archaic* **:** LADY — used as a form of respectful address
**2** *obsolete* **:** an Italian lady
**3 a :** VIRGIN MARY **b :** an artistic depiction (as a painting or statue) of the Virgin Mary
**Madonna lily** *noun* (1877)
**:** a widely cultivated lily (*Lilium candidum*) with bell-shaped to broad funnel-shaped white flowers
**ma·dras** \'ma-drəs; mə-'dras, -'dräs\ *noun* [*Madras*, India] (circa 1830)
**1 :** a large silk or cotton kerchief usually of bright colors that is often worn as a turban
**2 a :** a fine plain-woven shirting and dress fabric usually of cotton with varied designs (as plaid) in bright colors or in white **b :** a light open usually cotton fabric with a heavy design used for curtains
**mad·re·pore** \'ma-drə-,pōr, -,pȯr\ *noun* [French *madrépore*, from Italian *madrepora*, from *madre* mother (from Latin *mater*) + *poro* pore (from Latin *porus*) — more at MOTHER] (1751)
**:** any of various stony reef-building corals (order Madreporaria) of tropical seas that assume a variety of branching, encrusting, or massive forms
— **mad·re·po·ri·an** \,ma-drə-'pōr-ē-ən, -'pȯr-\ *adjective or noun*
— **mad·re·por·ic** \-'pōr-ik, -'pȯr-\ *adjective*
**mad·re·por·ite** \'ma-drə-,pōr-,īt, -,pȯr-\ *noun* [International Scientific Vocabulary *madrepore* + ¹-*ite* (segment); from the resemblances of the perforations to those of a madrepore] (1877)
**:** a perforated or porous body that is situated at the distal end of the stone canal in echinoderms
**mad·ri·gal** \'ma-dri-gəl\ *noun* [Italian *madrigale*, probably from Medieval Latin *matricale*, from neuter of (assumed) *matricalis* simple, from Late Latin, of the womb, from Latin *matric-, matrix* womb, from *mater* mother] (1588)
**1 :** a medieval short lyrical poem in a strict poetic form
**2 a :** a complex polyphonic unaccompanied vocal piece on a secular text developed especially in the 16th and 17th centuries **b :** PART-SONG; *especially* **:** GLEE
— **mad·ri·gal·ian** \,ma-drə-'ga-lē-ən, -'gā-\ *adjective*
— **mad·ri·gal·ist** \'ma-dri-gə-list\ *noun*

**ma·dri·lene** \,ma-drə-'len, -'län\ *noun* [French (*consommé*) *madrilène*, literally, Madrid consommé] (1907)
**:** a consommé flavored with tomato
**ma·dro·na** *or* **ma·dro·ne** *or* **ma·dro·no** \mə-'drō-nə\ *noun* [Spanish *madroño*] (1841)
**:** any of several evergreen trees (genus *Arbutus*) of the heath family; *especially* **:** one (*A. menziesii*) of the Pacific coast of North America with smooth bark, thick shining leaves, and edible red berries
**ma·du·ro** \mə-'dur-(,)ō\ *noun, plural* **-ros** [Spanish, from *maduro* ripe, from Latin *maturus* — more at MATURE] (1850)
**:** a dark-colored relatively strong cigar
**mad·wom·an** \'mad-,wü-mən\ *noun* (15th century)
**:** a woman who is or acts as if insane
**mad·wort** \-,wərt, -,wȯrt\ *noun* (1597)
**1 :** ALYSSUM 1
**2 :** a low hairy annual herb (*Asperugo procumbens*) of the borage family with blue flowers and a root used as a substitute for madder
**Mae·ce·nas** \mi-'sē-nəs\ *noun* [Latin, from Gaius *Maecenas* (died 8 B.C.) Roman statesman & patron of literature] (1542)
**:** a generous patron especially of literature or art
**mael·strom** \'mā(ə)l-strəm, -,sträm\ *noun* [obsolete Dutch (now *maalstroom*), from *malen* to grind + *strom* stream] (1682)
**1 :** a powerful often violent whirlpool sucking in objects within a given radius
**2 :** something resembling a maelstrom in turbulence
**mae·nad** \'mē-,nad\ *noun* [Latin *maenad-, maenas*, from Greek *mainad-, mainas*, from *mainesthai* to be mad; akin to Greek *menos* spirit — more at MIND] (1579)
**1 :** a woman participant in orgiastic Dionysian rites **:** BACCHANTE
**2 :** an unnaturally excited or distraught woman
— **mae·nad·ic** \mē-'na-dik\ *adjective*
**mae·sto·so** \mī-'stō-(,)sō, -(,)zō\ *adjective or adverb* [Italian, from Latin *majestosus*, from *majestas* majesty] (circa 1724)
**:** majestic and stately — used as a direction in music
**mae·stro** \'mī-(,)strō\ *noun, plural* **mae·stros** *or* **mae·stri** \-,strē\ [Italian, literally, master, from Latin *magister* — more at MASTER] (1724)
**:** a master usually in an art; *especially* **:** an eminent composer, conductor, or teacher of music
**Mae West** \'mā-'west\ *noun* [*Mae West* (died 1980) American actress noted for her full figure] (1940)
**:** an inflatable life jacket in the form of a collar extending down the chest that was worn by fliers in World War II
**maf·fick** \'ma-fik\ *intransitive verb* [back-formation from *Mafeking Night*, English celebration of the lifting of the siege of Mafeking, South Africa, May 17, 1900] (1900)
**:** to celebrate with boisterous rejoicing and hilarious behavior
**Ma·fia** \'mä-fē-ə, 'ma-\ *noun* [*Mafia, Maffia*, a Sicilian secret criminal society, from Italian dialect (Sicily)] (1875)
**1 a :** a secret criminal society of Sicily or Italy **b :** a similarly conceived criminal organization in the U.S.; *also* **:** a similar organization elsewhere ⟨the Japanese *Mafia*⟩ **c :** a criminal organization associated with a particular traffic ⟨the cocaine *Mafia*⟩
**2** *often not capitalized* **:** a group of people likened to the Mafia; *especially* **:** a group of people of similar interests or backgrounds prominent in a particular field or enterprise **:** CLIQUE
**maf·ic** \'ma-fik\ *adjective* [New Latin *magne*sium + Latin *f*errum iron + English -*ic*] (1912)
**:** of, relating to, or being a group of usually dark-colored minerals rich in magnesium and iron

**ma·fi·o·so** \ˌmä-fē-'ō-(ˌ)sō, ˌma-, -(ˌ)zō\ *noun, plural* **-si** \-(ˌ)sē, -(ˌ)zē\ [Italian, from *Mafia*] (1875)
: a member of the Mafia or a mafia

**mag** \'mag\ *noun* (1796)
: MAGAZINE

**mag·a·zine** \'ma-gə-ˌzēn, ˌma-gə-'\ *noun* [Middle French, from Old Provençal, from Arabic *makhāzin*, plural of *makhzan* storehouse] (1583)
**1** : a place where goods or supplies are stored : WAREHOUSE
**2** : a room in which powder and other explosives are kept in a fort or a ship
**3** : the contents of a magazine: as **a** : an accumulation of munitions of war **b** : a stock of provisions or goods
**4 a** : a periodical containing miscellaneous pieces (as articles, stories, poems) often illustrated **b** : a similar section of a newspaper usually appearing on Sunday **c** : a radio or television program presenting usually several short segments on a variety of topics
**5** : a supply chamber: as **a** : a holder in or on a gun for cartridges to be fed into the gun chamber **b** : a lightproof chamber for films or plates on a camera or for film on a motion-picture projector ◆

**mag·a·zin·ist** \-ˌzē-nist, -'zē-\ *noun* (1821)
: a person who writes for or edits a magazine

**mag·da·len** \'mag-də-lən\ *or* **mag·da·lene** \-ˌlēn\ *noun, often capitalized* [Mary *Magdalen* or *Magdalene* woman healed by Jesus of evil spirits (Luke 8:2), considered identical with a reformed prostitute (Luke 7:36–50)] (1697)
**1** : a reformed prostitute
**2** : a house of refuge or reformatory for prostitutes

**Mag·da·le·ni·an** \ˌmag-də-'lē-nē-ən\ *adjective* [French *magdalénien*, from *La Madeleine*, rock shelter in southwest France] (1885)
: of or relating to an Upper Paleolithic culture characterized by flint, bone, and ivory implements, carving, and paintings

**mage** \'māj\ *noun* [Middle English, from Latin *magus*] (14th century)
: MAGUS

**Mag·el·lan·ic Cloud** \ˌma-jə-'la-nik-, *chiefly British* ˌma-gə-\ *noun* [Ferdinand *Magellan*] (circa 1686)
: either of the two small galaxies that appear as conspicuous patches of light near the south celestial pole and are companions to the Milky Way galaxy

**Ma·gen Da·vid** \'mȯ-gən-'dȯ-vid, -'də-; 'mō-gən-'dā-vəd\ *noun* [Hebrew *māghēn Dāwīdh*, literally, shield of David] (circa 1904)
: a hexagram used as a symbol of Judaism

**ma·gen·ta** \mə-'jen-tə\ *noun* [*Magenta*, Italy] (1860)
**1** : FUCHSIN
**2** : a deep purplish red

**mag·got** \'ma-gət\ *noun* [Middle English *mathek, magotte*, of Scandinavian origin; akin to Old Norse *mathkr* maggot; akin to Old English *matha* maggot] (14th century)
**1** : a soft-bodied legless grub that is the larva of a dipterous insect (as the housefly)
**2** : a fantastic or eccentric idea : WHIM
— **mag·goty** \-gə-tē\ *adjective*

**magi** *plural of* MAGUS

**¹Ma·gi·an** \'mā-jē-ən\ *noun* (1578)
: MAGUS

**²Ma·gi·an** \-jē-ən, -ˌjī-\ *adjective* (1716)
: of or relating to the Magi
— **Ma·gi·an·ism** \-ə-ˌni-zəm\ *noun*

**¹mag·ic** \'ma-jik\ *noun* [Middle English *magique*, from Middle French, from Latin *magice*, from Greek *magikē*, feminine of *magikos* Magian, magical, from *magos* magus, sorcerer, of Iranian origin; akin to Old Persian *maguš* sorcerer] (14th century)
**1 a** : the use of means (as charms or spells) believed to have supernatural power over natural forces **b** : magic rites or incantations

**2 a** : an extraordinary power or influence seemingly from a supernatural source **b** : something that seems to cast a spell : ENCHANTMENT
**3** : the art of producing illusions by sleight of hand

**²magic** *adjective* (14th century)
**1** : of or relating to magic
**2 a** : having seemingly supernatural qualities or powers **b** : giving a feeling of enchantment
— **mag·i·cal** \'ma-ji-kəl\ *adjective*
— **mag·i·cal·ly** \-ji-k(ə-)lē\ *adverb*

**³magic** *transitive verb* **mag·icked; mag·ick·ing** (1906)
: to produce, remove, or influence by magic

**magic bullet** *noun* (1940)
: a substance or therapy capable of destroying pathogens (as bacteria or cancer cells) without deleterious side effects

**ma·gi·cian** \mə-'ji-shən\ *noun* (14th century)
**1** : one skilled in magic; *especially* : SORCERER
**2** : one who performs tricks of illusion and sleight of hand

**magic lantern** *noun* (1696)
: an early form of optical projector of still pictures using a transparent slide

**Magic Marker** *trademark*
— used for a felt-tipped pen

**magic realism** *noun* (1954)
: painting in a meticulously realistic style of imaginary or fantastic scenes or images
— **magic realist** *noun*

**magic square** *noun* (circa 1704)
: a square containing a number of integers arranged so that the sum of the numbers is the same in each row, column, and main diagonal and often in some or all of the other diagonals

**magic squares**

**Ma·gi·not Line** \'ma-zhə-ˌnō-, 'ma-jə-\ *noun* [André *Maginot* (died 1932) French minister of war] (1936)
: a line of defensive fortifications built before World War II to protect the eastern border of France but easily outflanked by German invaders

**mag·is·te·ri·al** \ˌma-jə-'stir-ē-əl\ *adjective* [Late Latin *magisterialis* of authority, from *magisterium* office of a master, from *magister*] (1632)
**1** (1) : of, relating to, or having the characteristics of a master or teacher : AUTHORITATIVE (2) : marked by an overbearingly dignified or assured manner or aspect **b** : of, relating to, or required for a master's degree
**2** : of or relating to a magistrate or a magistrate's office or duties
**synonym** *see* DICTATORIAL
— **mag·is·te·ri·al·ly** \-ē-ə-lē\ *adverb*

**mag·is·te·ri·um** \ˌma-jə-'stir-ē-əm\ *noun* [Latin] (1866)
: teaching authority especially of the Roman Catholic Church

**mag·is·tra·cy** \'ma-jə-strə-sē\ *noun, plural* **-cies** (circa 1585)
**1** : the state of being a magistrate
**2** : the office, power, or dignity of a magistrate
**3** : a body of magistrates
**4** : the district under a magistrate

**mag·is·tral** \'ma-jə-strəl, mə-'jis-trəl\ *adjective* [Late Latin *magistralis*, from Latin *magistr-, magister*] (1605)
: MAGISTERIAL 1a
— **mag·is·tral·ly** \-ē\ *adverb*

**mag·is·trate** \'ma-jə-ˌstrāt, -strət\ *noun* [Middle English *magestrat*, from Latin *magistratus* magistracy, magistrate, from *magistr-, magister* master, political superior — more at MASTER] (14th century)
: an official entrusted with administration of the laws: as **a** : a principal official exercising governmental powers over a major political

unit (as a nation) **b** : a local official exercising administrative and often judicial functions **c** : a local judiciary official having limited original jurisdiction especially in criminal cases
— **mag·is·trat·i·cal** \ˌma-jə-'stra-ti-kəl\ *adjective*
— **mag·is·trat·i·cal·ly** \-k(ə-)lē\ *adverb*

**magistrate's court** *noun* (1867)
**1** : POLICE COURT
**2** : a court that has minor civil and criminal jurisdiction

**mag·is·tra·ture** \'ma-jə-ˌstrā-chər, -strə-ˌchür\ *noun* (1672)
: MAGISTRACY

**mag·lev** \'mag-lev\ *noun, often attributive* [*magnetic levitation*] (1969)
**1** : the use of the physical properties of magnetic fields generated by superconducting magnets to cause an object (as a vehicle) to float above a solid surface
**2** : a train utilizing maglev technology

**mag·ma** \'mag-mə\ *noun* [Middle English, from Latin *magmat-, magma*, from Greek, thick unguent, from *massein* to knead — more at MINGLE] (15th century)
**1** *archaic* : DREGS, SEDIMENT
**2** : a thin pasty suspension (as of a precipitate in water)
**3** : molten rock material within the earth from which igneous rock results by cooling
— **mag·mat·ic** \mag-'ma-tik\ *adjective*

**Mag·na Car·ta** *or* **Mag·na Char·ta** \'mag-nə-'kär-tə\ *noun* [Middle English, from Medieval Latin, literally, great charter] (15th century)
**1** : a charter of liberties to which the English barons forced King John to give his assent in June 1215 at Runnymede
**2** : a document constituting a fundamental guarantee of rights and privileges

**mag·na cum lau·de** \ˌmäg-nə-(ˌ)kùm-'lau̇-də, -'lau̇-dē; ˌmag-nə-ˌkəm-'lȯ-dē\ *adverb or adjective* [Latin] (1900)
: with great distinction ⟨graduated *magna cum laude*⟩ — compare CUM LAUDE, SUMMA CUM LAUDE

**mag·na·nim·i·ty** \ˌmag-nə-'ni-mə-tē\ *noun, plural* **-ties** (14th century)
**1** : the quality of being magnanimous : loftiness of spirit enabling one to bear trouble

◇ WORD HISTORY

**magazine** In Arabic *makhzan* denotes a storehouse. From the plural form *makhāzin* medieval French borrowed *magasin* in the 14th century, most likely via Old Provençal. English in turn borrowed the word from French in the 16th century, in the same sense. The term then underwent various specializations of meaning, depending on what was being stored. An early development was the application of the word to storage places for weapons or gunpowder; a further extension applied *magazine* not to a building but to a chamber or clip to hold cartridges in a firearm. *Magazine* was also used in the titles of books with the implication "storehouse of knowledge." The word was thus used in 1731 for the first issue of *The Gentleman's Magazine: or, Monthly Intelligencer*, the suggestion being that the publication would present the general reader each month with a collection or "storehouse" of stories and articles. Other periodical publications began using *magazine* in their titles, and the word was soon used generically for a certain kind of periodical.

\ə\ **abut** \ᵊ\ **kitten** \ər\ **further** \a\ **ash** \ā\ **ace**
\ä\ **mop, mar** \au̇\ **out** \ch\ **chin** \e\ **bet** \ē\ **easy**
\g\ **go** \i\ **hit** \ī\ **ice** \j\ **job** \ŋ\ **sing** \ō\ **go**
\ȯ\ **law** \ȯi\ **boy** \th\ **thin** \t͟h\ **the** \ü\ **loot** \u̇\ **foot**
\y\ **yet** \zh\ **vision** *see also* Guide to Pronunciation

calmly, to disdain meanness and pettiness, and to display a noble generosity
**2 :** a magnanimous act
**mag·nan·i·mous** \mag-'na-nə-məs\ *adjective* [Latin *magnanimus,* from *magnus* great + *animus* spirit — more at MUCH, ANIMATE] (1584)
**1 :** showing or suggesting a lofty and courageous spirit ⟨the irreproachable lives and *magnanimous* sufferings of their followers — Joseph Addison⟩
**2 :** showing or suggesting nobility of feeling and generosity of mind ⟨too sincere for dissimulation, too *magnanimous* for resentment —Ellen Glasgow⟩
**— mag·nan·i·mous·ly** *adverb*
**— mag·nan·i·mous·ness** *noun*
**mag·nate** \'mag-ˌnāt, -nət\ *noun* [Middle English *magnates,* plural, from Late Latin, from Latin *magnus*] (15th century)
**:** a person of rank, power, influence, or distinction often in a specified area
**mag·ne·sia** \mag-'nē-shə, -zhə\ *noun* [New Latin, from *magnes carneus,* a white earth, literally, flesh magnet] (1755)
**:** MAGNESIUM OXIDE — compare MILK OF MAGNESIA
**— mag·ne·sian** \-shən, -zhən\ *adjective*
**mag·ne·site** \'mag-nə-ˌsīt\ *noun* (1815)
**:** native magnesium carbonate used especially in making refractories and magnesium oxide
**mag·ne·sium** \mag-'nē-zē-əm, -zhəm\ *noun* [New Latin, from *magnesia*] (1812)
**:** a silver-white light malleable ductile metallic element that occurs abundantly in nature and is used in metallurgical and chemical processes, in photography, signaling, and pyrotechnics because of the intense white light it produces on burning, and in construction especially in the form of light alloys — see ELEMENT table
**magnesium carbonate** *noun* (1903)
**:** a carbonate of magnesium; *especially* **:** a white crystalline salt $MgCO_3$ that occurs naturally as dolomite and magnesite
**magnesium chloride** *noun* (circa 1910)
**:** a bitter deliquescent salt $MgCl_2$ used especially as a source of magnesium metal
**magnesium hydroxide** *noun* (circa 1909)
**:** a slightly alkaline crystalline compound $Mg(OH)_2$ used especially as a laxative and gastric antacid
**magnesium oxide** *noun* (circa 1909)
**:** a white highly infusible compound MgO used especially in refractories, cements, insulation, and fertilizers, in rubber manufacture, and in medicine as an antacid and mild laxative
**magnesium sulfate** *noun* (circa 1890)
**:** a sulfate of magnesium: as **a :** a white salt $MgSO_4$ used in medicine and in industry **b :** EPSOM SALTS
**mag·net** \'mag-nət\ *noun* [Middle English *magnete,* from Middle French, from Latin *magnet-, magnes,* from Greek *magnēs (lithos),* literally, stone of Magnesia, ancient city in Asia Minor] (15th century)
**1 a :** LODESTONE **b :** a body having the property of attracting iron and producing a magnetic field external to itself; *specifically* **:** a mass of iron, steel, or alloy that has this property artificially imparted
**2 :** something that attracts ⟨a box-office *magnet*⟩
**magnet-** *or* **magneto-** *combining form* [Latin *magnet-, magnes*]
**1 :** magnetic force ⟨*magnet*ometer⟩
**2 :** magnetism **:** magnetic ⟨*magneto*electric⟩ ⟨*magneto*n⟩
**3 :** magnetoelectric ⟨*magneto*resistance⟩
**4 :** magnetosphere ⟨*magneto*pause⟩
**¹mag·net·ic** \mag-'ne-tik\ *adjective* (1611)
**1 :** possessing an extraordinary power or ability to attract ⟨a *magnetic* personality⟩

**2 a :** of or relating to a magnet or to magnetism **b :** of, relating to, or characterized by the earth's magnetism **c :** magnetized or capable of being magnetized **d :** actuated by magnetic attraction
**— mag·net·i·cal·ly** \-ti-k(ə-)lē\ *adverb*
**²magnetic** *noun* (1654)
**:** a magnetic substance
**magnetic bubble** *noun* (1969)
**:** a tiny movable magnetized cylindrical volume in a thin amorphous or crystalline magnetic material that along with other like volumes can be used to represent a bit of information (as in a computer)
**magnetic disk** *noun* (circa 1960)
**:** DISK 4c
**magnetic equator** *noun* (1832)
**:** an imaginary line roughly parallel to the geographical equator and passing through those points where a magnetic needle has no dip
**magnetic field** *noun* (1845)
**:** the portion of space near a magnetic body or a current-carrying body in which the magnetic forces due to the body or current can be detected
**magnetic flux** *noun* (1896)
**:** lines of force used to represent magnetic induction
**magnetic mirror** *noun* (1952)
**:** a magnetic field that confines a plasma by reflecting ions of the plasma back toward the main plasma concentration
**magnetic moment** *noun* (1865)
**:** a vector quantity that is a measure of the torque exerted on a magnetic system (as a bar magnet or dipole) when placed in a magnetic field and that for a magnet is the product of the distance between its poles and the strength of either pole
**magnetic north** *noun* (1812)
**:** the northerly direction in the earth's magnetic field indicated by the north-seeking pole of a compass needle
**magnetic pole** *noun* (1701)
**1 :** either of two small regions which are located respectively in the polar areas of the northern and southern hemispheres and toward which a compass needle points from any direction throughout adjacent regions; *also* **:** either of two comparable regions on a celestial body
**2 :** either of the poles of a magnet
**magnetic quantum number** *noun* (1923)
**:** an integer that expresses the component of the quantized angular momentum of an electron, atom, or molecule in the direction of an externally applied magnetic field
**magnetic recording** *noun* (1945)
**:** the process of recording sound, data (as for a computer), or a television program by producing varying local magnetization of a moving tape or disc
**— magnetic recorder** *noun*
**magnetic resonance** *noun* (1903)
**:** the response of electrons, atoms, molecules, or nuclei to various discrete radiation frequencies as a result of space quantization in a magnetic field
**magnetic resonance imaging** *noun* (1984)
**:** a noninvasive diagnostic technique that produces computerized images of internal body tissues and is based on nuclear magnetic resonance of atoms within the body induced by the application of radio waves — abbreviation MRI
**magnetic storm** *noun* (1860)
**:** a marked temporary disturbance of the earth's magnetic field held to be related to sunspots
**magnetic tape** *noun* (1937)
**:** a thin ribbon (as of plastic) coated with a magnetic material on which information (as sound or television images) may be stored
**mag·ne·tise** *British variant of* MAGNETIZE
**mag·ne·tism** \'mag-nə-ˌti-zəm\ *noun* (1616)

**1 a :** a class of physical phenomena that include the attraction for iron observed in lodestone and a magnet, are inseparably associated with moving electricity, are exhibited by both magnets and electric currents, and are characterized by fields of force **b :** a science that deals with magnetic phenomena
**2 :** an ability to attract or charm
**mag·ne·tite** \'mag-nə-ˌtīt\ *noun* (1851)
**:** a black isometric mineral of the spinel group that is an oxide of iron and an important iron ore
**mag·ne·ti·za·tion** \ˌmag-nə-tə-'zā-shən\ *noun* (1801)
**:** an instance of magnetizing or the state of being magnetized; *also* **:** the degree to which a body is magnetized
**mag·ne·tize** \'mag-nə-ˌtīz\ *transitive verb* **-tized; -tiz·ing** (1801)
**1 :** to induce magnetic properties in
**2 :** to attract like a magnet **:** CHARM
**— mag·ne·tiz·able** \-ˌtī-zə-bəl\ *adjective*
**— mag·ne·tiz·er** *noun*
**mag·ne·to** \mag-'nē-(ˌ)tō\ *noun, plural* **-tos** (1882)
**:** a magnetoelectric machine; *especially* **:** an alternator with permanent magnets used to generate current for the ignition in an internal-combustion engine
**mag·ne·to·elec·tric** \-ˌnē-tō-ə-'lek-trik, -ˌne-\ *adjective* (1831)
**:** relating to or characterized by electromotive forces developed by magnetic means
**mag·ne·to·flu·id·dy·nam·ics** \-ˌnē-tō-ˌflü-ə-dī-'na-miks, -ˌne-, -də-\ *noun plural but singular or plural in construction* (1962)
**:** the study of magnetohydrodynamic phenomena
**mag·ne·to·graph** \-ˌgraf\ *noun* (1847)
**:** an automatic instrument for recording measurements of a magnetic field (as of the earth or the sun)
**mag·ne·to·hy·dro·dy·nam·ic** \ˌmag-ˌnē-tō-ˌhī-drə-dī-'na-mik, -ˌne-, -də-\ *adjective* (1943)
**:** of, relating to, or being phenomena arising from the motion of electrically conducting fluids (as plasmas) in the presence of electric and magnetic fields
**— mag·ne·to·hy·dro·dy·nam·ics** \-miks\ *noun plural but singular or plural in construction*
**mag·ne·tom·e·ter** \ˌmag-nə-'tä-mə-tər\ *noun* (1827)
**:** an instrument used to detect the presence of a metallic object or to measure the intensity of a magnetic field
**— mag·ne·to·met·ric** \ˌmag-ˌnē-tə-'me-trik, -ˌne-\ *adjective*
**— mag·ne·tom·e·try** \ˌmag-nə-'tä-mə-trē\ *noun*
**mag·ne·to·mo·tive force** \mag-ˌnē-tə-'mō-tiv-, -ˌne-\ *noun* (1883)
**:** a force that is the cause of a flux of magnetic induction
**mag·ne·ton** \'mag-nə-ˌtän\ *noun* [International Scientific Vocabulary *magnet-* + ²-*on*] (1911)
**:** a unit of the quantized magnetic moment of a particle (as an atom)
**mag·ne·to·op·tic** \mag-ˌnē-tō-'äp-tik, -ˌne-\ *also* **mag·ne·to·op·ti·cal** \-ti-kəl\ *adjective* (1848)
**:** of or relating to the influence of a magnetic field upon light
**— mag·ne·to·op·tics** \-tiks\ *noun plural but singular or plural in construction*
**mag·ne·to·pause** \mag-'nē-tə-ˌpȯz, -ˌne-\ *noun* (1962)
**:** the outer boundary of a magnetosphere
**mag·ne·to·re·sis·tance** \-ˌnē-tō-ri-'zis-tən(t)s, -ˌne-\ *noun* (1927)
**:** a change in electrical resistance due to the presence of a magnetic field
**mag·ne·to·sphere** \mag-'nē-tə-ˌsfir, -ˌne-\ *noun* (1959)

: a region of space surrounding a celestial object (as the earth or a star) that is dominated by the object's magnetic field so that charged particles are trapped in it
— **mag·ne·to·spher·ic** \-,nē-tə-'sfir-ik, -'sfer-\ *adjective*

**mag·ne·to·stat·ic** \mag-,nē-tō-'sta-tik, -,ne-\ *adjective* (1893)
: of, relating to, or being a stationary magnetic field

**mag·ne·to·stric·tion** \-'strik-shən\ *noun* [International Scientific Vocabulary *magnet-* + *-striction* (as in *constriction*)] (1896)
: the change in the dimensions of a ferromagnetic body caused by a change in its state of magnetization
— **mag·ne·to·stric·tive** \-'strik-tiv\ *adjective*
— **mag·ne·to·stric·tive·ly** *adverb*

**mag·ne·tron** \'mag-nə-,trän\ *noun* [blend of *magnet* and *-tron*] (1924)
: a diode vacuum tube in which the flow of electrons is controlled by an externally applied magnetic field to generate power at microwave frequencies

**magnet school** *noun* (1968)
: a school with superior facilities and staff and specialized curricula designed to attract pupils from all segments of the community

**mag·nif·ic** \mag-'ni-fik\ *adjective* [Middle French *magnifique*, from Latin *magnificus*] (15th century)
1 : MAGNIFICENT 2
2 : imposing in size or dignity
3 a : SUBLIME, EXALTED b : characterized by grandiloquence : POMPOUS ⟨commenced the conversation in the most *magnific* style —S. T. Coleridge⟩
— **mag·nif·i·cal** \-fi-kəl\ *adjective*
— **mag·nif·i·cal·ly** \-k(ə-)lē\ *adverb*

**mag·nif·i·cat** \mag-'ni-fi-,kat, -,kät; män-'yi-fi-,kät\ *noun* [Middle English, from Latin, magnifies, from *magnificare* to magnify; from the first word of the canticle] (13th century)
1 *capitalized* a : the canticle of the Virgin Mary in Luke 1:46–55 b : a musical setting for the Magnificat
2 : an utterance of praise

**mag·ni·fi·ca·tion** \,mag-nə-fə-'kā-shən\ *noun* (15th century)
1 : the act of magnifying
2 a : the state of being magnified b : the apparent enlargement of an object by an optical instrument — called also *power*

**mag·nif·i·cence** \mag-'ni-fə-sən(t)s, məg-\ *noun* [Middle English, from Middle French, from Latin *magnificentia*, from *magnificus* noble in character, magnificent, from *magnus* great — more at MUCH] (14th century)
1 : the quality or state of being magnificent
2 : splendor of surroundings

**mag·nif·i·cent** \-sənt\ *adjective* (15th century)
1 : great in deed or exalted in place — used only of former famous rulers ⟨Lorenzo the *Magnificent*⟩
2 : marked by stately grandeur and lavishness ⟨a *magnificent* way of life⟩
3 : sumptuous in structure and adornment ⟨a *magnificent* cathedral⟩; *broadly* : strikingly beautiful or impressive ⟨a *magnificent* physique⟩
4 : impressive to the mind or spirit : SUBLIME ⟨*magnificent* prose⟩
5 : exceptionally fine ⟨a *magnificent* day⟩
**synonym** see GRAND
— **mag·nif·i·cent·ly** *adverb*

**mag·nif·i·co** \mag-'ni-fi-,kō\ *noun, plural* **-coes** *or* **-cos** [Italian, from *magnifico*, adjective, magnificent, from Latin *magnificus*] (1573)
1 : a nobleman of Venice
2 : a person of high position

**mag·ni·fi·er** \'mag-nə-,fī(-ə)r\ *noun* (1550)

: one that magnifies; *especially* : a lens or combination of lenses that makes something appear larger

**mag·ni·fy** \'mag-nə-,fī\ *verb* **-fied; -fy·ing** [Middle English *magnifien*, from Middle French *magnifier*, from Latin *magnificare*, from *magnificus*] (14th century)
*transitive verb*
1 a : EXTOL, LAUD b : to cause to be held in greater esteem or respect
2 a : to increase in significance : INTENSIFY b : EXAGGERATE
3 : to enlarge in fact or in appearance
*intransitive verb*
: to have the power of causing objects to appear larger than they are

**mag·nil·o·quence** \mag-'ni-lə-kwən(t)s\ *noun* [Latin *magniloquentia*, from *magniloquus* magniloquent, from *magnus* + *loqui* to speak] (circa 1623)
: the quality or state of being magniloquent

**mag·nil·o·quent** \-kwənt\ *adjective* [back-formation from *magniloquence*] (circa 1656)
: speaking in or characterized by a high-flown often bombastic style or manner
— **mag·nil·o·quent·ly** *adverb*

**mag·ni·tude** \'mag-nə-,tüd, -,tyüd\ *noun* [Middle English, from Latin *magnitudo*, from *magnus*] (15th century)
1 a : great size or extent b (1) : spatial quality : SIZE (2) : QUANTITY, NUMBER
2 : the importance, quality, or caliber of something
3 : a number representing the intrinsic or apparent brightness of a celestial body on a logarithmic scale in which an increase of one unit corresponds to a reduction in the brightness of light by a factor of 2.512
4 : a numerical quantitative measure expressed usually as a multiple of a standard unit

**mag·no·lia** \mag-'nōl-yə\ *noun* [New Latin, from Pierre *Magnol* (died 1715) French botanist] (1748)
: any of a genus (*Magnolia*) of the family Magnoliaceae, the magnolia family) of American and Asian shrubs and trees with entire evergreen or deciduous leaves and usually showy white, yellow, rose, or purple flowers usually appearing in early spring

magnolia

**mag·num** \'mag-nəm\ *noun* [Latin, neuter of *magnus* great] (1788)
: a large wine bottle holding about 1.5 liters

**mag·num opus** \'mag-nəm-'ō-pəs\ *noun* [Latin] (1791)
: a great work; *especially* : the greatest achievement of an artist or writer

¹**mag·pie** \'mag-,pī\ *noun* [*Mag* (nickname for *Margaret*) + ¹*pie*] (1598)
1 : any of various birds (especially *Pica pica*) related to the jays but having a long graduated tail and black-and-white or brightly colored plumage
2 : a person who chatters noisily
3 : one who collects indiscriminately

²**magpie** *adjective* (1808)
1 : collected indiscriminately : MISCELLANEOUS ⟨*magpie* compilations of unrelated tidbits —Helen R. Cross⟩
2 : given to indiscriminate collecting : ACQUISITIVE ⟨what possible *magpie* instinct had impelled me to retain them —S. J. Perelman⟩

**mag tape** \'mag-\ *noun* (1966)
: MAGNETIC TAPE

**ma·guey** \mə-'gā\ *noun* [Spanish, from Taino] (1589)
1 : any of various fleshy-leaved agaves (as the century plant)
2 : any of several hard fibers derived from magueys; *especially* : CANTALA

**ma·gus** \'mā-gəs\ *noun, plural* **ma·gi** \'mā-,jī\ [Latin, from Greek *magos* — more at MAGIC] (1621)
1 a : a member of a hereditary priestly class among the ancient Medes and Persians b *often capitalized* : one of the traditionally three wise men from the East paying homage to the infant Jesus
2 : MAGICIAN, SORCERER

**Mag·yar** \'mag-,yär, 'mäg-; 'mä-,jär\ *noun* [Hungarian] (1797)
1 : a member of the dominant people of Hungary
2 : HUNGARIAN 2
— **Magyar** *adjective*

**ma·ha·ra·ja** *or* **ma·ha·ra·jah** \,mä-hə-'rä-jə, -'rä-zhə\ *noun* [Sanskrit *mahārāja*, from *mahat* great + *rājan* raja; akin to Latin *rex* king — more at MUCH, ROYAL] (1698)
: a Hindu prince ranking above a raja

**ma·ha·ra·ni** *or* **ma·ha·ra·nee** \-'rä-nē\ *noun* [Hindi *mahārānī*, from *mahā* great (from Sanskrit *mahat*) + *rānī* rani] (circa 1855)
1 : the wife of a maharaja
2 : a Hindu princess ranking above a rani

**ma·ha·ri·shi** \,mä-hə-'rē-shē, -hä-, -'ri-\ *noun* [Sanskrit *mahārṣi*, from *mahat* + *ṛṣi* sage and poet] (1785)
: a Hindu teacher of mystical knowledge

**ma·hat·ma** \mə-'hät-mə, -'hat-\ *noun* [Sanskrit *mahātman*, from *mahātman* great-souled, from *mahat* + *ātman* soul — more at ATMAN] (1923)
1 : a person to be revered for high-mindedness, wisdom, and selflessness
2 : a person of great prestige in a field of endeavor

**Ma·ha·ya·na** \,mä-hə-'yä-nə\ *noun* [Sanskrit *mahāyāna*, literally, great vehicle] (1855)
: a liberal and theistic branch of Buddhism comprising sects chiefly in China and Japan, recognizing a large body of scripture in addition to the Pali canon, and teaching social concern and universal salvation — compare THERAVADA
— **Ma·ha·ya·nist** \-'yä-nist\ *noun or adjective*
— **Ma·ha·ya·nis·tic** \-yä-'nis-tik\ *adjective*

**Mah·di** \'mä-dē\ *noun* [Arabic *mahdīy*, literally, one rightly guided] (1800)
1 : the expected messiah of Muslim tradition
2 : a Muslim leader who assumes a messianic role
— **Mah·dism** \'mä-,di-zəm\ *noun*
— **Mah·dist** \'mä-dist\ *noun*

**Ma·hi·can** \mə-'hē-kən\ *noun, plural* **Mahican** *or* **Mahicans** [Mahican] (circa 1614)
1 : a member of an American Indian people of the upper Hudson River valley
2 : the extinct Algonquian language of the Mahican people

**ma·hi·ma·hi** \,mä-hē-'mä-(,)hē\ *noun* [Hawaiian, Tahitian, & Marquesan] (1943)
: the flesh of a dolphin (*Coryphaena hippurus*) used for food; *also* : the fish

**mah–jongg** *or* **mah·jong** \,mä-'zhäŋ, -'jäŋ, -'zhóŋ, -'jóŋ, 'mä-,\ *noun* [from *Mah-Jongg*, a trademark] (1920)
: a game of Chinese origin usually played by four persons with 144 tiles that are drawn and discarded until one player secures a winning hand

**mahl·stick** \'mól-\ *variant of* MAULSTICK

**ma·hoe** \mə-'hō, 'mä-,\ *noun* [French *maho*, from Taino] (1666)
: either of two tropical hibiscus trees (*Hibiscus elatus* and *H. tiliaceus*)

**ma·hog·a·ny** \mə-'hä-gə-nē\ *noun, plural* **-nies** [origin unknown] (circa 1660)

---

\ə\ abut \ᵊ\ kitten \ər\ further \a\ ash \ā\ ace
\ä\ mop, mar \aú\ out \ch\ chin \e\ bet \ē\ easy
\g\ go \i\ hit \ī\ ice \j\ job \ŋ\ sing \ō\ go
\ó\ law \ói\ boy \th\ thin \th\ the \ü\ loot \u̇\ foot
\y\ yet \zh\ vision *see also* Guide to Pronunciation

**1** : the wood of any of various chiefly tropical trees (family Meliaceae, the mahogany family): **a** (1) : the durable yellowish brown to reddish brown usually moderately hard and heavy wood of a West Indian tree (*Swietenia mahagoni*) that is widely used for cabinetwork and fine finish work (2) : a wood similar to mahogany from a congeneric tree (especially *S. macrophylla*) **b** (1) : the rather hard heavy usually odorless wood of any of several African trees (genus *Khaya*) (2) : the rather lightweight cedar-scented wood of any of several African trees (genus *Entandrophragma*) that varies in color from pinkish to deep reddish brown
**2** : any of various woods resembling or substituted for mahogany obtained from trees of the mahogany family
**3** : a tree that yields mahogany
**4** : a moderate reddish brown
**ma·ho·nia** \mə-'hō-nē-ə\ *noun* [New Latin, from Bernard McMahon (died 1816) American botanist] (1829)
: any of a genus (*Mahonia*) of American and Asian shrubs (as the Oregon grape) of the barberry family
**ma·hout** \mə-'haút\ *noun* [Hindi *mahāwat*, *mahāut*] (1662)
: a keeper and driver of an elephant
**Mah·rat·ta** *variant of* MARATHA
**maid** \'mād\ *noun* [Middle English *maide*, short for *maiden*] (13th century)
**1** : an unmarried girl or woman especially when young : VIRGIN
**2 a** : MAIDSERVANT **b** : a woman or girl employed to do domestic work
**¹maid·en** \'mā-d°n\ *noun* [Middle English, from Old English *mægden*, *mǣden*, diminutive of *mægeth*; akin to Old High German *magad* maiden, Old Irish *mug* serf] (before 12th century)
**1** : an unmarried girl or woman : MAID
**2** : a former Scottish beheading device resembling the guillotine
**3** : a horse that has never won a race
**²maiden** *adjective* (14th century)
**1 a** (1) : not married ⟨*maiden* aunt⟩ (2) : VIRGIN **b** *of a female animal* : never yet mated (2) : never having borne young
**2** : of, relating to, or befitting a maiden
**3** : FIRST, EARLIEST ⟨*maiden* voyage⟩ ⟨*maiden* flight of a spacecraft⟩
**maid·en·hair fern** \-,har-, -,her-\ *noun* (1833)
: any of a genus (*Adiantum*) of ferns with delicate palmately branched fronds — called also *maidenhair*
**maidenhair tree** *noun* (1773)
: GINKGO
**maid·en·head** \'mā-d°n-,hed\ *noun* [Middle English *maidenhed*, from *maiden* + *-hed* -hood; akin to Middle English *-hod* -hood] (13th century)
**1** : the quality or state of being a maiden : VIRGINITY
**2** : HYMEN
**maid·en·hood** \-,húd\ *noun* (before 12th century)
: the quality, state, or time of being a maiden
**maid·en·li·ness** \-lē-nəs\ *noun* (1555)
: conduct or traits befitting a maiden
**maid·en·ly** \-lē\ *adjective* (15th century)
: of, resembling, or suitable to a maiden
**maiden name** *noun* (1689)
: the surname of a woman before she marries
**maid·hood** \'mād-,húd\ *noun* (before 12th century)
: MAIDENHOOD
**maid-in-wait·ing** \'mā-d°n-'wā-tiŋ\ *noun*, *plural* **maids-in-wait·ing** \'mādz-\ (1953)

maidenhair fern

: a young woman of a queen's or princess's household appointed to attend her
**Maid Mar·i·an** \-'mer-ē-ən, -'mar-\ *noun*
: a companion of Robin Hood in some forms of his legend
**maid of honor** (circa 1586)
**1** : an unmarried lady usually of noble birth whose duty it is to attend a queen or a princess
**2** : a bride's principal unmarried wedding attendant
**maid·ser·vant** \'mād-,sər-vənt\ *noun* (14th century)
: a female servant
**ma·ieu·tic** \mā-'yü-tik, mī-\ *adjective* [Greek *maieutikos* of midwifery] (1655)
: relating to or resembling the Socratic method of eliciting new ideas from another
**¹mail** \'mā(ə)l\ *noun* [Middle English *male*, *maille*, from Old English *māl* agreement, pay, from Old Norse *māl* speech, agreement; akin to Old English *mǣl* speech] (before 12th century)
*chiefly Scottish* : PAYMENT, RENT
**²mail** *noun*, *often attributive* [Middle English *male*, from Old French, of Germanic origin; akin to Old High German *malaha* bag] (13th century)
**1** *chiefly Scottish* : BAG, WALLET
**2 a** : something sent or carried in the postal system **b** : a conveyance that transports mail **c** : messages sent electronically to an individual (as through a computer system)
**3** : a nation's postal system — often used in plural
**³mail** *transitive verb* (1827)
: to send by mail : POST
— **mail·abil·i·ty** \,mā-lə-'bi-lə-tē\ *noun*
— **mail·able** \'mā-lə-bəl\ *adjective*
**⁴mail** *noun* [Middle English *maille*, from Middle French, from Latin *macula* spot, mesh] (14th century)
**1** : armor made of metal links or sometimes plates
**2** : a hard enclosing covering of an animal (as a tortoise)
— **mailed** \'mā(ə)ld\ *adjective*
**mail·bag** \'mā(ə)l-,bag\ *noun* (1812)
**1** : a letter carrier's shoulder bag
**2** : a pouch used in the shipment of mail
**mail·box** \-,bäks\ *noun* (1872)
**1** : a public box for deposit of outgoing mail
**2** : a box at or near a dwelling for the occupant's mail
**3** : a computer file in which electronic mail is collected
**mail carrier** *noun* (1790)
: LETTER CARRIER
**mail drop** *noun* (1945)
**1** : an address used in transmitting secret communications
**2** : a receptacle or a slot for deposit of mail
**mai·le** \'mī-lē\ *noun* [Hawaiian] (1903)
: a Pacific island vine (*Alyxia olivaeformis*) of the dogbane family with fragrant leaves and bark that are used for decoration and in Hawaii for leis
**mailed fist** *noun* (1897)
: a threat of armed or overbearing force
**mail·er** \'mā-lər\ *noun* (1884)
**1** : one that mails
**2** : a container for mailing something
**3** : something (as an advertisement) sent by mail
**Mail·gram** \'māl-,gram\ *trademark*
— used for a message sent by wire to a post office that delivers it to the addressee
**mail·ing** \'mā-liŋ\ *noun* (1946)
: the mail dispatched at one time by a sender
**mail·lot** \mī-'ō, mä-'yō\ *noun* [French] (1888)
**1** : tights for dancers or gymnasts
**2** : JERSEY 2
**3** : a woman's one-piece bathing suit
**mail·man** \'mā(ə)l-,man\ *noun* (1881)
: a man who delivers mail — called also *postman*
**mail order** *noun* (1867)

: an order for goods that is received and filled by mail
— **mail-or·der** \-,or-dər\ *adjective*
**¹maim** \'mām\ *transitive verb* [Middle English *maynhen*, *maymen*, from Old French *maynier* — more at MAYHEM] (14th century)
**1** : to commit the felony of mayhem upon
**2** : to mutilate, disfigure, or wound seriously
☆
— **maim·er** *noun*
**²maim** *noun* (14th century)
**1** *obsolete* : serious physical injury; *especially* : loss of a member of the body
**2** *obsolete* : a serious loss
**¹main** \'mān\ *noun* [in sense 1, from Middle English, from Old English *mægen*; akin to Old High German *magan* strength, Old English *magan* to be able; in other senses, from ²*main* or by shortening — more at MAY] (before 12th century)
**1** : physical strength : FORCE — used in the phrase *with might and main*
**2 a** : MAINLAND **b** : HIGH SEA
**3** : the chief part : essential point ⟨they are in the *main* well-trained⟩
**4** : a pipe, duct, or circuit which carries the combined flow of tributary branches of a utility system
**5 a** : MAINMAST **b** : MAINSAIL
**²main** *adjective* [Middle English, from Old English *mægen-*, from *mægen* strength] (15th century)
**1** : CHIEF, PRINCIPAL ⟨the *main* idea⟩
**2** : fully exerted : SHEER ⟨*main* force⟩ ⟨by *main* strength⟩
**3** *obsolete* : of or relating to a broad expanse (as of sea)
**4** : connected with or located near the mainmast or mainsail
**5** : expressing the chief predication in a complex sentence ⟨the *main* clause⟩
**main chance** *noun* (1584)
: the best chance for personal or financial gain ⟨kept an eye on the *main chance*⟩
**Maine coon** *noun* (1935)
: any of a breed of large long-haired domestic cats that have a very full tapered tail — called also *coon cat, Maine cat*
**main·frame** \'mān-,frām\ *noun* (circa 1964)
: a computer with its cabinet and internal circuits; *also* : a large fast computer that can handle multiple tasks concurrently

**Maine coon**

**main·land** \'mān-,land, -lənd\ *noun* (14th century)
: a continent or the main part of a continent as distinguished from an offshore island or sometimes from a cape or peninsula

---

☆ **SYNONYMS**
**Maim, cripple, mutilate, batter, mangle** mean to injure so severely as to cause lasting damage. MAIM implies the loss or injury of a bodily member through violence ⟨*maimed* by a shark⟩. CRIPPLE implies the loss or serious impairment of an arm or leg ⟨*crippled* for life in an accident⟩. MUTILATE implies the cutting off or removal of an essential part of a person or thing thereby impairing its completeness, beauty, or function ⟨a tree *mutilated* by inept pruning⟩. BATTER implies a series of blows that bruise deeply, deform, or mutilate ⟨an old ship *battered* by fierce storms⟩. MANGLE implies a tearing or crushing that leaves deep extensive wounds ⟨a soldier's leg *mangled* by shrapnel⟩.

— **main·land·er** \-,lan-dər, -lən-\ *noun*

¹**main·line** \'mān-,līn\ (1938)
*transitive verb*
*slang* : to take by or as if by injecting into a principal vein
*intransitive verb*
*slang* : to mainline a narcotic drug

²**mainline** *adjective* (1941)
: being part of an established group; *also* : being in the mainstream

**main line** *noun* (1841)
**1** : a principal highway or railroad line
**2** *slang* : a principal vein of the circulatory system

**main·ly** \'mān-lē\ *adverb* (13th century)
**1** *obsolete* : in a forceful manner
**2** : for the most part : CHIEFLY

**main man** *noun* (1967)
**1** : best male friend
**2** : a man whose character or work is most admired
**3** : the most reliable or effective performer

**main·mast** \'mān-,mast, -məst\ *noun* (15th century)
: a sailing ship's principal mast usually second from the bow

**mains** \'mānz\ *adjective* (circa 1927)
*British* : of or relating to utility distribution mains ⟨*mains* voltage⟩ ⟨*mains* water⟩

**main·sail** \'mān-,sāl, 'mān(t)-səl\ *noun* (15th century)
: the principal sail on the mainmast — see SAIL illustration

**main sequence** *noun* (1925)
: the group of stars that on a graph of spectrum versus luminosity forms a band comprising 90% of stellar types and that includes stars believed to be representative of the stages a normal star passes through for the majority of its lifetime

**main·sheet** \'mān-,shēt\ *noun* (15th century)
: a rope by which the mainsail is trimmed and secured

**main·spring** \'mān-,spriŋ\ *noun* (1591)
**1** : the chief spring in a mechanism especially of a watch or clock
**2** : the chief or most powerful motive, agent, or cause

**main squeeze** *noun* (circa 1968)
*slang* : one's principal romantic partner

**main·stay** \'mān-,stā\ *noun* (15th century)
**1** : a ship's stay extending from the maintop forward usually to the foot of the foremast
**2** : a chief support

**main stem** *noun* (1832)
: a main trunk or channel: as **a** : the main course of a river or stream **b** : the main street of a city or town

¹**main·stream** \'mān-,strēm\ *noun* (1831)
: a prevailing current or direction of activity or influence
— **mainstream** *adjective*

²**main·stream** \'mān-'strēm\ *transitive verb* (1974)
: to place (as a handicapped child) in regular school classes

**Main Street** *noun* (circa 1743)
**1** : the principal street of a small town
**2 a** : the sections of a country centering about its small towns **b** : a place or environment characterized by materialistic self-complacent provincialism **c** : MIDDLE AMERICA 3
— **Main Street·er** \'mān-,strē-tər\ *noun*

**main·tain** \mān-'tān, mən-\ *transitive verb* [Middle English *mainteinen*, from Old French *maintenir*, from Medieval Latin *manutenēre*, from Latin *manu tenēre* to hold in the hand] (14th century)
**1** : to keep in an existing state (as of repair, efficiency, or validity) : preserve from failure or decline ⟨*maintain* machinery⟩
**2** : to sustain against opposition or danger : uphold and defend ⟨*maintain* a position⟩
**3** : to continue or persevere in : CARRY ON, KEEP UP ⟨couldn't *maintain* his composure⟩

**4 a** : to support or provide for ⟨has a family to *maintain*⟩ **b** : SUSTAIN ⟨enough food to *maintain* life⟩
**5** : to affirm in or as if in argument : ASSERT ⟨*maintained* that the earth is flat⟩ ☆
— **main·tain·abil·i·ty** \-,tā-nə-'bi-lə-tē\ *noun*
— **main·tain·able** \-'tā-nə-bəl\ *adjective*
— **main·tain·er** *noun*

**main·te·nance** \'mānt-nən(t)s, 'mān-tⁿn-ən(t)s\ *noun* [Middle English, from Middle French, from Old French, from *maintenir*] (14th century)
**1** : the act of maintaining : the state of being maintained : SUPPORT
**2** : something that maintains
**3** : the upkeep of property or equipment
**4** : an officious or unlawful intermeddling in a legal suit by assisting either party with means to carry it on

**main·top** \'mān-,täp\ *noun* (15th century)
: a platform about the head of the mainmast of a square-rigged ship

**main–top·mast** \mān-'täp-,mast, -məst\ *noun* (15th century)
: a mast next above the mainmast

**main yard** *noun* (15th century)
: the yard of a mainsail

**mair** \'mār\ *chiefly Scottish variant of* MORE

**mai·son·ette** \,mā-zⁿn-'et, -s°n-\ *noun* [French *maisonnette*, from Old French, diminutive of *maison* house, from Latin *mansion-, mansio* dwelling place — more at MANSION] (1793)
**1** : a small house
**2** : an apartment often on two floors

**maî·tre d'** *or* **mai·tre d'** \,mā-trə-'dē, ,me-, -tər-\ *noun, plural* **maître d's** *or* **maitre d's** \-'dēz\ (1950)
: MAÎTRE D'HÔTEL

**maî·tre d'hô·tel** \,mā-trə-(,)dō-'tel, ,me-; ,māt-dō-, ,met-\ *noun, plural* **maîtres d'hôtel** \*same*\ [French, literally, master of house] (1538)
**1 a** : MAJORDOMO **b** : HEADWAITER
**2** : a sauce of butter, parsley, salt, pepper, and lemon juice — called also *maître d'hôtel butter*

**maize** \'māz\ *noun* [Spanish *maíz*, from Taino *mahiz*] (1555)
: INDIAN CORN

**ma·jes·tic** \mə-'jes-tik\ *adjective* (1601)
: having or exhibiting majesty : STATELY
*synonym* see GRAND
— **ma·jes·ti·cal·ly** \-ti-k(ə-)lē\ *adverb*

**maj·es·ty** \'ma-jə-stē\ *noun, plural* **-ties** [Middle English *maieste*, from Middle French *majesté*, from Latin *majestat-, majestas;* akin to Latin *major* greater] (14th century)
**1** : sovereign power, authority, or dignity
**2** — used in addressing or referring to reigning sovereigns and their consorts ⟨Your *Majesty*⟩ ⟨Her *Majesty's* Government⟩
**3 a** : royal bearing or aspect : GRANDEUR **b** : greatness or splendor of quality or character

**ma·jol·i·ca** \mə-'jä-li-kə\ *also* **ma·iol·i·ca** \-'yä-\ *noun* [Italian *maiolica*, from Old Italian *Maiolica, Maiorica* Majorca] (1555)
**1** : earthenware covered with an opaque tin glaze and decorated on the glaze before firing; *especially* : an Italian ware of this kind
**2** : a 19th century earthenware modeled in naturalistic shapes and glazed in lively colors

¹**ma·jor** \'mā-jər\ *adjective* [Middle English *maiour*, from Latin *major*, comparative of *magnus* great, large — more at MUCH] (15th century)
**1** : greater in dignity, rank, importance, or interest ⟨one of the *major* poets⟩
**2** : greater in number, quantity, or extent ⟨the *major* part of his work⟩
**3** : having attained majority
**4** : notable or conspicuous in effect or scope : CONSIDERABLE ⟨a *major* improvement⟩
**5** : involving grave risk : SERIOUS ⟨a *major* illness⟩

**6** : of or relating to a subject of academic study chosen as a field of specialization
**7 a** : having half steps between the third and fourth and the seventh and eighth degrees ⟨*major* scale⟩ **b** : based on a major scale ⟨*major* key⟩ **c** : equivalent to the distance between the keynote and another tone (except the fourth and fifth) of a major scale ⟨*major* third⟩ **d** : having a major third above the root ⟨*major* triad⟩

²**major** *noun* (1616)
**1** : a person who has attained majority
**2 a** : one that is superior in rank, importance, size, or performance ⟨economic power of the oil *majors*⟩ **b** : a major musical interval, scale, key, or mode
**3** : a commissioned officer in the army, air force, or marine corps ranking above a captain and below a lieutenant colonel
**4 a** : an academic subject chosen as a field of specialization **b** : a student specializing in such a field ⟨a history *major*⟩
**5** *plural* : major league baseball — used with *the*

³**major** *intransitive verb* (1913)
: to pursue an academic major

**major axis** *noun* (1854)
: the axis passing through the foci of an ellipse

**ma·jor·do·mo** \,mā-jər-'dō-(,)mō\ *noun, plural* **-mos** [Spanish *mayordomo* or obsolete Italian *maiordomo*, from Medieval Latin *major domus*, literally, chief of the house] (1589)
**1** : a head steward of a large household (as a palace)
**2** : BUTLER, STEWARD
**3** : a person who speaks, makes arrangements, or takes charge for another

**ma·jor·ette** \,mā-jə-'ret\ *noun* (1940)
: DRUM MAJORETTE 2

**major general** *noun* [French *major général*, from *major*, noun + *général*, adjective, general] (1642)
: a commissioned officer in the army, air force, or marine corps who ranks above a brigadier general and whose insignia is two stars

**major histocompatibility complex** *noun* (1975)
: a group of genes in mammals that function especially in determining the histocompatibility antigens found on cell surfaces

**ma·jor·i·tar·i·an** \mə-,jȯr-ə-'ter-ē-ən, -,jär-\ *noun* (1942)
: a person who believes in or advocates majoritarianism
— **majoritarian** *adjective*

**ma·jor·i·tar·i·an·ism** \-ē-ə-,ni-zəm\ *noun* (1942)
: the philosophy or practice according to which decisions of an organized group should be made by a numerical majority of its members

---

☆ SYNONYMS
**Maintain, assert, defend, vindicate, justify** mean to uphold as true, right, just, or reasonable. MAINTAIN stresses firmness of conviction ⟨steadfastly *maintained* his innocence⟩. ASSERT suggests determination to make others accept one's claim ⟨*asserted* her rights⟩. DEFEND implies maintaining in the face of attack or criticism ⟨*defended* his voting record⟩. VINDICATE implies successfully defending ⟨his success *vindicated* our faith in him⟩. JUSTIFY implies showing to be true, just, or valid by appeal to a standard or to precedent ⟨the action was used to *justify* military intervention⟩.

---

\ə\ abut \°\ kitten \ər\ further \a\ ash \ā\ ace
\ä\ mop, mar \au̇\ out \ch\ chin \e\ bet \ē\ easy
\g\ go \i\ hit \ī\ ice \j\ job \ŋ\ sing \ō\ go
\ȯ\ law \ȯi\ boy \th\ thin \t̲h̲\ the \ü\ loot \u̇\ foot
\y\ yet \zh\ vision    *see also* Guide to Pronunciation

**ma·jor·i·ty** \mə-'jȯr-ə-tē, -'jär-\ *noun, plural* **-ties** (1552) **1** *obsolete* **:** the quality or state of being greater **2 a :** the age at which full civil rights are accorded **b :** the status of one who has attained this age **3 a :** a number greater than half of a total **b :** the excess of a majority over the remainder of the total **:** MARGIN **c :** the preponderant quantity or share **4 :** the group or political party whose votes preponderate **5 :** the military office, rank, or commission of a major — **majority** *adjective*

**majority leader** *noun* (1952) **:** a leader of the majority party in a legislative body (as the U.S. Senate)

**majority rule** *noun* (1893) **:** a political principle providing that a majority usually constituted by fifty percent plus one of an organized group will have the power to make decisions binding upon the whole

**major league** *noun* (1906) **1 :** a league of highest classification in U.S. professional baseball; *broadly* **:** a league of major importance in any of various sports **2 :** BIG TIME 2 — **major–league** *adjective*

**ma·jor·ly** \'mā-jər-lē\ *adverb* (1956) **:** in a major way **a :** PRIMARILY 1 ⟨was *majorly* a poet⟩ **b :** EXTREMELY 1 ⟨was *majorly* annoyed⟩

**major–medical** *adjective* (circa 1955) **:** of, relating to, or being a form of insurance designed to pay all or part of the medical bills of major illnesses usually after deduction of a fixed initial sum

**major order** *noun* (circa 1741) **:** one of the Roman Catholic or Eastern clerical orders that are sacramentally conferred and have a sacred character that implies major religious obligations (as clerical celibacy) — usually used in plural; compare MINOR ORDER

**major party** *noun* (1950) **:** a political party having electoral strength sufficient to permit it to win control of a government usually with comparative regularity and when defeated to constitute the principal opposition to the party in power

**major penalty** *noun* (circa 1936) **:** a 5-minute suspension of a player in ice hockey or lacrosse

**major premise** *noun* (1860) **:** the premise of a syllogism containing the major term

**major seminary** *noun* (1945) **:** a Roman Catholic seminary giving usually the entire six years of senior college and theological training required for major orders

**major suit** *noun* (1916) **:** either of the suits hearts or spades having superior scoring value in bridge

**major term** *noun* (1847) **:** the term of a syllogism constituting the predicate of the conclusion

**ma·jus·cule** \'ma-jəs-ˌkyü(ə)l, mə-'jəs-\ *noun* [French, from Latin *majusculus* rather large, diminutive of *major*] (circa 1825) **:** a large letter (as a capital) — **ma·jus·cu·lar** \mə-'jəs-kyə-lər\ *adjective* — **majuscule** *adjective*

**mak·able** *or* **make·able** \'mā-kə-bəl\ *adjective* (15th century) **:** capable of being made

**mak·ar** \'mä-kər, 'mā-\ *noun* [Middle English *maker*] (14th century) *chiefly Scottish* **:** POET

**¹make** \'māk\ *verb* **made** \'mād\; **mak·ing** [Middle English, from Old English *macian*; akin to Old High German *mahhōn* to prepare, make, Greek *magēnai* to be kneaded, Old Church Slavonic *mazati* to anoint, smear] (before 12th century)

*transitive verb* **1 a** *obsolete* **:** BEHAVE, ACT **b :** to seem to begin (an action) ⟨*made* to go⟩ **2 a :** to cause to happen to or be experienced by someone ⟨*made* trouble for us⟩ **b :** to cause to exist, occur, or appear **:** CREATE ⟨*make* a disturbance⟩ **c :** to favor the growth or occurrence of ⟨haste *makes* waste⟩ **d :** to fit, intend, or destine by or as if by creating ⟨was *made* to be an actor⟩ **3 a :** to bring into being by forming, shaping, or altering material **:** FASHION ⟨*make* a dress⟩ **b :** COMPOSE, WRITE ⟨*make* verses⟩ **c :** to lay out and construct ⟨*make* a road⟩ **4 :** to frame or formulate in the mind ⟨*make* plans⟩ **5 :** to put together from components **:** CONSTITUTE ⟨houses *made* of stone⟩ **6 a :** to compute or estimate to be **b :** to form and hold in the mind ⟨*make* no doubt of it⟩ **7 a :** to assemble and set alight the materials for (a fire) **b :** to set in order ⟨*make* beds⟩ **c :** PREPARE, FIX ⟨*make* dinner⟩ **d :** to shuffle (a deck of cards) in preparation for dealing **8 :** to prepare (hay) by cutting, drying, and storing **9 a :** to cause to be or become ⟨*made* them happy⟩ **b :** APPOINT ⟨*made* him bishop⟩ **10 a :** ENACT, ESTABLISH ⟨*make* laws⟩ **b :** to execute in an appropriate manner ⟨*make* a will⟩ **c :** SET, NAME ⟨*make* a price⟩ **11 a** *chiefly dialect* **:** SHUT ⟨the doors are *made* against you —Shakespeare⟩ **b :** to cause (an electric circuit) to be completed **12 a :** to conclude as to the nature or meaning of something ⟨what do you *make* of this development?⟩ **b :** to regard as being ⟨not the fool some *make* him⟩ **13 a :** to carry out (an action indicated or implied by the object) ⟨*make* war⟩ ⟨*make* a speech⟩ **b :** to perform with a bodily movement ⟨*make* a sweeping gesture⟩ **c :** to achieve by traversing ⟨*make* a detour⟩ ⟨*making* the rounds⟩ **14 a :** to produce as a result of action, effort, or behavior with respect to something ⟨*make* a mess of the job⟩ ⟨tried to *make* a thorough job of it⟩ **b** *archaic* **:** to turn into another language by translation **15 :** to cause to act in a certain way **:** COMPEL ⟨*make* her give it back⟩ **16 :** to cause or assure the success or prosperity of ⟨can either *make* you or break you⟩ **17 a :** to amount to in significance ⟨*makes* a great difference⟩ **b :** to form the essential being of ⟨clothes *make* the man⟩ **c :** to form by an assembling of individuals ⟨*make* a quorum⟩ **d :** to count as ⟨that *makes* the third time you've said it⟩ **18 a :** to be or be capable of being changed or fashioned into ⟨rags *make* the best paper⟩ **b :** to develop into ⟨she will *make* a fine judge⟩ **c :** FORM 6b **19 a :** REACH, ATTAIN — often used with *it* ⟨you'll never *make* it that far⟩; *also* **:** SURVIVE ⟨half the cubs won't *make* it through their first year⟩ **b :** to gain the rank of ⟨*make* major⟩ **c :** to gain a place on or in ⟨*make* the team⟩ ⟨the story *made* the papers⟩ **20 :** to gain (as money) by working, trading, or dealing ⟨*make* a living⟩ **21 a :** to act so as to win or acquire ⟨*makes* friends easily⟩ **b :** to score (points) in a game or sport **c :** to convert (a split) into a spare in bowling **22 a :** to fulfill (a contract) in a card game **b :** to win a trick with (a card) **23 a :** to include in a route or itinerary ⟨*make* New York on the return trip⟩ ⟨*make* it to the party⟩ **b :** CATCH 6b ⟨*made* the bus just in time⟩ **24 :** to persuade to consent to sexual intercourse **:** SEDUCE **25 :** to provide the most enjoyable or satisfying experience of ⟨meeting the star of the show really *made* our day⟩ *intransitive verb*

**1** *archaic* **:** to compose poetry **2 a :** BEHAVE, ACT **b :** to begin or seem to begin a certain action ⟨*made* as though to hand it to me⟩ **c :** to act so as to be or to seem to be ⟨*make* merry⟩ **d** *slang* **:** to play a part — usually used with *like* **3 :** SET OUT, HEAD ⟨*made* after the fox⟩ ⟨*made* straight for home⟩ **4 :** to increase in height or size ⟨the tide is *making* now⟩ **5 :** to reach or extend in a certain direction **6 :** to have considerable effect ⟨courtesy *makes* for safer driving⟩ **7 :** to undergo manufacture or processing ⟨the silk *makes* up beautifully⟩ — **make a face :** to distort one's features **:** GRIMACE — **make a mountain out of a molehill :** to treat a trifling matter as of great importance — **make away with 1 :** to carry off **:** STEAL **2 :** KILL — **make believe :** PRETEND, FEIGN — **make bold :** VENTURE, DARE — **make book :** to accept bets at calculated odds on all the entrants in a race or contest — **make common cause :** to unite to achieve a shared goal — **make do :** to get along or manage with the means at hand — **make ends meet :** to make one's means adequate to one's needs — **make eyes :** OGLE — **make fun of :** to make an object of amusement or laughter **:** RIDICULE, MOCK — **make good 1 :** to make valid or complete: as **a :** to make up for (a deficiency) **b :** INDEMNIFY ⟨*make good* the loss⟩ **c :** to carry out successfully ⟨*made good* his promise⟩ ⟨*make good* their escape⟩ **d :** PROVE ⟨*made good* a charge⟩ **2 :** to prove to be capable; *also* **:** SUCCEED — **make hay :** to make use of offered opportunity especially in gaining an early advantage — **make head 1 :** to make progress especially against resistance **2 :** to rise in armed revolt — **make it 1 :** to be successful ⟨trying to *make it* in the big time as a fashion photographer —Joe Kane⟩ ⟨the crème brûlée didn't quite *make it*⟩ **2 :** to have sexual intercourse — **make light of :** to treat as of little account — **make love 1 :** WOO, COURT **2 a :** NECK, PET **b :** to engage in sexual intercourse — **make much of 1 :** to treat as of importance **2 :** to treat with obvious affection or special consideration — **make no bones :** to be straightforward, unhesitating, or sure ⟨*makes no bones* about the seriousness of the matter⟩ — **make one's mark :** to achieve success or fame — **make public :** DISCLOSE — **make sail 1 :** to raise or spread sail **2 :** to set out on a voyage — **make shift :** to manage with difficulty — **make sport of :** RIDICULE, MOCK — **make the grade :** to measure up to some standard **:** be successful — **make the most of :** to show or use to the best advantage — **make the scene :** to be present at or participate in a usually specified activity or event — **make time 1 :** to travel fast **2 :** to gain time **3 :** to make progress toward winning favor ⟨trying to *make time* with the waitress⟩ — **make tracks 1 :** to proceed at a walk or run **2 :** to go in a hurry **:** RUN AWAY, FLEE — **make use of :** to put to use **:** EMPLOY — **make water 1** *of a boat* **:** LEAK **2 :** URINATE — **make waves :** to create a stir or disturbance

— **make way 1 :** to give room for passing, entering, or occupying **2 :** to make progress

— **make with** *slang* : PRODUCE, PERFORM — usually used with *the*

²**make** *noun* (14th century)
**1 a :** the manner or style in which a thing is constructed **b :** BRAND 4a
**2 :** the physical, mental, or moral constitution of a person ⟨men of his *make* are rare⟩
**3 a :** the action of producing or manufacturing **b :** the actual yield or amount produced over a specified period **:** OUTPUT
**4 :** the act of shuffling cards; *also* : turn to shuffle

— **on the make 1 :** in the process of forming, growing, or improving **2 :** in quest of a higher social or financial status **3 :** in search of sexual adventure

**make·bate** \'māk-ˌbāt\ *noun* [¹*make* + obsolete *bate* strife] (1529)
*archaic* **:** one that excites contention and quarrels

¹**make–be·lieve** \'māk-bə-ˌlēv\ *also* **make-be·lief** \-ˌlēf\ *noun* (1811)
**:** a pretending to believe

²**make–believe** *adjective* (1824)
**:** IMAGINARY, PRETENDED

**make–do** \'māk-ˌdü\ *adjective* (1923)
**:** MAKESHIFT
— **make–do** *noun*

**make·fast** \-ˌfast\ *noun* (1898)
**:** something (as a post or buoy) to which a boat can be fastened

**make off** *intransitive verb* (1709)
**:** to leave in haste
— **make off with :** to take away; *especially* : GRAB, STEAL

**make–or–break** \'mā-kər-'brāk\ *adjective* (1919)
**:** allowing no middle ground between success and failure

**make out** (15th century)
*transitive verb*
**1 :** to complete (as a printed form) by supplying required information ⟨*make out* a check⟩
**2 :** to find or grasp the meaning of ⟨tried to *make out* what had really happened⟩
**3 :** to form an opinion or idea about **:** CONCLUDE ⟨how do you *make* that *out*⟩
**4 a :** to represent as being ⟨*made* them *out* to be losers⟩ **b :** to pretend to be true ⟨*made out* that he had never heard of me⟩
**5 :** to represent or delineate in detail
**6 :** to see and identify with difficulty or effort **:** DISCERN ⟨*make out* a ship through the fog⟩
*intransitive verb*
**1 :** GET ALONG, FARE ⟨how are you *making out* with the new job⟩
**2 a :** to engage in sexual intercourse **b :** NECK 1

**make·over** \'mā-ˌkō-vər\ *noun* (1927)
**:** an act or instance of making over; *especially* : a changing of a person's appearance (as by the use of cosmetics or a different hairdo)

**make over** *transitive verb* (1546)
**1 :** to transfer the title of (property)
**2 :** REMAKE, REMODEL ⟨*made* the whole house *over*⟩

**mak·er** \'mā-kər\ *noun* (14th century)
**:** one that makes: as **a** *capitalized* : GOD 1 **b** *archaic* : POET **c** : a person who borrows money on a promissory note **d** : MANUFACTURER

**make–ready** \'māk-ˌre-dē\ *noun, plural* **-readies** (1887)
**:** final preparation (as of a form on a printing press) for running

**make·shift** \'māk-ˌshift\ *noun* (circa 1812)
**:** a usually crude and temporary expedient **:** SUBSTITUTE
*synonym* see RESOURCE
— **makeshift** *adjective*

**make·up** \'mā-ˌkəp\ *noun* (1821)
**1 a :** the way in which the parts or ingredients of something are put together **:** COMPOSITION **b** **:** physical, mental, and moral constitution

**2 a :** the operation of making up especially pages for printing **b :** design or layout of printed matter
**3 a** (1) **:** cosmetics used to color and beautify the face (2) **:** a cosmetic applied to other parts of the body **b :** materials (as wigs and cosmetics) used in making up or in special costuming (as for a play)
**4 :** REPLACEMENT; *specifically* : material added (as in a manufacturing process) to replace material that has been used up ⟨*makeup* water⟩
**5 :** a special examination in which a student may make up for absence or previous failure

**make up** (14th century)
*transitive verb*
**1 a :** to form by fitting together or assembling ⟨*make up* a train of cars⟩ **b :** to arrange typeset matter in (as pages) for printing
**2 a :** to combine to produce (a sum or whole) **b :** CONSTITUTE, COMPOSE ⟨10 chapters *make up* this volume⟩
**3 :** to make good (a deficiency)
**4 :** SETTLE, DECIDE ⟨*made up* my mind to depart⟩
**5 :** to wrap or fasten up ⟨*make* the books *up* into a parcel⟩
**6 a :** to prepare in physical appearance for a role **b :** to apply cosmetics to
**7 a :** INVENT, IMPROVISE ⟨*make up* a story⟩ **b :** to set in order ⟨rooms are *made up* daily⟩
*intransitive verb*
**1 :** to become reconciled ⟨quarreled but later *made up*⟩
**2 a :** to act ingratiatingly and flatteringly ⟨*made up* to his aunt for a new bicycle⟩ **b :** to make advances **:** COURT
**3 :** COMPENSATE ⟨*make up* for lost time⟩
**4 a :** to put on costumes or makeup (as for a play) **b :** to apply cosmetics

**make·weight** \'māk-ˌwāt\ *noun* (1695)
**1 a :** something thrown into a scale to bring the weight to a desired value **b :** something of little independent value thrown in to fill a gap
**2 :** COUNTERWEIGHT, COUNTERPOISE

**make–work** \'māk-ˌwərk\ *noun* (1923)
**:** work assigned or done chiefly to keep one busy

**ma·ki·mo·no** \ˌmä-ki-'mō-(ˌ)nō\ *noun, plural* **-nos** [Japanese, scroll, from *maki* roll + *mono* thing] (1882)
**:** a horizontal Japanese ornamental pictorial or calligraphic scroll

**mak·ing** \'mā-kiŋ\ *noun* [Middle English, from Old English *macung*, from *macian* to make] (12th century)
**1 :** the act or process of forming, causing, doing, or coming into being ⟨spots problems in the *making*⟩
**2 :** a process or means of advancement or success
**3 :** something made; *especially* : a quantity produced at one time **:** BATCH
**4 a :** POTENTIALITY — often used in plural ⟨had the *makings* of a great artist⟩ **b** *plural* **:** the material from which something is to be made; *especially* \usually \'mā-kənz\ **:** paper and tobacco for rolling cigarettes by hand

**ma·ko shark** \'mā-(ˌ)kō-, 'mä-\ *noun* [Maori *mako* mako shark] (1926)
**:** either of two mackerel sharks (*Isurus paucus* and *I. oxyrinchus*) that are notable sport fish and are considered dangerous to humans — called also *mako*; see SHARK illustration

**makuta** *plural of* LIKUTA

**mal-** *combining form* [Middle English, from Middle French, from Old French, from *mal* bad (from Latin *malus*) & *mal* badly, from Latin *male*, from *malus*]
**1 a :** bad ⟨*mal*practice⟩ **b :** badly ⟨*mal*odorous⟩
**2 a :** abnormal ⟨*mal*formation⟩ **b :** abnormally ⟨*mal*formed⟩
**3 a :** inadequate ⟨*mal*adjustment⟩ **b :** inadequately ⟨*mal*nourished⟩

**mal·ab·sorp·tion** \ˌma-ləb-'sȯrp-shən, -'zȯrp-\ *noun* (circa 1929)

**:** faulty absorption especially of nutrient materials from the alimentary canal

**ma·lac·ca** \mə-'la-kə\ *adjective* [*Malacca*, Malaya] (1844)
**:** made or comprised of the cane of an Asian rattan palm (*Calamus rotang*) ⟨an umbrella with a *malacca* handle⟩
— **malacca** *noun*

**Mal·a·chi** \'ma-lə-ˌkī\ *noun* [Hebrew *Mal'ākhī*]
**1** — used as the conventional name for the unidentified 5th century B.C. writer of the book of Malachi
**2 :** a prophetic book of canonical Jewish and Christian Scripture — see BIBLE table

**Mal·a·chi·as** \ˌma-lə-'kī-əs\ *noun* [Late Latin, from Hebrew *Mal'ākhī*]
**:** MALACHI

**mal·a·chite** \'ma-lə-ˌkīt\ *noun* [alteration of Middle English *melochites*, from Latin *molochites*, from Greek *molochitēs*, from *molochē*, *malachē* mallow] (1656)
**:** a mineral that is a green basic carbonate of copper used as an ore and for making ornamental objects

**mal·a·col·o·gy** \ˌma-lə-'kä-lə-jē\ *noun* [French *malacologie*, contraction of *malacozoologie*, from New Latin *Malacozoa*, zoological group including soft-bodied animals (from Greek *malakos* soft + New Latin *-zoa*) + French *-logie* -logy] (1836)
**:** a branch of zoology dealing with mollusks
— **mal·a·co·log·i·cal** \ˌma-lə-kə-'lä-ji-kəl\ *adjective*
— **mal·a·col·o·gist** \ˌma-lə-'kä-lə-jist\ *noun*

**mal·a·cos·tra·can** \ˌma-lə-'käs-tri-kən\ *noun* [ultimately from Greek *malakostrakos* soft-shelled, from *malakos* soft + *ostrakon* shell — more at MOLLIFY, OYSTER] (1835)
**:** any of a large subclass (Malacostraca) of crustaceans having a thorax consisting of eight segments usually covered by a carapace and including the decapods and isopods
— **malacostracan** *adjective*

**mal·ad·ap·ta·tion** \ˌma-ˌla-ˌdap-'tā-shən\ *noun* (1877)
**:** poor or inadequate adaptation

**mal·adapt·ed** \ˌma-lə-'dap-təd\ *adjective* (1943)
**:** unsuited or poorly suited (as to a particular use, purpose, or situation)

**mal·adap·tive** \-tiv\ *adjective* (1931)
**1 :** marked by poor or inadequate adaptation
**2 :** not conducive to adaptation

**mal·ad·just·ed** \ˌma-lə-'jəs-təd\ *adjective* (1886)
**:** poorly or inadequately adjusted; *specifically* **:** lacking harmony with one's environment from failure to adjust one's desires to the conditions of one's life

**mal·ad·jus·tive** \-'jəs-tiv\ *adjective* (1928)
**:** not conducive to adjustment

**mal·ad·just·ment** \-'jəs(t)-mənt\ *noun* (1833)
**:** poor, faulty, or inadequate adjustment

**mal·ad·min·is·tra·tion** \ˌma-ləd-ˌmi-nə-'strā-shən\ *noun* (1644)
**:** administration that is corrupt or incompetent (as that of a public office) or incorrect (as that of a drug)
— **mal·ad·min·is·ter** \-'mi-nə-stər\ *transitive verb*

**mal·adroit** \ˌma-lə-'drȯit\ *adjective* [French, from Middle French, from *mal-* + *adroit*] (1685)
**:** lacking adroitness **:** INEPT
*synonym* see AWKWARD
— **mal·adroit·ly** *adverb*
— **mal·adroit·ness** *noun*

---

\ə\ abut \ᵊ\ kitten \ər\ further \a\ ash \ā\ ace
\ä\ mop, mar \aȯ\ out \ch\ chin \e\ bet \ē\ easy
\g\ go \i\ hit \ī\ ice \j\ job \ŋ\ sing \ō\ go
\ȯ\ law \ȯi\ boy \th\ thin \th\ the \ü\ loot \u̇\ foot
\y\ yet \zh\ vision *see also* Guide to Pronunciation

**mal·a·dy** \'ma-lə-dē\ *noun, plural* **-dies** [Middle English *maladie*, from Old French, from *malade* sick, from Latin *male habitus* in bad condition] (13th century)
**1 :** a disease or disorder of the animal body
**2 :** an unwholesome or disordered condition
**ma·la fi·de** \ˌma-lə-'fī-dē, -də\ *adverb or adjective* [Late Latin] (1561)
**:** with or in bad faith
**Ma·la·ga** \'ma-lə-gə\ *noun* (1608)
**:** a sweet brown fortified wine from Málaga, Spain; *also* **:** a similar wine made elsewhere
**Mal·a·gasy** \ˌma-lə-'ga-sē; ˌmä-lə-'gä-sē, -shē\ *noun, plural* **Malagasy** *also* **Mal·a·gas·ies** (1839)
**1 :** a member of a people of Indonesian and African origin who inhabit Madagascar
**2 :** the Austronesian language of the Malagasy people
— **Malagasy** *adjective*
**ma·la·gue·na** \ˌma-lə-'gän-yə, ˌmä-\ *noun* [Spanish *malagueña*, from feminine of *malagueño* of Málaga, from *Málaga*] (circa 1883)
**1 :** a folk tune native to Málaga that is similar to a fandango
**2 :** a Spanish dance for couples that is similar to a fandango
**mal·aise** \mə-'lāz, ma-, -'lez\ *noun* [French *malaise*, from Old French, from *mal-* + *aise* comfort — more at EASE] (circa 1768)
**1 :** an indefinite feeling of debility or lack of health often indicative of or accompanying the onset of an illness
**2 :** a vague sense of mental or moral ill-being ⟨a *malaise* of cynicism and despair —Malcolm Boyd⟩
**mal·a·mute** \'ma-lə-ˌmyüt, -ˌmüt\ *noun* [*Malemute*, an Alaskan Eskimo people] (1898)
**:** a sled dog of northern North America; *especially* **:** ALASKAN MALAMUTE
**mal·a·pert** \ˌma-lə-'pərt\ *adjective* [Middle English, from Middle French, unskillful, from *mal-* + *apert* skillful, literally, open — more at PERT] (14th century)
**:** impudently bold **:** SAUCY
— **mal·a·pert·ly** *adverb*
— **mal·a·pert·ness** *noun*
**mal·ap·por·tioned** \ˌma-lə-'pōr-shənd, -'pȯr-\ *adjective* (1965)
**:** characterized by an inequitable or unsuitable apportioning of representatives to a legislative body
— **mal·ap·por·tion·ment** \-shən-mənt\ *noun*
**¹mal·a·prop** \'ma-lə-ˌpräp\ *noun* [Mrs. *Malaprop*] (1823)
**:** an example of malapropism ⟨was famed for *malaprops:* he always said "polo bears" and "Remember Pearl Island" and "neon stockings" —*Time*⟩
**²malaprop** *or* **mal·a·prop·ian** \ˌma-lə-'präpē-ən\ *adjective* (1840)
**:** using or marked by the use of malapropisms
**mal·a·prop·ism** \'ma-lə-ˌprä-ˌpi-zəm\ *noun* [Mrs. *Malaprop*, character noted for her misuse of words in R. B. Sheridan's comedy *The Rivals* (1775)] (1849)
**1 :** the usually unintentionally humorous misuse or distortion of a word or phrase; *especially* **:** the use of a word sounding somewhat like the one intended but ludicrously wrong in the context
**2 :** MALAPROP
— **mal·a·prop·ist** \-ˌprä-pist\ *noun*
**mal·ap·ro·pos** \ˌma-ˌla-prə-'pō\ *adverb* [French *mal à propos*] (1668)
**:** in an inappropriate or inopportune way
— **malapropos** *adjective*
**¹ma·lar** \'mā-lər, -ˌlär\ *adjective* [New Latin *malaris*, from Latin *mala* jawbone, cheek] (1782)
**:** of or relating to the cheek or the side of the head

**²malar** *noun* (circa 1828)
**:** ZYGOMATIC BONE — called also *malar bone*
**ma·lar·ia** \mə-'ler-ē-ə\ *noun* [Italian, from *mala aria* bad air] (1740)
**1** *archaic* **:** air infected with a noxious substance capable of causing disease; *especially* **:** MIASMA
**2 a :** a human disease that is caused by sporozoan parasites (genus *Plasmodium*) in the red blood cells, is transmitted by the bite of anopheline mosquitoes, and is characterized by periodic attacks of chills and fever **b :** any of various diseases of birds and mammals caused by blood protozoans
— **ma·lar·i·al** \-əl\ *adjective*
— **ma·lar·i·ous** \-əs\ *adjective*
**ma·lar·i·ol·o·gy** \-ˌler-ē-'ä-lə-jē\ *noun* (circa 1923)
**:** the scientific study of malaria
— **ma·lar·i·ol·o·gist** \-jist\ *noun*
**ma·lar·key** *also* **ma·lar·ky** \mə-'lär-kē\ *noun* [origin unknown] (1929)
**:** insincere or foolish talk **:** BUNKUM
**ma·late** \'ma-ˌlāt, 'mā-\ *noun* (1794)
**:** a salt or ester of malic acid
**mal·a·thi·on** \ˌma-lə-'thī-ən, -ˌän\ *noun* [from *Malathion*, a trademark] (1953)
**:** an insecticide $C_{10}H_{19}O_6PS_2$ with a lower mammalian toxicity than parathion
**Ma·lay** \mə-'lā, 'mā-ˌlā\ *noun* [obsolete Dutch *Malayo* (now *Maleier*), from Malay *Mĕlayu*] (1598)
**1 :** a member of a people of the Malay Peninsula, eastern Sumatra, parts of Borneo, and some adjacent islands
**2 :** the Austronesian language of the Malays
— **Malay** *adjective*
— **Ma·lay·an** \mə-'lā-ən, mā-; 'mā-ˌlā-\ *noun or adjective*
**Ma·la·ya·lam** \ˌma-lə-'yä-ləm, ˌmä-\ *noun* (1837)
**:** the Dravidian language of Kerala, southwest India, closely related to Tamil
**¹mal·con·tent** \ˌmal-kən-'tent\ *noun* (1581)
**:** a discontented person: **a :** one who bears a grudge from a sense of grievance or thwarted ambition **b :** one who is in active opposition to an established order or government **:** REBEL
**²malcontent** *adjective* [Middle French, from Old French, from *mal-* + *content* content] (1586)
**:** dissatisfied with the existing state of affairs **:** DISCONTENTED
**mal·con·tent·ed** \-'ten-təd\ *adjective* (1586)
**:** MALCONTENT
— **mal·con·tent·ed·ly** *adverb*
— **mal·con·tent·ed·ness** *noun*
**mal de mer** \ˌmal-də-'mer\ *noun* [French] (1778)
**:** SEASICKNESS
**mal·dis·tri·bu·tion** \ˌmal-ˌdis-trə-'byü-shən\ *noun* (1895)
**:** bad or faulty distribution **:** undesirable inequality or unevenness of placement or apportionment (as of population, resources, or wealth) over an area or among members of a group
**¹male** \'mā(ə)l\ *noun* [Middle English, from Middle French *masle*, *male*, adjective & noun, from Latin *masculus* — more at MASCULINE] (14th century)
**1 a :** a male person **:** a man or a boy **b :** an individual that produces small usually motile gametes (as spermatozoa or spermatozoids) which fertilize the eggs of a female
**2 :** a staminate plant
**²male** *adjective* (14th century)
**1 a** (1) **:** of, relating to, or being the sex that produces gametes which fertilize the eggs of a female (2) **:** STAMINATE; *especially* **:** having only staminate flowers and not producing fruit or seeds ⟨a *male* holly⟩ **b** (1) **:** of, relating to, or characteristic of the male sex ⟨a deep *male* voice⟩ (2) **:** made up of usually adult male individuals ⟨a *male* choir⟩
**2 :** MASCULINE 3a

**3 :** designed for fitting into a corresponding female part ⟨*male* hose coupling⟩
— **male·ness** \-nəs\ *noun*
**male alto** *noun* (circa 1879)
**:** COUNTERTENOR
**ma·le·ate** \ˌmā-lē-ˌāt, -lē-ət\ *noun* (1853)
**:** a salt or ester of maleic acid
**¹mal·e·dict** \ˌma-lə-'dikt\ *adjective* [Late Latin *maledictus*] (circa 1550)
*archaic* **:** ACCURSED
**²maledict** *transitive verb* (1623)
**:** CURSE, EXECRATE
**mal·e·dic·tion** \ˌma-lə-'dik-shən\ *noun* [Middle English *malediccioun*, from Late Latin *malediction-*, *maledictio*, from *maledicere* to curse, from Latin, to speak evil of, from *male* badly + *dicere* to speak, say — more at MAL-, DICTION] (14th century)
**:** CURSE, EXECRATION
— **mal·e·dic·to·ry** \-'dik-t(ə-)rē\ *adjective*
**mal·e·fac·tion** \ˌma-lə-'fak-shən\ *noun* (15th century)
**:** an evil deed **:** CRIME
**mal·e·fac·tor** \'ma-lə-ˌfak-tər\ *noun* [Middle English *malefactour*, from Latin *malefactor*, from *malefacere* to do evil, from *male* + *facere* to do — more at DO] (15th century)
**1 :** one who commits an offense against the law; *especially* **:** FELON
**2 :** one who does ill toward another
**male fern** *noun* (1562)
**:** a fern (*Dryopteris filix-mas*) producing an oleoresin used in expelling tapeworms
**ma·lef·ic** \mə-'le-fik\ *adjective* [Latin *maleficus* wicked, mischievous, from *male* + *-ficus* -fic] (1652)
**1 :** having malignant influence **:** BALEFUL
**2 :** MALICIOUS
**ma·lef·i·cence** \mə-'le-fə-sən(t)s\ *noun* [Italian *maleficenza*, from Latin *maleficentia*, from *maleficus*] (1598)
**1 a :** the act of committing harm or evil **b :** a harmful or evil act
**2 :** the quality or state of being maleficent
**ma·lef·i·cent** \-sənt\ *adjective* [back-formation from *maleficence*] (1678)
**:** working or productive of harm or evil **:** BALEFUL
**ma·le·ic acid** \mə-'lē-ik-, -'lā-\ *noun* [French *acide maléique*, alteration of *acide malique* malic acid; from its formation by dehydration of malic acid] (1857)
**:** a crystalline dicarboxylic acid $C_4H_4O_4$ that is isomeric with fumaric acid and is used especially in organic synthesis
**maleic anhydride** *noun* (1857)
**:** a caustic crystalline cyclic anhydride $C_4H_2O_3$ used especially in making resins
**maleic hydrazide** *noun* (1949)
**:** a crystalline cyclic hydrazide $C_4H_4N_2O_2$ used to retard plant growth
**mal·e·mute** *variant of* MALAMUTE
**male–ster·ile** \ˌmā(ə)l-'ster-əl\ *adjective* (1921)
**:** having male gametes lacking or nonfunctional
**ma·lev·o·lence** \mə-'le-və-lən(t)s\ *noun* (15th century)
**1 :** the quality or state of being malevolent
**2 :** malevolent behavior
*synonym* see MALICE
**ma·lev·o·lent** \-lənt\ *adjective* [Latin *malevolent-*, *malevolens*, from *male* badly + *volent-*, *volens*, present participle of *velle* to wish — more at MAL-, WILL] (1509)
**1 :** having, showing, or arising from intense often vicious ill will, spite, or hatred
**2 :** productive of harm or evil
— **ma·lev·o·lent·ly** *adverb*
**mal·fea·sance** \ˌmal-'fē-z°n(t)s\ *noun* [*mal-* + obsolete *feasance* doing, execution] (1696)
**:** wrongdoing or misconduct especially by a public official

**mal·for·ma·tion** \,mal-fȯr-'mā-shən, -fər-\ *noun* (1800)
: irregular, anomalous, abnormal, or faulty formation or structure

**mal·formed** \,mal-'fȯrmd\ *adjective* (1817)
: characterized by malformation : badly or imperfectly formed : MISSHAPEN

**mal·func·tion** \,mal-'fəŋ(k)-shən\ *intransitive verb* (1928)
: to function imperfectly or badly : fail to operate normally
— **malfunction** *noun*

**mal·gré** \mal-'grā, 'mal-,\ *preposition* [French, from Old French *maugré* — more at MAUGRE] (1608)
: DESPITE

**ma·lic** \'ma-lik, 'mā-\ *adjective* (circa 1909)
: involved in and especially catalyzing a reaction in which malic acid participates ⟨*malic* dehydrogenase⟩

**malic acid** *noun* [French *acide malique,* ultimately from Latin *malum* apple, from Greek *mēlon, malon*] (1797)
: a crystalline dicarboxylic acid $C_4H_6O_5$; *especially* : the optical isomer of malic acid that is found in various fruits (as apples) and is formed as an intermediate in the Krebs cycle

**mal·ice** \'ma-ləs\ *noun* [Middle English, from Middle French, from Latin *malitia,* from *malus* bad] (14th century)
**1** : desire to cause pain, injury, or distress to another
**2** : intent to commit an unlawful act or cause harm without legal justification or excuse ☆

**ma·li·cious** \mə-'li-shəs\ *adjective* (13th century)
: given to, marked by, or arising from malice
— **ma·li·cious·ly** *adverb*
— **ma·li·cious·ness** *noun*

**malicious mischief** *noun* (1769)
: willful, wanton, or reckless damage to or destruction of another's property

**¹ma·lign** \mə-'līn\ *adjective* [Middle English *maligne,* from Middle French, from Latin *malignus,* from *male* badly + *gignere* to beget — more at MAL-, KIN] (14th century)
**1 a** : evil in nature, influence, or effect : INJURIOUS **b** : MALIGNANT, VIRULENT
**2** : having or showing intense often vicious ill will : MALEVOLENT
**synonym** see SINISTER
— **ma·lign·ly** *adverb*

**²malign** *transitive verb* [Middle English, from Middle French *maligner* to act maliciously, from Late Latin *malignari,* from Latin *malignus*] (15th century)
: to utter injuriously misleading or false reports about : speak evil of ☆

**ma·lig·nance** \mə-'lig-nən(t)s\ *noun* (circa 1604)
: MALIGNANCY

**ma·lig·nan·cy** \-nən(t)-sē\ *noun, plural* **-cies** (1601)
**1** : the quality or state of being malignant
**2 a** : exhibition (as by a tumor) of malignant qualities : VIRULENCE **b** : a malignant tumor

**ma·lig·nant** \mə-'lig-nənt\ *adjective* [Late Latin *malignant-, malignans,* present participle of *malignari*] (circa 1545)
**1 a** *obsolete* : MALCONTENT, DISAFFECTED **b** : evil in nature, influence, or effect : INJURIOUS **c** : passionately and relentlessly malevolent : aggressively malicious
**2** : tending to produce death or deterioration ⟨*malignant* malaria⟩; *especially* : tending to infiltrate, metastasize, and terminate fatally ⟨*malignant* tumor⟩
— **ma·lig·nant·ly** *adverb*

**ma·lig·ni·ty** \mə-'lig-nə-tē\ *noun* (14th century)
**1** : MALIGNANCY, MALEVOLENCE
**2** : an instance of malignant or malicious behavior or nature
**synonym** see MALICE

**ma·li·hi·ni** \,mä-li-'hē-nē\ *noun* [Hawaiian] (1914)

: a newcomer or stranger among the people of Hawaii

**ma·lines** \mə-'lēn\ *noun, plural* **ma·lines** \-'lēn(z)\ [French, from *Malines* (Mechelen), Belgium] (1833)
**1** : MECHLIN
**2** *also* **ma·line** : a fine stiff net with a hexagonal mesh that is usually made of silk or rayon and that is often used for veils

**ma·lin·ger** \mə-'liŋ-gər\ *intransitive verb* **ma·lin·gered; ma·lin·ger·ing** \-g(ə-)riŋ\ [French *malingre* sickly] (1820)
: to pretend incapacity (as illness) so as to avoid duty or work
— **ma·lin·ger·er** \-gər-ər\ *noun*

**Ma·lin·ke** \mə-'liŋ-kē\ *noun, plural* **Malinke** or **Malinkes** (1883)
**1** : a member of a people of Mandingo affiliation widespread in the western part of Africa
**2** : the language of the Malinke people

**Ma·li·nois** \,ma-lən-'wä\ *noun* [French, one from Malines, from *Malines* (Mechelen), Belgium] (1929)
: BELGIAN MALINOIS

**mal·i·son** \'ma-lə-sən, -zən\ *noun* [Middle English, from Old French *maleiçon,* from Late Latin *malediction-, maledictio*] (13th century)
: CURSE, MALEDICTION

**mal·kin** \'mȯ(l)-kən, 'mal-\ *noun* [Middle English *malkyn* servant woman, from *Malkyn,* diminutive of the name *Maud*] (1586)
**1** *dialect chiefly British* : an untidy woman : SLATTERN
**2** *dialect chiefly British* **a** : CAT **b** : HARE

**¹mall** \'mȯl\ *variant of* MAUL

**²mall** \'mȯl, *especially British & for 1* 'mal\ *noun* [short for obsolete *pall-mall* mallet used in pall-mall] (1644)
**1** : an alley used for pall-mall
**2** [The *Mall,* promenade in London, originally a pall-mall alley] **a** : a usually public area often set with shade trees and designed as a promenade or as a pedestrian walk **b** : a usually paved or grassy strip between two roadways
**3 a** : an urban shopping area featuring a variety of shops surrounding a usually open-air concourse reserved for pedestrian traffic **b** : a usually large suburban building or group of buildings containing various shops with associated passageways ◆

**mal·lard** \'ma-lərd\ *noun, plural* **mallard** or **mallards** [Middle English, from Middle French *mallart*] (14th century)
: a common and widely distributed wild duck (*Anas platyrhynchos*) of the northern hemisphere the males of which have a green head and white-ringed neck

**mallard**

and which is the source of the domestic ducks

**mal·lea·ble** \'ma-lē-ə-bəl, 'mal-yə-bəl, 'ma-lə-bəl\ *adjective* [Middle English *malliable,* from Middle French or Medieval Latin; Middle French *malleable,* from Medieval Latin *malleabilis,* from *malleare* to hammer, from Latin *malleus* hammer — more at MAUL] (14th century)
**1** : capable of being extended or shaped by beating with a hammer or by the pressure of rollers
**2 a** : capable of being altered or controlled by outside forces or influences **b** : having a capacity for adaptive change
**synonym** see PLASTIC
— **mal·lea·bil·i·ty** \,ma-lē-ə-'bi-lə-tē, ,mal-yə-, ,ma-lə-\ *noun*

**mal·lee** \'ma-lē\ *noun* [Wuywurung (Australian aboriginal language of the Melbourne area, Victoria) *mali*] (1845)
**1** : any of various low-growing shrubby Aus-

tralian eucalypts (as *Eucalyptus dumosa* and *E. oleosa*)
**2** : a dense thicket or growth of mallees; *also* : land covered by such growth

---

☆ **SYNONYMS**

**Malice, malevolence, ill will, spite, malignity, spleen, grudge** mean the desire to see another experience pain, injury, or distress. MALICE implies a deep-seated often unexplainable desire to see another suffer ⟨felt no *malice* toward their former enemies⟩. MALEVOLENCE suggests a bitter persistent hatred that is likely to be expressed in malicious conduct ⟨a look of dark *malevolence*⟩. ILL WILL implies a feeling of antipathy of limited duration ⟨*ill will* provoked by a careless remark⟩. SPITE implies petty feelings of envy and resentment that are often expressed in small harassments ⟨petty insults inspired by *spite*⟩. MALIGNITY implies deep passion and relentlessness ⟨a life consumed by motiveless *malignity*⟩. SPLEEN suggests the wrathful release of latent spite or persistent malice ⟨venting his *spleen* against politicians⟩. GRUDGE implies a harbored feeling of resentment or ill will that seeks satisfaction ⟨never one to harbor a *grudge*⟩.

**Malign, traduce, asperse, vilify, calumniate, defame, slander** mean to injure by speaking ill of. MALIGN suggests specific and often subtle misrepresentation but may not always imply deliberate lying ⟨the most *maligned* monarch in British history⟩. TRADUCE stresses the resulting ignominy and distress to the victim ⟨so *traduced* the governor that he was driven from office⟩. ASPERSE implies continued attack on a reputation often by indirect or insinuated detraction ⟨both candidates *aspersed* the other's motives⟩. VILIFY implies attempting to destroy a reputation by open and direct abuse ⟨no criminal was more *vilified* in the press⟩. CALUMNIATE imputes malice to the speaker and falsity to the assertions ⟨falsely *calumniated* as a traitor⟩. DEFAME stresses the actual loss of or injury to one's good name ⟨sued them for *defaming* her reputation⟩. SLANDER stresses the suffering of the victim ⟨town gossips *slandered* their good name⟩.

---

◇ **WORD HISTORY**

**mall**   In 16th century Italy a popular alley game resembling croquet was known as *pallamaglio,* from *palla* "ball" and *maglic* "mallet." The game was adopted by the French as *pallemaille* and in the 17th century by the English as *pall-mall.* The alley on which the game was played came to be known as a *mall.* One of the best known of these alleys was located in London's St. James's Park and known as "The Mall." When still used as a playing field, the alley in St. James's had a hard sandy base covered with powdered cockleshells. After the game lost favor, The Mall at St. James's, as it continued to be called, was landscaped into a fashionable promenade lined with trees and flowers. Other similar, open-air places came to be called *malls* also. In the mid 20th century the word was applied to a variety of public spaces, ranging from an outdoor concourse between buildings to an enclosed shopping complex in which the stores and restaurants are linked by passageways.

---

\ə\ abut \ᵊ\ kitten \ər\ further \a\ ash \ā\ ace
\ä\ mop, mar \au̇\ out \ch\ chin \e\ bet \ē\ easy
\g\ go \i\ hit \ī\ ice \j\ job \ŋ\ sing \ō\ go
\ȯ\ law \ȯi\ boy \th\ thin \t̲h̲\ the \ü\ loot \u̇\ foot
\y\ yet \zh\ vision    *see also* Guide to Pronunciation

**mal·let** \'ma-lət\ *noun* [Middle English *mallet*, from Middle French, from Old French, diminutive of *mail* maul — more at MAUL] (15th century)
: a hammer with a typically barrel-shaped head: as **a** : a tool with a large head for driving another tool or for striking a surface without marring it **b** : a long-handled wooden implement used for striking a ball (as in polo or croquet) **c** : a light hammer with a small rounded or spherical usually padded head used in playing certain musical instruments (as a vibraphone)

**mal·le·us** \'ma-lē-əs\ *noun, plural* **mal·lei** \-lē-ˌī, -lē-ˌē\ [New Latin, from Latin, hammer] (1669)
: the outermost of a chain of three small bones of the mammalian middle ear — see EAR illustration

**mal·low** \'ma-(ˌ)lō\ *noun* [Middle English *malwe*, from Old English *mealwe*, from Latin *malva*] (before 12th century)
: any of a genus (*Malva* of the family Malvaceae, the mallow family) of herbs with palmately lobed or dissected leaves, usually showy flowers, and a disk-shaped fruit

**malm·sey** \'mäm-zē, 'mälm-, *New England also* 'mäm-\ *noun, often capitalized* [Middle English *malmesey*, from Medieval Latin *Malmasia* Monemvasia, village in Greece where a sweet wine was produced] (15th century)
: the sweetest variety of Madeira wine

**mal·nour·ished** \ˌmal-'nər-isht, -'nə-risht\ *adjective* (1927)
: UNDERNOURISHED

**mal·nu·tri·tion** \ˌmal-nü-'tri-shən, -nyü-\ *noun* (1862)
: faulty or inadequate nutrition

**mal·oc·clu·sion** \ˌma-lə-'klü-zhən\ *noun* (1888)
: improper occlusion; *especially* : abnormality in the coming together of teeth

**mal·odor** \ˌmal-'ō-dər\ *noun* (1825)
: an offensive odor

**mal·odor·ous** \-'ō-də-rəs\ *adjective* (1850)
**1** : having a bad odor
**2** : highly improper ⟨*malodorous* practices and chicanery in high financial places —*New Republic*⟩ ☆
— **mal·odor·ous·ly** *adverb*
— **mal·odor·ous·ness** *noun*

**ma·lo·lac·tic** \ˌma-lō-'lak-tik, ˌmä-\ *adjective* [*malic* + *-o-* + *lactic*] (1965)
: relating to or involved in the bacterial conversion of malic acid to lactic acid in wine ⟨*malolactic* fermentation⟩

**maloti** *plural of* LOTI

**Mal·pi·ghi·an corpuscle** \mal-'pi-gē-ən-, -'pē-\ *noun* [Marcello *Malpighi*] (1848)
: the part of a nephron that consists of a glomerulus and Bowman's capsule — called also *Malpighian body*

**Malpighian layer** *noun* (1878)
: the deeper part of the epidermis consisting of cells whose protoplasm has not yet changed into horny material

**Malpighian tubule** *noun* (1877)
: any of a group of long blind vessels opening into the posterior part of the alimentary canal in most insects and some other arthropods and functioning primarily as excretory organs — called also *Malpighian tube*

**mal·po·si·tion** \ˌmal-pə-'zi-shən\ *noun* (circa 1839)
: wrong or faulty position

**mal·prac·tice** \ˌmal-'prak-təs\ *noun* (1671)
**1** : a dereliction from professional duty or a failure to exercise an accepted degree of professional skill or learning by one (as a physician) rendering professional services which results in injury, loss, or damage
**2** : an injurious, negligent, or improper practice : MALFEASANCE

**mal·prac·ti·tio·ner** \ˌmal-prak-'ti-sh(ə-)nər\ *noun* (1800)
: one who engages in or commits malpractice

**¹malt** \'mȯlt\ *noun* [Middle English, from Old English *mealt;* akin to Old High German *malz* malt, Old English *meltan* to melt] (before 12th century)
**1** : grain (as barley) softened by steeping in water, allowed to germinate, and used especially in brewing and distilling
**2** : MALT LIQUOR
**3** : MALTED MILK
— **malty** \'mȯl-tē\ *adjective*

**²malt** (15th century)
*transitive verb*
**1** : to convert into malt
**2** : to make or treat with malt or malt extract
*intransitive verb*
**1** : to become malt
**2** : to make grain into malt

**malt·ase** \'mȯl-ˌtās, -ˌtāz\ *noun* (1890)
: an enzyme that catalyzes the hydrolysis of maltose to glucose

**malted milk** *noun* (1887)
**1** : a soluble powder prepared from dried milk and malted cereals
**2** : a beverage made by dissolving malted milk in milk and usually adding ice cream and flavoring — called also *malted*

**Mal·tese** \mȯl-'tēz, -'tēs\ *noun, plural* **Maltese** (1615)
**1** : a native or inhabitant of Malta
**2** : the Semitic language of the Maltese people
**3** : any of a breed of toy dogs with a long silky white coat, a black nose, and very dark eyes
— **Maltese** *adjective*

Maltese 3

**Maltese cross** *noun* (1877)
**1 a** : a cross formée **b** : a cross that resembles the cross formée but has the outer face of each arm indented in a V — see CROSS illustration
**2** : a Eurasian perennial (*Lychnis chalcedonica*) having scarlet or rarely white flowers in dense terminal heads

**Mal·thu·sian** \mal-'thü-zhən, mȯl-, -'thyü-\ *adjective* [Thomas R. *Malthus*] (1821)
: of or relating to Malthus or to his theory that population tends to increase at a faster rate than its means of subsistence and that unless it is checked by moral restraint or disaster (as disease, famine, or war) widespread poverty and degradation inevitably result
— **Malthusian** *noun*
— **Mal·thu·sian·ism** \-zhə-ˌni-zəm\ *noun*

**malt liquor** *noun* (1693)
: a fermented liquor (as beer) made with malt

**malt·ose** \'mȯl-ˌtōs, -ˌtōz\ *noun* [French, from English ¹*malt*] (1862)
: a crystalline dextrorotatory fermentable sugar $C_{12}H_{22}O_{11}$ formed especially from starch by amylase

**mal·treat** \ˌmal-'trēt\ *transitive verb* [part translation of French *maltraiter*, from Middle French, from *mal-* + *traiter* to treat, from Old French *traitier* — more at TREAT] (1708)
: to treat cruelly or roughly : ABUSE
— **mal·treat·er** \-'trē-tər\ *noun*
— **mal·treat·ment** \-'trēt-mənt\ *noun*

**malt·ster** \'mȯlt-stər\ *noun* (14th century)
: a maker of malt

**malt sugar** *noun* (1862)
: MALTOSE

**malt whiskey** *noun* (circa 1839)
: SCOTCH 3

**mal·ver·sa·tion** \ˌmal-vər-'sā-shən\ *noun* [Middle French, from *malverser* to be corrupt, from *mal* + *verser* to turn, handle, from Latin *versare*, frequentative of *vertere* to turn — more at WORTH] (1549)
**1** : misbehavior and especially corruption in an office, trust, or commission
**2** : corrupt administration

**ma·ma** *or* **mam·ma** \'mä-mə, *chiefly British* mə-'mä\ *noun* [baby talk] (1579)
**1** : MOTHER
**2** *slang* : WIFE, WOMAN

**mama's boy** *noun* (1850)
: a usually polite or timid boy or man who is extremely or excessively close to and solicitous of his mother

**mam·ba** \'mäm-bə, 'mam-\ *noun* [Zulu *imamba*] (1862)
: any of several chiefly arboreal venomous green or black elapid snakes (genus *Dendroaspis* synonym *Dendraspis*) of sub-Saharan Africa

**mam·bo** \'mäm-(ˌ)bō\ *noun, plural* **mambos** [American Spanish] (1948)
: a ballroom dance of Cuban origin that resembles the rumba and the cha-cha; *also* : the music for this dance
— **mambo** *intransitive verb*

**ma·mey** \ma-'mē\ *noun* [Spanish, from Taino] (1604)
: a tropical American tree (*Mammea americana* of the family Guttiferae) having an ovoid fruit with thick russet leathery rind and yellow or reddish juicy sweet flesh; *also* : the fruit

**Mam·luk** \'mam-ˌlük\ *or* **Mam·e·luke** \'ma-mə-ˌlük\ *noun* [Arabic *mamlūk*, literally, slave] (circa 1506)
**1** : a member of a politically powerful Egyptian military class occupying the sultanate from 1250 to 1517
**2** *often not capitalized* : a white or east Asian slave in Muslim countries

**mam·ma** \'ma-mə\ *noun, plural* **mam·mae** \'ma-ˌmē, -ˌmī\ [Latin, mother, breast, of baby-talk origin] (circa 1693)
: a mammary gland and its accessory parts

**mam·mal** \'ma-məl\ *noun* [New Latin *Mammalia*, from Late Latin, neuter plural of *mammalis* of the breast, from Latin *mamma* breast] (1826)
: any of a class (Mammalia) of warm-blooded higher vertebrates (as placentals, marsupials, or monotremes) that nourish their young with milk secreted by mammary glands, have the skin usually more or less covered with hair, and include humans
— **mam·ma·li·an** \mə-'mā-lē-ən, ma-\ *adjective or noun*

**mam·mal·o·gy** \mə-'ma-lə-jē, ma-'mä-, -'mä-\ *noun* [International Scientific Vocabulary, blend of *mammal* and *-logy*] (1835)
: a branch of zoology dealing with mammals
— **mam·mal·o·gist** \-jist\ *noun*

**mam·ma·ry** \'ma-mə-rē\ *adjective* (1682)
: of, relating to, lying near, or affecting the mammae

**mammary gland** *noun* (1831)
: any of the large compound modified sebaceous glands that in female mammals are modified to secrete milk, are situated ventrally in pairs, and usually terminate in a nipple

☆ **SYNONYMS**
**Malodorous, stinking, fetid, noisome, putrid, rank, fusty, musty** mean bad-smelling. MALODOROUS may range from the unpleasant to the strongly offensive (*malodorous* fertilizers). STINKING and FETID suggest the foul or disgusting (prisoners were held in *stinking* cells) (the *fetid* odor of skunk cabbage). NOISOME adds a suggestion of being harmful or unwholesome as well as offensive (a stagnant, *noisome* sewer). PUTRID implies particularly the sickening odor of decaying organic matter (the *putrid* smell of rotting fish). RANK suggests a strong unpleasant smell (*rank* cigar smoke). FUSTY and MUSTY suggest lack of fresh air and sunlight, FUSTY also implying prolonged uncleanliness, MUSTY stressing the effects of dampness, mildew, or age (a *fusty* attic) (the *musty* odor of a damp cellar).

**mam·mer** *intransitive verb* [Middle English *mameren* to stammer, of imitative origin] (circa 1555)
*obsolete* : WAVER, HESITATE

**mam·mil·la·ry** \'ma-mə-ˌler-ē, ma-'mi-lə-rē\ *adjective* [Latin *mammilla* breast, nipple, diminutive of *mamma*] (1669)
**1** : of, relating to, or resembling the breasts
**2** : studded with breast-shaped protuberances

**mam·mil·lat·ed** \'ma-mə-ˌlā-təd\ *adjective* [Late Latin *mammillatus*, from Latin *mammilla*] (1741)
**1** : having nipples or small protuberances
**2** : having the form of a bluntly rounded protuberance

**¹mam·mock** \'ma-mək\ *noun* [origin unknown] (circa 1529)
*chiefly dialect* : a broken piece : SCRAP

**²mammock** *transitive verb* (1607)
*chiefly dialect* : to tear into fragments : MANGLE

**mam·mo·gram** \'ma-mə-ˌgram\ *noun* [Latin *mamma* + English *-o-* + *-gram*] (1937)
: a photograph of the breasts made by X rays

**mam·mog·ra·phy** \ma-'mä-grə-fē\ *noun* (1937)
: X-ray examination of the breasts (as for early detection of cancer)
— **mam·mo·graph·ic** \ˌma-mə-'gra-fik\ *adjective*

**mam·mon** \'ma-mən\ *noun, often capitalized* [Late Latin *mammona*, from Greek *mamōna*, from Aramaic *māmōnā* riches] (15th century)
: material wealth or possessions especially as having a debasing influence ⟨you cannot serve God and *mammon* —Matthew 6:24 (Revised Standard Version)⟩
— **mam·mon·ism** \-mə-ˌni-zəm\ *noun*

**mam·mon·ist** \-mə-nist\ *noun* (1550)
*archaic* : one devoted to the ideal or pursuit of wealth

**¹mam·moth** \'ma-məth\ *noun* [Russian *mamont, mamot*] (1706)
**1** : any of a genus (*Mammuthus*) of extinct Pleistocene elephants distinguished from recent elephants by highly ridged molars, usually large size, very long tusks that curve upward, and well-developed body hair
**2** : something immense of its kind : GIANT ⟨a company that is a *mammoth* of the industry⟩

**²mammoth** *adjective* (1802)
: of very great size
**synonym** see ENORMOUS

**mam·my** \'ma-mē\ *noun, plural* **mammies** [alteration of *mamma*] (1523)
**1** : MAMA
**2** : a black woman serving as a nurse to white children especially formerly in the southern U.S.

**¹man** \'man, *in compounds* ˌman *or* mən\ *noun, plural* **men** \'men, *in compounds* ˌmen *or* mən\ [Middle English, from Old English *man, mon* human being, male human; akin to Old High German *man* human being, Sanskrit *manu*] (before 12th century)
**1 a** (1) : an individual human; *especially* : an adult male human (2) : a man belonging to a particular category (as by birth, residence, membership, or occupation) — usually used in combination ⟨council*man*⟩ (3) : HUSBAND (4) : LOVER **b** : the human race : MANKIND **c** : a bipedal primate mammal (*Homo sapiens*) that is anatomically related to the great apes but distinguished especially by notable development of the brain with a resultant capacity for articulate speech and abstract reasoning, is usually considered to form a variable number of freely interbreeding races, and is the sole representative of a natural family (Hominidæ); *broadly* : any living or extinct member of this family **d** (1) : one possessing in high degree the qualities considered distinctive of manhood (2) *obsolete* : the quality or state of being manly : MANLINESS **e** : FELLOW, CHAP **f** — used interjectionally to express intensity of feeling ⟨*man*, what a game⟩

**2 a** : INDIVIDUAL, PERSON ⟨a *man* could get killed there⟩ **b** : the individual who can fulfill or who has been chosen to fulfill one's requirements ⟨she's your *man*⟩
**3 a** : a feudal tenant : VASSAL **b** : an adult male servant **c** *plural* : the working force as distinguished from the employer and usually the management
**4 a** : one of the distinctive objects moved by each player in various board games **b** : one of the players on a team
**5** : an alumnus of or student at a college or university ⟨a Bowdoin *man*⟩
**6** *Christian Science* : the compound idea of infinite Spirit : the spiritual image and likeness of God : the full representation of Mind
**7** *often capitalized* : POLICE ⟨when I heard the siren, I knew it was the *Man* —*American Speech*⟩
**8** *often capitalized* : the white establishment : white society ⟨surprise that any black ... should take on so about The *Man* —Peter Goldman⟩
**9** : one extremely fond of or devoted to something specified ⟨a real vanilla ice cream *man*⟩
— **man·less** \'man-ləs\ *adjective*
— **man·like** \-ˌlīk\ *adjective*
— **as one man** : with the agreement and consent of all : UNANIMOUSLY
— **one's own man** : free from interference or control : INDEPENDENT
— **to a man** : without exception

**²man** *transitive verb* **manned; man·ning** (12th century)
**1 a** : to supply with people (as for service) ⟨*man* a fleet⟩ **b** : to station members of a ship's crew at ⟨*man* the capstan⟩ **c** : to serve in the force or complement of ⟨we'll *man* the concession stand while you sell tickets⟩
**2** : to accustom (as a hawk) to humans and the human environment
**3** : to furnish with strength or powers of resistance : BRACE

**ma·na** \'mä-nə\ *noun* [of Polynesian origin; akin to Hawaiian & Maori *mana* mana] (circa 1843)
**1** : the power of the elemental forces of nature embodied in an object or person
**2** : moral authority : PRESTIGE

**man–about–town** \ˌman-ə-ˌbaut-'taun\ *noun, plural* **men–about–town** \ˌmen-\ (1734)
: a worldly and socially active man

**¹man·a·cle** \'ma-ni-kəl\ *noun* [Middle English *manicle*, from Middle French, from Latin *manicula*, diminutive of *manus* hand — more at MANUAL] (14th century)
**1** : a shackle for the hand or wrist : HANDCUFF — usually used in plural
**2** : something used as a restraint

**²manacle** *transitive verb* **man·a·cled; man·a·cling** \-k(ə-)liŋ\ (14th century)
**1** : to confine (the hands) with manacles
**2** : to make fast or secure : BIND; *broadly* : to restrain from movement, progress, or action
**synonym** see HAMPER

**¹man·age** \'ma-nij\ *verb* **man·aged; man·ag·ing** [Italian *maneggiare*, from *mano* hand, from Latin *manus*] (1561)
*transitive verb*
**1** : to handle or direct with a degree of skill: as **a** : to make and keep compliant ⟨can't *manage* her child⟩ **b** : to treat with care : HUSBAND ⟨*managed* his resources carefully⟩ **c** : to exercise executive, administrative, and supervisory direction of ⟨*manage* a business⟩ ⟨*manage* a bond issue⟩ ⟨*manage* a baseball team⟩
**2** : to work upon or try to alter for a purpose ⟨*manage* the press⟩ ⟨*manage* stress⟩
**3** : to succeed in accomplishing : CONTRIVE ⟨*managed* to escape from prison⟩
**4** : to direct the professional career of ⟨an agency that *manages* entertainers⟩
*intransitive verb*
**1 a** : to direct or carry on business or affairs; *also* : to direct a baseball team **b** : to admit of being carried on

**2** : to achieve one's purpose
**synonym** see CONDUCT

**²manage** *noun* [Italian *maneggio* management, training of a horse, from *maneggiare*] (circa 1587)
**1 a** *archaic* : the action and paces of a trained riding horse **b** : the schooling or handling of a horse **c** : a riding school
**2** *obsolete* : MANAGEMENT

**man·age·able** \'ma-ni-jə-bəl\ *adjective* (1598)
: capable of being managed
— **man·age·abil·i·ty** \ˌma-ni-jə-'bi-lə-tē\ *noun*
— **man·age·able·ness** \'ma-ni-jə-bəl-nəs\ *noun*
— **man·age·ably** \-blē\ *adverb*

**man·age·ment** \'ma-nij-mənt\ *noun* (1598)
**1** : the act or art of managing : the conducting or supervising of something (as a business)
**2** : judicious use of means to accomplish an end
**3** : the collective body of those who manage or direct an enterprise
— **man·age·men·tal** \ˌma-nij-'men-t°l\ *adjective*

**man·ag·er** \'ma-ni-jər\ *noun* (1588)
: one that manages: as **a** : a person who conducts business or household affairs **b** : a person whose work or profession is management **c** (1) : a person who directs a team or athlete (2) : a student who in scholastic or collegiate sports supervises equipment and records under the direction of a coach
— **man·a·ge·ri·al** \ˌma-nə-'jir-ē-əl\ *adjective*
— **man·a·ge·ri·al·ly** \-ē-ə-lē\ *adverb*
— **man·ag·er·ship** \'ma-ni-jər-ˌship\ *noun*

**man·ag·er·ess** \'ma-ni-jə-rəs\ *noun* (1797)
: a woman who is a manager
**usage** see -ESS

**managing editor** *noun* (1865)
: an editor in executive and supervisory charge of all editorial activities of a publication (as a newspaper)

**¹ma·ña·na** \mən-'yä-nə\ *noun* [Spanish, literally, tomorrow, from (assumed) Vulgar Latin *maneana*, from feminine of *maneanus* early, from Latin *mane* early in the morning] (1845)
: an indefinite time in the future

**²mañana** *adverb* (1879)
: at an indefinite time in the future

**man ape** *noun* (circa 1864)
**1** : GREAT APE
**2** : any of various fossil primates intermediate in characters between recent humans and the great apes

**Ma·nas·seh** \mə-'na-sə\ *noun* [Hebrew *Měnashsheh*]
**1** : a son of Joseph and the traditional eponymous ancestor of one of the tribes of Israel
**2** : a king of Judah reigning in the 7th century B.C. and noted for his attempt to establish polytheism

**man–at–arms** \ˌman-ət-'ärmz\ *noun, plural* **men–at–arms** \ˌmen-\ (1581)
: SOLDIER; *especially* : a heavily armed and usually mounted soldier

**man·a·tee** \'ma-nə-ˌtē\ *noun* [Spanish *manatí*] (1555)
: any of a genus (*Trichechus*) of chiefly tropical aquatic herbivorous mammals that differ from the related dugong especially in having the tail rounded

**manatee**

**Man·ches·ter terrier** \'man-,ches-tər-, -chə-stər-\ *noun* [*Manchester*, England] (1891)
: any of a breed of small short-haired black-and-tan terriers developed in England

**man–child** \'man-,chīld\ *noun, plural* **men-chil-dren** \'men-,chil-drən, -dərn\ (14th century)
: a male child : SON

**man·chi·neel** \,man-chə-'nē(ə)l\ *noun* [French *mancenille*, from Spanish *manzanilla*, from diminutive of *manzana* apple] (1630)
: a poisonous tropical American tree (*Hippomane mancinella*) of the spurge family having a blistering milky juice and apple-shaped fruit

**Man·chu** \'man-,chü, man-'\ *noun, plural* **Manchu** *or* **Manchus** (1697)
1 : a member of an indigenous people of Manchuria who conquered China and established a dynasty there in 1644
2 : the Tungusic language of the Manchu people
— **Manchu** *adjective*

**man·ci·ple** \'man(t)-sə-pəl\ *noun* [Middle English, from Medieval Latin *mancipium* office of steward, from Latin, act of purchase, from *mancip-, manceps* purchaser — more at EMANCIPATE] (13th century)
: a steward or purveyor especially for a college or monastery

**-mancy** *noun combining form* [Middle English *-mancie*, from Old French, from Latin *-mantia*, from Greek *-manteia*, from *manteia*, from *mantis* diviner, prophet — more at MANTIS]
: divination ⟨oneiro*mancy*⟩

**Man·dae·an** \man-'dē-ən\ *noun* [Mandaean *mandayyā* having knowledge] (1875)
1 : a member of a Gnostic sect of the lower Tigris and Euphrates regions
2 : a form of Aramaic found in documents written by Mandaeans
— **Mandaean** *adjective*

**man·da·la** \'mən-də-lə\ *noun* [Sanskrit *maṇḍala* circle] (1859)
1 : a Hindu or Buddhist graphic symbol of the universe; *specifically* : a circle enclosing a square with a deity on each side
2 : a graphic and often symbolic pattern usually in the form of a circle divided into four separate sections or bearing a multiple projection of an image
— **man·dal·ic** \,mən-'da-lik\ *adjective*

**man·da·mus** \man-'dā-məs\ *noun* [Latin, we enjoin, from *mandare*] (1535)
: a writ issued by a superior court commanding the performance of a specified official act or duty

**Man·dan** \'man-,dan, -dən\ *noun, plural* **Mandan** *or* **Mandans** (1805)
1 : a member of an American Indian people of the Missouri River Valley in North Dakota
2 : the Siouan language of the Mandans

¹**man·da·rin** \'man-d(ə-)rən\ *noun* [Portuguese *mandarim*, from Malay *mĕntĕri*, from Sanskrit *mantrin* counselor, from *mantra* counsel — more at MANTRA] (1589)
1 a : a public official in the Chinese Empire of any of nine superior grades b (1) : a pedantic official (2) : BUREAUCRAT c : a person of position and influence often in intellectual or literary circles; *especially* : an elder and often traditionalist or reactionary member of such a circle
2 *capitalized* a : a form of spoken Chinese used by the court and the official classes of the Empire b : the group of closely related Chinese dialects that are spoken in about four fifths of the country and have a standard variety centering about Beijing
3 [French *mandarine*, from Spanish *mandarina*, probably from *mandarín* mandarin, from Portuguese *mandarim*; probably from the color of a mandarin's robes] a : a small spiny orange tree (*Citrus reticulata*) of southeastern Asia with yellow to reddish orange loose-

rinded fruits; *also* : a derivative of this tree developed in cultivation by artificial selection or hybridization b : the fruit of a mandarin
— **man·da·rin·ic** \,man-də-'ri-nik\ *adjective*
— **man·da·rin·ism** \'man-d(ə-)rə-,ni-zəm\ *noun*

²**mandarin** *adjective* (1604)
1 : of, relating to, or typical of a mandarin ⟨*mandarin* graces⟩
2 : marked by polished ornate complexity of language ⟨*mandarin* prose⟩

**man·da·rin·ate** \'man-d(ə-)rə-,nāt\ *noun* [probably from French *mandarinat*, from *mandarin* mandarin, from Portuguese *mandarim*] (circa 1741)
1 : the office or status of a mandarin
2 : a body of mandarins
3 : rule by mandarins

**mandarin collar** *noun* (1947)
: a narrow stand-up collar usually open in front

**mandarin orange** *noun* (1771)
: MANDARIN 3

**man·da·tary** \'man-də-,ter-ē\ *noun, plural* **-tar·ies** (15th century)
: MANDATORY

¹**man·date** \'man-,dāt\ *noun* [Middle French & Latin; Middle French *mandat*, from Latin *mandatum*, from neuter of *mandatus*, past participle of *mandare* to entrust, enjoin, probably irregular from *manus* hand + *-dere* to put — more at MANUAL, DO] (1501)
1 : an authoritative command; *especially* : a formal order from a superior court or official to an inferior one
2 : an authorization to act given to a representative ⟨accepted the *mandate* of the people⟩
3 a : an order or commission granted by the League of Nations to a member nation for the establishment of a responsible government over a former German colony or other conquered territory b : a mandated territory

²**mandate** *transitive verb* **man·dat·ed; man·dat·ing** (1919)
1 : to administer or assign (as a territory) under a mandate
2 : to make mandatory : ORDER; *also* : DIRECT, REQUIRE

**man·da·tor** \'man-,dā-tər\ *noun* (1681)
: one that gives a mandate

¹**man·da·to·ry** \'man-də-,tōr-ē, -,tor-\ *adjective* (1576)
1 : containing or constituting a command : OBLIGATORY ⟨*mandatory* retirement age⟩
2 : of, by, relating to, or holding a League of Nations mandate
— **man·da·to·ri·ly** \-,tōr-ə-lē, -,tor-\ *adverb*

²**mandatory** *noun, plural* **-ries** (1661)
: one given a mandate; *especially* : a nation holding a mandate from the League of Nations

**man–day** \'man-'dā\ *noun* (1925)
: a unit of one day's work by one person

**Man·de** \'män-,dā, män-'\ *noun* (1883)
1 : MANDINGO
2 : a branch of the Niger-Congo language family spoken primarily in Sierra Leone, Liberia, Guinea, Ivory Coast, Mali, and Burkina Faso

**man·di·ble** \'man-də-bəl\ *noun* [Middle French, from Late Latin *mandibula*, from Latin *mandere* to chew; probably akin to Greek *masasthai* to chew] (15th century)
1 a : JAW 1a; *especially* : a lower jaw consisting of a single bone or of completely fused bones b : the lower jaw with its investing soft parts c : either the upper or lower segment of the bill of a bird
2 : any of various invertebrate mouthparts serving to hold or bite food materials; *especially* : either member of the anterior pair of mouth appendages of an arthropod often forming strong biting jaws
— **man·dib·u·lar** \man-'di-byə-lər\ *adjective*
— **man·dib·u·late** \-lət\ *adjective*

**Man·din·go** \man-'diŋ-(,)gō\ *noun, plural* **Mandingo** *or* **Mandingoes** *or* **Mandingos** (1623)
1 : a member of a people of western Africa centering in the area of the upper Niger valley
2 : the language of the Mandingo people

**Man·din·ka** \man-'diŋ-kə\ *noun, plural* **Mandinka** *or* **Mandinkas** (1939)
: MALINKE

**man·di·o·ca** \,man-dē-'ō-kə\ *variant of* MANIOC

**man·do·la** \man-'dō-lə\ *noun* [Italian, from French *mandore*, modification of Late Latin *pandura* 3-stringed lute — more at BANDORE] (1758)
: a 16th and 17th century lute that is the ancestor of the smaller mandolin

**man·do·lin** \,man-də-'lin, 'man-d°l-ən\ *also* **man·do·line** \,man-də-'lēn, 'man-d°l-ən\ *noun* [Italian *mandolino*, diminutive of *mandola*] (1707)
1 : a musical instrument of the lute family that has a usually pear-shaped body and fretted neck and four to six pairs of strings
2 *usually* **mandoline** [French, from Italian *mandolino* mandolin] : a kitchen utensil with a blade for slicing and shredding
— **man·do·lin·ist** \,man-də-'li-nist\ *noun*

**man·drag·o·ra** \man-'dra-gə-rə\ *noun* [Middle English, from Old English, from Latin *mandragoras*, from Greek] (before 12th century)
: MANDRAKE 1

*mandolin 1*

**man·drake** \'man-,drāk\ *noun* [Middle English, probably alteration of *mandragora*] (14th century)
1 a : a Mediterranean herb (*Mandragora officinarum*) of the nightshade family with ovate leaves, yellowish or purple flowers, and a large forked root traditionally credited with human attributes b : the root of a mandrake formerly used especially to promote conception, as a cathartic, or as a narcotic and soporific
2 : MAYAPPLE

*mandrake 1*

**man·drel** *also* **man·dril** \'man-drəl\ *noun* [probably modification of French *mandrin*] (1665)
1 a : a usually tapered or cylindrical axle, spindle, or arbor inserted into a hole in a piece of work to support it during machining b : a metal bar that serves as a core around which material (as metal) may be cast, molded, forged, bent, or otherwise shaped
2 : the shaft and bearings on which a tool (as a circular saw) is mounted

**man·drill** \'man-drəl\ *noun* [probably from ¹*man* + ³*drill*] (1744)
: a large baboon (*Papio sphinx* synonym *Mandrillus sphinx*) of central Africa west of the Congo River with the male having a bright red and blue muzzle

**mane** \'mān\ *noun* [Middle English, from Old English *manu*; akin to Old High German *mana* mane, Latin *monile* necklace] (before 12th century)
1 : long and heavy hair growing about the neck and head of some mammals (as a horse or lion)
2 : long heavy hair on a person's head

*mandrill*

**— maned** \'mānd\ *adjective*
**man·eat·er** \'man-ˌē-tər\ *noun* (1600)
: one that is or is thought to have an appetite for human flesh: as **a** : CANNIBAL **b** : MACKEREL SHARK; *especially* : GREAT WHITE SHARK — called also *man-eater shark, man-eating shark* **c** : a large feline (as a lion or tiger) that has acquired the habit of feeding on human flesh
**— man–eat·ing** \-ˌē-tiŋ\ *adjective*
**maned wolf** *noun* (1903)
: a yellowish red wild canid (*Chrysocyon brachyurus*) inhabiting South American grasslands and having black coloration on the nape and lower legs
**ma·nège** *also* **ma·nege** \ma-'nezh, mə-, -'nāzh\ *noun* [French *manège*, from Italian *maneggio* training of a horse — more at MANAGE] (1644)
**1** : a school for teaching horsemanship and for training horses
**2** : the art of horsemanship or of training horses
**3** : the movements or paces of a trained horse
**ma·nes** \'mä-ˌnās, 'mā-ˌnēz\ *noun plural* [Latin]
**1** *often capitalized* : the deified spirits of the ancient Roman dead honored with graveside sacrifices
**2** : the venerated or appeased spirit of a dead person
**¹ma·neu·ver** \mə-'nü-vər, -'nyü-\ *noun* [French *manœuvre*, from Old French *maneuvre* work done by hand, from Medieval Latin *manuopera*, from Latin *manu operare* to work by hand] (1758)
**1 a** : a military or naval movement **b** : an armed forces training exercise; *especially* : an extended and large-scale training exercise involving military and naval units separately or in combination — often used in plural
**2** : a procedure or method of working usually involving expert physical movement
**3 a** : evasive movement or shift of tactics **b** : an intended and controlled variation from a straight and level flight path in the operation of an airplane
**4 a** : an action taken to gain a tactical end **b** : an adroit and clever management of affairs often using trickery and deception
*synonym* see TRICK
**²maneuver** *verb* **ma·neu·vered; ma·neu·ver·ing** \-'nü-və-riŋ, -'nyü-; -'n(y)üv-riŋ\ (1777)
*intransitive verb*
**1 a** : to perform a movement in military or naval tactics in order to secure an advantage **b** : to make a series of changes in direction and position for a specific purpose
**2** : to use stratagems : SCHEME
*transitive verb*
**1** : to cause to execute tactical movements
**2** : to manage into or out of a position or condition : MANIPULATE
**3 a** : to guide with adroitness and design **b** : to bring about or secure as a result of skillful management ◆
**— ma·neu·ver·abil·i·ty** \-ˌnü-və-rə-'bi-lə-tē, -ˌnyü-; -ˌn(y)üv-rə-\ *noun*
**— ma·neu·ver·able** \-'nü-və-rə-bəl, -'nyü-; -'n(y)üv-rə-bəl\ *adjective*
**— ma·neu·ver·er** \-'nü-vər-ər, -'nyü-\ *noun*
**man–for–man** \ˌman-fər-'man\ *adjective* (circa 1949)
: MAN-TO-MAN 2
**man Friday** *noun* [*Friday*, servant in *Robinson Crusoe* (1719), novel by Daniel Defoe] (1887)
: an efficient and devoted aide or employee : a right-hand man
**man·ful** \'man-fəl\ *adjective* (14th century)
: having or showing courage and resolution
**— man·ful·ly** \-fə-lē\ *adverb*
**— man·ful·ness** *noun*

**man·ga·bey** \'maŋ-gə-ˌbē\ *noun, plural* **-beys** [French, from *Mangabey*, region of Madagascar] (1774)
: any of a genus (*Cercocebus*) of slender long-tailed African monkeys
**mangan-** *combining form* [German *Mangan*, from French *manganèse*]
: manganese ⟨*manganate*⟩
**man·ga·nate** \'maŋ-gə-ˌnāt\ *noun* (1839)
**1** : a salt containing manganese in the anion MnO₄
**2** : MANGANITE
**man·ga·nese** \'maŋ-gə-ˌnēz, -ˌnēs\ *noun* [French *manganèse*, from Italian *manganese* manganese dioxide] (1783)
: a grayish white usually hard and brittle metallic element that resembles iron but is not magnetic — see ELEMENT table
**— man·ga·ne·sian** \ˌmaŋ-gə-'nē-zhən, -shən\ *adjective*
**manganese dioxide** *noun* (1882)
: a dark insoluble compound MnO₂ used especially as an oxidizing agent, as a depolarizer of dry cells, and in making glass and ceramics
**man·gan·ic** \man-'ga-nik, maŋ-\ *adjective* (circa 1828)
: of, relating to, or derived from manganese; *especially* : containing this element with a valence of three or six
**man·ga·nite** \'maŋ-gə-ˌnīt\ *noun* (1827)
**1** : an ore of manganese MnO(OH) that is a hydroxide of manganese usually in brilliant gray crystals
**2** : any of various unstable salts made by reaction of manganese dioxide with a base
**man·ga·nous** \-nəs\ *adjective* (1842)
: of, relating to, or derived from manganese; *especially* : containing this element with a valence of two
**mange** \'mānj\ *noun* [alteration of Middle English *manjewe*, from Middle French *mangene* itching, from *mangier* to eat] (1540)
: any of various persistent contagious skin diseases marked especially by eczematous inflammation and loss of hair, affecting domestic animals or sometimes humans, and caused by a minute parasitic mite — compare SARCOPTIC MANGE
**man·gel** \'maŋ-gəl\ *noun* [short for *mangelwurzel*] (1877)
: a large coarse yellow to reddish orange beet extensively grown as food for cattle
**man·gel–wur·zel** \-ˌwər-zəl\ *noun* [German, alteration of *Mangoldwurzel*, from *Mangold* beet + *Wurzel* root] (1767)
: MANGEL
**man·ger** \'mān-jər\ *noun* [Middle English *mangeour, manger*, from Middle French *maingeure*, from *mangier* to eat, from Latin *manducare* to chew, devour, from *manducus* glutton, from *mandere* to chew — more at MANDIBLE] (14th century)
: a trough or open box in a stable designed to hold feed or fodder for livestock
**¹man·gle** \'maŋ-gəl\ *transitive verb* **man·gled; man·gling** \-g(ə-)liŋ\ [Middle English, from Anglo-French *mangler*] (15th century)
**1** : to injure with deep disfiguring wounds by cutting, tearing, or crushing ⟨people . . . *mangled* by sharks —V. G. Heiser⟩
**2** : to spoil, injure, or make incoherent especially through ineptitude ⟨a story *mangled* beyond recognition⟩
*synonym* see MAIM
**— man·gler** \-g(ə-)lər\ *noun*
**²mangle** *noun* [Dutch *mangel*, from German, from Middle High German, diminutive of *mange* mangonel, mangle, from Latin *manganum*] (1774)
: a machine for ironing laundry by passing it between heated rollers
**³mangle** *transitive verb* **man·gled; man·gling** \-g(ə-)liŋ\ (1775)
: to press or smooth (as damp linen) with a mangle

**— man·gler** \-g(ə-)lər\ *noun*
**man·go** \'maŋ-ˌgō\ *noun, plural* **mangoes** *also* **mangos** [Portuguese *manga*, probably from Malayalam *māṅṅa*] (1582)
**1** : a tropical fruit commonly with a firm yellowish red skin, hard central stone, and juicy aromatic pulp; *also* : an evergreen tree (*Mangifera indica*) of the cashew family that bears mangoes
**2** : SWEET PEPPER
**man·go·nel** \'maŋ-gə-ˌnel\ *noun* [Middle English, from Old French, probably from Medieval Latin *manganellus*, diminutive of Late Latin *manganum* philter, mangonel, from Greek *manganon*] (13th century)
: a military engine formerly used to throw missiles
**man·go·steen** \'maŋ-gə-ˌstēn\ *noun* [modification of Malay *manggisutan*] (1598)
: a dark reddish brown fruit of southeastern Asia with a thick rind and juicy flesh having a flavor suggestive of both peach and pineapple; *also* : a tree (*Garcinia mangostana*) of the Saint-John's-wort family that bears mangosteens
**man·grove** \'man-ˌgrōv, 'maŋ-\ *noun* [probably from Portuguese *mangue* mangrove (from Spanish *mangle*, probably from Taino) + English *grove*] (1613)
**1** : any of a genus (*Rhizophora*, especially *R. mangle* of the family Rhizophoraceae) of tropical maritime trees or shrubs that send out many prop roots and form dense masses important in coastal land building
**2** : any of numerous trees (as of the genera *Avicennia* of the vervain family or *Sonneratia* of the family Sonneratiaceae) with growth habits like those of the true mangroves
**mangy** \'mān-jē\ *adjective* **mang·i·er; -est** (1540)
**1** : affected with or resulting from mange
**2** : having many worn or bare spots : SEEDY, SHABBY
**— man·gi·ness** \-jē-nəs\ *noun*
**man·han·dle** \'man-ˌhan-d³l\ *transitive verb* (circa 1865)
**1** : to handle roughly
**2** : to move or manage by human force ⟨*manhandled* the posts into place⟩
**man·hat·tan** \man-'ha-t³n, mən-\ *noun, often capitalized* [*Manhattan*, borough of New York City] (1890)

---

◇ WORD HISTORY
**maneuver** As peculiar as the connection seems, we owe both *maneuver* and *manure* to the same French source. The Old French verb *manovrer*, meaning "to work" or "to place with the hand," developed from *manu operare*, literally, "to work by hand," in the spoken Latin of Gaul. From an Anglo-French variant of this Old French verb such as *meinourer*, Middle English adopted *maynouren* or *manouren*, which had the senses "to take in hand, manage" and "to cultivate (land)." In the 16th century English derived on the basis of the latter sense the noun *manure*, meaning "material that fertilizes land." In the meantime, *manovrer* continued to go its own way in French. By the middle of the 18th century, its Modern French outcome *manœuvrer* (influenced in form by the noun *manœuvre*) had developed a new specific meaning "to perform a movement in military or naval tactics" and English reborrowed the word, quickly adapting it to several nonmilitary uses as well.

---

\ə\ abut \ᵊ\ kitten \ər\ further \a\ ash \ā\ ace
\ä\ mop, mar \au̇\ out \ch\ chin \e\ bet \ē\ easy
\g\ go \i\ hit \ī\ ice \j\ job \ŋ\ sing \ō\ go
\ȯ\ law \ȯi\ boy \th\ thin \th\ the \ü\ loot \u̇\ foot
\y\ yet \zh\ vision *see also* Guide to Pronunciation

: a cocktail consisting of vermouth, whiskey, and sometimes a dash of bitters

**man·hole** \'man-ˌhōl\ *noun* (1793)
: a hole through which one may go especially to gain access to an underground or enclosed structure

**man·hood** \'man-ˌhu̇d\ *noun* (13th century)
**1** : the condition of being a human being
**2** : qualities associated with men
**3** : the condition of being an adult male as distinguished from a child or female
**4** : adult males : MEN

**man–hour** \'man-'au̇(-ə)r\ *noun* (1912)
: a unit of one hour's work by one person that is used especially as a basis for cost accounting and wages

**man·hunt** \'man-ˌhənt\ *noun* (1846)
: an organized and usually intensive hunt for a person and especially for one charged with a crime

**ma·nia** \'mā-nē-ə, -nyə\ *noun* [Middle English, from Late Latin, from Greek, from *mainesthai* to be mad; akin to Greek *menos* spirit — more at MIND] (14th century)
**1** : excitement manifested by mental and physical hyperactivity, disorganization of behavior, and elevation of mood; *specifically* : the manic phase of manic-depressive psychosis
**2** : excessive or unreasonable enthusiasm ⟨a *mania* for saving things⟩; *also* : the object of such enthusiasm

**ma·ni·ac** \'mā-nē-ˌak\ *noun* [Late Latin *maniacus* maniacal, from Greek *maniakos,* from *mania*] (circa 1763)
**1** : MADMAN, LUNATIC
**2** : a person characterized by an inordinate or ungovernable enthusiasm for something

**ma·ni·a·cal** \mə-'nī-ə-kəl\ *also* **ma·ni·ac** \'mā-nē-ˌak\ *adjective* (1604)
**1** : affected with or suggestive of madness
**2** : characterized by ungovernable excitement or frenzy : FRANTIC
— **ma·ni·a·cal·ly** \mə-'nī-ə-k(ə-)lē\ *adverb*

**man·ic** \'ma-nik\ *adjective* (1902)
: affected with, relating to, or resembling mania
— **manic** *noun*
— **man·i·cal·ly** \-ni-k(ə-)lē\ *adverb*

**man·ic–de·pres·sive** \ˌma-nik-di-'pre-siv\ *adjective* (1902)
: characterized either by mania or by psychotic depression or by alternating mania and depression
— **manic–depressive** *noun*

**Man·i·chae·an** *or* **Man·i·che·an** \ˌma-nə-'kē-ən\ *or* **Man·i·chee** \'man-ə-ˌkē\ *noun* [Late Latin *manichaeus,* from Late Greek *manichaios,* from *Manichaios* Manes (died about 276 A.D.) Persian founder of the sect] (1556)
**1** : a believer in a syncretistic religious dualism originating in Persia in the 3d century A.D. and teaching the release of the spirit from matter through asceticism
**2** : a believer in religious or philosophical dualism
— **Manichaean** *adjective*
— **Man·i·chae·an·ism** \ˌma-nə-'kē-ə-ˌni-zəm\ *noun*
— **Man·i·chae·ism** \'ma-nə-(ˌ)kē-ˌi-zəm\ *noun*

**man·i·cot·ti** \ˌma-nə-'kä-tē\ *noun, plural* **manicotti** [Italian, plural of *manicotto* muff, from *manica* sleeve, from Latin, from *manus* hand] (1948)
: tubular pasta shells that may be stuffed with ricotta or a meat mixture; *also* : a dish of stuffed manicotti usually with tomato sauce

**¹man·i·cure** \'ma-nə-ˌkyu̇r\ *noun* [French, from Latin *manus* hand + French *-icure* (as in *pédicure* pedicure) — more at MANUAL] (1880)
**1** : MANICURIST
**2** : a treatment for the care of the hands and fingernails

**²manicure** *transitive verb* **-cured; -cur·ing** (circa 1890)
**1** : to do manicure work on; *especially* : to trim and polish the fingernails of
**2 a** : to trim closely and evenly ⟨*manicured* lawns⟩ **b** : GROOM 2 ⟨*manicured* flower beds⟩

**man·i·cur·ist** \-ˌkyu̇r-ist\ *noun* (1889)
: a person who gives manicures

**¹man·i·fest** \'ma-nə-ˌfest\ *adjective* [Middle English, from Middle French or Latin; Middle French *manifeste,* from Latin *manifestus* caught in the act, flagrant, obvious, perhaps from *manus* + *-festus* (akin to Latin in*festus* hostile)] (14th century)
**1** : readily perceived by the senses and especially by the sight
**2** : easily understood or recognized by the mind : OBVIOUS
*synonym* see EVIDENT
— **man·i·fest·ly** *adverb*

**²manifest** *transitive verb* (14th century)
: to make evident or certain by showing or displaying
*synonym* see SHOW
— **man·i·fest·er** *noun*

**³manifest** *noun* (1561)
**1** : MANIFESTATION, INDICATION
**2** : MANIFESTO
**3** : a list of passengers or an invoice of cargo for a vehicle (as a ship or plane)

**man·i·fes·tant** \ˌma-nə-'fes-tənt\ *noun* (1880)
: one who makes or participates in a manifestation

**man·i·fes·ta·tion** \ˌma-nə-fə-'stā-shən, -ˌfe-'stā-\ *noun* (15th century)
**1 a** : the act, process, or an instance of manifesting **b** : something that manifests or is manifest **c** : one of the forms in which an individual is manifested **d** : an occult phenomenon; *specifically* : MATERIALIZATION
**2** : a public demonstration of power and purpose

**manifest destiny** *noun, often M&D capitalized* (1845)
: a future event accepted as inevitable ⟨in the mid-19th century expansion to the Pacific was regarded as the *Manifest Destiny* of the United States⟩; *broadly* : an ostensibly benevolent or necessary policy of imperialistic expansion

**¹man·i·fes·to** \ˌma-nə-'fes-(ˌ)tō\ *noun, plural* **-tos** *or* **-toes** [Italian, denunciation, manifest, from *manifestare* to manifest, from Latin, from *manifestus*] (1647)
: a written statement declaring publically the intentions, motives, or views of its issuer

**²manifesto** *intransitive verb* (1748)
: to issue a manifesto

**¹man·i·fold** \'ma-nə-ˌfōld\ *adjective* [Middle English, from Old English *manigfeald,* from *manig* many + *-feald* -fold] (before 12th century)
**1 a** : marked by diversity or variety **b** : MANY
**2** : comprehending or uniting various features : MULTIFARIOUS
**3** : rightfully so-called for many reasons ⟨a *manifold* liar⟩
**4** : consisting of or operating many of one kind combined ⟨a *manifold* bellpull⟩
— **man·i·fold·ly** \-ˌfōl(d)-lē\ *adverb*
— **man·i·fold·ness** \-ˌfōl(d)-nəs\ *noun*

**²manifold** *adverb* (before 12th century)
: many times : a great deal ⟨will increase your blessings *manifold*⟩

**³manifold** (before 12th century)
*transitive verb*
**1** : to make manifold : MULTIPLY
**2** : to make several or many copies of
*intransitive verb*
: to make several or many copies

**⁴manifold** *noun* (1855)
: something that is manifold: as **a** : a whole that unites or consists of many diverse elements ⟨the *manifold* of aspirations, passions, frustrations —Harry Slochower⟩ **b** : a pipe fitting with several lateral outlets for connecting one pipe with others; *also* : a fitting on an

internal-combustion engine that directs a fuel and air mixture to or receives the exhaust gases from several cylinders **c** : SET 21 **d** : a topological space in which every point has a neighborhood that is homeomorphic to the interior of a sphere in Euclidean space of the same number of dimensions

**man·i·kin** *or* **man·ni·kin** \'ma-ni-kən\ *noun* [Dutch *mannekijn* little man, from Middle Dutch, diminutive of *man;* akin to Old English *man*] (circa 1536)
**1** : MANNEQUIN
**2** : a little man : DWARF, PYGMY

**ma·nila** *also* **ma·nil·la** \mə-'ni-lə\ *adjective* (1834)
**1** *capitalized* : made from Manila hemp
**2** : made of manila paper
— **manila** *noun*

**Manila hemp** *noun* [*Manila,* Philippine Islands] (circa 1847)
: ABACA

**manila paper** *noun, often M capitalized* (1873)
: a strong and durable paper of a brownish or buff color and smooth finish made originally from Manila hemp

**ma·nille** \mə-'nil\ *noun* [modification of Spanish *malilla*] (1674)
: the second highest trump in various card games (as in ombre)

**man in the street** (1831)
: an average or ordinary person

**man·i·oc** \'ma-nē-ˌäk\ *noun* [French *manioc* & Spanish *manioca,* from Portuguese *mandioca,* from Tupi *manioca*] (1568)
: CASSAVA

**man·i·ple** \'ma-nə-pəl\ *noun* [Middle English, from Medieval Latin *manipulus,* handful, from *manus* hand + *-pulus* (perhaps akin to Latin *plēre* to fill); from its having been originally held in the hand — more at MANUAL, FULL] (15th century)
**1** : a long narrow strip of silk worn at mass over the left arm by clerics of or above the order of subdeacon
**2** [Latin *manipulus,* from *manipulus* handful] : a subdivision of the Roman legion consisting of either 120 or 60 men

**ma·nip·u·la·ble** \mə-'ni-pyə-lə-bəl\ *adjective* (1881)
: capable of being manipulated
— **ma·nip·u·la·bil·i·ty** \-ˌni-pyə-lə-'bi-lə-tē\ *noun*

**ma·nip·u·lar** \mə-'ni-pyə-lər\ *adjective* (1623)
**1** : of or relating to the ancient Roman maniple
**2** : of, relating to, or performed by manipulation : MANIPULATIVE

**ma·nip·u·late** \mə-'ni-pyə-ˌlāt\ *transitive verb* **-lat·ed; -lat·ing** [back-formation from *manipulation,* from French, from *manipuler* to handle an apparatus in chemistry, ultimately from Latin *manipulus*] (1831)
**1** : to treat or operate with the hands or by mechanical means especially in a skillful manner
**2 a** : to manage or utilize skillfully **b** : to control or play upon by artful, unfair, or insidious means especially to one's own advantage
**3** : to change by artful or unfair means so as to serve one's purpose : DOCTOR
— **ma·nip·u·lat·able** \-ˌlā-tə-bəl\ *adjective*
— **ma·nip·u·la·tion** \-ˌni-pyə-'lā-shən\ *noun*
— **ma·nip·u·la·tive** \-'ni-pyə-ˌlā-tiv, -lə-\ *adjective*
— **ma·nip·u·la·tive·ly** *adverb*
— **ma·nip·u·la·tive·ness** *noun*
— **ma·nip·u·la·tor** \-ˌlā-tər\ *noun*
— **ma·nip·u·la·to·ry** \-lə-ˌtȯr-ē, -ˌtȯr-\ *adjective*

**man·i·tou** *or* **man·i·tu** \'ma-nə-ˌtü\ *also* **man·i·to** \-ˌtō\ *noun* [Ojibwa *manito`*] (1671)
: a supernatural force that according to an Algonquian conception pervades the natural world

**man jack** \'man-'jak\ *noun* (1840)
: individual man ⟨every *man jack*⟩

**man-kind** *noun singular but singular or plural in construction* (13th century)
**1** \'man-'kīnd, -,kīnd\ : the human race : the totality of human beings
**2** \-,kīnd\ : men especially as distinguished from women

**¹man-ly** \'man-lē\ *adverb* (before 12th century)
: in a manly manner

**²manly** *adjective* **man-li-er; -est** (13th century)
**1** : having qualities generally associated with a man : STRONG, VIRILE
**2** : appropriate in character to a man ⟨*manly* sports⟩
— **man-li-ness** *noun*

**man–made** \'man-'mād, -,mād\ *adjective* (circa 1718)
: manufactured, created, or constructed by human beings; *specifically* : SYNTHETIC ⟨*man-made* fibers⟩

**man-na** \'ma-nə\ *noun* [Middle English, from Old English, from Late Latin, from Greek, from Hebrew *mān*] (before 12th century)
**1 a** : food miraculously supplied to the Israelites in their journey through the wilderness **b** : divinely supplied spiritual nourishment **c** : a usually sudden and unexpected source of gratification, pleasure, or gain
**2 a** : the sweetish dried exudate of a European ash (especially *Fraxinus ornus*) that contains mannitol and has been used as a laxative and demulcent **b** : a similar product excreted by a scale insect (*Trabutina mannipara*) feeding on the tamarisk

**manna grass** *noun* (1597)
: any of a genus (*Glyceria*) of chiefly North American perennial grasses of wetland or aquatic habitats

**man-nan** \'ma-,nan, -nən\ *noun* [International Scientific Vocabulary *mannose* + ³-*an*] (1895)
: any of several polysaccharides that are polymers of mannose and occur especially in plant cell walls

**manned** \'mand\ *adjective* (1617)
: carrying or performed by a human being ⟨*manned* space-flight⟩

**man-ne-quin** \'ma-ni-kən\ *noun* [French, from Dutch *mannekijn* little man — more at MANIKIN] (1730)
**1** : an artist's, tailor's, or dressmaker's lay figure; *also* : a form representing the human figure used especially for displaying clothes
**2** : one employed to model clothing

**man-ner** \'ma-nər\ *noun* [Middle English *manere*, from Old French *maniere* way of acting, from (assumed) Vulgar Latin *manuaria*, from Latin, feminine of *manuarius* of the hand, from *manus* hand — more at MANUAL] (12th century)
**1 a** : KIND, SORT ⟨what *manner* of man is he⟩ **b** : KINDS, SORTS ⟨all *manner* of problems⟩
**2 a** (1) : a characteristic or customary mode of acting : CUSTOM (2) : a mode of procedure or way of acting : FASHION (3) : method of artistic execution or mode of presentation : STYLE **b** *plural* : social conduct or rules of conduct as shown in the prevalent customs ⟨Victorian *manners*⟩ **c** : characteristic or distinctive bearing, air, or deportment ⟨his poised gracious *manner*⟩ **d** *plural* (1) : habitual conduct or deportment : BEHAVIOR ⟨mind your *manners*⟩ (2) : good manners **e** : a distinguished or stylish air
*synonym* see BEARING, METHOD
— **man-ner-less** \-ləs\ *adjective*

**man-nered** \'ma-nərd\ *adjective* (14th century)
**1** : having manners of a specified kind ⟨well-*mannered*⟩
**2 a** : having or displaying a particular manner **b** : having an artificial or stilted character ⟨passages . . . so *mannered* as to be unintelligible —R. G. G. Price⟩

**man-ner-ism** \'ma-nə-,ri-zəm\ *noun* (1803)
**1 a** : exaggerated or affected adherence to a particular style or manner : ARTIFICIALITY, PRECIOSITY ⟨refined almost to the point of *mannerism* —Winthrop Sargeant⟩ **b** *often capitalized* : an art style in late 16th century Europe characterized by spatial incongruity and excessive elongation of the human figures
**2** : a characteristic and often unconscious mode or peculiarity of action, bearing, or treatment
*synonym* see POSE
— **man-ner-ist** \-rist\ *noun*
— **man-ner-is-tic** \,ma-nə-'ris-tik\ *adjective*

**man-ner-ly** \'ma-nər-lē\ *adjective* (circa 1529)
: showing good manners
— **man-ner-li-ness** *noun*
— **mannerly** *adverb*

**man-nish** \'ma-nish\ *adjective* (14th century)
**1** : resembling or suggesting a man rather than a woman
**2** : generally associated with or characteristic of a man rather than a woman ⟨her *mannish* clothes⟩
— **man-nish-ly** *adverb*
— **man-nish-ness** *noun*

**man-nite** \'ma-,nīt\ *noun* [French, from *manna*, from Late Latin] (1830)
: MANNITOL

**man-ni-tol** \'ma-nə-,tȯl, -,tōl\ *noun* [International Scientific Vocabulary] (1879)
: a slightly sweet crystalline alcohol $C_6H_{14}O_6$ found in many plants and used especially as a diuretic and in testing kidney function

**man-nose** \'ma-,nōs, -,nōz\ *noun* [International Scientific Vocabulary *mann*ite + ²-*ose*] (1888)
: an aldose $C_6H_{12}O_6$ whose dextrorotatory enantiomorph occurs especially as a structural unit of mannans from which it can be recovered by hydrolysis

**ma-no** \'mä-(,)nō\ *noun, plural* **manos** [Spanish, literally, hand, from Latin *manus* — more at MANUAL] (circa 1892)
: a stone used as the upper millstone for grinding foods (as Indian corn) by hand in a metate

**ma-noeu-vre** *chiefly British variant of* MANEUVER

**man of God** (1748)
: CLERGYMAN

**man of letters** (1645)
**1** : SCHOLAR
**2** : AUTHOR

**man of straw** (1624)
: STRAW MAN

**man of the house** (circa 1904)
: the chief male in a household

**man of the world** (15th century)
: a practical or worldly-wise man of wide experience

**man-of-war** \,ma-nə(v)-'wȯr\ *noun, plural* **men-of-war** \,men-\ (15th century)
: a combatant warship of a recognized navy

**ma-nom-e-ter** \mə-'nä-mə-tər\ *noun* [French *manomètre*, from Greek *manos* sparse, loose, rare (akin to Armenian *manr* small) + French -*mètre*] (circa 1730)
**1** : an instrument (as a pressure gauge) for measuring the pressure of gases and vapors
**2** : SPHYGMOMANOMETER
— **man-o-met-ric** \,ma-nə-'me-trik\ *adjective*
— **man-o-met-ri-cal-ly** \-tri-k(ə-)lē\ *adverb*
— **ma-nom-e-try** \mə-'nä-mə-trē\ *noun*

**man on horseback** (1860)
**1** : a usually military figure whose ambitions and popularity mark him as a potential dictator
**2** : DICTATOR

**man-or** \'ma-nər\ *noun* [Middle English *maner*, from Old French *manoir*, from *manoir* to sojourn, dwell, from Latin *manēre* — more at MANSION] (14th century)
**1 a** : the house or hall of an estate : MANSION **b** : a landed estate

**2 a** : a unit of English rural territorial organization; *especially* : such a unit in the Middle Ages consisting of an estate under a lord enjoying a variety of rights over land and tenants including the right to hold court **b** : a tract of land in North America occupied by tenants who pay a fixed rent in money or kind to the proprietor
— **ma-no-ri-al** \mə-'nȯr-ē-əl, -'nȯr-\ *adjective*
— **ma-no-ri-al-ism** \-ə-,li-zəm\ *noun*

**manor house** *noun* (1575)
: the house of the lord of a manor

**man-o'-war bird** \,ma-nə-'wȯr-\ *noun* (1707)
: FRIGATE BIRD

**man-pack** \'man-,pak\ *adjective* (1965)
: designed to be carried by one person

**man power** *noun* (1862)
**1** : power available from or supplied by the physical effort of human beings
**2** *usually* **man-pow-er** : the total supply of persons available and fitted for service

**man-qué** \mä^n-'kā\ *adjective* [French, from past participle of *manquer* to lack, fail, from Italian *mancare*, from *manco* lacking, left-handed, from Latin, having a crippled hand, probably from *manus*] (1778)
: short of or frustrated in the fulfillment of one's aspirations or talents — used postpositively ⟨a poet *manqué*⟩

**man-rope** \'man-,rōp\ *noun* (1769)
: a side rope (as to a ship's gangway or ladder) used as a handrail

**man-sard** \'man-,särd, -sərd\ *noun* [French *mansarde*, from François *Mansart* (died 1666) French architect] (circa 1734)
: a roof having two slopes on all sides with the lower slope steeper than the upper one — see ROOF illustration
— **man-sard-ed** \-,sär-dəd, -sər-\ *adjective*

**manse** \'man(t)s\ *noun* [Middle English *manss*, from Medieval Latin *mansa*, *mansus*, *mansum*, from Latin *mansus* lodging, from *manēre*] (15th century)
**1** *archaic* : the dwelling of a householder
**2** : the residence of a clergyman; *especially* : the house of a Presbyterian clergyman
**3** : a large imposing residence

**man-ser-vant** \'man-,sər-vənt\ *noun, plural* **men-ser-vants** \'men-,sər-vən(t)s\ (14th century)
: a male servant

**-manship** *noun suffix* [-*man* + -*ship* (as in *horsemanship*)]
**1** : art or practice of a competitive nature ⟨brink*manship*⟩
**2** : skilled engagement in a competitive activity ⟨grants*manship*⟩
*word history* see GAMESMANSHIP

**man-sion** \'man(t)-shən\ *noun* [Middle English, from Middle French, from Latin *mansion-, mansio*, from *manēre* to remain, dwell; akin to Greek *menein* to remain] (14th century)
**1 a** *obsolete* : the act of remaining or dwelling : STAY **b** *archaic* : DWELLING, ABODE
**2 a** (1) : the house of the lord of a manor (2) : a large imposing residence **b** : a separate apartment or lodging in a large structure
**3 a** : HOUSE 3b **b** : one of the 28 parts into which the moon's monthly course through the heavens is divided

**man-size** \'man-,sīz\ *or* **man-sized** \-,sīzd\ *adjective* (1913)
**1** : suitable for or requiring a man ⟨a *man-size* job⟩
**2** : larger than others of its kind ⟨constructed a *man-size* model⟩

**man-slaugh-ter** \'man-,slȯ-tər\ *noun* (15th century)

: the unlawful killing of a human being without express or implied malice

**man·slay·er** \-ˌslā-ər\ *noun* (14th century)
: one who commits homicide

**man's man** *noun* (1897)
: a man noted or admired for traditionally masculine interests and activities

**man·sue·tude** \'man(t)-swi-ˌtüd, man-'sü-ə-, -ˌtyüd\ *noun* [Middle English, from Latin *mansuetudo,* from *mansuescere* to tame, from *manus* hand + *suescere* to accustom; akin to Greek *ēthos* custom — more at MANUAL, SIB] (14th century)
: the quality or state of being gentle : MEEKNESS, TAMENESS

**man·ta** \'man-tə\ *noun* [Spanish, alteration of *manto* cloak, from Late Latin *mantus,* probably back-formation from Latin *mantellum* mantle] (1697)
**1** : a square piece of cloth or blanket used in southwestern U.S. and Latin America usually as a cloak or shawl
**2** [American Spanish, from Spanish; from its shape] : DEVILFISH 1

**man·tai·lored** \'man-ˌtā-lərd\ *adjective* (1922)
: made with the severe simplicity associated with men's coats and suits

**manta ray** *noun* (1936)
: DEVILFISH 1

**man·teau** \man-'tō, 'man-ˌ\ *noun* [French, from Old French *mantel*] (1671)
: a loose cloak, coat, or robe

**man·tel** \'man-t°l\ *noun* [Middle English, from Middle French, from Old French, mantle] (15th century)
**1 a** : a beam, stone, or arch serving as a lintel to support the masonry above a fireplace **b** : the finish around a fireplace
**2** : a shelf above a fireplace

**man·tel·et** \'mant-lət, 'man-t°l-ət, ˌman-t°l-'et\ *noun* [Middle English, from Middle French *mantlet,* diminutive of *mantel*] (14th century)
**1** : a very short cape or cloak
**2** *or* **mant·let** \'mant-lət\ : a movable shelter formerly used by besiegers as a protection when attacking

**man·tel·piece** \'man-t°l-ˌpēs\ *noun* (1686)
**1** : a mantel with its side elements
**2** : MANTEL 2

**man·tel·shelf** \-ˌshelf\ *noun* (circa 1828)
: MANTEL 2

**man·tic** \'man-tik\ *adjective* [Greek *mantikos,* from *mantis*] (1850)
: of or relating to the faculty of divination : PROPHETIC

**man·ti·core** \'man-ti-ˌkōr, -ˌkȯr\ *noun* [Middle English, from Latin *mantichora,* from Greek *mantichōras*] (14th century)
: a legendary animal with the head of a man, the body of a lion, and the tail of a dragon or scorpion

**man·tid** \'man-təd\ *noun* [New Latin *Mantidae,* group name, from *Mantis,* genus name] (1895)
: MANTIS

**man·til·la** \man-'tē-yə, -'ti-lə\ *noun* [Spanish, diminutive of *manta*] (1717)
**1** : a light scarf worn over the head and shoulders especially by Spanish and Latin-American women
**2** : a short light cape or cloak

**man·tis** \'man-təs\ *noun, plural* **man·tis·es** *or* **man·tes** \'man-ˌtēz\ [New Latin, from Greek, literally, diviner, prophet; akin to Greek *mainesthai* to be mad — more at MANIA] (1658)
: any of an order or suborder (Mantodea and especially family Mantidae) of large usually green insects that feed on other insects and clasp their prey in forelimbs held up as if in prayer

**man·tis·sa** \man-'ti-sə\ *noun* [Latin *mantisa, mantissa* makeweight, from Etruscan] (circa 1847)

: the part of a logarithm to the right of the decimal point

**¹man·tle** \'man-t°l\ *noun* [Middle English *mantel,* from Old French, from Latin *mantellum*] (13th century)
**1 a** : a loose sleeveless garment worn over other clothes : CLOAK **b** : a mantle regarded as a symbol of preeminence or authority ⟨invested his people with the *mantle* of universal champions of justice —Denis Goulet⟩
**2 a** : something that covers, enfolds, or envelops **b** (1) : a fold or lobe or pair of lobes of the body wall of a mollusk or brachiopod that in shell-bearing forms lines the shell and bears shell-secreting glands — see CLAM illustration (2) : the soft external body wall that lines the test or shell of a tunicate or barnacle **c** : the outer wall and casing of a blast furnace above the hearth; *broadly* : an insulated support or casing in which something is heated
**3** : the back, scapulars, and wings of a bird
**4** : a lacy hood or sheath of some refractory material that gives light by incandescence when placed over a flame
**5 a** : REGOLITH **b** : the part of the interior of a terrestrial planet and especially the earth that lies beneath the lithosphere and above the central core
**6** : MANTEL

**²mantle** *verb* **man·tled; man·tling** \'mant-liŋ, 'man-t°l-iŋ\ (13th century)
*transitive verb*
: to cover with or as if with a mantle : CLOAK ⟨the encroaching jungle growth that *mantled* the building —Sanka Knox⟩
*intransitive verb*
**1** : to become covered with a coating
**2** : to spread over a surface
**3** : BLUSH ⟨her rich face *mantling* with emotion —Benjamin Disraeli⟩

**man-to–man** \'man-tə-'man\ *adjective* (1902)
**1** : characterized by frankness and honesty ⟨a *man-to-man* talk⟩
**2** : of, relating to, or being a system of defense (as in football or basketball) in which each defensive player guards a specified opponent

**Man·toux test** \man-'tü-, 'män-\ *noun* [Charles *Mantoux* (died 1947) French physician] (circa 1923)
: an intracutaneous test for hypersensitivity to tuberculin that indicates past or present infection with tubercle bacilli

**man·tra** \'män-trə *also* 'man- *or* 'mən-\ *noun* [Sanskrit, sacred counsel, formula, from *manyate* he thinks; akin to Latin *mens* mind — more at MIND] (1808)
: a mystical formula of invocation or incantation (as in Hinduism); *also* : WATCHWORD 2
— **man·tric** \-trik\ *adjective*

**man·trap** \'man-ˌtrap\ *noun* (1788)
: a trap for catching humans : SNARE

**man·tua** \'man(t)-sh(ə-)wə, 'man-tə-wə\ *noun* [modification of French *manteau* mantle] (1678)
: a usually loose-fitting gown worn especially in the 17th and 18th centuries

**Manu** \'ma-ˌnü\ *noun* [Sanskrit]
: the progenitor of the human race and giver of the religious laws of Manu according to Hindu mythology

**¹man·u·al** \'man-yə-wəl, -yəl\ *adjective* [Middle English *manuel,* from Middle French, from Latin *manualis,* from *manus* hand; akin to Old English *mund* hand and perhaps to Greek *marē* hand] (15th century)

mantis

**1 a** : of, relating to, or involving the hands ⟨*manual* dexterity⟩ **b** : worked or done by hand and not by machine ⟨a *manual* transmission⟩ ⟨*manual* computation⟩ ⟨*manual* indexing⟩
**2** : requiring or using physical skill and energy ⟨*manual* labor⟩ ⟨*manual* workers⟩
— **man·u·al·ly** *adverb*

**²manual** *noun* (15th century)
**1** : a book that is conveniently handled; *especially* : HANDBOOK
**2** : the prescribed movements in the handling of a weapon or other military item during a drill or ceremony ⟨the *manual* of arms⟩
**3 a** : a keyboard for the hands; *specifically* : one of the several keyboards of an organ or harpsichord that controls a separate division of the instrument **b** : a device or apparatus intended for manual operation

**manual alphabet** *noun* (circa 1864)
: an alphabet especially for the deaf in which the letters are represented by finger positions

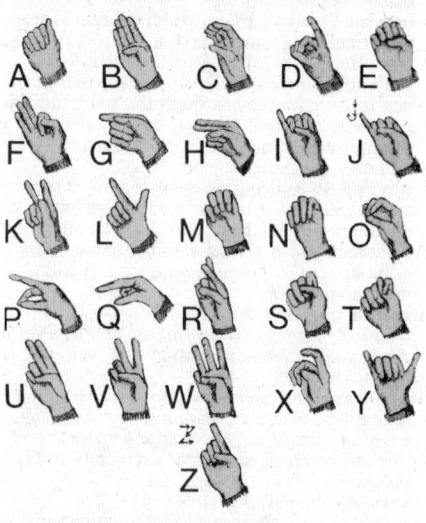

manual alphabet

**manual training** *noun* (1880)
: a course of training to develop skill in using the hands and to teach practical arts (as woodworking and metalworking)

**ma·nu·bri·um** \mə-'nü-brē-əm, -'nyü-\ *noun, plural* **-bria** \-brē-ə\ *also* **-bri·ums** [New Latin, from Latin, handle, from *manus*] (circa 1848)
: an anatomical process or part shaped like a handle: as **a** : the cephalic segment of the sternum of humans and many other mammals **b** : the process that bears the mouth of a hydrozoan : HYPOSTOME

**man·u·fac·to·ry** \ˌman-yə-'fak-t(ə-)rē, ˌma-nə-\ *noun* (1647)
: FACTORY 2a

**¹man·u·fac·ture** \ˌman-yə-'fak-chər, ˌma-nə-\ *noun* [Middle French, from Medieval Latin *manufactura,* from Latin *manu factus,* literally, made by hand] (1567)
**1** : something made from raw materials by hand or by machinery
**2 a** : the process of making wares by hand or by machinery especially when carried on systematically with division of labor **b** : a productive industry using mechanical power and machinery
**3** : the act or process of producing something

**²manufacture** *verb* **-tured; -tur·ing** \-'fak-chə-riŋ, -'fak-shriŋ\ (1683)
*transitive verb*
**1** : to make into a product suitable for use
**2 a** : to make from raw materials by hand or by machinery **b** : to produce according to an organized plan and with division of labor
**3** : INVENT, FABRICATE

**4 :** to produce as if by manufacturing **: CREATE** ⟨writers who *manufacture* stories for television⟩
*intransitive verb*
**:** to engage in manufacture
— **manufacturing** *noun*
**man·u·fac·tur·er** \-'fak-chər-ər, -'fak-shrər\ *noun* (1719)
**:** one that manufactures; *especially* **:** an employer of workers in manufacturing
**man·u·mis·sion** \ˌman-yə-'mi-shən\ *noun* [Middle English, from Middle French, from Latin *manumission-, manumissio,* from *manumittere*] (15th century)
**:** the act or process of manumitting; *especially* **:** formal emancipation from slavery
**man·u·mit** \ˌman-yə-'mit\ *transitive verb* **-mit·ted; -mit·ting** [Middle English *manumitten,* from Middle French *manumitter,* from Latin *manumittere,* from *manus* hand + *mittere* to let go, send] (15th century)
**:** to release from slavery
**synonym** see FREE
**¹ma·nure** \mə-'nur, -'nyur\ *transitive verb* **ma·nured; ma·nur·ing** [Middle English *manouren,* from Middle French *manouvrer,* literally, to do work by hand, from Latin *manu operare*] (15th century)
**1** *obsolete* **: CULTIVATE**
**2 :** to enrich (land) by the application of manure
***word history*** see MANEUVER
— **ma·nur·er** *noun*
**²manure** *noun* (1549)
**:** material that fertilizes land; *especially* **:** refuse of stables and barnyards consisting of livestock excreta with or without litter
— **ma·nu·ri·al** \-'n(y)ur-ē-əl\ *adjective*
**ma·nus** \'mā-nəs, 'mä-\ *noun, plural* **ma·nus** \-nəs, -ˌnüs\ [New Latin, from Latin, hand] (1826)
**:** the distal segment of the vertebrate forelimb from carpus to terminus
**¹man·u·script** \'man-yə-ˌskript\ *adjective* [Latin *manu scriptus*] (1597)
**:** written by hand or typed ⟨*manuscript* letters⟩
**²manuscript** *noun* (1600)
**1 :** a written or typewritten composition or document as distinguished from a printed copy; *also* **:** a document submitted for publication
**2 :** writing as opposed to print
**¹Manx** \'man(k)s\ *adjective* [alteration of *Maniske,* from (assumed) Old Norse *manskr,* from *Mana* Isle of Man] (1630)
**:** of, relating to, or characteristic of the Isle of Man, its people, or the Manx language
**²Manx** *noun* (1672)
**1 :** the Celtic language of the Manx people almost completely displaced by English
**2** *plural in construction* **:** the people of the Isle of Man
**3 : MANX CAT**
**Manx cat** *noun* (1859)
**:** any of a breed of shorthaired tailless domestic cats
**¹many** \'me-nē\ *adjective* **more** \'mōr, 'mȯr\; **most** \'mōst\ [Middle English, from Old English *manig;* akin to Old High German *manag* many, Old Church Slavonic *mŭnogŭ* much] (before 12th century)
**1 :** consisting of or amounting to a large but indefinite number ⟨worked for *many* years⟩
**2 :** being one of a large but indefinite number ⟨*many* a man⟩ ⟨*many* another student⟩
— **as many :** the same in number ⟨saw three plays in *as many* days⟩
**²many** *pronoun, plural in construction* (before 12th century)
**:** a large number of persons or things ⟨*many* are called⟩
**³many** *noun, plural in construction* (12th century)
**1 :** a large but indefinite number ⟨a good *many* of them⟩
**2 :** the great majority of people ⟨the *many*⟩

**man–year** \'man-'yir\ *noun* (1916)
**:** a unit of the work done by one person in a year composed of a standard number of working days
**many·fold** \ˌme-nē-'fōld\ *adverb* (14th century)
**:** by many times ⟨aid to research has increased *manyfold*⟩
**many–sid·ed** \ˌme-nē-'sī-dəd\ *adjective* (1570)
**1 :** having many sides or aspects
**2 :** having many interests or aptitudes
— **many–sid·ed·ness** *noun*
**many–val·ued** \ˌme-nē-'val-(ˌ)yüd, -yəd\ *adjective* (1934)
**1 :** possessing more than the customary two truth-values of truth and falsehood
**2 : MULTIPLE-VALUED**
**Man·za·nil·la** \ˌman-zə-'nē-yə, -'ni-lə\ *noun* [Spanish, diminutive of *manzana* apple] (1843)
**:** a pale very dry Spanish sherry
**man·za·ni·ta** \ˌman-zə-'nē-tə\ *noun* [American Spanish, diminutive of Spanish *manzana* apple] (1846)
**:** any of various western North American evergreen shrubs (genus *Arctostaphylos*) of the heath family with alternate leaves
**Mao·ism** \'mau̇-ˌi-zəm\ *noun* (1950)
**:** the theory and practice of Marxism-Leninism developed in China chiefly by Mao Tse-tung
— **Mao·ist** \'mau̇-ist\ *noun or adjective*
**Mao·ri** \'mau̇(ə)r-ē\ *noun, plural* **Maori** or **Maoris** (1843)
**1 :** a member of a Polynesian people native to New Zealand
**2 :** the Austronesian language of the Maori
**mao–tai** \'mau̇-'tī, -'dī\ *noun* [*Maotai,* town in China] (1943)
**:** a strong Chinese liquor made from sorghum
**¹map** \'map\ *noun* [Medieval Latin *mappa,* from Latin, napkin, towel] (1527)
**1 a :** a representation usually on a flat surface of the whole or a part of an area **b :** a representation of the celestial sphere or a part of it
**2 :** something that represents with a clarity suggestive of a map
**3 :** the arrangement of genes on a chromosome — called also *genetic map*
**4 : FUNCTION 5a**
— **map·like** \-ˌlīk\ *adjective*
— **on the map :** in a position of prominence or fame ⟨had put the fledgling university *on the map* —Lon Tinkle⟩
**²map** *verb* **mapped; map·ping** (1586)
*transitive verb*
**1 a :** to make a map of ⟨*map* the surface of the moon⟩ **b :** to delineate as if on a map ⟨sorrow was *mapped* on her face⟩ **c :** to make a survey of for or as if for the purpose of making a map **d :** to assign (as a set or element) in a mathematical correspondence ⟨*map* a set onto itself⟩ ⟨*map* picture elements to video memory⟩
**2 :** to plan in detail — often used with *out* ⟨*map* out a program⟩
**3 :** to locate (a gene) on a chromosome
*intransitive verb*
*of a gene* **:** to be located
— **map·pa·ble** \'ma-pə-bəl\ *adjective*
— **map·per** *noun*
**ma·ple** \'mā-pəl\ *noun* [Middle English, from Old English *mapul-;* akin to Old Norse *mǫpurr* maple] (14th century)
**:** any of a genus (*Acer* of the family Aceraceae, the maple family) of chiefly deciduous trees or shrubs with opposite leaves and a fruit of two united samaras; *also* **:** the hard light-colored close-grained wood of a maple used especially for flooring and furniture
**maple sugar** *noun* (1720)
**:** sugar made by boiling maple syrup
**maple syrup** *noun* (1849)
**:** syrup made by concentrating the sap of maple trees and especially the sugar maple
**map·mak·er** \'map-ˌmā-kər\ *noun* (1775)
**: CARTOGRAPHER**

— **map·mak·ing** \-kiŋ\ *noun*
**map·ping** \'ma-piŋ\ *noun* (circa 1775)
**1 :** the act or process of making a map
**2 : FUNCTION 5a** ⟨a one-to-one continuous *mapping*⟩
**ma·quette** \ma-'ket\ *noun* [French, from Italian *macchietta* sketch, diminutive of *macchia,* ultimately from Latin *macula* spot] (1903)
**:** a usually small preliminary model (as of a sculpture or a building)
**ma·qui·la·do·ra** \mə-ˌkē-lə-'dōr-ə, -'thȯr-\ *noun* [Mexican Spanish (*planta*) *maquiladora,* from *maquilar* to process ore for a fee, from *maquila* processing fee, multure, from Spanish, multure, from Arabic dialect *makīla* measure of grain] (1976)
**:** a foreign-owned factory in Mexico at which imported parts are assembled by lower-paid workers into products for export
**ma·quil·lage** \ˌma-kē-'yäzh\ *noun* [French] (1892)
**: MAKEUP 3**
**ma·quis** \ma-'kē, mä-\ *noun, plural* **ma·quis** \-'kē(z)\ [French, from Italian *macchie,* plural of *macchia* thicket, sketch, spot] (1858)
**1 :** thick scrubby underbrush of Mediterranean shores and especially of the island of Corsica; *also* **:** an area of such underbrush
**2** *often capitalized* **a :** a guerrilla fighter in the French underground during World War II **b :** a band of maquis
**¹mar** \'mär\ *transitive verb* **marred; mar·ring** [Middle English *marren,* from Old English *mierran* to obstruct, waste; akin to Old High German *merren* to obstruct] (before 12th century)
**1 :** to detract from the perfection or wholeness of **: SPOIL**
**2** *archaic* **a :** to inflict serious bodily harm on **b : DESTROY**
**synonym** see INJURE
**²mar** *noun* (1551)
**:** something that mars **: BLEMISH**
**mar·a·bou** *also* **mar·a·bout** \'mar-ə-ˌbü\ *noun* [French *marabout,* literally, marabout] (1823)

marabou 1b

**1 a :** a soft feathery fluffy material prepared from turkey feathers or the coverts of marabous and used especially for trimming women's hats or clothes **b** *marabou* **:** a large dark gray African stork (*Leptoptilos crumeniferus*) that has a distensible pouch of pink skin at the front of the neck and feeds especially on carrion — called also *marabou stork*
**2 a :** a thrown silk usually dyed in the gum **b :** a fabric made of this silk
**mar·a·bout** \'mar-ə-bü\ *noun, often capitalized* [French, from Portuguese *marabuto,* from Arabic *murābiṭ*] (1621)
**:** a dervish in Muslim Africa believed to have supernatural power
**ma·ra·ca** \mə-'rä-kə, -'ra-\ *noun* [Portuguese *maracá,* from Tupi] (1824)
**:** a rattle usually made from a gourd that is used as a percussion instrument
**mar·ag·ing steel** \'mär-ˌā-jiŋ-\ *noun* [*martensite* + *aging*] (1962)
**:** a strong tough low-carbon martensitic steel which contains up to 25 percent nickel and in which hardening precipitates are formed by aging

---

\ə\ abut \ᵊ\ kitten \ər\ further \a\ ash \ā\ ace \ä\ mop, mar \au̇\ out \ch\ chin \e\ bet \ē\ easy \g\ go \i\ hit \ī\ ice \j\ job \ŋ\ sing \ō\ go \ȯ\ law \ȯi\ boy \th\ thin \t̲h̲\ the \ü\ loot \u̇\ foot \y\ yet \zh\ vision *see also* Guide to Pronunciation

**mar·a·schi·no** \ˌmar-ə-'skē-(ˌ)nō, -'shē-\ *noun, plural* **-nos** *often capitalized* [Italian, from *marasca* bitter wild cherry, alteration of *amarasca*, from *amaro* bitter — more at AMARETTO] (circa 1793)
**1 :** a sweet liqueur distilled from the fermented juice of a bitter wild cherry
**2 :** a usually large cherry preserved in true or imitation maraschino

**ma·ras·mus** \mə-'raz-məs\ *noun* [Late Latin, from Greek *marasmos*, from *marainein* to waste away] (1656)
**:** a condition of chronic undernourishment occurring especially in children and usually caused by a diet deficient in calories and proteins
**— ma·ras·mic** \-'raz-mik\ *adjective*

**Ma·ra·tha** \mə-'rä-tə\ *noun* [Marathi *Marāṭhā* & Hindi *Marhaṭṭā*, from Sanskrit *Mahārāṣṭra* Maharashtra] (1748)
**:** a member of a people of the south central part of the subcontinent of India

**Ma·ra·thi** \mə-'rä-tē\ *noun* [Marathi *marāṭhī*] (1698)
**:** the chief Indo-Aryan language of the state of Maharashtra in India

**mar·a·thon** \'mar-ə-ˌthän\ *noun, often attributive* [*Marathon*, Greece, site of a victory of Greeks over Persians in 490 B.C. the news of which was carried to Athens by a long-distance runner] (1896)
**1 :** a long-distance race: **a :** a footrace run on an open course usually of 26 miles 385 yards (42.2 kilometers) **b :** a race other than a footrace marked especially by great length
**2 a :** an endurance contest **b :** something (as an event, activity, or session) characterized by great length or concentrated effort ◆

**mar·a·thon·er** \-ˌthä-nər\ *noun* (1923)
**:** one (as a runner) who takes part in a marathon
**— mar·a·thon·ing** \-niŋ\ *noun*

**ma·raud** \mə-'rȯd\ *verb* [French *marauder*] (1711)
*intransitive verb*
**:** to roam about and raid in search of plunder
*transitive verb*
**:** RAID, PILLAGE
**— ma·raud·er** *noun*

**¹mar·ble** \'mär-bəl\ *noun* [Middle English, from Old French *marbre*, from Latin *marmor*, from Greek *marmaros*] (12th century)
**1 a :** limestone that is more or less crystallized by metamorphism, that ranges from granular to compact in texture, that is capable of taking a high polish, and that is used especially in architecture and sculpture **b :** something (as a piece of sculpture) composed of or made from marble **c :** something suggesting marble (as in hardness, coldness, or smoothness) ⟨a heart of *marble*⟩
**2 a :** a little ball made of a hard substance (as glass) and used in various games **b** *plural but singular in construction* **:** any of several games played with these little balls
**3 :** MARBLING
**4** *plural* **:** elements of common sense; *especially* **:** SANITY ⟨persons who are born without all their *marbles* —Arthur Miller⟩
**— marble** *adjective*

**²marble** *transitive verb* **mar·bled; mar·bling** \-b(ə-)liŋ\ (1683)
**:** to give a veined or mottled appearance to ⟨*marble* the edges of a book⟩

**marble cake** *noun* (1871)
**:** a cake made with light and dark batter so as to have a mottled appearance

**mar·bled** \'mär-bəld\ *adjective* (1599)
**1** [¹*marble*] **a :** made of or covered with marble or marbling **b :** marked by an extensive use of marble as an architectural or decorative feature ⟨ancient *marbled* cities⟩
**2** [²*marble*] **:** marked by an intermixture of fat and lean ⟨well-*marbled* beef⟩

**mar·ble·ise** *British variant of* MARBLEIZE

**mar·ble·ize** \'mär-bə-ˌlīz\ *transitive verb* **-ized; -iz·ing** (circa 1859)
**:** MARBLE

**marbling** *noun* (circa 1752)
**1 :** the action or process of making like marble especially in coloration
**2 :** coloration or markings resembling or suggestive of marble
**3 :** an intermixture of fat and lean especially in a cut of meat when evenly distributed

**mar·bly** \-b(ə-)lē\ *adjective* (15th century)
**:** resembling or suggestive of marble

**marc** \'märk\ *noun* [French, from Middle French, from *marchier* to trample, march] (1601)
**1 :** the residue remaining after a fruit has been pressed; *broadly* **:** the organic residue from an extraction process ⟨the protein-rich cottonseed *marc*⟩
**2 :** brandy made from the residue of wine grapes after pressing

**mar·ca·site** \'mär-kə-ˌsīt, -ˌzīt; ˌmär-kə-'zēt\ *noun* [Middle English *marchasite*, from Medieval Latin *marcasita*] (15th century)
**1 a :** crystallized iron pyrites **b :** a mineral of the same composition and appearance as iron pyrites but of different crystalline organization and lower specific gravity
**2 :** a piece of marcasite used in jewelry

**mar·ca·to** \mär-'kä-(ˌ)tō\ *adverb or adjective* [Italian, past participle of *marcare* to mark, accent, of Germanic origin; akin to Old High German *marcōn* to mark] (circa 1840)
**:** with strong accentuation — used as a direction in music

**¹mar·cel** \mär-'sel\ *noun* [*Marcel* Grateau (died 1936) French hairdresser] (1895)
**:** a deep soft wave made in the hair by the use of a heated curling iron

**²marcel** *verb* **mar·celled; mar·cel·ing** (1906)
*transitive verb*
**:** to make a marcel in
*intransitive verb*
**:** to make a marcel

**¹march** \'märch\ *noun* [Middle English *marche*, from Old French, of Germanic origin; akin to Old High German *marha* boundary — more at MARK] (14th century)
**:** a border region **:** FRONTIER; *especially* **:** a district originally set up to defend a boundary — usually used in plural

**²march** *intransitive verb* (14th century)
**:** to have common borders or frontiers ⟨a region that *marches* with Canada in the north and the Pacific in the west⟩

**³march** \'märch, *imperatively often* 'härch *in the military*\ *verb* [Middle English, from Middle French *marchier* to trample, march, from Old French, to trample, probably of Germanic origin; akin to Old High German *marcōn* to mark] (15th century)
*intransitive verb*
**1 :** to move along steadily usually with a rhythmic stride and in step with others
**2 a :** to move in a direct purposeful manner **:** PROCEED **b :** to make steady progress **:** ADVANCE ⟨time *marches* on⟩
**3 :** to stand in orderly array suggestive of marching
*transitive verb*
**1 :** to cause to march ⟨*marched* the children off to bed⟩
**2 :** to cover by marching **:** TRAVERSE ⟨*marched* 10 miles⟩

**⁴march** \'märch\ *noun* (circa 1572)
**1 :** a musical composition that is usually in duple or quadruple time with a strongly accentuated beat and that is designed or suitable to accompany marching
**2 a** (1) **:** the action of marching (2) **:** the distance covered within a specific period of time by marching (3) **:** a regular measured stride or rhythmic step used in marching **b :** forward movement **:** PROGRESS ⟨the *march* of a movie toward the climax⟩

**3 :** an organized procession of demonstrators who are supporting or protesting something
**— march·like** \-ˌlīk\ *adjective*
**— on the march :** moving steadily **:** ADVANCING

**March** \'märch\ *noun* [Middle English, from Old French, from Latin *martius*, from *martius* of Mars, from *Mart-, Mars*] (13th century)
**:** the 3d month of the Gregorian calendar

**mär·chen** \'mer-kən\ *noun, plural* **märchen** [German] (1871)
**:** TALE; *especially* **:** FOLKTALE

**¹march·er** \'mär-chər\ *noun* (14th century)
**:** one who inhabits a border region

**²marcher** *noun* (1589)
**:** one that marches; *especially* **:** one that marches for a specific cause ⟨a peace *marcher*⟩

**mar·che·sa** \mär-'kā-zə\ *noun, plural* **-se** \-(ˌ)zā\ [Italian, feminine of *marchese*] (1797)
**:** an Italian woman holding the rank of a marchese **:** MARCHIONESS

**mar·che·se** \-(ˌ)zā\ *noun, plural* **-si** \-(ˌ)zē\ [Italian, from Medieval Latin *marcensis*, from *marca* border region, of Germanic origin; akin to Old High German *marha*] (1517)
**:** an Italian nobleman next in rank above a count **:** MARQUIS

**marching orders** *noun plural* (1780)
**:** authoritative orders or instructions especially to set out on or as if on a march

**mar·chio·ness** \'mär-sh(ə-)nəs\ *noun* [Medieval Latin *marchionissa*, from *marchion-, marchio* marquess, from *marca*] (circa 1599)
**1 :** the wife or widow of a marquess
**2 :** a woman who holds the rank of marquess in her own right

**march·pane** \'märch-ˌpān\ *noun* [Middle French *marcepain*, from Italian *marzapane*] (circa 1556)
**:** MARZIPAN

**march–past** \'märch-ˌpast\ *noun* (circa 1876)
**:** a filing by **:** PROCESSION

**Mar·cion·ism** \'mär-shə-ˌni-zəm, -sē-ə-, -shē-ə-\ *noun* [*Marcion* 2d century A.D. Christian Gnostic] (1882)
**:** the doctrinal system of a sect of the 2d and 3d centuries A.D. accepting some parts of the New Testament but denying Christ's corporality and humanity and condemning the Creator God of the Old Testament
**— Mar·cion·ite** \-ˌnīt\ *noun*

**Mar·co·ni** \mär-'kō-nē\ *adjective* [probably from the resemblance of the complex arrangement of stays and struts to that used to support

the antennae used in wireless telegraphy, invented by Guglielmo *Marconi*] (1912)
**:** of, having, or being a Bermuda rig
**Mar·di Gras** \'mär-dē-,grä, *in New Orleans commonly* -,grò\ *noun* [French, literally, fat Tuesday] (1699)
**1 a :** Shrove Tuesday often observed (as in New Orleans) with parades and festivities **b :** a carnival period climaxing on Shrove Tuesday
**2 :** a festive occasion resembling a pre-Lenten Mardi Gras
**¹mare** *noun* [Middle English, from Old English; akin to Old High German *mara* incubus, Serbo-Croatian *mora* nightmare] (before 12th century)
*obsolete* **:** an evil preternatural being causing nightmares
**²mare** \'mar, 'mer\ *noun* [Middle English, from Old English *mere;* akin to Old High German *merha* mare, Old English *mearh* horse, Welsh *march*] (before 12th century)
**:** a female horse or other equine animal especially when fully mature or of breeding age
**³ma·re** \'mär-(,)ā\ *noun, plural* **ma·ria** \'mär-ē-ā\ *also* **ma·res** \'mär-(,)āz\ [New Latin, from Latin, sea — more at MARINE] (1860)
**:** any of several mostly flat dark areas of considerable extent on the surface of the moon or Mars
**ma·re clau·sum** \'mär-(,)ā-'klaù-səm, -'klò-\ *noun* [New Latin, literally, closed sea] (1652)
**:** a navigable body of water (as a sea) that is under the jurisdiction of one nation and is closed to other nations
**Mar·ek's disease** \'mar-iks-, 'mer-\ *noun* [József *Marek* (died 1952) Hungarian veterinarian] (1947)
**:** a highly contagious viral disease of poultry that is characterized especially by proliferation of lymphoid cells and is caused by a herpesvirus
**ma·re li·be·rum** \'mär-(,)ā-'lē-bə-,rùm\ *noun* [New Latin, literally, free sea] (1652)
**1 :** a navigable body of water (as a sea) that is open to all nations
**2 :** FREEDOM OF THE SEAS
**ma·ren·go** \mə-'reŋ-(,)gō\ *adjective, often capitalized* [French, from *Marengo,* village in northwest Italy] (circa 1924)
**:** of, consisting of, or served with a sauce of mushrooms, tomatoes, olives, oil, and wine ⟨veal *marengo*⟩
**ma·re no·strum** \'mär-(,)ā-'nōs-trəm\ *noun* [New Latin, literally, our sea] (1941)
**:** a navigable body of water (as a sea) that belongs to a single nation or is mutually shared by two or more nations
**mare's nest** *noun, plural* **mare's nests** *or* **mares' nests** (1576)
**1 :** a false discovery, illusion, or deliberate hoax
**2 :** a place, condition, or situation of great disorder or confusion ⟨a *mare's nest* of spurious ambiguities to bewilder the simpleminded —J. H. Sledd⟩
**mare's tail** *noun, plural* **mare's tails** *or* **mares' tails** (circa 1762)
**1 a :** a common aquatic plant (*Hippuris vulgaris* of the family Hippuridaceae) with elongated shoots having dense whorls of narrow finely tapered leaves **b :** HORSEWEED 1
**2 :** a cirrus cloud that has a long slender flowing appearance
**Mar·fan's syndrome** \'mär-,fanz-\ *noun* [Antonin Bernard Jean *Marfan* (died 1942) French pediatrician] (circa 1923)
**:** a hereditary disorder of connective tissue that is characterized by abnormal elongation of the bones and often by ocular and circulatory defects — called also *Mar·fan syndrome* \'mär-,fan-\
**mar·ga·rine** \'mär-jə-rən, -,rēn; 'märj-,rən\ *noun* [French, ultimately from Greek *margaron* pearl, probably back-formation from *margarītēs*] (1873)

**:** a food product made usually from vegetable oils churned with ripened skim milk to a smooth emulsion and used like butter
**mar·ga·ri·ta** \,mär-gə-'rē-tə\ *noun* [from the Spanish feminine name *Margarita*] (1963)
**:** a cocktail consisting of tequila, lime or lemon juice, and an orange-flavored liqueur
**mar·ga·rite** \'mär-gə-,rīt\ *noun* [Middle English, from Middle French, from Latin *margarita,* from Greek *margarītēs*] (13th century)
*archaic* **:** PEARL
**mar·gay** \'mär-,gā, mär-'\ *noun* [French, from Tupi *maracaja*] (1781)
**:** a small American spotted cat (*Felis wiedii*) resembling the ocelot and ranging from southernmost Texas to Argentina

margay

**¹marge** \'märj\ *noun* [Middle French, from Latin *margo*] (1551)
*archaic* **:** MARGIN
**²marge** *noun* (1922)
*British* **:** MARGARINE
**mar·gent** \'mär-jənt\ *noun* (15th century)
*archaic* **:** MARGIN
**¹mar·gin** \'mär-jən\ *noun* [Middle English, from Latin *margin-, margo* border — more at MARK] (14th century)
**1 :** the part of a page or sheet outside the main body of printed or written matter
**2 :** the outside limit and adjoining surface of something **:** EDGE ⟨at the *margin* of the woods⟩ ⟨continental *margin*⟩
**3 a :** a spare amount or measure or degree allowed or given for contingencies or special situations ⟨left no *margin* for error⟩ **b (1) :** a bare minimum below which or an extreme limit beyond which something becomes impossible or is no longer desirable ⟨on the *margin* of good taste⟩ **(2) :** the limit below which economic activity cannot be continued under normal conditions
**4 a :** the difference which exists between net sales and the cost of merchandise sold and from which expenses are usually met or profit derived **b :** the excess market value of collateral over the face of a loan **c (1) :** cash or collateral that is deposited by a client with a commodity or securities broker to protect the broker from loss on a contract **(2) :** the client's equity in securities bought with the aid of credit obtained specifically (as from a broker) for that purpose **d :** a range about a specified figure within which a purchase is to be made
**5 :** measure or degree of difference ⟨the bill passed by a one-vote *margin*⟩
**— mar·gined** \-jənd\ *adjective*
**²margin** *transitive verb* (1715)
**1 a :** to provide with an edging or border **b :** to form a margin to **:** BORDER
**2 a :** to add margin to ⟨*margin* up an account⟩ **b (1) :** to use as margin ⟨*margin* bonds to buy stock⟩ **(2) :** to provide margin for ⟨*margin* a transaction⟩ **c :** to buy (securities) on margin
**mar·gin·al** \'märj-nəl, 'mär-jə-n°l\ *adjective* [Medieval Latin *marginalis,* from Latin *margin-, margo*] (1573)
**1 :** written or printed in the margin of a page or sheet ⟨*marginal* notes⟩
**2 a :** of, relating to, or situated at a margin or border **b :** not of central importance ⟨regards violence as a *marginal* rather than a central problem⟩ **c (1) :** occupying the borderland of a relatively stable territorial or cultural area ⟨*marginal* tribes⟩ **(2) :** characterized by the incorporation of habits and values from two divergent cultures and by incomplete assimilation in either ⟨the *marginal* cultural habits of

new immigrant groups⟩ **(3) :** excluded from or existing outside the mainstream of society, a group, or a school of thought ⟨*marginal* voters⟩
**3 :** located at the fringe of consciousness ⟨*marginal* sensations⟩
**4 a :** close to the lower limit of qualification, acceptability, or function **:** barely exceeding the minimum requirements ⟨a semiliterate person of *marginal* ability⟩ **b (1) :** having a character or capacity fitted to yield a supply of goods which when marketed at existing price levels will barely cover the cost of production ⟨*marginal* land⟩ **(2) :** of, relating to, or derived from goods produced and marketed with such result ⟨*marginal* profits⟩
**5 :** relating to or being a function of a random variable that is obtained from a function of several random variables by integrating or summing over all possible values of the other variables ⟨a *marginal* probability function⟩
**— mar·gin·al·i·ty** \,mär-jə-'na-lə-tē\ *noun*
**— mar·gin·al·ly** \'märj-nə-lē, 'mär-jə-n°l-ē\ *adverb*
**mar·gi·na·lia** \,mär-jə-'nā-lē-ə\ *noun plural* [New Latin, from Medieval Latin, neuter plural of *marginalis*] (1832)
**1 :** marginal notes (as in a book)
**2 :** nonessential items ⟨the meat and *marginalia* of American politics —Saturday Review⟩
**mar·gin·al·ize** \'märj-nə-,līz, 'mär-jə-n°l-,īz\ *transitive verb* **-ized; -iz·ing** (1970)
**:** to relegate to a marginal position within a society or group
**— mar·gin·al·i·za·tion** \,märj-nə-lə-'zā-shən, ,mär-jə-n°l-ə-\ *noun*
**marginal utility** *noun* (1890)
**:** the amount of additional utility provided by an additional unit of an economic good or service
**mar·gin·ate** \'mär-jə-,nāt\ *transitive verb* **-at·ed; -at·ing** (1623)
**1 :** MARGIN 1, 2a
**2 :** MARGINALIZE
**— mar·gin·ation** \,mär-jə-'nā-shən\ *noun*
**mar·gin·at·ed** \-,nā-təd\ *adjective* (circa 1727)
**:** having a distinct margin
**mar·gra·vate** \'mär-grə-,vāt\ *or* **mar·gra·vi·ate** \mär-'grā-vē-ət, -,āt\ *noun* (1802)
**:** the territory of a margrave
**mar·grave** \'mär-,grāv\ *noun* [Dutch *markgraaf,* from Middle Dutch *marcgrave;* akin to Old High German *marha* boundary and to Old High German *grāvo* count — more at MARK] (1551)
**1 :** the military governor especially of a German border province
**2 :** a member of the German nobility corresponding in rank to a British marquess
**— mar·gra·vi·al** \mär-'grā-vē-əl\ *adjective*
**mar·gra·vine** \'mär-grə-,vēn, ,mär-grə-'\ *noun* (1692)
**:** the wife of a margrave
**mar·gue·rite** \,mär-gə-'rēt, -gyə-\ *noun* [French, from Middle French *margarite* pearl, daisy — more at MARGARITE] (circa 1866)
**1 :** DAISY 1b
**2 :** any of various single-flowered chrysanthemums; *especially* **:** a chrysanthemum (*Chrysanthemum frutescens*) of the Canary Islands
**maria** *plural of* MARE
**ma·ri·a·chi** \,mär-ē-'ä-chē, mar-\ *noun* [Mexican Spanish, perhaps modification of French *mariage* marriage] (1927)
**1 :** a Mexican street band; *also* **:** a musician belonging to such a band
**2 :** the music performed by a mariachi
**Mar·i·an** \'mer-ē-ən, 'mar-ē-, 'mā-rē-\ *adjective* (1608)

**1 :** of or relating to Mary Tudor or her reign
**2 :** of or relating to the Virgin Mary

**Mar·i·an·ist** \-ə-nist\ *noun* (circa 1899)
**:** a member of the Roman Catholic Society of Mary of Paris founded by William Joseph Chaminade in France in 1817 and devoted especially to education

**Ma·ria The·re·sa dollar** \mə-ˈrē-ə-tə-ˈrā-sə-, -ˈrā-zə-\ *noun* (circa 1883)
**:** a 1780 silver trade coin used in the Middle East

**mari·cul·ture** \ˈmar-ə-ˌkəl-chər\ *noun* [Latin *mare* sea + English *-culture* (as in *agriculture*)] (circa 1909)
**:** the cultivation of marine organisms in their natural environment
— **mari·cul·tur·ist** \ˌmar-ə-ˈkəl-chə-rist, -ˈkəlch-rist\ *noun*

**mari·gold** \ˈmar-ə-ˌgōld, ˈmer-\ *noun* [Middle English, from *Mary*, mother of Jesus + Middle English *gold*] (14th century)
**1 :** POT MARIGOLD
**2 :** any of a genus (*Tagetes*) of composite herbs with showy yellow, orange, or maroon flower heads

**mar·i·jua·na** *also* **mar·i·hua·na** \ˌmar-ə-ˈwä-nə *also* -ˈhwä-\ *noun* [Mexican Spanish *mariguana, marihuana*] (1894)
**1 :** HEMP 1a, c
**2 :** the dried leaves and flowering tops of the pistillate hemp plant that yield THC and are smoked in cigarettes for their intoxicating effect — compare BHANG, CANNABIS, HASHISH

**ma·rim·ba** \mə-ˈrim-bə\ *noun* [of Bantu origin; akin to Kimbundu *marimba* xylophone] (1704)
**:** a xylophone of southern Africa and Central America with resonators beneath each bar; *also* **:** a modern form of this instrument
— **ma·rim·bist** \-bist\ *noun*

**ma·ri·na** \mə-ˈrē-nə\ *noun* [Italian & Spanish, seashore, from feminine of *marino*, adjective, marine, from Latin *marinus*] (1924)
**:** a dock or basin providing secure moorings for pleasure boats and often offering supply, repair, and other facilities

**¹mar·i·nade** \ˌmar-ə-ˈnād\ *noun* [French, from *mariner* to pickle, marinate, probably from Italian *marinare*] (1725)
**:** a savory usually acidic sauce in which meat, fish, or a vegetable is soaked to enrich its flavor or to tenderize it

**²marinade** *transitive verb* **-nad·ed; -nad·ing** (1727)
**:** MARINATE

**mar·i·na·ra** \ˌmar-ə-ˈnar-ə, ˌmer-ə-ˈner-, -ˈnär-\ *adjective* [Italian (*alla*) *marinara*, literally, in sailor style] (circa 1948)
**:** made with tomatoes, onions, garlic, and spices (*marinara* sauce); *also* **:** served with marinara sauce (spaghetti *marinara*)

**mar·i·nate** \ˈmar-ə-ˌnāt\ *verb* **-nat·ed; -nat·ing** [probably from Italian *marinato*, past participle of *marinare* to marinate, from *marino*] (circa 1645)
*transitive verb*
**:** to steep (meat, fish, or vegetables) in a marinade
*intransitive verb*
**:** to become marinated
— **mar·i·na·tion** \ˌmar-ə-ˈnā-shən\ *noun*

**¹ma·rine** \mə-ˈrēn\ *adjective* [Middle English, from Latin *marinus*, from *mare* sea; akin to Old English *mere* sea, pool, Old High German *meri* sea, Old Church Slavonic *morje*] (15th century)
**1 a :** of or relating to the sea (*marine* life) **b :** of or relating to the navigation of the sea **:** NAUTICAL (a *marine* chart) **c :** of or relating to the commerce of the sea **:** MARITIME (*marine* law) **d :** depicting the sea, seashore, or ships (a *marine* painter)
**2 :** of or relating to marines (*marine* barracks)

**²marine** *noun* (1669)

**1 a :** the mercantile and naval shipping of a country **b :** seagoing ships especially in relation to nationality or class
**2 :** one of a class of soldiers serving on shipboard or in close association with a naval force; *specifically* **:** a member of the U.S. Marine Corps
**3 :** an executive department (as in France) having charge of naval affairs
**4 :** a marine picture **:** SEASCAPE

**marine architect** *noun* (1949)
**:** NAVAL ARCHITECT
— **marine architecture** *noun*

**mar·i·ner** \ˈmar-ə-nər\ *noun* [Middle English, from Anglo-French *marinier*, from Medieval Latin *marinarius*, from *marinus*] (14th century)
**:** a person who navigates or assists in navigating a ship **:** SEAMAN, SAILOR

**mariner's compass** *noun* (1627)
**:** a compass used in navigation that consists of parallel magnetic needles or bundles of needles permanently attached to a card marked to indicate direction and degrees of a circle

**Mar·i·ol·a·try** \ˌmer-ē-ˈä-lə-trē, ˌmar-ē-, ˌmä-rē-\ *noun* (1612)
**:** excessive veneration of the Virgin Mary
— **Mar·i·ol·a·ter** \-ˈä-lə-tər\ *noun*

**Mar·i·ol·o·gy** \-ˈä-lə-jē\ *noun* (1857)
**:** study or doctrine relating to the Virgin Mary
— **Mar·i·o·log·i·cal** \-ə-ˈlä-ji-kəl\ *adjective*

**mar·i·o·nette** \ˌmar-ē-ə-ˈnet, ˌmer-\ *noun* [French *marionnette*, from Middle French *maryonete*, from *Marion*, diminutive of *Marie* Mary] (circa 1620)
**:** a small-scale usually wooden figure (as of a person) with jointed limbs that is moved from above by manipulation of the attached strings or wires ◆

**mar·i·po·sa lily** \ˌmar-ə-ˈpō-zə-, -sə-\ *noun* [probably from American Spanish *mariposa*, from Spanish, butterfly] (1882)
**:** any of a genus (*Calochortus*) of western North American plants of the lily family with showy flowers having three petals and three sepals — called also *mariposa tulip;* compare SEGO LILY

**mar·ish** \ˈmar-ish\ *noun* (15th century)
*archaic* **:** MARSH

**Mar·ist** \ˈmar-ist, ˈmer-\ *noun* [French *mariste*, from *Marie* Mary] (circa 1872)
**:** a member of the Roman Catholic Society of Mary founded by Jean Claude Colin in France in 1816 and devoted to education

**mar·i·tal** \ˈmar-ə-tᵊl\ *adjective* [Latin *maritalis*, from *maritus* married] (1603)
**1 :** of or relating to marriage or the married state (*marital* vows)
**2 :** of or relating to a husband and his role in marriage
— **mar·i·tal·ly** \-tᵊl-ē\ *adverb*

**mar·i·time** \ˈmar-ə-ˌtīm\ *adjective* [Latin *maritimus*, from *mare*] (1550)
**1 :** of, relating to, or bordering on the sea (a *maritime* province)
**2 :** of or relating to navigation or commerce on the sea
**3 :** having the characteristics of a mariner

**mar·jo·ram** \ˈmär-jə-rəm, ˈmärj-rəm\ *noun* [alteration of Middle English *mageram, majorane*, from Middle French *majorane*, from Medieval Latin *majorana*] (circa 1550)
**:** any of various usually fragrant and aromatic Old World mints (genus *Origanum*) often used in cookery

**¹mark** \ˈmärk\ *noun* [Middle English, from Old English *mearc* boundary, march, sign; akin to Old High German *marha* boundary, Latin *margo*] (before 12th century)
**1 :** a boundary land
**2 a** (1) **:** a conspicuous object serving as a guide for travelers (2) **:** something (as a line, notch, or fixed object) designed to record position **b :** one of the bits of leather or colored bunting placed on a sounding line at intervals

**c :** TARGET **d :** the starting line or position in a track event **e** (1) **:** GOAL, OBJECT (2) **:** an object of attack, ridicule, or abuse; *specifically* **:** a victim or prospective victim of a swindle (3) **:** the point under discussion (4) **:** condition of being correct or accurate (her observations are on the *mark*) **f :** a standard of performance, quality, or condition **:** NORM (not feeling up to the *mark* lately)
**3 a** (1) **:** SIGN, INDICATION (gave her the necklace as a *mark* of his esteem) (2) **:** an impression (as a scratch, scar, or stain) made on something (3) **:** a distinguishing trait or quality **:** CHARACTERISTIC (the *marks* of an educated person) **b :** a symbol used for identification or indication of ownership **c :** a cross made in place of a signature **d** (1) **:** TRADEMARK (2) *capitalized* — used with a numeral to designate a particular model of a weapon or machine (*Mark* II) **e :** a written or printed symbol (as a comma or colon) **f :** POSTMARK **g :** a symbol used to represent a teacher's estimate of a student's work or conduct; *especially* **:** GRADE **h :** a figure registering a point or level reached or achieved (the halfway *mark* in the first period of play); *especially* **:** RECORD
**4 a :** ATTENTION, NOTICE (nothing worthy of *mark*) **b :** IMPORTANCE, DISTINCTION (stands out as a person of *mark*) **c :** a lasting or strong impression (worked at several jobs but didn't make much of a *mark*) **d :** an assessment of merits **:** RATING (got high *marks* for honesty)
**synonym** see SIGN

**²mark** *verb* [Middle English, from Old English *mearcian;* akin to Old High German *marcōn* to mark, determine the boundaries of, Old English *mearc* boundary] (before 12th century)
*transitive verb*
**1 a** (1) **:** to fix or trace out the bounds or limits of (2) **:** to plot the course of **:** CHART **b :** to set apart by or as if by a line or boundary — usually used with *off*
**2 a** (1) **:** to designate as if by a mark (*marked* for greatness) (2) **:** to make or leave a mark on (3) **:** to furnish with natural marks (wings *marked* with white) (4) **:** to label so as to indicate price or quality (5) **:** to make notations in or on **b** (1) **:** to make note of in writing **:** JOT (*marking* the date in his journal) (2) **:** to indicate by a mark or symbol (*mark* an accent) (3) **:** REGISTER, RECORD (4) **:** to determine the value of by means of marks or symbols **:** GRADE (*mark* term papers) **c** (1) **:** CHARACTERIZE, DISTINGUISH (the flamboyance that *marks* her stage appearance) (2) **:** SIGNALIZE (this year *marks* our 50th anniversary)
**3 :** to take notice of **:** OBSERVE (*mark* my words)

◇ **WORD HISTORY**
**marionette** Puppet shows have been widespread in the world since ancient times, but the elaborately jointed and intricately wired figure known as the marionette was not perfected until the 19th century. At the time the word entered English in the 17th century, French *marionnette* denoted a much more rudimentary hand- or string-operated puppet. Nonetheless performances involving these figures were quite popular in France in the 16th century, when *marionette* is first attested in this sense in French. Puppet plays were performed in particular at the Feast of the Assumption of the Virgin Mary. This led to the puppets being called by a diminutive form of *Marie*, the French name of the Virgin Mary. (*Marionette* may be altered from a diminutive form of *mariole*, itself a diminutive of *Marie*, or formed directly from another diminutive, *Marion*.) Similar derivatives, such as *mariotte* and *mariole*, had been used to designate other objects associated with the Virgin, such as a 15th century coin bearing her image.

**4** : to pick up (one's golf ball) from a putting green and substitute a marker
*intransitive verb*
: to take careful notice
— **mark time 1** : to keep the time of a marching step by moving the feet alternately without advancing **2** : to maintain a static state of readiness ⟨the House was *marking* time while the Senate talked —F. L. Paxson⟩

³**mark** *noun* [Middle English, from Old English *marc*, probably of Scandinavian origin; akin to Old Norse *mǫrk* mark; akin to Old English *mearc* sign] (before 12th century)
**1** : any of various old European units of weight especially for gold and silver; *especially* : a unit equal to about 8 ounces (248 grams)
**2** : a unit of value: **a** : an old English unit equal to 13*s* 4*d* **b** : any one of various old Scandinavian or German units of value; *specifically* : a unit and corresponding silver coin of the 16th century worth ½ taler **c** (1) : DEUTSCHE MARK (2) : the basic monetary unit of East Germany replaced in 1990 by the West German deutsche mark **d** : MARKKA

**Mark** \'märk\ *noun* [Latin *Marcus*]
**1 a** : an early Jewish Christian traditionally identified as the writer of the Gospel of Mark — called also *John Mark* **b** : the second Gospel in the New Testament — see BIBLE table
**2** : a king of Cornwall, uncle of Tristram, and husband of Isolde

**mark·down** \'märk-ˌdau̇n\ *noun* (1880)
**1** : a lowering of price
**2** : the amount by which an original selling price is reduced

**mark down** *transitive verb* (1859)
: to put a lower price on

**marked** \'märkt\ *adjective* (before 12th century)
**1** : having an identifying mark ⟨a *marked* card⟩
**2** \or 'mär-kəd\ : having a distinctive or emphasized character : NOTICEABLE ⟨has a *marked* drawl⟩
**3 a** : enjoying fame or notoriety **b** : being an object of attack, suspicion, or vengeance ⟨a *marked* man⟩
**4** : overtly signaled by a linguistic feature ⟨with most English nouns the plural is the *marked* number⟩
— **mark·ed·ly** \'mär-kəd-lē\ *adverb*
— **mark·ed·ness** \'mär-kəd-nəs\ *noun*

**mark·er** \'mär-kər\ *noun* (15th century)
**1** : one that marks
**2** : something used for marking
**3** : SCORE 7; *specifically* : RUN
**4** : PROMISSORY NOTE, IOU
**5** : GENETIC MARKER

¹**mar·ket** \'mär-kət\ *noun, often attributive* [Middle English, from Old North French, from Latin *mercatus* trade, marketplace, from *mercari* to trade, from *merc-, merx* merchandise] (12th century)
**1 a** (1) : a meeting together of people for the purpose of trade by private purchase and sale and usually not by auction (2) : the people assembled at such a meeting **b** (1) : a public place where a market is held; *especially* : a place where provisions are sold at wholesale ⟨a farmers' *market*⟩ (2) : a retail establishment usually of a specified kind ⟨a fish *market*⟩
**2** *archaic* : the act or an instance of buying and selling
**3** : the rate or price offered for a commodity or security
**4 a** (1) : a geographical area of demand for commodities or services ⟨the foreign *market* for consulting firms⟩ (2) : a specified category of potential buyers ⟨the youth *market*⟩ **b** : the course of commercial activity by which the exchange of commodities is effected : extent of demand ⟨the *market* is dull⟩ **c** (1) : an opportunity for selling ⟨a good *market* for used cars⟩ (2) : the available supply of or potential demand for specified goods or services ⟨the la-

bor *market*⟩ **d** : the area of economic activity in which buyers and sellers come together and the forces of supply and demand affect prices ⟨producing goods for *market* rather than for consumption⟩
— **in the market** : in the position of being a potential buyer ⟨*in the market* for a house⟩
— **on the market** : available for purchase; *also* : up for sale ⟨put their house *on the market*⟩

²**market** (1635)
*intransitive verb*
: to deal in a market
*transitive verb*
**1** : to expose for sale in a market
**2** : SELL

**mar·ket·able** \'mär-kə-tə-bəl\ *adjective* (1600)
**1 a** : fit to be offered for sale in a market ⟨food that is not *marketable*⟩ **b** : wanted by purchasers or employers : SALABLE ⟨*marketable* securities⟩ ⟨*marketable* skills⟩
**2** : of or relating to buying or selling
— **mar·ket·abil·i·ty** \ˌmär-kə-tə-'bi-lə-tē\ *noun*

**market basket** *noun* (1943)
: a variety of consumer goods and services used to calculate a consumer price index

**mar·ke·teer** \ˌmär-kə-'tir\ *noun* (1832)
: a specialist in promoting or selling a product or service

**mar·ket·er** \'mär-kə-tər\ *noun* (1787)
: one that deals in a market; *specifically* : one that promotes or sells a product or service

**market garden** *noun* (1811)
*British* : TRUCK FARM
— **market gardener** *noun, British*
— **market gardening** *noun, British*

**mar·ket·ing** *noun* (1561)
**1 a** : the act or process of selling or purchasing in a market **b** : the process or technique of promoting, selling, and distributing a product or service
**2** : an aggregate of functions involved in moving goods from producer to consumer

**marketing research** *noun* (circa 1937)
: research into the means of promoting, selling, and distributing a product or service

**market order** *noun* (circa 1920)
: an order to buy or sell securities or commodities immediately at the best price obtainable in the market

**mar·ket·place** \'mär-kət-ˌplās\ *noun* (14th century)
**1 a** : an open square or place in a town where markets or public sales are held **b** : MARKET ⟨the *marketplace* is the interpreter of supply and demand⟩
**2** : the world of trade or economic activity : the everyday world ⟨a conviction that religion belongs in the *marketplace* —Current Biography⟩
**3** : a sphere in which intangible values compete for acceptance ⟨the *marketplace* of ideas⟩

**market price** *noun* (15th century)
: a price actually given in current market dealings

**market research** *noun* (1926)
: research into the size, location, and makeup of a product market
— **market researcher** *noun*

**market share** *noun* (1970)
: the percentage of the market for a product or service that a company supplies

**mark·ing** *noun* (14th century)
**1** : the act, process, or an instance of making or giving a mark
**2 a** : a mark made **b** : arrangement, pattern, or disposition of marks

**mark·ka** \'mär-ˌkä\ *noun, plural* **mark·kaa** \'mär-ˌkä\ *also* **mark·kas** \-ˌkäz\ [Finnish, from Swedish *mark*, a unit of value; akin to Old Norse *mǫrk* mark] (circa 1896)
— see MONEY table

**Markov chain** *noun* [A. A. *Markov* (died 1922) Russian mathematician] (1942)

: a usually discrete stochastic process (as a random walk) in which the probabilities of occurrence of various future states depend only on the present state of the system or on the immediately preceding state and not on the path by which the present state was achieved — called also *Markoff chain*

**Mar·kov·ian** \mär-'kō-vē-ən, -'kò-\ *or* **Mar·kov** \'mär-ˌkòf, -ˌkòv\ *also* **Mar·koff** \'mär-ˌkòf\ *adjective* (1950)
: of, relating to, or resembling a Markov process or Markov chain especially by having probabilities defined in terms of transition from the possible existing states to other states

**Markov process** *noun* (1939)
: a stochastic process (as Brownian motion) that resembles a Markov chain except that the states are continuous; *also* : MARKOV CHAIN — called also *Markoff process*

**marks·man** \'märks-mən\ *noun* (1660)
: a person skilled in shooting at a mark or target
— **marks·man·ship** \-ˌship\ *noun*

**marks·wom·an** \'märks-ˌwu̇-mən\ *noun* (1802)
: a woman skilled in shooting at a mark or target

**mark·up** \'mär-ˌkəp\ *noun* (1916)
**1** : an amount added to the cost price to determine the selling price; *broadly* : PROFIT
**2** : a U.S. Congressional committee session at which a bill is put into final form before it is reported out

**mark up** *transitive verb* (1869)
: to put a markup on

**marl** \'mär(-ə)l\ *noun* [Middle English, from Middle French *marle*, from Medieval Latin *margila*, diminutive of Latin *marga* marl, from Gaulish] (14th century)
: a loose or crumbling earthy deposit (as of sand, silt, or clay) that contains a substantial amount of calcium carbonate and is used especially as a fertilizer for soils deficient in lime
— **marly** \'mär-lē\ *adjective*

**mar·lin** \'mär-lən\ *noun* [short for *marlinspike*; from the appearance of its beak] (1917)
: any of several large marine billfishes (genera *Makaira* and *Tetrapturus*) that are notable sport fishes

**mar·line** *also* **mar·lin** \'mär-lən\ *noun* [Middle English *merlyn*, probably from Middle Low German *marlinc, merlinc*, from *mēren* to tie, moor] (15th century)
: a small usually tarred line of two strands twisted loosely left-handed that is used especially for seizing and as a covering for wire rope

**mar·line·spike** *also* **mar·lin·spike** \'mär-lən-ˌspīk\ *noun* (1626)
: a tool (as of wood or iron) that tapers to a point and is used to separate strands of rope or wire (as in splicing)

**marl·stone** \'mär(-ə)l-ˌstōn\ *noun* (circa 1839)
: a rock that consists of a mixture of clay materials and calcium carbonate and often contains kerogen

**mar·ma·lade** \'mär-mə-ˌlād\ *noun* [Portuguese *marmelada* quince conserve, from *marmelo* quince, from Latin *melimelum*, a sweet apple, from Greek *melimēlon*, from *meli* honey + *mēlon* apple — more at MELLIFLUOUS] (1524)
: a clear sweetened jelly in which pieces of fruit and fruit rind are suspended

**mar·mo·re·al** \mär-'mōr-ē-əl, -'mòr-\ *also* **mar·mo·re·an** \-ē-ən\ *adjective* [Latin *marmoreus*, from *marmor* marble] (1656)
: of, relating to, or suggestive of marble or a marble statue especially in coldness or aloofness

---

\ə\ abut  \ᵊ\ kitten  \ər\ further  \a\ ash  \ā\ ace
\ä\ mop, mar  \au̇\ out  \ch\ chin  \e\ bet  \ē\ easy
\g\ go  \i\ hit  \ī\ ice  \j\ job  \ŋ\ sing  \ō\ go
\ò\ law  \òi\ boy  \th\ thin  \th\ the  \ü\ loot  \u̇\ foot
\y\ yet  \zh\ vision   *see also* Guide to Pronunciation

— **mar·mo·re·al·ly** \-ē-ə-lē\ *adverb*

**mar·mo·set** \'mär-mə-,set, -,zet\ *noun* [Middle English *marmusette* kind of monkey, from Middle French *marmoset* grotesque figure, from *marmouser* to mumble, of imitative origin] (1679)
**:** any of numerous small soft-furred South and Central American monkeys (family Callithricidae) with claws instead of nails on all the digits except the great toe

marmoset

**mar·mot** \'mär-mət\ *noun* [French *marmotte*] (1607)
**:** any of a genus (*Marmota*) of stout-bodied short-legged chiefly herbivorous burrowing rodents with coarse fur, a short bushy tail, and very small ears — compare WOODCHUCK

marmot

**mar·o·cain** \'mar-ə-,kān\ *noun* [French (*crêpe*) *marocain,* literally, Moroccan crepe] (1922)
**:** a ribbed crepe fabric used in women's clothing

**Mar·o·nite** \'mar-ə-,nīt\ *noun* [Medieval Latin *maronita,* from *Maron-, Maro* 5th century A.D. Syrian monk] (circa 1511)
**:** a member of a Uniate church chiefly in Lebanon having a Syriac liturgy and married clergy

**¹ma·roon** \mə-'rün\ *noun* [French *maron, marron,* modification of American Spanish *cimarrón,* from *cimarrón* wild, savage] (1666)
**1** *capitalized* **:** a fugitive black slave of the West Indies and Guiana in the 17th and 18th centuries; *also* **:** a descendant of such a slave
**2 :** a person who is marooned ◆

**²maroon** *transitive verb* (circa 1709)
**1 :** to put ashore on a desolate island or coast and leave to one's fate
**2 :** to place or leave in isolation or without hope of ready escape

**³maroon** *noun* [French *marron* Spanish chestnut] (1791)
**:** a dark red

**mar·plot** \'mär-,plät\ *noun* (1764)
**:** one who frustrates or ruins a plan or undertaking by meddling

**¹marque** \'märk\ *noun* [Middle English, from Middle French, from Old Provençal *marca,* from *marcar* to mark, seize as pledge, of Germanic origin; akin to Old High German *marcōn* to mark] (15th century)
**1** *obsolete* **:** REPRISAL, RETALIATION
**2 :** LETTERS OF MARQUE

**²marque** *noun* [French, mark, brand, from Middle French, from *marquer* to mark, of Germanic origin; akin to Old High German *marcōn* to mark] (1906)
**:** a brand or make of a product (as a sports car)

**mar·quee** \mär-'kē\ *noun* [modification of French *marquise,* literally, marchioness] (1690)
**1** *chiefly British* **:** a large tent set up for an outdoor party, reception, or exhibition
**2 :** a permanent canopy often of metal and glass projecting over an entrance (as of a hotel or theater)
**3 :** BOX OFFICE 2 ⟨*marquee* value⟩

**Mar·que·san** \mär-'kā-z*ə*n, -s*ə*n\ *noun* (1799)
**1 :** a native or inhabitant of the Marquesas Islands
**2 :** the Austronesian language of the Marquesans
— **Marquesan** *adjective*

**mar·quess** \'mär-kwəs\ *or* **mar·quis** \'mär-kwəs, mär-'kē\ *noun, plural* **mar·quess·es** *or* **mar·quis·es** \-kwə-səz\ *or* **mar·quis** \-'kē(z)\ [Middle English *marquis, markis,* from Middle French *marquis,* alteration of *marchis,* from *marche* march] (14th century)
**1 :** a nobleman of hereditary rank in Europe and Japan
**2 :** a member of the British peerage ranking below a duke and above an earl
— **mar·quess·ate** \'mär-kwə-sət\ *or* **mar·quis·ate** \'mär-kwə-zət, -sət\ *noun*

**mar·que·try** *also* **mar·que·terie** \'mär-kə-trē\ *noun* [Middle French *marqueterie,* from *marqueter* to checker, inlay, from *marque* mark] (1563)
**:** decorative work in which elaborate patterns are formed by the insertion of pieces of material (as wood, shell, or ivory) into a wood veneer that is then applied to a surface (as of a piece of furniture)

**mar·quise** \mär-'kēz\ *noun, plural* **mar·quises** \-'kēz, -'kē-zəz\ [French, feminine of *marquis*] (1783)
**1 :** MARQUEE
**2 :** MARCHIONESS
**3 :** a gem or a ring setting or bezel usually elliptical in shape but with pointed ends

**mar·qui·sette** \,mär-kwə-'zet, -kə-\ *noun* [*marquise* + -*ette*] (1908)
**:** a sheer meshed fabric used for clothing, curtains, and mosquito nets

**mar·ram grass** \'mar-əm-\ *noun* [of Scandinavian origin; akin to Old Norse *maralmr,* a beach grass] (1834)
**:** any of several beach grasses (genus *Ammophila* and especially *A. arenaria*)

**Mar·ra·no** \mə-'rä-(,)nō\ *noun, plural* **-nos** [Spanish, literally, pig] (1583)
**:** a Christianized Jew of medieval Spain

**mar·riage** \'mar-ij *also* 'mer-\ *noun* [Middle English *mariage,* from Old French, from *marier* to marry] (14th century)
**1 a :** the state of being married **b :** the mutual relation of husband and wife **:** WEDLOCK **c :** the institution whereby men and women are joined in a special kind of social and legal dependence for the purpose of founding and maintaining a family
**2 :** an act of marrying or the rite by which the married status is effected; *especially* **:** the wedding ceremony and attendant festivities or formalities
**3 :** an intimate or close union ⟨the *marriage* of painting and poetry —J. T. Shawcross⟩
— **mar·riage·abil·i·ty** \,mar-i-jə-'bi-lə-tē *also* ,mer-\ *noun*
— **mar·riage·able** \'mar-i-jə-bəl *also* 'mer-\ *adjective*

**marriage of convenience** (1711)
**:** a marriage contracted for social, political, or economic advantage rather than for mutual affection; *broadly* **:** a union or cooperation formed solely for pragmatic reasons

**¹mar·ried** \'mar-ēd *also* 'mer-\ *adjective* (14th century)
**1 a :** being in the state of matrimony **:** WEDDED
**b :** of or relating to marriage **:** CONNUBIAL
**2 :** UNITED, JOINED

**²married** *noun, plural* **marrieds** *or* **married** (1890)
**:** a married person ⟨young *marrieds* are paid undue . . . attention —Paul Goodman⟩

**mar·ron** \ma-'rō*n*\ *noun* [French] (1594)
**1 :** a large Mediterranean chestnut (*Castanea sativa*) or its sweet edible nut — called also *Spanish chestnut*
**2 mar·rons** \-'rō*n*(z)\ *plural* **:** chestnuts preserved in vanilla-flavored syrup

**mar·rons gla·cés** \ma-'rō*n*-gla-'sā\ *noun plural* [French, literally, glazed marrons] (1871)
**:** MARRON 2

**¹mar·row** \'mar-(,)ō\ *noun* [Middle English *marowe,* from Old English *mearg;* akin to Old High German *marag* marrow, Sanskrit *majjan*] (before 12th century)

**1 a :** a soft highly vascular modified connective tissue that occupies the cavities and cancellous part of most bones — compare RED MARROW **b :** the substance of the spinal cord
**2 a :** the choicest of food **b :** the seat of animal vigor **c :** the inmost, best, or essential part **:** CORE ⟨personal liberty is the *marrow* of the American tradition —Clinton Rossiter⟩
**3** *chiefly British* **:** VEGETABLE MARROW
— **mar·rowy** \'mar-ə-wē\ *adjective*

**²marrow** *noun* [Middle English *marwe, marrow*] (1516)
*chiefly Scottish* **:** one of a pair

**mar·row·bone** \'mar-ə-,bōn, -ō-,bōn\ *noun* (14th century)
**1 :** a bone (as a shinbone) rich in marrow
**2** *plural* **:** KNEES

**mar·row·fat** \-ə-,fat, -ō-,fat\ *noun* (1733)
**:** any of several wrinkled-seeded garden peas

**¹mar·ry** \'mar-ē *also* 'mer-\ *verb* **mar·ried; mar·ry·ing** [Middle English *marien,* from Old French *marier,* from Latin *maritare,* from *maritus* married] (14th century)
*transitive verb*
**1 a :** to join as husband and wife according to law or custom **b :** to give in marriage ⟨*married* his daughter to his partner's son⟩ **c :** to take as spouse **:** WED ⟨*married* the girl next door⟩ **d :** to perform the ceremony of marriage for ⟨a priest will *marry* them⟩ **e :** to obtain by marriage ⟨*marry* wealth⟩
**2 :** to unite in close and usually permanent relation
*intransitive verb*
**1 :** to take a spouse **:** WED
**2 :** COMBINE, UNITE ⟨seafood *marries* with other flavors⟩
— **marry into :** to become a member of by marriage ⟨*married into* a prominent family⟩

**²marry** *interjection* [Middle English *marie,* from *Marie,* the Virgin Mary] (14th century)
*archaic* — used for emphasis and especially to express amused or surprised agreement

**Mars** \'märz\ *noun* [Latin *Mart-, Mars*]
**1 :** the Roman god of war — compare ARES
**2 :** the planet fourth in order from the sun and conspicuous for its red color — see PLANET table

**mar·sa·la** \mär-'sä-lə\ *noun, often capitalized* [*Marsala,* town in Sicily] (1806)
**:** a fortified Sicilian wine that varies from dry to sweet

**marse** \'märs\ *noun* [by shortening & alteration] (1869)
*Southern* **:** MASTER

**Mar·seilles** \mär-'sā(ə)lz\ *noun* [*Marseilles,* France] (1762)

---

: a firm cotton fabric that is similar to piqué

**¹marsh** \'märsh\ *noun, often attributive* [Middle English *mersh*, from Old English *merisc, mersc*; akin to Middle Dutch *mersch* marsh, Old English *mere* sea, pool — more at MARINE] (before 12th century)
: a tract of soft wet land usually characterized by monocotyledons (as grasses or cattails)

**¹mar·shal** *also* **mar·shall** \'mär-shəl\ *noun* [Middle English, from Old French *mareschal*, of Germanic origin; akin to Old High German *marahscalc* marshal, from *marah* horse + *scalc* servant] (13th century)
**1 a :** a high official in the household of a medieval king, prince, or noble originally having charge of the cavalry but later usually in command of the military forces **b :** a person who arranges and directs the ceremonial aspects of a gathering
**2 a :** FIELD MARSHAL **b :** a general officer of the highest military rank
**3 a :** an officer having charge of prisoners **b** (1) : a ministerial officer appointed for a judicial district (as of the U.S.) to execute the process of the courts and perform various duties similar to those of a sheriff (2) : a city law officer entrusted with particular duties **c :** the administrative head of a city police department or fire department ◆
— **mar·shal·cy** \-sē\ *noun*
— **mar·shal·ship** \-,ship\ *noun*

**²marshal** *also* **marshall** *verb* **-shaled** *or* **-shalled; -shal·ing** *or* **-shal·ling** \'märsh-(ə-)liŋ\ (15th century)
*transitive verb*
**1 :** to place in proper rank or position ⟨*marshaling* the troops⟩
**2 :** to bring together and order in an appropriate or effective way ⟨*marshal* arguments⟩
**3 :** to lead ceremoniously or solicitously : USHER ⟨*marshaling* her little group of children down the street⟩
*intransitive verb*
: to take form or order ⟨ideas *marshaling* neatly⟩
*synonym* SEE ORDER

**marshal of the Royal Air Force** (1947)
: the highest ranking officer in the British air force

**marsh elder** *noun* (circa 1775)
: any of a genus (*Iva*) of coarse shrubby composite plants of moist areas in eastern and central North America

**marsh gas** *noun* (1848)
: METHANE

**marsh hawk** *noun* (1772)
: NORTHERN HARRIER

**marsh hen** *noun* (1709)
**1 :** any of various American rails
**2 :** BITTERN

**marsh·land** \'märsh-,land\ *noun* (12th century)
: a marshy tract or area : MARSH

**marsh·mal·low** \'märsh-,me-lō, -,ma-\ *noun* (before 12th century)
**1 :** a pink-flowered European perennial herb (*Althaea officinalis*) of the mallow family that is naturalized in the eastern U.S. and has a mucilaginous root sometimes used in confectionery and in medicine
**2 :** a confection made from the root of the marshmallow or from corn syrup, sugar, albumen, and gelatin beaten to a light spongy consistency; *also* : a piece of partially dried marshmallow ⟨a bag of *marshmallows*⟩
— **marsh·mal·lowy** \-,me-lə-wē, -,ma-\ *adjective*

**marsh marigold** *noun* (1578)
: a swamp herb (*Caltha palustris*) of the buttercup family that occurs in Europe and North America and has bright yellow flowers — called also *cowslip, kingcup*

**marshy** \'mär-shē\ *adjective* **marsh·i·er; -est** (14th century)
**1 :** resembling or constituting a marsh ⟨*marshy* ground⟩

**2 :** relating to or occurring in marshes ⟨*marshy* vegetation⟩
— **marsh·i·ness** *noun*

**¹mar·su·pi·al** \mär-'sü-pē-əl\ *adjective* (1819)
**1 :** of, relating to, or being a marsupial
**2 :** of, relating to, or forming a marsupium

**²marsupial** *noun* [New Latin *Marsupialia*, from *marsupium*] (circa 1835)
: any of an order (Marsupialia) of mammals comprising kangaroos, wombats, bandicoots, opossums, and related animals that do not develop a true placenta and that usually have a pouch on the abdomen of the female which covers the teats and serves to carry the young

**mar·su·pi·um** \mär-'sü-pē-əm\ *noun, plural* **-pia** \-pē-ə\ [New Latin, from Latin, purse, pouch, from Greek *marsypion*] (1698)
**1 :** an abdominal pouch that is formed of a fold of the skin and encloses the mammary glands of most marsupials
**2 :** any of several structures in various invertebrates (as a bryozoan or mollusk) for enclosing or carrying eggs or young

**¹mart** \'märt\ *noun* [Middle English, from Middle Dutch *marct, mart*, probably from Old North French *market*] (15th century)
**1** *archaic* : a coming together of people to buy and sell : ⁵FAIR 1
**2** *obsolete* : the activity of buying and selling; *also* : BARGAIN
**3 :** MARKET

**²mart** *transitive verb* (1589)
: to deal in : SELL

**mar·tel·lo tower** \mär-'te-lō-\ *noun, often M capitalized* [Cape *Mortella*, Corsica] (1803)
: a circular masonry fort or blockhouse

**mar·ten** \'mär-t°n\ *noun, plural* **marten** *or* **martens** [Middle English *martryn*, from Middle French *martrine* marten fur, from Old French, from *martre* marten, of Germanic origin; akin to Old English *mearth* marten] (13th century)
**1 :** any of several semiarboreal slender-bodied carnivorous mammals (genus *Martes*) chiefly of the northern hemisphere that are larger than the related weasels
**2 :** the fur or pelt of a marten

**mar·tens·ite** \'mär-t°n-,zīt\ *noun* [Adolf *Martens* (died 1914) German metallurgist] (1898)
: the hard constituent that is the chief component of quenched steel
— **mar·tens·it·ic** \,mar-t°n-'zi-tik, -'si-\ *adjective*
— **mar·tens·it·i·cal·ly** \-ti-k(ə-)lē\ *adverb*

**Mar·tha** \'mär-thə\ *noun* [Late Latin, from Greek]
: a sister of Lazarus and Mary and friend of Jesus

**mar·tial** \'mär-shəl\ *adjective* [Middle English, from Latin *martialis* of Mars, from *Mart-, Mars*] (14th century)
**1 :** of, relating to, or suited for war or a warrior
**2 :** relating to an army or to military life
**3 :** experienced in or inclined to war : WARLIKE
— **mar·tial·ly** \-shə-lē\ *adverb*

**martial art** *noun* (1933)
: any of several arts of combat and self-defense (as karate and judo) that are widely practiced as sport
— **martial artist** *noun*

**martial law** *noun* (1568)
**1 :** the law applied in occupied territory by the military authority of the occupying power
**2 :** the law administered by military forces that is invoked by a government in an emergency when the civilian law enforcement agencies are unable to maintain public order and safety

**mar·tian** \'mär-shən\ *adjective, often capitalized* (1880)

: of or relating to the planet Mars or its hypothetical inhabitants
— **martian** *noun, often capitalized*

**mar·tin** \'mär-t°n\ *noun* [probably from Saint *Martin*] (1589)
**1 :** a small Eurasian swallow (*Delichon urbica*) with a forked tail, bluish black head and back, and white rump and underparts
**2 :** any of various swallows and flycatchers other than the martin

**mar·ti·net** \,mär-t°n-'et\ *noun* [Jean *Martinet*, 17th century French army officer] (1779)
**1 :** a strict disciplinarian
**2 :** a person who stresses a rigid adherence to the details of forms and methods

**mar·tin·gale** \'mär-t°n-,gāl, -tiŋ-\ *noun* [Middle French] (1589)
**1 :** a device for steadying a horse's head or checking its upward movement that typically consists of a strap fastened to the girth, passing between the forelegs, and bifurcating to end in two rings through which the reins pass
**2 a :** a lower stay of rope or chain for the jibboom used to sustain the strain of the forestays and fastened to or rove through the dolphin striker **b :** DOLPHIN STRIKER
**3 :** any of several systems of betting in which a player increases the stake usually by doubling each time a bet is lost

martingale 1

**mar·ti·ni** \mär-'tē-nē\ *noun* [probably alteration of *Martinez* (cocktail), from the name *Martinez*] (1894)
: a cocktail made of gin and dry vermouth; *also* : VODKA MARTINI

**Mar·tin Lu·ther King Day** \'mär-t°n-'lü-thər-'kiŋ-\ *noun* (1977)
: the third Monday in January observed as a legal holiday in some states of the U.S.

**Mar·tin·mas** \'mär-t°n-məs, -,mas\ *noun* [Middle English *martinmasse*, from Saint *Martin* + Middle English *masse* mass] (14th century)

---

◇ WORD HISTORY
**marshal** The French language is a direct descendant of Latin, but it has included since its earliest days a number of Germanic words. The Franks, a group of West Germanic peoples, entered Gaul in large numbers during the 5th century A.D. and left their name and some traces of their own speech to France. Old French *mareschal* is one of these words: etymologically it is a compound of two Frankish words, one meaning "horse" (and akin to Old English *mearh* "horse" and *mere* "mare"), and the other meaning "servant" (and akin to Old English *scealc* "servant"). The Old French word referred not only to a worker who shoed horses (a sense that survives in Modern French *maréchal-ferrant* "farrier"), but also to the officer of a noble household in charge of horses and by the 13th century to a royal officer in command of an army. This ascent in status of a man in charge of horses is paralleled by the history of *constable*, and Late Latin *comes stabuli*, the ultimate source of the word *constable*, may in fact be a loose translation of the Germanic compound underlying *marshal*. See in addition CONSTABLE.

---

\ə\ abut \°\ kitten \ər\ further \a\ ash \ā\ ace
\ä\ mop, mar \au̇\ out \ch\ chin \e\ bet \ē\ easy
\g\ go \i\ hit \ī\ ice \j\ job \ŋ\ sing \ō\ go
\ȯ\ law \ȯi\ boy \th\ thin \t̲h̲\ the \ü\ loot \u̇\ foot
\y\ yet \zh\ vision *see also* Guide to Pronunciation

: November 11 celebrated as the feast of Saint Martin

**mart·let** \'märt-lət\ *noun* [alteration of *martinet,* from Middle French, probably from Saint *Martin*] (1538)
: MARTIN 1

**¹mar·tyr** \'mär-tər\ *noun* [Middle English, from Old English, from Late Latin, from Greek *martyr-, martys,* literally, witness] (before 12th century)
**1 :** a person who voluntarily suffers death as the penalty of witnessing to and refusing to renounce a religion
**2 :** a person who sacrifices something of great value and especially life itself for the sake of principle
**3 :** VICTIM; *especially* **:** a great or constant sufferer ⟨a *martyr* to asthma all his life —A. J. Cronin⟩
— **mar·tyr·i·za·tion** \,mär-tə-rə-'zā-shən\ *noun*
— **mar·tyr·ize** \'mär-tə-,rīz\ *transitive verb*

**²martyr** *transitive verb* (before 12th century)
**1 :** to put to death for adhering to a belief, faith, or profession
**2 :** to inflict agonizing pain on **:** TORTURE

**mar·tyr·dom** \'mär-tər-dəm\ *noun* (before 12th century)
**1 :** the suffering of death on account of adherence to a cause and especially to one's religious faith
**2 :** AFFLICTION, TORTURE

**mar·tyr·ol·o·gist** \,mär-tə-'rä-lə-jist\ *noun* (1676)
: a writer of or a specialist in martyrology

**mar·tyr·ol·o·gy** \-jē\ *noun* (1599)
**1 :** a catalog of Roman Catholic martyrs and saints arranged by the dates of their feasts
**2 :** ecclesiastical history treating the lives and sufferings of martyrs

**mar·tyry** \'mär-tə-rē\ *noun, plural* **-tyr·ies** [Late Latin *martyrium,* from Late Greek *martyrion,* from Greek *martyr-, martys*] (circa 1722)
: a shrine erected in honor of a martyr

**¹mar·vel** \'mär-vəl\ *noun* [Middle English *mervel,* from Old French *merveille,* from Late Latin *mirabilia* marvels, from Latin, neuter plural of *mirabilis* wonderful, from *mirari* to wonder] (14th century)
**1 :** something that causes wonder or astonishment
**2 :** intense surprise or interest **:** ASTONISHMENT

**²marvel** *verb* **mar·veled** *or* **mar·velled; mar·vel·ing** *or* **mar·vel·ling** \'märv-liŋ, 'mär-və-\ (14th century)
*intransitive verb*
: to become filled with surprise, wonder, or amazed curiosity ⟨*marveled* at the magician's skill⟩
*transitive verb*
: to feel astonishment or perplexity at or about ⟨*marveled* that they had escaped⟩

**mar·vel·ous** *or* **mar·vel·lous** \'märv-(ə-)ləs\ *adjective* (14th century)
**1 :** causing wonder **:** ASTONISHING
**2 :** MIRACULOUS, SUPERNATURAL ⟨Gothic tales of the *marvelous* and the bizarre⟩
**3 :** of the highest kind or quality **:** notably superior ⟨has a *marvelous* way with children⟩
— **mar·vel·ous·ly** *adverb*
— **mar·vel·ous·ness** *noun*

**Marx·ian** \'märk-sē-ən\ *adjective* (1887)
: of, developed by, or influenced by the doctrines of Marx ⟨*Marxian* socialism⟩

**Marx·ism** \'märk-,si-zəm\ *noun* (1897)
: the political, economic, and social principles and policies advocated by Marx; *especially* **:** a theory and practice of socialism including the labor theory of value, dialectical materialism, the class struggle, and dictatorship of the proletariat until the establishment of a classless society
— **Marx·ist** \-sist\ *noun or adjective*

**Marx·ism–Le·nin·ism** \'märk-,si-zəm-'le-nə-,ni-zəm\ *noun* (1932)

: a theory and practice of communism developed by Lenin from doctrines of Marx
— **Marx·ist–Len·in·ist** \'märk-sist-'le-nə-nist\ *noun or adjective*

**Mary** \'mer-ē, 'mar-ē, 'mā-rē\ *noun* [Late Latin *Maria,* from Greek *Mariam, Maria,* from Hebrew *Miryām* Miriam]
**1 :** the mother of Jesus
**2 :** a sister of Lazarus and Martha and a friend of Jesus

**Mary Jane** \-'jān\ *noun* [by folk etymology (influenced by Spanish *Juana* Jane)] (1928)
*slang* **:** MARIJUANA

**Mary·knoll·er** \-,nō-lər\ *noun* (1943)
: a member of the Catholic Foreign Mission Society of America founded by T. F. Price and J. A. Walsh at Maryknoll, N.Y. in 1911

**Mary Mag·da·lene** \-'mag-də-lən, -,lēn; -,mag-də-'lē-nē\ *noun* [Late Latin *Magdalene,* from Greek *Magdalēnē*]
: a woman who was healed of evil spirits by Jesus and who saw the risen Christ near his sepulchre

**mar·zi·pan** \'märt-sə-,pän, -,pan; 'mär-zə-,pan\ *noun* [German, from Italian *marzapane*] (1542)
: a confection of crushed almonds or almond paste, sugar, and egg whites that is often shaped into various forms

**Ma·sai** \mä-'sī, 'mä-,\ *noun, plural* **Masai** *or* **Masais** (1857)
**1 :** a member of a pastoral and hunting people of Kenya and Tanzania
**2 :** the Nilotic language of the Masai people

**mas·cara** \ma-'skar-ə\ *noun* [probably from Italian *maschera* mask] (1886)
: a cosmetic especially for coloring the eyelashes

**mas·car·po·ne** \,mas-kär-'pō-(,)nā\ *noun* [Italian, from Italian dialect (Lombardy) *mascarpón,* augmentative of *mascarpa* cream cheese] (1932)
: an Italian cream cheese

**mas·con** \'mas-,kän\ *noun* [²*mass* + *concentration*] (1968)
: any of the high-density regions below the surface of lunar maria that are held to perturb the motion of spacecraft in lunar orbit

**mas·cot** \'mas-,kät *also* -kət\ *noun* [French *mascotte,* from Provençal *mascoto,* from *masco* witch, from Medieval Latin *masca*] (1881)
: a person, animal, or object adopted by a group as a symbolic figure especially to bring them good luck ⟨the team had a mountain lion as their *mascot*⟩ ◆

**¹mas·cu·line** \'mas-kyə-lən\ *adjective* [Middle English *masculin,* from Middle French, from Latin *masculinus,* from *masculus,* noun, male, diminutive of *mas* male] (14th century)
**1 a :** MALE **b :** having qualities appropriate to or usually associated with a man
**2 :** of, relating to, or constituting the gender that ordinarily includes most words or grammatical forms referring to males
**3 a :** having or occurring in a stressed final syllable ⟨*masculine* rhyme⟩ **b :** having the final chord occurring on a strong beat ⟨*masculine* cadence⟩
**4 :** of or forming the formal, active, or generative principle of the cosmos
— **mas·cu·line·ly** *adverb*
— **mas·cu·lin·i·ty** \,mas-kyə-'li-nə-tē\ *noun*

**²masculine** *noun* (14th century)
**1 :** the masculine gender
**2 :** a noun, pronoun, adjective, or inflectional form or class of the masculine gender
**3 :** a male person

**mas·cu·lin·ise** *British variant of* MASCULINIZE

**mas·cu·lin·ize** \'mas-kyə-lə-,nīz\ *transitive verb* **-ized; -iz·ing** (1912)
: to give a chiefly masculine character to; *especially* **:** to cause (a female) to take on male characteristics

— **mas·cu·lin·i·za·tion** \,mas-kyə-lə-nə-'zā-shən\ *noun*

**ma·ser** \'mā-zər\ *noun* [microwave *a*mplification by *s*timulated *e*mission of *r*adiation] (1955)
: a device or object that emits coherent microwave radiation produced by the natural oscillations of atoms or molecules between energy levels

**¹mash** \'mash\ *transitive verb* (13th century)
**1 a :** to reduce to a soft pulpy state by beating or pressure **b :** CRUSH, SMASH ⟨*mash* a finger⟩
**2 :** to subject (as crushed malt) to the action of water with heating and stirring in preparing wort

**²mash** *noun* [Middle English *mash-,* from Old English *māx-;* akin to Middle High German *meisch* mash] (1577)
**1 :** a mixture of ground feeds for livestock
**2 :** crushed malt or grain meal steeped and stirred in hot water to ferment (as for the production of beer or whiskey)
**3 :** a soft pulpy mass
**4** *British* **:** mashed potatoes

**³mash** *transitive verb* [origin unknown] (1879)
: to flirt with or seek the affection of

**⁴mash** *noun* (1880)
: CRUSH 4

**¹mash·er** \'ma-shər\ *noun* (circa 1500)
: one that mashes ⟨a potato *masher*⟩

**²masher** *noun* (1875)
: a man who makes passes at women

**¹mask** \'mask\ *noun* [Middle French *masque,* from Old Italian *maschera*] (1534)
**1 a** (1) **:** a cover or partial cover for the face used for disguise (2) **:** a person wearing a mask **:** MASKER **b** (1) **:** a figure of a head worn on the stage in antiquity to identify the character and project the voice (2) **:** a grotesque false face worn at carnivals or in rituals **c :** an often grotesque carved head or face used as an ornament (as on a keystone) **d :** a sculptured face or a copy of a face made by means of a mold
**2 a :** something that serves to conceal or disguise **:** PRETENSE, CLOAK ⟨aware of the *masks,* facades and defenses people erect to protect themselves —Kenneth Keniston⟩ **b :** something that conceals from view **c :** a translucent or opaque screen to cover part of the sensitive surface in taking or printing a photograph **d :** a pattern of opaque material used to shield selected areas of a surface (as of a semiconductor) in deposition or etching (as in producing an integrated circuit)

◇ WORD HISTORY
**mascot** The spoken Latin of Gaul, northern Italy, and the Iberian Peninsula had a root *mask-,* unattested in classical Latin. It overlapped two semantic fields, the color black and malevolent magic, that were strongly associated with each other in popular superstition. One outcome of this root in Occitan or Provençal, the Romance speech of southern France, was a feminine noun *masco* "sorceress, witch." *Mascoto* "enchantment, charm," a derivative of *masco,* was borrowed into French as *mascotte* and shortly thereafter provided English with the word *mascot.* Contemporary with the root *mask-* in spoken Latin was an extended form *maskar-,* which appears on the one hand in words such as Catalan *mascara* "lampblack, soot," and on the other in medieval Italian *maschera* "mask." The Italian word is the ultimate source of English *mask* and *masquerade,* both borrowed directly from French, and probably also of our *mascara,* which was originally theater argot.

**3 a :** a protective covering for the face **b :** GAS MASK **c :** a device covering the mouth and nose to facilitate inhalation **d :** a comparable device to prevent exhalation of infective material **e :** a cosmetic preparation for the skin of the face that produces a tightening effect as it dries
**4 a :** the head or face of an animal (as a fox or dog) **b :** an area (as the one around the eyes) of an animal's face that is distinguished by usually darker coloring

²**mask** (circa 1562)
*intransitive verb*
**1 :** to take part in a masquerade
**2 a :** to assume a mask **b :** to disguise one's true character or intentions
*transitive verb*
**1 :** to provide or conceal with a mask: as **a :** to conceal from view ⟨*mask* a gun battery⟩ **b :** to make indistinct or imperceptible ⟨*masks* undesirable flavors⟩ **c :** to cover up ⟨*masked* his real purpose⟩
**2 :** to cover for protection
**3 :** to modify the size or shape of (as a photograph) by means of an opaque border
**synonym** see DISGUISE
— **mask·like** \-ˌlīk\ *adjective*

**masked** \'maskt\ *adjective* (1585)
**1 :** marked by the use of masks ⟨a *masked* ball⟩
**2 :** failing to present or produce the usual symptoms **:** LATENT ⟨*masked* infection⟩ ⟨a *masked* virus⟩

**mask·er** \'mas-kər\ *noun* (circa 1548)
**:** a person who wears a mask; *especially* **:** a participant in a masquerade

**mask·ing tape** \'mas-kiŋ-\ *noun* (1936)
**:** a tape with adhesive on one side that has a variety of uses (as to cover a surface when painting an adjacent surface)

**mas·och·ism** \'ma-sə-ˌki-zəm, 'ma-zə- *also* 'mā-\ *noun* [International Scientific Vocabulary, from Leopold von Sacher-*Masoch* (died 1895) German novelist] (circa 1893)
**1 :** a sexual perversion characterized by pleasure in being subjected to pain or humiliation especially by a love object — compare SADISM
**2 :** pleasure in being abused or dominated **:** a taste for suffering
— **mas·och·ist** \-kist\ *noun*
— **mas·och·is·tic** \ˌma-sə-'kis-tik, ˌma-zə- *also* ˌmā-\ *adjective*
— **mas·och·is·ti·cal·ly** \-'kis-ti-k(ə-)lē\ *adverb*

**ma·son** \'mā-sᵊn\ *noun* [Middle English, from Old French *maçon*, of Germanic origin; akin to Old English *macian* to make] (13th century)
**1 :** a skilled worker who builds by laying units of substantial material (as stone or brick)
**2** *capitalized* **:** FREEMASON

**Ma·son·ic** \mə-'sä-nik\ *adjective* (1797)
**:** of, relating to, or characteristic of Freemasons or Freemasonry

**Ma·son·ite** \'mā-sᵊn-ˌīt\ *trademark*
— used for fiberboard made from steam-exploded wood fiber

**ma·son jar** \'mā-sᵊn-\ *noun, often M capitalized* [John L. *Mason,* 19th century American inventor] (1888)
**:** a widemouthed jar used especially for home canning

**ma·son·ry** \'mā-sᵊn-rē\ *noun, plural* **-ries** (13th century)
**1 a :** something constructed of materials used by masons **b :** the art, trade, or occupation of a mason **c :** work done by a mason
**2** *capitalized* **:** FREEMASONRY

**mason wasp** *noun* (1792)
**:** any of various solitary wasps that construct nests of hardened mud

**Ma·so·ra** *or* **Ma·so·rah** \mə-'sōr-ə, -'sör-\ *noun* [New Hebrew *mĕsōrāh,* from Late Hebrew *māsōreth* tradition, from Hebrew, bond] (1613)

**:** a body of notes on the textual traditions of the Hebrew Old Testament compiled by scribes during the 1st millennium of the Christian era

**Mas·o·rete** *or* **Mas·so·rete** \'ma-sə-ˌrēt\ *noun* [Middle French *massoreth,* from Late Hebrew *māsōreth*] (1587)
**:** one of the scribes who compiled the Masora
— **Mas·o·ret·ic** \ˌma-sə-'re-tik\ *adjective*

**masque** *also* **mask** \'mask\ *noun* [Middle French *masque* — more at MASK] (1514)
**1 :** MASQUERADE
**2 :** a short allegorical dramatic entertainment of the 16th and 17th centuries performed by masked actors

**masqu·er** \'mas-kər\ *variant of* MASKER

¹**mas·quer·ade** \ˌmas-kə-'rād\ *noun* [Middle French, from Old Italian dialect *mascarada,* from Old Italian *maschera* mask] (1587)
**1 a :** a social gathering of persons wearing masks and often fantastic costumes **b :** a costume for wear at such a gathering
**2 :** an action or appearance that is mere disguise or outward show

²**masquerade** *intransitive verb* **-ad·ed; -ad·ing** (1692)
**1 a :** to disguise oneself; *also* **:** to go about disguised **b :** to take part in a masquerade
**2 :** to assume the appearance of something one is not
— **mas·quer·ad·er** *noun*

¹**mass** \'mas\ *noun* [Middle English, from Old English *mæsse,* modification of (assumed) Vulgar Latin *messa,* literally, dismissal at the end of a religious service, from Late Latin *missa,* from Latin, feminine of *missus,* past participle of *mittere* to send] (before 12th century)
**1** *capitalized* **:** the liturgy of the Eucharist especially in accordance with the traditional Latin rite
**2** *often capitalized* **:** a celebration of the Eucharist ⟨Sunday *masses* held at three different hours⟩
**3 :** a musical setting for the ordinary of the Mass

²**mass** *noun* [Middle English *masse,* from Middle French, from Latin *massa,* from Greek *maza;* akin to Greek *massein* to knead — more at MINGLE] (15th century)
**1 a :** a quantity or aggregate of matter usually of considerable size **b** (1) **:** EXPANSE, BULK (2) **:** massive quality or effect ⟨impressed me with such *mass* and such vividness —F. M. Ford⟩ (3) **:** the principal part or main body ⟨the great *mass* of the continent is buried under an ice cap —Walter Sullivan⟩ (4) **:** AGGREGATE, WHOLE ⟨men in the *mass*⟩ **c :** the property of a body that is a measure of its inertia and that is commonly taken as a measure of the amount of material it contains and causes it to have weight in a gravitational field
**2 :** a large quantity, amount, or number ⟨a great *mass* of material⟩
**3 a :** a large body of persons in a compact group **:** a body of persons regarded as an aggregate **b :** the great body of the people as contrasted with the elite — often used in plural ⟨the underprivileged and disadvantaged *masses* —C. A. Buss⟩
**synonym** see BULK

³**mass** (14th century)
*transitive verb*
**:** to form or collect into a mass
*intransitive verb*
**:** to assemble in a mass ⟨three thousand students had *massed* in the plaza —A. E. Neville⟩

⁴**mass** *adjective* (1733)
**1 a :** of or relating to the mass of the people ⟨*mass* market⟩ ⟨*mass* education⟩ **b :** being one of or at one with the mass **:** AVERAGE, COMMONPLACE ⟨*mass* man⟩ **b :** participated in by or affecting a large number of individuals ⟨*mass* destruction⟩ ⟨*mass* demonstrations⟩ **c :** having a large-scale character **:** WHOLESALE ⟨*mass* production⟩

**2 :** viewed as a whole **:** TOTAL ⟨the *mass* effect of a design⟩

**mas·sa** \'ma-sə\ *noun* [by alteration] (1774) *Southern* **:** MASTER

**Mas·sa·chu·set** *or* **Mas·sa·chu·sett** \ˌma-sə-'chü-sət, -zət *also* ˌmas-'chü-\ *noun, plural* **Massachusets** *or* **Massachuset** *or* **Masachusetts** *or* **Massachusett** [Massachuset, a locality, literally, at the big hill] (1616)
**1 :** a member of an American Indian people of Massachusetts
**2 :** the extinct Algonquian language of the Massachuset people

¹**mas·sa·cre** \'ma-si-kər\ *noun* [Middle French] (circa 1578)
**1 :** the act or an instance of killing a number of usually helpless or unresisting human beings under circumstances of atrocity or cruelty
**2 :** a cruel or wanton murder
**3 :** a wholesale slaughter of animals
**4 :** an act of complete destruction ⟨the author's *massacre* of traditional federalist presuppositions —R. G. McCloskey⟩

²**massacre** *transitive verb* **mas·sa·cred; mas·sa·cring** \-k(ə-)riŋ\ (1581)
**1 :** to kill by massacre **:** SLAUGHTER
**2 :** MANGLE 2 ⟨words were misspelled and syntax *massacred* —Bice Clemow⟩
— **mas·sa·crer** \-kər-ər, -krər\ *noun*

¹**mas·sage** \mə-'säzh, -'säj\ *noun* [French, from *masser* to massage, from Arabic *massa* to stroke] (circa 1860)
**:** manipulation of tissues (as by rubbing, kneading, or tapping) with the hand or an instrument for therapeutic purposes

²**massage** *transitive verb* **mas·saged; mas·sag·ing** (1887)
**1 :** to subject to massage
**2 a :** to treat flatteringly **:** BLANDISH **b :** MANIPULATE 3, DOCTOR 2b ⟨researchers *massaged* the data to support their thesis⟩
— **mas·sag·er** *noun*

**massage parlor** *noun* (1913)
**:** an establishment that provides massage treatments; *also* **:** one offering sexual services in addition to or in lieu of massage

**mas·sa·sau·ga** \ˌma-sə-'sò-gə\ *noun* [Missisauga River, Ontario, Canada] (1835)
**:** a small North American rattlesnake (*Sistrurus catenatus*)

**mass card** *noun* (1948)
**:** a card notifying the recipient (as a bereaved family) that a mass is to be offered for the repose of the soul of a specified deceased person

**mass defect** *noun* (circa 1923)
**:** the difference between the mass of an isotope and its mass number

**mass driver** *noun* (1977)
**:** a large electromagnetic catapult designed to hurl material (as from an asteroid) into space

**mas·sé** \ma-'sā\ *noun* [French, from past participle of *masser* to make a massé shot, from *masse* sledgehammer, from Middle French *mace* mace] (1873)
**:** a shot in billiards or pool made by hitting the cue ball vertically or nearly vertically on the side to drive it around one ball in order to strike another

**mas·se·ter** \mə-'sē-tər, ma-\ *noun* [New Latin, from Greek *masētēr,* from *masasthai* to chew — more at MANDIBLE] (1666)
**:** a large muscle that raises the lower jaw and assists in mastication
— **mas·se·ter·ic** \ˌma-sə-'ter-ik\ *adjective*

**mas·seur** \ma-'sər, mə-\ *noun* [French, from *masser*] (1876)
**:** a man who practices massage

**mas·seuse** \-'sə(r)z, -'süz\ *noun* [French, feminine of *masseur*] (1876)

---

\ə\ abut   \ᵊ\ kitten   \ər\ further   \a\ ash   \ā\ ace
\ä\ mop, mar   \aů\ out   \ch\ chin   \e\ bet   \ē\ easy
\g\ go   \i\ hit   \ī\ ice   \j\ job   \ŋ\ sing   \ō\ go
\ò\ law   \òi\ boy   \th\ thin   \th\ the   \ü\ loot   \ů\ foot
\y\ yet   \zh\ vision    *see also* Guide to Pronunciation

**:** a woman who practices massage

**mas·sif** \ma-'sēf\ *noun* [French, from *massif*, adjective, from Middle French] (1885)
**1 :** a principal mountain mass
**2 :** a block of the earth's crust bounded by faults or flexures and displaced as a unit without internal change

**mas·sive** \'ma-siv\ *adjective* [Middle English *massiffe*, from Middle French *massif*, from *masse* mass] (15th century)
**1 :** forming or consisting of a large mass: **a :** BULKY **b :** WEIGHTY, HEAVY ⟨*massive* walls⟩ ⟨a *massive* volume⟩ **c :** impressively large or ponderous **d :** having no regular form but not necessarily lacking crystalline structure ⟨*massive* sandstone⟩
**2 a :** large, solid, or heavy in structure ⟨*massive* jaw⟩ **b :** large in scope or degree ⟨the feeling of frustration, of being ineffectual, is *massive* —David Halberstam⟩ **c** (1) **:** large in comparison to what is typical ⟨*massive* dose of penicillin⟩ (2) **:** being extensive and severe ⟨*massive* hemorrhage⟩ ⟨*massive* collapse of a lung⟩ (3) **:** imposing in excellence or grandeur **:** MONUMENTAL ⟨*massive* simplicity⟩
**3 :** having mass ⟨a *massive* boson⟩
— **mas·sive·ly** *adverb*
— **mas·sive·ness** *noun*

**mass·less** \'mas-ləs\ *adjective* (1879)
**:** having no mass ⟨a *massless* particle⟩

**mass–mar·ket** \'mas-'mär-kət\ *adjective* (1952)
**:** sold through such retail outlets as supermarkets and drugstores as well as through bookstores ⟨a *mass-market* paperback⟩; *also* **:** of, relating to, or publishing mass-market materials

**mass medium** *noun, plural* **mass media** (1923)
**:** a medium of communication (as newspapers, radio, or television) that is designed to reach the mass of the people — usually used in plural

**mass noun** *noun* (1933)
**:** a noun (as *sand* or *water*) that characteristically denotes in many languages a homogeneous substance or a concept without subdivisions and that in English is preceded in indefinite singular constructions by *some* rather than *a* or *an* — compare COUNT NOUN

**mass number** *noun* (1923)
**:** an integer that approximates the mass of an isotope and designates the number of nucleons in the nucleus

**mass–pro·duce** \,mas-prə-'düs, -'dyüs\ *transitive verb* [back-formation from *mass production*] (1923)
**:** to produce in quantity usually by machinery
— **mass production** *noun*

**mass spectrograph** *noun* (1920)
**:** an instrument used to separate and often to determine the masses of isotopes

**mass spectrometry** *noun* (1943)
**:** an instrumental method for identifying the chemical constitution of a substance by means of the separation of gaseous ions according to their differing mass and charge — called also *mass spectroscopy*
— **mass spectrometric** *adjective*
— **mass spectrometer** *noun*

**mass spectrum** *noun* (1920)
**:** the spectrum of a stream of gaseous ions separated according to their mass and charge

**massy** \'ma-sē\ *adjective* (14th century)
**:** MASSIVE

**¹mast** \'mast\ *noun* [Middle English, from Old English *mæst;* akin to Old High German *mast* mast, Latin *malus*] (before 12th century)
**1 :** a long pole or spar rising from the keel or deck of a ship and supporting the yards, booms, and rigging
**2 :** a slender vertical or nearly vertical structure (as an upright post in various cranes)
**3 :** a disciplinary proceeding at which the commanding officer of a naval unit hears and

disposes of cases against enlisted men — called also *captain's mast*
— **mast·ed** \'mas-təd\ *adjective*
— **before the mast 1 :** forward of the foremast **2 :** as a common sailor

**²mast** *transitive verb* (1627)
**:** to furnish with a mast

**³mast** *noun* [Middle English, from Old English *mæst;* akin to Old High German *mast* food, mast, and probably to Old English *mete* food — more at MEAT] (before 12th century)
**:** nuts (as acorns) accumulated on the forest floor and often serving as food for animals (as hogs)

**mas·ta·ba** \'mas-tə-bə\ *noun* [Arabic *maṣṭabah* stone bench] (1882)
**:** an Egyptian tomb of the time of the Memphite dynasties that is oblong in shape with sloping sides and a flat roof

**mast cell** \'mast-\ *noun* [part translation of German *Mastzelle,* from *Mast* food, mast (from Old High German) + *Zelle* cell] (circa 1890)
**:** a large cell that occurs especially in connective tissue and has basophilic granules containing substances (as histamine and heparin) which mediate allergic reactions

**mas·tec·to·my** \ma-'stek-tə-mē\ *noun, plural* **-mies** [Greek *mastos* breast + English *-ectomy*] (circa 1923)
**:** excision of the breast

**¹mas·ter** \'mas-tər\ *noun* [Middle English, from Old English *magister* & Old French *maistre,* both from Latin *magister;* akin to Latin *magnus* large — more at MUCH] (before 12th century)
**1 a** (1) **:** a male teacher (2) **:** a person holding an academic degree higher than a bachelor's but lower than a doctor's **b** *often capitalized* **:** a revered religious leader **c :** a worker or artisan qualified to teach apprentices **d** (1) **:** an artist, performer, or player of consummate skill (2) **:** a great figure of the past (as in science or art) whose work serves as a model or ideal
**2 a :** one having authority over another **:** RULER, GOVERNOR **b :** one that conquers or masters **:** VICTOR, SUPERIOR ⟨in this young, obscure challenger the champion found his *master*⟩ **c :** a person licensed to command a merchant ship **d** (1) **:** one having control (2) **:** an owner especially of a slave or animal **e :** the employer especially of a servant **f** (1) *dialect* **:** HUSBAND (2) **:** the male head of a household
**3 a** (1) *archaic* **:** MR. (2) **:** a youth or boy too young to be called *mister* — used as a title **b :** the eldest son of a Scottish viscount or baron
**4 a :** a presiding officer in an institution or society (as a college) **b :** any of several officers of court appointed to assist (as by hearing and reporting) a judge
**5 a :** a master mechanism or device **b :** an original from which copies can be made; *especially* **:** a master phonograph record or magnetic tape
— **mas·ter·ship** \-,ship\ *noun*

**²master** *adjective* (12th century)
**:** being or relating to a master: as **a :** having chief authority **:** DOMINANT **b :** SKILLED, PROFICIENT ⟨a prosperous *master* builder —*Current Biography*⟩ **c :** PRINCIPAL, PREDOMINANT **d :** SUPERLATIVE — often used in combination ⟨a *master*-liar⟩ **e :** being a device or mechanism that controls the operation of another mechanism or that establishes a standard (as a dimension or weight) **f :** being or relating to a master from which duplicates are made

**³master** *transitive verb* **mas·tered; mas·ter·ing** \-t(ə-)riŋ\ (13th century)
**1 :** to become master of **:** OVERCOME
**2 a :** to become skilled or proficient in the use of ⟨*master* a foreign language⟩ **b :** to gain a thorough understanding of ⟨had *mastered* every aspect of publishing —*Current Biography*⟩
**3 :** to produce a master phonograph record or magnetic tape of (as a musical rendition)

**master–at–arms** *noun, plural* **masters-at–arms** (1748)
**:** a petty officer charged with maintaining discipline aboard ship

**master bedroom** *noun* (1925)
**:** a large or principal bedroom

**master chief petty officer** *noun* (1958)
**:** an enlisted man in the navy or coast guard ranking above a senior chief petty officer

**master chief petty officer of the coast guard** (1966)
**:** the ranking petty officer in the coast guard serving as adviser to the commandant

**master chief petty officer of the navy** (1966)
**:** the ranking petty officer in the navy serving as adviser to the chief of naval operations

**master class** *noun* (1952)
**:** a seminar for advanced music students conducted by a master musician

**mas·ter·ful** \'mas-tər-fəl\ *adjective* (15th century)
**1 a :** inclined and usually competent to play the master **b :** suggestive of a domineering nature
**2 :** having or reflecting the power and skill of a master ☆ ■
— **mas·ter·ful·ly** \-fə-lē\ *adverb*
— **mas·ter·ful·ness** *noun*

**master gunnery sergeant** *noun* (1958)
**:** a noncommissioned officer in the marine corps ranking above a master sergeant

**master key** *noun* (1576)
**:** a key designed to open several different locks

**mas·ter·ly** \'mas-tər-lē\ *adjective* (15th century)
**:** suitable to or resembling that of a master; *especially* **:** indicating thorough knowledge or superior skill and power ⟨a *masterly* performance⟩

☆ SYNONYMS
**Masterful, domineering, imperious, peremptory, imperative** mean tending to impose one's will on others. MASTERFUL implies a strong personality and ability to act authoritatively ⟨her *masterful* personality soon dominated the movement⟩. DOMINEERING suggests an overbearing or arbitrary manner and an obstinate determination to enforce one's will ⟨children controlled by *domineering* parents⟩. IMPERIOUS implies a commanding nature or manner and often suggests arrogant assurance ⟨an *imperious* executive used to getting his own way⟩. PEREMPTORY implies an abrupt dictatorial manner coupled with an unwillingness to brook disobedience or dissent ⟨given a *peremptory* dismissal⟩. IMPERATIVE implies peremptoriness arising more from the urgency of the situation than from an inherent will to dominate ⟨an *imperative* appeal for assistance⟩.

□ USAGE
**masterful** Some commentators insist that use of *masterful* should be limited to sense 1 in order to preserve a distinction between it and *masterly.* The distinction is a modern one, excogitated by a 20th century pundit in disregard of the history of the word. Both words developed in a parallel manner but the earlier sense of *masterly,* equivalent to *masterful* 1, dropped out of use. Since *masterly* had but one sense, the pundit opined that it would be tidy if *masterful* were likewise limited to one sense and he forthwith condemned use of *masterful* 2 as an error. Sense 2 of *masterful,* which is slightly older than the sense of *masterly* intended to replace it, has continued in reputable use all along; it cannot rationally be called an error.

*usage* see MASTERFUL
— **mas·ter·li·ness** *noun*
— **masterly** *adverb*
¹**mas·ter·mind** \'mas-tər-ˌmīnd, ˌmas-tər-'\ *noun* (1720)
: a person who supplies the directing or creative intelligence for a project
²**mastermind** *transitive verb* (1940)
: to be the mastermind of
**master of arts** *often M&A capitalized* (15th century)
**1** : the recipient of a master's degree that usually signifies that the recipient has passed an integrated course of study in one or more of the humanities and sometimes has completed a thesis involving research or a creative project and that typically requires two years of work beyond a bachelor's degree
**2** : the degree making one a master of arts — abbreviation *M.A., A.M.*
**master of ceremonies** (1662)
**1** : a person who determines the forms to be observed on a public occasion
**2** : a person who acts as host at a formal event
**3** : a person who acts as host for a program of entertainment (as on television)
**master of science** *often M&S capitalized* (circa 1905)
**1** : the recipient of a master's degree that usually signifies that the recipient has passed an integrated course of study in one or more of the sciences and sometimes has completed a thesis involving research and that typically requires two years of work beyond a bachelor's degree
**2** : the degree making one a master of science — abbreviation *M.S., M.Sc.*
**mas·ter·piece** \'mas-tər-ˌpēs\ *noun* (1605)
**1** : a work done with extraordinary skill; *especially* : a supreme intellectual or artistic achievement
**2** : a piece of work presented to a medieval guild as evidence of qualification for the rank of master
**master plan** *noun* (circa 1930)
: a plan giving overall guidance
**master race** *noun* (1937)
: a people held to be racially preeminent and hence fitted to rule or enslave other peoples
**master's** *noun* (1939)
: a master's degree
**master sergeant** *noun* (circa 1934)
: a noncommissioned officer ranking in the army above a sergeant first class and below a staff sergeant major, in the air force above a technical sergeant and below a senior master sergeant, and in the marine corps above a gunnery sergeant and below a master gunnery sergeant
**mas·ter·sing·er** \'mas-tər-ˌsiŋ-ər\ *noun* (1810)
: MEISTERSINGER
**mas·ter·stroke** \-ˌstrōk\ *noun* (1679)
: a masterly performance or move
**mas·ter·work** \-ˌwərk\ *noun* (1617)
: MASTERPIECE
**mas·tery** \'mas-t(ə-)rē\ *noun* [Middle English *maistrie*, from Old French, from *maistre* master] (13th century)
**1 a** : the authority of a master : DOMINION **b** : the upper hand in a contest or competition : SUPERIORITY, ASCENDANCY
**2 a** : possession or display of great skill or technique **b** : skill or knowledge that makes one master of a subject : COMMAND
**mast·head** \'mast-ˌhed\ *noun* (1748)
**1** : the top of a mast
**2 a** : the printed matter in a newspaper or periodical that gives the title and pertinent details of ownership, advertising rates, and subscription rates **b** : the name of a publication (as a newspaper) displayed on the top of the first page
**mas·tic** \'mas-tik\ *noun* [Middle English *mastik*, from Latin *mastiche*, from Greek *mas-*

*tichē*, probably back-formation from *mastichan*] (14th century)
**1** : an aromatic resinous exudate from mastic trees used chiefly in varnishes
**2** : any of various pasty materials used as protective coatings or cements
**mas·ti·cate** \'mas-tə-ˌkāt\ *verb* **-cat·ed; -cat·ing** [Late Latin *masticatus*, past participle of *masticare*, from Greek *mastichan* to gnash the teeth; akin to Greek *masasthai* to chew — more at MANDIBLE] (1649)
*transitive verb*
**1** : to grind or crush (food) with or as if with the teeth in preparation for swallowing : CHEW
**2** : to soften or reduce to pulp by crushing or kneading
*intransitive verb*
: CHEW
— **mas·ti·ca·tion** \ˌmas-tə-'kā-shən\ *noun*
— **mas·ti·ca·tor** \'mas-tə-ˌkā-tər\ *noun*
¹**mas·ti·ca·to·ry** \'mas-ti-kə-ˌtōr-ē, -ˌtȯr-\ *adjective* (1694)
**1** : used for or adapted to chewing ⟨*masticatory* limbs of an arthropod⟩
**2** : of, relating to, or involving the organs of mastication ⟨*masticatory* paralysis⟩
²**masticatory** *noun, plural* **-ries** (circa 1611)
: a substance chewed to increase saliva
**mastic tree** *noun* (15th century)
: a small southern European evergreen tree (*Pistacia lentiscus*) of the cashew family that yields mastic
**mas·tiff** \'mas-təf\ *noun* [Middle English *mastif*, modification of Middle French *mastin*, from (assumed) Vulgar Latin *mansuetinus*, from Latin *mansuetus* tame — more at MANSUETUDE] (14th century)
: any of a breed of very large massive powerful smooth-coated dogs that are apricot, fawn, or brindle and are often used as guard dogs

* mastiff

**mas·ti·goph·o·ran** \ˌmas-tə-'gä-fə-rən\ *noun* [ultimately from Greek *mastig-, mastix* whip + *pherein* to carry — more at BEAR] (circa 1911)
: any of a subphylum (Mastigophora) of protozoans comprising forms with flagella and including many often treated as algae
— **mastigophoran** *adjective*
**mas·ti·tis** \ma-'stī-təs\ *noun, plural* **-tit·i·des** \-'sti-tə-ˌdēz\ [New Latin, from Greek *mastos* breast] (circa 1842)
: inflammation of the breast or udder usually caused by infection
— **mas·tit·ic** \-'sti-tik\ *adjective*
**mas·to·don** \'mas-tə-ˌdän, -dən\ *noun* [New Latin *mastodont-, mastodon*, from Greek *mastos* + *odont-, odōn, odous* tooth — more at TOOTH] (1813)
**1** : any of numerous extinct mammals (genus *Mastodon* synonym *Mammut*) that differ from the related mammoths and existing elephants chiefly in the form of the molar teeth
**2** : one that is unusually large
— **mas·to·don·ic** \ˌmas-tə-'dä-nik\ *adjective*
— **mas·to·dont** \'mas-tə-ˌdänt\ *adjective or noun*
¹**mas·toid** \'mas-ˌtȯid\ *adjective* [New Latin *mastoides* resembling a nipple, mastoid, from Greek *mastoeidēs*, from *mastos* breast] (1732)
**1** : being the process of the temporal bone behind the ear; *also* : being any of several bony elements that occupy a similar position in the skull of lower vertebrates
**2** : of, relating to, or occurring in the region of the mastoid process
²**mastoid** *noun* (1842)
: a mastoid bone or process
**mastoid cell** *noun* (1800)

: one of the small cavities in the mastoid process that develop after birth and are filled with air
**mas·toid·ec·to·my** \ˌmas-ˌtȯi-'dek-tə-mē\ *noun, plural* **-mies** [International Scientific Vocabulary] (1898)
: surgical removal of part of the mastoid process of the temporal bone
**mas·toid·itis** \ˌmas-ˌtȯi-'dī-təs\ *noun* [New Latin] (circa 1890)
: inflammation of the mastoid and especially of the mastoid cells
**mas·tur·bate** \'mas-tər-ˌbāt\ *verb* **-bat·ed; -bat·ing** [Latin *masturbatus*, past participle of *masturbari*] (1857)
*transitive verb*
: to practice masturbation on
*intransitive verb*
: to practice masturbation
— **mas·tur·ba·tor** \-ˌbā-tər\ *noun*
**mas·tur·ba·tion** \ˌmas-tər-'bā-shən\ *noun* (1766)
: erotic stimulation especially of one's own genital organs commonly resulting in orgasm and achieved by manual or other bodily contact exclusive of sexual intercourse, by instrumental manipulation, occasionally by sexual fantasies, or by various combinations of these agencies
**mas·tur·ba·to·ry** \'mas-tər-bə-ˌtōr-ē, -ˌtȯr-\ *adjective* (1864)
**1** : of, relating to, or involving masturbation ⟨*masturbatory* fantasies⟩
**2** : excessively self-absorbed or self-indulgent ⟨write tedious, *masturbatory* books . . . about themselves for people to read . . . with envy —D. R. Katz⟩
¹**mat** \'mat\ *noun* [Middle English, from Old English *meatte*, from Late Latin *matta*, of Semitic origin; akin to Hebrew *miṭṭāh* bed] (before 12th century)
**1 a** (1) : a piece of coarse, woven, plaited, or felted fabric used especially as a floor covering or a support (2) : a piece of material placed at a door for wiping soiled shoe soles **b** : a decorative piece of material used under a small item (as a dish) especially for support or protection **c** : a large thick pad or cushion used as a surface for wrestling, tumbling, and gymnastics
**2** : something made up of densely tangled or adhering strands especially of organic matter ⟨algal *mat*⟩ ⟨a *mat* of unkempt hair⟩
**3** : a large slab usually of reinforced concrete used as the supporting base of a building
²**mat** *verb* **mat·ted; mat·ting** (1549)
*transitive verb*
**1** : to provide with a mat or matting
**2 a** : to form into a tangled mass **b** : to pack down so as to form a dense mass
*intransitive verb*
: to become matted
³**mat** \'mat\ *transitive verb* **mat·ted; mat·ting** (1602)
**1** : to make (as a metal, glass, or color) matte
**2** : to provide (a picture) with a mat
⁴**mat** *variant of* ²MATTE
⁵**mat** *noun* [French *mat* dull color, unpolished surface, from *mat*, adjective — more at MATTE] (1845)
: a border going around a picture between picture and frame or serving as the frame
⁶**mat** *noun* (1904)
: MATRIX 2a
**mat·a·dor** \'ma-tə-ˌdȯr\ *noun* [Spanish, from *matar* to kill] (1681)
: a bullfighter who has the principal role and who kills the bull in a bullfight
¹**match** \'mach\ *noun* [Middle English *macche*, from Old English *gemæcca* mate,

\ə\ abut \ᵊ\ kitten \ər\ further \a\ ash \ā\ ace \ä\ mop, mar \au̇\ out \ch\ chin \e\ bet \ē\ easy \g\ go \i\ hit \ī\ ice \j\ job \ŋ\ sing \ō\ go \ȯ\ law \ȯi\ boy \th\ thin \t̲h̲\ the \ü\ loot \u̇\ foot \y\ yet \zh\ vision *see also* Guide to Pronunciation

equal; akin to Old English *macian* to make — more at MAKE] (before 12th century) **1 a :** a person or thing equal or similar to another **b :** one able to cope with another **c :** an exact counterpart **2 :** a pair suitably associated ⟨carpet and curtains are a *match*⟩ **3 a :** a contest between two or more parties ⟨a golf *match*⟩ ⟨a soccer *match*⟩ ⟨a shouting *match*⟩ **b :** a contest (as in tennis or volleyball) completed when one player or side wins a specified number of sets or games **4 a :** a marriage union **b :** a prospective partner in marriage

²**match** (14th century) *transitive verb* **1 a :** to encounter successfully as an antagonist **b** (1) **:** to set in competition or opposition (2) **:** to provide with a worthy competitor **c :** to set in comparison **2 :** to join or give in marriage **3 a** (1) **:** to put in a set possessing equal or harmonizing attributes (2) **:** to cause to correspond **:** SUIT **b** (1) **:** to be the counterpart of; *also* **:** to compare favorably with (2) **:** to harmonize with **c :** to provide with a counterpart **d :** to provide funds complementary to **4 :** to fit together or make suitable for fitting together **5 a :** to flip or toss (coins) and compare exposed faces **b :** to toss coins with *intransitive verb* **:** to be a counterpart
— **match·able** \'ma-chə-bəl\ *adjective*
— **match·er** *noun*

³**match** *noun* [Middle English *macche*, from Middle French *meiche*] (1549) **1 :** a chemically prepared wick or cord formerly used in firing firearms or powder **2 :** a short slender piece of flammable material (as wood) tipped with a combustible mixture that bursts into flame when slightly heated through friction (as by being scratched against a rough surface)

**match·board** \'mach-ˌbōrd, -ˌbȯrd\ *noun* (circa 1858) **:** a board with a groove cut along one edge and a tongue along the other so as to fit snugly with the edges of similarly cut boards

**match·book** \-ˌbu̇k\ *noun* (1944) **:** a small folder containing rows of paper matches

**match·box** \-ˌbäks\ *noun* (1786) **:** a box for matches

**match·less** \-ləs\ *adjective* (circa 1530) **:** having no equal **:** PEERLESS
— **match·less·ly** *adverb*

**match·lock** \-ˌläk\ *noun* (1637) **1 :** a slow-burning match lowered over a hole in the breech of a musket to ignite the charge **2 :** a musket equipped with a matchlock

**match·mak·er** \-ˌmā-kər\ *noun* (circa 1639) **:** one that arranges a match; *especially* **:** one who tries to bring two unmarried individuals together in an attempt to promote a marriage
— **match·mak·ing** \-kiŋ\ *noun*

**match play** *noun* (1893) **:** golf competition in which the winner is the person or team winning the greater number of holes — compare STROKE PLAY

**match point** *noun* (1921) **:** a situation (as in tennis) in which one player or side will win the match by winning the next point; *also* **:** the point itself

**match·stick** \'mach-ˌstik\ *noun* (1791) **1 :** a slender piece especially of wood from which a match is made **2 :** something resembling a matchstick especially in slenderness

**match·up** \-ˌəp\ *noun* (1964) **:** ¹MATCH

**match·wood** \-ˌwu̇d\ *noun* (1838) **:** small pieces of wood **:** SPLINTERS

¹**mate** \'māt\ *transitive verb* **mat·ed; mat·ing** [Middle English, from Middle French *mater*, from Old French *mat*, noun, checkmate, from Arabic *māt* (in *shāh māt*)] (14th century) **:** CHECKMATE 2

²**mate** *noun* (14th century) **:** CHECKMATE 1

³**mate** *noun* [Middle English, probably from Middle Low German *māt;* akin to Old English *gemetta* guest at one's table, *mete* food — more at MEAT] (14th century) **1 a** (1) **:** ASSOCIATE, COMPANION (2) *chiefly British* **:** an assistant to a more skilled worker **:** HELPER (3) *chiefly British* **:** FRIEND, BUDDY — often used as a familiar form of address **b** *archaic* **:** MATCH, PEER **2 :** a deck officer on a merchant ship ranking below the captain **3 :** one of a pair: as **a :** either member of a couple and especially a married couple **b :** either member of a breeding pair of animals **c :** either of two matched objects

⁴**mate** *verb* **mat·ed; mat·ing** (1509) *transitive verb* **1** *archaic* **:** EQUAL, MATCH **2 :** to join or fit together **:** COUPLE **3 a :** to join together as mates **b :** to provide a mate for *intransitive verb* **1 :** to become mated ⟨gears that *mate* well⟩ **2 :** COPULATE

**ma·té** *or* **ma·te** \'mä-ˌtā\ *noun* [French & American Spanish; French *maté*, from American Spanish *mate* maté, vessel for drinking it, from Quechua *mati* vessel] (1758) **1 :** a tealike beverage drunk especially in South America **2 :** a South American shrub or tree (*Ilex paraguariensis*) of the holly family whose leaves and shoots are used in making maté; *also* **:** these leaves and shoots

**mate·lot** \'mat-ˌlō, 'ma-tə-\ *noun* [French, from Middle French, from Middle Dutch *mattenoot*, literally, bedmate] (1911) *British* **:** SAILOR

**ma·te·lote** \ˌma-tᵊl-'ōt, mat-'lōt\ *noun* [French, literally, sailor's wife, from *matelot*] (circa 1736) **:** a stew made usually of fish in a seasoned wine sauce

**ma·ter** \'mā-tər\ *noun* [Latin — more at MOTHER] (circa 1859) *chiefly British* **:** MOTHER

**ma·ter·fa·mil·i·as** \ˌmä-tər-fə-'mi-lē-əs, ˌmä-\ *noun* [Latin, from *mater* + *familias*, archaic genitive of *familia* household — more at FAMILY] (1756) **:** a woman who is head of a household

¹**ma·te·ri·al** \mə-'tir-ē-əl\ *adjective* [Middle English *materiel*, from Middle French & Late Latin; Middle French, from Late Latin *materialis*, from Latin *materia* matter — more at MATTER] (14th century) **1 a** (1) **:** relating to, derived from, or consisting of matter; *especially* **:** PHYSICAL ⟨the *material* world⟩ (2) **:** BODILY ⟨*material* needs⟩ **b** (1) **:** of or relating to matter rather than form ⟨*material* cause⟩ (2) **:** of or relating to the subject matter of reasoning; *especially* **:** EMPIRICAL ⟨*material* knowledge⟩ **2 :** having real importance or great consequences ⟨facts *material* to the investigation⟩ **3 a :** being of a physical or worldly nature **b :** relating to or concerned with physical rather than spiritual or intellectual things ⟨*material* progress⟩ ☆
— **ma·te·ri·al·ly** \-ē-ə-lē\ *adverb*
— **ma·te·ri·al·ness** *noun*

²**material** *noun* (1556) **1 a** (1) **:** the elements, constituents, or substances of which something is composed or can be made (2) **:** matter that has qualities which give it individuality and by which it may be categorized ⟨sticky *material*⟩ ⟨explosive *materials*⟩ **b** (1) **:** something (as data) that may be worked into a more finished form ⟨*material* for a biography⟩ (2) **:** something used for or made the object of study ⟨*material* for the next semester⟩ (3) **:** a performer's repertoire ⟨a comedian's *material*⟩ **c :** MATTER 3b **d :** CLOTH **e :** a person potentially suited to some pursuit ⟨varsity *material*⟩ ⟨leadership *material*⟩ **2 a :** apparatus necessary for doing or making something ⟨writing *materials*⟩ **b :** MATÉRIEL

**ma·te·ri·al·ise** *British variant of* MATERIALIZE

**ma·te·ri·al·ism** \mə-'tir-ē-ə-ˌli-zəm\ *noun* (1748) **1 a :** a theory that physical matter is the only or fundamental reality and that all being and processes and phenomena can be explained as manifestations or results of matter **b :** a doctrine that the only or the highest values or objectives lie in material well-being and in the furtherance of material progress **c :** a doctrine that economic or social change is materially caused — compare HISTORICAL MATERIALISM **2 :** a preoccupation with or stress upon material rather than intellectual or spiritual things
— **ma·te·ri·al·ist** \-list\ *noun or adjective*
— **ma·te·ri·al·is·tic** \-ˌtir-ē-ə-'lis-tik\ *adjective*
— **ma·te·ri·al·is·ti·cal·ly** \-ti-k(ə-)lē\ *adverb*

**ma·te·ri·al·i·ty** \mə-ˌtir-ē-'a-lə-tē\ *noun, plural* **-ties** (1570) **1 :** the quality or state of being material **2 :** something that is material

**ma·te·ri·al·i·za·tion** \mə-ˌtir-ē-ə-lə-'zā-shən\ *noun* (1843) **1 :** the action of materializing or becoming materialized **2 :** something that has been materialized; *especially* **:** APPARITION

**ma·te·ri·al·ize** \mə-'tir-ē-ə-ˌlīz\ *verb* **-ized; -iz·ing** (1710) *transitive verb* **1 a :** to make material **:** OBJECTIFY **b :** to cause to appear in bodily form ⟨*materialize* the spirits of the dead⟩ **2 :** to cause to be materialistic *intransitive verb* **1 :** to assume bodily form **2 a :** to appear especially suddenly **b :** to come into existence
— **ma·te·ri·al·iz·er** *noun*

**materials science** *noun* (1961) **:** the scientific study of the properties and applications of materials of construction or manufacture (as ceramics, metals, polymers, and composites)
— **materials scientist** *noun*

---

☆ **SYNONYMS**
**Material, physical, corporeal, phenomenal, sensible, objective** mean of or belonging to actuality. MATERIAL implies formation out of tangible matter; used in contrast with *spiritual* or *ideal* it may connote the mundane, crass, or grasping ⟨*material* values⟩. PHYSICAL applies to what is perceived directly by the senses and may contrast with *mental, spiritual,* or *imaginary* ⟨the *physical* benefits of exercise⟩. CORPOREAL implies having the tangible qualities of a body such as shape, size, or resistance to force ⟨artists have portrayed angels as *corporeal* beings⟩. PHENOMENAL applies to what is known or perceived through the senses rather than by intuition or rational deduction ⟨scientists concerned with the *phenomenal* world⟩. SENSIBLE stresses the capability of readily or forcibly impressing the senses ⟨the earth's rotation is not *sensible* to us⟩. OBJECTIVE may stress material or independent existence apart from a subject perceiving it ⟨no *objective* evidence of damage⟩. See in addition RELEVANT.

**ma·te·ria med·i·ca** \mə-'tir-ē-ə-'me-di-kə\ *noun* [New Latin, literally, medical matter] (1699)
**1** : substances used in the composition of medical remedies : DRUGS, MEDICINE
**2 a** : a branch of medical science that deals with the sources, nature, properties, and preparation of drugs **b** : a treatise on materia medica
**ma·té·ri·el** *or* **ma·te·ri·el** \mə-,tir-ē-'el\ *noun* [French *matériel*, from *matériel*, adjective] (1814)
: equipment, apparatus, and supplies used by an organization or institution
**ma·ter·nal** \mə-'tər-n°l\ *adjective* [Middle English, from Middle French *maternel*, from Latin *maternus*, from *mater* mother — more at MOTHER] (15th century)
**1** : of, relating to, belonging to, or characteristic of a mother : MOTHERLY
**2 a** : related through a mother ⟨his *maternal* aunt⟩ **b** : inherited or derived from the female parent ⟨*maternal* genes⟩
— **ma·ter·nal·ly** \-n°l-ē\ *adverb*
¹**ma·ter·ni·ty** \mə-'tər-nə-tē\ *noun, plural* **-ties** (1611)
**1 a** : the quality or state of being a mother : MOTHERHOOD **b** : the qualities of a mother : MOTHERLINESS
**2** : a hospital facility designed for the care of women before and during childbirth and for the care of newborn babies
²**maternity** *adjective* (1893)
**1** : designed for wear during pregnancy ⟨a *maternity* dress⟩
**2** : effective for the period close to and including childbirth ⟨*maternity* leave⟩
**mat·ey** \'mā-tē\ *adjective* (1915)
*chiefly British* : COMPANIONABLE
— **mat·ey·ness** \-nəs\ *noun, chiefly British*
**math** \'math\ *noun* (circa 1878)
: MATHEMATICS
**math·e·mat·i·cal** \math-'ma-ti-kəl, ,ma-thə-\ *also* **math·e·mat·ic** \-tik\ *adjective* [Middle English *mathematicalle*, from Latin *mathematicus*, from Greek *mathēmatikos*, from *mathēmat-*, *mathēma* learning, mathematics, from *manthanein* to learn; probably akin to Gothic *mundon* to pay attention] (15th century)
**1** : of, relating to, or according with mathematics
**2 a** : rigorously exact : PRECISE **b** : CERTAIN
**3** : possible but highly improbable ⟨only a *mathematical* chance⟩
— **math·e·mat·i·cal·ly** \-ti-k(ə-)lē\ *adverb*
**mathematical expectation** *noun* (1838)
: EXPECTED VALUE
**mathematical induction** *noun* (1838)
: INDUCTION 2b
**mathematical logic** *noun* (1858)
: SYMBOLIC LOGIC
**math·e·ma·ti·cian** \math-mə-'ti-shən, ,ma-thə-\ *noun* (15th century)
: a specialist or expert in mathematics
**math·e·mat·ics** \math-'ma-tiks, ,ma-thə-\ *noun plural but usually singular in construction* (1581)
**1** : the science of numbers and their operations, interrelations, combinations, generalizations, and abstractions and of space configurations and their structure, measurement, transformations, and generalizations
**2** : a branch of, operation in, or use of mathematics ⟨the *mathematics* of physical chemistry⟩
**math·e·ma·ti·za·tion** \,math-mə-tə-'zā-shən, ,ma-thə-\ *noun* (1928)
: reduction to mathematical form
— **math·e·ma·tize** \'math-mə-,tiz, 'ma-thə-\ *verb*
**maths** \'maths\ *noun plural* (1911)
*chiefly British* : MATHEMATICS
**mat·in** \'ma-t°n\ *adjective* [Middle English, from Old French] (14th century)
: of or relating to matins or to early morning

**mat·in·al** \'ma-t°n-əl\ *adjective* (1803)
**1** : of or relating to matins
**2** : EARLY
**mat·i·nee** *or* **mat·i·née** \,ma-t°n-'ā\ *noun* [French *matinée*, literally, morning, from Old French, from *matin* morning, from Latin *matutinum*, from neuter of *matutinus* of the morning, from *Matuta*, goddess of morning; akin to Latin *maturus* ripe — more at MATURE] (1858)
: a musical or dramatic performance or social or public event held in the daytime and especially the afternoon
**matinee idol** *noun* (1902)
: a handsome male performer
**mat·ins** \'ma-t°nz\ *noun plural but singular or plural in construction, often capitalized* [Middle English *matines*, from Old French, from Late Latin *matutinae*, from Latin, feminine plural of *matutinus*] (14th century)
**1** : the night office forming with lauds the first of the canonical hours
**2** : MORNING PRAYER
**matr-** *or* **matri-** *or* **matro-** *combining form* [Latin *matr-*, *matri-*, from *matr-*, *mater*]
: mother ⟨*matriarch*⟩ ⟨*matronymic*⟩
**ma·tri·arch** \'mā-trē-,ärk\ *noun* (1606)
: a female who rules or dominates a family, group, or state; *specifically* : a mother who is head and ruler of her family and descendants
— **ma·tri·ar·chal** \,mā-trē-'är-kəl\ *adjective*
**ma·tri·ar·chate** \'mā-trē-,är-kət, -,kāt\ *noun* (1885)
: MATRIARCHY 1
**ma·tri·ar·chy** \'mā-trē-,är-kē\ *noun, plural* **-chies** (1885)
**1** : a family, group, or state governed by a matriarch
**2** : a system of social organization in which descent and inheritance are traced through the female line
**ma·tri·cide** \'ma-trə-,sīd, 'mā-\ *noun* (1594)
**1** [Latin *matricidium*, from *matr-* + *-cidium* -cide] : murder of a mother by her son or daughter
**2** [Latin *matricida*, from *matr-* + *-cida* -cide] : one that murders his or her mother
— **ma·tri·cid·al** \,ma-trə-'sī-d°l, ,mā-\ *adjective*
**ma·tric·u·late** \mə-'tri-kyə-,lāt\ *verb* **-lat·ed; -lat·ing** [Medieval Latin *matriculatus*, past participle of *matriculare*, from Late Latin *matricula* public roll, diminutive of *matric-*, *matrix* list, from Latin, breeding female] (1577)
*transitive verb*
: to enroll as a member of a body and especially of a college or university
*intransitive verb*
: to become matriculated
— **ma·tric·u·lant** \-lənt\ *noun*
— **ma·tric·u·la·tion** \-,tri-kyə-'lā-shən\ *noun*
**ma·tri·lin·eal** \,ma-trə-'li-nē-əl, ,mā-\ *adjective* (1904)
: relating to, based on, or tracing descent through the maternal line ⟨*matrilineal* society⟩
— **ma·tri·lin·eal·ly** \-nē-ə-lē\ *adverb*
**mat·ri·mo·nial** \,ma-trə-'mō-nē-əl, -nyəl\ *adjective* (15th century)
: of or relating to marriage, the married state, or married persons
— **mat·ri·mo·nial·ly** *adverb*
**mat·ri·mo·ny** \'ma-trə-,mō-nē\ *noun* [Middle English, from Middle French *matremoine*, from Latin *matrimonium*, from *matr-*, *mater* mother, matron — more at MOTHER] (14th century)
: the union of man and woman as husband and wife : MARRIAGE
**matrimony vine** *noun* (circa 1818)
: a shrub or vine (genus *Lycium*) of the nightshade family with often showy flowers and usually red berries

**ma·trix** \'mā-triks\ *noun, plural* **ma·tri·ces** \'mā-trə-,sēz, 'ma-\ *or* **ma·trix·es** \'mā-trik-səz\ [Latin, female animal used for breeding, parent plant, from *matr-*, *mater*] (1555)
**1** : something within or from which something else originates, develops, or takes form
**2 a** : a mold from which a relief surface (as a piece of type) is made **b** : DIE 3a(1) **c** : an engraved or inscribed die or stamp **d** : an electroformed impression of a phonograph record used for mass-producing duplicates of the original
**3 a** : the natural material (as soil or rock) in which something (as a fossil or crystal) is embedded **b** : material in which something is enclosed or embedded (as for protection or study)
**4 a** : the intercellular substance in which tissue cells (as of connective tissue) are embedded **b** : the thickened epithelium at the base of a fingernail or toenail from which new nail substance develops
**5 a** : a rectangular array of mathematical elements (as the coefficients of simultaneous linear equations) that can be combined to form sums and products with similar arrays having an appropriate number of rows and columns **b** : something resembling a mathematical matrix especially in rectangular arrangement of elements into rows and columns **c** : an array of circuit elements (as diodes and transistors) for performing a specific function
**6** : a main clause that contains a subordinate clause
**ma·tron** \'mā-trən\ *noun* [Middle English *matrone*, from Middle French, from Latin *matrona*, from *matr-*, *mater*] (14th century)
**1 a** : a married woman usually marked by dignified maturity or social distinction **b** : a woman who supervises women or children (as in a school or police station) **c** : the chief officer in a women's organization
**2** : a female animal kept for breeding
**ma·tron·ly** \'mā-trən-lē\ *adjective* (1656)
: having the character of or suitable to a matron
**matron of honor** (1903)
: a bride's principal married wedding attendant
**mat·ro·nym·ic** \,ma-trə-'ni-mik\ *noun* [*matr-* + *-onymic* (as in *patronymic*)] (1794)
: a name derived from that of the mother or a maternal ancestor
¹**matte** *or* **matt** \'mat\ *variant of* ³MAT
²**matte** *also* **matt** \'mat\ *adjective* [French *mat*, from Old French, faded, defeated] (circa 1648)
: lacking or deprived of luster or gloss: as **a** : having a usually smooth even surface free from shine or highlights ⟨*matte* metals⟩ ⟨*matte* finish⟩ **b** : having a rough or granular surface
³**matte** \'mat\ *noun* [French, from Middle French, crude metal, curdled milk, from feminine of *mat* thick, dull, matte] (1839)
**1** : a crude mixture of sulfides formed in smelting sulfide ores of metals (as copper, lead, or nickel)
**2** : a motion-picture effect in which part of a scene is blocked out and later replaced by footage containing other material (as a background painting)
¹**mat·ter** \'ma-tər\ *noun* [Middle English *matere*, from Old French, from Latin *materia* matter, physical substance, from *mater*] (13th century)

**1 a :** a subject under consideration **b :** a subject of disagreement or litigation **c** *plural* **:** the events or circumstances of a particular situation **d :** the subject or substance of a discourse or writing **e :** something of an indicated kind or having to do with an indicated field or situation ⟨this is a serious *matter*⟩ ⟨as a *matter* of policy⟩ ⟨*matters* of faith⟩ **f :** something to be proved in law **g** *obsolete* **:** sensible or serious material as distinguished from nonsense or drollery **h** (1) *obsolete* **:** REASON, CAUSE (2) **:** a source especially of feeling or emotion **i :** PROBLEM, DIFFICULTY
**2 a :** the substance of which a physical object is composed **b :** material substance that occupies space, has mass, and is composed predominantly of atoms consisting of protons, neutrons, and electrons, that constitutes the observable universe, and that is interconvertible with energy **c :** a material substance of a particular kind or for a particular purpose ⟨vegetable *matter*⟩ **d** (1) **:** material (as feces or urine) discharged from the living body (2) **:** material discharged by suppuration **:** PUS
**3 a :** the indeterminate subject of reality; *especially* **:** the element in the universe that undergoes formation and alteration **b :** the formless substratum of all things which exists only potentially and upon which form acts to produce realities
**4 :** a more or less definite amount or quantity ⟨cooks in a *matter* of minutes⟩
**5 :** something written or printed
**6 :** MAIL
**7** *Christian Science* **:** the illusion that the objects perceived by the physical senses have the reality of substance
**— for that matter :** so far as that is concerned
**— no matter :** without regard to **:** irrespective of ⟨points in the same direction *no matter* how it is tilted⟩
**— the matter :** WRONG ⟨nothing's *the matter* with me⟩
**²matter** *intransitive verb* (1530)
**1 :** to form or discharge pus **:** SUPPURATE ⟨*mattering* wound⟩
**2 :** to be of importance **:** SIGNIFY
**matter of course** (1739)
**:** something that is to be expected as a natural or logical consequence
**mat·ter–of–fact** \ˌma-tə-rə(v)-ˈfakt\ *adjective* (1712)
**:** adhering to the unembellished facts; *also* **:** being plain, straightforward, or unemotional
**— mat·ter–of–fact·ly** \-ˈfak(t)-lē\ *adverb*
**— mat·ter–of–fact·ness** \-ˈfak(t)-nəs\ *noun*
**mat·tery** \ˈma-tə-rē\ *adjective* (14th century)
**:** producing or containing pus or material resembling pus ⟨eyes all *mattery*⟩
**Mat·the·an** *or* **Mat·thae·an** \ma-ˈthē-ən, mə-\ *adjective* [Late Latin *Matthaeus*] (1897)
**:** of, relating to, or characteristic of the evangelist Matthew or the gospel ascribed to him
**Mat·thew** \ˈma-(ˌ)thyü *also* -(ˌ)thü\ *noun* [French *Mathieu*, from Late Latin *Matthaeus*, from Greek *Matthaios*, from Hebrew *Mattithyāh*]
**1 :** an apostle traditionally identified as the author of the first Gospel in the New Testament
**2 :** the first Gospel in the New Testament — see BIBLE table
**¹mat·ting** \ˈma-tiŋ\ *noun* (circa 1847)
**1 :** material for mats
**2 :** MATS
**²matting** *noun* [from gerund of ⁴*mat*] (1854)
**:** a dull lusterless surface (as on gilding, metalwork, or satin)
**mat·tins** *often capitalized, chiefly British variant of* MATINS
**mat·tock** \ˈma-tək\ *noun* [Middle English *mattok*, from Old English *mattuc*] (before 12th century)
**:** a digging and grubbing tool with features of an adze and an ax or pick

**mat·tress** \ˈma-trəs\ *noun* [Middle English *materas*, from Old French, from Arabic *maṭraḥ* place where something is thrown] (14th century)
**1 a :** a fabric case filled with resilient material (as cotton, hair, feathers, foam rubber, or an arrangement of coiled springs) used either alone as a bed or on a bedstead **b :** an inflatable airtight sack for use as a mattress
**2 :** a device (as of interwoven brush and poles) used to protect a shoreline, bank, or streambed from erosion
**mat·u·rate** \ˈma-chə-ˌrāt\ *verb* **-rat·ed; -rat·ing** (1622)
**:** MATURE
**mat·u·ra·tion** \ˌma-chə-ˈrā-shən\ *noun* (1541)
**1 a :** the process of becoming mature **b :** the emergence of personal and behavioral characteristics through growth processes **c :** the final stages of differentiation of cells, tissues, or organs
**2 a :** the entire process by which diploid gonocytes are transformed into haploid gametes that includes both meiosis and physiological and structural changes **b :** SPERMIOGENESIS
**— mat·u·ra·tion·al** \-shnəl, -shə-nᵊl\ *adjective*
**¹ma·ture** \mə-ˈtu̇r, -ˈtyu̇r *also* -ˈchu̇r\ *adjective* **ma·tur·er; -est** [Middle English, from Latin *maturus* ripe; akin to Latin *mane* in the morning, *manus* good] (15th century)
**1 :** based on slow careful consideration ⟨a *mature* judgment⟩
**2 a** (1) **:** having completed natural growth and development **:** RIPE (2) **:** having undergone maturation **b :** having attained a final or desired state ⟨*mature* wine⟩ **c :** having achieved a low but stable growth rate ⟨paper is a *mature* industry⟩
**3 a :** of or relating to a condition of full development **b :** characteristic of or suitable to a mature individual ⟨*mature* outlook⟩
**4 :** due for payment ⟨a *mature* loan⟩
**5 :** belonging to the middle portion of a cycle of erosion
**— ma·ture·ly** *adverb*
**²mature** *verb* **ma·tured; ma·tur·ing** (15th century)
*transitive verb*
**:** to bring to maturity or completion
*intransitive verb*
**1 :** to become fully developed or ripe
**2 :** to become due
**ma·tu·ri·ty** \mə-ˈtu̇r-ə-tē, -ˈtyu̇r- *also* -ˈchu̇r-\ *noun* (15th century)
**1 :** the quality or state of being mature; *especially* **:** full development
**2 :** termination of the period that an obligation has to run
**ma·tu·ti·nal** \ˌma-chu̇-ˈtī-nᵊl; mə-ˈtüt-nəl, -ˈtyüt-, -ˈtü-tᵊn-əl, -ˈtyü-\ *adjective* [Late Latin *matutinalis*, from Latin *matutinus* — more at MATINEE] (circa 1656)
**:** of, relating to, or occurring in the morning **:** EARLY
**— ma·tu·ti·nal·ly** *adverb*
**mat·zo** *or* **mat·zoh** \ˈmät-sə *also* -(ˌ)sō\ *noun, plural* **mat·zoth** \-ˌsōt, -ˌsōth, -sōs\ *or* **mat·zos** *or* **mat·zohs** \-səz, -səs *also* -ˌsōz\ [Yiddish *matse*, from Hebrew *maṣṣāh*] (circa 1846)
**1 :** unleavened bread eaten especially at the Passover
**2 :** a wafer of matzo
**matzo ball** *noun* (1952)
**:** a small ball-shaped dumpling made from matzo meal
**maud·lin** \ˈmȯd-lən\ *adjective* [alteration of Mary *Magdalene*; from her depiction as a weeping penitent] (1509)

mattock

**1 :** drunk enough to be emotionally silly
**2 :** weakly and effusively sentimental
**mau·gre** \ˈmȯ-gər\ *preposition* [Middle English, from Middle French *maugré*, from *maugré* displeasure, from *mau, mal* evil + *gré* pleasure] (13th century)
*archaic* **:** in spite of
**¹maul** \ˈmȯl\ *noun* [Middle English *malle* mace, maul, from Old French *mail*, from Latin *malleus;* akin to Old Church Slavonic *mlatŭ* hammer, Latin *molere* to grind — more at MEAL] (13th century)
**:** a heavy often wooden-headed hammer used especially for driving wedges; *also* **:** a tool like a sledgehammer with one wedge-shaped end that is used to split wood
**²maul** *transitive verb* (13th century)
**1 :** BEAT, BRUISE
**2 :** MANGLE 1
**3 :** to handle roughly
**— maul·er** *noun*
**maul·stick** \ˈmȯl-stik\ *noun* [part translation of Dutch *maalstok*, from obsolete Dutch *malen* to paint + Dutch *stok* stick, stock] (circa 1658)
**:** a stick used by painters as a rest for the hand while working
**mau-mau** \ˈmau̇-ˌmau̇\ *verb* **mau-maued; mau-mau·ing** *often both Ms capitalized* [*Mau Mau*, anti-European secret society in colonial Kenya] (1970)
*transitive verb*
**:** to intimidate (as an official) by hostile confrontation or threats
*intransitive verb*
**:** to engage in mau-mauing someone
**maun** \ˈmȯn, ˈmän, mən\ *verbal auxiliary* [Middle English *man,* from Old Norse, present of *munu* shall, will; akin to Old English *gemynd* mind — more at MIND] (13th century)
*chiefly Scottish* **:** MUST
**maun·der** \ˈmȯn-dər, ˈmän-\ *intransitive verb* **maun·dered; maun·der·ing** \-d(ə-)riŋ\ [probably imitative] (1621)
**1** *dialect British* **:** GRUMBLE
**2 :** to wander slowly and idly
**3 :** to speak indistinctly or disconnectedly
**— maun·der·er** \-dər-ər\ *noun*
**Maun·dy Thursday** \ˈmȯn-dē-, ˈmän-\ *noun* [Middle English *maunde* ceremony of washing the feet of the poor on Maundy Thursday, from Old French *mandé*, from Latin *mandatum* command; from Jesus' words in John 13:34 — more at MANDATE] (15th century)
**:** the Thursday before Easter observed in commemoration of the institution of the Eucharist
**mau·so·le·um** \ˌmȯ-sə-ˈlē-əm, ˌmȯ-zə-\ *noun, plural* **-leums** *or* **-lea** \-ˈlē-ə\ [Middle English, from Latin, from Greek *mausōleion*, from *Mausōlos* Mausolus (died about 353 B.C.) ruler of Caria] (15th century)

---

◇ WORD HISTORY

**maudlin** In the New Testament of the Bible one of the most devoted followers of Jesus is Mary Magdalene, who was so called because she was thought to have come from the Palestinian city of Magdala. The popular pronunciation of *Magdalene* in early Modern English is indicated by spellings such as *Maudlen* and *Mawdlin*, which represent borrowings from medieval French *Madelaine*, the French development of Late Latin *Magdalena*. By the 16th century it had become an artistic tradition in scenes of the crucifixion and burial of Jesus to portray Mary Magdalene as weeping. So identified with weeping did she become that by the 17th century *maudlin* had come to mean "tearful, lachrymose." Later the word was used to describe a tearful show of emotion and especially the overwrought display of emotion brought on by drunkenness.

**1 :** a large tomb; *especially* **:** a usually stone building with places for entombment of the dead above ground
**2 :** a large gloomy building or room ◆

**mauve** \'mōv, 'mōv\ *noun* [French, mallow, from Latin *malva*] (1859)
**1 a :** a moderate purple, violet, or lilac color **b :** a strong purple
**2 :** a dyestuff that produces a mauve color
— **mauve** *adjective*

**ma·ven** *or* **ma·vin** \'mā-vən\ *noun* [Yiddish *meyvn*, from Late Hebrew *mēbhīn*] (circa 1952)
**:** one who is experienced or knowledgeable **:** EXPERT; *also* **:** FREAK 4

**¹mav·er·ick** \'mav-rik, 'ma-və-\ *noun* [Samuel A. *Maverick* (died 1870) American pioneer who did not brand his calves] (1867)
**1 :** an unbranded range animal; *especially* **:** a motherless calf
**2 :** an independent individual who does not go along with a group or party ◆

**²maverick** *adjective* (1886)
**:** characteristic of, suggestive of, or inclined to be a maverick

**ma·vis** \'mā-vəs\ *noun* [Middle English, from Middle French *mauvis*] (14th century)
**:** SONG THRUSH

**ma·vour·neen** \mə-'vür-ˌnēn\ *noun* [Irish *mo mhuirnín*] (1800)
*Irish* **:** my darling

**maw** \'mȯ\ *noun* [Middle English, from Old English *maga;* akin to Old High German *mago* stomach, Lithuanian *makas* purse] (before 12th century)
**1 :** the receptacle into which food is taken by swallowing: **a :** STOMACH **b :** CROP
**2 a :** the throat, gullet, or jaws especially of a voracious animal **b :** something suggestive of a gaping maw

**mawk·ish** \'mȯ-kish\ *adjective* [Middle English *mawke* maggot, from Old Norse *mathkr* — more at MAGGOT] (circa 1697)
**1 :** having an insipid often unpleasant taste
**2 :** sickly or puerilely sentimental
— **mawk·ish·ly** *adverb*
— **mawk·ish·ness** *noun*

**max** \'maks\ *noun* (1968)
**:** MAXIMUM 1, 2
— **to the max :** to the greatest extent possible

**maxi** \'mak-sē\ *noun, plural* **max·is** [*maxi-*] (1967)
**:** a long skirt, dress, or coat

**maxi-** *combining form* [*maximum*]
**1 :** extra long ⟨*maxi*skirt⟩
**2 :** extra large ⟨*maxi*-problems⟩

**max·il·la** \mak-'si-lə\ *noun, plural* **max·il·lae** \-'si-(ˌ)lē, -ˌlī\ *or* **maxillas** [Latin, diminutive of *mala* jaw] (1676)
**1 a :** JAW 1a **b** (1) **:** an upper jaw especially of humans and other mammals in which the bony elements are closely fused (2) **:** either of the two bones that lie with one on each side of the upper jaw lateral to the premaxilla and that in higher vertebrates bear most of the teeth
**2 :** one of the first or second pair of mouthparts posterior to the mandibles in insects, myriapods, crustaceans, and closely related arthropods
— **max·il·lary** \'mak-sə-ˌler-ē, *chiefly Brit*ish mak-'si-lə-rē\ *adjective or noun*

**max·il·li·ped** \mak-'si-lə-ˌped\ *noun* [International Scientific Vocabulary *maxilli-* (from Latin *maxilla*) + *-ped*] (1846)
**:** any of the crustacean appendages that comprise the first pair or first three pairs situated next behind the maxillae

**max·il·lo·fa·cial** \mak-ˌsi-(ˌ)lō-'fā-shəl, ˌmak-sə-(ˌ)lō-\ *adjective* (circa 1923)
**:** of, relating to, or treating the maxilla and the face ⟨*maxillofacial* surgeons⟩

**max·im** \'mak-səm\ *noun* [Middle English *maxime*, from Middle French, from Medieval Latin *maxima*, from Latin, feminine of *maximus*, superlative of *magnus* large — more at MUCH] (1567)
**1 :** a general truth, fundamental principle, or rule of conduct
**2 :** a saying of proverbial nature

**max·i·mal** \'mak-s(ə-)məl\ *adjective* (1882)
**1 :** being an upper limit **:** HIGHEST
**2 :** most comprehensive **:** COMPLETE
— **max·i·mal·ly** *adverb*

**max·i·mal·ist** \-s(ə-)mə-list\ *noun* (1907)
**:** one who advocates immediate and direct action to secure the whole of a program or set of goals

**maxi·min** \'mak-sə-ˌmin\ *noun* [*maximum* + *minimum*] (1951)
**:** the maximum of a set of minima; *especially* **:** the largest of a set of minimum possible gains each of which occurs in the least advantageous outcome of a strategy followed by a participant in a situation governed by the theory of games — compare MINIMAX

**max·i·mise** *British variant of* MAXIMIZE

**max·i·mize** \'mak-sə-ˌmīz\ *transitive verb* **-mized; -miz·ing** (1802)
**1 :** to increase to a maximum
**2 :** to make the most of
**3 :** to find a maximum value of
— **max·i·mi·za·tion** \ˌmak-sə-mə-'zā-shən\ *noun*
— **max·i·miz·er** \'mak-sə-ˌmī-zər\ *noun*

**max·i·mum** \'mak-s(ə-)məm\ *noun, plural* **max·i·ma** \-sə-mə\ *or* **maximums** \-s(ə-)məmz\ [Latin, neuter of *maximus*] (1740)
**1 a :** the greatest quantity or value attainable or attained **b :** the period of highest, greatest, or utmost development
**2 :** an upper limit allowed (as by a legal authority) or allowable (as by the circumstances of a particular case)
**3 :** the largest of a set of numbers; *specifically* **:** the largest value assumed by a real-valued continuous function defined on a closed interval
— **maximum** *adjective*

**maximum likelihood** *noun* (1959)
**:** a statistical method for estimating population parameters (as the mean and variance) from sample data that selects as estimates those parameter values maximizing the probability of obtaining the observed data

**ma·xixe** \mə-'shēsh, -'shē-shə\ *noun, plural* **ma·xi·xes** \-'shē-shəz\ [Brazilian Portuguese] (1914)
**:** a ballroom dance of Brazilian origin that resembles the two-step

**max·well** \'maks-ˌwel, -wəl\ *noun* [James Clerk *Maxwell*] (1900)
**:** the centimeter-gram-second electromagnetic unit of magnetic flux equal to the flux per square centimeter of normal cross section in a region where the magnetic induction is one gauss **:** $10^{-8}$ weber

**¹may** \'mā\ *verbal auxiliary, past* **might** \'mīt\; *present singular & plural* **may** [Middle English (1st & 3d singular present indicative), from Old English *mæg;* akin to Old High German *mag* (1st & 3d singular present indicative) have power, am able (infinitive *magan*), and perhaps to Greek *mēchos* means, expedient] (before 12th century)
**1 a** *archaic* **:** have the ability to **b :** have permission to ⟨you *may* go now⟩ **:** be free to ⟨a rug on which children *may* sprawl —C. E. Silberman⟩ — used nearly interchangeably with *can* **c** — used to indicate possibility or probability ⟨you *may* be right⟩ ⟨things you *may* need⟩; sometimes used interchangeably with *can* ⟨one of those slipups that *may* happen from time to time —Jessica Mitford⟩ ⟨copula *may* optionally be deleted —J. D. McCawley⟩; sometimes used where *might* would be expected ⟨you *may* think from a little distance that the country was solid woods —Robert Frost⟩
**2** — used in auxiliary function to express a wish or desire especially in prayer, imprecation, or benediction ⟨long *may* he reign⟩
**3** — used in auxiliary function expressing purpose or expectation ⟨I laugh that I *may* not weep⟩ or contingency ⟨she'll do her duty come what *may*⟩ or concession ⟨he *may* be slow but he is thorough⟩ or choice ⟨the angler *may* catch them with a dip net, or he *may* cast a large, bare treble hook —Nelson Bryant⟩
**4 :** SHALL, MUST — used in law where the sense, purpose, or policy requires this interpretation
**usage** *see* CAN

**²may** \'mā\ *noun* [Middle English, from Old English *mæg* kinsman, kinswoman, maiden] (before 12th century)
*archaic* **:** MAIDEN

**May** \'mā\ *noun* [Middle English, from Old French & Latin; Old French *mai*, from Latin *Maius*, from *Maia*, Roman goddess] (12th century)
**1 :** the 5th month of the Gregorian calendar
**2** *often not capitalized* **:** the early vigorous blooming part of human life **:** PRIME
**3 :** the festivities of May Day

---

◇ WORD HISTORY

**mausoleum**   In the 4th century B.C. Mausolus was a satrap (governor) of the Persian empire who ruled over Caria, a region in what is now southwestern Turkey. Probably his most significant decision was moving his capital to Halicarnassus, where he conceived a building project that would assure the immortality of his name. This edifice, which he planned and his wife Artemisia completed, was his own tomb. It towered about 135 feet, had a rectangular base of white marble with a periphery of 411 feet, and was topped by an array of colossal statues, two of which portrayed Mausolus and Artemisia. Named the *Mausōleion* by the Greeks for its creator and occupant, this exercise in self-glorification was acclaimed as one of the Seven Wonders of the Ancient World. The Greek word later came to be used generically for any large and imposing burial structure.

**maverick**   Samuel Augustus Maverick (1803–70) was a South Carolina-born lawyer who emigrated to Texas in 1835 and was a prominent figure in the early years of the state's history. Maverick's consuming passion was not law or politics, however, but the acquisition of land; at his death he owned over 300,000 acres spread over 32 Texas counties. He was not a rancher and resided much of his life in San Antonio, but a minor episode in his career made his name part of every cowboy's vocabulary and a fixture of American English. In 1847 he bought a farm near Matagorda Bay with about 450 cattle that were left in charge of a single slave with no experience as a cowboy. Most of the calves were never penned and branded, and loss of animals led Maverick to move the herd to a ranch southeast of San Antonio in 1853 and finally to sell them in 1856. Presumably in the 1850s cowboys finding unbranded yearlings on land adjoining Maverick's began to call the animals *mavericks*. The vast extent of his land holdings and later legends about Maverick as a great cattle baron fostered the spread of the word throughout Texas and the West.

---

\ə\ abut   \ᵊ\ kitten   \ər\ further   \a\ ash   \ā\ ace
\ä\ mop, mar   \au̇\ out   \ch\ chin   \e\ bet   \ē\ easy
\g\ go   \i\ hit   \ī\ ice   \j\ job   \ŋ\ sing   \ō\ go
\ȯ\ law   \ȯi\ boy   \th\ thin   \t͟h\ the   \ü\ loot   \u̇\ foot
\y\ yet   \zh\ vision     *see also* Guide to Pronunciation

**4** *not capitalized* **a :** green or flowering branches used for May Day decorations **b :** a plant that yields may: as (1) **:** HAWTHORN (2) **:** a spring-flowering spirea

**ma·ya** \'mä-yə, 'mī-ə\ *noun* [Sanskrit *māyā*] (1788)
**:** the sense-world of manifold phenomena held in Vedanta to conceal the unity of absolute being; *broadly* **:** ILLUSION

**Ma·ya** \'mī-ə\ *noun, plural* **Maya** *or* **Mayas** [Spanish] (1825)
**1 a :** a Mayan language of the ancient Maya peoples recorded in inscriptions **b :** YUCATEC; *especially* **:** the older form of that language known from documents of the Spanish period **2 :** a member of a group of Indian peoples chiefly of Yucatán, Belize, and Guatemala whose languages are Mayan

**Ma·yan** \'mī-ən\ *noun* (1900)
**1 :** a member of the peoples speaking Mayan languages **2 :** an extensive language family of Central America and Mexico
— **Mayan** *adjective*

**Mayanist** \'mī-ə-nist\ *noun* (1950)
**:** a specialist in Mayan culture and history

**may·ap·ple** \'mā-ˌa-pəl\ *noun* [*May*] (circa 1733)
**:** a North American herb (*Podophyllum peltatum*) of the barberry family with a poisonous rootstock, one or two large-lobed peltate leaves, and a single large white flower followed by a yellow egg-shaped edible fruit; *also* **:** its fruit

**¹may·be** \'mā-bē *also* 'me-\ *adverb* (15th century)
**:** PERHAPS

**²maybe** *noun* (circa 1586)
**:** UNCERTAINTY

**May·day** \'mā-ˌdā\ [French *m'aider* help me] (1927)
— an international radio-telephone signal word used as a distress call

**May Day** \'mā-ˌdā\ *noun* (13th century)
**:** May 1 celebrated as a springtime festival and in some countries as Labor Day

**may·est** *or* **mayst** \'mā-əst, 'māst\ *archaic present 2d singular of* MAY

**may·flow·er** \'mā-ˌflaù(-ə)r\ *noun* (1594)
**:** any of various spring-blooming plants; *especially* **:** ARBUTUS 2

**may·fly** \'mā-flī\ *noun* (circa 1653)
**:** any of an order (Ephemeroptera) of insects with an aquatic nymph and a short-lived fragile adult having membranous wings and two or three long caudal styles — called also *ephemerid*

**mayfly**

**may·hap** \'mā-ˌhap, mā-'\ *adverb* [from the phrase *may hap*] (circa 1531)
**:** PERHAPS

**may·hem** \'mā-ˌhem, 'mā-əm\ *noun* [Middle English *mayme*, from Anglo-French *mahaim*, from Old French, loss of a limb, from *maynier* to maim, probably of Germanic origin; akin to Middle High German *meiden* gelding, Old Norse *meitha* to injure] (15th century)
**1 a :** willful and permanent deprivation of a bodily member resulting in the impairment of a person's fighting ability **b :** willful and permanent crippling, mutilation, or disfigurement of any part of the body **2 :** needless or willful damage or violence

**may·ing** \'mā-iŋ\ *noun, often capitalized* (14th century)
**:** the celebrating of May Day

**mayn't** \'mā-ənt, 'mānt\ (circa 1631)
**:** may not

**mayo** \'mā-(ˌ)ō\ *noun* (circa 1960)
**:** MAYONNAISE

**may·on·naise** \'mā-ə-ˌnāz, ˌmā-ə-'\ *noun* [French] (1841)
**:** a dressing made of egg yolks, vegetable oils, and vinegar or lemon juice

**may·or** \'mā-ər, 'me(-ə)r, *especially before names* (ˌ)mer\ *noun* [Middle English *maire*, from Old French, from Latin *major* greater — more at MAJOR] (14th century)
**:** an official elected or appointed to act as chief executive or nominal head of a city, town, or borough
— **may·or·al** \'mā-ə-rəl, 'me-ə-; ˌmā-'òr-əl\ *adjective*

**may·or·al·ty** \'mā-ə-rəl-tē, 'me-; 'mer-əl-\ *noun* [Middle English *mairaltee*, from Middle French *mairalté*, from Old French, from *maire*] (14th century)
**:** the office or term of office of a mayor

**may·or·ess** \'mā-ə-rəs, 'me-\ *noun* (15th century) *chiefly British*
**1 :** the wife or official hostess of a mayor **2 :** a woman holding the office of mayor
*usage* see -ESS

**may·pole** \'mā-ˌpōl\ *noun, often capitalized* (1554)
**:** a tall flower-wreathed pole forming a center for May Day sports and dances

**may·pop** \'mā-ˌpäp\ *noun* [alteration of *maracock*, perhaps from Virginia Algonquian] (1851)
**:** a climbing perennial passionflower (*Passiflora incarnata*) of the southern U.S. with a large ovoid yellow edible but insipid berry; *also* **:** its fruit

**May·time** \'mā-ˌtīm\ *noun* (14th century)
**:** the month of May

**maz·ard** \'ma-zərd\ *noun* [obsolete English *mazard* mazer, alteration of English *mazer*] (1602) *chiefly dialect* **:** HEAD, FACE

**¹maze** \'māz\ *transitive verb* **mazed; maz·ing** [Middle English] (13th century)
**1** *chiefly dialect* **:** STUPEFY, DAZE
**2 :** BEWILDER, PERPLEX

**²maze** *noun* (14th century)
**1 a :** a confusing intricate network of passages **b :** something intricately or confusingly elaborate or complicated (a *maze* of regulations)
**2** *chiefly dialect* **:** a state of bewilderment
— **maze·like** \-ˌlīk\ *adjective*

**ma·zer** \'mā-zər\ *noun* [Middle English, from Middle French *mazere*, of Germanic origin; akin to Old High German *masar* gnarled excrescence on a tree] (14th century)
**:** a large drinking bowl originally of a hard wood

**ma·zur·ka** \mə-'zər-kə, -'zùr-\ *also* **ma·zour·ka** \-'zùr-\ *noun* [Russian, from Polish *mazurek*, from *Mazury* Masuria, region of northeast Poland] (1818)
**1 :** a Polish folk dance in moderate triple measure **2 :** music for the mazurka or in its rhythm usually in moderate ¾ or ³⁄₈ time

**mazy** \'mā-zē\ *adjective* (1579)
**:** resembling a maze

**¹maz·zard** \'ma-zərd\ *noun* [origin unknown] (1578)
**:** SWEET CHERRY; *especially* **:** wild or seedling sweet cherry used as a rootstock for grafting

**²mazzard** *variant of* MAZARD

**mbi·ra** \em-'bir-ə\ *noun* [Shona] (circa 1911)
**:** an African musical instrument that consists of a wooden or gourd resonator and a varying number of tuned metal or wooden strips that vibrate when plucked

**MC** \ˌem-'sē\ *noun* (1790)
**:** MASTER OF CEREMONIES

**Mc·Car·thy·ism** \mə-'kär-thē-ˌi-zəm *also* -'kär-tē-\ *noun* [Joseph R. *McCarthy*] (1950)
**:** a mid-20th century political attitude characterized chiefly by opposition to elements held to be subversive and by the use of tactics involving personal attacks on individuals by means of widely publicized indiscriminate allegations especially on the basis of unsubstantiated charges
— **Mc·Car·thy·ite** \-ˌīt\ *noun or adjective*

**Mc·Coy** \mə-'kòi\ *noun* [alteration of *Mackay* (in the phrase *the real Mackay*), of unknown origin] (1922)
**:** something that is neither imitation nor substitute — often used in the phrase *the real McCoy*

**Mc·In·tosh** \'ma-kən-ˌtäsh\ *noun* [John *McIntosh* (flourished 1796) Canadian settler] (1878)
**:** a juicy bright red eating apple with a thin skin, white flesh, and aromatic slightly tart flavor

**M–day** \'em-ˌdā\ *noun* [*mobilization day*] (1924)
**:** a day on which a military mobilization is to begin

**me** \'mē\ *pronoun, objective case of* I [Middle English, from Old English *mē*; akin to Old High German *mīh* me, Latin *me*, Greek *me*, Sanskrit *mā*] □

**mea cul·pa** \ˌmā-ə-'kùl-pə, ˌmā-ä-, -'kùl-(ˌ)pä\ *noun* [Latin, through my fault] (1602)
**:** a formal acknowledgment of personal fault or error

**¹mead** \'mēd\ *noun* [Middle English *mede*, from Old English *medu*; akin to Old High German *metu* mead, Greek *methy* wine] (before 12th century)
**:** a fermented beverage made of water and honey, malt, and yeast

**²mead** *noun* [Middle English *mede*, from Old English *mǣd*] (before 12th century) *archaic* **:** MEADOW

**mead·ow** \'me-(ˌ)dō\ *noun, often attributive* [Middle English *medwe*, from Old English *mǣdwe*, oblique case form of *mǣd*; akin to Old English *māwan* to mow — more at MOW] (before 12th century)
**:** land in or predominantly in grass; *especially* **:** a tract of moist low-lying usually level grassland
— **mead·owy** \'me-də-wē\ *adjective*

**meadow beauty** *noun* (1840)
**:** any of a genus (*Rhexia* of the family Melastomaceae, the meadow-beauty family) of low perennial American herbs with showy solitary or cymose flowers

**meadow fescue** *noun* (1794)
**:** a tall vigorous perennial European fescue grass (*Festuca pratensis*) with broad flat leaves widely cultivated for permanent pasture and hay

**meadow grass** *noun* (13th century)
**:** any of various grasses (as of the genus *Poa*) that thrive in the presence of abundant moisture; *especially* **:** KENTUCKY BLUEGRASS

**mead·ow·land** \'me-dō-ˌland, -də-\ *noun* (1530)
**:** land that is or is used for meadow

□ USAGE
**me** *Me* is used in many constructions where strict grammarians prescribe *I*. This usage is not so much ungrammatical as indicative of the shrinking range of the nominative form: *me* began to replace *I* sometime around the 16th century largely because of the pressure of word order. *I* is now chiefly used as the subject of an immediately following verb. *Me* occurs in every other position: absolutely (who, *me*?), emphatically (*me* too), and after prepositions, conjunctions, and verbs, including *be* (come with *me*) (you're as big as *me*) (it's *me*). Almost all usage books recognize the legitimacy of *me* in these positions, especially in speech; some recommend *I* in formal and especially written contexts after *be* and after *as* and *than* when the first term of the comparison is the subject of a verb.

**mead·ow·lark** \'me-dō-,lärk, -də-\ *noun* (1611)
: any of several American songbirds (genus *Sturnella*) that are streaked brown above and in northernmost forms have a yellow breast marked with a black crescent

meadowlark

**meadow mouse** *noun* (1801)
: any of various voles (especially genus *Microtus*) that frequent open fields — called also *meadow vole*

**meadow mushroom** *noun* (1884)
: a common edible brown-spored agaric (*Agaricus campestris*) that occurs in moist open organically rich soil and is often cultivated

**meadow nematode** *noun* (1946)
: any of numerous plant-parasitic nematode worms (especially genus *Pratylenchus*) that destructively invade the roots of plants

**meadow rue** *noun* (1668)
: any of a genus (*Thalictrum*) of widely distributed plants of the buttercup family with decompound or compound leaves

**meadow saffron** *noun* (1578)
: AUTUMN CROCUS

**meadow spittlebug** *noun* (1942)
: a North American spittlebug (*Philaenus spumarius*) that does severe damage especially to grasses

**mead·ow·sweet** \'me-dō-,swēt, -də-\ *noun* (1530)
**1** : SPIREA 1; *especially* : a North American native or naturalized spirea (as *Spiraea alba* and *S. latifolia*)
**2** : any of a genus (*Filipendula*) of herbs closely related to the spireas

**mea·ger** *or* **mea·gre** \'mē-gər\ *adjective* [Middle English *megre*, from Middle French *maigre*, from Latin *macr-, macer* lean; akin to Old English *mæger* lean, Greek *makros* long] (14th century)
**1** : having little flesh : THIN
**2 a** : lacking desirable qualities (as richness or strength) ⟨leading a *meager* life⟩ **b** : deficient in quality or quantity ⟨a *meager* diet⟩ ☆
— **mea·ger·ly** *adverb*
— **mea·ger·ness** *noun*

**¹meal** \'mē(ə)l\ *noun* [Middle English *meel* appointed time, meal, from Old English *mæl*; akin to Old High German *māl* time, Latin *metiri* to measure — more at MEASURE] (before 12th century)
**1** : an act or the time of eating a portion of food to satisfy appetite
**2** : the portion of food eaten at a meal ◆

**²meal** *noun* [Middle English *mele,* from Old English *melu;* akin to Old High German *melo* meal, Latin *molere* to grind, Greek *mylē* mill] (before 12th century)
**1** : the usually coarsely ground and unbolted seeds of a cereal grass or pulse; *especially* : CORNMEAL
**2** : a product resembling seed meal especially in particle size or texture

**-meal** *adverb combining form* [Middle English *-mele,* from Old English *-mālum,* from *mālum,* dative plural of *māl*]
: by a (specified) portion or measure at a time ⟨piece*meal*⟩

**mea·lie** \'mē-lē\ *noun* [Afrikaans *mielie*] (1855)
*South African* : INDIAN CORN; *also* : an ear of Indian corn

**meals–on–wheels** *noun plural but singular in construction* (1961)
: a service that delivers daily hot meals to the homes of elderly or disabled people

**meal ticket** *noun* (circa 1899)
: one that serves as the ultimate source of one's income ⟨an advanced degree was his *meal ticket*⟩

**meal·time** \'mē(ə)l-,tīm\ *noun* (12th century)
: the usual time for serving a meal

**meal·worm** \-,wərm\ *noun* (1658)
: the larva of various beetles (genus *Tenebrio*) that infests and pollutes grain products but is often raised as food for insectivorous animals, for laboratory use, or as fishing bait

**mealy** \'mē-lē\ *adjective* **meal·i·er; -est** (1533)
**1** : soft, dry, and friable
**2** : containing meal : FARINACEOUS
**3 a** : covered with meal or with fine granules **b** : flecked with another color **c** : SPOTTY, UNEVEN **d** : PALLID, BLANCHED ⟨a *mealy* complexion⟩
**4** : MEALYMOUTHED

**mealy·bug** \'mē-lē-,bəg\ *noun* (1824)
: any of a family (Pseudococcidae) of scale insects that have a white powdery covering and are destructive pests especially of fruit trees

**mealy·mouthed** \'mē-lē-,maùthd, -,maùtht\ *adjective* (circa 1572)
: not plain and straightforward : DEVIOUS ⟨a *mealymouthed* politician⟩

**¹mean** \'mēn\ *verb* **meant** \'ment\; **mean·ing** \'mē-niŋ\ [Middle English *menen,* from Old English *mænan;* akin to Old High German *meinen* to have in mind, Old Church Slavonic *měniti* to mention] (before 12th century)
*transitive verb*
**1 a** : to have in the mind as a purpose : INTEND ⟨she *means* to win⟩ — sometimes used interjectionally with *I,* chiefly in informal speech for emphasis ⟨he throws, I *mean,* hard⟩ or to introduce a phrase restating the point of a preceding phrase ⟨we try to answer what we can, but I *mean* we're not God —Bobbie Ann Mason⟩ **b** : to design for or destine to a specified purpose or future ⟨I was *meant* to teach⟩
**2** : to serve or intend to convey, show, or indicate : SIGNIFY ⟨a red sky *means* rain⟩
**3** : to have importance to the degree of ⟨health *means* everything⟩
**4** : to direct to a particular individual
*intransitive verb*
: to have an intended purpose ⟨he *means* well⟩
— **mean·er** \'mē-nər\ *noun*
— **mean business** : to be in earnest

**²mean** *adjective* [Middle English *mene,* from *imene* common, shared, from Old English *gemǣne;* akin to Old High German *gimeini* common, Latin *communis* common, *munus* service, gift, Sanskrit *mayate* he exchanges] (14th century)
**1** : lacking distinction or eminence : HUMBLE
**2** : lacking in mental discrimination : DULL
**3 a** : of poor shabby inferior quality or status ⟨*mean* city streets⟩ **b** : worthy of little regard : CONTEMPTIBLE — often used in negative constructions as a term of praise ⟨no *mean* feat⟩
**4** : lacking dignity or honor : BASE
**5 a** : PENURIOUS, STINGY **b** : characterized by petty selfishness or malice **c** : causing trouble or bother : VEXATIOUS **d** : EXCELLENT, EFFECTIVE ⟨plays a *mean* trumpet⟩ ⟨a lean, *mean* athlete⟩
**6** : ASHAMED 1b ☆
— **mean·ness** \'mēn-nəs\ *noun*

**³mean** *adjective* [Middle English *mene,* from Middle French *meien,* from Latin *medianus* — more at MEDIAN] (14th century)
**1** : occupying a middle position : intermediate in space, order, time, kind, or degree
**2** : occupying a position about midway between extremes; *especially* : being the mean of a set of values : AVERAGE ⟨the *mean* temperature⟩
**3** : serving as a means : INTERMEDIARY
**synonym** see AVERAGE

**⁴mean** *noun* (14th century)
**1 a** (1) : something intervening or intermediate (2) : a middle point between extremes **b** : a value that lies within a range of values and is computed according to a prescribed law: as (1) : ARITHMETIC MEAN (2) : EXPECTED VALUE **c** (1) : either of the middle two terms of a proportion
**2** *plural but singular or plural in construction* : something useful or helpful to a desired end
**3** *plural* : resources available for disposal; *especially* : material resources affording a secure life
— **by all means** : most assuredly : CERTAINLY

---

☆ **SYNONYMS**
**Meager, scanty, scant, skimpy, spare, sparse** mean falling short of what is normal, necessary, or desirable. MEAGER implies the absence of elements, qualities, or numbers necessary to a thing's richness, substance, or potency ⟨a *meager* portion of meat⟩. SCANTY stresses insufficiency in amount, quantity, or extent ⟨supplies too *scanty* to last the winter⟩. SCANT suggests a falling short of what is desired or desirable rather than of what is essential ⟨in January the daylight hours are *scant*⟩. SKIMPY usually suggests niggardliness or penury as the cause of the deficiency ⟨tacky housing developments on *skimpy* lots⟩. SPARE may suggest a slight falling short of adequacy or merely an absence of superfluity ⟨a *spare,* concise style of writing⟩. SPARSE implies a thin scattering of units ⟨a *sparse* population⟩.

**Mean, ignoble, abject, sordid** mean being below the normal standards of human decency and dignity. MEAN suggests having such repellent characteristics as smallmindedness, ill temper, or cupidity ⟨*mean* and petty satire⟩. IGNOBLE suggests a loss or lack of some essential high quality of mind or spirit ⟨an *ignoble* scramble after material possessions⟩. ABJECT may imply degradation, debasement, or servility ⟨*abject* poverty⟩. SORDID is stronger than all of these in stressing physical or spiritual degradation and abjectness ⟨a *sordid* story of murder and revenge⟩.

---

◇ **WORD HISTORY**
**meal** It may be natural to suppose that the *meal* of "three meals a day" has some relation to the *meal* of "ground meal," since both words pertain to food, but in fact they are unrelated. The *meal* of "ground meal" is descended from Old English *melu,* a word akin to Old High German *malan* "to grind," as well as to Latin *molere* "to grind." Derived from *molere* is Latin *molina* "mill," the ultimate source of the English noun and verb *mill.* The *meal* of "three meals a day," on the other hand, is from Old English *mæl* or *mēl* "measure, appointed time, mealtime." It is akin to Old High German *mal* "time," and much more distantly to Latin *metiri* "to measure." As *mēl* became *meel* in Middle English, the word became more closely associated with food than with time or measurement. The modern senses and spelling were established by the end of the 17th century. A relative of this *meal* can be seen in *piecemeal,* where *-meal* is a suffix having the sense "by a specified portion or measure at a time."

---

\ə\ abut \ᵊ\ kitten \ər\ further \a\ ash \ā\ ace
\ä\ mop, mar \aù\ out \ch\ chin \e\ bet \ē\ easy
\g\ go \i\ hit \ī\ ice \j\ job \ŋ\ sing \ō\ go
\ò\ law \òi\ boy \th\ thin \th\ the \ü\ loot \ù\ foot
\y\ yet \zh\ vision    *see also* Guide to Pronunciation

**— by means of :** through the use of
**— by no means :** in no way : not at all
¹**me·an·der** \mē-'an-dər\ *noun* [Latin *maeander*, from Greek *maiandros*, from *Maiandros* (now *Menderes*), river in Asia Minor] (1576)
**1 :** a winding path or course; *especially* : LABYRINTH
**2 :** a turn or winding of a stream
**— me·an·drous** \-drəs\ *adjective*
²**meander** *intransitive verb* **-dered; -dering** \-d(ə-)riŋ\ (circa 1612)
**1 :** to follow a winding or intricate course
**2 :** to wander aimlessly or casually without urgent destination : RAMBLE
*synonym* see WANDER
**mean deviation** *noun* (1858)
**:** the mean of the absolute values of the numerical differences between the numbers of a set (as statistical data) and their mean or median
**mean distance** *noun* (circa 1889)
**:** the arithmetical mean of the maximum and minimum distances of an orbiting celestial object from its primary
**mean free path** *noun* (1879)
**:** the average distance traversed between collisions by particles (as molecules of a gas or free electrons in metal) in a system of agitated particles
**mean·ie** *also* **meany** \'mē-nē\ *noun, plural* **meanies** (1910)
**:** a mean or spiteful person
**mean·ing** \'mē-niŋ\ *noun* (14th century)
**1 a :** the thing one intends to convey especially by language : PURPORT **b :** the thing that is conveyed especially by language : IMPORT
**2 :** something meant or intended : AIM ⟨a mischievous *meaning* was apparent⟩
**3 :** significant quality; *especially* : implication of a hidden or special significance ⟨a glance full of *meaning*⟩
**4 a :** the logical connotation of a word or phrase **b :** the logical denotation or extension of a word or phrase
**— meaning** *adjective*
**— mean·ing·ly** \-niŋ-lē\ *adverb*
**mean·ing·ful** \-fəl\ *adjective* (1852)
**1 a :** having a meaning or purpose **b :** full of meaning : SIGNIFICANT ⟨a *meaningful* life⟩
**2 :** having an assigned function in a language system ⟨*meaningful* propositions⟩
**— mean·ing·ful·ly** \-fə-lē\ *adverb*
**— mean·ing·ful·ness** *noun*
**mean·ing·less** \'mē-niŋ-ləs\ *adjective* (1797)
**1 :** having no meaning; *especially* : lacking any significance
**2 :** having no assigned function in a language system
**— mean·ing·less·ly** *adverb*
**— mean·ing·less·ness** *noun*
¹**mean·ly** \'mēn-lē\ *adverb* (14th century)
*obsolete* : fairly well : MODERATELY
²**meanly** *adverb* (15th century)
**:** in a mean manner: as **a :** in a lowly manner : HUMBLY **b :** in an inferior manner : BADLY **c :** in a base or ungenerous manner
**mean proportional** *noun* (1571)
**:** GEOMETRIC MEAN; *especially* : the square root (as *x*) of the product of two numbers (as *a* and *b*) when expressed as the means of a proportion (as *a*/*x* = *x*/*b*)
**mean solar day** *noun* (1816)
**:** the interval between successive transits of a given meridian by the mean sun
**mean–spir·it·ed** \'mēn-'spir-ə-təd, ,mēn-\ *adjective* (1694)
**:** exhibiting or characterized by meanness of spirit
**— mean–spir·it·ed·ness** \-nəs\ *noun*
**mean square** *noun* (1845)
**:** the mean of the squares of a set of values
**mean square deviation** *noun* (1948)
**1 :** VARIANCE 5
**2 :** STANDARD DEVIATION
**means test** \'mēnz-\ *noun* (1930)

**:** an examination into the financial state of a person to determine his eligibility for public assistance
**— means–test·ed** \-,tes-təd\ *adjective*
**mean sun** *noun* (circa 1890)
**:** a fictitious sun used for timekeeping that moves uniformly along the celestial equator and maintains a constant rate of apparent motion equal to the average rate of apparent motion of the real sun
¹**mean·time** \'mēn-,tīm\ *noun* (14th century)
**:** the intervening time
²**meantime** *adverb* (1588)
**:** MEANWHILE
**mean time** *noun* (circa 1864)
**:** time that is based on the motion of the mean sun — called also *mean solar time*
**mean value theorem** *noun* (1902)
**1 :** a theorem in differential calculus: if a function of one variable is continuous on a closed interval and differentiable on the interval minus its endpoints there is at least one point where the derivative of the function is equal to the slope of the line joining the endpoints of the curve representing the function on the interval
**2 :** a theorem in integral calculus: if a function of one variable is continuous on a closed interval and differentiable on the interval minus its endpoints, there is at least one point in the interval where the product of the value of the function and the length of the interval is equal to the integral of the function over the interval
¹**mean·while** \'mēn-,hwīl, -,wīl\ *noun* (14th century)
**:** MEANTIME
²**meanwhile** *adverb* (14th century)
**1 :** during the intervening time
**2 :** at the same time
**mea·sle** \'mē-zəl\ *noun* [singular of *measles*] (1863)
**:** a cysticercus tapeworm larva; *specifically* : one found in the muscles of a domesticated mammal
**mea·sles** \'mē-zəlz\ *noun plural but singular or plural in construction* [Middle English *meseles*, plural of *mesel* measles, spot characteristic of measles; akin to Middle Dutch *masel* spot characteristic of measles] (14th century)
**1 a :** an acute contagious viral disease marked by an eruption of distinct red circular spots **b :** any of various eruptive diseases (as German measles)
**2** [Middle English *mesel* infested with tapeworms, literally, leprous, from Old French, from Medieval Latin *misellus* leper, from Latin, wretch, from *misellus,* diminutive of *miser* miserable] **:** infestation with or disease caused by larval tapeworms in the muscles and tissues
**mea·sly** \'mēz-lē, 'mē-zə-\ *adjective* **mea·sli·er; -est** (1687)
**1 :** infected with measles
**2 a :** containing larval tapeworms **b :** infested with trichinae
**3 :** contemptibly small
¹**mea·sure** \'me-zhər, 'mā-\ *noun* [Middle English *mesure,* from Old French, from Latin *mensura,* from *mensus,* past participle of *metiri* to measure; akin to Old English *mǣth* measure, Greek *metron*] (13th century)
**1 a** (1) **:** an adequate or due portion (2) **:** a moderate degree; *also* : MODERATION, TEMPERANCE (3) **:** a fixed or suitable limit : BOUNDS ⟨rich beyond *measure*⟩ **b :** the dimensions, capacity, or amount of something ascertained by measuring **c :** an estimate of what is to be expected (as of a person or situation) **d** (1) **:** a measured quantity (2) **:** AMOUNT, DEGREE
**2 a :** an instrument or utensil for measuring **b** (1) **:** a standard or unit of measurement — see WEIGHT table (2) **:** a system of standard units of measure ⟨metric *measure*⟩
**3 :** the act or process of measuring

**4 a** (1) **:** MELODY, TUNE (2) **:** DANCE; *especially* : a slow and stately dance **b :** rhythmic structure or movement : CADENCE: as (1) **:** poetic rhythm measured by temporal quantity or accent; *specifically* : METER (2) **:** musical time **c** (1) **:** a grouping of a specified number of musical beats located between two consecutive vertical lines on a staff (2) **:** a metrical unit : FOOT
**5 :** an exact divisor of a number
**6 :** a basis or standard of comparison ⟨wealth is not a *measure* of happiness⟩
**7 :** a step planned or taken as a means to an end; *specifically* : a proposed legislative act
**— for good measure :** in addition to the minimum required : as an extra
²**measure** *verb* **mea·sured; mea·sur·ing** \'me-zhə-riŋ, 'mā-; 'mezh-riŋ, 'māzh-\ (14th century)
*transitive verb*
**1 a :** to choose or control with cautious restraint : REGULATE ⟨*measure* his acts⟩ **b :** to regulate by a standard : GOVERN
**2 :** to allot or apportion in measured amounts ⟨*measure* out 3 cups⟩
**3 :** to lay off by making measurements
**4 :** to ascertain the measurements of
**5 :** to estimate or appraise by a criterion ⟨*measures* his skill against his rival⟩
**6** *archaic* : to travel over : TRAVERSE
**7 :** to serve as a means of measuring ⟨a thermometer *measures* temperature⟩
*intransitive verb*
**1 :** to take or make a measurement
**2 :** to have a specified measurement
**— mea·sur·abil·i·ty** \,me-zhə-rə-'bi-lə-tē, ,mā-; ,mezh-rə-, ,māzh-\ *noun*
**— mea·sur·able** \'me-zhə-rə-bəl, 'mā-; 'mezh-rə-, 'māzh-\ *adjective*
**— mea·sur·ably** \-blē\ *adverb*
**— mea·sur·er** \-zhər-ər\ *noun*
**mea·sured** \'me-zhərd, 'mā-\ *adjective* (14th century)
**1 :** marked by due proportion
**2 a :** marked by rhythm : regularly recurrent ⟨a *measured* gait⟩ **b :** METRICAL
**3 :** DELIBERATE, CALCULATED ⟨a *measured* response⟩
**— mea·sured·ly** *adverb*
**mea·sure·less** \-zhər-ləs\ *adjective* (14th century)
**1 :** having no observable limit : IMMEASURABLE ⟨the *measureless* universe⟩
**2 :** very great ⟨had *measureless* energy⟩
**mea·sure·ment** \'me-zhər-mənt, 'mā-\ *noun* (1751)
**1 :** the act or process of measuring
**2 :** a figure, extent, or amount obtained by measuring : DIMENSION
**3 :** MEASURE 2b
**measurement ton** *noun* (circa 1934)
**:** TON 1c
**measure up** *intransitive verb* (1910)
**1 :** to have necessary or fitting qualifications — often used with *to*
**2 :** to be the equal (as in ability) — used with *to*
**measuring worm** *noun* (1843)
**:** LOOPER 1
**meat** \'mēt\ *noun* [Middle English *mete,* from Old English; akin to Old High German *maz* food] (before 12th century)
**1 a :** FOOD; *especially* : solid food as distinguished from drink **b :** the edible part of something as distinguished from its covering (as a husk or shell)
**2 :** animal tissue considered especially as food: **a :** FLESH 2b **b :** FLESH 1a; *specifically* : flesh of domesticated animals
**3** *archaic* : ¹MEAL 1; *especially* : DINNER
**4 a :** the core of something : HEART **b :** PITH 2b ⟨a novel with *meat*⟩
**5 :** favorite pursuit or interest
**— meat·ed** \'mē-təd\ *adjective*
**— meat·less** *adjective*

**meat–and–potatoes** *adjective* (1949)
**1** : of fundamental importance : BASIC; *also* : concerned with or emphasizing the basic aspects of something
**2** : PRACTICAL; *also* : EVERYDAY
**3** : providing or preferring simple food (as meat and potatoes)

**meat and potatoes** *noun plural but singular or plural in construction* (1951)
: the most interesting or fundamental part : MEAT 4

**meat-ax** \'mēt-,aks\ *noun* (1834)
**1** : CLEAVER 1
**2** : an extreme or heavy-handed method of cutting or altering something

**meat·ball** \-,bȯl\ *noun* (circa 1838)
: a small ball of chopped or ground meat often mixed with bread crumbs and spices

**meat·head** \-,hed\ *noun* (1945)
: a stupid or bungling person

**meat loaf** *noun* (1899)
: a dish of ground meat seasoned and baked in the form of a loaf

**meat market** *noun* (1896)
: a depersonalizing environment in which people are treated as sexual or economic resources

**meat·pack·ing** \'mēt-,pa-kiŋ\ *noun* (1873)
: the wholesale meat industry

**me·a·tus** \mē-'ā-təs\ *noun, plural* **me·a·tus·es** \-tə-səz\ *or* **me·a·tus** \-'ā-təs, -,tüs\ [Late Latin, from Latin, going, passage, from *meatus*, past participle of *meare* to go — more at PERMEATE] (1665)
: a natural body passage

**meaty** \'mē-tē\ *adjective* **meat·i·er; -est** (circa 1787)
**1 a** : full of meat **b** : having the character of meat
**2** : rich especially in matter for thought : SUBSTANTIAL (actors looking for *meaty* roles)
— **meat·i·ness** *noun*

**mec·a·myl·amine** \,me-kə-'mi-lə-,mēn\ *noun* [from *Mecamylamine*, a trademark] (1955)
: a drug that in the hydrochloride $C_{11}H_{21}N \cdot HCl$ is used orally as a ganglionic blocking agent to effect a rapid lowering of severely elevated blood pressure

**mec·ca** \'me-kə\ *noun, often capitalized* [*Mecca*, Saudi Arabia, a destination of pilgrims in the Islamic world] (1850)
: a center of activity sought as a goal by people sharing a common interest

**mechan-** *or* **mechano-** *combining form* [Greek, from *mēchanē* machine — more at MACHINE]
: mechanical (*mechano*receptor)

**¹me·chan·ic** \mi-'ka-nik\ *adjective* [Middle English, probably from Middle French *mechanique*, adjective & noun, from Latin *mechanicus*, from Greek *mēchanikos*, from *mēchanē*] (14th century)
**1** : of or relating to manual work or skill
**2** : MECHANICAL 3a

**²mechanic** *noun* (1562)
**1** : a manual worker : ARTISAN
**2** : MACHINIST; *especially* : one who repairs machines

**¹me·chan·i·cal** \mi-'ka-ni-kəl\ *adjective* (15th century)
**1 a** (1) : of or relating to machinery or tools (*mechanical* applications of science) (a *mechanical* genius) (*mechanical* aptitude) (2) : produced or operated by a machine or tool (*mechanical* power) (a *mechanical* refrigerator) (a *mechanical* saw) **b** : of or relating to manual operations
**2** : of or relating to artisans or machinists (the *mechanical* trades)
**3 a** : done as if by machine : seemingly uninfluenced by the mind or emotions : AUTOMATIC (her singing was cold and *mechanical*) **b** : of or relating to technicalities or petty matters
**4 a** : relating to, governed by, or in accordance with the principles of mechanics (*me-*

*chanical* work) (*mechanical* energy) **b** : relating to the quantitative relations of force and matter (*mechanical* pressure of wind on a tower)
**5** : caused by, resulting from, or relating to a process that involves a purely physical as opposed to a chemical change (*mechanical* erosion of rock)
**synonym** see SPONTANEOUS
— **me·chan·i·cal·ly** \-ni-k(ə-)lē\ *adverb*

**²mechanical** *noun* (1590)
**1** *obsolete* : MECHANIC 1
**2** : a piece of finished copy consisting typically of type proofs and artwork positioned and mounted for photomechanical reproduction

**mechanical advantage** *noun* (1894)
: the advantage gained by the use of a mechanism in transmitting force; *specifically* : the ratio of the force that performs the useful work of a machine to the force that is applied to the machine

**mechanical drawing** *noun* (circa 1890)
**1** : drawing done with the aid of instruments
**2** : a drawing made with instruments

**mechanical engineering** *noun* (circa 1890)
: a branch of engineering concerned primarily with the industrial application of mechanics and with the production of tools, machinery, and their products

**mech·a·ni·cian** \,me-kə-'ni-shən\ *noun* (1570)
: MECHANIC, MACHINIST

**me·chan·ics** \mi-'ka-niks\ *noun plural but singular or plural in construction* (1648)
**1** : a branch of physical science that deals with energy and forces and their effect on bodies
**2** : the practical application of mechanics to the design, construction, or operation of machines or tools
**3** : mechanical or functional details or procedure

**mech·a·nism** \'me-kə-,ni-zəm\ *noun* (1662)
**1 a** : a piece of machinery **b** : a process or technique for achieving a result
**2** : mechanical operation or action : WORKING 2
**3** : a doctrine that holds natural processes (as of life) to be mechanically determined and capable of complete explanation by the laws of physics and chemistry
**4** : the fundamental physical or chemical processes involved in or responsible for an action, reaction, or other natural phenomenon (as organic evolution)

**mech·a·nist** \-nist\ *noun* (1606)
**1** *archaic* : MECHANIC
**2** : an adherent of the doctrine of mechanism

**mech·a·nis·tic** \,me-kə-'nis-tik\ *adjective* (1884)
**1** : mechanically determined (*mechanistic* universe)
**2** : of or relating to a mechanism or the doctrine of mechanism
**3** : MECHANICAL
— **mech·a·nis·ti·cal·ly** \-ti-k(ə-)lē\ *adverb*

**mech·a·nize** \'me-kə-,nīz\ *transitive verb* **-nized; -niz·ing** (1678)
**1** : to make mechanical; *especially* : to make automatic or routine
**2 a** : to equip with machinery especially to replace human or animal labor **b** : to equip with armed and armored motor vehicles **c** : to provide with mechanical power
**3** : to produce by or as if by machine
— **mech·a·niz·able** \-,nī-zə-bəl\ *adjective*
— **mech·a·ni·za·tion** \,me-kə-nə-'zā-shən\ *noun*
— **mech·a·niz·er** \'me-kə-,nī-zər\ *noun*

**mech·a·no·chem·is·try** \,me-kə-nō-'ke-mə-strē\ *noun* (1928)
: chemistry that deals with the conversion of chemical energy into mechanical work (as in the contraction of a muscle)

— **mech·a·no·chem·i·cal** \-'ke-mi-kəl\ *adjective*

**mech·a·no·re·cep·tor** \-ri-'sep-tər\ *noun* (1927)
: a neural end organ (as a tactile receptor) that responds to a mechanical stimulus (as a change in pressure)
— **mech·a·no·re·cep·tion** \-'sep-shən\ *noun*
— **mech·a·no·re·cep·tive** \-'sep-tiv\ *adjective*

**Mech·lin** \'me-klən\ *noun* [*Mechlin*, Belgium] (1699)
: a delicate bobbin lace used for dresses and millinery

**mec·li·zine** \'me-klə-,zēn\ *noun* [*methyl* + *chlor-* + *-izine* (alteration of *azine*)] (1954)
: a drug $C_{25}H_{27}ClN_2$ used usually in the form of its hydrochloride to treat nausea and vertigo

**me·co·ni·um** \mi-'kō-nē-əm\ *noun* [Latin, literally, poppy juice, from Greek *mēkōnion*, from *mēkōn* poppy; akin to Old High German *mago* poppy] (1706)
: a dark greenish mass that accumulates in the bowel during fetal life and is discharged shortly after birth

**med** \'med\ *adjective* (1891)
: MEDICAL (*med* school)

**me·da·ka** \mə-'dä-kə\ *noun* [Japanese] (1933)
: a small Japanese freshwater fish (*Oryzias latipes*) usually silvery brown in the wild but from pale yellow to deep red in aquarium strains

**med·al** \'me-d°l\ *noun* [Middle French *medaille*, from Old Italian *medaglia* coin worth half a denarius, medal, from (assumed) Vulgar Latin *medalis* half, alteration of Late Latin *medialis* middle, from Latin *medius* — more at MID] (circa 1578)
**1** : a small usually metal object bearing a religious emblem or picture
**2** : a piece of metal often resembling a coin and having a stamped design that is issued to commemorate a person or event or awarded for excellence or achievement

**Medal for Merit** (1942)
: a U.S. decoration awarded to civilians for exceptionally meritorious conduct in the performance of outstanding services

**med·al·ist** *or* **med·al·list** \'me-d°l-ist\ *noun* (circa 1757)
**1** : a designer, engraver, or maker of medals
**2** : a recipient of a medal as an award

**me·dal·lic** \mə-'da-lik\ *adjective* (1702)
: of, relating to, or shown on a medal

**me·dal·lion** \mə-'dal-yən\ *noun* [French *médaillon*, from Italian *medaglione*, augmentative of *medaglia*] (1658)
**1** : a large medal
**2** : something resembling a large medal; *especially* : a tablet or panel in a wall or window bearing a figure in relief, a portrait, or an ornament
**3** *also* **me·dail·lon** \mā-dà-yōⁿ\ : a small round or oval serving (as of meat)

**Medal of Freedom** (1945)
: a U.S. decoration awarded to civilians for meritorious achievement in any of various fields

**Medal of Honor** (1898)
: a U.S. military decoration awarded in the name of the Congress for conspicuous intrepidity at the risk of life in action with an enemy

**medal play** *noun* (1899)
: STROKE PLAY

**med·dle** \'me-d°l\ *intransitive verb* **med·dled; med·dling** \'med-liŋ, 'me-d°l-iŋ\ [Middle English *medlen*, from Middle French *mesler, medler*, from (assumed) Vulgar Latin

---

\ə\ abut \°\ kitten \ər\ further \a\ ash \ā\ ace
\ä\ mop, mar \aú\ out \ch\ chin \e\ bet \ē\ easy
\g\ go \i\ hit \ī\ ice \j\ job \ŋ\ sing \ō\ go
\ò\ law \òi\ boy \th\ thin \t̷h̷\ the \ü\ loot \ù\ foot
\y\ yet \zh\ vision   *see also* Guide to Pronunciation

*misculare,* from Latin *miscēre* to mix — more at MIX] (14th century)
**:** to interest oneself in what is not one's concern **:** interfere without right or propriety
— **med·dler** \'med-lər, 'me-d°l-ər\ *noun*
**med·dle·some** \'me-d°l-səm\ *adjective* (1615)
**:** given to meddling
*synonym* see IMPERTINENT
— **med·dle·some·ness** *noun*
**Mede** \'mēd\ *noun* [Middle English, from Latin *Medus,* from Greek *Mēdos*] (14th century)
**:** a native or inhabitant of ancient Media in Persia
**Me·dea** \mə-'dē-ə\ *noun* [Latin, from Greek *Mēdeia*]
**:** an enchantress noted in Greek mythology for helping Jason gain the Golden Fleece and for repeatedly resorting to murder to gain her ends
**med·e·vac** \'me-də-,vak, -dē-\ *noun* [*med*ical *evac*uation] (1966)
**1 :** emergency evacuation of the sick or wounded (as from a combat area)
**2 :** a helicopter used for medevac
**med·fly** \'med-,flī\ *noun, often capitalized* (1935)
**:** MEDITERRANEAN FRUIT FLY
**¹me·dia** \'mē-dē-ə\ *noun, plural* **me·di·ae** \-dē-,ē\ (1841)
**1** [Late Latin, from Latin, feminine of *medius;* from the voiced stops' being regarded as intermediate between the tenues and the aspirates] **:** a voiced stop
**2** [New Latin, from Latin] **:** the middle coat of the wall of a blood or lymph vessel consisting chiefly of circular muscle fibers
**²media** *noun, plural* **me·di·as** *often attributive* [plural of *medium*] (1923)
**1 :** a medium of cultivation, conveyance, or expression; *especially* **:** MEDIUM 2b
**2 a** *singular or plural in construction* **:** MASS MEDIA **b** *plural* **:** members of the mass media

**me·di·ad** \'mē-dē-,ad\ *adverb* (1878)
**:** toward the median line or plane of a body or part
**media event** *noun* (1972)
**:** a publicity event staged for coverage by the news media
**me·dia·gen·ic** \,mē-dē-ə-'je-nik\ *adjective* (1971)
**:** attractive or well-suited to the communications media
**me·di·al** \'mē-dē-əl\ *adjective* [Late Latin *medialis,* from Latin *medius*] (1570)
**1 :** MEAN, AVERAGE
**2 a :** being or occurring in the middle **b :** extending toward the middle
**3 :** situated between the extremes of initial and final in a word or morpheme
— **medial** *noun*
— **me·di·al·ly** \-ə-lē\ *adverb*
**¹me·di·an** \'mē-dē-ən\ *noun* (15th century)
**1 :** a medial part (as a vein or nerve)
**2 a :** a value in an ordered set of values below and above which there is an equal number of values or which is the arithmetic mean of the two middle values if there is no one middle number **b :** a vertical line that divides the histogram of a frequency distribution into two parts of equal area **c :** a value of a random variable for which all greater values make the distribution function greater than one half and all lesser values make it less than one half
**3 a :** a line from a vertex of a triangle to the midpoint of the opposite side **b :** a line joining the midpoints of the nonparallel sides of a trapezoid
**4 :** MEDIAN STRIP
*synonym* see AVERAGE
**²median** *adjective* [Middle French or Latin; Middle French, from Latin *medianus,* from *medius* middle — more at MID] (1645)

**1 :** being in the middle or in an intermediate position **:** MEDIAL
**2 :** lying in the plane dividing a bilateral animal into right and left halves
**3 :** relating to or constituting a statistical median
**4 :** produced without occlusion along the lengthwise middle line of the tongue
— **me·di·an·ly** *adverb*
**median strip** *noun* (1948)
**:** a paved or planted strip dividing a highway into lanes according to direction of travel
**me·di·ant** \'mē-dē-ənt\ *noun* [Italian *mediante,* from Late Latin *mediant-, medians,* present participle of *mediare* to be in the middle] (circa 1741)
**:** the third tone of a diatonic scale
**me·di·as·ti·num** \,mē-dē-ə-'stī-nəm\ *noun, plural* **-na** \-nə\ [New Latin, from Medieval Latin, neuter of *mediastinus* medial, from Latin *medius*] (1541)
**:** the space in the chest between the pleural sacs of the lungs that contains all the viscera of the chest except the lungs and pleurae; *also* **:** this space with its contents
— **me·di·as·ti·nal** \-'stī-n°l\ *adjective*
**¹me·di·ate** \'mē-dē-ət\ *adjective* [Middle English, from Late Latin *mediatus* intermediate, from past participle of *mediare*] (15th century)
**1 :** occupying a middle position
**2 a :** acting through an intervening agency **b :** exhibiting indirect causation, connection, or relation
— **me·di·a·cy** \-dē-ə-sē\ *noun*
— **me·di·ate·ly** *adverb*
**²me·di·ate** \'mē-dē-,āt\ *verb* **-at·ed; -at·ing** [Medieval Latin *mediatus,* past participle of *mediare,* from Late Latin, to be in the middle, from Latin *medius* middle] (1568)
*transitive verb*
**1 a :** to effect by action as an intermediary **b :** to bring accord out of by action as an intermediary
**2 a :** to act as intermediary agent in bringing, effecting, or communicating **:** CONVEY **b :** to transmit as intermediate mechanism or agency
*intransitive verb*
**1 :** to interpose between parties in order to reconcile them
**2 :** to reconcile differences
*synonym* see INTERPOSE
— **me·di·a·tive** \-,ā-tiv\ *adjective*
— **me·di·a·to·ry** \-ə-,tōr-ē, -,tôr-\ *adjective*
**me·di·a·tion** \,mē-dē-'ā-shən\ *noun* (14th century)
**:** the act or process of mediating; *especially* **:** intervention between conflicting parties to promote reconciliation, settlement, or compromise
— **me·di·a·tion·al** \-shnəl, -shə-n°l\ *adjective*
**me·di·a·tor** \'mē-dē-,ā-tər\ *noun* [Middle English, from Late Latin, from *mediare*] (14th century)
**1 :** one that mediates; *especially* **:** one that mediates between parties at variance
**2 :** a mediating agent in a physical, chemical, or biological process
**me·di·a·trix** \-'ā-triks\ *noun* [Middle English, from Late Latin, feminine of *mediator*] (15th century)
**:** a woman who is a mediator
**¹med·ic** \'me-dik\ *noun* [Middle English *medike,* from Latin *medica,* from Greek *mēdikē,* from feminine of *mēdikos,* from *Mēdia* Media] (15th century)
**:** any of a genus (*Medicago*) of leguminous herbs (as alfalfa)
**²medic** *noun* [Latin *medicus*] (1659)
**:** one engaged in medical work or study; *especially* **:** CORPSMAN
**med·i·ca·ble** \'me-di-kə-bəl\ *adjective* (circa 1616)
**:** CURABLE, REMEDIABLE

**med·ic·aid** \'me-di-,kād\ *noun, often capitalized* [*medic*al *aid*] (1966)
**:** a program of medical aid designed for those unable to afford regular medical service and financed by the state and federal governments
**med·i·cal** \'me-di-kəl\ *adjective* [French or Late Latin; French *médical,* from Late Latin *medicalis,* from Latin *medicus* physician, from *mederi* to remedy, heal; akin to Avestan *vīmad-* healer, Greek *medesthai* to be mindful of — more at METE] (1646)
**1 :** of, relating to, or concerned with physicians or the practice of medicine
**2 :** requiring or devoted to medical treatment
— **med·i·cal·ly** \-k(ə-)lē\ *adverb*
**medical examiner** *noun* (1877)
**:** a public officer who conducts autopsies of bodies to find the cause of death
**me·di·ca·ment** \mi-'di-kə-mənt, 'me-di-kə-\ *noun* [Middle French, from Latin *medicamentum,* from *medicare*] (1541)
**:** a substance used in therapy
— **me·di·ca·men·tous** \mi-,di-kə-'men-təs, ,me-di-kə-\ *adjective*
**medi·care** \'me-di-,ker, -,kar\ *noun, often capitalized* [blend of *medical* and *care*] (1955)
**:** a government program of medical care especially for the aged
**med·i·cate** \'me-də-,kāt\ *transitive verb* **-cat·ed; -cat·ing** [Latin *medicatus,* past participle of *medicare* to heal, from *medicus*] (circa 1623)
**1 :** to treat medicinally
**2 :** to impregnate with a medicinal substance ⟨*medicated* soap⟩
**med·i·ca·tion** \,me-də-'kā-shən\ *noun* (15th century)
**1 :** the act or process of medicating
**2 :** a medicinal substance **:** MEDICAMENT
**me·dic·i·na·ble** \mi-'dis-nə-bəl, -'di-s°n-ə-; *in Shakespeare* 'med-sə-nə-\ *adjective* (14th century)
**:** MEDICINAL
**me·dic·i·nal** \mə-'dis-nəl, -'di-s°n-əl; *in Shakespeare & Milton* ,me-di-'sī-n°l & 'med-sə-nəl\ *adjective* (14th century)
**1 :** tending or used to cure disease or relieve pain
**2 :** SALUTARY
— **medicinal** *noun*
— **me·dic·i·nal·ly** *adverb*
**medicinal leech** *noun* (circa 1890)
**:** a large European freshwater leech (*Hirudo medicinalis*) formerly used by physicians for bleeding patients
**med·i·cine** \'me-də-sən, *British usually* 'med-sən\ *noun* [Middle English, from Old French, from Latin *medicina,* from feminine of *medicinus* of a physician, from *medicus*] (13th century)
**1 a :** a substance or preparation used in treating disease **b :** something that affects well-being

---

□ USAGE
**media** The singular *media* and its plural *medias* seem to have originated in the field of advertising over 50 years ago; they are apparently still so used without stigma in that specialized field. In most other applications *media* is used as a plural of *medium.* The great popularity of the word in references to the agencies of mass communication is leading to the formation of a mass noun, construed as a singular ⟨there's no basis for it. You know, the news *media* gets on to something —Edwin Meese 3d⟩ ⟨the *media* is less interested in the party's policies —James Lewis, *Guardian Weekly*⟩. This use is not as well established as the mass-noun use of *data* and is likely to incur criticism especially in writing.

**2 a :** the science and art dealing with the maintenance of health and the prevention, alleviation, or cure of disease **b :** the branch of medicine concerned with the nonsurgical treatment of disease
**3 :** a substance (as a drug or potion) used to treat something other than disease
**4 :** an object held in traditional American Indian belief to give control over natural or magical forces; *also* **:** magical power or a magical rite
— **medicine** *transitive verb*
**medicine ball** *noun* (1895)
**:** a heavy stuffed leather-covered ball used for conditioning exercises
**medicine dropper** *noun* (1898)
**:** DROPPER 2
**medicine man** *noun* (1801)
**:** a priestly healer or sorcerer especially among the American Indians **:** SHAMAN
**medicine show** *noun* (circa 1906)
**:** a traveling show using entertainers to attract a crowd among which remedies or nostrums are sold
**med·i·co** \'me-di-ˌkō\ *noun, plural* **-cos** [Italian *medico* or Spanish *médico*, both from Latin *medicus*] (1689)
**:** a medical practitioner **:** PHYSICIAN; *also* **:** a medical student
**med·i·co·le·gal** \ˌme-di-kō-'lē-gəl\ *adjective* [New Latin *medicolegalis*, from Latin *medicus* medical + *-o-* + *legalis* legal] (1835)
**:** of or relating to both medicine and law
**¹me·di·e·val** *or* **me·di·ae·val** \mē-'dē-vəl, mi-, me-, -dē-'ē-vəl\ *adjective* [New Latin *medium aevum* Middle Ages] (1827)
**1 :** of, relating to, or characteristic of the Middle Ages
**2 :** extremely outmoded or antiquated
— **me·di·e·val·ly** *adverb*
**²medieval** *or* **mediaeval** *noun* (1856)
**:** a person of the Middle Ages
**me·di·e·val·ism** \-və-ˌli-zəm\ *noun* (1853)
**1 :** medieval quality, character, or state
**2 :** devotion to the institutions, arts, and practices of the Middle Ages
**me·di·e·val·ist** \-'dēv-list, -'dē-və-, -dē-'ēv-, -dē-'ē-və-\ *noun* (circa 1859)
**1 :** a specialist in medieval history and culture
**2 :** a connoisseur or devotee of medieval arts and culture
**Medieval Latin** *noun* (circa 1889)
**:** the Latin used especially for liturgical and literary purposes from the 7th to the 15th centuries inclusive
**me·di·na** \mə-'dē-nə\ *noun* [Arabic *madīna* city] (1906)
**:** the non-European part of a northern African city
**me·di·o·cre** \ˌmē-dē-'ō-kər\ *adjective* [Middle English, from Middle French, from Latin *mediocris*, from *medius* middle + Old Latin *ocris* stony mountain; akin to Latin *acer* sharp — more at EDGE] (circa 1586)
**:** of moderate or low quality, value, ability, or performance **:** ORDINARY, SO-SO
**me·di·oc·ri·ty** \ˌmē-dē-'ä-krə-tē\ *noun, plural* **-ties** (1531)
**1 a :** the quality or state of being mediocre **b :** moderate ability or value
**2 :** a mediocre person
**med·i·tate** \'me-də-ˌtāt\ *verb* **-tat·ed; -tat·ing** [Latin *meditatus*, past participle of *meditari*, frequentative of *mederi* to remedy — more at MEDICAL] (1560)
*intransitive verb*
**:** to engage in contemplation or reflection
*transitive verb*
**1 :** to focus one's thoughts on **:** reflect on or ponder over
**2 :** to plan or project in the mind **:** INTEND, PURPOSE
*synonym* see PONDER
— **med·i·ta·tor** \-ˌtā-tər\ *noun*
**med·i·ta·tion** \ˌme-də-'tā-shən\ *noun* (13th century)

**1 :** a discourse intended to express its author's reflections or to guide others in contemplation
**2 :** the act or process of meditating
**med·i·ta·tive** \'me-də-ˌtā-tiv\ *adjective* (circa 1656)
**1 :** disposed or given to meditation
**2 :** marked by or conducive to meditation
— **med·i·ta·tive·ly** *adverb*
— **med·i·ta·tive·ness** *noun*
**Med·i·ter·ra·nean** \ˌme-də-tə-'rā-nē-ən, -nyən\ *adjective* (15th century)
**1 a :** of, relating to, or characteristic of the Mediterranean Sea **b :** of, relating to, or characteristic of the peoples, lands, or cultures bordering the Mediterranean Sea
**2** *not capitalized* [Latin *mediterraneus*, from *medius* middle + *terra* land — more at TERRACE] **:** enclosed or nearly enclosed with land
**3 :** of or relating to a group or physical type of the Caucasian race characterized by medium or short stature, slender build, dolichocephaly, and dark complexion
**Mediterranean flour moth** *noun* (1895)
**:** a small largely gray and black nearly cosmopolitan pyralid moth (*Anagasta kuehniella*) whose larva destroys processed grain products
**Mediterranean fruit fly** *noun* (1907)
**:** a small widely distributed dipteran fly (*Ceratitis capitata*) with black-and-white markings whose larva lives and feeds in ripening fruit
**¹me·di·um** \'mē-dē-əm\ *noun, plural* **medi·ums** *or* **me·dia** \-dē-ə\ [Latin, from neuter of *medius* middle — more at MID] (1593)
**1 a :** something in a middle position **b :** a middle condition or degree **:** MEAN
**2 :** a means of effecting or conveying something: as **a** (1) **:** a substance regarded as the means of transmission of a force or effect (2) **:** a surrounding or enveloping substance (3) **:** the tenuous material (as gas and dust) in space that exists between large agglomerations of matter (as stars) ⟨interstellar *medium*⟩ **b** *plural usually* media (1) **:** a channel or system of communication, information, or entertainment — compare MASS MEDIUM (2) **:** a publication or broadcast that carries advertising (3) **:** a mode of artistic expression or communication (4) **:** something (as a magnetic disk) on which information may be stored **c :** GO-BETWEEN, INTERMEDIARY **d** *plural* mediums **:** an individual held to be a channel of communication between the earthly world and a world of spirits **e :** material or technical means of artistic expression
**3 a :** a condition or environment in which something may function or flourish **b** *plural* media (1) **:** a nutrient system for the artificial cultivation of cells or organisms and especially bacteria (2) **:** a fluid or solid in which organic structures are placed (as for preservation or mounting) **c :** a liquid with which pigment is mixed by a painter
*usage* see MEDIA
**²medium** *adjective* (1711)
**:** intermediate in quantity, quality, position, size, or degree
**medium frequency** *noun* (1920)
**:** a radio frequency between high frequency and low frequency — see RADIO FREQUENCY table
**me·di·um·is·tic** \ˌmē-dē-ə-'mis-tik\ *adjective* (1868)
**:** of, relating to, or having the qualities of a spiritualistic medium
**medium of exchange** (1714)
**:** something commonly accepted in exchange for goods and services and recognized as representing a standard of value
**me·di·um·ship** \'mē-dē-əm-ˌship\ *noun* (1868)
**:** the capacity, function, or profession of a spiritualistic medium
**med·lar** \'med-lər\ *noun* [Middle English *medeler*, from Middle French *medlier*, from *medle* medlar fruit, from Latin *mespilum*, from Greek *mespilon*] (14th century)

**:** a small Eurasian tree (*Mespilus germanica*) of the rose family whose fruit resembles a crab apple and is used in preserves; *also* **:** its fruit
**¹med·ley** \'med-lē\ *noun, plural* **medleys** [Middle English *medle*, from Middle French *medlee*, from feminine of *medlé*, past participle of *medler* to mix — more at MEDDLE] (14th century)
**1** *archaic* **:** MELEE
**2 :** a diverse assortment or mixture; *especially* **:** HODGEPODGE
**3 :** a musical composition made up of a series of songs or short musical pieces
**²medley** *adjective* (14th century)
**:** MIXED, MOTLEY
**medley relay** *noun* (1949)
**:** a relay race in swimming in which each member of a team uses a different stroke
**me·dul·la** \mə-'də-lə\ *noun, plural* **-las** *or* **-lae** \-(ˌ)lē, -ˌlī\ [Middle English, from Latin] (15th century)
**1** *plural* medullae **a :** MARROW 1 **b :** MEDULLA OBLONGATA
**2 a :** the inner or deep part of an animal or plant structure ⟨the adrenal *medulla*⟩ **b :** MYELIN SHEATH
**medulla ob·lon·ga·ta** \-ˌä-ˌblȯŋ-'gä-tə\ *noun, plural* **medulla oblongatas** *or* **medullae ob·lon·ga·tae** \-'gä-tē, -ˌtī\ [New Latin, literally, oblong medulla] (1676)
**:** the part of the vertebrate brain that is continuous posteriorly with the spinal cord and that contains the centers controlling involuntary vital functions — see BRAIN illustration
**med·ul·lary** \'me-dᵊl-ˌer-ē, 'me-jə-ˌler-; mə-'də-lə-rē\ *adjective* (1620)
**1 :** of or relating to the pith of a plant
**2 :** of or relating to a medulla and especially the medulla oblongata
**medullary ray** *noun* (1830)
**1 :** a primary tissue composed of radiating bands of parenchyma cells extending between the vascular bundles of herbaceous dicotyledonous stems and connecting the pith with the cortex
**2 :** VASCULAR RAY
**medullary sheath** *noun* (circa 1846)
**:** MYELIN SHEATH
**med·ul·lat·ed** \'me-dᵊl-ˌā-təd, 'me-jə-ˌlā-\ *adjective* (1867)
**1 :** MYELINATED
**2 :** having a medulla — used of fibers other than nerve fibers
**me·dul·lo·blas·to·ma** \mə-ˌdə-lō-ˌblas-'tō-mə\ *noun, plural* **-to·mas** *also* **-to·ma·ta** \-'tō-mə-tə\ [New Latin, from *medulla* + *-o-* + *blast-* + *-oma*] (1925)
**:** a malignant tumor of the central nervous system arising in the cerebellum especially in children
**me·du·sa** \mi-'dü-sə, -'dyü-, -zə\ *noun*
**1** *capitalized* [Latin, from Greek *Medousa*] **:** a mortal Gorgon who is slain when decapitated by Perseus
**2** *plural* **me·du·sae** \-ˌsē, -ˌzē, -ˌsī, -ˌzī\ [New Latin, from Latin] JELLYFISH 1a
— **me·du·san** \-sᵊn, -zᵊn\ *adjective or noun*
— **me·du·soid** \-ˌsȯid, -ˌzȯid\ *adjective or noun*
**meed** \'mēd\ *noun* [Middle English, from Old English *mēd*; akin to Old High German *miata* reward, Greek *misthos*] (before 12th century)
**1** *archaic* **:** an earned reward or wage
**2 :** a fitting return or recompense
**meek** \'mēk\ *adjective* [Middle English, of Scandinavian origin; akin to Old Norse *mjūkr* gentle; akin to Welsh *mwyth* soft] (13th century)

\ə\ abut \ᵊ\ kitten \ər\ further \a\ ash \ā\ ace
\ä\ mop, mar \au̇\ out \ch\ chin \e\ bet \ē\ easy
\g\ go \i\ hit \ī\ ice \j\ job \ŋ\ sing \ō\ go
\ȯ\ law \ȯi\ boy \th\ thin \th\ the \ü\ loot \u̇\ foot
\y\ yet \zh\ vision    *see also* Guide to Pronunciation

**1 :** enduring injury with patience and without resentment **:** MILD
**2 :** deficient in spirit and courage **:** SUBMISSIVE
**3 :** not violent or strong **:** MODERATE
— **meek·ly** *adverb*
— **meek·ness** *noun*

**meer·kat** \'mir-ˌkat\ *noun* [Afrikaans, from Dutch, a kind of monkey, from Middle Dutch *meercatte* monkey, from *meer* sea + *catte* cat] (1801)
**:** any of several African mongooses; *especially* **:** a burrowing highly social mammal (*Suricata suricatta*) of southern Africa that is chiefly grayish with inconspicuous black markings

**meer·schaum** \'mir-shəm, -ˌshȯm\ *noun* [German, from *Meer* sea + *Schaum* foam] (1784)
**1 :** a fine light white clayey mineral that is a hydrous magnesium silicate found chiefly in Asia Minor and is used especially for tobacco pipes
**2 :** a tobacco pipe of meerschaum

**¹meet** \'mēt\ *verb* **met** \'met\; **meet·ing** [Middle English *meten,* from Old English *mētan;* akin to Old English ge*mōt* assembly — more at MOOT] (before 12th century)
*transitive verb*
**1 a :** to come into the presence of **:** FIND **b :** to come together with especially at a particular time or place ⟨I'll *meet* you at the station⟩ **c :** to come into contact or conjunction with **:** JOIN **d :** to appear to the perception of
**2 :** to encounter as antagonist or foe **:** OPPOSE
**3 :** to enter into conference, argument, or personal dealings with
**4 :** to conform to especially with exactitude and precision ⟨a concept to *meet* all requirements⟩
**5 :** to pay fully **:** SETTLE
**6 :** to cope with ⟨was able to *meet* every social situation⟩
**7 :** to provide for ⟨enough money to *meet* our needs⟩
**8 :** to become acquainted with
**9 :** ENCOUNTER, EXPERIENCE
**10 :** to receive or greet in an official capacity
*intransitive verb*
**1 a :** to come face-to-face **b :** to come together for a common purpose **:** ASSEMBLE **c :** to come together as contestants, opponents, or enemies
**2 :** to form a junction or confluence ⟨the lines *meet* in a point⟩
**3 :** to occur together
— **meet·er** *noun*
— **meet halfway :** to compromise with
— **meet with :** to be subjected to **:** ENCOUNTER ⟨the proposal *met with* opposition⟩

**²meet** *noun* (circa 1834)
**1 :** the act of assembling for a hunt or for competitive sports
**2 :** a competition in which individuals (as athletes) match skills

**³meet** *adjective* [Middle English *mete,* from Old English ge*mǣte;* akin to Old English *metan* to mete] (14th century)
**:** precisely adapted to a particular situation, need, or circumstance **:** very proper
**synonym** see FIT
— **meet·ly** *adverb*

**meet·ing** \'mē-tiŋ\ *noun* (14th century)
**1 :** an act or process of coming together: as **a** **:** an assembly for a common purpose (as worship) **b :** a session of horse or dog racing
**2 :** a permanent organizational unit of the Society of Friends
**3 :** INTERSECTION, JUNCTION

**meet·ing·house** \-ˌhaủs\ *noun* (1632)
**:** a building used for public assembly and especially for Protestant worship

**meeting of minds** (1939)
**:** AGREEMENT, CONCORD

**mef·e·nam·ic acid** \ˌme-fə-'na-mik-\ *noun* [*dimethyl-* + *fen-* (by shortening & alteration from *phenyl*) + *aminobenzoic acid*] (circa 1964)

**:** a drug $C_{15}H_{15}NO_2$ used as an anti-inflammatory

**mega-** *or* **meg-** *combining form* [Greek, from *megas* large — more at MUCH]
**1 a :** great **:** large ⟨*mega*spore⟩ **b :** greatly surpassing others of its kind ⟨*mega*hit⟩
**2 :** million **:** multiplied by one million ⟨*meg*ohm⟩ ⟨*mega*cycle⟩

**mega·bar** \'me-gə-ˌbär\ *noun* [International Scientific Vocabulary] (1903)
**:** a unit of pressure equal to one million bars

**mega·bit** \-ˌbit\ *noun* (1956)
**:** one million bits

**mega·buck** \-ˌbək\ *noun* (1946)
**:** one million dollars; *also* **:** an indeterminately large sum of money — usually used in plural

**mega·byte** \-ˌbīt\ *noun* [from the fact that 1,048,576 ($2^{20}$) is the power of 2 closest to one million] (1970)
**:** a unit of computer information storage capacity equal to 1,048,576 bytes

**mega·city** \-ˌsi-tē\ *noun* (1968)
**:** MEGALOPOLIS 1

**mega·cor·po·ra·tion** \ˌme-gə-ˌkȯr-pə-'rā-shən\ *noun* (1973)
**:** a huge and powerful corporation

**mega·cy·cle** \'me-gə-ˌsī-kəl\ *noun* (1926)
**:** one million cycles; *especially* **:** MEGAHERTZ

**mega·deal** \-ˌdēl\ *noun* (1981)
**:** a business deal involving a lot of money

**mega·death** \-ˌdeth\ *noun* (1953)
**:** one million deaths — usually used as a unit in reference to nuclear warfare

**mega·dose** \-ˌdōs\ *noun* (1973)
**:** a large dose (as of a vitamin)

**mega·fau·na** \-ˌfȯ-nə, -ˌfä-\ *noun* (1935)
**:** fauna consisting of individuals large enough to be visible to the naked eye
— **mega·fau·nal** \-nᵊl\ *adjective*

**mega·ga·mete** \ˌme-gə-'ga-ˌmēt *also* -gə-'mēt\ *noun* (1891)
**:** MACROGAMETE

**mega·ga·me·to·phyte** \-gə-'mē-tə-ˌfīt\ *noun* (1933)
**:** the female gametophyte produced by a megaspore

**mega·hertz** \'me-gə-ˌhərts, -ˌherts\ *noun* [International Scientific Vocabulary] (1941)
**:** a unit of frequency equal to one million hertz — abbreviation *MHz*

**mega·hit** \-ˌhit\ *noun* (1982)
**:** something (as a motion picture) that is extremely successful

**mega·kar·yo·cyte** \ˌme-gə-'kar-ē-ō-ˌsīt\ *noun* (1890)
**:** a large cell that has a lobulated nucleus, is found especially in the bone marrow, and is the source of blood platelets
— **mega·kar·yo·cyt·ic** \-ˌkar-ē-ō-'si-tik\ *adjective*

**megal-** *or* **megalo-** *combining form* [New Latin, from Greek, from *megal-, megas* — more at MUCH]
**:** large **:** of giant size ⟨*megal*opolis⟩ **:** grandiose ⟨*megalo*mania⟩

**mega·lith** \'me-gə-ˌlith\ *noun* (1853)
**:** a very large usually rough stone used in prehistoric cultures as a monument or building block
— **mega·lith·ic** \ˌme-gə-'li-thik\ *adjective*

**meg·a·lo·blast** \'me-gə-lō-ˌblast\ *noun* (1899)
**:** a large erythroblast that appears in the blood especially in pernicious anemia
— **meg·a·lo·blas·tic** \ˌme-gə-lō-'blas-tik\ *adjective*

**megalith**

**meg·a·lo·ma·nia** \ˌme-gə-lō-'mā-nē-ə, -nyə\ *noun* [New Latin] (circa 1890)
**1 :** a mania for great or grandiose performance

**2 :** a delusional mental disorder that is marked by infantile feelings of personal omnipotence and grandeur
— **meg·a·lo·ma·ni·ac** \-'mā-nē-ˌak\ *adjective or noun*
— **meg·a·lo·ma·ni·a·cal** \-mə-'nī-ə-kəl\ *also* **meg·a·lo·man·ic** \-'ma-nik\ *adjective*
— **meg·a·lo·ma·ni·a·cal·ly** \-mə-'nī-ə-k(ə-)lē\ *adverb*

**meg·a·lop·o·lis** \ˌme-gə-'lä-pə-ləs\ *noun* (circa 1828)
**1 :** a very large city
**2 :** a thickly populated region centering in a metropolis or embracing several metropolises
— **meg·a·lo·pol·i·tan** \-lō-'pä-lə-tᵊn\ *noun or adjective*

**-megaly** *noun combining form* [New Latin *-megalia,* from Greek *megal-, megas*]
**:** abnormal enlargement ⟨hepato*megaly*⟩

**mega·par·sec** \ˌme-gə-'pär-ˌsek\ *noun* [International Scientific Vocabulary] (1933)
**:** a unit of measure for distances in intergalactic space equal to one million parsecs

**¹mega·phone** \'me-gə-ˌfōn\ *noun* (1878)
**:** a cone-shaped device used to intensify or direct the voice
— **mega·phon·ic** \ˌme-gə-'fä-nik\ *adjective*

**²megaphone** (1901)
*transitive verb*
**:** to transmit or address through or as if through a megaphone
*intransitive verb*
**:** to speak through or as if through a megaphone

**mega·proj·ect** \-ˌprä-ˌjekt, -jikt *also* -ˌprō-\ *noun* (1982)
**:** a major project or undertaking (as in business or construction)

**Me·gar·i·an** \mə-'gar-ē-ən, me-\ *adjective* (1603)
**:** of or relating to a Socratic school of philosophy founded by Euclid of Megara and noted for its subtle attention to logic
— **Megarian** *noun*

**Me·gar·ic** \-'gar-ik\ *adjective* (1656)
**:** MEGARIAN
— **Megaric** *noun*

**mega·scop·ic** \ˌme-gə-'skä-pik\ *adjective* [*mega-* + *-scopic* (as in *microscopic*)] (1879)
**1 :** MACROSCOPIC 1 ⟨*megascopic* features of leaves⟩
**2 :** based on or relating to observations made with the unaided eye
— **mega·scop·i·cal·ly** \-pi-k(ə-)lē\ *adverb*

**mega·spo·ran·gi·um** \ˌme-gə-spə-'ran-jē-əm\ *noun* [New Latin] (1886)
**:** a sporangium that develops only megaspores

**mega·spore** \'me-gə-ˌspȯr, -ˌspȯr\ *noun* [International Scientific Vocabulary] (1858)
**:** a spore in heterosporous plants that gives rise to female gametophytes and is generally larger than a microspore
— **mega·spor·ic** \ˌme-gə-'spȯr-ik, -'spȯr-\ *adjective*

**mega·spo·ro·gen·e·sis** \ˌme-gə-ˌspȯr-ə-'je-nə-səs, -ˌspȯr-\ *noun* [New Latin] (circa 1928)
**:** the formation and maturation of a megaspore

**mega·spo·ro·phyll** \-'spȯr-ə-ˌfil, -'spȯr-\ *noun* (circa 1899)
**:** a sporophyll that develops only megasporangia

**mega·star** \'me-gə-ˌstär\ *noun* (1975)
**:** SUPERSTAR

**mega·ton** \'me-gə-ˌtən\ *noun* (1952)
**:** an explosive force equivalent to that of one million tons of TNT

**mega·ton·nage** \-ˌtə-nij\ *noun* (1955)
**:** the destructive capability expressed in megatons especially of a collection of nuclear weapons

**mega·vi·ta·min** \ˌme-gə-'vī-tə-mən, *British usually* -'vi-\ *adjective* (1970)
**:** relating to or consisting of very large doses of vitamins ⟨*megavitamin* therapy⟩

**mega·vi·ta·mins** \-mənz\ *noun plural* (1974)
: a large quantity of vitamins

**mega·watt** \'me-gə-ˌwät\ *noun* [International Scientific Vocabulary] (circa 1900)
: one million watts

**me·gil·lah** \mə-'gi-lə\ *noun* [Yiddish *megile*, from Hebrew *mĕgillāh* scroll, volume (used especially of the Book of Esther, read aloud at the Purim celebration)] (circa 1952)
*slang* : a long involved story or account ⟨the whole *megillah*⟩

**me·gilp** \mə-'gilp\ *noun* [origin unknown] (1768)
: a gelatinous preparation commonly of linseed oil and mastic varnish that is used by artists as a vehicle for oil colors

**meg·ohm** \'meg-ˌōm\ *noun* [International Scientific Vocabulary] (circa 1868)
: one million ohms

**me·grim** \'mē-grəm\ *noun* [Middle English *migreime*, from Middle French *migraine* — more at MIGRAINE] (14th century)
**1 a** : MIGRAINE **b** : VERTIGO, DIZZINESS
**2 a** : FANCY, WHIM **b** *plural* : low spirits

**Mei·ji** \'mā-(ˌ)jē\ *noun* [Japanese, literally, enlightened rule] (1873)
: the period of the reign (1868–1912) of Emperor Mutsuhito of Japan

**mei·kle** \'mē-kəl\ *variant of* MICKLE

**mei·ny** *noun, plural* **meinies** [Middle English *meynie* — more at MENIAL] (13th century)
**1** \'mā-nē\ *archaic* : RETINUE, COMPANY
**2** \'men-yē\ *chiefly Scottish* : MULTITUDE

**mei·o·sis** \mī-'ō-səs\ *noun* [New Latin, from Greek *meiōsis* diminution, from *meioun* to diminish, from *meiōn* less; akin to Sanskrit *mīyate* he diminishes] (1550)
**1** : the presentation of a thing with underemphasis especially in order to achieve a greater effect : UNDERSTATEMENT
**2** : the cellular process that results in the number of chromosomes in gamete-producing cells being reduced to one half and that involves a reduction division in which one of each pair of homologous chromosomes passes to each daughter cell and a mitotic division — compare MITOSIS
— **mei·ot·ic** \mī-'ä-tik\ *adjective*
— **mei·ot·i·cal·ly** \-ti-k(ə-)lē\ *adverb*

**Meis·sen** \'mī-sᵊn\ *noun* [*Meissen*, Saxony, Germany] (1863)
: a ceramic ware made at Meissen near Dresden; *especially* : a European porcelain developed under the patronage of the king of Saxony about 1715 and used for both ornamental and table wares — called also *Meissen china, Meissen ware*

**Mei·ster·sing·er** \'mīs-tər-ˌsiŋ-ər, -ˌziŋ-\ *noun, plural* **Meistersinger** *or* **Meistersingers** [German, from Middle High German, from *meister* master + *singer* singer] (1845)
: a member of any of various German guilds formed chiefly in the 15th and 16th centuries by workingmen and craftsmen for the cultivation of poetry and music

**mel·a·mine** \'me-lə-ˌmēn\ *noun* [German *Melamin*] (circa 1835)
**1** : a white crystalline organic base $C_3H_6N_6$ with a high melting point that is used especially in melamine resins
**2** : a melamine resin or a plastic made from such a resin

**melamine resin** *noun* (1939)
: a thermosetting resin made from melamine and an aldehyde and used especially in molded or laminated products, adhesives, and coatings

**melan-** *or* **melano-** *combining form* [Middle English, from Middle French, from Late Latin, from Greek, from *melan-, melas*; perhaps akin to Lithuanian *mėlynas* blue, Sanskrit *malina* dirty]
**1** : black : dark ⟨*melanic*⟩ ⟨*melan*in⟩
**2** : melanin ⟨*melano*phore⟩

**mel·an·cho·lia** \ˌme-lən-'kō-lē-ə\ *noun* [New Latin, from Late Latin, melancholy] (circa 1693)
: a mental condition characterized by extreme depression, bodily complaints, and often hallucinations and delusions; *especially* : a manic-depressive psychosis
— **mel·an·cho·li·ac** \-lē-ˌak\ *noun*

**mel·an·chol·ic** \ˌme-lən-'kä-lik\ *adjective* (14th century)
**1** : of, relating to, or subject to melancholy : DEPRESSED
**2** : of or relating to melancholia
**3** : tending to depress the spirits : SADDENING
— **melancholic** *noun*

**¹mel·an·choly** \'me-lən-ˌkä-lē\ *noun, plural* **-chol·ies** [Middle English *malencolie*, from Middle French *melancolie*, from Late Latin *melancholia*, from Greek, from *melan-* + *cholē* bile — more at GALL] (14th century)
**1 a** : an abnormal state attributed to an excess of black bile and characterized by irascibility or depression **b** : BLACK BILE **c** : MELANCHOLIA
**2 a** : depression of spirits : DEJECTION **b** : a pensive mood

**²melancholy** *adjective* (14th century)
**1 a** : suggestive or expressive of melancholy ⟨sang in a *melancholy* voice⟩ **b** : causing or tending to cause sadness or depression of mind or spirit : DISMAL ⟨a *melancholy* thought⟩
**2 a** : depressed in spirits : DEJECTED, SAD **b** : PENSIVE

**Mel·a·ne·sian** \ˌme-lə-'nē-zhən, -shən\ *noun* (1849)
**1** : a language group consisting of the Austronesian languages of Melanesia
**2** : a member of the dominant native group of Melanesia
— **Melanesian** *adjective*

**mé·lange** \mā-'läⁿzh, -'länj\ *noun* [French, from Middle French, from *mesler, meler* to mix — more at MEDDLE] (1653)
: a mixture often of incongruous elements

**¹me·lan·ic** \mə-'la-nik\ *adjective* (1826)
**1** : MELANOTIC
**2** : affected with or characterized by melanism

**²melanic** *noun* (1952)
: a melanic individual

**mel·a·nin** \'me-lə-nən\ *noun* (1843)
: a dark brown or black animal or plant pigment

**mel·a·nism** \'me-lə-ˌni-zəm\ *noun* (1843)
**1** : an increased amount of black or nearly black pigmentation (as of skin, feathers, or hair) of an individual or kind of organism
**2** : intense human pigmentation of the skin, eyes, and hair
— **mel·a·nis·tic** \ˌme-lə-'nis-tik\ *adjective*

**mel·a·nite** \'me-lə-ˌnīt\ *noun* [German *Melanit*, from *melan-*] (circa 1807)
: a black andradite garnet
— **mel·a·nit·ic** \ˌme-lə-'ni-tik\ *adjective*

**mel·a·nize** \'me-lə-ˌnīz\ *transitive verb* **-nized; -niz·ing** (1885)
**1** : to convert into or infiltrate with melanin
**2** : to make dark or black
— **mel·a·ni·za·tion** \ˌme-lə-nə-'zā-shən\ *noun*

**me·la·no·blast** \mə-'la-nə-ˌblast, 'me-lə-nō-\ *noun* [International Scientific Vocabulary] (1901)
: a cell that is a precursor of a melanocyte or melanophore

**me·la·no·cyte** \mə-'la-nə-ˌsīt, 'me-lə-nō-\ *noun* [International Scientific Vocabulary] (circa 1890)
: an epidermal cell that produces melanin

**melanocyte–stimulating hormone** *noun* (1953)
: either of two vertebrate hormones of the pituitary gland especially of reptiles and amphibians that darken the skin by stimulating melanin dispersion in pigment-containing cells — called also *melanophore-stimulating hormone*

**me·la·no·gen·e·sis** \mə-ˌla-nə-'je-nə-səs, ˌme-lə-nō-\ *noun* [New Latin] (circa 1928)
: the formation of melanin

**mel·a·no·ma** \ˌme-lə-'nō-mə\ *noun, plural* **-mas** *also* **-ma·ta** \-mə-tə\ [New Latin] (1830)
: a usually malignant tumor containing dark pigment

**me·la·no·phore** \mə-'la-nə-ˌfōr, 'me-lə-nə-, -ˌför\ *noun* (1903)
: a melanin-containing cell especially of fishes, amphibians, and reptiles

**me·la·no·some** \-ˌsōm\ *noun* (1940)
: a melanin-producing granule in a melanocyte

**mel·a·not·ic** \ˌme-lə-'nä-tik\ *adjective* (1829)
: having or characterized by black pigmentation

**mel·a·to·nin** \ˌme-lə-'tō-nən\ *noun* [Greek *melas* black + *-tonin* (as in *serotonin*)] (1958)
: a vertebrate hormone of the pineal gland that produces lightening of the skin by causing concentration of melanin in pigment-containing cells

**mel·ba toast** \'mel-bə-\ *noun* [Nellie *Melba*] (1925)
: very thin crisp toast

**Mel·chite** *or* **Mel·kite** \'mel-ˌkīt\ *noun* [Medieval Latin *Melchita*, from Middle Greek *Melchitēs*, literally, royalist, from Syriac *malkā* king] (1619)
**1** : an Eastern Christian chiefly of Syria and Egypt adhering to Chalcedonian orthodoxy in preference to Monophysitism
**2** : a member of a Uniate body derived from the Melchites

**¹Mel·chiz·e·dek** \mel-'ki-zə-ˌdek\ *noun* [Greek *Melchisedek*, from Hebrew *Malkīṣedheq*]
: a priest-king of Jerusalem who prepared a ritual meal for Abraham and received tithes from him

**²Melchizedek** *adjective* (1842)
: of or relating to the higher order of the Mormon priesthood

**¹meld** \'meld\ *verb* [German *melden* to announce, from Old High German *meldōn*; akin to Old English *meldian* to announce, Lithuanian *malda* prayer] (1897)
*transitive verb*
: to declare or announce (a card or combination of cards) for a score in a card game especially by placing face up on the table
*intransitive verb*
: to declare a card or combination of cards as a meld

**²meld** *noun* (1897)
: a card or combination of cards that is or can be melded in a card game

**³meld** *verb* [blend of *melt* and *weld*] (1936)
: MERGE, BLEND

**⁴meld** *noun* (1954)
: BLEND, MIXTURE

**me·lee** *also* **mê·lée** \'mā-ˌlā, mā-'\ *noun* [French *mêlée*, from Old French *meslee*, from *mesler* to mix — more at MEDDLE] (circa 1648)
: a confused struggle; *especially* : a hand-to-hand fight among several people

**mel·ic** \'me-lik\ *adjective* [Latin *melicus*, from Greek *melikos*, from *melos* song — more at MELODY] (1699)
: of or relating to song : LYRIC; *especially* : of or relating to Greek lyric poetry of the 7th and 6th centuries B.C.

**mel·i·lot** \'me-lə-ˌlät\ *noun* [Middle English *mellilot*, from Old French *melilot*, from Latin *melilotos*, from Greek *melilōtos*, from *meli* honey + *lōtos* clover, lotus — more at MELLIFLUOUS] (14th century)

---

\ə\ abut \ᵊ\ kitten \ər\ further \a\ ash \ā\ ace
\ä\ mop, mar \au̇\ out \ch\ chin \e\ bet \ē\ easy
\g\ go \i\ hit \ī\ ice \j\ job \ŋ\ sing \ō\ go
\ȯ\ law \ȯi\ boy \th\ thin \t̲h̲\ the \ü\ loot \u̇\ foot
\y\ yet \zh\ vision *see also* Guide to Pronunciation

**:** SWEET CLOVER; *especially* **:** a yellow-flowered sweet clover (*Melilotus officinalis*)

**me·lio·rate** \'mēl-yə-ˌrāt, 'mē-lē-ə-\ *verb* **-rat·ed; -rat·ing** [Late Latin *melioratus*, past participle of *meliorare*, from Latin *melior* better; akin to Latin *multus* much, Greek *mala* very] (1542)
**:** AMELIORATE
— **me·lio·ra·tion** \ˌmēl-yə-'rā-shən, ˌmē-lē-ə-\ *noun*
— **me·lio·ra·tive** \'mēl-yə-ˌrā-tiv, 'mē-lē-ə-\ *adjective or noun*
— **me·lio·ra·tor** \-ˌrā-tər\ *noun*

**me·lio·rism** \'mēl-yə-ˌri-zəm, 'mē-lē-ə-\ *noun* (1877)
**:** the belief that the world tends to become better and that humans can aid its betterment
— **me·lio·rist** \-rist\ *adjective or noun*
— **me·lio·ris·tic** \ˌmēl-yə-'ris-tik, ˌmē-lē-ə-\ *adjective*

**me·lis·ma** \mi-'liz-mə\ *noun, plural* **-ma·ta** \-mə-tə\ [New Latin, from Greek, song, melody, from *melizein* to sing, from *melos* song] (circa 1880)
**1 :** a group of notes or tones sung on one syllable in plainsong
**2 :** melodic embellishment or ornamentation
**3 :** CADENZA
— **mel·is·mat·ic** \ˌme-ləz-'ma-tik\ *adjective*

**mell** \'mel\ *verb* [Middle English, from Middle French *mesler*] (14th century)
**:** MIX

**mel·lif·lu·ent** \me-'li-flə-wənt\ *adjective* [Late Latin *mellifluent-, mellifluens*, from Latin *mell-, mel* + *fluent-, fluens*, present participle of *fluere*] (1601)
**:** MELLIFLUOUS
— **mel·lif·lu·ent·ly** *adverb*

**mel·lif·lu·ous** \me-'li-flə-wəs, mə-\ *adjective* [Middle English *mellyfluous*, from Late Latin *mellifluus*, from Latin *mell-, mel* honey + *fluere* to flow; akin to Gothic *milith* honey, Greek *melit-, meli*] (15th century)
**1 :** having a smooth rich flow 〈a *mellifluous* voice〉
**2 :** filled with something (as honey) that sweetens ◆
— **mel·lif·lu·ous·ly** *adverb*
— **mel·lif·lu·ous·ness** *noun*

**mel·lo·phone** \'me-lə-ˌfōn\ *noun* [¹*mellow* + *-phone*] (1926)
**:** a valved brass instrument similar in form and range to the French horn

**mel·lo·tron** \'me-lə-ˌträn\ *noun* [from *Mellotron*, a trademark] (1967)
**:** an electronic keyboard instrument programmed to produce the tape-recorded sounds usually of orchestral instruments

**¹mel·low** \'me-(ˌ)lō\ *adjective* [Middle English *melowe*] (15th century)
**1 a** *of a fruit* **:** tender and sweet because of ripeness **b** *of a wine* **:** well aged and pleasingly mild
**2 a :** made gentle by age or experience **b :** rich and full but free from garishness or stridency **c :** warmed and relaxed by or as if by liquor **d :** PLEASANT, AGREEABLE **e :** LAID-BACK
**3** *of soil* **:** having a soft and loamy consistency
— **mel·low·ly** *adverb*
— **mel·low·ness** *noun*

**²mellow** (1572)
*transitive verb*
**:** to make mellow
*intransitive verb*
**:** to become mellow

**me·lo·de·on** \mə-'lō-dē-ən\ *noun* [German *Melodion*, from *Melodie* melody, from Old French] (1847)
**:** a small reed organ in which a suction bellows draws air inward through the reeds

**me·lod·ic** \mə-'lä-dik\ *adjective* (1823)
**:** of or relating to melody **:** MELODIOUS
— **me·lod·i·cal·ly** \-di-k(ə-)lē\ *adverb*

**me·lo·di·ous** \mə-'lō-dē-əs\ *adjective* (14th century)

**1 :** having a pleasing melody
**2 :** of, relating to, or producing melody
— **me·lo·di·ous·ly** *adverb*
— **me·lo·di·ous·ness** *noun*

**mel·o·dist** \'me-lə-dist\ *noun* (1789)
**1 :** SINGER
**2 :** a composer of melodies

**mel·o·dize** \'me-lə-ˌdīz\ *verb* **-dized; -diz·ing** (1662)
*intransitive verb*
**:** to compose a melody
*transitive verb*
**:** to make melodious **:** set to melody
— **mel·o·diz·er** *noun*

**melo·dra·ma** \'me-lə-ˌdrä-mə, -ˌdra-\ *noun* [modification of French *mélodrame*, from Greek *melos* song + French *drame* drama, from Late Latin *drama*] (1809)
**1 a :** a work (as a movie or play) characterized by extravagant theatricality and by the predominance of plot and physical action over characterization **b :** the genre of dramatic literature constituted by such works
**2 :** something resembling a melodrama or having a melodramatic quality
— **melo·dra·ma·tist** \ˌme-lə-'dra-mə-tist, -'drä-\ *noun*

**melo·dra·mat·ic** \ˌme-lə-drə-'ma-tik\ *adjective* (1816)
**1 :** of, relating to, or characteristic of melodrama
**2 :** appealing to the emotions **:** SENSATIONAL
**synonym** see DRAMATIC
— **melo·dra·mat·i·cal·ly** \-ti-k(ə-)lē\ *adverb*

**melo·dra·mat·ics** \-tiks\ *noun plural but singular or plural in construction* (1915)
**:** melodramatic conduct or writing

**melo·dra·ma·tise** *British variant of* MELODRAMATIZE

**melo·dra·ma·tize** \ˌme-lə-'dra-mə-ˌtīz, -'drä-\ *transitive verb* (1820)
**1 :** to make melodramatic 〈*melodramatize* a situation〉
**2 :** to make a melodrama of (as a novel)
— **melo·dra·ma·ti·za·tion** \-ˌdra-mə-tə-'zā-shən, -ˌdrä-\ *noun*

**mel·o·dy** \'me-lə-dē\ *noun, plural* **-dies** [Middle English *melodie*, from Old French, from Late Latin *melodia*, from Greek *melōidia* chanting, music, from *melos* limb, musical phrase, song (probably akin to Breton *mell* joint) + *aeidein* to sing — more at ODE] (13th century)
**1 :** a sweet or agreeable succession or arrangement of sounds **:** TUNEFULNESS
**2 :** a rhythmic succession of single tones organized as an aesthetic whole

**mel·on** \'me-lən\ *noun, often attributive* [Middle English, from Middle French, from Late Latin *melon-, melo*, short for Latin *melopepon-, melopepo*, from Greek *mēlopepōn*, from *mēlon* apple + *pepōn*, an edible gourd — more at PUMPKIN] (14th century)
**1 :** any of various gourds (as a muskmelon or watermelon) usually eaten raw as fruits
**2 :** something rounded like a melon: as **a :** the rounded organ in the front of the head of some cetaceans **b** *plural, slang* **:** large breasts
**3 a :** a surplus of profits available for distribution to stockholders **b :** a financial windfall

**mel·pha·lan** \'mel-fə-ˌlan\ *noun* [probably from *metha*nol + *ph*en*y*l*alani*ne] (circa 1964)
**:** an antineoplastic drug $C_{13}H_{18}Cl_2N_2O_2$

**Mel·pom·e·ne** \mel-'pä-mə-(ˌ)nē\ *noun* [Latin, from Greek *Melpomenē*]
**:** the Greek Muse of tragedy

**¹melt** \'melt\ *verb* [Middle English, from Old English *meltan*; akin to Old Norse *melta* to digest, Greek *meldein* to melt] (before 12th century)
*intransitive verb*
**1 :** to become altered from a solid to a liquid state usually by heat

**2 a :** DISSOLVE, DISINTEGRATE 〈the sugar *melted* in the coffee〉 **b :** to disappear as if by dissolving 〈her anger *melted* at his kind words〉
**3** *obsolete* **:** to become subdued or crushed (as by sorrow)
**4 :** to become mild, tender, or gentle
**5 :** to lose outline or distinctness **:** BLEND
*transitive verb*
**1 :** to reduce from a solid to a liquid state usually by heat
**2 :** to cause to disappear or disperse
**3 :** to make tender or gentle **:** SOFTEN
— **melt·abil·i·ty** \ˌmel-tə-'bi-lə-tē\ *noun*
— **melt·able** \'mel-tə-bəl\ *adjective*
— **melt·er** *noun*

**²melt** *noun* (1854)
**1 a :** material in the molten state **b :** the mass melted at a single operation or the quantity melted during a specified period
**2 a :** the action or process of melting or the period during which it occurs 〈the spring *melt*〉 **b :** the condition of being melted
**3 :** a sandwich with melted cheese 〈a tuna *melt*〉

**³melt** *noun* [Middle English *milte*, from Old English; akin to Old High German *miltzi* spleen] (before 12th century)
**:** SPLEEN; *especially* **:** spleen of slaughtered animals for use as feed or food

**melt·down** \'melt-ˌdaun\ *noun* (1963)
**1 :** the accidental melting of the core of a nuclear reactor
**2 :** a rapid or disastrous decline or collapse

**melt·ing** \'mel-tiŋ\ *adjective* (1565)
**:** TENDER, DELICATE 〈a love song's *melting* lyric〉
— **melt·ing·ly** *adverb*

**melting point** *noun* (1823)
**:** the temperature at which a solid melts

**melting pot** *noun* (1912)
**1 a :** a place where racial amalgamation and social and cultural assimilation are going on 〈long cherished the myth of the public school as the *melting pot* —M. R. Berube〉 **b :** the population of such a place
**2 :** a process of blending that often results in invigoration or novelty

**mel·ton** \'mel-tʳn\ *noun* [*Melton* Mowbray, town in England] (1823)
**:** a heavy smooth woolen fabric with short nap

**melt·wa·ter** \'melt-ˌwȯ-tər, -ˌwä-\ *noun* (1923)
**:** water derived from the melting of ice and snow

**mem** \'mem\ *noun* [Hebrew *mēm*, literally, water] (circa 1823)
**:** the 13th letter of the Hebrew alphabet — see ALPHABET table

**mem·ber** \'mem-bər\ *noun, often attributive* [Middle English *membre*, from Old French, from Latin *membrum*; akin to Gothic *mimz* flesh, Greek *mēros* thigh] (14th century)
**1 :** a body part or organ: as **a :** LIMB **b :** PENIS **c :** a unit of structure in a plant body
**2 :** one of the individuals composing a group
**3 :** a person baptized or enrolled in a church
**4 :** a constituent part of a whole: as **a :** a syntactic or rhythmic unit of a sentence **:** CLAUSE

---

◇ WORD HISTORY

**mellifluous**   Having a much longer history as a sweetener than cane sugar, honey has since ancient times been a symbol of sweetness. In English we continue to speak of those halcyon days following a wedding as a *honeymoon* and to refer to an eloquent orator as *honey-tongued*. Less obviously, we are using the same metaphor when we speak of a voice as being *mellifluous*. In Latin *mel* meant "honey" and *fluere* meant to "to flow," hence the Late Latin word *mellifluus* literally meant "flowing like honey."

**b :** one of the propositions of a syllogism **c :** one of the elements of a set or class **d :** either of the equated elements in a mathematical equation
**synonym** see PART
**mem·bered** \'mem-bərd\ *adjective* (14th century)
**:** made up of or divided into members
**mem·ber·ship** \'mem-bər-ˌship\ *noun* (1647)
**1 :** the state or status of being a member
**2 :** the body of members ⟨an organization with a large *membership*⟩
**3 :** the relation between an element of a set or class and the set or class — compare INCLUSION 3
**mem·brane** \'mem-ˌbrān\ *noun* [Middle English, from Latin *membrana* skin, parchment, from *membrum*] (15th century)
**1 :** a thin soft pliable sheet or layer especially of animal or plant origin
**2 :** a piece of parchment forming part of a roll
— **mem·braned** \'mem-ˌbrānd\ *adjective*
**mem·bra·nous** \'mem-brə-nəs\ *adjective* (1597)
**1 :** of, relating to, or resembling membrane
**2 :** thin, pliable, and often somewhat transparent ⟨*membranous* leaves⟩
**3 :** characterized or accompanied by the formation of a usually abnormal membrane or membranous layer ⟨*membranous* croup⟩
— **mem·bra·nous·ly** *adverb*
**membranous labyrinth** *noun* (1840)
**:** the sensory structures of the inner ear
**me·men·to** \mə-'men-(ˌ)tō, ÷mō-\ *noun, plural* **-tos** *or* **-toes** [Middle English, from Latin, remember, imperative of *meminisse* to remember; akin to Latin *ment-, mens* mind — more at MIND] (1580)
**:** something that serves to warn or remind; *also* **:** SOUVENIR ◻
**me·men·to mo·ri** \mə-'men-tō-'mōr-ē, -'mȯr-ē\ *noun, plural* **memento mori** [Latin, remember that you must die] (1596)
**:** a reminder of mortality; *especially* **:** DEATH'S-HEAD
**Mem·non** \'mem-ˌnän\ *noun* [Greek *Memnōn*]
**:** an Ethiopian king slain by Achilles at a late stage of the Trojan War
**memo** \'me-(ˌ)mō\ *noun, plural* **mem·os** (1889)
**:** MEMORANDUM
**mem·oir** \'mem-ˌwär, -ˌwȯr\ *noun* [Middle French *memoire*, from *memoire* memory, from Latin *memoria*] (1567)
**1 :** an official note or report **:** MEMORANDUM
**2 a :** a narrative composed from personal experience **b :** AUTOBIOGRAPHY — usually used in plural **c :** BIOGRAPHY
**3 a :** an account of something noteworthy **:** REPORT **b** *plural* **:** the record of the proceedings of a learned society
— **mem·oir·ist** \-ist\ *noun*
**mem·o·ra·bil·ia** \ˌme-mə-rə-'bi-lē-ə, -'bē-lē-ə, -'bil-yə\ *noun plural* [Latin, from neuter plural of *memorabilis*] (circa 1807)
**:** things that are remarkable and worthy of remembrance; *also* **:** things that stir recollection **:** MEMENTOS
**mem·o·ra·bil·i·ty** \-'bi-lə-tē\ *noun* (circa 1661)
**:** the quality or state of being easy to remember or worth remembering
**mem·o·ra·ble** \'mem-rə-bəl, 'mə-mə-rə-, 'me-mər-\ *adjective* [Middle English, from Latin *memorabilis*, from *memorare* to remind, mention, from *memor* mindful] (15th century)
**:** worth remembering **:** NOTABLE
— **mem·o·ra·ble·ness** *noun*
— **mem·o·ra·bly** \-blē\ *adverb*
**mem·o·ran·dum** \ˌme-mə-'ran-dəm\ *noun, plural* **-dums** *or* **-da** \-də\ [Middle English, to be remembered, from Latin, neuter of *memorandus*, gerundive of *memorare*] (circa 1543)
**1 :** an informal record; *also* **:** a written reminder

**2 :** an informal written note of a transaction or proposed instrument
**3 a :** an informal diplomatic communication **b :** a usually brief communication written for interoffice circulation **c :** a communication that contains directive, advisory, or informative matter ◻
**¹me·mo·ri·al** \mə-'mōr-ē-əl, -'mȯr-\ *adjective* [Middle English, from Latin *memorialis*, from *memoria* memory] (14th century)
**1 :** serving to preserve remembrance **:** COMMEMORATIVE
**2 :** of or relating to memory
— **me·mo·ri·al·ly** \-ə-lē\ *adverb*
**²memorial** *noun* (14th century)
**1 :** something that keeps remembrance alive: as **a :** MONUMENT **b :** something (as a speech or ceremony) that commemorates **c :** KEEPSAKE, MEMENTO
**2 a :** RECORD, MEMOIR ⟨language and literature . . . the *memorials* of another age —J. H. Fisher⟩ **b :** MEMORANDUM, NOTE; *specifically* **:** a legal abstract **c :** a statement of facts addressed to a government and often accompanied by a petition or remonstrance
**Memorial Day** *noun* (1869)
**1 :** May 30 formerly observed as a legal holiday in most states of the U.S. in remembrance of war dead
**2 :** the last Monday in May observed as a legal holiday in most states of the U.S.
**3 :** CONFEDERATE MEMORIAL DAY
**me·mo·ri·al·ise** *British variant of* MEMORIALIZE
**me·mo·ri·al·ist** \mə-'mōr-ē-ə-list, -'mȯr-\ *noun* (1706)
**1 :** a person who writes or signs a memorial
**2 :** a person who writes a memoir
**me·mo·ri·al·ize** \-ˌlīz\ *transitive verb* **-ized; -iz·ing** (1798)
**1 :** to address or petition by a memorial
**2 :** COMMEMORATE
**memorial park** *noun* (circa 1928)
**:** CEMETERY
**me·mo·ri·ter** \mə-'mȯr-ə-ˌter, -'mär-\ *adjective* [Latin, adverb, by memory, from *memor*] (circa 1812)
**:** marked by emphasis on memorization
**mem·o·rise** *British variant of* MEMORIZE
**mem·o·rize** \'me-mə-ˌrīz\ *transitive verb* **-rized; -riz·ing** (1838)
**:** to commit to memory **:** learn by heart
— **mem·o·riz·able** \ˌme-mə-'rī-zə-bəl\ *adjective*
— **mem·o·ri·za·tion** \ˌme-mə-rə-'zā-shən, ˌme-mə-(ˌ)rī-, ˌmem-rə-\ *noun*
— **mem·o·riz·er** *noun*
**mem·o·ry** \'mem-rē, 'me-mə-\ *noun, plural* **-ries** [Middle English *memorie*, from Middle French *memoire*, from Latin *memoria*, from *memor* mindful; akin to Old English *gemimor* well-known, Greek *mermēra* care, Sanskrit *smarati* he remembers] (14th century)
**1 a :** the power or process of reproducing or recalling what has been learned and retained especially through associative mechanisms **b :** the store of things learned and retained from an organism's activity or experience as evidenced by modification of structure or behavior or by recall and recognition
**2 a :** commemorative remembrance ⟨erected a statue in *memory* of the hero⟩ **b :** the fact or condition of being remembered ⟨days of recent *memory*⟩
**3 a :** a particular act of recall or recollection **b :** an image or impression of one that is remembered ⟨fond *memories* of her youth⟩ **c :** the time within which past events can be or are remembered ⟨within the *memory* of living men⟩
**4 a :** a device or a component of a device in which information especially for a computer can be inserted and stored and from which it may be extracted when wanted **b :** capacity for storing information ⟨four megabytes of *memory*⟩

**5 :** a capacity for showing effects as the result of past treatment or for returning to a former condition — used especially of a material (as metal or plastic) ☆
**memory lane** *noun* (1954)
**:** an imaginary path through the nostalgically remembered past — usually used in such phrases as *a walk down memory lane*
**memory trace** *noun* (1923)
**:** ENGRAM
**mem·sa·hib** \'mem-ˌsä-(ˌ)hib, -ˌsäb\ *noun* [Hindi, from English *ma'am* + Hindi *sahib* sahib] (1857)
**:** a white foreign woman of high social status living in India; *especially* **:** the wife of a British official
**men** *plural of* MAN
**men-** *or* **meno-** *combining form* [New Latin, from Greek *mēn* month — more at MOON]
**:** menstruation ⟨*menorrhagia*⟩
**¹men·ace** \'me-nəs\ *noun* [Middle English, from Middle French, from Latin *minacia*, from *minac-, minax* threatening, from *minari* to threaten — more at MOUNT] (14th century)
**1 :** a show of intention to inflict harm **:** THREAT

---

---

\ə\ abut  \ᵊ\ kitten  \ər\ further  \a\ ash  \ā\ ace
\ä\ mop, mar  \aు\ out  \ch\ chin  \e\ bet  \ē\ easy
\g\ go  \i\ hit  \ī\ ice  \j\ job  \ŋ\ sing  \ō\ go
\ȯ\ law  \ȯi\ boy  \th\ thin  \t̲h̲\ the  \ü\ loot  \ు\ foot
\y\ yet  \zh\ vision  *see also* Guide to Pronunciation

**2 a** : one that represents a threat : DANGER **b** : a person who causes annoyance
²**menace** *verb* **men·aced; men·ac·ing** (14th century)
*transitive verb*
**1** : to make a show of intention to harm
**2** : to represent or pose a threat to : ENDANGER
*intransitive verb*
: to act in a threatening manner
— **men·ac·ing·ly** \-nə-siŋ-lē\ *adverb*
**me·nad** *variant of* MAENAD
**men·a·di·one** \,me-nə-'dī-,ōn, -dī-'\ *noun* [*methyl* + *napthalene* + *di-* + *ketone*] (1941)
: a yellow crystalline compound $C_{11}H_8O_2$ with the biological activity of natural vitamin K
**mé·nage** \mā-'näzh\ *noun* [French, from Old French *mesnage* dwelling, from (assumed) Vulgar Latin *mansionaticum*, from Latin *mansion-, mansio* mansion] (1698)
: a domestic establishment : HOUSEHOLD; *also* : HOUSEKEEPING
**mé·nage à trois** \-ä-'trwä\ *noun* [French, literally, household for three] (1891)
: an arrangement in which three persons (as a married pair and the lover of one of the pair) share sexual relations especially while living together
**me·nag·er·ie** \mə-'naj-rē, -'na-jə- *also* -'nazh-rē, -'na-zhə-\ *noun* [French *ménagerie*, from Middle French, management of a household or farm, from *menage*] (1676)
**1 a** : a place where animals are kept and trained especially for exhibition **b** : a collection of wild or foreign animals kept especially for exhibition
**2** : a varied mixture ⟨a wonderful *menagerie* of royal hangers-on —V. S. Pritchett⟩
**men·ar·che** \'me-,när-kē\ *noun* [New Latin, from *men-* + Greek *archē* beginning] (1900)
: the beginning of the menstrual function; *especially* : the first menstrual period of an individual
— **men·ar·che·al** \,me-när-'kē-əl\ *adjective*
¹**mend** \'mend\ *verb* [Middle English, short for *amenden* — more at AMEND] (13th century)
*transitive verb*
**1** : to free from faults or defects: as **a** : to improve in manners or morals : REFORM **b** : to set right : CORRECT **c** : to put into good shape or working order again : patch up : REPAIR **d** : to improve or strengthen (as a relationship) by negotiation or conciliation — used chiefly in the phrase *mend fences* ⟨spends the weekend *mending* political fences —E. O. Hauser⟩ **e** : to restore to health : CURE
**2** : to make amends or atonement for ⟨least said, soonest *mended*⟩
*intransitive verb*
**1** : to improve morally : REFORM
**2** : to become corrected or improved
**3** : to improve in health; *also* : HEAL ☆
— **mend·able** \'men-də-bəl\ *adjective*
— **mend·er** *noun*
²**mend** *noun* (14th century)
**1** : an act of mending : REPAIR
**2** : a mended place
— **on the mend** : getting better : IMPROVING
**men·da·cious** \men-'dā-shəs\ *adjective* [Latin *mendac-, mendax* — more at AMEND] (1616)
: given to or characterized by deception or falsehood or divergence from absolute truth ⟨*mendacious* tales of his adventures⟩
**synonym** *see* DISHONEST
— **men·da·cious·ly** *adverb*
— **men·da·cious·ness** *noun*
**men·dac·i·ty** \men-'da-sə-tē\ *noun, plural* **-ties** (1646)
**1** : the quality or state of being mendacious
**2** : LIE
**Men·de** \'men-dē, -dā\ *noun, plural* **Mende** *or* **Mendes** (1732)
**1** : a Mande language of southern Sierra Leone and eastern Liberia

**2** : a member of a people speaking Mende
**men·de·le·vi·um** \,men-də-'lē-vē-əm, -'lā-\ *noun* [New Latin, from Dmitry *Mendeleyev*] (1955)
: a radioactive element that is artificially produced — see ELEMENT table
**Men·de·lian** \men-'dē-lē-ən, -'dēl-yən\ *adjective* (1901)
: of, relating to, or according with Mendel's laws or Mendelism
— **Mendelian** *noun*
**Mendelian factor** *noun* (1927)
: GENE
**Mendelian inheritance** *noun* (circa 1923)
: PARTICULATE INHERITANCE
**Men·del·ism** \'men-dªl-,i-zəm\ *noun* (1903)
: the principles or the operations of Mendel's laws; *also* : PARTICULATE INHERITANCE
— **Men·del·ist** \-dªl-ist\ *adjective or noun*
**Men·del's law** \'men-dªlz-\ *noun* [Gregor *Mendel*] (1903)
**1** : a principle in genetics: hereditary units occur in pairs that separate during gamete formation so that every gamete receives but one member of a pair — called also *law of segregation*
**2** : a principle in genetics limited and modified by the subsequent discovery of the phenomenon of linkage: the different pairs of hereditary units are distributed to the gametes independently of each other, the gametes combine at random, and the various combinations of hereditary pairs occur in the zygotes according to the laws of chance — called also *law of independent assortment*
**3** : a principle in genetics proved subsequently to be subject to many limitations: because one of each pair of hereditary units dominates the other in expression, characters are inherited alternatively on an all-or-nothing basis — called also *law of dominance*
**men·di·can·cy** \'men-di-kən(t)-sē\ *noun* (1790)
**1** : the condition of being a beggar
**2** : the practice of begging
**men·di·cant** \'men-di-kənt\ *noun* [Middle English, from Latin *mendicant-, mendicans*, present participle of *mendicare* to beg, from *mendicus* beggar — more at AMEND] (14th century)
**1** : BEGGAR 1
**2** *often capitalized* : a member of a religious order (as the Franciscans) combining monastic life and outside religious activity and originally owning neither personal nor community property : FRIAR
— **mendicant** *adjective*
**men·dic·i·ty** \men-'di-sə-tē\ *noun* [Middle English *mendicite*, from Middle French *mendicité*, from Latin *mendicitat-, mendicitas*, from *mendicus*] (15th century)
: MENDICANCY
**Men·e·la·us** \,me-nªl-'ā-əs\ *noun* [Latin, from Greek *Menelaos*]
: a king of Sparta, brother of Agamemnon, and husband of the abducted Helen of Troy
**men·folk** \'men-,fōk\ *or* **men·folks** \-,fōks\ *noun plural* (1802)
**1** : men in general
**2** : the men of a family or community
**men·ha·den** \men-'hā-dªn, mən-\ *noun, plural* **-den** *also* **-dens** [of Algonquian origin; akin to Narraganset *munnawhatteaûg* menhaden] (1792)
: a marine fish (*Brevoortia tyrannus*) of the herring family abundant along the Atlantic coast of the U.S. where it is used for bait or converted into oil and fertilizer; *also* : any of several congeneric fishes
**men·hir** \'men-,hir\ *noun* [French, from Breton, from *men* stone + *hir* long] (1840)
: a single upright rude monolith usually of prehistoric origin
¹**me·nial** \'mē-nē-əl, -nyəl\ *noun* (14th century)

: a person doing menial work; *specifically* : a domestic servant or retainer
²**menial** *adjective* [Middle English *meynial*, from *meynie* household, retinue, from Old French *mesnie*, from (assumed) Vulgar Latin *mansionata*, from Latin *mansion-, mansio* dwelling — more at MANSION] (15th century)
**1** : of or relating to servants : LOWLY
**2 a** : appropriate to a servant : HUMBLE, SERVILE ⟨answered in *menial* tones⟩ **b** : lacking interest or dignity ⟨a *menial* task⟩
— **me·nial·ly** *adverb*
**Mé·niè·re's disease** \mən-'yerz-, 'men-yərz-\ *noun* [Prosper *Ménière* (died 1862) French physician] (1876)
: a disorder of the membranous labyrinth of the inner ear that is marked by recurrent attacks of dizziness, tinnitus, and deafness — called also *Ménière's syndrome*
**mening-** *or* **meningo-** *also* **meningi-** *combining form* [New Latin, from *mening-, meninx*]
**1** : meninges ⟨*meningo*coccus⟩ ⟨*meningi*tis⟩
**2** : meninges and ⟨*meningo*encephalitis⟩
**men·in·ge·al** \me-nən-'jē-əl\ *adjective* (1829)
: of, relating to, or affecting the meninges
**meninges** *plural of* MENINX
**me·nin·gi·o·ma** \mə-,nin-jē-'ō-mə\ *noun, plural* **-mas** *or* **-ma·ta** \-'ō-mə-tə\ [New Latin] (1922)
: a slow-growing encapsulated tumor arising from the meninges and often causing damage by pressing upon the brain and adjacent parts
**men·in·gi·tis** \,me-nən-'jī-təs\ *noun, plural* **-git·i·des** \-'ji-tə-,dēz\ [New Latin] (1828)
**1** : inflammation of the meninges and especially of the pia mater and the arachnoid
**2** : a usually bacterial disease in which inflammation of the meninges occurs
— **men·in·git·ic** \-'ji-tik\ *adjective*
**me·nin·go·coc·cus** \mə-,nin-gə-'kä-kəs, -,nin-jə-\ *noun, plural* **-coc·ci** \-'käk-,sī, -,sē; -'kä-,kī, -,kē\ [New Latin] (circa 1893)
: the bacterium (*Neisseria meningitidis*) that causes cerebrospinal meningitis
— **me·nin·go·coc·cal** \-'kä-kəl\ *also* **me·nin·go·coc·cic** \-'käk-sik, -'kä-kik\ *adjective*
**me·nin·go·en·ceph·a·li·tis** \-gō-ən-,se-fə-'lī-təs, -jō-\ *noun, plural* **-lit·i·des** \-'li-tə-,dēz\ [New Latin] (circa 1860)
: inflammation of the brain and meninges
— **me·nin·go·en·ceph·a·lit·ic** \-'li-tik\ *adjective*
**me·ninx** \'mē-niŋ(k)s, 'me-\ *noun, plural* **me·nin·ges** \mə-'nin-(,)jēz\ [New Latin, from Greek *mēning-, mēninx* membrane] (1543)
: any of the three membranes that envelop the brain and spinal cord
**me·nis·cus** \mə-'nis-kəs\ *noun, plural* **me·nis·ci** \-'ni-,skī, -,skē, -,sī\ *also* **me·nis·cus·es** [New Latin, from Greek *mēniskos*, from diminutive of *mēnē* moon, crescent — more at MOON] (1693)
**1** : a concavo-convex lens
**2** : a crescent or crescent-shaped body
**3** : the curved upper surface of a column of liquid
**4** : a fibrous cartilage within a joint especially of the knee

---

☆ **SYNONYMS**
**Mend, repair, patch, rebuild** mean to put into good order something that has been injured, damaged, or defective. MEND implies making whole or sound something broken, torn, or injured ⟨*mended* the torn dress⟩. REPAIR applies to the fixing of more extensive damage or dilapidation ⟨*repaired* the back steps⟩. PATCH implies an often temporary fixing of a hole or break with new material ⟨*patch* worn jeans⟩. REBUILD suggests making like new without completely replacing ⟨a *rebuilt* automobile engine⟩.

**Men·no·nite** \'me-nə-ˌnīt\ *noun* [German *Mennonit*, from *Menno* Simons] (1565)
: a member of any of various Protestant groups derived from the Anabaptist movement in Holland and characterized by congregational autonomy and rejection of military service

**meno-** — see MEN-

**me·no mos·so** \ˌmā-nō-'mó(s)-(ˌ)sō\ *adverb* [Italian] (circa 1854)
: less rapid — used as a direction in music

**men·o·pause** \'me-nə-ˌpóz, 'mē-\ *noun* [French *ménopause*, from *méno-* men- + *pause* stop, pause] (1872)
: the period of natural cessation of menstruation occurring usually between the ages of 45 and 50
— **men·o·paus·al** \ˌme-nə-'pó-zəl, ˌmē-\ *adjective*

**me·no·rah** \mə-'nōr-ə, -'nór-\ *noun* [Hebrew *měnōrāh* candlestick] (1888)
: a candelabrum with seven or nine candles that is used in Jewish worship

**men·or·rha·gia** \ˌme-nə-'rā-j(ē-)ə, -'rä-zhə; -'rä-jə, -zhə\ *noun* [New Latin] (circa 1784)
: abnormally profuse menstrual flow

*menorah*

**men·sal** \'men-səl\ *adjective* [Middle English, from Late Latin *mensalis*, from Latin *mensa* table] (15th century)
: of, relating to, or done at the table

**mensch** \'men(t)sh\ *noun* [Yiddish *mentsh* human being, from Middle High German *mensch*, from Old High German *mennisco*; akin to Old English *man* human being, man] (1953)
: a person of integrity and honor

**¹mense** \'men(t)s\ *noun* [Middle English *menske* honor, from Old Norse *mennska* humanity; akin to Old English *man*] (circa 1500)
*chiefly Scottish* : PROPRIETY
— **mense·ful** \-fəl\ *adjective*
— **mense·less** \-ləs\ *adjective*

**²mense** *transitive verb* **mensed; mens·ing** (1540)
*chiefly Scottish* : to do honor to : GRACE

**men·ses** \'men-ˌsēz\ *noun plural but singular or plural in construction* [Latin, literally, months, plural of *mensis* month — more at MOON] (1597)
: the menstrual flow

**Men·she·vik** \'men(t)-shə-ˌvik, -ˌvēk\ *noun, plural* **Mensheviks** *or* **Men·she·vi·ki** \ˌmen(t)-shə-'vi-kē, -'vē-kē\ [Russian *men'shevik*, from *men'she* less; from their forming the minority group of the party] (1907)
: a member of a wing of the Russian Social Democratic party before and during the Russian Revolution believing in the gradual achievement of socialism by parliamentary methods in opposition to the Bolsheviks
— **Men·she·vism** \'men(t)-shə-ˌvi-zəm\ *noun*
— **Men·she·vist** \-vist\ *noun or adjective*

**mens rea** \menz-'rē-ə\ *noun* [New Latin, literally, guilty mind] (1861)
: criminal intent

**men's room** *noun* (1929)
: a room equipped with one or more sinks, toilets, and usually urinals for the use of men and boys

**men·stru·al** \'men(t)-strü-əl, -strəl\ *adjective* (14th century)
: of or relating to menstruation

**men·stru·ate** \'men(t)-strü-ˌwāt, 'men-ˌstrāt\ *intransitive verb* **-at·ed; -at·ing** [Late Latin *menstruatus*, past participle of *menstruari*, from Latin *menstrua* menses, from neuter plural of *menstruus* monthly, from *mensis*] (1800)
: to undergo menstruation

**men·stru·a·tion** \ˌmen(t)-strü-'wā-shən, men-'strä-\ *noun* (circa 1784)
: a discharging of blood, secretions, and tissue debris from the uterus that recurs in nonpregnant breeding-age primate females at approximately monthly intervals and that is considered to represent a readjustment of the uterus to the nonpregnant state following proliferative changes accompanying the preceding ovulation; *also* : PERIOD 6c

**men·stru·um** \'men(t)-strü-əm, -strəm\ *noun, plural* **-stru·ums** *or* **-strua** \-strü-ə, -strä\ [Medieval Latin, literally, menses, alteration of Latin *menstrua*] (1612)
: a substance that dissolves a solid or holds it in suspension : SOLVENT

**men·su·ra·ble** \'men(t)s-rə-bəl, 'men(t)sh-; 'men(t)-sə-rə-, -shə-\ *adjective* [Late Latin *mensurabilis*, from *mensurare* to measure, from Latin *mensura* measure — more at MEASURE] (1604)
**1** : capable of being measured : MEASURABLE
**2** : MENSURAL 1
— **men·sur·abil·i·ty** \ˌmen(t)s-rə-'bi-lə-tē, ˌmen(t)sh-; ˌmen(t)-sə-rə-, -shə-\ *noun*

**men·su·ral** \'men(t)s-rəl, 'men(t)sh-; 'men(t)-sə-rəl, -shə-\ *adjective* [Late Latin *mensuralis* measurable, from Latin *mensura*] (1609)
**1** : of, relating to, or being polyphonic music originating in the 13th century with each note having a definite and exact time value
**2** : of or relating to measure

**men·su·ra·tion** \ˌmen(t)-sə-'rā-shən, -shə-\ *noun* (1571)
**1** : the act of measuring : MEASUREMENT
**2** : geometry applied to the computation of lengths, areas, or volumes from given dimensions or angles

**mens·wear** \'menz-ˌwar, -ˌwer\ *noun* (1908)
: clothing for men

**-ment** \mənt\ *noun suffix* [Middle English, from Old French, from Latin *-mentum*; akin to Latin *-men*, suffix denoting concrete result, Greek *-mat-*, *-ma*]
**1 a** : concrete result, object, or agent of a (specified) action ⟨embank*ment*⟩ ⟨entangle*ment*⟩ **b** : concrete means or instrument of a (specified) action ⟨entertain*ment*⟩
**2 a** : action : process ⟨encircle*ment*⟩ ⟨develop*ment*⟩ **b** : place of a (specified) action ⟨encamp*ment*⟩
**3** : state or condition resulting from (a specified action) ⟨involve*ment*⟩

**¹men·tal** \'men-t°l\ *adjective* [Middle English, from Middle French, from Late Latin *mentalis*, from Latin *ment-*, *mens* mind — more at MIND] (15th century)
**1 a** : of or relating to the mind; *specifically* : of or relating to the total emotional and intellectual response of an individual to external reality ⟨*mental* health⟩ **b** : of or relating to intellectual as contrasted with emotional activity **c** : of, relating to, or being intellectual as contrasted with overt physical activity **d** : occurring or experienced in the mind : INNER ⟨*mental* anguish⟩ **e** : relating to the mind, its activity, or its products as an object of study : IDEOLOGICAL **f** : relating to spirit or idea as opposed to matter
**2 a** (1) : of, relating to, or affected by a psychiatric disorder ⟨a *mental* patient⟩ ⟨*mental* illness⟩ (2) : mentally disordered : MAD, CRAZY **b** : intended for the care or treatment of persons affected by psychiatric disorders ⟨*mental* hospitals⟩
**3** : of or relating to telepathic or mind-reading powers
— **men·tal·ly** \-t°l-ē\ *adverb*

**²mental** *adjective* [Latin *mentum* chin — more at MOUTH] (circa 1727)
: of or relating to the chin : GENIAL

**mental age** *noun* (1912)
: a measure used in psychological testing that expresses an individual's mental attainment in terms of the number of years it takes an average child to reach the same level

**mental deficiency** *noun* (1856)
: MENTAL RETARDATION

**men·tal·ist** \'men-t°l-ist\ *noun* (1930)
: MIND READER

**men·tal·is·tic** \ˌmen-t°l-'is-tik\ *adjective* (1882)
**1** : of or relating to any school of psychology or psychiatry that in contrast to behaviorism values subjective data (as those gained by introspection) in the study and explanation of behavior
**2** : of or relating to mental phenomena
— **men·tal·ism** \'men-t°l-ˌi-zəm\ *noun*

**men·tal·i·ty** \men-'ta-lə-tē\ *noun, plural* **-ties** (1691)
**1** : mental power or capacity : INTELLIGENCE
**2** : mode or way of thought : OUTLOOK

**mental retardation** *noun* (1914)
: subaverage intellectual ability that is equivalent to or less than an IQ of 70, is present from birth or infancy, and is manifested especially by abnormal development, by learning difficulties, and by problems in social adjustment

**men·ta·tion** \men-'tā-shən\ *noun* [Latin *ment-*, *mens* + English *-ation*] (1850)
: mental activity

**men·thol** \'men-ˌthól, -ˌthōl\ *noun* [German, ultimately from Latin *mentha* mint] (1876)
: a crystalline alcohol $C_{10}H_{20}O$ that occurs especially in mint oils and has the odor and cooling properties of peppermint

**men·tho·lat·ed** \'men(t)-thə-ˌlā-təd\ *adjective* (1922)
: containing or impregnated with menthol ⟨a *mentholated* salve⟩

**¹men·tion** \'men(t)-shən\ *noun* [Middle English *mencioun*, from Middle French *mention*, from Latin *mention-*, *mentio*; akin to Latin *meminisse* to remember, *ment-*, *mens* mind] (14th century)
**1** : the act or an instance of citing or calling attention to someone or something especially in a casual or incidental manner
**2** : formal citation for outstanding achievement

**²mention** *transitive verb* **men·tioned; men·tion·ing** \'men(t)-sh(ə-)niŋ\ (1530)
: to make mention of : refer to; *also* : to cite for outstanding achievement
— **men·tion·able** \'men(t)-sh(ə-)nə-bəl\ *adjective*
— **men·tion·er** \-sh(ə-)nər\ *noun*
— **not to mention** : to say nothing of

**¹men·tor** \'men-ˌtór, -tər\ *noun* [Latin, from Greek *Mentōr*]
**1** *capitalized* : a friend of Odysseus entrusted with the education of Odysseus' son Telemachus
**2 a** : a trusted counselor or guide **b** : TUTOR, COACH
— **men·tor·ship** \-ˌship\ *noun*

**²mentor** *transitive verb* (1983)
: to serve as a mentor for

**men·tum** \'men-təm\ *noun, plural* **men·ta** \-tə\ [Latin, chin — more at MOUTH] (1826)
: a median plate of the labium of an insect

**menu** \'men-(ˌ)yü, 'mān-\ *noun, plural* **menus** [French, from *menu* small, detailed, from Old French — more at MINUET] (1837)
**1 a** : a list of the dishes that may be ordered (as in a restaurant) or that are to be served (as at a banquet) **b** (1) : a comparable list or assortment of offerings ⟨a *menu* of television programs⟩ (2) : a list shown on the display of a computer from which a user can select the operation the computer is to perform

\ə\ abut \°\ kitten \ər\ further \a\ ash \ā\ ace
\ä\ mop, mar \aú\ out \ch\ chin \e\ bet \ē\ easy
\g\ go \i\ hit \ī\ ice \j\ job \ŋ\ sing \ō\ go
\ó\ law \ói\ boy \th\ thin \t͟h\ the \ü\ loot \ú\ foot
\y\ yet \zh\ vision *see also* Guide to Pronunciation

**2 :** the dishes available for or served at a meal; *also* **:** the meal itself ◆

**menu–driv·en** \-ˌdri-vən\ *adjective* (1977)
**:** relating to or being a computer program in which options are offered to the user via menus

**me·ow** \mē-ˈau̇\ *noun* [imitative] (1600)
**1 :** the cry of a cat
**2 :** a spiteful or malicious remark
— **meow** *intransitive verb*

**me·per·i·dine** \mə-ˈper-ə-ˌdēn\ *noun* [methyl + piperidine] (1947)
**:** a synthetic narcotic drug $C_{15}H_{21}NO_2$ used in the form of its hydrochloride as an analgesic, sedative, and antispasmodic

**Meph·is·toph·e·les** \ˌme-fə-ˈstä-fə-ˌlēz\ *noun* [German]
**:** a chief devil in the Faust legend
— **Me·phis·to·phe·lian** \ˌmef-ə-stə-ˈfēl-yən, mə-ˌfis-tə-\ *or* **Me·phis·to·phe·lean** \same, or ˌme-fə-ˌstä-fə-ˈlē-ən\ *adjective*

**me·phit·ic** \mə-ˈfi-tik\ *adjective* (circa 1623)
**:** of, relating to, or resembling mephitis **:** foul-smelling

**me·phi·tis** \mə-ˈfī-təs\ *noun* [Latin] (circa 1706)
**:** a noxious, pestilential, or foul exhalation from the earth; *also* **:** STENCH

**mep·ro·bam·ate** \ˌme-prō-ˈba-ˌmāt\ *noun* [methyl + *propyl* + dicar*bamate*] (1955)
**:** a bitter carbamate $C_9H_{18}N_2O_4$ used as a tranquilizer

**-mer** *noun combining form* [International Scientific Vocabulary, from Greek *meros* part — more at MERIT]
**:** member of a (specified) class ⟨mono*mer*⟩

**mer·bro·min** \ˌmər-ˈbrō-mən\ *noun* [*mercuric* + *brom-* + fluorescein] (1945)
**:** a green crystalline mercurial compound $C_{20}H_8Br_2HgNa_2O_6$ used as a topical antiseptic and germicide in the form of its red solution

**Mer·cal·li scale** \mer-ˈkä-lē-, (ˌ)mər-\ *noun* [Giuseppe *Mercalli* (died 1914) Italian priest and geologist] (1921)
**:** a scale of earthquake intensity ranging from I for an earthquake detected only by seismographs to XII for one causing total destruction of all buildings

**mer·can·tile** \ˈmər-kən-ˌtēl, -ˌtīl\ *adjective* [French, from Italian, from *mercante* merchant, from Latin *mercant-, mercans,* from present participle of *mercari* to trade — more at MARKET] (1642)
**1 :** of or relating to merchants or trading
**2 :** of, relating to, or having the characteristics of mercantilism ⟨*mercantile* system⟩

**mer·can·til·ism** \-ˌtē-ˌli-zəm, -ˌtī-, -tə-\ *noun* (1873)
**1 :** the theory or practice of mercantile pursuits **:** COMMERCIALISM
**2 :** an economic system developing during the decay of feudalism to unify and increase the power and especially the monetary wealth of a nation by a strict governmental regulation of the entire national economy usually through policies designed to secure an accumulation of bullion, a favorable balance of trade, the development of agriculture and manufactures, and the establishment of foreign trading monopolies
— **mer·can·til·ist** \-list\ *noun or adjective*
— **mer·can·til·is·tic** \ˌmər-kən-ˌtē-ˈlis-tik, -ˌtī-, -tə-\ *adjective*

**mer·cap·tan** \(ˌ)mər-ˈkap-ˌtan\ *noun* [German, from Danish, from Medieval Latin *mercurium captans,* literally, seizing mercury] (1835)
**:** any of various compounds that contain a thiol functional group **:** THIOL 1

**mer·cap·to·pu·rine** \(ˌ)mər-ˌkap-tə-ˈpyür-ˌēn\ *noun* [*mercapt*an + *-o-* + *purine*] (circa 1952)
**:** an antimetabolite $C_5H_4N_4S$ that interferes especially with the metabolism of purine bases

and the biosynthesis of nucleic acids and that is sometimes useful in the treatment of acute leukemia

**Mer·ca·tor** \(ˌ)mər-ˈkā-tər\ *adjective* (circa 1876)
**:** of, relating to, or drawn on the Mercator projection

**Mercator projection** *noun* [Gerardus *Mercator*] (circa 1881)
**:** a conformal map projection in the usual case of which the meridians are drawn parallel to each other and the parallels of latitude are straight lines whose distance from each other increases with their distance from the equator

**Mercator projection**

**¹mer·ce·nary** \ˈmər-sᵊn-ˌer-ē\ *noun, plural* **-nar·ies** [Middle English, from Latin *mercenarius,* irregular from *merced-, merces* wages — more at MERCY] (14th century)
**:** one that serves merely for wages; *especially* **:** a soldier hired into foreign service

**²mercenary** *adjective* (1532)
**1 :** serving merely for pay or sordid advantage **:** VENAL; *also* **:** GREEDY
**2 :** hired for service in the army of a foreign country
— **mer·ce·nar·i·ly** \ˌmər-sᵊn-ˈer-ə-lē\ *adverb*
— **mer·ce·nar·i·ness** \ˈmər-sᵊn-ˌer-ē-nəs\ *noun*

**mer·cer** \ˈmər-sər\ *noun* [Middle English, from Old French *mercier* merchant, from *mers* merchandise, from Latin *merc-, merx*] (13th century)
*British* **:** a dealer in usually expensive fabrics

**mer·cer·ise** *British variant of* MERCERIZE

**mer·cer·ize** \ˈmər-sə-ˌrīz\ *transitive verb* **-ized; -iz·ing** [John *Mercer* (died 1866) English calico printer] (1859)
**:** to give (as cotton yarn) luster, strength, and receptiveness to dyes by treatment under tension with caustic soda
— **mer·cer·i·za·tion** \ˌmərs-rə-ˈzā-shən, ˌmər-sə-\ *noun*

**mer·cery** \ˈmərs-rē, ˈmər-sə-\ *noun, plural* **-cer·ies** (14th century)
*British* **:** a mercer's wares, shop, or occupation

**¹mer·chan·dise** \ˈmər-chən-ˌdīz, -ˌdīs\ *noun* [Middle English *marchaundise,* from Old French *marcheandise,* from *marcheant*] (13th century)
**1** *archaic* **:** the occupation of a merchant **:** TRADE
**2 :** the commodities or goods that are bought and sold in business **:** WARES

**²mer·chan·dise** *also* **mer·chan·dize** \-ˌdīz\ *verb* **-dised** *also* **-dized; -dis·ing** *also* **diz·ing** (14th century)
*intransitive verb*
*archaic* **:** to carry on commerce **:** TRADE
*transitive verb*
**1 :** to buy and sell in business
**2 :** to promote for or as if for sale ⟨*merchandise* a movie star⟩
— **mer·chan·dis·er** *noun*

**mer·chan·dis·ing** *also* **mer·chan·diz·ing** \-ˌdī-ziŋ\ *noun* (1932)
**:** sales promotion as a comprehensive function including market research, development of

new products, coordination of manufacture and marketing, and effective advertising and selling

**¹mer·chant** \ˈmər-chənt\ *noun* [Middle English *marchant,* from Old French *marcheant,* from (assumed) Vulgar Latin *mercatant-, mercatans,* from present participle of *mercatare* to trade, frequentative of Latin *mercari* — more at MARKET] (13th century)
**1 :** a buyer and seller of commodities for profit **:** TRADER
**2 :** the operator of a retail business **:** STOREKEEPER
**3 :** one that is noted for a particular quality or activity **:** SPECIALIST ⟨a speed *merchant* on the base paths⟩
— **merchant** *adjective*

**²merchant** (14th century)
*intransitive verb*
*archaic* **:** to deal or trade as a merchant
*transitive verb*
**:** to deal or trade in

**mer·chant·able** \ˈmər-chən-tə-bəl\ *adjective* (15th century)
**:** of commercially acceptable quality **:** SALABLE
— **mer·chant·abil·i·ty** \ˌmər-chən-tə-ˈbi-lə-tē\ *noun*

**merchant bank** *noun* (1930)
*chiefly British* **:** a bank that specializes in bankers' acceptances and in underwriting or syndicating equity or bond issues
— **merchant banker** *noun*
— **merchant banking** *noun*

**mer·chant·man** \ˈmər-chənt-mən\ *noun* (15th century)
**1** *archaic* **:** MERCHANT
**2 :** a ship used in commerce

**merchant marine** *noun* (1855)
**1 :** the privately or publicly owned commercial ships of a nation
**2 :** the personnel of a merchant marine

**merchant ship** *noun* (15th century)
**:** MERCHANTMAN 2

**Mer·cian** \ˈmər-sh(ē-)ən\ *noun* (1513)
**1 :** a native or inhabitant of Mercia
**2 :** the Old English dialect of Mercia
— **Mercian** *adjective*

**mer·ci·ful** \ˈmər-si-fəl\ *adjective* (14th century)
**:** full of mercy **:** COMPASSIONATE; *also* **:** providing relief
— **mer·ci·ful·ness** \-fəl-nəs\ *noun*

**mer·ci·ful·ly** \-f(ə-)lē\ *adverb* (14th century)
**1 :** in a merciful manner
**2 :** FORTUNATELY 2 ⟨*mercifully* we didn't have to attend the meeting⟩

**mer·ci·less** \ˈmər-si-ləs\ *adjective* (14th century)
**:** having or showing no mercy **:** PITILESS
— **mer·ci·less·ly** *adverb*
— **mer·ci·less·ness** *noun*

**mer·cu·rate** \ˈmər-kyə-ˌrāt\ *transitive verb* **-rat·ed; -rat·ing** (1923)
**:** to combine or treat with mercury or a mercury salt
— **mer·cu·ra·tion** \ˌmər-kyə-ˈrā-shən\ *noun*

**¹mer·cu·ri·al** \(ˌ)mər-ˈkyu̇r-ē-əl\ *adjective* (14th century)

**1** : of, relating to, or born under the planet Mercury
**2** : having qualities of eloquence, ingenuity, or thievishness attributed to the god Mercury or to the influence of the planet Mercury
**3** : characterized by rapid and unpredictable changeableness of mood
**4** : of, relating to, containing, or caused by mercury
**synonym** see INCONSTANT
— **mer·cu·ri·al·ly** \-ē-ə-lē\ adverb
— **mer·cu·ri·al·ness** noun

**²mercurial** noun (1676)
: a pharmaceutical or chemical containing mercury

**mer·cu·ric** \(ˌ)mər-'kyur-ik\ adjective (circa 1828)
: of, relating to, or containing mercury; especially : containing mercury with a valence of two

**mercuric chloride** noun (1874)
: a heavy crystalline poisonous compound $HgCl_2$ used as a disinfectant and fungicide and in photography

**Mer·cu·ro·chrome** \(ˌ)mər-'kyur-ə-ˌkrōm\ trademark
— used for merbromin

**mer·cu·rous** \(ˌ)mər-'kyur-əs, 'mər-kyə-rəs\ adjective (circa 1865)
: of, relating to, or containing mercury; especially : containing mercury with a valence of one

**mercurous chloride** noun (circa 1885)
: CALOMEL

**mer·cu·ry** \'mər-kyə-rē, -k(ə-)rē\ noun, plural **-ries** [Latin Mercurius, Roman god and the planet]
**1 a** capitalized : a Roman god of commerce, eloquence, travel, cunning, and theft who serves as messenger to the other gods — compare HERMES **b** often capitalized, archaic : a bearer of messages or news or a conductor of travelers
**2** [Middle English mercurie, from Medieval Latin mercurius, from Latin, the god] **a** : a heavy silver-white poisonous metallic element that is liquid at ordinary temperatures and is used especially in scientific instruments — called also quicksilver; see ELEMENT table **b** : the mercury in a thermometer or barometer
**3** capitalized : the planet nearest the sun — see PLANET table

**mercury chloride** noun (circa 1885)
: a chloride of mercury: as **a** : CALOMEL **b** : MERCURIC CHLORIDE

**mercury–vapor lamp** noun (1904)
: an electric lamp in which the discharge takes place through mercury vapor — called also mercury lamp

**mer·cy** \'mər-sē\ noun, plural **mercies** [Middle English, from Old French merci, from Medieval Latin merced-, merces, from Latin, price paid, wages, from merc-, merx merchandise] (13th century)
**1 a** : compassion or forbearance shown especially to an offender or to one subject to one's power; also : lenient or compassionate treatment ⟨begged for mercy⟩ **b** : imprisonment rather than death imposed as penalty for first-degree murder
**2 a** : a blessing that is an act of divine favor or compassion **b** : a fortunate circumstance ⟨it was a mercy they found her before she froze⟩
**3** : compassionate treatment of those in distress ⟨works of mercy among the poor⟩ ☆ ◆
— **mercy** adjective
— **at the mercy of** : wholly in the power of : with no way to protect oneself against

**mercy killing** noun (1935)
: EUTHANASIA

**merde** \'merd, 'mard\ noun [French, from Old French, from Latin merda; perhaps akin to Lithuanian smirděti to stink] (1920)
: ²CRAP 1a, 2 — sometimes considered vulgar

**¹mere** \'mir\ noun [Middle English, from Old English — more at MARINE] (before 12th century)
chiefly British : an expanse of standing water : LAKE, POOL

**²mere** noun [Middle English, from Old English mære; akin to Old Norse landamæri borderland] (before 12th century)
: BOUNDARY; also : LANDMARK

**³mere** \'mir\ adjective, superlative **mer·est** [Middle English, from Latin merus; akin to Old English āmerian to purify and perhaps to Greek marmairein to sparkle — more at MORN] (1536)
**1** : having no admixture : PURE
**2** obsolete : being nothing less than : ABSOLUTE
**3** : being nothing more than ⟨a mere mortal⟩
— **mere·ly** adverb

**-mere** noun combining form [French -mère, from Greek meros part — more at MERIT]
: part : segment ⟨metamere⟩

**me·ren·gue** \mə-'reŋ-(ˌ)gā\ noun [American Spanish merengue & Haitian Creole méringue] (1936)
: a ballroom dance of Haitian and Dominican origin in which one foot is dragged on every step; also : the music for a merengue

**mer·e·tri·cious** \ˌmer-ə-'tri-shəs\ adjective [Latin meretricius, from meretric-, meretrix prostitute, from merēre to earn — more at MERIT] (circa 1626)
**1** : of or relating to a prostitute : having the nature of prostitution ⟨meretricious relationship⟩
**2 a** : tawdrily and falsely attractive ⟨the paradise they found was a piece of meretricious trash —Carolyn See⟩ **b** : superficially significant : PRETENTIOUS ⟨scholarly names to provide fig-leaves of respectability for meretricious but stylish books —Times Literary Supplement⟩
**synonym** see GAUDY
— **mer·e·tri·cious·ly** adverb
— **mer·e·tri·cious·ness** noun

**mer·gan·ser** \(ˌ)mər-'gan(t)-sər\ noun [New Latin, from Latin mergus, a waterfowl (from mergere) + anser goose — more at GOOSE] (1752)
: any of various fish-eating diving ducks (especially genus Mergus) with a slender bill hooked at the end and serrated along the margins and usually a crested head

**merganser**

**merge** \'mərj\ verb **merged; merg·ing** [Latin mergere; akin to Sanskrit majjati he dives] (1636)
transitive verb
**1** archaic : to plunge or engulf in something : IMMERSE
**2** : to cause to combine, unite, or coalesce
**3** : to blend gradually by stages that blur distinctions
intransitive verb
**1** : to become combined into one
**2** : to blend or come together without abrupt change ⟨merging traffic⟩
**synonym** see MIX
— **mer·gence** \'mər-jən(t)s\ noun

**merg·er** \'mər-jər\ noun [merge + -er (as in waiver)] (1728)
**1** law : the absorption of an estate, a contract, or an interest in another, of a minor offense in a greater, or of an obligation into a judgment
**2 a** : the act or process of merging **b** : absorption by a corporation of one or more others; also : any of various methods of combining two or more organizations (as business concerns)

**me·rid·i·an** \mə-'ri-dē-ən\ noun [Middle English, from Middle French meridien, from me-

ridien of noon, from Latin meridianus, from meridies noon, south, irregular from medius mid + dies day — more at MID, DEITY] (14th century)
**1** archaic : the hour of noon : MIDDAY
**2** : a great circle of the celestial sphere passing through its poles and the zenith of a given place
**3** : a high point
**4 a** (1) : a great circle on the surface of the earth passing through the poles (2) : the half of such a circle included between the poles **b** : a representation of such a circle or half circle numbered for longitude on a map or globe — see LONGITUDE illustration
— **meridian** adjective

**¹me·rid·i·o·nal** \mə-'ri-dē-ə-nᵊl\ adjective [Middle English, from Middle French meridional, from Late Latin meridionalis, from Latin meridies] (14th century)
**1** : of, relating to, or situated in the south : SOUTHERN
**2** : of, relating to, or characteristic of people living in the south especially of France
**3** : of, relating to, or situated on or along a meridian
— **me·rid·i·o·nal·ly** \-nᵊl-ē\ adverb

**²meridional** noun (1591)
: a native or inhabitant of southern Europe and especially southern France

**me·ringue** \mə-'raŋ\ noun [French] (1706)

---

☆ **SYNONYMS**

**Mercy, charity, clemency, grace, leniency** mean a disposition to show kindness or compassion. MERCY implies compassion that forbears punishing even when justice demands it ⟨threw himself on the mercy of the court⟩. CHARITY stresses benevolence and goodwill shown in broad understanding and tolerance of others ⟨show a little charity for the less fortunate⟩. CLEMENCY implies a mild or merciful disposition in one having the power or duty of punishing ⟨the judge refused to show clemency⟩. GRACE implies a benign attitude and a willingness to grant favors or make concessions ⟨by the grace of God⟩. LENIENCY implies lack of severity in punishing ⟨criticized the courts for excessive leniency⟩.

---

◇ **WORD HISTORY**

**mercy** Mercy is not something that can be bought or sold; yet it does have a connection with the marketplace. The word was borrowed into Middle English from Old French mercit or merci, which had about the same range of senses as English mercy. The Old French word is descended from Latin merces "price," "payment," or "reward," a derivative of merx "commodity, piece of merchandise." The basis of what is now the primary sense of mercy is to be found in the Latin of Christian writers, who began to use merces for the spiritual reward that derives from kindness to those who do not necessarily have a direct claim to it and from whom no recompense is to be expected. Thus, in a sense, the dispensation of mercy is a figurative form of trade, transacted in a less mundane currency than our daily negotiations. While English has retained most of the sense of Old French merci, by and large these senses have not survived in French itself, where today merci is used primarily to express thanks.

---

\ə\ abut \ᵊ\ kitten \ər\ further \a\ ash \ā\ ace
\ä\ mop, mar \au̇\ out \ch\ chin \e\ bet \ē\ easy
\g\ go \i\ hit \ī\ ice \j\ job \ŋ\ sing \ō\ go
\ȯ\ law \ȯi\ boy \th\ thin \th̲\ the \ü\ loot \u̇\ foot
\y\ yet \zh\ vision    see also Guide to Pronunciation

**1** : a dessert topping baked from a mixture of stiffly beaten egg whites and sugar
**2** : a shell made of meringue and filled with fruit or ice cream

**me·ri·no** \mə-'rē-(,)nō\ *noun, plural* **-nos** [Spanish] (1810)
**1** : any of a breed of fine-wooled white sheep originating in Spain and producing a heavy fleece of exceptional quality
**2** : a soft wool or wool and cotton clothing fabric resembling cashmere
**3** : a fine wool and cotton yarn used for hosiery and knitwear
— **merino** *adjective*

**-merism** *noun combining form* [International Scientific Vocabulary, from Greek *meros* part — more at MERIT]
: possession of (such) an arrangement of or relation among constituent chemical units (tautomerism)

**mer·i·stem** \'mer-ə-,stem\ *noun* [Greek *meristos* divided (from *merizein* to divide, from *meros*) + English *-em* (as in *system*)] (1874)
: a formative plant tissue usually made up of small cells capable of dividing indefinitely and giving rise to similar cells or to cells that differentiate to produce the definitive tissues and organs
— **mer·i·ste·mat·ic** \,mer-əs-tə-'ma-tik\ *adjective*
— **mer·i·ste·mat·i·cal·ly** \-ti-k(ə-)lē\ *adverb*

**me·ris·tic** \mə-'ris-tik\ *adjective* [Greek *meristos*] (1894)
**1** : SEGMENTAL
**2** : involving modification in number or in geometrical relation of body parts (*meristic* variation in flower petals)
— **me·ris·ti·cal·ly** \-ti-k(ə-)lē\ *adverb*

**¹mer·it** \'mer-ət\ *noun* [Middle English, from Middle French *merite*, from Latin *meritum*, from neuter of *meritus*, past participle of *merēre* to deserve, earn; akin to Greek *meiresthai* to receive as one's portion, *meros* part] (14th century)
**1 a** *obsolete* : reward or punishment due **b** : the qualities or actions that constitute the basis of one's deserts **c** : a praiseworthy quality : VIRTUE **d** : character or conduct deserving reward, honor, or esteem; *also* : ACHIEVEMENT
**2** : spiritual credit held to be earned by performance of righteous acts and to ensure future benefits
**3 a** *plural* : the intrinsic nature of a legal case apart from considerations of circumstance, jurisdiction, or procedure **b** : individual significance or justification

**²merit** (1526)
*transitive verb*
: to be worthy of or entitled or liable to : EARN
*intransitive verb*
**1** *obsolete* : to be entitled to reward or honor
**2** : DESERVE

**mer·i·toc·ra·cy** \,mer-ə-'tä-krə-sē\ *noun, plural* **-cies** [¹*merit* + *-o-* + *-cracy*] (1958)
**1** : a system in which the talented are chosen and moved ahead on the basis of their achievement
**2** : leadership selected on the basis of intellectual criteria
— **mer·i·to·crat·ic** \,mer-ə-tə-'kra-tik\ *adjective*

**mer·it·o·crat** \'mer-ə-tə-,krat\ *noun* (1960)
*chiefly British* : a person who advances through a meritocratic system

**mer·i·to·ri·ous** \,mer-ə-'tōr-ē-əs, -'tor-\ *adjective* (15th century)
: deserving of honor or esteem
— **mer·i·to·ri·ous·ly** *adverb*
— **mer·i·to·ri·ous·ness** *noun*

**merit system** *noun* (1879)
: a system by which appointments and promotions in the civil service are based on competence rather than political favoritism

**¹merle** *also* **merl** \'mər(-ə)l\ *noun* [Middle English, from Middle French, from Latin *merulus;* akin to Old English *ōsle* blackbird, Old High German *amsla*] (15th century)
: BLACKBIRD 1a

**²merle** *noun* [origin unknown] (1905)
: a bluish or reddish gray mixed with splotches of black that is the color of the coats of some dogs

**mer·lin** \'mər-lən\ *noun* [Middle English *merlioun*, from Anglo-French *merilun*, from Old French *esmerillon*, augmentative of *esmeril*, of Germanic origin; akin to Old High German *smiril* merlin] (14th century)
: a small compact Holarctic falcon (*Falco columbarius*) which has a broad dark terminal band on the tail and of which the upperparts are slate blue in males and dark brown in females — compare PIGEON HAWK 1

**Mer·lin** \'mər-lən\ *noun* [Medieval Latin *Merlinus*, from Middle Welsh *Myrddin*]
: a prophet and magician in Arthurian legend

**mer·lon** \'mər-lən\ *noun* [French, from Italian *merlone*, augmentative of *merlo* battlement, from Medieval Latin *merulus*, from Latin, merle] (circa 1704)
: any of the solid intervals between crenellations of a battlement — see BATTLEMENT illustration

**mer·lot** \mer-'lō\ *noun, often capitalized* [French] (circa 1941)
: a dry red wine made from a widely grown grape originally used in the Bordeaux region of France for blending

**mer·maid** \'mər-,mād\ *noun* [Middle English *mermayde*, from *mere* sea (from Old English) + *mayde* maid — more at MARINE] (14th century)
: a fabled marine creature with the head and upper body of a woman and the tail of a fish

**mer·man** \-,man, -mən\ *noun* (1601)
: a fabled marine creature with the head and upper body of a man and the tail of a fish

**mero-** *combining form* [International Scientific Vocabulary, from Greek, from *meros* part — more at MERIT]
: part : partial (*mero*blastic)

**mer·o·blas·tic** \,mer-ə-'blas-tik\ *adjective* [International Scientific Vocabulary] (1870)
: characterized by incomplete cleavage as a result of the presence of a mass of yolk material — compare HOLOBLASTIC
— **mer·o·blas·ti·cal·ly** \-ti-k(ə-)lē\ *adverb*

**mer·o·crine** \'mer-ə-krən, -,krīn, -,krēn\ *adjective* [International Scientific Vocabulary, from *mero-* + Greek *krinein* to separate — more at CERTAIN] (circa 1905)
: producing a secretion that is discharged without major damage to the secretory cells; *also* : produced by a merocrine gland

**mer·o·mor·phic** \,mer-ə-'mor-fik\ *adjective* (circa 1890)
: relating to or being a function of a complex variable that is analytic everywhere in a region except for singularities at each of which infinity is the limit and each of which is contained in a neighborhood where the function is analytic except for the singular point itself

**mer·o·my·o·sin** \,mer-ə-'mī-ə-sən\ *noun* (1952)
: either of two structural subunits of myosin that are obtained especially by tryptic digestion

**-merous** *adjective combining form* [New Latin *-merus*, from Greek *-merēs*, from *meros* — more at MERIT]
: having (such or so many) parts (di*merous*)

**Mer·o·vin·gian** \,mer-ə-'vin-j(ē-)ən\ *adjective* [French *mérovingien*, from Medieval Latin *Merovingi* Merovingians, from *Merovaeus* Merowig (died 458) Frankish founder of the dynasty] (circa 1694)
: of or relating to the first Frankish dynasty reigning from about A.D. 500 to 751
— **Merovingian** *noun*

**mer·o·zo·ite** \,mer-ə-'zō-,īt\ *noun* [International Scientific Vocabulary, from *mero-* + *zo-* + *-ite*] (1900)
: a sporozoan trophozoite produced by schizogony that is capable of initiating a new sexual or asexual cycle of development

**mer·ri·ment** \'mer-i-mənt\ *noun* (1576)
**1** : lighthearted gaiety or fun-making : HILARITY
**2** : a lively celebration or party : FESTIVITY

**mer·ry** \'mer-ē\ *adjective* **mer·ri·er; -est** [Middle English *mery*, from Old English *myrge, merge;* akin to Old High German *murg* short — more at BRIEF] (before 12th century)
**1** *archaic* : giving pleasure : DELIGHTFUL
**2** : full of gaiety or high spirits : MIRTHFUL
**3** : marked by festivity or gaiety
**4** : QUICK, BRISK (a *merry* pace) ☆
— **mer·ri·ly** \'mer-ə-lē\ *adverb*
— **mer·ri·ness** \'mer-ē-nəs\ *noun*

**mer·ry·an·drew** \,mer-ē-'an-(,)drü\ *noun, often M&A capitalized* [merry + Andrew, proper name] (1673)
: a person who clowns publicly

**mer·ry–go–round** \'mer-ē-gō-,raund, -gə-\ *noun* (1729)
**1** : an amusement park ride with seats often in the form of animals (as horses) revolving about a fixed center
**2** : a cycle of activity that is complex, fast-paced, or difficult to break out of (the corporate *merry-go-round*)

**mer·ry·mak·er** \'mer-ē-,mā-kər\ *noun* (1827)
: REVELER

**mer·ry·mak·ing** \-kiŋ\ *noun* (1714)
**1** : gay or festive activity : CONVIVIALITY
**2** : a convivial occasion : FESTIVITY

**mer·ry·thought** \'mer-ē-,thót\ *noun* (1607)
*chiefly British* : WISHBONE

**merry widow** *noun, often M&W capitalized* [*The Merry Widow,* operetta (1905) by Franz Lehár] (1964)
: a strapless corset or bustier usually having garters attached

**Mer·thi·o·late** \(,)mər-'thī-ə-,lāt, -lət\ *trademark*
— used for thimerosal

**mes-** *or* **meso-** *combining form* [Latin, from Greek, from *mesos* — more at MID]
**1** : mid : in the middle (*meso*carp)
**2** : intermediate (as in size or type) (*meso*morph) (*meson*)

**me·sa** \'mā-sə\ *noun* [Spanish, literally, table, from Latin *mensa*] (1759)
: an isolated relatively flat-topped natural elevation usually more extensive than a butte and less extensive than a plateau; *also* : a broad terrace with an abrupt slope on one side : BENCH

**més·al·li·ance** \,mā-,zal-'yäⁿs, ,mā-zə-'lī-ən(t)s\ *noun, plural* **mésalliances** \-'yäⁿs(-əz), -'lī-ən(t)-səz\ [French, from *més-* mis- + *alliance*] (1782)
: a marriage with a person of inferior social position

**mes·arch** \'me-,zärk, 'mē-, -,särk\ *adjective* (1891)
: having metaxylem developed both internal and external to the protoxylem

---

☆ **SYNONYMS**
**Merry, blithe, jocund, jovial, jolly** mean showing high spirits or lightheartedness. MERRY suggests cheerful, joyous, uninhibited enjoyment of frolic or festivity (a *merry* group of revelers). BLITHE suggests carefree, innocent, or even heedless gaiety (arrived late in his usual *blithe* way). JOCUND stresses elation and exhilaration of spirits (singing, dancing, and *jocund* feasting). JOVIAL suggests the stimulation of conviviality and good fellowship (dinner put them in a *jovial* mood). JOLLY suggests high spirits expressed in laughing, bantering, and jesting (our *jolly* host enlivened the party).

**mes·cal** \me-'skal, mə-\ *noun* [American Spanish *mezcal, mescal,* from Nahuatl *mexcalli* mescal liquor] (1702)
**1 :** a small cactus (*Lophophora williamsii*) with rounded stems covered with jointed tubercles that are used as a stimulant and antispasmodic especially among the Mexican Indians
**2 a :** a usually colorless Mexican liquor distilled especially from the central leaves of maguey plants **b :** a plant from which mescal is produced; *especially* **:** MAGUEY

mescal 1

**mescal button** *noun* (1888)
**:** one of the dried discoid tops of the mescal
**Mes·ca·le·ro** \mes-kə-'ler-(,)ō\ *noun, plural* **Mescalero** *or* **Mescaleros** [American Spanish, from *mezcal, mescal* maguey, mescal liquor] (1844)
**:** a member of an Apache people of Texas and New Mexico
**mes·ca·line** \'mes-kə-lən, -,lēn\ *noun* (1896)
**:** a hallucinatory crystalline alkaloid $C_{11}H_{17}NO_3$ that is the chief active principle in mescal buttons
**mesdames** *plural of* MADAM, *or of* MADAME, *or of* MRS.
**mesdemoiselles** *plural of* MADEMOISELLE
**me·seems** \mi-'sēmz\ *impersonal verb, past* **me·seemed** \-'sēmd\ (15th century)
*archaic* **:** it seems to me
**me·sem·bry·an·the·mum** \mə-,zem-brē-'an(t)-thə-məm\ *noun* [New Latin, irregular from Greek *mesēmbria* midday (from *mes-* + *hēmera* day) + *anthemon* flower, from *anthos* — more at ANTHOLOGY] (1753)
**:** any of a genus (*Mesembryanthemum*) of chiefly southern African fleshy-leaved herbs or subshrubs of the carpetweed family
**mes·en·ceph·a·lon** \,me-,zen-'se-fə-,län, ,mē-, -z°n-, -,sen-, -s°n-, -lən\ *noun* [New Latin] (1846)
**:** MIDBRAIN
— **mes·en·ce·phal·ic** \-,zen(t)-sə-'fa-lik, -z°n(t)-, -,sen(t)-, -s°n(t)-\ *adjective*
**mes·en·chy·mal** \mə-'zeŋ-kə-məl, -'seŋ-; ,me-z°n-'kī-məl, ,mē-, -s°n-\ *adjective* [International Scientific Vocabulary] (1886)
**:** of, resembling, or being mesenchyme
**mes·en·chyme** \'me-z°n-,kīm, 'mē-, -s°n-\ *noun* [German *Mesenchym,* from *mes-* + New Latin *-enchyma*] (1888)
**:** loosely organized undifferentiated mostly mesodermal cells that give rise to such structures as connective tissues, blood, lymphatics, bone, and cartilage
**mes·en·ter·on** \(,)me-'zen-tə-,rän, ,mē-, -'sen-, -rən\ *noun, plural* **-tera** \-tə-rə\ [New Latin] (1877)
**:** the part of the alimentary canal that is developed from the archenteron and is lined with hypoblast
**mes·en·tery** \'me-z°n-,ter-ē, -s°n-\ *noun, plural* **-ter·ies** [Middle English *mesenterie,* from Middle French & Medieval Latin; Middle French *mesentere,* from Medieval Latin *mesenterion,* from Greek, from *mes-* + *enteron* intestine — more at INTER-] (15th century)
**1 a :** one or more vertebrate membranes that consist of a double fold of the peritoneum and invest the intestines and their appendages and connect them with the dorsal wall of the abdominal cavity **b :** a fold of membrane comparable to a mesentery and supporting a viscus (as the heart) that is not a part of the digestive tract
**2 :** a support or partition in an invertebrate like the vertebrate mesentery
— **mes·en·ter·ic** \,me-z°n-'ter-ik, -s°n-\ *adjective*
**¹mesh** \'mesh\ *noun* [Middle English, probably from Middle Dutch *maesche;* akin to Old

High German *masca* mesh, Lithuanian *mazgos* knot] (14th century)
**1 :** one of the openings between the threads or cords of a net; *also* **:** one of the similar spaces in a network — often used to designate screen size as the number of openings per linear inch
**2 a :** the fabric of a net **b :** a woven, knit, or knotted material of open texture with evenly spaced holes **c :** an arrangement of interlocking metal links used especially for jewelry
**3 a :** an interlocking or intertwining arrangement or construction **:** NETWORK **b :** WEB, SNARE — usually used in plural
**4 :** working contact (as of the teeth of gears) ⟨in *mesh*⟩
— **meshed** \'mesht\ *adjective*
**²mesh** (circa 1547)
*transitive verb*
**1 a :** to catch in the openings of a net **b :** ENMESH, ENTANGLE
**2 :** to cause to resemble network
**3 a :** to cause (as gears) to engage **b :** to coordinate closely **:** INTERLOCK
*intransitive verb*
**1 :** to become entangled in or as if in meshes
**2 :** to be in or come into mesh — used especially of gears
**3 :** to fit or work together properly **:** COORDINATE
**me·shuga** *or* **me·shug·ge** *also* **me·shugah** *or* **me·shug·gah** \mə-'shü-gə\ *adjective* [Yiddish *meshuge,* from Hebrew *měshuggā'*] (1892)
**:** CRAZY, FOOLISH
**me·shug·gen·er** \-'shù-gə-nər\ *noun* [Yiddish *meshugener,* from *meshuge*] (1900)
**:** a foolish or crazy person
**mesh·work** \'mesh-,wərk\ *noun* (1830)
**:** NETWORK ⟨a vascular *meshwork*⟩
**me·si·al** \'mē-zē-əl, -sē-\ *adjective* (1803)
**1 :** MIDDLE, MEDIAN
**2 :** of, relating to, or being the surface of a tooth that is next to the tooth in front of it or that is closest to the middle of the front of the jaw — compare DISTAL 2
— **me·si·al·ly** \-ə-lē\ *adverb*
**¹me·sic** \'me-zik, 'mē-, -sik\ *adjective* [*mes-* + *-ic*] (1926)
**:** characterized by, relating to, or requiring a moderate amount of moisture ⟨a *mesic* habitat⟩ ⟨a *mesic* plant⟩ — compare HYDRIC, XERIC
**²mesic** *adjective* [*meson* + *-ic*] (1939)
**:** of or relating to a meson
**mes·mer·ic** \mez-'mer-ik *also* mes-\ *adjective* (1829)
**1 :** of, relating to, or induced by mesmerism
**2 :** FASCINATING, IRRESISTIBLE
— **mes·mer·i·cal·ly** \-i-k(ə-)lē\ *adverb*
**mes·mer·ise** *British variant of* MESMERIZE
**mes·mer·ism** \'mez-mə-,ri-zəm *also* 'mes-\ *noun* [F. A. *Mesmer*] (1784)
**1 :** hypnotic induction held to involve animal magnetism; *broadly* **:** HYPNOTISM
**2 :** hypnotic appeal
— **mes·mer·ist** \-rist\ *noun*
**mes·mer·ize** \-mə-,rīz\ *transitive verb* **-ized; -iz·ing** (1829)
**1 :** to subject to mesmerism; *also* **:** HYPNOTIZE
**2 :** SPELLBIND, FASCINATE ◆
— **mes·mer·iz·er** *noun*
**mesne** \'mēn\ *adjective* [Anglo-French, alteration of Middle French *meien* — more at MEAN] (1548)
**:** INTERMEDIATE, INTERVENING — used in law
**mesne lord** *noun* (1614)
**:** a feudal lord who holds land as tenant of a superior (as a king) but who is lord to his own tenant
**meso-** — see MES-
**me·so·carp** \'me-zə-,kärp, 'mē-, -sə-\ *noun* (1849)
**:** the middle layer of a pericarp — see ENDOCARP illustration
**me·so·cy·clone** \,me-zə-'sī-,klōn, ,mē-, -sə-'sī-\ *noun* (1975)

**:** a rapidly rotating air mass within a thunderstorm that often gives rise to a tornado
**me·so·derm** \'me-zə-,dərm, 'mē-, -sə-\ *noun* [International Scientific Vocabulary] (1873)
**:** the middle of the three primary germ layers of an embryo that is the source of many bodily tissues and structures (as bone, muscle, connective tissue, and dermis); *broadly* **:** tissue derived from this germ layer
— **me·so·der·mal** \,me-zə-'dər-məl, ,mē-, -sə-\ *adjective*
**me·so·glea** *or* **me·so·gloea** \,me-zə-'glē-ə, ,mē-, -sə-\ *noun* [New Latin, from *mes-* + Late Greek *gloia, glia* glue — more at CLAY] (1886)
**:** a gelatinous substance between the endoderm and ectoderm of sponges or coelenterates
**Me·so·lith·ic** \-'li-thik\ *adjective* [International Scientific Vocabulary] (1866)
**:** of, relating to, or being a transitional period of the Stone Age between the Paleolithic and the Neolithic
**me·so·mere** \'me-zə-,mir, 'mē-, -sə-\ *noun* (circa 1900)
**:** a blastomere of medium size; *also* **:** an intermediate part of the mesoderm
**me·so·morph** \'me-zə-,mórf, 'mē-, -sə-\ *noun* [*mesoderm* + *-morph*] (1940)
**:** a mesomorphic body or person
**me·so·mor·phic** \,me-zə-'mòr-fik, ,mē-, -sə-\ *adjective* [*mesoderm* + *-morphic;* from the predominance in such types of structures developed from the mesoderm] (1940)
**1 :** of or relating to the component in W. H. Sheldon's classification of body types that measures especially the degree of muscularity and bone development
**2 :** having a husky muscular body build
— **me·so·mor·phy** \'me-zə-,mòr-fē, -sə-\ *noun*
**me·son** \'me-,zän, 'mā-, 'mē-, -,sän\ *noun* [International Scientific Vocabulary *mes-* + *²-on*] (1939)
**:** any of a group of fundamental particles (as the pion and kaon) made up of a quark and an antiquark that are subject to the strong force

---

◇ **WORD HISTORY**
**mesmerize** Franz Anton Mesmer (1734–1815), from whose surname *mesmerize* is derived, was an Austrian physician. A graduate of a traditional medical school in Vienna, Mesmer early on formulated unorthodox medical beliefs. He claimed that a mysterious fluid, which he eventually called "animal magnetism," permeates all matter. Forced to leave Vienna for practicing "magic," Mesmer settled in Paris and soon put his theories of animal magnetism into practice. His therapy basically consisted of having patients sit around a tub of dilute sulfuric acid from which iron bars protruded. As the patients touched the previously "magnetized" bars, the outflowing current of animal magnetism, as well as a tap from Mesmer's magic wand, caused them to become highly agitated. Once the necessary crises had been produced, Mesmer effected the individual cures by having the animal magnetism flow from his body to the patient's. A royal commission's finding that the "cures" were entirely due to the imagination failed to dampen the rage for Mesmer's treatment. What Mesmer had discovered—or rediscovered—was the technique once called "artificial somnambulism" and now known as hypnotism.

---

\ə\ abut \°\ kitten \ər\ further \a\ ash \ā\ ace
\ä\ mop, mar \aù\ out \ch\ chin \e\ bet \ē\ easy
\g\ go \i\ hit \ī\ ice \j\ job \ŋ\ sing \ō\ go
\ò\ law \òi\ boy \th\ thin \th\ the \ü\ loot \ù\ foot
\y\ yet \zh\ vision *see also* Guide to Pronunciation

and have zero or an integer number of quantum units of spin

— **me·son·ic** \me-'zä-nik, mā-, mē-, -'sä-\ *adjective*

**me·so·neph·ros** \,me-zə-'ne-frəs, ,mē-, -sə-, -,fräs\ *noun, plural* **-neph·roi** \-,frói\ [New Latin, from *mes-* + Greek *nephros* kidney — more at NEPHRITIS] (1887)
: either member of the second and midmost of the three paired vertebrate renal organs that functions in adult fishes and amphibians but functions only in the embryo of reptiles, birds, and mammals in which it is replaced by a metanephros in the adult — compare METANEPHROS, PRONEPHROS
— **me·so·neph·ric** \-frik\ *adjective*

**me·so·pause** \'me-zə-,póz, 'mē-, -sə-\ *noun* [*meso*sphere + *pause*] (1950)
: the upper boundary of the mesosphere where the temperature of the atmosphere reaches its lowest point

**me·so·pe·lag·ic** \,me-zə-pə-'la-jik, ,mē-, -sə-\ *adjective* (1947)
: of or relating to oceanic depths from about 600 feet to 3000 feet (200 to 1000 meters)

**me·so·phyll** \'me-zə-,fil, 'mē-, -sə-\ *noun* [New Latin *mesophyllum*, from *mes-* + Greek *phyllon* leaf — more at BLADE] (1839)
: the parenchyma between the epidermal layers of a foliage leaf
— **me·so·phyl·lic** \,me-zə-'fi-lik, ,mē-, -sə-\ *or* **me·so·phyl·lous** \-ləs\ *adjective*

**me·so·phyte** \'me-zə-,fīt, 'mē-, -sə-\ *noun* [International Scientific Vocabulary] (1899)
: a plant that grows under medium conditions of moisture
— **me·so·phyt·ic** \,me-zə-'fi-tik, ,mē-, -sə-\ *adjective*

**me·so·scale** \'me-zə-,skāl, 'mē-, -sə-\ *adjective* (1956)
: of intermediate size; *especially* : of or relating to a meteorological phenomenon approximately 10 to 1000 kilometers in horizontal extent ⟨*mesoscale* cloud pattern⟩

**me·so·some** \-,sōm\ *noun* (1960)
: an organelle of bacteria that appears as an invagination of the plasma membrane and functions either in DNA replication and cell division or excretion of exoenzymes

**me·so·sphere** \-,sfir\ *noun* (1950)
: the part of the earth's atmosphere between the stratosphere and the thermosphere in which temperature decreases with altitude to the atmosphere's absolute minimum of about −112°F (−80°C)
— **me·so·spher·ic** \,me-zə-'sfir-ik, ,mē-, -sə-, -'sfer-\ *adjective*

**me·so·the·li·o·ma** \,me-zə-,thē-lē-'ō-mə, ,mē-, -sə-\ *noun, plural* **-mas** *or* **-ma·ta** \-mə-tə\ [New Latin] (circa 1899)
: a tumor derived from mesothelial tissue (as that lining the peritoneum or pleura)

**me·so·the·li·um** \-'thē-lē-əm\ *noun, plural* **-lia** \-lē-ə\ [New Latin, from *mes-* + epi*thelium*] (1886)
: epithelium derived from mesoderm that lines the body cavity of a vertebrate embryo and gives rise to epithelia (as of the peritoneum, pericardium, and pleurae), striated muscle, heart muscle, and several minor structures
— **me·so·the·li·al** \-lē-əl\ *adjective*

**me·so·tho·rac·ic** \-thə-'ra-sik\ *adjective* (1839)
: of or relating to the mesothorax

**me·so·tho·rax** \-'thōr-,aks, -'thór-\ *noun* [New Latin] (circa 1826)
: the middle of the three segments of the thorax of an insect — see INSECT illustration

**me·so·tro·phic** \,me-zə-'trō-fik, ,mē-, -sə-, -'trä-fik\ *adjective* (1940)
*of a body of water* : having a moderate amount of dissolved nutrients — compare EUTROPHIC, OLIGOTROPHIC

**Me·so·zo·ic** \-'zō-ik\ *adjective* (1840)
: of, relating to, or being an era of geological history comprising the interval between the

Permian and the Tertiary or the corresponding system of rocks that was marked by the presence of dinosaurs, marine and flying reptiles, ammonites, ferns, and gymnosperms and the appearance of angiosperms, mammals, and birds — see GEOLOGIC TIME table
— **Mesozoic** *noun*

**mes·quite** \mə-'skēt, me-\ *noun* [American Spanish, from Nahuatl *mizquitl*] (1759)
: any of several spiny leguminous trees or shrubs (genus *Prosopis* and especially *P. glandulosa*) chiefly of the southwestern U.S. that often form extensive thickets and have sweet pods eaten by livestock; *also* : the wood of the mesquite used especially in grilling food

¹**mess** \'mes\ *noun* [Middle English *mes*, from Middle French, from Late Latin *missus* course at a meal, from *missus*, past participle of *mittere* to put, from Latin, to send — more at SMITE] (14th century)
**1** : a quantity of food: **a** *archaic* : food set on a table at one time **b** : a prepared dish of soft food; *also* : a mixture of ingredients cooked or eaten together **c** : enough food of a specified kind for a dish or a meal ⟨picked a *mess* of peas for dinner⟩
**2 a** : a group of persons who regularly take their meals together; *also* : a meal so taken **b** : a place where meals are regularly served to a group : MESS HALL
**3 a** : a disordered, untidy, offensive, or unpleasant state or condition ⟨your room is in a *mess*⟩ **b** : one that is disordered, untidy, offensive, or unpleasant usually because of blundering, laxity, or misconduct ⟨[the movie] is a *mess*, as sloppy in concept as it is in execution —Judith Crist⟩ ⟨made a *mess* of his life⟩

²**mess** (14th century)
*transitive verb*
**1** : to provide with meals at a mess
**2 a** : to make dirty or untidy : DISARRANGE ⟨warned not to *mess* up your room⟩ **b** : to mix up : BUNGLE ⟨really *messed* up my life⟩
**3** : to interfere with ⟨magnetic storms that *mess* up communications —*Time*⟩
**4** : to rough up : MANHANDLE ⟨*mess* him up good so he won't double-cross us again⟩
*intransitive verb*
**1** : to take meals with a mess
**2** : to make a mess
**3 a** : PUTTER, TRIFLE ⟨small boys and girls who like to *mess* around with paints⟩ **b** : to handle or play with something especially carelessly ⟨don't *mess* with my camera⟩ — often used with *around* **c** : to take an active interest in something or someone ⟨*messing* around with new video techniques⟩; *also* : INTERFERE, MEDDLE ⟨*messing* in other people's affairs⟩ ⟨you'd better not *mess* with me⟩
**4** : to become confused or make an error — usually used with *up* ⟨got another chance and didn't want to *mess* up again⟩

¹**mes·sage** \'me-sij\ *noun* [Middle English, from Old French, from Medieval Latin *missaticum*, from Latin *missus*, past participle of *mittere*] (14th century)
**1** : a communication in writing, in speech, or by signals
**2** : a messenger's errand or function
**3** : an underlying theme or idea

²**message** *verb* **mes·saged; mes·sag·ing** (1583)
*transitive verb*
**1** : to send as a message or by messenger
**2** : to send a message to
*intransitive verb*
: to communicate by message

**mes·sa·line** \,me-sə-'lēn\ *noun* [French] (circa 1890)
: a soft lightweight silk dress fabric with a satin weave

**mes·san** \'me-s°n\ *noun* [Scottish Gaelic *measan*] (15th century)
*chiefly Scottish* : LAPDOG 1

**mess around** *intransitive verb* (circa 1932)
**1** : to waste time : DAWDLE, IDLE
**2 a** : ASSOCIATE ⟨don't *mess around* with admirals much —K. M. Dodson⟩ **b** : FLIRT, PHILANDER ⟨caught him *messing around* with my wife⟩

**messeigneurs** *plural of* MONSEIGNEUR

**mes·sen·ger** \'me-s°n-jər\ *noun* [Middle English *messangere*, from Old French *messagier*, from *message*] (14th century)
**1** : one who bears a message or does an errand: as **a** *archaic* : FORERUNNER, HERALD **b** : a dispatch bearer in government or military service **c** : an employee who carries messages
**2** : a light line used in hauling a heavier line (as between ships)
**3** : a substance (as a hormone) that mediates a biological effect
**4** : MESSENGER RNA

**messenger RNA** *noun* (1961)
: an RNA produced by transcription that carries the code for a particular protein from the nuclear DNA to a ribosome in the cytoplasm and acts as a template for the formation of that protein — compare TRANSFER RNA

**mess hall** *noun* (1862)
: a hall or building (as on an army post) in which mess is served

**mes·si·ah** \mə-'sī-ə\ *noun* [Hebrew *māshīaḥ* & Aramaic *měshīḥā*, literally, anointed]
**1** *capitalized* **a** : the expected king and deliverer of the Jews **b** : JESUS 1
**2** : a professed or accepted leader of some hope or cause
— **mes·si·ah·ship** \-,ship\ *noun*

**mes·si·an·ic** \,me-sē-'a-nik\ *adjective* [probably from French *messianique*, from *messianisme*] (circa 1834)
**1** : of or relating to a messiah
**2** : marked by idealism and an aggressive crusading spirit ⟨a *messianic* sense of historic mission —Edmond Taylor⟩

**mes·si·a·nism** \'me-sē-ə-,ni-zəm; mə-'sī-ə-, me-\ *noun* [French *messianisme*, from *messie* messiah + *-anisme* (as in *christianisme* Christianity)] (1876)
**1** : belief in a messiah as the savior of mankind
**2** : religious devotion to an ideal or cause

**Mes·si·as** \mə-'sī-əs\ *noun* [Middle English, from Late Latin, from Greek, from Aramaic *měshīḥā*]
: MESSIAH 1

**messieurs** *plural of* MONSIEUR

**mess jacket** *noun* (1891)
: a fitted waist-length man's jacket worn especially as part of a dress uniform

**mess kit** *noun* (circa 1877)
: a compact kit of nested cooking and eating utensils for use by soldiers and campers

**mess·mate** \'mes-,māt\ *noun* (1746)
: a person with whom one regularly takes mess (as on a ship)

**mess over** *transitive verb* (1965)
*slang* : to treat harshly or unfairly : ABUSE

**Messrs.** \'me-sərz\ *plural of* MR.
⟨*Messrs.* Jones, Brown, and Robinson⟩

**mes·suage** \'mes-wij\ *noun* [Middle English, from Anglo-French, probably alteration of Old French *mesnage* — more at MÉNAGE] (14th century)
: PREMISE 3b

**messy** \'me-sē\ *adjective* **mess·i·er; -est** (1843)
**1** : marked by confusion, disorder, or dirt : UNTIDY ⟨a *messy* room⟩
**2** : lacking neatness or precision : CARELESS, SLOVENLY ⟨*messy* thinking⟩
**3** : extremely unpleasant or trying ⟨*messy* lawsuits⟩
— **mess·i·ly** \'me-sə-lē\ *adverb*
— **mess·i·ness** \'me-sē-nəs\ *noun*

**mes·ti·za** \me-'stē-zə\ *noun* [Spanish, feminine of *mestizo*] (circa 1582)
: a woman who is a mestizo

**mes·ti·zo** \-(ˌ)zō\ *noun, plural* **-zos** [Spanish, from *mestizo*, adjective, mixed, from Late Latin *mixticius*, from Latin *mixtus*, past participle of *miscēre* to mix — more at MIX] (1582) : a person of mixed blood; *specifically* : a person of mixed European and American Indian ancestry

**mes·tra·nol** \'mes-trə-ˌnȯl, -ˌnōl\ *noun* [*meth-* + *estrogen* + *pregnane* (C₂₁H₃₆) + ¹-*ol*] (1962) : a synthetic estrogen $C_{21}H_{26}O_2$ used in oral contraceptives

**met** *past and past participle of* MEET

**meta-** *or* **met-** *prefix* [New Latin & Medieval Latin, from Latin or Greek; Latin, from Greek, among, with, after, from *meta* among, with, after; akin to Old English *mid, mith* with, Old High German *mit*] **1 a** : occurring later than or in succession to : after ⟨*metestrus*⟩ **b** : situated behind or beyond ⟨*metencephalon*⟩ ⟨*metacarpus*⟩ **c** : later or more highly organized or specialized form of ⟨*metaxylem*⟩ **2** : change : transformation **3** [*metaphysics*] : more comprehensive : transcending ⟨*metapsychology*⟩ — used with the name of a discipline to designate a new but related discipline designed to deal critically with the original one ⟨*metamathematics*⟩ **4 a** : involving substitution at or characterized by two positions in the benzene ring that are separated by one carbon atom ⟨*meta*-xylene⟩ **b** : derived from by loss of water ⟨*meta*phosphoric acid⟩

**met·a·bol·ic** \ˌme-tə-'bä-lik\ *adjective* (1845) : of, relating to, or based on metabolism — **met·a·bol·i·cal·ly** \-li-k(ə-)lē\ *adverb*

**me·tab·o·lism** \mə-'ta-bə-ˌli-zəm\ *noun* [International Scientific Vocabulary, from Greek *metabolē* change, from *metaballein* to change, from *meta-* + *ballein* to throw — more at DEVIL] (1872) **1 a** : the sum of the processes in the buildup and destruction of protoplasm; *specifically* : the chemical changes in living cells by which energy is provided for vital processes and activities and new material is assimilated **b** : the sum of the processes by which a particular substance is handled in the living body **c** : the sum of the metabolic activities taking place in a particular environment ⟨the *metabolism* of a lake⟩ **2** : METAMORPHOSIS 2 — usually used in combination ⟨holo*metabolism*⟩

**me·tab·o·lite** \-ˌlīt\ *noun* (1884) **1** : a product of metabolism **2** : a substance essential to the metabolism of a particular organism or to a particular metabolic process

**me·tab·o·lize** \-ˌlīz\ *verb* **-lized; -liz·ing** (1887) *transitive verb* : to subject to metabolism *intransitive verb* : to perform metabolism — **me·tab·o·liz·able** \mə-ˌta-bə-'lī-zə-bəl\ *adjective*

**¹meta·car·pal** \ˌme-tə-'kär-pəl\ *adjective* (1739) : of, relating to, or being the metacarpus or a metacarpal

**²metacarpal** *noun* (1854) : a bone of the part of the hand or forefoot between the carpus and the phalanges that typically contains five more or less elongated bones when all the digits are present

**meta·car·pus** \ˌme-tə-'kär-pəs\ *noun* [New Latin] (1676) : the part of the hand or forefoot that contains the metacarpals

**meta·cen·ter** \'me-tə-ˌsen-tər\ *noun* [French *métacentre*, from *méta-* meta- + *centre* center] (1794) : the point of intersection of the vertical through the center of buoyancy of a floating body with the vertical through the new center of buoyancy when the body is displaced

---

**meta·cen·tric** \ˌme-tə-'sen-trik\ *adjective* (1798) **1** : of or relating to a metacenter **2** : having the centromere medially situated so that the two chromosomal arms are of roughly equal length — **metacentric** *noun*

*metacenter: 1 center of gravity, 2 center of buoyancy, 3 new center of buoyancy when floating body is displaced, 4 point of intersection*

**meta·cer·car·ia** \ˌme-tə-(ˌ)sər-'kar-ē-ə, -'ker-\ *noun* [New Latin] (1928) : a tailless encysted late larva of a digenetic trematode that is usually the form which is infective for the definitive host — **meta·cer·car·i·al** \-ē-əl\ *adjective*

**meta·chro·mat·ic** \-krō-'ma-tik\ *adjective* (1876) **1** : staining or characterized by staining in a different color or shade from what is typical ⟨*metachromatic* granules in a bacterium⟩ **2** : having the capacity to stain different elements of a cell or tissue in different colors or shades ⟨*metachromatic* stains⟩

**meta·eth·ics** \-'e-thiks\ *noun plural but usually singular in construction* (1949) : the study of the meanings of ethical terms, the nature of ethical judgments, and the types of ethical arguments — **meta·eth·i·cal** \-thi-kəl\ *adjective*

**meta·fic·tion** \-'fik-shən\ *noun* (1978) : fiction which refers to or takes as its subject fictional writing and its conventions — **meta·fic·tion·al** \-shnəl, -shə-n³l\ *adjective* — **meta·fic·tion·ist** \-sh(ə-)nist\ *noun*

**meta·gal·axy** \-'ga-lək-sē\ *noun* [International Scientific Vocabulary] (1930) : the entire system of galaxies : UNIVERSE — **meta·ga·lac·tic** \-gə-'lak-tik\ *adjective*

**meta·gen·e·sis** \-'je-nə-səs\ *noun* [New Latin] (circa 1864) : alternation of generations in animals; *especially* : regular alteration of a sexual and an asexual generation — **meta·ge·net·ic** \-jə-'ne-tik\ *adjective*

**¹met·al** \'me-t³l\ *noun, often attributive* [Middle English, from Old French, from Latin *metallum* mine, metal, from Greek *metallon*] (14th century) **1** : any of various opaque, fusible, ductile, and typically lustrous substances that are good conductors of electricity and heat, form cations by loss of electrons, and yield basic oxides and hydroxides; *especially* : one that is a chemical element as distinguished from an alloy **2 a** : METTLE 1a **b** : the material or substance out of which a person or thing is made **3** : glass in its molten state **4 a** : printing type metal **b** : matter set in metal type **5** : ROAD METAL **6** : HEAVY METAL

**²metal** *transitive verb* **-aled** *or* **-alled; -al·ing** *or* **-al·ling** (1610) : to cover or furnish with metal

**meta·lan·guage** \'me-tə-ˌlaŋ-gwij\ *noun* (1936) : a language used to talk about language

**meta·lin·guis·tic** \'me-tə-liŋ-ˌgwis-tik\ *adjective* (1944) : of or relating to a metalanguage or to metalinguistics

**meta·lin·guis·tics** \-tiks\ *noun plural but singular in construction* (1949) : a branch of linguistics that deals with the relation between language and other cultural factors in a society

**metall-** *or* **metallo-** *combining form* [New Latin, from Latin *metallum*] : metal ⟨*metallo*phone⟩

---

**¹me·tal·lic** \mə-'ta-lik\ *adjective* (15th century) **1 a** : of, relating to, or being a metal **b** : made of or containing a metal **c** : having properties of a metal **2** : yielding metal **3** : resembling metal: as **a** : having iridescent and reflective properties ⟨*metallic* blond hair⟩ **b** : having an acrid quality like that of metal ⟨the tea has a *metallic* taste⟩ **4 a** : having a harsh resonance : GRATING ⟨a *metallic* voice⟩ **b** : having an impersonal or mechanical quality ⟨a *metallic* smile⟩ — **me·tal·li·cal·ly** \-li-k(ə-)lē\ *adverb*

**²metallic** *noun* (1952) : a fiber or yarn made of or coated with metal; *also* : a fabric made with this

**met·al·lif·er·ous** \ˌme-t³l-'i-f(ə-)rəs\ *adjective* [Latin *metallifer*, from *metallum* + *-fer* -ferous] (circa 1656) : yielding or containing metal

**met·al·lize** *also* **met·al·ize** \'me-t³l-ˌīz\ *transitive verb* **met·al·lized** *also* **met·al·ized; met·al·liz·ing** *also* **met·al·iz·ing** (1594) : to coat, treat, or combine with a metal — **met·al·li·za·tion** \ˌme-t³l-ə-'zā-shən\ *noun*

**met·al·log·ra·phy** \ˌme-t³l-'ä-grə-fē\ *noun* [International Scientific Vocabulary] (circa 1864) : a study of the structure of metals especially with the microscope — **met·al·log·ra·pher** \ˌme-t³l-'ä-grə-fər\ *noun* — **me·tal·lo·graph·ic** \mə-ˌta-lə-'gra-fik\ *adjective* — **me·tal·lo·graph·i·cal·ly** \-'gra-fi-k(ə-)lē\ *adverb*

**¹met·al·loid** \'me-t³l-ˌȯid\ *noun* (1832) **1** : a nonmetal that can combine with a metal to form an alloy **2** : an element intermediate in properties between the typical metals and nonmetals

**²metalloid** *also* **met·al·loi·dal** \ˌme-t³l-'ȯi-d³l\ *adjective* (circa 1850) **1** : resembling a metal **2** : of, relating to, or being a metalloid

**me·tal·lo·phone** \mə-'ta-lə-ˌfōn\ *noun* (circa 1883) : a percussion musical instrument consisting of a series of metal bars of varying pitch struck with hammers

**met·al·lur·gy** \'me-t³l-ˌər-jē, *especially British* mə-'ta-lər-\ *noun* [New Latin *metallurgia*, from *metall-* + *-urgia* -urgy] (circa 1704) : the science and technology of metals — **met·al·lur·gi·cal** \ˌme-t³l-'ər-ji-kəl\ *adjective* — **met·al·lur·gi·cal·ly** \-k(ə-)lē\ *adverb* — **met·al·lur·gist** \'me-t³l-ˌər-jist, *especially British* mə-'ta-lər-\ *noun*

**met·al·mark** \'me-t³l-ˌmärk\ *noun* (circa 1909) : any of a family (Riodinidae) of small or medium-sized usually brightly colored chiefly tropical butterflies that often have metallic coloration on the wings

**met·al·smith** \-ˌsmith\ *noun* (14th century) : a person skilled in metalworking

**met·al·ware** \-ˌwar, -ˌwer\ *noun* (1896) : ware made of metal; *especially* : metal utensils for household use

**met·al·work** \-ˌwərk\ *noun* (circa 1850) : the product of metalworking; *especially* : a metal object of artistic merit — **met·al·work·er** \-ˌwər-kər\ *noun*

**met·al·work·ing** \-ˌwər-kiŋ\ *noun* (1882) : the act or process of shaping things out of metal

---

\ə\ abut \³\ kitten \ər\ further \a\ ash \ā\ ace
\ä\ mop, mar \au̇\ out \ch\ chin \e\ bet \ē\ easy
\g\ go \i\ hit \ī\ ice \j\ job \ŋ\ sing \ō\ go
\ȯ\ law \ȯi\ boy \th\ thin \t̲h̲\ the \ü\ loot \u̇\ foot
\y\ yet \zh\ vision    *see also* Guide to Pronunciation

**meta·math·e·mat·ics** \'me-tə-ˌmath-'ma-tiks, -ma-thə-\ *noun plural but usually singular in construction* (circa 1890)
**:** a field of study concerned with the formal structure and properties (as the consistency and completeness of axioms) of mathematical systems
— **meta·math·e·mat·i·cal** \-ti-kəl\ *adjective*

**meta·mere** \'me-tə-ˌmir\ *noun* [International Scientific Vocabulary] (1877)
**:** any of a linear series of primitively similar segments into which the body of a higher invertebrate or vertebrate is divisible
— **meta·mer·ic** \ˌme-tə-'mer-ik, -'mir-\ *adjective*
— **meta·mer·i·cal·ly** \-i-k(ə-)lē\ *adverb*

**me·tam·er·ism** \mə-'ta-mə-ˌri-zəm\ *noun* (1877)
**:** the condition of having or the stage of evolutionary development characterized by a body made up of metameres

**meta·mor·phic** \ˌme-tə-'mòr-fik\ *adjective* (1816)
**1 :** of or relating to metamorphosis
**2** *of a rock* **:** of, relating to, or produced by metamorphism
— **meta·mor·phi·cal·ly** \-fi-k(ə-)lē\ *adverb*

**meta·mor·phism** \-'mòr-ˌfi-zəm\ *noun* (1845)
**:** a change in the constitution of rock; *specifically* **:** a pronounced change effected by pressure, heat, and water that results in a more compact and more highly crystalline condition

**meta·mor·phose** \-ˌfōz, -ˌfōs\ *verb* **-phosed; -phos·ing** [probably from Middle French *metamorphoser*, from *metamorphose* metamorphosis, from Latin *metamorphosis*] (1576)
*transitive verb*
**1 a :** to change into a different physical form especially by supernatural means **b :** to change strikingly the appearance or character of **:** TRANSFORM ⟨you are so *metamorphosed* I can hardly think you my master —Shakespeare⟩
**2 :** to cause (rock) to undergo metamorphism
*intransitive verb*
**1 :** to undergo metamorphosis
**2 :** to become transformed
**synonym** see TRANSFORM

**meta·mor·pho·sis** \ˌme-tə-'mòr-fə-səs\ *noun, plural* **-pho·ses** \-ˌsēz\ [Latin, from Greek *metamorphōsis*, from *metamorphoun* to transform, from *meta-* + *morphē* form] (1533)
**1 a :** change of physical form, structure, or substance especially by supernatural means **b :** a striking alteration in appearance, character, or circumstances
**2 :** a marked and more or less abrupt developmental change in the form or structure of an animal (as a butterfly or a frog) occurring subsequent to birth or hatching

**met·anal·y·sis** \ˌme-tə-'na-lə-səs\ *noun* (1914)
**:** a reanalysis of the division between sounds or words resulting in different constituents (as in the development of *an apron* from *a napron*)

**meta·neph·ros** \-'ne-frəs, -ˌfräs\ *noun, plural* **-roi** \-ˌfròi\ [New Latin, from *meta-* + Greek *nephros* kidney — more at NEPHRITIS] (1884)
**:** either member of the final and most caudal pair of the three successive pairs of vertebrate renal organs that functions as a permanent adult kidney in reptiles, birds, and mammals but is not present at all in lower forms — compare MESONEPHROS, PRONEPHROS
— **meta·neph·ric** \-frik\ *adjective*

**meta·phase** \'me-tə-ˌfāz\ *noun* [International Scientific Vocabulary] (1887)
**:** the stage of mitosis and meiosis in which the chromosomes become arranged in the equatorial plane of the spindle

**metaphase plate** *noun* (1939)
**:** a section in the equatorial plane of the metaphase spindle having the chromosomes oriented upon it

**met·a·phor** \'me-tə-ˌfòr *also* -fər\ *noun* [Middle French or Latin; Middle French *metaphore*, from Latin *metaphora*, from Greek, from *metapherein* to transfer, from *meta-* + *pherein* to bear — more at BEAR] (1533)
**1 :** a figure of speech in which a word or phrase literally denoting one kind of object or idea is used in place of another to suggest a likeness or analogy between them (as in *drowning in money*); *broadly* **:** figurative language — compare SIMILE
**2 :** an object, activity, or idea treated as a metaphor **:** SYMBOL 2
— **met·a·phor·ic** \ˌme-tə-'fòr-ik, -'fär-\ *or* **met·a·phor·i·cal** \-i-kəl\ *adjective*
— **met·a·phor·i·cal·ly** \-i-k(ə-)lē\ *adverb*

**meta·phos·phate** \ˌme-tə-'fäs-ˌfāt\ *noun* [International Scientific Vocabulary] (1833)
**:** a salt or ester of a metaphosphoric acid

**meta·phos·pho·ric acid** \-ˌfäs-'fòr-ik, -'fär-; -'fäs-f(ə-)rik-\ *noun* (1833)
**:** a glassy solid acid $HPO_3$ or $(HPO_3)_n$ formed by heating orthophosphoric acid

**meta·phrase** \'me-tə-ˌfrāz\ *noun* (1640)
**:** a literal translation

**meta·phys·ic** \ˌme-tə-'fi-zik\ *noun* [Middle English *metaphesyk*, from Medieval Latin *metaphysica*] (14th century)
**1 a :** METAPHYSICS **b :** a particular system of metaphysics
**2 :** the system of principles underlying a particular study or subject **:** PHILOSOPHY 3b
— **metaphysic** *adjective*

**meta·phys·i·cal** \-'fi-zi-kəl\ *adjective* (15th century)
**1 :** of or relating to metaphysics
**2 a :** of or relating to the transcendent or to a reality beyond what is perceptible to the senses **b :** SUPERNATURAL
**3 :** highly abstract or abstruse; *also* **:** THEORETICAL
**4** *often capitalized* **:** of or relating to poetry especially of the early 17th century that is highly intellectual and philosophical and marked by unconventional imagery
— **meta·phys·i·cal·ly** \-k(ə-)lē\ *adverb*

**Metaphysical** *noun* (1898)
**:** a metaphysical poet of the 17th century

**meta·phy·si·cian** \ˌme-tə-fə-'zi-shən\ *noun* (15th century)
**:** a student of or specialist in metaphysics

**meta·phys·ics** \-'fi-ziks\ *noun plural but singular in construction* [Medieval Latin *Metaphysica*, title of Aristotle's treatise on the subject, from Greek (*ta*) *meta* (*ta*) *physika*, literally, the (works) after the physical (works); from its position in his collected works] (1569)
**1 a (1) :** a division of philosophy that is concerned with the fundamental nature of reality and being and that includes ontology, cosmology, and often epistemology **(2) :** ONTOLOGY 2 **b :** abstract philosophical studies **:** a study of what is outside objective experience
**2 :** METAPHYSIC 2

**meta·pla·sia** \-'plā-zh(ē-)ə\ *noun* [New Latin] (1890)
**1 :** transformation of one tissue into another
**2 :** abnormal replacement of cells of one type by cells of another
— **meta·plas·tic** \-'plas-tik\ *adjective*

**meta·psy·chol·o·gy** \-sī-'kä-lə-jē\ *noun* [International Scientific Vocabulary] (circa 1909)
**:** speculative psychology concerned with postulating the structure (as the ego and id) and processes (as cathexis) of the mind which usually cannot be demonstrated objectively
— **meta·psy·cho·log·i·cal** \-ˌsī-kə-'lä-ji-kəl\ *adjective*

**meta·se·quoia** \-si-'kwòi-ə\ *noun* [New Latin] (1948)

**:** any of a genus (*Metasequoia*) of fossil and living deciduous coniferous trees of the bald cypress family that have leaves, buds, and branches arranged oppositely and flat leaves resembling needles

**meta·so·ma·tism** \-'sō-mə-ˌti-zəm\ *noun* (1886)
**:** metamorphism that involves changes in the chemical composition as well as in the texture of rock
— **meta·so·mat·ic** \-sō-'ma-tik\ *adjective*

**meta·sta·ble** \-'stā-bəl\ *adjective* [International Scientific Vocabulary] (1897)
**:** having or characterized by only a slight margin of stability ⟨a *metastable* compound⟩
— **meta·sta·bil·i·ty** \-stə-'bi-lə-tē\ *noun*
— **meta·sta·bly** \-'stā-b(ə-)lē\ *adverb*

**me·tas·ta·sis** \mə-'tas-tə-səs\ *noun, plural* **-ta·ses** \-ˌsēz\ [New Latin, from Late Latin, transition, from Greek, from *methistanai* to change, from *meta-* + *histanai* to set — more at STAND] (1663)
**:** change of position, state, or form: as **a :** transfer of a disease-producing agency from the site of disease to another part of the body **b :** a secondary metastatic growth of a malignant tumor
— **met·a·stat·ic** \ˌme-tə-'sta-tik\ *adjective*
— **met·a·stat·i·cal·ly** \-k(ə-)lē\ *adverb*

**me·tas·ta·size** \mə-'tas-tə-ˌsīz\ *intransitive verb* **-sized; -siz·ing** (1907)
**:** to spread by or as if by metastasis

**¹meta·tar·sal** \ˌme-tə-'tär-səl\ *adjective* (1739)
**:** of, relating to, or being the part of the human foot or of the hind foot in quadrupeds between the tarsus and the phalanges

**²metatarsal** *noun* (1854)
**:** a metatarsal bone

**meta·tar·sus** \ˌme-tə-'tär-səs\ *noun* [New Latin] (1676)
**:** the metatarsal part of a human foot or of a hind foot in quadrupeds

**me·ta·te** \mə-'tä-tē\ *noun* [Spanish, from Nahuatl *metatl*] (1834)
**:** a stone with a concave upper surface used as the lower millstone for grinding grains and especially maize

**me·tath·e·sis** \mə-'ta-thə-səs\ *noun, plural* **-e·ses** \-ˌsēz\ [Late Latin, from Greek, from *metatithenai* to transpose, from *meta-* + *tithenai* to place — more at DO] (1577)
**:** a change of place or condition: as **a :** transposition of two phonemes in a word (as in the development of *crud* from *curd* or the pronunciation \'pur-tē\ for *pretty*) **b :** a chemical reaction in which different kinds of molecules exchange parts to form other kinds of molecules
— **met·a·thet·i·cal** \ˌme-tə-'the-ti-kəl\ *or* **met·a·thet·ic** \-tik\ *adjective*
— **met·a·thet·i·cal·ly** \-ti-k(ə-)lē\ *adverb*

**meta·tho·rac·ic** \ˌme-tə-thə-'ra-sik\ *adjective* (circa 1839)
**:** of, relating to, or situated in or on the metathorax ⟨*metathoracic* legs⟩

**meta·tho·rax** \-'thōr-ˌaks, -'thòr-\ *noun* [New Latin] (1816)
**:** the posterior segment of the thorax of an insect — see INSECT illustration

**meta·xy·lem** \-'zī-ləm, -ˌlem\ *noun* (1902)
**:** the part of the primary xylem that differentiates after the protoxylem and that is distinguished typically by broader tracheids and vessels with pitted or reticulate walls

**meta·zo·al** \-'zō-əl\ *adjective* [New Latin *Metazoa*] (1928)
**:** of or relating to the metazoans

**meta·zo·an** \-'zō-ən\ *noun* [New Latin *Metazoa*, from *meta-* + *-zoa*] (1884)
**:** any of a group (*Metazoa*) that comprises all animals having the body composed of cells differentiated into tissues and organs and usually a digestive cavity lined with specialized cells
— **metazoan** *adjective*

**¹mete** \'mēt\ *transitive verb* **met·ed; met·ing** [Middle English, from Old English *metan*; akin to Old High German *mezzan* to measure, Latin *modus* measure, Greek *medesthai* to be mindful of] (before 12th century)
**1** *archaic* : MEASURE
**2** : to give out by measure : DOLE — usually used with *out* ⟨*mete* out punishment⟩

**²mete** *noun* [Middle English, from Anglo-French, from Latin *meta*] (15th century)
: BOUNDARY ⟨*metes* and bounds⟩

**me·tem·psy·cho·sis** \mə-,tem(p)-si-'kō-səs, ,me-təm-,sī-\ *noun* [Late Latin, from Greek *metempsychōsis*, from *metempsychousthai* to undergo metempsychosis, from *meta-* + *empsychos* animate, from *en-* + *psychē* soul — more at PSYCH-] (1591)
: the passing of the soul at death into another body either human or animal

**met·en·ceph·a·lon** \,met-en-'se-fə-,län, -lən\ *noun* [New Latin] (circa 1871)
: the anterior segment of the developing vertebrate hindbrain or the corresponding part of the adult brain composed of the cerebellum and pons
— **met·en·ce·phal·ic** \-,en(t)-sə-'fa-lik\ *adjective*

**me·te·or** \'mē-tē-ər, -,ȯr\ *noun* [Middle English, from Middle French *meteore*, from Medieval Latin *meteorum*, from Greek *meteōron*, from neuter of *meteōros* high in air, from *meta-* + *-eōros*, from *aeirein* to lift] (15th century)
**1** : an atmospheric phenomenon (as lightning or a snowfall)
**2 a** : any of the small particles of matter in the solar system that are directly observable only by their incandescence from frictional heating on entry into the atmosphere **b** : the streak of light produced by the passage of a meteor

**me·te·or·ic** \,mē-tē-'ȯr-ik, -'är-\ *adjective* (1789)
**1** : of, relating to, or derived from the earth's atmosphere ⟨*meteoric* water⟩
**2 a** : of or relating to a meteor **b** : resembling a meteor in speed or in sudden and temporary brilliance ⟨a *meteoric* rise to fame⟩
— **me·te·or·i·cal·ly** \-i-k(ə-)lē\ *adverb*

**me·te·or·ite** \'mē-tē-ə-,rīt\ *noun* (1824)
: a meteor that reaches the surface of the earth without being completely vaporized
— **me·te·or·it·ic** \,mē-tē-ə-'ri-tik\ *also* **me·te·or·it·i·cal** \-ti-kəl\ *adjective*

**me·te·or·it·ics** \,mē-tē-ə-'ri-tiks\ *noun plural but singular in construction* (circa 1930)
: a science that deals with meteors
— **me·te·or·it·i·cist** \-'ri-tə-sist\ *noun*

**me·te·or·oid** \'mē-tē-ə-,rȯid\ *noun* (1865)
**1** : a meteor particle itself without relation to the phenomena it produces when entering the earth's atmosphere
**2** : a meteor in orbit around the sun
— **me·te·or·oi·dal** \,mē-tē-ə-'rȯi-dᵊl\ *adjective*

**me·te·o·rol·o·gy** \,mē-tē-ə-'rä-lə-jē\ *noun* [French or Greek; French *météorologie*, from Middle French, from Greek *meteōrologia*, from *meteōron* + *-logia* -logy] (1620)
**1** : a science that deals with the atmosphere and its phenomena and especially with weather and weather forecasting
**2** : the atmospheric phenomena and weather of a region
— **me·te·o·ro·log·ic** \-rə-'lä-jik\ *or* **me·te·o·ro·log·i·cal** \-ji-kəl\ *adjective*
— **me·te·o·ro·log·i·cal·ly** \-ji-k(ə-)lē\ *adverb*
— **me·te·o·rol·o·gist** \-'rä-lə-jist\ *noun*

**¹me·ter** \'mē-tər\ *noun* [Middle English, from Old English & Middle French; Old English *mēter*, from Latin *metrum*, from Greek *metron* measure, meter; Middle French *metre*, from

Old French, from Latin *metrum* — more at MEASURE] (before 12th century)
**1 a** : systematically arranged and measured rhythm in verse: (1) : rhythm that continuously repeats a single basic pattern ⟨iambic *meter*⟩ (2) : rhythm characterized by regular recurrence of a systematic arrangement of basic patterns in larger figures ⟨ballad *meter*⟩ **b** : a measure or unit of metrical verse — usually used in combination ⟨penta*meter*⟩; compare FOOT 4 **c** : a fixed metrical pattern : verse form
**2** : the basic recurrent rhythmical pattern of note values, accents, and beats per measure in music

**²met·er** \'mē-tər\ *noun* [Middle English, from *meten* to mete] (14th century)
: one that measures; *especially* : an official measurer of commodities

**³me·ter** *noun* [French *mètre*, from Greek *metron* measure] (1797)
: the base unit of length in the International System of Units that is equal to the distance traveled by light in a vacuum in 1/299,792,458 second or to about 39.37 inches — see METRIC SYSTEM table

**⁴me·ter** *noun* [-*meter*] (1815)
**1** : an instrument for measuring and sometimes recording the time or amount of something ⟨a parking *meter*⟩ ⟨a gas *meter*⟩
**2** : POSTAGE METER; *also* : a postal marking printed by a postage meter

**⁵me·ter** *transitive verb* (1884)
**1** : to measure by means of a meter
**2** : to supply in a measured or regulated amount
**3** : to print postal indicia on by means of a postage meter

**-meter** *noun combining form* [French -*mètre*, from Greek *metron* measure]
: instrument or means for measuring ⟨baro*meter*⟩

**meter–kilogram–second** *adjective* (circa 1940)
: of, relating to, or being a system of units using the meter, kilogram, and second as its base units — abbreviation *mks*

**meter maid** *noun* (1957)
: a woman assigned by a police or traffic department to write tickets for parking violations

**me·ter·stick** \'mē-tər-,stik\ *noun* (1931)
: a measuring stick one meter long that is marked off in centimeters and usually millimeters

**met·es·trus** \,met-'es-trəs\ *noun* [New Latin] (1900)
: the period of regression that follows estrus

**meth-** *or* **metho-** *combining form* [International Scientific Vocabulary, from *methyl*]
: methyl ⟨*meth*acrylic⟩

**meth·ac·ry·late** \,me-'tha-krə-,lāt\ *noun* [International Scientific Vocabulary] (1865)
**1** : a salt or ester of methacrylic acid
**2** : an acrylic resin or plastic made from a derivative of methacrylic acid

**meth·acryl·ic acid** \,me-thə-'kri-lik-\ *noun* [International Scientific Vocabulary] (1865)
: an acid $C_4H_6O_2$ used especially in making acrylic resins or plastics

**meth·a·done** \'me-thə-,dōn\ *also* **meth·a·don** \-,dän\ *noun* [*meth*yl + *amino* + *diphenyl* + -*one*] (1947)
: a synthetic addictive narcotic drug $C_{21}H_{27}NO$ used especially in the form of its hydrochloride for the relief of pain and as a substitute narcotic in the treatment of heroin addiction

**meth·am·phet·amine** \,me-tham-'fe-tə-,mēn, -thəm-, -mən\ *noun* (1949)
: an amine $C_{10}H_{15}N$ used medically in the form of its crystalline hydrochloride especially in the treatment of obesity and often used illicitly as a stimulant — called also *methedrine*

**metha·na·tion** \,me-thə-'nā-shən\ *noun* (1926)

: the production of methane especially from carbon monoxide and hydrogen

**meth·ane** \'me-,thān, *British usually* 'mē-\ *noun* [International Scientific Vocabulary] (circa 1868)
: a colorless odorless flammable gaseous hydrocarbon $CH_4$ that is a product of decomposition of organic matter and of the carbonization of coal, is used as a fuel and as a starting material in chemical synthesis, and is the simplest of the alkanes

**meth·a·nol** \'me-thə-,nȯl, -,nōl\ *noun* [International Scientific Vocabulary] (1894)
: a light volatile flammable poisonous liquid alcohol $CH_3OH$ used especially as a solvent, antifreeze, or denaturant for ethyl alcohol and in the synthesis of other chemicals

**meth·aqua·lone** \me-'tha-kwə-,lōn\ *noun* [*meth-* + *-a-* (of unknown origin) + *quinoline* + *azole* + -*one*] (1961)
: a sedative and hypnotic nonbarbiturate drug $C_{16}H_{14}N_2O$ that is habit-forming — compare QUAALUDE

**meth·e·drine** \'me-thə-,drēn, -drən\ *noun* [from *Methedrine*, a trademark] (1939)
: METHAMPHETAMINE

**me·theg·lin** \mə-'the-glən\ *noun* [Welsh *meddyglyn*] (1533)
: ¹MEAD

**met·he·mo·glo·bin** \,met-'hē-mə-,glō-bən\ *noun* [International Scientific Vocabulary] (1870)
: a soluble brown crystalline basic blood pigment that differs from hemoglobin in containing ferric iron and in being unable to combine reversibly with molecular oxygen

**met·he·mo·glo·bi·ne·mia** \,met-,hē-mə-,glō-bə-'nē-mē-ə\ *noun* [New Latin] (1888)
: the presence of methemoglobin in the blood

**me·the·na·mine** \mə-'thē-nə-,mēn, -,mən\ *noun* [*methene* (methylene) + *amine*] (1926)
: hexamethylenetetramine especially when used as a urinary antiseptic

**meth·i·cil·lin** \,me-thə-'si-lən\ *noun* [*meth-* + *penicillin*] (1961)
: a semisynthetic penicillin $C_{17}H_{19}N_2O_6NaS$ that is especially effective against penicillinase-producing staphylococci

**me·thinks** \mi-'thiŋ(k)s\ *impersonal verb*, *past* **me·thought** \-'thȯt\ [Middle English *me thinketh*, from Old English *mē thincth*, from *mē* (dative of *ic* I) + *thincth* seems, from *thyncan* to seem — more at I, THINK] (before 12th century)
*archaic* : it seems to me

**me·thi·o·nine** \mə-'thī-ə-,nēn\ *noun* [International Scientific Vocabulary, from *methyl* + *thion-* + ²-*ine*] (1928)
: a crystalline sulfur-containing essential amino acid $C_5H_{11}NO_2S$

**meth·od** \'me-thəd\ *noun* [Middle French or Latin; Middle French *methode*, from Latin *methodus*, from Greek *methodos*, from *meta-* + *hodos* way] (1541)
**1** : a procedure or process for attaining an object: as **a** (1) : a systematic procedure, technique, or mode of inquiry employed by or proper to a particular discipline or art (2) : a systematic plan followed in presenting material for instruction **b** (1) : a way, technique, or process of or for doing something (2) : a body of skills or techniques
**2** : a discipline that deals with the principles and techniques of scientific inquiry
**3 a** : orderly arrangement, development, or classification : PLAN **b** : the habitual practice of orderliness and regularity
**4** *capitalized* : a dramatic technique by which an actor seeks to gain complete identification

---

\ə\ abut \ᵊ\ kitten \ər\ further \a\ ash \ā\ ace \ä\ mop, mar \au\ out \ch\ chin \e\ bet \ē\ easy \g\ go \i\ hit \ī\ ice \j\ job \ŋ\ sing \ō\ go \ȯ\ law \ȯi\ boy \th\ thin \th\ the \ü\ loot \u̇\ foot \y\ yet \zh\ vision    *see also* Guide to Pronunciation with the inner personality of the character being portrayed ☆

**me·thod·i·cal** \mə-'thä-di-kəl\ *also* **me·thod·ic** \-dik\ *adjective* (1570)
**1 :** arranged, characterized by, or performed with method or order ⟨a *methodical* treatment of the subject⟩
**2 :** habitually proceeding according to method **:** SYSTEMATIC ⟨*methodical* in his daily routine⟩
— **me·thod·i·cal·ly** \-di-k(ə-)lē\ *adverb*
— **me·thod·i·cal·ness** \-di-kəl-nəs\ *noun*

**meth·od·ise** *British variant of* METHODIZE

**meth·od·ism** \'me-thə-ˌdi-zəm\ *noun* (1739)
**1** *capitalized* **a :** the doctrines and practice of Methodists **b :** the Methodist churches
**2 :** methodical procedure

**meth·od·ist** \-dist\ *noun* (1593)
**1 :** a person devoted to or laying great stress on method
**2** *capitalized* **:** a member of one of the denominations deriving from the Wesleyan revival in the Church of England, having Arminian doctrine and in the U.S. modified episcopal polity, and stressing personal and social morality
— **methodist** *adjective, often capitalized*
— **meth·od·is·tic** \ˌme-thə-'dis-tik\ *adjective*

**meth·od·ize** \'me-thə-ˌdīz\ *transitive verb* **-ized; -iz·ing** (1589)
**:** to reduce to method **:** SYSTEMATIZE
*synonym* see ORDER

**method of fluxions** (circa 1719)
**:** DIFFERENTIAL CALCULUS

**meth·od·o·log·i·cal** \ˌme-thə-dᵊl-'ä-ji-kəl\ *adjective* (1849)
**:** of or relating to method or methodology
— **meth·od·o·log·i·cal·ly** \-k(ə-)lē\ *adverb*

**meth·od·ol·o·gist** \-thə-'dä-lə-jist\ *noun* (1865)
**:** a student of methodology

**meth·od·ol·o·gy** \ˌme-thə-'dä-lə-jē\ *noun, plural* **-gies** [New Latin *methodologia*, from Latin *methodus* + *-logia* -logy] (1800)
**1 :** a body of methods, rules, and postulates employed by a discipline **:** a particular procedure or set of procedures
**2 :** the analysis of the principles or procedures of inquiry in a particular field

**meth·o·trex·ate** \ˌme-thə-'trek-ˌsāt\ *noun* [*meth-* + *-trexate*, of unknown origin] (1955)
**:** a toxic anticancer drug $C_{20}H_{22}N_8O_5$ that is an analogue of folic acid and an antimetabolite

**me·thoxy·chlor** \me-'thäk-si-ˌklōr, -ˌklȯr\ *noun* [*meth-* + *oxy-* + *chlor-*] (1947)
**:** a chlorinated hydrocarbon insecticide $C_{16}H_{15}Cl_3O_2$

**me·thoxy·flu·rane** \me-ˌthäk-sē-'flu̇r-ˌān\ *noun* [*meth-* + *oxy-* + *fluor-* + *ethane*] (1962)
**:** a potent nonexplosive inhalational general anesthetic $C_3H_4Cl_2F_2O$ administered as a vapor

**Me·thu·se·lah** \mə-'thü-zə-lə, -'thyü-; -'th(y)üz-lə\ *noun* [Hebrew *Mĕthūšelah*]
**1 :** an ancestor of Noah held to have lived 969 years
**2 :** an oversize wine bottle holding about 6 liters

**meth·yl** \'me-thəl\ *noun* [International Scientific Vocabulary, back-formation from *methylene*] (circa 1844)
**:** an alkyl group $CH_3$ derived from methane by removal of one hydrogen atom
— **me·thyl·ic** \mə-'thi-lik\ *adjective*

**methyl acetate** *noun* (1885)
**:** a flammable fragrant liquid $C_3H_6O_2$ used as a solvent and paint remover and in organic synthesis

**methyl alcohol** *noun* (circa 1847)
**:** METHANOL

**me·thyl·amine** \ˌme-thə-lə-'mēn, -'la-mən; mə-'thi-lə-ˌmēn\ *noun* [International Scientific Vocabulary] (circa 1850)
**:** a flammable explosive gas $CH_3NH_2$ with a strong ammoniacal odor used especially in organic synthesis (as of dyes and insecticides)

**meth·yl·ase** \'me-thə-ˌlās, -ˌlāz\ *noun* (circa 1952)
**:** an enzyme that catalyzes methylation (as of RNA or DNA)

**meth·yl·ate** \'me-thə-ˌlāt\ *transitive verb* **-at·ed; -at·ing** (1861)
**:** to introduce the methyl group into
— **meth·yl·a·tion** \ˌme-thə-'lā-shən\ *noun*
— **meth·yl·a·tor** \'me-thə-ˌlā-tər\ *noun*

**methyl bromide** *noun* (circa 1897)
**:** a poisonous gaseous compound $CH_3Br$ used chiefly as a fumigant especially against rodents, worms, and insects

**meth·yl·cel·lu·lose** \ˌme-thəl-'sel-yə-ˌlōs, -ˌlōz\ *noun* (1921)
**:** any of various gummy products of cellulose methylation that swell in water and are used especially as emulsifiers, adhesives, thickeners, and bulk laxatives

**meth·yl·cho·lan·threne** \-kə-'lan-ˌthrēn\ *noun* [*methyl* + *cholic* acid + *anthracene*] (1937)
**:** a potent carcinogenic hydrocarbon $C_{21}H_{16}$

**meth·yl·do·pa** \ˌme-thəl-'dō-pə\ *noun* (1954)
**:** a drug $C_{10}H_{13}NO_4$ used to lower blood pressure

**meth·y·lene** \'me-thə-ˌlēn, -lən\ *noun* [French *méthylène*, from Greek *methy* wine + *hylē* wood — more at MEAD] (1835)
**:** a bivalent hydrocarbon group $CH_2$ derived from methane by removal of two hydrogen atoms

**methylene blue** *noun* (circa 1890)
**:** a basic thiazine dye $C_{16}H_{18}ClN_3S\cdot3H_2O$ used especially as a biological stain, an antidote in cyanide poisoning, and an oxidation-reduction indicator

**methylene chloride** *noun* (1880)
**:** a nonflammable liquid $CH_2Cl_2$ used especially as a solvent, paint remover, and aerosol propellant

**methyl ethyl ketone** *noun* (1876)
**:** a flammable liquid compound $C_4H_8O$ similar to acetone and used chiefly as a solvent — abbreviation *MEK*

**methyl isocyanate** *noun* (circa 1894)
**:** an extremely toxic chemical $CH_3NCO$ used especially in the manufacture of pesticides — abbreviation *MIC*

**meth·yl·mer·cury** \ˌme-thəl-'mər-kyə-rē, -'mər-k(ə-)rē\ *noun* (1919)
**:** any of various toxic compounds of mercury containing the complex $CH_3Hg-$ that often occur as pollutants which accumulate in living organisms (as fish) especially in higher levels of a food chain

**methyl methacrylate** *noun* (1933)
**:** a volatile flammable liquid $C_5H_8O_2$ that polymerizes readily and is used especially as a monomer for resins

**meth·yl·naph·tha·lene** \ˌme-thəl-'naf-thə-ˌlēn, -'nap-\ *noun* (circa 1885)
**:** either of two isomeric hydrocarbons $C_{11}H_{10}$; *especially* **:** an oily liquid used in determining cetane numbers

**methyl orange** *noun* (1881)
**:** an alkaline dye used as a chemical indicator that in dilute solution is yellow when neutral and pink when acid

**methyl parathion** *noun* (1957)
**:** a potent synthetic organophosphate insecticide $C_8H_{10}NO_5PS$ that is more toxic than parathion

**meth·yl·phe·ni·date** \ˌme-thəl-'fe-nə-ˌdāt, -'fē-\ *noun* [*methyl* + *phenyl* + piper*idine* + acet*ate*] (1958)
**:** a mild stimulant $C_{14}H_{19}NO_2$ of the central nervous system used in the form of its hydrochloride to treat narcolepsy and hyperkinetic behavior disorders in children

**meth·yl·pred·nis·o·lone** \-pred-'ni-sə-ˌlōn\ *noun* (1957)
**:** a glucocorticoid $C_{22}H_{30}O_5$ that is a derivative of prednisolone and is used as an antiinflammatory agent; *also* **:** any of several of its salts (as an acetate) used similarly

**meth·yl·xan·thine** \-'zan-ˌthēn\ *noun* (1949)
**:** a methylated xanthine derivative (as caffeine, theobromine, or theophylline)

**meth·y·ser·gide** \ˌme-thə-'sər-ˌjīd\ *noun* [*methyl* + ly*sergic* acid + am*ide*] (1962)
**:** a serotonin antagonist $C_{21}H_{27}N_3O_2$ used in the form of its maleate especially in the treatment and prevention of migraine headaches

**met·i·cal** \'me-ti-kəl\ *noun, plural* **met·i·cais** \-ˌ(ˌ)kī\ *also* **meticals** [Portuguese, from Arabic *mithqāl*] (1981)
— see MONEY table

**me·tic·u·lous** \mə-'ti-kyə-ləs\ *adjective* [Latin *meticulosus* fearful, irregular from *metus* fear] (1827)
**:** marked by extreme or excessive care in the consideration or treatment of details
*synonym* see CAREFUL
— **me·tic·u·los·i·ty** \-ˌti-kyə-'lä-sə-tē\ *noun*
— **me·tic·u·lous·ly** \-'ti-kyə-ləs-lē\ *adverb*
— **me·tic·u·lous·ness** \-nəs\ *noun*

**mé·tier** *also* **me·tier** \'me-ˌtyā, me-'\ *noun* [French, from (assumed) Vulgar Latin *misterium*, alteration of Latin *ministerium* work, ministry] (1792)
**1 :** VOCATION, TRADE
**2 :** an area of activity in which one excels **:** FORTE
*synonym* see WORK

**mé·tis** \mā-'tē(s)\ *noun, plural* **mé·tis** \-'tē(s), -'tēz\ [French, from Late Latin *mixticius* mixed — more at MESTIZO] (1816)
**:** one of mixed blood; *especially, often capitalized* **:** the offspring of an American Indian and a person of European ancestry

**met·o·nym** \'me-tə-ˌnim\ *noun* [back-formation from *metonymy*] (1862)
**:** a word used in metonymy

**me·ton·y·my** \mə-'tä-nə-mē\ *noun, plural* **-mies** [Latin *metonymia*, from Greek *metōnymia*, from *meta-* + *-ōnymon* -onym] (1547)
**:** a figure of speech consisting of the use of the name of one thing for that of another of which it is an attribute or with which it is associated (as "crown" in "lands belonging to the crown")
— **met·o·nym·ic** \ˌme-tə-'ni-mik\ *or* **met·o·nym·i·cal** \-mi-kəl\ *adjective*

**me–too** \'mē-'tü\ *adjective* (1926)
**1 :** marked by similarity to or by adoption of successful or persuasive policies or practices used or promoted by someone else
**2 :** similar or identical to an established product (as a drug) with no significant advantage over it
— **me–too·er** \-ər\ *noun*
— **me–too·ism** \-ˌi-zəm\ *noun*

**met·o·pe** \'me-tə-(ˌ)pē\ *noun* [Greek *metopē*, from *meta-* + *opē* opening; akin to Greek *ōps* eye, face — more at EYE] (1563)

☆ **SYNONYMS**
**Method, mode, manner, way, fashion, system** mean the means taken or procedure followed in achieving an end. METHOD implies an orderly logical effective arrangement usually in steps ⟨effective teaching *methods*⟩. MODE implies an order or course followed by custom, tradition, or personal preference ⟨the preferred *mode* of transportation⟩. MANNER is close to MODE but may imply a procedure or method that is individual or distinctive ⟨an odd *manner* of conducting⟩. WAY is very general and may be used for any of the preceding words ⟨has her own *way* of doing things⟩. FASHION may suggest a peculiar or characteristic way of doing something ⟨rushing about in his typical *fashion*⟩. SYSTEM suggests a fully developed or carefully formulated method often emphasizing the idea of rational orderliness ⟨a filing *system*⟩.

# METRIC SYSTEM[1]

## LENGTH

| Unit | Abbreviation | Number of Meters | Approximate U.S. Equivalent |
|---|---|---|---|
| kilometer | km | 1,000 | 0.62 mile |
| hectometer | hm | 100 | 328.08 feet |
| dekameter | dam | 10 | 32.81 feet |
| meter | m | 1 | 39.37 inches |
| decimeter | dm | 0.1 | 3.94 inches |
| centimeter | cm | 0.01 | 0.39 inch |
| millimeter | mm | 0.001 | 0.039 inch |
| micrometer | $\mu$m | 0.000001 | 0.000039 inch |

## AREA

| Unit | Abbreviation | Number of Square Meters | Approximate U.S. Equivalent |
|---|---|---|---|
| square kilometer | sq km *or* km$^2$ | 1,000,000 | 0.3861 square miles |
| hectare | ha | 10,000 | 2.47 acres |
| are | a | 100 | 119.60 square yards |
| square centimeter | sq cm *or* cm$^2$ | 0.0001 | 0.155 square inch |

## VOLUME

| Unit | Abbreviation | Number of Cubic Meters | Approximate U.S. Equivalent |
|---|---|---|---|
| cubic meter | m$^3$ | 1 | 1.307 cubic yards |
| cubic decimeter | dm$^3$ | 0.001 | 61.023 cubic inches |
| cubic centimeter | cu cm *or* cm$^3$ *also* cc | 0.000001 | 0.061 cubic inch |

## CAPACITY

| Unit | Abbreviation | Number of Liters | cubic | dry | liquid |
|---|---|---|---|---|---|
| kiloliter | kl | 1,000 | 1.31 cubic yards | | |
| hectoliter | hl | 100 | 3.53 cubic feet | 2.84 bushels | |
| dekaliter | dal | 10 | 0.35 cubic foot | 1.14 pecks | 2.64 gallons |
| liter | l | 1 | 61.02 cubic inches | 0.908 quart | 1.057 quarts |
| cubic decimeter | dm$^3$ | 1 | 61.02 cubic inches | 0.908 quart | 1.057 quarts |
| deciliter | dl | 0.10 | 6.1 cubic inches | 0.18 pint | 0.21 pint |
| centiliter | cl | 0.01 | 0.61 cubic inch | | 0.338 fluid ounce |
| milliliter | ml | 0.001 | 0.061 cubic inch | | 0.27 fluid dram |
| microliter | $\mu$l | 0.000001 | 0.000061 cubic inch | | 0,00027 fluid dram |

## MASS AND WEIGHT

| Unit | Abbreviation | Number of Grams | Approximate U.S. Equivalent |
|---|---|---|---|
| metric ton | t | 1,000,000 | 1.102 short tons |
| kilogram | kg | 1,000 | 2.2046 pounds |
| hectogram | hg | 100 | 3.527 ounces |
| dekagram | dag | 10 | 0.353 ounce |
| gram | g | 1 | 0.035 ounce |
| decigram | dg | 0.10 | 1.543 grains |
| centigram | cg | 0.01 | 0.154 grain |
| milligram | mg | 0.001 | 0.015 grain |
| microgram | $\mu$g | 0.000001 | 0.000015 grain |

[1]For metric equivalents of U.S. units, see Weights and Measures table

: the space between two triglyphs of a Doric frieze often adorned with carved work

**met·o·pon** \'me-tə-ˌpän\ *noun* [*meth-* + *hydro-* + *mor*phine + *-one*] (1941)
: a narcotic drug $C_{18}H_{21}NO_3$ that is derived from morphine and is used in the form of the hydrochloride to relieve pain

**me·tre** \'mē-tər\ *chiefly British variant of* METER

**[1]met·ric** \'me-trik\ *noun* [Greek *metrikē,* from feminine of *metrikos* in meter, by measure, from *metron* measure — more at MEASURE] (1760)
**1** *plural* : a part of prosody that deals with metrical structure
**2** : a standard of measurement ⟨no *metric* exists that can be applied directly to happiness —*Scientific Monthly*⟩
**3** : a mathematical function that associates with each pair of elements of a set a real nonnegative number with the general properties of distance such that the number is zero only if the two elements are identical, the number is the same regardless of the order in which the two elements are taken, and the number associated with one pair of elements plus that associated with one member of the pair and a third element is equal to or greater than the number associated with the other member of the pair and the third element

**[2]metric** *adjective* [French *métrique,* from *mètre* meter] (1864)
: of, relating to, or using the metric system ⟨a *metric* study⟩
— **met·ri·cal·ly** \-tri-k(ə-)lē\ *adverb*

**-metric** *or* **-metrical** *adjective combining form*
**1** : of, employing, or obtained by (such) a meter ⟨galvano*metric*⟩
**2** : of or relating to (such) an art, process, or science of measuring ⟨geo*metrical*⟩

**met·ri·cal** \'me-tri-kəl\ *or* **met·ric** \-trik\ *adjective* (15th century)
**1** : of, relating to, or composed in meter
**2** : of or relating to measurement
— **met·ri·cal·ly** \-tri-k(ə-)lē\ *adverb*

**met·ri·ca·tion** \ˌme-tri-'kā-shən\ *noun* (1965)
: the act or process of metricizing; *specifically* : conversion of an existent system of units into the metric system

**met·ri·cize** \'me-trə-ˌsīz\ *transitive verb* **-cized; -ciz·ing** (1873)
: to change into or express in the metric system

**metric space** *noun* (1927)
: a mathematical set for which a metric is defined for any pair of elements

**metric system** *noun* (1864)
: a decimal system of weights and measures based on the meter and on the kilogram

**metric ton** *noun* (circa 1890)
— see METRIC SYSTEM table

**me·trist** \'me-trist, 'mē-\ *noun* (1535)
**1** : a maker of verses
**2** : one skillful in handling meter
**3** : a student of meter or metrics

**[1]met·ro** \'me-(ˌ)trō, *in French context also* mā-'\ *noun, plural* **metros** [French *métro,* short for (*chemin de fer*) *métropolitain* metropolitan railroad] (1904)
: SUBWAY b

**[2]met·ro** \'me-(ˌ)trō\ *adjective* (1953)
: METROPOLITAN 2

**me·trol·o·gy** \me-'trä-lə-jē\ *noun* [French *métrologie,* from Greek *metrologia* theory of ratios, from *metron* measure — more at MEASURE] (1816)
**1** : the science of weights and measures or of measurement
**2** : a system of weights and measures
— **met·ro·log·i·cal** \ˌme-trə-'lä-ji-kəl\ *adjective*
— **me·trol·o·gist** \me-'trä-lə-jist\ *noun*

\ə\ abut \ᵊ\ kitten \ər\ further \a\ ash \ā\ ace
\ä\ mop, mar \aů\ out \ch\ chin \e\ bet \ē\ easy
\g\ go \i\ hit \ī\ ice \j\ job \ŋ\ sing \ō\ go
\ȯ\ law \ȯi\ boy \th\ thin \t̲h̲\ the \ü\ loot \ů\ foot
\y\ yet \zh\ vision *see also* Guide to Pronunciation

**met·ro·ni·da·zole** \,me-trə-'nī-də-,zōl\ *noun* [methyl + *-tron-* (probably alteration of *nitro-*) + im*ide* + *azole*] (1962)
**:** a drug $C_6H_9N_3O_3$ used especially in treating vaginal trichomoniasis

**met·ro·nome** \'me-trə-,nōm\ *noun* [Greek *metron* + *-nomos* controlling, from *nomos* law — more at NIMBLE] (1816)
**:** an instrument designed to mark exact time by a regularly repeated tick

**met·ro·nom·ic** \,me-trə-'nä-mik\ *also* **met·ro·nom·i·cal** \-mi-kəl\ *adjective* (1866)
**:** mechanically regular (as in action or tempo)
— **met·ro·nom·i·cal·ly** \-mi-k(ə-)lē\ *adverb*

**me·trop·o·lis** \mə-'trä-p(ə-)ləs\ *noun* [Middle English, from Late Latin, from Greek *mētropolis,* from *mētr-, mētēr* mother + *polis* city — more at MOTHER, POLICE] (14th century)
**1 :** the chief or capital city of a country, state, or region
**2 :** the city or state of origin of a colony (as of ancient Greece)
**3 a :** a city regarded as a center of a specified activity ⟨a great business *metropolis*⟩ **b :** a large important city ⟨the world's great *metropolises* —P. E. James⟩

**¹met·ro·pol·i·tan** \,me-trə-'pä-lə-t°n\ *noun* (14th century)
**1 :** the primate of an ecclesiastical province
**2 :** one who lives in a metropolis or displays metropolitan manners or customs

**²metropolitan** *adjective* [Middle English, from Late Latin *metropolitanus* of the see of a metropolitan, from *metropolita,* noun, metropolitan, from Late Greek *mētropolitēs,* from *mētropolis* see of a metropolitan, from Greek, capital] (15th century)
**1 :** of or constituting a metropolitan or his see
**2 :** of, relating to, or characteristic of a metropolis and sometimes including its suburbs
**3 :** of, relating to, or constituting a mother country as distinguished from a colony

**me·tror·rha·gia** \,mē-trə-'rā-j(ē-)ə, -'rā-zhə; -'rä-jə, -zhə\ *noun* [New Latin, from *metro-* womb (from Greek *mētra,* from *mētr-, mētēr* mother) + *-rrhagia* — more at MOTHER] (1879)
**:** profuse uterine bleeding especially between menstrual periods

**-metry** *noun combining form* [Middle English *-metrie,* from Middle French, from Latin *-metria,* from Greek, from *metrein* to measure, from *metron* — more at MEASURE]
**:** art, process, or science of measuring ⟨chronometry⟩ ⟨photometry⟩

**met·tle** \'me-t°l\ *noun* [alteration of *metal*] (1581)
**1 a :** vigor and strength of spirit or temperament ⟨suspected to have more tongue in his head than *mettle* in his bosom —Sir Walter Scott⟩ **b :** staying quality **:** STAMINA ⟨trucks had proved their *mettle* in army transport —*Pioneer & Pacemaker*⟩
**2 :** quality of temperament or disposition ⟨gentlemen of brave *mettle* —Shakespeare⟩
*synonym* see COURAGE
— **met·tled** \-t°ld\ *adjective*
— **on one's mettle :** aroused to do one's best

**met·tle·some** \'me-t°l-səm\ *adjective* (1662)
**:** full of mettle **:** SPIRITED

**meu·nière** \(,)mə(r)-'yer, mœn-\ *adjective* [French (*à la*) *meunière,* literally, in the manner of a miller's wife] (1903)
**:** rolled lightly in flour and sautéed in butter ⟨sole *meunière*⟩

**Meur·sault** \mə(r)-'sō, mœ-\ *noun* [French, from *Meursault,* commune in France] (1833)
**:** a dry white burgundy wine

**¹mew** \'myü\ *noun* [Middle English, from Old English *mǣw;* akin to Old Norse *mār* gull] (before 12th century)
**:** GULL; *especially* **:** the common European gull (*Larus canus*)

**²mew** *verb* [Middle English *mewen,* of imitative origin] (14th century)
*intransitive verb*
**:** to utter a mew or similar sound ⟨gulls *mewed* over the bay⟩
*transitive verb*
**:** to utter by mewing **:** MEOW

**³mew** *noun* (1596)
**:** MEOW

**⁴mew** *noun* [Middle English *mewe,* from Middle French *mue,* from *muer* to molt, from Latin *mutare* to change — more at MUTABLE] (14th century)
**1 :** an enclosure for trained hawks — usually used in plural
**2 :** a place for hiding or retirement
**3** *plural but singular or plural in construction, chiefly British* **a** (1) **:** stables usually with living quarters built around a court (2) **:** living quarters adapted from such stables **b :** back street **:** ALLEY

**⁵mew** *transitive verb* (15th century)
**:** to shut up **:** CONFINE — often used with *up*

**mewl** \'myü(ə)l\ *intransitive verb* [imitative] (1600)
**:** to cry weakly **:** WHIMPER

**Mex·i·can** \'mek-si-kən\ *noun* (1604)
**1 a :** a native or inhabitant of Mexico **b :** a person of Mexican descent **c** *Southwest* **:** a person of mixed Spanish and Indian descent
**2 :** NAHUATL
— **Mexican** *adjective*

**Mexican bean beetle** *noun* (1921)
**:** a spotted ladybug (*Epilachna varivestis*) that feeds on the leaves of beans

**Mexican jumping bean** *noun* (circa 1929)
**:** JUMPING BEAN

**Mexican Spanish** *noun* (1945)
**:** the Spanish used in Mexico

**Mexican standoff** *noun* (1891)
**:** a situation in which no one emerges a clear winner; *also* **:** DEADLOCK

**me·ze** \me-'zā, 'mā-(,)zā\ *noun, plural* **mezes** *also* **meze** [New Greek & Turkish; New Greek *mezes,* from Turkish *meze,* perhaps from Arabic dialect *mazza, māzza*] (1926)
**:** an appetizer in Greek or Middle Eastern cuisine often served with an aperitif

**me·ze·re·on** \mə-'zir-ē-ən\ *noun* [Middle English *mizerion,* from Medieval Latin *mezereon,* from Arabic *māzariyūn,* from Persian] (15th century)
**:** a small European shrub (*Daphne mezereum* of the family Thymelaeaceae, the mezereon family) with fragrant lilac purple flowers and poisonous emetic leaves, fruit, and bark

**me·zu·zah** *or* **me·zu·za** \mə-'zu̇-zə\ *noun, plural* **-zahs** *or* **-zas** *or* **-zot** \-'zu̇-,zōt\ [Hebrew *mĕzūzāh* doorpost] (1650)
**:** a small parchment scroll inscribed with Deuteronomy 6:4–9 and 11:13–21 and the name Shaddai and placed in a case fixed to the doorpost by some Jewish families as a sign and reminder of their faith

**mez·za·nine** \'me-z°n-,ēn, ,me-z°n-'\ *noun* [French, from Italian *mezzanino,* from *mezzano* middle, from Latin *medianus* middle, median] (1711)
**1 :** a low-ceilinged story between two main stories of a building; *especially* **:** an intermediate story that projects in the form of a balcony
**2 a :** the lowest balcony in a theater **b :** the first few rows of such a balcony

**mez·za vo·ce** \,met-sä-'vō-(,)chä, ,med-zä-\ *adverb or adjective* [Italian, half voice] (1775)
**:** with medium or half volume — used as a direction in music

**mez·zo** \'met-(,)sō, 'med-(,)zō\ *noun, plural* **mezzos** [Italian, literally, middle, moderate, half, from Latin *medius* — more at MID] (1832)

**:** MEZZO-SOPRANO

**mez·zo for·te** \,met-(,)sō-'fȯr-,tā, ,med-(,)zō-, -'fȯr-tē\ *adjective or adverb* [Italian] (1811)
**:** moderately loud — used as a direction in music

**mez·zo pia·no** \-pē-'ä-(,)nō\ *adjective or adverb* [Italian] (1811)
**:** moderately soft — used as a direction in music

**mez·zo-re·lie·vo** *or* **mez·zo-ri·lie·vo** \-ri-'lē-(,)vō, -rēl-'yā-(,)vō\ *noun, plural* **-vos** [Italian *mezzorilievo,* from *mezzo* + *rilievo* relief] (1598)
**:** sculptural relief intermediate between bas-relief and high relief

**mez·zo-so·pra·no** \-sə-'pra-(,)nō, -'prä-\ *noun* [Italian *mezzosoprano,* from *mezzo* + *soprano*] (circa 1753)
**1 :** a woman's voice with a range between that of the soprano and contralto
**2 :** a singer having a mezzo-soprano voice

**mez·zo·tint** \'met-sō-,tint, 'med-zō-\ *noun* [modification of Italian *mezzatinta,* from *mezza* (feminine of *mezzo*) + *tinta* tint] (1738)
**1 :** a manner of engraving on copper or steel by scraping or burnishing a roughened surface to produce light and shade
**2 :** an engraving produced by mezzotint

**mho** \'mō\ *noun, plural* **mhos** [backward spelling of *ohm*] (1883)
**:** a unit of conductance equal to the reciprocal of the ohm **:** SIEMENS

**mi** \'mē\ *noun* [Medieval Latin, from the syllable sung to this note in a medieval hymn to Saint John the Baptist] (15th century)
**:** the 3d tone of the diatonic scale in solmization

**MIA** \,em-(,)ī-'ā\ *noun* [*missing in action*] (1944)
**:** a member of the armed forces whose whereabouts following a combat mission are unknown and whose death cannot be established beyond reasonable doubt

**Mi·ami** \mī-'a-mē, -mə\ *noun, plural* **Mi·ami** *or* **Mi·am·is** (1722)
**:** a member of an American Indian people originally of Wisconsin and Indiana

**mi·aow** \mē-'au̇\ *variant of* MEOW

**mi·as·ma** \mī-'az-mə, mē-\ *noun, plural* **-mas** *also* **-ma·ta** \-mə-tə\ [New Latin, from Greek, defilement, from *miainein* to pollute] (1665)
**1 :** a vaporous exhalation formerly believed to cause disease; *also* **:** a heavy vaporous emanation or atmosphere ⟨a *miasma* of tobacco smoke⟩
**2 :** an influence or atmosphere that tends to deplete or corrupt ⟨freed from the *miasma* of poverty —Sir Arthur Bryant⟩; *also* **:** an atmosphere that obscures **:** FOG ⟨retreated into an asexual mental *miasma* —*Times Literary Supplement*⟩
— **mi·as·mal** \-məl\ *adjective*
— **mi·as·mat·ic** \,mī-əz-'ma-tik\ *adjective*
— **mi·as·mic** \mī-'az-mik, mē-\ *adjective*
— **mi·as·mi·cal·ly** \-mi-k(ə-)lē\ *adverb*

**mi·ca** \'mī-kə\ *noun* [New Latin, from Latin, grain, crumb; perhaps akin to Greek *mikros* small] (1777)
**:** any of various colored or transparent mineral silicates crystallizing in monoclinic forms that readily separate into very thin leaves
— **mi·ca·ceous** \mī-'kā-shəs\ *adjective*

**Mi·cah** \'mī-kə\ *noun* [Hebrew *Mīkhāh,* short for *Mīkhāyāh*]
**1 :** a Hebrew prophet of the 8th century B.C.
**2 :** a prophetic book of canonical Jewish and Christian Scripture — see BIBLE table

**Mi·caw·ber** \mi-'kȯ-bər, -'kä-\ *noun* [Wilkins *Micawber,* character in the novel *David Copperfield* (1849–50) by Charles Dickens] (1852)
**:** one who is poor but lives in optimistic expectation of better fortune
— **Mi·caw·ber·ish** \-bə-rish\ *adjective*

**mice** *plural of* MOUSE

**mi·celle** \mī-'sel\ *noun* [New Latin *micella*, from Latin *mica*] (1881)
**:** a unit of structure built up from polymeric molecules or ions: as **a :** an ordered region in a fiber (as of cellulose or rayon) **b :** a molecular aggregate that constitutes a colloidal particle
— **mi·cel·lar** \-'se-lər\ *adjective*

**Mi·chael** \'mī-kəl\ *noun* [Hebrew *Mīkhā'ēl*]
**:** one of the four archangels named in Hebrew tradition

**Mi·chae·lis constant** \mī-'kā-ləs-, mə-\ *noun* [Leonor *Michaelis* (died 1949) American biochemist] (1949)
**:** a constant that is a measure of the kinetics of an enzyme reaction and that is equivalent to the concentration of substrate at which the reaction takes place at one half its maximum rate

**Mich·ael·mas** \'mi-kəl-məs\ *noun* [Middle English *mychelmesse*, from Old English *Michaeles mæsse* Michael's mass] (before 12th century)
**:** September 29 celebrated as the feast of Saint Michael the Archangel

**Michaelmas daisy** *noun* (1785)
**:** a wild aster; *especially* **:** one blooming about Michaelmas

**Mi·che·as** \'mī-kē-əs, mī-'\ *noun* [Late Latin *Michaeas*, from Greek *Michaias*, from Hebrew *Mīkhāyāh*]
**:** MICAH

**mick** \'mik\ *noun, often capitalized* [*Mick*, nickname for *Michael*, common Irish given name] (1856)
**:** IRISHMAN — often taken to be offensive

**Mick·ey Finn** \mi-kē-'fin\ *noun* [probably from the name *Mickey Finn*] (1928)
**:** a drink of liquor doctored with a purgative or a drug

**Mickey Mouse** \'mi-kē-'maús\ *adjective* [*Mickey Mouse*, cartoon character created by Walt Disney] (1936)
**1** *often not capitalized* **:** being or performing insipid or corny popular music
**2 :** lacking importance **:** INSIGNIFICANT ⟨*Mickey Mouse* courses, where you don't work too hard —Willie Cager⟩
**3 :** annoyingly petty ⟨*Mickey Mouse* regulations⟩

**mick·le** \'mi-kəl\ *adjective* [Middle English *mikel*, from Old English *micel* — more at MUCH] (before 12th century)
*chiefly Scottish* **:** GREAT, MUCH
— **mickle** *adverb, chiefly Scottish*

**Mic·mac** \'mik-,mak\ *noun, plural* **Micmac** *or* **Micmacs** [Micmac *mi'kmaw*] (1830)
**1 :** a member of an American Indian people of eastern Canada
**2 :** the Algonquian language of the Micmac people

**micr-** *or* **micro-** *combining form* [Middle English *micro-*, from Latin, from Greek *mikr-*, *mikro-*, from *mikros, smikros* small, short; perhaps akin to Old English *smēalīc* careful, exquisite]
**1 a :** small **:** minute ⟨*micro*capsule⟩ **b :** used for or involving minute quantities or variations ⟨*micro*barograph⟩
**2 :** one millionth part of a (specified) unit ⟨*micro*gram⟩
**3 a :** using microscopy ⟨*micro*dissection⟩ **:** used in microscopy **b :** revealed by or having the structure discernible only by microscopic examination ⟨*micro*organism⟩
**4 :** abnormally small ⟨*micro*cyte⟩
**5 :** of or relating to a small area ⟨*micro*climate⟩
**6 :** employed in or connected with microphotographing or microfilming ⟨*micro*copy⟩

**¹mi·cro** \'mī-(,)krō\ *adjective* [*micr-*] (1923)
**1 :** very small; *especially* **:** MICROSCOPIC
**2 :** involving minute quantities or variations

**²micro** *noun, plural* **micros** (1971)
**1 :** MICROCOMPUTER
**2 :** MICROPROCESSOR

**mi·cro·am·pere** \,mī-krō-'am-,pir\ *noun* (circa 1890)
**:** a unit of current equal to one millionth of an ampere

**mi·cro·anal·y·sis** \-ə-'na-lə-səs\ *noun* (1856)
**:** chemical analysis on a small or minute scale that usually requires special, very sensitive, or small-scale apparatus
— **mi·cro·an·a·lyst** \-'a-nᵊl-ist\ *noun*
— **mi·cro·an·a·lyt·i·cal** \-'i-ti-kəl\ *also* **mi·cro·an·a·lyt·ic** \-,a-nᵊl-'i-tik\ *adjective*

**mi·cro·anat·o·my** \-ə-'na-tə-mē\ *noun* (circa 1899)
**:** HISTOLOGY
— **mi·cro·an·a·tom·i·cal** \-,a-nə-'tä-mi-kəl\ *adjective*

**mi·cro·bal·ance** \'mī-krō-,ba-lən(t)s\ *noun* (1903)
**:** a balance designed to measure very small weights

**mi·cro·baro·graph** \,mī-krō-'bar-ə-,graf\ *noun* [International Scientific Vocabulary] (1904)
**:** a barograph for recording small and rapid changes

**mi·crobe** \'mī-,krōb\ *noun* [International Scientific Vocabulary *micr-* + Greek *bios* life — more at QUICK] (1881)
**:** MICROORGANISM, GERM
— **mi·cro·bi·al** \mī-'krō-bē-əl\ *also* **mi·cro·bic** \-bik\ *adjective*

**mi·cro·beam** \'mī-krō-,bēm\ *noun* (1950)
**:** a beam of radiation of small cross section ⟨a focused laser *microbeam*⟩ ⟨a *microbeam* of electrons⟩

**mi·cro·bi·ol·o·gy** \,mī-krō-bī-'ä-lə-jē\ *noun* [International Scientific Vocabulary] (1888)
**:** a branch of biology dealing especially with microscopic forms of life
— **mi·cro·bi·o·log·i·cal** \-,bī-ə-'lä-ji-kəl\ *also* **mi·cro·bi·o·log·ic** \-'lä-jik\ *adjective*
— **mi·cro·bi·o·log·i·cal·ly** \-ji-k(ə-)lē\ *adverb*
— **mi·cro·bi·ol·o·gist** \-bī-'ä-lə-jist\ *noun*

**mi·cro·brew** \'mī-krō-,brü\ *noun* (1987)
**:** a beer produced by a microbrewery

**mi·cro·brew·ery** \,mī-krō-'brü-ə-rē, -'brü-(ə)r-ē\ *noun* (1984)
**:** a small brewery making specialty beer in limited quantities
— **mi·cro·brew·er** \'mī-krō-,brü-ər, -,brü-(ə)r\ *noun*
— **mi·cro·brew·ing** \-,brü-iŋ\ *noun*

**mi·cro·burst** \'mī-krō-,bərst\ *noun* (1982)
**:** a violent short-lived localized downdraft that creates extreme wind shears at low altitudes and is usually associated with thunderstorms

**mi·cro·bus** \-,bəs\ *noun* (1945)
**:** a station wagon shaped like a bus

**mi·cro·cal·o·rim·e·ter** \-,ka-lə-'ri-mə-tər\ *noun* (1911)
**:** an instrument for measuring very small quantities of heat
— **mi·cro·ca·lo·ri·met·ric** \-,ka-lə-rə-'me-trik; -kə-,lòr-ə-, -,lōr-, -,lär-\ *adjective*
— **mi·cro·cal·o·rim·e·try** \-,ka-lə-'ri-mə-trē\ *noun*

**mi·cro·cap·sule** \'mī-krō-,kap-səl, -(,)sül *also* -,syü(ə)l\ *noun* (1961)
**:** a tiny capsule containing material (as an adhesive or a medicine) that is released when the capsule is broken, melted, or dissolved

**mi·cro·cas·sette** \,mī-krō-kə-'set, -ka-\ *noun* (1979)
**:** a small cassette of magnetic tape that is used especially for dictation

**¹mi·cro·ce·phal·ic** \-sə-'fa-lik\ *adjective* (circa 1856)
**:** having a small head; *specifically* **:** having an abnormally small head

**²microcephalic** *noun* (circa 1873)
**:** one that is microcephalic

**mi·cro·ceph·a·ly** \-'se-fə-lē\ *noun* [New Latin *microcephalia*, from *microcephalus* microcephalic, from *micr-* + Greek *kephalē* head — more at CEPHALIC] (1863)
**:** a condition of abnormal smallness of the head usually associated with mental defects

**mi·cro·chip** \'mī-krō-,chip\ *noun* (1969)
**:** INTEGRATED CIRCUIT

**mi·cro·cir·cuit** \-,sər-kət\ *noun* (1959)
**:** a compact electronic circuit **:** INTEGRATED CIRCUIT
— **mi·cro·cir·cuit·ry** \,mī-krō-'sər-kə-trē\ *noun*

**mi·cro·cir·cu·la·tion** \,mī-krō-,sər-kyə-'lā-shən\ *noun* (1959)
**:** blood circulation in the microvascular system; *also* **:** the microvascular system itself
— **mi·cro·cir·cu·la·to·ry** \-'sər-kyə-lə-,tòr-ē, -,tòr-\ *adjective*

**mi·cro·cli·mate** \'mī-krō-,klī-mət\ *noun* [International Scientific Vocabulary] (1925)
**:** the essentially uniform local climate of a usually small site or habitat
— **mi·cro·cli·mat·ic** \,mī-krō-klī-'ma-tik\ *adjective*

**mi·cro·cline** \'mī-krō-,klīn\ *noun* [German *Mikroklin*, from *mikr-* micr- + Greek *klinein* to lean — more at LEAN] (1849)
**:** a triclinic mineral of the feldspar group that is like orthoclase in composition

**mi·cro·coc·cus** \,mī-krō-'kä-kəs\ *noun, plural* **-coc·ci** \-'käk-(,)sī, -(,)sē; -'kä-(,)kī, -(,)kē\ [New Latin] (1870)
**:** a small spherical bacterium; *especially* **:** any of a genus (*Micrococcus*) of gram-positive chiefly harmless bacteria that typically occur in irregular clusters
— **mi·cro·coc·cal** \-'kä-kəl\ *adjective*

**mi·cro·code** \'mī-krə-,kōd\ *noun* (circa 1962)
**:** the microinstructions especially of a microprocessor

**mi·cro·com·put·er** \'mī-krō-kəm-,pyü-tər\ *noun* (1971)
**1 :** a very small computer that uses a microprocessor to handle information
**2 :** MICROPROCESSOR

**mi·cro·copy** \'mī-krō-,kä-pē\ *noun* [International Scientific Vocabulary] (1935)
**:** a photographic copy in which graphic matter is reduced in size (as on microfilm)

**mi·cro·cosm** \'mī-krə-,kä-zəm\ *noun* [Middle English, from Medieval Latin *microcosmus*, modification of Greek *mikros kosmos*] (15th century)
**1 :** a little world; *especially* **:** the human race or human nature seen as an epitome of the world or the universe
**2 :** a community or other unity that is an epitome of a larger unity
— **mi·cro·cos·mic** \,mī-krə-'käz-mik\ *adjective*
— **mi·cro·cos·mi·cal·ly** \-mi-k(ə-)lē\ *adverb*
— **in microcosm :** in a greatly diminished size, form, or scale

**microcosmic salt** *noun* (1783)
**:** a white crystalline salt $NaNH_5PO_4 \cdot 4H_2O$ used as a flux in testing for metallic oxides and salts

**mi·cro·cos·mos** \'mī-krə-,käz-məs, -,mōs, -,mäs\ *noun* [Middle English *mycrocossmos*, from Medieval Latin *microcosmus*] (13th century)
**1 :** MICROCOSM
**2 :** the microscopic or submicroscopic world

**mi·cro·crys·tal** \'mī-krō-,kris-tᵊl\ *noun* (1886)
**:** a crystal visible only under the microscope
— **mi·cro·crys·tal·line** \,mī-krō-'kris-tə-lən *also* -,līn *or* -,lēn\ *adjective*
— **mi·cro·crys·tal·lin·i·ty** \-,kris-tə-'li-nə-tē\ *noun*

**mi·cro·cul·ture** \'mī-krō-,kəl-chər\ *noun* (1892)

**1 :** a microscopic culture of cells or organisms
**2 :** the culture of a small group of human beings with limited perspective
— **mi·cro·cul·tur·al** \ˌmī-krō-'kəlch-rəl, -'kəl-chə-\ *adjective*
**mi·cro·cu·rie** \'mī-krō-ˌkyùr-ē, ˌmī-krō-kyù-'rē\ *noun* (1911)
**:** a unit of quantity or of radioactivity equal to one millionth of a curie
**mi·cro·cyte** \'mī-krə-ˌsīt\ *noun* [International Scientific Vocabulary] (1876)
**:** a small red blood cell present especially in some anemias
— **mi·cro·cyt·ic** \ˌmī-krə-'si-tik\ *adjective*
**mi·cro·den·si·tom·e·ter** \'mī-krō-ˌden(t)-sə-'tä-mə-tər\ *noun* (1935)
**:** a densitometer for measuring the densities of very small areas of a photographic film or plate
— **mi·cro·den·si·to·met·ric** \-sə-tə-'me-trik\ *adjective*
— **mi·cro·den·si·tom·e·try** \-sə-'tä-mə-trē\ *noun*
**mi·cro·dis·sec·tion** \ˌmī-krō-di-'sek-shən, -dī-\ *noun* (1915)
**:** dissection under the microscope; *specifically* **:** dissection of cells and tissues by means of fine needles that are precisely manipulated by levers
**mi·cro·dot** \'mī-krə-ˌdät, -krō-\ *noun* (1946)
**:** a photographic reproduction of printed matter reduced to the size of a dot for ease or security of transmittal
**mi·cro·earth·quake** \ˌmī-krō-'ərth-ˌkwāk\ *noun* (1965)
**:** an earthquake of low intensity
**mi·cro·eco·nom·ics** \-ˌe-kə-'nä-miks, -ˌē-kə-\ *noun plural but usually singular in construction* (1947)
**:** a study of economics in terms of individual areas of activity (as a firm, household, or prices) — compare MACROECONOMICS
— **mi·cro·eco·nom·ic** \-'nä-mik\ *adjective*
**mi·cro·elec·trode** \ˌmī-krō-i-'lek-ˌtrōd\ *noun* (1917)
**:** a minute electrode; *especially* **:** one that is inserted in a living biological cell or tissue in studying its electrical characteristics
**mi·cro·elec·tron·ics** \-i-ˌlek-'trä-niks\ *noun plural* (1958)
**1** *singular in construction* **:** a branch of electronics that deals with the miniaturization of electronic circuits and components
**2 :** devices, equipment, or circuits produced using the methods of microelectronics
— **mi·cro·elec·tron·ic** \-nik\ *adjective*
— **mi·cro·elec·tron·i·cal·ly** \-ni-k(ə-)lē\ *adverb*
**mi·cro·elec·tro·pho·re·sis** \-i-ˌlek-trə-fə-'rē-səs\ *noun* [New Latin] (1936)
**:** electrophoresis in which the movement of single particles is observed in a microscope; *also* **:** electrophoresis in which micromethods are used
— **mi·cro·elec·tro·pho·ret·ic** \-'re-tik\ *adjective*
— **mi·cro·elec·tro·pho·ret·i·cal·ly** \-ti-k(ə-)lē\ *adverb*
**mi·cro·el·e·ment** \-'e-lə-mənt\ *noun* (1936)
**:** TRACE ELEMENT
**mi·cro·en·cap·su·late** \-in-'kap-sə-ˌlāt\ *transitive verb* (1963)
**:** to enclose in a microcapsule ⟨*microencapsulated* aspirin⟩
— **mi·cro·en·cap·su·la·tion** \-in-ˌkap-sə-'lā-shən\ *noun*
**mi·cro·en·vi·ron·ment** \-in-'vī-rən-mənt, -'vī(-ə)rn-\ *noun* (1938)
**:** a small or relatively small usually distinctly specialized and effectively isolated habitat (as a forest canopy) or environment (as of a nerve cell)
— **mi·cro·en·vi·ron·men·tal** \-ˌvī-rən-'men-t°l\ *adjective*

**mi·cro·evo·lu·tion** \-ˌe-və-'lü-shən *also* -ˌē-və-\ *noun* (1940)
**:** comparatively minor evolutionary change involving the accumulation of variations in populations usually below the species level
— **mi·cro·evo·lu·tion·ary** \-shə-ˌner-ē\ *adjective*
**mi·cro·far·ad** \'mī-krō-ˌfar-ˌad, -ˌfar-əd\ *noun* (1873)
**:** a unit of capacitance equal to one millionth of a farad
**mi·cro·fau·na** \ˌmī-krō-'fò-nə, -'fä-\ *noun* [New Latin] (1902)
**1 :** minute animals; *especially* **:** those invisible to the naked eye ⟨the soil *microfauna*⟩
**2 :** a small or strictly localized fauna (as of a microenvironment)
— **mi·cro·fau·nal** \-'fò-n°l, -'fä-\ *adjective*
**mi·cro·fi·bril** \-'fī-brəl, -'fi-\ *noun* (1938)
**:** a fine fibril; *especially* **:** one of the submicroscopic elongated bundles of cellulose of a plant cell wall
— **mi·cro·fi·bril·lar** \-brə-lər\ *adjective*
**mi·cro·fiche** \'mī-krō-ˌfēsh, -ˌfish\ *noun, plural* **-fiche** *or* **-fiches** \-ˌfēsh, -ˌfish, -fi-shəz, -ˌfish\ [French, from *micr-* micr- + *fiche* fiche] (1950)
**:** a sheet of microfilm containing rows of microimages of pages of printed matter
**mi·cro·fil·a·ment** \ˌmī-krō-'fi-lə-mənt\ *noun* (1963)
**:** any of the minute actin-containing protein filaments of eukaryotic cytoplasm that function in maintaining structure and in intracellular movement
**mi·cro·fi·lar·ia** \-fə-'lar-ē-ə, -'ler-\ *noun* [New Latin] (1878)
**:** a minute larval filaria
— **mi·cro·fi·lar·i·al** \-ē-əl\ *adjective*
¹**mi·cro·film** \'mī-krə-ˌfilm\ *noun* [International Scientific Vocabulary] (1927)
**:** a film bearing a photographic record on a reduced scale of printed or other graphic matter
²**microfilm** (1937)
*transitive verb*
**:** to reproduce on microfilm
*intransitive verb*
**:** to make microfilms
— **mi·cro·film·able** \ˌmī-krə-'fil-mə-bəl\ *adjective*
— **mi·cro·film·er** \'mī-krə-ˌfil-mər\ *noun*
**mi·cro·flo·ra** \ˌmī-krə-'flōr-ə, -'flòr-\ *noun* [New Latin] (1904)
**1 :** minute plants; *especially* **:** those invisible to the naked eye
**2 :** a small or strictly localized flora (as of a microenvironment)
— **mi·cro·flo·ral** \-əl\ *adjective*
**mi·cro·form** \'mī-krə-ˌfòrm\ *noun* (1958)
**1 :** a process for reproducing printed matter in a much reduced size ⟨documents in *microform*⟩
**2 a :** matter reproduced by microform **b :** MICROCOPY
**mi·cro·fos·sil** \ˌmī-krō-'fä-səl\ *noun* (1924)
**:** a fossil that can be studied only microscopically and that may be either a fragment of a larger organism or an entire minute organism
**mi·cro·fun·gus** \-'fəŋ-gəs\ *noun* [New Latin] (1874)
**:** a fungus (as a mold) with a microscopic fruiting body
**mi·cro·ga·mete** \-'ga-ˌmēt *also* -gə-'mēt\ *noun* [International Scientific Vocabulary] (circa 1891)
**:** the smaller and usually male gamete of a heterogamous organism
**mi·cro·ga·me·to·cyte** \-gə-'mē-tə-ˌsīt\ *noun* [International Scientific Vocabulary] (1902)
**:** a gametocyte producing microgametes
**mi·cro·gram** \'mī-krə-ˌgram\ *noun* [International Scientific Vocabulary] (circa 1890)
**:** one millionth of a gram — see METRIC SYSTEM table
**mi·cro·graph** \-ˌgraf\ *noun* [International Scientific Vocabulary] (1904)

**:** a graphic reproduction of the image of an object formed by a microscope
— **micrograph** *transitive verb*
**mi·cro·graph·ics** \ˌmī-krə-'gra-fiks\ *noun plural but singular in construction* (1969)
**:** the industry concerned with the manufacture and sale of graphic material in microform; *also* **:** the production of such material
— **mi·cro·graph·ic** \-fik\ *adjective*
— **mi·cro·graph·i·cal·ly** \-fi-k(ə-)lē\ *adverb*
**mi·cro·grav·i·ty** \-'gra-və-tē\ *noun* (1974)
**:** a condition in space in which only minuscule forces are experienced **:** virtual absence of gravity; *broadly* **:** a condition of weightlessness
**mi·cro·groove** \'mī-krō-ˌgrüv\ *noun* (1948)
**:** a narrow continuous V-shaped spiral track that has closely spaced turns and that is used on long-playing records
**mi·cro·hab·i·tat** \ˌmī-krō-'ha-bə-ˌtat\ *noun* (1933)
**:** the microenvironment in which an organism lives ⟨decaying wood creates a *microhabitat* for insects⟩
**mi·cro·im·age** \-'i-mij\ *noun* (1950)
**:** an image (as on a microfilm) that is greatly reduced in size
**mi·cro·inch** \-'inch\ *noun* (1941)
**:** one millionth of an inch
**mi·cro·in·jec·tion** \ˌmī-krō-in-'jek-shən\ *noun* (1921)
**:** injection under the microscope; *specifically* **:** injection into tissues by means of a fine mechanically controlled capillary tube
— **mi·cro·in·ject** \-'jekt\ *transitive verb*
**mi·cro·in·struc·tion** \-'strək-shən\ *noun* (1959)
**:** a computer instruction that activates the circuits necessary to perform a single machine operation usually as part of the execution of a machine-language instruction
**mi·cro·lep·i·dop·tera** \ˌmī-krō-ˌle-pə-'däp-tə-rə\ *noun plural* [New Latin] (1852)
**:** lepidopterous insects (as tortricids) that belong to families of minute or medium-sized moths
— **mi·cro·lep·i·dop·ter·ous** \-tə-rəs\ *adjective*
**mi·cro·li·ter** \'mī-krō-ˌlē-tər\ *noun* [International Scientific Vocabulary] (circa 1890)
**:** a unit of capacity equal to one millionth of a liter — see METRIC SYSTEM table
**mi·cro·lith** \'mī-krə-ˌlith\ *noun* [International Scientific Vocabulary] (1908)
**:** a tiny blade tool especially of the Mesolithic usually in a geometric shape (as that of a triangle) and often set in a bone or wooden haft
— **mi·cro·lith·ic** \ˌmī-krə-'li-thik\ *adjective*
**mi·cro·man·age** \ˌmī-krō-'ma-nij\ *transitive verb* (1979)
**:** to manage with great or excessive control or attention to details
— **mi·cro·man·age·ment** \-mənt\ *noun*
— **mi·cro·man·ag·er** \-'ma-ni-jər\ *noun*
**mi·cro·ma·nip·u·la·tion** \ˌmī-krō-mə-ˌni-pyə-'lā-shən\ *noun* (1921)
**:** the technique or practice of microdissection and microinjection
**mi·cro·ma·nip·u·la·tor** \-'ni-pyə-ˌlā-tər\ *noun* (1921)
**:** an instrument for micromanipulation
**mi·cro·mere** \'mī-krō-ˌmir\ *noun* [International Scientific Vocabulary] (1877)
**:** a small blastomere — see BLASTULA illustration
**mi·cro·me·te·or·ite** \ˌmī-krō-'mē-tē-ə-ˌrīt\ *noun* (1949)
**1 :** a meteorite so small that it can pass through the earth's atmosphere without becoming intensely heated
**2 :** a very small particle in interplanetary space
— **mi·cro·me·te·or·it·ic** \-ˌmē-tē-ə-'ri-tik\ *adjective*

**mi·cro·me·te·or·oid** \-'mē-tē-ə-,rȯid\ *noun* (1954)
: MICROMETEORITE 2

**mi·cro·me·te·o·rol·o·gy** \-,mē-tē-ə-'rä-lə-jē\ *noun* (1930)
: meteorology that deals with small-scale weather systems ranging up to several kilometers in diameter and confined to the lower troposphere
— **mi·cro·me·te·o·ro·log·i·cal** \-,mē-tē-,ȯr-ə-'lä-ji-kəl, -,är-ə-, -ə-rə-\ *adjective*
— **mi·cro·me·te·o·rol·o·gist** \-,mē-tē-ə-'rä-lə-jist\ *noun*

**¹mi·crom·e·ter** \mī-'krä-mə-tər\ *noun* [French *micromètre*, from *micr-* + *-mètre* -meter] (1670)
**1** : an instrument used with a telescope or microscope for measuring minute distances
**2** : a caliper for making precise measurements that has a spindle moved by a finely threaded screw

**micrometer 2**

**²mi·cro·me·ter** \'mī-krō-,mē-tər\ *noun* [International Scientific Vocabulary *micr-* + ³*meter*] (1880)
: a unit of length equal to one millionth of a meter — called also *micron*; see METRIC SYSTEM table

**mi·cro·meth·od** \'mī-krō-,me-thəd\ *noun* (1919)
: a method (as of microanalysis) that requires only very small quantities of material or that involves the use of the microscope

**mi·cro·mini** \,mī-krō-'mi-nē\ *noun* (1966)
: a very short miniskirt

**mi·cro·min·i·a·ture** \-'mi-nē-ə-,chu̇r, -'mi-ni-,chu̇r, -'min-yə-, -chər, -,tyu̇r, -,tu̇r\ *adjective* (1958)
**1** : MICROMINIATURIZED
**2** : suitable for use with microminiaturized parts

**mi·cro·min·i·a·tur·i·za·tion** \-,mi-nē-ə-,chu̇r-ə-'zā-shən, -,mi-ni-,chu̇r-, -,min-yə-,chu̇r-, -chər-, -,tyu̇r-, -,tu̇r-\ *noun* (1955)
: the process of producing microminiaturized things

**mi·cro·min·i·a·tur·ized** \-'mi-nē-ə-chə-,rīzd, -'mi-ni-chə-, -'min-yə-chə-, -,tyu̇-, -,tu̇-\ *adjective* (1959)
: reduced to or produced in a very small size and especially in a size smaller than one considered miniature

**mi·cro·mole** \'mī-krə-,mōl\ *noun* [International Scientific Vocabulary] (1936)
: one millionth of a mole
— **mi·cro·mo·lar** \,mī-krə-'mō-lər\ *adjective*

**mi·cro·mor·phol·o·gy** \,mī-krō-mȯr-'fä-lə-jē\ *noun* (1945)
: MICROSTRUCTURE
— **mi·cro·mor·pho·log·i·cal** \-fə-'lä-ji-kəl\ *adjective*

**mi·cron** \'mī-,krän\ *noun* [New Latin, from Greek *mikron*, neuter of *mikros* small — more at MICR-] (1885)
: ²MICROMETER

**Mi·cro·ne·sian** \,mī-krə-'nē-zhən, -shən\ *noun* (1847)
**1** : a native or inhabitant of Micronesia
**2** : a group of Austronesian languages spoken in the Micronesian islands
— **Micronesian** *adjective*

**mi·cron·ize** \'mī-krə-,nīz\ *transitive verb* **-ized; -iz·ing** [*micron*] (1940)
: to pulverize especially into particles a few micrometers in diameter

**mi·cro·nu·cle·us** \,mī-krō-'nü-klē-əs, -'nyü-\ *noun* [New Latin] (1892)
: a minute nucleus; *specifically* : one that is primarily concerned with reproductive and genetic functions in most ciliated protozoans

**mi·cro·nu·tri·ent** \-'nü-trē-ənt, -'nyü-\ *noun* (1939)

**1** : TRACE ELEMENT
**2** : an organic compound (as a vitamin) essential in minute amounts to the growth and health of an animal

**mi·cro·or·gan·ism** \-'ȯr-gə-,ni-zəm\ *noun* [International Scientific Vocabulary] (1880)
: an organism of microscopic or ultramicroscopic size

**mi·cro·pa·le·on·tol·o·gy** \-,pā-lē-,än-'tä-lə-jē, -lē-ən-, *especially British* -,pa-\ *noun* [International Scientific Vocabulary] (1883)
: the study of microscopic fossils
— **mi·cro·pa·le·on·to·log·i·cal** \-,än-t³l-'ä-ji-kəl\ *also* **mi·cro·pa·le·on·to·log·ic** \-jik\ *adjective*
— **mi·cro·pa·le·on·tol·o·gist** \-,än-'tä-lə-jist, -ən-\ *noun*

**mi·cro·par·ti·cle** \-'pär-ti-kəl\ *noun* (1929)
: a very small particle; *especially* : one that is microscopic in size

**mi·cro·phage** \'mī-krə-,fāj *also* -,fäzh\ *noun* [International Scientific Vocabulary] (1890)
: a small phagocyte

**mi·cro·phone** \'mī-krə-,fōn\ *noun* [International Scientific Vocabulary] (1878)
: an instrument whereby sound waves are caused to generate or modulate an electric current usually for the purpose of transmitting or recording sound (as speech or music)
— **mi·cro·phon·ic** \,mī-krə-'fä-nik\ *adjective*

**mi·cro·phon·ics** \,mī-krə-'fä-niks\ *noun plural* (1929)
: noises in a loudspeaker caused by mechanical shock or vibration of the electronic components

**mi·cro·pho·to·graph** \-'fō-tə-,graf\ *noun* [International Scientific Vocabulary] (1858)
**1** : a small photograph that is normally magnified for viewing : MICROCOPY
**2** : PHOTOMICROGRAPH
— **microphotograph** *transitive verb*
— **mi·cro·pho·tog·ra·pher** \-fə-'tä-grə-fər\ *noun*
— **mi·cro·pho·to·graph·ic** \-,fō-tə-'gra-fik\ *adjective*
— **mi·cro·pho·tog·ra·phy** \-fə-'tä-grə-fē\ *noun*

**mi·cro·pho·tom·e·ter** \-fō-'tä-mə-tər\ *noun* [International Scientific Vocabulary] (1899)
: an instrument for measuring the amount of light transmitted or reflected by small areas or for measuring the relative densities of spectral lines on a photographic film or plate
— **mi·cro·pho·to·met·ric** \-,fō-tə-'me-trik\ *adjective*
— **mi·cro·pho·to·met·ri·cal·ly** \-tri-k(ə-)lē\ *adverb*
— **mi·cro·pho·tom·e·try** \-fō-'tä-mə-trē\ *noun*

**mi·cro·phyll** \'mī-krə-,fil\ *noun* [International Scientific Vocabulary] (1935)
**1** : a small leaf
**2** : a leaf (as of a club moss) with single unbranched veins and no demonstrable gap around the leaf trace
— **mi·cro·phyl·lous** \,mī-krə-'fi-ləs\ *adjective*

**mi·cro·phys·ics** \,mī-krō-'fi-ziks\ *noun* (1885)
: the physics of molecules, atoms, and elementary particles
— **mi·cro·phys·i·cal** \-'fi-zi-kəl\ *adjective*
— **mi·cro·phys·i·cal·ly** \-k(ə-)lē\ *adverb*

**mi·cro·pi·pette** *or* **mi·cro·pi·pet** \-pī-'pet\ *noun* (1918)
**1** : a pipette for the measurement of minute volumes
**2** : a small and extremely fine-pointed pipette used in making microinjections

**mi·cro·plank·ton** \-'plaŋ(k)-tən, -,tän\ *noun* [International Scientific Vocabulary] (1903)
: microscopic plankton

**mi·cro·pore** \'mī-krə-,pōr, -,pȯr\ *noun* [International Scientific Vocabulary] (1884)
: a very fine pore

**mi·cro·po·ros·i·ty** \-pə-'rä-sə-tē, -pȯ-\ *noun*

**mi·cro·po·rous** \,mī-krə-'pōr-əs, -'pȯr-\ *adjective*

**mi·cro·prism** \'mī-krə-,pri-zəm\ *noun* (1966)
: a usually circular area on the focusing screen of a camera that is made up of tiny prisms and that causes the image in the viewfinder to blur if the subject is not in focus

**mi·cro·probe** \-,prōb\ *noun* (1944)
: a device for microanalysis that operates by exciting radiation in a minute area of material so that the composition may be determined from the emission spectrum

**mi·cro·pro·ces·sor** \,mī-krō-'prä-,se-sər, -'prō-\ *noun* (1970)
: a computer processor contained on an integrated-circuit chip; *also* : such a processor with memory and associated circuits

**mi·cro·pro·gram** \-'prō-,gram, -grəm\ *noun* (1953)
: a routine composed of microinstructions used in microprogramming

**mi·cro·pro·gram·ming** \-,gra-miŋ\ *noun* (1953)
: the use of routines stored in memory rather than specialized circuits to control a device (as a computer)

**mi·cro·pro·jec·tor** \-prə-'jek-tər\ *noun* (1927)
: a projector utilizing a compound microscope for projecting on a screen a greatly enlarged image of a microscopic object
— **mi·cro·pro·jec·tion** \-'jek-shən\ *noun*

**mi·cro·pub·lish·ing** \-'pə-bli-shiŋ\ *noun* (1966)
: publishing in microform
— **mi·cro·pub·lish·er** \-bli-shər\ *noun*

**mi·cro·pul·sa·tion** \-,pəl-'sā-shən\ *noun* (1949)
: a pulsation having a short period ⟨a *micropulsation* of the earth's magnetic field with a period in the range from a fraction of a second to several hundred seconds⟩

**mi·cro·punc·ture** \-'pəŋ(k)-chər\ *noun* (1948)
: an extremely small puncture (as of a nephron); *also* : an act of making a micropuncture

**mi·cro·pyle** \'mī-krə-,pīl\ *noun* [French, from *micr-* + Greek *pylē* gate] (1821)
**1** : a minute opening in the integument of an ovule of a seed plant
**2** : a differentiated area of surface in an egg through which a sperm enters
— **mi·cro·py·lar** \,mī-krə-'pī-lər\ *adjective*

**mi·cro·quake** \'mī-krō-,kwāk\ *noun* (1967)
: MICROEARTHQUAKE

**mi·cro·ra·di·og·ra·phy** \,mī-krō-,rā-dē-'ä-grə-fē\ *noun* (1913)
: radiography in which an X-ray photograph is prepared showing minute internal structure
— **mi·cro·ra·dio·graph** \-'rā-dē-ə-,graf\ *noun*
— **mi·cro·ra·dio·graph·ic** \-,rā-dē-ə-'gra-fik\ *adjective*

**mi·cro·read·er** \'mī-krō-,rē-dər\ *noun* (1949)
: an apparatus that gives an enlarged image of a microphotograph especially for reading

**mi·cro·re·pro·duc·tion** \,mī-krō-,rē-prə-'dək-shən\ *noun* (1938)
: the reproduction of written or printed matter in microform; *also* : an item so reproduced

**mi·cro·scale** \'mī-krō-,skāl\ *noun* (1931)
: a very small scale

**mi·cro·scope** \'mī-krə-,skōp\ *noun* [New Latin *microscopium*, from *micr-* + *-scopium* -scope] (1654)
**1** : an optical instrument consisting of a lens or combination of lenses for making enlarged

images of minute objects; *especially* **:** COMPOUND MICROSCOPE

**2 :** an instrument using radiations other than light or using vibrations for making enlarged images of minute objects ⟨acoustic *microscope*⟩

**mi·cro·scop·ic** \ˌmī-krə-ˈskä-pik\ *or* **mi·cro·scop·i·cal** \-pi-kəl\ *adjective* (1732)
**1 :** resembling a microscope especially in perception
**2 a :** invisible or indistinguishable without the use of a microscope **b :** very small or fine or precise
**3 :** of, relating to, or conducted with the microscope or microscopy
— **mi·cro·scop·i·cal·ly** \-pi-k(ə-)lē\ *adverb*

**mi·cros·co·py** \mī-ˈkräs-kə-pē\ *noun* (circa 1665)
**:** the use of or investigation with the microscope
— **mi·cros·co·pist** \-pist\ *noun*

**mi·cro·sec·ond** \ˈmī-krō-ˌse-kənd, -kənt\ *noun* [International Scientific Vocabulary] (1906)
**:** one millionth of a second

**mi·cro·seism** \ˈmī-krə-ˌsī-zəm\ *noun* [International Scientific Vocabulary *micr-* + Greek *seismos* earthquake — more at SEISMIC] (1887)
**:** a feeble rhythmically and persistently recurring earth tremor
— **mi·cro·seis·mic** \ˌmī-krə-ˈsīz-mik, -ˈsīs-\ *adjective*
— **mi·cro·seis·mic·i·ty** \-sīz-ˈmi-sə-tē, -sīs-\ *noun*

**mi·cro·some** \ˈmī-krə-ˌsōm\ *noun* [German *Mikrosom*, from *mikr-* micr- + *-som* -some] (1885)
**1 :** any of various minute cellular structures (as a ribosome)
**2 :** a particle in a particulate fraction that is obtained by heavy centrifugation of broken cells and consists of various amounts of ribosomes, fragmented endoplasmic reticulum, and mitochondrial cristae
— **mi·cro·som·al** \ˌmī-krə-ˈsō-məl\ *adjective*

**mi·cro·spec·tro·pho·tom·e·ter** \ˌmī-krə-ˌspek-trə-fō-ˈtä-mə-tər\ *noun* (1949)
**:** a spectrophotometer adapted to the examination of light transmitted by a very small specimen (as a single organic cell)
— **mi·cro·spec·tro·pho·to·met·ric** \-ˌfō-tə-ˈme-trik\ *adjective*
— **mi·cro·spec·tro·pho·tom·e·try** \-fō-ˈtä-mə-trē\ *noun*

**mi·cro·sphere** \ˈmī-krə-ˌsfir\ *noun* (1894)
**:** a minute sphere
— **mi·cro·spher·i·cal** \ˌmī-krə-ˈsfir-i-kəl, -ˈsfer-\ *adjective*

**mi·cro·spo·ran·gi·um** \ˌmī-krō-spə-ˈran-jē-əm\ *noun* [New Latin] (1881)
**:** a sporangium that develops only microspores
— **mi·cro·spo·ran·gi·ate** \-jē-ət\ *adjective*

**mi·cro·spore** \ˈmī-krə-ˌspōr, -ˌspȯr\ *noun* [International Scientific Vocabulary] (1858)
**:** any of the spores in heterosporous plants that give rise to male gametophytes and are generally smaller than the megaspore
— **mi·cro·spo·rous** \ˌmī-krə-ˈspōr-əs, -ˈspȯr-; mī-ˈkräs-pə-rəs\ *adjective*

**mi·cro·spo·ro·cyte** \-ˈspōr-ə-ˌsīt, -ˈspȯr-\ *noun* (1940)
**:** a microspore mother cell

**mi·cro·spo·ro·gen·e·sis** \ˌmī-krə-ˌspōr-ə-ˈje-nə-səs, -ˌspȯr-\ *noun* [New Latin] (1921)
**:** the formation and maturation of microspores

**mi·cro·spo·ro·phyll** \-ˌfil\ *noun* (circa 1890)
**:** a sporophyll that develops only microsporangia

**mi·cro·state** \ˈmī-krō-ˌstāt\ *noun* (1962)
**:** a nation that is extremely small in area and population

**mi·cro·struc·ture** \ˈmī-krō-ˌstrək-chər\ *noun* [International Scientific Vocabulary] (1885)
**:** the microscopic structure of a material (as a mineral or a biological cell)
— **mi·cro·struc·tur·al** \ˌmī-krō-ˈstrək-chə-rəl, -ˈstrək-shrəl\ *adjective*

**mi·cro·sur·gery** \ˌmī-krō-ˈsərj-rē, -ˈsər-jə-\ *noun* (1926)
**:** minute dissection or manipulation (as by a micromanipulator or laser beam) of living structures or tissue
— **mi·cro·sur·gi·cal** \-ˈsər-ji-kəl\ *adjective*

**mi·cro·switch** \-ˌswich\ *noun* (1940)
**:** a very small switch that is sensitive to minute motions and is used especially in automatic devices

**mi·cro·tech·nique** \ˌmī-krō-tek-ˈnēk\ *also* **mi·cro·tech·nic** \-ˈtek-nik, -tek-ˈnēk\ *noun* [International Scientific Vocabulary] (1892)
**:** any of various methods of handling and preparing material for microscopic observation and study

**mi·cro·tome** \ˈmī-krə-ˌtōm\ *noun* [International Scientific Vocabulary] (1856)
**:** an instrument for cutting sections (as of organic tissues) for microscopic examination

**mi·cro·tone** \ˈmī-krə-ˌtōn\ *noun* (1920)
**:** a musical interval smaller than a halftone
— **mi·cro·ton·al** \ˌmī-krə-ˈtō-nᵊl\ *adjective*
— **mi·cro·to·nal·i·ty** \-tō-ˈna-lə-tē\ *noun*
— **mi·cro·ton·al·ly** \-ˈtō-nᵊl-ē\ *adverb*

**mi·cro·tu·bule** \ˌmī-krō-ˈtü-(ˌ)byü(ə)l, -ˈtyü-\ *noun* (1961)
**:** any of the minute tubules in eukaryotic cytoplasm that are composed of the protein tubulin and form an important component of the cytoskeleton, mitotic spindle, cilia, and flagella
— **mi·cro·tu·bu·lar** \-byə-lər\ *adjective*

**mi·cro·vas·cu·lar** \-ˈvas-kyə-lər\ *adjective* (1959)
**:** of, relating to, or constituting the part of the circulatory system made up of minute vessels (as venules or capillaries) that average less than 0.3 millimeters in diameter
— **mi·cro·vas·cu·la·ture** \-lə-ˌchu̇r, -ˌtyu̇r, -ˌtu̇r\ *noun*

**mi·cro·vil·lus** \-ˈvi-ləs\ *noun* [New Latin] (1953)
**:** a microscopic projection of a tissue, cell, or cell organelle; *especially* **:** any of the fingerlike outward projections of some cell surfaces
— **mi·cro·vil·lar** \-ˈvi-lər\ *adjective*
— **mi·cro·vil·lous** \-ˈvi-ləs\ *adjective*

**mi·cro·volt** \ˈmī-krə-ˌvōlt\ *noun* (1868)
**:** one millionth of a volt

**mi·cro·watt** \-ˌwät\ *noun* (circa 1909)
**:** one millionth of a watt

**¹mi·cro·wave** \-ˌwāv\ *noun, often attributive* (1931)
**1 :** a comparatively short electromagnetic wave; *especially* **:** one between about 1 millimeter and 1 meter in wavelength
**2 :** MICROWAVE OVEN

**²microwave** *transitive verb* (1973)
**:** to cook or heat in a microwave oven
— **mi·cro·wav·able** *or* **mi·cro·wave·able** \ˌmī-krə-ˈwā-və-bəl\ *adjective*

**microwave oven** *noun* (1963)
**:** an oven in which food is cooked by the heat produced by the absorption of microwave energy by water molecules in the food

**mi·cro·world** \-ˌwər(-ə)ld\ *noun* (1955)
**:** a small universe; *specifically* **:** the natural universe observed at the microscopic or submicroscopic level

**mic·tu·rate** \ˈmik-chə-ˌrāt, ˈmik-tə-\ *intransitive verb* **-rat·ed; -rat·ing** [Latin *micturire* to desire to urinate, from *meiere* to urinate; akin to Old English *mīgan* to urinate, Greek *omeichein*] (1842)
**:** URINATE
— **mic·tu·ri·tion** \ˌmik-chə-ˈri-shən, ˌmik-tə-\ *noun*

**¹mid** \ˈmid\ *adjective* [Middle English, from Old English *midde*; akin to Old High German

*mitti* middle, Latin *medius*, Greek *mesos*] (before 12th century)
**1 :** being the part in the middle or midst ⟨in *mid* ocean⟩ — often used in combination ⟨*mid*-August⟩
**2 :** occupying a middle position ⟨the *mid* finger⟩
**3** *of a vowel* **:** articulated with the arch of the tongue midway between its highest and its lowest elevation
— **mid** *adverb*

**²mid** *preposition* (1808)
**:** AMID

**mid-air** \ˈmid-ˈar, -ˈer\ *noun* (1667)
**:** a point or region in the air not immediately adjacent to the ground ⟨planes collided in *midair*⟩

**Mi·das** \ˈmī-dəs\ *noun* [Latin, from Greek]
**:** a legendary Phrygian king who is given the power of turning everything he touches to gold

**Midas touch** *noun* (1883)
**:** an uncanny ability for making money in every venture

**mid·brain** \ˈmid-ˌbrān\ *noun* (1875)
**:** the middle of the three primary divisions of the developing vertebrate brain or the corresponding part of the adult brain — called also *mesencephalon*; see BRAIN illustration

**mid·course** \-ˈkōrs, -ˈkȯrs\ *adjective* (circa 1956)
**:** being or occurring in the middle part of a course (as of a spacecraft) ⟨a *midcourse* correction⟩

**mid·day** \ˈmid-ˌdā, -ˈdā\ *noun, often attributive* (before 12th century)
**:** the middle of the day

**mid·den** \ˈmi-dᵊn\ *noun* [Middle English *midding*, of Scandinavian origin; akin to Old Norse *myki* dung & Old Norse *dyngja* manure pile — more at DUNG] (14th century)
**1 :** DUNGHILL
**2 a :** a refuse heap; *especially* **:** KITCHEN MIDDEN **b :** a small pile (as of seeds, bones, or leaves) gathered by a rodent (as a pack rat)

**¹mid·dle** \ˈmi-dᵊl\ *adjective* [Middle English *middel*, from Old English; akin to Old English *midde*] (before 12th century)
**1 :** equally distant from the extremes **:** MEDIAL, CENTRAL ⟨the *middle* house in the row⟩
**2 :** being at neither extreme **:** INTERMEDIATE
**3** *capitalized* **a :** constituting a division intermediate between those prior and later or upper and lower ⟨*Middle* Paleozoic⟩ **b :** constituting a period of a language or literature intermediate between one called *Old* and one called *New* or *Modern* ⟨*Middle* Dutch⟩
**4** *of a verb form or voice* **:** typically asserting that a person or thing both performs and is affected by the action represented

**²middle** *noun* (before 12th century)
**1 :** a middle part, point, or position
**2 :** the central portion of the human body **:** WAIST
**3 :** the position of being among or in the midst of something
**4 :** something intermediate between extremes **:** MEAN
**5 :** the center of an offensive or defensive formation; *especially* **:** the area between the second baseman and the shortstop

**middle age** *noun* (14th century)
**:** the period of life from about 40 to about 60
— **mid·dle-aged** \ˌmi-dᵊl-ˈājd\ *adjective*
— **mid·dle-ag·er** \-ˈā-jər\ *noun*

**Middle Ages** *noun plural* (1616)
**:** the period of European history from about A.D. 500 to about 1500

**Middle America** *noun* (1898)
**1 :** the region of the western hemisphere including Mexico, Central America, often the West Indies, and sometimes Colombia and Venezuela
**2 :** the midwestern section of the U.S.

**3** : the middle-class segment of the U.S. population; *especially* : the traditional or conservative element of the middle class
— **middle–American** *adjective*
— **Middle American** *noun*

**mid·dle·brow** \'mi-d°l-ˌbraủ\ *noun* (1925)
: a person who is moderately but not highly cultivated
— **middlebrow** *adjective*

**middle C** *noun* (1840)
: the note designated by the first ledger line below the treble staff and the first above the bass staff

**mid·dle-class** \ˌmi-d°l-'klas\ *adjective* (1836)
: of or relating to the middle class; *especially* : characterized by a high material standard of living, sexual morality, and respect for property
— **mid·dle-class·ness** \-nəs\ *noun*

**middle class** *noun* (1766)
: a class occupying a position between the upper class and the lower class; *especially* : a fluid heterogeneous socioeconomic grouping composed principally of business and professional people, bureaucrats, and some farmers and skilled workers sharing common social characteristics and values

**middle distance** *noun* (1813)
**1** : a part of a pictorial representation or scene between the foreground and the background
**2** : any footrace distance usually from 800 to 1500 meters or from 880 yards to one mile

**Middle Dutch** *noun* (circa 1959)
: the Dutch language in use from about 1100 to about 1500 — see INDO-EUROPEAN LANGUAGES table

**middle ear** *noun* (1852)
: a small membrane-lined cavity that is separated from the outer ear by the eardrum and that transmits sound waves from the eardrum to the partition between the middle and inner ears through a chain of tiny bones

**Middle English** *noun* (1830)
: the English in use from the 12th to 15th centuries — see INDO-EUROPEAN LANGUAGES table

**middle finger** *noun* (before 12th century)
: the midmost of the five digits of the hand

**Middle French** *noun* (1889)
: the French in use from the 14th to 16th centuries — see INDO-EUROPEAN LANGUAGES table

**middle game** *noun* (1894)
: the middle phase of a board game; *specifically* : the part of a chess game after the pieces have been developed when players attempt to gain and exploit positional and material superiority — compare ENDGAME, OPENING

**Middle Greek** *noun* (1889)
: the Greek language used in the 7th to 15th centuries

**middle ground** *noun* (1801)
**1** : a standpoint midway between extremes
**2** : MIDDLE DISTANCE 1

**Middle High German** *noun* (1889)
: the High German in use from about 1100 to 1500 — see INDO-EUROPEAN LANGUAGES table

**Middle Irish** *noun* (1952)
: the Irish in use between the 10th and 13th centuries — see INDO-EUROPEAN LANGUAGES table

**middle lamella** *noun* (circa 1886)
: a layer of pectinaceous intercellular material lying between the walls of adjacent plant cells
— see CELL illustration

**Middle Low German** *noun* (circa 1889)
: the Low German in use from about 1100 to 1500 — see INDO-EUROPEAN LANGUAGES table

**mid·dle·man** \'mi-d°l-ˌman\ *noun* (1795)
: an intermediary or agent between two parties; *especially* : a dealer or agent intermediate between the producer of goods and the retailer or consumer

**middle management** *noun* (circa 1948)
: management personnel intermediate between operational supervisors and policy-making administrators
— **middle manager** *noun*

**middle name** *noun* (1835)
: a name between one's first name and surname

**middle–of–the–road** *adjective* (1894)
: standing for or following a course of action midway between extremes; *especially* : being neither liberal nor conservative in politics
— **mid·dle–of–the–road·er** \-'rō-dər\ *noun*
— **mid·dle–of–the–road·ism** \-'rō-ˌdi-zəm\ *noun*

**middle of the road** (1918)
: a course of action or a standpoint midway between extremes

**Middle Persian** *noun* (1930)
: any of the varieties of Persian in use from about 200 B.C. to about A.D. 1000

**mid·dler** \'mid-lər, 'mid-°l-ər\ *noun* (1882)
: one belonging to an intermediate group, division, or class: as **a** : a student in the second-year class of a three-year program (as at a seminary or law school) **b** : a student in the second- or third-year class in some private secondary schools having a four-year course **c** : a student in a division in some private schools that corresponds approximately to junior high school

**middle school** *noun* (1945)
: a school usually including grades 5 to 8 or 6 to 8
— **middle school·er** \-ˌskü-lər\ *noun*

**Middle Scots** *noun* (circa 1903)
: the Scots language in use between the latter half of the 15th and the early decades of the 17th centuries

**middle term** *noun* (1685)
: the term of a syllogism that occurs in both premises

**mid·dle·weight** \'mi-d°l-ˌwāt\ *noun* (1889)
: one of average weight; *specifically* : a boxer in a weight division having a maximum limit of 160 pounds for professionals and 165 pounds for amateurs — compare LIGHT HEAVYWEIGHT, WELTERWEIGHT

**Middle Welsh** *noun* (circa 1922)
: the Welsh in use from about 1150 to 1500 — see INDO-EUROPEAN LANGUAGES table

**¹mid·dling** \'mid-liŋ, -lən\ *noun* (1543)
**1** : any of various commodities of intermediate size, quality, or position
**2** *plural but singular or plural in construction* : a granular product of grain milling; *especially* : a wheat milling by-product used in animal feeds

**²middling** *adjective* (1550)
**1** : of middle, medium, or moderate size, degree, or quality
**2** : MEDIOCRE, SECOND-RATE
— **middling** *adverb*
— **mid·dling·ly** \-lē\ *adverb*

**mid·dor·sal** \'mid-'dȯr-səl\ *adjective* (1879)
: of, relating to, or situated in the middle part or median line of the back

**mid·dy** \'mi-dē\ *noun, plural* **middies** [by shortening & alteration] (1818)
**1** : MIDSHIPMAN
**2** : a loosely fitting blouse with a sailor collar worn by women and children

**mid·field** \'mid-ˌfēld, ˌmid-'\ *noun* (15th century)
**1** : the middle portion of a field; *especially* : the portion of a playing field (as in football) that is midway between goals
**2** : the players on a team (as in lacrosse or soccer) that normally play in the midfield

**mid·field·er** \-ˌfēl-dər, -'fēl-\ *noun* (1938)
: a member of a midfield

**Mid·gard** \'mid-ˌgärd\ *noun* [Old Norse *mithgarthr*]
: the abode of human beings in Norse mythology

**midge** \'mij\ *noun* [Middle English *migge*, from Old English *mycg*; akin to Old High German *mucka* midge, Greek *myia* fly, Latin *musca*] (before 12th century)
: a tiny dipteran fly (as a chironomid)

**midg·et** \'mi-jət\ *noun, often attributive* [*midge*] (1865)
**1** : a very small person; *specifically* : a person of unusually small size who is physically well-proportioned
**2** : something (as an animal) much smaller than usual
**3** : a front-engine, single-seat, open-wheel racing car smaller and of less engine displacement than standard cars of the type

**mid·gut** \'mid-ˌgət\ *noun* (1875)
: the middle part of an alimentary canal

**midi** \'mi-dē\ *noun* [¹mid + -i (as in *mini*)] (1967)
: a dress, skirt, or coat that usually extends to the mid-calf

**Mid·i·an·ite** \'mi-dē-ə-ˌnīt\ *noun* [*Midian*, son of Abraham] (1560)
: a member of an ancient northern Arabian people

**mid·land** \'mid-lənd, -ˌland\ *noun* (1555)
**1** : the interior or central region of a country
**2** *capitalized* **a** : the dialect of English spoken in the midland counties of England **b** : the dialect of English spoken in an area of the east central U.S. often divided into north Midland extending westward from an area including southern New Jersey; northern Delaware and Maryland; central and southern Pennsylvania; and central Ohio, Indiana, and Illinois and south Midland extending westward and southwestward from an area including the Appalachian regions of Virginia, North Carolina, South Carolina, and Georgia; Tennessee, Kentucky, West Virginia; and southern Ohio, Indiana, and Illinois
— **midland** *adjective, often capitalized*
— **Mid·land·er** \-lən-dər, -ˌlan-\ *noun*

**mid·lat·i·tudes** \'mid-'la-tə-ˌtüdz, ˌmid-, -ˌtyüdz\ *noun plural* (1925)
: latitudes of the temperate zones or from about 30 to 60 degrees north or south of the equator
— **mid·lat·i·tude** \-ˌtüd, -ˌtyüd\ *adjective*

**mid·life** \'mid-'līf\ *noun* (1898)
: MIDDLE AGE

**midlife crisis** *noun* (1965)
: a period of emotional turmoil in middle age characterized especially by a strong desire for change

**mid·line** \'mid-ˌlīn, -'līn\ *noun* (circa 1859)
: a median line; *especially* : the median line or median plane of the body or some part of the body

**mid·most** \-ˌmōst\ *adjective* (before 12th century)
**1** : being in or near the exact middle
**2** : most intimate : INNERMOST
— **midmost** *adverb or noun*

**mid·night** \'mid-ˌnīt\ *noun* (before 12th century)
**1** : the middle of the night; *specifically* : 12 o'clock at night
**2** : deep or extended darkness or gloom
— **midnight** *adjective*
— **mid·night·ly** *adverb or adjective*

**midnight blue** *noun* (1916)
: a deep blackish blue

**midnight sun** *noun* (1857)
: the sun above the horizon at midnight in the arctic or antarctic summer

**mid·point** \'mid-ˌpȯint, -'pȯint\ *noun* (14th century)
: a point at or near the center or middle

**mid·rash** \'mi-ˌdräsh\ *noun, plural* **mid·rash·im** \mi-'drä-shəm\ [Hebrew *midhrāsh* exposition, explanation] (1613)
**1** : a haggadic or halakic exposition of the underlying significance of a Bible text
**2** : a collection of midrashim

**3** *capitalized* **:** the midrashic literature written during the first Christian millennium
— **mid·rash·ic** \mi-'drä-shik\ *adjective, often capitalized*

**mid·rib** \'mid-,rib\ *noun* (1794)
**:** the central vein of a leaf

**mid·riff** \'mi-,drif\ *noun* [Middle English *midrif*, from Old English *midhrif*, from *midde* mid + *hrif* belly; akin to Old High German *href* body, and probably to Latin *corpus* body] (before 12th century)
**1 :** DIAPHRAGM 1
**2 :** the mid-region of the human torso
**3 a :** a section of a woman's garment that covers the midriff **b :** a woman's garment that exposes the midriff

**mid–rise** \'mid-,rīz, -'rīz\ *adjective* (1967)
**:** being approximately 5 to 10 stories high ⟨*mid-rise* condominiums⟩

**mid·sag·it·tal** \'mid-'sa-jə-t°l\ *adjective* (1947)
**:** median and sagittal

**mid·sec·tion** \-,sek-shən\ *noun* (1936)
**:** a section midway between the extremes; *especially* **:** MIDRIFF 2

**mid·ship·man** \'mid-,ship-mən, ,mid-'\ *noun* (1685)
**:** a person in training for a naval commission; *especially* **:** a student in a naval academy

**mid·ships** \'mid-,ships\ *adverb* (circa 1828)
**:** AMIDSHIPS

**mid·size** \-,sīz\ *also* **mid·sized** \-,sīzd\ *adjective* (1970)
**:** of intermediate size ⟨*midsize* car⟩

**mid·sole** \-,sōl\ *noun* (1926)
**:** a layer (as of leather or rubber) between the insole and the outsole of a shoe

**midst** \'midst, 'mitst\ *noun* [Middle English *middest*, alteration of *middes*, short for *amiddes* amid] (15th century)
**1 :** the interior or central part or point **:** MIDDLE ⟨in the *midst* of the forest⟩
**2 :** a position of proximity to the members of a group ⟨a traitor in our *midst*⟩
**3 :** the condition of being surrounded or beset ⟨in the *midst* of his troubles⟩
**4 :** a period of time about the middle of a continuing act or condition ⟨in the *midst* of a meal⟩
— **midst** *preposition*

**mid·stream** \'mid-'strēm, -,strēm\ *noun* (1669)
**1 :** the middle of a stream
**2 :** an intermediate stage in an act or process ⟨the tone changes in *midstream*⟩

**mid·sum·mer** \-'sə-mər, -,səm-\ *noun* (before 12th century)
**1 :** the middle of summer
**2 :** the summer solstice
— **midsummer** *adjective*

**Midsummer Day** *noun* (before 12th century)
**:** June 24 celebrated as the feast of the nativity of John the Baptist

**mid·term** \'mid-,tərm (*usual for 1b*), -'tərm\ *noun* (1906)
**1 a :** the middle of an academic term **b :** an examination at midterm
**2 :** the approximate middle of a term of office

**mid·town** \'mid-,taùn, -'taùn\ *noun* (1926)
**:** a central section of a city; *especially* **:** one situated between sections conventionally called *downtown* and *uptown*
— **midtown** *adjective*

**¹mid·way** \'mid-,wā, -'wā\ *adverb* (13th century)
**:** in the middle of the way or distance **:** HALFWAY

**²mid·way** \-,wā\ *noun* [*Midway* (*Plaisance*), Chicago, site of the amusement section of the Columbian Exposition 1893] (1893)
**:** an avenue at a fair, carnival, or amusement park for concessions and amusements

**mid·week** \-,wēk\ *noun* (1707)
**:** the middle of the week
— **midweek** *adjective or adverb*

— **mid·week·ly** \-,wē-klē, -'wē-\ *adjective or adverb*

**¹mid·wife** \'mid-,wīf\ *noun* [Middle English *midwif*, from *mid* with (from Old English) + *wif* woman] (14th century)
**1 :** a person who assists women in childbirth
**2 :** one that helps to produce or bring forth something

**²midwife** *transitive verb* **mid·wifed** \-,wīft\ *or* **mid·wived** \-,wīvd\; **mid·wif·ing** \-,wī-fiŋ\ *or* **mid·wiv·ing** \-,wī-viŋ\ (1638)
**:** to assist in producing, bringing forth, or bringing about

**mid·wife·ry** \,mid-'wi-f(ə)rē, -'wī-; 'mid-,wī-\ *noun* (15th century)
**1 :** the art or act of assisting at childbirth; *also* **:** OBSTETRICS
**2 :** the art, act, or process of producing, bringing forth, or bringing about

**mid·win·ter** \'mid-'win-tər, -,win-\ *noun* (before 12th century)
**1 :** the winter solstice
**2 :** the middle of winter
— **midwinter** *adjective*

**mid·year** \-,yir\ *noun* (1896)
**1 a :** an examination at the middle of an academic year **b** *plural* **:** the set of examinations at the middle of an academic year; *also* **:** the period of such examinations
**2 a :** the middle or middle portion of a calendar year **b :** the middle of an academic year
— **midyear** *adjective*

**mien** \'mēn\ *noun* [by shortening & alteration from ¹*demean*] (1513)
**1 :** air or bearing especially as expressive of attitude or personality **:** DEMEANOR ⟨of aristocratic *mien*⟩
**2 :** APPEARANCE, ASPECT ⟨the inherent dangers of government encroachment . . . presented such a distasteful *mien* —H. W. Baldwin⟩
*synonym* see BEARING

**¹miff** \'mif\ *noun* [origin unknown] (1623)
**1 :** a fit of ill humor
**2 :** a trivial quarrel

**²miff** *transitive verb* (1811)
**:** to put into an ill humor **:** OFFEND

**¹might** \'mīt\ [Middle English, from Old English *meahte, mihte;* akin to Old High German *mahta, mohta* could] *past of* MAY (before 12th century)
— used in auxiliary function to express permission, liberty, probability, possibility in the past ⟨the president *might* do nothing without the board's consent⟩ or a present condition contrary to fact ⟨if you were older you *might* understand⟩ or less probability or possibility than *may* ⟨*might* get there before it rains⟩ or as a polite alternative to *may* ⟨*might* I ask who is calling⟩ or to *ought* or *should* ⟨you *might* at least apologize⟩

**²might** *noun* [Middle English, from Old English *miht;* akin to Old High German *maht* might, *magan* to be able — more at MAY] (before 12th century)
**1 a :** the power, authority, or resources wielded (as by an individual or group) ⟨the *might* of the armed forces⟩ **b** (1) **:** bodily strength (2) **:** the power, energy, or intensity of which one is capable ⟨striving with *might* and main⟩
**2** *dialect* **:** a great deal
*synonym* see POWER

**might·i·ly** \'mī-t°l-ē\ *adverb* (before 12th century)
**1 :** in a mighty manner **:** VIGOROUSLY ⟨applauded *mightily*⟩
**2 :** very much ⟨depressed me *mightily*⟩

**might·i·ness** \'mī-tē-nəs\ *noun* (14th century)
**:** the quality or state of being mighty

**mightn't** \'mī-t°nt\ (1889)
**:** might not

**¹mighty** \'mī-tē\ *adjective* **might·i·er; -est** (before 12th century)
**1 :** possessing might **:** POWERFUL
**2 :** accomplished or characterized by might ⟨a *mighty* thrust⟩

**3 :** great or imposing in size or extent **:** EXTRAORDINARY

**²mighty** *adverb* (14th century)
**:** EXTREMELY, VERY ⟨a *mighty* handy gadget⟩ □

**mi·gnon** \mēn-'yōⁿ, min-'yòn\ *noun* (circa 1919)
**:** FILET MIGNON

**mi·gnon·ette** \,min-yə-'net\ *noun* [French *mignonnette*, from obsolete French, feminine of *mignonnet* dainty, from Middle French, from *mignon* darling] (1798)
**:** any of a genus (*Reseda* of the family Resedaceae, the mignonette family) of herbs; *especially* **:** a garden annual (*R. odorata*) bearing racemes of fragrant whitish flowers

**mi·graine** \'mī-,grān, *British often* 'mē-\ *noun* [French, modification of Late Latin *hemicrania* pain in one side of the head, from Greek *hēmikrania*, from *hēmi-* hemi- + *kranion* cranium] (15th century)
**1 :** a condition marked by recurrent severe headache often with nausea and vomiting
**2 :** an episode or attack of migraine
— **mi·grain·ous** \-,grā-nəs\ *adjective*

**mi·grant** \'mī-grənt\ *noun* [Latin *migrant-, migrans*, present participle of *migrare*] (1760)
**:** one that migrates: as **a :** a person who moves regularly in order to find work especially in harvesting crops **b :** an animal that shifts from one habitat to another
— **migrant** *adjective*

**mi·grate** \'mī-,grāt, mī-'\ *intransitive verb* **mi·grat·ed; mi·grat·ing** [Latin *migratus*, past participle of *migrare*; perhaps akin to Greek *ameibein* to change] (1697)
**1 :** to move from one country, place, or locality to another
**2 :** to pass usually periodically from one region or climate to another for feeding or breeding
**3 :** to change position in an organism or substance ⟨filarial worms *migrate* within the human body⟩
— **mi·gra·tion** \mī-'grā-shən\ *noun*
— **mi·gra·tion·al** \-shnəl, -shə-n°l\ *adjective*
— **mi·gra·tor** \'mī-,grā-tər, mī-'\ *noun*

**mi·gra·to·ry** \'mī-grə-,tōr-ē, -,tòr-\ *adjective* (1753)
**1 :** of, relating to, or characterized by migration
**2 :** WANDERING, ROVING

**mih·rab** \'mē-rəb\ *noun* [Arabic *miḥrāb*] (1816)
**:** a niche or chamber in a mosque indicating the direction of Mecca

**mi·ka·do** \mə-'kä-(,)dō\ *noun, plural* **-dos** [Japanese] (1727)
**:** an emperor of Japan

**¹mike** \'mīk\ *noun* [by shortening & alteration] (1924)
**:** MICROPHONE

**²mike** *transitive verb* **miked; mik·ing** (1939)
**:** to supply with a microphone

**Mike** \'mīk\ (1942)

---

□ USAGE

**mighty** The use of *mighty* as an intensive usually conveys a folksy down-home feeling ⟨plain and simple fare . . . but *mighty* filling and *mighty* satisfying —*Asheville (N.C.) Citizen-Times*⟩. It is used especially to create a chatty style ⟨turnip greens, corn bread and biscuits. That sounds *mighty* good to me —Julia Child⟩ or to stress a rural atmosphere ⟨a man must be *mighty* serious about his squirrel hunting —Stuart Williams, *Field & Stream*⟩. In a more formal context, *mighty* is used to create additional emphasis by drawing attention to itself ⟨the chairman made sure that there were *mighty* few of them —Mollie Panter-Downes⟩.

— a communications code word for the letter *m*

**¹mil** \'mil\ *noun* [Latin *mille* thousand] (1721)
**1** : THOUSAND ⟨found a salinity of 38.4 per *mil*⟩
**2** : a monetary unit formerly used in Cyprus equal to 1/1000 pound
**3** : a unit of length equal to ¹⁄₁₀₀₀ inch used especially in measuring thickness (as of plastic films)
**4** : a unit of angular measurement equal to ¹⁄₆₄₀₀ of 360 degrees and used especially in artillery

**²mil** *noun, plural* **military** [short for *million*] (circa 1955)
*slang* : a million dollars

**mi·la·dy** \mi-'lā-dē, *US also* mī-\ *noun* [French, from English *my lady*] (1839)
**1** : an Englishwoman of noble or gentle birth
**2** : a woman of fashion

**milch** \'milk, 'milch, 'milks\ *adjective* [Middle English *milche*, from Old English *-milce*; akin to Old English *melcan* to milk — more at EMULSION] (14th century)
: MILK

**mil·chig** \'mil-kik\ *adjective* [Yiddish *milkhik*, from *milkh* milk, from Middle High German, from Old High German *miluh* — more at MILK] (circa 1928)
: made of or derived from milk or dairy products — compare FLEISHIG, PAREVE

**mild** \'mī(ə)ld\ *adjective* [Middle English, from Old English *milde*; akin to Greek *malthakos* soft, Latin *mollis* — more at MELT] (before 12th century)
**1** : gentle in nature or behavior ⟨has a *mild* disposition⟩
**2 a** (1) : moderate in action or effect ⟨a *mild* cigar⟩ (2) : not sharp or bitter ⟨*mild* cheese⟩ ⟨*mild* ale⟩ **b** : not being or involving what is extreme ⟨an analysis under *mild* conditions⟩ ⟨a *mild* slope⟩
**3** : not severe : TEMPERATE ⟨a *mild* climate⟩ ⟨*mild* symptoms of disease⟩
— **mild·ly** \'mī(ə)l(d)-lē\ *adverb*
— **mild·ness** \'mī(ə)l(d)-nəs\ *noun*

**¹mil·dew** \'mil-,dü, -,dyü\ *noun* [Middle English, from Old English *meledēaw* honeydew; akin to Old High German *militou* honeydew] (14th century)
**1 a** : a superficial usually whitish growth produced especially on organic matter or living plants (as of the families Erysiphaceae and Peronosporaceae) **b** : a fungus producing mildew
**2** : a discoloration caused by fungi
— **mil·dewy** \-ē\ *adjective*

**²mildew** (circa 1552)
*transitive verb*
: to affect with or as if with mildew
*intransitive verb*
: to become affected with mildew

**mild steel** *noun* (1868)
: a low-carbon structural steel that is easily worked

**mile** \'mī(ə)l\ *noun* [Middle English, from Old English *mīl*, from Latin *milia* miles, from *milia passuum*, literally, thousands of paces, from *milia*, plural of *mille* thousand] (before 12th century)
**1** : any of various units of distance: as **a** : a unit equal to 5280 feet — see WEIGHT table **b** : NAUTICAL MILE
**2** : a race of a mile
**3** : a relatively great distance or interval — used chiefly adverbially in plural ⟨was *miles* too small⟩

**mile·age** \'mī-lij\ *noun* (1754)
**1** : an allowance for traveling expenses at a certain rate per mile
**2** : aggregate length or distance in miles: as **a** : the total miles traveled especially in a given period of time **b** : the amount of service that something will yield especially as expressed in terms of miles of travel **c** : the average number of miles a car will travel on a gallon of

gasoline that is used as a measure of fuel economy ⟨gets good *mileage*⟩
**3 a** : USEFULNESS ⟨got a lot of *mileage* left in her⟩ **b** : benefit derived from something ⟨got good political *mileage* from the debates⟩

**mile·post** \'mī(ə)l-,pōst\ *noun* (1768)
**1** : a post indicating the distance in miles from or to a given point; *also* : a post placed a mile from a similar post
**2** : MILESTONE 2

**mil·er** \'mī-lər\ *noun* (1889)
**1** : one that competes in mile races — often qualified in combination ⟨a quarter-*miler*⟩
**2** : one that is a specified number of miles in length — used in combination ⟨a 15-*miler*⟩

**mi·les glo·ri·o·sus** \'mē-,lās-,glōr-ə-'ō-səs, -,glȯr-\ *noun, plural* **mi·li·tes glo·ri·o·si** \'mē-lə-,tās-,glōr-ē-'ō-(,)sē, -,glȯr-\ [Latin] (1917)
: a boastful soldier; *especially* : a stock character of this type in comedy

**mile·stone** \'mī(ə)l-,stōn\ *noun* (circa 1746)
**1** : a stone serving as a milepost
**2** : a significant point in development

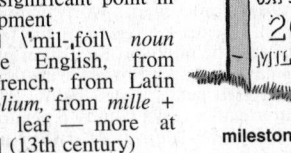
milestone 1

**mil·foil** \'mil-,fȯil\ *noun* [Middle English, from Old French, from Latin *millefolium*, from *mille* + *folium* leaf — more at BLADE] (13th century)
**1** : YARROW
**2** : WATER MILFOIL

**mil·i·ar·ia** \,mi-lē-'ar-ē-ə, -'er-\ *noun* [New Latin, from Latin, feminine of *miliarius*] (1807)
: an inflammatory disorder of the skin characterized by redness, eruption, burning or itching, and the release of sweat in abnormal ways (as by the eruption of vesicles) due to blockage of the ducts of the sweat glands; *especially* : PRICKLY HEAT
— **mil·i·ar·i·al** \-əl\ *adjective*

**mil·i·ary** \'mi-lē-,er-ē\ *adjective* [Latin *miliarius* of millet, from *milium* millet — more at MILLET] (1685)
: having or made up of many small projections or lesions ⟨*miliary* tubercles⟩

**mi·lieu** \mēl-'yə(r), -'yü; 'mēl-,yü, mē-lyœ̄\ *noun, plural* **milieus** *or* **mi·lieux** \-'yə(r)(z), -'yüz; -,yü(z), -lyœ̄(z)\ [French, from Old French, midst, from *mi* middle (from Latin *medius*) + *lieu* place, from Latin *locus* — more at MID, STALL] (1854)
: the physical or social setting in which something occurs or develops : ENVIRONMENT
*synonym* see BACKGROUND

**mil·i·tance** \'mi-lə-tən(t)s\ *noun* (circa 1947)
: MILITANCY

**mil·i·tan·cy** \-tən(t)-sē\ *noun* (1648)
: the quality or state of being militant

**mil·i·tant** \-tənt\ *adjective* (15th century)
**1** : engaged in warfare or combat : FIGHTING
**2** : aggressively active (as in a cause) : COMBATIVE ⟨*militant* conservationists⟩ ⟨a *militant* attitude⟩
*synonym* see AGGRESSIVE
— **militant** *noun*
— **mil·i·tant·ly** *adverb*
— **mil·i·tant·ness** *noun*

**mil·i·tar·ia** \,mi-lə-'ter-ē-ə\ *noun plural* (1964)
: military objects (as firearms and uniforms) of historical value or interest

**mil·i·tari·ly** \,mi-lə-'ter-ə-lē\ *adverb* (1660)
**1** : in a military manner
**2** : from a military standpoint

**mil·i·ta·rise** *British variant of* MILITARIZE

**mil·i·ta·rism** \'mi-lə-tə-,ri-zəm\ *noun* (1864)
**1 a** : predominance of the military class or its ideals **b** : exaltation of military virtues and ideals
**2** : a policy of aggressive military preparedness
— **mil·i·ta·rist** \-rist\ *noun or adjective*

— **mil·i·ta·ris·tic** \,mi-lə-tə-'ris-tik\ *adjective*
— **mil·i·ta·ris·ti·cal·ly** \-ti-k(ə-)lē\ *adverb*

**mil·i·ta·rize** \'mi-lə-tə-,rīz\ *transitive verb* **-rized; -riz·ing** (1880)
**1** : to equip with military forces and defenses
**2** : to give a military character to
**3** : to adapt for military use
— **mil·i·ta·ri·za·tion** \,mi-lə-t(ə-)rə-'zā-shən\ *noun*

**¹mil·i·tary** \'mi-lə-,ter-ē\ *adjective* [Middle English, from Middle French *militaire*, from Latin *militaris*, from *milit-, miles* soldier] (15th century)
**1 a** : of or relating to soldiers, arms, or war **b** : of or relating to armed forces; *especially* : of or relating to ground or sometimes ground and air forces as opposed to naval forces
**2 a** : performed or made by armed forces **b** : supported by armed force
**3** : of or relating to the army

**²military** *noun, plural* **military** *also* **mil·i·tar·ies** (1736)
**1** : military persons; *especially* : army officers
**2** : ARMED FORCES

**military–industrial complex** *noun* (1961)
: an informal alliance of the military and related government departments with defense industries that is held to influence government policy

**military police** *noun* (1827)
: a branch of an army that exercises guard and police functions

**military press** *noun* (1939)
: ¹PRESS 9

**military science** *noun* (circa 1830)
: the principles of military conflict

**military time** *noun* (1955)
: time measured in hours numbered to twenty-four (as 0100 or 2300) from one midnight to the next

**mil·i·tate** \'mi-lə-,tāt\ *intransitive verb* **-tat·ed; -tat·ing** [Latin *militatus*, past participle of *militare* to engage in warfare, from *milit-, miles*] (1642)
: to have weight or effect ⟨his boyish appearance *militated* against his getting an early promotion⟩
*usage* see MITIGATE

**mi·li·tia** \mə-'li-shə\ *noun* [Latin, military service, from *milit-, miles*] (circa 1660)
**1 a** : a part of the organized armed forces of a country liable to call only in emergency **b** : a body of citizens organized for military service
**2** : the whole body of able-bodied male citizens declared by law as being subject to call to military service

**mi·li·tia·man** \-mən\ *noun* (1780)
: a member of a militia

**mil·i·um** \'mi-lē-əm\ *noun, plural* **mil·ia** \-lē-ə\ [New Latin, from Latin, millet — more at MILLET] (1856)
: a small whitish lump in the skin due to retention of keratin in an oil gland duct — called *also* whitehead

**¹milk** \'milk\ *noun* [Middle English, from Old English *meolc, milc*; akin to Old High German *miluh* milk, Old English *melcan* to milk — more at EMULSION] (before 12th century)
**1 a** : a fluid secreted by the mammary glands of females for the nourishment of their young; *especially* : cow's milk used as a food by humans **b** : LACTATION ⟨cows in *milk*⟩
**2** : a liquid resembling milk in appearance: as **a** : the latex of a plant **b** : the juice of a coconut **c** : the contents of an unripe kernel of grain

**²milk** (before 12th century)
*transitive verb*

**1 a** (1) : to draw milk from the breasts or udder of (2) *obsolete* : SUCKLE **2 b :** to draw (milk) from the breast or udder **c :** SUCKLE 1 — used of lower mammals
**2 :** to draw something from as if by milking: as **a :** to induce (a snake) to eject venom **b :** to draw or coerce profit or advantage from illicitly or to an extreme degree : EXPLOIT
*intransitive verb*
: to draw or yield milk
**³milk** *adjective* (14th century)
: giving milk; *specifically* : bred or suitable primarily for milk production ⟨*milk* cows⟩
**milk–and–water** *adjective* (1783)
: WEAK, INSIPID
**milk chocolate** *noun* (1904)
: chocolate made with milk solids
**milk·er** \'mil-kər\ *noun* (15th century)
**1 :** one that milks an animal
**2 :** one that yields milk
**milk fever** *noun* (1758)
**1 :** a febrile disorder following parturition
**2 :** a disease of fresh cows, sheep, or goats that is caused by excessive drain on the body mineral reserves during the establishment of the milk flow
**milk·fish** \'milk-,fish\ *noun* (circa 1890)
: a large fork-tailed silvery herbivorous food fish (*Chanos chanos*) of warm parts of the Pacific and Indian oceans that is the sole living representative of its family (Chanidae)
**milk glass** *noun* (1874)
: an opaque and typically milky white glass used especially for novelty and ornamental objects
**milk house** *noun* (1589)
: a building for the cooling, handling, or bottling of milk
**milk leg** *noun* (circa 1860)
: a painful swelling of the leg caused by inflammation and clotting in the veins and affecting some postpartum women
**milk–liv·ered** \'milk-,li-vərd\ *adjective* (1605)
*archaic* : COWARDLY, TIMOROUS
**milk·maid** \-,mād\ *noun* (1552)
: DAIRYMAID
**milk·man** \-,man, -mən\ *noun* (1589)
: one who sells or delivers milk and milk products
**milk of magnesia** (1880)
: a milky white suspension of magnesium hydroxide in water used as an antacid and laxative
**milk punch** *noun* (1704)
: a mixed drink of alcoholic liquor, milk, and sugar
**milk run** *noun* [from the resemblance in regularity and uneventfulness to the morning delivery of milk] (1925)
: a short, routine, or uneventful flight
**milk shake** *noun* (1889)
: a thoroughly shaken or blended drink made of milk, a flavoring syrup, and often ice cream
**milk sickness** *noun* (1823)
**1 :** an acute disease characterized by weakness, vomiting, and constipation and caused by eating dairy products or meat from cattle poisoned by various plants
**2 :** TREMBLE 2
**milk snake** *noun* (1800)
: a common harmless grayish or tan American colubrid snake (*Lampropeltis triangulum*) having an arrow-shaped occipital marking and brown blotches on the body bordered with black or rings usually of black, red, and yellow; *broadly* : KING SNAKE
**milk·sop** \'milk-,säp\ *noun* [Middle English, literally, bread soaked in milk] (14th century)
: an unmanly man : MOLLYCODDLE
**milk sugar** *noun* (1846)
: LACTOSE
**milk tooth** *noun* (circa 1752)
: a deciduous tooth of a young mammal; *especially* : one of the human dentition including four incisors, two canines, and four molars in each jaw

**milk vein** *noun* (1844)
: a large subcutaneous vein that extends along the lower side of the abdomen of a cow and returns blood from the udder — see COW illustration
**milk vetch** *noun* [from the popular belief that it increases the milk yield of goats] (1597)
: any of a genus (*Astragalus*) of leguminous herbs; *especially* : an Old World perennial (*A. glycyphyllos*) that has sulfur yellow flowers in dense spikes
**milk·weed** \'milk-,wēd\ *noun* (circa 1598)
: any of various plants that secrete latex; *especially* : any of a genus (*Asclepias* of the family Asclepiadaceae, the milkweed family) of erect chiefly perennial herbs with milky juice and umbellate flowers
**milkweed bug** *noun* (1905)
: a large black red-marked bug (*Oncopeltus fasciatus*) cultured as a research organism
**milkweed butterfly** *noun* (1880)
: any of a family (Danaidae) or nymphalid subfamily (Danaine) of large butterflies feeding on plants of the milkweed family as larvae; *especially* : MONARCH BUTTERFLY
**milk·wort** \'milk-,wərt, -,wȯrt\ *noun* (1578)
: any of a genus (*Polygala* of the family Polygalaceae, the milkwort family) of plants typically having showy flowers with three sometimes crested petals united below into a tube and an irregular calyx with two petaloid sepals
**milky** \'mil-kē\ *adjective* **milk·i·er; -est** (14th century)
**1 :** resembling milk in color or consistency
**2 :** MILD, TIMOROUS
**3 a :** consisting of, containing, or abounding in milk **b :** yielding milk; *specifically* : having the characteristics of a good milk producer
— **milk·i·ness** *noun*
**milky disease** *noun* (circa 1940)
: a destructive bacterial disease of scarab beetle grubs and especially Japanese beetle larvae
**Milky Way** *noun*
**1 :** a broad luminous irregular band of light that stretches completely around the celestial sphere and is caused by the light of myriads of faint stars
**2 :** MILKY WAY GALAXY
**word history** see GALAXY
**Milky Way galaxy** *noun*
: the galaxy of which the sun and the solar system are a part and which contains the myriads of stars that comprise the Milky Way
**¹mill** \'mil\ *noun* [Middle English *mille*, from Old English *mylen*, from Late Latin *molina, molinum*, from feminine and neuter of *molinus* of a mill, of a millstone, from Latin *mola* mill, millstone; akin to Latin *molere* to grind — more at MEAL] (before 12th century)
**1 :** a building provided with machinery for grinding grain into flour
**2 a :** a machine or apparatus (as a quern) for grinding grain **b :** a machine for crushing or comminuting
**3 :** a machine that manufactures by the continuous repetition of some simple action
**4 :** a building or collection of buildings with machinery for manufacturing
**5 a :** a machine formerly used for stamping coins **b :** a machine for expelling juice from vegetable tissues by pressure or grinding
**6 :** MILLING MACHINE, MILLING CUTTER
**7 a :** a slow, laborious, or mechanical process or routine **b :** one that produces or processes people or things mechanically or in large numbers ⟨a diploma *mill*⟩ ⟨a rumor *mill*⟩
**8 :** a difficult and often educational experience — used in the phrase *through the mill*
**9** *slang* : the engine of an automobile or boat
**²mill** (1552)
*transitive verb*
**1 :** to subject to an operation or process in a mill: as **a :** to grind into flour, meal, or powder **b :** to shape or dress by means of a rotary cutter **c :** to mix and condition (as rubber) by passing between rotating rolls

**2 :** to give a raised rim or a ridged or corrugated edge to (a coin)
**3 :** to cut grooves in the metal surface of (as a knob)
*intransitive verb*
**1 :** to hit out with the fists
**2 :** to move in a circle or in an eddying mass; *also* : WANDER
**3 :** to undergo milling
**³mill** *noun* [Latin *mille* thousand] (1786)
: a money of account equal to ¹/₁₀ cent
**⁴mill** *variant of* ²MIL
**mill·age** \'mi-lij\ *noun* (1891)
: a rate (as of taxation) expressed in mills per dollar
**mill·dam** \'mil-,dam\ *noun* (12th century)
: a dam to make a millpond; *also* : MILLPOND
**mille** \'mil\ *noun* [Latin] (1894)
: THOUSAND
**mille–feuille** \mēl-'fwē\ *noun* [French, from *mille feuilles* a thousand leaves] (1895)
: a dish composed of puff pastry layered with a filling (as salmon or cream)
**mil·le·fi·o·ri** \,mi-lə-fē-'ōr-ē, -'ȯr-\ *noun* [Italian, from *mille fiori* a thousand flowers] (1849)
: ornamental glass produced by cutting cross sections of fused bundles of glass rods of various colors and sizes
**mille·fleur** *or* **mille·fleurs** \(,)mēl-'flər, -'flu̇r\ *adjective* [French *mille-fleurs*, from *mille fleurs* a thousand flowers] (1908)
: having an allover pattern of small flowers and plants ⟨*millefleur* tapestry⟩
**¹mil·le·nar·i·an** \,mi-lə-'ner-ē-ən\ *adjective* (1631)
**1 a :** of or relating to belief in a millennium **b :** APOCALYPTIC 2
**2 :** of or relating to 1000 years
**²millenarian** *noun* (circa 1674)
: one that believes in a millennium
**mil·le·nar·i·an·ism** \-ē-ə-,ni-zəm\ *noun* (circa 1847)
**1 :** belief in the millennium of Christian prophecy
**2 :** belief in a coming ideal society and especially one created by revolutionary action
**¹mil·le·na·ry** \'mi-lə-,ner-ē, mə-'le-nə-rē\ *noun, plural* **-ries** [Late Latin *millenarium*, from neuter of *millenarius* of a thousand, from Latin *milleni* one thousand each, from *mille*] (1550)
**1 a :** a group of 1000 units or things **b :** 1000 years : MILLENNIUM
**2 :** MILLENARIAN
**²millenary** *adjective* [Latin *millenarius*] (circa 1641)
**1 :** relating to or consisting of 1000
**2 :** suggesting a millennium
**mil·len·ni·al** \mə-'le-nē-əl\ *adjective* (1664)
: of or relating to a millennium
**mil·len·ni·al·ism** \-ē-ə-,li-zəm\ *noun* (1906)
: MILLENARIANISM
**mil·len·ni·al·ist** \-list\ *noun* (circa 1841)
: MILLENARIAN
**mil·len·ni·um** \mə-'le-nē-əm\ *noun, plural* **-nia** \-nē-ə\ *or* **-niums** [New Latin, from Latin *mille* thousand + New Latin *-ennium* (as in *biennium*)] (circa 1638)
**1 a :** the thousand years mentioned in Revelation 20 during which holiness is to prevail and Christ is to reign on earth **b :** a period of great happiness or human perfection
**2 a :** a period of 1000 years **b :** a 1000th anniversary or its celebration
**mill·er** \'mi-lər\ *noun* (14th century)
**1 :** one that operates a mill; *specifically* : one that grinds grain into flour
**2 :** any of various moths having powdery wings
**3 a :** MILLING MACHINE **b :** a tool for use in a milling machine
**mil·ler·ite** \'mi-lə-,rīt\ *noun* [German *Millerit*, from William H. *Miller* (died 1880) English mineralogist] (1854)

: sulfide of nickel NiS usually occurring as a mineral in capillary yellow crystals

**mill·er's–thumb** \\,mi-lərz-'thəm\ *noun* (15th century)
: any of several small freshwater spiny-finned sculpins (genus *Cottus*) of Europe and North America

**mil·les·i·mal** \mə-'le-sə-məl\ *noun* [Latin *millesimus*, adjective, thousandth, from *mille*] (1719)
: the quotient of a unit divided by 1000 : one of 1000 equal parts
— **millesimal** *adjective*
— **mil·les·i·mal·ly** \-mə-lē\ *adverb*

**mil·let** \'mi-lət\ *noun* [Middle English *milet*, from Middle French, diminutive of *mil*, from Latin *milium*; akin to Greek *melinē* millet] (15th century)
**1** : any of various small-seeded annual cereal and forage grasses: **a** : a grass (*Panicum miliaceum*) cultivated for its grain which is used for food **b** : any of several grasses related to common millet
**2** : the seed of a millet

**milli-** *combining form* [French, from Latin *milli-* thousand, from *mille*]
: thousandth ⟨*milliampere*⟩

**mil·li·am·pere** \,mi-lē-'am-,pir\ *noun* [International Scientific Vocabulary] (1885)
: one thousandth of an ampere

**mil·liard** \'mil-,yärd, 'mi-lē-,ärd\ *noun* [French, from Middle French *miliart*, from *mili-* (from *milion* million) (1793)
*British* : a thousand millions — see NUMBER table

**mil·li·ary** \'mi-lē-,er-ē\ *adjective* [Latin *miliarius, miliarius* consisting of a thousand, one mile long, from *mille* thousand, mile] (1644)
: marking the distance of a Roman mile

**mil·li·bar** \'mi-lə-,bär\ *noun* [International Scientific Vocabulary] (1910)
: a unit of atmospheric pressure equal to ¹⁄₁₀₀₀ bar or 1000 dynes per square centimeter

**mil·li·cu·rie** \,mi-lə-'kyúr-(,)ē, -kyú-'rē\ *noun* [International Scientific Vocabulary] (1910)
: one thousandth of a curie

**mil·li·de·gree** \-di-'grē\ *noun* (1942)
: one thousandth of a degree

**mil·lieme** \mē(l)-'yem\ *noun, plural* **mil·liemes** \-'yem(z)\ [French *millième* thousandth, from Middle French, from *mille* thousand, from Latin] (1902)
: a unit of value of Egypt and Sudan equal to ¹⁄₁₀₀₀ pound

**mil·li·gal** \'mi-lə-,gal\ *noun* [International Scientific Vocabulary] (1914)
: a unit of acceleration equivalent to ¹⁄₁₀₀₀ gal

**mil·li·gram** \-,gram\ *noun* [French *milligramme*, from *milli-* + *gramme* gram] (circa 1810)
— see METRIC SYSTEM table

**mil·li·hen·ry** \-,hen-rē\ *noun* [International Scientific Vocabulary] (1897)
: one thousandth of a henry

**mil·li·lam·bert** \-,lam-bərt\ *noun* (1916)
: one thousandth of a lambert

**mil·li·li·ter** \'mi-lə-,lē-tər\ *noun* [French *millilitre*, from *milli-* + *litre* liter] (circa 1810)
— see METRIC SYSTEM table

**mil·lime** \mə-'lēm\ *noun* [modification of Arabic *mallim*, from French *millième*] (circa 1919)
— see *dinar* at MONEY table

**mil·li·me·ter** \'mi-lə-,mē-tər\ *noun* [French *millimètre*, from *milli-* + *mètre* meter] (1807)
— see METRIC SYSTEM table

**mil·li·mi·cron** \,mi-lə-'mī-,krän\ *noun* [International Scientific Vocabulary] (1904)
: NANOMETER

**mil·li·mole** \'mi-lə-,mōl\ *noun* [International Scientific Vocabulary *milli-* + ⁵*mole*] (circa 1904)
: one thousandth of a mole (as of a substance)
— **mil·li·mo·lar** \-,mō-lər\ *adjective*

**mil·li·ner** \'mi-lə-nər\ *noun* [irregular from *Milan*, Italy; from the importation of women's finery from Italy in the 16th century] (1530)
: a person who designs, makes, trims, or sells women's hats ◆

**mil·li·nery** \'mi-lə-,ner-ē\ *noun* (circa 1688)
**1** : women's apparel for the head
**2** : the business or work of a milliner

**mill·ing** \'mi-liŋ\ *noun* (1817)
: a corrugated edge on a coin

**milling cutter** *noun* (1884)
: a rotary tool-steel cutter used in a milling machine for shaping and dressing metal surfaces

**milling machine** *noun* (1876)
: a machine tool on which work usually of metal secured to a carriage is shaped by rotating milling cutters

**mil·lion** \'mi(l)-yən\ *noun, plural* **millions** *or* **million** [Middle English *milioun*, from Middle French *milion*, from Old Italian *milione*, augmentative of *mille* thousand, from Latin] (14th century)
**1** — see NUMBER table
**2** : a very large number ⟨*millions* of cars on the road⟩
**3** : the mass of common people ⟨someone who writes for the *millions* —Bergen Evans⟩
— **million** *adjective*
— **mil·lion·fold** \-,fōld\ *adverb or adjective*
— **mil·lionth** \'mi(l)-yən(t)th\ *adjective or noun*

**mil·lion·aire** \,mi(l)-yə-'nar, -'ner, 'mi(l)-yə-,\ *noun* [French *millionnaire*, from *million*, from Middle French *milion*] (1826)
: a person whose wealth is estimated at a million or more (as of dollars or pounds)

**mil·lion·air·ess** \-'ar-əs, -'er-, -,ar-, -,er-\ *noun* (1881)
**1** : a woman who is a millionaire
**2** : the wife of a millionaire

**mil·li·os·mol** \,mi-lē-'äz-,mōl, -'äs-\ *noun* (1939)
: one thousandth of an osmol

**mil·li·pede** \'mi-lə-,pēd\ *noun* [Latin *millepeda*, a small crawling animal, from *mille* thousand + *ped-, pes* foot — more at FOOT] (1601)
: any of a class (Diplopoda) of myriapod arthropods having usually a cylindrical segmented body covered with hard integument, two pairs of legs on most apparent segments, and unlike centipedes no poison fangs

**mil·li·ra·di·an** \,mi-lə-'rā-dē-ən\ *noun* [International Scientific Vocabulary] (1954)
: one thousandth of a radian

**mil·li·rem** \'mi-lə-,rem\ *noun* (1947)
: one thousandth of a rem

**mil·li·roent·gen** \,mi-lə-'rent-gən, -'rənt-, -jən, -shən\ *noun* [International Scientific Vocabulary] (1947)
: one thousandth of a roentgen

**mil·li·sec·ond** \'mi-lə-,se-kənd, -kənt\ *noun* [International Scientific Vocabulary] (1909)
: one thousandth of a second

**mil·li·volt** \-,vōlt\ *noun* [International Scientific Vocabulary] (1861)
: one thousandth of a volt

**mil·li·watt** \-,wät\ *noun* [International Scientific Vocabulary] (circa 1914)
: one thousandth of a watt

**mill·pond** \'mil-,pänd\ *noun* (14th century)
: a pond created by damming a stream to produce a head of water for operating a mill

**mill·race** \-,rās\ *noun* (15th century)
: a canal in which water flows to and from a mill wheel; *also* : the current that drives the wheel

**mill·stone** \'mil-,stōn\ *noun* (before 12th century)
**1** : either of two circular stones used for grinding (as grain)
**2 a** : something that grinds or crushes **b** : a heavy burden

**mill·stream** \-,strēm\ *noun* (before 12th century)

**1** : a stream whose flow is utilized to run a mill
**2** : MILLRACE

**mill wheel** *noun* (before 12th century)
: a waterwheel that drives a mill

**mill·work** \'mil-,wərk\ *noun* (1899)
: woodwork (as doors, sashes, or trim) manufactured at a mill

**mill·wright** \-,rīt\ *noun* (14th century)
**1** : one whose occupation is planning and building mills or setting up their machinery
**2** : one who maintains and cares for mechanical equipment (as of a mill or factory)

**mi·lo** \'mī-(,)lō\ *noun, plural* **milos** [perhaps from Sesotho *maili*] (1882)
: a small usually early and drought-resistant grain sorghum with compact bearded heads of large yellow or whitish seeds

**mi·lord** \mi-'lòr(d)\ *noun* [French, from English *my lord*] (1596)
: an Englishman of noble or gentle birth

**mil·pa** \'mil-pə\ *noun* [Mexican Spanish, from Nahuatl *mīlpan*] (1844)
**1 a** : a small field in Mexico or Central America that is cleared from the forest, cropped for a few seasons, and abandoned for a fresh clearing **b** : a maize field in Mexico or Central America
**2** : the maize plant

**Milque·toast** \'milk-,tōst\ *noun* [Caspar *Milquetoast*, comic strip character created by H. T. Webster (died 1952) American cartoonist] (1935)
: a timid, meek, or unassertive person

**mil·reis** \mil-'rāsh, -'rās\ *noun, plural* **milreis** \*same or* -'rāz, -'räzh\ [Portuguese *milréis*] (1589)
**1** : a Portuguese unit of value equal before 1911 to 1000 reis
**2** : the basic monetary unit of Brazil until 1942
**3** : a coin representing one milreis

**milt** \'milt\ *noun* [probably from Middle Dutch *milte* milt of fish, spleen; akin to Old English *milte* spleen — more at MELT] (15th century)
: the sperm-containing fluid of a male fish

**mim** \'mim\ *adjective* [imitative of the act of pursing the lips] (1641)
*dialect* : affectedly shy or modest

**¹mime** \'mīm *also* 'mēm\ *noun* [Latin *mimus*, from Greek *mimos*] (1603)
**1** : an ancient dramatic entertainment representing scenes from life usually in a ridiculous manner
**2 a** : an actor in a mime **b** : one that practices mime
**3** : MIMIC 2
**4** : PANTOMIME 3a,b

**²mime** *verb* **mimed; mim·ing** (1616)

\ə\ abut \ᵊ\ kitten \ər\ further \a\ ash \ā\ ace
\ä\ mop, mar \au̇\ out \ch\ chin \e\ bet \ē\ easy
\g\ go \i\ hit \ī\ ice \j\ job \ŋ\ sing \ō\ go
\ȯ\ law \ȯi\ boy \th\ thin \th\ the \ü\ loot \u̇\ foot
\y\ yet \zh\ vision    *see also* Guide to Pronunciation

*intransitive verb*
**:** to act a part with mimic gesture and action usually without words
*transitive verb*
**1 :** MIMIC
**2 :** to act out in the manner of a mime
— **mim·er** *noun*
**mim·eo·graph** \'mi-mē-ə-ˌgraf\ *noun* [from *Mimeograph*, a trademark] (1889)
**:** a duplicator for making many copies that utilizes a stencil through which ink is pressed
— **mimeograph** *transitive verb*
**mi·me·sis** \mə-'mē-səs, mī-\ *noun* [Late Latin, from Greek *mimēsis*, from *mimeisthai*] (1550)
**:** IMITATION, MIMICRY
**mi·met·ic** \-'me-tik\ *adjective* [Late Latin *mimeticus*, from Greek *mimētikos*, from *mimeisthai* to imitate, from *mimos* mime] (1637)
**1 :** IMITATIVE
**2 :** relating to, characterized by, or exhibiting mimicry ⟨*mimetic* coloring of a butterfly⟩
— **mi·met·i·cal·ly** \-ti-k(ə-)lē\ *adverb*
**¹mim·ic** \'mi-mik\ *noun* (1590)
**1 :** MIME 2
**2 :** one that mimics
**²mimic** *adjective* [Latin *mimicus*, from Greek *mimikos*, from *mimos* mime] (1598)
**1 a :** IMITATIVE **b :** IMITATION, MOCK ⟨a *mimic* battle⟩
**2 :** of or relating to mime or mimicry
**³mimic** *transitive verb* **mim·icked** \-mikt\; **mim·ick·ing** (1687)
**1 :** to imitate closely **:** APE
**2 :** to ridicule by imitation
**3 :** SIMULATE
**4 :** to resemble by biological mimicry
**synonym** see COPY
**mim·ic·ry** \'mi-mi-krē\ *noun, plural* **-ries** (1687)
**1 a :** an instance of mimicking **b :** the action, practice, or art of mimicking
**2 :** a superficial resemblance of one organism to another or to natural objects among which it lives that secures it a selective advantage (as protection from predation)
**mi·mo·sa** \mə-'mō-sə, mī-, -zə\ *noun* [New Latin, from Latin *mimus* mime] (1751)
**1 :** any of a genus (*Mimosa*) of leguminous trees, shrubs, and herbs of tropical and warm regions with usually bipinnate often prickly leaves and globular heads of small white or pink flowers
**2 :** SILK TREE
**3 :** a mixed drink consisting of champagne and orange juice
**mi·na** \'mī-nə\ *noun* [Latin, from Greek *mna*, of Semitic origin; akin to Hebrew *māneh* mina] (circa 1580)
**:** an ancient unit of weight and value equal to ¹⁄₆₀ talent
**min·able** *or* **mine·able** \'mī-nə-bəl\ *adjective* (circa 1570)
**:** capable of being mined
**min·a·ret** \ˌmi-nə-'ret, 'mi-nə-ˌ\ *noun* [French, from Turkish *minare*, from Arabic *manārah* lighthouse] (1682)
**:** a tall slender tower of a mosque having one or more balconies from which the summons to prayer is cried by the muezzin
**mi·na·to·ry** \'mi-nə-ˌtōr-ē, 'mī-, -ˌtor-\ *adjective* [Late Latin *minatorius*, from Latin *minari* to threaten — more at MOUNT] (1532)
**:** having a menacing quality **:** THREATENING
**min·au·dière** \ˌmē-nōd-'yer\ *noun* [French, feminine of *minaudier* affected, coquettish, from *minauder* to mince] (1940)

**minaret**

**:** a small decorative case for carrying small articles (as cosmetics or jewelry)
**¹mince** \'min(t)s\ *verb* **minced; minc·ing** [Middle English, from Middle French *mincer*, from (assumed) Vulgar Latin *minutiare*, from Latin *minutia* smallness — more at MINUTIA] (14th century)
*transitive verb*
**1 a :** to cut or chop into very small pieces **b :** to subdivide minutely; *especially* **:** to damage by cutting up
**2 :** to utter or pronounce with affectation
**3 a** *archaic* **:** MINIMIZE **b :** to restrain (words) within the bounds of decorum
*intransitive verb*
**:** to walk with short steps in a prim affected manner
— **minc·er** *noun*
**²mince** *noun* (1600)
**1 :** small chopped bits (as of food); *specifically* **:** MINCEMEAT
**2** *British* **:** HAMBURGER 1a
**mince·meat** \'min(t)s-ˌmēt\ *noun* (1663)
**1 :** minced meat
**2 :** a finely chopped mixture (as of raisins, apples, and spices) sometimes with meat that is often used as pie filling
**3 :** a state of destruction or annihilation — used in the phrase *make mincemeat of*
**minc·ing** \'min(t)-siŋ\ *adjective* (1530)
**:** affectedly dainty or delicate
— **minc·ing·ly** \-siŋ-lē\ *adverb*
**¹mind** \'mīnd\ *noun* [Middle English, from Old English *gemynd;* akin to Old High German *gimunt* memory, Latin *ment-, mens* mind, *monēre* to remind, warn, Greek *menos* spirit, *mnasthai, mimnēskesthai* to remember] (before 12th century)
**1 :** RECOLLECTION, MEMORY ⟨keep that in *mind*⟩ ⟨time out of *mind*⟩
**2 a :** the element or complex of elements in an individual that feels, perceives, thinks, wills, and especially reasons **b :** the conscious mental events and capabilities in an organism **c :** the organized conscious and unconscious adaptive mental activity of an organism
**3 :** INTENTION, DESIRE ⟨I changed my *mind*⟩
**4 :** the normal or healthy condition of the mental faculties
**5 :** OPINION, VIEW
**6 :** DISPOSITION, MOOD
**7 a :** a person or group embodying mental qualities ⟨the public *mind*⟩ **b :** intellectual ability
**8** *capitalized, Christian Science* **:** GOD 1b
**9 :** a conscious substratum or factor in the universe
**²mind** (14th century)
*transitive verb*
**1** *chiefly dialect* **:** REMIND
**2** *chiefly dialect* **:** REMEMBER
**3 :** to attend to closely
**4 a** (1) **:** to become aware of **:** NOTICE (2) **:** to regard with attention **:** consider important — often used in the imperative with following *you* for emphasis ⟨I'm not against inspiration, *mind* you; I simply refuse to sit and stare at a blank page waiting for it —Dennis Whitcomb⟩ **b** *chiefly dialect* **:** INTEND, PURPOSE
**5 a :** to give heed to attentively in order to obey **b :** to follow the orders or instructions of
**6 a :** to be concerned about **b :** DISLIKE ⟨I don't *mind* going⟩
**7 a :** to be careful **:** SEE ⟨*mind* you finish it⟩ **b :** to be cautious about ⟨*mind* the broken rung⟩
**8 :** to give protective care to **:** TEND
*intransitive verb*
**1 :** to be attentive or wary
**2 :** to become concerned **:** CARE
**3 :** to pay obedient heed or attention
— **mind·er** *noun*
**mind–bend·ing** \'mīn(d)-ˌben-diŋ\ *adjective* (1965)
**:** MIND-BLOWING
**mind–blow·ing** \-ˌblō-iŋ\ *adjective* (1967)
**1 :** PSYCHEDELIC 1a

**2 :** MIND-BOGGLING
— **mind–blow·er** \-ˌblō(-ə)r\ *noun*
**mind–bog·gling** \-ˌbä-g(ə-)liŋ\ *adjective* (1964)
**:** mentally or emotionally exciting or overwhelming
— **mind–bog·gling·ly** \-lē\ *adverb*
**mind·ed** \'mīn-dəd\ *adjective* (15th century)
**1 :** INCLINED, DISPOSED
**2 :** having a mind especially of a specified kind or concerned with a specified thing — usually used in combination ⟨narrow-*minded*⟩ ⟨health-*minded*⟩
— **mind·ed·ness** \-dəd-nəs\ *noun*
**mind–ex·pand·ing** \'mīnd-ik-ˌspan-diŋ\ *adjective* (1963)
**:** PSYCHEDELIC 1a
**mind·ful** \'mīn(d)-fəl\ *adjective* (14th century)
**1 :** bearing in mind **:** AWARE
**2 :** inclined to be aware
— **mind·ful·ly** \-fə-lē\ *adverb*
— **mind·ful·ness** *noun*
**mind·less** \-ləs\ *adjective* (before 12th century)
**1 a :** marked by a lack of mind or consciousness ⟨a *mindless* sleep⟩ **b** (1) **:** marked by or displaying no use of the powers of the intellect ⟨*mindless* violence⟩ (2) **:** requiring little attention or thought; *especially* **:** not intellectually challenging or stimulating ⟨*mindless* work⟩ ⟨a *mindless* movie⟩
**2 :** not mindful **:** HEEDLESS ⟨*mindless* of the consequences⟩
— **mind·less·ly** *adverb*
— **mind·less·ness** *noun*
**mind reader** *noun* (1887)
**:** one that professes or is held to be able to perceive another's thought without normal means of communication
— **mind reading** *noun*
**mind–set** \'mīn(d)-ˌset\ *noun* (1926)
**1 :** a mental attitude or inclination
**2 :** a fixed state of mind
**mind's eye** *noun* (15th century)
**:** the mental faculty of conceiving imaginary or recollected scenes; *also* **:** the mental picture so conceived ⟨in the *mind's eye* one sees dinosaurs, mammoths, and sabertoothed tigers —F. P. Brooks Jr.⟩
**¹mine** \'mīn\ *adjective* [Middle English *min*, from Old English *mīn* — more at MY] (before 12th century)
**:** MY — used before a word beginning with a vowel or *h* ⟨this treasure in *mine* arms —Shakespeare⟩ or sometimes as a modifier of a preceding noun; archaic except in an elevated style
**²mine** *pronoun singular or plural in construction* (before 12th century)
**:** that which belongs to me — used without a following noun as a pronoun equivalent in meaning to the adjective *my*
**³mine** *noun* [Middle English, from Middle French, from (assumed) Vulgar Latin *mina*, probably of Celtic origin; akin to Welsh *mwyn* ore] (14th century)
**1 a :** a pit or excavation in the earth from which mineral substances are taken **b :** an ore deposit
**2 :** a subterranean passage under an enemy position
**3 :** an encased explosive that is placed in the ground or in water and set to explode when disturbed
**4 :** a rich source of supply
**⁴mine** *verb* **mined; min·ing** (14th century)
*transitive verb*
**1 a :** to dig under to gain access or cause the collapse of (an enemy position) **b :** UNDERMINE
**2 a :** to get (as ore) from the earth **b :** to extract from a source ⟨information *mined* from the files⟩
**3 :** to burrow beneath the surface of ⟨larva that *mines* leaves⟩
**4 :** to place military mines in, on, or under ⟨*mine* a harbor⟩

**5 a :** to dig into for ore or metal **b :** to process for obtaining a natural constituent ⟨*mine* the air for nitrogen⟩ **c :** to seek valuable material in *intransitive verb* **:** to dig a mine
— **min·er** *noun*

**mine·field** \ˈmīn-ˌfēld\ *noun* (1886)
**1 :** an area (as of water or land) set with mines
**2 :** something resembling a minefield especially in having many dangers or requiring extreme caution

**mine·lay·er** \-ˌlā-ər, -ˌle(-ə)r\ *noun* (1909)
**:** a naval vessel for laying underwater mines

**¹min·er·al** \ˈmin-rəl, ˈmi-nə-\ *noun* [Middle English, from Medieval Latin *minerale*, from neuter of *mineralis*] (15th century)
**1 :** ORE
**2 :** an inorganic substance (as in the ash of calcined tissue)
**3** *obsolete* **:** MINE
**4 :** something neither animal nor vegetable
**5 a :** a solid homogeneous crystalline chemical element or compound that results from the inorganic processes of nature; *broadly* **:** any of various naturally occurring homogeneous substances (as stone, coal, salt, sulfur, sand, petroleum, water, or natural gas) obtained usually from the ground **b :** a synthetic substance having the chemical composition and crystalline form and properties of a naturally occurring mineral
**6** *plural, British* **:** MINERAL WATER

**²mineral** *adjective* [Middle English, from Medieval Latin *mineralis*, from *minera* mine, ore, from Old French *miniere*, from *mine*] (15th century)
**1 :** of or relating to minerals; *also* **:** INORGANIC
**2 :** impregnated with mineral substances

**min·er·al·ise** *British variant of* MINERALIZE

**min·er·al·ize** \ˈmin-rə-ˌlīz, ˈmi-nə-\ *transitive verb* **-ized; -iz·ing** (1655)
**1 :** to transform (a metal) into an ore
**2 a :** to impregnate or supply with minerals or an inorganic compound **b :** to convert into mineral or inorganic form
**3 :** PETRIFY
— **min·er·al·iz·able** \ˌmin-rə-ˈlī-zə-bəl, ˌmi-nə-\ *adjective*
— **min·er·al·i·za·tion** \-rə-lə-ˈzā-shən\ *noun*
— **min·er·al·iz·er** \ˈmin-rə-ˌlī-zər, ˈmi-nə-\ *noun*

**mineral kingdom** *noun* (circa 1691)
**:** a basic group of natural objects that includes inorganic objects — compare ANIMAL KINGDOM, PLANT KINGDOM

**min·er·al·o·cor·ti·coid** \ˌmin-rə-lō-ˈkȯr-tə-ˌkȯid, ˌmi-nə-\ *noun* (1946)
**:** a corticosteroid (as aldosterone) that affects chiefly the electrolyte and fluid balance in the body — compare GLUCOCORTICOID

**min·er·al·o·gy** \ˌmi-nə-ˈrä-lə-jē, -ˈra-\ *noun* [probably from (assumed) New Latin *mineralogia*, irregular from Medieval Latin *minerale* + Latin *-logia* -logy] (1690)
**1 :** a science dealing with minerals, their crystallography, properties, classification, and the ways of distinguishing them
**2 :** the minerological characteristics of an area, a rock, or a rock formation
— **min·er·al·og·i·cal** \ˌmi-nə-rə-ˈlä-ji-kəl, ˌmin-rə-\ *also* **min·er·al·og·ic** \-ˈlä-jik\ *adjective*
— **min·er·al·og·i·cal·ly** \-ˈlä-ji-k(ə-)lē\ *adverb*
— **min·er·al·o·gist** \ˌmi-nə-ˈrä-lə-jist, -ˈra-\ *noun*

**mineral oil** *noun* (1805)
**:** an oil of mineral origin; *especially* **:** a refined petroleum oil used especially as a laxative

**mineral spirits** *noun plural but singular or plural in construction* (1927)
**:** a petroleum distillate that is used especially as a paint or varnish thinner

**mineral water** *noun* (1562)

---

**:** water naturally or artificially infused with mineral salts or gases (as carbon dioxide)

**mineral wax** *noun* (circa 1864)
**:** a wax of mineral origin; *especially* **:** OZOKERITE

**mineral wool** *noun* (circa 1881)
**:** any of various lightweight vitreous fibrous materials used especially in heat and sound insulation

**Mi·ner·va** \mə-ˈnər-və\ *noun* [Latin]
**:** the Roman goddess of wisdom — compare ATHENA

**min·e·stro·ne** \ˌmi-nə-ˈstrō-nē, -ˈstrōn\ *noun* [Italian, augmentative of *minestra*, from *minestrare* to serve, dish up, from Latin *ministrare*, from *minister* servant — more at MINISTER] (1891)
**:** a rich thick vegetable soup usually with dried beans and pasta (as macaroni or vermicelli)

**mine·sweep·er** \ˈmīn-ˌswē-pər\ *noun* (1905)
**:** a warship designed for removing or neutralizing mines by dragging
— **mine·sweep·ing** \-piŋ\ *noun*

**Ming** \ˈmiŋ\ *noun* [Chinese (Beijing) *míng* luminous] (1795)
**:** a Chinese dynasty dated 1368–1644 and marked by restoration of earlier traditions and in the arts by perfection of established techniques

**min·gle** \ˈmiŋ-gəl\ *verb* **min·gled; min·gling** \-g(ə-)liŋ\ [Middle English *menglen*, frequentative of *mengen* to mix, from Old English *mengan;* akin to Middle High German *mengen* to mix, Greek *massein* to knead] (15th century)
*transitive verb*
**1 :** to bring or mix together or with something else usually without fundamental loss of identity **:** INTERMIX
**2** *archaic* **:** to prepare by mixing **:** CONCOCT
*intransitive verb*
**1 :** to become mingled
**2 a :** to come into contact **:** ASSOCIATE **b :** to move about (as in a group) ⟨*mingled* with the guests⟩
**synonym** see MIX

**ming tree** \ˈmiŋ-\ *noun* [perhaps from *Ming*] (1948)
**:** a dwarfed evergreen conifer grown as bonsai; *also* **:** an artificial plant resembling this

**min·gy** \ˈmin-jē\ *adjective* **min·gi·er; -est** [perhaps blend of ¹*mean* and *stingy*] (1912)
**:** MEAN, STINGY

**¹mini** \ˈmi-nē\ *adjective* [mini-] (1954)
**1 :** small in relation to others of the same kind
**2 :** of short length or duration **:** BRIEF

**²mini** *noun, plural* **min·is** (1961)
**:** something small of its kind: as **a :** MINICAR **b :** MINISKIRT **c :** MINICOMPUTER

**mini-** *combining form* [miniature]
**:** smaller or briefer than usual, normal, or standard ⟨*mini*course⟩ ⟨*mini*bus⟩

**¹min·i·a·ture** \ˈmi-nē-ə-ˌchur, ˈmi-ni-ˌchur, ˈmin-yə-, -chər, -ˌtyur, -ˌtur\ *noun* [Italian *miniatura* art of illuminating a manuscript, from Medieval Latin, from Latin *miniatus*, past participle of *miniare* to color with minium, from *minium* red lead] (circa 1586)
**1 a :** a copy on a much reduced scale **b :** something small of its kind
**2 :** a painting in an illuminated book or manuscript
**3 :** the art of painting miniatures
**4 :** a very small portrait or other painting (as on ivory or metal) ◆
— **min·i·a·tur·ist** \-ˌchur-ist, -chər-, -ˌtyur-, -ˌtur\ *noun*
— **min·i·a·tur·is·tic** \ˌmi-nē-ə-chə-ˈris-tik, ˌmi-ni-, ˌmin-yə-, -ˌtyur-, -ˌtur-\ *adjective*
— **in miniature :** in a greatly diminished size, form, or scale

**²miniature** *adjective* (1714)
**:** being or represented on a small scale
**synonym** see SMALL

**miniature golf** *noun* (1915)

---

**:** a novelty golf game played with a putter on a miniature course usually having tunnels, bridges, sharp corners, and obstacles

**miniature pin·scher** \-ˈpin(t)-shər\ *noun* (1929)
**:** any of a breed of toy dogs that suggest a small Doberman pinscher and are 10 to 12½ inches (25 to 32 centimeters) in height at the withers

**miniature schnauzer** *noun* (circa 1929)
**:** any of a breed of schnauzers that are 12 to 14 inches (30 to 36 centimeters) in height at the withers and are classified as terriers

miniature schnauzer

**min·i·a·tur·ize** \ˈmi-nē-ə-chə-ˌrīz, ˈmi-ni-chə-, ˈmin-yə-chə-, -ˌtyu-, -ˌtu-\ *transitive verb* **-ized; -iz·ing** (1946)
**:** to design or construct in small size
— **min·i·a·tur·i·za·tion** \ˌmi-nē-ə-ˌchur-ə-ˈzā-shən, ˌmi-ni-, ˌmin-yə-, -chər-, -ˌtyur-, -ˌtur-\ *noun*

**mini·bike** \ˈmi-nē-ˌbīk\ *noun* (1962)
**:** a small one-passenger motorcycle with a low frame and raised handlebars
— **mini·bik·er** *noun*

**mini·bus** \-ˌbəs\ *noun* (1958)
**:** a small bus or van

**Mini·cam** \-ˌkam\ *trademark*
— used for a portable television camera

**mini·camp** \-ˌkamp\ *noun* (1979)
**:** a special abbreviated training camp for football players held especially in the spring or early summer

**mini·car** \-ˌkär\ *noun* (1949)
**:** a very small automobile; *especially* **:** SUBCOMPACT

**mini·com·put·er** \ˌmi-nē-kəm-ˈpyü-tər\ *noun* (1968)
**:** a small computer that is intermediate between a microcomputer and a mainframe in size, speed, and capacity, that can support time-sharing, and that is often dedicated to a single application

**mini·course** \ˈmi-nē-ˌkȯrs, -ˌkȯrs\ *noun* (1970)
**:** a brief course of study usually lasting less than a semester

\ə\ abut \ᵊ\ kitten \ər\ further \a\ ash \ā\ ace
\ä\ mop, mar \au̇\ out \ch\ chin \e\ bet \ē\ easy
\g\ go \i\ hit \ī\ ice \j\ job \ŋ\ sing \ō\ go
\ȯ\ law \ȯi\ boy \th\ thin \t͟h\ the \ü\ loot \u̇\ foot
\y\ yet \zh\ vision   *see also* Guide to Pronunciation

**min·ié ball** \'mi-nē-, ˌmi-nē-'ā-\ *noun* [Claude Étienne *Minié* (died 1879) French army officer] (1859)
: a rifle bullet with a conical head used in muzzle-loading firearms

**min·i·fy** \'mi-nə-ˌfī\ *transitive verb* **-fied; -fy·ing** [Latin *minus* less + English *-ify*] (1676)
: LESSEN

**min·i·kin** \'mi-ni-kən\ *noun* [obsolete Dutch *minneken* darling, ultimately from Middle Dutch *minne* love, beloved; akin to Old English *gemynd* mind, memory — more at MIND] (1761)
*archaic* : a small or dainty creature
— **minikin** *adjective*

**mini·lab** \'mi-nē-ˌlab\ *noun* (1982)
: a retail outlet offering rapid on-site film development and printing

**min·im** \'mi-nəm\ *noun* [Latin *minimus* least] (15th century)
**1** : HALF NOTE
**2** : something very minute
**3** — see WEIGHT table
— **minim** *adjective*

**min·i·mal** \'mi-nə-məl\ *adjective* (1666)
**1** : relating to or being a minimum: as **a** : the least possible ⟨a victory won with *minimal* loss of life⟩ **b** : barely adequate ⟨a *minimal* standard of living⟩ **c** : very small or slight ⟨a *minimal* interest in art⟩
**2** *often capitalized* : of, relating to, or being minimal art or minimalism
— **min·i·mal·ly** \-mə-lē\ *adverb*

**minimal art** *noun* (1965)
: abstract art consisting primarily of simple geometric forms executed in an impersonal style

**minimal brain dysfunction** *noun* (1972)
: ATTENTION DEFICIT DISORDER

**min·i·mal·ism** \'mi-nə-mə-ˌli-zəm\ *noun* (1969)
**1** : MINIMAL ART
**2** : a style or technique (as in music, literature, or design) that is characterized by extreme spareness and simplicity

**¹min·i·mal·ist** \-list\ *noun* (1907)
**1** : one who favors restricting the functions and powers of a political organization or the achievement of a set of goals to a minimum
**2 a** : a minimal artist **b** : an adherent of minimalism

**²minimalist** *adjective* (1967)
: of, relating to, or done in the style of minimalism

**minimal pair** *noun* (1942)
: two linguistic units that differ in a single distinctive feature or constituent (as voice in the initial consonants of *bat* and *pat*)

**mini·max** \'mi-ni-ˌmaks\ *noun* [*mini*mum + *max*imum] (1918)
: the minimum of a set of maxima; *especially* : the smallest of a set of maximum possible losses each of which occurs in the most unfavorable outcome of a strategy followed by a participant in a situation governed by the theory of games — compare MAXIMIN

**mini·mill** \'mi-nē-ˌmil\ *noun* (1969)
: a relatively small-scale steel mill that uses scrap metal as starting material

**min·i·mise** *British variant of* MINIMIZE

**min·i·mize** \'mi-nə-ˌmīz\ *transitive verb* **-mized; -miz·ing** (1802)
**1** : to reduce or keep to a minimum
**2** : to underestimate intentionally : play down : SOFT-PEDAL ⟨*minimizing* losses in our own forces while maximizing those of the enemy⟩
— **min·i·mi·za·tion** \ˌmi-nə-mə-'zā-shən\ *noun*
— **min·i·miz·er** \'mi-nə-ˌmī-zər\ *noun*

**min·i·mum** \'mi-nə-məm\ *noun, plural* **-i·ma** \-nə-mə\ *or* **-i·mums** [Latin, neuter of *minimus* smallest; akin to Latin *minor* smaller — more at MINOR] (1674)
**1** : the least quantity assignable, admissible, or possible

**2** : the least of a set of numbers; *specifically* : the smallest value assumed by a continuous function defined on a closed interval
**3 a** : the lowest degree or amount of variation (as of temperature) reached or recorded **b** : the lowest speed allowed on a highway
— **minimum** *adjective*

**minimum wage** *noun* (1860)
**1** : LIVING WAGE
**2** : the lowest wage paid or permitted to be paid; *specifically* : a wage fixed by legal authority or by contract as the least that may be paid either to employed persons generally or to a particular category of employed persons

**min·ing** \'mī-niŋ\ *noun* (1523)
: the process or business of working mines

**min·ion** \'min-yən\ *noun* [Middle French *mignon* darling] (1501)
**1** : a servile dependent, follower, or underling
**2** : one highly favored : IDOL
**3** : a subordinate or petty official

**mini·park** \'mi-nē-ˌpärk\ *noun* (1967)
: a small city park

**mini·school** \-ˌskül\ *noun* (1968)
: an experimental school offering specialized or individual instruction to its students

**min·is·cule** \'mi-nəs-ˌkyü(ə)l\ *variant of* MINUSCULE

**mini·se·ries** \'mi-nē-ˌsir-(ˌ)ēz\ *noun* (1973)
: a television production of a story presented in sequential episodes

**mini·skirt** \'mi-nē-ˌskərt\ *noun* (1965)
: a woman's short skirt with the hemline several inches above the knee
— **mini·skirt·ed** *adjective*

**mini·state** \-ˌstāt\ *noun* (1966)
: a small independent nation

**¹min·is·ter** \'mi-nə-stər\ *noun* [Middle English *ministre*, from Old French, from Latin *minister* servant; akin to Latin *minor* smaller] (14th century)
**1** : AGENT
**2 a** : one officiating or assisting the officiant in church worship **b** : a clergyman especially of a Protestant communion
**3 a** : the superior of one of several religious orders — called also *minister-general* **b** : the assistant to the rector or the bursar of a Jesuit house
**4** : a high officer of state entrusted with the management of a division of governmental activities
**5 a** : a diplomatic representative (as an ambassador) accredited to the court or seat of government of a foreign state **b** : a diplomatic representative ranking below an ambassador

**²minister** *intransitive verb* **-tered; -ter·ing** \-st(ə-)riŋ\ (14th century)
**1** : to perform the functions of a minister of religion
**2** : to give aid or service ⟨*minister* to the sick⟩

**min·is·te·ri·al** \ˌmi-nə-'stir-ē-əl\ *adjective* (1561)
**1** : of, relating to, or characteristic of a minister or the ministry
**2 a** : being or having the characteristics of an act or duty prescribed by law as part of the duties of an administrative office **b** : relating to or being an act done after ascertaining the existence of a specified state of facts in obedience to a legal order without exercise of personal judgment or discretion
**3** : acting or active as an agent : INSTRUMENTAL
— **min·is·te·ri·al·ly** \-ē-ə-lē\ *adverb*

**minister plenipotentiary** *noun, plural* **ministers plenipotentiary** (1796)
: a diplomatic agent ranking below an ambassador but possessing full power and authority

**minister resident** *noun, plural* **ministers resident** (1848)
: a diplomatic agent resident at a foreign court or seat of government and ranking below a minister plenipotentiary

**¹min·is·trant** \'mi-nə-strənt\ *adjective* (1667)

*archaic* : performing service in attendance on someone

**²ministrant** *noun* (1818)
: one that ministers

**min·is·tra·tion** \ˌmi-nə-'strā-shən\ *noun* (14th century)
: the act or process of ministering

**min·is·try** \'mi-nə-strē\ *noun, plural* **-tries** (14th century)
**1** : MINISTRATION
**2** : the office, duties, or functions of a minister
**3** : the body of ministers of religion : CLERGY
**4** : AGENCY 2, INSTRUMENTALITY
**5** : the period of service or office of a minister or ministry
**6** *often capitalized* **a** : the body of ministers governing a nation or state from which a smaller cabinet is sometimes selected **b** : the group of ministers constituting a cabinet
**7 a** : a government department presided over by a minister **b** : the building in which the business of a ministry is transacted

**mini·van** \'mi-nē-ˌvan\ *noun* (1960)
: a small van

**min·i·ver** \'mi-nə-vər\ *noun* [Middle English *meniver*, from Middle French *menu vair* small vair] (13th century)
: a white fur worn originally by medieval nobles and used chiefly for robes of state

**mink** \'miŋk\ *noun, plural* **mink** *or* **minks** [Middle English] (15th century)
**1** : soft fur or pelt of the mink varying in color from white to dark brown
**2** : either of two slender-bodied semiaquatic carnivorous mammals (*Mustela vison* of North America and *M. lutreola* of Eurasia) that resemble the related weasels and have partially webbed feet, a rather short bushy tail, and a soft thick coat

mink 2

**min·ke whale** \'miŋ-kə-\ *noun* [part translation of Norwegian *minkehval*, from *minke-* (perhaps from *Meincke*, a crewman of Svend Foyn (died 1894) Norwegian whaler) + *hval* whale] (1939)
: a small grayish baleen whale (*Balaenoptera acutorostrata*) with a whitish underside — called also *minke*

**min·ne·sing·er** \'mi-nə-ˌsiŋ-ər, -ˌziŋ-\ *noun* [German, from Middle High German, from *minne* love + *singer* singer] (1825)
: any of a class of German poets and musicians of the 12th to the 14th centuries

**Min·ne·so·ta Multiphasic Personality Inventory** \ˌmi-nə-'sō-tə-ˌməl-ti-'fā-zik-, -ˌməl-ˌtī-\ *noun* [University of *Minnesota*] (1943)
: a test of personal and social adjustment based on a complex scaling of the answers to an elaborate true or false test

**min·now** \'mi-(ˌ)nō\ *noun, plural* **minnows** *also* **minnow** [Middle English *menawe*; akin to Old English *myne* minnow, Old High German *munewa*, a kind of fish] (15th century)
**1 a** : a small cyprinid, killifish, or topminnow **b** : any of various small fish that are less than a designated size and are not game fish
**2** : a live or artificial minnow used as bait

**¹Mi·no·an** \mə-'nō-ən, mī-\ *adjective* [Latin *minous* of Minos, from Greek *minōios*, from *Minōs* Minos] (1894)
: of or relating to a Bronze Age culture of Crete (3000 B.C.–1100 B.C.)

**²Minoan** *noun* (1902)
: a native or inhabitant of ancient Crete

**¹mi·nor** \'mī-nər\ *adjective* [Latin, smaller, inferior; akin to Old High German *minniro* smaller, Latin *minuere* to lessen] (1526)
**1** : inferior in importance, size, or degree : comparatively unimportant
**2** : not having reached majority
**3 a** : having half steps between the second and third, the fifth and sixth, and sometimes the

seventh and eighth degrees ⟨*minor* scale⟩ **b** : based on a minor scale ⟨*minor* key⟩ **c** : less by a semitone than the corresponding major interval ⟨*minor* third⟩ **d** : having a minor third above the root ⟨*minor* triad⟩
**4** : not serious or involving risk to life ⟨*minor* illness⟩
**5** : of or relating to an academic subject requiring fewer courses than a major
**²minor** *noun* (1612)
**1** : a person who has not attained majority
**2** : a minor musical interval, scale, key, or mode
**3 a** : a minor academic subject **b** : a student taking a specified minor
**4** : a determinant or matrix obtained from a given determinant or matrix by eliminating the row and column in which a given element lies
**5** *plural* : minor league baseball — used with *the*
**³minor** *intransitive verb* (1926)
: to take courses in a minor subject
**minor axis** *noun* (1862)
: the chord of an ellipse passing through the center and perpendicular to the major axis
**minor element** *noun* (circa 1945)
: TRACE ELEMENT
**Mi·nor·ite** \'mī-nə-ˌrīt\ *noun* [from *Friar Minor* Franciscan] (circa 1587)
: FRANCISCAN
**mi·nor·i·ty** \mə-'nȯr-ə-tē, mī-, -'när-\ *noun, plural* **-ties** *often attributive* (1547)
**1 a** : the period before attainment of majority **b** : the state of being a legal minor
**2** : the smaller in number of two groups constituting a whole; *specifically* : a group having less than the number of votes necessary for control
**3 a** : a part of a population differing from others in some characteristics and often subjected to differential treatment **b** : a member of a minority group ⟨an effort to hire more *minorities*⟩
**minority leader** *noun* (1949)
: the leader of the minority party in a legislative body
**minor league** *noun* (1889)
: a league of professional clubs in a sport other than the recognized major leagues
**minor order** *noun* (1844)
: one of the Roman Catholic or Eastern clerical orders that are lower in rank and less sacred in character than major orders — usually used in plural
**minor party** *noun* (1949)
: a political party whose electoral strength is so small as to prevent its gaining control of a government except in rare and exceptional circumstances
**minor penalty** *noun* (1936)
: a two-minute suspension of a player in ice hockey with no substitute allowed
**minor planet** *noun* (1861)
: ASTEROID
**minor premise** *noun* (circa 1741)
: the premise of a syllogism that contains the minor term
**minor seminary** *noun* (circa 1948)
: a Roman Catholic seminary giving all or part of high school and junior college training with emphasis on preparing candidates for a major seminary
**minor suit** *noun* (1916)
: either of the suits diamonds or clubs having inferior scoring value in bridge
**minor term** *noun* (1843)
: the term of a syllogism that forms the subject of the conclusion
**Mi·nos** \'mī-nəs\ *noun* [Latin, from Greek *Mi-nōs*]
: a son of Zeus and Europa and king of Crete who for his just rule is made supreme judge in the underworld after his death
**Mi·no·taur** \'mi-nə-ˌtȯr, 'mī-\ *noun* [Middle English, from Middle French, from Latin *Minotaurus*, from Greek *Minōtauros*, from *Minōs* + *tauros* bull]

: a monster shaped half like a man and half like a bull, confined in the labyrinth built by Daedalus for Minos, and given a periodic tribute of youths and maidens as food until slain by Theseus
**mi·nox·i·dil** \mə-'näk-sə-ˌdil\ *noun* [perhaps from a*mino* + *oxi-* (alteration of *oxy-*) + piperi-*dine* + -*yl*] (1972)
: a peripheral vasodilator $C_9H_{15}N_5O$ used orally to treat hypertension and topically in a propylene glycol solution to promote hair regrowth in some forms of baldness
**min·ster** \'min(t)-stər\ *noun* [Middle English, monastery, church attached to a monastery, from Old English *mynster*, from Late Latin *monasterium* monastery] (before 12th century)
: a large or important church often having cathedral status
**min·strel** \'min(t)-strəl\ *noun* [Middle English *menestrel*, from Middle French, official, servant, minstrel, from Late Latin *ministerialis* imperial household officer, from Latin *ministerium* service, from *minister* servant — more at MINISTER] (14th century)
**1** : one of a class of medieval musical entertainers; *especially* : a singer of verses to the accompaniment of a harp
**2 a** : MUSICIAN **b** : POET
**3 a** : any of a troupe of performers typically giving a program of black American melodies, jokes, and impersonations and usually wearing blackface **b** : a performance by a troupe of minstrels
**min·strel·sy** \-sē\ *noun* [Middle English *minstralcie*, from Middle French *menestralsie*, from *menestrel*] (14th century)
**1** : the singing and playing of a minstrel
**2** : a body of minstrels
**3** : a group of songs or verse
**¹mint** \'mint\ *noun* [Middle English *minte*, from Old English, from Latin *mentha, menta*; akin to Greek *minthē* mint] (before 12th century)
**1** : any of a family (Labiatae, the mint family) of aromatic plants with a square stem and a 4-lobed ovary which produces four one-seeded nutlets in fruit; *especially* : any of a genus (*Mentha*) of mints that have white, purple, or pink verticillate flowers with a nearly regular corolla and four equal stamens and that include some used in flavoring and cookery
**2** : a confection flavored with mint
— **minty** \'min-tē\ *adjective*
**²mint** *noun* [Middle English *mynt* coin, money, from Old English *mynet*, from Latin *moneta* mint, coin, from *Moneta*, epithet of Juno; from the fact that the Romans coined money in the temple of Juno Moneta] (15th century)
**1** : a place where coins, medals, or tokens are made
**2** : a place where something is manufactured
**3** : a vast sum or amount
**³mint** *transitive verb* (1546)
**1** : to make (as coins) out of metal : COIN
**2** : CREATE, PRODUCE
— **mint·er** *noun*
**⁴mint** *adjective* (1902)
: unmarred as if fresh from a mint ⟨in *mint* condition⟩
**mint·age** \'min-tij\ *noun* (circa 1570)
**1** : the action or process of minting coins
**2** : an impression placed upon a coin
**3** : coins produced by minting or in a single period of minting
**mint julep** *noun* (1809)
: JULEP 2
**min·u·end** \'min-yə-ˌwend\ *noun* [Latin *minuendum*, neuter of *minuendus*, gerundive of *minuere* to lessen — more at MINOR] (1706)
: a number from which the subtrahend is to be subtracted
**min·u·et** \ˌmin-yə-'wet\ *noun* [French *menuet*, from obsolete French, tiny, from Old French, from *menu* small, from Latin *minutus*] (1673)

**1** : a slow graceful dance in ¾ time characterized by forward balancing, bowing, and toe pointing
**2** : music for or in the rhythm of a minuet
**¹mi·nus** \'mī-nəs\ *preposition* [Middle English, from Latin *minus*, adverb, less, from neuter of *minor* smaller — more at MINOR] (15th century)
**1** : diminished by : LESS ⟨seven *minus* four is three⟩
**2** : deprived of : WITHOUT ⟨*minus* his hat⟩
**²minus** *noun* (1654)
**1** : a negative quantity
**2** : DEFICIENCY, DEFECT
**³minus** *adjective* (1800)
**1** : algebraically negative ⟨a *minus* quantity⟩
**2** : having negative qualities
**3** : relating to or being a particular one of the two mating types that are required for successful fertilization in sexual reproduction in some lower plants (as a fungus)
**4** : falling low in a specified range ⟨B *minus*⟩
**¹mi·nus·cule** \'mi-nəs-ˌkyü(ə)l *also* mi-'nəs-\ *noun* [French, from Latin *minusculus* rather small, diminutive of *minor* smaller] (1705)
**1 a** : one of several ancient and medieval writing styles developed from cursive and having simplified and small forms **b** : a letter in this style
**2** : a lowercase letter
**²minuscule** *adjective* (circa 1741)
**1** : written in or in the size or style of minuscules
**2** : very small
**minus sign** *noun* (1668)
: a sign − used in mathematics to indicate subtraction (as in $8-6=2$) or a negative quantity (as in $-10°$)
**¹min·ute** \'mi-nət\ *noun* [Middle English, from Middle French, from Late Latin *minuta*, from Latin *minutus* small, from past participle of *minuere* to lessen — more at MINOR] (14th century)
**1** : a 60th part of an hour of time or of a degree : 60 seconds
**2** : the distance one can traverse in a minute
**3** : a short space of time : MOMENT
**4 a** : a brief note (as of summary or recommendation) **b** : MEMORANDUM, DRAFT **c** *plural* : the official record of the proceedings of a meeting
**²minute** *transitive verb* **min·ut·ed; min·ut·ing** (circa 1648)
: to make notes or a brief summary of
**³mi·nute** \mī-'nüt, mə-, -'nyüt\ *adjective* **mi·nut·er; -est** [Latin *minutus*] (circa 1626)
**1** : very small : INFINITESIMAL
**2** : of small importance : TRIFLING
**3** : marked by close attention to details
**synonym** see SMALL, CIRCUMSTANTIAL
— **mi·nute·ness** *noun*
**minute hand** *noun* (1726)
: the long hand that marks the minutes on the face of a watch or clock
**¹mi·nute·ly** \mī-'nüt-lē, mə-, -'nyüt-\ *adverb* (1599)
**1** : into very small pieces
**2** : in a minute manner or degree
**²min·ute·ly** \'mi-nət-lē\ *adjective* (1605)
*archaic* : minute by minute
**min·ute·man** \'mi-nət-ˌman\ *noun* (1774)
: a member of a group of armed men pledged to take the field at a minute's notice during and immediately before the American Revolution
**min·ute steak** \'mi-nət-\ *noun* (1921)
: a small thin steak that can be quickly cooked

\ə\ abut \ᵊ\ kitten \ər\ further \a\ ash \ā\ ace
\ä\ mop, mar \au̇\ out \ch\ chin \e\ bet \ē\ easy
\g\ go \i\ hit \ī\ ice \j\ job \ŋ\ sing \ō\ go
\ȯ\ law \ȯi\ boy \th\ thin \t̲h̲\ the \ü\ loot \u̇\ foot
\y\ yet \zh\ vision      *see also* Guide to Pronunciation

**mi·nu·tia** \mə-'nü-sh(ē-)ə, mī-, -'nyü-\ *noun, plural* **-ti·ae** \-shē-ˌē, -ˌī\ [Latin *minutiae* trifles, details, from plural of *minutia* smallness, from *minutus*] (1751)
: a minute or minor detail — usually used in plural

**minx** \'miŋ(k)s\ *noun* [origin unknown] (1592)
**1 :** a pert girl
**2** *obsolete* **:** a wanton woman

**min·yan** \'min-yən\ *noun, plural* **-ya·nim** \ˌmin-yə-'nēm\ *or* **-yans** [Hebrew *minyān,* literally, number, count] (1753)
: the quorum of 10 adult Jews required for communal worship

**Mio·cene** \'mī-ə-ˌsēn\ *adjective* [*mio-* (from Greek *meiōn* less) + *-cene* — more at MEIOSIS] (1831)
: of, relating to, or being an epoch of the Tertiary between the Pliocene and the Oligocene or the corresponding system of rocks — see GEOLOGIC TIME table
**— Miocene** *noun*

**mi·o·sis** \mī-'ō-səs, mē-\ *noun, plural* **mi·o·ses** \-ˌsēz\ [New Latin, from Greek *myein* to be closed (of the eyes) + New Latin *-osis*] (1819)
: excessive smallness or contraction of the pupil of the eye

**¹mi·ot·ic** \-'ä-tik\ *noun* (1864)
: an agent that causes miosis

**²miotic** *adjective* (1864)
: relating to or characterized by miosis

**mi·que·let** \ˌmi-kə-'let, ˌmē-\ *noun* [Spanish *miquelete*] (1827)
: a Spanish or French irregular soldier during the Peninsular War

**mir** \'mir\ *noun* [Russian] (1877)
: a village community in czarist Russia in which land was owned jointly but cultivated by individual families

**mi·ra·bi·le dic·tu** \mə-ˌrä-bə-lē-'dik-(ˌ)tü\ [Latin] (1831)
: wonderful to relate

**mi·ra·cid·i·um** \ˌmir-ə-'si-dē-əm, ˌmī-rə-\ *noun, plural* **-cid·ia** \-dē-ə\ [New Latin, from Greek *meirak-, meirax* youth, stripling + New Latin *-idium*] (1898)
: the free-swimming ciliated first larva of a digenetic trematode that seeks out and penetrates a suitable snail intermediate host in which it develops into a sporocyst
**— mi·ra·cid·i·al** \-dē-əl\ *adjective*

**mir·a·cle** \'mir-i-kəl\ *noun* [Middle English, from Old French, from Late Latin *miraculum,* from Latin, a wonder, marvel, from *mirari* to wonder at] (12th century)
**1 :** an extraordinary event manifesting divine intervention in human affairs
**2 :** an extremely outstanding or unusual event, thing, or accomplishment
**3** *Christian Science* **:** a divinely natural phenomenon experienced humanly as the fulfillment of spiritual law

**miracle drug** *noun* (1950)
: a drug usually newly discovered that elicits a dramatic response in a patient's condition — called also *wonder drug*

**miracle fruit** *noun* (1964)
: a tropical African shrub (*Synsepalum dulcificum*) of the sapodilla family whose fruit contains a glycoprotein that when applied to the tongue causes sour substances to taste sweet; *also* **:** its fruit

**miracle play** *noun* (circa 1852)
**1 :** a medieval drama based on episodes from the life of a saint or martyr
**2 :** MYSTERY PLAY

**mi·rac·u·lous** \mə-'ra-kyə-ləs\ *adjective* [Middle English, from Middle French *miraculeux,* from Medieval Latin *miraculosus,* from Latin *miraculum*] (15th century)
**1 :** of the nature of a miracle **:** SUPERNATURAL ⟨a *miraculous* event⟩
**2 :** suggesting a miracle **:** MARVELOUS ⟨gave proof of a *miraculous* memory —*Time*⟩

**3 :** working or able to work miracles ⟨*miraculous* power⟩
**— mi·rac·u·lous·ly** *adverb*
**— mi·rac·u·lous·ness** *noun*

**mir·a·dor** \'mir-ə-ˌdȯr, ˌmir-ə-'\ *noun* [Spanish, from Catalan, from *mirar* to look at, from Latin *mirari*] (1797)
: a turret, window, or balcony designed to command an extensive outlook

**mi·rage** \mə-'räzh\ *noun* [French, from *mirer* to look at, from Latin *mirari*] (1803)
**1 :** an optical effect that is sometimes seen at sea, in the desert, or over a hot pavement, that may have the appearance of a pool of water or a mirror in which distant objects are seen inverted, and that is caused by the bending or reflection of rays of light by a layer of heated air of varying density
**2 :** something illusory and unattainable like a mirage

**Mi·ran·da** \mə-'ran-də\ *adjective* [from *Miranda v. Arizona,* the U.S. Supreme Court ruling establishing such rights] (1972)
: of, relating to, or being the legal rights of an arrested person to have an attorney and to remain silent so as to avoid self-incrimination ⟨*Miranda* warnings⟩

**¹mire** \'mīr\ *noun* [Middle English, from Old Norse *mȳrr;* akin to Old English *mōs* marsh — more at MOSS] (14th century)
**1 :** wet spongy earth (as of a bog or marsh)
**2 :** heavy often deep mud or slush
**3 :** a troublesome or intractable situation ⟨found themselves in a *mire* of debt⟩
**— miry** \'mīr-ē\ *adjective*

**²mire** *verb* **mired; mir·ing** (15th century)
*transitive verb*
**1 a :** to cause to stick fast in or as if in mire **b :** to hamper or hold back as if by mire **:** ENTANGLE
**2 :** to cover or soil with mire
*intransitive verb*
: to stick or sink in mire

**mi·rex** \'mī-ˌreks\ *noun* [origin unknown] (1962)
: an organochlorine insecticide $C_{10}Cl_{12}$ used especially against ants

**mirk, mirky** *variant of* MURK, MURKY

**mir·li·ton** \ˌmir-lə-'tōⁿ\ *noun* [French] (circa 1909)
: CHAYOTE

**¹mir·ror** \'mir-ər\ *noun* [Middle English *mirour,* from Old French, from *mirer* to look at, from Latin *mirari* to wonder at] (13th century)
**1 :** a polished or smooth surface (as of glass) that forms images by reflection
**2 a :** something that gives a true representation **b :** an exemplary model
**— mir·rored** \-ərd\ *adjective*
**— mir·ror·like** \-ˌlīk\ *adjective*

**²mirror** *transitive verb* (1593)
: to reflect in or as if in a mirror

**mirror image** *noun* (1885)
: something that has its parts reversely arranged in comparison with another similar thing or that is reversed with reference to an intervening axis or plane

**mirth** \'mərth\ *noun* [Middle English, from Old English *myrgth,* from *myrge* merry — more at MERRY] (before 12th century)
: gladness or gaiety as shown by or accompanied with laughter
**— mirth·ful** \-fəl\ *adjective*
**— mirth·ful·ly** \-fə-lē\ *adverb*
**— mirth·ful·ness** *noun*
**— mirth·less** \-ləs\ *adjective*
**— mirth·less·ly** \-lē\ *adverb*

**¹MIRV** \'mərv\ *noun* [multiple independently targeted reentry vehicle] (1967)
: a missile with two or more warheads designed to strike separate enemy targets; *also* **:** any of the warheads of such a missile

**²MIRV** *verb* **MIRVed; MIRV·ing** (1969)
*transitive verb*
: to equip with MIRV warheads

*intransitive verb*
: to arm one's forces with MIRVs

**mis-** *prefix* [partly from Middle English, from Old English; partly from Middle English *mes-, mis-,* from Old French *mes-,* of Germanic origin; akin to Old English *mis-;* akin to Old English *missan* to miss]
**1 a :** badly **:** wrongly ⟨*mis*judge⟩ **b :** unfavorably ⟨*mis*esteem⟩ **c :** in a suspicious manner ⟨*mis*doubt⟩
**2 :** bad **:** wrong ⟨*mis*deed⟩
**3 :** opposite or lack of ⟨*mis*trust⟩
**4 :** not ⟨*mis*know⟩

| | |
|---|---|
| mis·act | mis·em·ploy |
| mis·ad·dress | mis·em·ploy·ment |
| mis·ad·just | mis·es·ti·mate |
| mis·ad·min·is·tra- | mis·es·ti·ma·tion |
| tion | mis·eval·u·ate |
| mis·ad·vise | mis·eval·u·a·tion |
| mis·aim | mis·field |
| mis·align | mis·file |
| mis·align·ment | mis·fo·cus |
| mis·al·lo·cate | mis·func·tion |
| mis·al·lo·ca·tion | mis·gauge |
| mis·anal·y·sis | mis·gov·ern |
| mis·ap·pli·ca·tion | mis·gov·ern·ment |
| mis·ap·ply | mis·grade |
| mis·ap·prais·al | mis·iden·ti·fi·ca·tion |
| mis·ar·tic·u·late | mis·iden·ti·fy |
| mis·as·sem·ble | mis·in·form |
| mis·as·sump·tion | mis·in·for·ma·tion |
| mis·at·trib·ute | mis·kick |
| mis·at·tri·bu·tion | mis·la·bel |
| mis·bal·ance | mis·learn |
| mis·be·have | mis·lo·cate |
| mis·be·hav·er | mis·lo·ca·tion |
| mis·bound | mis·man·age |
| mis·but·ton | mis·man·age·ment |
| mis·cal·cu·late | mis·mark |
| mis·cal·cu·la·tion | mis·mar·riage |
| mis·cap·tion | mis·match |
| mis·cat·a·log | mis·mate |
| mis·chan·nel | mis·or·der |
| mis·char·ac·ter·i·za- | mis·ori·ent |
| tion | mis·ori·en·ta·tion |
| mis·char·ac·ter·ize | mis·pack·age |
| mis·charge | mis·per·ceive |
| mis·choice | mis·per·cep·tion |
| mis·ci·ta·tion | mis·plan |
| mis·clas·si·fi·ca·tion | mis·po·si·tion |
| mis·clas·si·fy | mis·print |
| mis·code | mis·pro·gram |
| mis·com·pre·hen- | mis·quo·ta·tion |
| sion | mis·quote |
| mis·com·pu·ta·tion | mis·rec·ol·lec·tion |
| mis·com·pute | mis·re·cord |
| mis·con·ceive | mis·ref·er·ence |
| mis·con·ceiv·er | mis·reg·is·ter |
| mis·con·cep·tion | mis·reg·is·tra·tion |
| mis·con·nect | mis·re·late |
| mis·con·nec·tion | mis·re·mem·ber |
| mis·con·struc·tion | mis·ren·der |
| mis·con·strue | mis·re·port |
| mis·copy | mis·route |
| mis·cor·re·la·tion | mis·set |
| mis·cre·ate | mis·shape |
| mis·cre·a·tion | mis·shap·en |
| mis·cut | mis·shap·en·ly |
| mis·date | mis·sort |
| mis·deem | mis·strike |
| mis·de·fine | mis·throw |
| mis·de·scribe | mis·time |
| mis·de·scrip·tion | mis·ti·tle |
| mis·de·vel·op | mis·train |
| mis·di·ag·nose | mis·tran·scribe |
| mis·di·ag·no·sis | mis·tran·scrip·tion |
| mis·dial | mis·trans·late |
| mis·dis·tri·bu·tion | mis·trans·la·tion |
| mis·di·vi·sion | mis·truth |
| mis·draw | mis·tune |
| mis·ed·u·cate | mis·type |
| mis·ed·u·ca·tion | mis·uti·li·za·tion |
| mis·em·pha·sis | mis·vo·cal·i·za·tion |
| mis·em·pha·size | mis·write |

**mis·ad·ven·ture** \,mi-səd-'ven-chər\ *noun* [Middle English *mesaventure*, from Old French, from *mesavenir* to chance badly, from *mes-* mis- + *avenir* to chance, happen, from Latin *advenire* — more at ADVENTURE] (14th century)
: MISFORTUNE, MISHAP

**mis·al·li·ance** \,mi-sə-'lī-ən(t)s\ *noun* [modification of French *mésalliance*] (1738)
**1** : an improper alliance
**2 a** : MÉSALLIANCE **b** : a marriage between persons unsuited to each other

**mis·an·thrope** \'mi-sⁿn-,thrōp\ *noun* [Greek *misanthrōpos* hating mankind, from *misein* to hate + *anthrōpos* human being] (1683)
: a person who hates or distrusts mankind

**mis·an·throp·ic** \,mi-sⁿn-'thrä-pik\ *adjective* (1762)
**1** : of, relating to, or characteristic of a misanthrope
**2** : marked by a hatred or contempt for mankind
**synonym** see CYNICAL
— **mis·an·throp·i·cal·ly** \-pi-k(ə-)lē\ *adverb*

**mis·an·thro·py** \mi-'san(t)-thrə-pē\ *noun* (circa 1656)
: a hatred or distrust of mankind

**mis·ap·pre·hend** \(,)mis-,a-pri-'hend\ *transitive verb* (circa 1629)
: to apprehend wrongly : MISUNDERSTAND
— **mis·ap·pre·hen·sion** \-'hen(t)-shən\ *noun*

**mis·ap·pro·pri·ate** \,mi-sə-'prō-prē-,āt\ *transitive verb* (1857)
: to appropriate wrongly (as by theft or embezzlement)
— **mis·ap·pro·pri·a·tion** \-,prō-prē-'ā-shən\ *noun*

**mis·be·come** \,mis-bi-'kəm\ *transitive verb* **-came** \-'kām\; **-come; -com·ing** (1530)
: to be inappropriate or unbecoming to

**mis·be·got·ten** \-bi-'gä-tⁿn\ *adjective* (1554)
**1** : unlawfully conceived : ILLEGITIMATE ⟨a *misbegotten* child⟩
**2 a** : having a disreputable or improper origin : ill-conceived ⟨antiquated and *misbegotten* tax laws —R. M. Blough⟩ **b** : CONTEMPTIBLE, DEFORMED ⟨a *misbegotten* scoundrel⟩

**mis·be·lief** \,mis-bə-'lēf\ *noun* (13th century)
: erroneous or false belief

**mis·be·lieve** \-'lēv\ *intransitive verb* (14th century)
*obsolete* : to hold a false or unorthodox belief

**mis·be·liev·er** \-'lē-vər\ *noun* (15th century)
: HERETIC, INFIDEL

**mis·brand** \,mis-'brand\ *transitive verb* (circa 1930)
: to brand falsely or in a misleading way; *specifically* : to label in violation of statutory requirements

**mis·call** \,mis-'kȯl\ *transitive verb* (14th century)
: to call by a wrong name : MISNAME

**mis·car·riage** \,mis-'kar-ij, 'mis-,\ *noun* (circa 1652)
**1** : corrupt or incompetent management; *especially* : a failure in the administration of justice
**2** : spontaneous expulsion of a human fetus before it is viable and especially between the 12th and 28th weeks of gestation

**mis·car·ry** \,mis-'kar-ē, 'mis-,kar-ē\ *intransitive verb* (14th century)
**1** *obsolete* : to come to harm
**2** : to suffer miscarriage of a fetus
**3** : to fail to achieve the intended purpose : go wrong or amiss ⟨the plan *miscarried*⟩

**mis·cast** \,mis-'kast\ *transitive verb* **-cast; -cast·ing** (1925)
: to cast in an unsuitable role ⟨life had *miscast* her in the role of wife and mother —Edna Ferber⟩

**mis·ce·ge·na·tion** \(,)mi-,se-jə-'nā-shən, ,mi-si-jə-'nā-\ *noun* [irregular from Latin *miscēre* to mix + *genus* race — more at MIX, KIN] (1864)
: a mixture of races; *especially* : marriage or cohabitation between a white person and a member of another race
— **mis·ce·ge·na·tion·al** \-shnəl, -shə-nᵊl\ *adjective*

**mis·cel·la·nea** \,mi-sə-'lā-nē-ə, -nyə\ *noun plural* [Latin, from neuter plural of *miscellaneus*] (1571)
: a collection of miscellaneous objects or writings

**mis·cel·la·neous** \,mi-sə-'lā-nē-əs, -nyəs\ *adjective* [Latin *miscellaneus*, from *miscellus* mixed] (1637)
**1** : consisting of diverse things or members : HETEROGENEOUS
**2 a** : having various traits **b** : dealing with or interested in diverse subjects ⟨as a writer I was too *miscellaneous* —George Santayana⟩
— **mis·cel·la·neous·ly** *adverb*
— **mis·cel·la·neous·ness** *noun*

**mis·cel·la·nist** \'mi-sə-,lā-nist, *chiefly British* mi-'se-lə-nist\ *noun* (1810)
: a writer of miscellanies

**mis·cel·la·ny** \-nē\ *noun, plural* **-nies** [probably modification of French *miscellanées*, plural, from Latin *miscellanea*] (1615)
**1 a** *plural* : separate writings collected in one volume **b** : a collection of writings on various subjects
**2** : a mixture of various things

**mis·chance** \,mis-'chan(t)s\ *noun* [Middle English *mischaunce*, from Old French *meschance*, from *mes-* mis- + *chance* chance] (14th century)
**1** : bad luck
**2** : a piece of bad luck : MISHAP
**synonym** see MISFORTUNE

**mis·chief** \'mis-chəf, 'mish-\ *noun* [Middle English *meschief*, from Old French, calamity, from *mes-* + *chief* head, end — more at CHIEF] (14th century)
**1** : a specific injury or damage attributed to a particular agent
**2** : a cause or source of harm, evil, or irritation; *especially* : a person who causes mischief
**3 a** : action that annoys or irritates **b** : the quality or state of being mischievous : MISCHIEVOUSNESS ⟨had *mischief* in his eyes⟩

**mis·chie·vous** \'mis-chə-vəs, 'mish-; ÷mis-'chē-vē-əs, mish-\ *adjective* (14th century)
**1** : HARMFUL, INJURIOUS ⟨*mischievous* gossip⟩
**2 a** : able or tending to cause annoyance, trouble, or minor injury **b** : irresponsibly playful ⟨*mischievous* behavior⟩ □
— **mis·chie·vous·ly** *adverb*
— **mis·chie·vous·ness** *noun*

**misch metal** \'mish-\ *noun* [German *Mischmetall*, from *mischen* to mix + *Metall* metal] (1916)
: a complex alloy of rare earth metals used especially in tracer bullets and as a flint in lighters

**mis·ci·ble** \'mi-sə-bəl\ *adjective* [Medieval Latin *miscibilis*, from Latin *miscēre* to mix — more at MIX] (1570)
: capable of being mixed; *specifically* : capable of mixing in any ratio without separation of two phases ⟨*miscible* liquids⟩
— **mis·ci·bil·i·ty** \,mi-sə-'bi-lə-tē\ *noun*

**mis·com·mu·ni·ca·tion** \,mis-kə-,myü-nə-'kā-shən\ *noun* (1964)
: failure to communicate clearly

**mis·con·duct** \-'kän-(,)dəkt\ *noun* (1710)
**1** : mismanagement especially of governmental or military responsibilities
**2** : intentional wrongdoing; *specifically* : deliberate violation of a law or standard especially by a government official : MALFEASANCE
**3 a** : improper behavior **b** : ADULTERY
— **mis·con·duct** \-kən-'dəkt\ *transitive verb*

**mis·count** \-'kaunt\ *verb* [Middle English *misconten*, from Middle French *mesconter*, from *mes-* + *conter* to count] (14th century)
*intransitive verb*
: to make a wrong count
*transitive verb*
: to count wrongly : MISCALCULATE
— **miscount** \-'kaunt, 'mis-,\ *noun*

**¹mis·cre·ant** \'mis-krē-ənt\ *adjective* [Middle English *miscreaunt*, from Middle French *mescreant*, present participle of *mescroire* to disbelieve, from *mes-* + *croire* to believe, from Latin *credere* — more at CREED] (14th century)
**1** : UNBELIEVING, HERETICAL
**2** : DEPRAVED, VILLAINOUS

**²miscreant** *noun* (14th century)
**1** : INFIDEL, HERETIC
**2** : one who behaves criminally or viciously

**¹mis·cue** \,mis-'kyü, 'mis-,kyü\ *noun* (1873)
**1** : a faulty stroke in billiards in which the cue slips
**2** : MISTAKE, SLIP

**²miscue** *intransitive verb* (1894)
: to make a miscue

**mis·deal** \,mis-'dē(ə)l\ *verb* **-dealt** \-'delt\; **-deal·ing** (1850)
*intransitive verb*
: to deal cards incorrectly
*transitive verb*
: to deal incorrectly
— **misdeal** *noun*

**mis·deed** \-'dēd\ *noun* (before 12th century)
: a wrong deed : OFFENSE

**mis·de·mean·ant** \-di-'mē-nənt\ *noun* (1819)
: a person convicted of a misdemeanor

**mis·de·mean·or** \-di-'mē-nər\ *noun* (15th century)
**1** : a crime less serious than a felony
**2** : MISDEED

**mis·di·rect** \-də-'rekt, -(,)dī-\ *transitive verb* (1603)
**1** : to give a wrong direction to
**2** : to direct wrongly ⟨*misdirected* their energies⟩

**mis·di·rec·tion** \-'rek-shən\ *noun* (1768)
**1 a** : the act or an instance of misdirecting **b** : the state of being misdirected
**2** : a wrong direction

**mis·do** \,mis-'dü\ *verb* **-did** \-'did\; **-done** \-'dən\; **-do·ing** \-'dü-iŋ\; **-does** \-'dəz\ (before 12th century)
*intransitive verb*
*obsolete* : to act wrongly : transgress the laws of God ⟨the erring soul not wilfully *misdoing* —John Milton⟩
*transitive verb*
: to do (something) incorrectly or poorly
— **mis·do·er** \-'dü-ər\ *noun*

**misdoing** *noun* (15th century)
: the act or an instance of misbehaving : MISCONDUCT

**mis·doubt** \,mis-'daut\ *transitive verb* (circa 1540)
**1** : DOUBT
**2** : SUSPECT, FEAR
— **misdoubt** *noun*

\ə\ abut \ᵊ\ kitten \ər\ further \a\ ash \ā\ ace
\ä\ mop, mar \au̇\ out \ch\ chin \e\ bet \ē\ easy
\g\ go \i\ hit \ī\ ice \j\ job \ŋ\ sing \ō\ go
\ȯ\ law \ȯi\ boy \th\ thin \t̷h\ the \ü\ loot \u̇\ foot
\y\ yet \zh\ vision *see also* Guide to Pronunciation

**mise–en–scène** \,mē-zäⁿ-'sen, -'sän\ *noun,* *plural* **mise–en–scènes** \-'sen(z), -'sän(z)\ [French *mise en scène*] (1833)
**1 a** : the arrangement of actors and scenery on a stage for a theatrical production **b** : stage setting
**2 a** : the physical setting of an action : CONTEXT **b** : ENVIRONMENT, MILIEU
*synonym* see BACKGROUND

**mi·ser** \'mī-zər\ *noun* [Latin *miser* miserable] (circa 1560)
: a mean grasping person; *especially* : one who is extremely stingy with money

**mis·er·a·ble** \'mi-zər-bəl, 'miz-rə-, 'mi-zə-rə-\ *adjective* [Middle English, from Middle French, from Latin *miserabilis* wretched, pitiable, from *miserari* to pity, from *miser*] (15th century)
**1** : being in a pitiable state of distress or unhappiness (as from want or shame) ⟨*miserable* refugees⟩
**2 a** : wretchedly inadequate or meager ⟨a *miserable* hovel⟩ **b** : causing extreme discomfort or unhappiness ⟨a *miserable* situation⟩
**3** : being likely to discredit or shame ⟨his *miserable* neglect of his wife⟩ ⟨it was *miserable* of you to make fun of him⟩
— **miserable** *noun*
— **mis·er·a·ble·ness** *noun*
— **mis·er·a·bly** \-blē\ *adverb*

**mi·se·re·re** \,mi-zə-'rir-ē, -'rer-; ,mē-zə-'rā-(,)rā\ *noun* [Middle English, from Latin, be merciful, from *misereri* to be merciful, from *miser* wretched; from the first word of the Psalm] (13th century)
**1** *capitalized* : the 50th Psalm in the Vulgate
**2** : MISERICORD
**3** : a vocal complaint or lament

**mi·ser·i·cord** *also* **mi·ser·i·corde** \mə-'zer-ə-,kȯrd, -'ser-\ *noun* [Medieval Latin *misericordia* seat in church, from Latin, mercy, from *misericord-, misericors* merciful, from *misereri* + *cord-, cor* heart — more at HEART] (circa 1515)
: a small projection on the bottom of a hinged church seat that gives support to a standing worshiper when the seat is turned up

**mi·ser·ly** \'mī-zər-lē\ *adjective* (1593)
: of, relating to, or characteristic of a miser; *especially* : marked by grasping meanness and penuriousness
*synonym* see STINGY
— **mi·ser·li·ness** *noun*

**mis·ery** \'mi-zə-rē, 'miz-rē\ *noun,* *plural* **-er·ies** (14th century)
**1** : a state of suffering and want that is the result of poverty or affliction
**2** : a circumstance, thing, or place that causes suffering or discomfort
**3** : a state of great unhappiness and emotional distress
*synonym* see DISTRESS

**mis·es·teem** \,mi-sə-'stēm\ *transitive verb* (1611)
: to esteem wrongly; *especially* : to hold in too little regard

**mis·fea·sance** \mis-'fē-z°n(t)s\ *noun* [Middle French *mesfaisance,* from *mesfaire* to do wrong, from *mes-* mis- + *faire* to make, do, from Latin *facere* — more at DO] (1596)
: TRESPASS; *specifically* : the performance of a lawful action in an illegal or improper manner
— **mis·fea·sor** \-'fē-zər, -,zȯr\ *noun*

¹**mis·fire** \,mis-'fīr\ *intransitive verb* (1752)
**1** : to have the explosive or propulsive charge fail to ignite at the proper time ⟨the engine *misfired*⟩
**2** : to fail to fire ⟨the gun *misfired*⟩
**3** : to miss an intended effect or objective

²**mis·fire** \,mis-'fīr, 'mis-,\ *noun* (1839)
**1** : a failure (as of a cartridge or firearm) to fire
**2** : something that misfires

**mis·fit** \'mis-,fit *also* ,mis-'fit\ *noun* (circa 1823)
**1** : something that fits badly

**2** : one who is poorly adapted to a situation or environment ⟨social *misfits*⟩

**mis·for·tune** \,mis-'fȯr-chən\ *noun* (15th century)
**1 a** : an event or conjunction of events that causes an unfortunate or distressing result : bad luck ⟨by *misfortune* he fell into bad company⟩ ⟨had the *misfortune* to break his leg⟩ **b** : an unhappy situation ⟨always ready to help people in *misfortune*⟩
**2** : a distressing or unfortunate incident or event ⟨*misfortunes* never come singly⟩ ☆

**mis·give** \,mis-'giv\ *verb* **-gave** \-'gāv\; **-giv·en** \-'gi-vən\; **-giv·ing** (1513)
*transitive verb*
: to suggest doubt or fear to
*intransitive verb*
: to be fearful or apprehensive

**mis·giv·ing** \-'gi-viŋ\ *noun* (1601)
: a feeling of doubt or suspicion especially concerning a future event

**mis·guid·ance** \,mis-'gī-d°n(t)s\ *noun* (1640)
: MISDIRECTION

**mis·guide** \-'gīd\ *transitive verb* (14th century)
: to lead astray : MISDIRECT ⟨prejudice *misguides* our minds⟩
— **mis·guid·er** *noun*

**mis·guid·ed** \(,)mis-'gī-dəd\ *adjective* (1659)
: led or prompted by wrong or inappropriate motives or ideals ⟨well-meaning but *misguided* do-gooders⟩
— **mis·guid·ed·ly** \-lē\ *adverb*
— **mis·guid·ed·ness** \-nəs\ *noun*

**mis·han·dle** \-'han-d°l\ *transitive verb* (1530)
**1** : to treat roughly : MALTREAT
**2** : to deal with or manage wrongly or ignorantly

**mis·han·ter** \mi-'shän-tər\ *noun* [Middle English *misaunter,* alteration of *mesaventure*] (1742)
*chiefly Scottish* : MISADVENTURE

**mis·hap** \'mis-,hap, mis-'\ *noun* (14th century)
**1** : an unfortunate accident
**2** : bad luck : MISFORTUNE
*synonym* see MISFORTUNE

**mis·hear** \,mis-'hir\ *verb* **-heard** \-'hərd\; **-hear·ing** \-'hir-iŋ\ (before 12th century)
*transitive verb*
: to hear wrongly
*intransitive verb*
: to misunderstand what is heard

**mis·hit** \,mis-'hit\ *transitive verb* **-hit; -hit·ting** (1904)
: to hit in a faulty manner
— **mis·hit** \,mis-'hit, 'mis-,\ *noun*

**mish·mash** \'mish-,mash, -,mäsh\ *noun* [Middle English & Yiddish; Middle English *mysse masche,* perhaps reduplication of *mash* mash; Yiddish *mish-mash,* perhaps reduplication of *mishn* to mix] (15th century)
: HODGEPODGE, JUMBLE

**Mish·nah** *or* **Mish·na** \'mish-nə\ *noun* [Hebrew *mishnāh* instruction, oral law] (1610)
: the collection of mostly halakic Jewish traditions compiled about A.D. 200 and made the basic part of the Talmud
— **Mish·na·ic** \mish-'nā-ik\ *adjective*

**mis·im·pres·sion** \,mi-sim-'pre-shən\ *noun* (1670)
: a mistaken impression

**mis·in·ter·pret** \,mi-s°n-'tər-prət, -pət\ *transitive verb* (1547)
**1** : to explain wrongly
**2** : to understand wrongly
— **mis·in·ter·pre·ta·tion** \-,tər-prə-'tā-shən, -pə-\ *noun*

**mis·join·der** \,mis-'jȯin-dər\ *noun* (circa 1847)
: an improper union of parties or of causes of action in a single legal proceeding

**mis·judge** \,mis-'jəj\ (15th century)
*intransitive verb*
: to be mistaken in judgment
*transitive verb*
**1** : to estimate wrongly

**2** : to have an unjust opinion of
— **mis·judg·ment** \-'jəj-mənt\ *noun*

**Mi·ski·to** \mis-'kē-(,)tō\ *noun,* *plural* **Miskito** *or* **Miskitos** (1789)
**1** : a member of an American Indian people of the Atlantic coast of Nicaragua and Honduras
**2** : the language of the Miskito people

**mis·know** \,mis-'nō\ *transitive verb* **-knew** \-'nü, -'nyü\; **-known** \-'nōn\; **-know·ing** (1535)
: MISUNDERSTAND
— **mis·knowl·edge** \-'nä-lij\ *noun*

**mis·lay** \,mis-'lā\ *transitive verb* **-laid** \-'lād\; **-lay·ing** (1614)
: to put in an unremembered place : LOSE

**mis·lead** \,mis-'lēd\ *verb* **-led** \-'led\; **-lead·ing** (before 12th century)
*transitive verb*
: to lead in a wrong direction or into a mistaken action or belief often by deliberate deceit
*intransitive verb*
: to lead astray
*synonym* see DECEIVE
— **mis·lead·er** *noun*
— **mis·lead·ing·ly** \-'lē-diŋ-lē\ *adverb*

**mis·leared** \-'lird, -'lerd\ *adjective* [¹*mis-* + *lear* to learn] (1560)
*chiefly Scottish* : UNMANNERLY, ILL-BRED

**mis·like** \-'līk\ *transitive verb* (before 12th century)
**1** *archaic* : DISPLEASE
**2** : DISLIKE
— **mislike** *noun*

**mis·name** \-'nām\ *transitive verb* (1537)
: to name incorrectly : MISCALL

**mis·no·mer** \,mis-'nō-mər\ *noun* [Middle English *misnoumer,* from Middle French *mesnommer* to misname, from *mes-* mis- + *nommer* to name, from Latin *nominare* — more at NOMINATE] (15th century)
**1** : the misnaming of a person in a legal instrument
**2 a** : a use of a wrong name **b** : a wrong name or designation
— **mis·no·mered** \-mərd\ *adjective*

**mi·so** \'mē-(,)sō\ *noun* [Japanese] (1727)
: a high-protein food paste consisting chiefly of soybeans, salt, and usually fermented grain (as barley or rice) and ranging in taste from very salty to very sweet

**mi·sog·a·my** \mi-'sä-gə-mē, mī-\ *noun* [Greek *misein* to hate + English *-gamy*] (circa 1656)
: a hatred of marriage
— **mi·sog·a·mist** \-mist\ *noun*

**mi·sog·y·ny** \mə-'sä-jə-nē\ *noun* [Greek *misogynia,* from *misein* to hate + *gynē* woman — more at QUEEN] (circa 1656)
: a hatred of women
— **mi·sog·y·nic** \,mi-sə-'ji-nik, -'gī-\ *adjective*
— **mi·sog·y·nist** \mə-'sä-jə-nist\ *noun or adjective*
— **mi·sog·y·nis·tic** \mə-,sä-jə-'nis-tik\ *adjective*

**mi·sol·o·gy** \mə-'sä-lə-jē\ *noun* [Greek *misologia,* from *misein* + *-logia* -logy] (1833)

: a hatred of argument, reasoning, or enlightenment

**mis·o·ne·ism** \,mi-sə-'nē-,i-zəm\ *noun* [Italian *misoneismo*, from Greek *misein* + *neos* new + Italian *-ismo* -ism — more at NEW] (1886)
: a hatred, fear, or intolerance of innovation or change

**mis·place** \,mis-'plās\ *transitive verb* (1594)
**1 a** : to put in a wrong or inappropriate place ⟨*misplace* a comma⟩ **b** : MISLAY ⟨*misplaced* the keys⟩
**2** : to set on a wrong object or eventuality ⟨his trust had been *misplaced*⟩
— **mis·place·ment** \-'plās-mənt\ *noun*

**mis·play** \,mis-'plā\ *noun* (1867)
: a wrong or unskillful play : ERROR
— **mis·play** \,mis-'plā, 'mis-,\ *transitive verb*

¹**mis·pri·sion** \(,)mis-'pri-zhən\ *noun* [Middle English, from Middle French *mesprison* error, wrongdoing, from Old French, from *mesprendre* to make a mistake, from *mes-* mis- + *prendre* to take, from Latin *prehendere* to seize — more at GET] (15th century)
**1 a** : neglect or wrong performance of official duty **b** : concealment of treason or felony by one who is not a participant in the treason or felony **c** : seditious conduct against the government or the courts
**2** : MISUNDERSTANDING, MISINTERPRETATION

²**misprision** *noun* [*misprize*] (1586)
: CONTEMPT, SCORN

**mis·prize** \,mis-'prīz\ *transitive verb* [Middle French *mesprisier*, from *mes-* mis- + *prisier* to appraise — more at PRIZE] (14th century)
**1** : to hold in contempt : DESPISE
**2** : UNDERVALUE

**mis·pro·nounce** \,mis-prə-'naün(t)s\ *transitive verb* (1593)
: to pronounce incorrectly or in a way regarded as incorrect

**mis·pro·nun·ci·a·tion** \-,nən(t)-sē-'ā-shən *also* -,naün(t)-\ *noun* (1530)
: the act or an instance of mispronouncing

**mis·read** \,mis-'rēd\ *transitive verb* **-read** \-'red\; **-read·ing** \-'rē-diŋ\ (1809)
**1** : to read incorrectly
**2** : to misinterpret in or as if in reading ⟨totally *misread* the lesson of history —Christopher Hollis⟩

**mis·reck·on** \-'re-kən\ *verb* (circa 1525)
: MISCOUNT, MISCALCULATE

**mis·rep·re·sent** \(,)mis-,re-pri-'zent\ *transitive verb* (1647)
**1** : to give a false or misleading representation of usually with an intent to deceive or be unfair ⟨*misrepresented* the facts⟩
**2** : to serve badly or improperly as a representative of
— **mis·rep·re·sen·ta·tion** \(,)mis-,re-pri-,zen-'tā-shən, -zən-\ *noun*
— **mis·rep·re·sen·ta·tive** \-'zen-tə-tiv\ *adjective*

¹**mis·rule** \,mis-'rül\ *transitive verb* (14th century)
: to rule incompetently : MISGOVERN

²**misrule** *noun* (14th century)
**1** : the action of misruling : the condition of being misruled
**2** : DISORDER, ANARCHY

¹**miss** \'mis\ *verb* [Middle English, from Old English *missan*; akin to Old High German *missan* to miss] (before 12th century)
*transitive verb*
**1** : to fail to hit, reach, or contact
**2** : to discover or feel the absence of
**3** : to fail to obtain
**4** : ESCAPE, AVOID ⟨just *missed* hitting the other car⟩
**5** : to leave out : OMIT
**6** : to fail to comprehend, sense, or experience ⟨*missed* the point of the speech⟩
**7** : to fail to perform or attend ⟨had to *miss* school for a week⟩
*intransitive verb*

**1** *archaic* : to fail to get, reach, or do something
**2** : to fail to hit something
**3 a** : to be unsuccessful **b** : MISFIRE ⟨the engine *missed*⟩
— **miss·able** \'mi-sə-bəl\ *adjective*
— **miss a beat** : to deviate from regular smooth performance ⟨the company changed ownership without *missing a beat*⟩
— **miss out on** : to lose a good opportunity for ⟨*missed out on* a better job⟩
— **miss the boat** : to fail to take advantage of an opportunity

²**miss** *noun* (12th century)
**1** *chiefly dialect* : disadvantage or regret resulting from loss ⟨we know the *miss* of you, and even hunger . . . to see you —Samuel Richardson⟩
**2 a** : a failure to hit **b** : a failure to attain a desired result
**3** : MISFIRE

³**miss** *noun* [short for *mistress*] (circa 1667)
**1** *capitalized* **a** — used as a title prefixed to the name of an unmarried woman or girl **b** — used before the name of a place or of a line of activity or before some epithet to form a title for a usually young unmarried female who is representative of the thing indicated ⟨*Miss* America⟩
**2** : young lady — used without a name as a conventional term of address to a young woman
**3** : a young unmarried woman or girl

**mis·sa can·ta·ta** \,mi-sə-kən-'tä-tə\ *noun* [New Latin, sung mass] (circa 1903)
: HIGH MASS

**mis·sal** \'mi-səl\ *noun* [Middle English *messel*, from Middle French & Medieval Latin; Middle French, from Medieval Latin *missale*, from neuter of *missalis* of the mass, from Late Latin *missa* mass — more at MASS] (14th century)
: a book containing all that is said or sung at mass during the entire year

**mis·send** \,mis-'send\ *transitive verb* **-sent** \-'sent\; **-send·ing** (15th century)
: to send incorrectly ⟨*missent* mail⟩

**mis·sense** \'mis-,sen(t)s\ *noun* [¹*mis-* + *-sense* (as in *nonsense*)] (1961)
: genetic mutation involving alteration of one or more codons so that different amino acids are determined — compare ANTISENSE, NONSENSE

¹**mis·sile** \'mi-səl, *chiefly British* -,sīl\ *adjective* [Latin *missilis*, from *mittere* to throw, send] (1611)
**1** : capable of being thrown or projected to strike a distant object
**2** : adapted for throwing or hurling missiles

²**missile** *noun* (circa 1656)
: an object (as a weapon) thrown or projected usually so as to strike something at a distance ⟨stones, artillery shells, bullets, and rockets are *missiles*⟩: as **a** : GUIDED MISSILE **b** : BALLISTIC MISSILE

**mis·sil·eer** \,mi-sə-'lir\ *noun* (1958)
: MISSILEMAN

**mis·sile·man** \'mi-səl-mən\ *noun* (1951)
: one engaged in designing, building, or operating guided missiles

**mis·sile·ry** \'mi-səl-rē\ *noun* (1880)
: MISSILES; *especially* : GUIDED MISSILES

**miss·ing** \'mi-siŋ\ *adjective* (circa 1530)
: ABSENT; *also* : LOST ⟨*missing* in action⟩

**missing link** *noun* (1851)
**1** : an absent member needed to complete a series or resolve a problem
**2** : a hypothetical intermediate form between humans and their presumed simian progenitors

**mis·si·ol·o·gy** \,mi-sē-'ä-lə-jē\ *noun* [*mission* + *-logy*] (1924)
: the study of the church's mission especially with respect to missionary activity

¹**mis·sion** \'mi-shən\ *noun* [New Latin, Medieval Latin, & Latin; New Latin *mission-, missio* religious mission, from Medieval Latin,

task assigned, from Latin, act of sending, from *mittere* to send] (1606)
**1** *obsolete* : the act or an instance of sending
**2 a** : a ministry commissioned by a religious organization to propagate its faith or carry on humanitarian work **b** : assignment to or work in a field of missionary enterprise **c** (1) : a mission establishment (2) : a local church or parish dependent on a larger religious organization for direction or financial support **d** *plural* : organized missionary work **e** : a course of sermons and services given to convert the unchurched or quicken Christian faith
**3** : a body of persons sent to perform a service or carry on an activity: as **a** : a group sent to a foreign country to conduct diplomatic or political negotiations **b** : a permanent embassy or legation **c** : a team of specialists or cultural leaders sent to a foreign country
**4 a** : a specific task with which a person or a group is charged **b** (1) : a definite military, naval, or aerospace task ⟨a bombing *mission*⟩ ⟨a space *mission*⟩ (2) : a flight operation of an aircraft or spacecraft in the performance of a mission ⟨a *mission* to Mars⟩
**5** : CALLING, VOCATION

²**mission** *transitive verb* **mis·sioned; mis·sion·ing** \'mi-sh(ə-)niŋ\ (1692)
**1** : to send on or entrust with a mission
**2** : to carry on a religious mission among or in

³**mission** *adjective* (1904)
**1** : of or relating to a style used in the early Spanish missions of the southwestern U.S. ⟨*mission* architecture⟩
**2** : of, relating to, or having the characteristics of a style of plain heavy usually oak furniture originating in the U.S. in the early part of the 20th century

¹**mis·sion·ary** \'mi-shə-,ner-ē\ *adjective* (1644)
**1** : relating to, engaged in, or devoted to missions
**2** : characteristic of a missionary

²**missionary** *noun, plural* **-ar·ies** (circa 1656)
: a person undertaking a mission and especially a religious mission

**missionary position** *noun* [perhaps from the notion that missionaries insisted that this coital position is the only acceptable one] (1948)
: a coital position in which the female lies on her back with the male on top and with his face opposite hers

**mis·sion·er** \'mi-sh(ə-)nər\ *noun* (1654)
: MISSIONARY

**mis·sion·ize** \'mi-shə-,nīz\ *verb* **-ized; -iz·ing** (1826)
*intransitive verb*
: to carry on missionary work
*transitive verb*
: to do missionary work among
— **mis·sion·i·za·tion** \,mi-shə-nə-'zā-shən\ *noun*
— **mis·sion·iz·er** \'mi-shə-,nī-zər\ *noun*

**Mis·sis·sip·pi·an** \,mi-sə-'si-pē-ən, (,)mis-'si-\ *adjective* [*Mississippi* River] (1835)
**1** : of or relating to Mississippi, its people, or the Mississippi River
**2** : of, relating to, or being the period of the Paleozoic era in North America following the Devonian and preceding the Pennsylvanian or the corresponding system of rocks — see GEOLOGIC TIME table
— **Mississippian** *noun*

**mis·sive** \'mi-siv\ *noun* [Middle French *lettre missive*, literally, letter intended to be sent] (1501)
: a written communication : LETTER

**miss·out** \'mis-,aüt\ *noun* (1945)

\ə\ abut \ᵊ\ kitten \ər\ further \a\ ash \ā\ ace
\ä\ mop, mar \aü\ out \ch\ chin \e\ bet \ē\ easy
\g\ go \i\ hit \ī\ ice \j\ job \ŋ\ sing \ō\ go
\ȯ\ law \ȯi\ boy \th\ thin \th\ the \ü\ loot \ù\ foot
\y\ yet \zh\ vision *see also* Guide to Pronunciation

: a throw of dice that loses the main bet
**miss out** *transitive verb* (1870)
*British* : to leave out : OMIT
**mis·speak** \,mis-'spēk\ *verb* **-spoke** \-'spōk\;
**-spo·ken** \-'spō-kən\; **-speak·ing** (14th
century)
*transitive verb*
**1** : to speak (as a word) incorrectly
**2** : to express (oneself) imperfectly or incorrectly ⟨claims now that he *misspoke* himself⟩
*intransitive verb*
: to speak incorrectly : misspeak oneself
**mis·spell** \,mis-'spel\ *transitive verb* (1655)
: to spell incorrectly
**mis·spell·ing** \-'spe-liŋ\ *noun* (circa 1696)
: an incorrect spelling
**mis·spend** \,mis-'spend\ *transitive verb*
**-spent** \-'spent\; **-spend·ing** (14th century)
: to spend wrongly : SQUANDER ⟨a *misspent*
life⟩
**mis·state** \,mis-'stāt\ *transitive verb* (1650)
: to state incorrectly : give a false account of
— **mis·state·ment** \-mənt\ *noun*
**mis·step** \-'step\ *noun* (circa 1800)
**1** : a mistake in judgment or action : BLUNDER
**2** : a wrong step
**mis·sus** or **mis·sis** \'mi-səz, -səs, *especially
Southern* -zəz\ *noun* [alteration of *mistress*]
(1790)
**1** *dialect* : MISTRESS 1a
**2** : WIFE ⟨men spend money on themselves, but
argue over every dime the *missus* wants —W.
A. Lydgate⟩
**missy** \'mi-sē\ *noun* (1676)
: a young girl : MISS
**¹mist** \'mist\ *noun* [Middle English, from Old
English; akin to Middle Dutch *mist* mist,
Greek *omichlē*] (before 12th century)
**1** : water in the form of particles floating or
falling in the atmosphere at or near the surface
of the earth and approaching the form of rain
**2** : something that obscures understanding
⟨*mists* of antiquity⟩
**3** : a film before the eyes
**4 a** : a cloud of small particles or objects suggestive of a mist **b** : a suspension of a finely
divided liquid in a gas **c** : a fine spray
**5** : a drink of liquor served over cracked ice
**²mist** (before 12th century)
*intransitive verb*
**1** : to be or become misty
**2** : to become moist or blurred
*transitive verb*
: to cover or spray with or convert to mist
**mis·tak·able** \mə-'stā-kə-bəl\ *adjective*
(1646)
: capable of being misunderstood or mistaken
**¹mis·take** \mə-'stāk\ *verb* **mis·took** \-'stúk\;
**mis·tak·en** \-'stā-kən\; **mis·tak·ing** [Mid-
dle English, from Old Norse *mistaka* to take
by mistake, from *mis-* + *taka* to take — more
at TAKE] (14th century)
*transitive verb*
**1** : to blunder in the choice of ⟨*mistook* her
way in the dark⟩
**2 a** : to misunderstand the meaning or intention of : MISINTERPRET ⟨don't *mistake* me, I
mean exactly what I said⟩ **b** : to make a wrong
judgment of the character or ability of
**3** : to identify wrongly : confuse with another
⟨I *mistook* him for his brother⟩
*intransitive verb*
: to be wrong ⟨you *mistook* when you thought
I laughed at you —Thomas Hardy⟩
— **mis·tak·en·ly** *adverb*
— **mis·tak·er** *noun*
**²mistake** *noun* (1638)
**1** : a misunderstanding of the meaning or implication of something
**2** : a wrong action or statement proceeding
from faulty judgment, inadequate knowledge,
or inattention
**synonym** see ERROR
**¹mis·ter** \'mis-tər, *for 1* ,mis-tər *or in rapid
speech* (,)mis(t)\ *noun* [alteration of ¹*master*]
(1551)

**1** *capitalized* : MR. — used sometimes in writing instead of *Mr.*
**2** : SIR — used without a name as a generalized term of direct address of a man who is a
stranger ⟨hey, *mister*, do you want to buy a pa-
per⟩
**3** : a man not entitled to a title of rank or an
honorific or professional title ⟨though he was
only a *mister*, he was a greater scholar in his
field than any PhD⟩
**4** : HUSBAND
**²mis·ter** \'mis-tər\ *noun* [²*mist* + ²*-er*] (1973)
: a device for spraying a mist
**mis·think** \,mis-'thiŋk\ *verb* **-thought**
\-'thot\; **-think·ing** (circa 1530)
*intransitive verb*
*archaic* : to think mistakenly or unfavorably
*transitive verb*
*archaic* : to think badly or unfavorably of
**mis·tle·toe** \'mi-səl-,tō, *chiefly British* 'mi-
zəl-\ *noun* [Middle English *mistilto*, from Old
English *misteltān*, from *mistel* mistletoe + *tān*
twig; akin to Old High German & Old Saxon
*mistil* mistletoe and to Old High German *zein*
twig] (before 12th century)
: a European semiparasitic green shrub (*Viscum album* of the family Loranthaceae, the
mistletoe family) with thick leaves, small yellowish flowers, and waxy-white glutinous berries; *broadly* : any of various plants of the
mistletoe family (as of an American genus
*Phoradendron*) resembling the true mistletoe
**mis·tral** \'mis-trəl, mi-'sträl\ *noun* [French,
from Provençal, from *mistral* masterful, from
Late Latin *magistralis* of a teacher — more
at MAGISTRAL] (1604)
: a strong cold dry northerly wind of southern
France
**mis·treat** \,mis-'trēt\ *transitive verb* [Middle
English *mistreten*, probably from Middle
French *mestraitier*, from Old French, from
*mes-* mis- + *traitier* to treat — more at
TREAT] (15th century)
: to treat badly : ABUSE
— **mis·treat·ment** \-mənt\ *noun*
**mis·tress** \'mis-trəs\ *noun* [Middle English
*maistresse*, from Middle French, from Old
French, feminine of *maistre* master — more
at MASTER] (15th century)
**1** : a woman who has power, authority, or
ownership: as **a** : the female head of a household **b** : a woman who employs or supervises
servants **c** : a woman who is in charge of a
school or other establishment **d** : a woman of
the Scottish nobility having a status comparable to that of a master
**2 a** *chiefly British* : a female teacher or tutor **b**
: a woman who has achieved mastery in some
field
**3** : something personified as female that rules,
directs, or dominates ⟨when Rome was *mistress* of the world⟩
**4 a** : a woman other than his wife with whom
a married man has a continuing sexual relationship **b** *archaic* : SWEETHEART
**5 a** — used archaically as a title prefixed to
the name of a married or unmarried woman **b**
*chiefly Southern & Midland* : MRS. 1a
**mistress of ceremonies** (1952)
: a woman who presides at a public ceremony
or who acts as hostess of a stage, radio, or
television show
**mis·tri·al** \'mis-,trī(ə)l\ *noun* (1628)
: a trial that has no legal effect by reason of
some error or serious prejudicial misconduct
in the proceedings
**¹mis·trust** \,mis-'trəst\ *noun* (14th century)
: a lack of confidence : DISTRUST
**synonym** see UNCERTAINTY
— **mis·trust·ful** \-fəl\ *adjective*
— **mis·trust·ful·ly** \-fə-lē\ *adverb*
— **mis·trust·ful·ness** *noun*
**²mistrust** (14th century)
*transitive verb*
**1** : to have no trust or confidence in : SUSPECT
⟨*mistrusted* his neighbors⟩

**2** : to doubt the truth, validity, or effectiveness
of ⟨*mistrusted* his own judgment⟩
**3** : SURMISE ⟨your mind *mistrusted* there was
something wrong —Robert Frost⟩
*intransitive verb*
: to be suspicious
**misty** \'mis-tē\ *adjective* **mist·i·er; -est** (before 12th century)
**1 a** : obscured by mist **b** : consisting of or
marked by mist
**2 a** : INDISTINCT ⟨a *misty* recollection of the
event⟩ **b** : VAGUE, CONFUSED ⟨avoided the large,
vague, *misty* issues —Reuben Abel⟩
**3** : TEARFUL
— **mist·i·ly** \-tə-lē\ *adverb*
— **mist·i·ness** \-tē-nəs\ *noun*
**misty–eyed** \'mis-tē-,īd\ *adjective* (1928)
**1** : having tearful eyes
**2** : DREAMY, SENTIMENTAL ⟨*misty-eyed* recollec-
tions⟩
**mis·un·der·stand** \(,)mi-,sən-dər-'stand\
*transitive verb* **-stood** \-'stúd\; **-stand·ing**
(13th century)
**1** : to fail to understand
**2** : to interpret incorrectly
**mis·un·der·stand·ing** *noun* (15th century)
**1** : a failure to understand : MISINTERPRETA-
TION
**2** : QUARREL, DISAGREEMENT
**mis·us·age** \,mis-'yü-sij, ,mish-, -zij\ *noun*
[Middle French *mesusage*, from *mes-* mis- +
*usage* usage] (1532)
**1** : bad treatment : ABUSE
**2** : wrong or improper use (as of words)
**¹mis·use** \-'yüz\ *transitive verb* [Middle English, partly from *mis-* + *usen* to use; partly
from Middle French *mesuser* to abuse, from
Old French, from *mes-* + *user* to use] (14th
century)
**1** : to use incorrectly : MISAPPLY ⟨*misused* his
talents⟩
**2** : ABUSE, MISTREAT ⟨*misused* his servants⟩
— **mis·us·er** *noun*
**²mis·use** \-'yüs\ *noun* (14th century)
: incorrect or improper use : MISAPPLICATION
**¹mite** \'mīt\ *noun* [Middle English, from Old
English *mīte;* akin to Middle Dutch *mite* mite,
small copper coin and perhaps to Old High
German *meizan* to cut] (before 12th century)
: any of numerous small acarid arachnids that
often infest animals, plants, and stored foods
and include important disease vectors
**²mite** *noun* [Middle English, from Middle
French or Middle Dutch; Middle French,
small Flemish copper coin, from Middle
Dutch] (14th century)
**1** : a small coin or sum of money
**2 a** : a very little : BIT **b** : a very small object
or creature
— **a mite** : SOMEWHAT, RATHER ⟨could be
that I am *a mite* prejudiced —John Fischer⟩
**¹mi·ter** or **mi·tre** \'mī-tər\ *noun* [Middle English *mitre*, from Middle French, from Latin
*mitra* headband, turban, from Greek] (14th
century)
**1** : a liturgical
headdress worn
by bishops and
abbots
**2 a** : a surface
forming the
beveled end or
edge of a piece
where a joint is
made by cutting two pieces at an angle and fitting them together **b** : MITER JOINT
**²miter** or **mitre** *transitive verb* **mi·tered** or
**mi·tred; mi·ter·ing** or **mi·tring** \'mī-tə-
riŋ\ (14th century)
**1** : to confer a miter on
**2 a** : to match or fit together in a miter joint **b**
: to bevel the ends of for making a miter joint
— **mi·ter·er** \'mī-tər-ər\ *noun*
**miter box** *noun* (1678)
: a device for guiding a handsaw at the proper
angle in making a miter joint in wood

miter 2a: *1* plain, *2* milled,
*3* rabbeted

**miter joint** *noun* (1688)
: a joint made by fastening together usually perpendicularly parts with the ends cut at an angle

**miter square** *noun* (1678)
: a bevel with an immovable arm at an angle of 45 degrees for striking marking lines; *also*
: a square with an arm adjustable to any angle

**Mith·ra·ic** \mi-ˈthrā-ik\ *adjective* [Late Greek *mithraikos* of Mithras, ancient Persian god of light, from Greek *Mithras,* from Old Persian *Mithra*] (1678)
: of or relating to an oriental mystery cult for men flourishing in the late Roman empire
— **Mith·ra·ism** \ˈmith-rə-ˌi-zəm, -(ˌ)rā-\ *noun*
— **Mith·ra·ist** \mi-ˈthrā-ist\ *noun or adjective*

**mith·ri·date** \ˈmith-rə-ˌdāt\ *noun* [Medieval Latin *mithridatum,* from Late Latin *mithridatium,* from Latin, dogtooth violet (used as an antidote), from Greek *mithridation,* from *Mithridatēs* Mithridates VI] (1528)
: an antidote against poison; *especially* : an electuary held to be effective against poison

**mi·ti·cide** \ˈmī-tə-ˌsīd\ *noun* [*mite*] (circa 1946)
: an agent used to kill mites
— **mi·ti·cid·al** \ˌmī-tə-ˈsī-dᵊl\ *adjective*

**mit·i·gate** \ˈmi-tə-ˌgāt\ *transitive verb* **-gat·ed; -gat·ing** [Middle English, from Latin *mitigatus,* past participle of *mitigare* to soften, from *mitis* soft + *-igare* (akin to Latin *agere* to drive); akin to Old Irish *moíth* soft — more at AGENT] (15th century)
**1** : to cause to become less harsh or hostile : MOLLIFY ⟨aggressiveness may be *mitigated* or . . . channeled —Ashley Montagu⟩
**2 a** : to make less severe or painful : ALLEVIATE **b** : EXTENUATE ◻
*synonym* see RELIEVE
— **mit·i·ga·tion** \ˌmi-tə-ˈgā-shən\ *noun*
— **mit·i·ga·tive** \ˈmi-tə-ˌgā-tiv\ *adjective*
— **mit·i·ga·tor** \-ˌgā-tər\ *noun*
— **mit·i·ga·to·ry** \ˈmi-ti-gə-ˌtōr-ē, -ˌtȯr-\ *adjective*

**mi·to·chon·dri·on** \ˌmī-tə-ˈkän-drē-ən\ *noun, plural* **-dria** \-drē-ə\ [New Latin, from Greek *mitos* thread + *chondrion,* diminutive of *chondros* grain] (1901)
: any of various round or long cellular organelles of most eukaryotes that are found outside the nucleus, produce energy for the cell through cellular respiration, and are rich in fats, proteins, and enzymes — see CELL illustration
— **mi·to·chon·dri·al** \-drē-əl\ *adjective*

**mi·to·gen** \ˈmī-tə-jən\ *noun* [*mitosis* + *-gen*] (circa 1951)
: a substance that induces mitosis
— **mi·to·gen·ic** \ˌmī-tə-ˈje-nik\ *adjective*
— **mi·to·ge·nic·i·ty** \-jə-ˈni-sə-tē\ *noun*

**mi·to·my·cin** \ˌmī-tə-ˈmī-sᵊn\ *noun* [International Scientific Vocabulary *mito-* (probably from New Latin *mitosis*) + *-mycin*] (1956)
: a complex of antibiotic substances which is produced by a Japanese streptomyces (*Streptomyces caespitosus*) and one form of which acts directly on DNA and shows promise as an anticancer agent

**mi·to·sis** \mī-ˈtō-səs\ *noun, plural* **-to·ses** \-ˌsēz\ [New Latin, from Greek *mitos* thread] (1887)
**1** : a process that takes place in the nucleus of a dividing cell, involves typically a series of steps consisting of prophase, metaphase, anaphase, and telophase, and results in the formation of two new nuclei each having the same number of chromosomes as the parent nucleus — compare MEIOSIS
**2** : cell division in which mitosis occurs
— **mi·tot·ic** \-ˈtä-tik\ *adjective*
— **mi·tot·i·cal·ly** \-ti-k(ə-)lē\ *adverb*

**mi·tral** \ˈmī-trəl\ *adjective* (1610)
**1** : resembling a miter

**2** : of, relating to, being, or adjoining a mitral valve or orifice

**mitral valve** *noun* (1705)
: BICUSPID VALVE

**mi·tre·wort** *also* **mi·ter·wort** \ˈmī-tər-ˌwərt, -ˌwȯrt\ *noun* (circa 1818)
: any of a genus (*Mitella*) of rhizomatous perennial herbs of the saxifrage family that bear a capsule resembling a bishop's miter

**mitt** \ˈmit\ *noun* [short for *mitten*] (1765)
**1 a** : a woman's glove that leaves the fingers uncovered **b** : MITTEN 1 **c** : a baseball catcher's or first baseman's glove made in the style of a mitten
**2** *slang* : HAND

**mit·ten** \ˈmi-tᵊn\ *noun* [Middle English *mitain,* from Middle French *mitaine,* from Old French, from *mite* mitten] (14th century)
**1** : a covering for the hand and wrist having a separate section for the thumb only
**2** : MITT 1a

**mit·ti·mus** \ˈmi-tə-məs\ *noun* [Latin, we send, from *mittere* to send] (circa 1591)
: a warrant of commitment to prison

**mitz·vah** \ˈmits-və\ *noun, plural* **mitz·voth** \-ˌvōt, -ˌvōth, -ˌvōs\ *or* **mitz·vahs** [Hebrew *miṣwāh*] (1650)
**1** : a commandment of the Jewish law
**2** : a meritorious or charitable act

**¹mix** \ˈmiks\ *verb* [Middle English, back-formation from *mixte* mixed, from Middle French, from Latin *mixtus,* past participle of *miscēre* to mix; akin to Greek *mignynai* to mix] (15th century)
*transitive verb*
**1 a** (1) : to combine or blend into one mass (2) : to combine with another **b** : to bring into close association ⟨*mix* business with pleasure⟩
**2 a** : to form by mixing components ⟨*mix* a drink at the bar⟩ **b** : to produce (a sound recording) by electronically combining or adjusting sounds from more than one source
**3** : CONFUSE — often used with *up* ⟨*mixes* things up in his eagerness to speak out —Irving Howe⟩
*intransitive verb*
**1 a** : to become mixed **b** : to be capable of mixing
**2** : to enter into relations : ASSOCIATE
**3** : CROSSBREED
**4** : to become involved : PARTICIPATE ⟨decided not to *mix* in politics⟩ ☆
— **mix·able** \ˈmik-sə-bəl\ *adjective*
— **mix it up** : to engage in a fight, contest, or dispute

**²mix** *noun* (circa 1586)
**1** : an act or process of mixing
**2** : a product of mixing: as **a** : a commercially prepared mixture of food ingredients ⟨a cake *mix*⟩ **b** : a combination of different kinds ⟨the right *mix* of jobs, people and amenities —*London Times*⟩
**3** : MIXER 2b

**mixed** \ˈmikst\ *adjective* [Middle English *mixte*] (15th century)
**1** : combining characteristics of more than one kind; *specifically* : combining features of two or more systems of government ⟨a *mixed* constitution⟩
**2** : made up of or involving individuals or items of more than one kind: as **a** : made up of or involving persons differing in race, national origin, religion, or class **b** : made up of or involving individuals of both sexes ⟨*mixed* company⟩ ⟨a *mixed* school⟩
**3** : including or accompanied by inconsistent, incompatible, or contrary elements ⟨*mixed* emotions⟩ ⟨received *mixed* reviews⟩ ⟨a *mixed* blessing⟩
**4** : deriving from two or more races or breeds ⟨a stallion of *mixed* blood⟩

**mixed alphabet** *noun* (1931)
: an alphabet (as in a cryptographic system) that has been rearranged or disordered systematically or randomly

**mixed bag** *noun* (1926)

: a miscellaneous collection : ASSORTMENT

**mixed bud** *noun* (1900)
: a bud that produces a branch and leaves as well as flowers

**mixed drink** *noun* (1943)
: an alcoholic beverage prepared from two or more ingredients

**mixed farming** *noun* (1872)
: the growing of food or cash crops, feed crops, and livestock on the same farm

**mixed grill** *noun* (1913)
: meats (as lamb chop, kidney, and bacon) and vegetables broiled together and served on one plate

**mixed marriage** *noun* (1829)
: a marriage between persons of different races or religions

**mixed–media** *adjective* (1962)
: MULTIMEDIA

**mixed metaphor** *noun* (1800)
: a figure of speech combining inconsistent or incongruous metaphors

**mixed nerve** *noun* (1878)
: a nerve containing both sensory and motor fibers

**mixed number** *noun* (1542)
: a number (as 5⅔) composed of an integer and a fraction

**mixed–up** \ˈmikst-ˈəp\ *adjective* (1862)
: marked by bewilderment, perplexity, or disorder : CONFUSED

**mix·er** \ˈmik-sər\ *noun* (circa 1611)
**1** : one that mixes: as **a** (1) : one whose work is mixing the ingredients of a product (2) : one who balances and controls the dialogue, music, and sound effects to be recorded for or

---

☆ **SYNONYMS**
**Mix, mingle, commingle, blend, merge, coalesce, amalgamate, fuse**
mean to combine into a more or less uniform whole. MIX may or may not imply loss of each element's identity ⟨*mix* the salad greens⟩ ⟨*mix* a drink⟩. MINGLE usually suggests that the elements are still somewhat distinguishable or separately active ⟨fear *mingled* with anticipation in my mind⟩. COMMINGLE implies a closer or more thorough mingling ⟨a sense of duty *commingled* with a fierce pride drove her⟩. BLEND implies that the elements as such disappear in the resulting mixture ⟨*blended* several teas to create a balanced flavor⟩. MERGE suggests a combining in which one or more elements are lost in the whole ⟨in his mind reality and fantasy *merged*⟩. COALESCE implies an affinity in the merging elements and usually a resulting organic unity ⟨telling details that *coalesce* into a striking portrait⟩. AMALGAMATE implies the forming of a close union without complete loss of individual identities ⟨refugees who were readily *amalgamated* into the community⟩. FUSE stresses oneness and indissolubility of the resulting product ⟨a building in which modernism and classicism are *fused*⟩.

---

☐ **USAGE**
**mitigate** *Mitigate* is sometimes used as an intransitive (followed by *against*) where *militate* might be expected. Even though Faulkner used it ⟨some intangible and invisible social force that *mitigates* against him —William Faulkner⟩ and one critic thinks it should be called an American idiom, it is usually considered a mistake.

---

\ə\ **abut** \ᵊ\ **kitten** \ər\ **further** \a\ **ash** \ā\ **ace** \ä\ **mop, mar** \au̇\ **out** \ch\ **chin** \e\ **bet** \ē\ **easy** \g\ **go** \i\ **hit** \ī\ **ice** \j\ **job** \ŋ\ **sing** \ō\ **go** \ȯ\ **law** \ȯi\ **boy** \th\ **thin** \t̲h̲\ **the** \ü\ **loot** \u̇\ **foot** \y\ **yet** \zh\ **vision** *see also* Guide to Pronunciation

with a motion picture or television **b :** a container, device, or machine for mixing **c : a :** game, stunt, or dance used at a get-together to give members of the group an opportunity to meet one another in a friendly and informal atmosphere
**2 :** one that mixes with others: as **a :** a person considered in regard to casual sociability ⟨was shy and a poor *mixer*⟩ **b :** a nonalcoholic beverage (as ginger ale) used in a mixed drink
**mix·ol·o·gy** \mik-ˈsä-lə-jē\ *noun* (1948)
**:** the art or skill of preparing mixed drinks
— **mix·ol·o·gist** \-jist\ *noun*
**Mix·tec** \ˈmēs-ˌtek, mis-, mēsh-, mish-\ *noun, plural* **Mixtec** *or* **Mixtecs** [American Spanish *mixteco*] (1850)
**1 :** the language of the Mixtec people
**2 :** a member of an American Indian people of the state of Oaxaca, Mexico
**mix·ture** \ˈmiks-chər\ *noun* [Middle English, from Middle French, from Old French *misture*, from Latin *mixtura*, from *mixtus*] (15th century)
**1 a :** the act, the process, or an instance of mixing **b** (1) **:** the state of being mixed (2) **:** the relative proportions of constituents; *especially* **:** the proportion of fuel to air produced in a carburetor
**2 :** a product of mixing **:** COMBINATION: as **a :** a portion of matter consisting of two or more components in varying proportions that retain their own properties **b :** a fabric woven of variously colored threads **c :** a combination of several different kinds
**mix–up** \ˈmiks-ˌəp\ *noun* (1841)
**1 :** a state or instance of confusion
**2 :** MIXTURE
**3 :** CONFLICT, FIGHT
¹**miz·zen** *also* **miz·en** \ˈmi-zᵊn\ *noun* [Middle English *meson*, from Middle French *misaine* foremast sail, probably ultimately from Latin *medianus* of the middle — more at MEDIAN] (15th century)
**1 :** a fore-and-aft sail set on the mizzenmast
**2 :** MIZZENMAST
²**mizzen** *also* **mizen** *adjective* (15th century)
**:** of or relating to the mizzenmast
**miz·zen·mast** \-ˌmast, -məst\ *noun* (15th century)
**:** the mast aft or next aft of the mainmast in a ship
¹**miz·zle** \ˈmi-zəl\ *intransitive verb* **miz·zled; miz·zling** \ˈmi-zə-liŋ, ˈmiz-liŋ\ [Middle English *misellen;* akin to Flemish *mizzelen* to drizzle, Middle Dutch *mist* fog, mist] (15th century)
**:** to rain in very fine drops **:** DRIZZLE
— **mizzle** *noun*
— **miz·zly** \ˈmi-zə-lē, ˈmiz-lē\ *adjective*
²**mizzle** *intransitive verb* **miz·zled; miz·zling** \ˈmi-zə-liŋ, ˈmiz-liŋ\ [origin unknown] (1781)
*chiefly British* **:** to depart suddenly
¹**mne·mon·ic** \ni-ˈmä-nik\ *adjective* [Greek *mnēmonikos*, from *mnēmōn* mindful, from *mimnēskesthai* to remember — more at MIND] (1753)
**1 :** assisting or intended to assist memory; *also* **:** of or relating to mnemonics
**2 :** of or relating to memory
— **mne·mon·i·cal·ly** \-ni-k(ə-)lē\ *adverb*
²**mnemonic** *noun* (1858)
**:** a mnemonic device or code
**mne·mon·ics** \ni-ˈmä-niks\ *noun plural but singular in construction* (circa 1721)
**:** a technique of improving the memory
**Mne·mos·y·ne** \ni-ˈmä-sᵊn-ē, -ˈzᵊn-\ *noun* [Latin, from Greek *Mnēmosynē*]
**:** the Greek goddess of memory and mother of the Muses by Zeus
**-mo** *noun suffix* [duodeci*mo*]
— after numerals or their names to indicate the number of leaves made by folding a sheet of paper ⟨sixteen*mo*⟩ ⟨16*mo*⟩
**moa** \ˈmō-ə\ *noun* [Maori] (1842)

**:** any of various usually very large extinct flightless birds of New Zealand of a ratite family (Dinornithidae) including one (*Dinornis giganteus*) about 12 feet (3.7 meters) in height
**Mo·ab·ite** \ˈmō-ə-ˌbīt\ *noun* [Middle English, from Late Latin *Moabita, Moabites,* from Greek *Mōabitēs,* from *Mōab* Moab, ancient kingdom in Syria] (14th century)
**:** a member of an ancient Semitic people related to the Hebrews
— **Moabite** *or* **Mo·ab·it·ish** \-ˌbī-tish\ *adjective*
¹**moan** \ˈmōn\ *noun* [Middle English *mone,* from (assumed) Old English *mān*] (13th century)
**1 :** LAMENTATION, COMPLAINT
**2 :** a low prolonged sound of pain or of grief
²**moan** (14th century)
*transitive verb*
**1 :** to bewail audibly **:** LAMENT
**2 :** to utter with moans
*intransitive verb*
**1 :** LAMENT, COMPLAIN
**2 a :** to make a moan **:** GROAN **b :** to emit a sound resembling a moan ⟨the wind *moaned* in the trees⟩
— **moan·er** \ˈmō-nər\ *noun*
**moat** \ˈmōt\ *noun* [Middle English *mote,* probably from Middle French *motte* hill, mound] (14th century)
**1 :** a deep and wide trench around the rampart of a fortified place (as a castle) that is usually filled with water
**2 :** a channel resembling a moat (as about a seamount or for confinement of animals in a zoo)

**moat 1**

— **moat·ed** \ˈmō-təd\ *adjective*
— **moat·like** \-ˌlīk\ *adjective*
¹**mob** \ˈmäb\ *noun* [Latin *mobile vulgus* vacillating crowd] (1688)
**1 :** a large or disorderly crowd; *especially* **:** one bent on riotous or destructive action
**2 :** the lower classes of a community **:** MASSES, RABBLE
**3** *chiefly Australian* **:** a flock, drove, or herd of animals
**4 :** a criminal set **:** GANG; *especially, often capitalized* **:** MAFIA 1
**5** *chiefly British* **:** a group of people **:** CROWD
**synonym** see CROWD
— **mob·bish** \ˈmä-bish\ *adjective*
²**mob** *transitive verb* **mobbed; mob·bing** (1709)
**1 :** to crowd about and attack or annoy ⟨*mobbed* by autograph hunters⟩ ⟨a crow *mobbed* by songbirds⟩
**2 :** to crowd into or around ⟨customers *mob* the stores on sale days⟩
**mob·cap** \ˈmäb-ˌkap\ *noun* [*mob* woman's cap + *cap*] (1795)
**:** a woman's fancy indoor cap made with a high full crown and often tied under the chin
**mo·be pearl** *or* **mo·bé pearl** \ˈmō-ˌbā-, ˌmō-ˈ\ *noun, often M capitalized* [origin unknown] (1955)
**:** MABE
¹**mo·bile** \ˈmō-bəl, -ˌbīl *also* -ˌbēl\ *adjective* [Middle English *mobyll,* from Middle French *mobile,* from Latin *mobilis,* from *movēre* to move] (15th century)
**1 :** capable of moving or being moved **:** MOVABLE ⟨a *mobile* missile launcher⟩
**2 a :** changeable in appearance, mood, or purpose ⟨*mobile* face⟩ **b :** ADAPTABLE, VERSATILE
**3 :** MIGRATORY

**4 a :** characterized by the mixing of social groups **b :** having the opportunity for or undergoing a shift in status within the hierarchical social levels of a society ⟨socially *mobile* workers⟩
**5 :** marked by the use of vehicles for transportation ⟨*mobile* warfare⟩
**6 :** of or relating to a mobile
— **mo·bil·i·ty** \mō-ˈbi-lə-tē\ *noun*
²**mo·bile** \ˈmō-, -ˌbēl\ *noun* (1936)
**:** a construction or sculpture frequently of wire and sheet metal shapes with parts that can be set in motion by air currents; *also* **:** a similar structure (as of paper or plastic) suspended so that it moves in a current of air
**-mobile** *combining form* [auto*mobile*]
**1 :** motorized vehicle ⟨snow*mobile*⟩
**2 :** automotive vehicle bringing services to the public ⟨blood*mobile*⟩ ⟨book*mobile*⟩
**mobile home** *noun* (1949)
**:** a dwelling structure built on a steel chassis and fitted with wheels that is intended to be hauled to a usually permanent site — compare MOTOR HOME
**mo·bi·lise** *chiefly British variant of* MOBILIZE
**mo·bi·li·za·tion** \ˌmō-bə-lə-ˈzā-shən\ *noun* (1799)
**1 :** the act of mobilizing
**2 :** the state of being mobilized
**mo·bi·lize** \ˈmō-bə-ˌlīz\ *verb* **-lized; -liz·ing** (1838)
*transitive verb*
**1 a :** to put into movement or circulation ⟨*mobilize* financial assets⟩ **b :** to release (something stored in the organism) for bodily use
**2 a :** to assemble and make ready for war duty **b :** to marshal (as resources) for action ⟨*mobilize* support for a proposal⟩
*intransitive verb*
**:** to undergo mobilization
**Mö·bi·us strip** \ˈmœ-bē-əs-, ˈmə(r)-, ˈmō-\ *noun* [August F. *Möbius* (died 1868) German mathematician] (1904)
**:** a one-sided surface that is constructed from a rectangle by holding one end fixed, rotating the opposite end through 180 degrees, and joining it to the first end

**Möbius strip**

**mo·bled** \ˈmä-bəld\ *adjective* [past participle of *moble* to muffle, probably frequentative of *mob* to muffle, of unknown origin] (1603)
**:** being wrapped or muffled in or as if in a hood
**mob·oc·ra·cy** \mä-ˈbä-krə-sē\ *noun* (1754)
**1 :** rule by the mob
**2 :** the mob as a ruling class
— **mob·o·crat** \ˈmä-bə-ˌkrat\ *noun*
— **mob·o·crat·ic** \ˌmä-bə-ˈkra-tik\ *adjective*
**mob·ster** \ˈmäb-stər\ *noun* (1917)
**:** a member of a criminal gang
**moc** \ˈmäk\ *noun* (1948)
**:** MOCCASIN 1
**moc·ca·sin** \ˈmä-kə-sən\ *noun* [Virginia Algonquian *mockasin*] (circa 1612)
**1 a :** a soft leather heelless shoe or boot with the sole brought up the sides of the foot and over the toes where it is joined with a puckered seam to a U-shaped piece lying on top of the foot **b :** a regular shoe having a seam on the forepart of the vamp imitating the seam of a moccasin
**2 a :** WATER MOCCASIN **b :** a snake (as of the genus *Natrix*) resembling a water moccasin
**moccasin flower** *noun* (1680)
**:** any of several lady's slippers (genus *Cypripedium*); *especially* **:** a once common woodland orchid (*C. acaule*) of eastern North America with pink or white moccasin-shaped flowers
**mo·cha** \ˈmō-kə\ *noun* [*Mocha,* Yemen] (1773)

**1 a** (1) **:** a superior Arabian coffee consisting of small green or yellowish beans (2) **:** a coffee of superior quality **b :** a flavoring made of a strong coffee infusion or of a mixture of cocoa or chocolate with coffee
**2 :** a pliable suede-finished glove leather from African sheepskins
**3 :** a dark chocolate-brown color
**¹mock** \'mäk, 'mȯk\ *verb* [Middle English, from Middle French *mocquer*] (15th century)
*transitive verb*
**1 :** to treat with contempt or ridicule **:** DERIDE
**2 :** to disappoint the hopes of
**3 :** DEFY, CHALLENGE
**4 a :** to imitate (as a mannerism) closely **:** MIMIC **b :** to mimic in sport or derision
*intransitive verb*
**:** JEER, SCOFF
**synonym** see RIDICULE, COPY
**— mock·er** *noun*
**— mock·ing·ly** \'mä-kiŋ-lē, 'mȯ-\ *adverb*
**²mock** *noun* (15th century)
**1 :** an act of ridicule or derision **:** JEER
**2 :** one that is an object of derision or scorn
**3 :** MOCKERY
**4 a :** an act of imitation **b :** something made as an imitation
**³mock** *adjective* (1548)
**:** of, relating to, or having the character of an imitation **:** SIMULATED, FEIGNED ⟨the *mock* solemnity of the parody⟩
**⁴mock** *adverb* (circa 1619)
**:** in an insincere or counterfeit manner — usually used in combination ⟨*mock*-serious⟩
**mock·ery** \'mä-k(ə-)rē, 'mȯ-\ *noun, plural* **-er·ies** (15th century)
**1 :** insulting or contemptuous action or speech **:** DERISION
**2 :** a subject of laughter, derision, or sport
**3 a :** a counterfeit appearance **:** IMITATION **b :** an insincere, contemptible, or impertinent imitation ⟨makes a *mockery* of justice⟩
**4 :** something ridiculously or impudently unsuitable
**¹mock–he·ro·ic** \,mäk-hi-'rō-ik, ,mȯk-\ *adjective* (circa 1712)
**:** ridiculing or burlesquing heroic style, character, or action ⟨a *mock-heroic* poem⟩
**— mock–he·ro·ical·ly** \-i-k(ə-)lē\ *adverb*
**²mock–heroic** *noun* (1728)
**:** a mock-heroic composition — called also *mock-epic*
**mock·ing·bird** \'mä-kiŋ-,bərd, 'mȯ-\ *noun* (1676)
**:** a common grayish bird (*Mimus polyglottos*) especially of the southern U.S. that is remarkable for its exact imitations of the notes of other birds
**mock orange** *noun* (1731)
**1 :** any of a genus (*Philadelphus*) of ornamental shrubs of the saxifrage family of which several are widely grown for their showy white flowers — called also *philadelphus, syringa*
**2 :** any of several usually shrubby plants considered to resemble the orange
**mock turtle soup** *noun* (1783)
**:** a soup made of meat (as calf's head or veal), wine, and spices in imitation of green turtle soup
**mock–up** \'mäk-,əp, 'mȯk-\ *noun* (1920)
**:** a full-sized structural model built accurately to scale chiefly for study, testing, or display
**¹mod** \'mäd\ *noun* [probably from ²*mod*] (1960)
**:** one who wears mod clothes
**²mod** *adjective* [short for *modern*] (1964)
**1 :** of, relating to, or being the characteristic style of 1960s British youth culture
**2 :** HIP, TRENDY
**mod·acryl·ic fiber** \,mä-də-'kri-lik-\ *noun* [*mod*ified *acrylic*] (1960)
**:** any of various synthetic textile fibers that are long-chain polymers composed of 35 to 85 percent by weight of acrylonitrile units

**mod·al** \'mō-dᵊl\ *adjective* [Medieval Latin *modalis*, from Latin *modus*] (1569)
**1 :** of or relating to modality in logic
**2 :** containing provisions as to the mode of procedure or the manner of taking effect — used of a contract or legacy
**3 :** of or relating to a musical mode
**4 :** of or relating to structure as opposed to substance
**5 :** of, relating to, or constituting a grammatical form or category characteristically indicating predication of an action or state in some manner other than as a simple fact
**6 :** of or relating to a statistical mode
**— mod·al·ly** \-dᵊl-ē\ *adverb*
**modal auxiliary** *noun* (circa 1904)
**:** an auxiliary verb (as *can, must, might, may*) that is characteristically used with a verb of predication and expresses a modal modification and that in English differs formally from other verbs in lacking *-s* and *-ing* forms
**mo·dal·i·ty** \mō-'da-lə-tē\ *noun, plural* **-ties** (circa 1617)
**1 a :** the quality or state of being modal **b :** a modal quality or attribute **:** FORM
**2 :** the classification of logical propositions according to their asserting or denying the possibility, impossibility, contingency, or necessity of their content
**3 :** one of the main avenues of sensation (as vision)
**4 :** a usually physical therapeutic agency
**mod con** \,mäd-'kän\ *noun* [from *mod. con.*, abbreviation for *modern convenience*] (1934) *chiefly British* **:** a modern convenience — usually used in plural
**¹mode** \'mōd\ *noun* [Middle English *moede*, from Latin *modus* measure, manner, musical mode — more at METE] (14th century)
**1 a :** an arrangement of the eight diatonic notes or tones of an octave according to one of several fixed schemes of their intervals **b :** a rhythmical scheme (as in 13th and 14th century music)
**2 :** ²MOOD 2
**3** [Late Latin *modus*, from Latin] **a :** ²MOOD 1 **b :** the modal form of the assertion or denial of a logical proposition
**4 a :** a particular form or variety of something **b :** a form or manner of expression **:** STYLE
**5 :** a possible, customary, or preferred way of doing something ⟨explained in the usual solemn *mode*⟩
**6 a :** a manifestation, form, or arrangement of being; *specifically* **:** a particular form or manifestation of an underlying substance **b :** a particular functioning arrangement or condition **:** STATUS ⟨a spacecraft in reentry *mode*⟩ ⟨a computer operating in parallel *mode*⟩
**7 a :** the most frequent value of a set of data **b :** a value of a random variable for which a function of probabilities defined on it achieves a relative maximum
**8 :** any of various stationary vibration patterns of which an elastic body or oscillatory system is capable ⟨the vibration *mode* of an airplane propeller blade⟩ ⟨the vibrational *modes* of a molecule⟩
**synonym** see METHOD
**²mode** *noun* [French, from Latin *modus*] (circa 1645)
**:** a prevailing fashion or style (as of dress or behavior)
**synonym** see FASHION
**¹mod·el** \'mä-dᵊl\ *noun* [Middle French *modelle*, from Old Italian *modello*, from (assumed) Vulgar Latin *modellus*, from Latin *modulus* small measure, from *modus*] (1575)
**1** *obsolete* **:** a set of plans for a building
**2** *dialect British* **:** COPY, IMAGE
**3 :** structural design ⟨a home on the *model* of an old farmhouse⟩
**4 :** a usually miniature representation of something; *also* **:** a pattern of something to be made
**5 :** an example for imitation or emulation

**6 :** a person or thing that serves as a pattern for an artist; *especially* **:** one who poses for an artist
**7 :** ARCHETYPE
**8 :** an organism whose appearance a mimic imitates
**9 :** one who is employed to display clothes or other merchandise **:** MANNEQUIN
**10 a :** a type or design of clothing **b :** a type or design of product (as a car)
**11 :** a description or analogy used to help visualize something (as an atom) that cannot be directly observed
**12 :** a system of postulates, data, and inferences presented as a mathematical description of an entity or state of affairs
**13 :** VERSION ☆
**²model** *verb* **mod·eled** *or* **mod·elled; mod·el·ing** *or* **mod·el·ling** \'mäd-liŋ, 'mä-dᵊl-iŋ\ (1625)
*transitive verb*
**1 :** to plan or form after a pattern **:** SHAPE
**2** *archaic* **:** to make into an organization (as an army, government, or parish)
**3 a :** to shape or fashion in a plastic material **b :** to produce a representation or simulation of ⟨using a computer to *model* a problem⟩
**4 :** to construct or fashion in imitation of a particular model ⟨*modeled* its constitution on that of the U.S.⟩
**5 :** to display by wearing, using, or posing with ⟨*modeled* gowns⟩
*intransitive verb*
**1 :** to design or imitate forms **:** make a pattern ⟨enjoys *modeling* in clay⟩
**2 :** to work or act as a fashion model
**— mod·el·er** \'mäd-lər, 'mä-dᵊl-ər\ *noun*
**³model** *adjective* (1844)
**1 :** serving as or capable of serving as a pattern ⟨a *model* student⟩
**2 :** being a usually miniature representation of something ⟨a *model* airplane⟩
**mo·dem** \'mō-,dəm, -,dem\ *noun* [*modulator* + *demodulator*] (circa 1952)
**:** a device that converts signals produced by one type of device (as a computer) to a form compatible with another (as a telephone)
**¹mod·er·ate** \'mä-d(ə-)rət\ *adjective* [Middle English, from Latin *moderatus*, from past participle of *moderare* to moderate; akin to Latin *modus* measure] (15th century)
**1 a :** avoiding extremes of behavior or expression **:** observing reasonable limits ⟨a *moderate* drinker⟩ **b :** CALM, TEMPERATE
**2 a :** tending toward the mean or average amount or dimension **b :** having average or less than average quality **:** MEDIOCRE

---

☆ **SYNONYMS**
**Model, example, pattern, exemplar, ideal** mean someone or something set before one for guidance or imitation. MODEL applies to something taken or proposed as worthy of imitation ⟨a decor that is a *model* of good taste⟩. EXAMPLE applies to a person to be imitated or in some contexts on no account to be imitated but to be regarded as a warning ⟨children tend to follow the *example* of their parents⟩. PATTERN suggests a clear and detailed archetype or prototype ⟨American industry set a *pattern* for others to follow⟩. EXEMPLAR suggests either a faultless example to be emulated or a perfect typification ⟨cited Joan of Arc as the *exemplar* of courage⟩. IDEAL implies the best possible exemplification either in reality or in conception ⟨never found a job that matched his *ideal*⟩.

---

\ə\ **abut**  \ᵊ\ **kitten**  \ər\ **further**  \a\ **ash**  \ā\ **ace**
\ä\ **mop, mar**  \aú\ **out**  \ch\ **chin**  \e\ **bet**  \ē\ **easy**
\g\ **go**  \i\ **hit**  \ī\ **ice**  \j\ **job**  \ŋ\ **sing**  \ō\ **go**
\ȯ\ **law**  \ȯi\ **boy**  \th\ **thin**  \th̷\ **the**  \ü\ **loot**  \ú\ **foot**
\y\ **yet**  \zh\ **vision**    *see also* Guide to Pronunciation

**3 :** professing or characterized by political or social beliefs that are not extreme
**4 :** limited in scope or effect
**5 :** not expensive **:** reasonable or low in price
**6** *of a color* **:** of medium lightness and medium chroma
— **mod·er·ate·ly** *adverb*
— **mod·er·ate·ness** *noun*
²**mod·er·ate** \'mä-də-ˌrāt\ *verb* **-at·ed; -at·ing** (15th century)
*transitive verb*
**1 :** to lessen the intensity or extremeness of ⟨the sun *moderated* the chill⟩
**2 :** to preside over or act as chairman of
*intransitive verb*
**1 :** to act as a moderator
**2 :** to become less violent, severe, or intense
— **mod·er·a·tion** \ˌmä-də-'rā-shən\ *noun*
³**mod·er·ate** \'mä-d(ə-)rət\ *noun* (1794)
**:** one who holds moderate views or who belongs to a group favoring a moderate course or program
**moderate breeze** *noun* (circa 1881)
**:** wind having a speed of 13 to 18 miles (21 to 29 kilometers) per hour — see BEAUFORT SCALE table
**moderate gale** *noun* (1704)
**:** wind having a speed of 32 to 38 miles (51 to 61 kilometers) per hour — see BEAUFORT SCALE table
**mo·der·a·to** \ˌmä-də-'rä-(ˌ)tō\ *adverb or adjective* [Italian, from Latin *moderatus*] (circa 1724)
**:** MODERATE — used as a direction in music to indicate tempo
**mod·er·a·tor** \'mä-də-ˌrā-tər\ *noun* (circa 1560)
**1 :** one who arbitrates **:** MEDIATOR
**2 :** one who presides over an assembly, meeting, or discussion: as **a :** the presiding officer of a Presbyterian governing body **b :** the nonpartisan presiding officer of a town meeting **c :** the chairman of a discussion group
**3 :** a substance (as graphite) used for slowing down neutrons in a nuclear reactor
— **mod·er·a·tor·ship** \-ˌship\ *noun*
¹**mod·ern** \'mä-dərn, ÷'mä-d(ə-)rən\ *adjective* [Late Latin *modernus*, from Latin *modo* just now, from *modus* measure — more at METE] (1585)
**1 a :** of, relating to, or characteristic of the present or the immediate past **:** CONTEMPORARY **b :** of, relating to, or characteristic of a period extending from a relevant remote past to the present time
**2 :** involving recent techniques, methods, or ideas **:** UP-TO-DATE
**3** *capitalized* **:** of, relating to, or having the characteristics of the present or most recent period of development of a language
**4 :** of or relating to modernism **:** MODERNIST
— **mo·der·ni·ty** \mə-'dər-nə-tē, mä- *also* -'der-\ *noun*
— **mod·ern·ly** \'mä-dərn-lē\ *adverb*
— **mod·ern·ness** \-dərn-nəs\ *noun*
²**modern** *noun* (1585)
**1 a :** a person of modern times or views **b :** an adherent of modernism **:** MODERNIST
**2 :** a style of printing type distinguished by regularity of shape, precise curves, straight hairline serifs, and heavy downstrokes
**mo·derne** \mō-'dern, mə-\ *noun, often capitalized* [French, modern] (1955)
**:** ART DECO
**Modern Hebrew** *noun* (1949)
**:** NEW HEBREW
**mod·ern·i·sa·tion, mod·ern·ise** *British variant of* MODERNIZATION, MODERNIZE
**mod·ern·ism** \'mä-dər-ˌni-zəm\ *noun* (1737)
**1 :** a practice, usage, or expression peculiar to modern times
**2** *often capitalized* **:** a tendency in theology to accommodate traditional religious teaching to contemporary thought and especially to devalue supernatural elements

**3 :** modern artistic or literary philosophy and practice; *especially* **:** a self-conscious break with the past and a search for new forms of expression
— **mod·ern·ist** \-nist\ *noun or adjective*
— **mod·ern·is·tic** \ˌmä-dər-'nis-tik\ *adjective*
**mod·ern·i·za·tion** \ˌmä-dər-nə-'zā-shən\ *noun* (1770)
**1 :** the act of modernizing **:** the state of being modernized
**2 :** something modernized **:** a modernized version
**mod·ern·ize** \'mä-dər-ˌnīz\ *verb* **-ized; -iz·ing** (1748)
*transitive verb*
**:** to make modern (as in taste, style, or usage)
*intransitive verb*
**:** to adopt modern ways
— **mod·ern·iz·er** *noun*
**modern pentathlon** *noun* (circa 1912)
**:** a composite contest in which all contestants compete in a 300-meter freestyle swim, a 4000-meter cross-country run, a 5000-meter 30-jump equestrian steeplechase, épée fencing, and target shooting at 25 meters
**mod·est** \'mä-dəst\ *adjective* [Latin *modestus* moderate; akin to Latin *modus* measure] (1565)
**1 a :** placing a moderate estimate on one's abilities or worth **b :** neither bold nor self-assertive **:** tending toward diffidence
**2 :** arising from or characteristic of a modest nature
**3 :** observing the proprieties of dress and behavior **a :** DECENT
**4 a :** limited in size, amount, or scope **b :** UNPRETENTIOUS ⟨a *modest* cottage⟩
**synonym** see SHY, CHASTE
— **mod·est·ly** *adverb*
**mod·es·ty** \'mä-də-stē\ *noun* (1531)
**1 :** freedom from conceit or vanity
**2 :** propriety in dress, speech, or conduct
**mo·di·cum** \'mä-di-kəm *also* 'mō-\ *noun* [Middle English, from Latin, neuter of *modicus* moderate, from *modus* measure] (15th century)
**:** a small portion **:** a limited quantity
**mod·i·fi·ca·tion** \ˌmä-də-fə-'kā-shən\ *noun* (1603)
**1 :** the limiting of a statement **:** QUALIFICATION
**2 :** ¹MODE 6a
**3 :** the making of a limited change in something; *also* **:** the result of such a change **b :** a change in an organism caused by environmental factors
**4 :** a limitation or qualification of the meaning of a word by another word, by an affix, or by internal change
**mod·i·fi·er** \'mä-də-ˌfī(-ə)r\ *noun* (1583)
**1 :** one that modifies
**2 :** a word or phrase that makes specific the meaning of another word or phrase
**3 :** a gene that modifies the effect of another
**mod·i·fy** \'mä-də-ˌfī\ *verb* **-fied; -fy·ing** [Middle English *modifien*, from Middle French *modifier*, from Latin *modificare* to measure, moderate, from *modus*] (14th century)
*transitive verb*
**1 :** to make less extreme **:** MODERATE
**2 a :** to limit or restrict the meaning of especially in a grammatical construction **b :** to change (a vowel) by umlaut
**3 a :** to make minor changes in **b :** to make basic or fundamental changes in often to give a new orientation to or to serve a new end ⟨the wing of a bird is an arm *modified* for flying⟩
*intransitive verb*
**:** to undergo change
**synonym** see CHANGE
— **mod·i·fi·abil·i·ty** \ˌmä-də-ˌfī-ə-'bi-lə-tē\ *noun*
— **mod·i·fi·able** \'mä-də-ˌfī-ə-bəl\ *adjective*
**mo·dil·lion** \mō-'dil-yən\ *noun* [Italian *modiglione*] (1563)

**:** an ornamental block or bracket under the corona of the cornice (as in the Corinthian order)
**mod·ish** \'mō-dish\ *adjective* (1660)
**:** FASHIONABLE, STYLISH ⟨a *modish* hat⟩ ⟨a *modish* writer⟩
— **mod·ish·ly** *adverb*
— **mod·ish·ness** *noun*
**mo·diste** \mō-'dēst\ *noun* [French, from *mode* style, mode] (circa 1840)
**:** one who makes and sells fashionable dresses and hats for women
**Mo·dred** \'mō-dred\ *noun*
**:** a knight of the Round Table and nephew of King Arthur
**mod·u·la·bil·i·ty** \ˌmä-jə-lə-'bi-lə-tē\ *noun* (1928)
**:** the capability of being modulated
**mod·u·lar** \'mä-jə-lər\ *adjective* (1798)
**1 :** of, relating to, or based on a module or a modulus
**2 :** constructed with standardized units or dimensions for flexibility and variety in use
— **mod·u·lar·i·ty** \ˌmä-jə-'lar-ə-tē\ *noun*
— **mod·u·lar·ly** \'mä-jə-lər-lē\ *adverb*
**modular arithmetic** *noun* (1959)
**:** arithmetic that deals with whole numbers where the numbers are replaced by their remainders after division by a fixed number ⟨in a *modular arithmetic* with modulus 5, 3 multiplied by 4 is 2⟩
**mod·u·lar·ized** \'mä-jə-lə-ˌrīzd\ *adjective* (1959)
**1 :** containing or consisting of modules
**2 :** produced in the form of modules
**mod·u·late** \'mä-jə-ˌlāt\ *verb* **-lat·ed; -lat·ing** [Latin *modulatus*, past participle of *modulari* to play, sing, from *modulus* small measure, rhythm, diminutive of *modus* measure — more at METE] (1615)
*transitive verb*
**1 :** to tune to a key or pitch
**2 :** to adjust to or keep in proper measure or proportion **:** TEMPER
**3 :** to vary the amplitude, frequency, or phase of (a carrier wave or a light wave) for the transmission of intelligence (as by radio); *also* **:** to vary the velocity of electrons in an electron beam
*intransitive verb*
**1 :** to play or sing with modulation
**2 :** to pass from one musical key into another by means of intermediary chords or notes that have some relation to both keys
**3 :** to pass gradually from one state to another
— **mod·u·la·tor** \-ˌlā-tər\ *noun*
— **mod·u·la·to·ry** \-lə-ˌtōr-ē, -ˌtȯr-\ *adjective*
**mod·u·la·tion** \ˌmä-jə-'lā-shən\ *noun* (1531)
**1 :** a regulating according to measure or proportion **:** TEMPERING
**2 :** an inflection of the tone or pitch of the voice; *specifically* **:** the use of stress or pitch to convey meaning
**3 :** a change from one musical key to another by modulating
**4 :** the process of modulating a carrier or signal (as in radio); *also* **:** the result of this process
**mod·ule** \'mä-(ˌ)jü(ə)l\ *noun* [Latin *modulus*] (circa 1628)
**1 :** a standard or unit of measurement
**2 :** the size of some one part taken as a unit of measure by which the proportions of an architectural composition are regulated
**3 a :** any in a series of standardized units for use together: as (1) **:** a unit of furniture or architecture (2) **:** an educational unit which covers a single subject or topic **b :** a usually packaged functional assembly of electronic components for use with other such assemblies
**4 :** an independently-operable unit that is a part of the total structure of a space vehicle
**5 a :** a subset of an additive group that is also a group under addition **b :** a mathematical set that is a commutative group under addition and that is closed under multiplication which

is distributive from the left or right or both by elements of a ring and for which *a(bx)* = *(ab)x* or *(xb)a* = *x(ba)* or both where *a* and *b* are elements of the ring and *x* belongs to the set

**mod·u·lo** \'mä-jə-ˌlō\ *preposition* [New Latin, ablative of *modulus*] (1897)
: with respect to a modulus of ⟨19 and 54 are congruent *modulo* 7⟩
**mod·u·lus** \'mä-jə-ləs\ *noun, plural* **-li** \-ˌlī, -ˌlē\ [New Latin, from Latin, small measure] (1753)
**1 a** : the factor by which a logarithm of a number to one base is multiplied to obtain the logarithm of the number to a new base **b** : AB-SOLUTE VALUE 2 **c** (1) : the number (as a positive integer) or other mathematical entity (as a polynomial) in a congruence that divides the difference of the two congruent members without leaving a remainder — compare RES-IDUE b (2) : the number of different numbers used in a system of modular arithmetic
**2** : a constant or coefficient that expresses usually numerically the degree to which a body or substance possesses a particular property (as elasticity)
**mo·dus ope·ran·di** \ˌmō-dəs-ˌä-pə-ˌran-dē, -ˌdī\ *noun, plural* **mo·di operandi** \'mō-ˌdē-, 'mō-ˌdī-\ [New Latin] (1654)
: a method of procedure
**mo·dus vi·ven·di** \ˌmō-dəs-vi-'ven-dē, -ˌdī\ *noun, plural* **mo·di vivendi** \'mō-ˌdē-, 'mō-ˌdī-\ [New Latin, manner of living] (circa 1879)
**1** : a feasible arrangement or practical compromise; *especially* : one that bypasses difficulties
**2** : a manner of living : a way of life
**Mogen David** *variant of* MAGEN DAVID
**mog·gy** *also* **mog·gie** \'mä-gē\ *noun, plural* **mog·gies** [probably from *Moggy*, from *Mog*, nickname from the name *Margaret*] (circa 1911)
*British* : CAT
**¹mo·gul** \'mō-(ˌ)gəl\ *noun* [Persian *Mughul*, from Mongolian *mongɣol* Mongol] (1588)
**1** *or* **mo·ghul** *capitalized* : an Indian Muslim of or descended from one of several conquering groups of Mongol, Turkish, and Persian origin; *especially* : GREAT MOGUL
**2** : a great personage : MAGNATE
— **mogul** *adjective, often capitalized*
**²mo·gul** \'mō-gəl\ *noun* [German dialect; akin to German dialect (Viennese) *mugl* small hill] (1959)
: a bump in a ski run
**mo·hair** \'mō-ˌhar, -ˌher\ *noun* [modification of obsolete Italian *mocaiarro*, from Arabic *mukhayyar*, literally, choice] (1619)
: a fabric or yarn made wholly or in part of the long silky hair of the Angora goat; *also* : this hair
**Mo·ham·med·an** *variant of* MUHAMMADAN
**Mo·hawk** \'mō-ˌhok\ *noun, plural* **Mohawk** *or* **Mohawks** [of Algonquian origin; akin to Narraganset *or* Massachuset *Mohowawog* Mohawk, literally, cannibal] (1634)
**1** : a member of an American Indian people of the Mohawk River valley, New York
**2** : the Iroquoian language of the Mohawk people
**3** : a hairstyle with a narrow center strip of up-right hair and the sides shaved ◆
**Mo·he·gan** \mō-'hē-gən, mə-\ *or* **Mo·hi·can** \-'hē-kən\ *noun, plural* **Mohegan** *or* **Mohe-gans** *or* **Mohican** *or* **Mohicans** (1660)
: a member of an American Indian people of southeastern Connecticut
**Mo·hi·can** \mō-'hē-kən, mə-\ *variant of* MAHI-CAN
**Mo·ho** \'mō-ˌhō\ *noun* [short for *Mohorovicic discontinuity*, from Andrija *Mohorovičić* (died 1936) Yugoslavian geologist] (1952)
: the boundary layer between the earth's crust and mantle whose depth varies from about 3

miles (5 kilometers) beneath the ocean floor to about 25 miles (40 kilometers) beneath the continents
**Mo·hock** \'mō-ˌhäk\ *noun* [alteration of *Mohawk*] (circa 1712)
: one of a gang of aristocratic ruffians who assaulted and otherwise maltreated people in London streets in the early 18th century
— **Mo·hock·ism** \-ˌhä-ˌki-zəm\ *noun*
**Mo·ho·ro·vi·cic discontinuity** \ˌmō-hə-'rō-və-ˌchich-\ *noun* (1936)
: MOHO
**Mohs' scale** \'mōz-, 'mōs-, 'mō-səz-\ *noun* [Friedrich *Mohs* (died 1839) German mineralogist] (1879)
: a scale of hardness for minerals that ranges from a value of 1 for talc to 10 for diamond
**mo·hur** \'mō-(ə)r, mə-'hùr\ *noun* [Hindi *muhr* gold coin, seal, from Persian, from Middle Persian; akin to Sanskrit *mudrā* seal] (1690)
: a former gold coin of India and Persia equal to 15 rupees
**moi·e·ty** \'mòi-ə-tē\ *noun, plural* **-ties** [Middle English *moite*, from Middle French *moité*, from Late Latin *medietat-, medietas*, from Latin *medius* middle — more at MID] (15th century)
**1 a** : one of two equal parts : HALF **b** : one of two approximately equal parts
**2** : one of the portions into which something is divided : COMPONENT, PART
**3** : one of two basic complementary tribal subdivisions
**¹moil** \'mòi(ə)l\ *verb* [Middle English *moillen*, from Middle French *moillier*, from (assumed) Vulgar Latin *molliare*, from Latin *mollis* soft — more at MOLLIFY] (15th century)
*transitive verb*
*chiefly dialect* : to make wet or dirty
*intransitive verb*
**1** : to work hard : DRUDGE
**2** : to be in continuous agitation : CHURN, SWIRL
— **moil·er** *noun*
**²moil** *noun* (1612)
**1** : hard work : DRUDGERY
**2** : CONFUSION, TURMOIL
**moil·ing** \'mòi-liŋ\ *adjective* (1603)
**1 a** : requiring hard work **b** : INDUSTRIOUS ⟨*moiling* workers⟩
**2** : violently agitated : TURBULENT
— **moil·ing·ly** \-lē\ *adverb*
**Moi·rai** \'mòi-ˌrī\ *noun plural* [Greek, from plural of *moira* lot, fate; akin to Greek *meros* part — more at MERIT]
: FATE 4
**moire** \'mòi-(ə)r, 'mòr, 'mwär\ *noun* [French, from English *mohair*] (1660)
*archaic* : a watered mohair
**moi·ré** \mò-'rā, mwä-\ *or* **moire** \*same or* 'mòi-(ə)r, 'mòr, 'mwär\ *noun* [French *moiré*, from *moiré* like moire, from *moire*] (1818)
**1 a** : an irregular wavy finish on a fabric **b** : a ripple pattern on a stamp
**2** : a fabric having a wavy watered appearance
**3** : an independent usually shimmering pattern seen when two geometrically regular patterns (as two sets of parallel lines or two halftone screens) are superimposed especially at an acute angle
— **moiré** *or* **moire** *adjective*
**moist** \'mòist\ *adjective* [Middle English *moiste*, from Middle French, perhaps from (assumed) Vulgar Latin *muscidus*, alteration of Latin *mucidus* slimy, from *mucus* nasal mucus] (14th century)
**1** : slightly or moderately wet : DAMP
**2** : TEARFUL
**3** : characterized by high humidity
*synonym* see WET
— **moist·ly** *adverb*
— **moist·ness** \'mòis(t)-nəs\ *noun*
**moist·en** \'mòi-s°n\ *verb* **moist·ened;** **moist·en·ing** \'mòis-niŋ, 'mòi-s°n-iŋ\ (1580)
*transitive verb*
: to make moist

*intransitive verb*
: to become moist
— **moist·en·er** \'mòis-nər, 'mòi-s°n-ər\ *noun*
**mois·ture** \'mòis-chər, 'mòish-\ *noun* [Middle English, modification of Middle French *mois-tour*, from *moiste*] (14th century)
: liquid diffused or condensed in relatively small quantity
**mois·tur·ise** *British variant of* MOISTURIZE
**mois·tur·ize** \-chə-ˌrīz\ *transitive verb* **-ized;** **-iz·ing** (1945)
: to add moisture to ⟨*moisturize* the air⟩
— **mois·tur·iz·er** *noun*
**mo·jo** \'mō-(ˌ)jō\ *noun, plural* **mojoes** *or* **mojos** [probably of African origin; akin to Fulani *moco'o* medicine man] (1926)
: a magic spell, hex, or charm; *broadly* : magical power
**moke** \'mōk\ *noun* [origin unknown] (1848)
**1** *slang British* : DONKEY
**2** *slang Australian* : ¹NAG
**mol·al** \'mō-ləl\ *adjective* [⁵mole] (1905)
: of, relating to, or containing a mole of solute per 1000 grams of solvent
— **mo·lal·i·ty** \mō-'la-lə-tē\ *noun*
**¹mo·lar** \'mō-lər\ *noun* [Middle English *molares*, plural, from Latin *molaris*, from *molaris* of a mill, from *mola* millstone — more at MILL] (14th century)
: a tooth with a rounded or flattened surface adapted for grinding; *specifically* : one of the cheek teeth in mammals behind the incisors and canines — see TOOTH illustration
**²molar** *adjective* (1626)
**1** : pulverizing by friction : GRINDING
**2** : of, relating to, or located near the molar teeth
**³molar** *adjective* [⁵mole] (1902)
**1** : of or relating to a mole of a substance ⟨the *molar* volume of a gas⟩
**2** : containing one mole of solute in one liter of solution
— **mo·lar·i·ty** \mō-'lar-ə-tē\ *noun*
**mo·las·ses** \mə-'la-səz\ *noun* [modification of Portuguese *melaço*, from Late Latin *mella-ceum* grape juice, from Latin *mell-, mel* honey — more at MELLIFLUOUS] (1582)
**1** : the thick dark to light brown syrup that is separated from raw sugar in sugar manufacture

---

◇ WORD HISTORY

**Mohawk** The Mohawks are the eastern-most of the five Iroquois tribes that inhabited upstate New York in colonial times. These five tribes, joined in the 18th century by the Tuscarora, formed a remarkable confederacy, the League of the Iroquois, that ensured peace among its members; some have alleged that the example of the League influenced the framers of the U.S. Constitution. The English name *Mohawk*, like the names of a number of other Indian peoples, is based not on the Mohawks' own name for themselves, but rather on a designation applied to them by another people, in this case the New England Algonquian tribes who lived to the east of the Mohawks. This Algonquian name, which the colonist Roger Williams recorded from the Narragansetts as *Mohowa-wog*, means literally "man-eater." In part it was probably a literal accusation of cannibalism, and in part a reflection of the terror the Mohawks and other Iroquois inspired in their enemies. The Mohawks' self-designation is a word usually interpreted as "place of the gunflint."

---

**2 :** a syrup made from boiling down sweet vegetable or fruit juice ⟨citrus *molasses*⟩

¹**mold** \'mōld\ *noun* [Middle English, from Old English *molde;* akin to Old High German *molta* soil, Latin *molere* to grind — more at MEAL] (before 12th century)
**1 :** crumbling soft friable earth suited to plant growth **:** SOIL; *especially* **:** soil rich in humus — compare LEAF MOLD
**2** *dialect British* **a :** the surface of the earth **:** GROUND **b :** the earth of the burying ground
**3** *archaic* **:** earth that is the substance of the human body ⟨be merciful great Duke to men of *mold* —Shakespeare⟩

²**mold** *noun* [Middle English, modification of Old French *modle,* from Latin *modulus,* diminutive of *modus* measure — more at METE] (13th century)
**1 :** distinctive nature or character **:** TYPE
**2 :** the frame on or around which an object is constructed
**3 a :** a cavity in which a substance is shaped: as (1) **:** a matrix for casting metal (2) **:** a form in which food is given a decorative shape **b :** a molded object
**4 :** MOLDING
**5 a** *obsolete* **:** an example to be followed **b :** PROTOTYPE **c :** a fixed pattern **:** DESIGN

³**mold** *transitive verb* (14th century)
**1** *archaic* **:** to knead (dough) into a desired consistency or shape
**2 :** to give shape to ⟨the wind *molds* the waves⟩
**3 :** to form in a mold ⟨*mold* candles⟩
**4 :** to determine or influence the quality or nature of ⟨*mold* public opinion⟩
**5 :** to fit the contours of
**6 :** to ornament with molding or carving ⟨*molded* picture frames⟩
— **mold·able** \'mōl-də-bəl\ *adjective*
— **mold·er** *noun*

⁴**mold** *noun* [Middle English *mowlde,* perhaps alteration of *mowle,* from *moulen* to grow moldy, of Scandinavian origin; akin to Old Norse *mygla* to grow moldy] (14th century)
**1 :** a superficial often woolly growth produced especially on damp or decaying organic matter or on living organisms
**2 :** a fungus (as of the order Mucorales) that produces mold

⁵**mold** *intransitive verb* (1530)
**:** to become moldy

**mold·board** \'mōl(d)-,bōrd, -,bord\ *noun* (1508)
**1 :** a curved iron plate attached above a plowshare to lift and turn the soil
**2 :** the flat or curved blade (as of a bulldozer) that pushes material to one side as the machine advances

**mold·er** \'mōl-dər\ *intransitive verb* **mold·ered; mold·er·ing** \-d(ə-)riŋ\ [frequentative of ⁵*mold*] (1531)
**:** to crumble into particles **:** DISINTEGRATE, DECAY

**mold·ing** \'mōl-diŋ\ *noun* (14th century)
**1 a :** the art or occupation of a molder **b :** an object produced by molding
**2 a :** a decorative recessed or relieved surface **b :** a decorative plane or curved strip used for ornamentation or finishing

molding 2a: *1* fillet and fascia, *2* torus, *3* reeding, *4* cavetto, *5* scotia, *6* congé, *7* beak

**moldy** \'mōl-dē\ *adjective* **mold·i·er; -est** (14th century)
**1 :** of, resembling, or covered with a mold-producing fungus
**2 a :** being old and moldering **:** CRUMBLING **b :** ANTIQUATED, FUSTY ⟨*moldy* tradition⟩
— **mold·i·ness** *noun*

¹**mole** \'mōl\ *noun* [Middle English, from Old English *māl;* akin to Old High German *meil* spot] (14th century)
**:** a pigmented spot, mark, or small permanent protuberance on the human body; *especially* **:** NEVUS

²**mole** *noun* [Middle English; akin to Middle Low German *mol*] (14th century)
**1 :** any of numerous burrowing insectivores (especially family Talpidae) with tiny eyes, concealed ears, and soft fur
**2 :** one who works in the dark
**3 :** a machine for tunneling
**4 :** a spy (as a double agent) who establishes a cover long before beginning espionage

³**mole** *noun* [Middle English, from Latin *mola* mole, literally, mill, millstone — more at MILL] (15th century)
**:** an abnormal mass in the uterus especially when containing fetal tissues

⁴**mole** *noun* [Middle French, from Old Italian *molo,* from Late Greek *mōlos,* from Latin *moles,* literally, mass, exertion; akin to Greek *mōlos* exertion] (circa 1548)
**1 :** a massive work formed of masonry and large stones or earth laid in the sea as a pier or breakwater
**2 :** the harbor formed by a mole

⁵**mole** *also* **mol** \'mōl\ *noun* [German *Mol,* short for *Molekulargewicht* molecular weight, from *molekular* molecular + *Gewicht* weight] (1902)
**:** the base unit of amount of pure substance in the International System of Units that contains the same number of elementary entities as there are atoms in exactly 12 grams of the isotope carbon 12

⁶**mo·le** \'mō-lā\ *noun* [Mexican Spanish, from Nahuatl *mōlli* sauce] (1927)
**:** a spicy sauce made with chilies and usually chocolate and served with meat

**mo·lec·u·lar** \mə-'le-kyə-lər\ *adjective* (1823)
**1 :** of, relating to, or produced by molecules ⟨*molecular* oxygen⟩
**2 :** of or relating to simple or elementary organization
— **mo·lec·u·lar·ly** \-lē\ *adverb*

**molecular biology** *noun* (1938)
**:** a branch of biology dealing with the ultimate physicochemical organization of living matter and especially with the molecular basis of inheritance and protein synthesis
— **molecular biologist** *noun*

**molecular formula** *noun* (circa 1903)
**:** a chemical formula that is based on both analysis and molecular weight and gives the total number of atoms of each element in a molecule — compare STRUCTURAL FORMULA

**molecular mass** *noun* (1970)
**:** the mass of a molecule that is equal to the sum of the masses of all the atoms contained in the molecule

**molecular orbital** *noun* (1932)
**:** a solution of the Schrödinger equation that describes the probable location of an electron relative to the nuclei in a molecule and so indicates the nature of any bond in which the electron is involved

**molecular sieve** *noun* (1926)
**:** a crystalline substance (as a zeolite) characterized by uniformly sized pores of molecular dimension that can adsorb small molecules and is used especially in separations

**molecular weight** *noun* (1880)
**:** the average mass of a molecule of a compound compared to $1/12$ the mass of carbon 12 and calculated as the sum of the atomic weights of the constituent atoms

**mol·e·cule** \'mä-li-,kyü(ə)l\ *noun* [French *molécule,* from New Latin *molecula,* diminutive of Latin *moles* mass] (1794)
**1 :** the smallest particle of a substance that retains all the properties of the substance and is composed of one or more atoms
**2 :** a tiny bit **:** PARTICLE

**mole·hill** \'mōl-,hil\ *noun* (15th century)
**:** a little mound or ridge of earth pushed up by a mole

**mole·skin** \-,skin\ *noun* (1668)
**1 :** the skin of the mole used as fur
**2 a :** a heavy durable cotton fabric with a short thick velvety nap on one side **b :** a garment made of moleskin — usually used in plural

**mo·lest** \mə-'lest\ *transitive verb* [Middle English, from Middle French *molester,* from Latin *molestare,* from *molestus* burdensome, annoying; akin to Latin *moles* mass] (14th century)
**1 :** to annoy, disturb, or persecute especially with hostile intent or injurious effect
**2 :** to make annoying sexual advances to; *especially* **:** to force physical and usually sexual contact on
— **mo·les·ta·tion** \,mō-,les-'tā-shən, ,mä-, -ləs-\ *noun*
— **mo·lest·er** \mə-'les-tər\ *noun*

**mo·line** \mə-'lēn, -'līn\ *adjective* [(assumed) Anglo-French *moliné,* from Old French *molin* mill, from Late Latin *molinum* — more at MILL] (1562)
*of a heraldic cross* **:** having the end of each arm forked and recurved — see CROSS illustration

**moll** \'mäl, 'mȯl\ *noun* [probably from *Moll,* nickname for *Mary*] (1604)
**1 :** PROSTITUTE
**2 a :** DOLL 2 **b :** a gangster's girlfriend

**mol·li·fy** \'mä-lə-,fī\ *verb* **-fied; -fy·ing** [Middle English *mollifien,* from Middle French *mollifier,* from Late Latin *mollificare,* from Latin *mollis* soft; akin to Greek *amaldynein* to soften, Sanskrit *mṛdu* soft, and probably to Greek *malakos* soft, *amblys* dull, Old English *meltan* to melt] (15th century)
*transitive verb*
**1 :** to soothe in temper or disposition **:** APPEASE ⟨*mollified* the staff with a raise⟩
**2 :** to reduce the rigidity of **:** SOFTEN
**3 :** to reduce in intensity **:** ASSUAGE, TEMPER
*intransitive verb*
*archaic* **:** SOFTEN, RELENT
**synonym** see PACIFY
— **mol·li·fi·ca·tion** \,mä-lə-fə-'kā-shən\ *noun*

**mol·lus·ci·cide** \mə-'ləs-kə-,sīd, -'lə-sə-\ *noun* [New Latin *Mollusca* + English -*i*- + -*cide*] (circa 1947)
**:** an agent for destroying mollusks (as snails)
— **mol·lus·ci·cid·al** \-,ləs-kə-'sī-dᵊl, -,lə-sə-\ *adjective*

**mol·lusk** *or* **mol·lusc** \'mä-ləsk\ *noun* [French *mollusque,* from New Latin *Mollusca,* from Latin, neuter plural of *molluscus* thinshelled (of a nut), from *mollis*] (1783)
**:** any of a large phylum (Mollusca) of invertebrate animals (as snails, clams, or squids) with a soft unsegmented body usually enclosed in a calcareous shell; *broadly* **:** SHELLFISH
— **mol·lus·can** *also* **mol·lus·kan** \mə-'ləs-kən, mä-\ *adjective*

**mol·ly** *also* **mol·lie** \'mä-lē\ *noun, plural* **mollies** [by shortening from New Latin *Mollienisia,* former genus name, from Comte François N. *Mollien* (died 1850) French statesman] (circa 1933)
**:** any of several brightly colored live-bearers (genus *Poecilia* of the family Poeciliidae) highly valued as aquarium fishes

¹**mol·ly·cod·dle** \'mä-lē-,kä-dᵊl\ *noun* [*Molly,* nickname for *Mary*] (1833)
**:** a pampered or effeminate man or boy

²**mollycoddle** *transitive verb* **-cod·dled; -cod·dling** \-,käd-liŋ, -,kä-dᵊl-iŋ\ (1864)
**:** to surround with an excessive or absurd degree of indulgence and attention
**synonym** see INDULGE
— **mol·ly·cod·dler** \-,käd-lər, -,kä-dᵊl-ər\ *noun*

**Mo·loch** \'mä-lək, 'mō-,läk\ *noun* [Late Latin, from Greek, from Hebrew *Mōlekh*]

: a Semitic god to whom children were sacrificed

**Mo·lo·tov cocktail** \'mä-lə-ˌtȯf-, 'mȯ-, 'mō-, -ˌtȯv-\ *noun* [Vyacheslav M. *Molotov*] (1939)
: a crude bomb made of a bottle filled with a flammable liquid (as gasoline) and usually fitted with a wick (as a saturated rag) that is ignited just before the bottle is hurled

¹**molt** \'mōlt\ *verb* [alteration of Middle English *mouten,* from Old English *-mūtian* to change, from Latin *mutare* — more at MUTABLE] (1591)
*intransitive verb*
: to shed hair, feathers, shell, horns, or an outer layer periodically
*transitive verb*
: to cast off (an outer covering) periodically; *specifically* : to throw off (the old cuticle) — used of arthropods
— **molt·er** *noun*

²**molt** *noun* (1815)
: the act or process of molting; *specifically* : ECDYSIS

**mol·ten** \'mōl-tᵊn\ *adjective* [Middle English, from past participle of *melten* to melt] (14th century)
**1** *obsolete* : made by melting and casting
**2** : fused or liquefied by heat : MELTED ⟨*molten* lava⟩
**3** : having warmth or brilliance : GLOWING ⟨the *molten* sunlight of warm skies —T. B. Costain⟩

**mol·to** \'mōl-(ˌ)tō, 'mȯl-\ *adverb* [Italian, from Latin *multum,* from neuter of *multus* much] (circa 1801)
: MUCH, VERY — used in music directions ⟨*molto* vivace⟩

**mo·ly** \'mō-lē\ *noun* [Latin, from Greek *mōly*]
: a mythical herb with a black root, white blossoms, and magical powers

**mo·lyb·date** \mə-'lib-ˌdāt\ *noun* (1794)
: a salt of molybdenum containing the group $MoO_4$ or $Mo_2O_7$

**mo·lyb·de·nite** \mə-'lib-də-ˌnīt\ *noun* [New Latin *molybdena*] (1796)
: a blue usually foliated mineral consisting of molybdenum disulfide that is a source of molybdenum

**mo·lyb·de·num** \-nəm\ *noun* [New Latin, from *molybdena,* a lead ore, molybdenite, molybdenum, from Latin *molybdaena* galena, from Greek *molybdaina,* from *molybdos* lead] (1816)
: a metallic element that resembles chromium and tungsten in many properties, is used especially in strengthening and hardening steel, and is a trace element in plant and animal metabolism — see ELEMENT table

**molybdenum disulfide** *noun* (circa 1931)
: a compound $MoS_2$ used especially as a lubricant in grease

**mom** \'mäm, 'məm\ *noun* [short for *momma*] (circa 1894)
: MOTHER

**mom–and–pop** \'mäm-ən(d)-'päp\ *adjective* (1951)
: being a small owner-operated business

**mome** \'mōm\ *noun* [origin unknown] (1553)
*archaic* : BLOCKHEAD, FOOL

**mo·ment** \'mō-mənt\ *noun* [Middle English, from Middle French, from Latin *momentum* movement, particle sufficient to turn the scales, moment, from *movēre* to move] (14th century)
**1 a** : a minute portion or point of time : INSTANT **b** : a comparatively brief period of time
**2 a** : present time ⟨at the *moment* she is working on a novel⟩ **b** : a time of excellence or conspicuousness ⟨he has his *moments*⟩
**3** : importance in influence or effect ⟨a matter of great *moment*⟩
**4** *obsolete* : a cause or motive of action
**5** : a stage in historical or logical development

**6 a** : tendency or measure of tendency to produce motion especially about a point or axis **b** : the product of quantity (as a force) and the distance to a particular axis or point
**7 a** : the mean of the *n*th powers of the deviations of the observed values in a set of statistical data from a fixed value **b** : the expected value of a power of the deviation of a random variable from a fixed value
*synonym* see IMPORTANCE

**mo·men·tar·i·ly** \ˌmō-mən-'ter-ə-lē\ *adverb* (circa 1666)
**1** : for a moment
**2** *archaic* : INSTANTLY
**3** : at any moment : in a moment ■

**mo·men·tary** \'mō-mən-ˌter-ē\ *adjective* (15th century)
**1 a** : continuing only a moment : FLEETING **b** : having a very brief life
**2** : operative or recurring at every moment
*synonym* see TRANSIENT
— **mo·men·tar·i·ness** *noun*

**mo·ment·ly** \'mō-mənt-lē\ *adverb* (1676)
**1** : from moment to moment
**2** : at any moment
**3** : for a moment

*usage* see MOMENTARILY

**mo·men·to** *variant of* MEMENTO
*usage* see MEMENTO

**moment of inertia** (1830)
: a measure of the resistance of a body to angular acceleration about a given axis that is equal to the sum of the products of each element of mass in the body and the square of the element's distance from the axis

**moment of truth** (1932)
**1** : the final sword thrust in a bullfight
**2** : a moment of crisis on whose outcome much or everything depends

**mo·men·tous** \mō-'men-təs, mə-\ *adjective* (1652)
: IMPORTANT, CONSEQUENTIAL
— **mo·men·tous·ly** *adverb*
— **mo·men·tous·ness** *noun*

**mo·men·tum** \mō-'men-təm, mə-\ *noun, plural* **mo·men·ta** \-'men-tə\ *or* **momentums** [New Latin, from Latin, movement] (1610)
**1** : a property of a moving body that the body has by virtue of its mass and motion and that is equal to the product of the body's mass and velocity; *broadly* : a property of a moving body that determines the length of time required to bring it to rest when under the action of a constant force or moment
**2** : strength or force gained by motion or through the development of events : IMPETUS ⟨the campaign *momentum*⟩

**mom·ma** \'mä-mə, 'mə-mə\ *variant of* MAMA

**mom·my** \'mä-mē, 'mə-mə\ *noun, plural* **mom·mies** [alteration of *mammy*] (1899)
: MOTHER

**mommy track** *noun* (1989)
: a career path that allows a mother flexible or reduced work hours but tends to slow or block advancement

**Mo·mus** \'mō-məs\ *noun* [Latin, from Greek *Mōmos*]
: the Greek god of censure and mockery

**mon** \'män\ *dialect chiefly British variant of* MAN

**Mon** \'mōn\ *noun, plural* **Mon** *or* **Mons** (1798)
**1** : a member of the dominant native people of Pegu division, Myanmar (Burma)
**2** : the Mon-Khmer language of the Mon people

**mon-** *or* **mono-** *combining form* [Middle English, from Middle French & Latin; Middle French, from Latin, from Greek, from *monos* alone, single — more at MONK]
**1** : one : single : alone ⟨*mono*plane⟩ ⟨*mono*drama⟩
**2 a** : containing one (usually specified) atom, radical, or group ⟨*mono*hydroxy⟩ **b** : monomolecular ⟨*mono*layer⟩

**mon·a·chal** \'mä-ni-kəl\ *adjective* [Middle French or Late Latin; Middle French, from Late Latin *monachalis,* from *monachus* monk — more at MONK] (1587)
: MONASTIC
— **mon·a·chism** \'mä-nə-ˌki-zəm\ *noun*

**mo·nad** \'mō-ˌnad\ *noun* [Late Latin *monad-, monas,* from Greek, from *monos*] (1615)
**1 a** : UNIT, ONE **b** : ATOM **1 c** : an elementary individual substance which reflects the order of the world and from which material properties are derived
**2** : a flagellated protozoan (as of the genus *Monas*)
— **mo·nad·ic** \mō-'na-dik, mə-\ *adjective*
— **mo·nad·ism** \'mō-ˌna-ˌdi-zəm\ *noun*

**mon·adel·phous** \ˌmä-nə-'del-fəs\ *adjective* (1806)
*of stamens* : united by the filaments into one group usually forming a tube around the gynoecium

**mo·nad·nock** \mə-'nad-ˌnäk\ *noun* [Mount *Monadnock,* N.H.] (1893)
: INSELBERG

**mon·an·dry** \'mä-ˌnan-drē\ *noun, plural* **-dries** [*mon-* + *-andry* (as in *polyandry*)] (1855)
: a marriage form or custom in which a woman has only one husband at a time

**mon·arch** \'mä-nərk, -ˌnärk\ *noun* [Late Latin *monarcha,* from Greek *monarchos,* from *mon-* + *-archos* -arch] (15th century)
**1** : a person who reigns over a kingdom or empire: as **a** : a sovereign ruler **b** : a constitutional king or queen
**2** : one that holds preeminent position or power
**3** : MONARCH BUTTERFLY
— **mo·nar·chal** \mə-'när-kəl, mä-\ *or* **mo·nar·chi·al** \-kē-əl\ *adjective*

---

---

**monarch butterfly** *noun* (1890)
: a large migratory American butterfly (*Danaus plexippus*) that has orange-brown wings with black veins and borders and a larva that feeds on milkweed

monarch butterfly

**Mo·nar·chi·an** \mə-'när-kē-ən, mä-\ *noun* (1765)
: an adherent of one of two anti-Trinitarian groups of the 2d and 3d centuries A.D. teaching that God is one person as well as one being
— **Mo·nar·chi·an·ism** \-kē-ə-ˌni-zəm\ *noun*

**mo·nar·chi·cal** \mə-'när-ki-kəl, mä-\ *also* **mo·nar·chic** \-kik\ *adjective* (1576)
: of, relating to, suggestive of, or characteristic of a monarch or monarchy
— **mo·nar·chi·cal·ly** \-ki-k(ə-)lē\ *adverb*

**mon·ar·chism** \'mä-nər-ˌki-zəm, -ˌnär-\ *noun* (1838)
: monarchical government or principles
— **mon·ar·chist** \-kist\ *noun or adjective*

**mon·ar·chy** \'mä-nər-kē *also* -ˌnär-\ *noun, plural* **-chies** (14th century)
**1 :** undivided rule or absolute sovereignty by a single person
**2 :** a nation or state having a monarchical government
**3 :** a government having an hereditary chief of state with life tenure and powers varying from nominal to absolute

**mo·nar·da** \mə-'när-də\ *noun* [New Latin, from Nicolás *Monardes* (died 1588) Spanish botanist] (1712)
: any of a genus (*Monarda*) of coarse North American mints with a tubular many-nerved calyx and whorls of showy flowers

**mon·as·tery** \'mä-nə-ˌster-ē\ *noun, plural* **-ter·ies** [Middle English *monasterie*, from Late Latin *monasterium*, from Late Greek *monastērion*, from Greek, hermit's cell, from *monazein* to live alone, from *monos* single — more at MONK] (15th century)
: a house for persons under religious vows; *especially* : an establishment for monks

**mo·nas·tic** \mə-'nas-tik\ *adjective* (circa 1563)
**1 :** of or relating to monasteries or to monks or nuns
**2 :** resembling (as in seclusion or ascetic simplicity) life in a monastery
— **monastic** *noun*
— **mo·nas·ti·cal·ly** \-ti-k(ə-)lē\ *adverb*
— **mo·nas·ti·cism** \-tə-ˌsi-zəm\ *noun*

**mon·atom·ic** \ˌmä-nə-'tä-mik\ *adjective* (1848)
: consisting of one atom; *especially* : having but one atom in the molecule

**mon·au·ral** \(ˌ)mä-'nȯr-əl\ *adjective* (1931)
: MONOPHONIC 2
— **mon·au·ral·ly** \-ə-lē\ *adverb*

**mon·a·zite** \'mä-nə-ˌzīt\ *noun* [German *Monazit*, from Greek *monazein*] (1836)
: a mineral that is a yellow, red, or brown phosphate of cerium and other rare earth elements and thorium and is found often in sand and gravel deposits

**Mon·day** \'mən-dē, -(ˌ)dā\ *noun* [Middle English, from Old English *mōnandæg;* akin to Old High German *mānatag* Monday; akin to Old English *mōna* moon and to Old English *dæg* day] (before 12th century)
: the second day of the week
— **Mon·days** \-dēz\ *adverb*

**Monday–morning quarterback** *noun* [from a fan's usually critical rehashing of the weekend football game strategy] (1941)
: one who second-guesses

— **Monday–morning quarterbacking** *noun*

**mon·e·cious** *variant of* MONOECIOUS

**mo·ner·an** \mō-'nir-ən, mə-\ *noun* [New Latin *Monera*, kingdom comprising prokaryotes, ultimately from Greek *monērēs* single] (1869)
: PROKARYOTE
— **moneran** *adjective*

**M1 rifle** \'em-'wən-\ *noun* (1938)
: a .30 caliber gas-operated clip-fed semiautomatic rifle used by U.S. troops in World War II

**mon·es·trous** \(ˌ)mä-'nes-trəs\ *adjective* (1900)
: experiencing estrus once each year or breeding season

**mon·e·tar·ism** \'mä-nə-tə-ˌri-zəm *also* 'mən-\ *noun* (1969)
: a theory in economics that stable economic growth can be assured only by control of the rate of increase of the money supply to match the capacity for growth of real productivity
— **mon·e·tar·ist** \-rist\ *noun or adjective*

**mon·e·tary** \'mä-nə-ˌter-ē *also* 'mə-\ *adjective* [Late Latin *monetarius* of a mint, of money, from Latin *moneta*] (circa 1812)
: of or relating to money or to the mechanisms by which it is supplied to and circulates in the economy
— **mon·e·tar·i·ly** \ˌmä-nə-'ter-ə-lē *also* ˌmə-\ *adverb*

**monetary aggregate** *noun* (1979)
: one of the formal categories of money (as cash and demand deposits or bank credits) in a national economy that is used as a measure in predictions of economic growth

**monetary unit** *noun* (circa 1864)
: the standard unit of value of a currency

**mon·e·tize** \'mä-nə-ˌtīz *also* 'mə-\ *transitive verb* **-tized; -tiz·ing** [Latin *moneta*] (circa 1879)
**1 :** to coin into money; *also* : to establish as legal tender
**2 :** to purchase (public or private debt) and thereby free for other uses moneys that would have been devoted to debt service
— **mon·e·ti·za·tion** \ˌmä-nə-tə-'zā-shən *also* ˌmə-\ *noun*

**¹mon·ey** \'mə-nē\ *noun, plural* **moneys** *or* **mon·ies** \'mə-nēz\ *often attributive* [Middle English *moneye,* from Middle French *moneie,* from Latin *moneta* mint, money — more at MINT] (14th century)
**1 :** something generally accepted as a medium of exchange, a measure of value, or a means of payment: as **a :** officially coined or stamped metal currency **b :** MONEY OF ACCOUNT **c :** PAPER MONEY
**2 a :** wealth reckoned in terms of money **b** : an amount of money **c** *plural* : sums of money : FUNDS
**3 :** a form or denomination of coin or paper money
**4 a :** the first, second, and third place winners (as in a horse or dog race) — usually used in the phrases *in the money* or *out of the money* **b** : prize money ⟨his horse took third *money*⟩
**5 a :** persons or interests possessing or controlling great wealth **b** : a position of wealth ⟨born into *money*⟩ ◆
— **for one's money** : according to one's preference or opinion
— **on the money** : exactly right or accurate

**²money** *adjective* (1935)
: involving or reliable in a crucial situation ⟨a *money* player⟩ ⟨a *money* pitch⟩

**mon·ey–back** \-'bak\ *adjective* (1922)
: providing that the consumer is entitled to a refund if the purchased product is unsatisfactory ⟨a *money-back* guarantee⟩

**mon·ey–bags** \'mə-nē-ˌbagz\ *noun plural but singular or plural in construction* (1596)
**1 :** WEALTH
**2 :** a wealthy person

**money changer** *noun* (15th century)
**1 :** one whose business is the exchanging of kinds or denominations of currency
**2 :** a device for holding and dispensing sorted change

**mon·eyed** *also* **mon·ied** \'mə-nēd\ *adjective* (15th century)
**1 :** having money : WEALTHY
**2 :** consisting in or derived from money

**mon·ey·er** \'mə-nē-ər\ *noun* [Middle English, from Old French *monier,* from Late Latin *monetarius* master of a mint, coiner, from *monetarius* of a mint — more at MONETARY] (15th century)
: an authorized coiner of money : MINTER

**mon·ey–grub·ber** \'mə-nē-ˌgrə-bər\ *noun* (1840)
: a person bent on accumulating money
— **mon·ey–grub·bing** \-biŋ\ *adjective or noun*

**mon·ey·lend·er** \-ˌlen-dər\ *noun* (circa 1780)
: one whose business is lending money; *specifically* : PAWNBROKER

**mon·ey·mak·er** \-ˌmā-kər\ *noun* (1834)
**1 :** one that accumulates wealth
**2 :** one that produces profit
— **mon·ey·mak·ing** \-kiŋ\ *adjective or noun*

**mon·ey·man** \-ˌman\ *noun* (circa 1585)
: FINANCIER

**money market** *noun* (1950)
: the trade in short-term negotiable instruments (as certificates of deposit or U.S. Treasury securities)

**money of account** (1691)
: a denominator of value or basis of exchange which is used in keeping accounts and for which there may or may not be an equivalent coin or denomination of paper money

**money order** *noun* (1802)
: an order issued by a post office, bank, or telegraph office for payment of a specified sum of money usually at any branch of the organization

**mon·ey–spin·ner** \'mə-nē-ˌspi-nər\ *noun* (1859)
*chiefly British* : MONEYMAKER
— **mon·ey–spin·ning** \-niŋ\ *adjective or noun, chiefly British*

**mon·ey·wort** \-ˌwərt, -ˌwȯrt\ *noun* (1578)
: a trailing perennial herb (*Lysimachia nummularia*) of the primrose family with rounded opposite leaves and solitary yellow flowers in their axils

**¹mon·ger** \'məŋ-gər, 'mäŋ-\ *noun* [Middle English *mongere,* from Old English *mangere,* from Latin *mango-, mango,* of Greek origin; akin to Greek *manganon* charm, philter] (before 12th century)
**1 :** BROKER, DEALER — usually used in combination ⟨ale*monger*⟩

◇ WORD HISTORY
**money** One of the epithets of the goddess Juno, the wife of Jupiter in ancient Roman myth, was *Moneta.* When the Romans established a mint at the temple of Juno Moneta, this epithet became a generic Latin term for a place where money was made as well as for money itself. The English words *mint* and *money* are both ultimately borrowings from Latin *moneta.* The considerable difference between the two words may be accounted for by the widely different routes by which each came into English. *Mint,* continuing Old English *mynet,* as well as the German word *Münze* "coin" (continuing Old High German *munizza*), goes back to a prehistoric West Germanic borrowing from Latin *moneta. Money,* on the other hand, was borrowed from medieval French in the Middle English period as *moneye;* Old French *moneie,* in turn, is a Romance descendant of Latin *moneta.*

# MONEY

| NAME | SYMBOL | SUBDIVISION | COUNTRY | NAME | SYMBOL | SUBDIVISION | COUNTRY |
|---|---|---|---|---|---|---|---|
| afghani | Af | 100 puls | Afghanistan | lari | | 100 tetri | Republic of Georgia |
| baht or tical | B | 100 satang | Thailand | lats (pl lati or latu) | | 100 santimi or santimu (sing santims) | Latvia |
| balboa[1] | | 100 centesimos | Panama | | | | |
| birr | | 100 cents | Ethiopia | lek | | 100 qindarka | Albania |
| bolivar | B | 100 centimos | Venezuela | lempira | L | 100 centavos | Honduras |
| boliviano | $b | 100 centavos | Bolivia | leone | Le | 100 cents | Sierra Leone |
| cedi | ¢ | 100 pesewas | Ghana | leu | | 100 bani (sing ban) | Moldova |
| colón | C or ¢ | 100 centimos | Costa Rica | leu | | 100 bani (sing ban) | Romania |
| colón | ¢ | 100 centavos | El Salvador | lev | | 100 stotinki | Bulgaria |
| córdoba | C$ | 100 centavos | Nicaragua | lilangeni (pl emalangeni) | E | 100 cents | Swaziland |
| dalasi | | 100 bututs | Gambia | | | | |
| denar | | 100 deni[2] | Republic of Macedonia | lira | L or Lit | 100 centesimi[2] | Italy |
| deutsche mark | DM | 100 pfennig | Germany | lira or pound | £ or £M or Lm | 100 cents | Malta |
| dinar | DA | 100 centimes | Algeria | lira | TL | 100 kurus | Turkey |
| dinar | BD | 1000 fils | Bahrain | litas | | 100 centai or centu (sing centas) | Lithuania |
| dinar | ID | 1000 fils | Iraq | | | | |
| dinar | JD | 1000 fils | Jordan | livre—see POUND, below | | | |
| dinar | KD | 1000 fils | Kuwait | loti (pl maloti) | | 100 licente or lisente (sing sente) | Lesotho |
| dinar | LD | 1000 dirhams | Libya | | | | |
| dinar | | | Sudan | manat | | 100 gopik | Azerbaijan |
| dinar | D | 1000 millimes | Tunisia | mark—see DEUTSCHE MARK, above | | | |
| dinar | | 100 paras | Yugoslavia | markka | Fmk | 100 pennia | Finland |
| dirham | DH | 100 centimes | Morocco | metical | | 100 centavos | Mozambique |
| dirham | | 100 fils | United Arab Emirates | naira | ₦ | 100 kobo | Nigeria |
| dobra | Db | 100 centimos | São Tomé and Príncipe | nakfa | nfa | 100 cents | Eritrea |
| dollar | EC$[3] or $ | 100 cents | Antigua and Barbuda, Dominica, Grenada, St. Kitts-Nevis, St. Lucia, St. Vincent and the Grenadines | ngultrum | Nu | 100 chetrums | Bhutan |
| | | | | ouguiya | | 5 khoums | Mauritania |
| | | | | pa'anga | T$ | 100 seniti | Tonga |
| | | | | pataca | | 100 avos | Macao |
| dollar | $A or $ | 100 cents | Australia | peseta | PTA | 100 centimos[2] | Spain |
| dollar | $ or B$ | 100 cents | Bahamas | peso | | 100 centavos | Argentina |
| dollar | $ or Bds$ | 100 cents | Barbados | peso | | 100 centavos | Chile |
| dollar | $ | 100 cents | Belize | peso | | 100 centavos | Colombia |
| dollar | $ | 100 cents | Bermuda | peso | | 100 centavos | Cuba |
| dollar | B$ | 100 sen or cents | Brunei | peso | RD$ | 100 centavos | Dominican Republic |
| dollar | $ | 100 cents | Canada | peso | | 100 centavos | Guinea-Bissau |
| dollar | $ or F$ | 100 cents | Fiji | peso | $ | 100 centavos | Mexico |
| dollar | $ or G$ | 100 cents | Guyana | peso or piso | P | 100 sentimos or centavos | Philippines |
| dollar | $ or HK$ | 100 cents | Hong Kong | peso | $ | 100 centesimos | Uruguay |
| dollar | $ or J$ | 100 cents | Jamaica | pound | £ | 100 cents | Cyprus |
| dollar | L$ | 100 cents | Liberia | pound | £E | 100 piastres | Egypt |
| dollar | N$ | 100 cents | Namibia | pound | £ | 100 pence (sing penny) | Ireland |
| dollar | NZ$ | 100 cents | New Zealand | | | | |
| dollar | $ or S$ | 100 cents | Singapore | pound or livre | L | 100 piastres | Lebanon |
| dollar or yuan | NT$ | 100 cents | Taiwan | pound | | 100 piastres | Syria |
| dollar | $ or TT$ | 100 cents | Trinidad and Tobago | pound | £ | 100 pence (sing penny) | United Kingdom |
| dollar | $ | 100 cents | United States | | | | |
| dollar | $ or Z$ | 100 cents | Zimbabwe | pound—see LIRA, above | | | |
| dollar—see RINGGIT, below | | | | pula | P | 100 thebe | Botswana |
| dong | | 100 xu | Vietnam | quetzal | Q | 100 centavos | Guatemala |
| drachma | Dr | 100 lepta | Greece | rand | R | 100 cents | South Africa |
| dram | | 100 luma | Armenia | real | | 100 centavos | Brazil |
| escudo | | 100 centavos | Cape Verde | rial | R or Rl | 100 dinars | Iran |
| escudo | $ or Esc | 100 centavos | Portugal | rial | RO | 1000 baiza | Oman |
| florin—see GULDEN, below | | | | rial also riyal | YR or R | 100 fils | Yemen |
| forint | Ft | 100 filler | Hungary | rial—see RIYAL, below | | | |
| franc | BF or F or FR | 100 centimes | Belgium | riel | | 100 sen | Cambodia |
| franc | Fr or FR or F or CFA[4] | 100 centimes | Benin, Burkina Faso, Cameroon, Central African Republic, Chad, Republic of the Congo, Equatorial Guinea, Gabon, Ivory Coast, Mali, Niger, Senegal, Togo | ringgit or dollar | $ or M$ | 100 sen | Malaysia |
| | | | | riyal | QR | 100 dirhams | Qatar |
| | | | | riyal also rial | | 100 halala | Saudi Arabia |
| | | | | riyal—see RIAL, above | | | |
| | | | | ruble | | 100 kopecks | Russia |
| | | | | ruble | | 100 tanga | Tajikistan |
| | | | | rufiyaa | Rf | 100 laari | Maldives |
| franc | F or FBu | 100 centimes | Burundi | rupee | Re (pl Rs) | 100 paise | India |
| franc | Fr or F | 100 centimes | Djibouti | rupee | Re (pl Rs) | 100 cents | Mauritius |
| franc | Fr or F | 100 centimes | France | rupee | Re (pl Rs) | 100 paisa | Nepal |
| franc | GF | 100 centimes | Guinea | rupee | Re (pl Rs) | 100 paisa | Pakistan |
| franc | F or Flux | 100 centimes | Luxembourg | rupee | SR | 100 cents | Seychelles |
| franc | FMG | 100 centimes | Madagascar | rupee | Re (pl Rs) | 100 cents | Sri Lanka |
| franc | FR or RF | 100 centimes[2] | Rwanda | rupiah | Rp | 100 sen | Indonesia |
| franc | Fr or FR | 100 centimes or rappen | Switzerland | schilling | S or Sch | 100 groschen | Austria |
| | | | | shekel or sheqel | IS | 100 agorot | Israel |
| gourde | G | 100 centimes | Haiti | shilling | S or KSh | 100 cents | Kenya |
| guarani | G or | 100 centimos | Paraguay | shilling | | 100 cents | Somalia |
| gulden or guilder or florin | f or Fl or G | 100 cents | Netherlands | shilling | TSh | 100 cents | Tanzania |
| | | | | shilling | | 100 cents | Uganda |
| gulden or guilder or florin | Sf | 100 cents | Suriname | sol | | 100 centimos | Peru |
| | | | | som | | 100 tyiyn | Kyrgyzstan |
| hryvnia | | 100 kopiykas | Ukraine | sucre[1] | | 100 centavos | Ecuador |
| kina | K | 100 toea | Papua New Guinea | taka | Tk | 100 paisa or poisha | Bangladesh |
| kip | K | 100 at | Laos | tala | $ | 100 sene | Samoa |
| koruna | Kčs | 100 haleru | Czech Republic | tenge | | 100 tyin | Kazakstan |
| koruna | Kčs | 100 haleru | Slovakia | tical—see BAHT, above | | | |
| krona | KR | 100 aurar (sing eyrir) | Iceland | tolar | | 100 stotinov | Slovenia |
| | | | | tugrik | | 100 mongo | Mongolia |
| krona | SKr or KR | 100 ore | Sweden | vatu | | | Vanuatu |
| krone | DKr | 100 ore | Denmark | won | | 100 chon | North Korea |
| krone | KR or Nkr | 100 ore | Norway | won | | 100 chon | South Korea |
| kroon | EEK | 100 senti | Estonia | yen | ¥ | 100 sen[2] | Japan |
| kuna | | 100 lipa | Croatia | yuan | | 100 fen | China (mainland) |
| kwacha | K | 100 tambala | Malawi | yuan—see DOLLAR, above | | | |
| kwacha | K | 100 ngwee | Zambia | zaire | Z | 100 makuta (sing likuta) | Democratic Republic of the Congo |
| kwanza | | 100 lwei | Angola | | | | |
| kyat | K | 100 pyas | Myanmar | zloty | Zl | 100 groszy | Poland |

[1] A monetary unit in name only, replaced by the U.S. dollar in 2000.
[2] Now a subdivision in name only.
[3] Dollars issued by the Eastern Caribbean Central Bank, established to promote economic cooperation among the member nations.
[4] Francs issued by the African Financial Community (Communauté Financière Africaine), established to promote economic cooperation among member nations.

**2 :** a person who attempts to stir up or spread something that is usually petty or discreditable — usually used in combination ⟨war*monger*⟩

**²monger** *transitive verb* **mon·gered; mon·ger·ing** \-g(ə-)riŋ\ (circa 1864)
**:** PEDDLE

**mon·go** \'mäŋ-(ˌ)gō\ *noun, plural* **mongo** [Mongolian *möngö*] (1935)
— see *tugrik* at MONEY table

**Mon·gol** \'mäŋ-gəl; 'män-ˌgōl, 'mäŋ-\ *noun* [Mongolian *mongɣol*] (1698)
**1 :** a member of any of a group of traditionally pastoral peoples of Mongolia
**2 :** MONGOLIAN 1
**3 :** a person of Mongoloid racial stock
**4** *often not capitalized* **:** one affected with Down's syndrome
— **Mongol** *adjective*

**¹Mon·go·lian** \män-'gōl-yən, mäŋ-, -'gō-lē-ən\ *adjective* (1706)
**1 :** of, relating to, or constituting Mongolia, the Mongolian People's Republic, the Mongols, or Mongolian
**2 :** MONGOLOID 2

**²Mongolian** *noun* (1846)
**1 a :** the language of the Mongol people **b :** a family of Altaic languages that includes the languages of the Mongols and the Kalmucks
**2 a :** MONGOL 1 **b :** a person of Mongoloid racial stock **c :** a native or inhabitant of Mongolia

**Mongolian gerbil** *noun* (1948)
**:** a gerbil (*Meriones unguiculatus*) of Mongolia and northern China that has an external resemblance to a rat, has a high capacity for temperature regulation, and is used as an experimental laboratory animal

**Mon·gol·ic** \män-'gä-lik, mäŋ-\ *adjective* (1834)
**:** MONGOLOID 1

**mon·gol·ism** \'mäŋ-gə-ˌli-zəm\ *noun* (1900)
**:** DOWN'S SYNDROME

**Mon·gol·oid** \'mäŋ-gə-ˌlȯid\ *adjective* (1868)
**1 :** of, constituting, or characteristic of a major racial stock native to Asia as classified according to physical features (as the presence of an epicanthic fold) that includes peoples of northern and eastern Asia, Malaysians, Eskimos, and often American Indians
**2** *often not capitalized* **:** of, relating to, or affected with Down's syndrome
— **Mongoloid** *noun*

**mon·goose** \'män-ˌgüs, 'mäŋ-\ *noun, plural* **mon·goos·es** *also* **mon·geese** \-ˌgēs\ [Hindi & Marathi *māgūs*, from Prakrit *maṁgūsa*] (1698)
**:** any of the viverrid mammals that comprise two subfamilies (Herpestinae and Galidiinae) often grouped in a separate family (Herpestidae), that include agile ferret-

mongoose

sized mammals sometimes with bands or stripes, and that feed on small animals and fruits

**mon·grel** \'mäŋ-grəl, 'məŋ-\ *noun* [Middle English, probably from *mong* mixture, short for *ymong*, from Old English *gemong* crowd — more at AMONG] (15th century)
**1 :** an individual resulting from the interbreeding of diverse breeds or strains; *especially* **:** one of unknown ancestry
**2 :** a cross between types of persons or things
— **mongrel** *adjective*
— **mon·grel·i·za·tion** \ˌmäŋ-grə-lə-'zā-shən, ˌməŋ-\ *noun*
— **mon·grel·ize** \'mäŋ-grə-ˌlīz, 'məŋ-\ *transitive verb*

**monies** *plural of* MONEY

**mon·i·ker** *also* **mon·ick·er** \'mä-ni-kər\ *noun* [probably from Shelta (language of Irish itinerants) *munnik*, modification of Irish *ainm*] (1851)
**:** NAME, NICKNAME

**mo·ni·li·a·sis** \ˌmō-nə-'lī-ə-səs, ˌmä-\ *noun, plural* **-a·ses** \-ˌsēz\ [New Latin, from *Monilia*, genus of fungi, from Latin *monile* necklace] (1920)
**:** CANDIDIASIS

**mo·nil·i·form** \mə-'ni-lə-ˌfȯrm\ *adjective* [Latin *monile* necklace — more at MANE] (circa 1803)
**:** jointed or constricted at regular intervals so as to resemble a string of beads ⟨a *moniliform* root⟩ ⟨*moniliform* insect antennae⟩

**mon·ish** \'mä-nish\ *transitive verb* [Middle English *monesen*, alteration of *monesten*, from Old French *monester*, from (assumed) Vulgar Latin *monestare*, from Latin *monēre* to warn] (14th century)
**:** WARN

**mo·nism** \'mō-ˌni-zəm, 'mä-\ *noun* [German *Monismus*, from *mon-* + *-ismus* -ism] (1862)
**1 a :** a view that there is only one kind of ultimate substance **b :** the view that reality is one unitary organic whole with no independent parts
**2 :** MONOGENESIS
**3 :** a viewpoint or theory that reduces all phenomena to one principle
— **mo·nist** \'mō-nist, 'mä-\ *noun*
— **mo·nis·tic** \mō-'nis-tik, mä-\ *adjective*

**mo·ni·tion** \mō-'ni-shən, mə-\ *noun* [Middle English *monicioun*, from Middle French *monition*, from Latin *monition-, monitio*, from *monēre*] (14th century)
**1 :** WARNING, CAUTION
**2 :** an intimation of danger

**¹mon·i·tor** \'mä-nə-tər\ *noun* [Latin, one that warns, overseer, from *monēre* to warn — more at MIND] (1546)
**1 a :** a student appointed to assist a teacher **b :** one that warns or instructs **c :** one that monitors or is used in monitoring: as (1) **:** a cathode-ray tube used for display (as of television pictures or computer information) (2) **:** a device for observing a biological condition or function ⟨a heart *monitor*⟩
**2 :** any of various large tropical Old World lizards (genus *Varanus* of the family Varanidae) closely related to the iguanas
**3** [*Monitor*, first ship of the type] **a :** a heavily armored warship formerly used in coastal operations having a very low freeboard and one or more revolving gun turrets **b :** a small modern warship with shallow draft for coastal bombardment
**4 :** a raised central portion of a roof having low windows or louvers for providing light and air
— **mon·i·to·ri·al** \ˌmä-nə-'tōr-ē-əl, -'tȯr-\ *adjective*
— **mon·i·tor·ship** \'mä-nə-tər-ˌship\ *noun*

**²monitor** *transitive verb* **mon·i·tored; mon·i·tor·ing** \'mä-nə-t(ə-)riŋ\ (1924)
**:** to watch, keep track of, or check usually for a special purpose

**¹mon·i·to·ry** \'mä-nə-ˌtōr-ē, -ˌtȯr-\ *adjective* [Middle English, from Latin *monitorius*, from *monēre*] (15th century)
**:** giving admonition **:** WARNING

**²monitory** *noun, plural* **-ries** (15th century)
**:** a letter containing an admonition or warning

**¹monk** \'məŋk\ *noun* [Middle English, from Old English *munuc*, from Late Latin *monachus*, from Late Greek *monachos*, from Greek, adjective, single, from *monos* single, alone] (before 12th century)
**:** a man who is a member of a religious order and lives in a monastery; *also* **:** FRIAR

**²monk** *noun* (1843)
**:** MONKEY

**monk·ery** \'məŋ-kə-rē\ *noun, plural* **-er·ies** (1536)
**1 :** monastic life or practice **:** MONASTICISM

**2 :** a monastic house **:** MONASTERY

**¹mon·key** \'məŋ-kē\ *noun, plural* **monkeys** [probably of Low German origin; akin to *Moneke*, name of an ape, probably of Romance origin; akin to Old Spanish *mona* monkey] (circa 1530)
**1 :** a nonhuman primate mammal with the exception usually of the lemurs and tarsiers; *especially* **:** any of the smaller longer-tailed primates as contrasted with the apes
**2 a :** a person resembling a monkey **b :** a ludicrous figure **:** DUPE
**3 :** any of various machines, implements, or vessels; *especially* **:** the falling weight of a pile driver
**4 :** a desperate desire for or addiction to drugs — often used in the phrase *monkey on one's back; broadly* **:** a persistent or annoying encumbrance or problem

**²monkey** *verb* **mon·keyed; mon·key·ing** (1859)
*transitive verb*
**:** MIMIC, MOCK
*intransitive verb*
**1 :** to act in a grotesque or mischievous manner
**2 a :** FOOL, TRIFLE — often used with *around*
**b :** TAMPER — usually used with *with*

**monkey bars** *noun plural* (1955)
**:** a three-dimensional framework of horizontal and vertical bars from which children can hang and swing

**monkey business** *noun* (1883)
**:** SHENANIGAN 2

**monkey jacket** *noun* (1830)
**:** MESS JACKET

**mon·key·pod** \'məŋ-kē-ˌpäd\ *noun* (1888)
**1 :** an ornamental tropical leguminous tree (*Samanea saman* synonym *Pithecolobium saman*) that has bipinnate leaves, globose clusters of flowers with crimson stamens, sweet-pulp pods eaten by cattle, and wood used in carving — called also *rain tree*
**2 :** the wood of a monkeypod

**monkey puzzle** *noun* (1866)
**:** a tall araucaria (*Araucaria araucana*) that is native to Chile and western Argentina but widely grown elsewhere — called also *monkey puzzle tree*

**mon·key·shine** \'məŋ-kē-ˌshīn\ *noun* (circa 1832)
**:** PRANK — usually used in plural

**monkey wrench** *noun* (circa 1858)
**1 :** a wrench with one fixed and one adjustable jaw at right angles to a straight handle
**2 :** something that disrupts ⟨threw a *monkey wrench* into the peace negotiations⟩

**monk·fish** \'məŋk-ˌfish\ *noun* (1666)
**:** either of two goosefishes (*Lophius americanus* of America and *L. piscatorius* of Europe) used for food

**Mon–Khmer** \ˌmōn-kə-'mer\ *noun* (1887)
**:** a language family containing Mon, Khmer, and a number of other languages of southeast Asia

**monk·hood** \'məŋk-ˌhu̇d\ *noun* (before 12th century)
**1 :** the character, condition, or profession of a monk **:** MONASTICISM
**2 :** monks as a class

**monk·ish** \'məŋ-kish\ *adjective* (1546)
**1 :** of, relating to, or resembling a monk; *also* **:** resembling that of a monk
**2 :** inclined to disciplinary self-denial

**monk's cloth** *noun* (circa 1847)
**:** a coarse heavy fabric in basket weave made originally of worsted and used for monk's habits but now chiefly of cotton or linen and used for draperies

**monk seal** *noun* (1841)
**:** any of a genus (*Monachus*) of hair seals of Hawaii, the Mediterranean Sea, and formerly the Caribbean Sea

**monks·hood** \'məŋ(k)s-ˌhu̇d\ *noun* (1578)
**:** any of a genus (*Aconitum*) of usually bluish flowered poisonous herbs of the buttercup

family; *especially* : a poisonous Eurasian herb (*A. napellus*) often cultivated for its showy terminal racemes of white or purplish flowers — compare WOLFSBANE

**¹mono** \'mä-(ˌ)nō\ *noun, plural* **mon·os** [²*mono*] (1959)
: monophonic reproduction

**²mono** *adjective* (1961)
: MONOPHONIC 2

**³mono** *noun* (1962)
: INFECTIOUS MONONUCLEOSIS

**mono-** — see MON-

**mono·ac·id** \ˌmä-nō-'a-səd\ *noun* (1863)
: an acid having only one acid hydrogen atom

**mono·acid·ic** \-ə-'si-dik\ *adjective* (circa 1929)
: able to react with one molecule of a monobasic acid to form a salt or ester — used especially of bases

**mono·amine** \ˌmä-nō-ə-'mēn\ *noun* [International Scientific Vocabulary] (1951)
: an amine $RNH_2$ that has one organic substituent attached to the nitrogen atom; *especially* : one (as serotonin) that is functionally important in neural transmission

**monoamine oxidase** *noun* (1951)
: an enzyme that deaminates monoamines oxidatively and that functions in the nervous system by breaking down monoamine neurotransmitters oxidatively

**mono·am·in·er·gic** \ˌmä-nō-ˌa-mə-'nər-jik\ *adjective* (1966)
: liberating or involving monoamines (as serotonin or norepinephrine) in neural transmission 〈*monoaminergic* neurons〉 〈*monoaminergic* mechanisms〉

**mono·ba·sic** \ˌmä-nə-'bā-sik\ *adjective* [International Scientific Vocabulary] (1842)
*of an acid* : having only one replaceable hydrogen atom

**mono·car·box·yl·ic** \-ˌkär-(ˌ)bäk-'si-lik\ *adjective* (circa 1909)
: containing one carboxyl group 〈acetic acid is a *monocarboxylic* acid〉

**mono·car·pic** \-'kär-pik\ *adjective* [probably from (assumed) New Latin *monocarpicus*, from New Latin *mon-* + *-carpicus* -carpic] (1849)
: bearing fruit but once and then dying

**mono·cha·si·um** \ˌkä-zē-əm, -zhē-\ *noun, plural* **-sia** \-zē-ə, -zhē-\ [New Latin, from *mon-* + *-chasium* (as in *dichasium*)] (circa 1890)
: a cymose inflorescence that produces only one main axis
— **mono·cha·sial** \-zē-əl, -zhē-\ *adjective*

**mono·chord** \'mä-nə-ˌkȯrd\ *noun* [Middle English *monocorde*, from Middle French, from Medieval Latin *monochordum*, from Greek *monochordon*, from *mon-* + *chordē* string — more at YARN] (15th century)
: an instrument of ancient origin for measuring and demonstrating the mathematical relations of musical tones and that consists of a single string stretched over a sound box and a movable bridge set on a graduated scale

**mono·chro·mat** \'mä-nə-krō-ˌmat, ˌmä-nə-'\ *noun* [*mon-* + Greek *chrōmat-, chrōma*] (1902)
: a completely color-blind individual

**mono·chro·mat·ic** \ˌmä-nə-krō-'ma-tik\ *adjective* [Latin *monochromatos*, from Greek *monochrōmatos*, from *mon-* + *chrōmat-, chrōma* color] (1822)
**1 a** : having or consisting of one color or hue
**b** : MONOCHROME 2
**2** : consisting of radiation of a single wavelength or of a very small range of wavelengths
**3** : of, relating to, or exhibiting monochromatism
— **mono·chro·mat·i·cal·ly** \-ti-k(ə-)lē\ *adverb*
— **mono·chro·ma·tic·i·ty** \-ˌkrō-mə-'ti-sə-tē\ *noun*

**mono·chro·ma·tism** \-'krō-mə-ˌti-zəm\ *noun* (circa 1930)

: complete color blindness in which all colors appear as shades of gray

**mono·chro·ma·tor** \ˌmä-nə-'krō-ˌmä-tər\ *noun* [*monochromat*ic + illumin*ator*] (1909)
: a device for isolating a narrow portion of a spectrum

**¹mono·chrome** \'mä-nə-ˌkrōm\ *noun* [Medieval Latin *monochroma*, from Latin, feminine of *monochromos* of one color, from Greek *monochrōmos*, from *mon-* + *-chrōmos* -chrome] (1662)
: a painting, drawing, or photograph in a single hue
— **mono·chro·mic** \ˌmä-nə-'krō-mik\ *adjective*
— **mono·chrom·ist** \'mä-nə-ˌkrō-mist\ *noun*

**²monochrome** *adjective* (1849)
**1** : of, relating to, or made with a single color or hue
**2** : involving or producing visual images in a single color or in varying tones of a single color (as gray) 〈*monochrome* film〉 〈*monochrome* television monitor〉

**mon·o·cle** \'mä-ni-kəl\ *noun* [French, from Late Latin *monoculus* having one eye, from Latin *mon-* + *oculus* eye — more at EYE] (circa 1858)
: an eyeglass for one eye
— **mon·o·cled** \-kəld\ *adjective*

**mono·cline** \'mä-nə-ˌklīn\ *noun* (1879)
: an oblique geologic fold

**mono·clin·ic** \ˌmä-nə-'kli-nik\ *adjective* [International Scientific Vocabulary] (circa 1864)
: having one oblique intersection of the crystallographic axes

**monocle**

**monoclinic system** *noun* (1869)
: a crystal system characterized by three unequal axes with one oblique intersection

**mono·clo·nal** \ˌmä-nə-'klō-nᵊl\ *adjective* (1914)
: produced by, being, or composed of cells derived from a single cell 〈*monoclonal* antibodies〉 〈a *monoclonal* tumor〉
— **monoclonal** *noun*

**mono·coque** \'mä-nə-ˌkōk, -ˌkäk\ *noun* [French, from *mon-* + *coque* shell, probably from Latin *coccum* kermes — more at COCOON] (1913)
**1** : a type of construction (as of a fuselage) in which the outer skin carries all or a major part of the stresses
**2** : a type of vehicle construction (as of an automobile) in which the body is integral with the chassis

**mono·cot** \-ˌkät\ *noun* (1890)
: MONOCOTYLEDON

**mono·cot·y·le·don** \ˌmä-nə-ˌkä-tᵊl-'ē-dᵊn\ *noun* [ultimately from New Latin *mon-* + *cotyledon* cotyledon] (circa 1727)
: any of a class or subclass (Liliopsida or Monocotyledoneae) of chiefly herbaceous seedplants having an embryo with a single cotyledon, usually parallel-veined leaves, and floral organs arranged in cycles of three — compare DICOTYLEDON
— **mono·cot·y·le·don·ous** \-dᵊn-əs\ *adjective*

**mo·noc·ra·cy** \mä-'nä-krə-sē, mə-\ *noun* (1651)
: government by a single person
— **mono·crat** \'mä-nə-ˌkrat\ *noun*
— **mono·crat·ic** \ˌmä-nə-'kra-tik\ *adjective*

**mono·crys·tal** \'mä-nə-ˌkris-tᵊl\ *noun* (1926)
: a single crystal
— **monocrystal** *adjective*
— **mono·crys·tal·line** \ˌmä-nə-'kris-tə-lən *also* -ˌlīn, -ˌlēn\ *adjective*

**¹mon·oc·u·lar** \mä-'nä-kyə-lər, mə-\ *adjective* [Late Latin *monoculus* having one eye] (1640)
**1** : of, involving, or affecting a single eye

**2** : suitable for use with only one eye
— **mon·oc·u·lar·ly** *adverb*

**²monocular** *noun* (1936)
: a monocular device

**mono·cul·ture** \'mä-nə-ˌkəl-chər\ *noun* (1915)
**1** : the cultivation or growth of a single crop or organism especially on agricultural or forest land
**2** : a crop or a population of a single kind of organism grown on land in monoculture
— **mono·cul·tur·al** \ˌmä-nə-'kəlch-rəl, -'kəl-chə-\ *adjective*

**mono·cy·clic** \ˌmä-nə-'sī-klik, -'si-\ *adjective* [International Scientific Vocabulary] (1910)
: containing one ring in the molecular structure

**mono·cyte** \'mä-nə-ˌsīt\ *noun* [International Scientific Vocabulary] (circa 1913)
: a large white blood cell with finely granulated chromatin dispersed throughout the nucleus that is formed in the bone marrow, enters the blood, and migrates into the connective tissue where it differentiates into a macrophage
— **mono·cyt·ic** \ˌmä-nə-'si-tik\ *adjective*

**mono·dis·perse** \ˌmä-nō-dis-'pərs\ *adjective* [*mon-* + *disperse*, adjective, from *disperse*, verb] (1925)
: characterized by particles of uniform size in a dispersed phase

**mon·o·dist** \'mä-nə-dist\ *noun* (1751)
: a writer, singer, or composer of monody

**mono·dra·ma** \'mä-nə-ˌdrä-mə, -ˌdra-\ *noun* (1793)
: a drama acted or designed to be acted by a single person
— **mono·dra·mat·ic** \ˌmä-nə-drə-'ma-tik\ *adjective*

**mon·o·dy** \'mä-nə-dē\ *noun, plural* **-dies** [Medieval Latin *monodia*, from Greek *monōidia*, from *monōidos* singing alone, from *mon-* + *aeidein* to sing — more at ODE] (circa 1623)
**1** : an ode sung by one voice (as in a Greek tragedy)
**2** : an elegy or dirge performed by one person
**3 a** : a monophonic vocal piece **b** : the monophonic style of 17th century opera
— **mo·nod·ic** \mə-'nä-dik\ *or* **mo·nod·i·cal** \-di-kəl\ *adjective*
— **mo·nod·i·cal·ly** \-di-k(ə-)lē\ *adverb*

**mon·oe·cious** \mə-'nē-shəs, mä-\ *adjective* [ultimately from Greek *mon-* + *oikos* house — more at VICINITY] (1753)
**1** : having pistillate and staminate flowers on the same plant
**2** : having male and female sex organs in the same individual : HERMAPHRODITIC

**mon·oe·cism** \-'nē-ˌsi-zəm\ *noun* (1875)
: the condition of being monoecious

**mono·es·ter** \'mä-nō-ˌes-tər\ *noun* (1927)
: an ester (as of a dibasic acid) that contains only one ester group

**mono·fil·a·ment** \ˌmä-nə-'fi-lə-mənt\ *noun* (1940)
: a single untwisted synthetic filament (as of nylon)

**mo·nog·a·mist** \mə-'nä-gə-mist\ *noun* (1651)
: one who practices or upholds monogamy

**mo·nog·a·my** \-mē\ *noun* [French *monogamie*, from Late Latin *monogamia*, from Greek, from *monogamos* monogamous, from *mon-* + *gamos* marriage, from *gamein* to marry] (1612)
**1** *archaic* : the practice of marrying only once during a lifetime
**2** : the state or custom of being married to one person at a time

**3 :** the condition or practice of having a single mate during a period of time ⟨*monogamy* is common among birds⟩
— **mo·nog·a·mous** \mə-'nä-gə-məs\ *also* **mono·gam·ic** \ˌmä-nə-'ga-mik\ *adjective*
— **mo·nog·a·mous·ly** *adverb*
**mono·gas·tric** \ˌmä-nə-'gas-trik\ *adjective* (1814)
**:** having a stomach with only a single compartment ⟨swine, chicks, and human beings are *monogastric*⟩
**mono·ge·ne·an** \-'jē-nē-ən\ *noun* [New Latin *Monogenea,* group name] (1899)
**:** a monogenetic trematode
— **monogenean** *adjective*
**mono·gen·e·sis** \-'je-nə-səs\ *noun* [New Latin] (circa 1859)
**:** origin of diverse individuals or kinds (as of language) by descent from a single ancestral individual or kind
**mono·ge·net·ic** \-jə-'ne-tik\ *adjective* (1873)
**1 :** relating to or involving monogenesis
**2 :** of, relating to, or being any of a subclass (Monogenea) of trematode worms that ordinarily live as ectoparasites on a single host (as a fish or amphibian) throughout their entire life cycle
**mono·gen·ic** \-'je-nik\ *adjective* [International Scientific Vocabulary] (1939)
**:** of, relating to, or controlled by a single gene and especially by either of an allelic pair
— **mono·gen·i·cal·ly** \-ni-k(ə-)lē\ *adverb*
**mono·germ** \'mä-nə-ˌjərm\ *adjective* [mon- + germinate] (1950)
**:** producing or being a fruit that gives rise to a single plant ⟨a *monogerm* sugar beet⟩
**mono·glot** \-ˌglät\ *adjective* [mono- + -glot (as in *polyglot*)] (1830)
**:** MONOLINGUAL
— **monoglot** *noun*
**mono·glyc·er·ide** \ˌmä-nə-'gli-sə-ˌrīd\ *noun* (1860)
**:** any of various esters of glycerol in which only one of the three hydroxyl groups is esterified and which are often used as emulsifiers
**¹mono·gram** \'mä-nə-ˌgram\ *noun* [Late Latin *monogramma,* from Greek mon- + *gramma* letter — more at GRAM] (circa 1696)
**:** a sign of identity usually formed of the combined initials of a name
— **mono·gram·mat·ic** \ˌmä-nə-grə-'ma-tik\ *adjective*
**²monogram** *transitive verb* **-grammed; -gram·ming** (1868)
**:** to mark with a monogram
— **mono·gram·mer** \-ˌgra-mər\ *noun*
**¹mono·graph** \'mä-nə-ˌgraf\ *noun* (1821)
**:** a learned treatise on a small area of learning; *also* **:** a written account of a single thing
— **mono·graph·ic** \ˌmä-nə-'gra-fik\ *adjective*
**²monograph** *transitive verb* (1876)
**:** to write a monograph on
**mo·nog·y·nous** \mə-'nä-jə-nəs, mä-\ *adjective* (circa 1890)
**:** of, relating to, or living in monogyny
**mo·nog·y·ny** \-nē\ *noun* [International Scientific Vocabulary] (1876)
**:** the state or custom of having only one wife at a time
**mono·hull** \'mä-nə-ˌhəl\ *noun* (1967)
**:** a vessel (as a sailboat) with a single hull — compare MULTIHULL
**mono·hy·brid** \ˌmä-nō-'hī-brəd\ *noun* (1903)
**:** an individual or strain heterozygous for one specified gene
— **monohybrid** *adjective*
**mono·hy·dric** \-'hī-drik\ *adjective* (1880)
**:** MONOHYDROXY
**mono·hy·droxy** \-(ˌ)hī-'dräk-sē\ *adjective* [International Scientific Vocabulary *monohydroxy-,* from mon- + *hydroxy-*] (circa 1934)
**:** containing one hydroxyl group in the molecule
**mono·lay·er** \'mä-nō-ˌlā-ər, -ˌle(-ə)r\ *noun* (1926)

**:** a single continuous layer or film that is one cell or molecule in thickness
**mono·lin·gual** \ˌmä-nə-'liŋ-gwəl, ˌmō-, -'liŋ-gyə-wəl\ *adjective* (1926)
**:** knowing or using only one language
— **monolingual** *noun*
**mono·lith** \'mä-nᵊl-ˌith\ *noun* [French *monolithe,* from *monolithe* consisting of a single stone, from Latin *monolithus,* from Greek *monolithos,* from mon- + *lithos* stone] (1848)
**1 :** a single great stone often in the form of an obelisk or column
**2 :** a massive structure
**3 :** an organized whole that acts as a single unified powerful or influential force
**mono·lith·ic** \ˌmä-nᵊl-'i-thik\ *adjective* (1825)
**1 a :** of, relating to, or resembling a monolith **:** HUGE, MASSIVE **b** (1) **:** formed from a single crystal ⟨a *monolithic* silicon chip⟩ (2) **:** produced in or on a monolithic chip ⟨a *monolithic* circuit⟩
**2 a :** cast as a single piece ⟨a *monolithic* concrete wall⟩ **b :** formed or composed of material without joints or seams ⟨a *monolithic* floor covering⟩ ⟨a *monolithic* furnace lining⟩ **c :** consisting of or constituting a single unit
**3 a :** constituting a massive undifferentiated and often rigid whole ⟨a *monolithic* society⟩ **b :** exhibiting or characterized by often rigidly fixed uniformity ⟨*monolithic* party unity⟩
— **mono·lith·i·cal·ly** \-thi-k(ə-)lē\ *adverb*
**mono·logue** *also* **mono·log** \'mä-nᵊl-ˌóg, -ˌäg\ *noun* [Middle French *monologue,* from mon- + *-logue*] (1549)
**1 a :** SOLILOQUY **2 b :** a dramatic sketch performed by one actor **c :** the routine of a stand-up comic
**2 :** a literary composition written in the form of a soliloquy
**3 :** a long speech monopolizing conversation
— **mono·logu·ist** \-ˌó-gist, -ˌä-\ *or* **mo·nol·o·gist** \same *or* mə-'nä-lə-jist, -gist\ *noun*
**mono·ma·nia** \ˌmä-nə-'mā-nē-ə, -nyə\ *noun* [New Latin] (1823)
**1 :** mental illness especially when limited in expression to one idea or area of thought
**2 :** excessive concentration on a single object or idea
— **mono·ma·ni·ac** \-nē-ˌak\ *noun or adjective*
— **mono·ma·ni·a·cal** \-mə-'nī-ə-kəl\ *adjective*
— **mono·ma·ni·a·cal·ly** \-k(ə-)lē\ *adverb*
**mono·mer** \'mä-nə-mər\ *noun* [International Scientific Vocabulary] (1914)
**:** a chemical compound that can undergo polymerization
— **mo·no·mer·ic** \ˌmä-nə-'mer-ik, ˌmō-\ *adjective*
**mono·me·tal·lic** \ˌmä-nō-mə-'ta-lik\ *adjective* (1877)
**1 :** of or relating to monometallism
**2 :** consisting of or employing one metal
**mono·met·al·lism** \-'me-tᵊl-ˌi-zəm\ *noun* [International Scientific Vocabulary mon- + *-metallism* (as in *bimetallism*)] (1879)
**:** the adoption of one metal only in a currency
— **mono·met·al·list** \-tᵊl-ist\ *noun*
**mo·nom·e·ter** \mä-'nä-mə-tər, mə-\ *noun* [Late Latin, from Greek *monometros,* from mon- + *metron* measure — more at MEASURE] (circa 1846)
**:** a line of verse consisting of a single metrical foot or dipody
**mo·no·mi·al** \mä-'nō-mē-əl, mə-\ *noun* [blend of mon- and *-nomial* (as in *binomial*)] (circa 1706)
**1 :** a mathematical expression consisting of a single term
**2 :** a taxonomic name consisting of a single word or term
— **monomial** *adjective*
**mono·mo·lec·u·lar** \ˌmä-nə-mə-'le-kyə-lər\ *adjective* (1917)

**:** being only one molecule thick ⟨a *monomolecular* film⟩
— **mono·mo·lec·u·lar·ly** *adverb*
**mono·mor·phe·mic** \-mór-'fē-mik\ *adjective* (1936)
**:** consisting of only one morpheme ⟨the word *talk* is *monomorphemic* but *talked* is not⟩
**mono·mor·phic** \-'mór-fik\ *adjective* (circa 1879)
**:** having but a single form, structural pattern, or genotype ⟨a *monomorphic* species of insect⟩
— **mono·mor·phism** \-ˌfi-zəm\ *noun*
**mono·nu·cle·ar** \-'nü-klē-ər, -'nyü-, ÷-kyə-lər\ *adjective* [International Scientific Vocabulary] (1886)
**:** having only one nucleus ⟨a *mononuclear* cell⟩
— **mononuclear** *noun*
**mono·nu·cle·at·ed** \-'nü-klē-ˌā-təd, -'nyü-\ *also* **mono·nu·cle·ate** \-klē-ət, -ˌāt\ *adjective* (1890)
**:** MONONUCLEAR
**mono·nu·cle·o·sis** \-ˌnü-klē-'ō-səs, -ˌnyü-\ *noun* [New Latin, from International Scientific Vocabulary *mononuclear* + New Latin *-osis*] (1920)
**:** an abnormal increase of mononuclear white blood cells in the blood; *specifically* **:** INFECTIOUS MONONUCLEOSIS
**mono·nu·cle·o·tide** \-'nü-klē-ə-ˌtīd, -'nyü-\ *noun* (1908)
**:** a nucleotide that is derived from one molecule each of a nitrogenous base, a sugar, and a phosphoric acid
**mo·noph·a·gous** \mə-'nä-fə-gəs, mä-\ *adjective* (circa 1868)
**:** feeding on or utilizing a single kind of food; *especially* **:** feeding on a single kind of plant or animal
— **mo·noph·a·gy** \-fə-jē\ *noun*
**mono·pho·nic** \ˌmä-nə-'fä-nik, -'fō-\ *adjective* (circa 1864)
**1 :** having a single unaccompanied melodic line
**2 :** of or relating to sound transmission, recording, or reproduction involving a single transmission path
— **mono·pho·ni·cal·ly** \-ni-k(ə-)lē\ *adverb*
**mo·noph·o·ny** \mə-'nä-fə-nē, mä-\ *noun* (circa 1890)
**:** monophonic music
**mon·oph·thong** \'mä-nə(f)-ˌthóŋ\ *noun* [Late Greek *monophthongos* single vowel, from Greek mon- + *phthongos* sound] (1616)
**:** a vowel sound that throughout its duration has a single constant articulatory position
— **mon·oph·thon·gal** \ˌmä-nə(f)-'thóŋ-(g)əl\ *adjective*
**mono·phy·let·ic** \ˌmä-nō-fī-'le-tik\ *adjective* [International Scientific Vocabulary] (1874)
**:** of or relating to a single stock; *specifically* **:** developed from a single common ancestral form
— **mono·phy·ly** \'mä-nə-ˌfī-lē\ *noun*
**Mo·noph·y·site** \mə-'nä-fə-ˌsīt\ *noun* [Medieval Latin *Monophysita,* from Middle Greek *Monophysitēs,* from Greek mon- + *physis* nature — more at PHYSICS] (1698)
**:** one holding the doctrine that Christ's nature remains altogether divine and not human even though he has taken on an earthly and human body with its cycle of birth, life, and death
— **Monophysite** *or* **Mo·noph·y·sit·ic** \-ˌnä-fə-'si-tik\ *adjective*
— **Mo·noph·y·sit·ism** \-'nä-fə-ˌsī-ˌti-zəm\ *noun*
**mono·plane** \'mä-nə-ˌplān\ *noun* (1907)
**:** an airplane with only one main supporting surface
**¹mono·ploid** \'mä-nə-ˌplóid\ *adjective* (1928)
**1 :** HAPLOID
**2 :** having or being the basic haploid number of chromosomes in a polyploid series of organisms

**²monoploid** *noun* [International Scientific Vocabulary] (1944)
: a monoploid individual or organism

**mono·po·di·al** \ˌmä-nə-ˈpō-dē-əl\ *adjective* [New Latin *monopodium* main axis, from *mon-* + *-podium*] (1876)
: having or involving the formation of offshoots from a main axis
— **mono·po·di·al·ly** \-dē-ə-lē\ *adverb*

**mono·pole** \ˈmä-nə-ˌpōl\ *noun* (1937)
**1** : a single positive or negative electrical charge; *also* : a hypothetical north or south magnetic pole existing alone
**2** : a radio antenna consisting of a single often straight element

**mo·nop·o·lise** *British variant of* MONOPOLIZE

**mo·nop·o·list** \mə-ˈnä-pə-list\ *noun* (1601)
: one who monopolizes
— **mo·nop·o·lis·tic** \-ˌnä-pə-ˈlis-tik\ *adjective*
— **mo·nop·o·lis·ti·cal·ly** \-ti-k(ə-)lē\ *adverb*

**mo·nop·o·lize** \mə-ˈnä-pə-ˌlīz\ *transitive verb* **-lized; -liz·ing** (1611)
: to get a monopoly of : assume complete possession or control of ⟨*monopolize* a conversation⟩
— **mo·nop·o·li·za·tion** \-ˌnä-pə-lə-ˈzā-shən\ *noun*
— **mo·nop·o·liz·er** \-ˈnä-pə-ˌlī-zər\ *noun*

**mo·nop·o·ly** \mə-ˈnä-p(ə-)lē\ *noun, plural* **-lies** [Latin *monopolium*, from Greek *monopōlion*, from *mon-* + *pōlein* to sell] (1534)
**1** : exclusive ownership through legal privilege, command of supply, or concerted action
**2** : exclusive possession or control
**3** : a commodity controlled by one party
**4** : one that has a monopoly

**mono·pro·pel·lant** \ˌmä-nō-prə-ˈpe-lənt\ *noun* (circa 1945)
: a rocket propellant containing both the fuel and the oxidizer in a single substance

**mo·nop·so·ny** \mə-ˈnäp-sə-nē\ *noun, plural* **-nies** [*mon-* + *-opsony* (as in *oligopsony*)] (1933)
: an oligopsony limited to one buyer
— **mo·nop·so·nis·tic** \-ˌnäp-sə-ˈnis-tik\ *adjective*

**mono·rail** \ˈmä-nə-ˌrāl\ *noun* (1897)
: a single rail serving as a track for a wheeled vehicle; *also* : a vehicle traveling on such a track

**mon·or·chid** \mä-ˈnȯr-kəd\ *noun* [irregular from Greek *monorchis*, from *mon-* + *orchis* testicle — more at ORCHIS] (1874)
: an individual who has only one testis or only one descended into the scrotum
— **monorchid** *adjective*
— **mon·or·chi·dism** \-kə-ˌdi-zəm\ *noun*

**mono·rhyme** \ˈmä-nə-ˌrīm\ *noun* (1731)
: a strophe or poem in which all the lines have the same end rhyme
— **mono·rhymed** \-ˌrīmd\ *adjective*

**mono·sac·cha·ride** \ˌmä-nə-ˈsa-kə-ˌrīd\ *noun* [International Scientific Vocabulary] (1896)
: a sugar not decomposable to simpler sugars by hydrolysis

**mono·so·di·um glu·ta·mate** \ˌmä-nə-ˌsō-dē-əm-ˈglü-tə-ˌmāt\ *noun* (1929)
: a crystalline salt $C_5H_8O_4NaN$ used to enhance the flavor of food — *abbreviation* MSG

**mono·some** \ˈmä-nə-ˌsōm\ *noun* (circa 1909)
**1** : a chromosome lacking a synaptic mate; *especially* : an unpaired X chromosome
**2** : a single ribosome

**mono·so·mic** \ˌmä-nə-ˈsō-mik\ *adjective* (1926)
: having one less than the diploid number of chromosomes
— **monosomic** *noun*

**mono·so·my** \ˈmä-nə-ˌsō-mē\ *noun*

**mono·spe·cif·ic** \ˌmä-nō-spə-ˈsi-fik\ *adjective* (1947)
: specific for a single antigen or receptor site on an antigen
— **mono·spec·i·fic·i·ty** \-ˌspe-sə-ˈfi-sə-tē\ *noun*

**mono·stele** \ˈmä-nə-ˌstēl, ˌmä-nə-ˈstē-lē\ *noun* (circa 1900)
: PROTOSTELE
— **mono·ste·lic** \ˌmä-nə-ˈstē-lik\ *adjective*
— **mono·ste·ly** \ˌmä-nə-ˈstē-lē\ *noun*

**mono·syl·lab·ic** \ˌmä-nə-sə-ˈla-bik\ *adjective* [probably from French *monosyllabique*, from *monosyllabe*] (1768)
**1** : consisting of one syllable or of monosyllables
**2** : using or speaking only monosyllables
**3** : conspicuously brief in answering or commenting : TERSE
— **mono·syl·lab·i·cal·ly** \-bi-k(ə-)lē\ *adverb*
— **mono·syl·la·bic·i·ty** \-ˌsi-lə-ˈbi-sə-tē\ *noun*

**mono·syl·la·ble** \ˈmä-nə-ˌsi-lə-bəl, ˌmä-nə-ˈ\ *noun* [modification of Middle French or Late Latin; Middle French *monosyllabe*, from Late Latin *monosyllabon*, from Greek, from neuter of *monosyllabos* having one syllable, from *mon-* + *syllabē* syllable] (1533)
: a word of one syllable

**mono·syn·ap·tic** \ˌmä-nō-sə-ˈnap-tik\ *adjective* (1942)
: having or involving a single neural synapse
— **mono·syn·ap·ti·cal·ly** \-ti-k(ə-)lē\ *adverb*

**mono·ter·pene** \ˌmä-nə-ˈtər-ˌpēn\ *noun* (circa 1959)
: any of a class of terpenes $C_{10}H_{16}$ containing two isoprene units per molecule; *also* : a derivative of a monoterpene

**mono·the·ism** \ˈmä-nə-(ˌ)thē-ˌi-zəm\ *noun* (1660)
: the doctrine or belief that there is but one God
— **mono·the·ist** \-ˌthē-ist\ *noun*
— **mono·the·is·tic** \ˌmä-nə-thē-ˈis-tik\ *also* **mono·the·is·ti·cal** \-ti-kəl\ *adjective*
— **mono·the·is·ti·cal·ly** \-ti-k(ə-)lē\ *adverb*

**¹mono·tone** \ˈmä-nə-ˌtōn\ *noun* [Greek *monotonos* monotonous] (1644)
**1** : a succession of syllables, words, or sentences in one unvaried key or pitch
**2** : a single unvaried musical tone
**3** : a tedious sameness or reiteration
**4** : a person unable to produce or to distinguish between musical intervals

**²monotone** *adjective* (1769)
**1** : MONOTONIC 2
**2** : having a uniform color

**mono·ton·ic** \ˌmä-nə-ˈtä-nik\ *adjective* (1797)
**1** : characterized by the use of or uttered in a monotone
**2** : having the property either of never increasing or of never decreasing as the values of the independent variable or the subscripts of the terms increase ⟨*monotonic* functions⟩ ⟨a *monotonic* sequence⟩
— **mono·ton·i·cal·ly** \-ni-k(ə-)lē\ *adverb*
— **mono·to·nic·i·ty** \ˌmä-nə-tō-ˈni-sə-tē\ *noun*

**mo·not·o·nous** \mə-ˈnä-tᵊn-əs, -ˈnät-nəs\ *adjective* [Greek *monotonos*, from *mon-* + *tonos* tone] (1778)
**1** : uttered or sounded in one unvarying tone : marked by a sameness of pitch and intensity
**2** : tediously uniform or unvarying
— **mo·not·o·nous·ly** *adverb*
— **mo·not·o·nous·ness** *noun*

**mo·not·o·ny** \mə-ˈnä-tᵊn-ē, -ˈnät-nē\ *noun* (1706)
**1** : tedious sameness
**2** : sameness of tone or sound

**mono·treme** \ˈmä-nə-ˌtrēm\ *noun* [New Latin *Monotremata*, from Greek *mon-* + *trēmat-, trēma* hole — more at TREMATODE] (1835)
: any of an order (Monotremata) of egg-laying mammals comprising the platypuses and echidnas

**mono·type** \ˈmä-nə-ˌtīp\ *noun* (1882)
: an impression on paper of a design painted usually with the finger or a brush on a surface (as glass)

**Monotype** *trademark*
— used for a keyboard typesetting machine that casts and sets type in separate characters

**mono·typ·ic** \ˌmä-nə-ˈti-pik\ *adjective* [*mon-* + *type* + *-ic*] (circa 1859)
: including a single representative — used especially of a genus with only one species

**mono·un·sat·u·rat·ed** \ˌmä-nō-ˌən-ˈsa-chə-ˌrā-təd\ *adjective* (circa 1939)
: containing one double or triple bond per molecule — used especially of an oil or fatty acid; compare POLYUNSATURATED
— **mono·un·sat·u·rate** \-rət\ *noun*

**mono·va·lent** \ˌmä-nə-ˈvā-lənt\ *adjective* [International Scientific Vocabulary] (1869)
**1** : having a valence of one
**2** : containing antibodies specific for or antigens of a single strain of a microorganism ⟨a *monovalent* vaccine⟩

**mon·ovu·lar** \(ˌ)mä-ˈnäv-yə-lər, -ˈnōv-\ *adjective* (1929)
: MONOZYGOTIC

**mon·ox·ide** \mə-ˈnäk-ˌsīd\ *noun* [International Scientific Vocabulary] (1869)
: an oxide containing one atom of oxygen in a molecule

**mono·zy·got·ic** \ˌmä-nə-zī-ˈgä-tik\ *adjective* (1916)
: derived from a single egg ⟨*monozygotic* twins⟩

**Mon·roe Doctrine** \mən-ˈrō- *also* ˈmən- *or* ˈmän-\ *noun* [James *Monroe*] (1853)
: a statement of U.S. foreign policy expressing opposition to extension of European control or influence in the western hemisphere

**mon·sei·gneur** \ˌmōⁿ-ˌsän-ˈyər\ *noun, plural* **mes·sei·gneurs** \ˌmā-ˌsän-ˈyər(z)\ [French, literally, my lord] (1602)
: a French dignitary (as a prince or prelate) — used as a title preceding a title of office or rank

**mon·sieur** \məs-ˈyə(r), məsh-; mə-ˈsir\ *noun, plural* **mes·sieurs** \məs-ˈyə(r)(z), məsh-, mäs-; mə-ˈsir(z)\ [Middle French, literally, my lord] (1512)
: a Frenchman of high rank or station — used as a title equivalent to *Mister* and prefixed to the name of a Frenchman

**mon·si·gnor** \män-ˈsē-nyər, mən-\ *noun, plural* **monsignors** *or* **mon·si·gno·ri** \ˌmän-ˌsēn-ˈyȯr-ē, -ˈyȯr-\ [Italian *monsignore*, from French *monseigneur*] (1641)
: a Roman Catholic prelate having a dignity or titular distinction (as of domestic prelate or protonotary apostolic) usually conferred by the pope — used as a title prefixed to the surname or to the given name and surname
— **mon·si·gno·ri·al** \ˌmän-ˌsēn-ˈyȯr-ē-əl, -ˈyȯr-\ *adjective*

**mon·soon** \män-ˈsün, ˈmän-ˌ\ *noun* [obsolete Dutch *monssoen*, from Portuguese *monção*, from Arabic *mawsim* time, season] (1584)
**1** : a periodic wind especially in the Indian Ocean and southern Asia
**2** : the season of the southwest monsoon in India and adjacent areas that is characterized by very heavy rainfall
**3** : rainfall that is associated with the monsoon
— **mon·soon·al** \-ˈsü-nᵊl, -ˌsü-\ *adjective*

\ə\ **abut** \ᵊ\ **kitten** \ər\ **further** \a\ **ash** \ā\ **ace** \ä\ **mop, mar** \aú\ **out** \ch\ **chin** \e\ **bet** \ē\ **easy** \g\ **go** \i\ **hit** \ī\ **ice** \j\ **job** \ŋ\ **sing** \ō\ **go** \ȯ\ **law** \ȯi\ **boy** \th\ **thin** \t͟h\ **the** \ü\ **loot** \ú\ **foot** \y\ **yet** \zh\ **vision** *see also* Guide to Pronunciation

**mons pu·bis** \'mänz-'pyü-bəs\ *noun, plural*
**mon·tes pubis** \'män-tēz-\ [New Latin, pubic eminence] (circa 1903)
: a rounded eminence of fatty tissue upon the
pubic symphysis especially of the human female

¹**mon·ster** \'män(t)-stər\ *noun* [Middle English *monstre*, from Middle French, from Latin *monstrum* omen, monster, from *monēre* to
warn — more at MIND] (14th century)
**1 a :** an animal or plant of abnormal form or
structure **b :** one who deviates from normal or
acceptable behavior or character
**2 :** a threatening force
**3 a :** an animal of strange or terrifying shape
**b :** one unusually large for its kind
**4 :** something monstrous; *especially* **:** a person
of unnatural or extreme ugliness, deformity,
wickedness, or cruelty
**5 :** one that is highly successful
²**monster** *adjective* (1837)
: enormous or impressive in size, extent, or
numbers
**mon·strance** \'män(t)-strən(t)s\ *noun* [Mid-
dle English *monstrans*, from Middle French
*monstrance*, from Medieval Latin *monstran-
tia*, from Latin *monstrant-, monstrans*, present
participle of *monstrare* to show, from *monstrum*] (15th century)
: a vessel in which the consecrated Host is exposed for the adoration of the faithful
**mon·stros·i·ty** \män-'strä-sə-tē\
*noun, plural* **-ties** (15th century)
**1 a :** a malformation of a plant or
animal **b :** something deviating
from the normal **:** FREAK
**2 :** the quality or state of being
monstrous
**3 a :** an object of great and often
frightening size, force, or com-
plexity **b :** an excessively bad or shocking example

monstrance

**mon·strous** \'män(t)-strəs\ *adjective* (15th
century)
**1** *obsolete* **:** STRANGE, UNNATURAL
**2 :** having extraordinary often overwhelming
size **:** GIGANTIC
**3 a :** having the qualities or appearance of a
monster **b** *obsolete* **:** teeming with monsters
**4 a :** extraordinarily ugly or vicious **:** HORRI-
BLE **b :** shockingly wrong or ridiculous
**5 :** deviating greatly from the natural form or
character **:** ABNORMAL
**6 :** very great — used as an intensive ☆
— **mon·strous·ly** *adverb*
— **mon·strous·ness** *noun*
**mons ve·ne·ris** \'män(t)'ve-nə-rəs\ *noun, plural* **mon·tes veneris** \'män-ˌtēz-\ [New Latin, literally, eminence of Venus or of venery]
(1621)
: the mons pubis of the human female
**mon·ta·dale** \'män-tə-ˌdāl\ *noun* [*Montana*
state + *dale*] (1949)
: any of an American breed of white-faced
hornless sheep noted for heavy fleece and
good meat conformation
¹**mon·tage** \män-'täzh, mōⁿ(n)-, -'tàzh\ *noun*
[French, from *monter* to mount] (1929)
**1 :** the production of a rapid succession of images in a motion picture to illustrate an association of ideas
**2 a :** a literary, musical, or artistic composite
of juxtaposed more or less heterogeneous elements **b :** a composite picture made by combining several separate pictures
**3 :** a heterogeneous mixture **:** JUMBLE ⟨a *montage* of emotions⟩
²**montage** *transitive verb* **mon·taged;**
**mon·tag·ing** (1944)
: to combine into or depict in a montage
**mon·ta·gnard** \ˌmōⁿ-ˌtän-'yär(d)\ *noun, often
capitalized* [French, mountaineer, from *mon-
tagne* mountain, from Old French *montaigne*]
(1842)

: a member of any of various peoples inhabiting the highlands of central and southern Vietnam
— **montagnard** *adjective, often capitalized*
**Mon·ta·gue** \'män-tə-ˌgyü\ *noun*
: the family of Romeo in Shakespeare's
*Romeo and Juliet*
**mon·tane** \ˌmän-'tān, 'män-ˌ\ *adjective* [Latin
*montanus* of a mountain — more at MOUN-
TAIN] (1863)
**1 :** of, relating to, growing in, or being the
biogeographic zone of relatively moist cool
upland slopes below timberline dominated by
large coniferous trees
**2 :** of, relating to, or made up of montane
plants or animals
**Mon·ta·nist** \'män-tᵊn-ist\ *noun* [*Montanus*,
2d century A.D. Phrygian schismatic] (1577)
: an adherent of a Christian sect arising in the
late second century and stressing apocalyptic
expectations, the continuing prophetic gifts of
the Spirit, and strict ascetic discipline
— **Mon·ta·nism** \-tᵊn-ˌi-zəm\ *noun*
**mon·tan wax** \'män-tᵊn-\ *noun* [Latin *montanus* of a mountain] (1908)
: a hard brittle mineral wax obtained usually
from lignites by extraction and used especially
in polishes, carbon paper, and insulating compositions
**mon·te** \'män-tē\ *noun* [Spanish, bank, mountain, heap, from Italian, from Latin *mont-,
mons* mountain] (1824)
**1 :** a card game in which players select any
two of four cards turned face up in a layout
and bet that one of them will be matched before the other as cards are dealt one at a time
from the pack — called also *monte bank*
**2 :** THREE-CARD MONTE
**Mon·te Car·lo** \ˌmän-ti-'kär-(ˌ)lō\ *adjective*
[*Monte Carlo*, Monaco, famous for its gambling casino] (1949)
: of, relating to, or involving the use of random sampling techniques and often the use of
computer simulation to obtain approximate solutions to mathematical or physical problems
especially in terms of a range of values each
of which has a calculated probability of being
the solution ⟨*Monte Carlo* calculations⟩
**mon·teith** \män-'tēth\ *noun* [*Monteith*, 17th
century Scottish eccentric who wore a cloak
with a scalloped hem] (1683)
: a large silver punch bowl with scalloped rim
**Mon·te·rey cypress** \'män-tə-ˌrā-\ *noun*
[*Monterey*, California] (1873)
: a California cypress (*Cupressus macrocarpa*)
that is endemic to the Monterey and Carmel
seacoast and is often planted for ornament or
in a windbreak
**Monterey Jack** *noun* (circa 1947)
: a semisoft whole-milk cheese with high
moisture content
**Monterey pine** *noun* (1834)
: a pine (*Pinus radiata*) native to coastal California that is widely grown especially in the
southern hemisphere for its wood
**mon·te·ro** \män-'ter-(ˌ)ō\ *noun, plural* **-ros**
[Spanish, hunter, from *monte* mountain] (1622)
: a round hunter's cap with ear flaps
**Mon·te·zu·ma's revenge** \ˌmän-tə-'zü-
məz-\ *noun* [*Montezuma* II] (1962)
: diarrhea contracted in Mexico especially by
tourists
**month** \'mən(t)th\ *noun, plural* **months**
\'mən(t)s, 'mən(t)ths\ [Middle English, from
Old English *mōnath*; akin to Old High German *mānōd* month, Old English *mōna* moon]
(before 12th century)
**1 :** a measure of time corresponding nearly to
the period of the moon's revolution and
amounting to approximately 4 weeks or 30
days or ¹/₁₂ of a year
**2** *plural* **:** an indefinite usually extended period of time ⟨he has been gone for *months*⟩
**3 :** one ninth of the typical duration of human
pregnancy ⟨she was in her eighth *month*⟩

**month·long** \'mən(t)th-'lòŋ\ *adjective* (1843)
: lasting a month
¹**month·ly** \-lē\ *adverb* (circa 1534)
: once a month **:** by the month
²**monthly** *adjective* (1572)
**1 a :** of or relating to a month **b :** payable or
reckoned by the month
**2 :** lasting a month
**3 :** occurring or appearing every month
³**monthly** *noun, plural* **monthlies** (1833)
**1 :** a monthly periodical
**2** *plural* **:** a menstrual period
**Monthly Meeting** *noun* (circa 1772)
: a basic unit of an organization of Friends
**month's mind** *noun* (15th century)
: a Roman Catholic requiem mass held a
month after a person's death
**Mont·mo·ren·cy** \ˌmänt-mə-'ren(t)-sē\ *noun*
[French, from *Montmorency*, France] (1924)
: a cherry that is grown commercially for its
bright red sour fruit; *also* **:** the fruit
**mont·mo·ril·lon·ite** \ˌmänt-mə-'ri-lə-ˌnīt,
-'rē-ə-ˌnīt\ *noun* [French, from *Montmorillon*,
commune in western France] (1854)
: a soft clayey mineral that is a hydrous aluminum silicate with considerable capacity for exchanging part of the aluminum for magnesium
and bases
— **mont·mo·ril·lon·it·ic** \-ˌri-lə-'ni-tik,
-ˌrē-ə-'ni-\ *adjective*
**Mon·tra·chet** \ˌmōⁿ-trä-'she\ *noun* [French,
from *Montrachet*, vineyard in Burgundy,
France] (1833)
: a dry white burgundy wine
**mon·u·ment** \'män-yə-mənt\ *noun* [Middle
English, from Latin *monumentum*, literally,
memorial, from *monēre* to remind — more at
MIND] (13th century)
**1** *obsolete* **:** a burial vault **:** SEPULCHRE
**2 :** a written legal document or record **:** TREA-
TISE
**3 a** (1) **:** a lasting evidence, reminder, or example of someone or something notable or
great (2) **:** a distinguished person **b :** a memorial stone or a building erected in remembrance of a person or event
**4** *archaic* **:** an identifying mark **:** EVIDENCE;
*also* **:** PORTENT, SIGN
**5** *obsolete* **:** a carved statue **:** EFFIGY
**6 :** a boundary or position marker (as a stone)
**7 :** NATIONAL MONUMENT
**8 :** a written tribute
**mon·u·men·tal** \ˌmän-yə-'men-tᵊl\ *adjective*
(1604)
**1 :** of or relating to a monument
**2 :** serving as or resembling a monument
**:** MASSIVE; *also* **:** highly significant **:** OUT-
STANDING
**3 :** very great
— **mon·u·men·tal·i·ty** \-mən-'ta-lə-tē,
-ˌmen-\ *noun*
— **mon·u·men·tal·ly** \-tᵊl-ē\ *adverb*

---

☆ **SYNONYMS**
**Monstrous, prodigious, tremendous,
stupendous** mean extremely impressive.
MONSTROUS implies a departure from the
normal (as in size, form, or character) and
often carries suggestions of deformity, ugliness, or fabulousness ⟨the *monstrous* waste
of the project⟩. PRODIGIOUS suggests a mar-
velousness exceeding belief, usually in
something felt as going far beyond a previous maximum (as of goodness, greatness,
intensity, or size) ⟨made a *prodigious* effort
and rolled the stone aside⟩. TREMENDOUS
may imply a power to terrify or inspire awe
⟨the *tremendous* roar of the cataract⟩. STU-
PENDOUS implies a power to stun or astound,
usually because of size, numbers, complexity, or greatness beyond description ⟨a *stupendous* volcanic eruption⟩.

## MONTHS OF THE PRINCIPAL CALENDARS

### GREGORIAN[1]

| Name | Days |
|---|---|
| January | |
|   begins 10 days after the | |
|   winter solstice | 31 |
| February | 28 |
|   in leap years | 29 |
| March | 31 |
| April | 30 |
| May | 31 |
| June | 30 |
| July | 31 |
| August | 31 |
| September | 30 |
| October | 31 |
| November | 30 |
| December | 31 |

### JEWISH

| Name | Days |
|---|---|
| Tishri | |
|   in year 5753 began | |
|   Sept. 28, 1992 | 30 |
| Heshvan | 29 *or* 30 |
| Kislev | 29 *or* 30 |
| Tebet | 29 |
| Shebat | 30 |
| Adar[2] | 29 *or* 30 |
| Nisan[3] | 30 |
| Iyar | 29 |
| Sivan | 30 |
| Tammuz | 29 |
| Ab | 30 |
| Elul | 29 |

### ISLAMIC

| Name | Days |
|---|---|
| Muharram[4] | |
|   in A.H. 1413 began | |
|   July 2, 1992 | 30 |
| Safar | 29 |
| Rabi I | 30 |
| Rabi II | 29 |
| Jumada I | 30 |
| Jumada II | 29 |
| Rajab | 30 |
| Sha'ban | 29 |
| Ramadan | 30 |
| Shawwal | 29 |
| Dhu'l-Qa'dah | 30 |
| Dhu'l-Hijja | 29 |
|   in leap years | 30 |

[1] The equinoxes occur about March 21 and September 23, the solstices about June 22 and December 22.

[2] In leap years an intercalary month of 30 days takes the place of Adar, and is sometimes called Adar I. Adar then becomes the 29-day Veadar or Adar Sheni (sometimes called Adar II), and retains the usual festivals and holidays of Adar.

[3] The first month of the ecclesiastical year; anciently called Abib.

[4] Retrogresses through the seasons; the Islamic year is lunar and each month begins at the approximate new moon; the year 1 A.H. began on Friday, July 16, A.D. 622.

**mon·u·men·tal·ize** \-'men-t°l-,īz\ *transitive verb* **-ized; -iz·ing** (1857)
: to record or memorialize lastingly by a monument

**mon·u·ron** \'män-yə-,rän\ *noun* [*mon-* + *ur*ea + [1]-*on*] (circa 1957)
: a persistent herbicide $C_9H_{11}ClN_2O$ used especially to control broad-leaved weeds

**mon·zo·nite** \män-'zō-,nīt, 'män-zə-\ *noun*
[French, from Mount *Monzoni*, Italy] (1895)
: a granular igneous rock composed of plagioclase and orthoclase in about equal quantities together with augite and a little biotite

**moo** \'mü\ *intransitive verb* [imitative] (1549)
: to make the throat noise of a cow
— **moo** *noun*

**mooch** \'müch\ *verb* [probably from French dialect *muchier* to hide, lurk] (1851)
*intransitive verb*
**1** : to wander aimlessly : AMBLE; *also* : SNEAK
**2** : SPONGE, CADGE
*transitive verb*
**1** : to take surreptitiously : STEAL
**2** : BEG, CADGE
— **mooch·er** *noun*

**¹mood** \'müd\ *noun* [Middle English, from Old English *mōd;* akin to Old High German *muot* mood] (before 12th century)
**1** : a conscious state of mind or predominant emotion : FEELING; *also* : the expression of mood especially in art or literature
**2** *archaic* : a fit of anger : RAGE
**3 a** : a prevailing attitude : DISPOSITION **b** : a receptive state of mind predisposing to action **c** : a distinctive atmosphere or context : AURA

**²mood** *noun* [alteration of ¹*mode*] (1569)
**1** : the form of a syllogism as determined by the quantity and quality of its constituent propositions
**2** : distinction of form or a particular set of inflectional forms of a verb to express whether the action or state it denotes is conceived as fact or in some other manner (as command, possibility, or wish)
**3** : MODE 1b

**moody** \'mü-dē\ *adjective* **mood·i·er; -est** (1593)
**1** : subject to depression : GLOOMY
**2** : subject to moods : TEMPERAMENTAL
**3** : expressive of a mood
— **mood·i·ly** \'mü-d°l-ē\ *adverb*
— **mood·i·ness** \'mü-dē-nəs\ *noun*

**moo·la** *or* **moo·lah** \'mü-(,)lä, -lə\ *noun* [origin unknown] (1939)
*slang* : MONEY

**¹moon** \'mün\ *noun* [Middle English *mone*, from Old English *mōna;* akin to Old High German *māno* moon, Latin *mensis* month, Greek *mēn* month, *mēnē* moon] (before 12th century)
**1 a** *often capitalized* : the earth's natural satellite that shines by the sun's reflected light, revolves about the earth from west to east in about 29½ days with reference to the sun or about 27⅓ days with reference to the stars, and has a diameter of 2160 miles (3475 kilometers), a mean distance from the earth of about 238,900 miles (384,400 kilometers), and a mass about one eightieth that of the earth — usually used with *the* **b** : one complete moon cycle consisting of four phases **c** : SATELLITE 2; *specifically* : a natural satellite of a planet
**2** : an indefinite usually extended period of time 〈a labor of many *moons*〉
**3** : MOONLIGHT
**4** : something that resembles a moon: as **a** : a highly translucent spot on old porcelain **b** : LUNULE **c** *slang* : naked buttocks
**5** : something impossible or inaccessible 〈reach for the *moon*〉
— **moon·like** \-,līk\ *adjective*
— **over the moon** : very pleased : in high spirits

**²moon** (1836)
*transitive verb*
**1** : to spend in idle reverie : DREAM — used with *away*
**2** *slang* : to expose one's naked buttocks to
*intransitive verb*
: to spend time in idle reverie : behave abstractedly

**moon·beam** \'mün-,bēm\ *noun* (1590)
: a ray of light from the moon

**moon blindness** *noun* (circa 1720)
: a recurrent inflammation of the eye of the horse

**moon·calf** \'mün-,kaf, -,kàf\ *noun* (1614)
: a foolish or absentminded person : SIMPLETON

**moon·dust** \-,dəst\ *noun* (circa 1959)
: fine dry particles of the moon's soil

**moon·eye** \-,ī\ *noun* (1842)
: any of a genus (*Hiodon*) of silvery North American freshwater fishes that resemble shad

**moon-eyed** \-'īd\ *adjective* (1699)
: having the eyes wide open

**moon·faced** \-,fāst\ *adjective* (1855)
: having a round face

**moon·fish** \-,fish\ *noun, plural* **moonfish** *or* **moon·fish·es** (1646)
: any of various compressed often short deep-bodied silvery or yellowish marine fishes: as **a** : OPAH **b** : PLATY

**moon·flow·er** \-,flaù(-ə)r\ *noun* (circa 1909)
: a tropical American morning glory (*Calonyction aculeatum* synonym *Ipomoea alba*) with fragrant flowers; *also* : any of several related plants

**Moon·ie** \'mü-nē\ *noun* [Sun Myung *Moon* (born 1920) Korean evangelist] (1974)
: a member of the Unification Church founded by Sun Myung Moon

**moon·ish** \'mü-nish\ *adjective* (15th century)
: influenced by the moon; *also* : CAPRICIOUS
— **moon·ish·ly** *adverb*

**moon·less** \'mün-ləs\ *adjective* (1508)
: lacking the light of the moon

**moon·let** \-lət\ *noun* (1832)
: a small natural or artificial satellite

**¹moon·light** \-,līt\ *noun* (14th century)
: the light of the moon

**²moonlight** *intransitive verb* **moon·light·ed; moon·light·ing** [back-formation from *moonlighter*] (1957)
: to hold a second job in addition to a regular one
— **moon·light·er** *noun*

**moon·lit** \-,lit\ *adjective* (circa 1827)
: lighted by the moon

**moon·quake** \-,kwāk\ *noun* (1946)
: a seismic event on the moon

**moon·rise** \-,rīz\ *noun* (1728)
**1** : the rising of the moon above the horizon
**2** : the time of the moon's rising

**moon·scape** \-,skāp\ *noun* (1916)
: the surface of the moon as seen or as depicted; *also* : a landscape resembling this surface
*word history* see LANDSCAPE

**moon·seed** \-,sēd\ *noun* (1739)
: a twining plant (*Menispermum canadense* of the family Menispermaceae, the moonseed family) of eastern North America that has crescent-shaped seeds and black fruits

**moon·set** \-,set\ *noun* (1845)
**1** : the descent of the moon below the horizon
**2** : the time of the moon's setting

**moon shell** *noun* (1936)
: any of a cosmopolitan family (Naticidae) of carnivorous marine snails having smooth globose shells

moon shell

**moon·shine** \'mün-,shīn\ *noun* (15th century)
**1** : MOONLIGHT
**2** : empty talk : NONSENSE

**3 :** intoxicating liquor; *especially* **:** illegally distilled corn whiskey

**moon·shin·er** \-ˌshī-nər\ *noun* (1860)
**:** a maker or seller of illicit whiskey

**moon shot** *noun* (1958)
**:** a spacecraft mission to the moon

**moon·stone** \-ˌstōn\ *noun* (1632)
**:** a transparent or translucent feldspar of pearly or opaline luster used as a gem

**moon·struck** \-ˌstrək\ *adjective* (1674)
**:** affected by or as if by the moon: as **a :** mentally unbalanced **b :** romantically sentimental **c :** lost in fantasy or reverie

**moon·ward** \-wərd\ *adverb* (1855)
**:** toward the moon

**moony** \'mü-nē\ *adjective* (circa 1586)
**1 :** of or relating to the moon
**2 a :** crescent-shaped **b :** resembling the full moon **:** ROUND
**3 :** MOONLIT
**4 :** DREAMY, MOONSTRUCK

**¹moor** \'mu̇r\ *noun* [Middle English *mor,* from Old English *mōr;* akin to Old High German *muor* moor] (before 12th century)
**1** *chiefly British* **:** an expanse of open rolling infertile land
**2 :** a boggy area; *especially* **:** one that is peaty and dominated by grasses and sedges

**²moor** *verb* [Middle English *moren;* akin to Middle Dutch *meren, maren* to tie, moor] (15th century)
*transitive verb*
**:** to make fast with or as if with cables, lines, or anchors
*intransitive verb*
**1 :** to secure a boat by mooring **:** ANCHOR
**2 :** to be made fast

**Moor** \'mu̇r\ *noun* [Middle English *More,* from Middle French, from Latin *Maurus* inhabitant of Mauretania] (14th century)
**1 :** one of the Arab and Berber conquerors of Spain
**2 :** BERBER
— **Moor·ish** \-ish\ *adjective*

**moor·age** \'mu̇r-ij\ *noun* (1648)
**1 :** an act of mooring
**2 :** a place to moor

**moor·hen** \'mu̇r-ˌhen\ *noun* (14th century)
**:** the common gallinule (*Gallinula chloropus*) of the New World, Eurasia, and Africa

**moor·ing** \-iŋ\ *noun* (15th century)
**1 :** an act of making fast a boat or aircraft with lines or anchors
**2 a :** a place where or an object to which something (as a craft) can be moored **b :** a device (as a line or chain) by which an object is secured in place
**3 :** an established practice or stabilizing influence **:** ANCHORAGE 2 — usually used in plural

**moor·land** \-lənd, -ˌland\ *noun* (before 12th century)
**:** land consisting of moors **:** a stretch of moor

**moose** \'müs\ *noun, plural* **moose** [of Algonquian origin; akin to Massachuset *moos* moose] (1603)
**1 :** a ruminant mammal (*Alces alces*) with humped shoulders, long legs, and broadly palmated antlers that is the largest existing member of the deer family and inhabits forested areas of Canada, the northern U.S., Europe, and Asia

moose 1

**2** *capitalized* [Loyal Order of *Moose*] **:** a member of a major benevolent and fraternal order

**¹moot** \'müt\ *noun* [Middle English, from Old English *mōt, gemōt;* akin to Middle High German *muoze* meeting] (before 12th century)
**1 :** a deliberative assembly primarily for the administration of justice; *especially* **:** one held by the freemen of an Anglo-Saxon community
**2** *obsolete* **:** ARGUMENT, DISCUSSION

**²moot** *transitive verb* (before 12th century)
**1** *archaic* **:** to discuss from a legal standpoint **:** ARGUE
**2 a :** to bring up for discussion **:** BROACH **b :** DEBATE

**³moot** *adjective* (circa 1587)
**1 a :** open to question **:** DEBATABLE **b :** subjected to discussion **:** DISPUTED
**2 :** deprived of practical significance **:** made abstract or purely academic

**moot court** *noun* (1788)
**:** a mock court in which law students argue hypothetical cases for practice

**¹mop** \'mäp\ *noun* [Middle English *mappe*] (15th century)
**1 :** an implement made of absorbent material fastened to a handle and used especially for cleaning floors
**2 :** something that resembles a mop; *especially* **:** a thick mass of hair

**²mop** *verb* **mopped; mop·ping** (1709)
*transitive verb*
**:** to use a mop on: as **a :** to clean or clear away by mopping ⟨*mop* the floors⟩ — often used with *up* ⟨*mop* up the spillage⟩ **b :** to wipe as if with a mop ⟨*mopped* his brow with a handkerchief⟩
*intransitive verb*
**:** to clean a surface (as a floor) with a mop
— **mop·per** *noun*

**mop·board** \'mäp-ˌbōrd, -ˌbȯrd\ *noun* (1853)
**:** BASEBOARD

**¹mope** \'mōp\ *intransitive verb* **moped; mop·ing** [probably from obsolete *mop, mope* fool] (1568)
**1** *archaic* **:** to act in a dazed or stupid manner
**2 :** to give oneself up to brooding **:** become listless or dejected
**3 :** to move slowly or aimlessly **:** DAWDLE
— **mop·er** *noun*
— **mop·ey** \'mō-pē\ *adjective*

**²mope** *noun* (1693)
**1 :** one that mopes
**2** *plural* **:** BLUES 1

**mo·ped** \'mō-ˌped\ *noun* [Swedish, from *motor* motor + *pedal* pedal] (1955)
**:** a lightweight low-powered motorbike that can be pedaled

**mop·pet** \'mä-pət\ *noun* [obsolete English *mop* fool, child] (1601)
**1** *archaic* **:** BABY, DARLING
**2 :** CHILD

**mop–up** \'mäp-ˌəp\ *noun* (1900)
**:** a concluding action

**mop up** (circa 1811)
*transitive verb*
**1** *British* **:** to consume eagerly
**2 :** to gather as if by absorbing **:** GARNER ⟨*mopped up* all the awards⟩
**3 :** to overcome decisively **:** TROUNCE
**4 :** to clear (an area) of remaining pockets of resistance in the wake of a military offensive
*intransitive verb*
**:** to complete a project or transaction

**mo·quette** \mō-'ket\ *noun* [French] (1762)
**:** a carpet or upholstery fabric having a velvety pile

**mor** \'mȯr\ *noun* [Danish, literally, humus] (1931)
**:** forest humus that forms a layer of largely organic matter abruptly distinct from the mineral soil beneath

**mo·ra** \'mȯr-ə, 'mȯr-\ *noun, plural* **mo·rae** \'mȯr-ˌē, 'mȯr-, -ˌī\ *or* **mo·ras** [Latin, delay; akin to Old Irish *maraid* it lasts] (1832)
**:** the minimal unit of measure in quantitative verse equivalent to the time of an average short syllable

**mo·raine** \mə-'rān\ *noun* [French, from French dialect (Savoy) *morêna*] (1789)
**:** an accumulation of earth and stones carried and finally deposited by a glacier
— **mo·rain·al** \-'rā-nᵊl\ *adjective*
— **mo·rain·ic** \-'rā-nik\ *adjective*

**¹mor·al** \'mȯr-əl, 'mär-\ *adjective* [Middle English, from Middle French, from Latin *moralis,* from *mor-, mos* custom] (14th century)
**1 a :** of or relating to principles of right and wrong in behavior **:** ETHICAL ⟨*moral* judgments⟩ **b :** expressing or teaching a conception of right behavior ⟨a *moral* poem⟩ **c :** conforming to a standard of right behavior **d :** sanctioned by or operative on one's conscience or ethical judgment ⟨a *moral* obligation⟩ **e :** capable of right and wrong action ⟨a *moral* agent⟩
**2 :** probable though not proved **:** VIRTUAL ⟨a *moral* certainty⟩
**3 :** having the effects of such on the mind, confidence, or will ⟨a *moral* victory⟩ ⟨*moral* support⟩ ☆
— **mor·al·ly** \-ə-lē\ *adverb*

**²mor·al** \'mȯr-əl, 'mär-; *3 is* mə-'ral\ *noun* (15th century)
**1 a :** the moral significance or practical lesson (as of a story) **b :** a passage pointing out usually in conclusion the lesson to be drawn from a story
**2** *plural* **a :** moral practices or teachings **:** modes of conduct **b :** ETHICS
**3 :** MORALE

**mo·rale** \mə-'ral\ *noun* [in sense 1, from French, from feminine of *moral,* adjective; in other senses, modification of French *moral* morale, from *moral,* adjective] (1752)
**1 :** moral principles, teachings, or conduct
**2 a :** the mental and emotional condition (as of enthusiasm, confidence, or loyalty) of an individual or group with regard to the function or tasks at hand **b :** a sense of common purpose with respect to a group **:** ESPRIT DE CORPS
**3 :** the level of individual psychological well-being based on such factors as a sense of purpose and confidence in the future

**moral hazard** *noun* (circa 1917)
**:** the possibility of loss to an insurance company arising from the character or circumstances of the insured

**mor·al·ise** *British variant of* MORALIZE

**mor·al·ism** \'mȯr-ə-ˌli-zəm, 'mär-\ *noun* (1828)
**1 a :** the habit or practice of moralizing **b :** a conventional moral attitude or saying
**2 :** an often exaggerated emphasis on morality (as in politics)

**mor·al·ist** \-list\ *noun* (1621)
**1 :** one who leads a moral life
**2 :** a philosopher or writer concerned with moral principles and problems

---

☆ SYNONYMS
**Moral, ethical, virtuous, righteous, noble** mean conforming to a standard of what is right and good. MORAL implies conformity to established sanctioned codes or accepted notions of right and wrong ⟨the basic *moral* values of a community⟩. ETHICAL may suggest the involvement of more difficult or subtle questions of rightness, fairness, or equity ⟨committed to the highest *ethical* principles⟩. VIRTUOUS implies the possession or manifestation of moral excellence in character ⟨not a religious person, but *virtuous* nevertheless⟩. RIGHTEOUS stresses guiltlessness or blamelessness and often suggests the sanctimonious ⟨wished to be *righteous* before God and the world⟩. NOBLE implies moral eminence and freedom from anything petty, mean, or dubious in conduct and character ⟨had the *noblest* of reasons for seeking office⟩.

**3 :** one concerned with regulating the morals of others
**mor·al·is·tic** \ˌmȯr-ə-'lis-tik, ˌmär-\ *adjective* (1865)
**1 :** characterized by or expressive of a concern with morality
**2 :** characterized by or expressive of a narrow and conventional moral attitude
— **mor·al·is·ti·cal·ly** \-ti-k(ə-)lē\ *adverb*
**mo·ral·i·ty** \mə-'ra-lə-tē, mȯ-\ *noun, plural* **-ties** (14th century)
**1 a :** a moral discourse, statement, or lesson **b :** a literary or other imaginative work teaching a moral lesson
**2 a :** a doctrine or system of moral conduct **b** *plural* **:** particular moral principles or rules of conduct
**3 :** conformity to ideals of right human conduct
**4 :** moral conduct **:** VIRTUE
**morality play** *noun* (1929)
**1 :** an allegorical play popular especially in the 15th and 16th centuries in which the characters personify abstract qualities or concepts (as virtues, vices, or death)
**2 :** something which involves a direct conflict between right and wrong or good and evil and from which a moral lesson may be drawn
**mor·al·ize** \'mȯr-ə-ˌlīz, 'mär-\ *verb* **-ized; -iz·ing** (15th century)
*transitive verb*
**1 :** to explain or interpret morally
**2 a :** to give a moral quality or direction to **b :** to improve the morals of
*intransitive verb*
**:** to make moral reflections
— **mor·al·i·za·tion** \ˌmȯr-ə-lə-'zā-shən, ˌmär-\ *noun*
— **mor·al·iz·er** \'mȯr-ə-ˌlī-zər, 'mär-\ *noun*
**moral philosophy** *noun* (1606)
**:** ETHICS; *also* **:** the study of human conduct and values
**mo·rass** \mə-'ras, mȯ-\ *noun* [Dutch *moeras*, modification of Old French *maresc*, of Germanic origin; akin to Old English *mersc* marsh — more at MARSH] (1655)
**1 :** MARSH, SWAMP
**2 :** something that traps, confuses, or impedes ⟨a *morass* of troubles⟩
— **mo·rassy** \-'ra-sē\ *adjective*
**mor·a·to·ri·um** \ˌmȯr-ə-'tōr-ē-əm, ˌmär-, -'tȯr-\ *noun, plural* **-riums** *or* **-ria** \-ē-ə\ [New Latin, from Late Latin, neuter of *moratorius* dilatory, from Latin *morari* to delay, from *mora* delay] (1875)
**1 a :** a legally authorized period of delay in the performance of a legal obligation or the payment of a debt **b :** a waiting period set by an authority
**2 :** a suspension of activity
**Mo·ra·vi·an** \mə-'rā-vē-ən\ *noun* (1555)
**1 a :** a native or inhabitant of Moravia **b :** the group of Czech dialects spoken in Moravia
**2 :** a member of a Protestant denomination arising from a 15th century religious reform movement in Bohemia and Moravia
— **Moravian** *adjective*
**mo·ray eel** \mə-'rā-, 'mȯr-(ˌ)ā-\ *noun* [Portuguese *moréia*, from Latin *muraena*, from Greek *myraina*] (1926)
**:** any of numerous often brightly colored eels (family Muraenidae) that have sharp teeth capable of inflicting a severe bite, that occur in warm seas, and that include a chiefly Mediterranean eel (*Muraena helena*) sometimes used for food — called also *moray*
**mor·bid** \'mȯr-bəd\ *adjective* [Latin *morbidus* diseased, from *morbus* disease] (1656)
**1 a :** of, relating to, or characteristic of disease ⟨*morbid* anatomy⟩ **b :** affected with or induced by disease ⟨a *morbid* condition⟩ **c :** productive of disease ⟨*morbid* substances⟩
**2 :** abnormally susceptible to or characterized by gloomy or unwholesome feelings
**3 :** GRISLY, GRUESOME ⟨*morbid* details⟩ ⟨*morbid* curiosity⟩

— **mor·bid·ly** *adverb*
— **mor·bid·ness** *noun*
**mor·bid·i·ty** \mȯr-'bi-də-tē\ *noun* (circa 1721)
**1 :** the quality or state of being morbid
**2 :** the relative incidence of disease
**mor·ceau** \mȯr-'sō\ *noun, plural* **mor·ceaux** \-'sō(z)\ [French, from Old French *morsel* morsel] (1751)
**:** a short literary or musical piece
**mor·dan·cy** \'mȯr-dᵊn(t)-sē\ *noun* (circa 1656)
**1 :** a biting and caustic quality of style **:** INCISIVENESS
**2 :** a sharply critical or bitter quality of thought or feeling **:** HARSHNESS
**¹mor·dant** \'mȯr-dᵊnt\ *adjective* [Middle English, from Middle French, present participle of *mordre* to bite, from Latin *mordēre;* perhaps akin to Sanskrit *mṛdnāti* he presses, rubs] (15th century)
**1 :** biting and caustic in thought, manner, or style **:** INCISIVE ⟨a *mordant* wit⟩
**2 :** acting as a mordant
**3 :** BURNING, PUNGENT
**synonym** see CAUSTIC
— **mor·dant·ly** *adverb*
**²mordant** *noun* (1791)
**1 :** a chemical that fixes a dye in or on a substance by combining with the dye to form an insoluble compound
**2 :** a corroding substance used in etching
**³mordant** *transitive verb* (1836)
**:** to treat with a mordant
**Mor·de·cai** \'mȯr-di-ˌkī\ *noun* [Hebrew *Mordĕkhai*]
**:** a relative of Esther who gives advice on saving the Jews from the destruction planned by Haman
**mor·dent** \'mȯr-dᵊnt, mȯr-'dent\ *noun* [Italian *mordente*, from Latin *mordent-, mordens*, present participle of *mordēre*] (1806)
**:** a musical ornament made by a quick alternation of a principal tone with the tone immediately below it
**¹more** \'mȯr, 'mȯr\ *adjective* [Middle English, from Old English *māra;* akin to Old English *mā*, adverb, more, Old High German *mēr*, Old Irish *mó* more] (before 12th century)
**1 :** GREATER ⟨something *more* than she expected⟩
**2 :** ADDITIONAL, FURTHER ⟨*more* guests arrived⟩
**²more** *adverb* (before 12th century)
**1 a :** in addition ⟨a couple of times *more*⟩ **b :** MOREOVER
**2 :** to a greater or higher degree — often used with an adjective or adverb to form the comparative ⟨*more* evenly matched⟩
**³more** *noun* (before 12th century)
**1 :** a greater quantity, number, or amount ⟨liked the idea better the *more* I thought about it⟩
**2 :** something additional **:** an additional amount
**3** *obsolete* **:** persons of higher rank
**⁴more** *pronoun, singular or plural in construction* (13th century)
**:** additional persons or things or a greater amount ⟨*more* were found as the search continued⟩ ⟨*more* was spilled⟩
**more and more** *adverb* (13th century)
**:** to a progressively increasing extent
**mo·reen** \mə-'rēn, mȯ-\ *noun* [probably irregular from *moire*] (circa 1691)
**:** a strong fabric of wool, wool and cotton, or cotton with a plain glossy or moiré finish
**mo·rel** \mə-'rel, mȯ-\ *noun* [French *morille*, probably from (assumed) Vulgar Latin *mauricula*, from *maurus* brown, from Latin *Maurus* inhabitant of Mauretania] (1672)
**:** any of several edible fungi (genus *Morchella*, especially *M. esculenta*) having a cap with a highly pitted surface
**mo·rel·lo** \mə-'re-(ˌ)lō\ *noun, plural* **-los** [probably modification of Flemish *amarelle*,

*marelle*, from Medieval Latin *amarellum*, a sour cherry, from Latin *amarus* bitter, sour] (1598)
**:** a cultivated sour cherry (as the Montmorency) having a dark-colored skin and juice
**more or less** *adverb* (13th century)
**1 :** to a varying or undetermined extent or degree **:** SOMEWHAT ⟨they were *more or less* willing to help⟩
**2 :** with small variations **:** APPROXIMATELY ⟨contains 16 acres *more or less*⟩
**more·over** \mȯr-'ō-vər, mȯr-, 'mȯr-ˌ, 'mȯr-ˌ\ *adverb* (14th century)
**:** in addition to what has been said **:** BESIDES
**mo·res** \'mȯr-ˌāz, 'mȯr- *also* -(ˌ)ēz\ *noun plural* [Latin, plural of *mor-, mos* custom] (circa 1899)
**1 :** the fixed morally binding customs of a particular group
**2 :** moral attitudes
**3 :** HABITS, MANNERS ◼
**¹mo·resque** \mȯ-'resk, mə-\ *adjective, often capitalized* [French, from Spanish *morisco*, from *moro* Moor, from Latin *Maurus*] (circa 1611)
**:** having the characteristics of Moorish art or architecture
**²moresque** *noun, often capitalized* (circa 1752)
**:** an ornament or decorative motif in Moorish style
**mor·gan** \'mȯr-gən\ *noun* [Thomas Hunt *Morgan*] (1919)
**1 :** a unit of inferred distance between genes on a chromosome that is used in constructing genetic maps and is equal to the distance for which the frequency of crossing over between specific pairs of genes is 100 percent
**2 :** CENTIMORGAN
**Mor·gan** \'mȯr-gən\ *noun* [Justin *Morgan* (died 1798) American teacher] (1841)
**:** any of an American breed of light strong horses originated in Vermont from the progeny of one prepotent stallion of uncertain ancestry
**mor·ga·nat·ic** \ˌmȯr-gə-'na-tik\ *adjective* [New Latin *matrimonium ad morganaticam*, literally, marriage with morning gift] (circa 1741)
**:** of, relating to, or being a marriage between a member of a royal or noble family and a person of inferior rank in which the rank of the

□ USAGE
**mores** The pronunciation ending in \-(ˌ)ēz\ is now used by a minority of American and British speakers, but it was the original pronunciation of *mores* when the word first came into English about a century ago. Up until the middle of this century it was fashionable to anglicize words borrowed from another language, especially in British English. Thus, we do not pronounce *habeas corpus* according to the reconstructed Latin model as \'hä-bā-äs-'kȯr-pŭs\, but as a fully Englished form. One finds this tendency at work especially in the English of the Anglican Church, as in the church pronunciations of *Miserere, Venite, Kyrie,* and so forth. The word *mores* was thus also given a fully anglicized pronunciation at the start of its life in English, but when fashions changed and Latinate forms were given "Latin" pronunciations, the second syllable of *mores* became \-ˌāz\. Most of the evidence we have collected for the \-(ˌ)ēz\ pronunciation is from earlier decades, and it seems that among younger speakers the only recognized pronunciation ends in \-ˌāz\.

\ə\ abut \ᵊ\ kitten \ər\ further \a\ ash \ā\ ace
\ä\ mop, mar \au̇\ out \ch\ chin \e\ bet \ē\ easy
\g\ go \i\ hit \ī\ ice \j\ job \ŋ\ sing \ō\ go
\ȯ\ law \ȯi\ boy \th\ thin \th\ the \ü\ loot \u̇\ foot
\y\ yet \zh\ vision *see also* Guide to Pronunciation

inferior partner remains unchanged and the children of the marriage do not succeed to the titles, fiefs, or entailed property of the parent of higher rank

— **mor·ga·nat·i·cal·ly** \-ti-k(ə-)lē\ *adverb*

**mor·gan·ite** \'mȯr-gə-ˌnīt\ *noun* [J. P. Morgan (died 1913)] (1911)

: a rose-colored gem variety of beryl

**Morgan le Fay** \-lə-'fā\ *noun* [Old French *Morgain la fee* Morgan the fairy]

: a sorceress and sister of King Arthur

**mor·gen** \'mȯr-gə(n)\ *noun, plural* **morgen** [Dutch, literally, morning] (1626)

: a Dutch and southern African unit of land area equal to 2.116 acres (0.856 hectare)

**morgue** \'mȯrg\ *noun* [French] (1821)

**1 :** a place where the bodies of persons found dead are kept until identified and claimed by relatives or are released for burial
**2 :** a collection of reference works and files of reference material in a newspaper or news periodical office

**mor·i·bund** \'mȯr-ə-(ˌ)bənd, 'mär-\ *adjective* [Latin *moribundus,* from *mori* to die — more at MURDER] (circa 1721)

**1 :** being in the state of dying **:** approaching death
**2 :** being in a state of inactivity or obsolescence

— **mor·i·bun·di·ty** \ˌmȯr-ə-'bən-də-tē, ˌmär-\ *noun*

**¹mo·ri·on** \'mȯr-ē-ˌän, 'mȯr-\ *noun* [Middle French] (1563)

: a high-crested helmet with no visor

**²morion** *noun* [modification of Latin *mormorion*] (1748)

: a nearly black variety of smoky quartz

**Mo·ris·co** \mə-'ris-(ˌ)kō, mȯ-\ *noun, plural* **-cos** *or* **-coes** [Spanish, from *morisco,* adjective, from *moro* Moor] (1629)

**:** MOOR; *especially* **:** a Spanish Moor

— **Morisco** *adjective*

**Mor·mon** \'mȯr-mən\ *noun*

**1 :** the ancient redactor and compiler of the Book of Mormon presented as divine revelation by Joseph Smith
**2 :** LATTER-DAY SAINT; *especially* **:** a member of the Church of Jesus Christ of Latter-day Saints

— **Mor·mon·ism** \-mə-ˌni-zəm\ *noun*

**Mormon cricket** *noun* (1896)

: a large dark wingless katydid (*Anabrus simplex*) that resembles a cricket and is found in the arid parts of the western U.S. where it is occasionally an abundant pest of crops

**morn** \'mȯrn\ *noun* [Middle English, from Old English *morgen*; akin to Old High German *morgan* morning and perhaps to Greek *marmairein* to sparkle] (before 12th century)

**1 :** DAWN
**2 :** MORNING

**Mor·nay sauce** \mȯr-'nā-\ *noun* [Philippe de Mornay] (circa 1924)

: a cheese-flavored cream sauce

**morn·ing** \'mȯr-niŋ\ *noun* [Middle English, from *morn* + *-ing* (as in *evening*)] (13th century)

**1 a :** DAWN **b :** the time from sunrise to noon **c :** the time from midnight to noon
**2 :** a period of first development **:** BEGINNING

**morn·ing–after pill** \ˌmȯr-niŋ-'af-tər-\ *noun* [from its being taken after rather than before intercourse] (1966)

: an oral drug that interferes with pregnancy by blocking implantation of a fertilized egg in the human uterus

**morning glory** *noun* (1814)

: any of various usually twining plants (genus *Ipomoea* of the family Convolvulaceae, the morning-glory family) with showy trumpet-shaped flowers; *broadly* **:** a plant of the morning-glory family including herbs, shrubs, or trees with alternate leaves and regular pentamerous flowers

**morning line** *noun* (circa 1935)

: a bookmaker's list of entries for a race meet and the probable odds on each that is printed or posted before the betting begins

**Morning Prayer** *noun* (1552)

: a service of liturgical prayer used for regular morning worship in churches of the Anglican communion

**morn·ings** \'mȯr-niŋz\ *adverb* (1652)

: in the morning repeatedly **:** on any morning

**morning sickness** *noun* (1879)

: nausea and vomiting that occur on rising in the morning especially during the earlier months of pregnancy

**morning star** *noun* (1535)

: a bright planet (as Venus) seen in the eastern sky before or at sunrise

**Mo·ro** \'mōr-(ˌ)ō, 'mȯr-\ *noun, plural* **Moros** [Spanish, literally, Moor, from Latin *Maurus*] (1886)

**1 :** a member of any of several Muslim peoples of the southern Philippines
**2 :** any of the Austronesian languages of the Moro peoples

**mo·roc·co** \mə-'rä-(ˌ)kō\ *noun* [*Morocco,* Africa] (1634)

: a fine leather from goatskin tanned with sumac

**mo·ron** \'mōr-ˌän, 'mȯr-\ *noun* [irregular from Greek *mōros* foolish, stupid] (1910)

**1 :** a mentally retarded person who has a potential mental age of between 8 and 12 years and is capable of doing routine work under supervision
**2 :** a very stupid person

— **mo·ron·ic** \mə-'rä-nik, mȯ-\ *adjective*
— **mo·ron·i·cal·ly** \-ni-k(ə-)lē\ *adverb*
— **mo·ron·ism** \'mōr-ˌä-ˌni-zəm, 'mȯr-\ *noun*
— **mo·ron·i·ty** \mə-'rä-nə-tē, mȯ-\ *noun*

**mo·rose** \mə-'rōs, mȯ-\ *adjective* [Latin *morosus,* literally, capricious, from *mor-, mos* will] (1565)

**1 :** having a sullen and gloomy disposition
**2 :** marked by or expressive of gloom

*synonym* see SULLEN

— **mo·rose·ly** *adverb*
— **mo·rose·ness** *noun*
— **mo·ros·i·ty** \-'rä-sə-tē\ *noun*

**morph** \'mȯrf\ *noun* [back-formation from *morpheme*] (1947)

**1 a :** ALLOMORPH **b :** a distinctive collocation of phones (as a portmanteau form) that serves as the realization of more than one morpheme in a context (as the French *du* for the sequence of *de* and *le*)
**2 a :** a local population of a species that consists of interbreeding organisms and is distinguishable from other populations by morphology or behavior though capable of interbreeding with them **b :** a phenotypic variant of a species

**morph-** *or* **morpho-** *combining form* [German, from Greek, from *morphē*]

**1 :** form ⟨*morph*ogenesis⟩
**2 :** morpheme ⟨*morpho*phonemics⟩

**-morph** *noun combining form* [International Scientific Vocabulary, from *-morphous*]

: one having (such) a form ⟨iso*morph*⟩

**mor·phac·tin** \mȯr-'fak-tən\ *noun* [probably from *morph-* + *active* + *¹-in*] (1966)

: any of several synthetic fluorine-containing compounds that tend to produce morphological changes and suppress growth in plants

**mor·phal·lax·is** \ˌmȯr-fə-'lak-səs\ *noun, plural* **-lax·es** \-ˌsēz\ [New Latin, from *morph-* + Greek *allaxis* exchange, from *allassein* to change, exchange, from *allos* other — more at ELSE] (1901)

: regeneration of a part or organism from a fragment by reorganization without cell proliferation

**mor·pheme** \'mȯr-ˌfēm\ *noun* [French *morphème,* from Greek *morphē* form] (1926)

: a distinctive collocation of phonemes (as the free form *pin* or the bound form *-s* of *pins*) that contains no smaller meaningful parts

— **mor·phe·mic** \mȯr-'fē-mik\ *adjective*
— **mor·phe·mi·cal·ly** \-mi-k(ə-)lē\ *adverb*

**mor·phe·mics** \mȯr-'fē-miks\ *noun plural but singular in construction* (1947)

**1 :** a branch of linguistic analysis that consists of the study of morphemes
**2 :** the structure of a language in terms of morphemes

**Mor·pheus** \'mȯr-fē-əs, -ˌfyüs, -ˌfüs\ *noun* [Latin, from Greek]

: the Greek god of dreams

**mor·phia** \'mȯr-fē-ə\ *noun* [New Latin, from *Morpheus*] (1818)

**:** MORPHINE

**-morphic** *adjective combining form* [probably from French *-morphique,* from Greek *morphē*]

: having (such) a form ⟨endo*morphic*⟩

**mor·phine** \'mȯr-ˌfēn\ *noun* [French, from *Morpheus*] (1828)

: a bitter crystalline addictive narcotic base $C_{17}H_{19}NO_3$ that is the principal alkaloid of opium and is used in the form of a soluble salt (as a hydrochloride or a sulfate) as an analgesic and sedative ◆

**mor·phin·ism** \'mȯr-ˌfē-ˌni-zəm, -fə-\ *noun* (1882)

: a disordered condition of health produced by habitual use of morphine

**-morphism** *noun combining form* [Late Latin *-morphus* -morphous, from Greek *-morphos*]

: quality or state of having (such) a form ⟨hetero*morphism*⟩

**mor·pho** \'mȯr-(ˌ)fō\ *noun, plural* **morphos** [New Latin, from Greek *Morphō,* epithet of Aphrodite] (1853)

: any of a genus (*Morpho* of the family Morphoidae) of large showy tropical American butterflies that typically have a brilliant blue metallic luster on the upper surface of the wings

**mor·pho·gen** \'mȯr-fə-jən, -ˌjen\ *noun* (1950)

: a diffusible chemical substance that exerts control over morphogenesis especially by forming a gradient in concentration

**mor·pho·gen·e·sis** \ˌmȯr-fə-'je-nə-səs\ *noun* [New Latin] (circa 1890)

: the formation and differentiation of tissues and organs — compare ORGANOGENESIS

**mor·pho·ge·net·ic** \-jə-'ne-tik\ *adjective* (1884)

: relating to or concerned with the development of normal organic form ⟨*morphogenetic* movements of early embryonic cells⟩

— **mor·pho·ge·net·i·cal·ly** \-ti-k(ə-)lē\ *adverb*

**mor·pho·gen·ic** \-'je-nik\ *adjective* (circa 1890)

**:** MORPHOGENETIC

**mor·phol·o·gy** \mȯr-'fä-lə-jē\ *noun* [German *Morphologie,* from *morph-* + *-logie* -logy] (1830)

---

**1 a :** a branch of biology that deals with the form and structure of animals and plants **b :** the form and structure of an organism or any of its parts **2 a :** a study and description of word formation (as inflection, derivation, and compounding) in language **b :** the system of word-forming elements and processes in a language **3 a :** a study of structure or form **b :** STRUCTURE, FORM **4 :** the external structure of rocks in relation to the development of erosional forms or topographic features

— **mor·pho·log·i·cal** \ˌmȯr-fə-'lä-ji-kəl\ *also* **mor·pho·log·ic** \-'lä-jik\ *adjective*

— **mor·pho·log·i·cal·ly** \-k(ə-)lē\ *adverb*

— **mor·phol·o·gist** \mȯr-'fä-lə-jist\ *noun*

**mor·phom·e·try** \mȯr-'fä-mə-trē\ *noun* (circa 1856)
: measurement of external form

— **mor·pho·met·ric** \ˌmȯr-fə-'me-trik\ *adjective*

— **mor·pho·met·ri·cal·ly** \-tri-k(ə-)lē\ *adverb*

**mor·pho·pho·ne·mics** \ˌmȯr-fō-fə-'nē-miks\ *noun plural but singular in construction* (1939)
**1 :** a study of the phonemic differences between allomorphs of the same morpheme **2 :** the distribution of allomorphs in one morpheme **3 :** the structure of a language in terms of morphophonemics

**-morphous** *adjective combining form* [Greek -*morphos*, from *morphē*]
: having (such) a form ⟨iso*morphous*⟩

**-morphy** *noun combining form* [International Scientific Vocabulary, from -*morphous*]
: quality or state of having (such) a form ⟨endo*morphy*⟩

**mor·ris** \'mȯr-əs, 'mär-\ *noun* [Middle English *moreys daunce*, from *moreys* Moorish (from *More* Moor) + *daunce* dance] (1512)
: a vigorous English dance traditionally performed by men wearing costumes and bells

**morris chair** *noun* [William *Morris*] (1900)
: an easy chair with adjustable back and removable cushions

**mor·row** \'mär-(ˌ)ō, 'mȯr-\ *noun* [Middle English *morn, morwen* morn] (13th century)
**1** *archaic* **:** MORNING **2 :** the next day **3 :** the time immediately after a specified event

**Morse code** \'mȯrs-\ *noun* [Samuel F. B. *Morse*] (1867)
: either of two codes consisting of variously spaced dots and dashes or long and short sounds used for transmitting messages by audible or visual signals

morris chair

**¹mor·sel** \'mȯr-səl\ *noun* [Middle English, from Old French, diminutive of *mors* bite, from Latin *morsus*, from *mordēre* to bite — more at MORDANT] (14th century)
**1 :** a small piece of food **:** BITE **2 :** a small quantity **:** FRAGMENT **3 a :** a tasty dish **b :** something delectable and pleasing **4 :** a negligible person

**²morsel** *transitive verb* **-seled** *or* **-selled**; **-sel·ing** *or* **-sel·ling** (1598)
: to divide into or distribute in small pieces

**¹mort** \'mȯrt\ *noun* [probably alteration of Middle English *mot* horn note, from Middle French, word, horn note — more at MOT] (circa 1500)
**1 :** a note sounded on a hunting horn when a deer is killed **2 :** KILLING 1

---

## INTERNATIONAL MORSE CODE

| | | | |
|---|---|---|---|
| a | · — | á | · — · — |
| b | — · · · | ä | · — · — |
| c | — · — · | é | · · — · · |
| d | — · · | ñ | — — · — — |
| e | · | ö | — — — · |
| f | · · — · | ü | · · — — |
| g | — — · | 1 | · — — — — |
| h | · · · · | 2 | · · — — — |
| i | · · | 3 | · · · — — |
| j | · — — — | 4 | · · · · — |
| k | — · — | 5 | · · · · · |
| l | · — · · | 6 | — · · · · |
| m | — — | 7 | — — · · · |
| n | — · | 8 | — — — · · |
| o | — — — | 9 | — — — — · |
| p | · — — · | 0 | — — — — — |
| q | — — · — | , | — — · · — — (comma) |
| r | · — · | | |
| s | · · · | ? | · · — — · · |
| t | — | | |
| u | · · — | | |
| v | · · · — | ' | · — — — — · (apostrophe) |
| w | · — — | - | — · · · · — (hyphen) |
| x | — · · — | / | — · · — · |
| y | — · — — | ( | — · — — · (left parenthesis) |
| z | — — · · | ) | — · — — · — (right parenthesis) |

---

**²mort** *noun* [perhaps back-formation from ¹*mortal*] (1694)
: a great quantity or number

**mor·ta·del·la** \ˌmȯr-tə-'de-lə\ *noun* [Italian, from Latin *murtatum* sausage seasoned with myrtle berries, from *murtus* myrtle] (1613)
: a large smoked sausage made of beef, pork, and pork fat and seasoned with pepper and garlic

**¹mor·tal** \'mȯr-t°l\ *adjective* [Middle English, from Middle French, from Latin *mortalis*, from *mort-, mors* death — more at MURDER] (14th century)
**1 :** causing or having caused death **:** FATAL ⟨a *mortal* injury⟩ **2 a :** subject to death ⟨*mortal* man⟩ **b :** POSSIBLE, CONCEIVABLE ⟨have done every *mortal* thing⟩ **c :** DEADLY **3** ⟨waited three *mortal* hours⟩ **3 :** marked by unrelenting hostility **:** IMPLACABLE ⟨a *mortal* enemy⟩ **4 :** marked by great intensity or severity **:** EXTREME ⟨*mortal* fear⟩ ⟨a *mortal* shame⟩ **5 :** HUMAN ⟨*mortal* limitations⟩ **6 :** of, relating to, or connected with death ⟨*mortal* agony⟩

**synonym** see DEADLY

**²mortal** *adverb* (15th century)
*chiefly dialect* **:** MORTALLY

**³mortal** *noun* (1567)
: a human being

**mor·tal·i·ty** \mȯr-'ta-lə-tē\ *noun* (14th century)
**1 :** the quality or state of being mortal **2 :** the death of large numbers (as of people or animals) **3** *archaic* **:** DEATH **4 :** the human race **5 a :** the number of deaths in a given time or place **b :** the proportion of deaths to population **c :** the number lost or the rate of loss or failure

**mortality table** *noun* (1880)
: an actuarial table based on mortality statistics over a number of years

**mor·tal·ly** \'mȯr-t°l-ē\ *adverb* (14th century)
**1 :** in a deadly or fatal manner **:** to death ⟨*mortally* wounded⟩ **2 :** to an extreme degree **:** INTENSELY ⟨*mortally* afraid⟩

**mortal mind** *noun* (1875)
*Christian Science* **:** a belief that life, substance, and intelligence are in and of matter **:** ILLUSION

**mortal sin** *noun* (15th century)
: a sin (as murder) that is deliberately committed and is of such serious consequence according to Thomist theology that it deprives the soul of sanctifying grace — compare VENIAL SIN

**¹mor·tar** \'mȯr-tər\ *noun* [Middle English *morter*, from Old English *mortere* & Middle French *mortier*, from Latin *mortarium*] (before 12th century)
**1 :** a strong vessel in which material is pounded or rubbed with a pestle **2** [Middle French *mortier*] **a :** a muzzle-loading cannon having a tube short in relation to its caliber that is used to throw projectiles with low muzzle velocities at high angles **b :** any of several similar firing devices

**²mortar** *noun* [Middle English *morter*, from Old French *mortier*, from Latin *mortarium*] (14th century)
: a plastic building material (as a mixture of cement, lime, or gypsum plaster with sand and water) that hardens and is used in masonry or plastering

— **mor·tar·less** *adjective*

**³mortar** *transitive verb* (14th century)
: to plaster or make fast with mortar

**mor·tar·board** \'mȯr-tər-ˌbōrd, -ˌbȯrd\ *noun* (1854)
**1 a :** HAWK 2 **b :** a board or platform about three feet (one meter) square for holding mortar **2 :** an academic cap consisting of a closely fitting headpiece with a broad flat projecting square top

mortarboard 2

**¹mort·gage** \'mȯr-gij\ *noun* [Middle English *morgage*, from Middle French, from Old French, from *mort* dead (from Latin *mortuus*) + *gage* gage — more at MURDER] (15th century)
**1 :** a conveyance of or lien against property that is defeated upon payment or performance according to stipulated terms **2 a :** the instrument evidencing the mortgage **b :** the state of the property so mortgaged **c :** the interest of the mortgagee in such property

**²mortgage** *transitive verb* **mort·gaged; mort·gag·ing** (15th century)
**1 :** to grant or convey by a mortgage **2 :** to subject to a claim or obligation **:** PLEDGE

**mort·gag·ee** \ˌmȯr-gi-'jē\ *noun* (1584)
: a person to whom property is mortgaged

**mort·gag·or** \ˌmȯr-gi-'jȯr\ *also* **mort·gag·er** \'mȯr-gi-jər\ *noun* (1584)
: a person who mortgages property

**mor·ti·cian** \mȯr-'ti-shən\ *noun* [Latin *mort-, mors* death] (1895)
: UNDERTAKER 2

**mor·ti·fi·ca·tion** \ˌmȯr-tə-fə-'kā-shən\ *noun* (14th century)
**1 :** the subjection and denial of bodily passions and appetites by abstinence or self-inflicted pain or discomfort **2 :** NECROSIS, GANGRENE **3 a :** a sense of humiliation and shame caused by something that wounds one's pride or self-respect **b :** the cause of such humiliation

**mor·ti·fy** \'mȯr-tə-ˌfī\ *verb* **-fied; -fy·ing** [Middle English *mortifien*, from Middle French *mortifier*, from Late Latin *mortificare*, from Latin *mort-, mors*] (14th century)
*transitive verb*

---

**1** *obsolete* : to destroy the strength, vitality, or functioning of
**2** : to subdue or deaden (as the body or bodily appetites) especially by abstinence or self-inflicted pain or discomfort
**3** : to subject to severe and vexing embarrassment : SHAME
*intransitive verb*
**1** : to practice mortification
**2** : to become necrotic or gangrenous

**¹mor·tise** *also* **mor·tice** \'mȯr-təs\ *noun* [Middle English *mortays*, from Middle French *mortaise*] (15th century)
: a hole, groove, or slot into or through which some other part of an arrangement of parts fits or passes; *especially* : a cavity cut into a piece of material (as timber) to receive a tenon — see DOVETAIL illustration

**²mortise** *also* **mortice** *transitive verb* **mortised** *also* **morticed; mor·tis·ing** *also* **mor·tic·ing** (15th century)
**1** : to join or fasten securely; *specifically* : to join or fasten by a tenon and mortise
**2** : to cut or make a mortise in

**mort·main** \'mȯrt-ˌmān\ *noun* [Middle English *morte-mayne*, from Middle French *mortemain*, from Old French, from *morte* (feminine of *mort* dead) + *main* hand, from Latin *manus* — more at MANUAL] (15th century)
**1 a** : an inalienable possession of lands or buildings by an ecclesiastical or other corporation **b** : the condition of property or other gifts left to a corporation in perpetuity especially for religious, charitable, or public purposes
**2** : the influence of the past regarded as controlling the present

**¹mor·tu·ary** \'mȯr-chə-ˌwer-ē\ *adjective* [Latin *mortuarius* of the dead, from *mortuus* dead] (1514)
**1** : of or relating to the burial of the dead
**2** : of, relating to, or characteristic of death

**²mortuary** *noun, plural* **-ar·ies** (1865)
: a place in which dead bodies are kept until burial; *especially* : FUNERAL HOME

**mor·u·la** \'mȯr-(y)ə-lə, 'mär-\ *noun, plural* **-lae** \-ˌlē, -ˌlī\ [New Latin, from Latin *morum* mulberry, from Greek *moron*] (1874)
: a globular solid mass of blastomeres formed by cleavage of a zygote that typically precedes the blastula
— **mor·u·lar** \-lər\ *adjective*
— **mor·u·la·tion** \ˌmȯr-(y)ə-'lā-shən, ˌmär-\ *noun*

**¹mo·sa·ic** \mō-'zā-ik\ *noun* [Middle English *musycke*, from Middle French *mosaique*, from Old Italian *mosaico*, from Medieval Latin *musaicum*, alteration of Late Latin *musivum*, from Latin *museum, musaeum*] (15th century)
**1** : a surface decoration made by inlaying small pieces of variously colored material to form pictures or patterns; *also* : the process of making it
**2** : a picture or design made in mosaic
**3** : something resembling a mosaic ⟨a *mosaic* of visions and daydreams and memories —Lawrence Shainberg⟩
**4** : an organism or one of its parts composed of cells of more than one genotype : CHIMERA 3
**5** : a virus disease of plants characterized by diffuse light and dark green or yellow and green mottling of the foliage
**6** : a composite map made of photographs taken by an aircraft or spacecraft
**7** : the part of a television camera tube consisting of many minute photoelectric particles that convert light to an electric charge
— **mo·sa·ic·like** \-'zā-ik-ˌlīk\ *adjective*

**²mosaic** *adjective* (1585)
**1** : of, relating to, produced by, or resembling a mosaic
**2** : exhibiting mosaicism
**3** : DETERMINATE 5
— **mo·sa·i·cal·ly** \-'zā-ə-k(ə-)lē\ *adverb*

**³mosaic** *transitive verb* **-icked; -ick·ing** (1839)

**1** : to decorate with mosaics
**2** : to form into a mosaic

**Mo·sa·ic** \mō-'zā-ik\ *adjective* [New Latin *Mosaicus*, from *Moses* Moses] (1662)
: of or relating to Moses or the institutions or writings attributed to him

**mo·sa·i·cism** \mō-'zā-ə-ˌsi-zəm\ *noun* (1926)
: the condition of possessing cells of two or more different genetic constitutions

**mo·sa·i·cist** \-sist\ *noun* (1847)
**1 a** : a designer of mosaics **b** : a worker who makes mosaics
**2** : a dealer in mosaics

**mo·sa·saur** \'mō-zə-ˌsȯr\ *noun* [New Latin *Mosasaurus*, from Latin *Mosa* the river Meuse + Greek *sauros* lizard] (1841)
: any of a family (Mosasauridae) of very large extinct marine fish-eating lizards of the Upper Cretaceous with limbs modified into paddles that are related to the recent monitor lizards

**Mo·selle** \mō-'zel\ *noun* [German *Moselwein*, from *Mosel* Moselle, river in Germany + German *Wein* wine] (1693)
: a white wine from the Moselle valley

**Mo·ses** \'mō-zəz *also* -zəs\ *noun* [Latin, from Greek *Mōsēs*, from Hebrew *Mōsheh*]
: a Hebrew prophet who led the Israelites out of Egyptian slavery and at Mount Sinai delivered to them the Law establishing God's covenant with them

**mo·sey** \'mō-zē\ *intransitive verb* **mo·seyed; mo·sey·ing** [origin unknown] (1829)
**1** : to hurry away
**2** : to move in a leisurely or aimless manner : SAUNTER ⟨*moseyed* around the general store, testing the cheese straight off the round —Eric Sevareid⟩

**mo·shav** \mō-'shäv\ *noun, plural* **mo·sha·vim** \ˌmō-shə-'vēm\ [New Hebrew *mōshābh*, from Hebrew, dwelling] (1931)
: a cooperative settlement of small individual farms in Israel — compare KIBBUTZ

**Mos·lem** \'mäz-ləm *also* 'mäs-\ *variant of* MUSLIM

**Mo·so·tho** \mō-'sō-(ˌ)tō, -'sü-(ˌ)tü\ *noun, plural* **Ba·so·tho** \bä-\ (1952)
: a member of the Basotho people

**mosque** \'mäsk\ *noun* [Middle French *mosquee*, from Old Italian *moschea*, from Old Spanish *mezquita*, from Arabic *masjid* temple, from *sajada* to prostrate oneself, worship] (1711)
: a building used for public worship by Muslims

**mos·qui·to** \mə-'skē-(ˌ)tō\ *noun, plural* **-toes** *also* **-tos** [Spanish, diminutive of *mosca* fly, from Latin *musca* — more at MIDGE] (circa 1583)
: any of a family (Culicidae) of dipteran flies with females that have a set of slender organs in the proboscis adapted to puncture the skin of animals and to suck their blood and that are in some cases vectors of serious diseases
— **mos·qui·to·ey** \-'skē-tə-wē\ *adjective*

**mosquito fish** *noun* (1928)
: either of two North American live-bearers (*Gambusia affinis* and *Heterandria formosa* of the family Poeciliidae) used especially to exterminate mosquito larvae

**mosquito hawk** *noun* (1737)
: DRAGONFLY

**mosquito net** *noun* (1745)
: a net or screen for keeping out mosquitoes

**¹moss** \'mȯs\ *noun* [Middle English, from Old English *mos; akin to Old High German *mos* moss, Latin *muscus*] (before 12th century)
**1** *chiefly Scottish* : BOG, SWAMP; *especially* : a peat bog
**2 a** : any of a class (Musci) of bryophytic plants having a small leafy often tufted stem bearing sex organs at its tip; *also* : a clump or sward of these plants **b** : any of various plants resembling moss in appearance or habit of growth
**3** : a mossy covering

— **moss·like** \-ˌlīk\ *adjective*

**²moss** *transitive verb* (15th century)
: to cover or overgrow with moss

**moss agate** *noun* (1798)
: an agate mineral containing brown, black, or green mosslike or dendritic markings

**moss animal** *noun* (1881)
: BRYOZOAN

**moss·back** \'mȯs-ˌbak\ *noun* (1872)
**1** : a large sluggish fish (as a largemouth bass)
**2** : an extremely old-fashioned or reactionary person : FOGY
— **moss·backed** \-ˌbakt\ *adjective*

**moss green** *noun* (1884)
: a variable color averaging a moderate yellow-green

**moss–grown** \'mȯs-ˌgrōn\ *adjective* (14th century)
**1** : overgrown with moss
**2** : ANTIQUATED

**moss pink** *noun* (circa 1856)
: a low-growing perennial phlox (*Phlox subulata*) widely cultivated for its abundant usually pink or white flowers

**moss rose** *noun* (1776)
: an old-fashioned garden rose (*Rosa centifolia mucosa*) that has a glandular mossy calyx and flower stalk

**moss–troop·er** \'mȯs-ˌtrü-pər\ *noun* (1645)
**1** : one of a class of 17th century raiders in the marshy border country between England and Scotland
**2** : PIRATE
— **moss–troop·ing** \-piŋ\ *adjective*

**mossy** \'mȯ-sē\ *adjective* **moss·i·er; -est** (15th century)
**1** : resembling moss
**2** : covered with moss or something like moss
**3** : ANTIQUATED ⟨the *mossy* precepts of the . . . prescriptive grammarians —Thomas Pyles⟩

**mossy zinc** *noun* (1910)
: a granulated form of zinc made by pouring melted zinc into water

**¹most** \'mōst\ *adjective* [Middle English, from Old English *mæst; akin to Old High German *meist* most, Old English *māra* more — more at MORE] (before 12th century)
**1** : greatest in quantity, extent, or degree ⟨the *most* ability⟩
**2** : the majority of ⟨*most* people⟩

**²most** *adverb* (before 12th century)
**1** : to the greatest or highest degree — often used with an adjective or adverb to form the superlative ⟨the *most* challenging job he ever had⟩
**2** : to a very great degree ⟨was *most* persuasive⟩

**³most** *noun* (12th century)
: the greatest amount ⟨it's the *most* I can do⟩
— **at most** *or* **at the most** : as an extreme limit ⟨took him an hour *at most*⟩

**⁴most** *pronoun, singular or plural in construction* (13th century)
: the greatest number or part ⟨*most* become discouraged and quit⟩

**⁵most** *adverb* [by shortening] (circa 1584)
: ALMOST ⟨we'll be crossing the river *most* any time now —Hamilton Basso⟩ ◼

**-most** *adjective suffix* [Middle English, alteration of *-mest* (as in *formest* foremost)]
: most ⟨inner*most*⟩ : most toward ⟨head*most*⟩

**most·ly** \'mōst-lē\ *adverb* (1594)
: for the greatest part : MAINLY

□ USAGE
**most** Although considered by some to be unacceptable in all cases, *most* is often used to mean "almost" in both spoken and, to a lesser extent, written English to modify the adjectives *all, every,* and *any;* the pronouns *all, everyone, everything, everybody, anyone, anything,* and *anybody;* and the adverbs *everywhere, anywhere,* and *always.* Other uses of this sense of *most* are dialectal.

**Most Reverend** (15th century)
— used as a title for an archbishop or a Roman Catholic bishop

**mot** \'mō\ *noun, plural* **mots** \'mō(z)\ [French, word, saying, from Late Latin *muttum* grunt — more at MOTTO] (1631)
: a pithy or witty saying

¹**mote** \'mōt\ *verbal auxiliary* [Middle English, from Old English *mōtan* to be allowed to — more at MUST] (before 12th century)
*archaic* : MAY, MIGHT

²**mote** \'mōt\ *noun* [Middle English *mot*, from Old English; akin to Middle Dutch & Frisian *mot* sand] (before 12th century)
: a small particle : SPECK

**mo·tel** \mō-'tel\ *noun* [blend of *motor* and *hotel*] (1925)
: an establishment which provides lodging and parking and in which the rooms are usually accessible from an outdoor parking area

**mo·tet** \mō-'tet\ *noun* [Middle English, from Middle French, diminutive of *mot*] (14th century)
: a polyphonic choral composition on a sacred text usually without instrumental accompaniment

**moth** \'môth\ *noun, plural* **moths** \'môthz, 'môths\ [Middle English *mothe*, from Old English *moththe*; akin to Middle High German *motte* moth] (before 12th century)
**1** : CLOTHES MOTH
**2** : any of various usually nocturnal lepidopteran insects with antennae that are often feathery, with a stouter body, duller coloring, and proportionately smaller wings than the butterflies, and with larvae that are plant-eating caterpillars
— **moth·like** \-,līk\ *adjective*
— **mothy** \'mô-thē\ *adjective*

¹**moth·ball** \'môth-,bòl\ *noun* (1906)
**1** : a ball made formerly of camphor but now often of naphthalene and used to keep moths from clothing
**2** *plural* : a condition of protective storage ⟨put the ships in *mothballs* after the war⟩; *also* : a state of having been rejected for further use or dismissed from further consideration ⟨put that idea in *mothballs*⟩

²**mothball** *transitive verb* (1943)
**1** : to deactivate (as a ship) and prevent deterioration chiefly by dehumidification
**2** : to withdraw from use or service and keep in reserve

**moth bean** *noun* [probably by folk etymology from Marathi *math* moth bean] (1884)
: a bean (*Phaseolus aconitifolius*) that is cultivated especially in India for its cylindrical pods and small yellowish brown seeds

**moth–eat·en** \'môth-,ē-t°n\ *adjective* (14th century)
**1** : eaten into by moth larvae ⟨*moth-eaten* clothes⟩
**2 a** : DILAPIDATED **b** : ANTIQUATED, OUTMODED

¹**moth·er** \'mə-thər\ *noun* [Middle English *moder*, from Old English *mōdor*; akin to Old High German *muoter* mother, Latin *mater*, Greek *mētēr*, Sanskrit *mātṛ*] (before 12th century)
**1 a** : a female parent **b** (1) : a woman in authority; *specifically* : the superior of a religious community of women (2) : an old or elderly woman
**2** : SOURCE, ORIGIN ⟨necessity is the *mother* of invention⟩
**3** : maternal tenderness or affection
**4** [short for *motherfucker*] : one that is particularly impressive or contemptible — sometimes considered vulgar
— **moth·er·hood** \-,hůd\ *noun*
— **moth·er·less** \-ləs\ *adjective*
— **moth·er·less·ness** *noun*

²**mother** *adjective* (13th century)
**1 a** : of, relating to, or being a mother **b** : bearing the relation of a mother
**2** : derived from or as if from one's mother

**3** : acting as or providing parental stock — used without reference to sex

³**mother** *transitive verb* **moth·ered; moth·er·ing** \'mə-thə-riŋ, 'məth-riŋ\ (1548)
**1 a** : to give birth to **b** : to give rise to : PRODUCE
**2** : to care for or protect like a mother

⁴**mother** *noun* [archaic *mother* dregs, lees; akin to Middle Dutch *moeder* dregs] (circa 1828)
: MOTHER OF VINEGAR

**moth·er·board** \-,bōrd, -,bòrd\ *noun* (1972)
: the main circuit board especially of a microcomputer

**Mother Car·ey's chicken** \-'kar-ēz-, -'ker-\ *noun* [origin unknown] (1767)
: STORM PETREL

**mother cell** *noun* (1845)
: a cell that gives rise to other cells usually of a different sort

**mother country** *noun* (1587)
**1** : the country from which the people of a colony or former colony derive their origin
**2** : the country of one's parents or ancestors; *also* : FATHERLAND
**3** : a country that is the origin of something

**moth·er·fuck·er** \'mə-thər-,fə-kər\ *noun* (1959)
: one that is formidable, contemptible, or offensive — usually considered obscene; usually used as a generalized term of abuse
— **moth·er·fuck·ing** \-kiŋ\ *adjective*

**Mother Goose** *noun*
: the legendary author of a collection of nursery rhymes first published in London about 1760

**mother hen** *noun* (1954)
: a person who assumes an overly protective maternal attitude

**moth·er·house** \-,haůs\ *noun* (1661)
**1** : the convent in which the superior of a religious community resides
**2** : the original convent of a religious community

**Mother Hub·bard** \-'hə-bərd\ *noun* [probably from *Mother Hubbard*, character in a nursery rhyme] (1884)
: a loose usually shapeless dress

**moth·er–in–law** \'mə-thər-ən-,lò, 'məth-rən-, 'mə-thərn-\ *noun, plural* **moth·ers–in–law** \'mə-thər-zən-\ (14th century)
**1** : the mother of one's spouse
**2** *archaic* : STEPMOTHER

**moth·er·land** \'mə-thər-,land\ *noun* (1711)
**1** : a country regarded as a place of origin (as of an idea or a movement)
**2** : MOTHER COUNTRY 2

**mother lode** *noun* (1874)
**1** : the principal vein or lode of a region
**2** : a principal source or supply

**moth·er·ly** \-lē\ *adjective* (before 12th century)
**1** : of, relating to, or characteristic of a mother ⟨*motherly* advice⟩
**2** : resembling a mother : MATERNAL
— **moth·er·li·ness** *noun*

**moth·er–na·ked** \,mə-thər-'nā-kəd, *especially Southern* -'ne-kəd\ *adjective* (14th century)
: stark naked

**Mother Nature** *noun* (1601)
: nature personified as a woman considered as the source and guiding force of creation

**moth·er–of–pearl** \,mə-thə-rə(v)-'pər(-ə)l\ *noun* (circa 1510)
: the hard pearly iridescent substance forming the inner layer of a mollusk shell

**mother of vinegar** *noun* (1601)
: a slimy membrane composed of yeast and bacterial cells that develops on the surface of alcoholic liquids undergoing acetous fermentation and is added to wine or cider to produce vinegar — called also *mother*

**Mother's Day** *noun* (1908)
: the 2d Sunday in May appointed for the honoring of mothers

**mother tongue** *noun* (14th century)
**1** : one's native language
**2** : a language from which another language derives

**mother wit** *noun* (15th century)
: natural wit or intelligence

¹**moth·proof** \'môth-,prüf\ *adjective* (1893)
: impervious to penetration by moths ⟨*mothproof* wool⟩

²**mothproof** *transitive verb* (1925)
: to make mothproof
— **moth·proof·er** *noun*

**mo·tif** \mō-'tēf\ *noun* [French, motive, motif, from Middle French — more at MOTIVE] (1848)
**1** : a usually recurring salient thematic element (as in the arts); *especially* : a dominant idea or central theme
**2** : a single or repeated design or color
— **mo·tif·ic** \-'tē-fik, -'ti-\ *adjective*

¹**mo·tile** \'mō-t°l, -,tīl\ *adjective* [Latin *motus*, past participle of *movēre*] (circa 1859)
: exhibiting or capable of movement
— **mo·til·i·ty** \mō-'ti-lə-tē\ *noun*

²**motile** *noun* (1886)
: a person whose prevailing mental imagery takes the form of inner feelings of action

¹**mo·tion** \'mō-shən\ *noun* [Middle English *mocioun*, from Middle French *motion*, from Latin *motion-, motio* movement, from *movēre* to move] (14th century)
**1 a** : an act, process, or instance of changing place : MOVEMENT **b** : an active or functioning state or condition ⟨set the divorce proceedings in *motion*⟩
**2** : an impulse or inclination of the mind or will
**3 a** : a proposal for action; *especially* : a formal proposal made in a deliberative assembly **b** : an application made to a court or judge to obtain an order, ruling, or direction
**4** *obsolete* **a** : a puppet show **b** : PUPPET
**5** : MECHANISM
**6 a** : an act or instance of moving the body or its parts : GESTURE **b** *plural* : ACTIVITIES, MOVEMENTS
**7** : melodic change of pitch
— **mo·tion·al** \'mō-shnəl, -shə-n°l\ *adjective*
— **mo·tion·less** \'mō-shən-ləs\ *adjective*
— **mo·tion·less·ly** *adverb*
— **mo·tion·less·ness** *noun*
— **in motion** *of an offensive football player* : running parallel to the line of scrimmage before the snap

²**motion** *verb* **mo·tioned; mo·tion·ing** \'mō-sh(ə-)niŋ\ (1747)
*intransitive verb*
: to signal by a movement or gesture ⟨the pitcher *motioned* to the catcher⟩
*transitive verb*
: to direct by a motion ⟨*motioned* me to the seat⟩

**motion picture** *noun* (1896)
**1** : a series of pictures projected on a screen in rapid succession with objects shown in successive positions slightly changed so as to produce the optical effect of a continuous picture in which the objects move
**2** : a representation (as of a story) by means of motion pictures : MOVIE

**motion sickness** *noun* (1942)
: sickness induced by motion (as in travel by air, car, or ship) and characterized by nausea

**mo·ti·vate** \'mō-tə-,vāt\ *transitive verb* **-vat·ed; -vat·ing** (1885)
: to provide with a motive : IMPEL ⟨questions that excite and *motivate* youth⟩
— **mo·ti·va·tive** \-,vā-tiv\ *adjective*
— **mo·ti·va·tor** \-,vā-tər\ *noun*

---

\ə\ abut \°\ kitten \ər\ further \a\ ash \ā\ ace
\ä\ mop, mar \aů\ out \ch\ chin \e\ bet \ē\ easy
\g\ go \i\ hit \ī\ ice \j\ job \ŋ\ sing \ō\ go
\ò\ law \òi\ boy \th\ thin \th\ the \ü\ loot \ů\ foot
\y\ yet \zh\ vision *see also* Guide to Pronunciation

**mo·ti·va·tion** \ˌmō-tə-'vā-shən\ *noun* (1873)
**1 a :** the act or process of motivating **b :** the condition of being motivated
**2 :** a motivating force, stimulus, or influence **:** INCENTIVE, DRIVE
— **mo·ti·va·tion·al** \-shnəl, -shə-nᵊl\ *adjective*
— **mo·ti·va·tion·al·ly** *adverb*

**¹mo·tive** \'mō-tiv, 2 *is also* mō-'tēv\ *noun* [Middle English, from Middle French *motif*, from *motif*, adjective, moving, from Medieval Latin *motivus*, from Latin *motus*, past participle of *movēre* to move] (15th century)
**1 :** something (as a need or desire) that causes a person to act
**2 :** a recurrent phrase or figure that is developed through the course of a musical composition
**3 :** MOTIF ☆
— **mo·tive·less** \-ləs\ *adjective*
— **mo·tive·less·ly** *adverb*
— **mo·ti·vic** \mō-'tē-vik\ *adjective*

**²mo·tive** \'mō-tiv\ *adjective* [Middle French or Medieval Latin; Middle French *motif*, from Medieval Latin *motivus*] (1502)
**1 :** moving or tending to move to action
**2 :** of or relating to motion or the causing of motion ⟨*motive* energy⟩

**³mo·tive** \'mō-tiv\ *transitive verb* **mo·tived; mo·tiv·ing** (circa 1650)
**:** MOTIVATE

**motive power** *noun* (1889)
**1 :** an agency (as water or steam) used to impart motion especially to machinery
**2 :** something (as a locomotive or a motor) that provides motive power to a system

**mo·tiv·i·ty** \mō-'ti-və-tē\ *noun* (circa 1687)
**:** the power of moving or producing motion

**mot juste** \mō-zhœst\ *noun, plural* **mots justes** \*same*\ [French] (1912)
**:** the exactly right word or phrasing

**¹mot·ley** \'mät-lē\ *adjective* [Middle English, perhaps from *mot* mote, speck] (14th century)
**1 :** variegated in color ⟨a *motley* coat⟩
**2 :** composed of diverse often incongruous elements ⟨a *motley* crowd⟩

**²motley** *noun* [Middle English, probably from ¹*motley*] (14th century)
**1 :** a woolen fabric of mixed colors made in England between the 14th and 17th centuries
**2 :** a garment made of motley; *especially* **:** the characteristic dress of the professional fool
**3 :** JESTER, FOOL
**4 :** a mixture especially of incongruous elements

**mot·mot** \'mät-ˌmät\ *noun* [New Latin *momot, motmot*] (1837)
**:** any of a family (Momotidae) of long-tailed mostly green nonpasserine birds of Central and South American tropical forests

**mo·to·cross** \'mō-tō-ˌkrós\ *noun* [French, from *moto* motorcycle (short for *motocyclette*) + *cross*-country, from English] (1951)
**:** a closed-course motorcycle race over natural or simulated rough terrain (as with steep inclines, hairpin turns, and mud); *also* **:** the sport of engaging in motocross races

**mo·to·neu·ron** \ˌmō-tə-'nü-ˌrän, -'nyü-; -'nùr-ˌän, -'nyùr-\ *noun* [*motor* + *neuron*] (1908)
**:** a neuron that passes from the central nervous system or a ganglion toward a muscle and conducts an impulse that causes movement — called also *motor neuron*
— **mo·to·neu·ro·nal** \-'nùr-ə-nᵊl, -'nyùr-; -nù-'rō-nᵊl, -nyù-\ *adjective*

**¹mo·tor** \'mō-tər\ *noun* [Latin, from *movēre* to move] (1586)
**1 :** one that imparts motion; *specifically* **:** PRIME MOVER
**2 :** any of various power units that develop energy or impart motion: as **a :** a small compact engine **b :** INTERNAL COMBUSTION ENGINE; *especially* **:** a gasoline engine **c :** a rotating machine that transforms electrical energy into mechanical energy

**3 :** MOTOR VEHICLE; *especially* **:** AUTOMOBILE
— **mo·tor·dom** \-dəm\ *noun*
— **mo·tor·less** \-ləs\ *adjective*

**²motor** *adjective* (1840)
**1 a :** causing or imparting motion **b :** of, relating to, or being a motoneuron or a nerve containing motoneurons ⟨*motor* fiber⟩ **c :** of, relating to, concerned with, or involving muscular movement ⟨*motor* areas of the brain⟩
**2 a :** equipped with or driven by a motor **b :** of, relating to, or involving an automobile **c :** designed for motor vehicles or motorists

**³motor** (1896)
*intransitive verb*
**1 :** to travel by automobile **:** DRIVE
**2 :** to move or proceed at a vigorous steady pace ⟨*motored* down the field for a touchdown⟩
*transitive verb*
**:** to transport by automobile

**mo·tor·bike** \'mō-tər-ˌbīk\ *noun* (1903)
**:** a small usually lightweight motorcycle
— **motorbike** *intransitive verb*

**mo·tor·boat** \-ˌbōt\ *noun* (1902)
**:** a boat propelled usually by an internal combustion engine
— **mo·tor·boat·er** \-ˌbō-tər\ *noun*
— **mo·tor·boat·ing** \-tiŋ\ *noun*

**motor bus** *noun* (1901)
**:** BUS 1a — called also *motor coach*

**mo·tor·cade** \'mō-tər-ˌkād\ *noun* (1913)
**:** a procession of motor vehicles
— **motorcade** *intransitive verb*

**mo·tor·car** \-ˌkär\ *noun* (circa 1890)
**1 :** AUTOMOBILE
**2 :** *usually* **motor car :** a railroad car containing motors for propulsion

**motor court** *noun* (1936)
**:** MOTEL

**mo·tor·cy·cle** \'mō-tər-ˌsī-kəl\ *noun* [*motor* + bicycle] (1896)
**:** a 2-wheeled automotive vehicle having one or two saddles
— **motorcycle** *intransitive verb*
— **mo·tor·cy·clist** \-k(ə-)list\ *noun*

**motor home** *noun* (1965)
**:** a large motor vehicle equipped as living quarters — compare MOBILE HOME

**mo·tor·ic** \mō-'tòr-ik, -'tär-\ *adjective* (1930)
**:** MOTOR 1c
— **mo·tor·i·cal·ly** \-i-k(ə-)lē\ *adverb*

**motor inn** *noun* (1951)
**:** MOTEL; *especially* **:** a large multistory motel — called also *motor hotel*

**mo·tor·ise** *British variant of* MOTORIZE

**mo·tor·ist** \'mō-tə-rist\ *noun* (1896)
**:** a person who travels by automobile

**mo·tor·ize** \'mō-tə-ˌrīz\ *transitive verb* **-ized; -iz·ing** (circa 1913)
**1 :** to equip with a motor
**2 :** to equip with automobiles
— **mo·tor·i·za·tion** \ˌmō-tə-rə-'zā-shən\ *noun*

**motor lodge** *noun* (1949)
**:** MOTEL

**mo·tor·man** \'mō-tər-mən\ *noun* (1890)
**:** an operator of a motor-driven vehicle (as a streetcar or subway train)

**mo·tor·mouth** \-ˌmaùth\ *noun* (1971)
**:** a person who talks excessively

**motor pool** *noun* (1942)
**:** a group of motor vehicles centrally controlled (as by a governmental agency) and dispatched for use as needed

**motor sailer** *noun* (1923)
**:** a motorboat with sailing equipment

**motor scooter** *noun* (1919)
**:** a low 2- or 3-wheeled automotive vehicle resembling a child's scooter and having a seat so that the rider does not straddle the engine

**motor ship** *noun* (1915)
**:** a seagoing ship propelled by an internal combustion engine

**motor torpedo boat** *noun* (1940)
**:** PT BOAT

**mo·tor·truck** \'mō-tər-ˌtrək\ *noun* (1930)

**:** an automotive truck used especially for transporting freight

**motor unit** *noun* (1925)
**:** a motoneuron together with the muscle fibers on which it acts

**motor vehicle** *noun* (1890)
**:** an automotive vehicle not operated on rails; *especially* **:** one with rubber tires for use on highways

**mo·tor·way** \'mō-tər-ˌwā\ *noun* (1903)
*chiefly British* **:** SUPERHIGHWAY

**motte** \'mät\ *noun* [Middle English *mote*, from Old French *mote, motte*] (13th century)
**:** MOUND, HILL; *especially* **:** a hill serving as a site for a Norman castle in Britain

**motte and bailey** *noun* (1900)
**:** a medieval Norman castle consisting of two connecting ditched stockaded mounds with the higher mound surmounted by the keep and the lower one containing barracks and other buildings

**¹mot·tle** \'mä-tᵊl\ *noun* [probably back-formation from *motley*] (1676)
**1 :** a colored spot
**2 a :** a surface having colored spots or blotches **b :** the arrangement of such spots or blotches on a surface
**3 :** MOSAIC 5
— **mot·tled** \-tᵊld\ *adjective*

**²mottle** *transitive verb* **mot·tled; mot·tling** \'mät-liŋ, 'mä-tᵊl-iŋ\ (1676)
**:** to mark with spots or blotches of different color or shades of color as if stained
— **mot·tler** \'mät-lər, 'mä-tᵊl-ər\ *noun*

**mottled enamel** *noun* (1928)
**:** spotted tooth enamel caused by drinking water containing excessive fluorides during the time the teeth are calcifying

**mot·to** \'mä-(ˌ)tō\ *noun, plural* **mottoes** *also* **mottos** [Italian, from Late Latin *muttum* grunt, from Latin *muttire* to mutter] (1588)
**1 :** a sentence, phrase, or word inscribed on something as appropriate to or indicative of its character or use
**2 :** a short expression of a guiding principle

**moue** \'mü\ *noun* [French, from Middle French — more at MOW] (1850)
**:** a little grimace **:** POUT

**mou·flon** *also* **mouf·flon** \mü-'flōⁿ\ *noun* [French *mouflon*, from Italian dialect *muvrone*, from Late Latin *mufron-, mufro*] (1774)
**:** either of two wild sheep (*Ovis orientalis* and *O. musimon*) of the mountains of Sardinia, Corsica and western Asia that have large curling horns in the males and are sometimes included in a single species

mouflon

**mou·jik** \mü-'zhēk, -'zhik\ *variant of* MUZHIK

**mou·lage** \mü-'läzh\ *noun* [French, molding, from Middle French, from *mouler* to mold, from Old French *modle* mold — more at MOLD] (1902)
**1** : an impression or cast made for use especially as evidence in a criminal investigation
**2** : the taking of an impression for use as evidence in a criminal investigation

**mould** \'mōld\ *variant of* MOLD

**mould·ing** \'mōl-diŋ\ *variant of* MOLDING

**moult** \'mōlt\ *variant of* MOLT

**¹mound** \'maůnd\ *transitive verb* [origin unknown] (1515)
**1** *archaic* : to enclose or fortify with a fence or a ridge of earth
**2** : to form into a mound

**²mound** *noun, often attributive* [origin unknown] (1551)
**1** *archaic* : HEDGE, FENCE
**2 a** (1) : an artificial bank or hill of earth or stones; *especially* : one constructed over a burial or ceremonial site (2) : the slightly elevated ground on which a baseball pitcher stands **b** : a rounded hill or natural formation
**3 a** : HEAP, PILE ⟨*mounds* of work⟩ **b** : a small rounded mass ⟨a *mound* of mashed potatoes⟩

**Mound Builder** *noun* (1838)
: a member of a prehistoric American Indian people whose extensive earthworks are found from the Great Lakes down the Mississippi valley to the Gulf of Mexico

**¹mount** \'maůnt\ *noun* [Middle English, from Old English *munt* & Old French *mont*, both from Latin *mont-, mons*; akin to Welsh *mynydd* mountain, Latin *minari* to project, threaten] (before 12th century)
**1** : a high hill : MOUNTAIN — used especially before an identifying name ⟨*Mount* Everest⟩
**2** *archaic* : EARTHWORK 1
**3** : MOUND 2a(1)

**²mount** *verb* [Middle English, from Middle French *monter*, from (assumed) Vulgar Latin *montare*, from Latin *mont-, mons*] (14th century)
*intransitive verb*
**1** : RISE, ASCEND
**2** : to increase in amount or extent ⟨expenses began to *mount*⟩
**3** : to get up on something above the level of the ground; *especially* : to seat oneself (as on a horse) for riding
*transitive verb*
**1 a** : to go up : CLIMB **b** (1) : to seat or place oneself on (2) : COVER 6a
**2 a** : to lift up : RAISE **b** (1) : to put or have (as artillery) in position (2) : to have as equipment **c** (1) : to organize and equip (an attacking force) ⟨*mount* an army⟩ (2) : to launch and carry out (as an assault or a campaign)
**3** : to set on something that elevates
**4 a** : to cause to get on a means of conveyance **b** : to furnish with animals for riding
**5** : to post or set up for defense or observation ⟨*mounted* some guards⟩
**6 a** : to attach to a support **b** : to arrange or assemble for use or display
**7 a** : to prepare (as a specimen) for examination or display **b** : to prepare and supply with materials needed for performance or execution ⟨*mount* an opera⟩
— **mount·able** \'maůn-tə-bəl\ *adjective*
— **mount·er** *noun*

**³mount** *noun* (15th century)
**1** : an act or instance of mounting; *specifically* : an opportunity to ride a horse in a race
**2** : FRAME, SUPPORT: as **a** : the material (as cardboard) on which a picture is mounted **b** : a jewelry setting **c** (1) : an undercarriage or part on which a device (as a motor or an artillery piece) rests in service (2) : an attachment for an accessory **d** : a hinge, card, or acetate envelope for mounting a stamp **e** : a glass slide with its accessories on which objects are placed for examination with a microscope

**3** : a means of conveyance; *especially* : SADDLE HORSE

**moun·tain** \'maůn-tⁿn\ *noun, often attributive* [Middle English, from Old French *montaigne*, from (assumed) Vulgar Latin *montanea*, from feminine of *montaneus* of a mountain, alteration of Latin *montanus*, from *mont-, mons*] (13th century)
**1 a** : a landmass that projects conspicuously above its surroundings and is higher than a hill **b** : an elongated ridge
**2 a** : a great mass **b** : a vast number or quantity

**mountain ash** *noun* (1597)
: any of various trees or shrubs (genus *Sorbus*) of the rose family with pinnate leaves and red or orange-red fruits

**mountain bike** *noun* (1984)
: an all-terrain bicycle with wide knobby tires, straight handlebars, and typically 18 or 21 gears
— **mountain biker** *noun*
— **mountain biking** *noun*

**mountain bluebird** *noun* (1860)
: a bluebird (*Sialia currucoides*) of western North America having a blue-breasted rather than red-breasted male

**mountain cranberry** *noun* (1848)
: a low evergreen shrub (*Vaccinium vitis-idaea minus*) of north temperate uplands with red edible berries — called also *lingonberry*

**mountain dew** *noun* (1827)
: MOONSHINE 3

**moun·tain·eer** \,maůn-tⁿn-'ir\ *noun* (1610)
**1** : a native or inhabitant of a mountainous region
**2** : a person who climbs mountains for sport

**moun·tain·eer·ing** *noun* (1803)
: the sport or technique of scaling mountains

**mountain goat** *noun* (1833)
: a ruminant mammal (*Oreamnos americanus*) of mountainous northwestern North America that has a thick white coat and slightly curved horns and resembles a goat

mountain goat

**mountain gorilla** *noun* (1939)
: a gorilla (*Gorilla gorilla beringei*) inhabiting the Virunga mountain range

**mountain laurel** *noun* (1759)
: a North American evergreen shrub or small tree (*Kalmia latifolia*) of the heath family with glossy leaves and umbels of rose-colored or white flowers

**mountain lion** *noun* (1859)
: COUGAR

**mountain mahogany** *noun* (1810)
: any of a genus (*Cercocarpus*) of western North American evergreen shrubs or small trees of the rose family

**mountain man** *noun* (1839)
: an American frontiersman (as a trapper) at home in the wilderness

**moun·tain·ous** \'maůn-tⁿn-əs, 'maůnt-nəs\ *adjective* (14th century)
**1** : containing many mountains
**2** : resembling a mountain : HUGE
— **moun·tain·ous·ly** *adverb*
— **moun·tain·ous·ness** *noun*

**mountain sheep** *noun* (1802)
: any of various wild sheep (as bighorn, argali, or Dall sheep) inhabiting high mountains

**mountain sickness** *noun* (1848)
: altitude sickness experienced especially above 10,000 feet (3000 meters) and caused by insufficient oxygen in the air

**moun·tain·side** \'maůn-tⁿn-,sīd\ *noun* (14th century)
: the side of a mountain

**mountain time** *noun, often M capitalized* (1883)
: the time of the 7th time zone west of Greenwich that includes the Rocky mountain states of the U.S. — see TIME ZONE illustration

**moun·tain·top** \'maůn-tⁿn-,täp\ *noun* (1593)
: the summit of a mountain

**moun·tainy** \'maůn-tⁿn-ē, 'maůnt-nē\ *adjective* (1613)
**1** : MOUNTAINOUS
**2** : of, relating to, or living in mountains

**¹moun·te·bank** \'maůn-ti-,baŋk\ *noun* [Italian *montimbanco*, from *montare* to mount (from—assumed—Vulgar Latin) + *in* in, on (from Latin) + *banco, banca* bench — more at BANK] (1577)
**1** : a person who sells quack medicines from a platform
**2** : a boastful unscrupulous pretender : CHARLATAN
— **moun·te·bank·ery** \-,baŋ-k(ə-)rē\ *noun*

**²mountebank** (1607)
*transitive verb*
*obsolete* : to beguile or transform by trickery ⟨I'll *mountebank* their loves —Shakespeare⟩
*intransitive verb*
: to play the mountebank

**Mount·ie** \'maůn-tē\ *noun* [*mounted* policeman] (1914)
: a member of the Royal Canadian Mounted Police

**mount·ing** \'maůn-tiŋ\ *noun* (1563)
: ³MOUNT 2

**mourn** \'mōrn, 'mȯrn\ *verb* [Middle English, from Old English *murnan;* akin to Old High German *mornēn* to mourn, Greek *mermēra* care — more at MEMORY] (before 12th century)
*intransitive verb*
**1** : to feel or express grief or sorrow
**2** : to show the customary signs of grief for a death; *especially* : to wear mourning
**3** : to murmur mournfully — used especially of doves
*transitive verb*
**1** : to feel or express sorrow for
**2** : to utter mournfully
— **mourn·er** *noun*
— **mourn·ing·ly** \'mōr-niŋ-lē, 'mȯr-\ *adverb*

**mourn·ful** \'mōrn-fəl, 'mȯrn-\ *adjective* (15th century)
**1** : expressing sorrow : SORROWFUL
**2** : full of sorrow : SAD
**3** : causing sorrow or melancholy : GLOOMY
— **mourn·ful·ly** \-fə-lē\ *adverb*
— **mourn·ful·ness** *noun*

**mourn·ing** \'mōr-niŋ, 'mȯr-\ *noun* (13th century)
**1** : the act of sorrowing
**2 a** : an outward sign (as black clothes or an armband) of grief for a person's death **b** : a period of time during which signs of grief are shown

**mourning cloak** *noun* (1898)
: a blackish brown nymphalid butterfly (*Nymphalis antiopa*) with a broad yellow border on the wings found in temperate parts of Europe, Asia, and North America

**mourning dove** *noun* (1833)
: a wild American dove (*Zenaida macroura*) with a pointed tail and a plaintive coo

**¹mouse** \'maůs\ *noun, plural* **mice** \'mīs\ [Middle English, from Old English *mūs;* akin to Old High German *mūs* mouse, Latin *mus,* Greek *mys* mouse, muscle] (before 12th century)
**1** : any of numerous small rodents (as of the genus *Mus*) with pointed snout, rather small ears, elongated body, and slender tail
**2** : a timid person

\ə\ abut \ᵊ\ kitten \ər\ further \a\ ash \ā\ ace
\ä\ mop, mar \aů\ out \ch\ chin \e\ bet \ē\ easy
\g\ go \i\ hit \ī\ ice \j\ job \ŋ\ sing \ō\ go
\ȯ\ law \ȯi\ boy \th\ thin \th\ the \ü\ loot \ů\ foot
\y\ yet \zh\ vision *see also* Guide to Pronunciation

**3 :** a dark-colored swelling caused by a blow; *specifically* **:** BLACK EYE
**4 :** a small mobile manual device that controls movement of the cursor and selection of functions on a computer display
²**mouse** \'mau̇z\ *verb* **moused; mous·ing** (13th century)
*intransitive verb*
**1 :** to hunt for mice
**2 :** to search or move stealthily or slowly
*transitive verb*
**1** *obsolete* **a :** BITE, GNAW **b :** to toy with roughly
**2 :** to search for carefully — usually used with *out*
**mouse–ear** \'mau̇s-ˌir\ *noun* (13th century)
**1 :** a Eurasian hawkweed (*Hieracium pilosella*) that has soft hairy leaves and has been introduced into North America
**2 :** any of several plants other than mouse-ear that have soft hairy leaves
**mouse–ear chickweed** *noun* (1731)
**:** any of several hairy chickweeds (genus *Cerastium* and especially *C. vulgatum*)
**mous·er** \'mau̇-sər, *US also & chiefly British* -zər\ *noun* (15th century)
**:** a catcher of mice and rats; *especially* **:** a cat proficient at mousing
¹**mouse·trap** \'mau̇s-ˌtrap\ *noun* (15th century)
**1 :** a trap for mice
**2 :** a stratagem that lures one to defeat or destruction
**3 :** TRAP 2b
²**mousetrap** *transitive verb* (circa 1864)
**:** to snare in or as if in a mousetrap
**Mous·que·taire** \ˌmü-skə-'tar, -'ter\ *noun* [French — more at MUSKETEER] (1705)
**:** a French musketeer; *especially* **:** one of the royal musketeers of the 17th and 18th centuries conspicuous for their daring and their dandified dress
**mous·sa·ka** \ˌmü-sə-'kä\ *noun* [New Greek *mousakas*, from Turkish *musakka*] (1931)
**:** a Middle Eastern dish of ground meat (as lamb or beef) and sliced eggplant often topped with a seasoned sauce
¹**mousse** \'müs\ *noun* [French, literally, froth, moss, of Germanic origin; akin to Old High German *mos* moss — more at MOSS] (1892)
**1 :** a light spongy food usually containing cream or gelatin
**2 :** a molded chilled dessert made with sweetened and flavored whipped cream or egg whites and gelatin ⟨chocolate *mousse*⟩
**3 :** a foamy preparation used in styling hair
²**mousse** *transitive verb* **moussed; mouss·ing** (1984)
**:** to style (hair) with mousse
**mous·se·line** \ˌmü-sə-'lēn, ˌmüs-'lēn\ *noun* [French, literally, muslin — more at MUSLIN] (1696)
**1 :** a fine sheer fabric (as of rayon) that resembles muslin
**2 a :** a sauce (as hollandaise) to which whipped cream or beaten egg whites have been added **b :** MOUSSE 1 ⟨salmon *mousseline*⟩
**mousseline de soie** \-də-'swä\ *noun, plural* **mousselines de soie** \*same*\ [French, literally, silk muslin] (1850)
**:** a silk muslin having a crisp finish
**mous·tache** *variant of* MUSTACHE
**mous·ta·chio** *variant of* MUSTACHIO
**Mous·te·ri·an** \mü-'stir-ē-ən\ *adjective* [French *moustérien*, from Le *Moustier*, cave in Dordogne, France] (1890)
**:** of or relating to a Middle Paleolithic culture that is characterized by well-made flake tools often considered the work of Neanderthal man
**mousy** *or* **mous·ey** \'mau̇-sē, -zē\ *adjective* **mous·i·er; -est** (1853)
**:** of, relating to, or resembling a mouse: as **a :** QUIET, STEALTHY **b :** TIMID, RETIRING **c :** grayish brown
— **mous·i·ly** \-sə-lē, -zə-\ *adverb*
— **mous·i·ness** \-sē-nəs, -zē-\ *noun*

¹**mouth** \'mau̇th\ *noun, plural* **mouths** \'mau̇thz *also* 'mau̇s, 'mau̇ths; *in synecdochic compounds like "blabbermouths" this more frequently*\ *often attributive* [Middle English, from Old English *mūth;* akin to Old High German *mund* mouth and perhaps to Latin *mentum* chin] (before 12th century)
**1 a :** the natural opening through which food passes into the body of an animal and which in vertebrates is typically bounded externally by the lips and internally by the pharynx and encloses the tongue, gums, and teeth **b :** GRIMACE ⟨made a *mouth*⟩ **c :** an individual requiring food ⟨had too many *mouths* to feed⟩
**2 a :** VOICE, SPEECH ⟨finally gave *mouth* to her feelings⟩ **b :** MOUTHPIECE 3a **c** (1) **:** a tendency to excessive talk (2) **:** saucy or disrespectful language **:** IMPUDENCE
**3 :** something that resembles a mouth especially in affording entrance or exit: as **a :** the place where a stream enters a larger body of water **b :** the surface opening of an underground cavity **c :** the opening of a container **d :** an opening in the side of an organ flue pipe
— **mouth·like** \'mau̇th-ˌlīk\ *adjective*
— **down in the mouth :** DEJECTED, SULKY
²**mouth** \'mau̇th *also* 'mau̇th\ (14th century)
*transitive verb*
**1 a :** SPEAK, PRONOUNCE **b :** to utter bombastically **:** DECLAIM **c :** to repeat without comprehension or sincerity ⟨always *mouthing* platitudes⟩ **d :** to form soundlessly with the lips ⟨the librarian *mouthed* the word "quiet"⟩ **e :** to utter indistinctly **:** MUMBLE ⟨*mouthed* his words⟩
**2 :** to take into the mouth; *especially* **:** EAT
*intransitive verb*
**1 a :** to talk pompously **:** RANT — often used with *off* **b :** to talk insolently or impudently — usually used with *off*
**2 :** to move the mouth especially so as to make faces
— **mouth·er** *noun*
**mouth·breed·er** \'mau̇th-ˌbrē-dər\ *noun* (1927)
**:** any of several fishes that carry their eggs and young in the mouth; *especially* **:** a North African cichlid fish (*Haplochromis multicolor*) often kept in aquariums
**mouthed** \'mau̇thd, 'mau̇tht\ *adjective* (14th century)
**:** having a mouth especially of a specified kind — often used in combination ⟨a soft-*mouthed* fish⟩
**mouth·ful** \'mau̇th-ˌfu̇l\ *noun* (15th century)
**1 a :** as much as a mouth will hold **b :** the quantity usually taken into the mouth at one time
**2 :** a small quantity
**3 a :** a very long word or phrase **b :** a comment or a statement rich in meaning or substance
**mouth hook** *noun* (1937)
**:** one of a pair of hooked larval mouthparts of some dipteran flies that function as jaws
**mouth organ** *noun* (1866)
**:** HARMONICA 2
**mouth·part** \'mau̇th-ˌpärt\ *noun* (1799)
**:** a structure or appendage near the mouth (as of an insect) especially when adapted for use in gathering or eating food
**mouth·piece** \-ˌpēs\ *noun* (1683)
**1 :** something placed at or forming a mouth
**2 :** a part (as of an instrument) that goes in the mouth or to which the mouth is applied
**3 a :** one that expresses or interprets another's views **:** SPOKESMAN **b** *slang* **:** a criminal lawyer
**mouth–to–mouth** *adjective* (1941)
**:** of, relating to, or being a method of artificial respiration in which the rescuer's mouth is placed tightly over the victim's mouth in order to force air into the victim's lungs by blowing forcefully enough every few seconds to inflate them
**mouth·wash** \'mau̇th-ˌwȯsh, -ˌwäsh\ *noun* (1840)

**:** a usually antiseptic liquid preparation for cleaning the mouth and teeth or freshening the breath
**mouth·wa·ter·ing** \-ˌwȯ-tə-riŋ, -ˌwä-\ *adjective* (1900)
**:** arousing the appetite **:** tantalizingly delicious or appealing ⟨a *mouthwatering* aroma⟩
— **mouth·wa·ter·ing·ly** \-lē\ *adverb*
**mouthy** \'mau̇-thē, -thē\ *adjective* **mouth·i·er; -est** (1589)
**1 :** excessively talkative **:** GARRULOUS
**2 :** marked by bombast or back talk
**mou·ton** \'mü-ˌtän, mü-\ *noun* [French, sheep, sheepskin, from Middle French, ram — more at MUTTON] (1944)
**:** processed sheepskin that has been sheared and dyed to resemble beaver or seal
¹**mov·able** *or* **move·able** \'mü-və-bəl\ *adjective* (14th century)
**1 :** capable of being moved
**2 :** changing date from year to year ⟨*movable* holidays⟩
— **mov·abil·i·ty** \ˌmü-və-'bi-lə-tē\ *noun*
— **mov·able·ness** \'mü-və-bəl-nəs\ *noun*
— **mov·ably** \-blē\ *adverb*
²**movable** *or* **moveable** *noun* (15th century)
**:** something (as an article of furniture) that can be removed or displaced
¹**move** \'müv\ *verb* **moved; mov·ing** [Middle English, from Middle French *movoir*, from Latin *movēre;* probably akin to Sanskrit *mīvati* he moves, pushes] (13th century)
*intransitive verb*
**1 a** (1) **:** to go or pass to another place or in a certain direction with a continuous motion ⟨*moved* into the shade⟩ (2) **:** to proceed toward a certain state or condition ⟨*moving* up the executive ladder⟩ ⟨*moved* into second place in the tournament⟩ (3) **:** to become transferred during play ⟨checkers *move* along diagonally adjacent squares⟩ (4) **:** to keep pace ⟨*moving* with the times⟩ **b :** to start away from some point or place **:** DEPART **c :** to change one's residence or location
**2 :** to carry on one's life or activities in a specified environment ⟨*moves* in the best circles⟩
**3 :** to change position or posture **:** STIR ⟨told him to be quiet and not to *move*⟩
**4 :** to take action **:** ACT
**5 a :** to begin operating or functioning or working in a usual way **b :** to show marked activity ⟨after a brief lull things really began to *move*⟩ **c :** to move a piece (as in chess or checkers) during one's turn
**6 :** to make a formal request, application, or appeal
**7 :** to change hands by being sold or rented ⟨goods that were *moving* slowly⟩
**8** *of the bowels* **:** EVACUATE
*transitive verb*
**1 a** (1) **:** to change the place or position of (2) **:** to dislodge or displace from a fixed position **:** BUDGE **b :** to transfer (as a piece in chess) from one position to another
**2 a** (1) **:** to cause to go or pass from one place to another with a continuous motion ⟨*moved* the flag slowly up and down⟩ (2) **:** to cause to advance **b :** to cause to operate or function **:** ACTUATE ⟨this button *moves* the whole machine⟩ **c :** to put into activity or rouse up from inactivity
**3 :** to cause to change position or posture
**4 :** to prompt or rouse to the doing of something **:** PERSUADE ⟨the report *moved* the faculty to take action⟩
**5 a :** to stir the emotions, feelings, or passions of ⟨was deeply *moved* by such kindness⟩ **b :** to affect in such a way as to lead to an indicated show of emotion ⟨the story *moved* her to tears⟩
**6 a** *obsolete* **:** BEG **b :** to make a formal application to
**7 :** to propose formally in a deliberative assembly ⟨*moved* adjournment⟩
**8 :** to cause (the bowels) to void

**9** : to cause to change hands through sale or rent ☆

**²move** *noun* (1656)
**1 a** : the act of moving a piece (as in chess) **b** : the turn of a player to move
**2 a** : a step taken so as to gain an objective : MANEUVER ⟨a *move* to end the dispute⟩ **b** : the action of moving from a motionless position **c** : a change of residence or location **d** : an agile or deceptive action especially in sports
— **on the move 1** : in a state of moving about from place to place ⟨a salesman is constantly *on the move*⟩ **2** : in a state of moving ahead or making progress ⟨said that civilization is always *on the move*⟩
**move in** *intransitive verb* (1898)
: to occupy a dwelling or place of work
— **move in on** : to make advances or aggressive movements toward
**move·less** \'müv-ləs\ *adjective* (1578)
: being without movement : FIXED, IMMOBILE
— **move·less·ly** *adverb*
— **move·less·ness** *noun*
**move·ment** \'müv-mənt\ *noun* (14th century)
**1 a** (1) : the act or process of moving; *especially* : change of place or position or posture (2) : a particular instance or manner of moving **b** (1) : a tactical or strategic shifting of a military unit : MANEUVER (2) : the advance of a military unit **c** : ACTION, ACTIVITY — usually used in plural
**2 a** : TENDENCY, TREND ⟨detected a *movement* toward fairer pricing⟩ **b** : a series of organized activities working toward an objective; *also* : an organized effort to promote or attain an end ⟨the civil rights *movement*⟩
**3** : the moving parts of a mechanism that transmit a definite motion
**4 a** : MOTION 7 **b** : the rhythmic character or quality of a musical composition **c** : a distinct structural unit or division having its own key, rhythmic structure, and themes and forming part of an extended musical composition **d** : particular rhythmic flow of language : CADENCE
**5 a** : the quality (as in a painting or sculpture) of representing or suggesting motion **b** : the vibrant quality in literature that comes from elements that constantly hold a reader's interest (as a quickly moving action-filled plot)
**6 a** : an act of voiding the bowels **b** : matter expelled from the bowels at one passage
**mov·er** \'mü-vər\ *noun* (14th century)
: one that moves or sets something in motion; *especially* : one whose business or occupation is the moving of household goods from one residence to another
**mover and shaker** *noun, plural* **movers and shakers** (1951)
: a person who is active or influential in some field of endeavor
**mov·ie** \'mü-vē\ *noun* [*moving picture*] (1912)
**1** : MOTION PICTURE
**2** *plural* : a showing of a motion picture
**3** *plural* : the motion-picture medium or industry
**mov·ie·dom** \'mü-vē-dəm\ *noun* (1916)
: FILMDOM
**mov·ie·go·er** \-,gō(-ə)r\ *noun* (1923)
: FILMGOER
— **mov·ie·going** \-,gō-iŋ, -,gȯ(-)iŋ\ *noun*
**mov·ie·mak·er** \-,mā-kər\ *noun* (1915)
: one who makes movies
— **mov·ie·mak·ing** \-,mā-kiŋ\ *noun*
**mov·ing** *adjective* (14th century)
**1 a** : marked by or capable of movement **b** : of or relating to a change of residence ⟨*moving* expenses⟩ **c** : used for transferring furnishings from one residence to another ⟨a *moving* van⟩ **d** : involving a motor vehicle that is in motion ⟨a *moving* violation⟩
**2 a** : producing or transferring motion or action **b** : stirring deeply in a way that evokes a strong emotional response ⟨a *moving* story of a faithful dog⟩ ☆
— **mov·ing·ly** \'mü-viŋ-lē\ *adverb*

**moving picture** *noun* (1896)
: MOTION PICTURE
**Mov·i·ola** \,mü-vē-'ō-lə\ *trademark*
— used for a device for editing motion-picture film and synchronizing the sound
**¹mow** \'maü\ *noun* [Middle English, heap, stack, from Old English *müga;* akin to Old Norse *mügi* heap] (before 12th century)
**1** : a piled-up stack (as of hay or fodder); *also* : a pile of hay or grain in a barn
**2** : the part of a barn where hay or straw is stored
**²mow** \'mō\ *verb* **mowed; mowed** *or* **mown** \'mōn\; **mow·ing** [Middle English, from Old English *māwan;* akin to Old High German *māen* to mow, Latin *metere* to reap, mow, Greek *aman*] (before 12th century)
*transitive verb*
**1 a** : to cut down with a scythe or sickle or machine **b** : to cut the standing herbage (as grass) of
**2 a** (1) : to kill or destroy in great numbers or mercilessly ⟨machine guns *mowed* down the enemy⟩ (2) : to cause to fall : KNOCK DOWN **b** : to overcome swiftly and decisively : ROUT ⟨*mowed* down the opposing team⟩
*intransitive verb*
: to cut down standing herbage (as grass)
— **mow·er** \'mō(-ə)r\ *noun*
**³mow** \'maü, 'mō\ *noun* [Middle English *mowe,* from Middle French *moue,* of Germanic origin; akin to Middle Dutch *mouwe* protruding lip] (14th century)
: GRIMACE
**⁴mow** \'maü, 'mō\ *intransitive verb* (15th century)
: to make grimaces
**mox·ie** \'mäk-sē\ *noun* [from *Moxie,* a trademark for a soft drink] (1930)
**1** : ENERGY, PEP
**2** : COURAGE, DETERMINATION
**3** : KNOW-HOW, EXPERTISE
**moyen–âge** \mwȧ-ye-näzh\ *adjective* [French *moyen âge* Middle Ages] (1849)
: of or relating to medieval times
**moz·za·rel·la** \,mät-sə-'re-lə\ *noun* [Italian, diminutive of *mozza,* a kind of cheese, from *mozzare* to cut off, from *mozzo* cut off, docked, from (assumed) Vulgar Latin *mutius,* alteration of Latin *mutilus*] (1911)
: a moist white unsalted unripened cheese of mild flavor and a smooth rubbery texture
**moz·zet·ta** \mōt-'se-tə\ *noun* [Italian, probably from *mozzo* cut off] (1774)
: a short cape with a small ornamental hood worn over the rochet by Roman Catholic prelates
**M phase** *noun* [mitosis] (1945)
: the period in the cell cycle during which cell division takes place — compare G₁ PHASE, G₂ PHASE, S PHASE
**Mr.** \'mis-tər, *in rapid speech especially in sense 2* (,)mis(t)\ *noun, plural* **Messrs.** \'me-sərz\ [*Mr.* from Middle English, abbreviation of *maister* master; *Messrs.* abbreviation of *Messieurs,* from French, plural of *Monsieur*] (15th century)
**1** — used as a conventional title of courtesy except when usage requires the substitution of a title of rank or an honorific or professional title before a man's surname ⟨spoke to *Mr.* Doe⟩
**2** — used in direct address as a conventional title of respect before a man's title of office ⟨may I ask one more question, *Mr.* President⟩
**3** — used before the name of a place (as a country or city) or of a profession or activity (as a sport) or before some epithet (as *clever*) to form a title applied to a male viewed or recognized as representative of the thing indicated ⟨*Mr.* Baseball⟩
**Mr. Charlie** \-'chär-lē\ *noun* [*Charlie,* from *Charles,* proper name] (circa 1941)
: a white man : white people — usually used disparagingly

**mri·dan·ga** \mri-'dän-gə, ,mər-i-\ *or* **mri·dan·gam** \-gəm\ *noun* [Sanskrit *mṛdaṅga*] (1921)
: a drum of India that is shaped like an elongated barrel and has tuned heads of different diameters
**Mrs.** \'mi-səz, -səs, *especially Southern* 'mi-zəz, -zəs, *or in rapid speech in sense 1* (,)miz, *or before given names* (,)mis\ *noun, plural* **Mes·dames** \mā-'däm, -'dam\ [*Mrs.* abbreviation of *mistress; Mesdames* from French, plural of *Madame*] (1615)
**1 a** — used as a conventional title of courtesy except when usage requires the substitution of a title of rank or an honorific or professional title before a married woman's surname ⟨spoke to *Mrs.* Doe⟩ **b** — used before the name of a place (as a country or city) or of a profession or activity (as a sport) or before some epithet (as *clever*) to form a title applied to a married woman viewed or recognized as representative of the thing indicated ⟨*Mrs.* Golf⟩
**2** : WIFE ⟨took the *Mrs.* to dinner⟩
**Mrs. Grun·dy** \-'grən-dē\ *noun* [from a character alluded to in Thomas Morton's *Speed the Plough* (1798)] (1813)
: one marked by prudish conventionality in personal conduct
**Ms.** \'miz\ *noun, plural* **Mss.** *or* **Mses.** \'mi-zəz\ [probably blend of *Miss* and *Mrs.*] (1949)
— used instead of *Miss* or *Mrs.* (as when the marital status of a woman is unknown or irrelevant) ⟨*Ms.* Mary Smith⟩
**M16** \,em-(,)sik-'stēn\ *noun* [model *16*] (1968)
: a .223 caliber (5.56 mm.) gas-operated magazine-fed rifle for semiautomatic or automatic operation used by U.S. troops since the mid 1960s — called also *M16 rifle*
**mu** \'myü, 'mü\ *noun* [Greek *my*] (1823)
: the 12th letter of the Greek alphabet — see ALPHABET table

---

☆ **SYNONYMS**
**Move, actuate, drive, impel** mean to set or keep in motion. MOVE is very general and implies no more than the fact of changing position ⟨*moved* the furniture⟩. ACTUATE stresses transmission of power so as to work or set in motion ⟨turbines *actuated* by waterpower⟩. DRIVE implies imparting forward and continuous motion and often stresses the effect rather than the impetus ⟨a ship *driven* aground by hurricane winds⟩. IMPEL is usually figurative and suggests a great motivating impetus ⟨a candidate *impelled* by ambition⟩.

**Moving, impressive, poignant, affecting, touching, pathetic** mean having the power to produce deep emotion. MOVING may apply to any strong emotional effect including thrilling, agitating, saddening, or calling forth pity or sympathy ⟨a *moving* appeal for contributions⟩. IMPRESSIVE implies compelling attention, admiration, wonder, or conviction ⟨an *impressive* list of achievements⟩. POIGNANT applies to what keenly or sharply affects one's sensitivities ⟨a *poignant* documentary on the homeless⟩. AFFECTING is close to MOVING but most often suggests pathos ⟨an *affecting* deathbed reunion⟩. TOUCHING implies arousing tenderness or compassion ⟨the *touching* innocence in a child's eyes⟩. PATHETIC implies moving to pity or sometimes contempt ⟨*pathetic* attempts to justify misconduct⟩.

---

\ə\ abut \ə'\ kitten \ər\ further \a\ ash \ā\ ace
\ä\ mop, mar \aü\ out \ch\ chin \e\ bet \ē\ easy
\g\ go \i\ hit \ī\ ice \j\ job \ŋ\ sing \ō\ go
\ȯ\ law \ȯi\ boy \th\ thin \th\ the \ü\ loot \ü\ foot
\y\ yet \zh\ vision   *see also* Guide to Pronunciation

**muc-** *or* **muci-** *or* **muco-** *combining form* [Latin *muc-,* from *mucus*]
**1** : mucus ⟨*mucoprotein*⟩
**2** : mucous and ⟨*mucocutaneous*⟩

¹**much** \'məch\ *adjective* **more** \'mōr, 'mȯr\; **most** \'mōst\ [Middle English *muche* large, much, from *michel, muchel,* from Old English *micel, mycel;* akin to Old High German *mihhil* great, large, Latin *magnus,* Greek *megas,* Sanskrit *mahat*] (13th century)
**1** : great in quantity, amount, extent, or degree ⟨there is *much* truth in what you say⟩ ⟨taken too *much* time⟩
**2** *obsolete* : many in number
**3** : more than is expected or acceptable : more than enough ⟨eighty bedrooms, a bit *much* for a family of seven —Peter Dragadze⟩
— **too much 1** : WONDERFUL, EXCITING **2** : TERRIBLE, AWFUL

²**much** *adverb* **more; most** (13th century)
**1 a** (1) : to a great degree or extent : CONSIDERABLY ⟨*much* happier⟩ (2) : VERY **b** (1) : FREQUENTLY, OFTEN (2) : by or for a long time ⟨didn't get to work *much* before noon⟩ **c** : by far ⟨was *much* the brightest student⟩
**2** : NEARLY, APPROXIMATELY ⟨looks *much* the way his father did⟩
— **as much** : the same in quantity

³**much** *noun* (13th century)
**1** : a great quantity, amount, extent, or degree ⟨gave away *much*⟩
**2** : something considerable or impressive ⟨was not *much* to look at⟩

**mu·cha·cho** \mü-'chä-(ˌ)chō\ *noun, plural* **-chos** [Spanish, probably from *mocho* cropped, shorn] (1591)
**1** *chiefly Southwest* : a male servant
**2** *chiefly Southwest* : a young man

**much as** *conjunction* (circa 1699)
: however much : even though

**much less** *conjunction* (1710)
: to say nothing of — used especially in negative contexts to add to one item another denoting something less likely ⟨can hardly grow, *much less* ripen, till the stock is in the earth —Jonathan Swift⟩ ⟨he is never going to get out of the eighth grade, *much less* ever make it to college —Thomas Meehan⟩

**much·ness** \'məch-nəs\ *noun* (14th century)
: the quality or state of being great : GREATNESS
— **much of a muchness** : very much the same

**mu·ci·lage** \'myü-s(ə-)lij\ *noun* [Middle English *muscilage,* from Late Latin *mucilago* mucus, musty juice, from Latin *mucus*] (15th century)
**1** : a gelatinous substance of various plants (as legumes or seaweeds) that contains protein and polysaccharides and is similar to plant gums
**2** : an aqueous usually viscid solution (as of a gum) used especially as an adhesive

**mu·ci·lag·i·nous** \ˌmyü-sə-'la-jə-nəs\ *adjective* [Middle English *muscilaginous,* from Late Latin *mucilaginosus,* from *mucilagin-, mucilago*] (15th century)
**1** : STICKY, VISCID
**2** : of, relating to, full of, or secreting mucilage
— **mu·ci·lag·i·nous·ly** *adverb*

**mu·cin** \'myü-s°n\ *noun* [International Scientific Vocabulary *muc-*] (1846)
: any of various mucoproteins that occur especially in secretions of mucous membranes
— **mu·cin·ous** \-s°n-əs, 'myüs-nəs\ *adjective*

¹**muck** \'mək\ *noun* [Middle English *muk,* perhaps from Old English *-moc;* akin to Old Norse *myki* dung] (13th century)
**1** : soft moist farmyard manure
**2** : slimy dirt or filth
**3** : defamatory remarks or writings
**4 a** (1) : dark highly organic soil (2) : MIRE, MUD **b** : something resembling muck : GUNK

**5** : material removed in the process of excavating or mining
— **mucky** \'mə-kē\ *adjective*

²**muck** (14th century)
*transitive verb*
**1 a** : to clean up; *especially* : to clear of manure or filth — usually used with *out* **b** : to clear of muck
**2** : to dress (as soil) with muck
**3** : to dirty with or as if with muck : SOIL
*intransitive verb*
**1** : to move or load muck (as in a mine)
**2** : to engage in aimless activity — usually used with *about* or *around*
— **muck·er** *noun*

**muck-a-muck** \'mə-kə-ˌmək\ *or* **muck-ety-muck** \'mə-kə-tē-'mək\ *noun* (1912)
: HIGH-MUCK-A-MUCK

**muck·luck** *variant of* MUKLUK

**muck·rake** \'mək-ˌrāk\ *intransitive verb* [obsolete *muckrake,* noun, rake for dung] (1910)
: to search out and publicly expose real or apparent misconduct of a prominent individual or business ◆
— **muck·rak·er** *noun*

**muck up** *transitive verb* (1896)
: to make a mess of : BUNGLE, SPOIL

**mu·co·cu·ta·ne·ous** \ˌmyü-kō-kyü-'tā-nē-əs\ *adjective* (1898)
: made up of or involving both typical skin and mucous membrane

¹**mu·coid** \'myü-ˌkȯid\ *adjective* [International Scientific Vocabulary *muc-*] (1849)
: resembling mucus

²**mucoid** *noun* [International Scientific Vocabulary] (1900)
: MUCOPROTEIN

**mu·co·lyt·ic** \ˌmyü-kə-'li-tik\ *adjective* (circa 1923)
: hydrolyzing mucopolysaccharides : tending to break down or lower the viscosity of mucin-containing body secretions or components ⟨*mucolytic* enzymes⟩

**mu·co·pep·tide** \ˌmyü-kō-'pep-ˌtīd\ *noun* (1959)
: PEPTIDOGLYCAN

**mu·co·poly·sac·cha·ride** \'myü-kō-ˌpä-li-'sa-kə-ˌrīd\ *noun* [International Scientific Vocabulary] (1938)
: GLYCOSAMINOGLYCAN

**mu·co·pro·tein** \ˌmyü-kə-'prō-ˌtēn *also* -'prō-tē-ən\ *noun* (1925)
: any of various complex conjugated proteins (as mucins) that contain polysaccharides and occur in body fluids and tissues

**mu·co·sa** \myü-'kō-zə\ *noun, plural* **-sae** \-(ˌ)zē, -ˌzī\ *or* **-sas** [New Latin, from Latin, feminine of *mucosus* mucous] (1880)
: MUCOUS MEMBRANE
— **mu·co·sal** \-zəl\ *adjective*

**mu·cous** \'myü-kəs\ *adjective* [Latin *mucosus,* from *mucus*] (1646)
**1** : of, relating to, or resembling mucus
**2** : secreting or containing mucus
**3** : covered with or as if with mucus : SLIMY

**mucous membrane** *noun* (1812)
: a membrane rich in mucous glands; *specifically* : one that lines body passages and cavities which communicate directly or indirectly with the exterior

**mu·cro** \'myü-ˌkrō\ *noun, plural* **mu·cro·nes** \myü-'krō-(ˌ)nēz\ [New Latin *mucron-, mucro,* from Latin, point, edge] (1646)
: an abrupt sharp terminal point or tip or process (as of a leaf)
— **mu·cro·nate** \'myü-krə-ˌnāt\ *adjective*

**mu·cus** \'myü-kəs\ *noun* [Latin, nasal mucus; akin to Greek *myxa* mucus] (1661)
: a viscid slippery secretion that is usually rich in mucins and is produced by mucous membranes which it moistens and protects

¹**mud** \'məd\ *noun* [Middle English *mudde,* probably from Middle Low German] (14th century)

**1** : a slimy sticky mixture of solid material with a liquid and especially water; *especially* : soft wet earth
**2** : abusive and malicious remarks or charges ⟨political campaigners slinging *mud* at each other⟩
**3** : ANATHEMA 1b — usually used in the phrase *one's name is mud*

²**mud** *transitive verb* **mud·ded; mud·ding** (1593)
**1** : to make muddy or turbid
**2** : to treat or plaster with mud

**mud dauber** *noun* (1856)
: any of various wasps (especially family Sphecidae) that construct mud cells in which the female places an egg with spiders or insects paralyzed by a sting to serve as food for the larva

¹**mud·dle** \'mə-d°l\ *verb* **mud·dled; mud·dling** \'məd-liŋ, 'mə-d°l-iŋ\ [probably from obsolete Dutch *moddelen,* from Middle Dutch, from *modde* mud; akin to Middle Low German *mudde*] (1676)
*transitive verb*
**1** : to make turbid or muddy
**2** : to befog or stupefy especially with liquor
**3** : to mix confusedly
**4** : to make a mess of : BUNGLE
*intransitive verb*
: to think or act in a confused aimless way
— **mud·dler** \'məd-lər, 'mə-d°l-ər\ *noun*

²**muddle** *noun* (circa 1818)
**1** : a state of especially mental confusion
**2** : a confused mess
— **mud·dly** \'məd-lē, 'mə-d°l-ē\ *adjective*

**mud·dle·head·ed** \ˌmə-d°l-'he-dəd\ *adjective* (1759)
**1** : mentally confused
**2** : INEPT, BUNGLING
— **mud·dle·head·ed·ly** *adverb*
— **mud·dle·head·ed·ness** *noun*

**muddle through** *intransitive verb* (circa 1864)
: to achieve a degree of success without much planning or effort

¹**mud·dy** \'mə-dē\ *adjective* **mud·di·er; -est** (15th century)
**1** : morally impure : BASE
**2 a** : full of or covered with mud **b** : characteristic or suggestive of mud ⟨a *muddy* flavor⟩ ⟨*muddy* colors⟩ **c** : turbid with sediment
**3 a** : lacking in clarity or brightness : CLOUDY, DULL ⟨a *muddy* recording⟩ ⟨eyes *muddy* with sleep⟩ **b** : obscure in meaning : MUDDLED, CONFUSED ⟨*muddy* thinking⟩ ⟨a *muddy* style⟩

◇ WORD HISTORY
**muckrake**   John Bunyan's religious allegory *The Pilgrim's Progress* (1678) includes a character identified as "a man . . . with a Muckrake in his hand," who busies himself so much with raking the muck—that is, with attending to worldly things—that his gaze is always downward and he never sees a celestial crown held above him. The metaphor inspired some occasional uses of *muckrake* in the 19th century, most notably in political circles, but the word received its greatest boost when it was used by Theodore Roosevelt in an April 1906 speech criticizing the excesses of journalists who had achieved popularity by exposing the corruption of public figures and institutions. Roosevelt said, "The men with the muckrakes are often indispensable to the well-being of society; but only if they know when to stop raking the muck." The term *muckraker* quickly became established in popular use as a name for reform writers such as Lincoln Steffens, Ida M. Tarbell, Edwin Markham, and Upton Sinclair. Although originally meant to be pejorative, the word was adopted by the writers themselves, and it acquired connotations of courageous honesty and social conscience.

— **mud·di·ly** \'mə-d°l-ē\ *adverb*
— **mud·di·ness** \'mə-dē-nəs\ *noun*

²**muddy** *transitive verb* **mud·died; mud·dy·ing** (1601)
**1** : to soil or stain with or as if with mud
**2** : to make turbid
**3** : to make cloudy or dull
**4** : CONFUSE

**Mu·de·jar** \mü-'the-ˌhär, -ˌkär\ *noun, plural* **-ja·res** \-'the-hä-ˌräs, -kä-\ [Spanish *mudéjar*, from Arabic *mudajjan*, literally, allowed to remain] (1893)
: a Muslim living under a Christian king especially during the 8th to 11th centuries
— **Mudejar** *adjective*

**mud·flat** \'məd-ˌflat\ *noun* (1813)
: a level tract lying at little depth below the surface of water or alternately covered and left bare by the tide

**mud·flow** \-ˌflō\ *noun* (circa 1900)
: a moving mass of soil made fluid by rain or melting snow

**mud·guard** \-ˌgärd\ *noun* (1886)
**1 a** : FENDER d **b** : SPLASH GUARD
**2** : a strip of material applied to a shoe upper just above the sole for protection against dampness or as an ornament

**mud puppy** *noun* (1882)
: a large American salamander (*Necturus maculosus*) that has external gills and is gray to rusty brown usually with bluish black spots

mud puppy

**mu·dra** \mə-'drä\ *noun* [Sanskrit *mudrā*] (1811)
: one of the symbolic hand gestures used in religious ceremonies and dances of India

**mud·room** \'məd-ˌrüm, -ˌrùm\ *noun* (circa 1950)
: a room in a house designed especially for the shedding of dirty or wet footwear and clothing and located typically off the kitchen or in the basement

**mud·sill** \-ˌsil\ *noun* (1685)
**1** : a supporting sill (as of a building or bridge) resting directly on a base and especially the earth
**2** : a person of the lowest social level

**mud·skip·per** \-ˌski-pər\ *noun* (1860)
: any of several Asian and Polynesian gobies (genera *Periophthalmus* and *Boleophthalmus*) that are able to skip about actively over wet mud and sand

**mud·sling·er** \-ˌsliŋ-ər\ *noun* (circa 1890)
: one that uses offensive epithets and invective especially against a political opponent
— **mud·sling·ing** \-ˌsliŋ-iŋ\ *noun*

**mud·stone** \-ˌstōn\ *noun* (circa 1736)
: an indurated shale produced by the consolidation of mud

**mud turtle** *noun* (1785)
: any of a genus (*Kinosternon*) of bottom-dwelling freshwater turtles with two transverse hinges on the plastron

**Muen·ster** \'mən(t)-stər, 'mün(t)-, 'mùn(t)-, 'min(t)-\ *noun* [*Münster, Munster*, France] (1902)
: a semisoft cheese that may be bland or sharp in flavor

**mues·li** \'myüs-lē, 'myüz-\ *noun* [German dialect (Swiss) *Müsli*, diminutive of German *Mus* soft food, mush, from Old High German *muos*; akin to Old English *mōs* food and probably to Old English *mete* food — more at MEAT] (1939)
: a breakfast cereal of Swiss origin consisting of rolled oats, nuts, and fruit

**mu·ez·zin** \mü-'e-z°n, myü-; 'mwe-z°n\ *noun* [Arabic *mu'adhdhin*] (1585)
: a Muslim crier who calls the hour of daily prayers

¹**muff** \'məf\ *noun* [Dutch *mof*, from Middle French *moufle* mitten, from Medieval Latin *muffula*] (1599)
**1** : a warm tubular covering for the hands
**2** : a cluster of feathers on the side of the face of some domestic fowls

²**muff** *verb* [probably from ¹*muff*] (1827)
*transitive verb*
**1** : to handle awkwardly : BUNGLE
**2** : to fail to hold (a ball) when attempting a catch
*intransitive verb*
**1** : to act or do something stupidly or clumsily
**2** : to muff a ball — compare FUMBLE

³**muff** *noun* (1871)
**1** : a bungling performance
**2** : a failure to hold a ball in attempting a catch

**muf·fin** \'mə-fən\ *noun* [probably from Low German *muffen*, plural of *muffe* cake] (1703)
: a quick bread made of batter containing egg and baked in a muffin pan

**muf·fle** \'mə-fəl\ *transitive verb* **muf·fled; muf·fling** \'mə-f(ə-)liŋ\ [Middle English *muflen*] (15th century)
**1** : to wrap up so as to conceal or protect : ENVELOP
**2** *obsolete* : BLINDFOLD
**3 a** : to wrap or pad with something to dull the sound ⟨*muffle* the oarlocks⟩ **b** : to deaden the sound of
**4** : KEEP DOWN, SUPPRESS

**muf·fler** \'mə-flər\ *noun* (circa 1536)
**1 a** : a scarf worn around the neck **b** : something that hides or disguises
**2** : a device to deaden noise; *especially* : one forming part of the exhaust system of an automotive vehicle
— **muf·flered** *adjective*

¹**muf·ti** \'məf-tē, 'müf-\ *noun* [Arabic *muftī*] (1586)
: a professional jurist who interprets Muslim law

²**muf·ti** \'məf-tē\ *noun* [probably from ¹*mufti*] (1816)
: ordinary dress as distinguished from that denoting an occupation or station ⟨a priest in *mufti*⟩; *especially* : civilian clothes when worn by a person in the armed forces

¹**mug** \'məg\ *noun* [origin unknown] (1664)
**1** : a cylindrical drinking cup
**2 a** : the face or mouth of a person **b** : GRIMACE **c** : MUG SHOT
**3** *chiefly British* (1) : FOOL, BLOCKHEAD (2) : a person easily deceived **b** : PUNK, THUG
— **mug·ful** *noun*

²**mug** *verb* **mugged; mug·ging** (1855)
*intransitive verb*
: to pose or make faces especially to attract attention or for a camera
*transitive verb*
: PHOTOGRAPH

³**mug** *transitive verb* **mugged; mug·ging** [probably from earlier *mug* to strike in the face, perhaps from ¹*mug*] (circa 1864)
: to assault usually with intent to rob
— **mug·gee** \ˌmə-'gē\ *noun*

¹**mug·ger** \'mə-gər\ *noun* [Hindi *magar*, from Sanskrit *makara* water monster] (1844)
: a common usually harmless freshwater crocodile (*Crocodylus palustris*) of southeastern Asia

²**mugger** *noun* [³*mug*] (1863)
: one who attacks with intent to rob

³**mugger** *noun* [²*mug*] (1892)
: one that grimaces especially before an audience

**mug·gy** \'mə-gē\ *adjective* **mug·gi·er; -est** [English dialect *mug* drizzle] (1746)
: being warm, damp, and close
— **mug·gi·ness** \'mə-gē-nəs\ *noun*

muff 1

**Mu·ghal** *variant of* MOGUL

**mu·gho pine** \'mü-(ˌ)gō-, 'myü-\ *noun* [probably from French *mugho* mugho pine, from Italian *mugo*] (circa 1756)
: a shrubby spreading pine (*Pinus mugo mughus*) widely cultivated as an ornamental — called also *mugo pine*

**mug's game** \'məgz-\ *noun* (1910)
: a profitless or futile activity

**mug shot** *noun* (1950)
: a photograph of usually a person's head and especially face; *specifically* : a police photograph of a suspect's face or profile

**mug up** (circa 1860)
*intransitive verb*
*British* : to study intensively (as for an examination)
*transitive verb*
: to work up by study

**mug·wump** \'məg-ˌwəmp\ *noun* [obsolete slang *mugwump* kingpin, from Massachuset *mugquomp, muggumquomp* war leader] (1884)
**1** : a bolter from the Republican party in 1884
**2** : an independent in politics ◆

**Mu·ham·mad·an** \mō-'ha-mə-dən, -'hä- *also* mü-\ *adjective* (1681)
: of or relating to Muhammad or Islam
— **Muhammadan** *noun*
— **Mu·ham·mad·an·ism** \-də-ˌni-zəm\ *noun*

**Muhammadan calendar** *noun* (circa 1889)
: ISLAMIC CALENDAR

**Muhammadan era** *noun* (circa 1889)
: ISLAMIC ERA

**Mu·har·ram** \mü-'har-əm\ *noun* [Arabic *Muḥarram*] (circa 1615)
**1** : the 1st month of the Islamic year — see MONTH table
**2** : a Muslim festival held during Muharram

**mu·ja·hid·een** *or* **mu·ja·hed·in** *also* **mu·ja·hed·een** \mü-ˌja-hi-'dēn, mü-, -jä-\ *noun plural* [Arabic *mujāhidīn*, plural of *mujāhid*, literally, person who wages jihad] (1922)
: Islamic guerrilla fighters especially in the Middle East

**mu·jik** \mü-'zhēk, -'zhik\ *variant of* MUZHIK

**muk·luk** \'mək-ˌlək\ *noun* [Yupik *maklak* bearded seal] (1868)

\ə\ abut \°\ kitten \ər\ further \a\ ash \ā\ ace
\ä\ mop, mar \aù\ out \ch\ chin \e\ bet \ē\ easy
\g\ go \i\ hit \ī\ ice \j\ job \ŋ\ sing \ō\ go
\ò\ law \òi\ boy \th\ thin \th\ the \ü\ loot \ù\ foot
\y\ yet \zh\ vision *see also* Guide to Pronunciation

**1 :** a sealskin or reindeer-skin boot worn by Eskimos
**2 :** a boot often of duck with a soft leather sole and worn over several pairs of socks

**muk·tuk** \'mək-ˌtək\ *noun* [Inuit *maktak*] (1835)
**:** whale skin used for food

**mu·lat·to** \mə-'la-(ˌ)tō, mü-, myü-, -'lä-\ *noun*, *plural* **-toes** *or* **-tos** [Spanish *mulato*, from *mulo* mule, from Latin *mulus*] (1593)
**1 :** the first-generation offspring of a black person and a white person
**2 :** a person of mixed white and black ancestry

**mul·ber·ry** \'məl-ˌber-ē, -b(ə-)rē\ *noun* [Middle English *murberie, mulberie*, from Middle French *moure* mulberry (from Latin *morum*, from Greek *moron*) + Middle English *berie* berry] (14th century)
**1 :** any of a genus (*Morus* of the family Moraceae, the mulberry family) of trees with an edible usually purple multiple fruit that is an aggregate of juicy one-seeded drupes; *also* **:** the fruit
**2 :** a dark purple or purplish black

**mulch** \'məlch\ *noun* [perhaps irregular from English dialect *melch* soft, mild] (1657)
**:** a protective covering (as of sawdust, compost, or paper) spread or left on the ground to reduce evaporation, maintain even soil temperature, prevent erosion, control weeds, enrich the soil, or keep fruit (as strawberries) clean
**— mulch** *transitive verb*

**¹mulct** \'məlkt\ *noun* [Latin *multa, mulcta*] (1598)
**:** FINE, PENALTY

**²mulct** *transitive verb* (1611)
**1 :** to punish by a fine
**2 a :** to defraud especially of money **:** SWINDLE **b :** to obtain by fraud, duress, or theft

**¹mule** \'myü(ə)l\ *noun* [Middle English, from Old French *mul*, from Latin *mulus*] (13th century)
**1 a :** a hybrid between a horse and a donkey; *especially* **:** the offspring of a male donkey and a mare **b :** a self-sterile plant whether hybrid or not **c :** a usually sterile hybrid
**2 :** a very stubborn person
**3 :** a machine for simultaneously drawing and twisting fiber into yarn or thread and winding it into cops
**4** *slang* **:** a person who smuggles or delivers illicit drugs

**²mule** *noun* [Middle French, a kind of slipper, from Latin *mulleus* shoe worn by magistrates] (1562)
**:** a shoe or slipper without quarter or heel strap
**— compare** SCUFF

**mule deer** *noun* (1805)
**:** a long-eared deer (*Odocoileus hemionus*) of western North America that is larger and more heavily built than the common white-tail

**mule skinner** *noun* (1870)
**:** MULETEER

**mu·le·ta** \mü-'lā-tə, myü-\ *noun* [Spanish, crutch, muleta, diminutive of *mula* she-mule, from Latin, feminine of *mulus* mule] (1838)
**:** a small cloth attached to a short tapered stick and used by a matador in place of the large cape during the final stage of a bullfight

mule deer

**mu·le·teer** \ˌmyü-lə-'tir\ *noun* [French *muletier*, from *mulet*, from Old French, diminutive of *mul* mule] (1538)
**:** one who drives mules

**mu·ley** \'myü-lē, 'mü-, 'mü-\ *adjective* [of Celtic origin; akin to Irish & Scottish Gaelic *maol* bald, hornless, Welsh *moel*] (1840)

**:** POLLED, HORNLESS; *especially* **:** naturally hornless

**mu·li·eb·ri·ty** \ˌmyü-lē-'e-brə-tē\ *noun* [Late Latin *muliebritat-, muliebritas*, from Latin *muliebris* of a woman, from *mulier* woman] (1592)
**:** FEMININITY

**mul·ish** \'myü-lish\ *adjective* [¹*mule*] (1751)
**:** unreasonably and inflexibly obstinate
**synonym** see OBSTINATE
**— mul·ish·ly** *adverb*
**— mul·ish·ness** *noun*

**¹mull** \'məl\ *verb* [Middle English, from *mul, mol* dust, probably from Middle Dutch; akin to Old English *melu* meal — more at MEAL] (15th century)
*transitive verb*
**1 :** to grind or mix thoroughly **:** PULVERIZE
**2 :** to consider at length **:** PONDER — often used with *over*
*intransitive verb*
**:** MEDITATE, PONDER

**²mull** *transitive verb* [origin unknown] (1618)
**:** to heat, sweeten, and flavor (as wine or cider) with spices

**³mull** *noun* [by shortening & alteration from *mulmul* muslin, from Hindi *malmal*] (1798)
**:** a soft fine sheer fabric of cotton, silk, or rayon

**⁴mull** *noun* [German, from Danish *muld*, from Old Norse *mold* dust, soil; akin to Old High German *molta* dust, soil — more at MOLD] (1928)
**1 :** friable forest humus that forms a layer of mixed organic matter and mineral soil and merges gradually into the mineral soil beneath
**2 :** a finely powdered solid especially in a suspension

**mul·lah** \'mə-lə, 'mù-\ *noun* [Turkish *molla* & Persian & Hindi *mulla*, from Arabic *mawlā*] (1613)
**:** an educated Muslim trained in traditional religious law and doctrine and usually holding an official post
**— mul·lah·ism** \-lə-ˌi-zəm\ *noun*

**mul·lein** *also* **mul·len** \'mə-lən\ *noun* [Middle English *moleyne*, from Anglo-French *moleine*] (14th century)
**:** any of a genus (*Verbascum*) of usually woolly-leaved Eurasian herbs of the snapdragon family including some that are naturalized in North America

**mullein pink** *noun* (circa 1850)
**:** an Old World herb (*Lychnis coronaria*) of the pink family cultivated chiefly for its woolly herbage and crimson flowers

**mull·er** \'mə-lər\ *noun* [alteration of Middle English *molour*, probably from *mullen* to grind] (1612)
**:** a stone or piece of wood, metal, or glass used as a pestle for pounding or grinding

**Mül·le·ri·an** \myü-'lir-ē-ən, mi-, ˌmə-\ *adjective* [Fritz *Müller* (died 1897) German zoologist] (1899)
**:** of, relating to, or being mimicry that exists between two or more inedible or dangerous species (as of butterflies) and that is considered in evolutionary theory to be a mechanism reducing loss to predation by simplification of the recognition process

**mul·let** \'mə-lət\ *noun*, *plural* **mullet** *or* **mullets** [Middle English *molet*, from Middle French *mulet*, from Latin *mullus* red mullet, from Greek *myllos*] (14th century)
**:** any of a family (Mugilidae) of valuable chiefly marine food fishes with an elongate rather stout body

**mul·li·gan** \'mə-li-gən\ *noun* [probably from the name *Mulligan*] (circa 1949)
**:** a free shot sometimes given a golfer in informal play when the previous shot was poorly played

**mulligan stew** *noun* [probably from the name *Mulligan*] (1904)
**:** a stew made from whatever ingredients are available

**mul·li·ga·taw·ny** \ˌmə-li-gə-'tò-nē, -'tä-\ *noun* [Tamil *miḻakutaṇṇi*, from *miḻaku* pepper + *taṇṇi* water] (1784)
**:** a rich soup usually of chicken stock seasoned with curry

**mul·lion** \'məl-yən\ *noun* [probably alteration of *monial* mullion] (1567)
**:** a slender vertical member that forms a division between units of a window, door, or screen or is used decoratively
**— mullion** *transitive verb*

**mull·ite** \'mə-ˌlīt\ *noun* [*Mull*, island of the Inner Hebrides] (1924)
**:** a mineral that is an orthorhombic silicate of aluminum which is resistant to corrosion and heat and is used as a refractory

**multi-** *combining form* [Middle English, from Middle French or Latin; Middle French, from Latin, from *multus* much, many — more at MELIORATE]
**1 a :** many **:** multiple **:** much ⟨*multi*valent⟩ **b :** more than two ⟨*multi*lateral⟩ **c :** more than one ⟨*multi*parous⟩
**2 :** many times over ⟨*multi*millionaire⟩

| | |
|---|---|
| mul·ti·age | mul·ti·fre·quen·cy |
| mul·ti·agen·cy | mul·ti·func·tion |
| mul·ti·armed | mul·ti·func·tion·al |
| mul·ti·at·om | mul·ti·gen·er·a·tion·al |
| mul·ti·au·thor | |
| mul·ti·ax·i·al | mul·ti·gen·ic |
| mul·ti·band | mul·ti·grade |
| mul·ti·bank | mul·ti·grain |
| mul·ti·bar·rel | mul·ti·grid |
| mul·ti·bar·reled | mul·ti·group |
| mul·ti·bil·lion | mul·ti·hand·i·capped |
| mul·ti·bil·lion·aire | mul·ti·head·ed |
| mul·ti·blad·ed | mul·ti·hos·pi·tal |
| mul·ti·branched | mul·ti·hued |
| mul·ti·build·ing | mul·ti–in·dus·try |
| mul·ti·cam·pus | mul·ti–in·sti·tu·tion·al |
| mul·ti·car | |
| mul·ti·car·bon | mul·ti·lane |
| mul·ti·caus·al | mul·ti·lev·el |
| mul·ti·cell | mul·ti·lev·eled |
| mul·ti·celled | mul·ti·line |
| mul·ti·cel·lu·lar | mul·ti·lobed |
| mul·ti·cel·lu·lar·i·ty | mul·ti·manned |
| mul·ti·cen·ter | mul·ti·mega·ton |
| mul·ti·chain | mul·ti·mega·watt |
| mul·ti·cham·bered | mul·ti·mem·ber |
| mul·ti·chan·nel | mul·ti·me·tal·lic |
| mul·ti·char·ac·ter | mul·ti·mil·len·ni·al |
| mul·ti·city | mul·ti·mil·lion |
| mul·ti·cli·ent | mul·ti·mil·lion·aire |
| mul·ti·coat·ed | mul·ti·mode |
| mul·ti·col·or | mul·ti·mo·lec·u·lar |
| mul·ti·col·ored | mul·ti·na·tion |
| mul·ti·col·umn | mul·ti·nu·cle·ar |
| mul·ti·com·po·nent | mul·ti·nu·cle·ate |
| mul·ti·con·duc·tor | mul·ti·nu·cle·at·ed |
| mul·ti·copy | mul·ti·or·gas·mic |
| mul·ti·coun·ty | mul·ti·page |
| mul·ti·course | mul·ti·paned |
| mul·ti·cu·rie | mul·ti·pa·ram·e·ter |
| mul·ti·cur·ren·cy | mul·ti·part |
| mul·ti·di·a·lec·tal | mul·ti·par·ti·cle |
| mul·ti·di·men·sion·al | mul·ti·par·ty |
| mul·ti·di·men·sion·al·i·ty | mul·ti·path |
| | mul·ti·phase |
| mul·ti·di·rec·tion·al | mul·ti·phasic |
| mul·ti·dis·ci·plin·ary | mul·ti·pho·ton |
| mul·ti·dis·ci·pline | mul·ti·pic·ture |
| mul·ti·di·vi·sion·al | mul·ti·piece |
| mul·ti·do·main | mul·ti·pi·on |
| mul·ti·drug | mul·ti·pis·ton |
| mul·ti·elec·trode | mul·ti·plant |
| mul·ti·el·e·ment | mul·ti·play·er |
| mul·ti·em·ploy·er | mul·ti·pole |
| mul·ti·en·gine | mul·ti·pow·er |
| mul·ti·eth·nic | mul·ti·prob·lem |
| mul·ti·fac·et·ed | mul·ti·prod·uct |
| mul·ti·fam·i·ly | mul·ti·pur·pose |
| mul·ti·fil·a·ment | mul·ti·range |
| mul·ti·flash | mul·ti·re·gion·al |
| mul·ti·fo·cal | mul·ti·re·li·gious |

mul·ti·room
mul·ti·screen
mul·ti·ser·vice
mul·ti·sid·ed
mul·ti·site
mul·ti·size
mul·ti·skilled
mul·ti·source
mul·ti·spe·cies
mul·ti·speed
mul·ti·sport
mul·ti·stemmed
mul·ti·step
mul·ti·sto·ried
mul·ti·sto·ry
mul·ti·strand·ed
mul·ti·syl·lab·ic
mul·ti·sys·tem

mul·ti·tal·ent·ed
mul·ti·ter·mi·nal
mul·ti·tiered
mul·ti·ton
mul·ti·tone
mul·ti·tow·ered
mul·ti·track
mul·ti·tril·lion
mul·ti·union
mul·ti·unit
mul·ti·use
mul·ti·vi·ta·min
mul·ti·vol·ume
mul·ti·wall
mul·ti·war·head
mul·ti·wave·length
mul·ti·year

**mul·ti·cul·tur·al** \ˌməl-tē-'kəlch-rəl, -ˌtī-, -'kəl-chə-\ *adjective* (1941)
: of, relating to, reflecting, or adapted to diverse cultures ⟨a *multicultural* society⟩ ⟨*multicultural* education⟩ ⟨a *multicultural* menu⟩
— **mul·ti·cul·tur·al·ism** \-rə-ˌli-zəm\ *noun*

**mul·ti·en·zyme** \-'en-ˌzīm\ *adjective* (1961)
: composed of or involving two or more enzymes that function in a biosynthetic pathway ⟨*multienzyme* complex⟩

**mul·ti·fac·to·ri·al** \-fak-'tōr-ē-əl, -'tòr-\ *adjective* (1920)
**1** : having characters or a mode of inheritance dependent on a number of genes at different loci
**2** *or* **mul·ti·fac·tor** \-'fak-tər\ : having, involving, or produced by a variety of elements or causes
— **mul·ti·fac·to·ri·al·ly** \-fak-'tōr-ē-ə-lē, -'tòr-\ *adverb*

**mul·ti·far·i·ous** \ˌməl-tə-'far-ē-əs, -'fer-\ *adjective* [Medieval Latin *multifarius*, from Latin *multifariam* in many places] (1593)
: having or occurring in great variety : DIVERSE
— **mul·ti·far·i·ous·ness** *noun*

**mul·ti·flo·ra rose** \ˌməl-tə-'flōr-ə-, -'flòr-\ *noun* [New Latin *multiflora*, specific epithet, literally, having many flowers] (1829)
: a vigorous thorny rose (*Rosa multiflora*) with clusters of small flowers

**mul·ti·fold** \'məl-ti-ˌfōld\ *adjective* (1806)
: MANY, NUMEROUS

**mul·ti·form** \'məl-ti-ˌfòrm\ *adjective* [French *multiforme*, from Latin *multiformis*, from *multi-* + *-formis* -form] (1603)
: having many forms or appearances
— **mul·ti·for·mi·ty** \ˌməl-ti-'fòr-mə-tē\ *noun*

**mul·ti·germ** \ˌməl-ti-'jərm, -ˌtī-\ *adjective* [probably from *multi-* + *germinate*] (1950)
: producing or being a fruit cluster capable of giving rise to several plants ⟨a *multigerm* variety of sugar beet⟩

**mul·ti·hull** \'məl-ti-ˌhəl, -ˌtī-\ *noun* (1960)
: a vessel (as a catamaran or trimaran) with multiple side-by-side hulls — compare MONOHULL

**mul·ti·lat·er·al** \ˌməl-ti-'la-t(ə-)rəl, -ˌtī-\ *adjective* (1696)
**1** : having many sides
**2** : involving or participated in by more than two nations or parties ⟨*multilateral* agreements⟩
— **mul·ti·lat·er·al·ism** \-'la-t(ə-)rə-ˌli-zəm\ *noun*
— **mul·ti·lat·er·al·ist** \-list\ *noun*
— **mul·ti·lat·er·al·ly** *adverb*

**mul·ti·lay·ered** \-'lā-ərd, -'le(-ə)rd\ *or* **mul·ti·lay·er** \-'lā-ər, -'le(-ə)r\ *adjective* (1923)
: having or involving several distinct layers, strata, or levels

**mul·ti·lin·gual** \-'liŋ-gwəl, -'liŋ-gyə-wəl\ *adjective* (1838)
**1** : of, containing, or expressed in several languages ⟨a *multilingual* sign⟩ ⟨*multilingual* dictionaries⟩

**2** : using or able to use several languages ⟨*multilingual* translators⟩
— **mul·ti·lin·gual·ism** \-gwə-ˌli-zəm, -gyə-wə-\ *noun*
— **mul·ti·lin·gual·ly** \-gwə-lē, -gyə-wə-lē\ *adverb*

**mul·ti·me·dia** \-'mē-dē-ə\ *adjective* (1962)
: using, involving, or encompassing several media ⟨a *multimedia* approach to learning⟩
— **multimedia** *noun*

**mul·ti·mod·al** \-'mō-d°l\ *adjective* (1902)
: having or involving several modes, modalities, or maxima ⟨*multimodal* distributions⟩ ⟨*multimodal* responses⟩

**mul·ti·na·tion·al** \-'nash-nəl, -'na-shə-n°l\ *adjective* (1926)
**1** : of or relating to more than two nationalities ⟨a *multinational* society⟩
**2 a** : of, relating to, or involving more than two nations ⟨a *multinational* alliance⟩ **b** : having divisions in more than two countries ⟨a *multinational* corporation⟩
— **multinational** *noun*

**mul·ti·no·mi·al** \-'nō-mē-əl\ *noun* [*multi-* + *-nomial* (as in *binomial*)] (1674)
: a mathematical expression that consists of the sum of several terms : POLYNOMIAL
— **multinomial** *adjective*

**mul·tip·a·rous** \ˌməl-'ti-pə-rəs\ *adjective* [New Latin *multiparus*, from *multi-* + Latin *-parus* -parous] (1646)
**1** : producing many or more than one at a birth
**2** : having experienced one or more previous parturitions

**mul·ti·par·tite** \ˌməl-ti-'pär-ˌtīt\ *adjective* [Latin *multipartitus*, from *multi-* + *partitus*, past participle of *partire* to divide, from *part-*, *pars* part] (circa 1721)
**1** : divided into several or many parts
**2** : having numerous members or signatories ⟨a *multipartite* treaty⟩

**¹mul·ti·ple** \'məl-tə-pəl\ *adjective* [French, from Latin *multiplex*, from *multi-* + *-plex* -fold — more at -FOLD] (1647)
**1** : consisting of, including, or involving more than one ⟨*multiple* births⟩
**2** : MANY, MANIFOLD ⟨*multiple* achievements⟩
**3** : shared by many ⟨*multiple* ownership⟩
**4** : having numerous aspects or functions : VARIOUS
**5** : being a group of terminals which make a circuit available at a number of points
**6** : formed by coalescence of the ripening ovaries of several flowers ⟨a *multiple* fruit⟩

**²multiple** *noun* (1685)
**1 a** : the product of a quantity by an integer ⟨35 is a *multiple* of 7⟩ **b** : something in units of more than one or two
**2** : PARALLEL 4b
**3** *chiefly British* : CHAIN STORE

**multiple allele** *noun* (1938)
: an allele of a genetic locus having more than two allelic forms within a population

**multiple–choice** *adjective* (1926)
**1** : having several answers from which one is to be chosen ⟨a *multiple-choice* question⟩
**2** : composed of multiple-choice questions ⟨a *multiple-choice* test⟩

**multiple factor** *noun* (1915)
: one of a group of nonallelic genes that according to the multiple-factor hypothesis control various quantitative hereditary characters

**multiple myeloma** *noun* (1897)
: a disease of bone marrow that is characterized by the presence of numerous myelomas in various bones of the body

**multiple personality** *noun* (1901)
: an hysterical neurosis in which the personality becomes dissociated into two or more distinct but complex and socially and behaviorally integrated parts each of which becomes dominant and controls behavior from time to time to the exclusion of the others — compare SCHIZOPHRENIA, SPLIT PERSONALITY

**multiple regression** *noun* (1924)

: regression in which one variable is estimated by the use of more than one other variable

**multiple sclerosis** *noun* (1885)
: a demyelinating disease marked by patches of hardened tissue in the brain or the spinal cord and associated especially with partial or complete paralysis and jerking muscle tremor

**multiple star** *noun* (1850)
: several stars in close proximity that appear to form a single system

**multiple store** *noun* (1929)
*chiefly British* : CHAIN STORE

**mul·ti·plet** \'məl-tə-plət\ *noun* (1922)
**1** : a spectrum line having several components
**2** : a group of elementary particles that are different in charge but similar in other properties (as mass)

**multiple–valued** *adjective* (1882)
: having at least one and sometimes more of the values of the range associated with each value of the domain ⟨a *multiple-valued* function⟩ — compare SINGLE-VALUED

**¹mul·ti·plex** \'məl-tə-ˌpleks\ *adjective* [Latin] (1557)
**1** : MANY, MULTIPLE
**2** : being or relating to a system of transmitting several messages or signals simultaneously on the same circuit or channel

**²multiplex** (1907)
*transitive verb*
: to send (messages or signals) by a multiplex system
*intransitive verb*
: to multiplex messages or signals
— **mul·ti·plex·er** *also* **mul·ti·plex·or** \-ˌplek-sər\ *noun*

**³multiplex** *noun* (1985)
: a complex that houses several movie theaters

**mul·ti·pli·cand** \ˌməl-tə-plə-'kand\ *noun* [Latin *multiplicandus*, gerundive of *multiplicare*] (1594)
: the number that is to be multiplied by another

**mul·ti·pli·ca·tion** \ˌməl-tə-plə-'kā-shən\ *noun* [Middle English *multiplicacioun*, from Middle French *multiplication*, from Latin *multiplication-*, *multiplicatio*, from *multiplicare* to multiply] (14th century)
**1** : the act or process of multiplying : the state of being multiplied
**2 a** : a mathematical operation that at its simplest is an abbreviated process of adding an integer to itself a specified number of times and that is extended to other numbers in accordance with laws that are valid for integers **b** : any of various mathematical operations that are analogous in some way to multiplication of the real numbers but are defined for other or larger sets of elements (as complex numbers, vectors, matrices, or functions)

**multiplication sign** *noun* (1907)
: a symbol used to indicate multiplication: **a** : TIMES SIGN **b** : DOT 2b

**mul·ti·pli·ca·tive** \ˌməl-tə-'pli-kə-tiv, 'məl-tə-plə-ˌkā-tiv\ *adjective* (1653)
**1** : tending or having the power to multiply
**2** : of, relating to, or associated with a mathematical operation of multiplication ⟨the *multiplicative* property of 0 requires that $a \cdot 0 = 0$ and $0 \cdot a = 0$⟩
— **mul·ti·pli·ca·tive·ly** *adverb*

**multiplicative identity** *noun* (1958)
: an identity element (as 1 in the group of rational numbers without 0) that in a given mathematical system leaves unchanged any element by which it is multiplied

**multiplicative inverse** *noun* (1958)
: an element of a mathematical set that when multiplied by a given element yields the identity element — called also *reciprocal*

---

\ə\ abut \ᵊ\ kitten \ər\ further \a\ ash \ā\ ace
\ä\ mop, mar \aù\ out \ch\ chin \e\ bet \ē\ easy
\g\ go \i\ hit \ī\ ice \j\ job \ŋ\ sing \ō\ go
\ò\ law \òi\ boy \th\ thin \t͟h\ the \ü\ loot \ù\ foot
\y\ yet \zh\ vision    *see also* Guide to Pronunciation

**mul·ti·plic·i·ty** \ˌməl-tə-'pli-sə-tē\ *noun, plural* **-ties** [Middle English, from Middle French *multiplicité*, from Late Latin *multiplicitat-, multiplicitas*, from Latin *multiplic-, multiplex*] (15th century)
**1 a :** the quality or state of being multiple or various **b :** the number of components in a system (as a multiplet or a group of energy levels)
**2 :** a great number
**3 :** the number of times a root of an equation or zero of a function occurs when there is more than one root or zero ⟨the *multiplicity* of *x* = 2 for the equation (*x* − 2)³ = 0 is 3⟩
**mul·ti·pli·er** \'məl-tə-ˌplī-(-ə)r\ *noun* (15th century)
**:** one that multiplies: as **a :** a number by which another number is multiplied **b :** an instrument or device for multiplying or intensifying some effect **c :** a machine, mechanism, or circuit that multiplies figures
**¹mul·ti·ply** \'məl-tə-ˌplī\ *verb* **-plied; -ply·ing** [Middle English *multiplien*, from Old French *multiplier*, from Latin *multiplicare*, from *multiplic-, multiplex* multiple] (13th century)
*transitive verb*
**1 :** to increase in number especially greatly or in multiples **:** AUGMENT
**2 a :** to find the product of by multiplication ⟨*multiply* 7 and 8⟩ **b :** to use as a multiplicand in multiplication with another number ⟨*multiply* 7 by 8⟩
*intransitive verb*
**1 a :** to become greater in number **:** SPREAD **b :** BREED, PROPAGATE
**2 :** to perform multiplication
*synonym* see INCREASE
**²mul·ti·ply** \-plē\ *adverb* (1881)
**:** in a multiple manner **:** in several ways ⟨*multiply* handicapped children⟩
**mul·ti–ply** \ˌməl-ti-'plī, -ˌti-\ *adjective* (1926)
**:** composed of several plies
**mul·ti·po·lar** \-'pō-lər\ *adjective* [International Scientific Vocabulary] (1859)
**1 :** having several poles ⟨a *multipolar* generator⟩ ⟨*multipolar* mitoses⟩
**2 :** having several dendrites ⟨*multipolar* nerve cells⟩
**3 :** characterized by more than two centers of power or interest ⟨a *multipolar* world⟩
— **mul·ti·po·lar·i·ty** \-pō-'lar-ə-tē\ *noun*
**mul·ti·po·ten·tial** \-pə-'ten(t)-shəl\ *adjective* (1913)
**:** having the potential of becoming any of several mature cell types ⟨*multipotential* stem cell⟩
**mul·ti·pro·cess·ing** \-'prä-ˌse-siŋ, -'prō-, -sə-siŋ\ *noun* (1961)
**:** the processing of several computer programs at the same time especially by a computer system with two or more processors sharing a single memory
— **mul·ti·pro·ces·sor** \-sər\ *noun*
**mul·ti·pro·gram·ming** \-'prō-ˌgra-miŋ, -grə-\ *noun* (1959)
**:** the technique of utilizing several interleaved programs concurrently in a single computer system
**mul·ti·pronged** \-'prȯŋd\ *adjective* (1957)
**1 :** having several prongs ⟨*multipronged* fishing spears⟩
**2 :** having several distinct aspects or elements ⟨a *multipronged* attack on the problem⟩
**mul·ti·ra·cial** \-'rā-shəl\ *adjective* (1923)
**:** composed of, involving, or representing various races
— **mul·ti·ra·cial·ism** \-shə-ˌli-zəm\ *noun*
**mul·ti·sense** \'məl-ti-ˌsen(t)s\ *adjective* (1957)
**:** having several meanings ⟨*multisense* words⟩
**mul·ti·sen·so·ry** \ˌməl-ti-'sen(t)-sə-rē, -'sen(t)s-rē\ *adjective* (1949)
**:** relating to or involving several physiological senses ⟨*multisensory* teaching methods⟩ ⟨*multisensory* experience⟩

**mul·ti·spec·tral** \-'spek-trəl\ *adjective* (1965)
**:** of or relating to two or more ranges of frequencies or wavelengths in the electromagnetic spectrum
**mul·ti·stage** \'məl-ti-ˌstāj, -ˌtī-\ *adjective* (1904)
**1 :** having successive operating stages; *especially* **:** having propulsion units that operate in turn ⟨*multistage* rockets⟩
**2 :** conducted by or occurring in stages ⟨a *multistage* investigation⟩
**mul·ti·state** \-ˌstāt\ *adjective* (1944)
**1 :** having divisions in several states ⟨*multistate* enterprises⟩
**2 :** of, relating to, or involving several states ⟨a *multistate* attack on environmental pollution⟩
**mul·ti·task·ing** \-ˌtas-kiŋ\ *noun, often attributive* (1966)
**:** the concurrent performance of several jobs by a computer
**mul·ti·tude** \'məl-tə-ˌtüd, -ˌtyüd\ *noun* [Middle English, from Middle French or Latin; Middle French, from Latin *multitudin-, multitudo*, from *multus* much — more at MELIORATE] (14th century)
**1 :** the state of being many
**2 :** a great number **:** HOST
**3 :** a great number of people
**4 :** POPULACE, PUBLIC
**mul·ti·tu·di·nous** \ˌməl-tə-'tüd-nəs, -'tyüd-; -'tü-dᵊn-əs, -'tyü-\ *adjective* (1604)
**1 :** including a multitude of individuals **:** POPULOUS ⟨the *multitudinous* city⟩
**2 :** existing in a great multitude ⟨*multitudinous* opportunities⟩
**3 :** existing in or consisting of innumerable elements or aspects ⟨*multitudinous* applause⟩
— **mul·ti·tu·di·nous·ly** *adverb*
— **mul·ti·tu·di·nous·ness** *noun*
**mul·ti·us·er** \ˌməl-tī-'yü-zər, -tē-, -ti-\ *adjective* (1964)
**:** able to be used by more than one person simultaneously
**mul·tiv·a·lence** \ˌməl-ti-və-lən(t)s\ *noun* (circa 1881)
**:** the quality or state of having many values, meanings, or appeals
**mul·ti·va·lent** \ˌməl-ti-'vā-lənt, -ˌtī-, *especially in sense 3* ˌməl-'ti-və-\ *adjective* [International Scientific Vocabulary] (1874)
**1 :** POLYVALENT
**2 :** represented more than twice in the somatic chromosome number ⟨*multivalent* chromosomes⟩
**3 :** having many values, meanings, or appeals
— **multivalent** *noun*
**mul·ti·var·i·able** \ˌməl-ti-'ver-ē-ə-bəl, -ˌtī-, -'var-\ *adjective* (1963)
**:** MULTIVARIATE
**mul·ti·var·i·ate** \-'ver-ē-ət, -ˌāt\ *adjective* [*multi-* + *variable* + *³-ate*] (1951)
**:** having or involving a number of independent mathematical or statistical variables ⟨*multivariate* calculus⟩ ⟨*multivariate* data analysis⟩
**mul·ti·ver·si·ty** \-'vər-sə-tē, -stē\ *noun, plural* **-ties** [*multi-* + *-versity* (as in *university*)] (1963)
**:** a very large university with many component schools, colleges, or divisions and widely diverse functions
**mul·ti·vol·tine** \-'vȯl-ˌtēn, -'vȯl-\ *adjective* [*multi-* + *-voltine* having a given number of broods (from French, from Italian *volta* time, turn) — more at VOLT] (1874)
**:** having several broods in a season ⟨*multivoltine* insects⟩
**mul·ture** \'məl-chər, *Scottish usually* 'mü-tər\ *noun* [Middle English *multyr*, from Middle French *molture*, literally, grinding, from (assumed) Vulgar Latin *molitura*, from Latin *molitus*, past participle of *molere* to grind — more at MEAL] (14th century)

*chiefly Scottish* **:** a fee for grinding grain at a mill
**¹mum** \'məm\ *adjective* [probably imitative of a sound made with closed lips] (14th century)
**:** SILENT ⟨keep *mum*⟩
**²mum** *intransitive verb* **mummed; mumming** [Middle English *mommen*, from Middle French *momer* to go masked] (1530)
**1 :** to perform in a pantomime
**2 :** to go about merrymaking in disguise during festivals
**³mum** *noun* [German *Mumme*] (1640)
**:** a strong ale or beer
**⁴mum** *chiefly British variant of* MOM
**⁵mum** *noun* (1917)
**:** CHRYSANTHEMUM
**mum·ble** \'məm-bəl\ *verb* **mum·bled; mum·bling** \-b(ə-)liŋ\ [Middle English *momelen*, of imitative origin] (14th century)
*intransitive verb*
**:** to utter words in a low confused indistinct manner **:** MUTTER
*transitive verb*
**1 :** to utter with a low inarticulate voice
**2 :** to chew or bite with or as if with toothless gums
— **mumble** *noun*
— **mum·bler** \-b(ə-)lər\ *noun*
— **mum·bly** \-b(ə-)lē\ *adjective*
**mum·ble·ty–peg** \'məm-bəl-(tē-)ˌpeg, -blē-ˌpeg\ *also* **mum·ble–the–peg** \-bəl-(thə-)ˌpeg, -blē-ˌpeg\ *or* **mumble peg** \-bəl-ˌpeg, -blē-\ *noun* [from the phrase *mumble the peg*; from the loser's originally having to pull out with his teeth a peg driven into the ground] (1627)
**:** a game in which the players try to flip a knife from various positions so that the blade will stick into the ground
**mum·bo jum·bo** \ˌməm-bō-'jəm-(ˌ)bō\ *noun* [*Mumbo Jumbo*, a masked figure among Mandingo peoples of western Africa] (1738)
**1 :** an object of superstitious homage and fear
**2 a :** a complicated often ritualistic observance with elaborate trappings **b :** complicated activity usually intended to obscure and confuse
**3 :** unnecessarily involved and incomprehensible language **:** GIBBERISH
**mum·mer** \'mə-mər\ *noun* [Middle French *momeur*, from *momer* to go masked] (1502)
**1 :** a performer in a pantomime; *broadly* **:** ACTOR
**2 :** one who goes merrymaking in disguise during festivals
**mum·mery** \'mə-mə-rē\ *noun, plural* **-mer·ies** (circa 1530)
**1 :** a performance by mummers
**2 :** a ridiculous, hypocritical, or pretentious ceremony or performance
**mum·mi·chog** \'mə-mi-ˌchȯg, -ˌchäg\ *noun* [Narraganset *moamitteaúg*] (1787)
**:** a common American killifish (*Fundulus heteroclitus* of the family Cyprinodontidae)
**mum·mi·fy** \'mə-mi-ˌfī\ *verb* **-fied; -fy·ing** (1628)
*transitive verb*
**1 :** to embalm and dry as or as if a mummy
**2 a :** to make into or like a mummy **b :** to cause to dry up and shrivel
*intransitive verb*
**:** to dry up and shrivel like a mummy
— **mum·mi·fi·ca·tion** \ˌmə-mi-fə-'kā-shən\ *noun*
**¹mum·my** \'mə-mē\ *noun, plural* **mummies** [Middle English *mummie* powdered parts of a mummified body used as a drug, from Middle French *momie*, from Medieval Latin *mumia* mummy, powdered mummy, from Arabic *mūmiyah* bitumen, mummy, from Persian *mūm* wax] (1615)
**1 a :** a body embalmed or treated for burial with preservatives in the manner of the ancient

Egyptians **b :** a body unusually well preserved **2 :** one resembling a mummy

**²mummy** *chiefly British variant of* MOMMY

**mumps** \'məmps\ *noun plural but singular or plural in construction* [from plural of obsolete *mump* grimace] (1598)

**:** an acute contagious virus disease marked by fever and by swelling especially of the parotid gland

**munch** \'mənch\ *verb* [Middle English *monchen,* probably of imitative origin] (14th century)
*transitive verb*
**:** to eat with a chewing action ⟨many a mouthful is *munched* in private —Washington Irving⟩; *also* **:** to snack on ⟨drank coffee and *munched* homemade cookies —Lady Bird Johnson⟩
*intransitive verb*
**:** to eat or chew something; *also* **:** SNACK — usually used with *on*
— **munch·er** *noun*

**Mun·chau·sen syndrome** \'mən-,chaù-zən-, ,mən-'chaù-\ *noun* [Baron K. F. H. von *Münchausen* (died 1797) German soldier and proverbial teller of exaggerated tales] (1951)
**:** a condition characterized by the feigning of the symptoms of a disease or injury in order to undergo diagnostic tests, hospitalization, or medical or surgical treatment — called also *Munchausen's syndrome*

**munch·ies** \'mən-chēz\ *noun plural* (circa 1971)
**1 :** hunger pangs
**2 :** light snack foods

**munch·kin** \'mənch-,kin\ *noun* [the *Munchkins,* diminutive creatures in *The Wonderful Wizard of Oz* (1900) by L. Frank Baum] (1972)
**:** a person who is notably small and often endearing

**Mun·da** \'mùn-də\ *noun* (1901)
**:** a branch of the Austroasiatic language family spoken by tribal peoples of central and eastern India

**mun·dane** \,mən-'dān, 'mən-,\ *adjective* [Middle English *mondeyne,* from Middle French *mondain,* from Late Latin *mundanus,* from Latin *mundus* world] (15th century)
**1 :** of, relating to, or characteristic of the world
**2 :** characterized by the practical, transitory, and ordinary **:** COMMONPLACE ⟨the *mundane* concerns of day-to-day life⟩
*synonym* see EARTHLY
— **mun·dane·ly** *adverb*
— **mun·dane·ness** \-'dān-nəs, -,dān-\ *noun*
— **mun·dan·i·ty** \,mən-'dā-nə-tē\ *noun*

**mun·dun·gus** \,mən-'dəŋ-gəs\ *noun* [modification of Spanish *mondongo* tripe] (1641)
*archaic* **:** foul-smelling tobacco

**mung bean** \'məŋ-\ *noun* [Hindi *mū̃g,* from Sanskrit *mudga*] (1910)
**:** an erect bushy annual bean (*Phaseolus aureus*) that is widely cultivated in warm regions for its edible usually green or yellow seeds, for forage, and as the chief source of bean sprouts; *also* **:** the seed of the mung bean

**mun·go** \'məŋ-(,)gō\ *noun, plural* **mungos** [origin unknown] (1857)
**:** reclaimed wool of poor quality and very short staple

**mu·ni** \'myü-nē\ *noun* (1973)
**:** MUNICIPAL

**¹mu·nic·i·pal** \myù-'nis(-ə-)pəl *also* myə-, mə-, -'ni-sə-bəl, ÷,myü-nə-'si-pəl\ *adjective* [Latin *municipalis* of a municipality, from *municip-, municeps* inhabitant of a municipality, from *munus* duty, service + *capere* to take — more at MEAN, HEAVE] (circa 1540)
**1 :** of or relating to the internal affairs of a major political unit (as a nation)

**2 a :** of, relating to, or characteristic of a municipality **b :** having local self-government
**3 :** restricted to one locality

**²municipal** *noun* (1925)
**:** a security issued by a state or local government or by an authority set up by such a government — usually used in plural

**municipal court** *noun* (1828)
**1 :** a court that sits in some cities and larger towns and that usually has civil and criminal jurisdiction over cases arising within the municipality
**2 :** POLICE COURT

**mu·nic·i·pal·i·ty** \myù-,ni-sə-'pa-lə-tē\ *noun, plural* **-ties** (1790)
**1 :** a primarily urban political unit having corporate status and usually powers of self-government
**2 :** the governing body of a municipality

**mu·nic·i·pal·ize** \myù-'ni-sə-pə-,līz\ *transitive verb* **-ized; -iz·ing** (1880)
**:** to bring under municipal ownership or supervision
— **mu·nic·i·pal·i·za·tion** \-,ni-s(ə-)pə-lə-'zā-shən\ *noun*

**mu·nic·i·pal·ly** \myù-'ni-sə-p(ə-)lē\ *adverb* (circa 1842)
**:** by or in terms of a municipality

**mu·nif·i·cent** \myù-'ni-fə-sənt\ *adjective* [back-formation from *munificence,* from Latin *munificentia,* from *munificus* generous, from *munus* service, gift — more at MEAN] (1583)
**1 :** very liberal in giving or bestowing **:** LAVISH
**2 :** characterized by great liberality or generosity
*synonym* see LIBERAL
— **mu·nif·i·cence** \-sən(t)s\ *noun*
— **mu·nif·i·cent·ly** *adverb*

**mu·ni·ment** \'myü-nə-mənt\ *noun* [Middle English, from Anglo-French, from Middle French, defense, from Latin *munimentum,* from *munire* to fortify] (15th century)
**1 :** the evidence (as documents) that enables one to defend the title to an estate or a claim to rights and privileges — usually used in plural
**2** *archaic* **:** a means of defense

**mu·ni·tion** \myù-'ni-shən\ *noun* [Middle French, from Latin *munition-, munitio,* from *munire* to fortify, from *moenia* walls; akin to Latin *murus* wall and perhaps to Sanskrit *minoti* he builds, fastens] (1508)
**1** *archaic* **:** RAMPART, DEFENSE
**2 :** ARMAMENT, AMMUNITION
— **munition** *transitive verb*

**Mun·ster** *variant of* MUENSTER

**mun·tin** \'mən-t°n\ *noun* [alteration of *montant* vertical dividing bar, from French, from present participle of *monter* to rise — more at MOUNT] (1774)
**:** a strip separating panes of glass in a sash

**munt·jac** \'mən(t)-,jak, 'mən-,chak\ *noun* [Sundanese (Austronesian language of western Java) *mənyčak*] (circa 1798)
**:** any of a genus (*Muntiacus*) of small deer of southeastern Asia and the East Indies — called also *barking deer*

**mu·on** \'myü-,än\ *noun* [contraction of earlier *mu-meson,* from *mu*] (1952)
**:** an unstable lepton that is common in the cosmic radiation near the earth's surface, has a mass about 207 times that of the electron, and exists in negative and positive forms
— **mu·on·ic** \myü-'ä-nik\ *adjective*

**muntjac**

**mu·on·ium** \myü-'ō-nē-əm, -'ä-\ *noun* [New Latin] (1957)
**:** a short-lived quasi-atom consisting of an electron and a positive muon

**¹mu·ral** \'myùr-əl\ *adjective* [Latin *muralis,* from *murus* wall — more at MUNITION] (1586)
**1 :** of, relating to, or resembling a wall
**2 :** applied to and made integral with a wall or ceiling surface

**²mural** *noun* (1916)
**:** a mural work of art (as a painting)
— **mu·ral·ist** \-ə-list\ *noun*

**mu·ram·ic acid** \myù-'ra-mik-\ *noun* [Latin *murus* wall + English + glucosamine + ¹-*ic*] (1957)
**:** an amino sugar $C_9H_{17}NO_7$ that is a lactic acid derivative of glucosamine and is found especially in bacterial cell walls and in blue-green algae

**¹mur·der** \'mər-dər\ *noun* [partly from Middle English *murther,* from Old English *morthor*; partly from Middle English *murdre,* from Old French, of Germanic origin; akin to Old English *morthor*; akin to Old High German *mord* murder, Latin *mort-, mors* death, *mori* to die, *mortuus* dead, Greek *brotos* mortal] (before 12th century)
**1 :** the crime of unlawfully killing a person especially with malice aforethought
**2 a :** something very difficult or dangerous ⟨the traffic was *murder*⟩ **b :** something outrageous or blameworthy ⟨getting away with *murder*⟩

**²murder** *verb* **mur·dered; mur·der·ing** \'mər-d(ə-)riŋ\ (13th century)
*transitive verb*
**1 :** to kill (a human being) unlawfully and with premeditated malice
**2 :** to slaughter wantonly **:** SLAY
**3 a :** to put an end to **b :** TEASE, TORMENT **c :** MUTILATE, MANGLE ⟨*murders* French⟩ **d :** to defeat badly
*intransitive verb*
**:** to commit murder
*synonym* see KILL

**mur·der·ee** \,mər-də-'rē\ *noun* (1920)
**:** an actual or potential victim of a murder

**mur·der·er** \'mər-dər-ər\ *noun* (14th century)
**:** one who murders; *especially* **:** one who commits the crime of murder

**mur·der·ess** \'mər-də-rəs\ *noun* (14th century)
**:** a woman who murders

**mur·der·ous** \'mər-d(ə-)rəs\ *adjective* (1535)
**1 a :** having the purpose or capability of murder **b :** characterized by or causing murder or bloodshed
**2 :** having the ability or power to overwhelm **:** DEVASTATING ⟨*murderous* heat⟩
— **mur·der·ous·ly** *adverb*
— **mur·der·ous·ness** *noun*

**mu·rein** \'myùr-ē-ən, 'myùr-,ēn\ *noun* [muramic acid + *-ein,* alteration of ²-*ine*] (1964)
**:** PEPTIDOGLYCAN

**mu·rex** \'myùr-,eks\ *noun, plural* **mu·ri·ces** \'myùr-ə-,sēz\ *or* **mu·rex·es** [New Latin, from Latin, mollusk yielding a purple dye; akin to Greek *myak-, myax* mussel] (1589)
**:** any of a genus (*Murex*) of marine gastropod mollusks having a rough and often spinose shell, abounding in tropical seas, and yielding a purple dye

**mu·ri·ate** \'myùr-ē-,āt\ *noun* [French, back-formation from (*acide*) *muriatique* muriatic acid] (1790)
**:** CHLORIDE

**mu·ri·at·ic acid** \,myu̇r-ē-'a-tik-\ *noun* [French *muriatique*, from Latin *muriaticus* pickled in brine, from *muria* brine] (1790) **:** HYDROCHLORIC ACID

**mu·rid** \'myu̇r-əd\ *adjective* [ultimately from Latin *mur-, mus* mouse — more at MOUSE] (circa 1909) **:** of or relating to a family (Muridae) comprising the typical mice and rats — **murid** *noun*

**mu·rine** \'myu̇r-,īn\ *adjective* [ultimately from Latin *mur-, mus*] (1607) **:** of or relating to a murid genus (*Mus*) or its subfamily (Murinae) which includes the common household rats and mice; *also* **:** of, relating to, or involving these rodents and especially the house mouse — **murine** *noun*

**murine typhus** *noun* (1933) **:** a mild febrile disease that is marked by headache and rash, is caused by a rickettsia (*Rickettsia mooseri*), is widespread in nature in rodents, and is transmitted to humans by a flea

**murk** \'mərk\ *noun* [Middle English *mirke*, from Old English *mirce;* akin to Old Norse *myrkr* darkness] (before 12th century) **:** GLOOM, DARKNESS; *also* **:** FOG — **murk** *adjective, archaic*

**murky** \'mər-kē\ *adjective* **murk·i·er; -est** (14th century) **1 :** characterized by a heavy dimness or obscurity caused by or like that caused by overhanging fog or smoke **2 :** characterized by thickness and heaviness of air **:** FOGGY, MISTY **3 :** darkly vague or obscure ⟨*murky* official rhetoric⟩ — **murk·i·ly** \-kə-lē\ *adverb* — **murk·i·ness** \-kē-nəs\ *noun*

**¹mur·mur** \'mər-mər\ *noun* [Middle English *murmure*, from Middle French, from Latin *murmur* murmur, roar, of imitative origin] (14th century) **1 :** a half-suppressed or muttered complaint **:** GRUMBLING **2 a :** a low indistinct but often continuous sound **b :** a soft or gentle utterance **3 :** an atypical sound of the heart indicating a functional or structural abnormality

**²murmur** (14th century) *intransitive verb* **1 :** to make a murmur ⟨the breeze *murmured* in the pines⟩ **2 :** COMPLAIN, GRUMBLE *transitive verb* **:** to say in a murmur — **mur·mur·er** *noun*

**mur·mur·ous** \'mər-mə-rəs, 'mərm-rəs\ *adjective* (1582) **:** filled with or characterized by murmurs **:** low and indistinct — **mur·mur·ous·ly** *adverb*

**Mur·phy** \'mər-fē\ *noun* [Miss *Murphy*, nonexistent prostitute used to lure victims] (1959) **:** any of various confidence games; *especially* **:** one in which the victim believes he is paying for sex

**Murphy bed** *noun* [William L. *Murphy* (died 1959) American inventor] (1925) **:** a bed that may be folded or swung into a closet

**Murphy's Law** *noun* [Edward A. *Murphy* (born 1917) American engineer] (1958) **:** an observation: anything that can go wrong will go wrong

**mur·rain** \'mər-ən, 'mə-rən\ *noun* [Middle English *moreyne*, from Middle French *morine*, from *morir* to die, from Latin *mori* — more at MURDER] (14th century) **:** a pestilence or plague especially affecting domestic animals

**murre** \'mər\ *noun* [origin unknown] (1602) **:** any of a genus (*Uria*) of seabirds; *especially* **:** a common bird (*U. aalge*) of northern seas

**mur·rey** \'mər-ē, 'mə-rē\ *noun* [Middle English, from Middle French *moré*, from Medieval Latin *moratum*, from neuter of *moratus* mulberry colored, from Latin *morum* mulberry — more at MULBERRY] (15th century) **:** a purplish black **:** MULBERRY

**mur·ther** \'mər-thər\ *chiefly dialect variant of* MURDER

**mus·ca·det** \,məs-kə-'dā, -'de\ *noun, often capitalized* [French, from Provençal, muscadet grape, from *musc* musk] (circa 1899) **:** a dry white wine from the Loire valley of France

**mus·ca·dine** \'məs-kə-,dīn\ *noun* [probably alteration of *muscatel*] (circa 1785) **:** a grape (*Vitis rotundifolia*) of the southern U.S. with musky fruits borne in small clusters; *also* **:** the fruit

**mus·cae vo·li·tan·tes** \'məs-,kē-,vä-lə-'tan-,tēz, 'mə-,sē-\ *noun plural* [New Latin, literally, flying flies] (1797) **:** spots before the eyes due to cells and cell fragments in the vitreous humor and lens

**mus·ca·rine** \'məs-kə-,rēn\ *noun* [German *Muskarin*, from New Latin (*Amanita*) *muscaria* fly agaric] (1872) **:** a toxic ammonium base [$C_9H_{20}NO_2$]$^+$ that is biochemically related to acetylcholine, is found especially in fly agaric, and acts directly on smooth muscle

**mus·ca·rin·ic** \,məs-kə-'ri-nik\ *adjective* (1936) **:** relating to, resembling, producing, or mediating the parasympathetic effects (as a slowed heart rate and increased activity of smooth muscle) produced by muscarine ⟨*muscarinic* receptors⟩ — compare NICOTINIC

**mus·cat** \'məs-,kat, -kət\ *noun* [Middle French, from Old Provençal, from *muscat* musky, from *musc* musk, from Late Latin *muscus* — more at MUSK] (1548) **1 :** MUSCATEL **2 :** any of several cultivated grapes used in making wine and raisins

**mus·ca·tel** \,məs-kə-'tel\ *noun* [Middle English *muskadelle*, from Middle French *muscadel*, from Old Provençal, from *muscadel* resembling musk, from *muscat*] (15th century) **1 :** a sweet fortified wine from muscat grapes **2 :** a raisin from muscat grapes

**¹mus·cle** \'mə-səl\ *noun, often attributive* [Middle English, from Middle French, from Latin *musculus*, from diminutive of *mus* mouse — more at MOUSE] (14th century) **1 a :** a body tissue consisting of long cells that contract when stimulated and produce motion **b :** an organ that is essentially a mass of muscle tissue attached at either end to a fixed point and that by contracting moves or checks the movement of a body part **2 a :** muscular strength **:** BRAWN **b :** effective strength **:** POWER ⟨political *muscle*⟩ ◆

**²muscle** *verb* **mus·cled; mus·cling** \'mə-s(ə-)liŋ\ (1913) *transitive verb* **:** to move or force by or as if by muscular effort ⟨*muscled* him out of office⟩ *intransitive verb* **:** to make one's way by brute strength or by force

**mus·cle–bound** \'mə-səl-,bau̇nd\ *adjective* (1879) **1 :** having some of the muscles tense and enlarged and of impaired elasticity sometimes as a result of excessive exercise **2 :** lacking in flexibility **:** RIGID

**muscle car** \-,kär\ *noun* (1969) **:** any of a group of American-made 2-door sports coupes with powerful engines designed for high-performance driving

**mus·cled** \'mə-səld\ *adjective* (1644) **:** having muscles especially of a specified kind — often used in combination ⟨hard-*muscled* arms⟩

**muscle spindle** *noun* (1894) **:** a sensory end organ in a muscle that is sensitive to stretch in the muscle, consists of small striated muscle fibers richly supplied with nerve fibers, and is enclosed in a connective tissue sheath — called also *stretch receptor*

**mus·co·vite** \'məs-kə-,vīt\ *noun* [Medieval Latin or New Latin *Muscovia, Moscovia* Moscow] (1535) **1** *capitalized* **a :** a native or resident of the ancient principality of Moscow or of the city of Moscow **b :** RUSSIAN **2** [*muscovy (glass)*] **:** a mineral that is a colorless to pale brown potassium mica — **Muscovite** *adjective*

**Mus·co·vy duck** \'məs-,kō-vē-\ *noun* [*Muscovy*, principality of Moscow, Russia] (1657) **:** a large dark crested duck (*Cairina moschata*) of Central and South America that is widely kept in domestication

**muscul-** *or* **musculo-** *combining form* [Late Latin *muscul-*, from Latin *musculus*] **1 :** muscle ⟨*muscular*⟩ **2 :** muscular and ⟨*musculo*skeletal⟩

**mus·cu·lar** \'məs-kyə-lər\ *adjective* (1681) **1 a :** of, relating to, or constituting muscle **b :** of, relating to, or performed by the muscles **2 :** having well-developed musculature **3 a :** of or relating to physical strength **:** BRAWNY **b :** having strength of expression or character **:** VIGOROUS ⟨*muscular* prose⟩ — **mus·cu·lar·i·ty** \,məs-kyə-'lar-ə-tē\ *noun* — **mus·cu·lar·ly** \'məs-kyə-lər-lē\ *adverb*

**muscular dystrophy** *noun* (1886) **:** any of a group of hereditary diseases characterized by progressive wasting of muscles

**mus·cu·la·ture** \'məs-kyə-lə-,chu̇r, -chər, -,tyu̇r, -,tu̇r\ *noun* [French, from Latin *musculus*] (1875) **:** the muscles of all or a part of the animal body

**mus·cu·lo·skel·e·tal** \,məs-kyə-lō-'ske-lə-t³l\ *adjective* (circa 1944) **:** of, relating to, or involving both musculature and skeleton

**¹muse** \'myüz\ *verb* **mused; mus·ing** [Middle English, from Middle French *muser* to gape, idle, muse, from *muse* mouth of an animal, from Medieval Latin *musus*] (14th century) *intransitive verb* **1 :** to become absorbed in thought; *especially* **:** to turn something over in the mind meditatively and often inconclusively **2** *archaic* **:** WONDER, MARVEL

◇ **WORD HISTORY**
**muscle** The rippling muscles of a bodybuilder may not conjure in most people's imagination the image of a small rodent, but in a number of older Indo-European languages the word for "muscle" was identical with or a derivative of the word for "mouse." Hence Greek *mys* and Old English *mūs* mean both "mouse" and "muscle." Latin *musculus* (from which, via medieval French, comes English *muscle*) and Russian *myshtsa*, both words meaning "muscle," are derivatives of words meaning "mouse," respectively, *mus* and *mysh'*. (In some English dialects and in Scots, *mouse* continued to be applied to certain fleshy cuts of meat at least into the 19th century.) The usual explanation for this usage is that the lump of a contracting muscle in the upper arm or leg—perhaps more in the eyes of a child than an adult—has some resemblance to the furtive movement of a mouse. Alternatively, however, both the "mouse" and "muscle" senses of the word may reflect derivation from an Indo-European verbal base meaning "move," from which Latin *movēre* "to move" also descends.

*transitive verb*
**:** to think or say reflectively
**synonym** see PONDER
— **mus·er** *noun*
²**muse** *noun* (15th century)
**:** a state of deep thought or dreamy abstraction
³**muse** *noun* [Middle English, from Middle French, from Latin *Musa,* from Greek *Mousa*] (14th century)
**1** *capitalized* **:** any of the nine sister goddesses in Greek mythology presiding over song and poetry and the arts and sciences
**2 :** a source of inspiration; *especially* **:** a guiding genius
**3 :** POET
**mu·se·ol·o·gy** \,myü-zē-'ä-lə-jē\ *noun* [*museum* + *-logy*] (1885)
**:** the science or profession of museum organization and management
— **mu·seo·log·i·cal** \-ə-'lä-ji-kəl\ *adjective*
— **mu·se·ol·o·gist** \-'ä-lə-jist\ *noun*
**mu·sette** \myü-'zet\ *noun* [Middle English, from Middle French, diminutive of *muse* bagpipe, from *muser* to muse, play the bagpipe] (14th century)
**1 :** a bellows-blown bagpipe popular in France in the 17th and 18th centuries
**2 :** a small knapsack; *also* **:** a similar bag with one shoulder strap — called also *musette bag*
**mu·se·um** \myu̇-'zē-əm\ *noun* [Latin *Museum* place for learned occupation, from Greek *Mouseion,* from neuter of *Mouseios* of the Muses, from *Mousa*] (1672)
**:** an institution devoted to the procurement, care, study, and display of objects of lasting interest or value; *also* **:** a place where objects are exhibited
**museum piece** *noun* (1901)
**1 :** something preserved in or suitable for a museum
**2 :** one that is out-of-date **:** a thing of the past
¹**mush** \'məsh, *especially* 3 *also* 'mu̇sh\ *noun* [probably alteration of *mash*] (1671)
**1 :** a thick porridge made with cornmeal boiled in water or milk
**2 :** something soft and spongy or shapeless
**3 a :** weak sentimentality **:** DRIVEL **b :** mawkish amorousness
²**mush** (circa 1781)
*transitive verb*
*chiefly dialect* **:** to reduce to a crumbly mass
*intransitive verb*
*of an airplane* **:** to fly in a partly or nearly stalled condition
— **mush·er** *noun*
³**mush** *intransitive verb* [probably from French *marchons,* 1st plural imperative of *marcher* to move, march, from Middle French *marchier* — more at MARCH] (1897)
**:** to travel especially over snow with a sled drawn by dogs — often used as a command to a dog team
— **mush·er** *noun*
⁴**mush** *noun* (1902)
**:** a trip especially across snow with a dog team
¹**mush·room** \'məsh-,rüm, -,ru̇m; *chiefly Northern & Midland* -,rün; *dialect* 'mə-shə-,rüm, -,ru̇m, -,rün\ *noun* [alteration of Middle English *musseroun,* from Middle French *mousseron,* from Late Latin *mussirion-, mussirio*] (1533)
**1 a :** an enlarged complex aboveground fleshy fruiting body of a fungus (as a basidiomycete) that consists typically of a stem bearing a pileus; *especially* **:** one that is edible **b :** FUNGUS
**2 :** UPSTART
**3 :** something resembling a mushroom
²**mushroom** *intransitive verb* (1894)
**1 :** to collect wild mushrooms
**2 a :** to well up and spread out laterally from a central source **b :** to become enlarged or extended **:** GROW

**3 :** to spring up suddenly or multiply rapidly
**mushroom cloud** *noun* (circa 1909)
**:** a mushroom-shaped cloud; *specifically* **:** one caused by the explosion of a nuclear weapon
**mushy** \'mə-shē, *especially* 2 *also* 'mu̇-\ *adjective* **mush·i·er; -est** (1839)
**1 a :** having the consistency of mush **:** SOFT **b :** lacking in definition or precision
**2 :** excessively tender or emotional; *especially* **:** mawkishly amorous
— **mush·i·ly** \'mə-shə-lē, 'mu̇-\ *adverb*
— **mush·i·ness** \'mə-shē-nəs, 'mu̇-\ *noun*
**mu·sic** \'myü-zik\ *noun, often attributive* [Middle English *musik,* from Old French *musique,* from Latin *musica,* from Greek *mousikē* any art presided over by the Muses, especially music, from feminine of *mousikos* of the Muses, from *Mousa* Muse] (13th century)
**1 a :** the science or art of ordering tones or sounds in succession, in combination, and in temporal relationships to produce a composition having unity and continuity **b :** vocal, instrumental, or mechanical sounds having rhythm, melody, or harmony
**2 a :** an agreeable sound **:** EUPHONY ⟨her voice was *music* to my ears⟩ **b :** musical quality ⟨the *music* of verse⟩
**3 :** a musical accompaniment ⟨a play set to *music*⟩
**4 :** the score of a musical composition set down on paper
**5 :** a distinctive type or category of music ⟨there is a *music* for everybody —Eric Salzman⟩
¹**mu·si·cal** \'myü-zi-kəl\ *adjective* [Middle English, from Middle French, from Medieval Latin *musicalis,* from *musica*] (15th century)
**1 a :** of or relating to music **b :** having the pleasing harmonious qualities of music **:** MELODIOUS
**2 :** having an interest in or talent for music
**3 :** set to or accompanied by music
**4 :** of or relating to musicians or music lovers
— **mu·si·cal·ly** \-k(ə-)lē\ *adverb*
²**musical** *noun* (1823)
**1** *archaic* **:** MUSICALE
**2 :** a film or theatrical production typically of a sentimental or humorous nature that consists of musical numbers and dialogue based on a unifying plot
**musical box** *noun* (1829)
*chiefly British* **:** MUSIC BOX
**musical chairs** *noun plural but singular in construction* (1877)
**:** a game in which players march to music around a row of chairs numbering one less than the players and scramble for seats when the music stops; *also* **:** a situation or series of events suggesting the game of musical chairs (as in rapid change or confusing activity)
**musical comedy** *noun* (1765)
**:** MUSICAL 2
**mu·si·cale** \,myü-zi-'kal\ *noun* [French *soirée musicale,* literally, musical evening] (1872)
**:** a social entertainment with music as the leading feature
**mu·si·cal·ise** *British variant of* MUSICALIZE
**mu·si·cal·i·ty** \,myü-zi-'ka-lə-tē\ *noun* (1853)
**1 :** sensitivity to, knowledge of, or talent for music
**2 :** the quality or state of being musical **:** MELODIOUSNESS
**mu·si·cal·ize** \'myü-zi-kə-,līz\ *transitive verb* **-ized; -iz·ing** (1919)
**:** to set to music
— **mu·si·cal·i·za·tion** \,myü-zi-kə-lə-'zā-shən\ *noun*
**musical saw** *noun* (1927)
**:** a handsaw made to produce melody by bending the blade while sounding it with a hammer or violin bow
**music box** *noun* (1844)
**:** a container enclosing an apparatus that reproduces music mechanically when activated by a clockwork

**music drama** *noun* (1877)
**:** an opera in which the action is not interrupted by formal song divisions (as recitatives and arias) and the music is determined solely by dramatic appropriateness
**music hall** *noun* (1842)
**:** a vaudeville theater; *also* **:** VAUDEVILLE
**mu·si·cian** \myu̇-'zi-shən\ *noun* (14th century)
**:** a composer, conductor, or performer of music; *especially* **:** INSTRUMENTALIST
— **mu·si·cian·ly** \-lē\ *adjective*
— **mu·si·cian·ship** \-,ship\ *noun*
**music of the spheres** (1609)
**:** an ethereal harmony thought by the Pythagoreans to be produced by the vibration of the celestial spheres
**mu·si·col·o·gy** \,myü-zi-'kä-lə-jē\ *noun* [Italian *musicologia,* from Latin *musica* music + *-logia* -logy] (1909)
**:** a study of music as a branch of knowledge or field of research as distinct from composition or performance
— **mu·si·co·log·i·cal** \-kə-'lä-ji-kəl\ *adjective*
— **mu·si·col·o·gist** \-'kä-lə-jist\ *noun*
¹**mus·ing** \'myü-ziŋ\ *noun* (14th century)
**:** MEDITATION
²**musing** *adjective* (15th century)
**:** thoughtfully abstracted **:** MEDITATIVE
— **mus·ing·ly** \-lē\ *adverb*
**mu·sique con·crète** \myu̇-'zēk-kō̄ⁿ-'kret, mu̇-\ *noun* [French, literally, concrete music] (1952)
**:** a recorded montage of natural sounds often electronically modified and presented as a musical composition
**musk** \'məsk\ *noun* [Middle English *muske,* from Middle French *musc,* from Late Latin *muscus,* from Late Greek *moschos,* from (assumed) Middle Persian *mušk-,* from Sanskrit *muṣka* testicle, from diminutive of *mūṣ* mouse; akin to Old English *mūs* mouse] (14th century)
**1 a :** a substance with a penetrating persistent odor obtained from a sac beneath the abdominal skin of the male musk deer and used as a perfume fixative; *also* **:** a similar substance from another animal or a synthetic substitute **b :** the odor of musk; *also* **:** an odor resembling musk especially in heaviness or persistence
**2 :** any of various plants with musky odors; *especially* **:** MUSK PLANT
**musk deer** *noun* (1681)
**:** any of a genus (*Moschus*) of small heavy-limbed hornless deer of central Asian uplands with tusked musk-producing males
**mus·keg** \'məs-,keg, -,kāg\ *noun* [Cree *maske'k*] (1806)
**1 :** BOG; *especially* **:** a sphagnum bog of northern North America often with tussocks
**2 :** a usually thick deposit of partially decayed vegetable matter of wet boreal regions
**mus·kel·lunge** \'məs-kə-,lənj\ *noun, plural* **muskellunge** [alteration of Canadian French *maskinongé,* from Ojibwa *ma'skino'še'*] (1789)
**:** a large North American pike (*Esox masquinosy*) that has dark markings, may weigh over 60 pounds (27 kilograms), and is a valuable sport fish
**mus·ket** \'məs-kət\ *noun* [Middle French *mousquet,* from Old Italian *moschetto* small artillery piece, sparrow hawk, from diminutive of *mosca* fly, from Latin *musca* — more at MIDGE] (circa 1587)

\ə\ abut \ᵊ\ kitten \ər\ further \a\ ash \ā\ ace
\ä\ mop, mar \au̇\ out \ch\ chin \e\ bet \ē\ easy
\g\ go \i\ hit \ī\ ice \j\ job \ŋ\ sing \ō\ go
\ȯ\ law \ȯi\ boy \th\ thin \t͟h\ the \ü\ loot \u̇\ foot
\y\ yet \zh\ vision *see also* Guide to Pronunciation

: a heavy large-caliber muzzle-loading usually smoothbore shoulder firearm; *broadly* : a shoulder gun carried by infantry ◆

**mus·ke·teer** \ˌməs-kə-ˈtir\ *noun* [modification of Middle French *mousquetaire*, from *mousquet*] (1590)
**1** : a soldier armed with a musket
**2** [from the musketeers' friendship in the novel *Les Trois Mousquetaires* (1844) by Alexandre Dumas] : a good friend : BUDDY

**mus·ket·ry** \ˈməs-kə-trē\ *noun* (1646)
**1** : MUSKETS
**2** : MUSKETEERS
**3 a** : musket fire **b** : the art or science of using small arms especially in battle

**mus·kie** *or* **mus·ky** \ˈməs-kē\ *noun, plural* **muskies** (1894)
: MUSKELLUNGE

**musk·mel·on** \ˈməsk-ˌme-lən\ *noun* (1573)
: a usually sweet musky-odored edible melon that is the fruit of a trailing or climbing Asian herbaceous vine (*Cucumis melo*): as **a** : any of various melons of small or moderate size with netted skin that include most of the muskmelons cultivated in North America **b** : CANTALOUPE 1 **c** : WINTER MELON

**Mus·ko·ge·an** *or* **Mus·kho·ge·an** \(ˌ)məs-ˈkō-gē-ən\ *noun* (1891)
: a language family of southeastern U.S. that includes Muskogee

**Mus·ko·gee** \mə-ˈskō-gē\ *noun, plural* **Muskogee** *or* **Muskogees** (1775)
**1** : a member of an American Indian people of Georgia and eastern Alabama constituting the nucleus of the Creek confederacy
**2** : the language of the Muskogees and of some of the Seminoles

**musk ox** *noun* (1744)
: a heavyset shaggy-coated wild ox (*Ovibos moschatus*) now confined to Greenland and the barren northern lands of North America

**musk plant** *noun* (1852)
: a yellow-flowered North American herb (*Mimulus moschatus*) of the snapdragon family that has hairy foliage and sometimes a musky odor

**musk·rat** \ˈməs-ˌkrat\ *noun, plural* **muskrat** *or* **muskrats** [probably by folk etymology from a word of Algonquian origin; akin to Massachuset *musquash* muskrat] (1607)
: an aquatic rodent (*Ondatra zibethica*) of the U.S. and Canada with a long scaly laterally compressed tail, webbed hind feet, and dark glossy brown fur; *also* : its fur or pelt

**musk rose** *noun* (1577)
: a rose (*Rosa moschata*) of the Mediterranean region with white flowers having a musky odor

**musk thistle** *noun* (1731)
: a Eurasian thistle (*Carduus nutans*) that has nodding musky flower heads and is naturalized in eastern North America

**musk turtle** *noun* (1868)
: any of various small American freshwater turtles (genera *Sternotherus* and *Kinosternon*) that have musk glands; *especially* : a dark turtle (*S. odoratus*) having a strong musky odor

**musky** \ˈməs-kē\ *adjective* **musk·i·er; -est** (1613)
: having an odor of or resembling musk
— **musk·i·ness** *noun*

**Mus·lim** \ˈməz-ləm, ˈmus-, ˈmuz-\ *noun* [Arabic *muslim*, literally, one who surrenders (to God)] (1615)
**1** : an adherent of Islam
**2** : BLACK MUSLIM
— **Muslim** *adjective*

**Muslim era** *noun* (1948)
: ISLAMIC ERA

**mus·lin** \ˈməz-lən\ *noun* [French *mousseline*, from Italian *mussolina*, from Arabic *mawṣilīy* of Mosul, from al-*Mawṣil* Mosul, Iraq] (1609)
: a plain-woven sheer to coarse cotton fabric

**mus·quash** \ˈməs-ˌkwäsh, -ˌkwȯsh\ *noun* [Massachuset] (1633)
: MUSKRAT

**¹muss** \ˈməs\ *noun* [origin unknown] (1591)
**1** *obsolete* **a** : a game in which players scramble for small objects thrown to the ground **b** : SCRAMBLE
**2** *slang* : a confused conflict : ROW
**3** : a state of disorder : MESS

**²muss** *transitive verb* (1837)
: to make untidy : DISARRANGE

**mus·sel** \ˈmə-səl\ *noun* [Middle English *muscle*, from Old English *muscelle*, from (assumed) Vulgar Latin *muscula*, from Latin *musculus* muscle, mussel] (before 12th century)
**1** : a marine bivalve mollusk (especially genus *Mytilus*) usually having a dark elongated shell
**2** : a freshwater bivalve mollusk (as of *Unio*, *Anodonta*, or related genera) that is especially abundant in rivers of the central U.S. and has a shell with a lustrous nacreous lining

**Mus·sul·man** *also* **Mus·sal·man** \ˈmə-səl-mən\ *noun, plural* **Mus·sul·men** \-mən\ *or* **Mussulmans** [Turkish *müslüman* & Persian *musulmān*, modification of Arabic *muslim*] (circa 1583)
: MUSLIM

**mussy** \ˈmə-sē\ *adjective* **muss·i·er; -est** (circa 1859)
: characterized by clutter or muss : MESSY
— **muss·i·ly** \ˈmə-sə-lē\ *adverb*
— **muss·i·ness** \ˈmə-sē-nəs\ *noun*

**¹must** \ˈməs(t), ˈməst\ *verb, present & past all persons* **must** [Middle English *moste*, from Old English *mōste*, past indicative & subjunctive of *mōtan* to be allowed to, have to; akin to Old High German *muozan* to be allowed to, have to]
*verbal auxiliary*
(before 12th century)
**1 a** : be commanded or requested to ⟨you *must* stop⟩ **b** : be urged to : ought by all means to ⟨you *must* read that book⟩
**2** : be compelled by physical necessity to ⟨man *must* eat to live⟩ : be required by immediate or future need or purpose to ⟨we *must* hurry to catch the bus⟩
**3 a** : be obliged to : be compelled by social considerations to ⟨I *must* say you're looking well⟩ **b** : be required by law, custom, or moral conscience to ⟨we *must* obey the rules⟩ **c** : be determined to ⟨if you *must* go at least wait for me⟩ **d** : be unreasonably or perversely compelled to ⟨why *must* you be so stubborn⟩
**4** : be logically inferred or supposed to ⟨it *must* be time⟩
**5** : be compelled by fate or by natural law to ⟨what *must* be will be⟩
**6** : was or were presumably certain to : was or were bound to ⟨if he really was there I *must* have seen him⟩
**7** *dialect* : MAY, SHALL — used chiefly in questions
*intransitive verb*
*archaic* : to be obliged to go ⟨I *must* to Coventry —Shakespeare⟩

**²must** \ˈməst\ *noun* (1616)
**1** : an imperative need or duty : REQUIREMENT
**2** : an indispensable item : ESSENTIAL ⟨exercise is a *must*⟩

**³must** *noun* [Middle English, from Old English, from Latin *mustum*] (before 12th century)
: the expressed juice of fruit and especially grapes before and during fermentation; *also* : the pulp and skins of the crushed grapes

**⁴must** *noun* [Middle English (Scots) *moist*, from Middle French *must*, alteration of *musc* musk] (15th century)
**1** : MUSK
**2** : MOLD, MUSTINESS

**mus·tache** \ˈməs-ˌtash, (ˌ)mə-ˈstash\ *noun* [Middle French *moustache*, from Old Italian *mustaccio*, from Middle Greek *moustaki*, diminutive of Greek *mystak-, mystax* upper lip, mustache] (1585)
**1** : the hair growing on the human upper lip; *especially* : such hair grown and often trimmed in a particular style
**2** : hair or bristles about the mouth of a mammal
— **mus·tached** *adjective*

**mus·ta·chio** \(ˌ)mə-ˈsta-shē-ˌō, -ˈstä-, -shō\ *noun, plural* **-chios** [Spanish & Italian; Spanish *mostacho*, from Italian *mustaccio*, from Old Italian] (1588)
: MUSTACHE; *especially* : a large mustache
— **mus·ta·chioed** \-shē-ˌōd, -shōd\ *adjective*

**mus·tang** \ˈməs-ˌtaŋ\ *noun* [Mexican Spanish *mestengo*, from Spanish, stray, from *mesteño* strayed, from *mesta* annual roundup of cattle that disposed of strays, from Medieval Latin (*animalia*) *mixta* mixed animals] (1808)
**1** : the small hardy naturalized horse of the western plains directly descended from horses brought in by the Spaniards; *also* : BRONC
**2** *slang* : a commissioned officer (as in the U.S. Navy) who has risen from the ranks

**mus·tard** \ˈməs-tərd\ *noun* [Middle English, from Old French *mostarde*, from *moust* must, from Latin *mustum*] (13th century)
**1 a** : a pungent yellow powder of the seeds of any of several common mustards (*Brassica hirta, B. nigra,* or *B. juncea*) used as a condiment or in medicine as a stimulant and diuretic, an emetic, or a counterirritant **b** *slang* : ZEST
**2** : any of several herbs (genus *Brassica* of the family Cruciferae, the mustard family) with lobed leaves, yellow flowers, and linear beaked pods
**3** : a dark to moderate yellow
— **mus·tardy** \-tər-dē\ *adjective*

**mustard gas** *noun* (1917)
: an irritant vesicant oily liquid $C_4H_8Cl_2S$ used especially as a chemical weapon

**mustard plaster** *noun* (1810)
: a counterirritant and rubefacient plaster containing powdered mustard

**¹mus·ter** \ˈməs-tər\ *noun* [Middle English *mustre*, from Middle French *mostre, monstre,* from *monstrer*] (14th century)
**1** : a representative specimen : SAMPLE
**2 a** : an act of assembling; *specifically* : formal military inspection **b** : critical examination **c** : an assembled group : COLLECTION **d** : INVENTORY

**²muster** *verb* **mus·tered; mus·ter·ing** \-t(ə-)riŋ\ [Middle English *mustren* to show,

musk ox

muster, from Middle French *monstrer*, from Latin *monstrare* to show, from *monstrum* evil omen, monster — more at MONSTER] (15th century)
*transitive verb*
**1 a :** to cause to gather **:** CONVENE **b :** to enroll formally — usually used with *in* or *into* ⟨was *mustered* into the army⟩ **c :** to call the roll of
**2 a :** to bring together **:** COLLECT **b :** to call forth **:** ROUSE
**3 :** to amount to **:** COMPRISE
*intransitive verb*
**:** to come together **:** CONGREGATE
**synonym** see SUMMON
**muster out** *transitive verb* (1834)
**:** to discharge from service
**muster roll** *noun* (1605)
**:** INVENTORY, ROSTER; *specifically* **:** a register of the officers and men in a military unit or ship's company
**musth** *also* **must** \'məst\ *noun* [Hindi *mast* intoxicated, from Persian] (1878)
**:** a periodic state of the bull elephant characterized especially by aggressive behavior and usually connected with the rutting season
**mustn't** \'mə-s°nt\ (1741)
**:** must not
**must–see** \'məst-'sē\ *noun* (1946)
**:** something (as a film) that must or should be seen
— **must–see** *adjective*
**musty** \'məs-tē\ *adjective* **must·i·er; -est** (1530)
**1 a :** impaired by damp or mildew **:** MOLDY **b** **:** tasting of mold **c :** smelling of damp and decay **:** FUSTY
**2 a :** TRITE, STALE **b** (1) **:** ANTIQUATED (2) **:** SUPERANNUATED
**synonym** see MALODOROUS
— **must·i·ly** \'məs-tə-lē\ *adverb*
— **must·i·ness** \-tē-nəs\ *noun*
**mu·ta·ble** \'myü-tə-bəl\ *adjective* [Middle English, from Latin *mutabilis*, from *mutare* to change; akin to Old English *mīthan* to conceal, Sanskrit *mināti* he exchanges, deceives] (14th century)
**1 :** prone to change **:** INCONSTANT
**2 a :** capable of change or of being changed **b** **:** capable of or liable to mutation
— **mu·ta·bil·i·ty** \,myü-tə-'bi-lə-tē\ *noun*
— **mu·ta·bly** \'myü-tə-blē\ *adverb*
**mu·ta·gen** \'myü-tə-jən\ *noun* [International Scientific Vocabulary *mutation + -gen*] (1933)
**:** an agent (as mustard gas or various radiations) that tends to increase the frequency or extent of mutation
— **mu·ta·gen·ic** \,myü-tə-'je-nik\ *adjective*
— **mu·ta·gen·i·cal·ly** \-ni-k(ə-)lē\ *adverb*
**mu·ta·gen·e·sis** \,myü-tə-'je-nə-səs\ *noun* [New Latin] (1948)
**:** the occurrence or induction of mutation
**mu·ta·ge·nic·i·ty** \-jə-'ni-sə-tē\ *noun* (1956)
**:** the capacity to induce mutations
**mu·tant** \'myü-t°nt\ *adjective* [Latin *mutant-*, *mutans*, present participle of *mutare*] (1903)
**:** of, relating to, or produced by mutation
— **mutant** *noun*
**mu·tase** \'myü-,tās, -,tāz\ *noun* [International Scientific Vocabulary *mut-* (from Latin *mutare*) + *-ase*] (1938)
**:** any of various enzymes that catalyze molecular rearrangements and especially those involving the transfer of phosphate from one hydroxyl group to another in the same molecule
**mu·tate** \'myü-,tāt, myü-'\ *verb* **mu·tat·ed; mu·tat·ing** [Latin *mutatus*, past participle of *mutare*] (1818)
*intransitive verb*
**:** to undergo mutation
*transitive verb*
**:** to cause to undergo mutation
— **mu·ta·tive** \'myü-,tā-tiv, -tə-tiv\ *adjective*
**mu·ta·tion** \myü-'tā-shən\ *noun* (14th century)

**1 :** a significant and basic alteration **:** CHANGE
**2 :** UMLAUT
**3 a :** a relatively permanent change in hereditary material involving either a physical change in chromosome relations or a biochemical change in the codons that make up genes; *also* **:** the process of producing a mutation **b** **:** an individual strain or trait resulting from mutation
— **mu·ta·tion·al** \-shnəl, -shə-n°l\ *adjective*
— **mu·ta·tion·al·ly** *adverb*
**mu·ta·tis mu·tan·dis** \m(y)ü-'tä-təs-m(y)ü-'tän-dəs, -'tä-təs-, -'tan-\ *adverb* [Middle English, from Medieval Latin] (15th century)
**1 :** with the necessary changes having been made
**2 :** with the respective differences having been considered
**mutch·kin** \'məch-kən\ *noun* [Middle English (Scots) *muchekyn*] (15th century)
**:** a Scottish unit of liquid capacity equal to 0.90 pint (0.42 liter)
**¹mute** \'myüt\ *adjective* **mut·er; mut·est** [alteration of Middle English *muet*, from Middle French, from Old French *mu*, from Latin *mutus*, probably from *mu*, representation of a muttered sound] (1513)
**1 :** unable to speak **:** DUMB
**2 :** characterized by absence of speech: as **a** **:** felt or experienced but not expressed ⟨touched her hand in *mute* sympathy⟩ **b :** refusing to plead directly or stand trial ⟨the prisoner stands *mute*⟩
**3 :** remaining silent, undiscovered, or unrecognized
**4 a :** contributing nothing to the pronunciation of a word ⟨the *b* in *plumb* is *mute*⟩ **b :** contributing to the pronunciation of a word but not representing the nucleus of a syllable ⟨the *e* in *mate* is *mute*⟩
— **mute·ly** *adverb*
— **mute·ness** *noun*
**²mute** *noun* (1530)
**1 :** STOP 9
**2 :** a person who cannot or does not speak
**3 :** a device attached to a musical instrument to reduce, soften, or muffle its tone
**³mute** *transitive verb* **mut·ed; mut·ing** (1883)
**1 :** to muffle, reduce, or eliminate the sound of
**2 :** to tone down **:** SOFTEN, SUBDUE ⟨*mute* a color⟩
**⁴mute** *intransitive verb* **mut·ed; mut·ing** [Middle English, from Middle French *meutir*, short for *esmeutir*, from Old French *esmeltir*, of Germanic origin; akin to Middle Dutch *smelten* to melt, defecate (used of birds)] (15th century)
*of a bird* **:** to evacuate the cloaca
**mut·ed** \'myü-təd\ *adjective* (1861)
**1 :** provided with or produced or modified by the use of a mute
**2 a :** being mute **:** SILENT **b :** toned down **:** LOW-KEY, SUBDUED
— **mut·ed·ly** *adverb*
**mute swan** *noun* (1785)
**:** a common white swan (*Cygnus olor*) that produces no loud notes, is native to Europe and western Asia, and has been introduced into parts of the U.S.
**mu·ti·late** \'myü-t°l-,āt\ *transitive verb* **-lat·ed; -lat·ing** [Latin *mutilatus*, past participle of *mutilare*, from *mutilus* truncated, maimed] (1534)
**1 :** to cut up or alter radically so as to make imperfect ⟨the child *mutilated* the book with his scissors⟩
**2 :** to cut off or permanently destroy a limb or essential part of **:** CRIPPLE
**synonym** see MAIM
— **mu·ti·la·tion** \,myü-t°l-'ā-shən\ *noun*
— **mu·ti·la·tor** \'myü-t°l-,ā-tər\ *noun*
**mu·tine** \'myü-t°n\ *intransitive verb* **mu·tined; mu·tin·ing** [Middle French (*se*) *mutiner*] (1555)

*obsolete* **:** REBEL, MUTINY
**mu·ti·neer** \,myü-t°n-'ir\ *noun* (1610)
**:** one that mutinies
**mu·ti·nous** \'myü-t°n-əs, 'myüt-nəs\ *adjective* (1578)
**1 a :** disposed to or in a state of mutiny **:** REBELLIOUS **b :** TURBULENT, UNRULY
**2 :** of, relating to, or constituting mutiny
— **mu·ti·nous·ly** *adverb*
— **mu·ti·nous·ness** *noun*
**mu·ti·ny** \'myü-t°n-ē, 'myüt-nē\ *noun, plural* **-nies** [*mutine* to rebel, from Middle French (*se*) *mutiner*, from *mutin* mutinous, from *meute* revolt, from (assumed) Vulgar Latin *movita*, from feminine of *movitus*, alteration of Latin *motus*, past participle of *movēre* to move] (1567)
**1** *obsolete* **:** TUMULT, STRIFE
**2 :** forcible or passive resistance to lawful authority; *especially* **:** concerted revolt (as of a naval crew) against discipline or a superior officer
**synonym** see REBELLION
— **mutiny** *intransitive verb*
**mut·ism** \'myü-,ti-zəm\ *noun* [French *mutisme*, from Latin *mutus* mute] (1824)
**:** the condition of being mute
**mutt** \'mət\ *noun* [short for *muttonhead* dull-witted person] (1901)
**1 :** a stupid or insignificant person **:** FOOL
**2 :** a mongrel dog **:** CUR
**mut·ter** \'mə-tər\ *verb* [Middle English *muteren*, of imitative origin] (14th century)
*intransitive verb*
**1 :** to utter sounds or words indistinctly or with a low voice and with the lips partly closed
**2 :** to murmur complainingly or angrily **:** GRUMBLE
*transitive verb*
**:** to utter especially in a low or imperfectly articulated manner
— **mutter** *noun*
— **mut·ter·er** \-tər-ər\ *noun*
**mut·ton** \'mə-t°n\ *noun* [Middle English *motoun*, from Old French *moton* ram, wether, of Celtic origin; akin to Old Irish *molt* wether] (13th century)
**:** the flesh of a mature sheep used for food
— **mut·tony** \'mə-t°n-ē, 'mət-nē\ *adjective*
**mut·ton·chops** \'mə-t°n-,chäps\ *noun plural* (1865)
**:** side-whiskers that are narrow at the temple and broad and round by the lower jaws — called also *muttonchop whiskers*
**mut·ton·fish** \-,fish\ *noun* [from its flavor] (1735)
**:** a common snapper (*Lutjanus analis*) of the warmer parts of the western Atlantic that is usually olive green and sometimes nearly white or tinged with rosy red and that is a commercially important food and sport fish — called also *mutton snapper*
**mu·tu·al** \'myü-chə-wəl, -chəl; 'myüch-wəl\ *adjective* [Middle English, from Middle French *mutuel*, from Latin *mutuus* lent, borrowed, mutual, from *mutare* to change — more at MUTABLE] (15th century)
**1 a :** directed by each toward the other or the others ⟨*mutual* affection⟩ **b :** having the same feelings one for the other ⟨they had long been *mutual* enemies⟩ **c :** shared in common ⟨enjoying their *mutual* hobby⟩ **d :** JOINT
**2 :** characterized by intimacy
**3 :** of or relating to a plan whereby the members of an organization share in the profits and expenses; *specifically* **:** of, relating to, or taking the form of an insurance method in which

\ə\ abut \°\ kitten \ər\ further \a\ ash \ā\ ace
\ä\ mop, mar \aủ\ out \ch\ chin \e\ bet \ē\ easy
\g\ go \i\ hit \ī\ ice \j\ job \ŋ\ sing \ō\ go
\ȯ\ law \ȯi\ boy \th\ thin \<u>th</u>\ the \ü\ loot \ủ\ foot
\y\ yet \zh\ vision    *see also* Guide to Pronunciation

the policyholders constitute the members of the insuring company
— **mu·tu·al·ly** *adverb*

**mutual fund** *noun* (1934)
: an open-end investment company that invests money of its shareholders in a usually diversified group of securities of other corporations

**mu·tu·al·ism** \'myü-chə-wə-ˌli-zəm, 'myü-chə-ˌli-, 'myüch-wə-ˌli-\ *noun* (1849)
**1** : the doctrine or practice of mutual dependence as the condition of individual and social welfare
**2** : mutually beneficial association between different kinds of organisms
— **mu·tu·al·ist** \-list\ *noun*
— **mu·tu·al·is·tic** \ˌmyü-chə-wə-'lis-tik, ˌmyü-chə-'lis-, ˌmyüch-wə-'lis-\ *adjective*

**mu·tu·al·i·ty** \ˌmyü-chə-'wa-lə-tē\ *noun* (circa 1586)
**1** : the quality or state of being mutual
**2** : a sharing of sentiments : INTIMACY

**mu·tu·al·ize** \'myü-chə-wə-ˌlīz, 'myü-chə-ˌlīz, 'myüch-wə-ˌlīz\ *transitive verb* **-ized; -iz·ing** (1812)
: to make mutual
— **mu·tu·al·i·za·tion** \ˌmyü-chə-wə-lə-'zā-shən, ˌmyü-chə-lə-, ˌmyüch-wə-lə-\ *noun*

**mutually exclusive** *adjective* (1874)
: being related such that each excludes or precludes the other ⟨*mutually exclusive* events⟩; *also* : INCOMPATIBLE ⟨their outlooks were not *mutually exclusive*⟩

**mutuel** *noun* (1908)
: PARI-MUTUEL

**muu·muu** \'mü-ˌmü\ *noun* [Hawaiian *mu'umu'u*, from *mu'umu'u* cut off] (1923)
: a loose often long dress having bright colors and patterns and adapted from the dresses originally distributed by missionaries to the native women of Hawaii

**Mu·zak** \'myü-ˌzak\ *trademark*
— used for recorded background music transmitted by wire to the loudspeaker of a subscriber (as an office)

**mu·zhik** \mü-'zhēk, -'zhik\ *noun* [Russian] (1568)
: a Russian peasant

**¹muz·zle** \'mə-zəl\ *noun* [Middle English *musell*, from Middle French *musel*, from diminutive of *muse* mouth of an animal, from Medieval Latin *musus*] (15th century)
**1** : the projecting jaws and nose of an animal : SNOUT
**2 a** : a fastening or covering for the mouth of an animal used to prevent eating or biting **b** : something (as censorship) that restrains normal expression

muzzle 2a

**3** : the open end of an implement; *especially* : the discharging end of a weapon

**²muzzle** *transitive verb* **muz·zled; muz·zling** \'məz-liŋ, 'mə-zə-\ (15th century)
**1** : to fit with a muzzle
**2** : to restrain from expression : GAG
— **muz·zler** \-lər\ *noun*

**muz·zy** \'mə-zē\ *adjective* **muz·zi·er; -est** [perhaps blend of *muddled* and *fuzzy*] (circa 1728)
**1 a** : deficient in brightness : DULL, GLOOMY ⟨a *muzzy* day⟩ **b** : lacking in clarity and precision ⟨his conclusions can be *muzzy* and naive —*Times Literary Supplement*⟩
**2** : muddled or confused in mind
— **muz·zi·ly** \'mə-zə-lē\ *adverb*
— **muz·zi·ness** \'mə-zē-nəs\ *noun*

**MX** \ˌem-'eks\ *noun* [*m*issile, e*x*perimental] (1976)

: a mobile ICBM having up to 10 independently targeted nuclear warheads

**my** \'mī, mə\ *adjective* [Middle English, from Old English *mīn*, from *mīn*, suppletive genitive of *ic* I; akin to Old English *mē* me] (12th century)
**1** : of or relating to me or myself especially as possessor, agent, or object of an action ⟨*my* car⟩ ⟨*my* promise⟩ ⟨*my* injuries⟩
**2** — used interjectionally to express surprise and sometimes reduplicated ⟨*my* oh *my*⟩; used also interjectionally with names of various parts of the body to express doubt or disapproval ⟨*my* foot⟩

**my-** *or* **myo-** *combining form* [New Latin, from Greek, from *mys* mouse, muscle — more at MOUSE]
: muscle ⟨*myo*globin⟩ : muscle and ⟨*myo*neural⟩

**my·al·gia** \mī-'al-j(ē-)ə\ *noun* [New Latin] (1860)
: pain in one or more muscles
— **my·al·gic** \-jik\ *adjective*

**my·as·the·nia** \ˌmī-əs-'thē-nē-ə\ *noun* [New Latin] (circa 1856)
: muscular debility
— **my·as·then·ic** \-'the-nik\ *adjective or noun*

**myasthenia gra·vis** \-'gra-vəs, -'grä-\ *noun* [New Latin, literally, grave myasthenia] (1900)
: a disease characterized by progressive weakness and exhaustibility of voluntary muscles without atrophy or sensory disturbance and caused by an autoimmune attack on acetylcholine receptors at the neuromuscular junction

**myc-** *or* **myco-** *combining form* [New Latin, from Greek *mykēt-, mykēs* fungus; akin to Greek *myxa* nasal mucus]
: fungus ⟨*myco*logy⟩ ⟨*myco*sis⟩

**my·ce·li·um** \mī-'sē-lē-əm\ *noun, plural* **-lia** \-lē-ə\ [New Latin, from *myc-* + Greek *hēlos* nail, wart, callus] (1836)
: the mass of interwoven filamentous hyphae that forms especially the vegetative portion of the thallus of a fungus and is often submerged in another body (as of soil or organic matter or the tissues of a host); *also* : a similar mass of filaments formed by some bacteria (as streptomyces)
— **my·ce·li·al** \-əl\ *adjective*

**My·ce·nae·an** \ˌmī-sə-'nē-ən\ *also* **My·ce·ni·an** \mī-'sē-nē-ən\ *adjective* (1598)
**1** : of, relating to, or characteristic of Mycenae, its people, or the period (1400 to 1100 B.C.) of Mycenae's political ascendancy
**2** : characteristic of the Bronze Age Mycenaean culture of the eastern Mediterranean area
— **Mycenaean** *noun*

**my·ce·to·ma** \ˌmī-sə-'tō-mə\ *noun, plural* **-mas** *or* **-ma·ta** \-mə-tə\ [New Latin, from Greek *mykēt-, mykēs*] (1874)
: a condition marked by invasion of the deep subcutaneous tissues with fungi or actinomycetes; *also* : a tumorous mass occurring in such a condition
— **my·ce·to·ma·tous** \-mə-təs\ *adjective*

**my·ce·toph·a·gous** \ˌmī-sə-'tä-fə-gəs\ *adjective* [Greek *mykēt-, mykēs* + English *-phagous*] (circa 1890)
: feeding on fungi

**my·ce·to·zo·an** \mī-ˌsē-tə-'zō-ən\ *noun* [New Latin *Mycetozoa*, order of protozoans, from Greek *mykēt-, mykēs* + New Latin *-zoa*] (1881)
: SLIME MOLD
— **mycetozoan** *adjective*

**-mycin** *noun combining form* [*streptomycin*]
: substance obtained from a fungus-like bacterium ⟨erythro*mycin*⟩

**my·co·bac·te·ri·um** \ˌmī-kō-bak-'tir-ē-əm\ *noun* [New Latin] (1909)
: any of a genus (*Mycobacterium*) of nonmotile aerobic acid-fast bacteria that include nu-

merous saprophytes and the pathogens causing tuberculosis and leprosy
— **my·co·bac·te·ri·al** \-ē-əl\ *adjective*

**my·co·flo·ra** \ˌmī-kə-'flōr-ə, -'flȯr-\ *noun* [New Latin] (1945)
: the fungi characteristic of a region or special environment

**my·col·o·gy** \mī-'kä-lə-jē\ *noun* [New Latin *mycologia*, from *myc-* + Latin *-logia* -logy] (1836)
**1** : a branch of biology dealing with fungi
**2** : fungal life
— **my·co·log·i·cal** \ˌmī-kə-'lä-ji-kəl\ *adjective*
— **my·co·log·i·cal·ly** \ˌmī-kə-'lä-ji-k(ə-)lē\ *adverb*
— **my·col·o·gist** \mī-'kä-lə-jist\ *noun*

**my·coph·a·gist** \mī-'kä-fə-jist\ *noun* [*myco-phagy*, from *myc-* + *-phagy*] (1861)
: one that eats fungi (as mushrooms)
— **my·coph·a·gy** \-jē\ *noun*

**my·coph·a·gous** \-gəs\ *adjective* (circa 1909)
: feeding on fungi

**my·co·phile** \'mī-kō-ˌfīl\ *noun* (1953)
: a person whose hobby is hunting wild edible mushrooms

**my·co·plas·ma** \ˌmī-kō-'plaz-mə\ *noun, plural* **-mas** *or* **-ma·ta** \-mə-tə\ [New Latin] (1955)
: any of a genus (*Mycoplasma*) of minute pleomorphic gram-negative chiefly nonmotile microorganisms without cell walls that are intermediate in some respects between viruses and bacteria and are mostly parasitic usually in mammals — called also *pleuropneumonia-like organism*
— **my·co·plas·mal** \-məl\ *adjective*

**mycoplasma–like organism** *noun* (1968)
: any of a group of prokaryotic organisms that resemble mycoplasmas, cause disease in plants, are transmitted by insect vectors, and have proved extremely difficult to grow in artificial media

**my·cor·rhi·za** \ˌmī-kə-'rī-zə\ *noun, plural* **-zae** \-ˌzē\ *or* **-zas** [New Latin, from *myc-* + Greek *rhiza* root — more at ROOT] (1895)
: the symbiotic association of the mycelium of a fungus with the roots of a seed plant
— **my·cor·rhi·zal** \-zəl\ *adjective*

**my·co·sis** \mī-'kō-səs\ *noun, plural* **my·co·ses** \-ˌsēz\ [New Latin] (1876)
: infection with or disease caused by a fungus
— **my·cot·ic** \-'kä-tik\ *adjective*

**my·co·tox·in** \ˌmī-kə-'täk-sən\ *noun* (1962)
: a toxic substance produced by a fungus and especially a mold

**my·dri·a·sis** \mə-'drī-ə-səs\ *noun* [Latin, from Greek] (circa 1775)
: a long-continued or excessive dilatation of the pupil of the eye
— **myd·ri·at·ic** \ˌmi-drē-'a-tik\ *adjective or noun*

**myel-** *or* **myelo-** *combining form* [New Latin, from Greek, from *myelos*, probably from *myōn* cluster of muscles, from *mys* mouse, muscle — more at MOUSE]
: marrow : spinal cord ⟨*myel*encephalon⟩

**my·e·len·ceph·a·lon** \ˌmī-ə-len-'se-fə-ˌlän, -lən\ *noun* [New Latin] (1871)
: the posterior part of the developing vertebrate hindbrain or the corresponding part of the adult brain composed of the medulla oblongata
— **my·e·len·ce·phal·ic** \-ˌlen(t)-sə-'fa-lik\ *adjective*

**my·e·lin** \'mī-ə-lən\ *noun* [International Scientific Vocabulary] (1873)
: a soft white somewhat fatty material that forms a thick myelin sheath about the protoplasmic core of a myelinated nerve fiber
— **my·e·lin·ic** \ˌmī-ə-'li-nik\ *adjective*

**my·e·lin·at·ed** \'mī-ə-lə-ˌnā-təd\ *adjective* (1899)

: having a myelin sheath ⟨*myelinated* nerve fibers⟩

**myelin sheath** *noun* (1896)
: a layer of myelin surrounding some nerve fibers — called also *medullary sheath*

**my·e·li·tis** \ˌmī-ə-'lī-təs\ *noun, plural* **-lit·i·des** \-'li-tə-ˌdēz\ [New Latin] (1835)
: inflammation of the spinal cord or of the bone marrow

**my·e·lo·blast** \'mī-ə-lə-ˌblast\ *noun* [International Scientific Vocabulary] (circa 1904)
: a large mononuclear nongranular bone-marrow cell; *especially* : one that is a precursor of a myelocyte
— **my·e·lo·blas·tic** \ˌmī-ə-lə-'blas-tik\ *adjective*

**my·e·lo·cyte** \'mī-ə-lə-ˌsīt\ *noun* [International Scientific Vocabulary] (1891)
: a bone-marrow cell; *especially* : a motile cell with cytoplasmic granules that gives rise to the granulocytes of the blood and occurs abnormally in the circulating blood
— **my·e·lo·cyt·ic** \ˌmī-ə-lə-'si-tik\ *adjective*

**my·e·lo·fi·bro·sis** \ˌmī-ə-lō-fī-'brō-səs\ *noun* [New Latin] (1947)
: an anemic condition in which bone marrow becomes fibrotic and the liver and spleen usually exhibit a development of blood-cell precursors
— **my·e·lo·fi·brot·ic** \-'brä-tik\ *adjective*

**my·e·log·e·nous** \ˌmī-ə-'lä-jə-nəs\ *adjective* [International Scientific Vocabulary] (1876)
: of, relating to, originating in, or produced by the bone marrow ⟨*myelogenous* sarcoma⟩

**myelogenous leukemia** *noun* (1904)
: leukemia characterized by proliferation of myeloid tissue (as of the bone marrow and spleen) and an abnormal increase in the number of granulocytes, myelocytes, and myeloblasts in the circulating blood — called also *myelocytic leukemia, myeloid leukemia*

**my·e·loid** \'mī-ə-ˌlȯid\ *adjective* [International Scientific Vocabulary] (1857)
: of, relating to, or resembling bone marrow

**my·e·lo·ma** \ˌmī-ə-'lō-mə\ *noun* [New Latin] (circa 1857)
: a primary tumor of the bone marrow
— **my·e·lo·ma·tous** \-mə-təs\ *adjective*

**my·e·lop·a·thy** \-'lä-pə-thē\ *noun* [International Scientific Vocabulary] (circa 1891)
: a disease or disorder of the spinal cord or bone marrow
— **my·e·lo·path·ic** \ˌmī-ə-lō-'pa-thik\ *adjective*

**my·e·lo·pro·lif·er·a·tive** \'mī-ə-lō-prə-'lif(ə-)rə-tiv, -fə-ˌrā-\ *adjective* (1951)
: of, relating to, or being a disorder (as leukemia) marked by excessive proliferation of bone marrow elements and especially blood cell precursors

**my·i·a·sis** \mī-'ī-ə-səs, mē-\ *noun, plural* **my·i·a·ses** \-ˌsēz\ [New Latin, from Greek *myia* fly — more at MIDGE] (1837)
: infestation with fly maggots

**My·lar** \'mī-ˌlär\ *trademark*
— used for a polyester film

**my·nah** *or* **my·na** \'mī-nə\ *noun* [Hindi *mainā* hill mynah from Sanskrit *madana*, a kind of bird] (1769)
: any of various Asian starlings (especially genera *Acridotheres, Gracula,* and *Sturnus*); *especially* : a dark brown slightly crested bird (*A. tristis*) of southeastern Asia with a white tail tip and wing markings and bright yellow bill and feet — compare HILL MYNAH

**myn·heer** \mə-'ner\ *noun* [Dutch *mijnheer*, from *mijn* my + *heer* master, sir] (1652)
: a male Netherlander — used as a title equivalent to *Mr.*

**myo-** — see MY-

**myo·blast** \'mī-ə-ˌblast\ *noun* [International Scientific Vocabulary] (1884)

: an undifferentiated cell capable of giving rise to muscle cells

**myo·car·di·tis** \ˌmī-ə-(ˌ)kär-'dī-təs\ *noun* [New Latin] (1866)
: inflammation of the myocardium

**myo·car·di·um** \ˌmī-ə-'kär-dē-əm\ *noun* [New Latin, from *my-* + Greek *kardia* heart — more at HEART] (1879)
: the middle muscular layer of the heart wall
— **myo·car·di·al** \-dē-əl\ *adjective*

**myo·clo·nus** \ˌmī-'ä-klə-nəs\ *noun* [New Latin] (1883)
: irregular involuntary contraction of a muscle usually resulting from functional disorder of controlling motoneurons; *also* : a condition characterized by myoclonus
— **myo·clon·ic** \ˌmī-ə-'klä-nik\ *adjective*

**myo·elec·tric** \ˌmī-ō-i-'lek-trik\ *also* **myo·elec·tri·cal** \-tri-kəl\ *adjective* (circa 1919)
: of, relating to, or utilizing electricity generated by muscle

**myo·fi·bril** \ˌmī-ə-'fī-brəl, -'fi-\ *noun* [New Latin *myofibrilla*, from *my-* + *fibrilla* fibril] (1898)
: any of the longitudinal parallel contractile elements of a muscle cell that are composed of myosin and actin
— **myo·fi·bril·lar** \-brə-lər\ *adjective*

**myo·fil·a·ment** \-'fi-lə-mənt\ *noun* (1949)
: one of the individual filaments of actin or myosin that make up a myofibril

**myo·gen·ic** \-'je-nik\ *adjective* [International Scientific Vocabulary] (1904)
: taking place or functioning in ordered rhythmic fashion because of the inherent properties of cardiac muscle rather than specific neural stimuli ⟨a *myogenic* heartbeat⟩

**myo·glo·bin** \-'glō-bən, 'mī-ə-ˌ\ *noun* [International Scientific Vocabulary] (1925)
: a red iron-containing protein pigment in muscles that is similar to hemoglobin

**myo·ino·si·tol** \ˌmī-ō-i-'nō-sə-ˌtȯl, -ˌtōl\ *noun* (1951)
: a biologically active inositol that is a component of the vitamin B complex and a lipotropic agent

**my·ol·o·gy** \mī-'ä-lə-jē\ *noun* [French or New Latin; French *myologie*, from New Latin *myologia*, from *my-* + Latin *-logia* -logy] (1649)
: a scientific study of muscles

**my·o·ma** \mī-'ō-mə\ *noun, plural* **-mas** *or* **-ma·ta** \-mə-tə\ [New Latin] (1875)
: a tumor consisting of muscle tissue
— **my·o·ma·tous** \-mə-təs\ *adjective*

**myo·neu·ral** \ˌmī-ə-'nur-əl, -'nyur-\ *adjective* (1905)
: of, relating to, or connecting muscles and nerves ⟨*myoneural* junctions⟩

**my·op·a·thy** \mī-'ä-pə-thē\ *noun* [International Scientific Vocabulary] (circa 1849)
: a disorder of muscle tissue or muscles
— **myo·path·ic** \ˌmī-ə-'pa-thik\ *adjective*

**my·ope** \'mī-ˌōp\ *noun* [French, from Late Latin *myops* myopic, from Greek *myōps*, from *myein* to be closed + *ōps* eye, face — more at EYE] (1728)
: a myopic person

**my·o·pia** \mī-'ō-pē-ə\ *noun* [New Latin, from Greek *myōpia*, from *myōp-, myōps*] (circa 1752)
**1** : a condition in which the visual images come to a focus in front of the retina of the eye resulting especially in defective vision of distant objects
**2** : a lack of foresight or discernment : a narrow view of something
— **my·o·pic** \-'ō-pik, -'ä-\ *adjective*
— **my·o·pi·cal·ly** \-pi-k(ə-)lē\ *adverb*

**my·o·sin** \'mī-ə-sən\ *noun* [International Scientific Vocabulary *my-* + ²*-ose* + ¹*-in*] (1942)
: a fibrous globulin of muscle that can split ATP and that reacts with actin to form actomyosin

**my·o·sis, my·ot·ic** *variant of* MIOSIS, MIOTIC

**myo·si·tis** \ˌmī-ə-'sī-təs\ *noun* [New Latin, irregular from Greek *mys* muscle, mouse] (circa 1819)
: muscle soreness

**myo·tome** \'mī-ə-ˌtōm\ *noun* [International Scientific Vocabulary] (1894)
: the portion of an embryonic somite from which skeletal musculature is produced

**myo·to·nia** \ˌmī-ə-'tō-nē-ə\ *noun* [New Latin] (circa 1896)
: tonic spasm of one or more muscles; *also* : a condition characterized by such spasms
— **myo·ton·ic** \-'tä-nik\ *adjective*

**¹myr·i·ad** \'mir-ē-əd\ *noun* [Greek *myriad-, myrias,* from *myrioi* countless, ten thousand] (1555)
**1** : ten thousand
**2** : a great number ⟨a *myriad* of ideas⟩

**²myriad** *adjective* (1791)
**1** : INNUMERABLE ⟨those *myriad* problems⟩
**2** : having innumerable aspects or elements ⟨the *myriad* activity of the new land —Meridel Le Sueur⟩

**myr·ia·pod** *also* **myr·io·pod** \'mir-ē-ə-ˌpäd\ *noun* [ultimately from Greek *myrioi* + *pod-, pous* foot — more at FOOT] (1826)
: any of a group (Myriapoda) of arthropods having the body made up of numerous similar segments nearly all of which bear true jointed legs and including the millipedes and centipedes
— **myriapod** *also* **myriopod** *adjective*

**my·ris·tic acid** \mə-'ris-tik-, mī-\ *noun* [International Scientific Vocabulary, from New Latin *Myristica,* genus of trees] (1848)
: a crystalline fatty acid $C_{14}H_{28}O_2$ occurring especially in the form of glycerides in most fats

**myrmeco-** *combining form* [Greek *myrmēko-,* from *myrmēk-, myrmēx* — more at PISMIRE]
: ant ⟨*myrmeco*philous⟩

**myr·me·col·o·gy** \ˌmər-mə-'kä-lə-jē\ *noun* [International Scientific Vocabulary] (circa 1902)
: the scientific study of ants
— **myr·me·co·log·i·cal** \-kə-'lä-ji-kəl\ *adjective*
— **myr·me·col·o·gist** \-'kä-lə-jist\ *noun*

**myr·me·co·phile** \'mər-mi-kə-ˌfīl\ *noun* [International Scientific Vocabulary] (1898)
: an organism that habitually shares an ant nest

**myr·me·coph·i·lous** \ˌmər-mə-'kä-fə-ləs\ *adjective* (1866)
: fond of, associated with, or benefited by ants

**myr·mi·don** \'mər-mə-ˌdän, -dən\ *noun* [Middle English *Mirmydon,* Latin *Myrmidon-, Myrmido,* from Greek *Myrmidōn*] (15th century)
**1** *capitalized* : a member of a legendary Thessalian people who accompanied their king Achilles in the Trojan War
**2** : a loyal follower; *especially* : a subordinate who executes orders unquestioningly or unscrupulously

**my·rob·a·lan** \mī-'rä-bə-lən, mə-\ *noun* [Middle French *mirobolan,* from Latin *myrobalanus,* from Greek *myrobalanos,* from *myron* unguent + *balanos* acorn — more at GLAND] (circa 1530)
: the dried astringent fruit of an East Indian tree (genus *Terminalia* of the family Combretaceae) used chiefly in tanning and in inks

**myrrh** \'mər\ *noun* [Middle English *myrre,* from Old English, from Latin *myrrha,* from Greek, of Semitic origin; akin to Arabic *murr* myrrh] (before 12th century)
: a yellowish brown to reddish brown aromatic gum resin with a bitter slightly pungent taste obtained from a tree (especially *Commiphora*

---

\ə\ abut \ᵊ\ kitten \ər\ further \a\ ash \ā\ ace
\ä\ mop, mar \au̇\ out \ch\ chin \e\ bet \ē\ easy
\g\ go \i\ hit \ī\ ice \j\ job \ŋ\ sing \ō\ go
\ȯ\ law \ȯi\ boy \th\ thin \t͟h\ the \ü\ loot \u̇\ foot
\y\ yet \zh\ vision    *see also* Guide to Pronunciation

*abyssinica* of the family Burseraceae) of eastern Africa and Arabia; *also* : a mixture of myrrh and labdanum

**myr·tle** \ˈmər-t°l\ *noun, often attributive* [Middle English *mirtille*, from Middle French, from Medieval Latin *myrtillus*, from Latin *myrtus*, from Greek *myrtos*] (1562)
**1 a** : a common evergreen bushy shrub (*Myrtus communis*) of southern Europe with oval to lance-shaped shiny leaves, fragrant white or rosy flowers, and black berries **b** : any of a family (Myrtaceae, the myrtle family) of chiefly tropical shrubs or trees to which the common myrtle belongs
**2 a** : ¹PERIWINKLE 1a **b** : CALIFORNIA LAUREL

*myrtle 1a*

**my·self** \mī-ˈself, mə-, *Southern also* -ˈsef\ *pronoun* (before 12th century)
**1** : that identical one that is I — used reflexively ⟨I'm going to get *myself* a new suit⟩, for emphasis ⟨I *myself* will go⟩, or in absolute constructions ⟨*myself* a tourist, I nevertheless avoided other tourists⟩
**2** : my normal, healthy, or sane condition ⟨didn't feel *myself* yesterday⟩ ◻

**mys·ta·gogue** \ˈmis-tə-ˌgäg\ *noun* [Latin *mystagogus*, from Greek *mystagōgos*, from *mystēs* initiate (perhaps akin to Greek *myein* to be closed) + *agein* to lead — more at AGENT] (circa 1550)
**1** : one who initiates another into a mystery cult
**2** : one who understands or teaches mystical doctrines
— **mys·ta·go·gy** \-ˌgä-jē, -ˌgō-\ *noun*

**mys·te·ri·ous** \mis-ˈtir-ē-əs\ *adjective* (1600)
**1 a** : of, relating to, or constituting mystery ⟨the *mysterious* ways of God⟩ **b** : exciting wonder, curiosity, or surprise while baffling efforts to comprehend or identify : MYSTIFYING ⟨heard a *mysterious* noise⟩ ⟨a *mysterious* stranger⟩
**2** : stirred by or attracted to the inexplicable
— **mys·te·ri·ous·ly** *adverb*
— **mys·te·ri·ous·ness** *noun*

**¹mys·tery** \ˈmis-t(ə-)rē\ *noun, plural* **-ter·ies** [Middle English *mysterie*, from Latin *mysterium*, from Greek *mystērion*, from *mystēs* initiate] (14th century)
**1 a** : a religious truth that one can know only by revelation and cannot fully understand **b** (1) : any of the 15 events (as the Nativity, the Crucifixion, or the Assumption) serving as a subject for meditation during the saying of the rosary (2) *capitalized* : a Christian sacrament; *specifically* : EUCHARIST **c** (1) : a secret religious rite believed (as in Eleusinian and Mithraic cults) to impart enduring bliss to the initiate (2) : a cult devoted to such rites
**2 a** : something not understood or beyond understanding : ENIGMA **b** *obsolete* : a private secret **c** : the secret or specialized practices or ritual peculiar to an occupation or a body of people ⟨the *mysteries* of the tailor's craft⟩ **d** : a piece of fiction dealing usually with the solution of a mysterious crime
**3** : profound, inexplicable, or secretive quality or character ⟨the *mystery* of her smile⟩ ☆

**²mystery** *noun, plural* **-ter·ies** [Middle English, from Late Latin *misterium, mysterium*, alteration of *ministerium* service, occupation, from *minister* servant — more at MINISTER] (14th century)
**1** *archaic* : TRADE, CRAFT
**2** *archaic* : a body of persons engaged in a particular trade, business, or profession : GUILD
**3** : MYSTERY PLAY

**mystery play** *noun* [²*mystery*] (1852)
: a medieval drama based on scriptural incidents (as the creation of the world, the Flood,

or the life, death, and resurrection of Christ)
— compare MIRACLE PLAY

**¹mys·tic** \ˈmis-tik\ *adjective* [Middle English *mistik*, from Latin *mysticus* of mysteries, from Greek *mystikos*, from *mystēs* initiate] (14th century)
**1** : MYSTICAL 1a
**2** : of or relating to mysteries or esoteric rites : OCCULT
**3** : of or relating to mysticism or mystics
**4 a** : MYSTERIOUS **b** : OBSCURE, ENIGMATIC **c** : inducing a feeling of awe or wonder **d** : having magical properties

**²mystic** *noun* (1679)
**1** : a follower of a mystical way of life
**2** : an advocate of a theory of mysticism

**mys·ti·cal** \ˈmis-ti-kəl\ *adjective* (15th century)
**1 a** : having a spiritual meaning or reality that is neither apparent to the senses nor obvious to the intelligence ⟨the *mystical* food of the sacrament⟩ **b** : involving or having the nature of an individual's direct subjective communion with God or ultimate reality ⟨the *mystical* experience of the Inner Light⟩
**2** : MYSTERIOUS, UNINTELLIGIBLE
**3** : MYSTIC 2, 3
— **mys·ti·cal·ly** \-k(ə-)lē\ *adverb*

**mys·ti·cism** \ˈmis-tə-ˌsi-zəm\ *noun* (1736)
**1** : the experience of mystical union or direct communion with ultimate reality reported by mystics
**2** : the belief that direct knowledge of God, spiritual truth, or ultimate reality can be attained through subjective experience (as intuition or insight)
**3 a** : vague speculation : a belief without sound basis **b** : a theory postulating the possibility of direct and intuitive acquisition of ineffable knowledge or power

**mys·ti·fi·ca·tion** \ˌmis-tə-fə-ˈkā-shən\ *noun* (1815)
**1** : an act or instance of mystifying
**2** : the quality or state of being mystified
**3** : something designed to mystify

**mys·ti·fy** \ˈmis-tə-ˌfī\ *transitive verb* **-fied; -fy·ing** [French *mistifier*, from *mystère* mystery, from Latin *mysterium*] (circa 1734)
**1** : to perplex the mind of : BEWILDER
**2** : to make mysterious or obscure ⟨*mystify* an interpretation of a prophecy⟩
— **mys·ti·fi·er** \-ˌfī(-ə)r\ *noun*
— **mys·ti·fy·ing·ly** \-ˌfī-iŋ-lē\ *adverb*

**mys·tique** \mi-ˈstēk\ *noun* [French, from *mystique*, adjective, mystic, from Latin *mysticus*] (1891)
**1** : an air or attitude of mystery and reverence developing around something or someone
**2** : the special esoteric skill essential in a calling or activity

**myth** \ˈmith\ *noun* [Greek *mythos*] (1830)
**1 a** : a usually traditional story of ostensibly historical events that serves to unfold part of the world view of a people or explain a practice, belief, or natural phenomenon **b** : PARABLE, ALLEGORY
**2 a** : a popular belief or tradition that has grown up around something or someone; *especially* : one embodying the ideals and institutions of a society or segment of society ⟨seduced by the American *myth* of individualism —Orde Coombs⟩ **b** : an unfounded or false notion
**3** : a person or thing having only an imaginary or unverifiable existence
**4** : the whole body of myths

**myth·i·cal** \ˈmith-i-kəl\ *or* **myth·ic** \-ik\ *adjective* (1669)
**1** : based on or described in a myth especially as contrasted with history
**2** *usually* **mythical** : existing only in the imagination : FICTITIOUS, IMAGINARY ⟨sportswriters picked a *mythical* all-star team⟩

**3** *usually* **mythic** : having qualities suitable to myth : LEGENDARY ⟨the twilight of a *mythic* professional career —Clayton Riley⟩
**synonym** see FICTITIOUS
— **myth·i·cal·ly** \-thi-k(ə-)lē\ *adverb*

**myth·i·cize** \ˈmi-thə-ˌsīz\ *transitive verb* **-cized; -ciz·ing** (1840)
**1** : to turn into or envelop in myth
**2** : to treat as myth
— **myth·i·ciz·er** *noun*

**myth·mak·er** \ˈmith-ˌmā-kər\ *noun* (1871)
: a creator of myths or of mythical situations or lore
— **myth·mak·ing** \-kiŋ\ *noun*

**my·thog·ra·phy** \mi-ˈthä-grə-fē\ *noun* [Greek *mythographia*, from *mythos* + *-graphia* -graphy] (1851)
**1** : the representation of mythical subjects in art
**2** : a critical compilation of myths
— **my·thog·ra·pher** \-fər\ *noun*

**myth·o·log·i·cal** \ˌmi-thə-ˈlä-ji-kəl\ *also* **myth·o·log·ic** \-jik\ *adjective* (1614)
**1** : of or relating to mythology or myths : dealt with in mythology
**2** : lacking factual basis or historical validity : MYTHICAL, FABULOUS
— **myth·o·log·i·cal·ly** \-ji-k(ə-)lē\ *adverb*

**my·thol·o·gize** \mi-ˈthä-lə-ˌjīz\ *verb* **-gized; -giz·ing** (1603)
*transitive verb*
**1** *obsolete* : to explain the mythological significance of
**2** : to build a myth around : MYTHICIZE
*intransitive verb*
**1** : to relate, classify, and explain myths
**2** : to create or perpetuate myths

---

☆ SYNONYMS
**Mystery, problem, enigma, riddle, puzzle** mean something which baffles or perplexes. MYSTERY applies to what cannot be fully understood by human reason or less strictly to whatever resists or defies explanation ⟨the *mystery* of the stone monoliths⟩. PROBLEM applies to any question or difficulty calling for a solution or causing concern ⟨the *problems* created by high technology⟩. ENIGMA applies to utterance or behavior that is very difficult to interpret ⟨his suicide was an *enigma* his family never understood⟩. RIDDLE suggests an enigma or problem involving paradox or apparent contradiction ⟨the *riddle* of the reclusive pop star⟩. PUZZLE applies to an enigma or problem that challenges ingenuity for its solution ⟨the mechanisms of heredity were long a *puzzle* for scientists⟩.

---

◻ USAGE
**myself** *Myself* is often used where *I* or *me* might be expected: as subject ⟨to wonder what *myself* will say —Emily Dickinson⟩ ⟨others and *myself* continued to press for the legislation⟩, after *as, than,* or *like* ⟨an aversion to paying such people as *myself* to tutor⟩ ⟨was enough to make a better man than *myself* quail⟩ ⟨old-timers like *myself*⟩, and as object ⟨now here you see *myself* with the diver⟩ ⟨for my wife and *myself* it was a happy time⟩. Such uses almost always occur when the speaker or writer is referring to himself or herself as an object of discourse rather than as a participant in discourse. The other reflexive personal pronouns are similarly but less frequently used in the same circumstances. Critics have frowned on these uses since about the turn of the century, probably unaware that they serve a definite purpose. Users themselves are as unaware as the critics—they simply follow their instincts. These uses are standard.

— **my·thol·o·giz·er** *noun*

**my·thol·o·gy** \mi-'thä-lə-jē\ *noun, plural* **-gies** [French or Late Latin; French *mythologie,* from Late Latin *mythologia* interpretation of myths, from Greek, legend, myth, from *mythologein* to relate myths, from *mythos* + *logos* speech — more at LEGEND] (1603)
**1** : an allegorical narrative
**2** : a body of myths: as **a** : the myths dealing with the gods, demigods, and legendary heroes of a particular people **b** : MYTHOS 2 ⟨cold war *mythology*⟩
**3** : a branch of knowledge that deals with myth
**4** : a popular belief or assumption that has grown up around someone or something ⟨defective *mythologies* that ignore masculine depth of feeling —Robert Bly⟩
— **my·thol·o·ger** \-jər\ *noun*
— **my·thol·o·gist** \-jist\ *noun*

**mytho·ma·nia** \,mi-thə-'mā-nē-ə, -nyə\ *noun* [New Latin, from Greek *mythos* + Late Latin *mania* mania] (circa 1909)
: an excessive or abnormal propensity for lying and exaggerating
— **mytho·ma·ni·ac** \-nē-,ak\ *noun or adjective*

**mytho·poe·ia** \,mi-thə-'pē-ə\ *noun* [Late Latin, from Greek *mythopoiia,* from *mythopoiein* to make a myth, from *mythos* + *poiein* to make — more at POET] (1846)
: a creating of myth : a giving rise to myths
— **mytho·poe·ic** \-'pē-ik\ *also* **mytho·po·et·ic** \-pō-'e-tik\ *or* **mytho·po·et·i·cal** \-ti-kəl\ *adjective*

**my·thos** \'mi-,thōs, -,thäs\ *noun, plural* **my·thoi** \-,thòi\ [Greek] (1753)
**1 a** : MYTH 1a **b** : MYTHOLOGY 2a
**2** : a pattern of beliefs expressing often symbolically the characteristic or prevalent attitudes in a group or culture
**3** : THEME, PLOT

**mythy** \'mi-thē\ *adjective* (1931)
: resembling, concerned with, or of a subject for myth ⟨a *mythy* theme⟩

**my word** *interjection* (1841)
— used to express surprise or astonishment

**myx·ede·ma** \,mik-sə-'dē-mə\ *noun* [New Latin, from Greek *myxa* lamp wick, nasal mucus + New Latin *edema* edema — more at MUCUS] (1877)
: severe hypothyroidism characterized by firm inelastic edema, dry skin and hair, and loss of mental and physical vigor

— **myx·ede·ma·tous** \-'de-mə-təs, -'dē-\ *adjective*

**myx·o·ma** \mik-'sō-mə\ *noun, plural* **-mas** *or* **-ma·ta** \-mə-tə\ [New Latin, from Greek *myxa*] (1870)
: a soft tumor made up of gelatinous connective tissue like that of the umbilical cord
— **myx·o·ma·tous** \-mə-təs\ *adjective*

**myx·o·ma·to·sis** \mik-,sō-mə-'tō-səs\ *noun* [New Latin, from *myxomat-, myxoma*] (1927)
: a condition characterized by the presence of myxomas in the body; *specifically* : a severe virus disease of rabbits that is caused by a poxvirus transmitted by mosquitoes and that has been used in the biological control of rabbits in plague areas

**myxo·my·cete** \,mik-sō-'mī-,sēt, ,mik-sō-(,)mī-'\ *noun* [ultimately from Greek *myxa* + *mykēt-, mykēs* fungus — more at MYC-] (1877)
: SLIME MOLD

**myxo·vi·rus** \'mik-sə-,vī-rəs\ *noun* [New Latin, from Greek *myxa* + New Latin *virus* virus; from its affinity for certain mucins] (1955)
: any of a group of rather large RNA-containing viruses that includes the influenza viruses
— **myxo·vi·ral** \,mik-sə-'vī-rəl\ *adjective*

# N

N *is the fourteenth letter of the English alphabet. It came through the Latin by way of Etruscan from the Greek* nu, *which was borrowed from Phoenician* nun. *It represents either of two nasal consonant sounds: one, the* n *in* new, *is called an alveolar* n, *and is usually formed in English by bringing the tip of the tongue against the gums behind the upper front teeth; the other, called a velar* n, *occurs before* k *or* g *in such words as* sink *and* sing, *and is produced by pressing the back of the tongue against the velum (or rear roof of the mouth).* N *sometimes forms the nucleus of a syllable without a vowel, as in* hidden *and* listen. *It is silent in some words after* m, *as in* hymn. *Small* n *is believed to have evolved from an early Greek form of* nu *similar to the Roman capital* N *except that its cross-stroke slanted from the lower left to the upper right. Eventually this cross-stroke rose higher along the left side of the letter while the angle it formed on the right side rounded to a single curved line.*

**n** \'en\ *noun, plural* **n's** *or* **ns** \'enz\ *often capitalized, often attributive* (before 12th century)
**1 a :** the 14th letter of the English alphabet **b :** a graphic representation of this letter **c : a :** a speech counterpart of orthographic *n*
**2 :** a graphic device for reproducing the letter *n*
**3 a :** one designated *n* especially as the 14th in order or class **b :** an indefinite number; *especially* : a constant integer or a variable taking on integral values
**4 :** something shaped like the letter N
**5 :** the haploid or gametic number of chromosomes
**6 :** EN 2
**-n** — see -EN
**'n** \ən, ⁿn\ *conjunction* [by shortening]
**:** THAN
**'n'** *also* **'n** \ən, ⁿn\ *conjunction*
**:** AND ⟨fish *'n'* chips⟩
**naan** *variant of* NAN
**nab** \'nab\ *transitive verb* **nabbed; nab·bing** [perhaps alteration of English dialect *nap*] (1686)
**1 :** to catch or seize in arrest **:** APPREHEND
**2 :** to seize suddenly
**nabe** \'nāb\ *noun* [by shortening & alteration from *neighborhood*] (1935)
**:** a neighborhood theater — usually used in plural with *the*
**na·bob** \'nā-ˌbäb\ *noun* [Urdu *nawwāb*, from Arabic *nuwwāb*, plural of *nā'ib* governor] (1612)
**1 :** a provincial governor of the Mogul empire in India
**2 :** a person of great wealth or prominence
**Na·both** \'nā-ˌbäth\ *noun* [Hebrew *Nābhōth*]
**:** the owner of a vineyard coveted and seized by Ahab king of Israel
**na·celle** \nə-'sel\ *noun* [French, literally, small boat, from Late Latin *navicella*, diminutive of Latin *navis* ship — more at NAVE] (1904)
**:** a streamlined enclosure (as for an engine) on an aircraft
**na·cho** \'nä-(ˌ)chō\ *noun, plural* **nachos** [American Spanish, perhaps from Spanish *nacho* flat-nosed] (1969)
**:** a tortilla chip topped with melted cheese and often additional savory toppings (as hot peppers or refried beans)
**na·cre** \'nā-kər\ *noun* [Middle French, from Old Italian *naccara* drum, nacre, from Arabic *naqqārah* drum] (1718)
**:** MOTHER-OF-PEARL
— **na·cre·ous** \-krē-əs, -k(ə-)rəs\ *adjective*
**NAD** \ˌen-(ˌ)ā-'dē\ *noun* [*n*icotinamide *a*denine *d*inucleotide] (circa 1962)
**:** a coenzyme $C_{21}H_{27}N_7O_{14}P_2$ of numerous dehydrogenases that occurs in most cells and plays an important role in all phases of inter-

mediary metabolism as an oxidizing agent or when in the reduced form as a reducing agent for various metabolites — called also *nicotinamide adenine dinucleotide, diphosphopyridine nucleotide, DPN*
**na·da** \'nä-də\ *noun* [Spanish, from Latin (*res*) *nata* situation, circumstance, literally, a thing come into being] (1914)
**:** NOTHING
**Na–dene** *also* **Na–dé·né** \nä-'dā-(ˌ)nā, -'de-, -nē\ *noun, often D capitalized* [*na-* (from Haida *na* to dwell & Tlingit *na* people) + *Déné*] (1915)
**:** a hypothetically related group of American Indian languages that includes the Athabascan family, Tlingit, and Haida
**NADH** \en-(ˌ)ā-(ˌ)dē-'āch\ *noun* [*NAD* + *H*, symbol for hydrogen] (1965)
**:** the reduced form of NAD
**na·dir** \'nā-ˌdir, 'nā-dər\ *noun* [Middle English, from Middle French, from Arabic *nazīr* opposite] (14th century)
**1 :** the point of the celestial sphere that is directly opposite the zenith and vertically downward from the observer
**2 :** the lowest point
**NADP** \ˌen-(ˌ)ā-(ˌ)dē-'pē\ *noun* [*n*icotinamide *a*denine *d*inucleotide *p*hosphate] (circa 1962)
**:** a coenzyme $C_{21}H_{28}N_7O_{17}P_3$ of numerous dehydrogenases (as that acting on glucose-6-phosphate) that occurs especially in red blood cells and plays a role in intermediary metabolism similar to NAD but acting often on different metabolites — called also *nicotinamide adenine dinucleotide phosphate, TPN, triphosphopyridine nucleotide*
**NADPH** \ˌen-(ˌ)ā-(ˌ)dē-(ˌ)pē-'āch\ *noun* [*NADP* + *H*, symbol for hydrogen] (circa 1966)
**:** the reduced form of NADP
**¹nag** \'nag\ *noun* [Middle English *nagge*; akin to Dutch *negge* small horse] (15th century)
**:** HORSE; *especially* : one that is old or in poor condition
**²nag** *verb* **nagged; nag·ging** [probably of Scandinavian origin; akin to Old Norse *gnaga* to gnaw; akin to Old English *gnagan* to gnaw] (circa 1828)
*intransitive verb*
**1 :** to find fault incessantly **:** COMPLAIN
**2 :** to be a persistent source of annoyance or distraction
*transitive verb*
**1 :** to irritate by constant scolding or urging
**2 :** BADGER, WORRY
— **nag·ger** *noun*
— **nagging** *adjective*
— **nag·ging·ly** \'na-giŋ-lē\ *adverb*
**³nag** *noun* (1925)
**:** one who nags habitually

**na·ga·na** \nə-'gä-nə\ *noun* [Zulu *unakane, ulunakane*] (1895)
**:** trypanosomiasis (especially when caused by *Trypanosoma brucei*) of domestic animals
**nah** \'na, 'nä, 'ná\ *variant of* NO
**Na·huatl** \'nä-ˌwä-tᵊl\ *noun* [Spanish *náhuatl*, from Nahuatl *Nāhuatl*] (1822)
**:** a group of closely related Uto-Aztecan languages that includes the speech of several peoples (as the Aztecs) of central and southern Mexico and Central America
— **Na·huat·lan** \nä-'wät-lən\ *adjective or noun*
**Na·hum** \'nā-əm, -həm\ *noun* [Hebrew *Naḥūm*]
**1 :** a Hebrew prophet of the 7th century B.C.
**2 :** a prophetic book of canonical Jewish and Christian Scripture — see BIBLE table
**na·iad** \'nā-əd, 'nī-, -ˌad\ *noun, plural* **naiads** *or* **na·ia·des** \-ə-ˌdēz\ [Middle English, from Middle French or Latin; Middle French *naïade*, from Latin *naiad-, naias*, from Greek, from *nan* to flow — more at NOURISH] (14th century)
**1 :** any of the nymphs in classical mythology living in and giving life to lakes, rivers, springs, and fountains
**2 :** any of the aquatic young of a mayfly, dragonfly, damselfly, or stone fly — compare NYMPH 3
**3 :** any of a genus (*Najas* of the family Najadaceae) of submerged aquatic plants
**¹na·if** *or* **na·if** \nä-'ēf\ *adjective* [French] (1598)
**:** NAIVE
**²naïf** *or* **naif** *noun* (1893)
**:** a naive person
**¹nail** \'nā(ə)l\ *noun* [Middle English, from Old English *nægl*; akin to Old High German *nagal* nail, fingernail, Latin *unguis* fingernail, toenail, claw, Greek *onyx*] (before 12th century)
**1 a :** a horny sheath protecting the upper end of each finger and toe of humans and most other primates **b :** a structure (as a claw) that terminates a digit and corresponds to a nail
**2 :** a slender usually pointed and headed fastener designed to be pounded in
**²nail** *transitive verb* (before 12th century)
**1 :** to fasten with or as if with a nail
**2 :** to fix in steady attention ⟨*nailed* his eye on the crack⟩
**3 a :** CATCH, TRAP **b :** to detect and expose usually so as to discredit
**4 a :** STRIKE, HIT **b :** to put out (a runner) in baseball
**5 :** to perform or complete perfectly or impressively ⟨*nailed* a jump shot⟩
— **nail·er** *noun*
**nail–bit·er** \'nā(ə)l-ˌbī-tər\ *noun* (1971)
**:** something (as a close contest) that induces tension or anxiety ⟨lost a tough, 14-inning *nail-biter* —Steve Pate⟩
**nail·brush** \-ˌbrəsh\ *noun* (1802)
**:** a small firm-bristled brush for cleaning the hands and especially the fingernails
**nail down** *transitive verb* (1615)
**1 :** to gain or win decisively ⟨*nail down* his consent⟩
**2 :** to settle or establish clearly and unmistakably
**nail file** *noun* (1875)
**:** a small narrow instrument (as of metal or cardboard) with a rough or emery surface that is used for shaping fingernails
**nain·sook** \'nān-ˌsuk\ *noun* [Hindi *nainsukh*, from *nain* eye + *sukh* delight] (1790)
**:** a soft lightweight muslin
**nai·ra** \'nī-rə\ *noun* [alteration of *Nigeria*] (1972)
— see MONEY table
**na·ive** *or* **na·ïve** \nä-'ēv\ *adjective* **na·iv·er; -est** [French *naïve*, feminine of *naïf*, from Old French, inborn, natural, from Latin *nativus* native] (1654)
**1 :** marked by unaffected simplicity **:** ARTLESS, INGENUOUS

**2 a :** deficient in worldly wisdom or informed judgment; *especially* **:** CREDULOUS **b :** not previously subjected to experimentation or a particular experimental situation ⟨made the test with *naive* rats⟩; *also* **:** not having previously used a particular drug (as marijuana)
**3 :** SELF-TAUGHT, PRIMITIVE
**synonym** see NATURAL
— **na·ive·ly** *or* **na·ïve·ly** *adverb*
— **na·ive·ness** *noun*
**na·ïve·té** *also* **na·ive·te** *or* **na·ive·té** \(ˌ)nä-ˌēv-'tā, -ˌē-və-; nä-'ēv-ˌtā, -'ē-və-\ *noun* [French *naïveté*, from Old French, inborn character, from *naif*] (1673)
**1 :** a naive remark or action
**2 :** the quality or state of being naive
**na·ive·ty** *also* **na·ïve·ty** \nä-'ē-və-tē, -'ēv-tē\ *noun, plural* **-ties** (1708)
*chiefly British* **:** NAÏVETÉ
**na·ked** \'nā-kəd, *especially Southern* 'ne-kəd\ *adjective* [Middle English, from Old English *nacod*; akin to Old High German *nackot* naked, Latin *nudus*, Greek *gymnos*] (before 12th century)
**1 :** not covered by clothing **:** NUDE
**2 :** devoid of customary or natural covering **:** BARE: as **a :** not enclosed in a sheath or scabbard **b :** not provided with a shade **c** *of a plant or one of its parts* **:** lacking pubescence or enveloping or subtending parts **d :** lacking foliage or vegetation **e** *of an animal or one of its parts* **:** lacking an external covering (as of hair, feathers, or shell)
**3 a :** scantily supplied or furnished **b :** lacking embellishment **:** UNADORNED
**4 :** UNARMED, DEFENSELESS
**5 :** lacking confirmation or support
**6 :** devoid of concealment or disguise
**7 :** unaided by any optical device or instrument ⟨visible to the *naked* eye⟩
**8 :** not backed by the writer's ownership of the commodity contract or security
**synonym** see BARE
— **na·ked·ly** *adverb*
— **na·ked·ness** *noun*
**na·led** \'nā-ˌled\ *noun* [origin unknown] (circa 1962)
**:** a short-lived insecticide $C_4H_7Br_2Cl_2O_4P$ of relatively low toxicity to warm-blooded animals that is used especially to control crop pests and mosquitoes
**na·li·dix·ic acid** \ˌnā-lə-ˌdik-sik-\ *noun* [perhaps from *naphthyridine* ($C_8H_6N_2$ — from *naphth-* + *pyridine*) + carb*oxylic acid*] (1964)
**:** an antibacterial agent $C_{12}H_{12}N_2O_3$ that is used especially in the treatment of genitourinary infections
**na·lor·phine** \na-'lòr-ˌfēn\ *noun* [*N-allyl* + m*orphine*] (circa 1953)
**:** a white crystalline compound $C_{19}H_{21}NO_3$ that is derived from morphine and is used in the form of its hydrochloride as a respiratory stimulant to counteract poisoning by morphine and similar narcotic drugs
**nal·ox·one** \na-'läk-ˌsōn\ *noun* [*N-allyl* + hydr*oxy-* + *-one*] (1964)
**:** a potent antagonist $C_{19}H_{21}NO_4$ of narcotic drugs and especially morphine that is administered especially as the hydrochloride
**nal·trex·one** \nal-'trek-ˌsōn\ *noun* [*N-allyl* + *trex-* (as in *methotrexate*) + *-one*] (1973)
**:** a narcotic antagonist $C_{20}H_{23}NO_4$
**nam·by–pam·by** \ˌnam-bē-'pam-bē\ *adjective* [*Namby Pamby*, nickname given to Ambrose Philips] (1745)
**1 :** lacking in character or substance **:** INSIPID
**2 :** WEAK, INDECISIVE ◆
— **namby–pamby** *noun*
¹**name** \'nām\ *noun* [Middle English, from Old English *nama*; akin to Old High German *namo* name, Latin *nomen*, Greek *onoma*, *onyma*] (before 12th century)
**1 a :** a word or phrase that constitutes the distinctive designation of a person or thing **b :** a word or symbol used in logic to designate an entity

**2 :** a descriptive often disparaging epithet ⟨called him *names*⟩
**3 a :** REPUTATION ⟨gave the town a bad *name*⟩ **b :** an illustrious record **:** FAME ⟨made a *name* for himself in golf⟩ **c :** a person or thing with a reputation
**4 :** FAMILY, CLAN
**5 :** appearance as opposed to reality ⟨a friend in *name* only⟩
**6 :** one referred to by a name ⟨praise his holy *name*⟩
— **in the name of 1 :** by authority of ⟨open *in the name of* the law⟩ **2 :** for the reason of **:** using the excuse of ⟨called for reforms *in the name of* progress⟩
²**name** *transitive verb* **named; nam·ing** (before 12th century)
**1 :** to give a name to **:** CALL
**2 a :** to mention or identify by name **b :** to accuse by name
**3 :** to nominate for office **:** APPOINT
**4 :** to decide on **:** CHOOSE ⟨*name* the day for the wedding⟩
**5 :** to mention explicitly **:** SPECIFY ⟨unwilling to *name* a price⟩
— **nam·er** *noun*
³**name** *adjective* (1598)
**1 :** of, relating to, or bearing a name ⟨*name* tags⟩
**2 :** appearing in the name of a literary or theatrical production
**3 a :** having an established reputation **b :** featuring celebrities
**name·able** *also* **nam·able** \'nā-mə-bəl\ *adjective* (1780)
**1 :** worthy of being named **:** MEMORABLE
**2 :** capable of being named **:** IDENTIFIABLE
**name–call·ing** \'nām-ˌkò-liŋ\ *noun* (1853)
**:** the use of offensive names especially to win an argument or to induce rejection or condemnation (as of a person or project) without objective consideration of the facts
**name day** *noun* (1721)
**:** the church feast day of the saint after whom one is named
**name–drop·ping** \-ˌdrä-piŋ\ *noun* (1950)
**:** the practice of seeking to impress others by studied but apparently casual mention of prominent persons as associates
— **name–drop·per** \-pər\ *noun*
**name·less** \'nām-ləs\ *adjective* (14th century)
**1 :** OBSCURE, UNDISTINGUISHED
**2 :** not known by name **:** ANONYMOUS
**3 :** having no legal right to a name **:** ILLEGITIMATE
**4 :** not having been given a name **:** UNNAMED
**5 :** not marked with a name ⟨a *nameless* grave⟩
**6 a :** incapable of precise description **:** INDEFINABLE **b :** too repulsive or distressing to describe
— **name·less·ly** *adverb*
— **name·less·ness** *noun*
**name·ly** \'nām-lē\ *adverb* (14th century)
**:** that is to say **:** TO WIT
**name of the game** (1966)
**1 :** the essential quality or matter ⟨patience is the *name of the game* in coastal duck hunting —Dick Beals⟩
**2 :** the fundamental goal of an activity
**name·plate** \-ˌplāt\ *noun* (circa 1859)
**:** something (as a plate or plaque) bearing a name (as of a resident or manufacturer)
**name·sake** \-ˌsāk\ *noun* [probably from *name's sake*] (1646)
**:** one that has the same name as another; *especially* **:** one who is named after another or for whom another is named
**nan** \'nän, 'nan\ *noun* [Hindi & Persian; Hindi *nān*, from Persian] (1948)
**:** a round flat leavened bread especially of the Indian subcontinent
**nana** \'na-nə\ *noun* [probably of baby-talk origin] (circa 1844)
**:** GRANDMOTHER

**nance** \'nan(t)s\ *noun* [short for *nancy*, from the name *Nancy*] (1920)
**1 :** an effeminate male — often used disparagingly
**2 :** HOMOSEXUAL — often used disparagingly
**NAND** \'nand\ *noun* [*not AND*] (1958)
**:** a computer logic circuit that produces an output which is the inverse of that of an AND circuit
**nan·di·na** \nan-'dī-nə, -'dē-\ *noun* [New Latin, from Japanese *nanten*] (circa 1890)
**:** a widely cultivated Asian evergreen shrub (*Nandina domestica*) of the barberry family
**nan·keen** \nan-'kēn\ *noun* [*Nanking* (Nanjing), China] (1755)
**1 :** a durable brownish yellow cotton fabric originally loomed by hand in China
**2** *plural* **:** trousers made of nankeen
**Nan·kin** \'nan-'kin, 'nän-\ *or* **Nan·king** \-'kiŋ\ *noun* [*Nanking* (Nanjing), China] (1781)
**:** Chinese porcelain decorated in blue on a white ground
**nan·no·plank·ton** \ˌna-nō-'plaŋ(k)-tən, -ˌtän\ *noun* [New Latin, from Greek *nanos, nannos* dwarf + New Latin *plankton* plankton] (1912)
**:** the smallest plankton that consists of those organisms (as bacteria) passing through nets of very fine mesh silk cloth
**nan·ny** *also* **nan·nie** \'na-nē\ *noun, plural* **nannies** [probably of baby-talk origin] (1795)
**:** a child's nurse **:** NURSEMAID
**nanny goat** *noun* [*Nanny*, nickname for *Anne*] (1788)
**:** a female domestic goat
**nano-** *combining form* [International Scientific Vocabulary, from Greek *nanos* dwarf]
**:** one billionth ($10^{-9}$) part of ⟨*nanosecond*⟩
**nano·gram** \'na-nə-ˌgram\ *noun* [International Scientific Vocabulary] (1951)
**:** one billionth of a gram
**nano·me·ter** \'na-nə-ˌmē-tər\ *noun* [International Scientific Vocabulary] (1963)
**:** one billionth of a meter
**nano·sec·ond** \-ˌse-kənd, -kənt\ *noun* [International Scientific Vocabulary] (1959)
**:** one billionth of a second
**nano·tech·nol·o·gy** \ˌna-nō-tek-'nä-lə-jē\ *noun* (1987)
**:** the art of manipulating materials on an atomic or molecular scale especially to build microscopic devices (as robots)
**nano·tes·la** \'na-nō-ˌtes-lə\ *noun* (1968)
**:** a unit of magnetic flux density equal to $10^{-9}$ tesla
**Nan·tua sauce** \nä$^n$(n)-'twä-\ *noun* [*Nantua*, France] (circa 1961)

\ə\ abut \ᵊ\ kitten \ər\ further \a\ ash \ā\ ace \ä\ mop, mar \aù\ out \ch\ chin \e\ bet \ē\ easy \g\ go \i\ hit \ī\ ice \j\ job \ŋ\ sing \ō\ go \ò\ law \òi\ boy \th\ thin \ṯẖ\ the \ü\ loot \ù\ foot \y\ yet \zh\ vision *see also* Guide to Pronunciation

**:** a cream sauce flavored with shellfish (as lobster)

**Na·o·mi** \nā-'ō-mē\ *noun* [Hebrew *Nā'ŏmī*]
**:** the mother-in-law of the Old Testament heroine Ruth

¹**nap** \'nap\ *intransitive verb* **napped; napping** [Middle English *nappen*, from Old English *hnappian*; akin to Old High German *hnaffezen* to doze] (before 12th century)
**1 :** to sleep briefly especially during the day **: DOZE**
**2 :** to be off guard

²**nap** *noun* (14th century)
**:** a short sleep especially during the day **: SNOOZE**

³**nap** *noun* [Middle English *noppe*, from Middle Dutch, flock of wool, nap] (15th century)
**:** a hairy or downy surface (as on a fabric)
— **nap·less** \-ləs\ *adjective*
— **napped** \'napt\ *adjective*

⁴**nap** *transitive verb* **napped; nap·ping** (1620)
**:** to raise a nap on (fabric or leather)

⁵**nap** *noun* [from *to go nap* (to make all the points in the card game Napoleon)] (1895)
*British* **:** a pick or recommendation as a good bet to win a contest (as a horse race); *also* **:** one named in a nap

⁶**nap** *transitive verb* **napped; nap·ping** (1927)
*British* **:** to pick or single out in a nap

**napa cabbage** \'na-pə-\ *noun* [perhaps from Japanese dialect *nappa* greens] (1980)
**: CHINESE CABBAGE b**

**napa leather** *noun* [*Napa*, California] (1897)
**:** a glove leather made by tawing sheepskins with a soap-and-oil mixture; *also* **:** a similarly soft leather

¹**na·palm** \'nā-ˌpäm, -ˌpälm *also* 'na- *also* nə-'pä(l)m\ *noun* [*naphthene* + *palm*itate] (1942)
**1 :** a thickener consisting of a mixture of aluminum soaps used in jelling gasoline (as for incendiary bombs)
**2 :** fuel jelled with napalm

²**napalm** *transitive verb* (1950)
**:** to assault with napalm

**nape** \'nāp, 'nap\ *noun* [Middle English] (14th century)
**:** the back of the neck

**na·pery** \'nā-p(ə-)rē\ *noun* [Middle English, from Middle French *naperie*, from *nappe*, *nape* tablecloth — more at NAPKIN] (14th century)
**:** household linen; *especially* **: TABLE LINEN**

**Naph·ta·li** \'naf-tə-ˌlī\ *noun* [Hebrew *Naphtālī*]
**:** a son of Jacob and the traditional eponymous ancestor of one of the tribes of Israel

**naph·tha** \'naf-thə, ÷'nap-\ *noun* [Latin, from Greek, of Iranian origin; akin to Persian *neft* naphtha] (1572)
**1 :** any of various volatile often flammable liquid hydrocarbon mixtures used chiefly as solvents and diluents
**2 : PETROLEUM**

**naph·tha·lene** \-ˌlēn\ *noun* [alteration of earlier *naphthaline*, irregular from *naphtha*] (1821)
**:** a crystalline aromatic hydrocarbon $C_{10}H_8$ usually obtained by distillation of coal tar and used especially in organic synthesis

**naph·thene** \'naf-ˌthēn, ÷'nap-\ *noun* (1884)
**: CYCLOPARAFFIN**
— **naph·then·ic** \ˌnaf-'thē-nik, ÷nap-, -'the-\ *adjective*

**naph·thol** \'naf-ˌthȯl, ÷'nap-, -ˌthōl\ *noun* [International Scientific Vocabulary] (1849)
**1 :** either of two isomeric derivatives $C_{10}H_8O$ of naphthalene used as antiseptics and in the manufacture of dyes
**2 :** any of various hydroxy derivatives of naphthalene that resemble the simpler phenols

**naph·thyl·amine** \naf-'thi-lə-ˌmēn, ÷nap-\ *noun* [International Scientific Vocabulary] (1857)

**:** either of two isomeric crystalline bases $C_{10}H_9N$ used especially as dye intermediates

**na·pier grass** \'nā-pē-ər-\ *noun* [*Napier*, town in South Africa] (1914)
**:** a tall stout African perennial grass (*Pennisetum purpureum*) that resembles sugarcane and is widely grown for forage — called also *elephant grass*

**Na·pier·ian logarithm** \nə-'pir-ē-ən-, nā-\ *noun* [John *Napier*] (1816)
**: NATURAL LOGARITHM**

**Na·pier's bones** \'nā-pē-ərz-\ *noun* (circa 1658)
**:** a set of graduated rods (as of wood or bone) invented by John Napier and used for multiplication and division based on the principles of logarithms

**na·pi·form** \'nā-pə-ˌfȯrm\ *adjective* [Latin *napus* turnip (perhaps from Greek *napy, sinapy* mustard) + International Scientific Vocabulary *-iform*] (circa 1846)
**:** globular at the top and tapering off abruptly — used especially of roots

**nap·kin** \'nap-kən\ *noun* [Middle English *nappekin*, from *nappe* tablecloth, from Middle French, from Latin *mappa* napkin] (14th century)
**1 :** a piece of material (as cloth or paper) used at table to wipe the lips or fingers and protect the clothes
**2 :** a small cloth or towel: as **a** *dialect British* **: HANDKERCHIEF b** *chiefly Scottish* **: KERCHIEF c** *chiefly British* **: DIAPER 3**
**3 : SANITARY NAPKIN**

**na·po·leon** \nə-'pōl-yən, -'pō-lē-ən\ *noun* [French *napoléon*, from *Napoléon* Napoleon I] (1814)
**1 :** a former French 20-franc gold coin
**2 :** an oblong pastry with a filling of cream, custard, or jelly
**3** *capitalized* **:** one like Napoleon I (as in ambition)

**nappe** \'nap\ *noun* [French, tablecloth, sheet, nappe — more at NAPKIN] (1904)
**1 : SHEET 6**
**2 :** a large mass thrust over other rocks
**3 :** one of the two sheets that lie on opposite sides of the vertex and together make up a cone

¹**nap·py** \'na-pē\ *noun* [obsolete *nappy*, adjective, foaming] (1700)
*chiefly Scottish* **: LIQUOR;** *specifically* **: ALE**

²**nappy** *noun, plural* **nappies** [English dialect *nap* bowl, from Middle English, from Old English *hnæpp*; akin to Old High German *hnapf* bowl] (1864)
**:** a rimless shallow open serving dish

³**nappy** *noun, plural* **nappies** [*nap*kin + ⁴-*y*] (1927)
*chiefly British* **: DIAPER 3**

⁴**nappy** *adjective* **nap·pi·er; -est** [³*nap*] (1928)
**: KINKY 1**

**na·prap·a·thy** \nə-'pra-pə-thē\ *noun* [Czech *naprava* correction + English *-pathy*] (1909)
**:** a system of treatment by manipulation of connective tissue and adjoining structures (as ligaments, joints, and muscles) and by dietary measures that is held to facilitate the recuperative and regenerative processes of the body

**narc** \'närk\ *noun* [short for *narcotics agent*] (1967)
*slang* **:** a person (as a government agent) who investigates narcotics violations

**nar·cis·sism** \'när-sə-ˌsi-zəm\ *noun* [German *Narzissismus*, from *Narziss* Narcissus, from Latin *Narcissus*] (1822)
**1 : EGOISM, EGOCENTRISM**
**2 :** love of or sexual desire for one's own body ◆
— **nar·cis·sist** \'när-sə-sist\ *noun or adjective*
— **nar·cis·sis·tic** \ˌnär-sə-'sis-tik\ *adjective*

**nar·cis·sus** \när-'si-səs\ *noun* [Latin, from Greek *Narkissos*]

**1** *capitalized* **:** a beautiful youth in Greek mythology who pines away for love of his own reflection and is then turned into the narcissus flower
**2** *plural* **nar·cis·si** \-'si-ˌsī, -(ˌ)sē\ *or* **nar·cis·sus·es** *or* **narcissus** [New Latin, genus name, from Latin, narcissus, from Greek *narkissos*] **: DAFFODIL;** *especially* **:** one whose flowers have a short corona and are usually borne separately

**nar·co** \'när-(ˌ)kō\ *noun, plural* **narcos** (1955)
*slang* **: NARC**

**nar·co·lep·sy** \'när-kə-ˌlep-sē\ *noun, plural* **-sies** [International Scientific Vocabulary, from Greek *narkē*] (1880)
**:** a condition characterized by brief attacks of deep sleep
— **nar·co·lep·tic** \ˌnär-kə-'lep-tik\ *adjective*

**nar·co·lep·tic** \ˌnär-kə-'lep-tik\ *noun* (1928)
**:** a person who is subject to attacks of narcolepsy

**nar·co·sis** \när-'kō-səs\ *noun, plural* **-co·ses** \-ˌsēz\ [New Latin, from Greek *narkōsis*, action of benumbing, from *narkoun*] (circa 1693)
**:** a state of stupor, unconsciousness, or arrested activity produced by the influence of narcotics or other chemicals

¹**nar·cot·ic** \när-'kä-tik\ *noun* [Middle English *narkotik*, from Middle French *narcotique*, from *narcotique*, adjective, from Medieval Latin *narcoticus*, from Greek *narkōtikos*, from *narkoun* to benumb, from *narkē* numbness — more at SNARE] (14th century)
**1 a :** a drug (as opium) that in moderate doses dulls the senses, relieves pain, and induces profound sleep but in excessive doses causes stupor, coma, or convulsions **b :** a drug (as marijuana or LSD) subject to restriction similar to that of addictive narcotics whether physiologically addictive and narcotic or not
**2 :** something that soothes, relieves, or lulls

²**narcotic** *adjective* (1526)
**1 a :** having the properties of or yielding a narcotic **b :** inducing mental lethargy **: SOPORIFEROUS**
**2 :** of, induced by, or concerned with narcotics
**3 :** of, involving, or intended for narcotic addicts
— **nar·cot·i·cal·ly** \-ti-k(ə-)lē\ *adverb*

**nar·co·tize** \'när-kə-ˌtīz\ *verb* **-tized; -tiz·ing** [International Scientific Vocabulary] (1526)

◇ **WORD HISTORY**
**narcissism** The term *narcissism* represents the result of modern science finding a psychological truth in an ancient myth. In Greek mythology Narcissus was a youth so strikingly beautiful that he attracted many would-be lovers, both male and female. He spurned the attentions of all of them. Finally, Nemesis, the goddess of retribution, in response to the prayer of one rejected lover, contrived that Narcissus should catch sight of his own reflection in a pool on Mount Helicon. Narcissus became so entranced with his own beauty that he could not bear to tear himself away. He lay beside the pool day after day until he wasted away and finally expired. By an act of the gods his body was metamorphosed into the flower now known as the narcissus. Modern psychologists were reminded of the myth of Narcissus as they studied individuals morbidly interested in themselves or sexually attracted to their own bodies. In 1899 a German psychologist coined the term *Narzissmus* to describe this form of self-love. In 1905 Havelock Ellis, in his *Studies in the Psychology of Sex*, accepted this coinage and used *narcissism* as the English equivalent.

*transitive verb*
**1 a :** to treat with or subject to a narcotic **b
:** to put into a state of narcosis
**2 :** to soothe to unconsciousness or unawareness
*intransitive verb*
**:** to act as a narcotizing agent
**nard** \'närd\ *noun* [Middle English *narde,* from
Old English, from Latin *nardus,* from Greek
*nardos,* of Semitic origin; akin to Hebrew *nērd*
nard] (before 12th century)
**:** SPIKENARD 1b
**na·res** \'nar-(,)ēz, 'ner-\ *noun plural* [Middle
English, from Latin, plural of *naris;* akin to
Latin *nasus* nose — more at NOSE] (14th century)
**:** the pair of openings of the nose or nasal cavity of a vertebrate
**nar·ghi·le** \'när-gə-lē\ *or* **nar·gi·leh** \-,le\
*noun* [Persian *nārgīla,* from *nārgīl* coconut, of
Indo-Aryan origin; akin to Sanskrit *nārikela*
coconut; from the original material used in
making its bowl] (1758)
**:** a water pipe that originated in the Near East
**¹nark** \'närk\ *noun* [perhaps from Romany *nak*
nose] (circa 1860)
*British* **:** STOOL PIGEON
**²nark** *variant of* NARC
**³nark** *transitive verb* [origin unknown] (1888)
*British* **:** IRRITATE, ANNOY
**Nar·ra·gan·set** *or* **Nar·ra·gan·sett** \,nar-
ə-'gan(t)-sət\ *noun, plural* **Narraganset** *or*
**Narragansets** *or* **Narragansett** *or* **Narragansetts** (1622)
**1 :** a member of an American Indian people of
Rhode Island
**2 :** the Algonquian language of the Narraganset people
**nar·rate** \'nar-,āt, na-'rāt\ *transitive verb* **nar-
rat·ed; nar·rat·ing** [Latin *narratus,* past
participle of *narrare,* from Latin *gnarus*
knowing; akin to Latin *gnoscere, noscere* to
know — more at KNOW] (1656)
**:** to tell (as a story) in detail; *also* **:** to provide
spoken commentary for (as a movie or televi-
sion show)
— **nar·ra·tor** \'nar-,ā-tər; na-'rā-, nə-; 'nar-
ə-\ *noun*
**nar·ra·tion** \na-'rā-shən, nə-\ *noun* (15th century)
**1 :** the act or process or an instance of narrating
**2 :** STORY, NARRATIVE
— **nar·ra·tion·al** \-shnəl, -shə-n°l\ *adjective*
**nar·ra·tive** \'nar-ə-tiv\ *noun* (1566)
**1 :** something that is narrated **:** STORY
**2 :** the art or practice of narration
**3 :** the representation in art of an event or story; *also* **:** an example of such a representation
— **narrative** *adjective*
— **nar·ra·tive·ly** *adverb*
**nar·ra·tol·o·gy** \,nar-ə-'tä-lə-jē\ *noun* (1976)
**:** the study of structure in narratives
— **nar·ra·to·log·i·cal** \-tə-'lä-ji-kəl\ *adjective*
— **nar·ra·tol·o·gist** \-'tä-lə-jist\ *noun*
**¹nar·row** \'nar-(,)ō\ *adjective* [Middle English
*narowe,* from Old English *nearu;* akin to Old
High German *narwa* scar] (before 12th century)
**1 a :** of slender width **b :** of less than standard
width **c** *of a textile* **:** woven in widths less than
18 inches (46 centimeters)
**2 :** limited in size or scope
**3 a :** illiberal in views or disposition **:** PREJU-
DICED **b** *chiefly dialect* **:** STINGY, NIGGARDLY
**4 a :** barely sufficient **:** CLOSE **b :** barely successful
**5 :** minutely precise **:** METICULOUS
**6** *of a ration* **:** relatively rich in protein as
compared with carbohydrate and fat
**7 :** TENSE 3
— **nar·row·ly** *adverb*
— **nar·row·ness** *noun*
**²narrow** (before 12th century)

*transitive verb*
**1 :** to decrease the breadth or extent of **:** CON-
TRACT — often used with *down*
**2 :** to decrease the scope or sphere of **:** LIMIT
— often used with *down*
*intransitive verb*
**:** to lessen in width or extent **:** CONTRACT —
often used with *down*
**³narrow** *noun* (13th century)
**:** a narrow part or passage; *specifically* **:** a
strait connecting two bodies of water — usually used in plural but singular or plural in
construction
**nar·row·band** \'nar-ō-,band, 'nar-ə-\ *adjective*
(1950)
**:** operating at, responsive to, or including a
narrow range of frequencies
**narrow boat** *noun* (1949)
*British* **:** a barge with a beam of less than sev-
en feet (2.1 meters)
**nar·row·cast·ing** \'nar-ō-,kas-tiŋ, 'nar-ə-\
*noun* (1928)
**:** radio or television transmission aimed at a
narrowly defined area or audience (as paying
subscribers or night workers)
**nar·row–mind·ed** \,nar-ō-'mīn-dəd, ,nar-ə-\
*adjective* (1625)
**:** lacking in tolerance or breadth of vision **:**
PETTY
— **nar·row–mind·ed·ly** *adverb*
— **nar·row–mind·ed·ness** *noun*
**nar·thex** \'när-,theks\ *noun* [Late Greek
*narthēx,* from Greek, giant fennel, cane, cas-
ket] (circa 1673)
**1 :** the portico of an ancient church
**2 :** a vestibule leading to the nave of a church
**nar·whal** \'när-,wäl, -,hwäl, -wəl\ *also* **nar-
whale** \-,wāl, -,hwāl\ *noun* [Norwegian &
Danish *narhval* & Swedish *narval,* probably
modification of Icelandic *nárhvalur,* from Old
Norse *náhvalr,* from *nār* corpse + *hvalr* whale;
from its color] (1646)
**:** an arctic cetacean (*Monodon monoceros*)
about 20 feet (6 meters) long with the male
having a long twisted ivory tusk

**narwhal**

**nary** \'nar-ē, 'ner-\ *adjective* [alteration of *ne'er
a*] (1746)
**:** not any ⟨*nary* a person wanted to go⟩
**¹na·sal** \'nā-zəl\ *noun* [Middle English, from
Middle French, from Old French, from *nes*
nose, from Latin *nasus* — more at NOSE]
(14th century)
**1 :** the nosepiece of a helmet
**2 :** a nasal part
**3 :** a nasal consonant
**²nasal** *adjective* (1656)
**1 :** of or relating to the nose
**2 a :** uttered with the soft palate lowered and
with passage of air through the nose (as with
\m\, \n\, \ŋ\, \ōⁿ\, or \aⁿ\) **b :** characterized by
resonance produced through the nose
**3** *of a musical tone* **:** SHARP, PENETRATING
— **na·sal·i·ty** \nā-'za-lə-tē\ *noun*
— **na·sal·ly** \'nā-zə-lē, 'nāz-lē\ *adverb*
**na·sal·ize** \'nā-zə-,līz\ *verb* **-ized; -iz·ing**
(1817)
*transitive verb*
**:** to make nasal or pronounce as a nasal sound
— **na·sal·i·za·tion** \,nā-zə-lə-'zā-shən\
*noun*
**na·scence** \'na-s°n(t)s, 'nā-\ *noun* (1570)
**:** NASCENCY
**na·scen·cy** \-s°n(t)-sē\ *noun, plural* **-cies**
(1682)

**:** BIRTH, ORIGIN
**na·scent** \'na-s°nt, 'nā-\ *adjective* [Latin
*nascent-, nascens,* present participle of *nasci*
to be born] (circa 1624)
**:** coming or having recently come into existence
**naso-** *combining form* [Latin *nasus* nose]
**1 :** nose and ⟨*nasopharynx*⟩
**2 :** nasal ⟨*nasogastric*⟩
**na·so·gas·tric** \,nā-zō-'gas-trik\ *adjective*
(1942)
**:** being or performed by intubation of the
stomach through the nasal passages ⟨*nasogastric* tube⟩ ⟨*nasogastric* suction⟩
**na·so·pha·ryn·geal** \-fə-'rin-j(ē-)əl, -,far-ən-
'jē-əl\ *adjective* (1872)
**:** of, relating to, or affecting the nose and pharynx or the nasopharynx
**na·so·phar·ynx** \-'far-iŋ(k)s\ *noun* [New Lat-
in] (1877)
**:** the upper part of the pharynx continuous
with the nasal passages
**nas·tic** \'nas-tik\ *adjective* [Greek *nastos*
close-pressed, from *nassein* to press] (1908)
**:** of, relating to, or constituting a movement of
a plant part caused by disproportionate growth
or increase of turgor in one surface
**nas·tur·tium** \nə-'stər-shəm, na-\ *noun* [Latin,
a cress] (1704)
**:** any of a genus (*Tropaeolum*
of the family Tropaeolaceae,
the nasturtium family) of
herbs of Central and South
America with showy spurred
flowers and pungent seeds;
*especially* **:** either of two
widely cultivated ornamentals (*T. majus* and *T. minus*)
**nas·ty** \'nas-tē\ *adjective*
**nas·ti·er; -est** [Middle En-
glish] (14th century)
**1 a :** disgustingly filthy **b
:** physically repugnant
**2 :** INDECENT, OBSCENE
**3 :** MEAN, TAWDRY

**nasturtium**

**4 a :** extremely hazardous or harmful ⟨had a
*nasty* climb to reach the summit⟩ **b :** causing
severe pain or suffering ⟨a *nasty* wound⟩
**:** sharply unpleasant **:** DISAGREEABLE ⟨*nasty*
weather⟩
**5 a :** difficult to understand or deal with **:** VEX-
ATIOUS ⟨a *nasty* problem⟩ **b :** psychologically
unsettling **:** TRYING ⟨a *nasty* fear that she was
lost⟩
**6 :** lacking in courtesy or sportsmanship ⟨a
*nasty* trick⟩
**synonym** see DIRTY
— **nas·ti·ly** \-tə-lē\ *adverb*
— **nas·ti·ness** \-tē-nəs\ *noun*
— **nasty** *noun*
**na·tal** \'nā-t°l\ *adjective* [Middle English, from
Latin *natalis,* from *natus,* past participle of
*nasci* to be born — more at NATION] (15th
century)
**1 :** NATIVE
**2 :** of, relating to, or present at birth; *especially* **:** associated with one's birth ⟨a *natal* star⟩
**na·tal·i·ty** \nā-'ta-lə-tē, nə-\ *noun, plural*
**-ties** (1888)
**:** BIRTHRATE
**na·tant** \'nā-t°nt\ *adjective* [Middle English
*natand,* from Latin *natant-, natans,* present
participle of *natare* to swim; akin to Latin
*nare* to swim; akin to Greek *nein, nēchein* to
swim, Sanskrit *snāti* he bathes] (15th century)
**:** swimming or floating in water ⟨*natant* deca-
pods⟩
**na·ta·tion** \nā-'tā-shən, na-\ *noun* (1542)
**:** the action or art of swimming

**na·ta·to·ri·al** \ˌnā-tə-'tōr-ē-əl, ˌna-, -'tòr-\ *or* **na·ta·to·ry** \'nā-tə-ˌtōr-ē, 'na-, -ˌtòr-\ *adjective* (1816)
**1 :** of or relating to swimming
**2 :** adapted to or characterized by swimming ⟨a *natatorial* leg of an aquatic insect⟩
**na·ta·to·ri·um** \ˌnā-tə-'tōr-ē-əm, ˌna-, -'tòr-\ *noun* [Late Latin, from Latin *natare*] (circa 1890)
**:** an indoor swimming pool
**natch** \'nach\ *adverb* [by shortening & alteration from *naturally*] (circa 1945)
*slang* **:** of course **:** NATURALLY
**Natch·ez** \'na-chiz\ *noun, plural* **Natchez** (1845)
**1 :** a member of an American Indian people of southwestern Mississippi
**2 :** the language of the Natchez people
**na·tes** \'nā-ˌtēz\ *noun plural* [Latin, plural of *natis* buttock] (circa 1706)
**:** BUTTOCKS
**nathe·less** \'nāth-ləs\ *or* **nath·less** \'nath-\ *adverb* [Middle English, from Old English *nā thē læs* not the less] (before 12th century)
*archaic* **:** NEVERTHELESS, NOTWITHSTANDING
**na·tion** \'nā-shən\ *noun* [Middle English *nacioun*, from Middle French *nation*, from Latin *nation-, natio* birth, race, nation, from *nasci* to be born; akin to Latin *gignere* to beget — more at KIN] (14th century)
**1 a** (1) **:** NATIONALITY 5a (2) **:** a politically organized nationality (3) **:** a non-Jewish nationality ⟨why do the *nations* conspire —Psalms 2:1 (Revised Standard Version)⟩ **b :** a community of people composed of one or more nationalities and possessing a more or less defined territory and government **c :** a territorial division containing a body of people of one or more nationalities and usually characterized by relatively large size and independent status
**2** *archaic* **:** GROUP, AGGREGATION
**3 :** a tribe or federation of tribes (as of American Indians)
**¹na·tion·al** \'nash-nəl, 'na-shə-nᵊl\ *adjective* (1597)
**1 :** of or relating to a nation
**2 :** NATIONALIST
**3 :** comprising or characteristic of a nationality
**4 :** belonging to or maintained by the federal government
**5 :** of, relating to, or being a coalition government formed by most or all major political parties usually in a crisis
— **na·tion·al·ly** *adverb*
**²national** *noun* (1887)
**1 :** one that owes allegiance to or is under the protection of a nation without regard to the more formal status of citizen or subject
**2 :** a competition that is national in scope — usually used in plural
*synonym* see CITIZEN
**national bank** *noun* (1790)
**1 :** CENTRAL BANK
**2 :** a bank operating under federal charter and supervision
**national forest** *noun* (circa 1905)
**:** a usually forested area of considerable extent that is preserved by government decree from private exploitation and is harvested only under supervision
**National Guard** *noun* (1847)
**1 :** a militia force recruited by each state of the U.S., equipped by the federal government, and jointly maintained subject to the call of either
**2** *often not capitalized* **:** a military establishment serving as a national constabulary and defense force
**national income** *noun* (1878)
**:** the aggregate of earnings from a nation's current production including compensation of employees, interest, rental income, and profits of business after taxes
**na·tion·al·ise** *chiefly British variant of* NATIONALIZE

**na·tion·al·ism** \'nash-nə-ˌli-zəm, 'na-shə-nᵊl-ˌi-zəm\ *noun* (1844)
**:** loyalty and devotion to a nation; *especially* **:** a sense of national consciousness exalting one nation above all others and placing primary emphasis on promotion of its culture and interests as opposed to those of other nations or supranational groups
**¹na·tion·al·ist** \-list, -ist\ *noun* (1715)
**1 :** an advocate of or believer in nationalism
**2** *capitalized* **:** a member of a political party or group advocating national independence or strong national government
**²nationalist** *adjective* (1889)
**1 :** of, relating to, or advocating nationalism
**2** *capitalized* **:** of, relating to, or being a political group advocating or associated with nationalism
**na·tion·al·is·tic** \ˌnash-nə-'lis-tik, ˌna-shə-nᵊl-'is-tik\ *adjective* (1866)
**1 :** of, favoring, or characterized by nationalism ⟨*nationalistic* election speeches⟩
**2 :** NATIONAL 1
— **na·tion·al·is·ti·cal·ly** \-ti-k(ə-)lē\ *adverb*
**na·tion·al·i·ty** \ˌna-shə-'na-lə-tē, ˌnash-'na-\ *noun, plural* **-ties** (1691)
**1 :** national character
**2 :** NATIONALISM
**3 :** national status; *specifically* **:** a legal relationship involving allegiance on the part of an individual and usually protection on the part of the state **b :** membership in a particular nation
**4 :** political independence or existence as a separate nation
**5 a :** a people having a common origin, tradition, and language and capable of forming or actually constituting a nation-state **b :** an ethnic group constituting one element of a larger unit (as a nation)
**na·tion·al·ize** \'nash-nə-ˌlīz, 'na-shə-nᵊl-ˌīz\ *transitive verb* **-ized; -iz·ing** (1800)
**1 :** to give a national character to
**2 :** to invest control or ownership of in the national government
— **na·tion·al·i·za·tion** \ˌnash-nə-lə-'zā-shən, ˌna-shə-nᵊl-ə-\ *noun*
— **na·tion·al·iz·er** \'nash-nə-ˌlī-zər, ˌna-shə-nᵊl-ˌī-zər\ *noun*
**national monument** *noun* (1916)
**:** a place of historic, scenic, or scientific interest set aside for preservation usually by presidential proclamation
**national park** *noun* (1868)
**:** an area of special scenic, historical, or scientific importance set aside and maintained by a national government and in the U.S. by an act of Congress
**national seashore** *noun* (1962)
**:** a recreational area adjacent to a seacoast and maintained by the federal government
**national socialism** *noun, often N&S capitalized* (1931)
**:** NAZISM
— **national socialist** *adjective, often N&S capitalized*
**na·tion·hood** \'nā-shən-ˌhud\ *noun* (1850)
**:** NATIONALITY 1, 3a, 4
**na·tion-state** \'nā-shən-'stāt, -ˌstāt\ *noun* (1918)
**:** a form of political organization under which a relatively homogeneous people inhabits a sovereign state; *especially* **:** a state containing one as opposed to several nationalities
**¹na·tion·wide** \ˌnā-shən-'wīd\ *adjective* (1912)
**:** extending throughout a nation
**²nationwide** *adverb* (1926)
**:** throughout the nation
**¹na·tive** \'nā-tiv\ *adjective* [Middle English *natif*, from Middle French, from Latin *nativus*, from *natus*, past participle of *nasci* to be born — more at NATION] (14th century)
**1 :** INBORN, INNATE ⟨*native* talents⟩

**2 :** belonging to a particular place by birth ⟨*native* to Wisconsin⟩
**3** *archaic* **:** closely related
**4 :** belonging to or associated with one by birth
**5 :** NATURAL, NORMAL
**6 a :** grown, produced, or originating in a particular place or in the vicinity **:** LOCAL **b :** living or growing naturally in a particular region **:** INDIGENOUS
**7 :** SIMPLE, UNAFFECTED
**8 a :** constituting the original substance or source **b :** found in nature especially in an unadulterated form ⟨mining *native* silver⟩
**9** *chiefly Australian* **:** having a usually superficial resemblance to a specified English plant or animal ☆
— **na·tive·ly** *adverb*
— **na·tive·ness** *noun*
**²native** *noun* (1535)
**1 :** one born or reared in a particular place
**2 a :** an original or indigenous inhabitant **b :** something indigenous to a particular locality
**3 :** a local resident; *especially* **:** a person who has always lived in a place as distinguished from a visitor or a temporary resident
**Native American** *noun* (1925)
**:** AMERICAN INDIAN
— **Native American** *adjective*
**na·tiv·ism** \'nā-ti-ˌvi-zəm\ *noun* (1844)
**1 :** a policy of favoring native inhabitants as opposed to immigrants
**2 :** the revival or perpetuation of an indigenous culture especially in opposition to acculturation
— **na·tiv·ist** \-vist\ *noun or adjective*
— **na·tiv·is·tic** \ˌnā-ti-'vis-tik\ *adjective*
**na·tiv·i·ty** \nə-'ti-və-tē, nā-\ *noun, plural* **-ties** [Middle English *nativite*, from Middle French *nativité*, from Medieval Latin *nativitat-, nativitas*, from Late Latin, birth, from Latin *nativus*] (14th century)
**1 :** the process or circumstances of being born **:** BIRTH; *especially, capitalized* **:** the birth of Jesus
**2 :** a horoscope at or of the time of one's birth
**3 :** the place of origin
**na·tri·ure·sis** \ˌnā-trē-yủ-'rē-səs\ *noun* [New Latin, from *natrium* sodium (from International Scientific Vocabulary *natron*) + *uresis* urination, from Greek *ourēsis*, from *ourein* to urinate — more at URINE] (1957)
**:** excessive loss of sodium in the urine
— **na·tri·uret·ic** \-'re-tik\ *adjective or noun*
**na·tro·lite** \'nā-trə-ˌlīt\ *noun* [German *Natrolith*, from *Natron* (from French) + *-lith* -lite] (circa 1805)
**:** a hydrous silicate of sodium and aluminum that is related to zeolite
**na·tron** \'nā-ˌträn, -trən\ *noun* [French, from Spanish *natrón*, from Arabic *naṭrūn*, from Greek *nitron*] (1684)
**:** a hydrous native sodium carbonate used in ancient times in embalming, in ceramic pastes, and as a cleansing agent
**¹nat·ter** \'na-tər\ *intransitive verb* [probably imitative] (1942)
**:** CHATTER 2
**²natter** *noun* (1943)

---

☆ **SYNONYMS**
**Native, indigenous, endemic, aboriginal** mean belonging to a locality. NATIVE implies birth or origin in a place or region and may suggest compatibility with it (*native* tribal customs). INDIGENOUS applies to species or races and adds to NATIVE the implication of not having been introduced from elsewhere (maize is *indigenous* to America). ENDEMIC implies being peculiar to a region (edelweiss is *endemic* in the Alps). ABORIGINAL implies having no known race preceding in occupancy of the region (the *aboriginal* peoples of Australia).

*chiefly British* : idle talk or conversation : CHAT

**nat·ty** \'na-tē\ *adjective* **nat·ti·er; -est** [perhaps alteration of earlier *netty,* from obsolete *net* neat, clean] (1557)
: trimly neat and tidy : SMART
— **nat·ti·ly** \'na-t°l-ē\ *adverb*
— **nat·ti·ness** \'na-tē-nəs\ *noun*

**¹nat·u·ral** \'na-chə-rəl, 'nach-rəl\ *adjective* [Middle English, from Middle French, from Latin *naturalis* of nature, from *natura* nature] (14th century)
**1** : based on an inherent sense of right and wrong ⟨*natural* justice⟩
**2 a** : being in accordance with or determined by nature **b** : having or constituting a classification based on features existing in nature
**3 a** (1) : begotten as distinguished from adopted; *also* : LEGITIMATE (2) : being a relation by actual consanguinity as distinguished from adoption ⟨*natural* parents⟩ **b** : ILLEGITIMATE ⟨a *natural* child⟩
**4** : having an essential relation with someone or something : following from the nature of the one in question ⟨his guilt is a *natural* deduction from the evidence⟩
**5** : implanted or being as if implanted by nature : seemingly inborn ⟨a *natural* talent for art⟩
**6** : of or relating to nature as an object of study and research
**7** : having a specified character by nature ⟨a *natural* athlete⟩
**8 a** : occurring in conformity with the ordinary course of nature : not marvelous or supernatural ⟨*natural* causes⟩ **b** : formulated by human reason alone rather than revelation ⟨*natural* religion⟩ ⟨*natural* rights⟩ **c** : having a normal or usual character ⟨events followed their *natural* course⟩
**9** : possessing or exhibiting the higher qualities (as kindliness and affection) of human nature ⟨a noble . . . brother . . . ever most kind and *natural* —Shakespeare⟩
**10 a** : growing without human care; *also* : not cultivated ⟨*natural* prairie unbroken by the plow⟩ **b** : existing in or produced by nature : not artificial ⟨*natural* turf⟩ ⟨*natural* curiosities⟩ **c** : relating to or being natural food
**11 a** : being in a state of nature without spiritual enlightenment : UNREGENERATE ⟨*natural* man⟩ **b** : living in or as if in a state of nature untouched by the influences of civilization and society
**12 a** : having a physical or real existence as contrasted with one that is spiritual, intellectual, or fictitious ⟨a corporation is a legal but not a *natural* person⟩ **b** : of, relating to, or operating in the physical as opposed to the spiritual world ⟨*natural* laws describe phenomena of the physical universe⟩
**13 a** : closely resembling an original : true to nature **b** : marked by easy simplicity and freedom from artificiality, affectation, or constraint **c** : having a form or appearance found in nature
**14 a** : having neither flats nor sharps ⟨the *natural* scale of C major⟩ **b** : being neither sharp nor flat **c** : having the pitch modified by the natural sign
**15** : of an off-white or beige color ☆
— **nat·u·ral·ness** \-nəs\ *noun*

**²natural** *noun* (1533)
**1** : one born without the usual powers of reason and understanding
**2 a** : a sign ♮ placed on any degree of the musical staff to nullify the effect of a preceding sharp or flat **b** : a note or tone affected by the natural sign
**3** : a result or combination that immediately wins the stake in a game; *specifically* : a throw of 7 or 11 on the first cast in craps
**4 a** : one having natural skills, talents, or abilities **b** : something that is likely to become an immediate success **c** : one that is obviously suitable for a specific purpose

**5** : AFRO

**natural childbirth** *noun* (1933)
: a system of managing childbirth in which the mother receives preparatory education in order to remain conscious during and assist in delivery with minimal or no use of drugs or anesthetics

**natural family planning** *noun* (1975)
: a method of birth control that involves abstention from sexual intercourse during the period of ovulation which is determined through observation and measurement of bodily symptoms

**natural food** *noun* (1917)
: food that has undergone minimal processing and contains no preservatives or artificial additives

**natural gas** *noun* (1825)
**1** : gas issuing from the earth's crust through natural openings or bored wells; *especially* : a combustible mixture of methane and higher hydrocarbons used chiefly as a fuel and raw material
**2** : gas manufactured from organic matter (as coal)

**natural history** *noun* (1567)
**1** : a treatise on some aspect of nature
**2** : the natural development of something (as an organism or disease) over a period of time
**3** : the study of natural objects especially in the field from an amateur or popular point of view

**nat·u·ral·ise** *British variant of* NATURALIZE

**nat·u·ral·ism** \'na-chə-rə-,li-zəm, 'nach-rə-\ *noun* (circa 1641)
**1** : action, inclination, or thought based only on natural desires and instincts
**2** : a theory denying that an event or object has a supernatural significance; *specifically* : the doctrine that scientific laws are adequate to account for all phenomena
**3** : realism in art or literature; *specifically* : a theory in literature emphasizing scientific observation of life without idealization or the avoidance of the ugly

**nat·u·ral·ist** \-list\ *noun* (1587)
**1** : one that advocates or practices naturalism
**2** : a student of natural history; *especially* : a field biologist

**nat·u·ral·is·tic** \,na-chə-rə-'lis-tik, ,nach-rə-\ *also* **nat·u·ral·ist** \'na-chə-rə-list, 'nach-rə-\ *adjective* (1838)
: of, characterized by, or according with naturalism
— **nat·u·ral·is·ti·cal·ly** \,na-chə-rə-'lis-ti-k(ə-)lē, ,nach-rə-\ *adverb*

**nat·u·ral·ize** \'na-chə-rə-,līz, 'nach-rə-\ *verb* **-ized; -iz·ing** (1593)
*transitive verb*
**1** : to introduce into common use or into the vernacular
**2** : to bring into conformity with nature
**3** : to confer the rights of a national on; *especially* : to admit to citizenship
**4** : to cause (as a plant) to become established as if native
*intransitive verb*
: to become established as if native
— **nat·u·ral·i·za·tion** \,na-chə-rə-lə-'zā-shən, ,nach-rə-\ *noun*

**natural killer cell** *noun* (1975)
: a large granular lymphocyte capable of killing a tumor or microbial cell without prior exposure to the target cell and without having it presented with or marked by a histocompatibility antigen

**natural law** *noun* (15th century)
: a body of law or a specific principle held to be derived from nature and binding upon human society in the absence of or in addition to positive law

**natural logarithm** *noun* (1816)
: a logarithm with *e* as a base

**nat·u·ral·ly** \'na-chər-ə-lē, 'nach-rə-, 'na-chər-\ *adverb* (14th century)

**1** : by nature : by natural character or ability ⟨*naturally* timid⟩
**2** : according to the usual course of things : as might be expected ⟨we *naturally* dislike being hurt⟩
**3 a** : without artificial aid ⟨hair that curls *naturally*⟩ **b** : without affectation ⟨speak *naturally*⟩
**4** : with truth to nature : REALISTICALLY

**natural number** *noun* (1763)
: the number 1 or any number (as 3, 12, 432) obtained by adding 1 to it one or more times : a positive integer

**natural philosophy** *noun* (14th century)
: NATURAL SCIENCE; *especially* : PHYSICAL SCIENCE
— **natural philosopher** *noun*

**natural resource** *noun* (1870)
**1** *plural* : industrial materials and capacities (as mineral deposits and waterpower) supplied by nature
**2** : RESOURCE 1b

**natural science** *noun* (14th century)
: any of the sciences (as physics, chemistry, or biology) that deal with matter, energy, and their interrelations and transformations or with objectively measurable phenomena
— **natural scientist** *noun*

**natural selection** *noun* (1857)
: a natural process that results in the survival and reproductive success of individuals or groups best adjusted to their environment and that leads to the perpetuation of genetic qualities best suited to that particular environment

**natural theology** *noun* (1677)
: theology deriving its knowledge of God from the study of nature independent of special revelation

**na·ture** \'nā-chər\ *noun* [Middle English, from Middle French, from Latin *natura,* from *natus,* past participle of *nasci* to be born — more at NATION] (14th century)
**1 a** : the inherent character or basic constitution of a person or thing : ESSENCE **b** : DISPOSITION, TEMPERAMENT
**2 a** : a creative and controlling force in the universe **b** : an inner force or the sum of such forces in an individual
**3** : a kind or class usually distinguished by fundamental or essential characteristics ⟨documents of a confidential *nature*⟩ ⟨acts of a ceremonial *nature*⟩
**4** : the physical constitution or drives of an organism; *especially* : an excretory organ or function — used in phrases like *the call of nature*
**5** : a spontaneous attitude (as of generosity)

---

☆ **SYNONYMS**
**Natural, ingenuous, naive, unsophisticated, artless** mean free from pretension or calculation. NATURAL implies lacking artificiality and self-consciousness and having a spontaneousness suggesting the natural rather than the man-made world ⟨her unaffected, *natural* manner⟩. INGENUOUS implies inability to disguise or conceal one's feelings or intentions ⟨the *ingenuous* enthusiasm of children⟩. NAIVE suggests lack of worldly wisdom often connoting credulousness and unchecked innocence ⟨politically *naive*⟩. UNSOPHISTICATED implies a lack of experience and training necessary for social ease and adroitness ⟨*unsophisticated* adolescents⟩. ARTLESS suggests a naturalness resulting from unawareness of the effect one is producing on others ⟨*artless* charm⟩. See in addition REGULAR.

---

\ə\ abut  \°\ kitten  \ər\ further  \a\ ash  \ā\ ace
\ä\ mop, mar  \aú\ out  \ch\ chin  \e\ bet  \ē\ easy
\g\ go  \i\ hit  \ī\ ice  \j\ job  \ŋ\ sing  \ō\ go
\ò\ law  \òi\ boy  \th\ thin  \th\ the  \ü\ loot  \ú\ foot
\y\ yet  \zh\ vision  *see also* Guide to Pronunciation

**6 :** the external world in its entirety
**7 a :** humankind's original or natural condition **b :** a simplified mode of life resembling this condition
**8 :** the genetically controlled qualities of an organism
**9 :** natural scenery
**synonym** see TYPE
**na·tur·ism** \'nā-chə-,ri-zəm\ *noun* (1847)
**1 :** NATURALISM 1, 2
**2 :** the worship of the forces of nature
**3 :** NUDISM
— **na·tur·ist** \-rist\ *noun*
**na·tu·rop·a·thy** \,nā-chə-'rä-pə-thē\ *noun* (1901)
**:** a system of treatment of disease that avoids drugs and surgery and emphasizes the use of natural agents (as air, water, and sunshine) and physical means (as manipulation and electrical treatment)
— **na·tu·ro·path** \'nā-chər-ə-,path, 'na-\ *noun*
— **na·tu·ro·path·ic** \,nā-chər-ə-'pa-thik, ,na-; -nə-,tyùr-ə-, -'tùr-\ *adjective*
**Nau·ga·hyde** \'nò-gə-,hīd, 'nä-\ *trademark*
— used for vinyl-coated fabrics
**¹naught** \'nòt, 'nät\ *pronoun* [Middle English *nought,* from Old English *nāwiht,* from *nā* no + *wiht* creature, thing — more at NO, WIGHT] (before 12th century)
**:** NOTHING ⟨efforts came to *naught*⟩
**word history** see NAUGHTY
**²naught** *noun* (before 12th century)
**1 :** NOTHINGNESS, NONEXISTENCE
**2 :** the arithmetical symbol 0 : ZERO, CIPHER
**naugh·ty** \'nò-tē, 'nä-\ *adjective* **naugh·ti·er; -est** [Middle English *noughti,* from *nought*] (14th century)
**1 a** *archaic* **:** vicious in moral character **:** WICKED **b :** guilty of disobedience or misbehavior
**2 :** lacking in taste or propriety ◆
— **naugh·ti·ly** \'nò-t°l-ē, 'nä-\ *adverb*
— **naugh·ti·ness** \'nò-tē-nəs, 'nä-\ *noun*
**nau·ma·chia** \nò-'mā-kē-ə, -'ma-\ *noun, plural* **-chi·ae** \-kē-,ē, -kē-,ī\ *or* **-chi·as** [Latin, from Greek, naval battle, from *naus* ship + *machesthai* to fight — more at NAVE] (1596)
**1 :** an ancient Roman spectacle representing a naval battle
**2 :** a place for naumachiae
**nau·pli·us** \'nò-plē-əs\ *noun, plural* **-plii** \-plē-,ī, -,ē\ [New Latin, from Latin, a shellfish, from Greek *nauplios*] (1836)
**:** a crustacean larva in usually the first stage after leaving the egg and with three pairs of appendages, a median eye, and little or no segmentation
**nau·sea** \'nò-zē-ə, -sē-ə; 'nò-zhə, -shə\ *noun* [Latin, seasickness, nausea, from Greek *nautia, nausia,* from *nautēs* sailor] (1569)
**1 :** a stomach distress with distaste for food and an urge to vomit
**2 :** extreme disgust ◆
— **nau·se·ant** \-zhē-ənt, -shē-, -zē-, -sē-\ *noun or adjective*
**nau·se·ate** \'nò-zhē-,āt, -shē-, -zē-, -sē-\ *verb* **-at·ed; -at·ing** (1640)
*intransitive verb*
**1 :** to become affected with nausea
**2 :** to feel disgust
*transitive verb*
**:** to affect with nausea or disgust
**nauseating** *adjective* (1645)
**:** causing nausea or especially disgust
**usage** see NAUSEOUS
— **nau·se·at·ing·ly** *adverb*
**nau·seous** \'nò-shəs, 'nò-zē-əs\ *adjective* (1612)
**1 :** causing nausea or disgust **:** NAUSEATING
**2 :** affected with nausea or disgust ■
— **nau·seous·ly** *adverb*
— **nau·seous·ness** *noun*
**nautch** \'nòch\ *noun* [Hindi *nāc,* from Sanskrit *nṛtya,* from *nṛtyati* he dances] (1809)

**:** an entertainment in India consisting chiefly of dancing by professional dancing girls
**nau·ti·cal** \'nò-ti-kəl, 'nä-\ *adjective* [Latin *nauticus,* from Greek *nautikos,* from *nautēs* sailor, from *naus* ship — more at NAVE] (1552)
**:** of, relating to, or associated with seamen, navigation, or ships
— **nau·ti·cal·ly** \-k(ə-)lē\ *adverb*
**nautical mile** *noun* (1834)
**:** any of various units of distance used for sea and air navigation based on the length of a minute of arc of a great circle of the earth and differing because the earth is not a perfect sphere: as **a :** a British unit equal to 6080 feet (1853.2 meters) **b :** an international unit equal to 6076.115 feet (1852 meters) used officially in the U.S. since July 1, 1959
**nau·ti·loid** \'nò-t°l-,óid, 'nä-\ *noun* (circa 1847)
**:** any of a subclass (Nautiloidea) of shell-bearing cephalopods that were abundant in the Ordovician and especially the Silurian but are represented in the recent fauna only by the nautiluses
— **nautiloid** *adjective*
**nau·ti·lus** \'nò-t°l-əs, 'nä-\ *noun, plural* **-lus·es** *or* **-li** \-t°l-,ī, -,ē\ [New Latin, from Latin, paper nautilus, from Greek *nautilos,* literally, sailor, from *naus* ship] (1601)
**1 :** any of a genus (*Nautilus*) of cephalopod mollusks of the South Pacific and Indian Oceans with a spiral chambered shell that is pearly on the inside — called also *chambered nautilus*

**nautilus**

**2 :** PAPER NAUTILUS
**nav·aid** \'na-,vād\ *noun* [*navigation aid*] (1956)
**:** a device or system (as a radar beacon) that provides a navigator with navigational data
**Na·va·jo** *also* **Na·va·ho** \'na-və-,hō, 'nä-\ *noun, plural* **-jo** *or* **-jos** *also* **-ho** *or* **-hos** [Spanish (*Apache de*) *Navajó,* literally, Apache of Navajó, from *Navajó,* area occupied by Navajos, probably from Tewa (Pueblo Indian language of northern New Mexico) *navahu·,* literally, arroyo with planted fields] (1780)
**1 :** a member of an American Indian people of northern New Mexico and Arizona
**2 :** the language of the Navajo people
**na·val** \'nā-vəl\ *adjective* [Middle English, from Latin *navalis,* from *navis* ship] (15th century)
**1** *obsolete* **:** of or relating to ships or shipping
**2 a :** of or relating to a navy **b :** consisting of or involving warships
**naval architect** *noun* (circa 1885)
**:** one who designs ships
**naval stores** *noun plural* [from their former use in the construction and maintenance of wooden sailing vessels] (1678)
**:** products (as turpentine, pitch, and rosin) obtained from resinous conifers and especially pines
**¹nave** \'nāv\ *noun* [Middle English, from Old English *nafu;* akin to Old English *nafela* navel] (before 12th century)
**:** the hub of a wheel
**²nave** *noun* [Medieval Latin *navis,* from Latin, ship; akin to Old English *nōwend* sailor, Greek *naus* ship, Sanskrit *nau*] (1673)
**:** the main part of the interior of a church; *especially* **:** the long narrow central hall in a cruciform church that rises higher than the aisles flanking it to form a clerestory
**na·vel** \'nā-vəl\ *noun* [Middle English, from Old English *nafela;* akin to Old High German *nabalo* navel, Latin *umbilicus,* Greek *omphalos*] (before 12th century)

**1 :** a depression in the middle of the abdomen that marks the point of former attachment of the umbilical cord or yolk stalk
**2 :** the central point **:** MIDDLE
**navel orange** *noun* (1888)
**:** a seedless orange having a pit at the apex where the fruit encloses a small secondary fruit — called also *navel*
**¹na·vic·u·lar** \nə-'vi-kyə-lər\ *adjective* [Middle English *naviculare,* from Latin *navicula* boat, diminutive of *navis*] (15th century)
**1 :** shaped like a boat ⟨a *navicular* bone⟩
**2 :** of, relating to, or involving a navicular bone ⟨*navicular* disease⟩
**²navicular** *noun* [New Latin (*os*) *naviculare* navicular bone] (1816)
**:** a navicular bone; *especially* **:** one situated on the big-toe side of the tarsus

**nav·i·ga·ble** \'na-vi-gə-bəl\ *adjective* (15th century)
**1 :** deep enough and wide enough to afford passage to ships
**2 :** capable of being steered
— **nav·i·ga·bil·i·ty** \,na-vi-gə-'bi-lə-tē\ *noun*
— **nav·i·ga·bly** \'na-vi-gə-blē\ *adverb*

**nav·i·gate** \'na-və-,gāt\ *verb* **-gat·ed; -gat·ing** [Latin *navigatus,* past participle of *navigare,* from *navis* ship + *-igare* (from *agere* to drive) — more at AGENT] (1588)
*intransitive verb*
**1 :** to travel by water **:** SAIL
**2 :** to steer a course through a medium; *specifically* **:** to operate an airplane
**3 :** GET AROUND, MOVE
*transitive verb*
**1 a :** to sail over, on, or through **b :** to make one's way over or through **:** TRAVERSE
**2 a :** to steer or manage (a boat) in sailing **b :** to operate or control the course of (as an airplane)

**nav·i·ga·tion** \,na-və-'gā-shən\ *noun* (1547)
**1 :** the act or practice of navigating
**2 :** the science of getting ships, aircraft, or spacecraft from place to place; *especially* **:** the method of determining position, course, and distance traveled
**3 :** ship traffic or commerce
— **nav·i·ga·tion·al** \-shnəl, -shə-n°l\ *adjective*
— **nav·i·ga·tion·al·ly** *adverb*

**nav·i·ga·tor** \'na-və-,gā-tər\ *noun* (1590)
**:** one that navigates or is qualified to navigate

**nav·vy** \'na-vē\ *noun, plural* **navvies** [by shortening & alteration from *navigator* construction worker on a canal] (circa 1834)
*chiefly British* **:** an unskilled laborer

**na·vy** \'nā-vē\ *noun, plural* **navies** [Middle English *navie,* from Middle French, from Latin *navigia* ships, from *navigare*] (14th century)
**1 :** a group of ships **:** FLEET
**2 :** a nation's ships of war and of logistic support
**3** *often capitalized* **:** the complete naval establishment of a nation including yards, stations, ships, and personnel
**4 :** a dark grayish purplish blue

**navy bean** *noun* (1856)
**:** a white-seeded kidney bean grown especially for its nutritious seeds

**Navy Cross** *noun* (1919)
**:** a U.S. Navy decoration awarded for extraordinary heroism in operations against an armed enemy

**navy yard** *noun* (1771)
**:** a yard where naval vessels are built or repaired

**na·wab** \nə-'wäb\ *noun* [Urdu *nawwāb*] (1758)
**:** NABOB

¹**nay** \'nā\ *adverb* [Middle English, from Old Norse *nei,* from *ne* not + *ei* ever — more at NO, AYE] (13th century)
**:** NO

²**nay** *noun* (14th century)
**1 :** DENIAL, REFUSAL
**2 a :** a negative reply or vote **b :** one who votes no

³**nay** *conjunction* (1560)
**:** not merely this but also **:** not only so but 〈the letter made him happy, *nay,* ecstatic〉

**nay·say·er** \'nā-,sā-ər, -,se(-ə)r\ *noun* (1721)
**:** one who denies, refuses, opposes, or is skeptical or cynical about something
— **nay·say·ing** \-,sā-iŋ\ *noun*

**Naz·a·rene** \,na-zə-'rēn\ *noun* [Middle English *Nazaren,* from Late Latin *Nazarenus,* from Greek *Nazarēnos,* from *Nazareth* Nazareth, Palestine] (13th century)
**1 :** a native or resident of Nazareth
**2 a :** CHRISTIAN 1a **b :** a member of the Church of the Nazarene that is a Protestant denomination deriving from the merging of three holi-

ness groups, stressing sanctification, and following Methodist polity

**Na·zi** \'nät-sē, 'nat-\ *noun* [German, by shortening & alteration from *Nationalsozialist,* from *national* national + *Sozialist* socialist] (1930)
**1 :** a member of a German fascist party controlling Germany from 1933 to 1945 under Adolf Hitler
**2** *often not capitalized* **:** one who resembles a German Nazi
— **nazi** *adjective, often capitalized*
— **na·zi·fi·ca·tion** \,nät-si-fə-'kā-shən, ,nat-\ *noun, often capitalized*
— **na·zi·fy** \'nät-si-,fī, 'nat-\ *transitive verb, often capitalized*

**Naz·i·rite** *or* **Naz·a·rite** \'na-zə-,rīt\ *noun* [Late Latin *nazaraeus,* from Greek *naziraios, nazaraios,* from Hebrew *nāzīr,* literally, consecrated] (1560)
**:** a Jew of biblical times consecrated to God by a vow to avoid drinking wine, cutting the hair, and being defiled by the presence of a corpse
— **Naz·i·rit·ism** \-,rī-,ti-zəm\ *noun*

**Na·zism** \'nät-,si-zəm, 'nat-\ *or* **Na·zi·ism** \-sē-,i-zəm\ *noun* [*Nazi* + *-ism*] (1934)
**:** the body of political and economic doctrines held and put into effect by the National Socialist German Workers' party in the Third German Reich including the totalitarian principle of government, state control of all industry, predominance of groups assumed to be racially superior, and supremacy of the führer

**NCO** \,en-(,)sē-'ō\ *noun* (circa 1810)
**:** NONCOMMISSIONED OFFICER

**NC-17** \'en-'sē-,se-vən-'tēn\ *certification mark*
— used to certify that a motion picture is of such a nature that no one under the age of 17 can be admitted; compare G, PG, PG-13, R

**-nd** *symbol*
— used after the figure 2 to indicate the ordinal number *second* 〈2nd〉 〈72nd〉

**né** \'nā\ *adjective* [French, literally, born — more at NÉE] (1905)
**1** — used to indicate the original, former, or legal name of a man 〈Robert Roe, *né* John Doe〉
**2 :** originally or formerly called

**ne-** *or* **neo-** *combining form* [Greek, from *neos* new — more at NEW]
**1 a :** new **:** recent 〈*Neo*gene〉 **b :** new and different period or form of 〈*Neo*platonism〉 **:** in a new and different form or manner 〈*Neo*platonic〉 **c :** New World 〈*Neo*tropical〉 **d :** new and abnormal 〈*neo*plasm〉
**2 :** new chemical compound isomeric with or otherwise related to (such) a compound 〈*neo*stigmine〉

**Ne·an·der·thal** \nē-'an-dər-,tól, -,thól; nā-'än-dər-,täl\ *adjective* (1861)
**1** *also* **Ne·an·der·tal** \-,tól, -,täl\ **:** being, relating to, or resembling Neanderthal man
**2 :** suggesting a caveman in appearance, mentality, or behavior
— **Neanderthal** *noun*

**Neanderthal man** *noun* [*Neanderthal,* valley in western Germany] (1863)
**:** a Middle Paleolithic hominid (*Homo sapiens neanderthalensis*) known from skeletal remains in Europe, northern Africa, and western Asia
— **Ne·an·der·thal·oid** \-,tó-,lóid, -,thó-, -,tä-\ *adjective or noun*

¹**neap** \'nēp\ *adjective* [Middle English *neep,* from Old English *nēp* being at the stage of neap tide] (before 12th century)
**:** of, relating to, or constituting a neap tide

²**neap** *noun* (1584)
**:** NEAP TIDE

**Ne·a·pol·i·tan** \,nē-ə-'pä-lə-t°n\ *noun* [Middle English, from Latin *neapolitanus* of Naples, from Greek *neapolitēs* citizen of Naples, from *Neapolis* Naples] (15th century)
**:** a native or inhabitant of Naples, Italy
— **Neapolitan** *adjective*

**Neapolitan ice cream** *noun* (1895)

**:** a brick of from two to four layers of ice cream of different flavors

**neap tide** *noun* (circa 1548)
**:** a tide of minimum range occurring at the first and the third quarters of the moon

¹**near** \'nir\ *adverb* [Middle English *ner,* partly from *ner* nearer, from Old English *nēar,* comparative of *nēah* nigh; partly from Old Norse *nær* nearer, comparative of *nā-* nigh — more at NIGH] (13th century)
**1 :** at, within, or to a short distance or time
**2 :** ALMOST, NEARLY 〈*near* dead〉
**3 :** in a close or intimate manner **:** CLOSELY 〈*near* related〉
**4** *archaic* **:** in a frugal manner

²**near** *preposition* (13th century)
**:** close to

³**near** *adjective* (14th century)
**1 a :** not far distant in time, place, or degree 〈in the *near* future〉 **b :** almost happening **:** narrowly missed or avoided 〈a *near* win in the primary〉 〈a *near* midair collision〉 **c :** nearly not happening 〈a *near* escape〉
**2 :** closely related or intimately associated
**3 a :** being the closer of two 〈the *near* side〉 **b :** being the left-hand one of a pair 〈the *near* wheel of a cart〉
**4 :** DIRECT, SHORT 〈the *nearest* road〉
**5 :** STINGY, CLOSEFISTED
**6 a :** closely resembling the standard or typical 〈a *near* desert〉 **b :** approximating the genuine 〈*near* silk〉
— **near·ness** *noun*

⁴**near** *verb* (1513)
**:** APPROACH

**near beer** *noun* (1909)
**:** any of various malt liquors considered nonalcoholic because they contain less than a specified percentage of alcohol

**near·by** \nir-'bī, 'nir-,\ *adverb or adjective* (14th century)
**:** close at hand

**Ne·arc·tic** \nē-'ärk-tik, -'är-tik\ *adjective* (1858)
**:** of, relating to, or being the biogeographic subregion that includes Greenland and North America north of tropical Mexico

**near gale** *noun* (circa 1975)
**:** MODERATE GALE — see BEAUFORT SCALE table

**near–in·fra·red** \,nir-,in-frə-'red, -(,)frä-\ *adjective* (1950)
**:** of or relating to the shorter wavelengths of radiation in the infrared spectrum and especially to those between 0.7 and 2.5 micrometers

**near·ly** \'nir-lē\ *adverb* (1561)
**1 :** in a close manner or relationship 〈*nearly* related〉
**2 a :** almost but not quite 〈*nearly* identical〉 〈*nearly* a year later〉 **b :** to the least extent 〈not *nearly* as good as we expected〉

**near miss** *noun* (1940)
**1 a :** a miss (as with a bomb) close enough to cause damage **b :** something that falls just short of success
**2 a :** a near collision (as between aircraft) **b :** CLOSE CALL

**near money** *noun* (1942)
**:** assets (as savings accounts or government bonds) quickly and easily converted to cash

**near point** *noun* (1876)
**:** the point nearest the eye at which an object is accurately focused on the retina at full accommodation

**near·shore** \'nir-'shōr, -'shòr, 'nir-,\ *adjective* (1896)
**:** extending outward an indefinite but usually short distance from shore 〈*nearshore* sediments〉

\ə\ abut \ª\ kitten \ər\ further \a\ ash \ā\ ace
\ä\ mop, mar \aů\ out \ch\ chin \e\ bet \ē\ easy
\g\ go \i\ hit \ī\ ice \j\ job \ŋ\ sing \ō\ go
\ȯ\ law \ȯi\ boy \th\ thin \th\ the \ü\ loot \ů\ foot
\y\ yet \zh\ vision *see also* Guide to Pronunciation

**near·side** \-ˌsīd\ *adjective* (circa 1840)
*British* : LEFT-HAND 1
— **nearside** *noun*

**near·sight·ed** \-ˈsī-təd\ *adjective* (1686)
: able to see near things more clearly than distant ones : MYOPIC
— **near·sight·ed·ly** *adverb*
— **near·sight·ed·ness** *noun*

**near–ul·tra·vi·o·let** \ˌnir-ˌəl-trə-ˈvī-(ə-)lət\ *adjective* (1951)
: of, relating to, or being the longest wavelengths of radiation especially between 300 and 400 nanometers

**¹neat** \ˈnēt\ *noun, plural* **neat** *or* **neats** [Middle English *neet*, from Old English *nēat*; akin to Old High German *nōz* head of cattle, Old English *nēotan* to make use of, Lithuanian *nauda* use] (before 12th century)
: the common domestic bovine (*Bos taurus*)

**²neat** *adjective* [Middle French *net*, from Latin *nitidus* bright, neat, from *nitēre* to shine; probably akin to Middle Irish *níam* luster] (1542)
**1** : free from dirt and disorder : habitually clean and orderly
**2 a** : free from admixture or dilution : STRAIGHT ⟨*neat* brandy⟩ ⟨*neat* cement⟩ **b** : free from irregularity : SMOOTH ⟨*neat* silk⟩
**3** : marked by tasteful simplicity ⟨a *neat* outfit⟩
**4 a** : PRECISE, SYSTEMATIC **b** : marked by skill or ingenuity : ADROIT
**5** : NET ⟨*neat* profit⟩
**6** : FINE, ADMIRABLE
— **neat·ly** *adverb*
— **neat·ness** *noun*

**³neat** *adverb* (1649)
: without admixture or dilution : STRAIGHT

**neat·en** \ˈnē-tᵊn\ *transitive verb* **neat·ened; neat·en·ing** \ˈnēt-niŋ, ˈnē-tᵊn-iŋ\ (1898)
**1** : to set in order : make neat
**2** : to finish (as a piece of sewing) carefully

**neath** \ˈnēth\ *preposition* (1787)
*dialect* : BENEATH

**neat·herd** \ˈnēt-ˌhərd\ *noun* (14th century)
: HERDSMAN

**neat's–foot oil** \ˈnēts-ˌfut-\ *noun* (1787)
: a pale yellow fatty oil made especially from the bones of cattle and used chiefly as a leather dressing

**neb** \ˈneb\ *noun* [Middle English, from Old English; akin to Old Norse *nef* beak] (before 12th century)
**1 a** : the beak of a bird or tortoise : BILL **b** *chiefly dialect* : a person's mouth **c** : NOSE 1, SNOUT
**2** : NIB, TIP

**neb·bish** \ˈne-bish\ *noun* [Yiddish *nebekh* poor, unfortunate, from Czech *nebohý* ] (1951)
: a timid, meek, or ineffectual person
— **neb·bishy** \-bi-shē\ *adjective*

**ne·ben·kern** \ˈnā-bən-ˌkərn, -ˌkern\ *noun* [German, literally, subsidiary nucleus] (1898)
: a 2-stranded helical structure of the proximal tail region of a spermatozoon that is derived from mitochondria

**neb·u·la** \ˈne-byə-lə\ *noun, plural* **-lae** \-ˌlē, -ˌlī\ *also* **-las** [New Latin, from Latin, mist, cloud; akin to Old High German *nebul* fog, Greek *nephelē, nephos* cloud] (circa 1738)
**1** : any of numerous clouds of gas or dust in interstellar space
**2** : GALAXY; *especially* : a galaxy other than the Milky Way galaxy — not used technically
— **neb·u·lar** \-lər\ *adjective*

**nebular hypothesis** *noun* (1837)
: a hypothesis in astronomy: the solar system has evolved from a hot gaseous nebula

**neb·u·lize** \ˈne-byə-ˌlīz\ *transitive verb* **-lized; -liz·ing** [Latin *nebula*] (1872)
: to reduce to a fine spray
— **neb·u·li·za·tion** \ˌne-byə-lə-ˈzā-shən\ *noun*
— **neb·u·liz·er** \ˈne-byə-ˌlī-zər\ *noun*

**neb·u·los·i·ty** \ˌne-byə-ˈlä-sə-tē\ *noun, plural* **-ties** (1761)
**1** : the quality or state of being nebulous
**2** : nebulous matter; *also* : NEBULA 1

**neb·u·lous** \ˈne-byə-ləs\ *adjective* [Latin *nebulosus* misty, from *nebula*] (1784)
**1** : of, relating to, or resembling a nebula : NEBULAR
**2** : INDISTINCT, VAGUE
— **neb·u·lous·ly** *adverb*
— **neb·u·lous·ness** *noun*

**nec·es·sar·i·ly** \ˌne-sə-ˈser-ə-lē\ *adverb* (15th century)
**1** : of necessity : UNAVOIDABLY
**2** : as a logical result or consequence

**¹nec·es·sary** \ˈne-sə-ˌser-ē\ *adjective* [Middle English *necessarie*, from Latin *necessarius*, from *necesse* necessary, probably from *ne-* not + *cedere* to withdraw — more at NO] (14th century)
**1 a** : of an inevitable nature : INESCAPABLE **b** (1) : logically unavoidable (2) : that cannot be denied without contradiction **c** : determined or produced by the previous condition of things **d** : COMPULSORY
**2** : absolutely needed : REQUIRED

**²necessary** *noun, plural* **-sar·ies** (14th century)
: an indispensable item : ESSENTIAL

**necessary condition** *noun* (1817)
**1** : a proposition whose falsity assures the falsity of another
**2** : a state of affairs that must prevail if another is to occur : PREREQUISITE

**ne·ces·si·tar·i·an·ism** \ni-ˌse-sə-ˈter-ē-ə-ˌni-zəm\ *noun* (1854)
: the theory that results follow by invariable sequence from causes
— **ne·ces·si·tar·i·an** \-ˈter-ē-ən\ *adjective or noun*

**ne·ces·si·tate** \ni-ˈse-sə-ˌtāt\ *transitive verb* **-tat·ed; -tat·ing** (1628)
**1** : to make necessary : REQUIRE
**2** : FORCE, COMPEL
— **ne·ces·si·ta·tion** \-ˌse-sə-ˈtā-shən\ *noun*

**ne·ces·si·tous** \ni-ˈse-sə-təs\ *adjective* (1611)
**1** : NEEDY, IMPOVERISHED
**2** : URGENT, PRESSING
**3** : NECESSARY
— **ne·ces·si·tous·ly** *adverb*
— **ne·ces·si·tous·ness** *noun*

**ne·ces·si·ty** \ni-ˈse-sə-tē, -ˈses-tē\ *noun, plural* **-ties** [Middle English *necessite*, from Middle French *necessité*, from Latin *necessitat-, necessitas*, from *necesse*] (14th century)
**1** : the quality or state of being necessary
**2 a** : pressure of circumstance **b** : physical or moral compulsion **c** : impossibility of a contrary order or condition
**3** : the quality or state of being in need; *especially* : POVERTY
**4 a** : something that is necessary : REQUIREMENT **b** : an urgent need or desire
— **of necessity** : in such a way that it cannot be otherwise; *also* : as a necessary consequence

**¹neck** \ˈnek\ *noun* [Middle English *nekke*, from Old English *hnecca*; akin to Old High German *hnac* nape] (before 12th century)
**1 a** (1) : the part of an animal that connects the head with the body (2) : the siphon of a bivalve mollusk (as a clam) **b** : the part of a garment that covers or is next to the neck
**2** : a relatively narrow part suggestive of a neck: as **a** (1) : the constricted end of a bottle (2) : the slender proximal end of a fruit **b** : CERVIX 2 **c** : the part of a stringed musical instrument extending from the body and supporting the fingerboard and strings **d** : a narrow stretch of land : STRAIT 1b **f** : the part of a tooth between the crown and the root — see TOOTH illustration **g** : a column of solidified magma of a volcanic pipe or laccolith
**3** : a narrow margin ⟨won by a *neck*⟩
**4** : REGION, PART ⟨my *neck* of the woods⟩

**²neck** (1842)
*transitive verb*
**1** : to kiss and caress amorously
**2** : to reduce in diameter
*intransitive verb*
**1** : to engage in amorous kissing and caressing
**2** : to become constricted : NARROW

**neck and neck** *adverb or adjective* (1799)
: very close (as in a race)

**necked** \ˈnekt\ *adjective* (14th century)
: having a neck especially of a specified kind
— often used in combination ⟨long-*necked*⟩

**neck·er·chief** \ˈne-kər-chəf, -(ˌ)chif, -ˌchēf\ *noun, plural* **-chiefs** *also* **-chieves** \see HANDKERCHIEF plural\ [Middle English *nekkerchef*, from *nekke* + *kerchef* kerchief] (14th century)
: a kerchief for the neck

**neck·ing** \ˈne-kiŋ\ *noun* (1804)
**1** : a narrow molding near the top of a column or pilaster
**2** : the act or practice of kissing and caressing amorously

**neck·lace** \ˈne-kləs\ *noun* (circa 1590)
: an ornament worn around the neck

**neck·line** \ˈnek-ˌlīn\ *noun* (1904)
: the line of the neck opening of a garment

**neck–rein** \-ˌrān\ *noun* (1940)
*intransitive verb*
*of a saddle horse* : to respond to the pressure of a rein on one side of the neck by turning in the opposite direction
*transitive verb*
: to direct (a horse) by pressures of the rein on the neck

**neck·tie** \-ˌtī\ *noun* (1838)
: a narrow length of material worn about the neck and tied in front; *especially* : FOUR-IN-HAND

**neck·wear** \-ˌwar, -ˌwer\ *noun* (circa 1879)
: articles of clothing (as ties and scarves) worn about the neck

**necr-** *or* **necro-** *combining form* [Late Latin, from Greek *nekr-, nekro-*, from *nekros* dead body — more at NOXIOUS]
**1** : those that are dead ⟨*necrophilia*⟩
**2** : one that is dead ⟨*necropsy*⟩

**ne·crol·o·gy** \nə-ˈkrä-lə-jē, ne-\ *noun, plural* **-gies** [New Latin *necrologium*, from *necr-* + *-logium* (as in Medieval Latin *eulogium* eulogy)] (1799)
**1** : OBITUARY
**2** : a list of the recently dead
— **nec·ro·log·i·cal** \ˌne-krə-ˈlä-ji-kəl\ *adjective*
— **ne·crol·o·gist** \nə-ˈkrä-lə-jist, ne-\ *noun*

**nec·ro·man·cy** \ˈne-krə-ˌman(t)-sē\ *noun* [alteration of Middle English *nigromancie*, from Middle French, from Medieval Latin *nigromantia*, by folk etymology from Late Latin *necromantia*, from Late Greek *nekromanteia*, from Greek *nekr-* + *-manteia* -mancy] (1522)
**1** : conjuration of the spirits of the dead for purposes of magically revealing the future or influencing the course of events
**2** : MAGIC, SORCERY
— **nec·ro·man·cer** \-sər\ *noun*
— **nec·ro·man·tic** \ˌne-krə-ˈman-tik\ *adjective*
— **nec·ro·man·ti·cal·ly** \-ti-k(ə-)lē\ *adverb*

**ne·croph·a·gous** \nə-ˈkrä-fə-gəs, ne-\ *adjective* (1835)
: feeding on corpses or carrion ⟨*necrophagous* insects⟩

**nec·ro·phil·ia** \ˌne-krə-ˈfi-lē-ə\ *noun* [New Latin] (1892)
: obsession with and usually erotic interest in or stimulation by corpses
— **nec·ro·phil·i·ac** \-ˈfi-lē-ˌak\ *adjective or noun*
— **nec·ro·phil·ic** \-ˈfi-lik\ *adjective*

**ne·croph·i·lism** \nə-ˈkrä-fə-ˌli-zəm, ne-\ *noun* (1864)
: NECROPHILIA

**ne·crop·o·lis** \nə-'krä-pə-ləs, ne-\ *noun, plural* **-lis·es** *or* **-les** \-ləz\ *or* **-leis** \-ləs\ *or* **-li** \-,lī, -,lē\ [Late Latin, city of the dead, from Greek *nekropolis*, from *nekr*- + -*polis* -polis] (1819)
: CEMETERY; *especially* : a large elaborate cemetery of an ancient city

**¹nec·rop·sy** \'ne-,kräp-sē\ *noun, plural* **-sies** (1856)
: AUTOPSY 1

**²necropsy** *transitive verb* **-sied; -sy·ing** (1927)
: to perform an autopsy on

**ne·cro·sis** \nə-'krō-səs, ne-\ *noun, plural* **ne·cro·ses** \-,sēz\ [Late Latin, from Greek *nekrōsis*, from *nekroun* to make dead, from *nekros* dead body] (1665)
: usually localized death of living tissue
— **ne·crot·ic** \-'krä-tik\ *adjective*

**nec·ro·tiz·ing** \'ne-krə-,tī-ziŋ\ *adjective* [Greek *nekrōtikos* necrotic, from *nekroun*] (1899)
: causing, associated with, or undergoing necrosis ⟨*necrotizing* infections⟩ ⟨*necrotizing* tissue⟩

**nec·tar** \'nek-tər\ *noun* [Latin, from Greek *nektar*]
**1 a** : the drink of the Greek and Roman gods **b** : something delicious to drink **c** : a beverage of fruit juice and pulp ⟨apricot *nectar*⟩
**2** : a sweet liquid that is secreted by the nectaries of a plant and is the chief raw material of honey
— **nec·tar·ous** \-t(ə-)rəs\ *adjective*

**nec·tar·ine** \,nek-tə-'rēn\ *noun* [obsolete *nectarine*, adjective, like nectar] (1611)
: a peach with a smooth-skinned fruit that is a frequent somatic mutation of the normal peach; *also* : its fruit

**nec·tary** \'nek-t(ə-)rē\ *noun, plural* **-tar·ies** [New Latin *nectarium*, irregular from Latin *nectar* + -*arium* -ary] (1759)
: a plant gland that secretes nectar

**née** *or* **nee** \'nā\ *adjective* [French *née*, feminine of *né*, literally, born, past participle of *naître* to be born, from Latin *nasci* — more at NATION] (1758)
**1** — used to identify a woman by her maiden family name
**2** : originally or formerly called ⟨the Brewers *née* Pilots who also are in their third year —Fred Ciampa⟩

**¹need** \'nēd\ *noun* [Middle English *ned*, from Old English *nīed*, *nēd*; akin to Old High German *nōt* distress, need, Old Prussian *nautin* need] (before 12th century)
**1** : necessary duty : OBLIGATION
**2 a** : a lack of something requisite, desirable, or useful **b** : a physiological or psychological requirement for the well-being of an organism
**3** : a condition requiring supply or relief
**4** : lack of the means of subsistence : POVERTY

**²need** *verb* **need·ed; need·ing; needs** *or* (*auxiliary*) **need** (before 12th century)
*intransitive verb*
**1** : to be needful or necessary
**2** : to be in want
*transitive verb*
: to be in need of : REQUIRE
*verbal auxiliary*
: be under necessity or obligation to ⟨you *need* not answer⟩ ■

**¹need·ful** \'nēd-fəl\ *adjective* (12th century)
**1** : being in need
**2** : NECESSARY, REQUISITE
— **need·ful·ly** \-fə-lē\ *adverb*
— **need·ful·ness** *noun*

**²needful** *noun* (1709)
**1** : something needed or requisite
**2** : MONEY

**¹nee·dle** \'nē-dᵊl\ *noun* [Middle English *nedle*, from Old English *nǣdl*; akin to Old High German *nādala* needle, *nājan* to sew, Latin *nēre* to spin, Greek *nēn*] (before 12th century)
**1 a** : a small slender usually steel instrument that has an eye for thread or surgical sutures at

one end and that is used for sewing **b** : any of various devices for carrying thread and making stitches (as in crocheting or knitting) **c** (1) : a slender hollow instrument for introducing material into or removing material from the body parenterally (2) : any of various slender hollow devices used to introduce matter (as air) into or remove it from an object (as a ball)
**2 a** : a slender bar of magnetized steel that when allowed to turn freely (as in a compass) indicates the direction of a magnetic field (as of the earth) **b** : a slender usually sharp-pointed indicator on a dial
**3 a** : a slender pointed object resembling a needle: as (1) : a pointed crystal (2) : a sharp rock (3) : OBELISK **b** : a needle-shaped leaf (as of a conifer) **c** : a slender rod (as of jewel or steel) with a rounded tip used in a phonograph to transmit vibrations from a record : STYLUS **d** : a slender pointed rod controlling a fine inlet or outlet (as in a valve)
**4** : a teasing or gibing remark
— **nee·dle·like** \'nē-dᵊl-,(l)īk\ *adjective*

**²needle** *verb* **nee·dled; nee·dling** \'nēd-liŋ, 'nē-dᵊl-iŋ\ (circa 1715)
*transitive verb*
**1** : to sew or pierce with or as if with a needle
**2 a** : TEASE, TORMENT **b** : to incite to action by repeated gibes ⟨*needled* the boy into a fight⟩
*intransitive verb*
: SEW, EMBROIDER
— **nee·dler** \'nēd-lər, 'nē-dᵊl-ər\ *noun*

**nee·dle·fish** \'nē-dᵊl-,fish\ *noun* (1601)
**1** : any of a family (Belonidae) of elongate green and silvery chiefly marine bony fishes with long slender jaws
**2** : PIPEFISH

**needlefish 1**

**nee·dle·point** \-,point\ *noun* (1865)
**1** : lace worked with a needle over a paper pattern
**2** : embroidery done on canvas usually in simple even stitches across counted threads
— **needlepoint** *adjective*

**need·less** \'nēd-ləs\ *adjective* (14th century)
: not needed : UNNECESSARY ⟨*needless* waste⟩ ⟨*needless* to say⟩
— **need·less·ly** *adverb*
— **need·less·ness** *noun*

**nee·dle·wom·an** \'nē-dᵊl-,wu̇-mən\ *noun* (1535)
: a woman who does needlework; *especially* : SEAMSTRESS

**nee·dle·work** \-,wərk\ *noun* (14th century)
**1** : work done with a needle; *especially* : work (as embroidery) other than plain sewing
**2** : the occupation of one who does needlework
— **nee·dle·work·er** \-,wər-kər\ *noun*

**needn't** \'nē-dᵊnt\ (1865)
: need not

**needs** \'nēdz\ *adverb* [Middle English *nedes*, from Old English *nēdes*, from genitive of *nēd* need] (before 12th century)
: of necessity : NECESSARILY ⟨must *needs* be recognized⟩

**needy** \'nē-dē\ *adjective* **need·i·er; -est** (12th century)
: being in want : POVERTY-STRICKEN ⟨*needy* families⟩
— **need·i·ness** *noun*

**neem** \'nēm\ *noun* [Hindi *nīm*, from Sanskrit *nimba*] (1813)
: a large East Indian tree (*Azadirachta indica* of the family Meliaceae) whose trunk exudes a tenacious gum and has a bitter bark used as a tonic and whose fruit and seeds yield a medicinal aromatic oil

**neep** \'nēp\ *noun* [Middle English *nepe*, from Old English *nǣp*, from Latin *napus* — more at NAPIFORM] (before 12th century)
*chiefly Scottish* : TURNIP

**ne'er** \'nar, 'ner\ *adverb* (13th century)
: NEVER

**ne'er-do-well** \-dü-,wel\ *noun* (1736)
: an idle worthless person
— **ne'er-do-well** *adjective*

**ne·far·i·ous** \ni-'far-ē-əs, -'fer-\ *adjective* [Latin *nefarius*, from *nefas* crime, from *ne-* not + *fas* right, divine law; perhaps akin to Greek *themis* law, *tithenai* to place — more at DO] (circa 1609)
: flagrantly wicked or impious : EVIL
**synonym** see VICIOUS
— **ne·far·i·ous·ly** *adverb*

**ne·gate** \ni-'gāt\ *transitive verb* **ne·gat·ed; ne·gat·ing** [Latin *negatus*, past participle of *negare* to say no, deny, from *neg*- no, not (akin to *ne-* not) — more at NO] (circa 1623)
**1** : to deny the existence or truth of
**2** : to cause to be ineffective or invalid
**synonym** see NULLIFY
— **negate** *noun*
— **ne·ga·tor** \-'gā-tər\ *noun*

**ne·ga·tion** \ni-'gā-shən\ *noun* (15th century)
**1 a** : the action or logical operation of negating or making negative **b** : a negative statement, judgment, or doctrine; *especially* : a logical proposition formed by asserting the falsity of a given proposition
**2 a** : something that is the absence of something actual : NONENTITY **b** : something considered the opposite of something regarded as positive
— **ne·ga·tion·al** \-shnəl, -shə-nᵊl\ *adjective*

**¹neg·a·tive** \'ne-gə-tiv\ *adjective* (15th century)
**1 a** : marked by denial, prohibition, or refusal ⟨received a *negative* answer⟩; *also* : marked by absence, withholding, or removal of something positive ⟨the *negative* motivation of shame —Garrett Hardin⟩ **b** (1) : denying a predicate of a subject or a part of a subject ⟨"no A is B" is a *negative* proposition⟩ (2) : denoting the absence or the contradictory of something ⟨*nontoxic* is a *negative* term⟩ (3) : expressing negation ⟨*negative* particles such as *no* and *not*⟩ **c** : ADVERSE, UNFAVORABLE ⟨the reviews were mostly *negative*⟩
**2 a** : lacking positive qualities; *especially* : DISAGREEABLE **b** : marked by features of hostility, withdrawal, or pessimism that hinder or oppose constructive treatment or development ⟨a *negative* outlook⟩ ⟨*negative* criticism⟩

---

□ USAGE
**need**   Those who live in western Pennsylvania, central Ohio, Tennessee, or southeastern Colorado—somewhere in the area known as Midland to linguistic geographers—may have heard a curious idiom in which *need* is followed directly by a past participle, as in "the house needs painted," where the more widely used version would be "the house needs painting" or "the house needs to be painted." The idiom appears to be limited to the Midland area and, as far as we know now, is used almost exclusively in speech. A few people have told us that they have seen it in newspapers, but we have no printed evidence. One dictionary edited in England mentions the construction but says only that it is "widely disliked," which does not tell us much about possible dialectal restrictions. We do know that the construction exists in Scottish English, and it may be that the construction came from Scotland to this country. But 19th century use is only conjectural, so we cannot be sure.

---

**3 a** (1) **:** less than zero and opposite in sign to a positive number that when added to the given number yields zero ⟨−2 is a *negative* number⟩ (2) **:** having more outgo than income **:** constituting a loss ⟨*negative* cash flow⟩ ⟨*negative* worth⟩ **b :** extending or generated in a direction opposite to an arbitrarily chosen regular direction or position ⟨*negative* angle⟩
**4 a :** being, relating to, or charged with electricity of which the electron is the elementary unit **b :** having more electrons than protons ⟨a *negative* ion⟩ **c** (1) **:** having lower electric potential and constituting the part toward which the current flows from the external circuit ⟨the *negative* pole⟩ (2) **:** being the electron-emitting electrode of an electron tube
**5 a :** not affirming the presence of the organism or condition in question ⟨a *negative* TB test⟩ **b :** directed or moving away from a source of stimulation ⟨*negative* tropism⟩ **c :** less than the pressure of the atmosphere ⟨*negative* pressure⟩
**6 :** having the light and dark parts in approximately inverse order to those of the original photographic subject
**7** *of a lens* **:** diverging light rays and forming a virtual inverted image
— **neg·a·tive·ly** *adverb*
— **neg·a·tive·ness** *noun*
— **neg·a·tiv·i·ty** \ˌne-gə-'ti-və-tē\ *noun*

²**negative** *noun* (1571)
**1 a** (1) **:** a reply that indicates the withholding of assent **:** REFUSAL (2) *archaic* **:** a right of veto (3) *obsolete* **:** an adverse vote **:** VETO **b :** a proposition which denies or contradicts another; *especially* **:** the one of a pair of propositions in which negation is expressed
**2 a :** something that is the opposite or negation of something else **b :** DRAWBACK, LIABILITY
**3 a :** an expression (as the word *no*) of negation or denial **b :** a negative number
**4 :** the side that upholds the contradictory proposition in a debate
**5 :** a negative photographic image on transparent material used for printing positive pictures; *also* **:** the material that carries such an image
**6 :** a reverse impression taken from a piece of sculpture or ceramics

³**negative** *transitive verb* **-tived; -tiv·ing** (1706)
**1 a :** to refuse assent to **b :** to reject by or as if by a vote
**2 :** to demonstrate the falsity of
**3 :** to deny the truth, reality, or validity of
**4 :** NEUTRALIZE, COUNTERACT

**negative feedback** *noun* (1934)
**:** feedback that tends to stabilize a process by reducing its rate or output when its effects are too great

**negative income tax** *noun* (1966)
**:** a system of federal subsidy payments to families with incomes below a stipulated level

**negative transfer** *noun* (1921)
**:** the impeding of learning or performance in a situation by the carry-over of learned responses from another situation

**neg·a·tiv·ism** \'ne-gə-ti-ˌvi-zəm\ *noun* (1824)
**1 :** an attitude of mind marked by skepticism especially about nearly everything affirmed by others
**2 :** a tendency to refuse to do, to do the opposite of, or to do something at variance with what is asked
— **neg·a·tiv·ist** \-vist\ *noun or adjective*
— **neg·a·tiv·is·tic** \ˌne-gə-ti-'vis-tik\ *adjective*

¹**ne·glect** \ni-'glekt\ *transitive verb* [Latin *neglectus,* past participle of *neglegere, neclegere,* from *nec-* not (akin to *ne-* not) + *legere* to gather — more at NO, LEGEND] (1529)
**1 :** to give little attention or respect to **:** DISREGARD
**2 :** to leave undone or unattended to especially through carelessness ☆
— **ne·glect·er** *noun*

²**neglect** *noun* (1588)
**1 :** an act or instance of neglecting something
**2 :** the condition of being neglected

**ne·glect·ful** \ni-'glek(t)-fəl\ *adjective* (1644)
**:** given to neglecting **:** CARELESS, HEEDLESS
*synonym* see NEGLIGENT
— **ne·glect·ful·ly** \-fə-lē\ *adverb*
— **ne·glect·ful·ness** *noun*

**neg·li·gee** *also* **neg·li·gé** \ˌne-glə-'zhā, 'ne-glə-ˌ\ *noun* [French *négligé,* from past participle of *négliger* to neglect, from Latin *neglegere*] (1756)
**1 :** a woman's long flowing usually sheer dressing gown
**2 :** carelessly informal or incomplete attire

**neg·li·gence** \'ne-gli-jən(t)s\ *noun* (14th century)
**1 a :** the quality or state of being negligent **b :** failure to exercise the care that a prudent person usually exercises
**2 :** an act or instance of being negligent

**neg·li·gent** \-jənt\ *adjective* [Middle English, from Middle French & Latin; Middle French, from Latin *neglegent-, neglegens,* present participle of *neglegere*] (14th century)
**1 :** marked by or given to neglect especially habitually or culpably **:** not taking prudent care
**2 :** marked by a carelessly easy manner ☆
— **neg·li·gent·ly** *adverb*

**neg·li·gi·ble** \'ne-gli-jə-bəl\ *adjective* [Latin *neglegere, negligere*] (1829)
**:** so small or unimportant or of so little consequence as to warrant little or no attention **:** TRIFLING
— **neg·li·gi·bil·i·ty** \ˌne-gli-jə-'bi-lə-tē\ *noun*
— **neg·li·gi·bly** \'ne-gli-jə-blē\ *adverb*

**ne·go·tia·ble** \ni-'gō-sh(ē-)ə-bəl\ *adjective* (1758)
**:** capable of being negotiated: as **a :** transferable from one person to another by being delivered with or without endorsement so that the title passes to the transferee ⟨*negotiable* securities⟩ **b :** capable of being traversed, dealt with, or accomplished ⟨a difficult but *negotiable* road⟩ ⟨*negotiable* demands⟩ **c :** open to discussion or dispute
— **ne·go·tia·bil·i·ty** \-ˌgō-sh(ē-)ə-'bi-lə-tē\ *noun*

**ne·go·ti·ant** \-'gō-sh(ē-)ənt\ *noun* (circa 1611)
**:** one that negotiates

**ne·go·ti·ate** \ni-'gō-shē-ˌāt, ÷-sē-\ *verb* **-at·ed; -at·ing** [Latin *negotiatus,* past participle of *negotiari* to carry on business, from *negotium* business, from *neg-* not + *otium* leisure — more at NEGATE] (1599)
*intransitive verb*
**:** to confer with another so as to arrive at the settlement of some matter
*transitive verb*
**1 a :** to deal with (some matter or affair that requires ability for its successful handling) **:** MANAGE **b :** to arrange for or bring about through conference, discussion, and compromise ⟨*negotiate* a treaty⟩
**2 a :** to transfer (as a bill of exchange) to another by delivery or endorsement **b :** to convert into cash or the equivalent value ⟨*negotiate* a check⟩
**3 a :** to successfully travel along or over ⟨*negotiate* a turn⟩ **b :** COMPLETE, ACCOMPLISH ⟨*negotiate* the trip in two hours⟩
— **ne·go·ti·a·tor** \-ˌā-tər\ *noun*
— **ne·go·ti·a·to·ry** \-sh(ē-)ə-ˌtōr-ē, ÷-sē-, -ˌtòr-\ *adjective*

**ne·go·ti·a·tion** \ni-ˌgō-shē-'ā-shən, ÷-sē-\ *noun* (15th century)
**:** the action or process of negotiating or being negotiated — often used in plural

**Ne·gress** \'nē-grəs\ *noun* (1786)
**:** a black woman or girl — sometimes taken to be offensive

**Ne·gril·lo** \ni-'gri-(ˌ)lō, -'grē-(ˌ)yō\ *noun, plural* **-los** *or* **-loes** [Spanish, diminutive of *negro*] (1853)
**:** a member of a people (as Pygmies) belonging to a group of dark-skinned peoples of small stature that live in Africa

**Ne·gri·to** \nə-'grē-(ˌ)tō\ *noun, plural* **-tos** *or* **-toes** [Spanish, diminutive of *negro*] (1812)
**:** a member of a people (as the Andamanese) belonging to a group of dark-skinned peoples of small stature that live in Oceania and the southeastern part of Asia

**ne·gri·tude** \'ne-grə-ˌtüd, 'nē-, -ˌtyüd\ *noun* [French *négritude,* from *nègre* Negro + *-i-* + *-tude*] (1950)
**1 :** a consciousness of and pride in the cultural and physical aspects of the African heritage
**2 :** the state or condition of being black

**Ne·gro** \'nē-(ˌ)grō\ *noun, plural* **Negroes** [Spanish or Portuguese, from *negro* black, from Latin *nigr-, niger*] (1555)
**1 :** a member of the black race distinguished from members of other races by usually inherited physical and physiological characteristics without regard to language or culture; *especially* **:** a member of a people belonging to the African branch of the black race — sometimes taken to be offensive
**2 :** a person of Negro descent — sometimes taken to be offensive
— **Negro** *adjective*
— **Ne·gro·ness** \-grō-nəs\ *noun*

**ne·groid** \'nē-ˌgróid\ *adjective, often capitalized* (1859)
**:** of, resembling, related to, or characteristic of the Negro race
— **negroid** *noun, often capitalized*

**ne·gro·phobe** \'nē-grə-ˌfōb\ *noun, often capitalized* (1900)
**:** one who strongly dislikes or fears black people
— **ne·gro·pho·bia** \ˌnē-grə-'fō-bē-ə\ *noun, often capitalized*

---

☆ **SYNONYMS**
**Neglect, disregard, ignore, overlook, slight, forget** mean to pass over without giving due attention. NEGLECT implies giving insufficient attention to something that has a claim to one's attention ⟨habitually *neglected* his studies⟩. DISREGARD suggests voluntary inattention ⟨*disregarded* the wishes of other members⟩. IGNORE implies a failure to regard something obvious ⟨*ignored* the snide remark⟩. OVERLOOK suggests disregarding or ignoring through haste or lack of care ⟨in my rush I *overlooked* a key example⟩. SLIGHT implies contemptuous or disdainful disregarding or omitting ⟨*slighted* several major authors in her survey⟩. FORGET may suggest either a willful ignoring or a failure to impress something on one's mind ⟨*forget* what others say and listen to me⟩.

**Negligent, neglectful, lax, slack, remiss** mean culpably careless or indicative of such carelessness. NEGLIGENT implies inattention to one's duty or business ⟨*negligent* about writing a note of thanks⟩. NEGLECTFUL adds a more disapproving implication of laziness or deliberate inattention ⟨a society callously *neglectful* of the poor⟩. LAX implies a blameworthy lack of strictness, severity, or precision ⟨a reporter *lax* about accurate quotation⟩. SLACK implies want of due or necessary diligence or care ⟨*slack* workmanship and slipshod construction⟩. REMISS implies blameworthy carelessness shown in slackness, forgetfulness, or neglect ⟨had been *remiss* in her familial duties⟩.

**¹ne·gus** \'nē-gəs, ni-'güs\ *noun* [Amharic *nəgus*, from Ge'ez *nĕgūša nagašt* king of kings] (1594)
- KING — used as a title of the sovereign of Ethiopia

**²ne·gus** \'nē-gəs\ *noun* [Francis *Negus* (died 1732) English colonel] (1743)
: a beverage of wine, hot water, sugar, lemon juice, and spices

**Ne·he·mi·ah** \,nē-(h)ə-'mī-ə\ *noun* [Hebrew *Nĕḥemyāh*]
**1** : a Jewish leader of the 5th century B.C. who supervised the rebuilding of the Jerusalem city walls and instituted religious reforms in the city
**2** : a narrative and historical book of canonical Jewish and Christian Scripture — see BIBLE table

**Ne·he·mi·as** \-'mī-əs\ *noun* [Late Latin, from Hebrew *Nĕḥemyāh*]
: NEHEMIAH

**neigh** \'nā\ *intransitive verb* [Middle English *neyen,* from Old English *hnǣgan;* akin to Middle High German *nēgen* to neigh] (before 12th century)
: to make the prolonged cry of a horse
— **neigh** *noun*

**¹neigh·bor** \'nā-bər\ *noun* [Middle English, from Old English *nēahgebūr* (akin to Old High German *nāhgibūr*); akin to Old English *nēah* near and Old English *gebūr* dweller — more at NIGH, BOOR] (before 12th century)
**1** : one living or located near another
**2** : FELLOWMAN

**²neighbor** *adjective* (1530)
: being immediately adjoining or relatively near

**³neighbor** *verb* **neigh·bored; neigh·bor·ing** \-b(ə-)riŋ\ (circa 1586)
*transitive verb*
: to adjoin immediately or lie relatively near to
*intransitive verb*
**1** : to live or be located as a neighbor
**2** : to associate in a neighborly way

**neigh·bor·hood** \'nā-bər-,hůd\ *noun* (15th century)
**1** : neighborly relationship
**2** : the quality or state of being neighbors
: PROXIMITY
**3 a** : a place or region near : VICINITY **b** : an approximate amount, extent, or degree ⟨cost in the *neighborhood* of $10⟩
**4 a** : the people living near one another **b** : a section lived in by neighbors and usually having distinguishing characteristics
**5** : the set of all points belonging to a given set whose distances from a given point are less than a given positive number; *broadly* : a set that contains a neighborhood

**neigh·bor·ly** \-lē\ *adjective* (1558)
: of, relating to, or characteristic of congenial neighbors; *especially* : FRIENDLY
— **neigh·bor·li·ness** *noun*

**neigh·bour** \-bər\ *chiefly British variant of* NEIGHBOR

**¹nei·ther** \'nē-thər *also* 'nī-\ *conjunction* [Middle English, alteration (influenced by *either*) of *nauther, nother,* from Old English *nāhwæther, nōther,* from *nā, nō* not + *hwæther* which of two, whether] (12th century)
**1** : not either ⟨*neither* black nor white⟩
**2** : also not ⟨*neither* did I⟩ ■

**²neither** *pronoun* (13th century)
: not the one or the other of two or more ■

**³neither** *adjective* (14th century)
: not either ⟨*neither* hand⟩

**⁴neither** *adverb* (1551)
**1** *chiefly dialect* : EITHER ⟨are not to be understood *neither* —Earl of Chesterfield⟩
**2** : similarly not : also not ⟨just as the serf was not permitted to leave the land, so *neither* was his offspring —G. G. Coulton⟩

**nek·ton** \'nek-tən, -,tän\ *noun* [German *Nekton,* from Greek *nēkton,* neuter of *nēktos* swimming, from *nēchein* to swim — more at NATANT] (1893)
: free-swimming aquatic animals essentially independent of wave and current action
— **nek·ton·ic** \nek-'tä-nik\ *adjective*

**nel·son** \'nel-sən\ *noun* [probably from the name *Nelson*] (1889)
: a wrestling hold marked by the application of leverage against an opponent's arm, neck, and head — compare FULL NELSON, HALF NELSON

**nemat-** *or* **nemato-** *combining form* [New Latin, from Greek *nēmat-,* from *nēmat-, nēma,* from *nēn* to spin — more at NEEDLE]
**1** : thread ⟨*nemato*cyst⟩
**2** : nematode ⟨*nemato*logy⟩

**ne·mat·ic** \ni-'ma-tik\ *adjective* [International Scientific Vocabulary *nemat-* + ¹*-ic*] (1923)
: of, relating to, or being the phase of a liquid crystal characterized by arrangement of the long axes of the molecules in parallel lines but not layers — compare CHOLESTERIC, SMECTIC

**nem·a·to·cide** *or* **nem·a·ti·cide** \'ne-mə-tə-,sīd, ni-'ma-tə-\ *noun* (1898)
: a substance or preparation used to destroy nematodes
— **nem·a·to·ci·dal** *also* **nem·a·ti·ci·dal** \,ne-mə-tə-'sī-d²l, ni-,ma-tə-\ *adjective*

**nem·a·to·cyst** \-,sist\ *noun* [International Scientific Vocabulary] (1875)
: one of the stinging organelles of coelenterates used in catching prey

**nem·a·tode** \'ne-mə-,tōd\ *noun* [ultimately from Greek *nēmat-, nēma*] (1865)
: any of a phylum (Nematoda or Nemata) of elongated cylindrical worms parasitic in animals or plants or free-living in soil or water

**nem·a·tol·o·gy** \,ne-mə-'tä-lə-jē\ *noun* (circa 1916)
: a branch of zoology that deals with nematodes
— **nem·a·to·log·i·cal** \,ne-mə-t²l-'ä-ji-kəl\ *adjective*
— **nem·a·tol·o·gist** \,ne-mə-'tä-lə-jist\ *noun*

**Nem·bu·tal** \'nem-byə-,tȯl\ *trademark*
— used for the sodium salt of pentobarbital

**ne·mer·te·an** \ni-'mər-tē-ən\ *noun* [ultimately from Greek *Nēmertēs* Nemertes, one of the Nereids] (1861)
: any of a phylum (Nemertea synonym Rhynchocoela) of often vividly colored marine worms most of which burrow in the mud or sand along seacoasts — called also *ribbon worm*
— **nem·er·tine** \'ne-mər-,tīn\ *adjective or noun*

**nem·e·sis** \'ne-mə-səs\ *noun* [Latin, from Greek]
**1** *capitalized* : the Greek goddess of retributive justice
**2** *plural* **-e·ses** \-,sēz\ **a** : one that inflicts retribution or vengeance **b** : a formidable and usually victorious rival or opponent
**3** *plural* **-eses a** : an act or effect of retribution **b** : BANE 2

**ne·moph·i·la** \ni-'mä-fə-lə\ *noun* [New Latin, from Greek *nemos* wooded pasture + *philos* loving] (1838)
: any of a genus (*Nemophila*) of American annual herbs of the waterleaf family cultivated for their showy blue or white sometimes spotted flowers

**ne·ne** \'nā-(,)nā\ *noun* [Hawaiian *nēnē*] (1902)
: an endangered goose (*Branta sandvicensis* synonym *Nesochen sandvicensis*) of the Hawaiian Islands that usually inhabits waterless uplands and feeds on berries and vegetation

nene

**neo-** — see NE-

**neo·clas·sic** \,nē-ō-'kla-sik\ *or* **neo·clas·si·cal** \-si-kəl\ *adjective* (1877)
: of, relating to, or constituting a revival or adaptation of the classical especially in literature, music, art, or architecture
— **neo·clas·si·cism** \-'kla-sə-,si-zəm\ *noun*
— **neo·clas·si·cist** \-sist\ *noun or adjective*

**neo·co·lo·nial·ism** \,nē-ō-kə-'lōn-yə-,li-zəm, -'lō-nē-ə-,li-\ *noun* (1961)
: the economic and political policies by which a great power indirectly maintains or extends its influence over other areas or people
— **neo·co·lo·nial** \-'lōn-yəl, -'lō-nē-əl\ *adjective*
— **neo·co·lo·nial·ist** \-yə-list, -ə-list\ *noun or adjective*

**neo·con·ser·va·tive** \-kən-'sər-və-tiv\ *noun* (1955)
: a former liberal espousing political conservatism
— **neo·con·ser·va·tism** \-və-,ti-zəm\ *noun*
— **neoconservative** *adjective*

**neo·cor·tex** \,nē-ō-'kȯr-,teks\ *noun* [New Latin; from its being the cortex of the phylogenetically most recently developed part of the brain] (1909)
: the dorsal region of the cerebral cortex that is unique to mammals
**neo·cor·ti·cal** \-'kȯr-ti-kəl\ *adjective* (1909)
: of or relating to the neocortex

**neo–Dar·win·ian** \-där-'wi-nē-ən\ *adjective, often N capitalized* (1895)
: of or relating to neo-Darwinism

**neo–Dar·win·ism** \-'där-wə-,ni-zəm\ *noun, often N capitalized* (circa 1900)
: a theory of evolution that is a synthesis of Darwin's theory in terms of natural selection and modern population genetics
— **neo–Dar·win·ist** \-'där-wə-nist\ *noun, often N capitalized*

**neo·dym·i·um** \,nē-ō-'di-mē-əm\ *noun* [New Latin, from *ne-* + *-dymium* (from *didymium*)] (1885)
: a yellow metallic element of the rare-earth group that is used in magnets and lasers — see ELEMENT table

**neo–Ex·pres·sion·ism** \-ik-'spre-shə-,ni-zəm\ *noun, often N capitalized* (1961)
: a revival of expressionism in art characterized by intense colors, dramatic usually figural forms, and emotive subject matter
— **neo–Ex·pres·sion·ist** \-nist\ *noun or adjective, often N capitalized*

\ə\ abut \ᵊ\ kitten \ər\ further \a\ ash \ā\ ace \ä\ mop, mar \aů\ out \ch\ chin \e\ bet \ē\ easy \g\ go \i\ hit \ī\ ice \j\ job \ŋ\ sing \ō\ go \ȯ\ law \ȯi\ boy \th\ thin \th\ the \ü\ loot \ů\ foot \y\ yet \zh\ vision  *see also* Guide to Pronunciation

**neo-Freud·ian** \-'frói-dē-ən\ *adjective, often N capitalized* (1945)
**:** of or relating to a school of psychoanalysis that differs from Freudian orthodoxy in emphasizing the importance of social and cultural factors in the development of an individual's personality
— **neo-Freudian** *noun, often N capitalized*
**Neo·gene** \'nē-ə-,jēn\ *adjective* [International Scientific Vocabulary *ne-* + *-gene* (from Greek *-genēs* born) — more at -GEN] (1878)
**:** of, relating to, or being the later portion of the Tertiary including the Miocene and Pliocene or the corresponding system of rocks
— **Neogene** *noun*
**neo-Goth·ic** \,nē-ō-'gä-thik\ *adjective* (1892)
**:** of, relating to, or constituting a revival or adaptation of the Gothic especially in literature or architecture
**neo-im·pres·sion·ism** \,nē-ō-im-'pre-shə-,ni-zəm\ *noun, often N&I capitalized* [French *néo-impressionisme*, from *né-* ne- + *impressionisme* impressionism] (1892)
**:** a late 19th century French art theory and practice characterized by an attempt to make impressionism more precise in form and the use of a pointillist painting technique
— **neo-im·pres·sion·ist** \-'pre-sh(ə-)nist\ *adjective or noun, often N&I capitalized*
**Neo-Lat·in** \-'la-tᵊn\ *noun* [International Scientific Vocabulary] (1850)
**1 :** NEW LATIN
**2 :** ROMANCE 5
**neo·lib·er·al** \-'li-b(ə-)rəl\ *noun* (1945)
**:** a liberal who de-emphasizes traditional liberal doctrines in order to seek progress by more pragmatic methods
— **neoliberal** *adjective*
— **neo·lib·er·al·ism** \-b(ə-)rə-,li-zəm\ *noun*
**neo·lith** \'nē-ə-,lith\ *noun* [back-formation from *neolithic*] (1882)
**:** a Neolithic stone implement
**neo·lith·ic** \,nē-ə-'li-thik\ *adjective* (1865)
**1** *capitalized* **:** of or relating to the latest period of the Stone Age characterized by polished stone implements
**2 :** belonging to an earlier age and now outmoded
**neo·ol·o·gism** \nē-'ä-lə-,ji-zəm\ *noun* [French *néologisme*, from *ne-* + *log-* + *-isme* -ism] (1800)
**1 :** a new word, usage, or expression
**2 :** a meaningless word coined by a psychotic
— **ne·ol·o·gis·tic** \-,ä-lə-'jis-tik\ *adjective*
**neo·Mal·thu·sian** \,nē-ō-mal-'thü-zhən, -mȯl-, -'thyü-\ *adjective* (1896)
**:** advocating control of population growth (as by contraception)
— **neo-Malthusian** *noun*
— **neo·Mal·thu·sian·ism** \-zhə-,ni-zəm\ *noun*
**neo·my·cin** \,nē-ə-'mī-sᵊn\ *noun* (1949)
**:** a broad-spectrum highly toxic antibiotic or mixture of antibiotics produced by a streptomyces (*Streptomyces fradiae*) and used medically especially to treat local infections
**¹ne·on** \'nē-,än\ *noun* [Greek, neuter of *neos* new — more at NEW] (1898)
**1 :** a colorless odorless mostly inert gaseous element that is found in minute amounts in air and is used in electric lamps — see ELEMENT table
**2 a :** a discharge lamp in which the gas contains a large proportion of neon **b :** a sign composed of such lamps **c :** the illumination provided by such lamps or signs
— **ne·oned** \-,änd\ *adjective*
**²neon** *adjective* (1904)
**1 :** of, relating to, or using neon
**2 :** extremely bright **:** FLUORESCENT ⟨*neon* yellow⟩
**neo·na·tal** \,nē-ō-'nā-tᵊl\ *adjective* (1902)
**:** of, relating to, or affecting the newborn and especially the human infant during the first month after birth ⟨*neonatal* mortality⟩

— **neo·na·tal·ly** \-tᵊl-ē\ *adverb*
**ne·o·nate** \'nē-ə-,nāt\ *noun* [New Latin *neonatus*, from *ne-* + Latin *natus*, past participle of *nasci* to be born — more at NATION] (1932)
**:** a newborn child; *especially* **:** a child less than a month old
**neo·na·tol·o·gy** \,nē-ə-nā-'tä-lə-jē\ *noun* (1960)
**:** a branch of medicine concerned with the care, development, and diseases of newborn infants
— **neo·na·tol·o·gist** \-jist\ *noun*
**neo·Na·zi** \,nē-ō-'nät-sē, -'nat-\ *noun* (1938)
**:** a member of a group espousing the programs and policies of Hitler's Nazis
— **neo-Nazi** *adjective*
— **neo-Na·zism** \-'nät-,si-zəm, -'nat-\ *noun*
**neo·or·tho·dox** \,nē-ō-'ȯr-thə-,däks\ *adjective* (1946)
**:** of or relating to a 20th century movement in Protestant theology characterized by a reaction against liberalism and emphasis on various scripturally based Reformation doctrines
— **neo·or·tho·doxy** \-,däk-sē\ *noun*
**neo·phil·ia** \,nē-ə-'fi-lē-ə\ *noun* (circa 1947)
**:** love of or enthusiasm for what is new or novel
— **neo·phil·i·ac** \-lē-,ak\ *noun*
**neo·phyte** \'nē-ə-,fīt\ *noun* [Middle English, from Late Latin *neophytus*, from Greek *neophytos*, from *neophytos* newly planted, newly converted, from *ne-* + *phyein* to bring forth — more at BE] (14th century)
**1 :** a new convert **:** PROSELYTE
**2 :** NOVICE 1
**3 :** TYRO, BEGINNER
**neo·pla·sia** \,nē-ə-'plā-zh(ē-)ə\ *noun* [New Latin] (1890)
**1 :** the formation of tumors
**2 :** a tumorous condition
**neo·plasm** \'nē-ə-,pla-zəm\ *noun* [International Scientific Vocabulary] (1864)
**:** a new growth of tissue serving no physiological function **:** TUMOR
**neo·plas·tic** \,nē-ə-'plas-tik\ *adjective* [International Scientific Vocabulary] (circa 1890)
**1 :** of, relating to, or constituting a neoplasm or neoplasia
**2 :** of or relating to neoplasticism
**neo·plas·ti·cism** \-tə-,si-zəm\ *noun* [French *néo-plasticisme*, from *ne-* + *plastique* plastic + *-isme* -ism] (1933)
**:** DE STIJL
— **neo·plas·ti·cist** \-sist\ *noun*
**Neo·pla·to·nism** \,nē-ō-'plā-tᵊn-,i-zəm\ *noun* (1845)
**1 :** Platonism modified in later antiquity to accord with Aristotelian, post-Aristotelian, and oriental conceptions that conceives of the world as an emanation from an ultimate indivisible being with whom the soul is capable of being reunited in trance or ecstasy
**2 :** a doctrine similar to ancient Neoplatonism
— **Neo·pla·ton·ic** \-plə-'tä-nik, -plā-\ *adjective*
— **Neo·pla·to·nist** \-'plā-tᵊn-ist\ *noun*
**neo·prene** \'nē-ə-,prēn\ *noun* [*ne-* + chloroprene] (1937)
**:** a synthetic rubber made by the polymerization of chloroprene, characterized by superior resistance (as to oils), and used especially for special-purpose clothing (as gloves and wet suits)
**neo·re·al·ism** \,nē-ō-'rē-ə-,li-zəm, -'ri-ə-\ *noun* (1950)
**:** a movement especially in Italian filmmaking characterized by the simple direct depiction of lower-class life
— **neo·re·al·ist** \-list\ *adjective or noun*
— **neo·re·al·is·tic** \-,rē-ə-'lis-tik, -,ri-ə-\ *adjective*
**Neo·ri·can** \,nē-ō-'rē-kən\ *noun* [American Spanish *neorriqueño* Puerto Rican living in

New York City, blend of Spanish *neoyorquino* New Yorker and *puertorriqueño* Puerto Rican] (1970)
**:** a Puerto Rican who lives on the U.S. mainland or has lived there but has returned to Puerto Rico
**neo·scho·las·ti·cism** \,nē-ō-skə-'las-tə-,si-zəm\ *noun* (circa 1909)
**:** a movement among Catholic scholars aiming to restate medieval Scholasticism in a manner suited to present intellectual needs
**neo·stig·mine** \,nē-ə-'stig-,mēn\ *noun* [*ne-* + -stigmine (as in *physostigmine*)] (1941)
**:** a cholinergic drug used in the form of its bromide $C_{12}H_{19}BrN_2O_2$ or a methyl sulfate derivative $C_{13}H_{22}N_2O_6S$ especially in the treatment of some ophthalmic conditions and in the diagnosis and treatment of myasthenia gravis
**ne·ot·e·ny** \nē-'ä-tᵊn-ē\ *noun* [New Latin *neotenia*, from *ne-* + Greek *teinein* to stretch — more at THIN] (1901)
**1 :** retention of some larval or immature characters in adulthood
**2 :** attainment of sexual maturity during the larval stage
— **ne·o·ten·ic** \,nē-ə-'te-nik\ *adjective*
**ne·o·ter·ic** \,nē-ə-'ter-ik\ *adjective* [Late Latin *neotericus*, from Late Greek *neōterikos*, from Greek, youthful, from *neōterios*, comparative of *neos* new, young — more at NEW] (1596)
**:** recent in origin **:** MODERN
**Neo·trop·i·cal** \,nē-ō-'trä-pi-kəl\ *also* **Neo·trop·ic** \-pik\ *adjective* [International Scientific Vocabulary] (1858)
**:** of, relating to, or constituting the biogeographic region that extends south, east, and west from the central plateau of Mexico
**neo·trop·ics** \-'trä-piks\ *noun plural* (1923)
**:** the Neotropical region
**neo·type** \'nē-ə-,tīp\ *noun* (1905)
**:** a type specimen that is selected subsequent to the description of a species to replace a pre-existing type that has been lost or destroyed
**Ne·pali** \nə-'pȯ-lē, -'pä-, -'pa-\ *noun, plural* **Nepali** *also* **Ne·pal·is** [Hindi *naipālī* of Nepal, from Sanskrit *naipālīya*, from *Nepāla* Nepal] (circa 1885)
**1 :** a native or inhabitant of Nepal
**2 :** an Indo-Aryan language spoken in Nepal
— **Nepali** *adjective*
**ne·pen·the** \nə-'pen(t)-thē\ *noun* [Latin *nepenthes*, from Greek *nēpenthes*, neuter of *nēpenthēs* banishing pain and sorrow, from *nē-* not + *penthos* grief, sorrow; akin to Greek *pathos* suffering — more at NO, PATHOS] (1580)
**1 :** a potion used by the ancients to induce forgetfulness of pain or sorrow
**2 :** something capable of causing oblivion of grief or suffering
— **ne·pen·the·an** \-thē-ən\ *adjective*
**neph·e·line** \'ne-fə-,lēn\ *also* **neph·e·lite** \-,līt\ *noun* [French *néphéline*, from Greek *nephelē* cloud — more at NEBULA] (circa 1814)
**:** a hexagonal mineral that is a usually glassy crystalline silicate of sodium, potassium, and aluminum common in igneous rocks
— **neph·e·lin·ic** \,ne-fə-'li-nik\ *adjective*
**neph·e·lin·ite** \'ne-fə-lə-,nīt\ *noun* [International Scientific Vocabulary] (circa 1863)
**:** a silica-deficient igneous rock having nepheline as the predominant mineral
— **neph·e·lin·it·ic** \,ne-fə-lə-'ni-tik\ *adjective*
**neph·e·lom·e·ter** \,ne-fə-'lä-mə-tər\ *noun* [Greek *nephelē* cloud + International Scientific Vocabulary *-meter*] (1884)
**1 :** an instrument for measuring the extent or degree of cloudiness
**2 :** an instrument for determining the concentration or particle size of suspensions by means of transmitted or reflected light
— **neph·e·lo·met·ric** \,ne-fə-lō-'me-trik\ *adjective*

— **neph·e·lo·met·ri·cal·ly** \-tri-k(ə-)lē\ *adverb*

— **neph·e·lom·e·try** \-'lä-mə-trē\ *noun*

**neph·ew** \'ne-(,)fyü, *chiefly British* -(,)vyü\ *noun* [Middle English *nevew*, from Old French *neveu*, from Latin *nepot-*, *nepos* grandson, nephew; akin to Old English *nefa* grandson, nephew, Sanskrit *napāt* grandson] (14th century)
**1 a :** a son of one's brother or sister or of one's brother-in-law or sister-in-law **b :** an illegitimate son of an ecclesiastic
**2** *obsolete* **:** a lineal descendant; *especially* **:** GRANDSON

**nepho·scope** \'ne-fə-,skōp\ *noun* [Greek *nephos* cloud + International Scientific Vocabulary *-scope* — more at NEBULA] (1881)
**:** an instrument for observing the direction and velocity of clouds

**nephr-** *or* **nephro-** *combining form* [New Latin, from Greek, from *nephros* — more at NEPHRITIS]
**:** kidney ⟨*nephric*⟩ ⟨*nephrology*⟩

**ne·phrec·to·my** \ni-'frek-tə-mē\ *noun, plural* **-mies** [International Scientific Vocabulary] (1880)
**:** the surgical removal of a kidney
— **ne·phrec·to·mize** \-,mīz\ *transitive verb*

**neph·ric** \'ne-frik\ *adjective* (1887)
**:** RENAL

**ne·phrid·i·um** \ni-'fri-dē-əm\ *noun, plural* **-ia** \-dē-ə\ [New Latin] (1877)
**:** a tubular glandular excretory organ characteristic of various invertebrates
— **ne·phrid·i·al** \-dē-əl\ *adjective*

**neph·rite** \'ne-,frīt\ *noun* [German *Nephrit*, from Greek *nephros*; from its formerly being worn as a remedy for kidney diseases] (1794)
**:** a compact tremolite or actinolite that is the commoner and less valuable kind of jade and that varies in color from white to dark green or black

**ne·phrit·ic** \ni-'fri-tik\ *adjective* (1580)
**1 :** RENAL
**2 :** of, relating to, or affected with nephritis

**ne·phri·tis** \ni-'frī-təs\ *noun, plural* **ne·phrit·i·des** \-'fri-tə-,dēz\ [Late Latin, from Greek, from *nephros* kidney; probably akin to Middle English *nere* kidney] (1580)
**:** acute or chronic inflammation of the kidney caused by infection, degenerative process, or vascular disease

**ne·phrol·o·gy** \ni-'frä-lə-jē\ *noun* (circa 1842)
**:** a branch of medicine concerned with the kidneys
— **ne·phrol·o·gist** \-jist\ *noun*

**neph·ron** \'ne-,frän\ *noun* [German, from Greek *nephros*] (1932)
**:** a single excretory unit of the vertebrate kidney

**ne·phrop·a·thy** \ni-'frä-pə-thē\ *noun, plural* **-thies** [International Scientific Vocabulary] (circa 1900)
**:** an abnormal state of the kidney; *especially* **:** one associated with or secondary to some other pathological process
— **neph·ro·path·ic** \,ne-frə-'pa-thik\ *adjective*

**ne·phro·sis** \ni-'frō-səs\ *noun* [New Latin] (1916)
**:** a noninflammatory disease of the kidneys chiefly affecting function of the nephrons; *also* **:** NEPHROTIC SYNDROME
— **ne·phrot·ic** \-'frä-tik\ *adjective or noun*

**neph·ro·stome** \'ne-frə-,stōm\ *noun* [New Latin *nephrostoma*, from *nephr-* + *stoma* stoma] (1888)
**:** the ciliated funnel-shaped coelomic opening of a typical nephridium

**nephrotic syndrome** *noun* (1939)
**:** an abnormal condition that is marked by deficiency of albumin in the blood and its excretion in the urine due to altered permeability of the glomerular basement membranes

**neph·ro·tox·ic** \,ne-frə-'täk-sik\ *adjective* (1902)
**:** poisonous to the kidney ⟨*nephrotoxic* drugs⟩; *also* **:** resulting from or marked by poisoning of the kidney ⟨*nephrotoxic* effects⟩
— **neph·ro·tox·i·ci·ty** \-täk-'si-sə-tē\ *noun*

**ne plus ul·tra** \,nā-,pləs-'əl-trə, ,nē-\ *noun* [New Latin, (go) no more beyond] (1638)
**1 :** the highest point capable of being attained **:** ACME
**2 :** the most profound degree of a quality or state

**nep·o·tism** \'ne-pə-,ti-zəm\ *noun* [French *népotisme*, from Italian *nepotismo*, from *nepote* nephew, from Latin *nepot-*, *nepos* grandson, nephew — more at NEPHEW] (1670)
**:** favoritism (as in appointment to a job) based on kinship
— **nep·o·tis·tic** \,ne-pə-'tis-tik\ *adjective*

**Nep·tune** \'nep-,tün, -,tyün\ *noun* [Latin *Neptunus*]
**1 a :** the Roman god of the sea — compare POSEIDON **b :** OCEAN
**2 :** the planet 8th in order from the sun — see PLANET table
— **Nep·tu·ni·an** \nep-'tü-nē-ən, -'tyü-\ *adjective*

**nep·tu·ni·um** \nep-'tü-nē-əm, -'tyü-\ *noun* [New Latin, from International Scientific Vocabulary *Neptune*] (1941)
**:** a radioactive metallic element that is chemically similar to uranium and is obtained in nuclear reactors as a by-product in the production of plutonium — see ELEMENT table

**nerd** \'nərd\ *noun* [perhaps from *nerd*, a creature in the children's book *If I Ran the Zoo* (1950) by Dr. Seuss (Theodor Geisel)] (1951)
**:** an unstylish, unattractive, or socially inept person; *especially* **:** one slavishly devoted to intellectual or academic pursuits ⟨computer *nerds*⟩ ◆
— **nerd·ish** \'nər-dish\ *adjective*
— **nerdy** \-dē\ *adjective*

**ne·re·id** \'nir-ē-əd\ *noun* [New Latin *Nereidae*, from *Nereis*, a genus, from Latin, Nereid] (1840)
**:** any of a family (Nereidae) of polychaete worms; *especially* **:** any of a genus (*Nereis*) of usually large often dimorphic and greenish mostly marine worms
— **nereid** *adjective*

**Ne·re·id** \'nir-ē-əd\ *noun* [Latin *Nereid-, Nereis*, from Greek *Nēreid-, Nēreis*, from *Nēreus* Nereus] (1680)
**:** any of the sea nymphs fathered by Nereus

**Ne·re·us** \'nir-ē-əs\ *noun* [Latin, from Greek *Nēreus*]
**:** a sea-god in Greek mythology

**ne·rit·ic** \nə-'ri-tik\ *adjective* [International Scientific Vocabulary, perhaps from New Latin *Nerita*, genus of marine snails] (1891)
**:** of, relating to, inhabiting, or constituting the belt or region of shallow water adjoining the seacoast

**ne·rol** \'ner-,ōl, 'nir-\ *noun* [International Scientific Vocabulary *ner-* (from *neroli oil*) + *-ol*] (1869)
**:** a liquid alcohol $C_{10}H_{18}O$ that has a rose scent and is used in perfumery

**ner·o·li oil** \'ner-ə-lē-\ *noun* [French *néroli*, from Italian *neroli*, from Anna Maria de La Trémoille, princess of *Nerola* (flourished 1670)] (1849)
**:** a fragrant pale yellow essential oil obtained from orange flowers and used especially in cologne and as a flavoring

**nerts** \'nərts\ *noun plural* [alteration of *nuts*] (circa 1932)
*slang* **:** NONSENSE, NUTS — often used interjectionally

**ner·va·tion** \,nər-'vā-shən\ *noun* (1849)
**:** an arrangement or system of nerves; *also* **:** VENATION

**¹nerve** \'nərv\ *noun* [Latin *nervus* sinew, nerve; akin to Greek *neuron* sinew, nerve, *nēn* to spin — more at NEEDLE] (14th century)
**1 :** SINEW, TENDON ⟨strain every *nerve*⟩
**2 :** any of the filamentous bands of nervous tissue that connect parts of the nervous system with the other organs, conduct nervous impulses, and are made up of axons and dendrites together with protective and supportive structures
**3 a :** power of endurance or control **:** FORTITUDE, STRENGTH **b :** ASSURANCE, BOLDNESS; *also* **:** presumptuous audacity **:** GALL
**4 a :** a sore or sensitive point **b** *plural* **:** nervous disorganization or collapse **:** NERVOUSNESS
**5 :** VEIN 3
**6 :** the sensitive pulp of a tooth
*synonym* see TEMERITY

**²nerve** *transitive verb* **nerved; nerv·ing** (circa 1749)
**:** to give strength or courage to **:** supply with physical or moral force

**nerve cell** *noun* (1858)
**:** NEURON; *also* **:** CELL BODY

**nerve center** *noun* (1868)
**1 :** CENTER 2c
**2 :** a source of leadership, organization, control, or energy ⟨the financial *nerve center* of the nation⟩

**nerve cord** *noun* (1877)
**1 :** the pair of closely united ventral longitudinal nerves with their segmental ganglia that is characteristic of many elongate invertebrates (as earthworms)
**2 :** the dorsal tubular cord of nervous tissue above the notochord of a chordate that comprises or develops into the central nervous system

**nerved** \'nərvd\ *adjective* (1800)
**1 a :** VEINED ⟨a *nerved* wing⟩ **b :** having veins or nerves especially of a specified kind or number — used in combination ⟨fan-*nerved* leaves⟩
**2 :** showing courage or strength

**nerve ending** *noun* (circa 1890)
**:** a structure forming the distal end of a nerve axon

**nerve fiber** *noun* (circa 1847)
**:** any of the processes (as axons or dendrites) of a neuron

**nerve gas** *noun* (1940)

◇ WORD HISTORY
**nerd** The word *nerd* was first noted in an article on teenage slang that appeared in the October 8, 1951, issue of *Newsweek*: "In Detroit, someone who would once be called a drip or a square is now, regrettably, a nerd, or, in a less severe case, a scurve." No one knows if Detroit was actually the birthplace of *nerd*, but the word went on to a remarkably successful career in American English. It provided a label for a new character in postwar America: the student wholly devoted to intellectual interests and unable or unwilling to mix with the masses of young people for whom higher education was a less intensely serious matter. While the collegiate *nerd* was supplanted by *dweeb*, *dork*, *wonk*, and newer words, *nerd* expanded into adult realms, and the word became an only slightly derogatory epithet for a narrowly focused specialist, especially in the common collocation *computer nerd*. The origin of *nerd* remains unclear; the children's author Theodore Geisel ("Dr. Seuss") used *nerd* for an imaginary creature in *If I Ran the Zoo* (1950), but his coinage may be unrelated to the appearance of the word in 1951 Detroit.

\ə\ abut  \ᵊ\ kitten  \ər\ further  \a\ ash  \ā\ ace
\ä\ mop, mar  \au̇\ out  \ch\ chin  \e\ bet  \ē\ easy
\g\ go  \i\ hit  \ī\ ice  \j\ job  \ŋ\ sing  \ō\ go
\ȯ\ law  \ȯi\ boy  \th\ thin  \t̲h̲\ the  \ü\ loot  \u̇\ foot
\y\ yet  \zh\ vision  *see also* Guide to Pronunciation

**:** an organophosphate chemical weapon that interferes with normal nerve transmission and induces intense bronchial spasm with resulting inhibition of respiration

**nerve growth factor** *noun* (1962)
**:** a protein that promotes development of the sensory and sympathetic nervous systems and is required for maintenance of sympathetic neurons

**nerve impulse** *noun* (1900)
**:** the progressive physicochemical change in the membrane of a nerve fiber that follows stimulation and serves to transmit a record of sensation from a receptor or an instruction to act to an effector — called also *nervous impulse*

**nerve·less** \'nərv-ləs\ *adjective* (1742)
**1 :** lacking strength or courage **:** FEEBLE
**2 :** exhibiting control or balance **:** POISED, COOL
— **nerve·less·ly** *adverb*
— **nerve·less·ness** *noun*

**nerve net** *noun* (1904)
**:** a network of nerve cells apparently continuous with one another and conducting impulses in all directions; *also* **:** a primitive nervous system (as in a jellyfish) consisting of such a network

**nerve–rack·ing** *or* **nerve–wrack·ing** \'nərv-,ra-kiŋ\ *adjective* (1812)
**:** extremely trying on the nerves ⟨a *nerve-racking* ordeal⟩

**nerve trunk** *noun* (1851)
**:** a bundle of nerve fibers enclosed in a connective tissue sheath

**ner·vos·i·ty** \,nər-'vä-sə-tē\ *noun* (1787)
**:** the quality or state of being nervous

**ner·vous** \'nər-vəs\ *adjective* (14th century)
**1** *archaic* **:** SINEWY, STRONG
**2 :** marked by strength of thought, feeling, or style **:** SPIRITED ⟨a vibrant tight-packed *nervous* style of writing⟩
**3 :** of, relating to, or composed of neurons
**4 a :** of or relating to the nerves; *also* **:** originating in or affected by the nerves ⟨*nervous* energy⟩ **b :** easily excited or irritated **:** JUMPY **c :** TIMID, APPREHENSIVE ⟨a *nervous* smile⟩
**5 a :** tending to produce nervousness or agitation **:** UNEASY ⟨a *nervous* situation⟩ **b :** appearing or acting unsteady, erratic, or irregular — used of inanimate things
*synonym* see VIGOROUS
— **ner·vous·ly** *adverb*
— **ner·vous·ness** *noun*

**nervous breakdown** *noun* (1905)
**:** an attack of mental or emotional disorder especially when of sufficient severity to require hospitalization

**nervous Nel·lie** *or* **nervous Nel·ly** \-'ne-lē\ *noun, plural* **nervous Nellies** *often 1st N capitalized* [from the name *Nellie*] (1926)
**:** a timid or worrisome person

**nervous system** *noun* (1740)
**:** the bodily system that in vertebrates is made up of the brain and spinal cord, nerves, ganglia, and parts of the receptor organs and that receives and interprets stimuli and transmits impulses to the effector organs — compare CENTRAL NERVOUS SYSTEM; AUTONOMIC NERVOUS SYSTEM, PERIPHERAL NERVOUS SYSTEM

**ner·vure** \'nər-vyər\ *noun* [French, from *nerf* sinew, from Latin *nervus*] (1816)
**:** VEIN 3

**nervy** \'nər-vē\ *adjective* **nerv·i·er; -est** (1607)
**1** *archaic* **:** SINEWY, STRONG
**2 a :** showing calm courage **:** BOLD **b :** marked by effrontery or presumption **:** BRASH
**3 :** EXCITABLE, NERVOUS
— **nerv·i·ly** \-və-lē\ *adverb*
— **nerv·i·ness** \-vē-nəs\ *noun*

**ne·science** \'ne-sh(ē-)ən(t)s, 'nē-, -sē-ən(t)s\ *noun* [Late Latin *nescientia*, from Latin *nescient-, nesciens,* present participle of *nescire* not to know, from *ne-* not + *scire* to know — more at NO, SCIENCE] (1612)
**:** lack of knowledge or awareness **:** IGNORANCE

— **ne·scient** \-sh(ē-)ənt, -sē-ənt\ *adjective*

**ness** \'nes\ *noun* [Middle English *nasse,* from Old English *næss;* akin to Old English *nasu* nose — more at NOSE] (before 12th century)
**:** CAPE, PROMONTORY

**-ness** \nəs\ *noun suffix* [Middle English *-nes,* from Old English; akin to Old High German *-nissa* -ness]
**:** state **:** condition **:** quality **:** degree ⟨good*ness*⟩

**Nes·sel·rode** \'ne-səl-,rōd\ *noun* [Count Karl R. *Nesselrode* (died 1862) Russian statesman] (1845)
**:** a mixture of candied fruits, nuts, and maraschino used in puddings, pies, and ice cream

**Nes·sus** \'ne-səs\ *noun* [Latin, from Greek *Nessos*]
**:** a centaur slain by Hercules for trying to carry away Hercules' wife but avenged by means of a poisoned garment that causes Hercules to die in torment

**¹nest** \'nest\ *noun* [Middle English, from Old English; akin to Old High German *nest* nest, Latin *nidus*] (before 12th century)
**1 a :** a bed or receptacle prepared by an animal and especially a bird for its eggs and young **b :** a place or specially modified structure serving as an abode of animals and especially of their immature stages ⟨an ants' *nest*⟩ **c :** a receptacle resembling a bird's nest
**2 a :** a place of rest, retreat, or lodging **:** HOME ⟨grown children who have left the *nest*⟩ **b :** DEN, HANGOUT
**3 :** the occupants or frequenters of a nest
**4 a :** a group of similar things **:** AGGREGATION ⟨a *nest* of giant mountains —Helen MacInnes⟩ **b :** HOTBED 2 ⟨a *nest* of rebellion⟩
**5 :** a group of objects made to fit close together or one within another
**6 :** an emplaced group of weapons

**²nest** (13th century)
*intransitive verb*
**1 :** to build or occupy a nest **:** settle in or as if in a nest
**2 :** to fit compactly together or within one another **:** EMBED
*transitive verb*
**1 :** to form a nest for
**2 :** to pack compactly together
**3 :** to form a hierarchy, series, or sequence of with each member, element, or set contained in or containing the next ⟨*nested* subroutines in a computer program⟩

**nest egg** *noun* (14th century)
**1 :** a natural or artificial egg left in a nest to induce a fowl to continue to lay there
**2 :** a fund of money accumulated as a reserve

**nest·er** \'nes-tər\ *noun* (1880)
**1** *West* **:** a homesteader or squatter who takes up land on open range for a farm
**2 :** one that nests

**nes·tle** \'ne-səl\ *verb* **nes·tled; nes·tling** \-s(ə-)liŋ\ [Middle English, from Old English *nestlian,* from *nest*] (before 12th century)
*intransitive verb*
**1** *archaic* **:** NEST 1
**2 :** to settle snugly or comfortably
**3 :** to lie in an inconspicuous or sheltered manner
*transitive verb*
**1 :** to settle, shelter, or house in or as if in a nest ⟨the children were *nestled* all snug in their beds —Clement Moore⟩
**2 :** to press closely and affectionately ⟨*nestles* a kitten in her arms⟩
— **nes·tler** \-s(ə-)lər\ *noun*

**nest·ling** \'nest-liŋ\ *noun* (14th century)
**:** a young bird that has not abandoned the nest

**Nes·tor** \'nes-tər, -,tòr\ *noun* [Latin, from Greek *Nestōr*]
**1 :** a king of Pylos who serves in his old age as a counselor to the Greeks at Troy
**2** *often not capitalized* **:** one who is a patriarch or leader in a field

**Nes·to·ri·an** \ne-'stōr-ē-ən, -'stòr-\ *adjective* (1565)

**1 :** of or relating to the doctrine ascribed to Nestorius and ecclesiastically condemned in 431 that divine and human persons remained separate in the incarnate Christ
**2 :** of or relating to a church separating from Byzantine Christianity after 431, centering in Persia, and surviving chiefly in Asia Minor
— **Nestorian** *noun*
— **Nes·to·ri·an·ism** \-ə-,ni-zəm\ *noun*

**¹net** \'net\ *noun* [Middle English *nett,* from Old English; akin to Old High German *nezzi* net] (before 12th century)
**1 a :** an open-meshed fabric twisted, knotted, or woven together at regular intervals **b :** something made of net: as (1) **:** a device for catching fish, birds, or insects (2) **:** a fabric barricade which divides a court in half (as in tennis or volleyball) and over which a ball or shuttlecock must be hit to be in play (3) **:** the fabric that encloses the sides and back of the goal in various games (as soccer or hockey)
**2 :** an entrapping device or situation ⟨caught in the *net* of suspicious circumstances⟩
**3 :** something resembling a net in reticulation (as of lines, fibers, or figures)
**4 a :** a group of communications stations operating under unified control **b :** NETWORK 4
— **net·less** \-ləs\ *adjective*
— **net·like** \-,līk\ *adjective*
— **net·ty** \'ne-tē\ *adjective*

**²net** *transitive verb* **net·ted; net·ting** (1593)
**1 :** to cover or enclose with or as if with a net
**2 :** to catch in or as if in a net
**3 :** to cover with or as if with a network
**4 a :** to hit (a ball) into the net for the loss of a point in a racket game **b :** to hit (a ball or puck) into the goal for a score (as in hockey or soccer)
— **net·ter** *noun*

**³net** *adjective* [Middle English, clean, bright, from Middle French — more at NEAT] (15th century)
**1 :** free from all charges or deductions: as **a :** remaining after the deduction of all charges, outlay, or loss ⟨*net* earnings⟩ ⟨*net* worth⟩ — compare GROSS **b :** excluding all tare ⟨*net* weight⟩
**2 :** excluding all nonessential considerations **:** BASIC, FINAL ⟨the *net* result⟩ ⟨*net* effect⟩

**⁴net** *transitive verb* **net·ted; net·ting** (1758)
**1 a :** to receive by way of profit **:** CLEAR **b :** to produce by way of profit **:** YIELD
**2 :** to get possession of **:** GAIN

**⁵net** *noun* (circa 1904)
**1 :** a net amount, profit, weight, or price
**2 :** the score of a golfer in a handicap match after deducting his handicap from his gross
**3 :** ESSENCE, GIST

**neth·er** \'ne-thər\ *adjective* [Middle English, from Old English *nithera,* from *nither* down; akin to Old High German *nidar* down, Sanskrit *ni* ni] (before 12th century)
**1 :** situated down or below **:** LOWER ⟨the *nether* side⟩
**2 :** situated or believed to be situated beneath the earth's surface ⟨the *nether* regions⟩

**neth·er·most** \-,mōst\ *adjective* (14th century)
**:** farthest down **:** LOWEST

**neth·er·world** \-,wərld\ *noun* (1638)
**1 :** the world of the dead
**2 :** UNDERWORLD 4 ⟨the *netherworld* of deceit, subversion, and espionage —R. M. Nixon⟩

**net·mind·er** \'net-,mīn-dər\ *noun* (1937)
**:** GOALKEEPER

**net·su·ke** \'nets-(,)kā, -kē, -ke *also* 'net-sü\ *noun, plural* **netsuke** *or* **netsukes** [Japanese] (1876)
**:** a small and often intricately carved toggle (as of wood, ivory, or metal) used to fasten a small container to a kimono sash

**nett** *British variant of* NET

**net·ting** \'ne-tiŋ\ *noun* (1567)
**1 :** NETWORK 1

**2 :** the act or process of making a net or network

**3 :** the act, process, or right of fishing with a net

¹**net·tle** \'ne-t°l\ noun [Middle English, from Old English netel; akin to Old High German nazza nettle, Greek adikē] (before 12th century)
**1 :** any of a genus (Urtica of the family Urticaceae, the nettle family) of chiefly coarse herbs armed with stinging hairs
**2 :** any of various prickly or stinging plants other than the true nettles (genus Urtica)

²**nettle** transitive verb **net·tled; net·tling** \'net-liŋ, 'ne-t°l-iŋ\ (15th century)
**1 :** to strike or sting with or as if with nettles
**2 :** to arouse to sharp but transitory annoyance or anger
**synonym** see IRRITATE

**nettle rash** noun (1740)
**:** URTICARIA

**net·tle·some** \'ne-t°l-səm\ adjective (1766)
**:** causing vexation **:** IRRITATING

**net–veined** \'net-,vānd\ adjective (1861)
**:** having veins arranged in a fine network ⟨a net-veined leaf⟩ — compare PARALLEL-VEINED; see VENATION illustration
**— net venation** noun

**net–winged** \-,wiŋd\ adjective (circa 1890)
**:** having wings with a fine network of veins

¹**net·work** \'net-,wərk\ noun (1560)
**1 :** a fabric or structure of cords or wires that cross at regular intervals and are knotted or secured at the crossings
**2 :** a system of lines or channels resembling a network
**3 a :** an interconnected or interrelated chain, group, or system ⟨a network of hotels⟩ **b :** a system of computers, terminals, and databases connected by communications lines
**4 a :** a group of radio or television stations linked by wire or radio relay **b :** a radio or television company that produces programs for broadcast over such a network

²**network** (1887)
transitive verb
**1 :** to cover with or as if with a network ⟨a continent . . . so networked with navigable rivers and canals —Lamp⟩
**2** chiefly British **:** to distribute for broadcast on a television network; also **:** BROADCAST 3
**3 :** to join (as computers) in a network
intransitive verb
**:** to engage in networking

**net·work·ing** noun (1966)
**1 :** the exchange of information or services among individuals, groups, or institutions
**2 :** the establishment or use of a computer network

**Neuf·châ·tel** \,nü-shä-'tel, ,nyü-, ,nə(r)-\ noun [French, from Neufchâtel, France] (circa 1865)
**:** a soft unripened cheese similar to cream cheese but containing less fat and more moisture

**neume** \'nüm, 'nyüm\ noun [Middle English, from Medieval Latin pneuma, neuma, from Greek pneuma breath — more at PNEUMATIC] (14th century)
**:** any of various symbols used in the notation of Gregorian chant
**— neu·mat·ic** \nü-'ma-tik, nyü-\ adjective

**neur-** or **neuro-** combining form [New Latin, from Greek, nerve, sinew, from neuron — more at NERVE]
**1 :** nerve ⟨neural⟩ ⟨neurology⟩
**2 :** neural **:** neural and ⟨neuromuscular⟩

**neu·ral** \'nùr-əl, 'nyùr-\ adjective (circa 1847)
**1 :** of, relating to, or affecting a nerve or the nervous system
**2 :** situated in the region of or on the same side of the body as the brain and spinal cord **:** DORSAL
**— neu·ral·ly** \-ə-lē\ adverb

**neural arch** noun (circa 1860)

**:** the cartilaginous or bony arch enclosing the spinal cord on the dorsal side of a vertebra

**neural crest** noun (circa 1885)
**:** the ridge of one of the folds forming the neural tube that gives rise to the spinal ganglia and various structures of the autonomic nervous system

**neu·ral·gia** \nù-'ral-jə, nyù-\ noun [New Latin] (circa 1834)
**:** acute paroxysmal pain radiating along the course of one or more nerves usually without demonstrable changes in the nerve structure
**— neu·ral·gic** \-jik\ adjective

**neural net** noun (1949)
**:** a computer architecture in which a number of processors are interconnected in a manner suggestive of the connections between neurons in a human brain and which is able to learn by a process of trial and error — called also neural network

**neural plate** noun (1888)
**:** a thickened plate of ectoderm along the dorsal midline of the early vertebrate embryo that gives rise to the neural tube and crests

**neural tube** noun (1888)
**:** the hollow longitudinal dorsal tube formed by infolding and subsequent fusion of the opposite ectodermal folds in the vertebrate embryo that gives rise to the brain and spinal cord

**neur·amin·i·dase** \,nùr-ə-'mi-nə-,dās, ,nyùr-, -,dāz\ noun [neuraminic acid, an amino acid + -ide + -ase] (1956)
**:** a glycosidase that splits mucoproteins by breaking a glucoside link and occurs especially in influenza viruses as an antigen

**neur·as·the·nia** \,nùr-əs-'thē-nē-ə, ,nyùr-\ noun [New Latin] (1856)
**:** an emotional and psychic disorder that is characterized especially by easy fatigability and often by lack of motivation, feelings of inadequacy, and psychosomatic symptoms
**— neur·as·then·ic** \-'the-nik, -'thē-\ adjective or noun
**— neur·as·then·i·cal·ly** \-ni-k(ə-)lē\ adverb

**neu·ri·lem·ma** \,nùr-ə-'le-mə, ,nyùr-\ noun [New Latin, from neur- + Greek eilēma covering, coil, from eilein to wind; akin to Greek eilyein to roll — more at VOLUBLE] (1852)
**:** the plasma membrane surrounding a Schwann cell of a myelinated nerve fiber and separating layers of myelin
**— neu·ri·lem·mal** \-'le-məl\ adjective

**neu·ri·tis** \nù-'rī-təs, nyù-\ noun, plural **-rit·i·des** \-'ri-tə-,dēz\ or **-ri·tis·es** [New Latin] (1840)
**:** an inflammatory or degenerative lesion of a nerve marked especially by pain, sensory disturbances, and impaired or lost reflexes
**— neu·rit·ic** \-'ri-tik\ adjective or noun

**neu·ro·ac·tive** \,nùr-ō-'ak-tiv, ,nyùr-\ adjective (1961)
**:** stimulating neural tissue

**neu·ro·anat·o·my** \-ə-'na-tə-mē\ noun (circa 1899)
**:** the anatomy of nervous tissue and the nervous system
**— neu·ro·an·a·tom·i·cal** \-,a-nə-'tä-mi-kəl\ also **neu·ro·an·a·tom·ic** \-mik\ adjective
**— neu·ro·anat·o·mist** \-ə-'na-tə-mist\ noun

**neu·ro·bi·ol·o·gy** \-bī-'ä-lə-jē\ noun (1906)
**:** a branch of the life sciences that deals with the anatomy, physiology, and pathology of the nervous system
**— neu·ro·bi·o·log·i·cal** \-,bī-ə-'lä-ji-kəl\ adjective
**— neu·ro·bi·ol·o·gist** \-bī-'ä-lə-jist\ noun

**neu·ro·blas·to·ma** \-,blas-'tō-mə\ noun, plural **-mas** or **-ma·ta** \-mə-tə\ [New Latin, from International Scientific Vocabulary neuroblast embryonic ganglion cell, from neur- + -blast -blast] (1910)

**:** a malignant tumor formed of embryonic ganglion cells

**neu·ro·chem·is·try** \-'ke-mə-strē\ noun (1924)
**1 :** the study of the chemical makeup and activities of nervous tissue
**2 :** chemical processes and phenomena related to the nervous system
**— neu·ro·chem·i·cal** \-'ke-mi-kəl\ adjective or noun
**— neu·ro·chem·ist** \-'ke-mist\ noun

**neu·ro·de·gen·er·a·tive** \-di-'je-nə-rə-tiv, -'jen-ə-; -'je-nə-,rā-; -dē-\ adjective (1907)
**:** relating to or characterized by degeneration of nervous tissue

**neu·ro·en·do·crine** \-'en-də-krən, -,krīn, -,krēn\ adjective (1922)
**1 :** of, relating to, or being a hormonal substance that influences the activity of nerves
**2 :** of, relating to, or functioning in neurosecretion

**neu·ro·en·do·cri·nol·o·gy** \-,en-də-kri-'nä-lə-jē, -(,)krī-\ noun (1922)
**:** a branch of the life sciences dealing with neurosecretion and the physiological interaction between the central nervous system and the endocrine system
**— neu·ro·en·do·cri·no·log·i·cal** \-,kri-n°l-'ä-ji-kəl, -,krī-, -,krē-\ adjective
**— neu·ro·en·do·cri·nol·o·gist** \-kri-'nä-lə-jist, -(,)krī-\ noun

**neu·ro·fi·bril** \-'fī-brəl, -'fi-\ noun [New Latin neurofibrilla, from neur- + fibrilla fibril] (1898)
**:** a fine proteinaceous fibril that is found in cytoplasm (as of a neuron or a paramecium) and is capable of conducting excitation
**— neu·ro·fi·bril·lary** \-brə-,ler-ē\ adjective

**neu·ro·fi·bro·ma** \-fī-'brō-mə\ noun (1892)
**:** a fibroma composed of nervous and connective tissue and produced by proliferation of Schwann cells

**neu·ro·fi·bro·ma·to·sis** \-(,)fī-,brō-mə-'tō-səs\ noun [New Latin, from neurofibromat-, neurofibroma] (1896)
**:** a disorder inherited as an autosomal dominant and characterized especially by brown spots on the skin, neurofibromas of peripheral nerves, and deformities of subcutaneous tissue and bone

**neu·ro·gen·ic** \,nùr-ə-'je-nik, ,nyùr-\ adjective (1901)
**1 :** originating in or controlled by nervous tissue ⟨neurogenic heartbeat⟩
**2 :** induced or modified by nervous factors; especially **:** disordered because of abnormally altered neural relations
**— neu·ro·gen·i·cal·ly** \-ni-k(ə-)lē\ adverb

**neu·rog·lia** \nù-'rō-glē-ə, nyù-, -'rä-; ,n(y)ùr-ə-'glē-ə, -'glī-\ noun [New Latin, from neur- + Middle Greek glia glue — more at CLAY] (1873)
**:** supporting tissue intermingled with the essential elements of nervous tissue especially in the brain, spinal cord, and ganglia
**— neu·rog·li·al** \-əl\ adjective

**neu·ro·hor·mon·al** \,nùr-ō-hòr-'mō-n°l, ,nyùr-\ adjective (circa 1935)
**1 :** involving both neural and hormonal mechanisms
**2 :** of, relating to, or being a neurohormone

**neu·ro·hor·mone** \-'hòr-,mōn\ noun [International Scientific Vocabulary] (1935)
**:** a hormone (as acetylcholine or norepinephrine) produced by or acting on nervous tissue

**neu·ro·hu·mor** \-'hyü-mər, -'yü-\ noun (1932)
**:** NEUROHORMONE; especially **:** NEUROTRANSMITTER
**— neu·ro·hu·mor·al** \-mə-rəl\ adjective

**neu·ro·hy·poph·y·sis** \-hī-'pä-fə-səs\ *noun* [New Latin] (1912)
: the portion of the pituitary gland that is composed of the infundibulum and posterior lobe and is concerned with the secretion of various hormones
— **neu·ro·hy·po·phy·se·al** *or* **neu·ro·hy·po·phy·si·al** \-(,)hī-pə-fə-'sē-əl, -,hī-pə-fə-, -'zē-, ,hī-pə-'fi-zē-\ *adjective*

**neu·ro·lep·tic** \,nùr-ə-'lep-tik, ,nyùr-\ *noun* [French *neuroleptique*, from *neur-* + *-leptique* affecting, from Greek *lēptikos* seizing, from *lambanein* to take, seize — more at LATCH] (1958)
: any of the powerful tranquilizers (as the phenothiazines) used especially to treat psychosis and believed to act by blocking dopamine nervous receptors — called also *antipsychotic*
— **neuroleptic** *adjective*

**neu·rol·o·gist** \nù-'rä-lə-jist, nyù-\ *noun* (1832)
: one specializing in neurology; *especially* : a physician skilled in the diagnosis and treatment of disease of the nervous system

**neu·rol·o·gy** \-jē\ *noun* [New Latin *neurologia*, from *neur-* + *-logia* -logy] (circa 1681)
: the scientific study of the nervous system especially in respect to its structure, functions, and abnormalities
— **neu·ro·log·i·cal** \,nùr-ə-'lä-ji-kəl, ,nyùr-\ *or* **neu·ro·log·ic** \-jik\ *adjective*
— **neu·ro·log·i·cal·ly** \-ji-k(ə-)lē\ *adverb*

**neu·ro·ma** \nù-'rō-mə, nyù-\ *noun, plural* **-mas** *or* **-ma·ta** \-mə-tə\ [New Latin] (circa 1847)
: a tumor or mass growing from a nerve and usually consisting of nerve fibers

**neu·ro·mus·cu·lar** \,nùr-ō-'məs-kyə-lər, ,nyùr-\ *adjective* [International Scientific Vocabulary] (1864)
: of or relating to nerves and muscles; *especially* : jointly involving nervous and muscular elements ⟨a *neuromuscular* junction⟩

**neu·ron** \'nü-,rän, 'nyü-; 'nur-,än, 'nyùr-\ *also* **neu·rone** \-,rōn, -,ōn\ *noun* [New Latin *neuron*, from Greek, nerve, sinew — more at NERVE] (1891)
: a grayish or reddish granular cell with specialized processes that is the fundamental functional unit of nervous tissue
— **neu·ro·nal** \'nùr-ə-n°l, 'nyùr-; nù-'rō-n°l, nyù-\ *also* **neu·ron·ic** \nù-'rä-nik, nyù-\ *adjective*

**neu·ro·pa·thol·o·gy** \,nùr-ō-pə-'thä-lə-jē, ,nyùr-, -pa-\ *noun* [International Scientific Vocabulary] (1853)
: pathology of the nervous system
— **neu·ro·path·o·log·ic** \-,pa-thə-'lä-jik\ *or* **neu·ro·path·o·log·i·cal** \-ji-kəl\ *adjective*
— **neu·ro·pa·thol·o·gist** \-pə-'thä-lə-jist, -pa-\ *noun*

**neu·rop·a·thy** \nù-'rä-pə-thē, nyù-\ *noun, plural* **-thies** [International Scientific Vocabulary] (1857)
: an abnormal and usually degenerative state of the nervous system or nerves; *also* : a systemic condition that stems from a neuropathy
— **neu·ro·path·ic** \,nùr-ə-'pa-thik, ,nyùr-\ *adjective*
— **neu·ro·path·i·cal·ly** \-thi-k(ə-)lē\ *adverb*

**neu·ro·pep·tide** \,nùr-ə-'pep-,tīd, ,nyùr-\ *noun* (1975)
: an endogenous peptide that influences neural activity or functioning

**neu·ro·phar·ma·col·o·gy** \,nùr-ō-,fär-mə-'kä-lə-jē, ,nyùr-\ *noun* (1950)
**1** : a branch of medical science dealing with the action of drugs on and in the nervous system
**2** : the properties and reactions of a drug on and in the nervous system
— **neu·ro·phar·ma·co·log·i·cal** \-kə-'lä-ji-kəl\ *also* **neu·ro·phar·ma·co·log·ic** \-jik\ *adjective*

— **neu·ro·phar·ma·col·o·gist** \-'kä-lə-jist\ *noun*

**neu·ro·phys·i·ol·o·gy** \-,fi-zē-'ä-lə-jē\ *noun* (1868)
: physiology of the nervous system
— **neu·ro·phys·i·o·log·i·cal** \-ə-'lä-ji-kəl\ *also* **neu·ro·phys·i·o·log·ic** \-jik\ *adjective*
— **neu·ro·phys·i·o·log·i·cal·ly** \-ji-k(ə-)lē\ *adverb*
— **neu·ro·phys·i·ol·o·gist** \-'ä-lə-jist\ *noun*

**neu·ro·psy·chi·a·try** \-sə-'kī-ə-trē, -sī-\ *noun* (1918)
: a branch of medicine concerned with both neurology and psychiatry
— **neu·ro·psy·chi·at·ric** \-,sī-kē-'a-trik\ *adjective*
— **neu·ro·psy·chi·at·ri·cal·ly** \-tri-k(ə-)lē\ *adverb*
— **neu·ro·psy·chi·a·trist** \-sə-'kī-ə-trist, -sī-\ *noun*

**neu·ro·psy·chol·o·gy** \-sī-'kä-lə-jē\ *noun* (circa 1893)
: a science concerned with the integration of psychological observations on behavior and the mind with neurological observations on the brain and nervous system
— **neu·ro·psy·cho·log·i·cal** \-,sī-kə-'lä-ji-kəl\ *adjective*
— **neu·ro·psy·chol·o·gist** \-sī-'kä-lə-jist\ *noun*

**neu·rop·ter·an** \nù-'räp-tə-rən, nyù-\ *noun* [ultimately from Greek *neur-* + *pteron* wing — more at FEATHER] (circa 1842)
: any of an order (Neuroptera) of usually netwinged insects that include the lacewings and ant lions
— **neuropteran** *adjective*
— **neu·rop·ter·ous** \-rəs\ *adjective*

**neu·ro·ra·di·ol·o·gy** \,nùr-ō-,rā-dē-'ä-lə-jē, ,nyùr-\ *noun* (1938)
: radiology of the nervous system
— **neu·ro·ra·dio·log·i·cal** \-ə-'lä-ji-kəl\ *adjective*
— **neu·ro·ra·di·ol·o·gist** \-'ä-lə-jist\ *noun*

**neu·ro·sci·ence** \-'sī-ə̇n(t)s\ *noun* (1963)
: a branch (as neurophysiology) of the life sciences that deals with the anatomy, physiology, biochemistry, or molecular biology of nerves and nervous tissue and especially with their relation to behavior and learning
— **neu·ro·sci·en·tif·ic** \-,sī-ə̇n-'ti-fik\ *adjective*
— **neu·ro·sci·en·tist** \-'sī-ə̇n-tist\ *noun*

**neu·ro·se·cre·tion** \-si-'krē-shən\ *noun* (1941)
**1** : the process of producing a secretion by nerve cells
**2** : a secretion produced by neurosecretion
— **neu·ro·se·cre·to·ry** \-'krē-tə-rē\ *adjective*

**neu·ro·sen·so·ry** \-'sen(t)-sə-rē, -'sen(t)s-rē\ *adjective* (1929)
: of or relating to afferent nerves

**neu·ro·sis** \nù-'rō-səs, nyù-\ *noun, plural* **-ro·ses** \-,sēz\ [New Latin] (circa 1784)
: a mental and emotional disorder that affects only part of the personality, is accompanied by a less distorted perception of reality than in a psychosis, does not result in disturbance of the use of language, and is accompanied by various physical, physiological, and mental disturbances (as visceral symptoms, anxieties, or phobias)

**neu·ros·po·ra** \nù-'räs-p(ə-)rə, nyù-\ *noun* [New Latin, from *neur-* + *spora* spore] (1928)
: any of a genus (*Neurospora* of the family Sordariaceae) of ascomycetous fungi which are used extensively in genetic research and have black perithecia and persistent asci and some of which have salmon-pink or orange spore masses and are severe pests in bakeries

**neu·ro·sur·gery** \-'sər-jə-rē, -'sərj-rē\ *noun* (1904)
: surgery of nervous structures (as nerves, the brain, or the spinal cord)

— **neu·ro·sur·geon** \-'sər-jən\ *noun*
— **neu·ro·sur·gi·cal** \-'sər-ji-kəl\ *adjective*

**¹neu·rot·ic** \nù-'rä-tik\ *adjective* (1873)
: of, relating to, constituting, or affected with neurosis
— **neu·rot·i·cal·ly** \-ti-k(ə-)lē\ *adverb*

**²neurotic** *noun* (1896)
**1** : one affected with a neurosis
**2** : an emotionally unstable individual

**neu·rot·i·cism** \nù-'rä-tə-,si-zəm, nyù-\ *noun* (1900)
: a neurotic character, condition, or trait

**neu·ro·tox·ic** \,nùr-ō-'täk-sik, ,nyùr-\ *adjective* (circa 1903)
: toxic to the nerves or nervous tissue
— **neu·ro·tox·ic·i·ty** \-,täk-'si-sə-tē\ *noun*

**neu·ro·tox·in** \-'täk-sən\ *noun* [International Scientific Vocabulary] (1902)
: a poisonous complex especially of protein that acts on the nervous system

**neu·ro·trans·mis·sion** \-tran(t)s-'mi-shən, -tranz-\ *noun* (1961)
: the transmission of nerve impulses across a synapse

**neu·ro·trans·mit·ter** \-tran(t)s-'mi-tər, -tranz-\ *noun* (1961)
: a substance (as norepinephrine or acetylcholine) that transmits nerve impulses across a synapse

**neu·ro·trop·ic** \-'trä-pik\ *adjective* [International Scientific Vocabulary] (1903)
: having an affinity for or localizing selectively in nerve tissue ⟨a *neurotropic* virus⟩

**neu·ru·la** \'nùr-ə-lə, 'nyùr-, -yə-lə\ *noun, plural* **-lae** \-,lē\ *or* **-las** [New Latin, from *neur-* + Latin *-ula* -ule] (circa 1890)
: an early vertebrate embryo which follows the gastrula and in which nervous tissue begins to differentiate and the basic pattern of the vertebrate begins to emerge
— **neu·ru·la·tion** \,nùr-ə-'lā-shən, ,nyùr-, -yə-\ *noun*

**neus·ton** \'nü-,stän, 'nyü-\ *noun* [German, from Greek, neuter of *neustos* swimming, from *nein* to swim — more at NATANT] (1928)
: minute organisms that float in the surface film of water

**¹neu·ter** \'nü-tər, 'nyü-\ *adjective* [Middle English *neutre*, from Middle French & Latin; Middle French *neutre*, from Latin *neuter*, literally, neither, from *ne-* not + *uter* which of two — more at NO, WHETHER] (14th century)
**1 a** : of, relating to, or constituting the gender that ordinarily includes most words or grammatical forms referring to things classed as neither masculine nor feminine **b** : neither active nor passive : INTRANSITIVE
**2** : taking no side : NEUTRAL
**3** : lacking or having imperfectly developed or nonfunctional generative organs ⟨the worker bee is *neuter*⟩

**²neuter** *noun* (15th century)
**1 a** : a noun, pronoun, adjective, or inflectional form or class of the neuter gender **b** : the neuter gender
**2** : one that is neutral
**3 a** : WORKER 2 **b** : a spayed or castrated animal

**³neuter** *transitive verb* (1903)
: CASTRATE, ALTER

**¹neu·tral** \'nü-trəl, 'nyü-\ *noun* (15th century)
**1** : one that is neutral
**2** : a neutral color
**3** : a position of disengagement (as of gears)

**²neutral** *adjective* [Middle French, from (assumed) Medieval Latin *neutralis*, from Latin, of neuter gender, from *neutr-, neuter*] (1549)
**1** : not engaged on either side; *specifically* : not aligned with a political or ideological grouping ⟨a *neutral* nation⟩
**2** : of or relating to a neutral state or power ⟨*neutral* territory⟩

**3 a :** not decided or pronounced as to characteristics **:** INDIFFERENT **b** (1) **:** ACHROMATIC (2) **:** nearly achromatic **c** (1) **:** NEUTER 3 (2) **:** lacking stamens or pistils **d :** neither acid nor basic **e :** not electrically charged
**4 :** produced with the tongue in the position it has when at rest ⟨the *neutral* vowels of \ə-'bəv\ *above*⟩
— **neu·tral·ly** \-trə-lē\ *adverb*
— **neu·tral·ness** *noun*
**neu·tral·ise** *British variant of* NEUTRALIZE
**neu·tral·ism** \'nü-trə-ˌli-zəm, 'nyü-\ *noun* (1579)
**1 :** NEUTRALITY
**2 :** a policy or the advocacy of neutrality especially in international affairs
— **neu·tral·ist** \-list\ *noun*
— **neu·tral·is·tic** \ˌnü-trə-'lis-tik, ˌnyü-\ *adjective*
**neu·tral·i·ty** \nü-'tra-lə-tē, nyü-\ *noun* (15th century)
**:** the quality or state of being neutral; *especially* **:** refusal to take part in a war between other powers
**neu·tral·i·za·tion** \ˌnü-trə-lə-'zā-shən, ˌnyü-\ *noun* (1808)
**1 :** an act or process of neutralizing
**2 :** the quality or state of being neutralized
**neu·tral·ize** \'nü-trə-ˌlīz, 'nyü-\ *verb* **-ized; -iz·ing** (1759)
*transitive verb*
**1 :** to make chemically neutral
**2 a :** to counteract the activity or effect of **:** make ineffective ⟨propaganda that is difficult to *neutralize*⟩ **b :** KILL, DESTROY
**3 :** to make electrically inert by combining equal positive and negative quantities
**4 :** to invest (as a territory or a nation) with conventional or obligatory neutrality conferring inviolability during a war
**5 :** to make neutral by blending with the complementary color
**6 :** to give (as a pair of phonemes) a nondistinctive form or pronunciation ⟨\t\ and \d\ are *neutralized* when pronounced as flaps⟩
*intransitive verb*
**:** to undergo neutralization
— **neu·tral·iz·er** *noun*
**neutral red** *noun* (1890)
**:** a basic dye used chiefly as a biological stain and acid-base indicator
**neutral spirits** *noun plural but singular or plural in construction* (1919)
**:** ethyl alcohol of 190 or higher proof used especially for blending other alcoholic liquors
**neu·tri·no** \nü-'trē-(ˌ)nō, nyü-\ *noun, plural* **-nos** [Italian, from *neutro* neutral, neuter, from Latin *neutr-, neuter*] (1934)
**:** an uncharged elementary particle that is believed to be massless or to have a very small mass, that has any of three forms, and that interacts only rarely with other particles
— **neu·tri·no·less** \-ləs\ *adjective*
**neu·tron** \'nü-ˌträn, 'nyü-\ *noun* [probably from *neutral*] (1932)
**:** an uncharged elementary particle that has a mass nearly equal to that of the proton and is present in all known atomic nuclei except the hydrogen nucleus
— **neu·tron·ic** \nü-'trä-nik, nyü-\ *adjective*
**neutron activation analysis** *noun* (1951)
**:** an analytical method used to determine the chemical elements comprising a material by bombarding it with neutrons to produce radioactive atoms whose radiations are indicative of the elements present — called also *neutron activation*
**neutron bomb** *noun* (1959)
**:** a nuclear bomb designed to produce lethal neutrons but less blast and fire damage than other nuclear bombs
**neutron star** *noun* (1934)
**:** a hypothetical dense celestial object that consists primarily of closely packed neutrons and that results from the collapse of a much larger stellar body

**¹neu·tro·phil** \'nü-trə-ˌfil, 'nyü-\ *or* **neu·tro·phil·ic** \ˌnü-trə-'fi-lik, ˌnyü-\ *adjective* [International Scientific Vocabulary *neutro-* (from Latin *neutr-, neuter* neither) + *-phil*] (circa 1890)
**:** staining to the same degree with acid or basic dyes ⟨*neutrophil* granulocytes⟩
**²neutrophil** *noun* (1897)
**:** a granulocyte that is the chief phagocytic white blood cell of the blood
**né·vé** \nā-'vā\ *noun* [French dialect (Swiss), from (assumed) Vulgar Latin *nivatum*, from Latin *niv-, nix* snow — more at SNOW] (1843)
**:** the partially compacted granular snow that forms the surface part of the upper end of a glacier; *broadly* **:** a field of granular snow
**nev·er** \'ne-vər\ *adverb* [Middle English, from Old English *næfre*, from *ne* not + *æfre* ever — more at NO] (before 12th century)
**1 :** not ever **:** at no time ⟨*never* saw her before⟩
**2 :** not in any degree **:** not under any condition ⟨*never* the wiser for his experience⟩
**never mind** *conjunction* (1954)
**:** MUCH LESS, LET ALONE — used especially in negative contexts to add to one term another denoting something less likely ⟨with this knee I can hardly walk, *never mind* run⟩
**nev·er·more** \ˌne-vər-'mōr, -'mȯr\ *adverb* (12th century)
**:** never again
**nev·er–nev·er land** \ˌne-vər-'ne-vər-\ *noun* (1907)
**:** an ideal or imaginary place
**nev·er·the·less** \ˌne-vər-thə-'les\ *adverb* (14th century)
**:** in spite of that **:** HOWEVER ⟨her childish but *nevertheless* real delight —Richard Corbin⟩
**ne·vus** \'nē-vəs\ *noun, plural* **ne·vi** \-ˌvī\ [New Latin, from Latin *naevus*] (circa 1836)
**:** a congenital pigmented area on the skin **:** BIRTHMARK
**¹new** \'nü, *chiefly British* 'nyü, *in place names usually* (ˌ)nü *or* nə *or* (ˌ)ni\ *adjective* [Middle English, from Old English; akin to Old High German *niuwi* new, Latin *novus*, Greek *neos*] (before 12th century)
**1 :** having existed or having been made but a short time **:** RECENT, MODERN
**2 a** (1) **:** having been seen, used, or known for a short time **:** NOVEL ⟨rice was a *new* crop for the area⟩ (2) **:** UNFAMILIAR ⟨visit *new* places⟩ **b :** being other than the former or old ⟨a steady flow of *new* money⟩
**3 :** having been in a relationship or condition but a short time ⟨*new* to the job⟩
**4 a :** beginning as the resumption or repetition of a previous act or thing ⟨a *new* day⟩ ⟨the *new* edition⟩ **b :** made or become fresh ⟨awoke a *new* person⟩
**5 :** different from one of the same category that has existed previously ⟨*new* realism⟩
**6 :** of dissimilar origin and usually of superior quality ⟨introducing *new* blood⟩
**7** *capitalized* **:** MODERN 3; *especially* **:** having been in use after medieval times ☆
— **new·ish** \'nü-ish, 'nyü-\ *adjective*
— **new·ness** *noun*
**²new** *adverb* (before 12th century)
**:** NEWLY, RECENTLY — usually used in combination
**New Age** *adjective* (1956)
**1 :** of, relating to, or being a late 20th century social movement drawing on ancient concepts especially from Eastern and American Indian traditions and incorporating such themes as holism, concern for nature, spirituality, and metaphysics
**2 :** of, relating to, or being a soft soothing form of instrumental music often used to promote relaxation
**¹new·born** \-ˌbȯrn\ *adjective* (14th century)
**1 :** recently born
**2 :** born anew
**²newborn** *noun, plural* **newborn** *or* **newborns** (1879)
**:** a newborn individual

**New·burg** *or* **New·burgh** \'nü-ˌbərg, 'nyü-\ *adjective* [origin unknown] (1902)
**:** served with a sauce made of cream, butter, sherry, and egg yolks ⟨lobster *Newburg*⟩ ⟨shrimp *Newburg*⟩
**New·cas·tle disease** \'nü-ˌka-səl-, 'nyü-; n(y)ü-'\ *noun* [Newcastle upon Tyne, England] (1927)
**:** a destructive virus disease of birds and especially domestic fowl that involves respiratory and nervous symptoms
**new·com·er** \'nü-ˌkə-mər, 'nyü-\ *noun* (15th century)
**1 :** one recently arrived
**2 :** BEGINNER
**New Criticism** *noun* (1941)
**:** an analytic literary criticism that is marked by concentration on the language, imagery, and emotional or intellectual tensions in literary works
— **New Critic** *noun*
— **New Critical** *adjective*
**New Deal** *noun* [from the supposed resemblance to the situation of freshness and equality of opportunity afforded by a fresh deal in a card game] (1932)
**:** the legislative and administrative program of President F. D. Roosevelt designed to promote economic recovery and social reform during the 1930s; *also* **:** the period of this program
— **New Dealer** *noun*
— **New Deal·ish** \-'dē-lish\ *adjective*
— **New Deal·ism** \-'dē(ə)-ˌli-zəm\ *noun*
**new drug** *noun* (circa 1951)
**:** a drug that has not been declared safe and effective by qualified experts under the conditions prescribed, recommended, or suggested in the label and that may be a new chemical formula or an established drug prescribed for use in a new way
**new economics** *noun plural but usually singular in construction* (1928)
**:** an economic concept that is a logical extension of Keynesianism and that holds that appropriate fiscal and monetary maneuvering can maintain healthy economic growth and prosperity indefinitely
**new·el** \'nü-əl, 'nyü-\ *noun* [Middle English *nowell*, from Middle French *nouel* stone of a fruit, from Late Latin *nucalis* like a nut, from Latin *nuc-, nux* nut — more at NUT] (14th century)
**1 :** an upright post about which the steps of a circular staircase wind
**2 :** a post at the foot of a straight stairway or one at a landing
**New English Bible** *noun* (1957)
**:** a translation of the Bible by a British interdenominational committee first published in its entirety in 1970
**new·fan·gled** \nü-'faŋ-gəld\ *adjective* [Middle English, from *newefangel*, from *new* + (assumed) Old English *-fangol*, from Old English

---

☆ **SYNONYMS**
**New, novel, original, fresh** mean having recently come into existence or use. NEW may apply to what is freshly made and unused ⟨*new* brick⟩ or has not been known before ⟨*new* designs⟩ or not experienced before ⟨starts the *new* job⟩. NOVEL applies to what is not only new but strange or unprecedented ⟨a *novel* approach to the problem⟩. ORIGINAL applies to what is the first of its kind to exist ⟨a man without one *original* idea⟩. FRESH applies to what has not lost its qualities of newness such as liveliness, energy, brightness ⟨*fresh* towels⟩ ⟨a *fresh* start⟩.

---

\ə\ **abut** \ᵊ\ **kitten** \ər\ **further** \a\ **ash** \ā\ **ace** \ä\ **mop, mar** \au̇\ **out** \ch\ **chin** \e\ **bet** \ē\ **easy** \g\ **go** \i\ **hit** \ī\ **ice** \j\ **job** \ŋ\ **sing** \ō\ **go** \ȯ\ **law** \ȯi\ **boy** \th\ **thin** \t͟h\ **the** \ü\ **loot** \u̇\ **foot** \y\ **yet** \zh\ **vision** *see also* Guide to Pronunciation

*fōn* (past participle *fangen*) to take, seize — more at PACT] (14th century)
**1** : attracted to novelty
**2** : of the newest style or kind ⟨had many *new-fangled* gadgets in the kitchen⟩
— **new·fan·gled·ness** *noun*
**new–fash·ioned** \-'fa-shənd\ *adjective* (1592)
**1** : made in a new fashion or form
**2** : UP-TO-DATE
**new·found** \-'faùnd\ *adjective* (15th century)
: newly found ⟨a *newfound* friend⟩
**New·found·land** \'nü-fən(d)-lənd, 'nyü-, -,land; n(y)ü-'faùnd-lənd\ *noun* [*Newfoundland*, Canada] (1773)
: any of a breed of very large heavy highly intelligent, black, black and white, or bronze dogs developed in Newfoundland

Newfoundland

**New·gate** \'nü-,gāt, 'nyü-, -gət\ *noun* (14th century)
: a London prison razed in 1902
**New Greek** *noun* (circa 1958)
: Greek as used by the Greeks since the end of the medieval period
**New Hebrew** *noun* (circa 1959)
: the Hebrew language in use in present-day Israel
**new·ie** \'nü-ē, 'nyü-\ *noun* (circa 1945)
: something new
**New Jer·sey tea** \nü-'jər-zē-, nyü-\ *noun* [*New Jersey*, state of U.S.; from the use of its leaves as a substitute for tea during the American Revolution] (1759)
: a low deciduous shrub (*Ceanothus americanus*) of the buckthorn family that is found in the eastern U.S. and has dull green leaves and small white flowers borne in large terminal panicles
**New Je·ru·sa·lem** \-jə-'rü-s(ə-)ləm, -zə-ləm; -'rüz-ləm\ *noun* [from the phrase "the holy city, *New Jerusalem*" (Revelation 21:2)] (1535)
**1** : the final abode of souls redeemed by Christ
**2** : an ideal earthly community
**New Journalism** *noun* (1967)
: journalism that features the author's subjective responses to people and events and that often includes fictional elements meant to illuminate and dramatize those responses
**New Latin** *noun* (circa 1889)
: Latin as used since the end of the medieval period especially in scientific description and classification
**New Left** *noun* (1960)
: a political movement originating especially among students in the 1960s, favoring confrontational tactics, often breaking with traditional leftist ideologies, and associated especially with antiwar, antinuclear, feminist, and ecological issues
— **new leftist** *noun, often N&L capitalized*
**new·ly** \'nü-lē, 'nyü-\ *adverb* (before 12th century)
**1** : LATELY, RECENTLY ⟨a *newly* married couple⟩
**2** : ANEW, AFRESH
**new·ly·wed** \-,wed\ *noun* (1918)
: a person recently married
**new·mar·ket** \'nü-,mär-kət, 'nyü-\ *noun* [*Newmarket*, England] (1837)
: a long close-fitting coat worn in the 19th century
**new math** *noun* (1964)
: basic mathematics taught with emphasis on abstraction and the principles of set theory — called also *new mathematics*
**new moon** *noun* (before 12th century)
**1** : the moon's phase when it is in conjunction with the sun so that its dark side is toward the earth; *also* : the thin crescent moon seen shortly after sunset for a few days after the actual occurrence of the new moon phase
**2** : the first day of each Jewish month marked by a special liturgy
**New Right** *noun* (1966)
: a political movement made up especially of Protestants, opposed especially to secular humanism, and concerned with issues especially of church and state, patriotism, laissez-faire economics, pornography, and abortion
**news** \'nüz, 'nyüz\ *noun plural but singular in construction, often attributive* (15th century)
**1 a** : a report of recent events **b** : previously unknown information ⟨I've got *news* for you⟩
**2 a** : material reported in a newspaper or news periodical or on a newscast **b** : matter that is newsworthy
**3** : NEWSCAST ▢
— **news·less** \-ləs\ *adjective*
**news agency** *noun* (1873)
: an organization that supplies news to subscribing newspapers, periodicals, and newscasters
**news·agent** \'nüz-,ā-jənt, 'nyüz-\ *noun* (1851)
*chiefly British* : NEWSDEALER
**news·boy** \-,bòi\ *noun* (1764)
: one who delivers or sells newspapers
**news·break** \-,brāk\ *noun* (1944)
: a newsworthy event
**news·cast** \-,kast\ *noun* [*news* + broad*cast*] (circa 1939)
: a radio or television broadcast of news
— **news·cast·er** \-,kas-tər\ *noun*
**news conference** *noun* (1946)
: PRESS CONFERENCE
**news·deal·er** \-,dē-lər\ *noun* (1861)
: a dealer in newspapers, magazines, and often paperback books
**news·hound** \-,haùnd\ *noun* (1918)
: an aggressive journalist
**news·let·ter** \-,le-tər\ *noun* (1903)
: a small publication (as a leaflet or newspaper) containing news of interest chiefly to a special group
**news·mag·a·zine** \-,ma-gə-,zēn, -'zēn\ *noun* (1923)
**1** : a usually weekly magazine devoted chiefly to summarizing and analyzing news
**2** : MAGAZINE 4c
**news·man** \-mən, -,man\ *noun* (1596)
: one who gathers, reports, or comments on the news : REPORTER, CORRESPONDENT
**news·mon·ger** \-,mən-gər, -,mäŋ-\ *noun* (1592)
: one who is active in gathering and repeating news; *especially* : GOSSIP
**¹news·pa·per** \'nüz-,pā-pər, 'nyüz-, 'n(y)üs-\ *noun* (1670)
**1** : a paper that is printed and distributed usually daily or weekly and that contains news, articles of opinion, features, and advertising
**2** : an organization that publishes a newspaper
**3** : the paper of a newspaper : NEWSPRINT
**²newspaper** *intransitive verb* (1943)
: to do newspaper work
**news·pa·per·man** \-,man\ *noun* (1806)
: one who owns or is employed by a newspaper
**news·pa·per·wom·an** \-,wù-mən\ *noun* (1881)
: a woman who owns or is employed by a newspaper
**new·speak** \'nü-,spēk, 'nyü-\ *noun, often capitalized* [*Newspeak*, a language "designed to diminish the range of thought," in the novel *1984* (1949) by George Orwell] (1950)
: propagandistic language marked by euphemism, circumlocution, and the inversion of customary meanings : DOUBLE-TALK 2
**news·peo·ple** \'nüz-,pē-pəl, 'nyüz-\ *noun plural* (1972)
: REPORTERS
**news·per·son** \-,pər-s°n\ *noun* (1973)
: REPORTER
**news·print** \-,print\ *noun* (1909)
: paper made chiefly from groundwood pulp and used mostly for newspapers
**news·read·er** \-,rē-dər\ *noun* (1925)
*chiefly British* : one who broadcasts the news
**news·reel** \-,rēl\ *noun* (1916)
: a short movie dealing with current events
**news·room** \-,rüm, -,rùm\ *noun* (1929)
**1** : a place (as an office) where news is prepared for publication or broadcast
**2** : NEWSSTAND
**news·stand** \-,stand\ *noun* (1872)
: a place (as an outdoor stall) where newspapers and periodicals are sold
**New Style** *adjective* (1615)
: using or according to the Gregorian calendar
**news·week·ly** \-,wē-klē\ *noun* (1947)
: a weekly newspaper or newsmagazine
**news·wom·an** \-,wù-mən\ *noun* (1928)
: a woman who is a reporter
**news·wor·thy** \-,wər-thē\ *adjective* (1932)
: sufficiently interesting to the general public to warrant reporting (as in a newspaper)
— **news·wor·thi·ness** \-thē-nəs\ *noun*
**news·writ·ing** \-,rī-tiŋ\ *noun* (1916)
: JOURNALISM 1a
**newsy** \'nü-zē, 'nyü-\ *adjective* **news·i·er; -est** (1832)
**1** : containing or filled with news ⟨*newsy* letters⟩
**2** : NEWSWORTHY
— **news·i·ness** *noun*
**newt** \'nüt, 'nyüt\ *noun* [Middle English, alteration (resulting from misdivision of *an ewte*) of *ewte* — more at EFT] (15th century)
: any of various small semiaquatic salamanders (as of the genus *Triturus*)

newt

**New Testament** *noun* (14th century)
: the second part of the Christian Bible comprising the canonical Gospels and Epistles and also the book of Acts and book of Revelation — see BIBLE table
**new·ton** \'nü-t°n, 'nyü-\ *noun* [Sir Isaac *Newton*] (1904)
: the unit of force in the meter-kilogram-second system equal to the force required to impart an acceleration of one meter per second per second to a mass of one kilogram
**new town** *noun* (1918)
: an urban development comprising a small to medium-sized city with a broad range of housing and planned industrial, commercial, and recreational facilities
**new wave** *noun, often N&W capitalized* (1960)
**1** : a cinematic movement that is characterized by improvisation, abstraction, and subjective

symbolism and that often makes use of experimental photographic techniques
**2** : a new movement in a particular field
**3** : rock music characterized by cohesive ensemble playing and usually lyrics which express anger and social discontent
**4** : DERNIER CRI; *especially* : fashion that is strikingly outrageous
— **new–wave** \'nü-ˌwāv, 'nyü-, -ˌwāv\ *adjective*
— **new wav·er** \-'wā-vər\ *noun*
**New World** *noun* (1555)
: WESTERN HEMISPHERE; *especially* : the continental landmass of North and South America
**New Year** *noun* (13th century)
**1** : the calendar year about to start or recently started
**2 a** : NEW YEAR'S DAY **b** : the first days of a calendar year
**3** : ROSH HASHANAH
**New Year's Day** *noun* (13th century)
: the first day of the calendar year observed as a legal holiday in many countries
¹**next** \'nekst\ *adjective* [Middle English, from Old English *nīehst,* superlative of *nēah* nigh — more at NIGH] (before 12th century)
**1** : immediately adjacent (as in place, rank, or time)
**2** : any other considered hypothetically ⟨knew it as well as the *next* man⟩
²**next** *preposition* (before 12th century)
: nearest or adjacent to
³**next** *adverb* (14th century)
**1** : in the time, place, or order nearest or immediately succeeding ⟨*next* we drove home⟩ ⟨the *next* closest school⟩
**2** : on the first occasion to come ⟨when *next* we meet⟩
**next–door** \'neks(t)-'dōr, -'dȯr\ *adjective* (1749)
: located or living in the next building, house, apartment, or room; *broadly* : NEARBY, ADJACENT
**next door** *adverb* (1579)
: in or to the next building, house, apartment, or room ⟨lives *next door*⟩; *broadly* : in or at an adjacent place
— **next door to** : NEXT TO
**next friend** *noun* (1579)
: a person admitted to or appointed by a court to act for the benefit of a person (as an infant) lacking full legal capacity
**next of kin** (1766)
: one or more persons in the nearest degree of relationship to another person
¹**next to** *preposition* (1633)
**1** : immediately following or adjacent to
**2** : in comparison to ⟨*next to* you I'm wealthy⟩
²**next to** *adverb* (1667)
: very nearly : ALMOST ⟨it was *next to* impossible to see in the fog⟩
**nex·us** \'nek-səs\ *noun, plural* **nex·us·es** \-sə-səz\ *or* **nex·us** \-səs, -ˌsüs\ [Latin, from *nectere* to bind] (1663)
**1** : CONNECTION, LINK; *also* : a causal link
**2** : a connected group or series
**3** : CENTER, FOCUS
**Nez Percé** *or* **Nez Perce** \'nez-'pərs, 'nes-'pers, ÷'nā-per-'sā\ *noun, plural* **Nez Percé** *or* **Nez Per·cés** \same *or* -'pər-səz, -'per-; ÷-per-'sā(z)\ *or* **Nez Perce** *or* **Nez Per·ces** \same *or* -'pər-səz, -'per-\ [French, literally, pierced nose] (1812)
**1** : a member of an American Indian people of Idaho, Washington, and Oregon
**2** : the language of the Nez Percé people
**ngul·trum** \eŋ-'gùl-trəm, en-\ *noun* [Tibetan] (1973)
— see MONEY table
**ngwee** \eŋ-'gwē, en-\ *noun, plural* **ngwee** [Bemba, literally, bright] (1966)
— see *kwacha* at MONEY table
**ni·a·cin** \'nī-ə-sən\ *noun* [nicotinic *acid* + ¹-*in*] (1942)
: NICOTINIC ACID; *also* : NICOTINAMIDE

**ni·a·cin·amide** \ˌnī-ə-'si-nə-ˌmīd\ *noun* (1942)
: NICOTINAMIDE
**Ni·ag·a·ra** \nī-'a-g(ə-)rə\ *noun* [*Niagara* Falls] (1841)
: an overwhelming flood : TORRENT ⟨a *Niagara* of protests⟩
**ni·al·amide** \nī-'a-lə-ˌmīd\ *noun* [nicotinic acid + *amyl* + *amide*] (1959)
: a synthetic antidepressant drug $C_{16}H_{18}N_4O_2$ that is an inhibitor of monoamine oxidase
**nib** \'nib\ *noun* [probably alteration of *neb*] (1585)
**1** : BILL, BEAK
**2 a** : the sharpened point of a quill pen **b** : PEN POINT; *also* : each of the two divisions of a pen point
**3** : a small pointed or projecting part
¹**nib·ble** \'ni-bəl\ *verb* **nib·bled; nib·bling** \-b(ə-)liŋ\ [origin unknown] (circa 1512)
*transitive verb*
**1 a** : to bite gently **b** : to eat or chew in small bits
**2** : to take away bit by bit ⟨waves *nibbling* the shore⟩
*intransitive verb*
**1** : to take gentle, small, or cautious bites; *also* : SNACK
**2** : to deal with something as if by nibbling
— **nib·bler** \-b(ə-)lər\ *noun*
²**nibble** *noun* (1658)
**1** : an act of nibbling
**2** : a very small quantity or portion (as of food); *also* : SNACK
**3** : a tentative expression of interest
**Ni·be·lung** \'nē-bə-ˌlùŋ\ *noun, plural* **-lungs** *also* **-lung·en** \-ˌlùŋ-ən\ [German] (1861)
**1** : a member of a race of dwarfs in Germanic legend
**2** : any of the followers of Siegfried
**3** : any of the Burgundian kings in the medieval German *Nibelungenlied*
**nibs** \'nibz\ *noun plural but singular in construction* [origin unknown] (circa 1821)
: an important or self-important person — usually used in the phrases *his nibs* or *her nibs* as if a title of honor
**ni·cad** \'nī-ˌkad\ *noun* [¹nickel + *cad*mium] (1965)
: a rechargeable dry cell that has a nickel cathode and a cadmium anode
**nic·co·lite** \'ni-kə-ˌlīt\ *noun* [New Latin *niccolum* nickel, probably from Swedish *nickel*] (1868)
: a pale copper-red usually massive mineral of metallic luster that is essentially a nickel arsenide
**nice** \'nīs\ *adjective* **nic·er; nic·est** [Middle English, foolish, wanton, from Old French, from Latin *nescius* ignorant, from *nescire* not to know — more at NESCIENCE] (14th century)
**1** *obsolete* **a** : WANTON, DISSOLUTE **b** : COY, RETICENT
**2 a** : showing fastidious or finicky tastes : PARTICULAR **b** : exacting in requirements or standards : PUNCTILIOUS
**3** : possessing, marked by, or demanding great or excessive precision and delicacy
**4** *obsolete* : TRIVIAL
**5 a** : PLEASING, AGREEABLE ⟨a *nice* time⟩ ⟨a *nice* person⟩ **b** : well-executed ⟨*nice* shot⟩ **c** : APPROPRIATE, FITTING
**6 a** : socially acceptable : WELL-BRED **b** : VIRTUOUS, RESPECTABLE
**7** : POLITE, KIND ⟨that's *nice* of you to say⟩ ◆
**synonym** see CORRECT
— **nice** *adverb*
— **nice·ly** *adverb*
— **nice·ness** *noun*
**Ni·cene** \'nī-ˌsēn, nī-\ *adjective* [Middle English, from Late Latin *nicaenus,* from Latin *Nicaea* Nicaea, from Greek *Nikaia*] (14th century)
**1** : of or relating to Nicaea or the Nicaeans

**2** : of or relating to the ecumenical church council held in Nicaea in A.D. 325 or to the Nicene Creed
**Nicene Creed** *noun* (circa 1569)
: a Christian creed expanded from a creed issued by the first Nicene Council, beginning "I believe in one God," and used in liturgical worship
**nice-nel·ly** \'nīs-'ne-lē\ *adjective, often 2d N capitalized* [from the name *Nelly*] (1925)
**1** : marked by euphemism
**2** : PRUDISH
— **nice nelly** *noun, often 2d N capitalized*
— **nice-nel·ly·ism** \-ˌi-zəm\ *noun, often 2d N capitalized*
**nice·ty** \'nī-sə-tē, -stē\ *noun, plural* **-ties** [Middle English *nicete,* from Middle French *niceté* foolishness, from *nice,* adjective] (14th century)
**1** : the quality or state of being nice
**2** : an elegant, delicate, or civilized feature ⟨enjoy the *niceties* of life⟩
**3** : a fine point or distinction : SUBTLETY ⟨the *niceties* of table manners⟩
**4** : careful attention to details : delicate exactness : PRECISION
**5** : delicacy of taste or feeling : FASTIDIOUSNESS
¹**niche** \'nich, ÷'nēsh\ *noun* [French, from Middle French, from *nicher* to nest, from (assumed) Vulgar Latin *nidicare,* from Latin *nidus* nest — more at NEST] (1611)
**1 a** : a recess in a wall especially for a statue **b** : something that resembles a niche
**2 a** : a place, employment, status, or activity for which a person or thing is best fitted **b** : a habitat supplying the factors necessary for the existence of an organism or species **c** : the ecological role of an organism in a community especially in regard to food consumption **d** : a specialized market

niche 1a

²**niche** *transitive verb* **niched; nich·ing** (1752)
: to place in or as if in a niche
**Ni·chrome** \'nī-ˌkrōm\ *trademark*

\ə\ abut \ᵊ\ kitten \ər\ further \a\ ash \ā\ ace \ä\ mop, mar \aù\ out \ch\ chin \e\ bet \ē\ easy \g\ go \i\ hit \ī\ ice \j\ job \ŋ\ sing \ō\ go \ȯ\ law \ȯi\ boy \th\ thin \t͟h\ the \ü\ loot \ù\ foot \y\ yet \zh\ vision   *see also* Guide to Pronunciation

— used for an alloy of nickel, chromium, and iron that is commonly used in the heating elements of electrical appliances

¹**nick** \'nik\ *noun* [Middle English *nyke,* probably alteration of *nocke* nock] (15th century)

**1 a :** a small notch or groove **b :** a break in one strand of two-stranded DNA caused by a missing phosphodiester bond **c :** a small cut incurred in shaving

**2 :** a final critical moment ⟨in the *nick* of time⟩

**3** *slang British* **:** PRISON; *also* **:** POLICE STATION

**4** *British* **:** CONDITION ⟨in good *nick*⟩

²**nick** (1523)
*transitive verb*

**1 :** to jot down **:** RECORD

**2 a :** to make a nick in **:** NOTCH, CHIP **b :** to cut into or wound slightly ⟨a bullet *nicked* his leg⟩

**3 :** to cut short ⟨cold weather, which *nicked* steel and automobile output —*Time*⟩

**4 :** to catch at the right point or time

**5 :** CHEAT, OVERCHARGE

**6 a** *slang British* **:** ARREST **b** *slang British* **:** STEAL

*intransitive verb*

**1 :** to make petty attacks **:** SNIPE

**2 :** to complement one another genetically and produce superior offspring

**nick·el** *also* **nick·le** \'ni-kəl\ *noun* [probably from Swedish *nickel,* from German *Kupfernickel* niccolite, probably from *Kupfer* copper + *Nickel* goblin; from the deceptive copper color of niccolite] (1755)

**1 :** a silver-white hard malleable ductile metallic element capable of a high polish and resistant to corrosion that is used chiefly in alloys and as a catalyst — see ELEMENT table

**2 a** (1) **:** the U.S. 5-cent piece regularly containing 25 percent nickel and 75 percent copper (2) **:** the Canadian 5-cent piece **b :** five cents

**3 :** a pass defense in football that employs five defensive backs

¹**nick·el–and–dime** \,ni-kəl-ən-'dīm\ *adjective* (1950)

**1 :** involving or offering only a small amount of money

**2 :** SMALL-TIME

²**nickel–and–dime** *transitive verb* **nick·eled–and–dimed** \,ni-kəld-ən-'dīmd\ *or* **nick·el–and–dimed** \-ən-'dīmd\; **nick·el·ing–and–dim·ing** \-'dī-miŋ\ *or* **nickel–and–diming** (1961)

**:** to impair, weaken, or defeat gradually (as through a series of small incursions or excessive attention to detail)

**nick·el·if·er·ous** \,ni-kə-'li-f(ə-)rəs\ *adjective* (1821)

**:** containing nickel

**nick·el·ode·on** \,ni-kə-'lō-dē-ən\ *noun* [probably from *nickel* + *-odeon* (as in *melodeon* music hall)] (1907)

**1 :** an early movie theater to which admission usually cost five cents

**2 :** JUKEBOX

**nickel silver** *noun* (1860)

**:** GERMAN SILVER

¹**nick·er** \'ni-kər\ *intransitive verb* **nick·ered; nick·er·ing** \-k(ə-)riŋ\ [perhaps alteration of *neigh*] (1641)

**:** NEIGH, WHINNY

— **nicker** *noun*

²**nicker** *noun* [perhaps from *nicker* one that nicks] (1910)

*slang British* **:** ¹POUND 2a

**nick·nack** *variant of* KNICKKNACK

¹**nick·name** \'nik-,nām\ *noun* [Middle English *nekename* additional name, alteration (resulting from misdivision of *an ekename*) of *ekename,* from *eke* eke, *also* + *name* name] (15th century)

**1 :** a usually descriptive name given instead of or in addition to the one belonging to a person, place, or thing

**2 :** a familiar form of a proper name (as of a person or a city) ◆

²**nickname** *transitive verb* (1536)

**1 :** MISNAME, MISCALL

**2 :** to give a nickname to

— **nick·nam·er** *noun*

**ni·co·ti·a·na** \ni-,kō-shē-'a-nə, -'ä-nə, -'ā-nə\ *noun* [New Latin, from *herba nicotiana,* literally, Nicot's herb, from Jean *Nicot* (died 1600) French diplomat and scholar] (1600)

**:** any of several tobaccos (as *Nicotiana alata*) grown for their showy flowers

**nic·o·tin·amide** \,ni-kə-'tē-nə-,mīd, -'ti-\ *noun* [International Scientific Vocabulary] (1895)

**:** a compound $C_6H_6N_2O$ of the vitamin B complex found especially as a constituent of coenzymes and used similarly to nicotinic acid

**nicotinamide adenine dinucleotide** *noun* (1961)

**:** NAD

**nicotinamide adenine dinucleotide phosphate** *noun* (1962)

**:** NADP

**nic·o·tine** \'ni-kə-,tēn\ *noun* [French, from New Latin *nicotiana*] (1819)

**:** a poisonous alkaloid $C_{10}H_{14}N_2$ that is the chief active principle of tobacco and is used as an insecticide

**nic·o·tin·ic** \,ni-kə-'tē-nik, -'ti-\ *adjective* [International Scientific Vocabulary] (1873)

**:** relating to, resembling, producing, or mediating the effects produced by nicotine on nerve fibers at autonomic ganglia and at the neuromuscular junctions of voluntary muscle which increases activity in small doses and inhibits it in larger doses ⟨*nicotinic* receptors⟩

— compare MUSCARINIC

**nicotinic acid** *noun* (1873)

**:** an acid $C_6H_5NO_2$ of the vitamin B complex found widely in animals and plants and used especially against pellagra — called also *niacin*

**nic·ti·tate** \'nik-tə-,tāt\ *intransitive verb* **-tat·ed; -tat·ing** [alteration of *nictate* to wink, from Latin *nictatus,* past participle of *nictare* — more at CONNIVE] (circa 1834)

**:** WINK

**nictitating membrane** *noun* (1713)

**:** a thin membrane found in many vertebrates at the inner angle or beneath the lower lid of the eye and capable of extending across the eyeball

**ni·dic·o·lous** \nī-'di-kə-ləs\ *adjective* [Latin *nidus* nest + English *-colous* — more at NEST] (circa 1902)

**1 :** reared for a time in a nest

**2 :** sharing the nest of another kind of animal

**ni·di·fi·ca·tion** \,ni-də-fə-'kā-shən, ,nī-\ *noun* [Medieval Latin *nidification-, nidificatio,* from Latin *nidificare* to build a nest, from *nidus* nest] (1658)

**:** the act, process, or technique of building a nest

**ni·dif·u·gous** \nī-'di-fyə-gəs\ *adjective* [Latin *nidus* nest + *fugere* to flee — more at FUGITIVE] (1896)

**:** leaving the nest soon after hatching

**ni·dus** \'nī-dəs\ *noun, plural* **ni·di** \'nī-,dī\ *or* **ni·dus·es** [New Latin, from Latin] (1742)

**1 :** a nest or breeding place; *especially* **:** a place or substance in an animal or plant where bacteria or other organisms lodge and multiply

**2 :** a place where something originates, develops, or is located

**niece** \'nēs\ *noun* [Middle English *nece* granddaughter, niece, from Old French *niece,* from Late Latin *neptia,* from Latin *neptis;* akin to Latin *nepot-, nepos* grandson, nephew — more at NEPHEW] (14th century)

**1 :** a daughter of one's brother, sister, brother-in-law, or sister-in-law

**2 :** an illegitimate daughter of an ecclesiastic

¹**ni·el·lo** \nē-'e-(,)lō\ *noun, plural* **ni·el·li** \-(,)lē\ *or* **niellos** [Italian, from Medieval Latin *nigellum,* from neuter of Latin *nigellus* blackish, diminutive of *niger* black] (1816)

**1 :** any of several black enamel-like alloys usually of sulfur with silver, copper, and lead

**2 :** the art or process of decorating metal with incised designs filled with niello

**3 :** a piece of metal or an object decorated with niello

²**niello** *transitive verb* (1866)

**:** to inlay or ornament with niello

**ni·fed·i·pine** \nə-'fe-də-,pēn, -pən\ *noun* [probably *nitr-* + *-fe-* (from *phenyl*) + *-dipine* (by alteration & shortening from *pyridine*)] (1974)

**:** a calcium channel blocker $C_{17}H_{18}N_2O_6$ that is a coronary vasodilator used especially in the treatment of angina pectoris

**Nifl·heim** \'ni-vəl-,hām\ *noun* [Old Norse *Niflheimr*]

**:** the abode of the dead in Norse mythology

¹**nif·ty** \'nif-tē\ *adjective* **nif·ti·er; -est** [origin unknown] (1865)

**:** very good **:** very attractive **:** FINE ⟨*nifty* clothes⟩

— **nif·ti·ly** \'nif-tə-lē\ *adverb*

²**nifty** *noun, plural* **nifties** (1923)

**:** something that is nifty; *especially* **:** a clever or neatly turned phrase or joke

**Ni·ger–Con·go** \,nī-jər-'käŋ-(,)gō\ *noun* [*Niger* (river) + *Congo* (river)] (circa 1950)

**:** a language family that includes the Mande and Kwa branches and that is spoken by most of the indigenous peoples of west, central, and south Africa

¹**nig·gard** \'ni-gərd\ *noun* [Middle English, of Scandinavian origin; akin to Old Norse *hnøggr* niggardly; akin to Old English *hnēaw* niggardly] (14th century)

**:** a meanly covetous and stingy person **:** MISER

— **niggard** *adjective*

²**niggard** (circa 1600)
*intransitive verb*
*obsolete* **:** to act niggardly
*transitive verb*
*obsolete* **:** to treat in a niggardly manner

**nig·gard·ly** \-lē\ *adjective* (1571)

**1 :** grudgingly mean about spending or granting **:** BEGRUDGING

**2 :** provided in meanly limited supply

*synonym* see STINGY

— **nig·gard·li·ness** *noun*

— **niggardly** *adverb*

**nig·ger** \'ni-gər\ *noun* [alteration of earlier *neger,* from Middle French *negre,* from Spanish or Portuguese *negro,* from *negro* black, from Latin *niger*] (1700)

**1 :** a black person — usually taken to be offensive

**2 :** a member of any dark-skinned race — usually taken to be offensive

**3 :** a member of a socially disadvantaged class of persons ⟨it's time for somebody to lead all of America's *niggers* . . . all the people who feel left out of the political process —Ron Dellums⟩ ∎

¹**nig·gle** \'ni-gəl\ *verb* **nig·gled; nig·gling**

---

◇ WORD HISTORY

**nickname** The earliest sense of *nickname* is a descriptive name given to a person, or even a place, in addition to the proper name, while today it can also refer to a shortened or familiar form of a proper name. In Middle English the word expressed the first of these senses very explicitly. The noun *eke,* meaning "addition or extension," was combined with *name,* and thus an *ekename* was an additional name. By the 15th century an *ekename,* by misperception of the boundary between article and noun, was taken to be a *nekename,* and both *ekename* and *nekename* begin to appear in writing. The latter, in the modern form *nickname,* eventually superseded the former. The noun *eke* involved in the history of *nickname* is related both to the verb *eke,* as in "to eke out a living," and to the once common but now archaic adverb *eke* "too, also."

\-g(ə-)liŋ\ [origin unknown] (circa 1616)
*intransitive verb*
**1 a :** TRIFLE **b :** to spend too much effort on minor details
**2 :** to find fault constantly in a petty way **:** CARP ⟨she haggles, she *niggles,* she wears out our patience —Virginia Woolf⟩
**3 :** GNAW
*transitive verb*
**:** to give stingily or in tiny portions
— **nig·gler** \-g(ə-)lər\ *noun*
²**niggle** *noun* (1886)
*chiefly British* **:** a trifling doubt, objection, or complaint
**nig·gling** \'ni-g(ə-)liŋ\ *adjective* (1599)
**:** PETTY; *also* **:** bothersome or persistent especially in a petty or tiresome way ⟨*niggling* injuries⟩
— **niggling** *noun*
— **nig·gling·ly** \-lē\ *adverb*
¹**nigh** \'nī\ *adverb* [Middle English, from Old English *nēah;* akin to Old High German *nāh,* adverb, nigh, preposition, nigh, after, Old Norse *nā-* nigh] (before 12th century)
**1 :** near in place, time, or relationship — often used with *on, onto,* or *unto*
**2 :** NEARLY, ALMOST
²**nigh** *adjective* (before 12th century)
**1 :** CLOSE, NEAR
**2** *chiefly dialect* **:** DIRECT, SHORT
**3 :** being on the left side ⟨the *nigh* horse⟩
³**nigh** *preposition* (before 12th century)
**:** NEAR
⁴**nigh** (13th century)
*transitive verb*
**:** to draw or come near to **:** APPROACH
*intransitive verb*
**:** to draw near
¹**night** \'nīt\ *noun* [Middle English, from Old English *niht;* akin to Old High German *naht* night, Latin *noct-, nox,* Greek *nykt-, nyx*] (before 12th century)
**1 :** the time from dusk to dawn when no sunlight is visible
**2 a :** an evening or night taken as an occasion or point of time ⟨the opening *night*⟩ **b :** an evening set aside for a particular purpose
**3 a :** the quality or state of being dark **b :** a condition or period felt to resemble the darkness of night: as (1) **:** a period of dreary inactivity or affliction (2) **:** absence of moral values **c :** the beginning of darkness **:** NIGHTFALL
— **night·less** \-ləs\ *adjective*
²**night** *adjective* (before 12th century)
**1 :** of, relating to, or associated with the night ⟨*night* air⟩
**2 :** intended for use at night ⟨a *night* lamp⟩
**3 a :** existing, occurring, or functioning at night ⟨*night* baseball⟩ ⟨a *night* nurse⟩ **b :** active or functioning best at night ⟨*night* people⟩
**night and day** *adverb* (before 12th century)
**:** all the time **:** CONTINUALLY
**night blindness** *noun* (1754)
**:** reduced visual capacity in faint light (as at night)
— **night-blind** \'nīt-,blīnd\ *adjective*
**night–blooming cereus** *noun* (1832)
**:** any of several night-blooming cacti; *especially* **:** a slender sprawling or climbing cactus (*Selenicereus grandiflorus*) often cultivated for its large showy fragrant white flowers
**night·cap** \'nīt-,kap\ *noun* (14th century)
**1 :** a cloth cap worn with nightclothes
**2 :** a usually alcoholic drink taken at the end of the day
**3 :** the final race or contest of a day's sports; *especially* **:** the second game of a baseball doubleheader
**night·clothes** \-,klō(th)z\ *noun plural* (1602)
**:** garments for wear in bed
¹**night·club** \-,kləb\ *noun* (1894)
**:** a place of entertainment open at night usually serving food and liquor, having a floor

show, and providing music and space for dancing
²**nightclub** *intransitive verb* (1936)
**:** to patronize nightclubs
— **night·club·ber** *noun*
**night court** *noun* (1934)
**:** a criminal court in a large city that sits at night (as for the summary disposition of criminal charges and the granting of bail)
**night crawler** *noun* (1924)
**:** EARTHWORM; *especially* **:** a large earthworm found on the soil surface at night
**night·dress** \'nīt-,dres\ *noun* (circa 1714)
**1 :** NIGHTGOWN
**2 :** NIGHTCLOTHES
**night·fall** \'nīt-,fȯl\ *noun* (1700)
**:** the close of the day **:** DUSK
**night·glow** \-,glō\ *noun* (1951)
**:** airglow seen during the night
**night·gown** \-,gaủn\ *noun* (14th century)
**1** *archaic* **:** DRESSING GOWN
**2 :** a loose garment for wear in bed
**night·hawk** \-,hȯk\ *noun* (1611)
**1 a :** any of a genus (*Chordeiles*) of American nightjars related to the whippoorwill **b :** a common European nightjar (*Caprimulgus europaeus*)
**2 :** a person who habitually is active late at night

**nighthawk 1a**

**night heron** *noun* (1784)
**:** any of various widely distributed nocturnal or crepuscular herons (especially genus *Nycticorax*)
**night·ie** \'nī-tē\ *or* **nighty** *noun, plural* **night·ies** [*night*gown + -*ie*] (1871)
**:** a nightgown for a woman or child
**night·in·gale** \'nī-tⁿn-,gāl, -tiŋ-\ *noun* [Middle English, alteration of Old English *nihtegale,* from *niht* + *galan* to sing — more at YELL] (13th century)
**:** any of several Old World thrushes (genus *Erithacus* and especially *E. megarhynchos*) noted for the sweet usually nocturnal song of the male; *also* **:** any of various other birds that sing at night

**nightingale**

**night·jar** \'nīt-,jär\ *noun* [from its harsh sound] (1630)
**:** any of a family (Caprimulgidae) of medium-sized long-winged crepuscular or nocturnal birds (as the whippoorwills and nighthawks) having a short bill, short legs, and soft mottled plumage and feeding on insects which they catch on the wing — called also *goatsucker*
**night latch** *noun* (1854)
**:** a door lock having a spring bolt operated from the outside by a key and from the inside by a knob
**night letter** *noun* (1910)
**:** a telegram sent at night at a reduced rate for delivery the following morning
**night·life** \'nīt-,līf\ *noun* (1852)
**:** the activity of or entertainment provided for pleasure-seekers at night (as in nightclubs); *also* **:** establishments providing nightlife
**night–light** \-,līt\ *noun* (1839)
**:** a light kept burning throughout the night
¹**night–long** \-,lȯŋ\ *adjective* (1850)
**:** lasting the whole night ⟨*nightlong* festivities⟩
²**night–long** \-'lȯŋ\ *adverb* (1870)
**:** through the whole night
¹**night–ly** \-lē\ *adjective* (before 12th century)
**1 :** happening, done, or used by night or every night

**2 :** of or relating to the night or every night
²**nightly** *adverb* (15th century)
**:** every night; *also* **:** at or by night
**night·mare** \'nīt-,mar, -,mer\ *noun* [Middle English, from ¹*night* + ¹*mare*] (14th century)
**1 :** an evil spirit formerly thought to oppress people during sleep
**2 :** a frightening dream that usually awakens the sleeper
**3 :** something (as an experience, situation, or object) having the monstrous character of a nightmare or producing a feeling of anxiety or terror ◆
— **nightmare** *adjective*
— **night·mar·ish** \-,mar-ish, -,mer-\ *adjective*
— **night·mar·ish·ly** *adverb*
**night owl** *noun* (circa 1846)
**:** a person who keeps late hours at night
**night rail** \-,rāl\ *noun* [*night* + *rail,* a woman's loose garment] (1554)
*archaic* **:** NIGHTGOWN
**night raven** *noun* (before 12th century)
**:** a bird that cries at night
**night rider** *noun* (1877)
**:** a member of a secret band who ride masked at night doing acts of violence for the purpose of punishing or terrorizing
**nights** \'nīts\ *adverb* (before 12th century)
**:** in the nighttime repeatedly **:** on any night ⟨works *nights*⟩
**night·scope** \'nīt-,skōp\ *noun* (1972)
**:** an optical device usually using infrared radiation that enables a person to see objects in the dark better
**night·shade** \-,shād\ *noun* (before 12th century)
**1 :** any of a genus (*Solanum* of the family Solanaceae, the nightshade family) of herbs, shrubs, and trees having alternate leaves, cymose flowers, and fruits that are berries and including some poisonous weeds, various ornamentals, and important crop plants (as the potato and eggplant)
**2 :** BELLADONNA 1
**night·shirt** \-,shərt\ *noun* (1857)
**:** a nightgown resembling a shirt
**night·side** \-,sīd\ *noun* (1848)

□ USAGE
**nigger**  *Nigger* in senses 1 and 2 can be found in the works of such writers of the past as Joseph Conrad, Mark Twain, and Charles Dickens, but it now ranks as perhaps the most offensive and inflammatory racial slur in English. Its use by and among blacks is not always intended or taken as offensive, but, except in sense 3, it is otherwise a word expressive of racial hatred and bigotry.

◇ WORD HISTORY
**nightmare**  During the Middle Ages there was a widespread belief in an evil spirit that visits and lies on people as they sleep. Known as a *mare* in Old English, this evil spirit, or incubus, became known in Middle English as a *nightmare* after the time of its supposed visitation. It was not until the 16th century that the word *nightmare* came to refer to a frightening dream. Again, evil spirits were involved, for they were credited with causing such dreams. *Mare* in the sense of "a female horse," is an entirely different, unrelated word, though it too is from Old English.

\a\ abut   \ᵊ\ kitten   \ər\ **further**   \a\ **ash**   \ā\ **ace**
\ä\ **mop, mar**   \aủ\ **out**   \ch\ **chin**   \e\ **bet**   \ē\ **easy**
\g\ **go**   \i\ **hit**   \ī\ **ice**   \j\ **job**   \ŋ\ **sing**   \ō\ **go**
\ȯ\ **law**   \ȯi\ **boy**   \th\ **thin**   \th\ **the**   \ü\ **loot**   \ủ\ **foot**
\y\ **yet**   \zh\ **vision**   *see also* Guide to Pronunciation

: the side of a celestial body (as the earth, the moon, or a planet) not in daylight

**night soil** *noun* (circa 1774)
: human excrement used especially for fertilizing the soil

**night·spot** \'nīt-ˌspät\ *noun* (1936)
: NIGHTCLUB

**night·stand** \-ˌstand\ *noun* (1892)
: NIGHT TABLE

**night·stick** \-ˌstik\ *noun* (1887)
: a police officer's club

**night table** *noun* (1788)
: a small bedside table or stand

**night·time** \-ˌtīm\ *noun, often attributive* (14th century)
: the time from dusk to dawn

**night·walk·er** \-ˌwȯ-kər\ *noun* (15th century)
**1** : a person who roams about at night especially with criminal intent
**2** : PROSTITUTE, STREETWALKER

**ni·hil·ism** \'nī-(h)ə-ˌli-zəm, 'nē-\ *noun* [German *Nihilismus,* from Latin *nihil* nothing — more at NIL] (circa 1817)
**1 a** : a viewpoint that traditional values and beliefs are unfounded and that existence is senseless and useless **b** : a doctrine that denies any objective ground of truth and especially of moral truths
**2 a** (1) : a doctrine or belief that conditions in the social organization are so bad as to make destruction desirable for its own sake independent of any constructive program or possibility (2) *capitalized* : the program of a 19th century Russian party advocating revolutionary reform and using terrorism and assassination **b** : TERRORISM
— **ni·hil·ist** \-list\ *noun or adjective*
— **ni·hil·is·tic** \ˌnī-(h)ə-'lis-tik, ˌnē-\ *adjective*

**-nik** *noun suffix* [Yiddish, from Polish & Ukrainian]
: one connected with or characterized by being ⟨beat*nik*⟩

**Ni·ke** \'nī-kē\ *noun* [Greek *Nikē*]
: the Greek goddess of victory

**nil** \'nil\ *noun* [Latin, nothing, contraction of *nihil,* from Old Latin *nihilum,* from *ne-* not + *hilum* trifle — more at NO] (1833)
: NOTHING, ZERO
— **nil** *adjective*

**nile green** *noun, often N capitalized* [*Nile* River, Africa] (1871)
: a pale yellow green

**Nile perch** *noun* (1926)
: a large predaceous food fish (*Lates niloticus*) of the rivers and lakes of northern and central Africa that may exceed 200 pounds (91 kilograms) in weight

**nill** \'nil\ *verb* [Middle English *nilen,* from Old English *nyllan,* from *ne* not + *wyllan* to wish — more at NO, WILL] (before 12th century)
*intransitive verb*
*archaic* : to be unwilling : will not ⟨will you *nill* you, I will marry you —Shakespeare⟩
*transitive verb*
*archaic* : REFUSE

**Ni·lot·ic** \nī-'lä-tik\ *adjective* [Latin *Niloticus,* from Greek *Neilōtēs,* from *Neilos* Nile] (1653)
**1** : of or relating to the Nile or the peoples of the Nile basin
**2** : of, relating to, or being the languages of the Nilotic people

**nil·po·tent** \'nil-ˌpō-t°nt\ *adjective* [Latin *nil* nothing + *potent-, potens* having power — more at POTENT] (1870)
: equal to zero when raised to some power ⟨*nilpotent* matrices⟩

¹**nim** \'nim\ *verb* **nimmed; nim·ming** [earlier *nim* to take, from Middle English *nimen,* from Old English *niman*] (12th century)
*transitive verb*
*archaic* : STEAL, FILCH
*intransitive verb*
*archaic* : THIEVE

²**nim** *noun* [probably from ¹*nim*] (1901)

: any of various games in which counters are laid out in one or more piles and each player in turn draws one or more counters with the object of taking the last counter, forcing the opponent to take it, or taking the most or fewest counters

**nim·ble** \'nim-bəl\ *adjective* **nim·bler** \-b(ə-)lər\; **nim·blest** \-b(ə-)ləst\ [Middle English *nimel,* from Old English *numol* holding much, from *niman* to take; akin to Old High German *neman* to take, Greek *nemein* to distribute, manage, *nomos* pasture, *nomos* usage, custom, law] (14th century)
**1** : quick and light in motion : AGILE ⟨*nimble* fingers⟩
**2 a** : marked by quick, alert, clever conception, comprehension, or resourcefulness ⟨a *nimble* mind⟩ **b** : RESPONSIVE, SENSITIVE ⟨a *nimble* listener⟩
— **nim·ble·ness** \-bəl-nəs\ *noun*
— **nim·bly** \-blē\ *adverb*

**nim·bo·stra·tus** \ˌnim-bō-'strā-təs, -'stra-\ *noun* [New Latin, from Latin *nimbus* + New Latin *stratus* stratus] (circa 1909)
: a low dark gray rainy cloud layer — see CLOUD illustration

**nim·bus** \'nim-bəs\ *noun, plural* **nim·bi** \-ˌbī, -ˌbē\ *or* **nim·bus·es** [Latin, rainstorm, cloud; probably akin to Latin *nebula* cloud — more at NEBULA] (1616)
**1 a** : a luminous vapor, cloud, or atmosphere about a god or goddess when on earth **b** : a cloud or atmosphere (as of romance) about a person or thing
**2** : an indication (as a circle) of radiant light or glory about the head of a drawn or sculptured divinity, saint, or sovereign
**3 a** : a rain cloud **b** : THUNDERHEAD; *also* : CUMULUS 2

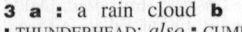
**nimbus 2**

**ni·mi·e·ty** \ni-'mī-ə-tē\ *noun, plural* **-ties** [Late Latin *nimietas,* from Latin *nimius* too much, adjective, from *nimis,* adverb] (circa 1564)
: EXCESS, REDUNDANCY

**nim·i·ny-pim·i·ny** \ˌni-mə-nē-'pi-mə-nē\ *adjective* [probably alteration of *namby-pamby*] (1786)
: affectedly refined : FINICKY

**Nim·rod** \'nim-ˌräd\ *noun* [Hebrew *Nimrōdh*]
**1** : a descendant of Ham represented in Genesis as a mighty hunter and a king of Shinar
**2** *not capitalized* : HUNTER

**nin·com·poop** \'nin-kəm-ˌpüp, 'niŋ-\ *noun* [origin unknown] (1676)
: FOOL, SIMPLETON
— **nin·com·poop·ery** \-ˌpü-pə-rē\ *noun*

**nine** \'nīn\ *noun* [Middle English, from *nyne,* adjective, from Old English *nigon;* akin to Old High German *niun* nine, Latin *novem,* Greek *ennea*] (before 12th century)
**1** — see NUMBER table
**2** : the ninth in a set or series ⟨wears a *nine*⟩
**3** : something having nine units or members: as **a** *capitalized* : the nine Muses **b** : a baseball team **c** : the first or last nine holes of an 18-hole golf course
— **nine** *adjective*
— **nine** *pronoun, plural in construction*
— **to the nines 1** : to perfection **2** : in a highly elaborate or showy manner ⟨dressed *to the nines*⟩

**nine days' wonder** *noun* (1594)
: something or someone that creates a short-lived sensation — called also *nine day wonder*

**nine·fold** \'nīn-ˌfōld, -'fōld\ *adjective* (before 12th century)
**1** : being nine times as great or as many
**2** : having nine units or members
— **nine·fold** \-'fōld\ *adverb*

**nine·pin** \-ˌpin\ *noun* (1580)

**1** *plural but singular in construction* : a bowling game resembling tenpins played without the headpin
**2** : a pin used in ninepins

**nine·teen** \nīn-'tēn, 'nīn-ˌ\ *noun* [Middle English *nynetene,* adjective, from Old English *nigontēne,* from *nigon* + *-tīene* (akin to Old English *tīen* ten) — more at TEN] (before 12th century)
— see NUMBER table
— **nineteen** *adjective*
— **nineteen** *pronoun, plural in construction*
— **nine·teenth** \-'tēn(t)th, -ˌtēn(t)th\ *adjective or noun*

**nine·ty** \'nīn-tē\ *noun, plural* **nineties** [Middle English *ninety,* adjective, from Old English *nigontig,* short for *hundnigontig,* from *hundnigontig,* noun, group of 90, from *hund-,* literally, hundred + *nigon* nine + *-tig* group of 10; akin to Old English *tīen* ten] (before 12th century)
**1** — see NUMBER table
**2** *plural* : the numbers 90 to 99; *specifically* : the years 90 to 99 in a lifetime or century
— **nine·ti·eth** \-tē-əth\ *adjective or noun*
— **ninety** *adjective*
— **ninety** *pronoun, plural in construction*

**nin·hy·drin** \nin-'hī-drən\ *noun* [from *Ninhydrin,* a trademark] (1913)
: a poisonous crystalline oxidizing agent $C_9H_6O_4$ used especially as an analytical reagent

**nin·ja** \'nin-jə, -(ˌ)jä\ *noun, plural* **ninja** *also* **ninjas** [Japanese, from *nin-* persevere + *-ja* person] (1975)
: a person trained in ancient Japanese martial arts and employed especially for espionage and assassinations

**nin·ny** \'ni-nē\ *noun, plural* **ninnies** [perhaps by shortening & alteration from *an innocent*] (1593)
: FOOL, SIMPLETON

**nin·ny·ham·mer** \'ni-nē-ˌha-mər\ *noun* (1592)
: NINNY

**ni·non** \'nē-ˌnän\ *noun* [probably from French *Ninon,* nickname for *Anne*] (1911)
: a smooth sheer fabric

**ninth** \'nīn(t)th\ *noun, plural* **ninths** \'nīn(t)s, 'nīn(t)ths\ (13th century)
**1** — see NUMBER table
**2 a** : a musical interval embracing an octave and a second **b** : the tone at this interval **c** : a chord containing a ninth
— **ninth** *adjective or adverb*

**ninth cranial nerve** *noun* (circa 1961)
: GLOSSOPHARYNGEAL NERVE

**ni·o·bate** \'nī-ə-ˌbāt\ *noun* [New Latin *niobium* + English ¹*-ate*] (1845)
: a salt containing an anionic grouping of niobium and oxygen

**Ni·o·be** \'nī-ə-bē\ *noun* [Latin, from Greek *Niobē*]
: a daughter of Tantalus and wife of Amphion who while weeping for her slain children is turned into a stone from which her tears continue to flow

**ni·o·bi·um** \nī-'ō-bē-əm\ *noun* [New Latin, from Latin *Niobe;* from its occurrence in tantalite] (1845)
: a lustrous light gray ductile metallic element that resembles tantalum chemically and is used in alloys — see ELEMENT table

¹**nip** \'nip\ *verb* **nipped; nip·ping** [Middle English *nippen;* akin to Old Norse *hnippa* to prod] (14th century)
*transitive verb*
**1 a** : to catch hold of and squeeze tightly between two surfaces, edges, or points : PINCH, BITE ⟨the dog *nipped* his ankle⟩ **b** : to pinch in (as a garment) ⟨a dress *nipped* at the waist⟩
**2 a** : to sever by or as if by pinching sharply **b** : to destroy the growth, progress, or fulfillment of ⟨*nipped* in the bud⟩
**3** : to injure or make numb with cold : CHILL

**4 :** SNATCH, STEAL
**5 :** to defeat by a small margin
*intransitive verb*
**1 :** to move briskly, nimbly, or quickly
**2** *chiefly British* **:** to make a quick trip
²**nip** *noun* (1549)
**1 :** something that nips: as **a** *archaic* **:** a sharp biting comment **b :** a sharp stinging cold ⟨a nip in the air⟩ **c :** a biting or pungent flavor **:** TANG ⟨cheese with a nip⟩
**2 :** the act of nipping **:** PINCH, BITE
**3 :** the region of a squeezing or crushing device (as a calender) where the rolls or jaws are closest together
**4 :** a small portion
³**nip** *noun* [probably from *nipperkin,* a liquor container] (circa 1796)
**:** a small quantity of liquor **:** SIP; *also* **:** a very small bottle of liquor
⁴**nip** *intransitive verb* **nipped; nip·ping** (1887)
**:** to take liquor in nips **:** TIPPLE
**ni·pa** \'nē-pə\ *noun* [probably from Italian, from Malay *nipah* nipa palm] (1779)
**:** thatch made of leaves of the nipa palm
**nip and tuck** \ˌnip-ən(d)-'tək\ *adjective or adverb* (1832)
**:** being so close that the lead or advantage shifts rapidly from one opponent to another
**nipa palm** *noun* (1882)
**:** a semiaquatic creeping palm (*Nipa fruticans*) found chiefly from India to Melanesia
**nip·per** \'ni-pər\ *noun* (1541)
**1 :** any of various devices (as pincers) for nipping — usually used in plural
**2 a** *chiefly British* **:** a boy employed as a helper (as of a carter or hawker) **b :** CHILD; *especially* **:** a small boy
**nip·ping** \'ni-piŋ\ *adjective* (1547)
**:** SHARP, CHILLING
— **nip·ping·ly** \-lē\ *adverb*
**nip·ple** \'ni-pəl\ *noun* [earlier *neble, nible,* probably diminutive of *neb, nib*] (1530)
**1 :** the protuberance of a mammary gland upon which in the female the lactiferous ducts open and from which milk is drawn
**2 a :** an artificial teat through which a bottle-fed infant nurses **b :** a device with an orifice through which the discharge of a liquid can be regulated
**3 a :** a protuberance resembling or suggesting the nipple of a breast **b :** a small projection through which oil or grease is injected into machinery
**4 :** a pipe coupling consisting of a short piece of threaded tubing
— **nip·pled** \-pəld\ *adjective*
**Nip·pon·ese** \ˌni-pə-'nēz, -'nēs\ *adjective* [*Nippon,* Japan] (1859)
**:** JAPANESE
— **Nipponese** *noun*
**nip·py** \'ni-pē\ *adjective* **nip·pi·er; -est** (1575)
**1 :** marked by a tendency to nip ⟨a *nippy* dog⟩
**2 :** brisk, quick, or nimble in movement **:** SNAPPY
**3 :** PUNGENT, SHARP
**4 :** CHILLY, CHILLING ⟨a *nippy* day⟩
— **nip·pi·ly** \'ni-pə-lē\ *adverb*
— **nip·pi·ness** \'ni-pē-nəs\ *noun*
**nip-up** \'nip-ˌəp\ *noun* (1938)
**:** a spring from a supine position to a standing position
**nir·va·na** \nir-'vä-nə, (ˌ)nər-\ *noun, often capitalized* [Sanskrit *nirvāṇa,* literally, act of extinguishing, from *nis-* out + *vāti* it blows — more at WIND] (1801)
**1 :** the final beatitude that transcends suffering, karma, and samsara and is sought especially in Buddhism through the extinction of desire and individual consciousness

nipa palm

**2 a :** a place or state of oblivion to care, pain, or external reality; *also* **:** BLISS. HEAVEN **b :** a goal hoped for but apparently unattainable **:** DREAM
— **nir·van·ic** \-'vä-nik, -'va-\ *adjective*
**Ni·san** \'ni-sᵊn, nē-'sän\ *noun* [Hebrew *Nīsān*] (14th century)
**:** the 7th month of the civil year or the 1st month of the ecclesiastical year in the Jewish calendar — see MONTH table
**ni·sei** \nē-'sā, 'nē-\ *noun, plural* **nisei** *often capitalized* [Japanese, literally, second generation, from *ni* second + *sei* generation] (1929)
**:** a son or daughter of Japanese immigrants who is born and educated in America and especially in the U.S.
**ni·si** \'nī-ˌsī\ *adjective* [Latin, unless, from *ne-* not + *si* if] (1836)
**:** taking effect at a specified time unless previously modified or avoided by cause shown, further proceedings, or a condition fulfilled ⟨a decree *nisi*⟩
**Nis·sen hut** \'ni-sᵊn-\ *noun* [Peter N. *Nissen* (died 1930) British mining engineer] (1932)
**:** a prefabricated shelter with a semicircular arching roof of corrugated iron sheeting and a concrete floor
**ni·sus** \'nī-səs\ *noun, plural* **ni·sus** \-səs, -ˌsüs\ [Latin, from *niti* to lean, rely, strive; akin to Latin *nictare* to wink — more at CONNIVE] (1699)
**:** a mental or physical effort to attain an end
**:** a perfective urge or endeavor
¹**nit** \'nit\ *noun* [Middle English *nite,* from Old English *hnitu;* akin to Old High German *hniz* nit, Greek *konid-, konios*] (before 12th century)
**:** the egg of a louse or other parasitic insect; *also* **:** the insect itself when young
²**nit** *noun* (circa 1941)
*chiefly British* **:** NITWIT
**nite** *variant of* NIGHT
**ni·ter** \'nī-tər\ *noun* [Middle English *nitre* natron, from Middle French, from Latin *nitrum,* from Greek *nitron,* from Egyptian *ntry*] (1684)
**1 :** POTASSIUM NITRATE
**2** *archaic* **:** CHILE SALTPETER
**nit·ery** *also* **nit·er·ie** \'nī-tə-rē\ *noun, plural* **nit·er·ies** [*nite* + *-ery* (as in *eatery*); *niterie* from *nite* + French *-erie* -ery] (circa 1934)
**:** NIGHTCLUB
**nit·id** \'ni-təd\ *adjective* [Latin *nitidus* — more at NEAT] (circa 1656)
**:** BRIGHT, LUSTROUS
**ni·ti·nol** \'nī-tᵊn-ˌōl, -ˌōl\ *noun* [nickel + titanium + *-nol* (from *Naval Ordnance Laboratory,* where it was created)] (1968)
**:** a nonmagnetic alloy of titanium and nickel that after being deformed returns to its original shape upon being reheated
**nit·pick** \'nit-ˌpik\ *verb* [back-formation from *nit-picking*] (1966)
*intransitive verb*
**:** to engage in nit-picking
*transitive verb*
**:** to criticize by nit-picking
— **nitpick** *noun*
— **nit·pick·er** *noun*
— **nit·picky** \-ˌpi-kē\ *adjective*
**nit-pick·ing** \'nit-ˌpi-kiŋ\ *noun* [¹*nit*] (1956)
**:** minute and usually unjustified criticism
**nitr-** *or* **nitro-** *combining form* [niter]
**1 :** nitrogen ⟨*nitride*⟩
**2** *usually* nitro- **:** containing the univalent group $NO_2$ composed of one nitrogen and two oxygen atoms ⟨*nitro*benzene⟩
**ni·trate** \'nī-ˌtrāt, -trət\ *noun* [French, from *nitrique*] (1794)
**1 :** a salt or ester of nitric acid
**2 :** sodium nitrate or potassium nitrate used as a fertilizer
**nitrate of soda** (1843)
**:** sodium nitrate used as a fertilizer
**ni·tra·tion** \nī-'trā-shən\ *noun* (1887)
**:** the process of adding a nitro group to an organic compound
— **ni·trate** \'nī-ˌtrāt\ *transitive verb*

— **ni·tra·tor** \-ˌtrā-tər\ *noun*
**ni·tre** *chiefly British variant of* NITER
**ni·tric acid** \'nī-trik-\ *noun* [French *nitrique,* from *nitre* niter, from Middle French] (1794)
**:** a corrosive liquid inorganic acid $HNO_3$ used especially as an oxidizing agent, in nitrations, and in making organic compounds (as fertilizers, explosives, and dyes)
**nitric oxide** *noun* (1807)
**:** a colorless poisonous gas NO formed by oxidation of nitrogen or ammonia
¹**ni·tride** \'nī-ˌtrīd\ *noun* [International Scientific Vocabulary] (1850)
**:** a binary compound of nitrogen with a more electropositive element
²**nitride** *transitive verb* **ni·trid·ed; ni·trid·ing** (1928)
**:** to case-harden (as steel) by causing the surface to absorb nitrogen
**ni·tri·fi·ca·tion** \ˌnī-trə-fə-'kā-shən\ *noun* (1827)
**:** the oxidation (as by bacteria) of ammonium salts to nitrites and the further oxidation of nitrites to nitrates
**ni·tri·fi·er** \'nī-trə-ˌfī(-ə)r\ *noun* (1903)
**:** any of the nitrifying bacteria
**ni·tri·fy·ing** \'nī-trə-ˌfī-iŋ\ *adjective* [French *nitrifier* to convert into nitrite, from *nitr-*] (1827)
**:** active in or relating to nitrification ⟨*nitrifying* organisms⟩ ⟨*nitrifying* activities⟩
**nitrifying bacteria** *noun plural* (1925)
**:** bacteria of a family (Nitrobacteraceae) comprising gram-negative bacteria commonly found in the soil and obtaining energy through the process of nitrification
**ni·trile** \'nī-trəl, -ˌtrīl\ *noun* [International Scientific Vocabulary *nitr-* + *-il, -ile* (from Latin *-ilis* ¹*-ile*)] (1848)
**:** an organic cyanide containing the group CN which on hydrolysis yields an acid with elimination of ammonia
**ni·trite** \'nī-ˌtrīt\ *noun* (1800)
**:** a salt or ester of nitrous acid
¹**ni·tro** \'nī-(ˌ)trō\ *adjective* [*nitr-*] (1892)
**:** containing or being the univalent group $NO_2$ united through nitrogen
²**nitro** *noun, plural* **nitros** (1903)
**:** any of various nitrated products; *specifically* **:** NITROGLYCERIN
**ni·tro·ben·zene** \ˌnī-trō-'ben-ˌzēn, -ben-'\ *noun* [International Scientific Vocabulary] (1868)
**:** a poisonous yellow insoluble oil $C_6H_5NO_2$ with an almond odor that is used especially as a solvent, as a mild oxidizing agent, and in making aniline
**ni·tro·cel·lu·lose** \-'sel-yə-ˌlōs, -ˌlōz\ *noun* [International Scientific Vocabulary] (1882)
**:** any of several nitric-acid esters of cellulose used especially for making explosives, plastics, and varnishes
**ni·tro·fu·ran** \ˌnī-trō-'fyúr-ˌan, -fyú-'ran\ *noun* (1930)
**:** any of several nitro derivatives of furan used as bacteria-inhibiting agents
**ni·tro·gen** \'nī-trə-jən\ *noun, often attributive* [French *nitrogène,* from *nitre* niter + *-gène* -gen] (1794)
**:** a colorless tasteless odorless element that as a diatomic gas is relatively inert and constitutes 78 percent of the atmosphere by volume and that occurs as a constituent of all living tissues — see ELEMENT table
— **ni·trog·e·nous** \nī-'trä-jə-nəs\ *adjective*
**ni·tro·ge·nase** \nī-'trä-jə-ˌnās, 'nī-trə-jə-, -ˌnāz\ *noun* (1934)
**:** an enzyme of various nitrogen-fixing bacteria that catalyzes the reduction of molecular nitrogen to ammonia

**nitrogen balance** *noun* (1944)
: the difference between nitrogen intake and nitrogen loss in the body or the soil

**nitrogen cycle** *noun* (1908)
: a continuous series of natural processes by which nitrogen passes successively from air to soil to organisms and back to air or soil involving principally nitrogen fixation, nitrification, decay, and denitrification

**nitrogen dioxide** *noun* (1885)
: a toxic reddish brown gas $NO_2$ that is a strong oxidizing agent, is produced by combustion (as of fossil fuels), and is an atmospheric pollutant

**nitrogen fixation** *noun* (1895)
: the metabolic assimilation of atmospheric nitrogen into ammonia by soil microorganisms and especially rhizobia

**nitrogen–fixer** *noun* (1912)
: any of various soil microorganisms that are involved in nitrogen fixation

**nitrogen–fixing** *adjective* (1899)
: capable of nitrogen fixation ⟨*nitrogen-fixing* bacteria⟩

**nitrogen mustard** *noun* (1943)
: any of various toxic blistering compounds analogous to mustard gas but containing nitrogen instead of sulfur

**nitrogen narcosis** *noun* (1937)
: a state of euphoria and exhilaration that occurs when nitrogen in normal air enters the bloodstream at approximately seven times atmospheric pressure (as in deep-water diving) — called also *rapture of the deep*

**nitrogen oxide** *noun* (circa 1934)
: any of several oxides of nitrogen most of which are produced in combustion and are considered to be atmospheric pollutants: as **a** : NITRIC OXIDE **b** : NITROGEN DIOXIDE **c** : NITROUS OXIDE

**nitrogen tetroxide** *noun* (1885)
: a colorless toxic gas $N_2O_4$ that is a dimer of nitrogen dioxide and that in liquid form is used as an oxidizer in rocket engines

**ni·tro·glyc·er·in** *or* **ni·tro·glyc·er·ine** \ˌnī-trə-ˈglis-rən, -ˈgli-sə-\ *noun* [International Scientific Vocabulary] (1857)
: a heavy oily explosive poisonous liquid $C_3H_5N_3O_9$ used chiefly in making dynamites and in medicine as a vasodilator

**ni·tro·meth·ane** \ˌnī-trō-ˈme-ˌthān, *British usually* -ˈmē-\ *noun* (1872)
: a liquid nitroparaffin $CH_3NO_2$ that is used as an industrial solvent, in chemical synthesis, and as a fuel for rockets and high-performance engines

**ni·tro·par·af·fin** \-ˈpar-ə-fən\ *noun* [International Scientific Vocabulary] (1892)
: any of various nitro derivatives of alkanes

**nitros-** *or* **nitroso-** *combining form* [New Latin *nitrosus* nitrous]
: containing the group NO ⟨*nitros*amine⟩

**ni·tro·sa·mine** \nī-ˈtrō-sə-ˌmēn\ *noun* (1878)
: any of various organic compounds which are characterized by the grouping NNO and some of which are powerful carcinogens

**ni·trous** \ˈnī-trəs\ *adjective* [New Latin *nitrosus*, from Latin, full of natron, from *nitrum* natron — more at NITER] (1601)
*archaic* : of, relating to, or containing niter

**nitrous acid** *noun* (1676)
: an unstable acid $HNO_2$ known only in solution or in the form of its salts

**nitrous oxide** *noun* (1800)
: a colorless gas $N_2O$ that when inhaled produces loss of sensibility to pain preceded by exhilaration and sometimes laughter and is used especially as an anesthetic in dentistry and that is an atmospheric pollutant produced by combustion and a suspected contributor to greenhouse warming — called also *laughing gas*

**nit·ty–grit·ty** \ˈni-tē-ˌgri-tē, ˌni-tē-ˈ\ *noun* [origin unknown] (1963)

: what is essential and basic : specific practical details ⟨get down to the *nitty-gritty* of the problem⟩
— **nitty–gritty** *adjective*

**nit·wit** \ˈnit-ˌwit\ *noun* [probably from German dialect *nit* not + English *wit*] (circa 1922)
: a scatterbrained or stupid person

**¹nix** \ˈniks\ *noun* [German *nichts* nothing] (1789)
: NOTHING

**²nix** *transitive verb* (circa 1934)
: VETO, REJECT ⟨the court *nixed* the merger⟩

**³nix** *adverb* (circa 1909)
: NO — used to express disagreement or the withholding of permission; often used with *on* ⟨they said *nix* on our plan⟩

**⁴nix** *noun* [German, from Old High German *nihhus*; akin to Old English *nicor* water monster and perhaps to Greek *nizein* to wash] (1833)
: a water sprite of Germanic folklore

**¹nix·ie** \ˈnik-sē\ *noun* [German *Nixe* female nix, from Old High German *nichessa*, feminine of *nihhus* nix] (1816)
: ⁴NIX

**²nix·ie** *also* **nixy** \ˈnik-sē\ *noun, plural* **nix·ies** [¹*nix* + -*ie*] (circa 1890)
: a piece of mail that is undeliverable because illegibly or incorrectly addressed

**Nix·ie** \ˈnik-sē\ *trademark*
— used for an electronic indicator tube

**ni·zam** \ni-ˈzäm, ˈnī-ˌzam, nī-ˈ\ *noun* [Hindi *nizām* order, governor, from Arabic *niẓām*] (1768)
: one of a line of sovereigns of Hyderabad, India, reigning from 1713 to 1950
— **ni·zam·ate** \ni-ˈzä-ˌmāt, nī-ˈza-\ *noun*

**¹no** \ˈnō\ *adverb* [Middle English, from Old English *nā*, from *ne* not + *ā* always; akin to Old Norse & Old High German *ne* not, Latin *ne*-, Greek *nē*- — more at AYE] (before 12th century)
**1 a** *chiefly Scottish* : NOT **b** — used as a function word to express the negative of an alternative choice or possibility ⟨shall we go out to dinner or *no*⟩
**2** : in no respect or degree — used in comparisons
**3** : not so — used to express negation, dissent, denial, or refusal ⟨*no*, I'm not going⟩
**4** — used with a following adjective to imply a meaning expressed by the opposite positive statement ⟨in *no* uncertain terms⟩
**5** — used as a function word to emphasize a following negative or to introduce a more emphatic, explicit, or comprehensive statement
**6** — used as an interjection to express surprise, doubt, or incredulity
**7** — used in combination with a verb to form a compound adjective ⟨*no*-bake pie⟩

**²no** *adjective* (12th century)
**1 a** : not any ⟨*no* parking⟩ ⟨*no* disputing the decision⟩ **b** : hardly any : very little ⟨finished in *no* time⟩
**2** : not a : quite other than a ⟨he's *no* expert⟩
**3** — used in combination with a noun to form a compound adjective ⟨a *no*-nonsense realist⟩

**³no** \ˈnō\ *noun, plural* **noes** *or* **nos** \ˈnōz\ (1588)
**1** : an act or instance of refusing or denying by the use of the word *no* : DENIAL
**2 a** : a negative vote or decision **b** *plural* : persons voting in the negative

**No** *or* **Noh** \ˈnō\ *noun, plural* **No** *or* **Noh** [Japanese *nō*, literally, talent] (1871)
: classic Japanese dance-drama having a heroic theme, a chorus, and highly stylized action, costuming, and scenery

**no–account** *adjective* (1845)
: of no account : TRIFLING ⟨her *no-account* relatives⟩

**No·a·chi·an** \nō-ˈā-kē-ən\ *adjective* [Hebrew *Nōah* Noah] (1678)
**1** : of or relating to the patriarch Noah or his time
**2** : ANCIENT, ANTIQUATED

**No·ah** \ˈnō-ə\ *noun* [Hebrew *Nōaḥ*]

: an Old Testament patriarch who built the ark in which he, his family, and living creatures of every kind survived the Flood

**¹nob** \ˈnäb\ *noun* [probably alteration of *knob*] (circa 1700)
**1** : HEAD 1
**2** : a jack of the same suit as the starter in cribbage that scores one point for the holder — usually used in the phrases *his nob* or *his nobs*

**²nob** *noun* [perhaps from ¹*nob*] (1703)
*chiefly British* : one in a superior position in life

**nob·ble** \ˈnä-bəl\ *transitive verb* **nob·bled;** **nob·bling** \-b(ə-)liŋ\ [perhaps irregular frequentative of *nab*] (1847)
**1** *British* : to incapacitate (a racehorse) especially by drugging
**2** *slang British* **a** : to win over to one's side **b** : STEAL **c** : SWINDLE, CHEAT **d** : to get hold of : CATCH
— **nob·bler** \-b(ə-)lər\ *noun*

**nob·by** \ˈnä-bē\ *adjective* **nob·bi·er; -est** (1788)
: CHIC, SMART

**No·bel·ist** \nō-ˈbe-list\ *noun* (1938)
: a winner of a Nobel prize

**no·bel·i·um** \nō-ˈbe-lē-əm\ *noun* [New Latin, from Alfred B. *Nobel*] (1957)
: a radioactive element produced artificially — see ELEMENT table

**No·bel prize** \nō-ˈbel-, ˈnō-ˌbel-\ *noun* (1900)
: any of various annual prizes (as in peace, literature, medicine) established by the will of Alfred Nobel for the encouragement of persons who work for the interests of humanity

**no·bil·i·ty** \nō-ˈbi-lə-tē\ *noun* [Middle English *nobilite*, from Middle French *nobilité*, from Latin *nobilitat-, nobilitas*, from *nobilis*] (14th century)
**1** : the quality or state of being noble in character, quality, or rank
**2** : the body of persons forming the noble class in a country or state : ARISTOCRACY

**¹no·ble** \ˈnō-bəl\ *adjective* **no·bler** \-b(ə-)lər\; **no·blest** \-b(ə-)ləst\ [Middle English, from Old French, from Latin *nobilis* well-known, noble, from *noscere* to come to know — more at KNOW] (13th century)
**1 a** : possessing outstanding qualities : ILLUSTRIOUS **b** : FAMOUS, NOTABLE ⟨*noble* deeds⟩
**2** : of high birth or exalted rank : ARISTOCRATIC
**3 a** : possessing very high or excellent qualities or properties ⟨*noble* wine⟩ **b** : very good or excellent
**4** : grand or impressive especially in appearance ⟨*noble* edifice⟩
**5** : possessing, characterized by, or arising from superiority of mind or character or of ideals or morals : LOFTY ⟨a *noble* ambition⟩
**6** : chemically inert or inactive especially toward oxygen ⟨a *noble* metal such as platinum⟩ — compare BASE 6a
**synonym** see MORAL
— **no·ble·ness** \-bəl-nəs\ *noun*
— **no·bly** \-blē *also* -bə-lē\ *adverb*

**²noble** *noun* (14th century)
**1** : a person of noble rank or birth
**2** : an old English gold coin equivalent to 6*s* 8*d*

**noble gas** *noun* (1902)
: any of a group of rare gases that include helium, neon, argon, krypton, xenon, and sometimes radon and that exhibit great stability and extremely low reaction rates — called also *inert gas*

**no·ble·man** \ˈnō-bəl-mən\ *noun* (14th century)
: a man of noble rank : PEER

**noble savage** *noun* (1672)
: a mythic conception of people belonging to non-European cultures as having innate natural simplicity and virtue uncorrupted by European civilization; *also* : a person exemplifying this conception

**no·blesse** \nō-'bles\ *noun* [Middle English, from Old French *noblesce,* from *noble*] (13th century)
**1** : noble birth or condition
**2** : the members especially of the French nobility

**no·blesse oblige** \nō-'bles-ə-'blēzh\ *noun* [French, literally, nobility obligates] (1837)
: the obligation of honorable, generous, and responsible behavior associated with high rank or birth

**no·ble·wom·an** \'nō-bəl-,wu̇-mən\ *noun* (13th century)
: a woman of noble rank : PEERESS

**¹no·body** \'nō-bə-dē, -,bä-dē\ *pronoun* (14th century)
: no person : not anybody ∎

**²nobody** *noun, plural* **no·bod·ies** (1581)
: a person of no influence or consequence

**no-brain·er** \'nō-'brā-nər\ *noun* (1973)
: something that requires a minimum of thought

**no·cent** \'nō-s°nt\ *adjective* [Middle English, from Latin *nocent-, nocens,* from present participle of *nocēre* to harm, hurt — more at NOXIOUS] (15th century)
: HARMFUL

**no·ci·cep·tive** \,nō-si-'sep-tiv\ *adjective* [Latin *nocēre* + English *-i-* + re*ceptive*] (1904)
**1** *of a stimulus* : PAINFUL, INJURIOUS
**2** : of, induced by, or responding to a nociceptive stimulus — used especially of receptors or protective reflexes

**¹nock** \'näk\ *noun* [Middle English *nocke* notched tip on the end of a bow; akin to Middle Dutch *nocke* summit] (14th century)
**1** : one of the notches cut in either of two tips of horn fastened on the ends of a bow or in the bow itself for holding the string
**2 a** : the part of an arrow having a notch for the bowstring **b** : the notch itself

**²nock** *transitive verb* (14th century)
**1** : to make a nock in (a bow or arrow)
**2** : to fit (an arrow) against the bowstring

**no contest** *noun* (1952)
: NOLO CONTENDERE

**noct·am·bu·list** \näk-'tam-byə-list\ *noun* [Latin *noct-, nox* night + *-ambulist* (as in *somnambulist*) — more at NIGHT] (circa 1731)
: SLEEPWALKER

**noc·ti·lu·cent cloud** \,näk-tə-'lü-s°nt-\ *noun* [*noctilucent* ultimately from Latin *noct-* + *lucent-, lucens* lucent] (1910)
: a luminous thin usually colored cloud seen especially at twilight at a height of about 50 miles (80 kilometers)

**noc·tu·id** \'näk-chə-wəd, 'näk-tə-\ *noun* [New Latin *Noctuidae,* from *Noctua,* genus of moths, from Latin, the little owl (*Athene noctua*); akin to Latin *nox* night] (1894)
: any of a large family (Noctuidae) of medium-sized often dull-colored moths with larvae (as cutworms and armyworms) that are often destructive agricultural pests
— **noctuid** *adjective*

**noc·turn** \'näk-,tərn\ *noun* [Middle English *nocturne,* from Middle French, from Medieval Latin *nocturna,* from Latin, feminine of *nocturnus*] (14th century)
: a principal division of the office of matins

**noc·tur·nal** \näk-'tər-n°l\ *adjective* [Middle English, from Middle French or Late Latin; Middle French, from Late Latin *nocturnalis,* from Latin *nocturnus* of night, nocturnal, from *noct-, nox* night] (15th century)
**1** : of, relating to, or occurring in the night ⟨a *nocturnal* journey⟩
**2** : active at night ⟨a *nocturnal* predator⟩
— **noc·tur·nal·ly** \-n°l-ē\ *adverb*

**noc·turne** \'näk-,tərn\ *noun* [French, adjective, nocturnal, from Latin *nocturnus*] (1862)
: a work of art dealing with evening or night; *especially* : a dreamy pensive composition for the piano — compare AUBADE 3

**noc·u·ous** \'nä-kyə-wəs\ *adjective* [Latin *nocuus,* from *nocēre* to harm — more at NOXIOUS] (1635)
: HARMFUL
— **noc·u·ous·ly** *adverb*

**¹nod** \'näd\ *verb* **nod·ded; nod·ding** [Middle English *nodden;* perhaps akin to Old High German *hnotōn* to shake] (14th century)
*intransitive verb*
**1** : to make a quick downward motion of the head whether deliberately (as in expressing assent, salutation, or command) or involuntarily (as from drowsiness)
**2** : to incline or sway from the vertical as though ready to fall
**3** : to bend or sway the upper part gently downward or forward : bob gently
**4** : to make a slip or error in a moment of abstraction
*transitive verb*
**1** : to incline (as the head) downward or forward
**2** : to bring, invite, or send by a nod ⟨*nodded* them into the room⟩
**3** : to signify by a nod ⟨*nodded* their approval⟩
— **nod·der** *noun*

**²nod** *noun* (circa 1541)
**1** : the act or an instance of nodding ⟨gave a *nod* of greeting⟩
**2** : an indication especially of approval or recognition ⟨received the party's *nod* as candidate for governor⟩

**nod·al** \'nō-d°l\ *adjective* (1831)
: being, relating to, or located at or near a node
— **no·dal·i·ty** \nō-'da-lə-tē\ *noun*
— **nod·al·ly** \'nō-d°l-ē\ *adverb*

**nodding** *adjective* (1590)
**1** : bending downward or forward : PENDULOUS, DROOPING ⟨a plant with *nodding* flowers⟩
**2** : SLIGHT, SUPERFICIAL ⟨a *nodding* acquaintance⟩

**nod·dle** \'nä-d°l\ *noun* [Middle English *nodle* back of the head or neck] (1579)
: HEAD, PATE

**nod·dy** \'nä-dē\ *noun, plural* **noddies** [probably short for obsolete *noddypoll,* alteration of *hoddypoll* fumbling inept person] (circa 1530)
**1** : a stupid person
**2** : any of several stout-bodied terns (especially genus *Anous*) of warm seas

**node** \'nōd\ *noun* [Middle English, from Latin *nodus* knot, node; akin to Middle Irish *naidm* bond] (15th century)
**1 a** : a pathological swelling or enlargement (as of a rheumatic joint) **b** : a discrete mass of one kind of tissue enclosed in tissue of a different kind
**2** : an entangling complication (as in a drama) : PREDICAMENT
**3** : either of the two points where the orbit of a planet or comet intersects the ecliptic; *also* : either of the points at which the orbit of an earth satellite crosses the plane of the equator
**4 a** : a point, line, or surface of a vibrating body or system that is free or relatively free from vibratory motion **b** : a point at which a wave has an amplitude of zero
**5 a** : a point at which subsidiary parts originate or center **b** : a point on a stem at which a leaf or leaves are inserted **c** : a point at which a curve intersects itself in such a manner that the branches have different tangents **d** : VERTEX 1b

**node of Ran·vier** \-'räⁿ-vē-,ā\ [Louis A. *Ranvier* (died 1922) French histologist] (circa 1885)
: a constriction in the myelin sheath of a myelinated nerve fiber

**nod off** *intransitive verb* (1914)
: to fall asleep

**no·dose** \'nō-,dōs\ *adjective* [Latin *nodosus,* from *nodus*] (circa 1721)
: having numerous or conspicuous protuberances
— **no·dos·i·ty** \nō-'dä-sə-tē\ *noun*

**nod·u·lar** \'nä-jə-lər\ *adjective* (1794)
: of, relating to, characterized by, or occurring in the form of nodules ⟨*nodular* lesions⟩

**nod·u·la·tion** \,nä-jə-'lā-shən\ *noun* (1872)
**1** : the process of forming nodules and especially root nodules containing symbiotic bacteria
**2** : NODULE

**nod·ule** \'nä-(,)jü(ə)l\ *noun* [Middle English, from Latin *nodulus,* diminutive of *nodus*] (15th century)
: a small mass of rounded or irregular shape: as **a** : a small rounded lump of a mineral or mineral aggregate **b** : a swelling on a leguminous root that contains symbiotic bacteria **c** : a small abnormal knobby bodily protuberance (as a tumorous growth or a calcification near an arthritic joint)

**no·dus** \'nō-dəs\ *noun, plural* **no·di** \'nō-,dī, -,dē\ [Latin, knot, node] (circa 1738)
: COMPLICATION, DIFFICULTY

**no·el** \nō-'el\ *noun* [French *noël* Christmas, carol, from Latin *natalis* birthday, from *natalis* natal] (1811)
**1** : a Christmas carol
**2** *capitalized* : CHRISTMAS

**noes** *plural of* NO

**no·et·ic** \nō-'e-tik\ *adjective* [Greek *noētikos* intellectual, from *noein* to think, from *nous* mind] (1653)
: of, relating to, or based on the intellect

**no–fault** *adjective* (1967)
**1** : of, relating to, or being a motor vehicle insurance plan under which someone involved in an accident is compensated usually up to a stipulated limit for actual losses (as for property damage, medical bills, and lost wages) by that person's own insurance company regardless of who is responsible for the accident
**2** : of, relating to, or being a divorce law under which neither party is held responsible for the breakup of the marriage
**3** : characterized by the absence of a prevailing sense of individual responsibility (as for behavior) ⟨a *no-fault* society⟩

**no–frills** \'nō-'frilz\ *adjective* (1960)
: offering or providing only the essentials : not fancy, elaborate, or luxurious

**nog** \'näg\ *noun* [origin unknown] (1693)
**1** : a strong ale formerly brewed in Norfolk, England
**2** [by shortening] : EGGNOG

**nog·gin** \'nä-gən\ *noun* [origin unknown] (1630)
**1** : a small mug or cup
**2** : a small quantity (as a gill) of drink
**3** : a person's head

▢ USAGE
**nobody** The indefinite pronouns *nobody* and *no one* share with other indefinite pronouns the characteristic of taking a singular verb and, more often than not, a plural pronoun in reference. The use of the plural pronoun—*they, their, them*—has traditionally been disapproved of by those who insist that agreement in number is more important than avoidance of gender-specific third-person singular pronouns. But the use of the plural pronouns has long been established ⟨*nobody* was in their right place —Jane Austen (1814)⟩ and increasing resistance to generic *he* may be easing their acceptance. Usage is still mixed ⟨*nobody* attains reality for my mother until he eats —Flannery O'Connor⟩ ⟨*nobody* naturally likes a mind quicker than their own —F. Scott Fitzgerald⟩.

\ə\ **abut** \ᵊ\ **kitten** \ər\ **further** \a\ **ash** \ā\ **ace**
\ä\ **mop, mar** \au̇\ **out** \ch\ **chin** \e\ **bet** \ē\ **easy**
\g\ **go** \i\ **hit** \ī\ **ice** \j\ **job** \ŋ\ **sing** \ō\ **go**
\ȯ\ **law** \ȯi\ **boy** \th\ **thin** \t͟h\ **the** \ü\ **loot** \u̇\ **foot**
\y\ **yet** \zh\ **vision** *see also* Guide to Pronunciation

**nog·ging** \'nä-gən, -giŋ\ *noun* [*nog* wooden block the size of a brick] (1825)
: rough brick masonry used to fill in the open spaces of a wooden frame

¹**no–good** \'nō-'gu̇d\ *adjective* (1908)
: having no worth, virtue, use, or chance of success

²**no–good** \'nō-,gu̇d\ *noun* (1924)
: a no-good person or thing

**Noh** *variant of* NO

**no–hit** *adjective* (1916)
: of, relating to, or being a baseball game or a part of a game in which a pitcher allows the opposition no base hits

**no–hit·ter** \,nō-'hi-tər\ *noun* (1947)
: a no-hit game in baseball

**no–holds–barred** \,nō-,hōl(d)z-'bärd\ *adjective* (1942)
: free of restrictions or hampering conventions ⟨a *no-holds-barred* contest⟩

**no–hop·er** \'nō-'hō-pər\ *noun* (circa 1943)
*chiefly British* : one that has no chance of success

**no·how** \'nō-,hau̇\ *adverb* (1775)
**1** : in no manner or way : not at all ⟨was *nohow* equal to the task⟩
**2** *dialect* : ANYHOW

**noil** \'nȯi(ə)l\ *noun* [origin unknown] (circa 1624)
: short fiber removed during the combing of a textile fiber and often separately spun into yarn

**noir** \'nwär\ *noun, often attributive* [short for *film noir*] (1980)
**1** : crime fiction featuring hard-boiled cynical characters and bleak sleazy settings
**2** : FILM NOIR
— **noir·ish** \-ish\ *adjective*

¹**noise** \'nȯiz\ *noun* [Middle English, from Old French, strife, quarrel, noise, from Latin *nausea* nausea] (13th century)
**1** : loud, confused, or senseless shouting or outcry
**2 a** : SOUND; *especially* : one that lacks agreeable musical quality or is noticeably unpleasant **b** : any sound that is undesired or interferes with one's hearing of something **c** : an unwanted signal or a disturbance (as static or a variation of voltage) in an electronic device or instrument (as radio or television); *broadly* : a disturbance interfering with the operation of a usually mechanical device or system **d** : electromagnetic radiation (as light or radio waves) that is composed of several frequencies and that involves random changes in frequency or amplitude **e** : irrelevant or meaningless data or output occurring along with desired information
**3** : common talk : RUMOR; *especially* : SLANDER
**4** : something that attracts attention ⟨the play . . . will make little *noise* in the world —Brendan Gill⟩
**5** : something spoken or uttered
— **noise·less** \-ləs\ *adjective*
— **noise·less·ly** *adverb*

²**noise** *verb* **noised; nois·ing** (14th century)
*intransitive verb*
**1** : to talk much or loudly
**2** : to make a noise
*transitive verb*
: to spread by rumor or report — usually used with *about* or *abroad* ⟨the scandal was quickly *noised* about⟩

**noise·mak·er** \'nȯiz-,mā-kər\ *noun* (1574)
: one that makes noise; *especially* : a device (as a horn or rattle) used to make noise at parties
— **noise·mak·ing** \-kiŋ\ *noun or adjective*

**noise pollution** *noun* (1966)
: annoying or harmful noise (as of automobiles or jet airplanes) in an environment

**noi·sette** \nwä-'zet, nwä-\ *noun* [French, diminutive of *nois* choice cut of meat, literally, nut, from Old French, from Latin *nux* — more at NUT] (1891)

: a small piece of lean meat

**noi·some** \'nȯi-səm\ *adjective* [Middle English *noysome*, from *noy* annoyance, from Old French *enui, anoi* — more at ENNUI] (14th century)
**1** : NOXIOUS, HARMFUL
**2 a** : offensive to the senses and especially to the sense of smell **b** : highly obnoxious or objectionable
*synonym* see MALODOROUS
— **noi·some·ly** *adverb*
— **noi·some·ness** *noun*

**noisy** \'nȯi-zē\ *adjective* **nois·i·er; -est** (1693)
**1** : making noise
**2** : full of or characterized by noise or clamor
**3** : noticeably showy, gaudy, or bright : CONSPICUOUS
— **nois·i·ly** \'nȯi-zə-lē\ *adverb*
— **nois·i·ness** \-zē-nəs\ *noun*

**no·li me tan·ge·re** \,nō-lē-(,)mē-'tan-jə-rē, -,lī-, -(,)mä-\ *noun* [Latin, do not touch me; from Jesus' words to Mary Magdalene (John 20:17)] (1591)
: a warning against touching or interference

**nol·le pro·se·qui** \,nä-lē-'prä-sə-,kwī\ *noun* [Latin, to be unwilling to pursue] (1681)
: an entry on the record of a legal action denoting that the prosecutor or plaintiff will proceed no further in an action or suit either as a whole or as to some count or as to one or more of several defendants

**no·lo** \'nō-(,)lō\ *noun* (1914)
: NOLO CONTENDERE

**no–load** \'nō-'lōd\ *adjective* (1963)
: charging no sales commission ⟨a *no-load* mutual fund⟩
— **no–load** \'nō-,lōd\ *noun*

**no·lo con·ten·de·re** \'nō-(,)lō-kən-'ten-də-rē\ *noun* [Latin, I do not wish to contend] (1872)
: a plea in a criminal prosecution that without admitting guilt subjects the defendant to conviction but does not preclude denying the truth of the charges in a collateral proceeding

**nol–pros** \'näl-'präs\ *transitive verb* **nol–prossed; nol–pros·sing** [*nol*le *pros*equi] (circa 1878)
: to discontinue by entering a nolle prosequi

**no·ma** \'nō-mə\ *noun* [New Latin, from Greek *nomē*, from *nemein* to spread (of an ulcer), literally, to graze, pasture — more at NIMBLE] (1834)
: a spreading invasive gangrene chiefly of the lining of the cheek and lips that is usually fatal and occurs most often in persons severely debilitated by disease or profound nutritional deficiency

**no·mad** \'nō-,mad, *British also* 'nä-\ *noun* [Latin *nomad-, nomas* member of a wandering pastoral people, from Greek, from *nemein*] (1579)
**1** : a member of a people who have no fixed residence but move from place to place usually seasonally and within a well-defined territory
**2** : an individual who roams about aimlessly
— **nomad** *adjective*
— **no·mad·ism** \'nō-,ma-,di-zəm\ *noun*

**no·mad·ic** \nō-'ma-dik\ *adjective* (circa 1818)
**1** : of, relating to, or characteristic of nomads ⟨a *nomadic* tribe⟩
**2** : roaming about from place to place aimlessly, frequently, or without a fixed pattern of movement

**no–man's–land** \'nō-,manz-,land\ *noun* (14th century)
**1 a** : an area of unowned, unclaimed, or uninhabited land **b** : an unoccupied area between opposing armies
**2** : an anomalous, ambiguous, or indefinite area especially of operation, application, or jurisdiction ⟨the *no-man's-land* between art and science⟩

**nom·bril** \'näm-brəl\ *noun* [Middle French, literally, navel, ultimately from Latin *umbilicus*] (1562)
: the center point of the lower half of an armorial escutcheon

**nom de guerre** \,näm-di-'ger\ *noun, plural* **noms de guerre** \,näm(z)-di-\ [French, literally, war name] (1679)
: PSEUDONYM

**nom de plume** \-'plüm\ *noun, plural* **noms de plume** \,näm(z)-di-\ [French, pen name; probably coined in English] (1823)
: PSEUDONYM, PEN NAME

**nome** \'nōm\ *noun* [Greek *nomos* pasture, district — more at NIMBLE] (circa 1727)
: a province of ancient Egypt

**no·men** \'nō-mən\ *noun, plural* **no·mi·na** \'nä-mə-nə, 'nō-\ [Latin *nomin-, nomen* name — more at NAME] (circa 1890)
: the second of the three usual names of an ancient Roman male

**no·men·cla·tor** \'nō-mən-,klā-tər\ *noun* [Latin, slave whose duty was to announce the names of persons met during a political campaign, from *nomen* + *calare* to call — more at LOW] (1585)
**1** : a book containing collections or lists of words
**2** *archaic* : one who announces the names of guests or of persons generally
**3** : one who gives names to or invents names for things

**no·men·cla·to·ri·al** \,nō-mən-klə-'tōr-ē-əl, -'tȯr-\ *adjective* (1885)
: relating to or connected with nomenclature

**no·men·cla·ture** \'nō-mən-,klā-chər *also* nō-'men-klə-,chu̇r, -'men-, -chər, -,tyu̇r, -,tu̇r\ *noun* [Latin *nomenclatura* assigning of names, from *nomen* + *calatus,* past participle of *calare*] (1610)
**1** : NAME, DESIGNATION
**2** : the act or process or an instance of naming
**3 a** : a system or set of terms or symbols especially in a particular science, discipline, or art **b** : an international system of standardized New Latin names used in biology for kinds and groups of kinds of animals and plants
— **no·men·cla·tur·al** \,nō-mən-'klāch-rəl, -'klā-chə-\ *adjective*

**no·men con·ser·van·dum** \'nō-mən-,kän(t)-sər-'van-dəm\ *noun, plural* **no·mi·na con·ser·van·da** \'nä-mə-nə-,kän(t)-sər-'van-də, 'nō-\ [New Latin, name to be kept] (circa 1925)
: a biological taxonomic name that is preserved by special sanction in exception to the usual rules

**nomen du·bi·um** \-'dü-bē-əm, -'dyü-\ *noun, plural* **nomina du·bia** \-bē-ə\ [New Latin, doubtful name] (1937)
: a taxonomic name that cannot be assigned with certainty to any taxonomic group because the description is insufficient for identification and the original specimens no longer exist

**nomen nu·dum** \-'nü-dəm, -'nyü-\ *noun, plural* **nomina nu·da** \-də\ [New Latin, bare name] (1900)
: a proposed taxonomic name that is invalid because the group designated is not described or illustrated sufficiently for recognition, that has no nomenclatural status, and that consequently can be used as though never previously proposed

¹**nom·i·nal** \'nä-mə-nºl, 'näm-nəl\ *adjective* [Middle English *nominalle,* from Medieval Latin *nominalis,* from Latin, of a name, from *nomin-, nomen* name — more at NAME] (15th century)
**1** : of, relating to, or being a noun or a word or expression taking a noun construction
**2 a** : of, relating to, or constituting a name **b** : bearing the name of a person
**3 a** : existing or being something in name or form only ⟨*nominal* head of his party⟩ **b** : of, being, or relating to a designated or theoretical

size that may vary from the actual **:** APPROXIMATE **c :** TRIFLING, INSIGNIFICANT
**4** *of a rate of interest* **a :** equal to the annual rate of simple interest that would obtain if interest were not compounded and paid for periods of less than a year **b :** equal to the percentage by which a repaid loan exceeds the principal borrowed with no adjustment made for inflation
**5 :** being according to plan **:** SATISFACTORY ⟨everything was *nominal* during the spacecraft launch⟩
— **nom·i·nal·ly** *adverb*
**²nominal** *noun* (1904)
**:** a word or word group functioning as a noun
**nom·i·nal·ism** \'nä-mə-nᵊl-ˌi-zəm, 'näm-nə-ˌli-zəm\ *noun* (1844)
**1 :** a theory that there are no universal essences in reality and that the mind can frame no single concept or image corresponding to any universal or general term
**2 :** the theory that only individuals and no abstract entities (as essences, classes, or propositions) exist — compare ESSENTIALISM, REALISM
— **nom·i·nal·ist** \-ist, -list\ *noun*
— **nominalist** *or* **nom·i·nal·is·tic** \ˌnä-mə-nᵊl-'is-tik, ˌnäm-nə-'lis-\ *adjective*
**nominal value** *noun* (circa 1901)
**:** PAR 1b
**nominal wages** *noun plural* (1898)
**:** wages measured in money as distinct from actual purchasing power
**nom·i·nate** \'nä-mə-ˌnāt\ *transitive verb* **-nat·ed; -nat·ing** [Latin *nominatus*, past participle of *nominare*, from *nomin-, nomen* name — more at NAME] (1545)
**1 :** DESIGNATE, NAME
**2 a :** to appoint or propose for appointment to an office or place **b :** to propose as a candidate for election to office **c :** to propose for an honor ⟨*nominate* her for player of the year⟩
**3 :** to enter (a horse) in a race
— **nom·i·na·tor** \-ˌnä-tər\ *noun*
**nom·i·na·tion** \ˌnä-mə-'nä-shən\ *noun* (15th century)
**1 :** the act, process, or an instance of nominating
**2 :** the state of being nominated
**nom·i·na·tive** \'näm-nə-tiv, 'nä-mə-; *2 & 3 are also* 'nä-mə-ˌnä-\ *adjective* [Middle English *nominatyf*, from Middle French or Latin; Middle French *nominatif*, from Latin (*casus*) *nominativus* nominative case, from *nominare*; from the traditional use of the nominative form in naming a noun] (14th century)
**1 a :** marking typically the subject of a verb especially in languages that have relatively full inflection ⟨*nominative case*⟩ **b :** of or relating to the nominative case ⟨a *nominative* ending⟩
**2 :** nominated or appointed by nomination
**3 :** bearing a person's name
— **nominative** *noun*
**nom·i·nee** \ˌnä-mə-'nē\ *noun* [*nominate*] (1688)
**:** a person who has been nominated
**no·mo·gram** \'nä-mə-ˌgram, 'nō-\ *noun* [Greek *nomos* law + International Scientific Vocabulary *-gram* — more at NIMBLE] (1908)
**:** a graphic representation that consists of several lines marked off to scale and arranged in such a way that by using a straightedge to connect known values on two lines an unknown value can be read at the point of intersection with another line
**no·mo·graph** \-ˌgraf\ *noun* (circa 1909)
**:** NOMOGRAM
— **no·mo·graph·ic** \ˌnä-mə-'gra-fik, ˌnō-\ *adjective*
— **no·mog·ra·phy** \nō-'mä-grə-fē\ *noun*
**no·mo·log·i·cal** \ˌnä-mə-'lä-ji-kəl, ˌnō-\ *adjective* [*nomology* science of physical and logical laws, from Greek *nomos* + English *-logy*] (1845)

**:** relating to or expressing basic physical laws or rules of reasoning ⟨*nomological* universals⟩
**no·mo·thet·ic** \-'the-tik\ *adjective* [Greek *nomothetikos* of legislation, from *nomothetēs* lawgiver, from *nomos* law + *-thetēs* one who establishes, from *tithenai* to put — more at DO] (1658)
**:** relating to, involving, or dealing with abstract, general, or universal statements or laws
**-nomy** *noun combining form* [Middle English *-nomie*, from Old French, from Latin *-nomia*, from Greek, from *nomos*]
**:** system of laws governing or sum of knowledge regarding a (specified) field ⟨agronomy⟩
**non-** \(')nän *also* ˌnən *or* 'nən *before* '-stressed syllable, ˌnän *also* ˌnən *before* ˌ-stressed or unstressed syllable; the variant with ə is also to be understood at pronounced entries, though not shown\ *prefix* [Middle English, from Middle French, from Latin *non* not, from Old Latin *noenum*, from *ne-* not + *oinom*, neuter of *oinos* one — more at NO, ONE]
**1 :** not **:** other than **:** reverse of **:** absence of
**2 :** of little or no consequence **:** unimportant **:** worthless ⟨*non*issues⟩ ⟨*non*system⟩
**3 :** lacking the usual especially positive characteristics of the thing specified ⟨*non*celebration⟩ ⟨*non*art⟩

non·abra·sive
non·ab·sorb·able
non·ab·sor·bent
non·ab·sorp·tive
non·ab·stract
non·ac·a·dem·ic
non·ac·cep·tance
non·ac·count·able
non·ac·cred·it·ed
non·ac·cru·al
non·achieve·ment
non·ac·id
non·acid·ic
non·ac·quis·i·tive
non·act·ing
non·ac·tion
non·ac·ti·vat·ed
non·ac·tor
non·adap·tive
non·ad·dict
non·ad·dic·tive
non·ad·he·sive
non·adi·a·bat·ic
non·ad·ja·cent
non·ad·mir·er
non·ad·mis·sion
non·aes·thet·ic
non·af·fil·i·at·ed
non·af·flu·ent
non–Af·ri·can
non·ag·gres·sion
non·ag·gres·sive
non·ag·ri·cul·tur·al
non·al·co·hol·ic
non·al·ler·gen·ic
non·al·ler·gic
non·al·pha·bet·ic
non·alu·mi·num
non·am·big·u·ous
non–Amer·i·can
non·an·a·lyt·ic
non·an·a·tom·ic
non·an·i·mal
non·an·swer
non·an·tag·o·nis·tic
non·an·thro·po·log·i·cal
non·an·thro·pol·o·gist
non·an·ti·bi·ot·ic
non·an·ti·gen·ic
non·ap·pear·ance
non·aquat·ic
non·aque·ous
non·ar·bi·trar·i·ness
non·ar·bi·trary

non·ar·chi·tect
non·ar·chi·tec·ture
non·ar·gu·ment
non·aris·to·crat·ic
non·ar·o·mat·ic
non·art
non·art·ist
non·ar·tis·tic
non·as·cet·ic
non·as·pi·rin
non·as·ser·tive
non·as·so·ci·at·ed
non·as·tro·nom·i·cal
non·ath·lete
non·ath·let·ic
non·atom·ic
non·at·tached
non·at·tach·ment
non·at·ten·dance
non·at·tend·er
non·au·di·to·ry
non·au·thor
non·au·thor·i·tar·i·an
non·au·to·mat·ed
non·au·to·mat·ic
non·au·to·mo·tive
non·au·ton·o·mous
non·avail·abil·i·ty
non·bac·te·ri·al
non·bar·bi·tu·rate
non·ba·sic
non·bear·ing
non·be·hav·ior·al
non·be·ing
non·be·lief
non·be·liev·er
non·bel·lig·er·en·cy
non·bel·lig·er·ent
non·bet·ting
non·bib·lio·graph·ic
non·bi·na·ry
non·bind·ing
non·bio·de·grad·able
non·bio·graph·i·cal
non·bi·o·log·i·cal
non·bi·o·log·i·cal·ly
non·bi·ol·o·gist
non·bit·ing
non·black
non·body
non·bond·ed
non·bot·a·nist
non·brand
non·break·able
non·breath·ing
non·breed·er
non·breed·ing

non·broad·cast
non·build·ing
non·burn·able
non·buy·ing
non·cab·i·net
non·cak·ing
non·call·able
non·cam·pus
non·can·cel·able
non·can·cer·ous
non·can·ni·bal·is·tic
non·cap·i·tal
non·cap·i·tal·ist
non·car·cin·o·gen
non·car·ci·no·gen·ic
non·car·di·ac
non·ca·reer
non·car·ri·er
non·cash
non·ca·su·al
non–Cath·o·lic
non·caus·al
non·cel·e·bra·tion
non·cel·e·bri·ty
non·cel·lu·lar
non·cel·lu·los·ic
non–Celt·ic
non·cen·tral
non·cer·tif·i·cat·ed
non·cer·ti·fied
non·char·ac·ter
non·char·is·mat·ic
non·chau·vin·ist
non·chem·i·cal
non–Chris·tian
non·chro·no·log·i·cal
non·church
non·church·go·er
non·cir·cu·lar
non·cir·cu·lat·ing
non·cit·i·zen
non·clan·des·tine
non·class
non·clas·si·cal
non·clas·si·fied
non·class·room
non·cler·i·cal
non·cling
non·clin·i·cal
non·clog·ging
non·co·er·cive
non·cog·ni·tive
non·co·her·ent
non·co·in·ci·dence
non·co·i·tal
non·cok·ing
non·co·la
non·col·lec·tor
non·col·lege
non·col·le·giate
non·col·lin·ear
non·col·or
non·col·ored
non·col·or·fast
non·com·bat
non·com·bat·ive
non·com·bus·ti·ble
non·com·mer·cial
non·com·mit·ment
non·com·mit·ted
non·com·mu·ni·cat·ing
non·com·mu·ni·ca·tion
non·com·mu·ni·ca·tive
non·com·mu·nist
non·com·mu·ni·ty
non·com·mu·ta·tive

non·com·mu·ta·tiv·i·ty
non·com·pa·ra·bil·i·ty
non·com·pa·ra·ble
non·com·pat·i·ble
non·com·pe·ti·tion
non·com·pet·i·tive
non·com·pet·i·tor
non·com·ple·men·ta·ry
non·com·plex
non·com·pli·ance
non·com·pli·cat·ed
non·com·ply·ing
non·com·pos·er
non·com·pound
non·com·pre·hen·sion
non·com·press·ible
non·com·put·er
non·com·put·er·ized
non·con·cep·tu·al
non·con·cern
non·con·clu·sion
non·con·cur·rent
non·con·dens·able
non·con·di·tioned
non·con·duct·ing
non·con·duc·tion
non·con·duc·tive
non·con·fer·ence
non·con·fi·dence
non·con·fi·den·tial
non·con·flict·ing
non·con·fron·ta·tion
non·con·fron·ta·tion·al
non·con·gru·ent
non·con·ju·gat·ed
non·con·nec·tion
non·con·scious
non·con·sec·u·tive
non·con·sen·su·al
non·con·ser·va·tion
non·con·ser·va·tive
non·con·sol·i·dat·ed
non·con·stant
non·con·sti·tu·tion·al
non·con·struc·tion
non·con·struc·tive
non·con·sum·er
non·con·sum·ing
non·con·sump·tion
non·con·sump·tive
non·con·tact
non·con·ta·gious
non·con·tem·po·rary
non·con·tig·u·ous
non·con·tin·gent
non·con·tin·u·ous
non·con·tract
non·con·trac·tu·al
non·con·tra·dic·tion
non·con·tra·dic·to·ry
non·con·trib·u·to·ry
non·con·trol·la·ble
non·con·trolled
non·con·trol·ling
non·con·tro·ver·sial
non·con·ven·tion·al
non·con·vert·ible
non·co·pla·nar
non·co·po·rate
non·cor·re·la·tion
non·cor·rod·ible
non·cor·rod·ing
non·cor·ro·sive
non·coun·try

non·coun·ty
non·cov·er·age
non·cre·a·tive
non·cre·a·tiv·i·ty
non·cre·den·tialed
non·crime
non·crim·i·nal
non·cri·sis
non·crit·i·cal
non·crush·able
non·crys·tal·line
non·cu·li·nary
non·cul·ti·vat·ed
non·cul·ti·va·tion
non·cul·tur·al
non·cu·mu·la·tive
non·cur·rent
non·cus·tom·er
non·cy·clic
non·cy·cli·cal
non·dance
non·danc·er
non–Dar·win·i·an
non·de·cep·tive
non·de·ci·sion
non·de·creas·ing
non·de·duc·tive
non·de·fer·ra·ble
non·de·form·ing
non·de·gen·er·ate
non·de·grad·able
non·de·gree
non·del·e·gate
non·de·lib·er·ate
non·de·lin·quent
non·de·liv·ery
non·de·mand·ing
non·dem·o·crat·ic
non·de·nom·i·na·
   tion·al
non·de·nom·i·na·
   tion·al·ism
non·de·part·men·tal
non·de·pen·dent
non·de·plet·able
non·de·plet·ing
non·de·po·si·tion
non·de·pressed
non·de·riv·a·tive
non·de·scrip·tive
non·de·sert
non·de·tach·able
non·de·ter·min·is·tic
non·de·vel·op·ment
non·de·vi·ant
non·di·a·bet·ic
non·di·a·lyz·able
non·di·dac·tic
non·dif·fus·ible
non·di·men·sion·al
non·dip·lo·mat·ic
non·di·rect·ed
non·di·rec·tion·al
non·dis·abled
non·dis·clo·sure
non·dis·count
non·dis·cre·tion·ary
non·dis·crim·i·na·
   tion
non·dis·crim·i·na·
   to·ry
non·dis·cur·sive
non·dis·per·sive
non·dis·rup·tive
non·di·ver·si·fied
non·doc·tor
non·doc·tri·naire
non·doc·u·men·ta·ry
non·dog·mat·ic
non·dol·lar
non·do·mes·tic
non·dom·i·nant
non·dra·mat·ic
non·driv·er
non·drug
non·du·ra·ble

non·earn·ing
non·ec·cle·si·as·ti·
   cal
non·econ·o·mist
non·ed·i·ble
non·ed·i·to·ri·al
non·ed·u·ca·tion
non·ed·u·ca·tion·al
non·ef·fec·tive
non·elas·tic
non·elect·ed
non·elec·tion
non·elec·tive
non·elec·tric
non·elec·tri·cal
non·elec·tron·ic
non·el·e·men·ta·ry
non·elite
non·emer·gen·cy
non·emo·tion·al
non·em·phat·ic
non·em·pir·i·cal
non·em·ploy·ee
non·em·ploy·ment
non·emp·ty
non·en·cap·su·lat·ed
non·end·ing
non·en·er·gy
non·en·force·abil·i·ty
non·en·force·ment
non·en·gage·ment
non·en·gi·neer·ing
non·en·ter·tain·ment
non·en·zy·mat·ic
non·en·zy·mic
non·equi·lib·ri·um
non·equiv·a·lence
non·equiv·a·lent
non·erot·ic
non·es·tab·lished
non·es·tab·lish·ment
non·es·ter·i·fied
non·eth·i·cal
non·eth·nic
non–Eu·ro·pe·an
non·eval·u·a·tive
non·ev·i·dence
non·ex·clu·sive
non·ex·ec·u·tive
non·ex·empt
non·ex·is·ten·tial
non·ex·ot·ic
non·ex·pend·able
non·ex·per·i·men·tal
non·ex·pert
non·ex·plan·a·to·ry
non·ex·ploi·ta·tion
non·ex·ploit·a·tive
non·ex·ploit·ive
non·ex·plo·sive
non·ex·posed
non·ex·tant
non·fact
non·fac·tor
non·fac·tu·al
non·fac·ul·ty
non·fad·ing
non·fa·mil·ial
non·fam·i·ly
non·fan
non·farm
non·farm·er
non·fa·tal
non·fat·ten·ing
non·fat·ty
non·fed·er·al
non·fed·er·at·ed
non·fem·i·nist
non·fil·a·men·tous
non·fil·ter·able
non·fi·nal
non·fi·nan·cial
non·fi·nite
non·fis·sion·able
non·flu·o·res·cent
non·fly·ing

non·food
non·for·feit·able
non·for·fei·ture
non·for·mal
non·fos·sil
non·frat·er·ni·za·tion
non·freez·ing
non·friv·o·lous
non·fro·zen
non·fuel
non·ful·fill·ment
non·func·tion·al
non·func·tion·ing
non·game
non·gas·eous
non·gay
non·ge·net·ic
non·gen·i·tal
non·geo·met·ri·cal
non·ghet·to
non·glam·or·ous
non·glare
non·golf·er
non·gov·ern·ment
non·gov·ern·men·tal
non·grad·ed
non·grad·u·ate
non·gram·mat·i·cal
non·gran·u·lar
non·grav·i·ta·tion·al
non·greasy
non·gre·gar·i·ous
non·grow·ing
non·growth
non·guest
non·ha·lo·ge·nat·ed
non·hand·i·capped
non·hap·pen·ing
non·har·dy
non·har·mon·ic
non·haz·ard·ous
non·heme
non·he·mo·lyt·ic
non·he·red·i·tary
non·hi·er·ar·chi·cal
non–His·pan·ic
non·his·tor·i·cal
non·home
non·ho·mo·ge·neous
non·ho·mol·o·gous
non·ho·mo·sex·u·al
non·hor·mon·al
non·hos·pi·tal
non·hos·pi·tal·ized
non·hos·tile
non·hous·ing
non·hu·man
non·hunt·er
non·hunt·ing
non·hy·gro·scop·ic
non·hys·ter·i·cal
non·ide·al
non·iden·ti·ty
non·ideo·log·i·cal
non·im·age
non·im·i·ta·tive
non·im·mi·grant
non·im·mune
non·im·pact
non·im·pli·ca·tion
non·im·por·ta·tion
non·in·clu·sion
non·in·creas·ing
non·in·cum·bent
non·in·de·pen·dence
non–In·di·an
non·in·dig·e·nous
non·in·di·vid·u·al
non–In·do–Eu·ro·
   pe·an
non·in·dus·tri·al
non·in·dus·tri·al·ized
non·in·dus·try
non·in·fect·ed
non·in·fec·tious
non·in·fec·tive

non·in·fest·ed
non·in·flam·ma·ble
non·in·flam·ma·to·ry
non·in·fla·tion·ary
non·in·flec·tion·al
non·in·flu·ence
non·in·for·ma·tion
non·ini·tial
non·ini·ti·ate
non·in·ju·ry
non·in·sect
non·in·sec·ti·cid·al
non·in·stall·ment
non·in·sti·tu·tion·al
non·in·sti·tu·tion·al·
   ized
non·in·struc·tion·al
non·in·stru·men·tal
non·in·sur·ance
non·in·sured
non·in·te·gral
non·in·te·grat·ed
non·in·tel·lec·tu·al
non·in·ter·act·ing
non·in·ter·ac·tive
non·in·ter·change·
   able
non·in·ter·course
non·in·ter·est
non·in·ter·fer·ence
non·in·ter·sect·ing
non·in·tim·i·dat·ing
non·in·tox·i·cant
non·in·tox·i·cat·ing
non·in·tru·sive
non·in·tu·i·tive
non·ion·iz·ing
non·ir·ra·di·at·ed
non·ir·ri·gat·ed
non·ir·ri·tant
non·ir·ri·tat·ing
non·is·sue
non–Jap·a·nese
non–Jew
non–Jew·ish
non·join·er
non·ju·di·cial
non·ju·ry
non·jus·ti·cia·ble
non·ko·sher
non·la·bor
non·land·own·er
non·lan·guage
non·law·yer
non·lead·ed
non·league
non·le·gal
non·le·gume
non·le·gu·mi·nous
non·le·thal
non·lex·i·cal
non·li·brar·i·an
non·li·brary
non·life
non·lin·e·al
non·lin·e·ar
non·lin·e·ar·i·ty
non·lin·guis·tic
non·liq·uid
non·lit·er·al
non·lit·er·ary
non·liv·ing
non·lo·cal
non·log·i·cal
non·lu·mi·nous
non·mag·net·ic
non·main·stream
non·ma·jor
non·ma·lig·nant
non·mal·lea·ble
non·man·age·ment
non·man·a·ge·ri·al
non·man·u·al
non·man·u·fac·tur·
   ing
non·mar·i·tal

non·mar·ket
non–Marx·ist
non·ma·te·ri·al
non·ma·te·ri·al·is·tic
non·math·e·mat·i·
   cal
non·math·e·ma·ti·
   cian
non·ma·tric·u·lat·ed
non·mean·ing·ful
non·mea·sur·able
non·meat
non·me·chan·i·cal
non·mech·a·nis·tic
non·med·i·cal
non·meet·ing
non·mem·ber
non·mem·ber·ship
non·men·tal
non·mer·cu·ri·al
non·meta·mer·ic
non·met·a·phor·i·cal
non·met·ric
non·met·ri·cal
non·met·ro
non·met·ro·pol·i·tan
non·mi·cro·bi·al
non·mi·grant
non·mi·gra·to·ry
non·mil·i·tant
non·mil·i·tary
non·mi·met·ic
non·mi·nor·i·ty
non·mo·bile
non·mo·lec·u·lar
non·mon·e·tar·ist
non·mon·e·tary
non·mon·ey
non·mo·nog·a·mous
non·mo·tile
non·mo·til·i·ty
non·mo·tor·ized
non·mov·ing
non·mu·nic·i·pal
non·mu·sic
non·mu·si·cal
non·mu·si·cian
non·mu·tant
non·my·e·lin·at·ed
non·mys·ti·cal
non·nar·ra·tive
non·na·tion·al
non·na·tive
non·nat·u·ral
non·ne·ces·si·ty
non·neg·li·gent
non·ne·go·tia·ble
non·net·work
non·news
non·ni·trog·e·nous
non·nor·ma·tive
non·nov·el
non·nu·cle·at·ed
non·nu·mer·i·cal
non·nu·tri·tious
non·nu·tri·tive
non·ob·scene
non·ob·ser·vance
non·ob·ser·vant
non·ob·vi·ous
non·oc·cu·pa·tion·al
non·oc·cur·rence
non·of·fi·cial
non·ohm·ic
non·oily
non·op·er·at·ic
non·op·er·at·ing
non·op·er·a·tion·al
non·op·er·a·tive
non·op·ti·mal
non·or·gan·ic
non·or·tho·dox
non·over·lap·ping
non·own·er
non·ox·i·diz·ing
non·paid

non·par·al·lel
non·par·a·sit·ic
non·par·tic·i·pant
non·par·tic·i·pat·ing
non·par·tic·i·pa·tion
non·par·tic·i·pa·to·ry
non·par·ty
non·pas·sive
non·past
non·pay·ing
non·pay·ment
non·per·for·mance
non·per·form·er
non·per·ish·able
non·per·mis·sive
non·per·son·al
non·pe·tro·leum
non·phi·los·o·pher
non·phil·o·soph·i·
   cal
non·pho·ne·mic
non·pho·net·ic
non·phos·phate
non·pho·to·graph·ic
non·phys·i·cian
non·pla·nar
non·plas·tic
non·play
non·play·ing
non·po·et·ic
non·poi·son·ous
non·po·lar·iz·able
non·po·lice
non·po·lit·i·cal
non·po·lit·i·cal·ly
non·po·lit·i·cian
non·pol·lut·ing
non·poor
non·po·rous
non·pos·ses·sion
non·prac·ti·cal
non·prac·tic·ing
non·preg·nant
non·print
non·prob·lem
non·pro·duc·ing
non·pro·fes·sion·al
non·pro·fes·sion·
   al·ly
non·pro·fes·so·ri·al
non·pro·gram
non·pro·gram·mer
non·pro·gres·sive
non·pro·pri·etary
non·psy·chi·at·ric
non·psy·chi·a·trist
non·psy·cho·log·i·
   cal
non·psy·chot·ic
non·pub·lic
non·pu·ni·tive
non·pur·po·sive
non·quan·ti·fi·able
non·quan·ti·ta·tive
non·ra·cial
non·ra·cial·ly
non·ra·dio·ac·tive
non·rail·road
non·ran·dom
non·ran·dom·ness
non·rat·ed
non·ra·tio·nal
non·re·ac·tive
non·re·ac·tor
non·re·al·is·tic
non·re·ap·point·
   ment
non·re·ceipt
non·re·cip·ro·cal
non·rec·og·ni·tion
non·re·cy·cla·ble
non·re·duc·ing
non·re·dun·dant
non·re·fill·able
non·re·flect·ing

non·reg·u·lat·ed
non·reg·u·la·tion
non·rel·a·tive
non·rel·e·vant
non·re·li·gious
non·re·new·able
non·re·new·al
non·re·pay·able
non·rep·re·sen·ta·tive
non·re·pro·duc·tive
non·res·i·den·tial
non·res·o·nant
non·re·spon·dent
non·re·spond·er
non·re·sponse
non·re·spon·sive
non·re·strict·ed
non·re·trac·tile
non·ret·ro·ac·tive
non·re·us·able
non·re·vers·ible
non·rev·o·lu·tion·ary
non·ri·ot·er
non·ri·ot·ing
non·ro·tat·ing
non·rou·tine
non·roy·al
non·rub·ber
non·rul·ing
non·ru·mi·nant
non–Rus·sian
non·sal·able
non·sa·line
non·sa·pon·i·fi·able
non·schiz·o·phren·ic
non·school
non·sci·en·tif·ic
non·sci·en·tist
non·sea·son·al
non·sec·re·tory
non·se·cure
non·sed·i·ment·able
non·seg·re·gat·ed
non·seg·re·ga·tion
non·se·lect·ed
non·se·lec·tive
non·self–gov·ern·ing
non·sen·sa·tion·al
non·sen·si·tive
non·sen·su·ous
non·sen·tence
non·sep·tate
non·se·quen·tial
non·se·ri·ous
non·sex·ist
non·sex·u·al
non·shrink
non·shrink·able
non·sign·er
non·si·mul·ta·neous
non·sink·able
non·skat·er
non·skel·e·tal
non·ski·er
non·smok·er
non·smok·ing
non·so·cial·ist
non·so·lar
non·so·lu·tion
non·spa·tial
non·speak·er
non·speak·ing
non·spe·cial·ist
non·spe·cif·ic
non·spe·cif·i·cal·ly
non·spec·tac·u·lar
non·spec·u·la·tive
non·speech
non·spher·i·cal
non·sta·tion·ary
non·sta·tis·ti·cal
non·steady
non·sto·ry
non·stra·te·gic

non·struc·tur·al
non·struc·tured
non·stu·dent
non·style
non·sub·ject
non·sub·jec·tive
non·sub·si·dized
non·suc·cess
non·sug·ar
non·su·per·im·pos·able
non·su·per·vi·so·ry
non·sur·gi·cal
non·swim·mer
non·sym·bol·ic
non·sym·met·ric
non·sym·met·ri·cal
non·syn·chro·nous
non·sys·tem·at·ic
non·sys·tem·ic
non·tar·iff
non·tax·able
non·teach·ing
non·tech·ni·cal
non·tem·po·ral
non·ten·ured
non·ter·mi·nal
non·the·at·ri·cal
non·the·ist
non·the·is·tic
non·theo·log·i·cal
non·the·o·ret·i·cal
non·ther·a·peu·tic
non·think·ing
non·threat·en·ing
non·tid·al
non·to·bac·co
non·ton·al
non·to·tal·i·tar·i·an
non·tox·ic
non·tra·di·tion·al
non·trans·fer·able
non·treat·ment
non·triv·i·al
non·trop·i·cal
non·tur·bu·lent
non·typ·i·cal
non·unan·i·mous
non·uni·form
non·uni·for·mi·ty
non·union·ized
non·unique
non·unique·ness
non·uni·ver·sal
non·uni·ver·si·ty
non·ur·ban
non·ur·gent
non·util·i·tar·i·an
non·util·i·ty
non·uto·pi·an
non·val·id
non·va·lid·i·ty
non·vas·cu·lar
non·veg·e·tar·i·an
non·ven·om·ous
non·vet·er·an
non·vi·a·ble
non·view·er
non·vi·ral
non·vir·gin
non·vis·cous
non·vi·su·al
non·vo·cal
non·vo·ca·tion·al
non·vol·ca·nic
non·vol·un·tary
non·vot·er
non·vot·ing
non·war
non·win·ning
non·woody
non·work
non·work·er
non·work·ing
non·writ·er
non·yel·low·ing

**non·ad·di·tive** \'nän-'a-də-tiv\ adjective (1926)
**1 :** not having a numerical value equal to the sum of values for the component parts
**2 :** of, relating to, or being a genic effect that is not additive
— **non·ad·di·tiv·i·ty** \,nän-,a-də-'ti-və-tē\ noun

**non·age** \'nä-nij, 'nō-\ noun [Middle English, from Middle French, from non- + age age] (15th century)
**1 :** MINORITY 1
**2 a :** a period of youth **b :** lack of maturity

**no·na·ge·nar·i·an** \,nō-nə-jə-'ner-ē-ən, ,nä-\ noun [Latin nonagenarius containing ninety, from nonageni ninety each, from nonaginta ninety, from nona- (akin to novem nine) + -ginta (akin to viginti twenty) — more at NINE, VIGESIMAL] (1804)
**:** a person whose age is in the nineties
— **nonagenarian** adjective

**no·na·gon** \'nō-nə-,gän\ noun [Latin nonus ninth + English -gon — more at NOON] (circa 1639)
**:** a polygon of nine angles and nine sides

**non·aligned** \,nän-ə-'līnd\ adjective (1960)
**:** not allied with other nations and especially with either the Communist or the non-Communist blocs
— **non·align·ment** \-mənt\ noun

**non·al·le·lic** \,nän-ə-'lē-lik, -'le-\ adjective (1945)
**:** not behaving as alleles toward one another ⟨nonallelic genes⟩

**non–A, non–B hepatitis** \'nän-'ā-'nän-'bē-\ noun (1976)
**:** hepatitis clinically and immunologically similar to hepatitis A and hepatitis B but caused by different viruses

**non·bank** \'nän-'baŋk\ noun, often attributive (1939)
**:** a business that is not an officially established bank but offers many similar services
— **non·bank·ing** \-'baŋ-kiŋ\ adjective

**non·bond·ing** \-'bän-diŋ\ adjective (1952)
**:** being or occupied by electrons especially of an atom's valence shell that are not involved in a chemical bond ⟨a nonbonding atomic orbital⟩

**¹non·book** \-'bùk\ adjective (1949)
**:** being something other than a book; especially **:** being a library holding (as a microfilm) that is not a book

**²non·book** \-,bùk\ noun (1960)
**:** a book of little literary merit which is often a compilation (as of pictures, press clippings, or speeches)

**non·busi·ness** \-'biz-nəs, -nəz\ adjective (1927)
**:** not related to business; especially **:** not related to one's primary business

**non·ca·lor·ic** \,nän-kə-'lór-ik, -'lór-\ adjective (1950)
**:** free from or very low in calories

**non·can·di·date** \'nän-'kan-də-,dāt, -'ka-nə-, -dət\ noun (1944)
**:** a person who is not a candidate; especially **:** one who has refused to be a candidate for a particular political office
— **non·can·di·da·cy** \-də-sē\ noun

**¹nonce** \'nän(t)s\ noun [Middle English nanes, alteration (from misdivision of then anes in such phrases as to then anes for the one purpose) of anes one purpose, irregular from an, on one — more at ONE] (13th century)
**1 :** the one, particular, or present occasion, purpose, or use ⟨for the nonce⟩
**2 :** the time being

**²nonce** adjective (1884)
**:** occurring, used, or made only once or for a special occasion ⟨a nonce word⟩

**non·cha·lance** \,nän-shə-'län(t)s; 'nän-shə-,län(t)s, -,län(t)s\ noun (1678)
**:** the quality or state of being nonchalant

**non·cha·lant** \-'länt, -,länt, -lənt\ adjective [French, from Old French, from present participle of nonchaloir to disregard, from non- + chaloir to concern, from Latin calēre to be warm — more at LEE] (circa 1734)
**:** having an air of easy unconcern or indifference
**synonym** see COOL
— **non·cha·lant·ly** adverb

**non·chro·mo·som·al** \,nän-,krō-mə-'sō-məl\ adjective (1960)
**1 :** not situated on a chromosome
**2 :** not involving chromosomes

**non·com** \'nän-,käm\ noun (1883)
**:** NONCOMMISSIONED OFFICER

**non·com·bat·ant** \,nän-kəm-'ba-t⁰nt also 'nän-'käm-bə-tənt\ noun (1811)
**:** one that does not engage in combat: as **a :** a member (as a chaplain) of the armed forces whose duties do not include fighting **b :** CIVILIAN
— **noncombatant** adjective

**non·com·mis·sioned officer** \,nän-kə-'mi-shənd-\ noun (1703)
**:** a subordinate officer (as a sergeant) in the army, air force, or marine corps appointed from among enlisted personnel

**non·com·mit·tal** \-kə-'mi-t⁰l\ adjective (1829)
**1 :** giving no clear indication of attitude or feeling
**2 :** having no clear or distinctive character
— **non·com·mit·tal·ly** \-t⁰l-ē\ adverb

**non com·pos men·tis** \,nän-,käm-pəs-'men-təs, ,nōn-\ adjective [Latin, literally, not having mastery of one's mind] (1607)
**:** not of sound mind

**non·con·cur** \,nän-kən-'kər\ intransitive verb (circa 1847)
**:** to refuse or fail to concur
— **non·con·cur·rence** \-'kər-ən(t)s, -'kə-rən(t)s\ noun

**non·con·duc·tor** \-kən-'dək-tər\ noun (1751)
**:** a substance that conducts heat, electricity, or sound only in very small degree

**non·con·form** \-kən-'fórm\ intransitive verb [back-formation from nonconformist] (1681)
**:** to fail to conform
— **non·con·form·er** noun

**non·con·for·mance** \-'fór-mən(t)s\ noun (1843)
**:** failure to conform

**non·con·form·ism** \-'fór-,mi-zəm\ noun (1844)
**:** NONCONFORMITY

**non·con·form·ist** \-'fór-mist\ noun (1619)
**1** often capitalized **:** a person who does not conform to an established church; especially **:** one who does not conform to the Church of England
**2 :** a person who does not conform to a generally accepted pattern of thought or action
— **nonconformist** adjective, often capitalized

**non·con·for·mi·ty** \-'fór-mə-tē\ noun (1618)
**1 a :** failure or refusal to conform to an established church **b** often capitalized **:** the movement or principles of English Protestant dissent **c** often capitalized **:** the body of English Nonconformists
**2 :** refusal to conform to an established or conventional creed, rule, or practice
**3 :** absence of agreement or correspondence

**non·co·op·er·a·tion** \,nän-kō-,ä-pə-'rā-shən\ noun (1795)
**:** failure or refusal to cooperate; specifically **:** refusal through civil disobedience of a people to cooperate with the government of a country
— **non·co·op·er·a·tion·ist** \-sh(ə-)nist\ noun
— **non·co·op·er·a·tor** \-'ä-pə-,rā-tər\ noun

**non·co·op·er·a·tive** \-'ä-p(ə-)rə-tiv, -pə-,rä-\ *adjective* (1922)
**:** of, relating to, or characterized by noncooperation

**non·cred·it** \'nän-'kre-dət\ *adjective* (1965)
**:** not offering credit toward a degree ⟨*noncredit* courses⟩

**non·cross·over** \-'krȯ,sō-vər\ *adjective* (1919)
**:** having or being chromosomes that have not participated in genetic crossing-over ⟨*noncrossover* offspring⟩

**non·cus·to·di·al** \-kə-'stō-dē-əl\ *adjective* (1973)
**:** of or being a parent who does not have legal custody of a child

**non·dairy** \-'der-ē, -'dar-; 'nän-,\ *adjective* (1968)
**:** containing no milk or milk products ⟨*nondairy* whipped topping⟩

**non·de·duct·ible** \,nän-di-'dək-tə-bəl\ *adjective* (1943)
**:** not deductible; *especially* **:** not deductible for income tax purposes
— **non·de·duct·ibil·i·ty** \-,dək-tə-'bi-lə-tē\ *noun*

**non·de·fense** \,nän-di-'fen(t)s\ *adjective* (1961)
**:** not used or intended for or associated with the military ⟨*nondefense* spending⟩

**non·de·script** \,nän-di-'skript\ *adjective* [*non-* + Latin *descriptus*, past participle of *describere* to describe] (circa 1807)
**1 :** belonging or appearing to belong to no particular class or kind **:** not easily described
**2 :** lacking distinctive or interesting qualities **:** DULL, DRAB
— **nondescript** *noun*

**non·de·struc·tive** \-di-'strək-tiv\ *adjective* (1926)
**:** not destructive; *specifically* **:** not causing destruction of material being investigated or treated ⟨*nondestructive* testing of metal⟩
— **non·de·struc·tive·ly** *adverb*
— **non·de·struc·tive·ness** *noun*

**non·dia·paus·ing** \,nän-,dī-ə-'pȯ-ziŋ\ *adjective* (1963)
**1 :** not having a diapause
**2 :** not being in a state of diapause

**non·di·rec·tive** \,nän-də-'rek-tiv, -(,)dī-\ *adjective* (1931)
**:** of, relating to, or being psychotherapy, counseling, or interviewing in which the counselor refrains from interpretation or explanation but encourages the client (as by repeating phrases) to talk freely

**non·dis·junc·tion** \,nän-dis-'jəŋ(k)-shən\ *noun* [International Scientific Vocabulary] (1913)
**:** failure of homologous chromosomes or sister chromatids to separate subsequent to metaphase in meiosis or mitosis so that one daughter cell has both and the other neither of the chromosomes
— **non·dis·junc·tion·al** \-shnəl, -shə-n°l\ *adjective*

**non·dis·tinc·tive** \-di-'stiŋ(k)-tiv\ *adjective* (1916)
*of a speech sound* **:** having no signaling value

**non·di·vid·ing** \,nän-də-'vī-diŋ\ *adjective* (1945)
**:** not undergoing cell division

**non·dor·mant** \'nän-'dȯr-mənt\ *adjective* (1940)
**1 :** being in such a condition that germination is possible ⟨*nondormant* seeds⟩
**2 :** being in active vegetative growth ⟨*nondormant* plants⟩

**non·drink·er** \-'driŋ-kər\ *noun* (1899)
**:** a person who abstains from alcoholic beverages
— **non·drink·ing** \-kiŋ\ *adjective*

**non·dry·ing oil** \-'drī-iŋ\ *noun* (1905)
**:** a highly saturated oil (as olive oil) that is unable to solidify when exposed in a thin film to air

¹**none** \'nən\ *pronoun, singular or plural in construction* [Middle English, from Old English *nān*, from *ne* not + *ān* one — more at NO, ONE] (before 12th century)
**1 :** not any
**2 :** not one **:** NOBODY
**3 :** not any such thing or person
**4 :** no part **:** NOTHING ▫

²**none** *adjective* (before 12th century)
*archaic* **:** not any **:** NO

³**none** *adverb* (1651)
**1 :** by no means **:** not at all ⟨*none* too soon to begin⟩
**2 :** in no way **:** to no extent ⟨*none* the worse for wear⟩

⁴**none** \'nōn\ *noun, often capitalized* [Late Latin *nona*, from Latin, 9th hour of the day from sunrise — more at NOON] (1845)
**:** the fifth of the canonical hours
*word history* SEE NOON

**non·eco·nom·ic** \,nän-,e-kə-'nä-mik, -,ē-kə-\ *adjective* (1920)
**:** not economic; *especially* **:** having no economic importance or implication

**non·elec·tro·lyte** \,nän-ə-'lek-trə-,līt\ *noun* (1891)
**:** a substance that does not readily ionize when dissolved or melted and is a poor conductor of electricity

**non·en·ti·ty** \-'en-tə-tē, -'e-nə-\ *noun* (circa 1600)
**1 :** something that does not exist or exists only in the imagination
**2 :** NONEXISTENCE
**3 :** a person of little consequence or significance

**nones** \'nōnz\ *noun plural but singular or plural in construction* [Middle English *nonys*, from Latin *nonae*, from feminine plural of *nonus* ninth] (14th century)
**1 :** the ninth day before the ides according to ancient Roman reckoning
**2** *often capitalized* **:** ⁴NONE
*word history* SEE NOON

**non·es·sen·tial** \,nän-i-'sen(t)-shəl\ *adjective* (1751)
**1 :** not essential
**2 :** synthesized by the body in sufficient quantity to satisfy dietary needs ⟨*nonessential* amino acids⟩
— **nonessential** *noun*

**none·such** \'nən-,səch\ *noun* (1590)
**:** a person or thing without an equal
— **nonesuch** *adjective*

**no·net** \nō-'net\ *noun* [Italian *nonetto*, from *nono* ninth, from Latin *nonus* — more at NOON] (1865)
**:** a combination of nine instruments or voices; *also* **:** a musical composition for such a combination

**none·the·less** \,nən-thə-'les\ *adverb* (1847)
**:** NEVERTHELESS

**non·eu·clid·e·an** \,nän-yu̇-'kli-dē-ən\ *adjective, often E capitalized* (circa 1864)
**:** not assuming or in accordance with all the postulates of Euclid's *Elements* ⟨*noneuclidean* geometry⟩

**non·event** \'nän-i-,vent, ,nän-i-'\ *noun* (1962)
**1 a :** an expected event that fails to take place or to satisfy expectations **b :** an often highly publicized event of little intrinsic interest or significance
**2 :** an occurrence that is officially ignored

**non·ex·is·tence** \,nän-ig-'zis-tən(t)s\ *noun* (1646)
**:** absence of existence **:** the negation of being
— **non·ex·is·tent** \-tənt\ *adjective*

**non·fat** \'nän-'fat\ *adjective* (1926)
**:** lacking fat solids **:** having fat solids removed ⟨*nonfat* milk⟩

**non·fea·sance** \'nän-'fē-z°n(t)s\ *noun* [*non-* + obsolete English *feasance* doing, execution] (1596)
**:** failure to act; *especially* **:** failure to do what ought to be done

**non·fer·rous** \-'fer-əs\ *adjective* (1887)

**1 :** not containing, including, or relating to iron
**2 :** of or relating to metals other than iron

**non·fic·tion** \-'fik-shən\ *noun* (1909)
**:** literature that is not fictional
— **non·fic·tion·al** \,nän-'fik-shnəl, -shə-n°l\ *adjective*

**non·fig·u·ra·tive** \'nän-'fi-gyə-rə-tiv, -'fi-gə-\ *adjective* (1927)
**:** NONOBJECTIVE 2

**non·flam·ma·ble** \-'fla-mə-bəl\ *adjective* (1915)
**:** not flammable; *specifically* **:** not easily ignited and not burning rapidly if ignited
— **non·flam·ma·bil·i·ty** \,nän-,fla-mə-'bi-lə-tē\ *noun*

**non·flow·er·ing** \'nän-'flau̇(-ə)r-iŋ\ *adjective* (circa 1934)
**:** producing no flowers; *specifically* **:** lacking a flowering stage in the life cycle

**non·flu·en·cy** \-'flü-ən(t)-sē\ *noun, plural* **-cies** (circa 1945)
**1 :** lack of fluency
**2 :** an instance of nonfluency

**non·gon·o·coc·cal** \,nän-,gä-nə-'kä-kəl\ *adjective* (1961)
**:** not caused by a gonococcus ⟨*nongonococcal* urethritis⟩

**non gra·ta** \,nän-'gra-tə, -'grä-\ *adjective* [*persona non grata*] (1925)
**:** not approved **:** UNWELCOME

**non·green** \'nän-'grēn\ *adjective* (1897)
**:** not green; *specifically* **:** containing no chlorophyll ⟨*nongreen* saprophytes⟩

**non·he·ro** \'nän-'hē-(,)rō, -'hir-(,)ō\ *noun* (1940)
**:** ANTI-HERO

**non·his·tone** \-'his-,tōn\ *adjective* (circa 1966)
**:** relating to or being any of the eukaryotic proteins (as DNA polymerase) that bind to nuclear DNA but are not histones

**non–Hodg·kin's lymphoma** \'nän-'häj-kənz-\ *noun* (1976)
**:** any of the numerous malignant lymphomas (as Burkitt's lymphoma) that are not classified as Hodgkin's disease

**non·iden·ti·cal** \ˌnän-(ˌ)ī-'den-ti-kəl, -ə-'den-\ *adjective* (1890)
**1** : DIFFERENT
**2** : FRATERNAL 2

**no·nil·lion** \nō-'nil-yən\ *noun, often attributive* [French, from Latin *nonus* ninth + French *-illion* (as in *million*) — more at NOON] (1690)
— see NUMBER table

**non·in·duc·tive** \ˌnän-in-'dək-tiv\ *adjective* (1896)
: not inductive; *especially* : having negligible inductance

**non·in·ter·ven·tion** \-ˌin-tər-'ven(t)-shən\ *noun* (1831)
: the state or policy of not intervening ⟨*nonintervention* in the affairs of other countries⟩
— **non·in·ter·ven·tion·ist** \-'ven(t)-sh(ə-)nist\ *noun or adjective*

**non·in·va·sive** \-in-'vā-siv, -ziv\ *adjective* (1971)
: not involving penetration (as by surgery or hypodermic needle) of the skin of the intact organism ⟨*noninvasive* diagnostic techniques⟩

**non·in·volve·ment** \-in-'välv-mənt, -'vōlv- *also* -'väv-, -'vòv-\ *noun* (1936)
: absence of involvement or emotional attachment
— **non·in·volved** \-'vä(l)vd, -'vò(l)vd\ *adjective*

**non·ion·ic** \-(ˌ)ī-'ä-nik\ *adjective* (1929)
: not ionic; *especially* : not dependent on a surface-active anion for effect ⟨*nonionic* surfactants⟩

**non·join·der** \'nän-'jòin-dər\ *noun* (1833)
: failure to include a necessary party to a suit at law

**non·judg·men·tal** \ˌnän-ˌjəj-'men-t°l\ *adjective* (1952)
: avoiding judgments based on one's personal and especially moral standards

**non·jur·ing** \'nän-'jùr-iŋ\ *adjective* [*non-* + Latin *jurare* to swear — more at JURY] (1691)
: not swearing allegiance — used especially of a member of a party in Great Britain that would not swear allegiance to William and Mary or to their successors

**non·ju·ror** \-'jùr-ər, -'jùr-ˌòr\ *noun* (1691)
: a person refusing to take an oath especially of allegiance, supremacy, or abjuration; *specifically* : one of the beneficed clergy in England and Scotland refusing to take an oath of allegiance to William and Mary or to their successors after the revolution of 1688

**non·lit·er·ate** \-'li-t(ə-)rət\ *adjective* (1947)
**1** : not literate
**2** : having no written language
— **nonliterate** *noun*

**non·met·al** \-'me-t°l\ *noun* (circa 1864)
: a chemical element (as boron, carbon, or nitrogen) that lacks the characteristics of a metal

**non·me·tal·lic** \ˌnän-mə-'ta-lik\ *adjective* (1815)
**1** : not metallic
**2** : of, relating to, or being a nonmetal

**non·mor·al** \'nän-'mòr-əl, -'mär-\ *adjective* (circa 1866)
: not falling into or existing in the sphere of morals or ethics

**non·neg·a·tive** \-'ne-gə-tiv\ *adjective* (1885)
: not negative: as **a** : being either positive or zero **b** : taking on nonnegative values ⟨a *nonnegative* function⟩

**non·nu·cle·ar** \-'nü-klē-ər, -'nyü-, ÷-kyə-lər\ *adjective* (1953)
**1** : not nuclear: as **a** : being a weapon whose destructive power is not derived from a nuclear reaction **b** : not operated by, using, or produced by nuclear energy **c** : not using or involving nuclear weapons
**2** : not having nuclear weapons ⟨a *nonnuclear* country⟩

**no–no** \'nō-ˌnō\ *noun, plural* **no–no's** *or* **no–nos** (circa 1942)
: something unacceptable or forbidden

**non·ob·jec·tive** \ˌnän-əb-'jek-tiv\ *adjective* (1905)
**1** : not objective
**2** : representing or intended to represent no natural or actual object, figure, or scene ⟨*nonobjective* art⟩
— **non·ob·jec·tiv·ism** \-ti-ˌvi-zəm\ *noun*
— **non·ob·jec·tiv·ist** \-vist\ *noun*
— **non·ob·jec·tiv·i·ty** \-ˌäb-ˌjek-'ti-və-tē, -əb-\ *noun*

**non ob·stan·te** \ˌnän-əb-'stan-tē, ˌnōn-\ *preposition* [Middle English, from Medieval Latin] (15th century)
: NOTWITHSTANDING

**non–oil** \'nän-'òi(ə)l\ *adjective* (1979)
**1** : not relating to, containing, or derived from oil
**2** : being a net importer of petroleum or petroleum products ⟨*non-oil* nations⟩

**no–nonsense** *adjective* (1928)
: tolerating no nonsense : SERIOUS, BUSINESSLIKE

**non·or·gas·mic** \ˌnän-òr-'gaz-mik\ *adjective* (1973)
: not capable of experiencing orgasm

**no·nox·y·nol–9** \nä-'näk-si-ˌnòl-'nīn, nə-, -ˌnòl-\ *noun* [*nonyl* (the radical C₉H₁₉) + *oxy-* + phe*nol* + *9* (from the fact that the compounds it contains have an average of nine ethylene oxide groups per molecule)] (1980)
: a spermicide used in contraceptive products

**non·para·met·ric** \-ˌpar-ə-'me-trik\ *adjective* (1942)
: not involving the estimation of parameters of a statistical function ⟨*nonparametric* statistical tests⟩

**¹non·pa·reil** \ˌnän-pə-'rel\ *adjective* [Middle English *nonparaille*, from Middle French *nonpareil*, from *non-* + *pareil* equal, from (assumed) Vulgar Latin *pariculus*, from Latin *par* equal] (15th century)
: having no equal

**²nonpareil** *noun* (1593)
**1** : an individual of unequaled excellence : PARAGON
**2 a** : a small flat disk of chocolate covered with white sugar pellets **b** : sugar in small pellets of various colors

**non·par·ti·san** \'nän-'pär-tə-zən, -sən\ *adjective* (1885)
: not partisan; *especially* : free from party affiliation, bias, or designation ⟨*nonpartisan* ballot⟩ ⟨a *nonpartisan* board⟩
— **non·par·ti·san·ship** \-ˌship\ *noun*

**non·pas·ser·ine** \-'pa-sə-ˌrīn\ *adjective* (circa 1909)
: not passerine; *especially* : of or relating to an order (Coraciiformes) of arboreal birds including the rollers, kingfishers, and hornbills

**non·patho·gen·ic** \ˌnän-ˌpa-thə-'je-nik\ *adjective* (1884)
: not capable of inducing disease — compare AVIRULENT

**non·peak** \'nän-'pēk\ *adjective* (circa 1914)
: OFF-PEAK

**non·per·form·ing** \ˌnän-pə(r)-'fòr-miŋ\ *adjective* (1979)
: not bringing in the expected return ⟨*nonperforming* loans⟩ ⟨*nonperforming* assets⟩

**non·per·sis·tent** \-pər-'sis-tənt, -'zis-\ *adjective* (1900)
: not persistent: as **a** : decomposed rapidly by environmental action ⟨*nonpersistent* insecticides⟩ **b** : capable of being transmitted by a vector for only a relatively short time ⟨*nonpersistent* viruses⟩

**non·per·son** \'nän-'pər-s°n\ *noun* (circa 1909)
: a person who is regarded as nonexistent: as **a** : UNPERSON **b** : one having no social or legal status

**non pla·cet** \'nän-'plā-sət, 'nōn-\ *noun* [Latin, it does not please] (1589)
: a negative vote

**¹non·plus** \ˌnän-'pləs\ *noun* [Latin *non plus* no more] (1582)
: a state of bafflement or perplexity : QUANDARY

**²nonplus** *transitive verb* **-plussed** *also* **-plused** \-'pləst\; **-plus·sing** *also* **-plus·ing** \-'plə-siŋ\ (1591)
: to cause to be at a loss as to what to say, think, or do : PERPLEX
*synonym* see PUZZLE

**non·point** \'nän-'pòint\ *adjective* (1977)
: not occurring at a single well-defined site; *specifically* : being pollution that cannot be traced to a single location

**non·po·lar** \'nän-'pō-lər\ *adjective* (1892)
: not polar; *especially* : consisting of molecules not having a dipole ⟨a *nonpolar* solvent⟩

**non pos·su·mus** \'nän-'pä-sə-məs, 'nōn-\ *noun* [Latin, we cannot] (1883)
: a statement expressing inability to do something

**non·pre·scrip·tion** \ˌnän-pri-'skrip-shən\ *adjective* (1958)
: capable of being bought without a doctor's prescription ⟨*nonprescription* drugs⟩

**non·pro·duc·tive** \-prə-'dək-tiv\ *adjective* (1901)
: not productive: as **a** : failing to produce or yield : UNPRODUCTIVE ⟨a *nonproductive* oil well⟩ **b** : not directly concerned with production ⟨the *nonproductive* labor of clerks and inspectors⟩ **c** *of a cough* : DRY
— **non·pro·duc·tive·ness** *noun*

**non·prof·it** \'nän-'prä-fət\ *adjective* (1903)
: not conducted or maintained for the purpose of making a profit ⟨a *nonprofit* organization⟩
— **nonprofit** *noun*

**non·pro·lif·er·a·tion** \ˌnän-prə-ˌli-fə-'rā-shən\ *adjective* (1964)
: providing for the stoppage of proliferation (as of nuclear arms) ⟨*nonproliferation* treaty⟩
— **nonproliferation** *noun*

**non·pros** \'nän-'präs\ *transitive verb* **non·prossed; non·pros·sing** [*non prosequitur*] (1755)
: to enter a non prosequitur against

**non pro·se·qui·tur** \ˌnän-prə-'se-kwə-tər, ˌnōn-\ *noun* [Late Latin, he does not prosecute] (1768)
: a judgment entered against the plaintiff in a suit in which that party does not appear to prosecute

**non·pro·tein** \'nän-'prō-ˌtēn, -'prō-tē-ən\ *adjective* (1926)
: not being or derived from protein ⟨the *nonprotein* part of an enzyme⟩ ⟨*nonprotein* nitrogen⟩

**non·read·er** \-'rē-dər\ *noun* (1924)
**1** : one who does not or cannot read
**2** : a child who is very slow in learning to read
— **non·read·ing** \-diŋ\ *adjective*

**non·re·com·bi·nant** \ˌnän-(ˌ)rē-'käm-bə-nənt\ *adjective* (1962)
: not exhibiting the results of genetic recombination
— **nonrecombinant** *noun*

**non·re·course** \'nän-'rē-ˌkòrs, -ˌkòrs, -ˌri-\ *adjective* (1926)
: being or based on an agreement in which the lender has no right of recourse to the borrower's assets beyond stated limits ⟨a *nonrecourse* note⟩ ⟨a *nonrecourse* loan⟩

**non·re·cur·rent** \ˌnän-ri-'kər-ənt, -'kə-rənt\ *adjective* (circa 1864)
: not recurring

**non·re·cur·ring** \-ri-'kər-iŋ, -'kə-riŋ\ *adjective* (circa 1864)
: NONRECURRENT; *specifically* : unlikely to happen again — used of financial transactions that affect a profit and loss statement abnormally

---

\ə\ abut \°\ kitten \ər\ further \a\ ash \ā\ ace \ä\ mop, mar \au\ out \ch\ chin \e\ bet \ē\ easy \g\ go \i\ hit \ī\ ice \j\ job \ŋ\ sing \ō\ go \ò\ law \òi\ boy \th\ thin \th\ the \ü\ loot \u\ foot \y\ yet \zh\ vision *see also* Guide to Pronunciation

**non·re·fund·able** \-ri-'fən-də-bəl\ *adjective* (1963)
: not subject to refunding or being refunded ⟨a *nonrefundable* bond⟩ ⟨a *nonrefundable* fee⟩

**non·rel·a·tiv·is·tic** \-,re-lə-ti-'vis-tik\ *adjective* (1930)
**1** : not based on or involving the theory of relativity ⟨*nonrelativistic* equations⟩ ⟨*nonrelativistic* kinematics⟩
**2** : of, relating to, or being a body moving at less than a relativistic velocity
— **non·rel·a·tiv·is·ti·cal·ly** \-'vis-ti-k(ə-)lē\ *adverb*

**non·rep·re·sen·ta·tion·al** \-,re-pri-,zen-'tā-shnəl, -zən-, -shə-nᵊl\ *adjective* (1923)
: NONOBJECTIVE 2
— **non·rep·re·sen·ta·tion·al·ism** \-shnə-,li-zəm, -shə-nᵊl-,i-zəm\ *noun*

**non·res·i·dence** \'nän-'re-zə-dən(t)s, -'rez-dən(t)s, -,den(t)s\ *noun* (1585)
: the state or fact of being nonresident

**non·res·i·den·cy** \-'re-zə-dən(t)-sē, -'rez-dən(t)-, -,den(t)-\ *noun* (1584)
: NONRESIDENCE

**non·res·i·dent** \-'re-zə-dənt, -'rez-dənt, -,dent\ *adjective* (1540)
: not residing in a particular place
— **nonresident** *noun*

**non·re·sis·tance** \,nän-ri-'zis-tən(t)s\ *noun* (1643)
: the principles or practice of passive submission to constituted authority even when unjust or oppressive; *also* : the principle or practice of not resisting violence by force

**non·re·sis·tant** \-tənt\ *adjective* (1702)
: not resistant; *specifically* : susceptible to the effects of a deleterious agent (as an insecticide, a pathogen, or an extreme environmental condition)
— **nonresistant** *noun*

**non·re·stric·tive** \-ri-'strik-tiv\ *adjective* (1916)
: not restrictive; *specifically* : not limiting the reference of a modified word or phrase

**nonrestrictive clause** *noun* (1916)
: a descriptive clause that is not essential to the definiteness of the meaning of the word it modifies (as *who is retired* in "my father, who is retired, does volunteer work")

**non·re·turn·able** \-ri-'tər-nə-bəl\ *adjective* (1903)
: not returnable; *specifically* : not returnable to a dealer in exchange for a deposit ⟨*nonreturnable* bottles⟩
— **nonreturnable** *noun*

**non·rig·id** \'nän-'ri-jəd\ *adjective* (1909)
: not rigid; *especially* : maintaining form by pressure of contained gas ⟨a *nonrigid* airship⟩

**non·sched·uled** \-'ske-(,)jü(ə)ld, -jəld\ *adjective* (1947)
: licensed to transport by air without a regular schedule ⟨*nonscheduled* airlines⟩

**¹non·sci·ence** \-'sī-ən(t)s\ *noun* (1855)
: something (as a discipline) that is not a science

**²nonscience** *adjective* (1944)
: of or relating to fields other than science

**non·se·cre·tor** \,nän-si-'krē-tər\ *noun* (1944)
: an individual of blood group A, B, or AB who does not secrete the antigens characteristic of these blood groups in bodily fluids (as saliva)

**non·sec·tar·i·an** \-(,)sek-'ter-ē-ən\ *adjective* (1831)
: not having a sectarian character : not affiliated with or restricted to a particular religious group

**non·self** \'nän-'self, *Southern also* -'sef\ *noun* (1963)
: material that is foreign to the body of an organism

**¹non·sense** \'nän-,sen(t)s, 'nän(t)-sən(t)s\ *noun* (1614)
**1 a** : words or language having no meaning or conveying no intelligible ideas **b** (1) : language, conduct, or an idea that is absurd or

contrary to good sense (2) : an instance of absurd action
**2 a** : things of no importance or value : TRIFLES **b** : affected or impudent conduct ⟨took no *nonsense* from subordinates⟩
**3** : genetic information consisting of one or more codons that do not code for any amino acid and usually cause termination of the molecular chain in protein synthesis — compare ANTISENSE, MISSENSE
— **non·sen·si·cal** \,nän-'sen(t)-si-kəl\ *adjective*
— **non·sen·si·cal·ly** \-k(ə-)lē\ *adverb*
— **non·sen·si·cal·ness** \-kəl-nəs\ *noun*

**²nonsense** *adjective* (1778)
**1** : consisting of an arbitrary grouping of speech sounds or symbols ⟨'shrŏg-,thī-əmpth\ is a *nonsense* word⟩ ⟨a *nonsense* syllable⟩
**2** : consisting of one or more codons that are genetic nonsense

**nonsense verse** *noun* (1799)
: humorous or whimsical verse that features absurd characters and actions and often contains evocative but meaningless nonce words

**non se·qui·tur** \'nän-'se-kwə-tər *also* -,tür\ *noun* [Latin, it does not follow] (1540)
**1** : an inference that does not follow from the premises; *specifically* : a fallacy resulting from a simple conversion of a universal affirmative proposition or from the transposition of a condition and its consequent
**2** : a statement (as a response) that does not follow logically from anything previously said

**non·sig·nif·i·cant** \,nän-sig-'ni-fi-kənt\ *adjective* (1902)
: not significant: as **a** : INSIGNIFICANT **b** : MEANINGLESS **c** : having or yielding a value lying within limits between which variation is attributed to chance ⟨a *nonsignificant* statistical test⟩
— **non·sig·nif·i·cant·ly** *adverb*

**non·sked** \'nän-'sked\ *noun* [by shortening & alteration from *nonscheduled*] (1949)
: a nonscheduled transport plane or airline

**non·skid** \-'skid\ *adjective* (1904)
: designed or equipped to prevent skidding

**non·slip** \-'slip\ *adjective* (1903)
: designed to reduce or prevent slipping

**non·so·cial** \-'sō-shəl\ *adjective* (1902)
: not socially oriented : lacking a social component

**non·sport·ing** \-'spōr-tiŋ, -'spȯr-\ *adjective* (1852)
: lacking the qualities characteristic of a hunting dog

**non·stan·dard** \-'stan-dərd\ *adjective* (1923)
**1** : not standard
**2** : not conforming in pronunciation, grammatical construction, idiom, or word choice to the usage generally characteristic of educated native speakers of a language — compare SUBSTANDARD

**non·start·er** \-'stär-tər\ *noun* (1902)
**1** : one that does not start
**2** : someone or something that is not productive or effective ⟨his son has been, in politics a *nonstarter* —Anthony Lejeune⟩

**non·ste·roi·dal** \,nän-stə-'rȯi-dᵊl\ *also* **non·ste·roid** \'nän-'stir-,ȯid, -'ster-\ *adjective* (1964)
: of, relating to, or being a compound and especially a drug that is not a steroid
— **nonsteroid** *noun*

**non·stick** \'nän-'stik\ *adjective* [³stick] (1958)
: allowing of easy removal of cooked food particles ⟨a *nonstick* coating in a frying pan⟩

**non·stop** \'nän-'stäp\ *adjective* (1902)
: done, made, or held without a stop : not easing or letting up
— **nonstop** *adverb*

**non·such** \'nən-,səch *also* 'nän-\ *variant of* NONESUCH

**non·suit** \'nän-'süt\ *noun* [Middle English, from Anglo-French *nounsuyte*, from *noun-* non- + Old French *siute* following, pursuit — more at SUIT] (14th century)

: a judgment against a plaintiff for failure to prosecute a case or inability to establish a prima facie case
— **nonsuit** *transitive verb*

**non·sup·port** \,nän-sə-'pōrt, -'pȯrt\ *noun* (1909)
: failure to support; *specifically* : failure (as of a parent) to honor a statutory or contractual obligation to provide maintenance

**non·syl·lab·ic** \-sə-'la-bik\ *adjective* (circa 1909)
: not constituting a syllable or the nucleus of a syllable ⟨the second vowel of a falling diphthong is *nonsyllabic* (as \i\ in \ȯi\)⟩

**non·sys·tem** \'nän-'sis-təm\ *noun* (1964)
: a system that lacks effective organization

**non·tar·get** \-'tär-gət\ *adjective* (1945)
: not being the intended object of action by a particular agent ⟨effect of insecticides on *nontarget* organisms⟩

**non·ter·mi·nat·ing** \-'tər-mə-,nā-tiŋ\ *adjective* (circa 1908)
: not terminating or ending; *especially* : being a decimal for which there is no place to the right of the decimal point such that all places farther to the right contain the entry 0 ⟨1/3 gives the *nonterminating* decimal .33333 . . .⟩

**non·ther·mal** \-'thər-məl\ *adjective* (circa 1964)
: not produced by heat; *specifically* : of, relating to, or being radiation having a spectrum that is not the spectrum of a blackbody

**non·ti·tle** \-'tī-tᵊl\ *adjective* (1968)
: of, relating to, or being an athletic contest in which a title is not at stake

**non trop·po** \'nän-'trȯ-(,)pō, 'nōn-\ *adverb or adjective* [Italian, literally, not too much] (circa 1854)
: without excess — used to qualify a direction in music

**non-U** \'nän-'yü\ *adjective* (1954)
: not characteristic of the upper classes

**non·union** \-'yün-yən\ *adjective* (1863)
**1** : not belonging to or connected with a trade union ⟨*nonunion* carpenters⟩
**2** : not recognizing or favoring trade unions or their members
**3** : not produced or worked on by members of a trade union ⟨*nonunion* lettuce⟩

**non·use** \'nän-'yüs\ *noun* (1542)
**1** : failure to use ⟨*nonuse* of available material⟩
**2** : the fact or condition of not being used

**non·us·er** \-'yü-zər\ *noun* (1926)
: one who does not make use of something (as an available public facility or a harmful drug)

**non·van·ish·ing** \-'va-ni-shiŋ\ *adjective* (1907)
: not zero or becoming zero

**non·vec·tor** \-'vek-tər\ *noun* (1956)
: an organism (as an insect) that does not transmit a particular pathogen (as a virus)

**non·ver·bal** \-'vər-bəl\ *adjective* (1924)
: not verbal: as **a** : being other than verbal ⟨*nonverbal* factors⟩ **b** : involving minimal use of language ⟨*nonverbal* tests⟩ **c** : ranking low in verbal skill
— **non·ver·bal·ly** \-bə-lē\ *adverb*

**non·vin·tage** \-'vin-tij\ *adjective* (1924)
: undated and usually blended to approximate a standard ⟨a *nonvintage* wine⟩

**non·vi·o·lence** \-'vī-ə-lən(t)s\ *noun* (1920)
**1** : abstention from violence as a matter of principle; *also* : the principle of such abstention
**2 a** : the quality or state of being nonviolent : avoidance of violence **b** : nonviolent demonstrations for the purpose of securing political ends ⟨studied the history and techniques of *nonviolence*⟩

**non·vi·o·lent** \-lənt\ *adjective* (1920)
: abstaining or free from violence
— **non·vi·o·lent·ly** *adverb*

**non·vol·a·tile** \-'vä-lə-tᵊl\ *adjective* (1866)

: not volatile: as **a** : not vaporizing readily ⟨a *nonvolatile* solvent⟩ **b** *of a computer memory* : retaining data when power is shut off

**non–West·ern** \-'wes-tərn\ *adjective* (1902)
**1** : not being part of the western tradition ⟨*non-Western* countries⟩
**2** : of or relating to non-Western societies ⟨*non-Western* values⟩

**non·white** \-'hwīt, -'wīt\ *noun* (1927)
: a person whose features and especially whose skin color are distinctively different from those of peoples of northwestern Europe; *especially* : one who has African ancestors of the black race
— **nonwhite** *adjective*

**non·word** \-'wərd\ *noun* (1961)
: a word that has no meaning, is not known to exist, or is disapproved

**non·wo·ven** \-'wō-vən\ *adjective* (1945)
**1** : made of fibers held together by interlocking or bonding (as by chemical or thermal means) : not woven, knitted, or felted ⟨*nonwoven* fabric⟩
**2** : made of nonwoven fabric ⟨a *nonwoven* dress⟩
— **nonwoven** *noun*

**non·ze·ro** \-'zē-(ˌ)rō, -'zir-(ˌ)ō\ *adjective* (1905)
**1** : being, having, or involving a value other than zero
**2** : having phonetic content ⟨*nonzero* affixes⟩

**¹noo·dle** \'nü-d⁰l\ *noun* [perhaps alteration of *noddle*] (1753)
**1** : a stupid person : SIMPLETON
**2** : HEAD, NOGGIN

**²noodle** *noun* [German *Nudel*] (1779)
: a food paste made with egg and shaped typically in ribbon form

**³noodle** *intransitive verb* **noo·dled; noo·dling** \'nüd-liŋ, 'nü-d⁰l-iŋ\ [imitative] (circa 1937)
: to improvise on an instrument in an informal or desultory manner

**nook** \'nuk\ *noun* [Middle English *noke, nok*] (14th century)
**1** *chiefly Scottish* : a right-angled corner
**2 a** : an interior angle formed by two meeting walls : RECESS **b** : a secluded or sheltered place or part ⟨searched every *nook* and cranny⟩

**nooky** \'nu-kē\ *noun* [perhaps from *nook* + ⁴-y] (1928)
**1** : SEXUAL INTERCOURSE — often considered vulgar
**2** : the female partner in sexual intercourse — often considered vulgar

**noon** \'nün\ *noun* [Middle English, from Old English *nōn* ninth hour from sunrise, from Latin *nona*, from feminine of *nonus* ninth; akin to Latin *novem* nine — more at NINE] (13th century)
**1** : MIDDAY; *specifically* : 12 o'clock at midday
**2** *archaic* : MIDNIGHT — used chiefly in the phrase *noon of night*
**3** : the highest point ◆

**noon·day** \-ˌdā\ *noun* (1535)
: MIDDAY

**no one** *pronoun* (before 12th century)
: no person : NOBODY
*usage* see NOBODY

**noon·ing** \'nü-niŋ, -nən\ *noun* (circa 1652)
**1** *chiefly dialect* : a meal eaten at noon
**2** *chiefly dialect* : a period at noon for eating or resting

**noon·tide** \'nün-ˌtīd\ *noun* (12th century)
**1** : NOONTIME
**2** : the culminating point

**noon·time** \-ˌtīm\ *noun* (14th century)
: the time of noon : MIDDAY

**¹noose** \'nüs, *British also* 'nüz\ *noun* [Middle English *nose*, perhaps of Provençal origin; akin to Provençal *nous* knot, from Latin *nodus* — more at NODE] (15th century)
**1** : a loop with a running knot that binds closer the more it is drawn
**2** : something that snares like a noose

**²noose** *transitive verb* **noosed; noos·ing** (1600)
**1** : to secure by a noose
**2** : to make a noose in or of

**noo·sphere** \'nō-ə-ˌsfir\ *noun* [International Scientific Vocabulary *noo-* mind (from Greek *noos, nous*) + *sphere* sphere] (1945)
: the sphere of human consciousness and mental activity especially in regard to its influence on the biosphere and in relation to evolution

**Noot·ka** \'nut-kə\ *noun, plural* **Nootka** *or* **Nootkas** (1841)
**1** : a member of a Wakashan people inhabiting the West Coast of Vancouver Island
**2** : the language of the Nootka people

**no·pal** \nō-'päl, -'pal; 'nō-pəl\ *noun* [Spanish, from Nahuatl *nohpalli*] (1730)
: any of a genus (*Nopalea*) of cacti of Mexico and Central America that differ from the prickly pears in having erect petals and scarlet flowers with the stamens much longer than the petals; *broadly* : PRICKLY PEAR

**no–par** *or* **no-par–value** *adjective* (1922)
: having no nominal value ⟨*no-par* stocks⟩

**nope** \'nōp, *or with glottal stop instead of* p\ *adverb* [by alteration] (1888)
: NO

**¹nor** \nər, 'nȯr, *Southern also* 'när\ *conjunction* [Middle English, contraction of *nother* neither, nor, from *nother*, pronoun & adjective, neither — more at NEITHER] (14th century)
**1** — used as a function word to introduce the second or last member or the second and each following member of a series of items each of which is negated ⟨neither here *nor* there⟩ ⟨not done by you *nor* me *nor* anyone⟩
**2** — used as a function word to introduce and negate a following clause or phrase
**3** *chiefly British* : NEITHER

**²nor** *conjunction* [Middle English, perhaps from ¹*nor*] (15th century)
*dialect* : THAN

**nor-** *combining form* [*nor*mal]
: homologue containing one less methyl group ⟨*nor*epinephrine⟩

**NOR** \'nȯr\ *noun* [*not OR*] (1957)
: a computer logic circuit that produces an output that is the inverse of that of an OR circuit

**nor·adren·a·line** *also* **nor·adren·a·lin** \ˌnȯr-ə-'dre-n⁰l-ən\ *noun* (1932)
: NOREPINEPHRINE

**nor·ad·ren·er·gic** \ˌnȯr-ˌa-drə-'nər-jik\ *adjective* [*noradrenaline* + *-ergic*] (1963)
: liberating, activated by, or involving norepinephrine in the transmission of nerve impulses ⟨*noradrenergic* nerve endings⟩ ⟨*noradrenergic* nerve fibers⟩

**¹Nor·dic** \'nȯr-dik\ *adjective* [French *nordique*, from *nord* north, from Old English *north*] (1898)
**1** : of or relating to the Germanic peoples of northern Europe and especially of Scandinavia
**2** : of or relating to a group or physical type of the Caucasian race characterized by tall stature, long head, light skin and hair, and blue eyes
**3 a** : of or relating to competitive ski events involving cross-country racing, ski jumping, or biathlon — compare ALPINE **b** : of, relating to, or being cross-country skiing

**²Nordic** *noun* (1901)
**1** : a native of northern Europe
**2** : a person of Nordic physical type
**3** : a member of the peoples of Scandinavia

**nor·epi·neph·rine** \ˌnȯr-ˌe-pə-'ne-frən\ *noun* (1945)
: a catecholamine $C_8H_{11}NO_3$ that is the chemical means of transmission across synapses in postganglionic neurons of the sympathetic nervous system and in some parts of the central nervous system, is a vasopressor hormone of the adrenal medulla, and is a precursor of epinephrine in its major biosynthetic pathway

**nor·eth·in·drone** \ˌnȯ-'re-thən-ˌdrōn\ *noun* [*nor-* + *ethinyl* + *hydr-* + *-one* (as in *progesterone*)] (1958)
: a synthetic progestational hormone $C_{20}H_{26}O_2$ used in oral contraceptives often in the form of its acetate

**Nor·folk jacket** \'nȯr-fək-, -ˌfȯk-\ *noun* [*Norfolk*, England] (1866)
: a loose-fitting belted single-breasted jacket with box pleats

**Norfolk terrier** *noun* (1964)
: any of a breed of dogs developed in England and resembling the Norwich terrier but having folded-over ears

**no·ri** \'nō-rē, 'nȯr-ē\ *noun* [Japanese] (1892)
: dried laver seaweed pressed into thin sheets and used especially as a seasoning or as a wrapper for sushi

**nor·land** \'nȯr-lənd\ *noun* (circa 1578)
*chiefly dialect* : NORTHLAND

**norm** \'nȯrm\ *noun* [Latin *norma*, literally, carpenter's square] (1674)
**1** : an authoritative standard : MODEL
**2** : a principle of right action binding upon the members of a group and serving to guide, control, or regulate proper and acceptable behavior
**3** : AVERAGE: as **a** : a set standard of development or achievement usually derived from the average or median achievement of a large group **b** : a pattern or trait taken to be typical in the behavior of a social group **c** : a widespread practice, procedure, or custom : RULE ⟨standing ovations became the *norm*⟩
**4 a** : a real-valued nonnegative function defined on a vector space and satisfying the conditions that the function is zero if and only if the vector is zero, the function of the product of a scalar and a vector is equal to the product of the absolute value of the scalar and the function of the vector, and the function of the sum of two vectors is less than or equal to the sum of the functions of the two vectors; *specifically* : the square root of the sum of the squares of the absolute values of the elements of a matrix or of the components of a vector **b** : the greatest distance between two successive points of a set of points that partition an interval into smaller intervals
**synonym** see AVERAGE

**¹nor·mal** \'nȯr-məl\ *adjective* [Latin *normalis*, from *norma*] (circa 1696)
**1** : PERPENDICULAR; *especially* : perpendicular to a tangent at a point of tangency

---

◇ **WORD HISTORY**
**noon** *Noon* has not always indicated that time of day at which the sun is most nearly overhead. According to the Roman method of reckoning time, the hours of the day were counted from sunrise to sunset, so that *nona*, short for *nona hora* "ninth hour," denoted the ninth hour of daylight, about 3 P.M. in modern reckoning. *Nona* was borrowed into Old English as *nōn*, which denoted either the ninth hour of the day or the liturgical office of nones that was read at this time. In early Middle English, however, *non* or *none* (later *noon*) was applied to a meal eaten before nones was read, perhaps originally an afternoon snack. If this was the case, however, the meaning seems soon to have shifted to the major midday meal, and then to midday itself, a sense that Modern English *noon* has retained. The word *none* or *nones* was later borrowed from Latin to refer specifically to the liturgical office.

---

\ə\ abut \ᵊ\ kitten \ər\ further \a\ ash \ā\ ace
\ä\ mop, mar \au̇\ out \ch\ chin \e\ bet \ē\ easy
\g\ go \i\ hit \ī\ ice \j\ job \ŋ\ sing \ō\ go
\ȯ\ law \ȯi\ boy \th\ thin \t̲h̲\ the \ü\ loot \u̇\ foot
\y\ yet \zh\ vision    *see also* Guide to Pronunciation

**2 a :** according with, constituting, or not deviating from a norm, rule, or principle **b :** conforming to a type, standard, or regular pattern **3 :** occurring naturally ⟨*normal* immunity⟩ **4 a :** of, relating to, or characterized by average intelligence or development **b :** free from mental disorder **: SANE 5 a** *of a solution* **:** having a concentration of one gram equivalent of solute per liter **b :** containing neither basic hydroxyl nor acid hydrogen ⟨*normal* silver phosphate⟩ **c :** not associated ⟨*normal* molecules⟩ **d :** having a straight-chain structure ⟨*normal* pentane⟩ ⟨*normal* butyl alcohol⟩ **6** *of a subgroup* **:** having the property that every coset produced by operating on the left by a given element is equal to the coset produced by operating on the right by the same element **7 :** relating to, involving, or being a normal curve or normal distribution ⟨*normal* approximation to the binomial distribution⟩ **8** *of a matrix* **:** having the property of commutativity under multiplication by the transpose of the matrix each of whose elements is a conjugate complex number with respect to the corresponding element of the given matrix ◆
**synonym** see REGULAR
— **nor·mal·i·ty** \nȯr-'ma-lə-tē\ *noun*
— **nor·mal·ly** \'nȯr-mə-lē\ *adverb*
**²normal** *noun* (circa 1738)
**1 a :** a normal line **b :** the portion of a normal line to a plane curve between the curve and the x-axis **2 :** one that is normal **3 :** a form or state regarded as the norm **: STANDARD**
**normal curve** *noun* (1894)
**:** the symmetrical bell-shaped curve of a normal distribution
**nor·mal·cy** \'nȯr-məl-sē\ *noun* (1857)
**:** the state or fact of being normal
**normal distribution** *noun* (1897)
**:** a probability density function that approximates the distribution of many random variables (as the proportion of outcomes of a particular sort in a large number of independent repetitions of an experiment in which the probabilities remain constant from trial to trial) and that has the form

$$f(x) = \frac{1}{\sigma\sqrt{2\pi}} e^{-\frac{1}{2}\left(\frac{x-\mu}{\sigma}\right)^2}$$

where $\mu$ is the mean and $\sigma$ is the standard deviation — compare NORMAL CURVE
**nor·mal·ise** *British variant of* NORMALIZE
**nor·mal·ize** \'nȯr-mə-ˌlīz\ *transitive verb* **-ized; -iz·ing** (1865)
**1 :** to make conform to or reduce to a norm or standard
**2 :** to make normal (as by a transformation of variables)
**3 :** to bring or restore (as relations between countries) to a normal condition
— **nor·mal·iz·able** \-ˌlī-zə-bəl\ *adjective*
— **nor·mal·i·za·tion** \ˌnȯr-mə-lə-'zā-shən\ *noun*
**nor·mal·iz·er** \'nȯr-mə-ˌlī-zər\ *noun* (1926)
**1 :** one that normalizes
**2 a :** a subgroup consisting of those elements of a group for which the group operation with regard to a given element is commutative **b :** the set of elements of a group for which the group operation with regard to every element of a given subgroup is commutative
**normal school** *noun* [translation of French *école normale;* from the fact that the first French school so named was intended to serve as a model] (1839)
**:** a usually 2-year school for training chiefly elementary teachers
**Nor·man** \'nȯr-mən\ *noun* [Middle English, from Old French *Normant,* from Old Norse *Northmann-, Northmathr* Norseman, from *northr* north + *mann-, mathr* man; akin to Old

English *north* north and to Old English *man* man] (13th century)
**1 :** a native or inhabitant of Normandy: **a :** one of the Scandinavian conquerors of Normandy in the 10th century **b :** one of the Norman-French conquerors of England in 1066
**2 :** NORMAN-FRENCH
— **Norman** *adjective*
**Norman architecture** *noun* (1797)
**:** a Romanesque style first appearing in and near Normandy about A.D. 950; *also* **:** architecture resembling or imitating this style
**nor·mande** \nȯr-'mand\ *adjective* [French, from feminine of *normand* Norman, from *Normandy,* France] (circa 1929)
**:** prepared with any of several foods traditionally associated with Normandy (as cream, apples, cider, or calvados) ⟨veal *normande*⟩
**Norman–French** *noun* (1605)
**1 :** the French language of the medieval Normans
**2 :** the modern dialect of Normandy
**nor·ma·tive** \'nȯr-mə-tiv\ *adjective* [French *normatif,* from *norme* norm, from Latin *norma*] (1878)
**1 :** of, relating to, or determining norms or standards ⟨*normative* tests⟩
**2 :** conforming to or based on norms ⟨*normative* behavior⟩ ⟨*normative* judgments⟩
**3 :** prescribing norms ⟨*normative* rules of ethics⟩ ⟨*normative* grammar⟩
— **nor·ma·tive·ly** *adverb*
— **nor·ma·tive·ness** *noun*
**normed** \'nȯrmd\ *adjective* (1935)
**:** being a mathematical entity upon which a norm is defined ⟨a *normed* vector space⟩
**nor·mo·ten·sive** \ˌnȯr-mō-'ten(t)-siv\ *adjective* [*normal* + *-o-* + *-tensive* (as in *hypotensive*)] (circa 1941)
**:** having blood pressure typical of the group to which one belongs
— **normotensive** *noun*
**nor·mo·ther·mia** \-'thər-mē-ə\ *noun* [New Latin, from *normalis* normal + *-o-* + *-thermia* -thermy] (1960)
**:** normal body temperature
— **nor·mo·ther·mic** \-mik\ *adjective*
**Norn** \'nȯrn\ *noun* [Old Norse]
**:** any of the three Norse goddesses of fate
**¹Norse** \'nȯrs\ *noun, plural* **Norse** [probably from obsolete Dutch *noorsch,* adjective, Norwegian, Scandinavian, alteration of obsolete Dutch *noordsch* northern, from Dutch *noord* north; akin to Old English *north* north] (circa 1688)
**1 a :** NORWEGIAN **2 b :** any of the western Scandinavian dialects or languages **c :** the Scandinavian group of Germanic languages
**2** *plural* **a :** SCANDINAVIANS **b :** NORWEGIANS
**²Norse** *adjective* (1768)
**1 :** of or relating to ancient Scandinavia or the language of its inhabitants
**2 :** NORWEGIAN
**Norse·man** \'nȯrs-mən\ *noun* (1817)
**:** any of the ancient Scandinavians
**¹north** \'nȯrth\ *adverb* [Middle English, from Old English; akin to Old High German *nord* north and perhaps to Greek *nerteros* lower, infernal] (before 12th century)
**:** to, toward, or in the north
**²north** *adjective* (before 12th century)
**1 :** situated toward or at the north ⟨the *north* entrance⟩
**2 :** coming from the north ⟨a *north* wind⟩
**³north** *noun* (13th century)
**1 a :** the direction of the north terrestrial pole **:** the direction to the left of one facing east **b :** the compass point directly opposite to south
**2** *capitalized* **a :** regions or countries lying to the north of a specified or implied point of orientation **b :** the industrially and economically developed nations of the world — compare SOUTH
**3** *often capitalized* **a :** the one of four positions at 90-degree intervals that lies to the

north or at the top of a diagram **b :** a person occupying this position in the course of a specified activity (as the game of bridge)
**north·bound** \'nȯrth-ˌbau̇nd\ *adjective* (1903)
**:** traveling or headed north
**north by east** (1725)
**:** a compass point that is one point east of due north **:** N11°15′E
**north by west** (circa 1771)
**:** a compass point that is one point west of due north **:** N11°15′W
**¹north·east** \nȯr-'thēst, *nautical* nȯ-'rēst\ *adverb* (before 12th century)
**:** to, toward, or in the northeast
**²northeast** *adjective* (before 12th century)
**1 :** coming from the northeast ⟨a *northeast* wind⟩
**2 :** situated toward or at the northeast ⟨the *northeast* corner⟩
**³northeast** *noun* (12th century)
**1 a :** the general direction between north and east **b :** the point midway between the north and east compass points
**2** *capitalized* **:** regions or countries lying to the northeast of a specified or implied point of orientation
**northeast by east** (circa 1771)
**:** a compass point that is one point east of due northeast **:** N56°15′E
**northeast by north** (circa 1771)
**:** a compass point that is one point north of due northeast **:** N33°45′E
**north·east·er** \nȯr-'thē-stər, nȯ-'rē-\ *noun* (1774)
**1 :** a storm northeast wind
**2 :** a storm with northeast winds
**north·east·er·ly** \nȯr-'thē-stər-lē\ *adverb or adjective* (1739)
**1 :** from the northeast
**2 :** toward the northeast
**north·east·ern** \-stərn\ *adjective* (14th century)
**1** *often capitalized* **:** of, relating to, or characteristic of a region conventionally designated Northeast
**2 :** lying toward or coming from the northeast
— **north·east·ern·most** \-stərn-ˌmōst\ *adjective*
**North·east·ern·er** \-stə(r)-nər\ *noun* (1961)
**:** a native or inhabitant of a northeastern region (as of the U.S.)
**¹north·east·ward** \nȯr-'thēs-twərd, nȯ-'rēs-\ *adverb or adjective* (1553)
**:** toward the northeast
— **north·east·wards** \-twərdz\ *adverb*
**²northeastward** *noun* (1892)
**:** NORTHEAST
**north·er** \'nȯr-thər\ *noun* (1820)
**1 :** a strong north wind
**2 :** a storm with north winds
**¹north·er·ly** \-lē\ *adjective or adverb* [*³north* + *-erly* (as in *easterly*)] (1551)

◇ WORD HISTORY
**normal** In Latin *norma* was the word for a carpenter's square, the tool which ensures that a carpenter can regularly reproduce corners and edges that are straight and that form right angles. *Norma* also had the extended sense "standard" or "pattern." Similarly, *normalis,* the Latin adjective formed from *norma,* had the literal meaning "forming a right angle" and by the Late Latin period the extended sense "according to rule." It is from this extended sense that we derive most of the English senses of *normal.* Incidentally, *normal school,* as a name for a college devoted to teacher training, is a translation of the French term *école normale.* The term derives from the fact that the first school named *école normale* was intended to serve as a standard or model for other teaching schools.

**1 :** situated toward or belonging to the north ⟨the *northerly* border⟩
**2 :** coming from the north ⟨a *northerly* wind⟩

**²northerly** *noun, plural* **-lies** (1955)
**:** a wind from the north

**¹north·ern** \'nȯr-thə(r)n\ *adjective* [Middle English *northerne,* from Old English; akin to Old High German *nordrōni* northern, Old English *north* north] (before 12th century)
**1** *capitalized* **a :** of, relating to, or characteristic of a region conventionally designated North **b :** of, relating to, or constituting the northern dialect
**2 a :** lying toward the north **b :** coming from the north ⟨a *northern* storm⟩
**— north·ern·most** \-ˌmōst\ *adjective*

**²northern** *noun* (1950)
**1** *capitalized* **:** the dialect of English spoken in the part of the U.S. north of a line running northwest through central New Jersey, below the northern tier of counties in Pennsylvania, through northern Ohio, Indiana, and Illinois, across central Iowa, and through the northwest corner of South Dakota
**2 :** ³PIKE 1a

**northern corn rootworm** *noun* (1952)
**:** a corn rootworm (*Diabrotica barberi* synonym *D. longicornis*) often destructive to Indian corn in the northern parts of the central and eastern U.S.

**Northern Cross** *noun*
**:** a cross formed by six stars in Cygnus

**North·ern·er** \'nȯr-thə(r)-nər\ *noun* (1599)
**:** a native or inhabitant of the North; *especially* **:** a native or resident of the northern part of the U.S.

**northern harrier** *noun* (1980)
**:** a widely distributed brown or grayish hawk (*Circus cyaneus*) that inhabits open and marshy regions and has a conspicuous white patch on the rump — called also *marsh hawk*

northern harrier

**northern hemisphere** *noun, often N&H capitalized* (circa 1771)
**:** the half of the earth that lies north of the equator

**northern lights** *noun plural* (14th century)
**:** AURORA BOREALIS

**northern oriole** *noun* (1974)
**:** an American oriole (*Icterus galbula*) that is characterized by the black and orange plumage of the male and that includes the Baltimore oriole of the eastern U.S. and a more western form (*I. g. bullockii*) with a black and orange head

**northern pike** *noun* (1856)
**:** ³PIKE 1a

**northern white cedar** *noun* (1926)
**:** an arborvitae (*Thuja occidentalis*) of eastern North America that has branchlets in horizontal planes; *also* **:** its wood — called also *white cedar*

**North Germanic** *noun* (circa 1930)
**:** a subdivision of the Germanic languages including Icelandic, Norwegian, Swedish, and Danish — see INDO-EUROPEAN LANGUAGES table

**north·ing** \'nȯr-thiŋ, -thiŋ\ *noun* (1669)
**1 :** difference in latitude to the north from the last preceding point of reckoning
**2 :** northerly progress

**north·land** \'nȯrth-ˌland, -lənd\ *noun, often capitalized* (before 12th century)
**:** land in the north **:** the north of a country

**North·man** \'nȯrth-mən\ *noun* (before 12th century)
**:** NORSEMAN

**north–north·east** \ˌnȯrth-ˌnȯr-'thēst, -ˌnȯ-'rēst\ *noun* (14th century)

**:** a compass point that is two points east of due north **:** N22°30′E

**north–north·west** \ˌnȯrth-ˌnȯr(th)-'west\ *noun* (14th century)
**:** a compass point that is two points west of due north **:** N22°30′W

**north pole** *noun* (14th century)
**1 a** *often N&P capitalized* **:** the northernmost point of the earth; *broadly* **:** the corresponding point of a celestial body (as a planet) **b :** the zenith of the heavens as viewed from the north terrestrial pole
**2** *of a magnet* **:** the pole that points toward the north when the magnet is freely suspended

**north–seeking pole** *noun* (circa 1920)
**:** NORTH POLE 2

**North Star** *noun*
**:** the star of the northern hemisphere toward which the axis of the earth points — called also *polestar*

**¹North·um·bri·an** \nȯr-'thəm-brē-ən\ *adjective* (1622)
**1 :** of, relating to, or characteristic of ancient Northumbria, its people, or its language
**2 :** of, relating to, or characteristic of Northumberland, its people, or its language

**²Northumbrian** *noun* (1752)
**1 :** a native or inhabitant of ancient Northumbria
**2 :** a native or inhabitant of Northumberland
**3 a :** the Old English dialect of Northumbria **b :** the Modern English dialect of Northumberland

**¹north·ward** \'nȯrth-wərd\ *adverb or adjective* (before 12th century)
**:** toward the north
**— north·wards** \-wərdz\ *adverb*

**²northward** *noun* (14th century)
**:** northward direction or part ⟨sail to the *northward*⟩

**¹north·west** \nȯrth-'west, *nautical* nȯr-'west\ *adverb* (before 12th century)
**:** to, toward, or in the northwest

**²northwest** *adjective* (before 12th century)
**1 :** coming from the northwest ⟨a *northwest* wind⟩
**2 :** situated toward or at the northwest ⟨the *northwest* corner⟩

**³northwest** *noun* (12th century)
**1 a :** the general direction between north and west **b :** the point midway between the north and west compass points
**2** *capitalized* **:** regions or countries lying to the northwest of a specified or implied point of orientation

**northwest by north** (circa 1771)
**:** a compass point that is one point north of due northwest **:** N33°45′W

**northwest by west** (circa 1771)
**:** a compass point that is one point west of due northwest **:** N56°15′W

**north·west·er** \nȯr(th)-'wes-tər\ *noun* (1737)
**:** a strong northwest wind

**north·west·er·ly** \-lē\ *adverb or adjective* (circa 1611)
**1 :** from the northwest
**2 :** toward the northwest

**north·west·ern** \-'wes-tərn\ *adjective* (1612)
**1** *often capitalized* **:** of, relating to, or characteristic of a region conventionally designated Northwest
**2 :** lying toward or coming from the northwest
**— north·west·ern·most** \-ˌmōst\ *adjective*

**North·west·ern·er** \-'wes-tə(r)-nər\ *noun* (1955)
**:** a native or inhabitant of the Northwest and especially of the northwestern part of the U.S.

**¹north·west·ward** \-'wes-twərd\ *adverb or adjective* (14th century)
**:** toward the northwest
**— north·west·wards** \-twərdz\ *adverb*

**²northwestward** *noun* (1796)
**:** NORTHWEST

**nor·trip·ty·line** \nȯr-'trip-tə-ˌlēn\ *noun* [*nor-* + *-tript-* (perhaps from *tricyclic* + *hepta-*) + *-yl* + ²*-ine*] (1964)
**:** a tricyclic antidepressant $C_{19}H_{21}N$

**Nor·way maple** \'nȯr-ˌwā-\ *noun* (1797)
**:** a European maple (*Acer platanoides*) with dark green or often reddish or red veined leaves that is much planted for shade in the U.S.

**Norway rat** *noun* (circa 1759)
**:** BROWN RAT

**Norway spruce** *noun* (1797)
**:** a widely cultivated spruce (*Picea abies*) that is native to northern Europe and has a pyramidal shape, spreading branches and pendulous branchlets, dark foliage, and long pendulous cones

**Nor·we·gian** \nȯr-'wē-jən\ *noun* [Medieval Latin *Norwegia* Norway] (1605)
**1 a :** a native or inhabitant of Norway **b :** a person of Norwegian descent
**2 :** the Germanic language of the Norwegian people
**— Norwegian** *adjective*

**Norwegian elkhound** *noun* (1930)
**:** any of a Norwegian breed of short-bodied medium-sized dogs with erect ears and a very heavy coat of gray hairs with black tips

**Nor·wich terrier** \'nȯr-(ˌ)wich-, *British* 'när-ich- *or* 'när-ij-\ *noun* [*Norwich,* England] (1931)
**:** any of an English breed of small active low-set terriers that have a long straight wiry coat and erect ears

Norwegian elkhound

**¹nose** \'nōz\ *noun* [Middle English, from Old English *nosu;* akin to Old High German *nasa* nose, Latin *nasus*] (before 12th century)
**1 a :** the part of the face that bears the nostrils and covers the anterior part of the nasal cavity; *broadly* **:** this part together with the nasal cavity **b :** the anterior part of the head at the top or end of the muzzle **:** SNOUT, PROBOSCIS
**2 a :** the sense of smell **:** OLFACTION **b :** AROMA, BOUQUET
**3 :** the vertebrate olfactory organ
**4 a :** the forward end or projection of something **b :** the projecting or working end of a tool
**5 :** the stem of a boat or its protective metal covering
**6 a :** the nose as a symbol of prying or meddling curiosity or interference **b :** a knack for discovery or understanding ⟨a keen *nose* for absurdity⟩
**— on the nose 1 a :** at or to a target point ⟨the bombs landed right *on the nose*⟩ **b** (1) **:** on target **:** ACCURATE (2) **:** ACCURATELY **2 :** to win — used of horse or dog racing bets

**²nose** *verb* **nosed; nos·ing** (circa 1587)
*transitive verb*
**1 :** to detect by or as if by smell **:** SCENT
**2 a :** to push or move with the nose **b :** to move (as a vehicle) ahead slowly or cautiously ⟨*nosed* my car into the parking space⟩
**3 :** to touch or rub with the nose **:** NUZZLE
*intransitive verb*
**1 :** to use the nose in examining, smelling, or showing affection
**2 :** to search impertinently **:** PRY
**3 :** to move ahead slowly or cautiously ⟨the boat *nosed* around the bend⟩

**nose·band** \'nōz-,band\ *noun* (1611)
: the part of a headstall that passes over a horse's nose

**nose·bleed** \-,blēd\ *noun* (1848)
: an attack of bleeding from the nose

**nose cone** *noun* (1949)
: a protective cone constituting the forward end of an aerospace vehicle

**nosed** \'nōzd\ *adjective* (1505)
: having a nose especially of a specified kind — usually used in combination ⟨snub-*nosed*⟩

**nose·dive** \'nōz-,dīv\ *noun* (1912)
**1** : a downward nose-first plunge of a flying object (as an airplane)
**2** : a sudden extreme drop ⟨stock prices took a *nosedive*⟩
— **nose-dive** *intransitive verb*

**no-see-um** \nō-'sē-əm\ *noun* [from the words (as supposedly spoken by American Indians) *no see um* you don't see them] (1848)
: BITING MIDGE

**nose·gay** \'nōz-,gā\ *noun* [Middle English, from *nose* nose + *gay* ornament, literally, something gay, from *gay*] (15th century)
: a small bunch of flowers : POSY

**nose·guard** \-,gärd\ *noun* (1950)
: a defensive lineman in football who plays opposite the offensive center

**nose job** *noun* (1963)
: RHINOPLASTY

**nose out** *transitive verb* (circa 1630)
**1** : to discover often by prying
**2** : to defeat by a narrow margin

**nose·piece** \-,pēs\ *noun* (1611)
**1** : a piece of armor for protecting the nose
**2** : the end piece of a microscope body to which an objective is attached
**3** : the bridge of a pair of eyeglasses

**nose tackle** *noun* (1977)
: NOSEGUARD

**nose·wheel** \-,hwēl, -,wēl\ *noun* (1934)
: a landing-gear wheel under the nose of an airplane

**nos·ey par·ker** \'nō-zē-'pär-kər\ *noun, often N&P capitalized* [probably from the name *Parker*] (1907)
*chiefly British* : BUSYBODY

**¹nosh** \'näsh\ *noun* (1952)
: a light meal : SNACK

**²nosh** *verb* [Yiddish *nashn*, from Middle High German *naschen* to eat on the sly] (1956)
*intransitive verb*
: to eat a snack
*transitive verb*
: CHEW, MUNCH
— **nosh·er** *noun*

**no-show** \'nō-,shō, -'shō\ *noun* (1941)
**1** : a person who reserves space (as on an airplane) but neither uses nor cancels the reservation
**2** : a person who buys a ticket (as to a sporting event) but does not attend; *broadly* : a person who is expected but who does not show up
**3** : failure to show up

**nos·ing** \'nō-ziŋ\ *noun* (circa 1775)
: the usually rounded edge of a stair tread that projects over the riser; *also* : a similar rounded projection

**nos·o·co·mi·al** \,nä-sə-'kō-mē-əl\ *adjective* [Late Latin *nosocomium* hospital, from Late Greek *nosokomeion*, from Greek *nosokomos* one who tends the sick, from *nosos* disease + -*komos*; akin to Greek *kamnein* to suffer, toil, Sanskrit *śāmyati* he tires] (circa 1843)
: originating or taking place in a hospital ⟨*nosocomial* infection⟩

**no·sol·o·gy** \nō-'sä-lə-jē, -'zä-\ *noun* [probably from New Latin *nosologia*, from Greek *nosos* disease + New Latin -*logia* -logy) (circa 1721)
**1** : a classification or list of diseases
**2** : a branch of medical science that deals with classification of diseases
— **no·so·log·i·cal** \,nō-sə-'lä-ji-kəl\ *or* **no·so·log·ic** \-jik\ *adjective*
— **no·so·log·i·cal·ly** \-ji-k(ə-)lē\ *adverb*

**nos·tal·gia** \nä-'stal-jə, nə- *also* nó-, nō-; nə-'stäl-\ *noun* [New Latin, from Greek *nostos* return home + New Latin -*algia*; akin to Greek *neisthai* to return, Old English *genesan* to survive, Sanskrit *nasate* he approaches] (1770)
**1** : the state of being homesick : HOMESICKNESS
**2** : a wistful or excessively sentimental yearning for return to or of some past period or irrecoverable condition; *also* : something that evokes nostalgia
— **nos·tal·gic** \-jik\ *adjective or noun*
— **nos·tal·gi·cal·ly** \-ji-k(ə-)lē\ *adverb*

**nos·tal·gist** \-jist\ *noun* (1953)
: a person given to nostalgia for the past

**nos·toc** \'näs-,täk\ *noun* [New Latin] (1650)
: any of a genus (*Nostoc*) of blue-green algae that fix nitrogen

**nos·tril** \'näs-trəl\ *noun* [Middle English *nosethirl*, from Old English *nosthyrl*, from *nosu* nose + *thyrel* hole; akin to Old English *thurh* through] (before 12th century)
**1** : either of the external nares; *broadly* : either of the nares with the adjoining passage on the same side of the septum
**2** : either fleshy lateral wall of the nose
*word history* see THRILL

**nos·trum** \'näs-trəm\ *noun* [Latin, neuter of *noster* our, ours, from *nos* we — more at US] (1602)
**1** : a medicine of secret composition recommended by its preparer but usually without scientific proof of its effectiveness
**2** : a usually questionable remedy or scheme : PANACEA

**nosy** *or* **nos·ey** \'nō-zē\ *adjective* **nos·i·er; -est** [¹*nose*] (1882)
: of prying or inquisitive disposition or quality : INTRUSIVE
— **nos·i·ly** \'nō-zə-lē\ *adverb*
— **nos·i·ness** \-zē-nəs\ *noun*

**not** \'nät\ *adverb* [Middle English, alteration of *nought*, from *nought*, pronoun — more at NAUGHT] (13th century)
**1** — used as a function word to make negative a group of words or a word
**2** — used as a function word to stand for the negative of a preceding group of words ⟨is sometimes hard to see and sometimes *not*⟩

**NOT** \'nät\ *noun* [*not*] (1947)
: a logical operator that produces a statement that is the inverse of an input statement

**nota** *plural of* NOTUM

**no·ta be·ne** \,nō-tə-'bē-nē, -'be-\ [Latin, mark well] (circa 1721)
— used to call attention to something important

**no·ta·bil·i·ty** \,nō-tə-'bi-lə-tē\ *noun, plural* -**ties** (1832)
: a notable or prominent person

**¹no·ta·ble** \'nō-tə-bəl, *for 2 also* 'nä-\ *adjective* (14th century)
**1 a** : worthy of note : REMARKABLE **b** : DISTINGUISHED, PROMINENT
**2** *archaic* : efficient or capable in performance of housewifely duties
— **no·ta·ble·ness** *noun*

**²no·ta·ble** \'nō-tə-bəl\ *noun* (1815)
**1** : a person of note : NOTABILITY
**2** *plural, often capitalized* : a group of persons summoned especially in monarchical France to act as a deliberative body

**no·ta·bly** \'nō-tə-blē\ *adverb* (14th century)
**1** : in a notable manner : to a high degree ⟨was *notably* impressed⟩
**2** : ESPECIALLY, PARTICULARLY ⟨other powers, *notably* Britain and the United States —C. A. Fisher⟩

**no·tar·i·al** \nō-'ter-ē-əl\ *adjective* (15th century)
**1** : of, relating to, or characteristic of a notary public
**2** : done or executed by a notary public
— **no·tar·i·al·ly** \-ə-lē\ *adverb*

**no·ta·ri·za·tion** \,nō-tə-rə-'zā-shən\ *noun* (1940)

**1** : the act, process, or an instance of notarizing
**2** : the notarial certificate appended to a document

**no·ta·rize** \'nō-tə-,rīz\ *transitive verb* -**rized; -riz·ing** (1926)
: to acknowledge or attest as a notary public

**no·ta·ry public** \'nō-tə-rē-\ *noun, plural* **no·taries public** *or* **notary publics** [Middle English *notary* clerk, notary public, from Latin *notarius* clerk, secretary, from *notarius* of shorthand, from *nota* note, shorthand character] (15th century)
: a public officer who attests or certifies writings (as a deed) to make them authentic and takes affidavits, depositions, and protests of negotiable paper — called also *notary*

**no·tate** \'nō-,tāt\ *transitive verb* **no·tat·ed; no·tat·ing** [back-formation from *notation*] (1903)
: to put into notation

**no·ta·tion** \nō-'tā-shən\ *noun* [Latin *notation-, notatio*, from *notare* to note] (1584)
**1** : ANNOTATION, NOTE
**2 a** : the act, process, method, or an instance of representing by a system or set of marks, signs, figures, or characters **b** : a system of characters, symbols, or abbreviated expressions used in an art or science or in mathematics or logic to express technical facts or quantities
— **no·ta·tion·al** \-shnəl, -shə-nᵊl\ *adjective*

**¹notch** \'näch\ *noun* [perhaps alteration (from misdivision of *an otch*) of (assumed) *otch*, from Middle French *oche*] (1577)
**1 a** : a V-shaped indentation **b** : a slit made to serve as a record **c** : a rounded indentation cut into the pages of a book on the edge opposite the spine
**2** : a deep close pass : GAP
**3** : DEGREE, STEP
— **notched** \'nächt\ *adjective*

**²notch** *transitive verb* (1600)
**1** : to cut or make a notch in
**2 a** : to mark or record by a notch **b** : SCORE, ACHIEVE — sometimes used with *up*

**notch·back** \'näch-,bak\ *noun* (1965)
: an automobile with a trunk whose lid forms a distinct deck; *also* : the back of such an automobile

**¹note** \'nōt\ *transitive verb* **not·ed; not·ing** [Middle English, from Old French *noter*, from Latin *notare* to mark, note, from *nota*] (13th century)
**1 a** : to notice or observe with care **b** : to record or preserve in writing
**2 a** : to make special mention of : REMARK **b** : INDICATE, SHOW
— **not·er** *noun*

**²note** *noun* [Middle English, from Old French, from Latin *nota* mark, character, written note] (13th century)
**1 a** (1) *obsolete* : MELODY, SONG (2) : TONE 2a (3) : CALL, SOUND; *especially* : the musical call of a bird **b** : a written symbol used to indicate duration and pitch of a tone by its shape and position on the staff
**2 a** : a characteristic feature (as of odor or flavor) **b** : something (as an emotion or disposition) like a note in tone or resonance ⟨a *note* of sadness⟩ ⟨end on a high *note*⟩
**3 a** (1) : MEMORANDUM (2) : a condensed or informal record **b** (1) : a brief comment or explanation (2) : a printed comment or reference

| | |
|---|---|
| | whole |
| | half |
| | quarter |
| | eighth |
| | sixteenth |
| | thirty-second |
| | sixty-fourth |

note 1b

set apart from the text **c** (1) **:** a written promise to pay a debt (2) **:** a piece of paper money **d** (1) **:** a short informal letter (2) **:** a formal diplomatic communication **e :** a scholarly or technical essay shorter than an article and restricted in scope **f :** a sheet of notepaper
**4 a :** DISTINCTION, REPUTATION ⟨a figure of international *note*⟩ **b :** OBSERVATION, NOTICE ⟨took full *note* of the proceedings⟩ **c :** KNOWLEDGE, INFORMATION
***synonym*** see SIGN
**note·book** \'nōt-ˌbuk\ *noun* (1579)
**1 :** a book for notes or memoranda
**2 :** a small portable microcomputer about the size of an ordinary loose-leaf binder
**note·case** \-ˌkās\ *noun* (1838)
*British* **:** WALLET 2a
**not·ed** \'nō-təd\ *adjective* (14th century)
**:** well-known by reputation **:** EMINENT, CELEBRATED
***synonym*** see FAMOUS
— **not·ed·ly** *adverb*
— **not·ed·ness** *noun*
**note·less** \'nōt-ləs\ *adjective* (circa 1616)
**:** not noticed **:** UNDISTINGUISHED
**note of hand** (circa 1738)
**:** PROMISSORY NOTE
**note·pad** \'nōt-ˌpad\ *noun* (1922)
**:** PAD 4
**note·pa·per** \-ˌpā-pər\ *noun* (1849)
**:** writing paper suitable for notes
**note·wor·thy** \-ˌwər-thē\ *adjective* (1552)
**:** worthy of or attracting attention especially because of some special excellence
— **note·wor·thi·ly** \-thə-lē\ *adverb*
— **note·wor·thi·ness** \-thē-nəs\ *noun*
**not–for–profit** *adjective* (circa 1973)
**:** NONPROFIT
**noth·er** *or* **'noth·er** \'nə-thər\ *adjective* [alteration (from misdivision of *another*) of *other*, adjective] (1956)
**:** OTHER — used especially in the phrase *a whole nother;* used chiefly in speech or informal prose
**¹noth·ing** \'nə-thin\ *pronoun* [Middle English, from Old English *nān thing*, *nāthing*, from *nān* no + *thing* thing — more at NONE] (before 12th century)
**1 :** not any thing **:** no thing ⟨leaves *nothing* to the imagination⟩
**2 :** no part
**3 :** one of no interest, value, or consequence ⟨they mean *nothing* to me⟩
— **nothing doing :** by no means **:** definitely no
— **nothing for it :** no alternative ⟨*nothing for it* but to start over⟩
**²nothing** *adverb* (12th century)
**:** not at all **:** in no degree
— **nothing like :** not nearly ⟨it's *nothing like* thorough enough⟩
**³nothing** *noun* (1535)
**1 a :** something that does not exist **b :** the absence of all magnitude or quantity; *also* **:** ZERO 1a **c :** NOTHINGNESS 3b
**2 :** someone or something of no or slight value or size
**⁴nothing** *adjective* (1611)
**:** of no account **:** WORTHLESS
**noth·ing·ness** \-nəs\ *noun* (circa 1631)
**1 :** the quality or state of being nothing: as **a :** NONEXISTENCE **b :** utter insignificance **c :** DEATH
**2 :** something insignificant or valueless
**3 a :** VOID, EMPTINESS **b :** a metaphysical entity opposed to and devoid of being and regarded by some existentialists as the ground of anxiety
**¹no·tice** \'nō-təs\ *noun* [Middle English, from Middle French, acquaintance, from Latin *notitia* knowledge, acquaintance, from *notus* known, from past participle of *noscere* to come to know — more at KNOW] (15th century)

**1 a** (1) **:** warning or intimation of something **:** ANNOUNCEMENT (2) **:** notification by one of the parties to an agreement or relation of intention of terminating it at a specified time (3) **:** the condition of being warned or notified — usually used in the phrase *on notice* **b :** INFORMATION, INTELLIGENCE
**2 a :** ATTENTION, HEED **b :** polite or favorable attention **:** CIVILITY
**3 :** a written or printed announcement
**4 :** a short critical account or examination
**²notice** *transitive verb* **no·ticed; no·tic·ing** (15th century)
**1 :** to give notice of
**2 a :** to comment upon **b :** REVIEW
**3 a :** to treat with attention or civility **b :** to take notice of **:** MARK
**4 :** to give a formal notice to
— **no·tic·er** *noun*
**no·tice·able** \'nō-tə-sə-bəl\ *adjective* (1796)
**1 :** worthy of notice
**2 :** capable of being noticed ☆
— **no·tice·ably** \-blē\ *adverb*
**notice board** *noun* (1854)
*chiefly British* **:** a board bearing a notice or on which notices may be posted; *especially* **:** BULLETIN BOARD
**no·ti·fi·able** \'nō-tə-ˌfī-ə-bəl, ˌnō-tə-'\ *adjective* (1889)
**:** required by law to be reported to official health authorities ⟨a *notifiable* disease⟩
**no·ti·fi·ca·tion** \ˌnō-tə-fə-'kā-shən\ *noun* (14th century)
**1 :** the act or an instance of notifying
**2 :** a written or printed matter that gives notice
**no·ti·fy** \'nō-tə-ˌfī\ *transitive verb* **-fied; -fy·ing** [Middle English *notifien*, from Middle French *notifier* to make known, from Late Latin *notificare*, from Latin *notus* known] (14th century)
**1** *obsolete* **:** to point out
**2 :** to give notice of or report the occurrence of ⟨he *notified* his intention to sue⟩
**3 :** to give formal notice to ⟨*notify* a family of the death of a relation⟩
***synonym*** see INFORM
— **no·ti·fi·er** \-ˌfī-(ə)r\ *noun*
**no–till** \'nō-'til\ *noun* (1968)
**:** NO-TILLAGE
**no–till·age** \-'ti-lij\ *noun* (1968)
**:** a system of farming that consists of planting a narrow slit trench without tillage and with the use of herbicides to suppress weeds
**no·tion** \'nō-shən\ *noun* [Latin *notion-, notio*, from *noscere*] (1537)
**1 a** (1) **:** an individual's conception or impression of something known, experienced, or imagined (2) **:** an inclusive general concept (3) **:** a theory or belief held by a person or group **b :** a personal inclination **:** WHIM
**2** *obsolete* **:** MIND, INTELLECT
**3** *plural* **:** small useful items **:** SUNDRIES
***synonym*** see IDEA
**no·tion·al** \'nō-shnəl, -shə-n°l\ *adjective* (1597)
**1 :** THEORETICAL, SPECULATIVE
**2 :** existing in the mind only **:** IMAGINARY
**3 :** given to foolish or fanciful moods or ideas
**4 a :** of, relating to, or being a notion or idea **:** CONCEPTUAL **b** (1) **:** presenting an idea of a thing, action, or quality ⟨*has* is *notional* in *he has luck*, relational in *he has gone*⟩ (2) **:** of or representing what exists or occurs in the world of things as distinguished from syntactic categories
— **no·tion·al·i·ty** \ˌnō-shə-'na-lə-tē\ *noun*
— **no·tion·al·ly** \'nō-shnə-lē, -shə-n°l-ē\ *adverb*
**no·to·chord** \'nō-tə-ˌkȯrd\ *noun* [Greek *nōton, nōtos* back + Latin *chorda* cord — more at CORD] (1848)
**:** a longitudinal flexible rod of cells that in the lowest chordates (as a lancelet or a lamprey) and in the embryos of the higher vertebrates forms the supporting axis of the body

— **no·to·chord·al** \ˌnō-tə-'kȯr-d°l\ *adjective*
**no·to·ri·e·ty** \ˌnō-tə-'rī-ə-tē\ *noun, plural* **-ties** [Middle French or Medieval Latin; Middle French *notorieté*, from Medieval Latin *notorietat-, notorietas*, from *notorius*] (circa 1650)
**1 :** the quality or state of being notorious
**2 :** a notorious person
**no·to·ri·ous** \nō-'tȯr-ē-əs, nə-, -'tȯr-\ *adjective* [Medieval Latin *notorius*, from Late Latin *notorium* information, indictment, from Latin *noscere* to come to know — more at KNOW] (1534)
**:** generally known and talked of; *especially* **:** widely and unfavorably known
***synonym*** see FAMOUS
**no·to·ri·ous·ly** \-lē\ *adverb* (1512)
**1 :** in a notorious manner
**2 :** it is notorious **:** as is very well known
**no–trump** *adjective* (1899)
**:** being a bid, contract, or hand suitable to play without any suit being trumps
— **no–trump** *noun*
**no·tum** \'nō-təm\ *noun, plural* **no·ta** \'nō-tə\ [New Latin, from Greek *nōton* back] (1877)
**:** the dorsal surface of a thoracic segment of an insect
**¹not·with·stand·ing** \ˌnät-with-'stan-din, -with-\ *preposition* [Middle English *notwithstonding*, from *not* + *withstonding*, present participle of *withstonden* to withstand] (14th century)
**:** DESPITE ⟨*notwithstanding* their lack of experience, they were an immediate success⟩ — often used after its object ⟨the motion passed, our objection *notwithstanding*⟩
**²notwithstanding** *adverb* (15th century)
**:** NEVERTHELESS, HOWEVER
**³notwithstanding** *conjunction* (15th century)
**:** ALTHOUGH
**nou·gat** \'nü-gət, *especially British* -ˌgä\ *noun* [French, from Provençal, from Old Provençal *nogat*, from *noga* nut, from (assumed) Vulgar Latin *nuca*, from Latin *nuc-, nux* — more at NUT] (1827)
**:** a confection of nuts or fruit pieces in a sugar paste
**nought** \'nȯt, 'nät\ *variant of* NAUGHT
***word history*** see NAUGHTY

---

☆ **SYNONYMS**
**Noticeable, remarkable, prominent, outstanding, conspicuous, salient, striking** mean attracting notice or attention. NOTICEABLE applies to something unlikely to escape observation ⟨a piano recital with no *noticeable* errors⟩. REMARKABLE applies to something so extraordinary or exceptional as to invite comment ⟨a film of *remarkable* intelligence and wit⟩. PROMINENT applies to something commanding notice by standing out from its surroundings or background ⟨a doctor who occupies a *prominent* position in the town⟩. OUTSTANDING applies to something that rises above and excels others of the same kind ⟨honored for her *outstanding* contributions to science⟩. CONSPICUOUS applies to something that is obvious and unavoidable to the sight or mind ⟨*conspicuous* bureaucratic waste⟩. SALIENT applies to something of significance that merits the attention given it ⟨the *salient* points of the speech⟩. STRIKING applies to something that impresses itself powerfully and deeply upon the observer's mind or vision ⟨the region's *striking* poverty⟩.

---

\ə\ abut \ə\ kitten \ər\ further \a\ ash \ā\ ace \ä\ mop, mar \aů\ out \ch\ chin \e\ bet \ē\ easy \g\ go \i\ hit \ī\ ice \j\ job \n\ sing \ō\ go \ȯ\ law \ȯi\ boy \th\ thin \th\ the \ü\ loot \ů\ foot \y\ yet \zh\ vision *see also* Guide to Pronunciation

**nou·me·non** \'nü-mə-ˌnän\ *noun, plural* **-na** \-nə, -ˌnä\ [German, from Greek *nooumenon* that which is apprehended by thought, from neuter of present passive participle of *noein* to think, conceive, from *nous* mind] (1796)
: a posited object or event as it appears in itself independent of perception by the senses — **nou·men·al** \-'mə-nᵊl\ *adjective*

**noun** \'naún\ *noun* [Middle English *nowne*, from Anglo-French *noun* name, noun, from Old French *nom*, from Latin *nomen* — more at NAME] (14th century)
: any member of a class of words that typically can be combined with determiners to serve as the subject of a verb, can be interpreted as singular or plural, can be replaced with a pronoun, and refer to an entity, quality, state, action, or concept

**noun phrase** *noun, often N&P capitalized* (1923)
: a phrase formed by a noun and all its modifiers and determiners; *broadly* : any syntactic element (as a clause, clitic, pronoun, or zero element) with a noun's function (as the subject of a verb or the object of a verb or preposition) — abbreviation *NP*

**nour·ish** \'nər-ish, 'nə-rish\ *transitive verb* [Middle English *nurishen*, from Old French *noriss-*, stem of *norrir*, from Latin *nutrire* to suckle, nourish; akin to Greek *nan* to flow, *noteros* damp, Sanskrit *snauti* it drips] (14th century)
**1** : NURTURE, REAR
**2** : to promote the growth of ⟨no occasions to exercise the feelings nor *nourish* passion —L. O. Coxe⟩
**3 a** : to furnish or sustain with nutriment : FEED **b** : MAINTAIN, SUPPORT ⟨their profits . . . *nourish* other criminal activities —Beverly Smith⟩
— **nour·ish·er** *noun*

**nour·ish·ing** *adjective* (14th century)
: giving nourishment : NUTRITIOUS

**nour·ish·ment** \'nər-ish-mənt, 'nə-rish-\ *noun* (15th century)
**1 a** : FOOD, NUTRIMENT **b** : SUSTENANCE 3 ⟨books for intellectual *nourishment*⟩
**2** : the act of nourishing : the state of being nourished

**nous** *noun* [Greek *noos, nous* mind] (1678)
**1** \'nüs *also* 'naús\ : MIND, REASON: as **a** : an intelligent purposive principle of the world **b** : the divine reason regarded in Neoplatonism as the first emanation of God
**2** \'naús\ *chiefly British* : COMMON SENSE, ALERTNESS

**nou·veau** \nü-'vō\ *adjective* [French, from Middle French *novel*] (1828)
: newly arrived or developed

**nou·veau riche** \ˌnü-ˌvō-'rēsh\ *noun, plural* **nou·veaux riches** \*same*\ [French, literally, new rich] (1813)
: a person newly rich : PARVENU

**nou·velle** \nü-'vel\ *adjective* [*nouvelle* cuisine] (1976)
: of or relating to nouvelle cuisine ⟨a *nouvelle* restaurant⟩

**nouvelle cuisine** *noun* [French, literally, new cuisine] (1975)
: a form of French cuisine that uses little flour or fat and stresses light sauces and the use of fresh seasonal produce; *also* : any national cuisine that stresses lightness and freshness in preparation ⟨American *nouvelle cuisine*⟩

**nouvelle vague** \-'väg, -'våg\ *noun* [French] (1959)
: NEW WAVE 1, 2

**no·va** \'nō-və\ *noun, plural* **novas** *or* **no·vae** \-(ˌ)vē, -ˌvī\ [New Latin, feminine of Latin *novus* new] (1927)
: a star that suddenly increases its light output tremendously and then fades away to its former obscurity in a few months or years
— **no·va·like** \-və-ˌlīk\ *adjective*

**no·vac·u·lite** \nō-'va-kyə-ˌlīt\ *noun* [Latin *novacula* razor] (1796)
: a very hard fine-grained siliceous rock used for whetstones and possibly of sedimentary origin

**no·va·tion** \nō-'vā-shən\ *noun* [Late Latin *novation-, novatio* renewal, legal novation, from Latin *novare* to make new, from *novus*] (1682)
: the substitution of a new legal obligation for an old one

**¹nov·el** \'nä-vəl\ *adjective* [Middle English, from Middle French, new, from Latin *novellus*, from diminutive of *novus* new — more at NEW] (15th century)
**1** : new and not resembling something formerly known or used
**2** : original or striking especially in conception or style ⟨a *novel* scheme to collect money⟩
**synonym** see NEW

**²novel** *noun* [Italian *novella*] (1639)
**1** : an invented prose narrative that is usually long and complex and deals especially with human experience through a usually connected sequence of events
**2** : the literary genre consisting of novels ◆
— **nov·el·is·tic** \ˌnä-və-'lis-tik\ *adjective*
— **nov·el·is·ti·cal·ly** \-ti-k(ə-)lē\ *adverb*

**nov·el·ette** \ˌnä-və-'let\ *noun* (1814)
: NOVELLA 2

**nov·el·ett·ish** \-'le-tish\ *adjective* (1904)
: of, relating to, or characteristic of a novelette; *especially* : SENTIMENTAL

**nov·el·ist** \'näv-list, 'nä-və-\ *noun* (1728)
: a writer of novels

**nov·el·ize** \'nä-və-ˌlīz\ *transitive verb* **-ized; -iz·ing** (1828)
: to convert into the form of a novel ⟨*novelize* a play⟩
— **nov·el·iza·tion** \ˌnä-və-lə-'zā-shən\ *noun*

**no·vel·la** \nō-'ve-lə\ *noun, plural* **novellas** *or* **no·vel·le** \-'ve-lē\ [Italian, from feminine of *novello* new, from Latin *novellus*] (1898)
**1** *plural* **novelle** : a story with a compact and pointed plot
**2** *plural usually* **novellas** : a work of fiction intermediate in length and complexity between a short story and a novel

**nov·el·ty** \'nä-vəl-tē\ *noun, plural* **-ties** [Middle English *novelte*, from Middle French *noveleté*, from *novel*] (14th century)
**1** : something new or unusual
**2** : the quality or state of being novel : NEWNESS
**3** : a small manufactured article intended mainly for personal or household adornment — usually used in plural

**¹No·vem·ber** \nō-'vem-bər, nə-\ *noun* [Middle English *Novembre*, from Old French, from Latin *November*, ninth month of the early Roman calendar, from *novem* nine — more at NINE] (13th century)
: the 11th month of the Gregorian calendar

**²November** (1956)
— a communications code word for the letter *n*

**no·vem·de·cil·lion** \ˌnō-ˌvem-di-'sil-yən\ *noun, often attributive* [Latin *novemdecim* nineteen (from *novem* + *decem* ten) + English *-illion* (as in *million*) — more at TEN] (circa 1934)
— see NUMBER table

**no·ve·na** \nō-'vē-nə\ *noun* [Medieval Latin, from Latin, feminine of *novenus* nine each, from *novem*] (1853)
: a Roman Catholic period of prayer lasting nine consecutive days

**nov·ice** \'nä-vəs\ *noun* [Middle English, from Middle French, from Medieval Latin *novicius*, from Latin, newly imported, from *novus* — more at NEW] (14th century)
**1** : a person admitted to probationary membership in a religious community
**2** : BEGINNER, TYRO

**no·vi·tiate** \nō-'vi-shət, nə-\ *noun* [French *noviciat*, from Medieval Latin *noviciatus*, from *novicius*] (1600)
**1** : the period or state of being a novice
**2** : a house where novices are trained
**3** : NOVICE

**no·vo·bi·o·cin** \ˌnō-və-'bī-ə-sən\ *noun* [*novo-* (perhaps modification of Latin *niveus* snowy, specific epithet of the bacterium *Streptomyces niveus*) + *bi-* + *-mycin*] (1956)
: a weak dibasic acid $C_{31}H_{36}N_2O_{11}$ that is highly toxic to humans and is used as an antimicrobial drug in some serious cases of staphylococcic and urinary tract infection

**No·vo·cain** \'nō-və-ˌkān\ *trademark*
— used for a preparation containing the hydrochloride of procaine

**no·vo·caine** \-ˌkān\ *noun* [International Scientific Vocabulary *novo-* (from Latin *novus* new) + *cocaine*] (1910)
: PROCAINE; *also* : its hydrochloride

**¹now** \'naú\ *adverb* [Middle English, from Old English *nū*; akin to Old High German *nū* now, Latin *nunc*, Greek *nyn*] (before 12th century)
**1 a** : at the present time or moment **b** : in the time immediately before the present ⟨thought of them just *now*⟩ **c** : in the time immediately to follow : FORTHWITH ⟨come in *now*⟩
**2** — used with the sense of present time weakened or lost to express command, request, or admonition ⟨*now* hear this⟩ ⟨*now* you be sure to write⟩
**3** — used with the sense of present time weakened or lost to introduce an important point or indicate a transition (as of ideas)
**4** : SOMETIMES ⟨*now* one and *now* another⟩
**5** : under the present circumstances
**6** : at the time referred to ⟨*now* the trouble began⟩

**²now** *conjunction* (before 12th century)
: in view of the fact that : SINCE — often followed by *that* ⟨*now* that we are here⟩

**³now** *noun* (12th century)
: the present time or moment ⟨been ill up to *now*⟩

**⁴now** *adjective* (14th century)
**1** : of or relating to the present time : EXISTING ⟨the *now* president⟩
**2 a** : excitingly new ⟨*now* clothes⟩ **b** : constantly aware of what is new ⟨*now* people⟩ ⟨the *now* generation⟩

**NOW account** \'naú-\ *noun* [*negotiable order of withdrawal*] (1974)
: a savings account on which checks may be drawn

**now·a·days** \'naú-(ə-)ˌdāz\ *adverb* [Middle English *now a dayes*, from ¹*now* + *a dayes* during the day] (14th century)
: at the present time

**now and then** *adverb* (15th century)

---

◇ WORD HISTORY

**novel** Italian *novella*, meaning literally "item of news," came to be applied in the 13th century to the short tales or fables that were becoming a popular literary form. Simple in plot and character development, these tales typically dealt with humorous, political, or amorous events, especially in a satiric way. Since similar tales were also becoming popular in England, English borrowed the word as *novel* in the 17th century. As the novel developed, however, the notion of brevity was abandoned and the narratives became considerably longer. During the 18th century the novel matured as a literary form, presenting psychologically developed characters in an extended, complex plot. At the end of the 19th century, English again borrowed the Italian word *novella*, this time intact to refer specifically to the medieval Italian stories of authors such as Boccaccio, and later to refer to a work of fiction intermediate in length between a short story and a novel.

: from time to time : OCCASIONALLY ⟨*now and then* we go off to the country⟩

**no·way** *adverb* (13th century)
**1** \'nō-ˌwā\ *or* **no·ways** \-ˌwāz\ : NOWISE
**2** *usually* **no way** \-'wā\ : NO — used emphatically

¹**no·where** \'nō-ˌhwer, -ˌhwar, -hwər *or without* h\ *adverb* (before 12th century)
**1** : not in or at any place
**2** : to no place

²**nowhere** *noun* (1831)
**1** : a nonexistent place
**2** : an unknown, distant, or obscure place or state ⟨rose to fame out of *nowhere*⟩
— **miles from nowhere** : in an extremely remote place

**nowhere near** *adverb* (15th century)
: not nearly

**no·wheres** \'nō-ˌhwerz, -ˌhwarz, -hwərz *or without* h\ *adverb* (circa 1866)
*chiefly dialect* : NOWHERE

**no·whith·er** \'nō-ˌhwi-thər, -ˌwi-thər; ˌnō-'\ *adverb* (before 12th century)
: to or toward no place

**no–win** \'nō-'win, -ˌwin\ *adjective* (1962)
: not likely to give victory, success, or satisfaction : that cannot be won ⟨a *no-win* situation⟩ ⟨a *no-win* war⟩

**no·wise** \'nō-ˌwīz\ *adverb* (14th century)
: not at all

**now·ness** \'naù-nəs\ *noun* (1674)
: the quality or state of existing or occurring in or belonging to the present time

**nowt** \'naùt *also* 'nōt\ *dialect English variant of* NOUGHT

**nox·ious** \'näk-shəs\ *adjective* [Middle English *noxius*, from Latin, from *noxa* harm; akin to Latin *nocēre* to harm, *nec-*, *nex* violent death, Greek *nekros* dead body] (15th century)
**1 a** : physically harmful or destructive to living beings ⟨*noxious* wastes that poison our streams⟩ **b** : constituting a harmful influence on mind or behavior : morally corrupting ⟨*noxious* doctrines⟩
**2** : DISTASTEFUL, OBNOXIOUS
*synonym* see PERNICIOUS
— **nox·ious·ly** *adverb*
— **nox·ious·ness** *noun*

**noz·zle** \'nä-zəl\ *noun* [diminutive of *nose*] (1683)
**1 a** : a projecting vent of something **b** : a short tube with a taper or constriction used (as on a hose) to speed up or direct a flow of fluid **c** : a part in a rocket engine that accelerates the exhaust gases from the combustion chamber to a high velocity
**2** *slang* : NOSE

**NSAID** \'en-ˌsed *also* -ˌsād\ *noun* [*nonsteroidal anti-inflammatory drug*] (1985)
: a nonsteroidal anti-inflammatory drug (as ibuprofen)

**-n't** *verb combining form*
: not ⟨*isn't*⟩

**nth** \'en(t)th\ *adjective* [*n* (indefinite number) + *-th*] (1852)
**1** : numbered with an unspecified or indefinitely large ordinal number ⟨for the *nth* time⟩
**2** : EXTREME, UTMOST ⟨to the *nth* degree⟩

**n-type** \'en-ˌtīp\ *adjective* [*negative* + *type*] (1946)
: relating to or being a semiconductor in which charge is carried by electrons — compare P-TYPE

**nu** \'nü, 'nyü\ *noun* [Greek *ny*, of Semitic origin; akin to Hebrew *nūn* nun] (circa 1823)
: the 13th letter of the Greek alphabet — see ALPHABET table

**nu·ance** \'nü-ˌän(t)s, 'nyü-, -ˌäⁿs; nù-', nyü-'\ *noun* [French, from Middle French, shade of color, from *nuer* to make shades of color, from *nue* cloud, from Latin *nubes*; perhaps akin to Welsh *nudd* mist] (1781)
**1** : a subtle distinction or variation
**2** : a subtle quality : NICETY

**3** : sensibility to, awareness of, or ability to express delicate shadings (as of meaning, feeling, or value)
— **nu·anced** \-ˌän(t)st, -'än(t)st\ *adjective*

**nub** \'nəb\ *noun* [alteration of English dialect *knub*, probably from Low German *knubbe*] (1727)
**1** : KNOB, LUMP
**2** : NUBBIN
**3** : GIST, POINT

**nub·bin** \'nə-bən\ *noun* [perhaps diminutive of *nub*] (1692)
**1** : something (as an ear of Indian corn) that is small for its kind, stunted, undeveloped, or imperfect
**2** : a small usually projecting part or bit
**3** : NUB 3

**nub·ble** \'nə-bəl\ *noun* [diminutive of *nub*] (1818)
: a small knob or lump
— **nub·bly** \-b(ə-)lē\ *adjective*

**nub·by** \'nə-bē\ *adjective* **nub·bi·er; -est** [*nub* + ¹*-y*] (circa 1876)
**1** : having or being like nubbles
**2** : having nubs ⟨a *nubby* knit fabric⟩

**Nu·bi·an** \'nü-bē-ən, 'nyü-\ *noun* (15th century)
**1 a** : a native or inhabitant of Nubia **b** : a member of one of the group of dark-skinned peoples that formed a powerful empire between Egypt and Ethiopia from the 6th to the 14th centuries
**2** : any of several languages spoken in central and northern Sudan
— **Nubian** *adjective*

**nu·bile** \'nü-ˌbīl, 'nyü-, -ˌbəl\ *adjective* [French, from Latin *nubilis*, from *nubere* to marry — more at NUPTIAL] (circa 1642)
**1** : of marriageable condition or age
**2** : sexually attractive — used of a young woman
— **nu·bil·i·ty** \nü-'bi-lə-tē, nyü-\ *noun*

**nu·cel·lus** \nü-'se-ləs, nyü-\ *noun, plural* **nu·cel·li** \-'se-ˌlī\ [New Latin, from Latin *nucella* small nut, from *nuc-*, *nux* nut — more at NUT] (1882)
: the central and chief part of a plant ovule that encloses the female gametophyte
— **nu·cel·lar** \-'se-lər\ *adjective*

**nu·chal** \'nü-kəl, 'nyü-\ *adjective* [Medieval Latin *nucha* nape, from Arabic *nukhāʿ* spinal marrow] (1835)
: of, relating to, or lying in the region of the nape

**nucle-** *or* **nucleo-** *combining form* [French *nuclé-*, *nucléo-*, from New Latin *nucleus*]
**1** : nucleus ⟨*nucleo*plasm⟩
**2** : nucleic acid ⟨*nucleo*protein⟩

**nu·cle·ar** \'nü-klē-ər, 'nyü-, ÷-kyə-lər\ *adjective* (1846)
**1** : of, relating to, or constituting a nucleus
**2 a** : of or relating to the atomic nucleus ⟨*nuclear* reaction⟩ ⟨*nuclear* physics⟩ **b** : used in or produced by a nuclear reaction (as fission) ⟨*nuclear* fuel⟩ ⟨*nuclear* waste⟩ ⟨*nuclear* energy⟩ **c** (1) : being a weapon whose destructive power derives from an uncontrolled nuclear reaction (2) : of, produced by, or involving nuclear weapons ⟨the *nuclear* age⟩ ⟨*nuclear* war⟩ (3) : armed with nuclear weapons ⟨*nuclear* powers⟩ **d** : of, relating to, or powered by nuclear energy ⟨a *nuclear* submarine⟩ ⟨the *nuclear* debate⟩ ⟨a *nuclear* plant⟩ ▪

**nuclear family** *noun* (1947)
: a family group that consists only of father, mother, and children

**nuclear magnetic resonance** *noun* (1942)
: the magnetic resonance of an atomic nucleus

**nuclear medicine** *noun* (1952)
: a branch of medicine dealing with the use of radioactive materials in the diagnosis and treatment of disease

**nuclear membrane** *noun* (1888)

: a double membrane enclosing a cell nucleus and having its outer part continuous with the endoplasmic reticulum — see CELL illustration

**nuclear–powered** *adjective* (1948)
: powered by nuclear energy

**nuclear resonance** *noun* (1940)
: the resonance absorption of a gamma ray by a nucleus identical to the nucleus that emitted the gamma ray

**nuclear sap** *noun* (1877)
: the clear homogeneous ground substance of a cell nucleus — called also *karyolymph*

**nuclear winter** *noun* (1983)
: the chilling of climate that is hypothesized to be a consequence of nuclear war and to result from the prolonged blockage of sunlight by high-altitude dust clouds produced by nuclear explosions

**nu·cle·ase** \'nü-klē-ˌās, 'nyü-, -ˌāz\ *noun* (1902)
: any of various enzymes that promote hydrolysis of nucleic acids

**nu·cle·ate** \'nü-klē-ˌāt, 'nyü-\ *verb* **-at·ed; -at·ing** [Late Latin *nucleatus*, past participle of *nucleare* to become stony, from Latin *nucleus*] (circa 1864)
*transitive verb*
**1** : to form into a nucleus : CLUSTER
**2** : to act as a nucleus for
**3** : to supply nuclei to
*intransitive verb*
**1** : to form a nucleus
**2** : to act as a nucleus
**3** : to begin to form
— **nu·cle·ation** \ˌnü-klē-'ā-shən, ˌnyü-\ *noun*
— **nu·cle·a·tor** \'nü-klē-ˌā-tər, 'nyü-\ *noun*

**nu·cle·at·ed** \'nü-klē-ˌā-təd, 'nyü-\ *or* **nu·cle·ate** \-klē-ət\ *adjective* [Latin *nucleatus*, from *nucleus* kernel] (1845)
**1** : having a nucleus or nuclei ⟨*nucleated* cells⟩
**2** *usually* **nucleate** : originating or occurring at nuclei ⟨*nucleate* boiling⟩

**nu·cle·ic acid** \nù-'klē-ik-, -'klā-, nyù-\ *noun* [from their occurrence in cell nuclei] (1892)
: any of various acids (as DNA or RNA) that are composed of nucleotide chains

**nu·cle·in** \'nü-klē-ən, 'nyü-\ *noun* (1878)
**1** : NUCLEOPROTEIN
**2** : NUCLEIC ACID

**nu·cle·o·cap·sid** \ˌnü-klē-ō-'kap-səd, ˌnyü-\ *noun* (1963)
: the nucleic acid and surrounding protein coat in a virus

**nu·cle·oid** \'nü-klē-ˌóid, 'nyü-\ *noun* (1938)
: the DNA-containing area of a prokaryotic cell (as a bacterium)

**nu·cle·o·lus** \nü-'klē-ə-ləs, nyü-\ *noun, plural* **-li** \-ˌlī\ [New Latin, from Latin, diminutive of *nucleus*] (1845)
: a spherical body of the nucleus of most eukaryotes that becomes enlarged during protein synthesis, is associated with a nucleolus organizer, and contains the DNA templates for ribosomal RNA — see CELL illustration

□ **USAGE**
**nuclear** Though disapproved of by many, pronunciations ending in \-kyə-lər\ have been found in widespread use among educated speakers including scientists, lawyers, professors, congressmen, U.S. cabinet members, and at least one U.S. president and one vice president. While most common in the U.S., these pronunciations have also been heard from British and Canadian speakers.

— **nu·cle·o·lar** \-lər\ *adjective*
**nucleolus organizer** *noun* (1939)
: the specific part of a chromosome with which a nucleolus is associated especially during its reorganization after nuclear division — called also *nucleolar organizer*
**nu·cle·on** \'nü-klē-,än, 'nyü-\ *noun* [International Scientific Vocabulary] (1923)
**1** : a nuclear particle: **a** : PROTON **b** : NEUTRON
**2** : a hypothetical single entity with one-half unit of isospin that can manifest itself as either a proton or a neutron
— **nu·cle·on·ic** \,nü-klē-'ä-nik, ,nyü-\ *adjective*
**nu·cle·on·ics** \,nü-klē-'ä-niks, ,nyü-\ *noun plural but singular or plural in construction* (1937)
: a branch of physical science that deals with nucleons or with all phenomena of the atomic nucleus
**nu·cle·o·phile** \'nü-klē-ə-,fīl, 'nyü-\ *noun* (1943)
: a nucleophilic substance (as an electron-donating reagent)
**nu·cle·o·phil·ic** \,nü-klē-ə-'fi-lik, ,nyü-\ *adjective* (1933)
**1** *of an atom, ion, or molecule* : having an affinity for atomic nuclei : being an electron donor
**2** : involving a nucleophilic species ⟨a *nucleophilic* reaction⟩ — compare ELECTROPHILIC
— **nu·cleo·phil·i·cal·ly** \-li-k(ə-)lē\ *adverb*
— **nu·cle·o·phi·lic·i·ty** \-klē-ō-fi-'li-sə-tē\ *noun*
**nu·cle·o·plasm** \'nü-klē-ə-,pla-zəm, 'nyü-\ *noun* [International Scientific Vocabulary] (1888)
: the protoplasm of a nucleus; *especially* : NUCLEAR SAP
— **nu·cle·o·plas·mic** \-klē-ə-'plaz-mik\ *adjective*
**nu·cle·o·pro·tein** \,nü-klē-ō-'prō-,tēn, ,nyü-, -'prō-tē-ən\ *noun* [International Scientific Vocabulary] (1907)
: a compound that consists of a protein (as a histone) conjugated with a nucleic acid (as a DNA) and that is the principal constituent of the hereditary material in chromosomes
**nu·cle·o·side** \'nü-klē-ə-,sīd, 'nyü-\ *noun* [International Scientific Vocabulary *nucle-* + -*ose* + -*ide*] (1911)
: a compound (as guanosine or adenosine) that consists of a purine or pyrimidine base combined with deoxyribose or ribose and is found especially in DNA or RNA
**nu·cle·o·some** \-,sōm\ *noun* (1962)
: any of the repeating globular subunits of chromatin that consist of a complex of DNA and histone
— **nu·cle·o·so·mal** \,nü-klē-ə-'sō-məl, ,nyü-\ *adjective*
**nu·cle·o·syn·the·sis** \,nü-klē-ō-'sin(t)-thə-səs, ,nyü-\ *noun* [New Latin] (1960)
: the production of a chemical element from simpler nuclei (as of hydrogen) especially in a star
— **nu·cle·o·syn·thet·ic** \-sin-'the-tik\ *adjective*
**nu·cle·o·tid·ase** \,nü-klē-ə-'tī-,dās, ,nyü-, -,dāz\ *noun* (1911)
: a phosphatase that promotes hydrolysis of a nucleotide (as into a nucleoside and phosphoric acid)
**nu·cle·o·tide** \'nü-klē-ə-,tīd, 'nyü-\ *noun* [International Scientific Vocabulary, irregular from *nucle-* + -*ide*] (1908)
: any of several compounds that consist of a ribose or deoxyribose sugar joined to a purine or pyrimidine base and to a phosphate group and that are the basic structural units of nucleic acids (as RNA and DNA) — compare NUCLEOSIDE
**nu·cle·us** \'nü-klē-əs, 'nyü-\ *noun, plural* **nu·clei** \-klē-,ī\ *also* **nu·cle·us·es** [New Latin,

from Latin, kernel, diminutive of *nuc-, nux* nut — more at NUT] (1704)
**1** : the small brighter and denser portion of a galaxy or of the head of a comet
**2** : a central point, group, or mass about which gathering, concentration, or accretion takes place: as **a** : a cellular organelle of eukaryotes that is essential to cell functions (as reproduction and protein synthesis), is composed of nuclear sap and a nucleoprotein-rich network from which chromosomes and nucleoli arise, and is enclosed in a definite membrane — see CELL illustration **b** : a mass of gray matter or group of nerve cells in the central nervous system **c** : a characteristic and stable complex of atoms or groups in a molecule; *especially* : RING ⟨the naphthalene *nucleus*⟩ **d** : the positively charged central portion of an atom that comprises nearly all of the atomic mass and that consists of protons and neutrons except in hydrogen which consists of one proton only
**3** : the peak of sonority in the utterance of a syllable
**nu·clide** \'nü-,klīd, 'nyü-\ *noun* [*nucleus* + Greek *eidos* form, species — more at IDOL] (1947)
: a species of atom characterized by the constitution of its nucleus and hence by the number of protons, the number of neutrons, and the energy content
— **nu·clid·ic** \nü-'kli-dik, nyü-\ *adjective*
¹**nude** \'nüd, 'nyüd\ *adjective* **nud·er; nud·est** [Latin *nudus* naked — more at NAKED] (1531)
**1** : lacking something essential especially to legal validity ⟨a *nude* contract⟩
**2 a** : devoid of a natural or conventional covering; *especially* : not covered by clothing or a drape **b** (1) : of the color of a white person's flesh (2) : giving the appearance of nudity ⟨a *nude* dress⟩ **c** : featuring nudes ⟨a *nude* movie⟩ **d** : frequented by naked people ⟨a *nude* beach⟩
**synonym** see BARE
— **nude** *adverb*
— **nude·ly** *adverb*
— **nude·ness** *noun*
— **nu·di·ty** \'nü-də-tē, 'nyü-\ *noun*
²**nude** *noun* (1708)
**1 a** : a representation of a nude human figure **b** : a nude person
**2** : the condition of being nude ⟨in the *nude*⟩
**nudge** \'nəj\ *verb* **nudged; nudg·ing** [origin unknown] (1675)
*transitive verb*
**1** : to touch or push gently; *especially* : to seek the attention of by a push of the elbow
**2** : to prod lightly : urge into action
**3** : APPROACH ⟨its circulation is *nudging* the four million mark —Bennett Cerf⟩
*intransitive verb*
: to give a nudge
— **nudge** *noun*
— **nudg·er** *noun*
**nu·di·branch** \'nü-də-,braŋk, 'nyü-\ *noun, plural* -**branchs** [New Latin *Nudibranchia*, from Latin *nudus* + Greek *branchia* gills] (1847)
: any of an order (Nudibranchia) of marine gastropod mollusks without a shell in the adult state and without true gills
— **nudibranch** *adjective*
**nud·ism** \'nü-,di-zəm, 'nyü-\ *noun* (1929)
: the practice of going nude especially in sexually mixed groups and during periods of time spent at specially secluded places
— **nud·ist** \'nü-dist, 'nyü-\ *adjective or noun*
**nud·nick** *or* **nud·nik** \'nud-nik\ *noun* [Yiddish *nudnik*, from *nudyen* to bore, from Polish *nudzić*, from *nuda* boredom] (1947)
: a person who is a bore or nuisance
**nu·ga·to·ry** \'nü-gə-,tōr-ē, 'nyü-, -,tȯr-\ *adjective* [Latin *nugatorius*, from *nugari* to trifle, from *nugae* trifles] (1603)
**1** : of little or no consequence : TRIFLING, INCONSEQUENTIAL

**2** : having no force : INOPERATIVE
**synonym** see VAIN
**nug·get** \'nə-gət\ *noun* [origin unknown] (1852)
**1** : a solid lump; *especially* : a native lump of precious metal
**2** : TIDBIT 2 ⟨*nuggets* of wisdom⟩
**3** : a small usually rounded piece of food ⟨chicken *nuggets*⟩
**nui·sance** \'nü-sᵊn(t)s, 'nyü-\ *noun* [Middle English *nusaunce*, from Anglo-French, from Old French *nuire* to harm, from Latin *nocēre* — more at NOXIOUS] (15th century)
**1** : HARM, INJURY
**2** : one that is annoying, unpleasant, or obnoxious : PEST
**nuisance tax** *noun* (1924)
: an excise tax collected in small amounts on a wide range of commodities directly from the consumer
¹**nuke** \'nük, 'nyük\ *noun* [by shortening & alteration from *nuclear*] (1959)
**1** : a nuclear weapon
**2** : a nuclear-powered electric generating station
²**nuke** *transitive verb* **nuked; nuk·ing** (1967)
**1** : to attack or destroy with or as if with nuclear bombs
**2** : MICROWAVE
¹**null** \'nəl\ *adjective* [Middle French *nul*, literally, not any, from Latin *nullus*, from *ne-* not + *ullus* any; akin to Latin *unus* one — more at NO, ONE] (circa 1567)
**1** : having no legal or binding force : INVALID
**2** : amounting to nothing : NIL
**3** : having no value : INSIGNIFICANT
**4 a** : having no elements ⟨*null* set⟩ **b** : having zero as a limit ⟨*null* sequence⟩ **c** *of a matrix* : having all elements equal to zero
**5 a** : indicating usually by a zero reading on a scale when a given quantity (as current or voltage) is zero or when two quantities are equal — used of an instrument **b** : being or relating to a method of measurement in which an unknown quantity (as of electric current) is compared with a known quantity of the same kind and found equal by a null detector
**6** : of, being, or relating to zero
**7** : ZERO 1c
²**null** *noun* (1605)
**1** : ZERO 3a(1)
**2 a** : a condition of a radio receiver when minimum or zero signal is received **b** : a minimum or zero value of an electric current or of a radio signal
³**null** *transitive verb* (1643)
: to make null
**nul·lah** \'nə-lə\ *noun* [Hindi *nālā*] (1776)
: GULLY, RAVINE
**null and void** *adjective* (1669)
: having no force, binding power, or validity
**null hypothesis** *noun* (1935)
: a statistical hypothesis to be tested and accepted or rejected in favor of an alternative; *specifically* : the hypothesis that an observed difference (as between the means of two samples) is due to chance alone and not due to a systematic cause
**nul·li·fi·ca·tion** \,nə-lə-fə-'kā-shən\ *noun* (1798)
**1** : the act of nullifying : the state of being nullified
**2** : the action of a state impeding or attempting to prevent the operation and enforcement within its territory of a law of the U.S.
— **nul·li·fi·ca·tion·ist** \-sh(ə-)nist\ *noun*
**nul·li·fi·er** \'nə-lə-,fī(-ə)r\ *noun* (1832)
: one that nullifies; *specifically* : one maintaining the right of nullification against the U.S. government
**nul·li·fy** \'nə-lə-,fī\ *transitive verb* -**fied; -fy·ing** [Late Latin *nullificare*, from Latin *nullus*] (1535)
**1** : to make null; *especially* : to make legally null and void

**2 :** to make of no value or consequence ☆

**nul·lip·a·rous** \,nə-'li-pə-rəs\ *adjective* [New Latin *nullipara* one who has never borne an offspring, from Latin *nullus* not any + *-para* -para] (1859)
**:** of, relating to, or being a female that has not borne offspring

**nul·li·ty** \'nə-lə-tē\ *noun, plural* **-ties** (1570)
**1 a :** the quality or state of being null; *especially* **:** legal invalidity **b** (1) **:** NOTHINGNESS; *also* **:** INSIGNIFICANCE (2) **:** a mere nothing **:** NONENTITY
**2 :** one that is null; *specifically* **:** an act void of legal effect
**3 :** the number of elements in a basis of a null-space

**null–space** \'nəl-,spās\ *noun* (1884)
**:** a subspace of a vector space consisting of vectors that under a given linear transformation are mapped onto zero

**numb** \'nəm\ *adjective* [Middle English *nomen*, from past participle of *nimen* to take — more at NIM] (14th century)
**1 :** devoid of sensation especially as a result of cold or anesthesia
**2 :** devoid of emotion **:** INDIFFERENT
— **numb** *transitive verb*
— **numb·ing·ly** \'nə-miŋ-lē\ *adverb*
— **numb·ly** \'nəm-lē\ *adverb*
— **numb·ness** *noun*

**¹num·ber** \'nəm-bər\ *noun* [Middle English *nombre*, from Old French, from Latin *numerus*] (14th century)
**1 a :** a sum of units **:** TOTAL (2) **:** COMPLEMENT 1b (3) **:** an indefinite usually large total ⟨a *number* of members were absent⟩ ⟨the *number* of elderly is rising⟩ (4) *plural* **:** a numerous group **:** MANY (5) **:** a numerical preponderance **b** (1) **:** the characteristic of an individual by which it is treated as a unit or of a collection by which it is treated in terms of units (2) **:** an ascertainable total ⟨bugs beyond *number*⟩ **c** (1) **:** a unit belonging to an abstract mathematical system and subject to specified laws of succession, addition, and multiplication; *especially* **:** NATURAL NUMBER (2) **:** an element (as π) of any of many mathematical systems obtained by extension of or analogy with the natural number system (3) *plural* **:** ARITHMETIC
**2 :** a distinction of word form to denote reference to one or more than one; *also* **:** a form or group of forms so distinguished
**3** *plural* **a** (1) **:** metrical structure **:** METER (2) **:** metrical lines **:** VERSES **b** *archaic* **:** musical sounds **:** NOTES
**4 a :** a word, symbol, letter, or combination of symbols representing a number **b :** a numeral or combination of numerals or other symbols used to identify or designate ⟨dialed the wrong *number*⟩ **c** (1) **:** a member of a sequence or collection designated by especially consecutive numbers (as an issue of a periodical) (2) **:** a position in a numbered sequence **d :** a group of one kind ⟨not of their *number*⟩
**5 :** one singled out from a group **:** INDIVIDUAL: as **a :** GIRL, WOMAN ⟨met an attractive *number* at the dance⟩ **b** (1) **:** a musical, theatrical, or literary selection or production (2) **:** ROUTINE, ACT **c :** an item of merchandise and especially clothing
**6 :** insight into a person's ability or character ⟨had my *number*⟩
**7** *plural but singular or plural in construction* **a :** a form of lottery in which an individual wagers on the appearance of a certain combination of digits (as in regularly published numbers) — called also *numbers game* **b :** ²POLICY 2a
**8** *plural* **a :** figures representing amounts of money usually in dollars spent, earned, or involved **b** (1) **:** STATISTICS 2; *especially* **:** individual statistics (as of an athlete) (2) **:** RATING 3c
**9 :** a person represented by a number or considered without regard to individuality ⟨at the

university I was just a *number*⟩
*usage* see AMOUNT
— **by the numbers 1 :** in unison to a specific count or cadence **2 :** in a systematic, routine, or mechanical manner
▶The Table of Numbers is on page 1254

**²number** *verb* **num·bered; num·ber·ing** \-b(ə-)riŋ\ (14th century)
*transitive verb*
**1 :** COUNT, ENUMERATE
**2 :** to claim as part of a total **:** INCLUDE
**3 :** to restrict to a definite number ⟨your days are *numbered*⟩
**4 :** to assign a number to
**5 :** to amount to in number **:** TOTAL ⟨the crew *numbers* 100⟩
*intransitive verb*
**1 :** to reach a total number
**2 :** to call off numbers in sequence ☐
— **num·ber·able** \-b(ə-)rə-bəl\ *adjective*
— **num·ber·er** \-bər-ər\ *noun*

**number cruncher** *noun* (1966)
**1 :** a computer that performs fast numerical calculations especially on large amounts of data
**2 :** a person concerned with complex numerical data (as statistics)
— **number crunching** *noun*

**num·ber·less** \'nəm-bər-ləs\ *adjective* (1573)
**:** INNUMERABLE, COUNTLESS

**number line** *noun* (1960)
**:** a line of infinite extent whose points correspond to the real numbers according to their distance in a positive or negative direction from a point arbitrarily taken as zero

**¹number one** *noun* (circa 1705)
**1 :** one's own interests or welfare **:** ONESELF ⟨looking out for *number one*⟩ — often written *No. 1*
**2 :** one that is first in rank, importance, or influence — often written *No. 1*

**²number one** *adjective* (1839)
**1 :** first in rank, importance, or influence **:** FOREMOST ⟨cancer is the country's *number one* killer⟩ — often written *No. 1*
**2 :** of highest or of high quality

**Num·bers** \'nəm-bərz\ *noun plural but singular in construction*
**:** the mainly narrative fourth book of canonical Jewish and Christian Scripture — see BIBLE table

**number theory** *noun* (1912)
**:** the study of the properties of integers
— **number theoretic** *adjective*
— **number theorist** *noun*

**numb·skull** \'nəm-,skəl\ *variant of* NUMSKULL
**nu·men** \'nü-mən, 'nyü-\ *noun, plural* **nu·mi·na** \-mə-nə\ [Latin, nod, divine will, numen; akin to Latin *nutare* to nod, Greek *neuein*] (1628)
**:** a spiritual force or influence often identified with a natural object, phenomenon, or place

**nu·mer·a·ble** \'nüm-rə-bəl, 'nü-mə-; 'nyüm-, 'nyü-mə-\ *adjective* [Latin *numerabilis*, from *numerare* to count] (1570)
**:** capable of being counted

**¹nu·mer·al** \'nüm-rəl, 'nü-mə-; 'nyüm-, 'nyü-mə-\ *adjective* [Middle English, from Middle French, from Late Latin *numeralis*, from Latin *numerus*] (14th century)
**1 :** of, relating to, or expressing numbers
**2 :** consisting of numbers or numerals
— **nu·mer·al·ly** *adverb*

**²numeral** *noun* (1686)
**1 :** a conventional symbol that represents a number
**2** *plural* **:** numbers that designate by year a school or college class and that are awarded for distinction in an extracurricular activity

**¹nu·mer·ate** \'nü-mə-,rāt, 'nyü-\ *transitive verb* **-at·ed; -at·ing** [Latin *numeratus*, past participle of *numerare* to count, from *numerus*] (circa 1721)
**:** ENUMERATE

**²nu·mer·ate** \'nüm-rət, 'nü-mə-; 'nyüm-, 'nyü-mə-\ *adjective* [Latin *numerus* number +

English *-ate* (as in *literate*)] (1959)
**:** marked by the capacity for quantitative thought and expression
— **nu·mer·a·cy** \'n(y)üm-rə-sē, 'n(y)ü-mə-\ *noun*

**nu·mer·a·tion** \,nü-mə-'rā-shən, ,nyü-\ *noun* (15th century)
**1 a :** the act or process or an instance of counting or numbering; *also* **:** a system of counting or numbering **b :** an act or instance of designating by a number
**2 :** the art of reading in words numbers expressed by numerals

**nu·mer·a·tor** \'nü-mə-,rā-tər, 'nyü-\ *noun* (1575)
**1 :** the part of a fraction that is above the line and signifies the number of parts of the denominator taken
**2 :** one that numbers

**¹nu·mer·ic** \nù-'mer-ik, nyù-\ *adjective* (circa 1828)
**:** NUMERICAL; *especially* **:** denoting a number or a system of numbers ⟨*numeric* code⟩ ⟨a *numeric* sign⟩

**²nu·mer·ic** *noun* (1879)
**:** NUMBER, NUMERAL

**nu·mer·i·cal** \nù-'mer-i-kəl, nyù-\ *adjective* [Latin *numerus*] (1628)
**1 :** of or relating to numbers ⟨the *numerical* superiority of the enemy⟩
**2 :** expressed in or involving numbers or a number system ⟨*numerical* standing in a class⟩ ⟨a *numerical* code⟩
— **nu·mer·i·cal·ly** \-k(ə-)lē\ *adverb*

---

☆ **SYNONYMS**
**Nullify, negate, annul, abrogate, invalidate** mean to deprive of effective or continued existence. NULLIFY implies counteracting completely the force, effectiveness, or value of something ⟨a penalty *nullified* the touchdown⟩. NEGATE implies the destruction or canceling out of each of two things by the other ⟨the arguments *negate* each other⟩. ANNUL suggests making ineffective or nonexistent often by legal or official action ⟨the treaty *annuls* all previous agreements⟩. ABROGATE is like ANNUL but more definitely implies a legal or official purposeful act ⟨a law to *abrogate* trading privileges⟩. INVALIDATE implies making something powerless or unacceptable by declaration of its logical or moral or legal unsoundness ⟨the court *invalidated* the statute⟩.

---

☐ **USAGE**
**number** There is a rule of thumb well-known in the newspaper business that *a number* takes a plural verb and *the number* a singular verb. Our files show that this rule is generally observed, even outside the newspaper business ⟨a *number* of celebrated modern manuscripts are available in published form —*New Yorker*⟩ ⟨the total *number* of emigrés is now estimated rather elastically —Barbara Tuchman⟩. When an adjective like *growing* or *increasing* is added, however, *a number* often takes a singular verb ⟨an increasing *number* of Ministers now believes the Government could be forced to go to the country —Ian Aitken⟩. We find some examples ⟨a large *number* of men was visible —Tom Clancy⟩ where the plural idea is belied by a singular verb; perhaps such instances are the result of uncritical copyediting. In this case, the rule of thumb is a good rule to follow.

---

\ə\ abut \ᵊ\ kitten \ər\ further \a\ ash \ā\ ace
\ä\ mop, mar \aù\ out \ch\ chin \e\ bet \ē\ easy
\g\ go \i\ hit \ī\ ice \j\ job \ŋ\ sing \ō\ go
\ȯ\ law \ȯi\ boy \th\ thin \t͟h\ the \ü\ loot \ù\ foot
\y\ yet \zh\ vision *see also* Guide to Pronunciation

# TABLE OF NUMBERS

## CARDINAL NUMBERS[1]

| NAME[2] | SYMBOL | |
| --- | --- | --- |
| | Hindu-Arabic | Roman[3] |
| zero or naught or cipher | 0 | |
| one | 1 | I |
| two | 2 | II |
| three | 3 | III |
| four | 4 | IV |
| five | 5 | V |
| six | 6 | VI |
| seven | 7 | VII |
| eight | 8 | VIII |
| nine | 9 | IX |
| ten | 10 | X |
| eleven | 11 | XI |
| twelve | 12 | XII |
| thirteen | 13 | XIII |
| fourteen | 14 | XIV |
| fifteen | 15 | XV |
| sixteen | 16 | XVI |
| seventeen | 17 | XVII |
| eighteen | 18 | XVIII |
| nineteen | 19 | XIX |
| twenty | 20 | XX |
| twenty-one | 21 | XXI |
| twenty-two | 22 | XXII |
| twenty-three | 23 | XXIII |
| twenty-four | 24 | XXIV |
| twenty-five | 25 | XXV |
| twenty-six | 26 | XXVI |
| twenty-seven | 27 | XXVII |
| twenty-eight | 28 | XXVIII |
| twenty-nine | 29 | XXIX |
| thirty | 30 | XXX |
| thirty-one | 31 | XXXI |
| thirty-two etc | 32 | XXXII |
| forty | 40 | XL |
| forty-one etc | 41 | XLI |
| fifty | 50 | L |
| sixty | 60 | LX |
| seventy | 70 | LXX |
| eighty | 80 | LXXX |
| ninety | 90 | XC |
| one hundred | 100 | C |
| on hundred and one or one hundred one | 101 | CI |
| one hundred and two etc | 102 | CII |
| two hundred | 200 | CC |
| three hundred | 300 | CCC |
| four hundred | 400 | CD |
| five hundred | 500 | D |
| six hundred | 600 | DC |
| seven hundred | 700 | DCC |
| eight hundred | 800 | DCCC |
| nine hundred | 900 | CM |
| one thousand or ten hundred etc | 1,000 | M |
| two thousand etc | 2,000 | MM |
| five thousand | 5,000 | V̄ |
| ten thousand | 10,000 | X̄ |
| one hundred thousand | 100,000 | C̄ |
| one million | 1,000,000 | M̄ |

## ORDINAL NUMBERS[4]

| NAME[5] | SYMBOL[6] |
| --- | --- |
| first | 1st |
| second | 2d or 2nd |
| third | 3d or 3rd |
| fourth | 4th |
| fifth | 5th |
| sixth | 6th |
| seventh | 7th |
| eighth | 8th |
| ninth | 9th |
| tenth | 10th |
| eleventh | 11th |
| twelfth | 12th |
| thirteenth | 13th |
| fourteenth | 14th |
| fifteenth | 15th |
| sixteenth | 16th |
| seventeenth | 17th |
| eighteenth | 18th |
| nineteenth | 19th |
| twentieth | 20th |
| twenty-first | 21st |
| twenty-second | 22d or 22nd |
| twenty-third | 23d or 23rd |
| twenty-fourth | 24th |
| twenty-fifth | 25th |
| twenty-sixth | 26th |
| twenty-seventh | 27th |
| twenty-eighth | 28th |
| twenty-ninth | 29th |
| thirtieth | 30th |
| thirty-first | 31st |
| thirty-second etc | 32d or 32nd |
| fortieth | 40th |
| forty-first | 41st |
| forty-second etc | 42d or 42nd |
| fiftieth | 50th |
| sixtieth | 60th |
| seventieth | 70th |
| eightieth | 80th |
| ninetieth | 90th |
| hundredth or one hundredth | 100th |
| hundred and first or one hundred first | 101st |
| hundred and seconds etc | 102d or 102nd |
| two hundredth | 200th |
| three hundredth | 300th |
| four hundredth | 400th |
| five hundredth | 500th |
| six hundredth | 600th |
| seven hundredth | 700th |
| eight hundredth | 800th |
| nine hundredth | 900th |
| thousandth or one thousandth | 1,000th |
| two thousandth etc | 2,000th |
| ten thousandth | 10,000th |
| hundred thousandth or one hundred thousandth | 100,000th |
| millionth or one millionth | 1,000,000th |

[1]The cardinal numbers are used in simple counting or in answer to "how many?" The words for these numbers may be used as nouns (he counted to *twelve*), as pronouns (*twelve* were found), or as adjectives (*twelve* boys).

[2]In formal contexts the numbers one to one hundred and in less formal contexts the numbers one to nine are commonly written out, while larger numbers are given in numerals. In nearly all contexts a number occurring at the beginning of a sentence is usually written out. Except in very formal contexts numerals are invariably used for dates. Hindu-Arabic numbers from 1,000 to 9,999 are often written without commas or spaces (1000, 9999). Year numbers are always written without commas (1783).

[3]The Roman numerals are written either in capitals or in lowercase letters.

[4]The ordinal numbers are used to show the order of succession in which such items as names, objects, and periods of time are considered (the *twelfth* month; the *fourth* row of seats; the *18th* century).

[5]Each of the terms for the ordinal numbers excepting *first* and *second* is used in designating one of a number of parts into which a whole may be divided (a *fourth*; a *sixth*; a *tenth*) and as the denominator in fractions designating the number of such parts constituting a certain portion of a whole (*one fourth*; *three fifths*). When used as nouns the fractions are usually written as two words, although they are regularly hyphenated as adjectives (a *two-thirds* majority). When fractions are written in numerals, the cardinal symbols are used (¼, ⅗, ⅚).

[6]The Hindu-Arabic symbols for the cardinal numbers may be read as ordinals in certain contexts (January 1 = January first; 2 Samuel = Second Samuel). The Roman numerals are sometimes read as ordinals (Henry IV = Henry the Fourth); sometimes they are written with the ordinal suffixes (XIXth Dynasty).

## DENOMINATIONS ABOVE ONE MILLION

| NAME | VALUE IN POWERS OF TEN | NUMBER OF ZEROS[2] | NUMBER OF GROUPS OF THREE 0'S AFTER 1,000 | NAME | VALUE IN POWERS OF TEN | NUMBER OF ZEROS[2] | POWERS OF 1,000,000 |
| --- | --- | --- | --- | --- | --- | --- | --- |
| billion | $10^9$ | 9 | 2 | milliard | $10^9$ | 9 | — |
| trillion | $10^{12}$ | 12 | 3 | billion | $10^{12}$ | 12 | 2 |
| quadrillion | $10^{15}$ | 15 | 4 | trillion | $10^{18}$ | 18 | 3 |
| quintillion | $10^{18}$ | 18 | 5 | quadrillion | $10^{24}$ | 24 | 4 |
| sextillion | $10^{21}$ | 21 | 6 | quintillion | $10^{30}$ | 30 | 5 |
| septillion | $10^{24}$ | 24 | 7 | sextillion | $10^{36}$ | 36 | 6 |
| octillion | $10^{27}$ | 27 | 8 | septillion | $10^{42}$ | 42 | 7 |
| nonillion | $10^{30}$ | 30 | 9 | octillion | $10^{48}$ | 48 | 8 |
| decillion | $10^{33}$ | 33 | 10 | nonillion | $10^{54}$ | 54 | 9 |
| undecillion | $10^{36}$ | 36 | 11 | decillion | $10^{60}$ | 60 | 10 |
| duodecillion | $10^{39}$ | 39 | 12 | undecillion | $10^{66}$ | 66 | 11 |
| tredecillion | $10^{42}$ | 42 | 13 | duodecillion | $10^{72}$ | 72 | 12 |
| quattuordecillion | $10^{45}$ | 45 | 14 | tredecillion | $10^{78}$ | 78 | 13 |
| quindecillion | $10^{48}$ | 48 | 15 | quattuordecillion | $10^{84}$ | 84 | 14 |
| sexdecillion | $10^{51}$ | 51 | 16 | quindecillion | $10^{90}$ | 90 | 15 |
| septendecillion | $10^{54}$ | 54 | 17 | sexdecillion | $10^{96}$ | 96 | 16 |
| octodecillion | $10^{57}$ | 57 | 18 | septendecillion | $10^{102}$ | 102 | 17 |
| novemdecillion | $10^{60}$ | 60 | 19 | octodecillion | $10^{108}$ | 108 | 18 |
| vigintillion | $10^{63}$ | 63 | 20 | novemdecillion | $10^{114}$ | 114 | 19 |
| centillion | $10^{303}$ | 303 | 100 | vigintillion | $10^{120}$ | 120 | 20 |
| | | | | centillion | $10^{600}$ | 600 | 100 |

[1]The American system of numeration for denominations above one million was modeled on the French system but more recently the French system has been changed to correspond to the German and British systems. In the American system each of the denominations above 1,000 millions (the American *billion*) is 1,000 times the preceding one (one trillion = 1,000 billions; one quadrillion = 1,000 trillions). In the British system the first denomination above one million (the British *milliard*) is 1,000 times the preceding one, but each of the denominations above 1,000 milliards (the British *billion*) is 1,000,000 times the preceding one (one trillion = 1,000,000 billions; one quadrillion = 1,000,000 trillions).

[2]For convenience in reading large numerals, the thousands, millions, etc., are usually separated by commas (21,530; 1,155,465) or especially in technical contexts by spaces (1 155 465). Serial numbers (as a social security number) are often written with hyphens (042-24-4705).

**numerical analysis** *noun* (1946)
: the study of quantitative approximations to the solutions of mathematical problems including consideration of the errors and bounds to the errors involved

**numerical taxonomy** *noun* (1963)
: taxonomy in which many quantitatively measured characters are given equal weight in the determination of taxa and the construction of diagrams indicating systematic relationships
— **numerical taxonomic** *adjective*
— **numerical taxonomist** *noun*

**nu·mer·ol·o·gy** \ˌnü-mə-ˈrä-lə-jē, ˌnyü-\ *noun* [Latin *numerus* + English *-o-* + *-logy*] (1911)
: the study of the occult significance of numbers
— **nu·mer·o·log·i·cal** \-mə-rə-ˈlä-ji-kəl\ *adjective*
— **nu·mer·ol·o·gist** \-mə-ˈrä-lə-jist\ *noun*

**nu·me·ro uno** \ˈnü-mə-rō-ˈü-(ˌ)nō, ˈnyü-\ *noun or adjective* [Italian *numero uno* or Spanish *número uno*] (1968)
: NUMBER ONE

**nu·mer·ous** \ˈnüm-rəs, ˈnü-mə-; ˈnyüm-, ˈnyü-mə-\ *adjective* [Middle English, from Middle French *numereux*, from Latin *numerosus*, from *numerus*] (15th century)
: consisting of great numbers of units or individuals ⟨born into a *numerous* family⟩; *also*
: MANY ⟨received *numerous* complaints⟩
— **nu·mer·ous·ly** *adverb*
— **nu·mer·ous·ness** *noun*

**nu·mi·nous** \ˈnü-mə-nəs, ˈnyü-\ *adjective* [Latin *numin-, numen* numen] (1647)
**1** : SUPERNATURAL, MYSTERIOUS
**2** : filled with a sense of the presence of divinity : HOLY
**3** : appealing to the higher emotions or to the aesthetic sense : SPIRITUAL
— **nu·mi·nous·ness** \-nəs\ *noun*

**nu·mis·mat·ic** \ˌnü-məz-ˈma-tik, -məs-, ˌnyü-\ *adjective* [French *numismatique*, from Latin *nomismat-, nomisma* coin, from Greek, current coin, from *nomizein* to use, from *nomos* custom, law — more at NIMBLE] (1792)
**1** : of or relating to numismatics
**2** : of or relating to currency : MONETARY
— **nu·mis·mat·i·cal·ly** \-ti-k(ə-)lē\ *adverb*

**nu·mis·mat·ics** \-tiks\ *noun plural but singular in construction* (circa 1828)
: the study or collection of coins, tokens, and paper money and sometimes related objects (as medals)
— **nu·mis·ma·tist** \nü-ˈmiz-mə-tist, nyü-\ *noun*

**num·mu·lar** \ˈnəm-yə-lər\ *adjective* [French *nummulaire*, from Latin *nummulus*, diminutive of *nummus* coin, probably from Greek *nomimos* customary, from *nomos*] (1846)
: characterized by circular or oval lesions or drops ⟨*nummular* dermatitis⟩

**num·mu·lit·ic limestone** \ˌnəm-yə-ˈli-tik-\ *noun* [New Latin *Nummulites*, genus of foraminifers, from Latin *nummulus*] (1833)
: the most widely distributed and distinctive formation of the Eocene in Europe, Asia, and northern Africa

**num·skull** \ˈnəm-ˌskəl\ *noun* [*numb* + *skull*] (1717)
**1** : a thick or muddled head
**2** : a dull or stupid person : DUNCE

**¹nun** \ˈnən\ *noun* [Middle English, from Old English *nunne*, from Late Latin *nonna*] (before 12th century)
: a woman belonging to a religious order; *especially* : one under solemn vows of poverty, chastity, and obedience
— **nun·like** \-ˌlīk\ *adjective*

**²nun** \ˈnün\ *noun* [Hebrew *nūn*] (circa 1823)
: the 14th letter of the Hebrew alphabet — see ALPHABET table

**nun·a·tak** \ˈnə-nə-ˌtak\ *noun* [Inuit (Greenland) *nunataq*] (1877)
: a hill or mountain completely surrounded by glacial ice

**Nunc Di·mit·tis** \ˌnəŋk-də-ˈmi-təs, ˌnùŋk-\ *noun* [Latin, now lettest thou depart; from the first words of the canticle] (1552)
: the prayer of Simeon in Luke 2:29–32 used as a canticle

**nun·cha·ku** \ˈnən-ˌchək, ˌnən-ˈchä-kü\ *noun* [Japanese dialect (Okinawa)] (1970)
: a weapon that consists of two hardwood sticks joined at their ends by a short length of rawhide, cord, or chain

**nun·ci·a·ture** \ˈnən(t)-sē-ə-ˌchùr, ˈnùn(t)-, -chər, -ˌtyùr, -ˌtùr\ *noun* [Italian *nunciatura*, from *nuncio*] (1652)
**1** : a papal diplomatic mission headed by a nuncio
**2** : the office or period of office of a nuncio

**nun·cio** \ˈnən(t)-sē-ˌō, ˈnùn(t)-\ *noun, plural* **-ci·os** [Italian, from Latin *nuntius* messenger, message] (1528)
: a papal legate of the highest rank permanently accredited to a civil government

**nun·cle** \ˈnəŋ-kəl\ *noun* [by alteration (from misdivision of *an uncle*)] (circa 1589), *chiefly dialect* : UNCLE

**nun·cu·pa·tive** \ˈnən-kyù-ˌpā-tiv, ˈnəŋ-; ˌnən-ˈkyü-pə-\ *adjective* [Medieval Latin *nuncupativus*, from Late Latin, so-called, from Latin *nuncupatus*, past participle of *nuncupare* to name, probably ultimately from *nomen* name + *capere* to take — more at NAME, HEAVE] (1546)
: not written : ORAL ⟨a *nuncupative* will⟩

**nun·nery** \ˈnən-rē, ˈnə-nə-\ *noun, plural* **-ner·ies** (14th century)
: a convent of nuns

**Nu·pe** \ˈnü-(ˌ)pā\ *noun, plural* **Nupe** *or* **Nupes** (1883)
**1** : the language of the Nupe people
**2** : a member of a people of west central Nigeria

**¹nup·tial** \ˈnəp-shəl, -chəl, ÷-shə-wəl, ÷-chə-wəl\ *adjective* [Latin *nuptialis*, from *nuptiae*, plural, wedding, from *nubere* to marry; perhaps akin to Greek *nymphē* bride, nymph] (15th century)
**1** : of or relating to marriage or the marriage ceremony
**2** : characteristic of or occurring in the breeding season ⟨*nuptial* flight⟩

**²nuptial** *noun* (circa 1555)
: MARRIAGE, WEDDING — usually used in plural

**nup·tial·i·ty** \ˌnəp-shē-ˈa-lə-tē, -chē-\ *noun, plural* **-ties** (1899)
: the marriage rate

**Nur·i·sta·ni** \ˌnùr-ə-ˈstä-nē, ˌnyùr-\ *noun* [*Nuristan*, Afghanistan] (1957)
: KAFIRI

**¹nurse** \ˈnərs\ *noun* [Middle English, from Old French *nurice*, from Late Latin *nutricia*, from Latin, feminine of *nutricius* nourishing — more at NUTRITIOUS] (13th century)
**1 a** : a woman who suckles an infant not her own : WET NURSE **b** : a woman who takes care of a young child : DRY NURSE
**2** : one that looks after, fosters, or advises
**3** : a person who is skilled or trained in caring for the sick or infirm especially under the supervision of a physician
**4 a** : a member of an insect society that belongs to the worker caste and cares for the young **b** : a female mammal used to suckle the young of another

**²nurse** *verb* **nursed; nurs·ing** [Middle English *nurshen* to suckle, nourish, contraction of *nurishen*] (14th century)
*transitive verb*
**1 a** : to nourish at the breast : SUCKLE **b** : to take nourishment from the breast of
**2** : REAR, EDUCATE
**3 a** : to promote the development or progress of **b** : to manage with care or economy ⟨*nursed* the business through hard times⟩ **c** : to take charge of and watch over
**4 a** : to care for and wait on (as a sick person) **b** : to attempt to cure by care and treatment
**5** : to hold in one's memory or consideration ⟨*nurse* a grievance⟩
**6 a** : to use, handle, or operate carefully so as to conserve energy or avoid injury or pain ⟨*nurse* a sprained ankle⟩ **b** : to use sparingly **c** : to consume slowly or over a long period ⟨*nurse* a cup of coffee⟩
*intransitive verb*
**1 a** : to feed an offspring from the breast **b** : to feed at the breast : SUCK
**2** : to act or serve as a nurse
— **nurs·er** *noun*

**nurse-maid** \ˈnərs-ˌmād\ *noun* (1657)
: a girl or woman who is regularly employed to look after children

**nurse–mid·wife** \-ˈmid-ˌwīf\ *noun* (1952)
: a registered nurse with additional training as a midwife who delivers infants and provides antepartum and postpartum care
— **nurse–mid·wife·ry** \-ˌmid-ˈwi-f(ə-)rē, -ˈwī-; -ˈmid-ˌwī-\ *noun*

**nurse–prac·ti·tion·er** \-prak-ˈti-sh(ə-)nər\ *noun* (1969)
: a registered nurse who is qualified through advanced training to assume some of the duties and responsibilities formerly assumed only by a physician

**nurs·ery** \ˈnərs-rē, ˈnər-sə-\ *noun, plural* **-er·ies** (14th century)
**1** *obsolete* : attentive care : FOSTERAGE
**2 a** : a child's bedroom **b** : a place where children are temporarily cared for in their parents' absence **c** : DAY NURSERY
**3 a** : something that fosters, develops, or promotes **b** : a place in which persons are trained or educated
**4** : an area where plants are grown for transplanting, for use as stocks for budding and grafting, or for sale
**5** : a place where young animals grow or are cared for

**nurs·ery·man** \-mən\ *noun* (1672)
: one whose occupation is the cultivation of plants (as trees and shrubs) especially for sale

**nursery rhyme** *noun* (1832)
: a short rhyme for children that often tells a story

**nursery school** *noun* (1835)
: a school for children usually under five years

**nurse's aide** *noun* (1943)
: a worker who assists trained nurses in a hospital by performing unspecialized services (as giving baths)

**nurse shark** *noun* [alteration of Middle English *nusse*] (1851)
: any of various sharks of a widely distributed family (Orectolobidae); *especially* : a shark (*Ginglymostoma cirratum*) of the warmer parts of the Atlantic Ocean

**nurs·ing** *noun* (1860)
**1** : the profession of a nurse ⟨schools of *nursing*⟩
**2** : the duties of a nurse ⟨proper *nursing* is difficult work⟩

**nursing home** *noun* (1896)
: a privately operated establishment providing maintenance and personal or nursing care for persons (as the aged or the chronically ill) who are unable to care for themselves properly

**nurs·ling** \ˈnərs-liŋ\ *noun* (1557)
**1** : one that is solicitously cared for
**2** : a nursing child

**nur·tur·ance** \ˈnər-chə-rən(t)s\ *noun* (circa 1938)
: affectionate care and attention
— **nur·tur·ant** \-rənt\ *adjective*

---

\ə\ abut \ᵊ\ kitten \ər\ further \a\ ash \ā\ ace
\ä\ mop, mar \aù\ out \ch\ chin \e\ bet \ē\ easy
\g\ go \i\ hit \ī\ ice \j\ job \ŋ\ sing \ō\ go
\ȯ\ law \ȯi\ boy \th\ thin \t͟h\ the \ü\ loot \ù\ foot
\y\ yet \zh\ vision    *see also* Guide to Pronunciation

¹**nur·ture** \'nər-chər\ *noun* [Middle English, from Middle French *norriture*, from Late Latin *nutritura* act of nursing, from Latin *nutritus*, past participle of *nutrire* to suckle, nourish — more at NOURISH] (14th century)
**1 :** TRAINING, UPBRINGING
**2 :** something that nourishes : FOOD
**3 :** the sum of the influences modifying the expression of the genetic potentialities of an organism

²**nurture** *transitive verb* **nur·tured; nur·tur·ing** \'nərch-riŋ, 'nər-chə-\ (15th century)
**1 :** to supply with nourishment
**2 :** EDUCATE
**3 :** to further the development of : FOSTER
— **nur·tur·er** \'nər-chər-ər\ *noun*

¹**nut** \'nət\ *noun* [Middle English *nute*, *note*, from Old English *hnutu*; akin to Old High German *nuz* nut and perhaps to Latin *nux* nut] (before 12th century)
**1 a** (1) **:** a hard-shelled dry fruit or seed with a separable rind or shell and interior kernel (2) **:** the kernel of a nut **b :** a dry indehiscent one-seeded fruit with a woody pericarp
**2 a :** a hard problem or undertaking **b :** CORE, HEART
**3 :** a perforated block usually of metal that has an internal screw thread and is used on a bolt or screw for tightening or holding something
**4 :** the ridge in a stringed instrument (as a violin) over which the strings pass on the upper end of the fingerboard
**5 :** a small lump (as of butter)
**6 a :** a foolish, eccentric, or crazy person **b :** ENTHUSIAST ⟨a movie *nut*⟩
**7** *plural* **:** NONSENSE — often used interjectionally
**8** *slang* **:** a person's head
**9 :** TESTIS — usually considered vulgar
**10 :** the amount of money that must be earned in order to break even
**11 :** EN 1
— **nut·like** \-,līk\ *adjective*

²**nut** *intransitive verb* **nut·ted; nut·ting** (1604)
**:** to gather or seek nuts

**nu·tate** \'nü-,tāt, 'nyü-\ *intransitive verb* **nu·tat·ed; nu·tat·ing** (1880)
**:** to exhibit or undergo nutation

**nu·ta·tion** \nü-'tā-shən, nyü-\ *noun* [Latin *nutation-*, *nutatio*, from *nutare* to nod, rock — more at NUMEN] (1612)
**1** *archaic* **:** the act of nodding the head
**2 :** oscillatory movement of the axis of a rotating body (as the earth) **:** WOBBLE
**3 :** a spontaneous usually spiral movement of a growing plant part
— **nu·ta·tion·al** \-shnəl, -shə-n°l\ *adjective*

**nut–brown** \'nət-'braùn\ *adjective* (14th century)
**:** of the color of a brown nut

**nut·case** \-,kās\ *noun* (1959)
**:** NUT 6a

**nut·crack·er** \-,kra-kər\ *noun* (circa 1548)
**:** an implement for cracking nuts

**nut·gall** \-,gól\ *noun* (15th century)
**:** a gall that resembles a nut; *especially* **:** a gall produced on oak

**nut grass** *noun* (1775)
**:** a perennial sedge (*Cyperus rotundus*) of wide distribution that has slender rootstocks bearing small edible tubers resembling nuts; *also* **:** a related sedge (*C. esculentus*)

**nut·hatch** \'nət-,hach\ *noun* [Middle English *notehache*, from *note* nut + *-hache* to*haccian* to hack — more at HACK] (14th century)
**:** any of various small tree-climbing chiefly insectivorous birds (family Sittidae and

nuthatch

especially genus *Sitta*) that have a compact body, a narrow bill, a short tail, and sometimes a black cap

**nut·house** \'nət-,haùs\ *noun* (1900)
*slang* **:** an insane asylum

**nut·let** \'nət-lət\ *noun* (1856)
**1 a :** a small nut **b :** a small fruit similar to a nut
**2 :** the stone of a drupelet

**nut·meg** \'nət-,meg, -,māg\ *noun* [Middle English *notemigge*, *notemuge*, ultimately from Old Provençal *noz muscada*, from *noz* nut (from Latin *nuc-*, *nux*) + *muscada*, feminine of *muscat* musky — more at MUSCAT] (15th century)
**:** an aromatic seed that is used as a spice and is produced by an evergreen tree (*Myristica fragrans* of the family Myristicaceae, the nutmeg family) native to the Moluccas; *also* **:** a tree yielding nutmeg

**nut·pick** \'nət-,pik\ *noun* (circa 1889)
**:** a small sharp-pointed implement for extracting the kernels from nuts

**nu·tria** \'nü-trē-ə, 'nyü-\ *noun* [American Spanish, from Spanish, otter, modification of Latin *lutra*; probably akin to Old English *oter* otter] (1820)
**1 :** the durable usually light brown fur of a nutria
**2 :** a large South American semiaquatic rodent (*Myocastor coypus*) with webbed hind feet that has been introduced into parts of Europe, Asia, and North America

¹**nu·tri·ent** \'nü-trē-ənt, 'nyü-\ *adjective* [Latin *nutrient-*, *nutriens*, present participle of *nutrire* to nourish — more at NOURISH] (1650)
**:** furnishing nourishment

²**nutrient** *noun* (circa 1828)
**:** a nutritive substance or ingredient

**nu·tri·ment** \'nü-trə-mənt, 'nyü-\ *noun* [Middle English, from Latin *nutrimentum*, from *nutrire*] (15th century)
**:** something that nourishes or promotes growth and repairs the natural wastage of organic life

**nu·tri·tion** \nù-'tri-shən, nyù-\ *noun* [Middle English *nutricioun*, from Middle French *nutrition*, from Late Latin *nutrition-*, *nutritio*, from Latin *nutrire*] (15th century)
**:** the act or process of nourishing or being nourished; *specifically* **:** the sum of the processes by which an animal or plant takes in and utilizes food substances
— **nu·tri·tion·al** \-'trish-nəl, -'tri-shə-n°l\ *adjective*
— **nu·tri·tion·al·ly** *adverb*

**nu·tri·tion·ist** \-'tri-sh(ə-)nist\ *noun* (1926)
**:** a specialist in the study of nutrition

**nu·tri·tious** \nù-'tri-shəs, nyü-\ *adjective* [Latin *nutricius*, from *nutric-*, *nutrix* nurse, from *nutrire* to nourish — more at NOURISH] (1665)
**:** NOURISHING
— **nu·tri·tious·ly** *adverb*
— **nu·tri·tious·ness** *noun*

**nu·tri·tive** \'nü-trə-tiv, 'nyü-\ *adjective* (14th century)
**1 :** of or relating to nutrition
**2 :** NOURISHING
— **nu·tri·tive·ly** *adverb*

**nutritive ratio** *noun* (1897)
**:** the ratio of digestible protein to other nutrients in a foodstuff or ration

**nuts** \'nəts\ *adjective* (1785)
**1 :** ENTHUSIASTIC, KEEN ⟨everyone seems *nuts* about it —Lois Long⟩
**2 :** INSANE, CRAZY ⟨said that it was a novel and all the people who said otherwise were *nuts* —Flannery O'Connor⟩ ◆

**nuts and bolts** *noun* (1967)
**1 :** the working parts or elements
**2 :** the practical workings of a machine or enterprise as opposed to theoretical considerations or speculative possibilities
— **nuts–and–bolts** *adjective*

**nut·sedge** \'nət-,sej\ *noun* (circa 1909)
**:** NUT GRASS

**nut·shell** \'nət-,shel\ *noun* (13th century)
**1 :** the hard external covering in which the kernel of a nut is enclosed
**2 :** something of small size, amount, or scope
— **in a nutshell :** in a very brief statement

**nut·ter** \'nə-tər\ *noun* (1958)
*slang British* **:** NUT 6a

**nut·ty** \'nə-tē\ *adjective* **nut·ti·er; -est** (15th century)
**1 :** having or producing nuts
**2 :** having a flavor like that of nuts
**3 :** ECCENTRIC, SILLY; *also* **:** mentally unbalanced
— **nut·ti·ly** \-tə-lē\ *adverb*
— **nut·ti·ness** *noun*

**nux vom·i·ca** \'nəks-'vä-mi-kə\ *noun*, *plural* **nux vomica** [New Latin, literally, emetic nut] (14th century)
**1 :** the poisonous seed of an Asian tree (*Strychnos nux-vomica* of the family Loganiaceae) that contains several alkaloids and especially strychnine and brucine; *also* **:** the tree yielding nux vomica
**2 :** a drug containing nux vomica

**nuz·zle** \'nə-zəl\ *verb* **nuz·zled; nuz·zling** \'nəz-liŋ, 'nə-zə-\ [Middle English *noselen* to bring the nose toward the ground, from *nose*] (1530)
*intransitive verb*
**1 :** to work with or as if with the nose; *especially* **:** to root, rub, or snuff something
**2 :** to lie close or snug **:** NESTLE
*transitive verb*
**1 :** to root, rub, or touch with or as if with the nose **:** NUDGE
**2 :** to rub or push gently (as one's face) against something ⟨*nuzzled* her face into the pillow⟩

**ny·a·la** \nē-'ä-lə\ *noun*, *plural* **nyalas** *or* **nyala** [of Bantu origin; akin to Venda *dzinyálà* nyala buck] (1894)
**:** an antelope (*Tragelaphus angasi*) of southeastern Africa with vertical white stripes on the sides of the body and with shaggy black hair along the male underside; *also* **:** a related antelope (*T. buxtoni*) of Ethiopia

**nyc·ta·lo·pia** \,nik-tə-'lō-pē-ə\ *noun* [New Latin, from

nyala

Latin *nyctalops* suffering from night blindness, from Greek *nyktalops*, from *nykt-, nyx* night + *alaos* blind + *ōp-, ōps* eye — more at NIGHT, EYE] (1684)
**:** NIGHT BLINDNESS

**ny·lon** \'nī-ˌlän\ *noun* [coined word] (1938)
**1 :** any of numerous strong tough elastic synthetic polyamide materials that are fashioned into fibers, filaments, bristles, or sheets and used especially in textiles and plastics
**2** *plural* **:** stockings made of nylon

**nymph** \'nim(p)f\ *noun* [Middle English *nimphe*, from Middle French, from Latin *nympha* bride, nymph, from Greek *nymphē* — more at NUPTIAL] (14th century)
**1 :** any of the minor divinities of nature in classical mythology represented as beautiful maidens dwelling in the mountains, forests, trees, and waters
**2 :** GIRL
**3 :** any of various immature insects; *especially* **:** a larva of an insect (as a grasshopper, true bug, or mayfly) with incomplete metamorphosis that differs from the imago especially in size and in its incompletely developed wings and genitalia — compare NAIAD 2
**— nymph·al** \'nim(p)-fəl\ *adjective*

**nym·pha·lid** \nim-'fa-ləd, 'nim-fə-ləd\ *noun* [New Latin *Nymphalidae*, ultimately from Latin *nympha* nymph] (1897)
**:** any of a family (Nymphalidae) of butterflies (as a mourning cloak or fritillary) with the first pair of legs reduced in size in both sexes and useless for walking
**— nymphalid** *adjective*

**nym·phet** *also* **nym·phette** \nim-'fet, 'nim(p)-fət\ *noun* (1955)
**:** a sexually precocious girl barely in her teens

**nym·pho** \'nim(p)-(ˌ)fō\ *noun, plural* **nymphos** [short for *nymphomaniac*] (circa 1910)
**:** a person affected by nymphomania **:** NYMPHOMANIAC

**nym·pho·lep·sy** \'nim(p)-fə-ˌlep-sē\ *noun* [*nympholept*, from Greek *nympholēptos* frenzied, literally, caught by nymphs, from *nymphē* + *lambanein* to seize — more at LATCH] (1775)
**1 :** a demoniac enthusiasm held by the ancients to seize one bewitched by a nymph
**2 :** a frenzy of emotion
**— nym·pho·lept** \-ˌlept\ *noun*
**— nym·pho·lep·tic** \ˌnim(p)-fə-'lep-tik\ *adjective*

**nym·pho·ma·nia** \ˌnim(p)-fə-'mā-nē-ə, -nyə\ *noun* [New Latin, from *nymphae* inner lips of the vulva (from Latin, plural of *nympha*) + Late Latin *mania* mania] (1775)
**:** excessive sexual desire by a female
**— nym·pho·ma·ni·ac** \-nē-ˌak\ *noun or adjective*
**— nym·pho·ma·ni·a·cal** \-mə-'nī-ə-kəl\ *adjective*

**Ny·norsk** \nü-'nȯrsk, nyü-, nœ-\ *noun* [Norwegian, literally, new Norwegian] (1931)
**:** a literary form of Norwegian based on the spoken dialects of Norway — compare BOKMÅL

**nys·tag·mus** \nis-'tag-məs\ *noun* [New Latin, from Greek *nystagmos* drowsiness, from *nystazein* to doze; probably akin to Lithuanian *snusti* to doze] (1822)
**:** a rapid involuntary oscillation of the eyeballs (as from dizziness)
**— nys·tag·mic** \-mik\ *adjective*

**nys·ta·tin** \'nis-tə-tən\ *noun* [*New York State* (where it was developed) + ¹-*in*] (1952)
**:** an antibiotic that is derived from a soil actinomycete (*Streptomyces noursei*) and is used especially in the treatment of candidiasis

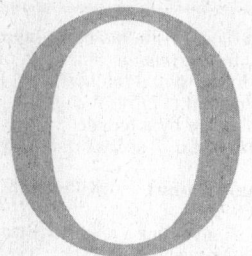

**O** *is the fifteenth letter of the English alphabet. It comes through Latin, via Etruscan, from Greek. The Greeks in turn took the letter from Phoenician, where it represented a consonant sound called 'ayin, sounding like an* h *pronounced harshly and with the vocal cords vibrating (rather like the sound one might make, for example, while being throttled). The Greeks, not having this consonant sound, assigned the letter-symbol to the short and long* o *vowel sounds. They later reassigned these two sounds to the separate letter-symbols* omicron *and* omega, *but the Romans continued to use one symbol for both.* O *stands for various sounds in English, the chief of which are its long sound, as in* bone, *its short sound, as in* nod, *and the sounds heard in the words* orb, son, do, *and* wolf. *With other vowels and with itself it forms several digraphs (*œ, œ, oi, oo, ou, *and* oy), *some representing simple vowels and others representing diphthongs. Small* o *developed by a simple reduction in the size of the capital form.*

**o** \'ō\ *noun, plural* **o's** *or* **os** \'ōz\ *often capitalized, often attributive* (before 12th century)
**1 a :** the 15th letter of the English alphabet **b :** a graphic representation of this letter **c :** a speech counterpart of orthographic *o*
**2 :** a graphic device for reproducing the letter *o*
**3 :** one designated *o* especially as the 15th in order or class
**4 :** something shaped like the letter O; *especially* **:** ZERO
**O** \'ō\ *variant of* OH
**o-** *or* **oo-** *combining form* [Greek *ōi-, ōio-,* from *ōion* — more at EGG]
**:** egg ⟨*oo*logy⟩; *specifically* **:** ovum ⟨*oo*gonium⟩
**-o-** [Middle English, from Old French, from Latin, from Greek, thematic vowel of many nouns and adjectives in combination]
— used as a connective vowel originally to join word elements of Greek origin and now also to join word elements of Latin or other origin ⟨speed*o*meter⟩ ⟨elast*o*mer⟩
**¹-o** *noun suffix* [perhaps from ¹*oh*]
**:** one that is, has the qualities of, or is associated with ⟨buck*o*⟩
**²-o** *interjection suffix* [probably from ¹*oh*]
— in interjections formed from other parts of speech ⟨cheeri*o*⟩ ⟨right*o*⟩
**o'** *also* **o** \ə, ō\ *preposition* [Middle English *o, o-,* contraction of *on* & *of*] (13th century)
**1** *chiefly dialect* **:** ON
**2 :** OF ⟨one *o*'clock⟩
**oaf** \'ōf\ *noun, plural* **oafs** [of Scandinavian origin; akin to Old Norse *alfr* elf — more at ELF] (1625)
**1 :** a stupid person **:** BOOB
**2 :** a big clumsy slow-witted person
— **oaf·ish** \'ō-fish\ *adjective*
— **oaf·ish·ly** *adverb*
— **oaf·ish·ness** *noun*
**oak** \'ōk\ *noun, plural* **oaks** *or* **oak** *often attributive* [Middle English *ook,* from Old English *āc;* akin to Old High German *eih* oak and perhaps to Greek *aigilōps,* a kind of oak] (before 12th century)
**1 a :** any of a genus (*Quercus*) of trees or shrubs of the beech family that produce acorns; *also* **:** any of various plants related to or resembling the oaks **b :** the tough hard durable wood of an oak tree
**2 :** the leaves of an oak used as decoration
— **oak·en** \'ō-kən\ *adjective*
**oak apple** *noun* (15th century)
**:** a large round gall produced on oak leaves and twigs by a gall wasp (especially *Amphibolips concluenta* or *Andricus quercuscalifornicus*)
**oak-leaf cluster** *noun* (1918)

**:** a bronze or silver cluster of oak leaves and acorns added to various military decorations to signify a second or subsequent award of the basic decoration
**oak·moss** \'ōk-,mós\ *noun* (1921)
**:** any of several lichens (as *Evernia prunastri*) that grow on oak trees and yield a resin used in perfumery
**oa·kum** \'ō-kəm\ *noun* [Middle English *okum,* from Old English *ācumba* tow, from *ā-* (separative & perfective prefix) + *-cumba* (akin to Old English *camb* comb) — more at ABIDE] (15th century)
**:** loosely twisted hemp or jute fiber impregnated with tar or a tar derivative and used in caulking seams and packing joints
**oak wilt** *noun* (1942)
**:** a destructive disease of oak trees that is caused by a fungus (*Ceratocystis fagacearum*) and is characterized by wilting, discoloration, and defoliation
**¹oar** \'ōr, 'ór\ *noun* [Middle English *oor,* from Old English *ār;* akin to Old Norse *ār* oar] (before 12th century)
**1 :** a long pole with a broad blade at one end used for propelling or steering a boat
**2 :** OARSMAN
— **oared** \'ōrd, 'órd\ *adjective*
**²oar** (1610)
*transitive verb*
**:** to propel with or as if with oars **:** ROW
*intransitive verb*
**:** to progress by or as if by using oars
**oar·fish** \'ōr-,fish, 'ór-\ *noun* (1860)
**:** any of several sea fishes (genus *Regalecus* and especially *R. glesne*) with narrow soft bodies from 20 to 30 feet (6 to 9 meters) long, a red dorsal fin running the entire length of the body, and red-tipped anterior rays rising above the head
**oar·lock** \-,läk\ *noun* (before 12th century)
**:** a usually U-shaped device for holding an oar in place
**oars·man** \'ōrz-mən, 'órz-\ *noun* (1701)
**:** one who rows especially in a racing crew
— **oars·man·ship** \-,ship\ *noun*
**oars·wom·an** \-,wù-mən\ *noun* (1882)
**:** a woman who rows especially in a racing crew
**oa·sis** \ō-'ā-səs\ *noun, plural* **oa·ses** \-,sēz\ [Late Latin, from Greek] (1613)
**1 :** a fertile or green area in an arid region (as a desert)
**2 :** something that provides refuge, relief, or pleasant contrast
**oast** \'ōst\ *noun* [Middle English *ost,* from Old English *āst;* akin to Middle Dutch *eest* kiln, Latin *aestus* heat, *aestas* summer — more at EDIFY] (before 12th century)

**:** a usually conical kiln used for drying hops, malt, or tobacco — called also *oast·house* \-,haùs\
**oat** \'ōt\ *noun, often attributive* [Middle English *ote,* from Old English *āte*] (before 12th century)
**1 a :** any of several grasses (genus *Avena*); *especially* **:** a widely cultivated cereal grass (*A. sativa*) **b :** a crop or plot of the oat; *also* **:** oat seed — usually used in plural but singular or plural in construction
**2** *archaic* **:** a reed instrument made of an oat straw
**oat·cake** \'ōt-,kāk\ *noun* (14th century)
**:** a thin flat oatmeal cake
**oat-cell** \-,sel\ *adjective* (1903)
**:** of, relating to, or being a highly malignant form of cancer especially of the lungs that is characterized by rapid proliferation of small anaplastic cells ⟨*oat-cell* carcinomas⟩

oat 1a

**oat·en** \'ōt-ᵊn\ *adjective* (14th century)
**:** of or relating to oats, oat straw, or oatmeal
**oat·er** \'ō-tər\ *noun* (1946)
**:** WESTERN 2
**oat grass** *noun* (1578)
**:** WILD OAT 1a; *broadly* **:** one of several grasses resembling the oat
**oath** \'ōth\ *noun, plural* **oaths** \'ōthz, 'ōths\ [Middle English *ooth,* from Old English *āth;* akin to Old High German *eid* oath, Middle Irish *oeth*] (before 12th century)
**1 a** (1) **:** a solemn usually formal calling upon God or a god to witness to the truth of what one says or to witness that one sincerely intends to do what one says (2) **:** a solemn attestation of the truth or inviolability of one's words **b :** something (as a promise) corroborated by an oath
**2 :** an irreverent or careless use of a sacred name; *broadly* **:** SWEARWORD
**oat·meal** \'ōt-,mēl, ōt-'mē(ə)l\ *noun* (14th century)
**1 a :** meal made from oats **b :** rolled oats
**2 :** porridge made from ground or rolled oats
**ob-** *prefix* [New Latin, from Latin, in the way, against, toward, from *ob* in the way of, on account of; akin to Old Church Slavonic *o, ob* on, around]
**:** inversely ⟨*ob*ovate⟩
**Oba·di·ah** \,ō-bə-'dī-ə\ *noun* [Hebrew *'Ōbhadhyāh*]
**1 :** a Hebrew prophet
**2 :** a prophetic book of canonical Jewish and Christian Scripture — see BIBLE table
**¹ob·li·ga·to** \,ä-blə-'gä-(,)tō\ *adjective* [Italian, obligatory, from past participle of *obbligare* to oblige, from Latin *obligare* — more at OBLIGE] (1794)
**:** not to be omitted **:** OBLIGATORY — used as a direction in music; compare AD LIBITUM
**²obbligato** *noun, plural* **-tos** *also* **-ti** \-'gä-tē\ (1845)
**1 :** an elaborate especially melodic part accompanying a solo or principal melody and usually played by a single instrument ⟨a song with violin *obbligato*⟩
**2 :** ACCOMPANIMENT 2b; *especially* **:** an attendant background sound
**ob·cor·date** \,äb-'kòr-,dāt\ *adjective* (1775)
**:** heart-shaped with the notch apical ⟨*obcordate* leaf⟩
**ob·du·ra·cy** \'äb-də-rə-sē, -dyə-; äb-'dùr-ə-, əb-, -'dyùr-\ *noun, plural* **-cies** (1597)
**:** the quality or state of being obdurate
**ob·du·rate** \'äb-də-rət, -dyə-; äb-'dùr-ət, əb-, -'dyùr-\ *adjective* [Middle English, from Latin *obduratus,* past participle of *obdurare* to harden, from *ob-* against + *durus* hard — more at DURING] (15th century)
**1 a :** stubbornly persistent in wrongdoing **b :** hardened in feelings

**2 :** resistant to persuasion or softening influences
**synonym** see INFLEXIBLE
— **ob·du·rate·ly** adverb
— **ob·du·rate·ness** noun
**obe·ah** \'ō-bē-ə\ also **obi** \'ō-bē\ noun, often capitalized [of African origin; akin to Twi *ɔ-bayifó* sorcerer, Ibo *díbìà* folk healer] (1760) : a system of belief among blacks chiefly of the British West Indies, the Guianas, and the southeastern U.S. that is characterized by the use of sorcery and magic ritual
**obe·di·ence** \ō-'bē-dē-ən(t)s, ə-\ noun (13th century)
**1 a :** an act or instance of obeying **b :** the quality or state of being obedient
**2 :** a sphere of jurisdiction; *especially* **:** an ecclesiastical or sometimes secular dominion
**obe·di·ent** \-ənt\ adjective [Middle English, from Old French, from Latin *oboedient-, oboediens,* from present participle of *oboedire* to obey] (13th century)
: submissive to the restraint or command of authority **:** willing to obey ☆
— **obe·di·ent·ly** adverb
**obei·sance** \ō-'bē-s°n(t)s, ə-, -'bā-\ noun [Middle English *obeisaunce* obedience, obeisance, from Middle French *obeissance,* from *obeissant,* present participle of *obeir* to obey] (14th century)
**1 :** a movement of the body made in token of respect or submission **:** BOW
**2 :** DEFERENCE, HOMAGE
— **obei·sant** \-s°nt\ adjective
— **obei·sant·ly** adverb
**obe·lia** \ō-'bēl-yə\ noun [New Latin] (1868) : any of a genus (*Obelia*) of small colonial marine hydroids with colonies branched like trees
**obe·lisk** \'ä-bə-,lisk also 'ō-\ noun [Middle French *obelisque,* from Latin *obeliscus,* from Greek *obeliskos,* from diminutive of *obelos*] (1569)
**1 :** an upright 4-sided usually monolithic pillar that gradually tapers as it rises and terminates in a pyramid
**2 a :** OBELUS **b :** DAGGER 2b
**obe·lize** \-,līz\ transitive verb **-lized; -liz·ing** (circa 1656) : to designate or annotate with an obelus
**obe·lus** \-ləs\ noun, plural **ob·e·li** \-,lī, -,lē\ [Middle English, from Late Latin, from Greek *obelos* spit, pointed pillar, obelus] (14th century)
**1 :** a symbol − or ÷ used in ancient manuscripts to mark a questionable passage
**2 :** the symbol ÷

obelisk

**Ober·on** \'ō-bə-,rän, -rən\ noun [French, from Old French *Auberon*] : the king of the fairies in medieval folklore
**obese** \ō-'bēs\ adjective [Latin *obesus,* from *ob-* against + *esus,* past participle of *edere* to eat — more at OB-, EAT] (1651) : excessively fat
**obe·si·ty** \ō-'bē-sə-tē\ noun (1611) : a condition characterized by excessive bodily fat
**obey** \ō-'bā, ə-\ verb **obeyed; obey·ing** [Middle English *obeien,* from Old French *obeir,* from Latin *oboedire,* from *ob-* toward + *-oedire* (akin to *audire* to hear) — more at OB-, AUDIBLE] (14th century)
*transitive verb*
**1 :** to follow the commands or guidance of
**2 :** to conform to or comply with ⟨*obey* an order⟩ ⟨falling objects *obey* the laws of physics⟩
*intransitive verb*
: to behave obediently
— **obey·er** noun

**ob·fus·cate** \'äb-fə-,skāt; äb-'fəs-,kāt, əb-\ transitive verb **-cat·ed; -cat·ing** [Late Latin *obfuscatus,* past participle of *obfuscare,* from Latin *ob-* in the way + *fuscus* dark brown — more at OB-, DUSK] (1577)
**1 a :** DARKEN **b :** to make obscure
**2 :** CONFUSE
— **ob·fus·ca·tion** \,äb-(,)fəs-'kā-shən\ noun
— **ob·fus·ca·to·ry** \äb-'fəs-kə-,tōr-ē, əb-, -,tȯr-\ adjective
**obi** \'ō-bē\ noun [Japanese] (1876) : a broad sash worn especially with a Japanese kimono
**Obie** \'ō-bē\ noun [*O.B.,* abbreviation for *off Broadway*] (1965) : an award presented annually by a professional organization for notable achievement in plays performed off-Broadway
**obit** \'ō-,bit, 'ō-bət, especially British 'ä-bit\ noun [Middle English, from Middle French, from Latin *obitus* death, from *obire* to go to meet, die, from *ob-* in the way + *ire* to go — more at ISSUE] (15th century) : OBITUARY
**obi·ter dic·tum** \,ō-bə-tər-'dik-təm, ,ä-\ noun, plural **obiter dic·ta** \-tə\ [Late Latin, literally, something said in passing] (1812)
**1 :** an incidental and collateral opinion that is uttered by a judge but is not binding
**2 :** an incidental remark or observation
**obit·u·ary** \ə-'bi-chə-,wer-ē, ō-, -'bi-chə-rē\ noun, plural **-ar·ies** [Medieval Latin *obituarium,* from Latin *obitus* death] (1738) : a notice of a person's death usually with a short biographical account
— **obit·u·ar·ist** \-'bi-chə-,wər-ist, -'bi-chə-rist\ noun
— **obituary** adjective
¹**ob·ject** \'äb-jikt, -(,)jekt\ noun [Middle English, from Medieval Latin *objectum,* from Latin, neuter of *objectus,* past participle of *obicere* to throw in the way, present, hinder, from *ob-* in the way + *jacere* to throw — more at OB-, JET] (14th century)
**1 a :** something material that may be perceived by the senses ⟨I see an *object* in the distance⟩ **b :** something that when viewed stirs a particular emotion (as pity) ⟨look to the tragic loading of this bed . . . the *object* poisons sight; let it be hid —Shakespeare⟩
**2 :** something mental or physical toward which thought, feeling, or action is directed ⟨an *object* for study⟩ ⟨the *object* of my affection⟩ ⟨delicately carved art *objects*⟩
**3 a :** the goal or end of an effort or activity **:** PURPOSE, OBJECTIVE ⟨their *object* is to investigate the matter thoroughly⟩ **b :** a cause for attention or concern ⟨money is no *object*⟩
**4 :** a thing that forms an element of or constitutes the subject matter of an investigation or science
**5 a :** a noun or noun equivalent (as a pronoun, gerund, or clause) denoting the goal or result of the action of a verb **b :** a noun or noun equivalent in a prepositional phrase
**synonym** see INTENTION
— **ob·ject·less** \-ləs\ adjective
— **ob·ject·less·ness** noun
²**ob·ject** \əb-'jekt\ verb [Middle English, from Latin *objectus,* past participle of *obicere* to throw in the way, object] (15th century)
*transitive verb*
: to put forth in opposition or as an objection ⟨*objected* that the statement was misleading⟩
*intransitive verb*
**1 :** to oppose something firmly and usually with words or arguments
**2 :** to feel distaste for something
— **ob·jec·tor** \-'jek-tər\ noun
**object ball** \'äb-jik(t)-, -(,)jek(t)-\ noun (1856) : the ball first struck by the cue ball in pool or billiards; *also* **:** a ball hit by the cue ball
**ob·jec·ti·fy** \əb-'jek-tə-,fī\ transitive verb **-fied; -fy·ing** (circa 1837)

**1 :** to treat as an object or cause to have objective reality
**2 :** to give expression to (as an abstract notion, feeling, or ideal) in a form that can be experienced by others ⟨it is the essence of the fairy tale to *objectify* differing facets of the child's emotional experience —John Updike⟩
— **ob·jec·ti·fi·ca·tion** \-,jek-tə-fə-'kā-shən\ noun
**ob·jec·tion** \əb-'jek-shən\ noun (14th century)
**1 :** an act of objecting
**2 a :** a reason or argument presented in opposition **b :** a feeling or expression of disapproval
**ob·jec·tion·able** \-sh(ə-)nə-bəl\ adjective (1781) : UNDESIRABLE, OFFENSIVE
— **ob·jec·tion·able·ness** noun
— **ob·jec·tion·ably** \-blē\ adverb
¹**ob·jec·tive** \əb-'jek-tiv, äb-\ adjective (1620)
**1 a :** relating to or existing as an object of thought without consideration of independent existence — used chiefly in medieval philosophy **b :** of, relating to, or being an object, phenomenon, or condition in the realm of sensible experience independent of individual thought and perceptible by all observers **:** having reality independent of the mind ⟨*objective* reality⟩ ⟨our reveries . . . are significantly and repeatedly shaped by our transactions with the *objective* world —Marvin Reznikoff⟩ — compare SUBJECTIVE 3a **c** *of a symptom of disease* **:** perceptible to persons other than the affected individual — compare SUBJECTIVE 4c **d :** involving or deriving from sense perception or experience with actual objects, conditions, or phenomena ⟨*objective* awareness⟩ ⟨*objective* data⟩
**2 :** relating to, characteristic of, or constituting the case of words that follow prepositions or transitive verbs
**3 a :** expressing or dealing with facts or conditions as perceived without distortion by personal feelings, prejudices, or interpretations ⟨*objective* art⟩ ⟨an *objective* history of the war⟩ ⟨an *objective* judgment⟩ **b** *of a test* **:** limited to choices of fixed alternatives and reducing subjective factors to a minimum
**synonym** see MATERIAL, FAIR
— **ob·jec·tive·ly** adverb
— **ob·jec·tive·ness** noun
— **ob·jec·tiv·i·ty** \,äb-,jek-'ti-və-tē, əb-\ noun
²**objective** noun (1835)
**1 :** a lens or system of lenses that forms an image of an object
**2 a :** something toward which effort is directed **:** an aim, goal, or end of action **b :** a strategic position to be attained or a purpose to be achieved by a military operation
**synonym** see INTENTION

---

☆ **SYNONYMS**
**Obedient, docile, tractable, amenable** mean submissive to the will of another. OBEDIENT implies compliance with the demands or requests of one in authority ⟨*obedient* to the government⟩. DOCILE implies a predisposition to submit readily to control or guidance ⟨a *docile* child⟩. TRACTABLE suggests having a character that permits easy handling or managing ⟨*tractable* beasts of burden⟩. AMENABLE suggests a willingness to yield or to cooperate either because of a desire to be agreeable or because of a natural open-mindedness ⟨*amenable* to new ideas⟩.

---

**objective complement** *noun* (1870)
: a noun, adjective, or pronoun used in the predicate as complement to a verb and as qualifier of its direct object (as *chairman* in "we elected him chairman")

**objective correlative** *noun* (1919)
: something (as a situation or chain of events) that symbolizes or objectifies a particular emotion and that may be used in creative writing to evoke a desired emotional response in the reader

**ob·jec·tiv·ism** \əb-'jek-ti-ˌvi-zəm, äb-\ *noun* (1854)
**1** : any of various theories asserting the validity of objective phenomena over subjective experience; *especially* : REALISM 2a
**2** : an ethical theory that moral good is objectively real or that moral precepts are objectively valid
**3** : a 20th century movement in poetry growing out of imagism and putting stress on form
— **ob·jec·tiv·ist** \-vist\ *adjective or noun*
— **ob·jec·tiv·is·tic** \-ˌjek-ti-ˈvis-tik\ *adjective*

**ob·ject language** \'äb-jikt-, -(ˌ)jekt-\ *noun* (1935)
: TARGET LANGUAGE

**ob·ject lesson** \'äb-jikt-, -(ˌ)jekt-\ *noun* (1831)
: something that serves as a practical example of a principle or abstract idea

**ob·jet d'art** \ˌȯb-ˌzhä-ˈdär\ *noun, plural* **objets d'art** \*same*\ [French, literally, art object] (1865)
**1** : an article of some artistic value
**2** : CURIO — called also *objet*

**ob·jet trou·vé** \ˈȯb-ˌzhä-trü-ˈvā\ *noun, plural* **objets trouvés** \*same*\ [French, literally, found object] (1937)
: a natural object (as a piece of driftwood) found by chance and held to have aesthetic value especially through the working of natural forces on it; *also* : an artifact not originally intended as art but held to have aesthetic value especially when displayed as a work of art

**ob·jur·ga·tion** \ˌäb-jər-ˈgā-shən\ *noun* [Middle English *objurgacyon*, from Middle French or Latin; Middle French *objurgation*, from Latin *objurgation-, objurgatio*, from *objurgare* to scold, blame, from *ob-* against + *jurgare* to quarrel, literally, to take to law, from *jur-, jus* law + *-igare* (from *agere* to lead) — more at OB-, JUST, AGENT] (15th century)
: a harsh rebuke
— **ob·jur·gate** \'äb-jər-ˌgāt\ *transitive verb*
— **ob·jur·ga·to·ry** \əb-ˈjər-gə-ˌtōr-ē, -ˌtȯr-\ *adjective*

**ob·lan·ceo·late** \(ˌ)äb-ˈlan(t)-sē-ə-ˌlāt\ *adjective* (1850)
: inversely lanceolate 〈an *oblanceolate* leaf〉
— see LEAF illustration

**ob·last** \'ä-ˌblast, 'ȯ-bləst\ *noun, plural* **oblasts** *also* **ob·las·ti** \-ˌblas-tē, -bləs-\ [Russian *oblast'*] (circa 1886)
: a political subdivision of Imperial Russia or of a republic in the U.S.S.R.

**¹ob·late** \ä-ˈblāt, 'ä-ˌ\ *adjective* [probably from New Latin *oblatus*, from *ob-* + *-latus* (as in *prolatus* prolate)] (1705)
: flattened or depressed at the poles 〈an *oblate* spheroid〉
— **ob·late·ness** *noun*

**²ob·late** \'ä-ˌblāt\ *noun* [Medieval Latin *oblatus*, literally, one offered up, from Latin, past participle of *offerre* — more at OFFER] (1864)
**1** : a layman living in a monastery under a modified rule and without vows
**2** : a member of one of several Roman Catholic communities of men or women

**ob·la·tion** \ə-ˈblā-shən, ō-\ *noun* [Middle English *oblacioun*, from Middle French *oblation*, from Late Latin *oblation-, oblatio*, from Latin *offerre*] (15th century)
**1** : the act of making a religious offering; *specifically, capitalized* : the act of offering the eucharistic elements to God

**2** : something offered in worship or devotion
: a holy gift offered usually at an altar or shrine

**¹ob·li·gate** \'ä-blə-ˌgāt\ *transitive verb* **-gat·ed; -gat·ing** [Latin *obligatus*, past participle of *obligare*] (1533)
**1** : to bind legally or morally : CONSTRAIN
**2** : to commit (as funds) to meet an obligation

**²ob·li·gate** \'ä-bli-gət, -blə-ˌgāt\ *adjective* (1887)
**1** : restricted to one particularly characteristic mode of life 〈an *obligate* parasite〉
**2** : biologically essential for survival 〈*obligate* mutualism〉
— **ob·li·gate·ly** *adverb*

**ob·li·ga·tion** \ˌä-blə-ˈgā-shən\ *noun* (14th century)
**1** : the action of obligating oneself to a course of action (as by a promise or vow)
**2 a** : something (as a formal contract, a promise, or the demands of conscience or custom) that obligates one to a course of action **b** : a debt security (as a mortgage or corporate bond) **c** : a commitment (as by a government) to pay a particular sum of money; *also* : an amount owed under such an obligation 〈unable to meet its *obligations*, the company went into bankruptcy〉
**3 a** : a condition or feeling of being obligated **b** : a debt of gratitude
**4** : something one is bound to do : DUTY, RESPONSIBILITY

**oblig·a·to·ry** \ə-ˈbli-gə-ˌtōr-ē, ä-, -ˌtȯr- *also* 'ä-bli-gə-\ *adjective* (15th century)
**1** : binding in law or conscience
**2** : relating to or enforcing an obligation 〈a writ *obligatory*〉
**3** : MANDATORY, REQUIRED 〈*obligatory* military service〉; *also* : so commonplace as to be a convention, fashion, or cliché 〈the *obligatory* death scene in opera〉
**4** : OBLIGATE 1
— **oblig·a·to·ri·ly** \ə-ˌbli-gə-ˈtōr-ə-lē, ä-, -ˌtȯr- *also* ˌä-bli-gə-\ *adverb*

**oblige** \ə-ˈblīj\ *verb* **obliged; oblig·ing** [Middle English, from Old French *obliger*, from Latin *obligare*, literally, to bind to, from *ob-* toward + *ligare* to bind — more at LIGATURE] (14th century)
*transitive verb*
**1** : to constrain by physical, moral, or legal force or by the exigencies of circumstance 〈*obliged* to find a job〉
**2 a** : to put in one's debt by a favor or service 〈we are much *obliged* for your help〉 **b** : to do a favor for 〈always ready to *oblige* a friend〉
*intransitive verb*
: to do something as or as if a favor
*synonym* see FORCE
— **oblig·er** *noun*

**ob·li·gee** \ˌä-blə-ˈjē\ *noun* (1574)
: one to whom another is obligated (as by a contract); *specifically* : one who is protected by a surety bond

**oblig·ing** \ə-ˈblī-jiŋ\ *adjective* (1632)
: willing to do favors : ACCOMMODATING
*synonym* see AMIABLE
— **oblig·ing·ly** \-jiŋ-lē\ *adverb*
— **oblig·ing·ness** *noun*

**ob·li·gor** \ˌä-blə-ˈgȯr, -ˈjȯr\ *noun* (1541)
: one who is bound by a legal obligation

**¹oblique** \ō-ˈblēk, ə-, -ˈblīk; *military usually* ī\ *adjective* [Middle English *oblike*, from Latin *obliquus*] (15th century)
**1 a** : neither perpendicular nor parallel : INCLINED **b** : having the axis not perpendicular to the base 〈an *oblique* cone〉 **c** : having no right angle 〈an *oblique* triangle〉
**2 a** : not straightforward : INDIRECT; *also* : OBSCURE **b** : DEVIOUS, UNDERHANDED
**3** : situated obliquely and having one end not inserted on bone 〈*oblique* muscles〉
**4** : taken from an airplane with the camera directed horizontally or diagonally downward 〈an *oblique* photograph〉
— **oblique·ly** *adverb*

— **oblique·ness** *noun*

**²oblique** *noun* (circa 1608)
**1** : something (as a line) that is oblique
**2** : any of several oblique muscles; *especially* : any of the thin flat muscles forming the middle and outer layers of the lateral walls of the abdomen

**³oblique** *adverb* (1667)
: at a 45 degree angle 〈to the right *oblique*, march〉

**oblique angle** *noun* (1695)
: an acute or obtuse angle

**oblique case** *noun* (1530)
: a grammatical case other than the nominative or vocative

**obliq·ui·ty** \ō-ˈbli-kwə-tē, ə-\ *noun, plural* **-ties** (15th century)
**1** : deviation from moral rectitude or sound thinking
**2 a** : deviation from parallelism or perpendicularity; *also* : the amount of such deviation **b** : the angle between the planes of the earth's equator and orbit having a value of about 23°27' 〈*obliquity* of the ecliptic〉
**3 a** : indirectness or deliberate obscurity of speech or conduct **b** : an obscure or confusing statement

**oblit·er·ate** \ə-ˈbli-tə-ˌrāt, ō-\ *transitive verb* **-at·ed; -at·ing** [Latin *oblitteratus*, past participle of *oblitterare*, from *ob-* ob- + *littera* letter] (1609)
**1** : to make undecipherable or imperceptible by obscuring or wearing away
**2 a** : to remove utterly from recognition or memory **b** : to remove from existence : destroy utterly all trace, indication, or significance of **c** : to cause to disappear (as a bodily part or a scar) or collapse (as a duct conveying body fluid) : REMOVE 4 〈a blood vessel *obliterated* by inflammation〉
**3** : CANCEL 4
— **oblit·er·a·tion** \-ˌbli-tə-ˈrā-shən\ *noun*
— **oblit·er·a·tor** \-'bli-tə-ˌrā-tər\ *noun*

**oblit·er·a·tive** \ə-ˈbli-tə-ˌrā-tiv, ō-, -rə-tiv\ *adjective* (circa 1812)
: inducing or characterized by obliteration: as **a** : causing or accompanied by closure or collapse of a lumen 〈*obliterative* arterial disease〉 **b** : tending to make inconspicuous 〈*obliterative* behavior〉

**obliv·i·on** \ə-ˈbli-vē-ən, ō-, ä-\ *noun* [Middle English, from Middle French, from Latin *oblivion-, oblivio*, from *oblivisci* to forget, perhaps from *ob-* in the way + *levis* smooth — more at OB-, LEVIGATE] (14th century)
**1** : the fact or condition of forgetting or having forgotten; *especially* : the condition of being oblivious
**2** : the condition or state of being forgotten or unknown

**obliv·i·ous** \-vē-əs\ *adjective* (15th century)
**1** : lacking remembrance, memory, or mindful attention
**2** : lacking active conscious knowledge or awareness — usually used with *of* or *to*
— **obliv·i·ous·ly** *adverb*
— **obliv·i·ous·ness** *noun*

**ob·long** \'ä-ˌblȯŋ\ *adjective* [Middle English, from Latin *oblongus*, from *ob-* toward + *longus* long — more at LONG] (15th century)
: deviating from a square, circular, or spherical form by elongation in one dimension 〈an *oblong* piece of paper〉 〈an *oblong* melon〉
— **oblong** *noun*

**ob·lo·quy** \'ä-blə-kwē\ *noun, plural* **-quies** [Middle English, from Late Latin *obloquium*, from *obloqui* to speak against, from *ob-* against + *loqui* to speak] (15th century)
**1** : a strongly condemnatory utterance : abusive language
**2** : the condition of one that is discredited : bad repute
*synonym* see ABUSE

**ob·nox·ious** \äb-'näk-shəs, əb-\ *adjective* [Latin *obnoxius,* from *ob* in the way of, exposed to + *noxa* harm — more at NOXIOUS] (1597)
**1** *archaic* **:** exposed to something unpleasant or harmful — used with *to*
**2** *archaic* **:** deserving of censure
**3 :** odiously or disgustingly objectionable **:** highly offensive
— **ob·nox·ious·ly** *adverb*
— **ob·nox·ious·ness** *noun*

**ob·nu·bi·late** \äb-'nü-bə-ˌlāt, -'nyü-\ *transitive verb* **-lat·ed; -lat·ing** [Latin *obnubilatus,* past participle of *obnubilare,* from *ob-* in the way + *nubilare* to be cloudy, from *nubilus* cloudy, from *nubes* cloud — more at OB-, NUANCE] (1583)
**:** BECLOUD, OBSCURE
— **ob·nu·bi·la·tion** \-ˌnü-bə-'lā-shən, -ˌnyü-\ *noun*

**oboe** \'ō-(ˌ)bō\ *noun* [Italian, from French *hautbois* — more at HAUTBOIS] (1794)
**:** a double-reed woodwind instrument having a conical tube, a brilliant penetrating tone, and a usual range from B flat below middle C upward for over 2½ octaves
— **obo·ist** \'ō-(ˌ)bō-ist\ *noun*

oboe

**obol** \'ä-bəl, 'ō-\ *noun* [Latin *obolus,* from Greek *obolos, obelos,* literally, spit] (1579)
**:** an ancient Greek coin or weight equal to ⅙ drachma

**ob·ovate** \(ˌ)äb-'ō-ˌvāt\ *adjective* (1785)
**:** ovate with the narrower end basal ⟨*obovate* leaves⟩ — see LEAF illustration

**ob·ovoid** \-ˌvȯid\ *adjective* (1819)
**:** ovoid with the broad end toward the apex ⟨an *obovoid* fruit⟩

**ob·scene** \äb-'sēn, əb-\ *adjective* [Middle French, from Latin *obscenus, obscaenus*] (1593)
**1 :** disgusting to the senses **:** REPULSIVE
**2 a :** abhorrent to morality or virtue; *specifically* **:** designed to incite to lust or depravity **b :** containing or being language regarded as taboo in polite usage ⟨*obscene* lyrics⟩ **c :** repulsive by reason of crass disregard of moral or ethical principles ⟨an *obscene* misuse of power⟩ **d :** so excessive as to be offensive ⟨*obscene* wealth⟩ ⟨*obscene* waste⟩
*synonym* see COARSE
— **ob·scene·ly** *adverb*

**ob·scen·i·ty** \-'se-nə-tē *also* -'sē-\ *noun, plural* **-ties** (1589)
**1 :** the quality or state of being obscene
**2 :** something (as an utterance or act) that is obscene

**ob·scur·ant** \äb-'skyu̇r-ənt, əb-\ *or* **ob·scu·ran·tic** \ˌäb-skyə-'ran-tik\ *adjective* (1878)
**:** tending to make obscure
— **obscurant** *noun*

**ob·scu·ran·tism** \äb-'skyu̇r-ən-ˌti-zəm, əb-; ˌäb-skyu̇-'ran-\ *noun* (1834)
**1 :** opposition to the spread of knowledge **:** a policy of withholding knowledge from the general public
**2 a :** a style (as in literature or art) characterized by deliberate vagueness or abstruseness **b :** an act or instance of obscurantism
— **ob·scu·ran·tist** \-ən-tist, -'ran-tist\ *noun or adjective*

**¹ob·scure** \äb-'skyu̇r, əb-\ *adjective* [Middle English, from Middle French *obscur,* from Latin *obscurus*] (15th century)
**1 a :** DARK, DIM **b :** shrouded in or hidden by darkness **c :** not clearly seen or easily distinguished **:** FAINT
**2 :** not readily understood or clearly expressed; *also* **:** MYSTERIOUS

**3 :** relatively unknown: as **a :** REMOTE, SECLUDED **b :** not prominent or famous ⟨an *obscure* poet⟩
**4 :** constituting the unstressed vowel \ə\ or having unstressed \ə\ as its value ☆
— **ob·scure·ly** *adverb*
— **ob·scure·ness** *noun*

**²obscure** *transitive verb* **ob·scured; ob·scur·ing** (15th century)
**1 :** to make dark, dim, or indistinct
**2 :** to conceal or hide by or as if by covering
**3 :** to reduce (a vowel) to the value \ə\
— **ob·scu·ra·tion** \ˌäb-skyu̇-'rā-shən\ *noun*

**³obscure** *noun* (1667)
**:** OBSCURITY

**ob·scu·ri·ty** \äb-'skyu̇r-ə-tē, əb-\ *noun, plural* **-ties** (14th century)
**1 :** one that is obscure
**2 :** the quality or state of being obscure

**ob·se·qui·ous** \əb-'sē-kwē-əs, äb-\ *adjective* [Middle English, compliant, from Latin *obsequiosus,* from *obsequium* compliance, from *obsequi* to comply, from *ob-* toward + *sequi* to follow — more at OB-, SUE] (15th century)
**:** marked by or exhibiting a fawning attentiveness
*synonym* see SUBSERVIENT
— **ob·se·qui·ous·ly** *adverb*
— **ob·se·qui·ous·ness** *noun*

**ob·se·quy** \'äb-sə-kwē\ *noun, plural* **-quies** [Middle English *obsequie,* from Middle French, from Medieval Latin *obsequiae* (plural), alteration of Latin *exsequiae,* from *exsequi* to follow out, execute — more at EXECUTION] (15th century)
**:** a funeral or burial rite — usually used in plural

**ob·serv·able** \əb-'zər-və-bəl\ *adjective* (1609)
**1 :** NOTEWORTHY
**2 :** capable of being observed **:** DISCERNIBLE
— **ob·serv·abil·i·ty** \-ˌzər-və-'bi-lə-tē\ *noun*
— **observable** *noun*
— **ob·serv·ably** \-'zər-və-blē\ *adverb*

**ob·ser·vance** \əb-'zər-vən(t)s\ *noun* (13th century)
**1 a :** a customary practice, rite, or ceremony ⟨Sabbath *observances*⟩ **b :** a rule governing members of a religious order
**2 :** an act or instance of following a custom, rule, or law ⟨*observance* of the speed limits⟩
**3 :** an act or instance of watching

**¹ob·ser·vant** \-vənt\ *adjective* (1602)
**1 a :** paying strict attention **:** WATCHFUL ⟨an *observant* spectator⟩ **b :** KEEN, PERCEPTIVE
**2 :** careful in observing (as rites, laws, or customs) **:** MINDFUL ⟨pious and religiously *observant* families —Sidney Hook⟩ ⟨always *observant* of the amenities⟩
— **ob·ser·vant·ly** *adverb*

**²observant** *noun* (1605)
*obsolete* **:** an assiduous or obsequious servant or attendant

**ob·ser·va·tion** \ˌäb-sər-'vā-shən, -zər-\ *noun* [Middle French, from Latin *observation-, observatio,* from *observare*] (1535)
**1 :** an act or instance of observing a custom, rule, or law **:** OBSERVANCE
**2 a :** an act of recognizing and noting a fact or occurrence often involving measurement with instruments ⟨weather *observations*⟩ **b :** a record or description so obtained
**3 :** a judgment on or inference from what one has observed; *broadly* **:** REMARK, STATEMENT
**4** *obsolete* **:** attentive care **:** HEED
**5 :** the condition of one that is observed ⟨under *observation* at the hospital⟩
— **ob·ser·va·tion·al** \-shnəl, -shə-nᵊl\ *adjective*
— **ob·ser·va·tion·al·ly** *adverb*

**ob·ser·va·to·ry** \əb-'zər-və-ˌtōr-ē, -ˌtȯr-\ *noun, plural* **-ries** [probably from New Latin *observatorium,* from Latin *observare*] (1676)
**1 :** a building or place given over to or equipped for observation of natural phenome-

na (as in astronomy); *also* **:** an institution whose primary purpose is making such observations
**2 :** a situation or structure commanding a wide view

**ob·serve** \əb-'zərv\ *verb* **ob·served; ob·serv·ing** [Middle English, from Middle French *observer,* from Latin *observare* to guard, watch, observe, from *ob-* in the way, toward + *servare* to keep — more at CONSERVE] (14th century)
*transitive verb*
**1 :** to conform one's action or practice to (as a law, rite, or condition) **:** comply with
**2 :** to inspect or take note of as an augury, omen, or presage
**3 :** to celebrate or solemnize (as a ceremony or festival) in a customary or accepted way
**4 a :** to watch carefully especially with attention to details or behavior for the purpose of arriving at a judgment **b :** to make a scientific observation on or of
**5 :** to come to realize or know especially through consideration of noted facts
**6 :** to utter as a remark
*intransitive verb*
**1 a :** to take notice **b :** to make observations **:** WATCH
**2 :** REMARK, COMMENT
*synonym* see KEEP
— **ob·serv·ing·ly** \-'zər-viŋ-lē\ *adverb*

**ob·serv·er** \əb-'zər-vər\ *noun* (circa 1550)
**:** one that observes: as **a :** a representative sent to observe but not participate officially in an activity (as a meeting or war) **b :** an expert analyst and commentator in a particular field ⟨political *observers*⟩

**ob·sess** \äb-'ses, əb-\ *verb* [Latin *obsessus,* past participle of *obsidēre* to frequent, besiege, from *ob-* against + *sedēre* to sit — more at OB-, SIT] (1531)
*transitive verb*
**:** to haunt or excessively preoccupy the mind of ⟨was *obsessed* with the idea⟩
*intransitive verb*
**:** to engage in obsessive thinking **:** become obsessed with an idea

**ob·ses·sion** \äb-'se-shən, əb-\ *noun* (1680)
**1 :** a persistent disturbing preoccupation with an often unreasonable idea or feeling; *broadly* **:** compelling motivation ⟨an *obsession* with profits⟩
**2 :** something that causes an obsession
— **ob·ses·sion·al** \-'sesh-nəl, -'se-shə-nᵊl\ *adjective*

---

☆ **SYNONYMS**
**Obscure, dark, vague, enigmatic, cryptic, ambiguous, equivocal** mean not clearly understandable. OBSCURE implies a hiding or veiling of meaning through some inadequacy of expression or withholding of full knowledge ⟨*obscure* poems⟩. DARK implies an imperfect or clouded revelation often with ominous or sinister suggestion ⟨muttered *dark* hints of revenge⟩. VAGUE implies a lack of clear formulation due to inadequate conception or consideration ⟨a *vague* sense of obligation⟩. ENIGMATIC stresses a puzzling, mystifying quality ⟨*enigmatic* occult writings⟩. CRYPTIC implies a purposely concealed meaning ⟨*cryptic* hints of hidden treasure⟩. AMBIGUOUS applies to language capable of more than one interpretation ⟨an *ambiguous* directive⟩. EQUIVOCAL applies to language left open to differing interpretations with the intention of deceiving or evading ⟨moral precepts with *equivocal* phrasing⟩.

---

\ə\ abut   \ᵊ\ kitten   \ər\ further   \a\ ash   \ā\ ace
\ä\ mop, mar   \au̇\ out   \ch\ chin   \e\ bet   \ē\ easy
\g\ go   \i\ hit   \ī\ ice   \j\ job   \ŋ\ sing   \ō\ go
\ȯ\ law   \ȯi\ boy   \th\ thin   \t̲h̲\ the   \ü\ loot   \u̇\ foot
\y\ yet   \zh\ vision   *see also* Guide to Pronunciation

— **ob·ses·sion·al·ly** *adverb*

**ob·ses·sive** \äb-'se-siv, əb-\ *adjective* (1901)
**1 a** : tending to cause obsession **b** : excessive often to an unreasonable degree
**2** : of, relating to, or characterized by obsession : deriving from obsession
— **obsessive** *noun*
— **ob·ses·sive·ly** *adverb*
— **ob·ses·sive·ness** *noun*

**obsessive–compulsive** *adjective* (1927)
: relating to or characterized by recurring obsessions and compulsions especially as symptoms of a neurotic state
— **obsessive–compulsive** *noun*

**ob·sid·i·an** \əb-'si-dē-ən\ *noun* [New Latin *obsidianus*, from Latin *obsidianus lapis*, false manuscript reading for *obsianus lapis*, literally, stone of Obsius, from *Obsius*, its supposed discoverer] (1796)
: a dark natural glass formed by the cooling of molten lava

**ob·so·lesce** \ˌäb-sə-'les\ *verb* **-lesced; -lesc·ing** [Latin *obsolescere*] (1873)
*intransitive verb*
: to be or become obsolescent
*transitive verb*
: to make obsolescent

**ob·so·les·cence** \-'le-sᵊn(t)s\ *noun* (circa 1841)
: the process of becoming obsolete or the condition of being nearly obsolete ⟨the gradual *obsolescence* of machinery⟩ ⟨reduced to *obsolescence*⟩

**ob·so·les·cent** \-sᵊnt\ *adjective* (1755)
: going out of use : becoming obsolete
— **ob·so·les·cent·ly** *adverb*

¹**ob·so·lete** \ˌäb-sə-'lēt, 'äb-sə-,\ *adjective* [Latin *obsoletus*, from past participle of *obsolescere* to grow old, become disused, perhaps from *ob-* toward + *solēre* to be accustomed] (1579)
**1 a** : no longer in use or no longer useful **b** : of a kind or style no longer current : OLD-FASHIONED
**2** *of a plant or animal part* : indistinct or imperfect as compared with a corresponding part in related organisms : VESTIGIAL
**synonym** see OLD
— **ob·so·lete·ly** *adverb*
— **ob·so·lete·ness** *noun*

²**obsolete** *transitive verb* **-let·ed; -let·ing** (1640)
: to make obsolete

**ob·sta·cle** \'äb-sti-kəl, -ˌsti-\ *noun* [Middle English, from Middle French, from Latin *obstaculum*, from *obstare* to stand in front of, from *ob-* in the way + *stare* to stand — more at OB-, STAND] (14th century)
: something that impedes progress or achievement

**obstacle course** *noun* (1943)
: a military training course filled with obstacles (as hurdles, fences, walls, and ditches) that must be negotiated; *broadly* : a series of obstacles that must be overcome

**ob·stet·ric** \əb-'ste-trik, äb-\ *or* **ob·stet·ri·cal** \-tri-kəl\ *adjective* [modification of Latin *obstetricius*, from *obstetric-, obstetrix* midwife, from *obstare*] (1742)
: of, relating to, or associated with childbirth or obstetrics
— **ob·stet·ri·cal·ly** \-tri-k(ə-)lē\ *adverb*

**ob·ste·tri·cian** \ˌäb-stə-'tri-shən\ *noun* (circa 1828)
: a physician specializing in obstetrics

**ob·stet·rics** \əb-'ste-triks, äb-\ *noun plural but singular or plural in construction* (circa 1819)
: a branch of medical science that deals with birth and with its antecedents and sequels

**ob·sti·na·cy** \'äb-stə-nə-sē\ *noun, plural* **-cies** (14th century)
**1 a** : the quality or state of being obstinate : STUBBORNNESS **b** : the quality or state of being difficult to remedy, relieve, or subdue ⟨the *obstinacy* of tuberculosis⟩

**2** : an instance of being obstinate

**ob·sti·nate** \'äb-stə-nət\ *adjective* [Middle English, from Latin *obstinatus*, past participle of *obstinare* to be resolved, from *ob-* in the way + *-stinare* (akin to *stare* to stand)] (14th century)
**1** : perversely adhering to an opinion, purpose, or course in spite of reason, arguments, or persuasion
**2** : not easily subdued, remedied, or removed ⟨*obstinate* fever⟩ ☆
— **ob·sti·nate·ly** *adverb*
— **ob·sti·nate·ness** *noun*

**ob·strep·er·ous** \əb-'stre-p(ə-)rəs, äb-\ *adjective* [Latin *obstreperus*, from *obstrepere* to clamor against, from *ob-* against + *strepere* to make a noise] (circa 1600)
**1** : marked by unruly or aggressive noisiness : CLAMOROUS ⟨*obstreperous* merriment⟩
**2** : stubbornly resistant to control : UNRULY
**synonym** see VOCIFEROUS
— **ob·strep·er·ous·ly** *adverb*
— **ob·strep·er·ous·ness** *noun*

**ob·struct** \əb-'strəkt, äb-\ *transitive verb* [Latin *obstructus*, past participle of *obstruere*, from *ob-* in the way + *struere* to build, heap up — more at OB-, STREW] (1590)
**1** : to block or close up by an obstacle
**2** : to hinder from passage, action, or operation : IMPEDE
**3** : to cut off from sight ⟨a wall *obstructs* the view⟩
**synonym** see HINDER
— **ob·struc·tive** \-'strək-tiv\ *adjective or noun*
— **ob·struc·tive·ness** *noun*
— **ob·struc·tor** \-tər\ *noun*

**ob·struc·tion** \əb-'strək-shən, äb-\ *noun* (1533)
**1 a** : an act of obstructing **b** : the state of being obstructed; *especially* : a condition of being clogged or blocked
**2** : something that obstructs

**ob·struc·tion·ism** \-shə-ˌni-zəm\ *noun* (1879)
: deliberate interference with the progress or business especially of a legislative body
— **ob·struc·tion·ist** \-sh(ə-)nist\ *noun or adjective*
— **ob·struc·tion·is·tic** \-ˌstrək-shə-'nis-tik\ *adjective*

**ob·tain** \əb-'tān, äb-\ *verb* [Middle English *obteinen*, from Middle French & Latin; Middle French *obtenir*, from Latin *obtinēre* to hold on to, possess, obtain, from *ob-* in the way + *tenēre* to hold — more at THIN] (15th century)
*transitive verb*
: to gain or attain usually by planned action or effort
*intransitive verb*
**1** *archaic* : SUCCEED
**2** : to be generally recognized or established : PREVAIL
— **ob·tain·abil·i·ty** \-ˌtā-nə-'bi-lə-tē\ *noun*
— **ob·tain·able** \-'tā-nə-bəl\ *adjective*
— **ob·tain·er** *noun*
— **ob·tain·ment** \-'tān-mənt\ *noun*

**ob·tect** \äb-'tekt, əb-\ *also* **ob·tect·ed** \-'tek-təd\ *adjective* [Latin *obtectus*, past participle of *obtegere* to cover over, from *ob-* in the way + *tegere* to cover — more at THATCH] (circa 1902)
: enclosed in or characterized by enclosure in a firm chitinous case or covering ⟨an *obtect* pupa⟩

**ob·trude** \əb-'trüd, äb-\ *verb* **ob·trud·ed; ob·trud·ing** [Latin *obtrudere* to thrust at, from *ob-* in the way + *trudere* to thrust — more at OB-, THREAT] (circa 1609)
*transitive verb*
**1** : to thrust out : EXTRUDE
**2** : to force or impose (as oneself or one's ideas) without warrant or request
*intransitive verb*
: to become unduly prominent or interfering : INTRUDE

— **ob·trud·er** *noun*

**ob·tru·sion** \-'trü-zhən\ *noun* [Late Latin *obtrusion-, obtrusio*, from Latin *obtrudere*] (1579)
**1** : an act of obtruding
**2** : something that is obtruded

**ob·tru·sive** \-'trü-siv, -ziv\ *adjective* (1667)
**1 a** : forward in manner or conduct ⟨*obtrusive* behavior⟩ **b** : undesirably prominent
**2** : thrust out : PROTRUDING
**synonym** see IMPERTINENT
— **ob·tru·sive·ly** *adverb*
— **ob·tru·sive·ness** *noun*

**ob·tund** \äb-'tənd\ *transitive verb* [Middle English, from Latin *obtundere*] (14th century)
: to reduce the edge or violence of : DULL ⟨*obtunded* reflexes⟩

**ob·tu·ra·tion** \ˌäb-tyə-'rā-shən, -tə-\ *noun* [Latin *obturation-, obturatio*, from *obturare* to obstruct] (1610)
: OBSTRUCTION, CLOSURE
— **ob·tu·rate** \'äb-tyə-ˌrāt, -tə-\ *transitive verb*

**ob·tu·ra·tor** \'äb-tyə-ˌrā-tər, -tə-\ *noun* [New Latin, from Latin *obturare*] (circa 1741)
: one that closes: as **a** : one (as a prosthetic device) that closes or blocks up an opening (as a fissure in the palate) **b** : a hooded swelling of the placenta that fits over the nucellus in some plants

**ob·tuse** \äb-'tüs, əb-, -'tyüs\ *adjective* **ob·tus·er; -est** [Middle English, from Latin *obtusus* blunt, dull, from past participle of *obtundere* to beat against, blunt, from *ob-* against + *tundere* to beat — more at OB-, CONTUSION] (15th century)
**1 a** : not pointed or acute : BLUNT **b** (1) *of an angle* : exceeding 90 degrees but less than 180 degrees (2) : having an obtuse angle ⟨an *obtuse* triangle⟩ — see TRIANGLE illustration **c** *of a leaf* : rounded at the free end
**2 a** : lacking sharpness or quickness of sensibility or intellect : INSENSITIVE, STUPID **b** : difficult to comprehend : not clear or precise in thought or expression
**synonym** see DULL
— **ob·tuse·ly** *adverb*
— **ob·tuse·ness** *noun*

¹**ob·verse** \äb-'vərs, əb-, 'äb-,\ *adjective* [Latin *obversus*, from past participle of *obvertere* to turn toward, from *ob-* toward + *vertere* to turn — more at OB-, WORTH] (circa 1656)
**1** : facing the observer or opponent
**2** : having the base narrower than the top ⟨an *obverse* leaf⟩
**3** : constituting the obverse of something : OPPOSITE
— **ob·verse·ly** *adverb*

²**ob·verse** \'äb-ˌvərs, äb-', əb-\ *noun* (1658)
**1** : the side of a coin or currency note bearing the chief device and lettering; *broadly* : a front or principal surface
**2** : a counterpart having the opposite orientation or force ⟨their rise was merely the *obverse* of the Empire's fall —A. J. Toynbee⟩; *also* : OPPOSITE 1 ⟨joy and its *obverse*, sorrow⟩

---

☆ **SYNONYMS**
**Obstinate, dogged, stubborn, pertinacious, mulish** mean fixed and unyielding in course or purpose. OBSTINATE implies usually an unreasonable persistence ⟨an *obstinate* proponent of conspiracy theories⟩. DOGGED suggests an admirable often tenacious and unwavering persistence ⟨pursued the story with *dogged* perseverance⟩. STUBBORN implies sturdiness in resisting change which may or may not be admirable ⟨a person too *stubborn* to admit error⟩. PERTINACIOUS suggests an annoying or irksome persistence ⟨a *pertinacious* salesclerk refusing to take no for an answer⟩. MULISH implies a thoroughly unreasonable obstinacy ⟨a *mulish* determination to have his own way⟩.

**3 :** a proposition inferred immediately from another by denying the opposite of what the given proposition affirms ⟨the *obverse* of "all *A* is *B*" is "no *A* is not *B*"⟩

**ob·vi·ate** \'äb-vē-,āt\ *transitive verb* **-at·ed; -at·ing** [Late Latin *obviatus*, past participle of *obviare* to meet, withstand, from Latin *obviam*] (1598)

**:** to anticipate and prevent (as a situation) or make unnecessary (as an action)
— **ob·vi·a·tion** \,äb-vē-'ā-shən\ *noun*

**ob·vi·ous** \'äb-vē-əs\ *adjective* [Latin *obvius*, from *obviam* in the way, from *ob* in the way of + *viam*, accusative of *via* way — more at OB-, VIA] (1603)
**1** *archaic* **:** being in the way or in front
**2 :** easily discovered, seen, or understood
**synonym** see EVIDENT
— **ob·vi·ous·ness** *noun*

**ob·vi·ous·ly** \-lē\ *adverb* (1638)
**1 :** in an obvious manner ⟨showed his anger *obviously*⟩
**2 :** as is plainly evident ⟨*obviously*, something is wrong⟩

**oca** \'ō-kə\ *noun* [Spanish, from Quechua *oqa*] (1604)
**:** either of two South American wood sorrels (*Oxalis crenata* and *O. tuberosa*) cultivated for their edible tubers; *also* **:** the tuber of an oca

**oc·a·ri·na** \,ä-kə-'rē-nə\ *noun* [Italian, from Italian dialect, diminutive of *oca* goose, from Late Latin *auca*, from Latin *avis* bird — more at AVIARY] (1877)
**:** a simple wind instrument typically having an oval body with finger holes and a projecting mouthpiece

ocarina

**Oc·cam's ra·zor** \'ä-kəmz-\ *noun* [William of *Occam*] (circa 1837)
**:** a scientific and philosophic rule that entities should not be multiplied unnecessarily which is interpreted as requiring that the simplest of competing theories be preferred to the more complex or that explanations of unknown phenomena be sought first in terms of known quantities

**¹oc·ca·sion** \ə-'kā-zhən\ *noun* [Middle English, from Middle French or Latin; Middle French, from Latin *occasion-, occasio*, from *occidere* to fall, fall down, from *ob-* toward + *cadere* to fall — more at OB-, CHANCE] (14th century)
**1 :** a favorable opportunity or circumstance ⟨did not have *occasion* to talk with them⟩
**2 a :** a state of affairs that provides a ground or reason ⟨the *occasion* of the discord was their mutual intolerance⟩ **b :** an occurrence or condition that brings something about; *especially* **:** the immediate inciting circumstance as distinguished from the fundamental cause ⟨his insulting remark was the *occasion* of a bitter quarrel⟩
**3 a :** HAPPENING, INCIDENT **b :** a time at which something happens **:** INSTANCE
**4 a :** a need arising from a particular circumstance **b** *archaic* **:** a personal want or need — usually used in plural
**5** *plural* **:** AFFAIRS, BUSINESS
**6 :** a special event or ceremony **:** CELEBRATION
— **on occasion :** from time to time

**²occasion** *transitive verb* **-sioned; -sion·ing** \-'kāzh-niŋ, -'kā-zhə-\ (15th century)
**:** BRING ABOUT, CAUSE

**oc·ca·sion·al** \-'kāzh-nəl, -'kā-zhə-n°l\ *adjective* (circa 1631)
**1 a :** of or relating to a particular occasion ⟨a budget able to meet *occasional* demands as well as regular ones⟩ **b :** created for a particular occasion ⟨*occasional* verse⟩

**2 :** acting as the occasion or contributing cause of something
**3 :** encountered, occurring, appearing, or taken at irregular or infrequent intervals ⟨*occasional* visitors⟩ ⟨an *occasional* vacation⟩
**4 :** acting in a specified capacity from time to time ⟨an *occasional* lecturer⟩
**5 :** designed or constructed to be used as the occasion demands ⟨*occasional* furniture⟩

**oc·ca·sion·al·ly** \-'kāzh-nə-lē, -'kā-zhə-n°l-ē\ *adverb* (1630)
**:** on occasion **:** NOW AND THEN

**Oc·ci·dent** \'äk-sə-dənt, -,dent\ *noun* [Middle English, from Middle French, from Latin *occident-, occidens*, from present participle of *occidere* to fall, set (of the sun)] (14th century)
**:** WEST 2a

**oc·ci·den·tal** \,äk-sə-'den-t°l\ *adjective, often capitalized* (14th century)
**1 :** of, relating to, or situated in the Occident **:** WESTERN
**2 :** of or relating to Occidentals
— **oc·ci·den·tal·ly** *adverb*

**Occidental** *noun* (1857)
**:** a member of one of the occidental peoples; *especially* **:** a person of European ancestry

**Oc·ci·den·tal·ism** \,äk-sə-'den-t°l-,i-zəm\ *noun* (1839)
**:** the characteristic features of occidental peoples or culture

**oc·ci·den·tal·ize** \-t°l-,īz\ *transitive verb* **-ized; -iz·ing** *often capitalized* (1870)
**:** to make occidental (as in culture)

**oc·cip·i·tal** \äk-'si-pə-t°l\ *adjective* (1541)
**:** of, relating to, or located within or near the occiput or the occipital bone
— **occipital** *noun*
— **oc·cip·i·tal·ly** *adverb*

**occipital bone** *noun* (1679)
**:** a compound bone that forms the posterior part of the skull and bears a condyle with which the skull articulates with the atlas

**occipital condyle** *noun* (circa 1860)
**:** an articular surface on the occipital bone by which the skull articulates with the atlas

**occipital lobe** *noun* (circa 1890)
**:** the posterior lobe of each cerebral hemisphere that bears the visual areas and has the form of a 3-sided pyramid

**oc·ci·put** \'äk-sə-(,)pət\ *noun, plural* **oc·ci·puts** *or* **oc·cip·i·ta** \äk-'si-pə-tə\ [Middle English, from Latin *occipit-, occiput*, from *ob-* against + *capit-, caput* head — more at OB-, HEAD] (14th century)
**:** the back part of the head or skull

**Oc·ci·tan** \'äk-sə-,tan\ *noun* [French, from Medieval Latin *occitanus*, from Old Provençal *oc* yes (contrasted with Old French *oïl* yes) + Medieval Latin *-itanus* (perhaps as in *aquitanus* of Aquitaine)] (1958)
**:** PROVENÇAL 2
— **Occitan** *adjective*

**oc·clude** \ə-'klüd, ä-\ *verb* **oc·clud·ed; oc·clud·ing** [Latin *occludere*, from *ob-* in the way + *claudere* to shut, close — more at CLOSE] (1597)
*transitive verb*
**1 :** to close up or block off **:** OBSTRUCT ⟨a thrombus *occluding* a coronary artery⟩; *also* **:** CONCEAL
**2 :** SORB
*intransitive verb*
**1 :** to come into contact with cusps of the opposing teeth fitting together ⟨his teeth do not *occlude* properly⟩
**2 :** to become occluded

**occluded front** *noun* (circa 1938)
**:** OCCLUSION 2

**oc·clu·sal** \ə-'klü-səl, ä-, -zəl\ *adjective* (1897)
**:** of or relating to the grinding or biting surface of a tooth or to occlusion of the teeth

**oc·clu·sion** \ə-'klü-zhən\ *noun* [Latin *occludere*] (circa 1645)
**1 :** the act of occluding **:** the state of being occluded: as **a :** the complete obstruction of the breath passage in the articulation of a speech sound **b :** the bringing of the opposing surfaces of the teeth of the two jaws into contact; *also* **:** the relation between the surfaces when in contact **c :** the inclusion or sorption of gas trapped during solidification of a material
**2 :** the front formed by a cold front overtaking a warm front and lifting the warm air above the earth's surface

**oc·clu·sive** \-siv, -ziv\ *adjective* [Latin *occlusus*, past participle of *occludere*] (1888)
**1 :** serving to occlude
**2 :** characterized by occlusion

**¹oc·cult** \ə-'kəlt, ä-\ *transitive verb* [Latin *occultare*, frequentative of *occulere*] (1500)
**:** to shut off from view or exposure **:** COVER, ECLIPSE
— **oc·cult·er** *noun*

**²oc·cult** \ə-'kəlt, ä-; 'ä-,kəlt\ *adjective* [Latin *occultus*, from past participle of *occulere* to cover up, from *ob-* in the way + *-culere* (akin to *celare* to conceal) — more at OB-, HELL] (1567)
**1 :** not revealed **:** SECRET
**2 :** not easily apprehended or understood **:** ABSTRUSE, MYSTERIOUS
**3 :** hidden from view **:** CONCEALED
**4 :** of or relating to the occult
**5 :** not manifest or detectable by clinical methods alone ⟨*occult* carcinoma⟩; *also* **:** not present in macroscopic amounts ⟨*occult* blood in a stool⟩
— **oc·cult·ly** *adverb*

**³occult** \*same as* ²\ *noun* (1923)
**:** matters regarded as involving the action or influence of supernatural or supernormal powers or some secret knowledge of them — used with *the*

**oc·cul·ta·tion** \,ä-(,)kəl-'tā-shən\ *noun* (15th century)
**1 :** the state of being hidden from view or lost to notice
**2 :** the interruption of the light from a celestial body or of the signals from a spacecraft by the intervention of a celestial body; *especially* **:** an eclipse of a star or planet by the moon

**oc·cult·ism** \ə-'kəl-,ti-zəm, ä-; 'ä-,kəl-\ *noun* (1881)
**:** occult theory or practice **:** belief in or study of the action or influence of supernatural or supernormal powers
— **oc·cult·ist** \-tist\ *noun*

**oc·cu·pan·cy** \'ä-kyə-pən(t)-sē\ *noun, plural* **-cies** (1596)
**1 :** the fact or condition of holding, possessing, or residing in or on something ⟨*occupancy* of the estate⟩
**2 :** the act or fact of taking or having possession (as of unowned land) to acquire ownership
**3 :** the fact or condition of being occupied ⟨*occupancy* by more than 400 persons is unlawful⟩
**4 :** the use to which a property is put ⟨industrial *occupancy*⟩
**5 :** a building or part of a building intended to be occupied (as by a tenant) ⟨multiple *occupancy* buildings⟩

**oc·cu·pant** \-pənt\ *noun* (1596)
**1 :** one who occupies a particular place; *especially* **:** RESIDENT
**2 :** one who acquires title by occupancy

**oc·cu·pa·tion** \,ä-kyə-'pā-shən\ *noun* [Middle English *occupacioun*, from Middle French *occupation*, from Latin *occupation-, occupatio*, from *occupare*] (14th century)

**1 a :** an activity in which one engages ⟨in the first three grades learning to read is perhaps the major *occupation* of the pupil —J. B. Conant⟩ **b :** the principal business of one's life **:** VOCATION
**2 a :** the possession, use, or settlement of land **:** OCCUPANCY **b :** the holding of an office or position
**3 a :** the act or process of taking possession of a place or area **:** SEIZURE **b :** the holding and control of an area by a foreign military force **c :** the military force occupying a country or the policies carried out by it
*synonym* see WORK
— **oc·cu·pa·tion·al** \-shnəl, -shə-nᵊl\ *adjective*
— **oc·cu·pa·tion·al·ly** *adverb*
**occupational therapy** *noun* (1915)
**:** therapy by means of activity; *especially* **:** creative activity prescribed for its effect in promoting recovery or rehabilitation
— **occupational therapist** *noun*
**oc·cu·py** \'ä-kyə-ˌpī\ *transitive verb* **-pied; -py·ing** [Middle English *occupien* to take possession of, occupy, modification of Middle French *occuper*, from Latin *occupare*, from *ob-* toward + *-cupare* (akin to *capere* to seize) — more at OB-, HEAVE] (14th century)
**1 :** to engage the attention or energies of
**2 a :** to take up (a place or extent in space) ⟨this chair is *occupied*⟩ ⟨the fireplace will *occupy* this corner of the room⟩ **b :** to take or fill (an extent in time) ⟨the hobby *occupies* all of my free time⟩
**3 a :** to take or hold possession or control of ⟨enemy troops *occupied* the ridge⟩ **b :** to fill or perform the functions of (an office or position)
**4 :** to reside in as an owner or tenant
— **oc·cu·pi·er** \-ˌpī-(-ə)r\ *noun*
**oc·cur** \ə-'kər\ *intransitive verb* **oc·curred; oc·cur·ring** \-'kər-iŋ, -'kə-riŋ\ [Latin *occurrere*, from *ob-* in the way + *currere* to run — more at OB-, CAR] (1534)
**1 :** to be found or met with **:** APPEAR
**2 :** to come into existence **:** HAPPEN
**3 :** to come to mind
**oc·cur·rence** \ə-'kər-ən(t)s, -'kə-rən(t)s\ *noun* (1539)
**1 :** something that occurs ⟨a startling *occurrence*⟩
**2 :** the action or instance of occurring ⟨the repeated *occurrence* of petty theft in the locker room⟩ ☆
¹**oc·cur·rent** \ə-'kər-ənt, -'kə-rənt\ *adjective* [Middle English, from Middle French, from Latin *occurrent-, occurrens*, present participle of *occurrere*] (15th century)
**1 :** occurring at a particular time or place **:** CURRENT
**2 :** INCIDENTAL
²**occurrent** *noun* (1535)
**:** something that occurs as distinguished from something that continues to exist
**ocean** \'ō-shən\ *noun, often attributive* [Middle English *occean*, from Latin *oceanus*, from Greek *Ōkeanos*, a river thought of as encircling the earth, ocean] (14th century)
**1 a :** the whole body of salt water that covers nearly three fourths of the surface of the globe **b :** any of the large bodies of water (as the Atlantic Ocean) into which the great ocean is divided
**2 :** a very large or unlimited space or quantity
**ocean·ar·i·um** \ˌō-shə-'nar-ē-əm, -'ner-\ *noun, plural* **-iums** *or* **-ia** \-ē-ə\ (1938)
**:** a large marine aquarium
**ocean·front** \'ō-shən-ˌfrənt\ *noun* (1919)
**:** a shore area on the ocean
**ocean·go·ing** \-ˌgō-iŋ\ *adjective* (1885)
**:** of, relating to, or designed for travel on the ocean
**oce·an·ic** \ˌō-shē-'a-nik\ *adjective* (1656)

**1 a :** of or relating to the ocean **b :** occurring in or frequenting the ocean and especially the open sea as distinguished from littoral or neritic waters
**2 :** VAST, GREAT
**Oce·anid** \ō-'sē-ə-nəd\ *noun* [Greek *ōkeanid-, ōkeanis*, from *Ōkeanos* Oceanus]
**:** any of the ocean nymphs that are daughters of Oceanus and Tethys in Greek mythology
**ocean·og·ra·phy** \ˌō-shə-'nä-grə-fē\ *noun* [International Scientific Vocabulary] (1859)
**:** a science that deals with the oceans and includes the delimitation of their extent and depth, the physics and chemistry of their waters, marine biology, and the exploitation of their resources
— **ocean·og·ra·pher** \-fər\ *noun*
— **ocean·o·graph·ic** \-nə-'gra-fik\ *also* **ocean·o·graph·i·cal** \-fi-kəl\ *adjective*
— **ocean·o·graph·i·cal·ly** \-fi-k(ə-)lē\ *adverb*
**ocean·ol·o·gy** \ˌō-shə-'nä-lə-jē\ *noun* (circa 1864)
**:** OCEANOGRAPHY; *specifically* **:** the science of marine resources and technology
— **ocean·ol·o·gist** \-'nä-lə-jist\ *noun*
**ocean perch** *noun* (1943)
**:** any of several marine scorpaenid food fishes (genus *Sebastes*): **a :** REDFISH a; *also* **:** a related food fish (*S. fasciatus*) **b :** one (*S. alutus*) abundant in the northeastern Pacific from Japan to the Bering Sea to southern California
**ocean sunfish** *noun* (1629)
**:** a large bony fish (*Mola mola* of the order Tetraodontiformes) having high dorsal and anal fins and a body nearly oval in outline and attaining a length of 10 feet (3 meters) and a weight in excess of 2 tons (1.8 metric tons)
**Oce·anus** \ō-'sē-ə-nəs\ *noun* [Latin, from Greek *Ōkeanos*]
**:** a Titan who rules over a great river encircling the earth in Greek mythology
**ocel·lus** \ō-'se-ləs\ *noun, plural* **ocel·li** \-'se-ˌlī, -(ˌ)lē\ [New Latin, from Latin, diminutive of *oculus* eye — more at EYE] (1819)
**1 :** a minute simple eye or eyespot of an invertebrate
**2 :** an eyelike colored spot (as on a peacock feather or the wings of some butterflies)
— **ocel·lar** \ō-'se-lər\ *adjective*
**oce·lot** \'ä-sə-ˌlät, 'ō-\ *noun* [French, from Nahuatl *ōcēlōtl* jaguar] (1774)
**:** a medium-sized American wildcat (*Felis pardalis*) that ranges from Texas to northern Argentina and has a tawny yellow or grayish coat dotted and striped with black
**ocher** *or* **ochre** \'ō-kər\ *noun* [Middle English *oker*, from Middle French *ocre*, from Latin *ochra*, from Greek *ōchra*, from feminine of *ōchros* yellow] (14th century)
**1 :** an earthy usually red or yellow and often impure iron ore used as a pigment
**2 :** the color of ocher; *especially* **:** the color of yellow ocher
— **ocher·ous** \'ō-k(ə-)rəs\ *or* **ochre·ous** \'ō-k(ə-)rəs, -krē-əs\ *adjective*
**och·loc·ra·cy** \ä-'klä-krə-sē\ *noun* [Greek & Middle French; Middle French *ochlocratie*, from Greek *ochlokratia*, from *ochlos* mob + *-kratia* -cracy] (1584)
**:** government by the mob **:** mob rule
— **och·lo·crat** \'ä-klə-ˌkrat\ *noun*
— **och·lo·crat·ic** \ˌä-klə-'kra-tik\ *or* **och·lo·crat·i·cal** \-ti-kəl\ *adjective*

ocelot

**-ock** *noun suffix* [Middle English *-oc*, from Old English]
**:** small one ⟨hill*ock*⟩
**Ock·ham's razor** \'ä-kəmz-\ *variant of* OCCAM'S RAZOR
**o'clock** \ə-'kläk, ō-\ *adverb* [contraction of *of the clock*] (circa 1601)
**1 :** according to the clock ⟨the time is three *o'clock*⟩
**2 —** used for indicating position or direction as if on a clock dial that is oriented vertically or horizontally ⟨an airplane approaching at six *o'clock*⟩
**oco·ti·llo** \ˌō-kə-'tē-(ˌ)yō\ *noun, plural* **-llos** [Mexican Spanish] (1856)
**:** a thorny scarlet-flowered candlewood (*Fouquieria splendens* of the family Fouquieriaceae) of the southwestern U.S. and Mexico
**octa-** *or* **octo-** *also* **oct-** *combining form* [Greek *okta-, oktō-, okt-* (from *oktō*) & Latin *octo-, oct-*, from *octo* — more at EIGHT]
**:** eight ⟨*octane*⟩ ⟨*octoroon*⟩

ocotillo

**oc·ta·gon** \'äk-tə-ˌgän\ *noun* [Latin *octagonum*, from Greek *oktagōnon*, from *okta-* + *-gōnon* -gon] (1639)
**:** a polygon of eight angles and eight sides
— **oc·tag·o·nal** \äk-'ta-gə-nᵊl\ *adjective*
— **oc·tag·o·nal·ly** \-nᵊl-ē\ *adverb*
**oc·ta·he·dral** \ˌäk-tə-'hē-drəl\ *adjective* (1758)
**1 :** having eight plane faces
**2 :** of, relating to, or formed in octahedrons
— **oc·ta·he·dral·ly** \-drə-lē\ *adverb*
**oc·ta·he·dron** \-drən\ *noun, plural* **-drons** *or* **-dra** \-drə\ [Greek *oktaedron*, from *okta-* + *-edron* -hedron] (1570)
**:** a solid bounded by eight plane faces
**oc·tal** \'äk-tᵊl\ *adjective* (1948)
**:** of, relating to, or being a number system with a base of eight
**oc·tam·e·ter** \äk-'ta-mə-tər\ *noun* [Late Latin, having eight feet, from Late Greek *oktametros*, from *okta-* + *metron* measure — more at MEASURE] (1889)
**:** a line of verse consisting of eight metrical feet
**oc·tane** \'äk-ˌtān\ *noun* [International Scientific Vocabulary] (circa 1872)
**1 :** any of several isomeric liquid alkanes $C_8H_{18}$
**2 :** OCTANE NUMBER
**octane number** *noun* (1931)
**:** a number that is used to measure the antiknock properties of a liquid motor fuel (as gasoline) with a higher number indicating a

smaller likelihood of knocking — called also *octane rating;* compare CETANE NUMBER

**oc·tant** \'äk-tənt\ *noun* [Latin *octant-, octans* eighth of a circle, from *octo*] (1731)
**1 :** an instrument for observing altitudes of a celestial body from a moving ship or aircraft
**2 :** any of the eight parts into which a space is divided by three coordinate planes

**oc·ta·pep·tide** \,äk-tə-'pep-,tīd\ *noun* (1961)
**:** a protein fragment or molecule (as oxytocin or vasopressin) that consists of eight amino acids linked in a polypeptide chain

**oc·tave** \'äk-tiv, -təv, -,tāv\ *noun* [Middle English, from Medieval Latin *octava,* from Latin, feminine of *octavus* eighth, from *octo* eight — more at EIGHT] (14th century)
**1 :** an 8-day period of observances beginning with a festival day
**2 a :** a stanza of eight lines **:** OTTAVA RIMA **b :** the first eight lines of an Italian sonnet
**3 a :** a musical interval embracing eight diatonic degrees **b :** a tone or note at this interval **c :** the harmonic combination of two tones an octave apart **d :** the whole series of notes, tones, or digitals comprised within this interval and forming the unit of the modern scale **e :** an organ stop giving tones an octave above those corresponding to the digitals
**4 :** the interval between two frequencies (as in an electromagnetic spectrum) having a ratio of 2 to 1
**5 :** a group of eight

**oc·ta·vo** \äk-'tā-(,)vō, -'tä-\ *noun, plural* **-vos** [Latin, ablative of *octavus* eighth] (1582)
**:** the size of a piece of paper cut eight from a sheet; *also* **:** a book, a page, or paper of this size

**oc·tet** \äk-'tet\ *noun* (1879)
**1 :** a group or set of eight: as **a :** OCTAVE 2b **b :** the performers of an octet
**2 :** a musical composition for eight instruments or voices

**oc·til·lion** \äk-'til-yən\ *noun* [French, from Middle French, from *oct-* octa- + *-illion* (as in *million*)] (1690)
— see NUMBER table

**Oc·to·ber** \äk-'tō-bər\ *noun* [Middle English *Octobre,* from Old English & Old French; Old English *October,* from Latin, 8th month of the early Roman calendar, from *octo;* Old French, from Latin *October*] (before 12th century)
**:** the 10th month of the Gregorian calendar

**oc·to·de·cil·lion** \,äk-tō-di-'sil-yən\ *noun* [Latin *octodecim* eighteen + English *-illion* (as in *million*)] (1939)
— see NUMBER table

**oc·to·ge·nar·i·an** \,äk-tə-jə-'ner-ē-ən\ *noun* [Latin *octogenarius* containing eighty, from *octogeni* eighty each, from *octoginta* eighty, from *octo* eight + *-ginta* (akin to viginti twenty) — more at VIGESIMAL] (1815)
**:** a person whose age is in the eighties
— **octogenarian** *adjective*

**oc·to·ploid** \'äk-tə-,plȯid\ *adjective* [International Scientific Vocabulary] (1925)
**:** having a chromosome number eight times the basic haploid chromosome number
— **octoploid** *noun*

**oc·to·pod** \'äk-tə-,päd\ *noun* [ultimately from Greek *oktōpod-, oktōpous* scorpion, from *oktō-* octa- + *pod-, pous* foot — more at FOOT] (circa 1836)
**:** any of an order (Octopoda) of cephalopod mollusks (as an octopus or argonaut) that have eight arms bearing sessile suckers
— **octopod** *adjective*

**oc·to·pus** \'äk-tə-pəs, -,pu̇s\ *noun, plural* **-pus·es** *or* **-pi** \-,pī\ [New Latin *Octopod-, Octopus,* from Greek *oktōpous*] (1758)
**1 :** any of a genus (*Octopus*) of cephalopod mollusks that have eight

octopus 1

muscular arms equipped with two rows of suckers; *broadly* **:** any octopod excepting the paper nautilus
**2 :** something that resembles an octopus especially in having many centrally directed branches

**oc·to·roon** \,äk-tə-'rün\ *noun* [*octa-* + *-roon* (as in *quadroon*)] (1861)
**:** a person of one-eighth black ancestry

**oc·to·syl·lab·ic** \,äk-tə-sə-'la-bik\ *adjective* [Late Latin *octosyllabus,* from Greek *oktasyllabos,* from *okta-* octa- + *syllabē* syllable] (circa 1771)
**1 :** consisting of eight syllables
**2 :** composed of verses of eight syllables
— **octosyllabic** *noun*

**oc·to·syl·la·ble** \'äk-tə-,si-lə-bəl, ,äk-tə-'\ *noun* (circa 1846)
**:** a word or line of eight syllables

**oc·to·thorp** \'äk-tə-,thȯrp, -tō-\ *noun* [*octo-* + *thorp,* of unknown origin; from the eight points on its circumference] (1971)
**:** the symbol #

**¹oc·u·lar** \'ä-kyə-lər\ *adjective* [Late Latin *ocularis* of eyes, from Latin *oculus* eye] (circa 1575)
**1 a :** done or perceived by the eye ⟨*ocular* inspection⟩ **b :** based on what has been seen ⟨*ocular* testimony⟩
**2 a :** of or relating to the eye ⟨*ocular* muscles⟩ **b :** resembling an eye in form or function

**²ocular** *noun* (1835)
**:** EYEPIECE

**oc·u·lar·ist** \'ä-kyə-lə-rist\ *noun* (1866)
**:** a person who makes and fits artificial eyes

**oc·u·list** \'ä-kyə-list\ *noun* [French *oculiste,* from Latin *oculus*] (1615)
**1 :** OPHTHALMOLOGIST
**2 :** OPTOMETRIST

**oc·u·lo·mo·tor** \,ä-kyə-lə-'mō-tər\ *adjective* [Latin *oculus* eye + English *-o-* + *motor*] (circa 1890)
**1 :** moving or tending to move the eyeball
**2 :** of or relating to the oculomotor nerve

**oculomotor nerve** *noun* (1881)
**:** either of the pair of chiefly motor nerves that comprise the 3d pair of cranial nerves, arise from the midbrain, and supply four muscles of the eye

**oc·u·lus** \'ä-kyə-ləs\ *noun, plural* **oc·u·li** \-,lī, -,lē\ [Latin, literally, eye — more at EYE] (1848)
**1 :** a circular or oval window
**2 :** a circular opening at the top of a dome

**od** *or* **odd** \'äd\ *interjection, often capitalized* [euphemism for *God*] (1695)
*archaic* — used as a mild oath

**¹OD** \,ō-'dē\ *noun* [overdose] (circa 1960)
**1 :** an overdose of a narcotic
**2 :** one who has taken an OD

**²OD** *intransitive verb* **OD'd** *or* **ODed; OD'-ing; OD's** (1966)
**1 :** to become ill or die of an OD
**2 :** to have or experience too much of something — used with *on* ⟨*OD* on television⟩

**oda·lisque** \'ō-d³l-,isk\ *noun* [French, from Turkish *odalık,* from *oda* room] (circa 1681)
**1 :** a female slave
**2 :** a concubine in a harem

**odd** \'äd\ *adjective* [Middle English *odde,* from Old Norse *oddi* point of land, triangle, odd number; akin to Old English *ord* point of a weapon] (14th century)
**1 a :** being without a corresponding mate ⟨an *odd* shoe⟩ **b** (1) **:** left over after others are paired or grouped (2) **:** separated from a set or series
**2 a :** somewhat more than the indicated approximate quantity, extent, or degree — usually used in combination ⟨300-*odd* pages⟩ **b** (1) **:** left over as a remainder ⟨had a few *odd* dollars for entertainment after paying his bills⟩ (2) **:** constituting a small amount ⟨had some *odd* change in her pocket⟩

**3 a :** being any of the integers (as −3, −1, +1, and +3) that are not exactly divisible by two **b :** marked by an odd number of units **c :** being a function such that $f(-x) = -f(x)$ where the sign is reversed but the absolute value remains the same if the sign of the independent variable is reversed
**4 a :** not regular, expected, or planned ⟨worked at *odd* jobs⟩ **b :** encountered or experienced from time to time **:** OCCASIONAL
**5 :** having an out-of-the-way location **:** REMOTE
**6 :** differing markedly from the usual or ordinary or accepted **:** PECULIAR ◆
  *synonym* see STRANGE
— **odd·ness** *noun*

**odd·ball** \'äd-,bȯl\ *noun* (1948)
**:** one that is eccentric
— **oddball** *adjective*

**Odd Fellow** *noun* [Independent Order of *Odd Fellows*] (1795)
**:** a member of a major benevolent and fraternal order

**odd·i·ty** \'ä-də-tē\ *noun, plural* **-ties** (1713)
**1 :** an odd person, thing, event, or trait
**2 :** the quality or state of being odd

**odd lot** *noun* (1897)
**:** a number or quantity other than the usual unit in transactions; *especially* **:** a quantity of less than 100 shares of stock

**odd·ly** \'äd-lē\ *adverb* (1610)
**1 :** in an odd manner
**2 :** it is odd that ⟨was quite happy, *oddly* enough⟩

**odd man out** *noun* (1923)
**:** a person who differs from the other members of a group

**odd·ment** \'äd-mənt\ *noun* (1796)
**1 a :** something left over **:** REMNANT **b** *plural* **:** ODDS AND ENDS
**2 :** something odd **:** ODDITY

**odd permutation** *noun* (1929)
**:** a permutation that is produced by the successive application of an odd number of interchanges of pairs of elements

**odd–pin·nate** \'äd-'pi-,nāt\ *adjective* (circa 1890)
**:** having leaflets on each side of the petiole and having a single leaflet at the tip of the petiole
— **odd–pin·nate·ly** *adverb*

**odds** \'ädz\ *noun plural but singular or plural in construction* (circa 1520)
**1 a** *archaic* **:** INEQUALITIES **b** *obsolete* **:** degree of unlikeness

---

◇ **WORD HISTORY**

**odd** Old Norse *oddi* originally meant "point of land." From the roughly triangular shape of a point of land, *oddi* was generalized to mean "triangle." A point of land can be seen as the apex of a triangle, with the other two angles forming a pair and the apex the unpaired angle, so *oddi* was extended to mean "odd number," the item of a threesome left over after the other two items are paired off. During the time when Scandinavians dominated northern and central England in the Middle Ages, *oddi* was presumably borrowed into English, though it is first recorded only in 14th century Middle English as the adjective *odde* "without a corresponding mate." Already in Middle English, *odde* could mean "unconforming, irregular," though in reference to people it usually meant "outstanding, illustrious." The modern sense "peculiar, eccentric" did not become widely used before the 17th century.

---

\ə\ **abut** \³\ **kitten** \ər\ **further** \a\ **ash** \ā\ **ace**
\ä\ **mop, mar** \au̇\ **out** \ch\ **chin** \e\ **bet** \ē\ **easy**
\g\ **go** \i\ **hit** \ī\ **ice** \j\ **job** \ŋ\ **sing** \ō\ **go**
\ȯ\ **law** \ȯi\ **boy** \th\ **thin** \t͟h\ **the** \ü\ **loot** \u̇\ **foot**
\y\ **yet** \zh\ **vision**    *see also* Guide to Pronunciation

**2 a :** an amount by which one thing exceeds or falls short of another ⟨won the election by considerable *odds*⟩ **b** (1) **:** a difference favoring one of two opposed things ⟨overwhelming *odds*⟩ (2) **:** a difference in terms of advantage or disadvantage ⟨what's the *odds*, if thinking so makes them happy —Flora Thompson⟩ **c** (1) **:** the probability that one thing is so or will happen rather than another **:** CHANCES ⟨the *odds* are against it⟩ (2) **:** the ratio of the probability of one event to that of an alternative event **3 :** DISAGREEMENT, VARIANCE — usually used with *at* ⟨faculty and administration often are at *odds* on everything —W. E. Brock (born 1930)⟩ **4 a :** special favor **:** PARTIALITY **b :** an allowance granted by one making a bet to one accepting the bet and designed to equalize the chances favoring one of the bettors **c :** the ratio between the amount to be paid off for a winning bet and the amount of the bet — **by all odds :** in every way **:** without question ⟨*by all odds* the best book of the year⟩

**odds and ends** *noun plural* (circa 1746) **1 a :** miscellaneous articles **b :** miscellaneous small matters (as of business) to be attended to **2 :** miscellaneous remnants or leftovers ⟨*odds and ends* of food⟩

**odds·mak·er** \'ädz-ˌmā-kər\ *noun* (circa 1949) **:** one who figures odds

**odds-on** \'ädz-'ȯn, -'än\ *adjective* (1890) **1 :** having or viewed as having a better than even chance to win ⟨the *odds-on* favorite⟩ **2 :** not involving much risk **:** pretty sure ⟨an *odds-on* bet⟩

**odd trick** *noun* (1897) **:** each trick in excess of six won by declarer's side at bridge — compare BOOK 9

**ode** \'ōd\ *noun* [Middle French or Late Latin; Middle French, from Late Latin, from Greek *ōidē*, literally, song, from *aeidein, aidein* to sing; akin to Greek *audē* voice] (1588) **:** a lyric poem usually marked by exaltation of feeling and style, varying length of line, and complexity of stanza forms — **od·ist** \-ist\ *noun*

**-ode** *noun combining form* [Greek *-odos,* from *hodos*] **1 :** way **:** path ⟨electr*ode*⟩ **2 :** electrode ⟨di*ode*⟩

**ode·um** \ō-'dē-əm, 'ō-dē-\ *noun, plural* **odea** \-ə\ [Latin & Greek; Latin, from Greek *ōideion,* from *ōidē* song] (1616) **1 :** a small roofed theater of ancient Greece and Rome used chiefly for competitions in music and poetry **2 :** a theater or concert hall

**od·ic** \'ō-dik\ *adjective* (1863) **:** of, relating to, or forming an ode

**Odin** \'ō-dᵊn\ *noun* [Danish, from Old Norse *Ōthinn*] **:** the supreme god and creator in Norse mythology

**odi·ous** \'ō-dē-əs\ *adjective* [Middle English, from Middle French *odieus,* from Latin *odiosus,* from *odium*] (14th century) **:** exciting or deserving hatred or repugnance ⟨*odious* associates⟩ ⟨an *odious* business⟩ — **odi·ous·ly** *adverb* — **odi·ous·ness** *noun*

**odi·um** \'ō-dē-əm\ *noun* [Latin, hatred, from *odisse* to hate; akin to Old English *atol* terrible, Greek *odyssasthai* to be angry] (1602) **1 :** the state or fact of being subjected to hatred and contempt as a result of a despicable act or blameworthy circumstance **2 :** hatred and condemnation accompanied by loathing or contempt **:** DETESTATION **3 :** disrepute or infamy attached to something **:** OPPROBRIUM

**odom·e·ter** \ō-'dä-mə-tər\ *noun* [French *odomètre,* from Greek *hodometron,* from *hodos* way, road + *metron* measure — more at MEASURE] (1791) **:** an instrument for measuring the distance traveled (as by a vehicle)

**odo·nate** \'ō-dᵊn-ˌāt, ō-'dä-(ˌ)nāt\ *noun* [irregular from Greek *odous, odōn* tooth] (1947) **:** any of an order (Odonata) of predaceous insects comprising the dragonflies and damselflies — **odonate** *adjective*

**odont-** *or* **odonto-** *combining form* [French, from Greek, *odont-, odous* — more at TOOTH] **:** tooth ⟨*odonto*blast⟩

**-odont** *adjective combining form* [Greek *odont-, odous* tooth] **:** having teeth of a (specified) nature ⟨acro*dont*⟩

**-odontia** *noun combining form* [New Latin, from Greek *odont-, odous*] **:** form, condition, or mode of treatment of the teeth ⟨orth*odontia*⟩

**odon·to·blast** \ō-'dän-tə-ˌblast\ *noun* [International Scientific Vocabulary] (1878) **:** any of the elongated radially arranged cells on the surface of the dental pulp that secrete dentin — **odon·to·blas·tic** \-ˌdän-tə-'blas-tik\ *adjective*

**odon·to·glos·sum** \ō-ˌdän-tə-'glä-səm\ *noun* [New Latin, from Greek *odont-* + *glōssa* tongue — more at GLOSS] (1880) **:** any of a genus (*Odontoglossum*) of widely cultivated tropical American orchids

**odon·toid process** \ō-'dän-ˌtȯid-\ *noun* (circa 1819) **:** a toothlike process projecting from the anterior end of the centrum of the axis vertebra on which the atlas vertebra rotates

**odor** \'ō-dər\ *noun* [Middle English *odour,* from Middle French, from Latin *odor;* akin to Latin *olēre* to smell, Greek *ozein* to smell, *osmē* smell, odor] (13th century) **1 a :** a quality of something that stimulates the olfactory organ **:** SCENT **b :** a sensation resulting from adequate stimulation of the olfactory organ **:** SMELL **2 a :** a characteristic or predominant quality **:** FLAVOR ⟨the *odor* of sanctity⟩ **b :** REPUTE, ESTIMATION ⟨in bad *odor*⟩ **3** *archaic* **:** something that emits a sweet or pleasing scent **:** PERFUME *synonym* see SMELL — **odored** \'ō-dərd\ *adjective* — **odor·less** \-dər-ləs\ *adjective*

**odor·ant** \'ō-də-rənt\ *noun* (1935) **:** an odorous substance; *especially* **:** one added to a dangerous odorless substance to warn of its presence

**odor·if·er·ous** \ˌō-də-'ri-f(ə-)rəs\ *adjective* (15th century) **1 :** yielding an odor **:** ODOROUS **2 :** morally offensive — **odor·if·er·ous·ly** *adverb* — **odor·if·er·ous·ness** *noun*

**odor·ize** \'ō-də-ˌrīz\ *transitive verb* **-ized; -iz·ing** (1884) **:** to make odorous **:** SCENT

**odor·ous** \'ō-də-rəs\ *adjective* (15th century) **:** having an odor: as **a :** FRAGRANT **b :** MALODOROUS ☆ — **odor·ous·ly** *adverb* — **odor·ous·ness** *noun*

**odour** *chiefly British variant of* ODOR

**Odys·se·an** \ō-'di-sē-ən ("*Odysseus*"), ˌä-də-'sē-ən ("*journey*")\ *adjective* (circa 1711) **:** of, relating to, or characteristic of Odysseus or his journey

**Odys·seus** \ō-'di-sē-əs, -'dis-yəs, -'di-shəs, -'di-ˌshüs\ *noun* [Greek] **:** a king of Ithaca and Greek leader in the Trojan War who after the war wanders 10 years before reaching home

**od·ys·sey** \'ä-də-sē\ *noun, plural* **-seys** [the *Odyssey,* epic poem attributed to Homer recounting the long wanderings of Odysseus] (1889) **1 :** a long wandering or voyage usually marked by many changes of fortune **2 :** an intellectual or spiritual wandering or quest

**oe·cu·men·i·cal** \*especially British* ˌē-\ *variant of* ECUMENICAL

**oe·de·ma** *chiefly British variant of* EDEMA

**oe·di·pal** \'e-də-pəl, 'ē-\ *adjective, often capitalized* (1939) **:** of, relating to, or resulting from the Oedipus complex — **oe·di·pal·ly** \-pə-lē\ *adverb, often capitalized*

**¹Oe·di·pus** \-pəs\ *noun* [Latin, from Greek *Oidipous*] **:** the son of Laius and Jocasta who in fulfillment of an oracle unknowingly kills his father and marries his mother

**²Oedipus** *adjective* (1910) **:** OEDIPAL

**Oedipus complex** *noun* (1910) **:** the positive libidinal feelings of a child toward the parent of the opposite sex and hostile or jealous feelings toward the parent of the same sex that may be a source of adult personality disorder when unresolved

**oeil-de-boeuf** \ˌə(r)-də-'bəf, ˌəi-\ *noun, plural* **oeils-de-boeuf** \*same*\ [French *œil-de-bœuf,* literally, ox's eye] (1849) **:** OCULUS 1

**oeil·lade** \ˌə(r)-'yäd, œ-yäd\ *noun* [Middle French *œillade,* from *œil* eye, from Latin *oculus* — more at EYE] (1592) **:** a glance of the eye; *especially* **:** OGLE

**OEM** \ˌō-(ˌ)ē-'em\ *noun* [*original equipment manufacturer*] (1968) **:** one that produces complex equipment (as a computer system) from components usually bought from other manufacturers

**oe·nol·o·gy** *variant of* ENOLOGY

**Oe·no·ne** \ē-'nō-nē\ *noun* [Latin, from Greek *Oinōnē*] **:** a nymph who is abandoned by her husband Paris for Helen of Troy

**oe·no·phile** \'ē-nə-ˌfīl\ *noun* [French *œnophile,* from *œno-* (from Greek *oinos* wine) + *-phile* -phile — more at WINE] (1930) **:** a lover or connoisseur of wine

**¹o'er** \'ȯr, 'ór\ *adverb* (1592) **:** OVER

**²o'er** *preposition* (1593) **:** OVER

**oer·sted** \'ər-stəd\ *noun* [Hans Christian *Oersted*] (1930) **:** the unit of magnetic field strength in the centimeter-gram-second system

**oe·soph·a·gus** *chiefly British variant of* ESOPHAGUS

**oestr-** *or* **oestro-** *chiefly British variant of* ESTR-

**oeu·vre** \œvrᵊ\ *noun, plural* **oeuvres** \*same*\ [French *œuvre,* literally, work, from Latin *opera* — more at OPERA] (1875) **:** a substantial body of work constituting the lifework of a writer, an artist, or a composer

---

☆ **SYNONYMS**
**Odorous, fragrant, redolent, aromatic** mean emitting and diffusing scent. ODOROUS applies to whatever has a strong distinctive smell whether pleasant or unpleasant ⟨*odorous* cheeses should be tightly wrapped⟩. FRAGRANT applies to things (as flowers or spices) with sweet or agreeable odors ⟨a *fragrant* rose⟩. REDOLENT applies usually to a place or thing impregnated with odors ⟨the kitchen was *redolent* of garlic and tomatoes⟩. AROMATIC applies to things emitting pungent often fresh odors ⟨an *aromatic* blend of tobaccos⟩.

**¹of** \əv, *before consonants also* ə; ˈəv, ˈäv\ *preposition* [Middle English, off, of, from Old English, adverb & preposition; akin to Old High German *aba* off, away, Latin *about* from, away, Greek *apo*] (before 12th century)
**1** — used as a function word to indicate a point of reckoning ⟨north *of* the lake⟩
**2 a** — used as a function word to indicate origin or derivation ⟨a man *of* noble birth⟩ **b** — used as a function word to indicate the cause, motive, or reason ⟨died *of* flu⟩ **c :** BY ⟨plays *of* Shakespeare⟩ **d :** on the part of ⟨very kind *of* you⟩
**3** — used as a function word to indicate the component material, parts, or elements or the contents ⟨throne *of* gold⟩ ⟨cup *of* water⟩
**4 a** — used as a function word to indicate the whole that includes the part denoted by the preceding word ⟨most *of* the army⟩ **b** — used as a function word to indicate a whole or quantity from which a part is removed or expended ⟨gave *of* his time⟩
**5 a :** relating to **:** ABOUT ⟨stories *of* her travels⟩ **b :** in respect to ⟨slow *of* speech⟩
**6 a** — used as a function word to indicate belonging or a possessive relationship ⟨king *of* England⟩ **b** — used as a function word to indicate relationship between a result determined by a function or operation and a basic entity (as an independent variable) ⟨a function *of x*⟩ ⟨the product *of* two numbers⟩
**7** — used as a function word to indicate something from which a person or thing is delivered ⟨eased *of* her pain⟩ or with respect to which someone or something is made destitute ⟨robbed *of* all their belongings⟩
**8 a** — used as a function word to indicate a particular example belonging to the class denoted by the preceding noun ⟨the city *of* Rome⟩ **b** — used as a function word to indicate apposition ⟨that fool *of* a husband⟩
**9 a** — used as a function word to indicate the object of an action denoted or implied by the preceding noun ⟨love *of* nature⟩ **b** — used as a function word to indicate the application of a verb ⟨cheats him *of* a dollar⟩ or of an adjective ⟨fond *of* candy⟩
**10** — used as a function word to indicate a characteristic or distinctive quality or possession ⟨a woman *of* courage⟩
**11 a** — used as a function word to indicate the position in time of an action or occurrence ⟨died *of* a Monday⟩ **b :** BEFORE ⟨quarter *of* ten⟩ **12** *archaic* **:** ON ⟨a plague *of* all cowards —Shakespeare⟩

**²of** \əv, *before consonants also* ə\ *verbal auxiliary* [by alteration] (1837)
*nonstandard* **:** HAVE — used in place of the contraction *'ve* often in representations of uneducated speech ⟨I could *of* beat them easy —Ring Lardner⟩

**ofay** \ˈō-ˌfā, ō-ˈ\ *noun* [origin unknown] (1925)
**:** a white person — usually used disparagingly ◆

**¹off** \ˈȯf\ *adverb* [Middle English *of*, from Old English — more at OF] (before 12th century)
**1 a** (1) — from a place or position ⟨march *off*⟩; *specifically* **:** away from land ⟨ship stood *off* to sea⟩ (2) **:** at a distance in space or time ⟨stood 10 paces *off*⟩ ⟨a long way *off*⟩ **b :** from a course **:** ASIDE ⟨turned *off* into a bypath⟩; *specifically* **:** away from the wind **c :** into an unconscious state ⟨dozed *off*⟩
**2 a :** so as to be separated from support ⟨rolled to the edge of the table and *off*⟩ or close contact ⟨blew the lid *off*⟩ ⟨the handle came *off*⟩ **b :** so as to be divided ⟨surface marked *off* into squares⟩
**3 a :** to a state of discontinuance or suspension ⟨shut *off* an engine⟩ **b** — used as an intensifier ⟨drink *off* a glass⟩ ⟨finish it *off*⟩
**4 :** in absence from or suspension of regular work or service ⟨take time *off* for lunch⟩
**5 :** OFFSTAGE

**²off** *preposition* (before 12th century)
**1 a** — used as a function word to indicate physical separation or distance from a position of rest, attachment, or union ⟨take it *off* the table⟩ ⟨a path *off* the main walk⟩ ⟨a shop just *off* the main street⟩ **b :** to seaward of ⟨two miles *off* shore⟩
**2** — used as a function word to indicate the object of an action ⟨borrowed a dollar *off* him⟩ ⟨dined *off* oysters⟩
**3 a** — used as a function word to indicate the suspension of an occupation or activity ⟨*off* duty⟩ ⟨*off* liquor⟩ **b :** below the usual standard or level of ⟨*off* his game⟩

**³off** *adjective* (1666)
**1 a :** more removed or distant ⟨the *off* side of the building⟩ **b :** SEAWARD **c :** RIGHT
**2 a :** started on the way ⟨*off* on a spree⟩ **b :** not taking place or staying in effect **:** CANCELED ⟨the deal was *off*⟩ **c :** not operating **d :** not placed so as to permit operation
**3 a :** not corresponding to fact **:** INCORRECT ⟨*off* in his reckoning⟩ **b :** POOR, SUBNORMAL **c :** not entirely sane **:** ECCENTRIC **d :** REMOTE, SLIGHT ⟨an *off* chance⟩
**4 a :** spent off duty ⟨reading on his *off* days⟩ **b :** SLACK ⟨*off* season⟩
**5 a :** OFF-COLOR **b :** INFERIOR ⟨*off* grade of oil⟩; *also* **:** affected with putrefaction **c :** DOWN ⟨stocks were *off*⟩
**6 :** CIRCUMSTANCED ⟨worse *off*⟩

**⁴off** (1717)
*intransitive verb*
**:** to go away **:** DEPART — used chiefly as an imperative ⟨*off*, or I'll shoot⟩
*transitive verb*
*slang* **:** KILL, MURDER

**of·fal** \ˈȯ-fəl, ˈä-\ *noun* [Middle English, from *of* off + *fall*] (14th century)
**1 :** the waste or by-product of a process: as **a :** trimmings of a hide **b :** the by-products of milling used especially for stock feeds **c :** the viscera and trimmings of a butchered animal removed in dressing
**2 :** RUBBISH

**off and on** *adverb* (1535)
**:** with periodic cessation **:** INTERMITTENTLY ⟨rained *off and on* all day⟩

**¹off·beat** \ˈȯf-ˌbēt\ *noun* (circa 1928)
**:** the unaccented beat of a musical measure

**²off·beat** \-ˈbēt\ *adjective* (1938)
**:** ECCENTRIC, UNCONVENTIONAL

**off Broadway** *noun, often O capitalized* [from its usually being produced in smaller theaters outside of the Broadway theatrical district] (1954)
**:** a part of the New York professional theater stressing fundamental and artistic values and formerly engaging in experimentation
— **off-Broadway** *adjective or adverb, often O capitalized*

**off·cast** \ˈȯf-ˌkast\ *adjective* (1571)
**:** cast off **:** DISCARDED
— **offcast** *noun*

**off·col·or** \ˈȯf-ˈkə-lər\ *or* **off-col·ored** \-lərd\ *adjective* (1860)
**1 a :** not having the right or standard color **b :** being out of sorts
**2 a :** of doubtful propriety **:** DUBIOUS **b :** verging on the indecent

**off·cut** \ˈȯf-ˌkət\ *noun* (circa 1664)
*chiefly British* **:** something that is cut off (as a waste piece of lumber)

**of·fend** \ə-ˈfend\ *verb* [Middle English, from Middle French *offendre*, from Latin *offendere* to strike against, offend, from *ob-* against + *-fendere* to strike — more at OB-, DEFEND] (14th century)
*intransitive verb*
**1 a :** to transgress the moral or divine law **:** SIN ⟨if it be a sin to covet honor, I am the most *offending* soul alive —Shakespeare⟩ **b :** to violate a law or rule **:** do wrong ⟨*offend* against the law⟩

**2 a :** to cause difficulty, discomfort, or injury ⟨took *off* his shoe and removed the *offending* pebble⟩ **b :** to cause dislike, anger, or vexation ⟨thoughtless words that *offend* needlessly⟩
*transitive verb*
**1 a :** VIOLATE, TRANSGRESS **b :** to cause pain to **:** HURT
**2** *obsolete* **:** to cause to sin or fall
**3 :** to cause to feel vexation or resentment usually by violation of what is proper or fitting ⟨was *offended* by their language⟩ ☆
— **of·fend·er** *noun*

**of·fense** *or* **of·fence** \ə-ˈfen(t)s, *especially for 3* ˈä-ˌfen(t)s, ˈȯ-\ *noun* [Middle English, from Middle French, from Latin *offensa*, from feminine of *offensus*, past participle of *offendere*] (14th century)
**1 a** *obsolete* **:** an act of stumbling **b** *archaic* **:** a cause or occasion of sin **:** STUMBLING BLOCK
**2 :** something that outrages the moral or physical senses
**3 a :** the act of attacking **:** ASSAULT **b :** the means or method of attacking or of attempting to score **c :** the offensive team or members of a team playing offensive positions **d :** scoring ability
**4 a :** the act of displeasing or affronting **b :** the state of being insulted or morally outraged ⟨takes *offense* at the slightest criticism⟩

---

☆ SYNONYMS
**Offend, outrage, affront, insult** mean to cause hurt feelings or deep resentment. OFFEND need not imply an intentional hurting but it may indicate merely a violation of the victim's sense of what is proper or fitting ⟨hoped that my remarks had not *offended* her⟩. OUTRAGE implies offending beyond endurance and calling forth extreme feelings ⟨*outraged* by their accusations⟩. AFFRONT implies treating with deliberate rudeness or contemptuous indifference to courtesy ⟨deeply *affronted* by his callousness⟩. INSULT suggests deliberately causing humiliation, hurt pride, or shame ⟨managed to *insult* every guest at the party⟩.

---

◇ WORD HISTORY
**ofay** *Ofay* is a derogatory word for a white person, now perhaps obsolescent, recorded in urban African-American speech since the 1920s. Soon after it first saw print, theories about the word's origin proliferated. Probably the most common is that *ofay* is a Pig Latin permutation of *foe*. However, if a word meaning "enemy" were to be so disguised, the rather literary word *foe* is an unlikely choice, and this explanation is most likely an after-the-fact guess that suits popular notions of what the underlying meaning of the word *should* be. More serious have been attempts to find an African source for *ofay;* the word sounds as if it could come from any of a number of West African languages, but none of the suggestions thus far put forward is entirely compelling. There is also the absence of any documentation for *ofay* before it appeared in a New York City newspaper, the *Inter-State Tattler,* in March, 1925, and shortly thereafter in essays by the Harlem Renaissance authors Rudolph Fisher and George S. Schuyler published in the magazine *American Mercury.* Perhaps we should look no further than 1920s Harlem, culturally creative in many respects, for this piece of linguistic creativity.

---

\ə\ *abut* \ᵊ\ *kitten* \ər\ *further* \a\ *ash* \ā\ *ace* \ä\ *mop, mar* \aů\ *out* \ch\ *chin* \e\ *bet* \ē\ *easy* \g\ *go* \i\ *hit* \ī\ *ice* \j\ *job* \ŋ\ *sing* \ō\ *go* \ȯ\ *law* \ȯi\ *boy* \th\ *thin* \t͟h\ *the* \ü\ *loot* \ů\ *foot* \y\ *yet* \zh\ *vision* *see also* Guide to Pronunciation

**5 a :** a breach of a moral or social code : SIN, MISDEED **b :** an infraction of law; *especially* : MISDEMEANOR ☆☆
— **of·fense·less** \-ləs\ *adjective*
¹**of·fen·sive** \ə-'fen(t)-siv, *especially for 1* 'ä-,fen(t)-, 'ȯ-\ *adjective* (circa 1548)
**1 a :** making attack : AGGRESSIVE **b :** of, relating to, or designed for attack ⟨*offensive* weapons⟩ **c :** of or relating to an attempt to score in a game or contest; *also* : of or relating to a team in possession of the ball or puck
**2 :** giving painful or unpleasant sensations : NAUSEOUS, OBNOXIOUS ⟨*offensive* odor of garbage⟩
**3 :** causing displeasure or resentment
— **of·fen·sive·ly** *adverb*
— **of·fen·sive·ness** *noun*
²**offensive** *noun* (1720)
**1 :** the act of an attacking party
**2 :** ATTACK
¹**of·fer** \'ȯ-fər, 'ä-\ *verb* **of·fered; of·fer·ing** \-f(ə-)riŋ\ [Middle English *offren*, in sense 1, from Old English *offrian*, from Late Latin *offerre*, from Latin, to present, tender, from *ob*-toward + *ferre* to carry; in other senses, from Old French *offrir*, from Latin *offerre* — more at BEAR] (before 12th century)
*transitive verb*
**1 a :** to present as an act of worship or devotion : SACRIFICE **b :** to utter (as a prayer) in devotion
**2 a :** to present for acceptance or rejection : TENDER ⟨was *offered* a job⟩ **b :** to present in order to satisfy a requirement ⟨candidates for degrees may *offer* French as one of their foreign languages⟩
**3 a :** PROPOSE, SUGGEST ⟨*offer* a solution to a problem⟩ **b :** to declare one's readiness or willingness ⟨*offered* to help me⟩
**4 a :** to try or begin to exert : PUT UP ⟨*offered* stubborn resistance⟩ **b :** THREATEN ⟨*offered* to strike him with his cane⟩
**5 :** to make available : AFFORD; *especially* : to place (merchandise) on sale
**6 :** to present in performance or exhibition
**7 :** to propose as payment : BID
*intransitive verb*
**1 :** to present something as an act of worship or devotion : SACRIFICE
**2** *archaic* : to make an attempt
**3 :** to present itself
**4 :** to make a proposal (as of marriage)
²**offer** *noun* (15th century)
**1 a :** a presenting of something for acceptance ⟨considering job *offers* from several firms⟩ ⟨an *offer* of marriage⟩ **b :** an undertaking to do an act or give something on condition that the party to whom the proposal is made do some specified act or make a return promise
**2** *obsolete* : OFFERING
**3 :** a price named by one proposing to buy : BID
**4 a :** ATTEMPT, TRY **b :** an action or movement indicating a purpose or intention
— **on offer** *chiefly British* : being offered especially for sale
**of·fer·ing** \'ȯ-f(ə-)riŋ, 'ä-\ *noun* (before 12th century)
**1 a :** the act of one who offers **b :** something offered; *especially* : a sacrifice ceremonially offered as a part of worship **c :** a contribution to the support of a church
**2 :** something offered for sale or patronage ⟨latest *offerings* of the leading novelists⟩
**3 :** a course of instruction or study
**of·fer·to·ry** \'ȯ-fə(r)-,tōr-ē, 'ä-, -,tȯr-\ *noun*, *plural* **-ries** [Medieval Latin *offertorium*, from Late Latin *offerre*] (1539)
**1** *often capitalized* **a :** the eucharistic offering of bread and wine to God before they are consecrated at Communion **b :** a verse from a Psalm said or sung at the beginning of the offertory
**2 a :** the period of collection and presentation of the offerings of the congregation at public

worship **b :** a musical composition played or sung during an offertory
¹**off·hand** \'ȯf-'hand, -,hand\ *adverb* (1694)
: without premeditation or preparation : EXTEMPORE ⟨couldn't give the figures *offhand*⟩
²**offhand** *adjective* (1708)
**1 :** CASUAL, INFORMAL ⟨a relaxed, *offhand* manner⟩
**2 :** done or made offhand ⟨*offhand* excuses⟩
**off·hand·ed** \-'han-dəd, -,han-\ *adjective* (1835)
: OFFHAND
— **off·hand·ed·ly** *adverb*
— **off·hand·ed·ness** *noun*
**off–hour** \'ȯf-,au̇(-ə)r\ *noun* (1932)
**1 :** a period of time other than a rush hour
**2 :** a period of time other than regular business hours
**of·fice** \'ä-fəs, 'ȯ-\ *noun* [Middle English, from Middle French, from Latin *officium* service, duty, office, from *opus* work + *facere* to make, do — more at OPERATE, DO] (13th century)
**1 a :** a special duty, charge, or position conferred by an exercise of governmental authority and for a public purpose : a position of authority to exercise a public function and to receive whatever emoluments may belong to it **b :** a postion of responsibility or some degree of executive authority
**2** [Middle English, from Old French, from Late Latin *officium*, from Latin] : a prescribed form or service of worship; *specifically*, *capitalized* : DIVINE OFFICE
**3 :** a religious or social ceremonial observance : RITE
**4 a :** something that one ought to do or must do : an assigned or assumed duty, task, or role **b :** the proper or customary action of something : FUNCTION **c :** something done for another : SERVICE
**5 :** a place where a particular kind of business is transacted or a service is supplied: as **a :** a place in which the functions of a public officer are performed **b :** the directing headquarters of an enterprise or organization **c :** the place in which a professional person conducts business
**6** *plural, chiefly British* : the apartments, attached buildings, or outhouses in which the activities attached to the service of a house are carried on
**7 a :** a major administrative unit in some governments ⟨British Foreign *Office*⟩ **b :** a subdivision of some government departments ⟨Patent *Office*⟩
*synonym* see FUNCTION
**office boy** *noun* (1846)
: a boy or man employed for odd jobs in a business office
**of·fice·hold·er** \-,hōl-dər\ *noun* (1818)
: one holding a public office
¹**of·fi·cer** \'ä-fə-sər, 'ȯ-\ *noun* [Middle English, from Middle French *officier*, from Medieval Latin *officiarius*, from Latin *officium*] (14th century)
**1 a** *obsolete* : AGENT **b :** one charged with police duties
**2 :** one who holds an office of trust, authority, or command ⟨the *officers* of the bank⟩
**3 a :** one who holds a position of authority or command in the armed forces; *specifically* : COMMISSIONED OFFICER **b :** the master or any of the mates of a merchant or passenger ship
²**officer** *transitive verb* (1670)
**1 :** to furnish with officers
**2 :** to command or direct as an officer
**officer of arms** *noun* (circa 1500)
: any of the officers (as king of arms, herald, or pursuivant) of a monarch or government responsible for devising and granting armorial bearings
¹**of·fi·cial** \ə-'fi-shəl *also* ō-\ *noun* (14th century)
**1 :** one who holds or is invested with an office : OFFICER ⟨government *officials*⟩
**2 :** one who administers the rules of a game or sport especially as a referee or umpire

²**official** *adjective* (circa 1604)
**1 :** of or relating to an office, position, or trust ⟨*official* duties⟩
**2 :** holding an office
**3 a :** AUTHORITATIVE, AUTHORIZED ⟨*official* statement⟩ **b :** prescribed or recognized as authorized ⟨an *official* language⟩ **c :** described by the U.S. Pharmacopeia or the National Formulary
**4 :** befitting or characteristic of a person in office ⟨extended an *official* greeting⟩
— **of·fi·cial·ly** \-'fi-sh(ə-)lē\ *adverb*
**of·fi·cial·dom** \-'fi-shəl-dəm\ *noun* (1863)
: officials as a class
**of·fi·cial·ese** \-,fi-shə-'lēz, -'lēs\ *noun* (1884)
: the characteristic language of official statements : wordy, pompous, or obscure language
**of·fi·cial·ism** \-'fi-shə-,li-zəm\ *noun* (1857)
: lack of flexibility and initiative combined with excessive adherence to regulations in the behavior of usually government officials
**of·fi·ci·ant** \ə-'fi-shē-ənt\ *noun* (1844)
: one (as a priest) that officiates at a religious rite
¹**of·fi·ci·ary** \ə-'fi-shē-,er-ē, ō-, ä-\ *noun*, *plural* **-ar·ies** [Medieval Latin *officiarius*] (1611)
**1 :** OFFICER, OFFICIAL
**2 :** a body of officers or officials
²**officiary** *adjective* (1612)
: connected with, derived from, or having a title or rank by virtue of holding an office ⟨*officiary* earl⟩
**of·fi·ci·ate** \ə-'fi-shē-,āt\ *verb* **-at·ed; -at·ing** (1631)
*transitive verb*
**1 :** to carry out (an official duty or function)
**2 :** to serve as a leader or celebrant of (a ceremony)
**3 :** to administer the rules of (a game or sport) especially as a referee or umpire
*intransitive verb*
**1 :** to perform a ceremony, function, or duty ⟨*officiate* at a wedding⟩
**2 :** to act in an official capacity : act as an official (as at a sports contest)
— **of·fi·ci·a·tion** \-,fi-shē-'ā-shən\ *noun*

---

☆ **SYNONYMS**
**Offense, resentment, umbrage, pique, dudgeon, huff** mean an emotional response to or an emotional state resulting from a slight or indignity. OFFENSE implies hurt displeasure ⟨takes deep *offense* at racial slurs⟩. RESENTMENT suggests a longer lasting indignation or smoldering ill will ⟨harbored a lifelong *resentment* of his brother⟩. UMBRAGE may suggest hurt pride, resentment, or suspicion of another's motives ⟨took *umbrage* at the offer of advice⟩. PIQUE applies to a transient feeling of wounded vanity ⟨in a *pique* I foolishly declined the invitation⟩. DUDGEON suggests an angry fit of indignation ⟨stormed out of the meeting in high *dudgeon*⟩. HUFF implies a peevish short-lived spell of anger usually at a petty cause ⟨in a *huff* he slammed the door⟩.

**Offense, sin, vice, crime, scandal** mean a transgression of law. OFFENSE applies to the infraction of any law, rule, or code ⟨at that school no *offense* went unpunished⟩. SIN implies an offense against moral or religious law ⟨the *sin* of blasphemy⟩. VICE applies to a habit or practice that degrades or corrupts ⟨regarded gambling as a *vice*⟩. CRIME implies a serious offense punishable by the law of the state ⟨the *crime* of murder⟩. SCANDAL applies to an offense that outrages the public conscience ⟨a career ruined by a sex *scandal*⟩.

**of·fi·ci·nal** \ə-'fi-sⁿn-əl, ò-, ä-; ˌò-fə-'sī-nⁿl, ˌä-\ *adjective* [Medieval Latin *officinalis* of a storeroom, from *officina* storeroom, from Latin, workshop, from *opific-, opifex* workman, from *opus* work + *facere* to do] (circa 1720) : MEDICINAL ⟨a monograph on *officinal* flora⟩

**of·fi·cious** \ə-'fi-shəs\ *adjective* [Latin *officiosus,* from *officium* service, office] (1565) **1** *archaic* **a** : KIND, OBLIGING **b** : DUTIFUL **2** : volunteering one's services where they are neither asked nor needed : MEDDLESOME **3** : INFORMAL, UNOFFICIAL *synonym* see IMPERTINENT
— **of·fi·cious·ly** *adverb*
— **of·fi·cious·ness** *noun*

**off·ing** \'ò-fiŋ, 'ä-\ *noun* [¹*off*] (1627) **1** : the part of the deep sea seen from the shore **2** : the near or foreseeable future ⟨in the *offing*⟩

**off·ish** \'ò-fish\ *adjective* [¹*off*] (1831) : STANDOFFISH
— **off·ish·ness** *noun*

**off-key** \'òf-'kē\ *adjective or adverb* (1927) **1** : varying in pitch from the proper tone of a melody **2** : IRREGULAR, ANOMALOUS

**off-kil·ter** \-'kil-tər\ *adjective* (circa 1944) : not in perfect balance : a bit askew

**off-lim·its** \'òf-'li-məts\ *adjective* (1945) : not to be entered or patronized by a designated class (as military personnel); *also* : not to be interfered with, considered, or spoken of ⟨the subject of sex was *off-limits* in her family⟩

**off-line** \-'līn\ *adjective* (1950) : not connected to or served by a system and especially a computer or telecommunications system; *also* : done independently of a system ⟨*off-line* computer storage⟩
— **off-line** *adverb*

**off·load** \(ˌ)òf-'lōd, 'òf-ˌ\ *verb* (1850) : UNLOAD

**off of** *preposition* (1593) : OFF ☐

**off-off-Broadway** *noun, often both Os capitalized* [from its relation to off Broadway being analogous to the relation of off Broadway to Broadway] (1965) : an avant-garde theatrical movement in New York
— **off-off-Broadway** *adjective or adverb, often both Os capitalized*

**off-peak** \'òf-'pēk\ *adjective* (1920) : not being in the period of maximum use or business : not peak ⟨telephone rates during *off-peak* hours⟩

**off-price** \'òf-'prīs\ *adjective* (1952) : of, relating to, selling, or being discounted merchandise ⟨an *off-price* store⟩ ⟨*off-price* apparel⟩

**off·print** \'òf-ˌprint\ *noun* (1885) : a separately printed excerpt (as a magazine article)
— **offprint** *transitive verb*

**off-put·ting** \-ˌpu̇-tiŋ\ *adjective* (1828) : that puts one off : REPELLENT, DISCONCERTING
— **off-put·ting·ly** \-lē\ *adverb*

**off-ramp** \-ˌramp\ *noun* (1954) : a ramp by which one leaves a limited-access highway

**off-road** \'òf-'rōd\ *adjective* (1968) : of, relating to, done with, or being a vehicle designed especially to operate away from public roads

**off·scour·ing** \-ˌska u̇(-ə)r-iŋ\ *noun* (1526) **1** : someone rejected by society : OUTCAST **2** : something that is scoured off : REFUSE

**off·screen** \'òf-'skrēn\ *adverb or adjective* (1935) **1** : out of sight of the motion picture or television viewer **2** : in private life

**off-sea·son** \'òf-ˌsē-zⁿn\ *noun* (1848) : a time of suspended or reduced activity; *especially* : the time during which an athlete is not training or competing

**¹off·set** \'òf-ˌset\ *noun* (circa 1555) **1 a** *archaic* : OUTSET, START **b** : CESSATION **2 a** (1) : a short prostrate lateral shoot arising from the base of a plant (2) : a small bulb arising from the base of another bulb **b** : a lateral or collateral branch (as of a family or race) : OFFSHOOT **c** : a spur from a range of hills **3 a** : a horizontal ledge on the face of a wall formed by a diminution of its thickness above **b** : DISPLACEMENT **c** : an abrupt change in the dimension or profile of an object or the part set off by such change **4** : something that sets off to advantage or embellishes something else : FOIL **5** : an abrupt bend in an object by which one part is turned aside out of line **6** : something that serves to counterbalance or to compensate for something else; *especially* : either of two balancing ledger items **7 a** : unintentional transfer of ink (as from a freshly printed sheet) **b** : a printing process in which an inked impression from a plate is first made on a rubber-blanketed cylinder and then transferred to the paper being printed
— **offset** *adjective or adverb*

**²off·set** \'òf-ˌset, *verb transitive senses are also* òf-\ *verb* **-set; -set·ting** (1792) *transitive verb* **1 a** : to place over against something : BALANCE ⟨credits *offset* debits⟩ **b** : to serve as a counterbalance for : COMPENSATE ⟨his speed *offset* his opponent's greater weight⟩ **2** : to form an offset in ⟨*offset* a wall⟩ *intransitive verb* : to become marked by offset

**off·shoot** \'òf-ˌshüt\ *noun* (1710) **1 a** : a collateral or derived branch, descendant, or member : OUTGROWTH **b** : a lateral branch (as of a mountain range) **2** : a branch of a main stem especially of a plant

**¹off·shore** \'òf-ˌshōr, -'shòr\ *adverb* (1720) **1** : from the shore : SEAWARD; *also* : at a distance from the shore **2** : outside the country : ABROAD

**²off·shore** \'òf-ˌ\ *adjective* (1845) **1** : coming or moving away from the shore toward the water ⟨an *offshore* breeze⟩ **2 a** : situated off the shore but within waters under a country's control ⟨*offshore* fisheries⟩ **b** : distant from the shore — compare INSHORE **3** : situated or operating in a foreign country ⟨*offshore* mutual funds⟩ ⟨*offshore* banking⟩

**³off·shore** \'òf-ˌ\ *preposition* (1965) : off the shore of

**off·side** \'òf-'sīd\ *adverb or adjective* (1867) : illegally in advance of the ball or puck

**off-site** \-'sīt\ *adjective or adverb* (1946) : not located or occurring at the site of a particular activity

**off-speed** \-'spēd\ *adjective* (1965) : being slower than usual or expected ⟨throwing *off-speed* pitches⟩

**off·spring** \'òf-ˌspriŋ\ *noun, plural* **offspring** *also* **offsprings** [Middle English *ofspring,* from Old English, from *of* off + *springan* to spring] (before 12th century) **1 a** : the progeny of an animal or plant : YOUNG **b** : CHILD **2 a** : PRODUCT, RESULT ⟨scholarly manuscripts —the labored *offsprings* of PhDs —Donna Martin⟩ **b** : OFFSHOOT 1a

**off·stage** \'òf-'stāj, -ˌstāj\ *adverb or adjective* (1921) **1** : on a part of the stage not visible to the audience **2** : in private life ⟨known *offstage* as a kindly person⟩ **3** : behind the scenes : out of the public view ⟨much of the important work of the conference was done *offstage*⟩

**off-the-books** *adjective* (1980) : not reported or recorded ⟨*off-the-books* transactions⟩ ⟨*off-the-books* covert operations⟩
— **off the books** *adverb*

**off-the-cuff** *adjective* (1938) : not prepared in advance : SPONTANEOUS, IN-FORMAL ⟨*off-the-cuff* remarks⟩
— **off-the-cuff** *adverb*

**off-the-peg** *adjective* (1959) *chiefly British* : READY-MADE 1

**off-the-rack** *adjective* (1965) : READY-MADE 1 ⟨*off-the-rack* suits⟩

**off-the-record** *adjective* (1933) : given or made in confidence and not for publication ⟨*off-the-record* comments⟩

**off-the-shelf** *adjective* (1950) : available as a stock item : not specially designed or custom-made ⟨made of *off-the-shelf* components⟩

**off-the-wall** *adjective* (circa 1966) : highly unusual : BIZARRE ⟨an *off-the-wall* sense of humor⟩

**off-track** \'òf-'trak\ *adverb or adjective* (1944) : away from a racetrack ⟨betting *offtrack*⟩ ⟨*offtrack* bookies⟩

**off-white** \'òf-'hwīt, -'wīt\ *noun* (1927) : a yellowish or grayish white

**off year** *noun* (1873) **1** : a year in which no major election is held **2** : a year of diminished activity or production ⟨an *off year* for auto sales⟩

**oft** \'òft\ *adverb* [Middle English, from Old English; akin to Old High German *ofto* often] (before 12th century) : OFTEN

**of·ten** \'ò-fən, ÷'òf-tən\ *adverb* [Middle English, alteration of *oft*] (14th century) : many times : FREQUENTLY

**of·ten·times** \-ˌtīmz\ *or* **oft·times** \'òf(t)-ˌtīmz\ *adverb* (14th century) : OFTEN, REPEATEDLY

**ogee** *also* **OG** \'ō-ˌjē\ *noun* [obsolete English *ogee* ogive; from the use of such moldings in ogives] (1677) **1** : a molding with an S-shaped profile **2** : a pointed arch having on each side a reversed curve near the apex — see ARCH illustration

**ogham** *or* **ogam** \'ä-gəm, 'ō-; 'ō(-ə)m\ *noun* [Irish *ogham,* from Middle Irish *ogom, ogum*] (1729) : the alphabetic system of 5th and 6th century Irish in which an alphabet of 20 letters is represented by notches for vowels and lines for consonants and which is known principally from inscriptions cut on the edges of rough standing tombstones
— **ogham·ic** \ä-'gä-mik, ō-; 'ō-(ə-)mik\ *adjective*
— **ogham·ist** \'ä-gə-mist, 'ō-; 'ō-(ə-)mist\ *noun*

**ogi·val** \ō-'jī-vəl\ *adjective* (1841) : of, relating to, or having the form of an ogive or an ogee

**ogive** \'ō-ˌjīv\ *noun* [Middle English *oggif* stone comprising an arch, from Middle French *augive* diagonal arch] (1611) **1 a** : a diagonal arch or rib across a Gothic vault **b** : a pointed arch **2** : a graph of a distribution function or a cumulative frequency distribution **3** : OGEE 1

**¹ogle** \'ō-gəl *also* 'ä-\ *verb* **ogled; ogling** \-g(ə-)liŋ\ [probably from Low German *oegeln,* from *oog* eye; akin to Old High German *ouga* eye — more at EYE] (1682)

\ə\ abut \ᵊ\ kitten \ər\ further \a\ ash \ā\ ace \ä\ mop, mar \au̇\ out \ch\ chin \e\ bet \ē\ easy \g\ go \i\ hit \ī\ ice \j\ job \ŋ\ sing \ō\ go \ò\ law \òi\ boy \th\ thin \th̷\ the \ü\ loot \u̇\ foot \y\ yet \zh\ vision *see also* Guide to Pronunciation

*intransitive verb*
: to glance with amorous invitation or challenge
*transitive verb*
**1** : to eye amorously or provocatively
**2** : to look at especially with greedy or interested attention
— **ogler** \-g(ə-)lər\ *noun*

**²ogle** *noun* (1711)
: an amorous or coquettish glance

**ogre** \'ō-gər\ *noun* [French, probably ultimately from Latin *Orcus,* god of the underworld] (1713)
**1** : a hideous giant of fairy tales and folklore that feeds on human beings : MONSTER
**2** : a dreaded person or object
— **ogre·ish** \'ō-g(ə-)rish\ *adjective*

**ogress** \'ō-g(ə-)rəs\ *noun* (1713)
: a female ogre

**¹oh** \(')ō\ *interjection* [Middle English *o*] (13th century)
**1** — used to express an emotion (as surprise or desire) or in response to physical stimuli
**2** — used in direct address ⟨*oh,* waiter! Will you come here, please?⟩
**3** — used to express acknowledgment or understanding of a statement
**4** — used to introduce an example or approximation

**²oh** \'ō\ *noun* [*o;* from the similarity of the symbol for zero (0) to the letter *O*] (1936)
: ZERO

**ohia** \ō-'hē-ə\ *noun* [Hawaiian *'ōhi'a*] (1824)
: LEHUA

**ohia lehua** *noun* [Hawaiian *'ōhi'a-lehua*] (1888)
: LEHUA

**ohm** \'ōm\ *noun* [Georg Simon *Ohm*] (1867)
: the practical meter-kilogram-second unit of electric resistance equal to the resistance of a circuit in which a potential difference of one volt produces a current of one ampere
— **ohm·ic** \'ō-mik\ *adjective*
— **ohm·i·cal·ly** \-mi-k(ə-)lē\ *adverb*

**ohm·me·ter** \'ō(m)-,mē-tər\ *noun* [International Scientific Vocabulary] (circa 1890)
: an instrument for indicating resistance in ohms directly

**Ohm's law** \'ōmz-\ *noun* (1863)
: a law in electricity: the strength of a direct current is directly proportional to the potential difference and inversely proportional to the resistance of the circuit

**-oic** *adjective suffix* [French *-oïque* (as in *acide caproïque* caproic acid)]
: containing carboxyl or a derivative ⟨benz*oic* acid⟩

**¹-oid** *noun suffix*
: something resembling a (specified) object or having a (specified) quality ⟨glob*oid*⟩

**²-oid** *adjective suffix* [Middle French & Latin; Middle French *-oïde,* from Latin *-oïdes,* from Greek *-oeidēs,* from *-o-* + *eidos* appearance, form — more at WISE]
: resembling : having the form or appearance of ⟨petal*oid*⟩

**oid·i·um** \ō-'id-ē-əm\ *noun, plural* **-ia** \-dē-ə\ [New Latin, from *o-* + *-idium*] (1857)
**1 a** : any of a genus (*Oidium* of the family Moniliaceae) of imperfect fungi many of which are now considered to be conidial stages of various powdery mildews **b** : one of the small conidia borne in chains by various fungi (as an oidium) — called also *arthrospore*
**2** : a powdery mildew caused by an oidium especially in the grape

**¹oil** \'ȯi(ə)l\ *noun, often attributive* [Middle English *oile,* from Old French, from Latin *oleum* olive oil, from Greek *elaion,* from *elaia* olive] (13th century)
**1 a** : any of numerous unctuous combustible substances that are liquid or can be liquefied easily on warming, are soluble in ether but not in water, and leave a greasy stain on paper or cloth **b** (1) : PETROLEUM (2) : the petroleum industry

**2** : a substance (as a cosmetic preparation) of oily consistency ⟨bath *oil*⟩
**3 a** : an oil color used by an artist **b** : a painting done in oil colors
**4** : unctuous or flattering speech

**²oil** (15th century)
*transitive verb*
: to smear, rub over, furnish, or lubricate with oil
*intransitive verb*
: to take on fuel oil
— **oil the hand** *or* **oil the palm** : BRIBE. TIP

**oil beetle** *noun* (1658)
: any of various blister beetles (genus *Meloe* or a related genus) that emit a yellowish liquid from the leg joints when disturbed

**oil·bird** \'ȯi(ə)l-,bərd\ *noun* (circa 1890)
: a nocturnal bird (*Steatornis caripensis*) of northern South America and Trinidad that is related to the nightjars, feeds chiefly on the fatty fruits of various palms, and has fatty young from which oil is extracted for use instead of butter — called also *guacharo*

**oil cake** *noun* (1743)
: the solid residue after extracting the oil from seeds (as of cotton)

**oil·can** \'ȯi(ə)l-,kan\ *noun* (1839)
: a can for oil; *especially* : a spouted can designed to release oil by drop (as for lubricating machinery)

**oil·cloth** \-,klȯth\ *noun* (1796)
: cloth treated with oil or paint and used for table and shelf coverings

**oil color** *noun* (1539)
**1** : a pigment used for oil paint
**2** : OIL PAINT

**oiled** \'ȯi(ə)ld\ *adjective* (1535)
**1** : lubricated, treated, or covered with or as if with oil ⟨*oiled* paper⟩
**2** *slang* : DRUNK 1a

**oil·er** \'ȯi-lər\ *noun* (circa 1846)
**1** : one (as a workman) that oils something
**2** : a receptacle or device for applying oil
**3** *plural* : OILSKIN 3
**4** : an auxiliary naval vessel used for refueling at sea

**oil field** *noun* (1894)
: a region rich in petroleum deposits; *especially* : one that has been brought into production

**oil gland** *noun* (circa 1836)
: a gland (as of the skin) that produces an oily secretion; *specifically* : UROPYGIAL GLAND

**oil·man** \'ȯi(ə)l-mən, -,man\ *noun* (1865)
**1** : an oil company executive
**2** : an oil field worker

**oil of vitriol** (1580)
: concentrated sulfuric acid

**oil of wintergreen** (1866)
: the methyl ester of salicylic acid that is used as a flavoring and as a counterirritant

**oil paint** *noun* (1790)
: paint in which a drying oil is the vehicle

**oil painting** *noun* (1782)
**1 a** : the act or art of painting in oil colors **b** : a picture painted in oils
**2** : painting that uses pigments originally ground in oil

**oil palm** *noun* (circa 1864)
: an African pinnate-leaved palm (*Elaeis guineensis*) cultivated for its clustered fruit whose flesh and seeds yield oil

**oil pan** *noun* (1908)
: the lower section of the crankcase used as a lubricating-oil reservoir on an internal combustion engine

**oil patch** *noun* (circa 1952)
**1** : OIL FIELD
**2** : the petroleum industry

**oil·seed** \'ȯi(ə)l-,sēd\ *noun* (1562)
: a seed or crop (as flaxseed) grown mainly for oil

**oil shale** *noun* (1873)
: a rock (as shale) from which oil can be recovered by distillation

**oil·skin** \'ȯi(ə)l-,skin\ *noun* (1812)

**1** : an oiled waterproof cloth used for coverings and garments
**2** : an oilskin raincoat
**3** *plural* : an oilskin suit of coat and trousers

**oil slick** *noun* (1889)
: a film of oil floating on water

**oil·stone** \'ȯi(ə)l-,stōn\ *noun* (1585)
: a whetstone for use with oil

**oil well** *noun* (1847)
: a well from which petroleum is obtained

**oily** \'ȯi-lē\ *adjective* **oil·i·er; -est** (14th century)
**1** : of, relating to, or consisting of oil
**2 a** : covered or impregnated with oil ⟨*oily* rags⟩ **b** : relatively high in naturally secreted oils ⟨*oily* skin⟩ ⟨*oily* hair⟩
**3** : excessively smooth or suave in manner
— **oil·i·ly** \'ȯi-lə-lē\ *adverb*
— **oil·i·ness** \-lē-nəs\ *noun*

**oink** \'ȯiŋk\ *noun* [imitative] (1941)
: the natural noise of a hog
— **oink** *intransitive verb*

**oint·ment** \'ȯint-mənt\ *noun* [Middle English, alteration of *oignement,* from Old French, ultimately from Latin *unguentum,* from *unguere* to anoint; akin to Old High German *ancho* butter, Sanskrit *anakti* he salves] (14th century)
: a salve or unguent for application to the skin

**oi·ti·ci·ca** \,ȯi-tə-'sē-kə\ *noun* [Portuguese, from Tupi] (1901)
: any of several South American trees; *especially* : a Brazilian tree (*Licania rigida*) with seeds that yield a drying oil similar to tung oil

**Ojib·wa** *or* **Ojib·way** \ō-'jib-(,)wä\ *noun, plural* **Ojibwa** *or* **Ojibwas** *or* **Ojibway** *or* **Ojibways** [Ojibwa *očipwe',* an Ojibwa band] (1700)
**1** : a member of an American Indian people of the region around Lake Superior and westward
**2** : an Algonquian language of the Ojibwa people

**¹OK** *or* **okay** \ō-'kā, *in assenting or agreeing also* 'ō-,kā\ *adverb or adjective* [abbreviation of *oll korrect,* facetious alteration of *all correct*] (1839)
: ALL RIGHT ◆

**²OK** *or* **okay** \ō-'kā\ *noun* (1841)
: APPROVAL, ENDORSEMENT

**³OK** *or* **okay** \ō-'kā\ *transitive verb* **OK'd** *or* **okayed; OK'·ing** *or* **okay·ing** (1888)
: APPROVE, AUTHORIZE

**oka** *variant of* OCA

---

◇ WORD HISTORY
**OK** *OK,* one of the most successful of all Americanisms, has long been the subject of etymological claims and counterclaims. According to the most plausible account, it arose in the late 1830s from a journalistic fad for reducing phrases to abbreviations. At the height of the fad it became fashionable to alter some of the abbreviations on the basis of pseudo-uneducated misspellings, so that *A.R.* for *all right* was transformed to *O.W.* on the basis of *oll wright,* and *N.G.* for *no go* to *K.G.* Hence *OK,* when it appeared in the Boston *Morning Post* on March 23, 1839— the earliest printed occurrence that anyone has yet found—is glossed as *oll korrect,* presumably a deliberate misspelling of *all correct. OK* might well have passed into oblivion with such other initialisms, but in the 1840 American presidential campaign it became associated with the Democratic O.K. Club, in which *O.K.* stood for *Old Kinderhook,* after Kinderhook, New York, the birthplace of the Democrats' candidate, Martin Van Buren. Humorous expansions of *OK,* including *oll korrect,* were bandied back and forth by both Democrats and Whigs. By 1841 *OK* had gone beyond the political arena to become an interjectional equivalent for "All right!"

**oka·pi** \ō-'kä-pē\ *noun* [Mvu'ba (language of northeast Zaire)] (1900)
: an ungulate mammal (*Okapia johnstoni*) of Zaire that is closely related to the giraffe but has a relatively short neck, a coat typically of solid reddish chestnut on the trunk, yellowish white on the cheeks, and purplish black and cream rings on the upper parts of the legs

okapi

**okey–doke** \ō-kē-'dōk\ *or* **okey–dokey** \-'dō-kē\ *adverb* [reduplication of *OK*] (circa 1932)
— used to express assent

**Okie** \'ō-kē\ *noun* [*Oklahoma* + *-ie*] (1938)
: a migrant agricultural worker; *especially* : one from Oklahoma in the 1930s — sometimes used disparagingly

**okra** \'ō-krə, *Southern also* -krē\ *noun* [of African origin; akin to Ibo *ókùrù* okra] (1679)
1 : a tall annual (*Abelmoschus esculentus*) of the mallow family that is cultivated for its mucilaginous green pods used especially in soups or stews; *also* : the pods of this plant
2 : ¹GUMBO 1

**¹-ol** *noun suffix* [International Scientific Vocabulary, from *alcohol*]
: chemical compound (as an alcohol or phenol) containing hydroxyl 〈glycer*ol*〉〈cres*ol*〉

**²-ol** — see -OLE

**³-ol** *noun combining form* [International Scientific Vocabulary, from Latin *oleum* oil — more at OIL]
: hydrocarbon chemically related to benzene 〈xyl*ol*〉

**¹old** \'ōld; *for sense 9 usually* 'ōl\ *adjective* [Middle English, from Old English *eald;* akin to Old High German *alt* old, Latin *alere* to nourish, *alescere* to grow, *altus* high, deep] (before 12th century)
1 a : dating from the remote past : ANCIENT 〈*old* traditions〉 b : persisting from an earlier time 〈an *old* ailment〉 〈they brought up the same *old* argument〉 c : of long standing 〈an *old* friend〉
2 a : distinguished from an object of the same kind by being of an earlier date 〈many still used the *old* name〉 b *capitalized* : belonging to an early period in the development of a language or literature 〈*Old* Persian〉
3 : having existed for a specified period of time 〈a girl three years *old*〉
4 : of, relating to, or originating in a past era 〈*old* chronicles record the event〉
5 a : advanced in years or age 〈an *old* man〉 b : showing the characteristics of age 〈looked *old* at 20〉
6 : EXPERIENCED 〈an *old* trooper speaking of the last war〉
7 : FORMER 〈his *old* students〉
8 a : showing the effects of time or use : WORN, AGED 〈*old* shoes〉 b : well advanced toward reduction by running water to the lowest level possible — used of topographic features c : no longer in use : DISCARDED 〈*old* rags〉 d : of a grayish or dusty color 〈*old* mauve〉 e : TIRESOME 〈gets *old* fast〉
9 a : long familiar 〈same *old* story〉 〈good *old* Joe〉 b — used as an intensive 〈a high *old* time〉 c — used to express an attitude of affection or amusement 〈a big *old* dog〉 〈flex the *old* biceps〉 〈any *old* time〉 ☆

**²old** *noun* (13th century)
1 : one of a specified age — usually used in combination 〈a 3-year-*old*〉
2 : old or earlier time — used in the phrase *of old* 〈mighty men of *old*〉

**old boy** *noun* (1868)
1 *often O&B capitalized, British* : an alumnus especially of a boys' school

2 : a man who is a member of a long-standing and usually influential clique especially in a professional, business, or social sphere

**Old Bulgarian** *noun* (1861)
: OLD CHURCH SLAVONIC

**Old Catholic** *noun* (1871)
: a member of one of various hierarchical and liturgical churches separating from the Roman Catholic Church at various times since the 18th century

**Old Christmas** *noun* (1863)
*chiefly Midland* : EPIPHANY 1

**Old Church Slavonic** *noun* (circa 1929)
: the Slavic language used in the liturgical and Biblical translations of Cyril and Methodius as attested in manuscripts of the 10th and 11th centuries — called also *Old Church Slavic*; see INDO-EUROPEAN LANGUAGES table

**old country** *noun, often O&C capitalized* (1782)
: an emigrant's country of origin; *especially* : one in Europe — usually used with *the*

**old·en** \'ōl-dən\ *adjective* (14th century)
: of or relating to a bygone era

**Old English** *noun* (13th century)
1 a : the language of the English people from the time of the earliest documents in the 7th century to about 1100 — see INDO-EUROPEAN LANGUAGES table b : English of any period before Modern English
2 : BLACK LETTER

**Old English sheepdog** *noun* (1891)
: any of a breed of tailless dogs developed in England and having a profuse blue-gray and white coat

**Old English sheepdog**

**old·fan·gled** \'ōl(d)-'faŋ-gəld\ *adjective* [*old* + *-fangled* (as in *newfangled*)] (1842)
: OLD-FASHIONED

**¹old–fash·ioned** \-'fa-shənd\ *adjective* (1596)
1 a : of, relating to, or characteristic of a past era 〈wears an *old-fashioned* black bow tie —Green Peyton〉 b : adhering to customs of a past era
2 : OUTMODED
— **old–fash·ioned·ly** \-shən(d)-lē\ *adverb*
— **old–fash·ioned·ness** \-nəs\ *noun*

**²old–fashioned** *noun* (1901)
: a cocktail usually made with whiskey, bitters, sugar, a twist of lemon peel, and a small amount of water or soda

**Old French** *noun* (1708)
: the French language from the 9th to the 16th century; *especially* : French from the 9th to the 13th century — see INDO-EUROPEAN LANGUAGES table

**Old Glory** *noun* (1862)
: the flag of the U.S.

**old gold** *noun* (1879)
: a dark yellow

**old guard** *noun, often O&G capitalized* (1850)
1 : a group of established prestige and influence
2 : the conservative members of an organization (as a political party)

**old hand** *noun* (circa 1785)
: HAND 10e

**old hat** *adjective* (1911)
1 : OLD-FASHIONED
2 : lacking in freshness : TRITE

**Old High German** *noun* (circa 1884)
: High German exemplified in documents prior to the 12th century — see INDO-EUROPEAN LANGUAGES table

**old·ie** \'ōl-dē\ *noun* (1874)
: one that is old; *especially* : a popular song of an earlier day

**Old Ionic** *noun* (circa 1889)
: the Greek dialect of the Homeric epics

**Old Iranian** *noun* (1939)
: any Iranian language in use in the period B.C.

**Old Irish** *noun* (circa 1884)
: the Irish in use from the 7th century to about 950 — see INDO-EUROPEAN LANGUAGES table

**old·ish** \'ōl-dish\ *adjective* (circa 1669)
: somewhat old or elderly

**old lady** *noun* (1836)
1 : WIFE
2 : MOTHER
3 : GIRLFRIEND; *especially* : one with whom a man cohabits

**Old Latin** *noun* (circa 1889)
: Latin used in the early inscriptions and in literature prior to the classical period

**old–line** \'ōl(d)-'līn\ *adjective* (1856)
1 a : having a reputation or authority based on length or proven quality of service 〈an *old-line* firm〉 b : of established prestige and influence 〈*old-line* families〉
2 : adhering to traditional policies or practices : CONSERVATIVE

**old maid** *noun* (circa 1530)
1 : SPINSTER 3
2 : a prim fussy person 〈he was a real *old maid* about burning rubbish —R. C. Ruark〉
3 : a simple card game in which cards are matched in pairs and the player holding the unmatched card at the end loses
— **old–maid·ish** \'ōl(d)-'mā-dish\ *adjective*
— **old–maid·ish·ness** \-nəs\ *noun*

**old man** *noun* (1768)
1 a : HUSBAND b : FATHER
2 *capitalized* : one in authority; *especially* : COMMANDING OFFICER
3 : BOYFRIEND; *especially* : one with whom a woman cohabits

**old–man's beard** \'ōl(d)-'manz-\ *noun* (1742)
1 : any of several clematises (especially *Clematis vitalba*) having plumose styles
2 : a greenish gray pendulous lichen (*Usnea barbata*) growing on trees

**old master** *noun* (1824)
: a work of art by an established master and especially by any of the distinguished painters of the 16th, 17th, or early 18th century; *also* : such an artist

**Old Nick** \'ōl(d)-'nik\ *noun* (1668)
— used as a name of the devil

---

☆ **SYNONYMS**

**Old, ancient, venerable, antique, antiquated, archaic, obsolete** mean having come into existence or use in the more or less distant past. OLD may apply to either actual or merely relative length of existence 〈*old* houses〉 〈an *old* sweater of mine〉. ANCIENT applies to occurrence, existence, or use in or survival from the distant past 〈*ancient* accounts of dragons〉. VENERABLE stresses the impressiveness and dignity of great age 〈the family's *venerable* patriarch〉. ANTIQUE applies to what has come down from a former or ancient time 〈collected *antique* Chippendale furniture〉. ANTIQUATED implies being discredited or outmoded or otherwise inappropriate to the present time 〈*antiquated* teaching methods〉. ARCHAIC implies having the character or characteristics of a much earlier time 〈the play used *archaic* language to convey a sense of period〉. OBSOLETE may apply to something regarded as no longer acceptable or useful even though it is still in existence 〈a computer that makes earlier models *obsolete*〉.

---

\ə\ abut \ᵊ\ kitten \ər\ further \a\ ash \ā\ ace
\ä\ mop, mar \au̇\ out \ch\ chin \e\ bet \ē\ easy
\g\ go \i\ hit \ī\ ice \j\ job \ŋ\ sing \ō\ go
\ȯ\ law \oi\ boy \th\ thin \t͟h\ the \ü\ loot \u̇\ foot
\y\ yet \zh\ vision *see also* Guide to Pronunciation

**Old Norse** *noun* (1844)
: the North Germanic language of the Scandinavian peoples prior to about 1350 — see INDO-EUROPEAN LANGUAGES table

**Old North French** *noun* (circa 1930)
: the northern dialects of Old French including especially those of Normandy and Picardy

**Old Persian** *noun* (circa 1909)
: an ancient Iranian language known from cuneiform inscriptions from the 5th and 6th centuries B.C. — see INDO-EUROPEAN LANGUAGES table

**Old Prussian** *noun* (1872)
: a Baltic language used in East Prussia until the 17th century — see INDO-EUROPEAN LANGUAGES table

**old rose** *noun* (1893)
: a variable color averaging a grayish red

**Old Saxon** *noun* (1841)
: the language of the Saxons of northwest Germany until about the 12th century — see INDO-EUROPEAN LANGUAGES table

**old school** *noun* (1749)
: adherents of traditional policies and practices

**old school tie** *noun* (1932)
**1 a :** an attitude of conservatism, aplomb, and upper-class solidarity associated with English public school graduates **b :** a necktie displaying the colors of an English public school
**2 :** clannishness among members of an established clique

**old–shoe** \'ōl(d)-'shü\ *adjective* (1944)
: characterized by familiarity or freedom from restraint : COMFORTABLE, UNPRETENTIOUS

**old sledge** *noun* (1830)
: SEVEN-UP

**old–squaw** \'ōl(d)-'skwȯ\ *noun* (1838)
: a common sea duck (*Clangula hyemalis*) of the more northern parts of the northern hemisphere

**old·ster** \'ōl(d)-stər\ *noun* (1848)
: an old or elderly person

**old style** *noun* (1617)
**1** *O&S capitalized* **:** a style of reckoning time used before the adoption of the Gregorian calendar
**2 :** a style of type distinguished by graceful irregularity among individual letters, bracketed serifs, and but slight contrast between light and heavy strokes

**Old Style** *adjective* (1678)
: using or according to the Julian calendar

**Old Swedish** *noun* (circa 1909)
: the Swedish language as exemplified in documents prior to about 1350

**Old Testament** *noun* (14th century)
: the first part of the Christian Bible containing the books of the Jewish canon of Scripture — see BIBLE table

**old–time** \'ōl(d)-'tīm\ *adjective* (1824)
**1 :** of, relating to, or characteristic of an earlier period ⟨*old-time* songs⟩
**2 :** of long standing ⟨*old-time* residents⟩

**old–tim·er** \-'tī-mər, -ˌtī-mər\ *noun* (1879)
**1 a :** VETERAN **b :** OLDSTER
**2 :** something that is old-fashioned : ANTIQUE

**old–timey** \'ōl(d)-'tī-mē\ *adjective* (1850)
: of a kind or style prevalent in or reminiscent of an earlier time ⟨*old-timey* music⟩

**Old Welsh** *noun* (1882)
: the Welsh language exemplified in documents prior to about 1150 — see INDO-EUROPEAN LANGUAGES table

**old·wife** \'ōl(d)-ˌwīf\ *noun* (1588)
**1 :** any of several marine fishes (as an alewife, menhaden, or triggerfish)
**2 :** OLD-SQUAW

**old wives' tale** *noun* (1656)
: an often traditional belief that is not based on fact : SUPERSTITION

**old–world** \'ōl(d)-'wər(-ə)ld\ *adjective* (1712)
: of, relating to, or characteristic of the Old World; *especially* **:** having the charm or picturesque qualities of the Old World ⟨narrow *old-world* streets⟩

**Old World** *noun* (circa 1596)
: the eastern hemisphere exclusive of Australia; *specifically* **:** Europe

**ole** \'ōl\ *adjective* [by alteration] (1844)
: OLD

**ole-** *or* **oleo-** *combining form* [French *olé-, oléo-,* from Latin *ole-,* from *oleum* — more at OIL]
: oil ⟨*oleo*graph⟩

**-ole** *also* **-ol** *noun combining form* [International Scientific Vocabulary, from Latin *oleum*]
**1 :** chemical compound containing a 5-membered usually heterocyclic ring ⟨pyrr*ole*⟩
**2 :** chemical compound not containing hydroxyl ⟨eucalypt*ol*⟩ — especially in names of ethers ⟨safr*ole*⟩

**olé** \ō-'lā\ *noun* [Spanish] (1922)
: ²BRAVO

**ole·ag·i·nous** \ˌō-lē-'a-jə-nəs\ *adjective* [Middle English, from Middle French *oleagineux,* from Latin *oleagineus* of an olive tree, from *olea* olive tree, from Greek *elaia*] (15th century)
**1 :** resembling or having the properties of oil : OILY; *also* **:** containing or producing oil
**2 :** marked by an offensively ingratiating manner or quality
— **ole·ag·i·nous·ly** *adverb*
— **ole·ag·i·nous·ness** *noun*

**ole·an·der** \'ō-lē-ˌan-dər, ˌō-lē-'\ *noun* [Medieval Latin, alteration of *arodandrum, lorandrum,* perhaps alteration of Latin *rhododendron* — more at RHODODENDRON] (1548)
: a poisonous evergreen shrub (*Nerium oleander*) of the dogbane family with fragrant white to red flowers

**ole·an·do·my·cin** \ˌō-lē-ˌan-də-'mī-sⁿn\ *noun* [*oleand*rose, a sugar derived from oleandrin (a glycoside contained in oleander leaves) + *-o- + -mycin*] (1956)
: an antibiotic $C_{35}H_{61}NO_{12}$ produced by a streptomyces (*Streptomyces antibioticus*)

**ole·as·ter** \'ō-lē-ˌas-tər, ˌō-lē-'\ *noun* [Middle English, from Latin, from *olea*] (14th century)
: any of several plants (genus *Elaeagnus* of the family Elaeagnaceae, the oleaster family) having alternate leaves and perfect flowers with four stamens; *especially* **:** RUSSIAN OLIVE

**ole·ate** \'ō-lē-ˌāt\ *noun* (circa 1823)
: a salt or ester of oleic acid

**olec·ra·non** \ō-'le-krə-ˌnän\ *noun* [New Latin, from Greek *ōlekranon,* from *ōlenē* elbow + *kranion* skull — more at ELL, CRANIUM] (circa 1741)
: the process of the ulna projecting behind the elbow joint

**ole·fin** \'ō-lə-fən\ *noun* [International Scientific Vocabulary, from French (*gaz*) *oléfiant* ethylene, from Latin *oleum*] (1860)
**1 :** ALKENE
**2 :** a synthetic fiber (as polypropylene) derived from an alkene
— **ole·fin·ic** \ˌō-lə-'fi-nik\ *adjective*

**oleic acid** *noun* (1819)
: a monounsaturated fatty acid $C_{18}H_{34}O_2$ found in natural fats and oils

**ole·in** \'ō-lē-ən\ *noun* [French *oléine,* from Latin *oleum*] (1838)
**1 :** an ester of glycerol and oleic acid
**2 :** the liquid portion of a fat

**oleo** \'ō-lē-ˌō\ *noun* [short for *oleomargarine*] (1884)
: MARGARINE

**oleo·graph** \'ō-lē-ə-ˌgraf\ *noun* [International Scientific Vocabulary] (1873)
: a chromolithograph printed on cloth to imitate an oil painting

**oleo·mar·ga·rine** \ˌō-lē-ō-'mär-jə-rən, -ˌrēn; -'märj-rən\ *noun* [French *oléomargarine,* from *olé- + margarine* margarine] (1873)
: MARGARINE

**oleo·res·in** \ˌō-lē-ō-'re-zⁿn\ *noun* [International Scientific Vocabulary] (circa 1846)

**1 :** a natural plant product (as copaiba) containing chiefly essential oil and resin; *especially* **:** TURPENTINE 1b
**2 :** a preparation consisting essentially of oil holding resin in solution
— **oleo·res·in·ous** \-'re-zⁿn-əs, -'rez-nəs\ *adjective*

**ole·um** \'ō-lē-əm\ *noun* [Latin, olive oil — more at OIL] (circa 1823)
**1** *plural* **olea** \-lē-ə\ **:** OIL
**2** *plural* **oleums :** a heavy oily strongly corrosive solution of sulfur trioxide in anhydrous sulfuric acid

**O level** *noun* (1949)
**1 :** the lowest of three levels of standardized British examinations in a secondary school subject; *also* **:** successful completion of an O-level examination in a particular subject — called also *Ordinary level;* compare A LEVEL, S LEVEL
**2 a :** the level of education required to pass an O-level examination **b :** a course leading to an O-level examination

**ol·fac·tion** \äl-'fak-shən, ōl-\ *noun* (circa 1846)
**1 :** the sense of smell
**2 :** the act or process of smelling

**ol·fac·tom·e·ter** \ˌäl-ˌfak-'tä-mə-tər, ˌōl-\ *noun* (1889)
: an instrument for measuring the sensitivity of the sense of smell

**ol·fac·to·ry** \äl-'fak-t(ə-)rē, ōl-\ *adjective* [Latin *olfactorius,* from *olfacere* to smell, from *olēre* to smell + *facere* to do — more at ODOR, DO] (circa 1658)
: of, relating to, or connected with the sense of smell

**olfactory bulb** *noun* (circa 1860)
: a bulbous anterior projection of the olfactory lobe that is the place of termination of the olfactory nerves and is especially well developed in lower vertebrates (as fishes)

**olfactory lobe** *noun* (circa 1860)
: an anterior projection of each cerebral hemisphere that is continuous anteriorly with the olfactory nerve

**olfactory nerve** *noun* (1670)
: either of the pair of nerves that are the first cranial nerves and that arise in the olfactory neurosensory cells of the nasal mucous membrane and pass to the anterior part of the cerebrum

**olig-** *or* **oligo-** *combining form* [Medieval Latin, from Greek, from *oligos;* perhaps akin to Armenian *aƚkat* scant]
: few ⟨*olig*ophagous⟩

**ol·i·garch** \'ä-lə-ˌgärk, 'ō-\ *noun* [Greek *oligarchēs,* from *olig- + -archēs* -arch] (circa 1610)
: a member or supporter of an oligarchy

**ol·i·gar·chic** \ˌä-lə-'gär-kik, ˌō-\ *or* **ol·i·gar·chi·cal** \-ki-kəl\ *adjective* (1586)
: of, relating to, or based on an oligarchy

**ol·i·gar·chy** \'ä-lə-ˌgär-kē, 'ō-\ *noun, plural* **-chies** (1542)
**1 :** government by the few
**2 :** a government in which a small group exercises control especially for corrupt and selfish purposes; *also* **:** a group exercising such control
**3 :** an organization under oligarchic control

**Ol·i·go·cene** \'ä-li-gō-ˌsēn, 'ō-; ə-'li-gə-\ *adjective* [International Scientific Vocabulary] (circa 1859)
: of, relating to, or being an epoch of the Tertiary between the Eocene and Miocene or the corresponding system of rocks — see GEOLOGIC TIME table
— **Oligocene** *noun*

**ol·i·go·chaete** \-ˌkēt\ *noun* [New Latin *Oligochaeta,* ultimately from Greek *olig- + chaitē* long hair] (1896)

: any of a class or order (Oligochaeta) of hermaphroditic terrestrial or aquatic annelids (as an earthworm) that lack a specialized head
— **oligochaete** *adjective*

**ol·i·go·clase** \'ä-li-gō-ˌklās, 'ō-, -ˌklāz; ə-'li-gə-\ *noun* [German *Oligoklas*, from *olig-* olig- + Greek *klasis* breaking, from *klan* to break — more at CLAST] (1832)
: a mineral of the plagioclase series

**ol·i·go·den·dro·cyte** \'ä-li-gō-'den-drə-ˌsīt, 'ō-; ə-ˌli-gə-\ *noun* [International Scientific Vocabulary, from *olig-* + *dendr-* + *-cyte*] (1932)
: a neuroglial cell resembling an astrocyte but smaller with few and slender processes having few branches

**ol·i·go·den·drog·lia** \-den-'drä-glē-ə, -'drò-\ *noun* [New Latin, from *oligodendro*cyte + *-glia* (form of neuroglia)] (1924)
: neuroglia made up of oligodendrocytes that is held to function in myelin formation in the central nervous system
— **ol·i·go·den·drog·li·al** \-glē-əl\ *adjective*

**olig·o·mer** \ə-'li-gə-mər\ *noun* (1952)
: a polymer or polymer intermediate containing relatively few structural units
— **olig·o·mer·ic** \-ˌli-gə-'mer-ik\ *adjective*
— **olig·o·mer·i·za·tion** \-mə-rə-'zā-shən\ *noun*

**ol·i·go·nu·cle·o·tide** \-'nü-klē-ə-ˌtīd, -'nyü-\ *noun* (1942)
: a chain of usually up to 20 nucleotides

**ol·i·goph·a·gous** \ˌä-lə-'gä-fə-gəs, ˌō-\ *adjective* (1920)
: eating only a few specific kinds of food
— **ol·i·goph·a·gy** \-'gä-fə-jē\ *noun*

**ol·i·gop·o·ly** \-'gä-pə-lē\ *noun* [*olig-* + *-poly* (as in *monopoly*)] (1895)
: a market situation in which each of a few producers affects but does not control the market
— **ol·i·gop·o·lis·tic** \-ˌgä-pə-'lis-tik\ *adjective*

**ol·i·gop·so·ny** \-'gäp-sə-nē\ *noun* [*olig-* + Greek *opsōnia* purchase of victuals, from *opsōnein* to purchase victuals, from *opson* food + *ōneisthai* to buy — more at VENAL] (1942)
: a market situation in which each of a few buyers exerts a disproportionate influence on the market
— **ol·i·gop·so·nis·tic** \-ˌgäp-sə-'nis-tik\ *adjective*

**ol·i·go·sac·cha·ride** \ˌä-li-gō-'sa-kə-ˌrīd, ˌō-; ə-'li-gə-\ *noun* [International Scientific Vocabulary] (1930)
: a saccharide (as a disaccharide) that contains a known small number of monosaccharide units

**ol·i·go·tro·phic** \-'trō-fik\ *adjective* [International Scientific Vocabulary] (1928)
: deficient in plant nutrients ⟨*oligotrophic* boggy acid soils⟩; *especially* : having abundant dissolved oxygen ⟨an *oligotrophic* body of water⟩ — compare EUTROPHIC, MESOTROPHIC

**olio** \'ō-lē-ˌō\ *noun, plural* **oli·os** [modification of Spanish *olla*] (circa 1643)
**1** : OLLA PODRIDA 1
**2 a** : a miscellaneous mixture : HODGEPODGE **b** : a miscellaneous collection (as of literary or musical selections)

**ol·i·va·ceous** \ˌä-lə-'vā-shəs\ *adjective* (1776)
: OLIVE 1

**¹ol·ive** \'ä-liv, -ləv\ *noun* [Middle English, from Old French, from Latin *oliva*, from Greek *elaia*] (13th century)
**1 a** : a Mediterranean evergreen tree (*Olea europaea* of the family Oleaceae, the olive family) cultivated for its drupaceous fruit that is an important food and source of oil; *also* : the fruit **b** : any of various shrubs and trees resembling the olive
**2** : any of several colors resembling that of the unripe fruit of the olive tree that are yellowish green

---

**3** : an oval eminence on each ventrolateral aspect of the medulla oblongata

**²olive** *adjective* (1657)
**1** : of the color olive or olive green
**2** : approaching olive in color or complexion

**olive branch** *noun* (14th century)
**1** : a branch of the olive tree especially when used as a symbol of peace
**2** : an offer or gesture of conciliation or goodwill

**olive drab** *noun* (1897)
**1** : a grayish olive
**2 a** : a wool or cotton fabric of an olive drab color **b** : a uniform of this fabric

**olive green** *noun* (circa 1757)
: a greenish olive

**oliv·en·ite** \ō-'li-və-ˌnīt\ *noun* [German *Olivenit*, from *oliven-*, *olive* olive] (1820)
: a mineral that is a basic arsenate of copper

**Ol·i·ver** \'ä-lə-vər\ *noun* [French *Olivier*]
: the close friend of Roland in the Charlemagne legends

**ol·iv·ine** \'ä-lə-ˌvēn\ *noun* [German *Olivin*, from Latin *oliva*] (1794)
: a usually greenish mineral that is a complex silicate of magnesium and iron used especially in refractories — compare PERIDOT
— **ol·iv·in·ic** \ˌä-lə-'vi-nik\ *or* **ol·iv·in·it·ic** \-və-'ni-tik\ *adjective*

**ol·la** \'ä-lə, 'ói-ə\ *noun* [Spanish, from Latin *olla*, *aulla* pot; akin to Sanskrit *ukhā* pot and probably to Gothic *auhns* oven] (1622)
: a large bulging widemouthed earthenware vessel sometimes with looped handles used (as by Pueblo Indians) for storage, cooking, or as a container for water

olla

**ol·la po·dri·da** \-pə-'drē-də\ *noun, plural* **olla podridas** \-'drē-dəz\ *also* **ollas podridas** [Spanish, literally, rotten pot] (1599)
**1** : a rich highly seasoned stew of meat and vegetables usually including sausage and chick-peas that is slowly simmered and is a traditional Spanish and Latin-American dish
**2** : HODGEPODGE

**olo·li·u·qui** \ˌō-ˌlō-lē-'ü-kē\ *noun* [Spanish *ololiuque*, from Nahuatl *ololiuhqui*, literally, something rolled into a ball] (1915)
: a woody stemmed Mexican vine (*Rivea corymbosa*) of the morning glory family having small fleshy fruits with single seeds that are used especially by the Indians for medicinal, narcotic, and religious purposes

**olo·ro·so** \ˌō-lə-'rō-(ˌ)sō\ *noun, plural* **-sos** [Spanish, from *oloroso* fragrant, from *olor* odor, from Latin *olēre* to smell — more at ODOR] (1876)
: a dry full-bodied Spanish sherry

**olym·pi·ad** \ə-'lim-pē-ˌad, ō-\ *noun, often capitalized* [Middle English, from Middle French *Olympiade*, from Latin *Olympiad-, Olympias*, from Greek, from *Olympia*, site of ancient Olympic Games] (14th century)
**1** : one of the 4-year intervals between Olympic Games by which time was reckoned in ancient Greece
**2** : a quadrennial celebration of the modern Olympic Games

**¹Olym·pi·an** \-pē-ən\ *adjective* (15th century)
**1** : of or relating to Mount Olympus in Thessaly
**2** : befitting or characteristic of an Olympian; *especially* : LOFTY ⟨his . . . formula of glib simplicity and *Olympian* arrogance —Richard Pollak⟩

**²Olympian** *adjective* (1593)
**1** : of or relating to the ancient Greek region of Olympia

---

**2** : of, relating to, or constituting the Olympic Games

**³Olympian** *noun* (1606)
: a participant in Olympic Games

**⁴Olympian** *noun* (1843)
**1** : one of the ancient Greek deities dwelling on Olympus
**2** : a being of lofty detachment or superior attainments

**Olympian Games** *noun plural* (1593)
: OLYMPIC GAMES 1

**Olym·pia oyster** \ə-'lim-pē-ə-, ō-\ *noun* [*Olympia*, Washington] (1908)
: a small flavorful native oyster (*Ostrea lurida*) of the Puget Sound area of the Pacific coast of North America — called also *Olympia*

**Olym·pic** \ə-'lim-pik, ō-\ *adjective* (1590)
**1** : ¹OLYMPIAN
**2** : of or relating to the Olympic Games

**Olympic Games** *noun plural* (circa 1610)
**1** : an ancient Panhellenic festival held every fourth year and made up of contests of sports, music, and literature with the victor's prize a crown of wild olive
**2** : a modified revival of the ancient Olympic Games consisting of international athletic contests that are held at separate winter and summer gatherings at four year intervals — called also *Olympics*

**Olym·pus** \ə-'lim-pəs, ō-\ *noun* [Latin, from Greek *Olympos*] (1580)
: a mountain in Thessaly that in Greek mythology is the abode of the gods

**om** \'ōm\ *noun* [Sanskrit] (1788)
: a mantra consisting of the sound \'ōm\ used in contemplation of ultimate reality

**-oma** *noun suffix, plural* **-omas** *or* **-omata** [Latin *omat-, -oma*, from Greek *-ōmat-, -ōma*, from *-ō-* (stem vowel of causative verbs in *-oun*) + *-mat-, -ma*, suffix denoting result — more at -MENT]
: tumor ⟨adeno*ma*⟩ ⟨fibro*ma*⟩

**Oma·ha** \'ō-mə-ˌhò, -ˌhä\ *noun, plural* **Omaha** *or* **Omahas** (1804)
: a member of an American Indian people of northeastern Nebraska

**oma·sum** \ō-'mā-səm\ *noun, plural* **oma·sa** \-sə\ [New Latin, from Latin, tripe of a bullock] (circa 1706)
: the third chamber of the ruminant stomach that is situated between the reticulum and the abomasum — compare RUMEN

**om·bre** \'äm-bər; 'äm-brē, 'əm-, -ˌbrā\ *noun* [French or Spanish; French *hombre*, from Spanish, literally, man — more at HOMBRE] (circa 1661)
: an old three-handed card game popular in Europe especially in the 17th and 18th centuries

**om·bré** \'äm-ˌbrā\ *adjective* [French, past participle of *ombrer* to shade, from Italian *ombrare* to shade, from *ombra* shade, from Latin *umbra* — more at UMBRAGE] (circa 1896)
: having colors or tones that shade into each other — used especially of fabrics in which the color is graduated from light to dark
— **ombré** *noun*

**om·buds·man** \'äm-ˌbùdz-mən, 'òm-, -bədz-, -ˌman; äm-'bùdz-, òm-\ *noun, plural* **-men** \-mən\ [Swedish, literally, representative, from Old Norse *umbothsmathr*, from *umboth* commission + *mathr* man] (1959)
**1** : a government official (as in Sweden or New Zealand) appointed to receive and investigate complaints made by individuals against abuses or capricious acts of public officials

**2 :** one that investigates reported complaints (as from students or consumers), reports findings, and helps to achieve equitable settlements ◆
— **om·buds·man·ship** \-,ship\ *noun*

**-ome** *noun suffix* [New Latin *-oma,* from Latin, *-oma*]
**:** mass ⟨phyll*ome*⟩

**ome·ga** \ō-'mā-gə, -'mē-, -'me-\ *noun* [Middle English, from Middle French, from Greek *ō mega,* literally, large o] (15th century)
**1 :** the 24th and last letter of the Greek alphabet — see ALPHABET table
**2 :** LAST, ENDING
**3 a :** a negatively charged elementary particle that has a mass 3270 times the mass of an electron — called also *omega minus* **b :** a very short-lived unstable meson with mass 1532 times the mass of an electron — called also *omega meson*

**ome·ga-3** \-'thrē\ *adjective* (1980)
**:** being or composed of polyunsaturated fatty acids that have the final double bond in the hydrocarbon chain between the third and fourth carbon atoms from one end of the molecule and that are found especially in fish, fish oils, vegetable oils, and green leafy vegetables

**om·e·lette** *or* **om·e·let** \'äm-lət, 'ä-mə-\ *noun* [French *omelette,* alteration of Middle French *alumelle,* literally, knife blade, modification of Latin *lamella,* diminutive of *lamina* thin plate] (circa 1611)
**:** beaten eggs cooked without stirring until set and served folded in half ◆

**omen** \'ō-mən\ *noun* [Latin *omin-, omen*] (1582)
**:** an occurrence or phenomenon believed to portend a future event **:** AUGURY

**omen·tum** \ō-'men-təm\ *noun, plural* **-ta** \-tə\ *or* **-tums** [Latin; perhaps akin to Latin *induere* to put on, *exuere* to take off — more at EXUVIAE] (1547)
**:** a fold of peritoneum connecting or supporting abdominal structures (as the viscera); *also* **:** a fold of peritoneum free at one end
— **omen·tal** \-'men-t°l\ *adjective*

**omer** \'ō-mər\ *noun* [Hebrew *'ōmer*] (circa 1608)
**1 :** an ancient Hebrew unit of dry capacity equal to ⅒ ephah
**2 a** *often capitalized* **:** the sheaf of barley traditionally offered in Jewish Temple worship on the second day of the Passover **b** *capitalized* **:** a 7-week liturgical period of expectancy between the second day of the Passover and Shabuoth

**om·i·cron** \'ä-mə-,krän, 'ō-, *British* ō-'mī-(,)krän\ *noun* [Middle English, from Middle French, from Greek *o mikron,* literally, small o] (15th century)
**:** the 15th letter of the Greek alphabet — see ALPHABET table

**om·i·nous** \'ä-mə-nəs\ *adjective* (1587)
**:** being or exhibiting an omen **:** PORTENTOUS; *especially* **:** foreboding or foreshowing evil **:** INAUSPICIOUS ☆
— **om·i·nous·ly** *adverb*
— **om·i·nous·ness** *noun*

**omis·si·ble** \ō-'mi-sə-bəl\ *adjective* (1816)
**:** that may be omitted

**omis·sion** \ō-'mi-shən, ə-\ *noun* [Middle English *omissioun,* from Late Latin *omission-, omissio,* from Latin *omittere*] (14th century)
**1 a :** something neglected or left undone **b :** apathy toward or neglect of duty
**2 :** the act of omitting **:** the state of being omitted

**omit** \ō-'mit, ə-\ *transitive verb* **omit·ted; omit·ting** [Middle English *omitten,* from Latin *omittere,* from *ob-* toward + *mittere* to let go, send — more at OB-] (15th century)
**1 :** to leave out or leave unmentioned
**2 :** to fail to perform or make use of **:** FORBEAR
**3** *obsolete* **:** DISREGARD
**4** *obsolete* **:** GIVE UP

**om·ma·tid·i·um** \,ä-mə-'ti-dē-əm\ *noun, plural* **-tid·ia** \-dē-ə\ [New Latin, from Greek *ommat-, omma* eye; akin to Greek *ōps* eye — more at EYE] (1884)
**:** one of the elements corresponding to a small simple eye that make up the compound eye of an arthropod
— **om·ma·tid·i·al** \-dē-əl\ *adjective*

**omni-** *combining form* [Latin, from *omnis*]
**:** all **:** universally ⟨*omni*directional⟩

**¹om·ni·bus** \'äm-ni-(,)bəs\ *noun* [French, from Latin, for all, dative plural of *omnis*] (1829)
**1 :** a usually automotive public vehicle designed to carry a large number of passengers **:** BUS
**2 :** a book containing reprints of a number of works

**²omnibus** *adjective* (1842)
**1 :** of, relating to, or providing for many things at once
**2 :** containing or including many items

**om·ni·com·pe·tent** \,äm-ni-'käm-pə-tənt\ *adjective* (1827)
**:** able to handle any situation; *especially* **:** having the authority or legal capacity to act in all matters
— **om·ni·com·pe·tence** \-tən(t)s\ *noun*

**om·ni·di·rec·tion·al** \,äm-ni-də-'rek-shnəl, -,nī-, -(,)dī-, -shə-n°l\ *adjective* (1927)
**:** being in or involving all directions; *especially* **:** receiving or sending radio waves equally well in all directions ⟨*omnidirectional* antenna⟩

**om·ni·far·i·ous** \,äm-nə-'far-ē-əs, -'fer-\ *adjective* [Late Latin *omnifarius,* from Latin *omni-* + *-farius* (as in *multifarius* diverse) — more at MULTIFARIOUS] (1653)
**:** of all varieties, forms, or kinds

**om·nif·i·cent** \äm-'ni-fə-sənt\ *adjective* [Latin *omni-* + English *-ficent* (as in *magnificent*)] (1677)
**:** unlimited in creative power

**om·nip·o·tence** \äm-'ni-pə-tən(t)s\ *noun* (15th century)
**1 :** the quality or state of being omnipotent
**2 :** an agency or force of unlimited power

**¹om·nip·o·tent** \-tənt\ *adjective* [Middle English, from Middle French, from Latin *omnipotent-, omnipotens,* from *omni-* + *potent-, potens* potent] (14th century)
**1** *often capitalized* **:** ALMIGHTY 1
**2 :** having virtually unlimited authority or influence
**3** *obsolete* **:** ARRANT
— **om·nip·o·tent·ly** *adverb*

**²omnipotent** *noun* (1600)
**1 :** one who is omnipotent
**2** *capitalized* **:** GOD 1

**om·ni·pres·ence** \,äm-ni-'pre-z°n(t)s\ *noun* (1601)
**:** the quality or state of being omnipresent **:** UBIQUITY

**om·ni·pres·ent** \-z°nt\ *adjective* (1609)
**:** present in all places at all times

**om·ni·range** \'äm-ni-,rānj\ *noun* (1946)
**:** a system of radio navigation in which any bearing relative to a special radio transmitter on the ground may be chosen and flown by an airplane pilot — called also *omnidirectional range*

**om·ni·science** \äm-'ni-shən(t)s\ *noun* [Medieval Latin *omniscientia,* from Latin *omni-* + *scientia* knowledge — more at SCIENCE] (1612)
**:** the quality or state of being omniscient

**om·ni·scient** \-shənt\ *adjective* [New Latin *omniscient-, omnisciens,* back-formation from Medieval Latin *omniscientia*] (1604)
**1 :** having infinite awareness, understanding, and insight
**2 :** possessed of universal or complete knowledge
— **om·ni·scient·ly** *adverb*

**om·ni·um–gath·er·um** \,äm-nē-əm-'ga-thə-rəm\ *noun, plural* **omnium–gatherums** [Latin *omnium* (genitive plural of *omnis*) + English *gather* + Latin *-um,* noun ending] (1530)
**:** a miscellaneous collection (as of things or persons)

**om·ni·vore** \'äm-ni-,vōr, -,vȯr\ *noun* [New Latin *omnivora,* neuter plural of *omnivorus,* from Latin] (1890)

---

☆ **SYNONYMS**
**Ominous, portentous, fateful** mean having a menacing or threatening aspect. OMINOUS implies having a menacing, alarming character foreshadowing evil or disaster ⟨*ominous* rumblings from a once-dormant volcano⟩. PORTENTOUS suggests being frighteningly big or impressive but now seldom definitely connotes forwarning of calamity ⟨an eerie and *portentous* stillness⟩. FATEFUL suggests being of momentous or decisive importance ⟨the *fateful* conference that led to war⟩.

---

◇ **WORD HISTORY**
**ombudsman** For a word that became current in late 20th century America, *ombudsman* has deep roots: it can be traced back to the Old Norse word *umbothsmathr.* Compounded from *umboth* "commission," and *mathr* "man," *umbothsmathr* had the meaning "commissary" or "manager." The word evolved into Modern Swedish *ombudsman,* acquiring the generic sense of "representative" or "commissioner." In 1809 the Swedish government established the office of *justitieombudsmannen,* or justice commissioner, who was empowered to investigate and redress the complaints of private citizens regarding abuse and maladministration on the part of public officials and bureaucrats. This functionary established a reputation as the one person to whom the victim of bureaucratic abuse could resort when other channels had failed. The concept of an ombudsman later spread to Finland, Denmark, and Norway. In 1962 New Zealand decided to appoint a comparably empowered official and to confer upon him the title of *ombudsman.* The establishment of the office of ombudsman in New Zealand inspired other parts of the English-speaking world to create their own officials with similar powers under this name.

**omelette** Although the word *omelette* bears little resemblance to the Latin word *lamina,* the shape of an omelette does resemble a thin plate, which is what *lamina,* the ultimate source of *omelette,* means. The Romans used the noun *lamella,* the diminutive form of *lamina,* to mean "thin metal plate." This diminutive became in Old French *lemelle* "blade of a knife." By a process somewhat similar to that which produced our *apron* from an earlier *napron, la lemelle* "the blade" was misinterpreted as *l'alemelle,* which accounts for the appearance of the initial vowel. In Middle French the word *alemelle* became *alumelle* and then was altered to *alumette,* by substitution of the suffix *-ette* for *-elle.* It also acquired the additional meaning "dish made with beaten eggs," since such a dish resembled a thin plate or blade. In turn, *alumette* was altered to *amelette* by transposition of the *l* and *m* sounds (a process called metathesis). It finally changed again (influenced by southern dialect words for "egg" descended from Old Provençal *ou*) to *omelette.* The word, now often written *omelet,* has been in English since the 17th century, when an omelette was described as "a pancake of egges."

: one that is omnivorous

**om·niv·o·rous** \äm-'niv-rəs, -'ni-və-\ *adjective* [Latin *omnivorus,* from *omni-* + *-vorus* -vorous] (circa 1656)
**1 :** feeding on both animal and vegetable substances
**2 :** avidly taking in everything as if devouring or consuming
— **om·niv·o·rous·ly** *adverb*

**om·pha·los** \'äm(p)-fə-ˌläs, -ləs\ *noun* [Greek, navel — more at NAVEL] (1855)
: a central point : HUB 2, FOCAL POINT

**om·pha·lo·skep·sis** \ˌäm(p)-fə-lō-'skep-səs\ *noun* [New Latin, from Greek *omphalos* + *skepsis* examination — more at SPY] (1925)
: contemplation of one's navel as an aid to meditation; *also* : INERTIA 2

**¹on** \'òn, 'än\ *preposition* [Middle English *an, on,* preposition & adverb, from Old English; akin to Old High German *ana* on, Greek *ana* up, on] (before 12th century)
**1 a** — used as a function word to indicate position in contact with and supported by the top surface of ⟨the book is lying *on* the table⟩ **b** — used as a function word to indicate position in or in contact with an outer surface ⟨the fly landed *on* the ceiling⟩ ⟨I have a cut *on* my finger⟩ ⟨paint *on* the wall⟩ **c** — used as a function word to indicate position in close proximity with ⟨a village *on* the sea⟩ ⟨stay *on* your opponent⟩ **d** — used as a function word to indicate direction or location with respect to something ⟨*on* the south⟩ ⟨the garden is *on* the side of the house⟩
**2 a** — used as a function word to indicate a source of attachment or support ⟨*on* a string⟩ ⟨stand *on* one foot⟩ ⟨hang it *on* a nail⟩ **b** — used as a function word to indicate a source of dependence ⟨you can rely *on* me⟩ ⟨feeds *on* insects⟩ ⟨lives *on* a pension⟩ **c** — used as a function word to indicate means of conveyance ⟨*on* the bus⟩ or presence within the confines or in possession of ⟨had a knife *on* him⟩
**3** — used as a function word to indicate a time frame during which something takes place ⟨a parade *on* Sunday⟩ or an instant, action, or occurrence when something begins or is done ⟨*on* cue⟩ ⟨*on* arriving home, I found your letter⟩ ⟨news *on* the hour⟩ ⟨cash *on* delivery⟩
**4** *archaic* : OF
**5 a** — used as a function word to indicate manner of doing something; often used with *the* ⟨*on* the sly⟩ ⟨keep everything *on* the up-and-up⟩ **b** — used as a function word to indicate means or agency ⟨cut myself *on* a knife⟩ ⟨talk *on* the telephone⟩ **c** — used as a function word to indicate a medium of expression; used originally to refer to physical position ⟨best show *on* television⟩
**6 a** (1) — used as a function word to indicate active involvement in a condition or status ⟨*on* fire⟩ ⟨*on* the increase⟩ ⟨*on* the lookout⟩ (2) : regularly using or showing the effects of using ⟨*on* drugs⟩ **b** — used as a function word to indicate involvement with the activity, work, or function of ⟨*on* tour⟩ ⟨*on* the jury⟩ ⟨*on* duty⟩ **c** — used as a function word to indicate position or status in proper relationship with a standard or objective ⟨*on* schedule⟩
**7 a** — used as a function word to indicate reason, ground, or basis (as for an action, opinion, or computation) ⟨I have it *on* good authority⟩ ⟨*on* one condition⟩ ⟨the interest will be 10 cents *on* the dollar⟩ **b** — used as a function word to indicate the cause or source ⟨profited *on* the sale of stock⟩ **c** — used as a function word to indicate the focus of obligation or responsibility ⟨drinks are *on* the house⟩ ⟨put the blame *on* my actions⟩
**8 a** — used as a function word to indicate the object of collision, opposition, or hostile action ⟨bumped my head *on* a limb⟩ ⟨an attack *on* religion⟩ ⟨pulled a gun *on* me⟩ **b** — used as a function word to indicate the object with respect to some disadvantage, handicap, or

detriment ⟨has three inches in height *on* me⟩ ⟨a 3-game lead *on* the second-place team⟩ ⟨the joke's *on* me⟩
**9 a** — used as a function word to indicate destination or the focus of some action, movement, or directed effort ⟨crept up *on* him⟩ ⟨feast your eyes *on* this⟩ ⟨working *on* my skiing⟩ ⟨made a payment *on* the loan⟩ **b** — used as a function word to indicate the focus of feelings, determination, or will ⟨have pity *on* me⟩ ⟨keen *on* sports⟩ ⟨a curse *on* you⟩ **c** — used as a function word to indicate the object with respect to some misfortune or disadvantageous event ⟨the crops died *on* them⟩ **d** — used as a function word to indicate the subject of study, discussion, or consideration ⟨a book *on* insects⟩ ⟨reflect *on* that a moment⟩ ⟨agree *on* price⟩
**10** — used as a function word to indicate reduplication or succession in a series ⟨loss *on* loss⟩

**²on** *adverb* (before 12th century)
**1 a :** in or into a position of contact with an upper surface especially so as to be positioned for use or operation ⟨put the plates *on*⟩ **b :** in or into a position of being attached to or covering a surface; *especially* : in or into the condition of being worn ⟨put his new shoes *on*⟩
**2 a :** forward or at a more advanced point in space or time ⟨went *on* home⟩ ⟨later *on*⟩ **b :** in continuance or succession ⟨rambled *on*⟩ ⟨and so *on*⟩
**3 :** into operation or a position permitting operation ⟨switched the light *on*⟩

**³on** *adjective* (circa 1541)
**1 :** engaged in an activity or function (as a dramatic role)
**2 a** (1) : being in operation ⟨the radio is *on*⟩ (2) : placed so as to permit operation ⟨the switch is *on*⟩ **b :** taking place ⟨the game is *on*⟩
**3 :** aware of something — usually used with *to* ⟨my boss was *on* to me⟩
**4 :** INTENDED, PLANNED ⟨has nothing *on* for tonight⟩
**5** *British* : talking or harping incessantly — used with *about*
**6** *chiefly British* : regarded as possible or feasible — usually used in negative constructions
**7 a :** engaged in or as if in a performance ⟨the comedian was always *on*⟩ **b :** being at a high level of performance

**¹-on** *noun suffix* [International Scientific Vocabulary, alteration of *-one*]
: chemical compound not a ketone or other oxo compound ⟨parathi*on*⟩

**²-on** *noun suffix* [from *-on* (in *ion*)]
**1 :** subatomic particle ⟨nucle*on*⟩
**2 a :** unit : quantum ⟨phot*on*⟩ ⟨magnet*on*⟩ **b :** basic hereditary component ⟨cistr*on*⟩ ⟨oper*on*⟩

**³-on** *noun suffix* [New Latin, from *-on* (in *argon*)]
: noble gas ⟨rad*on*⟩

**on–again, off–again** *adjective* (1948)
: existing briefly and then disappearing in an intermittent unpredictable way ⟨*on-again, off-again* fads⟩

**on·a·ger** \'ä-ni-jər\ *noun* [Middle English, wild ass, from Latin, from Greek *onagros,* from *onos* ass + *agros* field — more at ACRE] (14th century)
**1 :** an Asian wild ass (*Equus hemionus onager* synonym *E. onager*) that usually has a broad dorsal stripe and is related to the kiang
**2** [Late Latin, from Latin] : a heavy catapult used in ancient and medieval times

onager 2

**on and off** *adverb* (1855)
: OFF AND ON

— **on–and–off** *adjective*

**onan·ism** \'ō-nə-ˌni-zəm\ *noun* [probably from New Latin *onanismus,* from *Onan,* son of Judah (Genesis 38:9)] (circa 1741)
**1 :** MASTURBATION
**2 :** COITUS INTERRUPTUS
**3 :** SELF-GRATIFICATION
— **onan·is·tic** \ˌō-nə-'nis-tik\ *adjective*

**on·board** \'òn-ˌbòrd, 'än-, -'bòrd\ *adjective* (1960)
: carried within or occurring aboard a vehicle (as a satellite or spacecraft) ⟨an *onboard* computer⟩

**¹once** \'wən(t)s\ *adverb* [Middle English *ones,* from genitive of *on* one] (12th century)
**1 :** one time and no more
**2 :** at any one time : under any circumstances : EVER
**3 :** at some indefinite time in the past : FORMERLY
**4 :** by one degree of relationship
— **once and for all 1 :** with finality : DEFINITIVELY **2 :** for the last time

**²once** *noun* (13th century)
: one single time : one time at least
— **at once 1 :** at the same time : SIMULTANEOUSLY **2 :** IMMEDIATELY **3 :** ²BOTH

**³once** *adjective* (1691)
: that once was : FORMER

**⁴once** *conjunction* (1761)
: at the moment when : AS SOON AS

**once–over** \ˌwən(t)s-'ō-vər, 'wən(t)s-ˌ\ *noun* (1914)
: a swift examination or survey; *especially* : a swift comprehensive appraising glance

**once that** *conjunction* (1874)
: ONCE

**on·cho·cer·ci·a·sis** \ˌäŋ-kō-ˌsər-'kī-ə-səs\ *noun, plural* -**a·ses** \-ˌsēz\ [New Latin, from *Onchocerca,* genus of worms] (1911)
: infestation with or disease caused by filarial worms (genus *Onchocerca*); *especially* : a human disease caused by a worm (*O. volvulus*) that is native to Africa but now present in parts of tropical America and is transmitted by several blackflies

**on·cid·i·um** \än-'si-dē-əm, äŋ-'ki-\ *noun* [New Latin, from Greek *onkos* barbed hook — more at ANGLE] (circa 1868)
: any of a genus (*Oncidium*) of showy tropical American chiefly epiphytic orchids

**onco-** *combining form* [New Latin, from Greek *onkos* bulk, mass; akin to Greek *enenkein* to carry — more at ENOUGH]
: tumor ⟨*onco*logy⟩

**on·co·gene** \'äŋ-kō-ˌjēn\ *noun* (1969)
: a gene having the potential to cause a normal cell to become cancerous

**on·co·gen·e·sis** \ˌäŋ-kō-'je-nə-səs\ *noun* [New Latin] (circa 1932)
: the induction or formation of tumors

**on·co·gen·ic** \-'je-nik\ *adjective* (1936)
**1 :** relating to tumor formation
**2 :** tending to cause tumors

**on·co·ge·nic·i·ty** \-jə-'ni-sə-tē\ *noun* (1944)
: the capacity to induce or form tumors

**on·col·o·gy** \än-'kä-lə-jē, äŋ-\ *noun* (circa 1857)
: the study of tumors
— **on·co·log·i·cal** \ˌäŋ-kə-'lä-ji-kəl\ *also* **on·co·log·ic** \-jik\ *adjective*
— **on·col·o·gist** \än-'kä-lə-jist, äŋ-\ *noun*

**on·com·ing** \'òn-ˌkə-miŋ, 'än-\ *adjective* (1844)
**1 a :** coming nearer in time or space ⟨the *on-coming* year⟩ ⟨an *oncoming* car⟩ **b :** FUTURE ⟨looked forward to his *oncoming* visit⟩
**2 :** EMERGENT, RISING ⟨the *oncoming* generation⟩

\ə\ abut \ᵊ\ kitten \ər\ further \a\ ash \ā\ ace
\ä\ mop, mar \aú\ out \ch\ chin \e\ bet \ē\ easy
\g\ go \i\ hit \ī\ ice \j\ job \ŋ\ sing \ō\ go
\ò\ law \òi\ boy \th\ thin \th̲\ the \ü\ loot \ú\ foot
\y\ yet \zh\ vision *see also* Guide to Pronunciation

**on·cor·na·vi·rus** \än-ˌkȯr-nə-ˈvī-rəs\ *noun* [*onco-* + *RNA* + *virus*] (1970)
**:** any of a group of RNA-containing viruses that produce tumors

**¹one** \ˈwən\ *adjective* [Middle English *on, an,* from Old English *ān;* akin to Old High German *ein* one, Latin *unus* (Old Latin *oinos*), Sanskrit *eka*] (before 12th century)
**1 :** being a single unit or thing ⟨*one* day at a time⟩
**2 a :** being one in particular ⟨early *one* morning⟩ **b :** being preeminently what is indicated ⟨*one* fine person⟩
**3 a :** being the same in kind or quality ⟨both of *one* species⟩ **b** (1) **:** constituting a unified entity of two or more components ⟨the combined elements form *one* substance⟩ (2) **:** being in agreement or union ⟨am *one* with you on this⟩
**4 a :** SOME 1 ⟨will see you again *one* day⟩ **b :** being a certain individual specified by name ⟨*one* John Doe made a speech⟩
**5 :** ONLY 2 ⟨the *one* person she wanted to marry⟩

**²one** *noun* (before 12th century)
**1** — see NUMBER table
**2 :** the number denoting unity
**3 a :** the first in a set or series — often used with an attributive noun ⟨day *one*⟩ **b :** an article of clothing of a size designated *one* ⟨wears a *one*⟩
**4 :** a single person or thing ⟨has the *one* but needs the other⟩
**5 :** a one-dollar bill
**— at one :** at harmony **:** in a state of agreement
**— for one :** as one example ⟨I *for one* disagree⟩

**³one** *pronoun* (13th century)
**1 :** a certain indefinitely indicated person or thing ⟨saw *one* of his friends⟩
**2 a :** an individual of a vaguely indicated group ⟨*one* never knows⟩ **b :** used as a third person substitute for a first person pronoun ⟨I'd like to read more but *one* doesn't have the time⟩
**3 :** a single instance of a specified action ⟨felt like belting him *one* —John Casey⟩ ∎

**-one** *noun suffix* [International Scientific Vocabulary, alteration of *-ene*]
**:** ketone or related or analogous compound or class of compounds ⟨lact*one*⟩ ⟨quin*one*⟩

**one another** *pronoun* (1526)
**:** EACH OTHER
*usage* see EACH OTHER

**one–armed bandit** \ˈwən-ˈärm(d)-\ *also* **one–arm bandit** *noun* (1934)
**:** SLOT MACHINE 2

**one–bag·ger** \-ˈba-gər\ *noun* (1952)
**:** SINGLE 2

**one–di·men·sion·al** *adjective* (1883)
**1 :** having one dimension
**2 :** lacking depth **:** SUPERFICIAL ⟨*one-dimensional* characters⟩
**— one–di·men·sion·al·i·ty** *noun*

**one·fold** \ˈwən-ˌfōld, -ˈfōld\ *adjective* (before 12th century)
**:** constituting a single undivided whole

**one–hand·ed** \-ˈhan-dəd\ *adjective* (15th century)
**1 :** having or using only one hand ⟨could beat him up *one-handed*⟩
**2 a :** designed for or requiring the use of only one hand **b :** effected by the use of only one hand

**one–horse** \-ˈhȯrs\ *adjective* (1750)
**1 :** drawn or operated by one horse
**2 :** SMALL, SMALL-TIME ⟨a *one-horse* town⟩

**Onei·da** \ō-ˈnī-də\ *noun, plural* **Oneida** *or* **Oneidas** [Oneida *oneˑyóteˀ,* literally, standing rock] (1666)
**1 :** a member of an American Indian people originally of New York
**2 :** the Iroquoian language of the Oneida people

**onei·ric** \ō-ˈnī-rik\ *adjective* [Greek *oneiros* dream; akin to Armenian *anurǰ* dream] (1859)
**:** of or relating to dreams **:** DREAMY
**— onei·ri·cal·ly** \-ri-k(ə-)lē\ *adverb*

**onei·ro·man·cy** \ō-ˈnī-rə-ˌman(t)-sē\ *noun* [Greek *oneiros* + English *-mancy*] (1652)
**:** divination by means of dreams

**one–line octave** *noun* (1931)
**:** the musical octave that begins on middle C — see PITCH illustration

**one–lin·er** \ˌwən-ˈlī-nər\ *noun* (1967)
**:** a very succinct joke or witticism

**one–man** *adjective* (1842)
**:** of or relating to just one individual: as **a :** consisting of only one individual ⟨a *one-man* committee⟩ **b** (1) **:** done, presented, or produced by only one individual ⟨a *one-man* stage play⟩ (2) **:** featuring the work of a single artist (as a painter) ⟨a *one-man* show of oils⟩ **c :** designed for or limited to one individual

**one·ness** \ˈwən-nəs\ *noun* (1594)
**:** the quality or state or fact of being one: as **a :** SINGLENESS **b :** INTEGRITY, WHOLENESS **c :** HARMONY **d :** SAMENESS, IDENTITY **e :** UNITY, UNION

**one–night·er** \ˌwən-ˈnī-tər\ *noun* (circa 1937)
**:** ONE-NIGHT STAND

**one–night stand** *noun* (1880)
**1 :** a performance (as of a play or concert) given (as by a traveling group of actors or musicians) only once in each of a series of localities
**2 a :** a locality used for one-night stands **b :** a stopover for a one-night stand
**3 :** a sexual encounter limited to a single occasion; *also* **:** a partner in such an encounter

**one–note** \ˈwən-ˈnōt\ *adjective* (1973)
**:** unvarying in tone or emphasis **:** MONOTONOUS

**one–off** \ˌwən-ˈȯf\ *adjective* (1934)
*British* **:** limited to a single time, occasion, or instance **:** ONE-SHOT, UNIQUE
**— one–off** *noun*

**one–on–one** \ˌwən-ȯn-ˈwən, ˌwən-än-\ *adjective or adverb* (1967)
**1 :** playing directly against a single opposing player
**2 :** involving a direct encounter between one person and another

**one–piece** *adjective* (1880)
**:** consisting of or made in a single undivided piece ⟨a *one-piece* bathing suit⟩
**— one–piec·er** \ˈwən-ˈpē-sər\ *noun*

**oner·ous** \ˈä-nə-rəs, ˈō-\ *adjective* [Middle English, from Middle French *onereus,* from Latin *onerosus,* from *oner-, onus* burden; akin to Sanskrit *anas* cart] (14th century)
**1 :** involving, imposing, or constituting a burden **:** TROUBLESOME ⟨an *onerous* task⟩
**2 :** having legal obligations that outweigh the advantages ⟨*onerous* contract⟩ ☆
**— oner·ous·ly** *adverb*
**— oner·ous·ness** *noun*

**one·self** \(ˌ)wən-ˈself, *Southern also* -ˈsef\ *also* **one's self** \(ˌ)wən-, ˌwənz-\ *pronoun* (1548)
**1 :** a person's self **:** one's own self — used reflexively as object of a preposition or verb or for emphasis in various constructions
**2 :** one's normal, healthy, or sane condition or self
**— be oneself :** to conduct oneself in a usual or fitting manner

**one–shot** \ˈwən-ˌshät\ *adjective* (1927)
**1 :** that is complete or effective through being done or used or applied only once ⟨there is no easy *one-shot* answer to the problem⟩
**2 :** that is not followed by something else of the same kind ⟨a *one-shot* tax cut⟩
**— one–shot** *noun*

**one–sid·ed** \ˈwən-ˈsī-dəd\ *adjective* (1813)
**1 a** (1) **:** having one side prominent **:** LOPSIDED (2) **:** having or occurring on one side only **b :** limited to one side **:** PARTIAL ⟨a *one-sided* interpretation⟩
**2 :** UNILATERAL ⟨a *one-sided* decision⟩
**— one–sid·ed·ly** *adverb*
**— one–sid·ed·ness** *noun*

**ones place** *noun* (1976)
**:** UNITS PLACE

**one–step** \ˈwən-ˌstep\ *noun* (1911)
**1 :** a ballroom dance in ²/₄ time marked by quick walking steps backward and forward
**2 :** music used for the one-step
**— one–step** *intransitive verb*

**one–stop** \-ˈstäp\ *adjective* (1934)
**:** being or relating to a business that provides a complete range of goods or services of a particular kind

**one–tailed** \ˈwən-ˈtāl(d)\ *also* **one–tail** \-ˈtāl\ *adjective* (1947)
**:** being a statistical test for which the critical region consists of all values of the test statistic greater than a given value or less than a given value but not both — compare TWO-TAILED

**¹one–time** \ˈwən-ˈtīm\ *adjective* (1840)
**1 :** FORMER, SOMETIME ⟨a *onetime* actor⟩
**2 :** occurring only once **:** ONE-SHOT

**²onetime** *adverb* (1886)
**:** FORMERLY

**one–to–one** \ˌwən-tə-ˈwən, -də-\ *adjective* (1873)
**1 :** pairing each element of a set uniquely with an element of another set
**2 :** ONE-ON-ONE 2

**one–track** *adjective* (1926)
**:** marked by often narrowly restricted attention to or absorption in just one thing ⟨a *one-track* mind⟩

**one–two** \ˈwən-ˈtü, -ˌtü\ *noun* (1809)
**1 :** a combination of two quick blows in rapid succession in boxing; *especially* **:** a left jab followed at once by a hard blow with the right hand
**2** *or* **one–two punch :** a combination of two forces acting against something

**one–up** \ˌwən-ˈəp, ˈwən-\ *transitive verb* [back-formation from *one-upmanship*] (1963)
**:** to practice one-upmanship on

**one up** *adjective* (1919)

---

☆ SYNONYMS

**Onerous, burdensome, oppressive, exacting** mean imposing hardship. ONEROUS stresses being laborious and heavy especially because distasteful ⟨the *onerous* task of cleaning up the mess⟩. BURDENSOME suggests causing mental as well as physical strain ⟨*burdensome* responsibilities⟩. OPPRESSIVE implies extreme harshness or severity in what is imposed ⟨the *oppressive* tyranny of a police state⟩. EXACTING implies rigor or sternness rather than tyranny or injustice in the demands made or in the one demanding ⟨an *exacting* employer⟩.

---

□ USAGE

**one** Sense 2a is usually a sign of a formal style. A formal style excludes the participation of the reader or hearer; thus *one* is used where a less formal style might address the reader directly ⟨for the consequences of such choices, *one* has only oneself to thank —Walker Gibson⟩. This generic *one* has never been common in informal use in either British or American English, and people who start sentences with *one* often shift to another pronoun more natural to casual discourse ⟨when *one* is learning the river, he is not allowed to do or think about anything else —Mark Twain⟩. Use of *one* to replace a first-person pronoun—sense 2b—has occasionally been criticized. It is more common in British English than in American ⟨I'm watching this pretty carefully and I hope that the issue will come up in the Lords and *one* may be able to speak about it —Donald Coggan, Archbishop of Canterbury⟩. See in addition YOU.

: being in a position of advantage — usually used with *on*

**one·up·man·ship** \ˌwən-'əp-mən-ˌship\ *also* **one·ups·man·ship** \-'əps-mən-\ *noun* (1952)
: the art or practice of outdoing or keeping one jump ahead of a friend or competitor ⟨engaged in a round of verbal *one-upmanship*⟩
   **word history** see GAMESMANSHIP

**one–way** *adjective* (1824)
**1 :** that moves in or allows movement in only one direction ⟨*one-way* street⟩
**2 :** ONE-SIDED, UNILATERAL ⟨a *one-way* conversation⟩
**3 :** that functions in only one of two or more ways

**on·go·ing** \'ȯn-ˌgō-iŋ, 'än-, -ˌgȯ(-)iŋ\ *adjective* (1877)
**1 a :** being actually in process **b :** CONTINUING
**2 :** continuously moving forward **:** GROWING
  — **on·go·ing·ness** \-nəs\ *noun*

**on·ion** \'ən-yən\ *noun* [Middle English, from Middle French *oignon*, from Latin *union-, unio*] (14th century)
**1 :** a widely cultivated Asian herb (*Allium cepa*) of the lily family with pungent edible bulbs; *also* **:** its bulb
**2 :** any of various plants of the same genus as the onion
  — **on·iony** \-yə-nē\ *adjective*

**onion dome** *noun* (1941)
: a dome (as of a church) having the general shape of an onion
  — **onion–domed** *adjective*

**onion ring** *noun* (1946)
: a ring of sliced onion coated with batter or crumbs and fried

**on·ion·skin** \-ˌskin\ *noun* (1879)
: a thin strong translucent paper of very light weight

**oni·um** \'ō-nē-əm\ *adjective* [*-onium*] (1905)
: being or characterized by a usually complex cation

**-onium** *noun suffix* [New Latin, from *ammonium*]
: an ion having a positive charge ⟨hydr*onium*⟩ — compare -IUM 1b

**on–line** *adjective or adverb* (1950)
: connected to, served by, or available through a system and especially a computer or telecommunications system ⟨an *on-line* database⟩; *also* **:** done while connected to a system ⟨*on-line* computer storage⟩

**on·look·er** \'ȯn-ˌlu̇-kər, 'än-\ *noun* (1606)
: one that looks on; *especially* **:** a passive spectator
  — **on·look·ing** \-kiŋ\ *adjective*

**¹on·ly** \'ōn-lē\ *adjective* [Middle English, from Old English *ānlīc*, from *ān* one — more at ONE] (before 12th century)
**1 :** unquestionably the best **:** PEERLESS
**2 :** alone in its class or kind **:** SOLE ⟨an *only* child⟩

**²only** *adverb* (14th century)
**1 a :** as a single fact or instance and nothing more or different **:** MERELY ⟨has *only* lost one election —George Orwell⟩ **b :** SOLELY, EXCLUSIVELY ⟨known *only* to him⟩
**2 :** at the very least ⟨it was *only* too true⟩
**3 a :** in the final outcome ⟨will *only* make you sick⟩ **b :** with nevertheless the final result ⟨won the battles, *only* to lose the war⟩
**4 a :** as recently as ⟨*only* last week⟩ **b :** in the immediate past ⟨*only* just talked to her⟩ ◼

**³only** *conjunction* (14th century)
**1 a :** with the restriction that **:** BUT ⟨you may go, *only* come back early⟩ **b :** and yet **:** HOWEVER ⟨they look very nice, *only* we can't use them⟩
**2 :** were it not that **:** EXCEPT ⟨I'd introduce you to her, *only* you'd win her —Jack London⟩

**on·o·mas·tic** \ˌä-nə-'mas-tik\ *adjective* [Greek *onomastikos*, from *onomazein* to name, from *onoma* name — more at NAME] (1716)
: of, relating to, or consisting of a name or names

---

  — **on·o·mas·ti·cal·ly** \-ti-k(ə-)lē\ *adverb*
**on·o·mas·tics** \-tiks\ *noun plural but singular or plural in construction* (1930)
**1 a :** the science or study of the origins and forms of words especially as used in a specialized field **b :** the science or study of the origin and forms of proper names of persons or places
**2 :** the system underlying the formation and use of words especially for proper names or of words used in a specialized field
  — **on·o·mas·ti·cian** \ˌä-nə-mas-'ti-shən\ *noun*

**on·o·ma·tol·o·gy** \ˌä-nə-mə-'tä-lə-jē\ *noun* [French *onomatologie*, from Greek *onomat-, onoma* name + French *-logie* -logy] (circa 1847)
: ONOMASTICS
  — **on·o·ma·tol·o·gist** \-jist\ *noun*

**on·o·mato·poe·ia** \ˌä-nə-ˌmä-tə-'pē-ə, -ˌma-\ *noun* [Late Latin, from Greek *onomatopoiia*, from *onomat-, onoma* name + *poiein* to make — more at POET] (circa 1577)
**1 :** the naming of a thing or action by a vocal imitation of the sound associated with it (as *buzz, hiss*)
**2 :** the use of words whose sound suggests the sense
  — **on·o·mato·poe·ic** \-'pē-ik\ *or* **on·o·mato·po·et·ic** \-pō-'e-tik\ *adjective*
  — **on·o·mato·poe·i·cal·ly** \-'pē-ə-k(ə-)lē\ *or* **on·o·mato·po·et·i·cal·ly** \-pō-'e-ti-k(ə-)lē\ *adverb*

**On·on·da·ga** \ˌä-nə(n)-'dȯ-gə, -'dä-, -'dä-\ *noun, plural* **-ga** *or* **-gas** [Onondaga *onóʼtàʼke*, the chief Onondaga town] (1684)
**1 :** a member of an American Indian people of New York and Canada
**2 :** the Iroquoian language of the Onondaga people

**on–ramp** \'ȯn-ˌramp, 'än-\ *noun* (1958)
: a ramp by which one enters a limited-access highway

**on·rush** \-ˌrəsh\ *noun* (1844)
**1 :** a rushing forward or onward
**2 :** ONSET
  — **on·rush·ing** \-ˌrə-shiŋ\ *adjective*

**on–screen** \'ȯn-'skrēn, 'än-\ *adverb or adjective* (1955)
: in a motion picture or a television program

**on·set** \-ˌset\ *noun* (1535)
**1 :** ATTACK, ASSAULT ⟨withstand the *onset* of the army⟩
**2 :** BEGINNING, COMMENCEMENT ⟨the *onset* of winter⟩

**on·shore** \'ȯn-ˌshȯr, 'än-, -ˌshȯr\ *adjective* (1875)
**1 :** coming or moving from the water toward or onto the shore ⟨an *onshore* wind⟩
**2 a :** situated on or near the shore as distinguished from being in deep or open water **b :** situated on land
**3 :** DOMESTIC 2 ⟨*onshore* markets⟩
  — **on·shore** \'ȯn-', 'än-'\ *adverb*

**on·side** \-'sīd\ *adverb or adjective* (1871)
: not offside **:** in a position legally to play or receive the ball or puck

**onside kick** *noun* (1926)
: a kickoff in football in which the ball travels just far enough to be legally recoverable by the kicking team

**on–site** \-'sīt\ *adjective or adverb* (1946)
: carried out or located at the place connected with a particular activity ⟨*on-site* training in construction skills⟩

**on·slaught** \'än-ˌslȯt, 'ȯn-\ *noun* [modification of Dutch *aanslag* act of striking; akin to Old English *an* on and to Old English *slēan* to strike — more at SLAY] (circa 1625)
: an especially fierce attack; *also* **:** something resembling such an attack ⟨an *onslaught* of technological changes⟩

**on·stage** \'ȯn-'stāj, 'än-, -ˌstāj\ *adverb or adjective* (1925)
: on a part of the stage visible to the audience

---

**on·stream** \'ȯn-'strēm, 'än-\ *adverb or adjective* (1930)
: in or into production ⟨plants scheduled to come *onstream*⟩

**ont-** *or* **onto-** *combining form* [New Latin, from Late Greek, from Greek *ont-, ōn*, present participle of *einai* to be — more at IS]
**1 :** being **:** existence ⟨*ontology*⟩
**2 :** organism ⟨*ontogeny*⟩

**-ont** *noun combining form* [Greek *ont-, ōn*, present participle]
: cell **:** organism ⟨dipl*ont*⟩

**on–the–job** *adjective* (1946)
: of, relating to, or being something (as training or experience) learned, gained, or done while working at a job and often under supervision

**on·tic** \'än-tik\ *adjective* (1942)
: of, relating to, or having real being
  — **on·ti·cal·ly** \-ti-k(ə-)lē\ *adverb*

**¹on·to** \'ȯn-(ˌ)tü, 'än-\ *preposition* (1581)
**1 :** to a position on
**2 :** in or into a state of awareness about ⟨put me *onto* your methods⟩
**3 :** — used as a function word to indicate a set each element of which is the image of at least one element of another set ⟨a function mapping the set *S* onto the set *T*⟩

**²onto** *adjective* (1942)
: mapping elements in such a way that every element in one set is the image of at least one element in another set ⟨a function that is one-to-one and *onto*⟩

**on·to·gen·e·sis** \ˌän-tə-'je-nə-səs\ *noun* [New Latin] (1875)
: ONTOGENY

**on·to·ge·net·ic** \-jə-'ne-tik\ *adjective* [International Scientific Vocabulary] (1878)
**1 :** of, relating to, or appearing in the course of ontogeny
**2 :** based on visible morphological characters
  — **on·to·ge·net·i·cal·ly** \-ti-k(ə-)lē\ *adverb*

**on·tog·e·ny** \än-'tä-jə-nē\ *noun* [International Scientific Vocabulary] (1872)
: the development or course of development especially of an individual organism

**on·to·log·i·cal** \ˌän-tᵊl-'ä-ji-kəl\ *adjective* (1782)
**1 :** of or relating to ontology
**2 :** relating to or based upon being or existence
  — **on·to·log·i·cal·ly** \-k(ə-)lē\ *adverb*

**ontological argument** *noun* (1877)
: an argument for the existence of God based upon the meaning of the term *God*

**on·tol·o·gy** \än-'tä-lə-jē\ *noun* [New Latin *ontologia*, from *ont-* + *-logia* -logy] (circa 1721)
**1 :** a branch of metaphysics concerned with the nature and relations of being
**2 :** a particular theory about the nature of being or the kinds of existents

---

□ USAGE

**only**   The placement of *only* in a sentence has been a source of studious commentary since the 18th century, most of it intended to prove by force of argument that prevailing standard usage is wrong. After 200 years of preachment the following observations may be made: the position of *only* in standard spoken English is not fixed, since ambiguity is avoided through sentence stress; in casual prose that keeps close to the rhythms of speech *only* is often placed where it would be in speech; and in edited and more formal prose *only* tends to be placed immediately before the word or words it modifies.

---

\ə\ abut  \ᵊ\ kitten  \ər\ further  \a\ ash  \ā\ ace
\ä\ mop, mar  \au̇\ out  \ch\ chin  \e\ bet  \ē\ easy
\g\ go  \i\ hit  \ī\ ice  \j\ job  \ŋ\ sing  \ō\ go
\ȯ\ law  \ȯi\ boy  \th\ thin  \th̷\ the  \ü\ loot  \u̇\ foot
\y\ yet  \zh\ vision   *see also* Guide to Pronunciation

**— on·tol·o·gist** \-jist\ *noun*

**onus** \'ō-nəs\ *noun* (circa 1640)
**1** [Latin — more at ONEROUS] **a :** BURDEN **b** **:** a disagreeable necessity **:** OBLIGATION **c** **:** BLAME **d :** STIGMA
**2** [New Latin *onus* (*probandi*), literally, burden of proving] **:** BURDEN OF PROOF

**¹on·ward** \'òn-wərd, 'än-\ *also* **on·wards** \-wərdz\ *adverb* (1532)
**:** toward or at a point lying ahead in space or time **:** FORWARD

**²onward** *adjective* (1674)
**:** directed or moving onward **:** FORWARD

**on·y·choph·o·ran** \,ä-ni-'kä-fə-rən\ *noun* [New Latin *Onychophora*, group name, from Greek *onych-, onyx* claw + *-phoros* -phore] (circa 1890)
**:** PERIPATUS
**— onychophoran** *adjective*

**-onym** *noun combining form* [Middle English, from Latin *-onymum*, from Greek *-ōnymon*, from *onyma* — more at NAME]
**:** name **:** word ⟨ant*onym*⟩

**on·yx** \'ä-niks\ *noun* [Middle English *onix*, from Middle French & Latin; Middle French, from Latin *onych-, onyx*, from Greek, literally, claw, nail — more at NAIL] (14th century)
**:** a translucent chalcedony in parallel layers of different colors

**oo-** — see O-

**oo·cyst** \'ō-ə-,sist\ *noun* [International Scientific Vocabulary] (1875)
**:** ZYGOTE; *specifically* **:** a sporozoan zygote undergoing sporogenous development

**oo·cyte** \'ō-ə-,sīt\ *noun* [International Scientific Vocabulary] (1895)
**:** an egg before maturation **:** a female gametocyte

**oo·dles** \'ü-d°lz\ *noun plural but singular or plural in construction* [origin unknown] (1869)
**:** a great quantity **:** LOT

**oog·a·mous** \ō-'ä-gə-məs\ *adjective* (1888)
**:** having or involving a small motile male gamete and a large immobile female gamete
**— oog·a·my** \-mē\ *noun*

**oo·gen·e·sis** \,ō-ə-'je-nə-səs\ *noun* [New Latin] (circa 1879)
**:** formation and maturation of the egg
**— oo·ge·net·ic** \-jə-'ne-tik\ *adjective*

**oo·go·ni·um** \,ō-ə-'gō-nē-əm\ *noun, plural* **-nia** \-nē-ə\ [New Latin] (1867)
**1 :** a female sexual organ in various algae and fungi that corresponds to the archegonium of ferns and mosses
**2 :** a descendant of a primordial germ cell that gives rise to oocytes
**— oo·go·ni·al** \-nē-əl\ *adjective*

**¹ooh** \'ü\ *interjection* (1939)
**—** used to express amazement, joy, or surprise

**²ooh** *intransitive verb* (1951)
**:** to exclaim in amazement, joy, or surprise ⟨*oohing* and aahing over the new automobiles⟩
**— ooh** *noun*

**oo·lite** \'ō-ə-,līt\ *noun* [probably from French *oolithe*, from *oo-* o- + *-lithe* -lite] (1785)
**:** a rock consisting of small round grains usually of calcium carbonate cemented together
**— oo·lit·ic** \,ō-ə-'li-tik\ *adjective*

**ool·o·gist** \ō-'ä-lə-jist\ *noun* (1863)
**1 :** a person specializing in the study of birds' eggs
**2 :** a collector of birds' eggs
**— ool·o·gy** \-jē\ *noun*

**oo·long** \'ü-,lòn\ *noun* [Chinese (Beijing) *wūlóng*, literally, black dragon] (1850)
**:** tea made from leaves that have been partially fermented before firing

**oom·pah** \,üm-(,)pä, 'ùm-\ *also* **oom·pah-pah** \,üm-(,)pä-'pä, ,ùm-\ *noun* [imitative] (1877)
**:** a repeated rhythmic bass accompaniment especially in a band
**— oompah** *verb*

**oomph** \'ùm(p)f\ *noun* [imitative of a sound made under exertion] (1936)
**1 :** personal charm or magnetism **:** GLAMOUR
**2 :** SEX APPEAL
**3 :** PUNCH, VITALITY

**oo·pho·rec·to·my** \,ō-ə-fə-'rek-tə-mē\ *noun, plural* **-mies** [New Latin *oophoron* ovary (from *o-* + Greek *-phoron*, neuter of *-phoros* -phore) + English *-ectomy*] (1872)
**:** OVARIECTOMY

**oops** \'(w)ù(ə)ps\ *interjection* (1933)
**—** used typically to express mild apology, surprise, or dismay

**Oort cloud** \'òrt-, 'ort-\ *noun* [Jan *Oort* (died 1992) Dutch astronomer] (1968)
**:** a spherical shell of small frozen bodies believed to surround the sun far beyond the orbit of Pluto and from which some are dislodged when perturbed (as by a passing star) to fall toward the sun as comets

**oo·spore** \'ō-ə-,spōr, -,spòr\ *noun* [International Scientific Vocabulary] (1865)
**:** ZYGOTE; *especially* **:** a spore produced by heterogamous fertilization that yields a sporophyte

**oo·the·ca** \,ō-ə-'thē-kə\ *noun, plural* **oo·the·cae** \-'thē-(,)kē, -(,)sē\ [New Latin] (circa 1856)
**:** a firm-walled and distinctive egg case (as of a cockroach)
**— oo·the·cal** \-'thē-kəl\ *adjective*

**oo·tid** \'ō-ə-,tid\ *noun* [irregular from *o-* + *-id*] (1904)
**:** an egg cell after meiosis

**¹ooze** \'üz\ *noun* [Middle English *wose*, from Old English *wāse* mire; akin to Old Norse *veisa* stagnant water] (before 12th century)
**1 :** a soft deposit (as of mud, slime, or shells) on the bottom of a body of water
**2 :** a piece of soft wet plastic ground

**²ooze** *verb* **oozed; ooz·ing** [Middle English *wosen*, from *wose* sap] (14th century)
*intransitive verb*
**1 :** to pass or flow slowly through or as if through small openings or interstices
**2 :** to move slowly or imperceptibly ⟨the crowd began to *ooze* forward —Bruce Marshall⟩
**3 a :** to exude moisture **b :** to exude something often in a faintly repellent manner ⟨*ooze* with sympathy⟩
*transitive verb*
**1 :** to emit slowly
**2 :** EXUDE 2 ⟨*ooze* confidence⟩

**³ooze** *noun* [Middle English *wose* sap, juice, from Old English *wōs;* akin to Old High German *waso* damp] (circa 1581)
**1 :** a decoction of vegetable material used for tanning leather
**2 :** the act of oozing
**3 :** something that oozes

**oozy** \'ü-zē\ *adjective* **ooz·i·er; -est** (14th century)
**1 :** containing or composed of ooze **:** resembling ooze
**2 :** exuding moisture **:** SLIMY

**op** \'äp\ *noun* (1964)
**:** OPTICAL ART

**opac·i·ty** \ō-'pa-sə-tē\ *noun, plural* **-ties** [French *opacité* shadiness, from Latin *opacitat-, opacitas*, from *opacus* shaded, dark] (circa 1611)
**1 :** the quality or state of a body that makes it impervious to the rays of light; *broadly* **:** the relative capacity of matter to obstruct the transmission of radiant energy
**2 a :** obscurity of sense **:** UNINTELLIGIBLENESS **b :** the quality or state of being mentally obtuse **:** DULLNESS
**3 :** an opaque spot in a normally transparent structure (as the lens of the eye)

**opah** \'ō-pə, -,pä\ *noun* [perhaps from Ibo *úbà*] (1750)
**:** a large elliptical marine bony fish (*Lampris guttatus* of the family Lampridae) with brilliant colors

**opal** \'ō-pəl\ *noun* [Latin *opalus*, from Greek *opallios*, from Sanskrit *upala* stone, jewel] (1591)
**:** a mineral that is a hydrated amorphous silica softer and less dense than quartz and typically with definite and often marked iridescent play of colors

**opal·es·cent** \,ō-pə-'le-s°nt\ *adjective* (circa 1813)
**:** reflecting an iridescent light
**— opal·es·cence** \-s°n(t)s\ *noun*
**— opal·es·cent·ly** \-s°nt-lē\ *adverb*

**opal·ine** \'ō-pə-,līn, -,lēn\ *adjective* (1784)
**:** resembling opal

**opaque** \ō-'pāk\ *adjective* [Latin *opacus*] (1641)
**1 :** exhibiting opacity **:** blocking the passage of radiant energy and especially light
**2 a :** hard to understand or explain ⟨*opaque* prose⟩ **b :** OBTUSE, THICKHEADED
**— opaque** *noun*
**— opaque·ly** *adverb*
**— opaque·ness** *noun*

**opaque projector** *noun* (1951)
**:** a projector using reflected light for projecting an image of an opaque object or matter on an opaque support (as a photograph)

**op art** \'äp-\ *noun* (1964)
**:** OPTICAL ART
**— op artist** *noun*

**ope** \'ōp\ *verb* **oped; op·ing** (15th century)
*archaic* **:** OPEN

**op–ed** \'äp-'ed\ *noun, often O&E capitalized, often attributive* [short for *opposite editorial*] (1970)
**:** a page of special features usually opposite the editorial page of a newspaper

**¹open** \'ō-pən, -p°m\ *adjective* **open·er** \'ōp-nər, 'ō-pə-\; **open·est** \'ōp-nəst, 'ō-pə-\ [Middle English, from Old English; akin to Old High German *offan* open, Old English *ūp* up] (before 12th century)
**1 :** having no enclosing or confining barrier **:** accessible on all or nearly all sides ⟨cattle grazing on an *open* range⟩
**2 a** (1) **:** being in a position or adjustment to permit passage **:** not shut or locked ⟨an *open* door⟩ (2) **:** having a barrier (as a door) so adjusted as to allow passage ⟨the house was *open*⟩ **b :** having the lips parted ⟨stood there with his mouth wide *open*⟩ **c :** not buttoned or zipped ⟨an *open* shirt⟩
**3 a :** completely free from concealment **:** exposed to general view or knowledge ⟨their hostilities eventually erupted with *open* war⟩ **b** **:** exposed or vulnerable to attack or question **:** SUBJECT ⟨*open* to doubt⟩
**4 a :** not covered with a top, roof, or lid ⟨an *open* car⟩ ⟨her eyes were *open*⟩ **b :** having no protective covering ⟨*open* wiring⟩ ⟨an *open* wound⟩
**5 :** not restricted to a particular group or category of participants ⟨*open* to the public⟩ ⟨*open* housing⟩: as **a :** enterable by both amateur and professional contestants ⟨an *open* tournament⟩ **b :** enterable by a registered voter regardless of political affiliation ⟨an *open* primary⟩
**6 :** fit to be traveled over **:** presenting no obstacle to passage or view ⟨the *open* road⟩ ⟨*open* country⟩
**7 :** having the parts or surfaces laid out in an expanded position **:** spread out **:** UNFOLDED ⟨an *open* book⟩
**8 a** (1) **:** LOW 13 (2) **:** formed with the tongue in a lower position ⟨Italian has an *open* and a close *e*⟩ **b** (1) **:** having clarity and resonance unimpaired by undue tension or constriction of the throat ⟨an *open* vocal tone⟩ (2) *of a tone* **:** produced by an open string or on a wind instrument by the lip without the use of slides, valves, or keys
**9 a :** available to follow or make use of ⟨the only course *open* to us⟩ **b :** not taken up with duties or engagements ⟨keep an hour *open* on Friday⟩ **c :** not finally decided **:** subject to further consideration ⟨the salary is *open*⟩ ⟨an

*open* question⟩ **d** : available for a qualified applicant : VACANT ⟨the job is still *open*⟩ **e** : remaining available for use or filling until canceled ⟨an *open* order for more items⟩ **f** : available for future purchase ⟨these items are in *open* stock⟩

**10 a** : characterized by ready accessibility and usually generous attitude: as (1) : generous in giving (2) : willing to hear and consider or to accept and deal with : RESPONSIVE (3) : free from reserve or pretense : FRANK **b** : accessible to the influx of new factors (as foreign goods) ⟨an *open* market⟩

**11 a** : having openings, interruptions, or spaces: as (1) : being porous and friable ⟨*open* soil⟩ (2) : sparsely distributed : SCATTERED ⟨*open* population⟩ (3) *of a compound* : having components separated by a space in writing or printing (as *opaque projector*) **b** : not made up of a continuous closed circuit of channels ⟨the insect circulatory system is *open*⟩

**12 a** *of an organ pipe* : not stopped at the top **b** *of a string on a musical instrument* : not stopped by the finger

**13** : being in operation ⟨an *open* microphone⟩; *especially* : ready for business, patronage, or use ⟨the store is *open* from 9 to 5⟩ ⟨the new highway will be *open* next week⟩

**14 a** (1) : characterized by lack of effective regulation of various commercial enterprises ⟨an *open* town⟩ (2) : not repressed by legal controls ⟨*open* gambling⟩ **b** : free from checking or hampering restraints ⟨an *open* economy⟩ **c** : relatively unguarded by opponents ⟨passed to an *open* teammate⟩

**15** : having been opened by a first ante, bet, or bid ⟨the bidding is *open*⟩

**16** *of punctuation* : characterized by sparing use especially of the comma

**17 a** : containing none of its endpoints ⟨an *open* interval⟩ **b** : being a set or composed of sets each point of which has a neighborhood all of whose points are contained in the set ⟨the interior of a sphere is an *open* set⟩

**18 a** : being an incomplete electrical circuit **b** : not allowing the flow of electricity ⟨an *open* switch⟩

**synonym** see FRANK, LIABLE
— **open** *adverb*
— **open·ly** \'ō-pən-lē\ *adverb*
— **open·ness** \-pə(n)-nəs\ *noun*

²**open** *verb* **opened** \'ō-pənd, 'ō-pᵊmd\; **open·ing** \'ōp-niŋ, 'ō-pə-\ (before 12th century)
*transitive verb*
**1 a** : to move (as a door) from a closed position **b** : to make available for entry or passage by turning back (as a barrier) or removing (as a cover or an obstruction)
**2 a** : to make available for or active in a regular function ⟨*open* a new store⟩ **b** : to make accessible for a particular purpose ⟨*opened* new land for settlement⟩ ⟨*open* the way for changes⟩ **c** : to initiate access to (a computer file) prior to use
**3 a** : to disclose or expose to view : REVEAL **b** : to make more discerning or responsive : ENLIGHTEN ⟨must *open* our minds to the problems⟩ **c** : to bring into view or come in sight of by changing position
**4 a** : to make an opening in ⟨*opened* the boil⟩ **b** : to loosen and make less compact ⟨*open* the soil⟩
**5** : to spread out : UNFOLD ⟨*opened* the book⟩
**6 a** : to enter upon : BEGIN ⟨*opened* the meeting⟩ **b** : to commence action in a card game by making (a first bid), putting a first bet in (the pot), or playing (a card or suit) as first lead
**7** : to restore or recall (as an order) from a finally determined state to a state in which the parties are free to prosecute or oppose
*intransitive verb*
**1** : to become open ⟨the office *opened* early⟩
**2 a** : to spread out : EXPAND ⟨the wound *opened* under the strain⟩ **b** : to become disclosed ⟨a beautiful vista *opened* before us⟩

**3** : to become enlightened or responsive
**4** : to give access ⟨the rooms *open* onto a hall⟩
**5** : SPEAK OUT 2 ⟨finally he *opened* freely on the subject⟩
**6 a** : to begin a course or activity ⟨the play *opens* on Tuesday⟩ **b** : to make a bet, bid, or lead in commencing a round or hand of a card game
— **open·abil·i·ty** \ˌōp-nə-'bi-lə-tē, ˌō-pə-\ *noun*
— **open·able** \'ōp-nə-bəl, 'ō-pə-\ *adjective*

³**open** *noun* (13th century)
**1** : OPENING
**2** : open and unobstructed space: as **a** : OPEN AIR **b** : open water
**3** : an open contest, competition, or tournament
**4** : a public or unconcealed state or position

**open admission** *noun* (1969)
: OPEN ENROLLMENT 2

**open–air** *adjective* (1830)
: OUTDOOR

**open air** *noun* (15th century)
: the space where air is unconfined; *especially* : OUTDOORS

**open–and–shut** *adjective* (1841)
**1** : perfectly simple : OBVIOUS
**2** : easily settled ⟨an *open-and-shut* case⟩

**open bar** *noun* (1973)
: a bar (as at a wedding reception) at which drinks are served free — compare CASH BAR

**open·cast** \'ō-pən-ˌkast\ *adjective* (circa 1890)
*chiefly British* : worked from a surface open to the air ⟨an *opencast* mine⟩ ⟨*opencast* mining⟩

**open chain** *noun* (1884)
: an arrangement of atoms represented in a structural formula by a chain whose ends are not joined so as to form a ring

**open city** *noun* (1914)
: a city that is not occupied or defended by military forces and that is not allowed to be bombed under international law

**open dating** *noun* (1971)
: the marking of perishable food products with a clearly readable date indicating when the food was packaged or the last date on which it should be sold or used

**open door** *noun* (1526)
**1** : a recognized right of admittance : freedom of access
**2** : a policy giving opportunity for commercial relations with a country to all nations on equal terms
— **open–door** *adjective*

**open–end** *adjective* (1917)
: organized to allow for contingencies: as **a** : permitting additional debt to be incurred under the original indenture subject to specified conditions ⟨an *open-end* mortgage⟩ **b** : having a fluctuating capitalization of shares that are issued or redeemed at the current net asset value or at a figure in fixed ratio to this ⟨an *open-end* investment company⟩ — compare CLOSED-END

**open–end·ed** \ˌō-pən-'en-dəd\ *adjective* (1825)
: not rigorously fixed: as **a** : adaptable to the developing needs of a situation **b** : permitting or designed to permit spontaneous and unguided responses
— **open–end·ed·ness** *noun*

**open enrollment** *noun* (1964)
**1** : the voluntary enrollment of a student in a public school other than the one assigned on the basis of residence
**2** : enrollment on demand as a student in an institution of higher learning irrespective of formal qualifications

**open·er** \'ōp-nər, 'ō-pə-\ *noun* (15th century)
: one that opens ⟨a bottle *opener*⟩: as **a** *plural* : cards of sufficient value for a player to open the betting in a poker game **b** : the first item, contest, or event of a series
— **for openers** : to begin with

**open–eyed** \ˌō-pən-'īd\ *adjective* (1601)

**1** : having the eyes open
**2** : carefully observant : DISCERNING

**open–hand·ed** \-'han-dəd\ *adjective* (1593)
: GENEROUS, MUNIFICENT
— **open–hand·ed·ly** *adverb*
— **open–hand·ed·ness** *noun*

**open–heart** *adjective* (1960)
: of, relating to, or performed on a heart temporarily relieved of circulatory function and surgically opened for inspection and treatment ⟨*open-heart* surgery⟩

**open–heart·ed** \ˌō-pən-'här-təd\ *adjective* (1611)
**1** : candidly straightforward : FRANK
**2** : responsive to emotional appeal
— **open–heart·ed·ly** *adverb*
— **open–heart·ed·ness** *noun*

**open–hearth** *adjective* (1885)
: of, relating to, involving, or produced in the open-hearth process ⟨*open-hearth* steel⟩

**open–hearth process** *noun* (1882)
: a process of making steel from pig iron in a furnace of the regenerative reverberatory type

**open house** *noun* (15th century)
**1** : ready and usually informal hospitality or entertainment for all comers
**2** : a house or apartment open for inspection especially by prospective buyers or tenants

**open·ing** \'ōp-niŋ, 'ō-pə-\ *noun* (13th century)
**1 a** : an act or instance of making or becoming open **b** : an act or instance of beginning : COMMENCEMENT; *especially* : a formal and usually public event by which something new is put officially into operation
**2** : something that is open: as **a** (1) : BREACH, APERTURE (2) : an open width : SPAN **b** : an area without trees or with scattered usually mature trees that occurs as a break in a forest **c** : two pages that face one another in a book
**3** : something that constitutes a beginning: as **a** : a planned series of moves made at the beginning of a game of chess or checkers — compare ENDGAME, MIDDLE GAME **b** : a first performance
**4 a** : OCCASION, CHANCE **b** : an opportunity for employment

**open letter** *noun* (1878)
: a published letter of protest or appeal usually addressed to an individual but intended for the general public

**open loop** *noun* (1947)
: a control system for an operation or process in which there is no self-correcting action as there is in a closed loop

**open marriage** *noun* (1971)
: a marriage in which the partners agree to let each other have sexual partners outside the marriage

**open–mind·ed** \ˌō-pən-'mīn-dəd\ *adjective* (1828)
: receptive to arguments or ideas
— **open–mind·ed·ly** *adverb*
— **open–mind·ed·ness** *noun*

**open–mouthed** \ˌō-pən-'mau̇thd, -'mau̇tht\ *adjective* (15th century)
**1** : CLAMOROUS, VOCIFEROUS
**2** : having the mouth wide open
**3** : struck with amazement or wonder
— **open–mouth·ed·ly** \-'mau̇-thəd-lē, -thəd-\ *adverb*
— **open–mouth·ed·ness** \-'mau̇-thəd-nəs, -thəd-\ *noun*

**open–pol·li·nat·ed** \ˌō-pən-'pä-lə-ˌnā-təd\ *adjective* (1925)
: pollinated by natural agencies without human intervention

**open season** *noun* (circa 1890)
**1** : a period when it is legal to kill or catch game or fish protected at other times by law

**2 :** a time during which someone or something is the object of sustained attack or criticism

**open secret** *noun* (1828)
: a supposedly secret but generally known matter

**open sentence** *noun* (1937)
: a statement (as in mathematics) that contains at least one blank or unknown and that becomes true or false when the blank is filled or a quantity is substituted for the unknown

**open ses·a·me** \-'se-sə-mē\ *noun* [from *open sesame,* the magical command used by Ali Baba to open the door of the robbers' den in *Ali Baba and the Forty Thieves*] (circa 1837)
: something that unfailingly brings about a desired end

**open shop** *noun* (1903)
: an establishment in which eligibility for employment and retention on the payroll are not determined by membership or nonmembership in a labor union though there may be an agreement by which a union is recognized as sole bargaining agent

**open sight** *noun* (1591)
: a firearm rear sight having an open notch

**open stance** *noun* (1948)
: a stance (as in golf) in which the forward foot is farther from the line of play than the back foot — compare CLOSED STANCE

**open syllable** *noun* (1891)
: a syllable ended by a vowel or diphthong

**open up** (1582)
*transitive verb*
**1 :** to make available
**2 :** to make plain or visible **:** DISCLOSE
**3 :** to open by cutting into
*intransitive verb*
**1 :** to spread out or come into view ⟨the road *opens up* ahead⟩
**2 :** to commence firing
**3 :** to become communicative ⟨tried to get the patient to *open up*⟩

**open·work** \'ō-pən-,wərk\ *noun, often attributive* (1598)
: work constructed so as to show openings through its substance **:** work that is perforated or pierced ⟨wrought-iron *openwork*⟩
— **open–worked** \-,wərkt\ *adjective*

**¹opera** *plural of* OPUS

**²op·era** \'ä-p(ə-)rə, *Southern also* 'ä-prē\ *noun* [Italian, work, opera, from Latin, work, pains; akin to Latin *oper-, opus* — more at OPERATE] (1644)
**1 :** a drama set to music and made up of vocal pieces with orchestral accompaniment and orchestral overtures and interludes; *specifically* **:** GRAND OPERA
**2 :** the score of a musical drama
**3 :** the performance of an opera; *also* **:** a house where operas are performed

**op·er·a·ble** \'ä-p(ə-)rə-bəl\ *adjective* (1646)
**1 :** fit, possible, or desirable to use **:** PRACTICABLE
**2 :** likely to result in a favorable outcome upon surgical treatment ⟨an *operable* cancer⟩
— **op·er·a·bil·i·ty** \,ä-p(ə-)rə-'bi-lə-tē\ *noun*
— **op·er·a·bly** \'ä-p(ə-)rə-blē\ *adverb*

**op·éra bouffe** \'ō-pä-rä-'büf, 'ä-p(ə-)rə-\ *noun* [French, from Italian *opera buffa*] (1870)
: satirical comic opera

**opera buf·fa** \-'bü-fə\ *noun* [Italian, literally, comic opera] (1802)
: an 18th century farcical comic opera with dialogue in recitative

**opéra co·mique** \-kä-'mēk, -kō-\ *noun* [French, literally, comic opera] (1744)
: an opera characterized by spoken dialogue interspersed between the arias and ensemble numbers — compare GRAND OPERA

**opera glass** *noun* (1738)
: a small low-power binocular without prisms for use at the opera or theater — often used in plural

**op·era·go·er** \'ä-p(ə-)rə-,gō(-ə)r\ *noun* (1850)
: a person who frequently goes to operas
— **op·era·go·ing** \-,gō-iŋ, -,gó(-)iŋ\ *noun*

**opera hat** *noun* (1810)
: a man's collapsible top hat

opera glass

**opera house** *noun* (1720)
: a theater devoted principally to the performance of operas; *broadly* **:** THEATER

**op·er·and** \'ä-pə-'rand\ *noun* [Latin *operandum,* neuter of gerundive of *operari*] (1886)
: something (as a quantity or data) that is operated on (as in a mathematical operation); *also* **:** the address in a computer instruction of data to be operated on

**¹op·er·ant** \'ä-pə-rənt\ *adjective* (15th century)
**1 :** functioning or tending to produce effects **:** EFFECTIVE ⟨an *operant* conscience⟩
**2 :** of or relating to the observable or measurable
**3 :** of, relating to, or being an operant or operant conditioning ⟨*operant* behavior⟩
— **op·er·ant·ly** *adverb*

**²operant** *noun* (1937)
: behavior (as bar pressing by a rat to obtain food) that operates on the environment to produce rewarding and reinforcing effects

**operant conditioning** *noun* (1941)
: conditioning in which the desired behavior or increasingly closer approximations to it are followed by a rewarding or reinforcing stimulus — compare CLASSICAL CONDITIONING

**opera se·ria** \-'ser-ē-ə, -'sir-\ *noun* [Italian, literally, serious opera] (circa 1854)
: an 18th century opera with a heroic or legendary subject

**op·er·ate** \'ä-pə-,rāt, 'ä-,prāt\ *verb* **-at·ed; -at·ing** [Latin *operatus,* past participle of *operari* to work, from *oper-, opus* work; akin to Old English *efnan* to perform, Sanskrit *apas* work] (1588)
*intransitive verb*
**1 :** to perform a function **:** exert power or influence ⟨factors *operating* against our success⟩
**2 :** to produce an appropriate effect ⟨the drug *operated* quickly⟩
**3 a :** to perform an operation or a series of operations **b :** to perform surgery **c :** to carry on a military or naval action or mission
**4 :** to follow a course of conduct that is often irregular ⟨crooked gamblers *operating* in the club⟩
*transitive verb*
**1 :** BRING ABOUT, EFFECT
**2 a :** to cause to function **:** WORK **b :** to put or keep in operation
**3 :** to perform an operation on; *especially* **:** to perform surgery on

**op·er·at·ic** \,ä-pə-'ra-tik\ *adjective* (1749)
**1 :** of or relating to opera
**2 :** grand, dramatic, or romantic in style or effect
— **op·er·at·i·cal·ly** \-ti-k(ə-)lē\ *adverb*

**operating** *adjective* (1808)
: of, relating to, or used for or in operations ⟨*operating* expenses⟩ ⟨a hospital *operating* room⟩

**operating system** *noun* (1961)
: software that controls the operation of a computer and directs the processing of programs (as by assigning storage space in memory and controlling input and output functions)

**op·er·a·tion** \,ä-pə-'rā-shən\ *noun* [Middle English *operacioun,* from Middle French *operation,* from Latin *operation-, operatio,* from *operari*] (14th century)
**1 :** performance of a practical work or of something involving the practical application of principles or processes

**2 a :** an exertion of power or influence ⟨the *operation* of a drug⟩ **b :** the quality or state of being functional or operative ⟨the plant is now in *operation*⟩ **c :** a method or manner of functioning ⟨a machine of very simple *operation*⟩
**3 :** EFFICACY, POTENCY — archaic except in legal usage
**4 :** a procedure carried out on a living body usually with instruments especially for the repair of damage or the restoration of health
**5 :** any of various mathematical or logical processes (as addition) of deriving one entity from others according to a rule
**6 a :** a usually military action, mission, or maneuver including its planning and execution **b** *plural* **:** the office on the flight line of an airfield where pilots file clearance for flights and where flying from the field is controlled **c** *plural* **:** the agency of an organization charged with carrying on the principal planning and operating functions of a headquarters and its subordinate units
**7 :** a business transaction especially when speculative
**8 :** a single step performed by a computer in the execution of a program

**op·er·a·tion·al** \-shnəl, -shə-n°l\ *adjective* (circa 1909)
**1 :** of or relating to operation or to an operation ⟨the *operational* gap between planning and production⟩
**2 :** of, relating to, or based on operations
**3 a :** of, engaged in, or connected with execution of military or naval operations in campaign or battle **b :** ready for or in condition to undertake a destined function
— **op·er·a·tion·al·ly** *adverb*

**op·er·a·tion·al·ism** \-shnə-,li-zəm, -shə-n°l-,i-zəm\ *noun* (1931)
: a view that the concepts or terms used in nonanalytic scientific statements must be definable in terms of identifiable and repeatable operations
— **op·er·a·tion·al·ist** \-list, -ist\ *noun*
— **op·er·a·tion·al·is·tic** \-,rä-shnə-'lis-tik, -shə-n°l-'is-tik\ *adjective*

**op·er·a·tion·ism** \,ä-pə-'rä-shə-,ni-zəm\ *noun* (1935)
**:** OPERATIONALISM
— **op·er·a·tion·ist** \-sh(ə-)nist\ *noun*

**operations research** *noun* (1945)
: the application of scientific and especially mathematical methods to the study and analysis of problems involving complex systems — called also *operational research*

**¹op·er·a·tive** \'ä-p(ə-)rə-tiv, 'ä-pə-,rā-\ *adjective* (15th century)
**1 :** producing an appropriate effect **:** EFFICACIOUS
**2 :** exerting force or influence **:** OPERATING
**3 a :** having to do with physical operations (as of machines) **b :** WORKING ⟨an *operative* craftsman⟩
**4 :** based on or consisting of an operation ⟨*operative* dentistry⟩
— **op·er·a·tive·ly** *adverb*
— **op·er·a·tive·ness** *noun*

**²operative** *noun* (circa 1810)
**1 :** OPERATOR: as **a :** ARTISAN, MECHANIC **b :** a secret agent **c :** PRIVATE DETECTIVE

**op·er·a·tor** \'ä-pə-,rā-tər, 'ä-,prā-\ *noun* (1611)
**1 :** one that operates: as **a :** one that operates a machine or device **b :** one that operates a business **c :** one that performs surgical operations **d :** one that deals in stocks or commodities
**2 a :** MOUNTEBANK, FRAUD **b :** a shrewd and skillful person who knows how to circumvent restrictions or difficulties
**3 a :** something and especially a symbol that denotes or performs a mathematical or logical operation **b :** a mathematical function
**4 :** a binding site in a DNA chain at which a genetic repressor binds to inhibit the initiation of transcription of messenger RNA by one or more nearby structural genes — called also *operator gene;* compare OPERON

— **op·er·a·tor·less** *adjective*

¹**oper·cu·lar** \ō-'pər-kyə-lər\ *adjective* (1830)
: of, relating to, or constituting an operculum

²**opercular** *noun* (circa 1890)
: an opercular part (as a bone or scale)

**oper·cu·late** \ō-'pər-kyə-lət\ *also* **oper·cu·lat·ed** \-ˌlā-təd\ *adjective* (circa 1775)
: having an operculum

**oper·cu·lum** \ō-'pər-kyə-ləm\ *noun, plural* **-la** \-lə\ *also* **-lums** [New Latin, from Latin, cover, from *operire* to shut, cover] (1752)
**1** : a body process or part that suggests a lid: as **a** : a horny or shelly plate on the posterior dorsal surface of the foot in many gastropod mollusks that closes the shell when the animal is retracted **b** : the covering of the gills of a fish — see FISH illustration
**2** : a lid or covering flap (as of a moss capsule or a pyxidium in a seed plant)

**op·er·et·ta** \ˌä-pə-'re-tə\ *noun* [Italian, diminutive of *opera*] (1770)
: a usually romantic comic opera that includes songs and dancing

— **op·er·et·tist** \-'re-tist\ *noun*

**op·er·on** \'ä-pə-ˌrän\ *noun* [French *opéron*, from *opérer* to bring about, effect (from Latin *operari*) + *-on* ²-on] (1961)
: a group of closely linked genes that produces a single messenger RNA molecule in transcription and that consists of structural genes and regulating elements (as an operator and promoter)

**op·er·ose** \'ä-pə-ˌrōs\ *adjective* [Latin *operosus*, from *oper-, opus* work — more at OPERATE] (1678)
: TEDIOUS, WEARISOME

— **op·er·ose·ly** *adverb*
— **op·er·ose·ness** *noun*

**Ophe·lia** \ō-'fēl-yə\ *noun*
: the daughter of Polonius in Shakespeare's *Hamlet*

**ophid·i·an** \ō-'fi-dē-ən\ *adjective* [ultimately from Greek *ophis*] (1883)
: of, relating to, or resembling snakes

— **ophidian** *noun*

**Ophir** \'ō-fər\ *noun* [Hebrew *Ōphīr*]
: a biblical land of uncertain location but reputedly rich in gold

**ophit·ic** \ä-'fi-tik, ō-\ *adjective* [*ophite* serpentine (stone), from Latin *ophites*, from Greek *ophitēs* (*lithos*), from *ophitēs* snakelike, from *ophis* snake; akin to Sanskrit *ahi* snake and probably to Latin *anguis* snake, *anguilla* eel, Greek *enchelys* eel, *echidna* viper, *echinos* hedgehog, Old English *igil*] (1875)
: having or being a rock fabric in which lath-shaped plagioclase crystals are enclosed in later formed augite

**ophi·u·roid** \ˌō-fē-'yür-ˌoid, ˌä-\ *noun* [New Latin *Ophiuroidea*, group name, from *Ophiura*, genus name, from Greek *ophis* + *oura* tail — more at ASS] (circa 1879)
: BRITTLE STAR

— **ophiuroid** *adjective*

**ophthalm-** *or* **ophthalmo-** *combining form* [Greek, from *ophthalmos*]
: eye ⟨*ophthalmology*⟩

**oph·thal·mia** \äf-'thal-mē-ə, äp-\ *noun* [Middle English *obtalmia*, from Late Latin *ophthalmia*, from Greek, from *ophthalmos* eye; akin to Greek *ōps* eye — more at EYE] (14th century)
: inflammation of the conjunctiva or the eyeball

**oph·thal·mic** \-mik\ *adjective* (circa 1741)
**1** : of, relating to, or situated near the eye
**2** : supplying or draining the eye or structures in the region of the eye ⟨*ophthalmic* artery⟩

**oph·thal·mol·o·gist** \ˌäf-thə(l)-'mä-lə-jist, ˌäp-, -ˌthal-\ *noun* (1834)
: a physician that specializes in ophthalmology — compare OPTICIAN, OPTOMETRIST

**oph·thal·mol·o·gy** \-'mä-lə-jē\ *noun* (circa 1842)
: a branch of medical science dealing with the structure, functions, and diseases of the eye

— **oph·thal·mo·log·ic** \-mə-'lä-jik\ *or* **oph·thal·mo·log·i·cal** \-ji-kəl\ *adjective*
— **oph·thal·mo·log·i·cal·ly** \-ji-k(ə-)lē\ *adverb*

**oph·thal·mo·scope** \äf-'thal-mə-ˌskōp, äp-\ *noun* [International Scientific Vocabulary] (circa 1857)
: an instrument for use in viewing the interior of the eye and especially the retina

— **oph·thal·mo·scop·ic** \(ˌ)äf-ˌthal-mə-'skä-pik, (ˌ)äp-\ *adjective*
— **oph·thal·mos·co·py** \ˌäf-thəl-'mäs-kə-pē, äp-, -ˌthal-\ *noun*

**-opia** *noun combining form* [New Latin, from Greek *-ōpia*, from *ōps*]
**1** : condition of having (such) vision ⟨diplo*pia*⟩
**2** : condition of having (such) a visual defect ⟨hyper*opia*⟩

¹**opi·ate** \'ō-pē-ət, -ˌāt\ *noun* (15th century)
**1** : a preparation or derivative of opium; *broadly* : a narcotic or opioid peptide
**2** : something that induces rest or inaction or quiets uneasiness

²**opiate** *adjective* (1543)
**1 a** : containing or mixed with opium **b** : of, relating to, binding, or being an opiate ⟨*opiate* receptors⟩
**2 a** : inducing sleep : NARCOTIC **b** : causing dullness or inaction

**opine** \ō-'pīn\ *verb* **opined; opin·ing** [Middle English, from Middle French *opiner*, from Latin *opinari* to have an opinion] (15th century)
*intransitive verb*
: to express opinions
*transitive verb*
: to state as an opinion

**opin·ion** \ə-'pin-yən\ *noun* [Middle English, from Middle French, from Latin *opinion-, opinio*, from *opinari*] (14th century)
**1 a** : a view, judgment, or appraisal formed in the mind about a particular matter **b** : APPROVAL, ESTEEM
**2 a** : belief stronger than impression and less strong than positive knowledge **b** : a generally held view
**3 a** : a formal expression of judgment or advice by an expert **b** : the formal expression (as by a judge, court, or referee) of the legal reasons and principles upon which a legal decision is based ☆

— **opin·ioned** \-yənd\ *adjective*

**opin·ion·at·ed** \-yə-ˌnā-təd\ *adjective* (1601)
: unduly adhering to one's own opinion or to preconceived notions

— **opin·ion·at·ed·ly** *adverb*
— **opin·ion·at·ed·ness** *noun*

**opin·ion·a·tive** \-ˌnā-tiv\ *adjective* (1536)
**1** : of, relating to, or consisting of opinion : DOCTRINAL
**2** : OPINIONATED

— **opin·ion·a·tive·ly** *adverb*
— **opin·ion·a·tive·ness** *noun*

**opi·oid** \'ō-pē-ˌoid\ *adjective* (1957)
**1** : possessing some properties characteristic of opiate narcotics but not derived from opium
**2** : of, involving, or induced by an opioid substance or an opioid peptide

**opioid peptide** *noun* (1976)
: any of a group of endogenous neural polypeptides (as an endorphin or enkephalin) that bind especially to opiate receptors and mimic some of the pharmacological properties of opiate drugs — called also *opioid*

**opis·tho·branch** \ə-'pis-thə-ˌbraŋk\ *noun, plural* **-branchs** [New Latin *Opisthobranchia*, from Greek *opisthen* behind (akin to Greek *epi* on) + *branchia* gills — more at EPI-] (circa 1856)
: any of a subclass (Opisthobranchia) of marine gastropod mollusks that have the gills when present posterior to the heart and often lack a shell

— **opisthobranch** *adjective*

**opi·um** \'ō-pē-əm\ *noun* [Middle English, from Latin, from Greek *opion*, from diminutive of *opos* sap] (14th century)
**1** : a bitter brownish addictive narcotic drug that consists of the dried juice of the opium poppy
**2** : something having an effect like that of opium

**opium poppy** *noun* (1863)
: an annual Eurasian poppy (*Papaver somniferum*) cultivated since antiquity as the source of opium, for its edible oily seeds, or for its showy flowers

**opos·sum** \(ə-)'pä-səm\ *noun, plural* **opos·sums** *also* **opossum** [Virginia Algonquian, literally, white animal] (1610)
**1** : any of a family (Didelphidae) of American marsupials that usually have a pointed snout and prehensile tail; *especially* : a common omnivorous largely nocturnal and arboreal mammal (*Didelphis virginiana*) of North America having grayish to blackish fur with white on the cheeks

opossum 1

**2** : any of several Australian phalangers

¹**op·po·nent** \ə-'pō-nənt\ *noun* [Latin *opponent-, opponens*, present participle of *opponere*] (1588)
**1** : one that takes an opposite position (as in a debate, contest, or conflict)
**2** : a muscle that opposes or counteracts and limits the action of another

²**opponent** *adjective* (1647)
**1** : ANTAGONISTIC, OPPOSING
**2** : situated in front

**op·por·tune** \ˌä-pər-'tün, -'tyün\ *adjective* [Middle English, from Middle French *opportun*, from Latin *opportunus*, from *ob-* toward + *portus* port, harbor — more at OB-, FORD] (15th century)
**1** : suitable or convenient for a particular occurrence ⟨an *opportune* moment⟩
**2** : occurring at an appropriate time ⟨an *opportune* offer of assistance⟩

— **op·por·tune·ly** *adverb*
— **op·por·tune·ness** \-'t(y)ün-nəs\ *noun*

**op·por·tun·ism** \-'tü-ˌni-zəm, -'tyü-\ *noun* (1870)
: the art, policy, or practice of taking advantage of opportunities or circumstances often with little regard for principles or consequences

---

☆ **SYNONYMS**
**Opinion, view, belief, conviction, persuasion, sentiment** mean a judgment one holds as true. OPINION implies a conclusion thought out yet open to dispute ⟨each expert seemed to have a different *opinion*⟩. VIEW suggests a subjective opinion ⟨very assertive in stating his *views*⟩. BELIEF implies often deliberate acceptance and intellectual assent ⟨a firm *belief* in her party's platform⟩. CONVICTION applies to a firmly and seriously held belief ⟨the *conviction* that animal life is as sacred as human⟩. PERSUASION suggests a belief grounded on assurance (as by evidence) of its truth ⟨was of the *persuasion* that everything changes⟩. SENTIMENT suggests a settled opinion reflective of one's feelings ⟨her feminist *sentiments* are well-known⟩.

---

\ə\ abut \ˀ\ kitten ·ər\ further \a\ ash \ā\ ace
\ä\ mop, mar \au̇\ out \ch\ chin \e\ bet \ē\ easy
\g\ go \i\ hit \ī\ ice \j\ job \ŋ\ sing \ō\ go
\ȯ\ law \ȯi\ boy \th\ thin \th\ the \ü\ loot \u̇\ foot
\y\ yet \zh\ vision *see also* Guide to Pronunciation

— **op·por·tun·ist** \-'tü-nist, -'tyü-\ *noun or adjective*

**op·por·tu·nis·tic** \-tü-'nis-tik, -tyü-\ *adjective* (1892)
**:** taking advantage of opportunities as they arise: as **a :** exploiting opportunities with little regard to principle or consequences ⟨a politician considered *opportunistic*⟩ **b :** feeding on whatever food is available ⟨*opportunistic* feeders⟩ **c :** being or caused by a usually harmless microorganism that can become pathogenic when the host's resistance is impaired ⟨*opportunistic* infections⟩
— **op·por·tu·nis·ti·cal·ly** \-ti-k(ə-)lē\ *adverb*

**op·por·tu·ni·ty** \,ä-pər-'tü-nə-tē, -'tyü-\ *noun, plural* **-ties** (14th century)
**1 :** a favorable juncture of circumstances ⟨the halt provided an *opportunity* for rest and refreshment⟩
**2 :** a good chance for advancement or progress

**opportunity cost** *noun* (1911)
**:** the cost of making an investment that is the difference between the return on one investment and the return on an alternative

**op·pos·able** \ə-'pō-zə-bəl\ *adjective* (1667)
**1 :** capable of being opposed or resisted
**2 :** capable of being placed against one or more of the remaining digits of a hand or foot ⟨the *opposable* human thumb⟩
— **op·pos·abil·i·ty** \-,pō-zə-'bi-lə-tē\ *noun*

**op·pose** \ə-'pōz\ *transitive verb* **op·posed; op·pos·ing** [French *opposer*, from Latin *opponere* (perfect indicative *opposui*), from *ob-* against + *ponere* to place — more at OB-, POSITION] (1579)
**1 :** to place opposite or against something
**2 :** to place over against something so as to provide resistance, counterbalance, or contrast
**3 :** to offer resistance to ☆
— **op·pos·er** *noun*

**op·posed** \-'pōzd\ *adjective* (1596)
**:** set or placed in opposition **:** CONTRARY ⟨with politicians, as *opposed* to soap, you cannot return what you have bought —Felix G. Rohatyn⟩

**op·pose·less** \ə-'pōz-ləs\ *adjective* (1605)
*archaic* **:** IRRESISTIBLE

**¹op·po·site** \'ä-pə-zət, 'äp-sət\ *adjective* [Middle English, from Middle French, from Latin *oppositus,* past participle of *opponere*] (14th century)
**1 a :** set over against something that is at the other end or side of an intervening line or space ⟨*opposite* interior angles⟩ ⟨*opposite* ends of a diameter⟩ **b :** situated in pairs on an axis with each member being separated from the other by half the circumference of the axis ⟨*opposite* leaves⟩ — compare ALTERNATE
**2 a :** occupying an opposing and often antagonistic position ⟨*opposite* sides of the question⟩ **b :** diametrically different (as in nature or character) ⟨*opposite* meanings⟩
**3 :** contrary to one another or to a thing specified **:** REVERSE ⟨gave them *opposite* directions⟩
**4 :** being the other of a pair that are corresponding or complementary in position, function, or nature ⟨members of the *opposite* sex⟩
**5 :** of, relating to, or being the side of a baseball field that is near the first base line for a right-handed batter and near the third base line for a left-handed batter ☆
— **op·po·site·ly** *adverb*
— **op·po·site·ness** *noun*

**²opposite** *noun* (15th century)
**1 :** something that is opposed to some other often specified thing
**2 :** ANTONYM
**3 :** ADDITIVE INVERSE; *especially* **:** the additive inverse of a real number

**³opposite** *adverb* (1667)
**:** on or to an opposite side

**⁴opposite** *preposition* (1758)
**1 :** across from and usually facing or on the same level with ⟨sat *opposite* each other⟩

**2 :** in a role complementary to ⟨played *opposite* the leading man in the comedy⟩

**opposite number** *noun* (1906)
**:** a member of a system or class who holds relatively the same position as a particular member in a corresponding system or class **:** COUNTERPART

**op·po·si·tion** \,ä-pə-'zi-shən\ *noun* (14th century)
**1 :** a configuration in which one celestial body is opposite another in the sky or in which the elongation is near or equal to 180 degrees
**2 :** the relation between two propositions having the same subject and predicate but differing in quantity or quality or both
**3 :** an act of setting opposite or over against **:** the condition of being so set
**4 :** hostile or contrary action or condition
**5 a :** something that opposes; *specifically* **:** a body of persons opposing something **b** *often capitalized* **:** a political party opposing and prepared to replace the party in power
— **op·po·si·tion·al** \-'zish-nəl, -'zi-shə-nᵊl\ *adjective*

**op·po·si·tion·ist** \-'zi-sh(ə-)nist\ *noun* (1773)
**:** a member of an opposition
— **oppositionist** *adjective*

**op·press** \ə-'pres\ *transitive verb* [Middle English, from Middle French *oppresser,* from Latin *oppressus,* past participle of *opprimere,* from *ob-* against + *premere* to press — more at OB-, PRESS] (14th century)
**1 a** *archaic* **:** SUPPRESS **b :** to crush or burden by abuse of power or authority
**2 :** to burden spiritually or mentally **:** weigh heavily upon
*synonym* see WRONG
— **op·pres·sor** \-'pre-sər\ *noun*

**op·pres·sion** \ə-'pre-shən\ *noun* (14th century)
**1 a :** unjust or cruel exercise of authority or power **b :** something that oppresses especially in being an unjust or excessive exercise of power
**2 :** a sense of being weighed down in body or mind **:** DEPRESSION

**op·pres·sive** \ə-'pre-siv\ *adjective* (circa 1677)
**1 :** unreasonably burdensome or severe ⟨*oppressive* legislation⟩
**2 :** TYRANNICAL
**3 :** overwhelming or depressing to the spirit or senses ⟨an *oppressive* climate⟩
*synonym* see ONEROUS
— **op·pres·sive·ly** *adverb*
— **op·pres·sive·ness** *noun*

**op·pro·bri·ous** \ə-'prō-brē-əs\ *adjective* (14th century)
**1 :** expressive of opprobrium **:** SCURRILOUS ⟨*opprobrious* language⟩
**2 :** deserving of opprobrium **:** INFAMOUS
— **op·pro·bri·ous·ly** *adverb*
— **op·pro·bri·ous·ness** *noun*

**op·pro·bri·um** \-brē-əm\ *noun* [Latin, from *opprobrare* to reproach, from *ob* in the way of + *probrum* reproach; akin to Latin *pro* forward and to Latin *ferre* to carry, bring — more at OB-, FOR, BEAR] (1656)
**1 :** something that brings disgrace
**2 a :** public disgrace or ill fame that follows from conduct considered grossly wrong or vicious **b :** CONTEMPT, REPROACH

**op·pugn** \ə-'pyün, ä-\ *transitive verb* [Middle English, from Latin *oppugnare,* from *ob-* against + *pugnare* to fight — more at OB-, PUNGENT] (15th century)
**1 :** to fight against
**2 :** to call in question
— **op·pugn·er** *noun*

**Ops** \'äps\ *noun* [Latin]
**:** the Roman goddess of abundance and the wife of Saturn

**op·sin** \'äp-sən\ *noun* [probably from *rhodopsin*] (1951)
**:** any of various colorless proteins that in combination with retinal or a related prosthetic

group form a visual pigment (as rhodopsin) in a reaction which is reversed by light

**-opsis** *noun combining form, plural* **-opses** *or* **-opsides** [New Latin, from Greek, from *opsis* appearance, vision]
**:** structure resembling a (specified) thing ⟨cary*opsis*⟩

**op·son·ic** \äp-'sä-nik\ *adjective* (1903)
**:** of, relating to, or involving opsonin

**op·so·nin** \'äp-sə-nən\ *noun* [Latin *opsonare* to buy provisions, cater (from Greek *opsōnein*) + English ¹*-in* — more at OLIGOPSONY] (1903)
**:** an antibody of blood serum that makes foreign cells more susceptible to the action of the phagocytes

**-opsy** *noun combining form* [Greek *-opsia,* from *opsis*]
**:** examination ⟨necr*opsy*⟩

**opt** \'äpt\ *intransitive verb* [French *opter,* from Latin *optare*] (1877)
**:** to make a choice; *especially* **:** to decide in favor of something ⟨*opted* for a tax increase —Tom Wicker⟩

**op·ta·tive** \'äp-tə-tiv\ *adjective* (15th century)
**1 a :** of, relating to, or constituting a verbal mood that is expressive of wish or desire **b :** of, relating to, or constituting a sentence that is expressive of wish or hope
**2 :** expressing desire or wish
— **optative** *noun*
— **op·ta·tive·ly** *adverb*

**¹op·tic** \'äp-tik\ *adjective* [Middle English, from Middle French *optique,* from Medieval Latin *opticus,* from Greek *optikos,* from *opsesthai* to be going to see; akin to Greek *opsis* appearance, *ōps* eye — more at EYE] (14th century)
**:** of or relating to vision or the eye

**²optic** *noun* (1600)
**1 :** EYE
**2 a :** any of the elements (as lenses, mirrors, or light guides) of an optical instrument or system — usually used in plural **b :** an optical instrument

**op·ti·cal** \'äp-ti-kəl\ *adjective* (1570)
**1 :** of or relating to the science of optics
**2 a :** of or relating to vision **:** VISUAL **b :** VISIBLE 1 ⟨*optical* wavelength⟩ **c :** of, relating to, or being objects that emit light in the visible

---

range of frequencies ⟨an *optical* galaxy⟩ **d** : using the properties of light to aid vision ⟨an *optical* instrument⟩
**3 a** : of, relating to, or utilizing light especially instead of other forms of energy ⟨*optical* microscopy⟩ **b** : involving the use of light-sensitive devices to acquire information for a computer ⟨*optical* character recognition⟩
**4** : of or relating to optical art
— **op·ti·cal·ly** \-k(ə-)lē\ *adverb*

**optical activity** *noun* (1877)
: ability of a chemical substance to rotate the plane of vibration of polarized light to the right or left

**optical art** *noun* (1964)
: nonobjective art characterized by the use of straight or curved lines or geometric patterns often for an illusory effect (as of motion)

**optical bench** *noun* (1883)
: an apparatus that is fitted for the convenient location and adjustment of light sources and optical devices and that is used for the observation and measurement of optical phenomena

**optical disk** *noun* (1980)
: a disk with a plastic coating on which information (as music or visual images) is recorded digitally (as in the form of tiny pits) and which is read by using a laser

**optical fiber** *noun* (1962)
: a single fiber-optic strand

**optical glass** *noun* (1840)
: flint or crown glass of well-defined characteristics used especially for making lenses

**optical illusion** *noun* (1794)
: ILLUSION 2a(1)

**optically active** *adjective* (1885)
: capable of rotating the plane of polarization of light to the right or left — used of compounds, molecules, or atoms

**optical rotation** *noun* (1895)
: the angle through which the plane of vibration of polarized light that traverses an optically active substance is rotated

**optic axis** *noun* (1664)
: a line in a doubly refracting medium that is parallel to the direction in which all components of plane-polarized light travel with the same speed

**optic chiasma** *noun* (1872)
: the X-shaped partial decussation on the undersurface of the hypothalamus through which the optic nerves are continuous with the brain — called also *optic chiasm*

**optic cup** *noun* (circa 1885)
: the optic vesicle after invaginating to form a 2-layered cup from which the retina and pigmented layer of the eye will develop — called also *eyecup*

**optic disk** *noun* (circa 1890)
: BLIND SPOT 1a

**op·ti·cian** \äp-'ti-shən\ *noun* (1687)
**1** : a maker of or dealer in optical items and instruments
**2** : a person who reads prescriptions for visual correction, orders lenses, and dispenses spectacles and contact lenses — compare OPHTHALMOLOGIST, OPTOMETRIST

**optic lobe** *noun* (1854)
: either of two prominences of the midbrain concerned with vision

**optic nerve** *noun* (1615)
: either of the pair of nerves that comprise the 2d pair of cranial nerves, arise from the ventral part of the diencephalon, supply the retina, and conduct visual stimuli to the brain — see EYE illustration

**op·tics** \'äp-tiks\ *noun plural but singular in construction* (1579)
: a science that deals with the genesis and propagation of light, the changes that it undergoes and produces, and other phenomena closely associated with it

**optic vesicle** *noun* (circa 1885)
: an evagination of each lateral wall of the embryonic vertebrate forebrain from which the nervous structures of the eye develop

**op·ti·mal** \'äp-tə-məl\ *adjective* (1890)
: most desirable or satisfactory : OPTIMUM
— **op·ti·mal·i·ty** \,äp-tə-'ma-lə-tē\ *noun*
— **op·ti·mal·ly** \-mə-lē\ *adverb*

**op·ti·mi·sa·tion, op·ti·mise** *British variant of* OPTIMIZATION, OPTIMIZE

**op·ti·mism** \'äp-tə-,mi-zəm\ *noun* [French *optimisme*, from Latin *optimum*, noun, best, from neuter of *optimus* best; akin to Latin *ops* power — more at OPULENT] (1759)
**1** : a doctrine that this world is the best possible world
**2** : an inclination to put the most favorable construction upon actions and events or to anticipate the best possible outcome
— **op·ti·mist** \-mist\ *noun*
— **op·ti·mis·tic** \,äp-tə-'mis-tik\ *adjective*
— **op·ti·mis·ti·cal·ly** \-ti-k(ə-)lē\ *adverb*

**Op·ti·mist** \'äp-tə-mist\ *noun* [*Optimist (Club)*] (1911)
: a member of a major international service club

**op·ti·mi·za·tion** \,äp-tə-mə-'zā-shən\ *noun* (1857)
: an act, process, or methodology of making something (as a design, system, or decision) as fully perfect, functional, or effective as possible; *specifically* : the mathematical procedures (as finding the maximum of a function) involved in this

**op·ti·mize** \'äp-tə-,mīz\ *transitive verb* **-mized; -miz·ing** (1857)
: to make as perfect, effective, or functional as possible
— **op·ti·miz·er** \-,mī-zər\ *noun*

**op·ti·mum** \'äp-tə-məm\ *noun, plural* **-ma** \-mə\ *also* **-mums** [Latin] (1879)
**1** : the amount or degree of something that is most favorable to some end; *especially* : the most favorable condition for the growth and reproduction of an organism
**2** : greatest degree attained or attainable under implied or specified conditions
— **optimum** *adjective*

**¹op·tion** \'äp-shən\ *noun* [French, from Latin *option-, optio* free choice; akin to Latin *optare* to choose] (circa 1604)
**1** : an act of choosing
**2 a** : the power or right to choose : freedom of choice **b** : a privilege of demanding fulfillment of a contract on any day within a specified time **c** : a contract conveying a right to buy or sell designated securities, commodities, or property interest at a specified price during a stipulated period; *also* : the right conveyed by an option **d** : a right of an insured person to choose the form in which payments due on a policy shall be made or applied
**3** : something that may be chosen: as **a** : an alternative course of action ⟨didn't have many *options* open⟩ **b** : an item that is offered in addition to or in place of standard equipment
**4** : an offensive football play in which a back may choose whether to pass or run with the ball — called also *option play*
*synonym* SEE CHOICE

**²option** *transitive verb* (1926)
: to grant or take an option on

**op·tion·al** \'äp-shnəl, -shə-nᵊl\ *adjective* (1792)
: involving an option : not compulsory
— **op·tion·al·i·ty** \,äp-shə-'na-lə-tē\ *noun*
— **op·tion·al·ly** *adverb*

**opto-** *combining form* [Greek *optos*, verbal of *opsesthai* — more at OPTIC]
**1** : vision ⟨*opto*metry⟩
**2** : optic and ⟨*opto*electronics⟩

**op·to·elec·tron·ics** \,äp-(,)tō-i-lek-'trä-niks, -ē-lek-\ *noun plural but singular in construction* (1959)
: a branch of electronics that deals with electronic devices for emitting, modulating, transmitting, and sensing light
— **op·to·elec·tron·ic** \-nik\ *adjective*

**op·to·ki·net·ic** \,äp-tō-kə-'ne-tik, -kī-\ *adjective* (1925)

: of, relating to, or involving movements of the eyes

**op·tom·e·trist** \äp-'tä-mə-trist\ *noun* (1903)
: a specialist licensed to practice optometry — compare OPHTHALMOLOGIST, OPTICIAN

**op·tom·e·try** \-trē\ *noun* [International Scientific Vocabulary] (1886)
: the art or profession of examining the eye for defects and faults of refraction and prescribing correctional lenses or exercises
— **op·to·met·ric** \,äp-tə-'me-trik\ *adjective*

**opt out** *intransitive verb* (1951)
: to choose not to participate in something — often used with *of* ⟨*opted out* of the project⟩

**op·u·lence** \'ä-pyə-lən(t)s\ *noun* (circa 1510)
**1** : WEALTH, AFFLUENCE
**2** : ABUNDANCE, PROFUSION

**op·u·lent** \-lənt\ *adjective* [Latin *opulentus*, from *ops* power, help; akin to Latin *opus* work] (1601)
: exhibiting or characterized by opulence: as **a** : having a large estate or property : WEALTHY ⟨hoping to marry an *opulent* widow⟩ **b** : amply or plentifully provided or fashioned often to the point of ostentation ⟨living in *opulent* comfort⟩
*synonym* SEE RICH
— **op·u·lent·ly** *adverb*

**opun·tia** \ō-'pən(t)-sh(ē-)ə\ *noun* [Latin, a plant, from feminine of *opuntius* of Opus, from *Opunt-, Opus* Opus, ancient city in Greece] (1601)
: any of a large genus (*Opuntia*) of cacti with usually yellow flowers and flat or terete joints usually studded with tubercles bearing spines or prickly hairs — compare CHOLLA, PRICKLY PEAR

**opus** \'ō-pəs\ *noun, plural* **op·era** \'ō-pə-rə, 'ä-\ *also* **opus·es** \'ō-pə-səz\ [Latin *oper-, opus* — more at OPERATE] (1809)
: WORK; *especially* : a musical composition or set of compositions usually numbered in the order of its issue

**opus·cule** \ō-'pəs-(,)kyü(ə)l\ *noun* [French, from Latin *opusculum*, diminutive of *opus*] (circa 1656)
: a small or petty work : OPUSCULUM

**opus·cu·lum** \ō-'pəs-kyə-ləm\ *noun, plural* **-la** \-lə\ [Latin] (1654)
: a minor work (as of literature) — usually used in plural

**¹or** \ər, 'ȯr, *Southern also* 'är\ *conjunction* [Middle English, alteration of *other*, alteration of Old English *oththe*; akin to Old High German *eddo* or] (13th century)
**1** : — used as a function word to indicate an alternative ⟨coffee *or* tea⟩ ⟨sink *or* swim⟩, the equivalent or substitutive character of two words or phrases ⟨lessen *or* abate⟩, or approximation or uncertainty ⟨in five *or* six days⟩
**2** *archaic* : EITHER
**3** *archaic* : WHETHER
**4** : — used in logic as a sentential connective that forms a complex sentence which is true when at least one of its constituent sentences is true; compare DISJUNCTION

**²or** *preposition* [Middle English, from *or*, adverb, early, before, from Old Norse *ār*; akin to Old English *ǣr* early — more at ERE] (13th century)
*archaic* : BEFORE

**³or** *conjunction* (13th century)
*archaic* : BEFORE

**⁴or** \'ȯr\ *noun* [Middle English, from Middle French, gold, from Latin *aurum* — more at AUREUS] (15th century)
: the heraldic color gold or yellow

**OR** \'ȯr\ *noun* [¹*or*] (1947)
: a logical operator that requires either of two inputs to be present or conditions to be met for

---

\ə\ **abut** \ᵊ\ **kitten** \ər\ **further** \a\ **ash** \ā\ **ace**
\ä\ **mop, mar** \aù\ **out** \ch\ **chin** \e\ **bet** \ē\ **easy**
\g\ **go** \i\ **hit** \ī\ **ice** \j\ **job** \ŋ\ **sing** \ō\ **go**
\ȯ\ **law** \ȯi\ **boy** \th\ **thin** \t̲h̲\ **the** \ü\ **loot** \ù\ **foot**
\y\ **yet** \zh\ **vision** *see also* Guide to Pronunciation

an output to be made or a statement to be executed ⟨OR gate in a computer⟩

**¹-or** *noun suffix* [Middle English, from Old French *-eur, -eor* & Latin *-or;* Old French *-eur,* from Latin *-or;* Old French *-eor,* from Latin *-ator,* from *-a-,* verb stem + *-tor,* agent suffix; akin to Greek *-tōr,* agent suffix, Sanskrit *-tā*]
: one that does a (specified) thing ⟨grant*or*⟩

**²-or** *noun suffix* [Middle English, from Old French *-eur,* from Latin *-or*]
: condition : activity ⟨demean*or*⟩

**ora** *plural of* os

**or·ache** *or* **or·ach** \'ȯr-ich, 'är-\ *noun* [Middle English *orage, arage,* from Middle French *arrache,* from (assumed) Vulgar Latin *atrapic-, atrapex,* from Greek *atraphaxys*] (13th century)
: any of various herbs (genus *Atriplex*) of the goosefoot family that include some (as *A. hortensis*) used as potherbs

**or·a·cle** \'ȯr-ə-kəl\ *noun* [Middle English, from Middle French, from Latin *oraculum,* from *orare* to speak — more at ORATION] (15th century)
**1 a :** a person (as a priestess of ancient Greece) through whom a deity is believed to speak **b :** a shrine in which a deity reveals hidden knowledge or the divine purpose through such a person **c :** an answer or decision given by an oracle
**2 a :** a person giving wise or authoritative decisions or opinions **b :** an authoritative or wise expression or answer

**orac·u·lar** \ȯ-'ra-kyə-lər, ə-\ *adjective* [Latin *oraculum*] (1678)
**1 :** of, relating to, or being an oracle
**2 :** resembling an oracle (as in solemnity of delivery)
**synonym** see DICTATORIAL
**— orac·u·lar·i·ty** \-,ra-kyə-'lar-ə-tē\ *noun*
**— orac·u·lar·ly** \-'ra-kyə-lər-lē\ *adverb*

**¹oral** \'ȯr-əl, 'ȯr-, 'är-\ *adjective* [Latin *or-, os* mouth; akin to Old Norse *ōss* mouth of a river, Sanskrit *ās* mouth] (1628)
**1 a :** uttered by the mouth or in words : SPOKEN **b :** using speech or the lips especially in teaching the deaf
**2 a :** of, given through, or involving the mouth **b :** being on or relating to the same surface as the mouth
**3 a :** of, relating to, or characterized by the first stage of psychosexual development in psychoanalytic theory during which libidinal gratification is derived from intake (as of food), by sucking, and later by biting **b :** of, relating to, or characterized by personality traits of passive dependency and aggressiveness
**usage** see VERBAL
**— oral·i·ty** \ȯ-'ra-lə-tē, ō-\ *noun*
**— oral·ly** \'ȯr-ə-lē, 'ȯr-, 'är-\ *adverb*

**²oral** *noun* (1876)
: an oral examination — usually used in plural

**oral history** *noun* (1955)
**1 :** tape-recorded historical information obtained in interviews concerning personal experiences and recollections; *also* : the study of such information
**2 :** a written work based on oral history
**— oral historian** *noun*

**oral·ism** \'ȯr-ə-,li-zəm, 'ȯr-, 'är-\ *noun* (1883)
: advocacy or use of the oral method of teaching the deaf
**— oral·ist** \-list\ *noun*

**orang** \ə-'raŋ\ *noun* [by shortening] (1778)
: ORANGUTAN

**¹or·ange** \'är-inj, 'är-(ə-)nj; *chiefly Northern & Midland* 'ȯr-inj, 'ȯr-(ə)nj\ *noun* [Middle English, from Middle French, from Old Provençal *auranja,* from Arabic *nāranj,* from Persian *nārang,* from Sanskrit *nāraṅga* orange tree] (14th century)

**1 a :** a globose berry with a yellowish to reddish orange rind and a sweet edible pulp **b :** any of various rather small evergreen trees (genus *Citrus*) with ovate unifoliolate leaves, hard yellow wood, fragrant white flowers, and fruits that are oranges
**2 :** any of several trees or fruits resembling the orange
**3 :** any of a group of colors that lie midway between red and yellow in hue

**²orange** *adjective* (1542)
**1 :** of or relating to the orange
**2 :** of the color orange

**Orange** *adjective* (1795)
: of, relating to, or sympathizing with Orangemen
**— Or·ange·ism** \'är-in-,ji-zəm, 'är(ə)n-, 'ȯr-in-, 'ȯr(ə)-n-\ *noun*

**or·ange·ade** \,är-in-'jād, ,är-(ə)n-, ,ȯr-in-, ,ȯr(ə)n-\ *noun* [French, from *orange* + *-ade*] (1706)
: a beverage of sweetened orange juice mixed with water

**orange chromide** *noun* [*chromide,* ultimately from Greek *chromis,* a sea fish] (1933)
: a brilliant orange or yellow red-spotted fish (*Etroplus maculatus*) often kept in tropical aquariums

**orange hawkweed** *noun* (circa 1900)
: a European hawkweed (*Hieracium aurantiacum*) that has flower heads with bright orange-red rays and is a troublesome weed especially in northeastern North America

**Or·ange·man** \'är-inj-mən, 'är-(ə)nj-, 'ȯr-inj-, 'ȯr(ə)nj-\ *noun* [William III of England, prince of *Orange*] (1796)
**1 :** a member of a secret society organized in the north of Ireland in 1795 to defend the British sovereign and to support the Protestant religion
**2 :** a Protestant Irishman especially of Ulster

**orange peel** *noun* (circa 1909)
: a rough surface (as on porcelain) like that of an orange

**orange pekoe** *noun* (circa 1877)
: tea made from the smallest and youngest leaves of the shoot

**or·ange·ry** *also* **or·ange·rie** \'är-inj-rē, 'är-(ə)nj-, 'ȯr-inj-, 'ȯr(-ə)nj-\ *noun, plural* **-ries** (1664)
: a protected place and especially a greenhouse for raising oranges in cool climates

**or·ange·wood** \'är-inj-,wu̇d, 'är-(ə)nj-, 'ȯr-inj-, 'ȯr(-ə)nj-\ *noun* (1884)
: the wood of the orange tree used especially in turnery and carving

**or·ang·ish** \'är-in-jish, 'är-(ə)n-, 'ȯr-in-, 'ȯr(-ə)n-\ *adjective* (1967)
: somewhat orange

**orang·u·tan** \ə-'raŋ-ə-,taŋ, -'raŋ-gə-, -,taŋ\ *noun* [Bazaar Malay (Malay-based pidgin), from Malay *orang* man + *hutan* forest] (1691)
: a largely herbivorous arboreal anthropoid ape (*Pongo pygmaeus*) of Borneo and Sumatra that is about two thirds as large as the gorilla and has brown skin, long sparse reddish brown hair, and very long arms ◆

**or·angy** *or* **or·ang·ey** \'är-in-jē, 'är-(ə)n-, 'ȯr-in-, 'ȯr(-ə)n-\ *adjective* (1778)
: resembling or suggestive of an orange (as in flavor or color)

**orate** \ȯ-'rāt, ō-; 'ȯr-,āt, 'ȯr-\ *intransitive verb* **orat·ed; orat·ing** [back-formation from *oration*] (circa 1600)
: to speak in an elevated and often pompous manner

**ora·tion** \ə-'rā-shən, ȯ-\ *noun* [Latin *oration-, oratio* speech, oration, from *orare* to plead, speak, pray; akin to Hittite *ariya-* to consult an oracle and perhaps to Greek *ara* prayer] (1502)
: an elaborate discourse delivered in a formal and dignified manner

**ora·tor** \'ȯr-ə-tər, 'är-\ *noun* (15th century)
**1 :** one who delivers an oration
**2 :** one distinguished for skill and power as a public speaker

**Or·a·to·ri·an** \,ȯr-ə-'tȯr-ē-ən, ,är-, -'tȯr-\ *noun* (circa 1656)
: a member of the Congregation of the Oratory of Saint Philip Neri founded in Rome in 1575 and comprising independent communities of secular priests under obedience but without vows
**— Oratorian** *adjective*

**or·a·tor·i·cal** \,ȯr-ə-'tȯr-i-kəl, ,är-ə-'tär-\ *adjective* (1589)
: of, relating to, or characteristic of an orator or oratory
**— or·a·tor·i·cal·ly** \-k(ə-)lē\ *adverb*

**or·a·to·rio** \,ȯr-ə-'tȯr-ē-,ō, ,är-, -'tȯr-\ *noun, plural* **-ri·os** [Italian, from the *Oratorio* di San Filippo Neri (Oratory of Saint Philip Neri) in Rome] (circa 1738)
: a lengthy choral work usually of a religious nature consisting chiefly of recitatives, arias, and choruses without action or scenery

**¹or·a·to·ry** \'ȯr-ə-,tȯr-ē, 'är-, -,tȯr-\ *noun, plural* **-ries** [Middle English *oratorie,* from Late Latin *oratorium,* from Latin *orare*] (14th century)
**1 :** a place of prayer; *especially* : a private or institutional chapel
**2** *capitalized* **:** an Oratorian congregation, house, or church

**²oratory** *noun* [Latin *oratoria,* from feminine of *oratorius* oratorical, from *orare*] (1593)
**1 :** the art of speaking in public eloquently or effectively
**2 a :** public speaking that employs oratory **b :** public speaking that is characterized by the use of stock phrases and that appeals chiefly to the emotions

**¹orb** \'ȯrb\ *noun* [Middle English, from Middle French *orbe,* from Latin *orbis* circle, disk, orb] (14th century)
**1 :** any of the concentric spheres in old astronomy surrounding the earth and carrying the celestial bodies in their revolutions
**2** *archaic* **:** something circular : CIRCLE, ORBIT
**3 :** a spherical body; *especially* : a spherical celestial object
**4 :** EYE

---

◇ **WORD HISTORY**

**orangutan**   The orangutan, native to Borneo and Sumatra, has been known in western Europe since the 17th century. The name for the animal, similar in most European languages to the English word, is borrowed from two Malay words, *orang* "man, person," and *hutan* "forest," but the Malay word for "orangutan" is *mawas,* and the precise origin of the compound *orangutan* is not known. Presumably Europeans borrowed it from Bazaar Malay, a group of restructured forms of Malay used as common languages by the many non-Malay speakers of the Indonesian archipelago. Queried by Europeans about the name of the animal and not knowing the actual Malay word, inhabitants of the islands perhaps responded by making up *orangutan* on the spot, the sense "forest man" fitting well enough as a descriptive epithet. There has been a tendency ever since *orangutan* was borrowed to rhyme the second and last syllables (as if \raŋ\ and \taŋ\) and in some European languages including English a *g* is sometimes added to the last syllable.

orangutan

**5 :** a sphere surmounted by a cross symbolizing kingly power and justice
**²orb** (1600)
*transitive verb*
**1 :** to form into a disk or circle
**2** *archaic* **:** ENCIRCLE, SURROUND, ENCLOSE
*intransitive verb*
*archaic* **:** to move in an orbit
**or·bic·u·lar** \ȯr-'bi-kyə-lər\ *adjective* [Middle English *orbiculer*, from Middle French or Late Latin; Middle French *orbiculaire*, from Late Latin *orbicularis*, from Latin *orbiculus*, diminutive of *orbis*] (15th century)
**:** SPHERICAL, CIRCULAR
— **or·bic·u·lar·ly** \-'bi-kyə-lər-lē\ *adverb*
**or·bic·u·late** \ȯr-'bi-kyə-lət\ *adjective* (circa 1760)
**:** circular or nearly circular in outline ⟨an *orbiculate* leaf⟩ — see LEAF illustration
**¹or·bit** \'ȯr-bət\ *noun* [Middle English, from Medieval Latin *orbita*, from Latin, rut, track, probably from *orbis*] (15th century)
**:** the bony socket of the eye
— **or·bit·al** \'ȯr-bə-t°l\ *adjective*
**²orbit** *noun* [Latin *orbita* path, rut, orbit] (1696)
**1 a :** a path described by one body in its revolution about another (as by the earth about the sun or by an electron about an atomic nucleus); *also* **:** one complete revolution of a body describing such a path **b :** a circular path
**2 :** a range or sphere of activity or influence
**synonym** see RANGE
— **or·bit·al** \-t°l\ *adjective*
**³orbit** (1943)
*transitive verb*
**1 :** to revolve in an orbit around **:** CIRCLE
**2 :** to send up and make revolve in an orbit ⟨*orbit* a satellite⟩
*intransitive verb*
**:** to travel in circles
**or·bit·al** \'ȯr-bə-t°l\ *noun* [*orbital,* adjective] (1932)
**:** a subdivision of a nuclear shell containing zero, one, or two electrons
**or·bit·er** \-bə-tər\ *noun* (1951)
**:** one that orbits: as **a :** a spacecraft designed to orbit a celestial body without landing on its surface **b :** SPACE SHUTTLE
**orb weaver** *noun* (1889)
**:** any of a family (Araneidae) of North American spiders that have eight similar eyes and typically spin a large elaborate web
**or·ca** \'ȯr-kə\ *noun* [New Latin *Orca,* genus name, from Latin, a whale, probably modification of Greek *oryg-, oryx* — more at ORYX] (1866)
**:** KILLER WHALE
**Or·ca·di·an** \ȯr-'kā-dē-ən\ *noun* [Latin *Orcades* Orkney Islands] (1661)
**:** a native or inhabitant of the Orkney Islands
— **Orcadian** *adjective*
**or·chard** \'ȯr-chərd\ *noun* [Middle English, from Old English *ortgeard,* from *ort-* (from Latin *hortus* garden) + *geard* yard — more at YARD] (before 12th century)
**:** a planting of fruit trees, nut trees, or sugar maples; *also* **:** the trees of such a planting
**orchard grass** *noun* (1765)
**:** a widely grown tall stout hay and pasture grass (*Dactylis glomerata*) that grows in tufts and has loose open panicles
**or·chard·ist** \'ȯr-chər-dist\ *noun* (1794)
**:** an owner or supervisor of orchards
**or·ches·tra** \'ȯr-kəs-trə, -,kes-\ *noun* [Latin, from Greek *orchēstra,* from *orcheisthai* to dance; perhaps akin to Sanskrit *ṛghāyati* he trembles, he rages] (1606)
**1 a :** the circular space used by the chorus in front of the proscenium in an ancient Greek theater **b :** a corresponding semicircular space in a Roman theater used for seating important persons
**2 a :** the space in front of the stage in a modern theater that is used by an orchestra **b :** the forward section of seats on the main floor of a

theater **c :** the main floor of a theater
**3 :** a group of musicians including especially string players organized to perform ensemble music — compare BAND
**or·ches·tral** \ȯr-'kes-trəl\ *adjective* (circa 1811)
**1 :** of, relating to, or composed for an orchestra
**2 :** suggestive of an orchestra or its musical qualities
— **or·ches·tral·ly** \-trə-lē\ *adverb*
**or·ches·trate** \'ȯr-kə-,strāt\ *transitive verb* **-trat·ed; -trat·ing** (1880)
**1 a :** to compose or arrange (music) for an orchestra **b :** to provide with orchestration ⟨*orchestrate* a ballet⟩
**2 :** to arrange or combine so as to achieve a desired or maximum effect ⟨*orchestrated* preparations for the banquet⟩
— **or·ches·tra·tor** *also* **or·ches·trat·er** \-,strā-tər\ *noun*
**or·ches·tra·tion** \,ȯr-kə-'strā-shən\ *noun* (circa 1859)
**1 :** the arrangement of a musical composition for performance by an orchestra; *also* **:** orchestral treatment of a musical composition
**2 :** harmonious organization ⟨develop a world community through *orchestration* of cultural diversities —L. K. Frank⟩
— **or·ches·tra·tion·al** \-shnəl, -shə-n°l\ *adjective*
**or·chid** \'ȯr-kəd\ *noun* [irregular from New Latin *Orchis*] (1845)
**1 :** any of a large family (Orchidaceae, the orchid family) of perennial epiphytic or terrestrial monocotyledonous plants that usually have showy 3-petaled flowers with the middle petal enlarged into a lip and differing in shape and color from the others in shape and color
**2 :** a light purple
— **or·chid·like** \-,līk\ *adjective*

orchid 1

**or·chi·da·ceous** \,ȯr-kə-'dā-shəs\ *adjective* [New Latin *Orchidaceae,* family name, from *Orchis*] (1838)
**1 :** of, relating to, or resembling the orchids
**2 :** SHOWY, OSTENTATIOUS
**or·chis** \'ȯr-kəs\ *noun* [New Latin, from Latin, orchid, from Greek, testicle, orchid; akin to Middle Irish *uirgge* testicle] (1562)
**:** ORCHID; *especially* **:** any of a genus (*Orchis*) with fleshy roots and a spurred lip
**or·dain** \ȯr-'dān\ *verb* [Middle English *ordeinen,* from Old French *ordener,* from Late Latin *ordinare,* from Latin, to put in order, appoint, from *ordin-, ordo* order] (14th century)
*transitive verb*
**1 :** to invest officially (as by the laying on of hands) with ministerial or priestly authority
**2 a :** to establish or order by appointment, decree, or law **:** ENACT **b :** DESTINE, FOREORDAIN
*intransitive verb*
**:** to issue an order
— **or·dain·er** *noun*
— **or·dain·ment** \-'dān-mənt\ *noun*
**or·deal** \ȯr-'dē(-ə)l, 'ȯr-,\ *noun* [Middle English *ordal,* from Old English *ordāl;* akin to Old High German *urteil* judgment, Old English *dāl* division — more at DEAL] (before 12th century)
**1 :** a primitive means used to determine guilt or innocence by submitting the accused to dangerous or painful tests believed to be under supernatural control ⟨*ordeal* by fire⟩
**2 :** a severe trial or experience
**¹or·der** \'ȯr-dər\ *verb* **or·dered; or·der·ing** \'ȯr-d(ə-)riŋ\ [Middle English, from *ordre,* noun] (13th century)
*transitive verb*

**1 :** to put in order **:** ARRANGE
**2 a :** to give an order to **:** COMMAND **b :** DESTINE, ORDAIN **c :** to command to go or come to a specified place **d :** to give an order for ⟨*order* a meal⟩
*intransitive verb*
**1 :** to bring about order **:** REGULATE
**2 a :** to issue orders **:** COMMAND **b :** to give or place an order ☆
— **or·der·able** \-ə-bəl\ *adjective*
— **or·der·er** \-dər-ər\ *noun*
**²order** *noun* [Middle English, from Middle French *ordre,* from Medieval Latin & Latin; Medieval Latin *ordin-,* ordo ecclesiastical order, from Latin, arrangement, group, class; akin to Latin *ordiri* to lay the warp, begin] (14th century)
**1 a :** a group of people united in a formal way: as (1) **:** a fraternal society (the Masonic *Order*) (2) **:** a community under a religious rule; *especially* **:** one requiring members to take solemn vows **b :** a badge or medal of such a society; *also* **:** a military decoration
**2 a :** any of the several grades of the Christian ministry **b** *plural* **:** the office of a person in the Christian ministry **c** *plural* **:** ORDINATION
**3 a :** a rank, class, or special group in a community or society **b :** a class of persons or things grouped according to quality, value, or natural characteristics: as (1) **:** a category of taxonomic classification ranking above the family and below the class (2) **:** the broadest category in soil classification
**4 a** (1) **:** RANK, LEVEL ⟨a statesman of the first *order*⟩ (2) **:** CATEGORY, CLASS ⟨in emergencies of this *order* —R. B. Westerfield⟩ **b** (1) **:** the arrangement or sequence of objects or of events in time ⟨listed the items in *order* of importance⟩ (2) **:** a sequential arrangement of mathematical elements **c :** DEGREE 12a, b **d** (1) **:** the number of times differentiation is applied

order 8b: *1* Corinthian, *2* Doric, *3* Ionic

☆ **SYNONYMS**
**Order, arrange, marshal, organize, systematize, methodize** mean to put persons or things into their proper places in relation to each other. ORDER suggests a straightening out so as to eliminate confusion ⟨*ordered* her business affairs⟩. ARRANGE implies a setting in sequence, relationship, or adjustment ⟨*arranged* the files numerically⟩. MARSHAL suggests gathering and arranging in preparation for a particular operation or effective use ⟨*marshaling* the facts for argument⟩. ORGANIZE implies arranging so that the whole aggregate works as a unit with each element having a proper function ⟨*organized* the volunteers into teams⟩. SYSTEMATIZE implies arranging according to a predetermined scheme ⟨*systematized* billing procedures⟩. METHODIZE suggests imposing an orderly procedure rather than a fixed scheme ⟨*methodizes* every aspect of daily living⟩. See in addition COMMAND.

\ə\ abut \ᵊ\ kitten \ər\ further \a\ ash \ā\ ace \ä\ mop, mar \aů\ out \ch\ chin \e\ bet \ē\ easy \g\ go \i\ hit \ī\ ice \j\ job \ŋ\ sing \ō\ go \ȯ\ law \ȯi\ boy \th\ thin \t͟h\ the \ü\ loot \ů\ foot \y\ yet \zh\ vision *see also* Guide to Pronunciation

successively ⟨derivatives of higher *order*⟩ (2) *of a differential equation* **:** the order of the derivative of highest order **e :** the number of columns or rows or columns and rows in a magic square, determinant, or matrix ⟨the *order* of a matrix with 2 rows and 3 columns is 2 by 3⟩ **f :** the number of elements in a finite mathematical group

**5 a** (1) **:** a sociopolitical system ⟨was opposed to changes in the established *order*⟩ (2) **:** a particular sphere or aspect of a sociopolitical system ⟨the present economic *order*⟩ **b :** a regular or harmonious arrangement ⟨the *order* of nature⟩

**6 a :** a prescribed form of a religious service **:** RITE **b :** the customary mode of procedure especially in debate ⟨point of *order*⟩

**7 a :** the state of peace, freedom from confused or unruly behavior, and respect for law or proper authority ⟨promised to restore law and *order*⟩ **b :** a specific rule, regulation, or authoritative direction **:** COMMAND

**8 a :** a style of building **b :** a type of column and entablature forming the unit of a style

**9 a :** state or condition especially with regard to functioning or repair ⟨things were in terrible *order*⟩ **b :** a proper, orderly, or functioning condition ⟨their passports were in *order*⟩ ⟨the phone is out of *order*⟩

**10 a :** a written direction to pay money to someone **b :** a commission to purchase, sell, or supply goods or to perform work **c :** goods or items bought or sold **d :** an assigned or requested undertaking ⟨landing men on the moon was a large *order*⟩

**11 :** ORDER OF THE DAY ⟨flat roofs were the *order* in the small villages⟩

**— or·der·less** \-ləs\ *adjective*

**— in order :** APPROPRIATE, DESIRABLE ⟨an apology is *in order*⟩

**— in order to :** for the purpose of

**— on order :** in the process of being ordered

**— on the order of 1 :** after the fashion of **:** LIKE ⟨much *on the order of* Great Lakes bulk carriers —*Ships and the Sea*⟩ **2 :** ABOUT, APPROXIMATELY ⟨spent *on the order of* two million dollars⟩

**— to order :** according to the specifications of an order ⟨shoes made *to order*⟩

**order arms** *noun* [from the command *order arms!*] (1844)

**1 :** a position in the manual of arms in which the rifle is held vertically beside the right leg with the butt resting on the ground

**2 :** a command to return the rifle to order arms from present arms or to drop the hand from a hand salute

**or·dered** \'ȯr-dərd\ *adjective* (1579)

**:** characterized by order: as **a :** marked by regularity or discipline ⟨led an *ordered* life⟩ **b :** marked by regular or harmonious arrangement or disposition ⟨an *ordered* landscape⟩ ⟨the *ordered* crystal structure⟩ **c :** having elements arranged or identified according to a rule: as (1) **:** having the property that every pair of different elements is related by a transitive relationship that is not symmetric (2) **:** having elements labeled by ordinal numbers ⟨an *ordered* triple has a first, second, and third element⟩

**or·der·li·ness** \'ȯrd-ər-lē-nəs\ *noun* (1571)

**:** the quality or state of being orderly

**¹or·der·ly** \-lē\ *adjective* (circa 1577)

**1 a** (1) **:** arranged or disposed in some order or pattern **:** REGULAR ⟨*orderly* rows of houses⟩ (2) **:** not marked by disorder **:** TIDY ⟨keeps an *orderly* desk⟩ **b :** governed by law **:** REGULATED ⟨an *orderly* universe⟩ **c :** METHODICAL ⟨an *orderly* mind⟩

**2 :** well behaved **:** PEACEFUL ⟨an *orderly* crowd⟩

**— orderly** *adverb*

**²orderly** *noun, plural* **-lies** (1781)

**1 :** a soldier assigned to perform various services (as carrying messages) for a superior officer

**2 :** a hospital attendant who does routine or heavy work (as cleaning, carrying supplies, or moving patients)

**order of business** [*order of business* (predetermined sequence of matters to be dealt with by an assembly)] (circa 1890)

**:** a matter which must be dealt with **:** TASK ⟨the discipline problem was the first *order of business* at the meeting of the school board⟩

**order of magnitude** (1875)

**:** a range of magnitude extending from some value to ten times that value

**order of the day** (1698)

**1 :** the business or tasks appointed for an assembly for a given day

**2 :** the characteristic or dominant feature or activity ⟨growth and change are the *order of the day* in every field —Ruth G. Strickland⟩

**¹or·di·nal** \'ȯrd-nəl, 'ȯr-dᵊn-ᵊl\ *noun* (14th century)

**1** *capitalized* [Middle English, from Medieval Latin *ordinale*, from Late Latin, neuter of *ordinalis*] **:** a book of rites for the ordination of deacons, priests, and bishops

**2** [Late Latin *ordinalis*, from *ordinalis*, adjective] **:** ORDINAL NUMBER

**²ordinal** *adjective* [Late Latin *ordinalis*, from Latin *ordin-, ordo*] (1599)

**1 :** of a specified order or rank in a series

**2 :** of or relating to a taxonomic order

**ordinal number** *noun* (1607)

**1 :** a number designating the place (as first, second, or third) occupied by an item in an ordered sequence — see NUMBER table

**2 :** a number assigned to an ordered set that designates both the order of its elements and its cardinal number

**or·di·nance** \'ȯrd-nən(t)s, 'ȯr-dᵊn-ən(t)s\ *noun* [Middle English, from Middle French & Medieval Latin; Middle French *ordenance*, literally, act of arranging, from Medieval Latin *ordinantia*, from Latin *ordinant-, ordinans*, present participle of *ordinare* to put in order — more at ORDAIN] (14th century)

**1 :** an authoritative decree or direction **:** ORDER **b :** a law set forth by a governmental authority; *specifically* **:** a municipal regulation

**2 :** something ordained or decreed by fate or a deity

**3 :** a prescribed usage, practice, or ceremony

**synonym** see LAW

**or·di·nand** \'ȯr-dᵊn-'and\ *noun* [Late Latin *ordinandus*, gerundive of *ordinare* to ordain] (circa 1842)

**:** a candidate for ordination

**¹or·di·nary** \'ȯr-dᵊn-,er-ē\ *noun, plural* **-nar·ies** [Middle English *ordinarie*, from Anglo-French & Medieval Latin; Anglo-French, from Medieval Latin *ordinarius*, from Latin *ordinarius*, adjective] (14th century)

**1 a** (1) **:** a prelate exercising original jurisdiction over a specified territory or group (2) **:** a clergyman appointed formerly in England to attend condemned criminals **b :** a judge of probate in some states of the U.S.

**2** *often capitalized* **:** the parts of the Mass that do not vary from day to day

**3 :** the regular or customary condition or course of things — usually used in the phrase *out of the ordinary*

**4 a** *British* **:** a meal served to all comers at a fixed price **b** *chiefly British* **:** a tavern or eating house serving regular meals

**5 :** a common heraldic charge (as the bend) of simple form

**²ordinary** *adjective* [Middle English *ordinarie*, from Latin *ordinarius*, from *ordin-, ordo* order] (15th century)

**1 :** of a kind to be expected in the normal order of events **:** ROUTINE, USUAL

**2 :** having or constituting immediate or original jurisdiction; *also* **:** belonging to such jurisdiction

**3 a :** of common quality, rank, or ability **b :** deficient in quality **:** POOR, INFERIOR

**synonym** see COMMON

**— or·di·nar·i·ly** \,ȯr-dᵊn-'er-ə-lē\ *adverb*

**— or·di·nar·i·ness** \'ȯr-dᵊn-,er-ē-nəs\ *noun*

**ordinary–language philosophy** *noun* (1957)

**:** a trend in philosophical analysis that seeks to resolve philosophical perplexity by revealing sources of puzzlement in the misunderstanding of ordinary language

**Ordinary level** *noun* (1947)

**:** O LEVEL

**ordinary seaman** *noun* (1702)

**:** a seaman of some experience but not as skilled as an able seaman

**ordinary share** *noun* (1891)

*British* **:** a share of common stock

**or·di·nate** \'ȯrd-nət, 'ȯr-dᵊn-ət, -dᵊn-,āt\ *noun* [New Latin (*linea*) *ordinate* (*applicata*), literally, line applied in an orderly manner] (1676)

**:** the Cartesian coordinate obtained by measuring parallel to the y-axis — compare ABSCISSA

**or·di·na·tion** \,ȯr-dᵊn-'ā-shən\ *noun* (14th century)

**:** the act or an instance of ordaining **:** the state of being ordained

**ord·nance** \'ȯrd-nən(t)s\ *noun* [Middle English *ordinaunce*, from Middle French *ordenance*, literally, act of arranging] (14th century)

**1 a :** military supplies including weapons, ammunition, combat vehicles, and maintenance tools and equipment **b :** a service of the army charged with the procuring, distributing, and safekeeping of ordnance

**2 :** CANNON, ARTILLERY

**or·do** \'ȯr-(,)dō\ *noun, plural* **ordos** *or* **or·di·nes** \'ȯr-dᵊn-,ēz\ [Medieval Latin, from Latin, order] (1849)

**:** a list of offices and feasts of the Roman Catholic Church for each day of the year

**or·don·nance** \,ȯr-dᵊn-'äⁿs\ *noun* [French, alteration of Middle French *ordenance*] (1644)

**:** disposition of the parts (as of a literary composition) with regard to one another and the whole **:** ARRANGEMENT

**Or·do·vi·cian** \,ȯr-də-'vi-shən\ *adjective* [Latin *Ordovices*, ancient people in northern Wales] (1879)

**:** of, relating to, or being the period between the Cambrian and the Silurian or the corresponding system of rocks — see GEOLOGIC TIME table

**— Ordovician** *noun*

**or·dure** \'ȯr-jər\ *noun* [Middle English, from Middle French, from *ord* filthy, from Latin *horridus* horrid] (14th century)

**1 :** EXCREMENT

**2 :** something that is morally degrading

**¹ore** \'ȯr, 'ȯr\ *noun, often attributive* [Middle English *or, oor*, partly from Old English *ōra* ore; partly from Old English *ār* brass; akin to Old High German *ēr* bronze, Latin *aes* copper, bronze] (before 12th century)

**1 :** a mineral containing a valuable constituent (as metal) for which it is mined and worked

**2 :** a source from which valuable matter is extracted

**²ore** \'ər-ə\ *noun, plural* **ore** [Swedish *öre* & Danish & Norwegian *øre*] (1716)

**— see** *krona, krone* at MONEY table

**ore·ad** \'ȯr-ē-,ad, 'ȯr-, -ē-əd\ *noun* [Middle English *oreades*, plural, from Latin *oread-, oreas*, from Greek *oreiad-, oreias*, from *oreios* of a mountain, from *oros* mountain — more at ORIENT] (14th century)

**:** any of the nymphs of mountains and hills in Greek mythology

**ore dressing** *noun* (1862)

**:** mechanical preparation (as by crushing) and concentration (as by flotation) of ore

**oreg·a·no** \ə-'re-gə-ˌnō\ *noun* [American Spanish *orégano*, from Spanish, wild marjoram, from Latin *origanum* — more at ORIGANUM] (1771)
**1 :** a bushy perennial mint (*Origanum vulgare*) that is used as a seasoning and a source of aromatic oil — called also *origanum, wild marjoram*
**2 :** any of several plants (genera *Lippia* and *Coleus*) other than oregano of the vervain or mint families

**Or·e·gon grape** \'ȯr-i-gən-, ˌär-, -ˌgän-\ *noun* [*Oregon*, state of the U.S.] (1869)
**:** an evergreen shrub (*Mahonia aquifolium*) of the barberry family that has yellow flowers, bears edible bluish black berries, and is native to western North America

**Or·eo** \'ȯr-ē-(ˌ)ō, 'ȯr-, ˌär-\ *noun* [from *Oreo*, trademark for a chocolate cookie with a white cream filling] (1969)
**:** a black person who adopts the characteristic mentality and behavior of white middle-class society — usually used disparagingly

*Oregon grape*

**Ores·tes** \ə-'res-(ˌ)tēz, ȯ-\ *noun* [Latin, from Greek *Orestēs*]
**:** the son of Agamemnon and Clytemnestra who with his sister Electra avenges his father by killing his mother and her lover Aegisthus

**or·gan** \'ȯr-gən\ *noun* [Middle English, partly from Old English *organa*, from Latin *organum*, from Greek *organon*, literally, tool, instrument; partly from Old French *organe*, from Latin *organum*; akin to Greek *ergon* work — more at WORK] (before 12th century)
**1 a :** *archaic* : any of various musical instruments; *especially* : WIND INSTRUMENT **b** (1) **:** a wind instrument consisting of sets of pipes made to sound by compressed air and controlled by keyboards and producing a variety of musical effects — called also *pipe organ* (2) **:** REED ORGAN (3) **:** an instrument in which the sound and resources of the pipe organ are approximated by means of electronic devices (4) **:** any of various similar cruder instruments
**2 a :** a differentiated structure (as a heart, kidney, leaf, or stem) consisting of cells and tissues and performing some specific function in an organism **b :** bodily parts performing a function or cooperating in an activity ⟨the eyes and related structures that make up the visual *organs*⟩
**3 :** a subordinate group or organization that performs specialized functions ⟨the various *organs* of government⟩
**4 :** PERIODICAL

**organ-** *or* **organo-** *combining form* [Middle English, from Medieval Latin, from Latin *organum*]
**1 :** organ ⟨*organogenesis*⟩
**2 :** organic ⟨*organomercurial*⟩

**or·gan·dy** *also* **or·gan·die** \'ȯr-gən-dē\ *noun,* *plural* **-dies** [French *organdi*] (1835)
**:** a very fine transparent muslin with a stiff finish

**or·gan·elle** \ˌȯr-gə-'nel\ *noun* [New Latin *organella,* from Latin *organum*] (1920)
**:** a specialized cellular part (as a mitochondrion, lysosome, or ribosome) that is analogous to an organ

**or·gan–grind·er** \'ȯr-gən-ˌgrīn-dər\ *noun* (circa 1807)
**:** one that cranks a hand organ; *especially* **:** a street musician who operates a barrel organ

**¹or·gan·ic** \ȯr-'ga-nik\ *adjective* (1517)
**1** *archaic* **:** INSTRUMENTAL
**2 a :** of, relating to, or arising in a bodily organ **b :** affecting the structure of the organism

**3 a** (1) **:** of, relating to, or derived from living organisms (2) **:** of, relating to, yielding, or involving the use of food produced with the use of feed or fertilizer of plant or animal origin without employment of chemically formulated fertilizers, growth stimulants, antibiotics, or pesticides ⟨*organic* farming⟩ ⟨*organic* produce⟩ **b** (1) **:** of, relating to, or containing carbon compounds (2) **:** relating to, being, or dealt with by a branch of chemistry concerned with the carbon compounds of living beings and most other carbon compounds
**4 a :** forming an integral element of a whole **:** FUNDAMENTAL ⟨incidental music rather than *organic* parts of the action —Francis Fergusson⟩ **b :** having systematic coordination of parts **:** ORGANIZED ⟨an *organic* whole⟩ **c :** having the characteristics of an organism **:** developing in the manner of a living plant or animal ⟨society is *organic*⟩
**5 :** of, relating to, or constituting the law by which a government or organization exists
— **or·gan·i·cal·ly** \-ni-k(ə-)lē\ *adverb*
— **or·ga·nic·i·ty** \ˌȯr-gə-'ni-sə-tē\ *noun*

**²organic** *noun* (1942)
**:** an organic substance: as **a :** a fertilizer of plant or animal origin **b :** a pesticide whose active component is an organic compound or a mixture of organic compounds

**or·gan·i·cism** \ȯr-'ga-nə-ˌsi-zəm\ *noun* [International Scientific Vocabulary] (1883)
**1 a :** the explanation of life and living processes in terms of the levels of organization of living systems rather than in terms of the properties of their smallest components **b :** VITALISM
**2 :** any of various theories that attribute to society or the universe as a whole an existence or characteristics analogous to those of a biological organism
— **or·gan·i·cist** \-sist\ *noun or adjective*

**or·ga·ni·sa·tion, or·ga·nise, or·ga·nis·er** *British variant of* ORGANIZATION, ORGANIZE, ORGANIZER

**or·gan·ism** \'ȯr-gə-ˌni-zəm\ *noun* (circa 1774)
**1 :** a complex structure of interdependent and subordinate elements whose relations and properties are largely determined by their function in the whole
**2 :** an individual constituted to carry on the activities of life by means of organs separate in function but mutually dependent **:** a living being
— **or·gan·is·mic** \ˌȯr-gə-'niz-mik\ *also* **or·gan·is·mal** \-məl\ *adjective*
— **or·gan·is·mi·cal·ly** \-mi-k(ə-)lē\ *adverb*

**or·gan·ist** \'ȯr-gə-nist\ *noun* (1591)
**:** a person who plays the organ

**¹or·ga·ni·za·tion** \ˌȯr-gə-nə-'zā-shən, ˌȯrg-nə-\ *noun* (15th century)
**1 a :** the act or process of organizing or of being organized **b :** the condition or manner of being organized
**2 a :** ASSOCIATION, SOCIETY ⟨charitable *organizations*⟩ **b :** an administrative and functional structure (as a business or a political party); *also* **:** the personnel of such a structure

**²organization** *adjective* (1949)
**:** characterized by complete conformity to the standards and requirements of an organization ⟨an *organization* man⟩

**or·ga·ni·za·tion·al** \-shnəl, -shə-nᵊl\ *adjective* (1881)
**1 :** of or relating to an organization **:** involving organization ⟨the *organizational* state of a crystal⟩
**2 :** ORGANIZATION
— **or·ga·ni·za·tion·al·ly** *adverb*

**or·ga·nize** \'ȯr-gə-ˌnīz\ *verb* **-nized; -niz·ing** (15th century)
*transitive verb*
**1 :** to cause to develop an organic structure
**2 :** to form into a coherent unity or functioning whole **:** INTEGRATE ⟨trying to *organize* her thoughts⟩

**3 a :** to set up an administrative structure for **b** **:** to persuade to associate in an organization; *especially* **:** UNIONIZE
**4 :** to arrange by systematic planning and united effort
*intransitive verb*
**1 :** to undergo physical or organic organization
**2 :** to arrange elements into a whole of interdependent parts
**3 :** to form an organization; *specifically* **:** to form or persuade workers to join a union
**synonym** see ORDER
— **or·gan·iz·able** \ˌȯr-gə-'nī-zə-bəl\ *adjective*

**organized** *adjective* (1817)
**1 :** having a formal organization to coordinate and carry out activities ⟨*organized* baseball⟩ ⟨*organized* crime⟩
**2 :** affiliated by membership in an organization (as a union) ⟨*organized* steelworkers⟩

**or·ga·niz·er** \'ȯr-gə-ˌnī-zər\ *noun* (1849)
**1 :** one that organizes
**2 :** a region of a developing embryo or a substance produced by such a region that is capable of inducing a specific type of development in undifferentiated tissue — called also *inductor*

**or·gan·o·chlo·rine** \ˌȯr-gə-nō-'klȯr-ˌēn, ȯr-ˌga-nə-, -'klȯr-, -ən\ *adjective* (1961)
**:** of, relating to, or belonging to the chlorinated hydrocarbon pesticides (as aldrin, DDT, or dieldrin)
— **organochlorine** *noun*

**organ of Cor·ti** \-'kȯr-tē\ [Alfonso *Corti* (died 1876) Italian anatomist] (1882)
**:** a complex epithelial structure in the cochlea that rests on the internal surface of the basilar membrane and in mammals is the chief part of the ear by which sound is directly perceived

**or·gan·o·gen·e·sis** \ˌȯr-gə-nō-'je-nə-səs, ȯr-ˌga-nə-\ *noun* [New Latin] (circa 1860)
**:** the origin and development of bodily organs
— compare MORPHOGENESIS
— **or·gan·o·ge·net·ic** \-jə-'ne-tik\ *adjective*

**or·gan·o·lep·tic** \ȯr-gə-nō-'lep-tik, ȯr-ˌga-nə-\ *adjective* [French *organoleptique,* from *organ-* + Greek *lēptikos* disposed to take, from *lambanein* to take — more at LATCH] (1852)
**1 :** being, affecting, or relating to qualities (as taste, color, odor, and feel) of a substance (as a food or drug) that stimulate the sense organs
**2 :** involving use of the sense organs ⟨*organoleptic* evaluation of foods⟩
— **or·gan·o·lep·ti·cal·ly** \-ti-k(ə-)lē\ *adverb*

**or·ga·nol·o·gy** \ˌȯr-gə-'nä-lə-jē\ *noun* [International Scientific Vocabulary] (circa 1842)
**:** the study of the organs of plants and animals

**or·gan·o·mer·cu·ri·al** \ˌȯr-gə-nō-(ˌ)mər-'kyùr-ē-əl, ȯr-ˌga-nə-\ *noun* (1938)
**:** an organic compound or a pharmaceutical preparation containing mercury

**or·gan·o·me·tal·lic** \-mə-'ta-lik\ *adjective* [International Scientific Vocabulary] (1852)
**:** of, relating to, or being an organic compound that usually contains a metal or metalloid bonded directly to carbon
— **organometallic** *noun*

**or·ga·non** \'ȯr-gə-ˌnän\ *noun* [Greek, literally, tool — more at ORGAN] (1610)
**:** an instrument for acquiring knowledge; *specifically* **:** a body of principles of scientific or philosophic investigation

**or·gan·o·phos·phate** \ˌȯr-gə-nō-'fäs-ˌfāt, ȯr-ˌga-nō-\ *noun* (1949)
**:** an organophosphorus compound (as a pesticide)
— **organophosphate** *adjective*

---

**or·gan·o·phos·pho·rus** \-'fäs-f(ə-)rəs\ *also*
**or·gan·o·phos·pho·rous** \-fäs-'fōr-əs,
-'för-\ *adjective* (1950)
: of, relating to, or being a phosphorus-
containing organic compound and especially a
pesticide (as malathion) that acts by inhibiting
cholinesterase
— **organophosphorus** *noun*
**organ–pipe cactus** *noun* (1908)
: any of several tall upright cacti (as *Le-
maireocereus thurberi* or *L. marginatus*) of the
southwestern U.S. and adjacent Mexico that
usually branch at the base to form several upright stems
**or·ga·num** \'ȯr-gə-nəm\ *noun* [Medieval Latin, from Latin, organ] (1614)
**1** : ORGANON
**2** : early polyphony of the late Middle Ages
that consists of one or more voice parts accompanying the cantus firmus in parallel motion usually at a fourth, fifth, or octave above
or below; *also* : a composition in this style
**or·gan·za** \ȯr-'gan-zə\ *noun* [probably alteration of *Lorganza*, a trademark] (1820)
: a sheer dress fabric (as of silk or nylon) resembling organdy
**or·gan·zine** \'ȯr-gən-ˌzēn\ *noun* [French or
Italian; French *organsin*, from Italian *organ-
zino*] (1699)
: a raw silk yarn used for warp threads in fine
fabrics
**or·gasm** \'ȯr-ˌga-zəm\ *noun* [New Latin *orgas-
mus*, from Greek *orgasmos*, from *organ* to
grow ripe, be lustful; probably akin to Sanskrit
*ūrjā* sap, strength] (circa 1763)
: intense or paroxysmal excitement; *especially*
: the climax of sexual excitement that is usually accompanied by the ejaculation of semen in
the male and vaginal contractions in the female
— **or·gas·mic** \ȯr-'gaz-mik\ *also* **or·gas-
tic** \-'gas-tik\ *adjective*
**or·geat** \'ȯr-ˌzhä(t)\ *noun* [French, from Middle French, from *orge* barley, from Latin *hordeum;* akin to Old High German *gersta* bar-
ley] (1754)
: a sweet almond-flavored nonalcoholic syrup
used as a cocktail ingredient or food flavoring
**or·gi·as·tic** \ˌȯr-jē-'as-tik\ *adjective* [Greek
*orgiastikos*, from *orgiazein* to celebrate orgies,
from *orgia*] (1698)
**1** : of, relating to, or marked by orgies
**2** : characterized by unrestrained emotion
: FRENZIED
— **or·gi·as·ti·cal·ly** \-ti-k(ə-)lē\ *adverb*
**or·gone** \'ȯr-ˌgōn\ *noun* [probably from *orgasm* + *-one* (as in *hormone*)] (1942)
: a vital energy held to pervade nature and be
a factor in health in the theories of Wilhelm
Reich
**or·gu·lous** \'ȯr-gyə-ləs, -gə-\ *adjective* [Mid-
dle English, from Old French *orgueilleus*,
from *orgueil* pride, of Germanic origin; akin
to Old High German *urguol* distinguished]
(13th century)
: PROUD
**or·gy** \'ȯr-jē\ *noun, plural* **orgies** [Middle
French *orgie*, from Latin *orgia*, plural, from
Greek; akin to Greek *ergon* work — more at
WORK] (circa 1561)
**1** : secret ceremonial rites held in honor of an
ancient Greek or Roman deity and usually
characterized by ecstatic singing and dancing
**2 a** : drunken revelry **b** : a sexual encounter
involving many people; *also* : an excessive
sexual indulgence
**3** : something that resembles an orgy in lack
of control or moderation ⟨an *orgy* of destruc-
tion⟩
**-oria** *plural of* -ORIUM
**-orial** *adjective suffix* [Middle English, from
Latin *-orius* -ory + Middle English *-al*]
: of, belonging to, or connected with ⟨combi-
nat*orial*⟩
**orib·a·tid** \ȯ-'ri-bə-təd, ˌȯr-ə-'ba-təd\ *noun*
[New Latin *Oribatidae* (coextensive with *Ori-*

*batoidea*), from *Oribata*, genus name, from
Greek *oribatēs* walking the mountains, from
*oros* mountain + *-batēs*, from *bainein* to go —
more at ORIENT, COME] (1875)
: any of a superfamily (Oribatoidea) of small
oval eyeless nonparasitic mites having a
heavily sclerotized integument with a leathery
appearance
— **oribatid** *adjective*
**ori·el** \'ōr-ē-əl, 'ȯr-\ *noun* [Middle English,
porch, oriel, from Middle French *oriol* porch]
(14th century)
: a large bay window projecting from a wall
and supported by a corbel or bracket
¹**ori·ent** \'ōr-ē-ənt, 'ȯr-, -ˌent\ *noun* [Middle
English, from Middle French, from Latin
*orient-, oriens*, from present participle of *oriri*
to rise; akin to Sanskrit *ṛṇoti* he moves, arises,
Greek *ornynai* to rouse, *oros* mountain] (14th
century)
**1** *archaic* : EAST 1b
**2** *capitalized* : EAST 2
**3 a** : a pearl of great luster **b** : the luster of a
pearl ◆
²**orient** *adjective* (15th century)
**1** *archaic* : ORIENTAL 1
**2 a** : LUSTROUS, SPARKLING ⟨*orient* gems⟩ **b** *archaic* : RADIANT, GLOWING
**3** *archaic* : rising in the sky
³**ori·ent** \'ōr-ē-ˌent, 'ȯr-\ *transitive verb*
[French *orienter*, from Middle French, from
*orient*] (circa 1741)
**1 a** : to cause to face or point toward the east;
*specifically* : to build (a church or temple)
with the longitudinal axis pointing eastward
and the chief altar at the eastern end **b** : to set
or arrange in any determinate position especially in relation to the points of the compass
**c** : to ascertain the bearings of
**2 a** : to set right by adjusting to facts or principles **b** : to acquaint with the existing situation or environment
**3** : to direct (as a book or film) toward the interests of a particular group
**4** : to cause the axes of the molecules of to assume the same direction
*usage* see ORIENTATE
**ori·en·tal** \ˌōr-ē-'en-tᵊl, ˌȯr-\ *adjective* (14th
century)
**1** *often capitalized* : of, relating to, or situated
in the Orient
**2 a** : of superior grade, luster, or value **b** : being corundum or sapphire but simulating another gem in color
**3** *often capitalized* : of, relating to, or having
the characteristics of Orientals
**4** *capitalized* : of, relating to, or constituting
the biogeographic region that includes Asia
south and southeast of the Himalayas and the
Malay Archipelago west of Wallace's line
— **ori·en·tal·ly** \-tᵊl-ē\ *adverb*
**Oriental** *noun* (15th century)
: a member of one of the indigenous peoples
of the Orient
**oriental fruit moth** *noun* (1921)
: a small nearly cosmopolitan moth (*Gra-
pholita molesta*) probably of Japanese origin
whose larva is injurious to the twigs and fruit
of orchard trees and especially the peach —
called also *oriental peach moth*
**Ori·en·ta·lia** \ˌōr-ē-ən-'tāl-yə, ˌȯr-, -ˌen-, -'tā-
lē-ə\ *noun plural* [New Latin] (1903)
: materials concerning or characteristic of the
Orient
**ori·en·tal·ism** \ˌōr-ē-'en-tᵊl-ˌi-zəm\ *noun, often capitalized* (1769)
**1** : a trait, custom, or habit of expression characteristic of oriental peoples
**2** : scholarship or learning in oriental subjects
— **ori·en·tal·ist** \-tᵊl-ist\ *noun, often capitalized*
**ori·en·tal·ize** \-tᵊl-ˌīz\ *verb* **-ized; -iz·ing**
(1823)
*transitive verb*
*often capitalized* : to make oriental

*intransitive verb*
*often capitalized* : to become oriental
**Oriental poppy** *noun* (1731)
: an Asian perennial poppy (*Papaver orien-
tale*) that is commonly cultivated for its large
showy flowers
**Oriental rug** *noun* (1881)
: a handwoven or hand-knotted one-piece rug
or carpet made in the Orient — called also
*Oriental carpet*
**ori·en·tate** \'ōr-ē-ən-ˌtāt, 'ȯr-, -ˌen-\ *verb* **-tat-
ed; -tat·ing** (1849)
*transitive verb*
: ORIENT
*intransitive verb*
: to face or turn to the east ■
**ori·en·ta·tion** \ˌōr-ē-ən-'tā-shən, ˌȯr-, -ˌen-\
*noun* (1839)
**1 a** : the act or process of orienting or of being oriented **b** : the state of being oriented;
*broadly* : ARRANGEMENT, ALIGNMENT
**2** : a usually general or lasting direction of
thought, inclination, or interest
**3** : change of position by organs, organelles,
or organisms in response to external stimulus
— **ori·en·ta·tion·al** \-shnəl, -shə-nᵊl\ *adjective*
— **ori·en·ta·tion·al·ly** *adverb*
**ori·ent·ed** \'ōr-ē-ˌen-təd, 'ȯr-\ *adjective* (1944)
: intellectually, emotionally, or functionally directed ⟨humanistically *oriented* scholars⟩
**ori·en·teer** \ˌōr-ē-ən-'tir, ˌȯr-, -ˌen-\ *noun*
[back-formation from *orienteering*] (1965)
: one who engages in orienteering
**ori·en·teer·ing** \ˌōr-ē-ən-'tir-iŋ, ˌȯr-, -ˌen-\
*noun* [modification of Swedish *orientering*,
from *orientera* to orient] (1948)
: a cross-country race in which each participant uses a map and compass to navigate between checkpoints along an unfamiliar course

□ USAGE

**orientate** This back-formation from *orientation* had been in use for about a century
when it was first criticized as a needlessly
long variant of *orient*. A surprisingly large
number of handbooks and other commentators have subsequently disparaged *orientate*.
Since the whole controversy boils down to
three letters and one syllable, one might
think the matter too trivial to have drawn so
much attention. Both *orient* and *orientate* are
standard, but *orientate* is more common in
British English ⟨where the conservatives tend
to be clerically *orientated —Times Literary
Supplement*⟩ ⟨more emotionally or culturally
*orientated* toward Europe —Duke of Edin-
burgh⟩. *Orient* is the usual choice in American English.

◇ WORD HISTORY

**orient** As the ancient Romans did not
have magnetic compasses, they depended
upon the position of the rising sun to determine their daytime bearings. The direction
from which the sun rose was called *oriens*,
deriving from the present participle of the
verb *oriri*, meaning "to rise." The word *oriens*
also came to be used for the part of the
world in the direction from which the sun
rose, the East. After *oriens* was borrowed
into English as *Orient*, it became the name
for all the lands to the east of Europe, and
especially eastern Asia. With the spread of
Christianity across Europe it became customary to build churches with their longitudinal axes pointing eastward toward Jerusalem. This practice gave rise to the use of
*orient* as a verb meaning "to cause to face or
point toward the east." This sense served as
the basis for development of the verb's other
senses in English.

**or·i·fice** \ˈȯr-ə-fəs, ˈär-\ *noun* [Middle English, from Middle French, from Late Latin *orificium,* from Latin *or-, os* mouth + *facere* to make, do — more at ORAL, DO] (15th century) : an opening (as a vent, mouth, or hole) through which something may pass
— **or·i·fi·cial** \ˌȯr-ə-ˈfi-shəl, ˌär-\ *adjective*

**or·i·flamme** \ˈȯr-ə-ˌflam, ˈär-\ *noun* [Middle English *oriflamble,* the banner of Saint Denis, from Middle French, from Medieval Latin *aurea flamma,* literally, golden flame] (1600) : a banner, symbol, or ideal inspiring devotion or courage

**ori·ga·mi** \ˌȯr-ə-ˈgä-mē\ *noun* [Japanese, from *ori* fold + *kami* paper] (1956) : the Japanese art or process of folding squares of paper into representational shapes

**orig·a·num** \ə-ˈri-gə-nəm\ *noun* [Middle English, from Latin, wild marjoram, from Greek *origanon*] (14th century) : any of several aromatic mints (especially genus *Origanum*) used as seasonings; *especially* : OREGANO 1

**or·i·gin** \ˈȯr-ə-jən, ˈär-\ *noun* [Middle English *origine,* probably from Middle French, from Latin *origin-, origo,* from *oriri* to rise — more at ORIENT] (15th century)
**1** : ANCESTRY, PARENTAGE
**2 a** : rise, beginning, or derivation from a source **b** : the point at which something begins or rises or from which it derives ⟨the *origin* of the custom is forgotten⟩; *also* : something that creates, causes, or gives rise to another ⟨this spring is the *origin* of the brook⟩
**3** : the more fixed, central, or larger attachment of a muscle
**4** : the intersection of coordinate axes ☆

¹**orig·i·nal** \ə-ˈri-jə-nºl, -ˈrij-nəl\ *noun* (14th century)
**1** *archaic* : the source or cause from which something arises; *specifically* : ORIGINATOR
**2 a** : that from which a copy, reproduction, or translation is made **b** : a work composed first-hand
**3 a** : a person of fresh initiative or inventive capacity **b** : a unique or eccentric person

²**original** *adjective* (14th century)
**1** : of, relating to, or constituting an origin or beginning : INITIAL ⟨the *original* part of the house⟩
**2 a** : not secondary, derivative, or imitative **b** : being the first instance or source from which a copy, reproduction, or translation is or can be made
**3** : independent and creative in thought or action : INVENTIVE
**synonym** see NEW

**orig·i·nal·i·ty** \ə-ˌri-jə-ˈna-lə-tē\ *noun* (1742)
**1** : the quality or state of being original
**2** : freshness of aspect, design, or style
**3** : the power of independent thought or constructive imagination

**orig·i·nal·ly** \ə-ˈri-jə-nºl-ē; -ˈrij-nə-lē, -ˈri-jən-\ *adverb* (14th century)
**1** *archaic* : by origin or derivation : INHERENTLY
**2** : in the beginning : in the first place : INITIALLY
**3** : in a fresh or original manner

**original sin** *noun* (14th century) : the state of sin that according to Christian theology characterizes all human beings as a result of Adam's fall

**orig·i·nate** \ə-ˈri-jə-ˌnāt\ *verb* **-nat·ed; -nat·ing** (1667)
*transitive verb* : to give rise to : INITIATE
*intransitive verb* : to take or have origin : BEGIN
**synonym** see SPRING
— **orig·i·na·tion** \-ˌri-jə-ˈnā-shən\ *noun*
— **orig·i·na·tor** \-ˈri-jə-ˌnā-tər\ *noun*

**orig·i·na·tive** \ə-ˈri-jə-ˌnā-tiv, -nə-\ *adjective* (1827) : having ability to originate : CREATIVE
— **orig·i·na·tive·ly** *adverb*

**O–ring** \ˈō-ˌriŋ\ *noun* (1946) : a ring (as of synthetic rubber) used as a gasket

**ori·ole** \ˈōr-ē-ˌōl, ˈȯr-, -ē-əl\ *noun* [French *oriol,* from Latin *aureolus,* diminutive of *aureus* golden — more at AUREUS] (1776)
**1** : any of various usually brightly colored Old World passerine birds (family Oriolidae and especially genus *Oriolus*)
**2** : any of various New World passerine birds (family Icteridae and especially genus *Icterus*) of which the males are usually black and yellow or black and orange

oriole 2

**Ori·on** \ə-ˈrī-ən, ȯ-\ *noun* [Latin, from Greek *Ōriōn*]
**1** : a giant hunter slain by Artemis in Greek mythology
**2** [Latin (genitive *Orionis*)] : a constellation on the equator east of Taurus represented on charts by the figure of a hunter with belt and sword

**or·is·mol·o·gy** \ˌȯr-əz-ˈmä-lə-jē, ˌär-\ *noun* [Greek *horismos* definition (from *horizein* to define) + English *-logy* — more at HORIZON] (1816) : the science of defining technical terms
— **or·is·mo·log·i·cal** \ˌȯr-əz-mə-ˈlä-ji-kəl, ˌär-; ȯ-ˌriz-\ *adjective*

**or·i·son** \ˈȯr-ə-sən, ˈär-, -zən\ *noun* [Middle English, from Old French, from Late Latin *oration-, oratio,* from Latin, oration] (13th century) : PRAYER

**-orium** *noun suffix, plural* **-oriums** *or* **-oria** [Latin, from neuter of *-orius* -ory] : ¹-ORY ⟨haustor*ium*⟩

**Ori·ya** \ō-ˈrē-ə\ *noun* (1801) : the Indo-Aryan language of Orissa, India

**Or·lean·ist** \ˈȯr-lē-ə-nist, ȯr-ˈlē-(ə-)nist\ *noun* (1834) : a supporter of the Orleans family in its claim to the throne of France by descent from a younger brother of Louis XIV

**Or·lon** \ˈȯr-ˌlän\ *trademark* — used for an acrylic fiber

**or·lop deck** \ˈȯr-ˌläp-\ *noun* [Middle English *overlop* deck of a single decker, from Middle Low German *overlōp,* literally, something that overleaps] (1758) : the lowest deck in a ship having four or more decks

**Or·mazd** \ˈȯr-(ˌ)məzd, -ˌmazd\ *noun* [Persian *Urmazd,* from Middle Persian, from Avestan *Ahuramazdāh-*] (1603) : AHURA MAZDA

**or·mo·lu** \ˈȯr-mə-ˌlü\ *noun, often attributive* [French *or moulu,* literally, ground gold] (1765) : golden or gilded brass or bronze used for decorative purposes (as in mounts for furniture)

¹**or·na·ment** \ˈȯr-nə-mənt\ *noun* [Middle English, from Old French *ornement,* from Latin *ornamentum,* from *ornare*] (13th century)
**1** *archaic* : a useful accessory
**2 a** : something that lends grace or beauty **b** : a manner or quality that adorns
**3** : one whose virtues or graces add luster to a place or society
**4** : the act of adorning or being adorned
**5** : an embellishing note not belonging to the essential harmony or melody — called also *embellishment, fioritura*

²**or·na·ment** \-ˌment\ *transitive verb* (1720) : to provide with ornament : EMBELLISH
**synonym** see ADORN

¹**or·na·men·tal** \ˌȯr-nə-ˈmen-tºl\ *adjective* (1646)
: of, relating to, or serving as ornament; *specifically* : grown as an ornamental
— **or·na·men·tal·ly** \-tºl-ē\ *adverb*

²**ornamental** *noun* (1650) : a decorative object; *especially* : a plant cultivated for its beauty rather than for use

**or·na·men·ta·tion** \ˌȯr-nə-mən-ˈtā-shən, -ˌmen-\ *noun* (1851)
**1** : something that ornaments : EMBELLISHMENT
**2** : the act or process of ornamenting : the state of being ornamented

**or·nate** \ȯr-ˈnāt\ *adjective* [Middle English *ornat,* from Latin *ornatus,* past participle of *ornare* to furnish, embellish; akin to Latin *ordo* order — more at ORDER] (15th century)
**1** : marked by elaborate rhetoric or florid style
**2** : elaborately or excessively decorated
— **or·nate·ly** *adverb*
— **or·nate·ness** *noun*

**or·nery** \ˈȯr-nə-rē, ˈär-; ˈȯrn-rē, ˈärn-\ *adjective* **or·neri·er; -est** [alteration of *ordinary*] (1816) : having an irritable disposition : CANTANKEROUS ◆
— **or·neri·ness** *noun*

**ornith-** *or* **ornitho-** *combining form* [Latin, from Greek, from *ornith-, ornis* — more at ERNE] : bird ⟨*ornith*ology⟩

---

☆ **SYNONYMS**

**Origin, source, inception, root** mean the point at which something begins its course or existence. ORIGIN applies to the things or persons from which something is ultimately derived and often to the causes operating before the thing itself comes into being ⟨an investigation into the *origin* of baseball⟩. SOURCE applies more often to the point where something springs into being ⟨the *source* of the Nile⟩ ⟨the *source* of recurrent trouble⟩. INCEPTION stresses the beginning of something without implying causes ⟨the business has been a success since its *inception*⟩. ROOT suggests a first, ultimate, or fundamental source often not easily discerned ⟨the real *root* of the violence⟩.

---

◇ **WORD HISTORY**

**ornery** The word *ornery* was originally a vernacular, nonstandard pronunciation of *ordinary,* produced by loss of the syllable coming just after the initial primary stress—a common process in polysyllabic English words. The first hint of such a pronunciation is a three-syllable phonetic spelling of *ordinary* in *The English-School Reformed,* a guide to English spelling and pronunciation by one R. Brown published in 1700. It is not until the 19th century that the spelling *ornery* actually appears, in both British and American writing, presumably at the point that its meaning had shifted far enough from the "commonplace" sense of *ordinary* that its link with this spelling was forgotten and *ornery* was perceived as a distinct word. At first *ornery* is attested in the senses "of poor quality" or "unpleasant," though it soon is found with the meaning "cantankerous" that it usually has today. Spellings such as *o'n'ry* recorded in the 20th century show further phonetic loss: dropping of the first \r\ and deletion of the syllable following the primary stress.

---

**or·nith·ic** \ȯr-'ni-thik\ *adjective* [Greek *ornithikos*, from *ornith-*, *ornis*] (1854)
**:** of, relating to, or characteristic of birds

**or·ni·thine** \'ȯr-nə-ˌthēn\ *noun* [International Scientific Vocabulary *ornith*uric acid (a compound of which ornithine is a component, found in the urine of birds) + *²-ine*] (1881)
**:** a crystalline amino acid $C_5H_{12}N_2O_2$ that functions especially in urea production as a carrier by undergoing conversion to citrulline and then arginine in reaction with ammonia and carbon dioxide followed by recovery along with urea by enzymatic hydrolysis of arginine

**or·nith·is·chi·an** \ˌȯr-nə-'this-kē-ən\ *noun* [New Latin *Ornithischia*, from *ornith-* + *ischium*] (1933)
**:** any of an order (Ornithischia) of herbivorous dinosaurs (as a stegosaurus) that have the pubis of the pelvis rotated backward to a position parallel and close to the ischium — compare SAURISCHIAN
— **ornithischian** *adjective*

**or·ni·thol·o·gy** \ˌȯr-nə-'thä-lə-jē\ *noun, plural* **-gies** [New Latin *ornithologia*, from *ornith-* + *-logia* -logy] (1678)
**1 :** a branch of zoology dealing with birds
**2 :** a treatise on ornithology
— **or·ni·tho·log·i·cal** \-thə-'lä-ji-kəl\ *also* **or·ni·tho·log·ic** \-jik\ *adjective*
— **or·ni·tho·log·i·cal·ly** \-ji-k(ə-)lē\ *adverb*
— **or·ni·thol·o·gist** \-'thä-lə-jist\ *noun*

**or·nith·o·pod** \ȯr-'ni-thə-ˌpäd, 'ȯr-ni-thə-\ *noun* [ultimately from Greek *ornith-* + *pod-*, *pous* foot — more at FOOT] (circa 1890)
**:** any of a suborder (Ornithopoda) of bipedal ornithischian dinosaurs (as a hadrosaur) with digitigrade walking limbs usually having only three functional toes

**or·ni·thop·ter** \'ȯr-nə-ˌthäp-tər\ *noun* [International Scientific Vocabulary *ornith-* + *-pter* (as in *helicopter*)] (1908)
**:** an aircraft designed to derive its chief support and propulsion from flapping wings

**or·ni·tho·sis** \ˌȯr-nə-'thō-səs\ *noun, plural* **-tho·ses** \-ˌsēz\ [New Latin] (1939)
**:** PSITTACOSIS

**¹oro-** *combining form* [Greek *oros* — more at ORIENT]
**:** mountain ⟨*oro*graphy⟩

**²oro-** *combining form* [Latin *or-*, *os* — more at ORAL]
**:** mouth ⟨*oro*pharynx⟩

**oro·gen·e·sis** \ˌȯr-ə-'je-nə-səs, ˌōr-\ *noun* [New Latin] (1886)
**:** OROGENY
— **oro·ge·net·ic** \-jə-'ne-tik\ *adjective*

**orog·e·ny** \ȯ-'rä-jə-nē\ *noun* [International Scientific Vocabulary] (1890)
**:** the process of mountain formation especially by folding of the earth's crust
— **oro·gen·ic** \ˌȯr-ə-'je-nik, ˌōr-\ *adjective*

**oro·graph·ic** \ˌȯr-ə-'gra-fik, ˌōr-\ *also* **oro·graph·i·cal** \-fi-kəl\ *adjective* (circa 1803)
**:** of or relating to mountains; *especially* **:** associated with or induced by the presence of mountains ⟨*orographic* rainfall⟩

**orog·ra·phy** \ȯ-'rä-grə-fē\ *noun* [International Scientific Vocabulary] (circa 1846)
**:** a branch of physical geography that deals with mountains

**Oro·mo** \ȯ-'rō-(ˌ)mō, ō-\ *noun, plural* **Oromos** *or* **Oromo** (1893)
**1 :** a member of a Cushitic-speaking people of southern Ethiopia and adjacent parts of Kenya
**2 :** the Cushitic language of the Oromo

**oro·pha·ryn·geal** \ˌȯr-ə-ˌfar-ən-'jē-əl, ˌȯr-, -fə-'rin-j(ē-)əl\ *adjective* (1885)
**1 :** of or relating to the oropharynx
**2 :** of or relating to the mouth and pharynx

**oro·phar·ynx** \-'far-iŋ(k)s\ *noun* (1887)

**:** the part of the pharynx that is below the soft palate and above the epiglottis and is continuous with the mouth

**oro·tund** \'ȯr-ə-ˌtənd, 'är-, 'ōr-\ *adjective* [modification of Latin *ore rotundo*, literally, with round mouth] (circa 1799)
**1 :** marked by fullness, strength, and clarity of sound **:** SONOROUS
**2 :** POMPOUS, BOMBASTIC
— **oro·tun·di·ty** \ˌȯr-ə-'tən-də-tē, ˌär-, ˌōr-\ *noun*

**¹or·phan** \'ȯr-fən\ *noun* [Middle English, from Late Latin *orphanus*, from Greek *orphanos*; akin to Old High German *erbi* inheritance, Latin *orbus* orphaned] (15th century)
**1 :** a child deprived by death of one or usually both parents
**2 :** a young animal that has lost its mother
**3 :** one deprived of some protection or advantage ⟨*orphans* of the storm⟩
— **orphan** *adjective*
— **or·phan·hood** \-ˌhùd\ *noun*

**²orphan** *transitive verb* **or·phaned; or·phan·ing** \'ȯr-fə-niŋ, 'ȯrf-niŋ\ (1814)
**:** to cause to become an orphan

**or·phan·age** \'ȯr-fə-nij, 'ȯrf-nij\ *noun* (circa 1580)
**1 :** the state of being an orphan
**2 :** an institution for the care of orphans

**orphan drug** *noun* (1981)
**:** a drug that is not developed or marketed because its extremely limited use makes it unprofitable

**orphan's court** *noun* (1713)
**:** a probate court which in some states has jurisdiction over the affairs of minors and the administration of estates

**Or·pheus** \'ȯr-ˌfyüs, -fē-əs\ *noun* [Latin, from Greek]
**:** a poet and musician in Greek mythology who almost rescues his wife Eurydice from Hades by charming Pluto and Persephone with his lyre

**or·phic** \'ȯr-fik\ *adjective* (1678)
**1** *capitalized* **:** of or relating to Orpheus or the rites or doctrines ascribed to him
**2 :** MYSTIC, ORACULAR
**3 :** FASCINATING, ENTRANCING
— **or·phi·cal·ly** \-fi-k(ə-)lē\ *adverb*

**Or·phism** \'ȯr-ˌfi-zəm\ *noun* [*Orpheus*, its reputed founder] (1880)
**:** a mystic Greek religion offering initiates purification of the soul from innate evil and release from the cycle of reincarnation

**or·phrey** \'ȯr-frē\ *noun, plural* **orphreys** [Middle English *orfrey*, from Middle French *orfreis*, from Medieval Latin *aurifrigium*, from Latin *aurum* gold + *Phrygius* Phrygian — more at AUREUS] (13th century)
**1 a :** elaborate embroidery **b :** a piece of such embroidery
**2 :** an ornamental border or band especially on an ecclesiastical vestment

**or·pi·ment** \'ȯr-pə-mənt\ *noun* [Middle English, from Middle French, from Latin *auripigmentum*, from *aurum* + *pigmentum* pigment] (14th century)
**:** native orange to lemon-yellow arsenic trisulfide

**or·pine** \'ȯr-pən\ *noun* [Middle English *orpin*, from Middle French, from *orpiment*] (14th century)
**:** an herb (*Sedum telephium* of the family Crassulaceae, the orpine family) that has fleshy leaves and pink or purple flowers and was formerly used in folk medicine; *broadly* **:** SEDUM

**Or·ping·ton** \'ȯr-piŋ-tən\ *noun* [*Orpington*, England] (1897)
**:** any of an English breed of large deep-chested domestic fowls

**or·rery** \'ȯr-ər-ē, 'är-\ *noun, plural* **or·rer·ies** [Charles Boyle (died 1731) 4th Earl of *Orrery*] (1713)

**:** an apparatus showing the relative positions and motions of bodies in the solar system by balls moved by a clockwork

orrery

**or·ris** \'ȯr-əs, 'är-\ *noun* [probably alteration of Middle English *ireos*, from Medieval Latin, alteration of Latin *iris* iris] (1545)
**:** ORRISROOT

**or·ris·root** \-ˌrüt, -ˌrùt\ *noun* (1598)
**:** the fragrant rootstock of any of three European irises (*Iris florentina, I. germanica,* and *I. pallida*) used especially in perfumery

**ort** \'ȯrt\ *noun* [Middle English, from Middle Low German *orte*] (15th century)
**:** a morsel left at a meal **:** SCRAP

**orth-** *or* **ortho-** *combining form* [Middle English, from Middle French, straight, right, true, from Latin, from Greek, from *orthos*; akin to Sanskrit *ūrdhva* high, upright]
**1 :** straight **:** upright **:** vertical ⟨*ortho*grade⟩
**2 :** perpendicular ⟨*ortho*rhombic⟩
**3 :** correct **:** corrective ⟨*ortho*dontia⟩
**4 a :** hydrated or hydroxylated to the highest degree ⟨*ortho*phosphoric acid⟩ **b :** involving substitution at or characterized by or having the relationship of two neighboring positions in the benzene ring ⟨*ortho*-xylene⟩

**or·thi·con** \'ȯr-thi-ˌkän\ *noun* [International Scientific Vocabulary *orth-* + *icono*scope] (1939)
**:** a camera tube similar to but more sensitive than an iconoscope in which the charges are scanned by a low-velocity beam

**or·tho** \'ȯr-(ˌ)thō\ *adjective* (1904)
**:** ORTHOCHROMATIC

**or·tho·cen·ter** \'ȯr-thə-ˌsen-tər\ *noun* [International Scientific Vocabulary] (1869)
**:** the common intersection of the three altitudes of a triangle or their extensions or of the several altitudes of a polyhedron provided these latter exist and meet in a point

**or·tho·chro·mat·ic** \ˌȯr-thə-krō-'ma-tik\ *adjective* [International Scientific Vocabulary] (1887)
**1 :** of, relating to, or producing tone values of light and shade in a photograph that correspond to the tones in nature
**2 :** sensitive to all colors except red

**or·tho·clase** \'ȯr-thə-ˌklās, -ˌklāz\ *noun* [German *Orthoklas*, from *orth-* + Greek *klasis* breaking, from *klan* to break — more at CLAST] (1849)
**:** a mineral consisting of a monoclinic form of feldspar

**or·tho·don·tia** \ˌȯr-thə-'dän(t)-sh(ē-)ə\ *noun* [New Latin] (circa 1849)
**:** ORTHODONTICS

**or·tho·don·tics** \-'dän-tiks\ *noun plural but singular in construction* (1909)
**:** a branch of dentistry dealing with irregularities of the teeth and their correction (as by means of braces)
— **or·tho·don·tic** \-tik\ *adjective*
— **or·tho·don·ti·cal·ly** \-ti-k(ə-)lē\ *adverb*
— **or·tho·don·tist** \-'dän-tist\ *noun*

**¹or·tho·dox** \'ȯr-thə-ˌdäks\ *adjective* [Middle English *orthodoxe*, from Middle French or Late Latin; Middle French *orthodoxe*, from Late Latin *orthodoxus*, from Late Greek *orthodoxos*, from Greek *orth-* + *doxa* opinion — more at DOXOLOGY] (15th century)
**1 a :** conforming to established doctrine especially in religion **b :** CONVENTIONAL
**2** *capitalized* **:** of, relating to, or constituting any of various conservative religious or political groups: as **a :** EASTERN ORTHODOX **b :** of or relating to Orthodox Judaism
— **or·tho·dox·ly** *adverb*

**²orthodox** *noun, plural* **orthodox** *also* **or·tho·dox·es** (1587)
**1 :** one that is orthodox
**2** *capitalized* **:** a member of an Eastern Orthodox church

**Orthodox Judaism** *noun* (1904)
**:** Judaism that adheres to the Torah and Talmud as interpreted in an authoritative rabbinic law code and applies their principles and regulations to modern living — compare CONSERVATIVE JUDAISM, REFORM JUDAISM

**or·tho·doxy** \'ȯr-thə-ˌdäk-sē\ *noun, plural* **-dox·ies** (1630)
**1 :** the quality or state of being orthodox
**2 :** an orthodox belief or practice
**3** *capitalized* **a :** Eastern Orthodox Christianity **b :** ORTHODOX JUDAISM

**or·tho·epy** \'ȯr-thə-ˌwe-pē, ȯr-'thō-ə-pē\ *noun* [New Latin *orthoepia,* from Greek *orthoepeia,* from *orth-* + *epos* word — more at VOICE] (1668)
**1 :** the customary pronunciation of a language
**2 :** the study of the pronunciation of a language
— **or·tho·ep·ic** \ˌȯr-thə-'we-pik\ *adjective*
— **or·tho·ep·i·cal·ly** \-pi-k(ə-)lē\ *adverb*
— **or·tho·epist** \'ȯr-thə-ˌwe-pist, ȯr-'thō-ə-pist\ *noun*

**or·tho·gen·e·sis** \ˌȯr-thə-'je-nə-səs\ *noun* [New Latin] (1895)
**:** variation of organisms in successive generations that in some evolutionary theories takes place in some predestined direction and results in progressive evolutionary trends independent of external factors
— **or·tho·ge·net·ic** \-jə-'ne-tik\ *adjective*
— **or·tho·ge·net·i·cal·ly** \-ti-k(ə-)lē\ *adverb*

**or·thog·o·nal** \ȯr-'thä-gə-nᵊl\ *adjective* [Middle French, from Latin *orthogonius,* from Greek *orthogōnios,* from *orth-* + *gōnia* angle — more at -GON] (1612)
**1 a :** intersecting or lying at right angles **b :** having perpendicular slopes or tangents at the point of intersection ⟨*orthogonal* curves⟩
**2 :** having a sum of products or an integral that is zero or sometimes one under specified conditions: as **a** *of real-valued functions* **:** having the integral of the product of each pair of functions over a specific interval equal to zero **b** *of vectors* **:** having the scalar product equal to zero **c** *of a square matrix* **:** having the sum of products of corresponding elements in any two rows or any two columns equal to one if the rows or columns are the same and equal to zero otherwise **:** having a transpose with which the product equals the identity matrix
**3** *of a linear transformation* **:** having a matrix that is orthogonal **:** preserving length and distance
**4 :** composed of mutually orthogonal elements ⟨an *orthogonal* basis of a vector space⟩
**5 :** statistically independent
— **or·thog·o·nal·i·ty** \-ˌthä-gə-'na-lə-tē\ *noun*
— **or·thog·o·nal·ly** \-'thä-gə-nᵊl-ē\ *adverb*

**or·thog·o·nal·ize** \ȯr-'thä-gə-nᵊl-ˌīz\ *transitive verb* **-ized; -iz·ing** (1930)
**:** to make orthogonal
— **or·thog·o·nal·i·za·tion** \-ˌthä-gə-nᵊl-ə-'zā-shən\ *noun*

**or·tho·grade** \'ȯr-thə-ˌgrād\ *adjective* (1902)
**:** walking with the body upright or vertical

**or·tho·graph·ic** \ˌȯr-thə-'gra-fik\ *also* **or·tho·graph·i·cal** \-fi-kəl\ *adjective* (1706)
**1 :** of, relating to, being, or prepared by orthographic projection ⟨an *orthographic* map⟩
**2 a :** of or relating to orthography **b :** correct in spelling
— **or·tho·graph·i·cal·ly** \-fi-k(ə-)lē\ *adverb*

**orthographic projection** *noun* (1668)
**1 :** projection of a single view of an object (as a view of the front) onto a drawing surface in which the lines of projection are perpendicular to the drawing surface

**2 :** the representation of related views of an object as if they were all in the same plane and projected by orthographic projection

object *A* with top view, front view, and right view in orthographic projection

**or·thog·ra·phy** \ȯr-'thä-grə-fē\ *noun* [Middle English *or·tografie,* from Middle French, from Latin *orthographia,* from Greek, from *orth-* + *graphein* to write — more at CARVE] (15th century)
**1 a :** the art of writing words with the proper letters according to standard usage **b :** the representation of the sounds of a language by written or printed symbols
**2 :** a part of language study that deals with letters and spelling

**or·tho·mo·lec·u·lar** \ˌȯr-thə-mə-'le-kyə-lər\ *adjective* (1968)
**:** relating to, based on, using, or being a theory according to which disease and especially mental illness may be cured by restoring the optimum amounts of substances normally present in the body ⟨*orthomolecular* therapy⟩ ⟨an *orthomolecular* psychiatrist⟩

**or·tho·nor·mal** \ˌȯr-thə-'nȯr-məl\ *adjective* (1932)
**1** *of real-valued functions* **:** orthogonal with the integral of the square of each function over a specified interval equal to one
**2 :** being or composed of orthogonal elements of unit length ⟨*orthonormal* basis of a vector space⟩

**or·tho·pe·dic** *also* **or·tho·pae·dic** \ˌȯr-thə-'pē-dik\ *adjective* [French *orthopédique,* from *orthopédie* orthopedics, from *orth-* + Greek *paid-, pais* child — more at FEW] (1840)
**1 :** of, relating to, or employed in orthopedics
**2 :** marked by deformities or crippling
— **or·tho·pe·di·cal·ly** \-'pē-di-k(ə-)lē\ *adverb*

**or·tho·pe·dics** *also* **or·tho·pae·dics** \-'pē-diks\ *noun plural but singular or plural in construction* (circa 1853)
**:** a branch of medicine concerned with the correction or prevention of skeletal deformities
— **or·tho·pe·dist** \-'pē-dist\ *noun*

**or·tho·phos·phate** \ˌȯr-thə-'fäs-ˌfāt\ *noun* (1859)
**:** a salt or ester of orthophosphoric acid

**or·tho·phos·pho·ric acid** \ˌȯr-thə-ˌfäs-'fȯr-ik-, -'fär-; -'fäs-f(ə-)rik-\ *noun* [International Scientific Vocabulary] (1885)
**:** PHOSPHORIC ACID 1

**or·tho·psy·chi·a·try** \-sə-'kī-ə-trē, -(ˌ)sī-\ *noun* (circa 1927)
**:** prophylactic psychiatry concerned especially with incipient mental and behavioral disorders in youth
— **or·tho·psy·chi·at·ric** \-ˌsī-kē-'a-trik\ *adjective*
— **or·tho·psy·chi·a·trist** \-sə-'kī-ə-trist, -(ˌ)sī-\ *noun*

**or·thop·tera** \ȯr-'thäp-tə-rə\ *noun plural* [New Latin, order name, from *orth-* + Greek *pteron* wing — more at FEATHER] (1828)
**:** insects that are orthopterans

**or·thop·ter·an** \ȯr-'thäp-tə-rən\ *noun* [New Latin *Orthoptera*] (circa 1842)
**:** any of an order (Orthoptera) of insects (as crickets, grasshoppers, and sometimes mantises) that are characterized by biting mouthparts, two pairs of wings or none, and an incomplete metamorphosis
— **orthopteran** *adjective*
— **or·thop·ter·ist** \-rist\ *noun*
— **or·thop·ter·oid** \-ˌrȯid\ *noun or adjective*

**or·tho·rhom·bic** \ˌȯr-thə-'räm-bik\ *adjective* [International Scientific Vocabulary] (circa 1859)
**:** of, relating to, or constituting a system of crystallization characterized by three unequal axes at right angles to each other

**or·tho·scop·ic** \-'skä-pik\ *adjective* [International Scientific Vocabulary *orth-* + *-scopic* (as in *microscopic*)] (1853)
**:** giving an image in correct and normal proportions

**or·tho·sis** \ȯr-'thō-səs\ *noun, plural* **or·tho·ses** \-ˌsēz\ [New Latin, from Greek *orthōsis* straightening, from *orthoun* to straighten, from *orthos*] (1958)
**:** ORTHOTIC

**or·tho·stat·ic** \ˌȯr-thə-'sta-tik\ *adjective* (1902)
**:** of, relating to, or caused by erect posture ⟨*orthostatic* hypotension⟩

**or·thot·ic** \ȯr-'thä-tik\ *noun* [New Latin *orthosis*] (1955)
**:** a support or brace for weak or ineffective joints or muscles

**or·thot·ics** \-tiks\ *noun plural but singular in construction* (1957)
**:** a branch of mechanical and medical science that deals with the support and bracing of weak or ineffective joints or muscles
— **or·thot·ic** \-tik\ *adjective*
— **or·tho·tist** \ȯr-'thä-tist, 'ȯr-thə-tist\ *noun*

**or·thot·ro·pous** \ȯr-'thä-trə-pəs\ *adjective* [International Scientific Vocabulary] (1830)
**:** having the ovule straight so that the chalaza, hilum, and micropyle are in the same axial line

**or·to·lan** \'ȯr-tᵊl-ən\ *noun* [French or Italian; French, from Italian *ortolano,* literally, gardener, from Latin *hortulanus,* from *hortulus,* diminutive of *hortus* garden — more at YARD] (1656)
**:** an Old World bunting (*Emberiza hortulana*) having a greenish gray head and breast, streaky brown back and wings, and a yellow throat

**Or·vie·to** \ȯr-'vyā-(ˌ)tō\ *noun* [*Orvieto,* city in central Italy] (1846)
**:** a usually dry Italian white wine

**¹-ory** *noun suffix* [Middle English *-orie,* from Latin *-orium,* from neuter of *-orius,* adjective suffix]
**1 :** place of or for ⟨observat*ory*⟩
**2 :** something that serves for ⟨cremat*ory*⟩

**²-ory** *adjective suffix* [Middle English *-orie,* from Middle French & Latin; Middle French, from Latin *-orius*]
**1 :** of, relating to, or characterized by ⟨gustat*ory*⟩
**2 :** serving for, producing, or maintaining ⟨justificat*ory*⟩

**oryx** \'ȯr-iks, 'ȯr-, 'är-\ *noun, plural* **oryx** *or* **oryx·es** [New Latin, from Latin, a gazelle, from Greek, pickax, antelope, kind of whale, from *oryssein* to dig; akin to Latin *runcare* to grub up, weed, Sanskrit *luñcati* he plucks] (1535)
**:** any of a small genus (Oryx) of large heavily-built African and Arabian antelopes that have a light-colored coat with dark conspicuous markings especially on the face

oryx

**or·zo** \'ȯrd-(ˌ)zō\ *noun* [Italian, literally, barley, from Latin *hordeum* — more at ORGEAT] (circa 1929)
**:** rice-shaped pasta

**¹os** \'äs\ *noun, plural* **os·sa** \'ä-sə\ [Latin *oss-, os* — more at OSSEOUS] (15th century)
**:** BONE

**²os** \'ōs\ *noun, plural* **ora** \'ōr-ə, 'òr-ə\ [Latin *or-, os* — more at ORAL] (1737)
**:** MOUTH, ORIFICE

**Osage** \ō-'sāj, 'ō-\ *noun, plural* **Osag·es** or **Osage** (1698)
**1 :** a member of an American Indian people originally of Missouri
**2 :** the Siouan language of the Osage people

**Osage orange** *noun* (1817)
**:** an ornamental usually thorny American tree (*Maclura pomifera*) of the mulberry family with shiny ovate leaves and hard bright orange wood; *also* **:** its yellowish globose fruit

**Os·can** \'äs-kən\ *noun* [Latin *Oscus*] (1753)
**1 :** a member of a people of ancient Italy occupying Campania
**2 :** the language of the Oscan people — see INDO-EUROPEAN LANGUAGES table

**¹Os·car** \'äs-kər\ *trademark*
— used especially for any of a number of golden statuettes awarded annually by a professional organization for notable achievement in motion pictures

**²Oscar** (1952)
— a communications code word for the letter *o*

**os·cil·late** \'ä-sə-ˌlāt\ *intransitive verb* **-lat·ed; -lat·ing** [Latin *oscillatus*, past participle of *oscillare* to swing, from *oscillum* swing] (1726)
**1 a :** to swing backward and forward like a pendulum **b :** to move or travel back and forth between two points
**2 :** to vary between opposing beliefs, feelings, or theories
**3 :** to vary above and below a mean value
**synonym** see SWING
— **os·cil·la·to·ry** \'ä-sə-lə-ˌtōr-ē, -ˌtòr-\ *adjective*

**os·cil·la·tion** \ˌä-sə-'lā-shən\ *noun* (1658)
**1 :** the action or state of oscillating
**2 :** VARIATION, FLUCTUATION
**3 :** a flow of electricity changing periodically from a maximum to a minimum; *especially* **:** a flow periodically changing direction
**4 :** a single swing (as of an oscillating body) from one extreme limit to the other
— **os·cil·la·tion·al** \-shnəl, -shə-nᵊl\ *adjective*

**os·cil·la·tor** \'ä-sə-ˌlā-tər\ *noun* (1835)
**1 :** one that oscillates
**2 :** a device for producing alternating current; *especially* **:** a radio-frequency or audio-frequency generator

**oscillo-** *combining form* [International Scientific Vocabulary, from Latin *oscillare*]
**:** wave **:** oscillation ⟨*oscillo*scope⟩

**os·cil·lo·gram** \ä-'si-lə-ˌgram, ə-\ *noun* [International Scientific Vocabulary] (1903)
**:** a record made by an oscillograph or oscilloscope

**os·cil·lo·graph** \-ˌgraf\ *noun* [International Scientific Vocabulary] (1893)
**:** an instrument for recording alternating current wave forms or other electrical oscillations
— **os·cil·lo·graph·ic** \ä-ˌsi-lə-'gra-fik, ˌä-sə-lə-\ *adjective*
— **os·cil·lo·graph·i·cal·ly** \-fi-k(ə-)lē\ *adverb*
— **os·cil·log·ra·phy** \ˌä-sə-'lä-grə-fē\ *noun*

**os·cil·lo·scope** \ä-'si-lə-ˌskōp, ə-\ *noun* [International Scientific Vocabulary] (1906)
**:** an instrument in which the variations in a fluctuating electrical quantity appear temporarily as a visible wave form on the fluorescent screen of a cathode-ray tube
— **os·cil·lo·scop·ic** \ä-ˌsi-lə-'skä-pik, ˌä-sə-lə-\ *adjective*

**os·cine** \'ä-ˌsīn\ *adjective* [New Latin *Oscines*, suborder name, from Latin, plural of *oscin-, oscen* songbird, bird giving omens by its cry, from *obs-, ob-* in front of, in the way + *canere* to sing — more at OB-, CHANT] (1883)

**:** of or relating to a large suborder (Oscines) of passerine birds (as larks, shrikes, finches, orioles, and crows) characterized by a vocal apparatus highly specialized for singing
— **oscine** *noun*

**Os·co-Um·bri·an** \ˌäs-kō-'əm-brē-ən\ *noun* [Latin *Oscus* + English *Umbrian*] (1894)
**:** a subdivision of the Italic branch of the Indo-European language family containing Oscan and Umbrian

**os·cu·late** \'äs-kyə-ˌlāt\ *transitive verb* **-lat·ed; -lat·ing** [Latin *osculatus*, past participle of *osculari*, from *osculum* kiss, from diminutive of *os* mouth — more at ORAL] (circa 1656)
**:** KISS

**os·cu·la·tion** \ˌäs-kyə-'lā-shən\ *noun* (circa 1658)
**:** the act of kissing; *also* **:** KISS
— **os·cu·la·to·ry** \'äs-kyə-lə-ˌtōr-ē, -ˌtòr-\ *adjective*

**os·cu·lum** \'äs-kyə-ləm\ *noun* [New Latin, from Latin, diminutive of *os* mouth] (1887)
**:** an excurrent opening of a sponge

**¹-ose** *adjective suffix* [Middle English, from Latin *-osus*]
**:** full of **:** having **:** possessing the qualities of ⟨cym*ose*⟩

**²-ose** *noun suffix* [French, from *glucose*]
**1 :** carbohydrate ⟨amyl*ose*⟩; *especially* **:** sugar ⟨pent*ose*⟩
**2 :** primary hydrolysis product ⟨prote*ose*⟩

**Osee** \'ō-ˌzē, ō-'zä-ə\ *noun* [Late Latin, from Hebrew *Hōshēa'*]
**:** HOSEA

**osier** \'ō-zhər\ *noun* [Middle English, from Middle French, from Medieval Latin *auseria* osier bed] (14th century)
**1 :** any of various willows (especially *Salix viminalis*) whose pliable twigs are used for furniture and basketry
**2 :** a willow rod used in basketry
**3 :** any of several American dogwoods

**Osi·ris** \ō-'sī-rəs\ *noun* [Latin, from Greek, from Egyptian *Ws'r*]
**:** the Egyptian god of the underworld and husband and brother of Isis

**-osis** *noun suffix, plural* **-oses** or **-osises** [Middle English, from Latin, from Greek *-ōsis*, from *-ō-* (stem of causative verbs in *-oun*) + *-sis*]
**1 a :** action **:** process **:** condition ⟨hypn*osis*⟩ **b :** abnormal or diseased condition ⟨leuk*osis*⟩
**2 :** increase **:** formation ⟨leukocyt*osis*⟩

**Os·man·li** \äz-'man-lē\ *noun* [Turkish *osmanlı*, from *Osman*, founder of the Ottoman Empire] (1813)
**1 :** OTTOMAN 1
**2 :** TURKISH

**os·me·te·ri·um** \ˌäz-mə-'tir-ē-əm\ *noun, plural* **-ria** \-ē-ə\ [New Latin, irregular from Greek *osmē* odor] (1816)
**:** a protrusible forked glandular process that emits a disagreeable odor, is borne on the first thoracic segment of the larvae of many swallowtails and related butterflies, and is a defensive organ

**osmic acid** *noun* (1842)
**:** OSMIUM TETROXIDE

**os·mi·rid·i·um** \ˌäz-mə-'ri-dē-əm\ *noun* [Greek *osmē* + New Latin *iridium*] (1880)
**:** IRIDOSMINE

**os·mi·um** \'äz-mē-əm\ *noun* [New Latin, from Greek *osmē* odor] (1804)
**:** a hard brittle blue-gray or blue-black polyvalent metallic element of the platinum group with a high melting point that is the heaviest metal known and is used especially as a catalyst and in hard alloys — see ELEMENT table

**osmium tetroxide** *noun* (1876)
**:** a crystalline compound $OsO_4$ that is an oxide of osmium, has a poisonous irritating vapor, and is used as a catalyst, oxidizing agent, and biological fixative and stain

**os·mol** or **os·mole** \'äz-ˌmōl, 'äs-\ *noun* [blend of *osmosis* and *mol* (⁵mole)] (1942)

**:** a standard unit of osmotic pressure based on a one molal concentration of an ion in a solution

**os·mo·lal·i·ty** \ˌäz-mō-'la-lə-tē, ˌäs-\ *noun, plural* **-ties** [*osmol* + ¹*-al* + *-ity*] (circa 1944)
**:** the concentration of an osmotic solution especially when measured in osmols or milliosmols per 1000 grams of solvent
— **os·mo·lal** \äz-'mō-ləl, äs-\ *adjective*

**os·mo·lar·i·ty** \ˌäz-mō-'lar-ə-tē, ˌäs-\ *noun, plural* **-ties** [*osmol* + *-ar* + *-ity*] (1948)
**:** the concentration of an osmotic solution especially when measured in osmols or milliosmols per liter of solution
— **os·mo·lar** \äz-'mō-lər, äs-\ *adjective*

**os·mom·e·ter** \äz-'mä-mə-tər, äs-\ *noun* [*osmosis* + *-meter*] (1854)
**:** an apparatus for measuring osmotic pressure
— **os·mo·met·ric** \ˌäz-mə-'me-trik, ˌäs-\ *adjective*
— **os·mom·e·try** \äz-'mä-mə-trē\ *noun*

**os·mo·reg·u·la·tion** \ˌäz-mō-ˌre-gyə-'lā-shən, 'äs-\ *noun* [*osmosis* + *regulation*] (1927)
**:** regulation of osmotic pressure especially in the body of a living organism

**os·mo·reg·u·la·to·ry** \-'re-gyə-lə-ˌtōr-ē, -ˌtòr-\ *adjective* (circa 1911)
**:** of, relating to, or concerned with the maintenance of constant osmotic pressure

**os·mo·sis** \äz-'mō-səs, äs-\ *noun* [New Latin, short for *endosmosis*] (1867)
**1 :** movement of a solvent through a semipermeable membrane (as of a living cell) into a solution of higher solute concentration that tends to equalize the concentrations of solute on the two sides of the membrane
**2 :** a process of absorption or diffusion suggestive of the flow of osmotic action; *especially* **:** a usually effortless often unconscious assimilation ⟨learned a number of languages by *osmosis* —Roger Kimball⟩

**os·mot·ic** \-'mä-tik\ *adjective* (1854)
**:** of, relating to, or having the properties of osmosis
— **os·mot·i·cal·ly** \-ti-k(ə-)lē\ *adverb*

**osmotic pressure** *noun* (1888)
**:** the pressure produced by or associated with osmosis and dependent on molar concentration and absolute temperature: as **a :** the maximum pressure that develops in a solution separated from a solvent by a membrane permeable only to the solvent **b :** the pressure that must be applied to a solution to just prevent osmosis

**osmotic shock** *noun* (1950)
**:** a rapid change in the osmotic pressure (as by transfer to a medium of different concentration) affecting a living system

**os·mun·da** \äz-'mən-də\ *noun* [New Latin, from Medieval Latin, from Old French *osmonde*] (1789)
**:** any of a genus (*Osmunda*) of rather large ferns (as the cinnamon fern) with pinnate or bipinnate fronds and fibrous creeping rhizomes

**os·prey** \'äs-prē, -ˌprā\ *noun, plural* **ospreys** [Middle English *ospray*, from (assumed) Middle French *osfraie*, from Latin *ossifraga*, a bird of prey] (15th century)
**1 :** a large fish-eating hawk (*Pandion haliaetus*) that is a dark brown color or above and mostly pure white below
**2 :** a feather trimming used for millinery

osprey 1

**ossa** *plural of* OS

**os·se·in** \'ä-sē-ən\ *noun* [International Scientific Vocabulary, from Latin *oss-, os*] (1857)
**:** the collagen of bones

**os·se·ous** \'ä-sē-əs\ *adjective* [Latin *osseus,* from *oss-, os* bone; akin to Greek *osteon* bone, Sanskrit *asthi*] (1682)
**:** BONY 1

**Os·sete** \'ä-ˌsēt\ *also* **Os·set** \'ä-sət, -ˌset\ *noun* [Russian *osetin,* from *Osetiya* Ossetia, from Georgian *Oseti,* from *osi* Ossete] (1814)
**:** a member of a people of the central Caucasus
— **Os·se·tian** \ä-'sē-shən\ *adjective or noun*

**Os·set·ic** \ä-'se-tik\ *noun* (circa 1890)
**:** the Iranian language of the Ossetes

**Os·si·an·ic** \ˌä-sē-'a-nik, -shē-\ *adjective* (1808)
**:** of, relating to, or resembling the legendary Irish bard Ossian, the poems ascribed to him, or the rhythmic prose style used by James Macpherson in the poems he claimed to have translated from Ossian

**os·si·cle** \'ä-si-kəl\ *noun* [Latin *ossiculum,* diminutive of *oss-, os*] (1578)
**:** a small bone or bony structure (as the malleus, incus, or stapes)
— **os·sic·u·lar** \ä-'si-kyə-lər\ *adjective*

**os·si·fi·ca·tion** \ˌä-sə-fə-'kā-shən\ *noun* (1697)
**1 a :** the natural process of bone formation **b :** the hardening (as of muscular tissue) into a bony substance
**2 :** a mass or particle of ossified tissue
**3 :** a tendency toward or state of being molded into a rigid, conventional, sterile, or unimaginative condition

**os·si·frage** \'ä-sə-frij, -ˌfräj\ *noun* [Latin *ossifraga,* a bird of prey, from feminine of *ossifragus* bone-breaking, from *oss-, os* + *frangere* to break — more at BREAK] (1601)
**:** LAMMERGEIER

**os·si·fy** \'ä-sə-ˌfī\ *verb* **-fied; -fy·ing** [Latin *oss-, os* + English *-ify*] (1713)
*intransitive verb*
**1 :** to change into bone
**2 :** to become hardened or conventional and opposed to change
*transitive verb*
**1 :** to change (as cartilage) into bone
**2 :** to make rigidly conventional and opposed to change

**os·so bu·co** *also* **os·so buc·co** \ˌō-sō-'bü-(ˌ)kō, ˌó-sō-\ *noun* [Italian *ossobuco* veal shank, literally, pierced bone] (1935)
**:** braised veal shanks

**os·su·ary** \'ä-shə-ˌwer-ē, -syə-, -sə-\ *noun, plural* **-ar·ies** [Late Latin *ossuarium,* from Latin, neuter of *ossuarius* of bones, from Old Latin *ossua,* plural of *oss-, os*] (1658)
**:** a depository for the bones of the dead

**oste-** *or* **osteo-** *combining form* [New Latin, from Greek, from *osteon* — more at OSSEOUS]
**:** bone ⟨*osteal*⟩ ⟨*osteo*myelitis⟩

**os·te·al** \'äs-tē-əl\ *adjective* [International Scientific Vocabulary] (1877)
**:** of, relating to, or resembling bone; *also* **:** affecting or involving bone or the skeleton

**os·te·i·tis** \ˌäs-tē-'ī-təs\ *noun* [New Latin] (circa 1847)
**:** inflammation of bone

**os·ten·si·ble** \ä-'sten(t)-sə-bəl, ə-\ *adjective* [French, from Latin *ostensus,* past participle of *ostendere* to show, from *obs-, ob-* in the way + *tendere* to stretch — more at OB-, THIN] (circa 1771)
**1 :** intended for display **:** open to view
**2 :** being such in appearance **:** plausible rather than demonstrably true or real ⟨the *ostensible* purpose for the trip⟩
*synonym* see APPARENT

**os·ten·si·bly** \-blē\ *adverb* (1765)
**1 :** in an ostensible manner
**2 :** to all outward appearances

**os·ten·sive** \ä-'sten(t)-siv\ *adjective* (1782)
**1 :** OSTENSIBLE 2

**2 :** of, relating to, or constituting definition by exemplifying the thing or quality being defined
— **os·ten·sive·ly** *adverb*

**os·ten·so·ri·um** \ˌäs-tən-'sōr-ē-əm, -ˌten-, -'sór-\ *noun, plural* **-ria** \-ē-ə\ [Medieval Latin, from Latin *ostendere*] (circa 1772)
**:** MONSTRANCE

**os·ten·ta·tion** \ˌäs-tən-'tā-shən\ *noun* [Middle English *ostentacion,* from Middle French *ostentation,* from Latin *ostentation-, ostentatio,* from *ostentare* to display, frequentative of *ostendere*] (15th century)
**1 :** excessive display **:** PRETENTIOUSNESS
**2** *archaic* **:** an act of displaying

**os·ten·ta·tious** \-shəs\ *adjective* (1673)
**:** marked by or fond of conspicuous or vainglorious and sometimes pretentious display
*synonym* see SHOWY
— **os·ten·ta·tious·ly** *adverb*
— **os·ten·ta·tious·ness** *noun*

**os·te·o·ar·thri·tis** \ˌäs-tē-ō-är-'thrī-təs\ *noun* [New Latin] (1878)
**:** arthritis marked by degeneration of the cartilage and bone of joints
— **os·te·o·ar·thrit·ic** \-'thri-tik\ *adjective*

**os·te·o·blast** \'äs-tē-ə-ˌblast\ *noun* [International Scientific Vocabulary] (1875)
**:** a bone-forming cell
— **os·te·o·blas·tic** \ˌäs-tē-ə-'blas-tik\ *adjective*

**os·te·o·clast** \'äs-tē-ə-ˌklast\ *noun* [International Scientific Vocabulary *oste-* + Greek *klastos* broken — more at CLAST] (1872)
**:** any of the large multinucleate cells closely associated with areas of bone resorption
— **os·te·o·clas·tic** \ˌäs-tē-ə-'klas-tik\ *adjective*

**os·te·o·cyte** \'äs-tē-ə-ˌsīt\ *noun* (1942)
**:** a cell that is characteristic of adult bone and is isolated in a lacuna of the bone substance

**os·te·o·gen·e·sis** \ˌäs-tē-ə-'je-nə-səs\ *noun* [New Latin] (1830)
**:** development and formation of bone

**osteogenesis im·per·fec·ta** \-ˌim-(ˌ)pər-'fek-tə\ *noun* [New Latin, imperfect osteogenesis] (circa 1901)
**:** a hereditary disease marked especially by extreme brittleness of the long bones

**os·te·o·gen·ic** \ˌäs-tē-ə-'je-nik\ *adjective* (1867)
**1 :** producing bone
**2 :** originating in bone

**osteogenic sarcoma** *noun* (circa 1923)
**:** OSTEOSARCOMA

**¹os·te·oid** \'äs-tē-ˌóid\ *adjective* [International Scientific Vocabulary] (1840)
**:** resembling bone

**²osteoid** *noun* (1934)
**:** uncalcified bone matrix

**os·te·ol·o·gy** \ˌäs-tē-'ä-lə-jē\ *noun* [New Latin *osteologia,* from Greek, description of bones, from *oste-* + *-logia* -logy] (1670)
**1 :** a branch of anatomy dealing with the bones
**2 :** the bony structure of an organism
— **os·te·o·log·i·cal** \-tē-ə-'lä-ji-kəl\ *adjective*
— **os·te·ol·o·gist** \-tē-'ä-lə-jist\ *noun*

**os·te·o·ma** \ˌäs-tē-'ō-mə\ *noun, plural* **-mas** *or* **-ma·ta** \-mə-tə\ [New Latin] (circa 1849)
**:** a benign tumor composed of bone tissue

**os·te·o·ma·la·cia** \ˌäs-tē-ō-mə-'lā-sh(ē-)ə\ *noun* [New Latin, from *oste-* + Greek *malakia* softness, from *malakos* soft — more at MOLLIFY] (circa 1834)
**:** a disease of adults that is characterized by softening of the bones and is analogous to rickets in the immature

**os·te·o·my·e·li·tis** \-ˌmī-ə-'lī-təs\ *noun* [New Latin] (1854)
**:** an infectious inflammatory disease of bone often of bacterial origin that is marked by local death and separation of tissue

**os·te·o·path** \'äs-tē-ə-ˌpath\ *noun* (1897)
**:** a practitioner of osteopathy

**os·te·op·a·thy** \ˌäs-tē-'ä-pə-thē\ *noun* [New Latin *osteopathia,* from *oste-* + Latin *-pathia* -pathy] (1899)
**:** a system of medical practice based on a theory that diseases are due chiefly to loss of structural integrity which can be restored by manipulation of the parts supplemented by therapeutic measures (as use of medicine or surgery)
— **os·te·o·path·ic** \ˌäs-tē-ə-'pa-thik\ *adjective*
— **os·te·o·path·i·cal·ly** \-thi-k(ə-)lē\ *adverb*

**os·te·o·plas·ty** \'äs-tē-ə-ˌplas-tē\ *noun* (circa 1860)
**:** plastic surgery on bone; *especially* **:** replacement of lost bone tissue or reconstruction of defective bony parts
— **os·te·o·plas·tic** \ˌäs-tē-ə-'plas-tik\ *adjective*

**os·te·o·po·ro·sis** \ˌäs-tē-ō-pə-'rō-səs\ *noun, plural* **-ro·ses** \-ˌsēz\ [New Latin, from *oste-* + *porosis* rarefaction, from *porus* pore + *-osis*] (1846)
**:** a condition that affects especially older women and is characterized by decrease in bone mass with decreased density and enlargement of bone spaces producing porosity and fragility
— **os·te·o·po·rot·ic** \-'rä-tik\ *adjective*

**os·te·o·sar·co·ma** \-sär-'kō-mə\ *noun, plural* **-mas** *or* **-ma·ta** \-mə-tə\ [New Latin] (circa 1826)
**:** a sarcoma derived from bone or containing bone tissue

**osti·na·to** \ˌäs-tə-'nä-(ˌ)tō, ˌós-\ *noun, plural* **-tos** *also* **-ti** \-tē\ [Italian, obstinate, from Latin *obstinatus*] (circa 1876)
**:** a musical figure repeated persistently at the same pitch throughout a composition — compare IMITATION, SEQUENCE

**os·ti·ole** \'äs-tē-ˌōl\ *noun* [New Latin *ostiolum,* from Latin, diminutive of *ostium*] (circa 1857)
**:** a small bodily aperture, orifice, or pore

**os·ti·um** \'äs-tē-əm\ *noun, plural* **os·tia** \-tē-ə\ [New Latin, from Latin, door, mouth of a river; akin to Latin *os* mouth — more at ORAL] (1828)
**:** a mouthlike opening in a bodily organ

**os·tler** *variant of* HOSTLER

**ost·mark** \'ōst-ˌmärk, 'óst-\ *noun* [German, literally, East mark] (1948)
**:** the former East German mark

**os·to·my** \'äs-tə-mē\ *noun, plural* **-mies** [*colostomy*] (1957)
**:** an operation (as a colostomy) to create an artificial passage for bodily elimination

**-ostosis** *noun combining form, plural* **-ostoses** *or* **-ostosises** [New Latin, from Greek *-ostōsis,* from *osteon* bone — more at OSSEOUS]
**:** ossification of a (specified) part or to a (specified) degree ⟨hyper*ostosis*⟩

**os·tra·cise** *British variant of* OSTRACIZE

**os·tra·cism** \'äs-trə-ˌsi-zəm\ *noun* (1588)
**1 :** a method of temporary banishment by popular vote without trial or special accusation practiced in ancient Greece
**2 :** exclusion by general consent from common privileges or social acceptance

**os·tra·cize** \-ˌsīz\ *transitive verb* **-cized; -ciz·ing** [Greek *ostrakizein* to banish by voting with potsherds, from *ostrakon* shell, potsherd — more at OYSTER] (1649)
**1 :** to exile by ostracism

\ə\ abut \ᵊ\ kitten \ər\ further \a\ ash \ā\ ace
\ä\ mop, mar \aú\ out \ch\ chin \e\ bet \ē\ easy
\g\ go \i\ hit \ī\ ice \j\ job \ŋ\ sing \ō\ go
\ó\ law \ói\ boy \th\ thin \ṯẖ\ the \ü\ loot \ú\ foot
\y\ yet \zh\ vision *see also* Guide to Pronunciation

**2 :** to exclude from a group by common consent ◆

**os·tra·cod** \'äs-trə-ˌkäd\ *also* **os·tra·code** \-ˌkōd\ *noun* [ultimately from Greek *ostrakon*] (1865)
**:** any of a subclass (Ostracoda) of very small active mostly freshwater crustaceans that have the body enclosed in a bivalve carapace, the body segmentation obscured, the abdomen rudimentary, and only seven pairs of appendages

**os·tra·co·derm** \'äs-trə-kō-ˌdərm, äs-'tra-kə-\ *noun* [ultimately from Greek *ostrakon* + *derma* skin — more at DERM-] (1891)
**:** any of the early fossil jawless fishes of the Lower Paleozoic usually having a bony covering of plates or scales

**os·tra·con** \'äs-trə-ˌkän\ *noun, plural* **-tra·ca** \-trə-kə\ [Greek *ostrakon* potsherd, shell — more at OYSTER] (1883)
**:** a fragment (as of pottery) containing an inscription — usually used in plural

**os·trich** \'äs-trich, 'ȯs- *also* -trij\ *noun* [Middle English, from Old French *ostrusce*, from (assumed) Vulgar Latin *avis struthio*, from Latin *avis* bird + Late Latin *struthio* ostrich — more at STRUTHIOUS] (13th century)
**1 a :** a swift-footed 2-toed flightless ratite bird (*Struthio camelus*) of Africa that is the largest of existing birds and often weighs 300 pounds (140 kilograms) **b :** RHEA **c :** leather made from ostrich skin
**2** [from the belief that the ostrich when pursued hides its head in the sand and believes itself to be unseen] **:** one who attempts to avoid danger or difficulty by refusing to face it
— **os·trich·like** \-ˌlīk\ *adjective*

**Os·tro·goth** \'äs-trə-ˌgäth\ *noun* [Middle English, from Late Latin *Ostrogothi*, plural] (14th century)
**:** a member of the eastern division of the Goths
— **Os·tro·goth·ic** \ˌäs-trə-'gä-thik\ *adjective*

**Os·we·go tea** \ä-'swē-gō-\ *noun* [*Oswego* River, N. Y.] (1752)
**:** a North American mint (*Monarda didyma*) with showy scarlet irregular flowers

**ot-** *or* **oto-** *combining form* [Greek *ōt-, ōto-*, from *ōt-, ous* — more at EAR]
**:** ear ⟨*otitis*⟩ **:** ear and ⟨*oto*laryngology⟩

**Othel·lo** \ə-'the-(ˌ)lō, ō-\ *noun*
**:** a Moor in the military service of Venice, husband of Desdemona, and protagonist of Shakespeare's tragedy *Othello*

**¹oth·er** \'ə-thər\ *adjective* [Middle English, from Old English *ōther*; akin to Old High German *andar* other, Sanskrit *antara*] (before 12th century)
**1 a :** being the one (as of two or more) remaining or not included ⟨held on with one hand and waved with the *other* one⟩ **b :** being the one or ones distinct from that or those first mentioned or implied ⟨taller than the *other* boys⟩ **c :** SECOND ⟨every *other* day⟩
**2 :** not the same **:** DIFFERENT ⟨any *other* color would have been better⟩ ⟨something *other* than it seems to be⟩
**3 :** ADDITIONAL ⟨sold in the U.S. and 14 *other* countries⟩
**4 a :** recently past ⟨the *other* evening⟩ **b :** FORMER ⟨in *other* times⟩

**²other** *noun* (before 12th century)
**1 a :** one that remains of two or more **b :** a thing opposite to or excluded by something else ⟨went from one side to the *other*⟩
**2 :** a different or additional one ⟨the *others* came later⟩

**³other** *pronoun, sometimes plural in construction* (before 12th century)
**1** *obsolete* **a :** one of two that remains **b :** each preceding one
**2 :** a different or additional one ⟨something or *other*⟩

**⁴other** *adverb* (13th century)
**:** OTHERWISE — used with *than* ⟨was unable to see them *other* than by going to their home⟩

**oth·er–di·rect·ed** \ˌə-thər-də-'rek-təd, -dī-\ *adjective* (1950)
**:** directed in thought and action primarily by external norms rather than by one's own scale of values
— **oth·er–di·rect·ed·ness** *noun*

**oth·er·guess** \'ə-thər-ˌges\ *adjective* [alteration of English dialect *othergates*] (1632)
*archaic* **:** DIFFERENT

**oth·er·ness** \'ə-thər-nəs\ *noun* (1587)
**1 :** the quality or state of being other or different
**2 :** something that is other or different

**other than** *preposition* (1679)
**:** with the exception of **:** EXCEPT FOR, BESIDES ⟨*other than* that, nothing happened⟩

**oth·er·where** \-ˌhwer, -ˌhwar, -ˌwer, -ˌwar\ *adverb* (14th century)
**:** ELSEWHERE

**oth·er·while** \-ˌhwīl, -ˌwīl\ *also* **oth·er·whiles** \-ˌhwīlz, -ˌwīlz\ *adverb* (13th century)
*chiefly dialect* **:** at another time

**¹oth·er·wise** \-ˌwīz\ *pronoun* [Middle English, from Old English (*on*) *ōthre wīsan* in another manner] (before 12th century)
**:** something or anything else **:** something to the contrary ⟨do very little to enforce competition—and have never intended *otherwise* —Milton Viorst⟩

**²otherwise** *adverb* (13th century)
**1 :** in a different way or manner ⟨glossed over or *otherwise* handled —*Playboy*⟩
**2 :** in different circumstances ⟨might *otherwise* have left⟩
**3 :** in other respects ⟨an *otherwise* flimsy farce —*Current Biography*⟩
**4 :** if not ⟨do what I tell you, *otherwise* you'll be sorry⟩
**5 :** NOT — paired with an adjective, adverb, noun, or verb to indicate its contrary or to suggest an indefinite alternative ⟨people whose deeds, admirable or *otherwise* —John Fischer⟩ ⟨almost thirty thousand women, Irish and *otherwise* —J. M. Burns⟩ ⟨his opinion as to the success or *otherwise* of it —*Australian Dictionary of Biography*⟩

**³otherwise** *adjective* (14th century)
**:** DIFFERENT ⟨if conditions were *otherwise*⟩

**other woman** *noun* (1855)
**:** a woman with whom a married man has an affair — usually used with *the*

**oth·er·world** \'ə-thər-ˌwərld\ *noun* (13th century)
**:** a world beyond death or beyond present reality

**oth·er·world·ly** \ˌə-thər-'wərl(d)-lē\ *adjective* (1879)
**1 a :** of, relating to, or resembling that of a world other than the actual world **b :** devoted to preparing for a world to come
**2 :** devoted to intellectual or imaginative pursuits
— **oth·er·world·li·ness** *noun*

**¹-otic** *adjective suffix* [Greek *-ōtikos*, from *-ōtos*, ending of verbals, from *-o-* (stem of causative verbs in *-oun*) + *-tos*, suffix forming verbals — more at -ED]
**:** of, relating to, or characterized by a (specified) action, process, or condition ⟨symbi*otic*⟩

**²-otic** *adjective combining form* [Greek *ōtikos* of the ear, from *ōt-, ous* ear]
**:** having (such) a relationship to the ear ⟨di*chotic*⟩

**oti·ose** \'ō-shē-ˌōs, 'ō-tē-\ *adjective* [Latin *otiosus*, from *otium* leisure] (1794)
**1 :** producing no useful result **:** FUTILE
**2 :** being at leisure **:** IDLE
**3 :** lacking use or effect **:** FUNCTIONLESS
**synonym** see VAIN
— **oti·ose·ly** *adverb*
— **oti·ose·ness** *noun*
— **oti·os·i·ty** \ˌō-shē-'ä-sə-tē, ˌō-tē-\ *noun*

**oti·tis** \ō-'tī-təs\ *noun* [New Latin] (circa 1799)
**:** inflammation of the ear

**otitis me·dia** \-'mē-dē-ə\ *noun* [New Latin] (1874)

**:** inflammation of the middle ear marked by pain, fever, dizziness, and abnormalities of hearing

**oto·cyst** \'ō-tə-ˌsist\ *noun* [International Scientific Vocabulary; from its probable auditory function] (1877)
**:** a fluid-containing organ of many invertebrates that contains an otolith **:** STATOCYST
— **oto·cys·tic** \ˌō-tə-'sis-tik\ *adjective*

**oto·lar·yn·gol·o·gy** \ˌō-tō-ˌlar-ən-'gä-lə-jē\ *noun* (1897)
**:** a medical specialty concerned especially with the ear, nose, and throat
— **oto·lar·yn·go·log·i·cal** \-gə-'lä-ji-kəl\ *adjective*
— **oto·lar·yn·gol·o·gist** \-'gä-lə-jist\ *noun*

**oto·lith** \'ō-tᵊl-ˌith\ *noun* [French *otolithe*, from *ot-* + *-lithe* -lith] (circa 1836)
**:** a calcareous concretion in the inner ear of a vertebrate or in the otocyst of an invertebrate
— **oto·lith·ic** \ˌō-tᵊl-'i-thik\ *adjective*

**oto·rhi·no·lar·yn·gol·o·gy** \ˌō-tō-ˌrī-nō-ˌlar-ən-'gä-lə-jē\ *noun* (circa 1900)
**:** OTOLARYNGOLOGY
— **oto·rhi·no·lar·yn·go·log·i·cal** \-gə-'lä-ji-kəl\ *adjective*
— **oto·rhi·no·lar·yn·gol·o·gist** \-'gä-lə-jist\ *noun*

**oto·scle·ro·sis** \ˌō-tō-sklə-'rō-səs\ *noun* [New Latin] (1901)
**:** growth of spongy bone in the inner ear that causes progressively increasing deafness

**oto·tox·ic** \ˌō-tə-'täk-sik\ *adjective* (1951)
**:** producing, involving, or being adverse effects on organs or nerves involved in hearing or balance
— **oto·tox·ic·i·ty** \-täk-'si-sə-tē\ *noun*

**ot·ta·va** \ō-'tä-və\ *adverb or adjective* [Italian, octave, from Medieval Latin *octava*] (1848)
**:** at an octave higher or lower than written — used as a direction in music

**ottava ri·ma** \-'rē-mə\ *noun, plural* **ottava rimas** [Italian, literally, eighth rhyme] (1820)
**:** a stanza of eight lines of heroic verse with a rhyme scheme of *ababbcc*

**Ot·ta·wa** \'ä-tə-wə, -ˌwä, -ˌwȯ\ *noun, plural* **-was** *or* **-wa** (1687)
**:** a member of an American Indian people of Michigan and southern Ontario

**ot·ter** \'ä-tər\ *noun, plural* **otters** *also* **otter** [Middle English *oter*, from Old English *otor*; akin to Old High German *ottar* otter, Greek *hydōr* water — more at WATER] (before 12th century)
**1 :** any of various largely aquatic carnivorous mammals (as genus *Lutra* or *Enhydra*) that are

related to the weasels and minks and usually have webbed and clawed feet and dark brown fur

otter 1

**2** : the fur or pelt of an otter

**ot·ter   hound** *noun* [from its use in hunting otters] (1607)
: any of a British breed of large hounds that have a wiry water-resistant coat and a keen scent

**ot·to** \'ä-(,)tō\ *variant of* ATTAR

**ot·to·man** \'ä-tə-mən\ *noun* (1605)
**1** *capitalized* **a** : a member of a Turkish dynasty founded by Osman I that ruled the Ottoman Empire **b** : a citizen or functionary of the Ottoman Empire
**2** [French *ottomane,* from feminine of *ottoman,* adjective] **a** : an upholstered often overstuffed seat or couch usually without a back **b** : an overstuffed footstool
**3** : a heavy clothing fabric characterized by pronounced crosswise ribs

**Ot·to·man** \'ä-tə-mən\ *adjective* [French, adjective & noun, probably from Italian *ottomano,* from Arabic *'othmānī,* from *'Othmān* Osman I, founder of the Ottoman Empire] (1603)
: of or relating to the Ottoman Empire, its rulers, or its citizens or functionaries

**oua·bain** \wä-'bā-ən, 'wä-,bān\ *noun* [International Scientific Vocabulary, from French *ouabaïo,* an African tree, from Somali *waabayyo* arrow poison] (1893)
: a poisonous glycoside $C_{29}H_{44}O_{12}$ obtained from several African shrubs or trees (genera *Strophanthus* and *Acokanthera*) of the dogbane family and used medically like digitalis and in Africa as an arrow poison

**ou·bli·ette** \,ü-blē-'et\ *noun* [French, from Middle French, from *oublier* to forget, from (assumed) Vulgar Latin *oblitare,* frequentative of Latin *oblivisci* to forget — more at OBLIVION] (1819)
: a dungeon with an opening only at the top

**¹ouch** \'aúch\ *noun* [Middle English, alteration (from misdivision of *a nouche*) of *nouche,* from Middle French, of Germanic origin; akin to Old High German *nusca* clasp] (14th century)
**1** *obsolete* : CLASP, BROOCH
**2 a** : a setting for a precious stone **b** : JEWEL, ORNAMENT; *especially* : a buckle or brooch set with precious stones

**²ouch** *interjection* [origin unknown] (1838)
— used especially to express sudden pain

**oud** \'üd\ *noun* [Arabic *ūd,* literally, wood] (1738)
: a musical instrument of the lute family used in southwest Asia and northern Africa

**¹ought** \'ot\ *verbal auxiliary* [Middle English *oughte* (1st & 3d singular present indicative), from *oughte,* 1st & 3d singular past indicative & subjunctive of *owen* to own, owe — more at OWE] (12th century)
— used to express obligation ⟨*ought* to pay our debts⟩, advisability ⟨*ought* to take care of yourself⟩, natural expectation ⟨*ought* to be here by now⟩, or logical consequence ⟨the result *ought* to be infinity⟩

**²ought** \'ó(k)t\ *transitive verb* [Middle English *oughte,* 1st & 3d singular past indicative of *owen*] (13th century)
**1** *chiefly Scottish* : POSSESS
**2** *chiefly Scottish* : OWE

**³ought** \'ot\ *noun* (1678)
: moral obligation : DUTY

**⁴ought** \'ot, 'ät\ *variant of* AUGHT

**oughtn't** \'ó-t²nt\ (1884)
: ought not

**ou·gui·ya** \ü-'gwē-ə, -'gē-ə\ *noun, plural* **ou·guiya** [Arabic dialect *ūgīyah,* from Arabic *ūqīyah,* literally, ounce] (1973)

— see MONEY table

**Oui·ja** \'wē-jə, -jē\ *trademark*
— used for a board with the alphabet and other signs on it that is used with a planchette to seek spiritualistic or telepathic messages

**¹ounce** \'aún(t)s\ *noun* [Middle English, from Middle French *unce,* from Latin *uncia* 12th part, ounce, from *unus* one — more at ONE] (14th century)
**1 a** : a unit of weight equal to ¹⁄₁₂ troy pound — see WEIGHT table **b** : a unit of weight equal to ¹⁄₁₆ avoirdupois pound **c** : a small amount ⟨an *ounce* of common sense⟩
**2** : FLUIDOUNCE ◆

**²ounce** *noun* [Middle English *once* lynx, from Middle French, alteration (by misdivision, as if *l'once* the ounce) of *lonce,* from (assumed) Vulgar Latin *lyncea,* from Latin *lync-, lynx*] (1774)
: SNOW LEOPARD

**our** \är, 'aú(-ə)r\ *adjective* [Middle English *oure,* from Old English *ūre;* akin to Old High German *unsēr* our, Old English *ūs* us] (before 12th century)
: of or relating to us or ourselves or ourself especially as possessors or possessor, agents or agent, or objects or object of an action ⟨*our* throne⟩ ⟨*our* actions⟩ ⟨*our* being chosen⟩

**Our Father** *noun* [from the opening words] (1882)
: LORD'S PRAYER

**ours** \'aú(-ə)rz, ärz\ *pronoun, singular or plural in construction* (14th century)
: that which belongs to us — used without a following noun as a pronoun equivalent in meaning to the adjective *our*

**our·self** \är-'self, aú(-ə)r-\ *pronoun* (14th century)
: MYSELF — used to refer to the single-person subject when *we* is used instead of *I* (as by a sovereign) ⟨will keep *ourself* till supper time alone —Shakespeare⟩

**our·selves** \-'selvz\ *pronoun plural* (15th century)
**1** : those identical ones that are we — compare WE 1; used reflexively ⟨we're doing it solely for *ourselves*⟩, for emphasis ⟨we *ourselves* will never go⟩, or in absolute constructions ⟨*ourselves* no longer young, we can sympathize with those who are old⟩
**2** : our normal, healthy, or sane condition ⟨just not *ourselves* today⟩

**-ous** *adjective suffix* [Middle English, from Old French *-ous, -eus, -eux,* from Latin *-osus*]
**1** : full of : abounding in : having : possessing the qualities of ⟨clamor*ous*⟩ ⟨poison*ous*⟩
**2** : having a valence lower than in compounds or ions named with an adjective ending in *-ic* ⟨mercur*ous*⟩

**ou·sel** \'ü-zəl\ *variant of* OUZEL

**Ou·shak** \ü-'shäk\ *noun, often attributive* [from *Oushak, Ushak* (Uşak), town in Turkey] (1901)
: a heavy wool Oriental rug characterized especially by bright primary colors and an elaborate medallion pattern

**oust** \'aúst\ *transitive verb* [Middle English, from Anglo-French *ouster,* from Old French *oster,* from Late Latin *obstare* to ward off, from Latin, to stand in the way, from *ob-* in the way + *stare* to stand — more at OB-, STAND] (15th century)
**1 a** : to remove from or dispossess of property or position by legal action, by force, or by the compulsion of necessity **b** : to take away (as a right or authority) : BAR, REMOVE
**2** : to take the place of : SUPPLANT
*synonym* see EJECT

**oust·er** \'aús-tər\ *noun* [Anglo-French, to oust] (1531)
**1 a** : a wrongful dispossession **b** : a judgment removing an officer or depriving a corporation of a franchise
**2** : EXPULSION

**¹out** \'aút\ *adverb* [Middle English, from Old English *ūt;* akin to Old High German *ūz* out,

Greek *hysteros* later, Sanskrit *ud* up, out] (before 12th century)
**1 a** (1) : in a direction away from the inside or center ⟨went *out* into the garden⟩ (2) : OUTSIDE ⟨it's raining *out*⟩ **b** : from among others **c** : away from the shore **d** : away from home or work ⟨*out* to lunch⟩ **e** : away from a particular place
**2 a** : so as to be missing or displaced from the usual or proper place ⟨left a word *out*⟩ ⟨threw his shoulder *out*⟩ **b** : into the possession or control of another ⟨lend *out* money⟩ **c** : into a state of loss or defeat ⟨was voted *out*⟩ **d** : into a state of vexation ⟨they do not mark me, and that brings me *out* —Shakespeare⟩ **e** : into groups or shares ⟨sorted *out* her notes⟩ ⟨parceled *out* the farm⟩
**3 a** : to the point of depletion, extinction, or exhaustion ⟨the food ran *out*⟩ ⟨turn the light *out*⟩ ⟨all tuckered *out*⟩ **b** : to completion or satisfaction ⟨hear me *out*⟩ ⟨work the problem *out*⟩ **c** : to the full or a great extent or degree ⟨all decked *out*⟩ ⟨stretched *out* on the floor⟩
**4 a** : in or into the open ⟨the sun came *out*⟩ **b** : OUT LOUD ⟨cried *out*⟩ **c** : in or into public circulation ⟨the evening paper isn't *out* yet⟩ ⟨hand *out* pamphlets⟩ ⟨the library book is still *out*⟩
**5 a** : at an end ⟨before the day is *out*⟩ **b** : in or into an insensible or unconscious state ⟨she was *out* cold⟩ **c** : in or into a useless state ⟨landed the plane with one engine *out*⟩ **d** : so as to put a player or side *out* or to be put *out* in baseball
**6** — used on a two-way radio circuit to indicate that a message is complete and no reply is expected

**²out** (before 12th century)
*transitive verb*
: EJECT, OUST
*intransitive verb*
: to become publicly known ⟨the truth will *out*⟩

**³out** *preposition* (13th century)
— used as a function word to indicate an outward movement ⟨ran *out* the door⟩ ⟨looked *out* the window⟩

**⁴out** *adjective* (13th century)
**1 a** : situated outside : EXTERNAL **b** : OUT-OF-BOUNDS

◇ WORD HISTORY
**ounce**   The difficulty in determining and establishing standardized weights and measures is evidenced by the great variety of systems used in both ancient and modern times. The Romans used a system based on units divided into twelve parts. Thus Latin *uncia,* meaning "a twelfth part," was used to designate the twelfth part of a *pes* or "foot." A Germanic borrowing from *uncia* in this sense resulted in Old English *ince* or *ynce* and Modern English *inch.* The Roman pound, called *libra* in Latin (hence the English abbreviation *lb.*) was also divided into twelve parts similarly designated by the word *uncia.* In this sense *uncia* followed a different path, developing into *unce* in medieval French, which was borrowed into Middle English as *unce* or *ounce.* Why, then, do we have sixteen ounces in a pound? Unfortunately for the sake of consistency, two systems of weights were developed in the Middle Ages for weighing different sorts of material: one, the troy system, having twelve ounces, and the other, the avoirdupois system, which remains in use in the U.S. today, having sixteen ounces.

\ə\ **abut**   \²\ **kitten**   \ər\ **further**   \a\ **ash**   \ā\ **ace**
\ä\ **mop, mar**   \aú\ **out**   \ch\ **chin**   \e\ **bet**   \ē\ **easy**
\g\ **go**   \i\ **hit**   \ī\ **ice**   \j\ **job**   \ŋ\ **sing**   \ō\ **go**
\ò\ **law**   \òi\ **boy**   \th\ **thin**   \t͟h\ **the**   \ü\ **loot**   \ú\ **foot**
\y\ **yet**   \zh\ **vision**      *see also* Guide to Pronunciation

**2 :** situated at a distance **:** OUTLYING ⟨the *out* islands⟩

**3 :** not being in power

**4 :** ABSENT

**5 :** put out while at bat or baserunning in baseball

**6 :** directed outward or serving to direct something outward ⟨the *out* basket⟩

**7 :** not being in vogue or fashion

**8 :** not to be considered **:** out of the question

**9 :** DETERMINED 1 ⟨was *out* to get revenge⟩

**⁵out** *noun* (1717)

**1 :** OUTSIDE

**2 :** one who is out of office or power or on the outside ⟨a matter of *outs* versus ins⟩

**3 a :** an act or instance of putting a player out or of being put out in baseball **b :** a player that is put out

**4 :** a way of escaping from an embarrassing or difficult situation

— **on the outs :** on unfriendly terms **:** at variance

**out-** *prefix* [¹*out*]
**:** in a manner that exceeds or surpasses and sometimes overpowers or defeats ⟨*out*maneuver⟩

| | |
|---|---|
| out·achieve | out·or·ga·nize |
| out·act | out·pass |
| out·bar·gain | out·per·form |
| out·bid | out·pitch |
| out·bitch | out·play |
| out·bluff | out·plot |
| out·box | out·pol·i·tick |
| out·brag | out·poll |
| out·brawl | out·pop·u·late |
| out·bulk | out·pow·er |
| out·buy | out·pray |
| out·catch | out·preach |
| out·charge | out·price |
| out·climb | out·pro·duce |
| out·coach | out·prom·ise |
| out·com·pete | out·punch |
| out·dance | out·rate |
| out·daz·zle | out·re·bound |
| out·de·bate | out·re·pro·duce |
| out·de·liv·er | out·ri·val |
| out·de·sign | out·roar |
| out·drag | out·row |
| out·dress | out·rush |
| out·drink | out·sail |
| out·drive | out·scheme |
| out·du·el | out·scoop |
| out·earn | out·score |
| out·eat | out·shout |
| out·fight | out·sing |
| out·fig·ure | out·sit |
| out·fish | out·skate |
| out·fly | out·soar |
| out·fum·ble | out·spar·kle |
| out·gain | out·speed |
| out·glit·ter | out·sprint |
| out·gross | out·stride |
| out·hit | out·swear |
| out·ho·mer | out·swim |
| out·hunt | out·talk |
| out·hus·tle | out·think |
| out·in·trigue | out·throw |
| out·jump | out·trade |
| out·kick | out·vie |
| out·kill | out·vote |
| out·last | out·wait |
| out·leap | out·walk |
| out·learn | out·watch |
| out·man | out·wres·tle |
| out·ma·neu·ver | out·write |
| out·ma·nip·u·late | out·yell |
| out·march | out·yield |
| out·mus·cle | |

**out·age** \'aȯ-tij\ *noun* (1899)

**1 :** a quantity or bulk of something lost in transportation or storage

**2 a :** a failure or interruption in use or functioning **b :** a period of interruption especially of electric current

**out–and–out** \ˌaȯt-ᵊn(d)-'aȯt\ *adjective* (1813)
**:** being such completely at all times, in every way, or from every point of view ⟨an *out-and-out* fraud⟩

**out–and–out·er** \-'aȯ-tər\ *noun* (circa 1812)
**:** one who goes to extremes

**out·back** \'aȯt-ˌbak, -ˌbak\ *noun* (1893)
**:** isolated rural country especially of Australia

**out·bal·ance** \ˌaȯt-'ba-lən(t)s\ *transitive verb* (1644)
**:** OUTWEIGH

**¹out·board** \'aȯt-ˌbōrd, -ˌbȯrd\ *adjective* (circa 1823)

**1 :** situated outboard

**2 :** having, using, or limited to the use of an outboard motor

**²outboard** *adverb* (circa 1848)

**1 :** outside a ship's bulwarks **:** in a lateral direction from the hull

**2 :** in a position closer or closest to either of the wingtips of an airplane or to the sides of an automobile

**³outboard** *noun* (1935)

**1 :** OUTBOARD MOTOR

**2 :** a boat with an outboard motor

**outboard motor** *noun* (1909)
**:** a small internal combustion engine with propeller integrally attached for mounting at the stern of a small boat

**out·bound** \'aȯt-ˌbaȯnd\ *adjective* (1598)
**:** outward bound ⟨*outbound* traffic⟩

**out·brave** \ˌaȯt-'brāv\ *transitive verb* (1589)

**1 :** to face or resist defiantly

**2 :** to exceed in courage

**out·break** \'aȯt-ˌbrāk\ *noun* (1602)

**1 a :** a sudden or violent increase in activity or currency ⟨the *outbreak* of war⟩ **b :** a sudden rise in the incidence of a disease ⟨an *outbreak* of measles⟩ **c :** a sudden increase in numbers of a harmful organism and especially an insect within a particular area ⟨an *outbreak* of locusts⟩

**2 :** INSURRECTION, REVOLT

**out·breed** *transitive verb* **-bred** \-ˌbred, -'bred\; **-breed·ing** (circa 1909)

**1** \'aȯt-ˌbrēd\ **:** to subject to outbreeding

**2** \ˌaȯt-\ **:** to breed faster than

**out·breed·ing** \'aȯt-ˌbrē-diŋ\ *noun* (1901)
**:** the interbreeding of individuals or stocks that are relatively unrelated

**out·build·ing** \'aȯt-ˌbil-diŋ\ *noun* (1626)
**:** a building (as a stable or a woodshed) separate from but accessory to a main house

**out·burst** \-ˌbərst\ *noun* (1657)

**1 :** a violent expression of feeling ⟨an *outburst* of anger⟩

**2 :** a surge of activity or growth ⟨new *outbursts* of creative power —C. E. Montague⟩

**3 :** ERUPTION ⟨volcanic *outbursts*⟩

**out·bye** *or* **out·by** \ȯt-'bī\ *adverb* [Middle English (Scots) *out-by*, from *out* + *by*] (15th century)
*chiefly Scottish* **:** a short distance away; *also*
**:** OUTDOORS

**out·cast** \'aȯt-ˌkast\ *noun* (14th century)

**1 :** one that is cast out or refused acceptance (as by society) **:** PARIAH

**2** [Scots *cast out* to quarrel] *Scottish* **:** QUARREL
— **outcast** *adjective*

**out·caste** \-ˌkast\ *noun* (1876)

**1 :** a Hindu who has been ejected from his caste for violation of its customs or rules

**2 :** one who has no caste

**out·class** \ˌaȯt-'klas\ *transitive verb* (1870)
**:** to excel or surpass so decisively as to be or appear to be of a higher class

**out·come** \'aȯt-ˌkəm\ *noun* (1788)
**:** something that follows as a result or consequence

**¹out·crop** \'aȯt-ˌkräp\ *noun* (1805)

**1 :** a coming out of bedrock or of an unconsolidated deposit to the surface of the ground

**2 :** the part of a rock formation that appears at the surface of the ground

**²out·crop** \'aȯt-ˌkräp, ˌaȯt-'\ *intransitive verb* (circa 1847)

**1 :** to project from the surrounding soil ⟨ledges *outcropping* from the eroded slope⟩

**2 :** to come to the surface **:** APPEAR

**out·crop·ping** \'aȯt-ˌkrä-piŋ\ *noun* (1872)
**:** OUTCROP

**¹out·cross** \'aȯt-ˌkrȯs\ *noun* (1890)

**1 :** a cross between relatively unrelated individuals

**2 :** the progeny of an outcross

**²outcross** *transitive verb* (1918)
**:** to cross with a relatively unrelated individual or strain

**out·cry** \'aȯt-ˌkrī\ *noun* (14th century)

**1 a :** a loud cry **:** CLAMOR **b :** a vehement protest

**2 :** AUCTION

**out·dat·ed** \ˌaȯt-'dā-təd\ *adjective* (1616)
**:** no longer current **:** OUTMODED
— **out·dat·ed·ly** *adverb*
— **out·dat·ed·ness** *noun*

**out·dis·tance** \ˌaȯt-'dis-tən(t)s\ *transitive verb* (1857)
**:** to go far ahead of (as in a race) **:** OUTSTRIP

**out·do** \-'dü\ *transitive verb* **-did** \-'did\; **-done** \-'dən\; **-do·ing** \-'dü-iŋ\; **-does** \-'dəz\ (1607)

**1 :** to go beyond in action or performance

**2 :** DEFEAT, OVERCOME
**synonym** see EXCEED

**out·door** \'aȯt-ˌdȯr, -ˌdȯr; 'aȯt-'\ *also* **out·doors** \-ˌdȯrz, -ˌdȯrz; 'aȯt-'\ *adjective* [*out (of) door, out (of) doors*] (1748)

**1 :** of or relating to the outdoors

**2 a :** performed outdoors ⟨*outdoor* sports⟩ **b :** OUTDOORSY ⟨an *outdoor* couple⟩

**3 :** not enclosed **:** having no roof ⟨an *outdoor* restaurant⟩

**¹out·doors** \ˌaȯt-'dȯrz, -'dȯrz; 'aȯt-'\ *adverb* (1817)
**:** outside a building **:** in or into the open air

**²outdoors** *noun plural but singular in construction* (1844)

**1 :** a place or location away from the confines of a building

**2 :** the world away from human habitations

**out·doors·man** \-mən\ *noun* (1918)
**:** one who spends much time in the outdoors or in outdoor activities
— **out·doors·man·ship** \-ˌship\ *noun*

**out·doorsy** \ˌaȯt-'dȯr-zē, -'dȯr-\ *adjective* (1936)

**1 :** relating to, characteristic of, or appropriate for the outdoors ⟨*outdoorsy* clothing⟩

**2 :** fond of outdoor activities ⟨sounded rugged and *outdoorsy* —N.Y. Times⟩

**out·draw** \ˌaȯt-'drȯ\ *transitive verb* **-drew** \-'drü\; **-drawn** \-'drȯn\; **-draw·ing** (circa 1909)

**1 :** to attract a larger audience or following than

**2 :** to draw a handgun more quickly than

**out·er** \'aȯ-tər\ *adjective* [Middle English, from ⁴*out* + ¹*-er*] (13th century)

**1 :** existing independent of mind **:** OBJECTIVE

**2 a :** situated farther out ⟨the *outer* limits⟩ **b :** being away from a center **c :** situated or belonging on the outside ⟨the *outer* covering⟩

**out·er·coat** \'aȯ-tər-ˌkōt\ *noun* (1948)
**:** COAT 1a

**outer ear** *noun* (1935)
**:** the outer visible portion of the ear that collects and directs sound waves toward the eardrum by way of a canal which extends inward through the temporal bone

**out·er·most** \'aȯ-tər-ˌmōst\ *adjective* (14th century)
**:** farthest out

**outer planet** *noun* (1941)
**:** any of the planets Jupiter, Saturn, Uranus, Neptune, and Pluto whose orbits lie beyond the asteroid belt

**outer space** *noun* (1901)
**:** space immediately outside the earth's atmosphere; *broadly* **:** interplanetary or interstellar space

**out·er·wear** \'aȯ-tər-ˌwar, -ˌwer\ *noun* (1921)

: clothing for outdoor wear

**out·face** \ˌaut-ˈfās\ *transitive verb* (circa 1529)
**1** : to cause to waver or submit by or as if by staring
**2** : to confront unflinchingly : DEFY

**out·fall** \ˈaut-ˌfȯl\ *noun* (1629)
: the outlet of a body of water (as a river or lake); *especially* : the mouth of a drain or sewer

**out·field** \-ˌfēld\ *noun* (1868)
**1** : the part of a baseball field beyond the infield and between the foul lines
**2** : the baseball defensive positions comprising right field, center field, and left field; *also* : the players who occupy these positions
— **out·field·er** \-ˌfēl-dər\ *noun*

**¹out·fit** \ˈaut-ˌfit\ *noun* (circa 1769)
**1** : the act of fitting out or equipping (as for a voyage or expedition)
**2 a** : the tools or equipment for the practice of a trade **b** : wearing apparel with accessories usually for a special occasion or activity **c** : physical, mental, or moral endowments or resources
**3** : a group that works as a team : ORGANIZATION; *especially* : a military unit

**²outfit** *verb* **out·fit·ted; out·fit·ting** (1847)
*transitive verb*
**1** : to furnish with an outfit
**2** : SUPPLY ⟨*outfitting* every family with shoes —American Guide Series: Vermont⟩
*intransitive verb*
: to acquire an outfit
*synonym* see FURNISH

**out·fit·ter** \-ˌfi-tər\ *noun* (1846)
: one that outfits: as **a** : HABERDASHER **b** : a business providing equipment, supplies, and often trained guides (as for hunting trips); *also* : a guide working for such an outfitter

**out·flank** \ˌaut-ˈflaŋk\ *transitive verb* (1765)
**1** : to get around the flank of (an opposing force)
**2** : GET AROUND, CIRCUMVENT

**¹out·flow** \ˈaut-ˌflō, ˌaut-ˈ\ *intransitive verb* (circa 1580)
: to flow out

**²out·flow** \ˈaut-ˌflō\ *noun* (circa 1864)
**1** : a flowing out ⟨*outflow* of dollars⟩
**2** : something that flows out ⟨*outflow* of a sewage treatment plant⟩

**out·foot** \ˌaut-ˈfut\ *transitive verb* (1737)
: to outdo in speed : OUTSTRIP

**out·fox** \-ˈfäks\ *transitive verb* (1924)
: OUTSMART

**out–front** \-ˈfrənt\ *adjective* (1968)
: FRANK, OPEN

**out·gas** \ˈaut-ˌgas, ˌaut-ˈ\ (1925)
*transitive verb*
**1** : to remove occluded gases from usually by heating; *broadly* : to remove gases from
**2** : to remove (gases) from a material or a space
*intransitive verb*
: to lose gases

**out·gen·er·al** \ˌaut-ˈjen-rəl, -ˈje-nə-\ *transitive verb* (1767)
: to surpass in generalship : OUTMANEUVER

**¹out·giv·ing** \ˈaut-ˌgi-viŋ\ *noun* (1663)
: something that is given out; *especially* : a public statement or utterance

**²outgiving** *adjective* (1942)
: socially responsive and demonstrative

**¹out·go** \ˌaut-ˈgō\ *transitive verb* (1530)
: to go beyond : OUTDO

**²out·go** \ˈaut-ˌgō\ *noun, plural* **outgoes** (circa 1640)
**1** : something that goes out; *specifically* : EXPENDITURE
**2 a** : the act of going out **b** : DEPARTURE
**3** : OUTLET 1a

**out·go·ing** \ˈaut-ˌgō-iŋ, -ˌgȯ(-)iŋ\ *adjective* (1633)
**1 a** : going away : DEPARTING ⟨an *outgoing* ship⟩ **b** : retiring or withdrawing from a place or position ⟨the *outgoing* president⟩ **c** : directed to an intended recipient ⟨*outgoing* mail⟩

**2** : openly friendly and responsive : EXTROVERTED
— **out·go·ing·ness** *noun*

**out·go·ings** \-ˌgō-iŋz, -ˌgȯ(-)iŋz\ *noun plural* (1765)
*British* : costs incurred : EXPENSES

**out–group** \ˈaut-ˌgrüp\ *noun* (circa 1907)
: a group that is distinct from one's own and so usually an object of hostility or dislike — compare IN-GROUP 1

**out·grow** \ˌaut-ˈgrō\ *transitive verb* **-grew** \-ˈgrü\; **-grown** \-ˈgrōn\; **-grow·ing** (1594)
**1** : to grow or increase faster than ⟨mankind is *outgrowing* food supplies —R. C. Murphy⟩
**2** : to grow too large or too mature for ⟨*outgrew* his best suit⟩ ⟨the need to *outgrow* the habit of war —Norman Cousins⟩

**out·growth** \ˈaut-ˌgrōth\ *noun* (1837)
**1** : a process or product of growing out ⟨an *outgrowth* of hair⟩
**2** : CONSEQUENCE, BY-PRODUCT ⟨crime is often an *outgrowth* of poverty⟩

**out·guess** \ˌaut-ˈges\ *transitive verb* (1911)
: to anticipate the expectations, intentions, or actions of : OUTWIT

**out·gun** \-ˈgən\ *transitive verb* (1691)
: to surpass in firepower; *broadly* : OUTDO

**out·haul** \ˈaut-ˌhȯl\ *noun* (1840)
: a rope used to haul a sail taut along a spar

**out–Her·od** \ˌaut-ˈher-əd\ *transitive verb* [*out-* + *Herod* the Great, depicted in medieval mystery plays as a blustering tyrant] (1602)
: to exceed in violence or extravagance — usually used in the phrase *out-Herod Herod*

**out·house** \ˈaut-ˌhaus\ *noun* (14th century)
: OUTBUILDING; *especially* : PRIVY 1a

**out·ing** \ˈau-tiŋ\ *noun* (1821)
**1** : a brief usually outdoor pleasure trip
**2** : an athletic competition or race; *also* : an appearance therein
**3** : a usually public presentation or appearance (as in a particular role) ⟨her first *outing* as a novelist⟩
**4** : the public disclosure of the covert homosexuality of a prominent person by homosexual activists

**outing flannel** *noun* (1890)
: a flannelette sometimes having an admixture of wool

**out·land** \ˈaut-ˌland, -lənd\ *noun* (before 12th century)
**1** : a foreign land
**2** *plural* : the outlying regions of a country : PROVINCES
— **outland** *adjective*

**out·land·er** \-ˌlan-dər, -lən-\ *noun* (1598)
: a person who belongs to another region, culture, or group : FOREIGNER, STRANGER

**out·land·ish** \ˌaut-ˈlan-dish\ *adjective* (before 12th century)
**1** : of or relating to another country : FOREIGN
**2 a** : strikingly out of the ordinary : BIZARRE ⟨an *outlandish* costume⟩ **b** : exceeding proper or reasonable limits or standards
**3** : remote from civilization
*synonym* see STRANGE
— **out·land·ish·ly** *adverb*
— **out·land·ish·ness** *noun*

**¹out·law** \ˈaut-ˌlȯ\ *noun* [Middle English *outlawe*, from Old English *ūtlaga*, from Old Norse *ūtlagi*, from *ūt* out (akin to Old English *ūt* out) + *lag-, log* law — more at OUT, LAW] (before 12th century)
**1** : a person excluded from the benefit or protection of the law
**2 a** : a lawless person or a fugitive from law **b** : a person or organization under a ban or restriction **c** : one that is unconventional or rebellious
**3** : an animal (as a horse) that is wild and unmanageable
— **outlaw** *adjective*

**²outlaw** *transitive verb* (before 12th century)
**1 a** : to deprive of the benefit and protection of law : declare to be an outlaw **b** : to make illegal ⟨*outlawed* dueling⟩

**2** : to place under a ban or restriction
**3** : to remove from legal jurisdiction or enforcement
— **out·law·ry** \ˈaut-ˌlȯr-ē\ *noun*

**¹out·lay** \ˈaut-ˌlā, ˌaut-ˈ\ *transitive verb* **-laid** \-ˌlād, -ˈlād\; **-lay·ing** (1555)
: to lay out (money) : EXPEND

**²out·lay** \ˈaut-ˌlā\ *noun* (1798)
**1** : the act of expending
**2** : EXPENDITURE, PAYMENT ⟨*outlays* for national defense⟩

**out·let** \ˈaut-ˌlet, -lət\ *noun* [Middle English *utlete*, from *ut* out + *-lete* watercourse, from Old English *gelæt*, from *lætan* to let] (13th century)
**1 a** : a place or opening through which something is let out : EXIT, VENT **b** : a means of release or satisfaction for an emotion or impulse ⟨sexual *outlets*⟩ **c** : a medium of expression or publication
**2** : a stream flowing out of a lake or pond
**3 a** : a market for a commodity **b** : an agency (as a store or dealer) through which a product is marketed ⟨retail *outlets*⟩
**4** : a receptacle for the plug of an electrical device

**outlet pass** *noun* (circa 1975)
: a pass made in basketball by the player taking a defensive rebound to a teammate to start a fast break

**out·li·er** \-ˌlī(-ə)r\ *noun* (1676)
**1** : a person whose residence and place of business are at a distance
**2** : something (as a geological feature) that is situated away from or classed differently from a main or related body

**¹out·line** \ˈaut-ˌlīn\ *noun* (1662)
**1 a** : a line that marks the outer limits of an object or figure : BOUNDARY **b** : SHAPE
**2 a** : a style of drawing in which contours are marked without shading **b** : a sketch in outline
**3 a** : a condensed treatment of a particular subject ⟨an *outline* of world history⟩ **b** : a summary of a written work : SYNOPSIS
**4** : a preliminary account of a project : PLAN
**5** : a fishing line set out overnight : TROTLINE
☆

**²outline** *transitive verb* (circa 1790)
**1** : to draw the outline of
**2** : to indicate the principal features or different parts of ⟨*outlined* their responsibilities⟩

**out·live** \ˌaut-ˈliv\ *transitive verb* (15th century)
**1** : to live beyond or longer than ⟨*outlived* most of his friends⟩ ⟨*outlive* its usefulness⟩
**2** : to survive the effects of ⟨universities . . . *outlive* many political and social changes —J. B. Conant⟩

**out·look** \ˈaut-ˌluk\ *noun* (1667)

---

☆ **SYNONYMS**
**Outline, contour, profile, silhouette**
mean the line that bounds and gives form to something. OUTLINE applies to a line marking the outer limits or edges of a body or mass ⟨traced the *outline* of his hand⟩. CONTOUR stresses the quality of an outline or a bounding surface as being smooth, jagged, curving, or sharply angled ⟨a car with flowing *contours*⟩. PROFILE suggests a varied and sharply defined outline against a lighter background ⟨a portrait of her face in *profile*⟩. SILHOUETTE suggests a shape especially of a head or figure with all detail blacked out in shadow leaving only the outline clearly defined ⟨photograph in *silhouette* against a bright sky⟩.

---

\ə\ abut   \ᵊ\ kitten   \ər\ further   \a\ ash   \ā\ ace
\ä\ mop, mar   \au\ out   \ch\ chin   \e\ bet   \ē\ easy
\g\ go   \i\ hit   \ī\ ice   \j\ job   \ŋ\ sing   \ō\ go
\ȯ\ law   \ȯi\ boy   \th\ thin   \t̲h̲\ the   \ü\ loot   \u̇\ foot
\y\ yet   \zh\ vision    *see also* Guide to Pronunciation

**1 a** : a place offering a view **b** : a view from a particular place
**2** : POINT OF VIEW ⟨a positive *outlook* on life⟩
**3** : the act of looking out
**4** : the prospect for the future ⟨the *outlook* for steel demand in the U.S. —*Wall Street Journal*⟩
*synonym* see PROSPECT

**out loud** *adverb* (1821)
: loudly enough to be heard : ALOUD

**out·ly·ing** \'aut-ˌlī-iŋ\ *adjective* (circa 1690)
: remote from a center or main body ⟨*outlying* areas⟩

**out·match** \ˌaut-'mach\ *transitive verb* (1603)
: to prove superior to : OUTDO

**out·mi·grant** \'aut-ˌmī-grənt\ *noun* (1945)
: one that out-migrates

**out·mi·grate** \-ˌgrāt\ *intransitive verb* (1953)
: to leave one region or community in order to settle in another especially as part of a large-scale and continuing movement of population — compare IN-MIGRATE

**— out·mi·gra·tion** \ˌaut-mī-'grā-shən\ *noun*

**out·mode** \ˌaut-'mōd\ *transitive verb* **out·mod·ed; out·mod·ing** [*out* (*of*) *mode*] (1906)
: to make unfashionable or obsolete

**out·mod·ed** \-'mō-dəd\ *adjective* (1903)
**1** : not being in style
**2** : no longer acceptable, current, or usable ⟨*outmoded* customs⟩

**out·most** \'aut-ˌmōst\ *adjective* (12th century)
: farthest out : OUTERMOST

**out·num·ber** \ˌaut-'nəm-bər\ *transitive verb* (1670)
: to exceed in number

**out of** *preposition* (before 12th century)
**1 a** (1) — used as a function word to indicate direction or movement from within to the outside of ⟨walked *out of* the room⟩ (2) — used as a function word to indicate a change in quality, state, or form ⟨woke up *out of* a deep sleep⟩ **b** (1) — used as a function word to indicate a position or situation beyond the range, limits, or sphere of ⟨*out of* control⟩ (2) — used as a function word to indicate a position or state away from the usual or expected ⟨*out of* practice⟩
**2** — used as a function word to indicate origin, source, or cause ⟨a remarkable colt *out of* an ordinary mare⟩ ⟨built *out of* old lumber⟩ ⟨came *out of* fear⟩
**3** — used as a function word to indicate exclusion from or deprivation of ⟨cheated him *out of* his savings⟩ ⟨*out of* breath⟩
**4** — used as a function word to indicate choice or selection from a group ⟨one *out of* four survived⟩

**— out of it 1** : not part of a group, activity, or fashion **2** : in a dazed or confused state

**out-of-body** *adjective* (1970)
: relating to or involving a feeling of separation from one's body and of being able to view oneself and others from an external perspective ⟨an *out-of-body* experience⟩

**out-of-bounds** \ˌaut-ə(v)-'baun(d)z\ *adverb or adjective* (1857)
: outside the prescribed boundaries or limits

**out-of-date** \-'dāt\ *adjective* (1628)
: OUTMODED, OBSOLETE

**out-of-door** \-'dōr, -'dor\ *or* **out-of-doors** \-'dōrz, -'dorz\ *adjective* (1800)
: OUTDOOR

**out-of-doors** *noun plural but singular in construction* (1819)
: OUTDOORS

**out-of-pock·et** \-'pä-kət\ *adjective* (1885)
: requiring an outlay of cash ⟨*out-of-pocket* expenses⟩

**out-of-sight** \ˌau-də-'sīt\ *adjective* (1893)
*slang* : WONDERFUL

**out-of-the-way** \ˌaut-ə(v)-thə-'wā\ *adjective* (1704)
**1** : UNUSUAL ⟨*out-of-the-way* information⟩

**2** : being off the beaten track ⟨an *out-of-the-way* restaurant⟩

**out·pace** \ˌaut-'pās\ *transitive verb* (1611)
**1** : to surpass in speed
**2** : OUTDO

**out·pa·tient** \'aut-ˌpā-shənt\ *noun* (1715)
: a patient who is not hospitalized overnight but who visits a hospital, clinic, or associated facility for diagnosis or treatment — compare INPATIENT

**out·place·ment** \ˌaut-'plās-mənt, 'aut-ˌ\ *noun* (1970)
: the process of easing unwanted or unneeded executives out of a company by providing company-paid assistance in finding them new jobs

**out·point** \ˌaut-'point\ *transitive verb* (1883)
**1** : to sail closer to the wind than
**2** : to win more points than (as in a boxing match)

**out·port** \'aut-ˌpōrt, -ˌport\ *noun* (1642)
**1** *chiefly British* : a port other than the main port of a country
**2** : a small fishing village especially in Newfoundland

**out·post** \'aut-ˌpōst\ *noun* (1757)
**1 a** : a security detachment dispatched by a main body of troops to protect it from enemy surprise **b** : a military base established by treaty or agreement in another country
**2 a** : an outlying or frontier settlement **b** : an outlying branch or position of a main organization or group

**¹out·pour** \ˌaut-'pōr, -'por, 'aut-ˌ\ *transitive verb* (1671)
: to pour out

**²out·pour** \'aut-ˌpōr, -ˌpor\ *noun* (1864)
: OUTPOURING

**out·pour·ing** \'aut-ˌpōr-iŋ, -ˌpor-\ *noun* (15th century)
**1** : the act of pouring out
**2** : something that pours out or is poured out : OUTFLOW

**out·pull** \ˌaut-'pul\ *transitive verb* (1926)
: OUTDRAW 1

**¹out·put** \'aut-ˌput\ *noun* (circa 1858)
**1** : something produced: as **a** : mineral, agricultural, or industrial production ⟨steel *output*⟩ **b** : mental or artistic production ⟨literary *output*⟩ **c** : the amount produced by a person in a given time **d** : power or energy produced or delivered by a machine or system (as for storage or for conversion in kind or in characteristics) ⟨solar X-ray *output*⟩ **e** : the information produced by a computer
**2** : the act, process, or an instance of producing
**3** : the terminal for the output on an electrical device

**²output** *transitive verb* **out·put·ted** *or* **out·put; out·put·ting** (1858)
: to produce as output

**out·race** \ˌaut-'rās\ *transitive verb* (1657)
: OUTPACE

**¹out·rage** \'aut-ˌrāj\ *noun* [Middle English, from Middle French, excess, outrage, from *outre* beyond, in excess, from Latin *ultra* — more at ULTRA-] (14th century)
**1** : an act of violence or brutality
**2 a** : INJURY, INSULT ⟨do no *outrages* on silly women or poor passengers —Shakespeare⟩ **b** : an act that violates accepted standards of behavior or taste ⟨an *outrage* alike against decency and dignity —John Buchan⟩
**3** : the anger and resentment aroused by injury or insult ◆

**²outrage** *transitive verb* **out·raged; out·rag·ing** (1590)
**1 a** : RAPE **b** : to violate the standards or principles of ⟨he has *outraged* respectability past endurance —John Braine⟩
**2** : to arouse anger or resentment in usually by some grave offense
*synonym* see OFFEND

**out·ra·geous** \(ˌ)aut-'rā-jəs\ *adjective* (14th century)

**1 a** : exceeding the limits of what is usual **b** : not conventional or matter-of-fact : FANTASTIC
**2** : VIOLENT, UNRESTRAINED
**3 a** : going beyond all standards of what is right or decent ⟨an *outrageous* disregard of human rights⟩ **b** : deficient in propriety or good taste ⟨*outrageous* language⟩ ⟨*outrageous* manners⟩

**— out·ra·geous·ly** *adverb*
**— out·ra·geous·ness** *noun*

**ou·trance** \ü-'träⁿs\ *noun* [Middle English, from Middle French, from *outrer* to pass beyond, carry to excess, from *outre*] (15th century)
: the last extremity

**out·range** \ˌaut-'rānj\ *transitive verb* (1858)
: to surpass in range

**out·rank** \-'raŋk\ *transitive verb* (1842)
**1** : to rank higher than
**2** : to exceed in importance

**ou·tré** \ü-'trā\ *adjective* [French, from past participle of *outrer* to carry to excess] (1722)
: violating convention or propriety : BIZARRE
*word history* see OUTRAGE

**¹out·reach** \ˌaut-'rēch\ (circa 1568)
*transitive verb*
**1 a** : to surpass in reach **b** : EXCEED ⟨the demand *outreaches* the supply⟩
**2** : to get the better of by trickery
*intransitive verb*
**1** : to go too far
**2** : to reach out

**²out·reach** \'aut-ˌrēch\ *noun* (1870)
**1** : the act of reaching out
**2** : the extent or limit of reach ⟨the *outreach* of the Ohio floods —Clifton Johnson⟩
**3** : the extending of services or assistance beyond current or usual limits ⟨an *outreach* program⟩; *also* : the extent of such services or assistance

**¹out·ride** \ˌaut-'rīd\ *transitive verb* **-rode** \-'rōd\; **-rid·den** \-'ri-dᵊn\; **-rid·ing** \-'rī-diŋ\ (1530)
**1** : to ride better, faster, or farther than : OUTSTRIP
**2** : to ride out ⟨a storm⟩

**²out·ride** \'aut-ˌrīd\ *noun* (1880)
: an unstressed syllable or group of syllables added to a foot in sprung rhythm but not counted in the scansion

**out·rid·er** \-ˌrī-dər\ *noun* (1530)
**1** : a mounted attendant
**2** : one who escorts or clears the way for a vehicle or person
**3** : FORERUNNER, HARBINGER

**out·rig·ger** \'aut-ˌri-gər\ *noun* (1748)
**1 a** : a projecting spar with a shaped log at the end attached to a canoe to prevent upsetting **b** : a spar or projecting beam run out from a ship's side to help secure the masts or from a mast to extend a rope or sail **c** : a projecting support for an oarlock; *also* : a boat equipped with these supports
**2** : a projecting member run out from a main structure to provide additional stability or to

---

◇ **WORD HISTORY**

**outrage** Given the meaning of *outrage*, the assumption might be that the word is a compound of *out* and *rage*. Actually, such is not the case at all. The word's ultimate source is Latin *ultra* "beyond." *Ultra* developed into medieval French *outre*. To the adverb *outre* was appended the suffix *-age* to produce the noun *outrage*. Originally meaning "excess," *outrage* also developed the meaning "an act of violence or brutality." It was this sense that was borrowed into Middle English in the 14th century. In the 18th century English went back to a derivative of French *outre* once again, this time borrowing *outré* "bizarre," the past participle of the verb *outrer* "to carry to excess."

support something; *especially* **:** a projecting frame to support the elevator or tailplanes of an airplane or the rotor of a helicopter

**¹out·right** \aùt-'rīt\ *adverb* (14th century)
**1** *archaic* **:** straight ahead **:** DIRECTLY
**2 :** in entirety **:** COMPLETELY ⟨rejected the proposal *outright*⟩
**3 :** without restraint or reservation ⟨laughed *outright*⟩
**4 :** on the spot **:** INSTANTANEOUSLY ⟨was killed *outright*⟩
**5 :** without lien or encumbrance ⟨purchased the property *outright* for cash⟩
**²out·right** \'aùt-,rīt\ *adjective* (1532)
**1 a :** being completely or exactly what is stated ⟨an *outright* lie⟩ **b :** given without reservation ⟨*outright* grants for research⟩ **c :** made without encumbrance or lien ⟨*outright* sale⟩
**2** *archaic* **:** proceeding directly onward
— **out·right·ly** *adverb*

**out·run** \,aùt-'rən\ *transitive verb* **-ran** \-'ran\; **-run; -run·ning** (1526)
**1 :** to run faster than
**2 :** EXCEED, SURPASS ⟨his ambitions *outrun* his abilities⟩

**out·sell** \-'sel\ *transitive verb* **-sold** \-'sōld\; **-sell·ing** (1609)
**1** *archaic* **:** to exceed in value
**2 :** to exceed in number of items sold
**3 :** to surpass in selling or salesmanship

**out·set** \'aùt-,set\ *noun* (1759)
**:** BEGINNING, START

**out·shine** \,aùt-'shīn\ *verb* **-shone** \-'shōn, *especially British* -'shän\ *or* **-shined; -shin·ing** (1596)
*transitive verb*
**1 a :** to shine brighter than **b :** to excel in splendor or showiness
**2 :** OUTDO, SURPASS ⟨*outshone* most of the other films in quality —Kathleen Karr⟩
*intransitive verb*
**:** to shine out

**out·shoot** \,aùt-'shüt\ *transitive verb* **-shot** \-'shät\; **-shoot·ing** (1530)
**1 :** to surpass in shooting or making shots
**2 :** to shoot or go beyond

**¹out·side** \,aùt-'sīd, 'aùt-,\ *noun* (1505)
**1 a :** a place or region beyond an enclosure or boundary: as (1) **:** the world beyond the confines of an institution ⟨as a prison⟩ (2) *often capitalized, Alaska* **:** the world beyond the territory or state of Alaska; *especially* **:** the 48 contiguous states **b :** the area farthest from a specified point of reference: as (1) **:** the side of home plate farthest from the batter (2) **:** the part of a playing area toward the sidelines (3) **:** the part of a playing area away from the goal
**2 :** an outer side or surface
**3 :** an outer manifestation **:** APPEARANCE
**4 :** the extreme limit of a guess **:** MAXIMUM ⟨the crowd numbered 10,000 at the *outside*⟩
**²outside** *adjective* (1634)
**1 a :** of, relating to, or being on or toward the outer side or surface ⟨the *outside* edge⟩ **b :** of, relating to, or being on or toward the outer side of a curve or turn **c :** of, relating to, or being on or near the outside ⟨an *outside* pitch⟩
**2 a :** situated or performed outside a particular place **b :** connected with or giving access to the outside ⟨*outside* telephone line⟩
**3 :** MAXIMUM
**4 a :** not included or originating in a particular group or organization ⟨blamed the riot on *outside* agitators⟩ **b :** not belonging to one's regular occupation or duties ⟨*outside* interests⟩
**5 :** barely possible **:** REMOTE ⟨an *outside* chance⟩
**6 :** made or done from the outside ⟨borrowed a basketball and practiced his *outside* shot⟩
**³outside** *adverb* (1813)
**1 :** on or to the outside
**2 :** OUTDOORS
**⁴outside** *preposition* (1826)
**1** — used as a function word to indicate movement to or position on the outer side of

**2 :** beyond the limits of ⟨*outside* the scope of this report⟩ ⟨*outside* the law⟩
**3 :** EXCEPT
**outside of** *preposition* (circa 1840)
**1 :** OUTSIDE
**2 :** ASIDE FROM
**out·sid·er** \,aùt-'sī-dər, 'aùt-,\ *noun* (1800)
**1 :** a person who does not belong to a particular group
**2** *chiefly British* **:** a contender not expected to win
— **out·sid·er·ness** *noun*
**out·sight** \'aùt-,sīt\ *noun* (1605)
**:** the power or act of perceiving external things ⟨the clear-eyed insight and *outsight* of the born writer —*New Yorker*⟩
**¹out·size** \'aùt-,sīz\ *noun* (1845)
**:** an unusual size; *especially* **:** a size larger than the standard
**²outsize** *also* **out·sized** \-,sīzd\ *adjective* (1880)
**1 :** unusually large or heavy
**2 :** exaggerated or extravagant in size or degree
**out·skirt** \'aùt-,skərt\ *noun* (1596)
**:** a part remote from the center **:** BORDER — usually used in plural ⟨on the *outskirts* of town⟩
**out·slick** \,aùt-'slik\ *transitive verb* (1926)
**:** to get the better of especially by trickery or cunning
**out·smart** \,aùt-'smärt\ *transitive verb* (1924)
**:** to get the better of; *especially* **:** OUTWIT
**out·sole** \'aùt-,sōl\ *noun* (1884)
**:** the outside sole of a boot or shoe
**out·sourc·ing** \,aùt-,sōr-siŋ, -,sòr-\ *noun* (1982)
**:** the practice of subcontracting manufacturing work to outside and especially foreign or non-union companies
**out·speak** \,aùt-'spēk\ *transitive verb* **-spoke** \-'spōk\; **-spo·ken** \-'spō-kən\; **-speak·ing** (1603)
**1 :** to excel in speaking
**2 :** to declare openly or boldly
**out·spend** \-'spend\ *transitive verb* (1586)
**1 :** to exceed the limits of in spending ⟨*outspends* his income⟩
**2 :** to spend more than ⟨*outspent* the other candidates⟩
**out·spent** \-'spent\ *adjective* (1652)
**:** completely worn out **:** EXHAUSTED ⟨spurred him, like an *outspent* horse, to death —P. B. Shelley⟩
**out·spo·ken** \,aùt-'spō-kən\ *adjective* (circa 1808)
**1 :** direct and open in speech or expression **:** FRANK ⟨*outspoken* in his criticism —*Current Biography*⟩
**2 :** spoken or expressed without reserve ⟨his *outspoken* advocacy of gun control⟩
— **out·spo·ken·ly** *adverb*
— **out·spo·ken·ness** \-kən-nəs\ *noun*
**out·spread** \,aùt-'spred\ *transitive verb* **-spread; -spread·ing** (14th century)
**:** to spread out
**out·stand** \,aùt-'stand\ *verb* **-stood; -stand·ing** (1571)
*transitive verb*
**:** to endure beyond ⟨I have *outstood* my time —Shakespeare⟩
*intransitive verb*
**:** STAND OUT
**out·stand·ing** \aùt-'stan-diŋ, 'aùt-,\ *adjective* (1611)
**1 :** standing out **:** PROJECTING
**2 a :** UNPAID ⟨left several bills *outstanding*⟩ **b :** continuing to exist **:** UNRESOLVED ⟨a long *outstanding* problem in astronomy⟩ **c** *of securities* **:** publicly issued and sold
**3 a :** standing out from a group **:** CONSPICUOUS **b :** marked by eminence and distinction
**synonym** *see* NOTICEABLE
— **out·stand·ing·ly** \-diŋ-lē\ *adverb*
**out·stare** \,aùt-'star, -'ster\ *transitive verb* (1596)
**:** OUTFACE 1

**out·sta·tion** \'aùt-,stā-shən\ *noun* (1844)
**:** a remote or outlying station
**out·stay** \,aùt-'stā\ *transitive verb* (1600)
**1 :** OVERSTAY 1 ⟨*outstayed* their welcome⟩
**2 :** to surpass in staying power ⟨*outstayed* his competitors⟩
**out·stretch** \,aùt-'strech\ *transitive verb* (15th century)
**:** to stretch out **:** EXTEND
**out·strip** \,aùt-'strip\ *transitive verb* [*out-* + obsolete *strip* to move fast] (1580)
**1 :** to go faster or farther than
**2 :** to get ahead of **:** leave behind ⟨has civilization *outstripped* the ability of its users to use it? —Margaret Mead⟩
**synonym** *see* EXCEED
**out·take** \'aùt-,tāk\ *noun* (1902)
**1 :** a passage outward **:** FLUE, VENT
**2 :** something that is taken out: as **a :** a take that is not used in an edited version of a film or video tape **b :** a recorded musical selection not included in a record album
**out·turn** \'aùt-,tərn\ *noun* (1800)
**:** a quantity produced **:** OUTPUT
**¹out·ward** \'aùt-wərd\ *adjective* (before 12th century)
**1 :** moving, directed, or turned toward the outside or away from a center ⟨an *outward* flow⟩
**2 :** situated on the outside **:** EXTERIOR
**3 :** of or relating to the body or to appearances rather than to the mind or the inner life ⟨*outward* beauty⟩
**4 :** EXTERNAL
**²outward** *or* **out·wards** \-wərdz\ *adverb* (before 12th century)
**1 :** toward the outside
**2** *obsolete* **:** on the outside **:** EXTERNALLY
**³outward** *noun* (1606)
**:** external form, appearance, or reality
**out·ward–bound** \,aùt-wərd-'baùnd\ *adjective* (1602)
**:** bound in an outward direction or to foreign parts ⟨an *outward-bound* ship⟩
**out·ward·ly** \'aùt-wərd-lē\ *adverb* (14th century)
**1 a :** on the outside **:** EXTERNALLY **b :** toward the outside
**2 :** in outward state, behavior, or appearance ⟨was *outwardly* friendly⟩
**out·ward·ness** \-nəs\ *noun* (1580)
**1 :** the quality or state of being external
**2 :** concern with or responsiveness to outward things
**out·wash** \'aùt-,wòsh, -,wäsh\ *noun* (1894)
**:** detritus chiefly consisting of gravel and sand carried by running water from the melting ice of a glacier and laid down in stratified deposits
**out·wear** \,aùt-'war, -'wer\ *transitive verb* **-wore** \-'wōr, -'wòr\; **-worn** \-'wōrn, -'wòrn\; **-wear·ing** (circa 1541)
**1 :** WEAR OUT, EXHAUST
**2 :** to last longer than ⟨a fabric that *outwears* others⟩
**out·weigh** \-'wā\ *transitive verb* (1597)
**:** to exceed in weight, value, or importance ⟨the advantages *outweigh* the disadvantages⟩
**out·wit** \,aùt-'wit\ *transitive verb* **-wit·ted; -wit·ting** (1652)
**1 :** to get the better of by superior cleverness **:** OUTSMART
**2** *archaic* **:** to surpass in wisdom
**¹out·work** \,aùt-'wərk\ *transitive verb* (13th century)
**1 :** WORK OUT, COMPLETE
**2 :** to work harder, faster, or better than
**²out·work** \'aùt-,wərk\ *noun* (circa 1615)
**:** a minor defensive position constructed outside a fortified area
**out·work·er** \-,wər-kər\ *noun* (1813)

---

\ə\ abut \ᵊ\ kitten \ər\ further \a\ ash \ā\ ace
\ä\ mop, mar \aù\ out \ch\ chin \e\ bet \ē\ easy
\g\ go \i\ hit \ī\ ice \j\ job \ŋ\ sing \ō\ go
\ò\ law \òi\ boy \th\ thin \t͟h\ the \ü\ loot \ù\ foot
\y\ yet \zh\ vision    *see also* Guide to Pronunciation

*chiefly British* **:** a person who works at home for a business firm

**out·worn** \ˌaût-ˈwȯrn, -ˈwȯrn\ *adjective* (1565)
**:** no longer useful or acceptable **:** OUTMODED ⟨an *outworn* social system⟩

**out–year** \ˈaût-ˌyir\ *noun* (1981)
**:** the year beyond a current fiscal year — usually used in plural except when attributive

**ou·zel** \ˈü-zəl\ *noun* [Middle English *ousel*, from Old English *ōsle* — more at MERLE] (before 12th century)
**1 :** BLACKBIRD 1a; *also* **:** a related bird (*Turdus torquatus*)
**2 :** DIPPER 1

**ou·zo** \ˈü-(ˌ)zō, -(ˌ)zȯ\ *noun* [New Greek] (1898)
**:** a colorless anise-flavored unsweetened Greek liqueur

**ov-** *or* **ovi-** *or* **ovo-** *combining form* [Latin *ov-, ovi-*, from *ovum* — more at EGG]
**:** egg ⟨*ovicide*⟩ **:** ovum ⟨*oviduct*⟩

**ova** *plural of* OVUM

**¹oval** \ˈō-vəl\ *noun* (1570)
**1 :** an oval figure or object
**2 :** a racetrack in the shape of an oval or a rectangle having rounded corners

**²oval** *adjective* [Medieval Latin *ovalis*, from Late Latin, of an egg, from Latin *ovum*] (1577)
**:** having the shape of an egg; *also* **:** broadly elliptical
— **oval·i·ty** \ō-ˈva-lə-tē\ *noun*
— **oval·ly** \-ē-əl\ *adverb*
— **oval·ness** *noun*

**ov·al·bu·min** \ˌä-val-ˈbyü-mən, ˌō-\ *noun* (circa 1836)
**1 :** the principal albumin of white of egg; *especially* **:** the crystalline part of egg albumins
**2 :** dried whites of eggs

**Oval Office** *noun* [from the *Oval Office*, the U.S. president's office in the west wing of the White House] (1962)
**:** the seat of the executive department of the U.S. government

**oval window** *noun* (1683)
**:** FENESTRA 1a

**Ovam·bo** \ō-ˈvam-(ˌ)bō, -ˈväm-\ *noun, plural* **Ovambo** *or* **Ovambos** (1853)
**1 :** a member of a Bantu people of northern Namibia
**2 :** the Bantu language of the Ovambo people

**ovar·i·an** \ō-ˈvar-ē-ən, -ˈver-\ *also* **ovar·i·al** \-ē-əl\ *adjective* (circa 1834)
**:** of, relating to, or involving an ovary

**ovari·ec·to·my** \ō-ˌvar-ē-ˈek-tə-mē, -ˌver-\ *noun, plural* **-mies** (1889)
**:** the surgical removal of an ovary
— **ovari·ec·to·mized** \-ˌmīzd\ *adjective*

**ovar·i·ole** \ō-ˈvar-ē-ˌōl, -ˈver-\ *noun* [(assumed) New Latin *ovariolum*, diminutive of *ovarium*] (1877)
**:** one of the tubes of which the ovaries of most insects are composed

**ovar·i·ot·o·my** \ō-ˌvar-ē-ˈä-tə-mē, -ˌver-\ *noun, plural* **-mies** (1844)
**1 :** surgical incision of an ovary
**2 :** OVARIECTOMY

**ova·ry** \ˈō-və-rē, ˈōv-rē\ *noun, plural* **-ries** [New Latin *ovarium*, from Latin *ovum* egg] (1658)
**1 :** one of the typically paired essential female reproductive organs that produce eggs and in vertebrates female sex hormones
**2 :** the enlarged rounded usually basal portion of the pistil or gynoecium of an angiospermous plant that bears the ovules and consists of one or more carpels — see FLOWER illustration

**ovate** \ˈō-ˌvāt\ *adjective* (1760)
**1 :** shaped like an egg
**2 :** having an outline like a longitudinal section of an egg with the basal end broader ⟨*ovate* leaves⟩ — see LEAF illustration

**ova·tion** \ō-ˈvā-shən\ *noun* [Latin *ovation-, ovatio*, from *ovare* to exult; akin to Greek *euoi*, interjection used in bacchic revels] (1533)
**1 :** a ceremony attending the entering of Rome by a general who had won a victory of less importance than that for which a triumph was granted
**2 :** an expression or demonstration of popular acclaim especially by enthusiastic applause ⟨received a standing *ovation*⟩

**ov·en** \ˈə-vən\ *noun* [Middle English, from Old English *ofen*; akin to Old High German *ofan* oven and perhaps to Greek *ipnos* oven] (before 12th century)
**:** a chamber used for baking, heating, or drying

**ov·en·bird** \-ˌbərd\ *noun* [from the shape of its nest] (circa 1825)
**1 :** any of various South American small brown passerine birds (genus *Furnarius*)
**2 :** an American warbler (*Seiurus aurocapillus*) that builds a dome-shaped nest on the ground

ovenbird 2

**ov·en·proof** \-ˌprüf\ *adjective* (circa 1940)
**:** capable of withstanding the temperature range of a kitchen oven ⟨*ovenproof* dishes⟩

**¹over** \ˈō-vər\ *adverb* & *preposition*, from Old English *ofer*; akin to Old High German *ubar* (preposition) above, beyond, over, Latin *super*, Greek *hyper*] (before 12th century)
**1 a :** across a barrier or intervening space; *especially* **:** across the goal line in football **b :** forward beyond an edge or brink and often down ⟨wandered too near the cliff and fell *over*⟩ **c :** across the brim ⟨soup boiled *over*⟩ **d :** so as to bring the underside up ⟨turned his cards *over*⟩ **e :** from a vertical to a prone or inclined position ⟨knocked the lamp *over*⟩ **f :** from one person or side to another ⟨hand it *over*⟩ **g :** ACROSS ⟨got his point *over*⟩ **h :** to one's home ⟨invite some friends *over*⟩ **i :** on the other side of an intervening space ⟨the next town *over*⟩ **j :** to agreement or concord ⟨won them *over*⟩
**2 a** (1) **:** beyond some quantity, limit, or norm often by a specified amount or to a specified degree ⟨show ran a minute *over*⟩ (2) **:** in an excessive manner **:** INORDINATELY **b :** till a later time (as the next day) **:** OVERNIGHT ⟨stay *over*⟩ ⟨sleep *over*⟩
**3 a :** ABOVE **b :** so as to cover the whole surface ⟨windows boarded *over*⟩
**4** — used on a two-way radio circuit to indicate that a message is complete and a reply is expected
**5 a :** THROUGH ⟨read it *over*⟩; *also* **:** in an intensive or comprehensive manner **b :** once more **:** AGAIN ⟨do it *over*⟩

**²over** *preposition* (before 12th century)
**1** — used as a function word to indicate motion or situation in a position higher than or above another ⟨towered *over* his mother⟩ ⟨flew *over* the lake⟩ ⟨rode *over* the old Roman road⟩
**2 a** — used as a function word to indicate the possession of authority, power, or jurisdiction in regard to some thing or person ⟨respected those *over* him⟩ **b** — used as a function word to indicate superiority, advantage, or preference ⟨a big lead *over* the others⟩ **c** — used as a function word to indicate one that is overcome, circumvented, or disregarded ⟨passed *over* the governor's veto⟩
**3 a :** more than ⟨cost *over* $5⟩ **b :** ABOVE 4

**4 a** — used as a function word to indicate position upon or movement down upon ⟨laid a blanket *over* the child⟩ ⟨hit him *over* the head⟩ **b :** all through or throughout ⟨showed me *over* the house⟩ ⟨went *over* his notes⟩ (2) — used as a function word connecting one mathematical set and another whose elements are coefficients or values of parameters used to form elements of the first set ⟨polynomials *over* the field of real numbers⟩ **c** — used as a function word to indicate a particular medium or channel of communication ⟨*over* the radio⟩
**5** — used as a function word to indicate position on or motion to the other side or beyond ⟨lives *over* the way⟩ ⟨fell *over* the edge⟩
**6 a :** THROUGHOUT, DURING ⟨*over* the past 25 years⟩ **b :** until the end of ⟨stay *over* Sunday⟩
**7 a** — used as a function word to indicate an object of solicitude, interest, consideration, or reference ⟨the Lord watches *over* his own⟩ **b** — used as a function word to indicate the object of an expressed or implied occupation, activity, or concern ⟨trouble *over* money⟩ ⟨met with advisers *over* lunch⟩ ▫

**³over** *adjective* (before 12th century)
**1 a :** UPPER, HIGHER **b :** OUTER, COVERING **c :** EXCESSIVE ⟨*over* imagination⟩
**2 a :** not used up **:** REMAINING ⟨something *over* to provide for unusual requirements —J. A. Todd⟩ **b :** having or showing an excess or surplus
**3 :** being at an end ⟨the day is *over*⟩
**4 :** fried on both sides ⟨ordered two eggs *over*⟩
— **over easy :** fried on one side then turned and fried lightly on the other side ⟨eggs *over easy*⟩

**⁴over** *transitive verb* **overed; over·ing** \ˈō-və-riŋ, ˈōv-riŋ\ (1837)
**:** to leap over

**over-** *prefix*
**1 :** so as to exceed or surpass ⟨*over*achieve⟩
**2 :** EXCESSIVE ⟨*over*stimulation⟩
**3 :** to an excessive degree ⟨*over*thin⟩

| | |
|---|---|
| over·ab·stract | over·anx·ious |
| over·abun·dance | over·ap·pli·ca·tion |
| over·abun·dant | over·arous·al |
| over·ac·cen·tu·ate | over·ar·range |
| over·ad·just·ment | over·ar·tic·u·late |
| over·ad·ver·tise | over·as·sert |
| over·ag·gres·sive | over·as·ser·tion |
| over·alert | over·as·ser·tive |
| over·am·bi·tious | over·as·sess·ment |
| over·am·bi·tious- | over·at·ten·tion |
| ness | over·bake |
| over·am·pli·fied | over·beat |
| over·anal·y·sis | over·be·jew·eled |
| over·an·a·lyt·i·cal | over·bill |
| over·an·a·lyze | over·bleach |
| over·anx·i·ety | over·boil |

over·bold
over·bor·row
over·breath·ing
over·brief
over·bright
over·broad
over·browse
over·bru·tal
over·burn
over·busy
over·care·ful
over·cau·tion
over·cau·tious
over·cen·tral·i·za·tion
over·cen·tral·ize
over·chill
over·civ·i·lized
over·claim
over·clas·si·fi·ca·tion
over·clas·si·fy
over·clean
over·clear
over·coach
over·com·mer·cial·i·za·tion
over·com·mer·cial·ize
over·com·mu·ni·cate
over·com·mu·ni·ca·tion
over·com·plex
over·com·pli·ance
over·com·pli·cate
over·com·pli·cat·ed
over·com·press
over·con·cen·tra·tion
over·con·cern
over·con·cerned
over·con·fi·dence
over·con·fi·dent
over·con·fi·dent·ly
over·con·sci·en·tious
over·con·scious
over·con·ser·va·tive
over·con·struct
over·con·sume
over·con·sump·tion
over·con·trol
over·cook
over·cool
over·cor·rect
over·count
over·cred·u·lous
over·crit·i·cal
over·cul·ti·va·tion
over·cure
over·dec·o·rate
over·dec·o·ra·tion
over·de·mand·ing
over·de·pen·dence
over·de·pen·dent
over·de·sign
over·dif·fer·en·ti·a·tion
over·di·rect
over·dis·count
over·di·ver·si·ty
over·doc·u·ment
over·dra·mat·ic
over·dra·ma·tize
over·drink
over·dry
over·ea·ger
over·ea·ger·ness
over·ear·nest
over·ed·it
over·ed·u·cate
over·ed·u·cat·ed
over·ed·u·ca·tion
over·elab·o·rate
over·elab·o·ra·tion
over·em·bel·lish

over·emote
over·emo·tion·al
over·em·pha·sis
over·em·pha·size
over·em·phat·ic
over·en·am·ored
over·en·cour·age
over·en·er·get·ic
over·en·gi·neer
over·en·rolled
over·en·ter·tained
over·en·thu·si·asm
over·en·thu·si·as·tic
over·equipped
over·es·ti·mate
over·es·ti·ma·tion
over·eval·u·a·tion
over·ex·ag·ger·ate
over·ex·ag·ger·a·tion
over·ex·cite
over·ex·cit·ed
over·ex·er·cise
over·ex·ert
over·ex·er·tion
over·ex·pand
over·ex·pan·sion
over·ex·pec·ta·tion
over·ex·plain
over·ex·plic·it
over·ex·ploit
over·ex·ploi·ta·tion
over·ex·trac·tion
over·ex·trap·o·la·tion
over·ex·trav·a·gant
over·ex·u·ber·ant
over·fac·ile
over·fa·mil·iar
over·fa·mil·iar·i·ty
over·fas·tid·i·ous
over·fat
over·fa·vor
over·fer·til·i·za·tion
over·fer·til·ize
over·fo·cus
over·fond
over·ful·fill
over·fund
over·fussy
over·gen·er·al·i·za·tion
over·gen·er·al·ize
over·gen·er·os·i·ty
over·gen·er·ous
over·gen·er·ous·ly
over·glam·or·ize
over·gov·ern
over·han·dle
over·har·vest
over·hasty
over·ho·mog·e·nize
over·hunt
over·hunt·ing
over·hype
over·ide·al·ize
over·iden·ti·fi·ca·tion
over·iden·ti·fy
over·imag·i·na·tive
over·im·press
over·in·debt·ed·ness
over·in·dulge
over·in·dul·gence
over·in·dul·gent
over·in·dus·tri·al·ize
over·in·flate
over·in·flat·ed
over·in·fla·tion
over·in·form
over·in·formed
over·in·ge·nious
over·in·ge·nu·ity
over·in·sis·tent
over·in·tel·lec·tu·al·i·za·tion
over·in·tel·lec·tu·al·ize

over·in·tense
over·in·ten·si·ty
over·in·ter·pre·ta·tion
over·in·vest·ment
over·la·bor
over·la·bored
over·lad·en
over·large
over·lav·ish
over·lend
over·length
over·length·en
over·light
over·lit·er·al
over·lit·er·ary
over·load
over·long
over·loud
over·lush
over·man·age
over·man·nered
over·ma·ture
over·ma·tu·ri·ty
over·med·i·cate
over·med·i·ca·tion
over·mighty
over·milk
over·mine
over·mix
over·mod·est
over·mod·est·ly
over·mus·cled
over·nice
over·nour·ish
over·nu·tri·tion
over·ob·vi·ous
over·op·er·ate
over·opin·ion·at·ed
over·op·ti·mism
over·op·ti·mist
over·op·ti·mis·tic
over·op·ti·mis·ti·cal·ly
over·or·ches·trate
over·or·ga·nize
over·or·ga·nized
over·or·na·ment
over·pack·age
over·par·tic·u·lar
over·pay
over·pay·ment
over·ped·al
over·peo·ple
over·plan
over·plant
over·plot
over·po·tent
over·praise
over·pre·cise
over·pre·scribe
over·pre·scrip·tion
over·priv·i·leged
over·prize
over·pro·cess
over·pro·duce
over·pro·duc·tion
over·pro·gram
over·prom·ise
over·pro·mote
over·pro·tect
over·pro·tec·tion
over·pro·tec·tive
over·pro·tec·tive·ness
over·pump

**over·achiev·er** \ˌō-və-rə-'chē-vər\ noun (1952)
**:** one who achieves success over and above the standard or expected level especially at an early age
— **over·achieve** \-'chēv\ intransitive verb
— **over·achieve·ment** \-mənt\ noun
**over·act** \ˌō-vər-'akt\ (1611)
intransitive verb

over·rate
over·re·act
over·re·ac·tion
over·re·fined
over·re·fine·ment
over·reg·u·late
over·reg·u·la·tion
over·re·li·ance
over·re·port
over·re·spond
over·rich
over·rig·id
over·salt
over·san·guine
over·sat·u·rate
over·sat·u·ra·tion
over·sauce
over·scru·pu·lous
over·se·cre·tion
over·sen·si·tive
over·sen·si·tive·ness
over·sen·si·tiv·i·ty
over·se·ri·ous
over·se·ri·ous·ly
over·ser·vice
over·sim·plis·tic
over·smoke
over·so·lic·i·tous
over·so·phis·ti·cat·ed
over·spe·cial·i·za·tion
over·spe·cial·ize
over·spec·u·late
over·spec·u·la·tion
over·sta·bil·i·ty
over·staff
over·stim·u·late
over·stim·u·la·tion
over·stock
over·strain
over·stress
over·stretch
over·struc·tured
over·sub·tle
over·suds
over·sup·ply
over·sus·pi·cious
over·sweet
over·sweet·en
over·sweet·ness
over·swing
over·talk
over·talk·a·tive
over·tax
over·tax·a·tion
over·thin
over·think
over·tight·en
over·tip
over·tired
over·train
over·treat
over·treat·ment
over·use
over·uti·li·za·tion
over·uti·lize
over·vi·o·lent
over·viv·id
over·wa·ter
over·wea·ry
over·wind
over·with·hold
over·zeal·ous
over·zeal·ous·ness

**1 :** to act more than is necessary
**2 :** to overact a part
transitive verb
**:** to exaggerate in acting
— **over·ac·tion** \-'ak-shən\ noun
**over·ac·tive** \-'ak-tiv\ adjective (1854)
**:** excessively or abnormally active
— **over·ac·tiv·i·ty** \-ak-'ti-və-tē\ noun
**over against** preposition (1517)
**:** as opposed to **:** in contrast with
**¹over·age** \ˌō-vər-'āj\ also **over·aged** \-'ājd\ adjective [²over + age] (15th century)
**1 :** too old to be useful
**2 :** older than is normal for one's position, function, or grade
**²over·age** \'ō-və-rij, 'ōv-rij\ noun [³over + -age] (1909)
**:** SURPLUS, EXCESS
**¹over·all** \ˌō-vər-'ȯl\ adverb (13th century)
**1 :** ALL OVER 1 ⟨the pattern used overall⟩
**2 :** from one end to the other ⟨600 feet long overall⟩
**3 a :** in view of all the circumstances or conditions ⟨overall, the sale was a success⟩ **b :** as a whole : GENERALLY ⟨doesn't do as well overall⟩ **c :** with everyone or everything taken into account ⟨was third overall in earnings⟩ ⟨got 31 miles to the gallon overall⟩
**²over·all** \'ō-vər-,ȯl\ noun (1815)
**1** plural **a** archaic **:** loose protective trousers worn over regular clothes **b :** trousers of strong material usually with a bib and shoulder straps
**2** chiefly British **:** a loose-fitting protective smock worn over regular clothing
**³over·all** \ˌō-vər-'ȯl, 'ō-vər-,\ adjective (1894)
**1 :** including everything
**2 :** viewed as a whole **:** GENERAL
**over·alled** \'ō-vər-,ȯld\ adjective (1908)
**:** wearing overalls
**over and above** preposition (15th century)
**:** in addition to **:** BESIDES
**over and over** adverb (15th century)
**:** REPEATEDLY
**over·arch·ing** \ˌō-vər-'är-chiŋ\ adjective (1720)
**1 :** forming an arch overhead
**2 :** dominating or embracing all else ⟨overarching goals⟩
**over·arm** \'ō-vər-,ärm\ adjective (1864)
**1 :** OVERHAND
**2** of a swimming stroke **:** made with the arm lifted out of the water and stretched forward over the shoulder to begin the stroke
**over·awe** \ˌō-vər-'ȯ\ transitive verb (1579)
**:** to restrain or subdue by awe
**¹over·bal·ance** \ˌō-vər-'ba-lən(t)s\ transitive verb (1608)
**1 :** OUTWEIGH
**2 :** to cause to lose balance
**²over·bal·ance** \'ō-vər-,\ noun (1659)
**:** something more than an equivalent
**over·bear** \ˌō-vər-'bar, -'ber\ transitive verb **-bore** \-'bōr, -'bȯr\; **-borne** \-'bōrn, -'bȯrn\ also **-born** \-'bȯrn\; **-bear·ing** (1535)
**1 :** to bring down by superior weight or force **:** OVERWHELM
**2 a :** to domineer over **b :** to surpass in importance or cogency **:** OUTWEIGH
**overbearing** adjective (circa 1677)
**1 a :** tending to overwhelm **:** OVERPOWERING **b :** decisively important **:** DOMINANT
**2 :** harshly and haughtily arrogant
**synonym** see PROUD
— **over·bear·ing·ly** \-iŋ-lē\ adverb
**over·bid** \ˌō-vər-'bid\ verb **-bid; -bid·ding** (circa 1616)
intransitive verb
**1 :** to bid in excess of value

---

\ə\ abut \ᵊ\ kitten \ər\ further \a\ ash \ā\ ace
\ä\ mop, mar \aú\ out \ch\ chin \e\ bet \ē\ easy
\g\ go \i\ hit \ī\ ice \j\ job \ŋ\ sing \ō\ go
\ȯ\ law \ȯi\ boy \th\ thin \th\ the \ü\ loot \ú\ foot
\y\ yet \zh\ vision   see also Guide to Pronunciation

**2 a :** to bid more than the scoring capacity of a hand at cards **b** *British* **:** to make a higher bid than the preceding one
*transitive verb*
**:** to bid beyond or in excess of; *especially* **:** to bid more than the value of (one's hand at cards)
— **over·bid** \'ō-vər-ˌbid\ *noun*

**over·bite** \'ō-vər-ˌbīt\ *noun* (1887)
**:** the projection of the upper anterior teeth over the lower in the normal occlusal position of the jaws

**over·blouse** \-ˌblaús, -ˌblaúz\ *noun* (1921)
**:** a usually fitted or belted blouse worn untucked

**¹over·blown** \ˌō-vər-'blōn\ *adjective* [³*blow*] (1616)
**:** past the prime of bloom ⟨*overblown* roses⟩

**²overblown** *adjective* [¹*blow*] (1864)
**1 :** excessively large in girth **:** PORTLY
**2 :** INFLATED ⟨*overblown* claims⟩ ⟨*overblown* rhetoric⟩; *also* **:** PRETENTIOUS

**over·board** \'ō-vər-ˌbōrd, -ˌbórd\ *adverb* (before 12th century)
**1 :** over the side of a ship or boat into the water
**2 :** to extremes of enthusiasm
**3 :** into discard **:** ASIDE

**over·book** \ˌō-vər-'búk\ (1903)
*transitive verb*
**:** to issue reservations for (as an airplane flight) in excess of the space available
*intransitive verb*
**:** to issue reservations in excess of the space available

**over·bought** \-'bót\ *adjective* (1929)
**:** not likely to show an immediate rise in price because of prior heavy buying and accompanying price rises ⟨an *overbought* market⟩

**over·build** \-'bild\ *verb* **-built** \-'bilt\; **-building** (1601)
*transitive verb*
**:** to build beyond the actual demand of
*intransitive verb*
**:** to build houses or commercial developments in excess of demand

**¹over·bur·den** \-'bər-d°n\ *transitive verb* (1532)
**:** to place an excessive burden on

**²over·bur·den** \'ō-vər-ˌbər-d°n\ *noun* (1855)
**:** material overlying a deposit of useful geological materials or bedrock

**over·buy** \ˌō-vər-'bī\ *verb* **-bought** \-'bót\; **-buy·ing** (1745)
*transitive verb*
**:** to buy in excess of needs or demand
*intransitive verb*
**:** to make purchases beyond one's needs or in excess of one's ability to pay

**over·call** \-'kól\ (circa 1903)
*transitive verb*
**:** to make a higher bid than (the previous bid or bidder) in a card game
*intransitive verb*
**:** to bid over an opponent's bid in bridge when one's partner has not bid or doubled
— **over·call** \'ō-vər-ˌkól\ *noun*

**over·ca·pac·i·ty** \ˌō-vər-kə-'pa-sə-tē, -'pas-tē\ *noun* (1928)
**:** excessive capacity for production or services in relation to demand

**over·cap·i·tal·ize** \-'ka-pə-t°l-ˌīz, -'kap-t°l-\ *transitive verb* (1890)
**1 :** to put a nominal value on the capital of (a corporation) higher than actual cost or fair market value
**2 :** to capitalize beyond what the business or the profit-making prospects warrant
— **over·cap·i·tal·i·za·tion** \-ˌka-pə-t°l-ə-'zā-shən, -ˌkap-t°l-\ *noun*

**¹over·cast** *transitive verb* **-cast; -cast·ing** (14th century)
**1** \ˌō-vər-'kast, 'ō-vər-ˌ\ **:** DARKEN, OVERSHADOW

**2** \'ō-vər-ˌ\ **:** to sew (raw edges of a seam) with long slanting widely spaced stitches to prevent raveling

**²over·cast** \'ō-vər-ˌkast, ˌō-vər-'\ *adjective* (1536)
**:** clouded over ⟨an *overcast* day⟩

**³over·cast** \'ō-vər-ˌkast\ *noun* (1686)
**:** COVERING; *especially* **:** a covering of clouds over the sky

**over·cast·ing** \'ō-vər-ˌkas-tiŋ\ *noun* (1885)
**:** the act of stitching raw edges of fabric to prevent raveling; *also* **:** the stitching so done

**overcast stitch** *noun* (1891)
**:** a small close embroidery stitch sometimes done over a foundation thread and used to form outlines

overcast stitch

**over·charge** \ˌō-vər-'chärj\ (14th century)
*transitive verb*
**1 :** to charge too much or too fully
**2 :** to fill too full
**3 :** EXAGGERATE, OVERDRAW
*intransitive verb*
**:** to make an excessive charge
— **over·charge** \'ō-vər-ˌ\ *noun*

**over·cloud** \ˌō-vər-'klaúd\ *transitive verb* (1592)
**:** to overspread with or as if with clouds

**over·coat** \'ō-vər-ˌkōt\ *noun* (1802)
**1 :** a warm coat worn over indoor clothing
**2 :** a protective coating (as of paint)

**over·come** \ˌō-vər-'kəm\ *verb* **-came** \-'kām\; **-come; -com·ing** [Middle English, from Old English *ofercuman*, from *ofer* over + *cuman* to come] (before 12th century)
*transitive verb*
**1 :** to get the better of **:** SURMOUNT ⟨*overcome* difficulties⟩
**2 :** OVERWHELM
*intransitive verb*
**:** to gain the superiority **:** WIN
*synonym* see CONQUER
— **over·com·er** *noun*

**over·com·mit** \-kə-'mit\ *transitive verb* (1951)
**:** to commit excessively: as **a :** to obligate (as oneself) beyond the ability for fulfillment **b :** to allocate (resources) in excess of the capacity for replenishment
— **over·com·mit·ment** \-mənt\ *noun*

**over·com·pen·sa·tion** \-ˌkäm-pən-'sā-shən, -ˌpen-\ *noun* (1912)
**:** excessive compensation; *specifically* **:** excessive reaction to a feeling of inferiority, guilt, or inadequacy leading to an exaggerated attempt to overcome the feeling
— **over·com·pen·sate** \-'käm-pən-ˌsāt\ *verb*
— **over·com·pen·sa·to·ry** \-kəm-'pen(t)-sə-ˌtōr-ē, -ˌtór-\ *adjective*

**over·crowd** \ˌō-vər-'kraúd\ (1766)
*transitive verb*
**:** to cause to be too crowded
*intransitive verb*
**:** to crowd together too much

**over·cut** \-'kət\ *transitive verb* (1906)
**:** to cut excessively; *specifically* **:** to cut timber from (a forest) in excess of annual growth or an allotted annual amount

**over·de·ter·mined** \-di-'tər-mənd\ *adjective* (1915)
**1 :** excessively determined
**2 :** having more than one determining psychological factor

**over·de·vel·op** \-di-'ve-ləp\ *transitive verb* (1869)
**:** to develop excessively; *especially* **:** to subject (exposed photographic material) to a developing solution for excessive time or at excessive temperature, agitation, or concentration
— **over·de·vel·op·ment** \-mənt\ *noun*

**over·do** \ˌō-vər-'dü\ *verb* **-did** \-'did\; **-done** \-'dən\; **-do·ing** \-'dü-iŋ\; **-does** \-'dəz\ (before 12th century)
*transitive verb*
**1 a :** to do in excess **b :** to use to excess **c :** EXAGGERATE
**2 :** to cook too long
**3 :** EXHAUST
*intransitive verb*
**:** to go to extremes

**over·dog** \'ō-vər-ˌdóg\ *noun* [³*over* + *underdog*] (1938)
**:** one that is dominant or victorious

**over·dom·i·nance** \ˌō-vər-'dä-mə-nən(t)s, -'däm-nən(t)s\ *noun* (1947)
**:** the condition wherein a heterozygote produces a phenotype more extreme or better adapted than that of the homozygote
— **over·dom·i·nant** \-nənt\ *adjective*

**¹over·dose** \'ō-vər-ˌdōs\ *noun* (1700)
**1 :** too great a dose (as of a therapeutic agent); *also* **:** a lethal or toxic amount (as of a drug)
**2 :** an excessive quantity or amount ⟨an *overdose* of sports⟩
— **over·dos·age** \ˌō-vər-'dō-sij\ *noun*

**²over·dose** \ˌō-vər-'dōs\ (1727)
*transitive verb*
**:** to give an overdose or too many doses to
*intransitive verb*
**:** to take or experience an overdose — usually used with *on*

**over·draft** \'ō-vər-ˌdraft\ *noun* (1878)
**1 :** an act of overdrawing at a bank **:** the state of being overdrawn; *also* **:** the sum overdrawn
**2 :** LINE OF CREDIT

**over·draw** \ˌō-vər-'dró\ *verb* **-drew** \-'drü\; **-drawn** \-'drón\; **-draw·ing** (1734)
*transitive verb*
**1 :** to draw checks on (a bank account) for more than the balance ⟨the account was *overdrawn*⟩
**2 :** EXAGGERATE, OVERSTATE
*intransitive verb*
**:** to make an overdraft

**over·drawn** *adjective* (1866)
**:** having an overdrawn account

**¹over·dress** \ˌō-vər-'dres\ (1706)
*transitive verb*
**:** to dress or adorn to excess
*intransitive verb*
**:** to dress oneself to excess

**²over·dress** \'ō-vər-ˌdres\ *noun* (1812)
**:** a dress worn over another

**over·drive** \'ō-vər-ˌdrīv\ *noun* (1926)
**1 :** an automotive transmission gear that transmits to the drive shaft a speed greater than engine speed
**2 :** a state of heightened activity ⟨going into rhetorical *overdrive*⟩

**¹over·dub** \'ō-vər-ˌdəb\ *noun* (circa 1965)
**1 :** the act or an instance of overdubbing
**2 :** recorded sound that is overdubbed ⟨vocal *overdubs*⟩

**²over·dub** \ˌō-vər-'dəb\ *transitive verb* (1967)
**:** to transfer (recorded sound) onto a recording that bears sound recorded earlier in order to produce a combined effect

**over·due** \-'dü, -'dyü\ *adjective* (1845)
**1 a :** unpaid when due **b :** delayed beyond an appointed time
**2 :** too great **:** EXCESSIVE
**3 :** more than ready

**over·eat** \ˌō-vər-'ēt\ *intransitive verb* **over·ate** \-'āt\; **over·eat·en** \-'ē-t°n\; **over·eat·ing** (1599)
**:** to eat to excess
— **over·eat·er** \ˌō-vər-'ē-tər, 'ō-vər-ˌ\ *noun*

**over·ex·pose** \ˌō-vər-ik-'spōz\ *transitive verb* (1869)
**:** to expose excessively; *especially* **:** to expose (as film) to excessive radiation (as light)
— **over·ex·po·sure** \-'spō-zhər\ *noun*

**over·ex·tend** \ˌō-vər-ik-'stend\ *transitive verb* (1937)

: to extend or expand beyond a safe or reasonable point; *especially* : to commit (oneself) financially beyond what can be paid
— **over·ex·ten·sion** \-'sten(t)-shən\ *noun*
**over·fa·tigue** \ˌō-vər-fə-'tēg\ *noun* (1727)
: excessive fatigue especially when carried beyond the recuperative capacity of the individual
— **over·fa·tigued** \-'tēgd\ *adjective*
**over·feed** \ˌō-vər-'fēd\ *verb* **-fed** \-'fed\; **-feed·ing** (1608)
*transitive verb*
: to feed to excess
*intransitive verb*
: to eat to excess
**over·fill** \-'fil\ (13th century)
*transitive verb*
: to fill to overflowing
*intransitive verb*
: to become full to overflowing
**over·fish** \-'fish\ *transitive verb* (1867)
: to fish to the detriment of (a fishing ground) or to the depletion of (a kind of organism)
**over·flight** \'ō-vər-ˌflīt\ *noun* (1950)
: a passage over an area in an airplane
¹**over·flow** \ˌō-vər-'flō\ (before 12th century)
*transitive verb*
**1** : to cover with or as if with water : INUNDATE
**2** : to flow over the brim of
**3** : to cause to overflow
*intransitive verb*
**1** : to flow over bounds
**2** : to fill a space to capacity and spread beyond its limits ⟨the crowd *overflowed* into the street⟩
²**over·flow** \'ō-vər-ˌflō\ *noun* (1589)
**1** : a flowing over : INUNDATION
**2** : something that flows over : SURPLUS
**3** : an outlet or receptacle for surplus liquid
**over·fly** \ˌō-vər-'flī\ *transitive verb* **-flew** \-'flü\; **-flown** \-'flōn\; **-fly·ing** (14th century)
: to fly over; *especially* : to pass over in an airplane or spacecraft
**over·gar·ment** \'ō-vər-ˌgär-mənt\ *noun* (15th century)
: an outer garment
**over·glaze** \-ˌglāz\ *adjective* (1879)
: applied or suitable for applying on top of a fired glaze ⟨*overglaze* enamels⟩
— **overglaze** *noun*
**over·graze** \ˌō-vər-'grāz\ *transitive verb* (1919)
: to allow animals to graze (as a pasture) to the point of damaging vegetational cover
**over·grow** \ˌō-vər-'grō\ *verb* **-grew** \-'grü\; **-grown** \-'grōn\; **-grow·ing** (14th century)
*transitive verb*
**1** : to grow over so as to cover with herbage
**2** : to grow beyond or rise above : OUTGROW
*intransitive verb*
**1** : to grow excessively
**2** : to become grown over
— **over·growth** \'ō-vər-ˌgrōth\ *noun*
**overgrown** *adjective* (1604)
: grown abnormally or excessively large ⟨dismissed him as an *overgrown* adolescent⟩
¹**over·hand** \'ō-vər-ˌhand\ *adjective* (1656)
: made with the hand brought forward and down from above shoulder level
— **overhand** *adverb*
— **over·hand·ed** \ˌō-vər-'han-dəd\ *adverb or adjective*
²**overhand** *transitive verb* (1871)
: to sew with short vertical stitches
³**overhand** *noun* (circa 1934)
: an overhand stroke (as in handball)
**overhand knot** *noun* (1840)
: a small knot often used to prevent the end of a cord from fraying — see KNOT illustration
¹**over·hang** \'ō-vər-ˌhaŋ, ˌō-vər-'\ *verb* **-hung** \-ˌhəŋ, -'həŋ\; **-hang·ing** (1592)
*transitive verb*
**1** : to project over
**2** : to impend over : THREATEN

*intransitive verb*
: to project so as to be over something
²**over·hang** \'ō-vər-ˌhaŋ\ *noun* (1864)
**1** : the part of the bow or stern of a ship that projects over the water above the waterline
**2** : something that overhangs; *also* : the extent of the overhanging
**3** : a projection of the roof or upper story of a building beyond the wall of the lower part
**4** : an excess supply of a commodity that cannot be readily converted, sold, or disposed of ⟨dollar *overhang*⟩ ⟨inventory *overhang*⟩
**over·haul** \ˌō-vər-'hȯl\ *transitive verb* (1705)
**1 a** : to examine thoroughly **b** (1) : REPAIR (2) : to renovate, revise, or renew thoroughly
**2** : to haul or drag over
**3** : OVERTAKE
— **over·haul** \'ō-vər-ˌhȯl\ *noun*
¹**over·head** \ˌō-vər-'hed\ *adverb* (15th century)
: above one's head : ALOFT
²**over·head** \'ō-vər-ˌhed\ *adjective* (1874)
**1 a** : operating, lying, or coming from above **b** : having the driving part above the part driven ⟨valves operated by an *overhead* camshaft⟩
**2** : of or relating to overhead ⟨*overhead* costs⟩
³**over·head** \'ō-vər-ˌhed\ *noun* (1914)
**1** : business expenses (as rent, insurance, or heating) not chargeable to a particular part of the work or product
**2** : CEILING; *especially* : the ceiling of a ship's compartment
**3** : a stroke in a racket game made above head height : SMASH
**overhead projector** *noun* (1951)
: a projector for projecting onto a vertical screen magnified images of graphic material on a horizontal transparency illuminated from below — called also *overhead*
**over·hear** \ˌō-vər-'hir\ *verb* **-heard** \-'hərd\; **-hear·ing** \-'hir-iŋ\ (1549)
*transitive verb*
: to hear without the speaker's knowledge or intention
*intransitive verb*
: to overhear something
**over·heat** \-'hēt\ (14th century)
*transitive verb*
**1** : to heat to excess
**2** : to stimulate or agitate unduly
*intransitive verb*
: to become heated beyond a safe or desirable point
**over·heat·ed** \-'hē-təd\ *adjective* (1953)
: PERFERVID
**over·is·sue** \ˌō-vər-'i-(ˌ)shü\ *noun* (1803)
: an issue exceeding the limit of capital, credit, or authority
— **over·is·su·ance** \-'i-shə-wən(t)s\ *noun*
— **overissue** *transitive verb*
**over·joyed** \-'jȯid\ *adjective* (1594)
: feeling great joy
¹**over·kill** \ˌō-vər-'kil\ *transitive verb* (1957)
: to obliterate (a target) with more nuclear force than required
²**over·kill** \'ō-vər-ˌkil\ *noun* (1958)
**1** : a destructive capacity greatly exceeding that required for a given target
**2** : an excess of something (as a quantity or an action) beyond what is required or suitable for a particular purpose ⟨a propaganda *overkill*⟩ ⟨an *overkill* in weaponry⟩
**3** : killing in excess of what is intended or required
¹**over·land** \'ō-vər-ˌland, -lənd\ *adverb* (12th century)
: by, on, or across land
²**overland** *adjective* (1800)
: going or accomplished over the land instead of by sea ⟨*overland* emigrants⟩ ⟨an *overland* route⟩
**over·lap** \ˌō-vər-'lap\ (1726)
*transitive verb*
**1** : to extend over or past and cover a part of
**2** : to have something in common with
*intransitive verb*

**1** : to occupy the same area in part : lap over
**2** : to have something in common
— **over·lap** \'ō-vər-ˌlap\ *noun*
¹**over·lay** \ˌō-vər-'lā\ *transitive verb* **-laid** \-'lād\; **-lay·ing** (14th century)
**1 a** : to lay or spread over or across : SUPERIMPOSE **b** : to prepare an overlay for
**2** : OVERLIE 2
²**over·lay** \'ō-vər-ˌlā\ *noun* (1794)
: a covering either permanent or temporary: as **a** : an ornamental veneer **b** : a decorative and contrasting design or article placed on top of a plain one **c** : a transparent sheet containing graphic matter to be superimposed on another sheet
**over·leaf** \'ō-vər-ˌlēf, -'lēf\ *adverb* (1843)
: on the other side of a leaf (as of a book)
**over·leap** \ˌō-vər-'lēp\ *transitive verb* **-leaped** *or* **-leapt** \-'lēpt *also* -'lept\; **-leap·ing** \-'lē-piŋ\ (before 12th century)
**1** : to leap over or across
**2** : to defeat (oneself) by going too far
**over·learn** \-'lərn\ *transitive verb* (1874)
: to continue to study or practice after attaining proficiency
**over·lie** \-'lī\ *transitive verb* **-lay** \-'lā\; **-lain** \-'lān\; **-ly·ing** \-'lī-iŋ\ (13th century)
**1** : to lie over or upon
**2** : to cause the death of by lying upon
¹**over·look** \-'lu̇k\ *transitive verb* (14th century)
**1** : to look over : INSPECT
**2 a** : to look down upon from above **b** : to rise above or afford a view of
**3 a** : to look past : MISS **b** : IGNORE 1 **c** : EXCUSE 2
**4** : SUPERINTEND, OVERSEE
**5** : to look on with the evil eye : BEWITCH
*synonym* see NEGLECT
²**over·look** \'ō-vər-ˌlu̇k\ *noun* (1861)
: a place from which one may look down on a scene below ⟨plenty of *overlooks* and trails —Thelma H. Bell⟩
**over·lord** \'ō-vər-ˌlȯrd\ *noun* (13th century)
**1** : a lord over other lords : a lord paramount
**2 a** : an absolute or supreme ruler **b** : one having great power or authority ⟨a corporate *overlord*⟩
— **over·lord·ship** \-ˌship, ˌō-vər-'\ *noun*
**over·ly** \'ō-vər-lē\ *adverb* (1821)
: to an excessive degree
¹**over·man** \-mən, -ˌman\ *noun* (13th century)
**1** : a man in authority over others; *specifically* : FOREMAN
**2** \-ˌman\ [translation of German *Übermensch*] : SUPERMAN 1
²**over·man** \ˌō-vər-'man\ *transitive verb* (circa 1637)
: to have or get too many personnel for the needs of ⟨*overman* a ship⟩
**over·man·tel** \'ō-vər-ˌman-t°l\ *noun* (1882)
: an ornamental structure (as a painting) above a mantelpiece
— **overmantel** *adjective*
**over·mas·ter** \ˌō-vər-'mas-tər\ *transitive verb* (14th century)
: OVERPOWER, SUBDUE
**over·mas·ter·ing** \-'mas-tə-riŋ\ *adjective* (1645)
: DOMINANT ⟨*overmastering* behavior⟩ ⟨the *overmastering* question⟩
**over·match** \-'mach\ *transitive verb* (14th century)
**1** : to be more than a match for : DEFEAT
**2** : to match with a superior opponent
¹**over·much** \-'məch\ *adjective* (13th century)
: too much
²**overmuch** *adverb* (14th century)
: in too great a degree

³**over·much** \'ō-vər-,məch, ,ō-vər-'\ *noun*
(14th century)
: too great an amount

¹**over·night** \,ō-vər-'nīt\ *adverb* (14th century)
**1 a :** on the evening before **b :** during the
night ⟨stayed away *overnight*⟩
**2 :** very quickly or suddenly ⟨became famous
*overnight*⟩

²**overnight** *adjective* (1824)
**1 :** of, lasting, or staying the night
**2 :** SUDDEN, RAPID ⟨an *overnight* sensation⟩

³**over·night** \'ō-vər-,nīt, ,ō-vər-'\ *intransitive
verb* (1891)
: to stay overnight

⁴**over·night** \'ō-vər-,nīt\ *noun* (1959)
: an overnight stay

**overnight bag** *noun* (1925)
: a suitcase of a size to carry clothing and personal articles for an overnight trip — called
also *overnight case*

**over·night·er** \,ō-vər-'nī-tər\ *noun* (1949)
: OVERNIGHT BAG

¹**over·pass** \,ō-vər-'pas\ *transitive verb* (14th
century)
**1 :** to pass across, over, or beyond : CROSS;
*also* : SURPASS
**2 :** TRANSGRESS
**3 :** DISREGARD, IGNORE

²**over·pass** \'ō-vər-,pas\ *noun* (1929)
: a crossing of two highways or of a highway
and pedestrian path or railroad at different levels where clearance to traffic on the lower level is obtained by elevating the higher level;
*also* : the upper level of such a crossing

**over·per·suade** \,ō-vər-pər-'swād\ *transitive
verb* (1624)
: to persuade to act contrary to one's conviction or preference
— **over·per·sua·sion** \-'swā-zhən\ *noun*

**over·plaid** \'ō-vər-,plad\ *noun* (1926)
: a textile design consisting of a plaid pattern
superimposed on another plaid or on a textured ground; *also* : a fabric with such a design
— **over·plaid·ed** *adjective*

**over·play** \,ō-vər-'plā\ (1819)
*transitive verb*
**1 a :** to present (as a dramatic role) extravagantly : EXAGGERATE **b :** to place too much
emphasis on
**2 :** to rely too much on the strength of —
usually used in the phrase *overplay one's hand*
**3 :** to strike a golf ball beyond (a putting
green)
*intransitive verb*
: to exaggerate a part or effect

**over·plus** \'ō-vər-,pləs\ *noun* [Middle English,
part translation of Middle French *surplus*]
(14th century)
: SURPLUS

**over·pop·u·late** \,ō-vər-'päp-yə-,lāt\ (1868)
*transitive verb*
: to furnish or provide with more than the environment or market will bear
*intransitive verb*
: to become overly populous

**over·pop·u·la·tion** \,ō-vər-,pä-pyə-'lā-shən\
*noun* (1823)
: the condition of having a population so
dense as to cause environmental deterioration,
an impaired quality of life, or a population
crash

**over·pow·er** \,ō-vər-'paù-(-ə)r\ *transitive verb*
(1593)
**1 :** to overcome by superior force : SUBDUE
**2 :** to affect with overwhelming intensity ⟨the
stench *overpowered* us⟩
**3 :** to provide with more power than is needed
or desirable ⟨a dangerously *overpowered* car⟩
— **over·pow·er·ing·ly** \-'paù-(-ə)r-iŋ-lē\
*adverb*

**over·pres·sure** \'ō-vər-,pre-shər\ *noun*
(1644)
: pressure significantly above what is usual or
normal

**over·price** \,ō-vər-'prīs\ *transitive verb* (1605)

: to price too high

¹**over·print** \,ō-vər-'print\ *transitive verb*
(1863)
: to print over with something additional

²**over·print** \'ō-vər-,\ *noun* (1876)
: something added by or as if by overprinting;
*especially* : a printed marking added to a postage or revenue stamp especially to alter the
original or to commemorate a special event

**over·proof** \,ō-vər-'prüf\ *adjective* (1807)
: containing more alcohol than proof spirit

**over·pro·por·tion** \-prə-'pōr-shən, -'pór-\
*transitive verb* (1642)
: to make disproportionately large
— **overproportion** *noun*
— **over·pro·por·tion·ate** \-sh(ə-)nət\ *adjective*
— **over·pro·por·tion·ate·ly** *adverb*

**over·qual·i·fied** \-'kwä-lə-,fīd\ *adjective*
(1954)
: having more education, training, or experience than a job calls for

**over·reach** \,ō-və(r)-'rēch\ (14th century)
*transitive verb*
**1 :** to reach above or beyond : OVERTOP
**2 :** to defeat (oneself) by seeking to do or gain
too much
**3 :** to get the better of especially in dealing
and bargaining and typically by unscrupulous
or crafty methods
*intransitive verb*
**1** *of a horse* : to strike the forefoot with the
front part of the hind foot
**2 a :** to go to excess **b :** EXAGGERATE
**3 :** to overreach oneself
— **over·reach** \'ō-və(r)-,rēch, ,ō-və(r)-'\
*noun*
— **over·reach·er** \-,rē-chər, -'rē-chər\ *noun*

**over·rep·re·sent·ed** \'ō-və(r)-,re-pri-'zen-
təd\ *adjective* (1900)
: represented excessively; *especially* : having
representatives in a proportion higher than the
average
— **over·rep·re·sen·ta·tion** \-,re-pri-,zen-
'tā-shən, -zən-\ *noun*

¹**over·ride** \-'rīd\ *transitive verb* -**rode** \-'rōd\;
-**rid·den** \-'ri-d°n\; -**rid·ing** \-'rī-diŋ\ (before
12th century)
**1 :** to ride over or across : TRAMPLE
**2 :** to ride (as a horse) too much or too hard
**3 a :** to prevail over : DOMINATE **b :** to set
aside : ANNUL ⟨*override* a veto⟩ **c :** to neutralize the action of (as an automatic control)
**4 :** to extend or pass over; *especially* : OVER-
LAP

²**over·ride** \'o-və(r)-,rīd\ *noun* (1931)
**1 :** a commission paid to managerial personnel
on sales made by subordinates
**2 :** ROYALTY 5a
**3 :** a device or system used to override a control
**4 :** an act or an instance of overriding

**over·ripe** \,ō-və(r)-'rīp\ *adjective* (1671)
**1 :** passed beyond maturity or ripeness toward
decay
**2 a :** DECADENT **b :** lacking originality or vigor
— **over·ripe·ness** \-nəs\ *noun*

**over·rule** \-'rül\ *transitive verb* (1576)
**1 :** to rule over : GOVERN
**2 :** to prevail over : OVERCOME
**3 a :** to rule against or to set aside : REVERSE

¹**over·run** \-'rən\ *transitive verb* -**ran** \-'ran\;
-**run**; -**run·ning** (before 12th century)
**1 a** (1) **:** to defeat decisively and occupy the
positions of (2) **:** to invade and occupy or ravage **b :** to spread or swarm over : INFEST
**2 a :** to run or go beyond or past ⟨the plane
*overran* the runway⟩ **b :** EXCEED **c :** to readjust
(set type) by shifting letters or words from one
line into another
**3 :** to flow over

²**over·run** \'ō-və(r)-,rən\ *noun* (1898)
**1 :** an act or instance of overrunning; *especially* : an exceeding of the costs estimated in a
contract for development and manufacture of
new equipment

**2 :** the amount by which something overruns
**3 :** a run in excess of the quantity ordered by a
customer

**over·scale** \'ō-vər-,skāl\ *or* **over·scaled**
\-,skāld\ *adjective* (1953)
: OVERSIZE ⟨an *overscale* coat⟩ ⟨an *overscale*
sofa⟩

**over·sea** \,o-vər-'sē, 'ō-vər-,\ *adjective or adverb* (12th century)
*chiefly British* : OVERSEAS

¹**over·seas** \,ō-vər-'sēz\ *adverb* (1533)
: beyond or across the sea ⟨lived *overseas* for
a time⟩

²**over·seas** \'ō-vər-,sēz\ *adjective* (1892)
**1 :** of or relating to movement, transport, or
communication over the sea ⟨an *overseas* lin-
er⟩
**2 :** situated, originating in, or relating to lands
beyond the sea ⟨*overseas* installations⟩ ⟨*overseas* immigrants⟩

**over·see** \,ō-vər-'sē\ *transitive verb* -**saw**
\-'só\; -**seen** \-'sēn\; -**see·ing** (before 12th
century)
**1 :** SURVEY, WATCH
**2 a :** INSPECT, EXAMINE **b :** SUPERVISE

**over·seer** \'ō-və(r)-,sir, -,sē-ər, ,ō-və(r)-'\
*noun* (1523)
: SUPERVISOR, SUPERINTENDENT

**over·sell** \,ō-vər-'sel\ *transitive verb* -**sold**
\-'sōld\; -**sell·ing** (circa 1879)
**1 a :** to sell too much or too many to **b :** to
sell too much or too many of
**2 :** to make excessive claims for
— **over·sell** \'ō-vər-,sel\ *noun*

**over·set** \-'set\ *transitive verb* -**set**; -**setting** (1583)
**1 a :** to disturb mentally or physically : UPSET
**b :** to turn or tip over : OVERTURN
**2 :** to set too much type matter for
— **over·set** \'ō-vər-,set\ *noun*

**over·sexed** \,ō-vər-'sekst\ *adjective* (1898)
: exhibiting an excessive sexual drive or interest

**over·shad·ow** \-'sha-(,)dō\ *transitive verb*
(before 12th century)
**1 :** to cast a shadow over
**2 :** to exceed in importance : OUTWEIGH

**over·shirt** \'ō-vər-,shərt\ *noun* (1805)
: a shirt usually worn over another shirt without being tucked in

**over·shoe** \-,shü\ *noun* (1823)
: an outer shoe; *especially* : GALOSH

**over·shoot** \,ō-vər-'shüt\ *transitive verb*
-**shot** \-'shät\; -**shoot·ing** (14th century)
**1 :** to pass swiftly beyond
**2 :** to shoot or pass over or beyond so as to
miss
**3 :** to excel in shooting
— **over·shoot** \'ō-vər-,shüt\ *noun*

¹**over·shot** \'ō-vər-,shät\ *adjective* (circa
1535)
**1 :** actuated by the weight of water passing
over and flowing from above ⟨an *overshot* wa-
terwheel⟩
**2 a :** having the upper jaw extending beyond
the lower **b :** projecting beyond the lower jaw

²**overshot** *noun* (1945)
: a pattern or weave featuring filling threads
which pass two or more warp yarns before reentering the fabric

**over·sight** \'ō-vər-,sīt\ *noun* (15th century)
**1 a :** watchful and responsible care **b :** regulatory supervision ⟨congressional *oversight*⟩
**2 :** an inadvertent omission or error

**over·sim·ple** \,ō-vər-'sim-pəl\ *adjective* (15th
century)
: too simple : not thoroughgoing or exhaustive
⟨*oversimple* theories⟩
— **over·sim·ply** \-plē\ *adverb*

**over·sim·pli·fy** \-'sim-plə-,fī\ (1923)
*transitive verb*
: to simplify to such an extent as to bring
about distortion, misunderstanding, or error
*intransitive verb*
: to engage in undue or extreme simplification

— **over·sim·pli·fi·ca·tion** \-,sim-plə-fə-'kā-shən\ *noun*

**over·size** \'ō-vər-,sīz\ *or* **over·sized** \-'sīzd\ *adjective* (1853)
: being of more than standard or ordinary size ⟨*oversize* pillows⟩ ⟨an *oversize* shirt⟩

**over·skirt** \'ō-vər-,skərt\ *noun* (1870)
: a skirt worn over another skirt

**over·slaugh** \'ō-vər-'slȯ\ *transitive verb* [Dutch *overslaan* to pass over, omit, from Middle Dutch *overslaun*, from *over-* over- + *slaen* to strike] (1846)
: to pass over for appointment or promotion in favor of another

**over·sleep** \,ō-vər-'slēp\ *verb* **-slept** \-'slept\; **-sleep·ing** (14th century)
*intransitive verb*
: to sleep beyond the time for waking
*transitive verb*
: to allow (oneself) to oversleep

**over·slip** \,ō-vər-'slip\ *transitive verb* (15th century)
*obsolete* : ESCAPE

**over·sold** \,ō-vər-'sōld\ *adjective* (1926)
: likely to show a rise in price because of prior heavy selling and accompanying decline· in price ⟨an *oversold* stock⟩

**over·soul** \'ō-vər-,sōl\ *noun* (circa 1844)
: the absolute reality and basis of all existences conceived as a spiritual being in which the ideal nature imperfectly manifested in human beings is perfectly realized

**over·spend** \,ō-vər-'spend\ *verb* **-spent** \-'spent\; **-spend·ing** (circa 1618)
*transitive verb*
**1** : to spend or use to excess : EXHAUST
**2** : to exceed in expenditure
*intransitive verb*
: to spend beyond one's means
— **over·spend·er** *noun*

**over·spill** \'ō-vər-,spil\ *noun* (1884)
**1** : the act or an instance of spilling over
**2** *chiefly British* : the movement of excess urban population into less crowded areas

**over·spread** \,ō-vər-'spred\ *transitive verb* **-spread**; **-spread·ing** (before 12th century)
: to spread over or above
— **over·spread** \'ō-vər-,spred\ *noun*

**over·state** \-'stāt\ *transitive verb* (1803)
: to state in too strong terms : EXAGGERATE
— **over·state·ment** \-mənt\ *noun*

**over·stay** \-'stā\ *transitive verb* (1646)
: to stay beyond the time or the limits of

**over·steer** \'ō-vər-,stir\ *noun* (1951)
: the tendency of an automobile to steer into a sharper turn than the driver intends sometimes with a thrusting of the rear to the outside; *also*
: the action or an instance of oversteer

**over·step** \,ō-vər-'step\ *transitive verb* (before 12th century)
: EXCEED, TRANSGRESS

**over·sto·ry** \'ō-vər-,stōr-ē, -,stȯr-\ *noun* (1925)
**1** : the layer of foliage in a forest canopy
**2** : the trees contributing to an overstory

**over·strew** \,ō-vər-'strü\ *transitive verb* **-strewed**; **-strewed** *or* **-strewn** \-'strün\ **-strew·ing** (circa 1570)
**1** : to strew or scatter about
**2** : to cover here and there

**over·stride** \-'strīd\ *transitive verb* **-strode** \-'strōd\; **-strid·den** \-'strid-dᵊn\; **-strid·ing** \-'strī-diŋ\ (13th century)
**1 a** : to stride over, across, or beyond **b** : BESTRIDE
**2** : to stride faster than or beyond

**over·strung** \-'strəŋ\ *adjective* (1810)
: too highly strung : too sensitive

**over·stuff** \-'stəf\ *transitive verb* (1904)
**1** : to stuff too full
**2** : to cover (as a chair or sofa) completely and deeply with upholstery

**over·sub·scribe** \-səb-'skrīb\ *transitive verb* (1891)
: to subscribe for more of than is available

— **over·sub·scrip·tion** \-'skrip-shən\ *noun*

**overt** \ō-'vərt, 'ō-(,)vərt\ *adjective* [Middle English, from Middle French *ouvert, overt,* from past participle of *ouvrir* to open, from (assumed) Vulgar Latin *operire,* alteration of Latin *aperire*] (14th century)
: open to view : MANIFEST
— **overt·ly** *adverb*
— **overt·ness** *noun*

**over·take** \,ō-vər-'tāk\ *transitive verb* **-took** \-'tuk\; **-tak·en** \-'tā-kən\; **-tak·ing** [Middle English, from ¹*over* + *taken* to take] (13th century)
**1 a** : to catch up with **b** : to catch up with and pass by
**2** : to come upon suddenly

**over–the–counter** *adjective* (1921)
**1** : not traded or effected on an organized securities exchange ⟨*over-the-counter* transactions⟩ ⟨*over-the-counter* securities⟩
**2** : sold lawfully without prescription ⟨*over-the-counter* drugs⟩

**over–the–hill** *adjective* (1946)
**1** : past one's prime
**2** : advanced in age

**over–the–top** *adjective* (1985)
: extremely or excessively flamboyant or outrageous ⟨an *over-the-top* performance⟩

**over–the–transom** *adjective* (circa 1952)
: offered without prior arrangement especially for publication : UNSOLICITED ⟨an *over-the-transom* manuscript⟩

**over·throw** \,ō-vər-'thrō\ *transitive verb* **-threw** \-'thrü\; **-thrown** \-'thrōn\; **-throw·ing** (14th century)
**1** : OVERTURN, UPSET
**2** : to cause the downfall of : BRING DOWN, DEFEAT
**3** : to throw a ball over or past (as a base or a receiver)
— **over·throw** \'ō-vər-,thrō\ *noun*

**over·time** \'ō-vər-,tīm\ *noun* (1536)
**1** : time in excess of a set limit: as **a** : working time in excess of a standard day or week **b** : an extra period of play in a contest
**2** : the wage paid for overtime
— **overtime** *adverb*

**over·tone** \-,tōn\ *noun* (1867)
**1 a** : one of the higher tones produced simultaneously with the fundamental and that with the fundamental comprise a complex musical tone : HARMONIC 1a **b** : HARMONIC 2
**2** : the color of the light reflected (as by a paint)
**3** : a secondary effect, quality, or meaning : SUGGESTION 3, CONNOTATION

**over·top** \,ō-vər-'täp\ *transitive verb* (circa 1594)
**1** : to rise above the top of
**2** : to be superior to
**3** : SURPASS

**over·trade** \-'trād\ *intransitive verb* (1734)
: to trade beyond one's capital

**over·trick** \'ō-vər-,trik\ *noun* (1903)
: a card trick won in excess of the number bid

**over·trump** \,ō-vər-'trəmp\ (1746)
*transitive verb*
: to trump with a higher trump card than the highest previously played on the same trick
*intransitive verb*
: to play a higher trump card than the highest previously played on the same trick

¹**over·ture** \'ō-və(r)-,chur, -chər, -,tyur, -,tur\ *noun* [Middle English, literally, opening, from Middle French, from (assumed) Vulgar Latin *opertura,* alteration of Latin *apertura* — more at APERTURE] (15th century)
**1 a** : an initiative toward agreement or action : PROPOSAL **b** : something introductory : PRELUDE
**2 a** : the orchestral introduction to a musical dramatic work **b** : an orchestral concert piece written especially as a single movement in sonata form

²**overture** *transitive verb* **-tured; -tur·ing** (circa 1650)
**1** : to put forward as an overture
**2** : to make or present an overture to

¹**over·turn** \,ō-vər-'tərn\ (13th century)
*transitive verb*
**1** : to cause to turn over : UPSET
**2** : INVALIDATE, DESTROY
*intransitive verb*
: UPSET, TURN OVER

²**over·turn** \'ō-vər-,tərn\ *noun* (circa 1592)
**1** : the act of overturning : the state of being overturned
**2** : the sinking of surface water and rise of bottom water in a lake or sea that results from changes in temperature that commonly occur in spring and fall

**over·val·ue** \,ō-vər-'val-(,)yü\ *transitive verb* (1597)
: to assign an excessive or fictitious value to
— **over·val·u·a·tion** \-,val-yə-'wā-shən\ *noun*

**over·view** \'ō-vər-,vyü\ *noun* (1588)
: a general survey : SUMMARY

**over·volt·age** \,ō-vər-'vōl-tij\ *noun* (1907)
**1** : the excess potential required for the discharge of an ion at an electrode over and above the equilibrium potential of the electrode
**2** : voltage in excess of the normal operating voltage of a device or circuit

**over·wear** \-'war, -'wer\ *transitive verb* **-wore** \-'wōr, -'wȯr\; **-worn** \-'wōrn, -'wȯrn\; **-wear·ing** (1578)
: WEAR OUT, EXHAUST

**over·ween·ing** \-'wē-niŋ\ *adjective* [Middle English *overwening,* present participle of *overwenen* to be arrogant, from *over* + *wenen* to ween] (14th century)
**1** : ARROGANT, PRESUMPTUOUS
**2** : IMMODERATE, EXAGGERATED
— **over·ween·ing·ly** *adverb*

**over·weigh** \-'wā\ *transitive verb* (13th century)
**1** : to exceed in weight
**2** : OPPRESS 2

¹**over·weight** \'ō-vər-,wāt, 2 *is usually* ,ō-vər-'\ *noun* (1552)
**1** : weight over and above what is required or allowed
**2** : excessive or burdensome weight

²**over·weight** \,ō-vər-'wāt\ *transitive verb* (1603)
**1** : to give too much weight or consideration to
**2** : to weight excessively

³**over·weight** \,ō-vər-'wāt\ *adjective* (1638)
: exceeding expected, normal, or proper weight; *especially* : exceeding the bodily weight normal for one's age, height, and build

**over·whelm** \,ō-vər-'hwelm, -'welm\ *transitive verb* [Middle English, from ¹*over* + *whelmen* to turn over, cover up] (14th century)
**1** : UPSET, OVERTHROW
**2 a** : to cover over completely : SUBMERGE **b** : to overcome by superior force or numbers **c** : to overpower in thought or feeling

**over·whelm·ing** *adjective* (1742)
: tending or serving to overwhelm ⟨an *overwhelming* majority⟩; *also* : EXTREME, GREAT ⟨*overwhelming* indifference⟩
— **over·whelm·ing·ly** *adverb*

¹**over·win·ter** \,ō-vər-'win-tər\ *intransitive verb* (before 12th century)
: to survive the winter

²**overwinter** *adjective* (1900)
: occurring during the period spanning the winter

**over with** *adjective* (1915)
: being at an end : FINISHED, COMPLETED

**over·work** \ˌō-vər-'wərk\ (1818)
*transitive verb*
**1 :** to cause to work too hard, too long, or to exhaustion
**2 :** to decorate all over
**3 a :** to work too much on **: OVERDO b :** to make excessive use of
*intransitive verb*
**:** to work too much or too long **: OVERDO**
— **overwork** *noun*

**over·write** \ˌō-və(r)-'rīt\ *verb* **-wrote** \-'rōt\; **-writ·ten** \-'ri-tᵊn\; **-writ·ing** \-'rī-tiŋ\ (1699)
*transitive verb*
**1 :** to write over the surface of
**2 :** to write in inflated or overly elaborate style
*intransitive verb*
**:** to write too much or in an overly elaborate style

**over·wrought** \-'rȯt\ *adjective* [past participle of *overwork*] (1670)
**1 :** extremely excited **: AGITATED**
**2 :** elaborated to excess **: OVERDONE**

**ovi-** *or* **ovo-**
— see OV-

**ovi·cide** \'ō-və-ˌsīd\ *noun* [International Scientific Vocabulary] (1913)
**:** an agent that kills eggs; *especially* **:** an insecticide effective against the egg stage
— **ovi·cid·al** \ˌō-və-'sī-dᵊl\ *adjective*

**ovi·duct** \'ō-və-ˌdəkt\ *noun* [New Latin *oviductus,* from *ov-* + *ductus* duct] (1672)
**:** a tube that serves exclusively or especially for the passage of eggs from an ovary
— **ovi·duc·tal** \ˌō-və-'dək-tᵊl\ *adjective*

**ovine** \'ō-ˌvīn\ *adjective* [Late Latin *ovinus,* from Latin *ovis* sheep — more at EWE] (circa 1828)
**:** of, relating to, or resembling sheep
— **ovine** *noun*

**ovip·a·rous** \ō-'vi-p(ə-)rəs\ *adjective* [Latin *oviparus,* from *ov-* + *-parus* -parous] (1646)
**:** producing eggs that develop and hatch outside the maternal body; *also* **:** involving the production of such eggs

**ovi·pos·it** \'ō-və-ˌpä-zət, ˌō-və-'\ *intransitive verb* [probably back-formation from *ovipositor*] (1816)
**:** to lay eggs — used especially of insects
— **ovi·po·si·tion** \ˌō-və-pə-'zi-shən\ *noun*
— **ovi·po·si·tion·al** \-'zish-nəl, -'zi-shə-nᵊl\ *adjective*

**ovi·pos·i·tor** \'ō-və-ˌpä-zə-tər, ˌō-və-'\ *noun* [New Latin, from Latin *ov-* + *positor* one that places, from *ponere* to place — more at POSITION] (1816)
**:** a specialized organ (as of an insect) for depositing eggs — see INSECT illustration

**ovoid** \'ō-ˌvȯid\ *also* **ovoi·dal** \ō-'vȯi-dᵊl\ *adjective* [French *ovoïde,* from Latin *ovum* egg — more at EGG] (circa 1828)
**:** resembling an egg in shape **: OVATE**
— **ovoid** *noun*

**ovo·lo** \'ō-və-ˌlō\ *noun, plural* **-los** [Italian, diminutive of *uovo, ovo* egg, from Latin *ovum*] (1663)
**:** a rounded convex molding

**Ovon·ics** \ō-'vä-niks\ *noun plural but usually singular in construction* [Stanford R. Ovshinsky (born 1923) American inventor + *electronics*] (1968)
**:** a branch of electronics that deals with applications of the change from an electrically nonconducting state to a semiconducting state shown by glasses of special composition upon application of a certain minimum voltage
— **ovon·ic** \-nik\ *adjective*

**ovo·tes·tis** \ˌō-vō-'tes-təs\ *noun* [New Latin] (1877)
**:** a hermaphrodite gonad (as in some scale insects)

**ovo·vi·vip·a·rous** \'ō-vō-ˌvī-'vi-p(ə-)rəs\ *adjective* (1801)
**:** producing eggs that develop within the maternal body (as of various fishes or reptiles)

and hatch within or immediately after extrusion from the parent
— **ovo·vi·vip·a·rous·ly** *adverb*
— **ovo·vi·vip·a·rous·ness** *noun*

**ovu·late** \'äv-yə-ˌlāt, 'ōv-, -lət\ *adjective* (1861)
**:** bearing an ovule

**ovu·la·tion** \ˌäv-yə-'lā-shən, ˌōv-\ *noun* (1848)
**:** the discharge of a mature ovum from the ovary
— **ovu·late** \'äv-yə-ˌlāt, 'ōv-\ *verb*

**ovu·la·to·ry** \'äv-yə-lə-ˌtōr-ē, 'ōv-, -ˌtȯr-\ *adjective* (1931)
**:** of, relating to, or involving ovulation

**ovule** \'äv-(ˌ)yü(ə)l, 'ōv-\ *noun* [New Latin *ovulum,* diminutive of Latin *ovum*] (1830)
**1 :** an outgrowth of the ovary of a seed plant that is a megasporangium and encloses an embryo sac within a nucellus
**2 :** a small egg; *especially* **:** one in an early stage of growth

**ovum** \'ō-vəm\ *noun, plural* **ova** \-və\ [New Latin, from Latin, egg — more at EGG] (circa 1706)
**:** a female gamete **: MACROGAMETE**

**ow** \'aú, 'ü\ *interjection* [from *ow,* interjection expressing surprise, from Middle English] (circa 1911)
— used especially to express sudden pain

**owe** \'ō\ *verb* **owed; ow·ing** [Middle English, to possess, own, owe, from Old English *āgan;* akin to Old High German *eigun* (1st & 3d plural present indicative) possess, Sanskrit *īśe* he possesses] (before 12th century)
*transitive verb*
**1 a** *archaic* **: POSSESS, OWN b :** to have or bear (an emotion or attitude) to someone or something ⟨*owes* the boss a grudge⟩
**2 a** (1) **:** to be under obligation to pay or repay in return for something received **:** be indebted in the sum of ⟨*owes* me $5⟩ (2) **:** to be under obligation to render (as duty or service) ⟨I *owe* you a favor⟩ **b :** to be indebted to ⟨*owes* the grocer for supplies⟩
**3 :** to be indebted for ⟨*owed* his wealth to his father⟩ ⟨*owes* much to good luck⟩
*intransitive verb*
**1 :** to be in debt ⟨*owes* for his house⟩
**2 :** to be attributable ⟨an idea that *owes* to Greek philosophy⟩

**owing** *adjective* (15th century)
**:** due to be paid ⟨has bills *owing*⟩

**owing to** *preposition* (1695)
**: BECAUSE OF** ⟨delayed *owing to* a crash⟩

**owl** \'aú(ə)l\ *noun* [Middle English *owle,* from Old English *ūle;* akin to Old High German *uwila* owl] (before 12th century)
**:** any of an order (Strigiformes) of chiefly nocturnal birds of prey with a large head and eyes, short hooked bill, strong talons, and soft fluffy often mottled brown plumage

**owl·et** \'aú-lət\ *noun* (1542)
**:** a small or young owl

**owl·ish** \'aú-lish\ *adjective* (1611)
**:** resembling or suggesting an owl
— **owl·ish·ly** *adverb*
— **owl·ish·ness** *noun*

**¹own** \'ōn\ *adjective* [Middle English *owen,* from Old English *āgen;* akin to Old High German *eigan* own, Old Norse *eiginn,* Old English *āgan* to possess — more at OWE] (before 12th century)
**1 :** belonging to oneself or itself — usually used following a possessive case or possessive adjective ⟨cooked my *own* dinner⟩
**2 —** used to express immediate or direct kinship ⟨an *own* son⟩ ⟨an *own* sister⟩
**²own** (before 12th century)
*transitive verb*
**1 a :** to have or hold as property **: POSSESS b :** to have power over **: CONTROL** ⟨wanted to *own* his own life⟩
**2 :** to acknowledge to be true, valid, or as claimed **: ADMIT** ⟨*own* a debt⟩

*intransitive verb*
**:** to acknowledge something to be true, valid, or as claimed — used with *to* or *up*
**synonym** see ACKNOWLEDGE
— **own·er** \'ō-nər\ *noun*

**³own** *pronoun, singular or plural in construction* (before 12th century)
**:** one or ones belonging to oneself — used after a possessive and without a following noun ⟨gave out books so that each of us had our *own*⟩ ⟨a room of your *own*⟩
— **on one's own :** for or by oneself **:** independently of assistance or control

**own·er·ship** \'ō-nər-ˌship\ *noun* (1583)
**1 :** the state, relation, or fact of being an owner
**2 :** a group or organization of owners

**ox** \'äks\ *noun, plural* **ox·en** \'äk-sən\ *also* **ox** [Middle English, from Old English *oxa;* akin to Old High German *ohso* ox, Sanskrit *ukṣā* bull, and perhaps to Sanskrit *ukṣati* he moistens, Greek *hygros* wet — more at HUMOR] (before 12th century)
**1 :** a domestic bovine mammal (*Bos taurus*); *broadly* **:** a bovine mammal
**2 :** an adult castrated male domestic ox

**ox-** *or* **oxo-** *combining form* [French, from *oxygène*]
**:** oxygen ⟨*oxa*cillin⟩

**ox·a·cil·lin** \ˌäk-sə-'si-lən\ *noun* [*ox-* + *azole* + *penicillin*] (1962)
**:** a semisynthetic penicillin that is especially effective in the control of infections caused by penicillin-resistant staphylococci

**ox·a·late** \'äk-sə-ˌlāt\ *noun* (1791)
**:** a salt or ester of oxalic acid

**ox·al·ic acid** \(ˌ)äk-ˌsa-lik-\ *noun* [French *(acide) oxalique,* from Latin *oxalis*] (1791)
**:** a poisonous strong acid $(COOH)_2$ or $H_2C_2O_4$ that occurs in various plants as oxalates and is used especially as a bleaching or cleaning agent and as a chemical intermediate

**ox·al·is** \äk-'sa-ləs\ *noun* [New Latin, genus name, from Latin, wood sorrel, from Greek, from *oxys* sharp — more at OXYGEN] (circa 1706)
**: WOOD SORREL**

**ox·a·lo·ac·e·tate** \ˌäk-sə-lō-'a-sə-ˌtāt\ *also* **ox·al·ac·e·tate** \ˌäk-sə-'la-\ *noun* (1891)
**:** a salt or ester of oxaloacetic acid

**ox·a·lo·ace·tic acid** \ˌäk-sə-lō-ə-'sē-tik-\ *also* **ox·al·ace·tic acid** \ˌäk-sə-lə-'sē-tik-\ *noun* [*oxalic* + *acetic acid*] (1896)
**:** a crystalline acid $C_4H_4O_5$ that is formed by reversible oxidation of malic acid (as in carbohydrate metabolism via the Krebs cycle) and in reversible transamination reactions (as from aspartic acid)

**ox·a·lo·suc·cin·ic acid** \ˌäk-sə-lō-sək-ˌsi-nik-, ˌäk-'sa-lō-\ *noun* [*oxalic* + *succinic acid*] (1925)
**:** a tricarboxylic acid $C_6H_6O_7$ that is formed as an intermediate in the Krebs cycle

**ox·az·e·pam** \äk-'sa-zə-ˌpam\ *noun* [*hydroxy-* + *diazepam*] (1964)
**:** a tranquilizing drug $C_{15}H_{11}ClN_2O_2$

**ox·blood** \'äks-ˌbləd\ *noun* (1705)
**:** a moderate reddish brown

**ox·bow** \'äks-ˌbō\ *noun* (14th century)
**1 :** a U-shaped frame forming a collar about an ox's neck and supporting the yoke
**2 :** something (as a bend in a river) resembling an oxbow

oxbow 1

— **oxbow** *adjective*

**Ox·bridge** \'äks-ˌbrij\ *adjective* [*Ox*ford + *Cambridge*] (1960)
**:** of, relating to, or characteristic of Oxford and Cambridge Universities — compare PLATEGLASS, REDBRICK 2

**ox·cart** \-ˌkärt\ *noun* (1749)
**:** a cart drawn by oxen

**ox·eye** \-ˌī\ *noun* (15th century)

: any of several composite plants (as of the genera *Chrysanthemum* or *Heliopsis*) having heads with both disk and ray flowers; *especially* : DAISY 1b

**oxeye daisy** *noun* (circa 1763)
: DAISY 1b

**ox·ford** \'äks-fərd\ *noun* [*Oxford*, England] (circa 1890)
**1** : a low shoe laced or tied over the instep
**2** : a soft durable cotton or synthetic fabric made in plain or basket weaves — called also *oxford cloth*

**Oxford down** *noun, often D capitalized* [*Oxfordshire*, England] (1859)
: any of a Down breed of large hornless sheep developed by crossing Cotswolds and Hampshires — called also *Oxford*

**Oxford movement** *noun* (1841)
: a High Church movement within the Church of England begun at Oxford in 1833

**ox·heart** \'äks-,härt\ *noun* (1870)
: any of various large sweet cherries

**ox·i·dant** \'äk-sə-dənt\ *noun* (1884)
: OXIDIZING AGENT
— **oxidant** *adjective*

**ox·i·dase** \'äk-sə-,dās, -,dāz\ *noun* [International Scientific Vocabulary] (1896)
: any of various enzymes that catalyze oxidations; *especially* : one able to react directly with molecular oxygen
— **ox·i·da·sic** \,äk-sə-'dā-sik, -zik\ *adjective*

**ox·i·da·tion** \,äk-sə-'dā-shən\ *noun* [French, from *oxider, oxyder* to oxidize, from *oxide*] (1791)
**1** : the act or process of oxidizing
**2** : the state or result of being oxidized
— **ox·i·da·tive** \'äk-sə-,dā-tiv\ *adjective*
— **ox·i·da·tive·ly** *adverb*

**oxidation number** *noun* (1926)
: a positive or negative number that represents the effective charge of an atom or element and that indicates the extent or possibility of its oxidation ⟨the usual *oxidation number* of sodium is +1 and of oxygen −2⟩ — called also *oxidation state*

**oxidation–reduction** *noun* (1909)
: a chemical reaction in which one or more electrons are transferred from one atom or molecule to another

**oxidative phosphorylation** *noun* (1954)
: the synthesis of ATP by phosphorylation of ADP for which energy is obtained by electron transport and which takes place in the mitochondria during aerobic respiration

**ox·ide** \'äk-,sīd\ *noun* [French *oxide, oxyde,* from *ox-* (from *oxygène* oxygen) + *-ide* (from *acide* acid)] (1790)
: a binary compound of oxygen with a more electropositive element or group
— **ox·id·ic** \äk-'si-dik\ *adjective*

**ox·i·dize** \'äk-sə-,dīz\ *verb* **-dized; -diz·ing** (1806)
*transitive verb*
**1** : to combine with oxygen
**2** : to dehydrogenate especially by the action of oxygen
**3** : to change (a compound) by increasing the proportion of the electronegative part or change (an element or ion) from a lower to a higher positive valence : remove one or more electrons from (an atom, ion, or molecule)
*intransitive verb*
: to become oxidized
— **ox·i·diz·able** \,äk-sə-'dī-zə-bəl\ *adjective*

**ox·i·diz·er** \-,dī-zər\ *noun* (1875)
: OXIDIZING AGENT; *especially* : one used to support the combustion of a rocket propellant

**oxidizing agent** *noun* (1903)
: a substance that oxidizes something especially chemically (as by accepting electrons)

**ox·i·do·re·duc·tase** \'äk-sə-dō-ri-'dək-,tās, -,tāz\ *noun* [*oxidation* + *-o-* + *reduction* + *-ase*] (1922)

: an enzyme that catalyzes an oxidation-reduction reaction

**ox·ime** \'äk-,sēm\ *noun* [International Scientific Vocabulary *ox-* + *-ime* (from *imide*)] (circa 1890)
: any of various compounds obtained chiefly by the action of hydroxylamine on aldehydes and ketones and characterized by the bivalent grouping C=NOH

**ox·lip** \'äk-,slip\ *noun* [(assumed) Middle English *oxeslippe,* from Old English *oxanslyppe,* literally, ox dung, from *oxa* ox + *slypa, slyppe* paste — more at SLIP] (before 12th century)
: a Eurasian primula (*Primula elatior*) having usually yellow flowers

**oxo** \'äk-(,)sō\ *adjective* [*ox-*] (circa 1926)
: containing oxygen

**oxo-** — see OX-

**Ox·o·ni·an** \äk-'sō-nē-ən\ *noun* [Medieval Latin *Oxonia* Oxford] (circa 1540)
: a student or graduate of Oxford University
— **Oxonian** *adjective*

**ox·tail** \'äks-,tāl\ *noun* (15th century)
: the tail of a beef animal; *especially* : the skinned tail used for food (as in soup)

**ox·ter** \'äk-stər\ *noun* [Middle English (Scots), alteration of Old English *ōxta;* akin to Old English *eax* axis, axle — more at AXIS] (15th century)
**1** *chiefly Scottish & Irish* : ARMPIT 1
**2** *chiefly Scottish & Irish* : ARM

**ox·tongue** \'äks-,təŋ\ *noun* (14th century)
: a European hawkweed (*Picris echioides*) that has yellow flowers and is now naturalized in the eastern U.S.

**oxy** \'äk-sē\ *adjective* [French, from *oxygène* oxygen] (1910)
: containing oxygen or additional oxygen — often used in combination ⟨*oxy*hemoglobin⟩

**oxy·acet·y·lene** \,äk-sē-ə-'se-t°l-ən, -t°l-,ēn\ *adjective* [International Scientific Vocabulary] (1909)
: of, relating to, or utilizing a mixture of oxygen and acetylene ⟨an *oxyacetylene* torch⟩

**oxy·ac·id** \'äk-sē-,a-səd\ *noun* (circa 1841)
: an acid (as sulfuric acid) that contains oxygen — called also *oxygen acid*

**ox·y·gen** \'äk-si-jən\ *noun, often attributive* [French *oxygène,* from Greek *oxys,* adjective, acidic, literally, sharp + French *-gène* -gen; akin to Latin *acer* sharp — more at EDGE] (1790)
: a colorless tasteless odorless gaseous element that constitutes 21 percent of the atmosphere and is found in water, in most rocks and minerals, and in numerous organic compounds, that is capable of combining with all elements except the inert gases, that is active in physiological processes, and that is involved especially in combustion — see ELEMENT table
— **ox·y·gen·ic** \,äk-si-'je-nik\ *adjective*
— **ox·y·gen·less** \'äk-si-jən-ləs\ *adjective*

**ox·y·gen·ate** \'äk-si-jə-,nāt, äk-'si-jə-\ *transitive verb* **-at·ed; -at·ing** (1790)
: to impregnate, combine, or supply (as blood) with oxygen
— **ox·y·gen·a·tion** \,äk-si-jə-'nā-shən, äk-,si-jə-\ *noun*

**ox·y·gen·a·tor** \'äk-si-jə-,nā-tər, äk-'si-jə-\ *noun* (circa 1864)
: one that oxygenates; *specifically* : an apparatus that oxygenates the blood extracorporeally (as during open-heart surgery)

**oxygen cycle** *noun* (1935)
: the cycle whereby atmospheric oxygen is converted to carbon dioxide in animal respiration and regenerated by green plants in photosynthesis

**oxygen debt** *noun* (1923)
: a cumulative deficit of oxygen available for oxidative metabolism that develops during periods of intense bodily activity and must be made good when the body returns to rest

**oxygen demand** *noun* (1950)
: BIOCHEMICAL OXYGEN DEMAND

**oxygen mask** *noun* (1920)
: a device worn over the nose and mouth (as by pilots at high altitudes) through which oxygen is supplied from a storage tank

**oxygen tent** *noun* (1925)
: a canopy which can be placed over a bedridden person and within which a flow of oxygen can be maintained

**oxy·he·mo·glo·bin** \,äk-si-'hē-mə-,glō-bən\ *noun* [International Scientific Vocabulary] (1873)
: hemoglobin loosely combined with oxygen that it releases to the tissues

**oxy·hy·dro·gen** \-'hī-drə-jən\ *adjective* (1827)
: of, relating to, or utilizing a mixture of oxygen and hydrogen ⟨*oxyhydrogen* torch⟩

**ox·y·mo·ron** \,äk-si-'mōr-,än, -'mòr-\ *noun, plural* **-mo·ra** \-'mōr-ə, -'mòr-\ [Late Greek *oxymōron,* from neuter of *oxymōros* pointedly foolish, from Greek *oxys* sharp, keen + *mōros* foolish] (1657)
: a combination of contradictory or incongruous words (as *cruel kindness*)
— **ox·y·mo·ron·ic** \-mə-'rä-nik, -,mò-\ *adjective*
— **ox·y·mo·ron·i·cal·ly** \-ni-k(ə-)lē\ *adverb*

**oxy·phen·bu·ta·zone** \,äk-sē-,fen-'byü-tə-,zōn\ *noun* [*oxy* + *phenylbutazone*] (1961)
: a phenylbutazone derivative $C_{19}H_{20}N_2O_3$ used for its anti-inflammatory, analgesic, and antipyretic effects

**oxy·phil·ic** \,äk-si-'fi-lik\ *adjective* [Greek *oxys* acidic + English *-phil* — more at OXYGEN] (1901)
: ACIDOPHILIC

**oxy·tet·ra·cy·cline** \-,te-trə-'sī-,klēn\ *noun* (1953)
: a yellow crystalline broad-spectrum antibiotic $C_{22}H_{24}N_2O_9$ produced by a soil actinomycete (*Streptomyces rimosus*)

**oxy·to·cic** \,äk-si-'tō-sik\ *adjective* [International Scientific Vocabulary, from Greek *oxys* sharp, quick + *tokos* childbirth, from *tiktein* to bear — more at THANE] (1873)
: hastening parturition; *also* : inducing contraction of uterine smooth muscle
— **oxytocic** *noun*

**oxy·to·cin** \-'tō-s°n\ *noun* [International Scientific Vocabulary, from *oxytocic*] (1928)
: a pituitary octapeptide hormone $C_{43}H_{66}N_{12}O_{12}S_2$ that stimulates especially the contraction of uterine muscle and the secretion of milk

**oxy·uri·a·sis** \,äk-si-yü-'rī-ə-səs\ *noun* [New Latin, from *Oxyuris,* genus of worms] (circa 1909)
: infestation with or disease caused by pinworms (family Oxyuridae)

**oy·er and ter·mi·ner** \,òi-ər-ən(d)-'tər-mə-nər\ *noun* [Middle English, part translation of Anglo-French *oyer et terminer,* literally, to hear and determine] (15th century)
**1** : a commission authorizing a British judge to hear and determine a criminal case at the assizes
**2** : a high criminal court in some U.S. states

**¹oyez** \'ō-'yez, -'yā, 'ō-,yes, 'ō-,\ *verb imperative* [Middle English, from Anglo-French, hear ye, imperative plural of *oir* to hear, from Latin *audire* — more at AUDIBLE] (15th century)
— used by a court or public crier to gain attention before a proclamation

**²oyez** *noun, plural* **oyes·ses** \-'ye-səz, -,ye-səz\ (15th century)
: a cry of oyez

\ə\ **abut** \°\ **kitten** \ər\ **further** \a\ **ash** \ā\ **ace**
\ä\ **mop, mar** \aù\ **out** \ch\ **chin** \e\ **bet** \ē\ **easy**
\g\ **go** \i\ **hit** \ī\ **ice** \j\ **job** \ŋ\ **sing** \ō\ **go**
\ò\ **law** \òi\ **boy** \th\ **thin** \t̲h̲\ **the** \ü\ **loot** \ù\ **foot**
\y\ **yet** \zh\ **vision** *see also* Guide to Pronunciation

**oys·ter** \'ȯis-tər\ *noun, often attributive* [Middle English *oistre,* from Middle French, from Latin *ostrea,* from Greek *ostreon;* akin to Greek *ostrakon* shell, *osteon* bone — more at OSSEOUS] (13th century)
**1 a** : any of various marine bivalve mollusks (family Ostreidae) that have a rough irregular shell closed by a single adductor muscle and include commercially important shellfish **b** : any of various mollusks resembling or related to the oysters
**2** : something that is or can be readily made to serve one's personal ends ⟨the world was her *oyster*⟩
**3** : a small mass of muscle contained in a concavity of the pelvic bone on each side of the back of a fowl
**4** : an extremely taciturn person
**5** : a grayish-white color
**oyster bed** *noun* (1591)
: a place where oysters grow or are cultivated
**oys·ter·catch·er** \-ˌka-chər, -ˌke-\ *noun* (1731)
: any of a genus (*Haematopus*) of wading birds that have stout legs, a heavy wedge-shaped bill, and often black-and-white plumage
**oyster crab** *noun* (1756)
: a tiny crab (*Pinnotheres ostreum*) that lives as a commensal in the gill cavity of the oyster
**oyster cracker** *noun* (1873)
: a small salted usually round cracker
**oyster drill** *noun* (1925)
: DRILL 4a

**oys·ter·ing** \'ȯis-t(ə-)riŋ\ *noun* (1662)
: the act or business of taking oysters for the market or for food
**oys·ter·man** \'ȯis-tər-mən\ *noun* (1552)
: one who gathers, opens, breeds, or sells oysters
**oyster mushroom** *noun* (1875)
: an edible mushroom (*Pleurotus ostreatus*) that grows especially on deciduous trees and dead wood
**oyster plant** *noun* (1821)
: SALSIFY
**oysters Rocke·fel·ler** \-ˈrä-ki-ˌfe-lər\ *noun plural* [probably from John D. *Rockefeller* (died 1937)] (1939)
: a dish of oysters on the half shell cooked with various savory toppings typically including chopped spinach and a seasoned sauce
**ozo·ke·rite** \ˌō-zō-ˈkir-ˌīt\ *also* **ozo·ce·rite** \-ˈsir-\ *noun* [German *Ozokerit,* from Greek *ozein* to smell + *kēros* wax — more at CERUMEN] (circa 1837)
: a waxy mineral mixture of hydrocarbons that is colorless or white when pure and often of unpleasant odor and is used especially in making candles and in electrotyping
**ozon·a·tion** \ˌō-(ˌ)zō-ˈnā-shən\ *noun* (1854)
: the treatment or combination of a substance or compound with ozone
— **ozon·ate** \'ō-(ˌ)zō-ˌnāt, -zə-\ *transitive verb*
**ozone** \'ō-ˌzōn\ *noun* [German *Ozon,* from Greek *ozōn,* present participle of *ozein* to smell — more at ODOR] (circa 1840)

**1** : a triatomic very reactive form of oxygen that is a bluish irritating gas of pungent odor, that is formed naturally in the atmosphere by a photochemical reaction and is a major air pollutant in the lower atmosphere but a beneficial component of the upper atmosphere, and that is used for oxidizing, bleaching, disinfecting, and deodorizing
**2** : pure and refreshing air
— **ozo·nic** \ō-ˈzō-nik, -ˈzä-\ *adjective*
**ozone hole** *noun* (1986)
: an area of the ozone layer (as near the south pole) that is seasonally depleted of ozone
**ozone layer** *noun* (1929)
: an atmospheric layer at heights of about 20 to 30 miles (32 to 48 kilometers) that is normally characterized by high ozone content which blocks most solar ultraviolet radiation from entry into the lower atmosphere
**ozon·ide** \'ō-(ˌ)zō-ˌnīd\ *noun* (1867)
: a compound of ozone; *specifically* : a compound formed by the addition of ozone to the double or triple bond of an unsaturated organic compound
**ozon·ize** \-ˌnīz\ *transitive verb* **-ized; -iz·ing** (1850)
: to treat, impregnate, or combine with ozone
— **ozon·i·za·tion** \ˌō-(ˌ)zō-nə-ˈzā-shən\ *noun*
— **ozon·iz·er** \'ō-(ˌ)zō-ˌnī-zər\ *noun*
**ozo·no·sphere** \ō-ˈzō-nə-ˌsfir\ *noun* (1933)
: OZONE LAYER

**P** *is the sixteenth letter of the English alphabet. It comes through Latin, via Etruscan, from Greek* pi, *which in turn was borrowed from Phoenician* pê, *representing the sound which it has ever since retained, that of a voiceless bilabial stop (the* p *in English* pet*). P is sometimes silent in English, especially in the combinations* pn, ps, *and* pt *found at the beginning of certain words from Greek (for example,* pneumatic, *p*sychic, *and* ptomaine*). With* h *it unites to form the independent digraph* ph, *which represents the Greek* phi *and has the value of* f *in words from that language (such as* phrase *and gra*phic*). In related foreign words, English* p *corresponds to German* pf *or* f *and rarely to* b *in other Indo-European languages; compare, for example, English* plow *with German* Pflug *("plow") and English* deep *with German* tief *and Lithuanian* dubus *(both meaning "deep"). Small* p *was formed by reducing the size of the capital and placing the letter lower on the line.*

**p** \'pē\ *noun, plural* **p's** *or* **ps** \'pēz\ *often capitalized, often attributive* (before 12th century) **1 a :** the 16th letter of the English alphabet **b :** a graphic representation of this letter **c :** a speech counterpart of orthographic *p* **2 :** a graphic device for reproducing the letter *p* **3 :** one designated *p* especially as the 16th in order or class **4** [abbreviation for *pass*] **a :** a grade rating a student's work as passing **b :** one graded or rated with a P **5 :** something shaped like the letter P

**pa** \'pä, 'pò\ *noun* [short for *papa*] (1811) **:** FATHER

**PA** \(.)pē-'ā\ *noun* (1970) **:** PHYSICIAN'S ASSISTANT

**pa·an·ga** \pä-'äŋ-gə, -'äŋ-ə\ *noun* [Tongan, literally, seed from a species of vine] (1966) — see MONEY table

**PABA** \'pa-bə, 'pä-; ,pē-(,)ā-'bē-(,)ā\ *noun* [*para-aminobenzoic acid*] (1943) **:** PARA-AMINOBENZOIC ACID

**pab·lum** \'pa-bləm\ *noun* [from *Pablum,* a trademark for an infant cereal] (1948) **:** PABULUM 3

**pab·u·lum** \'pa-byə-ləm\ *noun* [Latin, food, fodder; akin to Latin *pascere* to feed — more at FOOD] (1733) **1 :** FOOD; *especially* **:** a suspension or solution of nutrients in a state suitable for absorption **2 :** intellectual sustenance **3 :** something (as writing or speech) that is insipid, simplistic, or bland

**pa·ca** \'pä-kə, 'pa-\ *noun* [Portuguese & Spanish, from Tupi *páka*] (1657) **:** either of two large chiefly Central and South American rodents that constitute a genus (*Agouti* synonym *Cuniculus*) and typically have a white-spotted brownish coat

paca

**¹pace** \'pās\ *noun* [Middle English *pas,* from Old French, step, from Latin *passus,* from *pandere* to spread — more at FATHOM] (14th century) **1 a :** rate of movement; *especially* **:** an established rate of locomotion **b :** rate of progress; *specifically* **:** parallel rate of growth or development ⟨supplies kept *pace* with demand⟩ **c :** an example to be emulated; *specifically* **:** first place in a competition ⟨three strokes off the *pace —Time*⟩ **d** (1) **:** rate of performance or delivery **:** TEMPO; *especially* **:** SPEED ⟨serves with great *pace*⟩ ⟨a *pace* bowler in cricket⟩ (2) **:** rhythmic animation **:** FLUENCY ⟨writes with color, with zest, and with *pace —*Amy Loveman⟩ **2 :** a manner of walking **:** TREAD **3 a :** STEP 2a(1) **b :** any of various units of distance based on the length of a human step **4 a** *plural* **:** an exhibition or test of skills or capacities ⟨the trainer put the tiger through its *paces*⟩ **b :** GAIT; *especially* **:** a fast 2-beat gait (as of the horse) in which the legs move in lateral pairs and support the animal alternately on the right and left legs

**²pace** *verb* **paced; pac·ing** (1513) *intransitive verb* **1 a :** to walk with often slow or measured tread **b :** to move along **:** PROCEED **2 :** to go at a pace — used especially of a horse *transitive verb* **1 a :** to measure by pacing — often used with *off* ⟨*paced* off a 10-yard penalty⟩ **b :** to cover at a walk ⟨could hear him *pacing* the floor⟩ **2 :** to cover (a course) by pacing — used of a horse **3 a :** to set or regulate the pace of ⟨taught them how to *pace* their solos for . . . impact *—*Richard Goldstein⟩; *also* **:** to establish a moderate or steady pace for (oneself) **b** (1) **:** to go before **:** PRECEDE (2) **:** to set an example for **:** LEAD **c :** to keep pace with

**³pace** \'pā-(,)sē; 'pä-(,)chā, -(,)kā\ *preposition* [Latin, ablative of *pac-, pax* peace, permission — more at PACT] (1863) **:** contrary to the opinion of — usually used as an expression of deference to someone's contrary opinion; usually italic ⟨easiness is a virtue in grammar, *pace* old-fashioned grammarians *—*Philip Howard⟩

**pace car** *noun* (1965) **:** an automobile that leads the field of competitors through a pace lap but does not participate in the race

**pace lap** *noun* (1971) **:** a lap of an auto racecourse by the entire field of competitors before the start of a race to allow the engines to warm up and to permit a flying start

**pace·mak·er** \'pās-,mā-kər\ *noun* (1884) **1 :** one that sets the pace for another **b :** one that takes the lead or sets an example **2 a :** a body part (as the sinoatrial node of the heart) that serves to establish and maintain a rhythmic activity **b :** an electrical device for stimulating or steadying the heartbeat or reestablishing the rhythm of an arrested heart — **pace·mak·ing** \-kiŋ\ *noun*

**pac·er** \'pā-sər\ *noun* (circa 1661) **1 :** one that paces; *specifically* **:** a horse whose predominant gait is the pace **2 :** PACEMAKER

**pace·set·ter** \'pās-,se-tər\ *noun* (1895) **:** PACEMAKER 1 — **pace·set·ting** \-tiŋ\ *adjective*

**pa·chi·si** \pə-'chē-zē\ *noun* [Hindi *pacīsī,* from *pacīs* twenty-five] (1867) **:** an ancient board game played with dice and counters on a cruciform board in which players attempt to be the first to reach the home square

**pa·chu·co** \pə-'chü-(,)kō\ *noun, plural* **-cos** [American Spanish] (1943) **:** a young Mexican-American having a taste for flashy clothes and a special jargon and usually belonging to a neighborhood gang

**pachy·derm** \'pa-ki-,dərm\ *noun* [French *pachyderme,* from Greek *pachydermos* thick-skinned, from *pachys* thick + *derma* skin; akin to Sanskrit *bahu* dense, much — more at DERM-] (1838) **:** any of various nonruminant hoofed mammals (as an elephant, a rhinoceros, or a pig) most of which have a thick skin

**pachy·der·ma·tous** \,pa-ki-'dər-mə-təs\ *adjective* [ultimately from Greek *pachys* + *dermat-, derma* skin] (1823) **1 :** of or relating to the pachyderms **2 a :** THICK, THICKENED ⟨*pachydermatous* skin⟩ **b :** CALLOUS, INSENSITIVE

**pach·y·san·dra** \,pa-ki-'san-drə\ *noun* [New Latin, irregular from Greek *pachys* + New Latin *-andrus* -androus] (1813) **:** any of a genus (*Pachysandra*) of shrubby evergreen plants of the box family often used as a ground cover

**pachy·tene** \'pa-ki-,tēn\ *noun* [International Scientific Vocabulary *pachy-* (from Greek *pachys*) + *-tene*] (1912) **:** the stage of meiotic prophase that immediately follows the zygotene and that is characterized by paired chromosomes thickened and visibly divided into chromatids and by the occurrence of crossing-over — **pachytene** *adjective*

**pa·cif·ic** \pə-'si-fik\ *adjective* [Middle English *pacifique,* from Latin *pacificus,* from *pac-, pax* peace + *-i-* + *-ficus* -fic — more at PACT] (circa 1548) **1 a :** tending to lessen conflict **:** CONCILIATORY **b :** rejecting the use of force as an instrument of policy **2 a :** having a soothing appearance or effect ⟨mild *pacific* breezes⟩ **b :** mild of temper **:** PEACEABLE **3** *capitalized* **:** of, relating to, bordering on, or situated near the Pacific Ocean — **pa·cif·i·cal·ly** \-fi-k(ə-)lē\ *adverb*

**pac·i·fi·ca·tion** \,pa-sə-fə-'kā-shən\ *noun* (15th century) **1 a :** the act or process of pacifying **:** the state of being pacified **b :** the act of forcibly suppressing or eliminating a population considered to be hostile **2 :** a treaty of peace

**pa·cif·i·ca·tor** \pə-'si-fə-,kā-tər\ *noun* (1539) **:** PACIFIER 1

**pac·i·fism** \pə-'si-fə-,si-zəm\ *noun* (1910) **:** PACIFISM — **pa·cif·i·cist** \-sist\ *noun*

**Pacific salmon** *noun* (1888) **:** any of several anadromous salmonid fishes (genus *Oncorhynchus*) chiefly of the northern Pacific including the sockeye, coho, chum salmon, and chinook salmon

**Pacific time** \pə-'si-fik-\ *noun* [*Pacific Ocean*] (1883) **:** the time of the 8th time zone west of Greenwich that includes the Pacific coastal region of the U.S. — see TIME ZONE illustration

**pac·i·fi·er** \'pa-sə-,fī(-ə)r\ *noun* (1533)

\ə\ abut \ᵊ\ kitten \ər\ further \a\ ash \ā\ ace \ä\ mop, mar \au̇\ out \ch\ chin \e\ bet \ē\ easy \g\ go \i\ hit \ī\ ice \j\ job \ŋ\ sing \ō\ go \ȯ\ law \ȯi\ boy \th\ thin \th\ the \ü\ loot \u̇\ foot \y\ yet \zh\ vision   *see also* Guide to Pronunciation

**1 :** one that pacifies
**2 :** a usually nipple-shaped device for babies to suck or bite on

**pac·i·fism** \'pa-sə-ˌfi-zəm\ *noun* [French *pacifisme*, from *pacifique* pacific] (1902)
**1 :** opposition to war or violence as a means of settling disputes; *specifically* **:** refusal to bear arms on moral or religious grounds
**2 :** an attitude or policy of nonresistance
— **pac·i·fist** \-fist\ *noun*
**pac·i·fist** \'pa-sə-fist\ *or* **pac·i·fis·tic** \ˌpa-sə-'fis-tik\ *adjective* (1908)
**1 :** of, relating to, or characteristic of pacifism or pacifists
**2 :** strongly and actively opposed to conflict and especially war
— **pac·i·fis·ti·cal·ly** \ˌpa-sə-'fis-ti-k(ə-)lē\ *adverb*
**pac·i·fy** \'pa-sə-ˌfi\ *transitive verb* **-fied; -fy·ing** [Middle English *pacifien*, from Latin *pacificare*, from *pac-, pax* peace] (15th century)
**1 a :** to allay the anger or agitation of **:** SOOTHE ⟨*pacify* a crying child⟩ **b :** APPEASE, PROPITIATE
**2 a :** to restore to a tranquil state **:** SETTLE ⟨made an attempt to *pacify* the commotion⟩ **b :** to reduce to a submissive state **:** SUBDUE ⟨forces moved in to *pacify* the country⟩ ☆
— **pac·i·fi·able** \ˌpa-sə-'fī-ə-bəl\ *adjective*
**Pa·cin·i·an corpuscle** \pə-'si-nē-ən-\ *noun* [Filippo *Pacini* (died 1883) Italian anatomist] (circa 1860)
**:** an oval capsule that terminates some sensory nerve fibers especially in the skin of the hands and feet

¹**pack** \'pak\ *noun, often attributive* [Middle English, of Low German or Dutch origin; akin to Middle Low German & Middle Dutch *pak* pack] (13th century)
**1 a :** a bundle arranged for convenience in carrying especially on the back **b :** a group or pile of related objects **c (1) :** a number of individual components packaged as a unit ⟨a *pack* of cigarettes⟩ **(2) :** CONTAINER **(3) :** a compact unitized assembly to perform a specific function **(4) :** a stack of magnetic disks in a container for use as a storage device
**2 a :** the contents of a bundle **b :** a large amount or number **:** HEAP ⟨a *pack* of lies⟩ **c :** a full set of playing cards
**3 a :** an act or instance of packing **b :** a method of packing
**4 a :** a set of persons with a common interest **:** CLIQUE **b :** an organized troop (as of Cub Scouts)
**5 a (1) :** a group of domesticated animals trained to hunt or run together **(2) :** a group of often predatory animals of the same kind ⟨a wolf *pack*⟩ **(3) :** a large group of individuals massed together (as in a race) **b :** WOLF PACK
**6 :** a concentrated or compacted mass (as of snow or ice)
**7 :** wet absorbent material for therapeutic application to the body
**8 a :** a cosmetic paste for the face **b :** an application or treatment of oils or creams for conditioning the scalp and hair
**9 :** material used in packing
²**pack** (14th century)
*transitive verb*
**1 a :** to make into a compact bundle **b :** to fill completely ⟨fans *packed* the stadium⟩ **c :** to fill with packing ⟨*pack* a joint in a pipe⟩ **d :** to load with a pack ⟨*pack* a mule⟩ **e :** to put in a protective container ⟨goods *packed* for shipment⟩
**2 a :** to crowd together **b :** to increase the density of **:** COMPRESS
**3 a :** to cause or command to go without ceremony ⟨*packed* him off to school⟩ **b :** to bring to an end **:** GIVE UP — used with *up* or *in* ⟨might *pack* up the assignment⟩; used especially in the phrase *pack it in*
**4 :** to gather into tight formation **:** make a pack of (as hounds)
**5 :** to cover or surround with a pack

**6 a :** to transport on foot or on the back of an animal ⟨*pack* a canoe overland⟩ **b :** to wear or carry as equipment ⟨*pack* a gun⟩ **c :** to be supplied or equipped with **:** POSSESS ⟨a storm *packing* hurricane winds⟩ **d :** to cause or be capable of making (an impact) ⟨a book that *packs* a man-sized punch —C. J. Rolo⟩
*intransitive verb*
**1 a :** to go away without ceremony **:** DEPART ⟨simply *packed* up and left⟩ **b :** QUIT, STOP — used with *up* or *in* ⟨why don't you *pack* in, before you kill yourself —Millard Lampell⟩
**2 a :** to stow goods and equipment for transportation **b :** to be suitable for packing ⟨a knit dress *packs* well⟩
**3 a :** to assemble in a group **:** CONGREGATE **b :** to crowd together
**4 :** to become built up or compacted in a layer or mass ⟨the ore *packed* into a stony mass⟩
**5 a :** to carry goods or equipment **b :** to travel with one's baggage (as by horse)
— **pack·abil·i·ty** \ˌpa-kə-'bi-lə-tē\ *noun*
— **pack·able** \'pa-kə-bəl\ *adjective*
³**pack** *transitive verb* [obsolete *pack* to make a secret agreement] (1587)
**1 :** to influence the composition of (as a political agency) so as to bring about a desired result ⟨*pack* a jury⟩
**2** *archaic* **:** to arrange (the cards in a pack) so as to cheat
⁴**pack** *adjective* [perhaps from obsolete *pack* to make a secret agreement] (1701)
*chiefly Scottish* **:** INTIMATE
¹**pack·age** \'pa-kij\ *noun* (1611)
**1** *archaic* **:** the act or process of packing
**2 a :** a small or moderate-sized pack **:** PARCEL **b :** a commodity or a unit of a product uniformly wrapped or sealed **c :** a preassembled unit
**3 :** a covering wrapper or container
**4 :** something that suggests a package: as **a :** PACKAGE DEAL **b :** a radio or television series offered for sale at a lump sum **c :** contract benefits gained through collective bargaining **d :** a ready-made computer program or collection of related software **e :** a travel arrangement contract that offers for a fixed price transportation, accommodations, and often sightseeing and entertainment **f :** a collection of related items; *especially* **:** one to be considered or acted on together ⟨presented his tax *package* to the nation⟩
²**package** *transitive verb* **pack·aged; pack·ag·ing** (1921)
**1 a :** to make into a package; *especially* **:** to produce as an entertainment package **b :** to present (as a product) in such a way as to heighten its appeal to the public
**2 :** to enclose in a package or covering
— **pack·ag·er** *noun*
**package deal** *noun* (circa 1948)
**1 :** an offer or agreement involving a number of related items or one making acceptance of one item dependent on the acceptance of another
**2 :** the items offered in a package deal
**package store** *noun* (circa 1918)
**:** a store that sells bottled or canned alcoholic beverages for consumption off the premises
**pack animal** *noun* (1847)
**:** an animal used for carrying packs
**pack·board** \'pak-ˌbȯrd, -ˌbȯrd\ *noun* (1939)
**:** a usually canvas-covered light wood or metal frame with shoulder straps used for carrying goods and equipment
**packed** \'pakt\ *adjective* (1777)
**1 a :** COMPRESSED ⟨hard-*packed* snow⟩ **b :** that is crowded or stuffed — often used in combination ⟨an action-*packed* story⟩
**2 :** filled to capacity ⟨played to a *packed* house⟩
**pack·er** \'pa-kər\ *noun* (14th century)
**1 :** one that packs: as **a :** one engaged in processing food (as meat) and distributing it to re-

tailers **b :** an automotive vehicle with a closed body and a compressing device (as for compacting rubbish) in the rear
**2 :** PORTER 1
**3 :** one that conveys goods by means of a pack
**pack·et** \'pa-kət\ *noun* [Middle English, from Middle French *pacquet*, of Germanic origin; akin to Middle Dutch *pak* pack] (15th century)
**1 a :** a small bundle or parcel **b :** a small thin package **c** *British* **(1) :** PAY ENVELOPE **(2) :** SALARY, PAYCHECK **d** *chiefly British* **:** a considerable amount ⟨that trip will cost you a *packet*⟩
**2 a :** a number of letters dispatched at one time **b :** a small group, cluster, or mass
**3 :** a passenger boat usually carrying mail and cargo
**4** *British* **:** a pack of cigarettes
**5 :** a short fixed-length section of data that is transmitted as a unit in an electronic communications network
**pack·horse** \'pak-ˌhȯrs\ *noun* (circa 1500)
**:** a horse used as a pack animal
**pack ice** *noun* (1850)
**:** sea ice formed into a mass by the crushing together of pans, floes, and brash
**pack·ing** \'pa-kiŋ\ *noun* (14th century)
**1 a :** the action or process of packing something; *also* **:** a method of packing **b :** the processing of food and especially meat for future sale
**2 :** material (as a covering or stuffing) used to protect packed goods (as for shipping); *also* **:** material used for making airtight or watertight ⟨*packing* for a faucet⟩
**pack·ing·house** \-ˌhau̇s\ *noun* (1834)
**:** an establishment for slaughtering livestock and processing and packing meat, meat products, and by-products; *also* **:** one for processing and packing other foodstuffs — called also *packing plant*
**pack·man** \'pak-mən\ *noun* (circa 1625)
**:** PEDDLER
**pack rat** *noun* (1885)
**1 :** WOOD RAT; *especially* **:** a bushy-tailed rodent (*Neotoma cinerea*) of the Rocky Mountain area that has well-developed cheek pouches and hoards food and miscellaneous objects
**2 :** one who collects or hoards especially unneeded items
**pack·sack** \'pak-ˌsak\ *noun* (1851)
**:** a case (as of canvas) held on the back by shoulder straps and used to carry gear when traveling on foot
**pack·sad·dle** \-ˌsa-d°l\ *noun* (14th century)
**:** a saddle designed to support loads on the backs of pack animals
**pack·thread** \-ˌthred\ *noun* (14th century)
**:** strong thread or small twine used for sewing or tying packs or parcels
**pact** \'pakt\ *noun* [Middle English, from Middle French, from Latin *pactum*, from neuter of *pactus*, past participle of *pacisci* to agree, contract; akin to Old English *fōn* to seize, Latin

*pax* peace, *pangere* to fix, fasten, Greek *pēgnynai*] (15th century)
: [4]COMPACT; *especially* : an international treaty
**¹pad** \'pad\ *verb* **pad·ded; pad·ding** [perhaps from Middle Dutch *paden* to follow a path, from *pad* path] (1553)
*transitive verb*
: to traverse on foot
*intransitive verb*
: to go on foot : WALK; *especially* : to walk with or as if with padded feet ⟨the dog *padded* along beside him⟩ ⟨*padding* around in bedroom slippers⟩
**²pad** *noun* [Middle Dutch *pad*] (1567)
**1** *dialect British* : PATH
**2** : a horse that moves along at an easy pace
**3** *archaic* : FOOTPAD
**³pad** *noun* [origin unknown] (1570)
**1 a** : a thin flat mat or cushion: as (1) : a piece of soft stuffed material used as or under a saddle (2) : padding used to shape an article of clothing (3) : a guard worn to shield body parts against impact (4) : a piece of usually folded absorbent material (as gauze) used as a surgical dressing or protective covering (5) : frictional material that presses against the disks in a disk brake **b** : a piece of material saturated with ink for inking the surface of a rubber stamp
**2 a** : the foot of an animal **b** : the cushioned thickening of the underside of the toes of an animal
**3** : a floating leaf of a water plant
**4** : a collection of sheets of paper glued together at one end
**5 a** (1) : a section of an airstrip used for warm-ups or turnarounds (2) : an area used for helicopter takeoffs and landings **b** : LAUNCHPAD **c** : a horizontal concrete surface (as for parking a mobile home)
**6 a** : BED **b** : living quarters
**⁴pad** *transitive verb* **pad·ded; pad·ding** (1827)
**1 a** : to furnish with a pad or padding **b** : MUTE, MUFFLE
**2** : to expand or increase especially with needless, misleading, or fraudulent matter ⟨*pad* an expense account⟩ — often used with *out* ⟨they *pad* out their bibliographies —J. P. Kenyon⟩
**⁵pad** *noun* [imitative] (1594)
: a soft muffled or slapping sound
**pad·ding** \'pa-diŋ\ *noun* (1828)
: material with which something is padded
**¹pad·dle** \'pa-dᵊl\ *intransitive verb* **pad·dled; pad·dling** \'pad-liŋ, 'pa-dᵊl-iŋ\ [origin unknown] (1530)
**1** : to move the hands or feet about in shallow water
**2** *archaic* : to use the hands or fingers in toying or caressing
**3** : TODDLE
— **pad·dler** \'pad-lər, 'pa-dᵊl-ər\ *noun*
**²paddle** *noun* [Middle English *padell* spade-shaped tool for cleaning a plow] (1624)
**1 a** : a usually wooden implement that has a long handle and a broad flattened blade and that is used to propel and steer a small craft (as a canoe) **b** : an implement often with a short handle and a broad flat blade that is used for stirring, mixing, or hitting; *especially* : one used to hit a ball in any of various games (as table tennis)
**2 a** : any of the broad boards at the circumference of a paddle wheel or waterwheel **b** : any of the broad blades attached to a shaft (as in an ice cream machine) and used for stirring
**3** : a computer input device with a dial used to control linear movement of a cursor on a computer display
**³paddle** *verb* **pad·dled; pad·dling** \'pad-liŋ, 'pa-dᵊl-iŋ\ (1677)
*intransitive verb*
: to go on or through water by or as if by means of a paddle or paddle wheel
*transitive verb*

**1 a** : to propel by a paddle **b** : to transport in a paddled craft ⟨*paddled* us to shore in his canoe⟩
**2 a** : to beat or stir with or as if with a paddle (as in washing or dyeing) **b** : to punish by or as if by beating with a paddle
— **pad·dler** \'pad-lər, 'pa-dᵊl-ər\ *noun*
**pad·dle·ball** \'pa-dᵊl-,bòl\ *noun* (1935)
: a game like handball played by hitting the ball with a paddle; *also* : the ball used in this game
**pad·dle·board** \-,bōrd, -,bòrd\ *noun* (1938)
: a long narrow buoyant board used for riding the surf or in rescuing swimmers
**pad·dle·boat** \-,bōt\ *noun* (1874)
: a boat propelled by a paddle wheel
**pad·dle·fish** \-,fish\ *noun* (1807)
: any of a family (Polyodontidae) of ganoid fishes; *especially* : a large fish (*Polyodon spathula*) of the Mississippi valley that has a long paddle-shaped snout

**paddlefish**

**paddle tennis** *noun* (1925)
: a game like tennis that is played with a paddle and rubber ball on a small court
**paddle wheel** *noun* (1685)
: a wheel with paddles around its circumference used to propel a boat
**paddle wheeler** *noun* (1924)
: a steamer propelled by a paddle wheel
**pad·dock** \'pa-dək, -dik\ *noun* [alteration of Middle English *parrok*, from Old English *pearroc*, from Medieval Latin *parricus*] (1622)
**1 a** : a usually enclosed area used especially for pasturing or exercising animals; *especially* : an enclosure where racehorses are saddled and paraded before a race **b** *Australian & New Zealand* : an often enclosed field
**2** : an area at an automobile racecourse where racing cars are parked
**pad·dy** *also* **padi** \'pa-dē\ *noun, plural* **paddies** *also* **pad·is** [Malay *padi*] (1623)
**1** : RICE; *especially* : threshed unmilled rice
**2** : wet land in which rice is grown
**Pad·dy** \'pa-dē\ *noun, plural* **Paddies** [from *Paddy*, Hiberno-English nickname for *Patrick*] (1780)
: IRISHMAN — often taken to be offensive
**pad·dy wagon** \'pa-dē-\ *noun* [probably from *Paddy*] (1930)
: an enclosed motortruck used by police to carry prisoners — called also *Black Maria, patrol wagon*
**pad·lock** \'pad-,läk\ *noun* [Middle English *padlok*, from *pad-* (of unknown origin) + *lok* lock] (15th century)
: a removable lock with a shackle that can be passed through a staple or link and then secured
— **padlock** *transitive verb*
**pa·dre** \'pä-(,)drā, -drē\ *noun* [Spanish or Italian or Portuguese, literally, father, from Latin *pater* — more at FATHER] (1584)
**1** : a Christian clergyman; *especially* : PRIEST
**2** : a military chaplain
**pa·dro·ne** \pə-'drō-nē\ *noun, plural* **-nes** *or* **-ni** \-nē\ [Italian, protector, owner, from Latin *patronus* patron] (1670)
**1 a** : MASTER **b** : an Italian innkeeper
**2** : one that secures employment especially for Italian immigrants
**pad·u·a·soy** \'pa-jə-wə-,sói, 'paj-wə-\ *noun* [alteration of earlier *poudesoy*, from French *pou-de-soie*] (1663)
: a corded silk fabric; *also* : a garment made of it
**pae·an** \'pē-ən\ *noun* [Latin, hymn of thanksgiving especially addressed to Apollo, from

Greek *paian, paiōn,* from *Paian, Paiōn,* epithet of Apollo in the hymn] (1589)
: a joyous song or hymn of praise, tribute, thanksgiving, or triumph; *broadly* : ENCOMIUM, TRIBUTE
**paed-** *or* **paedo-** — see PED-
**pae·di·at·ric, pae·di·a·tri·cian, pae·di·at·rics** *chiefly British variant of* PEDIATRIC, PEDIATRICIAN, PEDIATRICS
**pae·do·gen·e·sis** \,pē-dō-'je-nə-səs\ *noun* [New Latin] (circa 1871)
: reproduction by young or larval animals : NEOTENY
— **pae·do·ge·net·ic** \-jə-'ne-tik\ *or* **pae·do·gen·ic** \-'je-nik\ *adjective*
— **pae·do·ge·net·i·cal·ly** \-jə-'ne-ti-k(ə-)lē\ *adverb*
**pae·do·mor·phic** \,pē-də-'mòr-fik\ *adjective* (1891)
: of, relating to, or involving paedomorphosis or paedomorphism
**pae·do·mor·phism** \-'mòr-,fi-zəm\ *noun* (circa 1891)
: retention in the adult of infantile or juvenile characters
**pae·do·mor·pho·sis** \-'mòr-fə-səs\ *noun* [New Latin, from *paed-* + Greek *morphōsis* formation, from *morphoun* to form, from *morphē* form] (1922)
: phylogenetic change that involves retention of juvenile characters by the adult
**pa·el·la** \pä-'e-lə, -'ā-; -'äl-yə, -'ā-yə\ *noun* [Catalan, literally, pot, pan, from Middle French *paelle,* from Latin *patella* small pan — more at PATELLA] (circa 1892)
: a saffron-flavored dish containing rice, meat, seafood, and vegetables
**pae·on** \'pē-ən, -,än\ *noun* [Latin, from Greek *paiōn,* from *paian, paiōn* paean] (1603)
: a metrical foot of four syllables with one long and three short syllables (as in classical prosody) or with one stressed and three unstressed syllables (as in English prosody)
**pa·gan** \'pā-gən\ *noun* [Middle English, from Late Latin *paganus,* from Latin, country dweller, from *pagus* country district; akin to Latin *pangere* to fix — more at PACT] (14th century)
**1** : HEATHEN 1; *especially* : a follower of a polytheistic religion (as in ancient Rome)
**2** : one who has little or no religion and who delights in sensual pleasures and material goods : an irreligious or hedonistic person
— **pagan** *adjective*
— **pa·gan·ish** \-gə-nish\ *adjective*
**pa·gan·ism** \'pā-gə-,ni-zəm\ *noun* (15th century)
**1 a** : pagan beliefs or practices **b** : a pagan religion
**2** : the quality or state of being a pagan
**pa·gan·ize** \-,nīz\ *verb* **-ized; -iz·ing** (1615)
*transitive verb*
: to make pagan
*intransitive verb*
: to become pagan
— **pa·gan·iz·er** *noun*
**¹page** \'pāj\ *noun* [Middle English, from Middle French, from Old French] (14th century)
**1 a** (1) : a youth being trained for the medieval rank of knight and in the personal service of a knight (2) : a youth attendant on a person of rank especially in the medieval period **b** : a boy serving as an honorary attendant at a formal function (as a wedding)
**2** : one employed to deliver messages, assist patrons, serve as a guide, or attend to similar duties
**3** : an act or instance of paging ⟨a *page* came over the loudspeaker⟩

\ə\ abut \ᵊ\ kitten \ər\ further \a\ ash \ā\ ace \ä\ mop, mar \aù\ out \ch\ chin \e\ bet \ē\ easy \g\ go \i\ hit \ī\ ice \j\ job \ŋ\ sing \ō\ go \ò\ law \òi\ boy \th\ thin \ṯh\ the \ü\ loot \ù\ foot \y\ yet \zh\ vision   *see also* Guide to Pronunciation

²**page** *transitive verb* **paged; pag·ing** (15th century)
**1 :** to wait on or serve in the capacity of a page
**2 :** to summon by repeatedly calling out the name of

³**page** *noun* [Middle French, from Latin *pagina*; akin to Latin *pangere* to fix, fasten — more at PACT] (1589)
**1 a :** one of the leaves of a publication or manuscript; *also* : a single side of one of these leaves **b :** the material printed or written on a page
**2 a :** a written record **b :** a noteworthy event or period ⟨one of the brightest *pages* of my life⟩
**3 :** a sizable subdivision of computer memory; *also* : a block of information that fills a page and can be transferred as a unit between the internal and external storage of a computer

⁴**page** *verb* **paged; pag·ing** (1628)
*transitive verb*
**:** to number or mark the pages of
*intransitive verb*
**:** to turn the pages (as of a book or magazine) especially in a steady or haphazard manner — usually used with *through*

**pag·eant** \'pa-jənt\ *noun* [Middle English *pagyn, padgeant,* literally, scene of a play, from Medieval Latin *pagina,* perhaps from Latin, page] (14th century)
**1 a :** a mere show **:** PRETENSE **b :** an ostentatious display
**2 :** SHOW, EXHIBITION; *especially* : an elaborate colorful exhibition or spectacle often with music that consists of a series of tableaux, of a loosely unified drama, or of a procession usually with floats
**3 :** PAGEANTRY 1

**pag·eant·ry** \'pa-jən-trē\ *noun* (1608)
**1 :** pageants and the presentation of pageants
**2 :** colorful, rich, or splendid display **:** SPECTACLE
**3 :** mere show **:** empty display

**page boy** *noun* (1874)
**1 :** a boy serving as a page
**2** *usually* **pageboy :** an often shoulder-length hairdo with the ends of the hair turned under in a smooth roll

**pag·er** \'pā-jər\ *noun* (1901)
**:** one that pages; *especially* : BEEPER

**Pag·et's disease** \'pa-jəts-\ *noun* [Sir James Paget (died 1899) English surgeon] (1889)
**1 :** an eczematous inflammatory precancerous condition especially of the nipple and areola
**2 :** a chronic disease in which the bones become enlarged, weak, and deformed

**page–turn·er** \'pāj-,tər-nər\ *noun* (1972)
**:** an engrossing book or story

**pag·i·nate** \'pa-jə-,nāt\ *transitive verb* **-nat·ed; -nat·ing** [Latin *pagina* page] (1884)
**:** ⁴PAGE

**pag·i·na·tion** \,pa-jə-'nā-shən\ *noun* (1841)
**1 :** the action of paging **:** the condition of being paged
**2 a :** the numbers or marks used to indicate the sequence of pages (as of a book) **b :** the number and arrangement of pages or an indication of these

**pa·go·da** \pə-'gō-də\ *noun* [Portuguese *pagode* oriental idol, temple] (1588)
**:** a Far Eastern tower usually with roofs curving upward at the division of each of several stories and erected as a temple or memorial

**Pah·la·vi** \'pä-lə-(,)vē, 'pä-\ *noun* [Persian *pahlawī,* from *Pahlav* Parthia, from Old Persian *Parthava*] (1773)
**1 :** the Iranian language of Sassanian Persia — see INDO-EUROPEAN LANGUAGES table
**2 :** a script used for writing Pahlavi

**pagoda**

¹**paid** \'pād\ *past and past participle of* PAY

²**paid** *adjective* (1817)
**1 :** marked by the receipt of pay ⟨*paid* vacation time⟩
**2 :** being or having been paid or paid for ⟨a *paid* official⟩ ⟨a *paid* political announcement⟩

**pail** \'pā(ə)l\ *noun* [Middle English *payle, paille*] (14th century)
**1 :** a usually cylindrical container with a handle **:** BUCKET
**2 :** the quantity that a pail contains
— **pail·ful** \-,fúl\ *noun*

**pail·lard** \pī-'yär, pā-'yär\ *noun* [French *paillarde,* from *Paillard,* late 19th century French restaurateur] (1972)
**:** a piece of beef or veal usually pounded thin and grilled

**pail·lette** \pī-'yet, pā-'yet, pə-'let\ *noun* [French, from *paille* straw — more at PALLET] (circa 1890)
**1 :** a small shiny object (as a spangle) applied in clusters as a decorative trimming (as on women's clothing)
**2 :** a trimming made of paillettes

¹**pain** \'pān\ *noun* [Middle English, from Old French *peine,* from Latin *poena,* from Greek *poinē* payment, penalty; akin to Greek *tinein* to pay, *tinesthai* to punish, Avestan *kaēnā* revenge, Sanskrit *cayate* he revenges] (14th century)
**1 :** PUNISHMENT
**2 a :** usually localized physical suffering associated with bodily disorder (as a disease or an injury); *also* : a basic bodily sensation induced by a noxious stimulus, received by naked nerve endings, characterized by physical discomfort (as pricking, throbbing, or aching), and typically leading to evasive action **b :** acute mental or emotional distress or suffering **:** GRIEF
**3** *plural* **:** the throes of childbirth
**4** *plural* **:** trouble, care, or effort taken for the accomplishment of something ⟨was at *pains* to reassure us⟩
**5 :** one that irks or annoys or is otherwise troublesome — often used in such phrases as *pain in the neck*
— **pain·less** \-ləs\ *adjective*
— **pain·less·ly** *adverb*
— **pain·less·ness** *noun*
— **on pain of** *or* **under pain of :** subject to penalty or punishment of ⟨ordered not to leave the country *on pain of* death⟩

²**pain** (14th century)
*transitive verb*
**1 :** to make suffer or cause distress to **:** HURT
**2** *archaic* **:** to put (oneself) to trouble or exertion
*intransitive verb*
**1** *archaic* **:** SUFFER
**2 :** to give or have a sensation of pain

**pained** \'pānd\ *adjective* (14th century)
**1 :** feeling pain **:** HURT
**2 :** expressing or involving pain ⟨a *pained* expression⟩ ⟨with *pained* surprise⟩

**pain·ful** \'pān-fəl\ *adjective* **pain·ful·ler** \-fə-lər\; **pain·ful·lest** (14th century)
**1 a :** feeling or giving pain **b :** IRKSOME, ANNOYING
**2 :** requiring effort or exertion ⟨a long *painful* trip⟩
**3** *archaic* **:** CAREFUL, DILIGENT
— **pain·ful·ly** \-f(ə-)lē\ *adverb*
— **pain·ful·ness** \-fəl-nəs\ *noun*

**pain·kill·er** \-,ki-lər\ *noun* (1853)
**:** something (as a drug) that relieves pain
— **pain·kill·ing** \-liŋ\ *adjective*

¹**pains·tak·ing** \'pān-,stā-kiŋ\ *noun* (1538)
**:** the action of taking pains **:** diligent care and effort

²**painstaking** *adjective* (1696)
**:** taking pains **:** expending, showing, or involving diligent care and effort
— **pains·tak·ing·ly** \-kiŋ-lē\ *adverb*

¹**paint** \'pānt\ *verb* [Middle English, from Old French *peint,* past participle of *peindre,* from

Latin *pingere* to tattoo, embroider, paint; akin to Old English *fāh* variegated, Greek *poikilos* variegated, *pikros* sharp, bitter] (13th century)
*transitive verb*
**1 a** (1) **:** to apply color, pigment, or paint to (2) **:** to color with a cosmetic **b** (1) **:** to apply with a movement resembling that used in painting (2) **:** to treat with a liquid by brushing or swabbing ⟨*paint* the wound with iodine⟩
**2 a** (1) **:** to produce in lines and colors on a surface by applying pigments (2) **:** to depict by such lines and colors **b :** to decorate, adorn, or variegate by applying lines and colors **c :** to produce or evoke as if by painting ⟨*paints* glowing pictures of the farm⟩
**3 :** to touch up or cover over by or as if by painting
**4 :** to depict as having specified or implied characteristics ⟨*paints* them whiter than the evidence justifies —Oliver La Farge⟩
*intransitive verb*
**1 :** to practice the art of painting
**2 :** to use cosmetics

²**paint** *noun* (1602)
**1 :** the action of painting **:** something produced by painting
**2 :** MAKEUP; *especially* : a cosmetic to add color
**3 a** (1) **:** a mixture of a pigment and a suitable liquid to form a closely adherent coating when spread on a surface in a thin coat (2) **:** the pigment used in this mixture especially when in the form of a cake ⟨a box of *paints*⟩ **b :** an applied coating of paint
**4 :** PINTO
**5 :** FREE THROW LANE

**paint·brush** \'pānt-,brəsh\ *noun* (1827)
**1 :** a brush for applying paint
**2 a :** INDIAN PAINTBRUSH 1 **b :** ORANGE HAWKWEED

**painted bunting** *noun* (circa 1811)
**:** a brightly colored finch (*Passerina ciris*) that is found from the southern U.S. to Panama

**painted cup** *noun* (1787)
**:** INDIAN PAINTBRUSH 1

**painted lady** *noun* (1753)
**1 :** a migratory nymphalid butterfly (*Vanessa cardui*) with wings mottled in brown, orange, black, and white
**2 :** PROSTITUTE 1a

**painted trillium** *noun* (1855)
**:** a trillium (*Trillium undulatum*) of northeastern North America that has a solitary flower with white petals streaked with purple

**painted turtle** *noun* (1876)
**:** a North American turtle (*Chrysemys picta*) having a greenish to black carapace with yellow, red, or olive bordered scutes and a yellow plastron

¹**paint·er** \'pān-tər\ *noun* (14th century)
**:** one that paints: as **a :** an artist who paints **b :** one who applies paint especially as an occupation

²**paint·er** \'pān-tər\ *noun* [Middle English *paynter,* probably from Middle French *pendoir, pentoir* clothesline, from *pendre* to hang — more at PENDANT] (14th century)
**:** a line used for securing or towing a boat

³**paint·er** *noun* [alteration of *panther*] (circa 1764)
**:** COUGAR

**paint·er·ly** \'pān-tər-lē\ *adjective* (1586)
**:** of, relating to, or typical of a painter **:** ARTISTIC
— **paint·er·li·ness** *noun*

**painter's colic** *noun* (circa 1834)
**:** intestinal colic associated with obstinate constipation due to chronic lead poisoning

**paint·ing** \'pān-tiŋ\ *noun* (13th century)
**1 :** a product of painting; *especially* : a work produced through the art of painting
**2 :** the art or occupation of painting

**paint·work** \'pānt-,wərk\ *noun* (1888)
*chiefly British*
**1 :** work with paint
**2 :** PAINT 3b

**¹pair** \'par, 'per\ *noun, plural* **pairs** *or* **pair** [Middle English *paire*, from Old French, from Latin *paria* equal things, from neuter plural of *par* equal] (14th century) **1 a** (1) **:** two corresponding things designed for use together ⟨a *pair* of shoes⟩ (2) **:** two corresponding bodily parts or members ⟨a *pair* of hands⟩ **b :** something made up of two corresponding pieces ⟨a *pair* of trousers⟩ **2 a :** two similar or associated things: as (1) **:** two mated animals (2) **:** a couple in love, engaged, or married ⟨were a devoted *pair*⟩ (3) **:** two playing cards of the same value or denomination and especially of the same rank (4) **:** two horses harnessed side by side (5) **:** two members of a deliberative body that agree not to vote on a specific issue during a time agreed on; *also* **:** an agreement not to vote made by the two members **b :** a partnership especially of two players in a contest against another partnership **3** *chiefly dialect* **:** a set or series of small objects (as beads)

**²pair** (1606) *transitive verb* **1 a :** to make a pair of — often used with *off* or *up* ⟨*paired* off the animals⟩ **b :** to cause to be a member of a pair **c :** to arrange a voting pair between **2 :** to arrange in pairs *intransitive verb* **1 :** to constitute a member of a pair ⟨a sock that didn't *pair*⟩ **2 a :** to become associated with another — often used with *off* or *up* ⟨*paired* up with an old friend⟩ **b :** to become grouped or separated into pairs — often used with *off* ⟨*paired* off for the next dance⟩

**pair–bond** \-,bänd\ *noun* (1940) **:** a monogamous relationship — **pair–bond·ing** *noun*

**paired–associate learning** *noun* (1966) **:** the learning of syllables, digits, or words in pairs (as in the study of a foreign language) so that one member of the pair evokes recall of the other

**pair of compasses** (1563) **:** COMPASS 3c

**pair of virginals** (1542) **:** VIRGINAL

**pair production** *noun* (1934) **:** the transformation of a quantum of radiant energy simultaneously into an electron and a positron when the quantum interacts with the intense electric field near a nucleus

**pai·sa** \pī-'sä\ *noun* [ultimately from Hindi *paisā*, a quarter-anna coin] (1956) **1** *plural* **paisa** — see *rupee, taka* at MONEY table **2** *plural* **pai·se** \-'sā\ — see *rupee* at MONEY table

**pais·ley** \'pāz-lē\ *adjective, often capitalized* [*Paisley*, Scotland] (1824) **1 :** made typically of soft wool and woven or printed with colorful curved abstract figures **2 :** marked by designs, patterns, or figures typically used in paisley fabrics ⟨a *paisley* print⟩ — **paisley** *noun*

**Pai·ute** \'pī-,yüt\ *noun* (1827) **1 :** a member of an American Indian people originally of Utah, Arizona, Nevada, and California **2 :** either of the two Uto-Aztecan languages of the Paiute people

**pa·ja·ma** \pə-'jä-mə, -'ja-\ *noun* [Hindi *pājāma*, from Persian *pā* leg + *jāma* garment] (1883) **:** PAJAMAS — **pa·ja·maed** \-məd\ *adjective*

**pa·ja·mas** \-məz\ *noun plural* [plural of *pajama*] (1800) **1 :** loose lightweight trousers formerly much worn in the Near East **2 :** a loose usually two-piece lightweight suit designed especially for sleeping or lounging

**pak choi** \'päk-'choi, 'pak-\ *variant of* BOK CHOY

**pa·ke·ha** \'pä-kə-,hä, 'pa-kē-ə\ *noun, plural* **pakeha** *or* **pakehas** *often capitalized* [Maori] (1832) *chiefly New Zealand* **:** a person who is not of Maori descent; *especially* **:** a white person

**Paki** \'pa-kē, 'pä-\ *noun* [short for *Pakistani*] (1964) *chiefly British* **:** a Pakistani immigrant — usually used disparagingly

**¹pal** \'pal\ *noun* [Romany *phral, phal* brother, friend, from Sanskrit *bhrātr* brother; akin to Old English *brōthor* brother] (circa 1682) **:** a close friend — **pal·ship** \-,ship\ *noun*

**²pal** *intransitive verb* **palled; pal·ling** (1879) **:** to be or become pals **:** associate as pals ⟨they've *palled* around for years⟩

**¹pal·ace** \'pa-ləs\ *noun* [Middle English *palais*, from Old French, from Latin *palatium*, from *Palatium*, the Palatine Hill in Rome where the emperors' residences were built] (13th century) **1 a :** the official residence of a chief of state (as a monarch or a president) **b** *chiefly British* **:** the official residence of an archbishop or bishop **2 a :** a large stately house **b :** a large public building **c :** a highly decorated place for public amusement or refreshment ⟨a movie *palace*⟩ ◆

**²palace** *adjective* (14th century) **1 :** of or relating to a palace **2 :** of, relating to, or involving the intimates of a chief executive ⟨a *palace* revolution⟩ ⟨*palace* politics⟩ **3 :** LUXURIOUS, DELUXE

**pal·a·din** \'pa-lə-dən\ *noun* [French, from Italian *paladino*, from Medieval Latin *palatinus* courtier, from Late Latin, imperial official — more at PALATINE] (1592) **1 :** a trusted military leader (as for a medieval prince) **2 :** a leading champion of a cause

**palae-** *or* **palaeo-** *chiefly British variant of* PALE-

**pa·laes·tra** \pə-'les-trə\ *noun, plural* **-trae** \-,(,)trē\ [Middle English *palestre* arena, from Latin *palaestra* place for wrestling, from Greek *palaistra*, from *palaiein* to wrestle] (1580) **1 :** a school in ancient Greece or Rome for sports (as wrestling) **2 :** GYMNASIUM

**pa·lan·quin** \,pa-lən-'kēn, -'kwin, -'kin, 'pa-lən-,; pə-'laŋ-kwən\ *noun* [Portuguese *palanquim*, from Malay or Javanese *pelangki*, of Indo-Aryan origin; akin to Bengali *pālaṅka* bed] (1588) **:** a conveyance formerly used especially in eastern Asia usually for one person that consists of an enclosed litter borne on the shoulders of men by means of poles

**pal·at·able** \'pa-lə-tə-bəl\ *adjective* (1669) **1 :** agreeable to the palate or taste **2 :** agreeable or acceptable to the mind ☆ — **pal·at·abil·i·ty** \,pa-lə-tə-'bi-lə-tē\ *noun* — **pal·at·able·ness** *noun* — **pal·at·ably** \'pa-lə-tə-blē\ *adverb*

**pal·a·tal** \'pa-lə-t°l\ *adjective* (1728) **1 a :** formed with some part of the tongue near or touching the hard palate posterior to the teethridge ⟨the \sh\ and \y\ in English and the \k\ of *ich* \ik\ in German are examples of *palatal* consonants⟩ **b** *of a vowel* **:** FRONT 2 **2 :** of, relating to, forming, or affecting the palate — **palatal** *noun* — **pal·a·tal·ly** \-t°l-ē\ *adverb*

**pal·a·tal·i·za·tion** \,pa-lə-t°l-ə-'zā-shən\ *noun* (1863) **1 :** the quality or state of being palatalized **2 :** an act or instance of palatalizing an utterance ⟨in rapid speech the \t\ in *got* undergoes *palatalization* before *you* to yield \'gächə\⟩

**pal·a·tal·ize** \'pa-lə-t°l-,īz\ *transitive verb* **-ized; -iz·ing** (1867) **:** to pronounce as or change into a palatal sound

**pal·ate** \'pa-lət\ *noun* [Middle English, from Latin *palatum*] (14th century) **1 :** the roof of the mouth separating the mouth from the nasal cavity **2 a :** a usually intellectual taste or liking **b :** the sense of taste

**pa·la·tial** \pə-'lā-shəl\ *adjective* [Latin *palatium* palace] (1754) **1 :** of, relating to, or being a palace **2 :** suitable to a palace **:** MAGNIFICENT — **pa·la·tial·ly** \-shə-lē\ *adverb* — **pa·la·tial·ness** *noun*

**pal·at·i·nate** \pə-'la-t°n-ət\ *noun* (circa 1580) **:** the territory of a palatine

**¹pal·a·tine** \'pa-lə-,tīn\ *adjective* [Middle English, from Latin *palatinus* imperial, from *palatium*] (15th century) **1 a :** possessing royal privileges **b :** of or relating to a palatine or a palatinate **2 a :** of or relating to a palace especially of a Roman or Holy Roman emperor **b :** PALATIAL

**²palatine** \-,tīn, 3 *is also* -,tēn\ *noun* [Late Latin *palatinus* imperial official, from Latin *palatinus*, adjective] (1591)

---

☆ **SYNONYMS**
**Palatable, appetizing, savory, tasty, toothsome** mean agreeable or pleasant especially to the sense of taste. PALATABLE often applies to something that is found to be merely agreeable ⟨butterflies that birds find *palatable*⟩. APPETIZING suggests a whetting of the appetite and applies to aroma and appearance as well as taste ⟨*appetizing* hors d'oeuvres⟩. SAVORY applies to both taste and aroma and suggests piquancy and often spiciness ⟨dumplings with *savory* fillings⟩. TASTY implies a pronounced taste ⟨a tart and *tasty* pie⟩. TOOTHSOME stresses the notion of agreeableness and sometimes implies tenderness or daintiness ⟨an enticing array of *toothsome* desserts⟩.

---

◇ **WORD HISTORY**
**palace** The word *palace* conjures up images of kings and queens living in huge homes of splendor and luxury, often on high ground far above the common people. Although such palaces are the settings of fairy tales, they are not far removed from the first palaces of history. The *Palatium* or Palatine Hill, one of the seven hills of Rome, was the site of a number of large dwellings from about the 4th century B.C. Caesar Augustus took one of these homes as his residence, and the building of more imperial residences on the Palatine Hill by subsequent Roman emperors led to the use of *Palatium* to mean "the emperor's residence." In Late and Medieval Latin *palatium* became a generic noun denoting any royal or imperial residence, as well as the royal court and royal authority, and then any princely house or manor of a lord. When *paleis* or *palais*, the Old French outcome of *palatium*, first appeared, it referred simply to the luxurious residence of an important person, and this sense was carried into Middle English *palais* and Modern English *palace*, along with most of the other meanings of the Medieval Latin word.

---

\ə\ abut \ᵊ\ kitten \ər\ further \a\ ash \ā\ ace \ä\ mop, mar \aú\ out \ch\ chin \e\ bet \ē\ easy \g\ go \i\ hit \ī\ ice \j\ job \ŋ\ sing \ō\ go \ò\ law \òi\ boy \th\ thin \th\ the \ü\ loot \ú\ foot \y\ yet \zh\ vision    *see also* Guide to Pronunciation

**1 a :** a feudal lord having sovereign power within his domains **b :** a high officer of an imperial palace
**2** *capitalized* **:** a native or inhabitant of the Palatinate
**3** [French, from Elisabeth Charlotte of Bavaria (died 1722) Princess *Palatine*] **:** a fur cape or stole covering the neck and shoulders
³**pal·a·tine** \-ˌtīn\ *adjective* [French *palatin*, from Latin *palatum* palate] (circa 1656)
**:** of, relating to, or lying near the palate
⁴**pal·a·tine** \-ˌtīn\ *noun* (1854)
**:** either of a pair of bones that are situated behind and between the maxillae and in humans are of extremely irregular form
¹**pa·lav·er** \pə-ˈla-vər, -ˈlä-\ *noun* [Portuguese *palavra* word, speech, from Late Latin *parabola* parable, speech] (1735)
**1 a :** a long parley usually between persons of different cultures or levels of sophistication **b :** CONFERENCE, DISCUSSION
**2 a :** idle talk **b :** misleading or beguiling speech
²**palaver** *verb* **pa·lav·ered; pa·lav·er·ing** \pə-ˈla-və-riŋ, -ˈlä-; -ˈlav-riŋ, -ˈläv-\ (1773)
*intransitive verb*
**1 :** to talk profusely or idly
**2 :** PARLEY
*transitive verb*
**:** to use palaver to **:** CAJOLE
**pa·laz·zo** \pə-ˈlät-(ˌ)sō\ *noun, plural* **pa·laz·zi** \-(ˌ)sē\ [Italian, from Latin *palatium* palace] (circa 1666)
**:** a large imposing building (as a museum or a place of residence) especially in Italy
¹**pale** \ˈpā(ə)l\ *noun* [Middle English, from Middle French *pal* stake, from Latin *palus* — more at POLE] (12th century)
**1** *archaic* **:** PALISADE, PALING
**2 a :** one of the stakes of a palisade **b :** PICKET
**3 a :** a space or field having bounds **:** ENCLOSURE **b :** a territory or district within certain bounds or under a particular jurisdiction
**4 :** an area or the limits within which one is privileged or protected (as from censure) ⟨conduct that was beyond the *pale*⟩
**5 :** a perpendicular stripe on a heraldic shield
²**pale** *transitive verb* **paled; pal·ing** (14th century)
**:** to enclose with pales **:** FENCE
³**pale** *adjective* **pal·er; pal·est** [Middle English, from Middle French, from Latin *pallidus*, from *pallēre* to be pale — more at FALLOW] (14th century)
**1 :** deficient in color or intensity of color **:** PALLID ⟨a *pale* complexion⟩
**2 :** not bright or brilliant **:** DIM ⟨a *pale* sun shining through the fog⟩
**3 :** FEEBLE, FAINT ⟨a *pale* imitation⟩
**4 :** deficient in chroma ⟨a *pale* pink⟩
— **pale·ly** \ˈpā(ə)l-lē\ *adverb*
— **pale·ness** \-nəs\ *noun*
— **pal·ish** \ˈpā-lish\ *adjective*
⁴**pale** *verb* **paled; pal·ing** (14th century)
*intransitive verb*
**:** to become pale
*transitive verb*
**:** to make pale
**pale-** *or* **paleo-** *combining form* [Greek *palai-, palaio-* ancient, from *palaios*, from *palai* long ago; probably akin to Greek *tēle* far off, Sanskrit *carama* last]
**1 :** involving or dealing with ancient forms or conditions ⟨*paleo*botany⟩
**2 :** early **:** primitive **:** archaic ⟨*Paleo*lithic⟩
**pa·lea** \ˈpā-lē-ə\ *noun, plural* **pa·le·ae** \-lē-ˌē\ [New Latin, from Latin, chaff — more at PALLET] (1753)
**1 :** one of the chaffy scales on the receptacle of many composite plants
**2 :** the upper bract that with the lemma encloses the flower in grasses
— **pa·le·al** \-lē-əl\ *adjective*
**Pa·le·arc·tic** \ˌpā-lē-ˈärk-tik, -ˈär-tik\ *adjective* (1858)

**:** of, relating to, or being a biogeographic region or subregion that includes Europe, Asia north of the Himalayas, northern Arabia, and Africa north of the Sahara
**pale dry** *adjective* (1953)
**:** dry and light colored ⟨*pale dry* ginger ale⟩
**pale·face** \ˈpā(ə)l-ˌfās\ *noun* (1822)
**:** a white person
**pa·leo·an·thro·pol·o·gy** \ˌpā-lē-ō-ˌan(t)-thrə-ˈpä-lə-jē, *especially British* ˌpa-\ *noun* (1916)
**:** a branch of anthropology dealing with fossil hominids
— **pa·leo·an·thro·po·log·i·cal** \-pə-ˈlä-ji-kəl\ *adjective*
— **pa·leo·an·thro·pol·o·gist** \-ˈpä-lə-jist\ *noun*
**pa·leo·bi·ol·o·gy** \-bī-ˈä-lə-jē\ *noun* (1893)
**:** a branch of paleontology concerned with the biology of fossil organisms
— **pa·leo·bi·o·log·i·cal** \-bī-ə-ˈlä-ji-kəl\ *also* **pa·leo·bi·o·log·ic** \-ˈlä-jik\ *adjective*
— **pa·leo·bi·ol·o·gist** \-bī-ˈä-lə-jist\ *noun*
**pa·leo·bot·a·ny** \-ˈbä-tⁿn-ē, -ˈbät-nē\ *noun* [International Scientific Vocabulary] (1872)
**:** a branch of botany dealing with fossil plants
— **pa·leo·bo·tan·i·cal** \-bə-ˈta-ni-kəl\ *or* **pa·leo·bo·tan·ic** \-ˈta-nik\ *adjective*
— **pa·leo·bo·tan·i·cal·ly** \-ni-k(ə-)lē\ *adverb*
— **pa·leo·bot·a·nist** \-ˈbä-tⁿn-ist, -ˈbät-nist\ *noun*
**Pa·leo·cene** \ˈpā-lē-ə-ˌsēn, *especially British* ˈpa-\ *adjective* [International Scientific Vocabulary] (1877)
**:** of, relating to, or being the earliest epoch of the Tertiary or the corresponding system of rocks — see GEOLOGIC TIME table
— **Paleocene** *noun*
**pa·leo·cli·ma·tol·o·gy** \ˌpā-lē-ō-ˌklī-mə-ˈtä-lə-jē, *especially British* ˌpa-\ *noun* [International Scientific Vocabulary] (circa 1909)
**:** a science dealing with the climate of past ages
— **pa·leo·cli·ma·tol·o·gist** \-jist\ *noun*
**pa·leo·ecol·o·gy** \-i-ˈkä-lə-jē, -e-ˈkä-\ *noun* (1898)
**:** a branch of ecology that is concerned with the characteristics of ancient environments and with their relationships to ancient plants and animals
— **pa·leo·eco·log·i·cal** \-ˌē-kə-ˈlä-ji-kəl, -ˌe-kə-\ *also* **pa·leo·eco·log·ic** \-jik\ *adjective*
— **pa·leo·ecol·o·gist** \-i-ˈkä-lə-jist, -e-ˈkä-\ *noun*
**Pa·leo·gene** \ˈpā-lē-ə-ˌjēn, *especially British* ˈpa-\ *adjective* [German *Paläogen*, from *paläo-* pale- + *-gen* (from Greek *-genēs* born) — more at -GEN] (1882)
**:** of, relating to, or being the earlier part of the Tertiary including the Paleocene, Eocene, and Oligocene or the corresponding system of rocks
— **Paleogene** *noun*
**pa·leo·ge·og·ra·phy** \ˌpā-lē-ō-jē-ˈä-grə-fē, *especially British* ˌpa-\ *noun* [International Scientific Vocabulary] (1881)
**:** the geography of ancient times or of a particular past geological epoch
— **pa·leo·geo·graph·ic** \-ˌjē-ə-ˈgra-fik\ *or* **pa·leo·geo·graph·i·cal** \-fi-kəl\ *adjective*
— **pa·leo·geo·graph·i·cal·ly** \-fi-k(ə-)lē\ *adverb*
**pa·leo·graph·ic** \-ə-ˈgra-fik\ *or* **pa·leo·graph·i·cal** \-fi-kəl\ *adjective* (circa 1842)
**:** relating to writings of former times
— **pa·leo·graph·i·cal·ly** \-fi-k(ə-)lē\ *adverb*
**pa·le·og·ra·phy** \ˌpā-lē-ˈä-grə-fē, *especially British* ˌpa-\ *noun* [New Latin *palaeographia*, from Greek *palai-* pale- + *-graphia* -graphy] (circa 1818)
**1 :** the study of ancient writings and inscriptions

**2 a :** an ancient manner of writing **b :** ancient writings
— **pa·le·og·ra·pher** \-fər\ *noun*
**Pa·leo–In·di·an** \ˌpā-lē-ō-ˈin-dē-ən, *especially British* ˌpa-\ *noun* (1940)
**:** one of the early American hunting people of Asian origin extant in the late Pleistocene
— **Paleo–Indian** *adjective*
**Pa·leo·lith·ic** \ˌpā-lē-ə-ˈli-thik, *especially British* ˌpa-\ *adjective* [International Scientific Vocabulary] (1865)
**:** of or relating to the earliest period of the Stone Age characterized by rough or chipped stone implements
**pa·leo·mag·ne·tism** \ˌpā-lē-ō-ˈmag-nə-ˌti-zəm, *especially British* ˌpa-\ *noun* (1854)
**1 :** the intensity and direction of residual magnetization in ancient rocks
**2 :** a science that deals with paleomagnetism
— **pa·leo·mag·net·ic** \-mag-ˈne-tik\ *adjective*
— **pa·leo·mag·net·i·cal·ly** \-ti-k(ə-)lē\ *adverb*
— **pa·leo·mag·ne·tist** \-ˈmag-nə-tist\ *noun*
**pa·le·on·tol·o·gy** \ˌpā-lē-ˌän-ˈtä-lə-jē, -ən-, *especially British* ˌpa-\ *noun* [French *paléontologie*, from *palé-* pale- + Greek *onta* existing things (from neuter plural of *ont-, ōn*, present participle of *einai* to be) + French *-logie* -logy — more at IS] (1838)
**:** a science dealing with the life of past geological periods as known from fossil remains
— **pa·le·on·to·log·i·cal** \-ˌän-tⁿl-ˈä-ji-kəl\ *or* **pa·le·on·to·log·ic** \-jik\ *adjective*
— **pa·le·on·tol·o·gist** \-ˌän-ˈtä-lə-jist, -ən-\ *noun*
**pa·leo·pa·thol·o·gy** \ˌpā-lē-ō-pə-ˈthä-lə-jē, -pa-ˈthä-, *especially British* ˌpa-lē-\ *noun* (1893)
**:** a branch of pathology concerned with diseases of former times as evidenced especially in fossil or other remains
— **pa·leo·patho·log·i·cal** \-ˌpa-thə-ˈlä-ji-kəl\ *adjective*
— **pa·leo·pa·thol·o·gist** \-pə-ˈthä-lə-jist, -pa-\ *noun*
**Pa·leo·zo·ic** \ˌpā-lē-ə-ˈzō-ik, *especially British* ˌpa-\ *adjective* (1838)
**:** of, relating to, originating in, or being an era of geological history that extends from the beginning of the Cambrian to the close of the Permian and is marked by the culmination of nearly all classes of invertebrates except the insects and in the later epochs by the appearance of terrestrial plants, amphibians, and reptiles; *also* **:** relating to the corresponding system of rocks — see GEOLOGIC TIME table
— **Paleozoic** *noun*
**pa·leo·zo·ol·o·gy** \-zō-ˈä-lə-jē, -zə-ˈwä-\ *noun* [International Scientific Vocabulary] (1857)
**:** a branch of paleontology dealing with ancient and fossil animals
— **pa·leo·zoo·log·i·cal** \-ˌzō-ə-ˈlä-ji-kəl\ *adjective*
— **pa·leo·zo·ol·o·gist** \-jist\ *noun*
**pal·et** \ˈpā-lət, ˈpa-lət\ *noun* [*pale* palea + ¹*-et*] (circa 1880)
**:** PALEA
**pal·ette** \ˈpa-lət\ *noun* [French, from Middle French, diminutive of *pale* spade, from Latin *pala*; probably akin to Latin *pangere* to fix — more at PACT] (1622)
**1 :** a thin oval or rectangular board or tablet that a painter holds and mixes pigments on
**2 a :** the set of colors put on the palette **b** (1) **:** a particular range, quality, or use of color (2) **:** a comparable range, quality, or use of available elements especially in another art (as music)
**palette knife** *noun* (1759)
**:** a knife with usually a flexible steel blade and no cutting edge used to mix colors or to apply colors (as to a painting)

**pal·frey** \'pȯl-frē\ *noun, plural* **palfreys** [Middle English, from Old French *palefrei*, from Medieval Latin *palafredus*, from Late Latin *paraveredus* post-horse for secondary roads, from Greek *para-* beside, subsidiary + Late Latin *veredus* post-horse, from a Gaulish word akin to Welsh *gorwydd* horse; akin to Old Irish *réidid* he rides — more at PARA-, RIDE] (13th century) *archaic* : a saddle horse other than a warhorse; *especially* : a lady's light easy-gaited horse

**Pa·li** \'pä-lē\ *noun* [Sanskrit *pāli* row, series of Buddhist sacred texts] (1800) : an Indo-Aryan language used as the liturgical and scholarly language of Theravada Buddhism — see INDO-EUROPEAN LANGUAGES table

**pal·i·mo·ny** \'pa-lə-ˌmō-nē\ *noun* [blend of *pal* and *alimony*] (1979) : a court-ordered allowance paid by one member of a couple formerly living together out of wedlock to the other

**pa·limp·sest** \'pa-ləm(p)-ˌsest, pə-'lim(p)-\ *noun* [Latin *palimpsestus*, from Greek *palimpsēstos* scraped again, from *palin* + *psēn* to rub, scrape; akin to Sanskrit *psāti*, *babhasti* he chews] (1825) **1** : writing material (as a parchment or tablet) used one or more times after earlier writing has been erased **2** : something having usually diverse layers or aspects apparent beneath the surface

**pal·in·drome** \'pa-lən-ˌdrōm\ *noun* [Greek *palindromos* running back again, from *palin* back, again + *dramein* to run; akin to Greek *polos* axis, pole — more at POLE, DROMEDARY] (circa 1629) : a word, verse, or sentence (as "Able was I ere I saw Elba") or a number (as 1881) that reads the same backward or forward
— **pal·in·drom·ic** \ˌpa-lən-'drō-mik, -'drä-\ *adjective*
— **pal·in·drom·ist** \ˌpa-lən-ˌdrō-mist\ *noun*

**pal·ing** \'pā-liŋ\ *noun* (15th century) **1** : a fence of pales or pickets **2** : wood for making pales **3** : a pale or picket for a fence

**pal·in·gen·e·sis** \ˌpa-lən-'je-nə-səs\ *noun* [New Latin, from Greek *palin* again + Latin *genesis* genesis] (1818) : METEMPSYCHOSIS

**pal·in·ge·net·ic** \-jə-'ne-tik\ *adjective* (1833) : of or relating to palingenesis

**pal·in·ode** \'pa-lə-ˌnōd\ *noun* [Greek *palinōidia*, from *palin* + *aeidein* to sing — more at ODE] (1599) **1** : an ode or song recanting or retracting something in an earlier poem **2** : a formal retraction

**¹pal·i·sade** \ˌpa-lə-'sād\ *noun* [French *palissade*, ultimately from Latin *palus* stake — more at POLE] (1600) **1 a** : a fence of stakes especially for defense **b** : a long strong stake pointed at the top and set close with others as a defense **2** : a line of bold cliffs

**²palisade** *transitive verb* **-sad·ed; -sad·ing** (1632) : to fortify with palisades

**palisade cell** *noun* (1875) : a cell of the palisade layer

**palisade layer** *noun* (1914) : a layer of columnar cells rich in chloroplasts found beneath the upper epidermis of foliage leaves — called also *palisade mesophyll, palisade parenchyma, palisade tissue*; compare SPONGY PARENCHYMA

**¹pall** \'pȯl\ *verb* [Middle English, short for *appallen* to become pale — more at APPALL] (14th century) *intransitive verb* **1** : to lose strength or effectiveness **2** : to lose in interest or attraction ⟨his humor began to *pall* on us⟩ **3** : to become tired of something *transitive verb*

**1** : to cause to become insipid **2** : to deprive of pleasure in something by satiating
**synonym** see SATIATE

**²pall** *noun* [Middle English, cloak, mantle, from Old English *pæll*, from Latin *pallium*] (14th century) **1** : PALLIUM 1a **2 a** : a square of linen usually stiffened with cardboard that is used to cover the chalice **b** (1) : a heavy cloth draped over a coffin (2) : a coffin especially when holding a body **3** : something that covers or conceals; *especially* : an overspreading element that produces an effect of gloom ⟨a *pall* of thick black smoke⟩

**³pall** *transitive verb* (15th century) : to cover with a pall : DRAPE

**Pal·la·di·an** \pə-'lā-dē-ən, -'lä-\ *adjective* (1731) : of or relating to a revived classical style in architecture based on the works of Andrea Palladio
— **Pal·la·di·an·ism** \-ə-ˌni-zəm\ *noun*

**¹pal·la·di·um** \pə-'lā-dē-əm\ *noun* [Middle English, from Latin, from Greek *palladion*, from *Pallad-, Pallas*] **1** *capitalized* : a statue of Pallas whose preservation was believed to ensure the safety of Troy **2** *plural* **pal·la·dia** \-dē-ə\ : SAFEGUARD

**²palladium** *noun* [New Latin, from *Pallad-, Pallas,* an asteroid] (1803) : a silver-white ductile malleable metallic element of the platinum group that is used especially in electrical contacts, as a catalyst, and in alloys — see ELEMENT table
— **pal·la·dous** \pə-'lā-dəs\ *adjective*

**Pal·las** \'pa-ləs\ *noun* [Latin *Pallad-, Pallas,* from Greek] : ATHENA

**pall·bear·er** \'pȯl-ˌbar-ər, -ˌber-\ *noun* [²*pall*] (1707) : a person who helps to carry the coffin at a funeral; *also* : a member of the escort or honor guard of the coffin who does not actually help to carry it

**¹pal·let** \'pa-lət\ *noun* [Middle English *pailet*, from (assumed) Middle French *paillet*, from *paille* straw, from Latin *palea* chaff, straw; akin to Sanskrit *palāva* chaff] (14th century) **1** : a straw-filled tick or mattress **2** : a small, hard, or temporary bed

**²pallet** *noun* [Middle English *palette*, literally, small shovel, from Middle French — more at PALETTE] (1558) **1** : a wooden flat-bladed instrument **2** : a lever or surface in a timepiece that receives an impulse from the escapement wheel and imparts motion to a balance or pendulum **3** : a portable platform for handling, storing, or moving materials and packages (as in warehouses, factories, or vehicles)

**pal·let·ise** *British variant of* PALLETIZE

**pal·let·ize** \'pa-lə-ˌtīz\ *transitive verb* **-ized; -iz·ing** (1944) : to place on, transport, or store by means of pallets
— **pal·let·i·za·tion** \ˌpa-lə-tə-'zā-shən\ *noun*
— **pal·let·iz·er** \'pa-lə-ˌtī-zər\ *noun*

**pal·lette** \pa-'let\ *noun* [alteration of *palette*] (1834) : one of the plates at the armpits of a suit of armor — see ARMOR illustration

**pal·li·al** \'pa-lē-əl\ *adjective* [New Latin *pallium*] (1836) **1** : of, relating to, or produced by a mantle of a mollusk **2** : of or relating to the cerebral cortex

**pal·liasse** \pal-'yas\ *noun* [modification of French *paillasse*, from *paille* straw] (1763) : a thin straw mattress used as a pallet

**pal·li·ate** \'pa-lē-ˌāt\ *transitive verb* **-at·ed; -at·ing** [Middle English, from Late Latin *pal-*

*liatus,* past participle of *palliare* to cloak, conceal, from Latin *pallium* cloak] (15th century) **1** : to reduce the violence of (a disease) : ABATE **2** : to cover by excuses and apologies **3** : to moderate the intensity of ⟨trying to *palliate* the boredom⟩
— **pal·li·a·tion** \ˌpa-lē-'ā-shən\ *noun*
— **pal·li·a·tor** \'pa-lē-ˌā-tər\ *noun*

**¹pal·li·a·tive** \'pa-lē-ˌā-tiv, 'pal-yə-\ *adjective* (15th century) : serving to palliate ⟨*palliative* surgery⟩
— **pal·lia·tive·ly** *adverb*

**²palliative** *noun* (1724) : something that palliates

**pal·lid** \'pa-ləd\ *adjective* [Latin *pallidus* — more at PALE] (1590) **1** : deficient in color : WAN ⟨a *pallid* countenance⟩ **2** : lacking sparkle or liveliness : DULL ⟨a *pallid* entertainment⟩
— **pal·lid·ly** *adverb*
— **pal·lid·ness** *noun*

**pal·li·um** \'pa-lē-əm\ *noun, plural* **-lia** \-lē-ə\ *or* **-li·ums** [Middle English, from Latin] (12th century) **1 a** : a white woolen band with pendants in front and back worn over the chasuble by a pope or archbishop as a symbol of full episcopal authority **b** : a draped rectangular cloth worn as a cloak by men of ancient Greece and Rome **2** [New Latin, from Latin, cloak] **a** : CEREBRAL CORTEX **b** : the mantle of a mollusk, brachiopod, or bird

**pall–mall** \ˌpel-'mel, ˌpal-'mal, *US often* ˌpȯl-'mȯl\ *noun* [Middle French *pallemaille*, from Italian *pallamaglio*, from *palla* ball (of Germanic origin; akin to Old High German *balla* ball) + *maglio* mallet, from Latin *malleus* — more at BALL, MAUL] (1598) : a 17th century game in which each player attempts to drive a wooden ball with a mallet down an alley and through a raised ring in as few strokes as possible; *also* : the alley in which it is played

**pal·lor** \'pa-lər\ *noun* [Middle English, from Latin, from *pallēre* to be pale — more at FALLOW] (15th century) : deficiency of color especially of the face : PALENESS

**pal·ly** \'pa-lē\ *adjective* (1895) : sharing the relationship of pals : INTIMATE

**¹palm** \'päm, 'pälm, 'pȯm, 'pȯlm, *New England also* 'pȧm\ *noun* [Middle English, from Old English, from Latin *palma* palm of the hand, palm tree; from the resemblance of the tree's leaves to the outstretched hand; akin to Greek *palamē* palm of the hand, Old English *folm*, Old Irish *lám* hand] (before 12th century) **1** : any of a family (Palmae, the palm family) of mostly tropical or subtropical monocotyledonous trees, shrubs, or vines with usually a simple stem and a terminal crown of large pinnate or fan-shaped leaves **2** : a leaf of the palm as a symbol of victory or rejoicing; *also* : a branch (as of laurel) similarly used **3** : a symbol of triumph; *also* : VICTORY, TRIUMPH **4** : an addition to a military decoration in the form of a palm frond especially to indicate a second award of the basic decoration
— **palm–like** \-ˌlīk\ *adjective*

**²palm** *noun* [Middle English *paume*, from Middle French, from Latin *palma*] (14th century) **1** : the somewhat concave part of the human hand between the bases of the fingers and the

wrist or the corresponding part of the forefoot of a lower mammal
**2 :** a flat expanded part especially at the end of a base or stalk (as of an anchor)
**3** [Latin *palmus*, from *palma*] **:** a unit of length based on the breadth or length of the hand
**4 :** something (as a part of a glove) that covers the palm of the hand
**5 :** an act of palming (as of cards)
**³palm** *transitive verb* (1673)
**1 a :** to conceal in or with the hand ⟨*palm* a card⟩ **b :** to pick up stealthily
**2 :** to impose by fraud ⟨a second imposter to be *palmed* upon you —Sir Walter Scott⟩
**3 :** to touch with the palm: as **a :** to stroke with the palm or hand **b :** to shake hands with **c :** to allow (a basketball) to come to rest momentarily in the hand while dribbling thus committing a violation
**pal·mar** \'pal-mər, 'pä-, 'päl-, 'pȯ-, 'pȯl-\ *adjective* (1656)
**:** of, relating to, or involving the palm of the hand
**pal·ma·ry** \'pal-mə-rē, 'pä-, 'päl-, 'pȯ-, 'pȯl-\ *adjective* [Latin *palmarius* deserving the palm, from *palma*] (1657)
**:** OUTSTANDING, BEST
**pal·mate** \'pal-ˌmāt, 'pä-, 'päl-, 'pȯ-, 'pȯl-\ *also* **pal·mat·ed** \-ˌmā-təd\ *adjective* (circa 1760)
**:** resembling a hand with the fingers spread: as **a :** having lobes radiating from a common point ⟨a *palmate* leaf⟩ — see LEAF illustration **b :** having the distal portion broad, flat, and lobed ⟨a *palmate* antler⟩
— **pal·mate·ly** *adverb*
— **pal·ma·tion** \pal-'mā-shən, pä-, päl-, pȯ-, pȯl-\ *noun*
**palmed** \'pämd, 'pälmd, 'pȯmd, 'pȯlmd, *New England also* 'pämd\ *adjective* (15th century)
**:** having a palm of a specified kind — used in combination ⟨leather-*palmed* gloves⟩
**palm·er** \'pä-mər, 'päl-, 'pȯ-, 'pȯl-\ *noun* (13th century)
**:** a person wearing two crossed palm leaves as a sign of a pilgrimage made to the Holy Land
**palm·er·worm** \-ˌwərm\ *noun* (1560)
**:** a caterpillar that suddenly appears in great numbers devouring herbage
**palm·ette** \ˌpal-'met\ *noun* [French, from *palme* palm, from Latin *palma*] (1850)
**:** a decorative motif suggestive of a palm
**pal·met·to** \pal-'me-(ˌ)tō *also* pä-, päl-, pȯ-, pȯl-\ *noun, plural* **-tos** *or* **-toes** [modification of Spanish *palmito*, from *palma* palm, from Latin] (circa 1746)
**1 :** any of several usually low-growing fan-leaved palms; *especially* **:** CABBAGE PALMETTO
**2 :** strips of the leaf blade of a palmetto used in weaving
**palm·ist** \'pä-mist, 'päl-, 'pȯ-, 'pȯl-\ *noun* [probably back-formation from *palmistry*] (1886)
**:** one who practices palmistry

**palmetto 1**

**palm·ist·ry** \'pä-mə-strē, 'päl-, 'pȯ-, 'pȯl-\ *noun* [Middle English *pawmestry*, probably from *paume* palm + *maistrie* mastery] (15th century)
**:** the art or practice of reading a person's character or future from the lines on the palms
**pal·mi·tate** \'pal-mə-ˌtāt, 'pä-, 'päl-, 'pȯ-, 'pȯl-\ *noun* (1873)
**:** a salt or ester of palmitic acid
**pal·mit·ic acid** \(ˌ)pal-'mi-tik-, (ˌ)pä-, (ˌ)päl-, (ˌ)pȯ-, (ˌ)pȯl-\ *noun* [International Scientific Vocabulary, from *palmitin*] (1857)
**:** a waxy crystalline saturated fatty acid $C_{16}H_{32}O_2$ occurring free or in the form of es-

ters (as glycerides) in most fats and fatty oils and in several essential oils and waxes
**pal·mi·tin** \'pal-mə-tən, 'pä-, 'päl-, 'pȯ-, 'pȯl-\ *noun* [French *palmitine*, probably from *palmite* pith of the palm tree, from Spanish *palmito*] (1857)
**:** an ester of glycerol and palmitic acid; *especially* **:** a solid ester found in animal fats
**palm off** *transitive verb* (1822)
**1 :** to dispose of usually by trickery or guile
**2 :** PASS OFF 2
**palm oil** *noun* (1705)
**:** an edible fat obtained from the flesh of the fruit of several palms and used especially in soap and lubricating greases
**Palm Sunday** *noun* [from the palm branches strewn in Christ's way] (before 12th century)
**:** the Sunday before Easter celebrated in commemoration of Christ's triumphal entry into Jerusalem
**palmy** \'pä-mē, 'päl-, 'pȯ-, 'pȯl- *New England also* 'pä-mē\ *adjective* **palm·i·er; -est** (1602)
**1 :** marked by prosperity **:** FLOURISHING
**2 :** abounding in or bearing palms
**pal·my·ra** \pal-'mī-rə\ *noun* [Portuguese *palmeira*, from *palma* palm, from Latin] (1698)
**:** a tall fan-leaved palm (*Borassus flabellifer*) of India cultivated for its hard resistant wood, fiber, and sugar-rich sap — called also *palmyra palm*
**pal·o·mi·no** \ˌpa-lə-'mē-(ˌ)nō\ *noun, plural* **-nos** [American Spanish, from Spanish, like a dove, from Latin *palumbinus*, from *palumbes* ringdove; akin to Greek *peleia* dove, Latin *pallēre* to be pale — more at FALLOW] (1914)
**:** a horse that is pale cream to gold in color and has a flaxen or white mane and tail
**pa·loo·ka** \pə-'lü-kə\ *noun* [origin unknown] (1925)
**1 :** an inexperienced or incompetent boxer
**2 :** OAF, LOUT
**pal·o·ver·de** \ˌpa-lō-'ver-(ˌ)dā, ˌpä-, -'vər-\ *noun* [Mexican Spanish, literally, green tree] (1854)
**1 :** any of several small spiny leguminous trees or shrubs (genus *Cercidium*) that have greenish branches and are found chiefly in dry regions of the southwestern U.S. and Mexico
**2 :** JERUSALEM THORN
**palp** \'palp\ *noun* [New Latin *palpus*] (1842)
**:** PALPUS
**pal·pa·ble** \'pal-pə-bəl\ *adjective* [Middle English, from Late Latin *palpabilis*, from Latin *palpare* to stroke, caress — more at FEEL] (14th century)
**1 :** capable of being touched or felt **:** TANGIBLE
**2 :** easily perceptible **:** NOTICEABLE
**3 :** easily perceptible by the mind **:** MANIFEST
**synonym** see PERCEPTIBLE
— **pal·pa·bil·i·ty** \ˌpal-pə-'bi-lə-tē\ *noun*
— **pal·pa·bly** \'pal-pə-blē\ *adverb*
**pal·pate** \'pal-ˌpāt\ *transitive verb* **pal·pat·ed; pal·pat·ing** [probably back-formation from *palpation*, from Latin *palpation-, palpatio*, from *palpare*] (circa 1852)
**:** to examine by touch especially medically
— **pal·pa·tion** \pal-'pā-shən\ *noun*
**pal·pe·bral** \pal-'pē-brəl\ *adjective* [Late Latin *palpebralis*, from Latin *palpebra* eyelid; akin to Latin *palpare*] (1840)
**:** of, relating to, or located on or near the eyelids
**pal·pi·tant** \'pal-pə-tənt\ *adjective* (1837)
**:** marked by trembling or throbbing
**pal·pi·tate** \'pal-pə-ˌtāt\ *intransitive verb* **-tat·ed; -tat·ing** [Latin *palpitatus*, past participle of *palpitare*, frequentative of *palpare* to stroke] (circa 1623)
**:** to beat rapidly and strongly **:** THROB
— **pal·pi·ta·tion** \ˌpal-pə-'tā-shən\ *noun*
**pal·pus** \'pal-pəs\ *noun, plural* **pal·pi** \-ˌpī, -(ˌ)pē\ [New Latin, from Latin, caress, soft palm of the hand, from *palpare*] (1813)

**:** a segmented usually tactile or gustatory process on an arthropod mouthpart — see INSECT illustration
**pals·grave** \'pȯlz-ˌgräv\ *noun* [Dutch *paltsgrave*] (1539)
**:** COUNT PALATINE 1a
**pal·sied** \'pȯl-zēd\ *adjective* (1550)
**:** affected with or as if with palsy
**¹pal·sy** \'pȯl-zē\ *noun, plural* **palsies** [Middle English *parlesie*, from Middle French *paralisie*, from Latin *paralysis*] (14th century)
**1 :** PARALYSIS
**2 :** a condition marked by uncontrollable tremor of the body or a part
**²palsy** *transitive verb* **pal·sied; pal·sy·ing** (1615)
**:** to affect with or as if with palsy
**³palsy** \'pal-zē\ *adjective* (1951)
**:** PALSY-WALSY
**palsy–walsy** \ˌpal-zē-'wal-zē\ *adjective* [reduplication of *palsy*] (1943)
*slang* **:** being or appearing to be very intimate
**pal·ter** \'pȯl-tər\ *intransitive verb* **pal·tered; pal·ter·ing** \-t(ə-)riŋ\ [origin unknown] (1601)
**1 :** to act insincerely or deceitfully **:** EQUIVOCATE
**2 :** HAGGLE, CHAFFER
**synonym** see LIE
— **pal·ter·er** \-tər-ər\ *noun*
**pal·try** \'pȯl-trē\ *adjective* **pal·tri·er; -est** [obsolete *paltry* trash, from dialect *palt, pelt* piece of coarse cloth, trash; akin to Middle Low German *palte* rag] (1570)
**1 :** INFERIOR, TRASHY
**2 :** MEAN, DESPICABLE
**3 :** TRIVIAL
**4 :** MEAGER, MEASLY ⟨made a *paltry* donation⟩
— **pal·tri·ness** *noun*
**pa·lu·dal** \pə-'lü-d²l, 'pal-yə-d²l\ *adjective* [Latin *palud-, palus* marsh; akin to Sanskrit *palvala* pond] (circa 1820)
**:** of or relating to marshes or fens **:** MARSHY
**paly** \'pā-lē\ *adjective* (1560)
*archaic* **:** somewhat pale **:** PALLID
**pal·y·nol·o·gy** \ˌpa-lə-'nä-lə-jē\ *noun* [Greek *palynein* to sprinkle, from *palē* fine meal] (1944)
**:** a branch of science dealing with pollen and spores
— **pal·y·no·log·i·cal** \-nə-'lä-ji-kəl\ *also* **pal·y·no·log·ic** \-jik\ *adjective*
— **pal·y·no·log·i·cal·ly** \-ji-k(ə-)lē\ *adverb*
— **pal·y·nol·o·gist** \-'nä-lə-jist\ *noun*
**pam·pa** \'pam-pə, 'päm-\ *noun, plural* **pam·pas** \-pəz, -pəs\ [American Spanish, from Quechua] (1704)
**:** an extensive generally grass-covered plain of temperate South America east of the Andes **:** PRAIRIE
**pam·pas grass** \-pəz-, -pəs-\ *noun* (circa 1851)
**:** a South American grass (*Cortaderia selloana*) often grown for ornament that has showy white panicles borne on tall stems
**pam·pe·an** \'pam-pē-ən, 'päm-, pam-', päm-'\ *adjective* (1839)
**:** of or relating to the pampas of South America or their Indian inhabitants
**pam·per** \'pam-pər\ *transitive verb* **pam·pered; pam·per·ing** \-p(ə-)riŋ\ [Middle English, probably of Dutch origin; akin to Flemish *pamperen* to pamper] (14th century)
**1** *archaic* **:** to cram with rich food **:** GLUT
**2 a :** to treat with extreme or excessive care and attention ⟨*pampered* their guests⟩ **b :** GRATIFY, HUMOR ⟨enabled him to *pamper* his wanderlust —*New Yorker*⟩
**synonym** see INDULGE
— **pam·per·er** \-pər-ər\ *noun*
**pam·pe·ro** \pam-'per-(ˌ)ō, päm-\ *noun, plural* **-ros** [American Spanish, from *pampa*] (1818)
**:** a strong cold wind from the west or southwest that sweeps over the pampas

**pam·phlet** \'pam(p)-flət\ *noun* [Middle English *pamflet* unbound booklet, from *Pamphilus seu De Amore* Pamphilus or On Love, popular Latin love poem of the 12th century] (14th century)
: an unbound printed publication with no cover or with a paper cover ◆

¹**pam·phle·teer** \,pam(p)-flə-'tir\ *noun* (1642)
: a writer of pamphlets attacking something or urging a cause

²**pamphleteer** *intransitive verb* (1698)
**1** : to write and publish pamphlets
**2** : to engage in partisan arguments indirectly in writings

¹**pan** \'pan\ *noun* [Middle English *panne*, from Old English (akin to Old High German *phanna* pan), from Latin *patina*, from Greek *patanē*] (before 12th century)
**1 a** : a usually broad, shallow, and open container for domestic use (as for warming, baking, or frying) **b** : any of various similar usually metal receptacles: as (1) : the hollow part of the lock in a firelock or flintlock gun that receives the priming (2) : either of the receptacles in a pair of scales (3) : a round shallow metal container for separating metal (as gold) from waste by washing
**2 a** (1) : a natural basin or depression in land (2) : a similar artificial basin (as for evaporating brine) **b** : a drifting fragment of the flat thin ice that forms in bays or along the shore
**3** : HARDPAN 1
**4** *slang* : FACE
**5** : a harsh criticism

²**pan** *verb* **panned; pan·ning** (1839)
*transitive verb*
**1 a** : to wash in a pan for the purpose of separating heavy particles **b** : to separate (as gold) by panning **c** : to place in a pan
**2** : to criticize severely ⟨the show was *panned*⟩
*intransitive verb*
**1** : to wash material (as earth or gravel) in a pan in search of metal (as gold)
**2** : to yield precious metal in the process of panning — usually used with *out*

³**pan** \'pän\ *noun* [Hindi *pān*, from Sanskrit *parṇa* wing, leaf — more at FERN] (1616)
**1** : a betel leaf
**2** : a masticatory of betel nut, mineral lime, and pan

⁴**pan** \'pan\ *noun* [short for *panorama*] (circa 1922)
**1** : the process of panning a motion-picture or video camera
**2** : a shot in which the camera is panned

⁵**pan** \'pan\ *verb* **panned; pan·ning** (1930)
*transitive verb*
: to rotate (as a motion-picture camera) so as to keep an object in the picture or secure a panoramic effect
*intransitive verb*
**1** : to pan a motion-picture or video camera
**2** *of a camera* : to undergo panning

**Pan** \'pan\ *noun* [Latin, from Greek]
: a Greek god of pastures, flocks, and shepherds usually represented as having the legs, horns, and ears of a goat

**pan-** *combining form* [Greek, from *pan*, neuter of *pant-*, *pas* all, every; akin to Tocharian B *pont-* all]
**1** : all : completely ⟨*panchromatic*⟩
**2 a** : involving all of a (specified) group ⟨*Pan-American*⟩ **b** : advocating or involving the union of a (specified) group ⟨*Pan-Slavism*⟩
**3** : whole : general ⟨*panleukopenia*⟩

**pan·a·cea** \,pa-nə-'sē-ə\ *noun* [Latin, from Greek *panakeia*, from *panakēs* all-healing, from *pan-* + *akos* remedy] (1548)
: a remedy for all ills or difficulties : CURE-ALL
— **pan·a·ce·an** \-'sē-ən\ *adjective*

**pa·nache** \pə-'nash, -'näsh\ *noun* [Middle French *pennache*, from Old Italian *pennacchio*, from Late Latin *pinnaculum* small wing — more at PINNACLE] (1553)

**1** : an ornamental tuft (as of feathers) especially on a helmet
**2** : dash or flamboyance in style and action : VERVE ◆

**pa·na·da** \pə-'nä-də\ *noun* [Spanish, from *pan* bread, from Latin *panis* — more at FOOD] (circa 1598)
: a paste of flour or bread crumbs and water or stock used as a base for sauce or a binder for forcemeat or stuffing

**pan·a·ma** \'pa-nə-,mä, -,mȯ\ *noun, often capitalized* [American Spanish *panamá*, from *Panama*, Central America] (1848)
: a lightweight hat of natural-colored straw hand-plaited of narrow strips from the young leaves of the jipijapa; *also* : a machine-made imitation of this

**Panama Red** *noun* (1967)
: marijuana of a reddish tint that is of Panamanian origin and is held to be very potent

**Pan–Amer·i·can** \,pa-nə-'mer-ə-kən\ *adjective* (1889)
: of, relating to, or involving the independent republics of North and South America

**Pan–Amer·i·can·ism** \-kə-,ni-zəm\ *noun* (1901)
: a movement for greater cooperation among the Pan-American nations

**pan·a·tela** \,pa-nə-'te-lə\ *noun* [Spanish, from American Spanish, a long thin biscuit, ultimately from Latin *panis* bread] (1847)
: a long slender straight-sided cigar

¹**pan·cake** \'pan-,kāk\ *noun* (14th century)
: a flat cake made of thin batter and cooked (as on a griddle) on both sides

²**pancake** *verb* **pan·caked; pan·cak·ing** (1911)
*intransitive verb*
: to make a pancake landing
*transitive verb*
: to cause to pancake

**Pan–Cake** \'pan-,kāk\ *trademark*
— used for a cosmetic in semimoist cake form

**pancake landing** *noun* (1928)
: a landing in which the airplane is stalled usually unintentionally above the landing surface causing it to drop abruptly in an approximately horizontal position with little forward motion

**pan·cet·ta** \,(,)pan-'che-tə\ *noun* [Italian, from diminutive of *pancia* belly, paunch, from Latin *pantic-, pantex*] (1974)
: unsmoked bacon used especially in Italian cuisine

**pan·chax** \'pan-,kaks\ *noun* [New Latin] (1961)
: any of various small brilliantly colored Old World killifishes (genus *Aplocheilus*) often kept in the tropical aquarium

**Pan·chen Lama** \'pän-chən-\ *noun* [*Panchen* from Chinese (Beijing) *bānchán*] (1794)
: the lama who is the chief spiritual adviser of the Dalai Lama

**pan·chro·mat·ic** \,pan-krō-'ma-tik\ *adjective* [International Scientific Vocabulary] (1903)
: sensitive to light of all colors in the visible spectrum ⟨*panchromatic* film⟩

**pan·cra·ti·um** \pan-'krā-shē-əm\ *noun* [Latin, from Greek *pankration*, from *pan-* + *kratos* strength — more at HARD] (1603)
: an ancient Greek athletic contest involving both boxing and wrestling

**pan·cre·as** \'paŋ-krē-əs, 'pan-\ *noun* [New Latin, from Greek *pankreas* sweetbread, from *pan-* + *kreas* flesh, meat — more at RAW] (1578)
: a large lobulated gland of vertebrates that secretes digestive enzymes and the hormones insulin and glucagon
— **pan·cre·at·ic** \,paŋ-krē-'a-tik, ,pan-\ *adjective*

**pancreat-** *combining form* [New Latin, from Greek *pankreat-, pancreas*]
: pancreas ⟨*pancreatic*⟩

**pan·cre·a·tec·to·my** \,paŋ-krē-ə-'tek-tə-mē, ,pan-\ *noun* (circa 1900)
: surgical removal of all or part of the pancreas
— **pan·cre·a·tec·to·mized** \-,mīzd\ *adjective*

**pancreatic duct** *noun* (circa 1860)
: a duct leading from the pancreas and opening into the duodenum

**pancreatic juice** *noun* (circa 1666)
: a clear alkaline secretion of pancreatic enzymes (as trypsin and lipase) that flows into the duodenum and acts on food already acted on by the gastric juice and saliva

**pan·cre·a·tin** \pan-'krē-ə-tən; 'paŋ-krē-, 'pan-\ *noun* (circa 1860)
: a mixture of enzymes from the pancreatic juice; *also* : a preparation containing such a mixture

**pan·cre·a·ti·tis** \,paŋ-krē-ə-'tī-təs, ,pan-\ *noun, plural* **-tit·i·des** \-'ti-tə-,dēz\ [New Latin] (circa 1842)
: inflammation of the pancreas

**pan·cre·o·zy·min** \-krē-ō-'zī-mən\ *noun* [*pancreas* + *-o-* + *zym-* + ¹*-in*] (1943)
: CHOLECYSTOKININ

**pan·cy·to·pe·nia** \,pan-,sī-tə-'pē-nē-ə\ *noun* [New Latin, from *pan-* + *cyt-* + *-penia*] (circa 1941)

\ə\ abut   \ᵊ\ kitten   \ər\ further   \a\ ash   \ā\ ace
\ä\ mop, mar   \aú\ out   \ch\ chin   \e\ bet   \ē\ easy
\g\ go   \i\ hit   \ī\ ice   \j\ job   \ŋ\ sing   \ō\ go
\ȯ\ law   \ȯi\ boy   \th\ thin   \t̷h\ the   \ü\ loot   \ú\ foot
\y\ yet   \zh\ vision   *see also* Guide to Pronunciation

: an abnormal reduction in the number of erythrocytes, white blood cells, and blood platelets in the blood; *also* : a disorder (as aplastic anemia) characterized by such a reduction

**pan·da** \'pan-də\ *noun* [French, perhaps from a language of the southeast Himalayas] (1835)
**1** : a long-tailed largely herbivorous mammal (*Ailurus fulgens*) that is related to and resembles the American raccoon, has long rusty or chestnut fur, and is found from the Himalayas to China
**2** : GIANT PANDA

*A* panda 1, *B* giant panda

**panda car** *noun* [from its black and white coloration] (1967)
*British* : a police patrol car
**pan·da·nus** \pan-'dā-nəs, -'da-\ *noun, plural* **-ni** \-nī\ [New Latin, genus name, from Malay *pandan* screw pine] (1830)
: SCREW PINE; *also* : a fiber made from screwpine leaves and used for woven products (as mats)
**Pan·da·rus** \'pan-də-rəs\ *noun* [Latin, from Greek *Pandaros*]
: a Lycian archer in the Trojan War who in medieval legend procures Cressida for Troilus
**pan·dect** \'pan-ˌdekt\ *noun* [Late Latin *Pandectae*, the Pandects, digest of Roman civil law (6th century A.D.), from Latin, plural of *pandectes* encyclopedic work, from Greek *pandektēs* all-receiving, from *pan-* + *dechesthai* to receive; akin to Greek *dokein* to seem, seem good — more at DECENT] (1533)
**1** : a complete code of the laws of a country or system of law
**2** : a treatise covering an entire subject
¹**pan·dem·ic** \pan-'de-mik\ *adjective* [Late Latin *pandemus*, from Greek *pandēmos* of all the people, from *pan-* + *dēmos* people — more at DEMAGOGUE] (1666)
: occurring over a wide geographic area and affecting an exceptionally high proportion of the population ⟨*pandemic* malaria⟩
²**pandemic** *noun* (circa 1853)
: a pandemic outbreak of a disease
**Pan·de·mo·ni·um** \ˌpan-də-'mō-nē-əm\ *noun* [New Latin, from Greek *pan-* + *daimōn* evil spirit — more at DEMON]
**1** : the capital of Hell in Milton's *Paradise Lost*
**2** : the infernal regions : HELL
**3** *not capitalized* : a wild uproar : TUMULT
¹**pan·der** \'pan-dər\ *noun* [Middle English *Pandare* Pandarus, from Latin *Pandarus*] (1530)
**1 a** : a go-between in love intrigues **b** : PIMP
**2** : someone who caters to or exploits the weaknesses of others ◆
²**pander** *intransitive verb* **pan·dered; pan·der·ing** \-d(ə-)riŋ\ (1602)

: to act as a pander; *especially* : to provide gratification for others' desires ⟨films that *pander* to the basest emotions⟩
— **pan·der·er** \-dər-ər\ *noun*
**pan·dit** \'pan-dət, 'pən-\ *noun* [Hindi *paṇḍit*, from Sanskrit *paṇḍita*] (circa 1828)
: a wise or learned man in India — often used as an honorary title
**pan·do·ra** \pan-'dōr-ə, -'dȯr-\ *noun* [Italian, from Late Latin *pandura* 3-stringed lute, from Greek *pandoura*] (1597)
: BANDORE
**Pan·do·ra's box** \pan-'dȯr-əz-, -'dȯr-\ *noun* [from the box, sent by the gods to Pandora, which she was forbidden to open and which loosed a swarm of evils upon mankind when she opened it out of curiosity] (1579)
: a prolific source of troubles
**pan·dow·dy** \pan-'daù-dē\ *noun, plural* **-dies** [origin unknown] (1805)
: a deep-dish spiced apple dessert sweetened with sugar, molasses, or maple syrup and covered with a rich crust
**pan·dy** \'pan-dē\ *transitive verb* **pan·died; pan·dy·ing** [probably from Latin *pande*, imperative singular of *pandere* to spread out (the hand); command of the schoolmaster to the boy — more at FATHOM] (1863)
*British* : to punish (a schoolboy) with a blow on the palm of the hand especially with a ferule
**pane** \'pān\ *noun* [Middle English *pan, pane* strip of cloth, pane, from Middle French *pan*, from Latin *pannus* cloth, rag — more at VANE] (14th century)
: a piece, section, or side of something: as **a**
: a framed sheet of glass in a window or door **b** : one of the sections into which a sheet of postage stamps is cut for distribution
— **paned** \'pānd\ *adjective*
**pan·e·gy·ric** \ˌpa-nə-'jir-ik, -'jī-rik\ *noun* [Latin *panegyricus*, from Greek *panēgyrikos*, from *panēgyrikos* of or for a festival assembly, from *panēgyris* festival assembly, from *pan-* + *agyris* assembly; akin to Greek *ageirein* to gather] (1603)
: a eulogistic oration or writing; *also* : formal or elaborate praise
**synonym** see ENCOMIUM
— **pan·e·gy·ri·cal** \-'jir-i-kəl, -'jī-ri-\ *adjective*
— **pan·e·gy·ri·cal·ly** \-k(ə-)lē\ *adverb*
**pan·e·gy·rist** \ˌpa-nə-'jir-ist, -'jī-rist\ *noun* (1605)
: EULOGIST
¹**pan·el** \'pa-nᵊl\ *noun* [Middle English, piece of cloth, slip of parchment, jury schedule, from Middle French, piece of cloth, piece, from (assumed) Vulgar Latin *pannellus*, diminutive of Latin *pannus*] (14th century)
**1 a** (1) : a schedule containing names of persons summoned as jurors (2) : the group of persons so summoned (3) : JURY 1 **b** (1) : a group of persons selected for some service (as investigation or arbitration) ⟨a *panel* of experts⟩ (2) : a group of persons who discuss before an audience a topic of public interest; *also* : PANEL DISCUSSION (3) : a group of entertainers or guests engaged as players in a quiz or guessing game on a radio or television program
**2** : a separate or distinct part of a surface: as **a** : a fence section : HURDLE **b** (1) : a thin usually rectangular board set in a frame (as in a door) (2) : a usually sunken or raised section of a surface set off by a margin (3) : a flat usually rectangular piece of construction material (as plywood or precast masonry) made to form part of a surface **c** : a vertical section of fabric (as a gore) **d** : COMIC STRIP; *also* : a frame of a comic strip **e** : any of several units of construction of an airplane wing surface
**3** : a thin flat piece of wood on which a picture is painted; *also* : a painting on such a surface

**4 a** : a section of a switchboard **b** : a flat often insulating support (as for computer hardware or parts of an electrical device) usually with control handles on one face **c** : a usually vertical mount for controls or dials (as of instruments of measurement)
²**panel** *transitive verb* **-eled** *or* **-elled; -el·ing** *or* **-el·ling** (15th century)
: to furnish or decorate with panels ⟨*paneled* the living room⟩
**panel discussion** *noun* (circa 1938)
: a formal discussion by a panel
**paneling** *also* **panelling** *noun* (1824)
: panels joined in a continuous surface; *especially* : decorative wood panels so joined
**pan·el·ist** \'pa-nᵊl-ist\ *noun* (1951)
: a member of a discussion or advisory panel or of a radio or television panel
**panel truck** *noun* (1937)
: a small motortruck with a fully enclosed body
**pan·e·tela** *variant of* PANATELA
**pan·et·to·ne** \ˌpä-nə-'tō-nē, ˌpa-\ *noun* [Italian, from *panetto* small loaf, diminutive of *pane* bread, from Latin *panis* — more at FOOD] (1922)
: a usually yeast-leavened bread containing raisins and candied fruit
**pan·fish** \'pan-ˌfish\ *noun* (1805)
: a small food fish (as a sunfish) usually taken with hook and line and not available on the market
**pan·fry** \'pan-ˌfrī, pan-'frī\ *transitive verb* (circa 1929)
: to cook in a frying pan with a small amount of fat
**pan·ful** \'pan-ˌfùl\ *noun* (circa 1864)
: as much or as many as a pan will hold
¹**pang** \'paŋ\ *noun* [origin unknown] (15th century)
**1** : a brief piercing spasm of pain
**2** : a sharp attack of mental anguish ⟨*pangs* of remorse⟩ ⟨a *pang* of jealousy struck me —Graham Greene⟩
²**pang** *transitive verb* (1502)
: to cause to have pangs : TORMENT
**pan·ga** \'päŋ-gə\ *noun* [Swahili] (1925)
: MACHETE
**pan·gen·e·sis** \ˌpan-'je-nə-səs\ *noun* [New Latin] (1868)
: a disproven hypothetical mechanism of heredity in which the cells throw off particles that collect in the reproductive products or in buds so that the egg or bud contains particles from all parts of the parent
— **pan·ge·net·ic** \-jə-'ne-tik\ *adjective*
**Pan·gloss·ian** \pan-'glä-sē-ən, paŋ-, -'glȯ-\ *adjective* [*Pangloss*, optimistic tutor in Voltaire's *Candide* (1759)] (1831)

: marked by the view that all is for the best in this best of possible worlds **:** excessively optimistic

**pan·go·la grass** \pan-'gō-lə-, paŋ-\ *noun* [alteration of *Pongola grass,* from the *Pongola River,* South Africa] (1948)
: a rapid-growing perennial grass (*Digitaria decumbens*) of southern Africa that has been introduced into the southern U.S. as a pasture grass

**pan·go·lin** \'paŋ-gə-lən, 'pan-\ *noun* [Malay dialect *pĕngguling*] (1774)
: any of a family (Manidae) of Asian and African edentate mammals having the body covered with large imbricated horny scales

**pangolin**

**¹pan·han·dle** \'pan-,han-dᵊl\ *noun* (1856)
: a narrow projection of a larger territory (as a state) ⟨the Texas *panhandle*⟩

**²panhandle** *verb* **pan·han·dled; pan·han·dling** \-,han(d)-liŋ, -,han-dᵊl-iŋ\ [back-formation from *panhandler,* probably from *panhandle,* noun; from the extended forearm] (1903)
*intransitive verb*
: to stop people on the street and ask for food or money **:** BEG
*transitive verb*
**1 :** to accost on the street and beg from
**2 :** to get by panhandling
— **pan·han·dler** \-,han(d)-lər, -,han-dᵊl-ər\ *noun*

**Pan·hel·len·ic** \,pan-hə-'le-nik\ *adjective* (1847)
**1 :** of or relating to all Greece or all the Greeks
**2 :** of or relating to the Greek-letter sororities or fraternities in American colleges and universities or to an association representing them

**pan·hu·man** \,pan-'hyü-mən, -'yü-\ *adjective* (circa 1909)
: of or relating to all humanity ⟨the *panhuman* problem of evil —R. K. Merton⟩

**¹pan·ic** \'pa-nik\ *adjective* [French *panique,* from Greek *panikos,* literally, of Pan, from *Pan*] (1603)
**1 :** of, relating to, or resembling the mental or emotional state believed induced by the god Pan ⟨*panic* fear⟩
**2 :** of, relating to, or arising from a panic ⟨a wave of *panic* buying⟩
**3 :** of or relating to the god Pan

**²panic** *noun* (1708)
**1 :** a sudden overpowering fright; *especially* **:** a sudden unreasoning terror often accompanied by mass flight
**2 :** a sudden widespread fright concerning financial affairs that results in a depression of values caused by extreme measures for protection of property (as securities)
**3** *slang* **:** one that is very funny ◆
**synonym** see FEAR
— **pan·icky** \'pa-ni-kē\ *adjective*

**³panic** *verb* **pan·icked** \-nikt\; **pan·ick·ing** (1827)
*transitive verb*
**1 :** to affect with panic
**2 :** to produce demonstrative appreciation on the part of ⟨*panic* an audience with a gag⟩
*intransitive verb*
: to be affected with panic

**panic button** *noun* (circa 1950)
: something setting off a precipitous emergency response ⟨there was no pushing of *panic* buttons at the White House, no rushing of troops —J. C. Harsch⟩

**pan·ic grass** \'pa-nik-\ *noun* [Middle English *panik,* from Middle French or Latin; Middle French *panic* foxtail millet, from Latin *panicum,* from *panus* stalk of a panicle] (1597)

: any of various grasses (*Panicum* and related genera) including some important forage and cereal grasses

**pan·i·cle** \'pa-ni-kəl\ *noun* [Latin *panicula,* diminutive of *panus*] (1597)
**1 :** a compound racemose inflorescence — see INFLORESCENCE illustration
**2 :** a pyramidal loosely branched flower cluster
— **pan·i·cled** \-kəld\ *adjective*
— **pa·nic·u·late** \pa-'ni-kyə-lət, pə-\ *adjective*

**pan·ic–strick·en** \'pa-nik-,stri-kən\ *adjective* (1804)
: overcome with panic

**pan·i·cum** \'pa-ni-kəm\ *noun* [New Latin, from Latin, foxtail millet] (circa 1864)
: any of a large and widely distributed genus (*Panicum*) of grasses that have a very diverse habit and 1- to 2-flowered spikelets arranged in a panicle

**Pan·ja·bi** \,pən-'jä-bē, -'ja-\ *noun* [Hindi *pañjābī,* from *pañjābī* of Punjab] (1854)
**1 :** an Indo-Aryan language of the Punjab
**2 :** PUNJABI 2

**pan·jan·drum** \pan-'jan-drəm\ *noun, plural* **-drums** *also* **-dra** \-drə\ [Grand *Panjandrum,* burlesque title of an imaginary personage in some nonsense lines by Samuel Foote] (1755)
: a powerful personage or pretentious official

**pan·leu·ko·pe·nia** \,pan-,lü-kə-'pē-nē-ə\ *noun* [New Latin] (1940)
: an acute usually fatal viral epizootic disease especially of cats characterized by fever, diarrhea and dehydration, and extensive destruction of white blood cells

**pan·mic·tic** \,pan-'mik-tik\ *adjective* [*pan-* + Greek *miktos,* verbal of *mignynai* to mix] (1943)
: of, relating to, or exhibiting panmixia

**pan·mix·ia** \-'mik-sē-ə\ *noun* [New Latin, from *pan-* + Greek *mixis* act of mingling, mating, from *mignynai* to mix — more at MIX] (circa 1889)
: random mating within a breeding population

**panne** \'pan\ *noun* [French, from Old French *penne, panne* fur used for lining, from Latin *pinna* feather, wing — more at PEN] (circa 1794)
**1 :** a silk or rayon velvet with lustrous pile flattened in one direction — called also *panne velvet*
**2 :** a heavy silk or rayon satin with high luster and waxy smoothness

**pan·nier** *also* **pan·ier** \'pan-yər, 'pa-nē-ər\ *noun* [Middle English *panier,* from Middle French, from Latin *panarium,* from *panis* bread — more at FOOD] (13th century)
**1 :** a large container: as **a :** a basket often carried on the back of an animal or the shoulders of a person **b :** one of a pair of packs or baskets hung over the rear wheel of a vehicle (as a bicycle)
**2 a :** one of a pair of hoops formerly used to expand women's skirts at the sides **b :** an overskirt draped at the sides of a skirt for an effect of fullness

**pan·ni·kin** \'pa-ni-kən\ *noun* [¹*pan* + *-nikin* (as in *cannikin*)] (1823)
*British* **:** a small pan or cup

**pannier 2b**

**pa·no·cha** \pə-'nō-chə\ *or* **pa·no·che** \-chē\ *variant of* PENUCHE

**pan·o·plied** \'pa-nə-plēd\ *adjective* (1832)
: dressed in or having a panoply

**pan·op·tic** \,pa-'näp-tik\ *adjective* [Greek *panoptēs* all-seeing, from *pan-* + *opsesthai* to be going to see — more at OPTIC] (1826)
: being or presenting a comprehensive or panoramic view

**pan·o·ply** \'pa-nə-plē\ *noun, plural* **-plies** [Greek *panoplia,* from *pan-* + *hopla* arms, ar-

mor, plural of *hoplon* tool, weapon — more at HOPLITE] (1632)
**1 a :** a full suit of armor **b :** ceremonial attire
**2 :** something forming a protective covering
**3 a :** a magnificent or impressive array ⟨the full *panoply* of a military funeral⟩ **b :** a display of all appropriate appurtenances ⟨has the *panoply* of science fiction . . . but it is not true science fiction —Isaac Asimov⟩

**pan·o·rama** \,pa-nə-'ra-mə, -'rä-\ *noun* [*pan-* + Greek *horama* sight, from *horan* to see — more at WARY] (1796)
**1 a :** CYCLORAMA 1 **b :** a picture exhibited a part at a time by being unrolled before the spectator
**2 a :** an unobstructed or complete view of an area in every direction **b :** a comprehensive presentation of a subject ⟨a *panorama* of American history⟩ **c :** RANGE
**3 :** a mental picture of a series of images or events
— **pan·o·ram·ic** \-'ra-mik\ *adjective*
— **pan·o·ram·i·cal·ly** \-mi-k(ə-)lē\ *adverb*

**pan out** *intransitive verb* [²*pan*] (circa 1868)
: TURN OUT; *especially* **:** SUCCEED ⟨the signs revealed that the experiment wasn't *panning out* —Ronald Reagan⟩

**pan·pipe** \'pan-,pīp\ *noun* [*Pan,* its traditional inventor] (1820)
: a primitive wind instrument consisting of a series of short vertical pipes of graduated length bound together with the mouthpieces in an even row — often used in plural

**pan·sex·u·al** \,pan-'sek-sh(ə-)wəl, -shəl\ *adjective* (1926)
: exhibiting or implying many forms of sexual expression
— **pan·sex·u·al·i·ty** \,pan-,sek-shə-'wa-lə-tē\ *noun*

**panpipe**

**Pan–Slav·ism** \,pan-'slä-,vi-zəm, -'sla-\ *noun* (1850)
: a political and cultural movement originally emphasizing the cultural ties between the Slavic peoples but later associated with Russian expansionism
— **Pan–Slav·ic** \-'sla-vik, -'slä-\ *adjective*
— **Pan–Slav·ist** \-'slä-vist, -'sla-\ *noun*

**¹pan·sy** \'pan-zē\ *noun, plural* **pansies** [Middle English *pensee,* from Middle French *pensée,* from *pensee* thought, from feminine of *pensé,* past participle of *penser* to think, from Latin *pensare* to ponder — more at PENSIVE] (15th century)
**1 :** a garden plant (*Viola wittrockiana*) derived chiefly from the wild pansy (*Viola tricolor*) of Europe by hybridizing the latter with other wild violets; *also* **:** its flower

◇ **WORD HISTORY**
**panic** In ancient Greek religion Pan was the god of woodlands and pastures, flocks and shepherds. Although generally conceived as a pipe-playing, nymph-chasing pastoral deity, Pan was also recognized for his ability to induce terror. When accidentally awakened from his noontime slumber, he could give a great shout that would cause flocks to stampede. Athens became a seat of worship for Pan because its citizens believed that he had aided the Athenians against the Persians at the battle of Marathon. From this more formidable aspect of his nature later Greek authors derived the word *panikon* "groundless fear," the ultimate source of English *panic.*

\ə\ abut \ᵊ\ kitten \ər\ further \a\ ash \ā\ ace
\ä\ mop, mar \au̇\ out \ch\ chin \e\ bet \ē\ easy
\g\ go \i\ hit \ī\ ice \j\ job \ŋ\ sing \ō\ go
\ȯ\ law \ȯi\ boy \th\ thin \t͟h\ the \ü\ loot \u̇\ foot
\y\ yet \zh\ vision    *see also* Guide to Pronunciation

**2 a :** an effeminate man or boy — usually used disparagingly **b :** a male homosexual — usually used disparagingly
²**pansy** *adjective* (1929)
**:** EFFEMINATE 1; *also* : HOMOSEXUAL — usually used disparagingly
¹**pant** \'pant\ *verb* [Middle English, modification of Middle French *pantaisier*, from (assumed) Vulgar Latin *phantasiare* to have hallucinations, from Greek *phantasioun*, from *phantasia* appearance, imagination — more at FANCY] (14th century)
*intransitive verb*
**1 a :** to breathe quickly, spasmodically, or in a labored manner **b :** to run panting ⟨*panting* along beside the bicycle⟩ **c :** to move with or make a throbbing or puffing sound
**2 :** to long eagerly : YEARN
**3 :** THROB, PULSATE
*transitive verb*
**:** to utter with panting : GASP
²**pant** *noun* (1513)
**1 a :** a panting breath **b :** the visible movement of the chest accompanying such a breath
**2 :** a throbbing or puffing sound
³**pant** *noun* [short for *pantaloons*] (1840)
**1 :** an outer garment covering each leg separately and usually extending from the waist to the ankle — usually used in plural
**2** *plural, chiefly British* : men's underpants
**3** *plural* : PANTIE
***word history*** .see PANTALOON
— **with one's pants down :** in an embarrassing position (as of being unprepared to act)
⁴**pant** *adjective* (1899)
**:** of or relating to pants ⟨a *pant* leg⟩
**pant-** *or* **panto-** *combining form* [Middle French, from Latin, from Greek, from *pant-*, *pas* — more at PAN-]
**:** all ⟨*pantisocracy*⟩
**Pan·ta·gru·el** \,pan-tə-'grü-əl; pan-'ta-grə-wəl, -,wel\ *noun* [French]
**:** the huge son of Gargantua in Rabelais's *Pantagruel*
— **Pan·ta·gru·el·ian** \,pan-tə-grü-'e-lē-ən, (,)pan-,ta-grə-'we-\ *adjective*
— **Pan·ta·gru·el·ism** \,pan-tə-'grü-ə-,li-zəm; pan-'ta-grə-wə-,li-zəm, -,we-\ *noun*
— **Pan·ta·gru·el·ist** \-list\ *noun*
**pan·ta·lets** *or* **pan·ta·lettes** \,pan-tə-'lets\ *noun plural* [*pantaloons*] (1834)
**:** long drawers with a ruffle at the bottom of each leg worn especially by women and children in the first half of the 19th century
**pan·ta·loon** \,pan-tə-'lün\ *noun* [Middle French & Old Italian; Middle French *Pantalon*, from Old Italian *Pantaleone, Pantalone*] (circa 1590)
**1 a** *or* **pan·ta·lo·ne** \-tə-'lō-nē\ *capitalized* **:** a character in the commedia dell'arte that is usually a skinny old dotard who wears spectacles, slippers, and a tight-fitting combination of trousers and stockings **b :** a buffoon in pantomimes
**2** *plural* **a :** wide breeches worn especially in England during the reign of Charles II **b :** close-fitting trousers usually having straps passing under the instep and worn especially in the 19th century
**3 :** loose-fitting usually shorter than ankle-length trousers ◆
**pant·dress** \'pant-,dres\ *noun* (1964)
**:** a dress having a divided skirt
**pan·tech·ni·con** \pan-'tek-ni-kən\ *noun* [short for *pantechnicon van*, from *pantechnicon* storage warehouse] (1891)
*British* : ³VAN 1
**pan·the·ism** \'pan(t)-thē-,i-zəm\ *noun* [French *panthéisme*, from *panthéiste* pantheist, from English *pantheist*, from *pan-* + Greek *theos* god] (1732)
**1 :** a doctrine that equates God with the forces and laws of the universe
**2 :** the worship of all gods of different creeds, cults, or peoples indifferently; *also* : toleration

of worship of all gods (as at certain periods of the Roman empire)
— **pan·the·ist** \-thē-ist\ *noun*
— **pan·the·is·tic** \,pan(t)-thē-'is-tik\ *also*
**pan·the·is·ti·cal** \-ti-kəl\ *adjective*
— **pan·the·is·ti·cal·ly** \-ti-k(ə-)lē\ *adverb*
**pan·the·on** \'pan(t)-thē-,än, -ən\ *noun* [Middle English *Panteon*, a temple at Rome, from Latin *Pantheon*, from Greek *pantheion* temple of all the gods, from neuter of *pantheios* of all gods, from *pan-* + *theos* god] (14th century)
**1 :** a temple dedicated to all the gods
**2 :** a building serving as the burial place of or containing memorials to the famous dead of a nation
**3 :** the gods of a people; *especially* : the officially recognized gods
**4 :** a group of illustrious persons
**pan·ther** \'pan(t)-thər\ *noun, plural* **panthers** *also* **panther** [Middle English *pantere*, from Old French, from Latin *panthera*, from Greek *panthēr*] (13th century)
**1 :** LEOPARD: as **a :** a leopard of a hypothetical exceptionally large fierce variety **b :** a leopard of the black color phase
**2 :** COUGAR
**3 :** JAGUAR
**pant·ie** *or* **panty** \'pan-tē\ *noun, plural* **panties** [³*pant*] (1908)
**:** a woman's or child's undergarment covering the lower trunk and made with closed crotch — usually used in plural
***word history*** see PANTALOON
**pantie girdle** *noun* (1941)
**:** a woman's girdle having a sewed-in or detachable crotch and made with or without garters and bones
**pan·tile** \'pan-,tīl\ *noun* [¹*pan*] (1640)
**1 :** a roofing tile whose cross section is an ogee curve
**2 :** a roofing tile of which the cross section is an arc of a circle and which is laid with alternate convex and concave surfaces uppermost
— **pan·tiled** \-,tīld\ *adjective*
**pant·i·soc·ra·cy** \,pan-tə-'sä-krə-sē, ,pan-,tī-\ *noun, plural* **-cies** [*pant-* + *isocracy* equal rule, from Greek *isokratia*, from *is-* + *-kratia* -cracy] (1794)
**:** a utopian community in which all rule equally
— **pant·i·so·crat·ic** \,pan-,tī-sə-'kra-tik\ *or* **pant·i·so·crat·i·cal** \-'kra-ti-kəl\ *adjective*
— **pant·i·soc·ra·tist** \,pan-tə-'sä-krə-tist, ,pan-,tī-\ *noun*
**pan·to** \'pan-(,)tō\ *noun, plural* **pantos** (1852)
*British* : PANTOMIME 2c
**pan·to·fle** \pan-'tō-fəl, -'tä-, -'tü-; 'pan-tə-fəl\ *noun* [Middle English *pantufle*, from Middle French *pantoufle*] (15th century)
**:** SLIPPER
**pan·to·graph** \'pan-tə-,graf\ *noun* [French *pantographe*, from *pant-* + *-graphe* -graph] (1723)
**1 :** an instrument for copying (as a map) on a predetermined scale consisting of four light rigid bars jointed in parallelogram form; *also* : any of various extensible devices of similar construction (as for use as brackets or gates)
**2 :** an electrical trolley carried by a collapsible and adjustable frame
— **pan·to·graph·ic** \,pan-tə-'gra-fik\ *adjective*
¹**pan·to·mime** \'pan-tə-,mīm\ *noun* [Latin *pantomimus*, from *pant-* + *mimus* mime] (1589)
**1 :** PANTOMIMIST
**2 a :** an ancient Roman dramatic performance featuring a solo dancer and a narrative chorus

pantograph 1

**b :** any of various dramatic or dancing performances in which a story is told by expressive bodily or facial movements of the performers **c :** a British theatrical entertainment of the Christmas season based on a nursery tale and featuring topical songs, tableaux, and dances
**3 a :** conveyance of a story by bodily or facial movements especially in drama or dance **b :** the art or genre of conveying a story by bodily movements only
— **pan·to·mim·ic** \,pan-tə-'mi-mik\ *adjective*
²**pantomime** *verb* **-mimed; -mim·ing** (1768)
*intransitive verb*
**:** to engage in pantomime
*transitive verb*
**:** to represent by pantomime
**pan·to·mim·ist** \'pan-tə-,mī-mist, -,mi-\ *noun* (1838)
**1 :** an actor or dancer in pantomimes
**2 :** a composer of pantomimes
**pan·to·the·nate** \,pan-tə-'the-,nāt, pan-'tä-thə-,nāt\ *noun* (circa 1934)
**:** a salt or ester of pantothenic acid
**pan·to·then·ic acid** \,pan-tə-'the-nik-, -'thē-\ *noun* [Greek *pantothen* from all sides, from *pant-*, *pas* all — more at PAN-] (1933)
**:** a viscous oily acid $C_9H_{17}NO_5$ of the vitamin B complex found in all living tissues
**pan·trop·i·cal** \,pan-'trä-pi-kəl\ *also* **pan·trop·ic** \-pik\ *adjective* (1936)
**:** occurring or distributed throughout the tropical regions of the earth
**pan·try** \'pan-trē\ *noun, plural* **pantries** [Middle English *panetrie*, from Middle French *paneterie*, from Old French, from *panetier* servant in charge of the pantry, from *pan* bread, from Latin *panis* — more at FOOD] (14th century)
**1 :** a room or closet used for storing (as provisions) or from which food is brought to the table
**2 :** a room (as in a hotel or hospital) for preparation of foods on order
**pan·try·man** \-mən\ *noun* (circa 1567)
**:** a man in charge of or working in a pantry (as in a hotel or hospital)
**pants suit** *noun* (1964)
**:** PANTSUIT
**pant·suit** \'pant-,süt\ *noun* (1964)
**:** a woman's ensemble consisting usually of a long jacket and tailored pants of the same material
— **pant·suit·ed** *adjective*
**panty hose** *noun* (1963)

: a one-piece undergarment for women that consists of hosiery made with a panty-style top — usually plural in construction

**panty raid** *noun* (circa 1952)
: a raid on a women's dormitory by college men usually to obtain panties as trophies

**panty·waist** \'pan-tē-ˌwāst\ *noun* (circa 1936)
: SISSY
— **pantywaist** *adjective*

**Pan·urge** \'pa-ˌnərj, pa-'nůrzh\ *noun* [French]
: a witty rascal and companion of Pantagruel in Rabelais's *Pantagruel*

**pan·zer** \'pan-zər, 'pän(t)-sər\ *noun* [German *Panzer* tank, armor, coat of mail, from Middle High German *panzier*, from Old French *pancière*, from *pance, panche* belly — more at PAUNCH] (circa 1939)
: TANK 3; *specifically* : a German tank of World War II

**panzer division** *noun* (circa 1939)
: a German armored division

**¹pap** \'pap\ *noun* [Middle English *pappe*; of imitative origin] (13th century)
**1** *chiefly dialect* : NIPPLE, TEAT
**2** : something shaped like a nipple

**²pap** *noun* [Middle English] (15th century)
**1** : a soft food for infants or invalids
**2** : political patronage
**3** : something lacking solid value or substance

**pa·pa** \'pä-pə, *chiefly British* pə-'pä, -'pä\ *noun* [French (baby talk)] (1681)
: FATHER

**Pa·pa** \pə-'pä, 'pä-pə\ (1952)
— a communications code word for the letter *p*

**pa·pa·cy** \'pā-pə-sē\ *noun, plural* **-cies** [Middle English *papacie*, from Medieval Latin *papatia*, from Late Latin *papa* pope — more at POPE] (14th century)
**1** : the office of pope
**2** : a succession or line of popes
**3** : the term of a pope's reign
**4** *capitalized* : the system of government of the Roman Catholic Church of which the pope is the supreme head

**Pa·pa·go** \'pä-pə-ˌgō, 'pa-\ *noun, plural* **Papago** *or* **Papagos** (1839)
**1** : a member of an American Indian people of southwestern Arizona and northwestern Mexico
**2** : the Uto-Aztecan language of the Papago people

**pa·pa·in** \pə-'pā-ən, -'pī-ən\ *noun* [International Scientific Vocabulary, from *papaya*] (circa 1890)
: a protease in the juice of unripe papaya that is used especially as a tenderizer for meat and in medicine

**pa·pal** \'pā-pəl\ *adjective* [Middle English, from Middle French, from Medieval Latin *papalis*, from Late Latin *papa*] (14th century)
: of or relating to a pope or to the Roman Catholic Church; *also* : resembling a pope or that of a pope
— **pa·pal·ly** \-pə-lē\ *adverb*

**papal cross** *noun* (circa 1889)
: a figure of a cross having a long upright shaft and three crossbars with the longest at or somewhat above its middle and the two other successively shorter crossbars above the longest one — see CROSS illustration

**papal infallibility** *noun* (1870)
: the Roman Catholic doctrine that the pope cannot err when speaking ex cathedra in defining a doctrine of Christian faith or morals

**Pa·pa·ni·co·laou smear** \ˌpä-pə-pə-'nē-kə-ˌlaů-, ˌpa-pə-'ni-\ *noun* [George N. *Papanicolaou* (died 1962) American medical scientist] (1950)
: PAP SMEAR

**Papanicolaou test** *noun* (1946)
: PAP SMEAR

**pa·pa·raz·zo** \ˌpä-pə-pə-'rät-(ˌ)sō\ *noun, plural* **-raz·zi** \-(ˌ)sē\ [Italian] (1966)

: a free-lance photographer who aggressively pursues celebrities for the purpose of taking candid photographs

**pa·pav·er·ine** \pə-'pa-və-ˌrēn; -'pav-rən, -'pa-və-\ *noun* [International Scientific Vocabulary, from Latin *papaver* poppy] (1857)
: a crystalline alkaloid $C_{20}H_{21}NO_4$ that is found in opium and is used chiefly as an antispasmodic for its ability to relax smooth muscle

**pa·paw** *noun* [probably modification of Spanish *papaya*] (1624)
**1** \pə-'pȯ\ : PAPAYA
**2** \'pä-(ˌ)pȯ, 'pȯ-\ : a North American tree (*Asimina triloba*) of the custard-apple family with purple flowers and an edible fruit; *also* : its fruit

**pa·pa·ya** \pə-'pī-ə\ *noun* [Spanish, of American Indian origin; akin to Arawak *papáia*] (1598)
: a tropical American tree (*Carica papaya* of the family Caricaceae, the papaya family) with an oblong to globose yellow edible fruit; *also* : its fruit

**¹pa·per** \'pā-pər\ *noun* [Middle English *papir*, from Middle French *papier*, from Latin *papyrus* papyrus, paper, from Greek *papyros* papyrus] (14th century)
**1 a** (1) : a felted sheet of usually vegetable fibers laid down on a fine screen from a water suspension (2) : a similar sheet of other material (as plastic) **b** : a piece of paper
**2 a** : a piece of paper containing a written or printed statement : DOCUMENT (pedigree *papers*) **b** : a piece of paper containing writing or print **c** : a formal written composition often designed for publication and often intended to be read aloud (presented a scholarly *paper* at the meeting) **d** : a piece of written schoolwork
**3** : a paper container or wrapper
**4** : NEWSPAPER
**5** : the negotiable notes or instruments of commerce
**6** : WALLPAPER
**7** : TICKETS; *especially* : free passes
**8** : PAPERBACK
— **on paper 1** : in writing (wants these promises *on paper*) **2** : in theory (the plan looks good *on paper*) **3** : figured at face value (*on paper* the stock was worth nearly a million dollars)

**²paper** *verb* **pa·pered; pa·per·ing** \'pā-p(ə-)riŋ\ (1594)
*transitive verb*
**1** *archaic* : to put down or describe in writing
**2** : to fold or enclose in paper
**3** : to cover or line with paper; *especially* : to apply wallpaper to
**4** : to fill by giving out free passes (*paper* the theater for opening night)
**5** : to cover (an area) with advertising bills, circulars, or posters
*intransitive verb*
: to hang wallpaper
— **pa·per·er** \-pər-ər\ *noun*

**³paper** *adjective* (1594)
**1 a** : made of paper, paperboard, or papier-mâché (a *paper* bag) **b** : PAPERY
**2** : of or relating to clerical work or written communication
**3** : existing only in theory : NOMINAL (a *paper* blockade)
**4** : admitted by free passes (a *paper* audience)
**5** : finished with a crisp smooth surface similar to that of paper (*paper* taffeta)

**pa·per·back** \'pā-pər-ˌbak\ *noun* (1899)
: a book with a flexible paper binding
— **paperback** *also* **pa·per·backed** \-ˌbakt\ *adjective*

**paper birch** *noun* (1810)
: a North American birch (*Betula papyrifera*) with peeling white bark and toothed ovate leaves

**pa·per·board** \'pā-pər-ˌbȯrd, -ˌbȯrd\ *noun* (1549)

: a material made from cellulose fiber (as wood pulp) like paper but usually thicker

**pa·per·bound** \-ˌbaůnd\ *noun* (1950)
: PAPERBACK
— **paperbound** *adjective*

**pa·per·boy** \-ˌbȯi\ *noun* (1876)
: a boy who delivers newspapers : NEWSBOY

**paper chromatography** *noun* (1948)
: chromatography that uses paper strips or sheets as the adsorbent stationary phase through which a solution flows and that is used especially to separate amino acids

**paper clip** *noun* (1919)
: a piece of wire bent into flat loops that is used to hold papers together

**paper cutter** *noun* (circa 1828)
**1** : PAPER KNIFE
**2** : a machine or device for cutting or trimming sheets of paper to required dimensions

**pa·per·hang·er** \'pā-pər-ˌhaŋ-ər\ *noun* (1796)
**1** : one that applies wallpaper
**2** *slang* : one who passes worthless checks

**pa·per·hang·ing** \-ˌhaŋ-iŋ\ *noun* (1873)
: the act of applying wallpaper

**paper knife** *noun* (circa 1807)
**1** : a knife for slitting envelopes or uncut pages
**2** : the knife of a paper cutter

**pa·per·less** \'pā-pər-ləs\ *adjective* (1969)
: recording or relaying information by electronic media rather than on paper (*paperless* offices)

**pa·per·mak·er** \'pā-pər-ˌmā-kər\ *noun* (circa 1580)
: one that makes paper
— **pa·per·mak·ing** \-kiŋ\ *noun*

**paper money** *noun* (1691)
**1** : money consisting of government notes and banknotes
**2** : BANK MONEY

**paper mulberry** *noun* (1777)
: an Asian tree (*Broussonetia papyrifera*) of the mulberry family that is widely grown as a shade tree

**paper nautilus** *noun* (1835)
: a pelagic cephalopod (genus *Argonauta*) of which the female has a delicate papery shell

**paper nautilus**

**paper over** *transitive verb* (1955)
**1** : to gloss over, explain away, or patch up (as major differences or disparities) especially in order to maintain a semblance of unity or agreement
**2** : HIDE, CONCEAL

**paper profit** *noun* (1893)
: a profit that can be realized only by selling something (as a security) that has appreciated in market value

**paper-thin** *adjective* (1928)
: extremely thin (*paper-thin* partitions)

**paper tiger** *noun* (1850)
: one that is outwardly powerful or dangerous but inwardly weak or ineffectual

**paper trail** *noun* (1965)
: documents (as financial records or published materials) from which a person's actions may be traced or opinions learned

**pa·per-train** \'pā-pər-ˌtrān\ *transitive verb* (1971)
: to train (as a dog) to defecate and urinate on paper indoors

**pa·per·weight** \-ˌwāt\ *noun* (circa 1858)

: a usually small heavy object used to hold down loose papers (as on a desk)

**pa·per·work** \-,wərk\ noun (1889)
: routine clerical or record-keeping work often incidental to a more important task

**pa·pery** \'pā-p(ə-)rē\ adjective (1627)
: resembling paper in thinness or consistency ⟨papery leaves⟩ ⟨papery silk⟩
— **pa·per·i·ness** noun

**pa·pe·te·rie** \'pa-pə-trē, ,pa-pə-\ noun [French] (circa 1847)
: packaged fancy stationery

**¹Pa·phi·an** \'pā-fē-ən\ noun [Latin paphius, from Greek paphios, from Paphos, ancient city of Cyprus that was the center of worship of Aphrodite] (1598)
**1** often not capitalized : PROSTITUTE
**2** : a native or inhabitant of Paphos

**²Paphian** adjective (1605)
**1** : of or relating to illicit love : WANTON
**2** : of or relating to Paphos or its people

**Pa·pia·men·to** \,pä-pyä-'men-(,)tō\ also **Pa·pia·men·tu** \-(,)tü\ noun [Spanish, from Papiamento papya talk + -mentu -ment] (1923)
: a Spanish-based creole language of Netherlands Antilles

**pa·pier col·lé** \,pä-,pyä-(,)kò-'lā, ,pa-\ noun, plural **papiers collés** \-,pyä-(,)kò-'lā(z)\ [French, glued paper] (1935)
: COLLAGE

**¹pa·pier–mâ·ché** \,pā-pər-mə-'shā, ,pa-,pyä-mə-, -(,)ma-\ noun [French, literally, chewed paper] (1753)
: a light strong molding material of wastepaper pulped with glue and other additives

**²papier–mâché** adjective (1753)
**1** : formed of papier-mâché
**2** : UNREAL, ARTIFICIAL

**pa·pil·i·o·na·ceous** \pə-,pi-lē-ə-'nā-shəs\ adjective [Latin papilion-, papilio butterfly — more at PAVILION] (1668)
: having a corolla (as in the bean or pea) with usually five petals that include a large standard enclosing two lateral wings and a lower carina

**pa·pil·la** \pə-'pi-lə\ noun, plural **pa·pil·lae** \-'pi-(,)lē, -,lī\ [Latin, nipple, from diminutive of papula pimple; akin to Lithuanian papas nipple] (1713)
: a small projecting body part similar to a nipple in form: **a** : a vascular process of connective tissue extending into and nourishing the root of a hair, feather, or developing tooth **b** : any of the vascular protuberances of the dermal layer of the skin extending into the epidermal layer and often containing tactile corpuscles **c** : any of the small protuberances on the upper surface of the tongue
— **pap·il·lary** \'pa-pə-,ler-ē, especially British pə-'pi-lə-rē\ adjective
— **pa·pil·late** \'pa-pə-,lāt, pə-'pi-lət\ adjective
— **pa·pil·lose** \'pa-pə-,lōs, pə-'pi-,lōs\ adjective

**pap·il·lo·ma** \,pa-pə-'lō-mə\ noun, plural **-mas** or **-ma·ta** \-mə-tə\ [New Latin] (1866)
**1** : a benign tumor (as a wart) due to overgrowth of epithelial tissue on papillae of vascular connective tissue (as of the skin)
**2** : an epithelial tumor caused by a virus
— **pap·il·lo·ma·tous** \-'lō-mə-təs\ adjective

**pap·il·lo·ma·vi·rus** \-,vī-rəs\ noun [New Latin] (1960)
: any of a group of papovaviruses that cause papillomas

**pa·pil·lon** \,pä-pē-'yōⁿ, ,pa-\ noun [French, literally, butterfly, from Latin papilion-, papilio] (1907)
: any of a breed of small slender toy spaniels having large erect heavily fringed ears

**pa·pil·lote** \,pä-pē-'yōt, ,pa-\ noun [French, from papillon butterfly] (1818)
: a greased usually paper wrapper in which food (as meat or fish) is cooked

**pa·pist** \'pā-pist\ noun, often capitalized [Middle French or New Latin; Middle French papiste, from pape pope; New Latin papista, from Late Latin papa pope] (1534)
: ROMAN CATHOLIC — usually used disparagingly
— **papist** adjective

**pa·pist·ry** \'pā-pə-strē\ noun (1535)
: the Roman Catholic religion — usually used disparagingly

**pa·poose** \pa-'püs, pə-\ noun [Narraganset papoòs] (1634)
: a young child of American Indian parents

**pa·po·va·vi·rus** \pə-'pō-və-,vī-rəs\ noun [papilloma + polyoma + vacuolating + virus] (1962)
: any of a group of viruses that have a capsid composed of 72 subunits and that are associated with or responsible for various neoplasms (as some warts) of mammals

**pap·pose** \'pa-,pōs\ adjective (1691)
: having or being a pappus

**pap·pus** \'pa-pəs\ noun, plural **pap·pi** \'pa-,pī, -,pē\ [Latin, from Greek pappos] (circa 1704)
: an appendage or tuft of appendages that crowns the ovary or fruit in various seed plants and functions in dispersal of the fruit

**pap·py** \'pa-pē\ noun (1763)
chiefly Southern & Midland : PAPA

**pa·pri·ka** \pə-'prē-kə, pa-\ noun [Hungarian, from Serbo-Croation, from papar ground pepper, ultimately from Latin piper — more at PEPPER] (circa 1896)
: a usually mild red condiment consisting of the dried finely ground pods of various cultivated sweet peppers; also : a sweet pepper used for making paprika

**Pap smear** \'pap-\ noun [George N. Papanicolaou (died 1962) American medical scientist] (1952)
: a method for the early detection of uterine cancer that involves the staining of exfoliated cells using a special technique which differentiates diseased tissue — called also Papanicolaou smear, Papanicolaou test, Pap test

**Pap·u·an** \'pa-pyə-wən, -pə-\ noun (1814)
**1** : a native or inhabitant of Papua
**2** : a member of any of the native peoples of New Guinea and adjacent areas of Melanesia
**3** : any of a heterogeneous group of languages spoken in New Guinea, New Britain, and the Solomon islands
— **Papuan** adjective

**pap·u·lar** \'pa-pyə-lər\ adjective (circa 1820)
: consisting of or characterized by papules

**pap·ule** \'pa-(,)pyü(ə)l\ noun [Latin papula] (1864)
: a small solid usually conical elevation of the skin

**pap·y·rol·o·gy** \,pa-pə-'rä-lə-jē\ noun [International Scientific Vocabulary] (1898)
: the study of papyrus manuscripts
— **pap·y·rol·o·gist** \-jist\ noun

**pa·py·rus** \pə-'pī-rəs\ noun, plural **pa·py·ri** \-'pī-(,)rē, -rī\ or **pa·py·rus·es** [Middle English, from Latin — more at PAPER] (14th century)
**1** : a tall sedge (Cyperus papyrus) of the Nile valley
**2** : the pith of the papyrus plant especially when cut in strips and pressed into a material to write on
**3 a** : a writing on papyrus **b** : a written scroll made of papyrus

**¹par** \'pär\ noun [Latin, one that is equal, from par equal] (1622)
**1 a** : the established value of the monetary unit of one country expressed in terms of the monetary unit of another country using the same metal as the

papyrus 1

standard of value **b** : the face amount of an instrument of value (as a check or note): as (1) : the monetary value assigned to each share of stock in the charter of a corporation (2) : the principal of a bond
**2** : common level : EQUALITY — usually used with on ⟨judged the recording to be on a par with previous ones⟩
**3 a** : an amount taken as an average or norm **b** : an accepted standard; specifically : a usual standard of physical condition or health
**4** : the score standard for each hole of a golf course; also : a score equal to par
— **par** adjective
— **par for the course** : not unusual : NORMAL

**²par** transitive verb **parred; par·ring** (1950)
: to score par on (a hole)

**pa·ra** \'pär-ə\ noun, plural **paras** or **para** [Turkish, from Persian pārah, literally, piece] (1687)
**1 a** : any of several monetary units of the Turkish Empire **b** : a coin representing one para
**2** [Serbo-Croatian, from Turkish] — see dinar at MONEY table

**¹para- or par-** prefix [Middle English, from Middle French, from Latin, from Greek, from para; akin to Greek pro before — more at FOR]
**1** : beside : alongside of : beyond : aside from ⟨parathyroid⟩ ⟨parenteral⟩
**2 a** : closely related to ⟨paraldehyde⟩ **b** : involving substitution at or characterized by two opposite positions in the benzene ring that are separated by two carbon atoms ⟨paradichlorobenzene⟩
**3 a** : faulty : abnormal ⟨paresthesia⟩ **b** : associated in a subsidiary or accessory capacity ⟨paramedical⟩ **c** : closely resembling : almost ⟨paratyphoid⟩

**²para-** combining form [parachute]
: parachute ⟨paratrooper⟩

**-para** noun combining form, plural **-paras** or **-parae** [Latin, from parere to give birth to — more at PARE]
: woman delivered of (so many) children ⟨primipara⟩

**para–ami·no·ben·zo·ic acid** \,par-ə-ə-,mē-,nō-,ben-'zō-ik-, ,par-ə-,a-mə-(,)nō-\ noun [International Scientific Vocabulary] (1906)
: a colorless para-substituted aminobenzoic acid that is a growth factor of the vitamin B complex — called also PABA

**para–ami·no·sal·i·cyl·ic acid** \-,sa-lə-'si-lik-\ noun (1946)
: the white crystalline para-substituted isomer of aminosalicylic acid that is made synthetically and is used in the treatment of tuberculosis

**para·bi·o·sis** \,par-ə-(,)bī-'ō-səs, -bē-\ noun [New Latin] (1903)
**1** : reversible suspension of obvious vital activities
**2** : anatomical and physiological union of two organisms
— **para·bi·ot·ic** \-'ä-tik\ adjective
— **para·bi·ot·i·cal·ly** \-ti-k(ə-)lē\ adverb

**par·a·ble** \'par-ə-bəl\ noun [Middle English, from Middle French, from Late Latin parabola, from Greek parabolē comparison, from paraballein to compare, from para- + ballein to throw — more at DEVIL] (14th century)
: EXAMPLE; specifically : a usually short fictitious story that illustrates a moral attitude or a religious principle

**pa·rab·o·la** \pə-'ra-bə-lə\ noun [New Latin, from Greek parabolē, literally, comparison] (1579)
**1** : a plane curve generated by a point moving so that its distance from a fixed point is equal to its distance from a fixed line : the intersection of a right circular cone with a plane parallel to an element of the cone
**2** : something bowl-shaped (as an antenna or microphone reflector)

**par·a·bol·ic** \,par-ə-'bä-lik\ *adjective* [in sense 1, from Late Latin *parabola* parable; in sense 2, from New Latin *parabola*] (1669)
**1** : expressed by or being a parable : ALLEGORICAL
**2** : of, having the form of, or relating to a parabola ⟨motion in a *parabolic* curve⟩
— **par·a·bol·i·cal·ly** \-li-k(ə-)lē\ *adverb*
**pa·rab·o·loid** \pə-'ra-bə-,lȯid\ *noun* (circa 1702)
: a surface all of whose intersections by planes are either parabolas and ellipses or parabolas and hyperbolas

*parabola 1:*
*F* fixed point;
*CD* fixed line;
*x* moving point;
*AB* axis;
*xy* distance from *x* to *CD*;
*pp′* parabola

— **pa·rab·o·loi·dal** \-,ra-bə-'lȯi-d°l\ *adjective*
**¹par·a·chute** \'par-ə-,shüt\ *noun* [French, from *para-* (as in *parasol*) + *chute* fall — more at CHUTE] (1785)
**1** : a device for slowing the descent of a person or object through the air that consists of a usually hemispherical fabric canopy beneath which the person or object is suspended
**2** : PATAGIUM
**3** : a device or structure suggestive of a parachute in form, use, or operation
— **para·chut·ic** \,par-ə-'shü-tik\ *adjective*
**²parachute** *verb* **-chut·ed; -chut·ing** (1809)
*transitive verb*
: to convey by means of a parachute
*intransitive verb*
: to descend by means of a parachute
**para·chut·ist** \'par-ə-,shü-tist\ *noun* (1888)
: one that parachutes: as **a** : PARATROOPER **b** : a person who parachutes as a sport
**Par·a·clete** \'par-ə-,klēt\ *noun* [Middle English *Paraclyte*, from Late Latin *Paracletus, Paraclitus*, from Greek *Paráklētos*, literally, advocate, intercessor, from *parakalein* to invoke, from *para-* + *kalein* to call — more at LOW] (15th century)
: HOLY SPIRIT
**¹pa·rade** \pə-'rād\ *noun* [French, from Middle French, from *parer* to prepare — more at PARE] (circa 1656)
**1** : a pompous show : EXHIBITION
**2 a** : the ceremonial formation of a body of troops before a superior officer **b** : a place where troops assemble regularly for parade
**3 a** : an informal procession **b** : a public procession **c** : a showy array or succession ⟨a *parade* of tycoons' castles —Gail Sheehy⟩
**4 a** : a place for strolling **b** : those who promenade
**²parade** *verb* **pa·rad·ed; pa·rad·ing** (1686)
*transitive verb*
**1** : to cause to maneuver or march : MARSHAL
**2** : PROMENADE
**3** : to exhibit ostentatiously
*intransitive verb*
**1** : to march in or as if in a procession
**2** : PROMENADE
**3 a** : SHOW OFF **b** : MASQUERADE ⟨myths which *parade* as modern science —M. R. Cohen⟩
**synonym** see SHOW
— **pa·rad·er** *noun*
**para·di·chlo·ro·ben·zene** \,par-ə-,dī-,klȯr-ə-'ben-,zēn, -,klȯr-, ,ben-'\ *noun* [International Scientific Vocabulary] (1876)
: a white crystalline compound $C_6H_4Cl_2$ made by chlorinating benzene and used chiefly as a fumigant against clothes moths
**par·a·did·dle** \'par-ə-,di-d°l\ *noun* [origin unknown] (1927)
: a quick succession of drumbeats slower than a roll and alternating left- and right-hand strokes in a typical L-R-L-L, R-L-R-R pattern
**par·a·digm** \'par-ə-,dīm *also* -,dim\ *noun* [Late Latin *paradigma*, from Greek *para-*

*deigma*, from *paradeiknynai* to show side by side, from *para-* + *deiknynai* to show — more at DICTION] (15th century)
**1** : EXAMPLE, PATTERN; *especially* : an outstandingly clear or typical example or archetype
**2** : an example of a conjugation or declension showing a word in all its inflectional forms
**3** : a philosophical and theoretical framework of a scientific school or discipline within which theories, laws, and generalizations and the experiments performed in support of them are formulated
— **par·a·dig·mat·ic** \,par-ə-dig-'ma-tik\ *adjective*
— **par·a·dig·mat·i·cal·ly** \-ti-k(ə-)lē\ *adverb*
**par·a·di·sa·ic** \,par-ə-,dī-'sā-ik, -'zā-\ *adjective* [*paradise* + *-aic* (as in *Hebraic*)] (1754)
: PARADISIACAL
— **par·a·di·sa·i·cal** \-'sā-ə-kəl, -'zā-\ *adjective*
— **par·a·di·sa·i·cal·ly** \-ə-k(ə-)lē\ *adverb*
**par·a·dis·al** \,par-ə-'dī-səl, -zəl\ *adjective* (1560)
: PARADISIACAL
**par·a·dise** \'par-ə-,dīs, -,dīz\ *noun* [Middle English *paradis*, from Old French, from Late Latin *paradisus*, from Greek *paradeisos*, literally, enclosed park, of Iranian origin; akin to Avestan *pairi-daēza-* enclosure; akin to Greek *peri* around and to Greek *teichos* wall — more at PERI-, DOUGH] (12th century)
**1 a** : EDEN 2 **b** : an intermediate place or state where the righteous departed await resurrection and judgment **c** : HEAVEN
**2** : a place or state of bliss, felicity, or delight
— **par·a·dis·ial** \,par-ə-'di-sē-əl, -zē-\ *also* **par·a·dis·i·cal** \-si-kəl, -zi-\ *adjective*
**par·a·di·si·a·cal** \,par-ə-də-'sī-ə-kəl, -,dī-, -'zī-\ *or* **par·a·dis·i·ac** \-'di-zē-,ak, -sē-\ *adjective* [Late Latin *paradisiacus*, from *paradisus*] (1649)
: of, relating to, or resembling paradise
— **par·a·di·si·a·cal·ly** \-də-'sī-ə-k(ə-)lē, -,dī-, -'zī-\ *adverb*
**pa·ra·dor** \,pä-rä-'thȯr\ *noun* [Spanish, inn, from *parar* to stop, lodge for the night, from Latin *parare* to prepare — more at PARE] (1845)
: a usually government-operated hostelry found especially in Spain
**par·a·dox** \'par-ə-,däks\ *noun* [Latin *paradoxum*, from Greek *paradoxon*, from neuter of *paradoxos* contrary to expectation, from *para-* + *dokein* to think, seem — more at DECENT] (1540)
**1** : a tenet contrary to received opinion
**2 a** : a statement that is seemingly contradictory or opposed to common sense and yet is perhaps true **b** : a self-contradictory statement that at first seems true **c** : an argument that apparently derives self-contradictory conclusions by valid deduction from acceptable premises
**3** : something or someone with seemingly contradictory qualities or phases
**par·a·dox·i·cal** \,par-ə-'däk-si-kəl\ *adjective* (1581)
**1 a** : of the nature of a paradox **b** : inclined to paradoxes
**2** : not being the normal or usual kind ⟨*paradoxical* pulse⟩
— **par·a·dox·i·cal·i·ty** \-,däk-si-'ka-lə-tē\ *noun*
— **par·a·dox·i·cal·ly** \-'däk-si-k(ə-)lē\ *adverb*
— **par·a·dox·i·cal·ness** \-kəl-nəs\ *noun*
**paradoxical sleep** *noun* (1964)
: REM SLEEP
**par·aes·the·sia** *variant of* PARESTHESIA
**par·af·fin** \'par-ə-fən\ *noun* [German, from Latin *parum* too little (akin to Greek *pauros* little, *paid-, pais* child) + *affinis* bordering on — more at FEW, AFFINITY] (1838)
**1 a** : a waxy crystalline flammable substance obtained especially from distillates of wood,

coal, petroleum, or shale oil that is a complex mixture of hydrocarbons and is used chiefly in coating and sealing, in candles, in rubber compounding, and in pharmaceuticals and cosmetics **b** : any of various mixtures of similar hydrocarbons including mixtures that are semisolid or oily
**2** : ALKANE
**3** *chiefly British* : KEROSENE
— **par·af·fin·ic** \,par-ə-'fi-nik\ *adjective*
**para·for·mal·de·hyde** \,par-ə-fȯr-'mal-də-,hīd, -fər-\ *noun* (1894)
: a white powder $(CH_2O)_x$ that consists of a polymer of formaldehyde and is used especially as a fungicide
**para·gen·e·sis** \,par-ə-'je-nə-səs\ *noun* [New Latin] (1853)
: the formation of minerals in contact in such a manner as to affect one another's development
— **para·ge·net·ic** \-jə-'ne-tik\ *adjective*
— **para·ge·net·i·cal·ly** \-ti-k(ə-)lē\ *adverb*
**¹par·a·gon** \'par-ə-,gän, -gən\ *noun* [Middle French, from Old Italian *paragone*, literally, touchstone, from *paragonare* to test on a touchstone, from Greek *parakonan* to sharpen, from *para-* + *akonē* whetstone, from *akē* point; akin to Greek *akmē* point — more at EDGE] (circa 1548)
: a model of excellence or perfection
**²paragon** *transitive verb* (circa 1586)
**1** : to compare with : PARALLEL
**2** : to put in rivalry : MATCH
**3** *obsolete* : SURPASS
**¹par·a·graph** \'par-ə-,graf\ *noun* [Middle French & Medieval Latin; Middle French *paragraphe*, from Medieval Latin *paragraphus*, from Greek *paragraphos* line used to mark change of persons in a dialogue, from *paragraphein* to write alongside, from *para-* + *graphein* to write — more at CARVE] (1525)
**1 a** : a subdivision of a written composition that consists of one or more sentences, deals with one point or gives the words of one speaker, and begins on a new usually indented line **b** : a short composition or note that is complete in one paragraph
**2** : a character (as ¶) used to indicate the beginning of a paragraph and as a reference mark
— **par·a·graph·ic** \,par-ə-'gra-fik\ *adjective*
**²paragraph** (1764)
*transitive verb*
**1** : to write paragraphs about
**2** : to divide into paragraphs
*intransitive verb*
: to write paragraphs
**par·a·graph·er** \'par-ə-,gra-fər\ *noun* (1822)
: a writer of paragraphs especially for the editorial page of a newspaper
**para·in·flu·en·za virus** \,par-ə-,in-flü-'en-zə-\ *noun* (1959)
: any of several paramyxoviruses that are associated with or responsible for some respiratory infections especially in children — called also *parainfluenza*
**para·jour·nal·ism** \,par-ə-'jər-n°l-,i-zəm\ *noun* (1965)
: journalism that is heavily colored by the opinions of the reporter
**par·a·keet** \'par-ə-,kēt\ *noun* [Spanish & Middle French; Spanish *periquito*, from Middle French *perroquet* parrot] (1581)
: any of numerous usually small slender parrots with a long graduated tail
**para·lan·guage** \'par-ə-,laŋ-gwij\ *noun* (circa 1958)

**:** optional vocal effects (as tone of voice) that accompany or modify the phonemes of an utterance and that may communicate meaning

**par·al·de·hyde** \pa-'ral-də-ˌhīd, pə-\ *noun* (1857)
**:** a colorless liquid polymeric modification $C_6H_{12}O_3$ of acetaldehyde used as a hypnotic

**para·le·gal** \ˌpar-ə-'lē-gəl\ *adjective* (1971)
**:** of, relating to, or being a paraprofessional who assists a lawyer
— **para·le·gal** \'par-ə-ˌlē-gəl\ *noun*

**para·lin·guis·tics** \ˌpar-ə-liŋ-'gwis-tiks\ *noun* (circa 1958)
**:** the study of paralanguage
— **para·lin·guis·tic** \-tik\ *adjective*

**Par·a·li·pom·e·non** \ˌpar-ə-lə-'pä-mə-ˌnän, -lī-\ *noun* [Late Latin, from Greek *Paraleipomenōn*, genitive of *Paraleipomena*, literally, things left out, from neuter plural of passive present participle of *paraleipein* to leave out, from *para-* + *leipein* to leave; from its forming a supplement to Samuel and Kings — more at LOAN]
**:** CHRONICLES

**par·al·lac·tic** \ˌpar-ə-'lak-tik\ *adjective* [New Latin *parallacticus*, from Greek *parallaktikos*, from *parallaxis*] (1630)
**:** of, relating to, or due to parallax

**par·al·lax** \'par-ə-ˌlaks\ *noun* [Middle French *parallaxe*, from Greek *parallaxis*, from *parallassein* to change, from *para-* + *allassein* to change, from *allos* other] (1580)
**:** the apparent displacement or the difference in apparent direction of an object as seen from two different points not on a straight line with the object; *especially* **:** the angular difference in direction of a celestial body as measured from two points on the earth's orbit

**¹par·al·lel** \'par-ə-ˌlel, -ləl\ *adjective* [Latin *parallelus*, from Greek *parallēlos*, from *para* beside + *allēlōn* of one another, from *allos* . . . *allos* one . . . another, from *allos* other — more at ELSE] (1549)
**1 a :** extending in the same direction, everywhere equidistant, and not meeting ⟨*parallel* rows of trees⟩ **b :** everywhere equally distant ⟨concentric spheres are *parallel*⟩
**2 a :** having parallel sides ⟨a *parallel* reamer⟩ **b :** being or relating to an electrical circuit having a number of conductors in parallel **c :** arranged in parallel ⟨a *parallel* processor⟩ **d :** relating to or being a connection in a computer system in which the bits of a byte are transmitted over separate channels at the same time — compare SERIAL
**3 a :** similar, analogous, or interdependent in tendency or development **b :** readily compared **:** COMPANION **c :** having identical syntactical elements in corresponding positions; *also* **:** being such an element **d** (1) **:** having the same tonic — used of major and minor keys and scales (2) **:** keeping the same distance apart in musical pitch
**4 :** performed while keeping one's skis parallel ⟨*parallel* turns⟩
**synonym** see SIMILAR

**²parallel** *noun* (1551)
**1 a :** a parallel line, curve, or surface **b :** one of the imaginary circles on the surface of the earth paralleling the equator and marking the latitude; *also* **:** the corresponding line on a globe or map — see LATITUDE illustration **c :** a character ‖ used in printing especially as a reference mark
**2 a :** something equal or similar in all essential particulars **:** COUNTERPART **b :** SIMILARITY, ANALOGUE
**3 :** a comparison to show resemblance **:** a tracing of similarity
**4 a :** the state of being physically parallel **:** PARALLELISM **b :** an arrangement of electrical devices in a circuit in which the same potential difference is applied to two or more resistances with each resistance being on a different branch of the circuit — compare SERIES **c :** an arrangement or state that permits several

operations or tasks to be performed simultaneously rather than consecutively

**³parallel** *transitive verb* (1598)
**1 :** to indicate analogy of **:** COMPARE
**2 a :** to show something equal to **:** MATCH **b :** to correspond to
**3 :** to place so as to be parallel in direction with something
**4 :** to extend, run, or move in a direction parallel to

**⁴parallel** *adverb* (1787)
**:** in a parallel manner

**parallel bars** *noun plural* (1868)
**1 :** a pair of wooden bars supported horizontally above the floor at the same height or at different heights usually by a common base and used in gymnastics
**2 :** an event in gymnastics competition in which even or uneven parallel bars are used

**par·al·lel·e·pi·ped** \ˌpar-ə-ˌle-lə-'pī-pəd *also* -ˌle-'le-pə-ˌped\ *noun* [Greek *parallēlepipedon*, from *parallēlos* + *epipedon* plane surface, from neuter of *epipedos* flat, from *epi-* epi- + *pedon* ground; akin to Latin *ped-, pes* foot — more at FOOT] (1570)
**:** a 6-faced polyhedron all of whose faces are parallelograms lying in pairs of parallel planes

**par·al·lel·ism** \'par-ə-ˌle-ˌli-zəm, -lə-ˌli-\ *noun* (1610)
**1 :** the quality or state of being parallel
**2 :** RESEMBLANCE, CORRESPONDENCE
**3 :** repeated syntactical similarities introduced for rhetorical effect
**4 :** a theory that mind and matter accompany one another but are not causally related
**5 :** the development of similar new characters by two or more related organisms in response to similarity of environment — called also *parallel evolution*

**par·al·lel·o·gram** \ˌpar-ə-'le-lə-ˌgram\ *noun* [Late Latin or Greek; Late Latin *parallelogrammum*, from Greek *parallēlogrammon*, from neuter of *parallēlogrammos* bounded by parallel lines, from *parallēlos* + *grammē* line, from *graphein* to write — more at CARVE] (1570)
**:** a quadrilateral with opposite sides parallel and equal

**par·al·lel-veined** \ˌpar-ə-ˌlel-'vānd, -ləl-\ *adjective* (1861)
*of a leaf* **:** having veins arranged nearly parallel to one another — compare NET-VEINED

**pa·ral·o·gism** \pə-'ra-lə-ˌji-zəm\ *noun* [Middle French *paralogisme*, from Late Latin *paralogismus*, from Greek *paralogismos*, from *paralogos* unreasonable, from *para-* + *logos* speech, reason — more at LEGEND] (1565)
**:** a fallacious argument

**par·a·lyse** *British variant of* PARALYZE

**pa·ral·y·sis** \pə-'ra-lə-səs\ *noun, plural* **-y·ses** \-ˌsēz\ [Latin, from Greek, from *paralyein* to loosen, disable, from *para-* + *lyein* to loosen — more at LOSE] (1525)
**1 :** complete or partial loss of function especially when involving the motion or sensation in a part of the body
**2 :** loss of the ability to move
**3 :** a state of powerlessness or incapacity to act

**paralysis agi·tans** \-'a-jə-ˌtanz\ *noun* [New Latin, literally, shaking palsy] (1817)
**:** PARKINSON'S DISEASE

**¹par·a·lyt·ic** \ˌpar-ə-'li-tik\ *adjective* [Middle English *paralytyk*, from Middle French *paralitike*, from Latin *paralyticus*, from Greek *paralytikos*, from *paralyein*] (14th century)
**1 :** affected with or characterized by paralysis
**2 :** of, relating to, or resembling paralysis
— **par·a·lyt·i·cal·ly** \-ti-k(ə-)lē\ *adverb*

**²paralytic** *noun* (14th century)
**:** one affected with paralysis

**par·a·lyze** \'par-ə-ˌlīz\ *transitive verb* **-lyzed; -lyz·ing** [French *paralyser*, back-formation from *paralysie* paralysis, from Latin *paralysis*] (1804)
**1 :** to affect with paralysis

**2 :** to make powerless or ineffective
**3 :** UNNERVE
**4 :** STUN, STUPEFY
**5 :** to bring to an end **:** PREVENT, DESTROY
— **par·a·ly·za·tion** \ˌpar-ə-lə-'zā-shən\ *noun*
— **par·a·lyz·er** \'par-ə-ˌlī-zər\ *noun*
— **par·a·lyz·ing·ly** \-ˌlī-ziŋ-lē\ *adverb*

**para·mag·net** \'par-ə-ˌmag-nət\ *noun* [back-formation from *paramagnetic*] (circa 1900)
**:** a paramagnetic substance

**para·mag·net·ic** \ˌpar-ə-mag-'ne-tik\ *adjective* [International Scientific Vocabulary] (circa 1850)
**:** being or relating to a magnetizable substance (as aluminum) that has small but positive susceptibility which varies little with magnetizing force
— **para·mag·net·i·cal·ly** \-ti-k(ə-)lē\ *adverb*
— **para·mag·ne·tism** \-'mag-nə-ˌti-zəm\ *noun*

**par·a·me·cium** \ˌpar-ə-'mē-sh(ē-)əm, -sē-əm\ *noun, plural* **-cia** \-sh(ē-)ə, -sē-ə\ *also* **-ciums** [New Latin, from Greek *paramēkēs* oblong, from *para-* + *mēkos* length; akin to Greek *makros* long — more at MEAGER] (1752)
**:** any of a genus (*Paramecium*) of ciliate protozoans that have an elongate body rounded at the anterior end and an oblique funnel-shaped buccal groove bearing the mouth at the extremity

**para·med·ic** \ˌpar-ə-'me-dik\ *also* **para·med·i·cal** \-di-kəl\ *noun* (1967)
**1 :** a person who works in a health field in an auxiliary capacity to a physician (as by giving injections and taking X rays)
**2 :** a specially trained medical technician licensed to provide a wide range of emergency services (as defibrillation and the intravenous administration of drugs) before or during transportation to a hospital — compare EMT

**para·med·i·cal** \ˌpar-ə-'me-di-kəl\ *also* **para·med·ic** \-dik\ *adjective* (1921)
**:** concerned with supplementing the work of highly trained medical professionals ⟨*paramedical* aides and technicians⟩

**par·a·ment** \'par-ə-mənt\ *noun* [Middle English, from Medieval Latin *paramentum*, from *parare* to adorn, from Latin, to prepare — more at PARE] (15th century)
**:** an ornamental ecclesiastical hanging or vestment

**pa·ram·e·ter** \pə-'ram-ə-tər\ *noun* [New Latin, from *para-* + Greek *metron* measure — more at MEASURE] (1656)
**1 a :** an arbitrary constant whose value characterizes a member of a system (as a family of curves); *also* **:** a quantity (as a mean or variance) that describes a statistical population **b :** an independent variable used to express the coordinates of a variable point and functions of them — compare PARAMETRIC EQUATION
**2 :** any of a set of physical properties whose values determine the characteristics or behavior of something ⟨*parameters* of the atmosphere such as temperature, pressure, and density⟩
**3 :** something represented by a parameter **:** a characteristic element; *broadly* **:** CHARACTERISTIC, ELEMENT, FACTOR ⟨political dissent as a *parameter* of modern life⟩
**4 :** LIMIT, BOUNDARY — usually used in plural ⟨the *parameters* of science fiction⟩
— **para·met·ric** \ˌpar-ə-'me-trik\ *adjective*
— **para·met·ri·cal·ly** \-tri-k(ə-)lē\ *adverb*

**pa·ram·e·ter·ize** \pə-'ram-ə-tə-ˌrīz, -mə-ˌtrīz\ *or* **pa·ram·e·trize** \-'ra-mə-ˌtrīz\ *transitive verb* **-ter·ized** *or* **-trized; -ter·iz·ing** *or* **-triz·ing** (1940)
**:** to express in terms of parameters
— **pa·ram·e·ter·i·za·tion** \-ˌra-mə-tə-rə-'zā-shən, -mə-trə-\ *or* **pa·ram·e·tri·za·tion** \-mə-trə-\ *noun*

**parametric equation** *noun* (1909)

: any of a set of equations that express the co-ordinates of the points of a curve as functions of one parameter or that express the coordinates of the points of a surface as functions of two parameters

**para·mil·i·tary** \ˌpar-ə-ˈmi-lə-ˌter-ē\ *adjective* (1935)
: of, relating to, being, or characteristic of a force formed on a military pattern especially as a potential auxiliary military force ⟨a *paramilitary* border patrol⟩ ⟨*paramilitary* training⟩

**par·am·ne·sia** \ˌpar-ˌam-ˈnē-zhə, -əm-\ *noun* [New Latin, from *para-* + *-mnesia* (as in *amnesia*)] (1888)
: a disorder of memory; *especially* : DÉJÀ VU 1

¹**par·a·mount** \ˈpar-ə-ˌmaůnt\ *adjective* [Anglo-French *paramont*, from Old French *par* by (from Latin *per*) + *amont* above, from *a* to (from Latin *ad*) + *mont* mountain — more at FOR, AT, MOUNT] (1579)
: superior to all others : SUPREME
**synonym** see DOMINANT
— **par·a·mount·cy** \-ˌmaůn(t)-sē\ *noun*
— **par·a·mount·ly** \-ˌmaůnt-lē\ *adverb*

²**paramount** *noun* (1616)
: a supreme ruler

**par·amour** \ˈpar-ə-ˌmůr\ *noun* [Middle English, from *par amour* by way of love, from Middle French] (14th century)
: an illicit lover

**par·am·y·lum** \ˌpa-ˈra-mə-ləm\ *noun* [New Latin, from *para-* + Latin *amylum* starch — more at AMYL-] (1897)
: a reserve carbohydrate that is found in various protozoans and algae and resembles starch

**para·myxo·vi·rus** \ˌpar-ə-ˈmik-sə-ˌvī-rəs\ *noun* [New Latin] (1962)
: any of a group of RNA-containing viruses (as the mumps, measles, and parainfluenza viruses)

**pa·rang** \ˈpär-ˌaŋ\ *noun* [Malay] (1839)
: a short sword, cleaver, or machete common in Malaysia and Indonesia

**para·noia** \ˌpar-ə-ˈnȯi-ə\ *noun* [New Latin, from Greek, madness, from *paranous* demented, from *para-* + *nous* mind] (circa 1811)
**1** : a psychosis characterized by systematized delusions of persecution or grandeur usually without hallucinations
**2** : a tendency on the part of an individual or group toward excessive or irrational suspiciousness and distrustfulness of others
— **para·noi·ac** \-ˈnȯi-ˌak, -ˈnȯi-ik\ *also* **para·noic** \-ˈnȯi-(i)k, -ˈnō-ik\ *adjective or noun*
— **para·noi·cal·ly** \-ˈnȯi-(i)-k(ə-)lē, -ˈnō-i-k(ə-)lē\ *adverb*

**para·noid** \ˈpar-ə-ˌnȯid\ *also* **para·noi·dal** \ˌpar-ə-ˈnȯi-dᵊl\ *adjective* (1904)
**1** : characterized by or resembling paranoia
**2** : characterized by suspiciousness, persecutory trends, or megalomania
**3** : extremely fearful
— **paranoid** *noun*

**paranoid schizophrenia** *noun* (1940)
: schizophrenia characterized especially by persecutory or grandiose delusions or hallucinations or by delusional jealousy

**para·nor·mal** \ˌpar-ə-ˈnȯr-məl, ˈpar-ə-ˌ\ *adjective* (circa 1920)
: not scientifically explainable : SUPERNATURAL
— **paranormal** *noun*
— **para·nor·mal·i·ty** \ˌpar-ə-ˌnȯr-ˈma-lə-tē\ *noun*
— **para·nor·mal·ly** \-ˈnȯr-mə-lē\ *adverb*

**para·nymph** \ˈpar-ə-ˌnim(p)f\ *noun* [Late Latin *paranymphus*, from Greek *paranymphos*, from *para-* + *nymphē* bride — more at NUPTIAL] (1600)
**1** : a friend going with a bridegroom to fetch home the bride in ancient Greece; *also* : the bridesmaid conducting the bride to the bridegroom
**2 a** : BEST MAN **b** : BRIDESMAID

**par·a·pet** \ˈpar-ə-pət, -ˌpet\ *noun* [Italian *parapetto*, from *parare* to shield (from Latin, to

prepare) + *petto* chest, from Latin *pectus* — more at PARE, PECTORAL] (1590)
**1** : a wall, rampart, or elevation of earth or stone to protect soldiers : BREASTWORK
**2** : a low wall or railing to protect the edge of a platform, roof, or bridge — called also *parapet wall*
— **par·a·pet·ed** \-ˌpe-təd\ *adjective*

**pa·raph** \ˈpar-əf, pə-ˈraf\ *noun* [Middle French, from Latin *paragraphus* paragraph] (1584)
: a flourish at the end of a signature

**par·a·pher·na·lia** \ˌpar-ə-fə(r)-ˈnāl-yə\ *noun plural but singular or plural in construction* [Medieval Latin, ultimately from Greek *parapherna* bride's property beyond her dowry, from *para-* + *phernē* dowry, from *pherein* to bear — more at BEAR] (1651)
**1** : the separate real or personal property of a married woman that she can dispose of by will and sometimes according to common law during her life
**2** : personal belongings
**3 a** : articles of equipment : FURNISHINGS **b** : accessory items : APPURTENANCES

¹**para·phrase** \ˈpar-ə-ˌfrāz\ *noun* [Middle French, from Latin *paraphrasis*, from Greek, from *paraphrazein* to paraphrase, from *para-* + *phrazein* to point out] (1548)
**1** : a restatement of a text, passage, or work giving the meaning in another form
**2** : the use or process of paraphrasing in studying or teaching composition

²**paraphrase** *verb* **-phrased; -phras·ing** (1596)
*intransitive verb*
: to make a paraphrase
*transitive verb*
: to make a paraphrase of
— **para·phras·able** \ˌpar-ə-ˈfrā-zə-bəl\ *adjective*
— **para·phras·er** *noun*

**para·phras·tic** \ˌpar-ə-ˈfras-tik\ *adjective* [French *paraphrastique*, from Greek *paraphrastikos*, from *paraphrazein*] (circa 1623)
: having the nature of or being a paraphrase
— **para·phras·ti·cal·ly** \-ti-k(ə-)lē\ *adverb*

**par·aph·y·sis** \pə-ˈra-fə-səs\ *noun, plural* **-y·ses** \-ˌsēz\ [New Latin, from Greek, sucker, offshoot, from *paraphyein* to produce at the side, from *para-* + *phyein* to bring forth — more at BE] (1857)
: one of the slender sterile filaments borne among the sporogenous or gametogenous organs in cryptogamic plants

**para·ple·gia** \ˌpar-ə-ˈplē-j(ē-)ə\ *noun* [New Latin, from Greek *paraplēgiē* hemiplegia, from *para-* + *-plēgia* -plegia] (circa 1657)
: paralysis of the lower half of the body with involvement of both legs
— **para·ple·gic** \-jik\ *adjective or noun*

**para·po·di·um** \-ˈpō-dē-əm\ *noun, plural* **-dia** \-dē-ə\ [New Latin] (1877)
**1** : either of a pair of fleshy lateral processes borne by most segments of a polychaete worm
**2** : a lateral expansion on each side of the foot usually forming a broad swimming organ in some gastropods
— **para·po·di·al** \-dē-əl\ *adjective*

**para·pro·fes·sion·al** \-prə-ˈfesh-nəl, -ˈfe-shə-nᵊl\ *noun* (1965)
: a trained aide who assists a professional person (as a teacher or doctor)
— **paraprofessional** *adjective*

**para·psy·chol·o·gy** \ˌpar-ə-(ˌ)sī-ˈkä-lə-jē\ *noun* [International Scientific Vocabulary] (1925)
: a field of study concerned with the investigation of evidence for paranormal psychological phenomena (as telepathy, clairvoyance, and psychokinesis)
— **para·psy·cho·log·i·cal** \-ˌsī-kə-ˈlä-ji-kəl\ *adjective*
— **para·psy·chol·o·gist** \-(ˌ)sī-ˈkä-lə-jist\ *noun*

**para·quat** \ˈpar-ə-ˌkwät\ *noun* [*para-* + *quaternary*] (circa 1961)
: a highly toxic contact herbicide containing a salt of a cation $[C_{12}H_{14}N_2]^{2+}$

**para·ros·an·i·line** \ˌpar-ə-ˌrō-ˈza-nᵊl-ən\ *noun* [International Scientific Vocabulary] (circa 1879)
: a white crystalline base $C_{19}H_{19}N_3O$ that is the parent compound of many dyes; *also* : its red chloride used especially as a biological stain

**Pa·ra rubber** \ˈpar-ə-, pə-ˈrä-\ *noun* [*Pará*, Brazil] (1857)
: native rubber from South American rubber trees (genus *Hevea* and especially *H. brasiliensis*)

**Para rubber tree** *noun* (1930)
: a South American rubber tree (*Hevea brasiliensis*)

**para·sail·ing** \ˈpar-ə-ˌsā-liŋ\ *noun* (1967)
: the recreational sport of soaring in a parachute while being towed usually by a motorboat

**par·a·sang** \ˈpar-ə-ˌsaŋ\ *noun* [Latin *parasanga*, from Greek *parasangēs*, of Iranian origin; akin to Persian *farsung* parasang] (1594)
: any of various Persian units of distance; *especially* : an ancient unit of about four miles (six kilometers)

**para·sex·u·al** \-ˈsek-sh(ə-)wəl, -shəl\ *adjective* (1954)
: relating to or being reproduction that results in recombination of genes from different individuals but does not involve meiosis and formation of a zygote by fertilization as in sexual reproduction ⟨the *parasexual* cycle in some fungi⟩
— **para·sex·u·al·i·ty** \-ˌsek-shə-ˈwa-lə-tē\ *noun*

**pa·ra·shah** \ˈpär-ə-ˌshä\ *noun* [Hebrew *pārāshāh*, literally, explanation] (1624)
: a passage in Jewish Scripture dealing with a single topic; *specifically* : a section of the Torah assigned for weekly reading in synagogue worship

**par·a·site** \ˈpar-ə-ˌsīt\ *noun* [Middle French, from Latin *parasitus*, from Greek *parasitos*, from *para-* + *sitos* grain, food] (1539)
**1** : a person who exploits the hospitality of the rich and earns welcome by flattery
**2** : an organism living in, with, or on another organism in parasitism
**3** : something that resembles a biological parasite in dependence on something else for existence or support without making a useful or adequate return ☆

---

☆ **SYNONYMS**
**Parasite, sycophant, toady, leech, sponge** mean a usually obsequious flatterer or self-seeker. PARASITE applies to one who clings to a person of wealth, power, or influence or is useless to society ⟨a jet-setter with an entourage of *parasites*⟩. SYCOPHANT adds to this a strong suggestion of fawning, flattery, or adulation ⟨a powerful prince surrounded by *sycophants*⟩. TOADY emphasizes the servility and snobbery of the self-seeker ⟨cultivated leaders of society and became their *toady*⟩. LEECH stresses persistence in clinging to or bleeding another for one's own advantage ⟨a *leech* living off his family and friends⟩. SPONGE stresses the parasitic laziness, dependence, and opportunism of the cadger ⟨a shiftless *sponge*, always looking for a handout⟩.

---

\ə\ abut  \ᵊ\ kitten  \ər\ further  \a\ ash  \ā\ ace
\ä\ mop, mar  \aů\ out  \ch\ chin  \e\ bet  \ē\ easy
\g\ go  \i\ hit  \ī\ ice  \j\ job  \ŋ\ sing  \ō\ go
\ȯ\ law  \ȯi\ boy  \th\ thin  \t͟h\ the  \ü\ loot  \ů\ foot
\y\ yet  \zh\ vision  *see also* Guide to Pronunciation

— **par·a·sit·ic** \par-ə-'si-tik\ *also* **par·a·sit·i·cal** \-ti-kəl\ *adjective*
— **par·a·sit·i·cal·ly** \-ti-k(ə-)lē\ *adverb*
**par·a·sit·i·cid·al** \par-ə-si-tə-'sī-d²l\ *adjective* (1892)
: destructive to parasites
— **par·a·sit·i·cide** \-'si-tə-sīd\ *noun*
**par·a·sit·ise** *British variant of* PARASITIZE
**par·a·sit·ism** \'par-ə-sə-,ti-zəm, -,sī-\ *noun* (1611)
**1** : the behavior of a parasite
**2** : an intimate association between organisms of two or more kinds; *especially* : one in which a parasite obtains benefits from a host which it usually injures
**3** : PARASITOSIS
**par·a·sit·ize** \-sə-,tīz, -,sī-\ *transitive verb* **-ized; -iz·ing** (1890)
: to infest or live on or with as a parasite
— **par·a·sit·i·za·tion** \par-ə-sə-tə-'zā-shən, -,sī-\ *noun*
**par·a·sit·oid** \'par-ə-sə-,tóid, -,sī-\ *noun* (1922)
: an insect and especially a wasp that completes its larval development within the body of another insect eventually killing it and is free-living as an adult
— **parasitoid** *adjective*
**par·a·si·tol·o·gy** \par-ə-sə-'tä-lə-jē, -,sī-\ *noun* [Latin *parasitus* + International Scientific Vocabulary *-logy*] (1882)
: a branch of biology dealing with parasites and parasitism especially among animals
— **par·a·si·to·log·i·cal** \-si-t²l-'ä-ji-kəl, -,sī-\ *also* **par·a·si·to·log·ic** \-jik\ *adjective*
— **par·a·si·to·log·i·cal·ly** \-ji-k(ə-)lē\ *adverb*
— **par·a·si·tol·o·gist** \-sə-'tä-lə-jist, -,sī-\ *noun*
**par·a·sit·o·sis** \-sə-'tō-səs, -,sī-\ *noun, plural* **-o·ses** \-,sēz\ [New Latin] (circa 1899)
: infestation with or disease caused by parasites
**par·a·sol** \'par-ə-,sól, -,säl\ *noun* [French, from Old Italian *parasole*, from *parare* to shield + *sole* sun, from Latin *sol* — more at PARAPET, SOLAR] (1660)
: a lightweight umbrella used as a sunshade especially by women
**¹para·sym·pa·thet·ic** \par-ə-,sim-pə-'the-tik\ *adjective* [International Scientific Vocabulary] (1905)
: of, relating to, being, or acting on the parasympathetic nervous system
**²parasympathetic** *noun* (1925)
**1** : a parasympathetic nerve
**2** : PARASYMPATHETIC NERVOUS SYSTEM
**parasympathetic nervous system** *noun* (circa 1934)
: the part of the autonomic nervous system that contains chiefly cholinergic fibers, that tends to induce secretion, to increase the tone and contractility of smooth muscle, and to slow heart rate, and that consists of a cranial and a sacral part — compare SYMPATHETIC NERVOUS SYSTEM
**para·sym·pa·tho·mi·met·ic** \par-ə-,sim-pə-(,)thō-mī-'me-tik, -mə-\ *adjective* [International Scientific Vocabulary] (1942)
: simulating parasympathetic nervous action in physiological effect
**para·syn·the·sis** \par-ə-'sin(t)-thə-səs\ *noun* [New Latin] (1862)
: the formation of words by adding a derivative ending and prefixing a particle (as in *denationalize*)
— **para·syn·thet·ic** \-sin-'the-tik\ *adjective*
**para·tac·tic** \par-ə-'tak-tik\ *also* **para·tac·ti·cal** \-ti-kəl\ *adjective* (1871)
: of or relating to parataxis
— **para·tac·ti·cal·ly** \-ti-k(ə-)lē\ *adverb*
**para·tax·is** \par-ə-'tak-səs\ *noun* [New Latin, from Greek, act of placing side by side, from *paratassein* to place side by side, from *para-* + *tassein* to arrange] (circa 1842)

: the placing of clauses or phrases one after another without coordinating or subordinating connectives
**para·thi·on** \par-ə-'thī-ən, -,än\ *noun* [*para-* + *thiophosphate* + *¹-on*] (1947)
: an extremely toxic insecticide $C_{10}H_{14}NO_5PS$
**par·a·thor·mone** \par-ə-'thór-,mōn\ *noun* [from *Parathormone*, a trademark] (1925)
: PARATHYROID HORMONE
**¹para·thy·roid** \-'thī-,róid\ *noun* (1897)
: PARATHYROID GLAND
**²parathyroid** *adjective* [International Scientific Vocabulary] (1902)
: of, relating to, or produced by the parathyroid glands
**para·thy·roid·ec·to·my** \-,rói-'dek-tə-mē\ *noun, plural* **-mies** (1903)
: partial or complete excision of the parathyroid glands
— **para·thy·roid·ec·to·mized** \-,mīzd\ *adjective*
**parathyroid gland** *noun* [International Scientific Vocabulary] (circa 1903)
: any of usually four small endocrine glands that are adjacent to or embedded in the thyroid gland and produce parathyroid hormone
**parathyroid hormone** *noun* (1953)
: a hormone of the parathyroid gland that regulates the metabolism of calcium and phosphorus in the body
**para·troop·er** \'par-ə-,trü-pər\ *noun* (1927)
: a member of the paratroops
**para·troops** \-,trüps\ *noun plural* [²*para-*] (1940)
: troops trained and equipped to parachute from an airplane
— **para·troop** \-,trüp\ *adjective*
**¹para·ty·phoid** \par-ə-'tī-,fóid, -(,)tī-'\ *adjective* [International Scientific Vocabulary] (1902)
**1** : resembling typhoid fever
**2** : of or relating to paratyphoid or its causative organisms ⟨*paratyphoid* infection⟩
**²paratyphoid** *noun* (1903)
: a salmonellosis that resembles typhoid fever and is commonly contracted by eating contaminated food — called also *paratyphoid fever*
**para·vane** \'par-ə-,vān\ *noun* [French *para-* warding off (as in *parachute*) + English *vane*] (1919)
: a torpedo-shaped protective device with serrate teeth in its forward end used underwater by a ship in mined areas to sever the moorings of mines
**par·boil** \'pär-,bóil\ *transitive verb* [Middle English, from *parboilen* to boil thoroughly, from Middle French *parboillir*, from Late Latin *perbullire*, from Latin *per-* thoroughly (from *per* through) + *bullire* to boil, from *bulla* bubble — more at FOR] (14th century)
: to boil briefly as a preliminary or incomplete cooking procedure
**par·buck·le** \'pär-,bə-kəl\ *noun* [origin unknown] (1626)
: a purchase for hoisting or lowering a cylindrical object by making fast the middle of a long rope aloft and looping both ends around the object which rests in the loops and rolls in them as the ends are hauled up or paid out; *also* : a single line made fast at one end and passed around an object that is used similarly

**parbuckle**

— **parbuckle** *transitive verb*
**Par·cae** \'pär-,kī, -,sē\ *noun plural* [Latin]
: FATE 4
**¹par·cel** \'pär-səl\ *noun* [Middle English, from Middle French, from (assumed) Vulgar Latin

*particella*, from Latin *particula* small part — more at PARTICLE] (14th century)
**1 a** : FRAGMENT, PORTION **b** : a volume of a fluid (as air) considered as a single entity within a greater volume of the same fluid
**2** : a tract or plot of land
**3** : a company, collection, or group of persons, animals, or things : LOT ⟨the whole story was a *parcel* of lies⟩
**4 a** : a wrapped bundle : PACKAGE **b** : a unit of salable merchandise
**²parcel** *adverb* (15th century)
*archaic* : PARTLY
**³parcel** *adjective* (15th century)
: PART-TIME, PARTIAL
**⁴parcel** *transitive verb* **-celed** *or* **-celled; -cel·ing** *or* **-cel·ling** \'pär-s(ə-)liŋ\ (15th century)
**1** : to divide into parts : DISTRIBUTE — often used with *out*
**2** : to make up into a parcel : WRAP
**3** : to cover (as a rope) with strips of canvas or tape
**parcel post** *noun* (1837)
**1** : a mail service handling parcels
**2** : packages handled by parcel post
**par·ce·nary** \'pär-s²n-,er-ē\ *noun* [Anglo-French *parcenarie*, from Old French *parçonerie*, from *parçon* portion, from Latin *partition-, partitio* partition] (1544)
: COPARCENARY 1
**par·ce·ner** \'pärs-nər, 'pär-s²n-ər\ *noun* [Anglo-French, from Old French *parçonier*, from *parçon*] (1574)
: COPARCENER
**parch** \'pärch\ *verb* [Middle English] (14th century)
*transitive verb*
**1** : to toast under dry heat
**2** : to shrivel with heat
**3** : to dry or shrivel with cold
*intransitive verb*
: to become dry or scorched
**parched** \'pärcht\ *adjective* (circa 1552)
: deprived of natural moisture; *also* : THIRSTY
**Par·chee·si** \pär-'chē-zē, pər-, *especially British* -sē\ *trademark*
— used for a board game adapted from pachisi
**parch·ment** \'pärch-mənt\ *noun* [Middle English *parchemin*, from Middle French, modification of Latin *pergamena*, from Greek *pergamēnē*, from feminine of *Pergamēnos* of Pergamum, from *Pergamon* Pergamum] (14th century)
**1** : the skin of a sheep or goat prepared for writing on
**2** : strong, tough, and often somewhat translucent paper made to resemble parchment
**3** : a parchment manuscript; *also* : an academic diploma
**¹pard** \'pärd\ *noun* [Middle English *parde*, from Middle French, from Latin *pardus*, from Greek *pardos*] (14th century)
: LEOPARD
**²pard** *noun* [short for *pardner*] (1850)
*chiefly dialect* : PARTNER, CHUM
**par·die** *or* **par·di** *or* **par·dy** \pər-'dē, pär-\ *interjection* [Middle English *pardee*, from Old French *par Dé* by God] (14th century)
*archaic* — used as a mild oath
**pard·ner** \'pärd-nər\ *noun* [alteration of *partner*] (1795)
*chiefly dialect* : PARTNER, CHUM
**¹par·don** \'pär-d²n\ *noun* [Middle English, from Middle French, from *pardoner*] (14th century)
**1** : INDULGENCE 1
**2** : the excusing of an offense without exacting a penalty
**3 a** : a release from the legal penalties of an offense **b** : an official warrant of remission of penalty
**4** : excuse or forgiveness for a fault, offense, or discourtesy ⟨I beg your *pardon*⟩

²**pardon** *transitive verb* **par·doned; par·don·ing** \'pärd-niŋ, 'pär-dᵃn-iŋ\ [Middle English, from Middle French *pardoner,* from Late Latin *perdonare* to grant freely, from Latin *per-* thoroughly + *donare* to give — more at PARBOIL, DONATION] (15th century)
**1 a :** to absolve from the consequences of a fault or crime **b :** to allow (an offense) to pass without punishment : FORGIVE **c :** to relieve of a penalty improperly assessed
**2 :** TOLERATE
**synonym** see EXCUSE
**par·don·able** \'pärd-nə-bəl, 'pär-dᵃn-ə-bəl\ *adjective* (15th century)
**:** admitting of being pardoned : EXCUSABLE ⟨*pardonable* offenses⟩
— **par·don·able·ness** *noun*
— **par·don·ably** \-blē\ *adverb*
**par·don·er** \'pärd-nər, 'pär-dᵃn-ər\ *noun* (14th century)
**1 :** a medieval preacher delegated to raise money for religious works by soliciting offerings and granting indulgences
**2 :** one that pardons
**pare** \'par, 'per\ *transitive verb* **pared; par·ing** [Middle English, from Middle French *parer* to prepare, trim, from Latin *parare* to prepare, acquire; akin to Latin *parere* to give birth to, produce, Lithuanian *perėti* to hatch] (14th century)
**1 :** to trim off an outside, excess, or irregular part of ⟨*pare* apples⟩ ⟨*paring* his nails⟩
**2 :** to diminish or reduce by or as if by paring ⟨*pare* expenses⟩ ⟨the novel was *pared* down to 200 pages⟩
— **par·er** *noun*
**par·e·gor·ic** \,par-ə-'gȯr-ik, -'gōr-, -'gär-\ *noun* [French *parégorique* mitigating pain, from Late Latin *paregoricus,* from Greek *parēgorikos,* from *parēgorein* to talk over, soothe, from *para-* + *agora* assembly, from *ageirein* to gather] (circa 1847)
**:** camphorated tincture of opium used especially to relieve pain
**pa·ren·chy·ma** \pə-'reŋ-kə-mə\ *noun* [New Latin, from Greek, visceral flesh, from *parenchein* to pour in beside, from *para-* + *en-* en- + *chein* to pour — more at FOUND] (1651)
**1 :** a tissue of higher plants that consists of thin-walled living photosynthetic or storage cells capable of division even when mature and that makes up much of the substance of leaves and roots, the pulp of fruits, and parts of stems and supporting structures
**2 :** the essential and distinctive tissue of an organ or an abnormal growth as distinguished from its supportive framework
— **par·en·chy·ma·tous** \,par-ən-'kī-mə-təs, -'ki-\ *or* **pa·ren·chy·mal** \pə-'reŋ-kə-məl, ,par-ən-'kī\ *adjective*
¹**par·ent** \'par-ənt, 'per-\ *noun* [Middle English, from Middle French, from Latin *parent-, parens;* akin to Latin *parere* to give birth to] (15th century)
**1 a :** one that begets or brings forth offspring **b :** a person who brings up and cares for another
**2 a :** an animal or plant that is regarded in relation to its offspring **b :** the material or source from which something is derived **c :** a group from which another arises and to which it usually remains subsidiary ⟨a *parent* company⟩
— **parent** *adjective*
— **pa·ren·tal** \pə-'ren-tᵊl\ *adjective*
— **pa·ren·tal·ly** \-tᵊl-ē\ *adverb*
— **par·ent·less** \'par-ənt-ləs, 'per-\ *adjective*
²**parent** *transitive verb* (1663)
**:** to be or act as the parent of : ORIGINATE, PRODUCE
**par·ent·age** \'par-ən-tij, 'per-\ *noun* [Middle English, from Middle French, from *parent*] (15th century)

**1 a :** descent from parents or ancestors : LINEAGE ⟨a person of noble *parentage*⟩ **b :** DERIVATION, ORIGIN ⟨a tradition of uncertain *parentage*⟩
**2 :** PARENTHOOD
**par·en·ter·al** \pə-'ren-tə-rəl\ *adjective* [International Scientific Vocabulary *para-* + *enteral*] (circa 1910)
**:** situated or occurring outside the intestine; *especially* **:** introduced otherwise than by way of the intestines
— **par·en·ter·al·ly** \-rə-lē\ *adverb*
**pa·ren·the·sis** \pə-'ren(t)-thə-səs\ *noun, plural* **-the·ses** \-,sēz\ [Late Latin, from Greek, literally, act of inserting, from *parentithenai* to insert, from *para-* + *en-* en- + *tithenai* to place — more at DO] (circa 1550)
**1 a :** an amplifying or explanatory word, phrase, or sentence inserted in a passage from which it is usually set off by punctuation **b :** a remark or passage that departs from the theme of a discourse : DIGRESSION
**2 :** INTERLUDE, INTERVAL
**3 :** one or both of the curved marks ( ) used in writing and printing to enclose a parenthetical expression or to group a symbolic unit in a logical or mathematical expression
— **par·en·thet·i·cal** \,par-ən-'the-ti-kəl\ *also* **par·en·thet·ic** \-tik\ *adjective*
— **par·en·thet·i·cal·ly** \-ti-k(ə-)lē\ *adverb*
**pa·ren·the·size** \pə-'ren(t)-thə-,sīz\ *transitive verb* **-sized; -siz·ing** (1837)
**:** to make a parenthesis of **:** enclose within parentheses
**par·ent·hood** \'par-ənt-,hùd, 'per-\ *noun* (1856)
**:** the state of being a parent; *specifically* **:** the position, function, or standing of a parent
**par·ent·ing** \'par-ən-tiŋ, 'per-\ *noun* (1958)
**1 :** the raising of a child by its parents
**2 :** the act or process of becoming a parent
**3 :** the act of caring for someone in the manner of a parent
**parent–teacher association** *noun, often P&T&A capitalized* (1915)
**:** an organization of local groups of teachers and the parents of their pupils that works for the improvement of the schools and the benefit of the pupils
**pa·re·sis** \pə-'rē-səs, 'par-ə-\ *noun, plural* **pa·re·ses** \-,sēz\ [New Latin, from Greek, from *parienai* to let fall, from *para-* + *hienai* to let go, send — more at JET] (1693)
**1 :** slight or partial paralysis
**2 :** GENERAL PARESIS
— **pa·ret·ic** \pə-'re-tik\ *adjective or noun*
**par·es·the·sia** \,par-əs-'thē-zhə\ *noun* [New Latin, from *para-* + *-esthesia* (as in *anesthesia*)] (circa 1860)
**:** a sensation of pricking, tingling, or creeping on the skin that has no objective cause
— **par·es·thet·ic** \-'the-tik\ *adjective*
**pa·reu** *or* **pa·reo** \'pär-ā-(,)ü\ *noun* [Tahitian] (1860)
**:** a wraparound skirt usually made from a rectangular piece of printed cloth and worn by men and women throughout Polynesia
**pa·reve** \'pär-(ə-)və\ *adjective* [Yiddish *parev*] (1941)
**:** made without milk, meat, or their derivatives ⟨*pareve* margarine⟩ — compare FLEISHIG, MILCHIG
**par ex·cel·lence** \'pär-,ek-sə-'lä°s\ *adjective* [French, literally, by excellence] (1695)
**:** being the best of a kind : PREEMINENT ⟨a salesman *par excellence*⟩
**par·fait** \pär-'fā\ *noun* [French, literally, something perfect, from *parfait* perfect, from Latin *perfectus*] (1894)
**1 :** a flavored custard containing whipped cream and syrup frozen without stirring
**2 :** a cold dessert made of layers of fruit, syrup, ice cream, and whipped cream
**parfait glass** *noun* (circa 1951)
**:** a tall narrow glass with a short stem

**par·fleche** \'pär-,flesh\ *noun* [Canadian French *parflèche,* from French *parer* to ward off + *flèche* arrow] (1827)
**1 :** a raw hide soaked in lye to remove the hair and dried
**2 :** an article (as a bag or case) made of parfleche
**par·fo·cal** \'pär-'fō-kəl\ *adjective* [Latin *par* equal + English *focal*] (1886)
**:** being or having lenses or lens sets (as eyepieces) with the corresponding focal points all in the same plane
— **par·fo·cal·i·ty** \,pär-fō-'ka-lə-tē\ *noun*
— **par·fo·cal·ize** \,pär-'fō-kə-,līz\ *transitive verb*
**parge** \'pärj\ *transitive verb* **parged; parg·ing** (1701)
**:** PARGET
¹**par·get** \'pär-jət\ *transitive verb* **-get·ed** *or* **-get·ted; -get·ing** *or* **-get·ting** [Middle English *pargetten,* from Middle French *parjeter* to throw on top of, from *par-* thoroughly (from Latin *per-*) + *jeter* to throw — more at JET] (14th century)
**:** to coat with plaster; *especially* **:** to apply ornamental or waterproofing plaster to
²**parget** *noun* (14th century)
**1 :** plaster, whitewash, or roughcast for coating a wall
**2 :** plasterwork especially in raised ornamental figures on walls
**par·gy·line** \'pär-jə-,lēn\ *noun* [pro*pargyl* (an alcohol) + ²*-ine*] (1961)
**:** a monoamine oxidase inhibitor $C_{11}H_{13}N$ that is used in the hydrochloride especially as an antihypertensive agent
**parhelic circle** *noun* (1890)
**:** a luminous circle or halo parallel to the horizon at the altitude of the sun — called also *parhelic ring*
**par·he·lion** \pär-'hēl-yən\ *noun, plural* **-lia** \-yə\ [Latin *parelion,* from Greek *parēlion,* from *para-* + *hēlios* sun — more at SOLAR] (1647)
**:** any of several bright spots often tinged with color that often appear on the parhelic circle
— **par·he·lic** \-'hē-lik\ *adjective*
**pa·ri·ah** \pə-'rī-ə\ *noun* [Tamil *paraiyan,* literally, drummer] (1613)
**1 :** a member of a low caste of southern India
**2 :** OUTCAST 1
**par·i·an** \'par-ē-ən, 'per-\ *noun* [*Parian,* adjective; from its suitability for making statuettes] (1850)
**:** a porcelain composed essentially of kaolin and feldspar and usually used unglazed in ornamental articles
**Par·i·an** \'par-ē-ən, 'per-\ *adjective* (1611)
**:** of or relating to the island of Paros noted for its marble used extensively for sculpture in ancient times
**Parian ware** *noun* (1894)
**1 :** PARIAN
**2 :** articles made of parian
¹**pa·ri·e·tal** \pə-'rī-ə-tᵊl\ *adjective* [Middle French, from New Latin *pariet-, paries* wall of a cavity or hollow organ, from Latin, wall] (15th century)
**1 a :** of or relating to the walls of a part or cavity **b :** of, relating to, or forming the upper posterior wall of the head
**2 :** attached to the main wall rather than the axis or a cross wall of a plant ovary — used of an ovule or a placenta
**3 :** of or relating to college living or its regulation; *especially* **:** of or relating to parietals
²**parietal** *noun* (15th century)
**1 :** a parietal part (as a bone, scale, or plate)

**2** *plural* **:** the regulations governing the visiting privileges of members of the opposite sex in campus dormitories

**parietal bone** *noun* (15th century)
**:** either of a pair of bones of the roof of the skull between the frontal bones and the occipital bones

**parietal cell** *noun* (1875)
**:** any of the large oval cells of the gastric mucous membrane that secrete hydrochloric acid

**parietal lobe** *noun* (circa 1889)
**:** the middle division of each cerebral hemisphere that contains an area concerned with bodily sensations

**pari-mu-tu-el** \ˌpar-i-ˈmyü-chə-wəl, -chəl; -ˈmyüch-wəl\ *noun* [French *pari mutuel*, literally, mutual stake] (1888)
**1 :** a betting pool in which those who bet on competitors finishing in the first three places share the total amount bet minus a percentage for the management
**2 :** a machine for registering the bets and computing the payoffs in pari-mutuel betting

**par-ing** \ˈpar-iŋ, ˈper-\ *noun* (14th century)
**1 :** the act of cutting away an edge or surface
**2 :** something pared off ⟨apple *parings*⟩

**paring knife** *noun* (1591)
**:** a small short-bladed knife (as for paring fruit)

**pa-ri pas-su** \ˌpar-i-ˈpa-(ˌ)sü\ *adverb or adjective* [Latin, with equal step] (1567)
**:** at an equal rate or pace

**Par-is** \ˈpar-əs\ *noun* [Latin, from Greek]
**:** a son of Priam whose abduction of Helen leads to the Trojan War

**Par-is green** \ˈpar-əs-\ *noun* [*Paris*, France] (1868)
**1 :** a very poisonous copper-based bright green powder that is used as an insecticide and pigment
**2 :** a brilliant yellowish green

**par-ish** \ˈpar-ish\ *noun* [Middle English *parisshe*, from Middle French *parroche*, from Late Latin *parochia*, from Late Greek *paroikia*, from *paroikos* Christian, from Greek, stranger, from *para-* + *oikos* house — more at VICINITY] (14th century)
**1 a** (1) **:** the ecclesiastical unit of area committed to one pastor (2) **:** the residents of such an area **b** *British* **:** a subdivision of a county often coinciding with an original ecclesiastical parish and constituting the unit of local government
**2 :** a local church community composed of the members or constituents of a Protestant church
**3 :** a civil division of the state of Louisiana corresponding to a county in other states

**pa-rish-ion-er** \pə-ˈri-sh(ə-)nər\ *noun* [Middle English *parisshoner*, probably modification of Middle French *parrochien*, from *parroche*] (15th century)
**:** a member or inhabitant of a parish

**¹par-i-ty** \ˈpar-ə-tē\ *noun*, *plural* **-ties** [Latin *paritas*, from *par* equal] (circa 1609)
**1 :** the quality or state of being equal or equivalent
**2 a :** equivalence of a commodity price expressed in one currency to its price expressed in another **b :** equality of purchasing power established by law between different kinds of money at a given ratio
**3 :** an equivalence between farmers' current purchasing power and their purchasing power at a selected base period maintained by government support of agricultural commodity prices
**4 a :** the property of an integer with respect to being odd or even ⟨3 and 7 have the same *parity*⟩ **b** (1) **:** the state of being odd or even used as the basis of a method of detecting errors in binary-coded data (2) **:** PARITY BIT
**5 :** the property of oddness or evenness of a quantum mechanical function
**6 :** the symmetry of behavior in an interaction of a physical entity (as a subatomic particle) with that of its mirror image

**²parity** *noun* [*-parous*] (1878)
**:** the state or fact of having borne offspring; *also* **:** the number of children previously borne

**parity bit** *noun* (1957)
**:** a bit added to an array of bits (as on magnetic tape) to provide parity

**¹park** \ˈpärk\ *noun* [Middle English, from Old French *parc* enclosure, from Medieval Latin *parricus*] (13th century)
**1 a :** an enclosed piece of ground stocked with game and held by royal prescription or grant **b :** a tract of land that often includes lawns, woodland, and pasture attached to a country house and is used as a game preserve and for recreation
**2 a :** a piece of ground in or near a city or town kept for ornament and recreation **b :** an area maintained in its natural state as a public property
**3 a** *West* **:** a level valley between mountain ranges **b :** an open space and especially a grassland that is often all or partly surrounded by woodland and is suitable for cultivation or grazing
**4 a :** a space occupied by military animals, vehicles, or materials **b :** PARKING LOT
**5 :** an enclosed arena or stadium used especially for ball games
**6 :** an area designed for a specified industrial, commercial, or residential use ⟨amusement *park*⟩ ⟨industrial *park*⟩ ⟨mobile home *park*⟩
— **park-like** \ˈpärk-ˌlīk\ *adjective*

**²park** (1526)
*transitive verb*
**1 :** to enclose in a park
**2 a** (1) **:** to bring (a vehicle) to a stop and keep standing at the edge of a public way (2) **:** to leave temporarily on a public way or in a parking lot or garage **b :** to land and leave (as an airplane) **c :** to establish (as a satellite) in orbit
**3 a :** to set and leave temporarily ⟨*parked* his hat on the chair⟩ **b :** to place, settle, or establish especially for a considerable time ⟨kids *parked* in front of the TV⟩ ⟨*parked* her money in a savings account⟩
**4 :** to assemble (as equipment or stores) in a military dump or park
*intransitive verb*
**:** to park a vehicle
— **park-er** *noun*

**par-ka** \ˈpär-kə\ *noun* [Aleut, from Russian dialect, ultimately from Nenets (Samoyedic language of northern Russia)] (1780)
**1 :** a hooded fur pullover garment for arctic wear
**2 :** a usually lined fabric outerwear pullover or jacket

**parking lot** *noun* (1924)
**:** an area used for the parking of motor vehicles

**parking meter** *noun* (1936)
**:** a coin-operated device which registers the purchase of parking time for a motor vehicle

**par-kin-so-nian** \ˌpär-kən-ˈsō-nē-ən, -nyən\ *adjective* (1906)
**1 :** of or similar to that of parkinsonism
**2 :** affected with parkinsonism and especially Parkinson's disease

**par-kin-son-ism** \ˈpär-kən-sə-ˌni-zəm\ *noun* (circa 1923)
**1 :** PARKINSON'S DISEASE
**2 :** a nervous disorder that resembles Parkinson's disease

**Par-kin-son's disease** \ˈpär-kən-sənz-\ *noun* [James *Parkinson* (died 1824) English physician] (1877)
**:** a chronic progressive nervous disease chiefly of later life that is linked to decreased dopamine production in the substantia nigra and is marked by tremor and weakness of resting muscles and by a shuffling gait — called also *paralysis agitans*, *Parkinson's*, *Parkinson's syndrome*

**Parkinson's Law** *noun* [C. Northcote *Parkinson* (born 1909) English historian] (1955)
**1 :** an observation in office organization: the number of subordinates increases at a fixed rate regardless of the amount of work produced
**2 :** an observation in office organization: work expands so as to fill the time available for its completion

**park-land** \ˈpärk-ˌland\ *noun* (1907)
**:** land with clumps of trees and shrubs in cultivated condition used as or suitable for use as a park

**park-way** \ˈpärk-ˌwā\ *noun* (1887)
**:** a broad landscaped thoroughfare

**par-lance** \ˈpär-lən(t)s\ *noun* [Middle French, from Old French, from *parler*] (circa 1580)
**1 :** SPEECH; *especially* **:** formal debate or parley
**2 :** manner or mode of speech **:** IDIOM

**par-lan-do** \pär-ˈlän-(ˌ)dō\ *or* **par-lan-te** \-(ˌ)tā\ *adjective* [*parlando* from Italian, verbal of *parlare* to speak, from Medieval Latin *parabolare*; *parlante* from Italian, present participle of *parlare*] (circa 1854)
**:** delivered or performed in a style suggestive of speech — used as a direction in music

**¹par-lay** \ˈpär-ˌlā, -lē\ *transitive verb* [French *paroli*, noun, parlay, from Italian dialect, plural of *parolo*, perhaps from *paro* equal, from Latin *par*] (1828)
**1 :** to bet in a parlay
**2 a :** to exploit successfully **b :** to increase or otherwise transform into something of much greater value

**²parlay** *noun* (1904)
**:** a series of two or more bets so set up in advance that the original stake plus its winnings are risked on the successive wagers; *broadly* **:** the fresh risking of an original stake together with its winnings

**parle** \ˈpär(-ə)l\ *intransitive verb* **parled**; **parl-ing** [Middle English, to parley, from Middle French *parler*] (14th century)
*archaic* **:** PARLEY
— **parle** *noun*, *archaic*

**¹par-ley** \ˈpär-lē\ *noun*, *plural* **parleys** [Middle English *parlai* speech, probably from Middle French *parlee*, from feminine of *parlé*, past participle of *parler* to speak, from Medieval Latin *parabolare*, from Late Latin *parabola* speech, parable — more at PARABLE] (1581)
**1 a :** a conference for discussion of points in dispute **b :** a conference with an enemy
**2 :** DISCUSSION

**²par-ley** *intransitive verb* **par-leyed**; **par-ley-ing** (1591)
**:** to speak with another **:** CONFER; *specifically* **:** to discuss terms with an enemy

**par-lia-ment** \ˈpär-lə-mənt *also* ˈpärl-yə-\ *noun* [Middle English, from Old French *parlement*, from *parler*] (13th century)
**1 :** a formal conference for the discussion of public affairs; *specifically* **:** a council of state in early medieval England
**2 a :** an assemblage of the nobility, clergy, and commons called together by the British sovereign as the supreme legislative body in the United Kingdom **b :** a similar assemblage in another nation or state
**3 a :** the supreme legislative body of a usually major political unit that is a continuing institution comprising a series of individual assemblages **b :** the British House of Commons
**4 :** one of several principal courts of justice existing in France before the revolution of 1789

**par-lia-men-tar-i-an** \ˌpär-lə-ˌmen-ˈter-ē-ən, -mən- *also* ˌpärl-yə-\ *noun* (1644)
**1** *often capitalized* **:** an adherent of the parliament in opposition to the king during the English Civil War
**2 :** an expert in the rules and usages of a deliberative assembly (as a parliament)
**3 :** a member of a parliament

**par-lia-men-ta-ry** \-ˈmen-t(ə-)rē\ *adjective* (1616)

**1 a :** of or relating to a parliament **b :** enacted, done, or ratified by a parliament
**2 :** of or adhering to the parliament as opposed to the king during the English Civil War
**3 :** of, based on, or having the characteristics of parliamentary government
**4 :** of or relating to members of a parliament
**5 :** of or according to parliamentary law ⟨*parliamentary* procedure⟩

**parliamentary government** *noun* (1858)
**:** a system of government having the real executive power vested in a cabinet composed of members of the legislature who are individually and collectively responsible to the legislature

**parliamentary law** *noun* (1893)
**:** the rules and precedents governing the proceedings of deliberative assemblies and other organizations

**¹par·lor** \'pär-lər\ *noun* [Middle English *parlour*, from Old French, from *parler*] (13th century)
**1 :** a room used primarily for conversation or the reception of guests: as **a :** a room in a private dwelling for the entertainment of guests **b :** a conference chamber or private reception room **c :** a room in an inn, hotel, or club for conversation or semiprivate uses
**2 :** any of various business places ⟨a funeral *parlor*⟩ ⟨a beauty *parlor*⟩ ◆

**²parlor** *adjective* (1552)
**1 :** used in or suitable for a parlor ⟨*parlor* furniture⟩
**2 a :** fostered or advocated in comfortable seclusion without consequent action or application to affairs ⟨*parlor* bolshevism⟩ **b :** given to or characterized by fostering or advocating something (as a doctrine) in such a manner ⟨*parlor* socialist⟩

**parlor car** *noun* (1868)
**:** an extra-fare railroad passenger car for day travel equipped with individual chairs

**parlor game** *noun* (1872)
**:** a game suitable for playing indoors

**parlor grand** *noun* (1856)
**:** a grand piano intermediate in length between a concert grand and a baby grand

**par·lour** \'pär-lər\ *chiefly British variant of* PARLOR

**par·lous** \'pär-ləs\ *adjective* [Middle English, alteration of *perilous*] (14th century)
**1** *obsolete* **:** dangerously shrewd or cunning
**2 :** full of danger or risk **:** HAZARDOUS
— **par·lous·ly** *adverb*

**Par·me·san** \'pär-mə-ˌzän, -ˌzhän, -zən, -ˌzan\ *noun* [*Parmesan* of Parma, from Middle French *parmesan*, from Old Italian *parmigiano*] (1538)
**:** a very hard dry sharply flavored cheese that is sold grated or in wedges

**par·mi·gia·na** \ˌpär-mi-'jä-nə, -'zhän; 'pär-mi-ˌzhän, -ˌzän\ *or* **par·mi·gia·no** \-'jä-(ˌ)nō\ *adjective* [Italian *parmigiana*, feminine of *parmigiano* of Parma, from *Parma*] (1943)
**:** made or covered with Parmesan cheese ⟨veal *parmigiana*⟩

**Par·nas·si·an** \pär-'na-sē-ən\ *adjective* (circa 1644)
**1** [Latin *parnassius* of Parnassus, from Greek *parnasios*, from *Parnasos* Parnassus, mountain in Greece sacred to Apollo and the Muses] **:** of or relating to poetry
**2** [French *parnassien*, from *Parnasse* Parnassus; from *Le Parnasse contemporain* (1866), an anthology of poetry] **:** of or relating to a school of French poets of the second half of the 19th century emphasizing metrical form rather than emotion
— **Parnassian** *noun*

**pa·ro·chi·al** \pə-'rō-kē-əl\ *adjective* [Middle English *parochiall*, from Middle French *parochial*, from Late Latin *parochialis*, from *parochia* parish — more at PARISH] (14th century)
**1 :** of or relating to a church parish
**2 :** of or relating to a parish as a unit of local government

---

**3 :** confined or restricted as if within the borders of a parish **:** limited in range or scope (as to a narrow area or region) **:** PROVINCIAL, NARROW
— **pa·ro·chi·al·ly** \-kē-ə-lē\ *adverb*

**pa·ro·chi·al·ism** \-kē-ə-ˌli-zəm\ *noun* (1847)
**:** the quality or state of being parochial; *especially* **:** selfish pettiness or narrowness (as of interests, opinions, or views)

**parochial school** *noun* (1755)
**:** a private school maintained by a religious body usually for elementary and secondary instruction

**par·o·dist** \'par-ə-dist\ *noun* (1742)
**:** a writer of parodies

**¹par·o·dy** \'par-ə-dē\ *noun, plural* **-dies** [Latin *parodia*, from Greek *parōidia*, from *para-* + *aidein* to sing — more at ODE] (1598)
**1 :** a literary or musical work in which the style of an author or work is closely imitated for comic effect or in ridicule
**2 :** a feeble or ridiculous imitation
*synonym* see CARICATURE
— **pa·rod·ic** \pə-'rä-dik, pa-\ *adjective*
— **par·o·dis·tic** \ˌpar-ə-'dis-tik\ *adjective*

**²parody** *transitive verb* **-died; -dy·ing** (circa 1745)
**1 :** to compose a parody on ⟨*parody* a poem⟩
**2 :** to imitate in the manner of a parody

**par·ol** \'par-əl\ *noun* [Middle French *parole*] (1590)
**:** WORD OF MOUTH
— **parol** *adjective*

**¹pa·role** \pə-'rōl\ *noun* [French, speech, parole, from Middle French, from Late Latin *parabola* speech — more at PARABLE] (circa 1616)
**1 :** a promise made with or confirmed by a pledge of one's honor; *especially* **:** the promise of a prisoner of war to fulfill stated conditions in consideration of his release
**2 :** a watchword given only to officers of the guard and of the day
**3 :** a conditional release of a prisoner serving an indeterminate or unexpired sentence
**4 a :** language viewed as a specific individual usage **:** PERFORMANCE **b :** a linguistic act — compare LANGUE
— **parole** *adjective*

**²parole** *transitive verb* **pa·roled; pa·rol·ing** (1790)
**:** to release (a prisoner) on parole

**pa·rol·ee** \pə-ˌrō-'lē, -'rō-(ˌ); ˌpar-ə-'lē\ *noun* (1903)
**:** one released on parole

**par·o·no·ma·sia** \ˌpar-ə-nō-'mā-zh(ē-)ə, ˌpar-ˌä-nə-'mā-\ *noun* [Latin, from Greek, from *paronomazein* to call with a slight change of name, from *para-* + *onoma* name — more at NAME] (1577)
**:** a play on words **:** PUN
— **par·o·no·mas·tic** \-'mas-tik\ *adjective*

**par·o·nym** \'par-ə-ˌnim\ *noun* [Late Latin *paronymon*, from Greek *parōnymon*, neuter of *parōnymos*] (circa 1846)
**:** a paronymous word

**par·on·y·mous** \pə-'rä-nə-məs, pa-\ *adjective* [Greek *parōnymos*, from *para-* + *-ōnymos* (as in *homōnymos* homonymous)] (circa 1661)
**1 :** CONJUGATE 4
**2 a :** formed from a word in another language **b :** having a form similar to that of a cognate foreign word

**pa·rot·id** \pə-'rä-təd\ *adjective* [New Latin *parotid-, parotis* parotid gland, from Latin, tumor near the ear, from Greek *parōtid-, parōtis*, from *para-* + *ōt-, ous* ear — more at EAR] (1687)
**:** of or relating to the parotid gland

**parotid gland** *noun* (circa 1771)
**:** either of a pair of large serous salivary glands situated below and in front of the ear

**par·o·ti·tis** \ˌpar-ō-'tī-təs\ *noun* (1822)
**:** inflammation of the parotid glands; *also* **:** MUMPS

---

**par·ous** \'par-əs, 'per-\ *adjective* [-*parous*] (circa 1889)
**:** having produced offspring

**-parous** *adjective combining form* [Latin -*parus*, from *parere* to give birth to, produce — more at PARE]
**:** giving birth to **:** producing ⟨multi*parous*⟩

**Par·ou·sia** \ˌpär-ü-'sē-ə, pə-'rü-zē-ə\ *noun* [Greek, literally, presence, from *paront-, parōn*, present participle of *pareinai* to be present, from *para-* + *einai* to be — more at IS] (1875)
**:** SECOND COMING

**par·ox·ysm** \'par-ək-ˌsi-zəm *also* pə-'räk-\ *noun* [French & Medieval Latin; French *paroxysme*, from Medieval Latin *paroxysmus*, from Greek *paroxysmos*, from *paroxynein* to stimulate, from *para-* + *oxynein* to provoke, from *oxys* sharp — more at OXYGEN] (15th century)
**1 :** a fit, attack, or sudden increase or recurrence of symptoms (as of a disease) **:** CONVULSION ⟨a *paroxysm* of coughing⟩
**2 :** a sudden violent emotion or action **:** OUTBURST ⟨a *paroxysm* of rage⟩
— **par·ox·ys·mal** \ˌpar-ək-'siz-məl *also* pə-ˌräk-\ *adjective*

**¹par·quet** \pär-'kā\ *transitive verb* **par·queted** \-'kād\; **par·quet·ing** \-'kā-iŋ\ (1678)
**1 :** to furnish with a floor of parquet
**2 :** to make of parquetry

**²par·quet** \'pär-ˌkā, pär-'\ *noun* [French, from Middle French, small enclosure, from *parc* park] (1816)
**1 a :** a patterned wood surface (as flooring or paneling); *especially* **:** one made of parquetry
**b :** PARQUETRY
**2 :** the main floor of a theater; *specifically* **:** the part from the front of the stage to the parquet circle

**parquet circle** *noun* (1854)
**:** the part of the main floor of a theater that is beneath the galleries

**par·que·try** \'pär-kə-trē\ *noun, plural* **-tries** (circa 1842)

---

◇ **WORD HISTORY**

**parlor**   Within some medieval religious orders a rule of silence was enforced, and the members of a community belonging to the order could speak with each other or outsiders only in a special room. In 12th century Old French this room was called the *parlëure*, a derivative of the verb *parler* "to speak." The Old French word was borrowed at an early date into Middle English as *parlure* or *parlour*. In both French and English the sense of the word was extended to rooms such as a chamber for private conversation off the main hall of a manor house, or a room in a municipal building used for conferences. In England the *parlour* in an ordinary middle-class home developed into the best-furnished room in the house, often facing the street, where a family received guests; the word eventually became virtually synonymous with *drawing room* or *living room*. A late 19th century development originally unique to the U.S. was the use of *parlor* with a preceding attributive noun to denote a well-appointed commercial establishment. Though the *Oxford English Dictionary* labeled such usages as "commercial cant," no stigma is attached to *ice cream parlor, beauty parlor,* or *funeral parlor* in 20th century American English.

---

\ə\ abut   \ᵊ\ kitten   \ər\ further   \a\ ash   \ā\ ace
\ä\ mop, mar   \aú\ out   \ch\ chin   \e\ bet   \ē\ easy
\g\ go   \i\ hit   \ī\ ice   \j\ job   \ŋ\ sing   \ō\ go
\ò\ law   \òi\ boy   \th\ thin   \t͟h\ the   \ü\ loot   \ù\ foot
\y\ yet   \zh\ vision   *see also* Guide to Pronunciation

: work in the form of usually geometrically patterned wood laid or inlaid especially for floors

**parr** \'pär\ *noun, plural* **parr** *also* **parrs** [origin unknown] (circa 1722)
: a young salmon actively feeding in freshwater

**par·ra·keet** *variant of* PARAKEET

**par·rel** *or* **par·ral** \'par-əl\ *noun* [Middle English *perell*, from alteration of *parail* apparel, short for *apparail*, from Middle French *apareil*, from *apareillier* to prepare — more at APPAREL] (15th century)
: a rope loop or sliding collar by which a yard or spar is held to a mast in such a way that it may be hoisted or lowered

**par·ri·cid·al** \,par-ə-'sī-d°l\ *adjective* (1627)
: of, relating to, or guilty of parricide

**par·ri·cide** \'par-ə-,sīd\ *noun* (1554)
**1** [Latin *parricida* killer of a close relative, from *parri-* (perhaps akin to Greek *pēos* kinsman by marriage) + *-cida* -cide] : one that murders his or her father, mother, or a close relative
**2** [Latin *parricidium* murder of a close relative, from *parri-* + *-cidium* -cide] : the act of a parricide

**¹par·rot** \'par-ət\ *noun* [probably irregular from Middle French *perroquet*] (circa 1525)
**1** : any of numerous widely distributed tropical zygodactyl birds (order Psittaciformes and especially family Psittacidae) that have a distinctive stout curved hooked bill, are often crested and brightly variegated, and include some excellent mimics
**2** : a person who sedulously echoes another's words
— **parrot** *adjective*

**²parrot** *transitive verb* (1596)
: to repeat by rote

**parrot fever** *noun* (1930)
: PSITTACOSIS

**parrot fish** *noun* (1712)
: any of a family (Scaridae) of usually brightly colored chiefly tropical marine fishes that have the teeth in each jaw fused into a cutting plate like a beak

**par·ry** \'par-ē\ *verb* **par·ried; par·ry·ing** [probably from French *parez*, imperative of *parer* to parry, from Old Provençal *parar*, from Latin *parare* to prepare — more at PARE] (1672)
*intransitive verb*
**1** : to ward off a weapon or blow
**2** : to evade or turn aside something
*transitive verb*
**1** : to ward off (as a blow)
**2** : to evade especially by an adroit answer ⟨*parry* an embarrassing question⟩
— **parry** *noun*

**¹parse** \'pärs, *chiefly British* 'pärz\ *verb* **parsed; pars·ing** [Latin *pars orationis* part of speech] (1553)
*transitive verb*
**1 a** : to resolve (as a sentence) into component parts of speech and describe them grammatically **b** : to describe grammatically by stating the part of speech and explaining the inflection and syntactical relationships
**2** : to examine in a minute way : analyze critically ⟨*parses* appellate court opinions⟩
*intransitive verb*
**1** : to give a grammatical description of a word or a group of words
**2** : to admit of being parsed

**²parse** *noun* (1963)
: a product or an instance of parsing

**par·sec** \'pär-,sek\ *noun* [*parallax* + *second*] (1913)
: a unit of measure for interstellar space equal to the distance to an object having a parallax of one second or to 3.26 light-years

**pars·er** \'pär-sər\ *noun* (circa 1864)
: one that parses; *specifically* : a computer program that breaks down text into recognized strings of characters for further analysis

**Par·si** *also* **Par·see** \'pär-(,)sē\ *noun* [Persian *pārsī*, from *Pārs* Persia] (1615)
**1** : a Zoroastrian descended from Persian refugees settled principally at Bombay
**2** : the Iranian dialect of the Parsi religious literature
— **Par·si·ism** \-,i-zəm\ *noun*

**par·si·mo·ni·ous** \,pär-sə-'mō-nē-əs\ *adjective* (1598)
: exhibiting or marked by parsimony; *especially* : frugal to the point of stinginess
*synonym* see STINGY
— **par·si·mo·ni·ous·ly** *adverb*

**par·si·mo·ny** \'pär-sə-,mō-nē\ *noun* [Middle English *parcimony*, from Latin *parsimonia*, from *parsus*, past participle of *parcere* to spare] (15th century)
**1 a** : the quality of being careful with money or resources : THRIFT **b** : the quality or state of being stingy
**2** : economy in the use of means to an end; *especially* : economy of explanation in conformity with Occam's razor

**pars·ley** \'pär-slē\ *noun* [Middle English *persely*, from Old English *petersilie*, from (assumed) Vulgar Latin *petrosilium*, alteration of Latin *petroselinum*, from Greek *petroselinon*, from *petros* stone + *selinon* celery] (before 12th century)
: a European biennial herb (*Petroselinum crispum*) of the carrot family that is widely cultivated for its leaves which are used as a culinary herb or garnish

**pars·leyed** *also* **pars·lied** \-slēd\ *adjective* (1952)
: garnished or flavored with parsley ⟨*parsleyed* potatoes⟩

**pars·nip** \'pär-snəp\ *noun* [Middle English *pasnepe*, modification of Middle French *pasnaie*, from Latin *pastinaca*, from *pastinum* 2-pronged dibble] (14th century)
: a Eurasian biennial herb (*Pastinaca sativa*) of the carrot family with large pinnate leaves and yellow flowers that is cultivated for its long tapered edible root; *also* : the root

**par·son** \'pär-s°n\ *noun* [Middle English *persone*, from Old French, from Medieval Latin *persona*, literally, person, from Latin] (13th century)
**1** : RECTOR
**2** : CLERGYMAN; *especially* : a Protestant pastor
*word history* see PERSON

**par·son·age** \'pär-s(ə-)nij, 'pär-s°n-ij\ *noun* (15th century)
: the house provided by a church for its pastor

**Par·sons ta·ble** \'pär-s°nz-\ *noun* [*Parsons* School of Design, New York City] (1967)
: a usually rectangular table having straight legs that are flush with the edge of the top

**¹part** \'pärt\ *noun* [Middle English, from Old French & Old English, both from Latin *part-, pars*; perhaps akin to Latin *parare* to prepare — more at PARE] (before 12th century)
**1 a** (1) : one of the often indefinite or unequal subdivisions into which something is or is regarded as divided and which together constitute the whole (2) : an essential portion or integral element **b** : one of several or many equal units of which something is composed or into which it is divisible : an amount equal to another amount ⟨mix one *part* of the powder with three *parts* of water⟩ **c** (1) : an exact divisor of a quantity : ALIQUOT (2) : PARTIAL FRACTION **d** : one of the constituent elements of a plant or animal body: as (1) : ORGAN, MEMBER (2) *plural* : PRIVATE PARTS **e** : a division of a literary work **f** (1) : a vocal or instrumental line or melody in concerted music or in harmony (2) : a particular voice or instrument in concerted music; *also* : the score for it **g** : a constituent member of a machine or other apparatus; *also* : a spare part

**parsnip**

**2** : something falling to one in a division or apportionment : SHARE
**3** : one's share or allotted task (as in an action) ⟨one must do one's *part*⟩
**4** : one of the opposing sides in a conflict or dispute
**5** : a general area of indefinite boundaries — usually used in plural ⟨you're not from around these *parts*⟩ ⟨took off for *parts* unknown⟩
**6** : a function or course of action performed
**7 a** : an actor's lines in a play **b** : the role of a character in a play
**8** : a constituent of character or capacity : TALENT ⟨a man of many *parts*⟩
**9** : the line where the hair is parted ☆
— **for the most part** : in general : on the whole ⟨*for the most part* the crowd was orderly⟩
— **in part** : in some degree : PARTIALLY
— **on the part of** : with regard to the one specified

**²part** *verb* [Middle English, from Old French *partir*, from Latin *partire* to divide, from *part-, pars*] (13th century)
*intransitive verb*
**1 a** : to separate from or take leave of someone **b** : to take leave of one another
**2** : to become separated into parts
**3 a** : to go away : DEPART **b** : DIE
**4** : to become separated, detached, or broken
**5** : to relinquish possession or control ⟨hated to *part* with that money⟩
*transitive verb*
**1 a** : to divide into parts **b** : to separate by combing on each side of a line **c** : to break or suffer the breaking of (as a rope or anchor chain)
**2** : to divide into shares and distribute : APPORTION
**3 a** : to remove from contact or association ⟨if aught but death *part* thee and me —Ruth 1:17 (Authorized Version)⟩ **b** : to keep separate ⟨the narrow channel that *parts* England from France⟩ **c** : to hold (as brawlers) apart **d** : to separate by a process of extraction, elimination, or secretion
**4 a** *archaic* : LEAVE, QUIT **b** *dialect British* : RELINQUISH, GIVE UP
*synonym* see SEPARATE

**³part** *adverb* (1513)
: PARTLY

**⁴part** *adjective* (1818)
: PARTIAL 1

**par·take** \pär-'tāk, pər-\ *verb* **-took** \-'tůk\; **-tak·en** \-'tā-kən\; **-tak·ing** [back-formation from *partaker*, alteration of *part taker*] (circa 1585)
*intransitive verb*
**1** : to take part in or experience something along with others ⟨*partake* in the revelry⟩ ⟨*partake* of the good life⟩

---

☆ **SYNONYMS**
**Part, portion, piece, member, division, section, segment, fragment** mean something less than the whole. PART is a general term appropriate when indefiniteness is required ⟨they ran only *part* of the way⟩. PORTION implies an assigned or allotted part ⟨cut the pie into six *portions*⟩. PIECE applies to a separate or detached part of a whole ⟨a puzzle with 500 *pieces*⟩. MEMBER suggests one of the functional units composing a body ⟨a structural *member*⟩. DIVISION applies to a large or diversified part ⟨the manufacturing *division* of the company⟩. SECTION applies to a relatively small or uniform part ⟨the entertainment *section* of the newspaper⟩. SEGMENT applies to a part separated or marked out by or as if by natural lines of cleavage ⟨the retired *segment* of the population⟩. FRAGMENT applies to a part produced by or as if by breaking off or shattering ⟨only a *fragment* of the play still exists⟩.

**2** : to have a portion (as of food or drink)
**3** : to possess or share a certain nature or attribute ⟨the experience *partakes* of a mystical quality⟩
*transitive verb*
: to take part in
**synonym** see SHARE
— **par·tak·er** *noun*
**part and parcel** *noun* (15th century)
: an essential or integral component ⟨stress was *part and parcel* of the job⟩
**part·ed** \'pär-təd\ *adjective* (1590)
**1 a** : divided into parts **b** : cleft so that the divisions reach nearly but not quite to the base — usually used in combination ⟨a 3-*parted* corolla⟩
**2** *archaic* : DEAD
**par·terre** \pär-'ter\ *noun* [French, from Middle French, from *par terre* on the ground] (circa 1639)
**1** : an ornamental garden with paths between the beds
**2** : the part of the main floor of a theater that is behind the orchestra; *especially* : PARQUET CIRCLE
**par·the·no·car·py** \'pär-thə-nō-,kär-pē\ *noun* [International Scientific Vocabulary, from Greek *parthenos* virgin + *karpos* fruit — more at HARVEST] (1911)
: the production of fruits without fertilization ⟨bananas set fruit by *parthenocarpy* and without pollination⟩
— **par·the·no·car·pic** \,pär-thə-nō-'kär-pik\ *adjective*
**par·the·no·gen·e·sis** \,pär-thə-nō-'je-nə-səs\ *noun* [New Latin, from Greek *parthenos* + Latin *genesis* genesis] (1849)
: reproduction by development of an unfertilized usually female gamete that occurs especially among lower plants and invertebrate animals
**par·the·no·ge·net·ic** \-jə-'ne-tik\ *adjective* (1872)
: of, characterized by, or produced by parthenogenesis
— **par·the·no·ge·net·i·cal·ly** \-ti-k(ə-)lē\ *adverb*
**Par·the·non** \'pär-thə-,nän\ *noun* [Latin, from Greek *Parthenōn*] (circa 1841)
: a Doric temple of Athena built on the acropolis at Athens in the 5th century B.C.
**Par·thi·an** \'pär-thē-ən\ *adjective* (1579)
**1** : of, relating to, or characteristic of ancient Parthia or its people
**2** : relating to, being, or having the effect of a shot fired while in real or feigned retreat
— **Parthian** *noun*
¹**par·tial** \'pär-shəl\ *adjective* [Middle English *parcial*, from Middle French *partial*, from Medieval Latin *partialis*, from Late Latin, of a part, from Latin *part-, pars* part] (14th century)
**1** : of or relating to a part rather than the whole : not general or total ⟨a *partial* solution⟩
**2** : inclined to favor one party more than the other : BIASED
**3** : markedly fond of someone or something — used with *to* ⟨*partial* to pizza⟩
²**partial** *noun* (1880)
: OVERTONE 1a
**partial denture** *noun* (1860)
: a usually removable artificial replacement of one or more teeth
**partial derivative** *noun* (1889)
: the derivative of a function of several variables with respect to one of them and with the remaining variables treated as constants
**partial differential equation** *noun* (1889)
: a differential equation containing at least one partial derivative
**partial differentiation** *noun* (circa 1890)
: the process of finding a partial derivative
**partial fraction** *noun* (1816)
: one of the simpler fractions into the sum of which the quotient of two polynomials may be decomposed

**par·tial·i·ty** \,pär-shē-'a-lə-tē, pär-'sha-lə-tē\ *noun, plural* **-ties** (15th century)
**1** : the quality or state of being partial : BIAS
**2** : a special taste or liking
**par·tial·ly** \'pär-sh(ə-)lē\ *adverb* (15th century)
**1** *archaic* : in a biased manner : with partiality
**2** : to some extent : in some degree
**partially ordered** *adjective* (1941)
: having some or all elements connected by a relation that is reflexive, transitive, and antisymmetric
**partial pressure** *noun* (1857)
: the pressure exerted by a (specified) component in a mixture of gases
**partial product** *noun* (circa 1924)
: a product obtained by multiplying a multiplicand by one digit of a multiplier having more than one digit
**par·ti·ble** \'pär-tə-bəl\ *adjective* (14th century)
: capable of being parted : DIVISIBLE ⟨a *partible* inheritance⟩
— **par·ti·bil·i·ty** \,pär-tə-'bi-lə-tē\ *noun*
**par·tic·i·pant** \pär-'ti-sə-pənt, pər-\ *noun* (1562)
: one that participates
— **participant** *adjective*
**par·tic·i·pate** \pär-'ti-sə-,pāt, pər-\ *verb* **-pat·ed; -pat·ing** [Latin *participatus*, past participle of *participare*, from *particip-, particeps* participant, from *part-, pars* part + *capere* to take — more at HEAVE] (1531)
*transitive verb*
*archaic* : PARTAKE
*intransitive verb*
**1** : to possess some of the attributes of a person, thing, or quality
**2 a** : to take part ⟨always tried to *participate* in class discussions⟩ **b** : to have a part or share in something
**synonym** see SHARE
— **par·tic·i·pa·tor** \-,pā-tər\ *noun*
**par·tic·i·pa·tion** \(,)pär-,ti-sə-'pā-shən, pər-\ *noun* (14th century)
**1** : the act of participating
**2** : the state of being related to a larger whole
**par·tic·i·pa·tion·al** \-'pā-shnəl, -'pā-shə-n³l\ *adjective* (1959)
: PARTICIPATORY
**par·tic·i·pa·tive** \pär-'ti-sə-pə-tiv, pər-, -,pā-tiv\ *adjective* (1951)
: relating to or involving participation; *especially* : of, relating to, or being a style of management in which subordinates participate in decision making
**par·tic·i·pa·to·ry** \pär-'ti-sə-pə-,tōr-ē, pər-, -,tòr-\ *adjective* (1881)
: characterized by or involving participation; *especially* : providing the opportunity for individual participation ⟨*participatory* democracy⟩
**par·ti·cip·i·al** \,pär-tə-'si-pē-əl\ *adjective* [Latin *participialis*, from *participium*] (1591)
: of, relating to, or formed with or from a participle
— **par·ti·cip·i·al·ly** \-pē-ə-lē\ *adverb*
**par·ti·ci·ple** \'pär-tə-,si-pəl\ *noun* [Middle English, from Middle French, modification of Latin *participium*, from *particip-, particeps*] (14th century)
: a word having the characteristics of both verb and adjective; *especially* : an English verbal form that has the function of an adjective and at the same time shows such verbal features as tense and voice and capacity to take an object
**par·ti·cle** \'pär-ti-kəl\ *noun* [Middle English, from Latin *particula*, from diminutive of *part-, pars*] (14th century)
**1 a** : a minute quantity or fragment **b** : a relatively small or the smallest discrete portion or amount of something
**2** *archaic* : a clause or article of a composition or document
**3** : any of the basic units of matter and energy (as a molecule, atom, proton, electron, or photon)

**4** : a unit of speech expressing some general aspect of meaning or some connective or limiting relation and including the articles, most prepositions and conjunctions, and some interjections and adverbs ⟨the *particle up* has a perfective meaning in phrases such as *beat up* and *cut up*⟩
**5** : a small eucharistic wafer distributed to a Roman Catholic layman at Communion
**particle accelerator** *noun* (1946)
: ACCELERATOR d
**par·ti·cle·board** \-,bōrd, -,bòrd\ *noun* (circa 1957)
: a composition board made of very small pieces of wood bonded together
**particle physics** *noun* (1946)
: a branch of physics dealing with the constitution, properties, and interactions of elementary particles especially as revealed in experiments using particle accelerators — called also *high-energy physics*
— **particle physicist** *noun*
**par·ti·col·or** \'pär-tē-,kə-lər\ *or* **par·ti·col·ored** \-lərd\ *adjective* [obsolete English *party* parti-color, from Middle English *parti*, from Middle French, striped, from past participle of *partir* to divide] (1535)
: showing different colors or tints; *especially* : having a predominant color broken by patches of one or more other colors ⟨*parti-color* setters⟩
— **parti-color** *noun*
¹**par·tic·u·lar** \pə(r)-'ti-kyə-lər, -k(ə-)lər\ *adjective* [Middle English *particuler*, from Middle French, from Late Latin *particularis*, from Latin *particula* small part] (14th century)
**1** : of, relating to, or being a single person or thing ⟨the *particular* person I had in mind⟩
**2** *obsolete* : PARTIAL
**3** : of, relating to, or concerned with details ⟨gave us a very *particular* account of the trip⟩
**4 a** : distinctive among other examples or cases of the same general category : notably unusual ⟨suffered from measles of *particular* severity⟩ **b** : being one unit or element among others ⟨*particular* incidents in a story⟩
**5 a** : denoting an individual member or subclass in logic **b** : affirming or denying a predicate to a part of the subject — used of a proposition in logic ⟨"some men are wise" is a *particular* affirmative⟩
**6 a** : concerned over or attentive to details : METICULOUS ⟨a very *particular* gardener⟩ **b** : nice in taste : FASTIDIOUS **c** : hard to please : EXACTING
**synonym** see CIRCUMSTANTIAL, SPECIAL
²**particular** *noun* (15th century)
**1** *archaic* : a separate part of a whole
**2 a** : an individual fact, point, circumstance, or detail **b** : a specific item or detail of information or news ⟨bill of *particulars*⟩
**3 a** : an individual or a specific subclass (as in logic) falling under some general concept or term **b** : a particular proposition in logic
**synonym** see ITEM
— **in particular** : in distinction from others : SPECIFICALLY
**par·tic·u·lar·ise** *British variant of* PARTICULARIZE
**par·tic·u·lar·ism** \pə(r)-'ti-k(yə-)lə-,ri-zəm *also* pär-\ *noun* (1824)
**1** : exclusive or special devotion to a particular interest
**2** : a political theory that each political group has a right to promote its own interests and especially independence without regard to the interests of larger groups
**3** : a tendency to explain complex social phenomena in terms of a single causative factor

---

— **par·tic·u·lar·ist** \-rist\ *noun or adjective*

— **par·tic·u·lar·is·tic** \-,ti-k(yə-)lə-'ris-tik\ *adjective*

**par·tic·u·lar·i·ty** \pə(r)-,ti-kyə-'lar-ə-tē *also* (,)pär-\ *noun, plural* **-ties** (1528)
**1 a :** a minute detail **:** PARTICULAR **b :** an individual characteristic **:** PECULIARITY; *also* **:** SINGULARITY
**2 :** the quality or state of being particular as distinguished from universal
**3 a :** attentiveness to detail **:** EXACTNESS **b :** the quality or state of being fastidious in behavior or expression

**par·tic·u·lar·i·za·tion** \-,ti-k(yə-)lə-rə-'zā-shən\ *noun* (1657)
**:** the act of particularizing **:** the condition of being particularized

**par·tic·u·lar·ize** \pə(r)-'ti-k(yə-)lə-,rīz *also* pär-\ *verb* **-ized; -iz·ing** (1593)
*transitive verb*
**:** to state in detail **:** SPECIFY
*intransitive verb*
**:** to go into details

**par·tic·u·lar·ly** \pə(r)-'ti-kyə-(lər)lē, -kyə-lə-lē; pə(r)-'ti-k(ə-)lē; *also* pär-\ *adverb* (14th century)
**1 :** in a particular manner **:** in detail
**2 :** to an unusual degree
**3 :** in particular **:** SPECIFICALLY

¹**par·tic·u·late** \pär-'ti-kyə-lət *also* -,lāt\ *adjective* [Latin *particula*] (1871)
**:** of or relating to minute separate particles

²**particulate** *noun* (1942)
**:** a particulate substance

**particulate inheritance** *noun* (1889)
**:** inheritance of characters specifically transmitted by genes in accord with Mendel's laws

¹**part·ing** \'pär-tiŋ\ *noun* (15th century)
**:** a place or point where a division or separation occurs
— **parting of the ways 1 :** a point of separation or divergence **2 :** a place or time at which a choice must be made

²**parting** *adjective* (circa 1577)
**:** given, taken, or performed at parting ⟨a *parting* kiss⟩

**par·ti pris** \'pär-,tē-'prē\ *noun, plural* **partis pris** \-,tē-'prē(z)\ [French, literally, side taken] (1860)
**:** a preconceived opinion **:** PREJUDICE
— **parti pris** *adjective*

¹**par·ti·san** *also* **par·ti·zan** \'pär-tə-zən, -sən, -,zan, *chiefly British* ,pär-tə-'zan\ *noun* [Middle French *partisan*, from Old Italian *partigiano*, from *parte* part, party, from Latin *part-, pars* part] (1555)
**1 :** a firm adherent to a party, faction, cause, or person; *especially* **:** one exhibiting blind, prejudiced, and unreasoning allegiance
**2 a :** a member of a body of detached light troops making forays and harassing an enemy **b :** a member of a guerrilla band operating within enemy lines
**synonym** see FOLLOWER
— **partisan** *adjective*
— **par·ti·san·ly** \-lē\ *adverb*
— **par·ti·san·ship** \-,ship\ *noun*

²**par·ti·san** *or* **par·ti·zan** \'pär-tə-zən, -sən\ *noun* [Middle French *partisane*, from Old Italian *partigiana*, feminine of *partigiano*] (1556)
**:** a weapon of the 16th and 17th centuries with long shaft and broad blade

**par·ti·ta** \pär-'tē-tə\ *noun* [Italian, from *partire* to divide, from Latin — more at PART] (1880)
**1 :** VARIATION 4
**2 :** SUITE 2b(1)

**par·tite** \'pär-,tīt\ *adjective* [Latin *partitus*, from past participle of *partire*] (circa 1570)
**1 :** divided into a usually specified number of parts
**2 :** PARTED 1b ⟨a *partite* leaf⟩

¹**par·ti·tion** \pär-'ti-shən, pər-\ *noun* (15th century)
**1 :** the action of parting **:** the state of being parted **:** DIVISION

**2 :** something that divides; *especially* **:** an interior dividing wall
**3 :** one of the parts or sections of a whole

²**partition** *transitive verb* (1741)
**1 a :** to divide into parts or shares **b :** to divide (as a country) into two or more territorial units having separate political status
**2 :** to separate or divide by a partition (as a wall) — often used with *off*
— **par·ti·tion·er** \-'ti-sh(ə-)nər\ *noun*

**par·ti·tion·ist** \-'ti-sh(ə-)nist\ *noun* (circa 1900)
**:** an advocate of political partition

**par·ti·tive** \'pär-tə-tiv\ *adjective* (14th century)
**1 :** serving to part or divide into parts
**2 a :** of, relating to, or denoting a part ⟨a *partitive* construction⟩ **b :** serving to indicate the whole of which a part is specified ⟨*partitive* genitive⟩
— **par·ti·tive·ly** *adverb*

**part·let** \'pärt-lət\ *noun* [Middle English (Scots) *patelet*, from Middle French *patelette*, from diminutive of *patte* paw] (1519)
**:** a 16th century chemisette with a band or collar

**part·ly** \'pärt-lē\ *adverb* (1523)
**:** in some measure or degree **:** PARTIALLY

¹**part·ner** \'pärt-nər *also* 'pärd-\ *noun* [Middle English *partener*, alteration of *parcener*, from Anglo-French, coparcener — more at PARCENER] (14th century)
**1** *archaic* **:** one that shares **:** PARTAKER
**2 a :** one associated with another especially in an action **:** ASSOCIATE, COLLEAGUE **b :** either of two persons who dance together **c :** one of two or more persons who play together in a game against an opposing side **d :** either of two people living together; *especially* **:** SPOUSE
**3 :** a member of a partnership; *also* **:** such membership
**4 :** one of the heavy timbers that strengthen a ship's deck to support a mast — usually used in plural
— **part·ner·less** \-ləs\ *adjective*

²**partner** (1611)
*transitive verb*
**1 :** to join or associate with another as partner
**2 :** to provide with a partner
*intransitive verb*
**:** to act as a partner

**partners desk** *noun* (1946)
**:** a large desk with an open kneehole which allows use of the desk by two people seated opposite each other

**part·ner·ship** \-,ship\ *noun* (1576)
**1 :** the state of being a partner **:** PARTICIPATION
**2 a :** a legal relation existing between two or more persons contractually associated as joint principals in a business **b :** the persons joined together in a partnership
**3 :** a relationship resembling a legal partnership and usually involving close cooperation between parties having specified and joint rights and responsibilities

**part of speech** (1509)
**:** a traditional class of words distinguished according to the kind of idea denoted and the function performed in a sentence

**par·ton** \'pär-,tän\ *noun* [*particle* + ²-*on*] (1969)
**:** a hypothetical particle (as a quark or gluon) that is held to be a constituent of hadrons

**par·tridge** \'pär-trij, *dialect* 'pa-trij\ *noun, plural* **partridge** *or* **par·tridg·es** [Middle English *partrich*, modification of Old French *perdris*, modification of Latin *perdic-, perdix*, from Greek *perdik-, perdix*] (14th century)
**1 :** any of various typically medium-sized stout-bodied Old World gallinaceous game birds (*Perdix, Alectoris*, and related genera) with variegated plumage
**2 :** any of numerous gallinaceous birds (as the American ruffed grouse or bobwhite) somewhat like the Old World partridges in size, habits, or value as game

**par·tridge·ber·ry** \-,ber-ē\ *noun* (1714)
**:** an American trailing evergreen plant (*Mitchella repens*) of the madder family with insipid scarlet berries; *also* **:** its fruit

**part–song** \'pärt-,sȯŋ\ *noun* (1850)
**:** a usually unaccompanied song consisting of two or more voice parts with one part carrying the melody

**partridge 1**

**part–time** \'pärt-'tīm\ *adjective* (1891)
**:** involving or working less than customary or standard hours ⟨a *part-time* job⟩ ⟨*part-time* students⟩
— **part–time** *adverb*
— **part–tim·er** \-,tī-mər, -'tī-\ *noun*

¹**par·tu·ri·ent** \pär-'tur-ē-ənt, -'tyur-\ *adjective* [Latin *parturient-, parturiens*, present participle of *parturire* to be in labor, from *parere* to give birth to — more at PARE] (1592)
**1 :** bringing forth or about to bring forth young
**2 :** of or relating to parturition

²**parturient** *noun* (1947)
**:** a parturient individual

**par·tu·ri·tion** \,pär-chə-'ri-shən, ,pär-tyu-, ,pär-tə-\ *noun* [Late Latin *parturition-, parturitio*, from Latin *parturire*] (1646)
**:** the action or process of giving birth to offspring

**part·way** \'pärt-'wā\ *adverb* (1859)
**1 :** to some extent **:** PARTIALLY, PARTLY
**2 :** at a point in the way or distance ⟨*partway* through the trip they met some friends⟩

¹**par·ty** \'pär-tē\ *noun, plural* **parties** [Middle English *partie* part, party, from Old French, from *partir* to divide — more at PART] (14th century)
**1 :** a person or group taking one side of a question, dispute, or contest
**2 :** a group of persons organized for the purpose of directing the policies of a government
**3 :** a person or group participating in an action or affair ⟨mountain-climbing *party*⟩ ⟨a *party* to the transaction⟩
**4 :** a particular individual **:** PERSON ⟨an old *party* approaching 80⟩
**5 :** a detail of soldiers
**6 :** a social gathering; *also* **:** the entertainment provided for it
— **party** *adjective*

²**party** *intransitive verb* **par·tied; par·ty·ing** (1919)
**:** to attend or give parties; *broadly* **:** REVEL 1
— **par·ty·er** \-tē-ər\ *noun*

**party line** *noun* (1834)
**1 :** the policy or practice of a political party
**2 :** a single telephone circuit connecting two or more subscribers with the exchange — called also *party wire*
**3 :** the principles or policies of an individual or organization; *also* **:** the explanation or interpretation usually put forth ⟨the *party line* that her mother was a saint —Leslie Bennetts⟩
— **par·ty–lin·er** \,pär-tē-'lī-nər\ *noun*

**party poop·er** \-'pü-pər\ *noun* [³*poop* + -*er*] (1954)
**:** one who refuses to join in the fun of a party; *broadly* **:** one who refuses to go along with everyone else

**party wall** *noun* (circa 1798)
**:** a wall which divides two adjoining properties and in which each of the owners shares the rights

**pa·rure** \pə-'rur\ *noun* [French, literally, adornment, from Old French *pareure*, from *parer* to prepare, adorn — more at PARE] (1818)
**:** a matched set of ornaments (as jewelry)

**par value** *noun* (1807)
**:** PAR 1b(1)

**par·ve** \'pär-və\ *variant of* PAREVE

**par·ve·nu** \'pär-və-ˌnü, -ˌnyü\ *noun, plural* **-nus** \-ˌn(y)üz\ [French, from past participle of *parvenir* to arrive, from Latin *pervenire*, from *per* through + *venire* to come — more at FOR, COME] (1802)
: one that has recently or suddenly risen to an unaccustomed position of wealth or power and has not yet gained the prestige, dignity, or manner associated with it
— **parvenu** *adjective*

**par·ve·nue** \-ˌnü, -ˌnyü\ *noun* [French, from *parvenue,* feminine of *parvenum,* past participle] (1826)
: a woman who is a parvenu
— **parvenue** *adjective*

**par·vis** *also* **par·vise** \'pär-vəs\ *noun* [Middle English *parvis,* from Middle French, modification of Late Latin *paradisus* enclosed park — more at PARADISE] (14th century)
**1** : a court or enclosed space before a building (as a church)
**2** : a single portico or colonnade before a church

**par·vo** \'pär-ˌvō\ *noun* (1980)
: PARVOVIRUS 2

**par·vo·vi·rus** \'pär-vō-ˌvī-rəs\ *noun* [New Latin, from Latin *parvus* small (akin to Greek *pauros* small, *paid-, pais* child) + New Latin *-o-* + *virus* — more at FEW] (1965)
**1** : any of a group of small single-stranded DNA viruses pathogenic for vertebrates
**2** : a highly contagious febrile disease of dogs that is caused by a parvovirus and marked by loss of appetite, lethargy, often bloody diarrhea and vomiting, and sometimes death

**pas** \'pä\ *noun, plural* **pas** \'pä(z)\ [French, from Latin *passus* step — more at PACE] (1707)
**1** : the right of precedence
**2** : a dance step or combination of steps

**pas·cal** \pas-'kal, päs-'käl\ *noun* [Blaise *Pascal*] (1956)
**1** : a unit of pressure in the meter-kilogram-second system equivalent to one newton per square meter
**2** *usually P capitalized or all capitals* : a structured computer programming language developed from Algol and designed to process both numerical and textual data

**Pas·cal's triangle** \pas-'kalz-, päs-'kälz-\ *noun* (1886)
: a system of numbers triangularly arranged in rows that consist of the coefficients in the expansion of $(a + b)^n$ for $n = 0, 1, 2, 3, \ldots$

**Pasch** \'pask\ *also* **Pas·cha** \'päs-kə\ *noun* [Middle English *pasche* Passover, Easter, from Old French, from Late Latin *pascha,* from Late Greek, from Greek, Passover, from Hebrew *pesaḥ*] (12th century)
**1** : EASTER
**2** : PASSOVER
— **pas·chal** \'pas-kəl\ *adjective*

**paschal full moon** *noun* (1892)
: the 14th day of a lunar month occurring on or next after March 21 according to a fixed set of ecclesiastical calendar rules and without regard to the real moon

**Paschal Lamb** *noun* (15th century)
: AGNUS DEI 2

**pas de bour·rée** \ˌpä-də-bu̇-'rā\ *noun, plural* **pas de bourrée** \*same*\ *or* **pas de bour·rées** \-'rā(z)\ [French, literally, bourrée step] (1897)
: a walking or running ballet step usually executed on the points of the toes

**pas de chat** \-'sha\ *noun, plural* **pas de chat** \*same*\ [French, literally, cat's step] (1914)
: a forward leap in ballet

**pas de deux** \-'dœ(r), -'dü\ *noun, plural* **pas de deux** \-'dœr(z), -'də(z), -'dü(z)\ [French, literally, step for two] (circa 1762)
**1** : a dance or figure for two performers

**2** : an intricate relationship or activity involving two parties or things

**pas de qua·tre** \-'kat, -'ka-trə, -'kätrᵊ\ *noun, plural* **pas de quatre** \*same*\ [French, literally, step for four] (1884)
: a dance or figure for four performers

**pas de trois** \-'trwä, -'twä\ *noun, plural* **pas de trois** \-'trwä(z), -'twä(z)\ [French, literally, step for three] (circa 1762)
: a dance or figure for three performers

**pa·se** \'pä-(ˌ)sā\ *noun* [Spanish, literally, feint, from *pase* let him pass, from *pasar* to pass, from (assumed) Vulgar Latin *passare*] (1937)
: a movement of a cape by a matador in drawing a bull and taking his charge

**pa·seo** \pə-'sā-(ˌ)ō, pä-\ *noun, plural* **pa·se·os** [Spanish, from *pasear* to take a stroll, from *paso* passage, step, from Latin *passus*] (1832)
**1 a** : a leisurely stroll : PROMENADE **b** : a public walk or boulevard
**2** : a formal entrance march of bullfighters into an arena

**¹pash** \'pash\ *transitive verb* [Middle English *passhen*] (14th century)
*dialect English* : SMASH

**²pash** *noun* [origin unknown] (1611)
*dialect English* : HEAD

**pa·sha** \'pä-shə, 'pa-; pə-'shä, -'shò\ *noun* [Turkish *paşa*] (1646)
: a man of high rank or office (as in Turkey or northern Africa)

**Pash·to** \'pəsh-(ˌ)tō\ *noun* [Pashto *pašto*] (1784)
: the Iranian language of the Pashtuns

**Pash·tun** \ˌpəsh-'tün\ *noun, plural* **Pashtuns** *or* **Pashtun** (1815)
: a member of a people of eastern and southern Afghanistan and adjacent parts of Pakistan

**Pa·siph·aë** \pə-'si-fə-ˌē\ *noun* [Latin, from Greek *Pasiphaē*]
: the wife of Minos and mother of the Minotaur by a white bull

**pasque·flow·er** \'pask-ˌflau̇(-ə)r\ *noun* [modification of Middle French *passefleur,* from *passer* to pass (from Old French) + *fleur* flower, from Latin *flor-, flos* — more at BLOW] (1597)
: any of several low perennial herbs (genus *Anemone*) of the buttercup family with palmately compound leaves and large usually white or purple early spring flowers

**pas·qui·nade** \ˌpas-kwə-'nād\ *noun* [Middle French, from Italian *pasquinata,* from *Pasquino,* name given to a statue in Rome on which lampoons were posted] (1658)
**1** : a lampoon posted in a public place
**2** : satirical writing : SATIRE
— **pasquinade** *transitive verb*

**¹pass** \'pas\ *verb* [Middle English, from Old French *passer,* from (assumed) Vulgar Latin *passare,* from Latin *passus* step — more at PACE] (13th century)
*intransitive verb*
**1** : MOVE, PROCEED, GO
**2 a** : to go away : DEPART **b** : DIE — often used with *on*
**3 a** : to move in a path so as to approach and continue beyond something : move past; *especially* : to move past another vehicle going in the same direction **b** : to run the normal course — used of time or a period of time ⟨the hours *pass* quickly⟩
**4 a** : to go or make one's way through ⟨allow no one to *pass*⟩ **b** : to go uncensored, unchallenged, or seemingly unnoticed ⟨let the remark *pass*⟩
**5** : to go from one quality, state, or form to another ⟨*passes* from a liquid to a gaseous state⟩
**6 a** : to sit in inquest or judgment **b** (1) : to render a decision, verdict, or opinion ⟨the court *passed* on the legality of wiretapping⟩ (2) : to become legally rendered ⟨judgment *passed* for the plaintiff⟩
**7** : to go from the control, ownership, or possession of one person or group to that of an-

other ⟨the throne *passed* to the king's son⟩ ⟨title *passes* to the buyer upon payment in full⟩
**8 a** : HAPPEN, OCCUR **b** : to take place or be exchanged as or in a social, personal, or business interaction ⟨words *passed*⟩
**9 a** : to become approved by a legislature or body empowered to sanction or reject ⟨the proposal *passed*⟩ **b** : to undergo an inspection, test, or course of study successfully
**10 a** : to serve as a medium of exchange **b** : to be accepted or regarded ⟨drivel that *passes* for literature⟩ **c** : to identify oneself or be identified as something one isn't ⟨tried to *pass* as an adult⟩ ⟨Mom could *pass* as my sister⟩
**11 a** *obsolete* : to make a pass in fencing **b** : to throw or hit a ball or puck to a teammate — often used with *off*
**12 a** : to decline to bid, double, or redouble in a card game **b** : to withdraw from the current poker pot
*transitive verb*
**1** : to go beyond: as **a** : SURPASS, EXCEED ⟨*passes* all expectations⟩ **b** : to advance or develop beyond **c** : to go past (one moving in the same direction)
**2** : to omit a regularly scheduled declaration and payment of (a dividend)
**3 a** : to go across, over, or through : CROSS **b** : to live through (as an experience or peril) : UNDERGO **c** : to go through (as a test) successfully
**4 a** : to secure the approval of ⟨the bill *passed* the Senate⟩ **b** : to cause or permit to win approval or legal or official sanction ⟨*pass* a law⟩ **c** : to give approval or a passing grade to ⟨*pass* the students⟩
**5 a** : to let (as time or a period of time) go by especially while involved in a leisure activity ⟨I'll read to *pass* the time⟩ **b** : to let go unnoticed : OVERLOOK, DISREGARD
**6 a** : PLEDGE **b** : to transfer the right to or property in ⟨*pass* title to a house⟩
**7 a** : to put in circulation ⟨*pass* bad checks⟩ **b** (1) : to transfer or transmit from one to another (2) : to relay or communicate (as information) to another **c** : to cause or enable to go : TRANSPORT **d** : to throw or hit (a ball or puck) especially to a teammate
**8 a** : to pronounce (as a sentence or opinion) especially judicially **b** : UTTER ⟨*passed* a cutting remark⟩
**9 a** : to cause or permit to go past or through a barrier **b** : to move or cause to move in a particular manner or direction ⟨*passed* my hand over my face⟩ ⟨*pass* the rope through the loop⟩ **c** : to cause to march or go by in order ⟨*pass* the troops in review⟩
**10** : to emit or discharge from a bodily part and especially the bowels
**11 a** : to give a base on balls to **b** : to hit a ball past (an opponent) in a game (as tennis)
— **pass·er** *noun*
— **pass muster** : to gain approval or acceptance
— **pass the buck** : to shift a responsibility to someone else
— **pass the hat** : to take up a collection for money
— **pass the time of day** : to exchange greetings or engage in pleasant conversation

**²pass** *noun* [Middle English, from Middle French *pas,* from Latin *passus*] (14th century)
**1** : a means (as an opening, road, or channel) by which a barrier may be passed or access to a place may be gained; *especially* : a low place in a mountain range
**2** : a position to be held usually against odds

**³pass** *noun* [¹pass] (1523)
**1** : REALIZATION ⟨brought his dream to *pass*⟩
**2** : the act or an instance of passing : PASSAGE

\ə\ **abut** \ᵊ\ **kitten** \ər\ **further** \a\ **ash** \ā\ **ace** \ä\ **mop, mar** \au̇\ **out** \ch\ **chin** \e\ **bet** \ē\ **easy** \g\ **go** \i\ **hit** \ī\ **ice** \j\ **job** \ŋ\ **sing** \ō\ **go** \ȯ\ **law** \ȯi\ **boy** \th\ **thin** \t̲h̲\ **the** \ü\ **loot** \u̇\ **foot** \y\ **yet** \zh\ **vision**    *see also* Guide to Pronunciation

**3 :** a usually distressing or bad state of affairs ⟨what has brought you to such a *pass*?⟩
**4 a :** a written permission to move about freely in a place or to leave or enter it **b :** a written leave of absence from a military post or station for a brief period **c :** a permit or ticket allowing free transportation or free admission
**5** *archaic* **:** a thrust or lunge in fencing
**6 a :** a transference of objects by sleight of hand or other deceptive means **b :** a moving of the hands over or along something
**7** *archaic* **:** an ingenious sally (as of wit)
**8 :** the passing of an examination or course of study; *also* **:** the mark or certification of such passing
**9 :** a single complete mechanical operation; *also* **:** a single complete cycle of operations (as for processing, manufacturing, or printing)
**10 a** (1) **:** a transfer of a ball or a puck from one player to another on the same team (2) **:** a ball or puck so transferred **b :** PASSING SHOT
**11 :** BASE ON BALLS
**12 :** an election not to bid, bet, or draw an additional card in a card game
**13 :** a throw of dice in the game of craps that wins the bet for the shooter — compare ³CRAP 2, MISSOUT
**14 :** a single passage or movement (as of an airplane) over a place or toward a target
**15 a :** EFFORT, TRY **b :** a sexually inviting gesture or approach
**16 :** PASE

**pass·able** \'pa-sə-bəl\ *adjective* (15th century)
**1 a :** capable of being passed, crossed, or traveled on ⟨*passable* roads⟩ **b :** capable of being freely circulated
**2 :** good enough **:** ADEQUATE
**— pass·ably** \-blē\ *adverb*

**pas·sa·ca·glia** \ˌpä-sə-ˈkäl-yə, ˌpa-sə-ˈkal-yə\ *noun* [modification of Spanish *pasacalle*, from *pasar* to pass + *calle* street, from Latin *callis* path — more at PASE] (1659)
**1 a :** an old Italian or Spanish dance tune **b :** an instrumental musical composition consisting of variations usually on a ground bass in moderately slow triple time
**2 :** an old dance performed to a passacaglia

**pas·sa·do** \pə-ˈsä-(ˌ)dō\ *noun, plural* **-dos** *or* **-does** [modification of French *passade* (from Italian *passata*) or Italian *passata*, from *passare* to pass, from (assumed) Vulgar Latin] (1588)
*archaic* **:** a thrust in fencing with one foot advanced

**¹pas·sage** \'pa-sij\ *noun* (13th century)
**1 a :** a way of exit or entrance **:** a road, path, channel, or course by which something passes **b :** a corridor or lobby giving access to the different rooms or parts of a building or apartment
**2 a :** the action or process of passing from one place, condition, or stage to another **b :** DEATH 1 **c :** a continuous movement or flow ⟨the *passage* of time⟩
**3 a** (1) **:** a specific act of traveling or passing especially by sea or air (2) **:** a privilege of conveyance as a passenger **:** ACCOMMODATIONS **b :** the passing of a legislative measure or law **:** ENACTMENT
**4 :** a right, liberty, or permission to pass
**5 a :** something that happens or is done **:** INCIDENT **b :** something that takes place between two persons mutually
**6 a :** a usually brief portion of a written work or speech that is relevant to a point under discussion or noteworthy for content or style **b :** a phrase or short section of a musical composition **c :** a detail of a work of art (as a painting)
**7 :** the act or action of passing something or undergoing a passing
**8 :** incubation of a pathogen (as a virus) in culture, a living organism, or a developing egg

**²passage** *verb* **pas·saged; pas·sag·ing** (1824)
*intransitive verb*

**:** to go past or across **:** CROSS
*transitive verb*
**:** to subject to passage ⟨*passaged* a virus⟩

**pas·sage·way** \-ˌwā\ *noun* (1649)
**:** a way that allows passage

**pas·sage·work** \-ˌwərk\ *noun* (1865)
**:** a section of a musical composition characteristically unimportant thematically and consisting especially of ornamental figures

**pas·sant** \'pa-sᵊnt\ *adjective* [Middle English *passaunt*, from Middle French *passant*, from present participle of *passer* to pass] (15th century)
**:** walking with the farther forepaw raised — used of a heraldic animal

**pass away** *intransitive verb* (13th century)
**1 :** to go out of existence
**2 :** DIE 1

**pass·band** \'pas-ˌband\ *noun* (1922)
**:** a band of frequencies (as in a radio circuit or a light filter) that is transmitted with maximum efficiency

**pass·book** \-ˌbu̇k\ *noun* (1828)
**:** BANKBOOK

**pass degree** *noun* (1868)
**:** a bachelor's degree without honors that is taken at a British university

**pas·sé** \pa-ˈsā\ *adjective* [French, from past participle of *passer*] (1775)
**1 :** past one's prime
**2 a :** OUTMODED **b :** behind the times

**passed ball** *noun* (1861)
**:** a baseball pitch not hit by the batter that passes the catcher when it should have been caught and allows a base runner to advance — compare WILD PITCH

**passed pawn** *noun* (1797)
**:** a chess pawn that has no enemy pawn in front of it on its own or an adjacent file

**pas·sel** \'pa-səl\ *noun* [alteration of *parcel*] (1835)
**:** a large number or amount ◆

**passe·men·te·rie** \pas-ˈmen-t(ə-)rē\ *noun* [French, from *passement* ornamental braid, from *passer*] (1794)
**:** a fancy edging or trimming made of braid, cord, gimp, beading, or metallic thread

**pas·sen·ger** \'pa-sᵊn-jər\ *noun, often attributive* [Middle English *passager*, from Middle French, from *passager*, adjective, passing, from *passage* act of passing, from Old French, from *passer*] (14th century)
**1 :** WAYFARER
**2 :** a traveler in a public or private conveyance

**passenger pigeon** *noun* (1802)
**:** an extinct but formerly abundant North American migratory pigeon (*Ectopistes migratorius*)

**passe–par·tout** \ˌpas-pər-ˈtü, -ˌpär-\ *noun* [French, from *passe partout* pass everywhere] (1675)
**1 :** MASTER KEY
**2 a :** ⁵MAT **b :** a method of framing in which a picture, a mat, a glass, and a back (as of cardboard) are held together by strips of paper or cloth pasted over the edges
**3 :** a strong paper gummed on one side and used especially for mounting pictures

**pass·er·by** \ˌpa-sər-ˈbī, 'pa-sər-\ *noun, plural* **pass·ers·by** \-sərz-\ (1568)
**:** one who passes by

**pas·ser·ine** \'pa-sə-ˌrīn\ *adjective* [Latin *passerinus* of sparrows, from *passer* sparrow] (1776)
**:** of or relating to the largest order (Passeriformes) of birds which includes more than half of all living birds and consists chiefly of altricial songbirds of perching habits — compare OSCINE
**— passerine** *noun*

**pas seul** \pä-ˈsəl, -ˈsər-(ə)l\ *noun* [French, literally, solo step] (1813)
**:** a solo dance or dance figure

**pass–fail** \'pas-ˈfā(ə)l\ *adjective* (1959)

**:** being a system of grading whereby the grades "pass" and "fail" replace the traditional letter grades
**— pass–fail** *noun*

**pas·si·ble** \'pa-sə-bəl\ *adjective* [Middle English, from Middle French, from Late Latin *passibilis*, from Latin *passus*, past participle of *pati* to suffer — more at PATIENT] (14th century)
**:** capable of feeling or suffering

**pas·sim** \'pa-səm; 'pa-ˌsim, 'pä-\ *adverb* [Latin, from *passus* scattered, from past participle of *pandere* to spread — more at FATHOM] (1803)
**:** HERE AND THERE

**¹pass·ing** \'pa-siŋ\ *noun* (14th century)
**:** the act of one that passes or causes to pass; *especially* **:** DEATH 1
**— in passing :** by the way **:** INCIDENTALLY

**²passing** *adjective* (14th century)
**1 :** going by or past ⟨a *passing* pedestrian⟩
**2 :** having a brief duration ⟨a *passing* whim⟩
**3** *obsolete* **:** SURPASSING
**4 :** SUPERFICIAL ⟨a *passing* acquaintance⟩ ⟨a *passing* resemblance⟩
**5 a :** of, relating to, or used in or for the act or process of passing ⟨*passing* lanes⟩ **b :** given on satisfactory completion of an examination or course of study ⟨a *passing* grade⟩

**³passing** *adverb* (14th century)
**:** to a surpassing degree **:** EXCEEDINGLY ⟨*passing* strange⟩

**passing note** *noun* (1730)
**:** a nonharmonic tone interposed between essential harmonic tones of adjacent chords — called also *passing tone*

**passing shot** *noun* (circa 1949)
**:** a stroke (as in tennis) that drives the ball to one side and beyond the reach of an opponent

**pas·sion** \'pa-shən\ *noun* [Middle English, from Old French, from Late Latin *passion-*, *passio* suffering, being acted upon, from Latin *pati* to suffer — more at PATIENT] (13th century)
**1** *often capitalized* **a :** the sufferings of Christ between the night of the Last Supper and his death **b :** an oratorio based on a gospel narrative of the Passion
**2** *obsolete* **:** SUFFERING
**3 :** the state or capacity of being acted on by external agents or forces
**4 a** (1) **:** EMOTION ⟨his ruling *passion* is greed⟩ (2) *plural* **:** the emotions as distinguished from reason **b :** intense, driving, or overmastering feeling or conviction **c :** an outbreak of anger

◇ WORD HISTORY
**passel** The loss of the sound \r\ before \s\ inside a word probably took place in most areas of England during the late Middle Ages. (This change is distinct from the more general loss of \r\ before all consonants and at the end of words that now characterizes most people's speech in England and local speech in parts of the U.S.) In some words, such as *bass*, the fish, the pronunciation without \r\ has become standard and is reflected in spelling. In most words containing this sequence, however, the influence of orthography and other factors have made the \r\ forms standard and the forms without \r\, such as *fust* for *first* and *hoss* for *horse*, a mark of nonstandard or folk speech. In yet another set of words the form without \r\ is associated with distinctive senses of the source word or has developed new senses. The word *passel*, for example, meaning "large number," is akin to the "group" sense of *parcel* (as in a *parcel of lies*), but *passel* is used for none of the other senses of *parcel*, and, though it occurs in all varieties of writing, still has a slightly folksy tinge.

**5 a :** ardent affection **:** LOVE **b :** a strong liking or desire for or devotion to some activity, object, or concept **c :** sexual desire **d :** an object of desire or deep interest ☆
— **pas·sion·less** \-ləs\ *adjective*

**pas·sion·al** \'pa-shə-n°l, 'pash-nəl\ *adjective* (15th century)
**:** of, relating to, or marked by passion

**pas·sion·ate** \'pa-sh(ə-)nət\ *adjective* (15th century)
**1 a :** easily aroused to anger **b :** filled with anger **:** ANGRY
**2 a :** capable of, affected by, or expressing intense feeling **b :** ENTHUSIASTIC, ARDENT
**3 :** swayed by or affected with sexual desire
**synonym** see IMPASSIONED
— **pas·sion·ate·ly** *adverb*
— **pas·sion·ate·ness** *noun*

**pas·sion·flow·er** \'pa-shən-,flaù(-ə)r\ *noun* [from the fancied resemblance of parts of the flower to the instruments of Christ's crucifixion] (1633)
**:** any of a genus (*Passiflora* of the family Passifloraceae, the passionflower family) of chiefly tropical woody tendriled climbing vines or erect herbs with usually showy flowers and pulpy often edible berries

**passionflower**

**passion fruit** *noun* (1752)
**:** the edible fruit of a passionflower

**Pas·sion·ist** \'pa-sh(ə-)nist\ *noun* [Italian *passionista*, from *passione* passion, from Late Latin *passion-, passio*] (1832)
**:** a member of a Roman Catholic mendicant order founded by Saint Paul of the Cross in Italy in 1720 and devoted chiefly to missionary work and retreats

**passion play** *noun, often 1st P capitalized* (1870)
**:** a dramatic representation of the scenes connected with the passion and crucifixion of Christ

**Passion Sunday** *noun* (14th century)
**:** the fifth Sunday in Lent

**Pas·sion·tide** \'pa-shən-,tīd\ *noun* (1847)
**:** the last two weeks of Lent

**Passion Week** *noun* (15th century)
**1 :** HOLY WEEK
**2 :** the week between Passion Sunday and Palm Sunday

**pas·siv·ate** \'pa-si-,vāt\ *transitive verb* **-at·ed; -at·ing** (1913)
**1 :** to make inactive or less reactive ⟨*passivate* the surface of steel by chemical treatment⟩
**2 :** to protect (as a solid-state device) against contamination by coating or surface treatment
— **pas·siv·ation** \,pa-si-'vā-shən\ *noun*

**¹pas·sive** \'pa-siv\ *adjective* [Middle English, from Latin *passivus*, from *passus*, past participle] (14th century)
**1 a** (1) **:** acted upon by an external agency (2) **:** receptive to outside impressions or influences **b** (1) **:** asserting that the grammatical subject of a verb is subjected to or affected by the action represented by that verb (2) **:** containing or yielding a passive verb form **c** (1) **:** lacking in energy or will **:** LETHARGIC (2) **:** tending not to take an active or dominant part **d :** induced by an outside agency ⟨*passive* exercise of a paralyzed leg⟩
**2 a :** not active or operating **:** INERT **b :** of, relating to, or making direct use of the sun's heat usually without the intervention of mechanical devices ⟨*passive* technique⟩ ⟨*passive* solar house⟩ **c :** LATENT **d** (1) **:** of, relating to, or characterized by a state of chemical inactivity; *especially* **:** resistant to corrosion (2) **:** not involving expenditure of chemical energy

⟨*passive* transport across a cell membrane⟩ **e :** *of an electronic element* **:** exhibiting no gain or control **f :** operating solely by means of the power of an input signal ⟨a *passive* communication satellite that reflects television signals⟩ **g :** relating to the detection of an object through its emission of energy
**3 a :** receiving or enduring without resistance **:** SUBMISSIVE **b :** existing or occurring without being active, open, or direct ⟨*passive* support⟩
**4 :** of, relating to, or being business activity in which the investor does not have immediate control over income
**synonym** see INACTIVE
— **pas·sive·ly** *adverb*
— **pas·sive·ness** *noun*
— **pas·siv·i·ty** \pa-'si-və-tē\ *noun*

**²passive** *noun* (1530)
**1 :** a passive verb form
**2 :** the passive voice of a language □

**passive immunity** *noun* (1895)
**:** immunity acquired by transfer of antibodies (as by injection of serum from an individual with active immunity)
— **passive immunization** *noun*

**passive resistance** *noun* (1819)
**:** resistance especially to a government or an occupying power characterized mainly by noncooperation

**passive restraint** *noun* (1970)
**:** a restraint (as a self-locking seat belt) that acts automatically to protect an automobile rider during a crash

**passive smoking** *noun* (1971)
**:** the involuntary inhalation of tobacco smoke (as from another's cigarette) especially by a nonsmoker

**passive transfer** *noun* (1935)
**:** a local transfer of skin sensitivity from an allergic to a normal person by injection of serum from the former that is used especially for identifying specific allergens when a high degree of allergic sensitivity is suspected

**pas·siv·ism** \'pa-si-,vi-zəm\ *noun* (1872)
**:** a passive attitude, behavior, or way of life
— **pas·siv·ist** \-vist\ *noun*

**pass·key** \'pas-,kē\ *noun* (circa 1817)
**1 :** MASTER KEY
**2 :** SKELETON KEY

**pass off** *transitive verb* (1799)
**1 :** to make public or offer for sale with intent to deceive
**2 :** to give a false identity or character to

**pass out** (1899)
*intransitive verb*
**1 :** DIE 1
**2 :** to lose consciousness
*transitive verb*
**:** to reject (a deal in bridge) as unplayable because everyone has passed on the first round of bidding

**Pass·over** \'pas-,ō-vər\ *noun* [from the exemption of the Israelites from the slaughter of the firstborn in Egypt (Exodus 12:23–27)] (1530)
**:** a Jewish holiday beginning on the 14th of Nisan and commemorating the Hebrews' liberation from slavery in Egypt

**pass over** *transitive verb* (14th century)
**1 :** to ignore in passing
**2 :** to pay no attention to the claims of **:** DISREGARD

**pass·port** \'pas-,pōrt, -,pȯrt\ *noun* [Middle English (Scots) *pasport*, from Middle French *passeport*, from *passer* to pass + *port* port, from Latin *portus* — more at FORD] (15th century)
**1 a :** a formal document issued by an authorized official of a country to one of its citizens that is usually necessary for exit from and reentry into the country, that allows the citizen to travel in a foreign country in accordance with visa requirements, and that requests pro-

tection for the citizen while abroad **b :** a license issued by a country permitting a foreign citizen to pass or take goods through its territory **:** SAFE-CONDUCT **c :** a document of identification required by law to be carried by persons residing or traveling within a country

---

☆ **SYNONYMS**
**Passion, fervor, ardor, enthusiasm, zeal** mean intense emotion compelling action. PASSION applies to an emotion that is deeply stirring or ungovernable ⟨was a slave to his *passions*⟩. FERVOR implies a warm and steady emotion ⟨read the poem aloud with great *fervor*⟩. ARDOR suggests warm and excited feeling likely to be fitful or short-lived ⟨the *ardor* of their honeymoon soon faded⟩. ENTHUSIASM applies to lively or eager interest in or admiration for a proposal, cause, or activity ⟨never showed much *enthusiasm* for sports⟩. ZEAL implies energetic and unflagging pursuit of an aim or devotion to a cause ⟨preaches with the *zeal* of the converted⟩. See in addition FEELING.

---

□ **USAGE**
**passive** A passive sentence is made from an active sentence with a transitive verb by a transformation which makes the direct object, or sometimes the indirect object, into the subject, changes the active verb to a past participle with a form of *be,* and relegates the original subject to the status of agent. This transformation throws emphasis on the original object and de-emphasizes the original subject. For instance we can change the active "I broke the vase" to the passive "The vase was broken by me." The agent is optional in a passive construction; we can shorten it to "The vase was broken." These characteristics are turned into liabilities by many critics, who disparage the passive as wordy, weak, evasive, or vague. But these are not faults of the construction; they are faults of the writer. When the agent is omitted, the passive sentence is shorter than the active. And there are many times when the agent is better omitted, as when the doer is unknown ⟨the bank *was robbed* last night⟩ or is unimportant ⟨lawn mowers should not *be left* outside in the rain⟩ or is too obvious to need mentioning ⟨Clinton *was elected* president⟩. Sometimes the agent wants to be omitted ⟨I am sorry to inform you that your request *has been denied*⟩; this is commonly true in scientific and business reports where the authors are not supposed to use first person pronouns. Perhaps the most important thing to keep in mind is focus. One can write either "The car hit a pedestrian" or "A pedestrian was hit by the car"; the choice should be governed by whether the reader is meant to focus on the car or the pedestrian. The passive is useful for generalizing ⟨people *are imprisoned* for years without trial, or *shot* in the back of the neck or *sent* to die of scurvy in Arctic lumber camps —George Orwell⟩. Had Orwell, who wrote "Never use the passive where you can use the active," meant to be specific, he would probably have begun with "The Soviet secret police imprison . . ." or something similar. The point to remember is that the passive need not be avoided—it is much less commonly used than the active anyway—but it should be used where it best serves the writer's purpose.

---

\ə\ abut  \ə\ kitten  \ər\ further  \a\ ash  \ā\ ace
\ä\ mop, mar  \aù\ out  \ch\ chin  \e\ bet  \ē\ easy
\g\ go  \i\ hit  \ī\ ice  \j\ job  \ŋ\ sing  \ō\ go
\ȯ\ law  \ȯi\ boy  \th\ thin  \t̠h\ the  \ü\ loot  \ù\ foot
\y\ yet  \zh\ vision   *see also* Guide to Pronunciation

**2 a :** a permission or authorization to go somewhere **b :** something that secures admission, acceptance, or attainment ⟨education as a *passport* to success⟩

**pass–through** *noun* (1951)
**1 :** the act, action, or process of offsetting increased costs by raising prices
**2 :** an opening in a wall between two rooms through which something (as dishes) may be passed

**pass up** *transitive verb* (1896)
**:** to let go by without accepting or taking advantage of ⟨*pass up* a chance for promotion⟩; *also :* DECLINE, REJECT

**pass·word** \'pas-,wərd\ *noun* (circa 1817)
**1 :** something that enables one to pass or gain admission: as **a :** a spoken word or phrase required to pass by a guard **b :** a sequence of characters required for access to a computer system
**2 :** WATCHWORD

**¹past** \'past\ *adjective* [Middle English, from past participle of *passen* to pass] (14th century)
**1 a :** AGO ⟨12 years *past*⟩ **b :** just gone or elapsed ⟨for the *past* few months⟩
**2 :** having existed or taken place in a period before the present **:** BYGONE
**3 :** of, relating to, or constituting a verb tense that is expressive of elapsed time and that in English is usually formed by internal vowel change (as in *sang*) or by the addition of a suffix (as in *laughed*)
**4 :** having served as a specified officer in an organization ⟨*past* president⟩

**²past** *preposition* (14th century)
**1 a :** beyond the age for or of ⟨*past* playing with dolls⟩ **b :** AFTER ⟨half *past* two⟩
**2 a :** at the farther side of **:** BEYOND **b :** in a course or direction going close to and then beyond ⟨drove *past* the house⟩
**3** *obsolete* **:** more than
**4 :** beyond the capacity, range, or sphere of ⟨*past* belief⟩

**³past** *noun* (1590)
**1 a :** time gone by **b :** something that happened or was done in the past ⟨regret the *past*⟩
**2 a :** the past tense of a language **b :** a verb form in the past tense
**3 :** a past life, history, or course of action; *especially :* one that is kept secret
— **past·less** \'pas(t)-ləs\ *adjective*

**⁴past** *adverb* (1784)
**:** so as to reach and go beyond a point near at hand

**pas·ta** \'päs-tə *also* 'pas-\ *noun* [Italian, from Late Latin] (1874)
**1 :** paste in processed form (as spaghetti) or in the form of fresh dough (as ravioli)
**2 :** a dish of cooked pasta

**¹paste** \'pāst\ *noun* [Middle English, from Middle French, from Late Latin *pasta* dough, paste] (14th century)
**1 a :** a dough that contains a considerable proportion of fat and is used for pastry crust or fancy rolls **b :** a confection made by evaporating fruit with sugar or by flavoring a gelatin, starch, or gum arabic preparation **c :** a smooth food product made by evaporation or grinding ⟨tomato *paste*⟩ ⟨almond *paste*⟩ **d :** a shaped dough (as spaghetti or ravioli) prepared from semolina, farina, or wheat flour
**2 :** a soft plastic mixture or composition: as **a :** a preparation usually of flour or starch and water used as an adhesive or a vehicle for mordant or color **b :** clay or a clay mixture used in making pottery or porcelain
**3 :** a brilliant glass of high lead content used for the manufacture of artificial gems

**²paste** *transitive verb* **past·ed; past·ing** (1561)
**1 :** to cause to adhere by or as if by paste **:** STICK
**2 :** to cover with something pasted on

**³paste** *transitive verb* **past·ed; past·ing** [alteration of *baste*] (1846)

**1 :** to strike hard at
**2 :** to beat or defeat soundly

**¹paste·board** \'pās(t)-,bōrd, -,bȯrd\ *noun* (1562)
**1 :** a solid paperboard with a paper facing; *broadly :* PAPERBOARD
**2 :** TICKET

**²pasteboard** *adjective* (1599)
**1 :** made of pasteboard
**2 :** SHAM, UNSUBSTANTIAL ⟨prefabricated plots and *pasteboard* heroes —Peter Andrews⟩

**paste·down** \-,daún\ *noun* (circa 1888)
**:** the outer leaf of an endpaper that is pasted down to the inside of the front or back cover of a book

**¹pas·tel** \pa-'stel\ *noun* [French, from Italian *pastello*, from Late Latin *pastellus* woad, from diminutive of *pasta*] (1662)
**1 :** a paste made of powdered pigment ranging from pale to deep colors and used for making crayons; *also :* a crayon made of such paste
**2 a :** a drawing in pastel **b :** the process or art of drawing with pastels
**3 :** a light literary sketch
**4 :** any of various pale or light colors

**²pastel** *adjective* (1884)
**1 a :** of or relating to a pastel **b :** made with pastels
**2 :** pale and light in color
**3 :** lacking in body or vigor

**pas·tel·ist** *or* **pas·tel·list** \-'ste-list\ *noun* (1881)
**:** an artist who works with pastels

**pas·tern** \'pas-tərn\ *noun* [Middle French *pasturon*, from *pasture* tether attached to a horse's foot, alteration of (assumed) Old French *pastoire*, from Medieval Latin *pastoria*, from Latin, feminine of *pastorius* of a herdsman, from *pastor* herdsman — more at PASTOR] (circa 1530)
**1 :** a part of the foot of an equine extending from the fetlock to the top of the hoof — see HORSE illustration
**2 :** a part of the leg of an animal other than an equine that corresponds to the pastern

**paste·up** \'pāst-,əp\ *noun* (circa 1930)
**:** MECHANICAL; *also :* the process of making mechanicals

**pas·teur·ise** *British variant of* PASTEURIZE

**pas·teur·i·za·tion** \,pas-chə-rə-'zā-shən, ,pas-tyə-, -tə-\ *noun* (1886)
**1 :** partial sterilization of a substance and especially a liquid (as milk) at a temperature and for a period of exposure that destroys objectionable organisms without major chemical alteration of the substance
**2 :** partial sterilization of perishable food products (as fruit or fish) with radiation (as gamma rays)

**pas·teur·ize** \'pas-chə-,rīz, 'pas-tyə-, -tə-\ *transitive verb* **-ized; -iz·ing** [Louis *Pasteur*] (1881)
**:** to subject to pasteurization
— **pas·teur·iz·er** *noun*

**Pasteur treatment** *noun* (1926)
**:** a method of aborting rabies by stimulating production of antibodies through successive inoculations with attenuated virus of gradually increasing strength

**pas·tic·cio** \pa-'stē-ch(ē-,)ō, pä-\ *noun, plural* **-ci** \-(,)chē\ *or* **-cios** [Italian, literally, pasty, from (assumed) Vulgar Latin *pasticium*, from Late Latin *pasta*] (1752)
**:** PASTICHE

**pas·tiche** \pas-'tēsh, päs-\ *noun* [French, from Italian *pasticcio*] (1878)
**1 :** a literary, artistic, musical, or architectural work that imitates the style of previous work; *also :* such stylistic imitation
**2 a :** a musical, literary, or artistic composition made up of selections from different works **:** POTPOURRI **b :** HODGEPODGE
— **pas·ti·cheur** \,pas-tē-'shər, ,päs-\ *noun*

**past·ies** \'pās-tēz\ *noun plural* [²*paste*] (circa 1954)

**:** small round coverings for a woman's nipples worn especially by a stripteaser

**pas·tille** \pas-'tē(ə)l\ *also* **pas·til** \'pas-t°l\ *noun* [French *pastille*, from Latin *pastillus* small loaf, lozenge; akin to Latin *panis* bread — more at FOOD] (1658)
**1 :** a small mass of aromatic paste for fumigating or scenting the air of a room
**2 :** an aromatic or medicated lozenge **:** TROCHE

**pas·time** \'pas-,tīm\ *noun* (15th century)
**:** something that amuses and serves to make time pass agreeably **:** DIVERSION

**pas·ti·na** \'päs-tē-nə\ *noun* [Italian, diminutive of *pasta* pasta] (circa 1948)
**:** very small bits of pasta used in soup or broth

**pas·tis** \päs-'tēs\ *noun* [French, from French dialect (Marseilles), literally, jumble, kind of pastry, from Provençal, from Old Provençal *pastitz* cake, from (assumed) Vulgar Latin *pasticium*] (1926)
**:** a French liqueur flavored with aniseed

**past master** *noun* (1762)
**1 :** one who has held the office of worshipful master in a lodge of Freemasons or of master in a guild, club, or society
**2** [alteration of *passed master*] **:** one who is expert **:** ADEPT

**past·ness** \'pas(t)-nəs\ *noun* (1829)
**1 :** the quality or state of being past
**2 :** the subjective quality of something being remembered rather than immediately experienced

**¹pas·tor** \'pas-tər\ *noun* [Middle English *pastour*, from Middle French, from Latin *pastor* herdsman, from *pascere* to feed — more at FOOD] (14th century)
**:** a spiritual overseer; *especially :* a clergyman serving a local church or parish
— **pas·tor·ship** \-,ship\ *noun*

**²pastor** *transitive verb* **pas·tored; pas·tor·ing** \-t(ə-)riŋ\ (1623)
**:** to serve as pastor of (as a church)

**³pas·tor** \päs-'tór\ *noun* [Spanish, from Latin] (1849)
*chiefly Southwest :* HERDSMAN

**¹pas·to·ral** \'pas-t(ə-)rəl\ *adjective* [Middle English, from Latin *pastoralis*, from *pastor* herdsman] (15th century)
**1 a** (1) **:** of, relating to, or composed of shepherds or herdsmen (2) **:** devoted to or based on livestock raising **b :** of or relating to the countryside **:** not urban **c :** portraying or expressive of the life of shepherds or country people especially in an idealized and conventionalized manner ⟨*pastoral* poetry⟩ **d :** pleasingly peaceful and innocent **:** IDYLLIC
**2 a :** of or relating to spiritual care or guidance especially of a congregation **b :** of or relating to the pastor of a church
— **pas·to·ral·ly** \-t(ə-)rə-lē\ *adverb*
— **pas·to·ral·ness** *noun*

**²pastoral** \'pas-t(ə-)rəl; *1d is often* ,pas-tə-'räl, -'ral\ *noun* (1584)
**1 a :** a literary work (as a poem or play) dealing with shepherds or rural life in a usually artificial manner and typically drawing a contrast between the innocence and serenity of the simple life and the misery and corruption of city and especially court life **b :** pastoral poetry or drama **c :** a rural picture or scene **d :** PASTORALE 1b
**2 :** CROSIER 1
**3 :** a letter of a pastor to his charge: as **a :** a letter addressed by a bishop to his diocese **b :** a letter of the house of bishops of the Protestant Episcopal Church to be read in each parish

**pas·to·rale** \,pas-tə-'räl, -'ral *also* -'rä-lē\ *noun* [Italian, from *pastorale* of herdsmen, from Latin *pastoralis*] (1724)
**1 a :** an opera of the 16th or 17th centuries having a pastoral plot **b :** an instrumental or vocal composition having a pastoral theme
**2 :** PASTORAL 1a

**Pastoral Epistle** *noun* (1836)
: one of three New Testament letters including two addressed to Timothy and one to Titus that give advice on matters of church government and discipline

**pas·to·ral·ism** \'pas-t(ə-)rə-ˌli-zəm\ *noun* (1854)
1 : the quality or style characteristic of pastoral writing
2 a : livestock raising b : social organization based on livestock raising as the primary economic activity
— **pas·to·ral·ist** \-list\ *noun or adjective*

**pas·tor·ate** \'pas-t(ə-)rət\ *noun* (1795)
1 : the office, state, jurisdiction, or tenure of office of a pastor
2 : a body of pastors

**past participle** *noun* (1798)
: a participle that typically expresses completed action, that is traditionally one of the principal parts of the verb, that is traditionally used in English in the formation of perfect tenses in the active voice and of all tenses in the passive voice

**past perfect** *adjective* (1889)
: of, relating to, or constituting a verb tense that is traditionally formed in English with *had* and denotes an action or state as completed at or before a past time spoken of
— **past perfect** *noun*

**pas·tra·mi** *also* **pas·tromi** \pə-'strä-mē\ *noun* [Yiddish *pastrame*, from Romanian *pastramă* pressed and cured meat] (1936)
: a highly seasoned smoked beef prepared especially from shoulder cuts

**pas·try** \'pās-trē\ *noun, plural* **pastries** [¹*paste*] (circa 1538)
1 a : PASTE 1a b : sweet baked goods made of dough having a high fat content
2 : a piece of pastry

**past tense** *noun* (1813)
: a verb tense expressing action or state in or as if in the past: a : a verb tense expressive of elapsed time (as *wrote* in "on arriving I wrote a letter") b : a verb tense expressing action or state in progress or continuance or habitually done or customarily occurring at a past time (as *was writing* in "I was writing while he dictated" or *loved* in "their sons loved fishing")

**pas·tur·age** \'pas-chə-rij\ *noun* (circa 1533)
: PASTURE

**¹pas·ture** \'pas-chər\ *noun* [Middle English, from Middle French, from Late Latin *pastura*, from Latin *pastus*, past participle of *pascere* to feed — more at FOOD] (14th century)
1 : plants (as grass) grown for the feeding especially of grazing animals
2 : land or a plot of land used for grazing
3 : the feeding of livestock : GRAZING

**²pasture** *verb* **pas·tured; pas·tur·ing** (14th century)
*intransitive verb*
: GRAZE, BROWSE
*transitive verb*
1 : to feed (as cattle) on pasture
2 : to use as pasture

**pas·ture·land** \'pas-chər-ˌland\ *noun* (1591)
: PASTURE 2

**¹pas·ty** \'pas-tē\ *noun, plural* **pasties** [Middle English *pastee*, from Middle French *pasté*, from *paste* dough, paste] (13th century)
1 : ²PIE 1, 2; *especially* : a meat pie
2 : TURNOVER 5

**²pasty** \'pās-tē\ *adjective* **past·i·er; -est** (1659)
: resembling paste; *especially* : pallid and unhealthy in appearance
— **past·i·ness** \-nəs\ *noun*

**PA system** \ˌpē-'ā-\ *noun* (circa 1936)
: PUBLIC-ADDRESS SYSTEM

**¹pat** \'pat\ *noun* [Middle English *patte*, probably of imitative origin] (15th century)
1 : a light blow especially with the hand or a flat instrument
2 : a light tapping often rhythmical sound

3 : something (as butter) shaped into a small flat usually square individual portion
— **pat on the back** : an expression of approval

**²pat** *adverb* (1578)
: in a pat manner : APTLY, PERFECTLY

**³pat** *verb* **pat·ted; pat·ting** (1591)
*transitive verb*
1 : to strike lightly with a flat instrument
2 : to flatten, smooth, or put into place or shape with light blows
3 : to tap or stroke gently with the hand to soothe, caress, or show approval
*intransitive verb*
: to strike or beat gently

**⁴pat** *adjective* (1646)
1 a : exactly suited to the purpose or occasion b : APT b : suspiciously appropriate : CONTRIVED
2 : learned, mastered, or memorized exactly
3 : FIRM, UNYIELDING
4 : reduced to a simple or mechanical form : STANDARD, TRITE

**pa·ta·ca** \pə-'tä-kə\ *noun* [Portuguese] (1830)
— see MONEY table

**pat–a–cake** \'pa-də-ˌkāk, 'pat-ə-\ *variant of* PATTY-CAKE

**pa·ta·gi·um** \pə-'tā-jē-əm\ *noun, plural* **-gia** \-jē-ə\ [New Latin, from Latin, gold edging on a tunic] (1826)
1 : the fold of skin connecting the forelimbs and hind limbs of some tetrapods (as flying squirrels)
2 : the fold of skin in front of the main segments of a bird's wing

**¹patch** \'pach\ *noun* [Middle English *pacche*] (14th century)
1 : a piece of material used to mend or cover a hole or a weak spot
2 : a tiny piece of black silk or court plaster worn on the face or neck especially by women to hide a blemish or to heighten beauty
3 a : a piece of material (as adhesive plaster) used medically usually to cover a wound or repair a defect b : a shield worn over the socket of an injured or missing eye
4 a : a small piece : SCRAP b : a part or area distinct from that about it ⟨cabbage *patch*⟩ c : a period of time : SPELL ⟨was going through a rough *patch*⟩
5 : a piece of cloth sewed on a garment as an ornament or insignia; *especially* : SHOULDER PATCH
6 : a temporary connection in a communication system (as a telephone hookup)
7 : a minor usually temporary correction or modification in a computer program

**²patch** *transitive verb* (15th century)
1 : to mend, cover, or fill up a hole or weak spot in
2 : to provide with a patch
3 a : to make of patches or fragments b : to mend or put together especially in hasty or shabby fashion — usually used with *up* c : to make a patch in (a computer program)
4 : to connect (as circuits) by a patch cord
**synonym** see MEND

**³patch** *noun* [perhaps by folk etymology from Italian dialect *paccio*] (1549)
: FOOL, DOLT

**patch·board** \'pach-ˌbōrd, -ˌbȯrd\ *noun* (1934)
: a switchboard in which circuits are interconnected by patch cords

**patch cord** *noun* (1926)
: a wire with a plug at each end that is used to connect electrical devices

**patch·ou·li** *also* **patch·ou·ly** \'pa-chə-lē, pə-'chü-lē\ *noun* [Tamil *pacculi*] (1845)
: a heavy perfume made from a fragrant essential oil from an East Indian shrubby mint (*Pogostemon cablin*); *also* : the plant itself

**patch pocket** *noun* (1895)
: a flat pocket applied to the outside of a garment

**patch test** *noun* (1933)

: a test for determining allergic sensitivity that is made by applying to the unbroken skin small pads soaked with the allergen to be tested

**patch·work** \'pach-ˌwərk\ *noun, often attributive* (1692)
1 : something composed of miscellaneous or incongruous parts : HODGEPODGE
2 : pieces of cloth of various colors and shapes sewn together to form a covering

**patchwork quilt** *noun* (1840)
1 : a quilt made of patchwork
2 : PATCHWORK 1

*patchwork 2*

**patchy** \'pa-chē\ *adjective* **patch·i·er; -est** (1798)
1 : marked by, consisting of, or diversified with patches
2 : irregular in appearance, makeup, or quality
— **patch·i·ly** \'pa-chə-lē\ *adverb*
— **patch·i·ness** \'pa-chē-nəs\ *noun*

**pate** \'pāt\ *noun* [Middle English] (14th century)
1 : HEAD
2 : the crown of the head
3 : BRAIN — used chiefly disparagingly
— **pat·ed** \'pā-təd\ *adjective*

**pâte** \'pät\ *noun* [French, literally, paste, from Old French *paste*] (1863)
: PASTE 2b

**pâ·té** *also* **pate** \pä-'tā, pa-\ *noun* [French, from Middle French *pasté* — more at PASTY] (1706)
1 : a meat or fish pie or patty
2 : a spread of finely chopped or pureed seasoned meat ⟨chicken liver *pâté*⟩

**pâ·té de foie gras** \ˌ(ˌ)pä-ˌtā-də-ˌfwä-'grä, ˌ(ˌ)pä-\ *noun, plural* **pâ·tés de foie gras** \-ˌtā(z)-\ [French, literally, pâté of fat liver] (1827)
: a pâté of fat goose liver and usually truffles sometimes with added fat pork

**pa·tel·la** \pə-'te-lə\ *noun, plural* **-lae** \-'te-(ˌ)lē, -ˌlī\ *or* **-las** [Latin, from diminutive of *patina* shallow dish] (1693)
: a thick flat triangular movable bone that forms the anterior point of the knee and protects the front of the joint — called also *kneecap*
— **pa·tel·lar** \-'te-lər\ *adjective*

**pa·tel·li·form** \pə-'te-lə-ˌfȯrm\ *adjective* [New Latin *Patella*, genus including the limpet, from Latin, small shallow dish] (1819)
1 : resembling a limpet or limpet shell
2 : disk-shaped with a narrow rim

**pat·en** \'pa-tᵊn\ *noun* [Middle English, from Middle French *patene*, from Medieval Latin & Latin; Medieval Latin *patina*, from Latin, shallow dish, from Greek *patanē*] (14th century)
1 : a plate usually made of precious metal and used to carry the bread at the Eucharist
2 a : PLATE b : something (as a metal disk) resembling a plate

**pa·ten·cy** \'pa-tᵊn(t)-sē, 'pā-\ *noun* (1656)
: the quality or state of being patent

**¹pat·ent** \*1–3 are* 'pa-tᵊnt, *chiefly British* 'pā-; *4* 'pā-; *5* 'pā-, -pa-; *6–7* 'pa-, 'pā-, *British usually* 'pā-\ *adjective* [Middle English, from Middle French, from Latin *patent-, patens*, from present participle of *patēre* to be open — more at FATHOM] (14th century)
1 a : open to public inspection — used chiefly in the phrase *letters patent* b (1) : secured by letters patent or by a patent to the exclusive

control and possession of a particular individual or party (2) **:** protected by a patent **:** made under a patent ⟨*patent* locks⟩ **c :** protected by a trademark or a trade name so as to establish proprietary rights analogous to those conveyed by letters patent or a patent **:** PROPRIETARY ⟨*patent* drugs⟩
**2 :** of, relating to, or concerned with the granting of patents especially for inventions ⟨a *patent* lawyer⟩
**3 :** making exclusive or proprietary claims or pretensions
**4 :** affording free passage **:** UNOBSTRUCTED ⟨a *patent* opening⟩
**5 :** PATULOUS, SPREADING ⟨a *patent* calyx⟩
**6** *archaic* **:** ACCESSIBLE, EXPOSED
**7 :** readily visible or intelligible **:** OBVIOUS
**synonym** see EVIDENT
— **pat·ent·ly** *adverb*
²**pat·ent** \'pa-t⁼nt, *British also* 'pā-\ *noun* (14th century)
**1 :** an official document conferring a right or privilege **:** LETTERS PATENT
**2 a :** a writing securing to an inventor for a term of years the exclusive right to make, use, or sell an invention **b :** the monopoly or right so granted **c :** a patented invention
**3 :** PRIVILEGE, LICENSE
**4 :** an instrument making a conveyance of public lands; *also* **:** the land so conveyed
**5 :** PATENT LEATHER
³**pat·ent** *transitive verb* (1675)
**1 :** to obtain or grant a patent right to
**2 :** to grant a privilege, right, or license to by patent
**3 :** to obtain or secure by patent; *especially* **:** to secure by letters patent exclusive right to make, use, or sell
— **pat·ent·abil·i·ty** \,pa-t⁼n-tə-'bi-lə-tē, *British also* ,pā-\ *noun*
— **pat·ent·able** \'pa-t⁼n-tə-bəl, *British also* 'pā-\ *adjective*
**pat·ent·ed** \'pa-t⁼n-təd, *British also* 'pā-\ *adjective* (1951)
**:** originated by or peculiar to one person or group **:** INDIVIDUALIZED
**pat·en·tee** \,pa-t⁼n-'tē, *British also* ,pā-\ *noun* (15th century)
**:** one to whom a grant is made or a privilege secured by patent
**pat·ent flour** \'pa-t⁼n(t)-, *British also* 'pā-\ *noun* (1886)
**:** a high-grade wheat flour that consists solely of endosperm
**pat·ent leather** \'pa-t⁼n(t)-, *British usually* 'pā-\ *noun* (1829)
**:** a leather with a hard smooth glossy surface
**patent medicine** *noun* (1770)
**:** a packaged nonprescription drug which is protected by a trademark and whose contents are incompletely disclosed; *also* **:** any drug that is a proprietary
**patent office** *noun* (1696)
**:** a government office for examining claims to patents and granting patents
**pat·en·tor** \'pa-t⁼n-tər, ,pa-t⁼n-'tòr, *British also* 'pā-, ,pā-\ *noun* (circa 1890)
**:** one that grants a patent
**patent right** *noun* (1805)
**:** a right granted by letters patent; *especially* **:** the exclusive right to an invention
**pa·ter** *noun* (14th century)
**1** \'pä-,ter\ *often capitalized* **:** PATERNOSTER
**2** \'pā-tər\ [Latin] *chiefly British* **:** FATHER
**pa·ter·fa·mil·i·as** \,pa-tər-fə-'mi-lē-əs, ,pä-, ,pā-\ *noun, plural* **pa·tres·fa·mil·i·as** \,pā-,trēz-, ,pä-,träs-\ [Middle English, from Latin, from *pater* father + *familias,* archaic genitive of *familia* household — more at FATHER, FAMILY] (15th century)
**1 :** the male head of a household
**2 :** the father of a family
**pa·ter·nal** \pə-'tər-n⁼l\ *adjective* [Middle English, from Late Latin *paternalis,* from Latin *paternus* paternal, from *pater*] (15th century)

**1 a :** of or relating to a father **b :** like that of a father ⟨*paternal* benevolence⟩
**2 :** received or inherited from one's male parent
**3 :** related through one's father ⟨*paternal* grandfather⟩
— **pa·ter·nal·ly** \-n⁼l-ē\ *adverb*
**pa·ter·nal·ism** \pə-'tər-n⁼l-,i-zəm\ *noun* (1881)
**1 :** a system under which an authority undertakes to supply needs or regulate conduct of those under its control in matters affecting them as individuals as well as in their relations to authority and to each other
**2 :** a policy or practice based on or characteristic of paternalism
— **pa·ter·nal·ist** \-n⁼l-ist\ *noun or adjective*
— **pa·ter·nal·is·tic** \-,tər-n⁼l-'is-tik\ *adjective*
— **pa·ter·nal·is·ti·cal·ly** \-ti-k(ə-)lē\ *adverb*
**pa·ter·ni·ty** \pə-'tər-nə-tē\ *noun* (1582)
**1 :** the quality or state of being a father
**2 :** origin or descent from a father
**paternity test** *noun* (1926)
**:** a test especially of DNA or genetic traits to determine whether a given man could be the biological father of a given child
**pa·ter·nos·ter** \,pä-tər-'näs-tər, 'pa-tər-,, 'pä-,ter-', -'näs-,ter\ *noun* [Middle English, from Old English, from Medieval Latin, from Latin *pater noster* our father, from the opening words] (before 12th century)
**1** *often capitalized* **:** LORD'S PRAYER
**2 :** a word formula repeated as a prayer or magical charm
**path** \'path, 'pàth\ *noun, plural* **paths** \'pathz, 'paths, 'pàthz, 'pàths\ [Middle English, from Old English *pæth;* akin to Old High German *pfad* path] (before 12th century)
**1 :** a trodden way
**2 :** a track specially constructed for a particular use
**3 a :** COURSE, ROUTE **b :** a way of life, conduct, or thought
**4 a :** the continuous series of positions or configurations that can be assumed in any motion or process of change by a moving or varying system **b :** a sequence of arcs in a network that can be traced continuously without retracing any arc
**5 :** PATHWAY 2
**path-** *or* **patho-** *combining form* [New Latin, from Greek, from *pathos,* literally, suffering — more at PATHOS]
**:** pathological state **:** disease ⟨*patho*gen⟩
**-path** *noun combining form* [German, back-formation from *-pathie* *-pathy*]
**1 :** practitioner of a (specified) system of medicine that emphasizes one aspect of disease or its treatment ⟨naturo*path*⟩
**2** [International Scientific Vocabulary, from Greek *-pathēs,* adjective, suffering, from *pathos*] **a :** one suffering from a disorder (of such a part or system) ⟨psycho*path*⟩ **b :** one perceiving ⟨tele*path*⟩
**Pa·than** \pə-'tän, -pä-\ *noun* [Hindi *Paṭhān,* from Pashto (eastern dialect) *Pakhtana,* plural of *Pakhtun*] (1638)
**:** PASHTUN
**path·break·ing** \'path-,brā-kiŋ\ *adjective* (1914)
**:** TRAILBLAZING
**pa·thet·ic** \pə-'the-tik\ *adjective* [Middle French or Late Latin; Middle French *pathetique,* from Late Latin *patheticus,* from Greek *pathētikos* capable of feeling, pathetic, from *paschein* (aorist *pathein*) to experience, suffer — more at PATHOS] (1598)
**1 :** having a capacity to move one to either compassionate or contemptuous pity
**2 :** marked by sorrow or melancholy **:** SAD
**synonym** see MOVING
— **pa·thet·i·cal** \-ti-kəl\ *adjective*
— **pa·thet·i·cal·ly** \-ti-k(ə-)lē\ *adverb*

**pathetic fallacy** *noun* (1856)
**:** the ascription of human traits or feelings to inanimate nature (as in *cruel sea*)
**path·find·er** \'path-,fīn-dər, 'pàth-\ *noun* (1840)
**:** one that discovers a way; *especially* **:** one that explores untraversed regions to mark out a new route
— **path·find·ing** \-diŋ\ *noun or adjective*
**path·less** \-ləs\ *adjective* (1591)
**:** UNTRODDEN, TRACKLESS
— **path·less·ness** *noun*
**patho·bi·ol·o·gy** \,pa-thō-bī-'ä-lə-jē\ *noun* (circa 1909)
**:** PATHOLOGY
**path·o·gen** \'pa-thə-jən\ *noun* [International Scientific Vocabulary] (1880)
**:** a specific causative agent (as a bacterium or virus) of disease
**path·o·gen·e·sis** \,pa-thə-'je-nə-səs\ *noun* [New Latin] (1876)
**:** the origination and development of a disease
**path·o·ge·net·ic** \-jə-'ne-tik\ *adjective* [International Scientific Vocabulary] (1838)
**1 :** of or relating to pathogenesis
**2 :** PATHOGENIC 2
**path·o·gen·ic** \-'je-nik\ *adjective* [International Scientific Vocabulary] (1852)
**1 :** PATHOGENETIC 1
**2 :** causing or capable of causing disease
— **path·o·ge·nic·i·ty** \-jə-'ni-sə-tē\ *noun*
**pa·thog·no·mon·ic** \pa-thə(g)-nō-'mä-nik\ *adjective* [Greek *pathognōmonikos,* from *path-* + *gnōmonikos* fit to judge, from *gnōmōn* interpreter; akin to Greek *gignōskein* to know — more at KNOW] (1625)
**:** distinctively characteristic of a particular disease
**path·o·log·i·cal** \,pa-thə-'lä-ji-kəl\ *also* **path·o·log·ic** \-jik\ *adjective* (1688)
**1 :** of or relating to pathology
**2 :** altered or caused by disease
— **path·o·log·i·cal·ly** \-ji-k(ə-)lē\ *adverb*
**pa·thol·o·gist** \pə-'thä-lə-jist, pa-\ *noun* (1650)
**:** a specialist in pathology; *specifically* **:** one who interprets and diagnoses the changes caused by disease in tissues and body fluids
**pa·thol·o·gy** \-jē\ *noun, plural* **-gies** [New Latin *pathologia* & Middle French *pathologie,* from Greek *pathologia* study of the emotions, from *path-* + *-logia* *-logy*] (1611)
**1 :** the study of the essential nature of diseases and especially of the structural and functional changes produced by them
**2 :** something abnormal: **a :** the structural and functional deviations from the normal that constitute disease or characterize a particular disease **b :** deviation from propriety or from an assumed normal state of something nonliving or nonmaterial
**path·o·phys·i·ol·o·gy** \,pa-thō-,fi-zē-'ä-lə-jē\ *noun* (1947)
**:** the physiology of abnormal states; *specifically* **:** the functional changes that accompany a particular syndrome or disease
— **path·o·phys·i·o·log·i·cal** \-zē-ə-'lä-ji-kəl\ *also* **path·o·phys·i·o·log·ic** \-jik\ *adjective*
**pa·thos** \'pā-,thäs, -,thòs, -,thōs *also* 'pa-\ *noun* [Greek, suffering, experience, emotion, from *paschein* (aorist *pathein*) to experience, suffer; perhaps akin to Lithuanian *kęsti* to suffer] (1591)
**1 :** an element in experience or in artistic representation evoking pity or compassion
**2 :** an emotion of sympathetic pity
**path·way** \'path-,wā, 'pàth-\ *noun* (15th century)
**1 :** PATH, COURSE
**2 :** a line of communication over interconnecting neurons extending from one organ or center to another
**3 :** the sequence of enzyme catalyzed reactions by which an energy-yielding substance is utilized by protoplasm ⟨metabolic *pathways*⟩

**-pathy** *noun combining form* [Latin *-pathia*, from Greek *-patheia*, from *-pathēs* suffering, from *pathos*]
**1 :** feeling : suffering ⟨em*pathy*⟩ **:** perception ⟨tele*pathy*⟩
**2 :** disorder of (such) a part or kind ⟨neuro*pathy*⟩
**3 :** system of medicine based on (such) a factor ⟨osteo*pathy*⟩

**pa·tience** \'pā-shən(t)s\ *noun* (13th century)
**1 :** the capacity, habit, or fact of being patient
**2** *chiefly British* **:** SOLITAIRE 2

**¹pa·tient** \'pā-shənt\ *adjective* [Middle English *pacient*, from Middle French, from Latin *patient-, patiens*, from present participle of *pati* to suffer; perhaps akin to Greek *pēma* suffering] (14th century)
**1 :** bearing pains or trials calmly or without complaint
**2 :** manifesting forbearance under provocation or strain
**3 :** not hasty or impetuous
**4 :** steadfast despite opposition, difficulty, or adversity
**5 a :** able or willing to bear — used with *of* **b :** SUSCEPTIBLE, ADMITTING ⟨*patient* of one interpretation⟩
— **pa·tient·ly** *adverb*

**²patient** *noun* (14th century)
**1 a :** an individual awaiting or under medical care and treatment **b :** the recipient of any of various personal services
**2 :** one that is acted upon

**pa·ti·na** \pə-'tē-nə, 'pa-tə-nə\ *noun, plural* **pa·ti·nas** \-nəz\ *or* **pa·ti·nae** \-,nē, -,nī\ [Italian, from Latin, shallow dish — more at PATEN] (1748)
**1 a :** a usually green film formed naturally on copper and bronze by long exposure or artificially (as by acids) and often valued aesthetically for its color **b :** a surface appearance of something grown beautiful especially with age or use
**2 :** an appearance or aura that is derived from association, habit, or established character
**3 :** a superficial covering or exterior

**pat·i·nate** \'pa-tə-,nāt\ *verb* **-nat·ed; -nat·ing** (1880)
*transitive verb*
**:** to give a patina to
*intransitive verb*
**:** to take on a patina — usually used in the past participle ⟨*patinated* bronze⟩
— **pat·i·na·tion** \,pa-tə-'nā-shən\ *noun*

**¹pa·tine** \pa-'tēn\ *noun* [French, from Italian *patina*] (1883)
**:** PATINA

**²patine** *transitive verb* **pa·tined; pa·tin·ing** (1896)
**:** to cover with a patina

**pa·tio** \'pa-tē-,ō *also* 'pä-\ *noun, plural* **pa·ti·os** [Spanish] (1828)
**1 :** COURTYARD; *especially* **:** an inner court open to the sky
**2 :** a recreation area that adjoins a dwelling, is often paved, and is adapted especially to outdoor dining

**pa·tis·se·rie** *or* **pâ·tis·se·rie** \pə-'ti-sə-rē, pä-\ *noun* [French *pâtisserie*, from Middle French *pastiserie*, from *pasticier* to make pastry, from (assumed) Old French *pastitz* cake, from (assumed) Vulgar Latin *pasticium*, from Late Latin *pasta* dough] (1784)
**1 :** PASTRY
**2 :** a pastry shop

**pâ·tis·sier** *or* **pa·tis·sier** \pä-tis-'yā\ *noun* [French *pâtissier*, from Old French *pasticier*, from (assumed) Old French *pastitz* cake] (circa 1905)
**:** a pastry chef

**pa·tois** \'pa-,twä, 'pä-\ *noun, plural* **pa·tois** \-,twäz\ [French] (1643)
**1 a :** a dialect other than the standard or literary dialect **b :** uneducated or provincial speech
**2 :** the characteristic special language of an occupational or social group **:** JARGON

---

**patr-** *or* **patri-** *or* **patro-** *combining form* [*patr-, patri-* from Latin, from *patr-, pater; patr-, patro-* from Greek, from *patr-, patēr* — more at FATHER]
**:** father ⟨*patristic*⟩

**pa·tri·arch** \'pā-trē-,ärk\ *noun* [Middle English *patriarche*, from Old French, from Late Latin *patriarcha*, from Greek *patriarchēs*, from *patria* lineage (from *patr-, patēr* father) + *-archēs* -arch — more at FATHER] (13th century)
**1 a :** one of the scriptural fathers of the human race or of the Hebrew people **b :** a man who is father or founder **c (1) :** the oldest member or representative of a group **(2) :** a venerable old man **d :** a man who is head of a patriarchy
**2 a :** any of the bishops of the ancient or Eastern Orthodox sees of Constantinople, Alexandria, Antioch, and Jerusalem or the ancient and Western see of Rome with authority over other bishops **b :** the head of any of various Eastern churches **c :** a Roman Catholic bishop next in rank to the pope with purely titular or with metropolitan jurisdiction
**3 :** a Mormon of the Melchizedek priesthood empowered to perform the ordinances of the church and pronounce blessings within a stake or prescribed jurisdiction

**pa·tri·ar·chal** \,pā-trē-'är-kəl\ (15th century)
**:** of, relating to, or being a patriarch or patriarchy

**patriarchal cross** *noun* (circa 1727)
**:** a chiefly heraldic cross denoting a cardinal's or archbishop's rank and having two crossbars of which the lower is the longer and intersects the upright above or at its center — see CROSS illustration

**pa·tri·arch·ate** \'pā-trē-,är-kət, -,kāt\ *noun* (1617)
**1 a :** the office, jurisdiction, or time in office of a patriarch **b :** the residence or headquarters of a patriarch
**2 :** PATRIARCHY

**pa·tri·ar·chy** \-,är-kē\ *noun, plural* **-chies** (1632)
**1 :** social organization marked by the supremacy of the father in the clan or family, the legal dependence of wives and children, and the reckoning of descent and inheritance in the male line; *broadly* **:** control by men of a disproportionately large share of power
**2 :** a society or institution organized according to the principles or practices of patriarchy

**pa·tri·cian** \pə-'tri-shən\ *noun* [Middle English *patricion*, from Middle French *patricien*, from Latin *patricius*, from *patres* senators, from plural of *pater* father — more at FATHER] (15th century)
**1 :** a member of one of the original citizen families of ancient Rome
**2 a :** a person of high birth **:** ARISTOCRAT **b :** a person of breeding and cultivation
— **patrician** *adjective*

**pa·tri·ci·ate** \-'tri-shē-ət, -,āt\ *noun* (circa 1656)
**1 :** the position or dignity of a patrician
**2 :** a patrician class

**pat·ri·cide** \'pa-trə-,sīd\ *noun* (1593)
**1** [Latin *patricida*, from *patr-* + *-cida* -cide] **:** one who murders his or her own father
**2** [Late Latin *patricidium*, from Latin *patr-* + *-cidium* -cide] **:** the murder of one's own father
— **pat·ri·cid·al** \,pa-trə-'sī-d°l\ *adjective*

**pat·ri·lin·eal** \,pa-trə-'li-nē-əl\ *adjective* (1904)
**:** relating to, based on, or tracing descent through the paternal line ⟨*patrilineal* society⟩

**pat·ri·mo·ny** \'pa-trə-,mō-nē\ *noun* [Middle English *patrimonie*, from Middle French, from Latin *patrimonium*, from *patr-, pater* father] (14th century)
**1 a :** an estate inherited from one's father or ancestor **b :** anything derived from one's father or ancestors **:** HERITAGE

---

**2 :** an estate or endowment belonging by ancient right to a church
— **pat·ri·mo·ni·al** \,pa-trə-'mō-nē-əl\ *adjective*

**pa·tri·ot** \'pā-trē-ət, -,ät, *chiefly British* 'pa-trē-ət\ *noun* [Middle French *patriote* compatriot, from Late Latin *patriota*, from Greek *patriōtēs*, from *patria* lineage, from *patr-, patēr* father] (1605)
**:** one who loves his or her country and supports its authority and interests

**pa·tri·ot·ic** \,pā-trē-'ä-tik, *chiefly British* ,pa-\ *adjective* (1757)
**1 :** inspired by patriotism
**2 :** befitting or characteristic of a patriot
— **pa·tri·ot·i·cal·ly** \-ti-k(ə-)lē\ *adverb*

**pa·tri·ot·ism** \'pā-trē-ə-,ti-zəm, *chiefly British* 'pa-\ *noun* (circa 1726)
**:** love for or devotion to one's country

**Patriots' Day** *noun* (1897)
**:** the third Monday in April observed as a legal holiday in Maine and Massachusetts in commemoration of the battles of Lexington and Concord in 1775

**pa·tris·tic** \pə-'tris-tik\ *adjective* (circa 1828)
**:** of or relating to the church fathers or their writings
— **pa·tris·ti·cal** \-ti-kəl\ *adjective*

**pa·tris·tics** \-tiks\ *noun plural but singular in construction* (1847)
**:** the study of the writings and background of the church fathers

**Pa·tro·clus** \pə-'trō-kləs, -'trä-\ *noun* [Latin, from Greek *Patroklos*]
**:** a Greek hero and friend of Achilles slain by Hector at Troy

**¹pa·trol** \pə-'trōl\ *noun* (1664)
**1 a :** the action of traversing a district or beat or of going the rounds along a chain of guards for observation or the maintenance of security **b :** the person performing such an action **c :** a unit of persons or vehicles employed for reconnaissance, security, or combat
**2 :** a subdivision of a Boy Scout troop or Girl Scout troop

**²patrol** *verb* **pa·trolled; pa·trol·ling** [French *patrouiller*, from Middle French, to tramp around in the mud, from *patte* paw — more at PATTEN] (1691)
*intransitive verb*
**:** to carry out a patrol
*transitive verb*
**:** to carry out a patrol of
— **pa·trol·ler** *noun*

**pa·trol·man** \pə-'trōl-mən\ *noun* (1867)
**:** one who patrols; *especially* **:** a police officer assigned to a beat

**patrol wagon** *noun* (1887)
**:** PADDY WAGON

**pa·tron** \'pā-trən, *for 6 also* pa-'trōⁿ\ *noun* [Middle English, from Middle French, from Medieval Latin & Latin; Medieval Latin *patronus* patron saint, patron of a benefice, pattern, from Latin, defender, from *patr-, pater*] (14th century)
**1 a :** a person chosen, named, or honored as a special guardian, protector, or supporter **b :** a wealthy or influential supporter of an artist or writer **c :** a social or financial sponsor of a social function (as a ball or concert)
**2 :** one that uses wealth or influence to help an individual, an institution, or a cause
**3 :** one who buys the goods or uses the services offered especially by an establishment
**4 :** the holder of the right of presentation to an English ecclesiastical benefice
**5 :** a master in ancient times who freed his slave but retained some rights over him

---

**6** [French, from Middle French] **:** the proprietor of an establishment (as an inn) especially in France
**7 :** the chief male officer in some fraternal lodges having both men and women members
— **pa·tron·al** \'pā-trə-n°l; *British* pə-'trōn°l, pa-\ *adjective*
**pa·tron·age** \'pa-trə-nij, 'pā-\ *noun* (14th century)
**1 :** ADVOWSON
**2 :** the support or influence of a patron
**3 :** kindness done with an air of superiority
**4 :** business or activity provided by patrons ⟨the new branch library is expected to have a heavy *patronage*⟩
**5 a :** the power to make appointments to government jobs especially for political advantage **b :** the distribution of jobs on the basis of patronage **c :** jobs distributed by patronage
**pa·tron·ess** \'pā-trə-nəs\ *noun* (15th century)
**:** a woman who is a patron
**pa·tron·ise** *British variant of* PATRONIZE
**pa·tron·ize** \'pā-trə-nīz, 'pa-\ *transitive verb* **-ized; -iz·ing** (1589)
**1 :** to act as patron of **:** provide aid or support for
**2 :** to adopt an air of condescension toward **:** treat haughtily or coolly
**3 :** to be a frequent or regular customer or client of
— **pa·tron·i·za·tion** \,pā-trə-nə-'zā-shən, pa-\ *noun*
— **pa·tron·iz·ing·ly** \'pā-trə-,nī-ziŋ-lē, 'pa-\ *adverb*
**patron saint** *noun* (1717)
**1 :** a saint to whose protection and intercession a person, a society, a church, or a place is dedicated
**2 :** an original leader or prime exemplar
**pat·ro·nym·ic** \,pa-trə-'ni-mik\ *noun* [Late Latin *patronymicum,* from neuter of *patronymicus* of a patronymic, from Greek *patronymikos,* from *patronymia* patronymic, from *patr-* + *onyma* name — more at NAME] (1612)
**:** a name derived from that of the father or a paternal ancestor usually by the addition of an affix
— **patronymic** *adjective*
**pa·troon** \pə-'trün\ *noun* [French *patron* & Spanish *patrón,* from Medieval Latin *patronus,* from Latin, patron] (1743)
**1** *archaic* **:** the captain or officer commanding a ship
**2** [Dutch, from French *patron*] **:** the proprietor of a manorial estate especially in New York originally granted under Dutch rule but in some cases existing until the mid-19th century
**pat·sy** \'pat-sē\ *noun, plural* **pat·sies** [perhaps from Italian *pazzo* fool] (1903)
**:** a person who is easily manipulated or victimized **:** SUCKER
**pat·ten** \'pa-t°n\ *noun* [Middle English *patin,* from Middle French, from *patte* paw, hoof, from (assumed) Vulgar Latin *patta,* of imitative origin] (14th century)
**:** a clog, sandal, or overshoe often with a wooden sole or metal device to elevate the foot and increase the wearer's height or aid in walking in mud
**¹pat·ter** \'pa-tər\ *verb* [Middle English *patren,* from *paternoster*] (14th century)
*transitive verb*
**:** to say or speak in a rapid or mechanical manner
*intransitive verb*
**1 :** to recite prayers (as paternosters) rapidly or mechanically
**2 :** to talk glibly and volubly
**3 :** to speak or sing rapid-fire words in a theatrical performance
— **pat·ter·er** \-tər-ər\ *noun*
**²patter** *noun* (1758)
**1 :** a specialized lingo **:** CANT; *especially* **:** the jargon of criminals (as thieves)
**2 :** the spiel of a street hawker or of a circus barker

**3 :** empty chattering talk
**4 a** (1) **:** the rapid-fire talk of a comedian (2) **:** the talk with which an entertainer accompanies a routine **b :** the words of a comic song or of a rapidly spoken usually humorous monologue introduced into such a song
**³patter** *verb* [frequentative of ³*pat*] (1611)
*intransitive verb*
**1 :** to strike or pat rapidly and repeatedly
**2 :** to run with quick light-sounding steps
*transitive verb*
**:** to cause to patter
**⁴patter** *noun* (1844)
**:** a quick succession of light sounds or pats
**¹pat·tern** \'pa-tərn\ *noun* [Middle English *patron,* from Middle French, from Medieval Latin *patronus*] (14th century)
**1 :** a form or model proposed for imitation **:** EXEMPLAR
**2 :** something designed or used as a model for making things ⟨a dressmaker's *pattern*⟩
**3 :** a model for making a mold into which molten metal is poured to form a casting
**4 :** an artistic, musical, literary, or mechanical design or form
**5 :** a natural or chance configuration ⟨frost *pattern*⟩ ⟨the *pattern* of events⟩
**6 :** a length of fabric sufficient for an article (as of clothing)
**7 a :** the distribution of shrapnel, bombs on a target, or shot from a shotgun **b :** the grouping made on a target by bullets
**8 :** a reliable sample of traits, acts, tendencies, or other observable characteristics of a person, group, or institution ⟨behavior *pattern*⟩ ⟨spending *pattern*⟩
**9 a :** the flight path prescribed for an airplane that is coming in for a landing **b :** a prescribed route to be followed by a pass receiver in football
**10 :** TEST PATTERN
**11 :** a discernible coherent system based on the intended interrelationship of component parts ⟨foreign policy *patterns*⟩
**12 :** frequent or widespread incidence ⟨a *pattern* of dissent⟩
**synonym** *see* MODEL
— **pat·terned** \-tərnd\ *adjective*
— **pat·tern·less** *adjective*
**²pattern** (circa 1586)
*transitive verb*
**1** *dialect chiefly English* **a :** MATCH **b :** IMITATE
**2 :** to make, adapt, or fashion according to a pattern
**3 :** to furnish, adorn, or mark with a design
*intransitive verb*
**:** to form a pattern
**pat·tern·ing** \'pa-tər-niŋ\ *noun* (1862)
**1 :** decoration, composition, or configuration according to a pattern
**2 :** physiotherapy that is designed to improve malfunctioning nervous control by means of feedback from muscular activity imposed by an outside source or induced by other muscles
**pat·ty** *also* **pat·tie** \'pa-tē\ *noun, plural* **pat·ties** [French *pâté* pâté] (1710)
**1 :** a little pie
**2 a :** a small flat cake of chopped food ⟨a hamburger *patty*⟩ **b :** a small flat candy ⟨a peppermint *patty*⟩
**3 :** PATTY SHELL
**pat·ty-cake** \-,kāk\ *noun* [alteration of *pat-a-cake,* from the opening words of the rhyme] (1889)
**:** a game in which two participants (as mother and child) clap their hands together to the rhythm of an accompanying nursery rhyme
**pat·ty·pan** \-,pan\ *noun* [*pattypan* pan for baking patties] (1900)
**:** a summer squash having a scalloped edge — called also *cymling*
**patty shell** *noun* (1909)
**:** a shell of puff pastry made to hold a creamed meat, fish, or vegetable filling

**pat·u·lous** \'pa-chə-ləs\ *adjective* [Latin *patulus,* from *patēre* to be open — more at FATHOM] (1616)
**:** spreading widely from a center ⟨a tree with *patulous* branches⟩
**pat·zer** \'pät-sər, 'pat-\ *noun* [probably from German *Patzer* bungler, from *patzen* to blunder] (1959)
**:** an inept chess player
**pau·ci·ty** \'pò-sə-tē\ *noun* [Middle English *paucite,* from Middle French or Latin; Middle French *paucité,* from Latin *paucitat-, paucitas,* from *paucus* little — more at FEW] (15th century)
**1 :** smallness of number **:** FEWNESS
**2 :** smallness of quantity **:** DEARTH
**Paul** \'pòl\ *noun* [Latin *Paulus,* from Greek *Paulos*]
**:** an early Christian apostle and missionary and author of several New Testament epistles
**Paul Bun·yan** \-'bən-yən\ *noun*
**:** a giant lumberjack of American folklore
**Pau·li exclusion principle** \'paù-lē-\ *noun* [Wolfgang *Pauli*] (1926)
**:** EXCLUSION PRINCIPLE — called also *Pauli principle*
**Pau·line** \'pò-,līn\ *adjective* (1817)
**:** of or relating to the apostle Paul, his epistles, or the doctrine or theology implicit in his epistles
**Paul·ist** \'pò-list\ *noun* (circa 1883)
**:** a member of the Roman Catholic Congregation of the Missionary Priests of Saint Paul the Apostle founded by I. T. Hecker in the U.S. in 1858
**pau·low·nia** \pò-'lō-nē-ə\ *noun* [New Latin, from Anna *Pavlovna* (died 1865) Russian princess] (1843)
**:** any of a genus (*Paulownia*) of Chinese trees of the snapdragon family; *especially* **:** one (*P. tomentosa*) widely cultivated for its panicles of fragrant violet flowers
**paunch** \'pònch, 'pänch\ *noun* [Middle English, from Middle French *panche,* from Latin *pantic-, pantex*] (14th century)
**1 a :** the belly and its contents **b :** POTBELLY
**2 :** RUMEN
**paunchy** \'pòn-chē, 'pän-\ *adjective* **paunch·i·er; -est** (1598)
**:** having a potbelly
— **paunch·i·ness** *noun*
**pau·per** \'pò-pər\ *noun* [Latin, poor — more at POOR] (1516)
**1 :** a person destitute of means except such as are derived from charity; *specifically* **:** one who receives aid from funds designated for the poor
**2 :** a very poor person
— **pau·per·ism** \-pə-,ri-zəm\ *noun*
**pau·per·ize** \'pò-pə-,rīz\ *transitive verb* **-ized; -iz·ing** (1834)
**:** to reduce to poverty
**pau·piette** \pō-'pyet\ *noun* [French *paupiette,* from Italian *polpetta* meat croquette, diminutive of *polpa* pulp, flesh, from Latin *pulpa*] (1889)
**:** a thin slice of meat or fish wrapped around a forcemeat filling
**¹pause** \'pòz\ *noun* [Middle English, from Latin *pausa,* from Greek *pausis,* from *pauein* to stop] (15th century)
**1 :** a temporary stop
**2 a :** a break in a verse **b :** a brief suspension of the voice to indicate the limits and relations of sentences and their parts
**3 :** temporary inaction especially as caused by uncertainty **:** HESITATION
**4 a :** the sign denoting a fermata **b :** a mark (as a period or comma) used in writing or printing to indicate or correspond to a pause of voice
**5 :** a reason or cause for pausing (as to reconsider) ⟨a thought that should give one *pause*⟩
**²pause** *verb* **paused; paus·ing** (15th century)
*intransitive verb*

**1 :** to stop temporarily
**2 :** to linger for a time
*transitive verb*
**:** to cause to pause **:** STOP
**pa·vane** \pə-'vän, -'van\ *also* **pa·van** \*same
or* 'pa-vən\ *noun* [Middle French *pavane,* from
Italian dialect *pavana,* from feminine of *pa-
vano* of Padua, from *Pava* (Tuscan *Padova*)
Padua] (1535)
**1 :** a stately court dance by couples that was
introduced from southern Europe into England
in the 16th century
**2 :** music for the pavane; *also* **:** music having
the slow duple rhythm of a pavane
**pave** \'pāv\ *transitive verb* **paved; pav·ing**
[Middle English, from Middle French *paver,*
from Latin *pavire* to strike, pound; perhaps
akin to Greek *paiein* to strike] (14th century)
**1 :** to lay or cover with material (as asphalt or
concrete) that forms a firm level surface for
travel
**2 :** to cover firmly and solidly as if with paving material
**3 :** to serve as a covering or pavement of
— **pav·er** *noun*
— **pave the way :** to prepare a smooth
easy way **:** facilitate development
**pa·vé** \pa-'vā\ *also* **pa·véed** *or* **pa·véd** \pa-
'vād\ *or* **pa·ve** \pa-'vā\ *adjective* [*pavé* from
French, from past participle of *paver* to pave]
(1903)
*of jewels* **:** set as close together as possible to
conceal a metal base
**pave·ment** \'pāv-mənt\ *noun* [Middle English, from Old French, from Latin *pavimen-
tum,* from *pavire*] (13th century)
**1 :** a paved surface: as **a :** the artificially covered surface of a public thoroughfare **b** *chiefly
British* **:** SIDEWALK
**2 :** the material with which something is
paved
**3 :** something that suggests a pavement (as in
flatness, hardness, and extent of surface)
**pav·id** \'pa-vəd\ *adjective* [Latin *pavidus,* from
*pavēre* to be frightened; akin to Latin *pavire*]
(circa 1656)
**:** TIMID
**¹pa·vil·ion** \pə-'vil-yən\ *noun* [Middle English
*pavilon,* from Old French *paveillon,* from Latin *papilion-, papilio* butterfly; perhaps akin to
Old High German *fīfaltra* butterfly] (13th century)
**1 a :** a large often sumptuous tent **b :** something resembling a canopy or tent ⟨tree ferns
spread their delicate *pavilions* —Blanche E.
Baughan⟩
**2 a :** a part of a building projecting from the
rest **b :** one of several detached or semidetached units into which a building is sometimes divided
**3 a :** a light sometimes ornamental structure in
a garden, park, or place of recreation that is
used for entertainment or shelter **b :** a temporary structure erected at an exposition by an
individual exhibitor
**4 :** the lower faceted part of a brilliant below
the girdle
**²pavilion** *transitive verb* (14th century)
**:** to furnish or cover with or put in a pavilion
**pav·ing** \'pā-viŋ\ *noun* (15th century)
**:** PAVEMENT
**pav·ior** *or* **pav·iour** \'pāv-yər\ *noun* [Middle
English *pavier,* from *paven* to pave] (15th century)
*British* **:** one that paves
**pav·lo·va** \'pav-lə-və, pav-'lō-\ *noun, often
capitalized* [Anna *Pavlova*] (1926)
**:** a dessert of Australian and New Zealand origin consisting of a meringue shell topped with
whipped cream and usually fruit
**Pav·lov·i·an** \pav-'lò-vē-ən, -'lō-; -'lò-fē-\ *adjective* (1926)
**1 :** of or relating to Ivan Pavlov or to his work
and theories ⟨*Pavlovian* conditioning⟩

**2 :** being or expressing a conditioned or predictable reaction **:** AUTOMATIC ⟨the candidates
gave *Pavlovian* answers⟩
**¹paw** \'pò\ *noun* [Middle English, from Middle
French *poue*] (14th century)
**1 :** the foot of a quadruped (as a lion or dog)
that has claws; *broadly* **:** the foot of an animal
**2 :** a human hand especially when large or
clumsy
**²paw** (15th century)
*transitive verb*
**1 :** to touch or strike at with a paw
**2 :** to feel or touch clumsily, rudely, or sexually
**3 :** to scrape or beat with or as if with a hoof
**4 :** to flail at or grab for wildly
*intransitive verb*
**1 :** to beat or scrape something with or as if
with a hoof
**2 :** to touch or strike with a paw
**3 :** to feel or touch someone or something
clumsily, rudely, or sexually
**4 :** to flail or grab wildly
**paw·ky** \'pò-kē\ *adjective* [obsolete English
dialect *pawk* trick] (1676)
*chiefly British* **:** artfully shrewd **:** CANNY
**pawl** \'pòl\ *noun* [perhaps modification of
Dutch *pal* pawl] (1626)
**:** a pivoted tongue or sliding bolt on one part
of a machine that is adapted to fall into notches or interdental spaces on another part (as a
ratchet wheel) so as to permit motion in only
one direction — see RATCHET WHEEL illustration
**¹pawn** \'pòn, 'pän\ *noun* [Middle English
*pown,* from Middle French *poon,* from Medieval Latin *pedon-, pedo* foot soldier, from Late
Latin, one with broad feet, from Latin *ped-,
pes* foot — more at FOOT] (14th century)
**1 :** one of the chessmen of least value having
the power to move only forward ordinarily
one square at a time, to capture only diagonally forward, and to be promoted to any piece
except a king upon reaching the eighth rank
**2 :** one that can be used to further the purposes of another
**²pawn** *noun* [Middle English *paun,* modification of Middle French *pan*] (15th century)
**1 a :** something delivered to or deposited with
another as security for a loan **b :** HOSTAGE
**2 :** the state of being pledged
**3 :** something used as a pledge **:** GUARANTY
**4 :** the act of pawning
**³pawn** *transitive verb* (1570)
**:** to deposit in pledge or as security
— **pawn·er** \'pò-nər, 'pä-\ *or* **paw·nor**
\*same or* pò-'nòr, pä-\ *noun*
**pawn·bro·ker** \'pòn-,brō-kər, 'pän-\ *noun*
(1687)
**:** one who lends money on the security of personal property pledged in his keeping
— **pawn·bro·king** \-kiŋ\ *noun*
**Paw·nee** \pò-'nē, pä-\ *noun, plural* **Pawnee**
*or* **Pawnees** (1770)
**:** a member of an American Indian people
originally of Kansas and Nebraska
**pawn off** *transitive verb* (1832)
**:** to get rid of or pass off usually by deception
**:** PALM OFF
**pawn·shop** \'pòn-,shäp, 'pän-\ *noun* (1849)
**:** a pawnbroker's shop
**paw·paw** *variant of* PAPAW
**pax** \'paks, 'päks\ *noun* [Middle English, from
Medieval Latin, from Latin, peace — more at
PEACE] (14th century)
**1 :** a tablet decorated with a sacred figure (as
of Christ) and sometimes ceremonially kissed
by participants at mass
**2 :** the kiss of peace in the Mass
**3 :** PEACE; *especially, capitalized* **:** a period of
general stability in international affairs under
the influence of a dominant military power —
usually used in combination with a latinized
name ⟨*Pax* Americana⟩
**¹pay** \'pā\ *verb* **paid** \'pād\ *also in sense 7*
**payed; pay·ing** [Middle English, from Old

French *paier,* from Latin *pacare* to pacify,
from *pac-, pax* peace] (13th century)
*transitive verb*
**1 a :** to make due return to for services rendered or property delivered **b :** to engage for
money **:** HIRE ⟨you couldn't *pay* me to do that⟩
**2 a :** to give in return for goods or service
⟨*pay* wages⟩ **b :** to discharge indebtedness for
**:** SETTLE ⟨*pay* a bill⟩ **c :** to make a disposal or
transfer of (money)
**3 :** to give or forfeit in expiation or retribution
⟨*pay* the penalty⟩
**4 a :** to make compensation for **b :** to requite
according to what is deserved ⟨*pay* them back⟩
**5 :** to give, offer, or make freely or as fitting
⟨*pay* attention⟩ ⟨*pay* your respects⟩
**6 a :** to return value or profit to ⟨it *pays* you to
stay open⟩ **b :** to bring in as a return ⟨an investment *paying* five percent⟩
**7 :** to slacken (as a rope) and allow to run out
— used with *out*
*intransitive verb*
**1 :** to discharge a debt or obligation
**2 :** to be worth the expense or effort ⟨crime
doesn't *pay*⟩
**3 :** to suffer the consequences of an act ☆ ◆
— **pay one's dues 1 :** to earn a right or
position through experience, suffering, or hard
work **2** *also* **pay dues :** PAY *intransitive verb*
**3**

◇ WORD HISTORY
**pay** Etymologically speaking, to *pay* is "to
pacify." The Latin verb *pacare* "to pacify, impose a settlement on" is derived from *pax*
"pact, settlement, peace." In the Middle Ages
*pacare* was used specifically to mean "to appease (a creditor) by paying a debt" and
eventually in the more general sense "to
pay." Old French *paier,* descended from *pacare,* had both the original sense "to appease"
and the later meaning "to pay." Middle English *payen,* which was borrowed from
French in the late 12th or early 13th century,
was also used in both senses. The original
sense of *pay,* however, has long disappeared
from English usage.

— **pay one's way** or **pay one's own way** : to pay one's share of expenses
— **pay the piper** : to bear the cost of something
— **pay through the nose** : to pay exorbitantly or dearly

**²pay** *noun* (14th century)
**1** : something paid for a purpose and especially as a salary or wage : REMUNERATION
**2 a** : the act or fact of paying or being paid **b** : the status of being paid by an employer : EMPLOY
**3** : a person viewed with respect to reliability or promptness in paying debts or bills
**4 a** : ore or a natural situation that yields metal and especially gold in profitable amounts **b** : an oil-yielding stratum or zone
*synonym* see WAGE

**³pay** *adjective* (1856)
**1** : containing or leading to something precious or valuable
**2** : equipped with a coin slot for receiving a fee for use ⟨*pay* telephone⟩
**3** : requiring payment

**⁴pay** *transitive verb* **payed** *also* **paid; paying** [obsolete French *peier*, from Latin *picare*, from *pic-, pix* pitch — more at PITCH] (1627)
: to coat with a waterproof composition

**pay·able** \'pā-ə-bəl\ *adjective* (14th century)
**1** : that may, can, or must be paid
**2** : PROFITABLE

**pay–as–you–go** *adjective* (1840)
: of or relating to a system or policy of paying bills when due or of paying for goods and services when purchased

**pay·back** \'pā-ˌbak\ *noun* (1955)
**1** : a return on an investment equal to the original capital outlay; *also* : the period of time elapsed before an investment is recouped
**2** : REQUITAL

**pay·cable** *noun* (1975)
: pay-TV utilizing a cable television system

**pay·check** \'pā-ˌchek\ *noun* (1899)
**1** : a check in payment of wages or salary
**2** : WAGES, SALARY

**pay·day** \-ˌdā\ *noun* (1529)
: a regular day on which wages are paid

**pay dirt** *noun* (1856)
**1** : earth or ore that yields a profit to a miner
**2** : a useful or remunerative discovery or object

**pay·ee** \(ˌ)pā-'ē\ *noun* (1758)
: one to whom money is or is to be paid

**pay envelope** *noun* (1901)
: an envelope containing one's wages; *also* : WAGES

**pay·er** \'pā-ər\ *also* **pay·or** \'pā-ər, (ˌ)pā-'ȯr\ *noun* (14th century)
: one that pays; *especially* : the person by whom a bill or note has been or should be paid

**pay·load** \'pā-ˌlōd\ *noun* (circa 1922)
**1** : the load carried by a vehicle exclusive of what is necessary for its operation; *especially* : the load carried by an aircraft or spacecraft consisting of things (as passengers or instruments) necessary to the purpose of the flight
**2** : the weight of a payload

**pay·mas·ter** \-ˌmas-tər\ *noun* (1550)
: an officer or agent whose duty it is to pay salaries or wages

**pay·ment** \'pā-mənt\ *noun* (14th century)
**1** : the act of paying
**2** : something that is paid : PAY
**3** : REQUITAL

**pay·nim** \'pā-nəm\ *noun* [Middle English *painim*, from Old French *paienime* heathendom, from Late Latin *paganismus*, from *paganus* pagan] (13th century)
*archaic* : PAGAN; *especially* : MUSLIM

**¹pay·off** \'pā-ˌȯf\ *noun* (1905)
**1 a** : PROFIT, REWARD **b** : RETRIBUTION
**2** : the act or occasion of receiving money or material gain especially as compensation or as a bribe

**3** : the climax of an incident or enterprise; *specifically* : the denouement of a narrative
**4** : a decisive fact or factor resolving a situation or bringing about a definitive conclusion

**²payoff** *adjective* (1934)
: yielding results in the final test : DECISIVE

**pay off** (1710)
*transitive verb*
**1 a** : to give all due wages to; *especially* : to pay in full and discharge (an employee) **b** : to pay (a debt or a creditor) in full **c** : BRIBE
**2** : to inflict retribution on
**3** : to allow (a thread or rope) to run off a spool or drum
*intransitive verb*
: to yield returns

**pay·o·la** \pā-'ō-lə\ *noun* [¹*pay* + *-ola* (as in *Pianola*, trademark for a player piano)] (1938)
: undercover or indirect payment (as to a disc jockey) for a commercial favor (as for promoting a particular record)

**pay·out** \'pā-ˌaut\ *noun* (1943)
: the act of paying out : PAYOFF

**pay–per–view** *noun* (1980)
: a cable television service by which customers can order access to a single program for a fee

**pay phone** *noun* (1936)
: a usually coin-operated public telephone

**pay·roll** \'pā-ˌrōl\ *noun* (1740)
**1** : a paymaster's or employer's list of those entitled to pay and of the amounts due to each
**2** : the sum necessary for distribution to those on a payroll; *also* : the money to be distributed

**pay station** *noun* (1919)
: PAY PHONE

**pay–TV** *noun* (circa 1956)
: a service providing noncommercial television programming (as recent movies and entertainment specials) by means of a scrambled signal to subscribers who are provided with a decoder — called also *pay television;* compare PAY-CABLE, SUBSCRIPTION TV

**pay up** (15th century)
*intransitive verb*
: to pay what is due
*transitive verb*
: to pay in full

**PBB** \ˌpē-(ˌ)bē-'bē\ *noun* (circa 1975)
: POLYBROMINATED BIPHENYL

**PBX** \ˌpē-(ˌ)bē-'eks\ *noun* [*private branch exchange*] (circa 1961)
: a private telephone switchboard

**PC** \ˌpē-'sē\ *noun, plural* **PCs** *or* **PC's** (1978)
: PERSONAL COMPUTER

**PCB** \ˌpē-(ˌ)sē-'bē\ *noun* (1966)
: POLYCHLORINATED BIPHENYL

**PCP** \ˌpē-(ˌ)sē-'pē\ *noun* [*phenyl* + *cycl-* + *piperidine*] (circa 1970)
: PHENCYCLIDINE

**PDQ** \ˌpē-(ˌ)dē-'kyü\ *adverb, often not capitalized* [abbreviation of *pretty damned quick*] (1875)
: IMMEDIATELY

**pe** \'pā\ *noun* [Hebrew *pē*] (1823)
: the 17th letter of the Hebrew alphabet — see ALPHABET table

**pea** \'pē\ *noun, plural* **peas** *also* **pease** \'pēz\ *often attributive* [back-formation from Middle English *pease* (taken as a plural), from Old English *pise*, from Latin *pisa*, plural of *pisum*, from Greek *pison*] (1611)
**1 a** : a variable annual leguminous Eurasian vine (*Pisum sativum*) that is cultivated especially for its rounded smooth or wrinkled edible protein-rich seeds **b** : the seed of the pea **c** *plural* : the immature pods of the pea with their included seeds
**2** : any of various leguminous plants related to or resembling the pea — usually used in combination or with a qualifying term ⟨chickpea⟩ ⟨black-eyed *pea*⟩; *also* : the seed of such a plant
**3** : something resembling a pea (as in size or shape)

*word history* see SHERRY

**pea aphid** *noun* (1925)
: a widely distributed aphid (*Acyrthosiphon pisum*) that is a serious pest on legumes (as alfalfa, pea, and clover)

**pea bean** *noun* (circa 1887)
: any of various kidney beans cultivated for their small white seeds which are used dried (as for baking)

**¹peace** \'pēs\ *noun* [Middle English *pees*, from Old French *pais*, from Latin *pac-, pax*; akin to Latin *pacisci* to agree — more at PACT] (12th century)
**1** : a state of tranquillity or quiet: as **a** : freedom from civil disturbance **b** : a state of security or order within a community provided for by law or custom ⟨a breach of the *peace*⟩
**2** : freedom from disquieting or oppressive thoughts or emotions
**3** : harmony in personal relations
**4 a** : a state or period of mutual concord between governments **b** : a pact or agreement to end hostilities between those who have been at war or in a state of enmity
**5** — used interjectionally to ask for silence or calm or as a greeting or farewell
— **at peace** : in a state of concord or tranquillity

**²peace** *intransitive verb* (14th century)
*obsolete* : to be, become, or keep silent or quiet

**peace·able** \'pē-sə-bəl\ *adjective* (14th century)
**1 a** : disposed to peace : not contentious or quarrelsome **b** : quietly behaved
**2** : marked by freedom from strife or disorder
— **peace·able·ness** *noun*
— **peace·ably** \-blē\ *adverb*

**peace corps** *noun* (1960)
: a body of trained personnel sent as volunteers especially to assist underdeveloped nations

**peace·ful** \'pēs-fəl\ *adjective* (14th century)
**1** : PEACEABLE 1
**2** : untroubled by conflict, agitation, or commotion : QUIET, TRANQUIL
**3** : of or relating to a state or time of peace
**4** : devoid of violence or force
*synonym* see CALM
— **peace·ful·ly** \-fə-lē\ *adverb*
— **peace·ful·ness** *noun*

**peace·keep·ing** \'pēs-ˌkē-piŋ\ *noun* (1945)
: the preserving of peace; *especially* : international enforcement and supervision of a truce between hostile states or communities
— **peace·keep·er** \-pər\ *noun*

**peace·mak·er** \-ˌmā-kər\ *noun* (15th century)
: one who makes peace especially by reconciling parties at variance
— **peace·mak·ing** \-kiŋ\ *noun or adjective*

**peace·nik** \-ˌnik\ *noun* (1965)
: an opponent of the Vietnam War; *broadly* : PACIFIST

**peace offering** *noun* (circa 1530)
: a gift or service for the purpose of procuring peace or reconciliation

**peace officer** *noun* (1714)
: a civil officer (as a police officer) whose duty it is to preserve the public peace

**peace pipe** *noun* (1760)
: CALUMET

**peace sign** *noun* (1969)
**1** : a sign made by holding the palm outward and forming a V with the index and middle fingers and used to indicate the desire for peace
**2** : PEACE SYMBOL

**peace symbol** *noun* (1970)
: the symbol ⊕ used to signify peace

**peace·time** \'pēs-ˌtīm\ *noun* (1551)
: a time when a nation is not at war

**¹peach** \'pēch\ *noun* [Middle English *peche*, from Middle French (the fruit), from Late Latin *persica*, from Latin (*malum*) *persicum*, literally, Persian fruit] (14th century)
**1 a** : a low spreading freely branching Chi-

nese tree (*Prunus persica*) of the rose family that is widely cultivated in temperate areas and has lanceolate leaves, sessile usually pink flowers borne on the naked twigs in early spring, and a fruit which is a single-seeded drupe with a hard endocarp, a pulpy white or yellow mesocarp, and a thin downy epicarp **b** : the edible fruit of the peach **2** : a moderate yellowish pink **3** : one resembling a peach (as in sweetness, beauty, or excellence) ◆

²**peach** *verb* [Middle English *pechen*, short for *apechen* to accuse, from (assumed) Anglo-French *apecher*, from Late Latin *impedicare* to entangle — more at IMPEACH] (1570) *transitive verb* : to inform against : BETRAY *intransitive verb* : to turn informer : BLAB

**peach leaf curl** *noun* (1888) : leaf curl of the peach that is caused by a fungus (*Taphrina deformans*)

**peach tree borer** *noun* (1850) : a blue-black orange-marked clearwing moth (*Synanthedon exitiosa* synonym *Sanninoidea exitiosa*) whose white brown-headed larva bores in the wood of stone fruit trees (as the peach)

**peachy** \'pē-chē\ *adjective* **peach·i·er; -est** (1599) **1** : resembling a peach **2** : unusually fine : DANDY

¹**pea·cock** \'pē-ˌkäk\ *noun* [Middle English *pecok*, from *pe-* (from Old English *pēa* peafowl, from Latin *pavon-, pavo* peacock) + *cok* cock] (14th century) **1** : a male peafowl distinguished by a crest of upright plumules and by greatly elongated loosely webbed upper tail coverts which are mostly tipped with ocellated spots and can be erected and spread at will in a fan shimmering with iridescent color; *broadly* : PEAFOWL **2** : one making a proud display of himself : SHOW-OFF
— **pea·cock·ish** \-ˌkä-kish\ *adjective*
— **pea·cocky** \-kē\ *adjective*

²**peacock** (1586) *intransitive verb* : SHOW OFF

**peacock blue** *noun* (1881) : a moderate greenish blue

**peacock flower** *noun* (1884) : ROYAL POINCIANA

**pea·fowl** \'pē-ˌfaul\ *noun* [*pea-* (as in *peacock*) + *fowl*] (1804) : either of two very large terrestrial pheasants (*Pavo cristatus* and *P. muticus*) of southeastern Asia and the East Indies often reared as ornamental fowls

peafowl: *A* female; *B* male

**pea green** *noun* (1752) : a moderate yellow-green

**pea·hen** \'pē-ˌhen\ *noun* [Middle English *pehenne*, from *pe-* + *henne* hen] (15th century) : a female peafowl

**pea jacket** \'pē-\ *noun* [by folk etymology from Dutch *pijjekker*, from *pij*, a kind of cloth + *jekker* jacket] (1721) : a heavy woolen double-breasted jacket originally worn by sailors — called also *pea·coat* \'pē-ˌkōt\

¹**peak** \'pēk\ *noun* [perhaps alteration of *pike*] (1530) **1** : a pointed or projecting part of a garment; *especially* : the visor of a cap or hat **2** : PROMONTORY **3** : a sharp or pointed end

**4 a** (1) : the top of a hill or mountain ending in a point (2) : a prominent mountain usually having a well-defined summit **b** : something resembling a mountain peak **5 a** : the upper aftermost corner of a fore-and-aft sail **b** : the narrow part of a ship's bow or stern or the part of the hold in it **6 a** : the highest level or greatest degree **b** : a high point in a course of development especially as represented on a graph **7** : a point formed by the hair on the forehead *synonym* see SUMMIT

²**peak** (1577) *intransitive verb* : to reach a maximum (as of capacity, value, or activity) — often used with *out* *transitive verb* : to cause to come to a peak, point, or maximum

³**peak** *adjective* (1903) : being at or reaching the maximum

⁴**peak** *intransitive verb* [origin unknown] (1605) **1** : to grow thin or sickly **2** : to dwindle away

⁵**peak** *transitive verb* [from *apeak* held vertically] (1626) **1** : to set (as a gaff) nearer the perpendicular **2** : to hold (oars) with blades well raised

¹**peaked** \'pēkt *also* 'pē-kəd\ *adjective* (15th century) : having a peak : POINTED
— **peaked·ness** \'pēk(t)-nəs, 'pē-kəd-nəs\ *noun*

²**peak·ed** \'pē-kəd *also* 'pi-kəd\ *adjective* (1835) : being pale and wan or emaciated : SICKLY

**peaky** \'pē-kē\ *adjective* (1821) : ²PEAKED

¹**peal** \'pē(ə)l\ *noun* [Middle English, appeal, summons to church, short for *appel* appeal, from *appelen* to appeal] (14th century) **1 a** : the loud ringing of bells **b** : a complete set of changes on a given number of bells **c** : a set of bells tuned to the tones of the major scale for change ringing **2** : a loud sound or succession of sounds ⟨*peals* of laughter⟩

²**peal** (1632) *intransitive verb* : to give out peals *transitive verb* : to utter or give forth loudly

**pea·like** \'pē-ˌlīk\ *adjective* (1774) **1** : resembling a garden pea especially in size, firmness, and shape ⟨a *pealike* lump under the skin⟩ **2** *of a flower* : being showy and papilionaceous

¹**pea·nut** \'pē-(ˌ)nət\ *noun* (1802) **1** : a low-branching widely cultivated leguminous annual herb (*Arachis hypogaea*) with showy yellow flowers having a peduncle which elongates and bends into the soil where the ovary ripens into a pod containing one to three oily edible seeds; *also* : its seed or seed-containing pod **2** : an insignificant or tiny person **3** *plural* : a trifling amount

²**peanut** *adjective* (1836) : INSIGNIFICANT, PETTY ⟨*peanut* politics⟩

**peanut oil** *noun* (1882) : a colorless to yellow fatty nondrying oil that is obtained from peanuts and is used chiefly as a salad oil, in margarine, in soap, and as a vehicle in pharmaceutical preparations and cosmetics

**pear** \'par, 'per\ *noun* [Middle English *pere*, from Old English *peru*, from (assumed) Vulgar Latin *pira*, from Latin, plural of *pirum*] (before 12th century) **1** : a fleshy pome fruit that is borne by a tree (genus *Pyrus*, especially *P. communis*) of the rose family and is usually larger at the apical end **2** : a tree bearing pears

¹**pearl** \'pər(-ə)l\ *noun* [Middle English *perle*, from Middle French, probably from (assumed) Vulgar Latin *pernula*, diminutive of Latin *perna* upper leg, kind of sea mussel; akin to Old English *fiersn* heel, Greek *pternē*] (14th century) **1 a** : a dense variously colored and usually lustrous concretion formed of concentric layers of nacre as an abnormal growth within the shell of some mollusks and used as a gem **b** : MOTHER-OF-PEARL **2** : one that is very choice or precious **3** : something resembling a pearl intrinsically or physically **4** : a nearly neutral slightly bluish medium gray

²**pearl** (14th century) *transitive verb* **1** : to set or adorn with pearls **2** : to sprinkle or bead with pearly drops **3** : to form into small round grains **4** : to give a pearly color or luster to *intransitive verb* **1** : to form drops or beads like pearls **2** : to fish or search for pearls
— **pearl·er** \'pər-lər\ *noun*

³**pearl** *adjective* (1610) **1 a** : of, relating to, or resembling pearl **b** : made of or adorned with pearls **2** : having medium-sized grains

⁴**pearl** *noun or transitive verb* [alteration of *purl*] (1824) *British* : PICOT

**pearl·es·cent** \ˌpər-'le-sᵊnt\ *adjective* (1936) : having a pearly luster ⟨a *pearlescent* lacquer⟩
— **pearl·es·cence** \-sᵊn(t)s\ *noun*

**pearl essence** *noun* (circa 1909) : a translucent substance that occurs in the silvery scales of various fish (as herring) and is used in making artificial pearls, lacquers, and plastics

**pearl gray** *noun* (1796) **1** : a yellowish to light gray **2** : a pale blue

**Pearl Harbor** *noun* [*Pearl Harbor*, Oahu, Hawaii, American naval station attacked without warning by the Japanese on December 7, 1941] (1942) : a sneak attack often with devastating effect

**pearl·ite** \'pər(-ə)-ˌlīt\ *noun* [French *perlite*, from *perle* pearl] (1888) : the lamellar mixture of ferrite and cementite in slowly cooled iron-carbon alloys occurring normally as a principal constituent of both steel and cast iron
— **pearl·it·ic** \ˌpər-'li-tik\ *adjective*

**pearl·ized** \'pər(-ə)-ˌlīzd\ *adjective* (1937) : given a pearlescent surface or finish

**pearl millet** *noun* (circa 1890)

◇ WORD HISTORY

**peach**  When the peach, which is native to China, was introduced to the classical world in the first century A.D., it was known in Greek as *mēlon Persikon* and in Latin as *malum Persicum*. Both names literally meant "Persian apple." The fruit may not have reached the Mediterranean directly from Persia, and its attribution to that country in the name simply reflects a general sense that it was eastern in origin. The Latin *malum Persicum* was shortened to *persicum*, which was superseded in Late Latin by the feminine form *persica*. *Persica* developed into Old French *pesche*. In a Middle French form this word provided later Middle English with *peche*, the antecedent of Modern English *peach*.

: a tall cereal grass (*Pennisetum glaucum* synonym *P. americanum*) that has large leaves and dense round spikes and is widely grown for its seeds and for forage

**pearl onion** *noun* (circa 1890)
: a very small usually pickled onion used especially in appetizers and as a garnish

**pearly** \'pər-lē\ *adjective* **pearl·i·er; -est** (15th century)
**1** : resembling, containing, or adorned with pearls or mother-of-pearl
**2** : highly precious

**pearly everlasting** *noun* (1857)
: an everlasting (*Anaphalis margaritacea*) that has herbage covered with white woolly hairs and corymbose heads with white scarious involucres

**pearly nautilus** *noun* (1822)
: NAUTILUS 1

**pear psylla** *noun* (1904)
: a yellowish or greenish jumping plant louse (*Psylla pyricola*) that is often destructive to the pear

**pear–shaped** \'par-,shāpt, 'per-\ *adjective* (1758)
**1** : having an oval shape markedly tapering at one end
**2** *of a vocal tone* : free from harshness, thinness, or nasality

**peart** \'pirt\ *adjective* [alteration of *pert*] (1578)
*chiefly Southern & Midland* : being in good spirits : LIVELY
— **peart·ly** *adverb*

**peas·ant** \'pe-z°nt\ *noun* [Middle English *paissaunt*, from Middle French *paisant*, from Old French, from *païs* country, from Late Latin *pagensis* inhabitant of a district, from Latin *pagus* district] (15th century)
**1** : a member of a European class of persons tilling the soil as small landowners or as laborers; *also* : a member of a similar class elsewhere
**2** : a usually uneducated person of low social status

**peas·ant·ry** \-z°n-trē\ *noun* (circa 1553)
**1** : PEASANTS
**2** : the position, rank, or behavior of a peasant

**pease·cod** *or* **peas·cod** \'pēz-,käd\ *noun* [Middle English *pesecod*, from *pese* + *cod* bag, husk — more at CODPIECE] (14th century)
: a pea pod

**pea·shoot·er** \'pē-,shü-tər\ *noun* (1803)
: a toy blowgun that uses peas for projectiles

**pea soup** *noun* (1711)
**1** : a thick purée made of dried peas
**2** : a thick fog

**¹peat** \'pēt\ *noun, often attributive* [Middle English *pete*, from Medieval Latin *peta*] (14th century)
**1** : TURF 2b
**2** : partially carbonized vegetable tissue formed by partial decomposition in water of various plants (as mosses of the genus *Sphagnum*)
— **peaty** \'pē-tē\ *adjective*

**²peat** *noun* [origin unknown] (1599)
: a bold lively woman

**peat moss** *noun* (1880)
: SPHAGNUM

**pea·vey** *or* **pea·vy** \'pē-vē\ *noun, plural* **peaveys** *or* **peavies** [probably from the name *Peavey*] (1870)
: a lumberman's lever that has a pivoting hooked arm and metal spike at one end — called also *cant dog;* compare CANT HOOK

**¹peb·ble** \'pe-bəl\ *noun* [Middle English *pobble*, from Old English *papolstān*, from *papol-* (of unknown origin) + *stān* stone] (14th century)
**1** : a small usually rounded stone especially when worn by the action of water

*peavey*

**2** : transparent and colorless quartz : ROCK CRYSTAL
**3** : an irregular, crinkled, or grainy surface
— **peb·bly** \-b(ə-)lē\ *adjective*

**²pebble** *transitive verb* **peb·bled; peb·bling** \-b(ə-)liŋ\ (1605)
**1** : to pelt with pebbles
**2** : to pave or cover with pebbles or something resembling pebbles
**3** : to grain (as leather) so as to produce a rough and irregularly indented surface

**pec** \'pek\ *noun* (1966)
: PECTORAL MUSCLE

**pe·can** \pi-'kän, -'kan; 'pē-,kan\ *noun* [American French *pacane*, of Algonquian origin; akin to Ojibwa *paka'n*, a hard-shelled nut] (1712)
**1** : a large hickory (*Carya illinoensis*) that has roughish bark and hard but brittle wood and is widely grown in the warmer parts of the U.S. and in Mexico for its edible nut
**2** : the wood of the pecan tree
**3** : the smooth oblong thin-shelled nut of the pecan tree

**pec·ca·dil·lo** \,pe-kə-'di-(,)lō\ *noun, plural* **-loes** *or* **-los** [Spanish *pecadillo*, diminutive of *pecado* sin, from Latin *peccatum*, from neuter of *peccatus*, past participle of *peccare*] (1591)
: a slight offense

**pec·cant** \'pe-kənt\ *adjective* [Latin *peccant-, peccans*, present participle of *peccare* to stumble, sin] (circa 1604)
**1** : guilty of a moral offense : SINNING
**2** : violating a principle or rule : FAULTY
— **pec·cant·ly** *adverb*

**pec·ca·ry** \'pe-kə-rē\ *noun, plural* **-ries** [perhaps modification of Carib *baquira*] (1613)
: any of several largely nocturnal gregarious American mammals resembling the related pigs: as **a** : a grizzled animal (*Tayassu tajacu*) with an indistinct white collar **b** : a blackish animal (*Tayassu pecari*) with a whitish mouth region

**pec·ca·vi** \pe-'kä-(,)wē, -(,)vē; -'kä-,vī\ *noun* [Latin, I have sinned, from *peccare*] (1553)
: an acknowledgment of sin

**¹peck** \'pek\ *noun* [Middle English *pek*, from Middle French] (13th century)
**1** — see WEIGHT table
**2** : a large quantity or number

**²peck** *verb* [Middle English, perhaps from Middle Low German *pekken*] (14th century)
*transitive verb*
**1 a** : to strike or pierce especially repeatedly with the bill or a pointed tool **b** : to make by pecking 〈*peck* a hole〉
**2** : to pick up with the bill
*intransitive verb*
**1 a** : to strike, pierce, or pick up something with or as if with the bill **b** : CARP, NAG
**2** : to eat reluctantly and in small bites 〈*peck* at food〉

**³peck** *noun* (circa 1591)
**1** : an impression or hole made by pecking
**2** : a quick sharp stroke

**peck·er** \'pe-kər\ *noun* (1587)
**1** : one that pecks
**2** *chiefly British* : COURAGE
**3** : PENIS — often considered vulgar

**peck·er·wood** \'pe-kər-,wud\ *noun* [probably inversion of *woodpecker*] (1904)
: a rural white Southerner — often used disparagingly

**pecking order** *also* **peck order** *noun* (1928)
**1** : the basic pattern of social organization within a flock of poultry in which each bird pecks another lower in the scale without fear of retaliation and submits to pecking by one of higher rank; *broadly* : a dominance hierarchy in a group of social animals
**2** : a social hierarchy

**peck·ish** \'pe-kish\ *adjective* [²*peck*] (1785)
**1** *chiefly British* : HUNGRY
**2** : CROTCHETY

**Peck·sniff·ian** \pek-'sni-fē-ən\ *adjective* [Seth *Pecksniff*, character in *Martin Chuzzlewit* (1843–44) by Charles Dickens] (1851)
: unctuously hypocritical : PHARISAICAL

**pecky** \'pe-kē\ *adjective* [³*peck*] (1848)
**1** : marked by lenticular or finger-shaped pockets of decay caused by fungi 〈*pecky* cypress〉
**2** : containing discolored or shriveled grains 〈*pecky* rice〉

**pec·o·ri·no** \,pe-kə-'rē-(,)nō\ *noun, often capitalized* [Italian, from *pecorino* of sheep, from *pecora* sheep, ewe, from Latin, domestic animals, from plural of *pecus* cattle — more at FEE] (1912)
: any of various cheeses of Italian origin made from sheep's milk

**pec·ten** \'pek-tən\ *noun, plural* **pectens** [New Latin *pectin-, pecten*, from Latin, comb, scallop] (1682)
**1** : SCALLOP 1a
**2** *plural usually* **pec·ti·nes** \-tə-,nēz\ : a body part that resembles a comb; *especially* : a folded vascular pigmented membrane projecting into the vitreous humor in the eye of a bird or reptile

**pec·tic** \'pek-tik\ *adjective* [French *pectique*, from Greek *pēktikos* coagulating, from *pēgnynai* to fix, coagulate — more at PACT] (1831)
: of, relating to, or derived from pectin

**pectic acid** *noun* (1831)
: any of various water-insoluble substances formed by hydrolyzing the methyl ester groups of pectins

**pec·tin** \'pek-tən\ *noun* [French *pectine*, from *pectique*] (1838)
: any of various water-soluble substances that bind adjacent cell walls in plant tissues and yield a gel which is the basis of fruit jellies; *also* : a commercial product rich in pectins

**pec·ti·na·ceous** \,pek-tə-'nā-shəs\ *adjective* (circa 1844)
: of, relating to, or containing pectin

**pec·ti·nate** \'pek-tə-,nāt\ *adjective* [Latin *pectinatus*, from *pectin-, pecten* comb; akin to Greek *kten-, kteis* comb] (1793)
: having narrow parallel projections or divisions suggestive of the teeth of a comb 〈*pectinate* antennae〉
— **pec·ti·na·tion** \,pek-tə-'nā-shən\ *noun*

**pec·tin·es·ter·ase** \,pek-tə-'nes-tə-,rās, -,rāz\ *noun* (1945)
: an enzyme that catalyzes the hydrolysis of pectins into pectic acids and methanol

**¹pec·to·ral** \'pek-t(ə-)rəl\ *noun* (15th century)
: something worn on the breast

**²pectoral** *adjective* [Middle French or Latin; Middle French, from Latin *pectoralis*, from *pector-, pectus* breast; akin to Tocharian A *päśśäm* breasts, Old High German *ucht* breast] (1578)
**1** : of, situated in or on, or worn on the chest
**2** : coming from the breast or heart as the seat of emotion

**pectoral cross** *noun* (circa 1735)
: a cross worn on the breast especially by a prelate

**pectoral fin** *noun* (1769)
: either of the fins of a fish that correspond to the forelimbs of a quadruped

**pectoral girdle** *noun* (circa 1890)
: the bony or cartilaginous arch that supports the forelimbs of a vertebrate

**pectoral muscle** *noun* (1615)
: any of the muscles which connect the ventral walls of the chest with the bones of the upper arm and shoulder and of which there are two on each side of the human body

**pec·u·late** \'pe-kyə-,lāt\ *transitive verb* **-lat·ed; -lat·ing** [Latin *peculatus*, past participle of *peculari*, from *peculium*] (1802)
: EMBEZZLE
— **pec·u·la·tion** \,pe-kyə-'lā-shən\ *noun*
— **pec·u·la·tor** \'pe-kyə-,lā-tər\ *noun*

¹**pe·cu·liar** \pi-'kyül-yər\ *adjective* [Middle English *peculier*, from Latin *peculiaris* of private property, special, from *peculium* private property, from *pecu* cattle; akin to Latin *pecus* cattle — more at FEE] (15th century)
**1** : characteristic of only one person, group, or thing : DISTINCTIVE
**2** : different from the usual or normal: **a** : SPECIAL, PARTICULAR **b** : ODD, CURIOUS **c** : ECCENTRIC, QUEER ◆
**synonym** see CHARACTERISTIC, STRANGE
— **pe·cu·liar·ly** *adverb*

²**peculiar** *noun* (1562)
: something exempt from ordinary jurisdiction; *especially* : a church or parish exempt from the jurisdiction of the ordinary in whose territory it lies

**pe·cu·liar·i·ty** \pi-,kyül-'yar-ə-tē, -,kyü-lē-'ar-\ *noun, plural* **-ties** (1646)
**1** : the quality or state of being peculiar
**2** : a distinguishing characteristic
**3** : ODDITY, QUIRK

**pe·cu·niary** \pi-'kyü-nē-,er-ē\ *adjective* [Latin *pecuniarius*, from *pecunia* money — more at FEE] (1502)
**1** : consisting of or measured in money
**2** : of or relating to money : MONETARY
**word history** see PECULIAR
— **pe·cu·ni·ar·i·ly** \-,kyü-nē-'er-ə-lē\ *adverb*

**ped** \'ped\ *noun* [Greek *pedon* ground; akin to Latin *ped-, pes* foot — more at FOOT] (1951)
: a natural soil aggregate

**ped-** *or* **pedo-** *or* **paed-** *or* **paedo-** *combining form* [Greek *paid-, paido-,* from *paid-, pais* child, boy — more at FEW]
: child ⟨*pedi*atric⟩ : childhood ⟨*paedo*genesis⟩

**-ped** *or* **-pede** *noun combining form* [Latin *ped-, pes*]
: foot ⟨maxilli*ped*⟩

**ped·a·gog·i·cal** \,pe-də-'gä-ji-kəl, -'gō-\ *also* **ped·a·gog·ic** \-jik\ *adjective* (1619)
: of, relating to, or befitting a teacher or education
— **ped·a·gog·i·cal·ly** \-ji-k(ə-)lē\ *adverb*

**ped·a·gog·ics** \-jiks\ *noun plural but singular in construction* (circa 1859)
: PEDAGOGY

**ped·a·gogue** *also* **ped·a·gog** \'pe-də-,gäg\ *noun* [Middle English *pedagoge,* from Middle French, from Latin *paedagogus,* from Greek *paidagōgos,* slave who escorted children to school, from *paid-* ped- + *agōgos* leader, from *agein* to lead — more at AGENT] (14th century)
: TEACHER, SCHOOLMASTER; *especially* : a dull, formal, or pedantic teacher

**ped·a·go·gy** \'pe-də-,gō-jē *also* -,gä-, *especially British* -,gä-gē\ *noun* (1583)
: the art, science, or profession of teaching; *especially* : EDUCATION 2

¹**ped·al** \'pe-d²l\ *noun* [Middle French *pedale,* from Italian, from Latin *pedalis,* adjective] (1611)
**1** : a lever pressed by the foot in the playing of a musical instrument (as an organ or piano)
**2** : a foot lever or treadle by which a part is activated in a mechanism

²**ped·al** *adjective* [Latin *pedalis,* from *ped-, pes*] (1625)
**1** \'pe-d²l *also* 'pē-\ : of or relating to the foot
**2** \'pe-\ : of, relating to, or involving a pedal

³**ped·al** \'pe-d²l\ *verb* **ped·aled** *also* **pedalled; ped·al·ing** *also* **ped·al·ling** \'pe-d²l-iŋ, 'ped-liŋ\ (1888)
*intransitive verb*
**1** : to ride a bicycle
**2** : to use or work a pedal
*transitive verb*
: to work the pedals of

**pedal bone** *noun* (1881)
: COFFIN BONE

**pe·dal·fer** \pə-'dal-fər, -,fer\ *noun* [Greek *pedon* ground + English *alumen* + Latin *ferrum* iron] (1928)
: a soil that lacks a hardened layer of accumulated carbonates

**ped·al-note** \'pe-d²l-,nōt\ *noun* [from the playing of the lowest notes on the organ by means of pedals] (circa 1828)
**1** : PEDAL POINT
**2** : one of the lowest tones that can be sounded on a brass instrument being an octave below the normal usable range and representing the fundamental of the harmonic series

**ped·alo** \'pe-də-(,)lō\ *noun, plural* **-los** [French *pédalo,* from *pédale* pedal + *-o* (perhaps as in *meccano* children's construction set)] (1945)
*chiefly British* : a small recreational paddleboat powered by pedals

**pedal point** *noun* (1852)
: a single tone usually the tonic or dominant that is normally sustained in the bass and sounds against changing harmonies in the other parts

**pedal pushers** *noun plural* (1944)
: women's and girls' calf-length trousers

**pedal steel** *noun* (1969)
: a box-shaped musical instrument with legs that has usually 10 strings which can be altered in pitch by the use of pedals and which are plucked while being pressed with a movable steel bar — called also *pedal steel guitar*

**ped·ant** \'pe-d²nt\ *noun* [Middle French, from Italian *pedante*] (1588)
**1** *obsolete* : a male schoolteacher
**2 a** : one who makes a show of knowledge **b** : one who is unimaginative or who unduly emphasizes minutiae in the presentation or use of knowledge **c** : a formalist or precisionist in teaching

**pe·dan·tic** \pi-'dan-tik\ *adjective* (circa 1600)
**1** : of, relating to, or being a pedant
**2** : narrowly, stodgily, and often ostentatiously learned
**3** : UNIMAGINATIVE, PEDESTRIAN
— **pe·dan·ti·cal·ly** \-'dan-ti-k(ə-)lē\ *adverb*

**ped·ant·ry** \'pe-d²n-trē\ *noun, plural* **-ries** (1612)
**1** : pedantic presentation or application of knowledge or learning
**2** : an instance of pedantry

**ped·dle** \'pe-d²l\ *verb* **ped·dled; ped·dling** \'ped-liŋ, 'pe-d²l-iŋ\ [back-formation from *peddler,* from Middle English *pedlere*] (1532)
*intransitive verb*
**1** : to travel about with wares for sale; *broadly* : SELL
**2** : to be busy with trifles : PIDDLE
*transitive verb*
**1** : to sell or offer for sale from place to place : HAWK; *broadly* : SELL
**2** : to deal out or seek to disseminate

**ped·dler** *also* **ped·lar** \'ped-lər\ *noun* (14th century)
: one who peddles: as **a** : one who offers merchandise (as fresh produce) for sale along the street or from door to door **b** : one who deals in or promotes something intangible (as a personal asset or an idea) ⟨influence *peddlers*⟩

**ped·er·ast** \'pe-də-,rast\ *noun* [Greek *paiderastēs,* literally, lover of boys, from *paid-* ped- + *erastēs* lover, from *erasthai* to love — more at EROS] (circa 1736)
: one that practices anal intercourse especially with a boy
— **ped·er·as·tic** \,pe-də-'ras-tik\ *adjective*
— **ped·er·as·ty** \'pe-də-,ras-tē\ *noun*

¹**ped·es·tal** \'pe-dəs-t²l\ *noun* [Middle French *piedestal,* from Old Italian *piedestallo,* from *pie di stallo* foot of a stall] (1563)
**1 a** : the support or foot of a late classic or neoclassic column — see COLUMN illustration **b** : the base of an upright structure
**2** : BASE, FOUNDATION
**3** : a position of esteem

²**pedestal** *transitive verb* **-taled** *or* **-talled; -tal·ing** *or* **-tal·ling** (1648)
: to place on or furnish with a pedestal

¹**pe·des·tri·an** \pə-'des-trē-ən\ *adjective* [Latin *pedestr-, pedester,* literally, going on foot, from *ped-, pes* foot — more at FOOT] (1716)
**1** : COMMONPLACE, UNIMAGINATIVE
**2 a** : going or performed on foot **b** : of, relating to, or designed for walking ⟨a *pedestrian* mall⟩

²**pedestrian** *noun* (1793)
: a person going on foot : WALKER

**pe·des·tri·an·ism** \-ə-,ni-zəm\ *noun* (1809)
**1 a** : the practice of walking **b** : fondness for walking for exercise or recreation
**2** : the quality or state of being unimaginative or commonplace

**pe·di·at·ric** \,pē-dē-'a-trik\ *adjective* (1880)
: of or relating to pediatrics

**pe·di·a·tri·cian** \,pē-dē-ə-'tri-shən\ *or* **pe·di·a·trist** \,pē-dē-'a-trist, pē-'dī-ə-\ *noun* (circa 1903)
: a specialist in pediatrics

**pe·di·at·rics** \,pē-dē-'a-triks\ *noun plural but singular or plural in construction* (1884)
: a branch of medicine dealing with the development, care, and diseases of children

**pedi·cab** \'pe-di-,kab\ *noun* [Latin *ped-, pes* + English *cab*] (1945)
: a tricycle with a 2-seat passenger compartment covered by a usually folding top and a separate seat for a driver who pedals

**ped·i·cel** \'pe-də-,sel\ *noun* [New Latin *pedicellus,* diminutive of Latin *pediculus*] (1676)
: a slender basal part of an organism or one of its parts: as **a** : a plant stalk that supports a fruiting or spore-bearing organ **b** : a narrow basal attachment (as of the abdomen of an ant) of an animal organ or part
— **ped·i·cel·late** \,pe-də-'se-lət\ *adjective*

**ped·i·cle** \'pe-di-kəl\ *noun* [Latin *pediculus,* from diminutive of *ped-, pes*] (1626)
**1** : PEDICEL b
**2** : the part of a skin or tissue graft left attached to the original site during the preliminary stages of union
— **ped·i·cled** \-kəld\ *adjective*

**pe·dic·u·late** \pi-'di-kyə-lət\ *adjective* [ultimately from Latin *pediculus* little foot, pedicel] (circa 1890)

: of or relating to an order (Lophiiformes synonym Pediculati) of marine bony fishes with pectoral fins at the end of an armlike process and part of the dorsal fin modified into a lure
— **pediculate** *noun*

**pe·dic·u·lo·sis** \pi-ˌdi-kyə-'lō-səs\ *noun* [New Latin, from Latin *pediculus* louse, diminutive of *pedis* louse] (circa 1890)
: infestation with lice

**pe·dic·u·lous** \pi-'di-kyə-ləs\ *adjective* [Latin *pediculosus*, from *pediculus*] (circa 1550)
: infested with lice : LOUSY

**ped·i·cure** \'pe-di-ˌkyu̇r\ *noun* [French *pédicure*, from Latin *ped-*, *pes* foot + *curare* to take care, from *cura* care] (circa 1842)
**1** : one who practices chiropody
**2 a** : care of the feet, toes, and nails **b** : a single treatment of these parts
— **ped·i·cur·ist** \-ˌkyu̇r-ist\ *noun*

**ped·i·gree** \'pe-də-ˌgrē\ *noun* [Middle English *pedegru*, from Middle French *pie de grue* crane's foot; from the shape made by the lines of a genealogical chart] (15th century)
**1** : a register recording a line of ancestors
**2 a** : an ancestral line : LINEAGE **b** : the origin and the history of something
**3 a** : a distinguished ancestry **b** : the recorded purity of breed of an individual or strain
— **ped·i·greed** \-ˌgrēd\ *or* **pedigree** *adjective*

**ped·i·ment** \'pe-də-mənt\ *noun* [alteration of obsolete English *periment*, probably alteration of English *pyramid*] (1592)
**1** : a triangular space that forms the gable of a low-pitched roof and that is usually filled with relief sculpture in classical architecture; *also* : a similar form used as a decoration
**2** : a broad gently sloping bedrock surface with low relief that is situated at the base of a steeper slope and is usually thinly covered with alluvial gravel and sand
— **ped·i·men·tal** \ˌpe-də-'men-tᵊl\ *adjective*
— **ped·i·ment·ed** \'pe-də-ˌmen-təd\ *adjective*

**ped·i·palp** \'pe-də-ˌpalp\ *noun* [New Latin *pedipalpus*, from *ped-*, *pes* foot + *palpus* palpus] (1826)
: either of the second pair of appendages of an arachnid (as a spider) that are borne near the mouth and are often modified for a special (as sensory) function

**pedo-** — see PED-

**ped·o·cal** \'pe-də-ˌkal\ *noun* [Greek *pedon* earth + Latin *calc-*, *calx* lime — more at PED-, CHALK] (1928)
: a soil that includes a definite hardened layer of accumulated carbonates
— **ped·o·cal·ic** \ˌpe-də-'ka-lik\ *adjective*

**¹pe·do·gen·e·sis** \ˌpē-də-'je-nə-səs\ *variant of* PAEDOGENESIS

**²ped·o·gen·e·sis** \ˌpe-də-'je-nə-səs\ *noun* [New Latin, from Greek *pedon* + Latin *genesis*] (1936)
: the formation and development of soil
— **ped·o·gen·ic** \-'je-nik\ *also* **ped·o·ge·net·ic** \-jə-'ne-tik\ *adjective*

**pe·dol·o·gy** \pi-'dä-lə-jē, pe-\ *noun* [Greek *pedon* + International Scientific Vocabulary *-logy*] (1912)
: SOIL SCIENCE
— **ped·o·log·i·cal** \ˌpe-dᵊl-'ä-ji-kəl\ *also* **ped·o·log·ic** \-jik\ *adjective*
— **pe·dol·o·gist** \pi-'dä-lə-jist, pe-\ *noun*

**pe·dom·e·ter** \pi-'dä-mə-tər\ *noun* [French *pédomètre*, from Latin *ped-*, *pes* foot + French *-mètre* -meter — more at FOOT] (1723)
: an instrument usually in watch form that records the distance a person covers on foot by responding to the body motion at each step

**pe·do·phile** \'pē-də-ˌfīl\ *noun* (1951)
: one affected with pedophilia

**pe·do·phil·ia** \ˌpē-də-'fi-lē-ə\ *noun* [New Latin] (1906)
: sexual perversion in which children are the preferred sexual object

— **pe·do·phil·i·ac** \-'fi-lē-ˌak\ *or* **pe·do·phil·ic** \-'fi-lik\ *adjective*

**pe·dun·cle** \'pē-ˌdəŋ-kəl, pi-'\ *noun* [New Latin *pedunculus*, diminutive of Latin *ped-*, *pes*] (circa 1753)
**1** : a stalk bearing a flower or flower cluster or a fructification
**2** : a narrow part by which some larger part or the whole body of an organism is attached : STALK, PEDICEL
**3** : a narrow stalk by which a tumor or polyp is attached
— **pe·dun·cled** \-kəld\ *adjective*
— **pe·dun·cu·lar** \pi-'dəŋ-kyə-lər\ *adjective*

**pe·dun·cu·lat·ed** \pi-'dəŋ-kyə-ˌlā-təd\ *also* **pe·dun·cu·late** \-lət\ *adjective* [New Latin *pedunculus*] (1752)
: having, growing on, or being attached by a peduncle ⟨a *pedunculated* tumor⟩

**¹pee** \'pē\ *noun* (1612)
**1** : the letter *p*
**2** *plural* **pee** *British* : PENNY

**²pee** *intransitive verb* **peed**; **pee·ing** [euphemism from the initial letter of *piss*] (circa 1880)
: URINATE — sometimes considered vulgar

**³pee** *noun* (1946)
**1** : URINE — sometimes considered vulgar
**2** : an act of urination — sometimes considered vulgar

**¹peek** \'pēk\ *intransitive verb* [Middle English *piken*] (14th century)
**1 a** : to look furtively **b** : to peer through a crack or hole or from a place of concealment — often used with *in* or *out*
**2** : to take a brief look : GLANCE

**²peek** *noun* (1843)
**1** : a surreptitious look
**2** : a brief look : GLANCE

**¹peek·a·boo** \'pē-kə-ˌbü\ *noun* [¹*peek* + ¹*boo*] (1599)
: a game for amusing a baby by repeatedly hiding one's face or body and popping back into view exclaiming "Peekaboo!"

**²peekaboo** *adjective* (1895)
**1** : trimmed with eyelet embroidery ⟨a *peekaboo* blouse⟩
**2** : made of a sheer or transparent fabric
**3** : offering only limited display or disclosure especially of a teasing sort ⟨*peekaboo* publicity⟩

**¹peel** \'pē(ə)l\ *verb* [Middle English *pelen*, from Middle French *peler*, from Latin *pilare* to remove the hair from, from *pilus* hair] (13th century)
*transitive verb*
**1** : to strip off an outer layer of ⟨*peel* an orange⟩
**2** : to remove by stripping ⟨*peel* the label off the can⟩
*intransitive verb*
**1 a** : to come off in sheets or scales **b** : to lose an outer layer (as of skin) ⟨his face is *peeling*⟩
**2** : to take off one's clothes
**3** : to break away from a group or formation — often used with *off*
— **peel·able** \'pē-lə-bəl\ *adjective*

**²peel** *noun* (14th century)
**1** : the skin or rind of a fruit
**2** : a thin layer of organic material that is embedded in a film of collodion and stripped from the surface of an object (as a plant fossil) for microscopic study

**³peel** *noun* [Middle English *pele*, from Middle French, from Latin *pala*] (14th century)
: a usually long-handled spade-shaped instrument that is used chiefly by bakers for getting something (as bread or pies) into or out of the oven

**⁴peel** *noun* [Middle English *pel* stockade, stake, from Anglo-French, stockade & Middle French, stake, from Latin *palus* stake — more at POLE] (1726)

: a medieval small massive fortified tower along the Scottish-English border — called also *peel tower*

**¹peel·er** \'pē-lər\ *noun* (1597)
**1** : one that peels
**2** : a crab that is about to shed its shell
**3** : a log of wood (as Douglas fir) suitable for cutting into rotary veneer — called also *peeler log*

**²peeler** *noun* [Sir Robert *Peel*] (1817)
*British* : POLICE OFFICER

**peel·ing** \'pē-liŋ\ *noun* (1597)
: a peeled-off piece or strip

**peel off** *intransitive verb* (1941)
**1** : to veer away from an airplane formation especially for diving or landing
**2** : DEPART, LEAVE

**¹peen** \'pēn\ *transitive verb* (1513)
: to draw, bend, or flatten by or as if by hammering with a peen

**²peen** *noun* [probably of Scandinavian origin; akin to Norwegian *penn* peen] (1683)
: a usually hemispherical or wedge-shaped end of the head of a hammer that is opposite the face and is used especially for bending, shaping, or cutting the material struck

**¹peep** \'pēp\ *intransitive verb* [Middle English *pepen*, of imitative origin] (15th century)
**1** : to utter a feeble shrill sound as of a bird newly hatched : CHEEP
**2** : to utter the slightest sound

**²peep** *noun* (15th century)
**1** : a feeble shrill sound : CHEEP
**2** : a slight utterance especially of complaint or protest ⟨don't let me hear another *peep* out of you⟩
**3** : any of several small sandpipers

**³peep** *verb* [Middle English *pepen*, perhaps alteration of *piken* to peek] (15th century)
*intransitive verb*
**1 a** : to peer through or as if through a crevice **b** : to look cautiously or slyly
**2** : to begin to emerge from or as if from concealment : show slightly
*transitive verb*
: to put forth or cause to protrude slightly

**⁴peep** *noun* (1530)
**1** : a first glimpse or faint appearance ⟨at the *peep* of dawn⟩
**2 a** : a brief look : GLANCE **b** : a furtive look

**¹peep·er** \'pē-pər\ *noun* (1591)
**1** : one that makes a peeping sound
**2** : any of various tree frogs that peep shrilly; *especially* : SPRING PEEPER

**²peeper** *noun* (1652)
**1** : one that peeps; *specifically* : VOYEUR
**2** : EYE

**peep·hole** \'pēp-ˌhōl\ *noun* (1681)
: a hole or crevice to peep through

**Peeping Tom** \-'täm\ *noun* [*Peeping Tom*, legendary citizen of Coventry who watched Lady Godiva riding naked] (circa 1796)
: a pruriently prying person : VOYEUR
— **Peeping Tom·ism** \-'tä-ˌmi-zəm\ *noun*

**peep show** *noun* (1851)
: an entertainment (as a film) or object (as a small picture) that is viewed through a small opening or a magnifying glass and is usually sexually explicit

**peep sight** *noun* (1881)
: a rear sight for a gun having an adjustable metal piece pierced with a small hole to peep through in aiming

**¹peer** \'pir\ *noun* [Middle English, from Middle French *per*, from *per*, adjective, equal, from Latin *par*] (13th century)
**1** : one that is of equal standing with another : EQUAL; *especially* : one belonging to the same societal group especially based on age, grade, or status
**2** *archaic* : COMPANION
**3 a** : a member of one of the five ranks (as duke, marquess, earl, viscount, or baron) of the British peerage **b** : NOBLE 1
— **peer** *adjective*

**²peer** *transitive verb* (14th century)

*archaic* : RIVAL, MATCH

³**peer** *intransitive verb* [perhaps by shortening & alteration from *appear*] (1591)
**1** : to look narrowly or curiously; *especially* : to look searchingly at something difficult to discern
**2** : to come slightly into view : emerge partly

**peer·age** \'pir-ij\ *noun* (15th century)
**1** : the body of peers
**2** : the rank or dignity of a peer
**3** : a book containing a list of peers with their genealogy, history, and titles

**peer·ess** \'pir-əs\ *noun* (1689)
**1** : the wife or widow of a peer
**2** : a woman who holds in her own right the rank of a peer

**peer·less** \'pir-ləs\ *adjective* (14th century)
: MATCHLESS, INCOMPARABLE

¹**peeve** \'pēv\ *transitive verb* **peeved; peev·ing** [back-formation from *peevish*] (1908)
: to make peevish or resentful : ANNOY
**synonym** see IRRITATE

²**peeve** *noun* (1911)
**1** : a feeling or mood of resentment
**2** : a particular grievance or source of aggravation

**pee·vish** \'pē-vish\ *adjective* [Middle English *pevish* spiteful] (circa 1530)
**1** : querulous in temperament or mood : FRETFUL
**2** : perversely obstinate
**3** : marked by ill temper
— **pee·vish·ly** *adverb*
— **pee·vish·ness** *noun*

**pee·wee** \'pē-(ˌ)wē\ *noun* [imitative] (1806)
**1** : PEWEE
**2** : one that is diminutive or small; *especially* : a small child
— **peewee** *adjective*

**pee·wit** \'pē-ˌwit, 'pyü-ət\ *noun* [imitative] (circa 1529)
: any of several birds; *especially* : LAPWING

¹**peg** \'peg\ *noun* [Middle English *pegge*, probably from Middle Dutch] (15th century)
**1 a** : a small usually cylindrical pointed or tapered piece (as of wood) used to pin down or fasten things or to fit into or close holes : PIN, PLUG **b** *British* : CLOTHESPIN **c** : a predetermined level at which something (as a price) is fixed
**2 a** : a projecting piece used as a support or boundary marker **b** : something (as a fact or opinion) used as a support, pretext, or reason
**3 a** : one of the movable wooden pegs set in the head of a stringed instrument (as a violin) that are turned to regulate the pitch of the strings — see VIOLIN illustration **b** : a step or degree especially in estimation
**4** : a pointed prong or claw for catching or tearing
**5** *British* : DRINK ⟨poured himself out a stiff *peg* —Dorothy Sayers⟩
**6** : something (as a leg) resembling a peg
**7** : THROW; *especially* : a hard throw in baseball made in an attempt to put out a base runner

²**peg** *verb* **pegged; peg·ging** (1543)
*transitive verb*
**1 a** : to put a peg into **b** *British* : to pin (laundry) on a clothesline
**2** : to attach or fix as if with a peg: as **a** : to pin down : RESTRICT **b** : to fix or hold (as prices or wage increases) at a predetermined level or rate **c** : to place in a definite category : IDENTIFY
**3** : to mark by pegs
**4** : THROW
*intransitive verb*
**1** : to work steadily and diligently — often used with *away*
**2** : to move along vigorously or hastily : HUSTLE

³**peg** \'peg\ *or* **pegged** \'pegd\ *adjective* (1681)
: wide at the top and narrow at the bottom ⟨*peg* pants⟩

**Peg·a·sus** \'pe-gə-səs\ *noun* [Latin (genitive *Pegasi*, from Greek *Pēgasos*]
**1** : a winged horse that causes the stream Hippocrene to spring from Mount Helicon with a blow of his hoof
**2** : poetic inspiration
**3** : a northern constellation near the vernal equinoctial point

**Peg–Board** \'peg-ˌbōrd, -ˌbord\ *trademark*
— used for material (as fiberboard) with regularly spaced perforations into which hooks may be inserted for the storage or display of articles

**peg leg** *noun* [³*peg*] (1769)
: an artificial leg; *especially* : one fitted at the knee

**peg·ma·tite** \'peg-mə-ˌtīt\ *noun* [French, from Greek *pēgmat-, pēgma* something fastened together, from *pēgnynai* to fasten together — more at PACT] (circa 1828)
: a coarse variety of granite occurring in dikes or veins
— **peg·ma·tit·ic** \ˌpeg-mə-'ti-tik\ *adjective*

**peg–top** \'peg-'täp\ *or* **peg–topped** \-'täpt\ *adjective* (1858)
: PEG

**peg top** *noun* (1788)
**1** \'peg-ˌtäp\ : a pear-shaped top that is made to spin on the sharp metal peg in its base by the unwinding of a string wound round its center
**2** *plural* \-ˌtäps\ : peg trousers

**pei·gnoir** \pān-'wär, pen-\ *noun* [French, literally, garment worn while combing the hair, from Middle French, from *peigner* to comb the hair, from Latin *pectinare*, from *pectin-, pecten* comb — more at PECTINATE] (1835)
: a woman's loose negligee or dressing gown

**pein** *variant of* PEEN

¹**pe·jo·ra·tive** \pi-'jor-ə-tiv, -'jär- *also* 'pe-jə-rə-tiv *or* 'pē- *or* -ˌrā- *or* 'pej-rə- *or* 'pēj-\ *noun* (1882)
: a pejorative word or phrase

²**pejorative** *adjective* [Late Latin *pejoratus*, past participle of *pejorare* to make or become worse, from Latin *pejor* worse; akin to Sanskrit *padyate* he falls, Latin *ped-, pes* foot — more at FOOT] (circa 1888)
: having negative connotations; *especially* : tending to disparage or belittle : DEPRECIATORY
— **pe·jo·ra·tive·ly** *adverb*

**peke** \'pēk\ *noun, often capitalized* (1915)
: PEKINGESE 2

**Pe·kin** \pi-'kin, 'pē-ˌ\ *noun* [Pekin, Peking (Beijing), China] (1885)
: any of a breed of large white ducks of Chinese origin used for meat production

**Pe·king duck** \'pē-ˌkiŋ-\ *noun* (1955)
: a Chinese dish consisting of roasted duck meat and strips of crispy duck skin topped with scallions and sauce and wrapped in thin pancakes

**Pe·king·ese** *or* **Pe·kin·ese** \ˌpē-kə-'nēz, -'nēs; -ˌkiŋ-'ēz, -'ēs\ *noun, plural* **Pekingese** *or* **Pekinese** (1849)
**1 a** : the Chinese dialect of Beijing **b** : a native or resident of Beijing
**2** : any of a Chinese breed of small short-legged dogs with a broad flat face and a profuse long soft coat

Pekingese 2

**Peking man** *noun* (1926)
: an extinct Pleistocene hominid that is known from skeletal and cultural remains in cave deposits at Cho-k'ou-tien, China and is now classified with the pithecanthropines

**pe·koe** \'pē-(ˌ)kō *also* 'pe-\ *noun* [Chinese (Xiamen) *pek-ho*] (1712)
: a tea made from young leaves that are slightly larger than those of orange pekoe

**pel·age** \'pe-lij\ *noun* [French, from Middle French, from *poil* hair, from Latin *pilus*] (circa 1828)
: the hairy covering of a mammal

¹**Pe·la·gian** \pə-'lā-j(ē-)ən\ *noun* (15th century)
: one agreeing with Pelagius in denying original sin and consequently in holding that mankind has perfect freedom to do either right or wrong

²**Pelagian** *adjective* (15th century)
: of or relating to Pelagians or Pelagianism

**Pe·la·gian·ism** \-j(ē-)ə-ˌni-zəm\ *noun* (1583)
: the teaching of Pelagius or Pelagians

**pe·lag·ic** \pə-'la-jik\ *adjective* [Latin *pelagicus*, from Greek *pelagikos*, from *pelagos* sea — more at PLAGAL] (circa 1656)
: of, relating to, or living or occurring in the open sea : OCEANIC ⟨*pelagic* sediment⟩ ⟨*pelagic* birds⟩

**pel·ar·go·ni·um** \ˌpe-lär-'gō-nē-əm, -lər-\ *noun* [New Latin, from Greek *pelargos* stork (akin to Greek *pelios* livid, *polios* gray) + New Latin *-nium* (as in *Geranium*) — more at FALLOW] (circa 1819)
: any of a genus (*Pelargonium*) of southern African herbs (as a garden geranium) of the geranium family with showy flowers of various shades of red, pink, or white distinguished by a spurred calyx and irregular corolla

**Pe·las·gian** \pə-'laz-j(ē-)ən, -'laz-gē-ən\ *noun* [Greek *pelasgios*, adjective, Pelasgian, from *Pelasgoi* Pelasgians] (15th century)
: a member of an ancient people mentioned by classical writers as early inhabitants of Greece and the eastern islands of the Mediterranean
— **Pelasgian** *adjective*
— **Pe·las·gic** \-jik, -gik\ *adjective*

**pe·lec·y·pod** \pə-'le-sə-ˌpäd\ *noun* [New Latin *Pelecypoda*, group name, from Greek *pelekys* ax (akin to Sanskrit *paraśu* ax) + *pod-, pous* foot — more at FOOT] (circa 1890)
: LAMELLIBRANCH

**pel·er·ine** \ˌpe-lə-'rēn, 'pe-lə-rən\ *noun* [obsolete French, neckerchief, from French *pèlerine*, feminine of *pèlerin* pilgrim, from Late Latin *pelegrinus* — more at PILGRIM] (1744)
: a woman's narrow cape made of fabric or fur and usually with long ends hanging down in front

**Pe·leus** \'pēl-ˌyüs, 'pē-lē-əs\ *noun* [Latin, from Greek *Pēleus*]
: a son of Aeacus who becomes by the goddess Thetis the father of Achilles

**pelf** \'pelf\ *noun* [Middle English, from Middle French *pelfre* booty] (14th century)
: MONEY, RICHES

**pel·i·can** \'pe-li-kən\ *noun* [Middle English, from Old English *pellican*, from Late Latin *pelecanus*, from Greek *pelekan*] (before 12th century)
: any of a genus (*Pelecanus*) of large webfooted fish-eating birds with a very large bill and distensible gular pouch

**pe·lisse** \pə-'lēs, pe-\ *noun* [French, from Late Latin *pellicia*, from feminine of *pellicius* made of skin, from Latin *pellis* skin — more at FELL] (1717)
**1** : a long cloak or coat made of fur or lined or trimmed with fur
**2** : a woman's loose lightweight cloak with wide collar and fur trimming

**pel·la·gra** \pə-'la-grə, -'lā-, -'lä-\ *noun* [Italian, from *pelle* skin (from Latin *pellis*) + *-agra* (as in *podagra*, from Latin)] (circa 1811)
: a disease marked by dermatitis, gastrointestinal disorders, and central nervous symptoms and associated with a diet deficient in niacin

— **pel·la·grous** \-grəs\ *adjective*

**pel·la·grin** \-grən\ *noun* [irregular from *pellagra*] (1865)
: a person who is affected with pellagra

¹**pel·let** \'pel-lət\ *noun* [Middle English *pelote*, from Middle French, from (assumed) Vulgar Latin *pilota*, diminutive of Latin *pila* ball] (14th century)
**1** : a usually small rounded, spherical, or cylindrical body (as of food or medicine)
**2** : any of various projectiles fired from a weapon (as an air rifle)
— **pel·let·al** \-lə-t°l\ *adjective*

²**pellet** *transitive verb* (1597)
**1** : PELLETIZE
**2** : to strike with pellets

**pellet gun** *noun* (1952)
: AIR GUN 1

**pel·let·ise** *British variant of* PELLETIZE

**pel·let·ize** \'pe-lə-ˌtīz\ *transitive verb* **-ized; -iz·ing** (1942)
: to form or compact into pellets ⟨*pelletize* ore⟩
— **pel·let·i·za·tion** \ˌpe-lə-tə-'zā-shən\ *noun*
— **pel·let·iz·er** \'pe-lə-ˌtī-zər\ *noun*

**pel·li·cle** \'pe-li-kəl\ *noun* [Middle French *pellicule*, from Medieval Latin *pellicula*, from Latin, diminutive of *pellis*] (1541)
: a thin skin or film: as **a** : an outer membrane of some protozoans (as euglenoids or paramecia) **b** : a film that reflects a part of the light falling upon it and transmits the rest and that is used for dividing a beam of light (as in a photographic device)

¹**pel·li·to·ry** \'pe-lə-ˌtōr-ē, -ˌtor-\ *noun, plural* **-ries** [Middle English *peletre*, from Middle French *piretre*, from Latin *pyrethrum* — more at PYRETHRUM] (1533)
: a southern European composite plant (*Anacyclus pyrethrum*) resembling yarrow — called also *pellitory-of-Spain*

²**pellitory** *noun* [Middle English *paritorie*, from Middle French *paritaire*, from Late Latin *parietaria*, from feminine of *parietarius* of a wall, from Latin *pariet-, paries* wall] (1548)
: any of a genus (*Parietaria*) of herbs of the nettle family with alternate leaves and inconspicuous flowers — called also *pellitory-of-the-wall*

**pell–mell** \ˌpel-'mel\ *adverb* [Middle French *pelemele*] (1596)
**1** : in mingled confusion or disorder
**2** : in confused haste
— **pell–mell** *adjective or noun*

**pel·lu·cid** \pə-'lü-səd\ *adjective* [Latin *pellucidus*, from *per* through + *lucidus* lucid — more at FOR] (1619)
**1** : admitting maximum passage of light without diffusion or distortion
**2** : reflecting light evenly from all surfaces
**3** : easy to understand
— **pel·lu·cid·ly** \pə-'lü-səd-lē\ *adverb*

**pel·met** \'pel-mət\ *noun* [probably modification of French *palmette* palmette] (1821)
: a short valance or small cornice for concealing curtain fixtures

**Pe·lops** \'pē-ˌläps, 'pe-\ *noun* [Latin, from Greek]
: a son of Tantalus served by his father to the gods for food but later restored to life by them

**pe·lo·rus** \pə-'lōr-əs, -'lor-\ *noun* [origin unknown] (1854)
: a navigational instrument resembling a mariner's compass without magnetic needles and having two sight vanes by which bearings are taken

**pe·lo·ta** \pə-'lō-tə\ *noun* [Spanish, from Old French *pelote* little ball — more at PELLET] (1844)
**1** : a court game related to jai alai
**2** : the ball used in jai alai

¹**pelt** \'pelt\ *noun* [Middle English, perhaps back-formation from *peltry*] (15th century)
**1** : a usually undressed skin with its hair, wool, or fur
**2** : a skin stripped of hair or wool for tanning

²**pelt** *transitive verb* (1596)
: to strip off the skin or pelt of (an animal)

³**pelt** *verb* [Middle English] (15th century)
*transitive verb*
**1 a** : to strike with a succession of blows or missiles ⟨*pelted* him with stones⟩ **b** : to assail vigorously or persistently ⟨*pelted* her with accusations⟩
**2** : HURL, THROW ⟨*pelted* snowballs at them⟩
**3** : to beat or dash repeatedly against ⟨hailstones *pelting* the roof⟩
*intransitive verb*
**1** : to deliver a succession of blows or missiles
**2** : to beat incessantly
**3** : to move rapidly and vigorously : HURRY
— **pelt·er** *noun*

⁴**pelt** *noun* (1513)
: BLOW, WHACK

**pel·tate** \'pel-ˌtāt\ *adjective* [Latin *pelta* small shield, from Greek *peltē*] (circa 1760)
: shaped like a shield; *specifically* : having the stem or support attached to the lower surface instead of at the base or margin — see LEAF illustration

**pelt·ing** \'pel-tiŋ\ *adjective* [probably from English dialect *pelt* piece of trash] (1540)
*archaic* : PALTRY, INSIGNIFICANT

**pel·try** \'pel-trē\ *noun, plural* **peltries** [Middle English, from Anglo-French *pelterie*] (15th century)
: PELTS, FURS; *especially* : raw undressed skins — often used in plural

**pel·vic** \'pel-vik\ *adjective* (1830)
: of, relating to, or located in or near the pelvis
— **pelvic** *noun*

**pelvic fin** *noun* (circa 1909)
: one of the paired fins of a fish that are homologous with the hind limbs of a quadruped

**pelvic girdle** *noun* (1883)
: a bony or cartilaginous arch that supports the hind limbs of a vertebrate

**pelvic inflammatory disease** *noun* (1974)
: inflammation of the female reproductive tract and especially the fallopian tubes that is caused especially by sexually transmitted disease, occurs more often in women using IUDs, and is a leading cause of female sterility

**pel·vis** \'pel-vəs\ *noun, plural* **pel·vis·es** \-və-səz\ *or* **pel·ves** \-ˌvēz\ [New Latin, from Latin, basin; perhaps akin to Old English & Old Norse *full* cup] (1615)
**1** : a basin-shaped structure in the skeleton of many vertebrates that is formed by the pelvic girdle and adjoining bones of the spine
**2** : the cavity of the pelvis
**3** : the funnel-shaped cavity of the kidney into which urine is discharged

**pel·y·co·saur** \'pe-li-kə-ˌsor\ *noun* [ultimately from Greek *pelyc-, pelyx* bowl + *sauros* lizard] (1904)
: any of an order (Pelycosauria) of primitive Permian quadruped reptiles that resemble mammals and often have extreme development of the dorsal vertebral processes

**Pem·broke table** \'pem-ˌbrōk-, -ˌbrúk-\ *noun* [*Pembroke*, Wales] (1778)
: a small 4-legged table originating in the Georgian period and having two drop leaves and a drawer

**Pembroke Welsh corgi** *noun* (1938)
: any of a breed of Welsh corgis with pointed ears, straight forelegs, and a short tail — called also *Pembroke;* see WELSH CORGI illustration

**pem·mi·can** *also* **pem·i·can** \'pe-mi-kən\ *noun* [Cree *pimihka'n*] (1791)
: a concentrated food used by North American Indians and consisting of lean meat dried, pounded fine, and mixed with melted fat; *also* : a similar preparation (as of dried beef, flour, molasses, suet) used for emergency rations

**pem·o·line** \'pe-mə-ˌlēn\ *noun* [origin unknown] (1961)
: a synthetic organic drug $C_9H_8N_2O_2$ that is a mild stimulant of the central nervous system

**pem·phi·gus** \'pem(p)-fi-gəs, pem-'fī-\ *noun* [New Latin, from Greek *pemphig-, pemphix* pustule] (circa 1779)
: a disease characterized by large blisters on skin and mucous membranes and often by itching or burning

¹**pen** \'pen\ *transitive verb* **penned; penning** [Middle English *pennen*, from Old English *-pennian*] (13th century)
: to shut in or as if in a pen

²**pen** *noun* [Middle English, perhaps from *pennen*] (14th century)
**1 a** : a small enclosure for animals **b** : the animals in a pen ⟨a *pen* of sheep⟩
**2** : a small place of confinement or storage
**3** : a protected dock or slip for a submarine
**4** : BULL PEN 2

³**pen** *noun* [Middle English *penne*, from Middle French, feather, pen, from Latin *penna, pinna* feather; akin to Greek *pteron* wing — more at FEATHER] (14th century)
**1** : an implement for writing or drawing with ink or a similar fluid: as **a** : QUILL **b** : PEN POINT **c** : a penholder containing a pen point **d** : FOUNTAIN PEN **e** : BALLPOINT
**2 a** : a writing instrument regarded as a means of expression ⟨enlisted the *pens* of the best writers —F. H. Chase⟩ **b** : WRITER
**3** : the internal horny feather-shaped shell of a squid

⁴**pen** *transitive verb* **penned; pen·ning** (15th century)
: WRITE, INDITE ⟨*pen* a letter⟩

⁵**pen** *noun* [origin unknown] (1550)
: a female swan

⁶**pen** *noun* (1884)
: PENITENTIARY

**pe·nal** \'pē-n°l\ *adjective* [Middle English, from Middle French, from Latin *poenalis*, from *poena* punishment — more at PAIN] (15th century)
**1** : of, relating to, or involving punishment, penalties, or punitive institutions
**2** : liable to punishment ⟨a *penal* offense⟩
**3** : used as a place of confinement and punishment ⟨a *penal* colony⟩
— **pe·nal·ly** \-n°l-ē\ *adverb*

**penal code** *noun* (1845)
: a code of laws concerning crimes and offenses and their punishment

**pe·nal·ise** *British variant of* PENALIZE

**pe·nal·ize** \'pē-n°l-ˌīz, 'pe-\ *transitive verb* **-ized; -iz·ing** (1868)
**1** : to inflict a penalty on
**2** : to put at a serious disadvantage
— **pe·nal·i·za·tion** \-n°l-ə-'zā-shən\ *noun*

**pen·al·ty** \'pe-n°l-tē\ *noun, plural* **-ties** [Medieval Latin *poenalitas*, from Latin *poenalis*] (15th century)
**1** : the suffering in person, rights, or property that is annexed by law or judicial decision to the commission of a crime or public offense
**2** : the suffering or the sum to be forfeited in case to which a person agrees to be subjected in case of nonfulfillment of stipulations
**3 a** : disadvantage, loss, or hardship due to some action **b** : a disadvantage (as loss of yardage, time, or possession of the ball or an addition to or subtraction from the score) imposed on a team or competitor for violation of the rules of a sport
**4** : points scored in bridge by the side that defeats the opposing contract — usually used in plural
— **penalty** *adjective*

**penalty box** *noun* (1931)
: an area alongside an ice hockey rink to which penalized players are confined for the duration of their penalty

**penalty kick** (1889)
**1** : a free kick in rugby
**2** : a free kick at the goal in soccer made from a point 12 yards in front of the goal and allowed for certain violations within a designated area around the goal

**penalty shot** *noun* (circa 1948)
: an unhindered shot at the goal in ice hockey awarded to an individual for certain violations by an opponent

**¹pen·ance** \'pe-nən(t)s\ *noun* [Middle English, from Old French, from Medieval Latin *poenitentia* penitence] (14th century)
**1** : an act of self-abasement, mortification, or devotion performed to show sorrow or repentance for sin
**2** : a sacramental rite that is practiced in Roman, Eastern, and some Anglican churches and that consists of private confession, absolution, and a penance directed by the confessor
**3** : something (as a hardship or penalty) resembling an act of penance (as in compensating for an offense)

**²penance** *transitive verb* **pen·anced; pen·anc·ing** (1600)
: to impose penance on

**Pe·na·tes** \pə-'nā-tēz, -'nä-\ *noun plural* [Latin, from *penus* food, provisions]
: the Roman gods of the household worshiped in close connection with Vesta and with the Lares

**pence** \'pen(t)s\ *plural of* PENNY

**pen·cel** *or* **pen·cil** \'pen(t)-səl\ *noun* [Middle English *pencel,* modification of Old French *penoncel*] (13th century)
: PENNONCEL

**pen·chant** \'pen-chənt, *especially British* 'pä<sup>n</sup>-,shä<sup>n</sup>\ *noun* [French, from present participle of *pencher* to incline, from (assumed) Vulgar Latin *pendicare,* from Latin *pendere* to weigh] (1672)
: a strong and continued inclination; *broadly* : LIKING
**synonym** see LEANING

**¹pen·cil** \'pen(t)-səl\ *noun* [Middle English *pensel,* from Middle French *pincel,* from (assumed) Vulgar Latin *penicellus,* alteration of Latin *penicillus,* diminutive of *peniculus* brush, from diminutive of *penis* tail, penis] (14th century)
**1** : an artist's brush
**2** : an artist's individual skill or style
**3 a** : an implement for writing, drawing, or marking consisting of or containing a slender cylinder or strip of a solid marking substance **b** : a small medicated or cosmetic roll or stick for local applications
**4** : a set of geometric objects each pair of which has a common property (the lines in a plane through a point comprise a *pencil* of lines)
**5** : something (as a beam of radiation) long and thin like a pencil

**²pencil** *transitive verb* **-ciled** *or* **-cilled; -cil·ing** *or* **-cil·ling** \-s(ə-)liŋ\ (circa 1532)
: to paint, draw, write, or mark with a pencil

**pen·cil·ing** *or* **pen·cil·ling** *noun* (1706)
: the work of the pencil or brush; *also* : a product of this

**pencil pusher** *noun* (1881)
: a person who does predominantly paperwork

**pen·dant** *also* **pen·dent** \'pen-dənt; *3 & 4 are also* 'pen-ənt, *5 is also* pä<sup>n</sup>-dä<sup>n</sup>\ *noun* [Middle English *pendaunt,* from Middle French *pendant,* from present participle of *pendre* to hang, from (assumed) Vulgar Latin *pendere,* from Latin *pendēre;* akin to Latin *pendere* to weigh, estimate, pay, *pondus* weight] (14th century)
**1** : something suspended: as **a** : an ornament (as on a necklace) allowed to hang free **b** : an electrical fixture suspended from the ceiling
**2** : a hanging ornament of roofs or ceilings much used in the later styles of Gothic architecture
**3** : a length of line usually used as a connector on a boat or ship; *especially* : a short rope hanging from a spar and having at its free end a block or spliced thimble
**4** *chiefly British* : PENNANT 1a
**5 a** : COMPANION PIECE **b** : something secondary or supplementary

**pen·den·cy** \'pen-dən(t)-sē\ *noun* (1637)
: the state of being pending

**pen·dent** *or* **pen·dant** \'pen-dənt\ *adjective* [Middle English *pendaunt*] (14th century)
**1** : jutting or leaning over : OVERHANGING (a *pendent* cliff)
**2** : supported from above : SUSPENDED (icicles *pendent* from the eaves)
**3** : remaining undetermined : PENDING

**pen·den·tive** \pen-'den-tiv\ *noun* [French *pendentif,* from Latin *pendent-, pendens,* present participle of *pendēre*] (circa 1741)
: one of the concave triangular members that supports a dome over a square space

**¹pend·ing** \'pen-diŋ\ *preposition* [French *pendant,* from present participle of *pendre*] (1642)
**1** : DURING
**2** : while awaiting

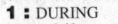

**1 pendentive**

**²pending** *adjective* (1797)
**1** : not yet decided : being in continuance
**2** : IMMINENT, IMPENDING

**pen·du·lar** \'pen-jə-lər, 'pen-dyə-, -də-\ *adjective* (1878)
: being or resembling the movement of a pendulum

**pen·du·lous** \-ləs\ *adjective* [Latin *pendulus,* from *pendēre* to hang] (circa 1605)
**1** *archaic* : poised without visible support
**2 a** : suspended so as to swing freely (branches hung with *pendulous* vines) **b** : inclined or hanging downward (*pendulous* jowls)
**3** : marked by vacillation, indecision, or uncertainty
— **pen·du·lous·ness** *noun*

**pen·du·lum** \-ləm\ *noun* [New Latin, from Latin, neuter of *pendulus*] (1660)
**1** : a body suspended from a fixed point so as to swing freely to and fro under the action of gravity and commonly used to regulate movements (as of clockwork)
**2** : something (as a state of affairs) that alternates between opposites

**Pe·nel·o·pe** \pə-'ne-lə-pē\ *noun* [Latin, from Greek *Pēnelopē*]
: the wife of Odysseus who waits faithfully for him during his 20 years' absence

**pe·ne·plain** *also* **pe·ne·plane** \'pē-ni-,plān, 'pe-\ *noun* [Latin *paene, pene* almost + English *plain* or *plane*] (1889)
: a land surface of considerable area and slight relief shaped by erosion

**pen·e·tra·ble** \'pe-nə-trə-bəl\ *adjective* (1538)
: capable of being penetrated
— **pen·e·tra·bil·i·ty** \,pe-nə-trə-'bi-lə-tē\ *noun*

**pen·e·tra·lia** \,pe-nə-'trā-lē-ə\ *noun plural* [Latin, neuter plural of *penetralis* inner, from *penetrare* to penetrate] (1668)
: the innermost or most private parts

**pen·e·trance** \'pe-nə-trən(t)s\ *noun* [International Scientific Vocabulary, from Latin *penetrare*] (1934)
: the proportion of individuals of a particular genotype that express its phenotypic effect in a given environment

**¹pen·e·trant** \-trənt\ *adjective* (1543)
: PENETRATING

**²penetrant** *noun* (circa 1734)
: one that penetrates or is capable of penetrating

**pen·e·trate** \'pe-nə-,trāt\ *verb* **-trat·ed; -trat·ing** [Latin *penetratus,* past participle of *penetrare,* from *penitus* deep within, far; akin to Latin *penus* provisions] (circa 1530)
*transitive verb*
**1 a** : to pass into or through **b** : to enter by overcoming resistance : PIERCE **c** : to gain entrance to

**2 a** : to see into or through **b** : to discover the inner contents or meaning of
**3** : to affect profoundly with feeling
**4** : to diffuse through or into
*intransitive verb*
**1 a** : to pass, extend, pierce, or diffuse into or through something **b** : to pierce something with the eye or mind
**2** : to affect deeply the senses or feelings
**synonym** see ENTER

**penetrating** *adjective* (1593)
**1** : having the power of entering, piercing, or pervading (a *penetrating* shriek)
**2** : ACUTE, DISCERNING (*penetrating* insights into life)
— **pen·e·trat·ing·ly** \-,trā-tiŋ-lē\ *adverb*

**pen·e·tra·tion** \,pe-nə-'trā-shən\ *noun* (1605)
**1 a** : the power to penetrate; *especially* : the ability to discern deeply and acutely **b** : the depth to which something penetrates **c** : the extent to which a commercial product or agency is familiar or sells in a market
**2** : the act or process of penetrating: as **a** : the act of entering a country so that actual establishment of influence is accomplished **b** : an attack that penetrates the enemy's front or territory
**synonym** see DISCERNMENT

**pen·e·tra·tive** \'pe-nə-,trā-tiv\ *adjective* (15th century)
**1** : tending to penetrate : PIERCING
**2** : ACUTE (*penetrative* observations)
**3** : IMPRESSIVE (a *penetrative* speaker)

**pen·e·trom·e·ter** \,pe-nə-'trä-mə-tər\ *noun* [Latin *penetrare* + International Scientific Vocabulary *-meter*] (1905)
: an instrument for measuring firmness or consistency (as of soil)

**pen·gö** \'peŋ-,gə(r), -,gœ\ *noun, plural* **pengö** *or* **pengös** [Hungarian *pengő,* literally, jingling] (1925)
: the basic monetary unit of Hungary from 1925 to 1946

**pen·guin** \'pen-gwən, 'peŋ-\ *noun* [obsolete English *penguin* great auk, perhaps from Welsh *pen gwyn* white head (applied to the bird in winter plumage)] (1588)
: any of various erect short-legged flightless aquatic birds (family Spheniscidae) of the southern hemisphere

**pen·hold·er** \'pen-,hōl-dər\ *noun* (1815)
: a holder or handle for a pen point

**-penia** *combining form* [New Latin, from Greek *penia*]
: deficiency (leuko*penia*)

**pen·i·cil·la·mine** \,pe-nə-'si-lə-,mēn\ *noun* [*penicillin* + *amine*] (1943)
: an amino acid $C_5H_{11}NO_2S$ that is obtained from penicillins and is used especially in the treatment of poisoning by metals (as copper or lead) and of cystinuria

**pen·i·cil·late** \,pe-nə-'si-lət, -,lāt\ *adjective* [Latin *penicillus* brush — more at PENCIL] (1819)
: furnished with a tuft of fine filaments (a *penicillate* stigma)

**pen·i·cil·lin** \,pe-nə-'si-lən\ *noun* [New Latin *Penicillium*] (1929)
**1** : any of several relatively nontoxic antibiotic acids of the general constitution $C_9H_{11}N_2O_4SR$ that are produced by molds (genus *Penicillium* and especially *P. notatum* or *P. chrysogenum*) or synthetically and are used especially against cocci; *also* : a mixture of such acids
**2** : a salt or ester of a penicillin or a mixture of such salts or esters

**pen·i·cil·lin·ase** \-'si-lə-,nās, -,nāz\ *noun* (1940)

: an enzyme found especially in staphylococcal bacteria that inactivates the penicillins by hydrolyzing them

**pen·i·cil·li·um** \-'si-lē-əm\ *noun, plural* **-lia** \-lē-ə\ [New Latin, from Latin *penicillus*] (1867)
: any of a genus (*Penicillium* of the family Moniliaceae) of fungi (as a blue mold) that are found chiefly on moist nonliving organic matter

**pe·nile** \'pē-,nīl\ *adjective* (circa 1861)
: of, relating to, or affecting the penis

**pen·in·su·la** \pə-'nin(t)-s(ə-)lə, -shə-lə\ *noun* [Latin *paeninsula*, from *paene* almost + *insula* island] (1538)
: a portion of land nearly surrounded by water and connected with a larger body by an isthmus; *also* : a piece of land jutting out into the water whether with or without a well-defined isthmus
— **pen·in·su·lar** \-s(ə-)lər, -shə-lər\ *adjective*

**pe·nis** \'pē-nəs\ *noun, plural* **pe·nes** \'pē-(,)nēz\ *or* **pe·nis·es** [Latin, penis, tail; akin to Old High German *faselt* penis, Greek *peos*] (1676)
: a male organ of copulation that in male mammals including humans usually functions as the channel by which urine leaves the body

**penis envy** *noun* (1924)
: the supposed coveting of the penis by a young human female which is held in Freudian psychoanalytic theory to lead to feelings of inferiority and defensive or compensatory behavior

**pen·i·tence** \'pe-nə-ten(t)s\ *noun* [Middle English, from Old French, from Medieval Latin *poenitentia*, alteration of Latin *paenitentia* regret, from *paenitent-, paenitens*, present participle] (13th century)
: the quality or state of being penitent : sorrow for sins or faults ☆

**¹pen·i·tent** \-tənt\ *adjective* [Middle English, from Middle French, from Latin *paenitent-, paenitens*, from present participle of *paenitēre* to cause regret, feel regret, perhaps from *paene* almost] (14th century)
: feeling or expressing humble or regretful pain or sorrow for sins or offenses : REPENTANT
— **pen·i·tent·ly** *adverb*

**²penitent** *noun* (14th century)
**1** : a person who repents of sin
**2** : a person under church censure but admitted to penance or reconciliation especially under the direction of a confessor

**pen·i·ten·tial** \,pe-nə-'ten(t)-shəl\ *adjective* (1508)
: of or relating to penitence or penance
— **pen·i·ten·tial·ly** \-'ten(t)-sh(ə-)lē\ *adverb*

**¹pen·i·ten·tia·ry** \,pe-nə-'ten(t)-sh(ə-)rē\ *noun, plural* **-ries** [Middle English *penitenciary*, from Medieval Latin *poenitentiarius*, from *poenitentia*] (15th century)
**1 a** : an officer in some Roman Catholic dioceses vested with power from the bishop to deal with cases of a nature normally handled only by the bishop **b** *capitalized* : a cardinal presiding over a tribunal of the Roman curia concerned with dispensations and indulgences
**2** : a public institution in which offenders against the law are confined for detention or punishment; *specifically* : a state or federal prison in the U.S.

**²pen·i·ten·tia·ry** \,pe-nə-'ten(t)-sh(ə-)rē, *1 also* -'ten(t)-shē-,er-ē\ *adjective* (1577)
**1** : PENITENTIAL
**2** : of, relating to, or incurring confinement in a penitentiary

**pen·knife** \'pen-,nīf\ *noun* [Middle English; from its original use for mending quill pens] (15th century)
: a small pocketknife usually with only one blade

**pen·light** *also* **pen·lite** \-,līt\ *noun* (1945)

: a small flashlight resembling a fountain pen in size or shape

**pen·man** \-mən\ *noun* (1539)
**1 a** : CALLIGRAPHER **b** : COPYIST, SCRIBE **c** : a person with a specified quality or kind of handwriting ⟨a poor *penman*⟩
**2** : AUTHOR

**pen·man·ship** \-,ship\ *noun* (1695)
**1** : the art or practice of writing with the pen
**2** : quality or style of handwriting

**pen name** *noun* (circa 1864)
: an author's pseudonym

**pen·nant** \'pe-nənt\ *noun* [alteration of *pendant*] (1698)
**1 a** : any of various nautical flags tapering usually to a point or swallowtail and used for identification or signaling **b** : a flag or banner longer in the fly than in the hoist; *especially* : one that tapers to a point
**2** : a flag emblematic of championship (as in a professional baseball league); *also* : the championship itself

**pen·nate** \'pe-,nāt\ *adjective* [irregular from New Latin *Pennales*] (1938)
: of, relating to, or being diatoms of an order (Pennales) usually characterized by a raphe or a structure resembling a raphe and by ornamentation of the valves that is bilaterally symmetrical

**pen·ne** \'pe(n)-(,)nā\ *noun, plural* **penne** [Italian, plural of *penna*, literally, quill, feather, pen, from Latin *pinna* feather & *penna* wing — more at PEN] (1974)
: short thick diagonally cut tubular pasta

**pen·ni** \'pe-nē\ *noun, plural* **pen·nia** \-nē-ə\ *also* **penni** *or* **pen·nis** \-nēz\ [Finnish] (circa 1893)
— see *markka* at MONEY table

**pen·ni·less** \'pe-ni-ləs, 'pe-nᵊl-əs\ *adjective* (14th century)
: destitute of money

**pen·non** \'pe-nən\ *noun* [Middle English, from Middle French *penon*, diminutive of *penne* quill, wing feather — more at PEN] (14th century)
**1 a** : a long usually triangular or swallow-tailed streamer typically attached to the head of a lance as an ensign **b** : PENNANT 1a
**2** : WING, PINION

**pen·non·cel** *or* **pen·on·cel** \'pe-nən-,sel\ *noun* [Middle English *penoncell*, from Middle French *penoncel*, diminutive of *penon*] (14th century)
: a small pennon used in late medieval or Renaissance times

**Penn·syl·va·nia Dutch** \,pen(t)-səl-'vā-nyə-, -nē-ə-\ *noun* (circa 1824)
**1** : a people living mostly in eastern Pennsylvania whose characteristic cultural traditions go back to the German migrations of the 18th century
**2** : a dialect of High German spoken in parts of Pennsylvania and Maryland
— **Pennsylvania Dutchman** *noun*

**Pennsylvania German** *noun* (1869)
: PENNSYLVANIA DUTCH

**Penn·syl·va·nian** \-'vā-nyən, -nē-ən\ *adjective* (1698)
**1** : of or relating to Pennsylvania or its people
**2** : of, relating to, or being the period of the Paleozoic era in North America between the Mississippian and Permian or the corresponding system of rocks — see GEOLOGIC TIME table
— **Pennsylvanian** *noun*

**pen·ny** \'pe-nē\ *noun, plural* **pennies** \-nēz\ *or* **pence** \'pen(t)s\ *often attributive* [Middle English, from Old English *penning, penig*; akin to Old High German *pfenning*, a coin] (before 12th century)
**1 a** : a monetary unit of the United Kingdom formerly equal to ¹⁄₂₄₀ pound but now equal to ¹⁄₁₀₀ pound **b** : a similar monetary unit of any of various other countries in or formerly in the Commonwealth — see *pound* at MONEY table
**c** : a coin representing one penny

**2** : DENARIUS
**3** *plural* **pennies** : CENT
**4** : a trivial amount
**5** : a piece or sum of money ⟨that will cost a pretty *penny*⟩

**-penny** *adjective combining form* [*penny*; perhaps from the original price per hundred]
: being a (designated) nail size ⟨an eight*penny* nail⟩

**pen·ny–an·te** \'pe-nē-'an-tē\ *adjective* (1868)
: SMALL-TIME, TWO-BIT

**penny ante** *noun* (1855)
: poker played for very low stakes

**penny arcade** *noun* (1908)
: an amusement center having coin-operated devices for entertainment

**pen·ny·cress** \'pe-nē-,kres\ *noun* (1713)
: a Eurasian herb (*Thlaspi arvense*) with round flat pods that is widely naturalized in the New World

**penny dreadful** *noun* (circa 1873)
: a novel of violent adventure or crime

**pen·ny–pinch·ing** \-,pin-chiŋ\ *noun* (1935)
: FRUGALITY, PARSIMONY
— **pen·ny–pinch·er** \-chər\ *noun*
— **penny–pinching** *adjective*

**pen·ny·roy·al** \,pen-ē-'rȯi(-ə)l, 'pe-ni-,rīl\ *noun* [probably by folk etymology from Middle French *poullieul*, modification of Latin *pulegium* fleabane, pennyroyal] (1530)
**1** : a European perennial mint (*Mentha pulegium*) with small aromatic leaves
**2** : an aromatic North American mint (*Hedeoma pulegioides*) that has blue or violet flowers borne in axillary tufts and yields an oil used in folk medicine or to drive away mosquitoes

**penny stock** *noun* (circa 1920)
: a usually unlisted highly speculative stock selling for a dollar or less

**pen·ny·weight** \'pe-nē-,wāt\ *noun* (14th century)
— see WEIGHT table

**pen·ny·whistle** \-,hwi-səl, -,wi-\ *noun* (1818)
**1** : a small fipple flute
**2** : a toy whistle

**pen·ny–wise** \-,wīz\ *adjective* [from the phrase *penny-wise and pound-foolish*] (1607)
: wise or prudent only in dealing with small sums or matters

**pen·ny·wort** \-,wərt, -,wȯrt\ *noun* (14th century)
: any of several usually round-leaved plants (as of the genus *Hydrocotyle* of the carrot family)

**pen·ny·worth** \'pe-nē-,wərth, *British often* 'pe-nərth\ *noun, plural* **pennyworth** *or* **pennyworths** (before 12th century)
**1** : a penny's worth
**2** : value for the money spent : BARGAIN
**3** : a small quantity : MODICUM

**Pe·nob·scot** \pə-'näb-,skät, -skət\ *noun, plural* **-scot** *or* **-scots** (1624)

---

☆ SYNONYMS
**Penitence, repentance, contrition, compunction, remorse** mean regret for sin or wrongdoing. PENITENCE implies sad and humble realization of and regret for one's misdeeds (absolution is dependent upon sincere *penitence*). REPENTANCE adds the implication of a resolve to change ⟨*repentance* accompanied by a complete change of character⟩. CONTRITION stresses the sorrowful regret that constitutes true penitence ⟨tearful expressions of *contrition*⟩. COMPUNCTION implies a painful sting of conscience especially for contemplated wrongdoing ⟨had no *compunctions* about taking back what is mine⟩. REMORSE suggests prolonged and insistent self-reproach and mental anguish for past wrongs and especially for those whose consequences cannot be remedied ⟨thieves untroubled by feelings of *remorse*⟩.

: a member of an American Indian people of the Penobscot river valley and Penobscot Bay region of Maine

**pe·no·che** \pə-'nō-chē\ *variant of* PENUCHE

**pe·nol·o·gy** \pi-'nä-lə-jē\ *noun* [Greek *poinē* penalty + English *-logy* — more at PAIN] (1838)
: a branch of criminology dealing with prison management and the treatment of offenders
— **pe·no·log·i·cal** \ˌpē-nə-'lä-ji-kəl\ *adjective*
— **pe·nol·o·gist** \pi-'nä-lə-jist\ *noun*

**pen pal** *noun* (1938)
: a friend made and kept through correspondence

**pen point** *noun* (circa 1864)
: a small thin convex metal device that tapers to a split point, fits into a holder, and is used for writing or drawing

**pen pusher** *noun* (circa 1905)
: PENCIL PUSHER

**¹pen·sion** \'pen(t)-shən\ *noun* [Middle English, from Middle French, from Latin *pension-, pensio,* from *pendere* to pay — more at PENDANT] (14th century)
**1** \'pen(t)-shən\ : a fixed sum paid regularly to a person: **a** *archaic* : WAGE **b** : a gratuity granted (as by a government) as a favor or reward **c** : one paid under given conditions to a person following retirement from service or to surviving dependents
**2** \päⁿs-yōⁿ\ [French, from Middle French] **a** : accommodations especially at a continental European hotel or boardinghouse : ROOM AND BOARD **b** *also* **pen·sio·ne** \ˌpen(t)-'syō-(ˌ)nā\ [*pensione,* from Italian] : a hotel or boardinghouse especially in continental Europe
— **pen·sion·less** \'pen(t)-shən-ləs\ *adjective*

**²pension** *transitive verb* **pen·sioned; pen·sion·ing** \'pen(t)-sh(ə-)niŋ\ (1702)
**1** : to grant or pay a pension to
**2** : to dismiss or retire from service with a pension ⟨*pensioned* off his faithful old servant⟩

**pen·sion·able** \'pen(t)-sh(ə-)nə-bəl\ *adjective* (1882)
*chiefly British* : of, relating to, qualified for, or qualifying for a pension ⟨*pensionable* employees⟩ ⟨a *pensionable* post⟩

**pen·sion·ary** \'pen(t)-shə-ˌner-ē\ *noun, plural* **-ar·ies** (1536)
: PENSIONER; *especially* : HIRELING
— **pensionary** *adjective*

**pen·sion·er** \'pen(t)-sh(ə-)nər\ *noun* (15th century)
**1** : a person who receives or lives on a pension
**2** *obsolete* **a** : GENTLEMAN-AT-ARMS **b** : RETAINER **c** : MERCENARY, HIRELING

**pen·sive** \'pen(t)-siv\ *adjective* [Middle English *pensif,* from Middle French, from *penser* to think, from Latin *pensare* to ponder, frequentative of *pendere* to weigh — more at PENDANT] (14th century)
**1** : musingly or dreamily thoughtful
**2** : suggestive of sad thoughtfulness
— **pen·sive·ly** *adverb*
— **pen·sive·ness** *noun*

**pen·ste·mon** \'pen-stə-mən, 'pen(t)-stə-\ *noun* [New Latin, from *penta-* + Greek *stēmōn* warp, thread — more at STAMEN] (1760)
: any of a genus (*Penstemon*) of chiefly American herbs of the snapdragon family with showy tubular flowers

**pen·stock** \'pen-ˌstäk\ *noun* (circa 1607)
**1** : a sluice or gate for regulating a flow (as of water)
**2** : a conduit or pipe for conducting water

**pent** \'pent\ *adjective* [probably from past participle of obsolete English *pend* to confine] (1550)
: shut up : CONFINED, REPRESSED ⟨a *pent* crowd⟩ ⟨*pent*-up feelings⟩

**penta-** *or* **pent-** *combining form* [Middle English, from Greek, from *pente* — more at FIVE]

**1** : five ⟨*penta*hedron⟩
**2** : containing five atoms or groups ⟨*pent*ane⟩

**pen·ta·chlo·ro·phe·nol** \ˌpen-tə-ˌklōr-ə-'fē-ˌnōl, -ˌklòr-, -fi-\ *noun* (1879)
: a crystalline compound $C_6Cl_5OH$ used especially as a wood preservative and fungicide and a disinfectant

**pen·ta·cle** \'pen-ti-kəl\ *noun* [(assumed) Medieval Latin *pentaculum,* probably from Greek *pente*] (1594)
: PENTAGRAM

**pen·tad** \'pen-ˌtad\ *noun* [Greek *pentad-, pentas,* from *pente*] (1653)
: a group of five

**pen·ta·gon** \'pen-tə-ˌgän\ *noun* [Greek *pentagōnon,* from neuter of *pentagōnos* pentagonal, from *penta-* + *gōnia* angle — more at -GON] (1571)
: a polygon of five angles and five sides

**Pentagon** *noun* [the *Pentagon* building, headquarters of the Department of Defense] (1941)
: the U.S. military leadership

**pen·tag·o·nal** \pen-'ta-gə-nᵊl\ *noun* (1571)
**1** : having five sides and five angles
**2** : having a pentagon as a cross section or as a base ⟨a *pentagonal* pyramid⟩
— **pen·tag·o·nal·ly** \-nᵊl-ē\ *adverb*

**Pen·ta·gon·ese** \ˌpen-tə-ˌgä-'nēz, -'nēs\ *noun* (1951)
: military jargon

**pen·ta·gram** \'pen-tə-ˌgram\ *noun* [Greek *pentagrammon,* from *penta-* + *-grammon* (akin to *gramma* letter) — more at GRAM] (1833)
: a figure of a 5-pointed star usually made with alternate points connected by a continuous line and used as a magic or occult symbol; *also* : a similar 6-pointed star (as a Solomon's seal)

**pen·ta·he·dron** \ˌpen-tə-'hē-drən\ *noun* [New Latin] (circa 1775)
: a solid bounded by five faces
— **pen·ta·he·dral** \-drəl\ *adjective*

**pen·tam·er·ous** \pen-'ta-mə-rəs\ *adjective* [New Latin *pentamerus,* from *penta-* (from Greek) + *-merus* -merous] (1826)
: divided into or consisting of five parts; *specifically* : having each floral whorl consisting of five or a multiple of five members

**pen·tam·e·ter** \pen-'ta-mə-tər\ *noun* [Latin, from Greek *pentametros* having five metrical feet, from *penta-* + *metron* measure — more at MEASURE] (1589)
: a line of verse consisting of five metrical feet

**pent·am·i·dine** \pen-'ta-mə-ˌdēn, -dən\ *noun* (1941)
: a drug $C_{19}H_{24}N_4O_2$ used especially to treat protozoal infections (as leishmaniasis) and to prevent AIDS-related pneumonia

**pen·tane** \'pen-ˌtān\ *noun* [International Scientific Vocabulary] (1877)
: any of three isomeric alkanes $C_5H_{12}$ that occur especially in petroleum

**pen·tan·gle** \'pent-ˌaŋ-gəl, 'pen-ˌtaŋ-\ *noun* (14th century)
: PENTAGRAM

**pen·ta·pep·tide** \ˌpen-tə-'pep-ˌtīd\ *noun* (1907)
: a polypeptide that contains five amino acid residues

**pen·ta·ploid** \'pen-tə-ˌplòid\ *adjective* (1921)
: having or being a chromosome number that is five times the basic number
— **pentaploid** *noun*
— **pen·ta·ploi·dy** \-ˌplòi-dē\ *noun*

**pen·tar·chy** \'pen-ˌtär-kē\ *noun* [Greek *pentarchia,* from *penta-* + *-archia* -archy] (1587)
: a group of five countries or districts each under its own ruler or government

**Pen·ta·teuch** \'pen-tə-ˌtük, -ˌtyük\ *noun* [Middle English *Penteteuke,* from Late Latin *Pentateuchus,* from Greek *Pentateuchos,* from *penta-* + *teuchos* tool, vessel, book, from *teuchein* to make — more at DOUGHTY] (15th century)

: the first five books of Jewish and Christian Scriptures

**pen·tath·lete** \pen-'tath-ˌlēt\ *noun* (1828)
: an athlete participating in a pentathlon

**pen·tath·lon** \pen-'tath-lən, -ˌlän\ *noun* [Greek, from *penta-* + *athlon* contest] (1603)
: an athletic contest involving participation by each contestant in five different events; *especially* : MODERN PENTATHLON

**pen·ta·ton·ic** \ˌpen-tə-'tä-nik\ *adjective* (1864)
: consisting of five tones; *specifically* : being or relating to a scale in which the tones are arranged like a major scale with the fourth and seventh tones omitted

**pen·ta·va·lent** \ˌpen-tə-'vā-lənt\ *adjective* (1871)
: having a valence of five

**pen·taz·o·cine** \pen-'ta-zə-ˌsēn\ *noun* [probably from *penta-* + *az-* + *octa-* + *²-ine*] (1963)
: an analgesic drug $C_{19}H_{27}NO$ that is less addictive than morphine

**Pen·te·cost** \'pen-ti-ˌkòst, -ˌkäst\ *noun* [Middle English, from Old English *pentecosten,* from Late Latin *pentecoste,* from Greek *pentēkostē,* literally, fiftieth day, from *pentēkostos* fiftieth, from *pentēkonta* fifty, from *penta-* + *-konta* (akin to Latin *viginti* twenty) — more at VIGESIMAL] (before 12th century)
**1** : SHABUOTH
**2** : a Christian feast on the seventh Sunday after Easter commemorating the descent of the Holy Spirit on the apostles — called also *Whitsunday*

**¹Pen·te·cos·tal** \ˌpen-ti-'käs-tᵊl, -'kòs-\ *adjective* (1663)
**1** : of, relating to, or suggesting Pentecost
**2** : of, relating to, or constituting any of various Christian religious bodies that emphasize individual experiences of grace, spiritual gifts (as glossolalia and faith healing), expressive worship, and evangelism
— **Pen·te·cos·tal·ism** \-tə-ˌli-zəm\ *noun*
— **Pen·te·cos·tal·ist** \-tə-list\ *noun or adjective*

**²Pentecostal** *noun* (1904)
: a member of a Pentecostal religious body

**pent·house** \'pent-ˌhaus\ *noun* [alteration of Middle English *pentis,* from Middle French *apentiz,* from *apent,* past participle of *apendre, appendre* to attach, hang against — more at APPEND] (1530)
**1 a** : a shed or roof attached to and sloping from a wall or building **b** : a smaller structure joined to a building : ANNEX
**2** : a structure or dwelling built on the roof of a building

**pent·land·ite** \'pent-lən-ˌdīt\ *noun* [French, from Joseph *Pentland* (died 1873) Irish scientist] (circa 1858)
: a bronzy yellow mineral that is an isometric nickel iron sulfide and the principal ore of nickel

**pen·to·bar·bi·tal** \ˌpen-tə-'bär-bə-ˌtòl\ *noun* [*penta-* + *-o-* + *barbital*] (1931)
: a granular barbiturate $C_{11}H_{18}N_2O_3$ used especially in the form of its sodium or calcium salt as a sedative, hypnotic, and antispasmodic

**pen·to·bar·bi·tone** \-ˌtōn\ *noun* [*penta-* + *-o-* + *barbitone*] (1938)
*British* : PENTOBARBITAL

**pen·to·san** \'pen-tə-ˌsan\ *noun* [International Scientific Vocabulary] (1892)
: any of various polysaccharides that yield only pentoses on hydrolysis and occur widely in plants

**pen·tose** \'pen-ˌtōs, -ˌtōz\ *noun* [International Scientific Vocabulary] (1890)
: a monosaccharide $C_5H_{10}O_5$ (as ribose) that contains five carbon atoms in the molecule

\ə\ abut \ᵊ\ kitten \ər\ further \a\ ash \ā\ ace \ä\ mop, mar \aú\ out \ch\ chin \e\ bet \ē\ easy \g\ go \i\ hit \ī\ ice \j\ job \ŋ\ sing \ō\ go \ò\ law \òi\ boy \th\ thin \t͟h\ the \ü\ loot \ú\ foot \y\ yet \zh\ vision *see also* Guide to Pronunciation

**Pen·to·thal** \'pen-tə-,thȯl\ *trademark*
— used for thiopental

**pent·ox·ide** \pent-'äk-,sīd\ *noun* [International-al Scientific Vocabulary] (circa 1872)
: an oxide containing five atoms of oxygen in the molecule

**pent·ste·mon** *variant of* PENSTEMON

**pen·tyl·ene·tet·ra·zol** \,pen-t⁰l-,ēn-'te-trə-,zȯl, -,zōl\ *noun* [*penta-* + methy*lene* + *tetra-zole* (CH₂N₄)] (1949)
: an analeptic drug $C_6H_{10}N_4$

**pe·nu·che** \pə-'nü-chē\ *noun* [Mexican Span-ish *panocha* raw sugar, from Spanish, ear of maize, ultimately from Latin *panicula* panicle — more at PANICLE] (1871)
: fudge made usually of brown sugar, butter, cream or milk, and nuts

**pe·nult** \'pē-,nəlt, pi-'\ *noun* [Latin *paenultima* penult, from feminine of *paenultimus* almost last, from *paene* almost + *ultimus* last — more at ULTIMATE] (1537)
: the next to the last member of a series; *especially* : the next to the last syllable of a word

**pen·ul·ti·ma** \pi-'nəl-tə-mə\ *noun* [Latin] (1589)
: PENULT

**pen·ul·ti·mate** \pi-'nəl-tə-mət\ *adjective* (1677)
**1** : next to the last ⟨the *penultimate* chapter of a book⟩
**2** : of or relating to a penult ⟨a *penultimate* ac-cent⟩
— **pen·ul·ti·mate·ly** *adverb*

**pen·um·bra** \pə-'nəm-brə\ *noun, plural* **-brae** \-(,)brē, -,brī\ *or* **-bras** [New Latin, from Latin *paene* almost + *umbra* shadow — more at UMBRAGE] (1666)
**1 a** : a space of partial illumination (as in an eclipse) between the perfect shadow on all sides and the full light **b** : a shaded region sur-rounding the dark central portion of a sunspot
**2** : a surrounding or adjoining region in which something exists in a lesser degree : FRINGE
**3** : a body of rights held to be guaranteed by implication in a civil constitution
— **pen·um·bral** \-brəl\ *adjective*

**pe·nu·ri·ous** \pə-'nu̇r-ē-əs, -'nyu̇r-\ *adjective* (1590)
**1** : marked by or suffering from penury
**2** : given to or marked by extreme stinting fru-gality
*synonym* see STINGY
— **pe·nu·ri·ous·ly** *adverb*
— **pe·nu·ri·ous·ness** *noun*

**pen·u·ry** \'pen-yə-rē\ *noun* [Middle English, from Latin *penuria, paenuria* want; perhaps akin to Latin *paene* almost] (14th century)
**1** : a cramping and oppressive lack of resourc-es (as money); *especially* : severe poverty
**2** : extreme and often niggardly frugality
*synonym* see POVERTY

**pe·on** \'pē-,än, -ən *also* pā-'ōn *for 2, British also* 'pyün *for 1*\ *noun, plural* **peons** *or* **pe·ones** \pā-'ō-nēz\ [Portuguese *peão* & French *pion*, from Medieval Latin *pedon-, pedo* foot soldier — more at PAWN] (1609)
**1** : any of various workers in India, Sri Lanka, or Malaysia: as **a** : INFANTRYMAN **b** : ORDERLY
**2** [Spanish *peón,* from Latin *pedon-, pedo*] : a member of the landless laboring class in Span-ish America
**3** *plural* **peons a** : a person held in compulso-ry servitude to a master for the working out of an indebtedness **b** : DRUDGE, MENIAL

**pe·on·age** \'pē-ə-nij\ *noun* (1844)
**1 a** : the use of laborers bound in servitude because of debt **b** : a system of convict labor by which convicts are leased to contractors
**2** : the condition of a peon

**pe·o·ny** \'pē-ə-nē\ *noun, plural* **-nies** [Middle English *piony,* from Middle French *pioine,* from Latin *paeonia,* from Greek *paiōnia,* from *Paiōn* Paeon, physician of the gods] (14th century)
: any of a genus (*Paeonia* of the family Paeo-niaceae) of chiefly Eurasian plants with large often double flowers

**¹peo·ple** \'pē-pəl\ *noun, plural* **people** [Mid-dle English *peple,* from Old French *peuple,* from Latin *populus*] (13th century)
**1** *plural* : human beings making up a group or assembly or linked by a common interest
**2** *plural* : HUMAN BEINGS, PERSONS — often used in compounds instead of *persons* ⟨sales-*people*⟩
**3** *plural* : the members of a family or kinship
**4** *plural* : the mass of a community as distin-guished from a special class ⟨disputes between the *people* and the nobles⟩ — often used by Communists to distinguish Communists from other people
**5** *plural* **peoples** : a body of persons that are united by a common culture, tradition, or sense of kinship, that typically have common language, institutions, and beliefs, and that of-ten constitute a politically organized group
**6** : lower animals usually of a specified kind or situation
**7** : the body of enfranchised citizens of a state
— **peo·ple·less** \-pə(l)-ləs\ *adjective*

**²people** *transitive verb* **peo·pled; peo·pling** \-p(ə-)liŋ\ [Middle French *peupler,* from Old French, from *peuple*] (15th century)
**1** : to supply or fill with people
**2** : to dwell in : INHABIT

**peo·ple·hood** \'pē-pəl-,hu̇d\ *noun* (circa 1899)
**1** : the quality or state of constituting a people
**2** : the awareness of the underlying unity that makes the individual a part of a people

**people mover** *noun* (1968)
: any of various rapid-transit systems (as of moving sidewalks or automated driverless cars) for shuttling people

**¹pep** \'pep\ *noun* [short for *pepper*] (1912)
: brisk energy or initiative and high spirits

**²pep** *transitive verb* **pepped; pep·ping** (1925)
: to inject pep into ⟨*pep* him up⟩

**pep·er·o·mia** \,pe-pə-'rō-mē-ə\ *noun* [New Latin, from Greek *peperi* pepper + *homoios* like, similar — more at HOMEO-] (1882)
: any of a genus (*Peperomia*) of fleshy tropical herbs of the pepper family often cultivated for their showy foliage

**pep·los** \'pe-pləs, -,pläs\ *also* **pep·lus** \-pləs\ *noun* [Latin *peplus,* from Greek *peplos*] (1776)
: a garment worn like a shawl by women of ancient Greece

**pep·lum** \-pləm\ *noun* [Latin, from Greek *pep-lon* peplos] (1866)
: a short section attached to the waistline of a blouse, jacket, or dress
— **pep·lumed** \-pləmd\ *ad-jective*

peplum

**pe·po** \'pē-(,)pō\ *noun, plural* **pepos** [Latin, a melon — more at PUMPKIN] (circa 1859)
: an indehiscent fleshy 1-celled or falsely 3-celled many-seeded berry (as a pumpkin, squash, melon, or cucumber) that has a hard rind and is the characteris-tic fruit of the gourd family

**¹pep·per** \'pe-pər\ *noun* [Middle English *peper,* from Old English *pipor,* from Latin *pi-per,* from Greek *peperi*] (before 12th century)
**1 a** : either of two pungent products from the fruit of an East Indian plant that are used as a condiment, carminative, or stimulant: (1) : BLACK PEPPER (2) : WHITE PEPPER **b** : any of a genus (*Piper* of the family Piperaceae, the pepper family) of tropical mostly jointed climbing shrubs with aromatic leaves; *espe-cially* : a woody vine (*P. nigrum*) with spicate flowers that is widely cultivated in the tropics for its red berries from which black pepper and white pepper are prepared

**2 a** : any of several products similar to pepper that are obtained from close relatives of the pepper plant **b** : any of various pungent condi-ments obtained from plants of other genera than that of the pepper
**3 a** : CAPSICUM 1; *especially* : a New World capsicum (*Capsicum annuum*) whose fruits are hot peppers or sweet peppers **b** : the fruit of a pepper that is usually red or yellow when ripe
— **pepper** *adjective*

**²pepper** *transitive verb* **pep·pered; pep·per·ing** \'pe-p(ə-)riŋ\ (1538)
**1 a** : to sprinkle, season, or cover with or as if with pepper **b** : to shower with or as if with shot or other missiles
**2** : to hit with rapid repeated blows
**3** : to sprinkle as if with pepper ⟨*peppered* the report with statistics⟩
— **pep·per·er** \-pər-ər\ *noun*

**pep·per-and-salt** \,pe-pər(-ə)n(d)-'sȯlt\ *ad-jective* (1774)
: SALT-AND-PEPPER

**pep·per·box** \'pe-pər-,bäks\ *noun* (1546)
**1** : a small usually cylindrical box or bottle with a perforated top used for sprinkling ground pepper on food
**2** : a pistol of the late 18th century with five or six revolving barrels

**pep·per·corn** \-,kȯrn\ *noun* (before 12th cen-tury)
: a dried berry of the black pepper

**peppered moth** *noun* (circa 1832)
: a European geometrid moth (*Biston betu-laria*) that typically has white wings with small black specks but also occurs as a solid black form especially in areas where the air is heavily polluted by industry

**pep·per·grass** \'pe-pər-,gras\ *noun* (15th cen-tury)
: any of a genus (*Lepidium*) of cresses; *espe-cially* : GARDEN CRESS

**pepper mill** *noun* (circa 1858)
: a hand mill for grinding peppercorns

**pep·per·mint** \-,mint, -mənt, *in rapid speech* 'pep-mənt *or* -⁰m-ənt\ *noun* (1696)
**1 a** : a pungent and aromatic mint (*Mentha pi-perita*) with dark green lanceolate leaves and whorls of small pink flowers in spikes **b** : any of several mints (as *M. arvensis*) that are relat-ed to the peppermint
**2** : candy flavored with peppermint
— **pep·per·minty** \'pe-pər-,min-tē\ *adjec-tive*

**pep·per·o·ni** \,pe-pə-'rō-nē\ *noun* [Italian *pe-peroni* cayenne peppers, plural of *peperone,* augmentative of *pepe* pepper, from Latin *piper* — more at PEPPER] (1921)
: a highly seasoned beef and pork sausage

**pepper pot** *noun* (1679)
**1** *British* : PEPPERBOX 1
**2 a** : a highly seasoned West Indian stew of vegetables and meat or fish **b** : a thick soup of tripe, meat, dumplings, and vegetables highly seasoned especially with crushed peppercorns — called also *Philadelphia pepper pot*

**pepper shaker** *noun* (1895)
: a container with a perforated top for sprin-kling pepper

**pep·per·tree** \'pe-pər-,trē\ *noun* (circa 1692)
: a Peruvian evergreen tree (*Schinus molle*) of the cashew family grown as a shade tree in mild regions

**pep·pery** \'pe-p(ə-)rē\ *adjective* (1699)
**1** : of, relating to, or having the qualities of pepper : HOT, PUNGENT ⟨a *peppery* taste⟩
**2** : having a hot temper : TOUCHY ⟨a *peppery* boss⟩
**3** : FIERY, STINGING ⟨a *peppery* satire⟩
— **pep·per·i·ness** \-nəs\ *noun*

**pep pill** *noun* (1937)
: any of various stimulant drugs in pill or tab-let form

**pep·py** \'pe-pē\ *adjective* **pep·pi·er; -est** (circa 1918)
: full of pep

— **pep·pi·ness** *noun*
**pep·sin** \'pep-sən\ *noun* [German, from Greek *pepsis* digestion, from *pessein*] (circa 1844)
**1** : a protease of the stomach that breaks down most proteins to polypeptides
**2** : a preparation containing pepsin that is obtained from the stomach especially of the hog and is used especially as a digestive
**pep·sin·o·gen** \pep-'si-nə-jən\ *noun* [International Scientific Vocabulary] (1878)
: a granular zymogen of the gastric glands that is readily converted into pepsin in a slightly acid medium
**pep talk** *noun* (1925)
: a usually brief, intense, and emotional talk designed to influence or encourage an audience
**pep·tic** \'pep-tik\ *adjective* [Latin *pepticus*, from Greek *peptikos*, from *peptos* cooked, from *peptein, pessein* to cook, digest — more at COOK] (1651)
**1** : relating to or promoting digestion : DIGESTIVE
**2** : of, relating to, producing, or caused by pepsin ⟨*peptic* digestion⟩
**3** : connected with or resulting from the action of digestive juices ⟨a *peptic* ulcer⟩
**pep·ti·dase** \'pep-tə-ˌdās, -ˌdāz\ *noun* (1918)
: an enzyme that hydrolyzes simple peptides or their derivatives
**pep·tide** \'pep-ˌtīd\ *noun* [International Scientific Vocabulary, from *peptone*] (1906)
: any of various amides that are derived from two or more amino acids by combination of the amino group of one acid with the carboxyl group of another and are usually obtained by partial hydrolysis of proteins
— **pep·tid·ic** \pep-'ti-dik\ *adjective*
**peptide bond** *noun* (1935)
: the chemical bond between carbon and nitrogen in a peptide linkage
**peptide linkage** *noun* (1925)
: the bivalent group CONH that unites the amino acid residues in a peptide
**pep·ti·do·gly·can** \ˌpep-tə-dō-'glī-ˌkan\ *noun* (1966)
: a polymer that is composed of polysaccharide and peptide chains and is found especially in bacterial cell walls — called also *mucopeptide, murein*
**pep·tone** \'pep-ˌtōn\ *noun* [German *Pepton*, from Greek, neuter of *peptos* cooked] (1860)
: any of various water-soluble products of partial hydrolysis of proteins
**Pe·quot** \'pē-ˌkwät\ *noun* [Narraganset *Pequttôog*] (1631)
: a member of an American Indian people of what is now eastern Connecticut
¹**per** \'pər\ *preposition* [Latin, through, by means of, by — more at FOR] (14th century)
**1** : by the means or agency of : THROUGH ⟨*per* bearer⟩
**2** : with respect to every member of a specified group : for each
**3** : according to — often used with *as* ⟨*per* instructions⟩ ⟨as *per* usual⟩ ◻
²**per** *adverb* (1899)
: for each : APIECE ⟨a bargain at $3.50 *per*⟩
**per-** *prefix* [Latin, through, throughout, thoroughly, detrimental to, from *per*]
**1** : throughout : thoroughly ⟨*peruse*⟩
**2 a** : containing the largest possible or a relatively large proportion of a (specified) chemical element ⟨*perchloroethylene*⟩ **b** : containing an element in its highest or a high oxidation state ⟨*perchloric* acid⟩
¹**per·ad·ven·ture** \'pər-əd-ˌven-chər, 'per-; ˌpər-əd-', ˌper-\ *adverb* [Middle English *per aventure*, from Old French, by chance] (14th century)
*archaic* : PERHAPS, POSSIBLY
²**peradventure** *noun* (1627)
**1** : DOUBT ⟨a fact established beyond *peradventure*⟩

**2** : CHANCE 4a ⟨beyond *peradventure* of doubt⟩
**per·am·bu·late** \pə-'ram-byə-ˌlāt\ *verb* **-lat·ed; -lat·ing** [Latin *perambulatus*, past participle of *perambulare*, from *per-* through + *ambulare* to walk] (1568)
*transitive verb*
**1** : to travel over or through especially on foot : TRAVERSE
**2** : to make an official inspection of (a boundary) on foot
*intransitive verb*
: STROLL
— **per·am·bu·la·tion** \-ˌram-byə-'lā-shən\ *noun*
— **per·am·bu·la·to·ry** \-'ram-byə-lə-ˌtōr-ē, -ˌtòr-\ *adjective*
**per·am·bu·la·tor** \pə-'ram-byə-ˌlā-tər, *for 2 also* 'pram-\ *noun* (1611)
**1** : one that perambulates
**2** *chiefly British* : a baby carriage
**per an·num** \(ˌ)pər-'a-nəm\ *adverb* [Medieval Latin] (1536)
: in or for each year
**per·bo·rate** \(ˌ)pər-'bōr-ˌāt, -'bòr-\ *noun* [International Scientific Vocabulary] (1881)
: a salt that is a compound of a borate with hydrogen peroxide
**per·cale** \(ˌ)pər-'kā(ə)l, 'pər-ˌ; (ˌ)pər-'kal\ *noun* [Persian *pargālah*] (1840)
: a fine closely woven cotton cloth variously finished for clothing, sheeting, and industrial uses
**per·ca·line** \ˌpər-kə-'lēn\ *noun* [French, from *percale*] (circa 1858)
: a lightweight cotton fabric; *especially* : a glossy fabric used for bookbindings
**per cap·i·ta** \(ˌ)pər-'ka-pə-tə\ *adverb or adjective* [Medieval Latin, by heads] (1682)
**1** : equally to each individual
**2** : per unit of population : by or for each person ⟨the highest income *per capita* of any state in the union⟩
**per·ceive** \pər-'sēv\ *transitive verb* **per·ceived; per·ceiv·ing** [Middle English, from Middle French *perceivre*, from Latin *percipere*, from *per-* thoroughly + *capere* to take — more at HEAVE] (14th century)
**1 a** : to attain awareness or understanding of **b** : to regard as being such ⟨*perceived* threats⟩ ⟨was *perceived* as a loser⟩
**2** : to become aware of through the senses; *especially* : SEE, OBSERVE
— **per·ceiv·able** \-'sē-və-bəl\ *adjective*
— **per·ceiv·ably** \-blē\ *adverb*
— **per·ceiv·er** *noun*
¹**per·cent** \pər-'sent\ *adverb* [earlier *per cent*, from *per* + Latin *centum* hundred — more at HUNDRED] (1568)
: in the hundred : of each hundred
²**percent** *noun, plural* **percent** *or* **per·cents** (1667)
**1** *plural percent* **a** : one part in a hundred **b** : PERCENTAGE ⟨a large *percent* of his income⟩
**2** *percents plural, British* : securities bearing a specified rate of interest
³**percent** *adjective* (1888)
**1** : reckoned on the basis of a whole divided into one hundred parts
**2** : paying interest at a specified percent
**per·cent·age** \pər-'sen-tij\ *noun* (circa 1789)
**1 a** : a part of a whole expressed in hundredths **b** : the result obtained by multiplying a number by a percent
**2 a** : a share of winnings or profits **b** : ADVANTAGE, PROFIT ⟨no *percentage* in going around looking like an old sack of laundry —Wallace Stegner⟩
**3** : an indeterminate part : PROPORTION
**4 a** : PROBABILITY **b** : favorable odds
**per·cen·tile** \pər-'sen-ˌtīl\ *noun* (1885)
: a value on a scale of one hundred that indicates the percent of a distribution that is equal to or below it ⟨a score in the 95th *percentile*⟩

**per cen·tum** \pər-'sen-təm\ *noun* [*per* + Latin *centum*] (circa 1565)
: PERCENT
**per·cept** \'pər-ˌsept\ *noun* [back-formation from *perception*] (1837)
: an impression of an object obtained by use of the senses : SENSE-DATUM
**per·cep·ti·ble** \pər-'sep-tə-bəl\ *adjective* (1603)
: capable of being perceived especially by the senses ⟨a *perceptible* change in her tone⟩ ⟨the light became increasingly *perceptible*⟩ ☆
— **per·cep·ti·bil·i·ty** \-ˌsep-tə-'bi-lə-tē\ *noun*
— **per·cep·ti·bly** \-blē\ *adverb*
**per·cep·tion** \pər-'sep-shən\ *noun* [Latin *perception-, perceptio* act of perceiving, from *percipere*] (14th century)
**1 a** : a result of perceiving : OBSERVATION **b** : a mental image : CONCEPT
**2** *obsolete* : CONSCIOUSNESS
**3 a** : awareness of the elements of environment through physical sensation ⟨color *perception*⟩ **b** : physical sensation interpreted in the light of experience
**4 a** : quick, acute, and intuitive cognition : APPRECIATION **b** : a capacity for comprehension
*synonym* see DISCERNMENT
— **per·cep·tion·al** \-shnəl, -shə-nᵊl\ *adjective*
**per·cep·tive** \pər-'sep-tiv\ *adjective* (1656)
**1** : responsive to sensory stimuli : DISCERNING ⟨a *perceptive* eye⟩
**2 a** : capable of or exhibiting keen perception : OBSERVANT ⟨a *perceptive* scholar⟩ **b** : characterized by sympathetic understanding or insight
— **per·cep·tive·ly** *adverb*
— **per·cep·tive·ness** *noun*
— **per·cep·tiv·i·ty** \(ˌ)pər-ˌsep-'ti-və-tē\ *noun*

---

☆ **SYNONYMS**
**Perceptible, sensible, palpable, tangible, appreciable, ponderable** mean apprehensible as real or existent. PERCEPTIBLE applies to what can be discerned by the senses often to a minimal extent ⟨a *perceptible* difference in sound to a careful listener⟩. SENSIBLE applies to whatever is clearly apprehended through the senses or impresses itself strongly on the mind ⟨an abrupt, *sensible* drop in temperature⟩. PALPABLE applies either to what has physical substance or to what is obvious and unmistakable ⟨the tension in the air was almost *palpable*⟩. TANGIBLE suggests what is capable of being handled or grasped both physically and mentally ⟨no *tangible* evidence of UFOs⟩. APPRECIABLE applies to what is distinctly discernible by the senses or definitely measurable ⟨an *appreciable* increase in income⟩. PONDERABLE suggests having definitely measurable weight or importance ⟨exerted a *ponderable* influence on world events⟩.

---

◻ **USAGE**
**per** *Per* occurs most frequently in business contexts; its use outside such contexts is often criticized but is quite widespread, especially in sense 2. Its most common and natural nonbusiness uses always involve figures, usually in relation to price ⟨$150 *per* performance⟩, automobiles ⟨32 miles *per* gallon⟩ ⟨55 miles *per* hour⟩, or sports ⟨averages 15 points and 9 rebounds *per* game⟩.

---

\ə\ abut \ᵊ\ kitten \ər\ further \a\ ash \ā\ ace
\ä\ mop, mar \aù\ out \ch\ chin \e\ bet \ē\ easy
\g\ go \i\ hit \ī\ ice \j\ job \ŋ\ sing \ō\ go
\ò\ law \òi\ boy \th\ thin \t̶h̶\ the \ü\ loot \ù\ foot
\y\ yet \zh\ vision *see also* Guide to Pronunciation

**per·cep·tu·al** \(ˌ)pər-ˈsep-chə-wəl, -chəl, -shwəl\ *adjective* [*percept* + *-ual* (as in *conceptual*)] (1878)
: of, relating to, or involving perception especially in relation to immediate sensory experience
— **per·cep·tu·al·ly** *adverb*

**Per·ce·val** \ˈpər-sə-vəl\ *noun* [Old French]
: a knight of King Arthur who wins a sight of the Holy Grail

**¹perch** \ˈpərch\ *noun* [Middle English *perche*, from Middle French, from Latin *pertica* pole] (14th century)
**1** : a bar or peg on which something is hung
**2 a** : a roost for a bird **b** : a resting place or vantage point : SEAT **c** : a prominent position ⟨his new *perch* as president⟩
**3** *chiefly British* : ROD 2

**²perch** (14th century)
*intransitive verb*
: to alight, settle, or rest on a perch, a height, or a precarious spot
*transitive verb*
: to place on a perch, a height, or a precarious spot

**³perch** *noun, plural* **perch** *or* **perch·es** [Middle English *perche*, from Middle French, from Latin *perca*, from Greek *perkē*; akin to Old High German *faro* colored, Latin *porcus*, a spiny fish] (14th century)
**1 a** : a small European freshwater bony fish (*Perca fluviatilis* of the family Percidae, the perch family) **b** : YELLOW PERCH
**2** : any of numerous bony fishes (as of the families Percidae, Centrarchidae, and Serranidae)

**per·chance** \pər-ˈchan(t)s\ *adverb* [Middle English *per chance*, from Middle French, by chance] (14th century)
: PERHAPS, POSSIBLY

**Per·che·ron** \ˈpər-chə-ˌrän, -shə-\ *noun* [French] (1875)
: any of a breed of powerful rugged draft horses that originated in the Perche region of France

**per·chlo·rate** \(ˌ)pər-ˈklōr-ˌāt, -ˈklȯr-, -ət\ *noun* [International Scientific Vocabulary] (1826)
: a salt or ester of perchloric acid

**Percheron**

**per·chlo·ric acid** \(ˌ)pər-ˈklōr-ik-, -ˈklȯr-\ *noun* (1818)
: a fuming corrosive strong acid $HClO_4$ that is the most highly oxidized acid of chlorine and a powerful oxidizing agent when heated

**per·chlo·ro·eth·y·lene** \(ˌ)pər-ˌklȯr-ō-ˈe-thə-ˌlēn, -ˌklȯr-\ *noun* (1873)
: a colorless nonflammable liquid $C_2Cl_4$ used often as a solvent in dry cleaning and for removal of grease from metals

**per·cip·i·ence** \pər-ˈsi-pē-ən(t)s\ *noun* (circa 1774)
: PERCEPTION 4

**¹per·cip·i·ent** \-ənt\ *noun* [Latin *percipient-, percipiens*, present participle of *percipere* to perceive] (1662)
**1** : one that perceives
**2** : a person on whose mind a telepathic impulse or message is held to fall

**²percipient** *adjective* (1692)
: capable of or characterized by perception
: DISCERNING
— **per·cip·i·ent·ly** *adverb*

**per·co·late** \ˈpər-kə-ˌlāt, ÷-kyə-\ *verb* **-lat·ed; -lat·ing** [Latin *percolatus*, past participle of *percolare*, from *per-* through + *colare* to sieve — more at PER-, COLANDER] (1626)
*transitive verb*
**1 a** : to cause (a solvent) to pass through a permeable substance (as a powdered drug) especially for extracting a soluble constituent **b** : to prepare (coffee) in a percolator
**2** : to be diffused through : PENETRATE
*intransitive verb*
**1** : to ooze or trickle through a permeable substance : SEEP
**2 a** : to become percolated **b** : to become lively or effervescent
**3** : to spread gradually ⟨allow the sunlight to *percolate* into our rooms —Norman Douglas⟩
**4** : SIMMER 2a
— **per·co·la·tion** \ˌpər-kə-ˈlā-shən\ *noun*

**per·co·la·tor** \ˈpər-kə-ˌlā-tər, ÷-kyə-\ *noun* (circa 1842)
: one that percolates; *specifically* : a coffeepot in which boiling water rising through a tube is repeatedly deflected downward through a perforated basket containing ground coffee beans to extract their essence

**per con·tra** \(ˌ)pər-ˈkän-trə\ *adverb* [Italian, by the opposite side (of the ledger)] (1554)
**1 a** : on the contrary **b** : by way of contrast
**2** : as an offset

**per cu·ri·am decision** \(ˌ)pər-ˈkyu̇r-ē-, ˌäm-, -ˈku̇r-\ *noun* [Medieval Latin *per curiam*, literally, by the court] (1927)
: a very brief usually unanimous decision of a court rendered without elaborate discussion

**per·cuss** \pər-ˈkəs\ *transitive verb* [Latin *percussus*, past participle of *percutere*] (1560)
: to tap sharply; *especially* : to practice percussion on

**per·cus·sion** \pər-ˈkə-shən\ *noun* [Middle English, from Latin *percussion-, percussio*, from *percutere* to beat, from *per-* thoroughly + *quatere* to shake] (15th century)
**1** : the act of percussing: as **a** : the striking of a percussion cap so as to set off the charge in a firearm **b** : the beating or striking of a musical instrument **c** : the act or technique of tapping the surface of a body part to learn the condition of the parts beneath by the resultant sound
**2** : the striking of sound on the ear
**3** : percussion instruments that form a section of a band or orchestra
— **percussion** *adjective*

**percussion cap** *noun* (1823)
: CAP 5

**percussion instrument** *noun* (1872)
: a musical instrument (as a drum, xylophone, or maraca) sounded by striking, shaking, or scraping

**per·cus·sion·ist** \pər-ˈkə-sh(ə-)nist\ *noun* (1939)
: one skilled in the playing of percussion instruments

**per·cus·sive** \pər-ˈkə-siv\ *adjective* (1793)
**1** : of or relating to percussion; *especially* : operative or operated by striking
**2** : having powerful impact
— **per·cus·sive·ly** *adverb*
— **per·cus·sive·ness** *noun*

**per·cu·ta·ne·ous** \ˌpər-kyu̇-ˈtā-nē-əs\ *adjective* (1887)
: effected or performed through the skin
— **per·cu·ta·ne·ous·ly** *adverb*

**per·die** \(ˌ)pər-ˈdē, per-\ *variant of* PARDIE

**¹per di·em** \(ˌ)pər-ˈdē-əm, -ˈdī-\ *adverb* [Medieval Latin] (1520)
: by the day : for each day

**²per diem** *adjective* (1809)
**1** : based on use or service by the day : DAILY
**2** : paid by the day

**³per diem** *noun, plural* **per diems** (1812)
**1** : a daily allowance
**2** : a daily fee

**per·di·tion** \pər-ˈdi-shən\ *noun* [Middle English *perdicion*, from Late Latin *perdition-, perditio*, from Latin *perdere* to destroy, from *per-* through + *dare* to give — more at PER-, DATE] (14th century)
**1 a** *archaic* : utter destruction **b** *obsolete*
: LOSS
**2 a** : eternal damnation **b** : HELL

**¹per·du** *or* **per·due** \ˈpər-(ˌ)dü, -(ˌ)dyü; (ˌ)pər-\ *noun* [French *sentinelle perdue*, literally, lost sentinel] (1605)
*obsolete* : a soldier assigned to extremely hazardous duty

**²per·du** *or* **per·due** \pər-ˈdœ\ *adjective* [French *perdu*, masculine, & *perdue*, feminine, from past participle of *perdre* to lose, from Latin *perdere*] (1624)
: remaining out of sight

**per·du·ra·ble** \(ˌ)pər-ˈdu̇r-ə-bəl, -ˈdyu̇r-; ˈpər-jə-rə-\ *adjective* [Middle English, from Middle French, from Late Latin *perdurabilis*, from Latin *perdurare* to endure, from *per-* throughout + *durare* to last — more at DURING] (14th century)
: very durable
— **per·du·ra·bil·i·ty** \(ˌ)pər-ˌdu̇r-ə-ˈbil-ət-ē, -ˌdyu̇r-; ˌpər-jə-rə-\ *noun*
— **per·du·ra·bly** \(ˌ)pər-ˈdu̇r-ə-blē, -ˈdyu̇r-; ˈpər-jə-rə-\ *adverb*

**per·dure** \(ˌ)pər-ˈdu̇r, -ˈdyu̇r\ *intransitive verb* **per·dured; per·dur·ing** [Middle English, from Latin *perdurare*] (15th century)
: to continue to exist : LAST

**per·e·gri·nate** \ˈper-ə-grə-ˌnāt\ *verb* **-nat·ed; -nat·ing** (1593)
*intransitive verb*
: to travel especially on foot : WALK
*transitive verb*
: to walk or travel over : TRAVERSE
— **per·e·gri·na·tion** \ˌper-ə-grə-ˈnā-shən\ *noun*

**¹per·e·grine** \ˈper-ə-grən, -ˌgrēn\ *adjective* [Middle English, from Medieval Latin *peregrinus*, from Latin, foreign — more at PILGRIM] (14th century)
: having a tendency to wander

**²peregrine** *noun* (1555)
: a swift nearly cosmopolitan falcon (*Falco peregrinus*) that is much used in falconry — called also *peregrine falcon*
**word history**
SEE PILGRIM

**peregrine**

**pe·rei·on** \pə-ˈrī-ˌän\ *or* **pe·re·on** \-ˈrē-\ *noun* [New Latin, from Greek *peraiōn*, present participle of *peraioun* to transport, from *peraios* situated beyond, from *pera* beyond; akin to Greek *poros* passage — more at FARE] (1855)
: the thorax or the seven metameres comprising the thorax of some crustaceans (as a decapod)

**pe·reio·pod** \pə-ˈrī-ə-ˌpäd\ *or* **pe·reo·pod** \-ˈrē-\ *noun* [New Latin *perion* + English *-pod*] (1893)
: an appendage of the pereion

**pe·remp·to·ry** \pə-ˈrem(p)-t(ə-)rē\ *adjective* [Late Latin & Latin; Late Latin *peremptorius*, from Latin, destructive, from *perimere* to take entirely, destroy, from *per-* thoroughly + *emere* to take — more at REDEEM] (15th century)
**1 a** : putting an end to or precluding a right of action, debate, or delay ⟨a *peremptory* mandamus⟩ **b** : admitting of no contradiction ⟨a *peremptory* conclusion based on absolute evidence⟩
**2** : expressive of urgency or command ⟨a *peremptory* call⟩
**3 a** : characterized by often imperious or arrogant self-assurance ⟨how insolent of late he is become, how proud, how *peremptory* —Shakespeare⟩ **b** : indicative of a peremptory attitude

or nature **:** HAUGHTY ⟨a *peremptory* tone⟩ ⟨*peremptory* disregard of an objection⟩

**synonym** see MASTERFUL
— **pe·remp·to·ri·ly** \-'rem(p)-t(ə-)rə-lē; -,rem(p)-'tōr-ə-lē, -'tōr-\ *adverb*
— **pe·remp·to·ri·ness** \-'rem(p)-t(ə-)rē-nəs\ *noun*

**peremptory challenge** *noun* (circa 1531)
**:** a challenge (as of a juror) made as of right without assigning any cause

**pe·ren·nate** \'per-ə-,nāt, pə-'re-,nāt\ *intransitive verb* **-nat·ed; -nat·ing** [Latin *perennatus*, past participle of *perennare*, from *perennis*] (circa 1623)
**:** to live over from season to season ⟨a *perennating* rhizome⟩
— **per·en·na·tion** \,per-ə-'nā-shən\ *noun*

**pe·ren·ni·al** \pə-'re-nē-əl\ *adjective* [Latin *perennis*, from *per-* throughout + *annus* year — more at PER-, ANNUAL] (1644)
**1 :** present at all seasons of the year
**2 :** persisting for several years usually with new herbaceous growth from a perennating part ⟨*perennial* asters⟩
**3 a :** PERSISTENT, ENDURING ⟨*perennial* traditions⟩ **b :** continuing without interruption **:** CONSTANT, PERPETUAL ⟨the *perennial* quest for certainty⟩ ⟨a *perennial* student⟩ **c :** regularly repeated or renewed **:** RECURRENT ⟨death is a *perennial* literary theme⟩

**synonym** see CONTINUAL
— **perennial** *noun*
— **pe·ren·ni·al·ly** \-nē-ə-lē\ *adverb*

**per·e·stroi·ka** \,per-ə-'stroi-kə\ *noun* [Russian *perestroĭka*, literally, restructuring] (1986)
**:** the policy of economic and governmental reform instituted by Mikhail Gorbachev in the Soviet Union during the mid-1980s

**¹per·fect** \'pər-fikt\ *adjective* [Middle English *parfit*, from Old French, from Latin *perfectus*, from past participle of *perficere* to carry out, perfect, from *per-* thoroughly + *facere* to make, do — more at DO] (14th century)
**1 a :** being entirely without fault or defect **:** FLAWLESS ⟨a *perfect* diamond⟩ **b :** satisfying all requirements **:** ACCURATE **c :** corresponding to an ideal standard or abstract concept ⟨a *perfect* gentleman⟩ **d :** faithfully reproducing the original; *specifically* **:** LETTER-PERFECT **e :** legally valid
**2 :** EXPERT, PROFICIENT ⟨practice makes *perfect*⟩
**3 a :** PURE, TOTAL **b :** lacking in no essential detail **:** COMPLETE **c :** SANE **d :** ABSOLUTE, UNEQUIVOCAL ⟨enjoys *perfect* happiness⟩ **e :** of an extreme kind **:** UNMITIGATED ⟨a *perfect* brat⟩ ⟨an act of *perfect* foolishness⟩
**4** *obsolete* **:** MATURE
**5 :** of, relating to, or constituting a verb form or verbal that expresses an action or state completed at the time of speaking or at a time spoken of
**6** *obsolete* **a :** CERTAIN, SURE **b :** CONTENTED, SATISFIED
**7** *of a musical interval* **:** belonging to the consonances unison, fourth, fifth, and octave which retain their character when inverted and when raised or lowered by a half step become augmented or diminished
**8 a :** sexually mature and fully differentiated ⟨a *perfect* insect⟩ **b :** having both stamens and pistils in the same flower ⟨a *perfect* flower⟩ ☆
■
— **per·fect·ness** \-fik(t)-nəs\ *noun*

**²per·fect** \pər-'fekt *also* 'pər-fikt\ *transitive verb* (14th century)
**1 :** to bring to final form
**2 :** to make perfect **:** IMPROVE, REFINE
— **per·fect·er** *noun*

**³per·fect** \'pər-fikt\ *noun* (1841)
**:** the perfect tense of a language; *also* **:** a verb form in the perfect tense

**per·fec·ta** \pər-'fek-tə\ *noun* [American Spanish *quiniela perfecta* perfect quiniela] (1967)
**:** a bet in which the bettor picks the first and

second place finishers in order — compare QUINIELA, TRIFECTA

**perfect binding** *noun* (1926)
**:** a book binding in which a layer of adhesive holds the pages and cover together
— **per·fect-bound** \'pər-fik(t)-'baünd\ *adjective*

**perfect game** *noun* (circa 1949)
**:** a baseball game in which a pitcher allows no hits, no runs, and no opposing batter to reach first base

**per·fect·ible** \pər-'fek-tə-bəl *also* 'pər-fik-\ *adjective* (1635)
**:** capable of improvement or perfection
— **per·fect·ibil·i·ty** \pər-,fek-tə-'bi-lə-tē *also* ,pər-fik-\ *noun*

**per·fec·tion** \pər-'fek-shən\ *noun* [Middle English *perfeccioun*, from Old French *perfection*, from Latin *perfection-, perfectio*, from *perficere*] (13th century)
**1 :** the quality or state of being perfect: as **a :** freedom from fault or defect **:** FLAWLESSNESS **b :** MATURITY **c :** the quality or state of being saintly
**2 a :** an exemplification of supreme excellence **b :** an unsurpassable degree of accuracy or excellence
**3 :** the act or process of perfecting

**per·fec·tion·ism** \-shə-,ni-zəm\ *noun* (circa 1846)
**1 a :** the doctrine that the perfection of moral character constitutes a person's highest good **b :** the theological doctrine that a state of freedom from sin is attainable on earth
**2 :** a disposition to regard anything short of perfection as unacceptable
— **per·fec·tion·ist** \-sh(ə-)nist\ *noun or adjective*
— **per·fec·tion·is·tic** \-,fek-shə-'nis-tik\ *adjective*

**per·fec·tive** \pər-'fek-tiv *also* 'pər-fik-\ *adjective* (1596)
**1** *archaic* **a :** tending to make perfect **b :** becoming better
**2 :** expressing action as complete or as implying the notion of completion, conclusion, or result ⟨*perfective* verb⟩
— **perfective** *noun*
— **per·fec·tive·ly** *adverb*
— **per·fec·tive·ness** *noun*
— **per·fec·tiv·i·ty** \pər-,fek-'ti-və-tē *also* ,pər-fik-\ *noun*

**per·fect·ly** \'pər-fik(t)-lē\ *adverb* (14th century)
**1 :** in a perfect manner
**2 :** to a complete or adequate extent **:** QUITE ⟨was *perfectly* happy until now⟩

**perfect number** *noun* (14th century)
**:** an integer (as 6 or 28) the sum of whose integral factors including 1 but excluding itself is equal to itself

**per·fec·to** \pər-'fek-(,)tō\ *noun, plural* **-tos** [Spanish, perfect, from Latin *perfectus*] (1894)
**:** a cigar that is thick in the middle and tapers at each end

**perfect participle** *noun* (1862)
**:** PAST PARTICIPLE

**perfect pitch** *noun* (1949)
**:** ABSOLUTE PITCH 2

**perfect square** *noun* (1856)
**:** an integer (as 9 or 36) whose square root is an integer

**per·fer·vid** \(,)pər-'fər-vəd, 'pər-\ *adjective* [New Latin *perfervidus*, from Latin *per-* thoroughly + *fervidus* fervid] (1856)
**:** marked by overwrought or exaggerated emotion **:** excessively fervent
**synonym** see IMPASSIONED

**per·fid·i·ous** \(,)pər-'fi-dē-əs\ *adjective* (1598)
**:** of, relating to, or characterized by perfidy
**synonym** see FAITHLESS
— **per·fid·i·ous·ly** *adverb*
— **per·fid·i·ous·ness** *noun*

**per·fi·dy** \'pər-fə-dē\ *noun, plural* **-dies** [Latin

*perfidia*, from *perfidus* faithless, from *per-* detrimental to + *fides* faith — more at PER-, FAITH] (1592)
**1 :** the quality or state of being faithless or disloyal **:** TREACHERY
**2 :** an act or an instance of disloyalty

**per·fo·li·ate** \,pər-'fō-lē-ət, 'pər-\ *adjective* [New Latin *perfoliata*, an herb having leaves pierced by the stem, from Latin *per* through + *foliata*, feminine of *foliatus* foliate] (1687)
**:** having the basal part naturally united around the stem ⟨a *perfoliate* leaf of a honeysuckle⟩

---

☆ **SYNONYMS**

**Perfect, whole, entire, intact** mean not lacking or faulty in any particular. PERFECT implies the soundness and the excellence of every part, element, or quality of a thing frequently as an unattainable or theoretical state ⟨a *perfect* set of teeth⟩. WHOLE suggests a completeness or perfection that can be sought, gained, or regained ⟨felt like a *whole* person again after vacation⟩. ENTIRE implies perfection deriving from integrity, soundness, or completeness of a thing ⟨the *entire* Beethoven corpus⟩. INTACT implies retention of perfection of a thing in its natural or original state ⟨the boat survived the storm *intact*⟩.

---

☐ **USAGE**

**perfect**  Can something be more perfect than something else? Can something be the most perfect of its kind? Writers and speakers of English have long thought so ⟨our sight is the most *perfect* and most delightful of all our senses —Joseph Addison (1712)⟩ ⟨some of their years were much more *perfect* than others —Benjamin Franklin (1752)⟩ ⟨the most *perfect* model of Roman discipline —Edward Gibbon (1776)⟩ ⟨the most *perfect* and precious . . . of antiquity —Thomas Jefferson (1786)⟩ ⟨in order to form a more *perfect* union —U.S. Constitution (1787)⟩. *Perfect* had been used in the comparative and superlative since the 14th century and, as the examples show, was common in the 18th century. Yet toward the end of the 18th century some grammarians decided that such use must be wrong in spite of its considerable literary authority. What is perfect is perfect, they said; the word does not admit of comparison. The argument claims to be based on logic. But did logicians agree ⟨man and the more *perfect* animals —John Stuart Mill (*A System of Logic*)⟩? The upshot of all this is that we have now inherited two traditions: a 200-year-old tradition of insisting that *perfect* cannot be compared and a 600-year-old tradition of using *perfect* in the comparative and superlative ⟨I was feeling more *perfect* with every Rainbow [trout] —Norman MacLean⟩ ⟨he felt . . . that circular motion was the most *perfect* —Stephen W. Hawking⟩. Resolution of this conflict lies in the fact that few things in reality are perfect, and when most people use *more perfect* or *most perfect* they are suggesting an approach to perfection. In other words, *more perfect* is equivalent to *more nearly perfect*. Sometimes writers find an excess of perfection ⟨it was perhaps too *perfect* in its unity —W. B. Yeats⟩ ⟨he is too *perfect* to believe —Lady Bird Johnson⟩. All of these uses are perfectly standard, but those who are diffident about *more perfect* can write, as some authors do, *more nearly perfect*.

---

\ə\ abut  \ᵊ\ kitten  \ər\ further  \a\ ash  \ā\ ace
\ä\ mop, mar  \aü\ out  \ch\ chin  \e\ bet  \ē\ easy
\g\ go  \i\ hit  \ī\ ice  \j\ job  \ŋ\ sing  \ō\ go
\o̊\ law  \o̊i\ boy  \th\ thin  \th\ the  \ü\ loot  \u̇\ foot
\y\ yet  \zh\ vision  *see also* Guide to Pronunciation

**per·fo·rate** \'pər-fə-ˌrāt\ verb **-rat·ed; -rat·ing** [Latin *perforatus,* past participle of *perforare* to bore through, from *per-* through + *forare* to bore — more at BORE] (1538)
*transitive verb*
**1 :** to make a hole through ⟨an ulcer *perforates* the duodenal wall⟩; *especially* **:** to make a line of holes in to facilitate separation
**2 :** to pass through or into by or as if by making a hole
*intransitive verb*
**:** to penetrate a surface
— **per·fo·rate** \'pər-f(ə-)rət, -fə-ˌrāt\ *adjective*
— **per·fo·ra·tor** \-fə-ˌrā-tər\ *noun*
**per·fo·rat·ed** \-fə-ˌrā-təd\ *adjective* (1597)
**1 :** having a hole or perforations; *especially* **:** having a specified number of perforations in 20 millimeters ⟨the stamps are *perforated* 10⟩
**2 :** characterized by perforation ⟨a *perforated* ulcer⟩
**per·fo·ra·tion** \ˌpər-fə-ˈrā-shən\ *noun* (15th century)
**1 :** the act or process of perforating
**2 a :** a hole or pattern made by or as if by piercing or boring **b :** one of the series of holes between rows of postage stamps in a sheet that serve as an aid in separation
**per·force** \pər-ˈfȯrs, -ˈfȯrs\ *adverb* [Middle English *par force,* from Middle French, by force] (14th century)
**1** *obsolete* **:** by physical coercion
**2 :** by force of circumstances
**per·form** \pə(r)-ˈfȯrm\ *verb* [Middle English, from Anglo-French *performer,* alteration of Old French *perfournir,* from *per-* thoroughly (from Latin) + *fournir* to complete — more at FURNISH] (14th century)
*transitive verb*
**1 :** to adhere to the terms of **:** FULFILL ⟨*perform* a contract⟩
**2 :** CARRY OUT, DO
**3 a :** to do in a formal manner or according to prescribed ritual **b :** to give a rendition of **:** PRESENT
*intransitive verb*
**1 :** to carry out an action or pattern of behavior **:** ACT, FUNCTION
**2 :** to give a performance **:** PLAY ☆
— **per·form·abil·i·ty** \-ˌfȯr-mə-ˈbi-lə-tē\ *noun*
— **per·form·able** \-ˈfȯr-mə-bəl\ *adjective*
— **per·form·er** \-ˈfȯr-mər\ *noun*
**per·for·mance** \pə(r)-ˈfȯr-mən(t)s\ *noun* (15th century)
**1 a :** the execution of an action **b :** something accomplished **:** DEED, FEAT
**2 :** the fulfillment of a claim, promise, or request **:** IMPLEMENTATION
**3 a :** the action of representing a character in a play **b :** a public presentation or exhibition ⟨a benefit *performance*⟩
**4 a :** the ability to perform **:** EFFICIENCY **b :** the manner in which a mechanism performs ⟨engine *performance*⟩
**5 :** the manner of reacting to stimuli **:** BEHAVIOR
**6 :** the linguistic behavior of an individual **:** PAROLE; *also* **:** the ability to speak a certain language — compare COMPETENCE 3
**performance art** *noun* (1971)
**:** a nontraditional art form that consists of or features a performance by the artist
— **performance artist** *noun*
**per·for·ma·tive** \-ˈfȯr-mə-tiv\ *adjective* (1955)
**:** being or relating to an expression that serves to effect a transaction or that constitutes the performance of the specified act by virtue of its utterance ⟨*performative* verbs such as *promise* and *congratulate*⟩ — compare CONSTATIVE

— **performative** *noun*
**per·for·ma·to·ry** \-mə-ˌtōr-ē, -ˌtȯr-\ *adjective* (1949)
**:** PERFORMATIVE; *also* **:** of or relating to performance
**performing** *adjective* (1889)
**:** of, relating to, or constituting an art (as drama) that involves public performance ⟨the *performing* arts⟩
**¹per·fume** \'pər-ˌfyüm, (ˌ)pər-ˈ\ *noun* [Middle French *perfum,* probably from Old Provençal, from *perfumar* to perfume, from *per-* thoroughly (from Latin) + *fumar* to smoke, from Latin *fumare,* from *fumus* smoke — more at FUME] (1533)
**1 :** the scent of something sweet-smelling
**2 :** a substance that emits a pleasant odor; *especially* **:** a fluid preparation of natural essences (as from plants or animals) or synthetics and a fixative used for scenting
*synonym* see FRAGRANCE
**²per·fume** \(ˌ)pər-ˈfyüm, ˈpər-\ *transitive verb* **per·fumed; per·fum·ing** (1538)
**:** to fill or imbue with an odor
**per·fum·er** \pə(r)-ˈfyü-mər, ˈpər-ˌ\ *noun* (circa 1580)
**:** one that makes or sells perfumes
**per·fum·ery** \pə(r)-ˈfyü-mə-rē, -ˈfyüm-rē\ *noun, plural* **-er·ies** (1800)
**1 a :** the art or process of making perfume **b :** the products made by a perfumer
**2 :** an establishment where perfumes are made
**per·func·to·ry** \pər-ˈfəŋ(k)-t(ə-)rē\ *adjective* [Late Latin *perfunctorius,* from Latin *perfungi* to accomplish, get through with, from *per-* through + *fungi* to perform — more at PER-, FUNCTION] (1593)
**1 :** characterized by routine or superficiality **:** MECHANICAL ⟨a *perfunctory* smile⟩
**2 :** lacking in interest or enthusiasm
— **per·func·to·ri·ly** \-t(ə-)rə-lē\ *adverb*
— **per·func·to·ri·ness** \-t(ə-)rē-nəs\ *noun*
**per·fus·ate** \(ˌ)pər-ˈfyü-ˌzāt, -zət\ *noun* (1915)
**:** a fluid (as a solution pumped through the heart) that is perfused
**per·fuse** \(ˌ)pər-ˈfyüz\ *transitive verb* **per·fused; per·fus·ing** [Middle English, from Latin *perfusus,* past participle of *perfundere* to pour over, from *per-* through + *fundere* to pour — more at FOUND] (15th century)
**1 :** SUFFUSE
**2 a :** to cause to flow or spread **:** DIFFUSE **b :** to force a fluid through (an organ or tissue) especially by way of the blood vessels
— **per·fu·sion** \-ˈfyü-zhən\ *noun*
**per·fu·sion·ist** \(ˌ)pər-ˈfyü-zhə-nist\ *noun* (1964)
**:** a certified medical technician responsible for extracorporeal oxygenation of the blood during open-heart surgery and for the operation and maintenance of equipment (as a heart-lung machine) controlling it
**per·go·la** \'pər-gə-lə, pər-ˈgō-\ *noun* [Italian, from Latin *pergula*] (1675)
**1 :** ARBOR, TRELLIS
**2 :** a structure usually consisting of parallel colonnades supporting an open roof of girders and cross rafters
**¹per·haps** \pər-ˈhaps, ˈpraps\ *adverb* [*per* + *hap*] (1528)
**:** possibly but not certainly **:** MAYBE
**²perhaps** *noun* (1534)
**:** something open to doubt or conjecture
**pe·ri** \'pir-ē\ *noun* [Persian *perī* fairy, genius, from Middle Persian *parīk;* akin to Avestan *pairikā* sorceress] (circa 1780)
**1 :** a supernatural being in Persian folklore descended from fallen angels and excluded from paradise until penance is accomplished
**2 :** a beautiful and graceful girl
**peri-** *prefix* [Latin, from Greek, around, in excess, from *peri;* akin to Greek *peran* to pass through — more at FARE]

**1 :** all around **:** about ⟨*periscope*⟩
**2 :** near ⟨*perihelion*⟩
**3 :** enclosing **:** surrounding ⟨*perineurium*⟩
**peri·anth** \'per-ē-ˌan(t)th\ *noun* [New Latin *perianthium,* from *peri-* + Greek *anthos* flower — more at ANTHOLOGY] (1828)
**:** the floral structure comprised of the calyx and corolla especially when the two whorls are fused — see FLOWER illustration
**peri·apt** \'per-ē-ˌapt\ *noun* [Middle French or Greek; Middle French *periapte,* from Greek *periapton,* from *periaptein* to fasten around (oneself), from *peri-* + *haptein* to fasten] (1584)
**:** AMULET
**peri·car·di·al** \ˌper-ə-ˈkär-dē-əl\ *adjective* (1654)
**:** of, relating to, or affecting the pericardium; *also* **:** situated around the heart
**peri·car·di·tis** \-ˌkär-ˈdī-təs\ *noun* [New Latin] (circa 1799)
**:** inflammation of the pericardium
**peri·car·di·um** \-ˈkär-dē-əm\ *noun, plural* **-dia** \-dē-ə\ [Middle English, from Medieval Latin, from Greek *perikardion,* neuter of *perikardios* around the heart, from *peri-* + *kardia* heart — more at HEART] (15th century)
**1 :** the conical sac of serous membrane that encloses the heart and the roots of the great blood vessels of vertebrates
**2 :** a cavity or space that contains the heart of an invertebrate and in arthropods is a part of the hemocoel
**peri·carp** \'per-ə-ˌkärp\ *noun* [New Latin *pericarpium,* from Greek *perikarpion* pod, from *peri-* + *-karpion* -carp] (1759)
**:** the ripened and variously modified walls of a plant ovary — see ENDOCARP illustration
**peri·chon·dri·um** \ˌper-ə-ˈkän-drē-əm\ *noun, plural* **-dria** \-drē-ə\ [New Latin, from *peri-* + Greek *chondros* grain, cartilage] (1741)
**:** the membrane of fibrous connective-tissue that invests cartilage except at joints
— **peri·chon·dral** \-drəl\ *adjective*
**pe·ric·o·pe** \pə-ˈri-kə-pē\ *noun* [Late Latin, from Greek *perikopē* section, from *peri-* + *kopē* act of cutting, from *koptein* to cut — more at CAPON] (1658)
**:** a selection from a book; *specifically* **:** LECTION 1
**peri·cra·ni·um** \ˌper-ə-ˈkrā-nē-əm\ *noun, plural* **-nia** \-nē-ə\ [Middle English *pericraneum,* from Medieval Latin, from Greek *perikranion,* neuter of *perikranios* around the skull, from *peri-* + *kranion* skull — more at CRANIUM] (15th century)

---

☆ **SYNONYMS**
**Perform, execute, discharge, accomplish, achieve, effect, fulfill** mean to carry out or into effect. PERFORM implies action that follows established patterns or procedures or fulfills agreed-upon requirements and often connotes special skill ⟨*performed* gymnastics⟩. EXECUTE stresses the carrying out of what exists in plan or in intent ⟨*executed* the hit-and-run⟩. DISCHARGE implies execution and completion of appointed duties or tasks ⟨*discharged* his duties⟩. ACCOMPLISH stresses the successful completion of a process rather than the means of carrying it out ⟨*accomplished* everything they set out to do⟩. ACHIEVE adds to ACCOMPLISH the implication of conquered difficulties ⟨*achieve* greatness⟩. EFFECT adds to ACHIEVE an emphasis on the inherent force in the agent capable of surmounting obstacles ⟨*effected* sweeping reforms⟩. FULFILL implies a complete realization of ends or possibilities ⟨*fulfilled* their ambitions⟩.

: the external periosteum of the skull

**peri·cy·cle** \'per-ə-ˌsī-kəl\ *noun* [French *péricycle,* from Greek *perikyklos* spherical, from *peri-* + *kyklos* circle — more at WHEEL] (circa 1892)
: a thin layer of parenchymatous or sclerenchymatous cells that surrounds the stele in most vascular plants
— **peri·cy·clic** \ˌper-ə-'sī-klik, -'si-\ *adjective*

**peri·derm** \'per-ə-ˌdərm\ *noun* [New Latin *peridermis,* from *peri-* + *-dermis*] (1849)
: an outer layer of tissue; *especially* : a cortical protective layer of many roots and stems that typically consists of phellem, phellogen, and phelloderm

**peri·rid·i·um** \pə-'ri-dē-əm\ *noun, plural* **peri·rid·ia** \-dē-ə\ [New Latin, from Greek *pēridion,* diminutive of *pēra* leather bag] (circa 1823)
: the outer envelope of the sporophore of many fungi

**peri·dot** \'per-ə-ˌdät, -ˌdō(t)\ *noun* [French *péridot,* from Old French *peritot*] (circa 1706)
: a deep yellowish green transparent olivine used as a gem
— **peri·do·tic** \ˌper-ə-'dä-tik, -'dō-\ *adjective*

**peri·do·tite** \pə-'ri-də-ˌtīt\ *noun* [French *péridotite,* from *péridot*] (1878)
: any of a group of granitoid igneous rocks composed of ferromagnesian minerals and especially olivine
— **peri·do·tit·ic** \pə-ˌri-də-'ti-tik\ *adjective*

**peri·gee** \'per-ə-(ˌ)jē\ *noun* [Middle French, from New Latin *perigeum,* from Greek *perigeion,* from neuter of *perigeios* near the earth, from *peri-* + *gē* earth] (1594)
: the point in the orbit of an object (as a satellite) orbiting the earth that is nearest to the center of the earth; *also* : the point nearest a planet or a satellite (as the moon) reached by an object orbiting it — compare APOGEE
— **peri·ge·an** \ˌper-ə-'jē-ən\ *adjective*

**peri·rig·y·nous** \pə-'ri-jə-nəs\ *adjective* [New Latin *perigynus,* from *peri-* + *-gynus* -gynous] (1807)
: borne on a ring or cup of the receptacle surrounding a pistil ⟨*perigynous* petals⟩; *also* : having perigynous stamens and petals ⟨*perigynous* flowers⟩
— **peri·rig·y·ny** \-nē\ *noun*

**peri·he·lion** \ˌper-ə-'hēl-yən\ *noun, plural* **-he·lia** \-'hēl-yə\ [New Latin, from *peri-* + Greek *hēlios* sun — more at SOLAR] (1666)
: the point in the path of a celestial body (as a planet) that is nearest to the sun — compare APHELION
— **peri·he·lial** \-'hēl-yəl\ *adjective*

**peri·kar·y·on** \-'kar-ē-ˌän, -ən\ *noun, plural* **-kar·ya** \-ē-ə\ [New Latin, from *peri-* + Greek *karyon* nut, kernel — more at CAREEN] (1897)
: CELL BODY
— **peri·kar·y·al** \-ē-əl\ *adjective*

**¹per·il** \'per-əl\ *noun* [Middle English, from Old French, from Latin *periculum* — more at FEAR] (13th century)
**1** : exposure to the risk of being injured, destroyed, or lost : DANGER ⟨fire put the city in *peril*⟩
**2** : something that imperils : RISK ⟨lessen the *perils* of the streets⟩

**²peril** *transitive verb* **-iled** *also* **-illed; -il·ing** *also* **-il·ling** (1567)
: to expose to danger

**pe·ril·la** \pə-'ri-lə\ *noun* [New Latin] (1900)
: any of a genus (*Perilla*) of Asian mints that have a bilabiate fruiting calyx and rugose nutlets

**perilla oil** *noun* (1917)
: a light yellow drying oil that is obtained

from seeds of perillas

**per·il·ous** \'per-ə-ləs\ *adjective* (14th century)
: full of or involving peril : HAZARDOUS
**synonym** see DANGEROUS
— **per·il·ous·ly** *adverb*
— **per·il·ous·ness** *noun*

**peri·lune** \'per-ə-ˌlün\ *noun* [*peri-* + Latin *luna* moon — more at LUNAR] (1960)
: the point in the path of a body orbiting the moon that is nearest to the center of the moon — compare APOLUNE

**peri·lymph** \-ˌlim(p)f\ *noun* [International Scientific Vocabulary] (circa 1839)
: the fluid between the membranous and bony labyrinths of the ear

**pe·rim·e·ter** \pə-'ri-mə-tər\ *noun* [Middle English *perimetre,* from Latin *perimetros,* from Greek, from *peri-* + *metron* measure — more at MEASURE] (15th century)
**1 a** : the boundary of a closed plane figure **b** : the length of a perimeter
**2** : a line or strip bounding or protecting an area
**3** : outer limits — often used in plural

**peri·my·si·um** \ˌper-ə-'mi-zhē-əm, -zē-\ *noun, plural* **-sia** \-zhē-ə, -zē-\ [New Latin, irregular from *peri-* + Greek *mys* mouse, muscle — more at MOUSE] (circa 1842)
: the connective-tissue sheath that surrounds a muscle and forms sheaths for the bundles of muscle fibers

**peri·na·tal** \-'nā-t°l\ *adjective* (1952)
: occurring in, concerned with, or being in the period around the time of birth ⟨*perinatal* mortality⟩ ⟨*perinatal* care⟩
— **peri·na·tal·ly** \-t°l-(l)ē\ *adverb*

**per·i·ne·um** \ˌper-ə-'nē-əm\ *noun, plural* **-nea** \-'nē-ə\ [Middle English, from Late Latin *perinaion,* from Greek, from *peri-* + *inan* empty out; perhaps akin to Sanskrit *iṣṇāti* he sets in motion] (15th century)
: an area of tissue that marks externally the approximate boundary of the outlet of the pelvis and gives passage to the urinogenital ducts and rectum; *also* : the area between the anus and the posterior part of the external genitalia
— **per·i·ne·al** \-'nē-əl\ *adjective*

**peri·neu·ri·um** \ˌper-ə-'nür-ē-əm, -'nyür-\ *noun, plural* **-ria** \-ē-ə\ [New Latin, from *peri-* + Greek *neuron* nerve — more at NERVE] (circa 1842)
: the connective-tissue sheath that surrounds a bundle of nerve fibers

**¹pe·ri·od** \'pir-ē-əd\ *noun* [Middle English *pariode,* from Middle French *periode,* from Medieval Latin, Latin, & Greek; Medieval Latin *periodus* period of time, punctuation mark, from Latin & Greek; Latin, rhetorical period, from Greek *periodos* circuit, period of time, rhetorical period, from *peri-* + *hodos* way] (circa 1530)
**1** : the completion of a cycle, a series of events, or a single action : CONCLUSION
**2 a** (1) : an utterance from one full stop to another : SENTENCE (2) : a well-proportioned sentence of several clauses (3) : PERIODIC SENTENCE **b** : a musical structure or melodic section usually composed of two or more contrasting or complementary phrases and ending with a cadence
**3 a** : the full pause with which the utterance of a sentence closes **b** : END, STOP
**4** *obsolete* : GOAL, PURPOSE
**5 a** : a point . used to mark the end (as of a declarative sentence or an abbreviation) — often used interjectionally to emphasize that no more need be said ⟨I don't remember — *period*⟩ **b** : a rhythmical unit in Greek verse composed of a series of two or more cola
**6 a** : a portion of time determined by some recurring phenomenon **b** (1) : the interval of time required for a cyclic motion or phenomenon to complete a cycle and begin to repeat it-

self (2) : a number *k* that does not change the value of a periodic function *f* when added to the independent variable; *especially* : the smallest such number **c** : a single cyclic occurrence of menstruation
**7 a** : a chronological division : STAGE **b** : a division of geologic time longer than an epoch and included in an era **c** : a stage of culture having a definable place in time and space
**8 a** : one of the divisions of the academic day **b** : one of the divisions of the playing time of a game ☆

**²period** *adjective* (1905)
: of, relating to, or representing a particular historical period ⟨*period* furniture⟩ ⟨*period* costumes⟩

**pe·ri·od·ic** \ˌpir-ē-'ä-dik\ *adjective* (1642)
**1** : occurring or recurring at regular intervals
**2 a** : consisting of or containing a series of repeated stages, processes, or digits : CYCLIC ⟨*periodic* decimals⟩ ⟨a *periodic* vibration⟩ **b** : being a function any value of which recurs at regular intervals
**3** : expressed in or characterized by periodic sentences

**per·iod·ic acid** \ˌpər-(ˌ)ī-'ä-dik-\ *noun* [International Scientific Vocabulary *per-* + *iodic*] (1836)
: any of the strongly oxidizing acids (as $H_5IO_6$ or $HIO_4$) that are the most highly oxidized acids of iodine

**¹pe·ri·od·i·cal** \ˌpir-ē-'ä-di-kəl\ *adjective* (1601)
**1** : PERIODIC 1
**2 a** : published with a fixed interval between the issues or numbers **b** : published in, characteristic of, or connected with a periodical

**²periodical** *noun* (1798)
: a periodical publication

**periodical cicada** *noun* (1890)
: SEVENTEEN-YEAR LOCUST

**pe·ri·od·i·cal·ly** \ˌpir-ē-'ä-di-k(ə-)lē\ *adverb* (1646)
**1** : at regular intervals of time
**2** : from time to time : FREQUENTLY

**pe·ri·od·ic·i·ty** \ˌpir-ē-ə-'di-sə-tē\ *noun* (1833)
: the quality, state, or fact of being regularly recurrent or having periods

**periodic law** *noun* (1872)
: a law in chemistry: the elements when arranged in the order of their atomic numbers show a periodic variation of atomic structure and of most of their properties

**periodic sentence** *noun* (circa 1928)
: a usually complex sentence that has no subordinate or trailing elements following its principal clause (as in "yesterday while I was walking down the street, I saw him")

---

☆ **SYNONYMS**
**Period, epoch, era, age** mean a division of time. PERIOD may designate an extent of time of any length ⟨*periods* of economic prosperity⟩. EPOCH applies to a period begun or set off by some significant or striking quality, change, or series of events ⟨the steam engine marked a new *epoch* in industry⟩. ERA suggests a period of history marked by a new or distinct order of things ⟨the *era* of global communications⟩. AGE is used frequently of a fairly definite period dominated by a prominent figure or feature ⟨the *age* of Samuel Johnson⟩.

---

\ə\ abut   \°\ kitten   \ər\ further   \a\ ash   \ā\ ace
\ä\ mop, mar   \au̇\ out   \ch\ chin   \e\ bet   \ē\ easy
\g\ go   \i\ hit   \ī\ ice   \j\ job   \ŋ\ sing   \ō\ go
\ȯ\ law   \ȯi\ boy   \th\ thin   \th̶\ the   \ü\ loot   \u̇\ foot
\y\ yet   \zh\ vision   *see also* Guide to Pronunciation

# PERIODIC TABLE

This is a common long form of the table. Roman numerals and letters heading the vertical columns indicate the groups (there are differences of opinion regarding the letter designations, those given here being probably the most generally used). The horizontal rows represent the periods, with two series removed from the two very long periods and represented below the main table. Atomic numbers are given above the symbols for the elements. Compare ELEMENT table.

| IA[1] | | | | | | | | | | | | | | | | VIIA[3] | Zero[4] |
|---|---|---|---|---|---|---|---|---|---|---|---|---|---|---|---|---|---|
| 1 H | IIA[2] | | | | | | | | | | | | | | | 1 H | 2 He |
| 3 Li | 4 Be | | | | | | | | | | | 5 B | 6 C | 7 N | 8 O | 9 F | 10 Ne |
| 11 Na | 12 Mg | IIIB | IVB | VB | VIB | VIIB | | VIII | | IB | IIB | 13 Al | 14 Si | 15 P | 16 S | 17 Cl | 18 Ar |
| 19 K | 20 Ca | 21 Sc | 22 Ti | 23 V | 24 Cr | 25 Mn | 26 Fe | 27 Co | 28 Ni | 29 Cu | 30 Zn | 31 Ga | 32 Ge | 33 As | 34 Se | 35 Br | 36 Kr |
| 37 Rb | 38 Sr | 39 Y | 40 Zr | 41 Nb | 42 Mo | 43 Tc | 44 Ru | 45 Rh | 46 Pd | 47 Ag | 48 Cd | 49 In | 50 Sn | 51 Sb | 52 Te | 53 I | 54 Xe |
| 55 Cs | 56 Ba | 57 *La | 72 Hf | 73 Ta | 74 W | 75 Re | 76 Os | 77 Ir | 78 Pt | 79 Au | 80 Hg | 81 Tl | 82 Pb | 83 Bi | 84 Po | 85 At | 86 Rn |
| 87 Fr | 88 Ra | 89 #Ac | 104 Rf | 105 Db | 106 Sg | 107 Bh | 108 Hs | 109 Mt | | | | | | | | | |

| *LANTHANIDE SERIES | 58 Ce | 59 Pr | 60 Nd | 61 Pm | 62 Sm | 63 Eu | 64 Gd | 65 Tb | 66 Dy | 67 Ho | 68 Er | 69 Tm | 70 Yb | 71 Lu |
|---|---|---|---|---|---|---|---|---|---|---|---|---|---|---|
| #ACTINIDE SERIES | 90 Th | 91 Pa | 92 U | 93 Np | 94 Pu | 95 Am | 96 Cm | 97 Bk | 98 Cf | 99 Es | 100 Fm | 101 Md | 102 No | 103 Lr |

[1] Group IA (excluding hydrogen) comprises the alkali metals.
[2] Group IIA comprises the alkaline-earth metals.
[3] Group VIIA (excluding hydrogen) comprises the halogens.
[4] Group Zero comprises the noble gases.

**periodic table** *noun* (1895)
: an arrangement of chemical elements based on the periodic law

**pe·ri·od·i·za·tion** \ˌpir-ē-ə-də-'zā-shən\ *noun* (1938)
: division (as of history) into periods

**peri·odon·tal** \ˌper-ē-ō-'dän-t°l\ *adjective* (1854)
**1** : investing or surrounding a tooth
**2** : of or affecting periodontal tissues or regions ⟨*periodontal* diseases⟩
— **peri·odon·tal·ly** \-t°l-ē\ *adverb*

**periodontal membrane** *noun* (circa 1903)
: the fibrous connective-tissue layer covering the cementum of a tooth and holding it in place in the jawbone

**peri·odon·tics** \-'dän-tiks\ *noun plural but singular or plural in construction* [New Latin *periodontium* periodontal tissue, from *peri-* + Greek *odont-, odous, odōn* tooth — more at TOOTH] (circa 1944)
: a branch of dentistry that deals with diseases of the supporting and investing structures of the teeth including the gums, cementum, periodontal membranes, and alveolar bone
— **peri·odon·tist** \-'dän-tist\ *noun*

**peri·odon·tol·o·gy** \-ˌdän-'tä-lə-jē\ *noun* (1914)
: PERIODONTICS

**period piece** *noun* (1940)
: a piece (as of fiction, art, furniture, or music) whose special value lies in its evocation of an historical period

**peri·onych·i·um** \ˌper-ē-ō-'ni-kē-əm\ *noun, plural* **-ia** \-kē-ə\ [New Latin, from *peri-* + Greek *onych-, onyx* nail — more at NAIL] (circa 1879)
: the tissue bordering the root and sides of a fingernail or toenail

**peri·os·te·al** \ˌper-ē-'äs-tē-əl\ *adjective* (1830)
**1** : situated around or produced external to bone
**2** : of, relating to, or involving the periosteum

**peri·os·te·um** \-tē-əm\ *noun, plural* **-tea** \-tē-ə\ [New Latin, from Late Latin *periosteon*, from Greek, neuter of *periosteos* around the bone, from *peri-* + *osteon* bone — more at OSSEOUS] (1597)
: the membrane of connective tissue that closely invests all bones except at the articular surfaces

**peri·os·ti·tis** \-ˌäs-'tī-təs\ *noun* [New Latin] (1843)
: inflammation of the periosteum

**¹peri·pa·tet·ic** \ˌper-ə-pə-'te-tik\ *noun* (15th century)
**1** *capitalized* : a follower of Aristotle or adherent of Aristotelianism
**2** : PEDESTRIAN, ITINERANT
**3** *plural* : movement or journeys hither and thither

**²peripatetic** *adjective* [Middle French & Latin; Middle French *peripatetique*, from Latin *peripateticus*, from Greek *peripatētikos*, from *peripatein* to walk up and down, discourse while pacing (as did Aristotle), from *peri-* + *patein* to tread; akin to Sanskrit *patha* path — more at FIND] (1566)
**1** *capitalized* : ARISTOTELIAN
**2 a** : of, relating to, or given to walking **b** : moving or traveling from place to place : ITINERANT
— **peri·pa·tet·i·cal·ly** \-ti-k(ə-)lē\ *adverb*
— **Peri·pa·tet·i·cism** \-'te-tə-ˌsi-zəm\ *noun*

**pe·rip·a·tus** \pə-'ri-pə-təs\ *noun* [New Latin, genus name, from Greek *peripatos* act of walking about, from *peri-* + *patein* to tread] (circa 1931)
: any of a class or phylum (Onychophora) of primitive tropical wormlike invertebrates that appear intermediate between annelid worms and arthropods

**peri·pe·teia** \ˌper-ə-pə-'tē-ə, -'tī-\ *noun* [Greek, from *peripiptein* to fall around, change suddenly, from *peri-* + *piptein* to fall — more at FEATHER] (1591)
: a sudden or unexpected reversal of circumstances or situation especially in a literary work

**pe·rip·e·ty** \pə-'ri-pə-tē\ *noun, plural* **-ties** (1753)
: PERIPETEIA

**¹pe·riph·er·al** \pə-'ri-f(ə-)rəl\ *adjective* (1808)
**1** : of, relating to, involving, or forming a periphery or surface part
**2** : of, relating to, or being part of the peripheral nervous system ⟨*peripheral* nerves⟩
**3** : of, relating to, or being the outer part of the field of vision ⟨good *peripheral* vision⟩
**4** : AUXILIARY, SUPPLEMENTARY ⟨*peripheral* equipment⟩; *also* : of or relating to computer peripherals
— **pe·riph·er·al·ly** *adverb*

**²peripheral** *noun* (1966)
: a device connected to a computer to provide communication (as input and output) or auxiliary functions (as additional storage)

**peripheral nervous system** *noun* (1935)
: the part of the nervous system that is outside the central nervous system and comprises the cranial nerves excepting the optic nerve, the spinal nerves, and the autonomic nervous system

**pe·riph·ery** \pə-'ri-f(ə-)rē\ *noun, plural* **-er·ies** [Middle French *peripherie*, from Late

Latin *peripheria*, from Greek *periphereia*, from *peripherein* to carry around, from *peri-* + *pherein* to carry — more at BEAR] (1571)
**1 :** the perimeter of a circle or other closed curve; *also* **:** the perimeter of a polygon
**2 :** the external boundary or surface of a body
**3 a :** the outward bounds of something as distinguished from its internal regions or center **:** CONFINES **b :** an area lying beyond the strict limits of a thing
**pe·riph·ra·sis** \pə-'ri-frə-səs\ *noun, plural* **-ra·ses** \-ˌsēz\ [Latin, from Greek, from *periphrazein* to express periphrastically, from *peri-* + *phrazein* to point out] (1533)
**1 :** use of a longer phrasing in place of a possible shorter form of expression
**2 :** an instance of periphrasis
**peri·phras·tic** \ˌper-ə-'fras-tik\ *adjective* (1805)
**1 :** of, relating to, or characterized by periphrasis
**2 :** formed by the use of function words or auxiliaries instead of by inflection ⟨*more fair* is a *periphrastic* comparative⟩
— **peri·phras·ti·cal·ly** \-ti-k(ə-)lē\ *adverb*
**pe·riph·y·ton** \pə-'ri-fə-ˌtän\ *noun* [New Latin, from Greek *periphytos* (verbal of *periphyein* to grow around, from *peri-* + *phyein* to bring forth, grow) + *-on* (as in *plankton*) — more at BE] (1945)
**:** organisms (as some algae) that live attached to underwater surfaces
— **peri·phyt·ic** \ˌper-ə-'fi-tik\ *adjective*
**peri·plast** \'per-ə-ˌplast\ *noun* (1853)
**:** PLASMA MEMBRANE; *also* **:** a proteinaceous subcellular layer below the plasma membrane especially of a euglena
**pe·rique** \pə-'rēk\ *noun* [Louisiana French *périque*] (1882)
**:** an aromatic fermented Louisiana tobacco used in smoking mixtures
**peri·sarc** \'per-ə-ˌsärk\ *noun* [International Scientific Vocabulary *peri-* + Greek *sark-, sarx* flesh — more at SARCASM] (circa 1871)
**:** the outer usually chitinous integument of a hydroid
**peri·scope** \-ˌskōp\ *noun* [International Scientific Vocabulary] (1879)
**:** a tubular optical instrument containing lenses and mirrors by which an observer obtains an otherwise obstructed field of view
**peri·scop·ic** \ˌper-ə-'skä-pik\ *adjective* (1804)
**1 :** providing a view all around or on all sides ⟨*periscopic* lens⟩
**2 :** of or relating to a periscope
**per·ish** \'per-ish\ *verb* [Middle English *perisshen*, from Old French *periss-*, stem of *perir*, from Latin *perire*, from *per-* detrimentally + *ire* to go — more at PER-, ISSUE] (13th century)
*intransitive verb*
**1 :** to become destroyed or ruined **:** DIE ⟨recollection of a past already long since *perished* —Philip Sherrard⟩ ⟨guard against your mistakes or your attempts (*perish* the thought) to cheat —C. B. Davis⟩
**2** *chiefly British* **:** DETERIORATE, SPOIL
*transitive verb*
**1** *chiefly British* **:** to cause to die **:** DESTROY
**2 :** WEAKEN, BENUMB
**per·ish·able** \'per-i-shə-bəl\ *adjective* (circa 1611)
**:** liable to perish **:** liable to spoil or decay ⟨such *perishable* products as fruit, vegetables, butter, and eggs⟩
— **per·ish·abil·i·ty** \ˌper-i-shə-'bi-lə-tē\ *noun*
— **perishable** *noun*
**pe·ris·so·dac·tyl** \pə-ˌri-sə-ˌdak-t²l\ *noun*

periscope

[New Latin *Perissodactyla*, from Greek *perissos* excessive, odd in number + *daktylos* finger, toe] (1849)
**:** any of an order (Perissodactyla) of nonruminant ungulate mammals (as a horse, a tapir, or a rhinoceros) that usually have an odd number of toes, molar teeth with transverse ridges on the grinding surface, and the posterior premolars resembling true molars
— **perissodactyl** *adjective*
**peri·stal·sis** \ˌper-ə-'stól-səs, -'stäl-, -'stal-\ *noun, plural* **-stal·ses** \-ˌsēz\ [New Latin, from Greek *peristaltikos* peristaltic] (1859)
**:** successive waves of involuntary contraction passing along the walls of a hollow muscular structure (as the esophagus or intestine) and forcing the contents onward
**peri·stal·tic** \-tik\ *adjective* [Greek *peristaltikos*, from *peristellein* to wrap around, from *peri-* + *stellein* to place] (1655)
**1 :** of, relating to, resulting from, or being peristalsis
**2 :** having an action suggestive of peristalsis
**peristaltic pump** *noun* (1962)
**:** a pump in which fluid is forced along by waves of contraction produced mechanically on flexible tubing
**peri·stome** \'per-ə-ˌstōm\ *noun* [New Latin *peristoma*, from *peri-* + Greek *stoma* mouth — more at STOMACH] (circa 1796)
**1 :** the fringe of teeth surrounding the orifice of a moss capsule
**2 :** the region around the mouth in various invertebrates
— **peri·sto·mi·al** \ˌper-ə-'stō-mē-əl\ *adjective*
**peri·style** \'per-ə-ˌstīl\ *noun* [French *péristyle*, from Latin *peristylum*, from Greek *peristylon*, from neuter of *peristylos* surrounded by a colonnade, from *peri-* + *stylos* pillar — more at STEER] (1612)
**1 :** a colonnade surrounding a building or court
**2 :** an open space enclosed by a colonnade
**peri·the·ci·um** \ˌper-ə-'thē-shē-əm, -sē-\ *noun, plural* **-cia** \-shē-ə, -sē-\ [New Latin, from *peri-* + Greek *thēkion*, diminutive of *thēkē* case — more at TICK] (circa 1832)
**:** a spherical, cylindrical, or flask-shaped hollow fruiting body in various ascomycetous fungi that contains the asci and usually opens by a terminal pore
— **peri·the·cial** \-'thē-sh(ē-)əl, -sē-əl\ *adjective*
**peri·to·ne·um** \ˌper-ə-t²n-'ē-əm\ *noun, plural* **-ne·ums** \-'ē-əmz\ *or* **-nea** \-'ē-ə\ [Middle English, from Late Latin, from Greek *peritonaion*, neuter of *peritonaios* stretched around, from *peri-* + *teinein* to stretch — more at THIN] (15th century)
**:** the smooth transparent serous membrane that lines the cavity of the abdomen of a mammal and is folded inward over the abdominal and pelvic viscera
— **peri·to·ne·al** \-'ē-əl\ *adjective*
— **peri·to·ne·al·ly** \-ə-lē\ *adverb*
**peri·to·ni·tis** \ˌper-ə-t²n-'ī-təs\ *noun* [New Latin] (1776)
**:** inflammation of the peritoneum
**pe·rit·ri·chous** \pə-'ri-tri-kəs\ *adjective* [*peri-* + Greek *trich-, thrix* hair] (1877)
**1 :** having flagella uniformly distributed over the body ⟨*peritrichous* bacteria⟩
**2 :** having a spiral line of modified cilia around the oral disk ⟨*peritrichous* protozoa⟩
— **pe·rit·ri·chous·ly** *adverb*
**peri·wig** \'per-i-ˌwig\ *noun* [modification of Middle French *perruque* — more at PERUKE] (1529)
**:** PERUKE
— **peri·wigged** \-ˌwigd\ *adjective*
**¹per·i·win·kle** \'per-i-ˌwiŋ-kəl\ *noun* [Middle English *perwinke*, from Old English *perwince*, from (assumed) Vulgar Latin *pervinca*, short for Latin *vincapervinca*] (before 12th century)
**1 :** any of several trailing or woody evergreen

herbs of the dogbane family: as **a :** a European creeper (*Vinca minor*) widely cultivated as a ground cover and for its blue or white flowers — called also *myrtle* **b :** a commonly cultivated subshrub (*Catharanthus roseus* synonym *Vinca rosea*) of the Old World tropics that is the source of several antineoplastic drugs — called also *Madagascar periwinkle*
**2 :** a light purplish blue — called also *periwinkle blue*
**²periwinkle** *noun* [(assumed) Middle English, alteration of Old English *pīnewincle*, from Latin *pina*, a kind of mussel (from Greek) + Old English *-wincle* (akin to Danish *vincle* snail shell)] (circa 1530)
**:** any of various gastropod mollusks: as **a :** any of a genus (*Littorina*) of edible littoral marine snails; *also* **:** any of various similar or related marine snails **b :** any of several North American freshwater snails
**per·jure** \'pər-jər\ *transitive verb*
**per·jured; per·jur·ing** \'pər-jə-riŋ, 'pərj-riŋ\ [Middle French *perjurer*, from Latin *perjurare*, from *per-* detrimentally, for the worse + *jurare* to swear — more at PER-, JURY] (1535)
**1 :** to make a perjurer of (oneself)
**2** *obsolete* **:** to cause to commit perjury
**per·jur·er** \'pər-jər-ər\ *noun* (15th century)
**:** a person guilty of perjury
**per·ju·ri·ous** \(ˌ)pər-'jùr-ē-əs\ *adjective* (1602)
**:** marked by perjury ⟨*perjurious* testimony⟩
— **per·ju·ri·ous·ly** *adverb*
**per·ju·ry** \'pər-jə-rē, 'pərj-rē\ *noun* (14th century)
**:** the voluntary violation of an oath or vow either by swearing to what is untrue or by omission to do what has been promised under oath **:** false swearing
**¹perk** \'pərk\ *verb* [Middle English] (14th century)
*intransitive verb*
**1 a :** to thrust up the head, stretch out the neck, or carry the body in a bold or insolent manner **b :** to stick up or out jauntily
**2 :** to gain in vigor or cheerfulness especially after a period of weakness or depression — usually used with *up* ⟨he's *perked* up noticeably⟩
*transitive verb*
**1 :** to make smart or spruce in appearance **:** FRESHEN, IMPROVE
**2 :** to thrust up quickly or impudently
**²perk** *intransitive verb* (1656)
**:** PERCOLATE
**³perk** *noun* (1824)
**:** PERQUISITE — usually used in plural
**perky** \'pər-kē\ *adjective* **perk·i·er; -est** (1855)
**1 :** briskly self-assured **:** COCKY
**2 :** JAUNTY ⟨a *perky* . . . waltz —*New Yorker*⟩
— **perk·i·ly** \-kə-lē\ *adverb*
— **perk·i·ness** \-kē-nəs\ *noun*
**per·lite** \'pər-ˌlīt\ *noun* [French, from *perle* pearl] (1833)
**:** volcanic glass that has a concentric shelly structure, appears as if composed of concretions, is usually grayish and sometimes spherulitic, and when expanded by heat forms a lightweight aggregate used especially in concrete and plaster and as a medium for potting plants
— **per·lit·ic** \ˌpər-'li-tik\ *adjective*
**¹perm** \'pərm\ *noun* (1927)
**:** PERMANENT
**²perm** *transitive verb* (1928)
**:** to give (hair) a permanent wave

\ə\ abut \ᵊ\ kitten \ər\ further \a\ ash \ā\ ace
\ä\ mop, mar \aù\ out \ch\ chin \e\ bet \ē\ easy
\g\ go \i\ hit \ī\ ice \j\ job \ŋ\ sing \ō\ go
\ò\ law \òi\ boy \th\ thin \t͟h\ the \ü\ loot \ù\ foot
\y\ yet \zh\ vision    *see also* Guide to Pronunciation

**per·ma·frost** \'pər-mə-ˌfròst\ *noun* [*permanent* + *frost*] (1943)
**:** a permanently frozen layer at variable depth below the surface in frigid regions of a planet (as earth)
**per·ma·nence** \'pər-mə-nən(t)s, 'pərm-nən(t)s\ *noun* (15th century)
**:** the quality or state of being permanent **:** DURABILITY
**per·ma·nen·cy** \-nən(t)-sē\ *noun, plural* **-cies** (1555)
**1 :** PERMANENCE
**2 :** something permanent
**¹per·ma·nent** \-nənt\ *adjective* [Middle English, from Middle French, from Latin *permanent-, permanens,* present participle of *permanēre* to endure, from *per-* throughout + *manēre* to remain — more at PER-, MANSION] (15th century)
**:** continuing or enduring without fundamental or marked change **:** STABLE
**synonym** see LASTING
— **per·ma·nent·ly** *adverb*
— **per·ma·nent·ness** *noun*
**²permanent** *noun* (1925)
**:** a long-lasting hair wave or straightening produced by mechanical and chemical means — called also *permanent wave*
**permanent magnet** *noun* (1828)
**:** a magnet that retains its magnetism after removal of the magnetizing force
**permanent press** *noun* (1964)
**1 :** the process of treating a fabric with a chemical (as a resin) and heat for setting the shape and for aiding wrinkle resistance
**2 :** material treated by permanent press
**3 :** the condition of material treated by permanent press
— **permanent–press** *adjective*
**permanent tissue** *noun* (circa 1928)
**:** plant tissue that has completed its growth and differentiation and is usually incapable of meristematic activity
**permanent tooth** *noun* (1836)
**:** any of the second set of teeth of a mammal that follow the milk teeth, typically persist into old age, and in humans are 32 in number
**per·man·ga·nate** \(ˌ)pər-'maŋ-gə-ˌnāt\ *noun* (1841)
**1 :** a salt containing the anion $MnO_4^-$; especially **:** POTASSIUM PERMANGANATE
**2 :** the anion $MnO_4^-$ of a permanganate
**per·me·abil·i·ty** \ˌpər-mē-ə-'bi-lə-tē\ *noun* (1759)
**1 :** the quality or state of being permeable
**2 :** the property of a magnetizable substance that determines the degree in which it modifies the magnetic flux in the region occupied by it in a magnetic field
**per·me·able** \'pər-mē-ə-bəl\ *adjective* (15th century)
**:** capable of being permeated **:** PENETRABLE; *especially* **:** having pores or openings that permit liquids or gases to pass through ⟨a *permeable* membrane⟩ ⟨*permeable* limestone⟩
**per·me·ase** \'pər-mē-ˌās, -ˌāz\ *noun* [International Scientific Vocabulary *perme-* (from *permeate*) + *-ase*] (1957)
**:** a substance that catalyzes the transport of another substance across a cell membrane
**per·me·ate** \'pər-mē-ˌāt\ *verb* **-at·ed; -at·ing** [Latin *permeatus,* past participle of *permeare,* from *per-* through + *meare* to go, pass; akin to Middle Welsh *mynet* to go, Czech *míjet* to pass] (1656)
*intransitive verb*
**:** to diffuse through or penetrate something
*transitive verb*
**1 :** to spread or diffuse through ⟨a room *permeated* with tobacco smoke⟩
**2 :** to pass through the pores or interstices of
— **per·me·ative** \-ˌā-tiv\ *adjective*
**per·me·ation** \ˌpər-mē-'ā-shən\ *noun* (circa 1623)
**1 :** the quality or state of being permeated
**2 :** the action or process of permeating

**per men·sem** \(ˌ)pər-'men(t)-səm\ *adverb* [Medieval Latin] (1647)
**:** by the month
**per·meth·rin** \(ˌ)pər-'me-thrən\ *noun* [*per-* + *methyl* + *pyrethrin*] (1976)
**:** a synthetic pyrethrin $C_{21}H_{20}Cl_2O_3$ used especially as an insecticide
**Perm·ian** \'pər-mē-ən, 'per-\ *adjective* [*Perm,* former province in eastern Russia] (1841)
**:** of, relating to, or being the last period of the Paleozoic era or the corresponding system of rocks — see GEOLOGIC TIME table
— **Permian** *noun*
**per mill** \(ˌ)pər-'mil\ *adverb* [*per* + Latin *mille* thousand] (1902)
**:** per thousand
— **per·mil·lage** \(ˌ)pər-'mi-lij\ *noun*
**per·mis·si·ble** \pər-'mi-sə-bəl\ *adjective* [Middle English, from Medieval Latin *permissibilis,* from Latin *permissus,* past participle of *permittere*] (15th century)
**:** that may be permitted **:** ALLOWABLE
— **per·mis·si·bil·i·ty** \-ˌmi-sə-'bi-lə-tē\ *noun*
— **per·mis·si·ble·ness** \-'mi-sə-bəl-nəs\ *noun*
— **per·mis·si·bly** \-blē\ *adverb*
**per·mis·sion** \pər-'mi-shən\ *noun* [Middle English, from Middle French, from Latin *permission-, permissio,* from *permittere*] (15th century)
**1 :** the act of permitting
**2 :** formal consent **:** AUTHORIZATION
**per·mis·sive** \pər-'mi-siv\ *adjective* [Middle English *permyssyf,* from Middle French *permissif,* from Latin *permissus*] (15th century)
**1** *archaic* **:** granted on sufferance **:** TOLERATED
**2 a :** granting or tending to grant permission **:** TOLERANT **b :** deficient in firmness or control **:** INDULGENT, LAX
**3 :** allowing discretion **:** OPTIONAL ⟨reduced the *permissive* retirement age from 65 to 62⟩
— **per·mis·sive·ly** *adverb*
— **per·mis·sive·ness** *noun*
**¹per·mit** \pər-'mit\ *verb* **per·mit·ted; per·mit·ting** [Middle English *permitten,* from Latin *permittere* to let through, permit, from *per-* through + *mittere* to let go, send] (15th century)
*transitive verb*
**1 :** to consent to expressly or formally ⟨*permit* access to records⟩
**2 :** to give leave **:** AUTHORIZE
**3 :** to make possible
*intransitive verb*
**:** to give an opportunity ⟨if time *permits*⟩
— **per·mit·tee** \pər-ˌmi(t)-'tē, ˌpər-mi(t)-\ *noun*
— **per·mit·ter** *noun*
**²per·mit** \'pər-ˌmit, pər-'\ *noun* (1682)
**1 :** a written warrant or license granted by one having authority ⟨a gun *permit*⟩
**2 :** PERMISSION
**³permit** *noun* [perhaps by folk etymology from Spanish *palometa,* a kind of pompano, from diminutive of *paloma* dove, from Latin *palumba, palumbes* — more at PALOMINO] (circa 1945)
**:** either of two pompanos (*Trachinotus falcatus* and *T. goodei*) that are important game fishes of temperate to tropical waters of the western Atlantic
**per·mit·tiv·i·ty** \ˌpər-ˌmi-'ti-və-tē, -mə-\ *noun* [*¹permit* + *-ivity* (as in *selectivity*)] (1887)
**:** the ability of a dielectric to store electrical potential energy under the influence of an electric field measured by the ratio of the capacitance of a condenser with the material as dielectric to its capacitance with vacuum as dielectric — called also *dielectric constant*
**per·mu·ta·tion** \ˌpər-myù-'tā-shən\ *noun* [Middle English *permutacioun* exchange, transformation, from Middle French *permutation,* from Latin *permutation-, permutatio,* from *permutare*] (14th century)
**1 :** often major or fundamental change (as in

character or condition) based primarily on rearrangement of existent elements ⟨land-owners and peasants . . . in the *permutations* of their tortured interdependence —P. E. Mosley⟩
**2 a :** the act or process of changing the lineal order of an ordered set of objects **b :** an ordered arrangement of a set of objects
— **per·mu·ta·tion·al** \-shnəl, -shə-nᵊl\ *adjective*
**permutation group** *noun* (1904)
**:** a group whose elements are permutations and in which the product of two permutations is a permutation whose effect is the same as the successive application of the first two
**per·mute** \pər-'myüt\ *transitive verb* **per·mut·ed; per·mut·ing** [Middle English, to exchange, from Middle French or Latin; Middle French *permuter,* from Latin *permutare,* from *per-* + *mutare* to change — more at MUTABLE] (1878)
**:** to change the order or arrangement of; *especially* **:** to arrange in all possible ways
— **per·mut·able** \-'myü-tə-bəl\ *adjective*
**per·ni·cious** \pər-'ni-shəs\ *adjective* [Middle English, from Middle French *pernicieus,* from Latin *perniciosus,* from *pernicies* destruction, from *per-* + *nec-, nex* violent death — more at NOXIOUS] (15th century)
**1 :** highly injurious or destructive **:** DEADLY
**2** *archaic* **:** WICKED ☆
— **per·ni·cious·ly** *adverb*
— **per·ni·cious·ness** *noun*
**pernicious anemia** *noun* (1874)
**:** a severe megaloblastic anemia marked by a progressive decrease in the number of red blood cells and by pallor, weakness, and gastrointestinal and nervous disturbances and associated with malabsorption of vitamin $B_{12}$ due to the absence of intrinsic factor
**per·nick·e·ty** \pər-'ni-kə-tē\ *adjective* [origin unknown] (circa 1818)
**:** PERSNICKETY
**Per·nod** \per-'nō, ˌpər-\ *trademark*
— used for a French liqueur
**pe·ro·ne·al** \ˌper-ō-'nē-əl, pə-'rō-nē-\ *adjective* [New Latin *peroneus,* from *perone* fibula, from Greek *peronē,* literally, pin, from *peirein* to pierce — more at DIAPIR] (1831)
**:** of, relating to, or located near the fibula
**per·oral** \(ˌ)pər-'ōr-əl, per-, -'òr-, -'är-\ *adjective* [International Scientific Vocabulary] (1908)
**:** occurring through or by way of the mouth
— **per·oral·ly** \-ə-lē\ *adverb*
**per·o·rate** \'per-ə-ˌrāt *also* 'pər-\ *intransitive verb* **-rat·ed; -rat·ing** [Latin *peroratus,* past participle of *perorare* to declaim at length, wind up an oration, from *per-* through + *orare* to speak — more at PER-, ORATION] (1603)
**1 :** to deliver a long or grandiloquent oration
**2 :** to make a peroration
**per·o·ra·tion** \ˌper-ə-'rā-shən *also* ˌpər-\ *noun* [Middle English *peroracyon,* from Latin *peroration-, peroratio,* from *perorare*] (15th century)

☆ **SYNONYMS**
**Pernicious, baneful, noxious, deleterious, detrimental** mean exceedingly harmful. PERNICIOUS implies irreparable harm done through evil or insidious corrupting or undermining ⟨the claim that pornography has a *pernicious* effect on society⟩. BANEFUL implies injury through poisoning or destroying ⟨the *baneful* notion that discipline destroys creativity⟩. NOXIOUS applies to what is both offensive and injurious to the health of a body or mind ⟨*noxious* chemical fumes⟩. DELETERIOUS applies to what has an often unsuspected harmful effect ⟨a diet found to have *deleterious* effects⟩. DETRIMENTAL implies obvious harmfulness to something specified ⟨the *detrimental* effects of excessive drinking⟩.

**1 :** the concluding part of a discourse and especially an oration
**2 :** a highly rhetorical speech
— **per·o·ra·tion·al** \ˌper-ə-'rā-shnəl, ˌpər-, -shə-n°l\ *adjective*

**pe·rov·skite** \pə-'räv-ˌskīt, -'räf-\ *noun* [German *Perowskit*, from Count L. A. *Perovskiĭ* (died 1856) Russian statesman] (1840)
**:** a yellow, brown, or grayish black mineral sometimes containing rare earth elements

**per·ox·i·dase** \pə-'räk-sə-ˌdās, -ˌdāz\ *noun* (1900)
**:** an enzyme that catalyzes the oxidation of various substances by peroxides

**¹per·ox·ide** \pə-'räk-ˌsīd\ *noun* [International Scientific Vocabulary] (1804)
**:** an oxide containing a high proportion of oxygen; *especially* **:** a compound (as hydrogen peroxide) in which oxygen is visualized as joined to oxygen
— **per·ox·id·ic** \-ˌräk-'si-dik\ *adjective*

**²peroxide** *transitive verb* **-id·ed; -id·ing** (1906)
**:** to treat with a peroxide; *especially* **:** to bleach (hair) with hydrogen peroxide

**³peroxide** *adjective* (1920)
**:** having or being bleached hair 〈a *peroxide* blonde〉

**per·ox·i·some** \pə-'räk-sə-ˌsōm\ *noun* [*peroxide* + ³-*some*] (1965)
**:** a cytoplasmic cell organelle containing enzymes (as catalase) which act in oxidative reactions and especially in the production and decomposition of hydrogen peroxide
— **per·ox·i·som·al** \-ˌräk-sə-'sō-məl\ *adjective*

**peroxy-** *combining form* [International Scientific Vocabulary *per-* + *oxy*]
**:** containing the bivalent group O—O 〈*peroxy*-acetyl nitrate〉

**per·oxy·ace·tyl nitrate** \pə-ˌräk-sē-ə-'sēt°l-; -'a-sə-t°l-, -ˌtēl-\ *noun* (1963)
**:** a toxic compound C₂H₃O₅N found especially in smog

**per·pend** \ˌpər-'pend\ *verb* [Middle English, from Latin *perpendere*, from *per-* thoroughly + *pendere* to weigh — more at PER-, PENDANT] (15th century)
*transitive verb*
**:** to reflect on carefully **:** PONDER
*intransitive verb*
**:** to be attentive **:** REFLECT

**¹per·pen·dic·u·lar** \ˌpər-pən-'di-kyə-lər\ *adjective* [Middle English *perpendiculer*, from Middle French, from Latin *perpendicularis*, from *perpendiculum* plumb line, from *per-* + *pendēre* to hang — more at PENDANT] (14th century)
**1 a :** standing at right angles to the plane of the horizon **:** exactly upright **b :** being at right angles to a given line or plane
**2 :** extremely steep **:** PRECIPITOUS
**3** *often capitalized* **:** of or relating to a medieval English Gothic style of architecture in which vertical lines predominate
**4 :** relating to, uniting, or consisting of individuals of dissimilar type or on different levels
*synonym* see VERTICAL
— **per·pen·dic·u·lar·i·ty** \-ˌdi-kyə-'lar-ə-tē\ *noun*
— **per·pen·dic·u·lar·ly** \-'di-kyə-lər-lē\ *adverb*

**²perpendicular** *noun* (1571)
**:** a line at right angles to a line or plane (as of the horizon)

**per·pe·trate** \'pər-pə-ˌtrāt\ *transitive verb* **-trat·ed; -trat·ing** [Latin *perpetratus*, past participle of *perpetrare*, from *per-* through + *patrare* to accomplish, from *pater* father — more at FATHER] (1537)
**:** to bring about or carry out (as a crime or deception) **:** COMMIT
— **per·pe·tra·tion** \ˌpər-pə-'trā-shən\ *noun*
— **per·pe·tra·tor** \'pər-pə-ˌtrā-tər\ *noun*

**per·pet·u·al** \pər-'pe-chə-wəl, -chəl\ *adjective* [Middle English *perpetuel*,

from Middle French, from Latin *perpetuus* uninterrupted, from *per-* through + *petere* to go to — more at FEATHER] (14th century)
**1 a :** continuing forever **:** EVERLASTING **b** (1) **:** valid for all time (2) **:** holding (as an office) for life or for an unlimited time
**2 :** occurring continually **:** indefinitely long-continued
**3 :** blooming continuously through the season
*synonym* see CONTINUAL
— **per·pet·u·al·ly** *adverb*

**perpetual calendar** *noun* (1895)
**:** a table for finding the day of the week for any one of a wide range of dates

**perpetual check** *noun* (circa 1909)
**:** an endless succession of checks to which an opponent's king may be subjected to force a draw in chess

**per·pet·u·ate** \pər-'pe-chə-ˌwāt\ *transitive verb* **-at·ed; -at·ing** [Latin *perpetuatus*, past participle of *perpetuare*, from *perpetuus*] (1530)
**:** to make perpetual or cause to last indefinitely 〈*perpetuate* the species〉
— **per·pet·u·a·tion** \-ˌpe-chə-'wā-shən\ *noun*
— **per·pet·u·a·tor** \-'pe-chə-ˌwā-tər\ *noun*

**per·pe·tu·i·ty** \ˌpər-pə-'tü-ə-tē, -'tyü-\ *noun, plural* **-ties** [Middle English *perpetuite*, from Middle French *perpetuité*, from Latin *perpetuitat-, perpetuitas*, from *perpetuus*] (15th century)
**1 :** ETERNITY 2
**2 :** the quality or state of being perpetual 〈bequeathed to them in *perpetuity*〉
**3 a :** the condition of an estate limited so that it will not take effect or vest within the period fixed by law **b :** an estate so limited
**4 :** an annuity payable forever

**per·phen·a·zine** \ˌpər-'fe-nə-ˌzēn, -'fe-\ *noun* [blend of *piperazine* and *phen-*] (1957)
**:** a tranquilizing drug C₂₁H₂₆ClN₃OS that is used to control tension, anxiety, and agitation especially in psychotic conditions

**per·plex** \pər-'pleks\ *transitive verb* [obsolete *perplex*, adjective, involved, perplexed, from Latin *perplexus*, from *per-* thoroughly + *plexus* involved, from past participle of *plectere* to braid, twine — more at PER-, PLY] (1593)
**1 :** to make unable to grasp something clearly or to think logically and decisively about something 〈her attitude *perplexes* me〉 〈a *perplexing* problem〉
**2 :** to make intricate or involved **:** COMPLICATE
*synonym* see PUZZLE

**per·plexed** \-'plekst\ *adjective* (15th century)
**1 :** filled with uncertainty **:** PUZZLED
**2 :** full of difficulty
— **per·plexed·ly** \-'plek-səd-lē, -'plekst-lē\ *adverb*

**per·plex·i·ty** \pər-'plek-sə-tē\ *noun, plural* **-ties** [Middle English *perplexite*, from Middle French *perplexité*, from Late Latin *perplexitat-, perplexitas*, from Latin *perplexus*] (14th century)
**1 :** the state of being perplexed
**2 :** something that perplexes
**3 :** ENTANGLEMENT

**per·qui·site** \'pər-kwə-zət\ *noun* [Middle English, property acquired by means other than inheritance, from Medieval Latin *perquisitum*, from neuter of *perquisitus*, past participle of *perquirere* to purchase, acquire, from Latin, to search for thoroughly, from *per-* thoroughly + *quaerere* to seek] (15th century)
**1 :** a privilege, gain, or profit incidental to regular salary or wages; *especially* **:** one expected or promised
**2 :** GRATUITY, TIP
**3 :** something held or claimed as an exclusive right or possession 〈concepts . . . not the *perquisites* of any particular groups —Gilbert Ryle〉

**per·ron** \'per-ən, pe-rōⁿ\ *noun* [French, from Old French, from *perre, pierre* rock, stone, from Latin *petra*, from Greek] (1723)

**:** an outdoor stairway leading up to a building entrance; *also* **:** a platform at its top

**per·ry** \'per-ē\ *noun* [Middle English *peirrie*, from Middle French *peré*, from (assumed) Vulgar Latin *piratum*, from Latin *pirum* pear] (14th century)
**:** fermented pear juice often made sparkling

**perse** \'pərs\ *adjective* [Middle English *pers*, from Middle French, from Medieval Latin *persus*] (15th century)
**:** of a dark grayish blue resembling indigo

**per se** \(ˌ)pər-'sā *also* per-'sä *or* (ˌ)pər-'sē\ *adverb* [Latin] (1572)
**:** by, of, or in itself or oneself or themselves **:** as such **:** INTRINSICALLY

**per second per second** *adverb* (1922)
**:** per second every second — used of acceleration

**per·se·cute** \'pər-si-ˌkyüt\ *transitive verb* **-cut·ed; -cut·ing** [Middle English, from Middle French *persecuter*, back-formation from *persecuteur* persecutor, from Late Latin *persecutor*, from *persequi* to persecute, from Latin, to pursue, from *per-* through + *sequi* to follow — more at SUE] (15th century)
**1 :** to harass in a manner designed to injure, grieve, or afflict; *specifically* **:** to cause to suffer because of belief
**2 :** to annoy with persistent or urgent approaches (as attacks, pleas, or importunities) **:** PESTER
*synonym* see WRONG
— **per·se·cu·tee** \ˌpər-si-ˌkyü-'tē\ *noun*
— **per·se·cu·tive** \'pər-si-ˌkyü-tiv\ *adjective*
— **per·se·cu·tor** \-ˌkyü-tər\ *noun*
— **per·se·cu·to·ry** \-kyü-ˌtōr-ē, -ˌtȯr-, -ˌkyü-tə-rē\ *adjective*

**per·se·cu·tion** \ˌpər-si-'kyü-shən\ *noun* (14th century)
**1 :** the act or practice of persecuting especially those who differ in origin, religion, or social outlook
**2 :** the condition of being persecuted, harassed, or annoyed

**Per·se·id** \'pər-sē-əd\ *noun* [Latin *Perseus*; from their appearing to radiate from a point in Perseus]
**:** any of a group of meteors that appear annually about August 11

**Per·seph·o·ne** \pər-'se-fə-nē\ *noun* [Latin, from Greek *Persephonē*]
**:** a daughter of Zeus and Demeter abducted by Pluto to reign with him over the underworld

**Per·seus** \'pər-ˌsüs, -sē-əs\ *noun* [Latin, from Greek]
**1 :** a son of Zeus and Danaë and slayer of Medusa
**2** [Latin (genitive *Persei*), from Greek] **:** a northern constellation between Taurus and Cassiopeia

**per·se·ver·ance** \ˌpər-sə-'vir-ən(t)s\ *noun* (14th century)
**:** the action or condition or an instance of persevering **:** STEADFASTNESS

**per·sev·er·a·tion** \pər-ˌse-və-'rā-shən\ *noun* [Latin *perseveration-, perseveratio*, from *perseverare*] (1910)
**:** continuation of something (as repetition of a word) usually to an exceptional degree or beyond a desired point
— **per·sev·er·ate** \-'se-və-ˌrāt\ *intransitive verb*

**per·se·vere** \ˌpər-sə-'vir\ *intransitive verb* **-vered; -ver·ing** [Middle English, from Middle French *perseverer*, from Latin *perseverare*, from *per-* through + *severus* severe] (14th century)
**:** to persist in a state, enterprise, or undertak-

\ə\ abut \ᵊ\ kitten \ər\ further \a\ ash \ā\ ace \ä\ mop, mar \aú\ out \ch\ chin \e\ bet \ē\ easy \g\ go \i\ hit \ī\ ice \j\ job \ŋ\ sing \ō\ go \ȯ\ law \ȯi\ boy \th\ thin \t͟h\ the \ü\ loot \ú\ foot \y\ yet \zh\ vision *see also* Guide to Pronunciation ing in spite of counterinfluences, opposition, or discouragement

— **per·se·ver·ing·ly** *adverb*

**Per·sian** \'pər-zhən, *especially British* -shən\ *noun* (14th century)
**1 :** one of the people of Persia: as **a :** one of the ancient Iranians who under Cyrus and his successors founded an empire in southwest Asia **b :** a member of one of the peoples forming the modern Iranian nationality
**2 a :** any of several Iranian languages dominant in Persia at different periods **b :** the modern language of Iran and western Afghanistan — see INDO-EUROPEAN LANGUAGES table
**3 :** a thin soft silk formerly used especially for linings
**4 :** PERSIAN CAT

— **Persian** *adjective*

**Persian cat** *noun* (1824)
**:** any of a breed of stocky round-headed domestic cats that have a long silky coat and thick ruff

**Persian lamb** *noun* (1889)
**1 :** a pelt that is obtained from karakul lambs older than those yielding broadtail and that is characterized by very silky tightly curled fur
**2 :** the young of the karakul sheep that furnishes skins used in furriery

**per·si·flage** \'pər-si-ˌfläzh, 'per-\ *noun* [French, from *persifler* to banter, from *per-* thoroughly + *siffler* to whistle, hiss, boo, ultimately from Latin *sibilare*] (1757)
**:** frivolous bantering talk **:** light raillery

Persian cat

Persian lamb 2

**per·sim·mon** \pər-'si-mən\ *noun* [Virginia Algonquian *pessemmin*] (1612)
**1 :** any of a genus (*Diospyros*) of trees of the ebony family with hard fine wood, oblong leaves, and small bell-shaped flowers; *especially* **:** an American tree (*D. virginiana*) or a Japanese tree (*D. kaki*)
**2 :** the usually orange several-seeded globular berry of a persimmon that is edible when fully ripe but usually extremely astringent when unripe

**per·sist** \pər-'sist, -'zist\ *intransitive verb* [Middle French *persister*, from Latin *persistere*, from *per-* + *sistere* to take a stand, stand firm; akin to Latin *stare* to stand — more at STAND] (1538)
**1 :** to go on resolutely or stubbornly in spite of opposition, importunity, or warning
**2** *obsolete* **:** to remain unchanged or fixed in a specified character, condition, or position
**3 :** to be insistent in the repetition or pressing of an utterance (as a question or an opinion)
**4 :** to continue to exist especially past a usual, expected, or normal time

**synonym** see CONTINUE

— **per·sist·er** *noun*

**per·sis·tence** \pər-'sis-tən(t)s, -'zis-\ *noun* (1546)
**1 :** the action or fact of persisting
**2 :** the quality or state of being persistent; *especially* **:** PERSEVERANCE

**per·sis·ten·cy** \-tən(t)-sē\ *noun* (1597)
**:** PERSISTENCE 2

**per·sis·tent** \-tənt\ *adjective* [Latin *persistent-, persistens*, present participle of *persistere*] (1826)
**1 :** existing for a long or longer than usual time or continuously: as **a :** retained beyond the usual period (a *persistent* leaf) **b :** continuing without change in function or structure (*persistent* gills) **c :** effective in the open for an appreciable time usually through slow vola-

tilizing (mustard gas is *persistent*) **d :** degraded only slowly by the environment (*persistent* pesticides) **e :** remaining infective for a relatively long time in a vector after an initial period of incubation (*persistent* viruses)
**2 a :** continuing or inclined to persist in a course **b :** continuing to exist in spite of interference or treatment (a *persistent* cough)

— **per·sis·tent·ly** *adverb*

**per·snick·e·ty** \pər-'sni-kə-tē\ *adjective* [alteration of *pernickety*] (circa 1905)
**1 a :** fussy about small details **:** FASTIDIOUS (a *persnickety* teacher) **b :** having the characteristics of a snob
**2 :** requiring great precision (a *persnickety* job)

— **per·snick·e·ti·ness** \-nəs\ *noun*

**per·son** \'pər-sᵊn\ *noun* [Middle English, from Old French *persone*, from Latin *persona* actor's mask, character in a play, person, probably from Etruscan *phersu* mask, from Greek *prosōpa*, plural of *prosōpon* face, mask — more at PROSOPOPOEIA] (13th century)
**1 :** HUMAN, INDIVIDUAL — sometimes used in combination especially by those who prefer to avoid *man* in compounds applicable to both sexes (chair*person*) (spokes*person*)
**2 :** a character or part in or as if in a play
**3 a :** one of the three modes of being in the Trinitarian Godhead as understood by Christians **b :** the unitary personality of Christ that unites the divine and human natures
**4 a** *archaic* **:** bodily appearance **b :** the body of a human being; *also* **:** the body and clothing (unlawful search of the *person*)
**5 :** the personality of a human being **:** SELF
**6 :** one (as a human being, a partnership, or a corporation) that is recognized by law as the subject of rights and duties
**7 :** reference of a segment of discourse to the speaker, to one spoken to, or to one spoken of as indicated by means of certain pronouns or in many languages by verb inflection ◆

— **per·son·hood** \-ˌhu̇d\ *noun*

— **in person :** in one's bodily presence

**per·so·na** \pər-'sō-nə, -ˌnä\ *noun, plural* **per·so·nae** \-(ˌ)nē, -ˌnī\ *or* **personas** [Latin] (1909)
**1 :** a character assumed by an author in a written work
**2 a** *plural* **personas** [New Latin, from Latin] **:** an individual's social facade or front that especially in the analytic psychology of C. G. Jung reflects the role in life the individual is playing — compare ANIMA **b :** the personality that a person (as an actor or politician) projects in public **:** IMAGE
**3** *plural* **personae :** a character in a fictional presentation (as a novel or play) — usually used in plural (comic *personae*)

**per·son·able** \'pərs-nə-bəl, 'pər-sᵊn-ə-bəl\ *adjective* (15th century)
**:** pleasant or amiable in person **:** ATTRACTIVE

— **per·son·able·ness** *noun*

**per·son·age** \'pərs-nij, 'pər-sᵊn-ij\ *noun* (15th century)
**1 :** a person of rank, note, or distinction; *especially* **:** one distinguished for presence and personal power
**2 :** a human individual **:** PERSON
**3 :** a dramatic, fictional, or historical character; *also* **:** IMPERSONATION

**per·so·na gra·ta** \pər-ˌsō-nə-'gra-tə, -'grä-\ *adjective* [New Latin, acceptable person] (1882)
**:** personally acceptable or welcome

**¹per·son·al** \'pərs-nəl, 'pər-sᵊn-əl\ *adjective* [Middle English, from Middle French, from Late Latin *personalis*, from Latin *persona*] (14th century)
**1 :** of, relating to, or affecting a person **:** PRIVATE, INDIVIDUAL (*personal* ambition)
**2 a :** done in person without the intervention of another; *also* **:** proceeding from a single person **b :** carried on between individuals directly (a *personal* interview)

**3 :** relating to the person or body
**4 :** relating to an individual or an individual's character, conduct, motives, or private affairs often in an offensive manner (a *personal* insult)
**5 a :** being rational and self-conscious (*personal*, responsive government is still possible —John Fischer) **b :** having the qualities of a person rather than a thing or abstraction (a *personal* devil)
**6 :** of, relating to, or constituting personal property (a *personal* estate)
**7 :** denoting grammatical person

**²personal** *noun* (1861)
**1 :** a short newspaper paragraph relating to the activities of a person or a group or to personal matters
**2 :** a short personal communication in a special column of the classified ads section of a newspaper or periodical
**3 :** PERSONAL FOUL

**personal computer** *noun* (1977)
**:** MICROCOMPUTER 1

**personal effects** *noun plural* (1843)
**:** privately owned items (as clothing and jewelry) normally worn or carried on the person

**personal equation** *noun* (1845)
**:** variation (as in observation) occasioned by the personal peculiarities of an individual; *also* **:** a correction or allowance made for such variation

**personal foul** *noun* (circa 1829)
**:** a foul in a game (as basketball) involving usually physical contact with or deliberate roughing of an opponent — compare TECHNICAL FOUL

**per·son·al·ise** *British variant of* PERSONALIZE

**per·son·al·ism** \'pərs-nə-ˌli-zəm, 'pər-sᵊn-ə-\ *noun* (circa 1846)
**:** a doctrine emphasizing the significance, uniqueness, and inviolability of personality

— **per·son·al·ist** \-list\ *noun or adjective*

— **per·son·al·is·tic** \ˌpərs-nə-'lis-tik, ˌpər-sᵊn-ə-\ *adjective*

**per·son·al·i·ty** \ˌpər-sᵊn-'a-lə-tē, ˌpər-'sna-\ *noun, plural* **-ties** [Middle English *personalite*, from Late Latin *personalitat-, personalitas*, from *personalis*] (15th century)
**1 a :** the quality or state of being a person **b :** personal existence
**2 a :** the condition or fact of relating to a particular person; *specifically* **:** the condition of referring directly to or being aimed disparagingly or hostilely at an individual **b :** an offensively personal remark (angrily resorted to *personalities*)

**3 :** the complex of characteristics that distinguishes an individual or a nation or group; *especially* **:** the totality of an individual's behavioral and emotional characteristics
**4 a :** distinction or excellence of personal and social traits; *also* **:** a person having such quality **b :** a person of importance, prominence, renown, or notoriety ⟨a TV *personality*⟩
**synonym** see DISPOSITION
**personality inventory** *noun* (1932)
**:** any of several tests that attempt to characterize the personality of an individual by objective scoring of replies to a large number of questions concerning his or her own behavior — compare MINNESOTA MULTIPHASIC PERSONALITY INVENTORY
**personality test** *noun* (1914)
**:** any of several tests that consist of standardized tasks designed to determine various aspects of the personality or the emotional status of the individual examined
**per·son·al·ize** \'pərs-nə-ˌlīz, 'pər-sᵊn-ə-\ *transitive verb* **-ized; -iz·ing** (circa 1741)
**1 :** PERSONIFY
**2 :** to make personal or individual; *specifically* **:** to mark as the property of a particular person ⟨*personalized* stationery⟩
— **per·son·al·i·za·tion** \ˌpərs-nə-lə-'zā-shən, ˌpər-sᵊn-ə-\ *noun*
**per·son·al·ly** \'pərs-nə-lē, 'pər-sᵊn-ə-\ *adverb* (14th century)
**1 :** in person ⟨attend to the matter *personally*⟩
**2 :** as a person **:** in personality ⟨*personally* attractive but not very trustworthy⟩
**3 :** for oneself **:** as far as oneself is concerned
**personal pronoun** *noun* (1668)
**:** a pronoun (as *I, you,* or *they*) that expresses a distinction of person
**personal property** *noun* (1838)
**:** property other than real property consisting of things temporary or movable **:** CHATTELS
**personal tax** *noun* (circa 1935)
**:** DIRECT TAX
**per·son·al·ty** \'pərs-nəl-tē, 'pər-sᵊn-əl-\ *noun, plural* **-ties** [Middle English, from Anglo-French *personalté,* from Late Latin *personalitat-, personalitas* personality] (15th century)
**:** PERSONAL PROPERTY
**per·so·na non gra·ta** \pər-'sō-nə-ˌnän-'grä-tə, -'grä-\ *adjective* [New Latin, unacceptable person] (1904)
**:** personally unacceptable or unwelcome
**per·son·ate** \'pər-sᵊn-ˌāt\ *transitive verb* **-at·ed; -at·ing** (1591)
**1 a :** IMPERSONATE, REPRESENT **b :** to assume without authority and with fraudulent intent (some character or capacity)
**2 :** to invest with personality or personal characteristics ⟨*personating* their gods ridiculous, and themselves past shame —John Milton⟩
— **per·son·a·tion** \ˌpər-sᵊn-'ā-shən\ *noun*
— **per·son·a·tive** \'pər-sᵊn-ˌā-tiv\ *adjective*
— **per·son·a·tor** \-ˌā-tər\ *noun*
**per·son–hour** \'pər-sᵊn-ˌau̇(-ə)r\ *noun* (1975)
**:** a unit of one hour's work by one person
**per·son·i·fi·ca·tion** \pər-ˌsä-nə-fə-'kā-shən\ *noun* (circa 1755)
**1 :** attribution of personal qualities; *especially* **:** representation of a thing or abstraction as a person or by the human form
**2 :** a divinity or imaginary being representing a thing or abstraction
**3 :** EMBODIMENT, INCARNATION
**per·son·i·fy** \pər-'sä-nə-ˌfī\ *transitive verb* **-fied; -fy·ing** (circa 1741)
**1 :** to conceive of or represent as a person or as having human qualities or powers
**2 :** to be the embodiment or personification of **:** INCARNATE ⟨a teacher who *personified* patience⟩
— **per·son·i·fi·er** \-ˌfī(-ə)r\ *noun*
**per·son·nel** \ˌpər-sᵊn-'el\ *noun* [French, from German *Personale, Personal,* from Medieval Latin *personale,* from Late Latin, neuter of *personalis* personal] (1837)

**1 a :** a body of persons usually employed (as in a factory, office, or organization) **b per·sonnel** *plural* **:** PERSONS
**2 :** a division of an organization concerned with personnel
**¹per·spec·tive** \pər-'spek-tiv\ *noun* [Middle English *perspectyf,* from Medieval Latin *perspectivum,* from neuter of *perspectivus* of sight, optical, from Latin *perspectus,* past participle of *perspicere* to look through, see clearly, from *per-* through + *specere* to look — more at PER-, SPY] (14th century)
*archaic* **:** an optical glass (as a telescope)
**²perspective** *noun* [Middle French, probably modification of Old Italian *prospettiva,* from *prospetto* view, prospect, from Latin *prospectus* — more at PROSPECT] (1563)
**1 a :** the technique or process of representing on a plane or curved surface the spatial relation of objects as they might appear to the eye; *specifically* **:** representation in a drawing or painting of parallel lines as converging in order to give the illusion of depth and distance **b :** a picture in perspective
**2 a :** the interrelation in which a subject or its parts are mentally viewed ⟨places the issues in proper *perspective*⟩; *also* **:** POINT OF VIEW **b :** the capacity to view things in their true relations or relative importance ⟨urge you to maintain your *perspective* and to view your own task in a larger framework —W. J. Cohen⟩
**3 a :** a visible scene; *especially* **:** one giving a distinctive impression of distance **:** VISTA **b :** a mental view or prospect ⟨to gain a broader *perspective* on the international scene —*Current Biography*⟩
**4 :** the appearance to the eye of objects in respect to their relative distance and positions
— **per·spec·tiv·al** \pər-'spek-ti-vəl, ˌpər-(ˌ)spek-'tī-vəl\ *adjective*
**³perspective** *adjective* [Middle English, optical, from Medieval Latin *perspectivus*] (1570)
**1** *obsolete* **:** aiding the vision ⟨his eyes should be like unto the wrong end of a *perspective* glass —Alexander Pope⟩
**2 :** of, relating to, employing, or seen in perspective ⟨*perspective* drawing⟩
— **per·spec·tive·ly** *adverb*
**Per·spex** \'pər-ˌspeks\ *trademark*
— used for an acrylic plastic consisting essentially of polymethyl methacrylate
**per·spi·ca·cious** \ˌpər-spə-'kā-shəs\ *adjective* [Latin *perspicac-, perspicax,* from *perspicere*] (1640)
**:** of acute mental vision or discernment **:** KEEN
**synonym** see SHREWD
— **per·spi·ca·cious·ly** *adverb*
— **per·spi·ca·cious·ness** *noun*
— **per·spi·cac·i·ty** \-'ka-sə-tē\ *noun*
**per·spic·u·ous** \pər-'spi-kyə-wəs\ *adjective* [Latin *perspicuus* transparent, perspicuous, from *perspicere*] (1586)
**:** plain to the understanding especially because of clarity and precision of presentation ⟨a *perspicuous* argument⟩
**synonym** see CLEAR
— **per·spi·cu·ity** \ˌpər-spə-'kyü-ə-tē\ *noun*
— **per·spic·u·ous·ly** \pər-'spi-kyə-wəs-lē\ *adverb*
— **per·spic·u·ous·ness** *noun*
**per·spi·ra·tion** \ˌpər-spə-'rā-shən\ *noun* (1626)
**1 :** the action or process of perspiring
**2 :** a saline fluid secreted by the sweat glands **:** SWEAT
**per·spi·ra·to·ry** \pər-'spī-rə-ˌtȯr-ē, 'pər-sp(ə-)rə-, -ˌtȯr-\ *adjective* (1725)
**:** of, relating to, secreting, or inducing perspiration
**per·spire** \pər-'spīr\ *intransitive verb* **per·spired; per·spir·ing** [French *perspirer,* from Middle French, from Latin *per-* through + *spirare* to blow, breathe — more at PER-] (circa 1682)
**:** to emit matter through the skin; *specifically*

**:** to secrete and emit perspiration
**per·suad·able** \pər-'swā-də-bəl\ *adjective* (circa 1598)
**:** capable of being persuaded
**per·suade** \pər-'swād\ *transitive verb* **per·suad·ed; per·suad·ing** [Latin *persuadēre,* from *per-* thoroughly + *suadēre* to advise, urge — more at SWEET] (15th century)
**1 :** to move by argument, entreaty, or expostulation to a belief, position, or course of action
**2 :** to plead with **:** URGE
— **per·suad·er** *noun*
**per·sua·si·ble** \-'swā-zə-bəl, -'swā-sə-\ *adjective* [Middle French, from Latin *persuasibilis* persuasive, from *persuasus,* past participle of *persuadēre*] (1502)
**:** PERSUADABLE
**per·sua·sion** \pər-'swā-zhən\ *noun* [Middle English *persuasioun,* from Middle French or Latin; Middle French *persuasion,* from Latin *persuasion-, persuasio,* from *persuadēre*] (14th century)
**1 a :** the act or process or an instance of persuading **b :** a persuading argument **c :** the ability to persuade **:** PERSUASIVENESS
**2 :** the condition of being persuaded
**3 a :** an opinion held with complete assurance **b :** a system of religious beliefs; *also* **:** a group adhering to a particular system of beliefs
**4 :** KIND, SORT
**synonym** see OPINION
**per·sua·sive** \-'swā-siv, -ziv\ *adjective* (15th century)
**:** tending to persuade
— **per·sua·sive·ly** *adverb*
— **per·sua·sive·ness** *noun*
**pert** \'pərt\ *adjective* [Middle English, open, bold, pert, modification of Old French *apert,* from Latin *apertus* open, from past participle of *aperire* to open] (14th century)
**1 a :** saucily free and forward **:** flippantly cocky and assured **b :** being trim and chic **:** JAUNTY ⟨a *pert* little hat⟩ **c :** piquantly stimulating ⟨is a *pert* notion⟩
**2 :** LIVELY, VIVACIOUS
— **pert·ly** *adverb*
— **pert·ness** *noun*
**per·tain** \pər-'tān\ *intransitive verb* [Middle English *perteinen,* from Middle French *partenir,* from Latin *pertinēre* to reach to, belong, from *per-* through + *tenēre* to hold — more at THIN] (14th century)
**1 a** (1) **:** to belong as a part, member, accessory, or product (2) **:** to belong as an attribute, feature, or function ⟨the destruction and havoc *pertaining* to war⟩ (3) **:** to belong as a duty or right ⟨responsibilities that *pertain* to fatherhood⟩ **b :** to be appropriate to something ⟨the criteria . . . will be different from those that *pertain* elsewhere —J. B. Conant⟩
**2 :** to have reference ⟨books *pertaining* to birds⟩
**per·ti·na·cious** \ˌpər-tᵊn-'ā-shəs\ *adjective* [Latin *pertinac-, pertinax,* from *per-* thoroughly + *tenac-, tenax* tenacious, from *tenēre*] (1626)
**1 a :** adhering resolutely to an opinion, purpose, or design **b :** perversely persistent
**2 :** stubbornly unyielding or tenacious
**synonym** see OBSTINATE
— **per·ti·na·cious·ly** *adverb*
— **per·ti·na·cious·ness** *noun*
— **per·ti·nac·i·ty** \-'a-sə-tē\ *noun*
**per·ti·nence** \'pər-tᵊn-ən(t)s, 'pərt-nən(t)s\ *noun* (1659)
**:** the quality or state of being pertinent **:** RELEVANCE
**per·ti·nen·cy** \-tᵊn-ən(t)-sē, -nən(t)-sē\ *noun* (1598)
**:** PERTINENCE

**per·ti·nent** \'pər-t⁸n-ənt, 'pərt-nənt\ *adjective* [Middle English, from Middle French, from Latin *pertinent-, pertinens*, present participle of *pertinēre*] (14th century)
: having a clear decisive relevance to the matter in hand
**synonym** see RELEVANT
— **per·ti·nent·ly** *adverb*
**per·turb** \pər-'tərb\ *transitive verb* [Middle English, from Middle French *perturber*, from Latin *perturbare* to throw into confusion, from *per-* + *turbare* to disturb — more at TURBID] (14th century)
**1** : to disturb greatly in mind : DISQUIET
**2** : to throw into confusion : DISORDER
**3** : to cause to experience a perturbation
**synonym** see DISCOMPOSE
— **per·turb·able** \-'tər-bə-bəl\ *adjective*
**per·tur·ba·tion** \,pər-tər-'bā-shən, ,pər-,tər-\ *noun* (14th century)
**1** : the action of perturbing : the state of being perturbed
**2** : a disturbance of motion, course, arrangement, or state of equilibrium; *especially* : a disturbance of the regular and usually elliptical course of motion of a celestial body that is produced by some force additional to that which causes its regular motion
— **per·tur·ba·tion·al** \-shnəl, -shə-n⁸l\ *adjective*
**per·tus·sis** \pər-'tə-səs\ *noun* [New Latin, from Latin *per-* thoroughly + *tussis* cough] (circa 1799)
: WHOOPING COUGH
**pe·ruke** \pə-'rük\ *noun* [Middle French *perruque*, from Old Italian *parrucca, perrucca* hair, wig] (circa 1573)
: WIG; *specifically* : one of a type popular from the 17th to the early 19th century
— **pe·ruked** \-'rükt\ *adjective*
**pe·ruse** \pə-'rüz\ *transitive verb* **pe·rused; pe·rus·ing** [Middle English, to use up, deal with in sequence, from Latin *per-* thoroughly + Middle English *usen* to use] (1532)
**1 a** : to examine or consider with attention and in detail : STUDY **b** : to look over or through in a casual or cursory manner
**2** : READ; *especially* : to read over in an attentive or leisurely manner ■
— **pe·rus·al** \-'rü-zəl\ *noun*
— **pe·rus·er** *noun*

peruke

**per·vade** \pər-'vād\ *transitive verb* **per·vad·ed; per·vad·ing** [Latin *pervadere* to go through, pervade, from *per-* through + *vadere* to go — more at PER-, WADE] (1659)
: to become diffused throughout every part of
**per·va·sion** \pər-'vā-zhən\ *noun* (1661)
: the action of pervading or condition of being pervaded
**per·va·sive** \pər-'vā-siv, -ziv\ *adjective* (circa 1750)
: that pervades or tends to pervade ⟨a *pervasive* odor⟩
— **per·va·sive·ly** *adverb*
— **per·va·sive·ness** *noun*
**per·verse** \(,)pər-'vərs, 'pər-\ *adjective* [Middle English, from Latin *perversus*, from past participle of *pervertere*] (14th century)
**1 a** : turned away from what is right or good : CORRUPT **b** : IMPROPER, INCORRECT **c** : contrary to the evidence or the direction of the judge on a point of law ⟨*perverse* verdict⟩
**2 a** : obstinate in opposing what is right, reasonable, or accepted : WRONGHEADED **b** : arising from or indicative of stubbornness or obstinacy
**3** : marked by peevishness or petulance : CRANKY

**synonym** see CONTRARY
— **per·verse·ly** *adverb*
— **per·verse·ness** *noun*
— **per·ver·si·ty** \pər-'vər-sə-tē, -stē\ *noun*
**per·ver·sion** \pər-'vər-zhən, -shən\ *noun* (14th century)
**1** : the action of perverting : the condition of being perverted
**2** : a perverted form; *especially* : an aberrant sexual practice especially when habitual and preferred to normal coitus
**per·ver·sive** \-'vər-siv, -ziv\ *adjective* (1817)
**1** : that perverts or tends to pervert
**2** : arising from or indicative of perversion
**¹per·vert** \pər-'vərt\ *transitive verb* [Middle English, from Middle French *pervertir*, from Latin *pervertere* to overturn, corrupt, pervert, from *per-* thoroughly + *vertere* to turn — more at PER-, WORTH] (14th century)
**1 a** : to cause to turn aside or away from what is good or true or morally right : CORRUPT **b** : to cause to turn aside or away from what is generally done or accepted : MISDIRECT
**2 a** : to divert to a wrong end or purpose : MISUSE **b** : to twist the meaning or sense of : MISINTERPRET
**synonym** see DEBASE
— **per·vert·er** *noun*
**²per·vert** \'pər-,vərt\ *noun* (circa 1661)
: one that has been perverted; *specifically* : one given to some form of sexual perversion
**per·vert·ed** \pər-'vər-təd\ *adjective* (14th century)
**1** : CORRUPT
**2** : marked by perversion
— **per·vert·ed·ly** *adverb*
— **per·vert·ed·ness** *noun*
**per·vi·ous** \'pər-vē-əs\ *adjective* [Latin *pervius*, from *per-* through + *via* way — more at PER-, WAY] (circa 1614)
**1** : ACCESSIBLE ⟨*pervious* to reason⟩
**2** : PERMEABLE ⟨*pervious* soil⟩
— **per·vi·ous·ness** *noun*
**Pe·sach** \'pä-,säk\ *noun* [Hebrew *pesaḥ*] (1613)
: PASSOVER
**pe·se·ta** \pə-'sā-tə\ *noun* [Spanish, from diminutive of *peso*] (1811)
— see MONEY table
**pe·se·wa** \pə-'sā-wə\ *noun* [Twi *pésɛwa*, literally, penny, penny's worth of gold dust] (1965)
— see *cedi* at MONEY table
**pes·ky** \'pes-kē\ *adjective* **pes·ki·er; -est** [probably irregular from *pest* + *-y*] (1775)
: TROUBLESOME, VEXATIOUS ⟨*pesky* issues⟩
**pe·so** \'pā-(,)sō, 'pe-\ *noun, plural* **pesos** [Spanish, literally, weight, from Latin *pensum* — more at POISE] (1555)
**1** : an old silver coin of Spain and Spanish America equal to eight reals
**2** — see MONEY table
**pes·sa·ry** \'pe-sə-rē\ *noun, plural* **-ries** [Middle English *pessarie*, from Late Latin *pessarium*, from *pessus, pessum* pessary, from Greek *pessos* oval stone for playing checkers, pessary] (14th century)
**1** : a vaginal suppository
**2** : a device worn in the vagina to support the uterus, remedy a malposition, or prevent conception
**pes·si·mism** \'pə-sə-,mi-zəm *also* 'pe-zə-\ *noun* [French *pessimisme*, from Latin *pessimus* worst — more at PEJORATIVE] (1815)
**1** : an inclination to emphasize adverse aspects, conditions, and possibilities or to expect the worst possible outcome
**2 a** : the doctrine that reality is essentially evil **b** : the doctrine that evil overbalances happiness in life
— **pes·si·mist** \-mist\ *noun*
**pes·si·mis·tic** \,pe-sə-'mis-tik *also* ,pe-zə-\ *adjective* (1868)
: of, relating to, or characterized by pessimism : GLOOMY
**synonym** see CYNICAL

— **pes·si·mis·ti·cal·ly** \-ti-k(ə-)lē\ *adverb*
**pest** \'pest\ *noun* [Middle French *peste*, from Latin *pestis*] (1553)
**1** : an epidemic disease associated with high mortality; *specifically* : PLAGUE
**2** : something resembling a pest in destructiveness; *especially* : a plant or animal detrimental to humans or human concerns (as agriculture or livestock production)
**3** : one that pesters or annoys : NUISANCE ◆
— **pesty** \'pes-tē\ *adjective*
**pes·ter** \'pes-tər\ *transitive verb* **pes·tered; pes·ter·ing** \-t(ə-)riŋ\ [modification of Middle French *empestrer* to hobble, embarrass, from (assumed) Vulgar Latin *impastoriare*, from Latin *in-* + Medieval Latin *pastoria* hobble — more at PASTERN] (1533)
**1** *obsolete* : OVERCROWD
**2** : to harass with petty irritations : ANNOY
**synonym** see WORRY
**pest·hole** \'pest-,hōl\ *noun* (1903)
: a place liable to epidemic disease
**pest·house** \-,haús\ *noun* (1611)
: a shelter or hospital for those infected with a pestilential or contagious disease
**pes·ti·cide** \'pes-tə-,sīd\ *noun* (circa 1925)
: an agent used to destroy pests

□ USAGE

**peruse** *Peruse* is a word with a literary flavor. It has been used in sense 2 since the time of Shakespeare and Marlowe, and it has been a useful alternative to the monosyllabic *read* for poets. It was probably a more ordinary word in the past than it is now, although it still has considerable use. About 1906 a writer on usage decided that *peruse* could mean only "to read with care and attention," for what reason we do not know. In time this opinion was echoed by a number of commentators, right down to the present. *Peruse* actually has been used in the "careful and attentive" sense, but writers almost always signal that meaning by a modifier ⟨have you with heed *perused* what I have written to you? —Shakespeare⟩ ⟨the lady in blue velvet, who so attentively *peruses* her book —Washington Irving⟩ ⟨each paragraph was carefully *perused* —Fred Allen⟩. And it has also been used, usually with a qualifier, to suggest casual or leisurely reading ⟨advertisements are now so numerous that they are very negligently *perused* —Samuel Johnson⟩ ⟨mirrors are gazed into, letters dreamily *perused* —Simon Schama⟩. But most of the time it simply means "to read" or "to read over or through" ⟨a magazine that the civilized reader may *peruse* without damage to his stomach —H. L. Mencken⟩ ⟨a dozen men, most of them huddled in dark suits at separate tables, *perusing* newspapers —A. N. Wilson⟩ ⟨these are what the bulk of the population *peruses* —Anthony Burgess⟩.

◇ WORD HISTORY

**pest** In contemporary usage a *pest* may be no more than a nuisance. Originally, however, the word meant something far more serious. In the 16th century when English borrowed *peste*, it was the French word for "plague." Although it could be used of any epidemic disease resulting in many deaths, the word customarily referred specifically to bubonic plague. The word *pest* had not been in English for very long before it was being used indiscriminately of anything destructive or troublesome. While French *peste* has retained all of its original force, the English word can be applied to persons or things that are only mildly irritating. *Pest* is now naturally associated with the verb *pester*, which is etymologically unrelated to it.

**pes·tif·er·ous** \pes-'ti-f(ə-)rəs\ *adjective* [Middle English, from Latin *pestifer* pestilential, noxious, from *pestis* + *-fer* -ferous] (15th century)
**1** : dangerous to society : PERNICIOUS
**2 a** : carrying or propagating infection : PESTILENTIAL **b** : infected with a pestilential disease
**3** : TROUBLESOME, ANNOYING
— **pes·tif·er·ous·ly** *adverb*
— **pes·tif·er·ous·ness** *noun*

**pes·ti·lence** \'pes-tə-lən(t)s\ *noun* (14th century)
**1** : a contagious or infectious epidemic disease that is virulent and devastating; *especially* : BUBONIC PLAGUE
**2** : something that is destructive or pernicious ⟨I'll pour this *pestilence* into his ear —Shakespeare⟩

**pes·ti·lent** \-lənt\ *adjective* [Middle English, from Latin *pestilent-, pestilens* pestilential, from *pestis*] (14th century)
**1** : destructive of life : DEADLY
**2** : injuring or endangering society : PERNICIOUS
**3** : causing displeasure or annoyance
**4** : INFECTIOUS, CONTAGIOUS ⟨*pestilent* disease⟩
— **pes·ti·lent·ly** *adverb*

**pes·ti·len·tial** \,pes-tə-'len(t)-shəl\ *adjective* (14th century)
**1 a** : causing or tending to cause pestilence : DEADLY **b** : of or relating to pestilence
**2** : morally harmful : PERNICIOUS
**3** : giving rise to vexation or annoyance : IRRITATING
— **pes·ti·len·tial·ly** \-'len(t)-sh(ə-)lē\ *adverb*

**¹pes·tle** \'pe-səl, 'pes-t³l\ *noun* [Middle English *pestel*, from Middle French, from Latin *pistillum*, from *pinsere* to pound, crush; akin to Greek *ptissein* to crush, Sanskrit *pinaṣṭi* he pounds] (14th century)
**1** : a usually club-shaped implement for pounding or grinding substances in a mortar
**2** : any of various devices for pounding, stamping, or pressing

**²pestle** *verb* **pes·tled; pes·tling** \'pe-s(ə-)liŋ, 'pes-t³l-iŋ\ (15th century)
*transitive verb*
*archaic* : to beat, pound, or pulverize with or as if with a pestle
*intransitive verb*
: to work with a pestle : use a pestle

pestle 1 (with mortar)

**pes·to** \'pes-(,)tō\ *noun* [Italian, from *pesto,* adjective, pounded, from *pestare* to pound, from Late Latin *pistare*, frequentative of Latin *pinsere*] (1937)
: a sauce made especially of fresh basil, garlic, oil, pine nuts, and grated cheese

**¹pet** \'pet\ *noun* [perhaps back-formation from Middle English *pety* small — more at PETTY] (1508)
**1 a** : a pampered and usually spoiled child **b** : a person who is treated with unusual kindness or consideration : DARLING
**2** : a domesticated animal kept for pleasure rather than utility

**²pet** *adjective* (1584)
**1** : kept or treated as a pet
**2** : expressing fondness or endearment ⟨a *pet* name⟩
**3** : FAVORITE ⟨a *pet* project⟩

**³pet** *verb* **pet·ted; pet·ting** (1629)
*transitive verb*
**1 a** : to treat as a pet **b** : to stroke in a gentle or loving manner
**2** : to treat with unusual kindness and consideration : PAMPER
*intransitive verb*
: to engage in amorous embracing, caressing, and kissing : NECK
— **pet·ter** *noun*

**⁴pet** *noun* [origin unknown] (1590)

: a fit of peevishness, sulkiness, or anger

**⁵pet** *intransitive verb* **pet·ted; pet·ting** (1629)
: to take offense : SULK

**peta-** *combining form* [International Scientific Vocabulary, modification of Greek *penta-*]
: quadrillion ⟨*peta*-electron volts⟩

**pet·al** \'pe-t³l\ *noun* [New Latin *petalum*, from Greek *petalon;* akin to Greek *petannynai* to spread out — more at FATHOM] (circa 1726)
: one of the modified often brightly colored leaves of the corolla of a flower — see FLOWER illustration
— **pet·aled** *or* **pet·alled** \-t³ld\ *adjective*
— **pet·al·like** \-t³l-,(l)īk\ *adjective*

**pet·al·oid** \'pe-t³l-,óid\ *adjective* (1730)
**1** : resembling a flower petal
**2** : consisting of petaloid elements

**pet·al·ous** \'pe-t³l-əs\ *adjective* (circa 1736)
**1** : having petals
**2** : having (such or so many) petals — used in combination ⟨poly*petalous*⟩

**pe·tard** \pə-'tär(d)\ *noun* [Middle French, from *peter* to break wind, from *pet* expulsion of intestinal gas, from Latin *peditum*, from neuter of *peditus*, past participle of *pedere* to break wind; akin to Greek *bdein* to break wind] (1598)
**1** : a case containing an explosive to break down a door or gate or breach a wall
**2** : a firework that explodes with a loud report

**pet·a·sos** *or* **pet·a·sus** \'pe-tə-səs\ *noun* [Latin & Greek; Latin *petasus,* from Greek *petasos;* akin to Greek *petannynai* to spread out] (1599)
: a broad-brimmed low-crowned hat worn by ancient Greeks and Romans; *especially* : the winged hat of Hermes

**pet·cock** \'pet-,käk\ *noun* [*pet-* (perhaps from *petty*) + *cock*] (circa 1864)
: a small cock, faucet, or valve for releasing a gas (as air) or draining

**pe·te·chia** \pə-'tē-kē-ə\ *noun, plural* **-chi·ae** \-kē-,ī\ [New Latin, from Italian *petecchia*, ultimately from Latin *impetigo*] (circa 1796)
: a minute reddish or purplish spot containing blood that appears in skin or mucous membrane especially in some infectious diseases (as typhoid fever)
— **pe·te·chi·al** \-kē-əl\ *adjective*

**¹pe·ter** \'pē-tər\ *intransitive verb* [origin unknown] (1846)
**1** : to diminish gradually and come to an end : GIVE OUT — usually used with *out* ⟨novelists whose creative impetus seems largely to have *petered* out —*Times Literary Supplement*⟩
**2** : to become exhausted — usually used with *out*

**²peter** *noun* [from the name *Peter*] (circa 1902)
: PENIS — often considered vulgar

**Pe·ter** \'pē-tər\ *noun* [Late Latin *Petrus,* from Greek *Petros,* from *petra* rock]
**1** : a fisherman of Galilee and one of the twelve apostles
**2** : either of two hortatory letters written to early Christians and included as books of the New Testament — see BIBLE table

**Peter Pan** \-'pan\ *noun*
**1** : a boy in Sir James Barrie's play *Peter Pan* who lives without growing older in a never-never land
**2** : an adult who doesn't want to grow up : one who hangs on to adolescent interests and attitudes

**Peter Pan collar** *noun* (1908)
: a usually small flat close-fitting collar with rounded ends that meet at the top in front

**Peter Principle** *noun* [Laurence J. *Peter* (born 1919) American (Canadian-born) educator] (1968)
: an observation: in a hierarchy employees tend to rise to the level of their incompetence

**Peter's pence** *noun plural but singular in construction* [Middle English; from the tradi-

tion that Saint Peter founded the papal see] (13th century)
**1** : an annual tribute of a penny formerly paid by each householder in England to the papal see
**2** : a voluntary annual contribution made by Roman Catholics to the pope

**pet·i·o·lar** \,pe-tē-'ō-lər\ *adjective* (1760)
: of, relating to, or proceeding from a petiole

Peter Pan collar

**pet·i·o·late** \'pe-tē-ə-,lāt, ,pe-tē-'ō-lət\ *adjective* (circa 1753)
: having a stalk or petiole

**pet·i·ole** \'pe-tē-,ōl\ *noun* [New Latin *petiolus,* from Latin *petiolus, peciolus* small foot, fruit stalk, probably alteration of (assumed) Latin *pediciolus,* diminutive of *pediculus,* diminutive of *ped-, pes* foot — more at FOOT] (1753)
**1** : a slender stem that supports the blade of a foliage leaf
**2** : PEDUNCLE; *specifically* : a slender abdominal segment joining the rest of the abdomen to the thorax in some insects
— **pet·i·oled** \-,ōld\ *adjective*

**pet·i·o·lule** \'pe-tē-ō-,lül, ,pe-tē-'ōl-(,)yü(ə)l\ *noun* [New Latin *petiolulus,* diminutive of *petiolus*] (1832)
: a stalk of a leaflet of a compound leaf

**pet·it** \'pe-tē\ *adjective* [Middle English, small, minor, from Middle French, small] (14th century)
: PETTY 1 — used chiefly in legal compounds

**pe·tit bourgeois** \pə-'tē-, ,pe-tē-\ *noun* [French, literally, small bourgeois] (1853)
**1** : a member of the petite bourgeoisie
**2** : PETITE BOURGEOISIE
— **petit bourgeois** *adjective*

**¹pe·tite** \pə-'tēt\ *adjective* [French, feminine of *petit*] (1784)
: having a small trim figure — usually used of a woman
— **pe·tite·ness** *noun*

**²petite** *noun* (circa 1929)
: a clothing size for short women

**petite bourgeoisie** *noun* [French, literally, small bourgeoisie] (1916)
: the lower middle class including especially small shopkeepers and artisans

**pe·tit four** \,pe-tē-'fór, pə-,tē-, -'fór; -'fúr\ *noun, plural* **petits fours** *or* **petit fours** \-'fórz, -'fórz, -'fúr(z)\ [French, literally, small oven] (1884)
: a small cake cut from pound or sponge cake and frosted

**¹pe·ti·tion** \pə-'ti-shən\ *noun* [Middle English, from Middle French, from Latin *petition-, petitio,* from *petere* to seek, request — more at FEATHER] (14th century)
**1** : an earnest request : ENTREATY
**2 a** : a formal written request made to an official person or organized body (as a court) **b** : a document embodying such a formal written request
**3** : something asked or requested
— **pe·ti·tion·ary** \-'ti-shə-,ner-ē\ *adjective*

**²petition** *verb* **pe·ti·tioned; pe·ti·tioning** \-'ti-sh(ə-)niŋ\ (1607)
*transitive verb*
: to make a request to : SOLICIT
*intransitive verb*
: to make a request; *especially* : to make a formal written request
— **pe·ti·tion·er** \-sh(ə-)nər\ *noun*

**pe·ti·tio prin·ci·pii** \pə-'tē-tē-,ō-(,)priŋ-'ki-pē-,ē\ *noun* [Medieval Latin, literally, postulation of the beginning, begging the question] (1531)
: a logical fallacy in which a premise is assumed to be true without warrant or in which what is to be proved is implicitly taken for granted

**pet·it jury** \'pe-tē-\ *noun* (15th century)
: a jury of 12 persons impaneled to try and to decide finally upon the facts at issue in causes for trial in a court

**petit larceny** *noun* (1587)
: larceny involving property of a value below a legally established minimum

**pe·tit–maî·tre** \pə-,tē-'mātr*ə*\ *noun, plural* **petits–maîtres** \*same*\ [French, literally, small master] (1711)
: DANDY, FOP

**pe·tit mal** \'pe-tē-,mal, -,mäl\ *noun* [French, literally, small illness] (1874)
: epilepsy characterized by mild convulsive seizure with transient clouding of consciousness — compare GRAND MAL

**pet·it point** \'pe-tē-,pȯint\ *noun* [French, literally, small point] (1882)
: TENT STITCH; *also* : embroidery made with this stitch

**pet peeve** *noun* (circa 1919)
: a frequent subject of complaint

**petr-** *or* **petri-** *or* **petro-** *combining form* [New Latin, from Greek *petr-, petro-,* from *petros* stone & *petra* rock]
**1** : stone : rock ⟨petrology⟩
**2** : petroleum ⟨petrodollar⟩

**pe·tra·le sole** \pə-'trä-lē-\ *noun* [*petrale* probably from Italian dialect, a flatfish] (1953)
: a flounder (*Eopsetta jordani*) chiefly of the Pacific waters of North America that is an important food fish — called also *petrale*

**Pe·trar·chan sonnet** \pi-'trär-kən-, ,pē-, (,)pe-\ *noun* [*Petrarch* (Francesco Petrarca)] (circa 1909)
: ITALIAN SONNET

**pe·trel** \'pe-trəl, 'pē-\ *noun* [alteration of earlier *pitteral*] (1676)
: any of numerous seabirds (especially families Procellariidae and Hydrobatidae); *especially* : one of the smaller long-winged birds that fly far from land — compare STORM PETREL

**pe·tri dish** \'pē-trē-\ *noun* [Julius R. *Petri* (died 1921) German bacteriologist] (1892)
: a small shallow dish of thin glass or plastic with a loose cover used especially for cultures in bacteriology

**pet·ri·fac·tion** \,pe-trə-'fak-shən\ *noun* (15th century)
**1** : the process of petrifying
**2** : something petrified
**3** : the quality or state of being petrified

**pet·ri·fi·ca·tion** \,pe-trə-fə-'kā-shən\ *noun* (circa 1611)
: PETRIFACTION

**pet·ri·fy** \'pe-trə-,fī\ *verb* **-fied; -fy·ing** [Middle French *petrifier,* from *petr-* + *-ifier* -ify] (1594)
*transitive verb*
**1** : to convert (organic matter) into stone or a substance of stony hardness by the infiltration of water and the deposition of dissolved mineral matter
**2** : to make rigid or inert like stone: **a** : to make lifeless or inactive : DEADEN ⟨slogans are apt to *petrify* a man's thinking —*Saturday Review*⟩ **b** : to confound with fear, amazement, or awe ⟨a novel about an airline pilot that will *petrify* you —Martin Levin⟩
*intransitive verb*
: to become stone or of stony hardness or rigidity

**Pe·trine** \'pē-,trīn\ *adjective* [Late Latin *Petrus* Peter] (1846)
**1** : of, relating to, or characteristic of the apostle Peter or the doctrines associated with his name

**2** : of, relating to, or characteristic of Peter the Great or his reign

**pet·ro·chem·i·cal** \,pe-trō-'ke-mi-kəl\ *noun* (1942)
: a chemical isolated or derived from petroleum or natural gas
— **pet·ro·chem·is·try** \-'ke-mə-strē\ *noun*

**pet·ro·dol·lar** \'pe-trō-,dä-lər\ *noun* (1974)
: a dollar's worth of foreign exchange obtained by a petroleum-exporting country through sales abroad — usually used in plural

**pet·ro·gen·e·sis** \,pe-trō-'je-nə-səs\ *noun* [New Latin] (1901)
: the origin or formation of rocks
— **pet·ro·ge·net·ic** \-jə-'ne-tik\ *adjective*

**pet·ro·glyph** \'pe-trə-,glif\ *noun* [French *pétroglyphe,* from *pétr-* petr- + *-glyphe* (as in *hiéroglyphe* hieroglyph)] (1870)
: a carving or inscription on a rock

**pe·trog·ra·phy** \pə-'trä-grə-fē, pe-\ *noun* [New Latin *petrographia,* from *petr-* + Latin *-graphia* -graphy] (1651)
: the description and systematic classification of rocks
— **pe·trog·ra·pher** \-fər\ *noun.*
— **pet·ro·graph·ic** \,pe-trə-'gra-fik\ *or* **pet·ro·graph·i·cal** \-fi-kəl\ *adjective*
— **pet·ro·graph·i·cal·ly** \-fi-k(ə-)lē\ *adverb*

**pet·rol** \'pe-trəl, -,träl\ *noun* [French *essence de pétrole,* literally, essence of petroleum] (1895)
*chiefly British* : GASOLINE

**pet·ro·la·tum** \,pe-trə-'lā-təm, -'lä-\ *noun* [New Latin, from Medieval Latin *petroleum*] (1887)
: PETROLEUM JELLY

**pe·tro·leum** \pə-'trō-lē-əm, -'trȯl-yəm\ *noun* [Middle English, from Medieval Latin, from Latin *petr-* + *oleum* oil — more at OIL] (15th century)
: an oily flammable bituminous liquid that may vary from almost colorless to black, occurs in many places in the upper strata of the earth, is a complex mixture of hydrocarbons with small amounts of other substances, and is prepared for use as gasoline, naphtha, or other products by various refining processes

**petroleum jelly** *noun* (1897)
: a neutral unctuous odorless tasteless substance obtained from petroleum and used especially in ointments and dressings

**pe·trol·o·gy** \pə-'trä-lə-jē, pe-\ *noun* [International Scientific Vocabulary] (1811)
: a science that deals with the origin, history, occurrence, structure, chemical composition, and classification of rocks
— **pet·ro·log·ic** \,pe-trə-'lä-jik\ *or* **pet·ro·log·i·cal** \-ji-kəl\ *adjective*
— **pet·ro·log·i·cal·ly** \-ji-k(ə-)lē\ *adverb*
— **pe·trol·o·gist** \pə-'trä-lə-jist, pe-\ *noun*

**pet·ro·nel** \'pe-trə-'nel\ *noun* [perhaps modification of Middle French *poitrinal, petrinal,* from *poitrinal* of the chest, from *poitrine* chest, derivative of Latin *pector-, pectus* — more at PECTORAL] (circa 1577)
: a portable firearm resembling a carbine of large caliber

**pe·tro·sal** \pə-'trō-səl\ *adjective* [New Latin *petrosa* petrous portion of the temporal bone, from Latin, feminine of *petrosus*] (1741)
: of, relating to, or situated in the region of the petrous portion of the temporal bone or capsule of the inner ear

**pe·trous** \'pe-trəs, 'pē-\ *adjective* [Middle English, from Middle French *petreux,* from Latin *petrosus,* from *petra* rock, from Greek] (14th century)
: of, relating to, or constituting the exceptionally hard and dense portion of the human temporal bone that contains the internal auditory organs

**¹pet·ti·coat** \'pe-tē-,kōt\ *noun* [Middle English *petycote* short tunic, petticoat, from *pety* small + *cote* coat] (15th century)
**1** : a skirt worn by women, girls, or young children: as **a** : an outer skirt formerly worn by women and small children **b** : a fancy skirt made to show below a draped-up overskirt **c** : an underskirt usually a little shorter than outer clothing and often made with a ruffled, pleated, or lace edge **d** *archaic* : the skirt of a woman's riding habit
**2 a** : a garment characteristic or typical of women ⟩ WOMAN
**3** : something (as a valance) resembling a petticoat
— **pet·ti·coat·ed** \-,kō-təd\ *adjective*

**²petticoat** *adjective* (1660)
: of, relating to, or exercised by women : FEMALE

**pet·ti·fog·ger** \'pe-tē-,fȯ-gər, -,fä-\ *noun* [probably from *petty* + obsolete English *fogger* pettifogger] (1576)
**1** : a lawyer whose methods are petty, underhanded, or disreputable : SHYSTER
**2** : one given to quibbling over trifles
— **pet·ti·fog·ging** \-giŋ\ *adjective or noun*
— **pet·ti·fog·gery** \-g(ə-)rē\ *noun*

**petting zoo** *noun* (1968)
: a collection of farm animals or gentle exotic animals for children to pet and feed

**pet·tish** \'pe-tish\ *adjective* [probably from ⁴*pet*] (circa 1591)
: FRETFUL, PEEVISH
— **pet·tish·ly** *adverb*
— **pet·tish·ness** *noun*

**pet·ti·toes** \'pe-tē-,tōz\ *noun plural* [plural of obsolete *pettytoe* offal] (1555)
**1** : the feet of a pig used as food
**2** : TOES, FEET

**pet·ty** \'pe-tē\ *adjective* **pet·ti·er; -est** [Middle English *pety* small, minor, alteration of *petit*] (14th century)
**1** : having secondary rank or importance : MINOR, SUBORDINATE
**2** : having little or no importance or significance
**3** : marked by or reflective of narrow interests and sympathies : SMALL-MINDED
— **pet·ti·ly** \'pe-t³l-ē\ *adverb*
— **pet·ti·ness** \'pe-tē-nəs\ *noun*

**petty cash** *noun* (1834)
: cash kept on hand for payment of minor items

**petty larceny** *noun* (1818)
: PETIT LARCENY

**petty officer** *noun* (1760)
: a subordinate officer in the navy or coast guard appointed from among the enlisted men — compare NONCOMMISSIONED OFFICER

**petty officer first class** *noun* (1942)
: an enlisted man in the navy or coast guard ranking above a petty officer second class and below a chief petty officer

**petty officer second class** *noun* (1942)
: an enlisted man in the navy or coast guard ranking above a petty officer third class and below a petty officer first class

**petty officer third class** *noun* (1942)
: an enlisted man in the navy or coast guard ranking above a seaman and below a petty officer second class

**pet·u·lance** \'pe-chə-lən(t)s\ *noun* (1610)
: the quality or state of being petulant : PEEVISHNESS

**pet·u·lan·cy** \-lən(t)-sē\ *noun* (1559)
*archaic* : PETULANCE

**pet·u·lant** \-lənt\ *adjective* [Latin or Middle French; Middle French, from Latin *petulant-, petulans;* akin to Latin *petere* to go to, attack, seek — more at FEATHER] (1605)
**1** : insolent or rude in speech or behavior
**2** : characterized by temporary or capricious ill humor : PEEVISH
— **pet·u·lant·ly** *adverb*

**pe·tu·nia** \pi-'tün-yə, -'tyün-\ *noun* [New Latin, from obsolete French *petun* tobacco, from Tupi *petima*] (1825)
: any of a genus (*Petunia*) of tropical American herbs of the nightshade family with flowers having funnel-shaped corollas

petunia

**pew** \'pyü\ *noun* [Middle English *pewe*, from Middle French *puie* balustrade, from Latin *podia*, plural of *podium* parapet, podium, from Greek *podion* base, diminutive of *pod-, pous* foot — more at FOOT] (14th century)
**1** : a compartment in the auditorium of a church providing seats for several persons
**2** : one of the benches with backs and sometimes doors fixed in rows in a church

**pe·wee** \'pē-(ˌ)wē\ *noun* [imitative] (1796)
: any of various small olivaceous flycatchers (genus *Contopus*)

**pew·hold·er** \'pyü-ˌhōl-dər\ *noun* (1845)
: a renter or owner of a pew

**pe·wit** *variant of* PEEWIT

**pew·ter** \'pyü-tər\ *noun* [Middle English, from Middle French *peutre*, from (assumed) Vulgar Latin *peltrum*] (14th century)
**1** : any of various alloys having tin as chief component; *especially* : a dull alloy with lead formerly used for domestic utensils
**2** : utensils of pewter
**3** : a bluish gray
— **pewter** *adjective*

**pew·ter·er** \'pyü-tər-ər\ *noun* (14th century)
: one that makes pewter utensils

**pey·o·te** \pā-'ō-tē\ *also* **pey·otl** \-'ō-tʰl\ *noun* [Mexican Spanish *peyote*, from Nahuatl *peyotl*] (1849)
**1** : a stimulant drug derived from mescal buttons
**2** : any of several American cacti (genus *Lophophora*); *especially* : MESCAL

**pfen·nig** \'fe-nig, -nik, *German* '(p)fe-nik\ *noun, plural* **pfennig** *also* **pfen·nigs** \'fe-nigz, -niks\ *or* **pfen·ni·ge** \'(p)fe-ni-gə, -niyə\ [German, from Old High German *pfenning*] (1547)
— more at PENNY
— see *deutsche mark* at MONEY table

**PG** \'pē-'jē\ *certification mark*
— used to certify that a motion picture is of such a nature that all ages may be allowed admission but parental guidance is suggested; compare G, NC-17, PG-13, R

**PG–13** \-ˌthər(t)-'tēn\ *certification mark*
— used to certify that a motion picture is of such a nature that persons of all ages may be admitted but parental guidance is suggested especially for children under 13; compare G, NC-17, PG, R

**pH** \'pē-'āch\ *noun* [German, from *Potenz* power + *H* (symbol for hydrogen)] (1909)
: a measure of acidity and alkalinity of a solution that is a number on a scale on which a value of 7 represents neutrality and lower numbers indicate increasing acidity and higher numbers increasing alkalinity and on which each unit of change represents a tenfold change in acidity or alkalinity and that is the negative logarithm of the effective hydrogen-ion concentration or hydrogen-ion activity in gram equivalents per liter of the solution; *also* : the condition represented by a pH number

**Phae·dra** \'fē-drə\ *noun* [Latin, from Greek *Phaidra*]
: a daughter of Minos who marries Theseus and falls in love with her stepson Hippolytus

**Pha·ë·thon** \'fā-ə-tʰn, -tən, -ˌthän\ *noun* [Latin, from Greek *Phaethōn*]
: a son of Helios who drives his father's sun-chariot through the sky but loses control and is struck down by a thunderbolt of Zeus

**pha·eton** \'fā-ə-tʰn\ *noun* [*Phaëthon*] (1742)

**1** : any of various light four-wheeled horse-drawn vehicles
**2** : TOURING CAR

**phage** \'fāj *also* 'fäzh\ *noun* [by shortening] (1926)
: BACTERIOPHAGE

**-phage** *noun combining form* [Greek *-phagos* one that eats, from *-phagos* -phagous]
: virus or cell that destroys cells ⟨bacterio*phage*⟩ ⟨micro*phage*⟩

**-phagia** *noun combining form* [New Latin, from Greek]
: -PHAGY ⟨dys*phagia*⟩

**phago·cyte** \'fa-gə-ˌsīt\ *noun* [International Scientific Vocabulary, from Greek *phagein* + New Latin *-cyta* -cyte] (circa 1884)
: a cell (as a white blood cell) that engulfs and consumes foreign material (as microorganisms) and debris
— **phago·cyt·ic** \ˌfa-gə-'si-tik\ *adjective*

**phago·cy·tize** \'fa-gə-sə-ˌtīz, -ˌsī-\ *transitive verb* **-tized; -tiz·ing** (1913)
: PHAGOCYTOSE

**phago·cy·tose** \-sə-ˌtōs, -sī-, -ˌtōz\ *transitive verb* **-tosed; -tos·ing** [back-formation from *phagocytosis*] (1912)
: to consume by phagocytosis

**phago·cy·to·sis** \ˌfa-gə-sə-'tō-səs, -sī-\ *noun, plural* **-to·ses** \-ˌsēz\ [New Latin] (1889)
: the engulfing and usually the destruction of particulate matter by phagocytes
— **phago·cy·tot·ic** \-'tä-tik\ *adjective*

**-phagous** *adjective combining form* [Greek *-phagos*, from *phagein* to eat — more at BAKSHEESH]
: eating ⟨sapro*phagous*⟩

**-phagy** *noun combining form, plural* **-phagies** [Greek *-phagia*, from *phagein*]
: eating of a (specified) type or substance ⟨geo*phagy*⟩

**pha·lange** \'fā-ˌlanj, fə-', fā-'\ *noun* [French, from Greek *phalang-, phalanx*] (circa 1860)
: PHALANX 2

**pha·lan·ge·al** \ˌfā-lən-'jē-əl, ˌfa-; fə-'lan-jē-, fā-\ *adjective* (1831)
: of or relating to a phalanx or the phalanges

**pha·lan·ger** \fə-'lan-jər, 'fā-ˌ\ *noun* [New Latin, from Greek *phalang-, phalanx*] (circa 1774)
: any of various small to medium-sized marsupial mammals (family Phalangeridae) of the Australian region that are chiefly arboreal and nocturnal and usually densely furred

**phal·an·stery** \'fa-lən-ˌster-ē\ *noun, plural* **-ster·ies** [French *phalanstère* dwelling of a Fourierist community, from Latin *phalang-, phalanx* + French *-stère* (as in *monastère* monastery)] (1846)
**1 a** : a Fourierist cooperative community **b** : a self-contained structure housing such a community
**2** : something resembling a Fourierist phalanstery

**pha·lanx** \'fā-ˌlaŋ(k)s, *British usually* 'fa-\ *noun, plural* **pha·lanx·es** *or* **pha·lan·ges** \fə-'lan-(ˌ)jēz, fā-, 'fā-ˌ, *British usually* fa-\ [Latin *phalang-, phalanx*, from Greek, battle line, digital bone, literally, log — more at BALK] (1553)
**1** : a body of heavily armed infantry in ancient Greece formed in close deep ranks and files; *broadly* : a body of troops in close array
**2** *plural phalanges* : one of the digital bones of the hand or foot of a vertebrate
**3** *plural usually phalanxes* **a** : a massed arrangement of persons, animals, or things **b** : an organized body of persons

**phal·a·rope** \'fa-lə-ˌrōp\ *noun, plural* **-ropes** *also* **-rope** [French, from New Latin *phalaropod-, phalaropus*, from Greek *phalaris* coot + *pod-, pous* foot; akin to Greek *phalios* having a white spot — more at BALD, FOOT] (circa 1776)
: any of a genus (*Phalaropus*) of small shorebirds that are related to sandpipers but have lobate toes and are good swimmers

**phal·lic** \'fa-lik\ *adjective* (1789)
**1** : of or relating to phallicism ⟨a *phallic* cult⟩
**2** : of, relating to, or resembling a phallus
**3** : relating to or being the stage of psychosexual development in psychoanalytic theory during which a child becomes interested in his or her own sexual organs
— **phal·li·cal·ly** \-li-k(ə-)lē\ *adverb*

**phal·li·cism** \'fa-lə-ˌsi-zəm\ *noun* (1884)
: the worship of the generative principle as symbolized by the phallus

**phal·lo·cen·tric** \ˌfa-lə-'sen-trik\ *adjective* (1927)
: centered on or emphasizing the masculine point of view

**phal·lus** \'fa-ləs\ *noun, plural* **phal·li** \'fa-ˌlī, -ˌlē\ *or* **phal·lus·es** [Latin, from Greek *phallos* penis, representation of the penis; probably akin to Latin *flare* to blow — more at BLOW] (circa 1613)
**1** : a symbol or representation of the penis
**2** : PENIS

**-phane** *noun combining form* [Greek *phanēs* appearing, from *phainein* to show — more at FANCY]
: substance having a (specified) form, quality, or appearance ⟨hydro*phane*⟩

**phan·er·o·gam** \'fa-nə-rə-ˌgam, fə-'ner-ə-\ *noun* [French *phanérogame*, ultimately from Greek *phaneros* visible (from *phainein*) + *gamos* marriage] (1861)
: a seed plant or flowering plant : SPERMATOPHYTE

**phan·er·o·phyte** \'fa-nə-rə-ˌfīt, fə-'ner-ə-\ *noun* [Greek *phaneros* + International Scientific Vocabulary *-phyte*] (1913)
: a perennial plant that bears its perennating buds well above the surface of the ground

**Phan·er·o·zo·ic** \ˌfa-nə-rə-'zō-ik\ *adjective* [Greek *phaneros* + English *²-zoic*] (1930)
: of, relating to, or being an eon of geologic history that comprises the Paleozoic, Mesozoic, and Cenozoic or the corresponding system of rocks — see GEOLOGIC TIME table
— **Phanerozoic** *noun*

**phan·tasm** \'fan-ˌta-zəm\ *noun* [Middle English *fantasme*, from Old French, from Latin *phantasma*, from Greek, from *phantazein* to present to the mind — more at FANCY] (13th century)
**1** : a product of fantasy: as **a** : delusive appearance : ILLUSION **b** : GHOST, SPECTER **c** : a figment of the imagination
**2** : a mental representation of a real object
— **phan·tas·mal** \fan-'taz-məl\ *adjective*
— **phan·tas·mic** \-mik\ *adjective*

**phan·tas·ma** \fan-'taz-mə\ *noun, plural* **-ma·ta** \-mə-tə\ [Latin] (1598)
: PHANTASM 1

**phan·tas·ma·go·ria** \(ˌ)fan-ˌtaz-mə-'gōr-ē-ə, -'gȯr-\ *noun* [French *phantasmagorie*, from *phantasme* phantasm (from Old French *fantasme*) + *-agorie* (perhaps from Greek *agora* assembly) — more at AGORA] (circa 1802)
**1** : an exhibition or display of optical effects and illusions
**2 a** : a constantly shifting complex succession of things seen or imagined **b** : a scene that constantly changes
**3** : a bizarre or fantastic combination, collection, or assemblage
— **phan·tas·ma·gor·ic** \-'gȯr-ik, -'gȯr-, -'gär-\ *or* **phan·tas·ma·gor·i·cal** \-i-kəl\ *adjective*

**phantasy** *variant of* FANTASY

**¹phan·tom** \'fan-təm\ *noun* [Middle English *fantosme, fantome*, from Middle French *fantosme*, modification of Latin *phantasma*] (14th century)

**1 a :** something (as a specter) apparent to sense but with no substantial existence **:** APPARITION **b :** something elusive or visionary **:** WILL-O'-THE-WISP **c :** an object of continual dread or abhorrence **:** BUGBEAR ⟨the *phantom* of disease and want⟩
**2 :** something existing in appearance only
**3 :** a representation of something abstract, ideal, or incorporeal ⟨she was a *phantom* of delight —William Wordsworth⟩
— **phan·tom·like** \-ˌlīk\ *adverb or adjective*
²**phantom** *adjective* (15th century)
**1 :** of the nature of, suggesting, or being a phantom **:** ILLUSORY
**2 :** FICTITIOUS, DUMMY ⟨*phantom* voters⟩
**pha·raoh** \'fer-(ˌ)ō, 'far-(ˌ)ō, 'fā-(ˌ)rō\ *noun, often capitalized* [Middle English *pharao*, from Old English, from Late Latin *pharaon-*, *pharao*, from Greek *pharaō*, from Hebrew *par'ōh*, from Egyptian *pr-'',*] (before 12th century)
**1 :** a ruler of ancient Egypt
**2 :** TYRANT
**pharaoh ant** *noun* (circa 1947)
**:** a little red ant (*Monomorium pharaonis*) that is a common household pest
**phar·a·on·ic** \ˌfer-ā-'ä-nik, ˌfar-\ *adjective, often capitalized* [French *pharaonique*, from *pharaon* pharaoh, from Late Latin *Pharaon-*, *Pharao*] (circa 1828)
**1 :** of, relating to, or characteristic of a pharaoh or the pharaohs
**2 :** enormous in size or magnitude ⟨*pharaonic* construction projects⟩
**phar·i·sa·ic** \ˌfar-ə-'sā-ik\ *adjective* [Late Latin *pharisaicus*, from Late Greek *pharisaikos*, from Greek *pharisaios* Pharisee] (1618)
**1 :** PHARISAICAL
**2** *capitalized* **:** of or relating to the Pharisees
**phar·i·sa·ical** \-'sā-ə-kəl\ *adjective* (1531)
**:** marked by hypocritical censorious self-righteousness
— **phar·i·sa·ical·ly** \-k(ə-)lē\ *adverb*
— **phar·i·sa·ical·ness** \-kəl-nəs\ *noun*
**phar·i·sa·ism** \'far-ə-(ˌ)sā-ˌi-zəm\ *noun* [New Latin *pharisaismus*, from Greek *pharisaios*] (1610)
**1** *capitalized* **:** the doctrines or practices of the Pharisees
**2** *often capitalized* **:** pharisaical character, spirit, or attitude **:** HYPOCRISY
**phar·i·see** \'far-ə-(ˌ)sē\ *noun* [Middle English *pharise*, from Old English *farise*, from Late Latin *pharisaeus*, from Greek *pharisaios*, from Aramaic *pĕrīshayyā*, plural of *pĕrīshā*, literally, separated] (before 12th century)
**1** *capitalized* **:** a member of a Jewish sect of the intertestamental period noted for strict observance of rites and ceremonies of the written law and for insistence on the validity of their own oral traditions concerning the law
**2 :** a pharisaical person
¹**phar·ma·ceu·ti·cal** \ˌfär-mə-'sü-ti-kəl\ *adjective* [Late Latin *pharmaceuticus*, from Greek *pharmakeutikos*, from *pharmakeuein* to administer drugs — more at PHARMACY] (1648)
**:** of, relating to, or engaged in pharmacy or the manufacture and sale of pharmaceuticals ⟨a *pharmaceutical* company⟩
— **phar·ma·ceu·ti·cal·ly** \-ti-k(ə-)lē\ *adverb*
²**pharmaceutical** *noun* (1881)
**:** a medicinal drug
**phar·ma·cist** \'fär-mə-sist\ *noun* (1834)
**:** a person licensed to engage in pharmacy
**pharmaco-** *combining form* [Greek *pharmako-*, from *pharmakon*]
**:** medicine **:** drug ⟨*pharmacology*⟩
**phar·ma·co·dy·nam·ics** \ˌfär-mə-kō-dī-'na-miks, -də-\ *noun plural but singular in construction* (circa 1842)
**:** a branch of pharmacology dealing with the reactions between drugs and living systems

— **phar·ma·co·dy·nam·ic** \-mik\ *adjective*
— **phar·ma·co·dy·nam·i·cal·ly** \-mi-k(ə-)lē\ *adverb*
**phar·ma·cog·no·sy** \ˌfär-mə-'käg-nə-sē\ *noun* [International Scientific Vocabulary, from Greek *pharmakon* + *-gnōsia* knowledge, from *gnōsis* — more at GNOSIS] (circa 1885)
**:** descriptive pharmacology dealing with crude drugs and simples
— **phar·ma·cog·nos·tic** \-ˌkäg-'näs-tik\ *or* **phar·ma·cog·nos·ti·cal** \-ti-kəl\ *adjective*
**phar·ma·co·ki·net·ics** \-kō-kə-'ne-tiks, -kō-kī-\ *noun plural but singular in construction* (1960)
**1 :** the study of the bodily absorption, distribution, metabolism, and excretion of drugs
**2 :** the characteristic interactions of a drug and the body in terms of its absorption, distribution, metabolism, and excretion
— **phar·ma·co·ki·net·ic** \-tik\ *adjective*
**phar·ma·col·o·gy** \ˌfär-mə-'kä-lə-jē\ *noun* (circa 1721)
**1 :** the science of drugs including materia medica, toxicology, and therapeutics
**2 :** the properties and reactions of drugs especially with relation to their therapeutic value
— **phar·ma·co·log·i·cal** \-kə-'lä-ji-kəl\ *also* **phar·ma·co·log·ic** \-jik\ *adjective*
— **phar·ma·co·log·i·cal·ly** \-ji-k(ə-)lē\ *adverb*
— **phar·ma·col·o·gist** \-'kä-lə-jist\ *noun*
**phar·ma·co·poe·ia** *also* **phar·ma·co·pe·ia** \-kə-'pē-ə\ *noun* [New Latin, from Late Greek *pharmakopoiia* preparation of drugs, from Greek *pharmako-* + *poiein* to make — more at POET] (1621)
**1 :** a book describing drugs, chemicals, and medicinal preparations; *especially* **:** one issued by an officially recognized authority and serving as a standard
**2 :** a collection or stock of drugs
— **phar·ma·co·poe·ial** *also* **phar·ma·co·pe·ial** \-əl\ *adjective*
**phar·ma·co·ther·a·py** \ˌfär-mə-kō-'ther-ə-pē\ *noun* (circa 1909)
**:** the treatment of disease and especially mental illness with drugs
**phar·ma·cy** \'fär-mə-sē\ *noun, plural* **-cies** [Late Latin *pharmacia* administration of drugs, from Greek *pharmakeia*, from *pharmakeuein* to administer drugs, from *pharmakon* magic charm, poison, drug] (1651)
**1 :** the art, practice, or profession of preparing, preserving, compounding, and dispensing medical drugs
**2 a :** a place where medicines are compounded or dispensed **b :** DRUGSTORE
**3 :** PHARMACOPOEIA 2
**pha·ryn·geal** \ˌfar-ən-'jē-əl, fə-'rin-j(ē-)əl\ *adjective* [New Latin *pharyngeus*, from *pharyng-*, *pharynx*] (1828)
**:** relating to or located or produced in the region of the pharynx
**phar·yn·gi·tis** \ˌfar-ən-'jī-təs\ *noun, plural* **-git·i·des** \-'ji-tə-ˌdēz\ (circa 1844)
**:** inflammation of the pharynx
**phar·ynx** \'far-iŋ(k)s\ *noun, plural* **pha·ryn·ges** \fə-'rin-(ˌ)jēz\ *also* **phar·ynx·es** [New Latin *pharyng-*, *pharynx*, from Greek, throat, pharynx; akin to Old Norse *barki* throat and probably to Latin *ferire* to strike — more at BORE] (circa 1693)
**1 :** the part of the vertebrate alimentary canal between the cavity of the mouth and the esophagus
**2 :** a differentiated part of the alimentary canal in some invertebrates that may be thickened and muscular, eversible and toothed, or adapted as a suctorial organ
¹**phase** \'fāz\ *noun* [New Latin *phasis*, from Greek, appearance of a star, phase of the moon, from *phainein* to show (middle voice, to appear) — more at FANCY] (1812)

**1 :** a particular appearance or state in a regularly recurring cycle of changes ⟨*phases* of the moon⟩
**2 a :** a distinguishable part in a course, development, or cycle ⟨the early *phases* of her career⟩ **b :** an aspect or part (as of a problem) under consideration
**3 :** the point or stage in a period of uniform circular motion, harmonic motion, or the periodic changes of any magnitude varying according to a simple harmonic law to which the rotation, oscillation, or variation has advanced considered in its relation to a standard position or assumed instant of starting
**4 :** a homogeneous, physically distinct, and mechanically separable portion of matter present in a nonhomogeneous physicochemical system
**5 :** an individual or subgroup distinguishably different in appearance or behavior from the norm of the group to which it belongs; *also* **:** the distinguishing peculiarity
— **pha·sic** \'fā-zik\ *adjective*
— **in phase :** in a synchronized or correlated manner
— **out of phase :** in an unsynchronized manner **:** not in correlation
²**phase** *transitive verb* **phased; phas·ing** (1904)
**1 :** to adjust so as to be in a synchronized condition
**2 :** to conduct or carry out by planned phases
**3 :** to introduce in stages — often used with *in* ⟨*phase* in new models⟩
**phase–contrast** *adjective* (1934)
**:** of or employing the phase-contrast microscope
**phase–contrast microscope** *noun* (1947)
**:** a microscope that translates differences in phase of the light transmitted through or reflected by the object into differences of intensity in the image — called also *phase microscope*
**phase·down** \'fāz-ˌdaùn\ *noun* (1964)
**:** a gradual reduction (as in operations)
**phase modulation** *noun* (1930)
**:** modulation of the phase of a radio carrier wave by voice or other signal
**phase·out** \'fā-ˌzaùt\ *noun* (1958)
**:** a gradual stopping of operations or production **:** a closing down by phases
**phase out** (1940)
*transitive verb*
**:** to discontinue the practice, production, or use of by phases ⟨*phase out* the old machinery⟩
*intransitive verb*
**:** to stop production or operation by phases
**-phasia** *noun combining form* [New Latin, from Greek, speech, from *phasis* utterance, from *phanai* to speak, say — more at BAN]
**:** speech disorder of a (specified) type ⟨dysphasia⟩
**phas·mid** \'faz-məd\ *noun* [New Latin *Phasmida*, group name, from *Phasma*, type genus, from Greek, apparition, from *phainein* to show — more at FANCY] (1872)
**:** any of an order (Phasmatodea synonym Phasmida) of large cylindrical or sometimes flattened chiefly tropical insects (as a walking stick) with long strong legs, strictly phytophagous habits, and slight metamorphosis
— **phasmid** *adjective*
**phat·ic** \'fa-tik\ *adjective* [Greek *phatos*, verbal of *phanai* to speak] (1923)
**:** of, relating to, or being speech used for social or emotive purposes rather than for communicating information
— **phat·i·cal·ly** \-ti-k(ə-)lē\ *adverb*
**pheas·ant** \'fe-zᵊnt\ *noun, plural* **pheasant** *or* **pheasants** [Middle English *fesaunt*, from Anglo-French, from Old French *fesan*, from Latin *phasianus*, from Greek *phasianos*, from *phasianos* of the Phasis River, from *Phasis*, river in Colchis] (13th century)

**1 :** any of numerous large often long-tailed and brightly colored Old World gallinaceous birds (*Phasianus* and related genera of the family Phasianidae) including many raised as ornamental or game birds
**2 :** any of various birds resembling a pheasant

**phel·lem** \'fe-,lem\ *noun* [Greek *phellos* cork + English *-em* (as in *phloem*)] (1887)
**:** a layer of usually suberized cells produced outwardly by a phellogen

**phel·lo·derm** \'fe-lə-,dərm\ *noun* [Greek *phellos* + International Scientific Vocabulary *-derm*] (1875)
**:** a layer of parenchyma produced inwardly by a phellogen

**phel·lo·gen** \'fe-lə-jən\ *noun* [Greek *phellos* + International Scientific Vocabulary *-gen*] (1875)
**:** a secondary meristem that initiates phellem and phelloderm in the periderm of a stem — called also *cork cambium*

**phen-** or **pheno-** *combining form* [obsolete *phene* benzene, from French *phène*, from Greek *phainein* to show; from its occurrence in illuminating gas — more at FANCY]
**1 :** related to or derived from benzene 〈*phe*nol〉
**2 :** containing phenyl 〈*pheno*barbital〉

**phe·na·caine** \'fē-nə-,kān, 'fe-\ *noun* [probably from *phen*etidine + *acet*- + *-caine*] (1907)
**:** a crystalline base $C_{18}H_{22}N_2O_2$ or its hydrochloride used as a local anesthetic

**phen·ac·e·tin** \fi-'na-sə-tən\ *noun* [International Scientific Vocabulary] (1887)
**:** a white crystalline compound $C_{10}H_{13}NO_2$ formerly used to ease pain or fever but withdrawn because of its serious side effects — called also *acetophenetidin*

**phen·a·kite** \'fe-nə-,kīt, 'fē-\ or **phen·a·cite** \-,sīt\ *noun* [German *Phenakit*, from Greek *phenak-, phenax* deceiver; from its being easily mistaken for quartz] (circa 1834)
**:** a glassy mineral that consists of a beryllium silicate and occurs in rhombohedral crystals

**phen·an·threne** \fə-'nan-,thrēn\ *noun* [International Scientific Vocabulary *phen-* + *an*thracene] (1882)
**:** a crystalline aromatic hydrocarbon $C_{14}H_{10}$ of coal tar isomeric with anthracene

**phen·a·zine** \'fe-nə-,zēn\ *noun* [International Scientific Vocabulary] (circa 1900)
**:** a yellowish crystalline base $C_{12}H_8N_2$ used especially in organic synthesis

**phen·cy·cli·dine** \(,)fen-'si-klə-,dēn, -'sī-, -dən\ *noun* [*phen-* + *cycl-* + *-idine*] (1959)
**:** a piperidine derivative $C_{17}H_{25}N$ used especially as a veterinary anesthetic and sometimes illicitly as a psychedelic drug — called also *angel dust, PCP*

**phe·net·ic** \fi-'ne-tik\ *adjective* [*phen*otype + *-etic* (as in *genetic*)] (1960)
**:** of or relating to taxonomic analysis that emphasizes the overall similarities of characteristics among biological taxa without regard to phylogenetic relationships

**phe·net·ics** \-tiks\ *noun plural but singular in construction* (circa 1960)
**:** a system of biological classification based on phenetic methods
— **phe·net·i·cist** \-'ne-tə-sist\ *noun*

**phen·met·ra·zine** \(,)fen-'me-trə-,zēn\ *noun* [*phen*yl + *methyl* + *tetra*- + *azine*] (1956)
**:** a sympathomimetic stimulant $C_{11}H_{15}NO$ used in the form of its hydrochloride as an appetite suppressant

**phe·no·bar·bi·tal** \,fē-nō-'bär-bə-,tȯl\ *noun* (1918)
**:** a crystalline barbiturate $C_{12}H_{12}N_2O_3$ used as a hypnotic and sedative

**phe·no·bar·bi·tone** \-bə-,tōn\ *noun* (circa 1932)
*chiefly British* **:** PHENOBARBITAL

**phe·no·copy** \'fē-nə-,kä-pē\ *noun* [International Scientific Vocabulary *phenotype* + *copy*] (1937)
**:** a phenotypic variation that is caused by unusual environmental conditions and resembles the normal expression of a genotype other than its own

**phe·no·cryst** \-,krist\ *noun* [French *phénocryste*, from Greek *phainein* to show + *krystallos* crystal — more at FANCY] (circa 1893)
**:** one of the prominent embedded crystals of a porphyry
— **phe·no·crys·tic** \,fē-nə-'kris-tik\ *adjective*

**phe·nol** \'fē-,nȯl, -,nȯl, fi-'\ *noun* [International Scientific Vocabulary *phen-* + ³-*ol*] (circa 1852)
**1 :** a corrosive poisonous crystalline acidic compound $C_6H_5OH$ present in coal tar and wood tar that in dilute solution is used as a disinfectant
**2 :** any of various acidic compounds analogous to phenol and regarded as hydroxyl derivatives of aromatic hydrocarbons

**phe·no·late** \'fē-nᵊl-,āt\ *noun* (1885)
**:** PHENOXIDE

**phe·no·lat·ed** \'fē-nᵊl-,ā-təd\ *adjective* (1923)
**:** treated, mixed, or impregnated with phenol

¹**phe·no·lic** \fi-'nō-lik, -'nä-\ *adjective* (1872)
**1 a :** of, relating to, or having the characteristics of a phenol **b :** containing or derived from a phenol
**2 :** of, relating to, or being a phenolic

²**phenolic** *noun* (1924)
**:** a usually thermosetting resin or plastic made by condensation of a phenol with an aldehyde and used especially for molding and insulating and in coatings and adhesives — called also *phenolic resin*

**phe·nol·o·gy** \fi-'nä-lə-jē\ *noun* [*phenomena* + *-logy*] (circa 1884)
**1 :** a branch of science dealing with the relations between climate and periodic biological phenomena (as bird migration or plant flowering)
**2 :** periodic biological phenomena (as of a kind of organism) that are correlated with climatic conditions
— **phe·no·log·i·cal** \,fē-nᵊl-'ä-ji-kəl\ *adjective*
— **phe·no·log·i·cal·ly** \-k(ə-)lē\ *adverb*

**phe·nol·phtha·lein** \,fē-nᵊl-'tha-lē-ən, -'tha-,lēn, -'thā-\ *noun* [International Scientific Vocabulary] (circa 1875)
**:** a white or yellowish white crystalline compound $C_{20}H_{14}O_4$ used in analysis as an indicator because its solution is brilliant red in alkalies and is decolorized by acids and in medicine as a laxative

**phenol red** *noun* (1916)
**:** a red crystalline compound $C_{19}H_{14}O_5S$ used especially as an acid-base indicator

**phe·nom** \'fē-,näm, fi-'näm\ *noun* (circa 1890)
**:** PHENOMENON; *especially* **:** a person of phenomenal ability or promise

**phe·nom·e·na** \fi-'nä-mə-nə, -,nä\ *noun, plural* **-nas** (1576)
*nonstandard* **:** PHENOMENON □

**phe·nom·e·nal** \fi-'nä-mə-nᵊl\ *adjective* (1825)
**:** relating to or being a phenomenon: as **a :** known through the senses rather than through thought or intuition **b :** concerned with phenomena rather than with hypotheses **c :** EXTRAORDINARY, REMARKABLE
*synonym* see MATERIAL
— **phe·nom·e·nal·ly** \-nᵊl-ē\ *adverb*

**phe·nom·e·nal·ism** \-nᵊl-,i-zəm\ *noun* (circa 1865)
**1 :** a theory that limits knowledge to phenomena only
**2 :** a theory that all knowledge is of phenomena and that what is construed to be perception of material objects is simply perception of sense-data
— **phe·nom·e·nal·ist** \-ist\ *noun or adjective*
— **phe·nom·e·nal·is·tic** \-,nä-mə-nᵊl-'is-tik\ *adjective*

— **phe·nom·e·nal·is·ti·cal·ly** \-ti-k(ə-)lē\ *adverb*

**phe·nom·e·no·log·i·cal** \fi-,nä-mə-nᵊl-'ä-ji-kəl\ *adjective* (circa 1858)
**1 :** of or relating to phenomenology
**2 :** PHENOMENAL
**3 :** of or relating to phenomenalism
— **phe·nom·e·no·log·i·cal·ly** \-k(ə-)lē\ *adverb*

**phe·nom·e·nol·o·gy** \fi-,nä-mə-nə-'nä-lə-jē\ *noun, plural* **-gies** [German *Phänomenologie*, from *Phänomenon* phenomenon + *-logie* *-logy*] (circa 1797)
**1 :** the study of the development of human consciousness and self-awareness as a preface to philosophy or a part of philosophy
**2 a (1) :** a philosophical movement that describes the formal structure of the objects of awareness and of awareness itself in abstraction from any claims concerning existence **(2) :** the typological classification of a class of phenomena 〈the *phenomenology* of religion〉 **b :** an analysis produced by phenomenological investigation
— **phe·nom·e·nol·o·gist** \-jist\ *noun*

**phe·nom·e·non** \fi-'nä-mə-,nän, -nən\ *noun, plural* **-na** \-nə, -,nä\ or **-nons** [Late Latin *phaenomenon*, from Greek *phainomenon*, from neuter of *phainomenos*, present participle of *phainesthai* to appear, middle voice of *phainein* to show — more at FANCY] (1605)
**1** *plural* **phenomena :** an observable fact or event
**2** *plural* **phenomena a :** an object or aspect known through the senses rather than by thought or intuition **b :** a temporal or spatiotemporal object of sensory experience as distinguished from a noumenon **c :** a fact or event of scientific interest susceptible of scientific description and explanation
**3 a :** a rare or significant fact or event **b** *plural* **phenomenons :** an exceptional, unusual, or abnormal person, thing, or occurrence
*usage* see PHENOMENA

**phe·no·thi·a·zine** \,fē-nō-'thī-ə-,zēn\ *noun* [International Scientific Vocabulary] (1894)
**1 :** a greenish yellow crystalline compound $C_{12}H_9NS$ used as an anthelmintic and insecticide especially in veterinary practice
**2 :** any of various phenothiazine derivatives (as chlorpromazine) that are used as tranquilizing agents especially in the treatment of schizophrenia

**phe·no·type** \'fē-nə-,tīp\ *noun* [German *Phänotypus*, from Greek *phainein* to show + *typos* type] (circa 1911)
**:** the visible properties of an organism that are produced by the interaction of the genotype and the environment
— **phe·no·typ·ic** \,fē-nə-'ti-pik\ *also* **phe·no·typ·i·cal** \-pi-kəl\ *adjective*
— **phe·no·typ·i·cal·ly** \-pi-k(ə-)lē\ *adverb*

---

☐ **USAGE**
**phenomena** *Phenomena* has been in occasional use as a singular for more than 400 years and its plural *phenomenas* for more than 350. Our evidence shows that it is primarily a speech form used by poets, critics, and professors, among others, but one that sometimes turns up in edited prose 〈the Borgia were, in modern terms, a media *phenomena* —*Economist*〉. It is etymologically no more irregular than *stamina, agenda,* and *candelabra,* but it has nowhere near the frequency of use that they have, and while they are standard, *phenomena* is still rather borderline.

---

\ə\ abut \ᵊ\ kitten \ər\ further \a\ ash \ā\ ace
\ä\ mop, mar \au̇\ out \ch\ chin \e\ bet \ē\ easy
\g\ go \i\ hit \ī\ ice \j\ job \ŋ\ sing \ō\ go
\ȯ\ law \ȯi\ boy \th\ thin \th\ the \ü\ loot \u̇\ foot
\y\ yet \zh\ vision *see also* Guide to Pronunciation

**phen·ox·ide** \fi-ˈnäk-ˌsīd\ *noun* (1888)
**:** a salt of a phenol especially in its capacity as a weak acid

**phen·tol·amine** \fen-ˈtä-lə-ˌmēn, -mən\ *noun* [*phen-* + *toluidine* + *amine*] (1952)
**:** an adrenergic blocking agent $C_{17}H_{19}N_3O$ that is used especially in the diagnosis and treatment of hypertension due to pheochromocytoma

**phe·nyl** \ˈfe-nᵊl, ˈfē-\ *noun* [International Scientific Vocabulary] (circa 1850)
**:** a univalent group $C_6H_5$ that is an aryl group derived from benzene by removal of one hydrogen atom — often used in combination — **phe·nyl·ic** \fi-ˈni-lik\ *adjective*

**phe·nyl·al·a·nine** \ˌfe-nᵊl-ˈa-lə-ˌnēn, ˌfē-\ *noun* [International Scientific Vocabulary] (1883)
**:** an essential amino acid $C_9H_{11}NO_2$ that is converted in the normal body to tyrosine

**phen·yl·bu·ta·zone** \ˌfe-nᵊl-ˈbyü-tə-ˌzōn\ *noun* [*phenyl* + *butyric acid* + *pyrazalone* $(C_3H_4N_2O)$] (1952)
**:** a drug $C_{19}H_{20}N_2O_2$ that is used for its analgesic and anti-inflammatory properties especially in the treatment of arthritis, gout, and bursitis

**phen·yl·eph·rine** \-ˈe-ˌfrēn, -frən\ *noun* [*phenyl* + *epinephrine*] (1947)
**:** a sympathomimetic agent $C_9H_{13}NO_2$ that is used in the form of the hydrochloride as a vasoconstrictor, a mydriatic, and by injection to raise the blood pressure

**phen·yl·eth·yl·amine** \ˌfe-nᵊl-ˌe-thəl-ˈa-ˌmēn, ˌfē-\ *noun* (1939)
**:** a neurotransmitter $C_8H_{11}N$ that is an amine resembling amphetamine in structure and pharmacological properties; *also* **:** any of its derivatives

**phe·nyl·ke·ton·uria** \ˌfe-nᵊl-ˌkē-tᵊn-ˈür-ē-ə, ˌfē-, -ˈyür-\ *noun* [New Latin, from International Scientific Vocabulary *phenyl* + *ketone* + New Latin *-uria*] (1935)
**:** an inherited human metabolic disease that is characterized by inability to oxidize a metabolic product of phenylalanine and by severe mental deficiency — abbreviation *PKU* — **phe·nyl·ke·ton·uric** \-ˈür-ik, -ˈyür-\ *noun or adjective*

**phen·yl·pro·pa·nol·amine** \ˌfe-nᵊl-ˌprō-pə-ˈnȯ-lə-ˌmēn, ˌfē-, -ˈnō-; -nȯ-ˈla-ˌmēn\ *noun* [*phenyl* + *propane* + *¹-ol* + *amine*] (1947)
**:** a sympathomimetic drug $C_9H_{13}NO$ used in the form of its hydrochloride especially as a nasal and bronchial decongestant and as an appetite suppressant

**phen·yl·thio·car·ba·mide** \ˌfe-nᵊl-ˌthī-ō-ˈkär-bə-ˌmīd, ˌfē-\ *noun* (1879)
**:** a crystalline compound $C_7H_8N_2S$ that is extremely bitter or tasteless depending on the presence or absence of a single dominant gene in the taster — called also *phenylthiourea, PTC*

**phen·yl·thio·urea** \-ˌthī-ō-yu̇-ˈrē-ə\ *noun* (1896)
**:** PHENYLTHIOCARBAMIDE

**phe·nyt·o·in** \fə-ˈni-tə-wən\ *noun* [di*phenyl*hydan*toin*] (1941)
**:** a crystalline anticonvulsant compound $C_{15}H_{12}N_2O_2$ used in the form of its sodium salt in the treatment of epilepsy — called also *diphenylhydantoin*

**pheo·chro·mo·cy·to·ma** \ˌfē-ə-ˌkrō-mə-sə-ˈtō-mə, -sī-\ *noun, plural* **-mas** *or* **-ma·ta** \-mə-tə\ [New Latin, from International Scientific Vocabulary *pheochromocyte* chromaffin cell + New Latin *-oma*] (circa 1929)
**:** a tumor that is derived from chromaffin cells and is usually associated with paroxysmal or sustained hypertension

**pher·o·mone** \ˈfer-ə-ˌmōn\ *noun* [International Scientific Vocabulary *phero-* (from Greek *pherein* to carry) + *-mone* (as in *hormone*) — more at BEAR] (1959)
**:** a chemical substance that is produced by an animal and serves especially as a stimulus to other individuals of the same species for one or more behavioral responses — **pher·o·mon·al** \ˌfer-ə-ˈmō-nᵊl\ *adjective*

**phew** \*a voiceless bilabial fricative usually followed by a voiceless* (y)ü *or* ʊ *sound; often read as* ˈf(y)ü\ *interjection* (1604)
**1** — used to express relief or fatigue
**2** — used to express disgust at or as if at an unpleasant odor

**phi** \ˈfī\ *noun* [Middle Greek, from Greek *phei*] (circa 1899)
**:** the 21st letter of the Greek alphabet — see ALPHABET table

**phi·al** \ˈfī-(ə)l\ *noun* [Middle English, from Latin *phiala*, from Greek *phialē*] (14th century)
**:** VIAL

**Phi Be·ta Kap·pa** \ˌfī-ˌbā-tə-ˈka-pə\ *noun* [*Phi Beta Kappa* (Society), from *phi* + *beta* + *kappa*, initials of the society's Greek motto *philosophia biou kybernētēs* philosophy the guide of life] (1912)
**:** a person winning high scholastic distinction in an American college or university and being elected to membership in a national honor society founded in 1776

**phil-** *or* **philo-** *combining form* [Middle English, from Old French, from Latin, from Greek, from *philos* dear, friendly]
**:** loving **:** having an affinity for ⟨*philo*progenitive⟩

**¹-phil** *or* **-phile** *noun combining form* [French *-phile*, from Greek *-philos* -philous]
**:** lover **:** one having an affinity for or a strong attraction to ⟨acido*phil*⟩ ⟨Slavo*phile*⟩

**²-phil** *or* **-phile** *adjective combining form* [New Latin *-philus*, from Latin, from Greek *-philos*]
**:** loving **:** having a fondness or affinity for ⟨Franco*phile*⟩

**Phil·a·del·phia lawyer** \ˌfi-lə-ˈdel-fyə-, -fē-ə-\ *noun* [*Philadelphia*, Pa.] (1788)
**:** a lawyer knowledgeable in even the most minute aspects of the law

**Philadelphia pepper pot** *noun* (1929)
**:** PEPPER POT 2b

**phil·a·del·phus** \ˌfi-lə-ˈdel-fəs\ *noun* [New Latin, from Greek *philadelphos* brotherly, from *phil-* + *adelphos* brother — more at -ADELPHOUS] (1950)
**:** MOCK ORANGE 1

**phi·lan·der** \fə-ˈlan-dər\ *intransitive verb* **-dered; -der·ing** \-d(ə-)riŋ\ [from obsolete *philander* lover, philanderer, probably from the name *Philander*] (1737)
**1 :** to make love to someone with whom marriage is impossible (as because of an existing marriage) or with no intention of proposing marriage
**2 :** to have many love affairs — **phi·lan·der·er** \-dər-ər\ *noun*

**phil·an·throp·ic** \ˌfi-lən-ˈthrä-pik\ *also* **phil·an·throp·i·cal** \-pi-kəl\ *adjective* (1789)
**1 :** of, relating to, or characterized by philanthropy **:** HUMANITARIAN
**2 :** dispensing or receiving aid from funds set aside for humanitarian purposes — **phil·an·throp·i·cal·ly** \-pi-k(ə-)lē\ *adverb*

**phi·lan·thro·pist** \fə-ˈlan(t)-thrə-pist\ *noun* (circa 1736)
**:** one who practices philanthropy

**phi·lan·thro·poid** \-ˌpȯid\ *noun* [blend of *philanthropist* and *anthropoid*] (1945)
**:** a person who works for a philanthropic organization

**phi·lan·thro·py** \-pē\ *noun, plural* **-pies** [Late Latin *philanthropia*, from Greek *philanthrōpia*, from *philanthrōpos* loving people, from *phil-* + *anthrōpos* human being] (circa 1623)
**1 :** goodwill to fellowmen; *especially* **:** active effort to promote human welfare
**2 a :** a philanthropic act or gift **b :** an organization distributing or supported by philanthropic funds

**phi·lat·e·list** \fə-ˈla-tᵊl-ist\ *noun* (circa 1865)
**:** a specialist in philately **:** one who collects or studies stamps

**phi·lat·e·ly** \fə-ˈla-tᵊl-ē\ *noun* [French *philatélie*, from *phil-* + Greek *ateleia* tax exemption, from *atelēs* free from tax, from *a-* + *telos* tax; perhaps akin to Greek *tlēnai* to bear; from the fact that a stamped letter frees the recipient from paying the mailing charges — more at TOLERATE] (circa 1865)
**:** the collection and study of postage and imprinted stamps **:** stamp collecting — **phil·a·tel·ic** \ˌfi-lə-ˈte-lik\ *adjective* — **phil·a·tel·i·cal·ly** \-li-k(ə-)lē\ *adverb*

**Phi·le·mon** \fə-ˈlē-mən, fī-\ *noun* [Greek *Philēmōn*]
**1 :** a friend and probable convert of the apostle Paul
**2 :** a letter written by Saint Paul to a Christian living in the area of Colossae and included as a book in the New Testament — see BIBLE table
**3 :** a poor aged Phrygian in Greek mythology who with his wife Baucis treats a disguised Zeus hospitably and is rewarded by him with a splendid temple

**phil·har·mon·ic** \ˌfi-lər-ˈmä-nik, -(ˌ)lär-; ˌfil-(ˌ)här-\ *noun* [French *philharmonique*, literally, loving harmony, from Italian *filarmonico*, from *fil-* phil- + *armonia* harmony, from Latin *harmonia*] (1843)
**:** SYMPHONY ORCHESTRA

**phil·hel·lene** \(ˌ)fil-ˈhe-ˌlēn\ *or* **phil·hel·len·ic** \ˌfil-hə-ˈle-nik\ *adjective* [Greek *philellēn*, from *phil-* + *Hellēn* Hellene] (circa 1825)
**:** admiring Greece or the Greeks — **philhellene** *noun* — **phil·hel·le·nism** \(ˌ)fil-ˈhe-lə-ˌni-zəm\ *noun* — **phil·hel·le·nist** \-nist\ *noun*

**-philia** *noun combining form* [New Latin, from Greek *philia* friendship, from *philos* dear]
**1 :** friendly feeling toward ⟨Franco*philia*⟩
**2 :** tendency toward ⟨hemo*philia*⟩
**3 :** abnormal appetite or liking for ⟨necro*philia*⟩

**-philiac** *noun combining form* [New Latin *-philia* + Greek *-akos*, adjective suffix]
**1 :** one having a tendency toward ⟨hemo*philiac*⟩
**2 :** one having an abnormal appetite or liking for ⟨copro*philiac*⟩

**-philic** *adjective combining form* [Greek *-philos* -philous]
**:** having an affinity for **:** loving ⟨acido*philic*⟩

**Phi·lip·pi·ans** \fə-ˈli-pē-ənz\ *noun plural but singular in construction* [short for *Epistle to the Philippians*]
**:** a hortatory letter written by Saint Paul to the Christians of Philippi and included as a book in the New Testament — see BIBLE table

**phi·lip·pic** \fə-ˈli-pik\ *noun* [Middle French *philippique*, from Latin & Greek; Latin *philippica, orationes philippicae*, speeches of Cicero against Mark Antony, translation of Greek *philippikoi logoi*, speeches of Demosthenes against Philip II of Macedon, literally, speeches relating to Philip] (1592)
**:** a discourse or declamation full of bitter condemnation **:** TIRADE

**Phil·ip·pine mahogany** \ˈfi-lə-ˌpēn-\ *noun* [*Philippine* Islands] (circa 1924)
**:** any of several Philippine dipterocarp timber trees (genera *Shorea, Parashorea,* and *Pentacme*) with wood resembling that of the true mahoganies; *also* **:** its wood

**phi·lis·tia** \fə-ˈlis-tē-ə\ *noun plural, often capitalized* [*Philistia,* ancient country of southwest Palestine] (1857)
**:** the class or world of cultural philistines

**Phi·lis·tine** \ˈfi-lə-ˌstēn; fə-ˈlis-tən, -ˌtēn; ˈfi-lə-stən\ *noun* (14th century)
**1 :** a native or inhabitant of ancient Philistia

**2** *often not capitalized* **a :** a person who is guided by materialism and is usually disdainful of intellectual or artistic values **b :** one uninformed in a special area of knowledge ◆
— **philistine** *adjective, often capitalized*
— **phi·lis·tin·ism** \-lə-ˌstē-ˌni-zəm; -ˈlis-tə-, -ˌtē-, -lə-stə\ *noun, often capitalized*

**Phil·lips** \ˈfi-ləps\ *adjective* [from *Phillips*, a trademark, from Henry M. *Phillips* 20th century American engineer] (1935)
**:** of, relating to, or being a screw having a head with a cross slot or the corresponding screwdriver

**phil·lu·men·ist** \fi-ˈlü-mə-nist\ *noun* [*phil-* + Latin *lumen* light — more at LUMINARY] (1943)
**:** one who collects matchbooks or matchbox labels

**Phi·loc·te·tes** \fi-ˈläk-tə-ˌtēz, ˌfi-läk-ˈtē-tēz\ *noun* [Greek *Philoktētēs*]
**:** a Greek archer who uses the bow of Hercules to slay Paris at Troy

**phil·o·den·dron** \ˌfi-lə-ˈden-drən\ *noun, plural* **-drons** *or* **-dra** \-drə\ [New Latin, from Greek, neuter of *philodendros* loving trees, from *phil-* + *dendron* tree — more at DENDR-] (1877)
**:** any of various aroid plants (as of the genus *Philodendron*) that are cultivated for their showy foliage

**phi·lol·o·gy** \fə-ˈlä-lə-jē *also* fī-\ *noun* [French *philologie*, from Latin *philologia* love of learning and literature, from Greek, from *philologos* fond of learning and literature, from *phil-* + *logos* word, speech — more at LEGEND] (1612)
**1 :** the study of literature and of disciplines relevant to literature or to language as used in literature
**2 a :** LINGUISTICS; *especially* **:** historical and comparative linguistics **b :** the study of human speech especially as the vehicle of literature and as a field of study that sheds light on cultural history
— **phil·o·log·i·cal** \ˌfi-lə-ˈlä-ji-kəl\ *adjective*
— **phil·o·log·i·cal·ly** \-k(ə-)lē\ *adverb*
— **phi·lol·o·gist** \fə-ˈlä-lə-jist *also* fī-\ *noun*

**Phil·o·mel** \ˈfi-lə-ˌmel\ *noun* [Latin *Philomela* Philomela, nightingale] (1579)
**:** NIGHTINGALE

**Phil·o·me·la** \ˌfi-lə-ˈmē-lə\ *noun* [Latin, from Greek *Philomēlē*]
**:** an Athenian princess in Greek mythology raped and deprived of her tongue by her brother-in-law Tereus, avenged by the killing of his son, and changed into a nightingale while fleeing from him

**phil·o·pro·gen·i·tive** \ˌfi-lə-prō-ˈje-nə-tiv\ *adjective* [*phil-* + Latin *progenitus*, past participle of *progignere* to beget — more at PROGENITOR] (1865)
**1 :** tending to produce offspring **:** PROLIFIC
**2 :** of, relating to, or characterized by love of offspring
— **phil·o·pro·gen·i·tive·ness** *noun*

**phi·lo·sophe** \ˌfē-lə-ˈzôf\ *noun* [French, literally, philosopher] (1779)
**:** one of the deistic or materialistic writers and thinkers of the 18th century French Enlightenment

**phi·los·o·pher** \fə-ˈlä-s(ə-)fər\ *noun* [Middle English, modification of Middle French *philosophe*, from Latin *philosophus*, from Greek *philosophos*, from *phil-* + *sophia* wisdom, from *sophos* wise] (14th century)
**1 a :** a person who seeks wisdom or enlightenment **:** SCHOLAR, THINKER **b :** a student of philosophy
**2 a :** a person whose philosophical perspective makes meeting trouble with equanimity easier **b :** an expounder of a theory in a particular area of experience **c :** one who philosophizes

**philosophers' stone** *noun* (14th century)

**:** an imaginary stone, substance, or chemical preparation believed to have the power of transmuting baser metals into gold and sought by alchemists — called also *philosopher's stone*

**phil·o·soph·i·cal** \ˌfi-lə-ˈsä-fi-kəl *also* -ˈzä-\ *or* **phil·o·soph·ic** \-fik\ *adjective* (14th century)
**1 a :** of or relating to philosophers or philosophy **b :** based on philosophy
**2 :** characterized by the attitude of a philosopher; *specifically* **:** calm or unflinching in face of trouble, defeat, or loss
— **phil·o·soph·i·cal·ly** \-fi-k(ə-)lē\ *adverb*

**philosophical analysis** *noun* (1936)
**:** ANALYTIC PHILOSOPHY

**phi·los·o·phise** *British variant of* 'PHILOSOPHIZE

**phi·los·o·phize** \fə-ˈlä-sə-ˌfīz\ *verb* **-phized; -phiz·ing** (1594)
*intransitive verb*
**1 :** to reason in the manner of a philosopher
**2 :** to expound a moralizing and often superficial philosophy
*transitive verb*
**:** to consider from or bring into conformity with a philosophical point of view
— **phi·los·o·phiz·er** *noun*

**phi·los·o·phy** \fə-ˈlä-s(ə-)fē\ *noun, plural* **-phies** [Middle English *philosophie*, from Old French, from Latin *philosophia*, from Greek, from *philosophos* philosopher] (14th century)
**1 a** (1) **:** all learning exclusive of technical precepts and practical arts (2) **:** the sciences and liberal arts exclusive of medicine, law, and theology ⟨a doctor of *philosophy*⟩ (3) **:** the 4-year college course of a major seminary **b** (1) *archaic* **:** PHYSICAL SCIENCE (2) **:** ETHICS **c :** a discipline comprising as its core logic, aesthetics, ethics, metaphysics, and epistemology
**2 a :** pursuit of wisdom **b :** a search for a general understanding of values and reality by chiefly speculative rather than observational means **c :** an analysis of the grounds of and concepts expressing fundamental beliefs
**3 a :** a system of philosophical concepts **b :** a theory underlying or regarding a sphere of activity or thought ⟨the *philosophy* of war⟩ ⟨*philosophy* of science⟩
**4 a :** the most general beliefs, concepts, and attitudes of an individual or group **b :** calmness of temper and judgment befitting a philosopher

**philosophy of life** (1853)
**1 :** an overall vision of or attitude toward life and the purpose of life
**2** [translation of German *Lebensphilosophie*] **:** any of various philosophies that emphasize human life or life in general

**-philous** *adjective combining form* [Greek *-philos*, from *philos* dear, friendly]
**:** loving **:** having an affinity for ⟨hygro*philous*⟩

**phil·ter** *or* **phil·tre** \ˈfil-tər\ *noun* [Middle French *philtre*, from Latin *philtrum*, from Greek *philtron*; akin to Greek *philos* dear] (circa 1587)
**1 :** a potion, drug, or charm held to have the power to arouse sexual passion
**2 :** a potion credited with magical power

**phi phenomenon** \ˈfī-\ *noun* (circa 1928)
**:** apparent motion resulting from an orderly sequence of stimuli (as lights flashed in rapid succession a short distance apart on a sign) without any actual motion being presented to the eye

**phiz** \ˈfiz\ *noun* [by shortening & alteration from *physiognomy*] (1688)
**:** FACE

**phleb-** *or* **phlebo-** *combining form* [Middle English *fleb-*, from Middle French, from Late Latin *phlebo-*, from Greek *phleb-*, *phlebo-*, from *phleb-*, *phleps*; perhaps akin to Greek *phlyein*, *phlyzein* to boil over — more at FLUID]
**:** vein ⟨*phlebitis*⟩

**phle·bi·tis** \fli-ˈbī-təs\ *noun* [New Latin] (circa 1834)
**:** inflammation of a vein

**phle·bo·gram** \ˈflē-bə-ˌgram\ *noun* [International Scientific Vocabulary] (1885)
**:** a figure of a vein or a record of its movements

**phle·bog·ra·phy** \fli-ˈbä-grə-fē\ *noun* [International Scientific Vocabulary] (1937)
**:** the process of making phlebograms
— **phle·bo·graph·ic** \ˌflē-bə-ˈgra-fik\ *adjective*

**phle·bol·o·gy** \fli-ˈbä-lə-jē\ *noun* [International Scientific Vocabulary] (1893)
**:** a branch of medicine concerned with the veins

**phle·bot·o·mus fever** \fli-ˈbä-tə-məs-\ *noun* [New Latin *Phlebotomus*, genus of sand flies] (circa 1923)
**:** SANDFLY FEVER

**phle·bot·o·my** \fli-ˈbä-tə-mē\ *noun, plural* **-mies** [Middle English *fleobotomie*, from Middle French *flebotomie*, from Late Latin *phlebotomia*, from Greek, from *phleb-* + *-tomia* -tomy] (14th century)
**:** the letting of blood for transfusion, diagnosis, or experiment, and especially formerly in the treatment of disease — called also *venesection*
— **phle·bot·o·mist** \-mist\ *noun*

**Phleg·e·thon** \ˈfle-gə-ˌthän\ *noun* [Latin, from Greek *Phlegethōn*]
**:** a river of fire in Hades

**phlegm** \ˈflem\ *noun* [Middle English *fleume*, from Middle French, from Late Latin *phlegmat-*, *phlegma*, from Greek, flame, inflammation, phlegm, from *phlegein* to burn — more at BLACK] (13th century)
**1 :** the one of the four humors in early physiology that was considered to be cold and moist and to cause sluggishness
**2 :** viscid mucus secreted in abnormal quantity in the respiratory passages
**3 a :** dull or apathetic coldness or indifference **b :** intrepid coolness or calm fortitude

◇ WORD HISTORY
**Philistine** In the Bible the *Philistines* are the perennial rivals and enemies of the neighboring Israelites. Biblical accounts portray the Philistines as a crude and warlike race. A figurative sense of *philistine* entered the English language as a result of a dispute between the townspeople and the university students in the German town of Jena in 1687. A bloody confrontation prompted a local clergyman to address the issue in a sermon to the townspeople on the value of education. For this sermon he chose his text from Judges 16:9 (Authorized Version): "The Philistines be upon these . . . ." *Philister*, the German word for *Philistine*, soon caught on with the students as an epithet first for the town militia and then for townsmen in general. Spreading more widely in German university slang, *Philister* came to be used for an outsider—someone who was not a member of the university community. Familiar with this usage, the English Victorian social and cultural critics Thomas Carlyle and Matthew Arnold, among others, used *Philistine* as an epithet for a materialist in various writings including Carlyle's *Sartor Resartus* (1831) and Arnold's *Culture and Anarchy* (1869). Since then, *philistine* has become widely used of any person who is indifferent or hostile to the arts and smugly accepts conventional values.

— **phleg·my** \'fle-mē\ adjective
**phleg·mat·ic** \fleg-'ma-tik\ adjective (14th century)
**1** : resembling, consisting of, or producing the humor phlegm
**2** : having or showing a slow and stolid temperament
**synonym** see IMPASSIVE
— **phleg·mat·i·cal·ly** \-ti-k(ə-)lē\ adverb

**phlo·em** \'flō-,em\ noun [German, from Greek phloios, phloos bark; perhaps akin to Greek phlein to teem, abound, phlyein, phlyzein to boil over — more at FLUID] (1875)
: a complex tissue in the vascular system of higher plants that consists mainly of sieve tubes and elongated parenchyma cells usually with fibers and that functions in translocation and in support and storage — compare XYLEM

**phloem necrosis** noun (1923)
: a pathological state in a plant characterized by brown discoloration and disintegration of the phloem; especially : a fatal disease of the American elm caused by a mycoplasma-like organism transmitted by a leafhopper (Scaphoideus luteolus)

**phloem ray** noun (1875)
: a vascular ray or part of a vascular ray that is located in phloem — compare XYLEM RAY

**phlo·gis·tic** \flō-'jis-tik\ adjective (1733)
**1** [New Latin phlogiston] : of or relating to phlogiston
**2** [Greek phlogistos] : of or relating to inflammations and fevers

**phlo·gis·ton** \-tən\ noun [New Latin, from Greek, neuter of phlogistos inflammable, from phlogizein to set on fire, from phlog-, phlox flame, from phlegein] (1733)
: the hypothetical principle of fire regarded formerly as a material substance

**phlog·o·pite** \'flä-gə-,pīt\ noun [German Phlogopit, from Greek phlogōpos fiery-looking, from phlog-, phlox + ōps face — more at EYE] (1850)
: a usually brown to red form of mica

**phlox** \'fläks\ noun, plural **phlox** or **phlox·es** [New Latin, from Latin, a flower, from Greek, flame, wallflower] (circa 1706)
: any of a genus (Phlox of the family Polemoniaceae, the phlox family) of American annual or perennial herbs that have red, purple, white, or variegated flowers, a salverform corolla with the stamens on its tube, and a 3-valved capsular fruit

phlox

**-phobe** noun combining form [Greek -phobos fearing]
: one fearing or averse to (something specified) ⟨Francophobe⟩

**pho·bia** \'fō-bē-ə\ noun [-phobia] (1786)
: an exaggerated usually inexplicable and illogical fear of a particular object, class of objects, or situation

**-phobia** noun combining form [New Latin, from Late Latin, from Greek, from -phobos fearing, from phobos fear, flight, from phebesthai to flee; akin to Lithuanian bėgti to flee, Old Church Slavonic běžati]
**1** : exaggerated fear of ⟨acrophobia⟩
**2** : intolerance or aversion for ⟨photophobia⟩

**pho·bic** \'fō-bik\ adjective (1897)
: of, relating to, affected with, or constituting phobia
— **phobic** noun

**-phobic** adjective combining form [French -phobique, from Late Latin -phobicus, from Greek -phobikos, from -phobia]
**1 a** : having an intolerance or aversion for ⟨photophobic⟩ ⟨Anglophobic⟩ **b** : exhibiting a phobia for ⟨claustrophobic⟩
**2** : lacking affinity for ⟨hydrophobic⟩

**phoe·be** \'fē-(,)bē\ noun [imitative] (1700)

: any of a genus (Sayornis) of American flycatchers; especially : one (S. phoebe) of the eastern U.S. that has a slight crest and is plain grayish brown above and yellowish white below

**Phoe·be** \'fē-bē\ noun [Latin, from Greek Phoibē, from phoibē, feminine of phoibos]
: ARTEMIS

**Phoe·bus** \'fē-bəs\ noun [Latin, from Greek Phoibos, from phoibos radiant]
**1** : APOLLO
**2** not capitalized : SUN

**Phoe·ni·cian** \fi-'nē-shən, -'ni-\ noun (14th century)
**1** : a native or inhabitant of ancient Phoenicia
**2** : the Semitic language of ancient Phoenicia
— **Phoenician** adjective

**phoe·nix** \'fē-niks\ noun [Middle English fenix, from Old English, from Latin phoenix, from Greek phoinix] (before 12th century)
: a legendary bird which according to one account lived 500 years, burned itself to ashes on a pyre, and rose alive from the ashes to live another period; also : a person or thing likened to the phoenix
— **phoe·nix·like** \-,līk\ adjective

**phon** \'fän\ noun [International Scientific Vocabulary, from Greek phōnē voice, sound] (1932)
: the unit of loudness on a scale beginning at zero for the faintest audible sound and corresponding to the decibel scale of sound intensity with the number of phons of a given sound being equal to the decibels of a pure 1000-cycle tone judged by the average listener to be equal in loudness to the given sound

**phon-** or **phono-** combining form [Latin, from Greek phōn-, phōno-, from phōnē — more at BAN]
: sound : voice : speech ⟨phonate⟩ ⟨phonograph⟩

**pho·nate** \'fō-,nāt\ intransitive verb **pho·nat·ed; pho·nat·ing** (1876)
: to produce vocal sounds and especially speech
— **pho·na·tion** \fō-'nā-shən\ noun

**¹phone** \'fōn\ noun [Greek phōnē] (circa 1866)
: a speech sound considered as a physical event without regard to its place in the sound system of a language

**²phone** noun [by shortening] (1884)
**1** : TELEPHONE
**2** : EARPHONE

**³phone** verb **phoned; phon·ing** (1889)
: TELEPHONE

**¹-phone** noun combining form [Greek -phōnos sounding, from phōnē]
**1** : sound ⟨homophone⟩ — often in names of musical instruments and sound-transmitting devices ⟨radiophone⟩ ⟨xylophone⟩
**2** : speaker of (a specified language) ⟨Francophone⟩

**²-phone** adjective combining form [French, from Greek -phōnos]
: of or relating to a population that speaks (a specified language) ⟨Francophone⟩

**phone-in** \'fōn-,in\ noun (1968)
: a call-in show (as on radio)

**pho·ne·mat·ic** \,fō-nē-'ma-tik\ adjective (1936)
: PHONEMIC

**pho·neme** \'fō-,nēm\ noun [French phonème, from Greek phōnēmat-, phōnēma speech sound, utterance, from phōnein to sound] (circa 1916)
: any of the abstract units of the phonetic system of a language that correspond to a set of similar speech sounds (as the velar \k\ of cool and the palatal \k\ of keel) which are perceived to be a single distinctive sound in the language

**pho·ne·mic** \fə-'nē-mik, fō-\ adjective (circa 1931)
**1** : of, relating to, or having the characteristics of a phoneme

**2 a** : constituting members of different phonemes (as \n\ and \m\ in English) **b** : DISTINCTIVE 2
— **pho·ne·mi·cal·ly** \-mi-k(ə-)lē\ adverb

**pho·ne·mics** \-miks\ noun plural but singular in construction (1936)
**1** : a branch of linguistic analysis that consists of the study of phonemes
**2** : the structure of a language in terms of phonemes
— **pho·ne·mi·cist** \-mə-sist\ noun

**pho·net·ic** \fə-'ne-tik\ adjective [New Latin phoneticus, from Greek phōnētikos, from phōnein to sound with the voice, from phōnē voice] (1826)
**1 a** : of or relating to spoken language or speech sounds **b** : of or relating to the science of phonetics
**2** : representing the sounds and other phenomena of speech: as **a** : constituting an alteration of ordinary spelling that better represents the spoken language, that employs only characters of the regular alphabet, and that is used in a context of conventional spelling **b** : representing speech sounds by means of symbols that have one value only **c** : employing for speech sounds more than the minimum number of symbols necessary to represent the significant differences in a speaker's speech
— **pho·net·i·cal·ly** \-ti-k(ə-)lē\ adverb

**phonetic alphabet** noun (1848)
**1** : a set of symbols (as IPA) used for phonetic transcription
**2** : any of various systems of identifying letters of the alphabet by means of code words in voice communication

**pho·ne·ti·cian** \,fō-nə-'ti-shən also ,fä-\ noun (1848)
: a specialist in phonetics

**pho·net·ics** \fə-'ne-tiks\ noun plural but singular in construction (1836)
**1** : the system of speech sounds of a language or group of languages
**2 a** : the study and systematic classification of the sounds made in spoken utterance **b** : the practical application of this science to language study

**pho·nic** \'fä-nik also 'fō-\ adjective (1823)
**1** : of, relating to, or producing sound : ACOUSTIC
**2 a** : of or relating to the sounds of speech **b** : of or relating to phonics
— **pho·ni·cal·ly** \-ni-k(ə-)lē\ adverb

**pho·nics** \'fä-niks, 1 is also 'fō-\ noun plural but singular in construction (circa 1684)
**1** : the science of sound : ACOUSTICS
**2** : a method of teaching beginners to read and pronounce words by learning the phonetic value of letters, letter groups, and especially syllables

**pho·no** \'fō-(,)nō\ noun, plural **phonos** (1909)
: PHONOGRAPH

**pho·no·car·dio·gram** \,fō-nə-'kär-dē-ə-,gram\ noun [International Scientific Vocabulary] (1912)
: a graphic record of heart sounds made by means of a microphone, amplifier, and galvanometer

**pho·no·car·di·og·ra·phy** \-,kär-dē-'ä-grə-fē\ noun (1916)
: the process of producing a phonocardiogram
— **pho·no·car·dio·graph** \-'kär-dē-ə-,graf\ noun
— **pho·no·car·dio·graph·ic** \-,kär-dē-ə-'gra-fik\ adjective

**pho·no·gram** \'fō-nə-,gram\ noun [International Scientific Vocabulary] (1860)
**1** : a character or symbol used to represent a word, syllable, or phoneme
**2** : a succession of orthographic letters that occurs with the same phonetic value in several words (as the ight of bright, fight, and flight)
— **pho·no·gram·mic** or **pho·no·gram·ic** \,fō-nə-'gra-mik\ adjective

— **pho·no·gram·mi·cal·ly** or **pho·no·gram·i·cal·ly** \-mi-k(ə-)lē\ adverb

**pho·no·graph** \'fō-nə-ˌgraf\ noun (1877)
: an instrument for reproducing sounds by means of the vibration of a stylus or needle following a spiral groove on a revolving disc or cylinder

**pho·nog·ra·pher** \fə-'nä-grə-fər, fō-\ noun (1845)
: a specialist in phonography

**pho·no·graph·ic** \ˌfō-nə-'gra-fik, 1 is also ˌfä-\ adjective (1828)
**1** : of or relating to phonography
**2** : of or relating to a phonograph
— **pho·no·graph·i·cal·ly** \-fi-k(ə-)lē\ adverb

**pho·nog·ra·phy** \fə-'nä-grə-fē, fō-\ noun (1701)
**1** : spelling based on pronunciation
**2** : a system of shorthand writing based on sound

**pho·no·lite** \'fō-nºl-ˌīt\ noun [French, from German Phonolith, from phon- + -lith; from its ringing sound when struck] (circa 1828)
: a gray or green volcanic rock consisting essentially of orthoclase and nepheline

**pho·nol·o·gy** \fə-'nä-lə-jē, fō-\ noun (1799)
**1** : the science of speech sounds including especially the history and theory of sound changes in a language or in two or more related languages
**2** : the phonetics and phonemics of a language at a particular time
— **pho·no·log·i·cal** \ˌfō-nºl-'ä-ji-kəl also ˌfä-\ also **pho·no·log·ic** \-jik\ adjective
— **pho·no·log·i·cal·ly** \-ji-k(ə-)lē\ adverb
— **pho·nol·o·gist** \fə-'nä-lə-jist, fō-\ noun

**pho·non** \'fō-ˌnän\ noun [phon- + ²-on] (1932)
: a quantum of vibrational energy (as in a crystal)

**pho·no·tac·tics** \ˌfo-nə-'tak-tiks\ noun plural but singular in construction (1956)
: the area of phonology concerned with the analysis and description of the permitted sound sequences of a language
— **pho·no·tac·tic** \-tik\ adjective

¹**pho·ny** or **pho·ney** \'fō-nē\ adjective **pho·ni·er; -est** [perhaps alteration of fawney gilded brass ring used in the fawney rig, a confidence game, from Irish fáinne ring, from Old Irish ánne — more at ANUS] (1900)
: not genuine or real: as **a** (1) : intended to deceive or mislead (2) : intended to defraud : COUNTERFEIT ⟨a phony $10 bill⟩ ⟨a phony check⟩ **b** : arousing suspicion : probably dishonest ⟨something phony about the story⟩ **c** : having no genuine existence : FICTITIOUS ⟨phony publicity stories⟩ **d** : FALSE, SHAM ⟨a phony name⟩ ⟨phony pearls⟩ **e** : making a false show: as (1) : HYPOCRITICAL (2) : SPECIOUS ⟨has a phony poetic elegance —New Republic⟩
— **pho·ni·ly** \'fō-ni-lē\ adverb
— **pho·ni·ness** \'fō-nē-nəs\ noun

²**phony** or **phoney** noun, plural **pho·nies** (1902)
: one that is phony

³**phony** or **phoney** transitive verb **pho·nied** or **pho·neyed; pho·ny·ing** or **pho·ney·ing** (circa 1942)
: COUNTERFEIT, FAKE — often used with up ⟨a paper phonied up on the spur of the moment —William Faulkner⟩

**-phony** also **-phonia** noun combining form [Middle English -phonie, from Old French, from Latin -phonia, from Greek -phōnia, from -phōnos sounding — more at -PHONE]
**1** : sound ⟨telephony⟩
**2** usually **-phonia** : speech disorder of a (specified) type ⟨dysphonia⟩

**phoo·ey** \'fü-ē\ interjection (1929)
— used to express repudiation or disgust

**pho·rate** \'fōr-ˌāt, 'fȯr-\ noun [phosphorus + thioate (salt of a thio acid)] (1959)
: a very toxic organophosphate systemic insecticide $C_7H_{17}O_2PS_3$ that is used especially in seed treatments

**-phore** noun combining form [New Latin -phorus, from Greek -phoros, from -phoros (adjective combining form) carrying, from pherein to carry — more at BEAR]
: carrier ⟨gametophore⟩

**-phoresis** noun combining form, plural **-phoreses** [New Latin, from Greek phorēsis act of carrying, from phorein to carry, wear, frequentative of pherein]
: transmission ⟨electrophoresis⟩

**phos·gene** \'fäz-ˌjēn\ noun [Greek phōs light + -genēs born, produced — more at FANCY, -GEN; from its originally having been obtained by the action of sunlight] (1812)
: a colorless gas $COCl_2$ of unpleasant odor that is a severe respiratory irritant

**phosph-** or **phospho-** combining form [phosphorus]
**1** : phosphorus ⟨phosphide⟩
**2** : phosphate ⟨phosphofructokinase⟩

**phos·pha·tase** \'fäs-fə-ˌtās, -ˌtāz\ noun (1912)
: an enzyme that accelerates the hydrolysis and synthesis of organic esters of phosphoric acid and the transfer of phosphate groups to other compounds: **a** : ALKALINE PHOSPHATASE **b** : ACID PHOSPHATASE

**phos·phate** \'fäs-ˌfāt\ noun [French, from acide phosphorique phosphoric acid] (1795)
**1 a** (1) : a salt or ester of a phosphoric acid (2) : the trivalent anion $PO_4^{3-}$ derived from phosphoric acid $H_3PO_4$ **b** : an organic compound of phosphoric acid in which the acid group is bound to nitrogen or a carboxyl group in a way that permits useful energy to be released (as in metabolism)
**2** : an effervescent drink of carbonated water with a small amount of phosphoric acid flavored with fruit syrup
**3** : a phosphatic material used for fertilizers

**phosphate rock** noun (1870)
: a rock that consists largely of calcium phosphate usually together with other minerals (as calcium carbonate), is used in making fertilizers, and is a source of phosphorus compounds

**phos·phat·ic** \fäs-'fa-tik, -'fā-\ adjective (1843)
: of, relating to, or containing phosphoric acid or phosphates ⟨phosphatic fertilizers⟩

**phos·pha·tide** \'fäs-fə-ˌtīd\ noun [International Scientific Vocabulary] (1884)
: PHOSPHOLIPID
— **phos·pha·tid·ic** \ˌfäs-fə-'ti-dik\ adjective

**phos·pha·ti·dyl** \ˌfäs-fə-'tī-dºl, fäs-'fa-tə-dºl\ noun (1941)
: any of several univalent groups $(RCOO)_2C_3H_5OPO(OH)$ that are derived from phosphatidic acids

**phos·pha·ti·dyl·cho·line** \ˌfäs-fə-ˌtī-dºl-'kō-ˌlēn, (ˌ)fäs-ˌfa-tə-dºl-\ noun (1954)
: LECITHIN

**phos·pha·ti·dyl·eth·a·nol·amine** \-ˌe-thə-'nä-lə-ˌmēn, -'nō-\ noun (1942)
: any of a group of phospholipids that occur especially in blood plasma and the white matter of the central nervous system — called also cephalin

**phos·pha·tize** \'fäs-fə-ˌtīz\ transitive verb **-tized; -tiz·ing** (1883)
**1** : to change to a phosphate or phosphates
**2** : to treat with phosphoric acid or a phosphate
— **phos·pha·ti·za·tion** \ˌfäs-fə-tə-'zā-shən, -ˌfā-\ noun

**phos·pha·tu·ria** \ˌfäs-fə-'tùr-ē-ə, -'tyùr-\ noun [New Latin, from International Scientific Vocabulary phosphate + New Latin -uria] (1876)
: the excessive discharge of phosphates in the urine

**phos·phene** \'fäs-ˌfēn\ noun [International Scientific Vocabulary phos- + Greek phainein to show — more at FANCY] (circa 1860)
: a luminous impression due to excitation of the retina

**phos·phide** \-ˌfīd\ noun [International Scientific Vocabulary] (1849)
: a binary compound of phosphorus with a more electropositive element or group

**phos·phine** \-ˌfēn\ noun [International Scientific Vocabulary] (1873)
**1** : a colorless poisonous flammable gas $PH_3$ that is a weaker base than ammonia and that is used especially to fumigate stored grain
**2** : any of various derivatives of phosphine analogous to amines but weaker as bases

**phos·phite** \-ˌfīt\ noun (1799)
: a salt or ester of phosphorous acid

**phos·pho·cre·a·tine** \ˌfäs-(ˌ)fō-'krē-ə-ˌtēn\ noun [International Scientific Vocabulary] (1927)
: a compound $C_4H_{10}N_3O_5P$ of creatine and phosphoric acid that is found especially in vertebrate muscle where it is an energy source for muscle contraction

**phos·pho·di·es·ter·ase** \-dī-'es-tə-ˌrās, -ˌrāz\ noun (1936)
: a phosphatase (as from snake venom) that acts on diesters (as some nucleotides) to hydrolyze only one of the two ester groups

**phos·pho·enol·pyr·uvate** \ˌfäs-fō-ə-ˌnȯl-pī-'rü-ˌvāt, -ˌnōl-, -ˌpīr-'yü-\ noun (1956)
: a salt or ester of phosphoenolpyruvic acid

**phos·pho·enol·pyr·uvic acid** \-pī-'rü-vik-, -ˌpīr-'yü-vik-\ noun (1959)
: the phosphate $H_2C=C(OPO_3H_2)COOH$ of the enol form of pyruvic acid that is formed as an intermediate in carbohydrate metabolism

**phos·pho·fruc·to·ki·nase** \ˌfäs-(ˌ)fō-ˌfrak-tō-'kī-ˌnās, -ˌfrük-, -frük-, -ˌnāz\ noun [phosph- + fructose + kinase] (1947)
: an enzyme that functions in carbohydrate metabolism and especially in glycolysis by catalyzing the transfer of a second phosphate (as from ATP) to fructose

**phos·pho·glu·co·mu·tase** \-ˌglü-kō-'myü-ˌtās, -ˌtāz\ noun (1938)
: an enzyme that is found in all plant and animal cells and that catalyzes the reversible isomerization of glucose-1-phosphate to glucose-6-phosphate

**phos·pho·glyc·er·al·de·hyde** \-ˌgli-sə-'ral-də-ˌhīd\ noun (1941)
: a phosphate of glyceraldehyde $C_3H_5O_3$-$(H_2PO_3)$ that is formed especially in anaerobic metabolism of carbohydrates by the splitting of a diphosphate of fructose

**phos·pho·glyc·er·ate** \ˌfäs-fō-'gli-sə-ˌrāt\ noun (1901)
: a salt or ester of phosphoglyceric acid

**phos·pho·glyc·er·ic acid** \-gli-'ser-ik-\ noun (1857)
: either of two isomeric phosphates HOOCC₃-$H_3(OH)OPO_3H_2$ of glyceric acid that are formed as intermediates in photosynthesis and in carbohydrate metabolism

**phos·pho·ki·nase** \ˌfäs-fō-'kī-ˌnās, -ˌnāz\ noun (1946)
: KINASE

**phos·pho·li·pase** \-'lī-ˌpās, -ˌpāz\ noun (1945)
: any of several enzymes that hydrolyze lecithins or phosphatidylethanolamines — called also lecithinase

**phos·pho·lip·id** \-'li-pəd\ noun (1928)
: any of numerous lipids (as lecithins and phosphatidylethanolamines) in which phosphoric acid as well as a fatty acid is esterified to glycerol and which are found in all living cells and in the bilayers of plasma membranes

**phos·pho·mono·es·ter·ase** \-ˌmä-nō-'es-tə-ˌrās, -ˌrāz\ noun (1933)
: a phosphatase that acts on monoesters

**phos·pho·ni·um** \fäs-'fō-nē-əm\ noun [New Latin] (1871)

---

: a univalent cation PH₄⁺ analogous to ammonium and derived from phosphine; *also* : an organic derivative of phosphonium (as (C₂H₅)₄P⁺)

**phos·pho·pro·tein** \ˌfäs-fō-ˈprō-ˌtēn, -ˈprō-tē-ən\ *noun* (circa 1908)
: any of various proteins (as casein) that contain combined phosphoric acid

**phos·phor** \ˈfäs-fər, -ˌfȯr\ *also* **phos·phore** \-ˌfȯr, -ˌfȯr, -fər\ *noun* [Latin *phosphorus*, from Greek *phōsphoros*, literally, light bringer, from *phōsphoros* light-bearing, from *phōs* light + *pherein* to carry, bring — more at FANCY, BEAR] (1705)
: a phosphorescent substance; *specifically* : a substance that emits light when excited by radiation

**phosphor bronze** *noun* (1875)
: a bronze of great hardness, elasticity, and toughness that contains a small amount of phosphorus

**phos·pho·resce** \ˌfäs-fə-ˈres\ *intransitive verb* **-resced; -resc·ing** [probably back-formation from *phosphorescent*] (1794)
: to exhibit phosphorescence

**phos·pho·res·cence** \-ˈre-sᵊn(t)s\ *noun* (1796)
1 : luminescence that is caused by the absorption of radiation at one wavelength followed by delayed reradiation at a different wavelength and that continues for a noticeable time after the incident radiation stops — compare FLUORESCENCE
2 : an enduring luminescence without sensible heat

**phos·pho·res·cent** \-sᵊnt\ *adjective* (1766)
: exhibiting phosphorescence
— **phos·pho·res·cent·ly** *adverb*

**phos·phor·ic** \fäs-ˈfȯr-ik, -ˈfär-; ˈfäs-f(ə-)rik\ *adjective* (1800)
: of, relating to, or containing phosphorus especially with a valence higher than in phosphorous compounds

**phosphoric acid** *noun* (1791)
1 : a syrupy or deliquescent tribasic acid H₃PO₄ used especially in preparing phosphates (as for fertilizers), in rust-proofing metals, and especially formerly as a flavoring in soft drinks — called also *orthophosphoric acid*
2 : a compound (as pyrophosphoric acid or metaphosphoric acid) consisting of phosphate groups linked directly to each other by oxygen

**phos·pho·rite** \ˈfäs-fə-ˌrīt\ *noun* (1796)
1 : a fibrous concretionary apatite
2 : PHOSPHATE ROCK
— **phos·pho·rit·ic** \ˌfäs-fə-ˈri-tik\ *adjective*

**phos·pho·rol·y·sis** \ˌfäs-fə-ˈrä-lə-səs\ *noun* [New Latin] (1937)
: a reversible reaction analogous to hydrolysis in which phosphoric acid functions in a manner similar to that of water with the formation of a phosphate (as glucose-1-phosphate in the breakdown of liver glycogen)
— **phos·pho·ro·lyt·ic** \-rō-ˈli-tik\ *adjective*

**phos·pho·rous** \ˈfäs-f(ə-)rəs; fäs-ˈfȯr-əs, -ˈfȯr-\ *adjective* (1815)
: of, relating to, or containing phosphorus especially with a valence lower than in phosphoric compounds

**phosphorous acid** *noun* (1794)
: a deliquescent crystalline acid H₃PO₃ used especially as a reducing agent and in making phosphites

**phos·pho·rus** \ˈfäs-f(ə-)rəs\ *noun, often attributive* [New Latin, from Greek *phōsphoros* light-bearing — more at PHOSPHOR] (1645)
1 : a phosphorescent substance or body; *especially* : one that shines or glows in the dark
2 : a nonmetallic element of the nitrogen family that occurs widely especially as phosphates — see ELEMENT table

**phos·pho·ryl** \ˈfäs-fə-ˌril\ *noun* [International Scientific Vocabulary] (1871)
: a usually trivalent group PO

**phos·phor·y·lase** \fäs-ˈfȯr-ə-ˌlās, -ˌlāz\ *noun* (1939)
: any of the enzymes that catalyze phosphorolysis with the formation of organic phosphates

**phos·phor·y·late** \-ˌlāt\ *transitive verb* **-lat·ed; -lat·ing** (1937)
: to cause (an organic compound) to take up or combine with phosphoric acid or a phosphorus-containing group
— **phos·phor·y·la·tive** \-ˌlā-tiv\ *adjective*

**phos·phor·y·la·tion** \ˌfäs-ˌfȯr-ə-ˈlā-shən\ *noun* (1925)
: the process of phosphorylating a chemical compound either by reaction with inorganic phosphate or by transfer of phosphate from another organic phosphate; *especially* : the enzymatic conversion of carbohydrates into their phosphoric esters in metabolic processes

**phot-** *or* **photo-** *combining form* [Greek *phōt-, phōto-*, from *phōt-, phōs* — more at FANCY]
1 : light : radiant energy ⟨*photon*⟩ ⟨*photo*graphy⟩
2 : photograph : photographic ⟨*photo*engraving⟩
3 : photoelectric ⟨*photo*cell⟩

**pho·tic** \ˈfō-tik\ *adjective* (1843)
1 : of, relating to, or involving light especially in relation to organisms
2 : penetrated by light especially of the sun ⟨the *photic* zone of the ocean⟩
— **pho·ti·cal·ly** \ˈfō-ti-k(ə-)lē\ *adverb*

**¹pho·to** \ˈfō-(ˌ)tō\ *noun, plural* **photos** (1860)
: PHOTOGRAPH

**²photo** *verb* (1868)
: PHOTOGRAPH

**³photo** *adjective* (1889)
: PHOTOGRAPHIC 1

**pho·to·au·to·troph** \ˌfō-tō-ˈȯ-tə-ˌtrōf\ *noun* (1949)
: a photoautotrophic organism

**pho·to·au·to·tro·phic** \-ˌȯ-tə-ˈtrō-fik\ *adjective* (1943)
: autotrophic and utilizing energy from light ⟨green plants are *photoautotrophic*⟩
— **pho·to·au·to·tro·phi·cal·ly** \-fi-k(ə-)lē\ *adverb*

**pho·to·bi·ol·o·gy** \ˌfō-tō-(ˌ)bī-ˈä-lə-jē\ *noun* [International Scientific Vocabulary] (1935)
: a branch of biology that deals with the effects on living beings of radiant energy (as light)
— **pho·to·bi·o·log·i·cal** \-ˌbī-ə-ˈlä-ji-kəl\ *also* **pho·to·bi·o·log·ic** \-ˈlä-jik\ *adjective*
— **pho·to·bi·ol·o·gist** \-(ˌ)bī-ˈä-lə-jist\ *noun*

**pho·to·cath·ode** \-ˈka-ˌthōd\ *noun* [International Scientific Vocabulary] (1930)
: a cathode that emits electrons when exposed to radiant energy and especially light

**pho·to·cell** \ˈfō-tə-ˌsel\ *noun* [International Scientific Vocabulary] (1891)
: PHOTOELECTRIC CELL

**pho·to·chem·i·cal** \ˌfō-tō-ˈke-mi-kəl\ *adjective* (1859)
1 : of, relating to, or resulting from the chemical action of radiant energy and especially light ⟨*photochemical* smog⟩
2 : of or relating to photochemistry ⟨*photochemical* studies⟩
— **pho·to·chem·i·cal·ly** \-k(ə-)lē\ *adverb*

**pho·to·chem·is·try** \-ˈke-mə-strē\ *noun* (1867)
1 : a branch of chemistry that deals with the effect of radiant energy in producing chemical changes
2 **a** : photochemical properties ⟨the *photochemistry* of gases⟩ **b** : photochemical processes ⟨*photochemistry* of vision⟩
— **pho·to·chem·ist** \-ˈke-mist\ *noun*

**pho·to·chro·mic** \ˌfō-tə-ˈkrō-mik\ *adjective* [*phot-* + *chrom-* + *¹-ic*] (1953)
1 : capable of changing color on exposure to radiant energy (as light) ⟨*photochromic* glass⟩

2 : of, relating to, or utilizing the change of color shown by a photochromic substance ⟨a *photochromic* process⟩
— **pho·to·chro·mism** \-ˌmi-zəm\ *noun*

**pho·to·co·ag·u·la·tion** \-kō-ˌa-gyə-ˈlā-shən\ *noun* (1961)
: a surgical process of coagulating tissue by means of a precisely oriented high-energy light source (as a laser)

**pho·to·com·pose** \ˌfō-tō-kəm-ˈpōz\ *transitive verb* (1929)
: to set (as reading matter) by photocomposition
— **pho·to·com·pos·er** *noun*

**pho·to·com·po·si·tion** \-ˌkäm-pə-ˈzi-shən\ *noun* (1929)
: composition of text directly on film or photosensitive paper for reproduction

**pho·to·con·duc·tive** \-kən-ˈdək-tiv\ *adjective* (1929)
: having, involving, or operating by photoconductivity

**pho·to·con·duc·tiv·i·ty** \-ˌkän-ˌdək-ˈti-və-tē, -kən-\ *noun* (1929)
: electrical conductivity that is affected by exposure to electromagnetic radiation (as light)

**¹pho·to·copy** \ˈfō-tə-ˌkä-pē\ *noun* [International Scientific Vocabulary] (circa 1909)
: a photographic reproduction of graphic matter

**²photocopy** (1944)
*transitive verb*
: to make a photocopy of
*intransitive verb*
: to make a photocopy
— **pho·to·cop·i·er** *noun*

**pho·to·cur·rent** \ˈfō-tō-ˌkər-ənt, -ˌkə-rənt\ *noun* (1913)
: a stream of electrons produced by photoelectric or photovoltaic effects

**pho·to·de·com·po·si·tion** \-ˌdē-ˌkäm-pə-ˈzi-shən\ *noun* (1888)
: chemical breaking down (as of a pesticide) by means of radiant energy

**pho·to·de·grad·able** \-di-ˈgrā-də-bəl\ *adjective* (1971)
: chemically degradable by the action of light ⟨*photodegradable* plastics⟩

**pho·to·de·tec·tor** \-di-ˈtek-tər\ *noun* (1947)
: any of various devices for detecting and measuring the intensity of radiant energy through photoelectric action

**pho·to·di·ode** \-ˈdī-ˌōd\ *noun* (1945)
: a photoelectric semiconductor device for detecting and often measuring radiant energy (as light)

**pho·to·dis·in·te·gra·tion** \-di-ˌsin-tə-ˈgrā-shən\ *noun* (1935)
: disintegration of the nucleus of an atom caused by absorption of radiant energy (as light)
— **pho·to·dis·in·te·grate** \-ˈsin-tə-ˌgrāt\ *transitive verb*

**pho·to·dis·so·ci·a·tion** \-di-ˌsō-sē-ˈā-shən, -shē-\ *noun* (1925)
: dissociation of the molecules of a substance (as water) caused by absorption of radiant energy
— **pho·to·dis·so·ci·ate** \-ˈsō-sē-ˌāt, -shē-\ *verb*

**pho·to·du·pli·ca·tion** \-ˌdü-plə-ˈkā-shən, -ˌdyü-\ *noun* (1941)
: the process of making photocopies
— **pho·to·du·pli·cate** \-ˈdü-plə-ˌkāt, -ˈdyü-\ *verb*
— **pho·to·du·pli·cate** \-pli-kət\ *noun*

**pho·to·dy·nam·ic** \-(ˌ)dī-ˈna-mik\ *adjective* [International Scientific Vocabulary] (1909)
: of, relating to, or having the property of intensifying or inducing a toxic reaction to light (as in the destruction of cancer cells stained with a light-sensitive dye) in a living system
— **pho·to·dy·nam·i·cal·ly** \-mi-k(ə-)lē\ *adverb*

**pho·to·elec·tric** \,fō-tō-i-'lek-trik\ *adjective* [International Scientific Vocabulary] (circa 1879)
**:** involving, relating to, or utilizing any of various electrical effects due to the interaction of radiation (as light) with matter
— **pho·to·elec·tri·cal·ly** \-tri-k(ə-)lē\ *adverb*

**photoelectric cell** *noun* (1891)
**:** an electronic device whose electrical properties are modified by the action of light

**photoelectric effect** *noun* (1892)
**:** the emission of free electrons from a metal surface when light strikes it

**pho·to·elec·tron** \,fō-tō-i-'lek-,trän\ *noun* [International Scientific Vocabulary] (1912)
**:** an electron released in photoemission
— **pho·to·elec·tron·ic** \-,lek-'trä-nik\ *adjective*

**pho·to·emis·sion** \-i-'mi-shən\ *noun* (1916)
**:** the release of electrons from a usually solid material (as a metal) by means of energy supplied by incidence of radiation and especially light
— **pho·to·emis·sive** \-'mi-siv\ *adjective*

**pho·to·en·grave** \-in-'grāv\ *transitive verb* [back-formation from *photoengraving*] (1892)
**:** to make a photoengraving of
— **pho·to·en·grav·er** *noun*

**pho·to·en·grav·ing** *noun* (1872)
**1 :** a photomechanical process for making linecuts and halftone cuts by photographing an image on a metal plate and then etching
**2 a :** a plate made by photoengraving **b :** a print made from such a plate

**pho·to·es·say** \'fō-tō-,e-,sā\ *noun* (1944)
**:** a group of photographs (as in a book or magazine) arranged to explore a theme or tell a story

**pho·to·ex·ci·ta·tion** \,fō-tō-,ek-,sī-'tā-shən, -,ek-sə-\ *noun* (1918)
**:** the process of exciting the atoms or molecules of a substance by the absorption of radiant energy
— **pho·to·ex·cit·ed** \-ik-'sī-təd, -ek-\ *adjective*

**photo finish** *noun* (1936)
**1 :** a race in which contestants are so close that a photograph of them as they cross the finish line has to be examined to determine the winner
**2 :** a close contest

**pho·to·fin·ish·er** \,fō-tō-'fi-ni-shər\ *noun* (circa 1934)
**:** one who develops and prints photographic film commercially
— **pho·to·fin·ish·ing** \-shiŋ\ *noun*

**pho·to·flash** \'fō-tō-,flash\ *noun* (1930)
**:** FLASH 6f

**pho·to·flood** \-,fləd\ *noun* (1933)
**:** an electric lamp that provides intense sustained illumination for taking photographs

**pho·to·flu·o·rog·ra·phy** \-flù-'rä-grə-fē, -flò-, -flō-\ *noun* (1941)
**:** the photography of the image produced on a fluorescent screen by X rays

**pho·tog** \fə-'täg\ *noun* [short for *photographer*] (circa 1906)
**:** one who takes photographs **:** PHOTOGRAPHER

**pho·to·ge·nic** \,fō-tə-'je-nik, -'jē-\ *adjective* (1839)
**1 :** produced or precipitated by light ⟨*photogenic* dermatitis⟩
**2 :** producing or generating light **:** PHOSPHORESCENT ⟨*photogenic* bacteria⟩
**3 :** suitable for being photographed ⟨a *photogenic* smile⟩
— **pho·to·ge·ni·cal·ly** \-ni-k(ə-)lē\ *adverb*

**pho·to·ge·ol·o·gy** \,fō-tō-jē-'ä-lə-jē\ *noun* (1941)
**:** a branch of geology concerned with the identification and study of geological features through the study of aerial or orbital photographs
— **pho·to·geo·log·ic** \-,jē-ə-'lä-jik\ *also* **pho·to·geo·log·i·cal** \-ji-kəl\ *adjective*

— **pho·to·ge·ol·o·gist** \-'ä-lə-jist\ *noun*

**pho·to·gram** \'fō-tə-,gram\ *noun* [International Scientific Vocabulary] (1859)
**:** a shadowlike photograph made by placing objects between light-sensitive paper and a light source

**pho·to·gram·me·try** \,fō-tə-'gra-mə-trē\ *noun* [International Scientific Vocabulary *photogram* photograph (from *phot-* + *-gram*) + *-metry*] (1875)
**:** the science of making reliable measurements by the use of photographs and especially aerial photographs (as in surveying)
— **pho·to·gram·met·ric** \-grə-'me-trik\ *adjective*
— **pho·to·gram·me·trist** \-'gra-mə-trist\ *noun*

**¹pho·to·graph** \'fō-tə-,graf\ *noun* (1839)
**:** a picture or likeness obtained by photography

**²photograph** (1839)
*transitive verb*
**:** to take a photograph of
*intransitive verb*
**1 :** to take a photograph
**2 :** to appear as an image in a photograph ⟨an actress who *photographs* well⟩

**pho·tog·ra·pher** \fə-'tä-grə-fər\ *noun* (1847)
**:** one who practices photography; *especially* **:** one who makes a business of taking photographs

**pho·to·graph·ic** \,fō-tə-'gra-fik\ *adjective* (1839)
**1 :** relating to, obtained by, or used in photography
**2 :** representing nature and human beings with the exactness of a photograph
**3 :** capable of retaining vivid impressions ⟨a *photographic* mind⟩
— **pho·to·graph·i·cal·ly** \-fi-k(ə-)lē\ *adverb*

**pho·tog·ra·phy** \fə-'tä-grə-fē\ *noun* (1839)
**:** the art or process of producing images on a sensitized surface (as a film) by the action of radiant energy and especially light

**pho·to·gra·vure** \,fō-tə-grə-'vyùr\ *noun* [French, from *phot-* + *gravure*] (1879)
**:** a process for printing from an intaglio plate prepared by photographic methods

**pho·to·in·duced** \,fō-tō-in-'düst, -'dyüst\ *adjective* (1947)
**:** induced by the action of light
— **pho·to·in·duc·tion** \-'dək-shən\ *noun*
— **pho·to·in·duc·tive** \-'dək-tiv\ *adjective*

**pho·to·in·ter·pre·ta·tion** \-in-,tər-prə-'tā-shən, -pə-\ *noun* (1923)
**:** the science of identifying and describing objects in photographs
— **pho·to·in·ter·pret·er** \-in-'tər-prə-tər, -pə-\ *noun*

**pho·to·ion·i·za·tion** \-,ī-ə-nə-'zā-shən\ *noun* (1914)
**:** ionization (as in the ionosphere) of a molecule or atom caused by absorption of radiant energy
— **pho·to·ion·ize** \-'ī-ə-,nīz\ *transitive verb*

**pho·to·jour·nal·ism** \,fō-tō-'jər-nºl-,i-zəm\ *noun* (1938)
**:** journalism in which written copy is subordinate to pictorial usually photographic presentation of news stories or in which a high proportion of pictorial presentation is used
— **pho·to·jour·nal·ist** \-nºl-ist\ *noun*
— **pho·to·jour·nal·is·tic** \-,jər-nºl-'is-tik\ *adjective*

**pho·to·ki·ne·sis** \-kə-'nē-səs, -kī-\ *noun* [New Latin] (1905)
**:** motion or activity induced by light
— **pho·to·ki·net·ic** \-'ne-tik\ *adjective*

**pho·to·li·thog·ra·phy** \-li-'thä-grə-fē\ *noun* [International Scientific Vocabulary] (1856)
**1 :** lithography in which photographically prepared plates are used
**2 :** a process involving the photographic transfer of a pattern to a surface for etching (as in producing an integrated circuit)

— **pho·to·lith·o·graph** \-'li-thə-,graf\ *noun or transitive verb*
— **pho·to·lith·o·graph·ic** \-,li-thə-'gra-fik\ *adjective*
— **pho·to·lith·o·graph·i·cal·ly** \-fi-k(ə-)lē\ *adverb*

**pho·tol·y·sis** \fō-'tä-lə-səs\ *noun* [New Latin] (1911)
**:** chemical decomposition by the action of radiant energy
— **pho·to·lyt·ic** \,fō-tºl-'i-tik\ *adjective*
— **pho·to·lyt·i·cal·ly** \-ti-k(ə-)lē\ *adverb*

**pho·to·lyze** \'fō-tºl-,īz\ *transitive verb* **-lyzed; -lyz·ing** (1936)
**:** to cause to undergo photolysis
— **pho·to·lyz·able** \-,ī-zə-bəl\ *adjective*

**pho·to·map** \'fō-tō-,map\ *noun* (1939)
**:** a photograph which is taken vertically from above (as from an airplane) and upon which a grid and data pertinent to maps have been added
— **photomap** *verb*

**pho·to·mask** \-,mask\ *noun* (1965)
**:** MASK 2d

**pho·to·me·chan·i·cal** \,fō-tō-mi-'ka-ni-kəl\ *adjective* [International Scientific Vocabulary] (circa 1889)
**:** relating to or involving any of various processes for producing printed matter from a photographically prepared surface
— **pho·to·me·chan·i·cal·ly** \-ni-k(ə-)lē\ *adverb*

**pho·tom·e·ter** \fō-'tä-mə-tər\ *noun* [New Latin *photometrum*, from *phot-* + *-metrum* -meter] (1778)
**:** an instrument for measuring luminous intensity, luminous flux, illumination, or brightness

**pho·to·met·ric** \,fō-tə-'me-trik\ *adjective* (circa 1828)
**:** of or relating to photometry or the photometer
— **pho·to·met·ri·cal·ly** \-tri-k(ə-)lē\ *adverb*

**pho·tom·e·try** \fō-'tä-mə-trē\ *noun* [New Latin *photometria*, from *phot-* + *-metria* -metry] (1824)
**:** a branch of science that deals with measurement of the intensity of light; *also* **:** the practice of using a photometer

**pho·to·mi·cro·graph** \,fō-tə-'mī-krə-,graf\ *noun* (1858)
**:** a photograph of a microscope image
— **pho·to·mi·cro·graph·ic** \-,mī-krə-'gra-fik\ *adjective*
— **pho·to·mi·crog·ra·phy** \-mī-'krä-grə-fē\ *noun*

**pho·to·mon·tage** \-män-'täzh, -mōⁿ(n)-, -'tàzh\ *noun* [International Scientific Vocabulary] (1931)
**:** montage using photographic images; *also* **:** a picture made by photomontage

**pho·to·mor·pho·gen·e·sis** \,fō-tə-,mòr-fə-'je-nə-səs\ *noun* [New Latin] (1959)
**:** plant morphogenesis controlled by radiant energy (as light)
— **pho·to·mor·pho·gen·ic** \-'je-nik\ *adjective*

**pho·to·mo·sa·ic** \-mō-'zā-ik\ *noun* (1942)
**:** a photographic mosaic; *especially* **:** one composed of aerial or orbital photographs

**pho·to·mul·ti·pli·er tube** \,fō-tō-'məl-tə-,plī(-ə)r-\ *noun* (1941)
**:** a vacuum tube that detects light especially from dim sources through the use of photoemission and successive instances of secondary emission to produce enough electrons to generate a useful current — called also *photomultiplier*

**pho·to·mu·ral** \-'myùr-əl\ *noun* (1927)

---

\ə\ abut \ᵊ\ kitten \ər\ further \a\ ash \ā\ ace
\ä\ mop, mar \aù\ out \ch\ chin \e\ bet \ē\ easy
\g\ go \i\ hit \ī\ ice \j\ job \ŋ\ sing \ō\ go
\ò\ law \òi\ boy \th\ thin \t̷h\ the \ü\ loot \ù\ foot
\y\ yet \zh\ vision *see also* Guide to Pronunciation

: an enlarged photograph usually several yards long used on walls especially as decoration

**pho·ton** \'fō-,tän\ noun [phot- + ²-on] (1916)
**1** : a unit of intensity of light at the retina equal to the illumination received per square millimeter of a pupillary area from a surface having a brightness of one candle per square meter
**2** : a quantum of electromagnetic radiation
— **pho·ton·ic** \fō-'tä-nik\ adjective

**pho·to·neg·a·tive** \,fō-tō-'ne-gə-tiv\ adjective (1914)
: exhibiting negative phototropism or phototaxis

**pho·ton·ics** \fō-'tä-niks\ noun plural but singular in construction (1952)
: a branch of physics that deals with the properties and applications of photons especially as a medium for transmitting information

**pho·to·nu·cle·ar** \,fō-tō-'nü-klē-ər, -'nyü-, ÷-kyə-lər\ adjective (1941)
: relating to or caused by the incidence of radiant energy (as gamma rays) on atomic nuclei

**pho·to·off·set** \-'of-,set\ noun (1926)
: offset printing from photolithographic plates

**photo opportunity** noun (1972)
: a situation or event that lends itself to and is often arranged expressly for the taking of pictures that favorably publicize the individuals photographed

**pho·to·ox·i·da·tion** \-,äk-sə-'dā-shən\ noun (1888)
: oxidation under the influence of radiant energy (as light)
— **pho·to·ox·i·da·tive** \-'äk-sə-,dā-tiv\ adjective
— **pho·to·ox·i·dize** \-'äk-sə-,dīz\ verb

**pho·to·pe·ri·od** \-'pir-ē-əd\ noun (1920)
: a recurring cycle of light and dark periods of constant length; also : PHOTOPHASE 2
— **pho·to·pe·ri·od·ic** \-,pir-ē-'ä-dik\ adjective
— **pho·to·pe·ri·od·i·cal·ly** \-di-k(ə-)lē\ adverb

**pho·to·pe·ri·od·ism** \-'pir-ē-ə-,di-zəm\ noun (circa 1911)
: a plant or animal's response or capacity to respond to photoperiod

**pho·to·phase** \'fō-tə-,fāz\ noun (1944)
**1** : LIGHT REACTION
**2** : the light period of a photoperiodic cycle of light and dark

**pho·to·pho·bia** \,fō-tə-'fō-bē-ə\ noun [New Latin] (circa 1799)
: intolerance to light; especially : painful sensitiveness to strong light

**pho·to·pho·bic** \-'fō-bik\ adjective (1858)
**1 a** : shunning or avoiding light **b** : growing best under reduced illumination
**2** : of or relating to photophobia

**pho·to·phore** \'fō-tə-,fōr, -,for\ noun [International Scientific Vocabulary] (1898)
: a light-emitting organ; especially : one of the luminous spots on various marine mostly deep-sea fishes

**pho·to·phos·phor·y·la·tion** \'fō-tō-,fäs-,fōr-ə-'lā-shən\ noun (1956)
: the synthesis of ATP from ADP and phosphate that occurs in a plant using radiant energy absorbed during photosynthesis

**phot·opic** \fōt-'ō-pik, -'ä-pik\ adjective [New Latin photopia, from phot- + -opia] (1915)
: relating to or being vision in bright light with light-adapted eyes that is mediated by the cones of the retina

**pho·to·play** \'fō-tō-,plā\ noun (1910)
: MOTION PICTURE 2

**pho·to·po·la·rim·e·ter** \,fō-tō-,pō-lə-'ri-mə-tər\ noun (circa 1890)
: an instrument used to measure the intensity and polarization of reflected light (as from clouds enveloping a planet)

**pho·to·poly·mer** \,fō-tō-'pä-lə-mər\ noun (1932)
: a photosensitive plastic used especially in the manufacture of printing plates

**pho·to·pos·i·tive** \-'pä-zə-tiv, -'päz-tiv\ adjective (1914)
: exhibiting positive phototropism or phototaxis

**pho·to·prod·uct** \-'prä-(,)dəkt\ noun (1926)
: a product of a photochemical reaction

**pho·to·pro·duc·tion** \-prə-'dək-shən\ noun (1949)
: the production of elementary particles (as mesons) as a result of the action of photons on atomic nuclei

**pho·to·re·ac·tion** \-rē-'ak-shən\ noun (1909)
: a photochemical reaction

**pho·to·re·ac·ti·va·tion** \-rē-,ak-tə-'vā-shən\ noun (1949)
: repair of DNA (as of a bacterium) especially by a light-dependent enzymatic reaction after damage by ultraviolet irradiation
— **pho·to·re·ac·ti·vat·ing** \-'ak-tə-,vā-tiŋ\ adjective

**photo–realism** noun (1961)
: realism in painting characterized by extremely meticulous depiction of detail
— **photo–realist** noun or adjective

**pho·to·re·cep·tion** \-ri-'sep-shən\ noun (1902)
: perception of waves in the range of visible light; specifically : VISION
— **pho·to·re·cep·tive** \-'sep-tiv\ adjective

**pho·to·re·cep·tor** \-'sep-tər\ noun (1906)
: a receptor for light stimuli

**pho·to·re·con·nais·sance** \-ri-'kä-nə-zən(t)s also -sən(t)s\ noun (1940)
: reconnaissance in which aerial photographs are taken

**pho·to·re·duc·tion** \-ri-'dək-shən\ noun (1888)
: chemical reduction under the influence of radiant energy (as light) : photochemical reduction
— **pho·to·re·duce** \-ri-'düs, -'dyüs\ transitive verb

**pho·to·re·pro·duc·tion** \-,rē-prə-'dək-shən\ noun (1939)
: reproduction by photographic means; also : PHOTOCOPY

**pho·to·re·sist** \'fō-tō-ri-,zist, ,fō-tō-ri-'\ noun (1953)
: a photosensitive resin that loses its resistance to chemical etching when exposed to radiation and is used especially in the transference of a circuit pattern to a semiconductor chip during the production of an integrated circuit

**pho·to·res·pi·ra·tion** \,fō-tō-,res-pə-'rā-shən\ noun (1945)
: oxidation involving production of carbon dioxide during photosynthesis

**pho·to·sen·si·tive** \-'sen(t)-s(ə-)tiv\ adjective (1886)
: sensitive or sensitized to the action of radiant energy
— **pho·to·sen·si·tiv·i·ty** \-,sen(t)-sə-'ti-və-tē\ noun

**pho·to·sen·si·ti·za·tion** \-,sen(t)-s(ə-)tə-'zā-shən\ noun (circa 1923)
**1** : the process of photosensitizing
**2** : the condition of being photosensitized; especially : the development of an abnormal capacity to react to sunlight typically by edematous swelling and dermatitis

**pho·to·sen·si·tize** \-'sen(t)-sə-,tīz\ transitive verb (circa 1923)
: to make sensitive to the influence of radiant energy and especially light
— **pho·to·sen·si·tiz·er** noun

**pho·to·set** \'fō-tō-,set\ transitive verb -set; -set·ting (1957)
: PHOTOCOMPOSE
— **pho·to·set·ter** noun

**pho·to·sphere** \'fō-tə-,sfir\ noun (1664)
**1** : a sphere of light or radiance
**2** : the luminous surface layer of the sun or a star
— **pho·to·spher·ic** \,fō-tə-'sfir-ik, -'sfer-\ adjective

**pho·to·stat** \'fō-tə-,stat\ transitive verb (1914)
: to copy by a Photostat device

**Photostat** trademark
— used for a device for making a photographic copy of graphic matter

**pho·to·stat·ic** \,fō-tə-'sta-tik\ adjective (1919)
: of, made by, or using a Photostat device ⟨a photostatic copy⟩ ⟨a photostatic process⟩

**pho·to·syn·thate** \,fō-tō-'sin-,thāt\ noun [photosynthesis + ¹-ate] (1913)
: a product of photosynthesis

**pho·to·syn·the·sis** \-'sin(t)-thə-səs\ noun [New Latin] (1898)
: synthesis of chemical compounds with the aid of radiant energy and especially light; especially : formation of carbohydrates from carbon dioxide and a source of hydrogen (as water) in the chlorophyll-containing tissues of plants exposed to light
— **pho·to·syn·the·size** \-,sīz\ intransitive verb
— **pho·to·syn·thet·ic** \-sin-'the-tik\ adjective
— **pho·to·syn·thet·i·cal·ly** \-ti-k(ə-)lē\ adverb

**pho·to·sys·tem** \'fō-tō-,sis-təm\ noun (1964)
: either of two photochemical reactions occurring in chloroplasts: **a** : one that proceeds best in long wavelength light — called also photosystem I **b** : one that proceeds best in short wavelength light — called also photosystem II

**pho·to·tac·tic** \,fō-tō-'tak-tik\ adjective [International Scientific Vocabulary] (1882)
: of, relating to, or exhibiting phototaxis
— **pho·to·tac·ti·cal·ly** \-ti-kə-lē\ adverb

**pho·to·tax·is** \-'tak-səs\ noun [New Latin] (circa 1890)
: a taxis in which light is the directive factor

**pho·to·te·leg·ra·phy** \-tə-'le-grə-fē\ noun [International Scientific Vocabulary] (1886)
: FACSIMILE 2

**pho·to·tox·ic** \-'täk-sik\ adjective (1942)
**1** : rendering the skin susceptible to damage (as sunburn or blisters) upon exposure to light and especially ultraviolet light
**2** : induced by a phototoxic substance
— **pho·to·tox·ic·i·ty** \-,täk-'si-sə-tē\ noun

**pho·to·tro·pic** \,fō-tə-'trō-pik, -'trä-\ adjective (circa 1890)
: of, relating to, or capable of phototropism
— **pho·to·tro·pi·cal·ly** \-pi-k(ə-)lē\ adverb

**pho·tot·ro·pism** \fō-'tä-trə-,pi-zəm\ noun [International Scientific Vocabulary] (1899)
: a tropism in which light is the orienting stimulus

**pho·to·tube** \'fō-tō-,tüb, -,tyüb\ noun (1930)
: an electron tube having a photoemissive cathode whose released electrons are drawn to the anode by reason of its positive potential

**pho·to·type·set·ting** \,fō-tō-'tīp-,se-tiŋ\ noun (1931)
: PHOTOCOMPOSITION; especially : photocomposition done on a keyboard or tape-operated composing machine
— **pho·to·type·set·ter** noun

**pho·to·vol·ta·ic** \-väl-'tā-ik, -vōl-\ adjective [International Scientific Vocabulary] (circa 1890)
: of, relating to, or utilizing the generation of a voltage when radiant energy falls on the boundary between dissimilar substances (as two different semiconductors)
— **photovoltaic** noun

**phrag·mo·plast** \'frag-mō-,plast\ noun [International Scientific Vocabulary phragmo- (from Greek phragmos fence, from phrassein to enclose) + -plast] (1912)
: the enlarged barrel-shaped spindle that is characteristic of the later stages of plant mitosis and within which the cell plate forms

**phras·al** \'frā-zəl\ adjective (1871)

: of, relating to, or consisting of a phrase ⟨*phrasal* prepositions⟩
— **phras·al·ly** \-zə-lē\ *adverb*

**¹phrase** \'frāz\ *noun* [Latin *phrasis*, from Greek, from *phrazein* to point out, explain, tell] (1530)
**1 :** a characteristic manner or style of expression **:** DICTION
**2 a :** a brief expression; *especially* **:** CATCHWORD **b :** WORD
**3 :** a short musical thought typically two to four measures long closing with a cadence
**4 :** a word or group of words forming a syntactic constituent with a single grammatical function ⟨an adverbial *phrase*⟩
**5 :** a series of dance movements comprising a section of a pattern

**²phrase** *transitive verb* **phrased; phrasing** (1570)
**1 a :** to express in words or in appropriate or telling terms **b :** to designate by a descriptive word or phrase
**2 :** to divide into melodic phrases

**phrase book** *noun* (1594)
: a book containing idiomatic expressions of a foreign language and their translation

**phrase·mak·er** \'frāz-,mā-kər\ *noun* (1822)
**1 :** one who coins impressive phrases
**2 :** one given to making fine-sounding but often hollow and meaningless phrases
— **phrase·mak·ing** \-kiŋ\ *noun*

**phrase·mon·ger** \-,məŋ-gər, -,mäŋ-\ *noun* (1815)
: PHRASEMAKER 2
— **phrase·mon·ger·ing** \-g(ə-)riŋ\ *noun*

**phra·se·o·log·i·cal** \,frā-zē-ə-'lä-ji-kəl\ *adjective* (1664)
**1 a :** expressed in formal often sententious phrases **b :** marked by frequently insincere use of such phrases
**2 :** of or relating to phraseology

**phra·se·ol·o·gist** \,frā-zē-'ä-lə-jist, frā-'zä-\ *noun* (1713)
: one who uses sententious or insincere phrases

**phra·se·ol·o·gy** \-jē\ *noun, plural* **-gies** [New Latin *phraseologia*, irregular from Greek *phrasis* + *-logia* -logy] (1664)
**1 :** a manner of organizing words and phrases into longer elements **:** STYLE
**2 :** choice of words

**phras·ing** \'frā-ziŋ\ *noun* (1611)
**1 :** style of expression **:** PHRASEOLOGY
**2 :** the act, method, or result of grouping notes into musical phrases

**phra·try** \'frā-trē\ *noun, plural* **phratries** [Greek *phratria*, from *phratēr* member of the same clan, member of a phratry — more at BROTHER] (1833)
**1 :** a kinship group forming a subdivision of a Greek phyle
**2 :** a tribal subdivision; *specifically* **:** an exogamous group typically comprising several totemic clans

**phre·at·ic** \frē-'a-tik\ *adjective* [Greek *phreat-, phrear* well; akin to Armenian *albiwr* spring, Old High German *brunno* — more at BURN] (circa 1890)
**1 :** of, relating to, or being groundwater
**2 :** of, relating to, or being an explosion caused by steam derived from groundwater

**phre·at·o·phyte** \frē-'a-tə-,fīt\ *noun* [Greek *phreat-, phrear* well + English *-o-* + *-phyte*] (1920)
: a deep-rooted plant that obtains its water from the water table or the layer of soil just above it
— **phre·at·o·phyt·ic** \-,a-tə-'fi-tik\ *adjective*

**phre·net·ic** *variant of* FRENETIC

**-phrenia** *noun combining form* [New Latin, from Greek *phren-, phrēn* diaphragm, mind]
: disordered condition of mental functions ⟨hebe*phrenia*⟩

**phren·ic** \'fre-nik\ *adjective* [New Latin *phrenicus*, from Greek *phren-, phrēn*] (1704)

**1 :** of or relating to the diaphragm
**2 :** of or relating to the mind

**phre·nol·o·gy** \fri-'nä-lə-jē\ *noun* [Greek *phren-, phrēn*] (1805)
: the study of the conformation of the skull based on the belief that it is indicative of mental faculties and character
— **phre·no·log·i·cal** \,fre-nᵊl-'ä-ji-kəl, ,frē-\ *adjective*
— **phre·nol·o·gist** \fri-'nä-lə-jist\ *noun*

**phren·sy** *variant of* FRENZY

**Phry·gian** \'fri-j(ē-)ən\ *noun* (15th century)
**1 :** a native or inhabitant of ancient Phrygia
**2 :** the extinct Indo-European language of the Phrygians — see INDO-EUROPEAN LANGUAGES table
— **Phrygian** *adjective*

**phthal·ic acid** \'tha-lik-\ *noun* [International Scientific Vocabulary, short for obsolete *naphthalic acid*, from *naphthalene*] (1857)
: any of three isomeric acids $C_8H_6O_4$ obtained by oxidation of various benzene derivatives

**phthalic anhydride** *noun* (1855)
: a crystalline cyclic acid anhydride $C_8H_4O_3$ used especially in making alkyd resins

**phtha·lo·cy·a·nine** \,tha-lō-'sī-ə-,nēn, ,thä-\ *noun* [International Scientific Vocabulary *phthalic acid* + *-o-* + *cyanine*] (1933)
: a bright greenish blue crystalline compound $C_{32}H_{18}N_8$; *also* **:** any of several metal derivatives that are brilliant fast blue to green dyes or pigments

**phthis·ic** \'ti-zik\ *noun* [Middle English *tisike*, from Middle French *tisique*, from *tisique* tubercular, from Latin *phthisicus*, from Greek *phthisikos*, from *phthisis*] (14th century)
: PHTHISIS
— **phthisic** *or* **phthis·i·cal** \-zi-kəl\ *adjective*

**phthi·sis** \'thī-səs, 'tī-, 'fthī-* or with* i *for* ī\ *noun, plural* **phthi·ses** \-,sēz\ [Latin, from Greek, from *phthinein* to waste away; akin to Sanskrit *kṣinoti* he destroys] (1526)
: a progressively wasting or consumptive condition; *especially* **:** pulmonary tuberculosis

**phyco-** *combining form* [Greek *phykos* seaweed]
: algae ⟨*phyco*logy⟩

**phy·co·cy·a·nin** \,fī-kō-'sī-ə-nən\ *noun* [International Scientific Vocabulary *phyco-* + *cyan-* + *¹-in*] (1875)
: any of various bluish green protein pigments in the cells of blue-green algae

**phy·co·er·y·thrin** \-'er-i-thrən\ *noun* [International Scientific Vocabulary *phyco-* + *erythr-* + *¹-in*] (circa 1868)
: any of the red protein pigments in the cells of red algae

**phy·col·o·gy** \fī-'kä-lə-jē\ *noun* (circa 1847)
: ALGOLOGY
— **phy·co·log·i·cal** \,fī-kə-'lä-ji-kəl\ *adjective*
— **phy·col·o·gist** \fī-'kä-lə-jist\ *noun*

**phy·co·my·cete** \,fī-kō-'mī-,sēt, -,mī-'sēt\ *noun* [ultimately from Greek *phykos* + *mykēt-, mykēs* fungus — more at MYC-] (circa 1900)
: any of a large class (Phycomycetes) of lower fungi that are in many respects similar to algae and are now often assigned to subdivisions (Mastigomycotina and Zygomycotina)
— **phy·co·my·ce·tous** \-,mī-'sē-təs\ *adjective*

**phyl-** *or* **phylo-** *combining form* [Latin, from Greek, from *phylē, phylon*; akin to Greek *phyein* to bring forth — more at BE]
: tribe **:** race **:** phylum ⟨*phylo*geny⟩

**phy·lac·tery** \fə-'lak-t(ə-)rē\ *noun, plural* **-ter·ies** [Middle English *philaterie*, from Medieval Latin *philaterium*, alteration of Late Latin *phylacterium*, from Greek *phylaktērion* amulet, phylactery, from *phylassein* to guard, from *phylak-, phylax* guard] (14th century)
**1 :** either of two small square leather boxes containing slips inscribed with scriptural passages and traditionally worn on the left arm

and on the head by Jewish men during morning weekday prayers
**2 :** AMULET

**phylactery 1**

**phy·le** \'fī-(,)lē\ *noun, plural* **phy·lae** \-,lē\ [Greek *phylē* tribe, phyle] (1863)
: the largest political subdivision among the ancient Athenians

**phy·let·ic** \fī-'le-tik\ *adjective* [International Scientific Vocabulary *phyl-* + *-etic* (as in *genetic*)] (1881)
: of or relating to evolutionary change in a single line of descent without branching
— **phy·let·i·cal·ly** \-ti-k(ə-)lē\ *adverb*

**phyll-** *or* **phyllo-** *combining form* [New Latin, from Greek, from *phyllon* — more at BLADE]
: leaf ⟨*phyllo*me⟩

**-phyll** *noun combining form* [New Latin *-phyllum*, from Greek *phyllon* leaf]
: leaf ⟨sporo*phyll*⟩

**phyl·la·ry** \'fi-lə-rē\ *noun, plural* **-ries** [New Latin *phyllarium*, from Greek *phyllarion*, diminutive of *phyllon* leaf] (1857)
: one of the involucral bracts subtending the flower head of a composite plant

**phyl·lo** \'fē-(,)lō, 'fī-\ *noun* [New Greek, sheet of pastry dough, literally, leaf, from Greek *phyllon*] (circa 1950)
: extremely thin pastry dough that is layered to produce a flaky pastry

**phyl·lo·clade** \'fi-lə-,klād\ *noun* [New Latin *phyllocladium*, from *phyll-* + Greek *klados* branch — more at HOLT] (1858)
: a flattened stem or branch (as a joint of a cactus) that functions as a leaf

**phyl·lode** \'fi-,lōd\ *noun* [New Latin *phyllodium*, from Greek *phyllōdēs* like a leaf, from *phyllon* leaf] (1848)
: a flat expanded petiole that replaces the blade of a foliage leaf, fulfills the same functions, and is analogous to a cladophyll

**phyl·lo·di·um** \fi-'lō-dē-əm\ *noun, plural* **-dia** \-dē-ə\ [New Latin] (circa 1847)
: PHYLLODE

**phyl·lome** \'fi-,lōm\ *noun* [International Scientific Vocabulary] (1875)
: a plant part that is a leaf or is phylogenetically derived from a leaf

**phyl·lo·tac·tic** \,fi-lə-'tak-tik\ *adjective* (1857)
: of or relating to phyllotaxis

**phyl·lo·tax·is** \,fi-lə-'tak-səs\ *also* **phyl·lo·taxy** \'fi-lə-,tak-sē\ *noun* [New Latin *phyllotaxis*, from *phyll-* + *-taxis*] (1857)
**1 :** the arrangement of leaves on a stem and in relation to one another
**2 :** the study of phyllotaxis and of the laws that govern it

**-phyllous** *adjective combining form* [New Latin *-phyllus*, from Greek *-phyllos*, from *phyllon* leaf — more at BLADE]
: having (such or so many) leaves, leaflets, or leaflike parts ⟨hetero*phyllous*⟩

**phyl·lox·e·ra** \,fi-,läk-'sir-ə, fə-'läk-sə-rə\ *noun* [New Latin, from *phyll-* + Greek *xēros* dry] (1868)
: any of various plant lice (especially genus *Phylloxera*) that differ from aphids especially in wing structure and in being continuously oviparous

**phy·lo·ge·net·ic** \,fī-lō-jə-'ne-tik\ *adjective* [International Scientific Vocabulary, from New

\ə\ **abut** \ᵊ\ **kitten** \ər\ **further** \a\ **ash** \ā\ **ace** \ä\ **mop, mar** \au̇\ **out** \ch\ **chin** \e\ **bet** \ē\ **easy** \g\ **go** \i\ **hit** \ī\ **ice** \j\ **job** \ŋ\ **sing** \ō\ **go** \o̊\ **law** \o̊i\ **boy** \th\ **thin** \t̶h̶\ **the** \ü\ **loot** \u̇\ **foot** \y\ **yet** \zh\ **vision** *see also* Guide to Pronunciation

Latin *phylogenesis* phylogeny, from *phyl-* + *genesis*] (1877)
**1 :** of or relating to phylogeny
**2 :** based on natural evolutionary relationships
**3 :** acquired in the course of phylogenetic development **:** RACIAL
— **phy·lo·ge·net·i·cal·ly** \-ti-k(ə-)lē\ *adverb*

**phy·log·e·ny** \fī-'lä-jə-nē\ *noun, plural* **-nies** [International Scientific Vocabulary] (1872)
**1 :** the evolutionary history of a kind of organism
**2 :** the evolution of a genetically related group of organisms as distinguished from the development of the individual organism
**3 :** the history or course of the development of something (as a word or custom)

**phy·lum** \'fī-ləm\ *noun, plural* **phy·la** \-lə\ [New Latin, from Greek *phylon* tribe, race — more at PHYL-] (1876)
**1 a :** a direct line of descent within a group **b :** a group that constitutes or has the unity of a phylum; *especially* **:** one of the usually primary divisions of the animal kingdom
**2 :** a group of languages related more remotely than those of a family or stock

**phys ed** \'fiz-'ed\ *noun* (1955)
**:** PHYSICAL EDUCATION

**physi-** *or* **physio-** *combining form* [Latin, from Greek, from *physis* — more at PHYSICS]
**1 :** nature ⟨*physio*graphy⟩
**2 :** physical ⟨*physio*therapy⟩

**phys·iat·rist** \,fī-zē-'a-trist\ *noun* [*physiatrics* physical medicine, from Greek *physis* + International Scientific Vocabulary *-iatrics*] (circa 1947)
**:** a physician who specializes in physical medicine

**¹phys·ic** \'fi-zik\ *noun* [Middle English *physik* natural science, art of medicine, from Old French *fisique*, from Latin *physica*, singular, natural science, from Greek *physikē*, from feminine of *physikos* — more at PHYSICS] (14th century)
**1 a :** the art or practice of healing disease **b :** the practice or profession of medicine
**2 :** a medicinal agent or preparation; *especially* **:** PURGATIVE
**3** *archaic* **:** NATURAL SCIENCE

**²physic** *transitive verb* **phys·icked; phys·ick·ing** (14th century)
**1 :** to treat with or administer medicine to; *especially* **:** PURGE
**2 :** HEAL, CURE

**¹phys·i·cal** \'fi-zi-kəl\ *adjective* [Middle English *phisicale* medical, from Medieval Latin *physicalis*, from Latin *physica*] (1597)
**1 a :** having material existence **:** perceptible especially through the senses and subject to the laws of nature ⟨everything *physical* is measurable by weight, motion, and resistance —Thomas De Quincey⟩ **b :** of or relating to material things
**2 a :** of or relating to natural science **b** (1) **:** of or relating to physics (2) **:** characterized or produced by the forces and operations of physics
**3 a :** of or relating to the body **b :** concerned or preoccupied with the body and its needs **:** CARNAL **c :** characterized by especially rugged and forceful physical activity **:** ROUGH ⟨a *physical* hockey game⟩ ⟨a *physical* player⟩
**synonym** see MATERIAL
— **phys·i·cal·ly** \-k(ə-)lē\ *adverb*
— **phys·i·cal·ness** \-kəl-nəs\ *noun*

**²physical** *noun* (1934)
**:** PHYSICAL EXAMINATION

**physical anthropology** *noun* (1873)
**:** anthropology concerned with the comparative study of human evolution, variation, and classification especially through measurement and observation — compare CULTURAL ANTHROPOLOGY
— **physical anthropologist** *noun*

**physical education** *noun* (1830)

**:** instruction in the development and care of the body ranging from simple calisthenic exercises to a course of study providing training in hygiene, gymnastics, and the performance and management of athletic games

**physical examination** *noun* (1884)
**:** an examination of the bodily functions and condition of an individual

**physical geography** *noun* (1808)
**:** geography that deals with the exterior physical features and changes of the earth

**phys·i·cal·ism** \'fi-zi-kə,li-zəm\ *noun* (circa 1931)
**:** a thesis that the descriptive terms of scientific language are reducible to terms which refer to spatiotemporal things or events or to their properties
— **phys·i·cal·ist** \-list\ *noun*
— **phys·i·cal·is·tic** \,fi-zi-kə-'lis-tik\ *adjective*

**phys·i·cal·i·ty** \,fi-zə-'ka-lə-tē\ *noun, plural* **-ties** (1660)
**1 :** intensely physical orientation **:** predominance of the physical usually at the expense of the mental, spiritual, or social
**2 :** a physical aspect or quality

**physical medicine** *noun* (1939)
**:** a branch of medicine concerned with the diagnosis and treatment of disease and disability by physical means (as radiation, heat, and electricity) — compare PHYSICAL THERAPY

**physical science** *noun* (1802)
**:** any of the natural sciences (as physics, chemistry, and astronomy) that deal primarily with nonliving materials
— **physical scientist** *noun*

**physical therapy** *noun* (1922)
**:** the treatment of disease by physical and mechanical means (as massage, regulated exercise, water, light, heat, and electricity)
— **physical therapist** *noun*

**phy·si·cian** \fə-'zi-shən\ *noun* [Middle English *fisicien*, from Old French, from *fisique* medicine] (13th century)
**1 :** a person skilled in the art of healing; *specifically* **:** a doctor of medicine
**2 :** one exerting a remedial or salutary influence

**physician's assistant** *noun* (1970)
**:** a person certified to provide basic medical services usually under the supervision of a licensed physician — called also *PA, physician assistant*

**phys·i·cist** \'fi-zə-sist, 'fiz-sist\ *noun* (1840)
**1 :** a specialist in physics
**2** *archaic* **:** a person skilled in natural science

**phys·i·co·chem·i·cal** \,fi-zi-kō-'ke-mi-kəl\ *adjective* (1664)
**1 :** being physical and chemical
**2 :** of or relating to chemistry that deals with the physicochemical properties of substances
— **phys·i·co·chem·i·cal·ly** \-k(ə-)lē\ *adverb*

**phys·ics** \'fi-ziks\ *noun plural but singular or plural in construction* [Latin *physica*, plural, natural science, from Greek *physika*, from neuter plural of *physikos* of nature, from *physis* growth, nature, from *phyein* to bring forth — more at BE] (1715)
**1 :** a science that deals with matter and energy and their interactions
**2 a :** the physical processes and phenomena of a particular system **b :** the physical properties and composition of something

**Phys·io·crat** \'fi-zē-ə-,krat\ *noun* [French *physiocrate*, from *physi-* physi- + *-crate* -crat] (1798)
**:** a member of a school of political economists founded in 18th century France and characterized chiefly by a belief that government policy should not interfere with the operation of natural economic laws and that land is the source of all wealth
— **phys·io·crat·ic** \,fi-zē-ə-'kra-tik\ *adjective, often capitalized*

**phys·i·og·nom·ic** \,fi-zē-ə(g)-'nä-mik\ *also* **phys·i·og·nom·i·cal** \-mi-kəl\ *adjective* (1588)
**:** of, relating to, or characteristic of physiognomy or the physiognomy
— **phys·i·og·nom·i·cal·ly** \-mi-k(ə-)lē\ *adverb*

**phys·i·og·no·my** \,fi-zē-'ä(g)-nə-mē\ *noun, plural* **-mies** [Middle English *phisonomie*, from Middle French, from Late Latin *physiognomonia, physiognomia,* from Greek *physiognōmonia,* from *physiognōmōn* judging character by the features, from *physis* nature, physique, appearance + *gnōmōn* interpreter — more at GNOMON] (14th century)
**1 :** the art of discovering temperament and character from outward appearance
**2 :** the facial features held to show qualities of mind or character by their configuration or expression
**3 :** external aspect; *also* **:** inner character or quality revealed outwardly

**phys·i·og·ra·phy** \,fi-zē-'ä-grə-fē\ *noun* [probably from French *physiographie,* from *physi-* + *-graphie* -graphy] (circa 1828)
**:** PHYSICAL GEOGRAPHY
— **phys·i·og·ra·pher** \-fər\ *noun*
— **phys·io·graph·ic** \,fi-zē-ō-'gra-fik\ *also* **phys·io·graph·i·cal** \-fi-kəl\ *adjective*

**phys·i·o·log·i·cal** \,fi-zē-ə-'lä-ji-kəl\ *or* **phys·i·o·log·ic** \-jik\ *adjective* (1814)
**1 :** of or relating to physiology
**2 :** characteristic of or appropriate to an organism's healthy or normal functioning
**3 :** differing in, involving, or affecting physiological factors ⟨a *physiological* strain of bacteria⟩
— **phys·i·o·log·i·cal·ly** \-ji-k(ə-)lē\ *adverb*

**physiological psychology** *noun* (1888)
**:** a branch of psychology that deals with the effects of normal and pathological physiological processes on mental life — called also *psychophysiology*

**physiological saline** *noun* (1896)
**:** a solution of a salt or salts that is essentially isotonic with tissue fluids or blood

**phys·i·ol·o·gy** \,fi-zē-'ä-lə-jē\ *noun* [Latin *physiologia* natural science, from Greek, from *physi-* + *-logia* -logy] (1597)
**1 :** a branch of biology that deals with the functions and activities of life or of living matter (as organs, tissues, or cells) and of the physical and chemical phenomena involved — compare ANATOMY
**2 :** the organic processes and phenomena of an organism or any of its parts or of a particular bodily process
— **phys·i·ol·o·gist** \-jist\ *noun*

**phys·io·pa·thol·o·gy** \'fi-zē-ō-pə-'thä-lə-jē, -pa-\ *noun* (circa 1889)
**:** a branch of biology or medicine that combines physiology and pathology especially in the study of altered bodily function in disease
— **phys·io·path·o·log·ic** \-,pa-thə-'lä-jik\ *or* **phys·io·path·o·log·i·cal** \-ji-kəl\ *adjective*

**phys·io·ther·a·py** \,fi-zē-ō-'ther-ə-pē\ *noun* [New Latin *physiotherapia,* from *physi-* + *therapia* therapy] (circa 1903)
**:** PHYSICAL THERAPY
— **phys·io·ther·a·pist** \-pist\ *noun*

**phy·sique** \fə-'zēk\ *noun* [French, from *physique* physical, bodily, from Latin *physicus* of nature, from Greek *physikos*] (1813)
**:** the form or structure of a person's body **:** bodily makeup

**phy·so·stig·mine** \,fī-sə-'stig-,mēn\ *noun* [International Scientific Vocabulary, from New Latin *Physostigma,* genus of vines that bear the Calabar bean] (1864)
**:** a crystalline tasteless alkaloid $C_{15}H_{21}N_3O_2$ from the Calabar bean that is used in medicine especially in the form of its salicylate for its anticholinesterase activity

**phyt-** *or* **phyto-** *combining form* [New Latin, from Greek, from *phyton*, from *phyein* to bring forth — more at BE]
: plant ⟨*phyto*phagous⟩

**phy·tane** \'fī-ˌtān\ *noun* (1907)
: an isoprenoid hydrocarbon $C_{20}H_{42}$ that is found especially associated with fossilized plant remains from the Precambrian and later eras

**-phyte** *noun combining form* [International Scientific Vocabulary, from Greek *phyton* plant]
: plant having a (specified) characteristic or habitat ⟨xero*phyte*⟩

**-phytic** *adjective combining form* [International Scientific Vocabulary, from Greek *phyton* plant]
: like a plant ⟨holo*phytic*⟩

**phy·to·alex·in** \ˌfī-tō-ə-'lek-sən\ *noun* [International Scientific Vocabulary *phyt-* + *alexin* substance combating infection, from Greek *alexein* to ward off, protect; akin to Sanskrit *rakṣati* he protects] (1949)
: a chemical substance produced by a plant to combat infection by a pathogen (as a fungus)

**phy·to·chem·i·cal** \-'ke-mi-kəl\ *adjective* (circa 1858)
: of, relating to, or being phytochemistry
— **phy·to·chem·i·cal·ly** \-mi-k(ə-)lē\ *adverb*

**phy·to·chem·is·try** \-'ke-mə-strē\ *noun* (1837)
: the chemistry of plants, plant processes, and plant products
— **phy·to·chem·ist** \-'ke-mist\ *noun*

**phy·to·chrome** \'fī-tə-ˌkrōm\ *noun* (circa 1893)
: a chromoprotein that is present in traces in many plants and that plays a significant role in initiating floral and developmental processes when activated by red or near-infrared radiation

**phy·to·fla·gel·late** \ˌfī-tō-'fla-jə-lət, -ˌlāt; -flə-'jə-\ *noun* (1935)
: any of various organisms (as dinoflagellates) that are considered a subclass (Phytomastigophora synonym Phytomastigina) usually of algae by botanists and of protozoans by zoologists and that have many characteristics in common with typical algae

**phy·to·ge·og·ra·phy** \ˌfī-tō-jē-'ä-grə-fē\ *noun* [International Scientific Vocabulary] (1847)
: the biogeography of plants
— **phy·to·ge·og·ra·pher** \-fər\ *noun*
— **phy·to·geo·graph·i·cal** \-ˌjē-ə-'gra-fi-kəl\ *or* **phy·to·geo·graph·ic** \-fik\ *adjective*
— **phy·to·geo·graph·i·cal·ly** \-fi-k(ə-)lē\ *adverb*

**phy·to·he·mag·glu·ti·nin** \-ˌhē-mə-'glüt-ᵊn-ən\ *noun* (1949)
: a proteinaceous hemagglutinin of plant origin used especially to induce mitosis (as in lymphocytes)

**phy·to·hor·mone** \-'hȯr-ˌmōn\ *noun* [International Scientific Vocabulary] (1933)
: PLANT HORMONE

**phy·ton** \'fī-ˌtän\ *noun* [New Latin, from Greek, plant] (1848)
1 : a structural unit of a plant consisting of a leaf and its associated portion of stem
2 : the smallest part of a stem, root, or leaf that when severed may grow into a new plant
— **phy·ton·ic** \fī-'tä-nik\ *adjective*

**phy·to·path·o·gen** \ˌfī-tō-'pa-thə-jən\ *noun* (circa 1930)
: an organism parasitic on a plant host
— **phy·to·path·o·gen·ic** \-ˌpa-thə-'je-nik\ *adjective*

**phy·to·pa·thol·o·gy** \-pə-'thä-lə-jē, -pa-\ *noun* [International Scientific Vocabulary] (circa 1859)
: plant pathology
— **phy·to·path·o·log·i·cal** \-ˌpa-thə-'lä-ji-kəl\ *adjective*

**phy·toph·a·gous** \fī-'tä-fə-gəs\ *adjective* (1826)
: feeding on plants ⟨a *phytophagous* insect⟩

**phy·to·plank·ter** \ˌfī-tō-'plaŋ(k)-tər\ *noun* (1944)
: a planktonic plant

**phy·to·plank·ton** \-'plaŋ(k)-tən, -ˌtän\ *noun* [International Scientific Vocabulary] (1897)
: planktonic plant life
— **phy·to·plank·ton·ic** \-ˌplaŋ(k)-'tä-nik\ *adjective*

**phy·to·so·ci·ol·o·gy** \-ˌsō-sē-'ä-lə-jē, -shē-\ *noun* (circa 1928)
: a branch of ecology concerned especially with the structure, composition, and interrelationships of plant communities
— **phy·to·so·cio·log·i·cal** \-sē-ə-'lä-ji-kəl\ *adjective*

**phy·tos·ter·ol** \fī-'täs-tə-ˌrȯl, -ˌrōl\ *noun* [International Scientific Vocabulary] (1898)
: any of various sterols derived from plants — compare ZOOSTEROL

**phy·to·tox·ic** \ˌfī-tə-'täk-sik\ *adjective* (1926)
: poisonous to plants
— **phy·to·tox·ic·i·ty** \-ˌtäk-'si-sə-tē\ *noun*

**¹pi** *also* **pie** \'pī\ *noun, plural* **pies** [origin unknown] (circa 1659)
1 : type that is spilled or mixed
2 : a pi character or matrix

**²pi** *also* **pie** *verb* **pied; pi·ing** *or* **pie·ing** (1870)
*transitive verb*
: to spill or throw (type or type matter) into disorder
*intransitive verb*
: to become pied

**³pi** *adjective* (circa 1940)
1 : not intended to appear in final printing ⟨*pi* lines⟩
2 : capable of being inserted only by hand ⟨*pi* characters⟩

**⁴pi** *noun, plural* **pis** \'pīz\ [Middle Greek, from Greek *pei*, of Semitic origin; akin to Hebrew *pē* pe] (1823)
1 : the 16th letter of the Greek alphabet — see ALPHABET table
2 a : the symbol π denoting the ratio of the circumference of a circle to its diameter **b** : the ratio itself : a transcendental number having a value to eight decimal places of 3.14159265

**pi·al** \'pī-əl, 'pē-\ *adjective* (1889)
: of or relating to the pia mater

**pia ma·ter** \'pī-ə-ˌmā-tər, 'pē-ə-ˌmä-\ *noun* [Middle English, from Medieval Latin, from Latin, tender mother] (14th century)
: the thin vascular membrane that invests the brain and spinal cord internal to the arachnoid and dura mater

**pi·a·nism** \'pē-ə-ˌni-zəm\ *noun* (1844)
1 : the art or technique of piano playing
2 : the composition or adaptation of music for the piano

**¹pi·a·nis·si·mo** \ˌpē-ə-'ni-sə-ˌmō\ *adverb or adjective* [Italian, from *piano* softly] (1724)
: very softly — used as a direction in music

**²pianissimo** *noun, plural* **-mi** \-(ˌ)mē\ *or* **-mos**
: a passage played, sung, or spoken very softly

**pi·a·nist** \pē-'a-nist, 'pē-ə-\ *noun* (circa 1828)
: one who plays the piano; *especially* : a skilled or professional performer on the piano

**pi·a·nis·tic** \ˌpē-ə-'nis-tik\ *adjective* (1881)
1 : of, relating to, or characteristic of the piano
2 : skilled in or well adapted to piano playing
— **pi·a·nis·ti·cal·ly** \-ti-k(ə-)lē\ *adverb*

**¹pi·a·no** \pē-'ä-(ˌ)nō\ *adverb or adjective* [Italian, from Late Latin *planus* smooth, from Latin, level — more at FLOOR] (1683)
: at a soft volume : SOFT — used as a direction in music

**²pi·a·no** \pē-'a-(ˌ)nō *also* -'ä-\ *noun, plural* **pi·a·nos** [Italian, short for *pianoforte*, from *gravicembalo col piano e forte*, literally, harpsi-

chord with soft and loud; from the fact that its tones could be varied in loudness] (1803)
: a musical instrument having steel wire strings that sound when struck by felt-covered hammers operated from a keyboard ◆

**piano accordion** *noun* (1860)
: an accordion with a keyboard for the right hand resembling and corresponding to the middle register of a piano keyboard

**pi·ano·forte** \pē-'a-nə-ˌfȯrt, -'ä-, -ˌfȯrt, -ˌfȯr-tē; -ˌa-nə-'fȯr-tē, -ˌä-\ *noun* [Italian] (1767)
1 : FORTEPIANO
2 : PIANO

**word history** see PIANO

**piano hinge** *noun* (1926)
: a hinge that has a thin pin joint and extends along the full length of the part to be moved

**pi·as·sa·va** \ˌpē-ə-'sä-və\ *noun* [Portuguese *piassaba*, from Tupi *piasawa*] (1835)
1 : any of several stiff coarse fibers obtained from palms and used especially in cordage or brushes
2 : a palm yielding piassava; *especially* : either of two Brazilian palms (*Attalia funifera* and *Leopoldinia piassaba*)

**pi·as·tre** *also* **pi·as·ter** \pē-'as-tər, -'äs-\ *noun* [French *piastre*, from Italian *piastra* thin metal plate, coin, from Latin *emplastra, emplastrum* plaster] (1592)
1 : PIECE OF EIGHT
2 — see *pound* at MONEY table

**pi·az·za** \pē-'a-zə, -'ä-, *1 is usually* -'at-sə, -'ät-\ *noun, plural* **piazzas** *or* **pi·az·ze** \-'at-(ˌ)sā, -'ät-\ [Italian, from Latin *platea* broad street — more at PLACE] (1563)
1 *plural* **piazze** : an open square especially in an Italian town
2 **a** : an arcaded and roofed gallery **b** *dialect* : VERANDA, PORCH

**pi·broch** \'pē-ˌbräk, -ˌbräk\ *noun* [Scottish Gaelic *piobaireachd* pipe music] (1719)
: a set of martial or mournful variations for the Scottish Highland bagpipe

**¹pic** \'pik\ *noun, plural* **pics** *or* **pix** \'piks\ [short for *picture*] (1884)
1 : PHOTOGRAPH
2 : MOTION PICTURE

**²pic** \'pik, 'pēk\ *noun* [Spanish *pica*, from *picar* to prick] (1926)
: the picador's lance

**¹pi·ca** \'pī-kə\ *noun* [New Latin, from Latin, magpie — more at PIE] (1563)
: an abnormal desire to eat substances (as chalk or ashes) not normally eaten

---

◇ **WORD HISTORY**
**piano** A harpsichord is played by means of a mechanism that plucks the strings, so it is not possible to achieve fine gradations of loudness. Feeling the need to overcome this drawback, Bartolomeo Cristofori (1655–1731), a Florentine instrument maker, invented a mechanism or action by means of which the strings of the instrument are struck by felt-covered hammers. This device allows the player to produce notes with varying degrees of loudness. In the first published notice of Cristofori's invention in 1711, it was called in Italian *gravicembalo col piano e forte*, "harpsichord with soft and loud." In English the terms *pianoforte* and *fortepiano* were used interchangeably in the 18th century. Eventually, both were largely replaced by *piano*, first attested in 1803, though scholars and performers continue to use *fortepiano* for 18th and early 19th century forms of the instrument.

---

²**pica** *noun* [probably from Medieval Latin, collection of church rules] (1588)
**1 :** 12-point type
**2 :** a unit of about ⅙ inch used in measuring typographic material
**3 :** a typewriter type providing 10 characters to the linear inch and six lines to the vertical inch

**pic·a·dor** \'pi-kə-ˌdȯr, ˌpi-kə-'\ *noun, plural* **picadors** \-ˌdȯrz, -'dȯrz\ *or* **pic·a·do·res** \ˌpi-kə-'dȯr-ēz, ˌdȯr-\ [Spanish, from *picar* to prick, from (assumed) Vulgar Latin *piccare* — more at PIKE] (1797)
**:** a horseman in a bullfight who jabs the bull with a lance to weaken its neck and shoulder muscles

**pi·ca·ra** \'pē-kä-ˌrä\ *noun* [Spanish *pícara*, feminine of *pícaro*] (circa 1930)
**:** a woman who is a rogue

¹**pic·a·resque** \ˌpi-kə-'resk, ˌpē-\ *adjective* [Spanish *picaresco*, from *pícaro*] (1810)
**:** of or relating to rogues or rascals; *also* **:** of, relating to, suggesting, or being a type of fiction dealing with the episodic adventures of a usually roguish protagonist ⟨a *picaresque* novel⟩

²**picaresque** *noun* (1895)
**:** one that is picaresque

**pi·ca·ro** \'pē-kä-ˌrō\ *noun, plural* **-ros** [Spanish *pícaro*] (1623)
**:** ROGUE, BOHEMIAN

¹**pic·a·roon** *or* **pick·a·roon** \ˌpi-kə-'rün\ *noun* [Spanish *picarón*, augmentative of *pícaro*] (1624)
**1 :** PIRATE
**2 :** PICARO

²**picaroon** *intransitive verb* (1675)
**:** to act as a pirate

¹**pic·a·yune** \ˌpi-kē-'yün\ *noun* [Provençal *picaioun*, a small coin, from *picaio* money, from *pica* to jingle, of imitative origin] (1804)
**1 a :** a Spanish half real piece formerly current in the South **b :** HALF DIME
**2 :** something trivial

²**picayune** *adjective* (1836)
**:** of little value **:** PALTRY; *also* **:** PETTY, SMALL-MINDED
— **pic·a·yun·ish** \-'yü-nish\ *adjective*

**pic·ca·lil·li** \ˌpi-kə-'li-lē\ *noun* [probably alteration of *pickle*] (1845)
**:** a relish of chopped vegetables and spices

¹**pic·co·lo** \'pi-kə-ˌlō\ *adjective* [Italian, small] (circa 1854)
**:** smaller than ordinary size ⟨a *piccolo* banjo⟩

²**piccolo** *noun, plural* **-los** [Italian, short for *piccolo flauto* small flute] (1856)
**:** a small shrill flute whose range is an octave higher than that of an ordinary flute
— **pic·co·lo·ist** \-ˌlō-ist\ *noun*

piccolo

**pice** \'pīs\ *noun, plural* **pice** [Hindi *paisā*] (1615)
**:** PAISA

**pi·ce·ous** \'pī-sē-əs\ *adjective* [Latin *piceus*, from *pic-, pix* pitch — more at PITCH] (1826)
**:** of, relating to, or resembling pitch; *especially* **:** glossy brownish black in color ⟨an insect with a *piceous* abdomen⟩

¹**pick** \'pik\ *verb* [Middle English *piken*, partly from (assumed) Old English *pīcian* (akin to Middle Dutch *picken* to prick); partly from Middle French *piquer* to prick — more at PIKE] (14th century)
*transitive verb*
**1 :** to pierce, penetrate, or break up with a pointed instrument ⟨*picked* the hard clay⟩
**2 a :** to remove bit by bit ⟨*pick* meat from bones⟩ **b :** to remove covering or adhering matter from ⟨*pick* the bones⟩
**3 a :** to gather by plucking ⟨*pick* apples⟩ **b :** CHOOSE, SELECT ⟨tried to *pick* the shortest route⟩ ⟨she *picked* out the most expensive

dress⟩ **c :** to make (one's way) slowly and carefully ⟨*picked* his way through the rubble⟩
**4 a :** PILFER, ROB ⟨*pick* pockets⟩ **b :** to obtain useful information from by questioning — used in such phrases as *pick the brains of*
**5 :** PROVOKE ⟨*pick* a quarrel⟩
**6 a :** to dig into **:** PROBE ⟨*pick* his teeth⟩ **b :** to pluck (as a guitar) with a pick or with the fingers **c :** to loosen or pull apart with a sharp point ⟨*pick* wool⟩
**7 :** to unlock with a device (as a wire) other than the key ⟨*pick* a lock⟩
*intransitive verb*
**1 :** to use or work with a pick
**2 :** to gather or harvest something by plucking
**3 :** PILFER — used in the phrase *picking and stealing*
**4 :** to eat sparingly or mincingly ⟨*picking* listlessly at his dinner⟩
— **pick and choose :** to select with care and deliberation
— **pick at :** to criticize repeatedly especially for minor faults **:** NAG
— **pick on :** to single out for criticism, teasing, or bullying ⟨*picked on* smaller boys⟩; *also* **:** to single out for a particular purpose or for special attention

²**pick** *noun* (15th century)
**1 :** a blow or stroke with a pointed instrument
**2 a :** the act or privilege of choosing or selecting **:** CHOICE ⟨take your *pick*⟩ **b :** the best or choicest one ⟨the *pick* of the herd⟩
**3 :** the portion of a crop gathered at one time ⟨the first *pick* of peaches⟩
**4 :** a screen in basketball

³**pick** *noun* [Middle English *pik*] (14th century)
**1 :** a heavy wooden-handled iron or steel tool pointed at one or both ends — compare MATTOCK
**2 a :** TOOTHPICK **b :** PICKLOCK **c :** a small thin piece (as of plastic or metal) used to pluck the strings of a stringed instrument
**3 :** one of the points on the forepart of the blade of a skate used in figure skating
**4 :** a comb with long widely spaced teeth used to give height to a hair style

pick 2c

⁴**pick** *transitive verb* [Middle English *pykken* to pitch (a tent); akin to Middle English *picchen* to pitch] (1523)
**1** *chiefly dialect* **:** to throw or thrust with effort **:** HURL
**2 :** to throw (a shuttle) across the loom

⁵**pick** *noun* (1627)
**1** *dialect English* **a :** the act of pitching or throwing **b :** something thrown
**2 a :** a throw of the shuttle **b :** a filling thread

**pick·a·back** \'pi-gē-ˌbak, 'pi-kə-\ *variant of* PIGGYBACK

**pick–and–roll** \'pik-ən(d)-'rōl\ *noun* (circa 1961)
**:** a basketball play in which a player sets a screen and then cuts toward the basket for a pass

**pick–and–shovel** *adjective* (1895)
**:** done with or as if with a pick and shovel **:** LABORIOUS

**pick·a·nin·ny** *or* **pic·a·nin·ny** \'pi-kə-ˌni-nē, ˌpi-kə-'\ *noun, plural* **-nies** [probably ultimately from Portuguese *pequenino*, diminutive of *pequeno* small] (1653)
**:** a black child — often taken to be offensive

**pick·ax** \'pik-ˌaks\ *noun* [Middle English *pecaxe*, alteration of *pikois*, from Old French *picois*, from *pic* pick, from Latin *picus* woodpecker — more at PIE] (15th century)
**:** ³PICK 1

¹**pick·ed** \'pi-kəd\ *adjective* [Middle English, from ³*pick*] (14th century)
*chiefly dialect* **:** POINTED, PEAKED

²**picked** \'pikt\ *adjective* [¹*pick*] (circa 1548)
**:** CHOICE, PRIME

**pick·eer** \pi-'kir\ *intransitive verb* [probably modification of French *picorer* to maraud, perhaps from Middle French *pecore* sheep, from Old Italian *pecora* — more at PECORINO] (circa 1645)
*archaic* **:** to skirmish in advance of an army; *also* **:** SCOUT, RECONNOITER

**pick·er** \'pi-kər\ *noun* (14th century)
**:** one that picks: as **a :** a worker who picks something (as crops) **b :** a tool, implement, or machine used in picking something **c :** a musician who picks a stringed instrument (as a banjo)

**pick·er·el** \'pi-k(ə-)rəl\ *noun, plural* **-el** *or* **-els** [Middle English *pikerel*, diminutive of *pike*] (13th century)
**1 a** *dialect chiefly British* **:** a young or small pike **b :** either of two fishes resembling but smaller than the related northern pike: (1) **:** CHAIN PICKEREL (2) **:** one (*Esox americanus*) having green or red fins and a black bar below and slanting away from the eye
**2 :** WALLEYE 3

**pick·er·el·weed** \-ˌwēd\ *noun* (1836)
**:** an American shallow-water monocotyledonous plant (*Pontederia cordata* of the family Pontederiaceae) with large leaves and a spike of blue flowers

¹**pick·et** \'pi-kət\ *noun* [French *piquet*, from Middle French, from *piquer* to prick — more at PIKE] (circa 1702)
**1 :** a pointed or sharpened stake, post, or pale
**2 a :** a detached body of soldiers serving to guard an army from surprise **b :** a detachment kept ready in camp for such duty **c :** SENTRY
**3 :** a person posted by a labor organization at a place of work affected by a strike; *also* **:** a person posted for a demonstration or protest

²**picket** (1745)
*transitive verb*
**1 :** to enclose, fence, or fortify with pickets
**2 a :** to guard with a picket **b :** to post as a picket
**3 :** TETHER
**4 a :** to post pickets at **b :** to walk or stand in front of as a picket
*intransitive verb*
**:** to serve as a picket
— **pick·et·er** *noun*

**pick·et·boat** \'pi-kət-ˌbōt\ *noun* (1866)
**:** a craft used (as by the coast guard) for harbor patrol

**picket line** *noun* (1856)
**1 :** a position held by a line of military pickets
**2 :** a line of people picketing a business, organization, or institution

**pick·ings** \'pi-kiŋz, -kənz\ *noun plural* (1642)
**:** something that is picked or picked up: as **a :** gleanable or eatable fragments **:** SCRAPS **b :** yield or return for effort expended

¹**pick·le** \'pi-kəl\ *noun* [Middle English *pekille*] (15th century)
**1 :** a solution or bath for preserving or cleaning: as **a :** a brine or vinegar solution in which foods are preserved **b :** any of various baths used in industrial cleaning or processing
**2 :** a difficult situation **:** PLIGHT ⟨could see no way out of the *pickle* I was in —R. L. Stevenson⟩
**3 :** an article of food that has been preserved in brine or in vinegar; *specifically* **:** a cucumber that has been so preserved
**4** *British* **:** a mischievous or troublesome person

²**pickle** *transitive verb* **pick·led; pick·ling** \-k(ə-)liŋ\ (1570)
**1 :** to treat, preserve, or clean in or with a pickle
**2 :** to give a light finish to (as furniture) by bleaching or painting and wiping

³**pickle** *noun* [perhaps from Scots *pickle* to trifle, pilfer] (1552)
**1** *Scottish* **:** GRAIN, KERNEL
**2** *Scottish* **:** a small quantity

**pickled** *adjective* (circa 1552)

**1 :** preserved in or cured with pickle ⟨*pickled* herring⟩
**2 :** DRUNK 1a ⟨gets thoroughly *pickled* before dinner —*New Yorker*⟩
**pick·lock** \'pik-,läk\ *noun* (1553)
**1 :** BURGLAR
**2 :** a tool for picking locks
**pick–me–up** \'pik-mē-,əp\ *noun* (1867)
**:** something that stimulates or restores **:** TONIC, BRACER
**pick·off** \'pik-,óf\ *noun* (1939)
**:** a baseball play in which a base runner is picked off
**pick off** *transitive verb* (1810)
**1 :** to shoot or bring down especially one by one
**2 :** to put out (a base runner who is off base) with a quick throw (as from the pitcher or catcher)
**3 :** INTERCEPT ⟨*picked off* a pass⟩
**pick out** *transitive verb* (1540)
**1 :** DISCERN, MAKE OUT
**2 :** to play the notes of by ear or one by one ⟨*picking out* tunes on the piano⟩
**pick over** *transitive verb* (1839)
**:** to examine in order to select the best or remove the unwanted
**pick·pock·et** \'pik-,pä-kət\ *noun* (1591)
**:** a thief who picks pockets
**pick·proof** \-,prüf\ *adjective* (1933)
**:** designed to prevent picking ⟨a *pickproof* lock⟩
**pick·thank** \-,thaŋk\ *noun* [from *pick a thank* to seek someone's favor] (15th century)
*archaic* **:** SYCOPHANT
¹**pick·up** \'pik-,əp\ *noun* (1848)
**1 :** one that is picked up: as **a :** a hitchhiker who is given a ride **b :** a temporary chance acquaintance
**2 :** the act or process of picking up: as **a :** a revival of business activity **b :** ACCELERATION
**3 :** the conversion of mechanical movements into electrical impulses in the reproduction of sound; *also* **:** a device (as on a phonograph) for making such conversion
**4 a** (1) **:** the reception of sound or an image into a radio or television transmitting apparatus for conversion into electrical signals (2) **:** interference (as with such reception) from an adjacent electrical circuit or system **b :** a device (as a microphone or a television camera) for converting sound or the image of a scene into electrical signals **c :** the place where a broadcast originates **d :** the electrical system for connecting to a broadcasting station a program produced outside the studio
**5 :** a light truck having an enclosed cab and an open body with low sides and tailgate — called also *pickup truck*
²**pickup** *adjective* (1909)
**:** utilizing or comprising local or available personnel especially without formal organization ⟨a *pickup* basketball game⟩
**pick up** (14th century)
*transitive verb*
**1 a :** to take hold of and lift up **b :** to gather together **:** COLLECT ⟨*picked up* all the pieces⟩ **c :** to clean up **:** TIDY
**2 :** to take (passengers or freight) into a vehicle
**3 a :** to acquire casually or by chance ⟨*picked up* a valuable antique at an auction⟩ **b :** to acquire by study or experience **:** LEARN ⟨*picking up* a great deal of knowledge in the process —Robert Schleicher⟩ **c :** to obtain especially by payment **:** BUY ⟨*picked up* some groceries⟩ **d :** to acquire (a player) especially from another team through a trade or by financial recompense **e :** to accept for the purpose of paying ⟨offered to *pick up* the tab⟩ **f :** to come down with **:** CATCH ⟨*picked up* a cold⟩ **g :** GAIN ⟨*picked up* a few yards on the last play⟩
**4 a :** to enter informally into conversation or companionship with (a previously unknown person) ⟨had a brief affair with a girl he *picked*

*up* in a bar⟩ **b :** to take into custody ⟨the police *picked up* the fugitive⟩
**5 a :** to catch sight of **:** PERCEIVE ⟨*picked up* the harbor lights⟩ **b :** to come to and follow ⟨*picked up* the outlaw's trail⟩ **c :** to bring within range of sight or hearing ⟨*pick up* distant radio signals⟩ **d :** UNDERSTAND, CATCH ⟨didn't *pick up* the hint⟩
**6 a :** REVIVE **b :** INCREASE
**7 :** to resume after a break **:** CONTINUE ⟨*pick up* the discussion tomorrow⟩
**8 :** to assume responsibility for guarding (an opponent) in an athletic contest
*intransitive verb*
**1 :** to recover speed, vigor, or activity **:** IMPROVE ⟨after the strike, business *picked up*⟩
**2 :** to put things in order ⟨was always *picking up* after her⟩
**3 :** to pack up one's belongings ⟨couldn't just *pick up* and leave⟩
**— pick up on 1 a :** UNDERSTAND, APPRECIATE **b :** to become aware of **:** NOTICE **2 :** to adopt as one's own **:** TAKE UP
**Pick·wick·ian** \(,)pik-'wi-kē-ən\ *adjective* [Samuel *Pickwick*, character in the novel *Pickwick Papers* (1836–37) by Charles Dickens] (1836)
**1 :** marked by simplicity and generosity
**2 :** intended or taken in a sense other than the obvious or literal one
**picky** \'pi-kē\ *adjective* **pick·i·er; -est** (1917)
**:** FUSSY, CHOOSY ⟨a *picky* eater⟩
**pi·clo·ram** \'pi-klə-,ram, 'pī-\ *noun* [*pic*oline + *chlor- + amine*] (1965)
**:** a systemic herbicide $C_6H_3Cl_3N_2O_2$ that breaks down only very slowly in the soil
¹**pic·nic** \'pik-(,)nik\ *noun, often attributive* [German or French; German *Picknick*, from French *pique-nique*] (1748)
**1 :** an excursion or outing with food usually provided by members of the group and eaten in the open; *also* **:** the food provided for a picnic
**2 a :** a pleasant or amusingly carefree experience ⟨I don't expect being married to be a *picnic* —Josephine Pinckney⟩ **b :** an easy task or feat
**3 :** a shoulder of pork with much of the butt removed
**— pic·nick·y** \-(,)ni-kē\ *adjective*
²**picnic** *intransitive verb* **pic·nicked; pic·nick·ing** (1842)
**:** to go on a picnic **:** eat in picnic fashion
**— pic·nick·er** *noun*
**pico-** *combining form* [International Scientific Vocabulary, probably from Spanish *pico* small amount, literally, peak, beak]
**1 :** one trillionth ($10^{-12}$) part of ⟨*pico*gram⟩
**2 :** very small ⟨*pico*rnavirus⟩
**pi·co·far·ad** \,pē-kō-'far-,ad, -əd\ *noun* [International Scientific Vocabulary] (circa 1926)
**:** one trillionth of a farad
**pi·co·gram** \'pē-kō-,gram, -kə-\ *noun* [International Scientific Vocabulary] (1951)
**:** one trillionth of a gram
**pic·o·line** \'pi-kə-,lēn, 'pī-\ *noun* [Latin *pic-*, *pix* pitch + International Scientific Vocabulary ¹*-ol* + ²*-ine* — more at PITCH] (1853)
**:** any of the three liquid pyridine bases $C_6H_7N$ used chiefly as solvents and in organic synthesis
**pi·co·mole** \'pē-kō-,mōl, -kə-\ *noun* (1968)
**:** one trillionth of a mole
**pi·cor·na·vi·rus** \(,)pē-,kór-nə-'vī-rəs\ *noun* [*pico-* + *RNA* + *virus*] (1962)
**:** any of a group of small RNA-containing viruses that includes the enteroviruses and rhinoviruses
**pi·co·sec·ond** \,pē-kō-'se-kənd, -kənt\ *noun* [International Scientific Vocabulary] (circa 1962)
**:** one trillionth of a second

¹**pi·cot** \'pē-(,)kō, pē-'\ *noun* [French, literally, small point, from Middle French, from *pic* prick, from *piquer* to prick — more at PIKE] (circa 1882)
**:** one of a series of small ornamental loops forming an edging on ribbon or lace
²**picot** *transitive verb* (1926)
**:** to finish with picots
**pic·o·tee** \,pi-kə-'tē\ *noun* [French *picoté* pointed, from *picoter* to mark with points, from *picot*] (1727)
**:** a flower (as some carnations or tulips) having one basic color with a margin of another color
**picr-** *or* **picro-** *combining form* [French, from Greek *pikr-*, *pikro-*, from *pikros* — more at PAINT]
**:** bitter ⟨*picr*ic acid⟩
**pic·ric acid** \'pi-krik-\ *noun* [International Scientific Vocabulary] (1852)
**:** a toxic explosive yellow crystalline strong acid $C_6H_3N_3O_7$ used especially in high explosives and as a dye
**pic·ro·tox·in** \,pi-krō-'täk-sən\ *noun* [International Scientific Vocabulary] (1815)
**:** a poisonous bitter crystalline stimulant and convulsive drug $C_{30}H_{34}O_{13}$ used intravenously as an antidote for barbiturate poisoning
**Pict** \'pikt\ *noun* [Middle English *Pictes*, plural, Picts, from Old English *Pihtas*, from Late Latin *Picti*] (before 12th century)
**:** a member of a people of the north of Scotland who are first noted in historical records in the late 3d century and who became amalgamated with the Scots in the mid-8th century
**— Pict·ish** \'pik-tish\ *adjective or noun*
**pic·to·gram** \'pik-tə-,gram\ *noun* [International Scientific Vocabulary *picto-* (from Latin *pictus*) + *-gram*] (1910)
**:** PICTOGRAPH
**pic·to·graph** \-,graf\ *noun* [Latin *pictus* + English *-o-* + *-graph*] (1851)
**1 :** an ancient or prehistoric drawing or painting on a rock wall
**2 :** one of the symbols belonging to a pictorial graphic system
**3 :** a diagram representing statistical data by pictorial forms
**— pic·to·graph·ic** \,pik-tə-'gra-fik\ *adjective*
**pic·tog·ra·phy** \pik-'tä-grə-fē\ *noun* (1851)
**:** use of pictographs **:** PICTURE WRITING 1
¹**pic·to·ri·al** \pik-'tōr-ē-əl, -'tór-\ *adjective* [Late Latin *pictorius*, from Latin *pictor* painter] (1646)
**1 :** of or relating to a painter, a painting, or the painting or drawing of pictures ⟨*pictorial* perspective⟩
**2 a :** of, relating to, or consisting of pictures ⟨*pictorial* records⟩ **b :** illustrated by pictures ⟨*pictorial* weekly⟩ **c :** consisting of or displaying the characteristics of pictographs **d :** suggesting or conveying visual images ⟨*pictorial* poetry⟩
**— pic·to·ri·al·ly** \-ē-ə-lē\ *adverb*
**— pic·to·ri·al·ness** *noun*
²**pictorial** *noun* (1844)
**:** a periodical having much pictorial matter
**pic·to·ri·al·ism** \-ē-ə-,li-zəm\ *noun* (1869)
**1 :** the use or creation of pictures or visual images
**2 :** a movement or technique in photography emphasizing artificial often romanticized pictorial qualities
**— pic·to·ri·al·ist** \-list\ *adjective or noun*
**pic·to·ri·al·ize** \pik-'tōr-ē-ə-,līz, -'tór-\ *transitive verb* **-ized; -iz·ing** (1870)
**:** to represent by a picture or illustrate with pictures

\ə\ **abut** \ᵊ\ **kitten** \ər\ **further** \a\ **ash** \ā\ **ace**
\ä\ **mop, mar** \au̇\ **out** \ch\ **chin** \e\ **bet** \ē\ **easy**
\g\ **go** \i\ **hit** \ī\ **ice** \j\ **job** \ŋ\ **sing** \ō\ **go**
\ȯ\ **law** \ȯi\ **boy** \th\ **thin** \t̲h̲\ **the** \ü\ **loot** \u̇\ **foot**
\y\ **yet** \zh\ **vision** *see also* Guide to Pronunciation

— **pic·to·ri·al·i·za·tion** \-ˌtōr-ē-ə-lə-'zā-shən, -ˌtòr-\ *noun*

**¹pic·ture** \'pik-chər\ *noun* [Middle English, from Latin *pictura*, from *pictus*, past participle of *pingere* to paint — more at PAINT] (15th century)
**1 :** a design or representation made by various means (as painting, drawing, or photography)
**2 a :** a description so vivid or graphic as to suggest a mental image or give an accurate idea of something ⟨the book gives a detailed *picture* of what is happening⟩ **b :** a mental image
**3 :** IMAGE, COPY ⟨the *picture* of his father⟩ ⟨the very *picture* of health⟩
**4 a :** a transitory visible image or reproduction **b :** MOTION PICTURE **c** *plural* **:** MOVIES
**5 :** TABLEAU 1, 2 ⟨stage *pictures*⟩
**6 :** SITUATION ⟨took a hard look at his financial *picture*⟩

**²picture** *transitive verb* **pic·tured; pic·tur·ing** \'pik-chə-riŋ, 'pik-shriŋ\ (15th century)
**1 :** to paint or draw a representation, image, or visual conception of **:** DEPICT; *also* **:** ILLUSTRATE
**2 :** to describe graphically in words
**3 :** to form a mental image of **:** IMAGINE

**picture–book** *adjective* (1922)
**:** suitable for or suggestive of a picture book: as **a :** PICTURESQUE **b :** PICTURE-PERFECT

**picture book** *noun* (1847)
**:** a book that consists wholly or chiefly of pictures

**picture hat** *noun* (1887)
**:** a woman's dressy hat with a broad brim

**picture–perfect** *adjective* (1981)
**:** completely flawless **:** PERFECT ⟨made a *picture-perfect* landing⟩

**pic·ture–phone** \'pik-chər-ˌfōn\ *noun* (1956)
**:** VIDEOPHONE

**picture–postcard** *adjective* (1907)
**:** PICTURESQUE, PICTURE-BOOK ⟨a *picture-postcard* village⟩

**picture puzzle** *noun* (1898)
**:** JIGSAW PUZZLE

**pic·tur·esque** \ˌpik-chə-'resk\ *adjective* [French & Italian; French *pittoresque*, from Italian *pittoresco*, from *pittore* painter, from Latin *pictor*, from *pingere*] (1703)
**1 a :** resembling a picture **:** suggesting a painted scene **b :** charming or quaint in appearance
**2 :** evoking mental images **:** VIVID
**synonym** see GRAPHIC
— **pic·tur·esque·ly** *adverb*
— **pic·tur·esque·ness** *noun*

**picture tube** *noun* (1937)
**:** a cathode-ray tube on which the picture appears in a television receiver

**picture window** *noun* (1938)
**:** an outsize usually single-paned window designed to frame an exterior view

**picture writing** *noun* (1741)
**1 :** the recording of events or expression of messages by pictures representing actions or facts
**2 :** the record or message represented by picture writing

**pic·tur·ize** \'pik-chə-ˌrīz\ *transitive verb* **-ized; -iz·ing** (circa 1846)
**:** to make a picture of **:** present in pictures; *especially* **:** to make into a motion picture
— **pic·tur·i·za·tion** \ˌpik-chə-rə-'zā-shən\ *noun*

**pid·dle** \'pi-dᵊl\ *intransitive verb* **pid·dled; pid·dling** \'pid-liŋ, 'pi-dᵊl-iŋ\ [origin unknown] (1545)
**1 :** DAWDLE, PUTTER
**2 :** URINATE

**pid·dling** \'pid-lən, -liŋ; 'pi-dᵊl-ən, -iŋ\ *adjective* (1559)
**:** TRIVIAL, PALTRY

**pid·dock** \'pi-dək, -dik\ *noun* [origin unknown] (1851)
**:** a bivalve mollusk (genus *Pholas* or family Pholadidae) that bores holes in wood, clay, and rocks

**pid·gin** \'pi-jən\ *noun* [*pidgin* English] (1876)
**:** a simplified speech used for communication between people with different languages ◆
— **pid·gin·i·za·tion** \ˌpi-jə-nə-'zā-shən\ *noun*
— **pid·gin·ize** \'pi-jə-ˌnīz\ *transitive verb*

**pidgin English** *noun, often P capitalized* [Chinese Pidgin English *pidgin* business] (1859)
**:** an English-based pidgin; *especially* **:** one originally used in parts of the Orient

**¹pie** \'pī\ *noun* [Middle English, from Old French, from Latin *pica;* akin to Latin *picus* woodpecker, Old High German *speh*] (13th century)
**:** MAGPIE

**²pie** *noun* [Middle English] (14th century)
**1 :** a meat dish baked with biscuit or pastry crust — compare POTPIE
**2 :** a dessert consisting of a filling (as of fruit or custard) in a pastry shell or topped with pastry or both
**3 a :** AFFAIR, BUSINESS ⟨she wanted her finger . . . in every possible social *pie* —Mary Deasy⟩ **b :** a whole regarded as divisible into shares ⟨giving the less fortunate . . . a larger share of the economic *pie* —R. M. Hutchins⟩

**³pie** *variant of* PI

**¹pie·bald** \'pī-ˌbóld\ *adjective* (1594)
**1 :** of different colors; *especially* **:** spotted or blotched with black and white
**2 :** composed of incongruous parts

**²piebald** *noun* (1765)
**:** a piebald animal (as a horse)

**¹piece** \'pēs\ *noun* [Middle English, from Old French, from (assumed) Vulgar Latin *pettia*, of Gaulish origin; akin to Welsh *peth* thing] (13th century)
**1 :** a part of a whole: as **a :** FRAGMENT ⟨*pieces* of broken glass⟩ **b :** any of the individual members comprising a unit — often used in combination ⟨a five-*piece* band⟩ ⟨a three-*piece* suit⟩
**2 :** an object or individual regarded as a unit of a kind or class ⟨a *piece* of fruit⟩
**3 :** a short distance ⟨down the road a *piece*⟩
**4 :** a standard quantity (as of length, weight, or size) in which something is made or sold
**5 :** a literary, journalistic, artistic, dramatic, or musical composition
**6 :** FIREARM
**7 :** COIN; *also* **:** TOKEN
**8 :** a man used in playing a board game; *specifically* **:** a chessman of superior rank
**9 :** OPINION, VIEW ⟨spoke his *piece*⟩
**10 a :** an act of copulation — usually considered vulgar **b :** the female partner in sexual intercourse — usually considered vulgar
**synonym** see PART
— **of a piece :** ALIKE, CONSISTENT
— **piece of one's mind :** a severe scolding **:** TONGUE-LASHING
— **piece of the action :** a share in activity or profit
— **to pieces 1 :** without reserve or restraint **:** COMPLETELY **2 :** into fragments; *also* **:** into component parts **3 :** out of control ⟨went *to pieces* from shock⟩

**²piece** *transitive verb* **pieced; piec·ing** (15th century)
**1 :** to repair, renew, or complete by adding pieces **:** PATCH
**2 :** to join into a whole — often used with *together* ⟨his new book . . . has been *pieced* together from talks —Merle Miller⟩
— **piec·er** *noun*

**piece by piece** *adverb* (1560)
**:** by degrees **:** PIECEMEAL

**pièce de ré·sis·tance** \pē-ˌes-də-rə-ˌzē-'stän(t)s, -ˌrā-, -'stä⁽ⁿ⁾s\ *noun, plural* **pièces de ré·sis·tance** \*same*\ [French, literally, piece of resistance] (1839)
**1 :** the chief dish of a meal
**2 :** an outstanding item or event **:** SHOWPIECE

**piece–dye** \'pēs-ˌdī\ *transitive verb* (1920)
**:** to dye after weaving or knitting

**piece goods** *noun plural* (1665)
**:** cloth fabrics sold from the bolt at retail in lengths specified by the customer — called also *yard goods*

**¹piece–meal** \'pēs-ˌmēl, -'mē(ə)l\ *adverb* (14th century)
**1 :** one piece at a time **:** GRADUALLY
**2 :** in pieces or fragments **:** APART

**²piecemeal** *adjective* (1600)
**:** done, made, or accomplished piece by piece or in a fragmentary way ⟨*piecemeal* reforms in the system⟩

**piece of cake** (1936)
**:** something easily done **:** CINCH, BREEZE

**piece of eight** (1610)
**:** an old Spanish peso of eight reals

**piece of work** (1928)
**:** a complicated, difficult, or eccentric person

**piece·wise** \'pēs-ˌwīz\ *adverb* (1674)
**:** with respect to a number of discrete intervals, sets, or pieces ⟨*piecewise* continuous functions⟩

**piece·work** \-ˌwərk\ *noun* (1549)
**:** work done by the piece and paid for at a set rate per unit
— **piece·work·er** \-ˌwər-kər\ *noun*

**pie chart** *noun* (1922)
**:** a circular chart cut by radii into segments illustrating relative magnitudes or frequencies — called also *circle graph*

**pie-crust** \'pī-ˌkrəst\ *noun* (1582)
**:** the pastry shell of a pie

**¹pied** \'pīd\ *adjective* (14th century)
**:** of two or more colors in blotches; *also* **:** wearing or having a parti-colored coat ⟨a *pied* horse⟩

**²pied** *past and past participle of* PI *or of* PIE

**pied–à–terre** \pē-ˌād-ə-'ter, -ˌād-ä-; ˌpyā-dä-\ *noun, plural* **pieds–à–terre** \*same*\ [French, literally, foot to the ground] (1829)
**:** a temporary or second lodging

**pied·mont** \'pēd-ˌmänt\ *adjective* [*Piedmont,* region of Italy] (1855)
**:** lying or formed at the base of mountains
— **piedmont** *noun*

**pied piper** *noun, often both Ps capitalized* [the *Pied Piper,* hero of a German folktale who charmed the rats of Hameln, Germany, into a river] (1925)
**1 :** one that offers strong but delusive enticement

**2 :** a leader who makes irresponsible promises

**3 :** a charismatic person who attracts followers

**pie–eyed** \'pī-,īd\ *adjective* (1904)

: INTOXICATED

**pie–faced** \-,fāst\ *adjective* (circa 1912)

: having a round, smooth, or blank face

**pieing** *present participle of* PI *or of* PIE

**pie in the sky** (1911)

: an unrealistic enterprise or prospect of prosperity

— **pie–in–the–sky** *adjective*

**pie-plant** \'pī-,plant\ *noun* (circa 1847)

: garden rhubarb

**pier** \'pir\ *noun* [Middle English *per*, from Old English, from Medieval Latin *pera*] (12th century)

**1 :** an intermediate support for the adjacent ends of two bridge spans

**2 :** a structure (as a breakwater) extending into navigable water for use as a landing place or promenade or to protect or form a harbor

**3 :** a vertical structural support: as **a :** the wall between two openings **b :** PILLAR, PILASTER **c** : a vertical member that supports the end of an arch or lintel **d :** an auxiliary mass of masonry used to stiffen a wall

**4 :** a structural mount (as for a telescope) usually of stonework, concrete, or steel

**pierce** \'pirs\ *verb* **pierced; pierc·ing** [Middle English *percen*, from Old French *percer*, from (assumed) Vulgar Latin *pertusiare*, from Latin *pertusus*, past participle of *pertundere* to perforate, from *per-* through + *tundere* to beat — more at PER-, CONTUSION] (14th century)

*transitive verb*

**1 a :** to run into or through as a pointed weapon does : STAB **b :** to enter or thrust into sharply or painfully

**2 :** to make a hole through : PERFORATE

**3 :** to force or make a way into or through

**4 :** to penetrate with the eye or mind : DISCERN

**5 :** to penetrate so as to move or touch the emotions of

*intransitive verb*

: to force a way into or through something

**synonym** see ENTER

**pierced** *adjective* (14th century)

**1 :** having holes; *especially* : decorated with perforations

**2 :** having the earlobe punctured for an earring ⟨*pierced* ears⟩

**3 :** designed for pierced ears ⟨*pierced* earrings⟩

**piercing** *adjective* (14th century)

: PENETRATING: as **a :** LOUD, SHRILL ⟨*piercing* cries⟩ **b :** PERCEPTIVE ⟨*piercing* eyes⟩ **c :** penetratingly cold : BITING ⟨a *piercing* wind⟩ **d** : CUTTING, INCISIVE ⟨*piercing* sarcasm⟩

— **pierc·ing·ly** \'pir-siŋ-lē\ *adverb*

**pier glass** *noun* (1703)

: a large high mirror; *especially* : one designed to occupy the wall space between windows — called also *pier mirror*

**Pi·eri·an** \pī-'ir-ē-ən, -'er-\ *adjective* (1591)

**1 :** of or relating to the region of Pieria in ancient Macedonia or to the Muses who were once worshiped there

**2 :** of or relating to learning or poetry

**pie-ro·gi** *also* **pi·ro·gi** \pə-'rō-gē, pi-\ *noun, plural* **-gi** *also* **-gies** [Polish, plural of *pieróg* dumpling, pierogi] (1927)

: a case of dough filled with a savory filling (as of meat, cheese, or vegetables) and cooked by boiling and then panfrying

**Pier·rot** \'pē-ə-,rō\ *noun* [French, diminutive of *Pierre* Peter] (circa 1770)

: a stock comic character of old French pantomime usually having a whitened face and wearing loose white clothes

**pier table** *noun* (1803)

: a table to be placed under a pier glass

**pies** *plural of* PI *or of* PIE

**pie safe** *noun* (1951)

: a cupboard whose doors have decoratively pierced tin panels for ventilation

**pie·tà** \,pē-(,)ā-'tä, pyä-\ *noun, often capitalized* [Italian, literally, pity, from Latin *pietat-, pietas*] (1644)

: a representation of the Virgin Mary mourning over the dead body of Christ

**pi·e·tism** \'pī-ə-,ti-zəm\ *noun* (1697)

**1** *capitalized* : a 17th century religious movement originating in Germany in reaction to formalism and intellectualism and stressing Bible study and personal religious experience

**2 a :** emphasis on devotional experience and practices **b :** affectation of devotion

— **pi·e·tist** \'pī-ə-tist\ *adjective or noun, often capitalized*

**pi·e·tis·tic** \,pī-ə-'tis-tik\ *adjective* (1830)

**1 :** of or relating to Pietism

**2 a :** of or relating to religious devotion or devout persons **b :** marked by overly sentimental or emotional devotion to religion : RELIGIOSE

— **pi·e·tis·ti·cal·ly** \-ti-k(ə-)lē\ *adverb*

**pi·e·ty** \'pī-ə-tē\ *noun, plural* **pi·e·ties** [French *pieté* piety, pity, from Latin *pietat-, pietas*, from *pius* dutiful, pious] (1565)

**1 :** the quality or state of being pious: as **a :** fidelity to natural obligations (as to parents) **b** : dutifulness in religion : DEVOUTNESS

**2 :** an act inspired by piety

**3 :** a conventional belief or standard : ORTHODOXY

**synonym** see FIDELITY

**piezo-** *combining form* [Greek *piezein* to press; perhaps akin to Sanskrit *pīḍayati* he squeezes] : pressure ⟨*piezo*meter⟩

**pi·e·zo·elec·tric** \pē-,ā-(,)zō-ə-'lek-trik, pē-,āt-(,)sō-\ *adjective* [International Scientific Vocabulary] (1883)

: of, relating to, marked by, or functioning by means of piezoelectricity

— **pi·e·zo·elec·tri·cal·ly** \-tri-k(ə-)lē\ *adverb*

**pi·e·zo·elec·tric·i·ty** \-,lek-'tri-s(ə-)tē\ *noun* [International Scientific Vocabulary] (1883)

: electricity or electric polarity due to pressure especially in a crystalline substance (as quartz)

**pi·e·zom·e·ter** \,pē-ə-'zä-mə-tər, pē-,āt-'sä-\ *noun* (1820)

: an instrument for measuring pressure or compressibility; *especially* : one for measuring the change of pressure of a material subjected to hydrostatic pressure

— **pi·e·zo·met·ric** \pē-,ā-zə-'me-trik, pē-,āt-sə-\ *adjective*

**¹pif·fle** \'pi-fəl\ *intransitive verb* **pif·fled; pif·fling** \-f(ə-)liŋ\ [perhaps blend of *piddle* and *trifle*] (circa 1878)

: to talk or act in a trivial, inept, or ineffective way

**²piffle** *noun* (1890)

: trivial nonsense ⟨pseudo-scientific *piffle*⟩

**pif·fling** \'pi-fləŋ, -f(ə-)liŋ\ *adjective* (1894)

: of little worth or importance : TRIVIAL

**¹pig** \'pig\ *noun, often attributive* [Middle English *pigge*] (13th century)

**1 :** a young swine not yet sexually mature; *broadly* : a wild or domestic swine

**2 a :** PORK **b :** the dressed carcass of a young swine weighing less than 130 pounds (60 kilograms) **c :** PIGSKIN

**3 a :** one that resembles a pig ⟨an unkempt . . . person is a *pig* —S. S. Hall⟩ **b :** an animal related to or resembling the pig

**4 :** a crude casting of metal (as iron)

**5** *slang* : an immoral woman

**6** *slang* : POLICE OFFICER — usually used disparagingly

— **pig·like** \-,līk\ *adjective*

**²pig** *verb* **pigged; pig·ging** (15th century)

*intransitive verb*

**1 :** FARROW

**2 :** to live like a pig ⟨*pig* it⟩

*transitive verb*

: FARROW

**pig·boat** \'pig-,bōt\ *noun* (1921)

: SUBMARINE

**¹pi·geon** \'pi-jən\ *noun* [Middle English, from Middle French *pijon*, from Late Latin *pipion-,*

*pipio* young bird, from Latin *pipire* to chirp] (14th century)

**1 :** any of a widely distributed family (Columbidae, order Columbiformes) of birds with a stout body, rather short legs, and smooth and compact plumage; *especially* : a member of any of numerous varieties of the rock dove that exist in domestication and in the feral state in cities and towns throughout most of the world

**2 :** a young woman

**3 :** an easy mark : DUPE

**4 :** CLAY PIGEON

**²pigeon** *noun* [alteration of *pidgin*] (1938)

: an object of special concern : BUSINESS

**pigeon breast** *noun* (1842)

: a deformity of the chest marked by sharp projection of the sternum

**pigeon hawk** *noun* (circa 1728)

**1 :** a falcon of the North American population of the merlin

**2 :** SHARP-SHINNED HAWK

**¹pi·geon·hole** \'pi-jən-,hōl\ *noun* (1577)

**1 :** a hole or small recess for pigeons to nest

**2 :** a small open compartment (as in a desk or cabinet) for keeping letters or documents

**3 :** a neat category which usually fails to reflect actual complexities

**²pigeonhole** *transitive verb* (1840)

**1 a :** to place in or as if in the pigeonhole of a desk **b :** to lay aside : SHELVE ⟨his reports continued to be *pigeonholed* and his advice not taken —Walter Mills⟩

**2 :** to assign to a category : CLASSIFY

— **pi·geon·hol·er** \-,hō-lər\ *noun*

**pi·geon·ite** \'pi-jə-,nīt\ *noun* [*Pigeon* Point, northeast Minn. + ¹-*ite*] (1900)

: a monoclinic mineral of the pyroxene group

**pi·geon–liv·ered** \'pi-jən-,li-vərd\ *adjective* (1602)

: GENTLE, MILD

**pigeon pea** *noun* (1725)

: a leguminous woody herb (*Cajanus cajan*) that has trifoliate leaves, yellow flowers, and somewhat flat pods and is much cultivated especially in the tropics; *also* : its small highly nutritious seed

**pi·geon–toed** \'pi-jən-,tōd\ *adjective* (1801)

: having the toes turned in

**pi·geon–wing** \-,wiŋ\ *noun* (circa 1808)

: a fancy dance step executed by jumping and striking the legs together

**pig·fish** \'pig-,fish\ *noun* (1860)

: a saltwater grunt (*Orthopristis chrysopterus*) that is a food fish found from Long Island southward

**pig·gery** \'pi-gə-rē\ *noun, plural* **-ger·ies** (1781)

**1 :** a place where swine are kept

**2 :** swinish behavior

**pig·gin** \'pi-gən\ *noun* [Middle English *pygyn*] (15th century)

: a small wooden pail with one stave extended upward as a handle

**pig·gish** \'pi-gish\ *adjective* (1792)

**1 :** of, relating to, or suggestive of a pig ⟨a *piggish* snort⟩

**2 :** having qualities (as greediness or stubbornness) associated with a pig

— **pig·gish·ly** *adverb*

— **pig·gish·ness** *noun*

**pig·gy** \'pi-gē\ *adjective* **pig·gi·er; -est** (circa 1845)

: PIGGISH

**¹pig·gy·back** \'pi-gē-,bak\ *adverb* [alteration of earlier *a pick pack*, of unknown origin] (1565)

**1 :** up on the back and shoulders

**2 :** on or as if on the back of another; *especially* : on a railroad flatcar

\ə\ abut \ᵊ\ kitten \ər\ further \a\ ash \ā\ ace
\ä\ mop, mar \au̇\ out \ch\ chin \e\ bet \ē\ easy
\g\ go \i\ hit \ī\ ice \j\ job \ŋ\ sing \ō\ go
\ȯ\ law \ȯi\ boy \th\ thin \th\ the \ü\ loot \u̇\ foot
\y\ yet \zh\ vision *see also* Guide to Pronunciation

**²piggyback** *noun* (circa 1590)
**1 :** the act of carrying piggyback
**2 :** the movement of loaded truck trailers on railroad flatcars

**³piggyback** *adjective* (1823)
**1 :** marked by being up on the shoulders and back ⟨a child needs hugging, tussling, and *piggyback* rides —Benjamin Spock⟩
**2 :** carried or transported piggyback: as **a :** of or relating to the hauling of truck trailers on railroad flatcars **b :** of, relating to, or being a radio or television commercial that is presented in addition to other commercials during one commercial break **c :** being or relating to something carried into space as an extra load by a vehicle (as a spacecraft)

**⁴piggyback** (1952)
*transitive verb*
**1 :** to carry up on the shoulders and back
**2 :** to haul (as a truck trailer) by railroad car
**3 :** to set up or cause to function in conjunction with something larger or more important
*intransitive verb*
**1 :** to haul truck trailers on railroad cars
**2 :** to function or be carried on or as if on the back of another

**piggy bank** *noun* (1941)
**:** a coin bank often in the shape of a pig

**pig·head·ed** \'pig-ˌhe-dəd\ *adjective* (1620)
**:** willfully or perversely unyielding **:** OBSTINATE
— **pig·head·ed·ly** *adverb*
— **pig·head·ed·ness** *noun*

**pig in a poke** (1562)
**:** something offered in such a way as to obscure its real nature or worth ⟨unwilling to buy a *pig in a poke*⟩

**pig iron** *noun* (1665)
**:** crude iron that is the direct product of the blast furnace and is refined to produce steel, wrought iron, or ingot iron

**pig latin** *noun, often L capitalized* (1931)
**:** a jargon that is made by systematic alteration of English (as *ipskay the ointjay* for *skip the joint*)

**pig·let** \'pi-glət\ *noun* (1883)
**:** a small usually young swine

**¹pig·ment** \'pig-mənt\ *noun* [Latin *pigmentum*, from *pingere* to paint — more at PAINT] (14th century)
**1 :** a substance that imparts black or white or a color to other materials; *especially* **:** a powdered substance that is mixed with a liquid in which it is relatively insoluble and used especially to impart color to coating materials (as paints) or to inks, plastics, and rubber
**2 :** a coloring matter in animals and plants especially in a cell or tissue; *also* **:** any of various related colorless substances
— **pig·men·tary** \-mən-ˌter-ē\ *adjective*

**²pig·ment** \-ˌment, -mənt\ *transitive verb* (1900)
**:** to color with or as if with pigment

**pig·men·ta·tion** \ˌpig-mən-'tā-shən, -ˌmen-\ *noun* (1866)
**:** coloration with or deposition of pigment; *especially* **:** an excessive deposition of bodily pigment

**pig·my** *variant of* PYGMY

**pi·gno·li** \pēn-'yō-lē\ *or* **pi·gno·lia** \-lē-ə\ *noun* [*pignoli* from Italian, plural of *pignolo*, *pinolo*, from *pigna*, *pina* pine cone, from Latin *pinea*; *pignolia* perhaps modification of *pignoli* — more at PINEAL] (1898)
**:** PINE NUT

**pig·nut** \'pig-ˌnət\ *noun* (1666)
**1 :** any of several bitter-flavored hickory nuts
**2 :** a hickory (as *Carya glabra* and *C. cordiformis*) bearing pignuts

**pig out** *intransitive verb* (1978)
*slang* **:** to eat greedily **:** GORGE
— **pig-out** \'pig-ˌaüt\ *noun*

**pig·pen** \-ˌpen\ *noun* (1803)
**1 :** a pen for pigs
**2 :** a dirty slovenly place

**pig·skin** \-ˌskin\ *noun* (1855)

**1 :** the skin of a swine or leather made of it
**2 a :** a jockey's saddle **b :** FOOTBALL 2a

**pig·stick** \-ˌstik\ *intransitive verb* (1891)
**:** to hunt the wild boar on horseback with a spear
— **pig·stick·er** *noun*

**pig·sty** \'pig-ˌstī\ *noun* (circa 1591)
**:** PIGPEN

**pig·tail** \-ˌtāl\ *noun* (1688)
**1 :** tobacco in small twisted strands or rolls
**2 :** a tight braid of hair

**pig·tailed** \-ˌtāld\ *adjective* (1754)
**:** wearing a pigtail ⟨*pigtailed* little girls⟩

**pig·weed** \-ˌwēd\ *noun* (circa 1801)
**:** any of various strongly growing weedy plants especially of the goosefoot or amaranth families

**piing** *present participle of* PI *or of* PIE

**pi·ka** \'pē-kə, 'pī-\ *noun* [perhaps from Evenki (Tungusic language of Siberia)] (1827)
**:** any of various short-eared small lagomorph mammals (family Ochotonidae) of rocky uplands of Asia and western North America with relatively short hind legs

pika

**pi·ka·ke** \'pē-kä-ˌkā\ *noun* [Hawaiian *pīkake*, literally, peacock, from English] (1938)
**:** an Asian vine (*Jasminum sambac*) cultivated for its profuse fragrant white flowers

**¹pike** \'pīk\ *noun* [Middle English, from Old English *pīc* pickax] (13th century)
**1 :** PIKESTAFF 1
**2 :** a sharp point or spike; *also* **:** the tip of a spear
— **piked** \'pīkt\ *adjective*

**²pike** *noun* [Middle English, perhaps of Scandinavian origin; akin to Norwegian dialect *pīk* pointed mountain] (13th century)
*dialect English* **:** a mountain or hill having a peaked summit — used especially in place names

**³pike** *noun, plural* **pike** *or* **pikes** [Middle English, from ¹*pike*] (14th century)
**1 a :** a large elongate long-snouted freshwater bony fish (*Esox lucius*) valued for food and sport and widely distributed in cooler parts of the northern hemisphere — called also *northern, northern pike* **b :** any of various fishes (family Esocidae) related to the pike: as (1) **:** MUSKELLUNGE (2) **:** PICKEREL
**2 :** any of various fishes resembling the pike in appearance or habits

**⁴pike** *noun* [Middle French *pique*, from *piquer* to prick, from (assumed) Vulgar Latin *piccare*, perhaps from Latin *picus* woodpecker — more at PIE] (circa 1511)
**:** a heavy spear with a very long shaft used by infantry especially in Europe from the Middle Ages to the 18th century

**⁵pike** *transitive verb* **piked; pik·ing** (1798)
**:** to pierce, kill, or wound with a pike

**⁶pike** *intransitive verb* **piked; pik·ing** [Middle English *pyken* (reflexive)] (1526)
**1 :** to leave abruptly ⟨get lonely and sore, and *pike* out —Sinclair Lewis⟩
**2 :** to make one's way ⟨*pike* along⟩

**⁷pike** *noun* (1812)
**1 :** TURNPIKE
**2 :** a railroad or railroad line or system
— **down the pike 1 :** in the course of events ⟨the greatest boxer to come *down the pike* in years⟩ **2 :** in the future ⟨today's advances only hint at what's *down the pike*⟩

**⁸pike** *noun* [perhaps from ³*pike*] (1928)
**:** a body position (as in diving) in which the hips are bent, the knees are straight, the head is pressed forward, and the hands touch the toes or clasp the legs behind or just above the knees

**pike·man** \'pīk-mən\ *noun* (1566)
**:** a soldier armed with a pike

**pike perch** *noun* (1842)
**:** a fish (as the walleye) of the perch group that resembles the pike

**pik·er** \'pī-kər\ *noun* [*pike* to play cautiously, of unknown origin] (1872)
**1 :** one who gambles or speculates with small amounts of money
**2 :** one who does things in a small way; *also* **:** TIGHTWAD, CHEAPSKATE

**pike·staff** \'pīk-ˌstaf\ *noun* (14th century)
**1 :** a spiked staff for use on slippery ground
**2 :** the staff of a foot soldier's pike

**pi·ki** \'pē-kē\ *noun* [Hopi *píki*] (circa 1889)
**:** bread made especially from blue cornmeal and baked in thin sheets by the Indians of the southwestern U.S.

**pi·laf** *or* **pi·laff** \pi-'läf, 'pē-ˌ\ *or* **pi·lau** \pi-'lō, -'lȯ, 'pē-ˌ\; *Southern often* 'pər-ˌ, -ˌ)lü, -ˌ)lō\ *noun* [Turkish & Persian; Turkish *pilav*, from Persian *pilāv*] (1612)
**:** a dish made of seasoned rice and often meat

**pi·las·ter** \pi-'las-tər, 'pī-ˌlas-\ *noun* [Middle French *pilastre*, from Italian *pilastro*] (1575)
**:** an upright architectural member that is rectangular in plan and is structurally a pier but architecturally treated as a column and that usually projects a third of its width or less from the wall

1 pilaster

**pil·chard** \'pil-chərd\ *noun* [origin unknown] (circa 1530)
**1 :** a fish (*Sardina pilchardus*) of the herring family resembling the herring and occurring in great schools along the coasts of Europe
**2 :** any of several sardines related to the European pilchard

**¹pile** \'pī(ə)l\ *noun* [Middle English, dart, stake, from Old English *pīl*, from Latin *pilum* javelin] (12th century)
**1 :** a long slender column usually of timber, steel, or reinforced concrete driven into the ground to carry a vertical load
**2 :** a wedge-shaped heraldic charge usually placed vertically with the broad end up
**3 a :** a target-shooting arrowhead without cutting edges **b :** [Latin *pilum*] **:** an ancient Roman foot soldier's heavy javelin

**²pile** *transitive verb* **piled; pil·ing** (15th century)
**:** to drive piles into

**³pile** *verb* **piled; pil·ing** [Middle English, from ⁴*pile*] (14th century)
*transitive verb*
**1 :** to lay or place in a pile **:** STACK
**2 a :** to heap in abundance **:** LOAD ⟨*piled* potatoes on his plate⟩ **b :** to collect little by little into a mass — usually used with *up*
*intransitive verb*
**1 :** to form a pile or accumulation — usually used with *up*
**2 :** to move or press forward in or as if in a mass **:** CROWD ⟨*piled* into a car⟩

**⁴pile** *noun* [Middle English, from Middle French, from Latin *pila* pillar] (15th century)
**1 a** (1) **:** a quantity of things heaped together (2) **:** a heap of wood for burning a corpse or a sacrifice **b :** any great number or quantity **:** LOT
**2 :** a large building or group of buildings
**3 :** a great amount of money **:** FORTUNE
**4 :** REACTOR 3b

**⁵pile** *noun* [Middle English, from Latin *pilus* hair] (15th century)
**1 :** a coat or surface of usually short close fine furry hairs

**2 :** a velvety surface produced by an extra set of filling yarns that form raised loops which are cut and sheared
— **pile·less** \'pī(ə)l-ləs\ *adjective*
⁶**pile** *noun* [Middle English, from Latin *pila* ball] (15th century)
**1 :** a single hemorrhoid
**2** *plural* : HEMORRHOIDS

**pi·le·at·ed** \'pī-lē-,ā-təd, 'pi-\ *adjective* (circa 1728)
**:** having a crest covering the pileum

**pileated woodpecker** *noun* (1782)
**:** a large red-crested North American woodpecker (*Dryocopus pileatus*) that is black with white on the face, neck, and undersides of the wings

**piled** \'pī(ə)ld\ *adjective* (15th century)
**:** having a pile ⟨a deep-*piled* rug⟩

**pile driver** *noun* (1772)
**:** a machine for driving down piles with a drop hammer or a steam or air hammer

**pi·le·um** \'pī-lē-əm\ *noun, plural* **pi·lea** \-lē-ə\ [New Latin, from Latin *pileus, pileum* felt cap; akin to Greek *pilos* felt] (1874)
**:** the top of the head of a bird from the bill to the nape

**pile·up** \'pī(ə)l-,əp\ *noun* (circa 1929)
**1 :** a collision involving usually several motor vehicles
**2 a :** a jammed tangled mass or pile (as of motor vehicles or people) resulting from collision or accumulation **b :** ACCUMULATION

**pi·le·us** \'pī-lē-əs\ *noun, plural* **pi·lei** \-lē-,ī\ [New Latin, from Latin] (1760)
**1 :** the convex, concave, or flattened spore-bearing structure of some basidiomycetes that is attached superiorly to the stem and typically is expanded with gills or pores on the underside — called also *cap*
**2** [Latin] **:** a pointed or close-fitting cap worn by ancient Romans

**pile·wort** \'pī(ə)l-,wərt, -,wȯrt\ *noun* [Middle English *pyle wort;* from its use in treating piles] (15th century)
**:** LESSER CELANDINE

**pil·fer** \'pil-fər\ *verb* **pil·fered; pil·fer·ing** \-f(ə-)riŋ\ [Middle French *pelfrer,* from *pelfre* booty] (circa 1548)
*intransitive verb*
**:** STEAL; *especially* **:** to steal stealthily in small amounts and often again and again
*transitive verb*
**:** STEAL; *especially* **:** to steal in small quantities
**synonym** see STEAL
— **pil·fer·able** \-f(ə-)rə-bəl\ *adjective*
— **pil·fer·age** \-f(ə-)rij\ *noun*
— **pil·fer·er** \-fər-ər\ *noun*
— **pil·fer·proof** \-,prüf\ *adjective*

**pil·gar·lic** \pil-'gär-lik\ *noun* [*pilled garlic*] (circa 1529)
**1 a :** a bald head **b :** a bald-headed man
**2 :** a man looked upon with humorous contempt or mock pity

**pil·grim** \'pil-grəm\ *noun* [Middle English, from Old French *peligrin,* from Late Latin *pelegrinus,* alteration of Latin *peregrinus* foreigner, from *peregrinus,* adjective, foreign, from *peregri* abroad, from *per* through + *agr-, ager* land — more at FOR, ACRE] (13th century)
**1 :** one who journeys in foreign lands **:** WAYFARER
**2 :** one who travels to a shrine or holy place as a devotee
**3** *capitalized* **:** one of the English colonists settling at Plymouth in 1620 ◆

¹**pil·grim·age** \'pil-grə-mij\ *noun* (14th century)
**1 :** a journey of a pilgrim; *especially* **:** one to a shrine or a sacred place
**2 :** the course of life on earth

²**pilgrimage** *intransitive verb* **-aged; -ag·ing** (14th century)
**:** to go on a pilgrimage

**pilgrim bottle** *noun* (1874)
**:** COSTREL

**pil·ing** \'pī-liŋ\ *noun* (15th century)
**:** a structure of piles; *also* **:** PILES

**Pi·li·pi·no** \,pi-lə-'pē-(,)nō, ,pē-\ *noun* [Tagalog, literally, Philippine, from Spanish *Filipino*] (1936)
**:** the Tagalog-based official language of the Republic of the Philippines

¹**pill** \'pil\ *verb* [Middle English *pilen, pillen,* partly from Old English *pilian* to peel, partly from Middle French *piller* to plunder] (12th century)
*intransitive verb*
*dialect chiefly English* **:** to come off in flakes or scales **:** PEEL
*transitive verb*
**1** *archaic* **:** to subject to depredation or extortion
**2** *dialect* **:** to peel or strip off

²**pill** *noun* [Middle English *pylle,* from Middle Dutch *pille,* ultimately from Latin *pilula,* diminutive of *pila* ball] (14th century)
**1 a :** medicine in a small rounded mass to be swallowed whole **b** *often capitalized* **:** an oral contraceptive — usually used with *the*
**2 :** something repugnant or unpleasant that must be accepted or endured
**3 :** something resembling a pill in size or shape
**4 :** a disagreeable or tiresome person

³**pill** (1736)
*transitive verb*
**1 :** to dose with pills
**2 :** BLACKBALL
*intransitive verb*
**:** to become rough with or mat into little balls ⟨brushed woolens often *pill*⟩

¹**pil·lage** \'pi-lij\ *noun* [Middle English, from Middle French, from *piller* to plunder, abuse] (14th century)
**1 :** the act of looting or plundering especially in war
**2 :** something taken as booty

²**pillage** *verb* **pil·laged; pil·lag·ing** (circa 1592)
*transitive verb*
**:** to plunder ruthlessly **:** LOOT
*intransitive verb*
**:** to take booty
**synonym** see RAVAGE
— **pil·lag·er** *noun*

¹**pil·lar** \'pi-lər\ *noun* [Middle English *piler,* from Old French, from Medieval Latin *pilare,* from Latin *pila*] (13th century)
**1 a :** a firm upright support for a superstructure **:** POST **b :** a usually ornamental column or shaft; *especially* **:** one standing alone for a monument
**2 :** a chief supporter **:** PROP
**3 :** a solid mass of coal, rock, or ore left standing to support a mine roof
**4 :** a body part that resembles a column
— **pil·lar·less** *adjective*
— **from pillar to post :** from one place or one predicament to another

²**pillar** *transitive verb* (1607)
**:** to provide or strengthen with or as if with pillars

**pil·lar-box** \'pi-lər-,bäks\ *noun* (1858)
*British* **:** a pillar-shaped mailbox

**pill-box** \'pil-,bäks\ *noun* (1730)
**1 :** a box for pills; *especially* **:** a shallow round box of pasteboard
**2 :** a small low concrete emplacement for machine guns and antitank weapons
**3 :** a small round hat without a brim; *specifically* **:** a woman's shallow hat with a flat crown and straight sides

**pill bug** *noun* [²*pill;* from its rolling into a ball when disturbed] (1843)
**:** WOOD LOUSE

¹**pil·lion** \'pil-yən\ *noun* [Scottish Gaelic or Irish; Scottish Gaelic *pillean,* diminutive of *peall* covering, couch; Irish *pillín,* diminutive of *peall* covering, couch] (1503)
**1 a :** a light saddle for women consisting chiefly of a cushion **b :** a pad or cushion put on behind a man's saddle chiefly for a woman to ride on
**2** *chiefly British* **:** a motorcycle or bicycle saddle for a passenger

²**pillion** *adverb* (1926)
*chiefly British* **:** on or as if on a pillion ⟨ride *pillion*⟩

¹**pil·lo·ry** \'pi-lə-rē, 'pil-rē\ *noun, plural* **-ries** [Middle English, from Old French *pilori*] (13th century)
**1 :** a device formerly used for publicly punishing offenders consisting of a wooden frame with holes in which the head and hands can be locked
**2 :** a means for exposing one to public scorn or ridicule

**pillory 1**

²**pillory** *transitive verb* **-ried; -ry·ing** (circa 1600)
**1 :** to set in a pillory as punishment
**2 :** to expose to public contempt, ridicule, or scorn

¹**pil·low** \'pi-(,)lō\ *noun* [Middle English *pilwe,* from Old English *pyle* (akin to Old High German *pfuliwi*), from Latin *pulvinus*] (before 12th century)
**1 a :** a support for the head of a reclining person; *especially* **:** one consisting of a cloth bag filled with feathers, down, sponge rubber, or plastic fiber **b :** something resembling a pillow especially in form
**2 :** a cushion or pad tightly stuffed and used as a support for the design and tools in making lace with a bobbin
— **pil·lowy** \'pi-lə-wē\ *adjective*

²**pillow** (1629)
*transitive verb*
**1 :** to rest or lay on or as if on a pillow
**2 :** to serve as a pillow for

◇ WORD HISTORY

**pilgrim** Latin *peregrinus* "foreigner, alien" is a derivative of *peregri* "abroad, away from home" itself formed from *per-* "through" and *ager* "field." In Late Latin and early Medieval Latin *peregrinus* was applied to wanderers directed by God, such as the Israelites after their departure from Egypt, prophets living in the wilderness, and those Church Fathers who like Saint Jerome left their homes for the desert or the Holy Land. From this use the word was extended to all wayfarers traveling to the Holy Land or the shrine of a saint as an act of faith or penance. *Peregrinus* became *pelegrinus* in Late Latin, the first of the two *r*s being altered by dissimilation. *Peregrinus* then became *pelerin* or *peligrin* in Old French. The latter form was borrowed into Middle English as *pilegrim* or *pilgrim.* Latin *peregrinus* reaches us more directly in *peregrine falcon* (in Medieval Latin *falco peregrinus*), so named because young birds were captured by falconers as "wanderers" from their nesting sites. Other birds of prey were taken directly from their nests, but the aerie of a peregrine falcon is typically on an inaccessible crag.

*intransitive verb*
**:** to lay or rest one's head on or as if on a pillow

**pillow block** *noun* (1844)
**:** a block or standard to support a journal (as of a shaft) **:** BEARING

**pil·low·case** \'pi-lə-ˌkās, -ˌlō-\ *noun* (1724)
**:** a removable covering for a pillow

**pillow lace** *noun* [from its being worked over a pillow on which the pattern is marked] (circa 1858)
**:** lace made with a bobbin

**pillow slip** *noun* (circa 1828)
**:** PILLOWCASE

**pillow talk** *noun* (1939)
**:** intimate conversation between lovers in bed

**pi·lo·car·pine** \ˌpī-lə-ˈkär-ˌpēn\ *noun* [International Scientific Vocabulary, from New Latin *Pilocarpus jaborandi*, species of tropical shrubs] (1875)
**:** a miotic alkaloid $C_{11}H_{16}N_2O_2$ that is obtained from jaborandi and used especially in the treatment of glaucoma

**pi·lose** \'pī-ˌlōs\ *adjective* [Latin *pilosus*, from *pilus* hair] (1753)
**:** covered with usually soft hair
— **pi·los·i·ty** \pī-ˈlä-sə-tē\ *noun*

**¹pi·lot** \'pī-lət\ *noun* [Middle French *pilote*, from Italian *pilota*, alteration of *pedota*, from (assumed) Middle Greek *pēdōtēs*, from Greek *pēda* steering oars, plural of *pēdon* oar; probably akin to Greek *pod-, pous* foot — more at FOOT] (1530)
**1 a :** one employed to steer a ship **:** HELMSMAN **b :** a person who is qualified and usually licensed to conduct a ship into and out of a port or in specified waters **c :** a person who flies or is qualified to fly an aircraft or spacecraft
**2 :** GUIDE, LEADER
**3 :** COWCATCHER
**4 :** a piece that guides a tool or machine part
**5 :** a television show produced and filmed or taped as a sample of a proposed series
**6 :** PILOT LIGHT 2
— **pi·lot·less** \-ləs\ *adjective*

**²pilot** *transitive verb* (1649)
**1 :** to act as a guide to **:** lead or conduct over a usually difficult course
**2 a :** to set and conn the course of ⟨*pilot* a ship⟩ **b :** to act as pilot of ⟨*pilot* a plane⟩
**synonym** see GUIDE

**³pilot** *adjective* (1802)
**:** serving as a guiding or tracing device, an activating or auxiliary unit, or a trial apparatus or operation ⟨a *pilot* study⟩

**pi·lot·age** \'pī-lə-tij\ *noun* (circa 1618)
**1 :** the action or business of piloting
**2 :** the compensation paid to a licensed ship's pilot

**pilot biscuit** *noun* (1836)
**:** HARDTACK — called also *pilot bread*

**pilot engine** *noun* (1838)
**:** a locomotive going in advance of a train to make sure that the way is clear

**pilot fish** *noun* (1634)
**:** a pelagic carangid fish (*Naucrates ductor*) that has dark stripes and often swims in company with a shark

**pi·lot·house** \'pī-lət-ˌhaus\ *noun* (1846)
**:** a deckhouse for a ship's helmsman containing the steering wheel, compass, and navigating equipment

**pilot light** *noun* (circa 1890)
**1 :** an indicator light showing where a switch or circuit breaker is located or whether a motor is in operation or power is on — called also *pilot lamp*
**2 :** a small permanent flame used to ignite gas at a burner

**pilot officer** *noun* (1919)
**:** a commissioned officer in the British air force who ranks with a second lieutenant in the army

**pilot whale** *noun* (1867)
**:** BLACKFISH 2

---

**pil·sner** *or* **pil·sen·er** \'pils-nər, 'pilz-, 'pil-zə-\ *noun* [German, literally, of Pilsen (Plzeň), city in the Czech Republic] (1877)
**1 :** a light beer with a strong flavor of hops
**2 :** a tall slender footed glass for beer

**Pilt·down man** \'pilt-ˌdaun-\ *noun* [*Piltdown*, East Sussex, England] (circa 1918)
**:** a supposedly very early hominid erroneously reconstructed from a combination of human and animal skeletal remains the latter of which were later found to have been planted by a hoaxer

**pil·u·lar** \'pil-yə-lər\ *adjective* (1802)
**:** of, relating to, or resembling a pill

**pil·ule** \'pil-(ˌ)yü(ə)l\ *noun* [Middle French, from Latin *pilula* pill — more at PILL] (1543)
**:** a little pill

**pi·lus** \'pī-ləs\ *noun, plural* **pi·li** \-ˌlī\ [Latin] (circa 1890)
**:** a hair or a structure (as of a bacterium) resembling a hair

**Pi·ma** \'pē-mə\ *noun, plural* **Pimas** *or* **Pima** (1850)
**1 :** a member of an American Indian people of southern Arizona and northern Mexico
**2 :** the Uto-Aztecan language of the Pima people
— **Pi·man** \-mən\ *adjective*

**pi·ma cotton** \'pē-mə-, 'pi-\ *noun* [*Pima* County, Arizona] (1925)
**:** a cotton that produces fiber of exceptional strength and firmness and that was developed in the southwestern U.S. by selection and breeding of Egyptian cottons

**pi·men·to** \pə-ˈmen-(ˌ)tō\ *noun, plural* **-tos** *or* **-to** [Spanish *pimienta* allspice, pepper, from Late Latin *pigmenta*, plural of *pigmentum* plant juice, from Latin, pigment] (1660)
**1 :** ALLSPICE
**2 :** PIMIENTO 1

**pimento cheese** *noun* (1916)
**:** a Neufchâtel, process, cream, or occasionally cheddar cheese to which ground pimientos have been added

**pi·me·son** \'pī-ˈme-ˌzän, -'mä-, -'mē-, -ˌsän\ *noun* [⁴pi] (1948)
**:** PION

**pi·mien·to** \pə-ˈmen-(ˌ)tō, pəm-ˈyen-\ *noun, plural* **-tos** [Spanish from *pimienta*] (1845)
**1 :** any of various bluntly conical thick-fleshed sweet peppers of European origin that have a distinctive mild sweet flavor and are used especially as a garnish, as a stuffing for olives, and as a source of paprika
**2 :** a plant that bears pimientos

**¹pimp** \'pimp\ *noun* [origin unknown] (1600)
**:** a man who solicits clients for a prostitute

**²pimp** *intransitive verb* (1636)
**:** to work as a pimp

**pim·per·nel** \'pim-pər-ˌnel, -pər-nəl\ *noun* [Middle English *pimpernele*, from Middle French *pimprenelle*, from Late Latin *pimpinella*, a medicinal herb] (14th century)
**:** any of a genus (*Anagallis*) of herbs of the primrose family; *especially* **:** SCARLET PIMPERNEL

**pimp·ing** \'pim-pən, -piŋ\ *adjective* [origin unknown] (1687)
**1 :** PETTY, INSIGNIFICANT
**2** *chiefly dialect* **:** PUNY, SICKLY

**pim·ple** \'pim-pəl\ *noun* [Middle English *pinple*] (14th century)
**1 :** a small inflamed elevation of the skin **:** PAPULE; *especially* **:** PUSTULE
**2 :** a swelling or protuberance like a pimple
— **pim·pled** \-pəld\ *adjective*
— **pim·ply** \-p(ə-)lē\ *adjective*

**pimp·mo·bile** \'pimp-mō-ˌbēl, -mə-\ *noun* (1971)
**:** an ostentatious luxury car of a kind characteristically used by a pimp

**¹pin** \'pin\ *noun* [Middle English, from Old English *pinn* (akin to Old High German *pfinn* peg), perhaps from Latin *pinna* quill, feather — more at PEN] (before 12th century)

---

**1 a :** a piece of solid material (as wood or metal) used especially for fastening separate articles together or as a support by which one article may be suspended from another **b** *obsolete* **:** the center peg of a target; *also* **:** the center itself **c :** something that resembles a pin especially in slender elongated form ⟨an electrical connector *pin*⟩ **d** (1) **:** one of the wooden pieces constituting the target in various games (as bowling) (2) **:** the peg at which a quoit is pitched (3) **:** the staff of the flag marking a hole on a golf course **e :** a peg for regulating the tension of the strings of a musical instrument **f :** the part of a key stem that enters a lock **g** (1) **:** THOLE 1 (2) **:** a belaying pin
**2 a** (1) **:** a small pointed piece of wire with a head used especially for fastening cloth (2) **:** something of small value **:** TRIFLE **b :** an ornament or emblem fastened to clothing with a pin **c** (1) **:** BOBBY PIN (2) **:** HAIRPIN (3) **:** SAFETY PIN
**3 :** LEG — usually used in plural ⟨wobbly on his *pins*⟩
**4 :** a fall in wrestling

**²pin** *transitive verb* **pinned; pin·ning** (14th century)
**1 a :** to fasten, join, or secure with a pin **b :** to hold fast or immobile **c :** to present (a young woman) with a fraternity pin as a pledge of affection
**2 a :** ATTACH, HANG ⟨*pinned* his hopes on a miracle⟩ **b :** to assign the blame or responsibility for ⟨*pin* the robbery on a night watchman⟩ **c :** to define or determine clearly or precisely — usually used with *down* ⟨it is hard to *pin* down exactly when things changed —Katharine Whittemore⟩
**3 a :** to make (a chess opponent's piece) unable to move without exposing the king to check or a valuable piece to capture **b** *of a wrestler* **:** to secure a fall over (an opponent)

**³pin** *adjective* (1523)
**1 :** of or relating to a pin
**2** *of leather* **:** having a grain suggesting the heads of pins

**pi·ña cloth** \'pēn-yə-\ *noun* [Spanish *piña* pineapple, pinecone, from Latin *pinea* pinecone — more at PINEAL] (circa 1858)
**:** a lustrous transparent cloth of Philippine origin that is woven of silky pineapple fibers

**pi·ña co·la·da** \ˌpēn-yə-kō-ˈlä-də, ˌpē-nə-\ *noun* [Spanish, literally, strained pineapple] (1923)
**:** a tall drink made of rum, cream of coconut, and pineapple juice mixed with ice

**pin·a·fore** \'pi-nə-ˌfōr, -ˌfòr\ *noun* [²pin + *afore*] (1782)
**:** a sleeveless usually low-necked garment fastened in the back and worn as an apron or dress
— **pin·a·fored** \-ˌfōrd, -ˌfòrd\ *adjective*

**pi·ña·ta** *or* **pi·na·ta** \pēn-ˈyä-tə\ *noun* [Spanish *piñata*, literally, pot, from Italian *pignatta*, probably from *pigna* pinecone — more at PIGNOLI] (1887)
**:** a decorated vessel (as a pottery jar) filled with candies, fruits, and gifts and hung from the ceiling to be broken with sticks by blindfolded persons as part of especially Latin-American festivities (as at Christmas or for a birthday party)

**pin·ball machine** \'pin-ˌbòl-\ *noun* (1936)
**:** an amusement device in which a ball propelled by a plunger scores points as it rolls down a slanting surface among pins and targets — called also *pinball game*

piñata

**pin·bone** \'pin-ˌbōn\ *noun* (1640)
**:** the hipbone especially of a quadruped — see COW illustration

**pince-nez** \paⁿs-'nā, pan(t)s-\ *noun, plural*
**pince–nez** \-'nā(z)\ [French, from *pincer* to
pinch + *nez* nose, from Latin *nasus* — more
at NOSE] (1876)
: eyeglasses clipped
to the nose by a
spring

pince-nez

**pin·cer** \'pin(t)-sər,
*especially for 1 US
often* 'pin-chər\ *noun*
[Middle English *pin-
ceour,* from (as-
sumed) Anglo-
French *pinceour,*
from Middle French
*pincier* to pinch,
from (assumed) Vul-
gar Latin *pinctiare, punctiare,* from Latin
*punctum* puncture — more at POINT] (14th
century)
**1** *plural but singular or plural in construction*
**a** : an instrument having two short handles
and two grasping jaws working on a pivot and
used for gripping things **b** : a claw (as of a
lobster) resembling a pair of pincers : CHELA
**2** : one part of a double envelopment in which
two military forces converge on opposite sides
of an enemy position
— **pin·cer·like** \-ˌlīk\ *adjective*

¹**pinch** \'pinch\ *verb* [Middle English, from
(assumed) Old North French *pinchier,* from
(assumed) Vulgar Latin *pinctiare* (14th century)
*transitive verb*
**1 a** : to squeeze between the finger and thumb
or between the jaws of an instrument **b** : to
prune the tip of (a plant or shoot) usually to
induce branching **c** : to squeeze or compress
painfully **d** : to cause physical or mental pain
to **e** (1) : to cause to appear thin or shrunken
(2) : to cause to shrivel or wither
**2 a** : to subject to strict economy or want
: STRAITEN **b** : to confine or limit narrowly
: CONSTRICT
**3 a** : STEAL **b** : ARREST
**4** : to sail too close to the wind
*intransitive verb*
**1** : COMPRESS, SQUEEZE
**2** : to be miserly or closefisted
**3** : to press painfully
**4** : NARROW, TAPER ⟨the road *pinched* down to a
trail —Cecelia Holland⟩
— **pinch pennies** : to practice strict economy

²**pinch** *noun* (15th century)
**1 a** : a critical juncture : EMERGENCY **b** (1)
: PRESSURE, STRESS (2) : HARDSHIP, PRIVATION **c**
: DEFICIT
**2 a** : an act of pinching : SQUEEZE **b** : as much
as may be taken between the finger and thumb
⟨a *pinch* of snuff⟩ **c** : a very small amount
**3** : a marked thinning of a vein or bed
**4 a** : THEFT **b** : a police raid; *also* : ARREST
**synonym** see JUNCTURE

³**pinch** *adjective* (1916)
**1** : SUBSTITUTE ⟨*pinch* runner⟩
**2** : hit by a pinch hitter ⟨*pinch* homer⟩
**pinch bar** *noun* (1837)
: a bar similar in form and use to a crowbar
and sometimes having an end adapted for pulling spikes or inserting under a heavy wheel
that is to be rolled
**pinch·beck** \'pinch-ˌbek\ *noun* [Christopher
*Pinchbeck* (died 1732) English watchmaker]
(1734)
**1** : an alloy of copper and zinc used especially
to imitate gold in jewelry
**2** : something counterfeit or spurious
— **pinchbeck** *adjective*
**pinch·er** \'pin-chər\ *noun* (15th century)
**1** : one that pinches
**2** *plural* : PINCERS
**pinch–hit** \'pinch-'hit, ˌpinch-\ *intransitive
verb* [back-formation from *pinch hitter*]
(1915)
**1** : to act or serve in place of another

**2** : to bat in the place of another player especially when a hit is particularly needed
**pinch hit** *noun* (1927)
: a hit made by a pinch hitter
**pinch hitter** *noun* (1912)
: one that pinch-hits
**pinch·pen·ny** \'pinch-ˌpe-nē\ *adjective* (1582)
: STINGY, NIGGARDLY
**pin curl** *noun* (1896)
: a curl made usually by dampening a strand
of hair with water or lotion, coiling it, and securing it by a hairpin or clip
**pin·cush·ion** \'pin-ˌku̇-shən\ *noun* (1632)
: a small cushion in which pins may be stuck
ready for use
¹**Pin·dar·ic** \pin-'dar-ik\ *adjective* (1640)
**1** : of or relating to the poet Pindar
**2** : written in the manner or style characteristic
of Pindar
²**Pindaric** *noun* (1685)
**1** : a Pindaric ode
**2** *plural* : loose irregular verses similar to
those used in Pindaric odes
**pin·dling** \'pin(d)-lən, -liŋ; 'pin-dᵊl-ən, -iŋ\ *adjective* [perhaps alteration of *spindling*] (1861)
*dialect* : PUNY, FRAIL
¹**pine** \'pīn\ *noun, often attributive* [Middle English, from Old English *pīn,* from Latin *pinus;*
probably akin to Greek *pitys* pine] (before
12th century)
**1** : any of a genus (*Pinus* of the family Pi-
naceae, the pine family) of coniferous evergreen trees that have slender elongated needles
and include some valuable timber trees and ornamentals
**2** : the straight-grained white or yellow usually durable and resinous wood of a pine varying from extreme softness in the white pine to
hardness in the longleaf pine
**3** : any of various Australian coniferous trees
(as of the genera *Callitris* or *Araucaria*)
**4** : PINEAPPLE
**5** : BENCH 1c
— **pin·ey** *also* **piny** \'pī-nē\ *adjective*
²**pine** *intransitive verb* **pined; pin·ing** [Mid-
dle English, from Old English *pīnian* to suffer,
from (assumed) Old English *pīn* punishment,
from Latin *poena* — more at PAIN] (14th century)
**1** : to lose vigor, health, or flesh (as through
grief) : LANGUISH
**2** : to yearn intensely and persistently especially for something unattainable ⟨they still
*pined* for their lost wealth⟩
**synonym** see LONG
**pi·ne·al** \'pī-nē-əl, pī-'\ *adjective* [French *piné-
al,* from Middle French, from Latin *pinea*
pinecone, from feminine of *pineus* of pine,
from *pinus*] (1681)
: of, relating to, or being the pineal gland
**pi·ne·al·ec·to·my** \ˌpī-nē-ə-'lek-tə-mē, pī-
ˌnē-\ *noun* (1915)
: surgical removal of the pineal gland
— **pi·ne·al·ec·to·mize** \-tə-ˌmīz\ *transitive verb*
**pineal gland** *noun* (1712)
: a small usually conical appendage of the
brain of all craniate vertebrates that functions
primarily as an endocrine organ and that in a
few reptiles has the essential structure of an
eye — called also *pineal, pineal body, pineal
organ*
**pine·ap·ple** \'pī-ˌna-pəl\ *noun* (1664)
**1 a** : a tropical monocotyledonous plant
(*Ananas comosus* of the family Bromeliaceae,
the pineapple family) that has rigid spiny-
margined recurved leaves and a short stalk
with a dense oblong head of small abortive
flowers **b** : the large edible multiple fruit of
the pineapple that consists of the sweet succulent fleshy inflorescence
**2** : a hand grenade
**pineapple guava** *noun* (circa 1924)
: FEIJOA
**pine·cone** \'pīn-ˌkōn\ *noun* (1695)
: a cone of a pine tree

**pine·drops** \'pīn-ˌdräps\ *noun plural but singular or plural in construction* (1857)
**1** : a purplish brown leafless saprophytic plant
(*Pterospora andromedea*) of the wintergreen
family with racemose drooping white flowers
**2** : BEECHDROPS
**pine·land** \'pīn-ˌland, -lənd\ *noun* (circa 1658)
: land naturally. dominated by pine forests
**pi·nene** \'pī-ˌnēn\ *noun* [International Scientific Vocabulary, from Latin *pinus*] (1885)
: either of two liquid isomeric unsaturated bicyclic terpene hydrocarbons $C_{10}H_{16}$ of which
one is a major constituent of wood turpentine
**pine nut** *noun* (before 12th century)
: the edible seed of any of several pines —
compare PIÑON
**pin·ery** \'pī-nə-rē, 'pīn-rē\ *noun, plural* **-er-
ies** (1758)
**1** : a hothouse or area where pineapples are
grown
**2** : a grove or forest of pine
**pine·sap** \'pīn-ˌsap\ *noun* (1840)
: any of several yellowish or reddish parasitic
or saprophytic herbs (genus *Monotropa*) of the
wintergreen family resembling the Indian pipe
**pine siskin** *noun* (1887)
: a North American finch (*Carduelis pinus*)
with streaked plumage
**pine snake** *noun* (1791)
**1** : a large constricting snake (*Pituophis mel-
anoleucus*) of the eastern U.S. that is typically
white and black and is found especially in
coastal regions from New Jersey southward
**2** : any of various snakes related to the pine
snake
**pine tar** *noun* (1880)
: tar obtained by destructive distillation of the
wood of the pine tree and used especially in
roofing and soaps and in the treatment of skin
diseases
**pi·ne·tum** \pī-'nē-təm\ *noun, plural* **pi·ne·ta**
\-'nē-tə\ [Latin, from *pinus*] (1842)
: a plantation of pine trees; *especially* : a scientific collection of living coniferous trees
**pine·wood** \'pīn-ˌwu̇d\ *noun* (1673)
**1** : a wood of pines — often used in plural
but singular or plural in construction
**2** : the wood of the pine tree
**piney woods** *noun plural* (1800)
: woodland of the southern U.S. in which
pines are the dominant tree
**pin·feath·er** \'pin-ˌfe-thər\ *noun* (circa 1775)
: a feather not fully developed; *especially* : a
feather just emerging through the skin
**pin·fish** \-ˌfish\ *noun* (1878)
: a small compressed dark green grunt (*La-
godon rhomboides*) that has sharp dorsal
spines and is found along the Atlantic coast
**pin·fold** \-ˌfōld\ *noun* [Middle English, from
Old English *pundfald,* from *pund-* enclosure +
*fald* fold] (13th century)
**1** : ²POUND 1a
**2** : a place of restraint
**ping** \'piŋ\ *noun* [imitative] (1835)
**1** : a sharp sound like that of a striking bullet
**2** : KNOCK 2b
— **ping** *intransitive verb*
**ping·er** \'piŋ-ər\ *noun* (1957)
: a device for producing pulses of sound (as
for marking an underwater site or detecting an
underwater object)
**pin·go** \'piŋ-(ˌ)gō\ *noun, plural* **pingos** [Inuit
*pinguq*] (1938)
: a low hill or mound forced up by hydrostatic
pressure in an area underlain by permafrost
**ping–pong** \'piŋ-ˌpäŋ, -ˌpȯŋ\ *verb* (1952)
: SHIFT, BOUNCE
**Ping-Pong** \'piŋ-ˌpäŋ, -ˌpȯŋ\ *trademark*
— used for table tennis
**pin·head** \'pin-ˌhed\ *noun* (1593)

**1 :** the head of a pin
**2 :** something very small or insignificant
**3 :** a very dull or stupid person : FOOL
**pin·head·ed** \-ˌhe-dəd\ *adjective* (1901)
**:** lacking intelligence or understanding : DULL, STUPID
— **pin·head·ed·ness** *noun*
**pin·hole** \-ˌhōl\ *noun* (1676)
**:** a small hole made by, for, or as if by a pin
**¹pin·ion** \'pin-yən\ *noun* [Middle English, from Middle French *pignon*, from (assumed) Vulgar Latin *pinnion-, pinnio*, from Latin *pinna* feather — more at PEN] (15th century)
**1 :** the terminal section of a bird's wing including the carpus, metacarpus, and phalanges; *broadly* : WING
**2 :** FEATHER, QUILL; *also* : FLIGHT FEATHERS
— **pin·ioned** \-yənd\ *adjective*
**²pinion** *transitive verb* (1558)
**1 a :** to disable or restrain by binding the arms **b :** to bind fast : SHACKLE
**2 :** to restrain (a bird) from flight especially by cutting off the pinion of one wing
**³pinion** *noun* [French *pignon*, from Middle French *peignon*, from *peigne* comb, from Latin *pecten* — more at PECTINATE] (1659)
**1 :** a gear with a small number of teeth designed to mesh with a larger wheel or rack
**2 :** the smaller of a pair or the smallest of a train of gear wheels
**¹pink** \'piŋk\ *noun* [Middle English, from Middle Dutch *pinke*] (15th century)
**:** a ship with a narrow overhanging stern — called also *pinkie*
**²pink** *noun* [origin unknown] (1573)
**1 :** any of a genus (*Dianthus* of the family Caryophyllaceae, the pink family) of herbs having a cylindrical many-veined calyx with bracts at its base
**2 a :** the very embodiment : PARAGON **b** (1) **:** one dressed in the height of fashion (2) **:** ELITE **c :** highest degree possible : HEIGHT ⟨keep their house in the *pink* of repair —Rebecca West⟩
— **in the pink :** in the best of health or condition
**³pink** *noun* (1678)
**1 :** any of a group of colors bluish red to red in hue, of medium to high lightness, and of low to moderate saturation
**2 a :** the scarlet color of a fox hunter's coat; *also* : a fox hunter's coat of this color **b :** pink-colored clothing **c** *plural* : light-colored trousers formerly worn by army officers
**3 :** PINKO
**⁴pink** *adjective* (1720)
**1 :** of the color pink
**2 :** holding moderately radical and usually socialistic political or economic views
**3 :** emotionally moved : EXCITED — often used as an intensive ⟨tickled *pink*⟩
— **pink·ness** *noun*
**⁵pink** *transitive verb* [Middle English, to thrust] (1503)
**1 a :** to perforate in an ornamental pattern **b :** to cut a saw-toothed edge on
**2 a :** PIERCE, STAB **b :** to wound by irony, criticism, or ridicule
**pink bollworm** *noun* (1906)
**:** a small dark brown moth (*Pectinophora gossypiella*) whose pinkish larva bores into the flowers and bolls of cotton and is a destructive pest in most cotton-growing regions
**pink–collar** *adjective* (1977)
**:** of, relating to, or constituting a class of employees in occupations (as nursing and clerical jobs) traditionally held by women
**pink elephants** *noun plural* (1940)
**:** hallucinations arising especially from heavy drinking or use of narcotics ⟨began to see *pink elephants*⟩
**pink·eye** \'piŋk-ˌī\ *noun* (1855)
**:** an acute highly contagious conjunctivitis of humans and various domestic animals

**¹pin·kie** \'piŋ-kē\ *noun* [probably from Dutch *pinkje* small pink, diminutive of *pink*, from Middle Dutch *pinke*] (1840)
**:** ¹PINK
**²pinkie** *or* **pin·ky** \'piŋ-kē\ *noun, plural* **pinkies** [probably from Dutch *pinkje*, diminutive of *pink* little finger] (circa 1808)
**:** LITTLE FINGER
**pinking shears** *noun plural* (circa 1939)
**:** shears with a saw-toothed inner edge on the blades for making a zigzag cut
**pink·ish** \'piŋ-kish\ *adjective* (1784)
**:** somewhat pink; *especially* : tending to be pink in politics
— **pink·ish·ness** *noun*
**pink lady** *noun* (1936)
**:** a cocktail consisting of gin, brandy, lemon juice, grenadine, and white of egg shaken with ice and strained
**pink·ly** \'piŋ-klē\ *adverb* (1836)
**:** in a pink manner : with a pink hue
**pin·ko** \'piŋ-(ˌ)kō\ *noun, plural* **pink·os** *also* **pink·oes** (1936)
**:** a person who holds advanced liberal or moderately radical political or economic views
**pink·root** \'piŋk-ˌrüt, -ˌrut\ *noun* (1763)
**:** any of several plants (genus *Spigelia*) related to the nux vomica and used as anthelmintics; *especially* : an American woodland herb (*S. marilandica*) sometimes cultivated for its showy red and yellow flowers
**pink salmon** *noun* (1905)
**:** a small spotted Pacific salmon (*Oncorhynchus gorbuscha*) native to the northern Pacific Ocean and adjacent rivers
**pink slip** *noun* (1915)
**:** a notice from an employer that a recipient's employment is being terminated
— **pink–slip** *transitive verb*
**pin money** *noun* (1697)
**1 a :** money given by a man to his wife for her own use **b :** money set aside for the purchase of incidentals
**2 :** a trivial amount of money ⟨worked for *pin money*⟩
**pin·na** \'pi-nə\ *noun, plural* **pin·nae** \'pi-ˌnē, -ˌnī\ *or* **pinnas** [New Latin, from Latin, feather, wing — more at PEN] (1785)
**1 :** a leaflet or primary division of a pinnate leaf or frond
**2 a :** a projecting body part (as a feather, wing, or fin) **b :** the largely cartilaginous projecting portion of the external ear — see EAR illustration
**pin·nace** \'pi-nəs\ *noun* [Middle French *pinace*, probably from Old Spanish *pinaza*, from *pino* pine, from Latin *pinus*] (1538)
**1 :** a light sailing ship; *especially* : one used as a tender
**2 :** any of various ship's boats
**¹pin·na·cle** \'pi-ni-kəl\ *noun* [Middle English *pinacle*, from Middle French, from Late Latin *pinnaculum* small wing, gable, from Latin *pinna* wing, battlement] (14th century)
**1 :** an upright architectural member generally ending in a small spire and used especially in Gothic construction to give weight especially to a buttress
**2 :** a structure or formation suggesting a pinnacle; *specifically* : a lofty peak
**3 :** the highest point of development or achievement : ACME
**synonym** see SUMMIT

*1 pinnacle 1*

**²pinnacle** *transitive verb* **-cled; -cling** \-k(ə-)liŋ\ (14th century)
**1 :** to surmount with a pinnacle
**2 :** to raise or rear on a pinnacle
**pin·nate** \'pi-ˌnāt\ *adjective* [New Latin *pinnatus*, from Latin, feathered, from *pinna* feather, wing, fin] (circa 1727)

**:** resembling a feather especially in having similar parts arranged on opposite sides of an axis like the barbs on the rachis of a feather ⟨*pinnate* leaf⟩ — see LEAF illustration
— **pin·nate·ly** *adverb*
**pin·nat·i·fid** \pə-'na-tə-fəd, -ˌfid\ *adjective* [New Latin *pinnatifidus*, from *pinnatus* + Latin *-fidus* -fid] (circa 1753)
**:** cleft in a pinnate manner ⟨a *pinnatifid* leaf⟩
**pin·ner** \'pi-nər\ *noun* (1652)
**1 :** a woman's cap with long lappets worn in the 17th and 18th centuries
**2 :** one that pins
**pin·ni·ped** \'pi-nə-ˌped\ *noun* [ultimately from Latin *pinna* + *ped-, pes* foot — more at FOOT] (circa 1842)
**:** any of a suborder (Pinnipedia) of aquatic carnivorous mammals (as a seal or walrus) with all four limbs modified into flippers
— **pinniped** *adjective*
**pin·nule** \'pin-(ˌ)yü(ə)l\ *noun* [New Latin *pinnula*, from Latin, diminutive of *pinna*] (1748)
**1 :** any of the secondary branches of a plumose organ especially of a crinoid
**2 :** one of the ultimate divisions of a twice pinnate leaf
**pin·ny** \'pi-nē\ *noun, plural* **pinnies** [by shortening & alteration] (1851)
*chiefly British* : PINAFORE
**pin oak** *noun* (1813)
**:** a pyramidally-crowned oak (*Quercus palustris*) of wet regions of the eastern U.S. that has deeply cleft toothed leaves and rather small nearly hemispherical acorns
**pi·noch·le** \'pē-ˌnə-kəl\ *noun* [modification of German dialect *Binokel*, a game resembling bezique, from French dialect *binocle*] (1864)
**:** a card game played with a 48-card pack containing two each of A, K, Q, J, 10, 9 in each suit with the object to score points by melding certain combinations of cards or by winning tricks that contain scoring cards; *also* : the meld of queen of spades and jack of diamonds scoring 40 points in this game
**pi·no·cy·to·sis** \ˌpi-nə-sə-'tō-səs, ˌpī-, -ˌsī-\ *noun, plural* **-to·ses** \-ˌsēz\ [New Latin, from Greek *pinein* to drink + New Latin *cyt-* + *-osis* — more at POTABLE] (1895)
**:** the uptake of fluid by a cell by invagination and pinching off of the plasma membrane
**pi·no·cy·tot·ic** \-'tä-tik\ *or* **pi·no·cyt·ic** \ˌpi-nə-'sī-tik, ˌpī-\ *adjective* (1959)
**:** of, relating to, or being pinocytosis
— **pi·no·cy·tot·i·cal·ly** \-ti-k(ə-)lē\ *adverb*
**pi·no·le** \pē-'nō-lē\ *noun* [American Spanish, from Nahuatl *pinolli*] (1842)
**1 :** a finely ground flour made from parched corn
**2 :** any of various flours resembling pinole and ground from the seeds of other plants
**pi·ñon** *or* **pin·yon** \'pin-ˌyōn, -ˌyän, -yən; pin-'yōn\ *noun, plural* **pi·ñons** *or* **pin·yons** *or* **pi·ño·nes** \pin-'yō-nēz\ [American Spanish *piñón*, from Spanish, pine nut, from *piña* pinecone, from Latin *pinea* — more at PINEAL] (1831)
**:** any of various low-growing pines (as *Pinus quadrifolia, P. cembroides, P. edulis,* and *P. monophylla*) of western North America with edible seeds; *also* : the edible seed of a piñon
**pi·not noir** \'pē-(ˌ)nō-'nwär, pē-'nō-\ *noun, often P&N capitalized* [French, literally, black Pinot (a grape variety)] (1941)
**:** a dry red wine produced from the same grape as French burgundy
**¹pin·point** \'pin-ˌpoint\ *noun* (1849)
**1 :** something that is extremely small or insignificant
**2 :** the point of a pin
**3 :** an extremely small or sharp point
**²pinpoint** *adjective* (1899)
**1 :** extremely fine or precise
**2 :** located, fixed, or directed with extreme precision ⟨*pinpoint* targets⟩
**3 :** small as a pinpoint
**³pinpoint** *transitive verb* (1917)

**1 :** to locate or aim with great precision or accuracy
**2 a :** to fix, determine, or identify with precision **b :** to cause to stand out conspicuously **:** HIGHLIGHT

**¹pin·prick** \'pin-ˌprik\ *noun* (1862)
**1 :** a small puncture made by or as if by a pin
**2 :** a petty irritation or annoyance

**²pinprick** (1899)
*transitive verb*
**:** to administer pinpricks to
*intransitive verb*
**:** to administer pinpricks

**pins and needles** *noun plural* (1813)
**:** a pricking tingling sensation in a limb growing numb or recovering from numbness
— **on pins and needles :** in a nervous or jumpy state of anticipation

**pin·set·ter** \'pin-ˌse-tər\ *noun* (1916)
**:** an employee or a mechanical device that spots pins in a bowling alley

**pin·spot·ter** \-ˌspä-tər\ *noun* (1946)
**:** PINSETTER

**pin·stripe** \-ˌstrīp\ *noun, often attributive* (1897)
**:** a very thin stripe especially on a fabric; *also*
**:** a suit with such stripes — often used in plural
— **pin·striped** \-ˌstrīpt\ *adjective*

**pint** \'pīnt\ *noun* [Middle English *pinte*, from Middle French, from Medieval Latin *pincta*, probably from (assumed) Vulgar Latin, feminine of *pinctus*, past participle of Latin *pingere* to paint — more at PAINT] (14th century)
**1 —** see WEIGHT table
**2 :** a pint pot or vessel

**¹pin·ta** \'pin-tə, -ˌtä\ *noun* [American Spanish, from Spanish, spot, mark, from (assumed) Vulgar Latin *pincta*] (1825)
**:** a chronic skin disease that is endemic in tropical America, that occurs successively as an initial papule, a generalized eruption, and a patchy loss of pigment, and that is caused by a spirochete (*Treponema careteum*) morphologically indistinguishable from the causative agent of syphilis

**²pinta** \'pīn-tə\ *noun* [*pint + -a* (as in *cuppa*)] (1959)
*British* **:** a pint of milk

**pin·ta·ble** \'pin-ˌtā-bəl\ *noun* (1936)
*British* **:** PINBALL MACHINE

**pin·tail** \'pin-ˌtāl\ *noun, plural* **pintail** *or* **pin·tails** (1768)
**:** a bird having elongated central tail feathers; *especially* **:** a slender duck (*Anas acuta*) of the northern hemisphere with the male having a brown head, a white breast with a white line continuing up the side of the neck, and chiefly gray upperparts

**pin·tle** \'pin-tᵊl\ *noun* [Middle English *pintel*, literally, penis, from Old English; akin to Middle Low German *pint* penis, Old English *pinn* pin] (15th century)
**:** a usually upright pivot pin on which another part turns

**¹pin·to** \'pin-(ˌ)tō\ *noun, plural* **pintos** *also* **pintoes** [American Spanish, from *pinto* spotted, from obsolete Spanish, from (assumed) Vulgar Latin *pinctus*] (1860)
**:** a horse or pony marked with patches of white and another color — compare PIEBALD, SKEWBALD

**²pinto** *adjective* (1865)
**:** PIED, MOTTLED

**pinto bean** *noun* (1916)
**:** a mottled kidney bean that is grown chiefly in the southwestern U.S. for food and for stock feed

**pint–size** \'pīnt-ˌsīz\ *or* **pint–sized** \-ˌsīzd\ *adjective* (1936)
**:** SMALL

**¹pin·up** \'pin-ˌəp\ *noun* (1943)

**:** something fastened to a wall: as **a :** a photograph or poster of a person considered to have glamorous qualities **b :** something (as a lamp) designed for wall attachment

**²pinup** *adjective* (1941)
**1 :** of or relating to pinups ⟨male *pinup* calendars⟩
**2 :** designed for hanging on a wall ⟨a *pinup* lamp⟩

**pinup girl** *noun* (1941)
**:** a girl or woman whose glamorous qualities make her a suitable subject for a pinup

**pin·wale** \'pin-ˌwāl\ *adjective* (1949)
*of a fabric* **:** made with narrow wales

**pin·weed** \-ˌwēd\ *noun* (1814)
**:** any of a genus (*Lechea*) of herbs of the rockrose family with slender stems, many small leaves, and tiny flowers

**¹pin·wheel** \-ˌhwēl, -ˌwēl\ *noun* (1869)
**1 :** a fireworks device in the form of a revolving wheel of colored fire
**2 :** a toy consisting of lightweight vanes that revolve at the end of a stick
**3 :** something (as a galaxy) shaped like a pinwheel

**²pinwheel** *intransitive verb* (circa 1934)
**:** to move like a pinwheel

**pin·worm** \-ˌwərm\ *noun* (circa 1864)
**1 :** any of numerous small nematode worms (family Oxyuridae) that infest the intestines and especially the cecum of various vertebrates; *especially* **:** a worm (*Enterobius vermicularis*) parasitic in humans
**2 :** any of several rather slender insect larvae that burrow in plant tissue

**pinx·ter flower** \'piŋ(k)-stər-\ *noun* [Dutch *pinkster* Whitsuntide] (1857)
**:** a deciduous pink-flowered azalea (*Rhododendron periclymenoides* synonym *R. nudiflorum*) that is native to rich moist woodlands of eastern North America

**pin·yin** \'pin-'yin\ *noun, often capitalized* [Chinese (Beijing) *pīnyīn*, from *pīn* to spell phonetically, from *pīn* to arrange + *yīn* sound, pronunciation] (1963)
**:** a system for romanizing Chinese ideograms in which tones are indicated by diacritics and unaspirated consonants are transcribed as voiced — compare WADE-GILES

**pi·on** \'pī-ˌän\ *noun* [contraction of *pi-meson*] (1950)
**:** any of four mesons that consist of combinations of two up or down quarks, that may be positive, negative, or neutral, that have a mass about 270 times that of the electron, and that are subject to the strong force
— **pi·on·ic** \pī-'ä-nik\ *adjective*

**¹pi·o·neer** \ˌpī-ə-'nir\ *noun* [Middle French *pionier*, from Old French *peonier* foot soldier, from *peon* foot soldier, from Medieval Latin *pedon-, pedo* — more at PAWN] (1523)
**1 :** a member of a military unit usually of construction engineers
**2 a :** a person or group that originates or helps open up a new line of thought or activity or a new method or technical development **b :** one of the first to settle in a territory
**3 :** a plant or animal capable of establishing itself in a bare, barren, or open area and initiating an ecological cycle ◆

**²pioneer** (1780)
*intransitive verb*
**:** to act as a pioneer ⟨*pioneered* in the development of airplanes⟩
*transitive verb*
**1 :** to open or prepare for others to follow; *also* **:** SETTLE
**2 :** to originate or take part in the development of

**³pioneer** *adjective* (1840)
**1 :** ORIGINAL, EARLIEST
**2 :** relating to or being a pioneer; *especially* **:** of, relating to, or characteristic of early settlers or their time

**pi·ous** \'pī-əs\ *adjective* [Middle English, from Latin *pius*] (15th century)

**1 a :** marked by or showing reverence for deity and devotion to divine worship **b :** marked by conspicuous religiosity ⟨a hypocrite—a thing all *pious* words and uncharitable deeds —Charles Reade⟩
**2 :** sacred or devotional as distinct from the profane or secular **:** RELIGIOUS ⟨a *pious* opinion⟩
**3 :** showing loyal reverence for a person or thing **:** DUTIFUL
**4 a :** marked by sham or hypocrisy **b :** marked by self-conscious virtue **:** VIRTUOUS
**5 :** deserving commendation **:** WORTHY ⟨a *pious* effort⟩
— **pi·ous·ly** *adverb*
— **pi·ous·ness** *noun*

**¹pip** \'pip\ *noun* [Middle English *pippe*, from Middle Dutch (akin to Old High German *pfiffiz*), from (assumed) Vulgar Latin *pipita*, alteration of Latin *pituita* phlegm, pip; perhaps akin to Greek *pitys* pine — more at PINE] (15th century)
**1 a :** a disorder of a bird marked by formation of a scale or crust on the tongue **b :** the scale or crust of this disorder
**2 a :** any of various human ailments; *especially* **:** a slight nonspecific disorder **b** *chiefly British* **:** a feeling of irritation or annoyance

**²pip** *verb* **pipped; pip·ping** [imitative] (1598)
*intransitive verb*
**1 :** ¹PEEP 1
**2 :** to break through the shell of the egg ⟨the chick *pipped*⟩
*transitive verb*
**:** to break open (the shell of an egg) in hatching

**³pip** *noun* [origin unknown] (1604)
**1 a :** one of the dots used on dice and dominoes to indicate numerical value **b :** SPOT 2c
**2 a :** SPOT, SPECK **b :** ¹SPIKE 6a; *also* **:** BLIP
**3 :** an individual rootstock of the lily of the valley
**4 :** a diamond-shaped insignia of rank worn by a second lieutenant, lieutenant, or captain in the British army

**⁴pip** *noun* [short for *pippin*] (1797)
**1 :** a small fruit seed; *especially* **:** one of a several-seeded fleshy fruit
**2 :** one extraordinary of its kind

◇ WORD HISTORY
**pioneer** Daniel Boone and the other pioneers who opened up the American West are heroic figures to many, but the origins of the word *pioneer* are somewhat less than grand. Medieval French *pēonier* or *pionier*, a derivative of *peon* "foot soldier," also originally meant "foot soldier," but later appeared in the sense "digger, excavator" and by the 14th century designated a solider who dug earthworks and prepared fortifications in advance of the troops who would occupy them. The word was borrowed by English in the latter sense as *pioner* in the 16th century, and with the modern spelling *pioneer* continues to refer to troops who build fortifications, roads, and bridges, though in the 20th century American army *engineer* has replaced it. In the figurative sense "forerunner" or "initiator," however, the English word has gone beyond its French source. Its specific application to a frontiersman first appeared in American English in the early 19th century, notably in the title of *The Pioneers*, a novel by James Fenimore Cooper published in 1823.

\ə\ abut \ᵊ\ kitten \ər\ further \a\ ash \ā\ ace
\ä\ mop, mar \au̇\ out \ch\ chin \e\ bet \ē\ easy
\g\ go \i\ hit \ī\ ice \j\ job \ŋ\ sing \ō\ go
\ȯ\ law \ȯi\ boy \th\ thin \t̷h\ the \ü\ loot \u̇\ foot
\y\ yet \zh\ vision    *see also* Guide to Pronunciation

**⁵pip** *transitive verb* **pipped; pip·ping** [probably from *pip* to blackball, from ³*pip* or ⁴*pip*] (1880)
*British* **:** to beat by a narrow margin
**⁶pip** *noun* [imitative] (1907)
*chiefly British* **:** a short high-pitched tone
**pip·age** *or* **pipe·age** \'pī-pij\ *noun* (1612)
**1 a :** transportation by means of pipes **b :** the charge for such transportation
**2 :** material for pipelines **:** PIPING
**pi·pal** \'pē-(ˌ)pəl\ *noun* [Hindi *pīpal,* from Sanskrit *pippala*] (1788)
**:** a large long-lived fig (*Ficus religiosa*) of India
**¹pipe** \'pīp\ *noun* [Middle English, from Old English *pīpa* (akin to Old High German *pfīfa* pipe), from (assumed) Vulgar Latin *pipa* pipe, from Latin *pipare* to peep, of imitative origin] (before 12th century)
**1 a :** a tubular wind instrument; *specifically* **:** a small fipple flute held in and played by the left hand **b :** one of the tubes of a pipe organ: (1) **:** FLUE PIPE (2) **:** REED PIPE **c :** BAGPIPE — usually used in plural **d** (1) **:** VOICE, VOCAL CORD — usually used in plural (2) **:** PIPING 1
**2 :** a long tube or hollow body for conducting a liquid, gas, or finely divided solid or for structural purposes
**3 a :** a tubular or cylindrical object, part, or passage **b :** a roughly cylindrical and vertical geological formation **c :** the eruptive channel opening into the crater of a volcano
**4 a :** a large cask of varying capacity used especially for wine and oil **b :** any of various units of liquid capacity based on the size of a pipe; *especially* **:** a unit equal to 2 hogsheads
**5 :** a device for smoking usually consisting of a tube having a bowl at one end and a mouthpiece at the other
**6 :** SNAP 2c, CINCH
— **pipe·ful** \-ˌfu̇l\ *noun*
— **pipe·less** \'pī-pləs\ *adjective*
— **pipe·like** \'pīp-ˌlīk\ *adjective*
**²pipe** *verb* **piped; pip·ing** (before 12th century)
*intransitive verb*
**1 a :** to play on a pipe **b :** to convey orders by signals on a boatswain's pipe
**2 a :** to speak in a high or shrill voice **b :** to emit a shrill sound
*transitive verb*
**1 a :** to play (a tune) on a pipe **b :** to utter in the shrill tone of a pipe
**2 a :** to lead or cause to go with pipe music **b** (1) **:** to call or direct by the boatswain's pipe (2) **:** to receive aboard or attend the departure of by sounding a boatswain's pipe
**3 :** to trim with piping
**4 :** to furnish or equip with pipes
**5 :** to convey by or as if by pipes; *especially* **:** to transmit by wire or coaxial cable
**6 :** NOTICE
**pipe clay** *noun* (1777)
**:** highly plastic grayish white clay used especially in making tobacco pipes and for whitening leather
**pipe cleaner** *noun* (1870)
**:** something used to clean the inside of a pipe; *specifically* **:** a piece of flexible wire in which tufted fabric is twisted and which is used to clean the stem of a tobacco pipe
**pipe cutter** *noun* (circa 1890)
**:** a tool or machine for cutting pipe; *especially* **:** a hand tool comprising a grasping device and one or more sharp-edged wheels that cut into the pipe as the tool is rotated
**pipe down** *intransitive verb* [²*pipe*] (1850)
**:** to stop talking or making noise
**pipe dream** *noun* [from the fantasies brought about by the smoking of opium] (1896)

**pipe cutter**

**:** an illusory or fantastic plan, hope, or story
**pipe·fish** \'pīp-ˌfish\ *noun* (1769)
**:** any of various fishes (family Syngnathidae) that are related to the sea horses and have a tube-shaped snout and a long slender body covered with bony plates
**pipe fitter** *noun* (circa 1883)
**:** a worker who installs and repairs piping
**pipe fitting** *noun* (circa 1890)
**1 :** a piece (as a coupling or elbow) used to connect pipes or as accessory to a pipe
**2 :** the work of a pipe fitter
**pipe·line** \'pīp-ˌlīn\ *noun* (1860)
**1 :** a line of pipe with pumps, valves, and control devices for conveying liquids, gases, or finely divided solids
**2 :** a direct channel for information
**3 :** the processes through which supplies pass from or as if from source to user
— **in the pipeline :** undergoing preparation, production, or completion **:** in the works
**pipe of peace** (1705)
**:** CALUMET
**pipe organ** *noun* (1885)
**:** ORGAN 1b(1)
**pip·er** \'pī-pər\ *noun* (before 12th century)
**:** one that plays on a pipe
**pi·per·a·zine** \pi-'per-ə-ˌzēn, pī-\ *noun* [International Scientific Vocabulary *piper*idine + *azine*] (1889)
**:** a crystalline heterocyclic base $C_4H_{10}N_2$ used especially as an anthelmintic
**pi·per·i·dine** \pi-'per-ə-ˌdēn, pī-\ *noun* [International Scientific Vocabulary *piper*ine + *-idine*] (1854)
**:** a liquid heterocyclic base $C_5H_{11}N$ that has a peppery ammoniacal odor and is obtained usually by hydrolysis of piperine
**pip·er·ine** \'pi-pə-ˌrēn\ *noun* [probably from French *pipérine,* from Latin *piper* pepper] (1820)
**:** a white crystalline alkaloid $C_{17}H_{19}NO_3$ that is the chief active constituent of pepper
**pi·per·o·nal** \pī-'per-ə-ˌnal\ *noun* [International Scientific Vocabulary *piper*ine + *-one* + ³*-al*] (1869)
**:** a crystalline aldehyde $C_8H_6O_3$ with an odor of heliotrope
**pi·per·o·nyl bu·tox·ide** \pī-'per-ə-ˌnil-byu̇-'täk-ˌsīd, -nᵊl-\ *noun* [*piperon*al + *-yl* + *but*yl + *oxide*] (1945)
**:** an insecticide $C_{19}H_{30}O_5$; *especially* **:** an oily liquid containing this compound that is used chiefly as a synergist (as for pyrethrum insecticides)
**pipe·stone** \'pīp-ˌstōn\ *noun* (circa 1805)
**:** a pink or mottled pink-and-white argillaceous stone used especially by American Indians to make carved objects (as tobacco pipes)
**pipe stop** *noun* (circa 1909)
**:** an organ stop composed of flue pipes
**pi·pette** *also* **pi·pet** \pī-'pet\ *noun* [French *pipette,* diminutive of *pipe* pipe, cask, from (assumed) Vulgar Latin *pipa, pippa* pipe] (1839)
**:** a small piece of apparatus which typically consists of a narrow tube into which fluid is drawn by suction (as for dispensing or measurement) and retained by closing the upper end
— **pipette** *also* **pipet** *verb*
**pipe up** *intransitive verb* (1889)
**:** SPEAK UP
**pipe wrench** *noun* (circa 1875)
**:** a wrench for gripping and turning a cylindrical object (as a pipe) usually by use of two serrated jaws so designed as to grip the pipe when turning in one direction only
**¹pip·ing** \'pī-piŋ\ *noun* (13th century)
**1 a :** a sound, note, or call like that of a pipe **b :** the music of a pipe
**2 :** a quantity or system of pipes
**3 :** trimming stitched in seams or along edges (as of clothing, slipcovers, or curtains)
**²piping** *adjective* (15th century)
**1 :** SHRILL ⟨a *piping* voice⟩

**2 :** TRANQUIL ⟨*piping* times of peace —Shakespeare⟩
**piping hot** *adjective* (14th century)
**:** very hot
**pip·it** \'pi-pət\ *noun* [imitative] (1768)
**:** any of various small singing birds (family Motacillidae and especially genus *Anthus*) resembling the lark
**pip·kin** \'pip-kən\ *noun* [perhaps from *pipe*] (1565)
**:** a small earthenware or metal pot usually with a horizontal handle
**pip·pin** \'pi-pən\ *noun* [Middle English *pepin,* from Middle French] (15th century)
**1 :** any of numerous apples that have usually yellow or greenish yellow skins strongly flushed with red and are used especially for cooking
**2 :** a highly admired or very admirable person or thing
**pip–pip** \ˌpi(p)-'pip\ *interjection* [probably from *pip-pip,* imitating the sound of a horn] (1907)
*British* — used to express farewell
**pip·sis·se·wa** \pip-'si-sə-ˌwȯ\ *noun* [perhaps from Eastern Abenaki *kpi-pskʷáhsawe,* literally, flower of the woods] (1789)
**:** any of a genus (*Chimaphila* and especially *C. umbellata*) of evergreen herbs of the wintergreen family with astringent leaves used as a tonic and diuretic
**pip–squeak** \'pip-ˌskwēk\ *noun* (1910)
**:** one that is small or insignificant
**pi·quance** \'pē-kən(t)s, -ˌkwən(t)s\ *noun* (1883)
**:** PIQUANCY
**pi·quan·cy** \'pē-kən(t)-sē, 'pē-ˌkwən(t)-\ *noun* (1664)
**:** the quality or state of being piquant
**pi·quant** \'pē-kənt, -ˌkänt; 'pi-kwənt\ *adjective* [Middle French, from present participle of *piquer*] (1630)
**1 :** agreeably stimulating to the palate; *especially* **:** SPICY
**2 :** engagingly provocative; *also* **:** having a lively arch charm
**synonym** see PUNGENT
— **pi·quant·ly** *adverb*
— **pi·quant·ness** *noun*
**¹pique** \'pēk\ *noun* (1592)
**:** a transient feeling of wounded vanity **:** RESENTMENT ⟨a fit of *pique*⟩
**synonym** see OFFENSE
**²pique** *transitive verb* **piqued; piqu·ing** [French *piquer,* literally, to prick — more at PIKE] (1669)
**1 :** to arouse anger or resentment in **:** IRRITATE ⟨what *piques* linguistic conservatives —T. H. Middleton⟩
**2 a :** to excite or arouse by a provocation, challenge, or rebuff ⟨sly remarks to *pique* their curiosity⟩ **b :** PRIDE ⟨he *piques* himself on his skill as a cook⟩
**synonym** see PROVOKE
**pi·qué** *or* **pi·que** \pi-'kā, pē-\ *noun* [French *piqué,* from past participle of *piquer* to prick, quilt] (1852)
**1 :** a durable ribbed clothing fabric of cotton, rayon, or silk
**2 :** decoration of a tortoiseshell or ivory object with inlaid fragments of gold or silver
**pi·quet** \pi-'kā, -'ket\ *noun* [French] (1646)
**:** a two-handed card game played with 32 cards
**pi·ra·cy** \'pī-rə-sē\ *noun, plural* **-cies** [Medieval Latin *piratia,* from Late Greek *peirateia,* from Greek *peiratēs* pirate] (1537)
**1 :** an act of robbery on the high seas; *also* **:** an act resembling such robbery
**2 :** robbery on the high seas
**3 :** the unauthorized use of another's production, invention, or conception especially in infringement of a copyright
**pi·ra·gua** \pə-'rä-gwə, -'ra-\ *noun* [Spanish] (1609)
**1 :** DUGOUT 1

**2 :** a 2-masted flat-bottomed boat

**pi·ra·nha** \pə-'rä-nə; -'rän-yə, -'ran-\ *noun* [Portuguese, from Tupi *pirāya*, from *pira* fish + *āya* tooth] (1869)
**:** any of various usually small South American characin fishes (genus *Serrasalmo*) having very sharp teeth and including some that may attack and inflict dangerous wounds upon humans and large animals — called also *caribe*

**pi·ra·ru·cu** \pi-ˌrär-ə-'kü\ *noun* [Portuguese, from Tupi *pirauruku*, from *pira* fish + *uruku* annatto] (1840)
**:** a very large edible bony fish (*Arapaima gigas* of the family Osteoglossidae) of the rivers of northern South America

**¹pi·rate** \'pī-rət\ *noun* [Middle English, from Middle French or Latin; Middle French, from Latin *pirata*, from Greek *peiratēs*, from *peiran* to attempt — more at FEAR] (14th century)
**:** one who commits or practices piracy
— **pi·rat·i·cal** \pə-'ra-ti-kəl, pī-\ *adjective*
— **pi·rat·i·cal·ly** \-k(ə-)lē\ *adverb*

**²pirate** *verb* **pi·rat·ed; pi·rat·ing** (1574)
*transitive verb*
**1 :** to commit piracy on
**2 :** to take or appropriate by piracy: as **a :** to reproduce without authorization especially in infringement of copyright **b :** to lure away from another employer by offers of betterment
*intransitive verb*
**:** to commit or practice piracy

**pirn** \'pərn, *2 is also* 'pirn\ *noun* [Middle English] (15th century)
**1 :** QUILL 1a(1)
**2** *chiefly Scottish* **:** a device resembling a reel

**pi·ro·gi** *variant of* PIEROGI

**pi·rogue** \'pē-ˌrōg\ *noun* [French, from Spanish *piragua*, from Carib *piraua*] (1666)
**1 :** DUGOUT 1
**2 :** a boat like a canoe

**piro·plasm** \'pir-ə-ˌpla-zəm\ *or* **piro·plas·ma** \ˌpir-ə-'plaz-mə\ *noun, plural* **piro·plasms** *or* **piro·plas·ma·ta** \ˌpir-ə-'plaz-mə-tə\ [New Latin *Piroplasma*, genus of piroplasms] (1901)
**:** BABESIA

**pi·rosh·ki** *or* **pi·rozh·ki** \pi-'rōsh-kē, -ˌpir-əsh-'kē\ *noun plural* [Russian *pirozhki*, plural of *pirozhok*, diminutive of *pirog* pastry] (1912)
**:** small pastries with meat, cheese, or vegetable filling

**pir·ou·ette** \ˌpir-ə-'wet\ *noun* [French, literally, teetotum] (1706)
**:** a rapid whirling about of the body; *especially* **:** a full turn on the toe or ball of one foot in ballet
— **pirouette** *intransitive verb*

**pis** *plural of* PI

**pis al·ler** \ˌpē-za-'lā\ *noun, plural* **pis al·lers** \-'lā(z)\ [French, literally, to go worst] (1676)
**:** a last resource or device **:** EXPEDIENT

**pis·ca·to·ri·al** \ˌpis-kə-'tōr-ē-əl, -'tòr-\ *adjective* (1828)
**:** PISCATORY

**pis·ca·to·ry** \'pis-kə-ˌtōr-ē, -ˌtòr-\ *adjective* [Latin *piscatorius*, from *piscari* to fish, from *piscis*] (1633)
**:** of, relating to, or dependent on fish or fishing

**Pis·ce·an** \'pī-sē-ən, 'pi-sē-, 'pis-kē-\ *noun* (1925)
**:** PISCES 2b

**Pis·ces** \'pī-(ˌ)sēz *also* 'pi-ˌsēz *or* 'pis-ˌkās\ *noun plural but singular in construction* [Middle English, from Latin (genitive *Piscium*), from plural of *piscis* fish — more at FISH]
**1 :** a zodiacal constellation directly south of Andromeda
**2 a :** the 12th sign of the zodiac in astrology — see ZODIAC table **b :** one born under this sign

**pis·ci·cul·ture** \'pī-sə-ˌkəl-chər, 'pi-sə-, 'pis-kə-\ *noun* [probably from French, from Latin *piscis* + French *culture* culture] (1859)
**:** fish culture

**pi·sci·na** \pə-'sē-nə, -'sī-\ *noun* [Medieval Latin, from Latin, fishpond, from *piscis*] (1793)
**:** a basin with a drain near the altar of a church for disposing of water from liturgical ablutions

**pi·scine** \'pī-ˌsēn, 'pi-ˌsīn, 'pis-ˌkīn\ *adjective* [Latin *piscinus*, from *piscis*] (1799)
**:** of, relating to, or characteristic of fish

**pi·sciv·o·rous** \pə-'si-və-rəs, pī-\ *adjective* [Latin *piscis* + English *-vorous*] (1668)
**:** feeding on fishes

**pish** \'pish\ *interjection* (1592)
**:** used to express disdain or contempt

**¹pi·si·form** \'pī-sə-ˌfòrm\ *adjective* [Latin *pisum* pea + English *-iform* — more at PEA] (1767)
**:** resembling a pea in size or shape

**²pisiform** *noun* (circa 1771)
**:** a bone on the ulnar side of the carpus in most mammals

**pis·mire** \'pis-ˌmīr, 'piz-\ *noun* [Middle English *pissemire*, from *pisse* urine + *mire* ant, of Scandinavian origin; akin to Old Norse *maurr* ant; akin to Latin *formica* ant, Greek *myrmēx*] (14th century)
**:** ANT

**pis·mo clam** \'piz-(ˌ)mō-\ *noun, often P capitalized* [*Pismo* Beach, Calif.] (1913)
**:** a thick-shelled clam (*Tivela stultorum*) of the southwest coast of North America used extensively for food

**pi·so** \'pē-(ˌ)sō\ *noun* [probably from Tagalog, from Spanish *peso*] (circa 1975)
**:** the peso of the Philippines

**pi·so·lite** \'pī-sə-ˌlīt\ *noun* [New Latin *pisolithus*, from Greek *pisos* pea + *-lithos* -lith] (1708)
**:** a limestone composed of pisiform concretions
— **pi·so·lit·ic** \ˌpī-sə-'li-tik\ *adjective*

**¹piss** \'pis\ *verb* [Middle English, from Old French *pissier*, from (assumed) Vulgar Latin *pissiare*, of imitative origin] (14th century)
*intransitive verb*
**:** URINATE — sometimes considered vulgar
*transitive verb*
**:** to urinate in or on — sometimes considered vulgar

**²piss** *noun* (14th century)
**1 :** URINE — sometimes considered vulgar
**2 :** an act of urinating — often used with *take*; sometimes considered vulgar

**piss·ant** \'pis-ˌant\ *noun, often attributive* [*pissant* ant, from ¹*piss* + *ant*] (circa 1946)
**:** one that is insignificant — used as a generalized term of abuse; sometimes considered vulgar

**piss away** *transitive verb* (1949)
**:** to fritter away **:** SQUANDER — sometimes considered vulgar

**pissed** \'pist\ *adjective* (1929)
**1** *chiefly British* **:** DRUNK 1a — sometimes considered vulgar
**2 :** ANGRY, IRRITATED — often used with *off*; sometimes considered vulgar

**piss off** (1953)
*intransitive verb*
*British* **:** to leave immediately **:** SCRAM — usually used as a command; sometimes considered vulgar
*transitive verb*
**:** ANGER, IRRITATE — sometimes considered vulgar

**pis·soir** \pi-'swär\ *noun* [French, from Middle French, from *pisser* to urinate, from Old French *pissier*] (1919)
**:** a public urinal usually located on the street in some European countries

**pis·ta·chio** \pə-'sta-sh(ē-ˌ)ō, -'stä-\ *noun, plural* **-chios** [Italian *pistacchio*, from Latin *pistacium* pistachio nut, from Greek *pistakion*, from *pistakē* pistachio tree, of Iranian origin; akin to Persian *pistah* pistachio tree] (1598)
**:** a small Asian tree (*Pistacia vera*) of the cashew family whose drupaceous fruit contains a greenish edible seed; *also* **:** its seed

**pis·ta·reen** \ˌpis-tə-'rēn\ *noun* [probably modification of Spanish *peseta* peseta] (1744)
**:** an old Spanish silver piece circulating at a debased rate

**piste** \'pēst\ *noun* [French, from Middle French, from Old Italian *pista*, from *pistare* to trample down, pound — more at PISTON] (circa 1741)
**:** TRAIL; *especially* **:** a downhill ski trail

**pis·til** \'pis-tᵊl\ *noun* [New Latin *pistillum*, from Latin, pestle — more at PESTLE] (1749)
**:** a single carpel or group of fused carpels usually differentiated into an ovary, style, and stigma — see FLOWER illustration

**pis·til·late** \'pis-tə-ˌlāt\ *adjective* (circa 1828)
**:** having pistils; *specifically* **:** having pistils but no stamens

**pis·tol** \'pis-tᵊl\ *noun* [Middle French *pistole*, from German, from Middle High German *pischulle*, from Czech *píšťala*, literally, pipe, fife; akin to Czech *pištět* to squeak] (circa 1570)
**:** a handgun whose chamber is integral with the barrel; *broadly* **:** HANDGUN
— **pistol** *transitive verb*

**pis·tole** \pis-'tōl\ *noun* [Middle French] (1592)
**:** an old gold 2-escudo piece of Spain; *also*
**:** any of several old gold coins of Europe of approximately the same value

**pis·tol·eer** \ˌpis-tə-'lir\ *noun* (1832)
**:** one who is armed with a pistol

**pistol grip** *noun* (1874)
**1 :** a grip of a shotgun or rifle shaped like a pistol stock
**2 :** a handle shaped like a pistol stock

**pistol–whip** *transitive verb* (circa 1942)
**:** to beat with a pistol

**pis·ton** \'pis-tən\ *noun* [French, from Italian *pistone*, from *pistare* to pound, from Old Italian, from Medieval Latin, from Latin *pistus*, past participle of *pinsere* to crush — more at PESTLE] (1704)
**1 :** a sliding piece moved by or moving against fluid pressure which usually consists of a short cylinder fitting within a cylindrical vessel along which it moves back and forth
**2 a :** a sliding valve moving in a cylinder in a brass instrument which when depressed by a finger knob serves to lower the instrument's pitch **b :** a button on an organ console to bring in a previously selected registration

**piston pin** *noun* (1897)
**:** WRIST PIN

**piston ring** *noun* (1867)
**:** a springy split metal ring for sealing the gap between a piston and the cylinder wall

**piston rod** *noun* (1786)
**:** CONNECTING ROD

**¹pit** \'pit\ *noun* [Middle English, from Old English *pytt* (akin to Old High German *pfuzzi* well), from Latin *puteus* well, pit] (before 12th century)
**1 a** (1) **:** a hole, shaft, or cavity in the ground (2) **:** MINE (3) **:** a scooped-out place used for burning something (as charcoal) **b :** an area often sunken or depressed below the adjacent floor area: as (1) **:** an enclosure in which animals are made to fight each other (2) **:** a space at the front of a theater for the orchestra (3) **:** an area in a securities or commodities exchange in which members trade (as stocks)
**2 a :** HELL — used with *the* **b :** a place or situation of futility, misery, or degradation **c** *plural* **:** WORST (it's the *pits*)
**3 :** a hollow or indentation especially in the surface of an organism: as **a :** a natural hollow in the surface of the body **b :** one of the indented scars left in the skin by a pustular disease **:** POCKMARK **c :** a minute depression in the secondary wall of a plant cell functioning

in the intercellular movement of water and dissolved material
**4 :** any of the areas alongside an auto racecourse used for refueling and repairing the cars during a race — often used in plural with *the*
²**pit** *verb* **pit·ted; pit·ting** (15th century)
*transitive verb*
**1 a :** to place, cast, bury, or store in a pit **b :** to make pits in; *especially* **:** to scar or mark with pits
**2 a :** to set (as gamecocks) into or as if into a pit to fight **b :** to set into opposition or rivalry — usually used with *against*
*intransitive verb*
**1 :** to become marked with pits; *especially* **:** to preserve for a time an indentation made by pressure
**2 :** to make a pit stop
³**pit** *noun* [Dutch, from Middle Dutch — more at PITH] (1841)
**:** the stone of a drupaceous fruit
⁴**pit** *transitive verb* **pit·ted; pit·ting** (1913)
**:** to remove the pit from (a fruit)
¹**pi·ta** \'pē-tə\ *noun* [Spanish & Portuguese] (1698)
**1 :** any of several fiber-yielding plants (as an agave)
**2 :** the fiber of a pita; *also* **:** any of several fibers from other sources
²**pita** *noun* [New Greek] (1951)
**:** a thin flat bread that can be separated easily into two layers to form a pocket — called also *pita bread*
**pit-a-pat** \,pit-i-'pat\ *noun* [imitative] (1582)
**:** PITTER-PATTER
— **pit-a-pat** *adverb or adjective*
— **pit-a-pat** *intransitive verb*
**pit boss** *noun* (1949)
**:** a person who supervises the gaming tables in a casino
**pit bull** *noun* (1930)
**:** a dog (as an American Staffordshire terrier) of any of several breeds or a real or apparent hybrid with one or more of these breeds that was developed and is now often trained for fighting and is noted for strength and stamina
**pit bull terrier** *noun* (1945)
**1 :** PIT BULL
**2 :** AMERICAN PIT BULL TERRIER
¹**pitch** \'pich\ *noun* [Middle English *pich*, from Old English *pic*, from Latin *pic-, pix;* akin to Greek *pissa* pitch, Old Church Slavonic *pĭcĭlŭ*] (before 12th century)
**1 :** a black or dark viscous substance obtained as a residue in the distillation of organic materials and especially tars
**2 :** any of various bituminous substances
**3 :** resin obtained from various conifers and often used medicinally
**4 :** any of various artificial mixtures resembling resinous or bituminous pitches
²**pitch** *transitive verb* (before 12th century)
**:** to cover, smear, or treat with or as if with pitch
³**pitch** *verb* [Middle English *pichen*] (13th century)
*transitive verb*
**1 :** to erect and fix firmly in place ⟨*pitch* a tent⟩
**2 :** to throw usually with a particular objective or toward a particular point ⟨*pitch* hay onto a wagon⟩: as **a :** to throw (a baseball) to a batter **b :** to toss (as coins) so as to fall at or near a mark ⟨*pitch* pennies⟩ **c :** to put aside or discard by or as if by throwing ⟨*pitched* the trash into the bin⟩ ⟨decided to *pitch* the whole idea⟩
**3 :** to present or advertise for sale especially in a high-pressure way
**4 a** (1) **:** to cause to be at a particular level or of a particular quality (2) **:** to set in a particular musical key **b :** to cause to be set at a particular angle **:** SLOPE
**5 :** to utter glibly and insincerely
**6 a :** to use as a starting pitcher **b :** to play as pitcher

**7 :** to hit (a golf ball) in a high arc with backspin so that it rolls very little after striking the green
*intransitive verb*
**1 a :** to fall precipitately or headlong **b** (1) *of a ship* **:** to have the bow alternately plunge precipitately and rise abruptly (2) *of an aircraft, missile, or spacecraft* **:** to turn about a lateral axis so that the forward end rises or falls in relation to the after end **c :** BUCK 1
**2 :** ENCAMP
**3 :** to hit upon or happen upon something ⟨*pitch* upon the perfect gift⟩
**4 :** to incline downward **:** SLOPE
**5 a :** to throw a ball to a batter **b :** to play ball as a pitcher **c :** to pitch a golf ball
**6 :** to make a sales pitch
*synonym* see THROW
— **pitch into 1 :** ATTACK, ASSAIL **2 :** to set to work on energetically
⁴**pitch** *noun* (1542)
**1 a :** SLOPE; *also* **:** degree of slope **:** RAKE **b :** the distance between any of various things: as (1) **:** distance between one point on a gear tooth and the corresponding point on the next tooth (2) **:** distance from any point on the thread of a screw to the corresponding point on an adjacent thread measured parallel to the axis **c :** the theoretical distance a propeller would advance longitudinally in one revolution **d :** the number of teeth or of threads per inch **e :** a unit of width of type based on the number of times a letter can be set in a linear inch
**2 :** the action or a manner of pitching; *especially* **:** an up-and-down movement — compare YAW
**3** *archaic* **:** TOP, ZENITH
**4 a :** the relative level, intensity, or extent of some quality or state ⟨tensions rose to a feverish *pitch*⟩ **b** (1) **:** the property of a sound and especially a musical tone that is determined by the frequency of the waves producing it **:** highness or lowness of sound (2) **:** a standard frequency for tuning instruments **c** (1) **:** the difference in the relative vibration frequency of the human voice that contributes to the total meaning of speech (2) **:** a definite relative pitch that is a significant phenomenon in speech
**5 :** a steep place **:** DECLIVITY
**6** *chiefly British* **a :** an outdoor site (as for camping or doing business) **b :** PLAYING FIELD 1
**7 :** an all-fours game in which the first card led is a trump
**8 a :** an often high-pressure sales presentation **b :** ADVERTISEMENT
**9 a :** the delivery of a baseball by a pitcher to a batter **b :** a baseball so thrown **c :** PITCHOUT 2
— **pitched** \'picht\ *adjective*
**pitch–black** \'pich-'blak\ *adjective* (1599)
**:** extremely dark or black
**pitch–blende** \'pich-,blend\ *noun* [part translation of German *Pechblende*, from *Pech* pitch + *Blende* blende] (1770)
**:** a brown to black mineral that consists of massive uraninite, has a distinctive luster, contains radium, and is the chief ore-mineral source of uranium
**pitch–dark** \'pich-'därk\ *adjective* (1827)
**:** extremely dark **:** PITCH-BLACK
**pitched battle** *noun* (1607)

staff notation of pitch 4b(1)

four-line octave
three-line octave
two-line octave
one-line octave
Middle C
small octave
great octave
contraoctave
subcontraoctave

**:** an intensely fought battle in which the opposing forces are locked in close combat
¹**pitch·er** \'pi-chər\ *noun* [Middle English *picher*, from Old French *pichier*, from Medieval Latin *bicarius* goblet] (13th century)
**1 :** a container for holding and pouring liquids that usually has a lip or spout and a handle
**2 :** a modified leaf of a pitcher plant in which the hollowed petiole and base of the blade form an elongated receptacle
— **pitch·er·ful** \-,fu̇l\ *noun*
²**pitcher** *noun* (circa 1722)
**:** one that pitches; *specifically* **:** the player that pitches in a game of baseball
**pitcher plant** *noun* (1819)
**:** a plant (especially family Sarraceniaceae, the pitcher-plant family) with leaves modified into pitchers in which insects are trapped and digested by means of liquids secreted by the leaves
**pitch·fork** \'pich-,fȯrk\ *noun* (13th century)
**:** a long-handled fork that has two or three long somewhat curved prongs and is used especially in pitching hay
— **pitchfork** *transitive verb*
**pitch in** *intransitive verb* (1843)
**1 :** to begin to work
**2 :** to contribute to a common endeavor
**pitch·man** \'pich-mən\ *noun* (circa 1926)
**:** one who makes a sales pitch: as **a :** one who sells merchandise on the streets or from a concession **b :** one who does radio or TV commercials
**pitch·out** \'pich-,au̇t\ *noun* (1912)
**1 :** a pitch in baseball deliberately out of reach of the batter to enable the catcher to put out a base runner especially with a throw
**2 :** a lateral pass in football between two backs behind the line of scrimmage
— **pitch out** *intransitive verb*
**pitch pine** *noun* (1676)
**1 :** any of several pines that yield pitch; *especially* **:** a 3-leaved pine (*Pinus rigida*) of eastern North America
**2 :** the wood of a pitch pine
**pitch pipe** *noun* (1711)
**:** a small reed pipe or flue pipe producing one or more tones to establish the pitch in singing or in tuning an instrument
**pitch·pole** \'pich-,pōl\ *verb* [*pitchpole* somersault, from ³*pitch* + *pole, poll* head] (1851)
*intransitive verb*
**:** to turn end over end ⟨the catamaran *pitchpoled*⟩
*transitive verb*
**:** to cause to turn end over end
**pitch·wom·an** \-,wu̇-mən\ *noun* (1957)
**:** a woman who makes a sales pitch
**pitchy** \'pi-chē\ *adjective* (15th century)
**1 a :** full of pitch **:** TARRY **b :** of, relating to, or having the qualities of pitch
**2 :** PITCH-BLACK
**pit·e·ous** \'pi-tē-əs\ *adjective* (14th century)
**:** of a kind to move to pity or compassion
— **pit·e·ous·ly** *adverb*
— **pit·e·ous·ness** *noun*
**pit·fall** \'pit-,fȯl\ *noun* (14th century)
**1 :** TRAP, SNARE; *specifically* **:** a pit flimsily covered or camouflaged and used to capture and hold animals or men
**2 :** a hidden or not easily recognized danger or difficulty
¹**pith** \'pith\ *noun* [Middle English, from Old English *pitha;* akin to Middle Dutch & Middle Low German *pit* pith, pit] (before 12th century)
**1 a :** a usually continuous central strand of spongy tissue in the stems of most vascular plants that probably functions chiefly in storage **b :** any of various loose spongy plant tissues that resemble true pith **c :** the soft or spongy interior of a part of the body
**2 a :** the essential part **:** CORE **b :** substantial quality (as of meaning)
**3 :** IMPORTANCE
²**pith** *transitive verb* (1805)

**1 a :** to kill (as cattle) by piercing or severing the spinal cord **b :** to destroy the spinal cord or central nervous system of (as a frog) usually by passing a wire or needle up and down the vertebral canal
**2 :** to remove the pith from (a plant stem)
**pit·head** \'pit-ˌhed\ noun (1839)
chiefly British **:** the top of a mining pit or coal shaft; also **:** the immediately adjacent ground and buildings
**pith·ec·an·thro·pine** \ˌpi-thi-'kan(t)-thrə-ˌpīn\ noun (1925)
**:** any of a group of Pleistocene hominids (as Java man, Peking man, and Heidelberg man) that have a smaller cranial capacity than modern humans (Homo sapiens) but a greater cranial capacity than the australopithecines, prominent eyebrow ridges, a receding forehead, constriction of the skull behind the eye sockets, and relatively large canine and incisor teeth and that were formerly considered to comprise a genus (Pithecanthropus) but are now grouped in a single species (Homo erectus)
**— pithecanthropine** adjective
**pith·ec·an·thro·pus** \-'kan(t)-thrə-pəs, -ˌkan-'thrō-\ noun, plural **-pi** \-ˌpī, -ˌpē\ [New Latin, from Greek pithēkos ape + anthrōpos human being] (1895)
**:** PITHECANTHROPINE
**pith helmet** noun (1889)
**:** TOPEE
**pith ray** noun (1902)
**:** MEDULLARY RAY
**pithy** \'pi-thē\ adjective **pith·i·er; -est** (1562)
**1 :** consisting of or abounding in pith
**2 :** having substance and point **:** tersely cogent
synonym see CONCISE
**— pith·i·ly** \'pi-thə-lē\ adverb
**— pith·i·ness** \'pi-thē-nəs\ noun
**piti·able** \'pi-tē-ə-bəl\ adjective (15th century)
**1 :** deserving or exciting pity **:** LAMENTABLE
**2 :** of a kind to evoke mingled pity and contempt especially because of inadequacy ⟨a pitiable excuse⟩
synonym see CONTEMPTIBLE
**— piti·able·ness** noun
**— piti·ably** \-blē\ adverb
**piti·er** \'pi-tē-ər\ noun (1601)
**:** one that pities
**piti·ful** \'pi-ti-fəl\ adjective (14th century)
**1** archaic **:** full of pity **:** COMPASSIONATE
**2 a :** deserving or arousing pity or commiseration **b :** exciting pitying contempt (as by meanness or inadequacy)
**— piti·ful·ly** \-f(ə-)lē\ adverb
**— piti·ful·ness** \-fəl-nəs\ noun
**piti·less** \'pi-ti-ləs, 'pi-t°l-əs\ adjective (15th century)
**:** devoid of pity **:** MERCILESS
**— piti·less·ly** adverb
**— piti·less·ness** noun
**pit·man** \'pit-mən\ noun (1703)
**1** plural **pit·men** \-mən\ **:** one who works in or near a pit (as in a coal mine)
**2** plural **pitmans :** CONNECTING ROD
**pi·ton** \'pē-ˌtän\ noun [French] (1893)
**:** a spike, wedge, or peg that is driven into a rock or ice surface as a support (as for a mountain climber)
**pi·tot-stat·ic tube** \pē-ˌtō-'sta-tik-\ noun, often P capitalized (1926)
**:** a device that consists of a pitot tube and a static tube and that measures pressures in such a way that the relative speed of a fluid can be determined
**pi·tot tube** \'pē-ˌtō-\ noun, often P capitalized [French (tube de) Pitot, from Henri Pitot (died 1771) French physicist] (circa 1859)
**1 :** a device that consists of a tube having a short right-angled bend which is placed vertically in a moving body of fluid with the mouth of the bent part directed upstream and that is used with a manometer to measure the velocity of fluid flow
**2 :** PITOT-STATIC TUBE

**pit saw** noun (1679)
**:** a handsaw worked by two persons one of whom stands on or above the log being sawed into planks and the other below it usually in a pit
**pit stop** noun (1932)
**1 :** a stop at the pits during an automobile race
**2 a :** a stop (as during a trip) for fuel, food, or rest or for use of a rest room **b** (1) **:** a place where a pit stop can be made (2) **:** an establishment providing food or drink
**pit·tance** \'pit-°n(t)s\ noun [Middle English pitance, from Old French, piety, pity, from Medieval Latin pietantia, from pietant-, pietans, present participle of pietari to be charitable, from Latin pietas piety — more at PITY] (14th century)
**:** a small portion, amount, or allowance; also **:** a meager wage or remuneration
**pit·ted** \'pi-təd\ adjective (before 12th century)
**:** marked with pits
**pit·ter-pat·ter** \'pi-tər-ˌpa-tər, 'pi-tē-ˌ\ noun [reduplication of ⁴patter] (15th century)
**:** a rapid succession of light sounds or beats **:** PATTER
**— pitter-patter** \ˌpi-tər-', ˌpi-tē-'\ adverb or adjective
**— pitter-patter** \same as adverb\ intransitive verb
**pit·ting** noun (1665)
**1 :** an arrangement of pits
**2 :** the action or process of forming pits
**3 :** the bringing of gamecocks together to fight
**pit·tos·po·rum** \pə-'täs-pə-rəm\ noun [New Latin, from Greek pitta, pissa pitch + spora seed — more at PITCH, SPORE] (1789)
**:** any of various Old World shrubs or trees (genus Pittosporum of the family Pittosporaceae) planted especially as ornamentals in warm regions
**¹pi·tu·i·tary** \pə-'tü-ə-ˌter-ē, -'tyü-\ adjective [Latin pituita phlegm; from the former belief that the pituitary gland secreted phlegm — more at PIP] (1615)
**1 :** of or relating to the pituitary gland
**2 :** caused or characterized by secretory disturbances of the pituitary gland ⟨a pituitary dwarf⟩
**²pituitary** noun, plural **-tar·ies** (1845)
**:** PITUITARY GLAND
**pituitary gland** noun (1825)
**:** a small oval endocrine organ that is attached to the infundibulum of the brain, consists of an epithelial anterior lobe joined by an intermediate part to a posterior lobe of nervous origin, and produces various internal secretions directly or indirectly impinging on most basic body functions — called also hypophysis, pituitary body; see BRAIN illustration
**pit viper** noun (circa 1885)
**:** any of various mostly New World venomous snakes (subfamily Crotalinae of the family Viperidae) with a sensory pit on each side of the head and hollow perforated fangs
**¹pity** \'pi-tē\ noun, plural **pit·ies** [Middle English pite, from Old French pité, from Latin pietat-, pietas piety, pity, from pius pious] (13th century)
**1 a :** sympathetic sorrow for one suffering, distressed, or unhappy **b :** capacity to feel pity
**2 :** something to be regretted ⟨it's a pity you can't go⟩ ☆
**²pity** verb **pit·ied; pity·ing** (15th century)
transitive verb
**:** to feel pity for
intransitive verb
**:** to feel pity
**pitying** adjective (1589)
**:** expressing or feeling pity
**— pity·ing·ly** \-iŋ-lē\ adverb
**pit·y·ri·a·sis** \ˌpi-ti-'rī-ə-səs\ noun [New Latin, from Greek, from pityron scurf] (circa 1693)
**:** a condition of humans or domestic animals marked by dry scaling or scurfy patches of skin

**più** \'pyü, pē-'ü\ adverb [Italian, from Latin plus] (1724)
**:** MORE — used to qualify an adverb or adjective used as a direction in music
**Pi·ute** variant of PAIUTE
**¹piv·ot** \'pi-vət\ noun [French] (1611)
**1 :** a shaft or pin on which something turns
**2 a :** a person, thing, or factor having a major or central role, function, or effect **b :** a key player or position; specifically **:** an offensive position of a basketball player standing usually with back to the basket to relay passes, shoot, or provide a screen for teammates
**3 :** the action of pivoting
**²pivot** adjective (1796)
**1 :** turning on or as if on a pivot
**2 :** PIVOTAL
**³pivot** (1841)
intransitive verb
**:** to turn on or as if on a pivot
transitive verb
**1 :** to provide with, mount on, or attach by a pivot
**2 :** to cause to pivot
**— pivot·able** \-və-tə-bəl\ adjective
**piv·ot·al** \'pi-və-t°l\ adjective (1844)
**1 :** of, relating to, or constituting a pivot
**2 :** vitally important **:** CRUCIAL
**— piv·ot·al·ly** \-t°l-ē\ adverb
**piv·ot·man** \'pi-vət-ˌman\ noun (circa 1814)
**:** one who plays the pivot; specifically **:** a center on a basketball team
**pivot tooth** noun (1842)
**:** an artificial crown attached to the root of a tooth by a usually metallic pin — called also pivot crown
**pix** plural of PIC
**pix·el** \'pik-səl, -ˌsel\ noun [pix + element] (1969)
**1 :** any of the small discrete elements that together constitute an image (as on a television screen)
**2 :** any of the detecting elements of a charge-coupled device used as an optical sensor
**¹pix·ie** or **pixy** \'pik-sē\ noun, plural **pix·ies** [origin unknown] (1746)
**:** FAIRY; specifically **:** a cheerful mischievous sprite
**— pix·ie·ish** \-sē-ish\ adjective
**²pixie** or **pixy** adjective (1943)
**:** playfully mischievous
**— pixi·ness** noun
**pix·i·lat·ed** or **pix·il·lat·ed** \'pik-sə-ˌlā-təd\ adjective [irregular from pixie] (1848)

---

\ə\ abut \°\ kitten \ər\ further \a\ ash \ā\ ace
\ä\ mop, mar \au̇\ out \ch\ chin \e\ bet \ē\ easy
\g\ go \i\ hit \ī\ ice \j\ job \ŋ\ sing \ō\ go
\ȯ\ law \ȯi\ boy \th\ thin \t̲h̲\ the \ü\ loot \u̇\ foot
\y\ yet \zh\ vision     see also Guide to Pronunciation

**1** : somewhat unbalanced mentally; *also* : BE-MUSED
**2** : WHIMSICAL
— **pix·i·la·tion** \ˌpik-sə-'lā-shən\ *noun*
**piz·za** \'pēt-sə\ *noun* [Italian, perhaps of Germanic origin; akin to Old High German *bizzo, pizzo* bite, bit, *bīzan* to bite — more at BITE] (1935)
: an open pie made typically of flattened bread dough spread with a savory mixture usually including tomatoes and cheese and often other toppings and baked — called also *pizza pie*
— **pizza·like** \-ˌlīk\ *adjective*
**piz·zazz** *or* **pi·zazz** \pə-'zaz\ *noun* [origin unknown] (1937)
: the quality of being exciting or attractive: as **a** : GLAMOUR **b** : VITALITY
— **piz·zazzy** *or* **pi·zazzy** \-'za-zē\ *adjective*
**piz·ze·ria** \ˌpēt-sə-'rē-ə\ *noun* [Italian, from *pizza*] (1943)
: an establishment where pizzas are made or sold
¹**piz·zi·ca·to** \ˌpit-si-'kä-(ˌ)tō\ *noun, plural* **-ca·ti** \-'kä-(ˌ)tē\ (1845)
: a note or passage played by plucking strings
²**pizzicato** *adverb or adjective* [Italian, past participle of *pizzicare* to pluck] (circa 1854)
: by means of plucking instead of bowing — used as a direction in music; compare ARCO
**piz·zle** \'pi-zəl\ *noun* [probably from Flemish *pezel;* akin to Low German *pesel* pizzle] (1523)
**1** : the penis of an animal
**2** : a whip made of a bull's pizzle
**pj's** \'pē-ˌjāz\ *noun plural* [*pajamas*] (1951)
: PAJAMAS
**PK** \ˌpē-'kā\ *noun* (1943)
: PSYCHOKINESIS
**pla·ca·ble** \'pla-kə-bəl, 'plā-\ *adjective* (1586)
: easily placated : TOLERANT, TRACTABLE
— **pla·ca·bil·i·ty** \ˌpla-kə-'bi-lə-tē, ˌplā-\ *noun*
— **pla·ca·bly** \'pla-kə-blē, 'plā-\ *adverb*
¹**plac·ard** \'pla-kərd, -ˌkärd\ *noun* [Middle English *placquart* formal document, from Middle French, from *plaquier* to plate — more at PLAQUE] (1560)
**1** : a notice posted in a public place : POSTER
**2** : a small card or metal plaque
²**plac·ard** \-ˌkärd, -kərd\ *transitive verb* (1813)
**1 a** : to cover with or as if with posters **b** : to post in a public place
**2** : to announce by or as if by posting
**pla·cate** \'plā-ˌkāt, 'pla-\ *transitive verb* **pla·cat·ed; pla·cat·ing** [Latin *placatus,* past participle of *placare* — more at PLEASE] (1678)
: to soothe or mollify especially by concessions : APPEASE
**synonym** see PACIFY
— **pla·cat·er** *noun*
— **pla·cat·ing·ly** \-ˌkā-tiŋ-lē\ *adverb*
— **pla·ca·tion** \plā-'kā-shən, pla-\ *noun*
— **pla·ca·tive** \'plā-ˌkā-tiv, 'pla-\ *adjective*
— **pla·ca·to·ry** \'plā-kə-ˌtōr-ē, 'pla-, -ˌtȯr-\ *adjective*
¹**place** \'plās\ *noun* [Middle English, from Old French, open space, from Latin *platea* broad street, from Greek *plateia* (*hodos*), from feminine of *platys* broad, flat; akin to Sanskrit *pṛthu* broad, Latin *planta* sole of the foot] (13th century)
**1 a** : physical environment : SPACE **b** : a way for admission or transit **c** : physical surroundings : ATMOSPHERE
**2 a** : an indefinite region or expanse ⟨all over the *place*⟩ **b** : a building or locality used for a special purpose ⟨a *place* of learning⟩ ⟨a fine eating *place*⟩ **c** *archaic* : the three-dimensional compass of a material object
**3 a** : a particular region, center of population, or location ⟨a nice *place* to visit⟩ **b** : a building, part of a building, or area occupied as a home ⟨our summer *place*⟩
**4** : a particular part of a surface or body : SPOT

**5** : relative position in a scale or series: as **a** : position in a social scale ⟨kept them in their *place*⟩ **b** : a step in a sequence ⟨in the first *place,* it's none of your business⟩ **c** : a position at the conclusion of a competition ⟨finished in last *place*⟩
**6 a** : a proper or designated niche ⟨the *place* of education in society⟩ **b** : an appropriate moment or point ⟨this is not the *place* to discuss compensation —Robert Moses⟩
**7 a** : an available seat or accommodation ⟨needs a *place* to stay⟩ **b** : an empty or vacated position ⟨new ones will take their *place*⟩
**8** : the position of a figure in relation to others of a row or series; *especially* : the position of a digit within a numeral
**9 a** : remunerative employment : JOB **b** : prestige accorded to one of high rank : STATUS ⟨an endless quest for preferment and *place* —*Time*⟩
**10** : a public square : PLAZA
**11** : a small street or court
**12** : second place at the finish (as of a horse race)
— **in place 1** : in an original or proper position **2** : in the same spot without forward or backward movement ⟨run *in place*⟩
²**place** *verb* **placed; plac·ing** (15th century)
*transitive verb*
**1 a** : to put in or as if in a particular place or position : SET **b** : to present for consideration ⟨a question *placed* before the group⟩ **c** : to put in a particular state ⟨*place* a performer under contract⟩ **d** : to direct to a desired spot **e** : to cause (the voice) to produce free and well resonated singing or speaking tones
**2 a** : to assign to a position in a series or category : RANK **b** : ESTIMATE ⟨*placed* the value of the estate too high⟩ **c** : to identify by connecting with an associated context ⟨couldn't quite *place* her face⟩ ⟨police *placed* them at the crime scene⟩
**3** : to distribute in an orderly manner : ARRANGE
**4** : to appoint to a position
**5** : to find a place (as a home or employment) for
**6 a** : to give (an order) to a supplier **b** : to give an order for ⟨*place* a bet⟩ **c** : to try to establish a connection for ⟨*place* a telephone call⟩
*intransitive verb*
: to earn a given spot in a competition; *specifically* : to come in second (as in a horse race)
— **place·able** \'plā-sə-bəl\ *adjective*
**pla·ce·bo** *noun, plural* **-bos** (13th century)
**1** \plä-'chā-(ˌ)bō\ [Middle English, from Latin, I shall please, from *placēre* to please — more at PLEASE] : the Roman Catholic vespers for the dead
**2** \plə-'sē-\ [Latin, I shall please] **a** (1) : a medication prescribed more for the mental relief of the patient than for its actual effect on a disorder (2) : an inert or innocuous substance used especially in controlled experiments testing the efficacy of another substance (as a drug) **b** : something tending to soothe
**placebo effect** *noun* (1950)
: improvement in the condition of a sick person that occurs in response to treatment but cannot be considered due to the specific treatment used
**place·hold·er** \'plās-ˌhōl-dər\ *noun* (1958)
: a symbol in a mathematical or logical expression that may be replaced by the name of any element of a set
¹**place·kick** \'plās-ˌkik\ *noun* (1856)
: the kicking of a ball (as a football) placed or held in a stationary position on the ground
²**placekick** *transitive verb* (1856)
**1** : to kick (a ball) from a stationary position
**2** : to score by means of a placekick
— **place·kick·er** *noun*
**place·less** \-ləs\ *adjective* (14th century)
: lacking a fixed location

— **place·less·ly** *adverb*
**place·man** \-mən\ *noun* (1741)
: a political appointee to a public office especially in 18th century Britain
**place mat** *noun* (1928)
: a small often rectangular table mat on which a place setting is laid
**place·ment** \'plās-mənt\ *noun* (1844)
**1** : an act or instance of placing: as **a** : an accurately hit ball (as in tennis) that an opponent cannot return **b** : the assignment of a person to a suitable place (as a job or a class in school)
**2** : PLACEKICK
**placement test** *noun* (1928)
: a test usually given to a student entering an educational institution to determine specific knowledge or proficiency in various subjects for the purpose of assignment to appropriate courses or classes
**place–name** \'plās-ˌnām\ *noun* (1868)
: the name of a geographical locality
**pla·cen·ta** \plə-'sen-tə\ *noun, plural* **-centas** *or* **-cen·tae** \-'sen-(ˌ)tē\ [New Latin, from Latin, flat cake, from Greek *plakoenta,* accusative of *plakoeis,* from *plak-, plax* flat surface — more at FLUKE] (1691)
**1** : the vascular organ in mammals except monotremes and marsupials that unites the fetus to the maternal uterus and mediates its metabolic exchanges through a more or less intimate association of uterine mucosal with chorionic and usually allantoic tissues; *also* : an analogous organ in another animal
**2** : a sporangium-bearing surface; *especially* : the part of the carpel bearing ovules
— **pla·cen·tal** \-'sen-t³l\ *adjective or noun*
**pla·cen·ta·tion** \ˌpla-s³n-'tā-shən, plə-ˌsen-\ *noun* (1760)
**1** : the arrangement of placentas and ovules in a plant ovary
**2 a** : the development of the placenta and attachment of the fetus to the uterus during pregnancy **b** : the morphological type of a placenta
¹**plac·er** \'plā-sər\ *noun* (1579)
: one that places: as **a** : one that deposits or arranges **b** : one of the winners in a competition
²**plac·er** \'pla-sər\ *noun* [Spanish, from Catalan, submarine plain, from *plaza* place, from Latin *platea* broad street — more at PLACE] (1848)
: an alluvial, marine, or glacial deposit containing particles of valuable mineral and especially of gold
**place setting** *noun* (1944)
: a table service for one person
**place value** *noun* (1911)
: the value of the place of a digit in a numeral
**plac·id** \'pla-səd\ *adjective* [Latin *placidus,* from *placēre* to please — more at PLEASE] (1626)
**1** : serenely free of interruption or disturbance ⟨*placid* skies⟩ ⟨a *placid* disposition⟩
**2** : COMPLACENT
**synonym** see CALM
— **pla·cid·i·ty** \pla-'si-də-tē, plə-\ *noun*
— **plac·id·ly** \'pla-səd-lē\ *adverb*
— **plac·id·ness** *noun*
**plack·et** \'pla-kət\ *noun* [origin unknown] (1605)
**1 a** : a slit in a garment (as a skirt) often forming the closure **b** *archaic* : a pocket especially in a woman's skirt
**2** *archaic* **a** : PETTICOAT **b** : WOMAN
**plac·oid** \'pla-ˌkȯid\ *adjective* [Greek *plak-, plax* flat surface] (1842)
: of, relating to, or being a scale of dermal origin with an enamel-tipped spine characteristic of the elasmobranchs
**pla·gal** \'plā-gəl\ *adjective* [Medieval Latin *plagalis,* ultimately from Greek *plagios* oblique, sideways, from *plagos* side; akin to Latin *plaga* net, region, Greek *pelagos* sea] (1597)
**1** *of a church mode* : having the keynote on the 4th scale step — compare AUTHENTIC 4a

**2** *of a cadence* **:** progressing from the subdominant chord to the tonic — compare AUTHENTIC 4b

**plage** \'pläzh\ *noun* [French, beach, luminous surface, from Italian *piaggia* beach, from Late Latin *plagia*, from Greek *plagios* oblique] (1888)
**1 :** the beach of a seaside resort
**2 :** a bright region on the sun caused by the light emitted by clouds of calcium or hydrogen and often associated with a sunspot
**pla·gia·rise** *British variant of* PLAGIARIZE
**pla·gia·rism** \'plā-jə-ˌri-zəm *also* -jē-ə-\ *noun* (1621)
**1 :** an act or instance of plagiarizing
**2 :** something plagiarized ◆
— **pla·gia·rist** \-rist\ *noun*
— **pla·gia·ris·tic** \ˌplā-jə-'ris-tik *also* -jē-ə-\ *adjective*
**pla·gia·rize** \'plā-jə-ˌrīz *also* -jē-ə-\ *verb* **-rized; -riz·ing** [*plagiary*] (1716)
*transitive verb*
**:** to steal and pass off (the ideas or words of another) as one's own **:** use (a created production) without crediting the source
*intransitive verb*
**:** to commit literary theft **:** present as new and original an idea or product derived from an existing source
— **pla·gia·riz·er** *noun*
**pla·gia·ry** \'plā-jē-ˌer-ē, -jə-rē\ *noun, plural* **-ries** [Latin *plagiarus*, literally, kidnapper, from *plagium* netting of game, kidnapping, from *plaga* net, trap] (1601)
**1** *archaic* **:** one that plagiarizes
**2 :** PLAGIARISM
**pla·gio·clase** \'plā-j(ē-)ə-ˌklās, 'plā-, -ˌklāz\ *noun* [Greek *plagios* oblique + *klasis* breaking, from *klan* to break — more at CLAST] (circa 1868)
**:** a triclinic feldspar; *especially* **:** one having calcium or sodium in its composition
**pla·gio·tro·pic** \ˌplā-j(ē-)ə-'trō-pik, ˌplā-, -'trä-\ *adjective* [Greek *plagios* + International Scientific Vocabulary *-tropic*] (1882)
**:** having the longer axis inclined away from the vertical
**¹plague** \'plāg\ *noun* [Middle English *plage*, from Middle French, from Late Latin *plaga*, from Latin, blow; akin to Latin *plangere* to strike — more at PLAINT] (14th century)
**1 a :** a disastrous evil or affliction **:** CALAMITY **b :** a destructively numerous influx ⟨a *plague* of locusts⟩
**2 a :** an epidemic disease causing a high rate of mortality **:** PESTILENCE **b :** a virulent contagious febrile disease that is caused by a bacterium (*Yersinia pestis*) and that occurs in bubonic, pneumonic, and septicemic forms — called also *black death*
**3 a :** a cause of irritation **:** NUISANCE **b :** a sudden unwelcome outbreak ⟨a *plague* of burglaries⟩
**²plague** *transitive verb* **plagued; plagu·ing** (15th century)
**1 :** to smite, infest, or afflict with or as if with disease, calamity, or natural evil
**2 a :** to cause worry or distress to **:** HAMPER, BURDEN **b :** to disturb or annoy persistently
*synonym* see WORRY
— **plagu·er** *noun*
**plagu·ey** *or* **plaguy** \'plā-gē, 'plē-\ *adjective* (1615)
**:** causing irritation or annoyance **:** TROUBLESOME
— **plaguey** *adverb*
— **plagu·i·ly** \-gə-lē\ *adverb*
**plaice** \'plās\ *noun, plural* **plaice** [Middle English *plaice*, from Middle French *plaïs*, from Late Latin *platessa*] (13th century)
**:** any of various flatfishes; *especially* **:** a large European flounder (*Pleuronectes platessa*) with red spots
**plaid** \'plad\ *noun* [Scottish Gaelic *plaide*] (1512)

**1 :** a rectangular length of tartan worn over the left shoulder as part of the Scottish national costume
**2 a :** a twilled woolen fabric with a tartan pattern **b :** a fabric with a pattern of tartan or an imitation of tartan
**3 a :** TARTAN 1 **b :** a pattern of unevenly spaced repeated stripes crossing at right angles
— **plaid** *adjective*
— **plaid·ed** \'pla-dəd\ *adjective*
**¹plain** \'plān\ *intransitive verb* [Middle English, from Old French *plaindre*, from Latin *plangere* to lament — more at PLAINT] (14th century)
*archaic* **:** COMPLAIN
**²plain** *noun* [Middle English, from Old French, from Latin *planum*, from neuter of *planus* flat, plain — more at FLOOR] (14th century)
**1 a :** an extensive area of level or rolling treeless country **b :** a broad unbroken expanse
**2 :** something free from artifice, ornament, or extraneous matter
**³plain** *adjective* (14th century)
**1** *archaic* **:** EVEN, LEVEL
**2 :** lacking ornament **:** UNDECORATED
**3 :** free of extraneous matter **:** PURE
**4 :** free of impediments to view **:** UNOBSTRUCTED
**5 a** (1) **:** evident to the mind or senses **:** OBVIOUS ⟨it's perfectly *plain* that they will resist⟩ (2) **:** CLEAR ⟨let me make my meaning *plain*⟩ **b :** marked by outspoken candor **:** free from duplicity or subtlety **:** BLUNT ⟨*plain* talk⟩
**6 a :** belonging to the great mass of humans **b :** lacking special distinction or affectation **:** ORDINARY
**7 :** characterized by simplicity **:** not complicated ⟨*plain* home-cooked meals⟩
**8 :** lacking beauty or ugliness
*synonym* see COMMON, EVIDENT, FRANK
— **plain·ly** *adverb*
— **plain·ness** \'plān-nəs\ *noun*
**⁴plain** *adverb* (14th century)
**:** in a plain manner ⟨saw them clearly and told you *plain* —*American Documentation*⟩
**⁵plain** *adverb* [partly from Middle English *plein* entire, complete, from Middle French, full, from Latin *plenus*; partly from ⁴*plain* — more at FULL] (1535)
**:** ABSOLUTELY ⟨it *plain* galled me to pay fancy prices —F. R. Buckley⟩
**plain·chant** \'plān-ˌchant\ *noun* [French *plain-chant*, literally, plain song] (circa 1741)
**:** PLAINSONG
**plain·clothes** \'plān-'klō(th)z\ *adjective* (1866)
**:** dressed in civilian clothes while on duty — used especially of a police officer
**plain·clothes·man** \'plān-'klō(th)z-mən, -ˌman\ *noun* (1899)
**:** a plainclothes police officer
**plain–Jane** \'plān-'jān\ *adjective* [from the name *Jane*] (1912)
**:** not fancy or glamorous **:** ORDINARY
**plain–laid** \'plān-'lād\ *adjective* (1881)
*of a rope* **:** consisting of three strands laid right-handed
**Plain People** *noun* (1904)
**:** members of any of various Protestant groups (as Mennonites) especially in the U.S. who wear distinctively plain clothes and adhere to a simple and traditional style of life excluding many conveniences of modern technology
**Plains** \'plānz\ *adjective* (1844)
**:** of or relating to North American Indians of the Great Plains or to their culture
**plain sailing** *noun* (1756)
**:** easy progress over an unobstructed course
**plains·man** \'plānz-mən\ *noun* [Great *Plains* + *man*] (1870)
**:** an inhabitant of the plains
**plain·song** \'plān-ˌsȯn\ *noun* (1513)
**:** a monophonic rhythmically free liturgical chant of any of various Christian rites; *especially* **:** GREGORIAN CHANT

**plain·spo·ken** \-'spō-kən\ *adjective* (1678)
**:** CANDID, FRANK
— **plain·spo·ken·ness** \-kən-nəs\ *noun*
**plaint** \'plānt\ *noun* [Middle English, from Middle French, from Latin *planctus*, from *plangere* to strike, beat one's breast, lament; akin to Old High German *fluokhōn* to curse, Greek *plēssein* to strike] (13th century)
**1 :** LAMENTATION, WAIL
**2 :** PROTEST, COMPLAINT
**plain·text** \'plān-ˌtekst\ *noun* (1918)
**:** the intelligible form of an encrypted text or of its elements — compare CIPHERTEXT
**plaint·ful** \'plānt-fəl\ *adjective* (14th century)
**:** MOURNFUL
**plain·tiff** \'plān-təf\ *noun* [Middle English *plaintif*, from Middle French, from *plaintif*, adjective] (14th century)
**:** a person who brings a legal action — compare DEFENDANT
**plain·tive** \'plān-tiv\ *adjective* [Middle English *plaintif* grieving, from Middle French, from *plaint*] (1579)
**:** expressive of suffering or woe **:** MELANCHOLY
— **plain·tive·ly** *adverb*
— **plain·tive·ness** *noun*
**plain–vanilla** *adjective* (1975)
**:** lacking special features or qualities **:** BASIC
**plain weave** *noun* (1888)
**:** a weave in which the threads interlace alternately
**plain–woven** *adjective* (1925)
**:** made in plain weave
**plais·ter** \'plas-tər, 'plās-\ *variant of* PLASTER
**¹plait** \'plāt, 'plat\ *noun* [Middle English *pleit*, from Middle French, from (assumed) Vulgar Latin *plicitum*, from neuter of Latin *plicitus*, past participle of *plicare* to fold — more at PLY] (14th century)
**1 :** PLEAT
**2 :** a braid of material (as hair or straw); *specifically* **:** PIGTAIL
**²plait** *transitive verb* (14th century)
**1 :** PLEAT 1
**2 a :** to interweave the strands or locks of **:** BRAID **b :** to make by plaiting
— **plait·er** *noun*
**plait·ing** *noun* (15th century)
**:** the interlacing of strands **:** BRAIDING
**¹plan** \'plan\ *noun* [French, plane, foundation, ground plan; partly from Latin *planum* level ground, from neuter of *planus* level; partly from French *planter* to plant, fix in place, from Late Latin *plantare* — more at FLOOR, PLANT] (1706)
**1 :** a drawing or diagram drawn on a plane: as **a :** a top or horizontal view of an object **b :** a large-scale map of a small area
**2 a :** a method for achieving an end **b :** an often customary method of doing something

---

◇ **WORD HISTORY**

**plagiarism** The Latin noun *plaga* denoted a hunting net or snare used for capturing game. The netting of such animals was termed *plagium*. By extension, this word was also used for the crime of kidnapping children or freemen and selling them as slaves. The kidnapper was called by the derivative noun *plagiarius*. We know that by the time of the poet Martial, who died about A.D. 103, *plagiarius* was also being used to refer to a literary thief or plagiarist. When Latin *plagiarius* was borrowed into English as *plagiary* in the 17th century, both the original and literary senses were carried over. Only the literary sense of *plagiary* appears in the English derivatives *plagiarism* and *plagiarize*.

---

\ə\ **abut** \ᵊ\ **kitten** \ər\ **further** \a\ **ash** \ā\ **ace**
\ä\ **mop, mar** \aú\ **out** \ch\ **chin** \e\ **bet** \ē\ **easy**
\g\ **go** \i\ **hit** \ī\ **ice** \j\ **job** \ŋ\ **sing** \ō\ **go**
\ȯ\ **law** \ȯi\ **boy** \th\ **thin** \t̷h\ **the** \ü\ **loot** \ú\ **foot**
\y\ **yet** \zh\ **vision** *see also* Guide to Pronunciation

## PLANETS

| NAME | SYMBOL | MEAN DISTANCE FROM THE SUN | | PERIOD OF REVOLUTION IN DAYS OR YEARS | EQUATORIAL DIAMETER IN MILES |
|------|--------|------------------|------------------|------------------|------------------|
| | | astronomical units | million miles | | |
| Mercury | ☿ | 0.387 | 36.0 | 87.97 days | 3,032 |
| Venus | ♀ | 0.723 | 67.2 | 224.70 days | 7,523 |
| Earth | ⊕ | 1.000 | 92.9 | 365.26 days | 7,928 |
| Mars | ♂ | 1.524 | 141.5 | 686.98 days | 4,218 |
| Jupiter | ♃ | 5.203 | 483.4 | 11.86 years | 88,900 |
| Saturn | ♄ | 9.522 | 884.6 | 29.46 years | 74,900 |
| Uranus | ⛢ | 19.201 | 1783.8 | 84.01 years | 31,800 |
| Neptune | ♆ | 30.074 | 2793.9 | 164.79 years | 30,800 |
| Pluto | ♇ | 39.725 | 3690.5 | 247.69 years | 1,400 |

**:** PROCEDURE **c :** a detailed formulation of a program of action **d :** GOAL, AIM **3 :** an orderly arrangement of parts of an overall design or objective **4 :** a detailed program (as for payment or the provision of some service) 〈pension *plan*〉 ☆
— **plan·less** \-ləs\ *adjective*
— **plan·less·ly** *adverb*
— **plan·less·ness** *noun*
**²plan** *verb* **planned; plan·ning** (1728) *transitive verb* **1 :** to arrange the parts of **:** DESIGN **2 :** to devise or project the realization or achievement of 〈*plan* a program〉 **3 :** to have in mind **:** INTEND *intransitive verb* **:** to make plans
— **plan·ner** *noun*
**plan-** *or* **plano-** *combining form* [Latin *planus*]
**1 :** flat 〈*plano*sol〉
**2 :** flat and 〈*plano*-concave〉
**pla·nar** \'plā-nər, -,när\ *adjective* (1850)
**1 :** of, relating to, or lying in a plane **2 :** two-dimensional in quality
— **pla·nar·i·ty** \plā-'nar-ə-tē\ *noun*
**pla·nar·ia** \plə-'nar-ē-ə, -'ner-\ *noun* [New Latin, from feminine of Late Latin *planarius* lying on a plane, from Latin *planum* plane] (circa 1909)
**:** PLANARIAN; *especially* **:** any of a genus (*Planaria*) of 2-eyed planarian worms
**pla·nar·i·an** \-ē-ən\ *noun* [New Latin *Planaria*] (circa 1858)
**:** any of various dark-colored freshwater triclad flatworms (family Planariidae) with two eyespots and a triangular head; *broadly* **:** TRICLAD
**pla·na·tion** \plā-'nā-shən\ *noun* (1877)
**:** the condition or process of becoming flattened
**plan·chet** \'plan-chət\ *noun* [diminutive of *planch* flat plate, from Middle French *planche*] (1611)
**1 :** a metal disk to be stamped as a coin **2 :** a small metal or plastic disk
**plan·chette** \plan-'shet\ *noun* [French, from diminutive of *planche* plank, from Latin *planca*] (1860)
**:** a small triangular or heart-shaped board supported on casters at two points and a vertical pencil at a third and believed to produce automatic writing when lightly touched by the fingers; *also* **:** a similar board without a pencil
**Planck's constant** \'pläŋ(k)s-, 'plaŋ(k)s-\ *noun* [Max K.E.L. *Planck*] (1910)
**:** a constant that gives the unvarying ratio of the energy of a quantum of radiation to its frequency and that has an approximate value of $6.626 \times 10^{-34}$ J·S — symbol *h*
**¹plane** \'plān\ *verb* **planed; plan·ing** [Middle English, from Middle French *planer*, from Late Latin *planare*, from Latin *planus* level — more at FLOOR] (14th century) *transitive verb* **1 a :** to make smooth or even **:** LEVEL **b :** to make smooth or even by use of a plane

**2 :** to remove by planing — often used with *away* or *off* *intransitive verb* **1 :** to work with a plane **2 :** to do the work of a plane
— **plan·er** *noun*
**²plane** *noun* [Middle English, from Middle French, from Latin *platanus*, from Greek *platanos*; probably akin to Greek *platys* broad — more at PLACE] (14th century)
**:** any of a genus (*Platanus* of the family Platanaceae, the plane-tree family) of trees with large palmately lobed leaves and flowers in globose heads — called also *buttonwood, plane tree, sycamore*
**³plane** *noun* [Middle English, from Middle French, from Late Latin *plana*, from *planare*] (14th century)
**:** a tool for smoothing or shaping a wood surface

**³plane**

**⁴plane** *noun* [Latin *planum*, from neuter of *planus* level] (1604)
**1 a :** a surface of such nature that a straight line joining two of its points lies wholly in the surface **b :** a flat or level surface **2 :** a level of existence, consciousness, or development 〈on the intellectual *plane*〉 **3 a :** one of the main supporting surfaces of an airplane **b** [by shortening] **:** AIRPLANE
**⁵plane** *adjective* [Latin *planus*] (1704)
**1 :** having no elevations or depressions **:** FLAT **2 a :** of, relating to, or dealing with geometric planes **b :** lying in a plane 〈a *plane* curve〉
**synonym** see LEVEL
**⁶plane** *intransitive verb* **planed; plan·ing** [Middle English, from Middle French *planer*, from *plain* level, plain] (15th century)
**1 a :** to fly while keeping the wings motionless **b :** to skim across the surface of the water **2 :** to travel by airplane
**plane angle** *noun* (1570)
**:** an angle that for a given dihedral angle is formed by two intersecting lines each of which lies on a face of the dihedral angle and is perpendicular to the edge of the face
**plane geometry** *noun* (1747)
**:** a branch of elementary geometry that deals with plane figures
**plane·load** \'plān-,lōd\ *noun* (1941)
**:** a load that fills an airplane
**plane of polarization** (1831)
**:** the plane in which the magnetic-vibration component of plane-polarized electromagnetic radiation lies
**plane–polarized** *adjective* (circa 1853)
**:** vibrating in a single plane 〈*plane*-polarized light waves〉
**pla·ner tree** \'plā-nər-\ *noun* [J. J. *Planer* (died 1789) German botanist] (circa 1810)
**:** a small-leaved North American tree (*Planera aquatica*) of the elm family with an oval ribbed fruit
**plan·et** \'pla-nət\ *noun* [Middle English *plan-*

*ete*, from Old French, from Late Latin *planeta*, modification of Greek *planēt-, planēs*, literally, wanderer, from *planasthai* to wander — more at FLOOR] (13th century)
**1 a :** any of the seven celestial bodies sun, moon, Venus, Jupiter, Mars, Mercury, and Saturn that in ancient belief have motions of their own among the fixed stars **b** (1) **:** any of the large bodies that revolve around the sun in the solar system (2) **:** a similar body associated with another star **c :** EARTH — usually used with *the*
**2 :** a celestial body held to influence the fate of human beings
**3 :** a person or thing of great importance **:** LUMINARY ◆
— **plan·et·like** \-,līk\ *adjective*
**plane table** *noun* (1607)
**:** an instrument consisting essentially of a drawing board on a tripod with a ruler pointed at the object observed and used for plotting the lines of a survey directly from observation
**plan·e·tar·i·um** \,pla-nə-'ter-ē-əm\ *noun, plural* **-i·ums** *or* **-ia** \-ē-ə\ (1860)
**1 :** a model or representation of the solar system
**2 a :** an optical device for projecting various celestial images and effects **b :** a building or room housing such a projector
**plan·e·tary** \'pla-nə-,ter-ē\ *adjective* (1607)
**1 a :** of, relating to, being, or resembling a planet **b :** ERRATIC, WANDERING **c :** having a motion like that of a planet 〈*planetary* electrons〉 **d :** IMMENSE 〈the scope of this project has reached *planetary* proportions〉

---

☆ **SYNONYMS**
**Plan, design, plot, scheme, project** mean a method devised for making or doing something or achieving an end. PLAN always implies mental formulation and sometimes graphic representation 〈*plans* for a house〉. DESIGN often suggests a particular pattern and some degree of achieved order or harmony 〈a *design* for a new dress〉. PLOT implies a laying out in clearly distinguished sections with attention to their relations and proportions 〈the *plot* of the play〉. SCHEME stresses calculation of the end in view and may apply to a plan motivated by craftiness and self-interest 〈a *scheme* to defraud the government〉. PROJECT often stresses imaginative scope and vision 〈a *project* to develop the waterfront〉.

---

◇ **WORD HISTORY**
**planet** In scanning the nighttime sky, ancient astronomers observed that while the vast majority of stars maintained fixed relative positions, there were five heavenly bodies that looked like bright stars but quite obviously changed their position in relation to each other and to the fixed stars. These five—Mercury, Venus, Mars, Jupiter, and Saturn—were called by the Greeks *planētes asteres* "wandering stars," or simply *planētes* "wanderers." The corresponding Latin expression was *stellae errantes* or *erraticae*, which also means "wandering stars." By the second century A.D. the borrowed Greek words *planētes* and *planētai* (the latter from a different noun derivative of the verb *planasthai* "to wander") were also appearing in Latin as *planetes* and *planetae* respectively; *planetae*, the singular of which was *planeta*, became the usual word in Late and Medieval Latin. Through medieval French, Middle English borrowed this word in the 14th century, which ultimately became *planet* in Modern English. Of course, we now know that the planets "wander" because they revolve around the sun, as does the earth.

**2 a :** of, relating to, or belonging to the earth : TERRESTRIAL **b :** GLOBAL, WORLDWIDE
**3 :** having or consisting of an epicyclic train of gear wheels
**planetary nebula** *noun* (1785)
: a usually compact luminous ring-shaped nebula that is composed of matter which has been ejected from a hot star at its center
**planetary science** *noun* (1969)
: PLANETOLOGY
— **planetary scientist** *noun*
**plan·e·tes·i·mal** \ˌpla-nə-ˈte-sə-məl, -zə-məl\ *noun* [*planet* + *-esimal* (as in *infinitesimal*)] (1903)
: any of numerous small solid celestial bodies that may have existed at an early stage of the development of the solar system
**planetesimal hypothesis** *noun* (1904)
: a hypothesis in astronomy: the planets have evolved by aggregation from planetesimals
**plan·et·oid** \ˈpla-nə-ˌtȯid\ *noun* (1803)
: a small body resembling a planet; *especially* : ASTEROID
— **plan·et·oi·dal** \ˌpla-nə-ˈtȯi-dᵊl\ *adjective*
**plan·et·ol·o·gy** \ˌpla-nə-ˈtä-lə-jē\ *noun, plural* **-gies** (1907)
: a branch of astronomy that deals with the condensed matter of the solar system and especially with the planets and their moons
— **plan·et·o·log·i·cal** \ˌpla-nə-tᵊl-ˈä-ji-kəl\ *adjective*
— **plan·et·ol·o·gist** \ˌpla-nə-ˈtä-lə-jist\ *noun*
**plan·et–strick·en** \ˈpla-nət-ˌstri-kən\ *or* **plan·et–struck** \-ˌstrək\ *adjective* (1599)
**1** *archaic* : affected by the influence of a planet
**2** *archaic* : PANIC-STRICKEN
**planet wheel** *noun* (1827)
: a gear wheel that revolves around the wheel with which it meshes in an epicyclic train
**plan·et–wide** \ˈpla-nət-ˈwīd\ *adjective* (1969)
: extending throughout or involving an entire planet
**plan·form** \ˈplan-ˌfȯrm\ *noun* (1908)
: the contour of an object (as an airplane) or mass as viewed from above
**plan·gen·cy** \ˈplan-jən(t)-sē\ *noun* (1858)
: the quality or state of being plangent
**plan·gent** \-jənt\ *adjective* [Latin *plangent-, plangens*, present participle of *plangere* to strike, lament — more at PLAINT] (1858)
**1 :** having a loud reverberating sound
**2 :** having an expressive and especially plaintive quality
— **plan·gent·ly** *adverb*
**pla·nim·e·ter** \plā-ˈni-mə-tər, plə-\ *noun* [French *planimètre*, from Latin *planum* plane + French *-mètre* -meter] (circa 1858)
: an instrument for measuring the area of a plane figure by tracing its boundary line
**pla·ni·met·ric** \ˌplā-nə-ˈme-trik\ *adjective* (circa 1828)
**1 :** of, relating to, or made by means of a planimeter ⟨*planimetric* measurements⟩
**2** *of a map* : having no indications of relief
— **pla·ni·met·ri·cal·ly** \-tri-k(ə-)lē\ *adverb*
**plan·ish** \ˈpla-nish\ *transitive verb* [Middle English *planysshen*, from Middle French *planiss-*, stem of *planir* to make smooth, from *plan* level, from Latin *planus* — more at FLOOR] (14th century)
: to smooth, toughen, and finish (metal) by hammering lightly
— **plan·ish·er** *noun*
**pla·ni·sphere** \ˈplā-nə-ˌsfir\ *noun* [alteration of Middle English *planisperie*, from Medieval Latin *planisphaerium*, from Latin *planum* plane + *sphaera* sphere] (1571)
: a representation of the circles of the sphere on a plane; *especially* : a polar projection of the celestial sphere and the stars on a plane with adjustable circles or other appendages for showing celestial phenomena for any given time

— **pla·ni·spher·ic** \ˌplā-nə-ˈsfir-ik, -ˈsfer-\ *adjective*
**¹plank** \ˈplaŋk\ *noun* [Middle English, from Old North French *planke*, from Latin *planca*] (13th century)
**1 a :** a heavy thick board; *especially* : one 2 to 4 inches (5 to 10 centimeters) thick and at least 8 inches (20 centimeters) wide **b :** an object made of a plank or planking **c :** PLANKING
**2 a :** an article in the platform of a political party **b :** a principal item of a policy or program
**²plank** *transitive verb* (15th century)
**1 :** to cover, build, or floor with planks
**2 :** SET DOWN 1, 2 — usually used with *down*
**3 :** to cook and serve on a board ⟨*planked* salmon⟩ ⟨*planked* steak⟩
**plank·ing** *noun* (15th century)
**1 :** the act or process of covering or fitting with planks
**2 :** a quantity of planks
**plank·ter** \ˈplaŋ(k)-tər\ *noun* [Greek *planktēr* wanderer, from *plazesthai*] (1935)
: a planktonic organism
**plank·ton** \ˈplaŋ(k)-tən, -ˌtän\ *noun* [German, from Greek, neuter of *planktos* drifting, from *plazesthai* to wander, drift, middle voice of *plazein* to drive astray; akin to Latin *plangere* to strike — more at PLAINT] (1891)
: the passively floating or weakly swimming usually minute animal and plant life of a body of water
— **plank·ton·ic** \plaŋ(k)-ˈtä-nik\ *adjective*
**Planned Parenthood** *service mark*
— used for research and dissemination of information on contraception
**plan·ning** *noun* (1748)
: the act or process of making or carrying out plans; *specifically* : the establishment of goals, policies, and procedures for a social or economic unit ⟨city *planning*⟩ ⟨business *planning*⟩
**plano–** — see PLAN-
**pla·no–con·cave** \ˌplā-nō-(ˌ)kän-ˈkāv, -ˈkän-ˌ\ *adjective* (1693)
: flat on one side and concave on the other
**pla·no–con·vex** \-(ˌ)kän-ˈveks, -ˈkän-ˌ, -kən-ˈ\ *adjective* (1665)
: flat on one side and convex on the other
**pla·nog·ra·phy** \plā-ˈnä-grə-fē, plə-\ *noun* (circa 1909)
: a process (as lithography) for printing from a plane surface
— **pla·no·graph·ic** \ˌplā-nə-ˈgra-fik\ *adjective*
**pla·no·sol** \ˈplā-nə-ˌsäl, -ˌsȯl\ *noun* [*plan-* + Latin *solum* ground, soil] (1938)
: any of an intrazonal group of soils that have a strongly leached upper layer over a compacted clay or silt and occur on smooth flat uplands
**plan position indicator** *noun* (1932)
: a radarscope having a sweep synchronized with a usually rotating antenna so that the radar return can be used to find range and bearing
**¹plant** \ˈplant\ *verb* [Middle English, from Old English *plantian*, from Late Latin *plantare* to plant, fix in place, from Latin, to plant, from *planta* plant] (before 12th century)
*transitive verb*
**1 a :** to put or set in the ground for growth ⟨*plant* seeds⟩ **b :** to set or sow with seeds or plants **c :** IMPLANT
**2 a :** ESTABLISH, INSTITUTE **b :** COLONIZE, SETTLE **c :** to place (animals) in a new locality **d :** to stock with animals
**3 a :** to place in or on the ground **b :** to place firmly or forcibly ⟨*planted* a hard blow on his chin⟩
**4 a :** CONCEAL **b :** to covertly place for discovery, publication, or dissemination
*intransitive verb*
: to plant something
— **plant·able** \ˈplan-tə-bəl\ *adjective*

**²plant** *noun* [Middle English *plante*, from Old English, from Latin *planta*] (before 12th century)
**1 a :** a young tree, vine, shrub, or herb planted or suitable for planting **b :** any of a kingdom (Plantae) of living things typically lacking locomotive movement or obvious nervous or sensory organs and possessing cellulose cell walls
**2 a :** the land, buildings, machinery, apparatus, and fixtures employed in carrying on a trade or an industrial business **b :** a factory or workshop for the manufacture of a particular product **c :** the total facilities available for production or service **d :** the buildings and other physical equipment of an institution
**3 :** an act of planting
**4 :** something or someone planted
— **plant–like** \-ˌlīk\ *adjective*
**Plan·tag·e·net** \plan-ˈta-jə-nət, -ˈtaj-nət\ *adjective* [*Plantagenet*, nickname of the family adopted as surname] (1868)
: of or relating to a royal house ruling England from 1154 to 1485
— **Plantagenet** *noun*
**¹plan·tain** \ˈplan-tᵊn\ *noun* [Middle English, from Old French, from Latin *plantagin-, plantago*, from *planta* sole of the foot; from its broad leaves — more at PLACE] (13th century)
: any of a genus (*Plantago* of the family Plantaginaceae, the plantain family) of short-stemmed elliptic-leaved herbs with spikes of minute greenish flowers
**²plantain** *noun* [Spanish *plántano, plátano* plane tree, banana tree, from Medieval Latin *plantanus* plane tree, alteration of Latin *platanus* — more at PLANE] (1555)
**1 :** a banana plant (*Musa paradisiaca*)
**2 :** the angular greenish starchy fruit of the plantain that is a staple food in the tropics when cooked
**plantain lily** *noun* (1882)
: any of a genus (*Hosta*) of perennial plants of the lily family with densely growing basal leaves and racemose white or violet flowers — called also *hosta, funkia*
**plan·tar** \ˈplan-tər, -ˌtär\ *adjective* [Latin *plantaris*, from *planta* sole — more at PLACE] (circa 1706)
: of or relating to the sole of the foot ⟨*plantar* wart⟩
**plan·ta·tion** \plan-ˈtā-shən\ *noun* (1569)
**1 :** a usually large group of plants and especially trees under cultivation
**2 :** a settlement in a new country or region ⟨Plymouth *Plantation*⟩
**3 a :** a place that is planted or under cultivation **b :** an agricultural estate usually worked by resident labor
**plant·er** \ˈplan-tər\ *noun* (14th century)
**1 :** one that cultivates plants: as **a** (1) : FARMER (2) : one who owns or operates a plantation **b :** a planting machine or implement
**2 :** one who settles or founds a place and especially a new colony
**3 :** a container in which ornamental plants are grown
**planter's punch** *noun* (1924)
: a punch of rum, lime or lemon juice, sugar, water, and sometimes bitters
**plant food** *noun* (1869)
**1 :** FOOD 1b
**2 :** FERTILIZER
**plant hormone** *noun* (1935)
: an organic substance other than a nutrient that in minute amounts modifies a plant physiological process; *especially* : one produced by a plant and active elsewhere than at the site of production

**plan·ti·grade** \'plan-tə-ˌgrād\ *adjective* [French, from Latin *planta* sole + French -*grade*] (1831)
**:** walking on the sole with the heel touching the ground ⟨humans are *plantigrade*⟩
— **plantigrade** *noun*

**plant·ing** (1632)
**:** an area where plants are grown for commercial or decorative purposes; *also* **:** the plants cultivated in such an area

**plant kingdom** *noun* (1884)
**:** a basic group of natural objects that includes all living and extinct plants — compare ANIMAL KINGDOM, MINERAL KINGDOM

**plant·let** \'plant-lət\ *noun* (1816)
**:** a small or young plant

**plant louse** *noun* (1805)
**:** APHID; *also* **:** any of various small insects (as a jumping plant louse) of similar habits

**plan·to·cra·cy** \plan-'tä-krə-sē\ *noun* [*planter* + -*o*- + -*cracy*] (circa 1846)
**1 :** a ruling class made up of planters
**2 :** government by planters

**plants·man** \'plants-mən, -ˌman\ *noun* (1881)
**:** a person skilled with plants **:** an expert gardener or horticulturist

**plan·u·la** \'plan-yə-lə\ *noun, plural* -**lae** \-ˌlē -ˌlī\ [New Latin, from Latin *planus* level, flat — more at FLOOR] (1870)
**:** the very young usually flattened oval or oblong free-swimming ciliated larva of a coelenterate

**plaque** \'plak\ *noun* [French, from Middle French, metal sheet, from *plaquier* to plate, from Middle Dutch *placken* to piece, patch; akin to Middle Dutch *placke* piece, Middle High German *placke* patch] (1848)
**1 a :** an ornamental brooch; *especially* **:** the badge of an honorary order **b :** a flat thin piece (as of metal) used for decoration **c :** a commemorative or identifying inscribed tablet
**2 a :** a localized abnormal patch on a body part or surface **b :** a film of mucus that harbors bacteria on a tooth **c :** an atherosclerotic lesion **d :** a histopathologic lesion of brain tissue that is characteristic of Alzheimer's disease and consists of a cluster of degenerating nerve endings and dendrites around a core of amyloid
**3 :** a clear area in a bacterial culture produced by destruction of cells by a virus

**¹plash** \'plash\ *noun* [probably imitative] (1513)
**:** SPLASH

**²plash** (1542)
*intransitive verb*
**:** to cause a splashing or spattering effect
*transitive verb*
**:** to break the surface of (water) **:** SPLASH

**-plasia** *or* **-plasy** *noun combining form* [New Latin -*plasia*, from Greek *plasis* molding, from *plassein*]
**:** development **:** formation ⟨hyper*plasia*⟩ ⟨homo*plasy*⟩

**plasm** \'pla-zəm\ *noun* [Late Latin *plasma* something molded] (1747)
**:** PLASMA

**plasm-** *or* **plasmo-** *combining form* [French, from New Latin *plasma*]
**:** plasma ⟨*plasmodium*⟩ ⟨*plasmolysis*⟩

**-plasm** *noun combining form* [German -*plasma*, from New Latin *plasma*]
**:** formative or formed material (as of a cell or tissue) ⟨endo*plasm*⟩

**plas·ma** \'plaz-mə\ *noun* [German, from Late Latin, something molded, from Greek, from *plassein* to mold — more at PLASTER] (1772)
**1 :** a green faintly translucent quartz
**2** [New Latin, from Late Latin] **a :** the fluid part of blood, lymph, or milk as distinguished from suspended material **b :** the juice that can be expressed from muscle
**3 :** PROTOPLASM
**4 :** a collection of charged particles (as in the atmospheres of stars or in a metal) containing about equal numbers of positive ions and elec-

trons and exhibiting some properties of a gas but differing from a gas in being a good conductor of electricity and in being affected by a magnetic field
— **plas·mat·ic** \plaz-'ma-tik\ *adjective*

**plasma cell** *noun* (1888)
**:** a lymphocyte that is a mature antibody-secreting B cell

**plas·ma·gel** \'plaz-mə-ˌjel\ *noun* (1923)
**:** gelated cytoplasm; *especially* **:** the outer firm zone of a pseudopodium

**plas·ma·gene** \-ˌjēn\ *noun* [International Scientific Vocabulary] (1939)
**:** an extranuclear determiner of hereditary characteristics with a capacity for replication similar to that of a nuclear gene

**plasma jet** *noun* (1957)
**:** a stream of very hot ionized plasma; *also* **:** a device for producing such a stream

**plas·ma·lem·ma** \ˌplaz-mə-'le-mə\ *noun* [New Latin, from *plasma* + Greek *lemma* husk — more at LEMMA] (1923)
**:** PLASMA MEMBRANE

**plasma membrane** *noun* (1900)
**:** a semipermeable limiting layer of cell protoplasm — called also *cell membrane;* see CELL illustration

**plas·ma·phe·re·sis** \ˌplaz-mə-fə-'rē-səs, -'fer-ə-səs\ *noun* [New Latin, from *plasm-* + Greek *aphairesis* taking off — more at APHAERESIS] (1914)
**:** a process for obtaining blood plasma without depleting the donor or patient of other blood constituents (as red blood cells) by separating out the plasma from the whole blood and returning the rest to the donor's or patient's circulatory system

**plas·ma·sol** \'plaz-mə-ˌsäl, -ˌsȯl, -ˌsōl\ *noun* (1923)
**:** cytoplasm in the form of a sol especially in a pseudopodium or amoeboid cell

**plasma torch** *noun* (1959)
**:** a device that heats a gas by electrical means to form a plasma for high-temperature operations (as melting metal)

**plas·mid** \'plaz-məd\ *noun* [*plasma* + -²*id*] (1952)
**:** an extrachromosomal ring of DNA especially of bacteria that replicates autonomously

**plas·min** \-mən\ *noun* (circa 1866)
**:** a proteolytic enzyme that dissolves the fibrin of blood clots

**plas·min·o·gen** \plaz-'mi-nə-jən\ *noun* (1945)
**:** the precursor of plasmin that is found in blood plasma and serum

**plas·mo·des·ma** \ˌplaz-mə-'dez-mə\ *also* **plas·mo·desm** \'plaz-mə-ˌde-zəm\ *noun, plural* -**des·ma·ta** \-'dez-mə-tə\ *or* -**des·mas** \-'dez-məz\ [New Latin *plasmodesma*, from *plasma* + Greek *desmat-*, *desma* bond, from *dein* to bind — more at DIADEM] (1905)
**:** one of the cytoplasmic strands that pass through openings in some plant cell walls and provide living bridges between cells

**plas·mo·di·um** \plaz-'mō-dē-əm\ *noun, plural* -**dia** \-dē-ə\ [New Latin, from *plasm-* + -*odium* thing resembling, from Greek -*ōdēs* like] (1875)
**1 a :** a motile multinucleate mass of protoplasm resulting from fusion of uninucleate amoeboid cells; *also* **:** an organism (as a stage of a slime mold) that consists of such a structure **b :** SYNCYTIUM 1
**2 :** an individual malaria parasite

**plas·mog·a·my** \plaz-'mä-gə-mē\ *noun* [International Scientific Vocabulary] (1912)
**:** fusion of the cytoplasm of two or more cells as distinguished from fusion of nuclei

**plas·mol·y·sis** \plaz-'mä-lə-səs\ *noun* [New Latin] (1883)
**:** shrinking of the cytoplasm away from the wall of a living cell due to outward osmotic flow of water
— **plas·mo·lyt·ic** \ˌplaz-mə-'li-tik\ *adjective*

**plas·mo·lyze** \'plaz-mə-ˌlīz\ *verb* -**lyzed; -lyz·ing** (1888)
*transitive verb*
**:** to subject to plasmolysis
*intransitive verb*
**:** to undergo plasmolysis

**-plast** *noun combining form* [Middle French -*plaste* thing molded, from Late Latin -*plastus*, from Greek -*plastos*, from *plastos* molded, from *plassein*]
**:** organized particle or granule **:** cell ⟨chromo*plast*⟩

**¹plas·ter** \'plas-tər\ *noun* [Middle English, from Old English, from Latin *emplastrum*, from Greek *emplastron*, from *emplassein* to plaster on, from *en-* + *plassein* to mold, plaster; perhaps akin to Latin *planus* level, flat — more at FLOOR] (before 12th century)
**1 :** a medicated or protective dressing that consists of a film (as of cloth or plastic) spread with a usually medicated substance ⟨adhesive *plaster*⟩; *broadly* **:** something applied to heal and soothe
**2 :** a pasty composition (as of lime, water, and sand) that hardens on drying and is used for coating walls, ceilings, and partitions
— **plas·tery** \-t(ə-)rē\ *adjective*

**²plaster** *verb* **plas·tered; plas·ter·ing** \-t(ə-)riŋ\ (14th century)
*transitive verb*
**1 :** to overlay or cover with plaster **:** COAT
**2 :** to apply a plaster to
**3 a :** to cover over or conceal as if with a coat of plaster **b :** to apply as a coating or incrustation **c :** to smooth down with a sticky or shiny substance ⟨*plastered* his hair down⟩
**4 :** to fasten or apply tightly to another surface
**5 :** to treat with plaster of paris
**6 :** to affix to or place on especially conspicuously or in quantity
**7 :** to inflict heavy damage or loss on especially by a concentrated or unremitting attack
*intransitive verb*
**:** to apply plaster
— **plas·ter·er** \-tər-ər\ *noun*

**plas·ter·board** \'plas-tər-ˌbȯrd, -ˌbȯrd\ *noun* (1897)
**:** a board made of several plies of fiberboard, paper, or felt usually bonded to a hardened gypsum plaster core and used especially as wallboard

**plaster cast** *noun* (1825)
**1 :** a sculptor's model in plaster of paris
**2 :** a rigid dressing of gauze impregnated with plaster of paris

**plas·tered** \'plas-tərd\ *adjective* (1902)
**:** DRUNK, INTOXICATED

**plastering** *noun* (15th century)
**1 :** a coating of or as if of plaster
**2 :** a decisive defeat

**plaster of par·is** \-'par-əs\ *often 2d P capitalized* [*Paris*, France] (15th century)
**:** a white powdery slightly hydrated calcium sulfate $CaSO_4 \cdot \frac{1}{2} H_2O$ or $2CaSO_4 \cdot H_2O$ made by calcining gypsum and used chiefly for casts and molds in the form of a quick-setting paste with water

**plaster saint** *noun* (1890)
**:** a person without human failings

**plas·ter·work** \'plas-tər-ˌwərk\ *noun* (1600)
**:** plastering often ornate in design used to finish architectural constructions

**¹plas·tic** \'plas-tik\ *adjective* [Latin *plasticus* of molding, from Greek *plastikos*, from *plassein* to mold, form] (1632)
**1 :** FORMATIVE, CREATIVE ⟨*plastic* forces in nature⟩
**2 a :** capable of being molded or modeled ⟨*plastic* clay⟩ **b :** capable of adapting to varying conditions **:** PLIABLE ⟨ecologically *plastic* animals⟩
**3 :** SCULPTURAL
**4 :** made of or consisting of a plastic
**5 :** capable of being deformed continuously and permanently in any direction without rupture

**6 :** of, relating to, or involving plastic surgery
**7 :** having a quality suggestive of mass-produced plastic goods; *especially* **:** ARTIFICIAL 4 ⟨*plastic* smiles⟩ ☆

²**plastic** *noun* (1905)
**1 :** a plastic substance; *specifically* **:** any of numerous organic synthetic or processed materials that are mostly thermoplastic or thermosetting polymers of high molecular weight and that can be made into objects, films, or filaments
**2 :** credit cards used for payment
— **plas·ticky** \'plas-ti-kē\ *adjective*

-**plastic** *adjective combining form* [Greek *-plastikos*, from *plassein*]
**1 :** developing **:** forming ⟨thrombo*plastic*⟩
**2 :** of or relating to (something designated by a term ending in *-plasm, -plast, -plasty,* or *-plasy*) ⟨homo*plastic*⟩ ⟨neo*plastic*⟩

**plas·ti·cal·ly** \'plas-ti-k(ə-)lē\ *adverb* (1835)
**1 :** in a plastic manner
**2 :** with respect to plastic qualities

**plastic art** *noun* (circa 1907)
**1 :** art (as sculpture or bas-relief) characterized by modeling **:** three-dimensional art
**2 :** visual art (as painting, sculpture, or film) especially as distinguished from art that is written (as poetry or music) — often used in plural

**plastic foam** *noun* (1943)
**:** EXPANDED PLASTIC

**plas·ti·cine** *also* **plas·ti·cene** \'plas-tə-ˌsēn\ *noun* [from *Plasticine*, a trademark] (1897)
**:** a plastic paste used for models and sculptures

**plas·tic·i·ty** \pla-'sti-sə-tē\ *noun* (circa 1783)
**1 :** the quality or state of being plastic; *especially* **:** capacity for being molded or altered
**2 :** the ability to retain a shape attained by pressure deformation
**3 :** the capacity of organisms with the same genotype to vary in developmental pattern, in phenotype, or in behavior according to varying environmental conditions

**plas·ti·cize** \'plas-tə-ˌsīz\ *transitive verb* **-cized; -ciz·ing** (1919)
**1 :** to make plastic
**2 :** to treat with a plastic ⟨a *plasticized* mattress cover⟩
— **plas·ti·ci·za·tion** \ˌplas-tə-sə-'zā-shən\ *noun*

**plas·ti·ciz·er** \'plas-tə-ˌsī-zər\ *noun* (1925)
**:** one that plasticizes; *specifically* **:** a chemical added especially to rubbers and resins to impart flexibility, workability, or stretchability

**plastic surgeon** *noun* (1946)
**:** a specialist in plastic surgery

**plastic surgery** *noun* (1842)
**:** surgery concerned with the repair, restoration, or improvement of lost, injured, defective, or misshapen body parts

**plas·tid** \'plas-təd\ *noun* [German, from Greek *plastos* molded] (1885)
**:** any of various cytoplasmic organelles (as an amyloplast or chloroplast) of photosynthetic cells that serve in many cases as centers of special metabolic activities
— **plas·tid·i·al** \pla-'sti-dē-əl\ *adjective*

**plas·ti·sol** \'plas-tə-ˌsäl, -ˌsol\ *noun* [*plastic* + ⁴*sol*] (1946)
**:** a substance consisting of a mixture of a resin and a plasticizer that can be molded, cast, or made into a continuous film by application of heat

**plas·to·cy·a·nin** \ˌplas-tō-'sī-ə-nən\ *noun* [Greek *plastos* + English *cyan-* + ¹*-in*] (1961)
**:** a copper-containing protein that acts as an intermediary in photosynthetic electron transport

**plas·to·qui·none** \ˌplas-(ˌ)tō-kwi-'nōn, -'kwi-ˌ\ *noun* [Greek *plastos* + English *quinone*] (1958)
**:** a plant substance that is related to vitamin K and plays a role in photosynthetic phosphorylation

**plas·tral** \'plas-trəl\ *adjective* (1889)
**:** of or relating to a plastron

**plas·tron** \'plas-trən\ *noun* [Middle French, from Old Italian *piastrone*, augmentative of *piastra* thin metal plate — more at PIASTRE] (circa 1507)
**1 a :** a metal breastplate formerly worn under the hauberk **b :** a quilted pad worn in fencing practice to protect the chest, waist, and the side on which the weapon is held
**2 :** the ventral part of the shell of a tortoise or turtle consisting typically of nine symmetrically placed bones overlaid by horny plates
**3 a :** a trimming like a bib for a woman's dress **b :** DICKEY 1a
**4 :** a thin film of air held by water-repellent hairs of some aquatic insects

-**plasty** *noun combining form* [French *-plastie*, from Late Greek *-plastia* molding, from Greek *-plastēs* molder, from *plassein*]
**:** plastic surgery ⟨osteo*plasty*⟩

-**plasy** — see -PLASIA

¹**plat** \'plat\ *transitive verb* **plat·ted; plat·ting** [Middle English, alteration of *plaiten*] (14th century)
**:** PLAIT

²**plat** *noun* (1535)
**:** PLAIT

³**plat** *noun* [probably alteration of *plot*] (15th century)
**1 :** a small piece of ground (as a lot or quadrat) **:** PLOT
**2 :** a plan, map, or chart of a piece of land with actual or proposed features (as lots); *also* **:** the land represented

⁴**plat** *transitive verb* **plat·ted; plat·ting** (1751)
**:** to make a plat of

**plat·an** \'pla-t⁽ᵉ⁾n\ *noun* [Middle English, from Latin *platanus* — more at PLANE] (14th century)
**:** ²PLANE

**plat du jour** \ˌplä-də-'zhŭr, ˌpla-\ *noun, plural* **plats du jour** \*same*\ [French, literally, plate of the day] (1906)
**:** a dish that is featured by a restaurant on a particular day

¹**plate** \'plāt\ *noun* [Middle English, from Old French, from *plate*, feminine of *plat* flat, from (assumed) Vulgar Latin *plattus*, probably from Greek *platys* broad, flat — more at PLACE] (14th century)
**1 a :** a smooth flat thin piece of material **b** (1) **:** forged, rolled, or cast metal in sheets usually thicker than ¼ inch (6 millimeters) (2) **:** a very thin layer of metal deposited on a surface of base metal by plating **c :** one of the broad metal pieces used in armor; *also* **:** armor of such plates **d** (1) **:** a lamina or plaque (as of bone or horn) that forms part of an animal body; *especially* **:** SCUTE (2) **:** the thin under portion of the forequarter of beef; *especially* **:** the fatty back part — see BEEF illustration **e :** HOME PLATE **f :** any of the large movable segments into which the earth's crust is divided according to the theory of plate tectonics
**2** [Middle English; partly from Old French *plate* plate, piece of silver; partly from Old Spanish *plata* silver, from (assumed) Vulgar Latin *platta* metal plate, from feminine of *plattus* flat] **a** *obsolete* **:** a silver coin **b :** precious metal; *especially* **:** silver bullion
**3** [Middle English, from Middle French *plat* dish, plate, from *plat* flat] **a :** domestic hollowware made of or plated with gold, silver, or base metals **b :** a shallow usually circular vessel from which food is eaten or served **c** (1) **:** a quantity to fill a plate **:** PLATEFUL (2) **:** a main course served on a plate (3) **:** food and service supplied to one person ⟨a dinner at $10 a *plate*⟩ **d** (1) **:** a prize given to the winner in a contest (2) *British* **:** a horse race in which the contestants compete for a prize of fixed value rather than stakes **e :** a dish or pouch passed in taking collections **f :** a flat glass dish used chiefly for culturing microorganisms

**4 a :** a prepared surface from which printing is done **b :** a sheet of material (as glass) coated with a light-sensitive photographic emulsion **c** (1) **:** the usually flat or grid-formed anode of an electron tube at which electrons collect (2) **:** a metallic grid with its interstices filled with active material that forms one of the structural units of a battery **d :** LICENSE PLATE
**5 :** a horizontal structural member that provides bearing and anchorage especially for the trusses of a roof or the rafters
**6 :** the part of a denture that fits to the mouth; *broadly* **:** DENTURE
**7 :** a full-page illustration often on different paper from the text pages
**8 :** a schedule of matters to deal with ⟨have a lot on my *plate* now⟩
— **plate·ful** \-ˌfŭl\ *noun*
— **plate·like** \-ˌlīk\ *adjective*

²**plate** *transitive verb* **plat·ed; plat·ing** (14th century)
**1 :** to cover or equip with plate: as **a :** to provide with armor plate **b :** to cover with an adherent layer mechanically, chemically, or electrically; *also* **:** to deposit (as a layer) on a surface
**2 :** to make a printing surface from or for
**3 :** to fix or secure with a plate
**4 :** to cause (as a runner) to score in baseball

¹**pla·teau** \pla-'tō, 'pla-ˌ\ *noun, plural* **plateaus** *or* **pla·teaux** \-'tōz, -ˌtōz\ [French, from Middle French, platter, from *plat* flat] (1796)
**1 a :** a usually extensive land area having a relatively level surface raised sharply above adjacent land on at least one side **:** TABLELAND **b :** a similar undersea feature
**2 a :** a region of little or no change in a graphic representation **b :** a relatively stable level, period, or condition
**3 :** a level of attainment or achievement ⟨the 500-point *plateau*⟩

²**plateau** *intransitive verb* (1939)
**:** to reach a level, period, or condition of stability

**plate-glass** \'plāt-'glas, -ˌglas\ *adjective, often capitalized* (1968)
**:** of, relating to, or being the British universities founded in the latter half of the twentieth century — compare OXBRIDGE, REDBRICK

**plate glass** *noun* (circa 1741)
**:** rolled, ground, and polished sheet glass

**plate·let** \'plāt-lət\ *noun* (1895)
**:** a minute flattened body (as of ice or a mineral); *especially* **:** BLOOD PLATELET

**plate·mak·er** \'plāt-ˌmā-kər\ *noun* (1904)

---

☆ **SYNONYMS**
**Plastic, pliable, pliant, ductile, malleable, adaptable** mean susceptible of being modified in form or nature. PLASTIC applies to substances soft enough to be molded yet capable of hardening into the desired fixed form ⟨*plastic* materials allow the sculptor greater freedom⟩. PLIABLE suggests something easily bent, folded, twisted, or manipulated ⟨*pliable* rubber tubing⟩. PLIANT may stress flexibility and sometimes connote springiness ⟨an athletic shoe with a *pliant* sole⟩. DUCTILE applies to what can be drawn out or extended with ease ⟨*ductile* metals such as copper⟩. MALLEABLE applies to what may be pressed or beaten into shape ⟨the *malleable* properties of gold enhance its value⟩. ADAPTABLE implies the capability of being easily modified to suit other conditions, needs, or uses ⟨computer hardware that is *adaptable*⟩.

---

\ə\ **abut** \ᵊ\ **kitten** \ər\ **further** \a\ **ash** \ā\ **ace**
\ä\ **mop, mar** \au̇\ **out** \ch\ **chin** \e\ **bet** \ē\ **easy**
\g\ **go** \i\ **hit** \ī\ **ice** \j\ **job** \ŋ\ **sing** \ō\ **go**
\ȯ\ **law** \ȯi\ **boy** \th\ **thin** \t͟h\ **the** \ü\ **loot** \u̇\ **foot**
\y\ **yet** \zh\ **vision** *see also* Guide to Pronunciation

: a machine for making printing plates and especially offset printing plates
— **plate·mak·ing** \-kiŋ\ *noun*

**plat·en** \'pla-tᵊn\ *noun* [Middle French *plateine*, from *plate*] (1541)
**1 :** a flat plate; *especially* **:** one that exerts or receives pressure (as in a printing press)
**2 :** the roller of a typewriter or printer

**plat·er** \'plā-tər\ *noun* (1777)
**1 :** one that plates
**2 a :** a horse that runs chiefly in plate races **b :** a racehorse that competes in the lowest grade of races

**plate rail** *noun* (1902)
: a rail or narrow shelf along the upper part of a wall for holding plates or ornaments

**plat·er·esque** \,pla-tə-'resk\ *adjective, often capitalized* [Spanish *plateresco*, from *platero* silversmith, from *plata* silver] (circa 1864)
: of, relating to, or being a 16th century Spanish architectural style characterized by elaborate ornamentation suggestive of silver plate

**plate tectonics** *noun plural but singular in construction* (1969)
: a theory in geology: the lithosphere of the earth is divided into a small number of plates which float on and travel independently over the mantle and much of the earth's seismic activity occurs at the boundaries of these plates — compare CONTINENTAL DRIFT

**plat·form** \'plat-,fôrm\ *noun, often attributive* [Middle French *plate-forme* diagram, map, literally, flat form] (1535)
**1 :** PLAN, DESIGN
**2 :** a declaration of the principles on which a group of persons stands; *especially* **:** a declaration of principles and policies adopted by a political party or a candidate
**3 a** (1) **:** a usually raised horizontal flat surface; *especially* **:** a raised flooring (as for speakers or performers) (2) **:** a device or structure incorporating or providing a platform; *especially* **:** such a structure on legs used for offshore drilling (as for oil) **b :** a place or opportunity for public discussion
**4 a :** a usually thick layer (as of cork) between the inner sole and outer sole of a shoe **b :** a shoe having such a sole
**5 :** a vehicle (as a satellite or aircraft) used for a particular activity or purpose or to carry a usually specified kind of equipment

**platform balance** *noun* (1811)
: a balance having a platform on which objects are weighed — called also *platform scale*

**platform rocker** *noun* (1944)
: a chair that rocks on a stable platform

**platform tennis** *noun* (1955)
: a variation of paddle tennis that is played on a platform enclosed by a wire fence

**pla·ti·na** \plə-'tē-nə\ *noun* [Spanish] (1750)
: PLATINUM

**plat·ing** \'plā-tiŋ\ *noun* (1831)
**1 :** the act or process of plating
**2 a :** a coating of metal plates **b :** a thin coating of metal

**plat·i·nize** \'pla-tᵊn-,īz\ *transitive verb* **-nized; -niz·ing** (1825)
: to cover, treat, or combine with platinum or a compound of platinum

**plat·i·no·cy·a·nide** \,pla-tᵊn-ō-'sī-ə-,nīd\ *noun* (1845)
: a fluorescent complex salt formed by the union of a compound of platinum and cyanide with another cyanide

**plat·i·num** \'plat-nəm, 'pla-tᵊn-əm\ *noun, often attributive* [New Latin, from Spanish *platina*, from diminutive of *plata* silver — more at PLATE] (1812)
**1 :** a heavy precious grayish white noncorroding ductile malleable metallic element that fuses with difficulty and is used especially in chemical ware and apparatus, as a catalyst, and in dental and jewelry alloys — see ELEMENT table
**2 :** a moderate gray

**platinum blonde** *noun* (1931)

**1 :** a person whose hair is of a pale silvery blonde color
**2 :** the color of the hair of a platinum blonde

**plat·i·tude** \'pla-tə-,tüd, -,tyüd\ *noun* [French, from *plat* flat, dull] (1812)
**1 :** the quality or state of being dull or insipid
**2 :** a banal, trite, or stale remark

**plat·i·tu·di·nal** \,pla-tə-'tüd-nəl, -'tyüd-; -'tü-dᵊn-əl, -'tyü-\ *adjective* (1870)
: PLATITUDINOUS

**plat·i·tu·di·nar·i·an** \-,tü-dᵊn-'er-ē-ən, -,tyü-\ *noun* (1855)
: one given to the use of platitudes

**plat·i·tu·di·nize** \-'tü-dᵊn-,īz, -'tyü-\ *intransitive verb* **-nized; -niz·ing** [*platitudinous*] (1885)
: to utter platitudes

**plat·i·tu·di·nous** \-'tüd-nəs, -'tyüd-; -'tü-dᵊn-əs, -'tyü-\ *adjective* [*platitude* + *-inous* (as in *multitudinous*)] (1862)
: having the characteristics of a platitude **:** full of platitudes ⟨*platitudinous* remarks⟩
— **plat·i·tu·di·nous·ly** *adverb*

**pla·ton·ic** \plə-'tä-nik, plā-\ *adjective* [Latin *platonicus*, from Greek *platōnikos*, from *Platōn* Plato] (1533)
**1** *capitalized* **:** of, relating to, or characteristic of Plato or Platonism
**2 a :** relating to or based on platonic love; *also* **:** experiencing or professing platonic love **b :** of, relating to, or being a relationship marked by the absence of romance or sex
**3 :** NOMINAL, THEORETICAL
— **pla·ton·i·cal·ly** \-ni-k(ə-)lē\ *adverb*

**platonic love** *noun, often P capitalized* (1631)
**1 :** love conceived by Plato as ascending from passion for the individual to contemplation of the universal and ideal
**2 :** a close relationship between two persons in which sexual desire is nonexistent or has been suppressed or sublimated

**Pla·to·nism** \'plā-tᵊn-,i-zəm\ *noun* (circa 1570)
**1 a :** the philosophy of Plato stressing especially that actual things are copies of transcendent ideas and that these ideas are the objects of true knowledge apprehended by reminiscence **b :** NEOPLATONISM
**2 :** PLATONIC LOVE
— **Pla·to·nist** \-tᵊn-ist\ *noun*
— **Pla·to·nis·tic** \,plā-tᵊn-'is-tik\ *adjective*

**Pla·to·nize** \'plā-tᵊn-,īz\ *verb* **-nized; -niz·ing** (1608)
*intransitive verb*
: to adopt, imitate, or conform to Platonic opinions
*transitive verb*
: to explain in accordance with or adapt to Platonic doctrines; *especially* **:** IDEALIZE

**¹pla·toon** \plə-'tün, pla-\ *noun* [French *peloton* small detachment, literally, ball, from Middle French *pelote* little ball — more at PELLET] (1637)
**1 :** a subdivision of a company-size military unit normally consisting of two or more squads or sections
**2 :** a group of persons sharing a common characteristic or activity ⟨a *platoon* of waiters⟩; *especially* **:** a group of football players who are trained for either offense or defense and are sent into or withdrawn from the game as a body

**²platoon** (1963)
*transitive verb*
: to play (one player) alternately with another player in the same position (as on a baseball team)
*intransitive verb*
**1 :** to alternate with another player at the same position
**2 :** to use alternate players at the same position

**platoon sergeant** *noun* (1915)

: a noncommissioned officer in the army ranking above a staff sergeant and below a first sergeant

**Platt·deutsch** \'plat-,dóich, 'plät-\ *noun* [German, from Dutch *Platduitsch*, literally, Low German, from *plat* flat, low + *duitsch* German] (1677)
: the Low German speech of northern Germany comprising several dialects

**plat·ter** \'pla-tər\ *noun* [Middle English *plater*, from Anglo-French, from Middle French *plat* plate] (13th century)
**1 a :** a large plate used especially for serving meat **b :** PLATE 3c(2)
**2 :** a phonograph record
— **plat·ter·ful** \-,fül\ *noun*
— **on a platter :** without effort **:** very easily ⟨can have the presidency *on a platter* —Jonathan Daniels⟩

**¹platy** \'plā-tē\ *adjective* (1533)
: resembling a plate; *also* **:** consisting of plates or flaky layers — used chiefly of soil or mineral formations

**²platy** \'pla-tē\ *noun, plural* **platy** *or* **plat·ys** *or* **plat·ies** [New Latin *Platypoecilus*, former genus name of the fish] (1931)
: either of two live-bearers (*Xiphophorus maculatus* and *X. variatus* of the family Poeciliidae) that are popular aquarium fishes and are noted for variability and brilliant color — called also *platy·fish* \-,fish\

**platy·hel·minth** \,pla-ti-'hel-,min(t)th\ *noun* [ultimately from Greek *platys* broad, flat + *helminth-, helmis* helminth] (circa 1890)
: any of a phylum (Platyhelminthes) of soft-bodied usually much flattened acoelomate worms (as the planarians, flukes, and tapeworms) — called also *flatworm*
— **platy·hel·min·thic** \-hel-'min(t)-thik, -'min-tik\ *adjective*

**platy·pus** \'pla-ti-pəs, -,pùs\ *noun, plural* **platy·pus·es** *also* **platy·pi** \-,pī, -,pē\ [New Latin, from Greek *platypous* flat-footed, from *platys* broad, flat + *pous* foot — more at PLACE, FOOT] (1799)
: a small carnivorous aquatic oviparous mammal (*Ornithorhynchus anatinus*) of eastern Australia and Tasmania that has a fleshy bill resembling that of a duck, dense fur, webbed feet, and a broad flattened tail

platypus

**plat·yr·rhine** \'pla-ti-,rīn\ *adjective* (1857)
**1** [New Latin *Platyrrhina*, from Greek *platyrrhin-, platyrrhis* broad-nosed, from *platys* + *rhin-, rhis* nose] **:** of, relating to, or being any of a division (Platyrrhina) of monkeys all of which are New World monkeys and are characterized by a broad nasal septum, usually 36 teeth, and often a prehensile tail
**2** [Greek *platyrrhin-, platyrrhis*] **:** having a short broad nose
— **platyrrhine** *noun*

**plau·dit** \'plô-dət\ *noun* [Latin *plaudite* applaud, plural imperative of *plaudere* to applaud] (1624)
**1 :** an act or round of applause
**2 :** enthusiastic approval — usually used in plural ⟨received the *plaudits* of the critics⟩

**plau·si·bil·i·ty** \,plô-zə-'bi-lə-tē\ *noun, plural* **-ties** (1649)
**1 :** the quality or state of being plausible
**2 :** something plausible

**plau·si·ble** \'plô-zə-bəl\ *adjective* [Latin *plausibilis* worthy of applause, from *plausus*, past participle of *plaudere*] (1565)
**1 :** superficially fair, reasonable, or valuable but often specious ⟨a *plausible* pretext⟩

**2** : superficially pleasing or persuasive ⟨a swindler . . . , then a quack, then a smooth, *plausible* gentleman —R. W. Emerson⟩
**3** : appearing worthy of belief ⟨the argument was both powerful and *plausible*⟩
— **plau·si·ble·ness** *noun*
— **plau·si·bly** \-blē\ *adverb*
**plau·sive** \'plȯ-ziv, -siv\ *adjective* [Latin *plausus*, past participle] (1600)
**1** : manifesting praise or approval
**2** *obsolete* : PLEASING
**3** *archaic* : SPECIOUS
**¹play** \'plā\ *noun* [Middle English, from Old English *plega*; akin to Old English *plegan* to play, Middle Dutch *pleyen*] (before 12th century)
**1 a** : SWORDPLAY **b** *archaic* : GAME, SPORT **c** : the conduct, course, or action of a game **d** : a particular act or maneuver in a game: as (1) : the action during an attempt to advance the ball in football (2) : the action in which a player is put out in baseball **e** : the action in which cards are played after bidding in a card game **f** : the moving of a piece in a board game (as chess) **g** : one's turn in a game ⟨it's your *play*⟩
**2 a** *obsolete* : SEXUAL INTERCOURSE **b** : amorous flirtation : DALLIANCE
**3 a** : recreational activity; *especially* : the spontaneous activity of children **b** : absence of serious or harmful intent : JEST ⟨said it in *play*⟩ **c** : the act or an instance of playing on words or speech sounds **d** : GAMING, GAMBLING
**4 a** (1) : an act, way, or manner of proceeding : MANEUVER ⟨that was a *play* to get your fingerprints —Erle Stanley Gardner⟩ (2) : DEAL, VENTURE **b** (1) : OPERATION, ACTIVITY ⟨other motives surely come into *play* —M. R. Cohen⟩ (2) : brisk, fitful, or light movement ⟨the gem presented a dazzling *play* of colors⟩ (3) : free or unimpeded motion (as of a part of a machine); *also* : the length or measure of such motion (4) : scope or opportunity for action
**5** : emphasis or publicity especially in the news media ⟨wished the country received a better *play* in the American press —Hugh Mac-Lennan⟩
**6** : a move or series of moves calculated to arouse friendly feelings — usually used with *make* ⟨made a big *play* for the girl —Will Herman⟩
**7 a** : the stage representation of an action or story **b** : a dramatic composition : DRAMA
**synonym** see FUN
— **in play** : in condition or position to be legitimately played
— **out of play** : not in play
**²play** (before 12th century)
*intransitive verb*
**1 a** : to engage in sport or recreation : FROLIC **b** : to have sexual relations; *especially* : to have promiscuous or illicit sexual relations — usually used in the phrase *play around* **c** (1) : to move aimlessly about : TRIFLE (2) : to toy or fiddle around with something ⟨*played* with her food⟩ (3) : to deal or behave frivolously or mockingly : JEST (4) : to deal in a light, speculative, or sportive manner (5) : to make use of double meaning or of the similarity of sound of two words for stylistic or humorous effect
**2 a** : to take advantage ⟨play on fears⟩ **b** (1) : FLUTTER, FRISK (2) : to move or operate in a lively, irregular, or intermittent manner **c** : to move or function freely within prescribed limits **d** : to produce a stream ⟨hoses *playing* on a fire⟩
**3 a** (1) : to perform music ⟨*play* on a violin⟩ (2) : to sound in performance ⟨the organ is *playing*⟩ (3) : to emit sounds ⟨the radio is *playing*⟩ (4) : to reproduce recorded sounds ⟨a record is *playing*⟩ **b** (1) : to act in a dramatic production (2) : SHOW, RUN ⟨what's *playing* at the theater⟩ **c** : to be suitable for dramatic performance **d** : to act with special consideration so as to gain favor, approval, or sympathy ⟨might *play* to popular prejudices to serve his

political ends —V. L. Parrington⟩ — often used in the phrase *play up to*
**4 a** : to engage or take part in a game **b** : to perform in a position in a specified manner ⟨the outfielders were *playing* deep⟩ **c** : to perform an action during one's turn in a game **d** : GAMBLE **e** (1) : to behave or conduct oneself in a specified way ⟨*play* safe⟩ (2) : to feign a specified state or quality ⟨*play* dead⟩ (3) : to take part in or assent to some activity : COOPERATE ⟨*play* along with his scheme⟩ (4) : to act so as to prove advantageous to another — usually used in the phrase *play into the hands of*
**5** : to gain approval : GO OVER ⟨her idea did not *play* well⟩
*transitive verb*
**1 a** (1) : to engage in or occupy oneself with ⟨*play* baseball⟩ (2) : to engage in (an activity) as a game (3) : to deal with, handle, or manage (4) : EXPLOIT, MANIPULATE **b** : to pretend to engage in the activities of ⟨*play* war⟩ ⟨children *playing* house⟩ **c** (1) : to amount to by one's efforts ⟨*played* an important role in their success⟩ (2) : to perform or execute for amusement or to deceive or mock ⟨*play* a trick⟩ (3) : WREAK ⟨*play* havoc⟩
**2 a** (1) : to put on a performance of (a play) (2) : to act in the character or part of (3) : to act or perform in ⟨*played* leading theaters⟩ **b** : to perform or act the part of ⟨*play* the fool⟩
**3 a** (1) : to contend against in or as if in a game (2) : to use as a contestant in a game ⟨the coach did not *play* him⟩ (3) : to perform the duties associated with (a certain position) ⟨*played* quarterback⟩ (4) : to guard or move into position to defend against (an opponent) in a specified manner **b** (1) : to wager in a game : STAKE (2) : to make wagers on ⟨*play* the races⟩ (3) : to speculate on or in ⟨*play* the stock market⟩ (4) : to operate on the basis of ⟨*play* a hunch⟩ **c** : to put into action in a game; *especially* : to remove (a playing card) from one's hand and place usually faceup on a table in one's turn either as part of a scoring combination or as one's contribution to a trick **d** : to catch or pick up (a batted ball) : FIELD ⟨*played* the ball bare-handed⟩ **e** : to direct the course of (as a ball) : HIT ⟨*played* a wedge shot to the green⟩; *also* : to cause (a ball or puck) to rebound ⟨*played* the ball off the backboard⟩
**4 a** : to perform (music) on an instrument ⟨*play* a waltz⟩ **b** : to perform music on ⟨*play* the violin⟩ **c** : to perform music of (a certain composer) **d** (1) : to cause (as a radio or phonograph) to emit sounds (2) : to cause the recorded sound or image of (as a record or a magnetic tape) to be reproduced
**5 a** : WIELD, PLY **b** : to discharge, fire, or set off with continuous effect ⟨*played* the hose on the burning building⟩ **c** : to cause to move or operate lightly and irregularly or intermittently **d** : to keep (a hooked fish) in action
— **play·abil·i·ty** \ˌplā-ə-'bi-lə-tē\ *noun*
— **play·able** \'plā-ə-bəl\ *adjective*
— **play ball** : COOPERATE
— **play both ends against the middle** : to set opposing interests against each other to one's own ultimate profit
— **play by ear** : to deal with something without previous planning or instructions
— **play games** : to try to hide the truth from someone by deceptive means
— **play one's cards** : to act with the means available to one
— **play possum** : to pretend to be asleep or dead
— **play second fiddle** : to take a subordinate position
— **play the field** : to date or have romantic connections with more than one person
— **play the game** : to act according to a code or set of standards
— **play with fire** : to do something risky or dangerous
— **play with oneself** : MASTURBATE

**pla·ya** \'plī-ə\ *noun* [Spanish, literally, beach, from Late Latin *plagia* — more at PLAGE] (1854)
: the flat-floored bottom of an undrained desert basin that becomes at times a shallow lake
**play–act** \'plā-ˌakt\ *verb* [back-formation from *playacting*] (1901)
*transitive verb*
: ACT OUT 1a
*intransitive verb*
**1 a** : to take part in theatrical performances especially as a professional **b** : to make believe
**2** : to engage in theatrical or insincere behavior
— **play·act·ing** *noun*
**play–action pass** *noun* (1964)
: a pass play in football in which the quarterback fakes a handoff before passing the ball — called also *play-action*
**play·back** \'plā-ˌbak\ *noun* (1929)
: an act or instance of reproducing recorded sound or pictures often immediately after recording
**play back** *transitive verb* (1949)
: to perform a playback of (a usually recently recorded disc or tape)
**play·bill** \'plā-ˌbil\ *noun* (1616)
: a bill advertising a play and usually announcing the cast
**Playbill** *trademark*
— used for a theater program
**play·book** \-ˌbu̇k\ *noun* (1535)
**1** : one or more plays in book form
**2** : a notebook containing diagrammed football plays
**play·boy** \-ˌbȯi\ *noun* (1907)
: a man who lives a life devoted chiefly to the pursuit of pleasure
**play–by–play** \ˌplā-ˌbī-'plā, ˌplā-ˌbī-'-\ *adjective* (1931)
**1** : being or giving a running commentary on a sports event
**2** : relating each event as it occurs
— **play–by–play** *noun*
**play down** *transitive verb* (1930)
: to attach little importance to : MINIMIZE
**played out** *adjective* (circa 1859)
**1** : worn out or used up
**2** : tired out : SPENT
**play·er** \'plā-ər\ *noun* (14th century)
: one that plays: as **a** : a person who plays a game **b** : MUSICIAN **c** : ACTOR **d** : a device that reproduces recorded material (as video images or music) from a usually specified medium **e** : one actively involved especially in a competitive field or process : PARTICIPANT
**player piano** *noun* (1907)
: a piano containing a mechanism by which it plays automatically
**play·fel·low** \'plā-ˌfe-(ˌ)lō\ *noun* (1513)
: PLAYMATE
**play·field** \-ˌfēld\ *noun* (1883)
: a playground for outdoor athletics
**play·ful** \'plā-fəl\ *adjective* (13th century)
**1** : full of play : FROLICSOME, SPORTIVE ⟨a *playful* kitten⟩
**2** : HUMOROUS, JOCULAR
— **play·ful·ly** \-fə-lē\ *adverb*
— **play·ful·ness** *noun*
**play·girl** \-ˌgər(-ə)l\ *noun* (1938)
: a woman who lives a life devoted chiefly to the pursuit of pleasure
**play·go·er** \-ˌgō-(ə)r\ *noun* (1822)
: a person who frequently attends plays
**play·ground** \-ˌgrau̇nd\ *noun* (1794)
**1** : a piece of land used for and usually equipped with facilities for recreation especially by children

**2 :** an area known or suited for activity of a specified sort ⟨a vacation *playground*⟩

**play·house** \-,haús\ *noun* (before 12th century)
**1 :** THEATER
**2 :** a small house for children to play in

**playing card** *noun* (1543)
**:** one of a set of 24 to 78 thin rectangular pieces of paperboard or plastic marked on one side to show its rank and suit and used in playing any of numerous games

**playing field** *noun* (circa 1584)
**1 :** a field for various games; *especially* **:** the part of a field officially marked off for play
**2 :** a set of conditions for competition (as in business) — usually used in such phrases as *a level playing field*

**play·land** \'plā-,land\ *noun* (1918)
**:** PLAYGROUND

**play·let** \-lət\ *noun* (1884)
**:** a short play

**play·list** \-,list\ *noun* (1972)
**:** a list of recordings to be played on the air by a radio station

**play·mak·er** \-,mā-kər\ *noun* (circa 1942)
**:** a player who leads the offense for a team (as in basketball or hockey)
— **play·mak·ing** \-kiŋ\ *noun or adjective*

**play·mate** \-,māt\ *noun* (1642)
**:** a companion in play

**play·off** \'plā-,óf\ *noun* (1895)
**1 :** a final contest or series of contests to determine the winner between contestants or teams that have tied
**2 :** a series of contests played after the end of the regular season to determine a championship

**play off** *transitive verb* (1807)
**1 a :** to set in opposition for one's own gain **b :** to set in contrast
**2 :** to complete the playing of (an interrupted contest)
**3 :** to break (a tie) by a play-off

**play out** (1596)
*transitive verb*
**1 a :** to perform to the end ⟨*play out* a role⟩ **b :** USE UP, FINISH
**2 :** UNREEL, UNFOLD ⟨*played out* a length of line —Gordon Webber⟩
*intransitive verb*
**:** to become spent or exhausted

**play·pen** \'plā-,pen\ *noun* (1931)
**:** a portable usually collapsible enclosure in which a baby or young child may play

**play·room** \-,rüm, -,rum\ *noun* (1819)
**:** RUMPUS ROOM

**play·suit** \-,süt\ *noun* (1908)
**:** a sports and play outfit for women or children that consists usually of a blouse and shorts

**play therapy** *noun* (1939)
**:** psychotherapy in which a child is encouraged to reveal feelings and conflicts in play rather than by verbalization

**play·thing** \'plā-,thiŋ\ *noun* (1675)
**:** TOY

**play·time** \-,tīm\ *noun* (1661)
**:** a time for play or diversion

**play up** *transitive verb* (1909)
**:** EMPHASIZE; *also* **:** EXAGGERATE, OVEREMPHASIZE

**play·wear** \'plā-,war, -,wer\ *noun* (1964)
**:** informal clothing worn for leisure activities

**play·wright** \'plā-,rīt\ *noun* [¹*play* + obsolete *wright* maker — more at WRIGHT] (1687)
**:** a person who writes plays

**play·writ·ing** *also* **play·wright·ing** \-,rī-tiŋ\ *noun* (1809)
**:** the writing of plays

**pla·za** \'pla-zə, 'plä-\ *noun* [Spanish, from Latin *platea* broad street — more at PLACE] (1683)
**1 a :** a public square in a city or town **b :** an open area usually located near urban buildings and often featuring walkways, trees and shrubs, places to sit, and sometimes shops

**2 :** a place on a thoroughfare (as a turnpike) at which all traffic must temporarily stop (as to pay tolls)
**3 :** an area adjacent to an expressway which has service facilities (as a restaurant, service station, and rest rooms)
**5 :** SHOPPING CENTER

**plea** \'plē\ *noun* [Middle English *plaid, plai,* from Old French *plait, plaid,* from Medieval Latin *placitum,* from Latin, decision, decree, from neuter of *placitus,* past participle of *placēre* to please, be decided — more at PLEASE] (13th century)
**1 :** a legal suit or action
**2 :** an allegation made by a party in support of a cause: as **a :** an allegation of fact — compare DEMURRER **b** (1) **:** a defendant's answer to a plaintiff's declaration in common-law practice (2) **:** an accused person's answer to a charge or indictment in criminal practice **c :** a plea of guilty to an indictment
**3 :** something offered by way of excuse or justification ⟨left early with the *plea* of a headache⟩
**4 :** an earnest entreaty **:** APPEAL ⟨their *plea* for understanding must be answered⟩
*synonym* see APOLOGY

**plea bargaining** *noun* (1964)
**:** the negotiation of an agreement between a prosecutor and a defendant whereby the defendant is permitted to plead guilty to a reduced charge
— **plea–bargain** *intransitive verb*
— **plea bargain** *noun*

**pleach** \'plēch, 'plach\ *transitive verb* [Middle English *plechen,* from Old North French *plechier,* from (assumed) Vulgar Latin *plactiare,* alteration of *plectere* to braid — more at PLY] (14th century)
**:** INTERLACE, PLAIT

**plead** \'plēd\ *verb* **plead·ed** \'plē-dəd\ *or* **pled** *also* **plead** \'pled\; **plead·ing** [Middle English *plaiden* to institute a lawsuit, from Middle French *plaidier,* from *plaid* plea] (13th century)
*intransitive verb*
**1 :** to argue a case or cause in a court of law
**2 a :** to make an allegation in an action or other legal proceeding; *especially* **:** to answer the previous pleading of the other party by denying facts therein stated or by alleging new facts **b :** to conduct pleadings
**3 :** to make a plea of a specified nature ⟨*plead* not guilty⟩
**4 :** to argue for or against a claim **b :** to entreat or appeal earnestly
*transitive verb*
**1 :** to maintain (as a case or cause) in a court of law or other tribunal
**2 :** to allege in or by way of a legal plea
**3 :** to offer as a plea usually in defense, apology, or excuse
— **plead·able** \'plē-də-bəl\ *adjective*
— **plead·er** *noun*
— **plead·ing·ly** \'plē-diŋ-lē\ *adverb*

**pleading** *noun* (14th century)
**1 :** advocacy of a cause in a court of law
**2 a :** one of the formal usually written allegations and counter allegations made alternately by the parties in a legal action or proceeding **b :** the action or process performed by the parties in presenting such formal allegations until a single point at issue is produced **c :** the introduction of one of these allegations and especially the first one **d :** the body of rules according to which these allegations are framed
**3 :** the act or an instance of making a plea
**4 :** a sincere entreaty

**pleas·ance** \'ple-z°n(t)s\ *noun* (14th century)
**1 :** a feeling of pleasure **:** DELIGHT
**2 :** a pleasant rest or recreation place usually attached to a mansion

**pleas·ant** \'ple-z°nt\ *adjective* [Middle English *plesaunt,* from Middle French *plaisant,* from present participle of *plaisir*] (14th century)

**1 :** having qualities that tend to give pleasure **:** AGREEABLE ⟨a *pleasant* day⟩
**2 :** having or characterized by pleasing manners, behavior, or appearance
— **pleas·ant·ly** *adverb*
— **pleas·ant·ness** *noun*

**pleas·ant·ry** \-z°n-trē\ *noun, plural* **-ries** (1655)
**1 :** an agreeable playfulness in conversation **:** BANTER
**2 :** a humorous act or remark **:** JEST
**3 :** a polite social remark (exchanged *pleasantries*)

**¹please** \'plēz\ *verb* **pleased; pleas·ing** [Middle English *plesen,* from Middle French *plaisir,* from Latin *placēre;* akin to Latin *placare* to placate and perhaps to Greek *plak-, plax* flat surface — more at FLUKE] (14th century)
*intransitive verb*
**1 :** to afford or give pleasure or satisfaction
**2 :** LIKE, WISH ⟨do as you *please*⟩
**3** *archaic* **:** to have the kindness ⟨will you *please* to enter the carriage —Charles Dickens⟩
*transitive verb*
**1 :** to give pleasure to **:** GRATIFY
**2 :** to be the will or pleasure of ⟨may it *please* your Majesty⟩
— **pleas·er** \'plē-zər\ *noun*

**²please** *adverb* (1667)
**1** — used as a function word to express politeness or emphasis in a request ⟨*please* come in⟩
**2** — used as a function word to express polite affirmation ⟨have some tea? *Please*⟩

**pleas·ing** \'plē-ziŋ\ *adjective* (14th century)
**:** giving pleasure **:** AGREEABLE ⟨the sun's *pleasing* warmth⟩
— **pleas·ing·ly** \-lē\ *adverb*
— **pleas·ing·ness** *noun*

**plea·sur·able** \'plezh-rə-bəl, 'plāzh-; 'ple-zhə-, 'plā-\ *adjective* (1579)
**:** PLEASANT, GRATIFYING
— **plea·sur·abil·i·ty** \,plezh-rə-'bi-lə-tē, ,plāzh-; ,ple-zhə-, ,plā-\ *noun*
— **plea·sur·able·ness** \'plezh-rə-bəl-nəs, 'plāzh-; 'ple-zhə-, 'plā-\ *noun*
— **plea·sur·ably** \-blē\ *adverb*

**¹plea·sure** \'ple-zhər, 'plā-\ *noun* [Middle English *plesure,* alteration of *plesir,* from Middle French *plaisir,* from *plaisir* to please] (14th century)
**1 :** DESIRE, INCLINATION ⟨wait upon his *pleasure* —Shakespeare⟩
**2 :** a state of gratification
**3 a :** sensual gratification **b :** frivolous amusement
**4 :** a source of delight or joy

**²pleasure** *verb* **plea·sured; plea·sur·ing** \'plezh-riŋ, 'plāzh-; 'ple-zhə-, 'plā-\ (1537)
*transitive verb*
**1 :** to give pleasure to **:** GRATIFY
**2 :** to give sexual pleasure to
*intransitive verb*
**1 :** to take pleasure **:** DELIGHT
**2 :** to seek pleasure

**pleasure dome** *noun* (1797)
**:** a place of pleasurable entertainment or recreation **:** RESORT

**plea·sure·less** \'ple-zhər-ləs, 'plā-\ *adjective* (1814)
**:** giving no pleasure

**pleasure principle** *noun* (1912)
**:** a tendency for individual behavior to be directed toward immediate satisfaction of instinctual drives and immediate relief from pain or discomfort

**¹pleat** \'plēt\ *transitive verb* [Middle English *pleten,* from *pleit, plete* plait] (14th century)
**1 :** FOLD; *especially* **:** to arrange in pleats ⟨*pleat* a skirt⟩
**2 :** PLAIT 2
— **pleat·er** *noun*

**²pleat** *noun* [Middle English *plete*] (15th century)

: a fold in cloth made by doubling material over on itself; *also* **:** something resembling such a fold
— **pleat·less** \-ləs\ *adjective*
**pleb** \'pleb\ *noun* (1865)
: PLEBEIAN
**plebe** \'plēb\ *noun* [obsolete *plebe* common people, from French *plèbe*, from Latin *plebs*] (1833)
: a freshman at a military or naval academy
**¹ple·be·ian** \pli-'bē-ən\ *noun* [Latin *plebeius* of the common people, from *plebs* common people] (1533)
**1 :** a member of the Roman plebs
**2 :** one of the common people
— **ple·be·ian·ism** \-ə-,ni-zəm\ *noun*
**²plebeian** *adjective* (1566)
**1 :** of or relating to plebeians
**2 :** crude or coarse in manner or style **:** COMMON
— **ple·be·ian·ly** *adverb*
**pleb·i·scite** \'ple-bə-,sīt, -sət *also* -,sēt\ *noun* [Latin *plebis scitum* law voted by the comitia, literally, decree of the common people] (1860)
: a vote by which the people of an entire country or district express an opinion for or against a proposal especially on a choice of government or ruler
— **ple·bi·sci·ta·ry** \ple-'bi-sə-,ter-ē, pli-; ,ple-bə-'sī-tə-rē\*adjective*
**plebs** \'plebz, 'pleps\ *noun, plural* **ple·bes** \'plē-(,)bēz, 'plā-,bās\ [Latin] (1647)
**1 :** the general populace
**2 :** the common people of ancient Rome
**ple·cop·ter·an** \pli-'käp-tə-rən\ *noun* [New Latin *Plecoptera*, group name, from Greek *plekein* to braid + *pteron* wing — more at PLY, FEATHER] (circa 1890)
: STONE FLY
— **plecopteran** *adjective*
**plec·trum** \'plek-trəm\ *noun, plural* **plec·tra** \-trə\ *or* **plectrums** [Latin, from Greek *plēktron*, from *plēssein* to strike — more at PLAINT] (1626)
: ³PICK 2c
**¹pledge** \'plej\ *noun* [Middle English, security, from Middle French *plege*, from Late Latin *plebium*, from (assumed) Late Latin *plebere* to pledge, probably of Germanic origin; akin to Old High German *pflegan* to take care of — more at PLIGHT] (14th century)
**1 a :** a bailment of a chattel as security for a debt or other obligation without involving transfer of title **b :** the chattel so delivered **c :** the contract incidental to such a bailment
**2 a :** the state of being held as a security or guaranty **b :** something given as security for the performance of an act
**3 :** a token, sign, or earnest of something else
**4 :** a gage of battle
**5 :** TOAST 3
**6 a :** a binding promise or agreement to do or forbear **b** (1) **:** a promise to join a fraternity, sorority, or secret society (2) **:** a person who has so promised
**²pledge** *transitive verb* **pledged; pledg·ing** (15th century)
**1 :** to make a pledge of; *especially* **:** PAWN
**2 :** to drink to the health of
**3 :** to bind by a pledge
**4 :** to promise the performance of by a pledge
— **pledg·er** \'ple-jər\ *or* **pled·gor** \'ple-jər, ple-'jŏr\ *noun*
**pledg·ee** \ple-'jē\ *noun* (1766)
: one to whom a pledge is given
**pled·get** \'ple-jət\ *noun* [origin unknown] (circa 1540)
: a compress or pad used to apply medication to or absorb discharges (as from a wound)
**-plegia** *noun combining form* [New Latin, from Greek *-plēgia*, from *plēssein* to strike — more at PLAINT]
: paralysis ⟨di*plegia*⟩
**ple·iad** \'plē-əd, 'plā-, -,ad, *chiefly British* 'plī-\ *noun* [French *Pléiade*, group of seven 16th century French poets, from Middle French,

group of seven tragic poets of ancient Alexandria, from Greek *Pleiad-, Pleias*, from singular of *Pleiades*] (circa 1839)
: a group of usually seven illustrious or brilliant persons or things
**Pleiad** *noun*
: any of the Pleiades
**Ple·ia·des** \'plē-ə-,dēz, 'plā-, *chiefly British* 'plī-\ *noun plural* [Latin, from Greek]
**1 :** the seven daughters of Atlas turned into a group of stars in Greek mythology
**2 :** a conspicuous cluster of stars in the constellation Taurus that includes six stars in the form of a very small dipper
**plein air** \,plān-'ar, -'er; ple-'när, -'ner\ *adjective* [French, open air] (1894)
**1 :** of or relating to painting in outdoor daylight
**2 :** of or relating to a branch of impressionism that attempts to represent outdoor light and air
— **plein-air·ism** \plā-'när,i-zəm, ple-, -'ner-\ *noun*
— **plein-air·ist** \-ist\ *noun*
**pleio-** *or* **pleo-** *or* **plio-** *combining form* [Greek *pleiōn, pleōn* — more at PLUS]
: more ⟨*pleio*tropic⟩ ⟨*pleo*morphic⟩ ⟨*Plio*cene⟩
**pleio·tro·pic** \,plī-ə-'trō-pik, -'trä-\ *adjective* (1938)
: producing more than one genic effect; *specifically* **:** having multiple phenotypic expressions ⟨a *pleiotropic* gene⟩
— **plei·ot·ro·py** \plī-'ä-trə-pē\ *noun*
**Pleis·to·cene** \'plīs-tə-,sēn\ *adjective* [Greek *pleistos* most + International Scientific Vocabulary *-cene*; akin to Greek *pleiōn* more] (1839)
: of, relating to, or being the earlier epoch of the Quaternary or the corresponding system of rocks — see GEOLOGIC TIME table
— **Pleistocene** *noun*
**ple·na·ry** \'plē-nə-rē, 'ple-\ *adjective* [Middle English, from Late Latin *plenarius*, from Latin *plenus* full — more at FULL] (15th century)
**1 :** complete in every respect **:** ABSOLUTE, UNQUALIFIED ⟨*plenary* power⟩
**2 :** fully attended or constituted by all entitled to be present ⟨a *plenary* session⟩
*synonym* see FULL
**plenary indulgence** *noun* (1675)
: a remission of the entire temporal punishment for sin
**ple·nip·o·tent** \pli-'ni-pə-tənt\ *adjective* [Late Latin *plenipotent-, plenipotens*, from Latin *plenus* + *potent-, potens* powerful — more at POTENT] (1658)
: PLENIPOTENTIARY
**¹plen·i·po·ten·tia·ry** \,ple-nə-pə-'ten(t)-sh(ə-)rē, -shē-,er-ē\ *adjective* [Medieval Latin *plenipotentiarius*, adjective & noun, from Late Latin *plenipotent-, plenipotens*] (circa 1645)
**1 :** invested with full power
**2 :** of or relating to a plenipotentiary
**²plenipotentiary** *noun, plural* **-ries** (circa 1656)
: a person and especially a diplomatic agent invested with full power to transact business
**plen·ish** \'ple-nish\ *transitive verb* [Middle English (Scots) *plenyssen* to fill up, from Middle French *pleniss-*, stem of *plenir*, from *plen* full, from Latin *plenus*] (1513)
*chiefly British* **:** EQUIP
**plen·i·tude** \'ple-nə-,tüd, -,tyüd\ *noun* [Middle English *plenitude*, from Middle French or Latin; Middle French, from Latin *plenitudo*, from *plenus*] (15th century)
**1 :** the quality or state of being full **:** COMPLETENESS
**2 :** a great sufficiency **:** ABUNDANCE
**plen·i·tu·di·nous** \,ple-nə-'tüd-nəs, -'tyüd-; -'tü-d°n-əs, -'tyü-\ *adjective* [Latin *plenitudin-, plenitudo*] (1895)
: characterized by plenitude
**plen·te·ous** \'plen-tē-əs\ *adjective* [Middle English *plentevous, plenteous*, from Middle French *plentiveus*, from *plentif* abundant, from *plenté* plenty] (14th century)

**1 :** FRUITFUL, PRODUCTIVE ⟨a *plenteous* harvest —J. G. Frazer⟩ — usually used with *in* or *of* ⟨the seasons had been *plenteous* in corn —George Eliot⟩
**2 :** constituting or existing in plenty ⟨*plenteous* grace with thee is found —Charles Wesley⟩
— **plen·te·ous·ly** *adverb*
— **plen·te·ous·ness** *noun*
**plen·ti·ful** \'plen-ti-fəl\ *adjective* (15th century)
**1 :** containing or yielding plenty ⟨a *plentiful* land⟩
**2 :** characterized by, constituting, or existing in plenty ☆
— **plen·ti·ful·ly** \-fə-lē\ *adverb*
— **plen·ti·ful·ness** *noun*
**plen·ti·tude** \'plen-tə-,tüd, -,tyüd\ *noun* [by alteration (influenced by *plenty*)] (1615)
: PLENITUDE
**¹plen·ty** \'plen-tē\ *noun* [Middle English *plente*, from Old French *plenté*, from Late Latin *plenitas-, plenitas*, from Latin, fullness, from *plenus* full — more at FULL] (13th century)
**1 a :** a full or more than adequate amount or supply ⟨had *plenty* of time to finish the job⟩ **b :** a large number or amount ⟨in *plenty* of trouble⟩
**2 :** the quality or state of being copious **:** PLENTIFULNESS
**²plenty** *adjective* (14th century)
**1 :** plentiful in amount, number, or supply ⟨if reasons were as *plenty* as blackberries —Shakespeare⟩
**2 :** AMPLE ⟨*plenty* work to be done —*Time*⟩ ▯
**³plenty** *adverb* (1842)
: more than sufficiently **:** to a considerable degree ⟨the nights were *plenty* cold —F. B. Gipson⟩ ▯

---

☆ **SYNONYMS**
**Plentiful, ample, abundant, copious** mean more than sufficient without being excessive. PLENTIFUL implies a great or rich supply ⟨peaches are *plentiful* this summer⟩. AMPLE implies a generous sufficiency to satisfy a particular requirement ⟨*ample* food to last the winter⟩. ABUNDANT suggests an even greater or richer supply than does PLENTIFUL ⟨streams *abundant* with fish⟩. COPIOUS stresses largeness of supply rather than fullness or richness ⟨*copious* examples of bureaucratic waste⟩.

---

---

\ə\ **abut** \ᵊ\ **kitten** \ər\ **further** \a\ **ash** \ā\ **ace**
\ä\ **mop, mar** \aú\ **out** \ch\ **chin** \e\ **bet** \ē\ **easy**
\g\ **go** \i\ **hit** \ī\ **ice** \j\ **job** \ŋ\ **sing** \ō\ **go**
\ò\ **law** \òi\ **boy** \th\ **thin** \ṯh\ **the** \ü\ **loot** \ú\ **foot**
\y\ **yet** \zh\ **vision** *see also* **Guide to Pronunciation**

**ple·num** \'ple-nəm, 'plē-\ *noun, plural* **-nums** *or* **-na** \-nə\ [New Latin, from Latin, neuter of *plenus*] (1678)
**1 a :** a space or all space every part of which is full of matter **b** (1) **:** a condition in which the pressure of the air in an enclosed space is greater than that of the outside atmosphere (2) **:** an enclosed space in which such a condition exists
**2 :** a general assembly of all members especially of a legislative body
**3 :** the quality or state of being full
**ple·och·ro·ism** \plē-'ä-krə-,wi-zəm\ *noun* [International Scientific Vocabulary *pleochroic,* from *pleio-* + Greek *chrōs* skin, color] (1857)
**:** the property of a crystal of showing different colors when viewed by light that vibrates parallel to different axes
— **pleo·chro·ic** \,plē-ə-'krō-ik\ *adjective*
**pleo·mor·phic** \,plē-ə-'mòr-fik\ *adjective* (1886)
**:** able to assume different forms **:** POLYMORPHIC ⟨*pleomorphic* bacteria⟩ ⟨a *pleomorphic* sarcoma⟩
— **pleo·mor·phism** \-,fi-zəm\ *noun*
**ple·o·nasm** \'plē-ə-,na-zəm\ *noun* [Late Latin *pleonasmus,* from Greek *pleonasmos,* from *pleonazein* to be excessive, from *pleiōn, pleōn* more — more at PLUS] (1610)
**1 :** the use of more words than those necessary to denote mere sense (as in *the man he said*) **:** REDUNDANCY
**2 :** an instance or example of pleonasm
— **ple·o·nas·tic** \,plē-ə-'nas-tik\ *adjective*
— **ple·o·nas·ti·cal·ly** \-ti-k(ə-)lē\ *adverb*
**ple·o·pod** \'plē-ə-,päd\ *noun* [Greek *plein* to sail + English *-o-* + *-pod;* from its use in swimming — more at FLOW] (circa 1890)
**:** an abdominal limb of a crustacean
**ple·ro·cer·coid** \,plir-ō-'sər-,kòid\ *noun* [Greek *plērēs* full + *kerkos* tail — more at FULL] (1906)
**:** the solid elongate infective larva of some tapeworms usually occurring in the muscles of fishes
**ple·si·o·saur** \'plē-sē-ə-,sòr, -zē-\ *noun* [ultimately from Greek *plēsios* close (akin to Greek *pelas* near) + *sauros* lizard] (1839)
**:** any of a suborder (Plesiosauria) of Mesozoic marine reptiles with dorsoventrally flattened bodies and limbs modified into paddles
**pleth·o·ra** \'ple-thə-rə\ *noun* [Medieval Latin, from Greek *plēthōra,* literally, fullness, from *plēthein* to be full — more at FULL] (1541)
**1 :** a bodily condition characterized by an excess of blood and marked by turgescence and a florid complexion
**2 :** EXCESS, SUPERFLUITY; *also* **:** PROFUSION, ABUNDANCE
— **ple·tho·ric** \plə-'thòr-ik, ple-, -'thär-; 'ple-thə-rik\ *adjective*
**ple·thys·mo·gram** \ple-'thiz-mə-,gram, plə-\ *noun* (1894)
**:** a tracing made by a plethysmograph
**ple·thys·mo·graph** \-,graf\ *noun* [International Scientific Vocabulary, from Greek *plēthysmos* increase, from *plēthynein* to increase, from *plēthys* mass, quantity, from *plēthein*] (1872)
**:** an instrument for determining and registering variations in the size of an organ or limb resulting from changes in the amount of blood present or passing through it
— **ple·thys·mo·graph·ic** \-,thiz-mə-'gra-fik\ *adjective*
— **ple·thys·mo·graph·i·cal·ly** \-fi-k(ə-)lē\ *adverb*
— **pleth·ys·mog·ra·phy** \,ple-thiz-'mä-grə-fē\ *noun*
**pleu·ra** \'plùr-ə\ *noun, plural* **pleu·rae** \'plùr-,ē, -,ī\ *or* **pleuras** [Middle English, from Medieval Latin, from Greek, rib, side] (15th century)

**:** the delicate serous membrane that lines each half of the thorax of mammals and is folded back over the surface of the lung of the same side
— **pleu·ral** \'plùr-əl\ *adjective*
**pleu·ri·sy** \'plùr-ə-sē\ *noun* [Middle English *pluresie,* from Middle French *pleuresie,* from Late Latin *pleurisis,* alteration of Latin *pleuritis,* from Greek, from *pleura* side] (14th century)
**:** inflammation of the pleura usually with fever, painful and difficult respiration, cough, and exudation of fluid or fibrinous material into the pleural cavity
— **pleu·rit·ic** \plù-'ri-tik\ *adjective*
**pleu·ro·pneu·mo·nia** \,plùr-ō-nù-'mō-nyə, -ò-nyù-\ *noun* [New Latin] (1725)
**1 :** combined inflammation of the pleura and lungs
**2 :** an acute febrile and often fatal respiratory disorder of cattle, goats, sheep, and related animals caused by a mycoplasma (*Mycoplasma mycoides*)
**pleuropneumonia–like organism** *noun* (1935)
**:** MYCOPLASMA
**pleus·ton** \'plü-stən, -,stän\ *noun* [International Scientific Vocabulary *pleus-* (irregular from Greek *plein* to sail, float) + *-on* (as in *plankton*)] (1943)
**:** organisms living in the thin surface layer existing at the air-water interface of a body of fresh water
— **pleus·ton·ic** \plü-'stä-nik\ *adjective*
**-plex** *noun combining form* [partly from Latin *-plex* (as in *duplex*); partly from *complex*]
**1 :** a figure of a given power ⟨googol*plex*⟩
**2 :** a building divided into an often specified number of spaces (as apartments or movie theaters) ⟨four*plex*⟩ ⟨multi*plex*⟩
**plex·i·form** \'plek-sə-,fòrm\ *adjective* [New Latin *plexus* + English *-iform*] (circa 1828)
**:** of, relating to, or having the form or characteristics of a plexus
**Plex·i·glas** \'plek-si-,glas\ *trademark*
— used for acrylic plastic sheets and molding powders
**plex·us** \'plek-səs\ *noun, plural* **plex·us·es** \-sə-səz\ [New Latin, from Latin *plectere* to braid — more at PLY] (1682)
**1 :** a network of anastomosing or interlacing blood vessels or nerves
**2 :** an interwoven combination of parts or elements in a structure or system
**pli·able** \'plī-ə-bəl\ *adjective* [Middle English, from Middle French, from *plier* to bend, fold — more at PLY] (14th century)
**1 a :** supple enough to bend freely or repeatedly without breaking **b :** yielding readily to others **:** COMPLAISANT
**2 :** adjustable to varying conditions
*synonym* see PLASTIC
— **pli·abil·i·ty** \,plī-ə-'bi-lə-tē\ *noun*
— **pli·able·ness** \'plī-ə-bəl-nəs\ *noun*
— **pli·ably** \-blē\ *adverb*
**pli·an·cy** \'plī-ən(t)-sē\ *noun* (1699)
**:** the quality or state of being pliant
**pli·ant** \'plī-ənt\ *adjective* (14th century)
**1 :** PLIABLE 1a
**2 :** easily influenced **:** YIELDING
**3 :** suitable for varied uses
*synonym* see PLASTIC
— **pli·ant·ly** *adverb*
— **pli·ant·ness** *noun*
**pli·ca** \'plī-kə\ *noun, plural* **pli·cae** \-,kē, -,sē\ [Medieval Latin, from Latin *plicare* to fold — more at PLY] (circa 1706)
**:** a fold or folded part; *especially* **:** a groove or fold of skin
**pli·cate** \'plī-,kāt\ *adjective* [Latin *plicatus,* past participle of *plicare*] (1760)
**1 :** folded lengthwise like a fan ⟨a *plicate* leaf⟩
**2 :** having the surface thrown up into or marked with parallel ridges ⟨*plicate* wing cases⟩
**pli·ca·tion** \plī-'kā-shən\ *noun* (14th century)

**1 :** the act or process of folding **:** the state of being folded
**2 :** FOLD
**plié** \plē-'ā\ *noun* [French, from past participle of *plier* to bend] (1892)
**:** a bending of the knees outward by a ballet dancer with the back held straight
**pli·ers** \'plī(-ə)rz\ *noun plural but singular or plural in construction* [²*ply*] (circa 1569)
**:** a small pincers for holding small objects or for bending and cutting wire
**¹plight** \'plīt\ *transitive verb* [Middle English, from Old English *plihtan* to endanger, from *pliht* danger; akin to Old English *plēon* to expose to danger, Old High German *pflegan* to take care of] (13th century)
**:** to put or give in pledge **:** ENGAGE ⟨*plight* one's troth⟩
— **plight·er** *noun*
**²plight** *noun* (13th century)
**:** a solemnly given pledge **:** ENGAGEMENT
**³plight** *noun* [Middle English *plit* condition, from Anglo-French, from (assumed) Vulgar Latin *plicitum* fold — more at PLAIT] (13th century)
**:** an unfortunate, difficult, or precarious situation
**plim·soll** \'plim(p)-səl, 'plim-,sòl\ *noun* [probably from the supposed resemblance of the upper edge of the shoe's mudguard to the Plimsoll mark on a ship] (1907)
*British* **:** SNEAKER 2
**Plimsoll mark** *noun* [Samuel *Plimsoll* (died 1898) English shipping reformer] (1884)
**:** a load line or a set of load-line markings on an oceangoing cargo ship — called also *Plimsoll line*
**¹plink** \'pliŋk\ *verb* [imitative] (1941)
*intransitive verb*
**1 :** to make a tinkling sound
**2 :** to shoot at random targets in an informal and noncompetitive manner
*transitive verb*
**1 :** to cause to make a tinkling sound
**2 :** to shoot at especially in a casual manner
— **plink·er** *noun*
**²plink** *noun* (1954)
**:** a tinkling metallic sound

**Plimsoll mark:** *TF* tropical freshwater mark; *F* freshwater mark; *T* tropical load line; *S* summer load line; *W* winter load line; *WNA* winter load line, North Atlantic

**plinth** \'plin(t)th\ *noun* [Latin *plinthus,* from Greek *plinthos*] (1601)
**1 a :** the lowest member of a base **:** SUBBASE **b :** a block upon which the moldings of an architrave or trim are stopped at the bottom
**2 :** a usually square block serving as a base; *broadly* **:** any of various bases or lower parts — see BASE illustration
**3 :** a course of stones forming a continuous foundation or base course
**plio-** — see PLEIO-
**Pli·o·cene** \'plī-ə-,sēn\ *adjective* (1831)
**:** of, relating to, or being the latest epoch of the Tertiary or the corresponding system of rocks — see GEOLOGIC TIME table
— **Pliocene** *noun*
**Plio·film** \'plī-ə-,film\ *trademark*
— used for a glossy membrane made of rubber hydrochloride and used especially for packaging
**plique–à–jour** \,plēk-(,)ä-'zhùr\ *noun* [French, literally, braid letting in daylight] (1878)
**:** a style of enameling in which usually transparent enamels are fused into the openings of a metal filigree to produce an effect suggestive of stained glass
**plis·kie** *or* **plis·ky** \'plis-kē\ *noun, plural* **pliskies** [origin unknown] (1706)
*chiefly Scottish* **:** PRACTICAL JOKE, TRICK

**plis·sé** or **plis·se** \pli-'sā\ noun [French plissé, from past participle of plisser to pleat, from Middle French, from pli fold, from plier to fold — more at PLY] (1873)
**1** : a textile finish of permanently puckered designs formed by treating with a sodium hydroxide solution
**2** : a fabric with a plissé finish

**plod** \'pläd\ verb **plod·ded; plod·ding** [origin unknown] (1562)
intransitive verb
**1** : to work laboriously and monotonously : DRUDGE
**2 a** : to walk heavily or slowly : TRUDGE **b** : to proceed slowly or tediously ⟨the movie just plods along⟩
transitive verb
: to tread slowly or heavily along or over
— **plod** noun
— **plod·der** noun
— **plod·ding·ly** \'plä-diŋ-lē\ adverb

**-ploid** adjective combining form [International Scientific Vocabulary, from diploid & haploid]
: having or being a chromosome number that bears (such) a relationship to or is (so many) times the basic chromosome number of a given group ⟨polyploid⟩

**ploi·dy** \'ploi-dē\ noun [from such words as diploidy, hexaploidy] (1939)
: degree of repetition of the basic number of chromosomes

**PL/1** \,pē-(,)el-'wən\ noun [programming language (version) 1] (1965)
: a general-purpose language for programming a computer

**¹plonk** \'pläŋk, 'plȯŋk\ variant of PLUNK

**²plonk** noun [short for earlier plink-plonk, perhaps modification of French vin blanc white wine] (1930)
chiefly British : cheap or inferior wine

**plop** \'pläp\ verb **plopped; plop·ping** [imitative] (1821)
intransitive verb
**1** : to fall, drop, or move suddenly with a sound like that of something dropping into water
**2** : to allow the body to drop heavily ⟨plopped into a chair⟩
transitive verb
: to set, drop, or throw heavily
— **plop** noun

**plo·sion** \'plō-zhən\ noun (1899)
: EXPLOSION 3

**plo·sive** \'plō-siv\ noun [short for explosive] (1899)
: STOP 9
— **plosive** adjective

**¹plot** \'plät\ noun [Middle English, from Old English] (before 12th century)
**1 a** : a small area of planted ground ⟨a vegetable plot⟩ **b** : a small piece of land in a cemetery **c** : a measured piece of land : LOT
**2** : GROUND PLAN, PLAT
**3** : the plan or main story of a literary work
**4** : a secret plan for accomplishing a usually evil or unlawful end : INTRIGUE
**5** : a graphic representation (as a chart) ☆
— **plot·less** \-ləs\ adjective
— **plot·less·ness** noun

**²plot** verb **plot·ted; plot·ting** (1588)
transitive verb
**1 a** : to make a plot, map, or plan of **b** : to mark or note on or as if on a map or chart
**2** : to lay out in plots
**3 a** : to locate (a point) by means of coordinates **b** : to locate (a curve) by plotted points **c** : to represent (an equation) by means of a curve so constructed
**4** : to plan or contrive especially secretly
**5** : to invent or devise the plot of (a literary work)
intransitive verb
**1** : to form a plot : SCHEME
**2** : to be located by means of coordinates ⟨the data plot at a single point⟩

**Plo·ti·nism** \plō-'tī-,ni-zəm, 'plō-t°n-,i-zəm\ noun (circa 1890)
: the Neoplatonic ideas of the philosopher Plotinus
— **Plo·ti·nist** \-'tī-nist, -t°n-ist\ noun

**plot·line** \'plät-,līn\ noun (1952)
: PLOT 3

**plot·tage** \'plä-tij\ noun (1936)
: the area included in a plot of land

**plot·ter** \'plä-tər\ noun (1588)
: one that plots: as **a** : a person who schemes or conspires **b** : a contriver of a literary plot **c** : a device for plotting; specifically : an instrument that graphs computer output

**plot·ty** \'plä-tē\ adjective **plot·ti·er; -est** (1897)
: marked by intricacy of plot or intrigue

**plough·man's lunch** \'plau̇-mənz-\ noun (1970)
: a cold lunch served especially in an English pub typically including bread, cheese, and pickled onions

**plo·ver** \'plə-vər, 'plō-\ noun, plural **plover** or **plovers** [Middle English, from Middle French, from (assumed) Vulgar Latin pluviarius, from Latin pluvia rain — more at PLUVIAL] (14th century)
**1** : any of a family (Charadriidae) of shore-inhabiting birds that differ from the sandpipers in having a short hard-tipped bill and usually a stouter more compact build
**2** : any of various birds (as a turnstone or sandpiper) related to the plovers

**¹plow** or **plough** \'plau̇\ noun [Middle English, from Old English plōh hide of land; akin to Old High German pfluog plow] (12th century)
**1** : an implement used to cut, lift, and turn over soil especially in preparing a seedbed
**2** : any of various devices (as a snowplow) operating like a plow

**²plow** or **plough** (15th century)
transitive verb
**1 a** : to turn, break up, or work with a plow **b** : to make (as a furrow) with a plow
**2** : to cut into, open, or make furrows or ridges in with or as if with a plow
**3** : to cleave the surface of or move through (water) ⟨whales plowing the ocean⟩
**4** : to clear away snow from with a snowplow ⟨plow the street⟩
intransitive verb
**1 a** : to use a plow **b** : to bear or admit of plowing
**2 a** : to move in a way resembling that of a plow ⟨the car plowed into a fence⟩ **b** : to proceed steadily and laboriously ⟨had to plow through a stack of letters⟩
— **plow·able** \-ə-bəl\ adjective
— **plow·er** \'plau̇(-ə)r\ noun

**plow back** transitive verb (1930)
: to reinvest (profits) in a business
— **plow·back** \'plau̇-,bak\ noun

**plow·boy** \'plau̇-,bȯi\ noun (1596)
**1** : a boy who leads the team drawing a plow
**2** : a country youth

**plow·man** \-mən, -,man\ noun (13th century)
**1** : a man who guides a plow
**2** : a farm laborer

**plow·share** \'plau̇-,sher, -,shar\ noun [Middle English ploughshare, from plough plow + schare plowshare — more at SHARE] (14th century)
: a part of a plow that cuts the furrow

**plow under** transitive verb (1900)
: to cause to disappear : BURY, OVERWHELM

**ploy** \'plȯi\ noun [probably from employ] (1722)
**1** : ESCAPADE, FROLIC
**2 a** : a tactic intended to embarrass or frustrate an opponent **b** : a devised or contrived move : STRATAGEM ⟨a ploy to get her to open the door —Robert B. Parker⟩

**¹pluck** \'plək\ verb [Middle English, from Old English pluccian; akin to Middle High German pflücken to pluck] (before 12th century)

transitive verb
**1** : to pull or pick off or out
**2 a** : to remove something (as hairs) from by or as if by plucking ⟨pluck one's eyebrows⟩ **b** : ROB, FLEECE
**3** : to move, remove, or separate forcibly or abruptly ⟨plucked the child from the middle of the street⟩
**4 a** : to pick, pull, or grasp at **b** : to play by sounding the strings with the fingers or a pick
intransitive verb
: to make a sharp pull or twitch
— **pluck·er** noun

**²pluck** noun (15th century)
**1** : an act or instance of plucking or pulling
**2** : the heart, liver, lungs, and windpipe of a slaughtered animal especially as an item of food
**3** : courageous readiness to fight or continue against odds : dogged resolution

**plucky** \'plə-kē\ adjective **pluck·i·er; -est** (1842)
: SPIRITED, BRAVE
— **pluck·i·ly** \'plə-kə-lē\ adverb
— **pluck·i·ness** \'plə-kē-nəs\ noun

**¹plug** \'pləg\ noun [Dutch, from Middle Dutch plugge; akin to Middle High German pfloc plug] (1627)
**1 a** : a piece used to fill a hole : STOPPER **b** : an obtruding or obstructing mass of material resembling a stopper
**2** : a flat compressed cake of tobacco
**3** : a small core or segment removed from a larger object
**4** : something inferior; especially : an inferior often aged or unsound horse; also : a quiet steady cold-blooded horse usually of light or moderate weight
**5 a** : HYDRANT, FIREPLUG **b** : SPARK PLUG
**6** : an artificial angling lure used primarily for casting and made with one or more sets of gang hooks
**7** : any of various devices resembling or functioning like a plug: as **a** : a male fitting for making an electrical connection to a live circuit by insertion in a receptacle (as an outlet) **b** : a device for connecting electric wires to a jack
**8** : a piece of favorable publicity or a favorable mention usually incorporated in general matter

**²plug** verb **plugged; plug·ging** (1630)
transitive verb
**1** : to stop, make tight, or secure by inserting a plug
**2** : to hit with a bullet : SHOOT
**3** : to advertise or publicize insistently
intransitive verb

---

☆ SYNONYMS

**Plot, intrigue, machination, conspiracy, cabal** mean a plan secretly devised to accomplish an evil or treacherous end. PLOT implies careful foresight in planning a complex scheme ⟨an assassination plot⟩. INTRIGUE suggests secret underhanded maneuvering in an atmosphere of duplicity ⟨backstairs intrigue⟩. MACHINATION implies a contriving of annoyances, injuries, or evils by indirect means ⟨the machinations of a party boss⟩. CONSPIRACY implies a secret agreement among several people usually involving treason or great treachery ⟨a conspiracy to fix prices⟩. CABAL typically applies to political intrigue involving persons of some eminence ⟨a cabal among powerful senators⟩. See in addition PLAN.

---

\ə\ abut \ᵊ\ kitten \ər\ further \a\ ash \ā\ ace
\ä\ mop, mar \au̇\ out \ch\ chin \e\ bet \ē\ easy
\g\ go \i\ hit \ī\ ice \j\ job \ŋ\ sing \ō\ go
\ȯ\ law \ȯi\ boy \th\ thin \th\ the \ü\ loot \u̇\ foot
\y\ yet \zh\ vision    see also Guide to Pronunciation

**1 :** to become plugged — usually used with *up*
**2 :** to work doggedly and persistently ⟨*plugged* away at her homework⟩
**3 :** to fire shots
**— plug·ger** *noun*
**— plug into :** to connect or become connected to by or as if by means of a plug ⟨the city was *plugged into* the new highway system⟩
**plugged** \'pləgd\ *adjective* (1694)
**1** *of a coin* **:** altered by the insertion of a plug of base metal
**2 :** closed by or as if by a plug **:** OBSTRUCTED
**plug hat** *noun* (1863)
**:** a man's stiff hat (as a bowler or top hat)
**plug-in** \'pləg-,in\ *adjective* (1922)
**:** designed to be connected to an electric circuit by plugging in ⟨a *plug-in* toy⟩
**— plug–in** *noun*
**plug in** (1903)
*intransitive verb*
**:** to establish an electric circuit by inserting a plug
*transitive verb*
**:** to attach or connect to a service outlet
**plug·o·la** \(,)plə-'gō-lə\ *noun* [*plug* + *-ola* (as in *payola*)] (1959)
**:** incidental advertising on radio or television that is not purchased like regular advertising
**plug-ug·ly** \'pləg-,əg-lē\ *noun* (1856)
**:** THUG, TOUGH; *especially* **:** one hired to intimidate
**plum** \'pləm\ *noun, often attributive* [Middle English, from Old English *plūme*, modification of Latin *prunum* plum, from Greek *proumnon*] (before 12th century)
**1 a :** any of numerous trees and shrubs (genus *Prunus*) with globular to oval smooth-skinned fruits that are drupes with oblong seeds **b :** the edible fruit of a plum
**2 :** any of various trees with edible fruits resembling plums; *also* **:** the fruit
**3 a :** a raisin when used in desserts **b :** SUGARPLUM
**4 :** something superior or very desirable; *especially* **:** something desirable given in return for a favor
**5 :** a dark reddish purple
**— plum·like** \-,līk\ *adjective*
**plum·age** \'plü-mij\ *noun* [Middle English, from Middle French, from Old French, from *plume* feather — more at PLUME] (14th century)
**:** the feathers of a bird
**— plum·aged** \-mijd\ *adjective*
**¹plumb** \'pləm\ *noun* [Middle English, from (assumed) Old French *plomb* lead, from Latin *plumbum*] (14th century)
**:** a lead weight attached to a line and used to indicate a vertical direction
**— out of plumb** *or* **off plumb :** out of vertical or true
**²plumb** *adverb* (15th century)
**1 :** straight down or up **:** VERTICALLY
**2** *chiefly dialect* **:** to a complete degree **:** ABSOLUTELY ⟨'you're *plumb* crazy', she remarked, with easy candor —*Harper's Weekly*⟩
**3 :** in a direct manner **:** EXACTLY; *also* **:** without interval of time **:** IMMEDIATELY
**³plumb** (15th century)
*transitive verb*
**1 :** to weight with lead
**2 a :** to measure the depth of with a plumb **b :** to examine minutely and critically ⟨*plumbing* the book's complexities⟩
**3 :** to adjust or test by a plumb line
**4 :** to seal with lead
**5** [back-formation from *plumber*] **:** to supply with or install as plumbing
*intransitive verb*
**:** to work as a plumber
**⁴plumb** *adjective* (15th century)
**1 :** exactly vertical or true
**2 :** THOROUGH, COMPLETE
**synonym** see VERTICAL

**plum·ba·go** \,pləm-'bā-(,)gō\ *noun, plural* **-gos** [Latin *plumbagin-, plumbago* galena, from *plumbum*] (1747)
**1** [New Latin, from Latin] **:** any of a genus (*Plumbago* of the family Plumbaginaceae, the plumbago family) of woody chiefly tropical plants with alternate leaves and spikes of showy flowers
**2 :** GRAPHITE 1
**plumb bob** *noun* (circa 1840)
**:** the metal bob of a plumb line
**plumb·er** \'pləm-ər\ *noun* [Middle English, from Middle French *plommier, plombier*, from Latin *plumbarius*, from *plumbum*] (15th century)
**1 :** a dealer or worker in lead
**2 :** one who installs, repairs, and maintains piping, fittings, and fixtures involved in the distribution and use of water in a building
**plumber's helper** *noun* (1952)
**:** PLUNGER d — called also *plumber's friend*
**plumber's snake** *noun* (1938)
**:** a long flexible rod or cable usually of steel that is used to free clogged pipes
**plumb·ing** \'plə-miŋ\ *noun* (1666)
**1 :** the act of using a plumb
**2 :** a plumber's occupation or trade
**3 a :** the apparatus (as pipes and fixtures) concerned in the distribution and use of water in a building **b :** an internal system that resembles plumbing; *especially* **:** one consisting of conduits or channels for conveying fluids
**plum·bism** \'pləm-,bi-zəm\ *noun* [Latin *plumbum* lead] (1876)
**:** lead poisoning especially when chronic
**plumb line** *noun* (15th century)
**1 :** a line (as of cord) that has at one end a weight (as a plumb bob) and is used especially to determine verticality
**2 :** a line directed to the center of gravity of the earth **:** a vertical line
**¹plume** \'plüm\ *noun* [Middle English, from Middle French, from Latin *pluma* small soft feather — more at FLEECE] (14th century)
**1 :** a feather of a bird: as **a :** a large conspicuous or showy feather **b :** CONTOUR FEATHER **c :** PLUMAGE **d :** a cluster of distinctive feathers
**2 a :** material (as a feather, cluster of feathers, or a tuft of hair) worn as an ornament **b :** a token of honor or prowess **:** PRIZE
**3 :** something resembling a feather (as in shape, appearance, or lightness): as **a :** a plumose appendage of a plant **b :** an elongated and usually open and mobile column or band (as of smoke, exhaust gases, or blowing snow) **c :** an animal structure having a main shaft bearing many hairs or filamentous parts; *especially* **:** a full bushy tail
**²plume** *transitive verb* **plumed; plum·ing** (15th century)
**1 a :** to provide or deck with feathers **b :** to array showily
**2 :** to indulge (oneself) in pride with an obvious or vain display of self-satisfaction
**3** *of a bird* **a :** to preen and arrange the feathers of (itself) **b :** to preen and arrange (feathers)
**plumed** \'plümd\ *adjective* (15th century)
**:** provided with or adorned with or as if with a plume. — often used in combination ⟨a white-*plumed* egret⟩
**plume·let** \'plüm-lət\ *noun* (circa 1847)
**:** a small tuft or plume
**plu·me·ria** \plü-'mir-ē-ə\ *noun* [New Latin, genus name, from Charles *Plumier* (died 1704) French botanist] (1753)
**:** FRANGIPANI
**¹plum·met** \'plə-mət\ *noun* [Middle English *plomet*, from Middle French *plombet* ball of lead, from *plomb* lead, from (assumed) Old French — more at PLUMB] (14th century)
**:** PLUMB; *also* **:** PLUMB LINE
**²plummet** *intransitive verb* (1937)
**1 :** to fall perpendicularly ⟨birds *plummeted* down⟩

**2 :** to drop sharply and abruptly ⟨prices *plummeted*⟩
**plum·my** \'plə-mē\ *adjective* **plum·mi·er; -est** (1759)
**1 a :** full of plums ⟨a rich *plummy* cake⟩ **b :** CHOICE, DESIRABLE ⟨got a *plummy* role in the movie⟩
**2 a :** having a plum color **b :** rich and mellow often to the point of affectation ⟨a *plummy* singing voice⟩
**plu·mose** \'plü-,mōs\ *adjective* (circa 1727)
**1 :** having feathers or plumes **:** FEATHERED
**2 :** FEATHERY
**¹plump** \'pləmp\ *verb* [Middle English] (14th century)
*intransitive verb*
**1 :** to drop, sink, or come in contact suddenly or heavily ⟨*plumped* down in the chair⟩
**2 :** to favor or decide in favor of someone or something strongly or emphatically — used with *for*
*transitive verb*
**1 :** to drop, cast, or place suddenly or heavily
**2 :** to give support and favorable publicity to
**²plump** *noun* (15th century)
**:** a sudden plunge, fall, or blow; *also* **:** the sound made by a plump
**³plump** *adverb* (1594)
**1 :** with a sudden or heavy drop
**2 a :** straight down **b :** straight ahead
**3 :** without qualification **:** DIRECTLY
**⁴plump** *noun* [Middle English *plumpe*] (15th century)
*chiefly dialect* **:** GROUP, FLOCK ⟨a *plump* of ducks rose at the same time —H. D. Thoreau⟩
**⁵plump** *verb* [⁶*plump*] (1533)
*transitive verb*
**:** to make plump
*intransitive verb*
**:** to become plump
**⁶plump** *adjective* [Middle English, dull, blunt, from Middle Dutch *plomp*] (1569)
**1 :** having a full rounded usually pleasing form ⟨a *plump* woman⟩
**2 :** AMPLE, ABUNDANT
**— plump·ish** \'pləm-pish\ *adjective*
**plump·en** \'pləm-pən\ *verb* (1687)
**:** ⁵PLUMP
**¹plump·er** \'pləm-pər\ *noun* [⁵*plump*] (1690)
**:** an object carried in the mouth to fill out the cheeks
**²plumper** *noun* [¹*plump*] (circa 1785)
*chiefly British* **:** a vote for only one candidate when two or more are to be elected to the same office
**¹plump·ly** \'pləm-plē\ *adverb* (1611)
**:** in a plump way ⟨a *plumply* pretty girl⟩
**²plumply** *adverb* [³*plump*] (1786)
**:** in a wholehearted manner and without hesitation or circumlocution **:** FORTHRIGHTLY
**¹plump·ness** \'pləmp-nəs\ *noun* (1545)
**:** the quality or state of being plump
**²plumpness** *noun* (1780)
**:** freedom from hesitation or circumlocution
**plum pudding** *noun* (1711)
**:** a rich boiled or steamed pudding containing fruits and spices
**plum tomato** *noun* (circa 1900)
**:** a small oblong tomato
**plu·mule** \'plü-(,)myü(ə)l\ *noun* [New Latin *plumula*, from Latin, diminutive of *pluma* small soft feather — more at FLEECE] (circa 1741)
**1 :** the primary bud of a plant embryo usually situated at the apex of the hypocotyl and consisting of leaves and an epicotyl
**2 :** a down feather
**plumy** \'plü-mē\ *adjective* **plum·i·er; -est** (1582)
**1 :** DOWNY
**2 :** having or resembling plumes

plumule of
morning
glory seedling:
*1* hypocotyl,
*2* plumule,
*3* cotyledons

**¹plun·der** \'plən-dər\ *verb* **plun·dered; plun·der·ing** \-d(ə-)riŋ\ [German *plündern*] (1632)
*transitive verb*
**1 a :** to take the goods of by force (as in war) **:** PILLAGE, SACK ⟨invaders *plundered* the town⟩ **b :** to take by force or wrongfully **:** STEAL, LOOT
**2 :** to make extensive use of as if by plundering **:** use or use up wrongfully ⟨*plunder* the land⟩
*intransitive verb*
**:** to commit robbery or looting
— **plun·der·er** \-dər-ər\ *noun*
**²plunder** *noun* (1643)
**1 :** an act of plundering **:** PILLAGING
**2 :** something taken by force, theft, or fraud **:** LOOT
**3** *chiefly dialect* **:** personal or household effects
*synonym* see SPOIL
**plun·der·ous** \-d(ə-)rəs\ *adjective* (1845)
**:** given to plundering
**¹plunge** \'plənj\ *verb* **plunged; plung·ing** [Middle English, from Middle French *plonger*, from (assumed) Vulgar Latin *plumbicare*, from Latin *plumbum* lead] (14th century)
*transitive verb*
**1 :** to cause to penetrate or enter quickly and forcibly into something
**2 :** to cause to enter a state or course of action usually suddenly, unexpectedly, or violently
*intransitive verb*
**1 :** to thrust or cast oneself into or as if into water
**2 a :** to become pitched or thrown headlong or violently forward and downward; *also* **:** to move oneself in such a manner **b :** to act with reckless haste **:** enter suddenly or unexpectedly **c :** to bet or gamble heavily and recklessly
**3 :** to descend or dip suddenly
**²plunge** *noun* (15th century)
**:** an act or instance of plunging **:** DIVE; *also* **:** SWIM
**plung·er** \'plən-jər\ *noun* (1611)
**:** one that plunges: as **a :** DIVER **b :** a reckless gambler or speculator **c** (1) **:** a sliding reciprocating piece driven by or against fluid pressure; *especially* **:** PISTON (2) **:** a piece with a motion more or less like that of a ram or piston **d :** a rubber suction cup on a handle used to free plumbing traps and waste outlets of obstructions
**plunk** \'pləŋk\ *verb* [imitative] (1805)
*transitive verb*
**1 :** to pluck or hit so as to produce a quick, hollow, metallic, or harsh sound
**2 :** to set down suddenly **:** PLUMP
*intransitive verb*
**1 :** to make a plunking sound
**2 :** to drop abruptly **:** DIVE
**3 :** to come out in favor of someone or something — used with *for*
— **plunk** *noun*
— **plunk·er** *noun*
**plunk down** (1891)
*intransitive verb*
**:** to drop abruptly **:** settle into position
*transitive verb*
**1 a :** to put down usually firmly or abruptly ⟨*plunked* the money *down* on the counter⟩ **b :** to settle (oneself) into position ⟨*plunked* himself *down* on the bench⟩
**2 :** to pay out
**plu·per·fect** \plü-'pər-fikt\ *adjective* [Middle English *pluperfyth*, modification of Late Latin *plusquamperfectus*, literally, more than perfect] (15th century)
**1 :** PAST PERFECT
**2 :** utterly perfect or complete
— **pluperfect** *noun*
**plu·ral** \'plur-əl\ *adjective* [Middle English, from Middle French & Latin; Middle French *plurel*, from Latin *pluralis*, from *plur-, plus* more — more at PLUS] (14th century)

**1 :** of, relating to, or constituting a class of grammatical forms usually used to denote more than one or in some languages more than two ⟨*genetics* is *plural* in form but takes a singular verb⟩
**2 :** relating to, consisting of, or containing more than one or more than one kind or class ⟨a *plural* society⟩
— **plural** *noun*
— **plu·ral·ly** \-ə-lē\ *adverb*
**plu·ral·ism** \'plur-ə-,li-zəm\ *noun* (1818)
**1 :** the holding of two or more offices or positions (as benefices) at the same time
**2 :** the quality or state of being plural
**3 a :** a theory that there are more than one or more than two kinds of ultimate reality **b :** a theory that reality is composed of a plurality of entities
**4 a :** a state of society in which members of diverse ethnic, racial, religious, or social groups maintain an autonomous participation in and development of their traditional culture or special interest within the confines of a common civilization **b :** a concept, doctrine, or policy advocating this state
— **plu·ral·ist** \-list\ *adjective or noun*
— **plu·ral·is·tic** \,plur-ə-'lis-tik\ *adjective*
— **plu·ral·is·ti·cal·ly** \-ti-k(ə-)lē\ *adverb*
**plu·ral·i·ty** \plu-'ra-lə-tē\ *noun, plural* **-ties** (14th century)
**1 a :** the state of being plural **b :** the state of being numerous **c :** a large number or quantity
**2 :** PLURALISM 1; *also* **:** a benefice held by pluralism
**3 a :** a number greater than another **b :** an excess of votes over those cast for an opposing candidate **c :** a number of votes cast for a candidate in a contest of more than two candidates that is greater than the number cast for any other candidate but not more than half the total votes cast
**plu·ral·ize** \'plur-ə-,līz\ *transitive verb* **-ized; -iz·ing** (1803)
**:** to make plural or express in the plural form
— **plu·ral·i·za·tion** \,plur-ə-lə-'zā-shən\ *noun*
**plu·rip·o·tent** \plu-'ri-pə-tənt\ *adjective* [Latin *plur-, plus* more + English *potent*] (1916)
**:** not fixed as to developmental potentialities **:** having developmental plasticity ⟨*pluripotent* stem cell⟩
**¹plus** \'pləs\ *adjective* [Latin, adverb, more, from neuter of *plur-, plus*, adjective; akin to Greek *pleion* more, Latin *plenus* full — more at FULL] (1579)
**1 :** algebraically positive
**2 :** having, receiving, or being in addition to what is anticipated
**3 a :** falling high in a specified range ⟨a grade of C *plus*⟩ **b :** greater than that specified **c :** possessing a specified quality to a high degree
**4 :** electrically positive
**5 :** relating to or being a particular one of the two mating types that are required for successful fertilization in sexual reproduction in some lower plants (as a fungus)
**²plus** *noun, plural* **plus·es** \'plə-səz\ *also* **plus·ses** (1654)
**1 :** PLUS SIGN
**2 :** an added quantity
**3 :** a positive factor or quality
**4 :** SURPLUS
**³plus** *preposition* (1668)
**1 :** increased by **:** with the addition of ⟨four *plus* five⟩ ⟨principal *plus* interest⟩ ⟨made twelve dollars a week *plus* room and board —E. L. Doctorow⟩
**2 :** BESIDES — used chiefly in speech and casual writing ⟨*plus* all this, as a sedative it has no equal —Groucho Marx⟩
**⁴plus** *conjunction* (circa 1950)
**1 :** AND ⟨the Smyth Report, *plus* an idea and some knowledge of bureaucracy, were all I needed —Pat Frank⟩ ⟨a box-office *plus* critical and artistic success —G. J. Nathan⟩ ⟨eats

alone, a hot beef sandwich *plus* a BLT *plus* apple pie —Garrison Keillor⟩
**2 :** in addition to which ⟨it was an achievement. *Plus*, I wrote the story and the musical score —Jackie Gleason⟩ ⟨it's also pretty on my open shelves, *plus* it smells good —Nikki Giovanni⟩ ◻
**plus fours** *noun plural* (1920)
**:** loose sports knickers made four inches longer than ordinary knickers
**¹plush** \'pləsh\ *noun* [Middle French *peluche*] (1594)
**:** a fabric with an even pile longer and less dense than velvet pile
**²plush** *adjective* (circa 1645)
**1 :** relating to, resembling, or made of plush
**2 :** notably luxurious
— **plush·ly** *adverb*
— **plush·ness** *noun*
**plushy** \'plə-shē\ *adjective* **plush·i·er; -est** (1611)
**1 :** having the texture of or covered with plush
**2 :** LUXURIOUS, SHOWY
— **plush·i·ness** *noun*
**plus·sage** \'plə-sij\ *noun* (1924)
**:** an amount over and above another amount
**plus sign** *noun* (circa 1907)
**:** a sign + denoting addition or a positive quantity
**Plu·to** \'plü-(,)tō\ *noun* [Latin *Pluton-, Pluto*, from Greek *Ploutōn*]
**1 :** the Greek god of the underworld — compare DIS
**2** [New Latin] **:** the planet with the farthest mean distance from the sun — see PLANET table
**plu·toc·ra·cy** \plü-'tä-krə-sē\ *noun, plural* **-cies** [Greek *ploutokratia*, from *ploutos* wealth; akin to Greek *plein* to sail, float — more at FLOW] (1652)
**1 :** government by the wealthy
**2 :** a controlling class of the wealthy
— **plu·to·crat** \'plü-tə-,krat\ *noun*
— **plu·to·crat·ic** \,plü-tə-'kra-tik\ *adjective*
— **plu·to·crat·i·cal·ly** \-ti-k(ə-)lē\ *adverb*
**plu·ton** \'plü-,tän\ *noun* [probably back-formation from *plutonic*] (1936)
**:** a typically large body of intrusive igneous rock
**plu·to·ni·an** \plü-'tō-nē-ən\ *adjective, often capitalized* (1667)
**:** of, relating to, or characteristic of Pluto or the lower world **:** INFERNAL
**plu·ton·ic** \plü-'tä-nik\ *adjective* [Latin *Pluton-, Pluto*] (1833)
**1 :** formed by solidification of magma deep within the earth and crystalline throughout ⟨*plutonic* rock⟩
**2** *often capitalized* **:** PLUTONIAN
**plu·to·ni·um** \plü-'tō-nē-əm\ *noun* [New Latin, from *Pluton-, Pluto*, the planet Pluto] (1942)
**:** a radioactive metallic element similar chemically to uranium that is formed as the isotope 239 by decay of neptunium and found in minute quantities in pitchblende, that undergoes slow disintegration with the emission of an alpha particle to form uranium 235, and

◻ USAGE
**plus** The preposition *plus* has long been used with a meaning equivalent to *and* (as in "two *plus* two"); it is not, therefore, very surprising that in time people have begun to use it as a conjunction much like *and*. Sense 2 is considered to be an adverb by some commentators. It is used chiefly in speech and in informal writing.

\ə\ abut \ə\ kitten \ər\ further \a\ ash \ā\ ace \ä\ mop, mar \aú\ out \ch\ chin \e\ bet \ē\ easy \g\ go \i\ hit \ī\ ice \j\ job \ŋ\ sing \ō\ go \ô\ law \ói\ boy \th\ thin \th\ the \ü\ loot \ú\ foot \y\ yet \zh\ vision *see also* Guide to Pronunciation that is fissionable with slow neutrons to yield atomic energy — see ELEMENT table

**¹plu·vi·al** \'plü-vē-əl\ *adjective* [Latin *pluvialis*, from *pluvia* rain, from feminine of *pluvius* rainy, from *pluere* to rain — more at FLOW] (circa 1656)
**1 a :** of or relating to rain **b :** characterized by abundant rain
**2** *of a geologic change* **:** resulting from the action of rain

**²pluvial** *noun* (1929)
**:** a prolonged period of wet climate

**¹ply** \'plī\ *verb* **plied; ply·ing** [Middle English *plien*, short for *applien* to apply] (14th century)
*transitive verb*
**1 a :** to use or wield diligently ⟨busily *plying* his pen⟩ **b :** to practice or perform diligently ⟨*ply* a trade⟩
**2 :** to keep furnishing or supplying something to ⟨*plied* us with liquor⟩
**3 a :** to make a practice of rowing or sailing over or on ⟨the boat *plies* the river⟩ **b :** to go or travel regularly over, on, or through ⟨jets *plying* the skies⟩
*intransitive verb*
**1 :** to apply oneself steadily
**2 :** to go or travel regularly ⟨a steamer *plying* between the towns⟩

**²ply** *noun, plural* **plies** [³*ply*] (1532)
**1 a :** one of several layers (as of cloth) usually sewn or laminated together **b :** one of the strands in a yarn **c :** one of the veneer sheets forming plywood **d :** a layer of a paper or paperboard
**2 :** INCLINATION, BIAS

**³ply** *transitive verb* **plied; ply·ing** [Middle English *plien* to fold, from Middle French *plier*, from Latin *plicare*; akin to Old High German *flehtan* to braid, Latin *plectere*, Greek *plekein*] (circa 1909)
**:** to twist together ⟨*ply* two single yarns⟩

**Plym·outh Rock** \'pli-məth-\ *noun* [*Plymouth Rock*, on which the Pilgrims are supposed to have landed in 1620] (1849)
**:** any of an American breed of medium-sized single-combed dual-purpose domestic fowls

**ply·wood** \'plī-ˌwu̇d\ *noun* (1907)
**:** a structural material consisting of sheets of wood glued or cemented together with the grains of adjacent layers arranged at right angles or at a wide angle

**-pnea** *or* **-pnoea** *noun combining form* [New Latin, from Greek *-pnoia*, from *pnoia*, from *pnein* to breathe]
**:** breath **:** breathing ⟨hyper*pnea*⟩ ⟨ap*noea*⟩

**pneum-** *or* **pneumo-** *combining form* [New Latin, partly from Greek *pneum-* (from *pneuma*); partly from Greek *pneumōn* lung]
**1 :** air **:** gas ⟨*pneumo*thorax⟩
**2 :** lung ⟨*pneumo*coniosis⟩
**3 :** respiration ⟨*pneumo*graph⟩
**4 :** pneumonia ⟨*pneumo*coccus⟩

**pneu·ma** \'nü-mə, 'nyü-\ *noun* [Greek] (1884)
**:** SOUL, SPIRIT

**pneumat-** *or* **pneumato-** *combining form* [Greek, from *pneumat-, pneuma*]
**1 :** air **:** vapor **:** gas ⟨*pneumato*lytic⟩
**2 :** respiration ⟨*pneumato*phore⟩

**pneu·mat·ic** \nu̇-'ma-tik, nyu̇-\ *adjective* [Latin *pneumaticus*, from Greek *pneumatikos*, from *pneumat-, pneuma* air, breath, spirit, from *pnein* to breathe — more at SNEEZE] (1659)
**1 :** of, relating to, or using gas (as air or wind): **a :** moved or worked by air pressure **b** (1) **:** adapted for holding or inflated with compressed air (2) **:** having air-filled cavities
**2 :** of or relating to the pneuma **:** SPIRITUAL
**3 :** having a well-proportioned feminine figure; *especially* **:** having a full bust
— **pneu·mat·i·cal·ly** \-ti-k(ə-)lē\ *adverb*
— **pneu·ma·tic·i·ty** \ˌnü-mə-'ti-sə-tē, ˌnyü-\ *noun*

**pneu·ma·tol·o·gy** \ˌnü-mə-'tä-lə-jē, ˌnyü-\ *noun* [New Latin *pneumatologia*, from Greek *pneumat-, pneuma* + New Latin *-logia* -logy] (1678)
**:** the study of spiritual beings or phenomena

**pneu·ma·to·lyt·ic** \ˌnü-mə-t°l-'i-tik, ˌnyü-; (ˌ)n(y)ü-ˌma-\ *adjective* [International Scientific Vocabulary] (1896)
**:** formed or forming by hot vapors or superheated liquids under pressure — used especially of minerals and ores

**pneu·mat·o·phore** \nu̇-'ma-tə-ˌfȯr, nyu̇-, -ˌfȯr\ *noun* [International Scientific Vocabulary] (1859)
**1 :** a muscular gas-containing sac that serves as a float on a siphonophore colony
**2 :** an erect root functioning as a respiratory organ in a wetland plant

**pneu·mo·coc·cus** \ˌnü-mə-'kä-kəs, ˌnyü-\ *noun, plural* **-coc·ci** \-'käk-ˌsī, -ˌsē; -'kä-ˌkī, -ˌkē\ [New Latin] (1890)
**:** a bacterium (*Streptococcus pneumoniae*) that causes an acute pneumonia involving one or more lobes of the lung
— **pneu·mo·coc·cal** \-'kä-kəl\ *adjective*

**pneu·mo·co·ni·o·sis** \ˌnü-mō-ˌkō-nē-'ō-səs, ˌnyü-\ *noun, plural* **-o·ses** \-ˌsēz\ [New Latin, from *pneum-* + Greek *konis* dust — more at INCINERATE] (1881)
**:** a disease of the lungs caused by the habitual inhalation of irritants (as mineral or metallic particles) — compare BLACK LUNG, SILICOSIS

**Pneu·mo·cys·tis ca·ri·nii pneumonia** \ˌnü-mə-'sis-təs-kə-'rī-nē-ˌē-, ˌnyü- ... \ *noun* [New Latin *Pneumocystis carinii*, species name] (1964)
**:** a pneumonia that affects individuals whose immunological defenses have been compromised, that is caused by a microorganism (*Pneumocystis carinii*), and that attacks especially the interstitial tissue of the lungs with marked thickening of the alveolar septa and alveoli

**pneu·mo·graph** \'nü-mə-ˌgraf, 'nyü-\ *noun* [International Scientific Vocabulary] (1878)
**:** an instrument for recording thoracic movements or volume change during respiration

**pneu·mo·nec·to·my** \ˌnü-mə-'nek-tə-mē, ˌnyü-\ *noun, plural* **-mies** [Greek *pneumōn* + International Scientific Vocabulary *-ectomy*] (circa 1895)
**:** excision of an entire lung or of one or more lobes of a lung

**pneu·mo·nia** \nu̇-'mō-nyə, nyu̇-\ *noun* [New Latin, from Greek, from *pneumōn* lung, alteration of *pleumōn* — more at PULMONARY] (1603)
**:** a disease of the lungs characterized by inflammation and consolidation followed by resolution and caused by infection or irritants

**pneu·mon·ic** \nu̇-'mä-nik, nyu̇-\ *adjective* [New Latin *pneumonicus*, from Greek *pneumonikos*, from *pneumōn*] (1675)
**1 :** of, relating to, or affecting the lungs **:** PULMONIC, PULMONARY
**2 :** of, relating to, or affected with pneumonia

**pneu·mo·ni·tis** \ˌnü-mə-'nī-təs, ˌnyü-\ *noun* [New Latin, from Greek *pneumōn*] (circa 1834)
**:** inflammation of the lungs

**pneu·mo·tho·rax** \ˌnü-mə-'thȯr-ˌaks, ˌnyü-, -'thȯr-\ *noun* [New Latin] (1821)
**:** a condition in which air or other gas is present in the pleural cavity and which occurs spontaneously as a result of disease or injury of lung tissue or puncture of the chest wall or is induced as a therapeutic measure to collapse the lung

**¹poach** \'pōch\ *transitive verb* [Middle English *pochen*, from Middle French *pocher*, from Old French *pochier*, literally, to put into a bag, from *poche* bag, pocket, of Germanic origin; akin to Old English *pocca* bag] (15th century)
**:** to cook in simmering liquid

**²poach** *verb* [Middle French *pocher*, of Germanic origin; akin to Middle English *poken* to poke] (1611)
*intransitive verb*
**1 :** to encroach upon especially for the purpose of taking something
**2 :** to trespass for the purpose of stealing game; *also* **:** to take game or fish illegally
*transitive verb*
**1 :** to trespass on ⟨a field *poached* too frequently by the amateur —*Times Literary Supplement*⟩
**2 a :** to take (game or fish) by illegal methods **b :** to appropriate (something) as one's own

**¹poach·er** \'pō-chər\ *noun* [²*poach*] (1614)
**1 :** one that trespasses or steals
**2 :** one who kills or takes wild animals (as game or fish) illegally

**²poacher** *noun* [¹*poach*] (1861)
**1 :** a covered pan containing a plate with depressions or shallow cups in each of which an egg can be cooked over steam rising from boiling water in the bottom of the pan
**2 :** a baking dish in which food (as fish) can be poached

**po'·boy** \'pō-ˌbȯi\ *variant of* POOR BOY

**po·chard** \'pō-chərd\ *noun* [origin unknown] (1552)
**:** any of numerous rather heavy-bodied diving ducks (especially genus *Aythya*) with a large head and with feet and legs placed far back under the body

**¹pock** \'päk\ *noun* [Middle English *pokke*, from Old English *pocc*; akin to Middle Low German & Middle Dutch *pocke* pock] (before 12th century)
**:** a pustule in an eruptive disease (as smallpox); *also* **:** a spot suggesting such a pustule

**²pock** *transitive verb* (1841)
**:** to mark with or as if with pocks **:** PIT

**¹pock·et** \'pä-kət\ *noun* [Middle English *poket*, from Old North French *pokete*, diminutive of *poke* bag, of Germanic origin; akin to Old English *pocca* bag] (15th century)
**1 a :** a small bag carried by a person **:** PURSE **b :** a small bag that is sewed or inserted in a garment so that it is open at the top or side ⟨coat *pocket*⟩
**2 :** supply of money **:** MEANS
**3 :** RECEPTACLE, CONTAINER: as **a :** an opening at the corner or side of a billiard table **b :** a superficial pouch in some animals
**4 :** a small often isolated area or group ⟨*pockets* of unemployment⟩ **: a** (1) **:** a cavity containing a deposit (as of gold, water, or gas) (2) **:** a small body of ore **b :** AIR POCKET
**5 :** a place for a batten made by sewing a strip on a sail
**6 a :** BLIND ALLEY **b :** the position of a contestant in a race hemmed in by others **c :** an area formed by blockers from which a football quarterback attempts to pass
**7 :** the concave area at the base of the finger sections of a baseball glove or mitt in which the ball is normally caught
— **pock·et·ful** \-ˌfu̇l\ *noun*
— **in one's pocket :** in one's control or possession
— **in pocket 1 :** provided with funds **2 :** in the position of having made a profit
— **out of pocket 1 :** low on money or funds **2 :** having suffered a loss

**²pocket** *transitive verb* (1589)
**1 a :** to put or enclose in or as if in one's pocket ⟨*pocketed* the change⟩ **b :** to appropriate to one's own use **:** STEAL **c :** to refuse assent to (a bill) by a pocket veto
**2 :** to put up with **:** ACCEPT
**3 :** to set aside **:** SUPPRESS ⟨*pocketed* his pride⟩
**4 a :** to hem in **b :** to drive (a ball) into a pocket of a pool table
**5 :** to cover or supply with pockets
— **pock·et·able** \'pä-kə-tə-bəl\ *adjective*

**³pocket** *adjective* (1612)

**1 a :** small enough to be carried in the pocket **b :** SMALL, MINIATURE ⟨a *pocket* park⟩ **2 a :** of or relating to money **b :** carried in or paid from one's own pocket

**pocket battleship** *noun* (1930)
**:** a small German battleship built so as to come within treaty limitations of tonnage and armament

**pocket billiards** *noun plural but usually singular in construction* (1913)
**:** POOL 2b

**¹pock·et·book** \'pä-kət-ˌbùk\ *noun* (1617)
**1** *often* **pocket book :** a small especially paperback book that can be carried in the pocket **2 :** a flat typically leather folding case for money or personal papers that can be carried in a pocket or handbag **3 a :** PURSE **b :** HANDBAG 2 **4 :** financial resources **:** INCOME

**²pocketbook** *adjective* (1894)
**:** relating to or involving economic interests ⟨*pocketbook* issues⟩

**pocket borough** *noun* (1856)
**:** an English constituency controlled before parliamentary reform by a single person or family

**pocket edition** *noun* (1715)
**1 :** POCKETBOOK 1 **2 :** a miniature form of something

**pocket gopher** *noun* (1873)
**:** GOPHER 2a

**pocket–handkerchief** *noun* (1645)
**:** a handkerchief carried in the pocket

**pock·et·knife** \'pä-kət-ˌnīf\ *noun* (1727)
**:** a knife that has one or more blades that fold into the handle and that can be carried in the pocket

**pocket money** *noun* (1632)
**:** money for small personal expenses

**pocket mouse** *noun* (1884)
**:** any of various nocturnal burrowing rodents (family Heteromyidae) that resemble mice, live in arid parts of western North America, and have long hind legs and tail and fur-lined cheek pouches

**pock·et·size** \'pä-kət-ˌsīz\ *also* **pock·et·sized** \-ˌsīzd\ *adjective* (1907)
**1 :** of a size convenient for carrying in the pocket **2 :** SMALL ⟨a *pocket-size* country⟩

pocket mouse

**pocket veto** *noun* (1842)
**:** an indirect veto of a legislative bill by an executive through retention of the bill unsigned until after adjournment of the legislature
**— pocket veto** *transitive verb*

**¹pock·mark** \'päk-ˌmärk\ *noun* (circa 1673)
**:** a mark, pit, or depressed scar caused by smallpox or acne; *also* **:** an imperfection or depression like a pockmark

**²pockmark** *transitive verb* (1756)
**:** to cover with or as if with pockmarks **:** PIT

**pocky** \'pä-kē\ *adjective* (14th century)
**:** covered with pocks

**po·co** \'pō-(ˌ)kō, 'pò-\ *adverb* [Italian, little, from Latin *paucus* — more at FEW] (1724)
**:** to a slight degree **:** SOMEWHAT — used to qualify a direction in music ⟨*poco* allegro⟩

**po·co a po·co** \'pō-kō-(ˌ)ä-'pō-(ˌ)kō, 'pò-kō-(ˌ)ä-'pò-\ *adverb* [Italian] (circa 1854)
**:** little by little **:** GRADUALLY — used as a direction in music

**po·co·cu·ran·te** \ˌpō-kō-kyù-'ran-tē, -kù-\ *adjective* [Italian *poco curante* caring little] (1815)
**:** INDIFFERENT, NONCHALANT
**— po·co·cu·ran·tism** \-'ran-ˌti-zəm\ *noun*

**po·co·sin** \pə-'kō-sᵊn\ *noun* [probably from Virginia or North Carolina Algonquian] (1634)
**:** an upland swamp of the coastal plain of the southeastern U.S.

**¹pod** \'päd\ *noun* [origin unknown] (1573)

**1 :** a bit socket in a brace **2 :** a straight groove or channel in the barrel of an auger

**²pod** *noun* [probably alteration of *cod* bag — more at CODPIECE] (1688)
**1 :** a dry dehiscent pericarp or fruit that is composed of one or more carpels; *especially* **:** LEGUME **2 a :** an anatomical pouch **b :** a grasshopper egg case **3 :** a tapered and roughly cylindrical body of ore or mineral **4 :** a usually protective container or housing: as **a :** a streamlined compartment (as for fuel) under the wings or fuselage of an aircraft **b :** a compartment (as for personnel, a power unit, or an instrument) on a ship or craft

**³pod** *intransitive verb* **pod·ded; pod·ding** (1734)
**:** to produce pods

**⁴pod** *noun* [origin unknown] (1832)
**:** a number of animals (as whales) clustered together

**-pod** *noun combining form* [Greek *-podos*, from *pod-, pous* foot — more at FOOT]
**:** foot **:** part resembling a foot ⟨pleo*pod*⟩

**po·dag·ra** \pə-'da-grə\ *noun* [Middle English, from Latin, from Greek, literally, foot trap, from *pod-, pous* + *agra* hunt, catch; probably akin to Greek *agein* to drive, lead — more at AGENT] (14th century)
**:** a painful condition of the big toe caused by gout

**pod corn** *noun* (1893)
**:** an Indian corn that has each kernel enclosed in a chaffy shell similar to that of other cereals

**po·de·sta** \ˌpō-də-'stä\ *noun* [Italian *podestà*, literally, power, from Latin *potestat-, potestas*, irregular from *potis* able — more at POTENT] (1548)
**:** a chief magistrate in a medieval Italian municipality

**podgy** \'pä-jē\ *adjective* **podg·i·er; -est** [*podge* something pudgy] (1846)
*chiefly British* **:** PUDGY

**po·di·a·try** \pə-'dī-ə-trē, pō-\ *noun* [Greek *pod-, pous* + English *-iatry*] (1914)
**:** the medical care and treatment of the human foot — called also *chiropody*
**— po·di·at·ric** \ˌpō-dē-'a-trik\ *adjective*
**— po·di·a·trist** \-'dī-ə-trist, pō-\ *noun*

**po·di·um** \'pō-dē-əm\ *noun, plural* **podiums** *or* **po·dia** \-dē-ə\ [Latin — more at PEW] (1743)
**1 :** a low wall serving as a foundation or terrace wall: as **a :** one around the arena of an ancient amphitheater serving as a base for the tiers of seats **b :** the masonry under the stylobate of a temple **2 a :** a dais especially for an orchestral conductor **b :** LECTERN ■

**-podium** *noun combining form, plural* **-podia** [New Latin, from Greek *podion*, diminutive of *pod-, pous* foot — more at FOOT]
**:** foot **:** part resembling a foot ⟨pseudo*podium*⟩

**podo·phyl·lin** \ˌpä-də-'fi-lən\ *noun* [International Scientific Vocabulary, from New Latin *Podophyllum*] (1851)
**:** a resin obtained from podophyllum and used in medicine as a caustic

**podo·phyl·lum** \-'fi-ləm\ *noun, plural* **-phyl·li** \-'fi-ˌlī\ *or* **-phyllums** [New Latin, from *Podophyllum*, genus of herbs including the mayapple] (1842)
**:** the dried rhizome and rootlet of the mayapple that is used as a caustic or as a source of the more effective podophyllin

**Po·dunk** \'pō-ˌdəŋk\ *noun* [*Podunk*, village in Mass. or locality in Conn.] (1846)
**:** a small, unimportant, and isolated town

**pod·zol** *also* **pod·sol** \'päd-ˌzòl\ *noun* [Russian] (1908)
**:** any of a group of zonal soils that develop in a moist climate especially under coniferous or mixed forest and have an organic mat and a thin organic-mineral layer above a light gray

leached layer resting on a dark illuvial horizon enriched with amorphous clay
**— pod·zol·ic** \päd-'zä-lik, -'zò-\ *adjective*

**pod·zol·i·za·tion** *also* **pod·sol·i·za·tion** \ˌpäd-ˌzò-lə-'zā-shən\ *noun* (1912)
**:** a process of soil formation especially in humid regions involving principally leaching of the upper layers with accumulation of material in lower layers and development of characteristic horizons; *specifically* **:** the development of a podzol
**— pod·zol·ize** \'päd-ˌzò-ˌlīz\ *verb*

**po·em** \'pō-əm, -im, 'pōm *also* 'pò(-)im, 'pō-ˌem\ *noun* [Middle French *poeme*, from Latin *poema*, from Greek *poiēma*, from *poiein*] (15th century)
**1 :** a composition in verse **2 :** something suggesting a poem (as in expressiveness, lyricism, or formal grace) ⟨the house we stayed in . . . was itself a *poem* —H. J. Laski⟩

**po·e·sy** \'pō-ə-zē, -sē\ *noun, plural* **po·e·sies** [Middle English *poesie*, from Middle French, from Latin *poesis*, from Greek *poiēsis*, literally, creation, from *poiein*] (14th century)
**1 a :** a poem or body of poems **b :** POETRY **c :** artificial or sentimentalized poetic writing **2 :** poetic inspiration

**po·et** \'pō-ət, -it *also* 'pò(-)it\ *noun* [Middle English, from Middle French *poete*, from Latin *poeta*, from Greek *poiētēs* maker, poet, from *poiein* to make; akin to Sanskrit *cinoti* he gathers, heaps up] (14th century)
**1 :** one who writes poetry **:** a maker of verses **2 :** one (as a creative artist) of great imaginative and expressive capabilities and special sensitivity to the medium

**po·et·as·ter** \'pō-ə-ˌtas-tər\ *noun* [New Latin, from Latin *poeta* + *-aster* -aster] (1599)
**:** an inferior poet

**po·et·ess** \'pō-ə-təs, 'pō-i- *also* 'pò(-)i-\ *noun* (1530)
**:** a girl or woman who is a poet
**usage** see -ESS

**po·et·ic** \pō-'e-tik\ *adjective* (1530)
**1 a :** of, relating to, or characteristic of poets or poetry **b :** given to writing poetry **2 :** written in verse

**po·et·i·cal** \-ti-kəl\ *adjective* (14th century)
**1 :** POETIC **2 :** being beyond or above the truth of history or nature **:** IDEALIZED ⟨had *poetical* ideas about love⟩
**— po·et·i·cal·ly** \-k(ə-)lē\ *adverb*
**— po·et·i·cal·ness** \-ti-kəl-nəs\ *noun*

**po·et·i·cism** \pō-'e-tə-ˌsi-zəm\ *noun* (1847)
**:** an archaic, trite, or strained expression in poetry

□ USAGE

**podium** Although critics sometimes complain that this or that writer does not know the difference between a podium and a lectern, sense 2b is standard ⟨the portable *podium* placed on a table at the end of the room —Stephen Coonts⟩ ⟨briskly seizes the *podium* in the still-humming law-school auditorium —*New England Monthly*⟩. It is a sort of in-joke among the critics that the man who seized the podium in the last quotation must be on his hands and knees. But the reading public never seems to be confused by the use. In general *on* is more likely to be used of musical conductors than of speakers; a speaker is often said to be standing *at* the podium ⟨Robert Frost, who was standing at this *podium* reading, suddenly slammed his book and threw it at me —Truman Capote⟩.

\ə\ abut \ᵊ\ kitten \ər\ further \a\ ash \ā\ ace
\ä\ mop, mar \aù\ out \ch\ chin \e\ bet \ē\ easy
\g\ go \i\ hit \ī\ ice \j\ job \ŋ\ sing \ō\ go
\ò\ law \òi\ boy \th\ thin \th\ the \ü\ loot \ù\ foot
\y\ yet \zh\ vision *see also* Guide to Pronunciation

**po·et·i·cize** \-,sīz\ *transitive verb* **-cized; -ciz·ing** (1804)
**:** to give a poetic quality to
**poetic justice** *noun* (circa 1890)
**:** an outcome in which vice is punished and virtue rewarded usually in a manner peculiarly or ironically appropriate
**poetic license** *noun* (1819)
**:** LICENSE 4
**po·et·ics** \pō-'e-tiks\ *noun plural but singular or plural in construction* (circa 1741)
**1 a :** a treatise on poetry or aesthetics **b** *also* **po·et·ic** \-tik\ **:** poetic theory or practice
**2 :** poetic feelings or utterances
**po·et·ize** \'pō-ə-,tīz\ *verb* **-ized; -iz·ing** (1581)
*intransitive verb*
**:** to compose poetry
*transitive verb*
**:** POETICIZE
— **po·et·iz·er** *noun*
**poet laureate** *noun, plural* **poets laure·ate** *or* **poet laureates** (15th century)
**1 :** a poet honored for achievement in his art
**2 :** a poet appointed for life by an English sovereign as a member of the royal household and formerly expected to compose poems for court and national occasions
**3 :** one regarded by a country or region as its most eminent or representative poet
**po·et·ry** \'pō-ə-trē, -i-trē *also* 'pȯ(-)i-trē\ *noun* (14th century)
**1 a :** metrical writing **:** VERSE **b :** the productions of a poet **:** POEMS
**2 :** writing that formulates a concentrated imaginative awareness of experience in language chosen and arranged to create a specific emotional response through meaning, sound, and rhythm
**3 a :** something likened to poetry especially in beauty of expression **b :** poetic quality or aspect ⟨the *poetry* of dance⟩
**po-faced** \'pō-,fāst\ *adjective* [perhaps from *po* chamber pot, toilet, from French *pot* pot] (1934)
*British* **:** having an assumed solemn, serious, or earnest expression or manner **:** piously or hypocritically solemn
**pog·o·nip** \'päg-ə-,nip\ *noun* [Shoshone *paɣinappih* cloud] (1865)
**:** a dense winter fog containing frozen particles that is formed in deep mountain valleys of the western U.S.
**po·go·noph·o·ran** \pō-gə-'nä-fə-rən\ *noun* [New Latin *Pogonophora,* from Greek *pōgōnophora,* neuter plural of *pōgōnophoros* wearing a beard, from *pōgōn* beard + *-phoros* -phore] (1963)
**:** any of a phylum (Pogonophora) of marine wormlike animals of uncertain systematic relationships that live in chitinous tubes, have obscure segmentation, and lack a mouth and digestive tract
— **pogonophoran** *adjective*
**po·go stick** \'pō-(,)gō-\ *noun* [from *Pogo,* a trademark] (1921)
**:** a pole with a strong spring at the bottom and two footrests on which a person stands and moves along with a series of jumps
**¹po·grom** \'pō-grəm, 'pä-; pō-'gräm, pə-\ *noun* [Yiddish, from Russian, literally, devastation] (1903)
**:** an organized massacre of helpless people; *specifically* **:** such a massacre of Jews
**²pogrom** *transitive verb* (1915)
**:** to massacre or destroy in a pogrom
**po·grom·ist** \'pō-grə-mist, 'pä-; pō-'grä-, pə-\ *noun* (1907)
**:** one who organizes or takes part in a pogrom
**po·gy** \'pō-gē\ *noun, plural* **pogies** [by shortening & alteration from *poghaden,* perhaps from Eastern Abenaki] (circa 1847)
**:** MENHADEN
**poi** \'pȯi\ *noun, plural* **poi** *or* **pois** [Hawaiian & Samoan] (1823)

**:** a Hawaiian food of taro root cooked, pounded, and kneaded to a paste and often allowed to ferment
**-poiesis** *noun combining form, plural* **-poieses** [New Latin, from Greek *poiēsis* creation — more at POESY]
**:** production **:** formation ⟨hemato*poiesis*⟩
**-poietic** *adjective combining form* [Greek *poiētikos* creative, from *poiētēs* maker — more at POET]
**:** productive **:** formative ⟨hemato*poietic*⟩
**poi·gnance** \'pȯi-nyən(t)s *sometimes* 'pȯi(g)-nən(t)s\ *noun* (1769)
**:** POIGNANCY
**poi·gnan·cy** \'pȯi-nyən(t)-sē *sometimes* 'pȯi(g)-nən(t)-sē\ *noun, plural* **-cies** (1730)
**1 :** the quality or state of being poignant
**2 :** an instance of poignancy
**poi·gnant** \'pȯi-nyənt *sometimes* 'pȯi(g)-nənt\ *adjective* [Middle English *poinaunt,* from Middle French *poignant,* present participle of *poindre* to prick, sting, from Latin *pungere* — more at PUNGENT] (14th century)
**1 :** pungently pervasive ⟨a *poignant* perfume⟩
**2 a (1) :** painfully affecting the feelings **:** PIERCING **(2) :** deeply affecting **:** TOUCHING **b :** designed to make an impression **:** CUTTING ⟨*poignant* satire⟩
**3 a :** pleasurably stimulating **b :** being to the point **:** APT
**synonym** see PUNGENT, MOVING
— **poi·gnant·ly** *adverb*
**poi·ki·lo·therm** \'pȯi-'kē-lə-,thərm, -'ki-\ *noun* [Greek *poikilos* variegated + International Scientific Vocabulary *-therm* — more at PAINT] (1920)
**:** an organism (as a frog) with a variable body temperature that is usually slightly higher than the temperature of its environment **:** a cold-blooded organism
— **poi·ki·lo·ther·mic** \,pȯi-kə-lō-'thər-mik\ *adjective*
**poi·lu** \pwäl-'yü, pwä-'lü; 'pwäl-,yü, 'pwä-,lü; pwä-lue\ *noun* [French, from *poilu* hairy, from Middle French, from *poil* hair, from Latin *pilus*] (1914)
**:** a French soldier; *especially* **:** a front-line soldier in World War I
**poin·ci·ana** \,pȯin(t)-sē-'a-nə, ,p(w)än(t)-\ *noun* [New Latin, from De *Poinci,* 17th century governor of part of the French West Indies] (1731)
**:** any of several ornamental tropical leguminous trees or shrubs (genera *Caesalpinia* and *Delonix*) formerly placed in their own genus (*Poinciana*) — compare ROYAL POINCIANA
**poin·set·tia** \pȯin-'se-tē-ə, ÷pȯint-, ÷-'se-tə\ *noun* [New Latin, from Joel R. *Poinsett* (died 1851) American diplomat] (1836)
**:** any of several spurges (genus *Euphorbia*) with flower clusters subtended by showy involucral bracts; *especially* **:** a showy Mexican and Central American plant (*E. pulcherrima*) with tapering usually scarlet bracts that suggest petals and surround small yellow flowers

**poinsettia**

**¹point** \'pȯint\ *noun* [Middle English, partly from Old French, puncture, small spot, point in time or space, from Latin *punctum,* from neuter of *punctus,* past participle of *pungere* to prick; partly from Old French *pointe* sharp end, from (assumed) Vulgar Latin *puncta,* from Latin, feminine of *punctus,* past participle — more at PUNGENT] (13th century)
**1 a (1) :** an individual detail **:** ITEM **(2) :** a distinguishing detail ⟨tact is one of her strong

*points*⟩ **b :** the most important essential in a discussion or matter ⟨missed the whole *point* of the joke⟩ **c :** COGENCY
**2** *obsolete* **:** physical condition
**3 :** an end or object to be achieved **:** PURPOSE ⟨did not see what *point* there was in continuing the discussion⟩
**4 a (1) :** a geometric element of which it is postulated that at least two exist and that two suffice to determine a line **(2) :** a geometric element determined by an ordered set of coordinates **b (1) :** a narrowly localized place having a precisely indicated position ⟨walked to a *point* 50 yards north of the building⟩ **(2) :** a particular place **:** LOCALITY ⟨have come from distant *points*⟩ **c (1) :** an exact moment ⟨at this *point* I was interrupted⟩ **(2) :** a time interval immediately before something indicated **:** VERGE ⟨at the *point* of death⟩ **d (1) :** a particular step, stage, or degree in development ⟨had reached the *point* where nothing seemed to matter anymore⟩ **(2) :** a definite position in a scale
**5 a :** the terminal usually sharp or narrowly rounded part of something **:** TIP **b :** a weapon or tool having such a part and used for stabbing or piercing: as **(1) :** ARROWHEAD **(2) :** SPEARHEAD **c (1) :** the contact or discharge extremity of an electric device (as a spark plug or distributor) **(2)** *chiefly British* **:** an electric outlet
**6 a :** a projecting usually tapering piece of land or a sharp prominence **b (1) :** the tip of a projecting body part **(2) :** TINE 2 **(3)** *plural* **:** the extremities or markings of the extremities of an animal especially when of a color differing from the rest of the body **c (1) :** a railroad switch **(2) :** the tip of the angle between two rails in a railroad frog **d :** the head of the bow of a stringed instrument
**7 :** a short musical phrase; *especially* **:** a phrase in contrapuntal music
**8 a :** a very small mark **b (1) :** PUNCTUATION MARK; *especially* **:** PERIOD **(2) :** DECIMAL POINT
**9 :** a lace for tying parts of a garment together used especially in the 16th and 17th centuries
**10 :** one of usually 11 divisions of a heraldic shield that determines the position of a charge
**11 a :** one of the 32 equidistant spots of a compass card **b :** the difference of 11¼ degrees between two such successive points
**12 :** a small detachment ahead of an advance guard or behind a rear guard
**13 a :** NEEDLEPOINT 1 **b :** lace made with a bobbin
**14 :** one of 12 spaces marked off on each side of a backgammon board
**15 :** a unit of measurement: as **a (1) :** a unit of counting in the scoring of a game or contest **(2) :** a unit used in evaluating the strength of a bridge hand **b :** a unit of academic credit **c (1) :** a unit used in quoting prices (as of stocks, bonds, and commodities) **(2)** *plural* **:** a percentage of the face value of a loan often added as a placement fee or service charge **(3) :** a percentage of the profits of a business venture (as a motion-picture production) **d :** a unit of about ¹/₇₂ inch used especially to measure the size of type
**16 :** the action of pointing: as **a :** the rigidly intent attitude of a hunting dog marking game for a gunner **b :** the action in dancing of extending one leg and arching the foot so that only the tips of the toes touch the floor
**17 :** a position of a player in various games (as lacrosse); *also* **:** the player of such a position
**18 :** a number thrown on the first roll of the dice in craps which the player attempts to repeat before throwing a seven — compare MISSOUT, PASS 13
**19 :** credit accruing from creating a good impression ⟨scored *points* for hard work⟩
— **beside the point :** IRRELEVANT
— **in point of :** with regard to **:** in the matter of ⟨*in point of* law⟩ ⟨*in point of* fact⟩

— **to the point :** RELEVANT, PERTINENT ⟨a suggestion that was *to the point*⟩

²**point** (14th century)
*transitive verb*
**1 a :** to furnish with a point : SHARPEN ⟨*pointing* a pencil with a knife⟩ **b :** to give added force, emphasis, or piquancy to ⟨*point* up a remark⟩
**2 :** to scratch out the old mortar from the joints of (as a brick wall) and fill in with new material
**3 a** (1) **:** to mark the pauses or grammatical divisions in : PUNCTUATE (2) **:** to separate (a decimal fraction) from an integer by a decimal point — usually used with *off* **b :** to mark (as Hebrew words) with diacritics (as vowel points)
**4 a** (1) **:** to indicate the position or direction of especially by extending a finger ⟨*point* the way home⟩ (2) **:** to direct someone's attention to ⟨*point* the way to new knowledge —Elizabeth Hall⟩ — usually used with *out* or *up* ⟨*point* out a mistake⟩ ⟨*points* up the difference⟩ **b** *of a hunting dog* **:** to indicate the presence and place of (game) by a point
**5 a :** to cause to be turned in a particular direction ⟨*point* a gun⟩ ⟨*pointed* the boat upstream⟩ **b :** to extend (a leg) and arch (the foot) in executing a point in dancing
*intransitive verb*
**1 a :** to indicate the fact or probability of something specified ⟨everything *points* to a bright future⟩ **b :** to indicate the position or direction of something especially by extending a finger ⟨*point* at the map⟩ **c :** to direct attention ⟨can *point* with pride to their own traditions⟩ **d :** to point game ⟨a dog that *points* well⟩
**2 a :** to lie extended, aimed, or turned in a particular direction ⟨a directional arrow that *pointed* to the north⟩ **b :** to execute a point in dancing
**3** *of a ship* **:** to sail close to the wind
**4 :** to train for a particular contest

**point–blank** \'point-'blank\ *adjective* (1591)
**1 a :** marked by no appreciable drop below initial horizontal line of flight **b :** so close to a target that a missile fired will travel in a straight line to the mark
**2 :** DIRECT, BLUNT ⟨a *point-blank* refusal⟩
— **point–blank** *adverb*

**point count** *noun* (1950)
**:** a method of evaluating the strength of a hand in bridge by counting points for each high card and usually for long or short suits; *also* **:** the value of a hand so evaluated

**point d'ap·pui** \,pwaⁿ(n)-da-'pwē\ *noun, plural* **points d'appui** \*same*\ [French, literally, point of support] (1819)
**:** FOUNDATION, BASE

**point–de·vice** \,point-di-'vīs\ *adjective* [Middle English *at point devis* at a fixed point] (1526)
*archaic* **:** marked by punctilious attention to detail : METICULOUS
— **point–device** *adverb, archaic*

**pointe** \'pwaⁿ(n)t\ *noun* [French *pointe* (*du pied*), literally, tiptoe] (1846)
**:** a ballet position in which the body is balanced on the extreme tip of the toe

¹**point·ed** \'poin-təd\ *adjective* (14th century)
**1 a :** having a point **b :** being an arch with a pointed crown; *also* **:** marked by the use of a pointed arch ⟨*pointed* architecture⟩
**2 a :** being to the point : PERTINENT **b :** aimed at a particular person or group
**3 :** CONSPICUOUS, MARKED ⟨*pointed* indifference⟩
— **point·ed·ly** *adverb*
— **point·ed·ness** *noun*

²**pointed** *adjective* [short for *appointed*] (1523)
*obsolete* **:** SET, FIXED

**poin·telle** \,poin-'tel\ *noun* [perhaps from ¹*point* + *-elle* (as in *dentelle* lace)] (1953)

**:** an openwork design (as in knitted fabric) typically in the shape of chevrons; *also* **:** a fabric with this design

**point·er** \'poin-tər\ *noun* (1574)
**1 a** *plural, capitalized* **:** the two stars in the Big Dipper a line through which points to the North Star **b :** one that points out; *especially* **:** a rod used to direct attention **c :** a computer memory address that contains another address (as of desired data)
**2 :** a large strong slender smooth-haired gundog that hunts by scent and indicates the presence of game by pointing
**3 :** one that furnishes with points
**4 :** a useful suggestion or hint : TIP

**point estimate** *noun* (1966)
**:** the single value assigned to a parameter in point estimation

**point estimation** *noun* (1962)
**:** estimation in which a single value is assigned to a parameter

**point guard** *noun* (1970)
**:** a guard in basketball who is chiefly responsible for running the offense

**poin·til·lism** \'pwaⁿ(n)-tē-,yi-zəm, 'poin-tᵊl-,i-zəm\ *noun, often capitalized* [French *pointillisme*, from *pointiller* to stipple, from *point* spot — more at POINT] (1901)
**:** the theory or practice in art of applying small strokes or dots of color to a surface so that from a distance they blend together
— **poin·til·list** \,pwaⁿ(n)-tē-'yēst, 'poin-tᵊl-ist\ *noun*

**poin·til·lis·tic** \,pwaⁿ(n)-tē-'yis-tik, ,poin-tᵊl-'is-\ *also* **point·til·lis·tic** \,pwaⁿ(n)-tē-'yēst, 'poin-tᵊl-ist\ *adjective* (1922)
**1 :** composed of many discrete details or parts
**2 :** of, relating to, or characteristic of pointillism or pointillists

**point lace** *noun* (1672)
**:** NEEDLEPOINT 1

**point·less** \'point-ləs\ *adjective* (1726)
**1 :** devoid of meaning : SENSELESS ⟨a *pointless* remark⟩
**2 :** devoid of effectiveness : FLAT ⟨*pointless* attempts to be funny⟩
— **point·less·ly** *adverb*
— **point·less·ness** *noun*

**point man** *noun* (1903)
**:** a soldier who goes ahead of a patrol; *broadly* **:** one who is in the forefront (as on a political issue)

**point mutation** *noun* (1925)
**:** mutation due to intramolecular gene reorganization (as by substitution, addition, or deletion of a nucleotide)

**point of accumulation** (1929)
**:** LIMIT POINT

**point of departure** (1857)
**:** a starting point especially in a discussion

**point of honor** (1612)
**:** a matter seriously affecting one's honor

**point of inflection** (1743)
**:** INFLECTION POINT

**point of no return** (1941)
**1 :** the point in the flight of an aircraft beyond which the remaining fuel will be insufficient for a return to the starting point with the result that the craft must proceed
**2 :** a critical point at which turning back or reversal is not possible

**point of view** (1720)
**:** a position from which something is considered or evaluated : STANDPOINT

**point set topology** *noun* (1957)
**:** a branch of topology concerned with the properties and theory of topological spaces and metric spaces developed with emphasis on set theory

**point source** *noun* (1903)
**:** a source of radiation (as light) that is concentrated at a point and considered as having no spatial extension

**point–to–point** *noun* (1898)
**:** a cross-country steeplechase

**pointy** \'poin-tē\ *adjective* **point·i·er; -est** (1644)
**1 :** coming to a rather sharp point
**2 :** having parts that stick out sharply here and there

**pointy–head** \'poin-tē-,hed\ *noun* (1968)
**:** INTELLECTUAL — usually used disparagingly
— **pointy–head·ed** \-,he-dəd\ *adjective*

¹**poise** \'poiz\ *noun* [Middle English *poyse* weight, heaviness, from Middle French *pois*, from Latin *pensum*, from neuter of *pensus*, past participle of *pendere* to weigh — more at PENDANT] (1555)
**1 :** a stably balanced state : EQUILIBRIUM ⟨a *poise* between widely divergent impulses —F. R. Leavis⟩
**2 a :** easy self-possessed assurance of manner **:** gracious tact in coping or handling; *also* **:** the pleasantly tranquil interaction between persons of poise ⟨no angry outbursts marred the *poise* of the meeting⟩ **b :** a particular way of carrying oneself **:** BEARING, CARRIAGE
*synonym* see TACT

²**poise** *verb* **poised; pois·ing** [Middle English, to weigh, ponder, from Middle French *pois-*, stem of *peser*, from Latin *pensare* — more at PENSIVE] (1598)
*transitive verb*
**1 a :** BALANCE; *especially* **:** to hold or carry in equilibrium ⟨carried a water jar *poised* on her head⟩ **b :** to hold supported or suspended without motion in a steady position ⟨*poised* her fork and gave her guest a knowing look —Louis Bromfield⟩
**2 :** to hold or carry (the head) in a particular way
**3 :** to put into readiness : BRACE
*intransitive verb*
**1 :** to become drawn up into readiness
**2 :** HOVER

³**poise** \'pwäz\ *noun* [French, from Jean Louis Marie *Poiseuille* (died 1869) French physician and anatomist] (1913)
**:** a centimeter-gram-second unit of viscosity equal to the viscosity of a fluid that would require a shearing force of one dyne to move a square-centimeter area of either of two parallel layers of fluid one centimeter apart with a velocity of one centimeter per second relative to the other layer with the space between the layers being filled with the fluid

**poised** \'poizd\ *adjective* (circa 1643)
**:** having poise: **a :** marked by balance or equilibrium **b :** marked by easy composure of manner or bearing

**poi·sha** \'poi-shə\ *noun, plural* **poisha** [Bengali, from Hindi *paisā*] (circa 1976)
**:** the paisa of Bangladesh

¹**poi·son** \'poi-zᵊn\ *noun* [Middle English, from Middle French, drink, poisonous drink, poison, from Latin *potion-*, *potio* drink — more at POTION] (13th century)
**1 a :** a substance that through its chemical action usually kills, injures, or impairs an organism **b** (1) **:** something destructive or harmful (2) **:** an object of aversion or abhorrence
**2 :** a substance that inhibits the activity of another substance or the course of a reaction or process ⟨a catalyst *poison*⟩
*word history* see VENOM

²**poison** *transitive verb* **poi·soned; poi·son·ing** \'poiz-niŋ, 'poi-zᵊn-iŋ\ (14th century)
**1 a :** to injure or kill with poison **b :** to treat, taint, or impregnate with or as if with poison
**2 :** to exert a baneful influence on : CORRUPT ⟨*poisoned* their minds⟩
**3 :** to inhibit the activity, course, or occurrence of
— **poi·son·er** \'poiz-nər, 'poi-zᵊn-ər\ *noun*

³**poison** *adjective* (1530)

**1** : POISONOUS, VENOMOUS ⟨a *poison* plant⟩ ⟨a *poison* tongue⟩
**2** : impregnated with poison : POISONED ⟨a *poison* arrow⟩

**poison gas** *noun* (1915)
: a poisonous gas or a liquid or a solid giving off poisonous vapors designed (as in chemical warfare) to kill, injure, or disable by inhalation or contact

**poison hemlock** *noun* (circa 1818)
**1** : a large branching biennial poisonous herb (*Conium maculatum*) of the carrot family with finely divided leaves and white flowers
**2** : WATER HEMLOCK

**poison ivy** *noun* (1784)
**1 a** : a climbing plant (*Rhus radicans*) of the cashew family that is especially common in the eastern and central U.S., that has ternate leaves, greenish flowers, and white berries, and that produces an acutely irritating oil causing a usually intensely itching skin rash **b** : any of several plants (as poison oak) closely related to poison ivy
**2** : a skin rash caused by poison ivy

poison ivy 1a

**poison oak** *noun* (1743)
**1** : any of several plants of the same genus (*Rhus*) as poison ivy that produce an oil with similar irritating properties: **a** : a bushy plant (*Rhus diversiloba*) of the Pacific coast **b** : a bushy plant (*Rhus toxicodendron* synonym *R. quercifolia*) of the southeastern U.S.
**2** : POISON IVY 1

**poi·son·ous** \'pȯiz-nəs, 'pȯi-z°n-əs\ *adjective* (circa 1580)
**1** : having the properties or effects of poison : VENOMOUS
**2** : DESTRUCTIVE, HARMFUL
**3** : SPITEFUL, MALICIOUS
— **poi·son·ous·ly** *adverb*

**poison–pen** *adjective* (1925)
: written with malice and spite and usually anonymously ⟨*poison-pen* letter⟩

**poison pill** *noun* (1983)
: a financial tactic (as increasing indebtedness) used by a company to deter an unwanted takeover

**poison sumac** *noun* (1817)
: a smooth American swamp shrub (*Rhus vernix*) that has pinnate leaves, greenish flowers, and greenish white berries and produces an irritating oil — called also *poison dogwood*

**poi·son·wood** \'pȯi-z°n-wu̇d\ *noun* (1721)
: a poisonous tree (*Metopium toxiferum*) of the cashew family that is native to Florida and the West Indies and has compound leaves, greenish paniculate flowers, and orange-yellow fruits

**Pois·son distribution** \pwä-'sō°-\ *noun* [Siméon D. *Poisson* (died 1840) French mathematician] (1922)
: a probability density function that is often used as a mathematical model of the number of outcomes obtained in a suitable interval of time and space, that is nearly equal to its variance, that is used as an approximation to the binomial distribution, and that has the form

$$f(x) = \frac{e^{-\mu}\mu^x}{x!} \text{ where } \mu$$

is the mean and *x* takes on nonnegative integral values

**Poisson's ratio** *noun* [S. *Poisson*] (1886)
: the ratio of transverse to longitudinal strain in a material under tension

**¹poke** \'pōk\ *noun* [Middle English, from Old North French — more at POCKET] (13th century)

**1** *chiefly Southern & Midland* : BAG, SACK
**2 a** : WALLET **b** : PURSE

**²poke** *verb* **poked; pok·ing** [Middle English; akin to Middle Dutch *poken* to poke] (14th century)
*transitive verb*
**1 a** (1) : PROD, JAB ⟨*poked* him in the ribs⟩ (2) : to urge or stir by prodding or jabbing (3) : to cause to prod : THRUST ⟨*poked* a stick at the snake⟩ **b** (1) : PIERCE, STAB (2) : to produce by piercing, stabbing, or jabbing ⟨*poke* a hole⟩ **c** (1) : HIT, PUNCH ⟨*poked* him in the nose⟩ (2) : to deliver (a blow) with the fist
**2 a** : to cause to project ⟨*poked* her head out of the window⟩ **b** : to make (one's way) by poking ⟨*poked* his way through the ruins⟩ **c** : to interpose or interject in a meddlesome manner ⟨asked him not to *poke* his nose into other people's business⟩
*intransitive verb*
**1 a** : to make a prodding, jabbing, or thrusting movement especially repeatedly **b** : to strike out at something
**2 a** : to look about or through something without system : RUMMAGE ⟨*poking* around in the attic⟩ **b** : MEDDLE
**3** : to move or act slowly or aimlessly ⟨just *poked* around and didn't accomplish much⟩
**4** : to become stuck out or forward : PROTRUDE
— **poke fun at** : RIDICULE, MOCK

**³poke** *noun* (circa 1796)
**1 a** : a quick thrust : JAB **b** : a blow with the fist : PUNCH
**2** : a projecting brim on the front of a woman's bonnet

**⁴poke** *noun* [perhaps modification of Virginia Algonquian *pocone*, *poughkone* puccoon] (1708)
: POKEWEED

**poke·ber·ry** \'pōk-,ber-ē\ *noun* (1774)
: the berry of the pokeweed; *also* : POKEWEED

**poke bonnet** *noun* (1820)
: a woman's bonnet with a projecting brim at the front

**¹pok·er** \'pō-kər\ *noun* (1534)
: one that pokes; *especially* : a metal rod for stirring a fire

**²po·ker** \'pō-kər\ *noun* [probably modification of French *poque*, a card game similar to poker] (1836)
: any of several card games in which a player bets that the value of his or her hand is greater than that of the hands held by others, in which each subsequent player must either equal or raise the bet or drop out, and in which the player holding the highest hand at the end of the betting wins the pot

poker hands in descending value: *1* five of a kind, *2* royal flush, *3* straight flush, *4* four of a kind, *5* full house, *6* flush, *7* straight, *8* three of a kind, *9* two pairs, *10* one pair

**poker face** *noun* [²*poker*; from the poker player's need to conceal emotions during play] (1885)
: an inscrutable face that reveals no hint of a person's thoughts or feelings
— **po·ker–faced** \'pō-kər-,fāst\ *adjective*

**poke·weed** \'pōk-,wēd\ *noun* (1751)
: a coarse American perennial herb (*Phytolacca americana* of the family Phytolaccaceae,

the pokeweed family) with racemose white flowers, dark purple juicy berries, a poisonous root, and young shoots sometimes used as potherbs

**po·key** \'pō-kē\ *noun, plural* **pokeys** [origin unknown] (circa 1919)
*slang* : JAIL

**poky** *or* **pok·ey** \'pō-kē\ *adjective* **pok·i·er; -est** [²*poke*] (1849)
**1** : small and cramped
**2** : SHABBY, DULL
**3** : annoyingly slow
— **pok·i·ly** \-kə-lē\ *adverb*
— **pok·i·ness** \-kē-nəs\ *noun*

**pol** \'päl\ *noun* (circa 1942)
: POLITICIAN

**Po·la·bi·an** \pō-'lä-bē-ən, -'lā-\ *noun* [*Polab*, ultimately from Polabian *po* on + *Lábí*, the Elbe River] (1866)
**1** *or* **Po·lab** \pō-'läb\ : a member of a Slavic people formerly dwelling in the basin of the Elbe and on the Baltic coast of Germany
**2** : the extinct West Slavic language of the Polabians

**Po·lack** \'pō-,läk, -,lak\ *noun* [Polish *polak*] (1574)
**1** *obsolete* : a native or inhabitant of Poland
**2** : a person of Polish birth or descent — usually used disparagingly

**Po·land Chi·na** \'pō-lən(d)-'chī-nə\ *noun* [*Poland*, Europe + *China*, Asia] (1879)
: any of an American breed of large white-marked black swine

**¹po·lar** \'pō-lər\ *adjective* [New Latin *polaris*, from Latin *polus* pole] (1551)
**1 a** : of or relating to a geographical pole or the region around it **b** : coming from or having the characteristics of such a region **c** (1) : passing over a celestial body's north and south poles ⟨a satellite in a *polar* orbit⟩ (2) : traveling in a polar orbit ⟨a *polar* satellite⟩
**2** : of or relating to one or more poles (as of a magnet)
**3** : serving as a guide
**4** : diametrically opposite
**5** : exhibiting polarity; *especially* : having a dipole or characterized by molecules having dipoles ⟨a *polar* solvent⟩
**6** : resembling a pole or axis around which all else revolves : PIVOTAL
**7** : of, relating to, or expressed in polar coordinates ⟨*polar* equations⟩; *also* : of or relating to a polar coordinate system

**²polar** *noun* (1848)
: a straight line related to a point; *specifically* : the straight line joining the points of contact of the tangents from a point exterior to a conic section

**polar bear** *noun* (1781)
: a large creamy-white bear (*Thalarctos maritimus* synonym *Ursus maritimus*) that inhabits arctic regions

polar bear

**polar body** *noun* (1888)
: a cell that separates from an oocyte during meiosis and that contains a nucleus produced in the first or second meiotic division but very little cytoplasm

**polar circle** *noun* (1551)
: either of the two parallels of latitude each at a distance from a pole of the earth equal to about 23 degrees 27 minutes

**polar coordinate** *noun* (1816)
: either of two numbers that locate a point in a plane by its distance from a fixed point on a line and the angle this line makes with a fixed line

**polar front** *noun* (1920)
: the boundary between the cold air of a polar region and the warmer air of lower latitudes

**po·lar·im·e·ter** \ˌpō-lə-ˈri-mə-tər\ *noun* [International Scientific Vocabulary, from *polarization*] (circa 1859)
**1 :** an instrument for determining the amount of polarization of light or the proportion of polarized light in a partially polarized ray
**2 :** a polariscope for measuring the amount of rotation of the plane of polarization especially by liquids
— **po·lar·i·met·ric** \pō-ˌlar-ə-ˈme-trik\ *adjective*
— **po·lar·im·e·try** \ˌpō-lə-ˈri-mə-trē\ *noun*
**Po·lar·is** \pə-ˈlar-əs, -ˈlär-\ *noun* [New Latin, from *polaris* polar]
**:** NORTH STAR
**po·lar·ise** *British variant of* POLARIZE
**po·lar·i·scope** \pō-ˈlar-ə-ˌskōp\ *noun* [International Scientific Vocabulary, from *polarization*] (1829)
**1 :** an instrument for studying the properties of or examining substances in polarized light
**2 :** POLARIMETER 2
— **po·lar·i·scop·ic** \-ˌlar-ə-ˈskä-pik\ *adjective*
**po·lar·i·ty** \pō-ˈlar-ə-tē, pə-\ *noun, plural* **-ties** (1646)
**1 :** the quality or condition inherent in a body that exhibits opposite properties or powers in opposite parts or directions or that exhibits contrasted properties or powers in contrasted parts or directions **:** the condition of having poles
**2 :** attraction toward a particular object or in a specific direction
**3 :** the particular state either positive or negative with reference to the two poles or to electrification
**4 a :** diametrical opposition **b :** an instance of such opposition
**po·lar·i·za·tion** \ˌpō-lə-rə-ˈzā-shən\ *noun* (1812)
**1 :** the action of polarizing or state of being or becoming polarized: as **a** (1) **:** the action or process of affecting radiation and especially light so that the vibrations of the wave assume a definite form (2) **:** the state of radiation affected by this process **b :** an increase in the resistance of an electrolytic cell often caused by the deposition of gas on one or both electrodes
**c :** MAGNETIZATION
**2 a :** division into two opposites **b :** concentration about opposing extremes of groups or interests formerly ranged on a continuum
**po·lar·ize** \ˈpō-lə-ˌrīz\ *verb* **-ized; -iz·ing** [French *polariser*, from New Latin *polaris* polar] (1811)
*transitive verb*
**1 :** to cause (as light waves) to vibrate in a definite pattern
**2 :** to give physical polarity to
**3 :** to break up into opposing factions or groupings ⟨a campaign that *polarized* the electorate⟩
**4 :** CONCENTRATE 1 ⟨recreate a cohesive rock community by *polarizing* . . . an amorphous, fragmented audience —Ellen Willis⟩
*intransitive verb*
**:** to become polarized
— **po·lar·iz·abil·i·ty** \ˌpō-lə-ˌrī-zə-ˈbi-lə-tē\ *noun*
— **po·lar·iz·able** \ˌpō-lə-ˈrī-zə-bəl\ *adjective*
**polar nucleus** *noun* (1882)
**:** either of the two nuclei of a seed plant embryo sac that are destined to form endosperm
**po·lar·og·ra·phy** \ˌpō-lə-ˈrä-grə-fē\ *noun* [International Scientific Vocabulary, from *polarization*] (1936)
**:** a method of qualitative or quantitative analysis based on current-voltage curves obtained during electrolysis of a solution with a steadily increasing electromotive force
— **po·lar·o·graph·ic** \pō-ˌlar-ə-ˈgra-fik\ *adjective*
— **po·lar·o·graph·i·cal·ly** \-fi-k(ə-)lē\ *adverb*

**Po·lar·oid** \ˈpō-lə-ˌròid\ *trademark*
— used especially for a light-polarizing material used especially in eyeglasses and lamps to prevent glare or for a camera that develops pictures instantly
**po·lar·on** \ˈpō-lə-ˌrän\ *noun* [International Scientific Vocabulary *polar* + ²-*on*] (1946)
**:** a conducting electron in an ionic crystal together with the induced polarization of the surrounding lattice
**pol·der** \ˈpōl-dər\ *noun* [Dutch] (1604)
**:** a tract of low land (as in the Netherlands) reclaimed from a body of water (as the sea)
**¹pole** \ˈpōl\ *noun* [Middle English, from Old English *pāl* stake, pole, from Latin *palus* stake; akin to Latin *pangere* to fix — more at PACT] (before 12th century)
**1 a :** a long slender usually cylindrical object (as a length of wood) **b :** a shaft which extends from the front axle of a wagon between wheelhorses and by which the wagon is drawn **:** TONGUE **c :** a long staff of wood, metal, or fiberglass used in the pole vault
**2 a :** a varying unit of length; *especially* **:** one measuring 16½ feet (5.03 meters) **b :** a unit of area equal to a square rod (25.293 square meters)
**3 :** a tree with a breast-high diameter of from 4 to 12 inches (10 to 30 centimeters)
**4 :** the inside front row position on the starting line for a race
**²pole** *verb* **poled; pol·ing** (1573)
*transitive verb*
**1 :** to act upon with a pole
**2 :** to impel or push with a pole
*intransitive verb*
**1 :** to propel a boat with a pole
**2 :** to use ski poles to gain speed
**³pole** *noun* [Middle English, from Latin *polus*, from Greek *polos* pivot, pole; akin to Greek *pelesthai* to become, Sanskrit *carati* he moves, wanders — more at WHEEL] (14th century)
**1 :** either extremity of an axis of a sphere and especially of the earth's axis
**2 a :** either of two related opposites **b :** a point of guidance or attraction
**3 a :** either of the two terminals of an electric cell, battery, generator, or motor **b :** one of two or more regions in a magnetized body at which the magnetic flux density is concentrated
**4 :** either of two morphologically or physiologically differentiated areas at opposite ends of an axis in an organism or cell — see BLASTULA illustration
**5 :** the fixed point in a system of polar coordinates that serves as the origin **b :** the point of origin of two tangents to a conic section that determine a polar
— **poles apart :** as diametrically opposed as possible
**Pole** \ˈpōl\ *noun* [German, of Slavic origin; akin to Polish *polak* Pole] (1535)
**1 :** a native or inhabitant of Poland
**2 :** a person of Polish descent
**¹pole·ax** \ˈpōl-ˌaks\ *noun* [Middle English *polax, pollax*, from *pol, polle* poll + *ax*] (14th century)
**1 :** a battle-ax with a short handle and often a hook or spike opposite the blade; *also* **:** one with a long handle used as an ornamental weapon
**2 :** an ax used in slaughtering cattle
**²poleax** *transitive verb* (1882)
**:** to attack, strike, or fell with or as if with a poleax
**pole bean** *noun* (circa 1770)
**:** a cultivated bean that is usually trained to grow upright on supports
**pole·cat** \ˈpōl-ˌkat\ *noun, plural* **polecats** *or* **polecat** [Middle English *polcat*, probably from Middle French *poul, pol* cock + Middle English *cat*; probably from its preying on poultry — more at PULLET] (14th century)
**1 :** any of several carnivorous mammals (as of the genera *Mustela* or *Vormela*) of the weasel

family; *especially* **:** a brown to black European mammal (*M. putorius*) from which the domesticated ferret is derived
**2 :** SKUNK
**word history** see FERRET
**poleis** *plural of* POLIS
**pole·less** \ˈpōl-ləs\ *adjective* (1647)
**:** having no pole
**po·lem·ic** \pə-ˈle-mik\ *noun* [French *polémique*, from Middle French, from *polemique* controversial, from Greek *polemikos* warlike, hostile, from *polemos* war; perhaps akin to Greek *pelemizein* to shake, Old English *ealfelo* baleful] (1638)
**1 a :** an aggressive attack on or refutation of the opinions or principles of another **b :** the art or practice of disputation or controversy — usually used in plural but singular or plural in construction
**2 :** an aggressive controversialist **:** DISPUTANT
— **po·lem·i·cist** \-ˈle-mə-sist\ *noun*
**po·lem·i·cal** \-mi-kəl\ *also* **po·lem·ic** \-mik\ *adjective* (1640)
**1 :** of, relating to, or being a polemic **:** CONTROVERSIAL
**2 :** engaged in or addicted to polemics **:** DISPUTATIOUS
— **po·lem·i·cal·ly** \-mi-k(ə-)lē\ *adverb*
**po·lem·i·cize** \-ˈle-mə-ˌsīz\ *intransitive verb* **-cized; -ciz·ing** (1950)
**:** to engage in controversy **:** deliver a polemic
**po·le·mist** \pə-ˈle-mist, ˈpä-lə-mist\ *noun* (1825)
**:** one skilled in or given to polemics
**pol·e·mize** \ˈpä-lə-ˌmīz\ *intransitive verb* **-mized; -miz·ing** (1828)
**:** POLEMICIZE
**pol·e·mo·ni·um** \ˌpä-lə-ˈmō-nē-əm\ *noun* [New Latin, from Greek *polemōnion*, a plant] (1900)
**:** JACOB'S LADDER 1
**po·len·ta** \pō-ˈlen-tə, pə-, -ˌtä\ *noun* [Italian, from Latin, crushed and hulled barley; akin to Latin *pollen* fine flour] (1764)
**:** mush made of chestnut meal, cornmeal, semolina, or farina
**pol·er** \ˈpō-lər\ *noun* (1848)
**:** one that poles; *especially* **:** one that poles a boat
**pole·star** \ˈpōl-ˌstär\ *noun*
**1 :** NORTH STAR
**2 a :** a directing principle **:** GUIDE **b :** a center of attraction
**pole vault** *noun* (circa 1890)
**:** a vault with the aid of a pole; *specifically* **:** a field event consisting of a vault for height over a crossbar
— **pole–vault** *intransitive verb*
— **pole–vaulter** *noun*
**pole·ward** \ˈpōl-wərd\ *adverb or adjective* (1875)
**:** toward or in the direction of a pole of the earth ⟨as the sun moves *poleward*⟩ ⟨*poleward* variation in temperature⟩
**¹po·lice** \pə-ˈlēs\ *transitive verb* **po·liced; po·lic·ing** [in sense 1, from Middle French *policier*, from *police* conduct of public affairs; in other senses, from ²*police*] (1589)
**1** *archaic* **:** GOVERN
**2 :** to control, regulate, or keep in order by use of police
**3 :** to make clean and put in order
**4 a :** to supervise the operation, execution, or administration of to prevent or detect and prosecute violations of rules and regulations **b :** to exercise such supervision over the policies and activities of
**5 :** to perform the functions of a police force in or over

**²police** *noun, plural* **police** *often attributive* [French, from Late Latin *politia* government, administration, from Greek *politeia*, from *politēs* citizen, from *polis* city, state; akin to Sanskrit *pur* rampart, Lithuanian *pilis* castle] (1716)
**1 a :** the internal organization or regulation of a political unit through exercise of governmental powers especially with respect to general comfort, health, morals, safety, or prosperity **b :** control and regulation of affairs affecting the general order and welfare of any unit or area **c :** the system of laws for effecting such control
**2 a :** the department of government concerned primarily with maintenance of public order, safety, and health and enforcement of laws and possessing executive, judicial, and legislative powers **b :** the department of government charged with prevention, detection, and prosecution of public nuisances and crimes
**3 a :** POLICE FORCE **b** *plural* **:** POLICE OFFICERS
**4 a :** a private organization resembling a police force ⟨campus *police*⟩ **b** *plural* **:** the members of a private police organization
**5 a :** the action or process of cleaning and putting in order **b :** military personnel detailed to perform this function
**police action** *noun* (1933)
**:** a localized military action undertaken without formal declaration of war by regular armed forces against persons (as guerrillas or aggressors) held to be violators of international peace and order
**police court** *noun* (1823)
**:** a court of record that has jurisdiction over various minor offenses (as breach of the peace) and the power to bind over for trial in a superior court or for a grand jury persons accused of more serious offenses
**police dog** *noun* (1908)
**1 :** a dog trained to assist police (as in drug detection)
**2 :** GERMAN SHEPHERD
**police force** *noun* (1838)
**:** a body of trained officers entrusted by a government with maintenance of public peace and order, enforcement of laws, and prevention and detection of crime
**po·lice·man** \pə-ˈlēs-mən\ *noun* (1801)
**1 :** a member of a police force
**2 :** one held to resemble a policeman ⟨making the United States the *policeman* for the whole wide world —R. B. Long⟩
**police officer** *noun* (1800)
**:** a member of a police force
**police power** *noun* (1827)
**:** the inherent power of a government to exercise reasonable control over persons and property within its jurisdiction in the interest of the general security, health, safety, morals, and welfare except where legally prohibited
**police procedural** *noun, plural* **police procedurals** (1967)
**:** a mystery story written from the point of view of the police investigating the crime
**police reporter** *noun* (1834)
**:** a reporter regularly assigned to cover police news (as crimes and arrests)
**police state** *noun* (1865)
**:** a political unit characterized by repressive governmental control of political, economic, and social life usually by an arbitrary exercise of power by police and especially secret police in place of regular operation of administrative and judicial organs of the government according to publicly known legal procedures
**police station** *noun* (1846)
**:** the headquarters of the police for a locality
**po·lice·wom·an** \pə-ˈlēs-ˌwu̇-mən\ *noun* (1853)
**:** a woman who is a member of a police force
**¹pol·i·cy** \ˈpä-lə-sē\ *noun, plural* **-cies** *often attributive* [Middle English *policie* government, policy, from Middle French, govern-

ment, regulation, from Late Latin *politia*] (15th century)
**1 a :** prudence or wisdom in the management of affairs **b :** management or procedure based primarily on material interest
**2 a :** a definite course or method of action selected from among alternatives and in light of given conditions to guide and determine present and future decisions **b :** a high-level overall plan embracing the general goals and acceptable procedures especially of a governmental body
**²policy** *noun, plural* **-cies** [alteration of earlier *police*, from Middle French, certificate, from Old Italian *polizza*, modification of Medieval Latin *apodixa* receipt, from Middle Greek *apodeixis*, from Greek, proof, from *apodeiknynai* to demonstrate — more at APODICTIC] (1565)
**1 :** a writing whereby a contract of insurance is made
**2 a :** a daily lottery in which participants bet that certain numbers will be drawn from a lottery wheel **b :** NUMBER 7a
**pol·i·cy·hold·er** \ˈpä-lə-sē-ˌhōl-dər\ *noun* (1851)
**:** the owner of an insurance policy
**policy science** *noun* (1950)
**:** a social science dealing with the making of high-level policy (as in a government or business)
**po·lio** \ˈpō-lē-ˌō\ *noun* (1931)
**:** POLIOMYELITIS
**po·lio·my·eli·tis** \ˌpō-lē-(ˌ)ō-ˌmī-ə-ˈlī-təs\ *noun* [New Latin, from Greek *polios* gray + *myelos* marrow — more at FALLOW, MYEL-] (1878)
**:** an acute infectious virus disease characterized by fever, motor paralysis, and atrophy of skeletal muscles often with permanent disability and deformity and marked by inflammation of nerve cells in the anterior gray matter in each lateral half of the spinal cord — called also *infantile paralysis*
**po·lio·vi·rus** \ˈpō-lē-(ˌ)ō-ˌvī-rəs\ *noun* [New Latin, from *polio*myelitis + *virus*] (1953)
**:** an enterovirus that occurs in several antigenically distinct forms and is the causative agent of human poliomyelitis
**po·lis** \ˈpä-ləs\ *noun, plural* **po·leis** \ˈpä-ˌlās\ [Greek — more at POLICE] (1894)
**:** a Greek city-state; *broadly* **:** a state or society especially when characterized by a sense of community
**-polis** *noun combining form* [Late Latin, from Greek, from *polis*]
**:** city ⟨megalo*polis*⟩
**¹pol·ish** \ˈpä-lish\ *verb* [Middle English *polisshen*, from Middle French *poliss-*, stem of *polir*, from Latin *polire*] (14th century)
*transitive verb*
**1 :** to make smooth and glossy usually by friction **:** BURNISH
**2 :** to smooth, soften, or refine in manners or condition
**3 :** to bring to a highly developed, finished, or refined state **:** PERFECT
*intransitive verb*
**:** to become smooth or glossy by or as if by friction
**— pol·ish·er** *noun*
**²polish** *noun* (1704)
**1 a :** a smooth glossy surface **:** LUSTER **b :** freedom from rudeness or coarseness **:** CULTURE **c :** a state of high development or refinement
**2 :** the action or process of polishing
**3 :** a preparation that is used to produce a gloss and often a color for the protection and decoration of a surface ⟨furniture *polish*⟩ ⟨nail *polish*⟩
**¹Pol·ish** \ˈpō-lish\ *adjective* [*Pole*] (1674)
**:** of, relating to, or characteristic of Poland, the Poles, or Polish
**²Polish** *noun* (1784)
**:** the Slavic language of the Poles

**polish off** *transitive verb* (1829)
**:** to finish off or dispose of rapidly or completely
**po·lit·bu·ro** \ˈpä-lət-ˌbyu̇r-(ˌ)ō, ˈpō-lət-, pə-ˈlit-\ *noun* [Russian *politbyuro*, from *politicheskoe byuro* political bureau] (1925)
**:** the principal policy-making and executive committee of a Communist party
**po·lite** \pə-ˈlīt\ *adjective* **po·lit·er; -est** [Latin *politus*, from past participle of *polire*] (1501)
**1 a :** of, relating to, or having the characteristics of advanced culture **b :** marked by refined cultural interests and pursuits especially in arts and belles lettres
**2 a :** showing or characterized by correct social usage **b :** marked by an appearance of consideration, tact, deference, or courtesy **c :** marked by a lack of roughness or crudities ⟨*polite* literature⟩
**synonym** SEE CIVIL
**— po·lite·ly** *adverb*
**— po·lite·ness** *noun*
**po·li·tesse** \ˌpä-li-ˈtes, ˌpō-\ *noun* [French, from Middle French, cleanness, from Old Italian *pulitezza*, from *pulito*, past participle of *pulire* to polish, clean, from Latin *polire*] (1717)
**:** formal politeness **:** DECOROUSNESS
**pol·i·tic** \ˈpä-lə-ˌtik\ *adjective* [Middle English *politik*, from Middle French *politique*, from Latin *politicus*, from Greek *politikos*, from *politēs* citizen — more at POLICE] (15th century)
**1 :** POLITICAL
**2 :** characterized by shrewdness in managing, contriving, or dealing
**3 :** sagacious in promoting a policy
**4 :** shrewdly tactful
**synonym** SEE EXPEDIENT, SUAVE
**po·lit·i·cal** \pə-ˈli-ti-kəl\ *adjective* [Latin *politicus*] (1551)
**1 a :** of or relating to government, a government, or the conduct of government **b :** of, relating to, or concerned with the making as distinguished from the administration of governmental policy
**2 :** of, relating to, involving, or involved in politics and especially party politics
**3 :** organized in governmental terms ⟨*political* units⟩
**4 :** involving or charged or concerned with acts against a government or a political system ⟨*political* prisoners⟩
**— po·lit·i·cal·ly** \-k(ə-)lē\ *adverb*
**political action committee** *noun* (1944)
**:** a group formed (as by an industry or an issue-oriented organization) to raise and contribute money to the campaigns of candidates likely to advance the group's interests
**political correctness** *noun* (1990)
**:** conformity to a belief that language and practices which could offend political sensibilities should be eliminated
**political economy** *noun* (1740)
**1 :** ECONOMICS
**2 :** the theory or study of the role of public policy in influencing the economic and social welfare of a political unit
**— political economist** *noun*
**po·lit·i·cal·ize** \pə-ˈli-ti-kə-ˌlīz\ *transitive verb* **-ized; -izing** (1869)
**:** POLITICIZE
**— po·lit·i·cal·i·za·tion** \-ˌli-ti-kə-lə-ˈzā-shən\ *noun*
**politically correct** *adjective* (1936)
**:** conforming to a belief that language and practices which could offend political sensibilities (as in matters of sex or race) should be eliminated
**political science** *noun* (1779)
**:** a social science concerned chiefly with the description and analysis of political and especially governmental institutions and processes
**— political scientist** *noun*
**pol·i·ti·cian** \ˌpä-lə-ˈti-shən\ *noun* (1589)

**1 :** a person experienced in the art or science of government; *especially* **:** one actively engaged in conducting the business of a government

**2 a :** a person engaged in party politics as a profession **b :** a person primarily interested in political office for selfish or other narrow usually short-sighted reasons

**po·lit·i·cise** *British variant of* POLITICIZE

**po·lit·i·cize** \pə-'li-tə-ˌsīz\ *transitive verb* **-cized; -ciz·ing** (1846)

**:** to give a political tone or character to ⟨an attempt to *politicize* the civil service⟩

— **po·lit·i·ci·za·tion** \-ˌli-tə-sə-'zā-shən\ *noun*

**pol·i·tick** \'pä-lə-ˌtik\ *intransitive verb* [back-formation from *politicking*, noun, from *politics* + ³*-ing*] (circa 1934)

**:** to engage in often partisan political discussion or activity

— **pol·i·tick·er** *noun*

**po·lit·i·co** \pə-'li-ti-ˌkō\ *noun, plural* **-cos** *also* **-coes** [Italian *politico* or Spanish *político*, ultimately from Latin *politicus* political] (1630)

**:** POLITICIAN 2

**pol·i·tics** \'pä-lə-ˌtiks\ *noun plural but singular or plural in construction* [Greek *politika*, from neuter plural of *politikos* political] (circa 1529)

**1 a :** the art or science of government **b :** the art or science concerned with guiding or influencing governmental policy **c :** the art or science concerned with winning and holding control over a government

**2 :** political actions, practices, or policies

**3 a :** political affairs or business; *especially* **:** competition between competing interest groups or individuals for power and leadership (as in a government) **b :** political life especially as a principal activity or profession **c :** political activities characterized by artful and often dishonest practices

**4 :** the political opinions or sympathies of a person

**5 a :** the total complex of relations between people living in society **b :** relations or conduct in a particular area of experience especially as seen or dealt with from a political point of view ⟨office *politics*⟩

**pol·i·ty** \'pä-lə-tē\ *noun, plural* **-ties** [Late Latin *politia* — more at POLICE] (1538)

**1 :** political organization

**2 :** a specific form of political organization

**3 :** a politically organized unit

**4 a :** the form or constitution of a politically organized unit **b :** the form of government of a religious denomination

**pol·ka** \'pōl-kə, 'pō-kə\ *noun* [Czech, from *Polka* Polish woman, feminine of *Polák* Pole] (1844)

**1 :** a vivacious couple dance of Bohemian origin in duple time with a basic pattern of hop-step-close-step

**2 :** a lively Bohemian dance tune in ²/₄ time

— **polka** *intransitive verb*

**pol·ka dot** \'pō-kə-ˌdät\ *noun* (1884)

**:** a dot in a pattern of regularly distributed dots in textile design

— **polka–dot** *or* **pol·ka–dot·ted** \-ˌdä-təd\ *adjective*

**¹poll** \'pōl\ *noun* [Middle English *pol, polle,* from Middle Low German] (14th century)

**1 :** HEAD

**2 a :** the top or back of the head **b :** NAPE

**3 :** the broad or flat end of a striking tool (as a hammer)

**4 a** (1) **:** the casting or recording of the votes of a body of persons (2) **:** a counting of votes cast **b :** the place where votes are cast or recorded — usually used in plural ⟨at the *polls*⟩ **c :** the period of time during which votes may be cast at an election **d :** the total number of votes recorded ⟨a heavy *poll*⟩

**5 a :** a questioning or canvassing of persons selected at random or by quota to obtain information or opinions to be analyzed **b :** a record of the information so obtained

**²poll** (14th century)

*transitive verb*

**1 a :** to cut off or cut short the hair or wool of **:** CROP, SHEAR **b :** to cut off or cut short (as wool)

**2 a :** to cut off or back the top of (as a tree); *specifically* **:** POLLARD **b :** to cut off or cut short the horns of (cattle)

**3 a :** to receive and record the votes of **b :** to request each member of to declare a vote individually ⟨*poll* the assembly⟩

**4 :** to receive (as votes) in an election

**5 :** to question or canvass in a poll

**6 :** to test (as several computer terminals sharing a single line) in sequence for messages to be transmitted

*intransitive verb*

**:** to cast one's vote at a poll

— **poll·ee** \pō-'lē\ *noun*

— **poll·er** \'pō-lər\ *noun*

**pol·lack** *or* **pol·lock** \'pä-lək\ *noun, plural* **pollack** *or* **pollock** [Middle English *poullok,* perhaps from Scottish Gaelic *pollag* or Irish *pollóg*] (15th century)

**1 :** a commercially important north Atlantic food fish (*Pollachius virens*) related to and resembling the cods but darker

**2 :** a commercially important northern Pacific food fish (*Theragra chalcogramma*) of the cod family that closely resembles the pollack — called also *walleye pollack*

**¹pol·lard** \'pä-lərd\ *noun* [²*poll*] (1611)

**:** a tree cut back to the trunk to promote the growth of a dense head of foliage

**²pollard** *transitive verb* (1670)

**:** to make a pollard of (a tree)

**polled** \'pōld\ *adjective* (1584)

**:** having no horns

**pol·len** \'pä-lən\ *noun* [New Latin *pollin-, pollen,* from Latin, fine flour] (1760)

**1 :** a mass of microspores in a seed plant appearing usually as a fine dust

**2 :** a dusty bloom on the body of an insect

**pollen basket** *noun* (1860)

**:** a smooth area on each hind tibia of a bee that is edged by a fringe of stiff hairs and serves to collect and transport pollen — called also *corbicula*

**pollen grain** *noun* (1835)

**:** one of the granular microspores that occur in pollen and give rise to the male gametophyte of a seed plant

**pol·len·iz·er** *also* **pol·lin·iz·er** \'pä-lə-ˌnī-zər\ *noun* [*pollenize* to pollinate] (1897)

**1 :** a plant that is a source of pollen

**2 :** POLLINATOR a

**pollen mother cell** *noun* (1884)

**:** a cell that is derived from the hypodermis of the pollen sac and that gives rise by meiosis to four cells each of which develops into a pollen grain

**pollen sac** *noun* (1875)

**:** one of the pouches of a seed plant anther in which pollen is formed

**pollen tube** *noun* (1835)

**:** a tube that is formed by a pollen grain and conveys the sperm nuclei to the embryo sac of an angiosperm or the archegonium of a gymnosperm

**pol·lex** \'pä-ˌleks\ *noun, plural* **pol·li·ces** \'pä-lə-ˌsēz\ [New Latin *pollic-, pollex,* from Latin, thumb, big toe] (circa 1836)

**:** the first digit of the forelimb **:** THUMB

**pollin-** *combining form* [New Latin *pollin-, pollen*]

**:** pollen ⟨*pollin*ate⟩

**pol·li·nate** \'pä-lə-ˌnāt\ *transitive verb* **-nat·ed; -nat·ing** (1875)

**1 :** to carry out the pollination of

**2 :** to mark or smudge with pollen

**pol·li·na·tion** \ˌpä-lə-'nā-shən\ *noun* (1875)

**:** the transfer of pollen from an anther to the stigma in angiosperms or from the microsporangium to the micropyle in gymnosperms

**pol·li·na·tor** \'pä-lə-ˌnā-tər\ *noun* (1903)

**:** one that pollinates: as **a :** an agent (as an insect) that pollinates flowers **b :** POLLENIZER 1

**pol·lin·i·um** \pä-'li-nē-əm\ *noun, plural* **-ia** \-nē-ə\ [New Latin, from *pollin-*] (1862)

**:** a coherent mass of pollen grains often with a stalk bearing an adhesive disk that clings to insects

**pol·li·no·sis** *or* **pol·len·osis** \ˌpä-lə-'nō-səs\ *noun* [New Latin *pollinosis,* from *pollin-*] (1925)

**:** an acute recurrent catarrhal disorder caused by allergic sensitivity to specific pollens

**poll·ster** \'pōl-stər\ *noun* (1939)

**:** one that conducts a poll or compiles data obtained by a poll

**poll tax** *noun* (1692)

**:** a tax of a fixed amount per person levied on adults

**pol·lut·ant** \pə-'lü-tᵊnt\ *noun* (1892)

**:** something that pollutes

**pol·lute** \pə-'lüt\ *transitive verb* **pol·lut·ed; pol·lut·ing** [Middle English, from Latin *pollutus,* past participle of *polluere,* from *por-* (akin to Latin *per* through) + *-luere* (akin to Latin *lutum* mud, Greek *lyma* dirt, defilement) — more at FOR] (14th century)

**1 a :** to make ceremonially or morally impure **:** DEFILE **b :** DEBASE 1 ⟨using language to deceive or mislead *pollutes* language —Linda C. Lederman⟩

**2 a :** to make physically impure or unclean **:** BEFOUL, DIRTY **b :** to contaminate (an environment) especially with man-made waste

**synonym** *see* CONTAMINATE

— **pol·lut·er** *noun*

— **pol·lut·ive** \-'lü-tiv\ *adjective*

**pol·lu·tion** \pə-'lü-shən\ *noun* (14th century)

**1 :** the action of polluting especially by environmental contamination with man-made waste; *also* **:** the condition of being polluted

**2 :** POLLUTANT

**Pol·lux** \'pä-ləks\ *noun* [Latin, modification of Greek *Polydeukēs*]

**1 :** one of the Dioscuri

**2 :** a first-magnitude star in the constellation Gemini

**Pol·ly·an·na** \ˌpä-lē-'a-nə\ *noun* [*Pollyanna,* heroine of the novel *Pollyanna* (1913) by Eleanor Porter (died 1920) American fiction writer] (1921)

**:** a person characterized by irrepressible optimism and a tendency to find good in everything

— **Pollyanna** *adjective*

— **Pol·ly·an·na·ish** \-'a-nə-ish\ *also* **Pol·ly·an·nish** \-'a-nish\ *adjective*

**pol·ly·wog** *or* **pol·li·wog** \'pä-lē-ˌwäg, -ˌwȯg\ *noun* [alteration of Middle English *polwygle,* probably from *pol* poll + *wiglen* to wiggle] (1832)

**:** TADPOLE

**po·lo** \'pō-(ˌ)lō\ *noun* [Balti, ball] (1872)

**1 :** a game played by teams of players on horseback using mallets with long flexible handles to drive a wooden ball through goalposts

**2 :** WATER POLO

— **po·lo·ist** \'pō-(ˌ)lō-ist\ *noun*

**polo coat** *noun* (1910)

**:** a tailored overcoat that is made especially of tan camel's hair and often has stitched edges and a half-belt on the back

**po·lo·naise** \ˌpä-lə-'nāz, ˌpō-\ *noun* [French, from feminine of *polonais* Polish, from *Pologne* Poland, from Medieval Latin *Polonia*] (1773)

\ə\ abut \ᵊ\ kitten \ər\ further \a\ ash \ā\ ace
\ä\ mop, mar \aú\ out \ch\ chin \e\ bet \ē\ easy
\g\ go \i\ hit \ī\ ice \j\ job \ŋ\ sing \ō\ go
\ȯ\ law \ȯi\ boy \th\ thin \t̲h̲\ the \ü\ loot \ù\ foot
\y\ yet \zh\ vision *see also* Guide to Pronunciation

**1 :** an elaborate overdress with a short-sleeved fitted waist and a draped cutaway overskirt
**2 a :** a stately Polish processional dance popular in 19th century Europe **b :** music for this dance in moderate ¾ time

**Po·lo·nia** \pə-'lō-nē-ə, -nyə\ *noun* [New Latin, Poland, from Medieval Latin] (1944)
**:** people of Polish descent living outside Poland

**po·lo·ni·um** \pə-'lō-nē-əm\ *noun* [New Latin, from Medieval Latin *Polonia*] (1898)
**:** a radioactive metallic element that is similar chemically to tellurium and bismuth, occurs especially in pitchblende and radium-lead residues, and emits an alpha particle to form an isotope of lead — see ELEMENT table

polonaise 1

**Po·lo·ni·us** \pə-'lō-nē-əs\ *noun*
**:** a garrulous courtier and father of Ophelia and Laertes in Shakespeare's *Hamlet*

**polo shirt** *noun* (1920)
**:** a close-fitting pullover often knit shirt with short or long sleeves and turnover collar or banded neck

**pol·ter·geist** \'pōl-tər-ˌgīst\ *noun* [German, from *poltern* to knock + *Geist* spirit] (1848)
**:** a noisy usually mischievous ghost held to be responsible for unexplained noises (as rappings)

**¹pol·troon** \päl-'trün\ *noun* [Middle French *poultron*, from Old Italian *poltrone*, probably akin to *poltro* colt, ultimately from Latin *pullus* young of an animal — more at FOAL] (circa 1529)
**:** a spiritless coward **:** CRAVEN

**²poltroon** *adjective* (1645)
**:** characterized by complete cowardice

**pol·troon·ery** \-'trü-nə-rē, -'trün-rē\ *noun* (1590)
**:** mean pusillanimity **:** COWARDICE

**poly** \'pä-lē\ *noun, plural* **pol·ys** \-lēz\ *often attributive* [short for *polymer*] (1942)
**:** a polymerized plastic or something made of this; *especially* **:** a polyester fiber, fabric, or garment

**poly-** *combining form* [Middle English, from Latin, from Greek, from *polys*; akin to Old High German *filu* many, Sanskrit *puru*, Latin *plenus* full — more at FULL]
**1 :** many **:** several **:** much **:** MULTI- ⟨*poly*chotomous⟩ ⟨*poly*gyny⟩
**2 a :** containing an indefinite number more than one of a (specified) substance ⟨*poly*sulfide⟩ **b :** polymeric **:** polymer of a (specified) monomer ⟨*poly*ethylene⟩ ⟨*poly*adenylic acid⟩

**poly-A** \ˌpä-lē-'ā\ *noun* [*poly-* + *a*denylic acid] (1957)
**:** RNA or a segment of RNA that is composed of a polynucleotide chain consisting entirely of adenylic acid residues and that codes for polylysine when functioning as messenger RNA in protein synthesis

**poly·acryl·amide** \ˌpä-lē-ə-'kri-lə-ˌmīd\ *noun* (1944)
**:** a polyamide of acrylic acid

**poly·ac·ry·lo·ni·trile** \ˌpä-lē-ˌa-krə-lō-'nī-trəl, -ˌtrēl\ *noun* (1935)
**:** a polymer of acrylonitrile used often as fibers

**poly·ad·e·nyl·ic acid** \ˌpä-lē-ˌa-dᵊn-'i-lik\ *noun* (1956)
**:** POLYA

**poly·al·co·hol** \ˌpä-lē-'al-kə-ˌhȯl\ *noun* (1900)
**:** an alcohol (as a diol) that contains more than one hydroxyl group

**poly·am·ide** \ˌpä-lē-'a-ˌmīd, -məd\ *noun* [International Scientific Vocabulary] (1929)
**:** a compound characterized by more than one amide group; *especially* **:** a polymeric amide (as nylon)

**poly·amine** \'pä-lē-ə-ˌmēn, ˌpä-lē-'a-ˌmēn\ *noun* (1861)
**:** a compound characterized by more than one amino group

**poly·an·dry** \'pä-lē-ˌan-drē\ *noun* [Greek *polyandros*, adjective, having many husbands, from *poly-* + *andr-*, *anēr* man, husband — more at ANDR-] (1780)
**:** the state or practice of having more than one husband or male mate at one time — compare POLYGAMY, POLYGYNY
— **poly·an·drous** \ˌpä-lē-'an-drəs\ *adjective*

**poly·an·tha** \ˌpä-lē-'an(t)-thə\ *noun* [New Latin, from Greek *polyanthos* blooming] (1889)
**:** any of numerous dwarf hybrid roses characterized by many large clusters of small flowers

**poly·an·thus** \-'an(t)-thəs\ *noun, plural* **-an·thus·es** *or* **-an·thi** \-'an-ˌthī, -ˌthē\ [New Latin, from Greek *polyanthos* blooming, from *poly-* + *anthos* flower — more at ANTHOLOGY] (circa 1727)
**1 :** any of various hybrid primroses
**2 :** a narcissus (*Narcissus tazetta*) having small white or yellow flowers arranged in umbels and having a spreading perianth

**poly·atom·ic** \-ə-'tä-mik\ *adjective* [International Scientific Vocabulary] (1857)
**:** containing more than one and especially more than two atoms ⟨*polyatomic* molecules⟩

**poly·bro·mi·nat·ed biphenyl** \ˌpä-lē-'brō-mə-ˌnā-təd-\ *noun* (1975)
**:** any of several compounds that are similar to polychlorinated biphenyls in environmental toxicity and in structure but that have various hydrogen atoms replaced by bromine rather than chlorine — called also *PBB*

**poly·bu·ta·di·ene** \-ˌbyü-tə-'dī-ˌēn, -ˌdī-'\ *noun* (1939)
**:** a synthetic rubber that has a high resistance to wear and is used especially in the manufacture of tires

**poly·car·bon·ate** \-'kär-bə-ˌnāt, -nət\ *noun* (1930)
**:** any of various tough transparent thermoplastics characterized by high impact strength and high softening temperature

**poly·cen·tric** \-'sen-trik\ *adjective* (1887)
**:** having more than one center (as of development or control): as **a :** having several centromeres ⟨*polycentric* chromosomes⟩ ⟨*polycentric* cells⟩ **b :** characterized by polycentrism

**poly·cen·trism** \-'sen-ˌtri-zəm\ *noun* (1956)
**:** the existence of many centers of communist ideological thought; *especially* **:** the existence of a number of autonomous national communist movements

**poly·chaete** \'pä-lē-ˌkēt\ *noun* [ultimately from Greek *polychaitēs* having much hair, from *poly-* + *chaitē* long hair] (1896)
**:** any of a class (Polychaeta) of chiefly marine annelid worms (as clam worms) usually with paired segmental appendages, separate sexes, and a free-swimming trochophore larva
— **polychaete** *adjective*

**poly·chlo·ri·nat·ed biphenyl** \ˌpä-lē-'klȯr-ə-ˌnā-təd-, -'klȯr-\ *noun* (1962)
**:** any of several compounds that are produced by replacing hydrogen atoms in biphenyl with chlorine, have various industrial applications, and are poisonous environmental pollutants which tend to accumulate in animal tissues — called also *PCB*

**poly·chot·o·mous** \-'kä-tə-məs\ *adjective* [*poly-* + *-chotomous* (as in *dichotomous*)] (circa 1858)
**:** dividing or marked by division into many parts, branches, or classes
— **poly·chot·o·my** \-mē\ *noun*

**poly·chro·mat·ic** \-krō-'ma-tik\ *adjective* [Greek *polychrōmatos*, from *poly-* + *chrōmat-*, *chrōma* color — more at CHROMATIC] (circa 1841)

**1 :** showing a variety or a change of colors **:** MULTICOLORED
**2 :** being or relating to radiation that is composed of more than one wavelength

**poly·chro·mato·phil·ic** \-ˌkrō-ˌma-tə-'fi-lik\ *adjective* (1897)
**:** stainable with more than one type of stain and especially with both acid and basic dyes ⟨*polychromatophilic* erythroblasts⟩
— **poly·chro·mato·phil·ia** \-'fi-lē-ə\ *noun*

**poly·chrome** \'pä-lē-ˌkrōm\ *adjective* [Greek *polychrōmos*, from *poly-* + *chrōma*] (1837)
**:** relating to, made with, or decorated in several colors ⟨*polychrome* pottery⟩
— **polychrome** *transitive verb*
— **poly·chro·my** \-ˌkrō-mē\ *noun*

**poly·cis·tron·ic** \ˌpä-lē-sis-'trä-nik\ *adjective* (1963)
**:** containing the genetic information of a number of cistrons ⟨*polycistronic* messenger RNA⟩

**poly·clin·ic** \-'kli-nik\ *noun* [International Scientific Vocabulary] (circa 1890)
**:** a clinic or hospital treating diseases of many sorts

**poly·clon·al** \-'klō-nəl\ *adjective* (1914)
**:** produced by or being cells derived from two or more cells of different ancestry or genetic constitution ⟨*polyclonal* antibodies⟩

**poly·con·den·sa·tion** \-ˌkän-ˌden-'sā-shən, -dən-\ *noun* [International Scientific Vocabulary] (1936)
**:** a chemical condensation leading to the formation of a compound of high molecular weight

**poly·con·ic projection** \ˌpä-lē-'kä-nik-\ *noun* (circa 1864)
**:** a map projection consisting of a composite series of concentric cones each of which before being unrolled has been placed over a sphere so as to be tangent to a different parallel of latitude

**poly·crys·tal·line** \-'kris-tə-lən\ *adjective* (1918)
**1 :** consisting of crystals variously oriented
**2 :** composed of more than one crystal
— **poly·crys·tal** \'pä-lē-ˌkris-tᵊl\ *noun*

**poly·cy·clic** \ˌpä-lē-'sī-klik, -'si-\ *adjective* [International Scientific Vocabulary] (1869)
**:** having more than one cyclic component; *especially* **:** having two or more rings in the molecule

**poly·cys·tic** \-'sis-tik\ *adjective* (1872)
**:** having or involving more than one cyst ⟨*polycystic* kidneys⟩ ⟨*polycystic* disease⟩

**poly·cy·the·mia** \-ˌ(ˌ)sī-'thē-mē-ə\ *noun* [New Latin, from *poly-* + *cyt-* + *-hemia*] (circa 1857)
**:** a condition marked by an abnormal increase in the number of circulating red blood cells; *specifically* **:** POLYCYTHEMIA VERA
— **poly·cy·the·mic** \-mik\ *adjective*

**polycythemia ve·ra** \-'vir-ə\ *noun* [New Latin, true polycythemia] (circa 1925)
**:** polycythemia of unknown cause that is characterized by increase in total blood volume and accompanied by nosebleed, distension of the circulatory vessels, and enlargement of the spleen — called also *erythremia*

**poly·cyt·i·dyl·ic acid** \ˌpä-lē-ˌsi-tə-'di-lik-\ *noun* (1965)
**:** RNA or a segment of RNA that is composed of a polynucleotide chain consisting entirely of cytosine-containing nucleotides and that codes for a polypeptide chain consisting of proline residues when functioning as messenger RNA in protein synthesis

**poly·dac·tyl** \-'dak-tᵊl\ *adjective* [Greek *polydaktylos*, from *poly-* + *daktylos* digit] (circa 1890)
**:** having or causing polydactyly

**poly·dac·ty·ly** \-'dak-tᵊl-ē\ *noun* (1886)
**:** the condition of having more than the normal number of fingers or toes

**poly·dip·sia** \-'dip-sē-ə\ *noun* [New Latin, from *poly-* + Greek *dipsa* thirst] (1660)
**:** excessive or abnormal thirst

— **poly·dip·sic** \-sik\ *adjective*

**poly·dis·perse** \-dis-'pərs\ *adjective* [*poly-* + Latin *dispersus* dispersed, from past participle of *dispergere* to disperse] (1915)
: of, relating to, or characterized by or as particles of varied sizes in the dispersed phase of a disperse system

— **poly·dis·per·si·ty** \-'pər-sə-tē\ *noun*

**poly·elec·tro·lyte** \,pä-lē-ə-'lek-trə-,līt\ *noun* (circa 1947)
: a substance of high molecular weight (as a protein) that is an electrolyte

**poly·em·bry·o·ny** \-'em-brē-ə-nē, -(,)em-'brī-\ *noun* [International Scientific Vocabulary *poly-* + *embryon-* + ²-y] (1849)
**1** : the condition of having several embryos
**2** : the production of two or more embryos from one ovule or egg

— **poly·em·bry·on·ic** \-,em-brē-'ä-nik\ *adjective*

**poly·ene** \'pä-lē-,ēn\ *noun* [International Scientific Vocabulary] (1928)
: an organic compound containing many double bonds; *especially* : one having the double bonds in a long aliphatic hydrocarbon chain

— **poly·enic** \,pä-lē-'ē-nik\ *adjective*

¹**poly·es·ter** \'pä-lē-,es-tər, ,pä-lē-'\ *noun* [International Scientific Vocabulary] (1929)
: any of a group of polymers that consist basically of repeated units of an ester and are used especially in making fibers or plastics

— **poly·es·ter·i·fi·ca·tion** \-e-,ster-ə-fə-'kā-shən\ *noun*

²**polyester** *adjective* (1975)
: characterized by inelegant or unsophisticated middle-class taste ⟨*polyester* suburbs⟩ ⟨*polyester* folks⟩

**poly·es·trous** \,pä-lē-'es-trəs\ *adjective* (1900)
: having more than one period of estrus in a year

**poly·eth·yl·ene** \-'e-thə-,lēn\ *noun* (circa 1862)
: a polymer of ethylene; *especially* : any of various partially crystalline lightweight thermoplastics ($CH_2CH_2$)$_x$ that are resistant to chemicals and moisture, have good insulating properties, and are used especially in packaging and insulation

**po·lyg·a·la** \pə-'li-gə-lə\ *noun* [New Latin, genus name, from Latin, milkwort, from Greek *polygalon*, from *poly-* + *gala* milk — more at GALAXY] (1578)
: MILKWORT

**poly·gam·ic** \,pä-lē-'ga-mik\ *adjective* (1819)
: POLYGAMOUS

**po·lyg·a·mous** \pə-'li-gə-məs\ *adjective* [Greek *polygamos*, from *poly-* + *-gamos* -gamous] (1613)
**1 a** : relating to or practicing polygamy **b** : having more than one mate at one time ⟨baboons are *polygamous*⟩
**2** : bearing both hermaphrodite and unisexual flowers on the same plant

**po·lyg·a·my** \-mē\ *noun* (circa 1591)
**1** : marriage in which a spouse of either sex may have more than one mate at the same time — compare POLYANDRY, POLYGYNY
**2** : the state of being polygamous

— **po·lyg·a·mist** \-mist\ *noun*
— **po·lyg·a·mize** \-,mīz\ *intransitive verb*

**poly·gene** \'pä-lē-,jēn\ *noun* [International Scientific Vocabulary] (1941)
: any of a group of nonallelic genes that collectively control the inheritance of a quantitative character or modify the expression of a qualitative character

— **poly·gen·ic** \,pä-lē-'jē-nik\ *adjective*

**poly·gen·e·sis** \,pä-lē-'je-nə-səs\ *noun* [New Latin] (circa 1882)
: development from more than one source

**poly·ge·net·ic** \-jə-'ne-tik\ *adjective* (1861)
**1** : POLYPHYLETIC
**2** : having many distinct sources

¹**poly·glot** \'pä-lē-,glät\ *noun* [²*polyglot*] (circa 1645)

**1** : one who is polyglot
**2** *capitalized* : a book containing versions of the same text in several languages; *especially* : the Scriptures in several languages
**3** : a mixture or confusion of languages or nomenclatures

²**polyglot** *adjective* [Greek *polyglōttos*, from *poly-* + *glōtta* language — more at GLOSS] (1656)
**1 a** : speaking or writing several languages : MULTILINGUAL **b** : composed of numerous linguistic groups ⟨a *polyglot* population⟩
**2** : containing matter in several languages ⟨a *polyglot* sign⟩
**3** : composed of elements from different languages
**4** : being widely diverse (as in ethnic or cultural origins) ⟨*polyglot* cuisine⟩

**poly·glot·ism** *or* **poly·glot·tism** \-,glä-,ti-zəm\ *noun* (1882)
: the use of many languages : the ability to speak many languages

**poly·gon** \'pä-lē-,gän\ *noun* [Late Latin *polygonum*, from Greek *polygōnon*, from neuter of *polygōnos* polygonal, from *poly-* + *gō-nia* angle — more at -GON] (1571)
**1** : a closed plane figure bounded by straight lines
**2** : a closed figure on a sphere bounded by arcs of great circles

— **po·lyg·o·nal** \pə-'li-gə-n°l\ *adjective*
— **po·lyg·o·nal·ly** \-n°l-ē\ *adverb*

**po·lyg·o·num** \pə-'li-gə-nəm\ *noun* [New Latin, from Greek *polygonon* knotgrass, from *poly-* + *gony* knee — more at KNEE] (circa 1706)
: any of a genus (*Polygonum*) of herbs of the buckwheat family with a prominent tubular sheath around the base of each petiole, thickened nodes, and flowers that are solitary and axillary or in spiked racemes — called also *knotweed*

**poly·graph** \'pä-lē-,graf\ *noun* (1871)
: an instrument for recording variations of several different pulsations (as of physiological variables) simultaneously; *broadly* : LIE DETECTOR

— **poly·graph·ic** \,pä-lē-'gra-fik\ *adjective*

**po·lyg·ra·pher** \'pä-lē-,gra-fər, pə-'li-grə-fər\ *noun* (circa 1934)
: one who operates a polygraph

**po·lyg·ra·phist** \'pä-lē-,gra-fist, pə-'li-grə-fist\ *noun* (1954)
: POLYGRAPHER

**po·lyg·y·nous** \pə-'li-jə-nəs\ *adjective* (1874)
: relating to or practicing polygyny

**po·lyg·y·ny** \-nē\ *noun* (1780)
: the state or practice of having more than one wife or female mate at one time — compare POLYANDRY, POLYGAMY

**polyhedral angle** *noun* (circa 1864)
: a portion of space partly enclosed by three or more planes whose intersections meet in a vertex

**poly·he·dron** \,pä-lē-'hē-drən\ *noun*, *plural* **-drons** *or* **-dra** \-drə\ [New Latin] (1570)
: a solid formed by plane faces

— **poly·he·dral** \-drəl\ *adjective*

**poly·he·dro·sis** \,pä-lē-hē-'drō-səs\ *noun*, *plural* **-dro·ses** \-,sēz\ [New Latin, from *polyhedron*] (1947)
: any of several virus diseases of insect larvae characterized by dissolution of tissues and accumulation of polyhedral granules in the resultant fluid

**poly·his·tor** \,pä-lē-'his-tər\ *noun* [Greek *polyistōr* very learned, from *poly-* + *istōr*, *histōr* learned — more at HISTORY] (1588)
: POLYMATH

— **poly·his·tor·ic** \-his-'tòr-ik, -'tär-\ *adjective*

**poly·hy·droxy** \-hī-'dräk-sē\ *adjective* (circa 1929)
: containing more than one hydroxyl group in the molecule

**Poly·hym·nia** \,pä-lē-'him-nē-ə\ *noun* [Latin, from Greek *Polymnia*]
: the Greek Muse of sacred song

**poly I:C** \,pä-lē-'ī-'sē\ *or* **poly I·poly C** \,pä-lē-'ī-,pä-lē-'sē\ *noun* [*poly-* + *inosinic acid* + *cytidylic acid*] (1969)
: a synthetic 2-stranded RNA composed of one strand of polyinosinic acid and one strand of polycytidylic acid that induces interferon formation and has been used experimentally as an anticancer and antiviral agent

**poly·ino·sin·ic acid** \,pä-lē-,i-nə-'si-nik-, -,ī-nə-\ *noun* [*poly-* + *inosinic acid* ($C_{10}H_{13}N_4$-$O_8P$), from Greek *in-*, *is* sinew + International Scientific Vocabulary ²-*ose* + ¹-*in* + ¹-*ic* + *acid*] (1965)
: RNA or a segment of RNA that is composed of a polynucleotide chain consisting entirely of inosinic acid residues

**poly·ly·sine** \,pä-lē-'lī-,sēn\ *noun* (1947)
: a protein whose polypeptide chain consists entirely of lysine residues

**poly·math** \'pä-lē-,math\ *noun* [Greek *polymathēs* very learned, from *poly-* + *manthanein* to learn — more at MATHEMATICAL] (1621)
: a person of encyclopedic learning

— **polymath** *or* **poly·math·ic** \,pä-lē-'ma-thik\ *adjective*
— **po·ly·ma·thy** \pə-'li-mə-thē, 'pä-lə-,ma-thē\ *noun*

**poly·mer** \'pä-lē-mər\ *noun* [International Scientific Vocabulary, back-formation from *polymeric*, from Greek *polymerēs* having many parts, from *poly-* + *meros* part — more at MERIT] (1866)
: a chemical compound or mixture of compounds formed by polymerization and consisting essentially of repeating structural units

— **poly·mer·ic** \,pä-lə-'mer-ik\ *adjective*
— **poly·mer·ism** \pə-'li-mə-,ri-zəm, 'pä-lə-mə-\ *noun*

**poly·mer·ase** \'pä-lə-mə-,rās, -,rāz\ *noun* (1958)
: any of several enzymes that catalyze the formation of DNA or RNA from precursor substances in the presence of preexisting DNA or RNA acting as a template

**polymerase chain reaction** *noun* (1987)
: an in vitro technique for rapidly synthesizing large quantities of a given DNA segment that involves separating the DNA into its two complementary strands, using DNA polymerase to synthesize two-stranded DNA from each single strand, and repeating the process

**po·ly·mer·i·sa·tion, po·ly·mer·ise** *chiefly British variant of* POLYMERIZATION, POLYMERIZE

**po·ly·mer·i·za·tion** \pə-,li-mə-rə-'zā-shən, ,pä-lə-mə-rə-\ *noun* [International Scientific Vocabulary] (1872)
**1** : a chemical reaction in which two or more molecules combine to form larger molecules that contain repeating structural units — compare ASSOCIATION 5
**2** : reduplication of parts in an organism

**po·ly·mer·ize** \pə-'li-mə-,rīz, 'pä-lə-mə-\ *verb* **-ized; -iz·ing** (1865)
*transitive verb*
: to subject to polymerization
*intransitive verb*
: to undergo polymerization

**poly·meth·yl methacrylate** \'pä-lē-,me-thəl-\ *noun* (1936)
: a thermoplastic resin of polymerized methyl methacrylate which is characterized by its optical clarity (as in a contact lens)

**poly·morph** \'pä-lē-,mòrf\ *noun* [International Scientific Vocabulary] (circa 1828)
**1** : a polymorphic organism; *also* : one of the several forms of such an organism

\ə\ abut \ᵊ\ kitten \ər\ further \a\ ash \ā\ ace \ä\ mop, mar \aù\ out \ch\ chin \e\ bet \ē\ easy \g\ go \i\ hit \ī\ ice \j\ job \ŋ\ sing \ō\ go \ò\ law \òi\ boy \th\ thin \t̲h̲\ the \ü\ loot \ù\ foot \y\ yet \zh\ vision   *see also* Guide to Pronunciation

**2** : any of the crystalline forms of a polymorphic substance

**poly·mor·phism** \,pä-lē-'mor-,fi-zəm\ noun (1839)

: the quality or state of being able to assume different forms: as **a** : existence of a species in several forms independent of the variations of sex **b** : the property of crystallizing in two or more forms with distinct structure
— **poly·mor·phic** \-fik\ adjective
— **poly·mor·phi·cal·ly** \-fi-k(ə-)lē\ adverb
**poly·mor·pho·nu·cle·ar** \-,mor-fə-'nü-klē-ər, -'nyü-\ adjective (1897)
of a leukocyte : having the nucleus complexly lobed
— **polymorphonuclear** noun
**poly·mor·phous** \-'mor-fəs\ adjective [Greek polymorphous, from poly- + -morphos -morphous] (1785)
: having, assuming, or occurring in various forms, characters, or styles : POLYMORPHIC ⟨a polymorphous rash⟩ ⟨polymorphous sexuality⟩
— **poly·mor·phous·ly** adverb
**polymorphous perverse** adjective (1909)
: relating to or exhibiting infantile sexual tendencies in which the genitals are not yet identified as the sole or principal sexual organs nor coitus as the goal of erotic activity
**poly·myx·in** \,pä-lē-'mik-sən\ noun [International Scientific Vocabulary, from New Latin polymyxa, from poly- + Greek myxa mucus — more at MUCUS] (1947)
: any of several toxic antibiotics obtained from a soil bacterium (Bacillus polymyxa) and active against gram-negative bacteria
**Poly·ne·sian** \,pä-lə-'nē-zhən, -shən\ noun (1807)
**1** : a member of any of the indigenous peoples of Polynesia
**2** : a group of Austronesian languages spoken in Polynesia
— **Polynesian** adjective
**poly·neu·ri·tis** \,pä-lē-nú-'rī-təs, -nyù-\ noun [New Latin] (1886)
: neuritis of several peripheral nerves at the same time
**Poly·ni·ces** \,pä-lə-'nī-sēz\ noun [Latin, from Greek Polyneikēs]
: a son of Oedipus for whom the Seven against Thebes mount their expedition
**¹poly·no·mi·al** \,pä-lə-'nō-mē-əl\ noun [poly- + -nomial (as in binomial)] (1674)
: a mathematical expression of one or more algebraic terms each of which consists of a constant multiplied by one or more variables raised to a nonnegative integral power (as $a + bx + cx^2$)
**²polynomial** adjective (circa 1704)
: relating to, composed of, or expressed as one or more polynomials ⟨polynomial functions⟩ ⟨polynomial equations⟩
**poly·nu·cle·ar** \,pä-lē-'nü-klē-ər, -'nyü-, ÷-kyə-lər\ adjective [International Scientific Vocabulary] (1908)
: chemically polycyclic especially with respect to the benzene ring — used chiefly of aromatic hydrocarbons that are important as pollutants and possibly as carcinogens
**poly·nu·cle·o·tide** \-'nü-klē-ə-,tīd, -'nyü-\ noun [International Scientific Vocabulary] (1911)
: a polymeric chain of nucleotides
**po·lyn·ya** \,pä-lən-'yä\ noun, plural **polyn·yas** also **po·lyn·yi** \-'yē\ [Russian polyn'ya] (1853)
: an area of open water in sea ice
**poly·ole·fin** \,pä-lē-'ō-lə-fən\ noun (1930)
: a polymer of an alkene (as polyethylene)
**poly·oma virus** \,pä-lē-'ō-mə-\ noun [New Latin polyoma, from poly- + -oma] (1958)
: a papovavirus of rodents that is associated with various kinds of tumors — called also polyoma
**poly·on·y·mous** \,pä-lē-'ä-nə-məs\ adjective [Greek polyōnymos, from poly- + onoma, onyma name — more at NAME] (1678)

: having or known by various names
**pol·yp** \'pä-ləp\ noun [Middle French polype octopus, nasal tumor, from Latin polypus, from Greek polypous, from poly- + pous foot — more at FOOT] (1742)
**1** : a coelenterate that has typically a hollow cylindrical body closed and attached at one end and opening at the other by a central mouth surrounded by tentacles armed with nematocysts
**2** : a projecting mass of swollen and hypertrophied or tumorous membrane
— **pol·yp·oid** \-lə-,poid\ adjective
**poly·pep·tide** \,pä-lē-'pep-,tīd\ noun [International Scientific Vocabulary] (1903)
: a molecular chain of amino acids
— **poly·pep·tid·ic** \-(,)pep-'ti-dik\ adjective
**poly·pet·al·ous** \-'pe-t°l-əs\ adjective [New Latin polypetalus, from poly- + petalum petal] (circa 1704)
: having or consisting of separate petals
**poly·pha·gia** \-'fā-j(ē-)ə\ noun [Greek polyphagia, from polyphagos] (circa 1693)
: excessive appetite or eating
**po·lyph·a·gous** \pə-'li-fə-gəs\ adjective [Greek polyphagos eating too much, from poly- + -phagos -phagous] (1815)
: feeding on or utilizing many kinds of food
— **po·lyph·a·gy** \-jē\ noun
**poly·phase** \'pä-lē-,fāz\ adjective [International Scientific Vocabulary] (1891)
: having or producing two or more phases ⟨a polyphase machine⟩ ⟨a polyphase current⟩
**poly·pha·sic** \,pä-lē-'fā-zik\ adjective (1922)
: consisting of two or more phases
**Poly·phe·mus** \,pä-lē-'fē-məs\ noun [Latin, from Greek Polyphēmos]
: a Cyclops whom Odysseus blinds in order to escape from his cave
**poly·phe·nol** \,pä-lē-'fē-,nol, -fi-\ noun [International Scientific Vocabulary] (1894)
: a polyhydroxy phenol
— **poly·phe·no·lic** \-fi-'nō-lik, -'nä-\ adjective
**poly·phil·o·pro·gen·i·tive** \-,fi-lə-prō-'je-nə-tiv\ adjective (1919)
: extremely prolific : PHILOPROGENITIVE
**poly·phone** \'pä-lē-,fōn\ noun (1872)
: a symbol or sequence of symbols having more than one phonemic value (as a in English)
**poly·phon·ic** \,pä-lē-'fä-nik\ or **po·lyph·o·nous** \pə-'li-fə-nəs\ adjective (1782)
**1** : of, relating to, or marked by polyphony
**2** : being a polyphone
— **poly·phon·i·cal·ly** \,pä-lē-'fä-ni-k(ə-)lē\ or **po·lyph·o·nous·ly** adverb
**polyphonic prose** noun (1916)
: a freely rhythmical prose employing characteristic devices of verse (as alliteration and assonance)
**po·lyph·o·ny** \pə-'li-fə-nē\ noun [Greek polyphōnia variety of tones, from polyphōnos having many tones or voices, from poly- + phōnē voice — more at BAN] (circa 1864)
: a style of musical composition in which two or more independent melodies are juxtaposed in harmony
**poly·phy·let·ic** \,pä-lē-(,)fī-'le-tik\ adjective [International Scientific Vocabulary, from Greek polyphylos of many tribes, from poly- + phylē tribe — more at PHYL-] (1875)
: of, relating to, or derived from different ancestral stocks; specifically : relating to or being a taxonomic group that includes members (as genera or species) from different ancestral lineages
— **poly·phy·let·i·cal·ly** \-ti-k(ə-)lē\ adverb
**pol·yp·ide** \'pä-lə-,pīd\ noun [polyp + Greek -idēs, patronymic suffix] (1850)
: one of the individual zooids of a bryozoan colony
**poly·ploid** \'pä-lē-,ploid\ adjective [International Scientific Vocabulary] (1920)

: having or being a chromosome number that is a multiple greater than two of the monoploid number
— **polyploid** noun
— **poly·ploi·dy** \-,ploi-dē\ noun
**po·lyp·nea** \pä-'lip-nē-ə, pə-\ noun [New Latin] (circa 1890)
: rapid or panting respiration
**poly·po·dy** \'pä-lē-,pō-dē\ noun, plural **-dies** [Middle English polypodie, from Latin polypodium, from Greek polypodion, from poly- + pod-, pous foot — more at FOOT] (14th century)
: any of a genus (Polypodium) of chiefly epiphytic ferns with creeping rhizomes; especially : either of two ferns (P. vulgare of Eurasia and P. virginianum of North America) with relatively narrow entire segments

**polypody**

**poly·pro·pyl·ene** \,pä-lē-'prō-pə-,lēn\ noun (1935)
: any of various thermoplastic plastics or fibers that are polymers of propylene
**po·lyp·tych** \'pä-ləp-,tik, pə-'lip-tik\ noun [Greek polyptychos having many folds, from poly- + ptychē fold, from ptyssein to fold] (1859)
: an arrangement of four or more panels (as of a painting) usually hinged and folding together
**poly·rhythm** \'pä-lē-,ri-thəm\ noun (1929)
: the simultaneous combination of contrasting rhythms in music
— **poly·rhyth·mic** \,pä-lē-'rith-mik\ adjective
— **poly·rhyth·mi·cal·ly** \-mi-k(ə-)lē\ adverb
**poly·ri·bo·nu·cle·o·tide** \,pä-lē-,rī-bō-'nü-klē-ə-,tīd, -'nyü-\ noun (1956)
: a polynucleotide in which the mononucleotides are ribonucleotides
**poly·ri·bo·some** \-'rī-bə-,sōm\ noun (1962)
: a cluster of ribosomes linked together by a molecule of messenger RNA and forming the site of protein synthesis
— **poly·ri·bo·som·al** \-,rī-bə-'sō-məl\ adjective
**poly·sac·cha·ride** \-'sa-kə-,rīd\ noun [International Scientific Vocabulary] (1892)
: a carbohydrate that can be decomposed by hydrolysis into two or more molecules of monosaccharides; especially : any of the more complex carbohydrates (as cellulose, starch, or glycogen)
**po·ly·se·mous** \,pä-lē-'sē-məs, pə-'li-sə-məs\ adjective [Late Latin polysemus, from Greek polysēmos, from poly- + sēma sign] (1884)
: having multiple meanings
— **po·ly·se·my** \-mē\ noun
**poly·some** \'pä-lē-,sōm\ noun (1962)
: POLYRIBOSOME
**poly·sor·bate** \,pä-lē-'sor-,bāt\ noun (1950)
: any of several emulsifiers used in the preparation of some pharmaceuticals or foods
**po·lys·ti·chous** \pə-'lis-ti-kəs\ adjective [Greek polystichos, from poly- + stichos row — more at DISTICH] (circa 1890)
: arranged in several rows
**poly·sty·rene** \,pä-lē-'stī-,rēn\ noun (1927)
: a polymer of styrene; especially : a rigid transparent thermoplastic that has good physical and electrical insulating properties and is used especially in molded products, foams, and sheet materials
**poly·sul·fide** \-'səl-,fīd\ noun [International Scientific Vocabulary] (1849)
: a sulfide containing two or more atoms of sulfur in the molecule
**poly·syl·lab·ic** \-sə-'la-bik\ adjective [Medieval Latin polysyllabus, from Greek polysyllabos, from poly- + syllabē syllable] (1782)
**1** : having more than one and usually more than three syllables

**2 :** characterized by words of many syllables
— **poly·syl·lab·i·cal·ly** \-bi-k(ə-)lē\ *adverb*

**poly·syl·la·ble** \'pä-lē-ˌsi-lə-bəl, ˌpä-lē-'\ *noun* (modification of Medieval Latin *polysyllaba,* from feminine of *polysyllabus*] (1570)
: a polysyllabic word

**poly·syn·ap·tic** \ˌpä-lē-sə-'nap-tik\ *adjective* (1964)
: involving two or more synapses in the central nervous system ⟨*polysynaptic* reflexes⟩
— **poly·syn·ap·ti·cal·ly** \-ti-k(ə-)lē\ *adverb*

**poly·syn·de·ton** \-'sin-də-ˌtän\ *noun* [New Latin, from Late Greek, neuter of *polysyndetos* using many conjunctions, from Greek *poly-* + *syndetos* bound together, conjunctive — more at ASYNDETON] (circa 1577)
: repetition of conjunctions in close succession (as in *we have ships and men and money and stores*)

**¹poly·tech·nic** \-'tek-nik\ *adjective* [French *polytechnique,* from Greek *polytechnos* skilled in many arts, from *poly-* + *technē* art — more at TECHNICAL] (1805)
: relating to or devoted to instruction in many technical arts or applied sciences

**²polytechnic** *noun* (1836)
: a polytechnic school

**poly·tene** \'pä-lē-ˌtēn\ *adjective* [International Scientific Vocabulary] (1935)
: relating to, being, or having chromosomes each of which consists of many strands with the corresponding chromomeres in contact
— **poly·te·ny** \-ˌtē-nē\ *noun*

**poly·the·ism** \'pä-lē-(ˌ)thē-ˌi-zəm\ *noun* [French *polytheisme,* from Late Greek *polytheos* polytheistic, from Greek, of many gods, from *poly-* + *theos* god] (1613)
: belief in or worship of more than one god
— **poly·the·ist** \-ˌthē-ist\ *adjective or noun*
— **poly·the·is·tic** \ˌpä-lē-thē-'is-tik\ *also* **poly·the·is·ti·cal** \-'is-ti-kəl\ *adjective*

**poly·thene** \'pä-lə-ˌthēn\ *noun* [by contraction] (1939)
*chiefly British* : POLYETHYLENE

**poly·to·nal·i·ty** \ˌpä-lē-tō-'na-lə-tē\ *noun* (1923)
: the simultaneous use of two or more musical keys
— **poly·ton·al** \-'tō-nᵊl\ *adjective*
— **poly·ton·al·ly** \-nᵊl-ē\ *adverb*

**poly·typ·ic** \ˌpä-lē-'ti-pik\ *adjective* (1888)
: represented by several or many types or subdivisions ⟨a *polytypic* species of organism⟩

**poly·un·sat·u·rat·ed** \ˌpä-lē-ˌən-'sa-chə-ˌrā-təd\ *adjective* (1932)
*of an oil or fatty acid* : having many double or triple bonds in a molecule — compare MONOUNSATURATED

**poly·ure·thane** \ˌpä-lē-'yùr-ə-ˌthān\ *noun* [International Scientific Vocabulary] (1944)
: any of various polymers that contain NHCOO linkages and are used especially in flexible and rigid foams, elastomers, and resins (as for coatings)

**poly·uria** \-'yùr-ē-ə\ *noun* [New Latin] (circa 1842)
: excessive secretion of urine

**poly·va·lent** \-'vā-lənt *also* pə-'li-və-lənt\ *adjective* [International Scientific Vocabulary] (1881)
**1 :** having a chemical valence greater usually than two
**2 :** effective against, sensitive toward, or counteracting more than one exciting agent (as a toxin or antigen)
— **poly·va·lence** \-lən(t)s\ *noun*

**poly·vi·nyl** \ˌpä-lē-'vī-nᵊl\ *adjective* [International Scientific Vocabulary] (1927)
: of, relating to, or being a polymerized vinyl compound, resin, or plastic — often used in combination

**polyvinyl chloride** *noun* (1933)

: a polymer of vinyl chloride used especially for electrical insulation, films, and pipes — abbreviation *PVC*

**poly·wa·ter** \'pä-lē-ˌwȯ-tər, -ˌwä-\ *noun* [*polymeric water*] (1969)
: water condensed into a glass capillary tube and formerly held to be a stable form with special properties

**Pom** \'päm\ *noun* (1912)
*Australian & New Zealand* : POMMY — usually used disparagingly

**pom·ace** \'pə-məs, 'pä-\ *noun* [Middle English *pomys,* probably from Medieval Latin *pomacium* cider, from Late Latin *pomum* apple, from Latin, fruit] (15th century)
**1 :** the dry or pulpy residue of material (as fruit, seeds, or fish) from which a liquid (as juice or oil) has been pressed or extracted
**2 :** something crushed to a pulpy mass

**po·ma·ceous** \pō-'mā-shəs\ *adjective* [New Latin *pomaceus,* from Late Latin *pomum*] (1708)
**1 :** of or relating to apples
**2** [*pome*] : resembling a pome

**po·made** \pō-'mäd, -'mād\ *noun* [Middle French *pommade* ointment formerly made from apples, from Italian *pomata,* from *pomo* apple, from Late Latin *pomum*] (1562)
: a perfumed ointment; *especially* : a fragrant hair dressing
— **pomade** *transitive verb*

**po·man·der** \'pō-ˌman-dər, pō-'\ *noun* [Middle English, modification of Middle French *pome d'ambre,* literally, apple or ball of amber] (15th century)
**1 :** a mixture of aromatic substances enclosed in a perforated bag or box and used to scent clothes and linens or formerly carried as a guard against infection; *also* : a clove-studded orange or apple used for the same purposes
**2 :** a box or hollow fruit-shaped ball for holding pomander

**po·ma·tum** \pō-'mā-təm, -'mä-\ *noun* [New Latin, from Late Latin *pomum* apple] (1562)
: POMADE

**pome** \'pōm\ *noun* [Middle English, from Middle French *pome, pomme* apple, pome, ball, ultimately from Late Latin *pomum*] (15th century)
: a fleshy fruit (as an apple or pear) consisting of an outer thickened fleshy layer and a central core with usually five seeds enclosed in a capsule

**pome·gran·ate** \'pä-mə-ˌgra-nət; 'päm-ˌgra-nət, 'pəm-\ *noun* [Middle English *poumgrenet,* from Middle French *pomme grenate,* literally, seedy apple] (14th century)
**1 :** a thick-skinned several-celled reddish berry that is about the size of an orange and has many seeds with pulpy crimson arils of tart flavor
**2 :** a widely cultivated tropical Old World tree (*Punica granatum* of the family Punicaceae) bearing pomegranates

**pomegranate**

**pom·e·lo** \'pä-mə-ˌlō\ *noun,* plural **-los** [alteration of earlier *pompelmous,* from Dutch *pompelmoes*] (1858)
**1 :** GRAPEFRUIT
**2 :** SHADDOCK

**Pom·er·a·nian** \ˌpä-mə-'rā-nē-ən, -nyən\ *noun* (1760)
**1 :** any of a breed of very small compact long-haired dogs
**2 :** a native or inhabitant of Pomerania
— **Pomeranian** *adjective*

**pom·mée** \pä-'mā, ˌpə-\ *adjective* [French, from Middle French *pomme* apple, ball] (1725)
*of a heraldic cross* : having the end of each arm terminating in a ball or disk — see CROSS illustration

**¹pom·mel** \'pə-məl, 'pä-\ *noun* [Middle English *pomel,* from Middle French, from (assumed) Vulgar Latin *pomellum* ball, knob, from diminutive of Late Latin *pomum* apple] (14th century)
**1 :** the knob on the hilt of a sword or saber
**2 :** the protuberance at the front and top of a saddle
**3 :** either of a pair of removable rounded or U-shaped handles used on the top of a pommel horse

**²pom·mel** \'pə-məl\ *transitive verb* **-meled** *or* **-melled; -mel·ing** *or* **-mel·ling** \'pə-mə-liŋ, 'pəm-liŋ\ [¹*pommel*] (1530)
: PUMMEL

**pommel horse** *noun* (1908)
**1 :** a gymnastics apparatus for swinging and balancing feats that consists of a padded rectangular or cylindrical form with two pommels on the top and that is supported in a horizontal position above the floor
**2 :** an event in which the pommel horse is used

**pommel horse 1**

**Pom·my** *or* **Pom·mie** \'pä-mē\ *noun,* plural **Pommies** [by shortening & alteration from *pomegranate,* alteration of *Jimmy Grant,* rhyming slang for *immigrant*] (1912)
*Australian & New Zealand* : BRITON; *especially* : an English immigrant — usually used disparagingly

**Po·mo** \'pō-(ˌ)mō\ *noun,* plural **Pomo** *or* **Pomos** (1852)
: a member of an American Indian people of northern California

**po·mol·o·gy** \pō-'mä-lə-jē\ *noun* [New Latin *pomologia,* from Latin *pomum* fruit + *-logia* -logy] (1818)
: the science and practice of fruit growing
— **po·mo·log·i·cal** \ˌpō-mə-'lä-ji-kəl\ *adjective*
— **po·mol·o·gist** \pō-'mä-lə-jist\ *noun*

**pomp** \'pämp\ *noun* [Middle English, from Middle French *pompe,* from Latin *pompa* procession, pomp, from Greek *pompē* act of sending, escort, procession, pomp, from *pempein* to send] (14th century)
**1 :** a show of magnificence : SPLENDOR ⟨every day begins . . . in a *pomp* of flaming colours —F. D. Ommanney⟩
**2 :** a ceremonial or festival display (as a train of followers or a pageant)
**3 a :** ostentatious display : VAINGLORY **b :** an ostentatious gesture or act

**pom·pa·dour** \'päm-pə-ˌdȯr, -ˌdȯr\ *noun* [Marquise de *Pompadour*] (1756)
**1 a :** a man's style of hairdressing in which the hair is combed into a high mound in front **b :** a woman's style of hairdressing in which the hair is brushed into a loose full roll around the face
**2 :** hair dressed in a pompadour
— **pom·pa·doured** \-ˌdȯrd, -ˌdȯrd\ *adjective*

**pom·pa·no** \'päm-pə-ˌnō, 'pəm-\ *noun,* plural **-no** *or* **-nos** [American Spanish *pámpano,* from Spanish, a percoid fish (*Sparus auratus*), literally, vine leaf, from Latin *pampinus*] (1778)
**1 :** a carangid food fish (*Trachinotus carolinus*) of the southern Atlantic and Gulf coasts of North America; *broadly* : any of several related fishes
**2 :** a small bluish or greenish butterfish (*Peprilus simillimus*) of the Pacific coast

**¹pom–pom** \'päm-,päm\ *noun* [alteration of *pompon*] (1897)
**1 :** an ornamental ball or tuft used especially on clothing, caps, or costumes
**2 :** a handheld usually brightly colored fluffy ball flourished by cheerleaders

**²pom–pom** *noun* [imitative; from the sound of its discharge] (1899)
**:** a multibarreled automatic antiaircraft gun of 20 to 40 millimeters mounted especially on ships

**pom·pon** \'päm-,pän\ *noun* [French, from Middle French *pompe* tuft of ribbons] (1753)
**1 :** ¹POM-POM 1
**2 :** a chrysanthemum or dahlia with small rounded flower heads

**pom·pos·i·ty** \päm-'pä-sə-tē\ *noun, plural* **-ties** (1620)
**1 :** pompous demeanor, speech, or behavior
**2 :** a pompous gesture, habit, or act

**pomp·ous** \'päm-pəs\ *adjective* (15th century)
**1 :** excessively elevated or ornate ⟨*pompous* rhetoric⟩
**2 :** having or exhibiting self-importance **:** ARROGANT ⟨a *pompous* politician⟩
**3 :** relating to or suggestive of pomp **:** MAGNIFICENT
— **pomp·ous·ly** *adverb*
— **pomp·ous·ness** *noun*

**ponce** \'pän(t)s\ *noun* [origin unknown] (1872)
*British* **:** PIMP; *also* **:** a male homosexual — usually used disparagingly

**pon·cho** \'pän-(,)chō\ *noun, plural* **ponchos** [American Spanish, from Araucanian] (1717)
**1 :** a blanket with a slit in the middle so that it can be slipped over the head and worn as a sleeveless garment
**2 :** a waterproof garment resembling a poncho and having an integral hood

**¹pond** \'pänd\ *noun* [Middle English *ponde* artificially confined body of water, probably alteration of *pounde* enclosure — more at POUND] (14th century)
**:** a body of water usually smaller than a lake

**²pond** (1694)
*transitive verb*
**:** to block (as a stream) to create a pond
*intransitive verb*
**:** to collect in or form a pond

**pon·der** \'pän-dər\ *verb* **pon·dered; pon·der·ing** \-d(ə-)riŋ\ [Middle English, from Middle French *ponderer*, from Latin *ponderare* to weigh, ponder, from *ponder-, pondus* weight — more at PENDANT] (14th century)
*transitive verb*
**1 :** to weigh in the mind **:** APPRAISE ⟨*pondered* their chances of success⟩
**2 :** to think about **:** reflect on ⟨*pondered* the events of the day⟩
*intransitive verb*
**:** to think or consider especially quietly, soberly, and deeply ☆
— **pon·der·er** \-dər-ər\ *noun*

**pon·der·a·ble** \'pän-d(ə-)rə-bəl\ *adjective* [Late Latin *ponderabilis*, from *ponderare*] (1813)
**:** significant enough to be worth considering **:** APPRECIABLE
*synonym* see PERCEPTIBLE

**pon·der·o·sa pine** \,pän-də-'rō-sə-, -zə-\ *noun* [New Latin *ponderosa*, specific epithet of *Pinus ponderosa*, from Latin, feminine of *ponderosus* ponderous] (1878)
**:** a tall pine (*Pinus ponderosa*) of western North America with long needles usually in groups of 2 or 3; *also* **:** its strong reddish straight-grained wood — called also *ponderosa*

**pon·der·ous** \'pän-d(ə-)rəs\ *adjective* [Middle English, from Middle French *pondereux*, from Latin *ponderosus*, from *ponder-, pondus* weight] (15th century)
**1 :** of very great weight
**2 :** unwieldy or clumsy because of weight and size

**3 :** oppressively or unpleasantly dull **:** LIFELESS ⟨*ponderous* prose⟩
*synonym* see HEAVY
— **pon·der·ous·ly** *adverb*
— **pon·der·ous·ness** *noun*

**pond lily** *noun* (1748)
**:** WATER LILY

**pond scum** *noun* (circa 1890)
**1 :** SPIROGYRA; *also* **:** any of various related algae
**2 :** a mass of tangled algal filaments in stagnant waters

**pond skater** *noun* (1895)
**:** WATER STRIDER

**pond·weed** \'pänd-,wēd\ *noun* (1578)
**:** any of a genus (*Potamogeton* of the family Potamogetonaceae, the pondweed family) of aquatic plants with jointed usually rooting stems, 2-ranked floating or submerged leaves, and spikes of greenish flowers

**pone** \'pōn\ *noun* [modification of Virginia Algonquian *appone*] (1634)
*Southern & Midland* **:** CORN PONE

**pon·gee** \,pän-'jē, 'pän-,\ *noun, often attributive* [Chinese (Beijing) *běnjī*, from *běn* own + *jī* loom] (1711)
**:** a thin soft fabric of Chinese origin woven from raw silk; *also* **:** an imitation of this fabric in cotton or a synthetic fiber (as of polyester or rayon)

**pon·gid** \'pän-jəd, 'päŋ-gəd\ *noun* [ultimately from Kongo *mpongi* ape] (1950)
**:** any of a family (Pongidae) of apes that includes the chimpanzee, gorilla, and orangutan
— **pongid** *adjective*

**¹pon·iard** \'pän-yərd\ *noun* [Middle French *poignard*, from *poing* fist, from Latin *pugnus* fist — more at PUNGENT] (1588)
**:** a dagger with a usually slender blade of triangular or square cross section

**²poniard** *transitive verb* (1601)
**:** to pierce or kill with a poniard

**pons** \'pänz\ *noun, plural* **pon·tes** \'pän-,tēz\ [New Latin, short for *pons Varolii*] (1831)
**:** a broad mass of chiefly transverse nerve fibers conspicuous on the ventral surface of the brain of man and lower mammals at the anterior end of the medulla oblongata — see BRAIN illustration

**pons asi·no·rum** \'pänz-,a-sə-'nōr-əm, -'nȯr-\ *noun* [New Latin, literally, asses' bridge, name applied to the proposition that the base angles of an isosceles triangle are equal] (1751)
**:** a critical test of ability or understanding; *also* **:** STUMBLING BLOCK

**pons Va·ro·lii** \-və-'rō-lē-,ī, -lē-,ē\ *noun* [New Latin, literally, bridge of Varoli, from Costanzo *Varoli* (died 1575) Italian surgeon and anatomist] (circa 1693)
**:** PONS

**pon·ti·fex** \'pän-tə-,feks\ *noun, plural* **pon·tif·i·ces** \pän-'ti-fə-,sēz\ [Latin *pontific-, pontifex*, from *pont-, pons* bridge + *facere* to make — more at FIND, DO] (circa 1580)
**:** a member of the council of priests in ancient Rome

**pon·tiff** \'pän-təf\ *noun* [French *pontif*, from Latin *pontific-, pontifex*] (1626)
**1 :** PONTIFEX
**2 :** BISHOP; *specifically* **:** POPE

**¹pon·tif·i·cal** \pän-'ti-fi-kəl\ *noun* (14th century)
**1 :** episcopal attire; *specifically* **:** the insignia of the episcopal order worn by a prelate when celebrating a pontifical mass — usually used in plural
**2 :** a book containing the forms for sacraments and rites performed by a bishop

**²pontifical** *adjective* [Middle English, from Latin *pontificalis*, from *pontific-, pontifex*] (15th century)
**1 a :** of or relating to a pontiff or pontifex **b :** celebrated by a prelate of episcopal rank with distinctive ceremonies ⟨*pontifical* mass⟩
**2 :** POMPOUS
**3 :** pretentiously dogmatic

— **pon·tif·i·cal·ly** \-k(ə-)lē\ *adverb*

**¹pon·tif·i·cate** \pän-'ti-fi-kət, -,kāt\ *noun* [Middle English, from Latin *pontificatus*, from *pontific-, pontifex*] (15th century)
**:** the state, office, or term of office of a pontiff

**²pon·tif·i·cate** \pän-'ti-fə-,kāt\ *intransitive verb* **-cat·ed; -cat·ing** [Medieval Latin *pontificatus*, past participle of *pontificare*, from Latin *pontific-, pontifex*] (1818)
**1 a :** to officiate as a pontiff **b :** to celebrate pontifical mass
**2 :** to speak or express opinions in a pompous or dogmatic way
— **pon·tif·i·ca·tion** \(,)pän-,ti-fə-'kā-shən\ *noun*
— **pon·tif·i·ca·tor** \-,kā-tər\ *noun*

**pon·til** \'pän-t'l\ *noun* [French, perhaps from Italian *puntello*, diminutive of *punto* point, from Latin *punctus* — more at POINT] (1832)
**:** PUNTY — called also *pontil rod*

**pon·tine** \'pän-,tīn\ *adjective* [New Latin *pont-, pons* pons] (1889)
**:** of or relating to the pons

**Pont l'É·vêque** \,pōⁿ-lā-'vek\ *noun* [*Pont l'Évêque*, town in France] (circa 1889)
**:** a soft surface-ripened cheese firmer, yellower, and having less surface mold than Camembert

**¹pon·toon** \pän-'tün\ *noun* [French *ponton*, from Latin *ponton-, ponto*] (1690)
**1 :** a flat-bottomed boat (as a lighter); *especially* **:** a flat-bottomed boat or portable float used in building a floating temporary bridge
**2 :** a float especially of a seaplane

**²pontoon** *noun* [perhaps alteration of *vingt-et-un*] (circa 1917)
*British* **:** BLACKJACK 5

**po·ny** \'pō-nē\ *noun, plural* **ponies** [probably from obsolete French *poulenet*, diminutive of French *poulain* colt, from Medieval Latin *pullanus*, from Latin *pullus* young of an animal, foal — more at FOAL] (1659)
**1 a :** a small horse; *especially* **:** one of any of several breeds of very small stocky animals noted for their gentleness and endurance **b :** a bronco, mustang, or similar horse of the western U.S. **c :** RACEHORSE — usually used in plural
**2 :** something smaller than standard: as **a :** a small beer glass **b :** a small liqueur glass typically holding one ounce
**3 :** a literal translation of a foreign language text; *especially* **:** one used surreptitiously by students in preparing or reciting lessons

**pony express** *noun, often P&E capitalized* (1860)
**:** a rapid postal and express system that operated across the western U.S. in 1860–1861 by relays of horses and riders

**po·ny·tail** \'pō-nē-,tāl\ *noun* (1951)
**:** a hairstyle in which the hair is pulled together and banded at the back of the head so as to resemble a pony's tail
— **po·ny·tailed** \-,tāld\ *adjective*

**po·ny up** \'pō-nē-\ *verb* **po·nied up; po·ny·ing up** [origin unknown] (1824)
*transitive verb*

---

☆ **SYNONYMS**
**Ponder, meditate, muse, ruminate** mean to consider or examine attentively or deliberately. PONDER implies a careful weighing of a problem or, often, prolonged inconclusive thinking about a matter ⟨*pondered* the course of action⟩. MEDITATE implies a definite focusing of one's thoughts on something so as to understand it deeply ⟨*meditated* on the meaning of life⟩. MUSE suggests a more or less focused daydreaming as in remembrance ⟨*mused* upon childhood joys⟩. RUMINATE implies going over the same matter in one's thoughts again and again but suggests little of either purposive thinking or rapt absorption ⟨*ruminated* on past disappointments⟩.

**:** to pay (money) especially in settlement of an account ⟨*ponied up* $12.50 for the fine —*Newsweek*⟩
*intransitive verb*
**:** PAY

**Pon·zi scheme** \'pän-zē-\ *noun* [Charles A. *Ponzi* (died 1949) American (Italian-born) swindler] (1973)
**:** an investment swindle in which some early investors are paid off with money put up by later ones in order to encourage more and bigger risks

**-poo** \,pü, 'pü\ *suffix* [origin unknown]
— used as a disparaging diminutive ⟨cutesy-*poo*⟩

**¹pooch** \'püch\ *verb* [alteration of ¹*pouch*] (circa 1923)
*chiefly dialect* **:** BULGE

**²pooch** *noun* [origin unknown] (1924)
**:** DOG

**pood** \'püd, 'püt\ *noun* [Russian *pud*, from Old Russian, from Old Norse *pund* pound — more at POUND] (1554)
**:** a Russian unit of weight equal to about 36.11 pounds (16.38 kilograms)

**poo·dle** \'pü-d°l\ *noun* [German *Pudel*, short for *Pudelhund*, from *pudeln* to splash + *Hund* dog] (1820)
**1 :** a dog of any of three breeds of active intelligent heavy-coated solid-colored dogs — compare TOY POODLE
**2 :** a fabric with a nubby or coarsely looped surface that resembles a poodle's coat — called also *poodle cloth*

**¹poof** \'püf, 'pûf\ *interjection* (1824)
— used to express disdain or dismissal or to suggest instantaneous occurrence

**²poof** *also* **poove** \'püv, 'pûv\ *noun, plural* **poofs** *also* **pooves** [perhaps alteration of ²*puff*] (circa 1860)
*British* **:** a male homosexual — usually used disparagingly

**poof·ter** \'püf-tər, 'pûf-\ *also* **poof·tah** \-tə\ *noun* [by alteration] (1903)
*British* **:** POOF — usually used disparagingly

**pooh** \'pü, 'pû\ *interjection* (1602)
— used to express contempt or disapproval

**pooh–bah** *also* **poo–bah** \'pü-,bä, -,bô\ *noun, often P&B capitalized* [*Pooh-Bah*, character in Gilbert and Sullivan's opera *The Mikado* (1885) bearing the title Lord-High-Everything-Else] (1888)
**1 :** a person holding many public or private offices
**2 :** a person in high position or of great influence

**pooh–pooh** \'pü-(,)pü, pü-\ *also* **pooh** \'pü\ *verb* [*pooh*] (1827)
*intransitive verb*
**:** to express contempt or impatience
*transitive verb*
**:** to express contempt for or make light of **:** PLAY DOWN, DISMISS

**¹pool** \'pü(ə)l\ *noun* [Middle English, from Old English *pōl;* akin to Old High German *pfuol* pool] (before 12th century)
**1 a** (1) **:** a small and rather deep body of usually fresh water (2) **:** a quiet place in a stream (3) **:** a body of water forming above a dam **b :** something resembling a pool ⟨a *pool* of light⟩
**2 :** a small body of standing liquid
**3 :** a continuous area of porous sedimentary rock that yields petroleum or gas
**4 :** SWIMMING POOL

**²pool** *intransitive verb* (1626)
**1 :** to form a pool
**2** *of blood* **:** to accumulate or become static (as in the veins of a bodily part)

**³pool** *noun* [French *poule*, literally, hen, from Old French, feminine of *poul* cock — more at PULLET] (circa 1712)
**1 a :** an aggregate stake to which each player of a game has contributed **b :** all the money bet by a number of persons on a particular event

**2 a :** a game played on an English billiard table in which each of the players stakes a sum and the winner takes all **b :** any of various games of billiards played on an oblong table having 6 pockets with usually 15 object balls
**3 :** an aggregation of the interests or property of different persons made to further a joint undertaking by subjecting them to the same control and a common liability
**4 :** a readily available supply: as **a :** the whole quantity of a particular material present in the body and available for function or the satisfying of metabolic demands **b :** a body product (as blood) collected from many donors and stored for later use **c :** a group of people available for some purpose ⟨a shrinking *pool* of applicants⟩ ⟨typing *pool*⟩
**5 :** GENE POOL

**⁴pool** *transitive verb* (1879)
**:** to combine (as resources) in a common fund or effort

**pool·room** \'pü(ə)l-,rüm, -,rûm\ *noun* (1861)
**1 :** a room in which bookmaking is carried on
**2 :** a room for the playing of pool

**pool·side** \-,sīd\ *noun* (1921)
**:** the area surrounding a swimming pool

**¹poop** \'püp\ *noun* [Middle English, from Middle French *poupe*, from Latin *puppis*] (15th century)
**1** *obsolete* **:** STERN
**2 :** an enclosed superstructure at the stern of a ship above the main deck

**²poop** *transitive verb* (1748)
**1 :** to break over the stern of
**2 :** to ship (a sea or wave) over the stern

**³poop** *verb* [origin unknown] (circa 1932)
*transitive verb*
*slang* **:** to put out of breath; *also* **:** to tire out
*intransitive verb*
*slang* **:** to become exhausted ⟨*poop* out⟩

**⁴poop** *noun* [perhaps from ⁵*poop*] (circa 1941)
*slang* **:** INFORMATION, SCOOP

**⁵poop** *noun* [*poop*, verb, to defecate, break wind, from Middle English *poupen* to make a gulping sound; of imitative origin] (1965)
**:** EXCREMENT

**poop deck** *noun* (1840)
**:** a partial deck above a ship's main afterdeck

**poop·er–scoop·er** \'pü-pər-,skü-pər\ *noun* [⁵*poop*] (1976)
**:** a device used for picking up the droppings of a pet (as a dog) for disposal

**poor** \'pûr, 'pōr\ *adjective* [Middle English *poure*, from Old French *povre*, from Latin *pauper;* akin to Latin *pauc*us little and to Latin *parere* to give birth to, produce — more at FEW, PARE] (13th century)
**1 a :** lacking material possessions **b :** of, relating to, or characterized by poverty
**2 a :** less than adequate **:** MEAGER **b :** small in worth
**3 :** exciting pity ⟨you *poor* thing⟩
**4 a :** inferior in quality or value **b :** HUMBLE, UNPRETENTIOUS **c :** MEAN, PETTY
**5 :** LEAN, EMACIATED
**6 :** BARREN, UNPRODUCTIVE — used of land
**7 :** INDIFFERENT, UNFAVORABLE
**8 :** lacking a normal or adequate supply of something specified — often used in combination ⟨oil-*poor* countries⟩
— **poor·ish** \-ish\ *adjective*
— **poor·ness** *noun*

**poor box** *noun* (1621)
**:** a box (as in a church) for alms for the poor

**poor boy** \'pō(r)-,bôi\ *noun* (circa 1941)
**:** SUBMARINE 2

**Poor Clare** \-'klar, -'kler\ *noun* (1608)
**:** a member of an austere order of nuns founded by Saint Clare under the direction of Saint Francis in Assisi, Italy, in 1212

**poor farm** \'pûr-,färm, 'pōr-\ *noun* (1852)
**:** a farm maintained at public expense for the support and employment of needy persons

**poor·house** \-,haûs\ *noun* (1792)
**:** a place maintained at public expense to house needy or dependent persons

**poor law** *noun* (1752)
**:** a law providing for or regulating the public relief or support of the poor

**¹poor·ly** \'pûr-lē, 'pōr-\ *adverb* (13th century)
**:** in a poor condition or manner; *especially* **:** in an inferior or imperfect way **:** BADLY ⟨sang *poorly*⟩

**²poor·ly** *adjective* (1750)
**:** somewhat ill **:** INDISPOSED

**poor–mouth** \'pûr-,maûth, 'pōr-, -,maûth\ (1964)
*intransitive verb*
**:** to plead poverty as a defense or excuse
*transitive verb*
**:** to speak disparagingly of

**poor mouth** \-,maûth\ *noun* (1822)
**:** an exaggerated claim of poverty

**poor–spir·it·ed** \-'spir-ə-təd\ *adjective* (1670)
**:** lacking zest, confidence, or courage
— **poor–spir·it·ed·ly** *adverb*
— **poor–spir·it·ed·ness** *noun*

**poor white** *noun* (1819)
**:** a member of an inferior or underprivileged white social group — often taken to be offensive

**¹pop** \'päp\ *verb* **popped; pop·ping** [Middle English *poppen*, of imitative origin] (15th century)
*transitive verb*
**1 :** to strike or knock sharply **:** HIT
**2 :** to push, put, or thrust suddenly and often deftly
**3 :** to cause to explode or burst open
**4 :** to fire at **:** SHOOT
**5 :** to take (pills) especially frequently or habitually
**6 :** to open with a pop ⟨*pop* a cold beer⟩
*intransitive verb*
**1 a :** to go, come, or appear suddenly — often used with *up* **b :** to escape or break away from something (as a point of attachment) usually suddenly or unexpectedly
**2 :** to make or burst with a sharp sound **:** EXPLODE
**3 :** to protrude from the sockets
**4 :** to shoot with a firearm
**5 :** to hit a pop fly — often used with *up* or *out*
— **pop the question :** to propose marriage

**²pop** *noun* (1591)
**1 :** a sharp explosive sound
**2 :** a shot from a gun
**3 :** SODA POP
**4 :** POP FLY
— **a pop :** for each one **:** APIECE ⟨tickets at $10 *a pop*⟩

**³pop** *adverb* (1621)
**:** like or with a pop **:** SUDDENLY

**⁴pop** *noun* [short for *poppa*] (1838)
**:** FATHER

**⁵pop** *adjective* [by shortening] (1880)
**1 :** POPULAR ⟨*pop* music⟩: as **a :** of or relating to popular music ⟨*pop* singer⟩ **b :** of or relating to the popular culture disseminated through the mass media ⟨*pop* psychology⟩ ⟨*pop* grammarians⟩ ⟨*pop* society⟩
**2 a :** of or relating to pop art ⟨*pop* painter⟩ **b :** having, using, or imitating themes or techniques characteristic of pop art ⟨*pop* movie⟩

**⁶pop** *noun* (1954)
**1 :** pop music
**2 :** POP ART
**3 :** pop culture

**pop art** *noun* (1957)
**:** art in which commonplace objects (as road signs, hamburgers, comic strips, or soup cans)

\ə\ abut \ə\ kitten \ər\ **further** \a\ ash \ā\ **ace**
\ä\ mop, mar \aû\ **out** \ch\ **chin** \e\ bet \ē\ **easy**
\g\ go \i\ hit \ī\ **ice** \j\ **job** \ŋ\ **sing** \ō\ **go**
\ô\ law \ôi\ **boy** \th\ **thin** \th\ **the** \ü\ **loot** \û\ **foot**
\y\ yet \zh\ **vision** *see also* Guide to Pronunciation

are used as subject matter and are often physically incorporated in the work
— **pop artist** *noun*

**pop·corn** \'päp-ˌkòrn\ *noun* (1823)
: an Indian corn (*Zea mays praecox*) whose kernels on exposure to heat burst open to form a white starchy mass; *also* : the kernels especially after popping

**pope** \'pōp\ *noun* [Middle English, from Old English *pāpa*, from Late Latin *papa*, from Greek *pappas, papas*, title of bishops, literally, papa] (before 12th century)
**1** *often capitalized* : a prelate who as bishop of Rome is the head of the Roman Catholic Church
**2** : one that resembles a pope (as in authority)
**3 a** : the Eastern Orthodox or Coptic patriarch of Alexandria **b** : a priest of an Eastern church

**pop·ery** \'pō-p(ə-)rē\ *noun* (circa 1534)
: ROMAN CATHOLICISM — usually used disparagingly

**pop eye** \'päp-ˌī\ *noun* [back-formation from *pop-eyed*] (1828)
: an eye staring and bulging (as from excitement)
— **pop–eyed** \-ˌīd\ *adjective*

**pop fly** *noun* (1887)
: a high fly ball in baseball

**pop·gun** \'päp-ˌgən\ *noun* (1622)
: a toy gun that usually shoots a cork and produces a popping sound

**pop·in·jay** \'pä-pən-ˌjā\ *noun* [Middle English *papejay* parrot, from Middle French *papegai, papejai*, from Arabic *babghā'*] (1528)
: a strutting supercilious person

**pop·ish** \'pō-pish\ *adjective* [*pope*] (1528)
: ROMAN CATHOLIC — often used disparagingly

**pop·lar** \'pä-plər\ *noun* [Middle English *poplere*, from Middle French *pouplier*, from *pouple* poplar, from Latin *populus*] (14th century)
**1 a** : any of a genus (*Populus*) of slender catkin-bearing quick-growing trees (as an aspen or cottonwood) of the willow family **b** : the wood of a poplar
**2** : TULIP TREE 1

**pop·lin** \'pä-plən\ *noun* [French *papeline*] (1710)
: a strong fabric in plain weave with crosswise ribs

**pop·li·te·al** \ˌpä-plə-'tē-əl *also* pä-'pli-tē-əl\ *adjective* [New Latin *popliteus*, from Latin *poplit-, poples* ham of the knee] (1786)
: of or relating to the back part of the leg behind the knee joint

**pop off** *intransitive verb* (1764)
**1 a** : to die unexpectedly **b** : to leave suddenly
**2** : to talk thoughtlessly and often loudly or angrily

**pop·over** \'päp-ˌō-vər\ *noun* (1876)
: a hollow quick bread shaped like a muffin and made from a thin batter of eggs, milk, and flour

**pop·pa** \'pä-pə\ *variant of* PAPA

**pop·per** \'pä-pər\ *noun* (1750)
**1** : one that pops; *especially* : a utensil for popping corn
**2** *slang* : a vial of amyl nitrite or butyl nitrite especially when used illicitly as an aphrodisiac

**pop·pet** \'pä-pət\ *noun* [Middle English *popet* — more at PUPPET] (15th century)
**1 a** *Midland* : DOLL **b** *obsolete* : MARIONETTE
**2** *chiefly British* : DEAR
**3 a** : an upright support or guide of a machine that is fastened at the bottom only **b** : a valve that rises perpendicularly to or from its seat

**pop·pied** \'pä-pēd\ *adjective* (1818)
**1** *archaic* : growing or overgrown with poppies
**2** : DROWSY

**¹pop·ple** \'pä-pəl\ *noun* [Middle English *popul*, from Old English, from Latin *populus*] (14th century)
*chiefly dialect* : POPLAR 1

**²popple** *noun* [*popple*, verb, from Middle English *poplen* to bubble, ripple, probably of imitative origin] (1875)
: a choppy sea

**pop·py** \'pä-pē\ *noun, plural* **poppies** [Middle English *popi*, from Old English *popæg, popig*, modification of Latin *papaver*] (before 12th century)
**1 a** : any of a genus (*Papaver* of the family Papaveraceae, the poppy family) of chiefly annual or perennial herbs with milky juice, showy regular flowers, and capsular fruits including the opium poppy and several forms cultivated as ornamentals **b** : an extract or decoction of poppy used medicinally
**2** : a strong reddish orange

**pop·py·cock** \'pä-pē-ˌkäk\ *noun* [Dutch dialect *pappekak*, literally, soft dung, from Dutch *pap* pap + *kak* dung] (1865)
: empty talk or writing : NONSENSE

**pop·py·head** \-ˌhed\ *noun* (1839)
: a raised ornament often in the form of a finial generally used on the tops of the upright ends of seats in Gothic churches

**poppy seed** *noun* (14th century)
: the seed of a poppy used chiefly as a topping or flavoring for baked goods

**pop quiz** *noun* (circa 1960)
: an unscheduled or unannounced quiz

**Pop·si·cle** \'päp-ˌsi-kəl, -sə-\ *trademark*
— used for flavored and colored water frozen on a stick

**pop–top** \'päp-ˌtäp\ *noun* (1965)
: a closure that can be pulled by hand to open a can

**pop·u·lace** \'pä-pyə-ləs\ *noun* [Middle French, from Italian *popolaccio* rabble, augmentative of *popolo* the people, from Latin *populus*] (1572)
**1** : the common people : MASSES
**2** : POPULATION

**pop·u·lar** \'pä-pyə-lər\ *adjective* [Latin *popularis*, from *populus* the people, a people] (1548)
**1** : of or relating to the general public
**2** : suitable to the majority: as **a** : adapted to or indicative of the understanding and taste of the majority ⟨a *popular* history of the war⟩ **b** : suited to the means of the majority : INEXPENSIVE ⟨sold at *popular* prices⟩
**3** : frequently encountered or widely accepted
**4** : commonly liked or approved ⟨a very *popular* girl⟩
**synonym** see COMMON
— **pop·u·lar·ly** *adverb*

**popular front** *noun, often P&F capitalized* (1936)
: a coalition especially of leftist political parties against a common opponent; *specifically* : one sponsored and dominated by Communists as a device for gaining power

**pop·u·lar·ise** *British variant of* POPULARIZE

**pop·u·lar·i·ty** \ˌpä-pyə-'lar-ə-tē\ *noun* (1601)
: the quality or state of being popular

**pop·u·lar·ize** \'pä-pyə-lə-ˌrīz\ *verb* **-ized; -iz·ing** (1593)
*intransitive verb*
: to cater to popular taste
*transitive verb*
: to make popular: as **a** : to cause to be liked or esteemed **b** : to present in generally understandable or interesting form
— **pop·u·lar·i·za·tion** \ˌpä-pyə-lə-rə-'zā-shən\ *noun*
— **pop·u·lar·iz·er** \'pä-pyə-lə-ˌrī-zər\ *noun*

**popular sovereignty** *noun* (1848)
**1** : a doctrine in political theory that government is created by and subject to the will of the people
**2** : a pre-Civil War doctrine asserting the right of the people living in a newly organized territory to decide by vote of their territorial legislature whether or not slavery would be permitted there

**pop·u·late** \'pä-pyə-ˌlāt\ *transitive verb* **-lat·ed; -lat·ing** [Medieval Latin *populatus*, past

participle of *populare* to people, from Latin *populus* people] (1578)
**1** : to have a place in : OCCUPY, INHABIT
**2 a** : to furnish or provide with inhabitants : PEOPLE **b** : to provide with members

**pop·u·la·tion** \ˌpä-pyə-'lā-shən\ *noun* [Late Latin *population-, populatio*, from Latin *populus*] (1612)
**1 a** : the whole number of people or inhabitants in a country or region **b** : the total of individuals occupying an area or making up a whole **c** : the total of particles at a particular energy level — used especially of atoms in a laser
**2** : the act or process of populating
**3 a** : a body of persons or individuals having a quality or characteristic in common **b** (1) : the organisms inhabiting a particular locality (2) : a group of interbreeding organisms that represents the level of organization at which speciation begins
**4** : a group of individual persons, objects, or items from which samples are taken for statistical measurement
— **pop·u·la·tion·al** \-shnəl, -shə-nᵊl\ *adjective*

**population explosion** *noun* (1953)
: a pyramiding of numbers of a biological population; *especially* : the recent great increase in human numbers resulting from increased survival and exponential population growth

**¹pop·u·list** \'pä-pyə-list\ *noun* [Latin *populus* the people] (1892)
**1** : a member of a political party claiming to represent the common people; *especially, often capitalized* : a member of a U.S. political party formed in 1891 primarily to represent agrarian interests and to advocate the free coinage of silver and government control of monopolies
**2** : a believer in the rights, wisdom, or virtues of the common people
— **pop·u·lism** \-ˌli-zəm\ *noun*
— **pop·u·lis·tic** \ˌpä-pyə-'lis-tik\ *adjective*

**²populist** *adjective* (1893)
**1** *often capitalized* : of, relating to, or characterized by populism
**2** : POPULAR 1, 2

**pop·u·lous** \'pä-pyə-ləs\ *adjective* [Middle English, from Latin *populosus*, from *populus* people] (15th century)
**1 a** : densely populated **b** : having a large population
**2 a** : NUMEROUS **b** : filled to capacity
— **pop·u·lous·ly** *adverb*
— **pop·u·lous·ness** *noun*

**pop–up** \'päp-ˌəp\ *noun* (1906)
: POP FLY

**por·bea·gle** \'pòr-ˌbē-gəl\ *noun* [Cornish *porgh-bugel*] (1758)
: a small viviparous shark (*Lamna nasus*) chiefly of the North Atlantic Ocean with a pointed nose and crescent-shaped tail

**por·ce·lain** \'pōr-s(ə-)lən, 'pòr-\ *noun* [Middle French *porcelaine* cowrie shell, porcelain, from Italian *porcellana*, from *porcello* vulva, literally, little pig, from Latin *porcellus*, diminutive of *porcus* pig, vulva; from the shape of the shell — more at FARROW] (circa 1530)
: a hard, fine-grained, sonorous, nonporous, and usually translucent and white ceramic ware that consists essentially of kaolin, quartz, and feldspar and is fired at high temperatures
— **por·ce·lain·like** \-ˌlīk\ *adjective*
— **por·ce·la·ne·ous** *or* **por·cel·la·ne·ous** \ˌpōr-sə-'lā-nē-əs, ˌpòr-\ *adjective*

**porcelain enamel** *noun* (1883)
: a fired-on opaque glassy coating on metal (as steel)

**por·ce·lain·ize** \'pōr-s(ə-)lə-ˌnīz, 'pòr-\ *transitive verb* **-ized; -iz·ing** (1951)
: to fire a glassy coating on (as steel)

**porch** \'pōrch, 'pòrch\ *noun* [Middle English *porche*, from Old French, from Latin *porticus* portico, from *porta* gate; akin to Latin *portus* port — more at FORD] (14th century)

**1 :** a covered area adjoining an entrance to a building and usually having a separate roof

**2** *obsolete* **:** PORTICO

**por·cine** \'pȯr-ˌsīn\ *adjective* [Latin *porcinus*, from *porcus* pig — more at FARROW] (circa 1656)

**:** of, relating to, or suggesting swine

**por·ci·no** \pȯr-'chē-(ˌ)nō\ *noun, plural* **-ni** \-(ˌ)nē\ [Italian, short for *fungo porcino*, literally, porcine mushroom] (1976)

**:** a wild edible boletus mushroom (especially *Boletus edulis*)

**por·cu·pine** \'pȯr-kyə-ˌpīn\ *noun, plural* **porcupines** *also* **porcupine** [Middle English *porkepin*, from Middle French *porc espin*, from Old Italian *porcospino*, from Latin *porcus* pig + *spina* spine, prickle] (15th century)

**:** any of various relatively large rodents having stiff sharp erectile bristles mingled with the hair and constituting an Old World terrestrial family (Hystricidae) and a New World arboreal family (Erethizontidae)

**porcupine fish** *noun* (1681)

**:** any of several bony fishes (family Diodontidae) having sharp spines covering the body; *especially* **:** a spotted chiefly tropical fish (*Diodon hystrix*) that is olive to brown above with white below

**¹pore** \'pȯr, 'pȯr\ *intransitive verb* **pored; por·ing** [Middle English *pouren*] (13th century)

**1 :** to gaze intently

**2 :** to read studiously or attentively — usually used with *over*

**3 :** to reflect or meditate steadily

**²pore** *noun* [Middle English, from Middle French, from Latin *porus*, from Greek *poros* passage, pore — more at FARE] (14th century)

**1 :** a minute opening especially in an animal or plant; *especially* **:** one by which matter passes through a membrane

**2 :** a small interstice (as in soil) admitting absorption or passage of liquid

— **pored** \'pȯrd, 'pȯrd\ *adjective*

**pore fungus** *noun* (1922)

**:** a fungus (family Boletaceae or Polyporaceae) having the spore-bearing surface within tubes or pores

**por·gy** \'pȯr-gē\ *noun, plural* **porgies** *also* **porgy** [alteration of *pargo*, from Spanish & Portuguese, from Latin *phager*, from Greek *phagros*] (1671)

**1 :** a blue-spotted crimson food fish (*Pagrus pagrus* of the family Sparidae) of the eastern and western Atlantic; *also* **:** any of various fishes of the same family

**2** [alteration of *pogy*] **:** any of various bony fishes (as a menhaden) of families other than that of the porgy

**pork** \'pȯrk, 'pȯrk\ *noun* [Middle English, from Old French *porc* pig, from Latin *porcus* — more at FARROW] (14th century)

**1 :** the fresh or salted flesh of swine when dressed for food

**2 :** government money, jobs, or favors used by politicians as patronage

**pork barrel** *noun* (1909)

**:** government projects or appropriations yielding rich patronage benefits; *also* **:** PORK 2

**pork belly** *noun* (circa 1950)

**:** an uncured side of pork

**pork·er** \'pȯr-kər, 'pȯr-\ *noun* (1657)

**:** HOG; *especially* **:** a young pig fattened for table use as fresh pork

**pork·pie hat** \'pȯrk-ˌpī-, 'pȯrk-\ *noun* [from its shape] (1860)

**:** a hat with a low telescoped crown, flat top, and brim turned up all around or up in back and down in front

**¹porky** \'pȯr-kē, 'pȯr-\ *adjective* **pork·i·er; -est** (1852)

**:** resembling a pig **:** FAT

**²por·ky** \'pȯr-kē\ *noun, plural* **porkies** (1900)

**:** PORCUPINE

**porn** \'pȯrn\ *also* **por·no** \'pȯr-(ˌ)nō\ *noun, often attributive* (1962)

**:** PORNOGRAPHY

**por·nog·ra·pher** \pȯr-'nä-grə-fər\ *noun* (1850)

**:** one who produces pornography

**por·nog·ra·phy** \-fē\ *noun* [Greek *pornographos*, adjective, writing about prostitutes, from *pornē* prostitute + *graphein* to write; akin to Greek *pernanai* to sell, *poros* journey — more at FARE, CARVE] (circa 1864)

**1 :** the depiction of erotic behavior (as in pictures or writing) intended to cause sexual excitement

**2 :** material (as books or a photograph) that depicts erotic behavior and is intended to cause sexual excitement

**3 :** the depiction of acts in a sensational manner so as to arouse a quick intense emotional reaction ⟨the *pornography* of violence⟩

— **por·no·graph·ic** \ˌpȯr-nə-'gra-fik\ *adjective*

— **por·no·graph·i·cal·ly** \-fi-k(ə-)lē\ *adverb*

**porny** \'pȯr-nē\ *adjective* **porn·i·er; -est** (1961)

**:** of, relating to, involved in, or being pornography

**po·ros·i·ty** \pə-'rä-sə-tē, pȯ-\ *noun, plural* **-ties** (14th century)

**1 a :** the quality or state of being porous **b :** the ratio of the volume of interstices of a material to the volume of its mass

**2 :** PORE

**po·rous** \'pȯr-əs, 'pȯr-\ *adjective* (14th century)

**1 a :** possessing or full of pores **b :** containing vessels ⟨hardwood is *porous*⟩

**2 a :** permeable to fluids **b :** permeable to outside influences ⟨his imagination is astonishingly *porous* —Elizabeth Hardwick⟩

**3 :** capable of being penetrated ⟨*porous* national boundaries⟩ ⟨a *porous* defense⟩

— **po·rous·ly** *adverb*

— **po·rous·ness** *noun*

**por·phyr·ia** \pȯr-'fir-ē-ə\ *noun* [New Latin, from International Scientific Vocabulary *porphyrin*] (1923)

**:** any of several usually hereditary abnormalities of porphyrin metabolism characterized by excretion of excess porphyrins in the urine

**por·phy·rin** \'pȯr-fə-rən\ *noun* [International Scientific Vocabulary, from Greek *porphyra* purple] (1910)

**:** any of various compounds with a structure that consists essentially of four pyrrole rings joined by four =CH— groups; *especially* **:** one (as chlorophyll or hemoglobin) containing a central metal atom and usually exhibiting biological activity

**por·phy·rit·ic** \ˌpȯr-fə-'ri-tik\ *adjective* [Medieval Latin *porphyriticus*, from Greek *porphyritikos*, from *porphyrītēs* (*lithos*) porphyry] (15th century)

**1 :** of or relating to porphyry

**2 :** having distinct crystals (as of feldspar) in a relatively fine-grained base

**por·phy·rop·sin** \ˌpȯr-fə-'räp-sən\ *noun* [Greek *porphyra* purple + English -opsin (as in *rhodopsin*)] (1930)

**:** a purple pigment in the retinal rods of freshwater fishes that resembles rhodopsin

**por·phy·ry** \'pȯr-f(ə-)rē\ *noun, plural* **-ries** [Middle English *porphiri*, from Medieval Latin *porphyrium*, alteration of Latin *porphyrites*, from Greek *porphyrītēs* (*lithos*), literally, stone like Tyrian purple, from *porphyra* purple] (15th century)

**1 :** a rock consisting of feldspar crystals embedded in a compact dark red or purple groundmass

**2 :** an igneous rock of porphyritic texture

**por·poise** \'pȯr-pəs\ *noun* [Middle English

*porpoys*, from Middle French *porpois*, from Medieval Latin *porcopiscis*, from Latin *porcus* pig + *piscis* fish — more at FARROW, FISH] (14th century)

**1 :** any of a family (Phocoenidae) of small gregarious toothed whales; *especially* **:** a blunt-snouted usually largely black whale (*Phocoena phocoena*) of the North Atlantic and Pacific 5 to 8 feet (1.5 to 2.4 meters) long

**2 :** DOLPHIN 1a

**por·rect** \pə-'rekt, pä-\ *adjective* [Latin *porrectus*, past participle of *porrigere* to stretch out, from *por-* forward + *regere* to direct — more at PORTEND, RIGHT] (15th century)

**:** extended forward ⟨*porrect* antennae⟩

**por·ridge** \'pȯr-ij, 'pär-\ *noun* [alteration of *pottage*] (circa 1643)

**:** a soft food made by boiling meal of grains or legumes in milk or water until thick

— **por·ridgy** \-i-jē\ *adjective*

**por·rin·ger** \-ən-jər\ *noun* [alteration of Middle English *poteger, potinger*, from Anglo-French *potageer*, from Middle French *potager* of pottage, from *potage* pottage] (1522)

**:** a low usually metal bowl with a single and usually flat and pierced handle

**¹port** \'pȯrt, 'pȯrt\ *noun* [Middle English, from Old English & Old French, from Latin *portus* — more at FORD] (before 12th century)

**1 :** a place where ships may ride secure from storms **:** HAVEN

**2 a :** a harbor town or city where ships may take on or discharge cargo **b :** AIRPORT

**3 :** PORT OF ENTRY

**²port** *noun* [Middle English *porte*, from Middle French, gate, door, from Latin *porta* passage, gate; akin to Latin *portus* port] (before 12th century)

**1** *chiefly Scottish* **:** GATE

**2 a :** an opening (as in a valve seat or valve face) for intake or exhaust of a fluid **b :** the area of opening in a cylinder face of a passageway for the working fluid in an engine; *also* **:** such a passageway

**3 a :** an opening in a vessel's side (as for admitting light or loading cargo) **b** *archaic* **:** the cover for a porthole

**4 :** a hole in an armored vehicle or fortification through which guns may be fired

**5 :** a hardware interface by which a computer communicates with another device or system

**³port** *noun* [Middle English, from Middle French, from *porter* to carry, from Latin *portare*] (14th century)

**1 :** the manner of bearing oneself

**2** *archaic* **:** STATE 3

**3 :** the position in which a military weapon is carried at the command *port arms*

**⁴port** *transitive verb* [⁵port] (1580)

**:** to turn or put (a helm) to the left — used chiefly as a command

**⁵port** *noun* [probably from ¹port or ²port] (circa 1625)

**:** the left side of a ship or aircraft looking forward — called also *larboard*; compare STARBOARD

> **word history** see STARBOARD

— **port** *adjective*

**⁶port** *noun* [*Oporto*, Portugal] (1691)

**:** a sweet fortified wine of rich taste and aroma made in Portugal; *also* **:** a similar wine made elsewhere

**¹por·ta·ble** \'pȯr-tə-bəl, 'pȯr-\ *adjective* [Middle English, from Middle French, from Late Latin *portabilis*, from Latin *portare* to carry — more at FARE] (15th century)

**1 a :** capable of being carried or moved about ⟨a *portable* TV⟩ ⟨a *portable* sawmill⟩ **b :** usable on many computers without modification ⟨*portable* software⟩

---

\ə\ abut \ᵊ\ kitten \ər\ further \a\ ash \ā\ ace
\ä\ mop, mar \au̇\ out \ch\ chin \e\ bet \ē\ easy
\g\ go \i\ hit \ī\ ice \j\ job \ŋ\ sing \ō\ go
\ȯ\ law \ȯi\ boy \th\ thin \t͟h\ the \ü\ loot \u̇\ foot
\y\ yet \zh\ vision   *see also* Guide to Pronunciation

**2** *archaic* : BEARABLE
— **por·ta·bil·i·ty** \ˌpȯr-tə-'bi-lə-tē, ˌpȯr-\ *noun*
— **por·ta·bly** \'pȯr-tə-blē, 'pȯr-\ *adverb*
²**portable** *noun* (1883)
: something that is portable
¹**por·tage** \'pȯr-tij, 'pȯr-, *3 is also* pȯr-'täzh\ *noun* [Middle English, from Middle French, from *porter* to carry] (15th century)
**1** : the labor of carrying or transporting
**2** *archaic* : the cost of carrying : PORTERAGE
**3 a** : the carrying of boats or goods overland from one body of water to another or around an obstacle (as a rapids) **b** : the route followed in making such a transfer
²**por·tage** \'pȯr-tij, 'pȯr-; pȯr-'täzh\ *verb* **por·taged; por·tag·ing** (1864)
*transitive verb*
: to carry over a portage
*intransitive verb*
: to move gear over a portage
¹**por·tal** \'pȯr-t³l, 'pȯr-\ *noun* [Middle English, from Middle French, from Medieval Latin *portale* city gate, porch, from neuter of *portalis* of a gate, from Latin *porta* gate — more at PORT] (14th century)
**1** : DOOR, ENTRANCE; *especially* : a grand or imposing one
**2** : the whole architectural composition surrounding and including the doorways and porches of a church
**3** : the approach or entrance to a bridge or tunnel
**4** : a communicating part or area of an organism; *specifically* : the point at which something (as a pathogen) enters the body
²**portal** *adjective* [New Latin *porta* transverse fissure of the liver, from Latin, gate] (1845)
**1** : of or relating to the transverse fissure on the underside of the liver where most of the vessels enter
**2** : of, relating to, or being a portal vein
**portal system** *noun* [*portal vein*] (1851)
: a system of veins that begins and ends in capillaries
**portal–to–portal** *adjective* (1943)
: of or relating to the time spent by a worker in traveling between the entrance to an employer's property and the worker's actual job site (as in a mine) ⟨*portal-to-portal* pay⟩
**portal vein** *noun* [²*portal*] (1845)
: a vein that collects blood from one part of the body and distributes it in another through capillaries; *especially* : a vein carrying blood from the digestive organs and spleen to the liver
**por·ta·men·to** \ˌpȯr-tə-'men-(ˌ)tō, ˌpȯr-\ *noun, plural* **-men·ti** \-(ˌ)tē\ [Italian, literally, act of carrying, from *portare* to carry, from Latin] (1771)
: a continuous gliding movement from one tone to another (as by the voice)
**por·ta·pak** *or* **por·ta·pack** \'pȯr-tə-ˌpak, 'pȯr-\ *noun* [*portable* + ¹*pack*] (1970)
: a small portable combined videotape recorder and camera
**port arms** *noun* [from the command *port arms!*] (circa 1890)
: a position in the manual of arms in which the rifle is held diagonally in front of the body with the muzzle pointing upward to the left; *also* : a command to assume this position
**por·ta·tive** \'pȯr-tə-tiv, 'pȯr-\ *adjective* [Middle English *portatif*, from Middle French, from Latin *portatus*, past participle of *portare*] (14th century)
: PORTABLE
**port·cul·lis** \pȯrt-'kə-ləs, 'pȯrt-\ *noun* [Middle English *port colice*, from Middle French *porte coleïce*, literally, sliding door] (14th century)
: a grating of iron hung over the gateway of a fortified place and lowered between grooves to prevent passage
**port de bras** \ˌpȯr-də-'brä\ *noun* [French, literally, carriage of the arm] (1912)

: the technique and practice of arm movement in ballet
**Port du Sa·lut** \ˌpȯr-də-sə-'lü, -sa-; -səl-'yü, -sal-\ *noun* [French *port-du-salut, port-salut*, from *Port du Salut*, Trappist abbey in northwest France] (1881)
: a semisoft pressed ripened cheese of usually mild flavor originated by Trappist monks in France

**portcullis**

**Porte** \'pȯrt, 'pȯrt\ *noun* [French, short for *Sublime Porte*, literally, sublime gate; from the gate of the sultan's palace where justice was administered] (15th century)
: the government of the Ottoman empire
**porte co·chere** \ˌpȯrt-kō-'sher, ˌpȯrt-\ *noun* [French *porte cochère*, literally, coach door] (1698)
**1** : a passageway through a building or screen wall designed to let vehicles pass from the street to an interior courtyard
**2** : a roofed structure extending from the entrance of a building over an adjacent driveway and sheltering those getting in or out of vehicles
**por·tend** \pȯr-'tend, pōr-\ *transitive verb* [Middle English, from Latin *portendere*, from *por-* forward (akin to *per* through) + *tendere* to stretch — more at FOR, THIN] (15th century)
**1** : to give an omen or anticipatory sign of : BODE
**2** : INDICATE, SIGNIFY
**por·tent** \'pȯr-ˌtent, 'pȯr-\ *noun* [Latin *portentum*, from neuter of *portentus*, past participle of *portendere*] (circa 1587)
**1** : something that foreshadows a coming event : OMEN
**2** : prophetic indication or significance
**3** : MARVEL, PRODIGY
**por·ten·tous** \pȯr-'ten-təs, pōr-\ *adjective* (15th century)
**1** : of, relating to, or constituting a portent
**2** : eliciting amazement or wonder : PRODIGIOUS
**3 a** : being a grave or serious matter ⟨*portentous* decisions⟩ **b** : self-consciously solemn or important : POMPOUS **c** : ponderously excessive ⟨that discipline's overwrought, *portentous* phrases —R. M. Coles⟩
*synonym* see OMINOUS
— **por·ten·tous·ly** *adverb*
— **por·ten·tous·ness** *noun*
¹**por·ter** \'pȯr-tər, 'pȯr-\ *noun* [Middle English, from Old French *portier*, from Late Latin *portarius*, from Latin *porta* gate — more at PORT] (13th century)
*chiefly British* : a person stationed at a door or gate to admit or assist those entering
²**porter** *noun* [Middle English *portour*, from Middle French *porteour*, from Late Latin *portator*, from Latin *portare* to carry — more at FARE] (14th century)
**1** : a person who carries burdens; *especially* : one employed to carry baggage for patrons at a hotel or transportation terminal
**2** : a parlor-car or sleeping-car attendant who waits on passengers and makes up berths
**3** [short for *porter's beer*] : a heavy dark brown beer brewed from browned or charred malt
**4** : a person who does routine cleaning (as in a hospital or office)
³**porter** (1609)
*transitive verb*
: to transport or carry as or as if by a porter
*intransitive verb*
: to act as a porter
**por·ter·age** \-tə-rij\ *noun* (15th century)
: a porter's work; *also* : the charge for it
**por·ter·house** \'pȯr-tər-ˌhaus, 'pȯr-\ *noun* (circa 1758)

**1** *archaic* : a house where malt liquor (as porter) is sold
**2** : a large steak cut from the thick end of the short loin to contain a T-shaped bone and a large piece of tenderloin — see BEEF illustration
**port·fo·lio** \pȯrt-'fō-lē-ˌō, pȯrt-\ *noun, plural* **-li·os** [Italian *portafoglio*, from *portare* to carry (from Latin) + *foglio* leaf, sheet, from Latin *folium* — more at BLADE] (1722)
**1** : a hinged cover or flexible case for carrying loose papers, pictures, or pamphlets
**2** [from the use of such a case to carry documents of state] : the office and functions of a minister of state or member of a cabinet
**3** : the securities held by an investor : the commercial paper held by a financial house (as a bank)
**4** : a set of pictures (as drawings or photographs) either bound in book form or loose in a folder
**port·hole** \'pȯrt-ˌhōl, 'pȯrt-\ *noun* [²*port*] (circa 1591)
**1** : an opening (as a window) with a cover or closure especially in the side of a ship or aircraft
**2** : a port through which to shoot
**3** : ²PORT 2
**Por·tia** \'pȯr-shə, 'pȯr-\ *noun*
: the heroine in Shakespeare's *The Merchant of Venice*
**por·ti·co** \'pȯr-ti-ˌkō, 'pȯr-\ *noun, plural* **-coes** *or* **-cos** [Italian, from Latin *porticus* — more at PORCH] (1605)
: a colonnade or covered ambulatory especially in classical architecture and often at the entrance of a building
**por·tiere** \pōr-'tyer, pȯr-, -'tir; 'pȯr-tē-ər, 'pȯr-\ *noun* [French *portière*, from Old French, feminine of *portier* porter, doorkeeper] (1843)
: a curtain hanging across a doorway
¹**por·tion** \'pȯr-shən, 'pȯr-\ *noun* [Middle English, from Old French, from Latin *portion-, portio;* akin to Latin *part-, pars* part] (14th century)
**1** : an individual's part or share of something: as **a** : a share received by gift or inheritance **b** : DOWRY **c** : enough food especially of one kind to serve one person at one meal
**2** : an individual's lot, fate, or fortune : one's share of good and evil
**3** : an often limited part set off or abstracted from a whole ⟨give but that *portion* which yourself proposed —Shakespeare⟩
*synonym* see PART, FATE
²**portion** *transitive verb* **por·tioned; por·tion·ing** \-sh(ə-)niŋ\ (14th century)
**1** : to divide into portions : DISTRIBUTE
**2** : to allot a dowry to : DOWER
**por·tion·less** \-shən-ləs\ *adjective* (1782)
: having no portion; *especially* : having no dowry or inheritance
**port·land cement** \'pȯrt-lən(d)-, 'pȯrt-\ *noun* [Isle of *Portland*, England; from its resemblance to a limestone found there] (1824)
: a hydraulic cement made by finely pulverizing the clinker produced by calcining to incipient fusion a mixture of clay and limestone or similar materials
**port·ly** \'pȯrt-lē, 'pȯrt-\ *adjective* **port·li·er; -est** [³*port*] (15th century)
**1** : DIGNIFIED, STATELY
**2** : heavy or rotund of body : STOUT
— **port·li·ness** *noun*
¹**port·man·teau** \pȯrt-'man-(ˌ)tō, 'pȯrt-\ *noun, plural* **-teaus** *or* **-teaux** \-(ˌ)tōz\ [Middle French *portemanteau*, from *porter* to carry + *manteau* mantle, from Latin *mantellum* — more at PORT] (1579)
**1** : a large suitcase
**2** : a word or morpheme whose form and meaning are derived from a blending of two or more distinct forms (as *smog* from *smoke* and *fog*)
²**portmanteau** *adjective* (1909)
**1** : combining more than one use or quality

**2** : being a portmanteau ⟨a *portmanteau* word⟩
**port of call** (1884)
**1** : an intermediate port where ships customarily stop for supplies, repairs, or transshipment of cargo
**2** : a stop included on an itinerary
**port of entry** (1840)
**1** : a place where foreign goods may be cleared through a customhouse
**2** : a place where an alien may be permitted to enter a country
**por·trait** \'pŏr-trət, 'pór-, -‚trāt\ *noun* [Middle French, from past participle of *portraire*] (1570)
**1** : PICTURE; *especially* : a pictorial representation (as a painting) of a person usually showing the face
**2** : a sculptured figure : BUST, STATUE
**3** : a graphic portrayal in words
**por·trait·ist** \-trə-tist, -‚trā-\ *noun* (1866)
: a maker of portraits
**por·trai·ture** \'pŏr-trə-‚chŭr, 'pór-, -chər, -‚tyŭr, -‚tŭr\ *noun* (14th century)
**1** : the making of portraits : PORTRAYAL
**2** : PORTRAIT
**por·tray** \pŏr-'trā, pór-, pər-\ *transitive verb* [Middle English *portraien*, from Middle French *portraire*, from Latin *protrahere* to draw forth, reveal, expose — more at PRO-TRACT] (14th century)
**1** : to make a picture of : DEPICT
**2 a** : to describe in words **b** : to play the role of : ENACT
**— por·tray·er** *noun*
**por·tray·al** \-'trā(-ə)l\ *noun* (circa 1847)
**1** : the act or process or an instance of portraying : REPRESENTATION
**2** : PORTRAIT
**por·tress** \'pŏr-trəs, 'pór-\ *noun* (15th century)
: a female porter: as **a** : a doorkeeper in a convent or apartment house **b** : CHARWOMAN
**Port Roy·al·ist** \pŏrt-'rói-ə-list, pórt-\ *noun* [French *port-royaliste*, from *Port-Royal*, a convent near Versailles, France] (circa 1741)
: a member or adherent of a 17th century French Jansenist lay community noted for its logicians and educators
**Port Sa·lut** \‚pór-sə-'lü, -sa-; -səl-'yü, -sal-\ *noun* (1902)
: PORT DU SALUT
**Por·tu·guese** \'pŏr-chə-‚gēz, 'pór-, -‚gēs; ‚pŏr-chə-', ‚pór-\ *noun, plural* **Portuguese** [Portuguese *português*, adjective & noun, from *Portugal*] (1534)
**1 a** : a native or inhabitant of Portugal **b** : one who is of Portuguese descent
**2** : the Romance language of Portugal and Brazil
**— Portuguese** *adjective*
**Portuguese man–of–war** *noun, plural* **Portuguese man–of–wars** *also* **Portuguese men–of–war** (1707)
: any of a genus (*Physalia*) of large tropical and subtropical pelagic siphonophores having a crested bladderlike float which bears the colony comprised of three types of zooids on the lower surface with one of the three having nematocyst-equipped tentacles
**por·tu·laca** \‚pŏr-chə-'la-kə, ‚pór-\ *noun* [New Latin, from Latin, purslane, from *portula*, diminutive of *porta* gate; from the lid of its capsule — more at PORT] (1548)
: any of a genus (*Portulaca*)

Portuguese man-of-war

of mainly tropical succulent herbs of the purslane family; *especially* : a widely cultivated plant (*P. grandiflora*) with showy flowers and small conical leaves
**port–wine stain** \'pŏrt-'wīn-, 'pórt-\ *noun* (circa 1909)

: a reddish purple superficial hemangioma of the skin commonly occurring as a birthmark
**po·sa·da** \pə-'sä-də\ *noun* [Spanish, from *posar* to lodge, from Late Latin *pausare*] (1763)
: an inn in Spanish-speaking countries
**¹pose** \'pōz\ *verb* **posed; pos·ing** [Middle English, from Middle French *poser*, from (assumed) Vulgar Latin *pausare*, from Late Latin, to stop, rest, pause, from Latin *pausa* pause] (14th century)
*transitive verb*
**1 a** : to present for attention or consideration ⟨let me *pose* a question⟩ **b** : to put or set forth : OFFER ⟨this attitude *poses* a threat to our hopes for peace⟩
**2 a** : to put or set in place **b** : to place (as a model) in a studied attitude
*intransitive verb*
**1** : to assume a posture or attitude usually for artistic purposes
**2** : to affect an attitude or character usually to deceive or impress
**²pose** *noun* (1818)
**1** : a sustained posture; *especially* : one assumed for artistic effect
**2** : an attitude, role, or characteristic assumed for effect ☆
**³pose** *transitive verb* **posed; pos·ing** [short for earlier *appose*, from Middle English *apposen*, alteration of *opposen* to oppose] (1593)
: PUZZLE, BAFFLE
**Po·sei·don** \pə-'sī-dªn\ *noun* [Latin, from Greek *Poseidōn*]
: the Greek god of the sea — compare NEP-TUNE
**¹pos·er** \'pō-zər\ *noun* [³*pose*] (1793)
: a puzzling or baffling question
**²poser** *noun* [¹*pose*] (1888)
: a person who poses
**po·seur** \pō-'zər\ *noun* [French, literally, poser, from *poser*] (1872)
: a person who pretends to be what he or she is not : an affected or insincere person
**posh** \'päsh\ *adjective* [origin unknown] (1918)
: ELEGANT, FASHIONABLE ◆
**— posh·ly** *adverb*
**— posh·ness** *noun*
**pos·it** \'pä-zət\ *transitive verb* **pos·it·ed** \'pä-zə-təd, 'päz-təd\; **pos·it·ing** \'pä-zə-tiŋ, 'päz-tiŋ\ [Latin *positus*, past participle of *ponere*] (1647)
**1** : to dispose or set firmly : FIX
**2** : to assume or affirm the existence of : POS-TULATE
**3** : to propose as an explanation : SUGGEST
**¹po·si·tion** \pə-'zi-shən\ *noun* [Middle English *posycion*, from Middle French *position*, from Latin *position-, positio*, from *ponere* to lay down, put, place, from (assumed) Old Latin *posinere*, from *po-* away (akin to Old Church Slavonic *po-*, perfective prefix, Greek *apo* away) + Latin *sinere* to leave — more at OF] (14th century)
**1** : an act of placing or arranging: as **a** : the laying down of a proposition or thesis **b** : arranging in order
**2** : a point of view adopted and held to ⟨made my *position* on the issue clear⟩
**3 a** : the point or area occupied by a physical object ⟨took her *position* at the head of the line⟩ **b** : a certain arrangement of bodily parts ⟨rose to a standing *position*⟩
**4** : a market commitment in securities or commodities; *also* : the inventory of a market trader
**5 a** : relative place, situation, or standing ⟨is now in a *position* to make decisions on his own⟩ **b** : social or official rank or status **c** : an employment for which one has been hired : JOB ⟨a *position* with a brokerage firm⟩ **d** : a situation that confers advantage or preference
**²position** *transitive verb* **po·si·tioned; po·si·tion·ing** \pə-'zi-sh(ə-)niŋ\ (1817)
: to put in proper position; *also* : LOCATE

**po·si·tion·al** \pə-'zi-sh(ə-)nəl\ *adjective* (1571)
**1** : of, relating to, or fixed by position ⟨*positional* astronomy⟩
**2** : involving little movement ⟨*positional* warfare⟩
**3** : dependent on position or environment or context ⟨the front-articulated \k\ in \kē\ *key* and the back-articulated \k\ in \kül\ *cool* are *positional* variants⟩
**— po·si·tion·al·ly** *adverb*
**positional notation** *noun* (1941)
: a system of expressing numbers in which the digits are arranged in succession, the position of each digit has a place value, and the number is equal to the sum of the products of each digit by its place value
**position effect** *noun* (1930)
: genetic effect that is due to interaction of adjacent genes and that is modified when the spatial relationships of the genes change (as by chromosomal inversion)
**position paper** *noun* (1949)
: a detailed report that recommends a course of action on a particular issue
**¹pos·i·tive** \'pä-zə-tiv, 'päz-tiv\ *adjective* [Middle English, from Middle French *positif*,

☆ SYNONYMS
**Pose, air, airs, affectation, mannerism** mean an adopted way of speaking or behaving. POSE implies an attitude deliberately assumed in order to impress others ⟨her shyness was just a *pose*⟩. AIR may suggest natural acquirement through environment or way of life ⟨a traveler's sophisticated *air*⟩. AIRS always implies artificiality and pretentiousness ⟨snobbish *airs*⟩. AFFECTATION applies to a trick of speech or behavior that strikes the observer as insincere ⟨the posh accent is an *affectation*⟩. MANNERISM applies to an acquired eccentricity that has become a habit ⟨gesturing with a cigarette was her most noticeable *mannerism*⟩.

◇ WORD HISTORY
**posh** The origin of the adjective *posh* "elegant, fashionable" is obscure, though dictionary editors have received hundreds of letters over the years claiming that *posh* comes from the first letters of the phrase "port out, starboard home." On the route from Suez to India taken by a British steamship line (the Peninsular and Oriental), the coolest cabins during the Red Sea passage were on the port side and the hottest cabins on the starboard side. On the return trip, the opposite was true. Hence the wealthiest and most important passengers supposedly took the cooler cabins and had the letters P.O.S.H. stamped on their tickets. Unfortunately, there is not a shred of evidence for this story from the P & O's archives, travelers' diaries, or any other source. Bookings for the homeward voyage were not issued when the outbound voyage was booked, so P.O.S.H. would not have appeared on tickets or documents, and there are no indications that first-class accommodations on one side of the ship were more desirable or expensive than accommodations on the other. Along with explanations of *cop* as "constable on patrol" and *news* as "north, east, west, south," the "port out, starboard home" theory for *posh* is most likely folklore.

\ə\ abut \ə\ kitten \ər\ further \a\ ash \ā\ ace
\ä\ mop, mar \au̇\ out \ch\ chin \e\ bet \ē\ easy
\g\ go \i\ hit \ī\ ice \j\ job \ŋ\ sing \ō\ go
\ȯ\ law \ȯi\ boy \th\ thin \t͟h\ the \ü\ loot \u̇\ foot
\y\ yet \zh\ vision    *see also* Guide to Pronunciation

from Latin *positivus,* from *positus,* past participle of *ponere*] (14th century)
**1 a :** formally laid down or imposed **:** PRE-SCRIBED ⟨*positive* laws⟩ **b :** expressed clearly or peremptorily ⟨her answer was a *positive no*⟩ **c :** fully assured **:** CONFIDENT
**2 a :** of, relating to, or constituting the degree of comparison that is expressed in English by the unmodified and uninflected form of an adjective or adverb and denotes no increase or diminution **b** (1) **:** independent of changing circumstances **:** UNCONDITIONED (2) **:** relating to or constituting a motion or device that is definite, unyielding, constant, or certain in its action ⟨a *positive* system of levers⟩ **c** (1) **:** IN-CONTESTABLE ⟨*positive* proof⟩ (2) **:** UNQUALI-FIED ⟨a *positive* disgrace⟩
**3 a :** not fictitious **:** REAL ⟨a *positive* influence for good in the community⟩ **b :** active and effective in social or economic function rather than merely maintaining peace and order ⟨a *positive* government⟩
**4 a :** having or expressing actual existence or quality as distinguished from deprivation or deficiency ⟨*positive* change in temperature⟩: as (1) **:** capable of being constructively applied (2) **:** not speculative **:** EMPIRICAL **b :** having rendition of light and shade similar in tone to the tones of the original subject ⟨a *positive* photographic image⟩ **c :** that is or is generated in a direction arbitrarily or customarily taken as that of increase or progression ⟨*positive* rotation of the earth⟩ ⟨we are making some *positive* progress⟩ **d :** directed or moving toward a source of stimulation ⟨a *positive* taxis⟩ **e :** real and numerically greater than zero ⟨+2 is a *positive* integer⟩
**5 a** (1) **:** being, relating to, or charged with electricity of which the proton is the elementary unit and which predominates in a glass body after being rubbed with silk (2) **:** having more protons than electrons ⟨a *positive* ion⟩ **b** (1) **:** having higher electric potential and constituting the part from which the current flows to the external circuit ⟨the *positive* terminal of a discharging storage battery⟩ (2) **:** being an electron-collecting electrode of an electron tube
**6 a :** marked by or indicating acceptance, approval, or affirmation **b :** affirming the presence of that sought or suspected to be present ⟨a *positive* test for blood⟩
**7** *of a lens* **:** converging light rays and forming a real inverted image
*synonym* see SURE
— **pos·i·tive·ly** \-lē, *for emphasis often* ˌpä-zə-'tiv-\ *adverb*
— **pos·i·tive·ness** \'pä-zə-tiv-nəs, 'päz-tiv-\ *noun*
²**positive** *noun* (1530)
**:** something positive: as **a** (1) **:** the positive degree of comparison in a language (2) **:** a positive form of an adjective or adverb **b :** something of which an affirmation can be made **:** REALITY **c :** a positive photograph or a print from a negative
**positive definite** *adjective* (1907)
**1 :** having a positive value for all values of the constituent variables ⟨*positive definite* quadratic forms⟩
**2** *of a matrix* **:** having the characteristic roots real and positive
**positive law** *noun* (14th century)
**:** law established or recognized by governmental authority — compare NATURAL LAW
**pos·i·tiv·ism** \'pä-zə-ti-ˌvi-zəm, 'päz-ti-\ *noun* [French *positivisme,* from *positif* positive + *-isme* -ism] (1847)
**1 a :** a theory that theology and metaphysics are earlier imperfect modes of knowledge and that positive knowledge is based on natural phenomena and their properties and relations as verified by the empirical sciences **b :** LOGICAL POSITIVISM
**2 :** the quality or state of being positive
— **pos·i·tiv·ist** \-vist\ *adjective or noun*

— **pos·i·tiv·is·tic** \ˌpä-zə-ti-'vis-tik, ˌpäz-ti-\ *adjective*
— **pos·i·tiv·is·ti·cal·ly** \-ti-k(ə-)lē\ *adverb*
**pos·i·tiv·i·ty** \ˌpä-zə-'ti-və-tē\ *noun, plural* **-ties** (1659)
**1 :** the quality or state of being positive
**2 :** something that is positive
**pos·i·tron** \'pä-zə-ˌträn\ *noun* [*posi*tive + *-tron* (as in *electron*)] (1933)
**:** a positively charged particle having the same mass and magnitude of charge as the electron and constituting the antiparticle of the electron
**positron–emission tomography** *noun* (1979)
**:** tomography in which a cross-sectional image of regional metabolism is obtained by a usually color-coded cathode-ray tube representation of the distribution of gamma radiation given off in the collision of electrons in cells with positrons emitted by radionuclides incorporated into metabolic substances
**pos·i·tro·ni·um** \ˌpä-zə-'trō-nē-əm\ *noun* (1945)
**:** a short-lived system that consists of a positron and an electron bound together and is suggestive of a hydrogen atom
**pos·se** \'pä-sē\ *noun* [Medieval Latin *posse comitatus,* literally, power or authority of the county] (1645)
**1 :** a large group often with a common interest
**2 :** a body of persons summoned by a sheriff to assist in preserving the public peace usually in an emergency
**3 :** a group of people temporarily organized to make a search (as for a lost child)
**pos·sess** \pə-'zes *also* -'ses\ *transitive verb* [Middle English, from Middle French *possesser* to have possession of, take possession of, from Latin *possessus,* past participle of *possidēre,* from *potis* able, having the power + *sedēre* to sit — more at POTENT, SIT] (14th century)
**1 a :** to have and hold as property **:** OWN **b :** to have as an attribute, knowledge, or skill
**2 a :** to take into one's possession **b :** to enter into and control firmly **:** DOMINATE ⟨was *possessed* by demons⟩ **c :** to bring or cause to fall under the influence, possession, or control of some emotional or intellectual reaction ⟨melancholy *possesses* her⟩
**3 a** *obsolete* **:** to instate as owner **b :** to make the owner or holder — used in passive construction to indicate simple possession ⟨*possessed* of riches⟩ ⟨*possessed* of knowledge and experience⟩
— **pos·ses·sor** *noun*
**pos·sessed** *adjective* (1534)
**1 a** (1) **:** influenced or controlled by something (as an evil spirit or a passion) (2) **:** MAD, CRAZED **b :** urgently desirous to do or have something
**2** *obsolete* **:** held as a possession
**3 :** SELF-POSSESSED, CALM
— **pos·sess·ed·ly** \-'ze-səd-lē, -'zest-lē *also* -'se-səd- *or* -'sest-\ *adverb*
— **pos·sess·ed·ness** \-'ze-səd-nəs, -'zest-nəs *also* -'se-səd- *or* -'sest-\ *noun*
**pos·ses·sion** \-'ze-shən *also* -'se-\ *noun* (14th century)
**1 a :** the act of having or taking into control **b :** control or occupancy of property without regard to ownership **c :** OWNERSHIP **d :** control of the ball or puck
**2 :** something owned, occupied, or controlled **:** PROPERTY
**3 a :** domination by something (as an evil spirit, a passion, or an idea) **b :** a psychological state in which an individual's normal personality is replaced by another **c :** the fact or condition of being self-controlled
— **pos·ses·sion·al** \-'zesh-nəl, -'ze-shə-n°l *also* -'sesh-nəl *or* -'se-shə-n°l\ *adjective*
— **pos·ses·sion·less** \-'ze-shən-ləs, -'se-\ *adjective*
¹**pos·ses·sive** \pə-'ze-siv *also* -'se-\ *adjective* (15th century)

**1 :** of, relating to, or constituting a word, a word group, or a grammatical case that denotes ownership or a relation analogous to ownership
**2 :** manifesting possession or the desire to own or dominate
— **pos·ses·sive·ly** *adverb*
— **pos·ses·sive·ness** *noun*
²**possessive** *noun* (15th century)
**1 :** a possessive word or word group
**2 a :** the possessive case **b :** a word in the possessive case
**possessive adjective** *noun* (1870)
**:** a pronominal adjective expressing possession
**possessive pronoun** *noun* (15th century)
**:** a pronoun that derives from a personal pronoun and denotes possession and analogous relationships
**pos·ses·so·ry** \pə-'ze-sə-rē, -'zes-rē *also* -'se-sə-rē *or* -'ses-rē\ *adjective* (15th century)
**1 :** of, arising from, or having the nature of possession ⟨*possessory* rights⟩
**2 :** having possession
**3 :** characteristic of a possessor **:** POSSESSIVE
**pos·set** \'pä-sət\ *noun* [Middle English *poshet, possot*] (15th century)
**:** a hot drink of sweetened and spiced milk curdled with ale or wine
**pos·si·bil·i·ty** \ˌpä-sə-'bi-lə-tē\ *noun, plural* **-ties** (14th century)
**1 :** the condition or fact of being possible
**2** *archaic* **:** one's utmost power, capacity, or ability
**3 :** something that is possible
**4 :** potential or prospective value — usually used in plural ⟨the house had great *possibilities*⟩
**pos·si·ble** \'pä-sə-bəl\ *adjective* [Middle English, from Middle French, from Latin *possibilis,* from *posse* to be able, from *potis, pote* able + *esse* to be — more at POTENT, IS] (14th century)
**1 a :** being within the limits of ability, capacity, or realization **b :** being what may be done or may occur according to nature, custom, or manners
**2 a :** being something that may or may not occur **b :** being something that may or may not be true or actual ⟨*possible* explanation⟩
**3 :** having an indicated potential ⟨a *possible* housing site⟩ ☆
**pos·si·bly** \-blē\ *adverb* (14th century)
**1 :** in a possible manner **:** by any possibility
**2 :** by merest chance **:** PERHAPS
**pos·sum** \'pä-səm\ *noun* (1613)
**:** OPOSSUM
¹**post** \'pōst\ *noun* [Middle English, from Old English, from Latin *postis;* probably akin to Latin *por-* forward and to Latin *stare* to stand — more at PORTEND, STAND] (before 12th century)
**1 :** a piece (as of timber or metal) fixed firmly in an upright position especially as a stay or support **:** PILLAR, COLUMN
**2 :** a pole or stake set up to mark or indicate something; *especially* **:** a pole that marks the starting or finishing point of a horse race
**3 :** a metallic fitting attached to an electrical device (as a storage battery) for convenience in making connections

☆ **SYNONYMS**
**Possible, practicable, feasible** mean capable of being realized. POSSIBLE implies that a thing may certainly exist or occur given the proper conditions ⟨a *possible* route up the west face of the mountain⟩. PRACTICABLE implies that something may be effected by available means or under current conditions ⟨a *practicable* route up the west face of the mountain⟩. FEASIBLE applies to what is likely to work or be useful in attaining the end desired ⟨commercially *feasible* for mass production⟩.

**4** : GOALPOST
**5** : the metal stem of a pierced earring
**²post** *transitive verb* (1633)
**1 a** : to publish, announce, or advertise by or as if by use of a placard **b** : to denounce by public notice **c** : to enter on a public listing **d** : to forbid (property) to trespassers under penalty of legal prosecution by notices placed along the boundaries **e** : SCORE ⟨*posted* a 70 in the final round⟩
**2** : to affix to a usual place (as a wall) for public notices : PLACARD
**³post** *noun* [Middle French *poste* relay station, courier, from Old Italian *posta* relay station, from feminine of *posto*, past participle of *porre* to place, from Latin *ponere* — more at POSITION] (1507)
**1** *obsolete* : COURIER
**2** *archaic* **a** : one of a series of stations for keeping horses for relays **b** : the distance between any two such consecutive stations : STAGE
**3** *chiefly British* **a** : a nation's organization for handling mail; *also* : the mail handled **b** : a single dispatch of mail **c** : POST OFFICE **d** : POSTBOX
**⁴post** (1533)
*intransitive verb*
**1** : to travel with post-horses
**2** : to ride or travel with haste : HURRY
**3** : to rise from the saddle and return to it in rhythm with a horse's trot
*transitive verb*
**1** *archaic* : to dispatch in haste
**2** : MAIL ⟨*post* a letter⟩
**3 a** : to transfer or carry from a book of original entry to a ledger **b** : to make transfer entries in
**4** : to make familiar with a subject : INFORM ⟨kept her *posted* on the latest gossip⟩
**⁵post** *adverb* (1549)
: with post-horses : EXPRESS
**⁶post** *noun* [Middle French *poste*, from Old Italian *posto*, from past participle of *porre* to place] (1598)
**1 a** : the place at which a soldier is stationed; *especially* : a sentry's beat or station **b** : a station or task to which one is assigned **c** : the place at which a body of troops is stationed : CAMP **d** : a local subdivision of a veterans' organization **e** : one of two bugle calls sounded (as in the British army) at tattoo
**2 a** : an office or position to which a person is appointed **b** : a player position in basketball that is the focal point of the offense; *specifically* : PIVOT 2b
**3 a** : TRADING POST, SETTLEMENT **b** : a trading station on the floor of a stock exchange
**⁷post** *transitive verb* (1683)
**1 a** : to station in a given place ⟨guards were *posted* at the doors⟩ **b** : to carry ceremoniously to a position ⟨*posting* the colors⟩
**2** *chiefly British* : to assign to a unit, position, or location (as in the military or civil service)
**3** : to put up (as bond)
**post-** *prefix* [Middle English, from Latin, from *post*; akin to Lithuanian *pas* at, Greek *apo* away from — more at OF]
**1 a** : after : subsequent : later ⟨*post*date⟩ **b** : behind : posterior : following after ⟨*post*lude⟩ ⟨*post*consonantal⟩
**2 a** : subsequent to : later than ⟨*post*operative⟩ **b** : posterior to ⟨*post*orbital⟩

post·abor·tion
post·ac·ci·dent
post·ad·o·les·cent
post·am·pu·ta·tion
post·apoc·a·lyp·tic
post·ar·rest
post·atom·ic
post·at·tack
post·bac·ca·lau·re·
    ate
post·base
post·bib·li·cal
post·bour·geois
post·burn
post·cap·i·tal·ist
post–Chris·tian
post·co·i·tal
post·col·lege
post·col·le·giate
post·co·lo·nial
post·con·cep·tion
post·con·cert
post·con·quest
post·con·so·nan·tal

post·con·ven·tion
post·cop·u·la·to·ry
post·cor·o·nary
post·coup
post·crash
post·cri·sis
post–Dar·win·i·an
post·dead·line
post·de·bate
post·deb·u·tante
post·de·liv·ery
post·de·po·si·tion·al
post·de·pres·sion
post·de·val·u·a·tion
post·dive
post·di·ves·ti·ture
post·di·vorce
post·drug
post·ed·it·ing
post–Ein·stein·ian
post·elec·tion
post·em·bry·o·nal
post·em·bry·on·ic
post·emer·gen·cy
post·en·ceph·a·lit·ic
post·ep·i·lep·tic
post·erup·tive
post·ex·er·cise
post·ex·pe·ri·ence
post·ex·per·i·men·tal
post·ex·po·sure
post·fault
post·fire
post·flight
post·frac·ture
post·freeze
post–Freud·ian
post·game
post·gla·cial
post·grad·u·a·tion
post·har·vest
post·hem·or·rhag·ic
post·hol·i·day
post·ho·lo·caust
post·hos·pi·tal
post·im·pact
post·im·pe·ri·al
post·in·au·gu·ral
post·in·de·pen·
    dence
post·in·dus·tri·al
post·in·fec·tion
post·in·jec·tion

post·in·oc·u·la·tion
post·ir·ra·di·a·tion
post·is·che·mic
post·iso·la·tion
post·land·ing
post·launch
post·lib·er·a·tion
post·mar·i·tal
post·mas·tec·to·my
post·mat·ing
post·me·di·e·val
post·mid·night
post·neo·na·tal
post·or·gas·mic
post·pol·li·na·tion
post·pres·i·den·tial
post·pri·ma·ry
post·pris·on
post·psy·cho·an·a·
    lyt·ic
post·pu·ber·ty
post·pu·bes·cent
post·race
post·re·ces·sion
post–Ref·or·ma·tion
post·res·ur·rec·tion
post·re·tire·ment
post·rev·o·lu·tion·
    ary
post·ri·ot
post·ro·man·tic
post·sea·son
post·sec·ond·ary
post·show
post·stim·u·la·tion
post·stim·u·la·to·ry
post·stim·u·lus
post·strike
post·sur·gi·cal
post·tax
post·teen
post·trau·mat·ic
post·treat·ment
post·trial
post·vac·ci·nal
post·vac·ci·na·tion
post·va·got·o·my
post·va·sec·to·my
post–Vic·to·ri·an
post·war
post·wean·ing
post·work·shop

**post·age** \'pōs-tij\ *noun* (1654)
**1** : the fee for postal service
**2** : adhesive stamps or printed indicia representing postal fees
**postage–due stamp** *noun* (1893)
: a special adhesive stamp that is applied by a post office to mail bearing insufficient postage
**postage meter** *noun* (1927)
: a machine that prints postal indicia on pieces of mail, records the amount of postage, and subtracts it from a total paid amount for which the machine has been set
**postage–stamp** *adjective* (1938)
: suggesting a postage stamp in size : very small ⟨*postage-stamp* yards⟩
**postage stamp** *noun* (1840)
: a government adhesive stamp or imprinted stamp for use on mail as evidence of prepayment of postage
**post·al** \'pōs-t°l\ *adjective* (1843)
**1** : of or relating to the mails or the post office
**2** : conducted by mail ⟨*postal* chess⟩
**postal card** *noun* (1872)
**1** : a card officially stamped and issued by the government for use in the mail
**2** : POSTCARD
**postal order** *noun* (1883)
*British* : MONEY ORDER
**postal service** *noun* (circa 1920)
: POST OFFICE 1
**postal union** *noun* (1875)

: an association of governments setting up uniform regulations and practices for international mail
**post·ax·i·al** \,pōst-'ak-sē-əl\ *adjective* (1872)
: of or relating to the ulnar side of the vertebrate forelimb or the fibular side of the hind limb; *also* : of or relating to the side of an animal or side of one of its limbs that is posterior or to the axis of its body or limb
**post·bag** \'pōs(t)-,bag\ *noun* (1813)
**1** *British* : MAILBAG
**2** *British* : a single batch of mail : LETTERS
**post·bel·lum** \,pōs(t)-'be-ləm\ *adjective* [Latin *post bellum* after the war] (1874)
: of, relating to, or characteristic of the period following a war and especially following the American Civil War
**post·box** \'pōs-,bäks\ *noun* (1754)
: MAILBOX; *especially* : a public mailbox
**post·boy** \-,bȯi\ *noun* (1707)
: POSTILION
**post·card** \'pōs(t)-,kärd\ *noun* (1870)
**1** : POSTAL CARD 1
**2** : a card on which a message may be written for mailing without an envelope and to which the sender must affix a stamp
— **post·card·like** \-,līk\ *adjective*
**post·ca·va** \,pōs(t)-'kä-və\ *noun* [New Latin] (1882)
: the inferior vena cava of vertebrates higher than fishes
— **post·ca·val** \-vəl\ *adjective*
**post chaise** *noun* (1712)
: a carriage usually having a closed body on four wheels and seating two to four persons
**post·clas·si·cal** \,pōs(t)-'kla-si-kəl\ *or* **post·clas·sic** \-sik\ *adjective* (1867)
: of or relating to a period (as in art, literature, or civilization) following a classical one
**post·code** \'pōs(t)-,kōd\ *noun* (1967)
: a code (as of numbers and letters) used similarly to the zip code especially in the United Kingdom and Australia
**post–com·mu·nion** \,pōs(t)-kə-'myü-nyən\ *noun, often P&C capitalized* [Medieval Latin *postcommunion-, postcommunio*, from Latin *post-* + Late Latin *communio* communion] (15th century)
: a liturgically variable prayer following the communion at Mass
**post·cra·ni·al** \-'krā-nē-əl\ *adjective* (1913)
: of or relating to the part of the body caudal to the head ⟨*postcranial* skeleton⟩ ⟨*postcranial* fossil remains⟩
— **post·cra·ni·al·ly** *adverb*
**post·date** \,pōs(t)-'dāt, 'pōs(t)-,\ *transitive verb* (1624)
**1 a** : to date with a date later than that of execution ⟨*postdate* a check⟩ **b** : to assign (an event) to a date subsequent to that of actual occurrence
**2** : to follow in time
**post·di·lu·vi·an** \,pōs(t)-də-'lü-vē-ən, -dī-\ *adjective* [*post-* + Latin *diluvium* flood — more at DELUGE] (1680)
: of or relating to the period after the flood described in the Bible
— **postdiluvian** *noun*
**¹post·doc** \'pōs(t)-,däk\ *noun* (1968)
: one engaged in postdoctoral study or research
**²postdoc** *adjective* (1970)
: POSTDOCTORAL
**post·doc·tor·al** \,pōs(t)-'däk-t(ə-)rəl, 'pōst-,\ *also* **post·doc·tor·ate** \-t(ə-)rət\ *adjective* (1936)
: being beyond the doctoral level: **a** : of or relating to advanced academic or professional work beyond a doctor's degree ⟨a *postdoctoral*

fellowship⟩ **b** : engaged in such work ⟨*post-doctoral* scholars⟩

**post·emer·gence** \ˌpōst-i-'mər-jən(t)s\ *adjective* (1940)
: used or occurring in the stage between the emergence of a seedling and the maturity of a crop plant ⟨*postemergence* herbicides⟩ ⟨*postemergence* development⟩

**¹post·er** \'pōs-tər\ *noun* [⁴*post*] (1605)
*archaic* : a swift traveler

**²poster** *noun* [²*post*] (1838)
: a bill or placard for posting often in a public place; *especially* : one that is decorative or pictorial

**poster color** *noun* (1925)
: an opaque watercolor paint with a gum or glue-size binder sold usually in jars — called also **poster paint**

**poste res·tante** \ˌpōst-res-'tänt\ *noun* [French, literally, waiting mail] (1768)
*chiefly British* : GENERAL DELIVERY

**¹pos·te·ri·or** \pō-'stir-ē-ər, pä-\ *adjective* [Latin, comparative of *posterus* coming after, from *post* after — more at POST-] (1534)
**1** : later in time : SUBSEQUENT
**2** : situated behind: as **a** : CAUDAL **b** *of the human body or its parts* : DORSAL
**3** *of a plant part* : ADAXIAL, SUPERIOR
— **pos·te·ri·or·ly** *adverb*

**²pos·te·ri·or** \pä-'stir-ē-ər, pō-\ *noun* (circa 1616)
: the hinder parts of the body; *specifically* : BUTTOCKS

**pos·te·ri·or·i·ty** \(ˌ)pō-ˌstir-ē-'ȯr-ə-tē, (ˌ)pä-ˌ-'är-\ *noun* (14th century)
: the quality or state of being later or subsequent

**pos·ter·i·ty** \pä-'ster-ə-tē\ *noun* [Middle English *posterite*, from Middle French *posterité*, from Latin *posteritat-, posteritas*, from *posterus* coming after] (14th century)
**1** : the offspring of one progenitor to the furthest generation
**2** : all future generations

**pos·tern** \'pōs-tərn, 'päs-\ *noun* [Middle English *posterne*, from Old French, alteration of *posterle*, from Late Latin *posterula*, diminutive of *postera* back door, from Latin, feminine of *posterus*] (14th century)
**1** : a back door or gate
**2** : a private or side entrance or way
— **postern** *adjective*

**pos·tero·lat·er·al** \ˌpäs-tə-rō-'la-t(ə-)rəl\ *adjective* [*posterior* + *-o-* + *lateral*] (1852)
: posterior and lateral in position or direction

**post exchange** *noun* (1892)
: a store at a military installation that sells merchandise and services to military personnel and authorized civilians

**post·ex·il·ic** \ˌpōst-(ˌ)eg-'zi-lik\ *adjective* (1871)
: of or relating to the period of Jewish history between the end of the exile in Babylon in 538 B.C. and A.D. 1

**post·face** \'pōs(t)-fəs, -ˌfās; pȯs-fás\ *noun* [French, from *post-* + *-face* (as in *préface* preface)] (1782)
: a brief article or note (as of explanation) placed at the end of a publication

**post·fem·i·nist** \ˌpōst-'fe-mə-nist\ *adjective* (1983)
: of, relating to, occurring in, or being the period following widespread advocacy and acceptance of feminism

**post·fix** \'pōs(t)-ˌfiks\ *adjective* [*post-* + *-fix* (as in *prefix*)] (1973)
: characterized by placement of an operator after its operand or after its two operands if it is a binary operator — compare INFIX, PREFIX

**post·free** \'pōs(t)-'frē\ *adjective* (1723)
*chiefly British* : POSTPAID

**post·gan·gli·on·ic** \ˌpōs(t)-ˌgaŋ-glē-'ä-nik\ *adjective* (1897)
: distal to a ganglion; *specifically* : of, relating to, or being an axon arising from a cell body

within an autonomic ganglion — compare PREGANGLIONIC

**¹post·grad·u·ate** \-'gra-jə-wət, -ˌwāt, -'graj-wət\ *adjective* (1858)
: GRADUATE 2

**²postgraduate** *noun* (circa 1890)
: a student continuing formal education after graduation from high school or college

**¹post·haste** \'pōst-'hāst\ *noun* [³*post*] (1545)
*archaic* : great haste

**²posthaste** *adverb* (1593)
: with all possible speed

**³posthaste** *adjective* (1604)
*obsolete* : SPEEDY, IMMEDIATE ⟨requires your · . . . *posthaste* appearance —Shakespeare⟩

**post hoc** \'pōst-'häk\ *adjective* [New Latin *post hoc, ergo propter hoc* after this, therefore because of this] (1704)
**1** : relating to or being the fallacy of arguing from temporal sequence to a causal relation
**2** : formulated after the fact ⟨a *post hoc* rationalization⟩

**post·hole** \'pōst-ˌhōl\ *noun* (1703)
: a hole dug for a post (as to support a fence or wall)

**post horn** *noun* (1675)
: a simple straight or coiled brass or copper wind instrument with cupped mouthpiece used especially by guards of mail coaches of the 18th and 19th centuries

**post horn**

**post–horse** \'pōst-ˌhȯrs\ *noun* [³*post*] (1527)
: a horse for use especially by couriers or mail carriers

**post·hu·mous** \'päs-chə-məs *also* -tə-, -tyə-, -thə-; päst-'hyü-məs, 'pōst-, -'yü-\ *adjective* [Latin *posthumus*, alteration of *postumus* lateborn, posthumous, from superlative of *posterus* coming after — more at POSTERIOR] (1619)
**1** : born after the death of the father
**2** : published after the death of the author
**3** : following or occurring after death ⟨*posthumous* fame⟩
— **post·hu·mous·ly** *adverb*
— **post·hu·mous·ness** *noun*

**post·hyp·not·ic** \ˌpōst-hip-'nä-tik, -ip-\ *adjective* [International Scientific Vocabulary] (1890)
: of, relating to, or characteristic of the period following a hypnotic trance

**pos·tiche** \pȯs-'tēsh\ *noun* [French, from Spanish *postizo*] (1886)
: WIG; *especially* : TOUPEE 2

**pos·til·ion** *or* **pos·til·lion** \pō-'stil-yən, pə-\ *noun* [Middle French *postillon* mail carrier using post-horses, from Italian *postiglione*, from *posta* post — more at POST] (circa 1611)
: one who rides as a guide on the near horse of one of the pairs attached to a coach or post chaise especially without a coachman

**Post·im·pres·sion·ism** \ˌpōst-im-'pre-shə-ˌni-zəm\ *noun* [French *postimpressionisme*, from *post-* + *impressionisme* impressionism] (1910)
: a theory or practice of art originating in France in the last quarter of the 19th century that in revolt against impressionism stresses variously volume, picture structure, or expressionism
— **Post·im·pres·sion·ist** \-'pre-sh(ə-)nist\ *adjective or noun*
— **Post·im·pres·sion·is·tic** \-ˌpre-shə-'nis-tik\ *adjective*

**¹post·ing** \'pōs-tiŋ\ *noun* [⁴*post*] (1682)
**1** : the act of transferring an entry or item from a book of original entry to the proper account in a ledger
**2** : the record in a ledger account resulting from the transfer of an entry or item from a book of original entry

**²posting** *noun* [⁷*post*] (1880)
: appointment to a post or a command

**post–Kant·ian** \ˌpōs(t)-'kan-tē-ən, -'kän-\ *adjective* (1843)
: of or relating to the idealist philosophers (as Fichte, Schelling, and Hegel) following Kant and developing some of his ideas

**post·lap·sar·i·an** \ˌlap-'ser-ē-ən\ *adjective* [*post-* + Latin *lapsus* slip, fall — more at LAPSE] (1733)
: of, relating to, or characteristic of the time or state after the fall of mankind

**post·lit·er·ate** \-'li-tə-rət *also* -'li-trət\ *adjective* (1965)
: relating to or occurring after the introduction of the electronic media

**post·lude** \'pōst-ˌlüd\ *noun* [*post-* + *-lude* (as in *prelude*)] (1851)
**1** : a closing piece of music; *especially* : an organ voluntary at the end of a church service
**2** : a closing phase (as of an epoch or a literary work)

**post·man** \'pōs(t)-mən, -ˌman\ *noun* (1529)
: MAILMAN

**¹post·mark** \-ˌmärk\ *noun* (1678)
: an official postal marking on a piece of mail; *specifically* : a mark showing the post office and date of mailing

**²postmark** *transitive verb* (1716)
: to put a postmark on

**post·mas·ter** \-ˌmas-tər\ *noun* (1513)
**1** : one who has charge of a post office
**2** : one who has charge of a station for the accommodation of travelers or who supplies post-horses
— **post·mas·ter·ship** \-ˌship\ *noun*

**postmaster general** *noun, plural* **postmasters general** (1626)
: an official in charge of a national post office department or agency

**post·men·o·paus·al** \ˌpōs(t)-ˌme-nə-'pȯ-zəl\ *adjective* (1928)
**1** : having undergone menopause
**2** : occurring after menopause

**post me·ri·di·em** \-mə-'ri-dē-əm, -ˌem\ *adjective* [Latin] (1647)
: being after noon — abbreviation *p.m.*

**post·mil·le·nar·i·an·ism** \-ˌmi-lə-'ner-ē-ə-ˌni-zəm\ *noun* (circa 1890)
: POSTMILLENNIALISM
— **postmillenarian** *adjective or noun*

**post·mil·len·ni·al** \-mə-'le-nē-əl\ *adjective* (1851)
**1** : coming after or relating to the period after the millennium
**2** : holding or relating to postmillennialism

**post·mil·len·ni·al·ism** \-ə-ˌli-zəm\ *noun* (1879)
: the theological doctrine that the second coming of Christ will occur after the millennium
— **post·mil·len·ni·al·ist** \-ə-list\ *noun*

**post·mis·tress** \'pōs(t)-ˌmis-trəs\ *noun* (1697)
: a woman who is a postmaster

**post·mod·ern** \ˌpōs(t)-'mä-dərn, ÷-'mä-d(ə-)rən\ *adjective* (1949)
: of, relating to, or being any of several movements (as in art, architecture, or literature) that are reactions against the philosophy and practices of modern movements and are typically marked by revival of traditional elements and techniques
— **post·mod·ern·ism** \-dər-ˌni-zəm\ *noun*
— **post·mod·ern·ist** \-nist\ *adjective or noun*

**¹post·mor·tem** \ˌpōs(t)-'mȯr-təm\ *adjective* [Latin *post mortem* after death] (circa 1836)
**1** : done, occurring, or collected after death ⟨*postmortem* tissue specimens⟩
**2** : following the event

**²postmortem** *noun* (1850)
**1** : an analysis or discussion of an event after it is over
**2** : AUTOPSY 1

**postmortem examination** *noun* (1837)
: AUTOPSY 1

**post·na·sal drip** \'pōst-ˌnā-zəl-\ *noun* (1949)

: flow of mucous secretion from the posterior part of the nasal cavity onto the wall of the pharynx occurring usually as a chronic accompaniment of an allergic state

**post·na·tal** \ˌpōs(t)-ˈnā-tᵊl\ *adjective* [International Scientific Vocabulary] (circa 1859)
: occurring or being after birth; *specifically* : of or relating to an infant immediately after birth ⟨*postnatal* care⟩
— **post·na·tal·ly** *adverb*

**post·nup·tial** \-ˈnəp-shəl, -chəl, ÷-chə-wəl\ *adjective* (1807)
: made or occurring after marriage or mating

**post oak** *noun* [¹post] (1775)
: an oak (*Quercus stellata*) of the eastern and central U.S. having hard durable wood

**¹post–obit** \ˌpōst-ˈō-bət, *especially British* -ˈä-bit\ *noun* (1751)
: POST-OBIT BOND

**²post–obit** *adjective* [Latin *post obitum* after death] (circa 1834)
: occurring or taking effect after death

**post–obit bond** *noun* (1788)
: a bond made by a reversioner to secure a loan and payable out of his reversion

**post office** *noun* (1652)
1 : a government department or agency handling the transmission of mail
2 : a local branch of a national post office handling the mail for a particular place or area
3 : a game in which a player acting as postmaster or postmistress may exact a kiss from one of the opposite sex as payment for the pretended delivery of a letter

**post·op·er·a·tive** \ˌpōst-ˈä-p(ə-)rə-tiv, -pə-ˌrā-\ *adjective* [International Scientific Vocabulary] (circa 1890)
1 : following a surgical operation ⟨*postoperative* care⟩
2 : having undergone a surgical operation ⟨*postoperative* patient⟩
— **post·op·er·a·tive·ly** *adverb*

**post·or·bit·al** \-ˈȯr-bə-tᵊl\ *adjective* (circa 1836)
: situated behind the eye socket

**post·paid** \ˈpōs(t)-ˈpād\ *adjective* (1653)
: having the postage paid by the sender and not chargeable to the receiver

**post·par·tum** \ˌpōs(t)-ˈpär-təm\ *adjective* [New Latin *post partum* after birth] (1846)
1 : following parturition ⟨*postpartum* period⟩
2 : being in the postpartum period ⟨*postpartum* mothers⟩
— **postpartum** *adverb*

**post·pone** \(ˌ)pōs(t)-ˈpōn\ *transitive verb* **post·poned; post·pon·ing** [Latin *postponere* to place after, postpone, from *post-* + *ponere* to place — more at POSITION] (circa 1520)
1 : to put off to a later time : DEFER
2 a : to place later (as in a sentence) than the normal position in English ⟨*postpone* an adjective⟩ b : to place later in order of precedence, preference, or importance
*synonym* see DEFER
— **post·pon·able** \-ˈpō-nə-bəl\ *adjective*
— **post·pone·ment** \-ˈpōn-mənt\ *noun*
— **post·pon·er** *noun*

**post·po·si·tion** \ˌpōs(t)-pə-ˈzi-shən, ˈpōs(t)-pə-ˌ\ *noun* [French, from *postposer* to place after, from Latin *postponere* (perfect indicative *postposui*)] (circa 1638)
: the placing of a grammatical element after a word to which it is primarily related in a sentence; *also* : such a word or particle especially when functioning as a preposition
— **post·po·si·tion·al** \ˌpōs(t)-pə-ˈzish-nəl, -ˈzi-shə-nᵊl\ *adjective*
— **post·po·si·tion·al·ly** *adverb*

**post·pos·i·tive** \-ˈpä-zə-tiv, -ˈpäz-tiv\ *adjective* (1786)
: placed after or at the end of another word
— **post·pos·i·tive·ly** *adverb*

**post·pran·di·al** \pōs(t)-ˈpran-dē-əl\ *adjective* (1820)
: occurring after a meal

**post·pro·duc·tion** \ˌpōs(t)-prə-ˈdək-shən, ˈpōs(t)-prə-ˌ, -prō-\ *noun* (1953)
: the period following filming or taping in which a motion picture or television show is readied for public presentation

**post road** *noun* (1657)
: a route over which mail is carried

**post·script** \ˈpōs(t)-ˌskript\ *noun* [New Latin *postscriptum*, from Latin, neuter of *postscriptus*, past participle of *postscribere* to write after, from *post-* + *scribere* to write — more at SCRIBE] (1551)
: a note or series of notes appended to a completed letter, article, or book

**post·syn·ap·tic** \ˌpōs(t)-sə-ˈnap-tik\ *adjective* (1909)
1 : occurring after synapsis ⟨a *postsynaptic* chromosome⟩
2 : relating to, occurring in, or being part of a nerve cell by which a wave of excitation is conveyed away from a synapse
— **post·syn·ap·ti·cal·ly** \-ti-k(ə-)lē\ *adverb*

**post·ten·sion** \-ˈten(t)-shən\ *transitive verb* (1950)
: to apply tension to (reinforcing steel) after concrete has set

**post·test** \ˈpōs(t)-ˌtest\ *noun* (circa 1951)
: a test given to students after completion of an instructional program or segment and often used in conjunction with a pretest to measure their achievement and the effectiveness of the program

**post time** *noun* [¹post] (1941)
: the designated time for the start of a horse race

**post·tran·scrip·tion·al** \ˌpōs(t)-tran(t)-ˈskrip-shnəl, -shə-nᵊl\ *adjective* (1969)
: occurring, acting, or existing after genetic transcription

**post·trans·fu·sion** \-tran(t)s-ˈfyü-zhən\ *adjective* (1944)
1 : caused by transfused blood
2 : occurring after blood transfusion ⟨*posttransfusion* shock⟩

**post·trans·la·tion·al** \-tran(t)s-ˈlā-shnəl, -shə-nᵊl\ *adjective* (1975)
: occurring or existing after genetic translation

**post–traumatic stress disorder** *noun* (1980)
: a psychological reaction occurring after a highly stressing event that is usually characterized by depression, anxiety, flashbacks, recurrent nightmares, and avoidance of reminders of the event — called also *post-traumatic stress syndrome*

**pos·tu·lan·cy** \ˈpäs-chə-lən(t)-sē\ *noun, plural* **-cies** (circa 1883)
1 : the quality or state of being a postulant
2 : the period during which a person remains a postulant

**pos·tu·lant** \ˈpäs-chə-lənt\ *noun* [French, petitioner, candidate, postulant, from Middle French, from present participle of *postuler* to demand, solicit, from Latin *postulare*] (1759)
1 : a person admitted to a religious order as a probationary candidate for membership
2 : a person on probation before being admitted as a candidate for holy orders in the Episcopal Church

**¹pos·tu·late** \ˈpäs-chə-ˌlāt\ *transitive verb* **-lat·ed; -lat·ing** [Latin *postulatus*, past participle of *postulare*; akin to Latin *poscere* to ask, Old High German *forscōn* to search, Sanskrit *pṛcchati* he asks — more at PRAY] (1593)
1 : DEMAND, CLAIM
2 a : to assume or claim as true, existent, or necessary : depend upon or start from the postulate of b : to assume as a postulate or axiom (as in logic or mathematics)
— **pos·tu·la·tion** \ˌpäs-chə-ˈlā-shən\ *noun*
— **pos·tu·la·tion·al** \-shnəl, -shə-nᵊl\ *adjective*

**²pos·tu·late** \ˈpäs-chə-lət, -ˌlāt\ *noun* [Medieval Latin *postulatum*, from neuter of *postula-*

*tus*, past participle of *postulare* to assume, from Latin, to demand] (1646)
1 : a hypothesis advanced as an essential presupposition, condition, or premise of a train of reasoning
2 : AXIOM 3

**pos·tu·la·tor** \-ˌlā-tər\ *noun* (1863)
: an official who presents a plea for beatification or canonization in the Roman Catholic Church — compare DEVIL'S ADVOCATE

**pos·tur·al** \ˈpäs-chə-rəl\ *adjective* (1857)
: of, relating to, or involving posture

**¹pos·ture** \ˈpäs-chər\ *noun* [French, from Italian *postura*, from Latin *positura*, from *positus*, past participle of *ponere* to place — more at POSITION] (circa 1586)
1 a : the position or bearing of the body whether characteristic or assumed for a special purpose ⟨erect *posture*⟩ b : the pose of a model or artistic figure
2 : state or condition at a given time especially with respect to capability in particular circumstances ⟨maintain a competitive *posture* in the market⟩ ⟨put the country in a *posture* of defense⟩
3 : a conscious mental or outward behavioral attitude ⟨takes a neutral *posture* toward the discussions⟩

**²posture** *verb* **pos·tured; pos·tur·ing** (circa 1645)
*transitive verb*
: to cause to assume a given posture : POSE
*intransitive verb*
1 : to assume a posture; *especially* : to strike a pose for effect
2 : to assume an artificial or pretended attitude : ATTITUDINIZE
— **pos·tur·er** \-chər-ər\ *noun*

**post·vo·cal·ic** \ˌpōs(t)-vō-ˈka-lik, -və-\ *adjective* [International Scientific Vocabulary] (1892)
: immediately following a vowel

**po·sy** \ˈpō-zē\ *noun, plural* **posies** [alteration of *poesy*] (1533)
1 : a brief sentiment, motto, or legend
2 a : BOUQUET, NOSEGAY b : FLOWER

**¹pot** \ˈpät\ *noun* [Middle English, from Old English *pott;* akin to Middle Low German *pot* pot] (before 12th century)
1 a : a usually rounded metal or earthen container used chiefly for domestic purposes (as in cooking or for holding liquids or growing plants); *also* : any of various technical or industrial vessels or enclosures resembling or likened to a household pot ⟨the *pot* of a still⟩ b : POTFUL ⟨a *pot* of coffee⟩
2 : an enclosed framework of wire, wood, or wicker for catching fish or lobsters
3 a : a large amount (as of money) b (1) : the total of the bets at stake at one time (2) : one round in a poker game c : the common fund of a group
4 : POTSHOT
5 : POTBELLY
6 : RUIN ⟨gone to *pot*⟩
7 *British* : a shot in snooker in which a ball is pocketed

**²pot** *verb* **pot·ted; pot·ting** (1616)
*transitive verb*
1 a : to place in a pot b : to pack or preserve (as cooked and chopped meat) in a sealed pot, jar, or can often with aspic
2 : to shoot with a potshot
3 : to make or shape (earthenware) as a potter
4 : to embed (as electronic components) in a container with an insulating or protective material (as plastic)
*intransitive verb*
: to take a potshot

---

\ə\ abut \ᵊ\ kitten \ər\ further \a\ ash \ā\ ace
\ä\ mop, mar \aú\ out \ch\ chin \e\ bet \ē\ easy
\g\ go \i\ hit \ī\ ice \j\ job \ŋ\ sing \ō\ go
\ȯ\ law \ȯi\ boy \th\ thin \th\ the \ü\ loot \ú\ foot
\y\ yet \zh\ vision *see also* Guide to Pronunciation

**³pot** *noun* [perhaps modification of Mexican Spanish *potiguaya*] (1938)
: MARIJUANA

**¹po·ta·ble** \'pō-tə-bəl\ *adjective* [Middle English, from Late Latin *potabilis*, from Latin *potare* to drink; akin to Latin *bibere* to drink, Greek *pinein*] (15th century)
: suitable for drinking
— **po·ta·bil·i·ty** \ˌpō-tə-'bi-lə-tē\ *noun*
— **po·ta·ble·ness** \'pō-tə-bəl-nəs\ *noun*

**²potable** *noun* (1623)
: a liquid that is suitable for drinking; *especially* : an alcoholic beverage

**po·tage** \pó-'täzh\ *noun* [Middle French, from Old French, pottage] (1567)
: a thick soup

**pot ale** *noun* (1812)
: the residue of fermented wort left in a still after the distillation of whiskey or alcohol and used for feeding swine

**pot·ash** \'pät-ˌash\ *noun* [singular of *pot ashes*] (circa 1648)
**1** : potassium carbonate especially from wood ashes
**2** : potassium or a potassium compound especially as used in agriculture or industry

**po·tas·sic** \pə-'ta-sik\ *adjective* (1858)
: of, relating to, or containing potassium

**po·tas·si·um** \pə-'ta-sē-əm\ *noun, often attributive* [New Latin, from *potassa* potash, from English *potash*] (circa 1807)
: a silver-white soft light low-melting univalent metallic element of the alkali metal group that occurs abundantly in nature especially combined in minerals — see ELEMENT table

**potassium–argon** *adjective* (1953)
: being or relating to a method of dating paleontological or geological materials based on the radioactive decay of potassium to argon that has taken place in a specimen

**potassium bromide** *noun* (1873)
: a crystalline salt KBr with a saline taste that is used as a sedative and in photography

**potassium carbonate** *noun* (1885)
: a white salt $K_2CO_3$ that forms a strongly alkaline solution and is used in making glass and soap

**potassium chlorate** *noun* (1885)
: a crystalline salt $KClO_3$ that is used as an oxidizing agent in matches, fireworks, and explosives

**potassium chloride** *noun* (1885)
: a crystalline salt KCl occurring as a mineral and in natural waters and used especially as a fertilizer

**potassium cyanide** *noun* (1885)
: a very poisonous crystalline salt KCN used especially in gold and silver extraction from ore

**potassium dichromate** *noun* (1885)
: a soluble salt $K_2Cr_2O_7$ forming large orange-red crystals used especially in dyeing, in photography, and as an oxidizing agent

**potassium hydroxide** *noun* (1885)
: a white deliquescent solid KOH that dissolves in water with much heat to form a strongly alkaline and caustic liquid and is used chiefly in making soap and as a reagent

**potassium nitrate** *noun* (1885)
: a crystalline salt $KNO_3$ that occurs as a product of nitrification in arable soils, is a strong oxidizer, and is used especially in making gunpowder, as a fertilizer, and in medicine

**potassium permanganate** *noun* (1869)
: a dark purple salt $KMnO_4$ used as an oxidizer and disinfectant

**potassium sorbate** *noun* (1960)
: a potassium salt $C_6H_7KO_2$ of sorbic acid used especially as a food preservative

**potassium sulfate** *noun* (1885)
: a white crystalline compound $K_2SO_4$ used especially as a fertilizer

**po·ta·tion** \pō-'tā-shən\ *noun* [Middle English *potacioun*, from Middle French *potation*, from Latin *potation-*, *potatio* act of drinking, from *potare* to drink — more at POTABLE] (15th century)
**1** : a usually alcoholic drink or brew
**2** : the act or an instance of drinking or inhaling; *also* : the portion taken in one such act

**po·ta·to** \pə-'tā-(ˌ)tō, -tə, *dialect* pə-'dā-, bə-\ *noun, plural* **-toes** *often attributive* [Spanish *batata*, from Taino] (1565)
**1** : SWEET POTATO
**2 a** : an erect South American herb (*Solanum tuberosum*) of the nightshade family widely cultivated as a vegetable crop
**b** : the edible starchy tuber of a potato — called also *Irish potato, white potato*
*usage* see TOMATO

**potato beetle** *noun* (1821)
: COLORADO POTATO BEETLE

**potato blight** *noun* (1879)
: any of several destructive fungus diseases of the potato

potato 2a

**potato bug** *noun* (1799)
: COLORADO POTATO BEETLE

**potato chip** *noun* (1878)
: a thin slice of white potato that has been fried until crisp and then usually salted

**potato leafhopper** *noun* (1921)
: a small green white-spotted leafhopper (*Empoasca fabae*) of the eastern and southern U.S. that is a serious pest on many cultivated plants and especially on the potato

**potato pancake** *noun* (1935)
: a fried flat cake of grated potato mixed with raw egg and usually grated onion and spices

**potato tu·ber·worm** \-'tü-bər-ˌwərm, -'tyü-\ *noun* (1920)
: a grayish brown moth (*Phthorimaea operculella* of the family Gelechiidae) whose larva mines the leaves and bores in the stems especially of potato and tobacco plants and commonly overwinters in potato tubers

**pot-au-feu** \ˌpät-ō-'fə(r), pȯ-tō-fœ\ *noun, plural* **pot-au-feu** [French, literally, pot on the fire] (1791)
: a French boiled dinner of meat and vegetables

**pot·bel·lied** \'pät-ˌbe-lēd\ *adjective* (1657)
: having a potbelly

**potbellied stove** *noun* (1933)
: a stove with a rounded or bulging body — called also *potbelly stove*

**pot·bel·ly** \'pät-ˌbe-lē\ *noun* (circa 1714)
**1** : an enlarged, swollen, or protruding abdomen
**2** : POTBELLIED STOVE

**pot·boil** \-ˌbȯil\ *intransitive verb* (1867)
: to produce potboilers

**pot·boil·er** \-ˌbȯi-lər\ *noun* (1864)
: a usually inferior work (as of art or literature) produced chiefly for profit

**pot–bound** \'pät-ˌbau̇nd\ *adjective* (1850)
*of a potted plant* : having roots so densely matted as to allow little or no space for further growth

**pot·boy** \-ˌbȯi\ *noun* (1795)
: a boy who serves drinks in a tavern

**pot cheese** *noun* (1812)
: COTTAGE CHEESE

**po·teen** *also* **po·theen** \pə-'tēn, -'chēn, -'tyēn, -'thēn\ *noun* [Irish *poitín*, literally, small pot, diminutive of *pota* pot] (1812)
: whiskey illicitly distilled in Ireland

**Po·tem·kin village** \pə-'tem(p)-kən-\ *noun* [Grigori *Potëmkin*, who supposedly built impressive fake villages along a route Catherine the Great was to travel] (1937)
: an impressive facade or show designed to hide an undesirable fact or condition ◆

**po·tence** \'pō-t⁽ᵊ⁾n(t)s\ *noun* (15th century)
: POTENCY

**po·ten·cy** \'pō-t⁽ᵊ⁾n(t)-sē\ *noun, plural* **-cies** (15th century)
**1 a** : FORCE, POWER **b** : the quality or state of being potent **c** : the ability or capacity to achieve or bring about a particular result
**2** : POTENTIALITY 1

**¹po·tent** \'pō-t⁽ᵊ⁾nt\ *adjective* [Middle English, from Latin *potent-*, *potens* (present participle of *posse* to be able), from Latin *potis*, *pote* able; akin to Gothic brūth*faths* bridegroom, Greek *posis* husband, Sanskrit *pati* master] (15th century)
**1** : having or wielding force, authority, or influence : POWERFUL
**2** : achieving or bringing about a particular result : EFFECTIVE
**3 a** : chemically or medicinally effective ⟨a *potent* vaccine⟩ **b** : rich in a characteristic constituent
**4** : able to copulate — usually used of the male
— **po·tent·ly** *adverb*

**²potent** *adjective* [obsolete English *potent* crutch] (1610)
*of a heraldic cross* : having flat bars across the ends of the arms — see CROSS illustration

**po·ten·tate** \'pō-t⁽ᵊ⁾n-ˌtāt\ *noun* (15th century)
: RULER, SOVEREIGN; *broadly* : one who wields great power or sway

**¹po·ten·tial** \pə-'ten(t)-shəl\ *adjective* [Middle English *potencial*, from Late Latin *potentialis*, from *potentia* potentiality, from Latin, power, from *potent-*, *potens*] (14th century)
**1** : existing in possibility : capable of development into actuality ⟨*potential* benefits⟩
**2** : expressing possibility; *specifically* : of, relating to, or constituting a verb phrase expressing possibility, liberty, or power by the use of an auxiliary with the infinitive of the verb (as in "it may rain")
*synonym* see LATENT
— **po·ten·tial·ly** \-'ten(t)-sh(ə-)lē\ *adverb*

**²potential** *noun* (1817)
**1 a** : something that can develop or become actual ⟨a *potential* for violence⟩ **b** : PROMISE 2
**2 a** : any of various functions from which the intensity or the velocity at any point in a field may be readily calculated **b** : the work required to move a unit positive charge from a reference point (as at infinity) to a point in question **c** : POTENTIAL DIFFERENCE

**potential difference** *noun* (1896)
: the difference in potential between two points that represents the work involved or the energy released in the transfer of a unit quantity of electricity from one point to the other

**potential energy** *noun* (1853)
: the energy that a piece of matter has because of its position or because of the arrangement of parts

**po·ten·ti·al·i·ty** \pə-ˌten(t)-shē-'a-lə-tē\ *noun, plural* **-ties** (1625)
**1** : the ability to develop or come into existence
**2** : POTENTIAL 1

◇ WORD HISTORY
**Potemkin village**   In 1787, according to an account by a Saxon diplomat named Helbig, the Russian Prince Grigory Aleksandrovich Potemkin arranged for the Empress Catherine the Great to take a grand tour of Ukraine and the newly conquered territory of Crimea. According to Helbig's account, Potemkin, in order to impress Catherine with the prosperity of her new acquisitions, erected whole villages along her traveling route. Fortunately, she was able to view these villages only from a distance, for they were mere facades. Though the story of the sham villages must be regarded as apocryphal, countless retellings have established *Potemkin village* as a general term for any imposing facade or display that masks an undesirable condition or fact.

**po·ten·ti·ate** \pə-'ten(t)-shē-ˌāt\ *transitive verb* **-at·ed; -at·ing** (1817)
: to make effective or active or more effective or more active; *also* : to augment the activity of (as a drug) synergistically
— **po·ten·ti·a·tion** \-ˌten(t)-shē-'ā-shən\ *noun*
— **po·ten·ti·a·tor** \-'ten(t)-shē-ˌā-tər\ *noun*
**po·ten·til·la** \ˌpō-t°n-'ti-lə\ *noun* [New Latin, from Medieval Latin, garden heliotrope, from Latin *potent-, potens*] (1548)
: CINQUEFOIL 1
**po·ten·ti·om·e·ter** \pə-ˌten(t)-shē-'ä-mə-tər\ *noun* [International Scientific Vocabulary *potential* + *-o-* + *-meter*] (1881)
**1** : an instrument for measuring electromotive forces
**2** : VOLTAGE DIVIDER
— **po·ten·ti·o·met·ric** \-sh(ē-)ə-'me-trik\ *adjective*
**pot·ful** \'pät-ˌfůl\ *noun* (14th century)
**1** : as much or as many as a pot will hold
**2** : a large amount ⟨makes a *potful* of money —John Corry⟩
**pot hat** *noun* (1798)
: a hat with a stiff crown; *especially* : DERBY
**pot·head** \'pät-ˌhed\ *noun* (1959)
: a person who smokes marijuana
**¹poth·er** \'pä-thər\ *noun* [origin unknown] (1591)
**1 a** : confused or fidgety flurry or activity : COMMOTION **b** : agitated talk or controversy usually over a trivial matter
**2** : a choking cloud of dust or smoke
**3** : mental turmoil
**²pother** *verb* **poth·ered; poth·er·ing** \'pä-thə-riŋ, 'päth-riŋ\ (1692)
*transitive verb*
: to put into a pother
*intransitive verb*
: to be in a pother
**pot·herb** \'pät-ˌərb, -ˌhərb\ *noun* (1538)
: a usually leafy herb that is cooked for use as greens; *also* : one (as mint) used to season food
**pot holder** *noun* (1944)
: a small cloth pad used for handling hot cooking utensils or containers
**pot·hole** \'pät-ˌhōl\ *noun* (1826)
**1 a** : a circular hole formed in the rocky bed of a river by the grinding action of stones or gravel whirled round by the water **b** : a sizable rounded often water-filled depression in land
**2** : a pot-shaped hole in a road surface
— **pot·holed** \-ˌhōld\ *adjective*
**pot·hook** \-ˌhůk\ *noun* (15th century)
**1** : an S-shaped hook for hanging pots and kettles over an open fire
**2** : a written character resembling a pothook
**pot·house** \-ˌhaůs\ *noun* (1724)
: TAVERN 1
**pot·hunt·er** \-ˌhən-tər\ *noun* (1781)
**1** : one who hunts game for food
**2** : an amateur archaeologist
— **pot·hunt·ing** \-tiŋ\ *noun*
**po·tion** \'pō-shən\ *noun* [Middle English *pocioun*, from Middle French *potion*, from Latin *potion-, potio* drink, potion, from *potare* to drink — more at POTABLE] (14th century)
: a mixture of liquids (as liquor or medicine)
**¹pot·latch** \'pät-ˌlach\ *noun* [Chinook Jargon *patlač*, from Nootka *p̌aX̌p̌ač*] (circa 1861)
**1** : a ceremonial feast of the American Indians of the northwest coast marked by the host's lavish distribution of gifts or sometimes destruction of property to demonstrate wealth and generosity with the expectation of eventual reciprocation
**2** *Northwest* : a social event or celebration
**²potlatch** (1898)
*transitive verb*
**1** : to give (as a gift) especially with the expectation of a gift in return
**2** : to hold or give a potlatch for (as a tribe or group)

*intransitive verb*
: to hold or give a potlatch
**pot lik·ker** \-'li-kər\ *Southern & Midland variant of* POT LIQUOR
**pot·line** \'pät-ˌlīn\ *noun* (1944)
: a row of electrolytic cells used in the production of aluminum
**pot liquor** *noun* (1744)
: the liquid left in a pot after cooking something
**pot·luck** \'pät-'lək, *1b also* -ˌlək\ *noun* (1592)
**1 a** : the regular meal available to a guest for whom no special preparations have been made **b** : a communal meal to which people bring food to share — usually used attributively ⟨a *potluck* supper⟩
**2** : whatever is offered or available in given circumstances or at a given time
**pot marigold** *noun* (1814)
: a calendula (*Calendula officinalis*) grown especially for ornament
**po·tom·e·ter** \pō-'tä-mə-tər\ *noun* [Greek *poton* drink (akin to Greek *pinein* to drink) + English *-meter* — more at POTABLE] (1884)
: an apparatus for measuring the rate of transpiration in a plant by determining the amount of water absorbed
**pot·pie** \'pät-'pī, -ˌpī\ *noun* (circa 1792)
: pastry-covered meat and vegetables cooked in a deep dish
**pot·pour·ri** \ˌpō-pů-'rē\ *noun* [French *pot pourri*, literally, rotten pot] (1749)
**1** : a mixture of flowers, herbs, and spices that is usually kept in a jar and used for scent
**2** : a miscellaneous collection : MEDLEY ⟨a *potpourri* of the best songs and sketches —*Current Biography*⟩ ◆
**pot roast** *noun* (1881)
: a piece of beef cooked by braising usually on top of the stove
**pot·sherd** \'pät-ˌshərd\ *noun* [Middle English *pot-sherd*, from *pot* + *sherd* shard] (14th century)
: a pottery fragment
**¹pot·shot** \-ˌshät\ *noun* [from the notion that such a shot is unsportsmanlike and worthy only of one whose object is to fill the cooking pot] (1858)
**1** : a shot taken from ambush or at a random or easy target
**2** : a critical remark made in a random or sporadic manner
**²potshot** *verb* **potshot; pot·shot·ting** (1918)
*intransitive verb*
: to take a potshot
*transitive verb*
: to attack or shoot with a potshot
**pot still** *noun* (1799)
: a still used especially in the distillation of Irish grain whiskey and Scotch malt whiskey in which the heat of the fire is applied directly to the pot containing the mash
**pot·stone** \'pät-ˌstōn\ *noun* (1771)
: a more or less impure steatite used especially in prehistoric times to make cooking vessels
**pot·tage** \'pä-tij\ *noun* [Middle English *potage*, from Old French, from *pot* pot, of Germanic origin; akin to Old English *pott* pot] (13th century)
: a thick soup of vegetables and often meat
**pot·ted** \'pä-təd\ *adjective* (1646)
**1** *chiefly British* : preserved in a pot, jar, or can
**2** : planted or grown in a pot
**3** *chiefly British* : briefly and superficially summarized ⟨a dull, pedestrian *potted* history —*Times Literary Supplement*⟩
**4** *slang* : DRUNK 1a
**¹pot·ter** \'pä-tər\ *noun* (before 12th century)
: one that makes pottery
**²potter** *intransitive verb* [probably frequentative of English dialect *pote* to poke] (1829)
: PUTTER
— **pot·ter·er** \'pä-tər-ər\ *noun*
— **pot·ter·ing·ly** \'pä-tə-riŋ-lē\ *adverb*

**potter's clay** *noun* (15th century)
: a plastic clay suitable for making pottery — called also *potter's earth*
**potter's field** *noun* [from the mention in Matthew 27:7 of the purchase of a potter's field for use as a graveyard] (1777)
: a public burial place for paupers, unknown persons, and criminals
**potter's wheel** *noun* (circa 1741)
: a usually horizontal disk revolving on a vertical spindle and carrying the clay being shaped by a potter
**pot·tery** \'pä-tə-rē\ *noun, plural* **-ter·ies** (15th century)
**1** : a place where clayware is made and fired
**2 a** : the art or craft of the potter **b** : the manufacture of clayware
**3** : CLAYWARE; *especially* : earthenware as distinguished on the one hand from porcelain and stoneware and on the other from brick and tile
**pot·tle** \'pä-t°l\ *noun* [Middle English *potel*, from Middle French, from *pot*] (14th century)
: a container holding a half gallon (1.9 liters)
**pot·to** \'pä-(ˌ)tō\ *noun, plural* **pottos** [perhaps from Wolof *pata*, a tailless monkey] (1705)
: any of several African primates (genera *Arctocebus* and *Perodicticus*); *especially* : a West African primate (*P. potto*) that has a vestigial index finger and tail
**Pott's disease** \'päts-\ *noun* [Percivall *Pott* (died 1788) English surgeon] (1835)
: tuberculosis of the spine with destruction of bone resulting in curvature of the spine
**¹pot·ty** \'pä-tē\ *adjective* **pot·ti·er; -est** [probably from ¹*pot*] (circa 1860)
**1** *British* : TRIVIAL, INSIGNIFICANT
**2** *chiefly British* : slightly crazy
**3** : SNOBBISH
**²potty** *noun, plural* **potties** (circa 1942)
: a small child's pot for urination or defecation
**pot·ty–chair** \-ˌcher, -ˌchar\ *noun* (1943)
: a child's chair having an open seat under which a receptacle in placed for toilet training
**pot·zer** \'pät-sər\ *variant of* PATZER
**¹pouch** \'paůch\ *noun* [Middle English *pouche*, from Middle French, of Germanic origin; akin to Old English *pocca* bag] (14th century)
**1** : a small drawstring bag carried on the person

---

◇ WORD HISTORY
**potpourri** A potpourri, which in ordinary usage alludes to a dried mixture of pleasant-smelling herbs or more broadly to any miscellaneous collection, is etymologically a "putrid pot." The original French *pot pourri* was a stew made of a variety of meats and vegetables cooked together. This was a traditional Spanish dish borrowed by the French, whose name for it is a loan translation of Spanish *olla podrida*. Just why the stew designated *olla podrida* was called "rotten" is not very clear. One explanation is that the Spanish adjective *podrido* has occasionally been used colloquially to mean "very full, teeming," a sense that would fit the nature of the dish. Though not common, similar uses of English *rotten* can be found (as, for example, in the passage "The country's rotten with money, if one could touch it" from a novel by Elizabeth Bowen). And *rotten* in the common idiom "to spoil a child rotten" means little more than "thoroughly."

---

| | | | | |
|---|---|---|---|---|
| \ə\ abut | \ᵊ\ kitten | \ər\ further | \a\ ash | \ā\ ace |
| \ä\ mop, mar | \aů\ out | \ch\ chin | \e\ bet | \ē\ easy |
| \g\ go | \i\ hit | \ī\ ice | \j\ job | \ŋ\ sing | \ō\ go |
| \ȯ\ law | \ȯi\ boy | \th\ thin | \th\ the | \ü\ loot | \ů\ foot |
| \y\ yet | \zh\ vision | *see also* Guide to Pronunciation | | |

**2 a :** a bag of small or moderate size for storing or transporting goods; *specifically* **:** a lockable bag for first-class mail or diplomatic dispatches **b** *chiefly Scottish* **:** POCKET **c :** PACKET **3 :** an anatomical structure resembling a pouch
— **pouched** \'pau̇cht\ *adjective*

**²pouch** (circa 1566)
*transitive verb*
**1 :** to put or form into or as if into a pouch
**2 :** to transmit by pouch
*intransitive verb*
**1 :** to bulge or stick out or down in a manner suggesting a pouch ⟨*pouching* cheeks⟩
**2 :** to transmit mail or dispatches by pouch

**pouchy** \'pau̇-chē\ *adjective* **pouch·i·er; -est** (1828)
**:** having, tending to have, or resembling a pouch ⟨*pouchy* insomniac eyes —Graham Greene⟩

**pouf** *also* **pouffe** \'püf\ *noun* [French *pouf,* something inflated, of imitative origin] (1817)
**1 :** PUFF 3b(3)
**2 :** a bouffant or fluffy part of a garment or accessory
**3 :** OTTOMAN
— **poufed** *or* **pouffed** \'püft\ *adjective*

**Pouil·ly–Fuis·sé** \pü-yē-fwē-'sā\ *noun* [Solutré-*Pouilly* and *Fuissé,* villages in France] (1927)
**:** a dry white burgundy from an area west of Mâcon, France

**Pouil·ly–Fu·mé** \pü-yē-fü-'mā, -fᵫ-\ *noun* [French, from *Pouilly*-sur-Loire, village in France + *fumé,* past participle of *fumer* to smoke, from Latin *fumare,* from *fumus* smoke — more at FUME] (1935)
**:** a dry white wine from the Loire valley of France

**pou·larde** *also* **pou·lard** \pü-'lärd\ *noun* [French *poularde*] (1732)
**:** a pullet sterilized to produce fattening

**poult** \'pōlt\ *noun* [Middle English *polet, pulte* young fowl — more at PULLET] (15th century)
**:** a young fowl; *especially* **:** a young turkey

**poul·ter·er** \'pōl-tər-ər\ *noun* [alteration of Middle English *pulter,* from Middle French *pouletier*] (1638)
**:** one that deals in poultry

**poul·ter's measure** \'pōl-tərz-\ *noun* [obsolete *poulter* poulterer; from Middle English *pulter;* from the former practice of occasionally giving one or two extra when counting eggs by dozens] (1576)
**:** a meter in which lines of 12 and 14 syllables alternate

**¹poul·tice** \'pōl-təs\ *noun* [Middle English *pultes,* from Medieval Latin, literally, pap, from Latin, plural of *pult-, puls* porridge] (15th century)
**:** a soft usually heated and sometimes medicated mass spread on cloth and applied to sores or other lesions

**²poultice** *transitive verb* **-ticed; -tic·ing** (1730)
**:** to apply a poultice to

**poul·try** \'pōl-trē\ *noun* [Middle English *pultrie,* from Middle French *pouleterie,* from Old French, from *pouletier* poulterer, from *poulet* — more at PULLET] (14th century)
**:** domesticated birds kept for eggs or meat

**poul·try·man** \-mən\ *noun* (circa 1574)
**1 :** one who raises domestic fowls especially on a commercial scale for the production of eggs and meat
**2 :** one who deals in poultry or poultry products

**¹pounce** \'pau̇n(t)s\ *noun* [Middle English, talon] (15th century)
**:** the claw of a bird of prey

**²pounce** *intransitive verb* **pounced; pounc·ing** (1744)

**1 a :** to swoop upon and seize something with or as if with talons **b :** to seize upon and make capital of something (as another's blunder or an opportunity)
**2 :** to make a sudden assault or approach

**³pounce** *noun* (1841)
**:** the act of pouncing

**⁴pounce** *transitive verb* **pounced; pounc·ing** [Middle French *poncer,* from *ponce*] (1535)
**:** to dust, rub, finish, or stencil with pounce

**⁵pounce** *noun* [French *ponce* pumice, from Middle French, from Late Latin *pomic-, pomex,* alteration of Latin *pumic-, pumex* — more at FOAM] (1706)
**1 :** a fine powder formerly used to prevent ink from spreading
**2 :** a fine powder for making stenciled patterns

**poun·cet–box** \'pau̇n(t)-sət-\ *noun* [probably from (assumed) Middle French *poncette* small pounce bag] (1596)
*archaic* **:** a box for carrying pomander

**¹pound** \'pau̇nd\ *noun, plural* **pounds** *also* **pound** [Middle English, from Old English *pund,* from Latin *pondo* pound, from ablative of *pondus* weight — more at PENDANT] (before 12th century)
**1 :** any of various units of mass and weight; *specifically* **:** a unit now in general use among English-speaking peoples equal to 16 avoirdupois ounces or 7000 grains or 0.45359237 kilogram — see WEIGHT table
**2 a :** the basic monetary unit of the United Kingdom — called also *pound sterling* **b :** any of numerous basic monetary units of other countries — see MONEY table **c :** ²LIRA

**²pound** *noun* [Middle English, enclosure, from Old English *pund-*] (14th century)
**1 a :** an enclosure for animals; *especially* **:** a public enclosure for stray or unlicensed animals ⟨a dog *pound*⟩ **b :** a depot for holding impounded personal property until redeemed by the owner ⟨a car *pound*⟩
**2 :** a place or condition of confinement
**3 :** an enclosure within which fish are kept or caught; *especially* **:** the inner compartment of a fish trap or pound net

**³pound** *noun* (1562)
**:** an act or sound of pounding

**⁴pound** *verb* [alteration of Middle English *pounen,* from Old English *pūnian*] (1594)
*transitive verb*
**1 :** to reduce to powder or pulp by beating
**2 a :** to strike heavily or repeatedly **b :** to produce or as if with repeated vigorous strokes — usually used with *out* ⟨*pound* out a story on the typewriter⟩ **c :** to inculcate by insistent repetition **:** DRIVE ⟨day after day the facts were *pounded* home to them —Ivy B. Priest⟩
**3 :** to move along heavily or persistently ⟨*pounded* the pavements looking for work⟩
*intransitive verb*
**1 :** to strike heavy repeated blows
**2 :** PULSATE, THROB ⟨my heart was *pounding*⟩
**3 a :** to move with or make a heavy repetitive sound **b :** to work hard and continuously — usually used with *away*

**¹pound·age** \'pau̇n-dij\ *noun* (circa 1500)
**1 :** a charge per pound of weight
**2 :** weight in pounds

**²poundage** *noun* (1554)
**:** IMPOUNDMENT 1

**pound·al** \'pau̇n-dᵊl\ *noun* [¹*pound* + *-al* (as in *quintal*)] (1879)
**:** a unit of force equal to the force that would give a free mass of one pound an acceleration of one foot per second per second

**pound cake** *noun* [from the original recipe prescribing a pound of each of the principal ingredients] (1747)
**:** a rich butter cake made with a large proportion of eggs and shortening

**¹pound·er** \'pau̇n-dər\ *noun* (before 12th century)
**1 :** one that pounds

**2 :** a tool used for pounding
**²pounder** *noun* (1684)
**1 :** a gun throwing a projectile of a specified weight — usually used in combination ⟨the ship was armed with six-*pounders*⟩
**2 :** one having a usually specified weight or value in pounds — usually used in combination ⟨caught a ten-*pounder*⟩

**pound–fool·ish** \'pau̇n(d)-'fü-lish\ *adjective* [from the phrase *penny-wise and pound-foolish*] (1607)
**:** imprudent in dealing with large sums or large matters

**pound mile** *noun* (1939)
**:** the transport of one pound of mail or express for one mile

**pound net** *noun* (1865)
**:** a fish trap consisting of a netting arranged into a directing wing and an enclosure with a narrow entrance

**pound sign** *noun* (1980)
**1 :** the symbol £
**2 :** the symbol #

**¹pour** \'pōr, 'pȯr\ *verb* [Middle English] (14th century)
*transitive verb*
**1 a :** to cause to flow in a stream **b :** to dispense from a container ⟨*poured* drinks for everyone⟩
**2 :** to supply or produce freely or copiously
**3 :** to give full expression to **:** VENT ⟨*poured* out his feelings⟩
*intransitive verb*
**1 :** to move with a continuous flow
**2 :** to rain hard
**3 :** to move or come continuously **:** STREAM ⟨complaints *poured* in⟩
— **pour·able** \'pōr-ə-bəl, 'pȯr-\ *adjective*
— **pour·er** \-ər\ *noun*
— **pour·ing·ly** \-iŋ-lē\ *adverb*

**²pour** *noun* (1790)
**1 :** the action of pouring **:** STREAM
**2 a :** an instance of pouring or an amount poured **b :** a heavy fall of rain **:** DOWNPOUR

**pour·boire** \pu̇r-'bwär\ *noun* [French, from *pour boire* for drinking] (1817)
**:** TIP, GRATUITY

**pour·par·ler** \pu̇r-pär-'lā\ *noun* [French, from Middle French, from *pourparler* to discuss, from Old French, from *pour* for, before + *parler* to speak — more at PURCHASE, PARLEY] (1795)
**:** a discussion preliminary to negotiations

**pour·point** \'pu̇r-pȯint, -pwänt\ *noun* [Middle English *purpoint,* from Middle French *pourpoint,* from Old French *porpoint,* from *porpoint,* adjective, quilted, alteration of (assumed) Vulgar Latin *perpunctus,* past participle of *perpungere* to perforate, from Latin *per* through + *pungere* to prick, pierce — more at PUNGENT] (14th century)
**:** a padded and quilted doublet

**pour point** \'pōr-pȯint, 'pȯr-\ *noun* (1922)
**:** the lowest temperature at which a substance flows under specified conditions

**pousse–ca·fé** \püs-(,)ka-'fā\ *noun* [French, literally, coffee chaser] (1880)
**:** an after-dinner drink consisting of several liqueurs of different colors and specific gravities poured so as to remain in separate layers

**pous·sette** \pü-'set\ *intransitive verb* **pous·sett·ed; pous·sett·ing** [French, game in which contestants cross pins with each attempting to get his pin on top, from *pousser* to push] (1812)
**:** to swing in a semicircle with hands joined with one's partner in a country-dance

**¹pout** \'pau̇t\ *verb* [Middle English] (14th century)
*intransitive verb*
**1 a :** to show displeasure by thrusting out the lips or wearing a sullen expression **b :** SULK
**2 :** PROTRUDE
*transitive verb*
**:** to cause to protrude ⟨*pouted* her lips⟩

**²pout** *noun* (1591)

**1** : a protrusion of the lips expressive of displeasure
**2** *plural* : a fit of pique
³**pout** *noun, plural* **pout** *or* **pouts** [probably from (assumed) Middle English *poute*, a fish with a large head, from Old English *-pūte*; akin to Middle English *pouten* to pout] (1591) : any of several large-headed fishes (as a bullhead or eelpout)
**pout·er** \'paú-tər\ *noun* (1725)
**1** : a domestic pigeon of a breed characterized by erect carriage and a dilatable crop
**2** : one that pouts
**pouty** \'paú-tē\ *adjective* (1863)
**1** : SULKY 1
**2** : expressive of displeasure
**pov·er·ty** \'pä-vər-tē\ *noun, often attributive* [Middle English *poverte*, from Old French *poverté*, from Latin *paupertat-, paupertas*, from *pauper* poor — more at POOR] (12th century)
**1 a** : the state of one who lacks a usual or socially acceptable amount of money or material possessions **b** : renunciation as a member of a religious order of the right as an individual to own property
**2** : SCARCITY, DEARTH
**3 a** : debility due to malnutrition **b** : lack of fertility ⟨*poverty* of the soil⟩ ☆
**poverty line** *noun* (1901) : a level of personal or family income below which one is classified as poor according to governmental standards — called also *poverty level*
**pov·er·ty–strick·en** \-ˌstri-kən\ *adjective* (1803) : very poor : DESTITUTE
¹**pow** \'pō, 'paú\ *noun* [alteration of *poll*] (1724) : HEAD, POLL
²**pow** \'paú\ *noun* [imitative] (1881) : a sound of a blow or explosion
**POW** \ˌpē-(ˌ)ō-'də-bəl-(ˌ)yü, -bə-(ˌ)yü; -'dəb-(ˌ)yü\ *noun* (circa 1919) : PRISONER OF WAR
¹**pow·der** \'paú-dər\ *verb* **pow·dered; pow·der·ing** \'paú-d(ə-)riŋ\ (13th century)
*transitive verb*
**1** : to sprinkle or cover with or as if with powder
**2** : to reduce or convert to powder
**3** : to hit (as a ball) very hard
*intransitive verb*
**1** : to become powder
**2** : to apply cosmetic powder
— **pow·der·er** \-dər-ər\ *noun*
²**powder** *noun, often attributive* [Middle English *poudre*, from Old French, from Latin *pulver-, pulvis* dust; probably akin to Sanskrit *palāva* chaff] (14th century)
**1** : matter in a finely divided state : particulate matter
**2 a** : a preparation in the form of fine particles especially for medicinal or cosmetic use **b** : fine dry light snow
**3** : any of various solid explosives used chiefly in gunnery and blasting
— **pow·der·less** \-ləs\ *adjective*
— **pow·der·like** \-ˌlīk\ *adjective*
**powder blue** *noun* (1896) : a pale blue
**powder horn** *noun* (1533) : a flask for carrying gunpowder; *especially* : one made of the horn of an ox or cow
**powder keg** *noun* (1855)
**1** : a small usually metal cask for holding gunpowder or blasting powder
**2** : something liable to explode
**powder metallurgy** *noun* (1933) : a branch of science or an art concerned with the production of powdered metals or of metallic objects by compressing a powdered metal or alloy with or without other materials and heating without thoroughly melting to solidify and strengthen
**powder monkey** *noun* (1682)

: one who carries or has charge of explosives (as in blasting operations)
**powder–puff** *adjective* (1939) : of, relating to, or being a competitive activity or event for women ⟨a *powder-puff* football game⟩
**powder puff** *noun* (circa 1704) : a small fluffy device (as a pad) for applying cosmetic powder
**powder room** *noun* (circa 1937)
**1** : a rest room for women
**2** : a lavatory in the main living area of a house
**pow·dery** \'paú-də-rē\ *adjective* (15th century)
**1 a** : resembling or consisting of powder ⟨*powdery* snow⟩ **b** : easily reduced to powder : CRUMBLING
**2** : covered with or as if with powder
**powdery mildew** *noun* (1889)
**1** : an ascomycetous fungus (family Erysiphaceae) producing abundant powdery conidia on the host
**2** : a plant disease caused by a powdery mildew
¹**pow·er** \'paú-(ə)r\ *noun, often attributive* [Middle English, from Old French *poeir*, from *poeir* to be able, from (assumed) Vulgar Latin *potēre*, alteration of Latin *posse* — more at POTENT] (13th century)
**1 a** (1) : ability to act or produce an effect (2) : ability to get extra-base hits (3) : capacity for being acted upon or undergoing an effect **b** : legal or official authority, capacity, or right
**2 a** : possession of control, authority, or influence over others **b** : one having such power; *specifically* : a sovereign state **c** : a controlling group : ESTABLISHMENT — often used in the phrase *the powers that be* **d** *archaic* : a force of armed men **e** *chiefly dialect* : a large number or quantity
**3 a** : physical might **b** : mental or moral efficacy **c** : political control or influence
**4** *plural* : an order of angels — see CELESTIAL HIERARCHY
**5 a** : the number of times as indicated by an exponent that a number occurs as a factor in a product; *also* : the product itself **b** : CARDINAL NUMBER 2
**6 a** : a source or means of supplying energy; *especially* : ELECTRICITY **b** : MOTIVE POWER **c** : the time rate at which work is done or energy emitted or transferred
**7** : MAGNIFICATION 2b
**8** : SCOPE, COMPREHENSIVENESS
**9** : the probability of rejecting the null hypothesis in a statistical test when a particular alternative hypothesis happens to be true ☆ ☆
²**power** (1540)
*transitive verb*
**1** : to supply with power and especially motive power
**2** : to give impetus to
*intransitive verb*
**1** : to move about by means of motive power
**2** : to move with great speed or force
³**power** *adjective* (1949)
**1** : relating to or utilizing power ⟨plays a *power* game⟩; *also* : POWERFUL 1 ⟨a *power* critic⟩
**2** : of, relating to, or being a meal at which influential people discuss business or politics
**power base** *noun* (1959) : a base of political support
**pow·er·boat** \'paú-(ə)r-ˌbōt\ *noun* (1908) : MOTORBOAT
**power broker** *noun* (1961) : a person (as in politics) able to exert strong influence through control of votes or individuals
**pow·er–dive** \-ˌdīv\ (1937)
*intransitive verb* : to make a power dive
*transitive verb* : to cause to power-dive
**power dive** *noun* (1930) : a dive of an airplane accelerated by the power of the engine

**pow·er·ful** \'paú-(ə)r-fəl\ *adjective* (15th century)
**1** : having great power, prestige, or influence
**2** : leading to many or important deductions ⟨a *powerful* set of postulates⟩
— **pow·er·ful·ly** \-f(ə-)lē\ *adverb*
**power function** *noun* (1957)
**1** : a function of a parameter under statistical test whose value for a particular value of the parameter is the probability of rejecting the null hypothesis if that value of the parameter happens to be true
**2** : a function (as $f(x) = ax^k$) that equals the product of a constant and a power of the independent variable
**pow·er·house** \'paú-(ə)r-ˌhaús\ *noun* (circa 1890)

---

☆ SYNONYMS
**Poverty, indigence, penury, want, destitution** mean the state of one with insufficient resources. POVERTY may cover a range from extreme want of necessities to an absence of material comforts ⟨the extreme *poverty* of the slum dwellers⟩. INDIGENCE implies seriously straitened circumstances ⟨the *indigence* of her years as a graduate student⟩. PENURY suggests a cramping or oppressive lack of money ⟨a catastrophic illness that condemned them to years of *penury*⟩. WANT and DESTITUTION imply extreme poverty that threatens life itself through starvation or exposure ⟨lived in a perpetual state of *want*⟩ ⟨the widespread *destitution* in countries beset by famine⟩.

**Power, authority, jurisdiction, control, command, sway, dominion** mean the right to govern or rule or determine. POWER implies possession of ability to wield force, permissive authority, or substantial influence ⟨the *power* to mold public opinion⟩. AUTHORITY implies the granting of power for a specific purpose within specified limits ⟨gave her attorney the *authority* to manage her estate⟩. JURISDICTION applies to official power exercised within prescribed limits ⟨the bureau having *jurisdiction* over alcohol and firearms⟩. CONTROL stresses the power to direct and restrain ⟨you are responsible for the students under your *control*⟩. COMMAND implies the power to make arbitrary decisions and compel obedience ⟨the army officer in *command*⟩. SWAY suggests the extent or scope of exercised power or influence ⟨an empire that extended its *sway* over the known world⟩. DOMINION stresses sovereign power or supreme authority ⟨given *dominion* over all the animals⟩.

**Power, force, energy, strength, might** mean the ability to exert effort. POWER may imply latent or exerted physical, mental, or spiritual ability to act or be acted upon ⟨the awesome *power* of flowing water⟩. FORCE implies the actual effective exercise of power ⟨used enough *force* to push the door open⟩. ENERGY applies to power expended or capable of being transformed into work ⟨a worker with boundless *energy*⟩. STRENGTH applies to the quality or property of a person or thing that makes possible the exertion of force or the withstanding of strain, pressure, or attack ⟨use weight training to build your *strength*⟩. MIGHT implies great or overwhelming power or strength ⟨the belief that *might* makes right⟩.

---

\ə\ **abut** \ᵊ\ **kitten** \ər\ **further** \a\ **ash** \ā\ **ace**
\ä\ **mop, mar** \aú\ **out** \ch\ **chin** \e\ **bet** \ē\ **easy**
\g\ **go** \i\ **hit** \ī\ **ice** \j\ **job** \ŋ\ **sing** \ō\ **go**
\ò\ **law** \òi\ **boy** \th\ **thin** \t̲h̲\ **the** \ü\ **loot** \ú\ **foot**
\y\ **yet** \zh\ **vision** *see also* Guide to Pronunciation

**1 a :** POWER PLANT 1 **b :** a source of influence or inspiration
**2 :** one having great power: as **a :** one having great drive, energy, or ability **b :** an athletic team characterized by strong aggressive play
**pow·er·less** \-ləs\ *adjective* (15th century)
**1 :** devoid of strength or resources
**2 :** lacking the authority or capacity to act
— **pow·er·less·ly** *adverb*
— **pow·er·less·ness** *noun*
**power mower** *noun* (1940)
: a motor-driven lawn mower
**power of attorney** (1747)
: a legal instrument authorizing one to act as the attorney or agent of the grantor
**power pack** *noun* (1936)
: a unit for converting a power supply (as from a battery or household electrical circuit) to a voltage suitable for an electronic device
**power plant** *noun* (1890)
**1 :** an electric utility generating station
**2 :** an engine and related parts supplying the motive power of a self-propelled object (as a rocket or automobile)
**power play** *noun* (1947)
**1 :** a military, diplomatic, political, or administrative maneuver in which power is brought to bear
**2 a :** a concentrated attack in football in which the ballcarrier is preceded by a mass of blockers **b :** a situation in ice hockey in which one team temporarily has more players on the ice than the other team because of a penalty
**power politics** *noun plural but singular or plural in construction* (1926)
: politics based primarily on the use of power (as military and economic strength) as a coercive force rather than on ethical precepts
**power series** *noun* (1893)
: an infinite series whose terms are successive integral powers of a variable multiplied by constants
**power shovel** *noun* (1909)
: a power-operated excavating machine consisting of a boom or crane that supports a lever arm with a large bucket at the end of it
**power station** *noun* (1901)
: POWER PLANT 1
**power steering** *noun* (1932)
: automotive steering with engine power used to amplify the torque applied at the steering wheel by the driver
**power structure** *noun* (1950)
**1 :** a group of persons having control of an organization : ESTABLISHMENT
**2 :** the hierarchical interrelationships existing within a controlling group
**power sweep** *noun* (1964)
: SWEEP 3e
**power take–off** *noun* (1929)
: a supplementary mechanism (as on a tractor) enabling the engine power to be used to operate nonautomotive apparatus (as a pump or saw)
**power train** *noun* (1943)
: the intervening mechanism by which power is transmitted from an engine to a propeller or axle that it drives
**power up** *transitive verb* (1970)
: to cause to operate ⟨*power up* the computer⟩
— **pow·er–up** \'paú(-ə)r-ˌəp\ *noun*
**¹pow·wow** \'paú-ˌwaú\ *noun* [Narraganset *powwaw* or Massachuset *pauwau*] (1625)
**1 :** an American Indian medicine man
**2 a :** an American Indian ceremony (as for victory in war) **b :** an American Indian social gathering or fair usually including competitive dancing
**3 a :** a social get-together **b :** a meeting for discussion
**²powwow** *intransitive verb* (1642)
: to hold a powwow
**¹pox** \'päks\ *noun, plural* **pox** *or* **pox·es** [alteration of *pocks*, plural of *pock*] (1550)

**1 a :** a virus disease (as chicken pox) characterized by pustules or eruptions **b** *archaic* : SMALLPOX **c :** SYPHILIS
**2 :** a disastrous evil : PLAGUE, CURSE ⟨a *pox* on him⟩
**²pox** *transitive verb* (1601)
*archaic* : to infect with a pox and especially with syphilis
**pox·vi·rus** \'päks-ˌvī-rəs\ *noun* (1941)
: any of a group of relatively large round, brick-shaped, or ovoid DNA-containing animal viruses (as the causative agent of smallpox) that have a fluffy appearance caused by a covering of tubules and threads
**poz·zo·la·na** \ˌpät-sə-'lä-nə\ *or* **poz·zo·lan** \'pät-sə-lən\ *noun* [Italian *pozzolana*] (1706)
: finely divided siliceous or siliceous and aluminous material that reacts chemically with slaked lime at ordinary temperature and in the presence of moisture to form a strong slow-hardening cement
— **poz·zo·la·nic** \ˌpät-sə-'la-nik, -'lä-\ *adjective*
**PPO** \ˌpē-(ˌ)pē-'ō\ *noun, plural* **PPOs** [*p*referred *p*rovider *o*rganization] (1983)
: an organization providing health care that gives economic incentives to the individual purchaser of a health-care contract to patronize certain physicians, laboratories, and hospitals that agree to supervision and reduced fees — compare HMO
**prac·ti·ca·ble** \'prak-ti-kə-bəl\ *adjective* (1670)
**1 :** capable of being put into practice or of being done or accomplished : FEASIBLE
**2 :** capable of being used : USABLE
**synonym** see POSSIBLE
— **prac·ti·ca·bil·i·ty** \ˌprak-ti-kə-'bi-lə-tē\ *noun*
— **prac·ti·ca·ble·ness** \'prak-ti-kə-bəl-nəs\ *noun*
— **prac·ti·ca·bly** \-blē\ *adverb*
**¹prac·ti·cal** \'prak-ti-kəl\ *adjective* [Middle English, from Late Latin *practicus*, from Greek *praktikos*, from *prassein* to pass over, fare, do; akin to Greek *peran* to pass through — more at FARE] (15th century)
**1 a :** of, relating to, or manifested in practice or action : not theoretical or ideal ⟨a *practical* question⟩ ⟨for all *practical* purposes⟩ **b :** being such in practice or effect : VIRTUAL ⟨a *practical* failure⟩
**2 :** actively engaged in some course of action or occupation ⟨a *practical* farmer⟩
**3 :** capable of being put to use or account : USEFUL ⟨he had a *practical* knowledge of French⟩
**4 a :** disposed to action as opposed to speculation or abstraction **b** (1) : qualified by practice or practical training ⟨a good *practical* mechanic⟩ (2) : designed to supplement theoretical training by experience
**5 :** concerned with voluntary action and ethical decisions ⟨*practical* reason⟩
— **prac·ti·cal·i·ty** \ˌprak-ti-'ka-lə-tē\ *noun*
— **prac·ti·cal·ness** \'prak-ti-kəl-nəs\ *noun*
**²practical** *noun* (1925)
: an examination requiring demonstration of some practical skill ⟨a zoology *practical*⟩
**practical art** *noun* (circa 1925)
: an art (as woodworking) that serves ordinary or material needs — usually used in plural
**practical joke** *noun* (circa 1847)
: a prank intended to trick or embarrass someone or cause physical discomfort
— **practical joker** *noun*
**prac·ti·cal·ly** \'prak-ti-k(ə-)lē\ *adverb* (1623)
**1 :** in a practical manner ⟨look *practically* at the problem⟩
**2 :** ALMOST, NEARLY ⟨*practically* everyone went to the party⟩
**practical nurse** *noun* (1921)
: a nurse who cares for the sick professionally without having the training or experience required of a registered nurse; *especially* : LICENSED PRACTICAL NURSE

**practical theology** *noun* (circa 1909)
: the study of the institutional activities of religion (as preaching, church administration, pastoral care, and liturgics)
**¹prac·tice** *or* **prac·tise** \'prak-təs\ *verb* **prac·ticed** *or* **prac·tised; prac·tic·ing** *or* **prac·tis·ing** [Middle English *practisen*, from Middle French *practiser*, from *practique*, *pratique* practice, noun, from Late Latin *practice*, from Greek *praktikē*, from feminine of *praktikos*] (14th century)
*transitive verb*
**1 a :** CARRY OUT, APPLY ⟨*practice* what you preach⟩ **b :** to do or perform often, customarily, or habitually ⟨*practice* politeness⟩ **c :** to be professionally engaged in ⟨*practice* medicine⟩
**2 a :** to perform or work at repeatedly so as to become proficient ⟨*practice* the act⟩ **b :** to train by repeated exercises ⟨*practice* pupils in penmanship⟩
**3** *obsolete* : PLOT
*intransitive verb*
**1 :** to do repeated exercises for proficiency
**2 :** to pursue a profession actively
**3** *archaic* : INTRIGUE
**4 :** to do something customarily
**5 :** to take advantage of someone ⟨he *practised* on their credulity with huge success —*Times Literary Supplement*⟩
— **prac·tic·er** *noun*
**²practice** *also* **practise** *noun* (15th century)
**1 a :** actual performance or application ⟨ready to carry out in *practice* what they advocated in principle⟩ **b :** a repeated or customary action ⟨had this irritating *practice*⟩ **c :** the usual way of doing something ⟨local *practices*⟩ **d :** the form, manner, and order of conducting legal suits and prosecutions
**2 a :** systematic exercise for proficiency ⟨*practice* makes perfect⟩ **b :** the condition of being proficient through systematic exercise ⟨get in *practice*⟩
**3 a :** the continuous exercise of a profession **b** : a professional business; *especially* : one constituting an incorporeal property
**synonym** see HABIT
**prac·ticed** *or* **prac·tised** \'prak-təst\ *adjective* (1568)
**1 :** EXPERIENCED, SKILLED
**2 :** learned by practice
**prac·tice–teach** \'prak-təs-'tēch\ *intransitive verb* **-taught** \-'tòt\; **-teach·ing** [back-formation from *practice teaching*] (1952)
: to engage in practice teaching
— **practice teacher** *noun*
**practice teaching** *noun* (circa 1913)
: teaching by a student under the supervision of an experienced teacher
**practicing** *or* **practising** *adjective* (1625)
: actively engaged in a specified career or way of life ⟨a *practicing* physician⟩
**prac·ti·cum** \'prak-ti-kəm\ *noun* [German *Praktikum*, from Late Latin *practicum*, neuter of *practicus* practical] (circa 1909)
: a course of study designed especially for the preparation of teachers and clinicians that involves the supervised practical application of previously studied theory
**prac·ti·tion·er** \prak-'ti-sh(ə-)nər\ *noun* [alteration of earlier *practician*, from Middle English (Scots) *pratician*, from Middle French *practicien*, from *pratique*] (1535)
**1 :** one who practices; *especially* : one who practices a profession
**2** *Christian Science* : an authorized healer
**prae·ci·pe** \'pre-sə-ˌpē, 'prē-\ *noun* [Middle English *presepe*, from Medieval Latin *praecipe*, from Latin, imperative of *praecipere* to instruct — more at PRECEPT] (15th century)
**1 :** any of various legal writs commanding a person to do something or to appear and show cause why he or she should not
**2 :** a written order requesting a clerk or prothonotary of a court to issue a writ and specifying the contents of the writ
**prae·di·al** *variant of* PREDIAL

**prae·mu·ni·re** \ˌprē-myù-'nīr-ē\ *noun* [Middle English *praemunire facias*, from Medieval Latin, that you cause to warn; from prominent words in the writ] (1529)
**:** an offense against the English Crown punishable chiefly by forfeiture and originally committed by asserting papal legal supremacy in England

**prae·no·men** \prē-'nō-mən\ *noun, plural* **-nomens** *or* **-no·mi·na** \-'nä-mə-nə, -'nō-\ [Latin, from *prae-* pre- + *nomen* name — more at NAME] (1706)
**:** the first of the usual three names of an ancient Roman male

**prae·sid·i·um** *variant of* PRESIDIUM

**prae·tor** \'prē-tər\ *noun* [Middle English *pretor*, from Latin *praetor*] (15th century)
**:** an ancient Roman magistrate ranking below a consul and having chiefly judicial functions
— **prae·to·ri·al** \prē-'tōr-ē-əl, -'tòr-\ *adjective*
— **prae·tor·ship** \'prē-tər-ˌship\ *noun*

**prae·to·ri·an** \prē-'tōr-ē-ən, -'tòr-\ *adjective* (15th century)
**1** *often capitalized* **:** of, forming, or resembling the Roman imperial bodyguard
**2 :** of or relating to a praetor
— **praetorian** *noun, often capitalized*

**prag·mat·ic** \prag-'ma-tik\ *also* **prag·mat·i·cal** \-ti-kəl\ *adjective* [Latin *pragmaticus* skilled in law or business, from Greek *pragmatikos*, from *pragmat-, pragma* deed, from *prassein* to do — more at PRACTICAL] (1616)
**1** *archaic* **a** (1) **:** BUSY (2) **:** OFFICIOUS **b :** OPINIONATED
**2 :** relating to matters of fact or practical affairs often to the exclusion of intellectual or artistic matters **:** practical as opposed to idealistic ⟨*pragmatic* men of power have had no time or inclination to deal with . . . social morality —K. B. Clark⟩
**3 :** relating to or being in accordance with philosophical pragmatism
— **pragmatic** *noun*
— **prag·mat·i·cal·ly** \-ti-k(ə-)lē\ *adverb*

**prag·mat·i·cism** \prag-'ma-tə-ˌsi-zəm\ *noun* (1905)
**:** the philosophic doctrine of C. S. Peirce
— **prag·mat·i·cist** \-sist\ *noun*

**prag·mat·ics** \prag-'ma-tiks\ *noun plural but singular or plural in construction* (1937)
**1 :** a branch of semiotic that deals with the relation between signs or linguistic expressions and their users
**2 :** linguistics concerned with the relationship of sentences to the environment in which they occur

**pragmatic sanction** *noun* (1643)
**:** a solemn decree of a sovereign on a matter of primary importance and with the force of fundamental law

**prag·ma·tism** \'prag-mə-ˌti-zəm\ *noun* (circa 1864)
**1 :** a practical approach to problems and affairs ⟨tried to strike a balance between principles and *pragmatism*⟩
**2 :** an American movement in philosophy founded by C. S. Peirce and William James and marked by the doctrines that the meaning of conceptions is to be sought in their practical bearings, that the function of thought is to guide action, and that truth is preeminently to be tested by the practical consequences of belief
— **prag·ma·tist** \-mə-tist\ *adjective or noun*
— **prag·ma·tis·tic** \ˌprag-mə-'tis-tik\ *adjective*

**prai·rie** \'prer-ē\ *noun, often attributive* [French, from (assumed) Vulgar Latin *prataria*, from Latin *pratum* meadow] (circa 1682)
**1 :** land in or predominantly in grass
**2 :** a tract of grassland: as **a :** a large area of level or rolling land in the Mississippi valley that in its natural uncultivated state usually has

deep fertile soil, a cover of tall coarse grasses, and few trees **b :** one of the dry treeless plateaus east of the Rocky Mountains that merge on their east side with the prairies proper and are characterized by shorter grasses and drier less fertile soil

**prairie chicken** *noun* (1691)
**:** a grouse (*Tympanuchus cupido*) chiefly of the prairies of the central U.S.; *also* **:** a closely related smaller grouse (*T. pallidicinctus*)

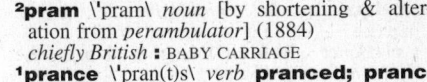

prairie chicken

**prairie dog** *noun* (1774)
**:** any of a genus (*Cynomys*) of gregarious burrowing rodents of the squirrel family chiefly of central and western U.S. plains; *especially* **:** a black-tailed rodent (*C. ludovicianus*) that usually lives in extensive colonial burrows

prairie dog

**prairie schooner** *noun* (1841)
**:** a covered wagon used by pioneers in cross-country travel — called also *prairie wagon*

**prairie soil** *noun* (1817)
**:** any of a zonal group of soils developed in a temperate relatively humid climate under tall grass

**prairie wolf** *noun* (1804)
**:** COYOTE

**¹praise** \'prāz\ *verb* **praised; prais·ing** [Middle English, from Old French *preisier* to prize, praise, from Late Latin *pretiare* to prize, from Latin *pretium* price — more at PRICE] (13th century)
*transitive verb*
**1 :** to express a favorable judgment of **:** COMMEND
**2 :** to glorify (a god or saint) especially by the attribution of perfections
*intransitive verb*
**:** to express praise
— **prais·er** *noun*

**²praise** *noun* (14th century)
**1 a :** an expression of approval **:** COMMENDATION **b :** WORSHIP
**2 a :** VALUE, MERIT **b** *archaic* **:** one that is praised

**praise·wor·thy** \'prāz-ˌwər-thē\ *adjective* (15th century)
**:** LAUDABLE
— **praise·wor·thi·ly** \-thə-lē\ *adverb*
— **praise·wor·thi·ness** \-thē-nəs\ *noun*

**Pra·krit** \'prä-ˌkrit, -krət\ *noun* [Sanskrit *prākṛta*, from *prākṛta* natural, vulgar] (1766)
**:** any or all of the ancient Indo-Aryan languages or dialects other than Sanskrit — see INDO-EUROPEAN LANGUAGES table

**pra·line** \'prä-ˌlēn, 'prā-, 'prò-\ *noun* [French, from Count Plessis-*Praslin* (died 1675) French soldier] (1723)
**:** a confection of nuts and sugar: **a :** almonds cooked in boiling sugar until brown and crisp **b :** a patty of creamy brown sugar and pecan meats

**prall·tril·ler** \'präl-ˌtri-lər\ *noun* [German, from *prallen* to rebound + *Triller* trill] (circa 1841)
**:** a musical ornament made by a quick alternation of a principal tone with the tone above

**¹pram** \'präm, 'pram\ *noun* [Middle Dutch *praem* & Middle Low German *prām*] (1548)
**:** a small lightweight nearly flat-bottomed boat with a broad transom and usually squared-off bow

**²pram** \'pram\ *noun* [by shortening & alteration from *perambulator*] (1884)
*chiefly British* **:** BABY CARRIAGE

**¹prance** \'pran(t)s\ *verb* **pranced; pranc·ing** [Middle English *praunen*] (14th century)
*intransitive verb*
**1 :** to spring from the hind legs or move by so doing
**2 :** to ride on a prancing horse
**3 :** to walk or move in a spirited manner **:** STRUT; *also* **:** to dance about
*transitive verb*
**:** to cause (a horse) to prance
— **pranc·er** \'pran(t)-sər\ *noun*

**²prance** *noun* (1751)
**:** an act or instance of prancing; *specifically* **:** a prancing movement

**pran·di·al** \'pran-dē-əl\ *adjective* [Latin *prandium* late breakfast, luncheon] (1820)
**:** of or relating to a meal

**prang** \'praŋ\ *transitive verb* [origin unknown] (1941)
*chiefly British* **:** to have an accident with **:** cause to crash
— **prang** *noun, chiefly British*

**¹prank** \'praŋk\ *noun* [obsolete *prank* to play tricks] (circa 1529)
**:** TRICK: **a** *obsolete* **:** a malicious act **b :** a mildly mischievous act **c :** a ludicrous act

**²prank** *verb* [probably from Dutch *pronken* to strut; akin to Middle High German ge*brunkel* glitter of metal] (15th century)
*intransitive verb*
**:** to show oneself off
*transitive verb*
**:** to dress or adorn gaily or showily

**prank·ish** \'praŋ-kish\ *adjective* (1827)
**1 :** full of pranks ⟨a *prankish* child⟩
**2 :** having the nature of a prank ⟨*prankish* acts⟩
— **prank·ish·ly** *adverb*
— **prank·ish·ness** *noun*

**prank·ster** \'praŋ(k)-stər\ *noun* (1927)
**:** a person who plays pranks

**prase** \'prāz, 'präs\ *noun* [French, from Latin *prasius*, from Greek *prasios*, from *prasios*, adjective, of the color of a leek from *prason* leek; akin to Latin *porrum* leek] (1788)
**:** a chalcedony that is translucent and yellowish green

**pra·seo·dym·i·um** \ˌprā-zē-ō-'di-mē-əm, ˌprā-sē-\ *noun* [New Latin, alteration of *praseodidymium*, irregular from Greek *prasios*, adjective + New Latin *didymium* didymium] (1885)
**:** a yellowish white trivalent metallic element of the rare-earth group used chiefly in the form of its salts in coloring glass greenish yellow — see ELEMENT table

**prate** \'prāt\ *intransitive verb* **prat·ed; prat·ing** [Middle English, from Middle Dutch; akin to Middle Low German *pratten* to pout] (15th century)
**:** to talk long and idly **:** CHATTER
— **prate** *noun*
— **prat·er** *noun*
— **prat·ing·ly** \'prā-tiŋ-lē\ *adverb*

**prat·fall** \'prat-ˌfòl\ *noun* [*prat* buttocks + *fall*] (1938)
**1 :** a fall on the buttocks
**2 :** a humiliating mishap or blunder

**pra·tin·cole** \'pra-tən-ˌkōl, 'prā-, -tiŋ-\ *noun* [ultimately from Latin *pratum* meadow + *incola* inhabitant, from *in-* + *colere* to cultivate — more at WHEEL] (1773)
**:** any of several Old World shore-inhabiting birds (genera *Glareolus* and *Stiltia* of the family Glareolidae) with a short bill and a forked tail

**pra·tique** \pra-'tēk\ *noun* [French, literally, practice — more at PRACTICE] (1609)
: clearance given an incoming ship by the health authority of a port

¹**prat·tle** \'pra-t°l\ *verb* **prat·tled; prat·tling** \'prat-liŋ, 'pra-t°l-iŋ\ [Low German *pratelen;* akin to Middle Dutch *praten* to prate] (1532)
*intransitive verb*
**1** : PRATE
**2** : to utter or make meaningless sounds suggestive of the chatter of children : BABBLE
*transitive verb*
: to say in an unaffected or childish manner
— **prat·tler** \'prat-lər, 'pra-t°l-ər\ *noun*
— **prat·tling·ly** \-liŋ-lē, -t°l-iŋ-\ *adverb*

²**prattle** *noun* (1555)
**1** : trifling or empty talk
**2** : a sound that is meaningless, repetitive, and suggestive of the chatter of children

**prau** \'prau̇, 'prä-ˌü\ *noun* [Malay *pĕrahu*] (1582)
: any of various Indonesian boats usually without a deck that are propelled especially by sails or paddles

¹**prawn** \'prȯn, 'prän\ *noun* [Middle English *prane*] (15th century)
: any of numerous widely distributed edible decapod crustaceans (as of the genera *Pandalus* and *Peneus*) that resemble shrimps and have large compressed abdomens; *also* : SHRIMP

²**prawn** *intransitive verb* (1886)
: to fish for or with prawns
— **prawn·er** *noun*

**prax·e·ol·o·gy** \ˌprak-sē-'ä-lə-jē\ *noun* [alteration of earlier *praxiology*, from *praxis* + *-o- + -logy*] (1904)
: the study of human action and conduct
— **prax·e·o·log·i·cal** \-sē-ə-'lä-ji-kəl\ *adjective*

**prax·is** \'prak-səs\ *noun, plural* **prax·es** \-ˌsēz\ [Medieval Latin, from Greek, doing, action, from *prassein* to do, practice — more at PRACTICAL] (1581)
: ACTION, PRACTICE: as **a** : exercise or practice of an art, science, or skill **b** : customary practice or conduct

**pray** \'prā\ *verb* [Middle English, from Old French *preier,* from Latin *precari,* from *prec-, prex* request, prayer; akin to Old High German *frāgēn* to ask, Sanskrit *pṛcchati* he asks] (13th century)
*transitive verb*
**1** : ENTREAT, IMPLORE — often used as a function word in introducing a question, request, or plea ⟨*pray* be careful⟩
**2** : to get or bring by praying
*intransitive verb*
**1** : to make a request in a humble manner
**2** : to address God or a god with adoration, confession, supplication, or thanksgiving

¹**prayer** \'prar, 'prer\ *noun, often attributive* [Middle English, from Middle French *preiere,* from Medieval Latin *precaria,* from Latin, feminine of *precarius* obtained by entreaty, from *prec-, prex*] (14th century)
**1 a** (1) : an address (as a petition) to God or a god in word or thought ⟨said a *prayer* for the success of the voyage⟩ (2) : a set order of words used in praying **b** : an earnest request or wish
**2** : the act or practice of praying to God or a god ⟨kneeling in *prayer*⟩
**3** : a religious service consisting chiefly of prayers — often used in plural
**4** : something prayed for
**5** : a slight chance ⟨haven't got a *prayer*⟩

²**pray·er** \'prā-ər, 'pre(-ə)r\ *noun* [Middle English *prayere,* from *prayen* to pray + ²*-er*] (14th century)
: one that prays : SUPPLIANT

**prayer beads** \'prar-, 'prer-\ *noun plural* (1630)
: a string of beads by which prayers are counted; *specifically* : ROSARY

**prayer book** *noun* (circa 1597)
: a book containing prayers and often other forms and directions for worship

**prayer·ful** \'prar-fəl, 'prer-\ *adjective* (1626)
**1** : DEVOUT
**2** : EARNEST, SINCERE
— **prayer·ful·ly** \-fə-lē\ *adverb*
— **prayer·ful·ness** *noun*

**prayer meeting** *noun* (1780)
: a usually informal gathering for worship and prayer; *especially* : a Protestant worship service usually held on a week night — called also *prayer service*

**prayer rug** *noun* (circa 1890)
: a small Oriental rug used by Muslims to kneel on when praying

**prayer shawl** *noun* (1905)
: TALLITH

**prayer wheel** *noun* (1814)
: a cylinder of wood or metal that revolves on an axis and contains written prayers and that is used in praying by Tibetan Buddhists

**praying mantis** *noun* (circa 1890)
: MANTIS; *especially* : a European mantis (*Mantis religiosa*) that has been introduced into the U.S. — called also *praying mantid*

**pre-** *prefix* [Middle English, from Old French & Latin; Old French, from Latin *prae-,* from *prae* in front of, before — more at FOR]
**1 a** (1) : earlier than : prior to : before ⟨*Pre*cambrian⟩ ⟨*pre*historic⟩ (2) : preparatory or prerequisite to ⟨*pre*medical⟩ **b** : in advance : beforehand ⟨*pre*cancel⟩ ⟨*pre*pay⟩
**2** : in front of : anterior to ⟨*pre*axial⟩ ⟨*pre*molar⟩

| | |
|---|---|
| pre·ad·mis·sion | pre·dis·cov·ery |
| pre·adult | pre·dive |
| pre·ag·ri·cul·tur·al | pre·drill |
| pre·an·es·thet·ic | pre·dy·nas·tic |
| pre·an·nounce | pre·elec·tion |
| pre·ap·prove | pre·elec·tric |
| pre·ar·range | pre·em·bar·go |
| pre·ar·range·ment | pre·em·ploy·ment |
| pre·as·sem·bled | pre·en·roll·ment |
| pre·as·sign | pre·erect |
| pre·bake | pre·es·tab·lish |
| pre·bat·tle | pre·eth·i·cal |
| pre·bib·li·cal | pre·ex·per·i·ment |
| pre·book | pre·fade |
| pre·break·fast | pre·fas·cist |
| pre·cap·i·tal·ist | pre·feu·dal |
| pre·chill | pre·fight |
| pre·Christ·mas | pre·file |
| pre·clear | pre·filled |
| pre·clear·ance | pre·fi·nance |
| pre·code | pre·fire |
| pre·co·i·tal | pre·flame |
| pre·col·lege | pre·flight |
| pre·col·le·giate | pre·for·mat |
| pre·co·lo·nial | pre·for·mu·late |
| pre·com·bus·tion | pre·fresh·man |
| pre·com·mit·ment | pre·fro·zen |
| pre·com·pute | pre·game |
| pre·com·put·er | pre·gen·i·tal |
| pre·con·cert | pre·har·vest |
| pre·con·quest | pre·head·ache |
| pre·con·so·nan·tal | pre·hir·ing |
| pre·con·struct·ed | pre·hol·i·day |
| pre·con·ven·tion | pre·hu·man |
| pre·con·vic·tion | pre·in·au·gu·ral |
| pre·cool | pre·in·cor·po·ra·tion |
| pre·cop·u·la·to·ry | pre·in·duc·tion |
| pre·crash | pre·in·dus·tri·al |
| pre·crease | pre·in·ter·view |
| pre·cri·sis | pre·in·va·sion |
| pre·cut | pre·kin·der·gar·ten |
| pre·dawn | pre·launch |
| pre·de·fine | pre·life |
| pre·de·liv·ery | pre·lit·er·ary |
| pre·de·par·ture | pre·log·i·cal |
| pre·des·ig·nate | pre·lunch |
| pre·de·val·u·a·tion | pre·lun·cheon |
| pre·de·vel·op·ment | pre·made |
| pre·din·ner | pre·man·u·fac·ture |
| pre·dis·charge | pre·mar·i·tal |

| | |
|---|---|
| pre·mar·i·tal·ly | pre·rev·o·lu·tion |
| pre·mar·ket | pre·rev·o·lu·tion·ary |
| pre·mar·ket·ing | pre·rinse |
| pre·mar·riage | pre·ri·ot |
| pre·meal | pre·rock |
| pre·mea·sure | pre·ro·man·tic |
| pre·me·di·e·val | pre·sale |
| pre·meet | pre·sched·ule |
| pre·mei·ot·ic | pre·screen |
| pre·men·o·paus·al | pre·sea·son |
| pre·merg·er | pre·sen·tence |
| pre·mi·gra·tion | pre·sen·tenc·ing |
| pre·mod·ern | pre·ser·vice |
| pre·mod·i·fi·ca·tion | pre·set |
| pre·mod·i·fy | pre·set·tle·ment |
| pre·moist·en | pre·show |
| pre·mold | pre·slaugh·ter |
| pre·molt | pre·sleep |
| pre·mor·al | pre·slice |
| pre·my·cot·ic | pre·song |
| pre·noon | pre·spec·i·fy |
| pre·no·ti·fi·ca·tion | pre·split |
| pre·no·ti·fy | pre·stamp |
| pre·num·ber | pre·ster·il·ize |
| pre·open·ing | pre·stor·age |
| pre·op·er·a·tion·al | pre·strike |
| pre·or·der | pre·struc·ture |
| pre·paste | pre·sum·mit |
| pre·per·for·mance | pre·sur·gery |
| pre·pill | pre·sweet·en |
| pre·plan | pre·symp·tom·at·ic |
| pre·por·tion | pre·tape |
| pre·pre·pared | pre·tax |
| pre·pres·i·den·tial | pre·tech·no·log·i·cal |
| pre·price | pre·tele·vi·sion |
| pre·pri·ma·ry | pre·ter·mi·na·tion |
| pre·pro·duc·tion | pre·the·a·ter |
| pre·pro·gram | pre·tour·na·ment |
| pre·psy·che·del·ic | pre·train |
| pre·pub·li·ca·tion | pre·trav·el |
| pre·punch | pre·treat |
| pre·pu·pal | pre·treat·ment |
| pre·pur·chase | pre·trial |
| pre·qual·i·fi·ca·tion | pre·trimmed |
| pre·qual·i·fy | pre·type |
| pre·race | pre·uni·fi·ca·tion |
| pre·re·ces·sion | pre·uni·ver·si·ty |
| pre·re·cord·ed | pre·vi·a·ble |
| pre·re·hears·al | pre·war |
| pre·re·lease | pre·warn |
| pre·re·quire | pre·wash |
| pre·re·tire·ment | pre·wean·ing |
| pre·re·turn | pre·work |
| pre·re·view | pre·wrap |
| pre·re·vi·sion·ist | |

**preach** \'prēch\ *verb* [Middle English *prechen,* from Old French *prechier,* from Late Latin *praedicare,* from Latin, to proclaim publicly, from *prae-* pre- + *dicare* to proclaim — more at DICTION] (13th century)
*intransitive verb*
**1** : to deliver a sermon
**2** : to urge acceptance or abandonment of an idea or course of action; *specifically* : to exhort in an officious or tiresome manner
*transitive verb*
**1** : to set forth in a sermon ⟨*preach* the gospel⟩
**2** : to advocate earnestly ⟨*preached* revolution⟩
**3** : to deliver (as a sermon) publicly
**4** : to bring, put, or affect by preaching ⟨*preached* the . . . church out of debt —*American Guide Series: Virginia*⟩
— **preach·er** *noun*
— **preach·ing·ly** \'prē-chiŋ-lē\ *adverb*

**preach·ify** \'prē-chə-ˌfī\ *intransitive verb* **-ified; -ify·ing** (1775)
: to preach ineptly or tediously

**preach·ment** \'prēch-mənt\ *noun* (14th century)
**1** : the act or practice of preaching
**2** : SERMON, EXHORTATION; *specifically* : a tedious or unwelcome one

**preachy** \'prē-chē\ *adjective* **preach·i·er; -est** (1819)

: marked by obvious moral exhortation : DIDACTIC
— **preach·i·ly** \-chə-lē\ *adverb*
— **preach·i·ness** \-chē-nəs\ *noun*
**pre·ad·ap·ta·tion** \ˌprē-ˌa-ˌdap-'tā-shən\ *noun* (1886)
**1** : the possession by an organism or taxonomic group of characters that are not adapted to the ancestral environment but favor survival in some other environment
**2** : a preadaptive character
**pre·adapt·ed** \ˌprē-ə-'dap-təd\ *adjective* (1915)
: characterized by preadaptation
**pre·adap·tive** \-'dap-tiv\ *adjective* (1915)
: of, relating to, or characterized by preadaptation
**pre·ad·o·les·cence** \ˌprē-ˌa-dᵊl-'e-sᵊn(t)s\ *noun* (1930)
: the period of human development just preceding adolescence; *specifically* : the period between the approximate ages of 9 and 12
— **pre·ad·o·les·cent** \-sᵊnt\ *adjective or noun*
**pre·am·ble** \'prē-ˌam-bəl, prē-'\ *noun* [Middle English, from Middle French *preambule*, from Medieval Latin *preambulum*, from Late Latin, neuter of *praeambulus* walking in front of, from Latin *prae-* + *ambulare* to walk] (14th century)
**1** : an introductory statement; *especially* : the introductory part of a constitution or statute that usually states the reasons for and intent of the law
**2** : an introductory fact or circumstance; *especially* : one indicating what is to follow
**pre·amp** \'prē-ˌamp\ *noun* (1949)
: PREAMPLIFIER
**pre·am·pli·fi·er** \(ˌ)prē-'am-plə-ˌfī(-ə)r\ *noun* (1935)
: an amplifier designed to amplify extremely weak electrical signals before they are fed to additional amplifier circuits
**pre·atom·ic** \ˌprē-ə-'tä-mik\ *adjective* (1914)
: of or relating to a time before the use of the atomic bomb and atomic energy
**pre·ax·i·al** \(ˌ)prē-'ak-sē-əl\ *adjective* (1872)
: situated in front of an axis of the body
**preb·end** \'pre-bənd\ *noun* [Middle English *prebende*, from Middle French, from Medieval Latin *praebenda*, from Late Latin, subsistence allowance granted by the state, from Latin, feminine of *praebendus*, gerundive of *praebēre* to offer, from *prae-* + *habēre* to hold — more at GIVE] (15th century)
**1** : a stipend furnished by a cathedral or collegiate church to a clergyman (as a canon) in its chapter
**2** : PREBENDARY
— **pre·ben·dal** \pri-'ben-dᵊl, 'pre-bən-\ *adjective*
**preb·en·dary** \'pre-bən-ˌder-ē\ *noun, plural* **-dar·ies** (15th century)
**1** : a clergyman receiving a prebend for officiating and serving in the church
**2** : an honorary canon in a cathedral chapter
**pre·bi·o·log·i·cal** \ˌprē-ˌbī-ə-'lä-ji-kəl\ *also* **pre·bi·o·log·ic** \-jik\ *adjective* (1953)
: of, relating to, or being chemical or environmental precursors of the origin of life (*prebiological* molecules)
**pre·bi·ot·ic** \ˌprē-bī-'ä-tik\ *adjective* (1958)
: PREBIOLOGICAL
**pre·cal·cu·lus** \(ˌ)prē-'kal-kyə-ləs\ *adjective* (1964)
: relating to or being mathematical prerequisites for the study of calculus
— **precalculus** *noun*
**Pre·cam·bri·an** \(ˌ)prē-'kam-brē-ən, -'kām-\ *adjective* (1864)
: of, relating to, or being the earliest era of geological history or the corresponding system of rocks characterized especially by the appearance of single-celled organisms and is equivalent to the Archean and Proterozoic eons — see GEOLOGIC TIME table

— **Precambrian** *noun*
**¹pre·can·cel** \(ˌ)prē-'kan(t)-səl\ *transitive verb* (1921)
: to cancel (a postage stamp) in advance of use
— **pre·can·cel·la·tion** \ˌprē-ˌkan(t)-sə-'lā-shən\ *noun*
**²precancel** *noun* (1929)
: a precanceled postage stamp
**pre·can·cer·ous** \(ˌ)prē-'kan(t)s-rəs, -'kan(t)-sə-\ *adjective* [International Scientific Vocabulary] (1882)
: tending to become cancerous (a *precancerous* lesion)
**pre·car·i·ous** \pri-'kar-ē-əs, -'ker-\ *adjective* [Latin *precarius* obtained by entreaty, uncertain — more at PRAYER] (1646)
**1** : depending on the will or pleasure of another
**2** : dependent on uncertain premises : DUBIOUS (*precarious* generalizations)
**3 a** : dependent on chance circumstances, unknown conditions, or uncertain developments **b** : characterized by a lack of security or stability that threatens with danger
**synonym** see DANGEROUS
— **pre·car·i·ous·ly** *adverb*
— **pre·car·i·ous·ness** *noun*
**pre·cast** \ˌprē-'kast, 'prē-ˌ\ *adjective* (1914)
: being concrete that is cast in the form of a structural element (as a panel or beam) before being placed in final position
**prec·a·to·ry** \'pre-kə-ˌtȯr-ē, -ˌtȯr-\ *adjective* [Late Latin *precatorius*, from Latin *precari* to pray — more at PRAY] (1636)
: expressing a wish
**pre·cau·tion** \pri-'kȯ-shən\ *noun* [French *précaution*, from Late Latin *praecaution-*, *praecautio*, from Latin *praecavēre* to guard against, from *prae-* + *cavēre* to be on one's guard — more at HEAR] (1603)
**1** : care taken in advance : FORESIGHT (warned of the need for *precaution*)
**2** : a measure taken beforehand to prevent harm or secure good : SAFEGUARD
— **pre·cau·tion·ary** \-shə-ˌner-ē\ *adjective*
**pre·cede** \pri-'sēd\ *verb* **pre·ced·ed; pre·ced·ing** [Middle English, from Middle French *preceder*, from Latin *praecedere*, from *prae-* pre- + *cedere* to go] (15th century) *transitive verb*
**1** : to surpass in rank, dignity, or importance
**2** : to be, go, or come ahead or in front of
**3** : to be earlier than
**4** : to cause to be preceded : PREFACE
*intransitive verb*
: to go or come before
**pre·ce·dence** \'pre-sə-dən(t)s, pri-'sē-dᵊn(t)s\ *noun* (1588)
**1 a** *obsolete* : ANTECEDENT **b** : the fact of preceding in time
**2 a** : the right to superior honor on a ceremonial or formal occasion **b** : the order of ceremonial or formal preference **c** : priority of importance (your safety takes *precedence*)
**pre·ce·den·cy** \-dən(t)-sē, -dᵊn(t)-sē\ *noun* (1612)
: PRECEDENCE
**¹pre·ce·dent** \pri-'sē-dᵊnt, 'pre-sə-dənt\ *adjective* [Middle English, from Middle French, from Latin *praecedent-*, *praecedens*, present participle of *praecedere*] (15th century)
: prior in time, order, arrangement, or significance
**²prec·e·dent** \'pre-sə-dənt\ *noun* (15th century)
**1** : an earlier occurrence of something similar
**2 a** : something done or said that may serve as an example or rule to authorize or justify a subsequent act of the same or an analogous kind (a verdict that had no *precedent*) **b** : the convention established by such a precedent or by long practice
**3** : a person or thing that serves as a model
**pre·ced·ing** \pri-'sē-diŋ\ *adjective* (15th century)

: that immediately precedes in time or place (the *preceding* day) (*preceding* paragraphs) ☆
**pre·cen·sor** \(ˌ)prē-'sen(t)-sər\ *transitive verb* (1942)
: to censor (a publication or film) before its release to the public
**pre·cen·tor** \pri-'sen-tər\ *noun* [Late Latin *praecentor*, from Latin *praecinere* to sing before, from *prae-* + *canere* to sing — more at CHANT] (1613)
: a leader of the singing of a choir or congregation
— **pre·cen·to·ri·al** \ˌprē-sen-'tȯr-ē-əl, -'tȯr-\ *adjective*
— **pre·cen·tor·ship** \pri-'sen-tər-ˌship\ *noun*
**pre·cept** \'prē-ˌsept\ *noun* [Middle English, from Latin *praeceptum*, from neuter of *praeceptus*, past participle of *praecipere* to take beforehand, instruct, from *prae-* + *capere* to take — more at HEAVE] (14th century)
**1** : a command or principle intended especially as a general rule of action
**2** : an order issued by legally constituted authority to a subordinate official
**synonym** see LAW
**pre·cep·tive** \pri-'sep-tiv\ *adjective* (15th century)
: giving precepts : DIDACTIC
**pre·cep·tor** \pri-'sep-tər, 'prē-ˌ\ *noun* (15th century)
**1 a** : TEACHER, TUTOR **b** : the headmaster or principal of a school
**2** : the head of a preceptory of Knights Templars
— **pre·cep·tor·ship** \-ˌship\ *noun*
**¹pre·cep·to·ri·al** \ˌprē-ˌsep-'tȯr-ē-əl, ˌprē-, -'tȯr-\ *adjective* (circa 1741)
: of, relating to, or making use of preceptors
**²preceptorial** *noun* (circa 1952)
: a college course that emphasizes independent reading, discussion in small groups, and individual conferences with the teacher
**pre·cep·to·ry** \pri-'sep-t(ə-)rē, 'prē-ˌ\ *noun, plural* **-ries** (1540)
**1** : a subordinate house or community of the Knights Templars; *broadly* : COMMANDERY 1
**2** : COMMANDERY 2
**pre·cess** \prē-'ses, 'prē-ˌ\ *verb* [back-formation from *precession*] (1892)
*intransitive verb*
: to progress with a movement of precession
*transitive verb*
: to cause to precess

---

☆ **SYNONYMS**
**Preceding, antecedent, foregoing, previous, prior, former, anterior** mean being before. PRECEDING usually implies being immediately before in time or in place (the *preceding* sentence). ANTECEDENT applies to order in time and may suggest a causal relation (conditions *antecedent* to the revolution). FOREGOING applies chiefly to statements (the *foregoing* remarks). PREVIOUS and PRIOR imply existing or occurring earlier, but PRIOR often adds an implication of greater importance (a child from a *previous* marriage) (a *prior* obligation). FORMER implies always a definite comparison or contrast with something that is latter (the *former* name of the company). ANTERIOR applies to position before or ahead of usually in space, sometimes in time or order (the *anterior* lobe of the brain).

---

\ə\ abut \ᵊ\ kitten \ər\ further \a\ ash \ā\ ace
\ä\ mop, mar \au̇\ out \ch\ chin \e\ bet \ē\ easy
\g\ go \i\ hit \ī\ ice \j\ job \ŋ\ sing \ō\ go
\ȯ\ law \ȯi\ boy \th\ thin \t͟h\ the \ü\ loot \u̇\ foot
\y\ yet \zh\ vision *see also* Guide to Pronunciation

**pre·ces·sion** \prē-'se-shən\ *noun* [New Latin *praecession-, praecessio,* from Medieval Latin, act of preceding, from Latin *praecedere* to precede] (1879)
: a comparatively slow gyration of the rotation axis of a spinning body about another line intersecting it so as to describe a cone
— **pre·ces·sion·al** \-'sesh-nəl, -'se-shə-nᵊl\ *adjective*

**precession of the equinoxes** (1621)
: a slow westward motion of the equinoxes along the ecliptic caused by the gravitational action of sun and moon upon the protuberant matter about the earth's equator

**pre–Chel·le·an** \(,)prē-'she-lē-ən\ *adjective* (1916)
: of or relating to a Lower Paleolithic culture preceding the Abbevillian and characterized by crudely flaked stone hand axes

**pre–Chris·tian** \-'kris-chən, -'krish-\ *adjective* (1828)
: of, relating to, or being a time before the beginning of the Christian era

**pré·cieux** \prā-syœ̄\ *or* **pré·cieuse** \-syœ̄z\ *adjective* [French *précieux,* masculine, & *précieuse,* feminine, literally, precious, from Middle French *precios*] (1727)
: PRECIOUS 3

**pre·cinct** \'prē-,siŋ(k)t\ *noun* [Middle English, from Medieval Latin *praecinctum,* from Latin, neuter of *praecinctus,* past participle of *praecingere* to gird about, from *prae-* pre- + *cingere* to gird — more at CINCTURE] (15th century)
**1** : a part of a territory with definite bounds or functions often established for administrative purposes : DISTRICT: as **a** : a subdivision of a county, town, city, or ward for election purposes **b** : a division of a city for police control
**2 a** : an enclosure bounded by the walls of a building — often used in plural **b** : a sphere of thought, action, or influence —, often used in plural
**3 a** *plural* : the region immediately surrounding a place : ENVIRONS **b** : PLACE, LOCALE
**4** : BOUNDARY — often used in plural ⟨a ruined tower within the *precincts* of the squire's grounds —T. L. Peacock⟩

**pre·ci·os·i·ty** \,pre-shē-'ä-sə-tē, -sē-\ *noun, plural* **-ties** (1866)
**1** : fastidious refinement
**2** : an instance of preciosity

¹**pre·cious** \'pre-shəs\ *adjective* [Middle English, from Middle French *precios,* from Latin *pretiosus,* from *pretium* price — more at PRICE] (13th century)
**1** : of great value or high price
**2** : highly esteemed or cherished
**3** : excessively refined : AFFECTED
**4** : GREAT, THOROUGHGOING ⟨*precious* scoundrel⟩
— **pre·cious·ness** *noun*

²**precious** *adverb* (1595)
: VERY, EXTREMELY ⟨has *precious* little to say⟩

**pre·cious·ly** *adverb* (14th century)
**1** : in a precious manner
**2** : PRECIOUS

**pre·ci·pe** *variant of* PRAECIPE

**prec·i·pice** \'pre-s(ə-)pəs\ *noun* [Middle French, from Latin *praecipitium,* from *praecipit-, praeceps* headlong, from *prae-* + *caput* head — more at HEAD] (1613)
**1** : a very steep or overhanging place
**2** : a hazardous situation; *broadly* : BRINK

**pre·cip·i·ta·ble** \pri-'si-pə-tə-bəl\ *adjective* (1670)
: capable of being precipitated

**pre·cip·i·tance** \pri-'si-pə-tən(t)s\ *noun* (1667)
: PRECIPITANCY

**pre·cip·i·tan·cy** \-tən(t)-sē\ *noun* (1646)
: undue hastiness or suddenness

¹**pre·cip·i·tant** \-tənt\ *adjective* (1671)
: PRECIPITATE
— **pre·cip·i·tant·ly** *adverb*
— **pre·cip·i·tant·ness** *noun*

²**precipitant** *noun* (circa 1685)
: a precipitating agent; *especially* : one that causes the formation of a precipitate

¹**pre·cip·i·tate** \pri-'si-pə-,tāt\ *verb* **-tat·ed; -tat·ing** [Latin *praecipitatus,* past participle of *praecipitare,* from *praecipit-, praeceps*] (1528)
*transitive verb*
**1 a** : to throw violently : HURL ⟨the quandaries into which the release of nuclear energy has *precipitated* mankind —A. B. Arons⟩ **b** : to throw down
**2** : to bring about especially abruptly ⟨*precipitate* a scandal that would end with his expulsion —John Cheever⟩
**3 a** : to cause to separate from solution or suspension **b** : to cause (vapor) to condense and fall or deposit
*intransitive verb*
**1 a** : to fall headlong **b** : to fall or come suddenly into some condition
**2** : to move or act precipitately
**3 a** : to separate from solution or suspension **b** : to condense from a vapor and fall as rain or snow
— **pre·cip·i·ta·tive** \-,tā-tiv\ *adjective*
— **pre·cip·i·ta·tor** \-,tā-tər\ *noun*

²**pre·cip·i·tate** \pri-'si-pə-tət, -,tāt\ *noun* [New Latin *praecipitatum,* from Latin, neuter of *praecipitatus*] (1594)
**1** : a substance separated from a solution or suspension by chemical or physical change usually as an insoluble amorphous or crystalline solid
**2** : a product, result, or outcome of some process or action

³**pre·cip·i·tate** \pri-'si-pə-tət\ *adjective* (1615)
**1 a** : falling, flowing, or rushing with steep descent **b** : PRECIPITOUS, STEEP
**2** : exhibiting violent or unwise speed ☆
— **pre·cip·i·tate·ly** *adverb*
— **pre·cip·i·tate·ness** *noun*

**pre·cip·i·ta·tion** \pri-,si-pə-'tā-shən\ *noun* (1502)
**1** : the quality or state of being precipitate : HASTINESS
**2** : an act, process, or instance of precipating; *especially* : the process of forming a precipitate
**3** : something precipitated: as **a** : a deposit on the earth of hail, mist, rain, sleet, or snow; *also* : the quantity of water deposited **b** : PRECIPITATE 1

**pre·cip·i·tin** \pri-'si-pə-tən\ *noun* [International Scientific Vocabulary, from *precipitate*] (1900)
: an antibody that forms a precipitate when it unites with its antigen

**pre·cip·i·tin·o·gen** \pri-,si-pə-'ti-nə-jən\ *noun* (1904)
: an antigen that stimulates the production of a specific precipitin

**pre·cip·i·tous** \pri-'si-pə-təs\ *adjective* [French *précipiteux,* from Middle French, from Latin *precipitium* precipice] (1613)
**1** : PRECIPITATE 2
**2 a** : very steep, perpendicular, or overhanging in rise or fall ⟨a *precipitous* slope⟩ **b** : having precipitous sides ⟨a *precipitous* gorge⟩ **c** : having a very steep ascent ⟨a *precipitous* street⟩
*synonym* see STEEP
— **pre·cip·i·tous·ly** *adverb*
— **pre·cip·i·tous·ness** *noun*

**pré·cis** \prā-'sē, 'prā-(,)sē\ *noun, plural* **pré·cis** \-'sēz, -(,)sēz\ [French, from *précis* precise] (1760)
: a concise summary of essential points, statements, or facts

**pre·cise** \pri-'sīs\ *adjective* [Middle English, from Middle French *precis,* from Latin *praecisus,* past participle of *praecidere* to cut off, from *prae-* + *caedere* to cut] (15th century)
**1** : exactly or sharply defined or stated
**2** : minutely exact

**3** : strictly conforming to a pattern, standard, or convention
**4** : distinguished from every other ⟨at just that *precise* moment⟩
*synonym* see CORRECT
— **pre·cise·ness** *noun*

**pre·cise·ly** *adverb* (14th century)
: EXACTLY ⟨*precisely* two o'clock⟩ — sometimes used as an intensive ⟨was popular *precisely* because he was so kind⟩

**pre·ci·sian** \pri-'si-zhən\ *noun* (1571)
**1** : a person who stresses or practices scrupulous adherence to a strict standard especially of religious observance or morality
**2** : PURITAN 1

¹**pre·ci·sion** \pri-'si-zhən\ *noun* (1740)
**1** : the quality or state of being precise : EXACTNESS
**2 a** : the degree of refinement with which an operation is performed or a measurement stated — compare ACCURACY 2b **b** : the accuracy (as in binary or decimal places) with which a number can be represented usually expressed in terms of the number of computer words available for representation ⟨double *precision* arithmetic permits the representation of an expression by two computer words⟩
**3** : RELEVANCE 2
— **pre·ci·sion·ist** \-'si-zhə-nist, -'sizh-nist\ *noun*

²**precision** *adjective* (1875)
**1** : adapted for extremely accurate measurement or operation
**2** : held to low tolerance in manufacture
**3** : marked by precision of execution

**pre·clin·i·cal** \(,)prē-'kli-ni-kəl\ *adjective* (1926)
**1** : of, relating to, or concerned with the period preceding clinical manifestations
**2** : of, relating to, or being the period in medical or dental education preceding the clinical study of medicine or dentistry

**pre·clude** \pri-'klüd\ *transitive verb* **pre·clud·ed; pre·clud·ing** [Latin *praecludere,* from *prae-* + *claudere* to close — more at CLOSE] (1629)
**1** *archaic* : CLOSE
**2** : to make impossible by necessary consequence : rule out in advance
— **pre·clu·sion** \-'klü-zhən\ *noun*
— **pre·clu·sive** \-'klü-siv, -ziv\ *adjective*
— **pre·clu·sive·ly** *adverb*

**pre·co·cial** \pri-'kō-shəl\ *adjective* [New Latin *praecoces* precocial birds, from Latin, plural of *praecoc-, precox*] (circa 1872)
: capable of a high degree of independent activity from birth ⟨ducklings are *precocial*⟩ — compare ALTRICIAL

**pre·co·cious** \pri-'kō-shəs\ *adjective* [Latin *praecoc-, praecox* early ripening, precocious, from *prae-* + *coquere* to cook — more at COOK] (1650)
**1** : exceptionally early in development or occurrence
**2** : exhibiting mature qualities at an unusually early age
— **pre·co·cious·ly** *adverb*
— **pre·co·cious·ness** *noun*

---

☆ **SYNONYMS**
**Precipitate, headlong, abrupt, impetuous, sudden** mean showing undue haste or unexpectedness. PRECIPITATE stresses lack of due deliberation and implies prematureness of action ⟨the army's *precipitate* withdrawal⟩. HEADLONG stresses rashness and lack of forethought ⟨a *headlong* flight from arrest⟩. ABRUPT stresses curtness and a lack of warning or ceremony ⟨an *abrupt* refusal⟩. IMPETUOUS stresses extreme impatience or impulsiveness ⟨an *impetuous* lover proposing marriage⟩. SUDDEN stresses unexpectedness and sharpness or violence of action ⟨flew into a *sudden* rage⟩.

— **pre·coc·i·ty** \pri-'kä-sə-tē\ *noun*
**pre·cog·ni·tion** \ˌprē-(ˌ)käg-'ni-shən\ *noun* [Late Latin *praecognition-, praecognitio*, from Latin *praecognoscere* to know beforehand, from *prae-* + *cognoscere* to know — more at COGNITION] (circa 1611)
: clairvoyance relating to an event or state not yet experienced
— **pre·cog·ni·tive** \(ˌ)prē-'käg-nə-tiv\ *adjective*
**pre–Co·lum·bi·an** \ˌprē-kə-'ləm-bē-ən\ *adjective* (1888)
: preceding or belonging to the time before the arrival of Columbus in America
**pre·con·ceive** \ˌprē-kən-'sēv\ *transitive verb* (1558)
: to form (as an opinion) prior to actual knowledge or experience ⟨*preconceived* notions⟩
**pre·con·cep·tion** \-kən-'sep-shən\ *noun* (1625)
**1** : a preconceived idea
**2** : PREJUDICE
**pre·con·cert** \ˌprē-kən-'sərt\ *transitive verb* (1748)
: to settle by prior agreement
**¹pre·con·di·tion** \-kən-'di-shən\ *noun* (1825)
: PREREQUISITE
**²precondition** *transitive verb* (1922)
: to put in a proper or desired condition or frame of mind especially in preparation
**¹pre·con·scious** \(ˌ)prē-'kän(t)-shəs\ *adjective* (1860)
: not present in consciousness but capable of being recalled without encountering any inner resistance or repression
— **pre·con·scious·ly** *adverb*
**²preconscious** *noun* (circa 1922)
: the preconscious part of the psyche especially in psychoanalysis
**pre·con·tact** \ˌprē-'kän-ˌtakt\ *adjective* (circa 1909)
: of or relating to the period before contact of an indigenous people with an outside culture
**pre·cook** \(ˌ)prē-'kůk\ *transitive verb* (1926)
: to cook partially or entirely before final cooking or reheating
**pre·crit·i·cal** \-'kri-ti-kəl\ *adjective* (1881)
: prior to the development of critical capacity
**pre·cur·sor** \pri-'kər-sər, 'prē-ˌ\ *noun* [Middle English *precursoure*, from Latin *praecursor*, from *praecurrere* to run before, from *prae-* pre- + *currere* to run — more at CURRENT] (15th century)
**1 a** : one that precedes and indicates the approach of another **b** : PREDECESSOR
**2** : a substance, cell, or cellular component from which another substance, cell, or cellular component is formed
**synonym** see FORERUNNER
— **pre·cur·so·ry** \-'kərs-rē, -'kər-sə-\ *adjective*
**pre·da·ceous** *or* **pre·da·cious** \pri-'dā-shəs\ *adjective* [Latin *praedari* to prey upon (from *praeda* prey) + English *-aceous* or *-acious* (as in *rapacious*) — more at PREY] (1713)
**1** : living by preying on other animals : PREDATORY
**2** *usually* **predacious** : tending to devour or despoil : RAPACIOUS
— **pre·da·ceous·ness** *noun*
— **pre·dac·i·ty** \-'da-sə-tē\ *noun*
**pre·date** \(ˌ)prē-'dāt\ *transitive verb* (circa 1864)
: ANTEDATE
**pre·da·tion** \pri-'dā-shən\ *noun* [Middle English *predacion*, from Latin *praedation-, praedatio*, from *praedari*] (15th century)
**1** : the act of preying or plundering : DEPREDATION
**2** : a mode of life in which food is primarily obtained by the killing and consuming of animals
**predation pressure** *noun* (1942)

: the effects of predation on a natural community especially with respect to the survival of species preyed upon
**pred·a·tor** \'pre-də-tər, -ˌtȯr\ *noun* (1912)
**1** : one that preys, destroys, or devours
**2** : an animal that lives by predation
**pred·a·to·ry** \'pre-də-ˌtȯr-ē, -ˌtȯr-\ *adjective* (1589)
**1 a** : of, relating to, or practicing plunder, pillage, or rapine **b** : inclined or intended to injure or exploit others for personal gain or profit ⟨*predatory* pricing practices⟩
**2** : living by predation : PREDACEOUS; *also* : adapted to predation
**pre·de·cease** \ˌprē-di-'sēs\ *verb* **-ceased; -ceas·ing** (1593)
*transitive verb*
: to die before (another person)
*intransitive verb*
: to die first
— **predecease** *noun*
**pre·de·ces·sor** \'pre-də-ˌse-sər, 'prē-ˌ; ˌpre-də-', ˌprē-\ *noun* [Middle English *predecessour*, from Middle French *predecesseur*, from Late Latin *praedecessor*, from Latin *prae-* pre- + *decessor* retiring governor, from *decedere* to depart, retire from office — more at DECEASE] (14th century)
**1** : one that precedes; *especially* : a person who has previously occupied a position or office to which another has succeeded
**2** *archaic* : ANCESTOR
**pre·des·ti·nar·i·an** \(ˌ)prē-ˌdes-tə-'ner-ē-ən, ˌprē-des-\ *noun* [*predestin*ation + *-arian*] (1667)
: one who believes in predestination
— **predestinarian** *adjective*
— **pre·des·ti·nar·i·an·ism** \-ē-ə-ˌni-zəm\ *noun*
**¹pre·des·ti·nate** \prē-'des-tə-nət, -ˌnāt\ *adjective* [Middle English, from Latin *praedestinatus*, past participle of *praedestinare*] (14th century)
: destined, fated, or determined beforehand
**²pre·des·ti·nate** \-ˌnāt\ *transitive verb* **-nat·ed; -nat·ing** [Middle English, from Latin *praedestinatus*, past participle] (15th century)
**1** : to foreordain to an earthly or eternal lot or destiny by divine decree
**2** *archaic* : PREDETERMINE
**pre·des·ti·na·tion** \(ˌ)prē-ˌdes-tə-'nā-shən, ˌprē-des-\ *noun* (14th century)
**1** : the act of predestinating : the state of being predestinated
**2** : the doctrine that God in consequence of his foreknowledge of all events infallibly guides those who are destined for salvation
**pre·des·ti·na·tor** \prē-'des-tə-ˌnā-tər\ *noun* (1579)
**1** *archaic* : PREDESTINARIAN
**2** : one that predestinates
**pre·des·tine** \(ˌ)prē-'des-tən\ *transitive verb* [Middle English, from Middle French or Latin; Middle French *predestiner*, from Latin *praedestinare*, from *prae-* + *destinare* to determine — more at DESTINE] (14th century)
: to destine, decree, determine, appoint, or settle beforehand; *specifically* : PREDESTINATE 1
**pre·de·ter·mi·na·tion** \ˌprē-di-ˌtər-mə-'nā-shən\ *noun* (1647)
**1** : the act of predetermining : the state of being predetermined: as **a** : the ordaining of events beforehand **b** : a fixing or settling in advance
**2** : a purpose formed beforehand
**pre·de·ter·mine** \-di-'tər-mən\ *transitive verb* [Late Latin *praedeterminare*, from Latin *prae-* + *determinare* to determine] (1625)
**1 a** : FOREORDAIN, PREDESTINE **b** : to determine beforehand
**2** : to impose a direction or tendency on beforehand
**pre·de·ter·min·er** \-di-'tər-mə-nər\ *noun* (1959)

: a limiting noun modifier (as *both* or *all*) characterized by occurrence before the determiner in a noun phrase
**pre·di·a·be·tes** \ˌprē-ˌdī-ə-'bē-tēz, -təs\ *noun* (1935)
: an inapparent abnormal state that precedes the development of clinically evident diabetes
— **pre·di·a·bet·ic** \-'be-tik\ *adjective or noun*
**pre·di·al** \'prē-dē-əl\ *adjective* [Middle English *prediall*, from Medieval Latin *praedialis*, from Latin *praedium* landed property, from *praed-, praes* bondsman, from *prae-* + *vad-, vas* surety — more at WED] (15th century)
: of or relating to land or its products
**¹pred·i·ca·ble** \'pre-di-kə-bəl\ *noun* [Medieval Latin *praedicabile*, from neuter of *praedicabilis*] (1551)
: something that may be predicated; *especially* : one of the five most general kinds of attribution in traditional logic that include genus, species, difference, property, and accident
**²predicable** *adjective* [Medieval Latin *praedicabilis*, from Late Latin *praedicare* to predicate] (circa 1598)
: capable of being asserted
**pre·dic·a·ment** \pri-'di-kə-mənt, *1 is usually* 'pre-di-kə-\ *noun* [Middle English, from Late Latin *praedicamentum*, from *praedicare*] (14th century)
**1** : the character, status, or classification assigned by a predication; *specifically* : CATEGORY 1
**2** : CONDITION, STATE; *especially* : a difficult, perplexing, or trying situation
**¹pred·i·cate** \'pre-di-kət\ *noun* [Middle English, from Late Latin *praedicatum*, from neuter of *praedicatus*] (15th century)
**1 a** : something that is affirmed or denied of the subject in a proposition in logic **b** : a term designating a property or relation
**2** : the part of a sentence or clause that expresses what is said of the subject and that usually consists of a verb with or without objects, complements, or adverbial modifiers
— **pred·i·ca·tive** \-kə-tiv, -ˌkā-\ *adjective*
— **pred·i·ca·tive·ly** *adverb*
**²pred·i·cate** \'pre-də-ˌkāt\ *transitive verb* **-cat·ed; -cat·ing** [Late Latin *praedicatus*, past participle of *praedicare* to assert, predicate logically, preach, from Latin, to proclaim publicly, assert — more at PREACH] (1552)
**1 a** : AFFIRM, DECLARE **b** *archaic* : PREACH
**2 a** : to assert to be a quality, attribute, or property — used with following *of* ⟨*predicates* intelligence of humans⟩ **b** : to make (a term) the predicate in a proposition
**3** : FOUND, BASE — usually used with *on* ⟨the theory is *predicated* on recent findings⟩
**4** : IMPLY
**³pred·i·cate** \'pre-di-kət\ *adjective* (1887)
: completing the meaning of a copula ⟨*predicate* adjective⟩ ⟨*predicate* noun⟩
**predicate calculus** *noun* (1950)
: the branch of symbolic logic that uses symbols for quantifiers and for arguments and predicates of propositions as well as for unanalyzed propositions and logical connectives — called also *functional calculus*; compare PROPOSITIONAL CALCULUS
**predicate nominative** *noun* (1887)
: a noun or pronoun in the nominative or common case completing the meaning of a copula
**pred·i·ca·tion** \ˌpre-də-'kā-shən\ *noun* [Middle English *predicacion*, from Middle French *predication*, from Latin *praedication-, praedicatio*, from *praedicare*] (14th century)
**1** *archaic* **a** : an act of proclaiming or preaching **b** : SERMON

**2 :** an act or instance of predicating: as **a :** the expression of action, state, or quality by a grammatical predicate **b :** the logical affirmation of something about another; *especially* **:** assignment of something to a class

**pred·i·ca·to·ry** \'pre-di-kə-ˌtȯr-ē, -ˌtȯr-\ *adjective* [Late Latin *praedicatorius,* from *praedicare* to preach] (1611)
**:** of or relating to preaching

**pre·dict** \pri-'dikt\ *verb* [Latin *praedictus,* past participle of *praedicere,* from *prae-* pre- + *dicere* to say — more at DICTION] (circa 1632)
*transitive verb*
**:** to declare or indicate in advance; *especially* **:** foretell on the basis of observation, experience, or scientific reason
*intransitive verb*
**:** to make a prediction
*synonym* see FORETELL
— **pre·dict·abil·i·ty** \-ˌdik-tə-'bi-lə-tē\ *noun*
— **pre·dict·able** \-'dik-tə-bəl\ *adjective*
— **pre·dic·tive** \-'dik-tiv\ *adjective*
— **pre·dic·tive·ly** \-lē\ *adverb*
— **pre·dic·tor** \-'dik-tər\ *noun*

**pre·dict·ably** \-'dik-tə-blē\ *adverb* (1914)
**1 :** in a manner that can be predicted ⟨works quickly and *predictably*⟩
**2 :** as one could predict **:** as one would expect ⟨*predictably,* the politicians howled⟩

**pre·dic·tion** \pri-'dik-shən\ *noun* (1561)
**1 :** an act of predicting
**2 :** something that is predicted **:** FORECAST

**pre·di·gest** \ˌprē-dī-'jest, -də-\ *transitive verb* (1663)
**1 :** to subject to predigestion
**2 :** to simplify for easy use ⟨*predigested* classics for children⟩

**pre·di·ges·tion** \-'jes-chən, -'jesh-\ *noun* (circa 1612)
**:** artificial or natural partial digestion of food ⟨enzymatic *predigestion*⟩ ⟨microbial *predigestion*⟩

**pre·di·lec·tion** \ˌpre-d°l-'ek-shən, ˌprē-\ *noun* [French *prédilection,* from Medieval Latin *praediligere* to love more, prefer, from Latin *prae-* + *diligere* to love — more at DILIGENT] (1742)
**:** an established preference for something ☆

**pre·dis·pose** \ˌprē-di-'spōz\ (1646)
*transitive verb*
**1 :** to dispose in advance ⟨a good teacher *predisposes* children to learn⟩
**2 :** to make susceptible ⟨malnutrition *predisposes* one to disease⟩
*intransitive verb*
**:** to bring about susceptibility
*synonym* see INCLINE
— **pre·dis·po·si·tion** \ˌprē-ˌdis-pə-'zi-shən\ *noun*

**pred·nis·o·lone** \pred-'ni-sə-ˌlōn\ *noun* [blend of *prednisone* and [1]-*ol*] (1955)
**:** a glucocorticoid $C_{21}H_{28}O_5$ that is a dehydrogenated analogue of hydrocortisone and is used especially as an anti-inflammatory drug

**pred·ni·sone** \'pred-nə-ˌsōn *also* -ˌzōn\ *noun* [probably from *pregnane* ($C_{21}H_{36}$) + *diene* (compound containing two double bonds) + *cortisone*] (1955)
**:** a glucocorticoid $C_{21}H_{26}O_5$ that is a dehydrogenated analogue of cortisone and is used as an anti-inflammatory agent especially in the treatment of arthritis, as an antineoplastic agent, and as an immunosuppressant

**pre·doc·tor·al** \(ˌ)prē-'däk-t(ə-)rəl\ *adjective* (1937)
**:** of, relating to, or engaged in academic study leading to the doctoral degree

**pre·dom·i·nance** \pri-'dä-mə-nən(t)s, -'dämnən(t)s\ *noun* (1602)
**:** the quality or state of being predominant

**pre·dom·i·nan·cy** \-nən(t)-sē\ *noun* (1598)
**:** PREDOMINANCE

**pre·dom·i·nant** \-nənt\ *adjective* [Middle French, from Medieval Latin *praedominant-,*

*praedominans,* present participle of *praedominari* to predominate, from Latin *prae-* + *dominari* to rule, govern — more at DOMINATE] (1576)
**1 :** having superior strength, influence, or authority **:** PREVAILING
**2 :** being most frequent or common
*synonym* see DOMINANT
*usage* see PREDOMINATE

**pre·dom·i·nant·ly** \-nənt-lē\ *adverb* (1681)
**:** for the most part **:** MAINLY
*usage* see PREDOMINATE

**¹pre·dom·i·nate** \-nət\ *adjective* [alteration of *predominant*] (1591)
**:** PREDOMINANT ▢
— **pre·dom·i·nate·ly** *adverb*

**²pre·dom·i·nate** \pri-'dä-mə-ˌnāt\ *verb* [Medieval Latin *praedominatus,* past participle of *praedominari*] (1594)
*intransitive verb*
**1 :** to hold advantage in numbers or quantity
**2 :** to exert controlling power or influence **:** PREVAIL
*transitive verb*
**:** to exert control over **:** DOMINATE
— **pre·dom·i·na·tion** \-ˌdä-mə-'nā-shən\ *noun*

**pree** \'prē\ *transitive verb* **preed; pree·ing** [alteration of *preve* to prove, test, from Middle English *preven,* from Old French *preuv-,* stem of *prover* to prove] (1680)
*Scottish* **:** to taste tentatively **:** SAMPLE

**pre·eclamp·sia** \ˌprē-i-'klam(p)-sē-ə\ *noun* [New Latin] (1923)
**:** a toxic condition developing in late pregnancy that is characterized by a sudden rise in blood pressure, excessive weight gain, generalized edema, albuminuria, severe headache, and visual disturbances
— **pre·eclamp·tic** \-'klam(p)-tik\ *adjective*

**pre·emer·gence** \ˌprē-ə-'mər-jən(t)s\ *adjective* (1935)
**:** used or occurring before emergence of seedlings above the ground ⟨*preemergence* herbicides⟩

**pre·emer·gent** \-jənt\ *adjective* (1959)
**:** PREEMERGENCE

**pree·mie** \'prē-mē\ *noun* [*prem*ature + -*ie*] (1927)
**:** a premature baby

**pre·em·i·nence** \prē-'e-mə-nən(t)s\ *noun* (13th century)
**:** the quality or state of being preeminent **:** SUPERIORITY

**pre·em·i·nent** \-nənt\ *adjective* [Middle English, from Late Latin *praeeminent-, praeeminens,* from Latin, present participle of *praeeminēre* to be outstanding, from *prae-* + *eminēre* to stand out — more at EMINENT] (15th century)
**:** having paramount rank, dignity, or importance **:** OUTSTANDING
— **pre·em·i·nent·ly** *adverb*

**pre·empt** \prē-'em(p)t\ *verb* [back-formation from *preemption*] (1850)
*transitive verb*
**1 :** to acquire (as land) by preemption
**2 :** to seize upon to the exclusion of others **:** take for oneself ⟨the movement was then *preempted* by a lunatic fringe⟩
**3 :** to replace with something considered to be of greater value or priority **:** take precedence over ⟨the program did not appear, having been *preempted* by a baseball game —Robert MacNeil⟩
**4 :** to gain a commanding or preeminent place in
**5 :** to prevent from happening or taking place **:** FORESTALL, PRECLUDE
*intransitive verb*
**:** to make a preemptive bid in bridge
— **pre·emp·tor** \-'em(p)-tər\ *noun*

**pre·emp·tion** \-'em(p)-shən\ *noun* [Medieval Latin *praeemption-, praeemptio* previous purchase, from *praeemere* to buy before, from

Latin *prae-* pre- + *emere* to buy — more at REDEEM] (1602)
**1 a :** the right of purchasing before others; *especially* **:** one given by the government to the actual settler upon a tract of public land **b :** the purchase of something under this right
**2 :** a prior seizure or appropriation **:** a taking possession before others

**pre·emp·tive** \-'em(p)-tiv\ *adjective* (1855)
**1 a :** of or relating to preemption **b :** having power to preempt
**2** *of a bid in bridge* **:** higher than necessary and intended to shut out bids by the opponents
**3 :** giving a stockholder first option to purchase new stock in an amount proportionate to his existing holdings
**4 :** marked by the seizing of the initiative **:** initiated by oneself ⟨a *preemptive* attack⟩
— **pre·emp·tive·ly** *adverb*

**¹preen** \'prēn\ *noun* [Middle English *prene,* from Old English *prēon;* akin to Middle High German *pfrieme* awl] (before 12th century)
**1** *dialect chiefly British* **:** PIN
**2** *dialect chiefly British* **:** BROOCH

**²preen** *transitive verb* (1572)
*chiefly Scottish* **:** PIN

**³preen** *verb* [Middle English *preinen*] (14th century)
*transitive verb*
**1 :** to dress or smooth (oneself) up **:** PRIMP
**2** *of a bird* **:** to trim or dress with a bill
**3 :** to pride or congratulate (oneself) for achievement
*intransitive verb*
**1 :** to make oneself sleek
**2 :** GLOAT, SWELL
— **preen·er** *noun*

**pre·en·gi·neered** \ˌprē-ˌen-jə-'nird\ *adjective* (1951)
**:** constructed of or employing prefabricated modules ⟨a *pre-engineered* building⟩

**pre·ex·il·ic** \ˌprē-eg-'zi-lik\ *adjective* (1880)
**:** previous to the exile of the Jews to Babylon in about 600 B.C.

**pre·ex·ist** \ˌprē-ig-'zist\ (1599)
*intransitive verb*

---

☆ **SYNONYMS**
**Predilection, prepossession, prejudice, bias** mean an attitude of mind that predisposes one to favor something. PREDILECTION implies a strong liking deriving from one's temperament or experience ⟨a *predilection* for horror movies⟩. PREPOSSESSION suggests a fixed conception likely to preclude objective judgment of anything counter to it ⟨a *prepossession* against technology⟩. PREJUDICE usually implies an unfavorable prepossession and connotes a feeling rooted in suspicion, fear, or intolerance ⟨a mindless *prejudice* against the unfamiliar⟩. BIAS implies an unreasoned and unfair distortion of judgment in favor of or against a person or thing ⟨the common *bias* against overweight people⟩.

---

▢ **USAGE**
**predominate** *Predominant* and *predominate* are synonymous adjectives. *Predominant* is the older and more common form. During this century a number of handbooks and commentators have held *predominate* to be a mistake—a few insisting that the word is only a verb. But they are wrong. As an adjective *predominate* is somewhat more likely to turn up in technical writing than in general writing. The adverbs *predominantly* and *predominately* are a more even match in frequency than their base adjectives are. *Predominately* seems to be more widely used than *predominate* and hence to be more often found in general writing.

: to exist earlier or before
*transitive verb*
: ANTEDATE

**pre·ex·is·tence** \-ig-'zis-tən(t)s\ *noun* (circa 1652)
: existence in a former state or previous to something else; *specifically* : existence of the soul before its union with the body
— **pre·ex·is·tent** \-tənt\ *adjective*

**pre·fab** \(ˌ)prē-'fab, 'prē-,\ *noun* (1937)
: a prefabricated structure
— **prefab** *adjective*

**pre·fab·ri·cate** \(ˌ)prē-'fa-bri-ˌkāt\ *transitive verb* (1932)
**1** : to fabricate the parts of at a factory so that construction consists mainly of assembling and uniting standardized parts
**2** : to produce artificially
— **pre·fab·ri·ca·tion** \ˌprē-ˌfa-bri-'kā-shən\ *noun*

**¹pref·ace** \'pre-fəs\ *noun* [Middle English, from Middle French, from Medieval Latin *prephatia*, alteration of Latin *praefation-, praefatio* foreword, from *praefari* to say beforehand, from *prae-* pre- + *fari* to say — more at BAN] (14th century)
**1** *often capitalized* : a variable doxology beginning with the Sursum Corda and ending with the Sanctus in traditional eucharistic liturgies
**2** : the introductory remarks of a speaker or author
**3** : APPROACH, PRELIMINARY

**²preface** *verb* **pref·aced; pref·ac·ing** (1619)
*intransitive verb*
: to make introductory remarks
*transitive verb*
**1** : to say or write as preface ⟨a note *prefaced* to the manuscript⟩
**2** : PRECEDE, HERALD
**3** : to introduce by or begin with a preface
**4** : to stand in front of ⟨a porch *prefaces* the entrance⟩
**5** : to be a preliminary to
— **pref·ac·er** *noun*

**pref·a·to·ry** \'pre-fə-ˌtōr-ē, -ˌtòr-\ *adjective* [Latin *praefari*] (1675)
**1** : of, relating to, or constituting a preface
**2** : located in front

**pre·fect** \'prē-ˌfekt\ *noun* [Middle English, from Middle French, from Latin *praefectus*, from past participle of *praeficere* to place at the head of, from *prae-* + *facere* to make — more at DO] (14th century)
**1** : any of various high officials or magistrates of differing functions and ranks in ancient Rome
**2** : a chief officer or chief magistrate
**3** : a student monitor in a private school

**prefect apostolic** *noun* (circa 1888)
: a Roman Catholic clergyman and usually a priest with quasi-episcopal jurisdiction over a district of a missionary territory

**pre·fec·ture** \'prē-ˌfek-chər\ *noun* (15th century)
**1** : the office or term of office of a prefect
**2** : the official residence of a prefect
**3** : the district governed by a prefect
— **pre·fec·tur·al** \'prē-ˌfek-chə-rəl, pri-'\ *adjective*

**prefecture apostolic** *noun* (1911)
: the district under a prefect apostolic

**pre·fer** \pri-'fər\ *transitive verb* **pre·ferred; pre·fer·ring** [Middle English *preferren*, from Middle French *preferer*, from Latin *praeferre* to put before, prefer, from *prae-* + *ferre* to carry — more at BEAR] (14th century)
**1** : to promote or advance to a rank or position
**2** : to like better or best ⟨*prefers* sports to reading⟩ ⟨*prefers* to watch TV⟩
**3** : to give (a creditor) priority
**4** *archaic* : to put or set forward or before someone : RECOMMEND
**5** : to bring or lay against someone ⟨won't *prefer* charges⟩

**6** : to bring forward or lay before one for consideration
— **pre·fer·rer** *noun*

**pref·er·a·ble** \'pre-f(ə-)rə-bəl, 'pre-fər-bəl *also* pri-'fər-ə-bəl\ *adjective* (1666)
: having greater value or desirability : being preferred
— **pref·er·a·bil·i·ty** \ˌpre-f(ə-)rə-'bi-lə-tē\ *noun*
— **pref·er·a·bly** \-blē\ *adverb*

**pref·er·ence** \'pre-fərn(t)s, 'pre-f(ə-)rən(t)s\ *noun* [Middle English *preferraunce*, from Middle French *preferance*, from Medieval Latin *praeferentia*, from Latin *praeferent-, praeferens*, present participle of *praeferre*] (15th century)
**1 a** : the act of preferring : the state of being preferred **b** : the power or opportunity of choosing
**2** : one that is preferred
**3** : the act, fact, or principle of giving advantages to some over others
**4** : priority in the right to demand and receive satisfaction of an obligation
**5** : ORIENTATION 2 ⟨sexual *preference*⟩
*synonym* see CHOICE

**pref·er·en·tial** \ˌpre-fə-'ren(t)-shəl\ *adjective* (1849)
**1** : showing preference
**2** : employing or creating a preference in trade relations
**3** : designed to permit expression of preference among candidates ⟨a *preferential* primary⟩
**4** : giving preference especially in hiring to union members ⟨a *preferential* shop⟩
— **pref·er·en·tial·ly** \-'ren(t)-sh(ə-)lē\ *adverb*

**pre·fer·ment** \pri-'fər-mənt\ *noun* (15th century)
**1 a** : advancement or promotion in dignity, office, or station **b** : a position or office of honor or profit
**2** : priority or seniority in right especially to receive payment or to purchase property on equal terms with others
**3** : the act of bringing forward (as charges)

**preferred stock** *noun* (circa 1859)
: stock guaranteed priority by a corporation's charter over common stock in the payment of dividends and usually in the distribution of assets

**pre·fig·u·ra·tion** \(ˌ)prē-ˌfi-gyə-'rā-shən, -gə-\ *noun* (14th century)
**1** : the act of prefiguring : the state of being prefigured
**2** : something that prefigures

**pre·fig·u·ra·tive** \ˌprē-'fi-gyə-rə-tiv, -gə-\ *adjective* (1504)
: of, relating to, or showing by prefiguration
— **pre·fig·u·ra·tive·ly** *adverb*
— **pre·fig·u·ra·tive·ness** *noun*

**pre·fig·ure** \ˌprē-'fi-gyər, *especially British* -'fi-gər\ *transitive verb* [Middle English, from Late Latin *praefigurare*, from Latin *prae-* + *figurare* to shape, picture, from *figura* figure] (15th century)
**1** : to show, suggest, or announce by an antecedent type, image, or likeness
**2** : to picture or imagine beforehand : FORESEE
— **pre·fig·ure·ment** \-mənt\ *noun*

**¹pre·fix** *transitive verb* [Middle English, from Middle French *prefixer*, from *pre-* + *fixer* to fix, from *fix* fixed, from Latin *fixus* — more at FIX] (15th century)
**1** \(ˌ)prē-'fiks\ : to fix or appoint beforehand
**2** \'prē-ˌ, prē-'\ [partly from ²*prefix*] : to place in front; *especially* : to add as a prefix ⟨*prefix* a syllable to a word⟩

**²pre·fix** \'prē-ˌfiks\ *noun* [New Latin *praefixum*, from Latin, neuter of *praefixus*, past participle of *praefigere* to fasten before, from *prae-* + *figere* to fasten — more at FIX] (1646)
**1** : an affix attached to the beginning of a word, base, or phrase and serving to produce a

derivative word or an inflectional form — compare SUFFIX
**2** : a title used before a person's name
— **pre·fix·al** \'prē-ˌfik-səl, prē-'\ *adjective*

**³pre·fix** \*same as* ²\ *adjective* (1971)
: characterized by placement of an operator before its operand or before its two operands if it is a binary operator — compare INFIX, POSTFIX

**pre·fo·cus** \(ˌ)prē-'fō-kəs\ *transitive verb* (1948)
: to focus beforehand (as automotive headlights before installation)

**pre·form** \'prē-ˌförm, (ˌ)prē-'\ *transitive verb* [Latin *praeformare*, from *prae-* + *formare* to form, from *forma* form] (1601)
**1** : to form or shape beforehand
**2** : to bring to approximate preliminary shape and size
— **pre·form** \'prē-ˌförm\ *noun*

**pre·for·ma·tion** \ˌprē-för-'mā-shən\ *noun* (1732)
**1** : previous formation
**2** : the now discredited theory that every germ cell contains the organism of its kind fully formed and that development involves merely an increase in size — compare EPIGENESIS 1, HOMUNCULUS 2
— **pre·for·ma·tion·ist** \-sh(ə-)nist\ *noun or adjective*

**¹pre·fron·tal** \(ˌ)prē-'frən-t°l\ *adjective* (1854)
: anterior to or involving the anterior part of a frontal structure ⟨a *prefrontal* bone⟩

**²prefrontal** *noun* (1854)
: a prefrontal part (as a bone)

**pre·gan·gli·on·ic** \ˌprē-ˌgaŋ-glē-'ä-nik\ *adjective* (1895)
: proximal to a ganglion; *specifically* : of, relating to, or being a usually medullated axon arising from a cell body in the central nervous system and terminating in an autonomic ganglion — compare POSTGANGLIONIC

**preg·na·ble** \'preg-nə-bəl\ *adjective* [alteration of Middle English *prenable*, from Middle French — more at IMPREGNABLE] (14th century)
: vulnerable to capture ⟨a *pregnable* fort⟩
— **preg·na·bil·i·ty** \ˌpreg-nə-'bi-lə-tē\ *noun*

**preg·nan·cy** \'preg-nən(t)-sē\ *noun, plural* **-cies** (15th century)
**1** : the quality of being pregnant (as in meaning)
**2** : the condition of being pregnant : GESTATION
**3** : an instance of being pregnant

**¹preg·nant** \'preg-nənt\ *adjective* [Middle English *preignant*, from Middle French, from present participle of *preindre* to press, from Latin *premere* — more at PRESS] (14th century)
*archaic* : COGENT

**²pregnant** *adjective* [Middle English, from Latin *praegnant-, praegnans*, alteration of *praegnas*, from *prae-* pre- + *-gnas* (akin to *gignere* to give birth to) — more at KIN] (15th century)
**1** : abounding in fancy, wit, or resourcefulness : INVENTIVE ⟨all this has been said . . . by great and *pregnant* artists —*Times Literary Supplement*⟩
**2** : rich in significance or implication : MEANINGFUL, PROFOUND ⟨the *pregnant* phrases of the Bible —Edmund Wilson⟩ ⟨a *pregnant* pause⟩
**3** : containing unborn young within the body : GRAVID
**4** : having possibilities of development or consequence : involving important issues : MOMENTOUS ⟨draw inspiration from the heroic achievements of that *pregnant* age —Kemp Malone⟩

\ə\ abut \ᵊ\ kitten \ər\ further \a\ ash \ā\ ace \ä\ mop, mar \au̇\ out \ch\ chin \e\ bet \ē\ easy \g\ go \i\ hit \ī\ ice \j\ job \ŋ\ sing \ō\ go \ò\ law \òi\ boy \th\ thin \t͟h\ the \ü\ loot \ u̇\ foot \y\ yet \zh\ vision *see also* Guide to Pronunciation

**5** *obsolete* : INCLINED, DISPOSED ⟨your own most *pregnant* and vouchsafed ear —Shakespeare⟩
**6** : FULL, TEEMING
— **preg·nant·ly** *adverb*

**preg·nen·o·lone** \preg-'ne-nᵊl-ˌōn\ *noun* [International Scientific Vocabulary *pregnene* (C₂₁H₃₄) + ¹-*ol* + -*one*] (1936)
: an unsaturated hydroxy steroid ketone C₂₁-H₃₂O₂ that is formed by the oxidation of steroids (as cholesterol) and yields progesterone on dehydrogenation

**pre·heat** \(ˌ)prē-'hēt\ *transitive verb* (1898)
: to heat beforehand; *especially* : to heat (an oven) to a designated temperature before using for cooking
— **pre·heat·er** *noun*

**pre·hen·sile** \prē-'hen(t)-səl, -'hen-ˌsīl\ *adjective* [French *préhensile*, from Latin *prehensus*, past participle of *prehendere* to seize — more at GET] (circa 1785)
**1** : adapted for seizing or grasping especially by wrapping around ⟨*prehensile* tail⟩
**2** : gifted with mental grasp or moral or aesthetic perception
— **pre·hen·sil·i·ty** \(ˌ)prē-ˌhen-'si-lə-tē\ *noun*

**pre·hen·sion** \prē-'hen(t)-shən\ *noun* (circa 1828)
**1** : the act of taking hold, seizing, or grasping
**2 a** : mental understanding : COMPREHENSION **b** : apprehension by the senses

**pre·His·pan·ic** \ˌprē-(h)i-'spa-nik\ *adjective* (1919)
: of, relating to, or being the time prior to Spanish conquests in the western hemisphere

**pre·his·to·ri·an** \ˌprē-(h)is-'tōr-ē-ən, -'tȯr-\ *noun* (1893)
: an archaeologist who specializes in prehistory

**pre·his·tor·ic** \ˌprē-(h)is-'tȯr-ik, -'tär-\ *also* **pre·his·tor·i·cal** \-i-kəl\ *adjective* (1851)
**1** : of, relating to, or existing in times antedating written history
**2** : of or relating to a language in a period of its development from which contemporary records of its sounds and forms have not been preserved
— **pre·his·tor·i·cal·ly** \-i-k(ə-)lē\ *adverb*

**pre·his·to·ry** \ˌprē-'his-t(ə-)rē\ *noun* (1871)
**1** : the study of prehistoric humankind
**2** : a history of the antecedents of an event, situation, or thing
**3** : the prehistoric period of human evolution

**pre·hom·i·nid** \-'hä-mə-nəd\ *noun* [ultimately from Latin *pre-* + *homin-, homo* human being — more at HOMAGE] (1939)
: any of various extinct primates resembling or ancestral to humans
— **prehominid** *adjective*

**pre·ig·ni·tion** \ˌprē-ig-'ni-shən\ *noun* (1898)
: ignition in an internal combustion engine while the inlet valve is open or before compression is completed

**pre·im·plan·ta·tion** \ˌprē-ˌim-ˌplan-'tā-shən\ *adjective* (1945)
: of, involving, or being an embryo before uterine implantation

**pre·judge** \(ˌ)prē-'jəj\ *transitive verb* [Middle French *prejuger*, from Latin *praejudicare*, from *prae-* + *judicare* to judge — more at JUDGE] (1579)
: to judge before hearing or before full and sufficient examination
— **pre·judg·er** *noun*
— **pre·judg·ment** \-'jəj-mənt\ *noun*

**¹prej·u·dice** \'pre-jə-dəs\ *noun* [Middle English, from Old French, from Latin *praejudicium* previous judgment, damage, from *prae-* + *judicium* judgment — more at JUDICIAL] (13th century)
**1** : injury or damage resulting from some judgment or action of another in disregard of one's rights; *especially* : detriment to one's legal rights or claims

**2 a** (1) : preconceived judgment or opinion (2) : an adverse opinion or leaning formed without just grounds or before sufficient knowledge **b** : an instance of such judgment or opinion **c** : an irrational attitude of hostility directed against an individual, a group, a race, or their supposed characteristics
*synonym* see PREDILECTION

**²prejudice** *transitive verb* **-diced; -dic·ing** (15th century)
**1** : to injure or damage by some judgment or action (as in a case of law)
**2** : to cause to have prejudice

**prej·u·diced** \-dəst\ *adjective* (1579)
: resulting from or having a prejudice or bias for or especially against

**prej·u·di·cial** \ˌpre-jə-'di-shəl\ *adjective* (15th century)
**1** : tending to injure or impair : DETRIMENTAL
**2** : leading to premature judgment or unwarranted opinion
— **prej·u·di·cial·ly** \-'di-sh(ə-)lē\ *adverb*
— **prej·u·di·cial·ness** \-shəl-nəs\ *noun*

**prel·a·cy** \'pre-lə-sē\ *noun, plural* **-cies** (14th century)
**1** : the office or dignity of a prelate
**2** : episcopal church government

**pre·lap·sar·i·an** \ˌprē-ˌlap-'ser-ē-ən\ *adjective* [*pre-* + Latin *lapsus* slip, fall — more at LAPSE] (1879)
: characteristic of or belonging to the time or state before the fall of mankind

**prel·ate** \'pre-lət *also* 'prē-ˌlāt\ *noun* [Middle English *prelat*, from Old French, from Medieval Latin *praelatus*, literally, one receiving preferment, from Latin (past participle of *praeferre* to prefer), from *prae-* + *latus*, past participle of *ferre* to carry — more at TOLERATE, BEAR] (13th century)
: an ecclesiastic (as a bishop or abbot) of superior rank

**prel·a·ture** \'pre-lə-ˌchu̇r, -chər, -ˌtyu̇r, -ˌtu̇r\ *noun* (1607)
**1** : PRELACY 1
**2** : a body of prelates

**pre·lect** \pri-'lekt\ *intransitive verb* [Latin *praelectus*, past participle of *praelegere*, from *prae-* + *legere* to read — more at LEGEND] (1785)
: to discourse publicly : LECTURE
— **pre·lec·tion** \-'lek-shən\ *noun*

**pre·li·ba·tion** \ˌprē-lī-'bā-shən\ *noun* [Latin *praelibation-, praelibatio*, from *praelibare* to taste beforehand, from *prae-* + *libare* to pour as an offering, taste — more at LIBATION] (1526)
: FORETASTE

**pre·lim** \'prē-ˌlim, pri-'\ *noun or adjective* (1891)
: PRELIMINARY

**¹pre·lim·i·nary** \pri-'li-mə-ˌner-ē\ *noun, plural* **-nar·ies** [French *préliminaires*, plural, from Medieval Latin *praeliminaris*, adjective, preliminary, from Latin *prae-* pre- + *limin-, limen* threshold] (1656)
: something that precedes or is introductory or preparatory: as **a** : a preliminary scholastic examination **b** *plural, British* : FRONT MATTER **c** : a preliminary heat or trial (as of a race) **d** : a minor match preceding the main event (as of a boxing card)

**²preliminary** *adjective* (circa 1667)
: coming before and usually forming a necessary prelude to something else
— **pre·lim·i·nar·i·ly** \-ˌli-mə-'ner-ə-lē\ *adverb*

**pre·lit·er·ate** \ˌprē-'li-t(ə-)rət\ *adjective* (1925)
**1 a** : not yet employing writing as a cultural medium **b** : lacking the use of writing
**2** : antedating the use of writing
— **preliterate** *noun*

**¹pre·lude** \'prel-ˌyüd, 'prāl-; 'pre-ˌlüd, 'prā-; *sense 1 also* ˌprē-'lüd\ *noun* [Middle French, from Medieval Latin *praeludium*, from Latin

*praeludere* to play beforehand, from *prae-* + *ludere* to play — more at LUDICROUS] (1561)
**1** : an introductory performance, action, or event preceding and preparing for the principal or a more important matter
**2 a** : a musical section or movement introducing the theme or chief subject (as of a fugue or suite) or serving as an introduction to an opera or oratorio **b** : an opening voluntary **c** : a separate concert piece usually for piano or orchestra and based entirely on a short motif

**²prelude** *verb* **pre·lud·ed; pre·lud·ing** (1655)
*transitive verb*
**1** : to serve as a prelude to
**2** : to play as a prelude
*intransitive verb*
: to give or serve as a prelude; *especially* : to play a musical introduction
— **pre·lud·er** *noun*

**pre·lu·sion** \pri-'lü-zhən\ *noun* [Latin *praelusion-, praelusio*, from *praeludere*] (1597)
: PRELUDE, INTRODUCTION

**pre·lu·sive** \-'lü-siv, -ziv\ *adjective* (1605)
: constituting or having the form of a prelude : INTRODUCTORY
— **pre·lu·sive·ly** *adverb*

**pre·ma·lig·nant** \ˌprē-mə-'lig-nənt\ *adjective* (circa 1897)
: PRECANCEROUS

**pre·man** \(ˌ)prē-'man, 'prē-ˌman\ *noun* (1921)
: any of several extinct primates ancestral to humans and especially recent humans

**pre·ma·ture** \ˌprē-mə-'tyu̇r, -'tu̇r, -'chu̇r *also* ˌpre-\ *adjective* [Latin *praematurus* too early, from *prae-* + *maturus* ripe, mature] (circa 1529)
: happening, arriving, existing, or performed before the proper, usual, or intended time; *especially* : born after a gestation period of less than 37 weeks ⟨*premature* babies⟩
— **premature** *noun*
— **pre·ma·ture·ly** *adverb*
— **pre·ma·ture·ness** *noun*
— **pre·ma·tu·ri·ty** \-'tyu̇r-ə-tē, -'tu̇r-, -'chu̇r-\ *noun*

**pre·max·il·la** \ˌprē-mak-'si-lə\ *noun* [New Latin] (1866)
: either of a pair of bones of the upper jaw of vertebrates between and in front of the maxillae
— **pre·max·il·lary** \(ˌ)prē-'mak-sə-ˌler-ē, *chiefly British* ˌprē-mak-'si-lə-rē\ *adjective or noun*

**¹pre·med** \(ˌ)prē-'med, 'prē-ˌmed\ *noun* (circa 1928)
: a premedical student or course of study

**²premed** *adjective* (1950)
: PREMEDICAL

**pre·med·i·cal** \(ˌ)prē-'me-di-kəl\ *adjective* (1904)
: preceding and preparing for the professional study of medicine

**pre·med·i·tate** \(ˌ)prē-'me-də-ˌtāt\ *verb* [Latin *praemeditatus*, past participle of *praemeditari*, from *prae-* + *meditari* to meditate] (circa 1548)
*transitive verb*
: to think about and revolve in the mind beforehand
*intransitive verb*
: to think, consider, or deliberate beforehand
— **pre·med·i·ta·tor** \-ˌtā-tər\ *noun*

**pre·med·i·tat·ed** *adjective* (1590)
: characterized by fully conscious willful intent and a measure of forethought and planning ⟨*premeditated* murder⟩
— **pre·med·i·tat·ed·ly** *adverb*

**pre·med·i·ta·tion** \(ˌ)prē-ˌme-də-'tā-shən\ *noun* (15th century)
: an act or instance of premeditating; *specifically* : consideration or planning of an act beforehand that shows intent to commit that act

**pre·med·i·ta·tive** \(ˌ)prē-'me-də-ˌtā-tiv\ *adjective* (1858)
: given to or characterized by premeditation

**pre·men·stru·al** \(ˌ)prē-'men(t)-strə-wəl, -strəl\ *adjective* (1885)
: of, relating to, occurring in, or being the period just preceding menstruation ⟨*premenstrual* tension⟩ ⟨*premenstrual* women⟩
— **pre·men·stru·al·ly** *adverb*
**premenstrual syndrome** *noun* (1982)
: a varying group of symptoms manifested by some women prior to menstruation that may include emotional instability, irritability, insomnia, fatigue, anxiety, depression, headache, edema, and abdominal pain — abbreviation *PMS*
**pre·mie** *variant of* PREEMIE
**¹pre·mier** \pri-'mir, -'myir, -'mē-ər; 'prē-ˌ, 'pre-\ *adjective* [Middle English *primier,* from Middle French *premier* first, chief, from Latin *primarius* of the first rank — more at PRIMARY] (15th century)
**1** : first in position, rank, or importance
**2** : first in time : EARLIEST
**²premier** *noun* [French, from *premier,* adjective] (1711)
: PRIME MINISTER
— **pre·mier·ship** \-ˌship\ *noun*
**pre·mier dan·seur** \prə-myā-dän-sœr\ *noun* [French] (1828)
: the principal male dancer in a ballet company
**¹pre·miere** \pri-'myer, -'mir, -'mē-ər; ˌpri-mē-'er\ *adjective* [alteration of ¹*premier*] (1768)
: PREMIER
**²premiere** *also* **pre·mière** \*same as* ¹PREMIERE\ *noun* [French *première,* from feminine of *premier* first] (1889)
**1** : a first performance or exhibition ⟨the *premiere* of a play⟩
**2** : the chief actress of a theatrical cast
**³premiere** *also* **pre·mière** *or* **pre·mier** \*same as* ¹PREMIERE\ *verb* **premiered** *also* **pre·mièred; pre·mier·ing** *also* **pre·mièr·ing** (1933)
*transitive verb*
: to give a first public performance of
*intransitive verb*
**1** : to have a first public performance
**2** : to appear for the first time as a star performer
**pre·mière dan·seuse** \prə-myer-dän-sœz\ *noun* [French] (1828)
: PRIMA BALLERINA
**pre·mil·le·nar·i·an·ism** \ˌprē-ˌmi-lə-'ner-ē-ə-ˌni-zəm\ *noun* (1844)
: PREMILLENNIALISM
— **pre·mil·le·nar·i·an** \-ē-ən\ *adjective or noun*
**pre·mil·len·ni·al** \ˌprē-mə-'le-nē-əl\ *adjective* (1846)
**1** : coming before a millennium
**2** : holding or relating to premillennialism
— **pre·mil·len·ni·al·ly** \-nē-ə-lē\ *adverb*
**pre·mil·len·ni·al·ism** \-nē-ə-ˌli-zəm\ *noun* (circa 1883)
: the view that Christ's return will usher in a future millennium of Messianic rule mentioned in Revelation
— **pre·mil·len·ni·al·ist** \-nē-ə-list\ *noun*
**¹prem·ise** *also* **pre·miss** \'pre-məs\ *noun* [in sense 1, from Middle English *premisse,* from Middle French, from Medieval Latin *praemissa,* from Latin, feminine of *praemissus,* past participle of *praemittere* to place ahead, from *prae-* pre- + *mittere* to send; in other senses, from Middle English *premisses,* from Medieval Latin *praemissa,* from Latin, neuter plural of *praemissus*] (14th century)
**1 a** : a proposition antecedently supposed or proved as a basis of argument or inference; *specifically* : either of the first two propositions of a syllogism from which the conclusion is drawn **b** : something assumed or taken for granted : PRESUPPOSITION
**2** *plural* : matters previously stated; *specifically* : the preliminary and explanatory part of a deed or of a bill in equity

**3** *plural* [from its being identified in the premises of the deed] **a** : a tract of land with the buildings thereon **b** : a building or part of a building usually with its appurtenances (as grounds)
**²pre·mise** \'pre-məs *also* pri-'mīz\ *transitive verb* **pre·mised; pre·mis·ing** (1526)
**1 a** : to set forth beforehand as an introduction or a postulate **b** : to offer as a premise in an argument
**2** : POSTULATE
**3** : to base on certain assumptions
**¹pre·mi·um** \'prē-mē-əm\ *noun* [Latin *praemium* booty, profit, reward, from *prae-* + *emere* to take, buy — more at REDEEM] (1601)
**1 a** : a reward or recompense for a particular act **b** : a sum over and above a regular price paid chiefly as an inducement or incentive **c** : a sum in advance of or in addition to the nominal value of something ⟨bonds callable at a *premium* of six percent⟩ **d** : something given free or at a reduced price with the purchase of a product or service
**2** : the consideration paid for a contract of insurance
**3** : a high value or a value in excess of that normally or usually expected ⟨put a *premium* on accuracy⟩
**²premium** *adjective* (1844)
: of exceptional quality or amount; *also* : higher-priced
**¹pre·mix** \(ˌ)prē-'miks, 'prē-\ *transitive verb* (1927)
: to mix before use
**²pre·mix** \'prē-ˌmiks\ *noun* (1937)
: a mixture of ingredients designed to be mixed with other ingredients before use
**pre·mo·lar** \(ˌ)prē-'mō-lər\ *adjective* (circa 1859)
: situated in front of or preceding the molar teeth; *especially* : being or relating to those teeth of a mammal in front of the true molars and behind the canines when the latter are present
— **premolar** *noun*
**pre·mon·ish** \-'mä-nish\ (1526)
*transitive verb*
*archaic* : FOREWARN
*intransitive verb*
*archaic* : to give warning in advance
**pre·mo·ni·tion** \ˌprē-mə-'ni-shən, ˌpre-\ *noun* [Middle English, from Middle French, from Late Latin *praemonition-, praemonitio,* from Latin *praemonēre* to warn in advance, from *prae-* + *monēre* to warn — more at MIND] (15th century)
**1** : previous notice or warning : FOREWARNING
**2** : anticipation of an event without conscious reason : PRESENTIMENT
**pre·mon·i·to·ry** \pri-'mä-nə-ˌtōr-ē, -ˌtòr-\ *adjective* (1647)
: giving warning ⟨a *premonitory* symptom⟩
— **pre·mon·i·to·ri·ly** \-ˌmä-nə-'tòr-ə-lē, -'tòr-\ *adverb*
**Pre·mon·stra·ten·sian** \ˌprē-ˌmän(t)-strə-'ten(t)-shən\ *noun* [Medieval Latin *praemonstratensis,* from *praemonstratensis* of Prémontré, from *Praemonstratus* Prémontré] (1695)
: a member of an order of canons regular founded by Saint Norbert at Prémontré near Laon, France, in 1120
**pre·mune** \(ˌ)prē-'myün\ *adjective* [back-formation from *premunition*] (1948)
: exhibiting premunition
**pre·mu·ni·tion** \ˌprē-myù-'ni-shən\ *noun* [Latin *praemunition-, praemunitio* advance fortification, from *praemunire* to fortify in advance, from *prae-* + *munire* to fortify — more at MUNITION] (1607)
**1** *archaic* : an advance provision of protection
**2 a** : resistance to a disease due to the existence of its causative agent in a state of physiological equilibrium in the host **b** : immunity to a particular infection due to previous presence of the causative agent

**pre·name** \'prē-ˌnām\ *noun* (1894)
: FORENAME
**pre·na·tal** \(ˌ)prē-'nā-tᵊl\ *adjective* (1826)
**1** : occurring, existing, or performed before birth ⟨*prenatal* care⟩ ⟨the *prenatal* period⟩
**2** : providing or receiving prenatal medical care ⟨a *prenatal* clinic⟩ ⟨*prenatal* patients⟩
— **pre·na·tal·ly** \-tᵊl-ē\ *adverb*
**¹pre·nom·i·nate** \(ˌ)prē-'nä-mə-nət\ *adjective* [Late Latin *praenominatus,* past participle of *praenominare* to name before, from Latin *prae-* + *nominare* to name — more at NOMINATE] (1513)
*obsolete* : previously mentioned
**²pre·nom·i·nate** \-ˌnāt\ *transitive verb* (1547)
*obsolete* : to mention previously
— **pre·nom·i·na·tion** \(ˌ)prē-ˌnä-mə-'nā-shən\ *noun, obsolete*
**pre·no·tion** \(ˌ)prē-'nō-shən, 'prē-\ *noun* [Latin *praenotion-, praenotio* preconception, from *prae-* + *notio* idea, conception — more at NOTION] (1588)
**1** : PRESENTIMENT, PREMONITION
**2** : PRECONCEPTION
**¹pren·tice** \'pren-təs\ *noun* [Middle English *prentis,* short for *apprentis*] (14th century)
: APPRENTICE 1, LEARNER
— **prentice** *adjective*
**²prentice** *transitive verb* **pren·ticed; pren·tic·ing** (1598)
: APPRENTICE
**pre·nup·tial** \(ˌ)prē-'nəp-shəl, -chəl, ÷-chə-wəl\ *adjective* (1869)
: made or occurring before marriage ⟨a *prenuptial* agreement⟩
**pre·oc·cu·pan·cy** \(ˌ)prē-'ä-kyə-pən(t)-sē\ *noun* (circa 1755)
**1** : an act or the right of taking possession before another
**2** : the condition of being completely busied or preoccupied
**pre·oc·cu·pa·tion** \(ˌ)prē-ˌä-kyə-'pā-shən\ *noun* (1603)
**1** : an act of preoccupying : the state of being preoccupied
**2 a** : extreme or excessive concern with something **b** : something that preoccupies one
**pre·oc·cu·pied** \(ˌ)prē-'ä-kyə-ˌpīd\ *adjective* (1842)
**1** : previously applied to another group and unavailable for use in a new sense — used of a biological generic or specific name
**2 a** : lost in thought; *also* : absorbed in some preoccupation **b** : already occupied
**pre·oc·cu·py** \-ˌpī\ *transitive verb* [Latin *praeoccupare,* literally, to seize in advance, from *prae-* + *occupare* to seize, occupy] (1567)
**1** : to engage or engross the interest or attention of beforehand or preferentially
**2** : to take possession of or fill beforehand or before another
**pre·op·er·a·tive** \(ˌ)prē-'ä-p(ə-)rə-tiv, -pə-ˌrā-\ *adjective* (1904)
: occurring before a surgical operation
— **pre·op·er·a·tive·ly** *adverb*
**pre·or·dain** \ˌprē-òr-'dān\ *transitive verb* (1533)
: to decree or ordain in advance : FOREORDAIN
— **pre·or·dain·ment** \-mənt\ *noun*
— **pre·or·di·na·tion** \(ˌ)prē-ˌòr-dᵊn-'ā-shən\ *noun*
**pre·ovu·la·to·ry** \(ˌ)prē-'äv-yə-lə-ˌtōr-ē, -ˌtòr-, -'ōv-\ *adjective* (1935)
: occurring or existing in or typical of the period immediately preceding ovulation ⟨*preovulatory* oocytes⟩ ⟨a *preovulatory* surge of luteinizing hormone⟩
**pre-owned** \(ˌ)prē-'ōnd, 'prē-\ *adjective* (1964)

**: SECONDHAND**

**¹prep** \'prep\ *noun* (1862)
**1 :** PREPARATION
**2 :** PREPARATORY SCHOOL
**3 :** a preliminary trial for a racehorse

**²prep** *verb* **prepped; prep·ping** (1915)
*intransitive verb*
**1 :** to attend preparatory school
**2** [short for *prepare*] **:** to get ready
*transitive verb*
**:** PREPARE; *especially* **:** to prepare for operation or examination

**pre·pack·age** \(ˌ)prē-'pa-kij\ *transitive verb* (1945)
**:** to package (as food or a manufactured article) before offering for sale to the consumer

**prep·a·ra·tion** \ˌpre-pə-'rā-shən\ *noun* [Middle English *preparacion*, from Middle French *preparation*, from Latin *praeparation-*, *praeparatio*, from *praeparare* to prepare] (14th century)
**1 :** the action or process of making something ready for use or service or of getting ready for some occasion, test, or duty
**2 :** a state of being prepared **:** READINESS
**3 :** a preparatory act or measure
**4 :** something that is prepared; *specifically* **:** a medicinal substance made ready for use ⟨a *preparation* for colds⟩

**¹pre·par·a·tive** \pri-'par-ə-tiv\ *noun* (14th century)
**:** something that prepares the way for or serves as a preliminary to something else **:** PREPARATION

**²preparative** *adjective* (circa 1530)
**:** PREPARATORY
**— pre·par·a·tive·ly** *adverb*

**pre·par·a·tor** \pri-'par-ə-tər\ *noun* (1762)
**:** one that prepares; *specifically* **:** a person who prepares scientific specimens or museum displays

**pre·pa·ra·to·ry** \pri-'par-ə-ˌtōr-ē, -ˌtȯr- *also* 'pre-p(ə-)rə-\ *adjective* (15th century)
**:** preparing or serving to prepare for something **:** INTRODUCTORY
**— pre·pa·ra·to·ri·ly** \pri-ˌpar-ə-'tōr-ə-lē, -'tȯr- *also* ˌpre-p(ə-)rə-\ *adverb*

**preparatory school** *noun* (1822)
**1 :** a usually private school preparing students primarily for college
**2** *British* **:** a private elementary school preparing students primarily for British public schools

**preparatory to** *preposition* (1649)
**:** in preparation for

**pre·pare** \pri-'par, -'per\ *verb* **pre·pared; pre·par·ing** [Middle English, from Middle French *preparer*, from Latin *praeparare*, from *prae-* pre- + *parare* to procure, prepare — more at PARE] (15th century)
*transitive verb*
**1 a :** to make ready beforehand for some purpose, use, or activity ⟨*prepare* food for dinner⟩ **b :** to put in a proper state of mind ⟨is *prepared* to listen⟩
**2 :** to work out the details of **:** plan in advance ⟨*preparing* strategy for the coming campaign⟩
**3 a :** to put together **:** COMPOUND ⟨*prepare* a prescription⟩ **b :** to put into written form ⟨*prepare* a report⟩
*intransitive verb*
**:** to get ready ⟨*preparing* for a career⟩
**— pre·par·er** *noun*

**prepared** *adjective* (1663)
**:** subjected to a special process or treatment
**— pre·pared·ly** \-'pärd-lē, -'perd-; -'par-əd-, -'per-\ *adverb*

**pre·pared·ness** \pri-'par-əd-nəs, -'per- *also* -'pärd-nəs *or* -'perd-nəs\ *noun* (1590)
**:** the quality or state of being prepared; *especially* **:** a state of adequate preparation in case of war

**pre·pay** \(ˌ)prē-'pā\ *transitive verb* **-paid** \-'pād\; **-pay·ing** (1839)
**:** to pay or pay the charge on in advance
**— pre·pay·ment** \-'pā-mənt\ *noun*

**pre·pense** \pri-'pen(t)s\ *adjective* [by shortening & alteration from earlier *purpensed*, from Middle English, past participle of *purpensen* to deliberate, premeditate, from Middle French *purpenser*, from Old French, from *pur-* for + *penser* to think — more at PURCHASE, PENSIVE] (1702)
**:** planned beforehand **:** PREMEDITATED — usually used postpositively ⟨malice *prepense*⟩
**— pre·pense·ly** *adverb*

**pre·plant** \ˌprē-'plant, 'prē-ˌ\ *also* **pre·plant·ing** \-'plan-tiŋ\ *adjective* (1961)
**:** occurring or used before planting a crop ⟨*preplant* soil fertilization⟩

**pre·pon·der·ance** \pri-'pän-d(ə-)rən(t)s\ *noun* (1681)
**1 :** a superiority in weight, power, importance, or strength
**2 a :** a superiority or excess in number or quantity **b :** MAJORITY

**pre·pon·der·an·cy** \-d(ə-)rən(t)-sē\ *noun* (1646)
**:** PREPONDERANCE

**pre·pon·der·ant** \pri-'pän-d(ə-)rənt\ *adjective* (15th century)
**1 :** having superior weight, force, or influence
**2 :** having greater prevalence
*synonym* see DOMINANT
**— pre·pon·der·ant·ly** *adverb*

**¹pre·pon·der·ate** \pri-'pän-də-ˌrāt\ *verb* **-at·ed; -at·ing** [Latin *praeponderatus*, past participle of *praeponderare*, from *prae-* + *ponder-*, *pondus* weight — more at PENDANT] (1623)
*intransitive verb*
**1 :** to exceed in weight
**2 :** to exceed in influence, power, or importance
**3 :** to exceed in numbers
*transitive verb*
**1** *archaic* **:** OUTWEIGH
**2** *archaic* **:** to weigh down
**— pre·pon·der·a·tion** \-ˌpän-də-'rā-shən, ˌprē-\ *noun*

**²pre·pon·der·ate** \-'pän-də-rət\ *adjective* (1802)
**:** PREPONDERANT
**— pre·pon·der·ate·ly** *adverb*

**prep·o·si·tion** \ˌpre-pə-'zi-shən\ *noun* [Middle English *preposicioun*, from Latin *praeposition-*, *praepositio*, from *praeponere* to put in front, from *prae-* pre- + *ponere* to put — more at POSITION] (14th century)
**:** a function word that typically combines with a noun phrase to form a phrase which usually expresses a modification or predication ■
**— prep·o·si·tion·al** \-'zish-nəl, -'zi-shə-n°l\ *adjective*
**— prep·o·si·tion·al·ly** *adverb*

**pre·pos·i·tive** \pri-'pä-zə-tiv, -'päz-tiv\ *adjective* [Late Latin *praepositivus*, from Latin *praepositus*, past participle of *praeponere*] (1583)
**:** put before **:** PREFIXED
**— pre·pos·i·tive·ly** *adverb*

**pre·pos·sess** \ˌprē-pə-'zes *also* -'ses\ *transitive verb* (1614)
**1** *obsolete* **:** to take previous possession of
**2 :** to cause to be preoccupied
**3 :** to influence beforehand especially favorably

**pre·pos·sess·ing** *adjective* (1642)
**1** *archaic* **:** creating prejudice
**2 :** tending to create a favorable impression **:** ATTRACTIVE

**pre·pos·ses·sion** \ˌprē-pə-'ze-shən *also* -'se-\ *noun* (1648)
**1** *archaic* **:** prior possession
**2 :** an attitude, belief, or impression formed beforehand **:** PREJUDICE
**3 :** an exclusive concern with one idea or object **:** PREOCCUPATION
*synonym* see PREDILECTION

**pre·pos·ter·ous** \pri-'päs-t(ə-)rəs\ *adjective* [Latin *praeposterus*, literally, in the wrong order, from *prae-* + *posterus* hinder, following — more at POSTERIOR] (1542)
**:** contrary to nature, reason, or common sense **:** ABSURD
**— pre·pos·ter·ous·ly** *adverb*
**— pre·pos·ter·ous·ness** *noun*

**pre·po·ten·cy** \(ˌ)prē-'pō-t°n(t)-sē\ *noun* (1646)
**1 :** the quality or state of being prepotent **:** PREDOMINANCE
**2 :** unusual ability of an individual or strain to transmit its characters to offspring because of homozygosity for numerous dominant genes

**pre·po·tent** \-t°nt\ *adjective* [Middle English, from Latin *praepotent-*, *praepotens*, from *prae-* + *potens* powerful — more at POTENT] (15th century)
**1 a :** having exceptional power, authority, or influence **b :** exceeding others in power
**2 :** exhibiting genetic prepotency
**— pre·po·tent·ly** *adverb*

**¹prep·py** *or* **prep·pie** \'pre-pē\ *noun, plural* **prep·pies** [¹*preposition*] (1967)
**1 :** a student at or a graduate of a preparatory school
**2 :** a person deemed to dress or behave like a preppy

**²preppy** *or* **preppie** *adjective* (1967)
**1 :** relating to, characteristic of, or being a preppy
**2 :** relating to or being a style of dress characterized especially by classic clothing and neat appearance
**— prep·pi·ly** \'pre-pə-lē\ *adverb*
**— prep·pi·ness** \'pre-pē-nəs\ *noun*

**pre·pran·di·al** \(ˌ)prē-'pran-dē-əl\ *adjective* (1822)
**:** of, relating to, or suitable for the time just before dinner ⟨a *preprandial* drink⟩

**pre·preg** \ˌprē-'preg, 'prē-\ *noun* [*pre-* + im*preg*nated] (1954)
**:** a reinforcing or molding material (as paper or glass cloth) already impregnated with a synthetic resin

**¹pre·print** \'prē-ˌprint, ˌprē-'print\ *noun* (1889)
**1 :** an issue of a technical paper often in preliminary form before its publication in a journal
**2 :** something (as an advertisement) printed before the rest of the publication in which it is to appear

---

□ **USAGE**

**preposition** Is it all right to end a sentence with a preposition? The answer is yes, even though many people cherish the notion that it is not. The notion of the inappropriateness of the deferred preposition goes back to the middle of the 17th century and is probably based on Latin grammar. But modern commentators know that the construction is standard. It is even required by these constructions: a restrictive clause introduced by *that* (the magazine that I most wanted to have a story published *in* —Truman Capote), a restrictive clause from which *that* has been omitted (as soon as I finish the short story I'm working *on* —F. Scott Fitzgerald), a clause introduced by *what* (we can only speculate what they might have been *about* —Elizabeth Drew), an infinitive clause (both bought new suits to be married *in* —Russell Baker), a participial clause (relatively new and therefore worth keeping track *of* —Kenneth G. Wilson), and a passive construction (people deficient in learning were looked down *on* —Cynthia Ozick). Questions, too, require the deferred preposition ⟨has the car been paid *for*?⟩ ⟨what does she look *like*?⟩. The preposition at the end is so natural that consciously avoiding it can cause mistakes ⟨a young man *with* whom most Americans could identify *with* —Herbert Warren Wind⟩.

²**pre·print** \(ˌ)prē-'print\ *transitive verb* (1926)
: to print in advance for later use

**pre·pro·cess** \(ˌ)prē-'prä-ˌses, -'prō-, -səs\ *transitive verb* (1942)
: to do preliminary processing of (as data)
— **pre·pro·ces·sor** \-ˌse-sər; -sə-sər, -ˌsòr\ *noun*

**pre·pro·fes·sion·al** \ˌprē-prə-'fesh-nəl, -'fe-shə-nᵊl\ *adjective* (1926)
: of or relating to the period preceding specific study for or practice of a profession

**prep school** *noun* (1895)
: PREPARATORY SCHOOL

**pre·pu·ber·al** \(ˌ)prē-'pyü-b(ə-)rəl\ *adjective* (circa 1935)
: PREPUBERTAL

**pre·pu·ber·tal** \-bər-tᵊl\ *adjective* (1859)
: of or relating to prepuberty

**pre·pu·ber·ty** \-bər-tē\ *noun* (1922)
: the period immediately preceding puberty

**pre·pu·bes·cence** \ˌprē-pyü-'be-sᵊn(t)s\ *noun* (1916)
: PREPUBERTY

**pre·pu·bes·cent** \-sᵊnt\ *adjective* (1904)
: PREPUBERTAL
— **prepubescent** *noun*

**pre·puce** \'prē-ˌpyüs\ *noun* [Middle English, from Middle French, from Latin *praeputium*] (15th century)
: FORESKIN; *also* : a similar fold investing the clitoris
— **pre·pu·tial** \prē-'pyü-shəl\ *adjective*

**pre·quel** \'prē-kwəl\ *noun* [*pre-* + *-quel* (as in *sequel*)] (1972)
: a literary or dramatic work whose story precedes that of an earlier work

**Pre-Ra·pha·el·ite** \(ˌ)prē-'ra-fē-ə-ˌlīt, -'rä-, -'rä-\ *noun* (1850)
**1 a** : a member of a brotherhood of artists formed in England in 1848 to restore the artistic principles and practices regarded as characteristic of Italian art before Raphael **b** : an artist or writer influenced by this brotherhood
**2** : a modern artist dedicated to restoring early Renaissance ideals or methods
— **Pre-Raphaelite** *adjective*
— **Pre-Ra·pha·el·it·ism** \-ˌlī-ˌti-zəm\ *noun*

**pre·reg·is·tra·tion** \ˌprē-ˌre-jə-'strā-shən\ *noun* (1967)
: a special registration (as for returning students) prior to an official registration period
— **pre·reg·is·ter** \(ˌ)prē-'re-jə-stər\ *intransitive verb*

**pre·req·ui·site** \(ˌ)prē-'re-kwə-zət\ *noun* (1633)
: something that is necessary to an end or to the carrying out of a function
— **prerequisite** *adjective*

**pre·rog·a·tive** \pri-'rä-gə-tiv\ *noun* [Middle English, from Middle French & Latin; Middle French, from Latin *praerogativa*, Roman century voting first in the comitia, privilege, from feminine of *praerogativus* voting first, from *praerogatus*, past participle of *praerogare* to ask for an opinion before another, from *prae-* + *rogare* to ask — more at RIGHT] (15th century)
**1 a** : an exclusive or special right, power, or privilege: as (1) : one belonging to an office or an official body (2) : one belonging to a person, group, or class of individuals (3) : one possessed by a nation as an attribute of sovereignty **b** : the discretionary power inhering in the British Crown
**2** : a distinctive excellence
— **pre·rog·a·tived** \-tivd\ *adjective*

¹**pres·age** \'pre-sij, *also* pri-'sāj\ *noun* [Middle English, from Latin *praesagium*, from *praesagus* having a foreboding, from *prae-* + *sagus* prophetic — more at SEEK] (14th century)
**1** : something that foreshadows or portends a future event : OMEN
**2** : an intuition or feeling of what is going to happen in the future

**3** *archaic* : PROGNOSTICATION
**4** : warning or indication of the future
— **pre·sage·ful** \pri-'sāj-fəl\ *adjective*

²**pre·sage** \'pre-sij, pri-'sāj\ *verb* **pre·saged; pre·sag·ing** (1562)
*transitive verb*
**1** : to give an omen or warning of : FORESHADOW
**2** : FORETELL, PREDICT
*intransitive verb*
: to make or utter a prediction
— **pre·sag·er** *noun, obsolete*

**pre·sanc·ti·fied** \(ˌ)prē-'saŋ(k)-ti-ˌfīd\ *adjective* (1758)
: consecrated at a previous service — used of eucharistic elements

**pres·by·ope** \'prez-bē-ˌōp; 'pres-bē-, -pē-\ *noun* [probably from French, from Greek *presbys* old man + *ōps* eye — more at EYE] (circa 1857)
: one affected with presbyopia

**pres·by·o·pia** \ˌprez-bē-'ō-pē-ə, ˌpres-\ *noun* [New Latin] (1793)
: a visual condition which becomes apparent especially in middle age and in which loss of elasticity of the lens of the eye causes defective accommodation and inability to focus sharply for near vision
— **pres·by·o·pic** \-'ō-pik, -'ä-\ *adjective or noun*

**pres·by·ter** \'prez-bə-tər, 'pres-\ *noun* [Late Latin, elder, priest, from Greek *presbyteros*, comparative of *presbys* old man, elder; akin to Greek *pro* before and Greek *bainein* to go — more at FOR, COME] (1597)
**1** : a member of the governing body of an early Christian church
**2** : a member of the order of priests in churches having episcopal hierarchies that include bishops, priests, and deacons
**3** : ELDER 4b
— **pres·byt·er·ate** \ˌprez-'bi-tə-rət, pres-, -ˌrāt\ *noun*

¹**pres·by·te·ri·al** \ˌprez-bə-'tir-ē-əl, ˌpres-\ *adjective* (circa 1600)
: of or relating to presbyters or a presbytery
— **pres·by·te·ri·al·ly** \-ē-ə-lē\ *adverb*

²**presbyterial** *noun, often capitalized* (1928)
: an organization of Presbyterian women associated with a presbytery

¹**Pres·by·te·ri·an** \-ē-ən\ *noun* (1640)
: a member of a Presbyterian church

²**Presbyterian** *adjective* (1641)
**1** *often not capitalized* : characterized by a graded system of representative ecclesiastical bodies (as presbyteries) exercising legislative and judicial powers
**2** : of, relating to, or constituting a Protestant Christian church that is presbyterian in government and traditionally Calvinistic in doctrine
— **Pres·by·te·ri·an·ism** \-ē-ə-ˌni-zəm\ *noun*

**pres·by·tery** \'prez-bə-ˌter-ē, 'pres-, -bə-trē\ *noun, plural* **-ter·ies** [Middle English & Late Latin; Middle English *presbytory* part of church reserved for clergy, from Late Latin *presbyterium* group of presbyters, part of church reserved for clergy, from Greek *presbyterion* group of presbyters, from *presbyteros* elder, priest] (15th century)
**1** : the part of a church reserved for the officiating clergy
**2** : a ruling body in presbyterian churches consisting of the ministers and representative elders from congregations within a district
**3** : the jurisdiction of a presbytery
**4** : the house of a Roman Catholic parish priest

¹**pre·school** \'prē-ˌskül, (ˌ)prē-'\ *adjective* (1914)
: of, relating to, or constituting the period in a child's life from infancy to the age of five or six that ordinarily precedes attendance at elementary school

²**pre·school** \'prē-ˌskül\ *noun* (circa 1925)

: NURSERY SCHOOL, KINDERGARTEN

**pre·school·er** \-ˌskü-lər\ *noun* (1946)
**1** : a child not yet old enough for school
**2** : a child attending a preschool

**pre·science** \'pre-sh(ē-)ən(t)s, 'prē-, -s(ē-)ən(t)s\ *noun* [Middle English, from Late Latin *praescientia*, from Latin *praescient-, praesciens*, present participle of *praescire* to know beforehand, from *prae-* + *scire* to know — more at SCIENCE] (14th century)
: foreknowledge of events: **a** : divine omniscience **b** : human anticipation of the course of events : FORESIGHT
— **pre·scient** \-sh(ē-)ənt, -s(ē-)ənt\ *adjective*
— **pre·scient·ly** *adverb*

**pre·sci·en·tif·ic** \ˌprē-ˌsī-ən-'ti-fik\ *adjective* (1858)
: of, relating to, or having the characteristics of a period before the rise of modern science or a state prior to the application of the scientific method

**pre·scind** \pri-'sind\ *verb* [Latin *praescindere* to cut off in front, from *prae-* + *scindere* to cut — more at SHED] (1650)
*intransitive verb*
: to withdraw one's attention
*transitive verb*
: to detach for purposes of thought

**pre·score** \(ˌ)prē-'skōr, -'skòr\ *transitive verb* (1937)
: to record (as sound) in advance for use when the corresponding scenes are photographed in making movies

**pre·scribe** \pri-'skrīb\ *verb* **pre·scribed; pre·scrib·ing** [Middle English, from Latin *praescribere* to write at the beginning, dictate, order, from *prae-* + *scribere* to write — more at SCRIBE] (15th century)
*intransitive verb*
**1** : to lay down a rule : DICTATE
**2** [Middle English, from Medieval Latin *praescribere*, from Latin, to write at the beginning] : to claim a title to something by right of prescription
**3** : to write or give medical prescriptions
**4** : to become by prescription invalid or unenforceable
*transitive verb*
**1 a** : to lay down as a guide, direction, or rule of action : ORDAIN **b** : to specify with authority
**2** : to designate or order the use of as a remedy
— **pre·scrib·er** *noun*

**pre·script** \'prē-ˌskript, pri-'\ *adjective* [Middle English, from Latin *praescriptus*, past participle] (circa 1540)
: prescribed as a rule
— **pre·script** \'prē-ˌskript\ *noun*

**pre·scrip·tion** \pri-'skrip-shən\ *noun* [partly from Middle English *prescripcion* establishment of a claim, from Middle French *prescription*, from Late Latin *praescription-, praescriptio*, from Latin, act of writing at the beginning, order, limitation of subject matter, from *praescribere*; partly from Latin *praescription-, praescriptio* order] (14th century)
**1 a** : the establishment of a claim of title to something under common law usually by use and enjoyment for a period fixed by statute **b** : the right or title acquired under common law by such possession
**2** : the process of making claim to something by long use and enjoyment
**3** : the action of laying down authoritative rules or directions
**4 a** : a written direction for a therapeutic or corrective agent; *specifically* : one for the

preparation and use of a medicine **b** : a prescribed medicine **c** : something like a doctor's prescription ⟨*prescriptions* for economic recovery⟩
**5 a** : ancient or long continued custom **b** : a claim founded upon ancient custom or long continued use
**6** : something prescribed as a rule
**prescription drug** *noun* (1951)
: a drug that can be obtained only by means of a physician's prescription
**pre·scrip·tive** \pri-'skrip-tiv\ *adjective* (1748)
**1** : serving to prescribe ⟨*prescriptive* rules of usage⟩
**2** : acquired by, founded on, or determined by prescription or by long-standing custom
— **pre·scrip·tive·ly** *adverb*
**pre·se·lect** \,prē-sə-'lekt\ *transitive verb* (circa 1859)
: to choose in advance usually on the basis of a particular criterion
— **pre·se·lec·tion** \-'lek-shən\ *noun*
**pre·sell** \(,)prē-'sel\ *transitive verb* **-sold** \-'sōld\; **-sell·ing** (1947)
**1** : to precondition (as a customer) for subsequent purchase or create advance demand for (as a product) especially through marketing strategies
**2** : to sell in advance ⟨raised money to publish the book by *preselling* film rights⟩
**pres·ence** \'pre-z°n(t)s\ *noun* (14th century)
**1** : the fact or condition of being present
**2 a** : the part of space within one's immediate vicinity **b** : the neighborhood of one of superior especially royal rank
**3** *archaic* : COMPANY 2a
**4** : one that is present: as **a** : the actual person or thing that is present **b** : something present of a visible or concrete nature
**5 a** : the bearing, carriage, or air of a person; *especially* : stately or distinguished bearing **b** : a quality of poise and effectiveness that enables a performer to achieve a close relationship with his audience
**6** : something (as a spirit) felt or believed to be present
**presence of mind** (1665)
: self-control so maintained in an emergency or in an embarrassing situation that one can say or do the right thing
¹**pres·ent** \'pre-z°nt\ *noun* [Middle English, from Old French, from *presenter*] (13th century)
: something presented : GIFT
²**pre·sent** \pri-'zent\ *verb* [Middle English, from Old French *presenter*, from Latin *praesentare*, from *praesent-, praesens,* adjective] (14th century)
*transitive verb*
**1 a** (1) : to bring or introduce into the presence of someone especially of superior rank or status (2) : to introduce socially **b** : to bring (as a play) before the public
**2** : to make a gift to
**3** : to give or bestow formally
**4 a** : to lay (as a charge) before a court as an object of inquiry **b** : to bring a formal public charge, indictment, or presentment against
**5** : to nominate to a benefice
**6 a** : to offer to view : SHOW **b** : to bring to one's attention ⟨this *presents* a problem⟩
**7** : to act the part of : PERFORM
**8** : to aim, point, or direct (as a weapon) so as to face something or in a particular direction
*intransitive verb*
**1** : to present a weapon
**2** : to become manifest
**3** : to come forward as a patient
**4** : to make a presentation
**synonym** see GIVE
— **pres·ent·er** *noun*
³**pres·ent** \'pre-z°nt\ *adjective* [Middle English, from Old French, from Latin *praesent-, praesens,* from present participle of *praeesse* to be before one, from *prae-* pre- + *esse* to be — more at IS] (14th century)

**1** : now existing or in progress
**2 a** : being in view or at hand **b** : existing in something mentioned or under consideration
**3** : constituting the one actually involved, at hand, or being considered
**4** : of, relating to, or constituting a verb tense that is expressive of present time or the time of speaking
**5** *obsolete* : ATTENTIVE
**6** *archaic* : INSTANT, IMMEDIATE
— **pres·ent·ness** *noun*
⁴**pres·ent** \'pre-z°nt\ *noun* (14th century)
**1 a** *obsolete* : present occasion or affair **b** *plural* : the present words or statements; *specifically* : the legal instrument or other writing in which these words are used
**2 a** : the present tense of a language **b** : a verb form in the present tense
**3** : the present time
— **at present** : at or during this time : NOW
**pre·sent·able** \pri-'zen-tə-bəl\ *adjective* (circa 1626)
**1** : capable of being presented
**2** : being in condition to be seen or inspected especially by the critical
— **pre·sent·abil·i·ty** \-,zen-tə-'bi-lə-tē\ *noun*
— **pre·sent·able·ness** \-'zen-tə-bəl-nəs\ *noun*
— **pre·sent·ably** \-blē\ *adverb*
**pre·sent arms** \pri-'zent-\ *noun* [from the command *present arms!*] (circa 1884)
**1** : a position in the manual of arms in which the rifle is held vertically in front of the body
**2** : a command to assume the position of present arms or to give a hand salute
**pre·sen·ta·tion** \,prē-,zen-'tā-shən, ,pre-z°n-, ,prē-z°n-\ *noun* (15th century)
**1 a** : the act of presenting **b** : the act, power, or privilege especially of a patron of applying to the bishop or ordinary for instituting someone into a benefice
**2** : something presented: as **a** : a symbol or image that represents something **b** : something offered or given : GIFT **c** : something set forth for the attention of the mind **d** : a descriptive or persuasive account (as by a salesman of a product)
**3** : the position in which the fetus lies in the uterus in labor with respect to the mouth of the uterus
**4** : an immediate object of perception, cognition, or memory
**5** *often capitalized* : a church feast on November 21 celebrating the presentation of the Virgin Mary in the temple
**6** : the method by which radio, navigation, or radar information is given to the operator (as the pilot of an airplane)
— **pre·sen·ta·tion·al** \-shnəl, -shə-n°l\ *adjective*
**pre·sen·ta·tive** \pri-'zen-tə-tiv, 'pre-z°n-,tā-\ *adjective* (circa 1842)
: known, knowing, or capable of being known directly rather than through cogitation
**pres·ent–day** \'pre-z°nt-'dā\ *adjective* (1887)
: now existing or occurring
**pre·sen·tee** \,pre-z°n-'tē, pri-,zen-\ *noun* (15th century)
: one who is presented or to whom something is presented
**pre·sen·tient** \pri-'sen(t)-sh(ē-)ənt, 'prē-; pri-'zen(t)-\ *adjective* [Latin *praesentient-, praesentiens,* present participle of *praesentire*] (1814)
: having a presentiment
**pre·sen·ti·ment** \pri-'zen-tə-mənt\ *noun* [French *pressentiment,* from Middle French, from *pressentir* to have a presentiment, from Latin *praesentire* to feel beforehand, from *prae-* + *sentire* to feel — more at SENSE] (1714)
: a feeling that something will or is about to happen : PREMONITION

— **pre·sen·ti·men·tal** \-,zen-tə-'men-t°l\ *adjective*
**pres·ent·ism** \'pre-z°n-,ti-zəm\ *noun* [³*present*] (1923)
: an outlook dominated by present-day attitudes and experiences
— **pres·ent·ist** \-z°n-tist\ *adjective*
**pres·ent·ly** \'pre-z°nt-lē\ *adverb* (14th century)
**1 a** *archaic* : at once **b** : before long : without undue delay
**2** : at the present time : NOW ▪
**pre·sent·ment** \pri-'zent-mənt\ *noun* (14th century)
**1** : the act of presenting to an authority a formal statement of a matter to be dealt with; *specifically* : the notice taken or statement made by a grand jury of an offense from their own knowledge without a bill of indictment laid before them
**2** : the act of offering at the proper time and place a document (as a bill of exchange) that calls for acceptance or payment by another
**3 a** : the act of presenting to view or consciousness **b** : something set forth, presented, or exhibited **c** : the aspect in which something is presented
**present participle** *noun* (1864)
: a participle that typically expresses present action in relation to the time expressed by the finite verb in its clause and that in English is formed with the suffix *-ing* and is used in the formation of the progressive tenses
**present perfect** *adjective* (1887)
: of, relating to, or constituting a verb tense that is formed in English with *have* and that expresses action or state completed at the time of speaking
— **present perfect** *noun*
**present tense** *noun* (14th century)
: the tense of a verb that expresses action or state in the present time and is used of what occurs or is true at the time of speaking and of what is habitual or characteristic or is always or necessarily true, that is sometimes used to refer to action in the past, and that is sometimes used for future events
**present value** *noun* (1831)
: the sum of money which if invested now at a given rate of compound interest will accumulate exactly to a specified amount at a specified future date
**pres·er·va·tion·ist** \,pre-zər-'vā-sh(ə-)nist\ *noun* (1927)
: one who advocates preservation (as of a biological species or a historical landmark)
¹**pre·ser·va·tive** \pri-'zər-və-tiv\ *adjective* (14th century)
: having the power of preserving
²**preservative** *noun* (15th century)
: something that preserves or has the power of preserving; *specifically* : an additive used to protect against decay, discoloration, or spoilage

---

□ USAGE
**presently**   Both senses 1b and 2 are flourishing in current English, but many commentators have objected to sense 2. Since this sense has been in continuous use since the 15th century, it is not clear why it is objectionable. Perhaps a note in the *Oxford English Dictionary* (1909) that the sense has been obsolete since the 17th century in literary English is to blame, but the note goes on to observe that the sense is in regular use in most English dialects. The last citation in that dictionary is from a 1901 Leeds newspaper, written in Standard English. Sense 2 is most common in contexts relating to business and politics ⟨the fastest-rising welfare cost is Medicaid, *presently* paid by the states and cities —William Safire⟩

**¹pre·serve** \pri-'zərv\ *verb* **pre·served; pre·serv·ing** [Middle English, from Middle French *preserver,* from Medieval Latin *praeservare,* from Late Latin, to observe beforehand, from Latin *prae-* + *servare* to keep, guard, observe — more at CONSERVE] (14th century)
*transitive verb*
**1 :** to keep safe from injury, harm, or destruction **:** PROTECT
**2 a :** to keep alive, intact, or free from decay **b :** MAINTAIN
**3 a :** to keep or save from decomposition **b :** to can, pickle, or similarly prepare for future use
**4 :** to keep up and reserve for personal or special use
*intransitive verb*
**1 :** to make preserves
**2 :** to raise and protect game for purposes of sport
**3 :** to be able to be preserved (as by canning)
— **pre·serv·abil·i·ty** \-,zər-və-'bi-lə-tē\ *noun*
— **pre·serv·able** \-'zər-və-bəl\ *adjective*
— **pres·er·va·tion** \,pre-zər-'vā-shən\ *noun*
— **pre·serv·er** \pri-'zər-vər\ *noun*

**²preserve** *noun* (1600)
**1 :** fruit canned or made into jams or jellies or cooked whole or in large pieces in a syrup so as to keep its shape — often used in plural
**2 :** an area restricted for the protection and preservation of natural resources (as animals or trees); *especially* **:** one used primarily for regulated hunting or fishing
**3 :** something regarded as reserved for certain persons

**pre·shrink** \(,)prē-'shriŋk, *especially Southern* -'sriŋk\ *transitive verb* **-shrank** \-'shraŋk, -'sraŋk\; **-shrunk** \-'shrəŋk, -'srəŋk\ (1926)
**:** to shrink (as a fabric) before making into a garment so that it will not shrink much when washed

**pre·side** \pri-'zīd\ *intransitive verb* **pre·sid·ed; pre·sid·ing** [Latin *praesidēre* to guard, preside over, from *prae-* + *sedēre* to sit — more at SIT] (1608)
**1 :** to exercise guidance, direction, or control
**2 a :** to occupy the place of authority **:** act as president, chairman, or moderator **b :** to occupy a position similar to that of a president or chairman
**3 :** to occupy a position of featured instrumental performer — usually used with *at* ⟨*presided* at the organ⟩
— **pre·sid·er** *noun*

**pres·i·den·cy** \'pre-zə-dən(t)-sē, 'prez-dən(t)- *also* 'pre-zə-,den(t)-sē\ *noun, plural* **-cies** (1591)
**1 a :** the office of president **b** (1) **:** the office of president of the U.S. (2) **:** the American governmental institution comprising the office of president and various associated administrative and policy-making agencies
**2 :** the term during which a president holds office
**3 :** the action or function of one that presides **:** SUPERINTENDENCE
**4 :** a Mormon executive council of the church or a stake consisting of a president and two counselors

**pres·i·dent** \'pre-zə-dənt, 'prez-dənt, 'pre-zə-,dent *in rapid speech* 'pre-z°nt\ *noun* [Middle English, from Middle French, from Latin *praesident-, praesidens,* from present participle of *praesidēre*] (14th century)
**1 :** an official chosen to preside over a meeting or assembly
**2 :** an appointed governor of a subordinate political unit
**3 :** the chief officer of an organization (as a corporation or institution) usually entrusted with the direction and administration of its policies
**4 :** the presiding officer of a governmental body

**5 a :** an elected official serving as both chief of state and chief political executive in a republic having a presidential government **b :** an elected official having the position of chief of state but usually only minimal political powers in a republic having a parliamentary government
— **pres·i·den·tial** \,pre-zə-'den(t)-shəl, ,prez-'den(t)-\ *adjective*
— **pres·i·den·tial·ly** \-sh(ə-)lē\ *adverb*
— **pres·i·dent·ship** \'pre-zə-dənt-,ship, 'prez-dənt-, 'pre-zə-,dent-\ *noun*

**presidential government** *noun* (1902)
**:** a system of government in which the president is constitutionally independent of the legislature

**Presidents' Day** *noun* (1952)
**:** WASHINGTON'S BIRTHDAY 2

**pre·sid·i·al** \pri-'si-dē-əl, prī-, -'zi-\ *adjective* [Late Latin *praesidialis,* from Latin *praesidium* garrison, from *praesid-, praeses* guard, governor, from *praesidēre*] (1611)
**1** [French *présidial,* from Middle French, alteration of *presidal,* from Late Latin *praesidialis* of a provincial governor, from Latin *praesid-, praeses*] **:** PROVINCIAL 1
**2 :** of, having, or constituting a garrison
**3 :** of or relating to a president **:** PRESIDENTIAL

**pre·sid·i·ary** \-dē-,er-ē\ *adjective* (1599)
**:** PRESIDIAL 2

**pre·si·dio** \pri-'sē-dē-,ō, -'si-, -'zē-, -'zi-\ *noun, plural* **-di·os** [Spanish, from Latin *praesidium*] (1763)
**:** a garrisoned place; *especially* **:** a military post or fortified settlement in areas currently or originally under Spanish control

**pre·sid·i·um** \pri-'si-dē-əm, prī-, -'zi-\ *noun, plural* **-ia** \-dē-ə\ *or* **-iums** [Russian *prezidium,* from Latin *praesidium* garrison] (1920)
**1 :** a permanent executive committee selected especially in Communist countries to act for a larger body
**2 :** a nongovernmental executive committee

**pre·sig·ni·fy** \(,)prē-'sig-nə-,fī\ *transitive verb* [Latin *praesignificare,* from *prae-* + *significare* to signify] (1586)
**:** to intimate or signify beforehand **:** PRESAGE

**¹pre·soak** \(,)prē-'sōk\ *transitive verb* (1919)
**:** to soak beforehand

**²pre·soak** \'prē-,sōk\ *noun* (1919)
**1 :** an instance of presoaking
**2 :** a preparation used in presoaking clothes

**pre–So·crat·ic** \,prē-sə-'kra-tik, -sō-\ *adjective* (1871)
**:** of or relating to Greek philosophers before Socrates
— **pre-Socratic** *noun*

**pre·sort** \(,)prē-'sȯrt\ *transitive verb* (1951)
**:** to sort (outgoing mail) by zip code usually before delivery to a post office

**¹press** \'pres\ *noun* [Middle English *presse,* from Old French, from *presser* to press] (13th century)
**1 a :** a crowd or crowded condition **:** THRONG **b :** a thronging or crowding forward or together
**2 a :** an apparatus or machine by which a substance is cut or shaped, an impression of a body is taken, a material is compressed, pressure is applied to a body, liquid is expressed, or a cutting tool is fed into the work by pressure **b :** a building containing presses or a business using presses
**3 :** CLOSET, CUPBOARD
**4 a :** an action of pressing or pushing **:** PRESSURE **b :** an aggressive pressuring defense employed in basketball often over the entire court area
**5 :** the properly smoothed and creased condition of a freshly pressed garment ⟨out of *press*⟩
**6 a :** PRINTING PRESS **b :** the act or the process of printing **c :** a printing or publishing establishment
**7 a :** the gathering and publishing or broadcasting of news **:** JOURNALISM **b :** newspapers, periodicals, and often radio and television

news broadcasting **c :** news reporters, publishers, and broadcasters **d :** comment or notice in newspapers and periodicals ⟨is getting a good *press*⟩
**8 :** any of various pressure devices (as one for keeping sporting gear from warping when not in use)
**9 :** a lift in weight lifting in which the weight is raised to shoulder height and then smoothly extended overhead without assist from the legs
— compare CLEAN AND JERK, SNATCH

**²press** *verb* [Middle English, from Middle French *presser,* from Latin *pressare,* frequentative of *premere* to press; probably akin to Russian na*peret'* to press] (14th century)
*transitive verb*
**1 :** to act upon through steady pushing or thrusting force exerted in contact **:** SQUEEZE
**2 a :** ASSAIL, HARASS **b :** AFFLICT, OPPRESS
**3 a :** to squeeze out the juice or contents of **b :** to squeeze with apparatus or instruments to a desired density, smoothness, or shape
**4 a :** to exert influence on **:** CONSTRAIN **b :** to try hard to persuade **:** BESEECH, ENTREAT
**5 :** to move by means of pressure
**6 a :** to lay stress or emphasis on **b :** to insist on or request urgently
**7 :** to follow through (a course of action)
**8 :** to clasp in affection or courtesy
**9 :** to make (a phonograph record) from a matrix
*intransitive verb*
**1 :** to crowd closely **:** MASS
**2 :** to force or push one's way
**3 :** to seek urgently **:** CONTEND
**4 :** to require haste or speed in action
**5 :** to exert pressure
**6 :** to take or hold a press
**7 :** to employ a press in basketball
— **press·er** *noun*
— **press the flesh :** to greet and shake hands with people especially while campaigning for political office

**³press** *verb* [alteration of obsolete *prest* to enlist by giving pay in advance] (1578)
*transitive verb*
**1 :** to force into service especially in an army or navy **:** IMPRESS
**2 a :** to take by authority especially for public use **:** COMMANDEER **b :** to take and force into any usually emergency service
*intransitive verb*
**:** to impress men as soldiers or sailors

**⁴press** *noun* (1599)
**1 :** impressment into service especially in a navy
**2** *obsolete* **:** a warrant for impressing recruits

**press agent** *noun* [¹*press*] (1883)
**:** an agent employed to establish and maintain good public relations through publicity
— **press–agent** *verb*
— **press–agent·ry** \-'ā-jən-trē\ *noun*

**press·board** \'pres-,bȯrd, -,bȯrd\ *noun* (1849)
**1 :** IRONING BOARD; *especially* **:** a small one for sleeves
**2 :** a strong highly glazed composition board resembling vulcanized fiber

**press box** *noun* (1889)
**:** a space reserved for reporters (as at a stadium)

**press cloth** *noun* (1899)
**:** a cloth used between an iron and a garment

**press conference** *noun* (1937)
**:** an interview or announcement given by a public figure to the press by appointment

**press–gang** \'pres-,gaŋ\ *noun* [⁴*press*] (1693)
**:** a detachment of men under command of an officer empowered to force men into military or naval service

— **press–gang** *transitive verb*
**press·ing** *adjective* (1616)
**1 :** urgently important **:** CRITICAL
**2 :** EARNEST, WARM
— **press·ing·ly** \'pre-siŋ-lē\ *adverb*
**press kit** *noun* (1968)
**:** a collection of promotional materials for distribution to the press
**press·man** \'pres-mən, -ˌman\ *noun* (1598)
**1 :** an operator of a press; *especially* **:** the operator of a printing press
**2** *British* **:** NEWSPAPERMAN
**press·mark** \-ˌmärk\ *noun* [¹*press* (closet)] (1802)
*chiefly British* **:** a mark or number assigned to a book to indicate its location in a library
**press of sail** (1794)
**:** the fullest amount of sail that a ship can crowd on — called also *press of canvas*
**pres·sor** \'pre-ˌsȯr, -sər\ *adjective* [Late Latin, one that presses, from Latin *premere* to press — more at PRESS] (circa 1890)
**:** raising or tending to raise blood pressure; *also* **:** involving vasoconstriction
**press·room** \'pres-ˌrüm, -ˌrum\ *noun* (1683)
**1 :** a room in a printing plant containing the printing presses
**2 :** a room (as at the White House) for the use of members of the press
**press·run** \-ˌrən\ *noun* (1945)
**:** a continuous operation of a printing press producing a specified number of copies; *also* **:** the number of copies printed
**press secretary** *noun* (1951)
**:** a person officially in charge of press relations for a usually prominent public figure ⟨the President's *press secretary*⟩
**press–up** \'pres-ˌəp\ *noun* (1936)
*British* **:** PUSH-UP
**¹pres·sure** \'pre-shər\ *noun* [Middle English, from Late Latin *pressura*, from Latin, action of pressing, pressure, from *pressus*, past participle of *premere*] (14th century)
**1 a :** the burden of physical or mental distress **b :** the constraint of circumstance **:** the weight of social or economic imposition
**2 :** the application of force to something by something else in direct contact with it **:** COMPRESSION
**3** *archaic* **:** IMPRESSION, STAMP
**4 a :** the action of a force against an opposing force **b :** the force or thrust exerted over a surface divided by its area **c :** ELECTROMOTIVE FORCE
**5 :** the stress or urgency of matters demanding attention **:** EXIGENCY ⟨people who work well under *pressure*⟩
**6 :** the force of selection that results from one or more agents and tends to reduce a population of organisms ⟨population *pressure*⟩ ⟨predation *pressure*⟩
**7 :** atmospheric pressure
**8 :** a sensation aroused by moderate compression of a body part or surface
— **pres·sure·less** *adjective*
**²pressure** *transitive verb* **pres·sured; pres·sur·ing** \'pre-sh(ə-)riŋ\ (1938)
**1 :** to apply pressure to
**2 :** PRESSURIZE
**3 :** to cook in a pressure cooker
**pressure cabin** *noun* (1935)
**:** a pressurized cabin
**pressure cooker** *noun* (1915)
**1 :** an airtight utensil for quick cooking or preserving of foods by means of superheated steam under pressure
**2 :** a situation or environment that is fraught with emotional or social pressures
— **pressure–cook** *verb*
**pressure gauge** *noun* (1862)
**:** a gauge for indicating fluid pressure
**pressure group** *noun* (1928)
**:** an interest group organized to influence public and especially government policy but not to elect candidates to office

**pressure point** *noun* (1909)
**:** a point where a blood vessel runs near a bone and can be compressed (as to check bleeding) by the application of pressure against the bone
**pressure suit** *noun* (1936)
**:** an inflatable suit for high-altitude or space flight to protect the body from low pressure
**pressure wave** *noun* (1942)
**:** a wave (as a sound wave) in which the propagated disturbance is a variation of pressure in a material medium — called also *P-wave*
**pres·sur·ise** *British variant of* PRESSURIZE
**pres·sur·ize** \'pre-shə-ˌrīz\ *transitive verb* **-ized; -iz·ing** (1938)
**1 :** to confine the contents of under a pressure greater than that of the outside atmosphere; *especially* **:** to maintain near-normal atmospheric pressure in during high-altitude or spaceflight (as by means of a supercharger)
**2 :** to apply pressure to
**3 :** to design to withstand pressure
— **pres·sur·i·za·tion** \ˌpre-sh(ə-)rə-'zā-shən\ *noun*
— **pres·sur·iz·er** *noun*
**press·work** \'pres-ˌwərk\ *noun* (1771)
**:** the operation, management, or product of a printing press; *especially* **:** the branch of printing concerned with the actual transfer of ink from form or plates to paper
**prest** \'prest\ *adjective* [Middle English, from Old French *prest*, from Latin *praestus* — more at PRESTO] (14th century)
*obsolete* **:** READY
**pres·ti·dig·i·ta·tion** \ˌpres-tə-ˌdi-jə-'tā-shən\ *noun* [French, from *prestidigitateur* prestidigitator, from *preste* nimble, quick (from Italian *presto*) + Latin *digitus* finger — more at DIGIT] (1859)
**:** SLEIGHT OF HAND, LEGERDEMAIN
— **pres·ti·dig·i·ta·tor** \-'di-jə-ˌtā-tər\ *noun*
**pres·tige** \pre-'stēzh, -'stēj\ *noun, often attributive* [French, from Middle French, conjuror's trick, illusion, from Latin *praestigiae*, plural, conjuror's tricks, from *praestringere* to graze, blunt, constrict, from *prae-* + *stringere* to bind tight — more at STRAIN] (1829)
**1 :** standing or estimation in the eyes of people **:** weight or credit in general opinion
**2 :** commanding position in people's minds ◆
**synonym** see INFLUENCE
— **pres·tige·ful** \-fəl\ *adjective*
**pres·ti·gious** \pre-'sti-jəs, -'stē- *also* prə-\ *adjective* [Latin *praestigiosus*, from *praestigiae*] (1546)
**1** *archaic* **:** of, relating to, or marked by illusion, conjuring, or trickery
**2 :** having prestige **:** HONORED
— **pres·ti·gious·ly** *adverb*
— **pres·ti·gious·ness** *noun*
**pres·tis·si·mo** \pre-'sti-sə-ˌmō\ *adverb or adjective* [Italian, from *presto* + *-issimo*, suffix denoting a high degree] (circa 1724)
**:** faster than presto — used as a direction in music
**¹pres·to** \'pres-(ˌ)tō\ *adverb or adjective* [Italian, quick, quickly, from Latin *praestus* ready, from *praesto*, adverb, on hand; akin to Latin *prae* before — more at FOR] (circa 1599)
**1 :** suddenly as if by magic **:** IMMEDIATELY
**2 :** at a rapid tempo — used as a direction in music
**²presto** *noun, plural* **prestos** (1869)
**:** a presto musical passage or movement
**¹pre·stress** \(ˌ)prē-'stres\ *transitive verb* (1934)
**:** to introduce internal stresses into (as a structural beam) to counteract the stresses that will result from applied load (as in incorporating cables under tension in concrete)
**²pre·stress** \'prē-ˌstres, ˌprē-'\ *noun* (1934)
**1 :** the stresses introduced in prestressing
**2 :** the process of prestressing

**3 :** the condition of being prestressed
**pre·sum·able** \pri-'zü-mə-bəl\ *adjective* (1692)
**:** capable of being presumed **:** acceptable as an assumption
**pre·sum·ably** \-blē\ *adverb* (1846)
**:** by reasonable assumption
**pre·sume** \pri-'züm\ *verb* **pre·sumed; pre·sum·ing** [Middle English, from Late Latin & Middle French; Late Latin *praesumere* to dare, from Latin, to anticipate, assume, from *prae-* + *sumere* to take; Middle French *presumer* to assume, from Latin *praesumere* — more at CONSUME] (14th century)
*transitive verb*
**1 :** to undertake without leave or clear justification **:** DARE
**2 :** to expect or assume especially with confidence
**3 :** to suppose to be true without proof ⟨*presumed* innocent until proved guilty⟩
**4 :** to take for granted **:** IMPLY
*intransitive verb*
**1 :** to act or proceed presumptuously or on a presumption
**2 :** to go beyond what is right or proper
— **pre·sumed·ly** \-'zü-məd-lē, -'zümd-lē\ *adverb*
— **pre·sum·er** *noun*
**presuming** *adjective* (15th century)
**:** PRESUMPTUOUS
— **pre·sum·ing·ly** \-'zü-miŋ-lē\ *adverb*
**pre·sump·tion** \pri-'zəm(p)-shən\ *noun* [Middle English *presumpcioun*, from Old French *presumption*, from Late Latin & Latin; Late Latin *praesumption-*, *praesumptio* presumptuous attitude, from Latin, assumption, from *praesumere*] (13th century)
**1 :** presumptuous attitude or conduct **:** AUDACITY
**2 a :** an attitude or belief dictated by probability **:** ASSUMPTION **b :** the ground, reason, or evidence lending probability to a belief
**3 :** a legal inference as to the existence or truth of a fact not certainly known that is drawn from the known or proved existence of some other fact
**pre·sump·tive** \-'zəm(p)-tiv\ *adjective* (15th century)
**1 :** based on probability or presumption
**2 :** giving grounds for reasonable opinion or belief
**3 :** being an embryonic precursor with the potential for forming a particular structure or tissue in the normal course of development ⟨*presumptive* retina⟩
— **pre·sump·tive·ly** *adverb*
**pre·sump·tu·ous** \pri-'zəm(p)-chə-wəs, -chəs, -shəs\ *adjective* [Middle English, from Middle French *presumptueux*, from Late Latin *praesumptuosus*, irregular from *praesumptio*] (14th century)

---

◇ WORD HISTORY
**prestige** The word *prestige* has witnessed a curious change in sense over the course of its history. French *prestige*, the immediate source of the English word, is a learned borrowing from Latin *praestigiae* "conjurer's tricks." Consequently its original meaning was "illusion produced by magic" or "enchantment, charm," hence by extension "charm of a dazzling personality, glamour," and then more generally "ability to create an impression." English borrowed the original French meaning "illusion" in the 17th century and the sense "ability to create an impression" in the 19th century, but the English and French words are no longer accurate translations for each other. English *prestige* now usually means "standing or estimation in the eyes of people," and a person or thing can be of either low or high prestige.

: overstepping due bounds (as of propriety or courtesy) : taking liberties
— **pre·sump·tu·ous·ly** adverb
— **pre·sump·tu·ous·ness** noun
**pre·sup·pose** \ˌprē-sə-'pōz\ transitive verb [Middle English, from Middle French presupposer, from Medieval Latin praesupponere (perfect indicative praesupposui), from Latin prae- + Medieval Latin supponere to suppose — more at SUPPOSE] (15th century)
**1** : to suppose beforehand
**2** : to require as an antecedent in logic or fact
— **pre·sup·po·si·tion** \ˌ(ˌ)prē-ˌsə-pə-'zi-shən\ noun
— **pre·sup·po·si·tion·al** \-'zish-nəl, -'zi-shə-n°l\ adjective
**pre·syn·ap·tic** \ˌprē-sə-'nap-tik\ adjective (1909)
: situated or occurring just before a nerve synapse
— **pre·syn·ap·ti·cal·ly** \-ti-k(ə-)lē\ adverb
**pret-a-por·ter** or **prêt-à-por·ter** \ˌpret-ä-pȯr-'tā\ noun [French, ready to wear] (1959)
: ready-to-wear clothes
**¹pre·teen** \'prē-ˌtēn, -ˌtēn\ noun (1952)
: a boy or girl not yet 13 years old
**²preteen** adjective (1954)
**1** : relating to or produced for children especially in the 9 to 12 year-old age group ⟨preteen fashions⟩
**2** : being younger than 13
**pre·teen·ag·er** \ˌ(ˌ)prē-tē-nā-jər\ noun (1965)
: PRETEEN
**¹pre·tend** \pri-'tend\ verb [Middle English, from Latin praetendere to allege as an excuse, literally, to stretch out, from prae- pre- + tendere to stretch — more at THIN] (15th century)
transitive verb
**1** : to give a false appearance of being, possessing, or performing ⟨does not pretend to be a psychiatrist⟩
**2 a** : to make believe : FEIGN ⟨he pretended deafness⟩ **b** : to claim, represent, or assert falsely ⟨pretending an emotion he could not really feel⟩
**3** archaic : VENTURE, UNDERTAKE
intransitive verb
**1** : to feign an action, part, or role in play
**2** : to put in a claim
**synonym** see ASSUME
**²pretend** adjective (1911)
: IMAGINARY, MAKE-BELIEVE
**pre·tend·ed** adjective (15th century)
: professed or avowed but not genuine ⟨pretended affection⟩
— **pre·tend·ed·ly** adverb
**pre·tend·er** \pri-'ten-dər\ noun (1609)
: one that pretends: as **a** : one who lays claim to something; specifically : a claimant to a throne who is held to have no just title **b** : one who makes a false or hypocritical show
**pre·tense** or **pre·tence** \'prē-ˌten(t)s, pri-'\ noun [Middle English, from Middle French pretensse, from (assumed) Medieval Latin praetensa, from Late Latin, feminine of praetensus, past participle of Latin praetendere] (15th century)
**1** : a claim made or implied; especially : one not supported by fact
**2 a** : mere ostentation : PRETENTIOUSNESS ⟨confuse dignity with pomposity and pretense —Bennett Cerf⟩ **b** : a pretentious act or assertion
**3** : an inadequate or insincere attempt to attain a certain condition or quality
**4** : professed rather than real intention or purpose : PRETEXT ⟨was there under false pretenses⟩
**5** : MAKE-BELIEVE, FICTION
**6** : false show : SIMULATION ⟨saw through his pretense of indifference⟩

**¹pre·ten·sion** \pri-'ten(t)-shən\ noun (15th century)
**1** : an allegation of doubtful value : PRETEXT
**2** : a claim or an effort to establish a claim
**3** : a claim or right to attention or honor because of merit
**4** : an aspiration or intention that may or may not reach fulfillment ⟨has serious literary pretensions⟩
**5** : VANITY, PRETENTIOUSNESS
**synonym** see AMBITION
— **pre·ten·sion·less** \-ləs\ adjective
**²pretension** \prē-'ten(t)-shən\ transitive verb [pre- + ²tension] (1937)
: PRESTRESS
**pre·ten·tious** \pri-'ten(t)-shəs\ adjective [French prétentieux, from prétention pretension, from Medieval Latin praetention-, praetentio, from Latin praetendere] (1837)
**1** : characterized by pretension: as **a** : making usually unjustified or excessive claims (as of value or standing) ⟨the pretentious fraud who assumes a love of culture that is alien to him —Richard Watts⟩ **b** : expressive of affected, unwarranted, or exaggerated importance, worth, or stature ⟨pretentious language⟩ ⟨pretentious houses⟩
**2** : making demands on one's skill, ability, or means : AMBITIOUS ⟨the pretentious daring of the Green Mountain Boys in crossing the lake —American Guide Series: Vermont⟩
**synonym** see SHOWY
— **pre·ten·tious·ly** adverb
— **pre·ten·tious·ness** noun
**¹pret·er·it** or **pret·er·ite** \'pre-tə-rət\ adjective [Middle English preterit, from Middle French, from Latin praeteritus, from past participle of praeterire to go by, pass, from praeter beyond, past, by (from comparative of prae before) + ire to go — more at FOR, ISSUE] (14th century)
archaic : BYGONE, FORMER
**²preterit** or **preterite** noun (14th century)
: PAST TENSE
**pre·term** \ˌ(ˌ)prē-'tərm, 'prē-ˌ\ adjective (1928)
: of, relating to, being, or brought forth by premature birth ⟨preterm infant⟩ ⟨preterm labor⟩
**pre·ter·mi·nal** \ˌ(ˌ)prē-'tərm-nəl, -'tər-mə-\ adjective (1947)
: occurring before death ⟨preterminal cancer⟩
**pre·ter·mis·sion** \ˌprē-tər-'mi-shən\ noun [Latin praetermission-, praetermissio, from praetermittere] (1583)
: the act or an instance of pretermitting : OMISSION
**pre·ter·mit** \-'mit\ transitive verb **-mit·ted; -mit·ting** [Latin praetermittere, from praeter by, past + mittere to let go, send] (1538)
**1** : to let pass without mention or notice : OMIT
**2** : to leave undone : NEGLECT
**3** : SUSPEND, BREAK OFF
**pre·ter·nat·u·ral** \ˌprē-tər-'na-chə-rəl, -'nach-rəl\ adjective [Medieval Latin praeternaturalis, from Latin praeter naturam beyond nature] (1580)
**1** : existing outside of nature
**2** : exceeding what is natural or regular : EXTRAORDINARY ⟨wits trained to preternatural acuteness by the debates —G. L. Dickinson⟩
**3** : inexplicable by ordinary means; especially : PSYCHIC ⟨preternatural phenomena⟩
— **pre·ter·nat·u·ral·ly** \-'na-chə-rə-lē, -'nach-rə-, -'na-chər-\ adverb
— **pre·ter·nat·u·ral·ness** \-'na-chə-rəl-nəs, -'nach-rəl-\ noun
**pre·test** \'prē-ˌtest\ noun (1926)
: a preliminary test: as **a** : a test of the effectiveness or safety of a product prior to its sale **b** : a test to evaluate the preparedness of students for further studies
— **pre·test** \ˌ(ˌ)prē-'test\ transitive verb
**pre·text** \'prē-ˌtekst\ noun [Latin praetextus, from praetexere to assign as a pretext, screen,

extend in front, from prae- + texere to weave — more at TECHNICAL] (1513)
: a purpose or motive alleged or an appearance assumed in order to cloak the real intention or state of affairs
**synonym** see APOLOGY
**pre·tor, pre·to·ri·an** variant of PRAETOR, PRAETORIAN
**pret·ti·fy** \'pri-ti-ˌfī, 'pȯr-, 'prù-\ transitive verb **-fied; -fy·ing** (1850)
: to make pretty
— **pret·ti·fi·ca·tion** \ˌpri-ti-fə-'kā-shən, ˌpȯr-, ˌprù-\ noun
— **pret·ti·fi·er** \'pri-ti-ˌfī(-ə)r, 'pȯr-, 'prù-\ noun
**pret·ti·ness** \'pri-tē-nəs, 'pȯr-, 'prù-\ noun (1649)
**1** : the quality or state of being pretty
**2** : something pretty
**¹pret·ty** \'pri-tē, 'pȯr- also 'prù-\ adjective **pret·ti·er; -est** [Middle English praty, prety, from Old English prættig tricky, from prætt trick; akin to Old Norse prettr trick] (15th century)
**1 a** : ARTFUL, CLEVER **b** : PAT, APT
**2 a** : pleasing by delicacy or grace **b** : having conventionally accepted elements of beauty **c** : appearing or sounding pleasant or nice but lacking strength, force, manliness, purpose, or intensity ⟨pretty words that make no sense —Elizabeth B. Browning⟩
**3 a** : MISERABLE, TERRIBLE ⟨a pretty mess you've gotten us into⟩ **b** chiefly Scottish : STOUT
**4** : moderately large : CONSIDERABLE ⟨a very pretty profit⟩ ⟨cost a pretty penny⟩
**synonym** see BEAUTIFUL
— **pret·ti·ly** \-t°l-ē\ adverb
— **pret·ty·ish** \-tē-ish\ adjective
**²pret·ty** \'pȯr-tē, 'pər-tē, 'pri-tē also 'prù-tē; before "near(ly)" often 'pərt or 'prit or 'prùt\ adverb (1565)
**1** : in some degree : MODERATELY ⟨pretty cold weather⟩
**2** : in a pretty manner : PRETTILY ⟨pop vocalists who can sing pretty —Gerald Levitch⟩ ■
**³pret·ty** \'pri-tē, 'pȯr-tē also 'prù-tē\ noun, plural **pretties** (1736)
**1** plural : dainty clothes; especially : LINGERIE
**2** : a pretty person or thing
**⁴pret·ty** \same as ³\ transitive verb **prettied; pret·ty·ing** (1909)
: to make pretty — usually used with up ⟨curtains to pretty up the room⟩
**pret·zel** \'pret-səl\ noun [German Brezel, ultimately from Latin brachiatus having branches like arms, from brachium arm — more at BRACE] (circa 1838)

\ə\ abut \ᵊ\ kitten \ər\ further \a\ ash \ā\ ace \ä\ mop, mar \aù\ out \ch\ chin \e\ bet \ē\ easy \g\ go \i\ hit \ī\ ice \j\ job \ŋ\ sing \ō\ go \ȯ\ law \ȯi\ boy \th\ thin \th\ the \ü\ loot \ù\ foot \y\ yet \zh\ vision see also Guide to Pronunciation

: a brittle or chewy glazed usually salted slender bread often shaped like a loose knot ◆

**pre·vail** \pri-'vā(ə)l\ *intransitive verb* [Middle English, from Latin *praevalēre,* from *prae-* pre- + *valēre* to be strong — more at WIELD] (15th century)
**1** : to gain ascendancy through strength or superiority : TRIUMPH
**2** : to be or become effective or effectual
**3** : to use persuasion successfully ⟨*prevailed* on him to sing⟩
**4** : to be frequent : PREDOMINATE ⟨the west winds that *prevail* in the mountains⟩
**5** : to be or continue in use or fashion : PERSIST ⟨a custom that still *prevails*⟩

**prev·a·lence** \'pre-və-lən(t)s, 'prev-lən(t)s\ *noun* (1713)
**1** : the quality or state of being prevalent
**2** : the degree to which something is prevalent; *especially* : the percentage of a population that is affected with a particular disease at a given time

**prev·a·lent** \-lənt\ *adjective* [Latin *praevalent-, praevalens* very powerful, from present participle of *praevalēre*] (1576)
**1** *archaic* : POWERFUL
**2** : being in ascendancy : DOMINANT
**3** : generally or widely accepted, practiced, or favored : WIDESPREAD
**— prevalent** *noun*
**— prev·a·lent·ly** *adverb*

**pre·var·i·cate** \pri-'var-ə-ˌkāt\ *intransitive verb* **-cat·ed; -cat·ing** [Latin *praevaricatus,* past participle of *praevaricari* to active in collusion, literally, to straddle, from *prae-* + *vari·care* to straddle, from *varus* bowlegged] (circa 1631)
: to deviate from the truth : EQUIVOCATE
*synonym* see LIE
**— pre·var·i·ca·tion** \-ˌvar-ə-'kā-shən\ *noun*
**— pre·var·i·ca·tor** \-'var-ə-ˌkā-tər\ *noun*

**pre·ve·nient** \pri-'vēn-yənt\ *adjective* [Latin *praevenient-, praeveniens,* present participle of *praevenire*] (circa 1656)
: ANTECEDENT, ANTICIPATORY
**— pre·ve·nient·ly** *adverb*

**pre·vent** \pri-'vent\ *verb* [Middle English, to anticipate, from Latin *praeventus,* past participle of *praevenire* to come before, anticipate, forestall, from *prae-* + *venire* to come — more at COME] (15th century)
*transitive verb*
**1** *archaic* **a** : to be in readiness for (as an occasion) **b** : to meet or satisfy in advance **c** : to act ahead of **d** : to go or arrive before
**2** : to deprive of power or hope of acting or succeeding
**3** : to keep from happening or existing ⟨steps to *prevent* war⟩
**4** : to hold or keep back : HINDER, STOP — often used with *from*
*intransitive verb*
: to interpose an obstacle ☆
**— pre·vent·abil·i·ty** \-ˌven-tə-'bi-lə-tē\ *noun*
**— pre·vent·able** *also* **pre·vent·ible** \-'ven-tə-bəl\ *adjective*
**— pre·vent·er** *noun*

**pre·ven·ta·tive** \-'ven-tə-tiv\ *adjective or noun* (circa 1666)
: PREVENTIVE

**pre·ven·tion** \pri-'ven(t)-shən\ *noun* (1582)
: the act of preventing or hindering

**¹pre·ven·tive** \-'ven-tiv\ *noun* (circa 1639)
: something that prevents; *especially* : something used to prevent disease

**²preventive** *adjective* (1639)
**1** : devoted to or concerned with prevention : PRECAUTIONARY ⟨*preventive* steps against soil erosion⟩
**2** : undertaken to forestall anticipated hostile action ⟨a *preventive* coup⟩
**— pre·ven·tive·ly** *adverb*
**— pre·ven·tive·ness** *noun*

**pre·ver·bal** \(ˌ)prē-'vər-bəl\ *adjective* (1921)

**1** : occurring before the verb
**2** : having not yet acquired the faculty of speech ⟨a *preverbal* child⟩

**¹pre·view** \'prē-ˌvyü\ *transitive verb* (1607)
**1** : to see beforehand; *specifically* : to view or to show in advance of public presentation
**2** : to give a preliminary survey of
**— pre·view·er** \-ˌvyü-ər\ *noun*

**²preview** *noun* (1922)
**1** : an advance showing or performance (as of a motion picture or play)
**2** *also* **pre·vue** \-ˌvyü\ : a showing of snatches from a motion picture advertised for appearance in the near future — called also *trailer*
**3** : an advance statement, sample, or survey

**pre·vi·ous** \'prē-vē-əs\ *adjective* [Latin *praevius* leading the way, from *prae-* pre- + *via* way — more at WAY] (1625)
**1** : going before in time or order : PRIOR
**2** : acting too soon : PREMATURE
*synonym* see PRECEDING
**— pre·vi·ous·ly** *adverb*
**— pre·vi·ous·ness** *noun*

**previous question** *noun* (circa 1715)
: a parliamentary motion to put the pending question to an immediate vote without further debate or amendment that if defeated has the effect of permitting resumption of debate

**previous to** *preposition* (1702)
: PRIOR TO, BEFORE

**¹pre·vi·sion** \prē-'vi-zhən\ *noun* [Middle English *previsioun,* from Old French *prevision,* from Late Latin *praevision-, praevisio,* from Latin *praevidēre* to foresee, from *prae-* + *vidēre* to see — more at WIT] (15th century)
**1** : FORESIGHT, PRESCIENCE
**2** : FORECAST, PROGNOSTICATION
**— pre·vi·sion·al** \-'vizh-nəl, -'vi-zhə-n°l\ *adjective*
**— pre·vi·sion·ary** \-'vi-zhə-ˌner-ē\ *adjective*

**²prevision** *transitive verb* **pre·vi·sioned; pre·vi·sion·ing** \-'vi-zhə-niŋ, -'vizh-niŋ\ (1891)
: FORESEE

**pre·vo·cal·ic** \ˌprē-vō-'ka-lik, -və-\ *adjective* [International Scientific Vocabulary] (1899)
: immediately preceding a vowel

**pre·vo·ca·tion·al** \ˌprē-vō-'kā-shnəl, -shə-n°l\ *adjective* (1914)
: given or required before admission to a vocational school

**pre·writ·ing** \'prē-ˌrī-tiŋ\ *noun* (1968)
: the formulation and organization of ideas preparatory to writing

**prexy** \'prek-sē\ *also* **prex** \'preks\ *noun, plural* **prex·ies** *also* **prex·es** [*prexy* from *prex,* by shortening & alteration from *president*] (1871)
*slang* : PRESIDENT — used chiefly of a college president

**¹prey** \'prā\ *noun, plural* **prey** *also* **preys** [Middle English *preie,* from Old French, from Latin *praeda;* akin to Latin *prehendere* to grasp, seize — more at GET] (13th century)
**1** *archaic* : SPOIL, BOOTY
**2 a** : an animal taken by a predator as food **b** : one that is helpless or unable to resist attack : VICTIM ⟨was *prey* to his own appetites⟩
**3** : the act or habit of preying

**²prey** *intransitive verb* **preyed; prey·ing** [Middle English, from Old French *preier,* from Latin *praedari,* from *praeda*] (14th century)
**1** : to make raids for the sake of booty
**2 a** : to seize and devour prey **b** : to commit violence or robbery or fraud
**3** : to have an injurious, destructive, or wasting effect
**— prey·er** *noun*

**prez** \'prez\ *noun, plural* **prez·es** \'pre-zəz\ [by shortening & alteration] (1892)
*slang* : PRESIDENT

**Pri·am** \'prī-əm, -ˌam\ *noun* [Latin *Priamus,* from Greek *Priamos*]

: the father of Hector and Paris and king of Troy during the Trojan War

**pri·a·pic** \prī-'ā-pik, -'a-\ *adjective* [Latin *priapus* lecher, from *Priapus*] (1786)
**1** : PHALLIC
**2** : relating to or preoccupied with virility

**Pri·a·pus** \prī-'ā-pəs\ *noun* [Latin, from Greek *Priapos*]
: a Greek and Roman god of gardens and male generative power

**¹price** \'prīs\ *noun* [Middle English *pris,* from Old French, from Latin *pretium* price, money; probably akin to Sanskrit *prati-* against, in return — more at PROS-] (13th century)
**1** *archaic* : VALUE, WORTH
**2 a** : the quantity of one thing that is exchanged or demanded in barter or sale for another **b** : the amount of money given or set as consideration for the sale of a specified thing
**3** : the terms for the sake of which something is done or undertaken: as **a** : an amount sufficient to bribe one ⟨believed every man had his *price*⟩ **b** : a reward for the apprehension or death of a person ⟨an outlaw with a *price* on his head⟩
**4** : the cost at which something is obtained ⟨the *price* of freedom is restraint —J. Irwin Miller⟩

**²price** *transitive verb* **priced; pric·ing** (15th century)
**1** : to set a price on
**2** : to find out the price of
**3** : to drive by raising prices excessively ⟨*priced* themselves out of the market⟩
**— pric·er** *noun*

**price–cut·ter** \'prīs-ˌkə-tər\ *noun* (1901)
: one that reduces prices especially to a level designed to cripple competition
**— price–cut·ting** \-tiŋ\ *noun*

**priced** \'prīst\ *adjective* (1722)
: having a specified price — used in combination ⟨low-*priced* merchandise⟩

---

☆ **SYNONYMS**
**Prevent, anticipate, forestall** mean to deal with beforehand. PREVENT implies taking advance measures against something possible or probable ⟨measures taken to *prevent* leaks⟩. ANTICIPATE may imply merely getting ahead of another by being a precursor or forerunner or it may imply checking another's intention by acting first ⟨*anticipated* the question by making a statement⟩. FORESTALL implies a getting ahead so as to stop or interrupt something in its course ⟨hoped to *forestall* the sale⟩.

---

◇ **WORD HISTORY**
**pretzel** Pretzels were apparently known to Americans by 1856, when the word *pretzel,* borrowed from German *Prezel* or *Brezel,* appears in a Sacramento, California, newspaper among a list of items claimed to be typical of German cuisine, such as wurst and lager beer. This familiar hard, knot-shaped bread has been baked, at least in Germanic countries, for centuries, as is evidenced by its appearance in a painting by the 16th century Flemish artist Pieter Brueghel. The origins of the pretzel, however, are even earlier, for the word is found in Old High German glosses as *brecila* or *brezitela.* These words were borrowed from the same vernacular Latin source that yielded Medieval Latin *bracidellus* and 15th century Italian *bracciatello.* These were names for a sweet, ring-shaped pastry—all ultimately from derivatives of Latin *brachiatus* "branched, having branches like arms." Twisted pastries were apparently so called because of the similarity between their knotted shape and a pair of folded arms.

**price–earnings ratio** *noun* (1961)
: a measure of the value of a common stock determined as the ratio of its market price to its earnings per share and usually expressed as a simple numeral

**price–fix·ing** \'prīs-,fik-siŋ\ *noun* (1920)
: the setting of prices artificially (as by producers or government) contrary to free market operations

**price index** *noun* (1886)
: an index number expressing the level of a group of commodity prices relative to the level of the prices of the same commodities during an arbitrarily chosen base period and used to indicate changes in the level of prices from one period to another

**price·less** \'prīs-ləs\ *adjective* (1593)
**1 a :** having a value beyond any price **:** INVALUABLE **b :** costly because of rarity or quality **:** PRECIOUS
**2 :** having worth in terms of other than market value
**3 :** delightfully amusing, odd, or absurd
— **price·less·ly** *adverb*

**price support** *noun* (1945)
: artificial maintenance of prices (as of a raw material) at some predetermined level usually through government action

**price tag** *noun* (1881)
**1 :** a tag on merchandise showing the price at which it is offered for sale
**2 :** PRICE, COST

**price war** *noun* (1925)
: commercial competition characterized by the repeated cutting of prices below those of competitors

**pric·ey** *also* **pricy** \'prī-sē\ *adjective* **pric·i·er; -est** (1932)
**:** EXPENSIVE

**¹prick** \'prik\ *noun* [Middle English *prikke*, from Old English *prica*; akin to Middle Dutch *pric* prick] (before 12th century)
**1 :** a mark or shallow hole made by a pointed instrument
**2 a :** a pointed instrument or weapon **b :** a sharp projecting organ or part
**3 :** an instance of pricking or the sensation of being pricked: as **a :** a nagging or sharp feeling of remorse, regret, or sorrow **b :** a slight sharply localized discomfort ⟨the *prick* of a needle⟩
**4 :** PENIS — usually considered vulgar
**5 :** a spiteful or contemptible man often having some authority — usually considered vulgar

**²prick** (before 12th century)
*transitive verb*
**1 :** to pierce slightly with a sharp point
**2 :** to affect with anguish, grief, or remorse ⟨doubt began to *prick* him —Philip Hale⟩
**3 :** to ride, guide, or urge on with or as if with spurs **:** GOAD
**4 :** to mark, distinguish, or note by means of a small mark
**5 :** to trace or outline with punctures
**6 :** to remove (a young seedling) from the seedbed to another suitable for further growth — usually used with *out*
**7 :** to cause to be or stand erect ⟨a dog *pricking* its ears⟩
*intransitive verb*
**1 a :** to prick something or cause a pricking sensation **b :** to feel discomfort as if from being pricked
**2 a :** to urge a horse with the spur **b :** to ride fast
**3 :** THRUST
**4 :** to become directed upward **:** POINT
— **prick up one's ears :** to listen intently

**prick·er** \'pri-kər\ *noun* (14th century)
**1 :** one that pricks: as **a :** a rider of horses **b :** a military light horseman
**2 a :** THORN, PRICKLE **b :** BRIER

**prick·et** \'pri-kət\ *noun* [Middle English *priket*, from *prikke*] (15th century)

**1 a :** a spike on which a candle is stuck **b :** a candlestick with such a point
**2 :** a buck in the second year of life

**¹prick·le** \'pri-kəl\ *noun* [Middle English *prikle*, from Old English *pricle;* akin to Old English *prica* prick] (15th century)
**1 :** a fine sharp process or projection; *especially* **:** a sharp pointed emergence arising from the epidermis or bark of a plant
**2 :** a prickling or tingling sensation

**²prickle** *verb* **prick·led; prick·ling** \-k(ə-)liŋ\ (1513)
*transitive verb*
**1 :** to prick slightly
**2 :** to produce prickles in
*intransitive verb*
**:** to cause or feel a prickling, tingling, or stinging sensation

**prick·ly** \'pri-k(ə-)lē\ *adjective* **prick·li·er; -est** (1578)
**1 :** full of or covered with prickles; *especially* **:** distinguished from related kinds by the presence of prickles
**2 :** marked by prickling **:** STINGING ⟨a *prickly* sensation⟩
**3 a :** TROUBLESOME, VEXATIOUS ⟨*prickly* issues⟩ **b :** easily irritated ⟨had a *prickly* disposition⟩
— **prick·li·ness** *noun*

**prickly ash** *noun* (1709)
: a prickly aromatic shrub or small tree (*Zanthoxylum americanum*) of the rue family with yellowish flowers

**prickly heat** *noun* (1736)
: a noncontagious cutaneous eruption of red pimples with intense itching and tingling caused by inflammation around the sweat ducts

**prickly pear** *noun* (1612)
**1 :** OPUNTIA; *especially* **:** any of those with flat spiny joints — called also *prickly pear cactus;* compare CHOLLA
**2 :** the pulpy pear-shaped edible fruit of various prickly pears (as *Opuntia ficus= indica*)

**prickly poppy** *noun* (1724)
: any of a genus (*Argemone*) of plants of the poppy family with white or yellow flowers and prickly leaves and fruits

**¹pride** \'prīd\ *noun* [Middle English, from Old English *prȳde*, from *prūd* proud — more at PROUD] (before 12th century)
**1 :** the quality or state of being proud: as **a :** inordinate self-esteem **:** CONCEIT **b :** a reasonable or justifiable self-respect **c :** delight or elation arising from some act, possession, or relationship ⟨parental *pride*⟩
**2 :** proud or disdainful behavior or treatment **:** DISDAIN
**3 a :** ostentatious display **b :** highest pitch **:** PRIME
**4 :** a source of pride **:** the best in a group or class
**5 :** a company of lions
**6 :** a showy or impressive group ⟨a *pride* of dancers⟩

**²pride** *transitive verb* **prid·ed; prid·ing** (13th century)
: to indulge (as oneself) in pride

**pride·ful** \'prīd-fəl\ *adjective* (15th century)
: full of pride: as **a :** DISDAINFUL, HAUGHTY **b :** EXULTANT, ELATED
— **pride·ful·ly** \-fə-lē\ *adverb*
— **pride·ful·ness** *noun*

**pride of place** (1605)
: the highest or first position

**prie–dieu** \(,)prē-'dyə(r), prē-dyœ̄\ *noun, plural* **prie–dieux** \-'dyə(r)(z), -dyœ̄(z)\ [French, literally, pray God] (1760)
**1 :** a kneeling bench designed for use by a person at prayer and fitted with a raised shelf on which the elbows or a book may be rested

**2 :** a low armless upholstered chair with a high straight back

prie-dieu 1

**pri·er** \'prī(-ə)r\ *noun* (1552)
: one that pries; *especially* **:** an inquisitive person

**priest** \'prēst\ *noun* [Middle English *preist*, from Old English *prēost*, ultimately from Late Latin *presbyter* —more at PRESBYTER] (before 12th century)
: one authorized to perform the sacred rites of a religion especially as a mediatory agent between humans and God; *specifically* **:** an Anglican, Eastern Orthodox, or Roman Catholic clergyman ranking below a bishop and above a deacon

**priest·ess** \'prēs-təs\ *noun* (1693)
**1 :** a woman authorized to perform the sacred rites of a religion
**2 :** a woman regarded as a leader (as of a movement)
*usage* see -ESS

**priest·hood** \'prēst-,hu̇d, 'prē-,stu̇d\ *noun* (before 12th century)
**1 :** the office, dignity, or character of a priest
**2 :** the whole body of priests

**priest·ly** \'prēst-lē\ *adjective* (before 12th century)
**1 :** of or relating to a priest or the priesthood **:** SACERDOTAL
**2 :** characteristic of or befitting a priest
— **priest·li·ness** *noun*

**priest–rid·den** \'prēst-,ri-d°n\ *adjective* (1653)
: controlled or oppressed by a priest

**¹prig** \'prig\ *noun* [*prig* to steal] (1610)
**:** THIEF

**²prig** *noun* [probably from ¹*prig*] (1676)
**1** *archaic* **:** FOP
**2** *archaic* **:** FELLOW, PERSON
**3 :** one who offends or irritates by observance of proprieties (as of speech or manners) in a pointed manner or to an obnoxious degree
— **prig·gery** \-gə-rē\ *noun*
— **prig·gish** \'pri-gish\ *adjective*
— **prig·gish·ly** *adverb*
— **prig·gish·ness** *noun*

**prig·gism** \'pri-,gi-zəm\ *noun* (circa 1805)
: stilted adherence to convention

**¹prill** \'pril\ *transitive verb* [origin unknown] (1944)
: to convert (as a molten solid) into spherical pellets usually by forming into drops in a spray and allowing the drops to solidify

**²prill** *noun* (1952)
: a pellet made by prilling

**¹prim** \'prim\ *transitive verb* **primmed; prim·ming** [origin unknown] (1706)
**1 :** to give a prim or demure expression to ⟨*primming* her thin lips after every mouthful —John Buchan⟩
**2 :** to dress primly

**²prim** *adjective* **prim·mer; prim·mest** (1709)
**1 a :** stiffly formal and proper **:** DECOROUS **b :** PRUDISH
**2 :** NEAT, TRIM ⟨*prim* hedges⟩
— **prim·ly** *adverb*
— **prim·ness** *noun*

**pri·ma bal·le·ri·na** \'prē-mə-\ *noun* [Italian, leading ballerina] (1870)
: the principal female dancer in a ballet company

**pri·ma·cy** \'prī-mə-sē\ *noun* (14th century)
**1 :** the state of being first (as in importance, order, or rank) **:** PREEMINENCE ⟨the *primacy* of

prickly pear 1

intellectual and esthetic over materialistic values —T. R. McConnell⟩
**2 :** the office, rank, or preeminence of an ecclesiastical primate

**pri·ma don·na** \ˌpri-mə-ˈdä-nə, ˌprē-\ *noun, plural* **prima donnas** [Italian, literally, first lady] (1782)
**1 :** a principal female singer in an opera or concert organization
**2 :** an extremely sensitive, vain, or undisciplined person

**¹pri·ma fa·cie** \ˌprī-mə-ˈfā-shə, -shē, -sē *also* -shē-ˌē, -sē-ˌē\ *adverb* [Middle English, from Latin] (15th century)
**:** at first view **:** on the first appearance

**²prima facie** *adjective* (1800)
**1 :** true, valid, or sufficient at first impression **:** APPARENT ⟨the theory . . . gives a *prima facie* solution —R. J. Butler⟩
**2 :** SELF-EVIDENT
**3 :** legally sufficient to establish a fact or a case unless disproved ⟨*prima facie* evidence⟩

**pri·mal** \ˈprī-məl\ *adjective* [Medieval Latin *primalis*, from Latin *primus* first — more at PRIME] (1602)
**1 :** ORIGINAL, PRIMITIVE ⟨village life continued in its *primal* innocence —Van Wyck Brooks⟩
**2 :** first in importance **:** FUNDAMENTAL ⟨our *primal* concern⟩

**pri·mal·i·ty** \prī-ˈma-lə-tē\ *noun* (1919)
**:** the property of being a prime number

**primal scream therapy** *noun* (1971)
**:** psychotherapy in which the patient recalls and reenacts a particularly disturbing past experience usually occurring early in life and expresses normally repressed anger or frustration especially through spontaneous and unrestrained screams, hysteria, or violence — called also *primal therapy*

**pri·mar·i·ly** \prī-ˈmer-ə-lē *also* prə-, *chiefly British* ˈprī-mər-ə-lē\ *adverb* (1601)
**1 :** for the most part **:** CHIEFLY ⟨has now become *primarily* a residential town —S. P. B. Mais⟩
**2 :** in the first place **:** ORIGINALLY

**¹pri·ma·ry** \ˈprī-ˌmer-ē, ˈprī-mə-rē, ˈprīm-rē\ *adjective* [Middle English, from Late Latin *primarius* basic, primary, from Latin, principal, from *primus*] (15th century)
**1 a :** first in order of time or development **:** PRIMITIVE ⟨the *primary* stage of civilization⟩ **b :** of or relating to formations of the Paleozoic and earlier periods
**2 a :** of first rank, importance, or value **:** PRINCIPAL ⟨the *primary* purpose⟩ **b :** BASIC, FUNDAMENTAL ⟨security is a *primary* need⟩ **c :** of, relating to, or constituting the principal quills of a bird's wing **d :** of or relating to agriculture, forestry, and the extractive industries or their products **e :** expressive of present or future time ⟨*primary* tense⟩ **f :** of, relating to, or constituting the strongest of the three or four degrees of stress recognized by most linguists ⟨the first syllable of *basketball* carries *primary* stress⟩
**3 a :** DIRECT, FIRSTHAND ⟨*primary* sources of information⟩ **b :** not derivable from other colors, odors, or tastes **c :** preparatory to something else in a continuing process ⟨*primary* instruction⟩ **d :** of or relating to a primary school ⟨*primary* education⟩ **e :** belonging to the first group or order in successive divisions, combinations, or ramifications ⟨*primary* nerves⟩ **f :** of, relating to, or constituting the inducing current or its circuit in an induction coil or transformer **g :** directly derived from ores ⟨*primary* metals⟩ **h :** of, relating to, or being the amino acid sequence in proteins ⟨*primary* protein structure⟩
**4 :** resulting from the substitution of one of two or more atoms or groups in a molecule; *especially* **:** being or characterized by a carbon atom having a bond to only one other carbon atom

**5 :** of, relating to, involving, or derived from primary meristem ⟨*primary* tissue⟩ ⟨*primary* growth⟩
**6 :** of, relating to, or involved in the production of organic substances by green plants ⟨*primary* productivity⟩

**²primary** *noun, plural* **-ries** (circa 1772)
**1 :** something that stands first in rank, importance, or value **:** FUNDAMENTAL — usually used in plural
**2 :** the celestial body around which one or more other celestial bodies revolve; *especially* **:** the more massive usually brighter component of a binary star system
**3 :** one of the usually 9 or 10 strong quills on the distal joint of a bird's wing — see WING illustration
**4 a :** PRIMARY COLOR **b :** a primary-color sensation
**5 a :** CAUCUS **b :** an election in which qualified voters nominate or express a preference for a particular candidate or group of candidates for political office, choose party officials, or select delegates for a party convention
**6 :** the coil that is connected to the source of electricity in an induction coil or transformer — called also *primary coil*

**primary atypical pneumonia** *noun* (circa 1944)
**:** any of a group of pneumonias (as Q fever and psittacosis) caused especially by viruses, mycoplasmas, rickettsias, and chlamydias

**primary cell** *noun* (1902)
**:** a cell that converts chemical energy into electrical energy by irreversible chemical reactions

**primary color** *noun* (1612)
**:** any of a set of colors from which all other colors may be derived

**primary meristem** *noun* (1875)
**:** meristem (as procambium) derived from the apical meristem

**primary root** *noun* (circa 1890)
**:** the root of a plant that develops first and originates from the radicle

**primary school** *noun* (1802)
**1 :** a school usually including the first three grades of elementary school but sometimes also including kindergarten
**2 :** ELEMENTARY SCHOOL

**primary syphilis** *noun* (circa 1890)
**:** the first stage of syphilis that is marked by the development of a chancre and the spread of the causative spirochete in the tissues of the body

**primary tooth** *noun* (circa 1898)
**:** MILK TOOTH

**primary wall** *noun* (circa 1933)
**:** the first-formed wall of a plant cell that is produced around the protoplast and usually has plasmodesmata

**pri·mate** \ˈprī-ˌmāt *or especially for 1* -mət\ *noun* [Middle English *primat*, from Old French, from Medieval Latin *primat-, primas* archbishop, from Latin, leader, from *primus*] (13th century)
**1** *often capitalized* **:** a bishop who has precedence in a province, group of provinces, or a nation
**2** *archaic* **:** one first in authority or rank **:** LEADER
**3** [New Latin *Primates,* from Latin, plural of *primat-, primas*] **:** any of an order (Primates) of mammals comprising humans, apes, monkeys, and related forms (as lemurs and tarsiers)
— **pri·mate·ship** \-ˌship\ *noun*
— **pri·ma·tial** \prī-ˈmā-shəl\ *adjective*

**pri·ma·tol·o·gy** \ˌprī-mə-ˈtä-lə-jē\ *noun* (1926)
**:** the study of primates especially other than recent humans (*Homo sapiens*)
— **pri·ma·to·log·i·cal** \-mə-tᵊl-ˈä-ji-kəl\ *adjective*
— **pri·ma·tol·o·gist** \-mə-ˈtä-lə-jist\ *noun*

**¹prime** \ˈprīm\ *noun* [Middle English, from Old English *prīm,* from Latin *prima hora* first hour] (before 12th century)
**1 a** *often capitalized* **:** the second of the canonical hours **b :** the first hour of the day usually considered either as 6 a.m. or the hour of sunrise
**2 a :** the earliest stage **b :** SPRING **c :** YOUTH
**3 :** the most active, thriving, or successful stage or period ⟨in the *prime* of his life⟩
**4 :** the chief or best individual or part **:** PICK ⟨*prime* of the flock, and choicest of the stall —Alexander Pope⟩
**5 :** PRIME NUMBER
**6 a :** the first note or tone of a musical scale **:** TONIC **b :** the interval between two notes on the same staff degree
**7 :** the symbol ′
**8 :** PRIME RATE

**²prime** *adjective* [Middle English, from Middle French, feminine of *prin* first, from Latin *primus;* akin to Latin *prior*] (14th century)
**1 :** first in time **:** ORIGINAL
**2 a :** of, relating to, or being a prime number — compare RELATIVELY PRIME **b :** having no polynomial factors other than itself and no monomial factors other than 1 ⟨a *prime* polynomial⟩ **c :** expressed as a product of prime factors (as prime numbers and prime polynomials) ⟨a *prime* factorization⟩
**3 a :** first in rank, authority, or significance **:** PRINCIPAL **b :** having the highest quality or value ⟨*prime* farmland⟩ **c :** of the highest grade regularly marketed — used of meat and especially beef
**4 :** not deriving from something else **:** PRIMARY
— **prime·ly** *adverb*
— **prime·ness** *noun*

**³prime** *verb* **primed; prim·ing** [probably from ¹*prime*] (1513)
*transitive verb*
**1 :** FILL, LOAD
**2 a :** to prepare for firing by supplying with priming **b :** to insert a primer into (a cartridge case)
**3 :** to apply the first color, coating, or preparation to ⟨*prime* a wall⟩
**4 :** to put into working order by filling or charging with something ⟨*prime* a pump with water⟩
**5 :** to instruct beforehand **:** COACH ⟨*primed* the witness⟩
**6 :** STIMULATE
*intransitive verb*
**:** to become prime
— **prime the pump :** to take steps to encourage the growth or functioning of something

**prime cost** *noun* (1718)
**:** the combined total of raw material and direct labor costs incurred in production; *broadly* **:** cost less vendor's or agent's commission for charges

**prime meridian** *noun* (circa 1859)
**:** the meridian of 0 degrees longitude which runs through the original site of the Royal Observatory at Greenwich, England, and from which other longitudes are reckoned

**prime minister** *noun* (1655)
**1 :** the chief minister of a ruler or state
**2 :** the official head of a cabinet or ministry; *especially* **:** the chief executive of a parliamentary government
— **prime ministerial** *adjective*
— **prime ministership** *noun*
— **prime ministry** *noun*

**prime mover** *noun* [translation of Medieval Latin *primus motor*] (1809)
**1 a :** an initial source of motive power (as a windmill, waterwheel, turbine, or internal combustion engine) designed to receive and modify force and motion as supplied by some

natural source and apply them to drive machinery **b** : a powerful tractor or truck usually with all-wheel drive

**2** : the self-moved being that is the source of all motion

**3** : the original or most effective force in an undertaking or work ⟨education is . . . a *prime mover* of cultural and societal change —R. C. Buck⟩

**prime number** *noun* (1570)
: any integer other than 0 or ± 1 that is not divisible without remainder by any other integers except ± 1 and ± the integer itself

**¹prim·er** \'pri-mər, *chiefly British* 'prī-mər\ *noun* [Middle English, from Medieval Latin *primarium,* from Late Latin, neuter of *primarius* primary] (14th century)
**1** : a small book for teaching children to read
**2** : a small introductory book on a subject

**²prim·er** \'prī-mər\ *noun* (1819)
**1** : a device for priming; *especially* : a cap, tube, or wafer containing percussion powder or compound used to ignite an explosive charge
**2** : material used in priming a surface — called also *prime coat*
**3** : a molecule (as a short strand of RNA or DNA) whose presence is required for formation of another molecule (as a longer chain of DNA)

**prime rate** *noun* (1958)
: an interest rate formally announced by a bank to be the lowest available at a particular time to its most credit-worthy customers — called also *prime interest rate*

**pri·me·ro** \pri-'mer-(,)ō, -'mir-\ *noun* [modification of Spanish *primera,* from feminine of *primer* first, from Latin *primarius*] (1533)
: a card game popular in the 16th and 17th centuries

**prime time** *noun* (1958)
**1** : the time period when the television or radio audience is the largest; *also* : prime-time television
**2** : the choicest or busiest time
— **prime–time** *adjective*

**pri·me·val** \prī-'mē-vəl\ *adjective* [Latin *primaevus,* from *primus* first + *aevum* age — more at AYE] (1662)
**1** : of or relating to the earliest ages (as of the world or human history) : ANCIENT, PRIMITIVE ⟨100 acres of *primeval* forest which has never felt an ax —Mary R. Zimmer⟩
**2** : PRIMORDIAL 1b
— **pri·me·val·ly** \-və-lē\ *adverb*

**priming** *noun* (15th century)
**1** : the act of one that primes
**2** : the explosive used in priming a charge
**3** : ²PRIMER 2

**pri·mip·a·ra** \prī-'mi-pə-rə\ *noun, plural* **-ras** *or* **-rae** \-,rē, -,rī\ [Latin, from *primus* first + *-para* -para] (circa 1842)
**1** : an individual bearing a first offspring
**2** : an individual that has borne only one offspring
— **pri·mip·a·rous** \prī-'mi-pə-rəs\ *adjective*

**¹prim·i·tive** \'pri-mə-tiv\ *adjective* [Middle English *primitif,* from Latin *primitivus* first formed, from *primitiae* first fruits, from *primus* first — more at PRIME] (14th century)
**1 a** : not derived : ORIGINAL, PRIMARY **b** : assumed as a basis; *especially* : AXIOMATIC ⟨*primitive* concepts⟩
**2 a** : of or relating to the earliest age or period : PRIMEVAL ⟨the *primitive* church⟩ **b** : closely approximating an early ancestral type : little evolved ⟨*primitive* mammals⟩ **c** : belonging to or characteristic of an early stage of development : CRUDE, RUDIMENTARY ⟨*primitive* technology⟩ **d** : of, relating to, or constituting the assumed parent speech of related languages ⟨*primitive* Germanic⟩
**3 a** : ELEMENTAL, NATURAL ⟨our *primitive* feelings of vengeance —John Mackwood⟩ **b** : of, relating to, or produced by a people or culture that is nonindustrial and often nonliterate and

tribal ⟨*primitive* art⟩ **c** : NAIVE **d** (1) : SELF-TAUGHT, UNTUTORED ⟨*primitive* craftsmen⟩ (2) : produced by a self-taught artist ⟨a *primitive* painting⟩
— **prim·i·tive·ly** *adverb*
— **prim·i·tive·ness** *noun*
— **prim·i·tiv·i·ty** \,pri-mə-'ti-və-tē\ *noun*

**²primitive** *noun* (15th century)
**1 a** : something primitive; *specifically* : a primitive idea, term, or proposition **b** : a root word
**2 a** (1) : an artist of an early period of a culture or artistic movement (2) : a later imitator or follower of such an artist **b** (1) : a self-taught artist (2) : an artist whose work is marked by directness and naïveté **c** : a work of art produced by a primitive artist **d** : a typically rough or simple usually handmade and antique home accessory or furnishing
**3 a** : a member of a primitive people **b** : an unsophisticated person

**prim·i·tiv·ism** \'pri-mə-ti-,vi-zəm\ *noun* (1861)
**1 a** : belief in the superiority of a simple way of life close to nature **b** : belief in the superiority of nonindustrial society to that of the present
**2** : the style of art of primitive peoples or primitive artists
— **prim·i·tiv·ist** \-vist\ *noun or adjective*
— **prim·i·tiv·is·tic** \,pri-mə-ti-'vis-tik\ *adjective*

**¹pri·mo** \'prē-(,)mō\ *noun, plural* **primos** [Italian, from *primo* first, from Latin *primus*] (1792)
: the first or leading part (as in a duet or trio)

**²pri·mo** \'prē-(,)mō, 'prī-\ *adverb* [Latin, from *primus*] (circa 1901)
: in the first place

**³pri·mo** \'prē-(,)mō\ *adjective* [probably from Italian, chief, first] (1972)
*slang* : of the finest quality : EXCELLENT

**pri·mo·gen·i·tor** \,prī-mō-'je-nə-tər\ *noun* [Late Latin, from Latin *primus* + *genitor* begetter, from *gignere* to beget — more at KIN] (1654)
: ANCESTOR, FOREFATHER

**pri·mo·gen·i·ture** \-,chùr, -chər, -,tyùr, -,tùr\ *noun* [Late Latin *primogenitura,* from Latin *primus* + *genitura* birth, from *genitus,* past participle of *gignere*] (1602)
**1** : the state of being the firstborn of the children of the same parents
**2** : an exclusive right of inheritance belonging to the eldest son

**pri·mor·di·al** \prī-'mòr-dē-əl\ *adjective* [Middle English, from Late Latin *primordialis,* from Latin *primordium* origin, from *primus* first + *ordiri* to begin — more at PRIME, ORDER] (14th century)
**1 a** : first created or developed : PRIMEVAL 1 **b** : existing in or persisting from the beginning (as of a solar system or universe) ⟨a *primordial* gas cloud⟩ **c** : earliest formed in the growth of an individual or organ : PRIMITIVE
**2** : FUNDAMENTAL, PRIMARY ⟨*primordial* human joys —Sir Winston Churchill⟩
— **pri·mor·di·al·ly** \-dē-ə-lē\ *adverb*

**pri·mor·di·um** \-dē-əm\ *noun, plural* **-dia** \-dē-ə\ [New Latin, from Latin] (1671)
: the rudiment or commencement of a part or organ

**primp** \'primp\ *verb* [perhaps alteration of ¹*prim*] (1801)
*transitive verb*
: to dress, adorn, or arrange in a careful or finicky manner
*intransitive verb*
: to dress or groom oneself carefully ⟨*primps* for hours before a date⟩

**prim·rose** \'prim-,rōz\ *noun* [Middle English *primerose,* from Middle French, from *prime* (feminine of *prin* prime) + *rose* rose — more at PRIME, ROSE] (14th century)
: any of a genus (*Primula* of the family Primulaceae, the primrose family) of perennial herbs

with large tufted basal leaves and showy variously colored flowers — compare EVENING PRIMROSE

**primrose path** *noun* (1602)
**1** : a path of ease or pleasure and especially sensual pleasure ⟨himself the *primrose path* of dalliance treads —Shakespeare⟩
**2** : a path of least resistance

**primrose yellow** *noun* (1882)
**1** : a light to moderate greenish yellow
**2** : a light to moderate yellow

**prim·u·la** \'prim-yə-lə\ *noun* [Medieval Latin, from *primula veris,* literally, first fruit of spring] (1753)
: PRIMROSE

**pri·mum mo·bi·le** \'prī-məm-'mō-bə-lē, 'prē-\ *noun, plural* **primum mobiles** [Middle English, from Medieval Latin, literally, first moving thing] (15th century)
: the outermost concentric sphere conceived in medieval astronomy as carrying the spheres of the fixed stars and the planets in its daily revolution

**pri·mus** \'prī-məs\ *noun, often capitalized* [Medieval Latin, one who is first, magnate, from Latin, first — more at PRIME] (1724)
: the presiding bishop of the Scottish Episcopal Church

**pri·mus in·ter pa·res** \'prī-məs-,in-tər-'par-ēz, 'prē-məs-\ *noun* [Latin] (1813)
: first among equals

**prince** \'prin(t)s\ *noun* [Middle English, from Old French, from Latin *princip-, princeps* leader, initiator, from *primus* first + *capere* to take — more at HEAVE] (13th century)
**1 a** : MONARCH, KING **b** : the ruler of a principality or state
**2** : a male member of a royal family; *especially* : a son of the sovereign
**3** : a nobleman of varying rank and status
**4** : one likened to a prince; *especially* : a man of high rank or of high standing in his class or profession
— **prince·ship** \'prin(t)s-,ship\ *noun*

**Prince Al·bert** \-'al-bərt\ *noun* [Prince Albert Edward (later Edward VII king of England)] (1884)
: a double-breasted frock coat with the upper part fitted to the body

**Prince Charming** *noun* [*Prince Charming,* hero of the fairy tale *Cinderella* by Charles Perrault] (1862)
: a suitor who fulfills the dreams of his beloved; *also* : a man of often specious charm toward women

**prince consort** *noun, plural* **princes consort** (1861)
: the husband of a reigning queen

**prince·dom** \'prin(t)s-dəm, -təm\ *noun* (1560)
**1** : the jurisdiction, sovereignty, rank, or estate of a prince
**2** : PRINCIPALITY 3 — usually used in plural

**prince·let** \'prin(t)s-lət\ *noun* (1682)
: PRINCELING

**prince·li·ness** \-lē-nəs\ *noun* (1571)
**1** : princely conduct or character
**2** : LUXURY, MAGNIFICENCE

**prince·ling** \'prin(t)s-liŋ\ *noun* (1794)
: a petty or insignificant prince

**prince·ly** \'prin(t)s-lē\ *adjective* **prince·li·er; -est** (15th century)
**1** : of or relating to a prince : ROYAL
**2** : befitting a prince : NOBLE, MAGNIFICENT ⟨*princely* manners⟩ ⟨a *princely* sum⟩
— **princely** *adverb*

Prince Albert

**Prince of Wales** \-'wā(ə)lz\ (15th century)
: the male heir apparent to the British throne — used as a title only after it has been specifically conferred by the sovereign

**prince's–feath·er** \'prin(t)-səz-ˌfe-thər\ noun (1629)
: a showy widely cultivated annual plant (*Amaranthus hybridus erythrostachys*) of the amaranth family having dense usually red spikes of flowers

¹**prin·cess** \'prin(t)-səs, 'prin-ˌses, (*British usually*) prin-'ses\ noun (14th century)
**1** *archaic* : a woman having sovereign power
**2** : a female member of a royal family; *especially* : a daughter or granddaughter of a sovereign
**3** : the consort of a prince
**4** : one likened to a princess; *especially* : a woman of high rank or of high standing in her class or profession ⟨a pop music *princess*⟩

²**princess** \*same as* ¹\ *or* **prin·cesse** \prin-'ses\ adjective [French *princesse* princess, from *prince*] (1867)
: close-fitting and usually with gores from neck to flaring hemline ⟨a *princess* gown⟩

**Princess Royal** noun, plural **Princesses Royal** (circa 1649)
: the eldest daughter of a British sovereign — a title granted for life and used only after it has been specifically conferred by the sovereign

¹**prin·ci·pal** \'prin(t)-s(ə-)pəl, -sə-bəl\ adjective [Middle English, from Old French, from Latin *principalis*, from *princip-, princeps*] (14th century)
**1** : most important, consequential, or influential : CHIEF
**2** : of, relating to, or constituting principal or a principal
*usage* see PRINCIPLE
— **prin·ci·pal·ly** \-sə-p(ə-)lē, -sə-bə-lē, -splē\ adverb

²**principal** noun (14th century)
**1** : a person who has controlling authority or is in a leading position: as **a** : a chief or head man or woman **b** : the chief executive officer of an educational institution **c** : one who employs another to act as agent subject to the employer's general control and instruction; *specifically* : the person from whom an agent's authority derives **d** : the chief or an actual participant in a crime **e** : the person primarily or ultimately liable on a legal obligation **f** : a leading performer : STAR
**2** : a matter or thing of primary importance: as **a** (1) : a capital sum placed at interest, due as a debt, or used as a fund (2) : the corpus of an estate, portion, devise, or bequest **b** : the construction that gives shape and strength to a roof and is usually one of several trusses; *broadly* : the most important member of a piece of framing
*usage* see PRINCIPLE
— **prin·ci·pal·ship** \'prin(t)-s(ə-)pəl-ˌship, -sə-bəl-\ noun

**principal diagonal** noun (1965)
: the diagonal in a square matrix that runs from upper left to lower right

**prin·ci·pal·i·ty** \ˌprin(t)-sə-'pa-lə-tē\ noun, plural **-ties** (14th century)
**1 a** : the state, office, or authority of a prince **b** : the position or responsibilities of a principal (as of a school)
**2** : the territory or jurisdiction of a prince : the country that gives title to a prince
**3** *plural* : an order of angels — see CELESTIAL HIERARCHY

**principal parts** noun plural (1870)
: a series of verb forms from which all the other forms of a verb can be derived including in English the infinitive, the past tense, and the present and past participles

**prin·cip·i·um** \prin-'si-pē-əm, prin-'ki-\ noun, plural **-ia** \-pē-ə\ [Latin, beginning, basis] (1600)
: a fundamental principle

**prin·ci·ple** \'prin(t)-s(ə-)pəl, -sə-bəl\ noun [Middle English, modification of Middle French *principe*, from Latin *principium* beginning, from *princip-, princeps* initiator — more at PRINCE] (14th century)
**1 a** : a comprehensive and fundamental law, doctrine, or assumption **b** (1) : a rule or code of conduct (2) : habitual devotion to right principles ⟨a man of *principle*⟩ **c** : the laws or facts of nature underlying the working of an artificial device
**2** : a primary source : ORIGIN
**3 a** : an underlying faculty or endowment ⟨such *principles* of human nature as greed and curiosity⟩ **b** : an ingredient (as a chemical) that exhibits or imparts a characteristic quality
**4** *capitalized, Christian Science* : a divine principle : GOD ▪
— **in principle** : with respect to fundamentals ⟨prepared to accept the proposition *in principle*⟩

**prin·ci·pled** \-s(ə-)pəld, -sə-bəld\ adjective (1642)
: exhibiting, based on, or characterized by principle — often used in combination

**prin·cox** \'prin-ˌkäks, 'priṅ-\ noun [origin unknown] (1540)
*archaic* : a pert youth : COXCOMB

**prink** \'priṅk\ verb [probably alteration of ²*prank*] (1576)
: PRIMP
— **prink·er** noun

¹**print** \'print\ noun [Middle English *preinte*, from Middle French, from *preint*, past participle of *preindre* to press, from Latin *premere* — more at PRESS] (14th century)
**1 a** : a mark made by pressure : IMPRESSION **b** : something impressed with a print or formed in a mold
**2 a** : printed state or form **b** : the printing industry
**3 a** : PRINTED MATTER **b** *plural* : printed publications
**4** : printed letters : TYPE
**5 a** (1) : a copy made by printing (2) : a reproduction of an original work of art (as a painting) made by a photomechanical process (3) : an original work of art (as a woodcut, etching, or lithograph) intended for graphic reproduction and produced by or under the supervision of the artist who designed it **b** : cloth with a pattern or figured design applied by printing; *also* : an article of such cloth **c** : a photographic or motion-picture copy; *especially* : one made from a negative
— **in print** : procurable from the publisher
— **out of print** : not procurable from the publisher

²**print** (14th century)
*transitive verb*
**1 a** : to impress something in or on **b** : to stamp (as a mark) in or on something
**2 a** : to make a copy of by impressing paper against an inked printing surface **b** (1) : to impress (as wallpaper) with a design or pattern (2) : to impress (a pattern or design) on something **c** : to publish in print **d** : PRINT OUT; *also* : to display on a surface (as a computer screen) for viewing
**3** : to write in letters shaped like those of ordinary roman text type
**4** : to make (a positive picture) on a sensitized photographic surface from a negative or a positive
*intransitive verb*
**1 a** : to work as a printer **b** : to produce printed matter
**2** : to produce something in printed form
**3** : to write or hand-letter in imitation of unjoined printed characters

³**print** adjective (1953)
: of, relating to, or writing for printed publications ⟨*print* journalists⟩

**print·able** \'prin-tə-bəl\ adjective (1837)
**1** : capable of being printed or of being printed from

**2** : considered fit to publish
— **print·abil·i·ty** \ˌprin-tə-'bi-lə-tē\ noun

**printed circuit** noun (1946)
: a circuit for electronic apparatus made by depositing conductive material in continuous paths from terminal to terminal on an insulating surface

**printed matter** noun (1876)
: matter printed by any of various mechanical processes that is eligible for mailing at a special rate

**print·er** \'prin-tər\ noun (1504)
: one that prints: as **a** : a person engaged in printing **b** : a device used for printing; *especially* : a machine for printing from photographic negatives **c** : a device (as a dot matrix printer) that produces printout

**printer's devil** noun (1763)
: an apprentice in a printing office

**print·ery** \'prin-tə-rē\ noun, plural **-er·ies** (1638)
: PRINTING OFFICE

**print·head** \'print-ˌhed\ noun (1968)
: a usually movable part of a computer printer that contains the printing elements

**print·ing** noun (14th century)
**1** : the act or product of one that prints
**2** : reproduction in printed form
**3** : the art, practice, or business of a printer
**4** : IMPRESSION 4c
**5** *plural* : paper to be printed on

**printing office** noun (1733)
: an establishment where printing is done

**printing press** noun (1588)
: a machine that produces printed copies

**print·less** \'print-ləs\ adjective (1610)
: making, bearing, or taking no imprint

**print·mak·ing** \-ˌmā-kiṅ\ noun (1928)
: the design and production of prints by an artist
— **print·mak·er** \-kər\ noun

**print·out** \'print-ˌaut\ noun (1953)
: a printed record produced automatically (as by a computer)

**print out** transitive verb (1953)
: to make a printout of

**pri·on** \'prē-ˌän\ noun [*pro*tinaceous + *in*fectious + ²-*on*] (1982)
: a protein particle that lacks nucleic acid and is sometimes held to be the cause of various infectious diseases of the nervous system (as scrapie and Creutzfeldt-Jakob disease)

¹**pri·or** \'prī-(ə)r\ noun [Middle English, from Old English & Old French; both from Medieval Latin, from Late Latin, administrator, from Latin, former, superior] (before 12th century)
**1** : the superior ranking next to the abbot of a monastery
**2** : the superior of a house or group of houses of any of various religious communities
— **pri·or·ate** \'prī-ə-rət\ noun
— **pri·or·ship** \'prī-(ə)r-ˌship\ noun

²**prior** adjective [Latin, former, superior, comparative of Old Latin *pri* before; akin to Latin *priscus* ancient, *prae* before — more at FOR] (1714)
**1** : earlier in time or order : PREVIOUS ⟨by *prior* agreement⟩
**2** : taking precedence (as in importance)
*synonym* see PRECEDING
— **pri·or·ly** adverb

**pri·or·ess** \'prī-ə-rəs\ noun (14th century)
: a nun corresponding in rank to a prior

**pri·or·i·tize** \prī-'ȯr-ə-ˌtīz, -'är-; 'prī-ə-rə-\ *transitive verb* **-tized; -tiz·ing** (1964) : to list or rate (as projects or goals) in order of priority
*usage* see -IZE
— **pri·or·i·ti·za·tion** \prī-ˌȯr-ə-tə-'zā-shən, -är-; ˌprī-ə-rə-\ *noun*
**pri·or·i·ty** \prī-'ȯr-ə-tē, -'är-\ *noun, plural* **-ties** (14th century)
**1 a** (1) : the quality or state of being prior (2) : precedence in date or position of publication — used of taxa **b** (1) : superiority in rank, position, or privilege (2) : legal precedence in exercise of rights over the same subject matter
**2** : a preferential rating; *especially* : one that allocates rights to goods and services usually in limited supply ⟨that project has top *priority*⟩
**3** : something given or meriting attention before competing alternatives
**prior restraint** *noun* (1951) : governmental prohibition imposed on expression before the expression actually takes place
**prior to** *preposition* (1714) : in advance of : BEFORE □
**pri·o·ry** \'prī-(ə-)rē\ *noun, plural* **-ries** [Middle English *priorie*, from Anglo-French, from Medieval Latin *prioria*, from *prior*] (13th century) : a religious house under a prior or prioress
**prise** \'prīz\ *chiefly British variant of* ⁵PRIZE
**prism** \'pri-zəm\ *noun* [Late Latin *prismat-, prisma*, from Greek, literally, anything sawn, from *priein* to saw] (1570)
**1** : a polyhedron with two polygonal faces lying in parallel planes and with the other faces parallelograms
**2 a** : a transparent body that is bounded in part by two nonparallel plane faces and is used to refract or disperse a beam of light **b** : a prism-shaped decorative glass luster
**3** : a crystal form whose faces are parallel to one axis; *especially* : one whose faces are parallel to the vertical axis
**4** : a medium that distorts, slants, or colors whatever is viewed through it
**pris·mat·ic** \priz-'ma-tik\ *adjective* (1709)
**1** : relating to, resembling, or constituting a prism
**2 a** : formed by a prism **b** : resembling the colors formed by refraction of light through a prism ⟨*prismatic* effects⟩
**3** : highly colored : BRILLIANT ⟨*prismatic* lyrics⟩
**4** : having such symmetry that a general form with faces cutting all axes at unspecified intercepts is a prism ⟨*prismatic* crystals⟩
— **pris·mat·i·cal·ly** \-ti-k(ə-)lē\ *adverb*
**pris·ma·toid** \'priz-mə-ˌtȯid\ *noun* [Late Latin *prismat-, prisma* prism] (circa 1890) : a polyhedron that has all of its vertices in two parallel planes
**pris·moid** \'priz-ˌmȯid\ *noun* (circa 1704) : a prismatoid whose parallel bases have the same number of sides
— **pris·moi·dal** \priz-'mȯi-d°l\ *adjective*
¹**pris·on** \'pri-z°n\ *noun* [Middle English, from Old French, from Latin *prehension-, prehensio* act of seizing, from *prehendere* to seize — more at GET] (12th century)
**1** : a state of confinement or captivity
**2** : a place of confinement especially for lawbreakers; *specifically* : an institution (as one under state jurisdiction) for confinement of persons convicted of serious crimes — compare JAIL
²**prison** *transitive verb* (14th century) : IMPRISON, CONFINE
**prison camp** *noun* (circa 1908)
**1** : a camp for the confinement of reasonably trustworthy prisoners usually employed on government projects
**2** : a camp for prisoners of war or political prisoners
**pris·on·er** \'priz-nər, 'pri-z°n-ər\ *noun* (14th century)

**1** : a person deprived of liberty and kept under involuntary restraint, confinement, or custody; *especially* : one on trial or in prison
**2** : someone restrained as if in prison ⟨a *prisoner* of her own conscience⟩
**prisoner of war** (1678) : a person captured in war; *especially* : a member of the armed forces of a nation who is taken by the enemy during combat
**prisoner's base** *noun* (circa 1773) : a game in which players on each of two teams seek to tag and imprison players of the other team who have ventured out of their home territory
**pris·sy** \'pri-sē\ *adjective* **pris·si·er; -est** [probably blend of *prim* and *sissy*] (1895) : being prim and precise : FINICKY
— **pris·si·ly** \'pri-sə-lē\ *adverb*
— **pris·si·ness** \'pri-sē-nəs\ *noun*
**pris·tane** \'pris-ˌtān\ *noun* [Latin *pristis* shark, sawfish; from its occurrence in the liver oils of sharks] (1923) : an isoprenoid hydrocarbon $C_{19}H_{40}$ that usually accompanies phytane
**pris·tine** \'pris-ˌtēn, pri-'stēn, *especially British* 'pris-ˌtīn\ *adjective* [Latin *pristinus*; akin to Latin *prior*] (1534)
**1** : belonging to the earliest period or state : ORIGINAL ⟨the hypothetical *pristine* lunar atmosphere⟩
**2 a** : not spoiled, corrupted, or polluted (as by civilization) : PURE ⟨a *pristine* forest⟩ **b** : fresh and clean as or as if new ⟨*pristine* hard-backs in uniform editions to fill our built-in bookcases —Michiko Kakutani⟩
— **pris·tine·ly** *adverb*
**prith·ee** \'pri-thē, -thē\ *interjection* [alteration of (*I*) *pray thee*] (circa 1591)
*archaic* — used to express a wish or request
**pri·va·cy** \'prī-və-sē, *especially British* 'pri-\ *noun, plural* **-cies** (15th century)
**1 a** : the quality or state of being apart from company or observation : SECLUSION **b** : freedom from unauthorized intrusion ⟨one's right to *privacy*⟩
**2** *archaic* : a place of seclusion
**3 a** : SECRECY **b** : a private matter : SECRET
**pri·vat·do·cent** *or* **pri·vat·do·zent** \pri-'vät-(ˌ)dō(t)-ˌsent\ *noun* [German *Privatdozent*, from *privat* private + *Dozent* teacher, from Latin *docent-, docens*, present participle of *docēre* to teach — more at DOCILE] (1854) : an unsalaried university lecturer or teacher in German-speaking countries remunerated directly by students' fees
¹**pri·vate** \'prī-vət\ *adjective* [Middle English *privat*, from Latin *privatus*, from past participle of *privare* to deprive, release, from *privus* private, individual; probably akin to Latin *pro* for, in front of — more at FOR] (14th century)
**1 a** : intended for or restricted to the use of a particular person, group, or class ⟨a *private* park⟩ **b** : belonging to or concerning an individual person, company, or interest ⟨a *private* house⟩ **c** (1) : restricted to the individual or arising independently of others ⟨*private* opinion⟩ (2) : carried on by the individual independently of the usual institutions ⟨*private* study⟩; *also* : being educated by independent study or a tutor or in a private school ⟨*private* students⟩ **d** : not general in effect ⟨a *private* statute⟩ **e** : of, relating to, or receiving hospital service in which the patient has more privileges than a semiprivate or ward patient
**2 a** (1) : not holding public office or employment ⟨a *private* citizen⟩ (2) : not related to one's official position : PERSONAL ⟨*private* correspondence⟩ **b** : being a private ⟨a *private* soldier⟩
**3 a** : withdrawn from company or observation : SEQUESTERED ⟨a *private* retreat⟩ **b** : not known or intended to be known publicly : SECRET **c** : preferring to keep personal affairs to oneself : valuing privacy highly **d** : unsuitable for public use or display

**4** : not having shares that can be freely traded on the open market ⟨a *private* company⟩
— **pri·vate·ly** *adverb*
— **pri·vate·ness** *noun*
²**private** *noun* (15th century)
**1** *archaic* : one not in public office
**2** *obsolete* : PRIVACY
**3** *plural* : PRIVATE PARTS
**4 a** : a person of low rank in various organizations (as a police or fire department) **b** : an enlisted man of the lowest rank in the marine corps or of one of the two lowest ranks in the army
— **in private** : not openly or in public
**private detective** *noun* (1868) : PRIVATE INVESTIGATOR
**private enterprise** *noun* (1844) : FREE ENTERPRISE
**pri·va·teer** \ˌprī-və-'tir\ *noun* (1664) : an armed private ship licensed to attack enemy shipping; *also* : a sailor on such a ship
— **privateer** *intransitive verb*
**private eye** *noun* (1938) : PRIVATE INVESTIGATOR
**private first class** *noun* (1918) : an enlisted man ranking in the army above a private and below a corporal and in the marine corps above a private and below a lance corporal
**private investigator** *noun* (1940) : a person not a member of a police force who is licensed to do detective work (as investigation of suspected wrongdoing or searching for missing persons)
**private law** *noun* (1773) : a branch of law concerned with private persons, property, and relationships — compare PUBLIC LAW
**private parts** *noun plural* (1785) : the external genital and excretory organs
**private school** *noun* (1857) : a school that is established, conducted, and primarily supported by a nongovernmental agency
**private treaty** *noun* (1858) : a sale of property on terms determined by conference of the seller and buyer — compare AUCTION
**pri·va·tion** \prī-'vā-shən\ *noun* [Middle English *privacion*, from Middle French *privation*, from Latin *privation-, privatio*, from *privare* to deprive] (14th century)
**1** : an act or instance of depriving : DEPRIVATION
**2** : the state of being deprived; *especially* : lack of what is needed for existence
**pri·va·tise** *British variant of* PRIVATIZE
**pri·va·tism** \'prī-və-ˌti-zəm\ *noun* [*private*] (1950) : the attitude of being uncommitted to or avoiding involvement in anything beyond one's immediate interests

\ə\ **abut** \ᵊ\ **kitten** \ər\ **further** \a\ **ash** \ā\ **ace** \ä\ **mop, mar** \aú\ **out** \ch\ **chin** \e\ **bet** \ē\ **easy** \g\ **go** \i\ **hit** \ī\ **ice** \j\ **job** \ŋ\ **sing** \ō\ **go** \ȯ\ **law** \ȯi\ **boy** \th\ **thin** \t͟h\ **the** \ü\ **loot** \ú\ **foot** \y\ **yet** \zh\ **vision** *see also* Guide to Pronunciation

**¹priv·a·tive** \'pri-və-tiv\ *adjective* (14th century)
**:** constituting or predicating privation or absence of a quality (as the prefixes *a-, un-, non-*)
— **priv·a·tive·ly** *adverb*
**²priv·a·tive** *noun* (1588)
**:** a privative term, expression, or proposition; *also* **:** a privative prefix or suffix
**pri·vat·ize** \'prī-və-ˌtīz\ *transitive verb* (1948)
**:** to make private; *especially* **:** to change (as a business or industry) from public to private control or ownership
— **pri·vat·iza·tion** \ˌprī-və-tə-'zā-shən\ *noun*
**priv·et** \'pri-vət\ *noun* [origin unknown] (1542)
**:** a European deciduous shrub (*Ligustrum vulgare*) of the olive family with semievergreen leaves and small white flowers that is widely used for hedges; *broadly* **:** any of various congeneric shrubs
**¹priv·i·lege** \'priv-lij, 'pri-və-\ *noun* [Middle English, from Old French, from Latin *privilegium* law for or against a private person, from *privus* private + *leg-, lex* law] (12th century)
**:** a right or immunity granted as a peculiar benefit, advantage, or favor **:** PREROGATIVE; *especially* **:** such a right or immunity attached specifically to a position or an office
**²privilege** *transitive verb* **-leged; -leg·ing** (14th century)
**:** to grant a privilege to
**priv·i·leged** \-lijd\ *adjective* (14th century)
**1 :** having or enjoying one or more privileges ⟨*privileged* classes⟩
**2 :** not subject to the usual rules or penalties because of some special circumstance; *especially* **:** not subject to disclosure in a court of law ⟨a *privileged* communication⟩
**priv·i·ty** \'pri-və-tē\ *noun, plural* **-ties** [Middle English *privite* privacy, secret, from Old French *privité*, from Medieval Latin *privitat-, privitas*, from Latin *privus* private — more at PRIVATE] (1523)
**1 a :** a relationship between persons who successively have a legal interest in the same right or property **b :** an interest in a transaction, contract, or legal action to which one is not a party arising out of a relationship to one of the parties
**2 :** private or joint knowledge of a private matter; *especially* **:** cognizance implying concurrence
**¹privy** \'pri-vē\ *adjective* [Middle English *prive*, from Old French *privé*, from Latin *privatus* private] (14th century)
**1 a :** PRIVATE, WITHDRAWN **b :** SECRET
**2 :** belonging or relating to a person in one's individual rather than official capacity
**3 :** admitted as one sharing in a secret ⟨*privy* to the conspiracy⟩
— **priv·i·ly** \-və-lē\ *adverb*
**²privy** *noun, plural* **priv·ies** (14th century)
**1 a :** a small building having a bench with holes through which the user may defecate or urinate **b :** TOILET 3b
**2 :** a person having a legal interest of privity
**privy council** *noun* (14th century)
**1** *archaic* **:** a secret or private council
**2** *P&C capitalized* **:** a body of officials and dignitaries chosen by the British monarch as an advisory council to the Crown usually functioning through its committees
**3 :** a usually appointive advisory council to an executive
— **privy councillor** *noun*
**privy purse** *noun* (1765)
**:** an allowance for the private expenses of the British sovereign
**prix fixe** \ˌprē-'fēks, -'fiks\ *noun* [French, fixed price] (1883)
**:** a complete meal offered at a fixed price; *also* **:** the price charged

**¹prize** \'prīz\ *noun* [Middle English *pris* prize, price — more at PRICE] (14th century)
**1 :** something offered or striven for in competition or in contests of chance; *also* **:** PREMIUM 1d
**2 :** something exceptionally desirable
**3** *archaic* **:** a contest for a reward **:** COMPETITION
**²prize** *adjective* (1803)
**1 a :** awarded or worthy of a prize **b :** awarded as a prize **c :** entered for the sake of a prize ⟨a *prize* drawing⟩
**2 :** outstanding of a kind ⟨raised *prize* hogs⟩
**³prize** *transitive verb* **prized; priz·ing** [Middle English *prisen*, from Middle French *prisier*, from Late Latin *pretiare*, from Latin *pretium* price, value — more at PRICE] (14th century)
**1 :** to estimate the value of **:** RATE
**2 :** to value highly **:** ESTEEM
*synonym* see APPRECIATE
**⁴prize** *noun* [Middle English *prise*, from Middle French, act of taking, from *prendre* to take, from Latin *prehendere* — more at GET] (14th century)
**1 :** something taken by force, stratagem, or threat; *especially* **:** property lawfully captured at sea in time of war
**2 :** an act of capturing or taking; *especially* **:** the wartime capture of a ship and its cargo at sea
*synonym* see SPOIL
**⁵prize** *transitive verb* **prized; priz·ing** [*prize* lever] (1686)
**:** to press, force, or move with a lever **:** PRY
**prize·fight** \'prīz-ˌfīt\ *noun* (1824)
**:** a professional boxing match
— **prize·fight·er** \-ˌfī-tər\ *noun*
**prize·fight·ing** \-ˌfī-tiŋ\ *noun* (1706)
**:** professional boxing
**prize money** *noun* (1748)
**1 :** a part of the proceeds of a captured ship formerly divided among the officers and men making the capture
**2 :** money offered in prizes
**priz·er** \'prī-zər\ *noun* (1599)
*archaic* **:** one that contends for a prize
**prize·win·ner** \'prīz-ˌwi-nər\ *noun* (1893)
**:** a winner of a prize
**prize·win·ning** \-ˌwi-niŋ\ *adjective* (1919)
**:** having won or of a quality to win a prize ⟨a *prizewinning* design⟩
**¹pro** \'prō\ *noun, plural* **pros** [Middle English, from Latin, preposition, for — more at FOR] (15th century)
**1 :** an argument or evidence in affirmation ⟨an appraisal of the *pros* and cons⟩
**2 :** the affirmative side or one holding it
**²pro** *adverb* [*pro-*] (15th century)
**:** on the affirmative side **:** in affirmation ⟨much has been written *pro* and con⟩
**³pro** *preposition* [Latin] (1837)
**:** in favor of **:** FOR
**⁴pro** *noun or adjective* (1866)
**:** PROFESSIONAL
**¹pro-** *prefix* [Middle English, from Old French, from Latin, from Greek, before, forward, forth, for, from *pro* — more at FOR]
**1 a :** earlier than **:** prior to **:** before ⟨*pro*thalamion⟩ **b :** rudimentary **:** PROT- ⟨*pro*nucleus⟩ **c :** precursory **:** ⟨*pro*insulin⟩
**2 a :** located in front of or at the front of **:** anterior to ⟨*pro*cephalic⟩ ⟨*pro*ventriculus⟩ **b :** front **:** anterior ⟨*pro*thorax⟩
**3 :** projecting ⟨*pro*gnathous⟩
**²pro-** *prefix* [Latin *pro* in front of, before, for, forward — more at FOR]
**1 :** taking the place of **:** substituting for ⟨*pro*cathedral⟩ ⟨*pro*caine⟩
**2 :** favoring **:** supporting **:** championing ⟨*pro*American⟩
**proa** \'prō-ə\ *variant of* PRAU
**pro·abor·tion** \ˌprō-ə-'bȯr-shən\ *adjective* (1972)
**:** favoring the legalization of abortion
— **pro–abor·tion·ist** \-sh(ə-)nist\ *noun*

**pro·ac·tive** \(ˌ)prō-'ak-tiv\ *adjective* (1933)
**1** [¹*pro-*] **:** relating to, caused by, or being interference between previous learning and the recall or performance of later learning ⟨*proactive* inhibition of memory⟩
**2** [²*pro-* + *re*active] **:** acting in anticipation of future problems, needs, or changes
**prob·a·bi·lism** \'prä-bə-bə-ˌli-zəm\ *noun* [French *probabilisme*, from Latin *probabilis* probable] (circa 1843)
**1 :** a theory that in disputed moral questions any solidly probable course may be followed even though an opposed course is or appears more probable
**2 :** a theory that certainty is impossible especially in the sciences and that probability suffices to govern belief and action
— **prob·a·bi·list** \-list\ *adjective or noun*
**prob·a·bi·lis·tic** \ˌprä-bə-bə-'lis-tik\ *adjective* (1864)
**1 :** of or relating to probabilism
**2 :** of, relating to, or based on probability
— **prob·a·bi·lis·ti·cal·ly** *adverb*
**prob·a·bil·i·ty** \ˌprä-bə-'bi-lə-tē\ *noun, plural* **-ties** (15th century)
**1 :** the quality or state of being probable
**2 :** something (as an event or circumstance) that is probable
**3 a** (1) **:** the ratio of the number of outcomes in an exhaustive set of equally likely outcomes that produce a given event to the total number of possible outcomes (2) **:** the chance that a given event will occur **b :** a branch of mathematics concerned with the study of probabilities
**4 :** a logical relation between statements such that evidence confirming one confirms the other to some degree
**probability density** *noun* (1939)
**:** PROBABILITY DENSITY FUNCTION; *also* **:** a particular value of a probability density function
**probability density function** *noun* (1957)
**1 :** PROBABILITY FUNCTION
**2 :** a function of a continuous random variable whose integral over an interval gives the probability that its value will fall within the interval
**probability distribution** *noun* (1937)
**:** PROBABILITY FUNCTION; *also* **:** PROBABILITY DENSITY FUNCTION 2
**probability function** *noun* (1906)
**:** a function of a discrete random variable that gives the probability that a specified value will occur
**¹prob·a·ble** \'prä-bə-bəl, 'prä(b)-bəl\ *adjective* [Middle English, provable, from Middle French, from Latin *probabilis* commendable, probable, from *probare* to test, approve, prove — more at PROVE] (1606)
**1 :** supported by evidence strong enough to establish presumption but not proof ⟨a *probable* hypothesis⟩
**2 :** establishing a probability ⟨*probable* evidence⟩
**3 :** likely to be or become true or real ⟨*probable* events⟩
**²probable** *noun* (1647)
**:** one that is probable
**probable cause** *noun* (circa 1676)
**:** a reasonable ground for supposing that a charge is well-founded
**prob·a·bly** \'prä-bə-blē, 'prä(b)-blē\ *adverb* (1613)
**:** insofar as seems reasonably true, factual, or to be expected **:** without much doubt ⟨is *probably* happy⟩ ⟨it will *probably* rain⟩
**pro·band** \'prō-ˌband, prō-'\ *noun* [Latin *probandus*, gerundive of *probare*] (circa 1929)
**:** SUBJECT 3c(2)
**pro·bang** \'prō-ˌbaŋ\ *noun* [origin unknown] (1657)
**:** a slender flexible rod with a sponge on one end used especially for removing obstructions from the esophagus
**¹pro·bate** \'prō-ˌbāt, *British also* -bit\ *noun* [Middle English *probat*, from Latin *probatum*,

neuter of *probatus*, past participle of *probare*] (15th century)
**1 a :** the action or process of proving before a competent judicial authority that a document offered for official recognition and registration as the last will and testament of a deceased person is genuine **b :** the judicial determination of the validity of a will
**2 :** the officially authenticated copy of a probated will
²**pro·bate** \-ˌbāt\ *transitive verb* **pro·bat·ed; pro·bat·ing** (1570)
**1 :** to establish (a will) by probate as genuine and valid
**2 :** to put (a convicted offender) on probation
**probate court** *noun* (circa 1847)
**:** a court that has jurisdiction chiefly over the probate of wills and administration of deceased persons' estates
**pro·ba·tion** \prō-'bā-shən\ *noun* [Middle English *probacioun*, from Middle French *probation*, from Latin *probation-, probatio*, from *probare*] (15th century)
**1 :** critical examination and evaluation or subjection to such examination and evaluation
**2 a :** subjection of an individual to a period of testing and trial to ascertain fitness (as for a job or school) **b :** the action of suspending the sentence of a convicted offender and giving the offender freedom during good behavior under the supervision of a probation officer **c :** the state or a period of being subject to probation
— **pro·ba·tion·al** \-shnəl, -shə-nᵊl\ *adjective*
— **pro·ba·tion·al·ly** *adverb*
— **pro·ba·tion·ary** \-shə-ˌner-ē\ *adjective*
**pro·ba·tion·er** \-sh(ə-)nər\ *noun* (1603)
**1 :** a person (as a newly admitted student nurse) whose fitness is being tested during a trial period
**2 :** a convicted offender on probation
**probation officer** *noun* (1880)
**:** an officer appointed to investigate, report on, and supervise the conduct of convicted offenders on probation
**pro·ba·tive** \'prō-bə-tiv\ *adjective* (15th century)
**1 :** serving to test or try **:** EXPLORATORY
**2 :** serving to prove **:** SUBSTANTIATING
**pro·ba·to·ry** \'prō-bə-ˌtōr-ē, -ˌtòr-\ *adjective* (1625)
**:** PROBATIVE
¹**probe** \'prōb\ *noun* [Medieval Latin *proba* examination, from Latin *probare*] (1580)
**1 :** a slender medical instrument used especially for exploration (as of a wound or bodily cavity)
**2 a :** any of various testing devices or substances: as (1) **:** a pointed metal tip for making electrical contact with a circuit element being checked (2) **:** a usually small object that is inserted into something so as to test conditions at a given point (3) **:** a device used to penetrate or send back information especially from outer space or a celestial body (4) **:** a device (as an ultrasound generator) or a substance (as DNA in genetic research) used to obtain specific information for diagnostic or experimental purposes **b :** a pipe on the receiving airplane thrust into the drogue of the delivering airplane in air refueling
**3 a :** the action of probing **b :** a penetrating or critical investigation **c :** a tentative exploratory advance or survey
²**probe** *verb* **probed; prob·ing** (1649)
*transitive verb*
**1 :** to search into and explore with great thoroughness **:** subject to a penetrating investigation
**2 :** to examine with a probe ⟨unmanned vehicles *probed* space⟩
*intransitive verb*
**:** to make a searching exploratory investigation
*synonym* see ENTER

— **prob·er** *noun*
**pro·ben·e·cid** \prō-'be-nə-səd\ *noun* [irregular from *propyl* + *benzoic* a*cid*] (1950)
**:** a drug $C_{13}H_{19}NO_4S$ that acts on renal tubular function and is used to increase the concentration of some drugs (as penicillin) in the blood by inhibiting their excretion and to increase the excretion of urates in gout
**prob·it** \'prä-bət\ *noun* [*prob*ability un*it*] (1934)
**:** a unit of measurement of statistical probability based on deviations from the mean of a normal distribution
**pro·bi·ty** \'prō-bə-tē\ *noun* [Middle English *probite*, from Middle French *probité*, from Latin *probitat-, probitas*, from *probus* honest — more at PROVE] (15th century)
**:** adherence to the highest principles and ideals **:** UPRIGHTNESS
*synonym* see HONESTY
¹**prob·lem** \'prä-bləm, -bᵊm, -ˌblem\ *noun* [Middle English *probleme*, from Middle French, from Latin *problema*, from Greek *problēma*, literally, obstacle, from *proballein* to throw forward, from *pro-* forward + *ballein* to throw — more at PRO-, DEVIL] (14th century)
**1 a :** a question raised for inquiry, consideration, or solution **b :** a proposition in mathematics or physics stating something to be done
**2 a :** an intricate unsettled question **b :** a source of perplexity, distress, or vexation **c :** difficulty in understanding or accepting ⟨I have a *problem* with your saying that⟩
*synonym* see MYSTERY
²**problem** *adjective* (1894)
**1 :** dealing with a problem of conduct or social relationship ⟨a *problem* play⟩
**2 :** difficult to deal with ⟨a *problem* child⟩
¹**prob·lem·at·ic** \ˌprä-blə-'ma-tik\ *or* **prob·lem·at·i·cal** \-ti-kəl\ *adjective* (1609)
**1 a :** posing a problem **:** difficult to solve or decide **b :** not definite or settled **:** UNCERTAIN ⟨their future remains *problematic*⟩ **c :** open to question or debate **:** QUESTIONABLE
**2 :** expressing or supporting a possibility
*synonym* see DOUBTFUL
— **prob·lem·at·i·cal·ly** \-ti-k(ə-)lē\ *adverb*
²**problematic** *noun* (1957)
**:** something that is problematic **:** a problematic aspect or concern
**pro bono** \ˌprō-'bō-(ˌ)nō\ *adjective* [Latin *pro bono publico* for the public good] (1970)
**:** being, involving, or doing legal work donated especially for the public good ⟨*pro bono* work⟩
**pro·bos·ci·de·an** \prə-ˌbä-sə-'dē-ən\ *or* **pro·bos·cid·i·an** \prə-ˌbä-'si-dē-ən, (ˌ)prō-\ *noun* [ultimately from Latin *proboscid-, proboscis*] (circa 1859)
**:** any of an order (Proboscidea) of large mammals comprising the elephants and extinct related forms
— **proboscidean** *adjective*
**pro·bos·cis** \prə-'bä-səs, -'bäs-kəs\ *noun, plural* **-bos·cis·es** *also* **-bos·ci·des** \-'bä-sə-ˌdēz\ [Latin, from Greek *proboskis*, from *pro-* + *boskein* to feed] (1576)
**1 a :** the trunk of an elephant; *also* **:** any long flexible snout **b :** the human nose especially when prominent
**2 :** any of various elongated or extensible tubular processes (as the sucking organ of a butterfly) of the oral region of an invertebrate
**pro·caine** \'prō-ˌkān\ *noun* [International Scientific Vocabulary ²*pro-* + *-caine*] (1918)
**:** a basic ester $C_{13}H_{20}N_2O_2$ of para-aminobenzoic acid; *also* **:** its crystalline hydrochloride used as a local anesthetic
**pro·cam·bi·um** \(ˌ)prō-'kam-bē-əm\ *noun* [New Latin] (1875)
**:** the part of the primary meristem of a plant that forms cambium and primary vascular tissues
— **pro·cam·bi·al** \-bē-əl\ *adjective*

**pro·car·ba·zine** \prō-'kär-bə-ˌzēn, -zən\ *noun* [*propyl* + *carbamic acid* + *azine*] (1965)
**:** an antineoplastic drug $C_{12}H_{19}N_3O$ that is a monoamine oxidase inhibitor used in the form of its hydrochloride especially in the palliative treatment of Hodgkin's disease
**pro·cary·ote** *variant of* PROKARYOTE
**pro·ca·the·dral** \ˌprō-kə-'thē-drəl\ *noun* (1868)
**:** a parish church used as a cathedral
¹**pro·ce·dur·al** \prə-'sē-jə-rəl, -'sēj-rəl\ *adjective* (1889)
**:** of or relating to procedure; *especially* **:** of or relating to the procedure used by courts or other bodies administering substantive law
— **pro·ce·dur·al·ly** *adverb*
²**procedural** *noun* (1974)
**:** a realist crime novel with a specific focus ⟨a courtroom *procedural*⟩; *especially* **:** POLICE PROCEDURAL
**procedural due process** *noun* (1938)
**:** DUE PROCESS 1
**pro·ce·dure** \prə-'sē-jər\ *noun* [French *procédure*, from Middle French, from *proceder*] (circa 1611)
**1 a :** a particular way of accomplishing something or of acting **b :** a step in a procedure
**2 a :** a series of steps followed in a regular definite order ⟨legal *procedure*⟩ ⟨a surgical *procedure*⟩ **b :** a series of instructions for a computer that has a name by which it can be called into action
**3 a :** a traditional or established way of doing things **b :** PROTOCOL 3a
**pro·ceed** \prō-'sēd, prə-\ *intransitive verb* [Middle English *proceden*, from Middle French *proceder*, from Latin *procedere*, from *pro-* forward + *cedere* to go — more at PRO-] (14th century)
**1 :** to come forth from a source **:** ISSUE
**2 a :** to continue after a pause or interruption **b :** to go on in an orderly regulated way
**3 a :** to begin and carry on an action, process, or movement **b :** to be in the process of being accomplished
**4 :** to move along a course **:** ADVANCE
*synonym* see SPRING
**pro·ceed·ing** *noun* (15th century)
**1 :** legal action ⟨a divorce *proceeding*⟩
**2 :** PROCEDURE
**3** *plural* **:** EVENTS, HAPPENINGS
**4 :** TRANSACTION
**5** *plural* **:** an official record of things said or done
**pro·ceeds** \'prō-ˌsēdz\ *noun plural* (1665)
**1 :** the total amount brought in ⟨the *proceeds* of a sale⟩
**2 :** the net amount received (as for a check or from an insurance settlement) after deduction of any discount or charges
**pro·ce·phal·ic** \ˌprō-sə-'fa-lik\ *adjective* (1874)
**:** relating to, forming, or situated on or near the front of the head
**pro·cer·coid** \(ˌ)prō-'sər-ˌkoid\ *noun* [*pro-* + Greek *kerkos* tail] (1926)
**:** the solid first parasitic larva of some tapeworms that develops usually in the body cavity of a copepod
¹**pro·cess** \'prä-ˌses, 'prō-, -səs\ *noun, plural* **pro·cess·es** \-ˌse-səz, -sə-, -ˌsēz\ [Middle English *proces*, from Middle French, from Latin *processus*, from *procedere*] (14th century)
**1 a :** PROGRESS, ADVANCE ⟨in the *process* of time⟩ **b :** something going on **:** PROCEEDING
**2 a** (1) **:** a natural phenomenon marked by gradual changes that lead toward a particular

result ⟨the *process* of growth⟩ (2) **:** a natural continuing activity or function ⟨such life *processes* as breathing⟩ **b :** a series of actions or operations conducing to an end; *especially* **:** a continuous operation or treatment especially in manufacture **3 a :** the whole course of proceedings in a legal action **b :** the summons, mandate, or writ used by a court to compel the appearance of the defendant in a legal action or compliance with its orders **4 :** a prominent or projecting part of an organism or organic structure ⟨a bone *process*⟩ **5 :** ⁵CONK

²**process** *transitive verb* (1532) **1 a :** to proceed against by law **:** PROSECUTE **b** (1) **:** to take out a summons against (2) **:** to serve a summons on **2 a :** to subject to a special process or treatment (as in the course of manufacture) **b** (1) **:** to subject to or handle through an established usually routine set of procedures ⟨*process* insurance claims⟩ (2) **:** to subject to examination or analysis ⟨computers *process* data⟩ **c :** to work (hair) into a conk

³**process** *adjective* (1888) **1 :** treated or made by a special process especially when involving synthesis or artificial modification **2 :** made by or used in a mechanical or photomechanical duplicating process **3 :** of or involving illusory effects usually introduced during processing of the film

⁴**pro·cess** \prə-'ses\ *intransitive verb* [back-formation from ¹*procession*] (1814) *chiefly British* **:** to move in a procession

**process cheese** *noun* (1926) **:** a cheese made by blending several lots of cheese — called also *processed cheese*

**pro·cess·ible** *or* **pro·cess·able** \'prä-ˌse-sə-bəl, 'prō-\ *adjective* (1954) **:** suitable for processing **:** capable of being processed

— **pro·cess·ibil·i·ty** *or* **pro·cess·abil·i·ty** \ˌprä-ˌse-sə-'bi-lə-tē, ˌprō-\ *noun*

¹**pro·ces·sion** \prə-'se-shən\ *noun* [Middle English *processioun*, from Old French *procession*, from Late Latin & Latin; Late Latin *procession-*, *processio* religious procession, from Latin, act of proceeding, from *procedere*] (12th century) **1 a :** a group of individuals moving along in an orderly often ceremonial way **b :** SUCCESSION, SEQUENCE **2 a :** continuous forward movement **:** PROGRESSION **b :** EMANATION ⟨the Holy Spirit's *procession* from the Father⟩

²**procession** *intransitive verb* (1691) *archaic* **:** to go in procession

¹**pro·ces·sion·al** \prə-'sesh-nəl, -'se-shə-nᵊl\ *noun* (15th century) **1 :** a book containing material for a procession **2 :** a musical composition (as a hymn) designed for a procession **3 :** a ceremonial procession

²**processional** *adjective* (circa 1611) **:** of, relating to, or moving in a procession

— **pro·ces·sion·al·ly** *adverb*

**pro·ces·sor** \'prä-ˌse-sər, 'prō-\ *noun* (1909) **1 :** one that processes ⟨scrap *processor*⟩ ⟨agricultural *processor*⟩ **2 a** (1) **:** COMPUTER (2) **:** the part of a computer system that operates on data — called also *central processing unit* **b :** a computer program (as a compiler) that puts another program into a form acceptable to the computer **3 :** FOOD PROCESSOR

**pro·cès–ver·bal** \ˌprō-ˌsā-vər-'bäl, -(ˌ)ver-\ *noun,* plural **pro·cès–ver·baux** \-'bō\ [French, literally, verbal trial] (1635) **:** an official written record

**pro–choice** \(ˌ)prō-'chois\ *adjective* (1975) **:** favoring the legalization of abortion

— **pro–choic·er** \-'choi-sər\ *noun*

**pro·claim** \prō-'klām, prə-\ *transitive verb* [Middle English *proclamen*, from Middle

French or Latin; Middle French *proclamer*, from Latin *proclamare*, from *pro-* before + *clamare* to cry out — more at PRO-, CLAIM] (14th century) **1 a :** to declare publicly, typically insistently, proudly, or defiantly and in either speech or writing **:** ANNOUNCE **b :** to give outward indication of **:** SHOW **2 :** to declare or declare to be solemnly, officially, or formally ⟨*proclaim* an amnesty⟩ ⟨*proclaim* the country a republic⟩ **3 :** to praise or glorify openly or publicly **:** EXTOL

*synonym* see DECLARE

— **pro·claim·er** *noun*

**proc·la·ma·tion** \ˌprä-klə-'mā-shən\ *noun* [Middle English *proclamacion*, from Middle French *proclamation*, from Latin *proclamation-*, *proclamatio*, from *proclamare*] (14th century) **1 :** the action of proclaiming **:** the state of being proclaimed **2 :** something proclaimed; *specifically* **:** an official formal public announcement

**pro·clit·ic** \(ˌ)prō-'kli-tik\ *noun* [New Latin *procliticus*, from Greek *pro-* + Late Latin *-cliticus* (as in *encliticus* enclitic)] (circa 1864) **:** a clitic that is associated with a following word

— **proclitic** *adjective*

**pro·cliv·i·ty** \prō-'kli-və-tē\ *noun,* plural **-ties** [Latin *proclivitas*, from *proclivis* sloping, prone, from *pro-* forward + *clivus* slope — more at PRO-, DECLIVITY] (circa 1591) **:** an inclination or predisposition toward something; *especially* **:** a strong inherent inclination toward something objectionable

*synonym* see LEANING

**Proc·ne** \'präk-nē\ *noun* [Latin, from Greek *Proknē*] **:** the wife of Tereus who is changed into a swallow while fleeing from him

**pro·con·sul** \(ˌ)prō-'kän(t)-səl\ *noun* [Middle English, from Latin, from *pro consule* for a consul] (14th century) **1 :** a governor or military commander of an ancient Roman province **2 :** an administrator in a modern colony, dependency, or occupied area usually with wide powers

— **pro·con·su·lar** \-s(ə-)lər\ *adjective*
— **pro·con·su·late** \-s(ə-)lət\ *noun*
— **pro·con·sul·ship** \-səl-ˌship\ *noun*

**pro·cras·ti·nate** \prə-'kras-tə-ˌnāt, prō-\ *verb* **-nat·ed; -nat·ing** [Latin *procrastinatus,* past participle of *procrastinare,* from *pro-* forward + *crastinus* of tomorrow, from *cras* tomorrow] (1588) *transitive verb* **:** to put off intentionally and habitually *intransitive verb* **:** to put off intentionally the doing of something that should be done

*synonym* see DELAY

— **pro·cras·ti·na·tion** \-ˌkras-tə-'nā-shən\ *noun*
— **pro·cras·ti·na·tor** \-'kras-tə-ˌnā-tər\ *noun*

**pro·cre·ant** \'prō-krē-ənt\ *adjective* (1588) **1 :** producing offspring **2** *archaic* **:** of or relating to procreation

**pro·cre·ate** \-ˌāt\ *verb* **-at·ed; -at·ing** [Latin *procreatus,* past participle of *procreare,* from *pro-* forth + *creare* to create — more at PRO-, CREATE] (1536) *transitive verb* **:** to beget or bring forth (offspring) **:** PROPAGATE *intransitive verb* **:** to beget or bring forth offspring **:** REPRODUCE

— **pro·cre·ation** \ˌprō-krē-'ā-shən\ *noun*
— **pro·cre·ative** \'prō-krē-ˌā-tiv\ *adjective*
— **pro·cre·ator** \-ˌā-tər\ *noun*

**pro·crus·te·an** \prə-'krəs-tē-ən, prō-\ *adjective, often capitalized* (circa 1846) **1 :** of, relating to, or typical of Procrustes

**2 :** marked by arbitrary often ruthless disregard of individual differences or special circumstances

**procrustean bed** *noun, often P capitalized* (1844) **:** a scheme or pattern into which someone or something is arbitrarily forced

**Pro·crus·tes** \prə-'krəs-(ˌ)tēz, prō-\ *noun* [Latin, from Greek *Prokroustēs*] **:** a villainous son of Poseidon in Greek mythology who forces travelers to fit into his bed by stretching their bodies or cutting off their legs

**pro·cryp·tic** \(ˌ)prō-'krip-tik\ *adjective* [*pro-* (as in *protect*) + *cryptic*] (1891) **:** of, relating to, or being a concealing pattern or shade of coloring especially in insects

**proc·to·dae·um** \ˌpräk-tə-'dē-əm\ *noun, plural* **-daea** \-'dē-ə\ *or* **-dae·ums** [New Latin, from Greek *prōktos* anus + *hodos* way] (1878) **:** the posterior ectodermal part of the alimentary canal formed in the embryo by invagination of the outer body wall

**proc·tol·o·gy** \präk-'tä-lə-jē\ *noun* [Greek *prōktos* + English *-logy*] (1899) **:** a branch of medicine dealing with the structure and diseases of the anus, rectum, and sigmoid colon

— **proc·to·log·ic** \ˌpräk-tə-'lä-jik\ *or* **proc·to·log·i·cal** \-ji-kəl\ *adjective*
— **proc·tol·o·gist** \präk-'tä-lə-jist\ *noun*

**proc·tor** \'präk-tər\ *noun* [Middle English *procutour* procurator, proctor, alteration of *procuratour*] (14th century) **:** SUPERVISOR, MONITOR; *specifically* **:** one appointed to supervise students (as at an examination)

— **proctor** *verb*
— **proc·to·ri·al** \präk-'tōr-ē-əl, -'tor-\ *adjective*
— **proc·tor·ship** \'präk-tər-ˌship\ *noun*

**pro·cum·bent** \prō-'kəm-bənt\ *adjective* [Latin *procumbent-, procumbens,* present participle of *procumbere* to fall or lean forward, from *pro-* forward + *-cumbere* to lie down] (1668) **1 :** being or having stems that trail along the ground without rooting **2 :** lying face down

**proc·u·ra·tion** \ˌpräk-yə-'rā-shən\ *noun* [Middle English *procuratioun,* from Middle French *procuration,* from Latin *procuration-, procuratio,* from *procurare*] (15th century) **1 a :** the act of appointing another as one's agent or attorney **b :** the authority vested in one so appointed **2 :** the action of obtaining something (as supplies) **:** PROCUREMENT

**proc·u·ra·tor** \'präk-yə-ˌrā-tər\ *noun* (14th century) **1 :** one that manages another's affairs **:** AGENT **2 :** an officer of the Roman empire entrusted with management of the financial affairs of a province and often having administrative powers as agent of the emperor

— **proc·u·ra·to·ri·al** \ˌpräk-yə-rə-'tōr-ē-əl, -'tor-\ *adjective*

**pro·cure** \prə-'kyùr, prō-\ *verb* **pro·cured; pro·cur·ing** [Middle English, from Late Latin *procurare,* from Latin, to take care of, from *pro-* for + *cura* care] (14th century) *transitive verb* **1 a :** to get possession of **:** obtain by particular care and effort **b :** to get and make available for promiscuous sexual intercourse **2 :** BRING ABOUT, ACHIEVE *intransitive verb* **:** to procure women

— **pro·cur·able** \-'kyùr-ə-bəl\ *adjective*
— **pro·cure·ment** \-'kyùr-mənt\ *noun*

**pro·cur·er** \-'kyùr-ər\ *noun* (1538) **:** one that procures; *especially* **:** PANDER

**Pro·cy·on** \'prō-sē-ˌän, 'prä-, -ən\ *noun* [Latin, from Greek *Prokyōn,* literally, fore-dog; from its rising before Sirius]

: the brightest star in the constellation Canis Minor

**¹prod** \'präd\ *verb* **prod·ded; prod·ding** [origin unknown] (1535)
*transitive verb*
**1 a :** to thrust a pointed instrument into **:** PRICK **b :** to incite to action **:** STIR
**2 :** to poke or stir as if with a prod
*intransitive verb*
**:** to urge someone on
— **prod·der** *noun*

**²prod** *noun* (circa 1787)
**1 :** a pointed instrument used to prod
**2 :** an incitement to act

**¹prod·i·gal** \'prä-di-gəl\ *adjective* [Latin *prodigus*, from *prodigere* to drive away, squander, from *pro-, prod-* forth + *agere* to drive — more at PRO-, AGENT] (circa 1520)
**1 :** recklessly extravagant
**2 :** characterized by wasteful expenditure **:** LAVISH
**3 :** yielding abundantly **:** LUXURIANT — often used with *of* ⟨nature has been so *prodigal* of her bounty —H. T. Buckle⟩
*synonym* see PROFUSE
— **prod·i·gal·i·ty** \,prä-də-'ga-lə-tē\ *noun*
— **prod·i·gal·ly** \'prä-di-g(ə-)lē\ *adverb*

**²prodigal** *noun* (1596)
**:** one who spends or gives lavishly and foolishly

**pro·di·gious** \prə-'di-jəs\ *adjective* (15th century)
**1 a** *obsolete* **:** being an omen **:** PORTENTOUS **b** *archaic* **:** resembling or befitting a prodigy **:** STRANGE, UNUSUAL
**2 :** exciting amazement or wonder
**3 :** extraordinary in bulk, quantity, or degree **:** ENORMOUS
*synonym* see MONSTROUS
— **pro·di·gious·ly** *adverb*
— **pro·di·gious·ness** *noun*

**prod·i·gy** \'prä-də-jē\ *noun, plural* **-gies** [Middle English, from Latin *prodigium* omen, monster, from *pro-, prod-* + *-igium* (akin to *aio* I say) — more at ADAGE] (15th century)
**1 a :** a portentous event **:** OMEN **b :** something extraordinary or inexplicable
**2 a :** an extraordinary, marvelous, or unusual accomplishment, deed, or event **b :** a highly talented child or youth

**pro·dro·mal** \(,)prō-'drō-məl\ *adjective* (1716)
**:** PRECURSORY; *especially* **:** marked by prodromes

**pro·drome** \'prō-,drōm\ *noun* [French, literally, precursor, from Greek *prodromos*, from *pro-* before + *dromos* act of running, racecourse — more at PRO-, DROMEDARY] (circa 1834)
**:** a premonitory symptom of disease

**¹pro·duce** \prə-'düs, prō-, -'dyüs\ *verb* **pro·duced; pro·duc·ing** [Middle English (Scots), from Latin *producere*, from *pro-* forward + *ducere* to lead — more at TOW] (15th century)
*transitive verb*
**1 :** to offer to view or notice
**2 :** to give birth or rise to **:** YIELD
**3 :** to extend in length, area, or volume ⟨*produce* a side of a triangle⟩
**4 :** to present to the public on the stage or screen or over radio or television
**5 a :** to cause to have existence or to happen **:** BRING ABOUT **b :** to give being, form, or shape to **:** MAKE; *especially* **:** MANUFACTURE
**6 :** to compose, create, or bring out by intellectual or physical effort
**7 :** to cause to accrue
*intransitive verb*
**:** to bear, make, or yield something
— **pro·duc·ible** \-'dü-sə-bəl, -'dyü-\ *adjective*

**²pro·duce** \'prä-(,)düs, 'prō- *also* -(,)dyüs\ *noun* (1695)
**1 a :** something produced **b :** the amount produced **:** YIELD

**2 :** agricultural products and especially fresh fruits and vegetables as distinguished from grain and other staple crops
**3 :** the progeny usually of a female animal

**pro·duc·er** \prə-'dü-sər, prō-, -'dyü-\ *noun* (1513)
**1 :** one that produces; *especially* **:** one that grows agricultural products or manufactures crude materials into articles of use
**2 :** a furnace or apparatus that produces combustible gas to be used for fuel by circulating air or a mixture of air and steam through a layer of incandescent fuel
**3 :** a person who supervises or finances the production of a stage or screen production or radio or television program
**4 :** any of various organisms (as a green plant) which produce their own organic compounds from simple precursors (as carbon dioxide and inorganic nitrogen) and many of which are food sources for other organisms — compare CONSUMER

**producer gas** *noun* (1895)
**:** a fuel gas made in a producer and consisting chiefly of carbon monoxide, hydrogen, and nitrogen

**producer goods** *noun plural* (1948)
**:** goods (as tools and raw materials) used to produce other goods and satisfy human wants only indirectly

**prod·uct** \'prä-(,)dəkt\ *noun* [in sense 1, from Middle English, from Medieval Latin *productum*, from Latin, something produced, from neuter of *productus*, past participle of *producere*; in other senses, from Latin *productum*] (15th century)
**1 :** the number or expression resulting from the multiplication together of two or more numbers or expressions
**2 a :** something produced **b :** something resulting from or necessarily following from a set of conditions ⟨a *product* of his environment⟩
**3 :** the amount, quantity, or total produced
**4 :** CONJUNCTION 5

**pro·duc·tion** \prə-'dək-shən, prō-\ *noun* (15th century)
**1 a :** something produced **:** PRODUCT **b** (1) **:** a literary or artistic work (2) **:** a work presented on the stage or screen or over the air **c :** something exaggerated out of proportion to its importance
**2 a :** the act or process of producing **b :** the creation of utility; *especially* **:** the making of goods available for use
**3 :** total output especially of a commodity or an industry
— **pro·duc·tion·al** \-shnəl, -shə-n°l\ *adjective*

**production control** *noun* (1929)
**:** systematic planning, coordinating, and directing of all manufacturing activities and influences to insure having goods made on time, of adequate quality, and at reasonable cost

**production line** *noun* (1935)
**:** LINE 6j

**pro·duc·tive** \prə-'dək-tiv, prō-\ *adjective* (1612)
**1 :** having the quality or power of producing especially in abundance ⟨*productive* fishing waters⟩
**2 :** effective in bringing about ⟨investigating committees have been *productive* of much good —R. K. Carr⟩
**3 a :** yielding results, benefits, or profits **b :** yielding or devoted to the satisfaction of wants or the creation of utilities
**4 :** continuing to be used in the formation of new words or constructions ⟨*un-* is a *productive* prefix⟩
**5 :** raising mucus or sputum (as from the bronchi) ⟨a *productive* cough⟩
— **pro·duc·tive·ly** *adverb*
— **pro·duc·tive·ness** *noun*

**pro·duc·tiv·i·ty** \,prō-dək-'ti-və-tē, ,prä-, prə-, ,dək-\ *noun* (circa 1810)

**1 :** the quality or state of being productive
**2 :** rate of production especially of food by the utilization of solar energy by producer organisms

**pro·em** \'prō-,em, -əm\ *noun* [Middle English *proheme*, from Middle French, from Latin *prooemium*, from Greek *prooimion*, from *pro-* + *oimē* song; probably akin to Hittite *išamai-* song, Sanskrit *syati* he binds — more at SINEW] (14th century)
**1 :** preliminary comment **:** PREFACE
**2 :** PRELUDE
— **pro·emi·al** \prō-'ē-mē-əl, -'e-\ *adjective*

**pro·en·zyme** \(,)prō-'en-,zīm\ *noun* [International Scientific Vocabulary] (circa 1900)
**:** ZYMOGEN

**pro·es·trus** \(,)prō-'es-trəs\ *noun* [New Latin] (1923)
**:** a period immediately preceding estrus characterized by preparatory physiological changes

**prof** \'präf\ *noun* (1838)
**:** PROFESSOR

**pro·fam·i·ly** \,prō-'fam-lē, -'fa-mə-\ *adjective* (1926)
**1 :** favoring or encouraging traditional family structures and values
**2 :** opposing abortion and often birth control

**prof·a·na·tion** \,prä-fə-'nā-shən, ,prō-\ *noun* (1552)
**:** the act or an instance of profaning

**pro·fa·na·to·ry** \prō-'fa-nə-,tōr-ē, prə-, -'fä-, -,tȯr-\ *adjective* (1853)
**:** tending to profane **:** DESECRATING

**¹pro·fane** \prō-'fān, prə-\ *transitive verb* **pro·faned; pro·fan·ing** [Middle English *prophanen*, from Latin *profanare*, from *profanus*] (14th century)
**1 :** to treat (something sacred) with abuse, irreverence, or contempt **:** DESECRATE
**2 :** to debase by a wrong, unworthy, or vulgar use
— **pro·fan·er** *noun*

**²profane** *adjective* [Middle English *prophane*, from Middle French, from Latin *profanus*, from *pro-* before + *fanum* temple — more at PRO-, FEAST] (15th century)
**1 :** not concerned with religion or religious purposes **:** SECULAR
**2 :** not holy because unconsecrated, impure, or defiled **:** UNSANCTIFIED
**3 :** serving to debase or defile what is holy **:** IRREVERENT
**4 a :** not being among the initiated **b :** not possessing esoteric or expert knowledge
— **pro·fane·ly** *adverb*
— **pro·fane·ness** \-'fān-nəs\ *noun*

**pro·fan·i·ty** \prō-'fa-nə-tē, prə-\ *noun, plural* **-ties** (1607)
**1 a :** the quality or state of being profane **b :** the use of profane language
**2 a :** profane language **b :** an utterance of profane language

**pro·fess** \prə-'fes, prō-\ *verb* [in sense 1, from Middle English, from *profes,* adjective, having professed one's vows, from Middle French, from Late Latin *professus,* from Latin, past participle of *profitēri* to profess, confess, from *pro-* before + *fatēri* to acknowledge; in other senses, from Latin *professus,* past participle — more at CONFESS] (14th century)
*transitive verb*
**1 :** to receive formally into a religious community following a novitiate by acceptance of the required vows
**2 a :** to declare or admit openly or freely **:** AFFIRM **b :** to declare in words or appearances only **:** PRETEND, CLAIM
**3 :** to confess one's faith in or allegiance to

**4 a :** to practice or claim to be versed in (a calling or profession) **b :** to teach as a professor
*intransitive verb*
**1 :** to make a profession or avowal
**2** *obsolete* **:** to profess friendship
**pro·fessed** \-'fest\ *adjective* (circa 1569)
**1 :** openly and freely declared or acknowledged **:** AFFIRMED
**2 :** professing to be qualified; *also* **:** EXPERT
**pro·fess·ed·ly** \prə-'fe-səd-lē, -'fest-lē\ *adverb* (1570)
**1 :** by profession or declaration **:** AVOWEDLY
**2 :** with pretense **:** ALLEGEDLY
**pro·fes·sion** \prə-'fe-shən\ *noun* [Middle English *professioun*, from Old French *profession*, from Late Latin & Latin; Late Latin *profession-*, *professio*, from Latin, public declaration, from *profitēri*] (13th century)
**1 :** the act of taking the vows of a religious community
**2 :** an act of openly declaring or publicly claiming a belief, faith, or opinion **:** PROTESTATION
**3 :** an avowed religious faith
**4 a :** a calling requiring specialized knowledge and often long and intensive academic preparation **b :** a principal calling, vocation, or employment **c :** the whole body of persons engaged in a calling
¹**pro·fes·sion·al** \prə-'fesh-nəl, -'fe-shə-nᵊl\ *adjective* (circa 1748)
**1 a :** of, relating to, or characteristic of a profession **b :** engaged in one of the learned professions **c** (1) **:** characterized by or conforming to the technical or ethical standards of a profession (2) **:** exhibiting a courteous, conscientious, and generally businesslike manner in the workplace
**2 a :** participating for gain or livelihood in an activity or field of endeavor often engaged in by amateurs ⟨a *professional* golfer⟩ **b :** having a particular profession as a permanent career ⟨a *professional* soldier⟩ **c :** engaged in by persons receiving financial return ⟨*professional* football⟩
**3 :** following a line of conduct as though it were a profession ⟨a *professional* patriot⟩
— **pro·fes·sion·al·ly** *adverb*
²**professional** *noun* (1811)
**:** one that is professional; *especially* **:** one that engages in a pursuit or activity professionally
**professional corporation** *noun* (1970)
**:** a corporation organized by one or more licensed individuals (as a doctor or lawyer) especially for the purpose of providing professional services and obtaining tax advantages
**pro·fes·sion·al·ism** \-'fesh-nə-ˌli-zəm, -'fe-shə-nᵊl-ˌi-\ *noun* (1856)
**1 :** the conduct, aims, or qualities that characterize or mark a profession or a professional person
**2 :** the following of a profession (as athletics) for gain or livelihood
**pro·fes·sion·al·ize** \-ˌlīz, -ˌīz\ *transitive verb* **-ized; -iz·ing** (1856)
**:** to give a professional character to
— **pro·fes·sion·al·i·za·tion** \-ˌfesh-nə-lə-'zā-shən, -ˌfe-shə-nᵊl-ə-\ *noun*
**pro·fes·sor** \prə-'fe-sər\ *noun* (14th century)
**1 :** one that professes, avows, or declares
**2 a :** a faculty member of the highest academic rank at an institution of higher education **b :** a teacher at a university, college, or sometimes secondary school **c :** one that teaches or professes special knowledge of an art, sport, or occupation requiring skill
— **pro·fes·so·ri·al** \ˌprō-fə-'sōr-ē-əl, ˌprä-, -'sòr-\ *adjective*
— **pro·fes·so·ri·al·ly** \-ē-ə-lē\ *adverb*
— **pro·fes·sor·ship** \prə-'fe-sər-ˌship\ *noun*
**pro·fes·sor·ate** \prə-'fe-sə-rət\ *noun* (1860)
**:** the office, term of office, or position of a professor

**pro·fes·so·ri·at** \ˌprō-fə-'sōr-ē-ət, ˌprä-, -'sòr-, -ē-ˌat\ *or* **pro·fes·so·ri·ate** \-ət, -ˌāt\ *noun* [modification of French *professorat*, from *professeur* professor, from Latin *professor*, from *profitēri*] (1858)
**1 :** the body of college and university teachers at an institution or in society
**2 :** the office, duties, or position of a professor
¹**prof·fer** \'prä-fər\ *transitive verb* **proffered; prof·fer·ing** \-f(ə-)riŋ\ [Middle English *profren*, from Anglo-French *profrer*, from Old French *poroffrir*, from *por-* forth (from Latin *pro-*) + *offrir* to offer — more at PRO-] (14th century)
**:** to present for acceptance **:** TENDER, OFFER
²**proffer** *noun* (14th century)
**:** OFFER, SUGGESTION
**pro·fi·cien·cy** \prə-'fi-shən(t)-sē\ *noun* (1544)
**1 :** advancement in knowledge or skill **:** PROGRESS
**2 :** the quality or state of being proficient
**pro·fi·cient** \-shənt\ *adjective* [Latin *proficient-*, *proficiens*, present participle of *proficere* to go forward, accomplish, from *pro-* forward + *facere* to make — more at PRO-, DO] (circa 1590)
**:** well advanced in an art, occupation, or branch of knowledge ☆
— **proficient** *noun*
— **pro·fi·cient·ly** *adverb*
¹**pro·file** \'prō-ˌfīl\ *noun* [Italian *profilo*, from *profilare* to draw in outline, from *pro-* forward (from Latin) + *filare* to spin, from Late Latin — more at FILE] (circa 1656)
**1 :** a representation of something in outline; *especially* **:** a human head or face represented or seen in a side view
**2 :** an outline seen or represented in sharp relief **:** CONTOUR
**3 :** a side or sectional elevation: as **a :** a drawing showing a vertical section of the ground **b :** a vertical section of a soil from the ground surface to the underlying unweathered material
**4 :** a set of data often in graphic form portraying the significant features of something ⟨a corporation's earnings *profile*⟩; *especially* **:** a graph representing the extent to which an individual exhibits traits or abilities as determined by tests or ratings
**5 :** a concise biographical sketch
**6 :** degree or level of public exposure ⟨trying to keep a low *profile*⟩ ⟨a job with a high *profile*⟩
**synonym** see OUTLINE
²**profile** *transitive verb* **pro·filed; pro·fil·ing** (1715)
**1 :** to represent in profile or by a profile **:** produce (as by drawing, writing, or graphing) a profile of
**2 :** to shape the outline of by passing a cutter around
— **pro·fil·er** *noun*
¹**prof·it** \'prä-fət\ *noun, often attributive* [Middle English, from Middle French, from Latin *profectus* advance, profit, from *proficere*] (14th century)
**1 :** a valuable return **:** GAIN
**2 :** the excess of returns over expenditure in a transaction or series of transactions; *especially* **:** the excess of the selling price of goods over their cost
**3 :** net income usually for a given period of time
**4 :** the ratio of profit for a given year to the amount of capital invested or to the value of sales
**5 :** the compensation accruing to entrepreneurs for the assumption of risk in business enterprise as distinguished from wages or rent
— **prof·it·less** \-ləs\ *adjective*
— **prof·it·wise** \-ˌwīz\ *adverb*
²**profit** (14th century)
*intransitive verb*
**1 :** to be of service or advantage **:** AVAIL
**2 :** to derive benefit **:** GAIN

**3 :** to make a profit
*transitive verb*
**:** to be of service to **:** BENEFIT
**prof·it·able** \'prä-fə-tə-bəl, 'präf-tə-bəl\ *adjective* (14th century)
**:** affording profits **:** yielding advantageous returns or results
— **prof·it·abil·i·ty** \ˌprä-fə-tə-'bi-lə-tē\ *noun*
— **prof·it·able·ness** \'prä-fə-tə-bəl-nəs\ *noun*
— **prof·it·ably** \-blē\ *adverb*
**profit and loss** *noun* (1588)
**:** a summary account used at the end of an accounting period to collect the balances of the nominal accounts so that the net profit or loss may be shown
**prof·i·teer** \ˌprä-fə-'tir\ *noun* (1912)
**:** one who makes what is considered an unreasonable profit especially on the sale of essential goods during times of emergency
— **profiteer** *intransitive verb*
**pro·fit·er·ole** \prə-'fi-tə-ˌrōl\ *noun* [French, perhaps from *profit* profit] (1884)
**:** a miniature cream puff with a sweet or savory filling
**profit sharing** *noun* (1881)
**:** a system or process under which employees receive a part of the profits of an industrial or commercial enterprise
**profit system** *noun* (1945)
**:** FREE ENTERPRISE
**prof·li·ga·cy** \'prä-fli-gə-sē\ *noun* (1738)
**:** the quality or state of being profligate
¹**prof·li·gate** \'prä-fli-gət, -ˌgāt\ *adjective* [Latin *profligatus*, from past participle of *profligare* to strike down, from *pro-* forward, down + *-fligare* (akin to *fligere* to strike); akin to Greek *phlibein* to squeeze] (1647)
**1 :** completely given up to dissipation and licentiousness
**2 :** wildly extravagant **:** PRODIGAL
— **prof·li·gate·ly** *adverb*
²**profligate** *noun* (1709)
**:** a person given to wildly extravagant and usually grossly self-indulgent expenditure
**pro·flu·ent** \'prä-ˌflü-ənt, 'prō-; prō-'flü-\ *adjective* [Middle English, from Latin *profluent-*, *profluens*, present participle of *profluere* to flow forth, from *pro-* forth + *fluere* to flow — more at PRO-, FLUID] (15th century)
**:** flowing copiously or smoothly
**pro for·ma** \(ˌ)prō-'fòr-mə\ *adjective* [Latin, for form] (circa 1580)
**1 :** made or carried out in a perfunctory manner or as a formality
**2 :** provided in advance to prescribe form or describe items ⟨*pro forma* invoice⟩
¹**pro·found** \prə-'faùnd, prō-\ *adjective* [Middle English, from Middle French *profond* deep, from Latin *profundus*, from *pro-* before + *fundus* bottom — more at PRO-, BOTTOM] (14th century)
**1 a :** having intellectual depth and insight **b :** difficult to fathom or understand
**2 a :** extending far below the surface **b :** coming from, reaching to, or situated at a depth **:** DEEP-SEATED ⟨a *profound* sigh⟩

---

☆ **SYNONYMS**
**Proficient, adept, skilled, skillful, expert** mean having great knowledge and experience in a trade or profession. PROFICIENT implies a thorough competence derived from training and practice ⟨*proficient* in translating foreign languages⟩. ADEPT implies special aptitude as well as proficiency ⟨*adept* at doing long division⟩. SKILLED stresses mastery of technique ⟨a *skilled* surgeon⟩. SKILLFUL implies individual dexterity in execution or performance ⟨*skillful* drivers⟩. EXPERT implies extraordinary proficiency and often connotes knowledge as well as technical skill ⟨*expert* in the evaluation of wines⟩.

**3 a :** characterized by intensity of feeling or quality **b :** all encompassing : COMPLETE ⟨*profound* sleep⟩
— **pro·found·ly** \-'fau̇n(d)-lē\ *adverb*
— **pro·found·ness** \-'fau̇n(d)-nəs\ *noun*
**²profound** *noun* (1621)
*archaic* : something that is very deep; *specifically* : the depths of the sea
**pro·fun·di·ty** \prə-'fən-də-tē\ *noun, plural* **-ties** [Middle English *profundite,* from Middle French *profundité,* from Latin *profunditat-, profunditas* depth, from *profundus*] (15th century)
**1 a :** intellectual depth **b :** something profound or abstruse
**2 :** the quality or state of being profound or deep
**pro·fuse** \prə-'fyüs, prō-\ *adjective* [Middle English, from Latin *profusus,* past participle of *profundere* to pour forth, from *pro-* forth + *fundere* to pour — more at FOUND] (15th century)
**1 :** pouring forth liberally : EXTRAVAGANT ⟨*profuse* in their thanks⟩
**2 :** exhibiting great abundance : BOUNTIFUL ⟨a *profuse* harvest⟩ ☆
— **pro·fuse·ly** *adverb*
— **pro·fuse·ness** *noun*
**pro·fu·sion** \-'fyü-zhən\ *noun* (1545)
**1 :** lavish expenditure : EXTRAVAGANCE
**2 :** the quality or state of being profuse
**3 :** great quantity : lavish display or supply ⟨snow falling in *profusion*⟩
**¹prog** \'präg\ *intransitive verb* **progged; prog·ging** [origin unknown] (1624)
*chiefly dialect* : to search about; *especially* : FORAGE
**²prog** *noun* (1655)
*chiefly dialect* : FOOD, VICTUALS
**pro·gen·i·tor** \prō-'je-nə-tər, prə-\ *noun* [Middle English, from Middle French *progeniteur,* from Latin *progenitor,* from *progignere* to beget, from *pro-* forth + *gignere* to beget — more at KIN] (14th century)
**1 a :** an ancestor in the direct line : FOREFATHER **b :** a biologically ancestral form
**2 :** PRECURSOR, ORIGINATOR ⟨*progenitors* of socialist ideas —*Times Literary Supplement*⟩
**prog·e·ny** \'prä-jə-nē\ *noun, plural* **-nies** [Middle English *progenie,* from Middle French, from Latin *progenies,* from *progignere*] (14th century)
**1 a :** DESCENDANTS, CHILDREN **b :** offspring of animals or plants
**2 :** OUTCOME, PRODUCT
**3 :** a body of followers, disciples, or successors
**pro·ges·ta·tion·al** \ˌprō-ˌjes-'tā-shnəl, -shə-nᵊl\ *adjective* (1923)
: preceding pregnancy or gestation; *especially* : of, relating to, inducing, or constituting the modifications of the female mammalian system associated especially with ovulation and corpus luteum formation ⟨*progestational* hormones⟩
**pro·ges·ter·one** \prō-'jes-tə-ˌrōn\ *noun* [*progestin* + *-sterone*] (1935)
: a female steroid sex hormone $C_{21}H_{30}O_2$ that is secreted by the corpus luteum to prepare the endometrium for implantation and later by the placenta during pregnancy to prevent rejection of the developing embryo or fetus
**pro·ges·tin** \-'jes-tən\ *noun* [*pro-* + *gestation* + *¹-in*] (1930)
: a progestational hormone; *especially* : PROGESTERONE
**pro·ges·to·gen** \-'jes-tə-jən\ *noun* [*progestational* + *-ogen* (as in *estrogen*)] (1942)
: any of several progestational steroids (as progesterone)
— **pro·ges·to·gen·ic** \-ˌjes-tə-'je-nik\ *adjective*
**pro·glot·tid** \(ˌ)prō-'glä-təd\ *noun* [New Latin *proglottis*] (1878)
: a segment of a tapeworm containing both male and female reproductive organs

**pro·glot·tis** \(ˌ)prō-'glä-təs\ *noun, plural* **-glot·ti·des** \-'glä-tə-ˌdēz\ [New Latin *proglottid-, proglottis,* from Greek *proglōttis* tip of the tongue, from *pro-* + *glōtta* tongue — more at GLOSS] (1855)
: PROGLOTTID
**prog·na·thism** \'präg-nə-ˌthi-zəm, präg-'nā-\ *noun* (circa 1864)
: prognathous condition
**prog·na·thous** \-thəs\ *adjective* (1836)
: having the jaws projecting beyond the upper part of the face
**prog·no·sis** \präg-'nō-səs\ *noun, plural* **-no·ses** \-ˌsēz\ [Late Latin, from Greek *prognōsis,* literally, foreknowledge, from *progignōskein* to know before, from *pro-* + *gignōskein* to know — more at KNOW] (1655)
**1 :** the prospect of recovery as anticipated from the usual course of disease or peculiarities of the case
**2 :** FORECAST, PROGNOSTICATION
**¹prog·nos·tic** \präg-'näs-tik\ *noun* [Middle English *pronostique,* from Middle French, from Latin *prognosticum,* from Greek *prognōstikon,* from neuter of *prognōstikos* foretelling, from *progignōskein*] (14th century)
**1 :** something that foretells : PORTENT
**2 :** PROGNOSTICATION, PROPHECY
**²prognostic** *adjective* (1603)
: of, relating to, or serving as ground for prognostication or a prognosis ⟨*prognostic* weather charts⟩ ⟨favorable *prognostic* signs⟩
**prog·nos·ti·cate** \präg-'näs-tə-ˌkāt\ *transitive verb* **-cat·ed; -cat·ing** (15th century)
**1 :** to foretell from signs or symptoms : PREDICT
**2 :** PRESAGE
**synonym** see FORETELL
— **prog·nos·ti·ca·tive** \-ˌkā-tiv\ *adjective*
— **prog·nos·ti·ca·tor** \-ˌkā-tər\ *noun*
**prog·nos·ti·ca·tion** \(ˌ)präg-ˌnäs-tə-'kā-shən\ *noun* (15th century)
**1 :** an indication in advance : FORETOKEN
**2 a :** an act, the fact, or the power of prognosticating : FORECAST **b :** FOREBODING
**pro·grade** \'prō-ˌgrād\ *adjective* [Latin *pro-* forward + English *-grade* (as in *retrograde*)] (1967)
: having or being a direction of rotation or revolution that is counterclockwise as viewed from the north pole of the sky or a planet
**¹pro·gram** \'prō-ˌgram, -grəm\ *noun* [French *programme* agenda, public notice, from Greek *programma,* from *prographein* to write before, from *pro-* before + *graphein* to write — more at CARVE] (1633)
**1 :** [Late Latin *programma,* from Greek] : a public notice
**2 a :** a brief usually printed outline of the order to be followed, of the features to be presented, and the persons participating (as in a public exercise or performance) **b :** the performance of a program; *especially* : a performance broadcast on radio or television
**3 :** a plan or system under which action may be taken toward a goal
**4 :** CURRICULUM
**5 :** PROSPECTUS, SYLLABUS
**6 a :** a plan for the programming of a mechanism (as a computer) **b :** a sequence of coded instructions that can be inserted into a mechanism (as a computer); *also* : such a sequence that is part of an organism's genotype or behavioral repertoire
**²program** *also* **programme** *transitive verb* **-grammed** *or* **-gramed; -gram·ming** *or* **-gram·ing** (1896)
**1 a :** to arrange or furnish a program of or for : BILL **b :** to enter in a program
**2 :** to work out a sequence of operations to be performed by (a mechanism) : provide with a program

**3 a :** to insert a program for (a particular action) into or as if into a mechanism **b :** to control by or as if by a program **c** (1) : to code in an organism's program (2) : to provide with a biological program ⟨cells *programmed* to synthesize hemoglobin⟩
**4 :** to predetermine the thinking, behavior, or operations of as if by computer programming ⟨children are *programmed* into violence —Lisa A. Richette⟩
— **pro·gram·ma·bil·i·ty** \(ˌ)prō-ˌgra-mə-'bi-lə-tē\ *noun*
— **pro·gram·ma·ble** \'prō-ˌgra-mə-bəl\ *adjective or noun*
**program director** *noun* (1953)
: one in charge of planning and scheduling program material for a radio or television station or network
**pro·gram·mat·ic** \ˌprō-grə-'ma-tik\ *adjective* (1896)
**1 :** relating to program music
**2 :** of, relating to, resembling, or having a program
— **pro·gram·mat·i·cal·ly** \-ti-k(ə-)lē\ *adverb*
**programme** *chiefly British variant of* PROGRAM
**programmed instruction** *noun* (1962)
: instruction through information given in small steps with each requiring a correct response by the learner before going on to the next step
**pro·gram·mer** *also* **pro·gram·er** \'prō-ˌgra-mər, -grə-\ *noun* (circa 1890)
: one that programs: as **a :** a person who prepares and tests programs for devices (as computers) **b :** one that programs a mechanism **c** : one that prepares instructional or educational programs
**pro·gram·ming** *also* **pro·gram·ing** \-miŋ\ *noun* (1940)
**1 :** the planning, scheduling, or performing of a program
**2 a :** the process of instructing or learning by means of an instructional program **b :** the process of preparing an instructional program
**program music** *noun* (1879)
: music intended to suggest a sequence of images or incidents
**program trading** *noun* (1985)
: computerized trading of large blocks of stocks in one market against stock index futures in another
**¹prog·ress** \'prä-grəs, -ˌgres, *US also & British usually* 'prō-ˌgres\ *noun* [Middle English, from Latin *progressus* advance, from *progredi* to go forth, from *pro-* forward + *gradi* to go — more at PRO-, GRADE] (15th century)

---

☆ **SYNONYMS**
**Profuse, lavish, prodigal, luxuriant, lush, exuberant** mean giving or given out in great abundance. PROFUSE implies pouring forth without restraint ⟨uttered *profuse* apologies⟩. LAVISH suggests an unstinted or unmeasured profusion ⟨a *lavish* wedding reception⟩. PRODIGAL implies reckless or wasteful lavishness threatening to lead to early exhaustion of resources ⟨*prodigal* spending⟩. LUXURIANT suggests a rich and splendid abundance ⟨*luxuriant* sidewhiskers⟩. LUSH suggests rich, soft luxuriance ⟨a *lush* green lawn⟩. EXUBERANT implies marked vitality or vigor in what produces abundantly ⟨an *exuberant* imagination⟩.

---

\ə\ abut  \ᵊ\ kitten  \ər\ further  \a\ ash  \ā\ ace
\ä\ mop, mar  \au̇\ out  \ch\ chin  \e\ bet  \ē\ easy
\g\ go  \i\ hit  \ī\ ice  \j\ job  \ŋ\ sing  \ō\ go
\o̊\ law  \o̊i\ boy  \th\ thin  \t̲h̲\ the  \ü\ loot  \u̇\ foot
\y\ yet  \zh\ vision  *see also* Guide to Pronunciation

**1 a** (1) **:** a royal journey marked by pomp and pageant (2) **:** a state procession **b :** a tour or circuit made by an official (as a judge) **c :** an expedition, journey, or march through a region **2 :** a forward or onward movement (as to an objective or to a goal) **:** ADVANCE **3 :** gradual betterment; *especially* **:** the progressive development of mankind
— **in progress :** going on **:** OCCURRING
²**pro·gress** \prə-'gres\ *intransitive verb* (1539)
**1 :** to move forward **:** PROCEED
**2 :** to develop to a higher, better, or more advanced stage
**pro·gres·sion** \prə-'gre-shən\ *noun* (15th century)
**1 :** a sequence of numbers in which each term is related to its predecessor by a uniform law **2 a :** the action or process of progressing **:** ADVANCE **b :** a continuous and connected series **:** SEQUENCE
**3 a :** succession of musical tones or chords **b :** the movement of musical parts in harmony **c :** SEQUENCE 2c
— **pro·gres·sion·al** \-'gresh-nəl, -'gre-shə-n°l\ *adjective*
¹**pro·gres·sive** \prə-'gre-siv\ *adjective* (circa 1612)
**1 a :** of, relating to, or characterized by progress **b :** making use of or interested in new ideas, findings, or opportunities **c :** of, relating to, or constituting an educational theory marked by emphasis on the individual child, informality of classroom procedure, and encouragement of self-expression
**2 :** of, relating to, or characterized by progression
**3 :** moving forward or onward **:** ADVANCING
**4 a :** increasing in extent or severity ⟨a *progressive* disease⟩ **b :** increasing in rate as the base increases ⟨a *progressive* tax⟩
**5** *often capitalized* **:** of or relating to political Progressives
**6 :** of, relating to, or constituting a verb form that expresses action or state in progress at the time of speaking or a time spoken of
— **pro·gres·sive·ly** *adverb*
— **pro·gres·sive·ness** *noun*
²**progressive** *noun* (1846)
**1 a :** one that is progressive **b :** one believing in moderate political change and especially social improvement by governmental action
**2** *capitalized* **:** a member of any of various U.S. political parties: as **a :** a member of a predominantly agrarian minor party that around 1912 split off from the Republicans; *specifically* **:** BULL MOOSE **b :** a follower of Robert M. La Follette in the presidential campaign of 1924 **c :** a follower of Henry A. Wallace in the presidential campaign of 1948
**Progressive Conservative** *adjective* (1944)
**:** of or relating to a major political party in Canada traditionally advocating economic nationalism and close ties with the United Kingdom and the Commonwealth
— **Progressive Conservative** *noun*
**pro·gres·siv·ism** \prə-'gre-si-ˌvi-zəm\ *noun* (1892)
**1 :** the principles, beliefs, or practices of progressives
**2** *capitalized* **:** the political and economic doctrines advocated by the Progressives
**3 :** the theories of progressive education
— **pro·gres·siv·ist** \-vist\ *noun or adjective*
— **pro·gres·siv·is·tic** \-ˌgre-si-'vis-tik\ *adjective*
**pro·gres·siv·i·ty** \ˌprō-(ˌ)gre-'si-və-tē\ *noun* (1883)
**:** the quality or state of being a progressive tax
**pro·hib·it** \prō-'hi-bət, prə-\ *transitive verb* [Middle English, from Latin *prohibitus,* past participle of *prohibēre* to keep off, from *pro-* forward + *habēre* to hold — more at PRO-, GIVE] (15th century)
**1 :** to forbid by authority **:** ENJOIN

**2 a :** to prevent from doing something **b :** PRECLUDE
*synonym* see FORBID
**pro·hi·bi·tion** \ˌprō-ə-'bi-shən *also* ˌprō-hə-\ *noun* (14th century)
**1 :** the act of prohibiting by authority
**2 :** an order to restrain or stop
**3** *often capitalized* **:** the forbidding by law of the manufacture, transportation, and sale of alcoholic liquors except for medicinal and sacramental purposes
**pro·hi·bi·tion·ist** \-sh(ə-)nist\ *noun* (circa 1846)
**:** one who favors prohibition; *especially, capitalized* **:** a member of a minor U.S. political party advocating prohibition
**pro·hib·i·tive** \prō-'hi-bə-tiv, prə-\ *adjective* (15th century)
**1 :** tending to prohibit or restrain
**2 :** tending to preclude use or purchase ⟨*prohibitive* costs⟩
**3 :** almost certain to perform as predicted ⟨a *prohibitive* favorite⟩
— **pro·hib·i·tive·ly** *adverb*
— **pro·hib·i·tive·ness** *noun*
**pro·hib·i·to·ry** \-'hi-bə-ˌtōr-ē, -ˌtȯr-\ *adjective* (circa 1591)
**:** PROHIBITIVE
**pro·insulin** \(ˌ)prō-'in(t)-s(ə-)lən\ *noun* (1916)
**:** a single-chain pancreatic polypeptide precursor of insulin that gives rise to the double chain of insulin by loss of the middle part of the molecule
¹**proj·ect** \'prä-ˌjekt, -jikt *also* 'prō-\ *noun* [Middle English *proiecte,* from Medieval Latin *projectum,* from Latin, neuter of *projectus,* past participle of *proicere* to throw forward, from *pro-* + *jacere* to throw — more at JET] (15th century)
**1 :** a specific plan or design **:** SCHEME
**2** *obsolete* **:** IDEA
**3 :** a planned undertaking: as **a :** a definitely formulated piece of research **b :** a large usually government-supported undertaking **c :** a task or problem engaged in usually by a group of students to supplement and apply classroom studies
**4 :** a usually public housing development consisting of houses or apartments built and arranged according to a single plan
*synonym* see PLAN
²**pro·ject** \prə-'jekt\ *verb* [partly modification of Middle French *projeter,* from Old French *porjeter* to throw forward, from *por-* (from Latin *porro* forward; akin to Greek *pro* forward) + *jeter* to throw; partly from Latin *projectus,* past participle — more at FOR, JET] (15th century)
*transitive verb*
**1 a :** to devise in the mind **:** DESIGN **b :** to plan, figure, or estimate for the future ⟨*project* expenditures for the coming year⟩
**2 :** to throw or cast forward **:** THRUST
**3 :** to put or set forth **:** present for consideration
**4 :** to cause to protrude
**5 :** to cause (light or shadow) to fall into space or (an image) to fall on a surface ⟨*project* a beam of light⟩
**6 :** to reproduce (as a point, line, or area) on a surface by motion in a prescribed direction
**7 :** to display outwardly especially to an audience ⟨*project* an image⟩ ⟨an actress who could *project* amorality *—Current Biography*⟩
**8 :** to attribute (one's own ideas, feelings, or characteristics) to other people or to objects ⟨a nation is an entity on which one can *project* many of the worst of one's instincts *—Times Literary Supplement*⟩
*intransitive verb*
**1 :** to jut out **:** PROTRUDE
**2 a :** to come across vividly **:** give an impression **b :** to make oneself heard clearly
— **pro·ject·able** \-'jek-tə-bəl\ *adjective*
¹**pro·jec·tile** \prə-'jek-t°l, -ˌtīl, *chiefly British* 'prä-jik-ˌtīl\ *noun* (1665)

**1 :** a body projected by external force and continuing in motion by its own inertia; *especially* **:** a missile for a weapon (as a firearm)
**2 :** a self-propelling weapon (as a rocket)
²**projectile** *adjective* (1715)
**1 :** projecting or impelling forward ⟨a *projectile* force⟩
**2 :** capable of being thrust forward
**pro·jec·tion** \prə-'jek-shən\ *noun* (1557)
**1 a :** a systematic presentation of intersecting coordinate lines on a flat surface upon which features from the curved surface of the earth or the celestial sphere may be mapped **b :** the process or technique of reproducing a spatial object upon a plane or curved surface or a line by projecting its points; *also* **:** a graph or figure so formed
**2 :** a transforming change
**3 :** the act of throwing or thrusting forward
**4 :** the forming of a plan **:** SCHEMING
**5 a** (1) **:** a jutting out (2) **:** a part that juts out **b :** a view of a building or architectural element
**6 a :** the act of perceiving a mental object as spatially and sensibly objective; *also* **:** something so perceived **b :** the attribution of one's own ideas, feelings, or attitudes to other people or to objects; *especially* **:** the externalization of blame, guilt, or responsibility as a defense against anxiety
**7 :** the display of motion pictures by projecting an image from them upon a screen
**8 a :** the act of projecting especially to an audience **b :** control of the volume, clarity, and distinctness of a voice to gain greater audibility
**9 :** an estimate of future possibilities based on a current trend ☆
— **pro·jec·tion·al** \-shnəl, -shə-n°l\ *adjective*
**projection booth** *noun* (circa 1928)
**:** a booth in a theater or hall for housing and operating a projector and especially a motion-picture projector
**pro·jec·tion·ist** \prə-'jek-sh(ə-)nist\ *noun* (1922)
**:** one that makes projections: as **a :** CARTOGRAPHER **b :** a person who operates a motion-picture projector or television equipment
**pro·jec·tive** \prə-'jek-tiv\ *adjective* (1682)
**1 :** relating to, produced by, or involving geometric projection
**2 :** of or relating to something that indicates the psychodynamic constitution of an individual ⟨*projective* tests⟩
— **pro·jec·tive·ly** *adverb*
**projective geometry** *noun* (1885)
**:** a branch of geometry that deals with the properties of configurations that are unaltered by projection
**pro·jec·tor** \prə-'jek-tər\ *noun* (1596)
**1 :** one that plans a project; *specifically* **:** PROMOTER
**2 :** one that projects: as **a :** a device for projecting a beam of light **b :** an optical instrument for projecting an image upon a surface **c :** a machine for projecting motion pictures on a screen
**3 :** an imagined line from an object to a surface along which projection takes place

---

☆ **SYNONYMS**
**Projection, protrusion, protuberance, bulge** mean an extension beyond the normal line or surface. PROJECTION implies a jutting out especially at a sharp angle ⟨those *projections* along the wall are safety hazards⟩. PROTRUSION suggests a thrusting out so that the extension seems a deformity ⟨the bizarre *protrusions* of a coral reef⟩. PROTUBERANCE implies a growing or swelling out in rounded form ⟨a skin disease marked by warty *protuberances*⟩. BULGE suggests an expansion caused by internal pressure ⟨*bulges* in the tile floor⟩.

**pro·jet** \prō-'zhā, 'prō-\ *noun, plural* **projets** \-'zhā(z), -,zhā(z)\ [French, from Middle French *pourget*, from *pourjeter*, *projeter*] (1808)
**1 :** PLAN; *especially* **:** a draft of a proposed measure or treaty
**2 :** a projected or proposed design

**pro·kary·ote** \(,)prō-'kar-ē-,ōt\ *noun* [New Latin *Prokaryotes*, proposed subdivision of protists, from ¹*pro-* + *kary-* + *-otes*, plural noun suffix, from Greek *-ōtos* — more at -OTIC] (1963)
**:** a cellular organism (as a bacterium or a blue-green alga) that does not have a distinct nucleus — compare EUKARYOTE
**— pro·kary·ot·ic** \-,kar-ē-'ä-tik\ *adjective*

**pro·lac·tin** \prō-'lak-tən\ *noun* [²*pro-* + *lact-* + ¹*-in*] (1932)
**:** a protein hormone of the anterior lobe of the pituitary that induces lactation

**pro·la·min** *or* **pro·la·mine** \'prō-lə-mən, -,mēn\ *noun* [International Scientific Vocabulary *proline* + *ammonia* + ¹*-in*, ²*-ine*] (1908)
**:** any of various simple proteins (as zein) that are found especially in seeds and are insoluble in absolute alcohol or water

**pro·lan** \'prō-,lan\ *noun* [German, from Latin *proles* progeny — more at PROLETARIAN] (1931)
**:** either of two gonadotrophic hormones: **a :** FOLLICLE-STIMULATING HORMONE **b :** LUTEINIZING HORMONE

**¹pro·lapse** \prō-'laps, 'prō-\ *noun* [New Latin *prolapsus*, from Late Latin, fall, from Latin *prolabi* to fall or slide forward, from *pro-* forward + *labi* to slide — more at PRO-, SLEEP] (circa 1834)
**:** the falling down or slipping of a body part from its usual position or relations

**²pro·lapse** \prō-'laps\ *intransitive verb* **pro·lapsed; pro·laps·ing** (1876)
**:** to undergo prolapse

**pro·late** \'prō-,lāt\ *adjective* [Latin *prolatus* (past participle of *proferre* to bring forward, extend) from *pro-* forward + *latus*, past participle of *ferre* to carry — more at BEAR, TOLERATE] (1694)
**:** EXTENDED; *especially* **:** elongated in the direction of a line joining the poles ⟨a *prolate* spheroid⟩

**prole** \'prōl\ *noun or adjective* (1887)
**:** PROLETARIAN

**pro·leg** \'prō-,leg, -,lāg\ *noun* (1816)
**:** a fleshy leg that occurs on an abdominal segment of some insect larvae but not in the adult

**pro·le·gom·e·non** \,prō-li-'gä-mə-,nän, -nən\ *noun, plural* **-e·na** \-nə\ [Greek, neuter present passive participle of *prolegein* to say beforehand, from *pro-* before + *legein* to say — more at LEGEND] (circa 1652)
**:** prefatory remarks; *specifically* **:** a formal essay or critical discussion serving to introduce and interpret an extended work
**— pro·le·gom·e·nous** \-nəs\ *adjective*

**pro·lep·sis** \prō-'lep-səs\ *noun, plural* **-lep·ses** \-,sēz\ [Greek *prolēpsis*, from *prolambanein* to take beforehand, from *pro-* before + *lambanein* to take — more at LATCH] (1578)
**:** ANTICIPATION: as **a :** the representation or assumption of a future act or development as if presently existing or accomplished **b :** the application of an adjective to a noun in anticipation of the result of the action of the verb (as in "while yon slow oxen turn the *furrowed* plain")
**— pro·lep·tic** \-'lep-tik\ *adjective*
**— pro·lep·ti·cal·ly** \-ti-k(ə-)lē\ *adverb*

**pro·le·tar·i·an** \,prō-lə-'ter-ē-ən\ *noun* [Latin *proletarius*, from *proles* progeny, from *pro-* forth + *-oles* (akin to *alere* to nourish) — more at OLD] (1658)
**:** a member of the proletariat
**— proletarian** *adjective*

**pro·le·tar·i·an·ise** *British variant of* PROLETARIANIZE

**pro·le·tar·i·an·ize** \-'ter-ē-ə-,nīz\ *transitive verb* **-ized; -iz·ing** (1887)
**:** to reduce to a proletarian status or level
**— pro·le·tar·i·an·i·za·tion** \-,ter-ē-ə-nə-'zā-shən\ *noun*

**pro·le·tar·i·at** \,prō-lə-'ter-ē-ət, -'tar-, -ē-,at\ *noun* [French *prolétariat*, from Latin *proletarius*] (1853)
**1 :** the lowest social or economic class of a community
**2 :** the laboring class; *especially* **:** the class of industrial workers who lack their own means of production and hence sell their labor to live

**pro–life** \(,)prō-'līf\ *adjective* (1961)
**:** ANTIABORTION
**— pro–lif·er** \-'lī-fər\ *noun*

**pro·lif·er·ate** \prə-'li-fə-,rāt\ *verb* **-at·ed; -at·ing** [back-formation from *proliferation*, from French *prolifération*, from *proliférer* to proliferate, from *prolifère* reproducing freely, from Latin *proles* + *-fer* -ferous] (1873)
*intransitive verb*
**1 :** to grow by rapid production of new parts, cells, buds, or offspring
**2 :** to increase in number as if by proliferating **:** MULTIPLY
*transitive verb*
**:** to cause to grow by proliferating
**— pro·lif·er·a·tion** \-,li-fə-'rā-shən\ *noun*
**— pro·lif·er·a·tive** \-'li-fə-,rā-tiv, -f(ə-)rə-tiv\ *adjective*

**pro·lif·ic** \prə-'li-fik\ *adjective* [French *prolifique*, from Latin *proles*] (1650)
**1 :** producing young or fruit especially freely **:** FRUITFUL
**2** *archaic* **:** causing abundant growth, generation, or reproduction
**3 :** marked by abundant inventiveness or productivity ⟨a *prolific* composer⟩
*synonym* see FERTILE
**— pro·lif·i·ca·cy** \-'li-fi-kə-sē\ *noun*
**— pro·lif·i·cal·ly** \-fi-k(ə-)lē\ *adverb*
**— pro·lif·ic·ness** \-fik-nəs\ *noun*

**pro·li·fic·i·ty** \,prō-lə-'fi-sə-tē\ *noun* (1725)
**:** prolific power or character

**pro·line** \'prō-,lēn\ *noun* [German *Prolin*] (1904)
**:** an amino acid $C_5H_9NO_2$ that can be synthesized by animals from glutamate

**pro·lix** \prō-'liks, 'prō-(,)\ *adjective* [Middle English, from Middle French & Latin; Middle French *prolixe*, from Latin *prolixus* extended, from *pro-* forward + *liquēre* to be fluid — more at LIQUID] (15th century)
**1 :** unduly prolonged or drawn out **:** too long
**2 :** marked by or using an excess of words
*synonym* see WORDY
**— pro·lix·i·ty** \prō-'lik-sə-tē\ *noun*
**— pro·lix·ly** *adverb*

**pro·loc·u·tor** \prō-'lä-kyə-tər\ *noun* [Middle English, from Latin, from *pro-* for + *locutor* speaker, from *loqui* to speak] (15th century)
**1 :** one who speaks for another **:** SPOKESMAN
**2 :** presiding officer **:** CHAIRMAN

**pro·lo·gize** \'prō-,lō-,gīz, -,lä-; -lə-,jīz\ *or* **pro·lo·gu·ize** \-,lō-,gīz, -,lä-\ *intransitive verb* **-log·ized** *or* **-logu·ized; -log·iz·ing** *or* **-logu·iz·ing** (1608)
**:** to write or speak a prologue

**pro·logue** *also* **pro·log** \'prō-,lóg, -,läg\ *noun* [Middle English *prolog*, from Middle French *prologue*, from Latin *prologus* preface to a play, from Greek *prologos* part of a Greek play preceding the entry of the chorus, from *pro-* before + *legein* to speak — more at PRO-, LEGEND] (14th century)
**1 :** the preface or introduction to a literary work
**2 a :** a speech often in verse addressed to the audience by an actor at the beginning of a play **b :** the actor speaking such a prologue
**3 :** an introductory or preceding event or development

**pro·long** \prə-'lóŋ\ *transitive verb* [Middle English, from Middle French *prolonguer*, from Late Latin *prolongare*, from Latin *pro-* forward + *longus* long] (15th century)
**1 :** to lengthen in time **:** CONTINUE
**2 :** to lengthen in extent, scope, or range
*synonym* see EXTEND
**— pro·long·er** \-'lóŋ-ər\ *noun*

**pro·lon·ga·tion** \(,)prō-,lóŋ-'gā-shən, prə-\ *noun* (15th century)
**1 :** an extension or lengthening in time or duration
**2 :** an expansion or continuation in extent, scope, or range

**pro·lu·sion** \prō-'lü-zhən\ *noun* [Latin *prolusion-, prolusio*, from *proludere* to play beforehand, from *pro-* before + *ludere* to play — more at LUDICROUS] (1601)
**1 :** a preliminary trial or exercise **:** PRELUDE
**2 :** an introductory and often tentative discourse
**— pro·lu·so·ry** \-'lü-sə-rē, -zə-; -'lüz-rē, -'lüz-\ *adjective*

**prom** \'präm\ *noun* [short for *promenade*] (1894)
**1 :** a formal dance given by a high school or college class
**2** *British* **:** PROMENADE 2

**¹prom·e·nade** \,prä-mə-'nād, -'näd\ *verb* **-nad·ed; -nad·ing** [²*promenade*] (1588)
*intransitive verb*
**1 :** to take or go on a promenade
**2 :** to perform a promenade in a dance
*transitive verb*
**:** to walk about in or on
**— prom·e·nad·er** *noun*

**²promenade** *noun* [French, from *promener* to take for a walk, from Latin *prominare* to drive forward, from *pro-* forward + *minare* to drive — more at AMENABLE] (1648)
**1 :** a place for strolling
**2 :** a leisurely walk or ride especially in a public place for pleasure or display
**3 a :** a ceremonious opening of a formal ball consisting of a grand march of all the guests **b :** a figure in a square dance in which couples move counterclockwise in a circle

◇ **WORD HISTORY**
**proletariat** The Latin adjective *proletarius* "pertaining to the lowest class of citizens" was a derivative of *proles* "offspring, progeny," the Roman conception apparently being that the humblest citizens had nothing to contribute to the state but their offspring. *Proletarius* was borrowed into French as *prolétaire*, which in the writing of early French socialists such as Saint-Simon was applied to the working class, that is, those people who did not own property and lived solely off their wages. In 1832 the socialist philosopher Pierre Leroux first used the derivative noun *prolétariat* to refer to this class. The concept of the proletariat was refined by Karl Marx, whose "scientific socialism" ousted French utopianism, and French *prolétariat* was borrowed into nearly every language of Europe, including English. The phrase *dictature du prolétariat* "dictatorship of the proletariat," which apparently first surfaced in Paris in 1850, in a manifesto of a revolutionary group inspired by the agitator Louis-Auguste Blanqui, was taken up by Marx in the same year and became a staple of communism. Under Lenin it was synonymous with the dictatorship of the party and became a license for ruthless suppression of dissent in the name of the proletariat.

**promenade deck** *noun* (1829)
: an upper deck or an area on a deck of a passenger ship where passengers stroll

**Pro·me·the·an** \prə-'mē-thē-ən\ *adjective* (1588)
: of, relating to, or resembling Prometheus, his experiences, or his art; *especially* : daringly original or creative

**Pro·me·theus** \-thē-əs, -,thyüs\ *noun* [Latin, from Greek *Promētheus*]
: a Titan who is chained and tortured by Zeus for stealing fire from heaven and giving it to mankind

**pro·me·thi·um** \-thē-əm\ *noun* [New Latin, from Latin *Prometheus*] (1948)
: a radioactive metallic element of the rare-earth group obtained as a fission product of uranium or from neutron-irradiated neodymium — see ELEMENT table

**prom·i·nence** \'prä-mə-nən(t)s, 'präm-nən(t)s\ *noun* (1598)
**1** : something prominent : PROJECTION ⟨a rocky *prominence*⟩
**2** : the quality, state, or fact of being prominent or conspicuous
**3** : a mass of gas resembling a cloud that arises from the chromosphere of the sun

**prom·i·nent** \-nənt\ *adjective* [Middle English *promynent*, from Latin *prominent-, prominens*, from present participle of *prominēre* to jut forward, from *pro-* forward + *-minēre* (akin to *mont-, mons* mountain) — more at MOUNT] (15th century)
**1** : standing out or projecting beyond a surface or line : PROTUBERANT
**2 a** : readily noticeable : CONSPICUOUS **b** : widely and popularly known : LEADING
**synonym** see NOTICEABLE
— **prom·i·nent·ly** *adverb*

**pro·mis·cu·i·ty** \,prä-mə-'skyü-ə-tē, ,prō-\ *noun, plural* **-ties** (circa 1849)
**1** : a miscellaneous mixture or mingling of persons or things
**2** : promiscuous sexual behavior

**pro·mis·cu·ous** \prə-'mis-kyə-wəs\ *adjective* [Latin *promiscuus*, from *pro-* forth + *miscēre* to mix — more at PRO-, MIX] (1603)
**1** : composed of all sorts of persons or things
**2** : not restricted to one class, sort, or person : INDISCRIMINATE ⟨education . . . cheapened through the *promiscuous* distribution of diplomas —Norman Cousins⟩
**3** : not restricted to one sexual partner
**4** : CASUAL, IRREGULAR ⟨*promiscuous* eating habits⟩
— **pro·mis·cu·ous·ly** *adverb*
— **pro·mis·cu·ous·ness** *noun*

**¹prom·ise** \'prä-məs\ *noun* [Middle English *promis*, from Latin *promissum*, from neuter of *promissus*, past participle of *promittere* to send forth, promise, from *pro-* forth + *mittere* to send] (15th century)
**1 a** : a declaration that one will do or refrain from doing something specified **b** : a legally binding declaration that gives the person to whom it is made a right to expect or to claim the performance or forbearance of a specified act
**2** : reason to expect something ⟨little *promise* of relief⟩; *especially* : ground for expectation of success, improvement, or excellence ⟨shows considerable *promise*⟩
**3** : something that is promised

**²promise** *verb* **prom·ised; prom·is·ing** (15th century)
*transitive verb*
**1** : to pledge to do, bring about, or provide ⟨*promise* aid⟩
**2** *archaic* : WARRANT, ASSURE
**3** *chiefly dialect* : BETROTH
**4** : to suggest beforehand : give promise of ⟨dark clouds *promise* rain⟩
*intransitive verb*
**1** : to make a promise

**2** : to give ground for expectation : be imminent
— **prom·is·ee** \,prä-mə-'sē\ *noun*
— **prom·i·sor** \-'sòr\ *also* **prom·is·er** \'prä-mə-sər\ *noun*

**promised land** *noun* (1667)
: something and especially a place or condition believed to promise final satisfaction or realization of hopes

**prom·is·ing** \'prä-mə-siŋ\ *adjective* (1601)
: full of promise : likely to succeed or to yield good results
— **prom·is·ing·ly** \-siŋ-lē\ *adverb*

**prom·is·so·ry** \'prä-mə-,sōr-ē, -,sòr-\ *adjective* [Middle English *promissorye*, from Medieval Latin *promissorius*, from Latin *promittere*] (15th century)
: containing or conveying a promise or assurance

**promissory note** *noun* (1710)
: a written promise to pay at a fixed or determinable future time a sum of money to a specified individual or to bearer

**pro·mo** \'prō-(,)mō\ *noun, plural* **promos** *often attributive* [short for *promotional*] (1946)
: a promotional announcement, blurb, or appearance

**prom·on·to·ry** \'prä-mən-,tōr-ē, -,tòr-\ *noun, plural* **-ries** [Latin *promunturium, promontorium*; probably akin to *prominēre* to jut forth — more at PROMINENT] (1548)
**1 a** : a high point of land or rock projecting into a body of water **b** : a prominent mass of land overlooking or projecting into a lowland
**2** : a bodily prominence

**pro·mote** \prə-'mōt\ *transitive verb* **pro·mot·ed; pro·mot·ing** [Middle English, from Latin *promotus*, past participle of *promovēre*, literally, to move forward, from *pro-* forward + *movēre* to move] (14th century)
**1 a** : to advance in station, rank, or honor : RAISE **b** : to change (a pawn) into a piece in chess by moving to the eighth rank **c** : to advance (a student) from one grade to the next higher grade
**2 a** : to contribute to the growth or prosperity of : FURTHER ⟨*promote* international understanding⟩ **b** : to help bring (as an enterprise) into being : LAUNCH **c** : to present (merchandise) for buyer acceptance through advertising, publicity, or discounting
**3** *slang* : to get possession of by doubtful means or by ingenuity
**synonym** see ADVANCE
— **pro·mot·abil·i·ty** \-,mō-tə-'bi-lə-tē\ *noun*
— **pro·mot·able** \-'mō-tə-bəl\ *adjective*

**pro·mot·er** \-'mō-tər\ *noun* (14th century)
**1** : one that promotes; *especially* : one who assumes the financial responsibilities of a sporting event (as a boxing match) including contracting with the principals, renting the site, and collecting gate receipts
**2** *obsolete* : PROSECUTOR
**3** : a substance that in very small amounts is able to increase the activity of a catalyst
**4** : a binding site in a DNA chain at which RNA polymerase binds to initiate transcription of messenger RNA by one or more nearby structural genes

**pro·mo·tion** \prə-'mō-shən\ *noun* (15th century)
**1** : the act or fact of being raised in position or rank : PREFERMENT
**2** : the act of furthering the growth or development of something; *especially* : the furtherance of the acceptance and sale of merchandise through advertising, publicity, or discounting
— **pro·mo·tion·al** \-shnəl, -shə-n°l\ *adjective*

**pro·mo·tive** \-'mō-tiv\ *adjective* (1644)
: tending or serving to promote
— **pro·mo·tive·ness** *noun*

**¹prompt** \'präm(p)t\ *transitive verb* [Middle English, from Medieval Latin *promptare*, from Latin *promptus* prompt] (14th century)
**1** : to move to action : INCITE
**2** : to assist (one acting or reciting) by suggesting or saying the next words of something forgotten or imperfectly learned : CUE
**3** : to serve as the inciting cause of
— **prompt·er** *noun*

**²prompt** *adjective* (1784)
: of or relating to prompting actors

**³prompt** *adjective* [Middle English, from Middle French or Latin; Middle French, from Latin *promptus* ready, prompt, from past participle of *promere* to bring forth, from *pro-* forth + *emere* to take — more at REDEEM] (15th century)
**1** : being ready and quick to act as occasion demands
**2** : performed readily or immediately ⟨*prompt* assistance⟩
**synonym** see QUICK
— **prompt·ly** \'präm(p)t-lē, 'präm-plē\ *adverb*
— **prompt·ness** \'präm(p)t-nəs, 'prämp-nəs\ *noun*

**⁴prompt** *noun, plural* **prompts** \'präm(p)ts, 'prämps\ (1597)
**1** [¹*prompt*] : something that prompts : REMINDER
**2** [³*prompt*] : a limit of time given for payment of an account for goods purchased; *also* : the contract by which this time is fixed

**prompt·book** \'präm(p)t-,bùk, 'prämp-,bùk\ *noun* (1809)
: a copy of a play with directions for performance used by a theater prompter

**promp·ti·tude** \'präm(p)-tə-,tüd, -,tyüd\ *noun* [Middle English, from Middle French or Late Latin; Middle French, from Late Latin *promptitudo*, from Latin *promptus*] (15th century)
: the quality or habit of being prompt : PROMPTNESS

**prompt side** *noun* (1824)
**1** : the side of the stage adjacent to the prompter's corner
**2** : the side of the stage to the right of an actor facing the audience

**pro·mul·gate** \'prä-məl-,gāt; prō-'məl-, prə-', 'prō-(,)\ *transitive verb* **-gat·ed; -gat·ing** [Latin *promulgatus*, past participle of *promulgare*, from *pro-* forward + *-mulgare* (probably akin to *mulgēre* to milk, extract) — more at EMULSION] (1530)
**1** : to make known by open declaration : PROCLAIM
**2 a** : to make known or public the terms of (a proposed law) **b** : to put (a law) into action or force
**synonym** see DECLARE
— **pro·mul·ga·tion** \,prä-məl-'gā-shən; ,prō-(,)məl-, (,)prō-\ *noun*
— **pro·mul·ga·tor** \'prä-məl-,gā-tər; prō-'məl-, prə-', 'prō-(,)\ *noun*

**pro·na·tion** \prō-'nā-shən\ *noun* [*pronate*, from Late Latin *pronatus*, past participle of *pronare* to bend forward, from Latin *pronus*] (1666)
**1** : rotation of the hand and forearm so that the palm faces backwards or downwards
**2** : rotation of the medial bones in the midtarsal region of the foot inward and downward so that in walking the foot tends to come down on its inner margin
— **pro·nate** \'prō-,nāt\ *verb*

**pro·na·tor** \'prō-,nā-tər\ *noun* (circa 1741)
: a muscle that produces pronation

**prone** \'prōn\ *adjective* [Middle English, from Latin *pronus* bent forward, tending; akin to Latin *pro* forward — more at FOR] (14th century)
**1** : having a tendency or inclination : being likely ⟨*prone* to forget names⟩ ⟨accident-*prone*⟩

**2 a :** having the front or ventral surface downward **b :** lying flat or prostrate ☆ ■
— **prone** *adverb*
— **prone·ly** *adverb*
— **prone·ness** \'prōn-nəs\ *noun*
**pro·neph·ros** \(,)prō-'ne-frəs, -,fräs\ *noun* [New Latin, from Greek *pro-* + *nephros* kidney — more at NEPHRITIS] (1881)
**:** either member of the first and most anterior pair of the three successive paired vertebrate renal organs that functions in the adults of amphioxus and some lampreys, functions temporarily in larval fishes and amphibians, and is present but nonfunctional in embryos of reptiles, birds, and mammals — compare MESONEPHROS, METANEPHROS
— **pro·neph·ric** \-frik\ *adjective*
**¹prong** \'prȯŋ, 'präŋ\ *noun* [Middle English *pronge*] (15th century)
**1 :** FORK
**2 :** a tine of a fork
**3 :** a slender pointed or projecting part: as **a** **:** a fang of a tooth **b :** a point of an antler
**4 :** something resembling a prong
**²prong** *transitive verb* (1848)
**:** to stab, pierce, or break up with a pronged device
**pronged** \'prȯŋd, 'präŋd\ *adjective* (1767)
**1 :** having a usually specified number of prongs — usually used in combination ⟨a three-*pronged* fork⟩
**2 :** having a usually specified number of parts or approaches ⟨a two-*pronged* strategy⟩
**prong·horn** \'prȯŋ-,hȯrn, 'präŋ-\ *noun, plural* **pronghorn** *or* **pronghorns** (1823)
**:** a ruminant mammal (*Antilocapra americana*) of treeless parts of western North America that resembles an antelope — called also *pronghorn antelope*
**pro·nom·i·nal** \prō-'nä-mə-nᵊl, -'näm-nəl\ *adjective* [Late Latin *pronominalis*, from Latin *pronomin-, pronomen*] (1680)

**pronghorn**

**1 :** of, relating to, or constituting a pronoun
**2 :** resembling a pronoun in identifying or specifying without describing ⟨the *pronominal* adjective *this* in *this* dog⟩
— **pro·nom·i·nal·ly** *adverb*
**pro·noun** \'prō-,naun\ *noun* [Middle English *pronom*, from Latin *pronomin-, pronomen*, from *pro-* for + *nomin-, nomen* name — more at PRO-, NAME] (1530)
**:** any of a small set of words in a language that are used as substitutes for nouns or noun phrases and whose referents are named or understood in the context
**pro·nounce** \prə-'naun(t)s\ *verb* **pro·nounced; pro·nounc·ing** [Middle English, from Middle French *prononcier*, from Latin *pronuntiare*, from *pro-* forth + *nuntiare* to report, from *nuntius* messenger — more at PRO-] (14th century)
*transitive verb*
**1 :** to declare officially or ceremoniously ⟨the minister *pronounced* them husband and wife⟩
**2 :** to declare authoritatively or as an opinion ⟨doctors *pronounced* him fit to resume duties⟩
**3 a :** to employ the organs of speech to produce ⟨*pronounce* these words⟩; *especially* **:** to say correctly ⟨I can't *pronounce* his name⟩ **b :** to represent in printed characters the spoken counterpart of (an orthographic representation) ⟨both dictionaries *pronounce clique* the same⟩
**4 :** RECITE ⟨speak the speech, I pray you, as I *pronounced* it to you —Shakespeare⟩
*intransitive verb*
**1 :** to pass judgment
**2 :** to produce the components of spoken language

— **pro·nounce·abil·i·ty** \-,naun(t)-sə-'bi-lə-tē\ *noun*
— **pro·nounce·able** \-'naun(t)-sə-bəl\ *adjective*
— **pro·nounc·er** *noun*
**pro·nounced** \-'naun(t)st\ *adjective* (circa 1741)
**:** strongly marked **:** DECIDED
— **pro·nounc·ed·ly** \-'naun(t)-səd-lē, -'naun(t)st-lē\ *adverb*
**pro·nounce·ment** \prə-'naun(t)s-mənt\ *noun* (1593)
**1 :** a usually formal declaration of opinion
**2 :** an authoritative announcement
**pronouncing** *adjective* (1764)
**:** relating to or indicating pronunciation ⟨a *pronouncing* dictionary⟩
**pron·to** \'prän-,tō\ *adverb* [Spanish, from Latin *promptus* prompt] (circa 1740)
**:** without delay
**¹pro·nu·clear** \(,)prō-'nü-klē-ər, -'nyü-, ÷-kyə-lər\ *adjective* [*pronucleus*] (circa 1890)
**:** of, relating to, or resembling a pronucleus
**²pronuclear** *adjective* [²*pro-* + *nuclear*] (1971)
**:** advocating the use of nuclear-powered generating stations
**pro·nu·cle·us** \(,)prō-'nü-klē-əs, -'nyü-\ *noun* [New Latin] (1880)
**:** the haploid nucleus of a male or female gamete (as an egg or sperm) up to the time of fusion with that of another gamete in fertilization
**pro·nun·ci·a·men·to** \prō-,nən(t)-sē-ə-'men-(,)tō\ *noun, plural* **-tos** *or* **-toes** [modification of Spanish *pronunciamiento*, from *pronunciar* to pronounce, from Latin *pronuntiare*] (1835)
**:** PROCLAMATION, PRONOUNCEMENT
**pro·nun·ci·a·tion** \prə-,nən(t)-sē-'ā-shən *also* ÷-,naun(t)-\ *noun* [Middle English *pronunciacion*, from Middle French *prononciation*, from Latin *pronuntiation-, pronuntiatio*, from *pronuntiare*] (15th century)
**:** the act or manner of pronouncing something ■
— **pro·nun·ci·a·tion·al** \-shnəl, -shə-nᵊl\ *adjective*
**¹proof** \'prüf\ *noun* [Middle English, alteration of *preove*, from Old French *preuve*, from Late Latin *proba*, from Latin *probare* to prove — more at PROVE] (13th century)
**1 a :** the cogency of evidence that compels acceptance by the mind of a truth or a fact **b :** the process or an instance of establishing the validity of a statement especially by derivation from other statements in accordance with principles of reasoning
**2** *obsolete* **:** EXPERIENCE
**3 :** something that induces certainty or establishes validity
**4** *archaic* **:** the quality or state of having been tested or tried; *especially* **:** unyielding hardness
**5 :** evidence operating to determine the finding or judgment of a tribunal
**6 a** *plural* **proofs** *or* **proof :** a copy (as of typeset text) made for examination or correction **b :** a test impression of an engraving, etching, or lithograph **c :** a coin that is struck from a highly-polished die on a polished planchet, is not intended for circulation, and sometimes differs in metallic content from coins of identical design struck for circulation **d :** a test photographic print made from a negative
**7 :** a test applied to articles or substances to determine whether they are of standard or satisfactory quality
**8 a :** the minimum alcoholic strength of proof spirit **b :** strength with reference to the standard for proof spirit; *specifically* **:** alcoholic strength indicated by a number that is twice the percent by volume of alcohol present ⟨whiskey of 90 *proof* is 45% alcohol⟩

**²proof** *adjective* (1592)
**1 :** able to resist or repel ⟨boots that were . . . *proof* against cold and wet —Robertson Davies⟩ — often used in combination ⟨wind-*proof*⟩
**2 :** used in proving or testing or as a standard of comparison

☆ **SYNONYMS**
**Prone, supine, prostrate, recumbent** mean lying down. PRONE implies a position with the front of the body turned toward the supporting surface ⟨push-ups require a *prone* position⟩. SUPINE implies lying on one's back and suggests inertness or abjectness ⟨lying *supine* on the couch⟩. PROSTRATE implies lying full-length as in submission, defeat, or physical collapse ⟨a runner fell *prostrate* at the finish line⟩. RECUMBENT implies the posture of one sleeping or resting ⟨a patient comfortably *recumbent* in a hospital bed⟩. See in addition LIABLE.

□ **USAGE**
**prone** Most commentators insist on the distinction between *prone* and *supine* spelled out in the synonymy paragraph above. The distinction is indeed observed by those writing on physiology and anatomy, and *prone* always means lying on one's belly to those who shoot guns and write about it: But *prone* has wider application: it is used of inanimate objects to mean simply "lying flat" ⟨the *prone* golden autumn harvest of leaves —Michael P. O'Connor⟩ and is also used of the body when its orientation is uncertain or unimportant ⟨I caught sight of the large *prone* figure in bed —D. H. Lawrence⟩ ⟨I too have been *prone* on my couch this week, a victim of the common cold —Flannery O'Connor⟩. Sometimes it is used where *supine* could be used ⟨he lies *prone*, his face to the sky —James Joyce⟩; such use may come from a conscious avoidance of the pejorative overtones of sense 2 of *supine*. *Supine* is a relatively rare word, so apparently most writers find a way around it. Both *prone* and *supine* are more commonly used in their figurative senses.

**pronunciation** As if to prove the inherently controversial nature of English pronunciation, the very word *pronunciation* has given rise to not one, but two disputes. The first has to do with the sound of the letter *c* before *i*: should it be articulated as an \s\ as in *précis* or as an \sh\ as in *specialty*? The *ci* sequence in *species, uncial, preciosity*, and *sociologist* is heard both ways, though in many familiar words of Latin derivation the *c* before *i* is pronounced only as \sh\: *special, precious, superficial, judicious*. No fast rule obtains for the Latinate *ci*, though, and thus common usage has dictated the \s\ sound for *pronunciation*. The second issue is that some substitute the syllable \-,naun(t)-\ for \-,nən(t)-\, perhaps wanting unconsciously to preserve the relatedness of *pronounce* and *pronunciation*. The same speakers do not, however, extend the analogy to the pronunciation of *annunciation* or *denunciation*. The \-,naun(t)-\ variant has never established itself as an accepted form. Again, common usage overwhelmingly dictates the *pronunciation* \prə-,nən(t)-sē-'ā-shən\.

\ə\ abut \ᵊ\ kitten \ər\ further \a\ ash \ā\ ace
\ä\ mop, mar \au̇\ out \ch\ chin \e\ bet \ē\ easy
\g\ go \i\ hit \ī\ ice \j\ job \ŋ\ sing \ō\ go
\ȯ\ law \ȯi\ boy \th\ thin \th\ the \ü\ loot \u̇\ foot
\y\ yet \zh\ vision *see also* Guide to Pronunciation

## PROOFREADERS' MARKS

| | |
|---|---|
| ℰ or γ or ℒ | delete; take it out |
| ⌒ | close up; print as one word |
| ℰ⌒ | delete and close up |
| ∧ or ⟩ or ⋏ | caret; insert here ⟨something⟩ |
| # | insert a space |
| eq# | space evenly where indicated |
| stet | let marked text stand as set |
| tr | transpose change order the |
| / | used to separate two or more marks and often as a concluding stroke at the end of an insertion |
| ⊏ ⌊ | set farther to the left |
| ⊐ set⌋ | farther to the right |
| ⌢ | set æ or fl as ligatures æ or fl |
| = | straighten alignment |
| ‖ ⦀ | straighten or align |
| ✗ | imperfect or broken character |
| ⊓ | indent or insert em quad space |
| ¶ | begin a new paragraph |
| SP | spell out ⟨set 5 lbs as five pounds⟩ |
| cap | set in capitals ⟨CAPITALS⟩ |
| sm cap or s.c. | set in small capitals ⟨SMALL CAPITALS⟩ |
| lc | set in lowercase ⟨lowercase⟩ |

| | |
|---|---|
| ital | set in italic ⟨italic⟩ |
| rom | set in roman ⟨roman⟩ |
| bf | set in boldface ⟨**boldface**⟩ |
| = or -/ or ⌒ or /H/ | hyphen |
| 1/N or en or /N/ | en dash ⟨1965–72⟩ |
| 1/M or em or /M/ | em — or long — dash |
| ∨ | superscript or superior ⟨∨2 as in πr²⟩ |
| ∧ | subscript or inferior ⟨∧2 as in H₂O⟩ |
| ∨ or ⋎ | centered ⟨⊙for a centered dot in p · q⟩ |
| ↻ | comma |
| ∨ | apostrophe |
| ⊙ | period |
| ; or ;/ | semicolon |
| : or ⊙ | colon |
| or | quotation marks |
| (/) | parentheses |
| ⌊/⌋ | brackets |
| OK/? | query to author: has this been set as intended? |
| ⊥ or ⊥¹ | push down a work-up |
| ↺¹ | turn over an inverted letter |
| wf¹ | wrong font; a character of the wrong size or esp. style |

¹ The last three symbols are unlikely to be needed in marking proofs of photocomposed matter.

---

**3 :** of standard strength or quality or alcoholic content

**³proof** *transitive verb* (1745)
**1 a :** to make or take a proof or test of **b :** PROOFREAD
**2 :** to give a resistant quality to
**3 :** to activate (yeast) by mixing with water and sometimes sugar or milk
**— proof·er** *noun*

**proof·read** \'prüf-ˌrēd\ *transitive verb* **-read** \-ˌred\; **-read·ing** [back-formation from *proofreader*] (1920)
**:** to read and mark corrections in (as a proof)

**proof·read·er** \-ˌrē-dər\ *noun* (1832)
**:** a person who proofreads

**proof·room** \'prüf-ˌrüm, -ˌrùm\ *noun* (1903)
**:** a room for proofreading

**proof spirit** *noun* (1790)
**:** an alcoholic liquor or mixture of ethanol and water that contains 50% ethanol by volume at 60°F (16°C)

**¹prop** \'präp\ *noun* [Middle English *proppe*, from Middle Dutch, stopper; akin to Middle Low German *proppe* stopper] (15th century)
**:** something that props or sustains : SUPPORT

**²prop** *transitive verb* **propped; prop·ping** (1538)
**1 a :** to support by placing something under or against — often used with *up* **b :** to support by placing against something
**2 :** SUSTAIN, STRENGTHEN

**³prop** *noun* (1841)
**:** PROPERTY 3

**⁴prop** *noun* (1914)
**:** PROPELLER

**prop-** *combining form* [International Scientific Vocabulary, from *propionic (acid)*]
**:** related to propionic acid ⟨*propane*⟩ ⟨*propyl*⟩

**pro·pae·deu·tic** \ˌprō-pi-'dü-tik, -'dyü-\ *noun* [Greek *propaideuein* to teach beforehand,

from *pro-* before + *paideuein* to teach, from *paid-, pais* child — more at PRO-, FEW] (1798)
**:** preparatory study or instruction
**— propaedeutic** *adjective*

**pro·pa·gan·da** \ˌprä-pə-'gan-də, ˌprō-\ *noun* [New Latin, from *Congregatio de propaganda fide* Congregation for propagating the faith, organization established by Pope Gregory XV (died 1623)] (1718)
**1** *capitalized* **:** a congregation of the Roman curia having jurisdiction over missionary territories and related institutions
**2 :** the spreading of ideas, information, or rumor for the purpose of helping or injuring an institution, a cause, or a person
**3 :** ideas, facts, or allegations spread deliberately to further one's cause or to damage an opposing cause; *also* **:** a public action having such an effect ◆
**— pro·pa·gan·dist** \-dist\ *noun or adjective*
**— pro·pa·gan·dis·tic** \-ˌgan-'dis-tik\ *adjective*
**— pro·pa·gan·dis·ti·cal·ly** \-ti-k(ə-)lē\ *adverb*

**pro·pa·gan·dize** \-'gan-ˌdīz\ *verb* **-dized; -diz·ing** (1844)
*transitive verb*
**:** to subject to propaganda; *also* **:** to carry on propaganda for
*intransitive verb*
**:** to carry on propaganda
**— pro·pa·gan·diz·er** \-ˌdī-zər\ *noun*

**prop·a·gate** \'prä-pə-ˌgāt\ *verb* **-gat·ed; -gat·ing** [Latin *propagatus*, past participle of *propagare* to set slips, propagate, from *propages* slip, offspring, from *pro-* before + *pangere* to fasten — more at PRO-, PACT] (circa 1570)
*transitive verb*

**1 :** to cause to continue or increase by sexual or asexual reproduction
**2 :** to pass along to offspring
**3 a :** to cause to spread out and affect a greater number or greater area : EXTEND **b :** to foster

◇ WORD HISTORY
**propaganda** In 1622, in an effort to centralize the missionary activities of the Roman Catholic Church overseas, Pope Gregory XV issued a bull by which he established the *Congregatio de propaganda fide* ("Congregation for the Propagation of the Faith"), a committee of cardinals charged with the administration of ecclesiastical affairs in non-Catholic countries. The name of the office was informally shortened to *Propaganda,* a word that became current in several European vernaculars, including English. During the French Revolution, the French form *propagande* was generalized to mean any group whose purpose was to spread views or principles, especially of a political nature, and then to mean the activity of spreading such views. The latter meaning of the word was taken up by English, German, Russian, and other languages. The association of *propaganda* in various languages with the promulgation of subversive political or economic ideas by revolutionary groups gave it a negative connotation in the 19th and 20th centuries. In extremist circles of both the left and right, though, it simply came to mean "inculcation of correct political views," and German *Propaganda* was a positive term to both the Nazis and the Communist regime that succeeded the Nazis in eastern Germany.

growing knowledge of, familiarity with, or acceptance of (as an idea or belief) **:** PUBLICIZE **c** **:** to transmit (as sound or light) through a medium
*intransitive verb*
**1 :** to multiply sexually or asexually
**2 :** INCREASE, EXTEND
**3 :** to travel through space or a material — used of wave energy (as light, sound, or radio waves)
— **prop·a·ga·ble** \'prä-pə-gə-bəl\ *adjective*
— **prop·a·ga·tive** \-,gā-tiv\ *adjective*
— **prop·a·ga·tor** \-,gā-tər\ *noun*
**prop·a·ga·tion** \,prä-pə-'gā-shən\ *noun* (15th century)
**:** the act or action of propagating: as **a :** increase (as of a kind of organism) in numbers **b :** the spreading of something (as a belief) abroad or into new regions **c :** enlargement or extension (as of a crack) in a solid body
**prop·a·gule** \'prä-pə-,gyü(ə)l\ *noun* [New Latin *propagulum*, from Latin *propages* slip] (1858)
**:** a structure (as a cutting, a seed, or a spore) that propagates a plant
**pro·pane** \'prō-,pān\ *noun* [International Scientific Vocabulary *prop- + -ane*] (1866)
**:** a heavy flammable gaseous alkane $C_3H_8$ found in crude petroleum and natural gas and used especially as fuel and in chemical synthesis
**pro·pel** \prə-'pel\ *transitive verb* **pro·pelled; pro·pel·ling** [Middle English *propellen*, from Latin *propellere*, from *pro-* before + *pellere* to drive — more at FELT] (15th century)
**:** to drive forward or onward by or as if by means of a force that imparts motion
¹**pro·pel·lant** *also* **pro·pel·lent** \-'pe-lənt\ *adjective* (1644)
**:** capable of propelling
²**propellant** *also* **propellent** *noun* (1814)
**:** something that propels: as **a :** an explosive for propelling projectiles **b :** fuel plus oxidizer used by a rocket engine **c :** a gas kept under pressure in a bottle or can for expelling the contents when the pressure is released
**pro·pel·ler** *also* **pro·pel·lor** \prə-'pe-lər\ *noun* (1780)
**:** one that propels; *especially* **:** a device that consists of a central hub with radiating blades placed and twisted so that each forms part of a helical surface and that is used to propel a vehicle (as a ship or airplane)
**pro·pend** \prō-'pend\ *intransitive verb* [Latin *propendēre*, from *pro-* before + *pendēre* to hang — more at PENDANT] (1545)
*obsolete* **:** INCLINE
**pro·pense** \prō-'pen(t)s\ *adjective* [Latin *propensus*, past participle of *propendēre*] (1528)
*archaic* **:** leaning or inclining toward **:** DISPOSED
**pro·pen·si·ty** \prə-'pen(t)-sə-tē\ *noun, plural* **-ties** (1570)
**:** an often intense natural inclination or preference
*synonym* see LEANING
¹**prop·er** \'prä-pər\ *adjective* [Middle English *propre* proper, own, from Middle French, from Latin *proprius* own] (14th century)
**1 a :** referring to one individual only **b :** belonging to one **:** OWN **c :** appointed for the liturgy of a particular day **d :** represented heraldically in natural color
**2 :** belonging characteristically to a species or individual **:** PECULIAR
**3** *chiefly dialect* **:** GOOD-LOOKING, HANDSOME
**4 :** very good **:** EXCELLENT
**5** *chiefly British* **:** UTTER, ABSOLUTE
**6 :** strictly limited to a specified thing, place, or idea ⟨the city *proper*⟩
**7 a :** strictly accurate **:** CORRECT **b** *archaic* **:** VIRTUOUS, RESPECTABLE **c :** strictly decorous **:** GENTEEL
**8 :** marked by suitability, rightness, or appropriateness **:** FIT

**9 :** being a mathematical subset (as a subgroup) that does not contain all the elements of the inclusive set from which it is derived
*synonym* see FIT
— **prop·er·ly** *adverb*
— **prop·er·ness** *noun*
²**proper** *noun* (15th century)
**1 :** the parts of the Mass that vary according to the liturgical calendar
**2 :** the part of a missal or breviary containing the proper of the Mass and the offices proper to the holy days of the liturgical year
³**proper** *adverb* (15th century)
*chiefly dialect* **:** in a thorough manner **:** COMPLETELY
**proper adjective** *noun* (1905)
**:** an adjective that is formed from a proper noun and that is usually capitalized in English
**pro·per·din** \prō-'pər-d°n\ *noun* [probably from ¹*pro-* + Latin *perdere* to destroy + English ¹*-in* — more at PERDITION] (1954)
**:** a serum protein that participates in destruction of bacteria, neutralization of viruses, and lysis of red blood cells
**proper fraction** *noun* (1674)
**:** a fraction in which the numerator is less or of lower degree than the denominator
**proper noun** *noun* (circa 1890)
**:** a noun that designates a particular being or thing, does not take a limiting modifier, and is usually capitalized in English — called also *proper name*
**prop·er·tied** \'prä-pər-tēd\ *adjective* (circa 1772)
**:** possessing property
**prop·er·ty** \'prä-pər-tē\ *noun, plural* **-ties** [Middle English *proprete*, from Middle French *propreté*, from Latin *proprietat-, proprietas*, from *proprius* own] (14th century)
**1 a :** a quality or trait belonging and especially peculiar to an individual or thing **b :** an effect that an object has on another object or on the senses **c :** VIRTUE **3 d :** an attribute common to all members of a class
**2 a :** something owned or possessed; *specifically* **:** a piece of real estate **b :** the exclusive right to possess, enjoy, and dispose of a thing **:** OWNERSHIP **c :** something to which a person or business has a legal title **d :** one (as a performer) under contract whose work is especially valuable
**3 :** an article or object used in a play or motion picture except painted scenery and costumes
*synonym* see QUALITY
— **prop·er·ty·less** \-ləs\ *adjective*
— **prop·er·ty·less·ness** \-nəs\ *noun*
**property damage insurance** *noun* (circa 1946)
**:** insurance protecting against all or part of an individual's legal liability for damage done (as by his or her automobile) to the property of another
**property right** *noun* (1903)
**:** a legal right or interest in or against specific property
**property tax** *noun* (1808)
**:** a tax levied on real or personal property
**pro·phage** \'prō-,fāj, -,fäzh\ *noun* (1951)
**:** an intracellular form of a bacteriophage in which it is harmless to the host, is usually integrated into the hereditary material of the host, and reproduces when the host does
**pro·phase** \-,fāz\ *noun* [International Scientific Vocabulary] (1884)
**1 :** the initial stage of mitosis and of the mitotic division of meiosis characterized by the condensation of chromosomes consisting of two chromatids, disappearance of the nucleolus and nuclear membrane, and formation of mitotic spindle
**2 :** the initial stage of the first division of meiosis in which the chromosomes become visible, homologous pairs of chromosomes undergo synapsis and crossing over, chiasmata appear, chromosomes condense with homo-

logues visible as tetrads, and the nuclear membrane and nucleolus disappear — compare DIAKINESIS, DIPLOTENE, LEPTOTENE, PACHYTENE, ZYGOTENE
— **pro·pha·sic** \(,)prō-'fā-zik\ *adjective*
**proph·e·cy** *also* **proph·e·sy** \'prä-fə-sē\ *noun, plural* **-cies** *also* **-sies** [Middle English *prophecie*, from Old French, from Late Latin *prophetia*, from Greek *prophēteia*, from *prophētēs* prophet] (13th century)
**1 :** an inspired utterance of a prophet
**2 :** the function or vocation of a prophet; *specifically* **:** the inspired declaration of divine will and purpose
**3 :** a prediction of something to come
**proph·e·sy** \'prä-fə-,sī\ *verb* **-sied; -sy·ing** [Middle English *prophesien*, from Middle French *prophesier*, from Old French, from *prophecie*] (14th century)
*transitive verb*
**1 :** to utter by or as if by divine inspiration
**2 :** to predict with assurance or on the basis of mystic knowledge
**3 :** PREFIGURE
*intransitive verb*
**1 :** to speak as if divinely inspired
**2 :** to give instruction in religious matters **:** PREACH
**3 :** to make a prediction
*synonym* see FORETELL
— **proph·e·si·er** \-,sī(-ə)r\ *noun*
**proph·et** \'prä-fət\ *noun* [Middle English *prophete*, from Old French, from Latin *propheta*, from Greek *prophētēs*, from *pro* for + *phanai* to speak — more at FOR, BAN] (12th century)
**1 :** one who utters divinely inspired revelations; *specifically, often capitalized* **:** the writer of one of the prophetic books of the Old Testament
**2 :** one gifted with more than ordinary spiritual and moral insight; *especially* **:** an inspired poet
**3 :** one who foretells future events **:** PREDICTOR
**4 :** an effective or leading spokesman for a cause, doctrine, or group
**5** *Christian Science* **a :** a spiritual seer **b :** disappearance of material sense before the conscious facts of spiritual Truth
— **proph·et·hood** \-,hůd\ *noun*
**proph·et·ess** \'prä-fə-təs\ *noun* (14th century)
**:** a woman who is a prophet
**pro·phet·ic** \prə-'fe-tik\ *also* **pro·phet·i·cal** \-'fe-ti-kəl\ *adjective* (15th century)
**1 :** of, relating to, or characteristic of a prophet or prophecy
**2 :** foretelling events **:** PREDICTIVE
— **pro·phet·i·cal·ly** \-ti-k(ə-)lē\ *adverb*
**Proph·ets** \'prä-fəts\ *noun plural*
**:** the second part of the Jewish scriptures — see BIBLE table
¹**pro·phy·lac·tic** \,prō-fə-'lak-tik *also* ,prä-\ *adjective* [Greek *prophylaktikos*, from *prophylassein* to be on guard, from *pro-* before + *phylassein* to guard, from *phylak-, phylax* guard] (1574)
**1 :** guarding from or preventing disease
**2 :** tending to prevent or ward off **:** PREVENTIVE
— **pro·phy·lac·ti·cal·ly** \-ti-k(ə-)lē\ *adverb*
²**prophylactic** *noun* (1642)
**:** something prophylactic; *especially* **:** a device and especially a condom for preventing venereal infection or conception
**pro·phy·lax·is** \-'lak-səs\ *noun, plural* **-lax·es** \-'lak-,sēz\ [New Latin, from Greek *prophylaktikos*] (circa 1842)

: measures designed to preserve health (as of an individual or of society) and prevent the spread of disease

¹**pro·pine** \prə-'pēn, -'pīn\ *transitive verb* **pro·pined; pro·pin·ing** [Middle English, from Middle French *propiner*, from Latin *propinare* to present, drink to someone's health, from Greek *propinein* literally, to drink first, from *pro-* + *pinein* to drink — more at POTABLE] (15th century)
*chiefly Scottish* : to present or give especially as a token of friendship

²**propine** *noun* (15th century)
*Scottish* : a gift in return for a favor

**pro·pin·qui·ty** \prə-'piŋ-kwə-tē\ *noun* [Middle English *propinquite*, from Latin *propinquitat-, propinquitas* kinship, proximity, from *propinquus* near, akin, from *prope* near — more at APPROACH] (14th century)
**1** : nearness of blood : KINSHIP
**2** : nearness in place or time : PROXIMITY

**pro·pi·o·nate** \'prō-pē-ə-ˌnāt\ *noun* [International Scientific Vocabulary] (1862)
: a salt or ester of propionic acid

**pro·pi·on·ic acid** \ˌprō-pē-'ä-nik-\ *noun* [International Scientific Vocabulary ¹*pro-* + Greek *pīōn* fat; akin to Sanskrit *pīvan* swelling, fat] (1850)
: a liquid sharp-odored fatty acid $C_3H_6O_2$ found in milk and distillates of wood, coal, and petroleum

**pro·pi·ti·ate** \prō-'pi-shē-ˌāt\ *transitive verb* **-at·ed; -at·ing** [Latin *propitiatus*, past participle of *propitiare*, from *propitius* propitious] (1583)
: to gain or regain the favor or goodwill of : APPEASE, CONCILIATE
**synonym** see PACIFY
— **pro·pi·ti·a·tor** \-ˌā-tər\ *noun*

**pro·pi·ti·a·tion** \prō-ˌpi-shē-'ā-shən\ *noun* (14th century)
**1** : the act of propitiating
**2** : something that propitiates; *specifically* : an atoning sacrifice

**pro·pi·ti·a·to·ry** \prō-'pi-sh(ē-)ə-ˌtōr-ē, -ˌtȯr-\ *adjective* (1551)
**1** : intended to propitiate : EXPIATORY
**2** : of or relating to propitiation

**pro·pi·tious** \prə-'pi-shəs\ *adjective* [Middle English *propicious*, from Latin *propitius*, probably from *pro-* for + *petere* to seek — more at PRO-, FEATHER] (15th century)
**1** : favorably disposed : BENEVOLENT
**2** : being of good omen : AUSPICIOUS ⟨*propitious* sign⟩
**3** : tending to favor : ADVANTAGEOUS
**synonym** see FAVORABLE
— **pro·pi·tious·ly** *adverb*
— **pro·pi·tious·ness** *noun*

**pro·plas·tid** \(ˌ)prō-'plas-təd\ *noun* [International Scientific Vocabulary] (1922)
: a minute cytoplasmic body from which a plastid is formed

**prop·man** \'präp-ˌman\ *noun* (circa 1937)
: a man in charge of stage properties

**prop·o·lis** \'prä-pə-ləs\ *noun* [Middle English *propoleos*, from Medieval Latin, alteration of Latin *propolis*, from Greek, from *pro-* for + *polis* city — more at PRO-, POLICE] (15th century)
: a brownish resinous material of waxy consistency collected by bees from the buds of trees and used as a cement

**pro·pone** \prə-'pōn\ *transitive verb* **pro·poned; pro·pon·ing** [Middle English (Scots), from Latin *proponere* — more at PROPOUND] (14th century)
**1** *Scottish* : PROPOSE, PROPOUND
**2** *Scottish* : to put forward (a defense)

**pro·po·nent** \prə-'pō-nənt, 'prō-ˌ\ *noun* [Latin *proponent-, proponens*, present participle of *proponere*] (1588)
: one who argues in favor of something : ADVOCATE

¹**pro·por·tion** \prə-'pōr-shən, -'pȯr-\ *noun* [Middle English *proporcion*, from Middle French *proportion*, from Latin *proportion-, proportio*, from *pro* for + *portion-, portio* portion — more at FOR] (14th century)
**1** : harmonious relation of parts to each other or to the whole : BALANCE, SYMMETRY
**2 a** : proper or equal share ⟨each did her *proportion* of the work⟩ **b** : QUOTA, PERCENTAGE
**3** : the relation of one part to another or to the whole with respect to magnitude, quantity, or degree : RATIO
**4** : SIZE, DIMENSION
**5** : a statement of equality between two ratios in which the first of the four terms divided by the second equals the third divided by the fourth (as in 4/2=10/5) — compare EXTREME 1b, MEAN 1c
— **in proportion** : PROPORTIONAL 1

²**proportion** *transitive verb* **pro·por·tioned; pro·por·tion·ing** \-sh(ə-)niŋ\ (14th century)
**1** : to adjust (a part or thing) in size relative to other parts or things
**2** : to make the parts of harmonious or symmetrical
**3** : APPORTION, ALLOT

**pro·por·tion·able** \-sh(ə-)nə-bəl\ *adjective* (14th century)
: PROPORTIONAL, PROPORTIONATE
— **pro·por·tion·ably** \-blē\ *adverb, archaic*

¹**pro·por·tion·al** \prə-'pōr-shnəl, -'pȯr-, -shə-nᵊl\ *noun* (14th century)
: a number or quantity in a proportion

²**proportional** *adjective* (15th century)
**1 a** : corresponding in size, degree, or intensity **b** : having the same or a constant ratio ⟨corresponding sides of similar triangles are *proportional*⟩
**2** : regulated or determined in size or degree with reference to proportions ⟨a *proportional* system of immigration quotas⟩
— **pro·por·tion·al·i·ty** \-ˌpōr-shə-'na-lə-tē, -ˌpȯr-\ *noun*
— **pro·por·tion·al·ly** \-'pōr-shnə-lē, -'pȯr-, -shə-nᵊl-ē\ *adverb*

**proportional parts** *noun plural* (circa 1890)
: fractional parts of the difference between successive entries in a table for use in linear interpolation

**proportional representation** *noun* (1870)
: an electoral system designed to represent in a legislative body each political group or party in proportion to its actual voting strength in the electorate

**proportional tax** *noun* (circa 1943)
: a tax in which the tax rate remains constant regardless of the amount of the tax base

¹**pro·por·tion·ate** \prə-'pōr-sh(ə-)nət, -'pȯr-\ *adjective* (14th century)
: PROPORTIONAL 1
— **pro·por·tion·ate·ly** *adverb*

²**pro·por·tion·ate** \-shə-ˌnāt\ *transitive verb* **-at·ed; -at·ing** (1570)
: to make proportionate : PROPORTION

**pro·pos·al** \prə-'pō-zəl\ *noun* (1653)
**1** : an act of putting forward or stating something for consideration
**2 a** : something proposed : SUGGESTION **b** : OFFER; *specifically* : an offer of marriage

**pro·pose** \prə-'pōz\ *verb* **pro·posed; pro·pos·ing** [Middle English, from Middle French *proposer*, from Latin *proponere* (perfect indicative *proposui*) — more at PROPOUND] (14th century)
*intransitive verb*
**1** : to form or put forward a plan or intention ⟨man *proposes*, but God disposes⟩
**2** *obsolete* : to engage in talk or discussion
**3** : to make an offer of marriage
*transitive verb*
**1 a** : to set before the mind (as for discussion, imitation, or action) ⟨*propose* a plan for settling the dispute⟩ **b** : to set before someone and especially oneself as an aim or intent ⟨*proposed* to spend the summer in Italy⟩

**2 a** : to set forth for acceptance or rejection ⟨*propose* terms for peace⟩ ⟨*propose* a topic for debate⟩ **b** : to recommend to fill a place or vacancy : NOMINATE ⟨*propose* them for membership⟩ **c** : to offer as a toast ⟨*propose* the happiness of the couple⟩
— **pro·pos·er** *noun*

¹**prop·o·si·tion** \ˌprä-pə-'zi-shən\ *noun* (14th century)
**1 a** (1) : something offered for consideration or acceptance : PROPOSAL (2) : a request for sexual intercourse **b** : the point to be discussed or maintained in argument usually stated in sentence form near the outset **c** : a theorem or problem to be demonstrated or performed
**2 a** : an expression in language or signs of something that can be believed, doubted, or denied or is either true or false **b** : the objective meaning of a proposition
**3** : something of an indicated kind ⟨getting there is a tough *proposition*⟩ ⟨the farm was never a paying *proposition*⟩
— **prop·o·si·tion·al** \-'zish-nəl, -'zi-shə-nᵊl\ *adjective*

²**proposition** *transitive verb* **-si·tioned; -si·tion·ing** \-'zi-sh(ə-)niŋ\ (1924)
: to make a proposal to; *especially* : to suggest sexual intercourse to

**propositional calculus** *noun* (1903)
: the branch of symbolic logic that uses symbols for unanalyzed propositions and logical connectives only — called also *sentential calculus*; compare PREDICATE CALCULUS

**propositional function** *noun* (1903)
**1** : SENTENTIAL FUNCTION
**2** : something that is designated or expressed by a sentential function

**pro·pos·i·tus** \prō-'pä-zə-təs\ *noun, plural* **-i·ti** \-ˌtī\ [New Latin, from Latin, past participle of *proponere*] (1899)
: the person immediately concerned : SUBJECT

**pro·pound** \prə-'paůnd\ *transitive verb* [alteration of earlier *propone*, from Middle English (Scots) *proponen*, from Latin *proponere* to display, propound, from *pro-* before + *ponere* to put, place — more at PRO-, POSITION] (1537)
: to offer for discussion or consideration
— **pro·pound·er** *noun*

**pro·poxy·phene** \prō-'päk-sə-ˌfēn\ *noun* [*prop-* + *oxy* + *-phene* (alteration of *phenyl*)] (1955)
: an analgesic $C_{22}H_{29}NO_2$ structurally related to methadone but less addicting that is administered in the form of its hydrochloride

**pro·prae·tor** *or* **pro·pre·tor** \(ˌ)prō-'prē-tər\ *noun* [Latin *propraetor*, from *pro-* (as in *proconsul*) + *praetor*] (circa 1580)
: a praetor of ancient Rome sent out to govern a province

**pro·pran·o·lol** \prō-'pra-nə-ˌlȯl, -ˌlōl\ *noun* [*propyl* + *propanol* + ¹*-ol*] (1964)
: a beta-adrenergic blocking agent $C_{16}H_{21}NO_2$ used in the form of its hydrochloride in the treatment of abnormal heart rhythms and angina pectoris

¹**pro·pri·e·tary** \prə-'prī-ə-ˌter-ē\ *noun, plural* **-tar·ies** (15th century)
**1** : one that possesses, owns, or holds exclusive right to something; *specifically* : PROPRIETOR 1
**2** : something that is used, produced, or marketed under exclusive legal right of the inventor or maker; *specifically* : a drug (as a patent medicine) that is protected by secrecy, patent, or copyright against free competition as to name, product, composition, or process of manufacture
**3** : a business secretly owned by and run as a cover for an intelligence organization

²**proprietary** *adjective* [Late Latin *proprietarius*, from Latin *proprietas* property — more at PROPERTY] (1589)
**1** : of, relating to, or characteristic of a proprietor ⟨*proprietary* rights⟩
**2** : used, made, or marketed by one having the exclusive legal right ⟨a *proprietary* process⟩

**3 :** privately owned and managed and run as a profit-making organization ⟨a *proprietary* clinic⟩

**pro·pri·e·tor** \prə-'prī-ə-tər\ *noun* [alteration of ¹*proprietary*] (1637)
**1 :** one granted ownership of a colony (as one of the original American colonies) and full prerogatives of establishing a government and distributing land
**2 a :** one who has the legal right or exclusive title to something : OWNER **b :** one having an interest (as control or present use) less than absolute and exclusive right
— **pro·pri·e·tor·ship** \-,ship\ *noun*

**pro·pri·e·to·ri·al** \prə-,prī-ə-'tōr-ē-əl, prō-, -'tȯr-\ *adjective* (1851)
**:** PROPRIETARY 1

**pro·pri·e·tress** \-'prī-ə-trəs\ *noun* (1692)
**:** a woman who is a proprietor

**pro·pri·e·ty** \prə-'prī-ə-tē\ *noun, plural* **-ties** [Middle English *propriete*, from Middle French *proprieté, propreté* property, quality of a person or thing — more at PROPERTY] (14th century)
**1** *obsolete* **:** true nature
**2** *obsolete* **:** a special characteristic : PECULIARITY
**3 :** the quality or state of being proper : APPROPRIATENESS
**4 a :** conformity to what is socially acceptable in conduct or speech **b :** fear of offending against conventional rules of behavior especially between the sexes **c** *plural* **:** the customs and manners of polite society

**pro·pri·o·cep·tion** \,prō-prē-ō-'sep-shən\ *noun* [proprioceptive + -ion] (1906)
**:** the reception of stimuli produced within the organism

**pro·pri·o·cep·tive** \-'sep-tiv\ *adjective* [Latin *proprius* own + English *-ceptive* (as in *receptive*)] (1906)
**:** of, relating to, or being stimuli arising within the organism

**pro·pri·o·cep·tor** \-tər\ *noun* [New Latin, from Latin *proprius* + New Latin *-ceptor* (as in *receptor*)] (1906)
**:** a sensory receptor (as a muscle spindle) excited by proprioceptive stimuli

**prop root** *noun* (1905)
**:** a root that serves as a prop or support to the plant

**prop·to·sis** \präp-'tō-səs, prō-'tō-\ *noun* [New Latin, from Late Latin, falling forward, from Greek *proptōsis*, from *propiptein* to fall forward, from *pro-* forward + *piptein* to fall — more at PRO-, FEATHER] (1676)
**:** forward projection or displacement especially of the eyeball

**pro·pul·sion** \prə-'pəl-shən\ *noun* [Latin *propellere* to propel] (1626)
**1 :** the action or process of propelling
**2 :** something that propels

**pro·pul·sive** \-'pəl-siv\ *adjective* [Latin *propulsus*] (1758)
**:** tending or having power to propel

**pro·pyl** \'prō-pəl\ *noun, often attributive* [International Scientific Vocabulary *prop-* + *-yl*] (1850)
**:** either of two isomeric alkyl groups $C_3H_7$ derived from propane — often used in combination

**pro·py·lae·um** \,prä-pə-'lē-əm, ,prō-\ *noun, plural* **-laea** \-'lē-ə\ [Latin, from Greek *propylaion*, from *pro-* before + *pylē* gate — more at PRO-] (circa 1706)
**:** a vestibule or entrance of architectural importance before a building or enclosure — often used in plural

**pro·pyl·ene** \'prō-pə-,lēn\ *noun* (1850)
**:** a flammable gaseous hydrocarbon $C_3H_6$ obtained by cracking petroleum hydrocarbons and used chiefly in organic synthesis

**propylene glycol** *noun* (1885)

**:** a sweet hygroscopic viscous liquid $C_3H_8O_2$ made especially from propylene and used especially as an antifreeze and solvent and in brake fluids

**pro ra·ta** \(,)prō-'rä-tə, -'rä-, -'ra-\ *adverb* [Latin] (1575)
**:** proportionately according to an exactly calculable factor (as share or liability)
— **pro rata** *adjective*

**pro·rate** \(,)prō-'rāt, 'prō-,\ *verb* **pro·rat·ed; pro·rat·ing** [pro rata] (1860)
*transitive verb*
**:** to divide, distribute, or assess proportionately
*intransitive verb*
**:** to make a pro rata distribution
— **pro·ra·tion** \prō-'rā-shən\ *noun*

**pro·ro·gate** \'prō-rə-,gāt\ *transitive verb* **-gat·ed; -gat·ing** (1534)
**:** PROROGUE
— **pro·ro·ga·tion** \,prō-rə-'gā-shən\ *noun*

**pro·rogue** \prō-'rōg\ *verb* **pro·rogued; pro·rogu·ing** [Middle English *prorogen*, from Middle French *proroguer*, from Latin *prorogare*, from *pro-* before + *rogare* to ask — more at PRO-, RIGHT] (15th century)
*transitive verb*
**1 :** DEFER, POSTPONE
**2 :** to terminate a session of (as a British parliament) by royal prerogative
*intransitive verb*
**:** to suspend or end a legislative session

**pros** *plural of* PRO

**pros-** *prefix* [Late Latin, from Greek, from *proti, pros* face to face with, toward, in addition to, near; akin to Sanskrit *prati-* near, toward, against, in return, Greek *pro* before — more at FOR]
**:** in front ⟨*pros*encephalon⟩

**pro·sa·ic** \prō-'zā-ik\ *adjective* [Late Latin *prosaicus*, from Latin *prosa* prose] (circa 1656)
**1 a :** characteristic of prose as distinguished from poetry : FACTUAL **b :** DULL, UNIMAGINATIVE
**2 :** EVERYDAY, ORDINARY
— **pro·sa·i·cal·ly** \-'zā-ə-k(ə-)lē\ *adverb*

**pro·sa·ism** \'prō-(,)zā-,i-zəm\ *noun* (1787)
**1 :** a prosaic manner, style, or quality
**2 :** a prosaic expression

**pro·sa·ist** *noun* [Latin *prosa* prose] (1803)
**1** \'prō-(,)zā-ist, -zā-,ist\ **:** a prose writer
**2** \prō-'zā-ist\ **:** a prosaic person

**pro·sa·teur** \,prō-zə-'tər\ *noun* [French, from Italian *prosatore*, from Medieval Latin *prosator*, from Latin *prosa*] (1880)
**:** a writer of prose

**pro·sau·ro·pod** \prō-'sȯr-ə-,päd\ *noun* [New Latin *Prosauropoda*, from ¹*pro-* + *Sauropoda* — more at SAUROPOD] (1941)
**:** any of a group (Prosauropoda) of chiefly herbivorous Triassic dinosaurs that are probably ancestral to sauropods

**pro·sce·ni·um** \prō-'sē-nē-əm\ *noun* [Latin, from Greek *proskēnion* front of the building forming the background for a dramatic performance, stage, from *pro-* + *skēnē* building forming the background for a dramatic performance — more at SCENE] (1606)
**1 a :** the stage of an ancient Greek or Roman theater **b :** the part of a modern stage in front of the curtain **c :** the wall that separates the stage from the auditorium and provides the arch that frames it
**2 :** FOREGROUND

**pro·sciut·to** \prō-'shü-(,)tō\ *noun, plural* **-ti** \-(,)tē\ *or* **-tos** [Italian, alteration of *presciutto*, from *pre-* (from Latin *prae-* pre-) + *asciutto* dried out, from Latin *exsuctus*, from past participle of *exsugere* to suck out, from *ex-* + *sugere* to suck — more at SUCK] (circa 1929)
**:** dry-cured spiced Italian ham usually sliced thin

**pro·scribe** \prō-'skrīb\ *transitive verb* **proscribed; pro·scrib·ing** [Latin *proscribere*

to publish, proscribe, from *pro-* before + *scribere* to write — more at SCRIBE] (1560)
**1 :** to condemn or forbid as harmful or unlawful : PROHIBIT
**2 :** to publish the name of as condemned to death with the property of the condemned forfeited to the state
— **pro·scrib·er** *noun*

**pro·scrip·tion** \prō-'skrip-shən\ *noun* [Middle English *proscripcion*, from Latin *proscription-, proscriptio*, from *proscribere*] (14th century)
**1 :** the act of proscribing : the state of being proscribed
**2 :** an imposed restraint or restriction : PROHIBITION
— **pro·scrip·tive** \-'skrip-tiv\ *adjective*
— **pro·scrip·tive·ly** *adverb*

**¹prose** \'prōz\ *noun* [Middle English, from Middle French, from Latin *prosa*, from feminine of *prorsus, prosus*, straightforward, being in prose, contraction of *proversus*, past participle of *provertere* to turn forward, from *pro-* forward + *vertere* to turn — more at PRO-, WORTH] (14th century)
**1 a :** the ordinary language people use in speaking or writing **b :** a literary medium distinguished from poetry especially by its greater irregularity and variety of rhythm and its closer correspondence to the patterns of everyday speech
**2 :** a prosaic style, quality, or condition

**²prose** *adjective* (14th century)
**1 :** of, relating to, or written in prose
**2 :** PROSAIC

**³prose** *intransitive verb* **prosed; pros·ing** (1642)
**1 :** to write prose
**2 :** to write or speak in a prosaic manner

**pro·sec·tor** \prō-'sek-tər\ *noun* [probably from French *prosecteur*, from Late Latin *prosector* anatomist, from Latin *prosecare* to cut away, from *pro-* forth + *secare* to cut — more at PRO-, SAW] (circa 1857)
**:** a person who makes dissections for anatomic demonstrations

**pros·e·cute** \'prä-si-,kyüt\ *verb* **-cut·ed; -cut·ing** [Middle English, from Latin *prosecutus*, past participle of *prosequi* to pursue — more at PURSUE] (15th century)
*transitive verb*
**1 :** to follow to the end : pursue until finished ⟨was . . . ordered to *prosecute* the war with . . . vigor —Marjory S. Douglas⟩
**2 :** to engage in : PERFORM
**3 a :** to bring legal action against for redress or punishment of a crime or violation of law ⟨*prosecuted* them for fraud⟩ **b :** to institute legal proceedings with reference to ⟨*prosecute* a claim⟩
*intransitive verb*
**:** to institute and carry on a legal suit or prosecution
— **pros·e·cut·able** \,prä-sə-'kyü-tə-bəl\ *adjective*

**prosecuting attorney** *noun* (1832)
**:** an attorney who conducts proceedings in a court on behalf of the government : DISTRICT ATTORNEY

**pros·e·cu·tion** \,prä-si-'kyü-shən\ *noun* (1567)
**1 :** the act or process of prosecuting; *specifically* **:** the institution and continuance of a criminal suit involving the process of pursuing formal charges against an offender to final judgment
**2 :** the party by whom criminal proceedings are instituted or conducted
**3** *obsolete* **:** PURSUIT

\ə\ abut  \ᵊ\ kitten  \ər\ further  \a\ ash  \ā\ ace
\ä\ mop, mar  \au̇\ out  \ch\ chin  \e\ bet  \ē\ easy
\g\ go  \i\ hit  \ī\ ice  \j\ job  \ŋ\ sing  \ō\ go
\ȯ\ law  \ȯi\ boy  \th\ thin  \t̷h\ the  \ü\ loot  \u̇\ foot
\y\ yet  \zh\ vision      *see also* Guide to Pronunciation

**pros·e·cu·tor** \'prä-si-ˌkyü-tər\ *noun* (circa 1670)
**1 :** a person who institutes an official prosecution before a court
**2 :** PROSECUTING ATTORNEY
**pros·e·cu·to·ri·al** \ˌprä-si-kyü-'tōr-ē-əl, -'tòr-\ *adjective* (1968)
**:** of, relating to, or being a prosecutor or prosecution
¹**pros·e·lyte** \'prä-sə-ˌlīt\ *noun* [Middle English *proselite*, from Late Latin *proselytus* proselyte, alien resident, from Greek *prosēlytos*, from *pros* near + *-ēlytos* (akin to *ēlythe* he went) — more at PROS-, ELASTIC] (14th century)
**:** a new convert; *specifically* **:** a convert to Judaism
²**proselyte** *verb* **-lyt·ed; -lyt·ing** (1624)
**:** PROSELYTIZE
**pros·e·ly·tise** *British variant of* PROSELYTIZE
**pros·e·ly·tism** \'prä-sə-ˌlī-ˌti-zəm, 'prä-s(ə-)lə-\ *noun* (circa 1660)
**1 :** the act of becoming or condition of being a proselyte **:** CONVERSION
**2 :** the act or process of proselytizing
**pros·e·ly·tize** \'prä-s(ə-)lə-ˌtīz\ *verb* **-tized; -tiz·ing** (1679)
*intransitive verb*
**1 :** to induce someone to convert to one's faith
**2 :** to recruit someone to join one's party, institution, or cause
*transitive verb*
**:** to recruit or convert especially to a new faith, institution, or cause
— **pros·e·ly·ti·za·tion** \ˌprä-s(ə-)lə-tə-'zā-shən, ˌprä-sə-ˌlī-tə-\ *noun*
— **pros·e·ly·tiz·er** \'prä-s(ə-)lə-ˌtī-zər\ *noun*
**pro·sem·i·nar** \(ˌ)prō-'se-mə-ˌnär\ *noun* (circa 1922)
**:** a directed course of study like a graduate seminar but often open to advanced undergraduates
**pros·en·ceph·a·lon** \ˌpräs-ˌen-'se-fə-ˌlän, -lən\ *noun* [New Latin] (1846)
**:** FOREBRAIN
— **pros·en·ce·phal·ic** \-sə-'fa-lik\ *adjective*
**prose poem** *noun* (1842)
**:** a composition in prose that has some of the qualities of a poem
— **prose poet** *noun*
**pros·er** \'prō-zər\ *noun* (1627)
**1 :** a writer of prose
**2 :** one who talks or writes tediously
**Pro·ser·pi·na** \prə-'sər-pə-nə\ *or* **Pros·er·pine** \'prä-sər-ˌpīn\ *noun* [Latin]
**:** PERSEPHONE
**pro·sim·i·an** \prō-'si-mē-ən\ *noun* [New Latin *Prosimii*, from ¹*pro-* + Latin *simia* ape — more at SIMIAN] (circa 1890)
**:** any of a suborder (Prosimii) of lower primates (as lemurs)
— **prosimian** *adjective*
**pro·sit** \'prō-zət, -sət\ *or* **prost** \'prōst\ *interjection* [German, from Latin *prosit* may it be beneficial, from *prodesse* to be useful — more at PROUD] (1846)
— used to wish good health especially before drinking
**pro·so** \'prō-(ˌ)sō\ *noun* [Russian] (1917)
**:** MILLET 1a
**pros·o·branch** \'prä-sə-ˌbraŋk\ *noun, plural* **-branchs** [New Latin *Prosobranchia*, from *proso-* in front (from Greek *prosō* forward) + *branchia* gills (from Greek)] (1851)
**:** any of a subclass (Prosobranchia) of gastropod mollusks that have the loop of visceral nerves twisted into a figure eight, the sexes usually separate, and usually an operculum
— **prosobranch** *adjective*
**pro·sod·ic** \prə-'sä-dik *also* -'zä-\ *or* **pro·sod·i·cal** \-di-kəl\ *adjective* (1774)
**:** of or relating to prosody
— **pro·sod·i·cal·ly** \-di-k(ə-)lē\ *adverb*

**pros·o·dy** \'prä-sə-dē, -zə-\ *noun, plural* **-dies** [Middle English, from Latin *prosodia* accent of a syllable, from Greek *prosōidia* song sung to instrumental music, accent, from *pros* in addition to + *ōidē* song — more at PROS-, ODE] (15th century)
**1 :** the study of versification; *especially* **:** the systematic study of metrical structure
**2 :** a particular system, theory, or style of versification
**3 :** the rhythmic and intonational aspect of language
— **pros·o·dist** \-dist\ *noun*
**pro·so·ma** \(ˌ)prō-'sō-mə\ *noun* [New Latin, from Greek *pro-* + *sōma* body] (1872)
**:** the anterior region of the body of an invertebrate when not readily analyzable into its primitive segmentation; *especially* **:** CEPHALOTHORAX
**pros·o·pog·ra·phy** \ˌprä-sə-'pä-grə-fē\ *noun* [New Latin *prosopographia*, from Greek *prosōpon* person + *-graphia* -graphy] (1929)
**:** a study that identifies and relates a group of persons or characters within a particular historical or literary context
— **pros·o·po·graph·i·cal** \-pə-'gra-fi-kəl\ *adjective*
**pro·so·po·poe·ia** \prə-ˌsō-pə-'pē-ə, ˌprä-sə-pə-\ *noun* [Latin, from Greek *prosōpopoiia*, from *prosōpon* mask, person (from *pros-* + *ōps* face) + *poiein* to make — more at EYE, POET] (circa 1555)
**1 :** a figure of speech in which an imaginary or absent person is represented as speaking or acting
**2 :** PERSONIFICATION
¹**pros·pect** \'prä-ˌspekt\ *noun* [Middle English, from Latin *prospectus* view, prospect, from *prospicere* to look forward, exercise foresight, from *pro-* forward + *specere* to look — more at PRO-, SPY] (15th century)
**1 :** EXPOSURE 3b
**2 a** (1) **:** an extensive view (2) **:** a mental consideration **:** SURVEY **b :** a place that commands an extensive view **:** LOOKOUT **c :** something extended to the view **:** SCENE **d** *archaic* **:** a sketch or picture of a scene
**3** *obsolete* **:** ASPECT
**4 a :** the act of looking forward **:** ANTICIPATION **b :** a mental picture of something to come **:** VISION **c :** something that is awaited or expected **:** POSSIBILITY **d** *plural* (1) **:** financial expectations (2) **:** CHANCES
**5 :** a place showing signs of containing a mineral deposit
**6 a :** a potential buyer or customer **b :** a likely candidate ☆
— **in prospect :** possible or likely for the future
²**pros·pect** \'prä-ˌspekt, *chiefly British* prə-'\ (1841)
*intransitive verb*
**:** to explore an area especially for mineral deposits
*transitive verb*
**:** to inspect (a region) for mineral deposits; *broadly* **:** EXPLORE
— **pros·pec·tor** \-ˌspek-tər, -'spek-\ *noun*
**pro·spec·tive** \prə-'spek-tiv *also* 'prä-ˌ, prō-', prä-'\ *adjective* (circa 1699)
**1 :** relating to or effective in the future
**2 a :** likely to come about **:** EXPECTED ⟨the *prospective* benefits of this law⟩ **b :** likely to be or become ⟨a *prospective* mother⟩
— **pro·spec·tive·ly** *adverb*
**pro·spec·tus** \prə-'spek-təs, prä-\ *noun, plural* **-tus·es** [Latin, prospect] (1765)
**1 :** a preliminary printed statement that describes an enterprise (as a business or publication) and that is distributed to prospective buyers, investors, or participants
**2 :** something (as a statement or situation) that forecasts the course or nature of something
**pros·per** \'prä-spər\ *verb* **pros·pered; pros·per·ing** \-p(ə-)riŋ\ [Middle English, from Middle French *prosperer*, from Latin *prosper-*

*are* to cause to succeed, from *prosperus* favorable] (14th century)
*intransitive verb*
**1 :** to succeed in an enterprise or activity; *especially* **:** to achieve economic success
**2 :** to become strong and flourishing
*transitive verb*
**:** to cause to succeed or thrive
**pros·per·i·ty** \prä-'sper-ə-tē\ *noun* (13th century)
**:** the condition of being successful or thriving; *especially* **:** economic well-being
**Pros·pero** \'präs-pə-ˌrō\ *noun*
**:** the rightful duke of Milan in Shakespeare's *The Tempest*
**pros·per·ous** \'präs-p(ə-)rəs\ *adjective* [Middle English, from Middle French *prospereus*, from Latin *prosperus*] (15th century)
**1 :** AUSPICIOUS, FAVORABLE
**2 a :** marked by success or economic well-being **b :** enjoying vigorous and healthy growth **:** FLOURISHING
— **pros·per·ous·ly** *adverb*
— **pros·per·ous·ness** *noun*
**pross** \'präs\ *or* **pros·sie** \'prä-sē\ *or* **pros·tie** \'prä-stē\ *noun* (circa 1902) *slang* **:** PROSTITUTE 1a
**pros·ta·cy·clin** \ˌpräs-tə-'sī-klən\ *noun* [*prosta-* (as in *prostaglandin*) + *cycl-* + ¹*-in*] (1976)
**:** a prostaglandin that is a metabolite of arachidonic acid, inhibits platelet aggregation, and dilates blood vessels
**pros·ta·glan·din** \ˌpräs-tə-'glan-dən\ *noun* [*prosta*te *gland* + ¹*-in;* from its occurrence in the seminal fluid of animals] (1936)
**:** any of various oxygenated unsaturated cyclic fatty acids of animals that perform a variety of hormonelike actions (as in controlling blood pressure or smooth muscle contraction)
**pros·tate** \'präs-ˌtāt\ *noun* [New Latin *prostata* prostate gland, from Greek *prostatēs*, from *proïstanai* to put in front, from *pro-* before + *histanai* to cause to stand — more at PRO-, STAND] (1646)
**:** PROSTATE GLAND
— **pros·tat·ic** \prä-'sta-tik\ *adjective*
**pros·ta·tec·to·my** \ˌpräs-tə-'tek-tə-mē\ *noun, plural* **-mies** (circa 1890)
**:** surgical removal or resection of the prostate gland
**prostate gland** *noun* (1828)
**:** a firm partly muscular partly glandular body that is situated about the base of the mammalian male urethra and secretes an alkaline viscid fluid which is a major constituent of the ejaculatory fluid
**pros·ta·tism** \'präs-tə-ˌti-zəm\ *noun* (circa 1900)
**:** disease of the prostate; *especially* **:** a disorder resulting from obstruction of the bladder neck by an enlarged prostate
**pros·ta·ti·tis** \ˌpräs-tə-'tī-təs\ *noun* [New Latin] (circa 1844)
**:** inflammation of the prostate gland
**pros·the·sis** \'präs-ˌthē-səs, 'präs-thə-\ *noun, plural* **-the·ses** \-ˌsēz\ [New Latin, from Greek, addition, from *prostithenai* to add to,

from *pros-* in addition to + *tithenai* to put — more at PROS-, DO] (circa 1900)
**:** an artificial device to replace a missing part of the body
**pros·thet·ic** \präs-'the-tik\ *adjective* (circa 1890)
**1 :** of or relating to a prosthesis or prosthetics
**2 :** of, relating to, or constituting a nonprotein group of a conjugated protein
— **pros·thet·i·cal·ly** \-ti-k(ə-)lē\ *adverb*
**pros·thet·ics** \-tiks\ *noun plural but singular or plural in construction* (circa 1894)
**:** the surgical or dental specialty concerned with the design, construction, and fitting of prostheses
**pros·thet·ist** \'präs-thə-tist\ *noun* (1902)
**:** a specialist in prosthetics
**pros·tho·don·tics** \,präs-thə-'dän-tiks\ *noun plural but singular or plural in construction* [New Latin *prosthodontia,* from *prosthesis* + *-odontia*] (1947)
**:** prosthetic dentistry
**pros·tho·don·tist** \-'dän-tist\ *noun* (1917)
**:** a specialist in prosthodontics
**¹pros·ti·tute** \'präs-tə-,tüt, -,tyüt\ *transitive verb* **-tut·ed; -tut·ing** [Latin *prostitutus,* past participle of *prostituere,* from *pro-* before + *statuere* to station — more at PRO-, STATUTE] (1530)
**1 :** to offer indiscriminately for sexual intercourse especially for money
**2 :** to devote to corrupt or unworthy purposes **:** DEBASE ⟨*prostitute* one's talents⟩
— **pros·ti·tu·tor** \-,tü-tər, -,tyü-\ *noun*
**²prostitute** *adjective* (1563)
**:** devoted to corrupt purposes **:** PROSTITUTED
**³prostitute** *noun* (1613)
**1 a :** a woman who engages in promiscuous sexual intercourse especially for money **:** WHORE **b :** a male who engages in sexual and especially homosexual practices for money
**2 :** a person (as a writer or painter) who deliberately debases his or her talents (as for money)
**pros·ti·tu·tion** \,präs-tə-'tü-shən, -'tyü-\ *noun* (1553)
**1 :** the act or practice of indulging in promiscuous sexual relations especially for money
**2 :** the state of being prostituted **:** DEBASEMENT
**pro·sto·mi·um** \prō-'stō-mē-əm\ *noun, plural* **-mia** \-mē-ə\ [New Latin, from Greek *pro-* + *stoma* mouth — more at STOMACH] (1870)
**:** the portion of the head of various worms that is situated in front of the mouth
— **pro·sto·mi·al** \-mē-əl\ *adjective*
**¹pros·trate** \'prä-,strāt\ *adjective* [Middle English *prostrat,* from Latin *prostratus,* past participle of *prosternere,* from *pro-* before + *sternere* to spread out, throw down — more at STREW] (14th century)
**1 :** stretched out with face on the ground in adoration or submission; *also* **:** lying flat
**2 :** completely overcome and lacking vitality, will, or power to rise ⟨was *prostrate* from the heat⟩
**3 :** trailing on the ground **:** PROCUMBENT ⟨*prostrate* shrub⟩
**synonym** see PRONE
**²pros·trate** \'prä-,strāt, *especially British* prä-'\ *transitive verb* **pros·trat·ed; pros·trat·ing** (15th century)
**1 :** to throw or put into a prostrate position
**2 :** to put (oneself) in a humble and submissive posture or state ⟨the whole town had to *prostrate* itself in official apology —Claudia Cassidy⟩
**3 :** to reduce to submission, helplessness, or exhaustion ⟨was *prostrated* with grief⟩
**pros·tra·tion** \prä-'strā-shən\ *noun* (14th century)
**1 a :** the act of assuming a prostrate position **b :** the state of being in a prostrate position **:** ABASEMENT

**2 a :** complete physical or mental exhaustion **:** COLLAPSE **b :** the process of being made powerless or the condition of powerlessness ⟨the country suffered economic *prostration* after the war⟩
**prosy** \'prō-zē\ *adjective* **pros·i·er; -est** [¹*prose*] (1814)
**:** lacking in qualities that seize the attention or strike the imagination **:** COMMONPLACE; *especially* **:** tediously dull in speech or manner
— **pros·i·ly** \-zə-lē\ *adverb*
— **pros·i·ness** \-zē-nəs\ *noun*
**prot-** *or* **proto-** *combining form* [Middle English *protho-,* from Middle French, from Late Latin *proto-,* from Greek *prōt-, prōto-,* from *prōtos;* akin to Greek *pro* before — more at FOR]
**1 a :** first in time ⟨*proto*history⟩ **b :** beginning **:** giving rise to ⟨*proto*planet⟩
**2 :** parent substance of a (specified) substance ⟨*prot*actinium⟩
**3 :** first formed **:** primary ⟨*proto*xylem⟩
**4** *capitalized* **:** relating to or constituting the recorded or assumed language that is ancestral to a language or to a group of related languages or dialects ⟨*Proto*-Indo-European⟩
**prot·ac·tin·i·um** \,prō-,tak-'ti-nē-əm\ *noun* [New Latin] (1918)
**:** a shiny radioactive metallic element of relatively short life — see ELEMENT table
**pro·tag·o·nist** \prō-'ta-gə-nist\ *noun* [Greek *prōtagōnistēs,* from *prōt-* prot- + *agōnistēs* competitor at games, actor, from *agōnizesthai* to compete, from *agōn* contest, competition at games — more at AGONY] (1671)
**1 a :** the principal character in a literary work (as a drama or story) **b :** a leading actor, character, or participant in a literary work or real event
**2 :** a leader, proponent, or supporter of a cause **:** CHAMPION
**3 :** a muscle that by its contraction actually causes a particular movement
**prot·amine** \'prō-tə-,mēn\ *noun* [International Scientific Vocabulary *prot-* + *amine*] (1874)
**:** any of various strongly basic proteins of relatively low molecular weight that are rich in arginine and are found associated especially with DNA in place of histone in the sperm cells of various animals (as fish)
**prot·a·sis** \'prä-tə-səs\ *noun, plural* **-a·ses** \-,sēz\ [Late Latin, from Greek, premise of a syllogism, conditional clause, from *proteinein* to stretch out before, put forward, from *pro-* + *teinein* to stretch — more at THIN] (circa 1568)
**1 :** the introductory part of a play or narrative poem
**2 :** the subordinate clause of a conditional sentence — compare APODOSIS
— **pro·tat·ic** \prä-'ta-tik, prō-\ *adjective*
**prote-** *or* **proteo-** *combining form* [International Scientific Vocabulary, from French *protéine*]
**:** protein ⟨*prote*olysis⟩ ⟨*prote*ose⟩
**pro·tea** \'prō-tē-ə\ *noun* [New Latin, from Latin *Proteus* Proteus] (1825)
**:** any of a genus (*Protea* of the family Proteaceae, the protea family) of evergreen shrubs often grown for their showy bracts and dense flower heads
**pro·te·an** \'prō-tē-ən, prō-'tē-\ *adjective* (1598)
**1 :** of or resembling Proteus in having a varied nature or ability to assume different forms
**2 :** displaying great diversity or variety **:** VERSATILE

protea

**pro·te·ase** \'prō-tē-,ās, -,āz\ *noun* [International Scientific Vocabulary] (1903)
**:** any of numerous enzymes that hydrolyze proteins and are classified according to the

most prominent functional group (as serine or cysteine) at the active site — called also *proteinase*
**pro·tect** \prə-'tekt\ *transitive verb* [Middle English, from Latin *protectus,* past participle of *protegere,* from *pro-* in front + *tegere* to cover — more at PRO-, THATCH] (15th century)
**1 :** to cover or shield from exposure, injury, or destruction **:** GUARD
**2 :** to maintain the status or integrity of especially through financial or legal guarantees: as **a :** to save from contingent financial loss **b :** to foster or shield from infringement or restriction ⟨salesmen with *protected* territories⟩; *specifically* **:** to restrict competition for (as domestic industries) by means of tariffs or trade controls
**synonym** see DEFEND
— **pro·tec·tive** \-'tek-tiv\ *adjective*
— **pro·tec·tive·ly** *adverb*
— **pro·tec·tive·ness** *noun*
**pro·tec·tant** \prə-'tek-tənt\ *noun* (1935)
**:** a protecting agent
**pro·tec·tion** \prə-'tek-shən\ *noun* (14th century)
**1 :** the act of protecting **:** the state of being protected
**2 a :** one that protects **b :** supervision or support of one that is smaller and weaker
**3 :** the freeing of the producers of a country from foreign competition in their home market by restrictions (as high duties) on foreign competitive goods
**4 a :** immunity from prosecution purchased by criminals through bribery **b :** money extorted by racketeers posing as a protective association
**5 :** COVERAGE 1a
**pro·tec·tion·ist** \-sh(ə-)nist\ *noun* (1844)
**:** an advocate of government economic protection for domestic producers through restrictions on foreign competitors
— **pro·tec·tion·ism** \-shə-,ni-zəm\ *noun*
— **protectionist** *adjective*
**protective tariff** *noun* (1838)
**:** a tariff intended primarily to protect domestic producers rather than to yield revenue
**pro·tec·tor** \prə-'tek-tər\ *noun* (14th century)
**1 a :** one that protects **:** GUARDIAN **b :** a device used to prevent injury **:** GUARD
**2 a :** one having the care of a kingdom during the king's minority **:** REGENT **b :** the executive head of the Commonwealth of England, Scotland, and Ireland from 1653 to 1659 — called also *Lord Protector of the Commonwealth*
— **pro·tec·tor·ship** \-,ship\ *noun*
**pro·tec·tor·al** \-'tek-t(ə-)rəl\ *adjective* (1657)
**:** of or relating to a protector or protectorate
**pro·tec·tor·ate** \-'tek-t(ə-)rət\ *noun* (1692)
**1 a :** government by a protector **b** *capitalized* **:** the government of England (1653–59) under the Cromwells **c :** the rank, office, or period of rule of a protector
**2 a :** the relationship of superior authority assumed by one power or state over a dependent one **b :** the dependent political unit in such a relationship
**pro·tec·to·ry** \-'tek-t(ə-)rē\ *noun, plural* **-ries** (1885)
**:** an institution for the protection and care usually of homeless or delinquent children
**pro·tec·tress** \-'tek-trəs\ *noun* (1570)
**:** a woman who is a protector
**pro·té·gé** \'prō-tə-,zhā, ,prō-tə-'\ *noun* [French, from past participle of *protéger* to protect, from Latin *protegere*] (1787)

\ə\ abut \ᵊ\ kitten \ər\ further \a\ ash \ā\ ace
\ä\ mop, mar \aů\ out \ch\ chin \e\ bet \ē\ easy
\g\ go \i\ hit \ī\ ice \j\ job \ŋ\ sing \ō\ go
\ȯ\ law \ȯi\ boy \th\ thin \t̲h̲\ the \ü\ loot \ů\ foot
\y\ yet \zh\ vision *see also* Guide to Pronunciation

: one who is protected or trained or whose career is furthered by a person of experience, prominence, or influence

**pro·té·gée** \'prō-tə-ˌzhā, ˌprō-tə-'\ *noun* [French, feminine of *protégé*] (1778)
: a female protégé

**pro·tein** \'prō-ˌtēn *also* 'prō-tē-ən\ *noun, often attributive* [French *protéine,* from Late Greek *prōteios* primary, from Greek *prōtos* first — more at PROT-] (circa 1844)
**1 :** any of numerous naturally occurring extremely complex substances that consist of amino-acid residues joined by peptide bonds, contain the elements carbon, hydrogen, nitrogen, oxygen, usually sulfur, and occasionally other elements (as phosphorus or iron), and include many essential biological compounds (as enzymes, hormones, or immunoglobulins)
**2 :** the total nitrogenous material in plant or animal substances

**pro·tein·a·ceous** \ˌprō-tᵊn-'ā-shəs; ˌprō-ˌtē(-ə)-'nā-shəs\ *adjective* (circa 1844)
: of, relating to, resembling, or being protein

**pro·tein·ase** \'prō-tᵊn-ˌās, -ˌāz; 'prō-ˌtē(-ə)-ˌnās, -ˌnāz\ *noun* [International Scientific Vocabulary] (circa 1929)
**:** PROTEASE

**pro·tein·uria** \ˌprō-tᵊn-'ùr-ē-ə, -'yùr-; ˌprō-ˌtē(-ə)-'nùr-ē-ə, -'nyùr-\ *noun* [New Latin, from International Scientific Vocabulary *protein* + New Latin *-uria*] (1911)
: the presence of excess protein in the urine

**pro tem** \(ˌ)prō-'tem\ *adverb* (1828)
**:** PRO TEMPORE

**pro tem·po·re** \prō-'tem-pə-ˌrē\ *adverb* [Middle English, from Latin] (15th century)
: for the time being

**pro·tend** \prō-'tend\ *verb* [Middle English, from Latin *protendere,* from *pro-* + *tendere* to stretch — more at THIN] (15th century)
*transitive verb*
**1** *archaic* **:** to stretch forth
**2** *archaic* **:** EXTEND
*intransitive verb*
*archaic* **:** STICK OUT, PROTRUDE

**pro·ten·sive** \-'ten(t)-siv\ *adjective* [Latin *protensus,* past participle of *protendere*] (1671)
**1** *archaic* **:** having continuance in time
**2** *archaic* **:** having lengthwise extent or extensiveness
**— pro·ten·sive·ly** *adverb*

**pro·teo·gly·can** \ˌprō-tē-ə-'glī-ˌkan\ [International Scientific Vocabulary] (1968)
: any of a class of glycoproteins of high molecular weight that are found especially in the extracellular matrix of connective tissue

**pro·te·ol·y·sis** \ˌprō-tē-'ä-lə-səs\ *noun* [New Latin] (1880)
: the hydrolysis of proteins or peptides with formation of simpler and soluble products

**pro·teo·lyt·ic** \ˌprō-tē-ə-'li-tik\ *adjective* (1877)
: of, relating to, or producing proteolysis
**— pro·teo·lyt·i·cal·ly** \-ti-k(ə-)lē\ *adverb*

**pro·te·ose** \'prō-tē-ˌōs, -ˌōz\ *noun* [International Scientific Vocabulary] (circa 1890)
: any of various water-soluble protein derivatives formed by partial hydrolysis of proteins

**Pro·te·ro·zo·ic** \ˌprä-tə-rə-'zō-ik, ˌprō-\ *adjective* [Greek *proteros* former, earlier (from *pro* before) + International Scientific Vocabulary *-zoic* — more at FOR] (1899)
: of, relating to, or being the eon of geologic time or the corresponding system of rocks that includes the interval between the Archean and Phanerozoic eons, perhaps exceeds in length all of subsequent geological time, and is marked by rocks that contain fossils indicating the first appearance of eukaryotic organisms (as algae) — see GEOLOGIC TIME table
**— Proterozoic** *noun*

---

**¹pro·test** \'prō-ˌtest\ *noun* [Middle English, from Middle French, from *protester*] (15th century)
**1 :** a solemn declaration of opinion and usually of dissent: as **a :** a sworn declaration that payment of a note or bill has been refused and that all responsible signers or debtors are liable for resulting loss or damage **b :** a declaration made especially before or while paying that a tax is illegal and that payment is not voluntary
**2 :** the act of objecting or a gesture of disapproval ⟨resigned in *protest*⟩; *especially* **:** a usually organized public demonstration of disapproval
**3 :** a complaint, objection, or display of unwillingness usually to an idea or a course of action ⟨went under *protest*⟩
**4 :** an objection made to an official or a governing body of a sport

**²pro·test** \prə-'test, 'prō-ˌ, prō-'\ *verb* [Middle English, from Middle French *protester,* from Latin *protestari,* from *pro-* forth + *testari* to call to witness — more at PRO-, TESTAMENT] (15th century)
*transitive verb*
**1 :** to make solemn declaration or affirmation of ⟨*protest* my innocence⟩
**2 :** to execute or have executed a formal protest against (as a bill or note)
**3 :** to make a statement or gesture in objection to ⟨*protested* the abuses of human rights⟩
*intransitive verb*
**1 :** to make a protestation
**2 :** to make or enter a protest
**synonym** *see* ASSERT
**— pro·test·er** *or* **pro·tes·tor** \-'tes-tər, -ˌtes-\ *noun*

**¹prot·es·tant** \'prä-təs-tənt, 2 *is also* prə-'tes-\ *noun* [Middle French, from Latin *protestant-, protestans,* present participle of *protestari*] (1539)
**1** *capitalized* **a :** any of a group of German princes and cities presenting a defense of freedom of conscience against an edict of the Diet of Spires in 1529 intended to suppress the Lutheran movement **b :** a member of any of several church denominations denying the universal authority of the Pope and affirming the Reformation principles of justification by faith alone, the priesthood of all believers, and the primacy of the Bible as the only source of revealed truth; *broadly* **:** a Christian not of a Catholic or Eastern church
**2 :** one who makes or enters a protest
**— Prot·es·tant·ism** \'prä-təs-tən-ˌti-zəm\ *noun*

**²protestant** *adjective* (1539)
**1** *capitalized* **:** of or relating to Protestants, their churches, or their religion
**2 :** making or sounding a protest ⟨the two *protestant* ladies up and marched out —*Time*⟩

**Protestant ethic** *noun* (1926)
: an ethic that stresses the virtue of hard work, thrift, and self-discipline

**pro·tes·ta·tion** \ˌprä-təs-'tā-shən, ˌprō-, -ˌtes-\ *noun* (14th century)
: the act of protesting **:** a solemn declaration or avowal

**pro·te·us** \'prō-tē-əs\ *noun, plural* **-tei** \-tē-ˌī\ [New Latin, from Latin, Proteus] (1896)
: any of a genus (*Proteus*) of aerobic usually motile enterobacteria that include saprophytes in decaying organic matter and forms associated with urinary tract infections

**Pro·teus** \'prō-ˌtyüs, -tē-əs, -ˌtüs\ *noun* [Latin, from Greek *Prōteus*]
: a Greek sea god capable of assuming different forms

**pro·tha·la·mi·on** \ˌprō-thə-'lā-mē-ən, -ˌän\ *or* **pro·tha·la·mi·um** \-mē-əm\ *noun, plural* **-mia** \-mē-ə\ [New Latin, from Greek *pro-* + *-thalamion* (as in *epithalamion*)] (1597)
: a song in celebration of a marriage

---

**pro·thal·li·um** \prō-'tha-lē-əm\ *noun, plural* **-thal·lia** \-lē-ə\ [New Latin, from *pro-* + *thallus*] (1858)
**1 :** the gametophyte of a pteridophyte (as a fern) that is typically a small flat green thallus attached to the soil by rhizoids
**2 :** a greatly reduced structure of a seed plant corresponding to the pteridophyte prothallium

**pro·thal·lus** \(ˌ)prō-'tha-ləs\ *noun* [New Latin] (1854)
**:** PROTHALLIUM

**proth·e·sis** \'prä-thə-səs\ *noun, plural* **-e·ses** \-ˌsēz\ [Late Latin, alteration of *prosthesis,* from Greek, literally, addition — more at PROSTHESIS] (circa 1550)
: the addition of a sound to the beginning of a word (as in Old French *estat*—whence English *estate*—from Latin *status*)
**— pro·thet·ic** \prä-'the-tik\ *adjective*

**pro·tho·no·ta·ry** \prō-'thä-nə-ˌter-ē, ˌprō-thə-'nō-tə-rē\ *or* **pro·to·no·ta·ry** \prō-'tä-nə-ˌter-ē, ˌprō-tə-'nō-tə-rē\ *noun, plural* **-ries** [Middle English *prothonotarie,* from Late Latin *protonotarius,* from *prot-* + Latin *notarius* stenographer — more at NOTARY PUBLIC] (15th century)
: a chief clerk of any of various courts of law
**— pro·tho·no·tar·i·al** \prō-ˌthä-nə-'ter-ē-əl, ˌprō-thə-nō-'ter-ē-əl\ *adjective*

**pro·tho·rac·ic** \ˌprō-thə-'ra-sik\ *adjective* (1826)
: of or relating to the prothorax

**prothoracic gland** *noun* (1887)
: one of a pair of thoracic endocrine organs in some insects that control molting

**pro·tho·rax** \(ˌ)prō-'thor-ˌaks, -'thor-\ *noun* [New Latin *prothorac-, prothorax,* from ¹*pro-* + *thorax*] (1826)
: the anterior segment of the thorax of an insect — see INSECT illustration

**pro·throm·bin** \(ˌ)prō-'thräm-bən\ *noun* [International Scientific Vocabulary] (1898)
: a plasma protein produced in the liver in the presence of vitamin K and converted into thrombin in the clotting of blood

**pro·tist** \'prō-(ˌ)tist\ *noun* [New Latin *Protista,* from Greek, neuter plural of *prōtistos* very first, primal, from superlative of *prōtos* first — more at PROT-] (1889)
: any of a taxonomic group and especially a kingdom (Protista) of unicellular, colonial, or multicellular organisms usually including the protozoans and most algae and in various classifications prokaryotes, some or all fungi, and the sponges
**— pro·tis·tan** \prō-'tis-tən\ *adjective or noun*

**pro·ti·um** \'prō-tē-əm, 'prō-shē-\ *noun* [New Latin, from Greek *prōtos* first] (1933)
: the ordinary light hydrogen isotope of atomic mass 1

**proto-** — *see* PROT-

**pro·to·col** \'prō-tə-ˌkol, -ˌkōl, -ˌkäl, -kəl\ *noun* [Middle French *prothocole,* from Medieval Latin *protocollum,* from Late Greek *prōtokollon* first sheet of a papyrus roll bearing data of manufacture, from Greek *prōt-* prot- + *kollan* to glue together, from *kolla* glue; perhaps akin to Middle Dutch *helen* to glue] (1541)
**1 :** an original draft, minute, or record of a document or transaction
**2 a :** a preliminary memorandum often formulated and signed by diplomatic negotiators as a basis for a final convention or treaty **b :** the records or minutes of a diplomatic conference or congress that show officially the agreements arrived at by the negotiators
**3 a :** a code prescribing strict adherence to correct etiquette and precedence (as in diplomatic exchange and in the military services) **b :** a set of conventions governing the treatment and especially the formatting of data in an electronic communications system

**4 :** a detailed plan of a scientific or medical experiment, treatment, or procedure ◆

**pro·to·derm** \'prō-tə-ˌdərm\ *noun* [International Scientific Vocabulary] (circa 1932)
**:** the outer primary meristem of a plant or plant part

**pro·to·gal·axy** \ˌprō-tō-'ga-lək-sē\ *noun* (1950)
**:** a cloud of gas believed to be the precursor to a galaxy

**pro·to·his·to·ry** \-'his-t(ə-)rē\ *noun* [International Scientific Vocabulary] (1903)
**:** the study of human beings in the times that immediately antedate recorded history
— **pro·to·his·to·ri·an** \-(h)is-'tōr-ē-ən, -'tȯr-\ *noun*
— **pro·to·his·tor·ic** \-'tȯr-ik, -'tär-\ *adjective*

**pro·to·hu·man** \-'hyü-mən, -'yü-\ *adjective* (circa 1909)
**:** of, relating to, or resembling an early hominid (as an australopithecine)
— **protohuman** *noun*

**pro·to·lan·guage** \'prō-tō-ˌlaŋ-gwij\ *noun* (1948)
**:** an assumed or recorded ancestral language

**pro·to·mar·tyr** \'prō-tō-ˌmär-tər\ *noun* [Middle English *prothomartir*, from Middle French, from Late Latin *protomartyr*, from Late Greek *prōtomartyr-, prōtomartys*, from Greek *prōt- + martyr-, martys* martyr] (15th century)
**:** the first martyr in a cause or region

**pro·ton** \'prō-ˌtän\ *noun* [Greek *prōton*, neuter of *prōtos* first — more at PROT-] (1920)
**:** an elementary particle that is identical with the nucleus of the hydrogen atom, that along with neutrons is a constituent of all other atomic nuclei, that carries a positive charge numerically equal to the charge of an electron, and that has a mass of $1.673 \times 10^{-24}$ gram
— **pro·ton·ic** \prō-'tä-nik\ *adjective*

**pro·ton·ate** \'prō-tə-ˌnāt\ *verb* **-at·ed; -at·ing** (1945)
*transitive verb*
**:** to add a proton to
*intransitive verb*
**:** to acquire an additional proton
— **pro·ton·ation** \ˌprō-tə-'nā-shən\ *noun*

**pro·to·ne·ma** \ˌprō-tə-'nē-mə\ *noun, plural* **-ne·ma·ta** \-'nē-mə-tə, -'ne-\ [New Latin *protonemat-, protonema*, from *prot-* + Greek *nēma* thread — more at NEMAT-] (1857)
**:** the primary usually filamentous thalloid stage of the gametophyte in mosses and in some liverworts comparable to the prothallium in ferns
— **pro·to·ne·mal** \-'nē-məl\ *adjective*
— **pro·to·ne·ma·tal** \-'nē-mə-tᵊl, -'ne-\ *adjective*

**protonotary apostolic** *or* **prothonotary apostolic** *noun, plural* **protonotaries apostolic** *or* **prothonotaries apostolic** (1682)
**:** a priest of the chief college of the papal curia who keeps records of consistories and canonizations and signs papal bulls; *also* **:** an honorary member of this college

**proton synchrotron** *noun* (1947)
**:** a synchrotron in which protons are accelerated by means of frequency modulation of the radio-frequency accelerating voltage so that they have energies of billions of electron volts

**pro·to·path·ic** \ˌprō-tə-'pa-thik\ *adjective* [International Scientific Vocabulary, from Middle Greek *prōtopathēs* affected first, from Greek *prōt-* prot- + *pathos* experience, suffering — more at PATHOS] (1905)
**:** of, relating to, or being cutaneous sensory reception responsive only to rather gross stimuli

**pro·to·phlo·em** \-'flō-ˌem\ *noun* (1884)
**:** the first-formed phloem that develops from procambium, consists of narrow thin-walled cells capable of a limited amount of stretching, and is usually associated with a region of rapid growth

**pro·to·plan·et** \'prō-tō-ˌpla-nət\ *noun* (1949)

**:** a hypothetical whirling gaseous mass within a giant cloud of gas and dust that rotates around a sun and is believed to give rise to a planet
— **pro·to·plan·e·tary** \ˌprō-tō-'pla-nə-ˌter-ē\ *adjective*

**pro·to·plasm** \'prō-tə-ˌpla-zəm\ *noun* [German *Protoplasma*, from *prot-* + New Latin *plasma*] (1848)
**1 :** the organized colloidal complex of organic and inorganic substances (as proteins and water) that constitutes the living nucleus, cytoplasm, plastids, and mitochondria of the cell
**2 :** CYTOPLASM
— **pro·to·plas·mic** \ˌprō-tə-'plaz-mik\ *adjective*

**pro·to·plast** \'prō-tə-ˌplast\ *noun* [Middle French *protoplaste*, from Late Latin *protoplastus* first human, from Greek *prōtoplastos* first formed, from *prōt-* prot- + *plastos* formed, from *plassein* to mold — more at PLASTER] (1532)
**1 :** one that is formed first **:** PROTOTYPE
**2 :** a plant cell that has had its cell wall removed; *also* **:** the nucleus, cytoplasm, and plasma membrane of a cell as distinguished from inert walls and inclusions

**pro·to·por·phy·rin** \ˌprō-tō-'pȯr-f(ə-)rən\ *noun* [International Scientific Vocabulary] (1925)
**:** a purple porphyrin acid $C_{34}H_{34}N_4O_4$ obtained from hemin or heme by removal of bound iron

**pro·to·star** \'prō-tō-ˌstär\ *noun* (1947)
**:** a cloud of gas and dust in space believed to develop into a star

**pro·to·stele** \'prō-tə-ˌstēl, ˌprō-tə-'stē-lē\ *noun* (1901)
**:** a stele forming a solid rod with the phloem surrounding the xylem
— **pro·to·ste·lic** \ˌprō-tə-'stē-lik\ *adjective*

**pro·to·stome** \'prō-tə-ˌstōm\ *noun* [New Latin *Protostomia*, from *prot-* + Greek *stoma* mouth — more at STOMACH] (circa 1961)
**:** any of a major group (Protostomia) of bilateral metazoan animals (as mollusks, annelids, and arthropods) characterized in typical forms by determinate and spiral cleavage, formation of a mouth and anus directly from the blastopore, and formation of the coelom by splitting of the embryonic mesoderm — compare DEUTEROSTOME

**pro·to·troph** \'prō-tə-ˌtrōf, -ˌträf\ *noun* [backformation from *prototrophic*] (1946)
**:** a prototrophic individual

**pro·to·tro·phic** \ˌprō-tə-'trō-fik\ *adjective* [International Scientific Vocabulary] (1900)
**:** having the nutritional requirements of the normal or wild type
— **pro·to·tro·phy** \prō-'tä-trə-fē\ *noun*

**pro·to·typ·al** \ˌprō-tə-'tī-pəl\ *adjective* (circa 1693)
**:** PROTOTYPICAL

**pro·to·type** \'prō-tə-ˌtīp\ *noun* [French, from Greek *prōtotypon*, from neuter of *prōtotypos* archetypal, from *prōt-* + *typos* type] (1552)
**1 :** an original model on which something is patterned **:** ARCHETYPE
**2 :** an individual that exhibits the essential features of a later type
**3 :** a standard or typical example
**4 :** a first full-scale and usually functional form of a new type or design of a construction (as an airplane)

**pro·to·typ·i·cal** \ˌprō-tə-'ti-pi-kəl\ *also* **pro·to·typ·ic** \-pik\ *adjective* (1650)
**:** of, relating to, or being a prototype
— **pro·to·typ·i·cal·ly** \-pi-k(ə-)lē\ *adverb*

**pro·to·xy·lem** \ˌprō-tə-'zī-ləm, -ˌlem\ *noun* (1887)
**:** the first-formed xylem developing from procambium and consisting of narrow cells with annular, spiral, or scalariform wall thickenings

**pro·to·zo·al** \ˌprō-tə-'zō-əl\ *adjective* (1890)
**:** of or relating to protozoans

**pro·to·zo·an** \-'zō-ən\ *noun* [New Latin *Protozoa*, from *prot-* + *-zoa*] (circa 1864)
**:** any of a phylum or subkingdom (Protozoa) of chiefly motile and heterotrophic unicellular protists (as amoebas, trypanosomes, sporozoans, and paramecia) that are represented in almost every kind of habitat and include some pathogenic parasites of humans and domestic animals
— **protozoan** *adjective*

**pro·to·zo·ol·o·gy** \-zō-'ä-lə-jē, -zə-'wä-\ *noun* [New Latin *Protozoa* + International Scientific Vocabulary *-logy*] (1904)
**:** a branch of zoology dealing with protozoans
— **pro·to·zo·ol·o·gist** \-zō-'ä-lə-jist, -zə-'wä-\ *noun*

**pro·to·zo·on** \-'zō-ˌän\ *noun, plural* **-zoa** \-'zō-ə\ [New Latin, from singular of *Protozoa*] (circa 1853)
**:** PROTOZOAN

**pro·tract** \prō-'trakt, prə-\ *transitive verb* [Latin *protractus*, past participle of *protrahere*, literally, to draw forward, from *pro-* forward + *trahere* to draw — more at PRO-] (1540)
**1** *archaic* **:** DELAY, DEFER
**2 :** to prolong in time or space **:** CONTINUE
**3 :** to extend forward or outward — compare RETRACT 1
**synonym** see EXTEND
— **pro·trac·tive** \-'trak-tiv\ *adjective*

**protracted meeting** *noun* (1832)
**:** a protracted revival meeting

**pro·trac·tile** \-'trak-tᵊl, -ˌtīl\ *adjective* [Latin *protractus*] (1828)
**:** capable of being thrust out ⟨*protractile* jaws⟩

**pro·trac·tion** \-'trak-shən\ *noun* [Late Latin *protraction-, protractio* act of drawing out, from *protrahere*] (1535)
**1 :** the act of protracting **:** the state of being protracted
**2 :** the drawing to scale of an area of land

**pro·trac·tor** \-'trak-tər\ *noun* (circa 1611)
**1 a :** one that protracts **b :** a muscle that extends a part
**2 :** an instrument for laying down and measuring angles in drawing and plotting

◇ WORD HISTORY
**protocol** In ancient Greece a book consisted of papyrus sheets glued together along their edges to form a roll. The first sheet in the roll was known in Late Greek as the *protokollon*, from *proto-*, "first, beginning," and *-kollon*, a derivative of Greek *kolla* "glue." From *protokollon* came Medieval Latin *protocollum* and hence Middle French *prothocole*. By the time this ancient Greek word made its way into English via French in the 16th century as *protocol*, it had come to denote a "first" document of a different kind: the original draft, minute, or record of a transaction. A century later the word referred specifically to the first draft or record of a diplomatic document, such as a treaty or declaration. The diplomatic connection was reinforced in the 19th century when the official records or minutes of a diplomatic conference or congress also came under the rubric of *protocol*. Not long afterward, the French used *protocole* in the name of a department within the Ministry of Foreign Affairs whose province was the etiquette to be observed in official ceremonies and diplomatic relations. This use by the French is responsible for what is now the most familiar meaning of *protocol* in English.

**pro·trep·tic** \prō-'trep-tik\ *noun* [Late Latin *protrepticus* hortatory, encouraging, from Greek *protreptikos*, from *protrepein* to turn forward, urge on, from *pro-* + *trepein* to turn] (circa 1656)
: an utterance (as a speech) designed to instruct and persuade
— **protreptic** *adjective*

**pro·trude** \prō-'trüd\ *verb* **pro·trud·ed; pro·trud·ing** [Latin *protrudere*, from *pro-* + *trudere* to thrust — more at THREAT] (1620)
*transitive verb*
**1** *archaic* : to thrust forward
**2** : to cause to project
*intransitive verb*
: to jut out from the surrounding surface or context ⟨a handkerchief *protruding* from his breast pocket⟩
— **pro·tru·si·ble** \-'trü-sə-bəl, -zə-\ *adjective*

**pro·tru·sion** \prō-'trü-zhən\ *noun* [Latin *protrudere*] (1646)
**1** : the act of protruding : the state of being protruded
**2** : something (as a part or excrescence) that protrudes
**synonym** see PROJECTION

**pro·tru·sive** \-'trü-siv, -ziv\ *adjective* (1676)
**1** *archaic* : thrusting forward
**2** : PROMINENT, PROTUBERANT ⟨a *protrusive* jaw⟩
**3** : OBTRUSIVE, PUSHING ⟨a coarse *protrusive* manner⟩
— **pro·tru·sive·ly** *adverb*
— **pro·tru·sive·ness** *noun*

**pro·tu·ber·ance** \prō-'tü-b(ə-)rən(t)s, -'tyü-\ *noun* (1646)
**1** : something that is protuberant
**2** : the quality or state of being protuberant
**synonym** see PROJECTION

**pro·tu·ber·ant** \-b(ə-)rənt\ *adjective* [Late Latin *protuberant-, protuberans*, present participle of *protuberare* to bulge out, from Latin *pro-* forward + *tuber* excrescence, swelling; perhaps akin to Latin *tumēre* to swell — more at THUMB] (1646)
**1** : thrusting out from a surrounding or adjacent surface often as a rounded mass : PROMINENT
**2** : forcing itself into consciousness : OBTRUSIVE
— **pro·tu·ber·ant·ly** *adverb*

**proud** \praud\ *adjective* [Middle English, from Old English *prūd*, probably from Old French *prod, prud, prou* capable, good, valiant, from Late Latin *prode* advantage, advantageous, back-formation from Latin *prodesse* to be advantageous, from *pro-, prod-* for, in favor + *esse* to be — more at PRO-, IS] (before 12th century)
**1** : feeling or showing pride: as **a** : having or displaying excessive self-esteem **b** : much pleased : EXULTANT **c** : having proper self-respect
**2 a** : marked by stateliness : MAGNIFICENT **b** : giving reason for pride : GLORIOUS ⟨the *proudest* moment in her life⟩
**3** : VIGOROUS, SPIRITED ⟨a *proud* steed⟩
**4** *chiefly British* : raised above a surrounding area ⟨a *proud* design on a stamp⟩ ☆
— **proud·ly** *adverb*

**proud flesh** *noun* (14th century)
: an excessive growth of granulation tissue (as in an ulcer)

**proud·ful** \praud-fəl\ *adjective* (14th century)
*chiefly dialect* : marked by or full of pride

**proud-heart·ed** \-'här-təd\ *adjective* (14th century)
: proud in spirit : HAUGHTY

**proust·ite** \'prü-ˌstīt\ *noun* [French, from Joseph L. Proust (died 1826) French chemist] (1835)
: a mineral that consists of a red silver arsenic sulfide and occurs in crystals or massively

**pro·vas·cu·lar** \(ˌ)prō-'vas-kyə-lər\ *adjective* (circa 1948)
: of, relating to, or being procambium

**prove** \'prüv\ *verb* **proved; proved** *or* **prov·en** \'prü-vən, *British also* 'prō-\; **prov·ing** \'prü-viŋ\ [Middle English, from Old French *prover*, from Latin *probare* to test, approve, prove, from *probus* good, honest, from *pro-* for, in favor + *-bus* (akin to Old English *bēon* to be) — more at PRO-, BE] (13th century)
*transitive verb*
**1** *archaic* : to learn or find out by experience
**2 a** : to test the truth, validity, or genuineness of ⟨the exception *proves* the rule⟩ ⟨*prove* a will at probate⟩ **b** : to test the worth or quality of; *specifically* : to compare against a standard — sometimes used with *up* or *out* **c** : to check the correctness of (as an arithmetic result)
**3 a** : to establish the existence, truth, or validity of (as by evidence or logic) ⟨*prove* a theorem⟩ ⟨the charges were never *proved* in court⟩ **b** : to demonstrate as having a particular quality or worth ⟨the vaccine has been *proven* effective after years of tests⟩ ⟨*proved* herself a great actress⟩
**4** : to show (oneself) to be worthy or capable ⟨eager to *prove* myself in the new job⟩
*intransitive verb*
: to turn out especially after trial or test ⟨the new drug *proved* effective⟩ ▪
— **prov·able** \'prü-və-bəl\ *adjective*
— **prov·able·ness** *noun*
— **prov·ably** \-blē\ *adverb*
— **prov·er** \'prü-vər\ *noun*

**prov·e·nance** \'präv-nən(t)s, 'prä-və-ˌnän(t)s\ *noun* [French, from *provenir* to come forth, originate, from Latin *provenire*, from *pro-* forth + *venire* to come — more at PRO-, COME] (1785)
**1** : ORIGIN, SOURCE
**2** : the history of ownership of a valued object or work of art or literature

**¹Pro·ven·çal** \ˌprō-vän-'säl, ˌprä-vən-, *sense 1 also* prə-'ven(t)-səl\ *adjective* [Middle French, from *Provence* Provence] (1589)
**1** : of, relating to, or characteristic of Provence or the people of Provence
**2** *or* **Pro·ven·çale** : cooked with garlic, onion, mushrooms, tomato, olive oil, and herbs ⟨scallops *Provençal*⟩

**²Pro·ven·çal** \ˌprō-vän-'säl, ˌprä-vən-\ *noun* (1600)
**1** : a native or inhabitant of Provence
**2** : a Romance language spoken in southern France; *especially* : the dialect of this language spoken in Provence

**prov·en·der** \'prä-vən-dər\ *noun* [Middle English, from Middle French *provende, provendre*, from Medieval Latin *provenda*, alteration of *praebenda* prebend] (14th century)
**1** : dry food for domestic animals : FEED
**2** : FOOD, VICTUALS

**pro·ve·nience** \prə-'vē-nyən(t)s, -nē-ən(t)s\ *noun* [alteration of *provenance*] (1882)
: ORIGIN, SOURCE

**prov·en·ly** \'prü-vən-lē, *British also* 'prō-\ *adverb* (1887)
: demonstrably as stated : without doubt or uncertainty

**pro·ven·tric·u·lus** \ˌprō-ven-'tri-kyə-ləs\ *noun, plural* **-li** \-ˌlī, -ˌlē\ [New Latin] (circa 1836)
**1** : the glandular or true stomach of a bird that is situated between the crop and gizzard
**2** : a muscular dilatation of the foregut in most mandibulate insects that is armed internally with chitinous teeth or plates for triturating food
**3** : the thin-walled sac in front of the gizzard of an earthworm

**prove out** *intransitive verb* (1941)
: to turn out to be satisfactory or as expected

**¹prov·erb** \'prä-ˌvərb\ *noun* [Middle English *proverbe*, from Middle French, from Latin *proverbium*, from *pro-* + *verbum* word — more at WORD] (14th century)
**1** : a brief popular epigram or maxim : ADAGE

**2** : BYWORD 4

**²proverb** *transitive verb* (14th century)
**1** : to speak of proverbially
**2** *obsolete* : to provide with a proverb

**pro·verb** \'prō-ˌvərb, -'vərb\ *noun* (1907)
: a form of the verb *do* used to avoid repetition of a verb (as *do* in "act as I do")

**pro·ver·bi·al** \prə-'vər-bē-əl\ *adjective* (1548)
**1** : of, relating to, or resembling a proverb
**2** : that has become a proverb or byword : commonly spoken of ⟨the *proverbial* smoking gun⟩
— **pro·ver·bi·al·ly** \-ə-lē\ *adverb*

**Prov·erbs** \'prä-vərbz\ *noun plural but singular in construction*
: a collection of moral sayings and counsels forming a book of canonical Jewish and Christian Scripture — see BIBLE table

**pro·vide** \prə-'vīd\ *verb* **pro·vid·ed; pro·vid·ing** [Middle English, from Latin *providēre*, literally, to see ahead, from *pro-* forward + *vidēre* to see — more at PRO-, WIT] (15th century)
*intransitive verb*
**1** : to take precautionary measures ⟨*provide* for the common defense —U.S. Constitution⟩
**2** : to make a proviso or stipulation ⟨the constitution . . . *provides* for an elected two-chamber legislature —Current Biography⟩
**3** : to make preparation to meet a need ⟨*provide* for entertainment⟩; *especially* : to supply something for sustenance or support ⟨*provides* for the poor⟩
*transitive verb*
**1** *archaic* : to prepare or get ready in advance

**2 a :** to supply or make available (something wanted or needed) ⟨*provided* new uniforms for the band⟩; *also :* AFFORD ⟨curtains *provide* privacy⟩ **b :** to make something available to ⟨*provide* the children with free balloons⟩ **3 :** to have as a condition : STIPULATE ⟨the contract *provides* that certain deadlines will be met⟩

**provided** *conjunction* [Middle English, past participle of *providen* to provide] (15th century)
: on condition that : with the understanding : IF
*usage* see PROVIDING

**prov·i·dence** \'prä-və-dən(t)s, -,den(t)s\ *noun* [Middle English, from Middle French, from Latin *providentia*, from *provident-, providens*] (14th century)
**1 a** *often capitalized :* divine guidance or care **b** *capitalized :* God conceived as the power sustaining and guiding human destiny **2 :** the quality or state of being provident

**prov·i·dent** \-dənt, -,dent\ *adjective* [Middle English, from Latin *provident-, providens*, from present participle of *providēre*] (15th century)
**1 :** making provision for the future : PRUDENT **2 :** FRUGAL, SAVING
— **prov·i·dent·ly** *adverb*

**prov·i·den·tial** \,prä-və-'den(t)-shəl\ *adjective* (1648)
**1 :** of, relating to, or determined by Providence **2** *archaic :* marked by foresight : PRUDENT **3 :** occurring by or as if by an intervention of Providence ⟨a *providential* escape⟩
*synonym* see LUCKY
— **prov·i·den·tial·ly** \-'den(t)-sh(ə-)lē\ *adverb*

**pro·vid·er** \prə-'vī-dər\ *noun* (1523)
: one that provides; *especially :* BREADWINNER

**providing** *conjunction* [Middle English, present participle of *providen*] (15th century)
: on condition that : in case ■

**prov·ince** \'prä-vən(t)s\ *noun* [Middle English, from Middle French, from Latin *provincia*] (14th century)
**1 a :** a country or region brought under the control of the ancient Roman government **b :** an administrative district or division of a country **c** *plural :* all of a country except the metropolises **2 a :** a division of a country forming the jurisdiction of an archbishop or metropolitan **b :** a territorial unit of a religious order **3 a :** a biogeographic division of less rank than a region **b :** an area that exhibits essential continuity of geological history; *also :* one characterized by particular structural or petrological features **4 a :** proper or appropriate function or scope : SPHERE **b :** a department of knowledge or activity
*synonym* see FUNCTION

**¹pro·vin·cial** \prə-'vin(t)-shəl\ *noun* [in sense 1, from Middle English, from Middle French or Medieval Latin; Middle French, from Medieval Latin *provincialis*, from *provincia* ecclesiastical province; in other senses, from Latin *provincialis*, from *provincia* province] (14th century)
**1 :** the superior of a province of a Roman Catholic religious order **2 :** one living in or coming from a province **3 a :** a person of local or restricted interests or outlook **b :** a person lacking urban polish or refinement

**²provincial** *adjective* (14th century)
**1 :** of, relating to, or coming from a province **2 a :** limited in outlook : NARROW **b :** lacking the polish of urban society : UNSOPHISTICATED **3 :** of or relating to a decorative style (as in furniture) marked by simplicity, informality, and relative plainness; *especially :* FRENCH PROVINCIAL
— **pro·vin·cial·ly** \-'vin(t)-sh(ə-)lē\ *adverb*
**pro·vin·cial·ism** \-shə-,li-zəm\ *noun* (1770)

**1 :** a dialectal or local word, phrase, or idiom **2 :** the quality or state of being provincial

**pro·vin·cial·ist** \-'vin(t)-sh(ə-)list\ *noun* (1656)
: a native or inhabitant of a province

**pro·vin·ci·al·i·ty** \prə-,vin(t)-shē-'a-lə-tē\ *noun, plural* **-ties** (1782)
**1 :** PROVINCIALISM 2 **2 :** an act or instance of provincialism

**pro·vin·cial·ize** \-'vin(t)-shə-,līz\ *transitive verb* **-ized; -iz·ing** (1829)
: to make provincial
— **pro·vin·cial·i·za·tion** \-,vin(t)-sh(ə-)lə-'zā-shən\ *noun*

**proving ground** *noun* (circa 1890)
**1 :** a place for scientific experimentation or testing (as of vehicles or weapons) **2 :** a place where something is developed or tried out

**pro·vi·rus** \(,)prō-'vī-rəs\ *noun* [New Latin] (1949)
: a form of a virus that is integrated into the genetic material of a host cell and by replicating with it can be transmitted from one cell generation to the next without causing lysis
— **pro·vi·ral** \-rəl\ *adjective*

**¹pro·vi·sion** \prə-'vi-zhən\ *noun* [Middle English, from Middle French, from Late Latin & Latin; Late Latin *provision-, provisio* act of providing, from Latin, foresight, from *providēre* to see ahead — more at PROVIDE] (14th century)
**1 a :** the act or process of providing **b :** the fact or state of being prepared beforehand **c :** a measure taken beforehand to deal with a need or contingency : PREPARATION ⟨made *provision* for replacements⟩ **2 :** a stock of needed materials or supplies; *especially :* a stock of food — usually used in plural **3 :** PROVISO, STIPULATION

**²provision** *transitive verb* **pro·vi·sioned; pro·vi·sion·ing** \-'vi-zhə-niŋ, -'vizh-niŋ\ (1809)
: to supply with provisions

**¹pro·vi·sion·al** \prə-'vizh-nəl, -'vi-zhə-nᵊl\ *adjective* (1601)
: serving for the time being : TEMPORARY
— **pro·vi·sion·al·ly** *adverb*

**²provisional** *noun* (1886)
: a postage stamp for use until a regular issue appears — compare DEFINITIVE

**pro·vi·sion·ary** \prə-'vi-zhə-,ner-ē\ *adjective* (1617)
: PROVISIONAL

**pro·vi·sion·er** \-'vi-zhə-nər, -'vizh-nər\ *noun* (1866)
: a furnisher of provisions

**pro·vi·so** \prə-'vī-(,)zō\ *noun, plural* **-sos** or **-soes** [Middle English, from Medieval Latin *proviso quod* provided that] (15th century)
**1 :** an article or clause (as in a contract) that introduces a condition **2 :** a conditional stipulation

**pro·vi·so·ry** \-'vī-zə-rē, -'vīz-rē\ *adjective* (circa 1611)
**1 :** containing or subject to a proviso : CONDITIONAL **2 :** PROVISIONAL

**pro·vi·ta·min** \(,)prō-'vī-tə-mən\ *noun* (1927)
: a precursor of a vitamin convertible into the vitamin in an organism

**Pro·vo** \'prō-(,)vō\ *noun, plural* **Provos** [*Provisional* I.R.A., name of the faction + ¹*-o*] (1971)
: a member of the extremist faction of the Irish Republican Army

**pro·vo·ca·teur** \prō-,vä-kə-'tər\ *noun* (1919)
: AGENT PROVOCATEUR

**prov·o·ca·tion** \,prä-və-'kā-shən\ *noun* [Middle English *provocacioun*, from Middle French *provocation*, from Latin *provocation-, provocatio*, from *provocare*] (14th century)
**1 :** the act of provoking : INCITEMENT **2 :** something that provokes, arouses, or stimulates

**pro·voc·a·tive** \prə-'vä-kə-tiv\ *adjective* (15th century)
: serving or tending to provoke, excite, or stimulate
— **provocative** *noun*
— **pro·voc·a·tive·ly** *adverb*
— **pro·voc·a·tive·ness** *noun*

**pro·voke** \prə-'vōk\ *transitive verb* **pro·voked; pro·vok·ing** [Middle English, from Middle French *provoquer*, from Latin *provocare*, from *pro-* forth + *vocare* to call, from *voc-, vox* voice — more at PRO-, VOICE] (14th century)
**1 a** *archaic :* to arouse to a feeling or action **b :** to incite to anger **2 a :** to call forth (as a feeling or action) : EVOKE ⟨*provoke* laughter⟩ **b :** to stir up purposely ⟨*provoke* a fight⟩ **c :** to provide the needed stimulus for ⟨will *provoke* a lot of discussion⟩ ☆
— **pro·vok·er** *noun*

**pro·vok·ing** \-'vō-kiŋ\ *adjective* (1642)
: causing mild anger : ANNOYING
— **pro·vok·ing·ly** \-kiŋ-lē\ *adverb*

**pro·vo·lo·ne** \,prō-və-'lō-nē\ *noun* [Italian, augmentative of *provola*, a kind of cheese] (1912)
: a usually firm pliant often smoked cheese of Italian origin

**pro·vost** \'prō-,vōst, 'prä-vəst, 'prō-vəst, *especially attributive* ,prō-(,)vō\ *noun* [Middle English, from Old English *profost* & Old French *provost*, from Medieval Latin *propositus*, alteration of *praepositus*, from Latin, one in charge, director, from past participle of *praeponere* to place at the head — more at PREPOSITION] (before 12th century)
**1 :** the chief dignitary of a collegiate or cathedral chapter **2 :** the chief magistrate of a Scottish burgh **3 :** the keeper of a prison **4 :** a high-ranking university administrative officer

**provost court** *noun* (1864)
: a military court usually for the trial of minor offenses within an occupied hostile territory

**provost guard** *noun* (1862)
: a police detail of soldiers under the authority of the provost marshal

**provost marshal** *noun* (1535)
: an officer who supervises the military police of a command

---

☆ **SYNONYMS**
**Provoke, excite, stimulate, pique, quicken** mean to arouse as if by pricking. PROVOKE directs attention to the response called forth ⟨my stories usually *provoke* laughter⟩. EXCITE implies a stirring up or moving profoundly ⟨news that *excited* anger and frustration⟩. STIMULATE suggests a rousing out of lethargy, quiescence, or indifference ⟨*stimulating* conversation⟩. PIQUE suggests stimulating by mild irritation or challenge ⟨that remark *piqued* my interest⟩. QUICKEN implies beneficially stimulating and making active or lively ⟨the high salary *quickened* her desire to have the job⟩. See in addition IRRITATE.

---

□ **USAGE**
**providing** Although occasionally still disapproved, *providing* is as well established as a conjunction as *provided* is. *Provided* is more common.

---

\ə\ abut \ᵊ\ kitten \ər\ further \a\ ash \ā\ ace
\ä\ mop, mar \au̇\ out \ch\ chin \e\ bet \ē\ easy
\g\ go \i\ hit \ī\ ice \j\ job \ŋ\ sing \ō\ go
\ȯ\ law \ȯi\ boy \th\ thin \th̲\ the \ü\ loot \u̇\ foot
\y\ yet \zh\ vision *see also* Guide to Pronunciation

**¹prow** \'prau̇\ *adjective* [Middle English, from Middle French *prou* — more at PROUD] (14th century)

*archaic* **:** VALIANT, GALLANT

**²prow** \'prau̇, *archaic* 'prō\ *noun* [Middle French *proue*, probably from Old Italian dialect *prua*, from Latin *prora*, from Greek *prōira*] (1555)

**1 :** the bow of a ship **:** STEM

**2 :** a pointed projecting front part

**prow·ess** \'prau̇-əs *also* 'prō-\ *noun* [Middle English *prouesse*, from Old French *proesse*, from *prou*] (13th century)

**1 :** distinguished bravery; *especially* **:** military valor and skill

**2 :** extraordinary ability ⟨his *prowess* on the football field⟩

**¹prowl** \'prau̇(ə)l\ *verb* [Middle English *prollen*] (14th century)

*intransitive verb*

**:** to move about or wander stealthily in or as if in search of prey

*transitive verb*

**:** to roam over in a predatory manner

— **prowl·er** \'prau̇-lər\ *noun*

**²prowl** *noun* (1803)

**:** an act or instance of prowling

— **on the prowl :** in the act of prowling; *also* **:** in search of something ⟨his fourth wife had just left him, and he was *on the prowl* again —Mary McCarthy⟩

**prowl car** *noun* (1937)

**:** SQUAD CAR

**prox·e·mics** \präk-'sē-miks\ *noun plural but singular or plural in construction* [*proximity* + *-emics* (as in *phonemics*)] (1963)

**:** the study of the nature, degree, and effect of the spatial separation individuals naturally maintain (as in various social and interpersonal situations) and of how this separation relates to environmental and cultural factors

— **prox·e·mic** \-mik\ *adjective*

**prox·i·mal** \'präk-sə-məl\ *adjective* [Latin *proximus*] (1727)

**1 :** situated close to **:** PROXIMATE

**2 :** next to or nearest the point of attachment or origin, a central point, or the point of view; *especially* **:** located toward the center of the body — compare DISTAL

**3 :** of, relating to, or being the mesial and distal surfaces of a tooth

— **prox·i·mal·ly** \-mə-lē\ *adverb*

**proximal convoluted tubule** *noun* (circa 1899)

**:** the convoluted portion of the vertebrate nephron that lies between Bowman's capsule and the loop of Henle and functions especially in the resorption of sugar, sodium and chloride ions, and water from the glomerular filtrate — called also *proximal tubule*

**prox·i·mate** \'präk-sə-mət\ *adjective* [Latin *proximatus*, past participle of *proximare* to approach, from *proximus* nearest, next, superlative of *prope* near — more at APPROACH] (1661)

**1 :** immediately preceding or following (as in a chain of events, causes, or effects) ⟨*proximate*, rather than ultimate, goals —Reinhold Niebuhr⟩

**2 a :** very near **:** CLOSE **b :** soon forthcoming **:** IMMINENT

— **prox·i·mate·ly** *adverb*

— **prox·i·mate·ness** *noun*

**prox·im·i·ty** \präk-'si-mə-tē\ *noun* [Middle French *proximité*, from Latin *proximitat-*, *proximitas*, from *proximus*] (15th century)

**:** the quality or state of being proximate **:** CLOSENESS

**proximity fuze** *noun* (1945)

**:** a fuze for a projectile that uses the principle of radar to detect the presence of a target within the projectile's effective range

**prox·i·mo** \'präk-sə-ˌmō\ *adjective* [Latin *proximo mense* in the next month] (1855)

**:** of or occurring in the next month after the present

**proxy** \'präk-sē\ *noun, plural* **prox·ies** [Middle English *procucie*, contraction of *procuracie*, from Anglo-French, from Medieval Latin *procuratia*, alteration of Latin *procuratio* procuration] (15th century)

**1 :** the agency, function, or office of a deputy who acts as a substitute for another

**2 a :** authority or power to act for another **b :** a document giving such authority; *specifically* **:** a power of attorney authorizing a specified person to vote corporate stock

**3 :** a person authorized to act for another **:** PROCURATOR

— **proxy** *adjective*

**proxy marriage** *noun* (1900)

**:** a marriage celebrated in the absence of one of the contracting parties who is represented at the ceremony by a proxy

**prude** \'prüd\ *noun* [French, good woman, prudish woman, short for *prudefemme* good woman, from Old French *prode femme*] (1704)

**:** a person who is excessively or priggishly attentive to propriety or decorum; *especially* **:** a woman who shows or affects extreme modesty

**pru·dence** \'prüd-ᵊn(t)s\ *noun* [Middle English, from Middle French, from Latin *prudentia*, alteration of *providentia* — more at PROVIDENCE] (14th century)

**1 :** the ability to govern and discipline oneself by the use of reason

**2 :** sagacity or shrewdness in the management of affairs

**3 :** skill and good judgment in the use of resources

**4 :** caution or circumspection as to danger or risk

**pru·dent** \-dᵊnt\ *adjective* [Middle English, from Middle French, from Latin *prudent-*, *prudens*, contraction of *provident-*, *providens* — more at PROVIDENT] (14th century)

**:** characterized by, arising from, or showing prudence: as **a :** marked by wisdom or judiciousness **b :** shrewd in the management of practical affairs **c :** marked by circumspection **:** DISCREET **d :** PROVIDENT, FRUGAL

**synonym** SEE WISE

— **pru·dent·ly** *adverb*

**pru·den·tial** \prü-'den(t)-shəl\ *adjective* (15th century)

**1 :** of, relating to, or proceeding from prudence

**2 :** exercising prudence especially in business matters

— **pru·den·tial·ly** \-'den(t)-sh(ə-)lē\ *adverb*

**prud·ery** \'prü-d(ə-)rē\ *noun, plural* **-er·ies** (1709)

**1 :** the characteristic quality or state of a prude

**2 :** a prudish act or remark

**prud·ish** \'prü-dish\ *adjective* (1717)

**:** marked by prudery **:** PRIGGISH

— **prud·ish·ly** *adverb*

— **prud·ish·ness** *noun*

**pru·i·nose** \'prü-ə-ˌnōs\ *adjective* [Latin *pruinosus* covered with hoarfrost, from *pruina* hoarfrost — more at FREEZE] (circa 1826)

**:** covered with whitish dust or bloom ⟨*pruinose* stems⟩

**¹prune** \'prün\ *noun* [Middle English, from Middle French, plum, from Latin *prunum* — more at PLUM] (14th century)

**:** a plum dried or capable of drying without fermentation

**²prune** *verb* **pruned; prun·ing** [Middle English *prouynen*, from Middle French *proignier*, probably alteration of *provigner* to layer, from *provain* layer, from Latin *propagin-*, *propago*, from *pro-* forward + *pangere* to fix — more at PRO-, PACT] (15th century)

*transitive verb*

**1 a :** to reduce especially by eliminating superfluous matter ⟨*pruned* the text⟩ ⟨*prune* the budget⟩ **b :** to remove as superfluous ⟨*prune* away all ornamentation⟩

**2 :** to cut off or cut back parts of for better shape or more fruitful growth

*intransitive verb*

**:** to cut away what is unwanted or superfluous

— **prun·er** *noun*

**pru·nel·la** \prü-'ne-lə\ *also* **pru·nelle** \-'nel\ *noun* [French *prunelle*, literally, sloe, from diminutive of *prune* plum] (1670)

**1 :** a twilled woolen dress fabric

**2 :** a heavy woolen fabric used for the uppers of shoes

**pruning hook** *noun* (1611)

**:** a pole bearing a curved blade for pruning plants

**pru·nus** \'prü-nəs\ *noun* [New Latin, from Latin, plum tree, from Greek *proumnē*] (1901)

**:** any of a genus (*Prunus*) of drupaceous trees or shrubs of the rose family that have showy clusters of usually white or pink flowers first appearing in the spring often before the leaves including many grown for ornament or for their fruit (as the plum, cherry, or apricot)

**pru·ri·ence** \'pru̇r-ē-ən(t)s\ *noun* (1781)

**:** the quality or state of being prurient

**pru·ri·en·cy** \-ən(t)-sē\ *noun* (1795)

**:** PRURIENCE

**pru·ri·ent** \-ənt\ *adjective* [Latin *prurient-*, *pruriens*, present participle of *prurire* to itch, crave; akin to Latin *pruna* glowing coal, Sanskrit *ploṣati* he singes, and probably to Latin *pruina* hoarfrost — more at FREEZE] (1592)

**:** marked by or arousing an immoderate or unwholesome interest or desire; *especially* **:** marked by, arousing, or appealing to unusual sexual desire

— **pru·ri·ent·ly** *adverb*

**pru·ri·go** \prü-'rī-(ˌ)gō, -'rē-\ *noun* [New Latin, from Latin, itch, from *prurire*] (circa 1646)

**:** a chronic inflammatory skin disease marked by itching papules

**pru·rit·ic** \-'ri-tik\ *adjective* (1899)

**:** of, relating to, or marked by itching

**pru·ri·tus** \-'rī-təs, -'rē-\ *noun* [Latin, from *prurire*] (1653)

**:** ITCH 1a

**Prus·sian blue** \'prə-shən-\ *noun* [*Prussia*, Germany] (1724)

**1 :** any of numerous blue iron pigments formerly regarded as ferric ferrocyanide

**2 :** a dark blue crystalline hydrated ferric ferrocyanide $Fe_4[Fe(CN)_6]_3 \cdot xH_2O$ used as a test for ferric iron

**3 :** a greenish blue

**prus·sian·ise** *British variant of* PRUSSIANIZE

**Prus·sian·ism** \'prə-shə-ˌni-zəm\ *noun* (1856)

**:** the practices or policies (as the advocacy of militarism) held to be typically Prussian

**prus·sian·ize** \-ˌnīz\ *transitive verb* **-ized; -iz·ing** *often capitalized* (1861)

**:** to make Prussian in character or principle (as in authoritarian control or rigid discipline)

— **prus·sian·i·za·tion** \ˌprə-shə-nə-'zā-shən\ *noun*

**pru·tah** *or* **pru·ta** \'prü-'tä\ *noun, plural* **pru·toth** \-'tōt, -'tōth, -'tōs\ *or* **pru·tot** \-'tōt, -'tōs\ [New Hebrew *pĕrūṭāh*, from Late Hebrew, a small coin] (1949)

**1 :** a former monetary unit of Israel equivalent to ¹/₁₀₀₀ pound

**2 :** a coin representing one prutah

**¹pry** \'prī\ *intransitive verb* **pried; pry·ing** [Middle English *prien*] (14th century)

**:** to look closely or inquisitively; *also* **:** to make a nosy or presumptuous inquiry

**²pry** *transitive verb* **pried; pry·ing** [probably back-formation from ⁵*prize*] (circa 1806)

**1 :** to raise, move, or pull apart with a lever **:** PRIZE

**2 :** to extract, detach, or open with difficulty ⟨*pried* the secret out of my sister⟩

**³pry** *noun* (1823)

**1 :** a tool for prying

**2 :** LEVERAGE

**pry·er** *variant of* PRIER

**prying** *adjective* (1552)

: impertinently or officiously inquisitive or interrogatory

**synonym** see CURIOUS

— **pry·ing·ly** \-iŋ-lē\ adverb

**Prze·wal·ski's horse** \pshə-'väl-skēz-, shə-, ‚pər-zhə-'väl-\ noun [Nikolaĭ M. Przhevalskiĭ (died 1888) Russian soldier & explorer] (1881)

: a small stocky bay- or dun-colored wild horse (Equus caballus przewalskii synonym E. przewalskii) of central Asia having a large head and short erect mane — called also Prze·wal·ski horse \-skē-\

**psalm** \'säm, 'sälm, 'sóm, 'sólm, New England also 'sàm\ noun, often capitalized [Middle English, from Old English psealm, from Late Latin psalmus, from Greek psalmos, literally, twanging of a harp, from psallein to pluck, play a stringed instrument] (before 12th century)

: a sacred song or poem used in worship; especially : one of the biblical hymns collected in the Book of Psalms

**psalm·book** \-‚búk\ noun (12th century)
archaic : PSALTER

**psalm·ist** \'sä-mist, 'säl-, 'sò-, 'sól-, New England also 'sà-mist\ noun (15th century)

: a writer or composer of especially biblical psalms

**psalm·o·dy** \'sä-mə-dē, 'säl-, 'sò-, 'sól, New England also 'sà-mə-dē\ noun [Middle English psalmodie, from Late Latin psalmodia, from Late Greek psalmōidia, literally, singing to the harp, from Greek psalmos + aidein to sing — more at ODE] (14th century)

1 : the act, practice, or art of singing psalms in worship

2 : a collection of psalms

**Psalms** \'sämz, 'sälmz, 'sómz, 'sólmz, New England also 'sàmz\ noun plural but singular in construction

: a collection of sacred poems forming a book of canonical Jewish and Christian Scripture — see BIBLE table

**Psal·ter** \'sàl-tər, 'sòl-\ noun [Middle English, from Old English psalter & Old French psaltier, from Late Latin psalterium, from Late Greek psaltērion, from Greek, psaltery (before 12th century)

: the Book of Psalms; also : a collection of Psalms for liturgical or devotional use

**psal·te·ri·um** \säl-'tir-ē-əm, sòl-\ noun, plural -ria \-ē-ə\ [New Latin, from Late Latin, psalter; from the resemblance of the folds to the pages of a book] (circa 1846)

: OMASUM

**psal·tery** also **psal·try** \'sàl-t(ə-)rē, 'sòl-\ noun, plural -ter·ies also -tries [Middle English psalterie, from Middle French, from Latin psalterium, from Greek psaltērion, from psallein to play on a stringed instrument] (14th century)

: an ancient musical instrument resembling the zither

**p's and q's** \‚pēz-ən-'kyüz\ noun plural [from the phrase mind one's p's and q's, alluding to the difficulty a child learning to write has in distinguishing between p and q] (1779)

1 : something (as one's manners) that one should be mindful of ⟨better watch his p's and q's when I get a six-gun of my own —Jean Stafford⟩

2 : best behavior ⟨being on her p's and q's for two solid days was too much —Guy McCrone⟩

**pse·phol·o·gy** \sē-'fä-lə-jē\ noun [Greek psēphos pebble, ballot, vote; from the use of pebbles by the ancient Greeks in voting] (1952)

: the scientific study of elections

— **pse·pho·log·i·cal** \‚sē-fə-'lä-ji-kəl\ adjective

— **pse·phol·o·gist** \sē-'fä-lə-jist\ noun

**pseud** \'süd\ noun [short for pseudo-intellectual] (1964)
British : a person who pretends to be an intellectual

**pseud-** or **pseudo-** combining form [Middle English, from Late Latin, from Greek, from pseudēs, from pseudesthai to lie; akin to Armenian sut lie and probably to Greek psychein to breathe — more at PSYCH-]

: false : spurious ⟨pseudoclassic⟩ ⟨pseudopodium⟩

**pseud·ep·i·graph** \sü-'de-pə-‚graf\ noun (1884)

: PSEUDEPIGRAPHON 2

**pseud·epig·ra·phon** \‚sü-di-'pi-grə-‚fän\ noun, plural -pha \-fə\ [New Latin, singular of pseudepigrapha, from Greek, neuter plural of pseudepigraphos falsely inscribed, from pseud- + epigraphein to inscribe — more at EPIGRAM] (1692)

1 plural : APOCRYPHA

2 : any of various pseudonymous or anonymous Jewish religious writings of the period 200 B.C. to 200 A.D.; especially : one of such writings (as the Psalms of Solomon) not included in any canon of biblical Scripture — usually used in plural

**pseud·epig·ra·phy** \-fē\ noun [Greek pseudepigraphos] (circa 1842)

: the ascription of false names of authors to works

**pseu·do** \'sü-(‚)dō\ adjective [Middle English, from pseudo-] (15th century)

: being apparently rather than actually as stated : SHAM, SPURIOUS ⟨distinction between true and pseudo humanism —K. F. Reinhardt⟩

**pseu·do·al·lele** \‚sü-dō-ə-'lē(ə)l\ noun (1948)

: any of two or more closely linked genes that act usually as if a single member of an allelic pair but occasionally undergo crossing-over and recombination

**pseu·do·cho·lin·es·ter·ase** \'sü-dō-‚kō-lə-'nes-tə-‚rās, -‚rāz\ noun (1943)

: CHOLINESTERASE 2

**pseu·do·clas·sic** \‚sü-dō-'kla-sik\ adjective (1899)

: pretending to be or erroneously regarded as classic

— **pseudoclassic** noun

**pseu·do·clas·si·cism** \-'kla-sə-‚si-zəm\ noun (1871)

: imitative representation of classicism in literature and art

**pseu·do·coel** \'sü-də-‚sēl\ noun (1887)

: a body cavity that is not a product of gastrulation and is not lined with a well-defined mesodermal membrane

**pseu·do·coe·lom·ate** \‚sü-dō-'sē-lə-‚māt\ noun (1940)

: an invertebrate (as a nematode or rotifer) having a body cavity that is a pseudocoel

— **pseudocoelomate** adjective

**pseu·do·cy·e·sis** \-sī-'ē-səs\ noun [New Latin, from pseud- + cyesis pregnancy, from Greek kyēsis, from kyein to be pregnant — more at CYME] (circa 1817)

: a psychosomatic state that occurs without conception and is marked by some of the physical symptoms and changes in hormonal balance of pregnancy

**pseu·do·mo·nad** \‚sü-də-'mō-‚nad, -nəd\ noun [New Latin Pseudomonad-, Pseudomonas] (1921)

: any of a genus (Pseudomonas) of gram-negative rod-shaped motile bacteria including some that produce a greenish fluorescent water-soluble pigment and some that are saprophytes or plant or animal pathogens

**pseu·do·mo·nas** \-nəs\ noun, plural -mo·na·des \-'mō-nə-‚dēz, -'mä-\ [New Latin, from pseud- + monad-, monas monad] (1903)

: PSEUDOMONAD

**pseu·do·morph** \'sü-də-‚mòrf\ noun [probably from French pseudomorphe, from pseud- + -morphe -morph] (1849)

1 : a mineral having the characteristic outward form of another species

2 : a deceptive or irregular form

— **pseu·do·mor·phic** \‚sü-də-'mòr-fik\ adjective

— **pseu·do·mor·phism** \-‚fi-zəm\ noun
— **pseu·do·mor·phous** \-fəs\ adjective

**pseu·do·nym** \'sü-d°n-‚im\ noun [French pseudonyme, from Greek pseudōnymos bearing a false name, from pseud- + onyma name — more at NAME] (1833)

: a fictitious name; especially : PEN NAME

**pseu·do·nym·i·ty** \‚sü-d°n-'i-mə-tē\ noun (1877)

: the use of a pseudonym; also : the fact or state of being signed with a pseudonym

**pseu·don·y·mous** \sü-'dä-nə-məs\ adjective [Greek pseudōnymos] (circa 1706)

: bearing or using a fictitious name ⟨a pseudonymous report⟩; also : being a pseudonym

— **pseu·don·y·mous·ly** adverb
— **pseu·don·y·mous·ness** noun

**pseu·do·pa·ren·chy·ma** \‚sü-dō-pə-'reŋ-kə-mə\ noun [New Latin] (1875)

: compactly interwoven short-celled filaments in a thallophyte that resemble parenchyma of higher plants

— **pseu·do·par·en·chy·ma·tous** \-‚par-ən-'ki-mə-təs, -'kī-\ adjective

**pseu·do·pod** \'sü-də-‚päd\ noun [New Latin pseudopodium] (1874)

: PSEUDOPODIUM

— **pseu·dop·o·dal** \sü-'dä-pə-d°l\ or **pseu·do·po·di·al** \‚sü-də-'pō-dē-əl\ adjective

**pseu·do·po·di·um** \‚sü-də-'pō-dē-əm\ noun, plural -po·dia \-dē-ə\ [New Latin] (1854)

1 : a temporary protrusion or retractile process of the cytoplasm of a cell that functions (as in an amoeba) especially in a locomotor or food gathering capacity — see AMOEBA illustration

2 : a slender leafless branch of the gametophyte in various mosses that often bears gemmae

**pseu·do·preg·nan·cy** \‚sü-dō-'preg-nən(t)-sē\ noun (1860)

1 : PSEUDOCYESIS

2 : an anestrous state resembling pregnancy that occurs in various mammals usually after an infertile copulation

— **pseu·do·preg·nant** \-nənt\ adjective

**pseu·do·ran·dom** \-'ran-dəm\ adjective (1949)

: being or involving entities (as numbers) that are selected by a definite computational process but that satisfy one or more standard tests for statistical randomness

**pseu·do·sci·ence** \‚sü-dō-'sī-ən(t)s\ noun (1844)

: a system of theories, assumptions, and methods erroneously regarded as scientific

— **pseu·do·sci·en·tif·ic** \-‚sī-ən-'ti-fik\ adjective

— **pseu·do·sci·en·tist** \-'sī-ən-tist\ noun

**pseu·do·scor·pi·on** \-'skòr-pē-ən\ noun [New Latin Pseudoscorpiones, from pseud- + Latin scorpion-, scorpio scorpion] (1835)

: any of a widely distributed order (Pseudoscorpionida synonym Pseudoscorpiones) of tiny arachnids that have no caudal stinger and feed on tiny invertebrates (as insects and mites)

**pseu·do·so·phis·ti·ca·tion** \'sü-dō-sə-‚fis-tə-'kā-shən\ noun (1965)

: false or feigned sophistication

— **pseu·do·so·phis·ti·cat·ed** \-sə-'fis-ti-‚kā-təd\ adjective

**pseu·do·tu·ber·cu·lo·sis** \-‚tü-‚bər-kyə-'lō-səs, -tyü-\ noun [New Latin] (1900)

: any of several diseases that are characterized by the formation of granulomas resembling tubercular nodules but are not caused by the tubercle bacillus

**pshaw** \'shò\ interjection (1673)

— used to express irritation, disapproval, contempt, or disbelief

**¹psi** \'sī, 'psī\ *noun* [Middle English, from Medieval Latin, from Late Greek, from Greek *psei*] (15th century)
: the 23d letter of the Greek alphabet — see ALPHABET table

**²psi** \'sī\ *noun* [probably by shortening & alteration from *psychic*] (circa 1946)
: parapsychological psychic phenomena or powers

**psi·lo·cy·bin** \ˌsī-lə-'sī-bən\ *noun* [New Latin *Psilocybe*, fungus genus + ¹-*in*] (1958)
: a hallucinogenic indole $C_{12}H_{17}N_2O_4P$ obtained from a fungus (*Psilocybe mexicana*)

**psi·lo·phyte** \'sī-lə-ˌfīt\ *noun* [New Latin *Psilophyton*, genus of plants, from Greek *psilos* bare, mere (probably akin to Greek *psēn* to rub) + *phyton* plant — more at PHYT-] (circa 1911)
: any of an order (Psilophytales) of extinct simple dichotomously branched plants from the Paleozoic of Europe and eastern Canada that include the oldest known land plants with vascular structure
— **psi·lo·phyt·ic** \ˌsī-lə-'fi-tik\ *adjective*

**psi particle** \'sī-, 'psī-\ *noun* (1974)
: J/PSI PARTICLE

**psit·ta·cine** \'si-tə-ˌsīn\ *adjective* [Latin *psittacinus*, from *psittacus* parrot, from Greek *psittakos*] (1874)
: of or relating to the parrots
— **psittacine** *noun*

**psit·ta·co·sis** \ˌsi-tə-'kō-səs\ *noun* [New Latin, from Latin *psittacus*] (1897)
: an infectious disease of birds caused by a bacterium (*Chlamydia psittaci*), marked by diarrhea and wasting, and transmissible to humans in whom it usually occurs as an atypical pneumonia accompanied by high fever
— **psit·ta·cot·ic** \-'kä-tik, -'kō\ *adjective*

**pso·cid** \'sō-səd\ *noun* [ultimately from New Latin *Psocus*, genus of lice] (1891)
: any of an order (Psocoptera synonym Corrodentia) of minute usually winged primitive insects (as a book louse)

**pso·ri·a·sis** \sə-'rī-ə-səs\ *noun* [New Latin, from Greek *psōriasis*, from *psōrian* to have the itch, from *psōra* itch; akin to Greek *psēn* to rub] (circa 1684)
: a chronic skin disease characterized by circumscribed red patches covered with white scales
— **pso·ri·at·ic** \ˌsōr-ē-'a-tik, ˌsòr-\ *adjective or noun*

**psych** *also* **psyche** \'sīk\ *transitive verb*
**psyched; psych·ing** [by shortening] (1917)
**1** : PSYCHOANALYZE
**2 a** : to anticipate correctly the intentions or actions of : OUTGUESS **b** : to analyze or figure out (as a problem or course of action) ⟨I *psyched* it all out by myself and decided —David Hulburd⟩
**3 a** : to make psychologically uneasy : INTIMIDATE, SCARE ⟨pressure doesn't *psych* me —Jerry Quarry⟩ — often used with *out* **b** : to make (as oneself) psychologically ready especially for performance — often used with *up* ⟨*psyched* herself up for the race⟩

**psych-** *or* **psycho-** *combining form* [Greek, from *psychē* breath, principle of life, life, soul, from *psychein* to breathe; akin to Sanskrit *babhasti* he blows]
**1** : mind : mental processes and activities ⟨*psycho*dynamic⟩ ⟨*psycho*logy⟩
**2** : psychological methods ⟨*psycho*analysis⟩ ⟨*psycho*therapy⟩
**3** : brain ⟨*psycho*surgery⟩
**4** : mental and ⟨*psycho*somatic⟩

**psych·as·the·nia** \ˌsī-kəs-'thē-nē-ə\ *noun* [New Latin] (1900)
: a neurotic state characterized especially by phobias, obsessions, or compulsions that one knows are irrational

— **psych·as·then·ic** \-'the-nik\ *adjective or noun*

**Psy·che** \'sī-kē\ *noun* [Latin, from Greek *psychē* soul]
**1** : a princess loved by Cupid
**2** *not capitalized* [Greek *psychē*] **a** : SOUL, SELF **b** : MIND

**psy·che·de·lia** \ˌsī-kə-'dēl-yə\ *noun* [New Latin, from English *psychedelic*] (1967)
: the world of people, phenomena, or items associated with psychedelic drugs

**¹psy·che·del·ic** \ˌsī-kə-'de-lik\ *noun* [irregular from *psych-* + Greek *dēloun* to show, from *dēlos* evident; akin to Sanskrit *dīdeti* it shines, Latin *dies* day — more at DEITY] (1956)
: a psychedelic drug (as LSD)

**²psychedelic** *adjective* (1957)
**1 a** : of, relating to, or being drugs (as LSD) capable of producing abnormal psychic effects (as hallucinations) and sometimes psychic states resembling mental illness **b** : produced by or associated with the use of psychedelic drugs ⟨a *psychedelic* experience⟩
**2** : imitating, suggestive of, or reproducing effects (as distorted or bizarre images or sounds) resembling those produced by psychedelic drugs ⟨*psychedelic* color schemes⟩
— **psy·che·del·i·cal·ly** \-'de-li-k(ə-)lē\ *adverb*

**psy·chi·a·try** \sə-'kī-ə-trē, sī-\ *noun* [probably from French *psychiatrie*, from *psychiatre* psychiatrist, from *psych-* psych- + Greek *iatros* physician — more at -IATRY] (circa 1846)
: a branch of medicine that deals with mental, emotional, or behavioral disorders
— **psy·chi·at·ric** \ˌsī-kē-'a-trik\ *adjective*
— **psy·chi·at·ri·cal·ly** \-tri-k(ə-)lē\ *adverb*
— **psy·chi·a·trist** \sə-'kī-ə-trist, sī-\ *noun*

**¹psy·chic** \'sī-kik\ *also* **psy·chi·cal** \-ki-kəl\ *adjective* [Greek *psychikos* of the soul, from *psychē* soul] (1642)
**1** : of or relating to the psyche : PSYCHOGENIC
**2** : lying outside the sphere of physical science or knowledge : immaterial, moral, or spiritual in origin or force
**3** : sensitive to nonphysical or supernatural forces and influences : marked by extraordinary or mysterious sensitivity, perception, or understanding
— **psy·chi·cal·ly** \-ki-k(ə-)lē\ *adverb*

**²psychic** *noun* (1871)
**1 a** : a person apparently sensitive to nonphysical forces **b** : MEDIUM 2d
**2** : psychic phenomena

**psy·cho** \'sī-(ˌ)kō\ *noun, plural* **psychos** [short for *psychopath*] (1942)
: a deranged or psychopathic person — not used technically
— **psycho** *adjective*

**psy·cho·acous·tics** \ˌsī-kō-ə-'kü-stiks\ *noun plural but singular in construction* (1948)
: a branch of science dealing with hearing, the sensations produced by sounds, and the problems of communication
— **psy·cho·acous·tic** \-stik\ *adjective*

**psy·cho·ac·tive** \ˌsī-kō-'ak-tiv\ *adjective* (1961)
: affecting the mind or behavior ⟨*psychoactive* drugs⟩

**psy·cho·anal·y·sis** \ˌsī-kō-ə-'na-lə-səs\ *noun* [New Latin] (1906)
: a method of analyzing psychic phenomena and treating emotional disorders that involves treatment sessions during which the patient is encouraged to talk freely about personal experiences and especially about early childhood and dreams
— **psy·cho·an·a·lyst** \-'a-nᵊl-ist\ *noun*

**psy·cho·an·a·lyt·ic** \-ˌa-nᵊl-'i-tik\ *also* **psy·cho·an·a·lyt·i·cal** \-ti-kəl\ *adjective* (1906)
: of, relating to, or employing psychoanalysis or its principles and techniques
— **psy·cho·an·a·lyt·i·cal·ly** \-ti-k(ə-)lē\ *adverb*

**psy·cho·an·a·lyze** \-'a-nᵊl-ˌīz\ *transitive verb* (1911)

: to treat by means of psychoanalysis

**psy·cho·bab·ble** \'sī-kō-ˌba-bəl\ *noun* (1975)
: a predominantly metaphorical language for expressing one's feelings; *also* : psychological jargon
— **psy·cho·bab·bler** \-ˌba-blər\ *noun*

**psy·cho·bi·og·ra·phy** \ˌsī-kō-bī-'ä-grə-fē, -bē-\ *noun* (1931)
: a biography written from a psychodynamic or psychoanalytical point of view; *also* : the application of such a point of view when writing a biography
— **psy·cho·bi·og·ra·pher** \-fər\ *noun*
— **psy·cho·bio·graph·i·cal** \-ˌbī-ə-'grafi-kəl\ *adjective*

**psy·cho·bi·ol·o·gy** \-bī-'ä-lə-jē\ *noun* [International Scientific Vocabulary] (1902)
: the study of mental functioning and behavior in relation to other biological processes
— **psy·cho·bi·o·log·i·cal** \-ˌbī-ə-'lä-ji-kəl\ *also* **psy·cho·bi·o·log·ic** \-jik\ *adjective*
— **psy·cho·bi·ol·o·gist** \-bī-'ä-lə-jist\ *noun*

**psy·cho·chem·i·cal** \-'ke-mi-kəl\ *noun* (1956)
: a psychoactive chemical
— **psychochemical** *adjective*

**psy·cho·dra·ma** \-'drä-mə, -'dra-\ *noun* (1937)
**1** : an extemporized dramatization designed to afford catharsis and social relearning for one or more of the participants from whose life history the plot is abstracted
**2** : a dramatic narrative or event characterized by psychological overtones
— **psy·cho·dra·mat·ic** \-drə-'ma-tik\ *adjective*

**psy·cho·dy·nam·ics** \-dī-'na-miks, -də-\ *noun plural but singular or plural in construction* (1874)
**1** : the psychology of mental or emotional forces or processes developing especially in early childhood and their effects on behavior and mental states
**2** : explanation or interpretation (as of behavior or mental states) in terms of mental or emotional forces or processes
**3** : motivational forces acting especially at the unconscious level
— **psy·cho·dy·nam·ic** \-mik\ *adjective*
— **psy·cho·dy·nam·i·cal·ly** \-mi-k(ə-)lē\ *adverb*

**psy·cho·gen·e·sis** \-'je-nə-səs\ *noun* [New Latin] (1838)
**1** : the origin and development of mental functions, traits, or states
**2** : development from mental as distinguished from physical origins
— **psy·cho·ge·net·ic** \-jə-'ne-tik\ *adjective*

**psy·cho·gen·ic** \-'je-nik\ *adjective* (1902)
: originating in the mind or in mental or emotional conflict
— **psy·cho·gen·i·cal·ly** \-ni-k(ə-)lē\ *adverb*

**psy·cho·graph** \'sī-kə-ˌgraf\ *noun* (1916)
: PSYCHOBIOGRAPHY

**psy·cho·his·to·ry** \'sī-kō-ˌhis-t(ə-)rē\ *noun* (1934)
: historical analysis or interpretation employing psychological and psychoanalytic methods; *also* : a work of history employing such methods
— **psy·cho·his·to·ri·an** \ˌsī-kō-(h)is-'tōr-ē-ən, -'tòr-, -'tär-\ *noun*
— **psy·cho·his·to·ri·cal** \-'tòr-i-kəl, -'tär-\ *adjective*

**psy·cho·ki·ne·sis** \ˌsī-kō-kə-'nē-səs, -kī-\ *noun* [New Latin] (1914)
: movement of physical objects by the mind without use of physical means — compare PRECOGNITION, TELEKINESIS
— **psy·cho·ki·net·ic** \-'ne-tik\ *adjective*

**psy·cho·lin·guis·tics** \ˌsī-kō-liŋ-'gwis-tiks\ *noun plural but singular in construction* (1936)

: the study of the mental faculties involved in the perception, production, and acquisition of language
— **psy·cho·lin·guist** \-'liŋ-gwist\ *noun*
— **psy·cho·lin·guis·tic** \-tik\ *adjective*
**psy·cho·log·i·cal** \ˌsī-kə-'lä-ji-kəl\ *also* **psy·cho·log·ic** \-jik\ *adjective* (circa 1688)
**1 a :** of or relating to psychology **b :** MENTAL
**2 :** directed toward the will or toward the mind specifically in its conative function ⟨*psychological* warfare⟩
— **psy·cho·log·i·cal·ly** \-ji-k(ə-)lē\ *adverb*
**psychological moment** *noun* (1871)
: the occasion when the mental atmosphere is most certain to be favorable to the full effect of an action or event
**psy·chol·o·gise** *British variant of* PSYCHOLOGIZE
**psy·chol·o·gism** \sī-'kä-lə-ˌji-zəm\ *noun* (1858)
: a theory that applies psychological conceptions to the interpretation of historical events or logical thought
**psy·chol·o·gize** \-ˌjīz\ *verb* **-gized; -gizing** (1810)
*intransitive verb*
: to speculate in psychological terms or on psychological motivations
*transitive verb*
: to explain or interpret in psychological terms
**psy·chol·o·gy** \-jē\ *noun, plural* **-gies** [New Latin *psychologia*, from *psych-* + *-logia* -logy] (1653)
**1 :** the science of mind and behavior
**2 a :** the mental or behavioral characteristics of an individual or group **b :** the study of mind and behavior in relation to a particular field of knowledge or activity
**3 :** a treatise on psychology
— **psy·chol·o·gist** \-jist\ *noun*
**psy·cho·met·ric** \ˌsī-kə-'me-trik\ *adjective* (1854)
: of or relating to psychometrics or psychometry
— **psy·cho·met·ri·cal·ly** \-tri-k(ə-)lē\ *adverb*
**psy·cho·me·tri·cian** \-mə-'tri-shən\ *noun* (circa 1939)
**1 :** a person (as a clinical psychologist) who is skilled in the administration and interpretation of objective psychological tests
**2 :** a psychologist who devises, constructs, and standardizes psychometric tests
**psy·cho·met·rics** \-'me-triks\ *noun plural but singular in construction* (circa 1924)
: the psychological theory or technique of mental measurement
**psy·chom·e·try** \sī-'kä-mə-trē\ *noun* (circa 1842)
**1 :** divination of facts concerning an object or its owner through contact with or proximity to the object
**2 :** PSYCHOMETRICS
**psy·cho·mo·tor** \ˌsī-kə-'mō-tər\ *adjective* [International Scientific Vocabulary] (1878)
: of or relating to motor action directly proceeding from mental activity
**psy·cho·neu·ro·sis** \ˌsī-kō-nu̇-'rō-səs, -nyu̇-\ *noun* [New Latin] (1883)
: NEUROSIS; *especially* : a neurosis based on emotional conflict in which an impulse that has been blocked seeks expression in a disguised response or symptom
— **psy·cho·neu·rot·ic** \-'rä-tik\ *adjective or noun*
**psy·cho·path** \'sī-kə-ˌpath\ *noun* [International Scientific Vocabulary] (1885)
: a mentally ill or unstable person; *especially* : a person having a psychopathic personality
**¹psy·cho·path·ic** \ˌsī-kə-'pa-thik\ *adjective* (1847)
: of, relating to, or characterized by psychopathy
— **psy·cho·path·i·cal·ly** \-thi-k(ə-)lē\ *adverb*

**²psychopathic** *noun* (circa 1890)
: PSYCHOPATH
**psychopathic personality** *noun* (circa 1923)
**1 :** an emotionally and behaviorally disordered state characterized by clear perception of reality except for the individual's social and moral obligations and often by the pursuit of immediate personal gratification in criminal acts, drug addiction, or sexual perversion
**2 :** an individual having a psychopathic personality
**psy·cho·pa·thol·o·gy** \ˌsī-kō-pə-'thä-lə-jē, -pa-\ *noun* [International Scientific Vocabulary] (1847)
: the study of psychological and behavioral dysfunction occurring in mental disorder or in social disorganization; *also* : such dysfunction
— **psy·cho·path·o·log·ic** \-ˌpa-thə-'lä-jik\ *or* **psy·cho·path·o·log·i·cal** \-ji-kəl\ *adjective*
— **psy·cho·path·o·log·i·cal·ly** \-ji-k(ə-)lē\ *adverb*
— **psy·cho·pa·thol·o·gist** \-pə-'thä-lə-jist, -pa-\ *noun*
**psy·chop·a·thy** \sī-'kä-pə-thē\ *noun* [International Scientific Vocabulary] (1847)
: mental disorder; *especially* : extreme mental disorder marked usually by egocentric and antisocial activity
**psy·cho·phar·ma·col·o·gy** \ˌsī-kō-ˌfär-mə-'kä-lə-jē\ *noun* (1920)
: the study of the effect of drugs on the mind and behavior
— **psy·cho·phar·ma·co·log·i·cal** \-mə-kə-'lä-ji-kəl\ *or* **psy·cho·phar·ma·co·log·ic** \-jik\ *adjective*
— **psy·cho·phar·ma·col·o·gist** \-'kä-lə-jist\ *noun*
**psy·cho·phys·i·cal** \ˌsī-kō-'fi-zi-kəl\ *adjective* (1847)
: of or relating to psychophysics; *also* : sharing mental and physical qualities
— **psy·cho·phys·i·cal·ly** \-k(ə-)lē\ *adverb*
**psychophysical parallelism** *noun* (1894)
: PARALLELISM 4
**psy·cho·phys·ics** \ˌsī-kō-'fi-ziks\ *noun plural but singular in construction* [International Scientific Vocabulary] (1878)
: a branch of psychology concerned with the effect of physical processes (as intensity of stimulation) on the mental processes of an organism
— **psy·cho·phys·i·cist** \-'fi-zə-sist, -'fiz-ˌsist\ *noun*
**psy·cho·phys·i·o·log·i·cal** \ˌsī-kō-ˌfi-zē-ə-'lä-ji-kəl\ *also* **psy·cho·phys·i·o·log·ic** \-jik\ *adjective* (1839)
**1 :** of or relating to physiological psychology
**2 :** combining or involving mental and bodily processes
— **psy·cho·phys·i·o·log·i·cal·ly** \-ji-k(ə-)lē\ *adverb*
**psy·cho·phys·i·ol·o·gy** \-ˌfi-zē-'ä-lə-jē\ *noun* [International Scientific Vocabulary] (1839)
: PHYSIOLOGICAL PSYCHOLOGY
— **psy·cho·phys·i·ol·o·gist** \-jist\ *noun*
**psy·cho·sex·u·al** \-'sek-shə-wəl, -shwəl, -shəl\ *adjective* (1897)
**1 :** of or relating to the mental, emotional, and behavioral aspects of sexual development
**2 :** of or relating to mental or emotional attitudes concerning sexual activity
**3 :** of or relating to the physiological psychology of sex
— **psy·cho·sex·u·al·ly** *adverb*
**psy·cho·sex·u·al·i·ty** \-ˌsek-shə-'wa-lə-tē\ *noun* (1910)
: the psychic factors of sex
**psy·cho·sis** \sī-'kō-səs\ *noun, plural* **-cho·ses** \-ˌsēz\ [New Latin] (1847)
: fundamental mental derangement (as schizophrenia) characterized by defective or lost contact with reality

**psy·cho·so·cial** \ˌsī-kō-'sō-shəl\ *adjective* (1899)
**1 :** involving both psychological and social aspects ⟨*psychosocial* adjustment in marriage⟩
**2 :** relating social conditions to mental health ⟨*psychosocial* medicine⟩
— **psy·cho·so·cial·ly** \-'sō-sh(ə-)lē\ *adverb*
**psy·cho·so·mat·ic** \-sə-'ma-tik\ *adjective* [International Scientific Vocabulary] (1863)
**1 :** of, relating to, concerned with, or involving both mind and body ⟨the *psychosomatic* nature of man —Herbert Ratner⟩
**2 :** of, relating to, involving, or concerned with bodily symptoms caused by mental or emotional disturbance ⟨*psychosomatic* illness⟩ ⟨*psychosomatic* medicine⟩
— **psy·cho·so·mat·i·cal·ly** \-ti-k(ə-)lē\ *adverb*
**psy·cho·so·mat·ics** \-sə-'ma-tiks\ *noun plural but singular in construction* (1938)
: a branch of medical science dealing with interrelationships between the mind or emotions and the body and especially with the relation of psychic conflict to somatic symptomatology
**psy·cho·sur·gery** \-'sər-jə-rē, -'sərj-rē\ *noun* (1936)
: cerebral surgery employed in treating psychic symptoms
— **psy·cho·sur·geon** \-'sər-jən\ *noun*
— **psy·cho·sur·gi·cal** \-'sər-ji-kəl\ *adjective*
**psy·cho·syn·the·sis** \-'sin(t)-thə-səs\ *noun* (1919)
: a form of psychotherapy combining psychoanalytic techniques with meditation and exercise
**psy·cho·ther·a·peu·tic** \-ˌther-ə-'pyü-tik\ *adjective* [International Scientific Vocabulary] (circa 1888)
: of, relating to, or used in psychotherapy
— **psy·cho·ther·a·peu·ti·cal·ly** \-ti-k(ə-)lē\ *adverb*
**psy·cho·ther·a·py** \-'ther-ə-pē\ *noun* [International Scientific Vocabulary] (circa 1890)
: treatment of mental or emotional disorder or of related bodily ills by psychological means
— **psy·cho·ther·a·pist** \-pist\ *noun*
**psy·chot·ic** \sī-'kä-tik\ *adjective* (circa 1890)
: of, relating to, marked by, or affected with psychosis ⟨a *psychotic* patient⟩ ⟨*psychotic* behavior⟩
— **psychotic** *noun*
— **psy·chot·i·cal·ly** \-ti-k(ə-)lē\ *adverb*
**psy·cho·to·mi·met·ic** \ˌsī-ˌkä-tō-mə-'me-tik, -mī-\ *adjective* [*psychot*ic + *-o-* + *mimetic*] (1957)
: of, relating to, involving, or inducing psychotic alteration of behavior and personality ⟨*psychotomimetic* drugs⟩
— **psychotomimetic** *noun*
— **psy·cho·to·mi·met·i·cal·ly** \-ti-k(ə-)lē\ *adverb*
**psy·cho·tro·pic** \ˌsī-kə-'trō-pik\ *adjective* (1948)
: acting on the mind ⟨*psychotropic* drugs⟩
— **psychotropic** *noun*
**psych–out** \'sīk-ˌau̇t\ *noun* (1971)
: an act or an instance of psyching someone out
**psychro-** *combining form* [Greek, from *psychros*, from *psychein* to cool]
: cold ⟨*psychro*meter⟩
**psy·chrom·e·ter** \sī-'krä-mə-tər\ *noun* [International Scientific Vocabulary] (1838)
: a hygrometer consisting essentially of two similar thermometers with the bulb of one being kept wet so that the cooling that results from evaporation makes it register a lower

---

\ə\ abut \ᵊ\ kitten \ər\ further \a\ ash \ā\ ace
\ä\ mop, mar \au̇\ out \ch\ chin \e\ bet \ē\ easy
\g\ go \i\ hit \ī\ ice \j\ job \ŋ\ sing \ō\ go
\ȯ\ law \ȯi\ boy \th\ thin \t͟h\ the \ü\ loot \u̇\ foot
\y\ yet \zh\ vision *see also* Guide to Pronunciation

temperature than the dry one and with the difference between the readings constituting a measure of the dryness of the atmosphere
— **psy·chro·met·ric** \ˌsī-krə-'me-trik\ *adjective*
— **psy·chrom·e·try** \sī-'krä-mə-trē\ *noun*
**psy·chro·phil·ic** \ˌsī-krō-'fi-lik\ *adjective* (circa 1903)
: thriving at a relatively low temperature ⟨*psychrophilic* bacteria⟩
**psyl·la** \'si-lə\ *noun* [New Latin, genus name, from Greek, flea; akin to Latin *pulex* flea, Sanskrit *pluṣi*] (1852)
: any of various plant lice (family Psyllidae) including economically important plant pests
— compare PEAR PSYLLA
**psyl·lid** \'si-lad\ *noun* [ultimately from New Latin *Psylla*] (1899)
: PSYLLA
— **psyllid** *adjective*
**psyl·li·um seed** \'si-lē-əm-\ *noun* [New Latin *psyllium*, from Greek *psyllion* fleawort, from *psylla*] (1897)
: the seed of a fleawort (especially *Plantago psyllium*) that has the property of swelling and becoming gelatinous when moist and is used as a mild laxative — called also *psyllium*
**psy·war** \'sī-ˌwȯr\ *noun* [by shortening] (1951)
: psychological warfare
**ptar·mi·gan** \'tär-mi-gən\ *noun, plural* **-gan** *or* **-gans** [modification of Scottish Gaelic *tarmachan*] (1599)
: any of various grouses (genus *Lagopus*) of northern regions with completely feathered feet
**PT boat** \ˌpē-'tē-, 'pē-ˌ\ *noun* [*patrol torpedo*] (1941)
: a small fast patrol craft usually armed with torpedoes, machine guns, and depth charges — called also *PT*
**PTC** \ˌpē-(ˌ)tē-'sē\ *noun* (1932)
: PHENYLTHIOCARBAMIDE

ptarmigan: *A* summer plumage; *B* winter plumage

**pter·an·o·don** \tə-'ra-nə-ˌdän, -'rä-\ *noun* [New Latin, from Greek *pteron* wing + *anodōn* toothless from *an-* + *odōn, odous* tooth — more at FEATHER, TOOTH] (1897)
: any of a genus (*Pteranodon*) of Cretaceous pterosaurs having a backwardly directed bony crest on the skull and a wingspan of about 25 feet (7.7 meters)
**pterid-** *or* **pterido-** *combining form* [Greek *pterid-, pteris;* akin to Greek *pteron* wing, feather]
: fern ⟨*pteridology*⟩
**pter·i·dine** \'ter-ə-ˌdēn\ *noun* [International Scientific Vocabulary *pter*in + *-idine*] (circa 1943)
: a yellow crystalline bicyclic base $C_6H_4N_4$ that is a structural constituent especially of various animal pigments
**pter·i·dol·o·gy** \ˌter-ə-'dä-lə-jē\ *noun* (1855)
: the study of ferns
— **pter·i·do·log·i·cal** \ˌter-ə-də-'lä-ji-kəl\ *adjective*
— **pter·i·dol·o·gist** \-'dä-lə-jist\ *noun*
**pte·ri·do·phyte** \tə-'ri-də-ˌfīt, 'ter-ə-dō-\ *noun* [New Latin *Pteridophyta*, from Greek *pterid-, pteris* fern + *phyton* plant — more at PHYT-] (1880)
: any of a division (Pteridophyta) of vascular plants (as a fern) that have roots, stems, and leaves but lack flowers or seeds
**pte·ri·do·sperm** \tə-'ri-də-ˌspərm, 'ter-ə-dō-\ *noun* [International Scientific Vocabulary] (1904)
: SEED FERN

**pter·in** \'ter-ən\ *noun* [International Scientific Vocabulary *pter-* (from Greek *pteron* wing) + [1]*-in*; from its being a factor in the pigments of butterfly wings] (1934)
: any of various compounds that contain the bicyclic ring system characteristic of pteridine
**ptero·dac·tyl** \ˌter-ə-'dak-t[ə]l\ *noun* [New Latin *Pterodactylus*, genus of reptiles, from Greek *pteron* wing + *daktylos* finger — more at FEATHER] (1830)
: any of various pterosaurs (suborder Pterodactyloidea) of the Late Jurassic and Cretaceous having a rudimentary tail and a beak with reduced dentition; *broadly* : PTEROSAUR
**ptero·pod** \'ter-ə-ˌpäd\ *noun* [New Latin *Pteropoda*, group name, from Greek *pteron* wing + New Latin *-poda*] (1835)
: any of the opisthobranch mollusks comprising two orders (Thecosomata and Gymnosomata) and having the anterior lobes of the foot expanded into broad thin winglike swimming organs
**ptero·saur** \'ter-ə-ˌsȯr\ *noun* [New Latin *Pterosauria*, from Greek *pteron* wing + *sauros* lizard] (1862)
: any of an order (Pterosauria) of extinct flying reptiles existing from the Late Triassic throughout the Jurassic and most of the Cretaceous and having a featherless wing membrane extending from the side of the body along the arm to the end of the greatly elongated fourth digit
**pter·o·yl·glu·tam·ic acid** \ˌter-ə-ˌwil-glü-'ta-mik-\ *noun* [International Scientific Vocabulary *pteroyl* (the radical $(C_{13}H_{11}N_6O)CO$) + *glutamic acid*] (1943)
: FOLIC ACID
[1]**pter·y·goid** \'ter-ə-ˌgȯid\ *adjective* [New Latin *pterygoides*, from Greek *pterygoeidēs*, literally, shaped like a wing, from *pteryg-, pteryx* wing; akin to Greek *pteron* wing — more at FEATHER] (1722)
: of, relating to, or lying in the region of the inferior part of the sphenoid bone of the vertebrate skull
[2]**pterygoid** *noun* (1831)
: a pterygoid part (as a bone, muscle, or nerve)
**pterygoid process** *noun* (1741)
: a process extending downward from each side of the sphenoid bone in humans and other mammals
**pter·y·la** \'ter-ə-lə\ *noun, plural* **-lae** \-ˌlē, -ˌlī\ [New Latin, from Greek *pteron* + *hylē* wood, forest] (1867)
: one of the definite areas of the skin of a bird on which feathers grow
**Ptol·e·ma·ic** \ˌtä-lə-'mā-ik\ *adjective* [Greek *Ptolemaikos*, from *Ptolemaios* Ptolemy] (1674)
**1** : of or relating to Ptolemy the geographer and astronomer who flourished at Alexandria about A.D. 130
**2** : of or relating to the Greco-Egyptian Ptolemies ruling Egypt from 323 to 30 B.C.
**Ptolemaic system** *noun* (circa 1771)
: the system of planetary motions according to which the earth is at the center with the sun, moon, and planets revolving around it
**pto·maine** \'tō-ˌmān, tō-'\ *noun* [Italian *ptomaina*, from Greek *ptōma* fall, fallen body, corpse, from *piptein* to fall — more at FEATHER] (1880)
: any of various organic bases which are formed by the action of putrefactive bacteria on nitrogenous matter and some of which are poisonous
**ptomaine poisoning** *noun* (1893)
: food poisoning caused by bacteria or bacterial products
**pto·sis** \'tō-səs\ *noun, plural* **pto·ses** \-ˌsēz\ [New Latin, from Greek *ptōsis* act of falling, from *piptein*] (1743)
: a sagging or prolapse of an organ or part; *especially* : a drooping of the upper eyelid

**pty·a·lin** \'tī-ə-lən\ *noun* [Greek *ptyalon* saliva, from *ptyein* to spit — more at SPEW] (1845)
: an amylase found in the saliva of many animals that converts starch into sugar
**pty·a·lism** \-ˌli-zəm\ *noun* [New Latin *ptyalismus*, from Greek *ptyalismos*, from *ptyalizein* to salivate, from *ptyalon*] (1676)
: an excessive flow of saliva
**p–type** \'pē-ˌtīp\ *adjective* [*positive type*] (1946)
: relating to or being a semiconductor in which charge is carried by holes — compare N-TYPE
**pub** \'pəb\ *noun* (circa 1859)
**1** *chiefly British* : PUBLIC HOUSE 2
**2** : an establishment where alcoholic beverages are sold and consumed
**pub crawler** *noun* (1910)
: one who goes from bar to bar
— **pub–crawl** *intransitive verb*
— **pub crawl** *noun*
**pu·ber·tal** \'pyü-bər-t[ə]l\ *or* **pu·ber·al** \'pyü-bə-rəl\ *adjective* [*pubertal* from *puberty; puberal* from Medieval Latin *puberalis;* from Latin *puber*] (circa 1837)
: of or relating to puberty
**pu·ber·ty** \'pyü-bər-tē\ *noun* [Middle English *puberte*, from Latin *pubertas*, from *puber* pubescent] (14th century)
**1** : the condition of being or the period of becoming first capable of reproducing sexually marked by maturing of the genital organs, development of secondary sex characteristics, and in the human and in higher primates by the first occurrence of menstruation in the female
**2** : the age at which puberty occurs often construed legally as 14 in boys and 12 in girls
**pu·ber·u·lent** \pyü-'ber-ə-lənt, -yə-lənt\ *adjective* [Latin *puber* pubescent + English *-ulent* (as in *pulverulent*)] (circa 1859)
: covered with fine pubescence
**pu·bes** \'pyü-(ˌ)bēz\ *noun, plural* **pubes** [New Latin, from Latin, manhood, body hair, pubic region; akin to Latin *puber* pubescent] (circa 1570)
**1** : the hair that appears on the lower part of the hypogastric region at puberty
**2** : the pubic region
**pu·bes·cence** \pyü-'be-s[ə]n(t)s\ *noun* (15th century)
**1** : the quality or state of being pubescent
**2** : a pubescent covering or surface
**pu·bes·cent** \-s[ə]nt\ *adjective* [Latin *pubescent-, pubescens*, present participle of *pubescere* to reach puberty, become covered as with hair, from *pubes*] (1646)
**1 a** : arriving at or having reached puberty **b** : of or relating to puberty
**2** : covered with fine soft short hairs — compare VILLOUS
**pu·bic** \'pyü-bik\ *adjective* (1831)
: of, relating to, or situated in or near the region of the pubes or the pubis
**pu·bis** \'pyü-bəs\ *noun, plural* **pu·bes** \-(ˌ)bēz\ [New Latin *os pubis*, literally, bone of the pubic region] (1597)
: the ventral and anterior of the three principal bones composing either half of the pelvis — called also *pubic bone*
[1]**pub·lic** \'pə-blik\ *adjective* [Middle English *publique*, from Middle French, from Latin *publicus;* akin to Latin *populus* the people] (14th century)
**1 a** : exposed to general view : OPEN **b** : WELL-KNOWN, PROMINENT **c** : PERCEPTIBLE, MATERIAL
**2 a** : of, relating to, or affecting all the people or the whole area of a nation or state ⟨*public* law⟩ **b** : of or relating to a government **c** : of, relating to, or being in the service of the community or nation
**3 a** : of or relating to people in general : UNIVERSAL **b** : GENERAL, POPULAR
**4** : of or relating to business or community interests as opposed to private affairs : SOCIAL

**5 :** devoted to the general or national welfare **:** HUMANITARIAN
**6 a :** accessible to or shared by all members of the community **b :** capitalized in shares that can be freely traded on the open market — often used with *go*
— **pub·lic·ness** *noun*

**²public** *noun* (15th century)
**1 :** a place accessible or visible to the public — usually used in the phrase *in public*
**2 :** the people as a whole **:** POPULACE
**3 :** a group of people having common interests or characteristics; *specifically* **:** the group at which a particular activity or enterprise aims

**public–address system** *noun* (1923)
**:** an apparatus including a microphone and loudspeakers used for broadcasting to a large audience in an auditorium or outdoors

**pub·li·can** \'pə-bli-kən\ *noun* [Middle English, from Old French, from Latin *publicanus* tax farmer, from *publicum* public revenue, from neuter of *publicus*] (13th century)
**1 a :** a Jewish tax collector for the ancient Romans **b :** a collector of taxes or tribute
**2** *chiefly British* **:** the licensee of a public house

**public assistance** *noun* (1884)
**:** government aid to needy, blind, aged, or disabled persons and to dependent children

**pub·li·ca·tion** \,pə-blə-'kā-shən\ *noun* [Middle English *publicacioun*, from Middle French *publication*, from Latin *publication-, publicatio*, from *publicare*, from *publicus* public] (14th century)
**1 :** the act or process of publishing
**2 :** a published work

**public defender** *noun* (1918)
**:** a lawyer usually holding public office whose duty is to defend accused persons unable to pay for legal assistance

**public domain** *noun* (1832)
**1 :** land owned directly by the government
**2 :** the realm embracing property rights that belong to the community at large, are unprotected by copyright or patent, and are subject to appropriation by anyone

**public health** *noun* (1617)
**:** the art and science dealing with the protection and improvement of community health by organized community effort and including preventive medicine and sanitary and social science

**public house** *noun* (1658)
**1 :** INN, HOSTELRY
**2** *chiefly British* **:** a licensed saloon or bar

**pub·li·cise** *British variant of* PUBLICIZE

**pub·li·cist** \'pə-blə-sist\ *noun* (1792)
**1 a :** an expert in international law **b :** an expert or commentator on public affairs
**2 :** one that publicizes; *specifically* **:** PRESS AGENT

**pub·lic·i·ty** \(,)pə-'bli-sə-tē, -'blis-tē\ *noun* (1791)
**1 :** the quality or state of being public
**2 a :** an act or device designed to attract public interest; *specifically* **:** information with news value issued as a means of gaining public attention or support **b :** the dissemination of information or promotional material **c :** paid advertising **d :** public attention or acclaim

**pub·li·cize** \'pə-blə-,sīz\ *transitive verb* **-cized; -ciz·ing** (1925)
**:** to bring to the attention of the public **:** ADVERTISE

**public land** *noun* (1789)
**:** land owned by a government; *specifically* **:** that part of the U.S. public domain subject to sale or disposal under the homestead laws

**public law** *noun* (1773)
**1 :** a legislative enactment affecting the public at large
**2 :** a branch of law concerned with regulating the relations of individuals with the government and the organization and conduct of the government itself — compare PRIVATE LAW

**pub·lic·ly** \'pə-bli-klē\ *also* **pub·li·cal·ly** \-li-k(ə-)lē\ *adverb* (1567)
**1 :** in a manner observable by or in a place accessible to the public **:** OPENLY
**2 a :** by the people generally **b :** by a government

**public officer** *noun* (1925)
**:** a person who has been legally elected or appointed to office and who exercises governmental functions

**public relations** *noun plural but usually singular in construction, often attributive* (1807)
**:** the business of inducing the public to have understanding for and goodwill toward a person, firm, or institution; *also* **:** the degree of understanding and goodwill achieved

**public sale** *noun* (1678)
**:** AUCTION 1

**public school** *noun* (1580)
**1 :** an endowed secondary boarding school in Great Britain offering a classical curriculum and preparation for the universities or public service
**2 :** a free tax-supported school controlled by a local governmental authority

**public servant** *noun* (1676)
**:** a government official or employee

**public service** *noun* (circa 1576)
**1 :** the business of supplying a commodity (as electricity or gas) or service (as transportation) to any or all members of a community
**2 :** a service rendered in the public interest
**3 :** governmental employment; *especially* **:** CIVIL SERVICE

**public–service corporation** *noun* (1904)
**:** a quasi-public corporation

**public speaking** *noun* (1762)
**1 :** the act or process of making speeches in public
**2 :** the art of effective oral communication with an audience

**public–spirited** *adjective* (1677)
**:** motivated by devotion to the general welfare
— **pub·lic–spir·it·ed·ness** *noun*

**public television** *noun* (1965)
**:** television supported by public funds and private contributions rather than by commercials

**public utility** *noun* (1903)
**:** a business organization (as an electric company) performing a public service and subject to special governmental regulation

**public works** *noun plural* (1676)
**:** works (as schools, highways, docks) constructed for public use or enjoyment especially when financed and owned by the government

**pub·lish** \'pə-blish\ *verb* [Middle English, modification of Middle French *publier*, from Latin *publicare*, from *publicus* public] (14th century)
*transitive verb*
**1 a :** to make generally known **b :** to make public announcement of
**2 a :** to disseminate to the public **b :** to produce or release for distribution; *specifically* **:** PRINT 2c **c :** to issue the work of (an author)
*intransitive verb*
**1 :** to put out an edition
**2 :** to have one's work accepted for publication
— **pub·lish·able** \-bli-shə-bəl\ *adjective*

**pub·lish·er** \'pə-bli-shər\ *noun* (15th century)
**:** one that publishes something; *especially* **:** a person or corporation whose business is publishing

**pub·lish·ing** \-shiŋ\ *noun* (1580)
**:** the business or profession of the commercial production and issuance of literature, information, musical scores or sometimes recordings, or art ⟨newspaper *publishing*⟩ ⟨software *publishing*⟩

**puc·coon** \(,)pə-'kün\ *noun* [Virginia Algonquian *poughkone*] (1612)
**1 :** any of several American plants (as bloodroot) yielding a red or yellow pigment
**2 :** a pigment from a puccoon

**puce** \'pyüs\ *noun* [French, literally, flea, from Latin *pulic-, pulex* — more at PSYLLA] (1882)
**:** a dark red

**¹puck** \'pək\ *noun* [Middle English *puke*, from Old English *pūca*; akin to Old Norse *pūki* devil] (before 12th century)
**1** *archaic* **:** an evil spirit **:** DEMON
**2 :** a mischievous sprite **:** HOBGOBLIN; *specifically, capitalized* **:** ROBIN GOODFELLOW

**²puck** *noun* [English dialect *puck* to poke, hit, probably from Irish *poc* butt, stroke in hurling, literally, buck (male deer)] (1891)
**:** a vulcanized rubber disk used in ice hockey

**pucka** *variant of* PUKKA

**¹puck·er** \'pə-kər\ *verb* **puck·ered; puck·er·ing** \-k(ə-)riŋ\ [probably irregular from ¹*poke*] (1598)
*intransitive verb*
**:** to become wrinkled or constricted
*transitive verb*
**:** to contract into folds or wrinkles

**²pucker** *noun* (circa 1750)
**:** a fold or wrinkle in a normally even surface

**puck·ery** \'pə-k(ə-)rē\ *adjective* (1830)
**:** that puckers or causes puckering

**puck·ish** \'pə-kish\ *adjective* [¹*puck*] (1874)
**:** IMPISH, WHIMSICAL
— **puck·ish·ly** *adverb*
— **puck·ish·ness** *noun*

**pud** \'pùd\ *noun* (1706)
*British* **:** PUDDING

**pud·ding** \'pù-diŋ\ *noun* [Middle English] (13th century)
**1 :** BLOOD SAUSAGE
**2 a** (1) **:** a boiled or baked soft food usually with a cereal base ⟨corn *pudding*⟩ (2) **:** a dessert of a soft, spongy, or thick creamy consistency ⟨chocolate *pudding*⟩ (3) *British* **:** DESSERT
**1 b :** a dish often containing suet or having a suet crust and originally boiled in a bag ⟨steak and kidney *pudding*⟩

**pudding stone** *noun* (1753)
**:** CONGLOMERATE

**¹pud·dle** \'pə-dªl\ *noun* [Middle English *podel*; akin to Low German *pudel* puddle, Old English *pudd* ditch] (14th century)
**1 :** a very small pool of usually dirty or muddy water
**2 a :** an earthy mixture (as of clay, sand, and gravel) worked while wet into a compact mass that becomes impervious to water when dry **b :** a thin mixture of soil and water for puddling plants

**²puddle** *verb* **pud·dled; pud·dling** \'pəd-liŋ, 'pə-dªl-iŋ\ (15th century)
*intransitive verb*
**:** to dabble or wade around in a puddle
*transitive verb*
**1 :** to make muddy or turbid **:** MUDDLE
**2 a :** to work (a wet mixture of earth or concrete) into a dense impervious mass **b :** to subject (iron) to the process of puddling
**3 a :** to strew with puddles **b :** to compact (soil) especially by working when too wet **c :** to dip the roots of (a plant) in a thin mud before transplanting
— **pud·dler** \'pəd-lər, 'pə-dªl-ər\ *noun*

**puddle duck** *noun* (1877)
**:** DABBLER b

**puddle jumper** *noun* (1942)
*slang* **:** LIGHTPLANE

**pud·dling** \'pəd-liŋ, 'pə-dªl-iŋ\ *noun* (1839)
**:** the process of converting pig iron into wrought iron or rarely steel by subjecting it to heat and frequent stirring in a furnace in the presence of oxidizing substances

**pu·den·cy** \'pyü-dªn(t)-sē\ *noun* [Latin *pudentia*, from *pudent-, pudens*, present participle of *pudēre* to be ashamed, make ashamed] (1611)
**:** MODESTY

\ə\ abut \ª\ kitten \ər\ further \a\ ash \ā\ ace
\ä\ mop, mar \aù\ out \ch\ chin \e\ bet \ē\ easy
\g\ go \i\ hit \ī\ ice \j\ job \ŋ\ sing \ō\ go
\ò\ law \òi\ boy \th\ thin \ṯẖ\ the \ü\ loot \ù\ foot
\y\ yet \zh\ vision *see also* Guide to Pronunciation

**pu·den·dum** \pyù-'den-dəm\ *noun, plural* **-da** \-də\ [New Latin, singular of Latin *pudenda*, from neuter plural of *pudendus*, gerundive of *pudēre* to be ashamed] (1634)
: the external genital organs of a human being and especially of a woman — usually used in plural
— **pu·den·dal** \-d°l\ *adjective*

**pudgy** \'pə-jē\ *adjective* **pudg·i·er; -est** [origin unknown] (1836)
: being short and plump : CHUBBY
— **pudg·i·ness** *noun*

**pu·di·bund** \'pyü-də-,bənd\ *adjective* [Latin *pudibundus*, from *pudēre* to be ashamed + *-bundus* (as in *moribundus* moribund)] (circa 1656)
: PRUDISH

**pueb·lo** \'pwe-(,)blō; pü-'e-, pyü-\ *noun, plural* **-los** [Spanish, village, literally, people, from Latin *populus*] (1808)
**1 a** : the communal dwelling of an Indian village of Arizona, New Mexico, and adjacent areas consisting of contiguous flat-roofed stone or adobe houses in groups sometimes several stories high **b** : an Indian village of the southwestern U.S.
**2** *capitalized* : a member of a group of Indian peoples of the southwestern U.S.

**pu·er·ile** \'pyù(-ə)r-əl, -,īl\ *adjective* [French or Latin; French *puéril*, from Latin *puerilis*, from *puer* boy, child; akin to Sanskrit *putra* son, child and perhaps to Greek *pais* boy, child — more at FEW] (1661)
**1** : JUVENILE
**2** : CHILDISH, SILLY ⟨*puerile* remarks⟩
— **pu·er·ile·ly** \-ə(l)-lē, -,īl-lē\ *adverb*
— **pu·er·il·i·ty** \,pyü-ə-'ri-l-ə-tē\ *noun*

**pu·er·il·ism** \'pyù(-ə)r-ə-,li-zəm, 'pyü(-ə)r-,ī-\ *noun* (1924)
: childish behavior especially as a symptom of mental disorder

**pu·er·per·al** \pyü-'ər-p(ə-)rəl\ *adjective* [Latin *puerpera* woman in childbirth, from *puer* child + *parere* to give birth to — more at PARE] (1768)
: of, relating to, or occurring during childbirth or the period immediately following ⟨*puerperal* infection⟩ ⟨*puerperal* depression⟩

**puerperal fever** *noun* (1768)
: an abnormal condition that results from infection of the placental site following delivery or abortion and is characterized in mild form by fever but in serious cases the infection may spread through the uterine wall or pass into the bloodstream — called also *childbed fever, puerperal sepsis*

**pu·er·pe·ri·um** \,pyü-ər-'pir-ē-əm\ *noun, plural* **-ria** \-ē-ə\ [Latin, from *puerpera*] (circa 1890)
: the period between childbirth and the return of the uterus to its normal size

**¹puff** \'pəf\ *verb* [Middle English, from Old English *pyffan*, of imitative origin] (before 12th century)
*intransitive verb*
**1 a** (1) : to blow in short gusts (2) : to exhale forcibly **b** : to breathe hard : PANT **c** : to emit small whiffs or clouds (as of smoke) often as an accompaniment to vigorous action ⟨*puff* at a pipe⟩
**2** : to speak or act in a scornful, conceited, or exaggerated manner
**3 a** : to become distended : SWELL — usually used with *up* **b** : to open or appear in or as if in a puff
**4** : to form a chromosomal puff
*transitive verb*
**1 a** : to emit, propel, blow, or expel by or as if by puffs : WAFT **b** : to draw on (as a cigar, cigarette, or pipe) with intermittent exhalations of smoke
**2 a** : to distend with or as if with air or gas : INFLATE **b** : to make proud or conceited : ELATE **c** (1) : to praise extravagantly and usually with exaggeration : ADVERTISE

**²puff** *noun* (13th century)

**1 a** : an act or instance of puffing : WHIFF **b** : a slight explosive sound accompanying a puff **c** : a perceptible cloud or aura emitted in a puff **d** : DRAW 1a
**2** : a light round hollow pastry
**3 a** : a slight swelling : PROTUBERANCE **b** : a fluffy mass: as (1) : POUF 2 (2) : a small fluffy pad for applying cosmetic powder (3) : a soft loose roll of hair (4) : a quilted bed covering
**4** : a commendatory or promotional notice or review
**5** : an enlarged region of a chromosome that is associated with intensely active genes involved in RNA synthesis
— **puff·i·ness** \'pə-fē-nəs\ *noun*
— **puffy** \'pə-fē\ *adjective*

**puff adder** *noun* (1789)
**1** : a thick-bodied extremely venomous African viper (*Bitis arietans*)
**2** : HOGNOSE SNAKE

**puff·ball** \'pəf-,bȯl\ *noun* (1649)
: any of various globose and often edible fungi (especially family Lycoperdaceae) that discharge ripe spores in a smokelike cloud when pressed or struck

**puff·er** \'pə-fər\ *noun* (1629)
**1** : one that puffs
**2 a** : any of a family (Tetraodontidae) of chiefly tropical marine bony fishes which can distend themselves to a globular form and most of which are highly poisonous — called also *blowfish, globefish* **b** : any of various fish of the same order (Tetraodontiformes synonym Plectognathi) as the puffers

**puff·ery** \'pə-f(ə-)rē\ *noun* (1782)
: exaggerated commendation especially for promotional purposes : HYPE

**puf·fin** \'pə-fən\ *noun* [Middle English *pophyn*] (14th century)
: any of several seabirds (genera *Fratercula* and *Lunda*) having a short neck and a deep grooved parti-colored laterally compressed bill

**puff pastry** *noun* (1611)
: a pastry dough containing many alternating layers of butter and dough or the light flaky pastry made from it — called also *puff paste*

puffin

**¹pug** \'pəg\ *noun* [obsolete *pug* hobgoblin, monkey] (1789)
**1** : a small sturdy compact dog of a breed of Asian origin with a close coat, tightly curled tail, and broad wrinkled face
**2 a** : PUG NOSE **b** : a close knot or coil of hair : BUN

**²pug** *transitive verb* **pugged; pug·ging** [origin unknown] (1843)
: to work and mix (as clay) when wet especially to make more homogeneous and easier to handle (as in throwing or molding wares)

pug 1

**³pug** *noun* [by shortening & alteration from *pugilist*] (1858)
: ¹BOXER 1

**⁴pug** *noun* [Hindi *pag* foot] (1865)
: FOOTPRINT; *especially* : a print of a wild mammal

**pug·ga·ree** *or* **pug·a·ree** *or* **pug·gree** \'pə-g(ə-)rē\ *noun* [Hindi *pagṛī* turban] (1665)
: a light scarf wrapped around a sun helmet or used as a hatband

**pu·gi·lism** \'pyü-jə-,li-zəm\ *noun* [Latin *pugil* boxer; akin to Latin *pugnus* fist — more at PUNGENT] (1791)
: ²BOXING
— **pu·gi·lis·tic** \,pyü-jə-'lis-tik\ *adjective*

**pu·gi·list** \'pyü-jə-list\ *noun* (1790)

: FIGHTER; *especially* : a professional boxer

**pug·mark** \'pəg-,märk\ *noun* (1922)
: ⁴PUG

**pug mill** *noun* [²*pug*] (1824)
: a machine in which materials (as clay and water) are mixed, blended, or kneaded into a desired consistency

**pug·na·cious** \,pəg-'nā-shəs\ *adjective* [Latin *pugnac-, pugnax*, from *pugnare* to fight — more at PUNGENT] (1642)
: having a quarrelsome or combative nature : TRUCULENT
***synonym*** see BELLIGERENT
— **pug·na·cious·ly** *adverb*
— **pug·na·cious·ness** *noun*
— **pug·nac·i·ty** \-'na-sə-tē\ *noun*

**pug nose** *noun* [¹*pug*] (1778)
: a nose having a slightly concave bridge and flattened nostrils
— **pug–nosed** \'pəg-,nōzd\ *adjective*

**puis·ne** \'pyü-nē\ *adjective* [Middle French *puisné* younger — more at PUNY] (1688)
*chiefly British* : inferior in rank ⟨*puisne* judge⟩
— **puisne** *noun*

**puis·sance** \'pwi-s°n(t)s, 'pyü-ə-sən(t)s, pyü-'i-s°n(t)s\ *noun* [Middle English, from Middle French, from Old French, from *puissant* powerful, from *poeir* to be able, be powerful — more at POWER] (15th century)
: STRENGTH, POWER

**puis·sant** \-s°nt, -sənt\ *adjective* (15th century)
: having puissance : POWERFUL

**puke** \'pyük\ *verb* **puked; puk·ing** [origin unknown] (1600)
: VOMIT
— **puke** *noun*

**puk·ka** \'pə-kə\ *adjective* [Hindi *pakkā* cooked, ripe, solid, from Sanskrit *pakva*; akin to Greek *pessein* to cook — more at COOK] (1698)
: GENUINE, AUTHENTIC; *also* : FIRST-CLASS

**pul** \'pül\ *noun, plural* **puls** \'pülz\ *or* **pul** [Persian *pūl*] (1927)
— see *afghani* at MONEY table

**pu·la** \'pü-lə, 'pyü-\ *noun, plural* **pula** [Tswana, literally, rain (used as a greeting)] (1976)
— see MONEY table

**Pu·las·ki** \pə-'las-kē, pyü-\ *noun* [Edward C. Pulaski, 20th century American forest ranger] (1924)
: a single-bit ax with an adze-shaped hoe extending from the back

**pul·chri·tude** \'pəl-krə-,tüd, -,tyüd\ *noun* [Middle English, from Latin *pulchritudin-, pulchritudo*, from *pulchr-, pulcher* beautiful] (15th century)
: physical comeliness
— **pul·chri·tu·di·nous** \,pəl-krə-'tüd-nəs, -'tyüd-; -'tü-d°n-əs, -'tyü-\ *adjective*

**pule** \'pyü(ə)l\ *intransitive verb* **puled; pul·ing** [probably imitative] (1534)
: WHINE, WHIMPER

**pu·li** \'pü-lē, 'pyü-\ *noun, plural* **pu·lik** \-lik\ *or* **pulis** \-lēz\ [Hungarian] (1936)
: any of a breed of medium-sized Hungarian sheepdogs with a thick woolly coat hanging in long thin cords

**Pu·lit·zer prize** \'pu̇-lət-sər-, 'pyü-\ *noun* (1918)
: any of various annual prizes (as for outstanding literary or journalistic achievement) established by the will of Joseph Pulitzer — called also *Pulitzer*

**¹pull** \'pul *also* 'pəl\ *verb* [Middle English, from Old English *pullian*; akin to Middle Low German *pulen* to shell, cull] (before 12th century)
*transitive verb*
**1 a** : to exert force upon so as to cause or tend to cause motion toward the force **b** : to stretch (cooling candy) repeatedly ⟨*pull* taffy⟩ **c** : to strain abnormally ⟨*pull* a tendon⟩ **d** : to hold back (a racehorse) from winning **e** : to work (an oar) by drawing back strongly

**2 a :** to draw out from the skin ⟨*pull* feathers from a rooster's tail⟩ **b :** to pluck from a plant or by the roots ⟨*pull* flowers⟩ ⟨*pull* turnips⟩ **c :** EXTRACT ⟨*pull* a tooth⟩
**3 :** to hit (a ball) toward the left from a right-handed swing or toward the right from a left-handed swing — compare PUSH
**4 :** to draw apart : REND, TEAR
**5 :** to print (as a proof) by impression
**6 :** to remove from a place or situation ⟨*pull* the engine⟩ ⟨*pulled* the pitcher in the third inning⟩ ⟨*pulled* the show⟩
**7 :** to bring (a weapon) into the open ⟨*pulled* a knife⟩
**8 a :** COMMIT, PERPETRATE ⟨*pull* a robbery⟩ ⟨*pull* a prank⟩ **b :** to carry out as an assignment or duty
**9 :** PUT ON, ASSUME ⟨*pull* a grin⟩
**10 a :** to draw the support or attention of : ATTRACT ⟨*pull* votes⟩ — often used with *in* **b :** OBTAIN, SECURE ⟨*pulled* a B in the course⟩
**11 :** to demand or obtain an advantage over someone by the assertion of ⟨*pull* rank⟩
*intransitive verb*
**1 a :** to use force in drawing, dragging, or tugging **b :** to move especially through the exercise of mechanical energy ⟨the car *pulled* clear of the rut⟩ **c** (1) **:** to take a drink (2) **:** to draw hard in smoking ⟨*pulled* at a pipe⟩ **d :** to strain against the bit
**2 :** to draw a gun
**3 :** to admit of being pulled
**4 :** to feel or express strong sympathy : ROOT ⟨*pulling* for my team to win⟩
**5** *of an offensive lineman in football* **:** to move back from the line of scrimmage and toward one flank to provide blocking for a ballcarrier
— **pull·er** *noun*
— **pull a fast one :** to perpetrate a trick or fraud
— **pull punches** *also* **pull a punch :** to refrain from using all the force at one's disposal
— **pull oneself together :** to regain one's composure
— **pull one's leg :** to deceive someone playfully : HOAX
— **pull one's weight :** to do one's full share of the work
— **pull out all the stops :** to use all one's resources without restraint
— **pull stakes** *or* **pull up stakes :** to move out : LEAVE
— **pull strings** *also* **pull wires :** to exert hidden influence or control
— **pull the plug 1 :** to disconnect a medical life-support system **2 :** to withdraw essential and especially financial support
— **pull the rug from under :** to weaken or unsettle especially by removing support or assistance from
— **pull the string :** to throw a change-up
— **pull the wool over one's eyes :** to blind to the true situation : HOODWINK
— **pull together :** to work in harmony : COOPERATE
**²pull** *noun, often attributive* (14th century)
**1 a :** the act or an instance of pulling **b** (1) **:** a draft of liquid (2) **:** an inhalation of smoke **c :** the effort expended in moving ⟨a long *pull* uphill⟩ **d :** force required to overcome resistance to pulling ⟨trigger *pull*⟩
**2 a :** ADVANTAGE **b :** special influence
**3 :** PROOF 6a
**4 :** a device for pulling something or for operating by pulling ⟨drawer *pull*⟩
**5 :** a force that attracts, compels, or influences : ATTRACTION
**6 :** an injury resulting from abnormal straining or stretching ⟨a muscle *pull*⟩ ⟨a groin *pull*⟩
**pull away** *intransitive verb* (circa 1934)
**1 :** to draw oneself back or away : WITHDRAW
**2 :** to move off or ahead
**pull·back** \ˈpu̇l-ˌbak\ *noun* (1668)
**:** a pulling back; *especially* **:** an orderly withdrawal of troops from a position or area

**pull down** *transitive verb* (15th century)
**1 a :** DEMOLISH, DESTROY **b :** to hunt down : OVERCOME
**2 a :** to bring to a lower level : REDUCE **b :** to depress in health, strength, or spirits
**3 :** to draw as wages or salary
**pul·let** \ˈpu̇-lət\ *noun* [Middle English *polet* young fowl, from Middle French *poulet*, from Old French, diminutive of *poul* cock, from Late Latin *pullus*, from Latin, young of an animal, chicken, sprout — more at FOAL] (14th century)
**:** a young hen; *specifically* **:** a hen of the domestic chicken less than a year old
**pul·ley** \ˈpu̇-lē\ *noun, plural* **pulleys** [Middle English *pouley*, from Middle French *poulie*, probably ultimately from Greek *polos* axis, pole — more at POLE] (14th century)
**1 :** a sheave or small wheel with a grooved rim and with or without the block in which it runs used singly with a rope or chain to change the direction and point of application of a pulling force and in various combinations to increase the applied force especially for lifting weights
**2 :** a pulley or pulleys with ropes to form a tackle that constitutes one of the simple machines
**3 :** a wheel used to transmit power by means of a band, belt, cord, rope, or chain passing over its rim
**pull in** (1605)
*transitive verb*
**1 :** CHECK, RESTRAIN
**2 :** ARREST
*intransitive verb*
**:** to arrive at a destination or come to a stop
**Pull·man** \ˈpu̇l-mən\ *noun* [George M. *Pullman*] (1867)
**1 :** a railroad passenger car with specially comfortable furnishings for day or especially for night travel
**2 :** a large suitcase
**pull off** *transitive verb* (1883)
**:** to carry out despite difficulties : accomplish successfully against odds
**pul·lo·rum disease** \pə-ˈlȯr-əm-, -ˈlȯr-\ *noun* [New Latin *pullorum* (specific epithet of *Salmonella pullorum*), from Latin, of chickens (genitive plural of *pullus*)] (1929)
**:** a destructive typically diarrheal salmonellosis especially of young domestic chickens that is caused by a bacterium (*Salmonella pullorum*)
**pull·out** \ˈpu̇l-ˌau̇t\ *noun* (1825)
**1 :** the act or an instance of pulling out: as **a :** the action in which an airplane goes from a dive to horizontal flight **b :** PULLBACK
**2 :** something that can be pulled out
**pull out** *intransitive verb* (1855)
**1 :** LEAVE, DEPART
**2 :** WITHDRAW
**¹pull·over** \ˈpu̇l-ˌō-vər\ *noun* (1899)
**:** a pullover garment (as a sweater)
**²pullover** *adjective* (1907)
**:** put on by being pulled over the head
**pull over** (1930)
*intransitive verb*
**:** to steer one's vehicle to the side of the road
*transitive verb*
**:** to cause to pull over ⟨*pulled* him *over* for speeding⟩
**pull round** (1891)
*intransitive verb*
*chiefly British* **:** to regain one's health
*transitive verb*
*chiefly British* **:** to restore to good health
**pull tab** *noun* (1963)
**:** a metal tab (as on a can) pulled to open the container
**pull through** (1852)
*intransitive verb*
**:** to survive a dangerous or difficult situation
*transitive verb*
**:** to help survive a dangerous or difficult situation

**pul·lu·late** \ˈpəl-yə-ˌlāt\ *intransitive verb* **-lat·ed; -lat·ing** [Latin *pullulatus*, past participle of *pullulare*, from *pullulus*, diminutive of *pullus* chicken, sprout — more at FOAL] (1619)
**1 a :** GERMINATE, SPROUT **b :** to breed or produce freely
**2 :** SWARM, TEEM
— **pul·lu·la·tion** \ˌpəl-yə-ˈlā-shən\ *noun*
**pull-up** \ˈpu̇l-ˌəp\ *noun* (1938)
**:** CHIN-UP
**pull up** (1623)
*transitive verb*
**1 :** to bring to a stop : HALT
**2 :** CHECK, REBUKE
*intransitive verb*
**1 a :** to check oneself **b :** to come to an often abrupt halt : STOP
**2 :** to draw even with others in a race
**pul·mo·nary** \ˈpu̇l-mə-ˌner-ē, ˈpəl-\ *adjective* [Latin *pulmonarius*, from *pulmon-*, *pulmo* lung; akin to Greek *pleumōn* lung, Sanskrit *kloman* right lung] (1704)
**1 :** relating to, functioning like, or associated with the lungs
**2 :** PULMONATE
**3 :** carried on by the lungs
**pulmonary artery** *noun* (1704)
**:** an artery that conveys venous blood from the heart to the lungs — see HEART illustration
**pulmonary circulation** *noun* (circa 1890)
**:** the passage of blood from the right side of the heart through arteries to the lungs where it picks up oxygen and is returned to the left side of the heart by veins
**pulmonary vein** *noun* (1704)
**:** a valveless vein that returns oxygenated blood from the lungs to the heart
**¹pul·mo·nate** \ˈpu̇l-mə-ˌnāt, ˈpəl-\ *adjective* [Latin *pulmon-*, *pulmo* lung] (circa 1859)
**1 :** having lungs or organs resembling lungs
**2 :** of or relating to a subclass (Pulmonata) of gastropod mollusks having a respiratory sac and comprising most land snails and slugs and many freshwater snails
**²pulmonate** *noun* (1883)
**:** a pulmonate gastropod
**pul·mon·ic** \pu̇l-ˈmä-nik, ˌpəl-\ *adjective* [Latin *pulmon-*, *pulmo*] (1661)
**:** PULMONARY
**pul·mo·tor** \ˈpu̇l-ˌmō-tər, ˈpəl-\ *noun* [from *Pulmotor*, a trademark] (1911)
**:** a respiratory apparatus for pumping oxygen or air into and out of the lungs (as of an asphyxiated person)
**¹pulp** \ˈpəlp\ *noun* [Middle English *pulpe*, from Middle French *poulpe*, from Latin *pulpa* flesh, pulp] (14th century)
**1 a** (1) **:** the soft, succulent part of a fruit usually composed of mesocarp (2) **:** stem pith when soft and spongy **b :** a soft mass of vegetable matter (as of apples) from which most of the water has been extracted by pressure **c :** the soft sensitive tissue that fills the central cavity of a tooth — see TOOTH illustration **d :** a material prepared by chemical or mechanical means from various materials (as wood or rags) for use in making paper and cellulose products
**2 :** pulverized ore mixed with water
**3 a :** pulpy condition or character **b :** something in such a condition or having such a character
**4 :** a magazine or book printed on cheap paper (as newsprint) and often dealing with sensational material
— **pulp·i·ness** \ˈpəl-pē-nəs\ *noun*
— **pulpy** \ˈpəl-pē\ *adjective*
**²pulp** (1683)
*transitive verb*
**1 :** to reduce to pulp : cause to appear pulpy

\ə\ **abut** \ᵊ\ **kitten** \ər\ **further** \a\ **ash** \ā\ **ace**
\ä\ **mop, mar** \au̇\ **out** \ch\ **chin** \e\ **bet** \ē\ **easy**
\g\ **go** \i\ **hit** \ī\ **ice** \j\ **job** \ŋ\ **sing** \ō\ **go**
\ȯ\ **law** \ȯi\ **boy** \th\ **thin** \t͟h\ **the** \ü\ **loot** \u̇\ **foot**
\y\ **yet** \zh\ **vision** *see also* Guide to Pronunciation

**2 :** to deprive of the pulp
**3 :** to produce or reproduce (written matter) in pulp form
*intransitive verb*
**:** to become pulp or pulpy
— **pulp·er** *noun*

**pulp·al** \'pəl-pəl\ *adjective* (1903)
**:** of or relating to pulp especially of a tooth ⟨a *pulpal* abscess⟩
— **pulp·al·ly** \'pəl-pə-lē\ *adverb*

**pul·pit** \'pùl-,pit *also* 'pəl-, -pət\ *noun* [Middle English, from Late Latin *pulpitum*, from Latin, staging, platform] (14th century)
**1 :** an elevated platform or high reading desk used in preaching or conducting a worship service
**2 a :** the preaching profession **b :** a preaching position

**pulp·wood** \'pəlp-,wùd\ *noun* (1885)
**:** a wood (as of aspen, hemlock, pine, or spruce) used in making pulp for paper

**pul·que** \'pùl-,kā; 'pül-kē, 'pùl-\ *noun* [Mexican Spanish] (1693)
**:** a Mexican alcoholic beverage made from the fermented sap of various agaves (as *Agave atrovirens*)

**pul·sant** \'pəl-sənt\ *adjective* (1709)
**:** pulsating with activity

**pul·sar** \'pəl-,sär\ *noun* [*pulse* + *-ar* (as in *quasar*)] (1968)
**:** a celestial source of pulsating electromagnetic radiation (as radio waves) characterized by a short relatively constant interval (as .033 second) between pulses that is held to be a rotating neutron star

**pul·sate** \'pəl-,sāt *also* ,pəl-'\ *intransitive verb*
**pul·sat·ed; pul·sat·ing** [Latin *pulsatus*, past participle of *pulsare*, frequentative of *pellere*] (1794)
**1 :** to exhibit a pulse or pulsation **:** BEAT
**2 :** to throb or move rhythmically **:** VIBRATE

**pul·sa·tile** \'pəl-sə-t³l, -,tīl\ *adjective* (1541)
**:** of or marked by pulsation

**pul·sa·tion** \,pəl-'sā-shən\ *noun* (1541)
**1 :** rhythmical throbbing or vibrating (as of an artery); *also* **:** a single beat or throb
**2 :** a periodically recurring alternate increase and decrease of a quantity (as pressure, volume, or voltage)

**pul·sa·tor** \'pəl-,sā-tər, ,pəl-'\ *noun* (1890)
**:** something that beats or throbs in working

**¹pulse** \'pəls\ *noun* [Middle English *puls*, from Old French *pouls* porridge, from Latin *pult-, puls*, probably from Greek *poltos*] (13th century)
**:** the edible seeds of various leguminous crops (as peas, beans, or lentils); *also* **:** a plant yielding pulse

**²pulse** *noun* [Middle English *puls*, from Middle French *pouls*, from Latin *pulsus*, literally, beating, from *pellere* to drive, push, beat — more at FELT] (14th century)
**1 a :** a regular throbbing caused in the arteries by the contractions of the heart **:** the palpable beat resulting from such pulse as detected in a superficial artery; *also* **:** the number of individual beats in a specified time period (as one minute) ⟨a resting *pulse* of 70⟩
**2 a :** underlying sentiment or opinion or an indication of it **b :** VITALITY
**3 a :** rhythmical beating, vibrating, or sounding **b :** BEAT, THROB
**4 a :** a transient variation of a quantity (as electrical current or voltage) whose value is normally constant **b** (1) **:** an electromagnetic wave or modulation thereof of brief duration (2) **:** a brief disturbance of pressure in a medium; *especially* **:** a sound wave or short train of sound waves
**5 :** a dose of a substance especially when applied over a short period of time ⟨*pulse*-labeled DNA⟩

**³pulse** *verb* **pulsed; puls·ing** (15th century)
*intransitive verb*
**:** to exhibit a pulse or pulsation **:** THROB
*transitive verb*

**1 :** to drive by or as if by a pulsation
**2 :** to cause to pulsate
**3 a :** to produce or modulate (as electromagnetic waves) in the form of pulses ⟨*pulsed* waves⟩ **b :** to cause (an apparatus) to produce pulses
— **puls·er** *noun*

**pulse–jet engine** \'pəls-'jet-\ *noun* (1949)
**:** a jet engine designed to produce a pulsating thrust by the intermittent flow of hot gases

**pul·ver·a·ble** \'pəl-və-rə-bəl, 'pəlv-rə-\ *adjective* (circa 1617)
**:** capable of being pulverized

**pul·ver·ise** *British variant of* PULVERIZE

**pul·ver·ize** \'pəl-və-,rīz\ *verb* **-ized; -iz·ing** [Middle English, from Middle French *pulveriser*, from Late Latin *pulverizare*, from Latin *pulver-, pulvis* dust, powder — more at POWDER] (15th century)
*transitive verb*
**1 :** to reduce (as by crushing, beating, or grinding) to very small particles **:** ATOMIZE
**2 :** ANNIHILATE, DEMOLISH
*intransitive verb*
**:** to become pulverized
— **pul·ver·iz·able** \,pəl-və-'rī-zə-bəl\ *adjective*
— **pul·ver·i·za·tion** \,pəl-və-rə-'zā-shən, ,pəlv-rə-\ *noun*
— **pul·ver·iz·er** \'pəl-və-,rī-zər\ *noun*

**pul·ver·u·lent** \,pəl-'ver-yə-lənt, -'ver-ə-\ *adjective* [Latin *pulverulentus* dusty, from *pulver-, pulvis*] (circa 1656)
**1 :** consisting of or reducible to fine powder
**2 :** being or looking dusty **:** CRUMBLY

**pul·vil·lus** \,pəl-'vi-ləs\ *noun, plural* **-vil·li** \-'vi-,lī, -(,)lē\ [New Latin, from Latin, diminutive of *pulvinus*] (circa 1826)
**:** one of the lobed hairy adhesive organs that terminate the feet of dipteran flies

**pul·vi·nus** \,pəl-'vī-nəs, -'vē-\ *noun, plural* **-vi·ni** \-'vī-,nī, -'vē-(,)nē\ [New Latin, from Latin, cushion] (1857)
**:** a mass of large thin-walled cells surrounding a vascular strand at the base of a petiole or petiolule and functioning in turgor movements of leaves or leaflets

**pu·ma** \'pü-mə, 'pyü-\ *noun, plural* **pumas** *also* **puma** [Spanish, from Quechua] (1777)
**:** COUGAR; *also* **:** the fur or pelt of a cougar

**pum·ice** \'pə-məs\ *noun* [Middle English *pomis*, from Middle French, from Latin *pumic-, pumex* — more at FOAM] (15th century)
**:** a volcanic glass full of cavities and very light in weight used especially in powder form for smoothing and polishing
— **pu·mi·ceous** \pyü-'mi-shəs, ,pə-\ *adjective*

**pum·ic·ite** \'pə-mə-,sīt\ *noun* (1916)
**:** PUMICE

**pum·mel** \'pə-məl\ *verb* **-meled** *also* **-melled; -mel·ing** *also* **-mel·ling** \'pə-mə-liŋ, 'pəm-liŋ\ [alteration of *pommel*] (1548)
**:** POUND, BEAT

**pum·me·lo** *variant of* POMELO 2

**¹pump** \'pəmp\ *noun* [Middle English *pumpe, pompe*, from Middle Low German *pumpe* or Middle Dutch *pompe*, perhaps from Spanish *bomba*, of imitative origin] (15th century)
**1 :** a device that raises, transfers, or compresses fluids or that attenuates gases especially by suction or pressure or both
**2 :** HEART
**3 :** an act or the process of pumping
**4 :** an energy source (as light) for pumping atoms or molecules
**5 :** a mechanism (as the sodium pump) for pumping atoms, ions, or molecules

**²pump** (1508)
*intransitive verb*
**1 :** to work a pump **:** raise or move a fluid with a pump
**2 :** to exert oneself to pump or as if to pump something
**3 :** to move in a manner that resembles the action of a pump handle

*transitive verb*
**1 a :** to raise (as water) with a pump **b :** to draw fluid from with a pump
**2 :** to pour forth, deliver, or draw with or as if with a pump ⟨*pumped* money into the economy⟩ ⟨*pump* new life into the classroom⟩
**3 a :** to question persistently **b :** to elicit by persistent questioning
**4 a :** to operate by manipulating a lever **b :** to manipulate as if operating a pump handle ⟨*pumped* my hand warmly⟩ **c :** to cause to move with an action resembling that of a pump handle ⟨a runner *pumping* her arms⟩
**5 :** to transport (as ions) against a concentration gradient by the expenditure of energy
**6 a :** to excite (as atoms or molecules) especially so as to cause emission of coherent monochromatic electromagnetic radiation (as in a laser) **b :** to energize (as a laser) by pumping
— **pump iron :** to lift weights

**³pump** *noun* [origin unknown] (1555)
**:** a shoe that grips the foot chiefly at the toe and heel; *especially* **:** a close-fitting woman's dress shoe with a moderate to high heel

**pumped storage** *noun* (1927)
**:** a hydroelectric system in which electricity is generated during periods of high demand by the use of water that has been pumped into a reservoir at a higher altitude during periods of low demand

**pump·er** \'pəm-pər\ *noun* (1660)
**:** one that pumps; *especially* **:** a fire truck equipped with a pump

**pum·per·nick·el** \'pəm-pər-,ni-kəl\ *noun* [German, from *pumpern* to break wind + *Nickel* goblin; from its reputed indigestibility] (1756)
**:** a dark coarse sourdough bread made of unbolted rye flour

**pump·kin** \'pəm(p)-kən, ÷'pəŋ-kən\ *noun, often attributive* [alteration of earlier *pumpion*, modification of French *popon, pompon* melon, pumpkin, from Latin *pepon-, pepo*, from Greek *pepōn*, from *pepōn* ripened; akin to Greek *pessein* to cook, ripen — more at COOK] (1654)
**1 a :** the usually round orange fruit of a vine (*Cucurbita pepo*) of the gourd family widely cultivated as food **b :** WINTER CROOKNECK **c** *British* **:** any of various large-fruited winter squashes (*C. maxima*)
**2 :** a usually hairy prickly vine that produces pumpkins

**pump·kin·seed** \-,sēd\ *noun* (1814)
**:** a brilliantly colored North American freshwater sunfish (*Lepomis gibbosus*) with a reddish spot on the operculum

**pump priming** *noun* (1936)
**:** government investment expenditures designed to induce a self-sustaining expansion of economic activity

**pump up** *transitive verb* (1791)
**1 a :** to fill with enthusiasm or excitement **b :** to fill with or as if with air **:** INFLATE
**2 :** INCREASE 1

**¹pun** \'pən\ *noun* [perhaps from Italian *puntiglio* fine point, quibble — more at PUNCTILIO] (1662)
**:** the usually humorous use of a word in such a way as to suggest two or more of its meanings or the meaning of another word similar in sound

**²pun** *intransitive verb* **punned; pun·ning** (1670)
**:** to make puns

**pu·na** \'pü-nə\ *noun* [American Spanish, from Quechua] (1613)
**:** a treeless windswept tableland or basin in the higher Andes

**¹punch** \'pənch\ *verb* [Middle English, from Middle French *poinçonner* to prick, stamp, from *poinçon* puncheon] (14th century)
*transitive verb*

**1 a :** PROD, POKE **b :** DRIVE, HERD ⟨*punching* cattle⟩
**2 a :** to strike with a forward thrust especially of the fist **b :** to drive or push forcibly by or as if by a punch **c :** to hit (a ball) with less than a full swing
**3 :** to emboss, cut, perforate, or make with or as if with a punch
**4 a :** to push down so as to produce a desired result ⟨*punch* buttons on a jukebox⟩ **b :** to hit or press down the operating mechanism of ⟨*punch* a time clock⟩ ⟨*punch* a typewriter⟩ **c :** to produce by or as if by punching keys ⟨*punch* out a tune on the piano⟩ **d :** to enter (as data) by punching keys
**5 :** to give emphasis to
*intransitive verb*
**:** to perform the action of punching something
— **punch·er** *noun*

**²punch** *noun* (14th century)
**1 :** the action of punching
**2 :** a quick blow with or as if with the fist
**3 :** effective energy or forcefulness ⟨a story that packs a *punch*⟩ ⟨political *punch*⟩
— **punch·less** \'pənch-ləs\ *adjective*
— **to the punch :** to the first blow or to decisive action — usually used with *beat*

**³punch** *noun* [probably short for *puncheon*] (14th century)
**1 a :** a tool usually in the form of a short rod of steel that is variously shaped at one end for different operations (as forming, perforating, embossing, or cutting) **b :** a short tapering steel rod for driving the heads of nails below a surface **c :** a steel die faced with a letter in relief that is forced into a softer metal to form an intaglio matrix from which foundry type is cast **d :** a device or machine for cutting holes or notches (as in paper or cardboard)
**2 :** a hole or notch from a perforating operation

**⁴punch** *noun* [perhaps from Hindi *pãc* five, from Sanskrit *pañca*; akin to Greek *pente* five; from its originally having five ingredients — more at FIVE] (1632)
**:** a hot or cold drink that is usually a combination of hard liquor, wine, or beer and nonalcoholic beverages; *also* **:** a drink that is a mixture of nonalcoholic beverages

**Punch–and–Judy show** \,pənch-ən-'jü-dē-\ *noun* (1876)
**:** a traditional puppet show in which the little hook-nosed humpback Punch fights comically with his wife Judy

**punch·ball** \'pənch-,bȯl\ *noun* (1932)
**:** baseball adapted for small areas in which a rubber ball is hit with a fist instead of a bat

**punch·board** \-,bȯrd, -,bȯrd\ *noun* (1912)
**:** a small board that has many holes each filled with a rolled-up printed slip to be punched out on payment of a nominal sum in an effort to obtain a slip that entitles the player to a designated prize

**punch bowl** *noun* (1692)
**:** a large bowl from which a beverage (as punch) is served

**punch–drunk** \'pənch-,drəŋk\ *adjective* [²*punch*] (1918)
**1 :** suffering cerebral injury from many minute brain hemorrhages as a result of repeated head blows received in boxing
**2 :** behaving as if punch-drunk **:** DAZED, CONFUSED

**punched card** \'pəncht-\ *noun* (1919)
**:** a card in which holes are punched in designated positions to represent data — called also *Hollerith card, punch card*

**¹pun·cheon** \'pən-chən\ *noun* [Middle English *ponson*, from Middle French *poinçon* pointed tool, king post, from (assumed) Vulgar Latin *punction-, punctio* pointed tool, from Latin, action of pricking, from *pungere* to prick — more at PUNGENT] (14th century)
**1 :** a pointed tool for piercing or for working on stone

**2 a :** a short upright framing timber **b :** a split log or heavy slab with the face smoothed

**²puncheon** *noun* [Middle English *poncion*, from Middle French *ponchon, poinçon*, of unknown origin] (15th century)
**:** a large cask of varying capacity

**punch in** *intransitive verb* (1926)
**:** to record the time of one's arrival or beginning work by punching a time clock

**pun·chi·nel·lo** \,pən-chə-'ne-(,)lō\ *noun* [modification of Italian dialect *polecenella*] (1666)
**1** *capitalized* **:** a fat short humpbacked clown or buffoon in Italian puppet shows
**2** *plural* **-los :** a squat grotesque person

**punching bag** *noun* (1886)
**:** a stuffed or inflated bag that is usually suspended for free movement and that is punched for exercise or for training in boxing

**punch line** *noun* (1921)
**:** the sentence, statement, or phrase (as in a joke) that makes the point

**punch–out** \'pənch-,aut\ *noun* (1928)
**:** FISTFIGHT

**punch out** (1973)
*intransitive verb*
**1 :** to record the time of one's stopping work or departure by punching a time clock
**2 :** to bail out of an aircraft using an ejection seat
*transitive verb*
**1 :** to beat up
**2 :** STRIKE OUT

**punch press** *noun* (1911)
**:** a press equipped with cutting, shaping, or combination dies for working on material (as metal)

**punch–up** \'pənch-,əp\ *noun* (1958)
*chiefly British* **:** FISTFIGHT

**punch up** *transitive verb* (circa 1959)
**:** to give energy or forcefulness to ⟨jokes added to *punch up* a speech⟩

**punchy** \'pən-chē\ *adjective* **punch·i·er; -est** (1917)
**1 :** having punch **:** FORCEFUL, SPIRITED
**2 :** PUNCH-DRUNK

**punc·tate** \'pəŋk-,tāt\ *adjective* [New Latin *punctatus*, from Latin *punctum* point — more at POINT] (circa 1760)
**1 :** marked with minute spots or depressions ⟨a *punctate* leaf⟩
**2 :** characterized by dots or points ⟨*punctate* skin lesions⟩
— **punc·ta·tion** \,pəŋk-'tā-shən\ *noun*

**punc·til·io** \,pəŋk-'ti-lē-,ō\ *noun, plural* **-i·os** [Italian & Spanish; Italian *puntiglio* point of honor, scruple, from Spanish *puntillo*, from diminutive of *punto* point, from Latin *punctum*] (1596)
**1 :** a minute detail of conduct in a ceremony or in observance of a code
**2 :** careful observance of forms (as in social conduct)

**punc·til·i·ous** \-lē-əs\ *adjective* (1634)
**:** marked by or concerned about precise accordance with the details of codes or conventions
*synonym* see CAREFUL
— **punc·til·i·ous·ly** *adverb*
— **punc·til·i·ous·ness** *noun*

**punc·tu·al** \'pəŋk-chə-wəl, -chəl\ *adjective* [Middle English, having a sharp point, from Medieval Latin *punctualis*, of a point, from Latin *punctus* pricking, point, from *pungere* to prick — more at PUNGENT] (1675)

**:** being on time **:** PROMPT
— **punc·tu·al·i·ty** \,pəŋk-chə-'wa-lə-tē\ *noun*
— **punc·tu·al·ly** \'pəŋk-chə-wə-lē, -chə-lē\ *adverb*

**punc·tu·ate** \'pəŋk-chə-,wāt\ *verb* **-at·ed; -at·ing** [Medieval Latin *punctuatus*, past participle of *punctuare* to point, provide with punctuation marks, from Latin *punctus* point] (circa 1818)
*transitive verb*
**1 :** to mark or divide (written matter) with punctuation marks
**2 :** to break into or interrupt at intervals ⟨the steady click of her needles *punctuated* the silence —Edith Wharton⟩
**3 :** ACCENTUATE, EMPHASIZE
*intransitive verb*
**:** to use punctuation marks
— **punc·tu·a·tor** \-,wā-tər\ *noun*

**punctuated equilibrium** *noun* (1978)
**:** evolution that is characterized by long periods of stability in the characteristics of an organism and short periods of rapid change during which new forms appear especially from small subpopulations of the ancestral form in restricted parts of its geographic range; *also* **:** a theory or model of evolution emphasizing this — compare GRADUALISM 2

**punc·tu·a·tion** \,pəŋk-chə-'wā-shən\ *noun* (circa 1539)
**1 :** the act of punctuating **:** the state of being punctuated
**2 :** the act or practice of inserting standardized marks or signs in written matter to clarify the meaning and separate structural units; *also* **:** a system of punctuation
**3 :** something that contrasts or accentuates

**punctuation mark** *noun* (1860)
**:** any of various standardized marks or signs used in punctuation

## PUNCTUATION MARKS

| | |
|---|---|
| . | period (*or* full stop) |
| , | comma |
| ; | semicolon |
| : | colon |
| ' | apostrophe |
| ' ' | quotation marks, single (*or chiefly British* inverted commas) |
| " " | quotation marks, double (*or chiefly British* inverted commas) |
| « » | guillemets |
| ? | question mark (*or* interrogation point) |
| ¿ ? | question marks, Spanish |
| ! | exclamation point |
| ¡ ! | exclamation points, Spanish |
| ‽ | interrobang |
| / | slash (*or* diagonal *or* slant *or* solidus *or* virgule) |
| . . . *or* . . . . | ellipsis (*or* suspension points) |
| - | hyphen |
| ⸗ | double hyphen |
| – | dash (*or* en dash) |
| — | dash (*or* em dash) |
| ~ | swung dash |
| ( ) | parentheses (*or* brackets) |
| [ ] | brackets, square (*or* braces) |
| ⟨ ⟩ | brackets, angle |
| { } | braces (*or* curly brackets) |

Punchinello

\ə\ **abut** \ᵊ\ **kitten** \ər\ **further** \a\ **ash** \ā\ **ace**
\ä\ **mop, mar** \au̇\ **out** \ch\ **chin** \e\ **bet** \ē\ **easy**
\g\ **go** \i\ **hit** \ī\ **ice** \j\ **job** \ŋ\ **sing** \ō\ **go**
\ȯ\ **law** \ȯi\ **boy** \th\ **thin** \t̲h̲\ **the** \ü\ **loot** \u̇\ **foot**
\y\ **yet** \zh\ **vision** *see also* Guide to Pronunciation

**¹punc·ture** \'pəŋk-chər\ *noun* [Middle English, from Latin *punctura*, from *punctus*, past participle of *pungere*] (14th century)
**1** : an act of puncturing
**2** : a hole, wound, or perforation made by puncturing
**3** : a minute depression

**²puncture** *verb* **punc·tured; punc·tur·ing** \'pəŋk-chə-riŋ, 'pəŋk-shriŋ\ (1699)
*transitive verb*
**1** : to pierce with or as if with a pointed instrument or object
**2** : to make useless or ineffective as if by a puncture : DEFLATE
*intransitive verb*
: to become punctured

**puncture vine** *noun* (1911)
: an Old World annual prostrate herb (*Tribulus terrestris*) of the caltrop family that has hard spiny pods and is a troublesome weed especially in the western U.S. — called also *caltrop, puncture-weed*

**pun·dit** \'pən-dət\ *noun* [Hindi *paṇḍit*, from Sanskrit *paṇḍita*, from *paṇḍita* learned] (1672)
**1** : PANDIT
**2** : a learned man : TEACHER
**3** : one who gives opinions in an authoritative manner : CRITIC
— **pun·dit·ry** \-də-trē\ *noun*

**pung** \'pəŋ\ *noun* [short for earlier *tow-pong*, of Algonquian origin; akin to Micmac *tobâgun* drag made with skin] (1825)
*New England* : a sleigh with a box-shaped body

**pun·gen·cy** \'pən-jən(t)-sē\ *noun* (1649)
: the quality or state of being pungent

**pun·gent** \-jənt\ *adjective* [Latin *pungent-, pungens,* present participle of *pungere* to prick, sting; akin to Latin *pugnus* fist, *pugnare* to fight, Greek *pygmē* fist] (1597)
**1** : sharply painful
**2** : having a stiff and sharp point ⟨*pungent* leaves⟩
**3 a** : marked by a sharp incisive quality : CAUSTIC ⟨a *pungent* critic⟩ ⟨*pungent* language⟩ **b** : being sharp and to the point
**4** : causing a sharp or irritating sensation; *especially* : ACRID ☆
— **pun·gent·ly** *adverb*

**pun·gle** \'pən-gəl\ *verb* **pun·gled; pun·gling** \'pən-g(ə-)liŋ\ [Spanish *póngale* put it down] (1851)
*transitive verb*
: to make a payment or contribution of (money) — usually used with *up*
*intransitive verb*
: PAY, CONTRIBUTE — usually used with *up*

**¹Pu·nic** \'pyü-nik\ *adjective* [Latin *punicus*, from *Poenus* inhabitant of Carthage; akin to Greek *Phoinix* Phoenician] (1533)
**1** : of or relating to Carthage or the Carthaginians
**2** : FAITHLESS, TREACHEROUS

**²Punic** *noun* (1673)
: the Phoenician dialect of ancient Carthage

**pun·ish** \'pə-nish\ *verb* [Middle English *punisshen*, from Middle French *puniss-*, stem of *punir*, from Latin *punire*, from *poena* penalty — more at PAIN] (14th century)
*transitive verb*
**1 a** : to impose a penalty on for a fault, offense, or violation **b** : to inflict a penalty for the commission of (an offense) in retribution or retaliation
**2 a** : to deal with roughly or harshly **b** : to inflict injury on : HURT
*intransitive verb*
: to inflict punishment ☆
— **pun·ish·abil·i·ty** \,pə-nish-ə-'bi-lə-tē\ *noun*
— **pun·ish·able** \'pə-nish-ə-bəl\ *adjective*
— **pun·ish·er** *noun*
**pun·ish·ment** \'pə-nish-mənt\ *noun* (15th century)

**1** : the act of punishing
**2 a** : suffering, pain, or loss that serves as retribution **b** : a penalty inflicted on an offender through judicial procedure
**3** : severe, rough, or disastrous treatment

**pu·ni·tion** \pyü-'ni-shən\ *noun* [Middle English *punicion*, from Middle French *punition*, from Latin *punition-, punitio*, from *punire*] (15th century)
: PUNISHMENT

**pu·ni·tive** \'pyü-nə-tiv\ *adjective* [French *punitif*, from Medieval Latin *punitivus*, from Latin *punitus*, past participle of *punire*] (1624)
: inflicting, involving, or aiming at punishment
— **pu·ni·tive·ly** *adverb*
— **pu·ni·tive·ness** *noun*

**punitive damages** *noun plural* (circa 1890)
: damages awarded in excess of normal compensation to the plaintiff to punish a defendant for a serious wrong

**Pun·jabi** \,pən-'jä-bē, -'ja-\ *noun* [Hindi *pañjābī*, from *pañjābī* of Punjab, from Persian *panjābī*, from *Panjāb* Punjab] (1846)
**1** : PANJABI 1
**2** : a native or inhabitant of the Punjab region of the northwestern Indian subcontinent
— **Punjabi** *adjective*

**¹punk** \'pəŋk\ *noun* [origin unknown] (1596)
**1** *archaic* : PROSTITUTE
**2** [probably partly from ³*punk*] : NONSENSE, FOOLISHNESS
**3 a** : a young inexperienced person : BEGINNER, NOVICE; *especially* : a young man **b** : a usually petty gangster, hoodlum, or ruffian **c** : a youth used as a homosexual partner
**4 a** : PUNK ROCK **b** : a punk rock musician **c** : one who affects punk styles

**²punk** *adjective* (1896)
**1** : very poor : INFERIOR ⟨played a *punk* game⟩
**2** : being in poor health ⟨said that she was feeling *punk*⟩
**3 a** : of or relating to punk rock **b** : relating to or being a style (as of dress or hair) inspired by punk rock
— **punk·ish** \'pən-kish\ *adjective*

**³punk** *noun* [perhaps alteration of *spunk*] (1687)
**1** : wood so decayed as to be dry, crumbly, and useful for tinder
**2** : a dry spongy substance prepared from fungi (genus *Fomes*) and used to ignite fuses especially of fireworks

**pun·kah** \'pən-kə\ *noun* [Hindi *pākhā*] (1787)
: a fan used especially in India that consists of a canvas-covered frame suspended from the ceiling and that is operated by a cord

**punk·er** \'pən-kər\ *noun* (1977)
: ¹PUNK 4b, c

**pun·kie** *also* **pun·ky** \'pən-kē\ *noun, plural* **punkies** [New York Dutch *punki*, modification of Delaware (Munsee) *pónkwəs*] (1769)
: BITING MIDGE

**pun·kin** \'pən-kən\ *variant of* PUMPKIN

**punk rock** *noun* (1971)
: rock music marked by extreme and often deliberately offensive expressions of alienation and social discontent
— **punk rocker** *noun*

**¹punky** \'pən-kē\ *adjective* **punk·i·er; -est** [³*punk*] (1872)
: resembling punk in being soft or rotted
— **punk·i·ness** *noun*

**²punky** *adjective* [¹*punk*] (1972)
: resembling or typical of a punk

**pun·net** \'pə-nət\ *noun* [origin unknown] (circa 1822)
*British* : a small basket for fruits or vegetables

**Pun·nett square** \'pə-nət-\ *noun* [Reginald C. Punnett (died 1967) English geneticist] (1942)
: an $n \times n$ square used in genetics to calculate the frequencies of the different genotypes and phenotypes among the offspring of a cross

**pun·ny** \'pə-nē\ *adjective* **pun·ni·er; -est** (1947)

: constituting or involving a pun

**pun·ster** \'pən(t)-stər\ *noun* (1700)
: one who is given to punning

**¹punt** \'pənt\ *noun* [(assumed) Middle English, from Old English, from Latin *ponton-, ponto*] (before 12th century)
: a long narrow flat-bottomed boat with square ends usually propelled with a pole

**²punt** *transitive verb* (1816)
: to propel (as a punt) with a pole

**³punt** *intransitive verb* [French *ponter*, from *ponte* point in some games, play against the banker, from Spanish *punto* point, from Latin *punctum* — more at POINT] (1712)
**1** : to play at a gambling game against the banker
**2** *British* : GAMBLE

**⁴punt** *verb* [origin unknown] (1845)
*transitive verb*
: to kick (a football or soccer ball) with the top of the foot before the ball which is dropped from the hands hits the ground
*intransitive verb*
: to punt a ball

**⁵punt** *noun* (1845)
: the act or an instance of punting a ball

**⁶punt** \'pùnt\ *noun* [Irish, pound, from English *pound*] (1975)
: the monetary pound of Ireland

**punt·er** \'pən-tər\ *noun* (circa 1706)
: one that punts: as **a** *chiefly British* : a person who gambles; *especially* : one who bets against a bookmaker **b** : one who uses a punt in boating **c** : one who punts a ball

**punt formation** *noun* (1949)
: an offensive football formation in which a back making a punt stands approximately 10 yards behind the line and the other backs are in blocking position close to the line

**pun·ty** \'pən-tē\ *noun, plural* **punties** [French *pontil*] (1662)
: a metal rod used for fashioning hot glass

**pu·ny** \'pyü-nē\ *adjective* **pu·ni·er; -est** [Middle French *puisné* younger, literally, born afterward, from *puis* afterward + *né* born] (1593)

---

☆ **SYNONYMS**
**Pungent, piquant, poignant, racy** mean sharp and stimulating to the mind or the senses. PUNGENT implies a sharp, stinging, or biting quality especially of odors ⟨a cheese with a *pungent* odor⟩. PIQUANT suggests a power to whet the appetite or interest through tartness or mild pungency ⟨a *piquant* sauce⟩. POIGNANT suggests something is sharply or piercingly effective in stirring one's consciousness or emotions ⟨felt a *poignant* sense of loss⟩. RACY implies having a strongly characteristic natural quality fresh and unimpaired ⟨spontaneous, *racy* prose⟩.

**Punish, chastise, castigate, chasten, discipline, correct** mean to inflict a penalty on in requital for wrongdoing. PUNISH implies subjecting to a penalty for wrongdoing ⟨*punished* for stealing⟩. CHASTISE may apply to either the infliction of corporal punishment or to verbal censure or denunciation ⟨*chastised* his son for neglecting his studies⟩. CASTIGATE usually implies a severe, typically public censure ⟨an editorial *castigating* the entire city council⟩. CHASTEN suggests any affliction or trial that leaves one humbled or subdued ⟨*chastened* by a landslide election defeat⟩. DISCIPLINE implies a punishing or chastening in order to bring under control ⟨parents must *discipline* their children⟩. CORRECT implies punishing aimed at reforming an offender ⟨the function of prison is to *correct* the wrongdoer⟩.

: slight or inferior in power, size, or importance : WEAR ◆
— **pu·ni·ly** \'pyü-nᵊl-ē\ *adverb*
— **pu·ni·ness** \'pyü-nē-nəs\ *noun*
¹**pup** \'pəp\ *noun* [short for *puppy*] (1773)
: a young dog; *also* : one of the young of various animals (as a seal or rat)
²**pup** *intransitive verb* **pupped; pup·ping** (1787)
: to give birth to pups
**pu·pa** \'pyü-pə\ *noun, plural* **pu·pae** \-(,)pē *also* -,pī\ *or* **pupas** [New Latin, from Latin *pupa* doll] (1815)
: an intermediate usually quiescent stage of a metamorphic insect (as a bee, moth, or beetle) that occurs between the larva and the imago, is usually enclosed in a cocoon or protective covering, and undergoes internal changes by which larval structures are replaced by those typical of the imago
*word history* see LARVA
— **pu·pal** \'pyü-pəl\ *adjective*
**pu·par·i·um** \pyü-'par-ē-əm, -'per-\ *noun, plural* **pu·par·ia** \-ē-ə\ [New Latin, from *pupa*] (1815)
: a rigid outer shell formed from the larval skin that covers some pupae (as of a dipteran fly)
**pu·pate** \'pyü-,pāt\ *intransitive verb* **pu·pat·ed; pu·pat·ing** (circa 1879)
: to become a pupa : pass through a pupal stage
— **pu·pa·tion** \pyü-'pā-shən\ *noun*
**pup·fish** \'pəp-,fish\ *noun* (1949)
: any of several killifishes (genus *Cyprinodon* of the family Cyprinodontidae) especially of warm streams and springs of the western U.S.
¹**pu·pil** \'pyü-pəl\ *noun* [Middle English *pupille* minor ward, from Middle French, from Latin *pupillus* male ward (from diminutive of *pupus* boy) & *pupilla* female ward, from diminutive of *pupa* girl, doll] (1536)
**1** : a child or young person in school or in the charge of a tutor or instructor : STUDENT
**2** : one who has been taught or influenced by a famous or distinguished person ◆
²**pupil** *noun* [Middle French *pupille*, from Latin *pupilla*, from diminutive of *pupa* doll; from the tiny image of oneself seen reflected in another's eye] (1567)
: the contractile aperture in the iris of the eye ◆
— **pu·pil·lary** \'pyü-pə-,ler-ē\ *adjective*
**pu·pil·age** *or* **pu·pil·lage** \'pyü-pə-lij\ *noun* (circa 1599)
: the state or period of being a pupil
**pup·pet** \'pə-pət\ *noun, often attributive* [Middle English *popet*, from Middle French *poupette*, diminutive of (assumed) *poupe* doll, from Latin *pupa*] (1538)
**1 a** : a small-scale figure (as of a person or animal) usually with a cloth body and hollow head that fits over and is moved by the hand **b** : MARIONETTE
**2** : DOLL 1
**3** : one whose acts are controlled by an outside force or influence
— **pup·pet·like** \-,līk\ *adjective*
**pup·pe·teer** \,pə-pə-'tir\ *noun* (circa 1923)
: one who manipulates puppets
**pup·pet·ry** \'pə-pə-trē\ *noun, plural* **-ries** (1528)
**1** : the production or creation of puppets or puppet shows
**2** : the art of manipulating puppets
**pup·py** \'pə-pē\ *noun, plural* **puppies** [Middle English *popi*, from Middle French *poupée* doll, toy, from (assumed) *poupe* doll] (1591)
: a young domestic dog; *specifically* : one less than a year old
— **pup·py·hood** \-,hud\ *noun*
— **pup·py·ish** \-ish\ *adjective*
— **pup·py·like** \-,līk\ *adjective*
**puppy dog** *noun* (1595)
: a domestic dog; *especially* : one having the lovable attributes of a puppy
**puppy love** *noun* (1834)

: transitory affection felt by a boy or girl for one of the opposite sex
**pup tent** *noun* (1863)
: a low small tent for two persons usually consisting of two halves fastened together
**Pu·ra·na** \pu-'rä-nə\ *noun, often capitalized* [Sanskrit *purāṇa*, from *purāṇa* ancient, from *purā* formerly; akin to Sanskrit *pura* before, Greek *para* beside, *pro* before — more at FOR] (1696)
: one of a class of Hindu sacred writings chiefly from A.D. 300 to A.D. 750 comprising popular myths and legends and other traditional lore
— **Pu·ra·nic** \-nik\ *adjective*
**pur·blind** \'pər-,blīnd\ *adjective* [Middle English *pur blind*, from *pur* purely, wholly, from *pur* pure] (14th century)
**1 a** *obsolete* : wholly blind **b** : partly blind
**2** : lacking in vision, insight, or understanding : OBTUSE
— **pur·blind·ly** \-,blīn(d)-lē\ *adverb*
— **pur·blind·ness** \-,blīn(d)-nəs\ *noun*
¹**pur·chase** \'pər-chəs\ *verb* **pur·chased; pur·chas·ing** [Middle English *purchacen*, from Old French *purchacier* to seek to obtain, from *por-, pur-* for, forward (modification of Latin *pro-*) + *chacier* to pursue, chase — more at PRO-] (14th century)
*transitive verb*
**1 a** *archaic* : GAIN, ACQUIRE **b** : to acquire (real estate) by means other than descent or inheritance **c** : to obtain by paying money or its equivalent : BUY **d** : to obtain by labor, danger, or sacrifice
**2** : to apply a device for obtaining a mechanical advantage to (as something to be moved); *also* : to move by a purchase
**3** : to constitute the means for buying ⟨our dollars *purchase* less each year⟩
*intransitive verb*
: to purchase something
— **pur·chas·able** \-chə-sə-bəl\ *adjective*
— **pur·chas·er** *noun*
²**purchase** *noun* (14th century)
**1** : an act or instance of purchasing
**2** : something obtained especially for a price in money or its equivalent
**3 a** (1) : a mechanical hold or advantage applied to the raising or moving of heavy bodies (2) : an apparatus or device by which advantage is gained **b** (1) : an advantage (as a firm hold or position) used in applying one's power ⟨clutching the steering wheel for more *purchase* —Barry Crump⟩ (2) : a means of exerting power
**pur·dah** \'pər-də\ *noun* [Hindi *parda*, literally, screen, veil] (1865)
**1** : seclusion of women from public observation among Muslims and some Hindus especially in India
**2** : a state of seclusion or concealment
**pure** \'pyur\ *adjective* **pur·er; pur·est** [Middle English *pur*, from Old French, from Latin *purus*; akin to Old High German *fowen* to sift, Sanskrit *punāti* he cleanses, Middle Irish *ur* fresh, new] (14th century)
**1 a** (1) : unmixed with any other matter ⟨*pure* gold⟩ (2) : free from dust, dirt, or taint ⟨*pure* food⟩ (3) : SPOTLESS, STAINLESS **b** : free from harshness or roughness and being in tune — used of a musical tone **c** *of a vowel* : characterized by no appreciable alteration of articulation during utterance
**2 a** : being thus and no other : SHEER, UNMITIGATED ⟨*pure* folly⟩ **b** (1) : ABSTRACT, THEORETICAL (2) : A PRIORI ⟨*pure* mechanics⟩ **c** : not directed toward exposition of reality or solution of practical problems ⟨*pure* literature⟩ **d** : being nonobjective and to be appraised on formal and technical qualities only ⟨*pure* form⟩

**3 a** (1) : free from what vitiates, weakens, or pollutes (2) : containing nothing that does not properly belong **b** : free from moral fault or guilt **c** : marked by chastity : CONTINENT **d** (1) : of pure blood and unmixed ancestry (2) : homozygous in and breeding true for one or more characters **e** : ritually clean
*synonym* see CHASTE
— **pure·ness** *noun*
**pure–blood·ed** \'pyur-,blə-dəd\ *or* **pure-blood** \-,bləd\ *adjective* (1821)
: FULL-BLOODED 1
— **pure–blood** \-,bləd\ *noun*
**pure·bred** \-'bred, -,bred\ *adjective* (1868)
: bred from members of a recognized breed, strain, or kind without admixture of other blood over many generations
— **pure·bred** \-,bred\ *noun*
**pure democracy** *noun* (circa 1910)
: democracy in which the power is exercised directly by the people rather than through representatives
¹**pu·ree** *or* **pu·rée** \pyu-'rā, -'rē\ *noun* [French *purée*, from Middle French, from feminine of *puré*, past participle of *purer* to purify, strain, from Latin *purare* to purify, from *purus*] (1707)
**1** : a paste or thick liquid suspension usually made from cooked food ground finely
**2** : a thick soup made of pureed vegetables
²**puree** *transitive verb* **pu·reed; pu·ree·ing** (1928)
: to make a puree of
**pure imaginary** *noun* (1947)

---

◇ WORD HISTORY
**puny** In medieval French *puisné*, literally "born afterward," was used to mean "younger" in reference to the relationship between two people. When borrowed into English, *puisne* and the phonetic spelling *puny* came to be used of anyone in a lesser position relative to others. From this use a specific legal sense developed. A *puisne* (or *puny*) judge became the designation for a junior or subordinate judge in the superior courts. By Shakespeare's time *puny* had largely lost its implication of relative rank and become nearly synonymous with "weak" or "feeble," a sense the word retains.

**pupil** If you look into another person's eyes, you see reflected within the iris a tiny image of your own face. The Romans, comparing this image of a miniature human to a doll, called the opening in the iris that seems to hold the image *pupilla*, a diminutive of the word *pupa*, meaning "doll." This Latin word, via medieval French *pupille*, was borrowed into English as *pupil*. Another sense of Latin *pupa* was "girl," and a young girl, typically an orphan, who was under the care of a guardian was called by the same diminutive form *pupilla* as the pupil of the eye. The masculine counterpart of *pupilla* was *pupillus*, a diminutive of *pupus*, meaning "boy." In medieval French and later in Middle English, the word *pupille* served for both sexes. It had about the same meaning as the Latin word, an orphan in a guardian's care, though in the 15th century *pupille* began to be used in French for any child being instructed by a tutor. English *pupil* adopted this meaning in the 16th century, but it has gradually expanded in scope to include the children under instruction in an elementary school (for which the Modern French counterpart is *élève*.)

---

\ə\ abut \ᵊ\ kitten \ər\ further \a\ ash \ā\ ace
\ä\ mop, mar \au̇\ out \ch\ chin \e\ bet \ē\ easy
\g\ go \i\ hit \ī\ ice \j\ job \ŋ\ sing \ō\ go
\o̊\ law \o̊i\ boy \th\ thin \ṯh\ the \ü\ loot \u̇\ foot
\y\ yet \zh\ vision    *see also* Guide to Pronunciation

: a complex number that is the product of a real number other than zero and the imaginary unit

**— pure imaginary** *adjective*

**pure·ly** \'pyu̇r-lē\ *adverb* (14th century)
**1 :** WHOLLY, COMPLETELY ⟨a selection based *purely* on merit⟩
**2 :** without admixture of anything injurious or foreign
**3 :** SIMPLY, MERELY ⟨read *purely* for relaxation⟩
**4 :** in a chaste or innocent manner

**pur·fle** \'pər-fəl\ *transitive verb* **pur·fled; pur·fling** \-f(ə-)liŋ\ [Middle English *purfilen*, from Middle French *porfiler*, from (assumed) Vulgar Latin *profilare*, from Latin *pro-* forward + Late Latin *filare* to spin — more at PRO-, FILE] (14th century)
: to ornament the border or edges of
**— purfle** *noun*

**pur·ga·tion** \ˌpər-'gā-shən\ *noun* (14th century)
: the act or result of purging

**¹pur·ga·tive** \'pər-gə-tiv\ *adjective* [Middle English *purgatif*, from Middle French, from Late Latin *purgativus*, from Latin *purgatus*, past participle] (15th century)
: purging or tending to purge

**²purgative** *noun* (1626)
: a purging medicine : CATHARTIC

**pur·ga·to·ri·al** \ˌpər-gə-'tōr-ē-əl, -'tȯr-\ *adjective* (15th century)
**1 :** of, relating to, or suggestive of purgatory
**2 :** cleansing of sin : EXPIATORY

**pur·ga·to·ry** \'pər-gə-ˌtōr-ē, -ˌtȯr-\ *noun, plural* **-ries** [Middle English, from Anglo-French or Medieval Latin; Anglo-French *purgatorie*, from Medieval Latin *purgatorium*, from Late Latin, neuter of *purgatorius* purging, from Latin *purgare*] (13th century)
**1 :** an intermediate state after death for expiatory purification; *specifically* : a place or state of punishment wherein according to Roman Catholic doctrine the souls of those who die in God's grace may make satisfaction for past sins and so become fit for heaven
**2 :** a place or state of temporary suffering or misery

**¹purge** \'pərj\ *verb* **purged; purg·ing** [Middle English, from Middle French *purgier*, from Latin *purigare, purgare* to purify, purge, from *purus* pure + *-igare* (akin to *agere* to drive, do) — more at ACT] (14th century)
*transitive verb*
**1 a :** to clear of guilt **b :** to free from moral or ceremonial defilement
**2 a :** to cause evacuation from (as the bowels) **b** (1) : to make free of something unwanted ⟨*purge* a manhole of gas⟩ ⟨*purge* yourself of fear⟩ (2) : to free (as a boiler) of sediment or relieve (as a steam pipe) of trapped air by bleeding **c** (1) : to rid (as a nation or party) by a purge (2) : to get rid of ⟨the leaders had been *purged*⟩ ⟨*purge* money-losing operations⟩
*intransitive verb*
**1 :** to become purged
**2 :** to have or produce frequent evacuations
**3 :** to cause purgation
**— purg·er** *noun*

**²purge** *noun* (1563)
**1 :** something that purges; *especially* : PURGATIVE
**2 a :** an act or instance of purging **b :** the removal of elements or members regarded as undesirable and especially as treacherous or disloyal

**pu·ri** \'pu̇r-ē\ *noun, plural* **puri** *or* **puris** [Hindi *pūrī*, from Sanskrit *pūra*] (circa 1885)
: a puffy fried wheat cake of India

**pu·ri·fi·ca·tion** \ˌpyu̇r-ə-fə-'kā-shən\ *noun* (14th century)
: the act or an instance of purifying or of being purified

**pu·ri·fi·ca·tor** \'pyu̇r-ə-fə-ˌkā-tər\ *noun* (1853)
**1 :** a linen cloth used to wipe the chalice after celebration of the Eucharist
**2 :** one that purifies

**pu·ri·fi·ca·to·ry** \pyu̇r-'i-fi-kə-ˌtōr-ē, 'pyu̇r-(ə-)fə-kə-, -ˌtȯr-\ *adjective* (1610)
: serving, tending, or intended to purify

**pu·ri·fy** \'pyu̇r-ə-ˌfī\ *verb* **-fied; -fy·ing** [Middle English *purifien*, from Middle French *purifier*, from Latin *purificare*, from Latin *purus* + *-ificare* -ify] (14th century)
*transitive verb*
: to make pure: as **a :** to clear from material defilement or imperfection **b :** to free from guilt or moral or ceremonial blemish **c :** to free from undesirable elements
*intransitive verb*
: to grow or become pure or clean
**— pu·ri·fi·er** \-ˌfī(-ə)r\ *noun*

**Pu·rim** \'pu̇r-im, 'pyu̇r-, -ˌēm; pu̇-'rim, pyu̇-, -'rēm\ *noun* [Hebrew *pūrīm*, literally, lots; from the casting of lots by Haman (Esther 9:24–26)] (1535)
: a Jewish holiday celebrated on the 14th of Adar in commemoration of the deliverance of the Jews from the massacre plotted by Haman

**pu·rine** \'pyu̇r-ˌēn\ *noun* [German *Purin*, from Latin *purus* pure + New Latin *uricus* uric (from English *uric*) + German *-in* ²-ine] (1898)
**1 :** a crystalline base $C_5H_4N_4$ that is the parent of compounds of the uric-acid group
**2 :** a derivative of purine; *especially* : a base (as adenine or guanine) that is a constituent of DNA or RNA

**pur·ism** \'pyu̇r-ˌi-zəm\ *noun* (1803)
**1 :** an example of rigid adherence to or insistence on purity or nicety especially in use of words; *especially* : a word, phrase, or sense used chiefly by purists
**2 :** the quality or practice of adherence to purity especially in language

**pur·ist** \'pyu̇r-ist\ *noun* (circa 1706)
: one who adheres strictly and often excessively to a tradition; *especially* : one preoccupied with the purity of a language and its protection from the use of foreign or altered forms
**— pu·ris·tic** \pyu̇-'ris-tik\ *adjective*
**— pu·ris·ti·cal·ly** \-ti-k(ə-)lē\ *adverb*

**¹pu·ri·tan** \'pyu̇r-ə-t°n\ *noun* [probably from Late Latin *puritas* purity] (1572)
**1** *capitalized* : a member of a 16th and 17th century Protestant group in England and New England opposing as unscriptural the ceremonial worship and the prelacy of the Church of England
**2 :** one who practices or preaches a more rigorous or professedly purer moral code than that which prevails

**²puritan** *adjective, often capitalized* (1589)
: of or relating to puritans, the Puritans, or puritanism

**pu·ri·tan·i·cal** \ˌpyu̇r-ə-'ta-ni-kəl\ *adjective* (1607)
**1 :** PURITAN
**2 :** of, relating to, or characterized by a rigid morality
**— pu·ri·tan·i·cal·ly** \-k(ə-)lē\ *adverb*

**pu·ri·tan·ism** \'pyu̇r-ə-t°n-ˌi-zəm\ *noun* (1573)
**1** *capitalized* : the beliefs and practices characteristic of the Puritans
**2 :** strictness and austerity especially in matters of religion or conduct

**pu·ri·ty** \'pyu̇r-ə-tē\ *noun* [Middle English *purete*, from Old French *pureté*, from Late Latin *puritat-, puritas*, from Latin *purus* pure] (13th century)
**1 :** the quality or state of being pure
**2 :** SATURATION 4a

**Pur·kin·je cell** \(ˌ)pər-'kin-jē-\ *noun* [Jan Purkinje] (circa 1890)
: any of numerous nerve cells that occupy the middle layer of the cerebellar cortex and are characterized by a large globose body with massive dendrites directed outward and a single slender axon directed inward

**Purkinje fiber** *noun* (circa 1890)
: any of the modified cardiac muscle fibers that have few nuclei, granulated central cyto-

plasm, and sparse peripheral striations and make up a network of conducting tissue in the myocardium

**¹purl** \'pər(-ə)l\ *noun* [Middle English] (14th century)
**1 :** gold or silver thread or wire for embroidering or edging
**2 :** the intertwisting of thread that knots a stitch usually along an edge
**3 :** PURL STITCH

**²purl** (1526)
*transitive verb*
**1 a :** to embroider with gold or silver thread **b :** to edge or border with gold or silver embroidery
**2 :** to knit in purl stitch
*intransitive verb*
: to do knitting in purl stitch

**³purl** *noun* [perhaps of Scandinavian origin; akin to Norwegian *purla* to ripple] (circa 1522)
**1 :** a purling or swirling stream or rill
**2 :** a gentle murmur or movement (as of purling water)

**⁴purl** *intransitive verb* (1591)
**1 :** EDDY, SWIRL
**2 :** to make a soft murmuring sound like that of a purling stream

**pur·lieu** \'pərl-(ˌ)yü, 'pər-(ˌ)lü\ *noun* [Middle English *purlewe* land severed from an English royal forest by perambulation, from Anglo-French *puralé* perambulation, from Old French *puraler* to go through, from *pur-* for, through + *aler* to go — more at PURCHASE] (15th century)
**1 a :** an outlying or adjacent district **b** *plural* : ENVIRONS, NEIGHBORHOOD
**2 a :** a frequently visited place : HAUNT **b** *plural* : CONFINES, BOUNDS

**pur·lin** \'pər-lən\ *noun* [origin unknown] (15th century)
: a horizontal member in a roof

**pur·loin** \(ˌ)pər-'lȯin; 'pər-ˌ\ *transitive verb* [Middle English, to put away, misappropriate, from Anglo-French *purloigner*, from Old French *porloigner* to put off, delay, from *por-* forward + *loing* at a distance, from Latin *longe*, from *longus* long — more at PURCHASE, LONG] (15th century)
: to appropriate wrongfully and often by a breach of trust
**synonym** see STEAL
**— pur·loin·er** *noun*

**purl stitch** *noun* [¹purl] (1885)
: a knitting stitch usually made with the yarn at the front of the work by inserting the right needle into the front of a loop on the left needle from the right, catching the yarn with the right needle, and bringing it through to form a new loop — compare KNIT STITCH

**pu·ro·my·cin** \ˌpyu̇r-ō-'mī-s°n\ *noun* [*purine* + *-o-* + *-mycin*] (1953)
: an antibiotic $C_{22}H_{29}N_7O_5$ that is obtained from an actinomycete (*Streptomyces alboniger*) and is used especially as a potent inhibitor of protein synthesis

**¹pur·ple** \'pər-pəl\ *adjective* **pur·pler** \-p(ə-)lər\; **pur·plest** \-p(ə-)ləst\ [Middle English *purpel*, alteration of *purpur*, from Old English *purpuran* of purple, genitive of *purpure* purple color, from Latin *purpura*, from Greek *porphyra*] (before 12th century)
**1 :** REGAL, IMPERIAL
**2 :** of the color purple
**3 a :** highly rhetorical : ORNATE **b :** marked by profanity

**²purple** *noun* (15th century)
**1 a** (1) : cloth dyed purple (2) : a garment of such color; *especially* : a purple robe worn as an emblem of rank or authority **b** (1) : TYRIAN PURPLE (2) : any of various colors that fall about midway between red and blue in hue **c** (1) : a mollusk (as of the genus *Purpura*) yielding a purple dye and especially the Tyrian purple of ancient times (2) : a pigment or dye that colors purple

**2 a** : imperial or regal rank or power **b** : high rank or station

³**purple** *verb* **pur·pled; pur·pling** \-p(ə-)liŋ\ (15th century)
*transitive verb*
: to make purple
*intransitive verb*
: to become purple

**pur·ple·heart** \'pər-pəl-ˌhärt\ *noun* (1796)
: a strong durable purplish wood that is obtained from various leguminous trees (genus *Peltogyne*); *also* : a tree producing such wood

**Purple Heart** *noun* (1932)
: a U.S. military decoration awarded to any member of the armed forces wounded or killed in action

**purple loosestrife** *noun* (1548)
: an Old World marsh herb (*Lythrum salicaria*) of the loosestrife family that is naturalized in the eastern U.S. and has long spikes of purple flowers

**purple martin** *noun* (1743)
: a large swallow (*Progne subis*) of North America the males of which have bluish black plumage

**purple passage** *noun* [translation of Latin *pannus purpureus* purple patch; from the traditional splendor of purple cloth as contrasted with plainer materials] (1895)
**1** : a passage conspicuous for brilliance or effectiveness in a work that is dull, commonplace, or uninspired
**2** *chiefly British* : a piece of obtrusively ornate writing — called also *purple patch*

**purple scale** *noun* (circa 1909)
: a brownish or purplish armored scale (*Lepidosaphes beckii*) that is destructive to citrus fruit

**pur·plish** \'pər-p(ə-)lish\ *adjective* (1562)
: somewhat purple

**pur·ply** \'pər-p(ə-)lē\ *adjective* (1725)
: PURPLISH

¹**pur·port** \'pər-ˌpōrt, -ˌpȯrt\ *noun* [Middle English, from Anglo-French, content, tenor, from *purporter* to contain, from Old French *porporter* to convey, from *por-* forward + *porter* to carry — more at PURCHASE, PORT] (15th century)
: meaning conveyed, professed, or implied
: IMPORT; *also* : SUBSTANCE, GIST

²**pur·port** \(ˌ)pər-'pōrt, -'pȯrt\ *transitive verb* (1528)
**1** : to have the often specious appearance of being, intending, or claiming (something implied or inferred) ⟨a book that *purports* to be an objective analysis⟩; *also* : CLAIM ⟨foreign novels which he *purports* to have translated —Mary McCarthy⟩
**2** : INTEND, PURPOSE

**pur·port·ed** \-'pōr-təd, -'pȯr-\ *adjective* (1894)
: REPUTED, ALLEGED ⟨took gullible tourists to *purported* ancient sites⟩

**pur·port·ed·ly** \-lē\ *adverb* (1942)
: it is purported : OSTENSIBLY, ALLEGEDLY

¹**pur·pose** \'pər-pəs\ *noun* [Middle English *purpos*, from Old French, from *purposer* to purpose, from Latin *proponere* (perfect indicative *proposui*) to propose — more at PROPOUND] (14th century)
**1 a** : something set up as an end to be attained : INTENTION **b** : RESOLUTION, DETERMINATION
**2** : a subject under discussion or an action in course of execution
**synonym** see INTENTION
— **on purpose** : by intent : INTENTIONALLY

²**purpose** *transitive verb* **pur·posed; pur·pos·ing** (14th century)
: to propose as an aim to oneself

**pur·pose–built** \ˌpər-pəs-'bilt\ *adjective* (1954)
*chiefly British* : built for a particular purpose

**pur·pose·ful** \'pər-pəs-fəl\ *adjective* (1853)
**1** : having a purpose: as **a** : MEANINGFUL ⟨*purposeful* activities⟩ **b** : INTENTIONAL ⟨*purposeful* ambiguity⟩

**2** : full of determination ⟨a *purposeful* man⟩
— **pur·pose·ful·ly** \-fə-lē\ *adverb*
— **pur·pose·ful·ness** *noun*

**pur·pose·less** \-ləs\ *adjective* (circa 1552)
: having no purpose : AIMLESS, MEANINGLESS
— **pur·pose·less·ly** *adverb*
— **pur·pose·less·ness** *noun*

**pur·pose·ly** \-lē\ *adverb* (15th century)
: with a deliberate or express purpose

**pur·po·sive** \'pər-pə-siv, (ˌ)pər-'pō-\ *adjective* (1855)
**1** : serving or effecting a useful function though not as a result of planning or design
**2** : having or tending to fulfill a conscious purpose or design : PURPOSEFUL
— **pur·po·sive·ly** *adverb*
— **pur·po·sive·ness** *noun*

**pur·pu·ra** \'pər-pyə-rə, -pə-rə\ *noun* [New Latin, from Latin, purple color] (1753)
: any of several hemorrhagic states characterized by patches of purplish discoloration resulting from extravasation of blood into the skin and mucous membranes
— **pur·pu·ric** \ˌpər-'pyur-ik\ *adjective*

**pur·pure** \'pər-pyər\ *noun* [Middle English, from Old English, purple] (1535)
: the heraldic color purple

¹**purr** \'pər\ *noun* [imitative] (1601)
: a low vibratory murmur typical of an apparently contented or pleased cat

²**purr** *intransitive verb* (1620)
**1** : to make a purr or a sound like a purr ⟨cars *purring* along the highway⟩
**2 a** : to speak in a manner that resembles a purr **b** : to speak in a malicious catty manner
— **purr·ing·ly** \-iŋ-lē\ *adverb*

¹**purse** \'pərs\ *noun* [Middle English *purs*, from Old English, modification of Medieval Latin *bursa*, from Late Latin, ox hide, from Greek *byrsa*] (before 12th century)
**1 a** (1) : a small bag for money (2) : a receptacle (as a pocketbook) for carrying money and often other small objects **b** : a receptacle (as a pouch) shaped like a purse
**2 a** : RESOURCES, FUNDS **b** : a sum of money offered as a prize or present; *also* : the total amount of money offered in prizes for a given event
— **purse·like** \-ˌlīk\ *adjective*

²**purse** *transitive verb* **pursed; purs·ing** (14th century)
**1** : to put into a purse
**2** : PUCKER, KNIT

**purse–proud** \'pərs-ˌprau̇d\ *adjective* (1681)
: proud because of one's wealth especially in the absence of other distinctions

**purs·er** \'pər-sər\ *noun* [Middle English, from *purs* purse] (15th century)
**1** : an official on a ship responsible for papers and accounts and on a passenger ship also for the comfort and welfare of passengers
**2** : a steward on an airliner

**purse seine** *noun* (1870)
: a large seine designed to be set by two boats around a school of fish and so arranged that after the ends have been brought together the bottom can be closed

**purse seine**

— **purse seiner** *noun*
— **purse seining** *noun*

**purse strings** *noun plural* (15th century)
: financial resources; *also* : control over these resources

**purs·lane** \'pər-slən, -ˌslān\ *noun* [Middle English, from Middle French *porcelaine*, from Late Latin *porcillagin-, porcillago*, alteration of Latin *porcillaca*, alteration of *portulaca*] (14th century)
: any of a family (Portulacaceae, the purslane family) of cosmopolitan usually succulent herbs; *especially* : a fleshy-leaved trailing plant (*Portulaca oleracea*) with tiny yellow

flowers that is a common troublesome weed but is sometimes eaten as a potherb or in salads

**pur·su·ance** \pər-'sü-ən(t)s\ *noun* (1605)
: the act of pursuing; *especially* : a carrying out or into effect : PROSECUTION ⟨in *pursuance* of his duties⟩

**pur·su·ant to** \-ənt-\ *preposition* (1648)
: in carrying out : in conformity with : ACCORDING TO

**pur·sue** \pər-'sü, -'syü\ *verb* **pur·sued; pur·su·ing** [Middle English, from Anglo-French *pursuer*, from Old French *poursuir*, from Latin *prosequi*, from *pro-* forward + *sequi* to follow — more at PRO-, SUE] (14th century)
*transitive verb*
**1** : to follow in order to overtake, capture, kill, or defeat
**2** : to find or employ measures to obtain or accomplish : SEEK ⟨*pursue* a goal⟩
**3** : to proceed along ⟨*pursues* a northern course⟩
**4 a** : to engage in ⟨*pursue* a hobby⟩ **b** : to follow up or proceed with ⟨*pursue* an argument⟩
**5** : to continue to afflict : HAUNT ⟨was *pursued* by horrible memories⟩
**6** : ²CHASE 1c ⟨*pursued* by dozens of fans⟩
*intransitive verb*
: to go in pursuit
**synonym** see CHASE
— **pur·su·er** *noun*

**pur·suit** \pər-'süt, -'syüt\ *noun* [Middle English, from Middle French *poursuite*, from *poursuir*] (14th century)
**1** : the act of pursuing
**2** : an activity that one engages in as a vocation, profession, or avocation : OCCUPATION
**synonym** see WORK

**pursuit plane** *noun* (circa 1918)
: a fighter plane especially of the period before World War II

**pur·sui·vant** \'pər-si-vənt, -swi-\ *noun* [Middle English *pursevant* attendant of a herald, from Middle French *poursuivant*, literally, follower, from present participle of *poursuir, poursuivre* to pursue] (14th century)
**1** : an officer of arms ranking below a herald but having similar duties
**2** : FOLLOWER, ATTENDANT

¹**pur·sy** \'pə-sē, 'pər-sē\ *adjective* **pur·si·er; -est** [Middle English, from Anglo-French *pursif*, alteration of Middle French *polsif*, from *poulser, polser* to beat, push, pant — more at PUSH] (15th century)
**1** : short-winded especially because of corpulence
**2** : FAT
— **pur·si·ness** *noun*

²**pursy** \'pər-sē\ *adjective* **purs·i·er; -est** [¹*purse*] (1552)
**1** : having a puckered appearance
**2** : PURSE-PROUD

**pur·te·nance** \'pərt-nən(t)s, 'pər-tᵊn-ən(t)s\ *noun* [Middle English, literally, appendage, modification of Middle French *partenance*, from *partenir* to pertain — more at PERTAIN] (15th century)
: ENTRAILS, PLUCK

**pu·ru·lence** \'pyur-ə-lən(t)s, 'pyur-yə-\ *noun* (1597)
: the quality or state of being purulent; *also* : PUS

**pu·ru·lent** \-lənt\ *adjective* [Latin *purulentus*, from *pur-, pus* pus] (1597)
**1** : containing, consisting of, or being pus ⟨a *purulent* discharge⟩
**2** : accompanied by suppuration

**pur·vey** \(ˌ)pər-ˈvā, ˈpər-\ *transitive verb* **pur·veyed; pur·vey·ing** [Middle English *purveien,* from Middle French *porveeir,* from Latin *providēre* to provide] (14th century) **1 :** to supply (as provisions) usually as a matter of business **2 :** PEDDLE 2

**pur·vey·ance** \-ən(t)s\ *noun* (14th century) **:** the act or process of purveying or procuring

**pur·vey·or** \-ər\ *noun* (14th century) **1 :** one that purveys **2 :** VICTUALLER, CATERER

**pur·view** \ˈpər-ˌvyü\ *noun* [Middle English *purveu,* from Anglo-French *purveu est* it is provided (opening phrase of a statute)] (15th century) **1 a :** the body or enacting part of a statute **b :** the limit, purpose, or scope of a statute **2 :** the range or limit of authority, competence, responsibility, concern, or intention **3 :** range of vision, understanding, or cognizance

**pus** \ˈpəs\ *noun* [Latin *pur-, pus* — more at FOUL] (1541) **:** thick opaque usually yellowish white fluid matter formed by suppuration and composed of exudate containing white blood cells, tissue debris, and microorganisms

**Pu·sey·ism** \ˈpyü-zē-ˌi-zəm, -sē-\ *noun* [Edward Bouverie *Pusey*] (1838) **:** TRACTARIANISM
— **Pu·sey·ite** \-ˌīt\ *noun*

**¹push** \ˈpu̇sh\ *verb* [Middle English *pusshen,* from Middle French *poulser* to beat, push, from Old French, from Latin *pulsare,* frequentative of *pellere* to drive, strike — more at FELT] (13th century) *transitive verb* **1 a :** to press against with force in order to drive or impel **b :** to move or endeavor to move away or ahead by steady pressure without striking **2 a :** to thrust forward, downward, or outward **b :** to cause to increase **:** RAISE ⟨*push* prices to record levels⟩ **c :** to hit (a ball) toward the right from a right-handed swing or toward the left from a left-handed swing — compare PULL **3 a :** to press or urge forward to completion **b :** to urge or press the advancement, adoption, or practice of ⟨*pushed* a bill in the legislature⟩; *especially* **:** to make aggressive efforts to sell ⟨we're *pushing* ham this week⟩ **c :** to engage in the illicit sale of (narcotics) **4 :** to bear hard upon so as to involve in difficulty ⟨poverty *pushed* them to the breaking point⟩ **5 :** to approach in age or number ⟨grandmother must be *pushing* 75⟩ *intransitive verb* **1 :** to press against something with steady force in or as if in order to impel **2 :** to press forward energetically against opposition **3 :** to exert oneself continuously, vigorously, or obtrusively to gain an end ⟨*pushing* for higher wages⟩
— **push one's luck :** to take an increasing risk

**²push** *noun* (1563) **1 :** a vigorous effort to attain an end **:** DRIVE: **a :** a military assault or offensive **b :** an advance that overcomes obstacles **c :** a campaign to promote a product **2 :** a time for action **:** EMERGENCY **3 a :** an act of pushing **:** SHOVE **b** (1) **:** a physical force steadily applied in a direction away from the body exerting it (2) **:** a nonphysical pressure **:** INFLUENCE, URGE **c :** vigorous enterprise or energy **4 a :** an exertion of influence to promote another's interests **b :** stimulation to activity **:** IMPETUS
— **push comes to shove :** a decisive moment comes ⟨backed down when *push came to shove*⟩

**push around** *transitive verb* (1923) **:** to impose on contemptuously

**push-ball** \ˈpu̇sh-ˌbȯl\ *noun* (1896) **:** a game in which each of two sides endeavors to push an inflated originally leather-covered ball six feet (1.8 meters) in diameter across its opponents' goal; *also* **:** the ball used

**push–bike** \-ˌbīk\ *noun* (1913) *British* **:** BICYCLE — called also *push bicycle*

**push broom** *noun* (1926) **:** a long-handled wide brush that is designed to be pushed and is used for sweeping

**push–button** *adjective* (1916) **1 :** operated or done by means of push buttons ⟨a *push-button* phone⟩ **2 :** using or dependent on complex and more or less self-operating mechanisms that are put in operation by a simple act comparable to pushing a button ⟨*push-button* warfare⟩

**push button** *noun* (1878) **:** a small button or knob that when pushed operates something especially by closing an electric circuit

**push·cart** \ˈpu̇sh-ˌkärt\ *noun* (1893) **:** a cart or barrow pushed by hand

**push–chair** \-ˌcher, -ˌchar\ *noun* (1921) *chiefly British* **:** STROLLER

**push–down** \-ˌdau̇n\ *noun* (1961) **:** a store of data (as in a computer) from which the most recently stored item must be the first retrieved — called also *pushdown list, pushdown stack*

**push·er** \ˈpu̇-shər\ *noun* (1591) **:** one that pushes; *especially* **:** one that pushes illegal drugs

**push·ful** \-fəl\ *adjective* (1896) *chiefly British* **:** PUSHING
— **push·ful·ness** *noun, chiefly British*

**push·ing** *adjective* (1692) **1 :** marked by ambition, energy, enterprise, and initiative **2 :** marked by tactless forwardness or officious intrusiveness

**push off** *intransitive verb* (1925) **:** SET OUT ⟨we *pushed off* for home⟩

**push on** *intransitive verb* (1718) **:** to continue on one's way **:** PROCEED

**push·over** \ˈpu̇sh-ˌō-vər\ *noun* (1906) **1 :** something accomplished without difficulty **:** SNAP **2 :** an opponent who is easy to defeat or a victim who is capable of no effective resistance **3 :** someone unable to resist an attraction or appeal **:** SUCKER

**push·pin** \-ˌpin\ *noun* (1907) **:** a pin that has a roughly cylindrical head and that is easily inserted and withdrawn (as from a bulletin board)

**push–pull** \-ˈpu̇l\ *adjective* (1922) **:** relating to or being an arrangement of two electronic circuit elements (as transistors) such that an alternating input causes them to send current through a load alternately ⟨a *push-pull* circuit⟩
— **push–pull** *noun*

**Push·tu** \ˈpəsh-(ˌ)tü\ *variant of* PASHTO

**Push·tun** *variant of* PASHTUN

**push–up** \ˈpu̇sh-ˌəp\ *noun* (1942) **:** a conditioning exercise performed in a prone position by raising and lowering the body with the straightening and bending of the arms while keeping the back straight and supporting the body on the hands and toes

**pushy** \ˈpu̇-shē\ *adjective* **push·i·er; -est** (1936) **:** aggressive often to an objectionable degree **:** FORWARD
— **push·i·ly** \ˈpu̇-shə-lē\ *adverb*
— **push·i·ness** \ˈpu̇-shē-nəs\ *noun*

**pu·sil·la·nim·i·ty** \ˌpyü-sə-lə-ˈni-mə-tē *also* ˌpyü-slə-\ *noun* (14th century) **:** the quality or state of being pusillanimous **:** COWARDLINESS

**pu·sil·lan·i·mous** \-ˈla-nə-məs\ *adjective* [Late Latin *pusillanimis,* from Latin *pusillus* very small (diminutive of *pusus* boy) + *animus* spirit; perhaps akin to Latin *puer* child — more at PUERILE, ANIMATE] (1586) **:** lacking courage and resolution **:** marked by contemptible timidity
*synonym* see COWARDLY
— **pu·sil·lan·i·mous·ly** *adverb*

**¹puss** \ˈpu̇s\ *noun* [origin unknown] (circa 1530) **1 :** CAT **2 :** GIRL

**²puss** *noun* [Irish *pus* mouth] (circa 1890) *slang* **:** FACE

**puss·ley** \ˈpəs-lē\ *noun* [by alteration] (1833) **:** PURSLANE

**¹pussy** \ˈpu̇-sē\ *noun, plural* **puss·ies** [¹*puss*] (1726) **1 :** CAT **2 :** a catkin of the pussy willow

**²pus·sy** \ˈpu̇-sē\ *noun, plural* **pussies** [perhaps of Low German or Scandinavian origin; akin to Old Norse *pūss* pocket, pouch, Low German *pūse* vulva, Old English *pusa* bag] (circa 1879) **1 :** VULVA — usually considered vulgar **2 a :** SEXUAL INTERCOURSE — usually considered vulgar **b :** the female partner in sexual intercourse — usually considered vulgar

**³pus·sy** \ˈpə-sē\ *adjective* **pus·si·er; -est** (circa 1890) **:** full of or resembling pus

**⁴pus·sy** \ˈpə-sē\ *variant of* ¹PURSY

**pussy·cat** \ˈpu̇-sē-ˌkat\ *noun* (1805) **1 :** CAT **2 :** one that is weak, compliant, or amiable **:** SOFTY

**pussy·foot** \ˈpu̇-sē-ˌfu̇t\ *intransitive verb* (1903) **1 :** to tread or move warily or stealthily **2 :** to refrain from committing oneself
— **pussy·foot·er** *noun*

**pussy·toes** \ˈpu̇-sē-ˌtōz\ *or* **puss·y's–toes** \-ˌsēz-\ *noun plural but singular or plural in construction* (1892) **:** any of a genus (*Antennaria*) of woolly or hoary chiefly temperate composite herbs that have small usually whitish discoid flower heads and a pappus formed of club-shaped bristles

**pussy willow** \ˈpu̇-sē-\ *noun* (1869) **:** a willow (as the American *Salix discolor*) having large cylindrical silky aments

*pussy willow*

**¹pus·tu·lant** \ˈpəs-chə-lənt; ˈpəs-tyə-, -tə-\ *noun* (1871) **:** an agent (as a chemical) that induces pustule formation

**²pustulant** *adjective* (circa 1890) **:** producing pustules

**pus·tu·lar** \-lər\ *adjective* (1739) **1 :** of, relating to, or resembling pustules **2 :** covered with pustular prominences **:** PUSTULATED

**pus·tu·lat·ed** \-ˌlā-təd\ *adjective* (1732) **:** covered with pustules

**pus·tu·la·tion** \ˌpəs-chə-ˈlā-shən, ˌpəs-tyə-, -tə-\ *noun* (circa 1860) **1 :** the act of producing pustules **:** the state of having pustules **2 :** PUSTULE

**pus·tule** \ˈpəs-(ˌ)chü(ə)l, -(ˌ)tyü(ə)l, -(ˌ)tü(ə)l\ *noun* [Middle English, from Latin *pustula;* akin to Lithuanian *pusti* to blow, Greek *physa* breath] (14th century) **1 :** a small circumscribed elevation of the skin containing pus and having an inflamed base **2 :** a small often distinctively colored elevation or spot resembling a blister or pimple

**¹put** \ˈpu̇t\ *verb* **put; put·ting** [Middle English *putten;* akin to Old English *putung* instigation, Middle Dutch *poten* to plant] (12th century) *transitive verb*

**1 a :** to place in a specified position or relationship : LAY ⟨*put* the book on the table⟩ **b :** to move in a specified direction **c** (1) **:** to send (as a weapon or missile) into or through something : THRUST (2) **:** to throw with an overhand pushing motion ⟨*put* the shot⟩ **d :** to bring into a specified state or condition ⟨a reapportionment . . . that was *put* into effect at the September primaries —*Current Biography*⟩
**2 a :** to cause to endure or suffer something : SUBJECT ⟨*put* traitors to death⟩ **b :** IMPOSE, INFLICT ⟨*put* a special tax on luxuries⟩
**3 a :** to set before one for judgment or decision ⟨*put* the question⟩ **b :** to call for a formal vote on ⟨*put* the motion⟩
**4 a** (1) **:** to convey into another form ⟨want to *put* my feelings into words⟩ (2) **:** to translate into another language or style ⟨*put* the poem into English⟩ (3) **:** ADAPT ⟨lyrics *put* to music⟩ **b :** EXPRESS, STATE ⟨*putting* it mildly⟩
**5 a :** to devote (oneself) to an activity or end ⟨*put* himself to winning back their confidence⟩ **b :** APPLY ⟨*put* her mind to the problem⟩ **c :** ASSIGN ⟨*put* them to work⟩ **d :** to cause to perform an action : URGE ⟨*put* the horse over the fence⟩ **e :** IMPEL, INCITE ⟨*put* them into a frenzy⟩
**6 a :** REPOSE, REST ⟨*puts* his faith in reason⟩ **b :** INVEST ⟨*put* her money in the company⟩
**7 a :** to give as an estimate ⟨*put* the time as about eleven⟩ **b :** ATTACH, ATTRIBUTE ⟨*puts* a high value on their friendship⟩ **c :** IMPUTE ⟨*put* the blame on the partners⟩
**8 :** BET, WAGER ⟨*put* $2 on the favorite⟩
*intransitive verb*
**1 :** to start in motion : GO; *especially* **:** to leave in a hurry
**2** *of a ship* **:** to take a specified course ⟨*put* down the river⟩
— **put forth 1 a :** ASSERT, PROPOSE **b :** to make public : ISSUE **2 :** to bring into action : EXERT **3 :** to produce or send out by growth ⟨*put forth* leaves⟩ **4 :** to start out
— **put forward :** PROPOSE ⟨*put forward* a theory⟩
— **put in mind :** REMIND
— **put one's finger on :** IDENTIFY ⟨*put his finger on* the cause of the trouble⟩
— **put one's foot down :** to take a firm stand
— **put one's foot in one's mouth :** to make a tactless or embarrassing blunder
— **put paid to** *British* **:** to finish off : WIPE OUT
— **put the arm on** *or* **put the bite on :** to ask for money
— **put the finger on :** to inform on ⟨*put the finger on* . . . heroin pushers —Barrie Zwicker⟩
— **put the make on :** to make sexual advances toward
— **put to bed :** to make the final preparations for printing (as a newspaper)
— **put together 1 :** to create as a unified whole : CONSTRUCT **2 :** ADD, COMBINE
— **put to it :** to give difficulty to : press hard ⟨had been *put to it* to keep up⟩
**²put** *noun* (14th century)
**1 :** a throw made with an overhand pushing motion; *specifically* **:** the act or an instance of putting the shot
**2 :** an option to sell a specified amount of a security (as a stock) or commodity (as wheat) at a fixed price at or within a specified time — compare CALL 3d
**³put** *adjective* (1848)
**:** being in place : FIXED, SET ⟨stay *put* until I call⟩
**put about** (1748)
*intransitive verb*
*of a ship* **:** to change direction : go on another tack
*transitive verb*
**:** to cause to change course or direction
**put across** *transitive verb* (1919)
**1 :** PUT OVER 3

**2 :** to convey effectively or forcefully
**put-and-take** \ˌpu̇t-ᵊn-ˈtāk\ *noun* (1922)
**:** any of various games of chance played with a teetotum or with dice in which players contribute to a pool and take from it according to the instructions on the top or dice
**pu·ta·tive** \ˈpyü-tə-tiv\ *adjective* [Middle English, from Late Latin *putativus*, from Latin *putatus*, past participle of *putare* to think] (15th century)
**1 :** commonly accepted or supposed
**2 :** assumed to exist or to have existed
— **pu·ta·tive·ly** *adverb*
**put away** *transitive verb* (14th century)
**1 a :** DISCARD, RENOUNCE ⟨to *put* grief *away* is disloyal to the memory of the departed —H. A. Overstreet⟩ **b :** DIVORCE
**2 :** to eat or drink up : CONSUME
**3 a :** to confine especially in a mental institution **b :** BURY **c :** KILL
**put by** *transitive verb* (15th century)
**1** *archaic* **:** REJECT
**2 :** to lay aside : SAVE
**put-down** \ˈpu̇t-ˌdau̇n\ *noun* (1962)
**:** an act or instance of putting down; *especially* **:** a humiliating remark : SQUELCH
**put down** *transitive verb* (14th century)
**1 :** to bring to an end : STOP ⟨*put down* a riot⟩
**2 a :** DEPOSE, DEGRADE **b :** DISPARAGE, BELITTLE ⟨mentioned his poetry only to *put* it *down*⟩ **c :** DISAPPROVE, CRITICIZE ⟨was *put down* for the way she dressed⟩ **d :** HUMILIATE, SQUELCH ⟨*put* him *down* with a sharp retort⟩
**3 :** to make ineffective : CHECK ⟨*put down* the gossip⟩
**4 :** to do away with (as an injured, sick, or aged animal) : DESTROY
**5 a :** to put in writing ⟨*put* it *down* truthfully⟩ **b :** to enter in a list ⟨*put* me *down* for a donation⟩
**6 a :** to place in a category ⟨I *put* him *down* as a hypochondriac —O. S. J. Gogarty⟩ **b :** ATTRIBUTE ⟨*put* it *down* to inexperience⟩
**7 :** to pack or preserve for future use
**8 :** CONSUME ⟨*putting down* helping after helping —Carson McCullers⟩
— **put down roots :** to establish a permanent residence
**put in** (15th century)
*transitive verb*
**1 :** to make a formal offer or declaration of ⟨*put in* a plea of guilty⟩
**2 :** to come in with : INTERPOSE ⟨*put in* a word for his brother⟩
**3 :** to spend (time) especially at some occupation or job ⟨*put in* six hours at the office⟩
**4 :** PLANT ⟨*put in* a crop⟩
*intransitive verb*
**1 :** to call at or enter a place; *especially* **:** to enter a harbor or port
**2 :** to make an application, request, or offer — often used with *for* ⟨had to retire and *put in* for a pension —Seymour Nagan⟩
**put·log** \ˈpu̇t-ˌlȯg, ˈpət-, -ˌläg\ *noun* [probably alteration of earlier *putlock*, perhaps from ³*put* + ²*lock*] (1645)
**:** one of the short timbers that support the flooring of a scaffold
**put off** *transitive verb* (14th century)
**1 a :** DISCONCERT **b :** REPEL
**2 a :** to hold back to a later time **b :** to induce to wait ⟨*put* the bill collector *off*⟩
**3 :** to rid oneself of : TAKE OFF
**4 :** to sell or pass fraudulently
**¹put-on** \ˈpu̇t-ˌȯn, -ˌän\ *adjective* (1621)
**:** PRETENDED, ASSUMED
**²put-on** \ˈpu̇t-ˌȯn, -ˌän\ *noun* (circa 1927)
**1 :** an instance of putting someone on ⟨conversational *put-ons* are related to old-fashioned joshing —Jacob Brackman⟩
**2 :** PARODY, SPOOF ⟨a kind of *put-on* of every pretentious film ever made —C. A. Ridley⟩
**put on** *transitive verb* (15th century)
**1 a :** to dress oneself in : DON **b :** to make part of one's appearance or behavior **c :** FEIGN ⟨*put* a saintly manner *on*⟩

**2 :** to cause to act or operate : APPLY ⟨*put on* more speed⟩
**3 a :** ADD ⟨*put on* weight⟩ **b :** EXAGGERATE, OVERSTATE ⟨he's *putting* it *on* when he makes such claims⟩
**4 :** PERFORM, PRODUCE ⟨*put on* a play⟩
**5 a :** to mislead deliberately especially for amusement ⟨the interviewer . . . must be put down — or possibly, *put on* —Melvin Maddocks⟩ **b :** KID ⟨you're *putting* me *on*⟩
**put·out** \ˈpu̇t-ˌau̇t\ *noun* (1885)
**:** the retiring of a base runner or batter by a defensive player in baseball
**put out** (14th century)
*transitive verb*
**1 :** EXTINGUISH ⟨*put* the fire *out*⟩
**2 :** EXERT, USE ⟨*put out* considerable effort⟩
**3 :** PUBLISH, ISSUE
**4 :** to produce for sale
**5 a :** DISCONCERT, EMBARRASS **b :** ANNOY, IRRITATE **c :** INCONVENIENCE ⟨don't *put* yourself *out* for us⟩
**6 :** to cause to be out (as in baseball or cricket)
*intransitive verb*
**1 :** to set out from shore
**2 :** to make an effort
**3 :** to engage in sexual intercourse
**put over** *transitive verb* (1528)
**1 :** POSTPONE, DELAY
**2 :** PUT ACROSS 2
**3 :** to achieve or carry through by deceit or trickery ⟨*put one over on* me⟩
**pu·tre·fac·tion** \ˌpyü-trə-ˈfak-shən\ *noun* [Middle English *putrefaccion*, from Late Latin *putrefaction-, putrefactio*, from Latin *putrefacere*] (14th century)
**1 :** the decomposition of organic matter; *especially* **:** the typically anaerobic splitting of proteins by bacteria and fungi with the formation of foul-smelling incompletely oxidized products
**2 :** the state of being putrefied : CORRUPTION
— **pu·tre·fac·tive** \-ˈfak-tiv\ *adjective*
**pu·tre·fy** \ˈpyü-trə-ˌfī\ *verb* **-fied; -fy·ing** [Middle English *putrefien*, from Middle French & Latin; Middle French *putrefier*, from Latin *putrefacere*, from *putrēre* to be rotten + *facere* to make — more at DO] (14th century)
*transitive verb*
**:** to make putrid
*intransitive verb*
**:** to undergo putrefaction
*synonym* see DECAY
**pu·tres·cence** \pyü-ˈtre-sᵊn(t)s\ *noun* (1646)
**:** the state of being putrescent
**pu·tres·cent** \-sᵊnt\ *adjective* [Latin *putrescent-, putrescens*, present participle of *putrescere* to grow rotten, inchoative of *putrēre*] (1732)
**1 :** undergoing putrefaction : becoming putrid
**2 :** of or relating to putrefaction
**pu·tres·ci·ble** \-ˈtre-sə-bəl\ *adjective* (1797)
**:** liable to become putrid
**pu·tres·cine** \-ˈtre-ˌsēn\ *noun* [International Scientific Vocabulary, from Latin *putrescere*] (1887)
**:** a crystalline slightly poisonous ptomaine $C_4H_{12}N_2$ that occurs in small amounts in virtually all living things
**pu·trid** \ˈpyü-trəd\ *adjective* [Latin *putridus*, from *putrēre* to be rotten, from *puter, putris* rotten; akin to Latin *putēre* to stink — more at FOUL] (1598)
**1 a :** being in a state of putrefaction : ROTTEN **b :** of, relating to, or characteristic of putrefaction : FOUL ⟨a *putrid* odor⟩
**2 a :** morally corrupt **b :** totally objectionable
*synonym* see MALODOROUS
— **pu·trid·i·ty** \pyü-ˈtri-də-tē\ *noun*

— **pu·trid·ly** \'pyü-trəd-lē\ *adverb*

**putsch** \'pu̇ch\ *noun* [German] (1920)
: a secretly plotted and suddenly executed attempt to overthrow a government

**putsch·ist** \'pu̇-chist\ *noun* (1898)
: one who takes part in a putsch

**putt** \'pət\ *noun* [Scots, literally, shove, gentle push, from *putt, put* to put] (1743)
: a golf stroke made on a putting green to cause the ball to roll into or near the hole
— **putt** *verb*

**put·tee** \pə-'tē, pu̇-; 'pə-tē\ *noun* [Hindi *paṭṭī* strip of cloth, from Sanskrit *paṭṭikā*] (1886)
**1** : a cloth strip wrapped around the leg from ankle to knee
**2** : a usually leather legging secured by a strap or catch or by laces

**¹putt·er** \'pu̇t-ər\ *noun* (14th century)
: one that puts ⟨a *putter* of questions⟩

**²putt·er** \'pə-tər\ *noun* (1743)
**1** : a golf club used in putting
**2** : one that putts

**³put·ter** \'pə-tər\ *intransitive verb* [alteration of *potter*] (circa 1877)
**1** : to move or act aimlessly or idly
**2** : to work at random : TINKER
— **put·ter·er** \-tər-ər\ *noun*

**put through** *transitive verb* (1852)
**1** : to carry to a successful conclusion ⟨*put through* a number of reforms⟩
**2 a** : to make a telephone connection for **b** : to obtain a connection for (a telephone call)

**putt·ing green** \'pə-tiŋ-\ *noun* (1841)
: a smooth grassy area at the end of a golf fairway containing the hole; *also* : a similar area usually with many holes that is used for practice

**put·to** \'pü-(ˌ)tō\ *noun, plural* **put·ti** \-(ˌ)tē\ [Italian, literally, boy, from (assumed) Vulgar Latin *puttus,* alteration of Latin *putus;* akin to Latin *puer* boy — more at PUERILE] (1644)
: a figure of an infant boy especially in European art of the Renaissance — usually used in plural

**¹put·ty** \'pə-tē\ *noun, plural* **putties** [French *potée* potter's glaze, literally, potful, from Old French, from *pot* pot — more at POTTAGE] (circa 1706)
**1 a** : a doughlike material typically made of whiting and linseed oil that is used especially to fasten glass in window frames and to fill crevices in woodwork **b** : any of various substances resembling putty in appearance, consistency, or use
**2** : a light brownish gray to light grayish brown color
**3** : one who is easily manipulated ⟨is *putty* in her hands⟩
— **put·ty·less** *adjective*
— **put·ty·like** *adjective*

**²putty** *transitive verb* **put·tied; put·ty·ing** (1734)
: to use putty on or apply putty to

**putty knife** *noun* (1858)
: an implement with a broad flat metal blade used especially for applying putty and for scraping

**put·ty·root** \'pə-tē-ˌrüt, -ˌru̇t\ *noun* (1817)
: a North American orchid (*Aplectrum hyemale*) having a slender naked rootstock and producing a solitary leaf and a scape bearing a raceme of brownish flowers

**put–up** \'pu̇t-ˌəp\ *adjective* (1810)
: arranged secretly beforehand

**put up** (14th century)
*transitive verb*
**1 a** : to place in a container or receptacle ⟨*put* his lunch *up* in a bag⟩ **b** : to put away (a sword) in a scabbard : SHEATHE **c** : to prepare so as to preserve for later use : CAN **d** : to put in storage
**2** : to start (game) from cover
**3** : to nominate for election
**4** : to offer up (as a prayer)
**5** : SET 16

**6** : to offer for public sale ⟨*put* their possessions *up* for auction⟩
**7** : to give food and shelter to : ACCOMMODATE
**8** : to arrange (as a plot or scheme) with others ⟨*put up* a job to steal the jewels⟩
**9** : BUILD, ERECT
**10 a** : to make a display of ⟨*put up* a bluff⟩ **b** : to engage in ⟨*put up* a struggle against odds⟩
**11 a** : CONTRIBUTE, PAY **b** : to offer as a prize or stake
**12** *chiefly British* : to increase the amount of : RAISE
*intransitive verb*
: LODGE
— **put up to** : INCITE, INSTIGATE ⟨they *put* him *up to* playing the prank⟩
— **put up with** : to endure or tolerate without complaint or attempt at reprisal

**put-up·on** \'pu̇t-ə-ˌpȯn, -ˌpän\ *adjective* (1920)
: imposed upon : taken advantage of

**¹puz·zle** \'pə-zəl\ *verb* **puz·zled; puz·zling** \'pə-zə-liŋ, 'pəz-liŋ\ [origin unknown] (1602)
*transitive verb*
**1** : to offer or represent to (as a person) a problem difficult to solve or a situation difficult to resolve : challenge mentally; *also* : to exert (as oneself) over such a problem or situation ⟨they *puzzled* their wits to find a solution⟩
**2** *archaic* : COMPLICATE, ENTANGLE
**3** : to solve with difficulty or ingenuity ⟨*puzzle* out an answer to a riddle⟩
*intransitive verb*
**1** : to be uncertain as to action or choice
**2** : to attempt a solution of a puzzle by guesswork or experiment ☆
— **puz·zler** \'pə-zə-lər, 'pəz-lər\ *noun*

**²puzzle** *noun* (circa 1612)
**1** : the state of being puzzled : PERPLEXITY
**2 a** : something that puzzles **b** : a question, problem, or contrivance designed for testing ingenuity
**synonym** see MYSTERY

**puz·zle·head·ed** \'pə-zəl-ˌhe-dəd\ *adjective* (circa 1784)
: having or based on confused attitudes or ideas
— **puz·zle·head·ed·ness** *noun*

**puz·zle·ment** \'pə-zəl-mənt\ *noun* (1822)
**1** : the state of being puzzled : PERPLEXITY
**2** : PUZZLE

**puzzling** *adjective* (1666)
: difficult to understand or solve
— **puz·zling·ly** *adverb*

**P-wave** \'pē-ˌwāv\ *noun* [by shortening] (1936)
: PRESSURE WAVE

**py-** *or* **pyo-** *combining form* [Greek, from *pyon* pus — more at FOUL]
: pus ⟨*pyemia*⟩ ⟨*pyorrhea*⟩

**pya** \'pyä, pē-'ä\ *noun* [Burmese] (1952)
— see *kyat* at MONEY table

**pyc·nid·i·um** \pik-'ni-dē-əm\ *noun, plural* **-ia** \-dē-ə\ [New Latin, from Greek *pyknos* dense] (1857)
: a flask-shaped fruiting body bearing conidiophores and conidia on the interior and occurring in various imperfect fungi and ascomycetes
— **pyc·nid·i·al** \-dē-əl\ *adjective*

**pyc·no·go·nid** \pik-'nä-gə-nəd, ˌpik-nə-'gä-nəd\ *noun* [ultimately from Greek *pyknos* + *gony* knee — more at KNEE] (1881)
: SEA SPIDER

**pyc·nom·e·ter** \pik-'nä-mə-tər\ *noun* [Greek *pyknos* + International Scientific Vocabulary *-meter*] (1858)
: a standard vessel often provided with a thermometer for measuring and comparing the densities of liquids or solids

**pye–dog** \'pī-ˌdȯg\ *noun* [perhaps from Hindi *pāhī* outsider] (1864)
: a half-wild dog common about Asian villages

**pyel-** *or* **pyelo-** *combining form* [New Latin, pelvis, from Greek *pyelos* basin; akin to Greek *plynein* to wash, *plein* to sail — more at FLOW]
: renal pelvis ⟨*pyelitis*⟩

**py·eli·tis** \ˌpī-ə-'lī-təs\ *noun* [New Latin] (circa 1842)
: inflammation of the lining of the renal pelvis

**py·elo·ne·phri·tis** \ˌpī-(ə-)lō-ni-'frī-təs\ *noun* [New Latin] (1866)
: inflammation of both the lining of the pelvis and the parenchyma of the kidney
— **py·elo·ne·phrit·ic** \-'fri-tik\ *adjective*

**py·emia** \pī-'ē-mē-ə\ *noun* [New Latin] (circa 1857)
: septicemia caused by pus-forming bacteria and accompanied by multiple abscesses

**py·gid·i·um** \pī-'ji-dē-əm\ *noun, plural* **-ia** \-dē-ə\ [New Latin, from Greek *pygidion,* diminutive of *pygē* rump] (circa 1849)
: a caudal structure or the terminal body region of various invertebrates
— **py·gid·i·al** \-dē-əl\ *adjective*

**pyg·mae·an** *or* **pyg·me·an** \pig-'mē-ən, 'pig-mē-\ *adjective* [Latin *pygmaeus*] (1667)
: PYGMY

**Pyg·ma·lion** \pig-'māl-yən, -'mā-lē-ən\ *noun* [Latin, from Greek *Pygmaliōn*]
: a king of Cyprus who makes a female figure of ivory that is brought to life for him by Aphrodite

**pyg·moid** \'pig-ˌmȯid\ *adjective* (circa 1930)
: resembling or having the characteristics of the Pygmies

**pyg·my** \'pig-mē\ *noun, plural* **pygmies** [Middle English *pigmei,* from Latin *pygmaeus* of a pygmy, dwarfish, from Greek *pygmaios,* from *pygmē* fist, measure of length — more at PUNGENT] (14th century)
**1** *often capitalized* : any of a race of dwarfs described by ancient Greek authors
**2** *capitalized* : any of a small people of equatorial Africa ranging under five feet (1.5 meters) in height
**3 a** : a short insignificant person : DWARF **b** : something very small of its kind
— **pygmy** *adjective*

**pygmy chimpanzee** *noun* (1962)
: an anthropoid ape (*Pan paniscus*) of Zaire that has a lighter build than the related common chimpanzee (*P. troglodytes*) — called also *pygmy chimp*

**py·ja·mas** \pə-'jä-məz\ *chiefly British variant of* PAJAMAS

**pyk·nic** \'pik-nik\ *adjective* [International Scientific Vocabulary, from Greek *pyknos* dense, stocky] (1925)

---

☆ **SYNONYMS**
**Puzzle, perplex, bewilder, distract, nonplus, confound, dumbfound** mean to baffle and disturb mentally. PUZZLE implies existence of a problem difficult to solve ⟨the persistent fever *puzzled* the doctor⟩. PERPLEX adds a suggestion of worry and uncertainty especially about making a necessary decision ⟨a behavior that *perplexed* her friends⟩. BEWILDER stresses a confusion of mind that hampers clear and decisive thinking ⟨a *bewildering* number of possibilities⟩. DISTRACT implies agitation or uncertainty induced by conflicting preoccupations or interests ⟨*distracted* by personal problems⟩. NONPLUS implies a bafflement that makes orderly planning or deciding impossible ⟨the remark left us utterly *nonplussed*⟩. CONFOUND implies temporary mental paralysis caused by astonishment or profound abasement ⟨the tragic news *confounded* us all⟩. DUMBFOUND suggests intense but momentary confounding; often the idea of astonishment is so stressed that it becomes a near synonym of *astound* ⟨was at first too *dumbfounded* to reply⟩.

: characterized by shortness of stature, broadness of girth, and powerful muscularity **:** ENDOMORPHIC 2

— **pyknic** *noun*

**py·lon** \'pī-ˌlän, -lən\ *noun* [Greek *pylōn*, from *pylē* gate] (1850)
**1 a :** a usually massive gateway **b :** an ancient Egyptian gateway building in a truncated pyramidal form **c :** a monumental mass flanking an entranceway or an approach to a bridge
**2 a** *chiefly British* **:** a tower for supporting either end of usually a number of wires over a long span **b :** any of various towerlike structures
**3 a :** a post or tower marking a prescribed course of flight for an airplane **b :** TRAFFIC CONE
**4 :** a rigid structure on the outside of an aircraft for supporting something (as an engine or missile) — see AIRPLANE illustration

**py·lo·ric** \pī-'lȯr-ik, pə-, -'lȯr-\ *adjective* (1807)
**:** of or relating to the pylorus; *also* **:** of, relating to, or situated in or near the posterior part of the stomach

**py·lo·rus** \-əs\ *noun, plural* **py·lo·ri** \-'lȯr-ˌī, -ˌ)ē\ [Late Latin, from Greek *pylōros*, literally, gatekeeper, from *pylē*] (1615)
**:** the opening from the vertebrate stomach into the intestine

**pyo·der·ma** \ˌpī-ə-'dər-mə\ *noun* [New Latin] (1930)
**:** a bacterial skin inflammation marked by pus-filled lesions

**pyo·gen·ic** \-'je-nik\ *adjective* [International Scientific Vocabulary] (circa 1847)
**:** producing pus ⟨*pyogenic* bacteria⟩; *also* **:** marked by pus production ⟨*pyogenic* meningitis⟩

**py·or·rhea** \ˌpī-ə-'rē-ə\ *noun* [New Latin] (1878)
**:** purulent inflammation of the sockets of the teeth leading usually to loosening of the teeth

**pyr-** *or* **pyro-** *combining form* [Middle English, from Middle French, from Late Latin, from Greek, from *pyr* — more at FIRE]
**1 :** fire **:** heat ⟨*pyro*meter⟩ ⟨*pyr*heliometer⟩
**2 a :** produced by or as if by the action of heat ⟨*pyro*electricity⟩ **b :** derived from a corresponding ortho acid by loss usually of one molecule of water from two molecules of acid ⟨*pyro*phosphoric acid⟩
**3 :** fever ⟨*pyro*genic⟩

**pyr·acan·tha** \ˌpī-rə-'kan(t)-thə\ *noun* [New Latin, from Greek *pyrakantha*, a tree, from *pyr-* + *akantha* thorn] (1705)
**:** any of a small genus (*Pyracantha*) of Eurasian thorny evergreen or semievergreen shrubs of the rose family with alternate leaves, corymbs of white flowers, and small red or orange pomes

**py·ral·id** \'pī-rə-ləd\ *noun* [ultimately from Latin *pyralis*, fly fabled as living in fire, from Greek, from *pyr* fire] (circa 1890)
**:** any of a very large heterogeneous family (Pyralidae) of mostly small slender long-legged moths

— **pyralid** *adjective*

**¹pyr·a·mid** \'pir-ə-ˌmid\ *noun* [Latin *pyramid-, pyramis*, from Greek] (1549)
**1 a :** an ancient massive structure found especially in Egypt having typically a square ground plan, outside walls in the form of four triangles that meet in a point at the top, and inner sepulchral chambers **b :** a structure or object of similar form
**2 :** a polyhedron having for its base a polygon and for faces triangles with a common vertex — see VOLUME table

pyramid 2

**3 :** a crystalline form each face of which intersects the vertical axis and either two lateral axes or in the tetragonal system one lateral axis
**4 :** an anatomical structure resembling a pyramid: as **a :** any of the conical masses that project from the renal medulla into the kidney pelvis **b :** either of two large bundles of motor fibers from the cerebral cortex that reach the medulla oblongata and are continuous with the pyramidal tracts of the spinal cord
**5 :** an immaterial structure built on a broad supporting base and narrowing gradually to an apex ⟨the socioeconomic *pyramid*⟩

— **py·ra·mi·dal** \pə-'ra-mə-dᵊl, ˌpir-ə-'mi-\ *adjective*
— **py·ra·mi·dal·ly** *adverb*
— **pyr·a·mid·i·cal** \ˌpir-ə-'mi-di-kəl\ *adjective*

**²pyramid** (circa 1900)
*intransitive verb*
**1 :** to speculate (as on a security or commodity exchange) by using paper profits as margin for additional transactions
**2 :** to increase rapidly and progressively step by step on a broad base
*transitive verb*
**1 :** to arrange or build up as if on the base of a pyramid
**2 :** to use (as profits) in speculative pyramiding
**3 :** to increase the impact of (as a tax assessed at the production level) on the ultimate consumer by treating as a cost subject to markup

**pyramidal tract** *noun* (circa 1890)
**:** any of four columns of motor fibers that run in pairs on each side of the spinal cord and are continuations of the pyramids of the medulla oblongata

**Pyr·a·mus** \'pir-ə-məs\ *noun* [Latin, from Greek *Pyramos*]
**:** a legendary youth of Babylon who dies for love of Thisbe

**py·ran** \'pīr-ˌan\ *noun* [International Scientific Vocabulary] (1904)
**:** either of two cyclic compounds $C_5H_6O$ that contain five carbon atoms and one oxygen atom in the ring

**py·ra·nose** \'pī-rə-ˌnōs, -ˌnōz\ *noun* [International Scientific Vocabulary] (1927)
**:** a monosaccharide in the form of a cyclic hemiacetal containing a pyran ring

**py·ran·o·side** \pī-'ra-nə-ˌsīd\ *noun* (1932)
**:** a glycoside containing the pyran ring

**pyr·ar·gy·rite** \pī-'rär-jə-ˌrīt\ *noun* [German *Pyrargyrit*, from Greek *pyr-* + *argyros* silver — more at ARGENT] (1849)
**:** a mineral consisting of silver antimony sulfide that occurs in rhombohedral crystals or in massive form and has a dark red or black color or with a metallic luster

**pyre** \'pīr\ *noun* [Latin *pyra*, from Greek, from *pyr* fire — more at FIRE] (1658)
**:** a combustible heap for burning a dead body as a funeral rite; *broadly* **:** a pile of material to be burned ⟨a *pyre* of dead leaves⟩

**py·re·noid** \pī-'rē-ˌnȯid, 'pī-rə-\ *noun* [International Scientific Vocabulary, from New Latin *pyrena* stone of a fruit, from Greek *pyrēnoun*; akin to Greek *pyros* wheat grain, wheat — more at FURZE] (circa 1875)
**:** one of the protein bodies in the chromatophores of various lower organisms (as some algae) that act as centers for starch deposition

**py·re·thrin** \pī-'rē-thrən, -'re-\ *noun* [International Scientific Vocabulary, from Latin *pyrethrum*] (1924)
**:** either of two oily liquid esters $C_{21}H_{28}O_3$ and $C_{22}H_{28}O_5$ having insecticidal properties and occurring especially in the flowers of pyrethrum

**py·re·throid** \-'rē-ˌthrȯid, -'re-\ *noun* [*pyrethrin* + *-oid*] (1949)
**:** any of various synthetic compounds that are related to the pyrethrins and resemble them in insecticidal properties

— **pyrethroid** *adjective*

**py·re·thrum** \pī-'rē-thrəm, -'re-\ *noun* [Latin, pellitory, from Greek *pyrethron*, from *pyr* fire] (circa 1543)
**1 :** any of several chrysanthemums with finely divided often aromatic leaves including ornamentals as well as important sources of insecticides
**2 :** an insecticide made from the dried heads of any of several Old World chrysanthemums

**py·ret·ic** \pī-'re-tik\ *adjective* [New Latin *pyreticus*, from Greek *pyretikos*, from *pyretos* fever, from *pyr*] (circa 1858)
**:** of or relating to fever **:** FEBRILE

**Py·rex** \'pīr-ˌeks\ *trademark*
— used for borosilicate glass and glassware resistant to heat, chemicals, and electricity

**py·rex·ia** \pī-'rek-sē-ə\ *noun* [New Latin, from Greek *pyressein* to be feverish, from *pyretos*] (1769)
**:** abnormal elevation of body temperature **:** FEVER

— **py·rex·i·al** \-sē-əl\ *adjective*
— **py·rex·ic** \-sik\ *adjective*

**pyr·he·li·om·e·ter** \ˌpīr-ˌhē-lē-'ä-mə-tər, ˌpir-\ *noun* [International Scientific Vocabulary] (1863)
**:** an instrument for measuring the sun's radiant energy as received at the earth

— **pyr·he·lio·met·ric** \-lē-ə-'me-trik\ *adjective*

**py·ric** \'pī-rik, 'pir-ik\ *adjective* [French *pyrique*, from Greek *pyr*] (1946)
**:** resulting from, induced by, or associated with burning

**pyr·i·dine** \'pir-ə-ˌdēn\ *noun* [*pyr-* + *-ide* + *²-ine*] (1851)
**:** a toxic water-soluble flammable liquid base $C_5H_5N$ of pungent odor that is the parent of many naturally occurring organic compounds and is used as a solvent and as a denaturant for alcohol and in the manufacture of pharmaceuticals and waterproofing agents

**pyr·i·dox·al** \ˌpir-ə-'däk-ˌsal\ *noun* [International Scientific Vocabulary, from *pyridoxine*] (1944)
**:** a crystalline aldehyde $C_8H_9NO_3$ of the vitamin $B_6$ group that occurs as a phosphate and is active as a coenzyme

**pyr·i·dox·amine** \ˌpir-ə-'däk-sə-ˌmēn\ *noun* [International Scientific Vocabulary *pyridox*ine + *amine*] (1944)
**:** a crystalline amine $C_8H_{12}N_2O_2$ of the vitamin $B_6$ group that occurs as a phosphate and is active as a coenzyme

**pyr·i·dox·ine** \ˌpir-ə-'däk-ˌsēn, -sən\ *noun* [*pyridine* + *ox-* + *²-ine*] (1939)
**:** a crystalline phenolic alcohol $C_8H_{11}NO_3$ of the vitamin $B_6$ group found especially in cereals and convertible in the organism into pyridoxal and pyridoxamine

**pyr·i·form** \'pir-ə-ˌfȯrm\ *adjective* [New Latin *pyriformis*, from Medieval Latin *pyrum* pear (alteration of Latin *pirum*) + Latin *-iformis* *-iform*] (1741)
**:** having the form of a pear

**py·ri·meth·amine** \ˌpir-ə-'me-thə-ˌmēn\ *noun* [*pyrimidine* + *ethyl* + *amine*] (1952)
**:** a folic acid antagonist $C_{12}H_{13}ClN_4$ used in the treatment of malaria and of toxoplasmosis

**py·rim·i·dine** \pī-'ri-mə-ˌdēn, pə-\ *noun* [International Scientific Vocabulary, alteration of *pyridine*] (1885)
**1 :** a feeble organic base $C_4H_2N_2$ of penetrating odor
**2 :** a derivative of pyrimidine; *especially* **:** a base (as cytosine, thymine, or uracil) that is a constituent of DNA or RNA

**py·rite** \'pī-ˌrīt\ *noun* [Latin *pyrites*] (1588)

: a common mineral that consists of iron disulfide, has a pale brass-yellow color and metallic luster, and is burned in making sulfur dioxide and sulfuric acid

**py·rites** \pə-ˈrī-tēz, pī-; ˈpī-ˌrīts\ *noun, plural* **pyrites** [Latin, flint, from Greek *pyritēs* of or in fire, from *pyr* fire] (1543)
: any of various metallic-looking sulfides of which pyrite is the commonest
— **py·rit·ic** \-ˈri-tik\ *adjective*

**py·ro·cat·e·chol** \ˌpī-rō-ˈka-tə-ˌkȯl, -ˌkōl\ *noun* [International Scientific Vocabulary] (1890)
: a crystalline phenol $C_6H_6O_2$ obtained by pyrolysis of various natural substances (as resins and lignins) but usually made synthetically and used especially as a photographic developer and in organic synthesis

**py·ro·clas·tic** \-ˈklas-tik\ *adjective* (1887)
: formed by or involving fragmentation as a result of volcanic or igneous action

**py·ro·elec·tric·i·ty** \ˈpī-rō-ə-ˌlek-ˈtri-sə-tē, -ˈtris-tē\ *noun* [International Scientific Vocabulary] (circa 1834)
: a state of electrical polarization produced (as in a crystal) by a change of temperature
— **py·ro·elec·tric** \-ˈlek-trik\ *adjective*

**py·ro·gal·lol** \ˌpī-rō-ˈga-ˌlȯl, -ˌlōl; -ˈgȯ-\ *noun* [International Scientific Vocabulary *pyro-* + *gallic* (acid) + *1-ol*] (1876)
: a poisonous bitter crystalline phenol $C_6H_6O_3$ with weak acid properties that is obtained usually by pyrolysis of gallic acid and used especially as a mild reducing agent (as in photographic developing)

**py·ro·gen** \ˈpī-rə-jən\ *noun* [International Scientific Vocabulary] (circa 1890)
: a fever-producing substance

**py·ro·gen·ic** \ˌpī-rō-ˈje-nik\ *adjective* [International Scientific Vocabulary] (1853)
**1** : producing or produced by heat or fever
**2** : of or relating to igneous origin
— **py·ro·ge·nic·i·ty** \ˌpī-rō-jə-ˈni-sə-tē\ *noun*

**py·ro·la** \pī-ˈrō-lə\ *noun* [New Latin, probably from Latin *pirum* pear] (1578)
: WINTERGREEN 1

**py·ro·lig·ne·ous acid** \ˌpī-rō-ˈlig-nē-əs-\ *noun* [French *pyroligneux*, from *pyr-* + *ligneux* woody, from Latin *lignosus*, from *lignum* wood — more at LIGNEOUS] (circa 1790)
: an acid reddish brown aqueous liquid containing chiefly acetic acid, methanol, wood oils, and tars that is obtained by destructive distillation of wood

**py·ro·lu·site** \ˈpī-rō-ˈlü-ˌsīt\ *noun* [German *Pyrolusit*, from Greek *pyr-* + *lousis* washing, from *louein* to wash — more at LYE] (1828)
: a mineral consisting of manganese dioxide that is of an iron-black or dark steel-gray color and metallic luster, is usually soft, and is the most important ore of manganese

**py·rol·y·sate** \pī-ˈrä-lə-ˌzāt, -ˌsāt\ *or* **py·rol·y·zate** \-ˌzāt\ *noun* (1944)
: a product of pyrolysis

**py·rol·y·sis** \pī-ˈrä-lə-səs\ *noun* [New Latin] (circa 1890)
: chemical change brought about by the action of heat
— **py·ro·lyt·ic** \ˌpī-rə-ˈli-tik\ *adjective*
— **py·ro·lyt·i·cal·ly** \-ti-k(ə-)lē\ *adverb*

**py·ro·lyze** *also* **py·ro·lize** \ˈpī-rə-ˌlīz\ *transitive verb* **-lyzed** *also* **-lized; -lyz·ing** *also* **-liz·ing** (1932)
: to subject to pyrolysis
— **py·ro·lyz·able** \ˌpī-rə-ˈlī-zə-bəl\ *adjective*
— **py·ro·lyz·er** *noun*

**py·ro·man·cy** \-ˌman(t)-sē\ *noun* [Middle English *pyromancie*, from Middle French, from Late Latin *pyromantia*, from Greek *pyromanteia*, from *pyr* fire + *manteia* divination — more at -MANCY] (14th century)
: divination by means of fire or flames

**py·ro·ma·nia** \ˌpī-rō-ˈmā-nē-ə, -nyə\ *noun* [New Latin] (circa 1842)
: an irresistible impulse to start fires
— **py·ro·ma·ni·ac** \-nē-ˌak\ *noun*
— **py·ro·ma·ni·a·cal** \-mə-ˈnī-ə-kəl\ *adjective*

**py·ro·met·al·lur·gy** \-ˈme-tᵊl-ˌər-jē, *especially British* -mə-ˈta-lər-\ *noun* [International Scientific Vocabulary] (1908)
: chemical metallurgy depending on heat action (as roasting and smelting)
— **py·ro·met·al·lur·gi·cal** \-ˌme-tᵊl-ˈər-ji-kəl\ *adjective*

**py·rom·e·ter** \pī-ˈrä-mə-tər\ *noun* [International Scientific Vocabulary] (1796)
: an instrument for measuring temperatures especially when beyond the range of mercurial thermometers
— **py·ro·met·ric** \ˌpī-rə-ˈme-trik\ *adjective*
— **py·ro·met·ri·cal·ly** \-tri-k(ə-)lē\ *adverb*
— **py·rom·e·try** \pī-ˈrä-mə-trē\ *noun*

**py·ro·mor·phite** \ˌpī-rə-ˈmȯr-ˌfīt\ *noun* [German *Pyromorphit*, from Greek *pyr-* + *morphē* form] (circa 1814)
: a mineral consisting essentially of a lead chloride and phosphate

**py·ro·nine** \ˈpī-rə-ˌnēn\ *noun* [International Scientific Vocabulary, irregular from *pyr-* + *2-ine*] (1895)
: any of several basic xanthene dyes used chiefly as biological stains

**py·ro·nin·o·phil·ic** \ˌpī-rə-ˌnē-nə-ˈfi-lik\ *adjective* (1946)
: staining selectively with pyronines ⟨*pyroninophilic* cells⟩

**py·rope** \ˈpī-ˌrōp\ *noun* [Middle English *pirope*, a red gem, from Middle French, from Latin *pyropus*, a red bronze, from Greek *pyrōpos*, literally, fiery-eyed, from *pyr-* + *ōp-, ōps* eye — more at EYE] (1804)
: a magnesium-aluminum garnet that is deep red in color and is frequently used as a gem

**py·ro·phor·ic** \ˌpī-rə-ˈfȯr-ik, -ˈfär-\ *adjective* [New Latin *pyrophorus*, from Greek *pyrophoros* fire-bearing, from *pyr-* + *-phoros* carrying — more at -PHORE] (1836)
**1** : igniting spontaneously
**2** : emitting sparks when scratched or struck especially with steel

**py·ro·phos·phate** \-ˈfäs-ˌfāt\ *noun* (1836)
: a salt or ester of pyrophosphoric acid

**py·ro·phos·pho·ric acid** \-fäs-ˈfȯr-ik-, -ˈfär-; -ˈfäs-f(ə-)rik-\ *noun* [International Scientific Vocabulary] (1832)
: a crystalline acid $H_4P_2O_7$ formed when orthophosphoric acid is heated or prepared in the form of salts by heating acid salts of orthophosphoric acid

**py·ro·phyl·lite** \ˌpī-rō-ˈfi-ˌlīt, pī-ˈrä-fə-ˌlīt\ *noun* [German *Pyrophyllit*, from Greek *pyr-* + *phyllon* leaf — more at BLADE] (1830)
: a white or greenish mineral that is a hydrous aluminum silicate, resembles talc, occurs in a foliated form or in compact masses, and is used especially in ceramic wares

**py·ro·sis** \pī-ˈrō-səs\ *noun* [New Latin, from Greek *pyrōsis* burning, from *pyroun* to burn, from *pyr* fire — more at FIRE] (1789)
: HEARTBURN

**1py·ro·tech·nic** \ˌpī-rō-ˈtek-nik\ *also* **py·ro·tech·ni·cal** \-ni-kəl\ *adjective* [French *pyrotechnique*, from Greek *pyr* fire + *technē* art — more at TECHNICAL] (1825)
: of or relating to pyrotechnics
— **py·ro·tech·ni·cal·ly** \-ni-k(ə-)lē\ *adverb*

**2pyrotechnic** *noun* (1840)
**1 a** : FIREWORK **b** : any of various similar devices (as for igniting a rocket or producing an explosion)
**2** : a combustible substance used in a firework

**py·ro·tech·nics** \ˌpī-rə-ˈtek-niks\ *noun plural* (1729)
**1** *singular or plural in construction* : the art of making or the manufacture and use of fireworks
**2 a** : a display of fireworks **b** : a spectacular display (as of extreme virtuosity) ⟨verbal *pyrotechnics*⟩ ⟨keyboard *pyrotechnics*⟩
— **py·ro·tech·nist** \-ˈtek-nist\ *noun*

**py·rox·ene** \pī-ˈräk-ˌsēn, pə-\ *noun* [French *pyroxène*, from Greek *pyr-* + *xenos* stranger] (1800)
: any of a group of igneous-rock-forming silicate minerals that contain calcium, sodium, magnesium, iron, or aluminum, usually occur in short prismatic crystals or massive form, are often laminated, and vary in color from white to dark green or black
— **py·rox·e·nic** \ˌpī-ˌräk-ˈsē-nik, pə-, -ˈse-\ *adjective*
— **py·rox·e·noid** \pī-ˈräk-sə-ˌnȯid, pə-\ *adjective or noun*

**py·rox·e·nite** \pī-ˈräk-sə-ˌnīt, pə-\ *noun* (circa 1862)
: an igneous rock that is free from olivine and is composed essentially of pyroxene
— **py·rox·e·nit·ic** \-ˌräk-sə-ˈni-tik\ *adjective*

**py·rox·y·lin** \pī-ˈräk-sə-lən, pə-\ *noun* [International Scientific Vocabulary *pyr-* + Greek *xylon* wood] (circa 1847)
**1** : a flammable mixture of nitrocelluloses used especially in making plastics and water-repellent coatings (as lacquers)
**2** : a pyroxylin product

**Pyr·rha** \ˈpir-ə\ *noun* [Latin, from Greek]
: the wife of Deucalion

**pyr·rhic** \ˈpir-ik\ *noun* [Latin *pyrrhichius*, from Greek (*pous*) *pyrrhichios*, from *pyrrhichē*, a kind of dance] (1626)
: a metrical foot consisting of two short or unaccented syllables

**Pyr·rhic** \ˈpir-ik\ *adjective* [*Pyrrhus*, king of Epirus who sustained heavy losses in defeating the Romans] (1885)
: achieved at excessive cost ⟨a *Pyrrhic* victory⟩; *also* : costly to the point of negating or outweighing expected benefits ⟨a great but *Pyrrhic* act of ingenuity⟩

**Pyr·rho·nism** \ˈpir-ə-ˌni-zəm\ *noun* [French *pyrrhonisme*, from *Pyrrhon* Pyrrho, 4th century B.C. Greek philosopher, from Greek *Pyrrhōn*] (circa 1670)
**1** : the doctrines of a school of ancient extreme skeptics who suspended judgment on every proposition — compare ACADEMICISM
**2** : total or radical skepticism
— **Pyr·rho·nist** \-nist\ *noun*

**pyr·rho·tite** \ˈpir-ə-ˌtīt\ *noun* [modification of German *Pyrrhotin*, from Greek *pyrrhotēs* redness, from *pyrrhos* red, from *pyr* fire — more at FIRE] (1868)
: a bronze-colored mineral of metallic luster that consists of ferrous sulfide and is attracted by a magnet

**Pyr·rhus** \ˈpir-əs\ *noun* [Latin, from Greek *Pyrrhos*]
: a son of Achilles and slayer of Priam at the taking of Troy

**pyr·role** \ˈpir-ˌōl\ *noun* [Greek *pyrrhos*] (1835)
: a toxic liquid heterocyclic compound $C_4H_5N$ that has a ring consisting of four carbon atoms and one nitrogen atom, polymerizes readily in air, and is the parent compound of many biologically important substances (as bile pigments, porphyrins, and chlorophyll); *broadly* : a derivative of pyrrole
— **pyr·rol·ic** \pir-ˈrō-lik\ *adjective*

**py·ru·vate** \pī-ˈrü-ˌvāt\ *noun* (1855)
: a salt or ester of pyruvic acid

**py·ru·vic acid** \pī-ˈrü-vik-\ *noun* [International Scientific Vocabulary *pyr-* + Latin *uva* grapes; from its importance in fermentation — more at UVULA] (1838)
: a 3-carbon keto acid $C_3H_4O_3$ that in carbo-

hydrate metabolism is an important intermediate product formed as pyruvate by glycolysis

**¹Py·thag·o·re·an** \pə-ˌtha-gə-ˈrē-ən, ˌ(ˌ)pī-\ *noun* (1550)
: any of a group professing to be followers of the Greek philosopher Pythagoras

**²Pythagorean** *adjective* (circa 1580)
: of, relating to, or associated with the Greek philosopher Pythagoras, his philosophy, or the Pythagoreans

**Py·thag·o·re·an·ism** \-ˈrē-ə-ˌni-zəm\ *noun* (circa 1727)
: the doctrines and theories of Pythagoras and the Pythagoreans who developed some basic principles of mathematics and astronomy, originated the doctrine of the harmony of the spheres, and believed in metempsychosis, the eternal recurrence of things, and the mystical significance of numbers

**Pythagorean theorem** *noun* (circa 1909)
: a theorem in geometry: the square of the length of the hypotenuse of a right triangle equals the sum of the squares of the lengths of the other two sides

**Pyth·i·ad** \ˈpi-thē-ˌad, -əd\ *noun* [Greek *Pythia,* the Pythian games, from neuter plural of *pythios*] (1842)
: the 4-year period between celebrations of the Pythian games in ancient Greece

**¹Pyth·i·an** \ˈpi-thē-ən\ *adjective* [Latin *pythius* of Delphi, from Greek *pythios,* from *Pythō* Pytho, name for Delphi, Greece] (1603)
**1** : of or relating to games celebrated at Delphi every four years
**2** : of or relating to Delphi or its oracle of Apollo

**²Pythian** *noun* (1903)
: KNIGHT OF PYTHIAS

**Pyth·i·as** \ˈpi-thē-əs\ *noun* [Greek]
: a friend of Damon condemned to death by Dionysius of Syracuse

**py·thon** \ˈpī-ˌthän, -thən\ *noun* [Latin, monstrous serpent killed by Apollo, from Greek *Pythōn,* from *Pythō* Delphi] (1836)
: any of various large constricting snakes (as a boa); *especially* : any of the large oviparous snakes (subfamily Pythoninae of the family Boidae) of Africa, Asia, Australia, and adjacent islands that include some of the largest existing snakes

python

**py·tho·ness** \ˈpī-thə-nəs, ˈpi-\ *noun* [Middle English *Phitonesse,* from Middle French *pithonisse,* from Late Latin *pythonissa,* from Greek *Pythōn,* spirit of divination, perhaps from *Pythō,* seat of the Delphic oracle] (14th century)
**1** : a woman who practices divination
**2** : a prophetic priestess of Apollo
— **py·thon·ic** \pī-ˈthä-nik\ *adjective*

**py·uria** \pī-ˈyůr-ē-ə\ *noun* [New Latin] (circa 1811)
: pus in the urine; *also* : a condition characterized by pus in the urine

**pyx** \ˈpiks\ *noun* [Middle English, from Medieval Latin *pyxis,* from Latin, box, from Greek, from *pyxos* box (shrub)] (15th century)
**1** : a container for the reserved host; *especially* : a small round metal receptacle used to carry the Eucharist to the sick
**2** : a box used in a mint for deposit of sample coins reserved for testing weight and fineness

**pyx·ie** \ˈpik-sē\ *noun* [by shortening & alteration from New Latin *Pyxidanthera*] (1882)
: a creeping evergreen dicotyledonous shrub (*Pyxidanthera barbulata* of the family Diapensiaceae) of the sandy pine barrens of the Atlantic coast of the U.S. that has white or pink pentamerous flowers

**pyx·is** \ˈpik-səs\ *noun, plural* **pyx·i·des** \-sə-ˌdēz\ [New Latin, from Latin, box] (1845)
: a capsular fruit that dehisces so that the upper part falls off like a cap

*Q is the seventeenth letter of the English alphabet. It comes from Phoenician* qōph, *representing a guttural* k *sound, which survived in a western Greek alphabet as* koppa *and passed through Etruscan and Latin into English as* Q. *In English, as in Latin, this sign is normally used in combination with* u *to represent the sound of* kw, *as in* quiet. *In some English words of French origin, however,* qu *has the sound of plain* k, *as in antique.* Q *seldom appears without* u, *except in the transliteration of the Semitic letter* koph (*Arabic* qāf), *as in* Iraq. Q *is rarely found in Old English, where the usual spelling for the* kw- *sound was* cw *or* cu (*as in* cwēn *"queen"*). Qu *became the usual form in Middle English, under the influence of French and Latin. The small form of* q *developed in the late Roman period when scribes began forming the capital letter with one pen stroke, making its tail extend vertically along the right side of the letter.*

**q** \'kyü\ *noun, plural* **q's** *or* **qs** \'kyüz\ *often capitalized, often attributive* (before 12th century)
**1 a** : the 17th letter of the English alphabet **b** : a graphic representation of this letter **c** : a speech counterpart of orthographic *q*
**2** : a graphic device for reproducing the letter *q*
**3** : one designated *q* especially as the 17th in order or class
**4** : something shaped like the letter Q
**Q–boat** \'kyü-,bōt\ *noun* (1918)
: Q-SHIP
**Q fever** \'kyü-\ *noun* [query] (1937)
: a disease that is characterized by high fever, chills, and muscular pains, is caused by a rickettsial bacterium (*Coxiella burnetii*), and is transmitted by raw milk, by droplet infection, or by ticks
**qin·tar** \kyin-'tär, kin-\ *noun, plural* **qin·dar·ka** \-'där-kə\ *also* **qintars** *or* **qin·dars** \-'därz\ [Albanian] (circa 1929)
— see *lek* at MONEY table
**qi·vi·ut** \'kē-vē-ət, -vē-,üt\ *noun* [Inuit] (1958)
: the wool of the undercoat of the musk ox
**qoph** \'kōf\ *noun* [Hebrew *qōph*] (circa 1823)
: the 19th letter of the Hebrew alphabet — see ALPHABET table
**Q–ship** \'kyü-,ship\ *noun* (1919)
: an armed ship disguised as a merchant or fishing ship to decoy enemy submarines into gun range
**q.t.** \,kyü-'tē\ *noun, often Q&T capitalized* [abbreviation] (circa 1887)
: QUIET — usually used in the phrase *on the q.t.*
**qua** \'kwä *also* 'kwā\ *preposition* [Latin, which way, as, from ablative singular feminine of *qui* who — more at WHO] (1647)
: in the capacity or character of : AS ⟨confusion of the role of scientist *qua* scientist with that of scientist as citizen —Philip Handler⟩
**quaa·lude** \'kwā-,lüd\ *noun* [from *Quaalude*, a trademark] (1966)
: a tablet or capsule of methaqualone
**¹quack** \'kwak\ *intransitive verb* [alteration of *queck* to quack, from Middle English *queken*, from *queke*, interjection, of imitative origin] (14th century)
: to make the characteristic cry of a duck
**²quack** *noun* (1839)
: a noise made by quacking
**³quack** *intransitive verb* [⁴*quack*] (1628)
: to act like a quack
**⁴quack** *noun* [short for *quacksalver*] (1638)
**1** : CHARLATAN 2
**2** : a pretender to medical skill
— **quack·ish** \'kwa-kish\ *adjective*
**⁵quack** *adjective* (1653)

: of, relating to, or characteristic of a quack; *especially* : pretending to cure diseases
**quack·ery** \'kwa-k(ə-)rē\ *noun* (circa 1711)
: the practices or pretensions of a quack
**quack grass** \'kwak-\ *noun* [alteration of *quick* (grass), alteration of *quitch* (grass)] (circa 1818)
: a European grass (*Agropyron repens*) that is naturalized throughout North America as a weed and spreads by creeping rhizomes — called also *couch grass, quitch, twitch, witch-grass*
**quack·sal·ver** \'kwak-,sal-vər\ *noun* [obsolete Dutch (now *kwakzalver*)] (1579)
: CHARLATAN, QUACK
**¹quad** \'kwäd\ *noun* (1820)
: QUADRANGLE
**²quad** *noun* [short for *quadrat*] (circa 1879)
: a type-metal space that is 1 en or more in width
**³quad** *transitive verb* **quad·ded; quad·ding** (1888)
: to fill out (as a typeset line) with blank space
**⁴quad** *noun* (1896)
: QUADRUPLET
**⁵quad** *adjective* (1970)
: QUADRAPHONIC
**⁶quad** *noun* (1971)
: quadraphonic sound
**⁷quad** *noun* [short for *quadrillion*] (1974)
: a unit of energy equal to one quadrillion British thermal units
**quad·ran·gle** \'kwä-,draŋ-gəl\ *noun* [Middle English, from Middle French, from Late Latin *quadriangulum*, from Latin, neuter of *quadriangulus* quadrangular, from *quadri-* + *angulus* angle] (15th century)
**1** : QUADRILATERAL
**2 a** : a 4-sided enclosure especially when surrounded by buildings **b** : the buildings enclosing a quadrangle
**3** : a tract of country represented by one of a series of map sheets (as published by the U.S. Geological Survey)
— **qua·dran·gu·lar** \kwä-'draŋ-gyə-lər\ *adjective*
**quad·rant** \'kwä-drənt\ *noun* [Middle English, from Latin *quadrant-, quadrans* fourth part; akin to Latin *quattuor* four — more at FOUR] (15th century)
**1 a** : an instrument for measuring altitudes consisting commonly of a graduated arc of 90 degrees with an index or vernier and usually having a plumb line or spirit level for fixing the vertical or horizontal direc-

tion **b** : a device or mechanical part shaped like or suggestive of the quadrant of a circle
**2 a** : an arc of 90 degrees that is one quarter of a circle **b** : the area bounded by a quadrant and two radii
**3 a** : any of the four parts into which a plane is divided by rectangular coordinate axes lying in that plane **b** : any of the four quarters into which something is divided by two real or imaginary lines that intersect each other at right angles
— **qua·dran·tal** \kwä-'dran-t°l\ *adjective*
**Qua·dran·tid** \kwä-'dran-təd\ *noun* [New Latin *Quadrant-, Quadrans* (*Muralis*) mural quadrant, a group of stars in the constellation Draco from which the shower appears to radiate]
: any of a group of meteors that appear annually about January 3
**quad·ra·phon·ic** *also* **quad·ri·phon·ic** \,kwä-drə-'fä-nik\ *adjective* [irregular from *quadri-* + *-phonic* (as in *stereophonic*)] (circa 1970)
: of, relating to, or using four channels for the transmission, recording, or reproduction of sound
— **quad·ra·phon·ics** *or* **quad·ri·phon·ics** \-niks\ *noun plural but singular in construction*
**quad·rat** \'kwä-drət, -,drat\ *noun* [alteration of ²*quadrate*] (1683)
**1** : ²QUAD
**2** : a usually rectangular plot used for ecological or population studies
**¹quad·rate** \'kwä-,drāt, -drət\ *adjective* [Middle English, from Latin *quadratus*, past participle of *quadrare* to make square, fit, from *quadrum* square; akin to Latin *quattuor* four] (14th century)
**1** : being square or approximately square
**2** *of a heraldic cross* : expanded into a square at the junction of the arms — see CROSS illustration
**3** : of, relating to, or constituting a bony or cartilaginous element of each side of the skull to which the lower jaw is articulated in most vertebrates below mammals
**²quadrate** *noun* (15th century)
**1** : an approximately square or cubical area, space, or body
**2** : a quadrate bone
**qua·drat·ic** \kwä-'dra-tik\ *adjective* (1668)
: involving terms of the second degree at most ⟨*quadratic* function⟩ ⟨*quadratic* equations⟩
— **quadratic** *noun*
— **qua·drat·i·cal·ly** \-ti-k(ə-)lē\ *adverb*
**quadratic form** *noun* (1859)
: a homogeneous polynomial (as $x^2 + 5xy + y^2$) of the second degree
**quad·ra·ture** \'kwä-drə-,chùr, -chər, -,tyùr, -,tùr\ *noun* (1591)
**1** : a configuration in which two celestial bodies (as the moon and the sun) have an angular separation of 90 degrees as seen from the earth
**2** : the process of finding a square equal in area to a given area
**qua·dren·ni·al** \kwä-'dre-nē-əl\ *adjective* (circa 1656)
**1** : consisting of or lasting for four years
**2** : occurring or being done every four years
— **quadrennial** *noun*
— **qua·dren·ni·al·ly** \-nē-ə-lē\ *adverb*
**qua·dren·ni·um** \-nē-əm\ *noun, plural* **-ni·ums** *or* **-nia** \-nē-ə\ [Latin *quadriennium*, from *quadri-* + *annus* year — more at ANNUAL] (1754)
: a period of four years
**quadri-** *or* **quadr-** *or* **quadru-** *combining form* [Middle English, from Latin; akin to Latin *quattuor* four]
**1 a** : four ⟨*quadri*lateral⟩ ⟨*quadru*manous⟩ **b** : square ⟨*quadri*c⟩
**2** : fourth ⟨*quadri*centennial⟩
**quad·ric** \'kwä-drik\ *adjective* [International Scientific Vocabulary] (1858)

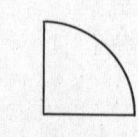

**quadrant 2**

: QUADRATIC ⟨*quadric* surface⟩ — used where there are more than two variables
— **quadric** *noun*

**quad·ri·cen·ten·ni·al** \‚kwä-drə-sen-'te-nē-əl\ *noun* (1882)
: a 400th anniversary or its celebration

**quad·ri·ceps** \'kwä-drə-‚seps\ *noun* [New Latin *quadricipit-, quadriceps,* from *quadri-* + *-cipit-, -ceps* (as in *bicipit-, biceps* biceps)] (1840)
: the greater extensor muscle of the front of the thigh that is divided into four parts

**qua·dri·ga** \kwä-'drē-gə\ *noun, plural* **-gae** \-‚gī\ [Latin, singular of *quadrigae* team of four, contraction of *quadrijugae,* feminine plural of *quadrijugus* yoked four abreast, from *quadri-* + *jungere* to yoke, join — more at YOKE] (circa 1741)
: a chariot drawn by four horses abreast

¹**quad·ri·lat·er·al** \‚kwä-drə-'la-t(ə-)rəl\ *noun* [Latin *quadrilaterus* four-sided, from *quadri-* + *later-, latus* side] (1650)
: a polygon of four sides

²**quadrilateral** *adjective* (1656)
: having four sides

¹**qua·drille** \kwä-'dril, kwə-, kə-\ *noun* [French, group of knights engaged in a carousel, from Spanish *cuadrilla* troop, from diminutive of *cuadra* square, from Latin *quadra, quadrum*] (1726)
**1** : a four-handed variant of ombre popular especially in the 18th century
**2** : a square dance for four couples made up of five or six figures chiefly in ⅝ and ¾ time; *also* : music for this dance

²**quadrille** *adjective* [French *quadrillé*] (circa 1885)
: marked with squares or rectangles

**qua·dril·lion** \kwä-'dril-yən\ *noun* [French, from Middle French, from *quadri-* + *-illion* (as in *million*)] (1674)
— see NUMBER table
— **quadrillion** *adjective*
— **qua·dril·lionth** \-yən(t)th\ *adjective or noun*

**quad·ri·par·tite** \‚kwä-drə-'pär-‚tīt\ *adjective* [Middle English, from Latin *quadripartitus,* from *quadri-* + *partitus,* past participle of *partire* to divide, from *part-, pars* part] (15th century)
**1** : consisting of or divided into four parts
**2** : shared or participated in by four parties or persons ⟨a *quadripartite* agreement⟩

**quad·ri·ple·gic** \‚kwä-drə-'plē-jik\ *noun* [*quadriplegia,* from New Latin] (1921)
: one affected with paralysis of both arms and both legs
— **quad·ri·ple·gia** \-j(ē-)ə\ *noun*

¹**quad·ri·va·lent** \‚kwä-drə-'vā-lənt, *in sense* 2 kwä-'dri-və-lənt\ *adjective* [International Scientific Vocabulary] (1865)
**1** : TETRAVALENT
**2** : composed of four homologous chromosomes synapsed in meiotic prophase

²**quadrivalent** *noun* (1923)
: a quadrivalent chromosomal group

**qua·driv·i·al** \kwä-'dri-vē-əl\ *adjective* (15th century)
**1** : of or relating to the quadrivium
**2** : having four ways or roads meeting in a point

**qua·driv·i·um** \-vē-əm\ *noun* [Late Latin, from Latin, crossroads, from *quadri-* + *via* way — more at WAY] (1804)
: a group of studies consisting of arithmetic, music, geometry, and astronomy and forming the upper division of the seven liberal arts in medieval universities — compare TRIVIUM

**qua·droon** \kwä-'drün\ *noun* [modification of Spanish *cuarterón,* from *cuarto* fourth, from Latin *quartus* — more at QUART] (1707)
: a person of one-quarter black ancestry

**qua·dru·ma·nous** \kwä-'drü-mə-nəs\ *adjective* [ultimately from Latin *quadri-* + *manus* hand — more at MANUAL] (1819)

: of, relating to, or being the primates excluding humans which are distinguished by hand-shaped feet

**qua·drum·vir** \kwä-'drəm-vər\ *noun* [back-formation from *quadrumvirate*] (1790)
: a member of a quadrumvirate

**qua·drum·vi·rate** \-və-rət\ *noun* [*quadri-* + *-umvirate* (as in *triumvirate*)] (1752)
: a group or association of four

**quad·ru·ped** \'kwä-drə-‚ped\ *noun* [Latin *quadruped-, quadrupes,* from *quadruped-, quadrupes,* adjective, having four feet, from *quadri-* + *ped-, pes* foot — more at FOOT] (1646)
: an animal having four feet
— **quadruped** *adjective*
— **qua·dru·pe·dal** \kwä-'drü-pə-d°l, ‚kwä-drə-'pe-\ *adjective*

¹**qua·dru·ple** \kwä-'drü-pəl, -'drə-; 'kwä-drə-\ *verb* **qua·dru·pled; qua·dru·pling** \-p(ə-)liŋ\ (14th century)
*transitive verb*
: to make four times as great or as many
*intransitive verb*
: to become four times as great or as numerous

²**quadruple** *noun* (15th century)
: a sum four times as great as another

³**quadruple** *adjective* [Middle French or Latin; Middle French, from Latin *quadruplus,* from *quadri-* + *-plus* multiplied by — more at -FOLD] (1557)
**1** : having four units or members
**2** : being four times as great or as many
**3** : marked by four beats per measure ⟨*quadruple* meter⟩
— **qua·dru·ply** \-'drü-plē, -'drə-, -drə-\ *adverb*
— **qua·dru·plic·i·ty** \‚kwä-drù-'pli-sə-tē\ *noun*

**qua·dru·plet** \kwä-'drü-plət, -'drə-; 'kwä-drə-plət\ *noun* (1787)
**1** : one of four offspring born at one birth
**2** : a combination of four of a kind
**3** : a group of four musical notes to be performed in the time ordinarily given to three of the same kind

¹**qua·dru·pli·cate** \kwä-'drü-pli-kət\ *adjective* [Latin *quadruplicatus,* past participle of *quadruplicare* to quadruple, from *quadruplic-, quadruplex* fourfold, from *quadri-* + *-plic-, -plex* fold — more at -FOLD] (1657)
**1** : consisting of or existing in four corresponding or identical parts or examples ⟨*quadruplicate* invoices⟩
**2** : being the fourth of four things exactly alike

²**qua·dru·pli·cate** \-plə-‚kāt\ *transitive verb* **-cat·ed; -cat·ing** (circa 1661)
**1** : to make quadruple or fourfold
**2** : to prepare in quadruplicate
— **qua·dru·pli·ca·tion** \-‚drü-plə-'kā-shən\ *noun*

³**qua·dru·pli·cate** \kwä-'drü-pli-kət\ *noun* (1790)
**1** : four copies all alike — used with *in* ⟨typed in *quadruplicate*⟩
**2** : one of four things exactly alike; *specifically* : one of four identical copies

**quad·ru·pole** \'kwä-drù-‚pōl\ *noun* [International Scientific Vocabulary *quadri-* + *pole*] (1922)
: a system composed of two dipoles of equal but oppositely directed moment

**quae·re** \'kwir-ē, 'kwer-\ *noun* [Latin, imperative of *quaerere* to seek, question] (1589)
*archaic* : QUERY

**quaes·tor** \'kwe-stər, 'kwē-\ *noun* [Middle English *questor,* from Latin *quaestor,* from *quaerere*] (14th century)
: one of numerous ancient Roman officials concerned chiefly with financial administration

**quaff** \'kwäf, 'kwaf\ *verb* [origin unknown] (1523)
*intransitive verb*
: to drink deeply

*transitive verb*
: to drink (a beverage) deeply
— **quaff** *noun*
— **quaff·er** *noun*

**quag** \'kwag, 'kwäg\ *noun* [origin unknown] (1589)
: MARSH, BOG

**quag·ga** \'kwa-gə, 'kwä-\ *noun* [obsolete Afrikaans (now *kwagga*), from Khoikhoi *quácha*] (1785)
: an extinct mammal (*Equus quagga*) of southern Africa related to the zebras

**quag·gy** \'kwa-gē, 'kwä-\ *adjective* (1610)
**1** : MARSHY
**2** : FLABBY

**quag·mire** \'kwag-‚mīr, 'kwäg-\ *noun* (circa 1580)
**1** : soft miry land that shakes or yields under the foot
**2** : a difficult, precarious, or entrapping position : PREDICAMENT

**qua·hog** *also* **qua·haug** \'kō-‚hòg, 'kwò-, 'kwō-, -‚häg\ *noun* [Narraganset *poquaûhock*] (1753)
: a thick-shelled edible clam (*Mercenaria mercenaria*) of the U.S.

**quai** \'kā\ *noun* [French, from Middle French *cai* — more at QUAY] (1862)
: QUAY

**quaich** *or* **quaigh** \'kwāk\ *noun* [Scottish Gaelic *cuach*] (1546)
*chiefly Scottish* : a small shallow drinking vessel with ears for use as handles

¹**quail** \'kwā(ə)l\ *noun, plural* **quail** *or* **quails** [Middle English *quaille,* from Middle French, from Medieval Latin *quaccula,* of imitative origin] (14th century)
: any of numerous small gallinaceous birds: as **a** : an Old World migratory game bird (*Coturnix coturnix*) **b** : BOB-WHITE

²**quail** *verb* [Middle English, from Middle Dutch *quelen*] (15th century)
*intransitive verb*
**1 a** *chiefly dialect* : WITHER, DECLINE **b** : to give way : FALTER ⟨his courage never *quailed*⟩
**2** : to recoil in dread or terror : COWER ⟨the strongest *quail* before financial ruin —Samuel Butler (died 1902)⟩
*transitive verb*
*archaic* : to make fearful
**synonym** see RECOIL

**quaint** \'kwānt\ *adjective* [Middle English *cointe,* from Old French, from Latin *cognitus,* past participle of *cognoscere* to know — more at COGNITION] (13th century)
**1** *obsolete* : EXPERT, SKILLED
**2 a** : marked by skillful design ⟨*quaint* with many a device in India ink —Herman Melville⟩ **b** : marked by beauty or elegance
**3 a** : unusual or different in character or appearance : ODD ⟨figures of fun, *quaint* people —Herman Wouk⟩ **b** : pleasingly or strikingly old-fashioned or unfamiliar
**synonym** see STRANGE
— **quaint·ly** *adverb*
— **quaint·ness** *noun*

¹**quake** \'kwāk\ *intransitive verb* **quaked; quak·ing** [Middle English, from Old English *cwacian*] (before 12th century)
**1** : to shake or vibrate usually from shock or instability
**2** : to tremble or shudder usually from cold or fear

²**quake** *noun* (14th century)

quail

---

\ə\ abut \ᵊ\ kitten \ər\ further \a\ ash \ā\ ace \ä\ mop, mar \aù\ out \ch\ chin \e\ bet \ē\ easy \g\ go \i\ hit \ī\ ice \j\ job \ŋ\ sing \ō\ go \ò\ law \òi\ boy \th\ thin \t͟h\ the \ü\ loot \ù\ foot \y\ yet \zh\ vision *see also* Guide to Pronunciation

**:** an instance of shaking or trembling (as of the earth or moon); *especially* **:** EARTHQUAKE

**quak·er** \'kwā-kər\ *noun* (1597)
**1 :** one that quakes
**2** *capitalized* **:** FRIEND 5
— **Quak·er·ish** \'kwā-k(ə-)rish\ *adjective*
— **Quak·er·ism** \-kə-ˌri-zəm\ *noun*
— **Quak·er·ly** \-kər-lē\ *adjective*

**Quaker gun** *noun* [from opposition to war as a basic Quaker tenet] (1809)
**:** a dummy piece of artillery usually made of wood

**quak·er–la·dies** \ˌkwā-kər-'lā-dēz\ *noun plural* (1871)
**:** BLUETS

**quaking aspen** *noun* (1843)
**:** an aspen (*Populus tremuloides*) chiefly of the U.S. and Canada that has small nearly circular leaves with flattened petioles and finely serrate margins

**qua·le** \'kwä-lē, -ˌlā\ *noun, plural* **qua·lia** \'kwä-lē-ə\ [Latin, neuter of *qualis* of what kind] (1675)
**1 :** a property (as redness) considered apart from things having the property **:** UNIVERSAL
**2 :** a property as it is experienced as distinct from any source it might have in a physical object

**qual·i·fi·able** \ˌkwä-lə-'fī-ə-bəl\ *adjective* (1611)
**:** capable of qualifying or being qualified

**qual·i·fi·ca·tion** \ˌkwä-lə-fə-'kā-shən\ *noun* (circa 1544)
**1 :** a restriction in meaning or application **:** a limiting modification ⟨this statement stands without *qualification*⟩
**2 a** *obsolete* **:** NATURE **b** *archaic* **:** CHARACTERISTIC
**3 a :** a quality or skill that fits a person (as for an office) ⟨the applicant with the best *qualifications*⟩ **b :** a condition or standard that must be complied with (as for the attainment of a privilege) ⟨a *qualification* for membership⟩

**qual·i·fied** \'kwä-lə-ˌfīd\ *adjective* (1558)
**1 a :** fitted (as by training or experience) for a given purpose **:** COMPETENT **b :** having complied with the specific requirements or precedent conditions (as for an office or employment) **:** ELIGIBLE
**2 :** limited or modified in some way ⟨*qualified* approval⟩
— **qual·i·fied·ly** \-ˌfī(-ə)d-lē\ *adverb*

**qual·i·fi·er** \-ˌfī(-ə)r\ *noun* (1561)
**:** one that qualifies: as **a :** one that satisfies requirements or meets a specified standard **b :** a word (as an adjective) or word group that limits or modifies the meaning of another word (as a noun) or word group

**qual·i·fy** \'kwä-lə-ˌfī\ *verb* **-fied; -fy·ing** [Middle French *qualifier*, from Medieval Latin *qualificare*, from Latin *qualis*] (1533)
*transitive verb*
**1 a :** to reduce from a general to a particular or restricted form **:** MODIFY **b :** to make less harsh or strict **:** MODERATE **c :** to alter the strength or flavor of **d :** to limit or modify the meaning of (as a noun)
**2 :** to characterize by naming an attribute **:** DESCRIBE ⟨cannot *qualify* it as . . . either glad or sorry —T. S. Eliot⟩
**3 a :** to fit by training, skill, or ability for a special purpose **b** (1) **:** to declare competent or adequate **:** CERTIFY (2) **:** to invest with legal capacity **:** LICENSE
*intransitive verb*
**1 :** to be or become fit (as for an office) **:** meet the required standard
**2 :** to acquire legal or competent power or capacity ⟨has just *qualified* as a lawyer⟩
**3 a :** to exhibit a required degree of ability in a preliminary contest ⟨*qualified* for the finals⟩ **b :** to shoot well enough to earn a marksmanship badge

**qual·i·ta·tive** \'kwä-lə-ˌtā-tiv\ *adjective* (1607)
**:** of, relating to, or involving quality or kind

— **qual·i·ta·tive·ly** *adverb*

**qualitative analysis** *noun* (1842)
**:** chemical analysis designed to identify the components of a substance or mixture

**¹qual·i·ty** \'kwä-lə-tē\ *noun, plural* **-ties** [Middle English *qualite*, from Old French *qualité*, from Latin *qualitat-*, *qualitas*, from *qualis* of what kind; akin to Latin *qui* who — more at WHO] (14th century)
**1 a :** peculiar and essential character **:** NATURE ⟨her ethereal *quality* —Gay Talese⟩ **b :** an inherent feature **:** PROPERTY ⟨had a *quality* of stridence, dissonance —Roald Dahl⟩ **c :** CAPACITY, ROLE ⟨in the *quality* of reader and companion —Joseph Conrad⟩
**2 a :** degree of excellence **:** GRADE ⟨the *quality* of competing air service —*Current Biography*⟩ **b :** superiority in kind ⟨merchandise of *quality*⟩
**3 a :** social status **:** RANK **b :** ARISTOCRACY
**4 a :** a distinguishing attribute **:** CHARACTERISTIC ⟨possesses many fine *qualities*⟩ **b** *archaic* **:** an acquired skill **:** ACCOMPLISHMENT
**5 :** the character in a logical proposition of being affirmative or negative
**6 :** vividness of hue
**7 a :** TIMBRE **b :** the identifying character of a vowel sound determined chiefly by the resonance of the vocal chambers in uttering it
**8 :** the attribute of an elementary sensation that makes it fundamentally unlike any other sensation ☆

**²quality** *adjective* (1701)
**:** being of high quality

**quality assurance** *noun* (1982)
**:** a program for the systematic monitoring and evaluation of the various aspects of a project, service, or facility to ensure that standards of quality are being met

**quality circle** *noun* (1980)
**:** a group of employees who volunteer to meet regularly to discuss and propose solutions to problems (as of quality or productivity) in the workplace

**quality control** *noun* (1935)
**:** an aggregate of activities (as design analysis and inspection for defects) designed to ensure adequate quality especially in manufactured products
— **quality controller** *noun*

**quality point** *noun* (1948)
**:** GRADE POINT

**quality point average** *noun* (circa 1972)
**:** GRADE POINT AVERAGE

**qualm** \'kwäm *also* 'kwȯm *or* 'kwälm\ *noun* [origin unknown] (circa 1530)
**1 :** a sudden attack of illness, faintness, or nausea
**2 :** a sudden access of usually disturbing emotion (as doubt or fear)
**3 :** a feeling of uneasiness about a point especially of conscience or propriety ☆
— **qualmy** *adjective*

**qualm·ish** \'kwä-mish *also* 'kwȯ- *or* 'kwäl-\ *adjective* (1548)
**1 a :** feeling qualms **:** NAUSEATED **b :** overly scrupulous **:** SQUEAMISH
**2 :** of, relating to, or producing qualms
— **qualm·ish·ly** *adverb*
— **qualm·ish·ness** *noun*

**qua·mash** \'kwä-mish\ *variant of* CAMAS

**quan·da·ry** \'kwän-d(ə-)rē\ *noun, plural* **-ries** [origin unknown] (1579)
**:** a state of perplexity or doubt

**quan·tal** \'kwän-tᵊl\ *adjective* (1933)
**1** [Latin *quanti* how many, plural of *quantus*] **:** of, relating to, or having only two experimental alternatives (as dead or alive, all or none)
**2** [*quantum*] **:** of or relating to a quantum

**quan·ti·fi·ca·tion** \ˌkwän-tə-fə-'kā-shən\ *noun* (circa 1840)
**:** the operation of quantifying
— **quan·ti·fi·ca·tion·al** \-shnəl, -shə-nᵊl\ *adjective*
— **quan·ti·fi·ca·tion·al·ly** *adverb*

**quan·ti·fi·er** \'kwän-tə-ˌfī(-ə)r\ *noun* (1876)
**:** one that quantifies: as **a :** a prefixed operator that binds the variables in a logical formula by specifying their quantity **b :** a limiting noun modifier (as *five* in "the five young men") expressive of quantity and characterized by occurrence before the descriptive adjectives in a noun phrase

**quan·ti·fy** \-ˌfī\ *transitive verb* **-fied; -fy·ing** [Medieval Latin *quantificare*, from Latin *quantus* how much] (circa 1840)
**1 a** (1) **:** to limit by a quantifier (2) **:** to bind by prefixing a quantifier **b :** to make explicit the logical quantity of
**2 :** to determine, express, or measure the quantity of
— **quan·ti·fi·able** \ˌkwän-tə-'fī-ə-bəl\ *adjective*

**quan·ti·tate** \'kwän-tə-ˌtāt\ *transitive verb* **-tat·ed; -tat·ing** [back-formation from *quantitative*] (1927)
**1 :** to measure or estimate the quantity of; *especially* **:** to measure or determine precisely
**2 :** to express in quantitative terms
— **quan·ti·ta·tion** \ˌkwän-tə-'tā-shən\ *noun*

**quan·ti·ta·tive** \'kwän-tə-ˌtā-tiv\ *adjective* [Medieval Latin *quantitativus*, from Latin *quantitat-*, *quantitas* quantity] (1581)
**1 :** of, relating to, or expressible in terms of quantity
**2 :** of, relating to, or involving the measurement of quantity or amount
**3 :** based on quantity; *specifically, of classical verse* **:** based on temporal quantity or duration of sounds
— **quan·ti·ta·tive·ly** *adverb*
— **quan·ti·ta·tive·ness** *noun*

**quantitative analysis** *noun* (circa 1847)
**:** chemical analysis designed to determine the amounts or proportions of the components of a substance

**quantitative inheritance** *noun* (circa 1929)
**:** genic inheritance of a character (as human skin color) controlled by polygenes

**quan·ti·ty** \'kwän-tə-tē\ *noun, plural* **-ties** [Middle English *quantite*, from Middle French *quantité*, from Latin *quantitat-*, *quantitas*, from *quantus* how much, how large; akin to Latin *quam* how, as, *quando* when, *qui* who — more at WHO] (14th century)

---

☆ **SYNONYMS**
**Quality, property, character, attribute** mean an intelligible feature by which a thing may be identified. QUALITY is a general term applicable to any trait or characteristic whether individual or generic ⟨material with a silky *quality*⟩. PROPERTY implies a characteristic that belongs to a thing's essential nature and may be used to describe a type or species ⟨the *property* of not conducting heat⟩. CHARACTER applies to a peculiar and distinctive quality of a thing or a class ⟨remarks of an unseemly *character*⟩. ATTRIBUTE implies a quality ascribed to a thing or a being ⟨the traditional *attributes* of a military hero⟩.

**Qualm, scruple, compunction, demur** mean a misgiving about what one is doing or going to do. QUALM implies an uneasy fear that one is not following one's conscience or better judgment ⟨no *qualms* about plagiarizing⟩. SCRUPLE implies doubt of the rightness of an act on grounds of principle ⟨no *scruples* against buying stolen goods⟩. COMPUNCTION implies a spontaneous feeling of responsibility or compassion for a potential victim ⟨had *compunctions* about lying⟩. DEMUR implies hesitation caused by objection to an outside suggestion or influence ⟨accepted her decision without *demur*⟩.

**1 a :** an indefinite amount or number **b :** a determinate or estimated amount **c :** total amount or number **d :** a considerable amount or number — often used in plural ⟨generous *quantities* of luck —H. E. Putsch⟩
**2 a :** the aspect in which a thing is measurable in terms of greater, less, or equal or of increasing or decreasing magnitude **b :** the subject of a mathematical operation **c :** an individual considered with respect to a given situation ⟨an unknown *quantity* . . . as attorney general —Tom Wicker⟩
**3 a :** duration and intensity of speech sounds as distinct from their individual quality or phonemic character; *specifically* **:** the relative length or brevity of a prosodic syllable in some languages (as Greek and Latin) **b :** the relative duration or time length of a speech sound or sound sequence
**4 :** the character of a logical proposition as being universal, particular, or singular

**quantity theory** *noun* (1888)
**:** a theory in economics: changes in the price level tend to vary directly with the amount of money in circulation and the rate of its circulation

**quan·tize** \'kwän-ˌtīz\ *transitive verb* **quantized; quan·tiz·ing** [*quantum*] (1922)
**1 :** to subdivide (as energy) into small but measurable increments
**2 :** to calculate or express in terms of quantum mechanics
— **quan·ti·za·tion** \ˌkwän-tə-'zā-shən\ *noun*
— **quan·tiz·er** \'kwän-ˌtī-zər\ *noun*

**¹quan·tum** \'kwän-təm\ *noun, plural* **quanta** \'kwän-tə\ [Latin, neuter of *quantus* how much] (1567)
**1 a :** QUANTITY, AMOUNT **b :** PORTION, PART **c :** gross quantity **:** BULK
**2 a :** any of the very small increments or parcels into which many forms of energy are subdivided **b :** any of the small subdivisions of a quantized physical magnitude (as magnetic moment)

**²quantum** *adjective* (1942)
**:** LARGE, SIGNIFICANT ⟨a *quantum* improvement⟩

**quantum chromodynamics** *noun plural but singular in construction* (1975)
**:** a theory of fundamental particles based on the assumption that quarks are distinguished by differences in color and are held together (as in hadrons) by an exchange of gluons

**quantum electrodynamics** *noun plural but usually singular in construction* (1927)
**:** quantum mechanics applied to electrical interactions (as between nuclear particles)

**quantum field theory** *noun* (1948)
**:** a theory in physics: the interaction of two separate physical systems (as particles) is attributed to a field that extends from one to the other and is manifested in a particle exchange between the two systems

**quantum jump** *noun* (1926)
**1 :** an abrupt transition (as of an electron, an atom, or a molecule) from one discrete energy state to another
**2 :** QUANTUM LEAP

**quantum leap** *noun* (1956)
**:** an abrupt change, sudden increase, or dramatic advance

**quantum mechanics** *noun plural but singular or plural in construction* (1922)
**:** a theory of matter that is based on the concept of the possession of wave properties by elementary particles, that affords a mathematical interpretation of the structure and interactions of matter on the basis of these properties, and that incorporates within it quantum theory and the uncertainty principle — called also *wave mechanics*
— **quantum mechanical** *adjective*
— **quantum mechanically** *adverb*

**quantum number** *noun* (1902)
**:** any of a set of integers or half odd integers that indicate the magnitude of various discrete

quantities (as electric charge) of a particle or system and that serve to define its state

**quantum theory** *noun* (1912)
**:** a theory in physics based on the concept of the subdivision of radiant energy into finite quanta and applied to numerous processes involving transference or transformation of energy in an atomic or molecular scale

**¹quar·an·tine** \'kwȯr-ən-ˌtēn, 'kwär-\ *noun* [partly modification of French *quarantaine*, from Old French, from *quarante* forty, from Latin *quadraginta*, from *quadra-* (akin to *quattuor* four) + *-ginta* (akin to *viginti* twenty); partly modification of Italian *quarantena* quarantine of a ship, from *quaranta* forty, from Latin *quadraginta* — more at FOUR, VIGESIMAL] (1609)
**1 :** a period of 40 days
**2 a :** a term during which a ship arriving in port and suspected of carrying contagious disease is held in isolation from the shore **b :** a regulation placing a ship in quarantine **c :** a place where a ship is detained during quarantine
**3 a :** a restraint upon the activities or communication of persons or the transport of goods designed to prevent the spread of disease or pests **b :** a place in which those under quarantine are kept
**4 :** a state of enforced isolation

**²quarantine** *verb* **-tined; -tin·ing** (1804)
*transitive verb*
**1 :** to detain in or exclude by quarantine
**2 :** to isolate from normal relations or communication ⟨*quarantine* an aggressor⟩
*intransitive verb*
**:** to establish or declare a quarantine

**quare** \'kwar, 'kwer, 'kwär\ *dialect variant of* ¹QUEER

**quark** \'kwȯrk, 'kwärk\ *noun* [coined by Murray Gell-Mann] (1964)
**:** any of several elementary particles that are postulated to come in pairs (as in the up and down varieties) of similar mass with one member having a charge of +⅔ and the other a charge of −⅓ and are held to make up hadrons ◆

**¹quar·rel** \'kwȯr-(ə-)l, 'kwär-(ə-)l\ *noun* [Middle English, from Old French, square-headed arrow, building stone, from (assumed) Vulgar Latin *quadrellum*, diminutive of Latin *quadrum* square — more at QUADRATE] (13th century)
**:** a square-headed bolt or arrow especially for a crossbow

**²quarrel** *noun* [Middle English *querele*, from Middle French, complaint, from Latin *querela*, from *queri* to complain] (14th century)
**1 :** a ground of dispute or complaint ⟨have no *quarrel* with a different approach⟩
**2 :** a usually verbal conflict between antagonists **:** ALTERCATION

**³quarrel** *intransitive verb* **-reled** *or* **-relled; -rel·ing** *or* **-rel·ling** (14th century)
**1 :** to find fault ⟨many people *quarrel* with the idea —Johns Hopkins Magazine⟩
**2 :** to contend or dispute actively ⟨*quarreled* frequently with his superiors —London Calling⟩
— **quar·rel·er** *or* **quar·rel·ler** *noun*

**quar·rel·some** \'kwȯr-(ə-)l-səm, 'kwär-(ə-)l-\ *adjective* (1596)
**:** apt or disposed to quarrel in an often petty manner **:** CONTENTIOUS
**synonym** see BELLIGERENT
— **quar·rel·some·ly** *adverb*
— **quar·rel·some·ness** *noun*

**quar·ri·er** \'kwȯr-ē-ər, 'kwär-\ *noun* (14th century)
**:** a worker in a stone quarry

**¹quar·ry** \'kwȯr-ē, 'kwär-\ *noun, plural* **quarries** [Middle English *querre* entrails of game given to the hounds, from Middle French *cuiree*, from *cuir* skin, hide (on which the entrails were placed), from Latin *corium* — more at CUIRASS] (14th century)

**1** *obsolete* **:** a heap of the game killed in a hunt
**2 :** GAME; *specifically* **:** game hunted with hawks
**3 :** one that is sought or pursued **:** PREY ◆

**²quarry** *noun, plural* **quarries** [Middle English *quarey*, alteration of *quarrere*, from Middle French *quarriere*, from (assumed) Old French *quarre* squared stone, from Latin *quadrum* square] (14th century)
**1 :** an open excavation usually for obtaining building stone, slate, or limestone
**2 :** a rich source

**³quarry** *verb* **quar·ried; quar·ry·ing** (1774)
*transitive verb*
**1 :** to dig or take from or as if from a quarry ⟨*quarry* marble⟩
**2 :** to make a quarry in ⟨*quarry* a hill⟩
*intransitive verb*
**:** to delve in or as if in a quarry

**⁴quarry** *noun, plural* **quarries** [alteration of ¹*quarrel*] (1555)
**:** a diamond-shaped pane of glass, stone, or tile

**quarrying** *noun* (circa 1828)
**:** the business, occupation, or act of extracting useful material (as building stone) from quarries

**quar·ry·man** \'kwȯr-ē-mən, 'kwär-\ *noun* (15th century)
**:** QUARRIER

**quart** \'kwȯrt\ *noun* [Middle English, one fourth of a gallon, from Middle French *quarte*, from Old French, from feminine of *quart*, adjective, fourth, from Latin *quartus;* akin to Latin *quattuor* four — more at FOUR] (14th century)

**1** : see WEIGHT table

**2** : a vessel or measure having a capacity of one quart

**¹quar·tan** \'kwȯr-t°n\ *adjective* [Middle English *quarteyne,* from Middle French (*fievre*) *quartaine* quartan fever, from Latin (*febris*) *quartana,* from *quartanus* of the fourth, from *quartus*] (14th century)

: occurring every fourth day reckoning inclusively; *specifically* : recurring at approximately 72-hour intervals

**²quartan** *noun* (14th century)

: an intermittent fever that recurs at approximately 72-hour intervals; *especially* : a quartan malaria

**¹quar·ter** \'kwȯ(r)-tər *also* 'kȯ(r)-\ *noun* [Middle English, from Old French *quartier,* from Latin *quartarius,* from *quartus* fourth] (14th century)

**1** : one of four equal parts into which something is divisible : a fourth part ⟨in the top *quarter* of his class⟩

**2** : any of various units of capacity or weight equal to or derived from one fourth of some larger unit

**3** : any of various units of length or area equal to one fourth of some larger unit

**4** : the fourth part of a measure of time: as **a** : one of a set of four 3-month divisions of a year ⟨business was up during the third *quarter*⟩ **b** : a school term of about 12 weeks **c** : QUARTER HOUR ⟨a *quarter* after three⟩

**5 a** : a coin worth a quarter of a dollar **b** : the sum of 25 cents

**6 a** : one limb of a quadruped with the adjacent parts; *especially* : one fourth part of the carcass of a slaughtered animal including a leg **b** *plural, British* : HINDQUARTER 2

**7 a** : the region or direction lying under any of the four divisions of the horizon **b** : one of the four parts into which the horizon is divided or the cardinal point corresponding to it **c** : a compass point or direction other than the cardinal points **d** (1) : an unspecified person or group ⟨financial help from many *quarters* —*Current Biography*⟩ (2) : a point, direction, or place not definitely identified ⟨the view to the rear *quarter* —*Consumer Reports*⟩

**8 a** : a division or district of a town or city ⟨he describes the immigrant *quarter* —Alfred Kazin⟩ **b** : the inhabitants of such a quarter

**9 a** : an assigned station or post **b** *plural* : an assembly of a ship's company for ceremony, drill, or emergency **c** *plural* : living accommodations : LODGINGS ⟨show you to your *quarters*⟩

**10** : merciful consideration of an opponent; *specifically* : the clemency of not killing a defeated enemy

**11** : a fourth part of the moon's period

**12** : the side of a horse's hoof between the toe and the heel — see HOOF illustration

**13 a** : any of the four parts into which a heraldic field is divided **b** : a bearing or charge occupying the first fourth part of a heraldic field

**14** : the state of two machine parts that are exactly at right angles to one another or are spaced about a circle so as to subtend a right angle at the center of the circle

**15 a** : the stern area of a ship's side **b** : the part of the yardarm outside the slings

**16** : one side of the upper of a shoe or boot from heel to vamp

**17** : one of the four equal periods into which the playing time of some games is divided

**²quarter** (14th century)

*transitive verb*

**1 a** : to cut or divide into four equal or nearly equal parts ⟨*quarter* an apple⟩ ⟨condemned to be hanged, drawn, and *quartered*⟩ **b** *archaic* : DIVIDE

**2** : to provide with lodging or shelter

**3** : to crisscross (an area) in many directions

**4 a** : to arrange or bear (as different coats of arms) quarterly on one escutcheon **b** : to add (a coat of arms) to others on one escutcheon **c** : to divide (a shield) into distinct sections (as by stripes)

**5** : to adjust or locate (as cranks) at right angles in a machine

*intransitive verb*

**1** : LODGE, DWELL

**2** : to crisscross a district

**3** : to change from one quarter to another ⟨the moon *quarters*⟩

**4** : to strike on a ship's quarter ⟨the wind was *quartering*⟩

**³quarter** *adjective* (14th century)

: consisting of or equal to a quarter

**quar·ter·age** \'kwȯ(r)-tə-rij\ *noun* (14th century)

: a quarterly payment, tax, wage, or allowance

**¹quar·ter·back** \'kwȯ(r)-tər-,bak\ *noun* (1879)

**1** : an offensive back in football who usually lines up behind the center, calls the signals, and directs the offensive play of the team

**2** : one who gives direction and leadership

**²quarterback** (1944)

*transitive verb*

**1** : to direct the offensive play of (as a football team)

**2** : to give executive direction to : BOSS ⟨*quarterbacked* the original buying syndicate —*Time*⟩

*intransitive verb*

: to play quarterback

**quarterback sneak** *noun* (circa 1923)

: a usually quick run with the ball by a quarterback into the middle of the offensive line

**quar·ter·bound** \'kwȯ(r)-tər-'baùnd\ *adjective* (circa 1888)

*of a book* : bound in material of two qualities with the material of better quality on the spine only

— **quarter binding** *noun*

**quarter day** *noun* (15th century)

*chiefly British* : the day which begins a quarter of the year and on which a quarterly payment often falls due

**quar·ter·deck** \'kwȯ(r)-tər-,dek\ *noun* (1627)

**1** : the stern area of a ship's upper deck

**2** : a part of a deck on a naval vessel set aside by the captain for ceremonial and official use

**¹quar·ter·fi·nal** \,kwȯ(r)-tər-'fī-n°l\ *noun* (1927)

**1** *plural* : a quarterfinal round

**2** : a quarterfinal match

— **quar·ter·fi·nal·ist** \-n°l-ist\ *noun*

**²quarterfinal** *adjective* (circa 1934)

**1** : immediately preceding the semifinal in an elimination tournament

**2** : of or participating in a quarterfinal

**quarter horse** *noun* [from its high speed for distances up to a quarter of a mile] (1834)

: any of a breed of compact muscular saddle horses characterized by great endurance and by high speed for short distances

quarter horse

**quarter hour** *noun* (1883)

**1** : any of the quarter points of an hour

**2** : fifteen minutes

**3** : a unit of academic credit representing an hour of class (as lecture class) or three hours of laboratory work each week for an academic quarter

**¹quar·ter·ing** \'kwȯ(r)-tə-riŋ\ *noun* (15th century)

**1 a** : the division of an escutcheon containing different coats of arms into four or more com-

partments **b** : a quarter of an escutcheon or the coat of arms on it

**2** : a line of usually noble or distinguished ancestry

**²quartering** *adjective* (circa 1692)

**1** : coming from a point well abaft the beam of a ship but not directly astern ⟨*quartering* waves⟩

**2** : lying at right angles

**¹quar·ter·ly** \'kwȯ(r)-tər-lē\ *adverb* (14th century)

**1** : in heraldic quarters or quarterings

**2** : at 3-month intervals

**²quarterly** *adjective* (15th century)

**1** : computed for or payable at 3-month intervals ⟨*quarterly* premium⟩

**2** : recurring, issued, or spaced at 3-month intervals

**3** : divided into heraldic quarters or compartments

**³quarterly** *noun, plural* **-lies** (1830)

: a periodical published four times a year

**Quarterly Meeting** *noun* (1675)

: an organizational unit of the Society of Friends usually composed of several Monthly Meetings

**quar·ter·mas·ter** \'kwȯ(r)-tər-,mas-tər\ *noun* (15th century)

**1** : a petty officer who attends to a ship's helm, binnacle, and signals

**2** : an army officer who provides clothing and subsistence for a body of troops

**quar·tern** \'kwȯ(r)-tərn\ *noun* [Middle English *quarteron,* from Old French, quarter of a pound, quarter of a hundred, from *quartier* quarter] (14th century)

: a fourth part (as of a unit of measurement)

**quarter note** *noun* (1763)

: a musical note with the time value of ¼ of a whole note — see NOTE illustration

**quarter rest** *noun* (circa 1890)

: a musical rest corresponding in time value to a quarter note — see REST illustration

**quar·ter·sawn** \'kwȯ(r)-tər-'sȯn\ *also* **quar·ter·sawed** \-'sȯd\ *adjective* (circa 1890)

: sawed from quartered logs so that the annual rings are nearly at right angles to the wide face — used of boards and planks

**quarter section** *noun* (1804)

: a tract of land that is half a mile square and contains 160 acres in the U.S. government system of land surveying

**quarter sessions** *noun plural* (1577)

: a former English local court with limited original and appellate criminal and sometimes civil jurisdiction and often administrative functions held quarterly usually by two justices of the peace in a county or by a recorder in a borough

**quar·ter·staff** \'kwȯ(r)-tər-,staf\ *noun, plural* **-staves** \-,stavz, -,stāvz\ (1550)

: a long stout staff formerly used as a weapon and wielded with one hand in the middle and the other between the middle and the end

**quarter tone** *noun* (circa 1776)

**1** : a musical interval of one half a semitone

**2** : a tone at an interval of one quarter

**quar·tet** *also* **quar·tette** \kwȯr-'tet\ *noun* [Italian *quartetto,* from *quarto* fourth, from Latin *quartus* — more at QUART] (1773)

**1** : a musical composition for four instruments or voices

**2** : a group or set of four; *especially* : the performers of a quartet

**quar·tic** \'kwȯr-tik\ *adjective* [Latin *quartus* fourth] (circa 1890)

: of the fourth degree ⟨*quartic* equation⟩

— **quartic** *noun*

**quar·tile** \'kwȯr-,tīl, -t°l\ *noun* [International Scientific Vocabulary, from Latin *quartus*] (1879)

: any of the three values that divide the items of a frequency distribution into four classes with each containing one fourth of the total population; *also* : any one of the four classes

**quar·to** \'kwȯr-(,)tō\ *noun, plural* **quartos** [Latin, ablative of *quartus* fourth] (1589)
**1 :** the size of a piece of paper cut four from a sheet; *also* **:** paper or a page of this size
**2 :** a book printed on quarto pages

**quartz** \'kwȯrts\ *noun* [German *Quarz*] (circa 1631)
**1 :** a mineral consisting of silicon dioxide occurring in colorless and transparent or colored hexagonal crystals or in crystalline masses
**2 :** a quartz crystal that when placed in an electric field oscillates at a constant frequency and is used to control devices which require precise regulation ⟨a *quartz* watch⟩
— **quartz·ose** \'kwȯrt,sōs\ *adjective*

**quartz glass** *noun* (1903)
**:** vitreous silica prepared from pure quartz and noted for its transparency to ultraviolet radiation

**quartz heater** *noun* (1980)
**:** a portable electric radiant heater that has heating elements sealed in quartz-glass tubes producing infrared radiation in front of a reflective backing

**quartz–iodine lamp** *noun* (circa 1964)
**:** an incandescent lamp that has a quartz bulb and a tungsten filament with the bulb containing iodine which reacts with the vaporized tungsten to prevent excessive blackening of the bulb

**quartz·ite** \'kwȯrt-,sīt\ *noun* [International Scientific Vocabulary] (circa 1847)
**:** a compact granular rock composed of quartz and derived from sandstone by metamorphism
— **quartz·it·ic** \kwȯrt-'si-tik\ *adjective*

**qua·sar** \'kwā-,zär *also* -,sär\ *noun* [*quasi*-stell*ar*] (1964)
**:** any of a class of celestial objects that resemble stars but whose large redshift and apparent brightness imply extreme distance and huge energy output

**¹quash** \'kwäsh, 'kwȯsh\ *transitive verb* [Middle English *quashen* to smash, from Middle French *quasser, casser*, from Latin *quassare* to shake violently, shatter, frequentative of *quatere* to shake] (13th century)
**:** to suppress or extinguish summarily and completely ⟨*quash* a rebellion⟩

**²quash** *transitive verb* [Middle English *quassen*, from Middle French *casser, quasser* to annul, from Late Latin *cassare*, from Latin *cassus* void] (14th century)
**:** to nullify especially by judicial action ⟨*quash* an indictment⟩

**qua·si** \'kwā-,zī, -,sī; 'kwä-zē, -sē\ *adjective* [*quasi*-] (1642)
**1 :** having some resemblance usually by possession of certain attributes ⟨a *quasi* corporation⟩
**2 :** having a legal status only by operation or construction of law and without reference to intent ⟨a *quasi* contract⟩

**quasi-** *combining form* [Latin *quasi* as if, as it were, approximately, from *quam* as + *si* if — more at QUANTITY, SO]
**1 :** in some sense or degree ⟨*quasi*periodic⟩
**2 :** resembling in some degree ⟨*quasi*particle⟩

**qua·si–ju·di·cial** \,kwä-,zī-jü·'di-shəl, -,sī-, ,kwä-zē-, -sē-\ *adjective* (1836)
**1 :** having a partly judicial character by possession of the right to hold hearings and conduct investigations into disputed claims and alleged infractions of rules and regulations and to make decisions in the general manner of courts ⟨*quasi-judicial* bodies⟩
**2 :** essentially judicial in character but not within the judicial power or function especially as constitutionally defined ⟨*quasi-judicial* review⟩
— **qua·si–ju·di·cial·ly** \-'di-sh(ə-)lē\ *adverb*

**qua·si–leg·is·la·tive** \-'le-jəs-,lā-tiv\ *adjective* (circa 1934)
**1 :** having a partly legislative character by possession of the right to make rules and regu-

lations having the force of law ⟨a *quasi-legislative* agency⟩
**2 :** essentially legislative in character but not within the legislative power or function especially as constitutionally defined ⟨*quasi-legislative* powers⟩

**Qua·si·mo·do** \,kwä-si-'mō-(,)dō, ,kwä-zi-\ *noun* [Medieval Latin *quasi modo geniti infantes* as newborn babes (words of the introit for Low Sunday)] (circa 1847)
**:** LOW SUNDAY

**qua·si·par·ti·cle** \,kwä-,zī-'pär-ti-kəl, -,sī-, ,kwä-zē-, -sē-\ *noun* (1957)
**:** a composite entity (as a vibration in a solid) that is analogous in its behavior to a single particle

**qua·si·pe·ri·od·ic** \-,pir-ē-'ä-dik\ *adjective* (circa 1890)
**:** almost but not quite periodic; *especially* **:** periodic on a small scale but unpredictable at some larger scale
— **qua·si·pe·ri·od·ic·i·ty** \-,pir-ē-ə-'di-sə-tē\ *noun*

**qua·si–pub·lic** \-'pə-blik\ *adjective* (1888)
**:** essentially public (as in services rendered) although under private ownership or control

**qua·si–stel·lar object** \-'ste-lər-\ *noun* (1964)
**:** QUASAR

**quas·sia** \'kwä-shə\ *noun* [New Latin, genus name of a South American tree, from *Quassi* 18th century Surinam slave who discovered the medicinal value of quassia] (1770)
**:** a drug from the heartwood of various tropical trees of the ailanthus family used especially as a bitter tonic and remedy for roundworms in children and as an insecticide

**qua·ter·cen·te·na·ry** \,kwä-tər-sen-'te-nə-rē, -'sen-tⁿn-,er-ē, -sen-'tē-nə-rē\ *noun* [Latin *quater* four times + English *centenary* — more at QUATERNION] (1883)
**:** a year marking a 400th anniversary

**¹qua·ter·na·ry** \'kwä-tə(r)-,ner-ē, kwə-'tər-nə-rē\ *adjective* [Latin *quaternarius*, from *quaterni* four each] (1605)
**1 a :** of, relating to, or consisting of four units or members **b :** of, relating to, or being a number system with a base of four
**2** *capitalized* **:** of, relating to, or being the geological period from the end of the Tertiary to the present time or the corresponding system of rocks — see GEOLOGIC TIME table
**3 :** consisting of, containing, or being an atom bonded to four other atoms

**²quaternary** *noun, plural* **-ries** (1880)
**1** *capitalized* **:** the Quaternary period or system of rocks
**2 :** a member of a group fourth in order or rank

**quaternary ammonium compound** *noun* (circa 1934)
**:** any of numerous strong bases and their salts derived from ammonium by replacement of the hydrogen atoms with organic radicals and important especially as surface-active agents, disinfectants, and drugs

**qua·ter·ni·on** \kwə-'tər-nē-ən, kwä-\ *noun* [Middle English *quaternyoun*, from Late Latin *quaternion-, quaternio*, from Latin *quaterni* four each, from *quater* four times; akin to Latin *quattuor* four — more at FOUR] (14th century)
**1 :** a set of four parts, things, or persons
**2 a :** a generalized complex number that is composed of a real number and a vector and that depends on one real and three imaginary units **b** *plural* **:** the calculus of quaternions

**qua·ter·ni·ty** \kwä-'tər-nə-tē, kwə-\ *noun, plural* **-ties** [Late Latin *quaternitas*, from Latin *quaterni* four each] (1529)
**:** a union of a group or set of four

**qua·train** \'kwä-,trān, kwä-'\ *noun* [Middle French, from *quatre* four, from Latin *quattuor*] (1582)
**:** a unit or group of four lines of verse

**qua·tre·foil** \'ka-tər-,fȯil, 'ka-trə-\ *noun* [Middle English *quaterfoil* set of four leaves, from Middle French *quatre* + Middle English *-foil* (as in *trefoil*)] (15th century)
**1 :** a conventionalized representation of a flower with four petals or of a leaf with four leaflets
**2 :** a 4-lobed foliation in architecture

**quat·tro·cen·to** \,kwä-trō-'chen-(,)tō\ *noun, often capitalized* [Italian, literally, four hundred, from *quattro* four (from Latin *quattuor*) + *cento* hundred — more at CINQUECENTO] (circa 1854)
**:** the 15th century especially with reference to Italian literature and art

**quat·tu·or·de·cil·lion** \,kwä-tə-,wȯr-di-'sil-yən, *noun, often attributive* [Latin *quattuordecim* fourteen (from *quattuor* four + *decem* ten) + English *-illion* (as in *million*) — more at TEN] (circa 1903)
— see NUMBER table

**¹qua·ver** \'kwā-vər\ *verb* **qua·vered; qua·ver·ing** \'kwā-və-riŋ, 'kwāv-riŋ\ [Middle English, frequentative of *quaven* to tremble] (15th century)
*intransitive verb*
**1 :** TREMBLE
**2 :** TRILL
**3 :** to utter sound in tremulous tones
*transitive verb*
**:** to utter quaveringly
— **qua·ver·ing·ly** *adverb*
— **qua·very** \'kwā-və-rē, 'kwāv-rē\ *adjective*

**²quaver** *noun* (1570)
**1 :** EIGHTH NOTE
**2 :** TRILL 1
**3 :** a tremulous sound

**quay** \'kē, 'kā, 'kwā\ *noun* [alteration of earlier *key*, from Middle English, from Middle French dialect *cai*, probably of Celtic origin; akin to Breton *kae* hedge, enclosure; akin to Old English *hecg* hedge] (1696)
**:** a structure built parallel to the bank of a waterway for use as a landing place

**quay·age** \-ij\ *noun* (circa 1756)
**1 :** a charge for use of a quay
**2 :** room on or for quays
**3 :** a system of quays

**quay·side** \-,sīd\ *noun* (1903)
**:** land bordering a quay

**quean** \'kwēn, 'kwān\ *noun* [Middle English *quene*, from Old English *cwene*; akin to Old English *cwēn* woman, queen] (before 12th century)
**1 :** a disreputable woman; *specifically* **:** PROSTITUTE
**2** *chiefly Scottish* **:** WOMAN; *especially* **:** one that is young or unmarried

**quea·sy** *also* **quea·zy** \'kwē-zē\ *adjective* **quea·si·er; -est** [Middle English *coysy, qwesye*] (15th century)
**1 a :** causing nausea ⟨*queasy* motion⟩ **b :** suffering from nausea **:** NAUSEATED
**2 :** full of doubt **:** HAZARDOUS
**3 a :** causing uneasiness **b** (1) **:** DELICATE, SQUEAMISH (2) **:** ill at ease
— **quea·si·ly** \-zə-lē\ *adverb*
— **quea·si·ness** \-zē-nəs\ *noun*

**Que·bec** \kwi-'bek *also* ki-\ (1952)
— a communications code word for the letter *q*

**Que·be·cois** *or* **Qué·bé·cois** *or* **Qué·be·cois** \kā-bə-'kwä, -,be-\ *noun, plural* **Que·becois** *or* **Qué·bé·cois** *or* **Qué·be·cois** \-'kwä(z)\ [French *québecois, québécois*, from *Québec* Quebec] (1873)
**:** a native or inhabitant of Quebec; *specifically* **:** a French-speaking native or inhabitant of Quebec

---

\ə\ **abut** \ᵊ\ **kitten** \ər\ **further** \a\ **ash** \ā\ **ace**
\ä\ **mop, mar** \aú\ **out** \ch\ **chin** \e\ **bet** \ē\ **easy**
\g\ **go** \i\ **hit** \ī\ **ice** \j\ **job** \ŋ\ **sing** \ō\ **go**
\ȯ\ **law** \ȯi\ **boy** \th\ **thin** \t̲h̲\ **the** \ü\ **loot** \ú\ **foot**
\y\ **yet** \zh\ **vision** *see also* Guide to Pronunciation

**— Quebecois** or **Québécois** or **Québe-cois** adjective

**que·bra·cho** \kä-'brä-(,)chō, ki-\ noun [American Spanish, alteration of quiebracha, from Spanish quiebra it breaks + hacha ax] (circa 1881)
**1 :** any of several trees of southern South America with hard wood: as **a :** a tree (Aspidosperma quebracho) of the dogbane family which occurs in Argentina and Chile and whose dried bark is used as a respiratory sedative in dyspnea and in asthma **b :** a chiefly Argentine tree (Schinopsis lorentzii) of the cashew family with dense wood rich in tannins **2 a :** the wood of a quebracho **b :** a tannin-rich extract of the Argentine quebracho used in tanning leather
**Que·chua** \'ke-chə-wə, 'kech-wə\ noun, plural **Quechua** or **Quechuas** [Spanish, probably from Southern Peruvian Quechua qheswa (simi), literally, valley speech] (1840)
**1 :** a family of languages spoken by Indian peoples of Peru, Bolivia, Ecuador, Chile, and Argentina
**2 a :** a member of an Indian people of central Peru **b :** a group of peoples forming the dominant element of the Inca Empire
**— Que·chu·an** \-wən\ adjective or noun
**¹queen** \'kwēn\ noun [Middle English quene, from Old English cwēn woman, wife, queen; akin to Gothic qens wife, Greek gynē woman, Sanskrit jani] (before 12th century)
**1 a :** the wife or widow of a king **b :** the wife or widow of a tribal chief
**2 a :** a female monarch **b :** a female chieftain
**3 a :** a woman eminent in rank, power, or attractions (a movie queen) **b :** a goddess or a thing personified as female and having supremacy in a specified realm **c :** an attractive girl or woman; especially : a beauty contest winner
**4 :** the most privileged piece of each color in a set of chessmen having the power to move in any direction across any number of unoccupied squares
**5 :** a playing card marked with a stylized figure of a queen
**6 :** the fertile fully developed female of social bees, ants, and termites whose function is to lay eggs
**7 :** a mature female cat kept especially for breeding
**8 :** a male homosexual; especially : an effeminate one — often used disparagingly
**²queen** (1611)
intransitive verb
**1 :** to act like a queen; especially : to put on airs — usually used with it (queens it over her friends)
**2 :** to become a queen in chess
transitive verb
**:** to promote (a pawn) to a queen in chess
**Queen Anne** \-'an\ adjective [Queen Anne of England] (1863)
**1 :** of, relating to, or having the characteristics of a style of furniture originating in England under Dutch influence especially during the first half of the 18th century that is marked by extensive use of upholstery, marquetry, and oriental fabrics
**2 :** of, relating to, or having the characteristics of a style of English building of the early 18th century characterized by modified classic ornament and the use of red brickwork in which even relief ornament is carved
**Queen Anne's lace** noun (1895)
**:** a widely naturalized Eurasian biennial herb (Daucus carota) which has a whitish acrid taproot and from which the cultivated carrot originated — called also wild carrot
**queen consort** noun, plural **queens consort** (1765)
**:** the wife of a reigning king
**queen·ly** \'kwēn-lē\ adjective **queen·li·er; -est** (15th century)
**1 :** of, relating to, or befitting a queen

**2 :** having royal rank
**3 :** MONARCHICAL
**— queen·li·ness** noun
**— queenly** adverb
**queen mother** noun (1577)
**:** a queen dowager who is mother of the reigning sovereign
**queen post** noun (1823)
**:** one of two vertical tie post in a truss (as of a roof)
**queen regnant** noun, plural **queens regnant** (circa 1639)
**:** a queen reigning in her own right

de gf queen posts

**Queen's Bench** noun (circa 1809)
**:** a division of the English superior courts system that hears civil and criminal court cases — used during the reign of a queen
**Queen's Counsel** noun (circa 1860)
**:** a barrister selected to serve as counsel to the British crown — used during the reign of a queen
**queen·ship** \'kwēn-,ship\ noun (1536)
**1 :** the rank, dignity, or state of being a queen
**2 :** a regal quality like that of a queen
**queen·side** \-,sīd\ noun (1897)
**:** the side of a chessboard containing the file on which the queen sits at the beginning of the game
**queen–size** adjective (1959)
**1 :** having dimensions of approximately 60 inches by 80 inches (about 1.5 by 2.0 meters) — used of a bed; compare FULL-SIZE, KING-SIZE, TWIN-SIZE
**2 :** of a size that fits a queen-size bed (a queen-size sheet)
**queen substance** noun (1954)
**:** a pheromone secreted by queen bees that is consumed by worker bees and inhibits ovary development
**¹queer** \'kwir\ adjective [origin unknown] (1508)
**1 a :** WORTHLESS, COUNTERFEIT (queer money) **b :** QUESTIONABLE, SUSPICIOUS
**2 a :** differing in some odd way from what is usual or normal **b** (1) : ECCENTRIC, UNCONVENTIONAL (2) : mildly insane : TOUCHED **c :** absorbed or interested to an extreme or unreasonable degree : OBSESSED **d :** HOMOSEXUAL — usually used disparagingly
**3 :** not quite well
synonym see STRANGE
**— queer·ish** \-ish\ adjective
**— queer·ly** adverb
**— queer·ness** noun
**²queer** transitive verb (circa 1812)
**1 :** to spoil the effect or success of (queer one's plans)
**2 :** to put or get into an embarrassing or disadvantageous situation
**³queer** noun (circa 1812)
**:** one that is queer; especially : HOMOSEXUAL — usually used disparagingly
**¹quell** \'kwel\ transitive verb [Middle English, to kill, quell, from Old English cwellan to kill; akin to Old High German quellen to torture, kill, quāla torment, Lithuanian gelti to hurt] (13th century)
**1 :** to thoroughly overwhelm and reduce to submission or passivity (quell a riot)
**2 :** QUIET, PACIFY (quell fears)
**— quell·er** noun
**²quell** noun [Middle English, from quellen to kill] (15th century)
**1** obsolete : SLAUGHTER
**2** archaic : the power of quelling
**quench** \'kwench\ verb [Middle English, from Old English -cwencan; akin to Old English -cwincan to vanish, Old Frisian quinka] (12th century)
transitive verb

**1 a :** PUT OUT, EXTINGUISH **b :** to put out the light or fire of (quench glowing coals with water) **c :** to cool (as heated metal) suddenly by immersion (as in oil or water) **d :** to cause to lose heat or warmth (you have quenched the warmth of France toward you —Alfred Tennyson)
**2 a :** to bring (something immaterial) to an end typically by satisfying, damping, cooling, or decreasing (a rational understanding of the laws of nature can quench impossible desires —Lucius Garvin) (the praise that quenches all desire to read the book —T. S. Eliot) **b :** to terminate by or as if by destroying : ELIMINATE (the Commonwealth party quenched a whole generation of play-acting —Margery Bailey) (quench a rebellion) **c :** to relieve or satisfy with liquid (quenched his thirst at a wayside spring)
intransitive verb
**1 :** to become extinguished : COOL
**2 :** to become calm : SUBSIDE
**— quench·able** \'kwen-chə-bəl\ adjective
**— quench·er** noun
**— quench·less** \'kwench-ləs\ adjective
**que·nelle** \kə-'nel\ noun [French, from German Knödel dumpling, from Middle High German; akin to Old High German knoto knot — more at KNOT] (1845)
**:** a poached oval dumpling of pureed forcemeat (as of pike) often served in a cream sauce
**quer·ce·tin** \'kwər-sə-tən\ noun [International Scientific Vocabulary, from Latin quercetum oak forest, from quercus oak — more at FIR] (1857)
**:** a yellow crystalline pigment $C_{15}H_{10}O_7$ occurring usually in the form of glycosides in various plants
**quer·cit·ron** \'kwər-,si-trən, ,kwər-'\ noun [blend of New Latin Quercus and International Scientific Vocabulary citron] (1794)
**1 :** a large timber oak (Quercus velutina) of the eastern and central U.S.
**2 :** the bark of the quercitron that is rich in tannin and a dye containing quercetin; also : the dye
**que·rist** \'kwir-əst, 'kwer-\ noun [Latin quaerere to ask] (1633)
**:** one who inquires
**quern** \'kwərn\ noun [Middle English, from Old English cweorn; akin to Old High German quirn quirn, Old Church Slavonic žrŭny] (before 12th century)
**:** a primitive hand mill for grinding grain
**quer·u·lous** \'kwer-yə-ləs, -ə-ləs also 'kwir-\ adjective [Middle English querelose, from Latin querulus, from queri to complain] (15th century)
**1 :** habitually complaining
**2 :** FRETFUL, WHINING (a querulous voice)
**— quer·u·lous·ly** adverb
**— quer·u·lous·ness** noun
**¹que·ry** \'kwir-ē, 'kwer-\ noun, plural **queries** [alteration of earlier quere, from Latin quaere, imperative of quaerere to ask] (circa 1635)
**1 :** QUESTION, INQUIRY
**2 :** a question in the mind : DOUBT
**3 :** QUESTION MARK
**²query** transitive verb **que·ried; que·ry·ing** (1654)
**1 :** to ask questions of especially with a desire for authoritative information
**2 :** to ask questions about especially in order to resolve a doubt
**3 :** to put as a question
**4 :** to mark with a query
synonym see ASK
**— que·ri·er** noun
**que·sa·dil·la** \,kā-sə-'dē-ə also -'thē- or -'thēl-yə\ noun [Mexican Spanish, from Spanish, cheese pastry, diminutive of quesada, from queso cheese, from Latin caseus] (1944)

: a wheat tortilla filled with a savory mixture, folded, fried in deep fat, and topped with cheese

**¹quest** \'kwest\ *noun* [Middle English, search, pursuit, investigation, inquest, from Middle French *queste* search, pursuit, from (assumed) Vulgar Latin *quaesta,* from Latin, feminine of *quaestus,* past participle of *quaerere*] (14th century)
**1 a :** a jury of inquest **b :** INVESTIGATION
**2 :** an act or instance of seeking: **a :** PURSUIT, SEARCH **b :** a chivalrous enterprise in medieval romance usually involving an adventurous journey
**3** *obsolete* **:** a person or group of persons who search or make inquiry

**²quest** (14th century)
*intransitive verb*
**1** *of a dog* **a :** to search a trail **b :** BAY
**2 :** to go on a quest
*transitive verb*
**1 :** to search for
**2 :** to ask for
**— quest·er** *noun*

**¹ques·tion** \'kwes-chən, 'kwesh-\ *noun* [Middle English, from Middle French, from Latin *quaestion-, quaestio,* from *quaerere* to seek, ask] (14th century)
**1 a** (1) **:** an interrogative expression often used to test knowledge (2) **:** an interrogative sentence or clause **b :** a subject or aspect in dispute or open for discussion **:** ISSUE; *broadly* **:** PROBLEM, MATTER **c** (1) **:** a subject or point of debate or a proposition to be voted on in a meeting (2) **:** the bringing of such to a vote **d :** the specific point at issue
**2 a :** an act or instance of asking **:** INQUIRY **b :** INTERROGATION; *also* **:** a judicial or official investigation **c :** torture as part of an examination **d** (1) **:** OBJECTION (true beyond *question*) (2) **:** room for doubt or objection (little *question* of his skill) (3) **:** CHANCE, POSSIBILITY (no *question* of escape)

**²question** (15th century)
*transitive verb*
**1 :** to ask a question of or about
**2 :** to interrogate intensively **:** CROSS-EXAMINE
**3 a :** DOUBT, DISPUTE **b :** to subject to analysis **:** EXAMINE
*intransitive verb*
**:** to ask questions **:** INQUIRE
**synonym** see ASK
**— ques·tion·er** *noun*

**ques·tion·able** \'kwes-chə-nə-bəl, 'kwesh-, *in rapid speech* 'kwesh-nə-\ *adjective* (1590)
**1** *obsolete* **:** inviting inquiry
**2** *obsolete* **:** liable to judicial inquiry or action
**3 :** affording reason for being doubted, questioned, or challenged **:** not certain or exact **:** PROBLEMATIC (milk of *questionable* purity) (a *questionable* decision)
**4 :** attended by well-grounded suspicions of being immoral, crude, false, or unsound **:** DUBIOUS (*questionable* motives)
**synonym** see DOUBTFUL
**— ques·tion·able·ness** *noun*
**— ques·tion·ably** \-blē\ *adverb*

**ques·tion·ary** \'kwes-chə-,ner-ē, 'kwesh-\ *noun, plural* **-ar·ies** (1887)
**:** QUESTIONNAIRE

**ques·tion·less** \'kwes-chən-ləs, 'kwesh-\ *adjective* (1532)
**1 :** INDUBITABLE, UNQUESTIONABLE
**2 :** UNQUESTIONING

**question mark** *noun* (1869)
**1 :** something unknown, unknowable, or uncertain
**2 :** a mark ? used in writing and printing at the conclusion of a sentence to indicate a direct question

**ques·tion·naire** \,kwes-chə-'nar, -'ner, ,kwesh-\ *noun* [French, from *questionner* to question, from Middle French, from *question,* noun] (1899)

**1 :** a set of questions for obtaining statistically useful or personal information from individuals
**2 :** a written or printed questionnaire often with spaces for answers
**3 :** a survey made by the use of a questionnaire

**question time** *noun* (1885)
**:** a period in a session of a British parliamentary body during which members may put questions to ministers on matters concerning their departments

**ques·tor** \'kwes-tər\ *variant of* QUAESTOR

**quet·zal** \ket-'säl, -'sal\ *noun, plural* **quet·zals** *or* **quet·za·les** \-'sä-(,)läs, -'sa-\ [American Spanish, from Nahuatl *quetzalli* tail coverts of the quetzal] (1827)
**1 :** a Central American trogon (*Pharomachrus mocinno*) that has brilliant green plumage above, a red breast, and in the male long upper tail coverts
**2** *plural* **quetzales** — see MONEY table

**Quet·zal·co·a·tl** \,kwet-səl-kə-'wä-t°l, ,ket-, -səl-'kwä-; ket-,säl-, -,sal-\ *noun* [Nahuatl *Quetzalcōātl*]
**:** a chief Toltec and Aztec god identified with the wind and air and represented by a feathered serpent

quetzal 1

**¹queue** \'kyü\ *noun* [French, literally, tail, from Latin *cauda, coda*] (1748)
**1 :** a braid of hair usually worn hanging at the back of the head
**2 :** a waiting line especially of persons or vehicles
**3 a :** a sequence of messages or jobs held in auxiliary storage awaiting transmission or processing **b :** a data structure that consists of a list of records such that records are added at one end and removed from the other

**²queue** *verb* **queued; queu·ing** *or* **queue·ing** (1777)
*transitive verb*
**:** to arrange or form in a queue
*intransitive verb*
**:** to line up or wait in a queue — often used with *up*
**— queu·er** *noun*

**¹quib·ble** \'kwi-bəl\ *verb* **quib·bled; quib·bling** \-b(ə-)liŋ\ (1656)
*intransitive verb*
**1 :** to evade the point of an argument by caviling about words
**2 a :** CAVIL, CARP **b :** BICKER
*transitive verb*
**:** to subject to quibbles
**— quib·bler** \-b(ə-)lər\ *noun*

**²quibble** *noun* [probably diminutive of obsolete *quib* quibble] (1670)
**1 :** an evasion of or shift from the point
**2 :** a minor objection or criticism

**quiche** \'kēsh\ *noun* [French, from French dialect (Lorraine)] (1941)
**:** an unsweetened custard pie usually having a savory filling (as spinach, mushrooms, or ham)

**quiche lor·raine** \-lə-'rän, -lò-\ *noun, often L capitalized* [French, quiche of Lorraine] (1941)
**:** a quiche containing cheese and bacon bits

**¹quick** \'kwik\ *adjective* [Middle English *quik,* from Old English *cwic;* akin to Old Norse *kvikr* living, Latin *vivus* living, *vivere* to live, Greek *bios, zōē* life] (before 12th century)
**1 :** not dead **:** LIVING, ALIVE
**2 :** acting or capable of acting with speed: as **a** (1) **:** fast in understanding, thinking, or learning **:** mentally agile (a *quick* wit) (*quick*

thinking) (2) **:** reacting to stimuli with speed and keen sensitivity (3) **:** aroused immediately and intensely (*quick* tempers) **b** (1) **:** fast in development or occurrence (a *quick* succession of events) (2) **:** done or taking place with rapidity (gave them a *quick* look) **c :** marked by speed, readiness, or promptness of physical movement (walked with *quick* steps) **d :** inclined to hastiness (as in action or response) (*quick* to criticize) **e :** capable of being easily and speedily prepared (a *quick* and tasty dinner)
**3** *archaic* **a :** not stagnant **:** RUNNING, FLOWING **b :** MOVING, SHIFTING (*quick* mud)
**4** *archaic* **:** FIERY, GLOWING
**5** *obsolete* **a :** PUNGENT **b :** CAUSTIC
**6** *archaic* **:** PREGNANT
**7 :** having a sharp angle (a *quick* turn in the road) ☆
**— quick·ly** *adverb*
**— quick·ness** *noun*

**²quick** *noun* (before 12th century)
**1** *quick plural* **:** living beings
**2** [probably of Scandinavian origin; akin to Old Norse *kvika* sensitive flesh, from *kvikr* living] **a :** a painfully sensitive spot or area of flesh (as that underlying a fingernail or toenail) **b :** the inmost sensibilities (hurt to the *quick* by the remark) **c :** the very center of something **:** HEART
**3** *archaic* **:** LIFE 11

**³quick** *adverb* (14th century)
**:** in a quick manner

**quick assets** *noun plural* (1891)
**:** cash, accounts receivable, and other current assets excluding inventories

**quick bread** *noun* (1918)
**:** bread made with a leavening agent (as baking powder or baking soda) that permits immediate baking of the dough or batter mixture

**quick·en** \'kwi-kən\ *verb* **quick·ened; quick·en·ing** \'kwi-kə-niŋ, 'kwik-niŋ\ (14th century)
*transitive verb*
**1 a :** to make alive **:** REVIVE **b :** to cause to be enlivened **:** STIMULATE
**2** *archaic* **a :** KINDLE **b :** to cause to burn more intensely
**3 :** to make more rapid **:** HASTEN, ACCELERATE (*quickened* her steps)
**4 a :** to make (a curve) sharper **b :** to make (a slope) steeper
*intransitive verb*
**1 :** to quicken something
**2 :** to come to life; *especially* **:** to enter into a phase of active growth and development (seeds *quickening* in the soil)
**3 :** to reach the stage of gestation at which fetal motion is felt

---

☆ **SYNONYMS**
**Quick, prompt, ready, apt** mean able to respond without delay or hesitation or indicative of such ability. QUICK stresses instancy of response and is likely to connote native rather than acquired power (*quick* reflexes) (a keen *quick* mind). PROMPT is more likely to connote training and discipline that fits one for instant response (*prompt* emergency medical care). READY suggests facility or fluency in response (backed by a pair of *ready* assistants). APT stresses the possession of qualities (as intelligence, a particular talent, or a strong bent) that makes quick effective response possible (an *apt* student) (her answer was *apt* and to the point). See in addition FAST.

---

\ə\ abut \ᵊ\ kitten \ər\ further \a\ ash \ā\ ace
\ä\ mop, mar \aú\ out \ch\ chin \e\ bet \ē\ easy
\g\ go \i\ hit \ī\ ice \j\ job \ŋ\ sing \ō\ go
\ò\ law \òi\ boy \th\ thin \th\ the \ü\ loot \ù\ foot
\y\ yet \zh\ vision *see also* Guide to Pronunciation

**4 :** to shine more brightly ⟨watched the dawn *quickening* in the east⟩
**5 :** to become more rapid ⟨her pulse *quickened* at the sight⟩ ☆
— **quick·en·er** \'kwi-kə-nər, 'kwik-nər\ *noun*

**quick fix** *noun* (1970)
**:** an expedient usually temporary or inadequate solution to a problem

**quick–freeze** \'kwik-'frēz\ *transitive verb* **-froze** \-'frōz\; **-fro·zen** \-'frō-z°n\; **-freez·ing** (1930)
**:** to freeze (food) for preservation so rapidly that ice crystals formed are too small to rupture the cells and the natural juices and flavor are preserved

**quick·ie** \'kwi-kē\ *noun, often attributive* (circa 1926)
**:** something done or made in a hurry: as **a :** a quickly and usually cheaply produced work (as a motion picture or book) **b :** a hastily performed act of sexual intercourse

**quick kick** *noun* (circa 1940)
**:** a punt in football on first, second, or third down made from a running or passing formation and designed to take the opposing team by surprise

**quick·lime** \'kwik-,līm\ *noun* (14th century)
**:** ¹LIME 2a

**quick·sand** \'kwik-,sand\ *noun* (14th century)
**1 :** sand readily yielding to pressure; *especially* **:** a deep mass of loose sand mixed with water into which heavy objects readily sink
**2 :** something that entraps or frustrates

**quick·set** \-,set\ *noun* (15th century)
*chiefly British* **:** plant cuttings set in the ground to grow especially in a hedgerow; *also* **:** a hedge or thicket especially of hawthorn grown from quickset

**¹quick·sil·ver** \-,sil-vər\ *noun* (before 12th century)
**:** MERCURY 2a ◆

**²quicksilver** *adjective* (1655)
**:** resembling or suggestive of quicksilver; *especially* **:** MERCURIAL 3

**quick·step** \-,step\ *noun* (circa 1811)
**:** a spirited march tune usually accompanying a march in quick time

**quick–tem·pered** \-'tem-pərd\ *adjective* (1830)
**:** easily angered **:** IRASCIBLE

**quick time** *noun* (circa 1802)
**:** a rate of marching in which 120 steps each 30 inches in length are taken in one minute

**quick–wit·ted** \'kwik-'wi-təd\ *adjective* (1530)
**:** quick in perception and understanding **:** mentally alert
*synonym* see INTELLIGENT
— **quick–wit·ted·ly** *adverb*
— **quick–wit·ted·ness** *noun*

**¹quid** \'kwid\ *noun, plural* **quid** *also* **quids** [origin unknown] (1688)
*British* **:** a pound sterling

**²quid** *noun* [English dialect, cud, from Middle English *quide*, from Old English *cwidu, cwudu* — more at CUD] (circa 1727)
**:** a cut or wad of something chewable

**quid·di·ty** \'kwi-də-tē\ *noun, plural* **-ties** [Middle English *quidite*, from Medieval Latin *quidditat-, quidditas* essence, from Latin *quid* what, neuter of *quis* who — more at WHO] (14th century)
**1 :** whatever makes something the type that it is **:** ESSENCE
**2 a :** a trifling point **:** QUIBBLE **b :** CROTCHET, ECCENTRICITY

**quid·nunc** \'kwid-,nəŋk\ *noun* [Latin *quid nunc* what now?] (1709)
**:** a person who seeks to know all the latest news or gossip **:** BUSYBODY

**quid pro quo** \,kwid-,prō-'kwō\ *noun* [New Latin, something for something] (1591)
**:** something given or received for something else; *also* **:** a deal arranging a quid pro quo

**qui·es·cence** \kwī-'e-s°n(t)s, kwē-\ *noun* (circa 1631)
**:** the quality or state of being quiescent

**qui·es·cent** \-s°nt\ *adjective* [Latin *quiescent-, quiescens*, present participle of *quiescere* to become quiet, rest, from *quies*] (1605)
**1 :** marked by inactivity or repose **:** tranquilly at rest
**2 :** causing no trouble or symptoms ⟨*quiescent* gallstones⟩
*synonym* see LATENT
— **qui·es·cent·ly** *adverb*

**¹qui·et** \'kwī-ət\ *noun* [Middle English, from Latin *quiet-, quies* rest, quiet — more at WHILE] (14th century)
**:** the quality or state of being quiet **:** TRANQUILLITY
— **on the quiet :** in a secretive manner **:** in secret

**²quiet** *adjective* [Middle English, from Middle French, from Latin *quietus*, from past participle of *quiescere*] (14th century)
**1 a :** marked by little or no motion or activity **:** CALM ⟨a *quiet* sea⟩ **b :** GENTLE, EASYGOING ⟨a *quiet* temperament⟩ **c :** not interfered with ⟨*quiet* reading⟩ **d :** enjoyed in peace and relaxation ⟨a *quiet* cup of tea⟩
**2 a :** free from noise or uproar **:** STILL **b :** UNOBTRUSIVE, CONSERVATIVE ⟨*quiet* clothes⟩
**3 :** SECLUDED ⟨a *quiet* nook⟩
— **qui·et·ly** *adverb*
— **qui·et·ness** *noun*

**³quiet** *adverb* (1573)
**:** in a quiet manner ⟨a *quiet*-running engine⟩

**⁴quiet** *verb* [Middle English, from Late Latin *quietare* to set free, to calm, from Latin *quietus*] (14th century)
*transitive verb*
**1 :** to cause to be quiet **:** CALM
**2 :** to make secure by freeing from dispute or question ⟨*quiet* title to a property⟩
*intransitive verb*
**:** to become quiet — usually used with *down*
— **qui·et·er** *noun*

**qui·et·en** \'kwī-ə-t°n\ *verb* **qui·et·ened; qui·et·en·ing** \'kwī-ət-niŋ, 'kwī-ə-t°n-iŋ\ (circa 1828)
*chiefly British* **:** QUIET

**qui·et·ism** \'kwī-ə-,ti-zəm\ *noun* (1687)
**1 a :** a system of religious mysticism teaching that perfection and spiritual peace are attained by annihilation of the will and passive absorption in contemplation of God and divine things **b :** a passive withdrawn attitude or policy toward the world or worldly affairs
**2 :** a state of calmness or passivity
— **qui·et·ist** \-tist\ *adjective or noun*
— **qui·et·ist·ic** \,kwī-ə-'tis-tik\ *adjective*

**qui·etude** \'kwī-ə-,tüd, -,tyüd\ *noun* [Middle French, from Late Latin *quietudo*, from Latin *quietus*] (1597)
**:** a quiet state **:** REPOSE

**qui·etus** \kwī-'ē-təs, -'ā-\ *noun* [Middle English *quietus est*, from Medieval Latin, he is quit, formula of discharge from obligation] (1540)
**1 :** final settlement (as of a debt)
**2 :** removal from activity; *especially* **:** DEATH
**3 :** something that quiets or represses

**quiff** \'kwif\ *noun* [origin unknown] (circa 1890)
*British* **:** a prominent forelock

**¹quill** \'kwil\ *noun* [Middle English *quil* hollow reed, bobbin; akin to Middle High German *kil* large feather] (15th century)
**1 a (1) :** a bobbin, spool, or spindle on which filling yarn is wound **(2) :** a hollow shaft often surrounding another shaft and used in various mechanical devices **b :** a roll of dried bark ⟨cinnamon *quills*⟩
**2 a (1) :** the hollow horny shaft of a feather — see FEATHER illustration **(2) :** FEATHER; *especially* **:** one of the large stiff feathers of the wing or tail **b :** one of the hollow sharp spines of a porcupine or hedgehog **c :** ³PEN 3

**3 :** something made from or resembling the quill of a feather; *especially* **:** a pen for writing
**4 :** a float for a fishing line

**²quill** *transitive verb* (1783)
**1 :** to pierce with quills
**2 a :** to wind (thread or yarn) on a quill **b :** to make a series of small rounded ridges in (cloth)

**quill·back** \'kwil-,bak\ *noun, plural* **quillback** *or* **quillbacks** (1882)
**:** any of several suckers; *especially* **:** a small fish (*Carpiodes cyprinus*) of central and eastern North America that has the first ray of the dorsal fin much elongated

**quill·work** \-,wərk\ *noun* (1843)
**:** ornamental work in porcupine or bird quills

**¹quilt** \'kwilt\ *noun* [Middle English *quilte* mattress, quilt, from Old French *cuilte*, from Latin *culcita* mattress] (14th century)
**1 :** a bed coverlet of two layers of cloth filled with padding (as down or batting) held in place by ties or stitched designs
**2 :** something that is quilted or resembles a quilt

**²quilt** (1555)
*transitive verb*
**1 a :** to fill, pad, or line like a quilt **b (1) :** to stitch, sew, or cover with lines or patterns like those used in quilts **(2) :** to stitch (designs) through layers of cloth **c :** to fasten between two pieces of material
**2 :** to stitch or sew in layers with padding in between
*intransitive verb*
**1 :** to make quilts
**2 :** to do quilted work
— **quilt·er** *noun*

**quilt·ing** *noun* (1609)
**1 :** material that is quilted or used for making quilts
**2 :** the process of quilting

**quin·a·crine** \'kwi-nə-,krēn\ *noun* [*quin*ine + *acridine*] (circa 1934)
**:** an antimalarial drug derived from acridine and used especially in the form of its dihydrochloride $C_{23}H_{30}ClN_3O \cdot 2HCl \cdot 2H_2O$

**quince** \'kwin(t)s\ *noun* [Middle English *quynce* quinces, plural of *coyn, quyn* quince,

---

☆ **SYNONYMS**
**Quicken, animate, enliven, vivify**
mean to make alive or lively. QUICKEN stresses a sudden renewal of life or activity especially in something inert ⟨the arrival of spring *quickens* the earth⟩. ANIMATE emphasizes the imparting of motion or vitality to what is or might be mechanical or artificial ⟨happiness *animated* his conversation⟩. ENLIVEN suggests a stimulus that arouses from dullness or torpidity ⟨*enlivened* her lectures with humorous anecdotes⟩. VIVIFY implies a freshening or energizing through renewal of vitality ⟨new blood needed to *vivify* the dying club⟩. See in addition PROVOKE.

---

◇ **WORD HISTORY**
**quicksilver** The silver-colored metal known as mercury is, unlike other metallic elements, liquid at room temperature. Its ready fluidity has long suggested a semblance of life. Fittingly, the ancient Romans called the metal *argentum vivum* "living silver." Our English word is a loan translation of the Latin phrase. First attested in the Old English form *cwicseolfor*, *quicksilver* represents a use of *quick* in its original sense "alive, living." The chemical symbol for mercury, Hg, and the less common name *hydrargyrum*, of which the symbol is an abbreviation, are ultimately from Greek *hydrargyros*, literally, "watery silver."

from Middle French *coin,* from Latin *cotoneum,* alteration *cydonium,* from Greek *kydōnion*] (14th century)
**1 :** the fruit of a central Asian tree (*Cydonia oblonga*) of the rose family that resembles a hard-fleshed yellow apple and is used especially in preserves
**2 :** a tree that bears quinces

quince 1

**quin·cen·te·na·ry** \ˌkwin-sen-ˈte-nə-rē, -ˈsen-tᵊn-,er-ē, *especially British* -sen-ˈtē-nə-rē\ *noun* [Latin *quinque* five + English *centenary*] (1879)
**:** a 500th anniversary or its celebration
**— quincentenary** *adjective*

**quin·cen·ten·ni·al** \-sen-ˈte-nē-əl\ *noun* [Latin *quinque* five + English *centennial*] (1884)
**:** QUINCENTENARY
**— quincentennial** *adjective*

**quin·cunx** \ˈkwin-ˌkəŋ(k)s\ *noun* [Latin *quincunc-, quincunx,* literally, five twelfths, from *quinque* five + *uncia* twelfth part — more at FIVE, OUNCE] (1658)
**:** an arrangement of five things in a square or rectangle with one at each corner and one in the middle
**— quin·cun·cial** \kwin-ˈkən(t)-shəl\ *or* **quin·cunx·ial** \-ˈkəŋk-sē-əl\ *adjective*

**quin·de·cil·lion** \ˌkwin-di-ˈsil-yən\ *noun, often attributive* [Latin *quindecim* fifteen (from *quinque* five + *decem* ten) + English *-illion* (as in *million*) — more at TEN] (1903)
**—** see NUMBER table

**quin·i·dine** \ˈkwi-nə-ˌdēn\ *noun* [International Scientific Vocabulary, from *quinine*] (1836)
**:** an alkaloid $C_{20}H_{24}N_2O_2$ that is stereoisomeric with quinine and is used in treating cardiac rhythm irregularities

**qui·nie·la** \kwin-ˈye-lə\ *or* **qui·nel·la** \kwi-ˈne-lə\ *noun* [American Spanish *quiniela,* a game of chance resembling a lottery] (1905)
**:** a bet in which the bettor picks the first and second place finishers but need not designate their order of finish in order to win — compare PERFECTA

**qui·nine** \ˈkwī-ˌnīn *also* ˈkwi- *or* kwi-ˈnīn *or* ki-ˈnēn *or* kwi-ˈnēn\ *noun* [Spanish *quina* cinchona, from Quechua *kina* bark] (1826)
**1 :** a bitter crystalline alkaloid $C_{20}H_{24}N_2O_2$ from cinchona bark used in medicine
**2 :** a salt of quinine used especially as an antipyretic, antimalarial, and bitter tonic

**quinine water** *noun* (1953)
**:** TONIC WATER

**qui·noa** \ˈkēn-ˌwä\ *noun* [Spanish, from Quechua *kinua*] (1625)
**:** a pigweed (*Chenopodium quinoa*) of the high Andes whose seeds are ground and widely used as food in Peru

**quin·o·line** \ˈkwi-nᵊl-ˌēn\ *noun* [International Scientific Vocabulary *quinine* + ³*-ol* + ²*-ine*] (1845)
**1 :** a pungent oily nitrogenous base $C_9H_7N$ obtained usually by distillation of coal tar or by synthesis from aniline that is the parent compound of many alkaloids, drugs, and dyes
**2 :** a derivative of quinoline

**qui·none** \kwi-ˈnōn, ˈkwi-ˌ\ *noun* [International Scientific Vocabulary *quinine* + *-one*] (1853)
**1 :** either of two isomeric cyclic crystalline compounds $C_6H_4O_2$ that are di-keto derivatives of dihydro-benzene
**2 :** any of various usually yellow, orange, or red quinonoid compounds including several that are biologically important as coenzymes, hydrogen acceptors, or vitamins

**qui·no·noid** \kwi-ˈnō-ˌnóid, ˈkwi-nə-\ *or* **quin·oid** \ˈkwi-ˌnóid\ *adjective* (1878)

**:** resembling quinone especially in having a benzene nucleus containing two double bonds within the nucleus

**quin·quen·ni·al** \kwin-ˈkwe-nē-əl, kwiŋ-\ *adjective* (15th century)
**1 :** consisting of or lasting for five years
**2 :** occurring or being done every five years
**— quinquennial** *noun*
**— quin·quen·ni·al·ly** \-nē-ə-lē\ *adverb*

**quin·quen·ni·um** \-nē-əm\ *noun, plural* **-ni·ums** *or* **-nia** \-nē-ə\ [Latin, from *quinque* five + *annus* year — more at FIVE, ANNUAL] (1621)
**:** a period of five years

**quin·sy** \ˈkwin-zē\ *noun* [Middle English *quinesie,* from Middle French *quinancie,* from Late Latin *cynanche,* from Greek *kynanchē,* from *kyn-, kyōn* dog + *anchein* to strangle — more at HOUND, ANGER] (14th century)
**:** an abscess in the tissue around a tonsil usually resulting from bacterial infection and often accompanied by pain and fever

**quint** \ˈkwint\ *noun* (1935)
**:** QUINTUPLET

**quin·ta** \ˈkin-tə, ˈkēn-\ *noun* [Spanish & Portuguese, quinta, farm rented at one fifth of its income, from Latin, feminine of *quintus* fifth] (1754)
**:** a country villa or estate especially in Portugal or Latin America

**quin·tain** \ˈkwin-tᵊn\ *noun* [Middle English *quintaine,* from Middle French, perhaps from Latin *quintana* street in a Roman camp separating the fifth maniple from the sixth where a market was held, from feminine of *quintanus* fifth in rank, from *quintus* fifth] (15th century)
**:** an object to be tilted at; *especially* **:** a post with a revolving crosspiece that has a target at one end and a sandbag at the other end

**quin·tal** \ˈkwin-tᵊl, ˈkan-\ *noun* [Middle English, from Middle French, from Medieval Latin *quintale,* from Arabic *qinṭār,* from Late Greek *kentēnarion,* from Late Latin *centenarium,* from Latin, neuter of *centenarius* consisting of a hundred — more at CENTENARY] (15th century)
**1 :** HUNDREDWEIGHT
**2 :** a unit of weight equal to 100 kilograms (about 220 pounds)

**quin·tes·sence** \kwin-ˈte-sᵊn(t)s\ *noun* [Middle English, from Middle French *quinte essence,* from Medieval Latin *quinta essentia,* literally, fifth essence] (15th century)
**1 :** the fifth and highest element in ancient and medieval philosophy that permeates all nature and is the substance composing the celestial bodies
**2 :** the essence of a thing in its purest and most concentrated form
**3 :** the most typical example or representative
◇
**— quin·tes·sen·tial** \ˌkwin-tə-ˈsen(t)-shəl\ *adjective*
**— quin·tes·sen·tial·ly** *adverb*

**quin·tet** *also* **quin·tette** \kwin-ˈtet\ *noun* [*quintet* from Italian *quintetto,* from *quinto* fifth, from Latin *quintus; quintette* from French, from Italian *quintetto*] (1811)
**1 :** a musical composition or movement for five instruments or voices
**2 :** a group or set of five: as **a :** the performers of a quintet **b :** a basketball team

¹**quin·tic** \ˈkwin-tik\ *adjective* [Latin *quintus* fifth] (1853)
**:** of the fifth degree

²**quintic** *noun* (1856)
**:** a polynomial or a polynomial equation of the fifth degree

**quin·tile** \ˈkwin-ˌtīl\ *noun* [Latin *quintus* + English ²*-ile*] (circa 1928)
**:** any of the four values that divide the items of a frequency distribution into five classes with each containing one fifth of the total population; *also* **:** any one of the five classes

**quin·til·lion** \kwin-ˈtil-yən\ *noun* [Latin *quintus* + English *-illion* (as in *million*)] (1674)

**—** see NUMBER table
**— quintillion** *adjective*
**— quin·til·lionth** \-yən(t)th\ *adjective or noun*

¹**quin·tu·ple** \kwin-ˈtü-pəl, -ˈtyü-, -ˈtə-; ˈkwin-tə-\ *adjective* [Middle French, from Medieval Latin *quintuplus,* from Latin *quintus* fifth + *-plus* -fold; akin to Latin *quinque* five — more at FIVE, -FOLD] (1570)
**1 :** being five times as great or as many
**2 :** having five units or members
**3 :** marked by five beats per measure ⟨*quintuple* meter⟩
**— quintuple** *noun*

²**quintuple** *verb* **quin·tu·pled; quin·tu·pling** \-p(ə-)liŋ\ (1639)
*transitive verb*
**:** to make five times as great or as many
*intransitive verb*
**:** to become five times as much or as numerous

**quin·tu·plet** \kwin-ˈtə-plət, -ˈtü-, -ˈtyü-; ˈkwin-tə-\ *noun* (1873)
**1 :** a combination of five of a kind
**2 :** one of five offspring born at one birth

¹**quin·tu·pli·cate** \kwin-ˈtü-pli-kət, -ˈtyü-\ *adjective* [Medieval Latin *quintuplicatus,* past participle of *quintuplicare* to quintuple, from *quintuplus* quintuple] (1656)
**1 :** consisting of or existing in five corresponding or identical parts or examples ⟨*quintuplicate* invoices⟩
**2 :** being the fifth of five things exactly alike ⟨file the *quintuplicate* copy⟩

²**quintuplicate** *noun* (1851)
**1 :** one of five things exactly alike; *specifically* **:** one of five identical copies
**2 :** five copies all alike — used with *in* ⟨typed in *quintuplicate*⟩

³**quin·tu·pli·cate** \-plə-ˌkāt\ *transitive verb* **-cat·ed; -cat·ing** (circa 1890)
**1 :** to make quintuple or fivefold
**2 :** to prepare in quintuplicate

¹**quip** \ˈkwip\ *noun* [earlier *quippy,* perhaps from Latin *quippe* indeed, to be sure (often ironic), from *quid* what — more at QUIDDITY] (1532)
**1 a :** a clever usually taunting remark **:** GIBE **b :** a witty or funny observation or response usually made on the spur of the moment

◇ WORD HISTORY

**quintessence** Before the advent of modern science it was thought by those who speculated about nature's secrets that there were four elements: earth, air, fire, and water. These combined in varying proportions to form all the different substances found on Earth. The stars and planets, however, seemed to be composed of an altogether different, less substantial element. This fifth substance or *quintessence* (from Medieval Latin *quinta essentia,* itself a loan translation of Greek *pemptē ouisa* "fifth substance" or "fifth essence") was believed to permeate all space beyond the earth's atmosphere. The quintessence was conceived by some as being composed of pure and invisible light or fire. Alchemists believed that the quintessence was innate in all matter, and so they labored in vain to extract it from other materials. The hope was that the quintessence might provide a panacea for disease or even for mortality itself. Though discarded long ago, this alchemistic belief gave rise to the customary meaning of the word today: "the essence of a thing in its purest and most concentrated form."

**2 :** QUIBBLE, EQUIVOCATION
**3 :** something strange, droll, curious, or eccentric **:** ODDITY

**²quip** *verb* **quipped; quip·ping** (1579)
*intransitive verb*
**:** to make quips **:** GIBE
*transitive verb*
**:** to jest or gibe at
— **quip·per** \'kwi-pər\ *noun*

**quip·ster** \'kwip-stər\ *noun* (1876)
**:** one who is given to quipping

**qui·pu** \'kē-(ˌ)pü\ *noun* [Spanish *quipo*, from Quechua *khipu*] (1704)
**:** a device made of a main cord with smaller varicolored cords attached and knotted and used by the ancient Peruvians (as for calculating)

**¹quire** \'kwīr\ *noun* [Middle English *quair* four sheets of paper folded once, collection of sheets, from Middle French *quaer*, from (assumed) Vulgar Latin *quaternum* set of four, from Latin *quaterni* four each, set of four — more at QUATERNION] (15th century)
**:** a collection of 24 or sometimes 25 sheets of paper of the same size and quality **:** one twentieth of a ream

**²quire** *variant of* CHOIR

**Qui·ri·nus** \kwə-'rī-nəs, -'rē-\ *noun* [Latin]
**:** an early state god of the Romans later identified with Romulus

**¹quirk** \'kwərk\ *noun* [origin unknown] (1565)
**1 a :** an abrupt twist or curve **b :** a peculiar trait **:** IDIOSYNCRASY **c :** ACCIDENT, VAGARY ⟨a *quirk* of fate⟩
**2 :** a groove separating a bead or other molding from adjoining members
— **quirk·i·ly** \'kwər-kə-lē\ *adverb*
— **quirk·i·ness** \-kē-nəs\ *noun*
— **quirk·ish** \'kwər-kish\ *adjective*
— **quirky** \-kē\ *adjective*

**²quirk** *verb* (1596)
**:** CURVE, TWIST ⟨*quirked* his eyebrows⟩

**¹quirt** \'kwərt\ *noun* [Mexican Spanish *cuarta*] (1845)
**:** a riding whip with a short handle and a rawhide lash

**²quirt** *transitive verb* (1887)
**:** to strike or drive with a quirt

**quis·ling** \'kwiz-liŋ\ *noun, often attributive* [Vidkun *Quisling* (died 1945) Norwegian politician who collaborated with the Nazis] (1940)
**:** TRAITOR 2, COLLABORATOR
— **quis·ling·ism** \-liŋ-ˌi-zəm\ *noun*

**¹quit** \'kwit\ *adjective* [Middle English *quite, quit*, from Old French *quite*] (13th century)
**:** released from obligation, charge, or penalty; *especially* **:** FREE

**²quit** *verb* **quit** *also* **quit·ted; quit·ting** [Middle English *quiten, quitten*, from Middle French *quiter, quitter*, from Old French, from *quite* free of, released, literally, at rest, from Latin *quietus* quiet, at rest] (13th century)
*transitive verb*
**1 :** to make full payment of **:** PAY UP ⟨*quit* a debt⟩
**2 :** to set free **:** RELIEVE, RELEASE ⟨*quit* oneself of fear⟩
**3 :** CONDUCT, ACQUIT ⟨the youths *quit* themselves like men⟩
**4 a :** to depart from or out of **b :** to leave the company of **c :** GIVE UP 1, 2 ⟨*quit* a job⟩ ⟨*quit* smoking⟩
*intransitive verb*
**1 :** to cease normal, expected, or necessary action
**2 :** to give up employment
**3 :** to admit defeat **:** GIVE UP
**synonym** see STOP

**³quit** *noun* (circa 1923)
**:** the act or an instance of quitting a job

**quitch** \'kwich\ *noun* [(assumed) Middle English *quicche*, from Old English *cwice*; akin to Old High German *quecca* couch grass] (before 12th century)
**:** QUACK GRASS

**quit·claim** \'kwit-ˌklām\ *transitive verb* (14th century)
**:** to release or relinquish a legal claim to; *especially* **:** to release a claim to or convey by a quitclaim deed
— **quitclaim** *noun*

**quitclaim deed** *noun* (1756)
**:** a legal instrument used to release one person's right, title, or interest to another without providing a guarantee or warranty of title

**quite** \'kwīt\ *adverb* [Middle English, from *quite*, adjective, quit] (14th century)
**1 :** WHOLLY, COMPLETELY ⟨not *quite* finished⟩
**2 :** to an extreme **:** POSITIVELY ⟨*quite* sure⟩ — often used as an intensifier with *a* ⟨*quite* a swell guy⟩ ⟨*quite* a beauty⟩
**3 :** to a considerable extent **:** RATHER ⟨*quite* near⟩
*usage* see PLENTY
— **quite a bit :** a considerable amount
— **quite a few :** MANY

**quit·rent** \'kwit-ˌrent\ *noun* (15th century)
**:** a fixed rent payable to a feudal superior in commutation of services; *specifically* **:** a fixed rent due from a socage tenant

**quits** \'kwits\ *adjective* [Middle English, quit, probably from Medieval Latin *quittus*, alteration of Latin *quietus* at rest] (15th century)
**:** being on even terms by repayment or requital

**quit·tance** \'kwi-t°n(t)s\ *noun* (14th century)
**1 a :** discharge from a debt or an obligation **b :** a document evidencing quittance
**2 :** RECOMPENSE, REQUITAL

**quit·ter** \'kwi-tər\ *noun* (1611)
**:** one that quits; *especially* **:** one that gives up too easily **:** DEFEATIST

**quit·tor** \'kwi-tər\ *noun* [Middle English *quiture* pus, probably from Old French, act of boiling, from Latin *coctura*, from *coctus*, past participle of *coquere* to cook — more at COOK] (1703)
**:** a purulent inflammation of the feet especially of horses and donkeys

**¹quiv·er** \'kwi-vər\ *noun* [Middle English, from Middle French *quivre*, of Germanic origin; akin to Old English *cocer* quiver, Old High German *kohhari*] (14th century)
**1 :** a case for carrying or holding arrows
**2 :** the arrows in a quiver

**²quiver** *intransitive verb* **quiv·ered; quiv·er·ing** \'kwi-və-riŋ, 'kwiv-riŋ\ [Middle English, probably from *quiver* agile, quick; akin to Old English *cwiferlice* zealously] (15th century)
**:** to shake or move with a slight trembling motion
— **quiv·er·ing·ly** *adverb*

**³quiver** *noun* (1786)
**:** the act or action of quivering **:** TREMOR

**qui vive** \kē-'vēv\ *noun* [French *qui-vive*, from *qui vive?* long live who?, challenge of a French sentry] (1726)
**:** ALERT, LOOKOUT — used in the phrase *on the qui vive*

**qui·xote** \'kwik-sət, kē-'hō-tē, -'ō-\ *noun, often capitalized* [Don *Quixote*, hero of the novel *Don Quixote de la Mancha* (1605, 1615) by Cervantes] (1648)
**:** a quixotic person
— **quix·o·tism** \'kwik-sə-ˌti-zəm\ *noun*
— **quix·o·try** \-sə-trē\ *noun*

**quix·ot·ic** \kwik-'sä-tik\ *adjective* [Don *Quixote*] (1815)
**1 :** foolishly impractical especially in the pursuit of ideals; *especially* **:** marked by rash lofty romantic ideas or extravagantly chivalrous action
**2 :** CAPRICIOUS, UNPREDICTABLE ◆
**synonym** see IMAGINARY
— **quix·ot·i·cal** \-ti-kəl\ *adjective*
— **quix·ot·i·cal·ly** \-ti-k(ə-)lē\ *adverb*

**¹quiz** \'kwiz\ *noun, plural* **quiz·zes** [origin unknown] (1749)

**1 :** an eccentric person
**2 :** PRACTICAL JOKE
**3 :** the act or action of quizzing; *specifically* **:** a short oral or written test

**²quiz** *transitive verb* **quizzed; quiz·zing** (1794)
**1 :** to make fun of **:** MOCK
**2 :** to look at inquisitively
**3 :** to question closely
— **quiz·zer** *noun*

**quiz·mas·ter** \'kwiz-ˌmas-tər\ *noun* (1943)
**:** one who puts the questions to contestants in a quiz show

**quiz show** *noun* (1944)
**:** an entertainment program (as on radio or television) in which contestants answer questions — called also *quiz program*

**quiz·zi·cal** \'kwi-zi-kəl\ *adjective* (1800)
**1 :** comically quaint
**2 :** mildly teasing or mocking ⟨a *quizzical* remark⟩
**3 :** expressive of puzzlement, curiosity, or disbelief ⟨raised a *quizzical* eyebrow⟩
— **quiz·zi·cal·i·ty** \ˌkwi-zə-'ka-lə-tē\ *noun*
— **quiz·zi·cal·ly** \'kwi-zi-k(ə-)lē\ *adverb*

**quod** \'kwäd\ *noun* [origin unknown] (circa 1700)
*slang British* **:** PRISON

**quod·li·bet** \'kwäd-lə-ˌbet\ *noun* [Middle English, from Medieval Latin *quodlibetum*, from Latin *quodlibet*, neuter of *quilibet* any whatever, from *qui* who, what + *libet* it pleases, from *libēre* to please — more at WHO, LOVE] (14th century)
**1 :** a philosophical or theological point proposed for disputation; *also* **:** a disputation on such a point
**2 :** a whimsical combination of familiar melodies or texts

**¹quoin** \'kȯin, 'kwȯin\ *noun* [alteration of ¹*coin*] (1532)
**1 a :** a solid exterior angle (as of a building) **b :** one of the members (as a block) forming a quoin and usually differentiated from the adjoining walls by material, texture, color, size, or projection
**2 :** the keystone or a voussoir of an arch
**3 :** a wooden or expandable metal block used by printers to lock up a form within a chase

quoin 1b

**²quoin** *transitive verb* (1683)
**1 :** to equip (a type form) with quoins
**2 :** to provide with quoins ⟨*quoined* walls⟩

**¹quoit** \'kȯit, 'kwȯit, 'kwāt\ *noun* [Middle English *coite*] (15th century)
**1 :** a flattened ring of iron or circle of rope used in a throwing game

---

◇ WORD HISTORY
**quixotic** The word *quixotic* reflects the lasting place in world literature held by Miguel de Cervantes Saavedra's novel *Don Quixote de la Mancha* (1605 and 1615). The story concerns Alonso Quijano, who, inspired by the romantic ideals of the days of chivalry, sets out determined to have his own chivalric adventures and in the process undo the wrongs of the world. With the title of Don Quixote and the viewpoint of a romantic idealist, he undergoes a series of adventures that turn into comic misadventures. The would-be knight returns to his home in La Mancha a tired and disillusioned old man. *Don Quixote* was translated into English not long after its Spanish publication and within a few decades gave rise to *Quixote* as a synonym for an impractical idealist. The 19th century derivative *quixotic* now evokes the unrealizable schemes of modern Don Quixotes.

**2** *plural but singular in construction* **:** a game in which the quoits are thrown at an upright pin in an attempt to ring the pin or come as near to it as possible

**²quoit** *transitive verb* (1597)
**:** to throw like a quoit

**quon·dam** \'kwän-dəm, -,dam\ *adjective* [Latin, at one time, formerly, from *quom, cum* when; akin to Latin *qui* who — more at WHO] (1539)
**:** FORMER, SOMETIME ⟨a *quondam* friend⟩

**Quon·set** \'kwän(t)-sət, 'kwän-zət\ *trademark* — used for a prefabricated shelter set on a foundation of bolted steel trusses and built of a semicircular arching roof of corrugated metal insulated with wood fiber

**quo·rum** \'kwōr-əm, 'kwòr-\ *noun* [Middle English, quorum of justices of the peace, from Latin, of whom, genitive plural of *qui* who; from the wording of the commission formerly issued to justices of the peace] (1602)
**1 :** a select group
**2 :** the number (as a majority) of officers or members of a body that when duly assembled is legally competent to transact business
**3 :** a Mormon body comprising those in the same grade of priesthood

**quo·ta** \'kwō-tə\ *noun* [Medieval Latin, from Latin *quota pars* how great a part] (1618)
**1 :** a proportional part or share; *especially* **:** the share or proportion assigned to each in a division or to each member of a body
**2 :** the number or amount constituting a proportional share

**quot·able** \'kwō-tə-bəl *also* 'kō-\ *adjective* (1811)
**:** fit for or worth quoting
**— quot·abil·i·ty** \,kwō-tə-'bi-lə-tē *also* ,kō-\ *noun*

**quo·ta·tion** \kwō-'tā-shən *also* kō-\ *noun* (1646)
**1 a :** the act or process of quoting **b** (1) **:** the naming or publishing of current bids and offers or prices of securities or commodities (2) **:** the bids, offers, or prices so named or published; *especially* **:** the highest bid and lowest offer for a particular security in a given market at a given time
**2 :** something that is quoted; *especially* **:** a passage referred to, repeated, or adduced

**quotation mark** *noun* (circa 1859)
**:** one of a pair of punctuation marks " " or ' ' used chiefly to indicate the beginning and the end of a quotation in which the exact phraseology of another or of a text is directly cited

**¹quote** \'kwōt *also* 'kōt\ *verb* **quot·ed; quot·ing** [Medieval Latin *quotare* to mark the number of, number references, from Latin *quotus* of what number or quantity, from *quot* how many, (as) many as; akin to Latin *qui* who — more at WHO] (1582)
*transitive verb*
**1 a :** to speak or write (a passage) from another usually with credit acknowledgment **b :** to repeat a passage from especially in substantiation or illustration
**2 :** to cite in illustration ⟨*quote* cases⟩
**3 a :** to state (the current price or bid-offer spread) for a commodity, stock, or bond **b :** to give exact information on
**4 :** to set off by quotation marks
*intransitive verb*
**:** to inform a hearer or reader that matter following is quoted
**— quot·er** *noun*

**²quote** *noun* (1888)
**1 :** QUOTATION
**2 :** QUOTATION MARK — often used orally to indicate the beginning of a direct quotation

**quoth** \'kwōth *also* 'kōth\ *verb past* [Middle English, past of *quethen* to say, from Old English *cwethan;* akin to Old High German *quedan* to say] (before 12th century)
*archaic* **:** SAID — used chiefly in the first and third persons with a postpositive subject

**quotha** \'kwō-thə\ *interjection* [alteration of *quoth he*] (1519)
*archaic* — used especially to express surprise or contempt

**quo·tid·i·an** \kwō-'ti-dē-ən\ *adjective* [Middle English *cotidian*, from Middle French, from Latin *quotidianus, cotidianus,* from *quotidie* every day, from *quot* (as) many as + *dies* day — more at DEITY] (14th century)
**1 :** occurring every day ⟨*quotidian* fever⟩
**2 a :** belonging to each day **:** EVERYDAY ⟨*quotidian* routine⟩ **b :** COMMONPLACE, ORDINARY ⟨*quotidian* drabness⟩
**— quotidian** *noun*

**quo·tient** \'kwō-shənt\ *noun* [Middle English *quocient*, modification of Latin *quotiens* how many times, from *quot* how many] (15th century)
**1 :** the number resulting from the division of one number by another
**2 :** the numerical ratio usually multiplied by 100 between a test score and a measurement on which that score might be expected largely to depend
**3 :** QUOTA, SHARE

**quotient group** *noun* (1893)
**:** a group whose elements are the cosets of a normal subgroup of a given group — called also *factor group*

**quotient ring** *noun* (circa 1958)
**:** a ring whose elements are the cosets of an ideal in a given ring

**quo war·ran·to** \,kwō-wə-'rän-(,)tō, -'ran-; -'wòr-ən-,tō, -'wär-\ *noun* [Middle English *quo waranto*, from Medieval Latin *quo warranto* by what warrant; from the wording of the writ] (15th century)
**1 a :** an English writ formerly requiring a person to show by what authority he exercises a public office, franchise, or liberty **b :** a legal proceeding for a like purpose begun by an information
**2 :** the legal action begun by a quo warranto

**Qur·an** *also* **Qur·an** \kə-'ran, -'rän; kù-'ran, -'rän\ *variant of* KORAN

**QWER·TY** \'kwər-tē, 'kwer-\ *noun, often not capitalized* [from the first six letters in the second row of the keyboard] (1929)
**:** a standard typewriter keyboard — called also *QWERTY keyboard*

# R

R *is the eighteenth letter of the English alphabet. It came through Latin by way of Etruscan from Greek* rhō, *which originated as a borrowing of Phoenician* rês. *In English* r *usually denotes the consonant shared by* run, dry, *and* very. *In words derived from Greek the letter* h *that is usually written after* r *to represent* rhō *with a rough breathing mark over it (as in* rhapsody *and* rhetoric*) does not affect the pronunciation of the English word. In many regional dialects of the United States (as those of eastern New England, metropolitan New York, and the South) and in England, an* r *sound at the end of a syllable is "dropped," that is, either it is not pronounced and the preceding vowel is lengthened slightly or it is pronounced as the neutral schwa sound with little or no* r *quality in it. The small* r *form developed in the late Roman period through the gradual degeneration of the loop and tail of the capital form.*

**r** \ˈär\ *noun, plural* **r's** *or* **rs** \ˈärz\ *often capitalized, often attributive* (before 12th century)
**1 a :** the 18th letter of the English alphabet **b :** a graphic representation of this letter **c :** a speech counterpart of orthographic *r*
**2 :** a graphic device for reproducing the letter *r*
**3 :** one designated *r* especially as the 18th in order or class
**4 :** something shaped like the letter R
**R** *certification mark*
— used to certify that a motion picture is of such a nature that admission is restricted to persons over a specified age (as 17) unless accompanied by a parent or guardian; compare G, NC-17, PG, PG-13
**Ra** \ˈrä\ *noun* [Egyptian *rʿ*]
**:** the Egyptian sun-god and chief deity
**ra·ba·to** \rə-ˈbä-(ˌ)tō\ *noun, plural* **-tos** [modification of Middle French *rabat*, literally, act of turning down, from *rabattre*] (1591)
**:** a wide lace-edged collar of the early 17th century often stiffened to stand high at the back
**¹rab·bet** \ˈra-bət\ *noun* [Middle English *rabet*, from Middle French *rabat* act of beating down, from Old French *rabattre* to beat down, reduce — more at REBATE] (14th century)
**:** a channel, groove, or recess cut out of the edge or face of a surface; *especially* **:** one that is intended to receive another member (as a panel)
**²rabbet** (15th century)
*transitive verb*
**1 :** to unite the edges of in a rabbet joint
**2 :** to cut a rabbet in
*intransitive verb*
**:** to become joined by a rabbet
**rabbet joint** *noun* (circa 1828)
**:** a joint formed by fitting together rabbeted boards or timbers
**rab·bi** \ˈra-ˌbī\ *noun* [Middle English, from Old English, from Late Latin, from Greek *rhabbi*, from Hebrew *rabbī* my master, from *rabh* master + *-ī* my] (before 12th century)
**1 :** MASTER, TEACHER — used by Jews as a term of address
**2 :** a Jew qualified to expound and apply the halakah and other Jewish law
**3 :** a Jew trained and ordained for professional religious leadership; *specifically* **:** the official leader of a Jewish congregation
**rab·bin** \ˈra-bən\ *noun* [French] (1579)
**:** RABBI
**rab·bin·ate** \ˈra-bə-nət, -ˌnāt\ *noun* (1702)

**rabbet joint**

**1 :** the office or tenure of a rabbi
**2 :** the whole body of rabbis
**rab·bin·ic** \rə-ˈbi-nik, ra-\ *or* **rab·bin·i·cal** \-ni-kəl\ *adjective* (1612)
**1 :** of or relating to rabbis or their writings
**2 :** of or preparing for the rabbinate
**3 :** comprising or belonging to any of several sets of Hebrew characters simpler than the square Hebrew letters
— **rab·bin·i·cal·ly** \-ni-k(ə-)lē\ *adverb*
**Rabbinic Hebrew** *noun* (circa 1909)
**:** the Hebrew used especially by medieval rabbis
**rab·bin·ism** \ˈra-bə-ˌni-zəm\ *noun* (1652)
**:** rabbinic teachings and traditions
**¹rab·bit** \ˈra-bət\ *noun, plural* **rabbit** *or* **rabbits** *often attributive* [Middle English *rabet*, probably from Middle French dialect (Walloon) *robett*, from Middle Dutch *robe*] (14th century)
**1 :** any of a family (Leporidae) of long-eared short-tailed lagomorph mammals with long hind legs: **a :** any of various lagomorphs that are born naked, blind, and helpless, and that are sometimes gregarious, and that include especially the cottontails of the New World and a small Old World mammal (*Oryctolagus cuniculus*) that is the source of various domestic breeds **b :** HARE
**2 :** the pelt of a rabbit
**3 :** WELSH RABBIT
**4 a :** a figure of a rabbit sped mechanically along the edge of a dog track as an object of pursuit **b :** a runner in a long-distance race who sets a fast pace for the field in the first part of the race
— **rab·bity** \-bə-tē\ *adjective*
**²rabbit** *intransitive verb* (1852)
**:** to hunt rabbits
— **rab·bit·er** *noun*
**rab·bit·brush** \ˈra-bət-ˌbrəsh\ *noun* (circa 1890)
**:** any of several low branching composite shrubs (genus *Chrysothamnus* and especially *C. nauseosus*) of the alkali plains of western North America that are characterized by linear entire leaves and clusters of golden yellow or white flowers
**rabbit ears** *noun plural* (1952)
**:** an indoor dipole television antenna consisting of two usually extensible rods connected to a base to form a V shape
**rabbit fever** *noun* (1925)
**:** TULAREMIA
**rabbit punch** *noun* (1915)
**:** a short chopping blow delivered to the back of the neck or the base of the skull
— **rabbit-punch** *transitive verb*
**rab·bit·ry** \ˈra-bə-trē\ *noun, plural* **-ries** (1838)

**:** a place where domestic rabbits are kept; *also*
**:** a rabbit-raising enterprise
**¹rab·ble** \ˈra-bəl\ *noun* [Middle English *rabel* pack of animals] (14th century)
**1 :** a disorganized or confused collection of things
**2 a :** a disorganized or disorderly crowd of people **:** MOB **b :** the lowest class of people
**²rabble** *transitive verb* **rab·bled; rab·bling** \-b(ə-)liŋ\ (1644)
**:** to insult or assault by or as a mob
**rab·ble·ment** \ˈra-bəl-mənt\ *noun* (1548)
**1 :** RABBLE
**2 :** DISTURBANCE
**rab·ble-rous·er** \ˈra-bəl-ˌrau̇-zər\ *noun* (1843)
**:** one that stirs up (as to hatred or violence) the masses of the people **:** DEMAGOGUE
— **rab·ble-rous·ing** \-ziŋ\ *noun or adjective*
**Ra·be·lai·sian** \ˌra-bə-ˈlā-zhən, -zē-ən\ *adjective* (1817)
**1 :** of, relating to, or characteristic of Rabelais or his works
**2 :** marked by gross robust humor, extravagance of caricature, or bold naturalism
**Ra·bi** \ˈrə-bē\ *noun* [Arabic *rabīʿ*] (circa 1769)
**:** either of two months of the Islamic year: **a :** the 3d month **b :** the 4th month — see MONTH table
**ra·bic** \ˈrā-bik\ *adjective* (1885)
**:** of or relating to rabies
**ra·bid** \ˈra-bəd *also* ˈrā-\ *adjective* [Latin *rabidus* mad, from *rabere*] (1611)
**1 a :** extremely violent **:** FURIOUS **b :** going to extreme lengths in expressing or pursuing a feeling, interest, or opinion
**2 :** affected with rabies
— **ra·bid·i·ty** \rə-ˈbi-də-tē, ra-, rā-\ *noun*
— **ra·bid·ly** \ˈra-bəd-lē *also* ˈrā-\ *adverb*
— **ra·bid·ness** *noun*
**ra·bies** \ˈrā-bēz\ *noun, plural* **rabies** [New Latin, from Latin, madness, from *rabere* to rave — more at RAGE] (circa 1598)
**:** an acute virus disease of the nervous system of warm-blooded animals usually transmitted through the bite of a rabid animal and typically characterized by increased salivation, abnormal behavior, and eventual paralysis and death
**rac·coon** \ra-ˈkün *also* rə-\ *noun, plural* **raccoon** *or* **raccoons** [Virginia Algonquian *raugroughcun, arocoun*] (1608)
**1 a :** a small nocturnal carnivore (*Procyon lotor*) of North America that is chiefly gray, has a black mask and bushy ringed tail, lives chiefly in trees, and has a varied diet including small animals, fruits, and nuts **b :** the pelt of this animal

**raccoon 1a**

**2 :** any of several animals resembling or related to the raccoon ◆
**raccoon dog** *noun* (1868)
**:** a small omnivorous canid (*Nyctereutes procyonoides*) of eastern Asia having a long yellowish brown coat and facial markings resembling that of a raccoon — called also *tanuki*
**¹race** \ˈrās\ *noun* [Middle English *ras*, from Old Norse *rās*; akin to Old English *rǣs* rush] (14th century)
**1** *chiefly Scottish* **:** the act of running
**2 a :** a strong or rapid current of water flowing through a narrow channel **b :** a watercourse used industrially **c :** the current flowing in such a course

**3 a :** a set course or duration of time **b :** the course of life
**4 a :** a contest of speed **b** *plural* **:** a meeting in which several races (as for horses) are run **c :** a contest or rivalry involving progress toward a goal ⟨pennant *race*⟩
**5 :** a track or channel in which something rolls or slides; *specifically* **:** a groove (as for the balls) in a bearing — see ROLLER BEARING illustration
²**race** *verb* **raced; rac·ing** (15th century)
*intransitive verb*
**1 :** to compete in a race
**2 :** to go or move at top speed or out of control
**3 :** to revolve too fast under a diminished load
*transitive verb*
**1 :** to engage in a race with
**2 a :** to enter in a race **b :** to drive or ride at high speed **c :** to transport or propel at maximum speed
**3 :** to speed (as an engine) without a working load or with the transmission disengaged
³**race** *noun* [Middle French, generation, from Old Italian *razza*] (1580)
**1 :** a breeding stock of animals
**2 a :** a family, tribe, people, or nation belonging to the same stock **b :** a class or kind of people unified by community of interests, habits, or characteristics ⟨the English *race*⟩
**3 a :** an actually or potentially interbreeding group within a species; *also* **:** a taxonomic category (as a subspecies) representing such a group **b :** BREED **c :** a division of mankind possessing traits that are transmissible by descent and sufficient to characterize it as a distinct human type
**4** *obsolete* **:** inherited temperament or disposition
**5 :** distinctive flavor, taste, or strength
**race·course** \'rās-ˌkōrs, -ˌkȯrs\ *noun* (1764)
**1 :** a course for racing
**2 :** RACEWAY 1
**race·horse** \-ˌhȯrs\ *noun* (circa 1626)
**:** a horse bred or kept for racing
**ra·ce·mate** \rā-'sē-ˌmāt, rə-; 'ra-sə-\ *noun* (1907)
**:** a racemic compound or mixture
**ra·ceme** \rā-'sēm, rə-\ *noun* [Latin *racemus* bunch of grapes; probably akin to Greek *rhag-, rhax* grape] (1785)
**:** a simple inflorescence (as in the lily-of-the-valley) in which the flowers are borne on short stalks of about equal length at equal distances along an elongated axis and open in succession toward the apex — see INFLORESCENCE illustration
**ra·ce·mic** \-'sē-mik\ *adjective* (1892)
**:** of, relating to, or constituting a compound or mixture that is composed of equal amounts of dextrorotatory and levorotatory forms of the same compound and is not optically active
**ra·ce·mi·za·tion** \rā-ˌsē-mə-'zā-shən, rə-; ˌra-sə-mə-\ *noun* (1895)
**:** the action or process of changing from an optically active compound into a racemic compound or mixture
**— ra·ce·mize** \rā-'sē-ˌmīz, rə-; 'ra-sə-\ *verb*
**ra·ce·mose** \rā-'sē-ˌmōs; rā-'sē-, rə-\ *adjective* [Latin *racemosus* full of clusters, from *racemus*] (1698)
**:** having or growing in the form of a raceme
**rac·er** \'rā-sər\ *noun* (1649)
**1 :** one that races or is used for racing
**2 :** any of various active American colubrid snakes (genus *Coluber* and *Mastigophis*); *especially* **:** BLACK RACER
**race riot** *noun* (1890)
**:** a riot caused by racial dissensions or hatreds
**race runner** *noun* (1915)
**:** a North American lizard (*Cnemidophorus sexlineatus*) that moves swiftly
**race·track** \'rās-ˌtrak\ *noun* (1859)

**:** a usually oval course for racing
**race·track·er** \-ˌtra-kər\ *noun* (1953)
**:** one who frequents a racetrack
**race·walk·ing** \-ˌwȯ-kiŋ\ *noun* (1962)
**:** the competitive sport of racing at a fast walk while maintaining continuous foot contact with the ground and keeping the supporting leg straight
**— race·walk·er** \-kər\ *noun*
**race·way** \-ˌwā\ *noun* (1828)
**1 :** a canal for a current of water
**2 :** a channel for loosely holding electrical wires in buildings
**3 :** ¹RACE 5
**4 :** a course for racing; *especially* **:** a track for harness racing
**rach·et** \'ra-chət\ *variant of* RATCHET
**ra·chis** \'rā-kəs, 'ra-\ *noun, plural* **ra·chis·es** *also* **ra·chi·des** \'ra-kə-ˌdēz, 'rā-\ [New Latin *rachid-, rachis*, from Greek *rhachis*; akin to Greek *rhachos* thorn, Lithuanian *ražas* dry twig, tine] (1842)
**1 :** SPINAL COLUMN
**2 :** an axial structure: as **a** (1) **:** the elongated axis of an inflorescence (2) **:** an extension of the petiole of a compound leaf that bears the leaflets **b :** the distal part of the shaft of a feather that bears the web
**ra·chit·ic** \rə-'ki-tik\ *adjective* [New Latin *rachitis* rickets, from Greek *rhachitis* spinal disease, from *rhachis*] (1797)
**:** RICKETY
**ra·cial** \'rā-shəl\ *adjective* (1862)
**1 :** of, relating to, or based on a race
**2 :** existing or occurring between races
**— ra·cial·ly** \-shə-lē\ *adverb*
**ra·cial·ism** \'rā-shə-ˌli-zəm\ *noun* (1907)
**:** RACISM
**— ra·cial·ist** \-list\ *noun or adjective*
**— ra·cial·is·tic** \ˌrā-shə-'lis-tik\ *adjective*
**rac·ing** \'rā-siŋ\ *noun* (1680)
**:** the sport or profession of engaging in or holding races
**racing form** *noun* (1946)
**:** an information sheet giving details of past performance (as for racehorses) for use by bettors
**rac·ism** \'rā-ˌsi-zəm *also* -ˌshi-\ *noun* (1936)
**1 :** a belief that race is the primary determinant of human traits and capacities and that racial differences produce an inherent superiority of a particular race
**2 :** racial prejudice or discrimination
**— rac·ist** \-sist *also* -shist\ *noun or adjective*
¹**rack** \'rak\ *noun* [Middle English *rak*, probably of Scandinavian origin; akin to Swedish dialect *rak* wreck; akin to Old English *wrecan* to drive — more at WREAK] (14th century)
**:** a wind-driven mass of high often broken clouds
²**rack** *intransitive verb* (1590)
**:** to fly or scud in high wind
³**rack** *noun* [Middle English, probably from Middle Dutch *rec* framework; akin to Old English *reccan* to stretch, Greek *oregein* — more at RIGHT] (14th century)
**1 :** a framework for holding fodder for livestock
**2 :** an instrument of torture on which a body is stretched
**3 a** (1) **:** a cause of anguish or pain (2) **:** acute suffering **b :** the action of straining or wrenching
**4 :** a framework, stand, or grating on or in which articles are placed
**5 :** a frame placed in a stream to stop fish and floating or suspended matter
**6 a :** a bar with teeth on one face for gearing with a pinion or worm gear to transform rotary motion to linear motion or vice versa (as in an automobile steering mechanism or microscope

drawtube) **b :** a notched bar used as a ratchet to engage with a pawl, click, or detent
**7 :** a pair of antlers
**8 :** a triangular frame used to set up the balls in a pool game; *also* **:** the balls as set up
**— rack·ful** \-ˌfu̇l\ *noun*
**— on the rack** **:** under great mental or emotional stress
⁴**rack** (15th century)
*transitive verb*
**1 :** to torture on the rack
**2 :** to cause to suffer torture, pain, or anguish
**3 a :** to stretch or strain violently ⟨*racked* his brains⟩ **b :** to raise (rents) oppressively **c :** to harass or oppress with high rents or extortions
**4 :** to work or treat (material) on a rack
**5 :** to work by a rack and pinion or worm so as to extend or contract ⟨*rack* a camera⟩
**6 :** to seize (as parallel ropes of a tackle) together
**7 :** to place (as pool balls) in a rack
*intransitive verb*
**:** to become forced out of shape or out of plumb
**synonym** see AFFLICT
**— rack·er** *noun*
**— rack·ing·ly** \'ra-kiŋ-lē\ *adverb*
⁵**rack** *transitive verb* [Middle English *rakken*, from Old Provençal *arraca*, from *raca* stems and husks of pressed grapes] (15th century)
**:** to draw off (as wine) from the lees
⁶**rack** *intransitive verb* [probably alteration of ¹*rock*] (1530)
*of a horse* **:** to go at a rack
⁷**rack** *noun* (1580)
**:** either of two gaits of a horse: **a :** PACE 4b **b :** a fast showy 4-beat gait
⁸**rack** *noun* [perhaps from ³*rack*] (1570)
**1 :** the neck and spine of a forequarter of veal, pork, or especially mutton
**2 :** the rib section of a foresaddle of lamb used for chops or as a roast — see LAMB illustration
⁹**rack** *noun* [alteration of *wrack*] (1599)
**:** DESTRUCTION ⟨*rack* and ruin⟩
¹**rack·et** *also* **rac·quet** \'ra-kət\ *noun* [Mid-

---

◇ **WORD HISTORY**
**raccoon** The Algonquian-speaking Indians of tidewater Virginia contributed to American history one of its oldest stock images, the young princess Pocahontas beseeching her father Powhatan to spare the life of the English colonist John Smith—a tale related by Smith himself and the subject of much fictional elaboration later. Descendants of Powhatan's people still live in parts of Virginia, though, like the tribes of southern New England who were also very early victims of white colonization, they maintain few traces of their original culture, and their language has long been extinct. Before its demise, however, Virginia Algonquian contributed to English some of the oldest and best known loanwords from Native American languages, including *hickory, hominy, moccasin, opossum*, and *tomahawk*. Another familiar word from Virginia Algonquian is *raccoon*, which John Smith first recorded as *aroughcun*, *rarowcun*, and *raugroughcun*. Like the opossum, the raccoon was unknown to Europeans, who borrowed the indigenous name for it, as is clear from John Smith's remark in describing the animal to his readers: "There is a beast they call *Aroughcun*, much like a badger."

---

\ə\ abut \ᵊ\ kitten \ər\ further \a\ ash \ā\ ace
\ä\ mop, mar \au̇\ out \ch\ chin \e\ bet \ē\ easy
\g\ go \i\ hit \ī\ ice \j\ job \ŋ\ sing \ō\ go
\ȯ\ law \ȯi\ boy \th\ thin \t̲h̲\ the \ü\ loot \u̇\ foot
\y\ yet \zh\ vision *see also* Guide to Pronunciation

dle French *raquette*, ultimately from Arabic *rāḥah* palm of the hand) (circa 1520)
**1 :** a lightweight implement that consists of a netting (as of nylon) stretched in a usually oval open frame with a handle attached and that is used for striking the ball or shuttlecock in various games (as tennis, racquets, or badminton)

racket 1: *A* tennis, *B* racquetball, *C* badminton

**2** *usually* **racquets** *plural but singular in construction* **:** a game for two or four players with ball and racket on a 4-walled court

²**racket** *noun* [origin unknown] (1565)
**1 :** confused clattering noise **:** CLAMOR
**2 a :** social whirl or excitement **b :** the strain of exciting or trying experiences
**3 a :** a fraudulent scheme, enterprise, or activity **b :** a usually illegitimate enterprise made workable by bribery or intimidation **c :** an easy and lucrative means of livelihood **d** *slang* **:** OCCUPATION, BUSINESS

³**racket** *intransitive verb* (1609)
**1 :** to engage in active social life
**2 :** to move with or make a racket

¹**rack·e·teer** \ˌra-kə-ˈtir\ *noun* (1928)
**:** one who obtains money by an illegal enterprise usually involving intimidation

²**racketeer** (1928)
*intransitive verb*
**:** to carry on a racket
*transitive verb*
**:** to practice extortion on

**rack·ety** \ˈra-kə-tē\ *adjective* (1773)
**1 :** NOISY
**2 :** FLASHY, ROWDY
**3 :** RICKETY

**rack·le** \ˈra-kəl\ *adjective* [Middle English *rakel*] (14th century)
*chiefly Scottish* **:** IMPETUOUS

**rack railway** *noun* (1884)
**:** a railway having between its rails a rack that meshes with a gear wheel or pinion of the locomotive for traction on steep grades

**rack–rent** *transitive verb* (1748)
**:** to subject to rack rent

**rack rent** *noun* [⁴*rack*] (1607)
**1 :** an excessive or unreasonably high rent
**2** *British* **:** the highest rent that can be earned on a property

**rack–rent·er** \ˈrak-ˌren-tər\ *noun* (1680)
**:** one that pays or exacts rack rent

**rack up** *transitive verb* (1949)
**:** ACCUMULATE, GAIN ⟨*racked up* their tenth victory⟩

**ra·clette** \ra-ˈklet, rä-\ *noun* [French, literally, scraper, from *racler* to scrape, from Middle French, from Old Provençal *rasclar*, from (assumed) Vulgar Latin *rasiculare*, from Latin *rasus*, past participle of *radere* to scrape — more at RODENT] (circa 1949)
**:** a Swiss dish consisting of cheese melted over a fire and then scraped onto bread or boiled potatoes; *also* **:** the cheese used in this dish

**ra·con** \ˈrā-ˌkän\ *noun* [*radar* bea*con*] (1945)
**:** RADAR BEACON

**ra·con·teur** \ˌra-ˌkän-ˈtər, -kən-\ *noun* [French, from Middle French, from *raconter* to tell, from Old French, from *re-* + *aconter*, *acompter* to tell, count — more at ACCOUNT] (1828)
**:** a person who excels in telling anecdotes

**ra·coon** *variant of* RACCOON

**rac·quet·ball** \ˈra-kət-ˌbȯl\ *noun* (1968)
**:** a game similar to handball that is played on a

4-walled court with a short-handled racket and a larger ball

¹**racy** \ˈrā-sē\ *adjective* **rac·i·er; -est** [³*race*] (circa 1650)
**1 a :** full of zest or vigor **b :** having a strongly marked quality **:** PIQUANT ⟨a *racy* flavor⟩ **c :** RISQUÉ, SUGGESTIVE
**2 :** having the distinctive quality of something in its original or most characteristic form
**synonym** see PUNGENT
— **rac·i·ly** \ˈrā-sə-lē\ *adverb*
— **rac·i·ness** \-sē-nəs\ *noun*

²**racy** *adjective* **rac·i·er; -est** [¹*race*] (1841)
**:** having a body fitted for racing **:** long-bodied and lean

¹**rad** \ˈrad\ *noun* [*radiation absorbed dose*] (1918)
**:** a unit of absorbed dose of ionizing radiation equal to an energy of 100 ergs per gram of irradiated material

²**rad** *adjective* (1982)
*slang* **:** COOL 7, RADICAL

**ra·dar** \ˈrā-ˌdär\ *noun, often attributive* [*radio detecting and ranging*] (1941)
**:** a device or system consisting usually of a synchronized radio transmitter and receiver that emits radio waves and processes their reflections for display and is used especially for detecting and locating objects (as aircraft) or surface features (as of a planet)

**radar astronomy** *noun* (1959)
**:** astronomy in which celestial bodies in the solar system are studied by analyzing the return of radio waves directed at them

**radar beacon** *noun* (1945)
**:** a radar transmitter that upon receiving a radar signal emits a signal which reinforces the normal reflected signal or which introduces a code into the reflected signal especially for identification purposes

**ra·dar·scope** \ˈrā-ˌdär-ˌskōp\ *noun* [*radar* + *oscilloscope*] (1945)
**:** the oscilloscope or screen serving as the visual indicator in a radar receiver

¹**rad·dle** \ˈra-d²l\ *noun* [Middle English *radel*, from diminutive of *rad-*, *red* red] (14th century)
**:** RED OCHER

²**raddle** *transitive verb* **rad·dled; rad·dling** \ˈrad-liŋ, ˈra-d²l-iŋ\ (1631)
**:** to mark or paint with raddle

³**raddle** *transitive verb* **rad·dled; rad·dling** \ˈrad-liŋ, ˈra-d²l-iŋ\ [English dialect *raddle* supple stick interwoven with others as in making a fence] (1671)
**:** to twist together **:** INTERWEAVE

**rad·dled** \ˈra-d²ld\ *adjective* [origin unknown] (1694)
**1 :** being in a state of confusion **:** lacking composure
**2 :** BROKEN-DOWN, WORN

**radi-** *or* **radio-** *combining form* [French, from Latin *radius* ray] (1694)
**1 :** radiant energy **:** radiation ⟨*radio*active⟩ ⟨*radio*paque⟩
**2 :** radioactive ⟨*radio*element⟩
**3 :** radium **:** X rays ⟨*radio*therapy⟩
**4 :** radioactive isotopes especially as produced artificially ⟨*radio*carbon⟩
**5 :** radio ⟨*radio*telegraphy⟩

¹**ra·di·al** \ˈrā-dē-əl\ *adjective* [Medieval Latin *radialis*, from Latin *radius* ray] (1570)
**1 :** arranged or having parts arranged like rays
**2 a :** relating to, placed like, or moving along a radius **b :** characterized by divergence from a center
**3 :** of, relating to, or adjacent to a bodily radius
**4 :** developing uniformly around a central axis
— **ra·di·al·ly** \-ə-lē\ *adverb*

²**radial** *noun* (1872)
**1 a :** a radial part **b :** RAY
**2 :** a body part (as an artery) lying near or following the course of the radius

**3 :** a pneumatic tire in which the ply cords that extend to the beads are laid at approximately 90 degrees to the centerline of the tread — called also *radial-ply tire*, *radial tire*

**radial cleavage** *noun* (1973)
**:** holoblastic cleavage that is typical of deuterostomes and that is characterized by arrangement of the blastomeres of each upper tier directly over those of the next lower tier resulting in radial symmetry around the pole to pole axis of the embryo — compare SPIRAL CLEAVAGE

**radial engine** *noun* (1909)
**:** a usually internal combustion engine with cylinders arranged radially like the spokes of a wheel

**radial ker·a·tot·o·my** \-ˌker-ə-ˈtä-tə-mē\ *noun* (1980)
**:** multiple incision of the cornea in a radial pattern that is performed to correct myopia

**radial symmetry** *noun* (circa 1890)
**:** the condition of having similar parts regularly arranged around a central axis
— **radially symmetrical** *adjective*

**ra·di·an** \ˈrā-dē-ən\ *noun* (1879)
**:** a unit of plane angular measurement that is equal to the angle at the center of a circle subtended by an arc equal in length to the radius

**ra·di·ance** \ˈrā-dē-ən(t)s\ *noun* (1601)
**1 :** the quality or state of being radiant
**2 :** a deep pink
**3 :** the flux density of radiant energy per unit solid angle and per unit projected area of radiating surface

**ra·di·an·cy** \-ən(t)-sē\ *noun* (1646)
**:** RADIANCE

¹**ra·di·ant** \ˈrā-dē-ənt\ *adjective* (15th century)
**1 a :** radiating rays or reflecting beams of light **b :** vividly bright and shining **:** GLOWING
**2 :** marked by or expressive of love, confidence, or happiness ⟨a *radiant* smile⟩
**3 a :** emitted or transmitted by radiation **b** **:** emitting or relating to radiant heat
**synonym** see BRIGHT
— **ra·di·ant·ly** *adverb*

²**radiant** *noun* (circa 1741)
**:** something that radiates: as **a :** a point in the heavens at which the visible parallel paths of meteors appear to meet when traced backward **b :** the part of a gas or electric heater that becomes incandescent

**radiant energy** *noun* (circa 1890)
**:** energy traveling as electromagnetic waves

**radiant flux** *noun* (1917)
**:** the rate of emission or transmission of radiant energy

**radiant heat** *noun* (1794)
**:** heat transmitted by radiation as contrasted with that transmitted by conduction or convection

¹**ra·di·ate** \ˈrā-dē-ˌāt\ *verb* **-at·ed; -at·ing** [Latin *radiatus*, past participle of *radiare*, from *radius* ray] (circa 1619)
*intransitive verb*
**1 :** to proceed in a direct line from or toward a center
**2 :** to send out rays **:** shine brightly
**3 a :** to issue in or as if in rays **b :** to evolve by adaptive radiation
*transitive verb*
**1 :** to send out in or as if in rays
**2 :** IRRADIATE, ILLUMINATE
**3 :** to spread abroad or around as if from a center

²**ra·di·ate** \ˈrā-dē-ət, -ˌāt\ *adjective* (1668)
**:** having rays or radial parts: as **a :** having ray flowers **b :** characterized by radial symmetry **:** radially symmetrical
— **ra·di·ate·ly** *adverb*

**ra·di·a·tion** \ˌrā-dē-ˈā-shən\ *noun* (15th century)
**1 a :** the action or process of radiating **b :** the process of emitting radiant energy in the form

of waves or particles **c** (1) : the combined processes of emission, transmission, and absorption of radiant energy (2) : the transfer of heat by radiation — compare CONDUCTION, CONVECTION
**2 a** : something that is radiated **b** : energy radiated in the form of waves or particles
**3** : radial arrangement
**4** : ADAPTIVE RADIATION
**5** : RADIATOR
— **ra·di·a·tion·al** \-shnəl, -shə-n°l\ adjective
— **ra·di·a·tion·less** \-shən-ləs\ adjective
— **ra·di·a·tive** \'rā-dē-ˌā-tiv\ adjective
**radiation sickness** noun (1924)
: sickness that results from exposure to radiation and is commonly marked by fatigue, nausea, vomiting, loss of teeth and hair, and in more severe cases by damage to blood-forming tissue with decrease in red and white blood cells and with bleeding
**ra·di·a·tor** \'rā-dē-ˌā-tər, dialect 'ra-\ noun (1836)
: one that radiates: as **a** : any of various devices (as a nest of pipes or tubes) for transferring heat from a fluid within to an area or object outside **b** : a transmitting antenna
**¹rad·i·cal** \'ra-di-kəl\ adjective [Middle English, from Late Latin radicalis, from Latin radic-, radix root — more at ROOT] (14th century)
**1** : of, relating to, or proceeding from a root: as **a** (1) : of or growing from the root of a plant ⟨radical tubers⟩ (2) : growing from the base of a stem, from a rootlike stem, or from a stem that does not rise above the ground ⟨radical leaves⟩ **b** : of, relating to, or constituting a linguistic root **c** : of or relating to a mathematical root **d** : designed to remove the root of a disease or all diseased tissue ⟨radical surgery⟩
**2** : of or relating to the origin : FUNDAMENTAL
**3 a** : marked by a considerable departure from the usual or traditional : EXTREME **b** : tending or disposed to make extreme changes in existing views, habits, conditions, or institutions **c** : of, relating to, or constituting a political group associated with views, practices, and policies of extreme change **d** : advocating extreme measures to retain or restore a political state of affairs ⟨the radical right⟩
**4** slang : EXCELLENT, COOL ◆
— **rad·i·cal·ness** noun
**²radical** noun (1641)
**1 a** : a root part **b** : a basic principle : FOUNDATION
**2 a** : ROOT 6 **b** : a sound or letter belonging to a radical
**3** : one who is radical
**4** : FREE RADICAL; also : a group of atoms bonded together that is considered an entity in various kinds of reactions
**5 a** : a mathematical expression indicating a root by means of a radical sign **b** : RADICAL SIGN
**radical chic** noun (1970)
: a fashionable practice among socially prominent people of associating with radicals or members of minority groups
**rad·i·cal·ise** British variant of RADICALIZE
**rad·i·cal·ism** \'ra-di-kə-ˌli-zəm\ noun (1820)
**1** : the quality or state of being radical
**2** : the doctrines or principles of radicals
**rad·i·cal·ize** \-kə-ˌlīz\ transitive verb **-ized; -iz·ing** (1830)
: to make radical especially in politics
— **rad·i·cal·i·za·tion** \ˌra-di-kə-lə-'zā-shən\ noun
**rad·i·cal·ly** \'ra-di-k(ə-)lē\ adverb (15th century)
**1** : in origin or essence
**2** : in a radical or extreme manner
**radical sign** noun (1668)
: the sign √ or √ placed before an expression to denote that the square root is to be ex-

tracted or that the root marked by an index (as in ³√ or ³√ for the cube root) is to be extracted
**rad·i·cand** \ˌra-də-'kand\ noun [Latin radicandum, neuter of radicandus, gerundive of radicari] (circa 1890)
: the quantity under a radical sign
**ra·dic·chio** \ra-'di-kē-ō\ noun [Italian, chicory, from (assumed) Vulgar Latin radiculus, alteration of Latin radicula] (1968)
: a chicory of a red variety with variegated leaves that is used as a salad green
**radices** plural of RADIX
**rad·i·cle** \'ra-di-kəl\ noun [Latin radicula, diminutive of radic-, radix] (1671)
**1** : the lower part of the axis of a plant embryo or seedling: **a** : the embryonic root of a seedling **b** : HYPOCOTYL **c** : the hypocotyl and the root together
**2** : RADICAL
**ra·dic·u·lar** \rə-'di-kyə-lər, ra-\ adjective (1830)
**1** : of or relating to a plant radicle
**2** : of, relating to, or involving a nerve root ⟨radicular pain⟩
**radii** plural of RADIUS
**¹ra·dio** \'rā-dē-ˌō\ adjective [²radio or radio-] (1887)
**1** : of, relating to, or operated by radiant energy
**2** : of or relating to electric currents or phenomena (as electromagnetic radiation) of frequencies between about 15,000 and 10¹¹ hertz
**3 a** : of, relating to, or used in radio or a radio set **b** : specializing in radio or associated with the radio industry **c** (1) : transmitted by radio (2) : making or participating in radio broadcasts **d** : controlled or directed by radio
**²radio** noun, plural **ra·di·os** [short for radiotelegraphy] (1903)
**1 a** : the wireless transmission and reception of electric impulses or signals by means of electromagnetic waves **b** : the use of these waves for the wireless transmission of electric impulses into which sound is converted
**2** : a radio message
**3** : a radio receiving set
**4 a** : a radio transmitting station **b** : a radio broadcasting organization **c** : the radio broadcasting industry **d** : communication by radio
**³radio** (1913)
transitive verb
**1** : to send or communicate by radio
**2** : to send a radio message to
intransitive verb
: to send or communicate something by radio
**radio-** — see RADI-
**ra·dio·ac·tive** \ˌrā-dē-ō-'ak-tiv\ adjective [International Scientific Vocabulary] (1898)
: of, caused by, or exhibiting radioactivity
— **ra·dio·ac·tive·ly** adverb
**ra·dio·ac·tiv·i·ty** \-ak-'ti-və-tē\ noun [International Scientific Vocabulary] (1899)
: the property possessed by some elements (as uranium) or isotopes (as carbon 14) of spontaneously emitting energetic particles (as electrons or alpha particles) by the disintegration of their atomic nuclei; also : the rays emitted
**ra·dio·al·ler·go·sor·bent** \ˌrā-dē-ō-ə-,lər-gō-'sȯr-bənt\ adjective [radi- + allergen + -o- + sorbent] (1967)
: relating to or being a blood analysis that tests for allergen-specific antibodies and is used to detect allergic reactions
**radio astronomy** noun (1948)
: astronomy dealing with radio waves received from outside the earth's atmosphere
— **radio astronomer** noun
— **radio astronomical** adjective
**ra·dio·au·to·graph** \ˌrā-dē-ō-'ȯ-tə-ˌgraf\ noun (1941)
: AUTORADIOGRAPH
— **ra·dio·au·to·graph·ic** \-ˌȯ-tə-'gra-fik\ adjective

— **ra·dio·au·tog·ra·phy** \-ȯ-'tä-grə-fē\ noun
**radio beacon** noun (1919)
: a radio transmitting station that transmits special radio signals for use (as on a landing field) in determining the direction or position of those receiving them
**ra·dio·bi·ol·o·gy** \ˌrā-dē-ō-bī-'ä-lə-jē\ noun (1919)
: a branch of biology dealing with the effects of radiation or radioactive materials on biological systems
— **ra·dio·bi·o·log·i·cal** \-ˌbī-ə-'lä-ji-kəl\ also **ra·dio·bi·o·log·ic** \-jik\ adjective
— **ra·dio·bi·o·log·i·cal·ly** \-ji-k(ə-)lē\ adverb
— **ra·dio·bi·ol·o·gist** \-bī-'ä-lə-jist\ noun
**radio car** noun (1925)
: an automobile equipped with radio communication
**ra·dio·car·bon** \ˌrā-dē-ō-'kär-bən\ noun, often attributive [International Scientific Vocabulary] (1939)
: radioactive carbon; especially : CARBON 14
**radiocarbon dating** noun (1951)
: CARBON DATING
— **radiocarbon–date** \-'dāt\ transitive verb
**ra·dio·chem·is·try** \ˌrā-dē-ō-'ke-mə-strē\ noun (1904)
: a branch of chemistry dealing with radioactive substances and phenomena including tracer studies
— **ra·dio·chem·i·cal** \-'ke-mi-kəl\ adjective
— **ra·dio·chem·i·cal·ly** \-k(ə-)lē\ adverb
— **ra·dio·chem·ist** \-'ke-mist\ noun
**ra·dio·chro·ma·to·gram** \-krō-'ma-tə-ˌgram, -krə-\ noun (1951)
: a chromatogram revealing one or more radioactive substances
**radio compass** noun (1918)
: a direction finder used in navigation
**ra·dio·ecol·o·gy** \ˌrā-dē-ō-i-'kä-lə-jē\ noun (1956)
: the study of the effects of radiation and radioactive substances on ecological communities
**ra·dio·el·e·ment** \-'e-lə-mənt\ noun [International Scientific Vocabulary] (1903)
: a radioactive element
**radio frequency** noun (1915)
: any of the electromagnetic wave frequencies that lie in the range extending from below 3 kilohertz to about 300 gigahertz and that in-

◇ WORD HISTORY

**radical** The Late Latin adjective radicalis "rooted, having roots," a derivative of Latin radix "root," was borrowed into later Middle English as radical. Aside from its literal meaning "of a root," radical in the 16th century meant "primary" or "fundamental," that is, effecting the "root" of something. In the 17th and 18th centuries radical increasingly began to modify nouns such as change or cure and gradually shifted from the sense "fundamental" to "thorough" and then "extreme." This shift was complete by about the year 1800, when radical reform became a political catchphrase, and an advocate of radical reform was called a radical. In the 20th century radical, when applied to opinions or to advocates of a particular cause, is practically synonymous with extremist.

\ə\ abut \ᵊ\ kitten \ər\ further \a\ ash \ā\ ace \ä\ mop, mar \aú\ out \ch\ chin \e\ bet \ē\ easy \g\ go \i\ hit \ī\ ice \j\ job \ŋ\ sing \ō\ go \ȯ\ law \ȯi\ boy \th\ thin \th\ the \ü\ loot \ú\ foot \y\ yet \zh\ vision    see also Guide to Pronunciation

## RADIO FREQUENCIES

| CLASS | ABBREVIATION | RANGE |
|---|---|---|
| extremely low frequency | ELF | below 3 kilohertz |
| very low frequency | VLF | 3 to 30 kilohertz |
| low frequency | LF | 30 to 300 kilohertz |
| medium frequency | MF | 300 to 3000 kilohertz |
| high frequency | HF | 3 to 30 megahertz |
| very high frequency | VHF | 30 to 300 megahertz |
| ultrahigh frequency | UHF | 300 to 3000 megahertz |
| superhigh frequency | SHF | 3 to 30 gigahertz |
| extremely high frequency | EHF | 30 to 300 gigahertz |

clude the frequencies used for radio and television transmission

**radio galaxy** *noun* (1960)
: a galaxy that is a powerful source of radio waves

**ra·dio·gen·ic** \,rā-dē-ō-'je-nik\ *adjective* (1935)
: produced by or determined from radioactivity ⟨*radiogenic* isotopes⟩ ⟨*radiogenic* tumors⟩

**ra·dio·gram** \'rā-dē-ō-,gram\ *noun* (1896)
**1** : RADIOGRAPH
**2** : a message transmitted by radiotelegraphy
**3** [short for *radiogramophone*] *British* : a combined radio receiver and record player

**¹ra·dio·graph** \-,graf\ *noun* (1896)
: a picture produced on a sensitive surface by a form of radiation other than visible light; *specifically* : an X-ray or gamma ray photograph
— **ra·dio·graph·ic** \,rā-dē-ō-'gra-fik\ *adjective*
— **ra·dio·graph·i·cal·ly** \-fi-k(ə-)lē\ *adverb*

**²radiograph** *transitive verb* (1896)
: to make a radiograph of

**ra·di·og·ra·phy** \,rā-dē-'ä-grə-fē\ *noun* [International Scientific Vocabulary] (1896)
: the art, act, or process of making radiographs

**ra·dio·im·mu·no·as·say** \,rā-dē-ō-,i-myə-nō-'a-,sā, -i-,myü-, -a-'sā\ *noun* (1961)
: immunoassay of a substance that has been radioactively labeled
— **ra·dio·im·mu·no·as·say·able** \-ə-bəl\ *adjective*

**ra·dio·iso·tope** \,rā-dē-ō-'ī-sə-,tōp\ *noun* [International Scientific Vocabulary] (1946)
: a radioactive isotope
— **ra·dio·iso·to·pic** \-,ī-sə-'tä-pik, -'tō-\ *adjective*
— **ra·dio·iso·to·pi·cal·ly** \-pi-k(ə-)lē\ *adverb*

**ra·dio·la·bel** \-'lā-bəl\ *transitive verb* (1953)
: to label with a radioactive atom or substance

**ra·di·o·lar·i·an** \,rā-dē-ō-'lar-ē-ən, -'ler-\ *noun* [ultimately from Late Latin *radiolus* small sunbeam, from diminutive of Latin *radius* ray — more at RAY] (1877)
: any of three classes (Acantharia, Polycystina, and Phaeodaria) of usually spherical marine protozoans having radiating threadlike pseudopodia and often a siliceous skeleton of spicules
— **radiolarian** *adjective*

**ra·dio·log·i·cal** \,rā-dē-ə-'lä-ji-kəl\ *or* **ra·dio·log·ic** \-jik\ *adjective* (1909)

**1** : of or relating to radiology
**2** : of or relating to nuclear radiation
— **ra·dio·log·i·cal·ly** \-k(ə-)lē\ *adverb*

**ra·di·ol·o·gist** \,rā-dē-'ä-lə-jist\ *noun* (1906)
: a physician specializing in the use of radiant energy for diagnostic and therapeutic purposes

**ra·di·ol·o·gy** \-jē\ *noun* (1900)
**1** : a branch of medicine concerned with the use of radiant energy (as X rays and radium) in the diagnosis and treatment of disease
**2** : the science of radioactive substances and high-energy radiations

**ra·dio·lu·cent** \,rā-dē-ō-'lü-s°nt\ *adjective* (1917)
: partly or wholly permeable to radiation ⟨*radiolucent* tissues⟩
— **ra·dio·lu·cen·cy** \-s°n(t)-sē\ *noun*

**ra·di·ol·y·sis** \,rā-dē-'ä-lə-səs\ *noun* [New Latin] (1948)
: chemical decomposition by the action of radiation
— **ra·dio·lyt·ic** \-dē-ə-'li-tik\ *adjective*

**ra·dio·man** \'rā-dē-ō-,man\ *noun* (1921)
: a radio operator or technician

**ra·di·om·e·ter** \,rā-dē-'ä-mə-tər\ *noun* (1875)
: an instrument for measuring the intensity of radiant energy by the torsional twist of suspended vanes that are blackened on one side and exposed to a source of radiant energy; *also* : an instrument for measuring electromagnetic or acoustic radiation
— **ra·di·om·e·try** \-mə-trē\ *noun*

**radiometer**

**ra·dio·met·ric** \,rā-dē-ō-'me-trik\ *adjective* [International Scientific Vocabulary] (1877)
**1** : relating to, using, or measured by a radiometer
**2** : of or relating to the measurement of geologic time by means of the rate of disintegration of radioactive elements
— **ra·dio·met·ri·cal·ly** \-tri-k(ə-)lē\ *adverb*

**ra·dio·mi·met·ic** \-mə-'me-tik, -mī-\ *adjective* [International Scientific Vocabulary] (1947)
: producing effects similar to those of radiation

**ra·dio·nu·clide** \,rā-dē-ō-'nü-,klīd, -'nyü-\ *noun* (1947)
: a radioactive nuclide

**ra·di·opaque** \,rā-dē-ō-'pāk\ *adjective* (circa 1923)
: being opaque to various forms of radiation (as X rays)

**ra·dio·phar·ma·ceu·ti·cal** \,rā-dē-ō-,fär-mə-'sü-ti-kəl\ *noun* (1952)
: a radioactive drug used for diagnostic or therapeutic purposes
— **radiopharmaceutical** *adjective*

**ra·dio·phone** \'rā-dē-ə-,fōn\ *noun* (1919)
: RADIOTELEPHONE

**ra·dio·pho·to** \,rā-dē-ō-'fō-(,)tō\ *noun* (1929)
: a picture transmitted by radio

**ra·dio·pro·tec·tive** \-prə-'tek-tiv\ *adjective* (1956)
: serving to protect or aiding in protecting against the injurious effect of radiations ⟨*radioprotective* drugs⟩
— **ra·dio·pro·tec·tion** \-'tek-shən\ *noun*

**radio range** *noun* (1929)
: a radio facility for aircraft navigation

**ra·dio·sen·si·tive** \,rā-dē-ō-'sen(t)-sə-tiv, -'sen(t)-stiv\ *adjective* (1920)
: sensitive to the effects of radiant energy ⟨*radiosensitive* cancer cells⟩
— **ra·dio·sen·si·tiv·i·ty** \-,sen(t)-sə-'ti-və-tē\ *noun*

**ra·dio·sonde** \'rā-dē-ō-,sänd\ *noun* [International Scientific Vocabulary] (1937)
: a miniature radio transmitter that is carried aloft (as by an unmanned balloon) with instruments for broadcasting the humidity, temperature, and pressure

**radio spectrum** *noun* (1929)
: the region of the electromagnetic spectrum usually including frequencies below 30,000 megahertz in which radio or radar transmission and detection techniques may be used

**radio star** *noun* (1948)
: a cosmic radio source; *especially* : a point source of radio emissions

**ra·dio·stron·tium** \,rā-dē-ō-'strän(t)-sh(ē-)əm, -'strän-tē-əm\ *noun* [New Latin] (1941)
: radioactive strontium; *especially* : STRONTIUM 90

**ra·dio·tele·graph** \-'te-lə-,graf\ *noun* [International Scientific Vocabulary] (1903)
: WIRELESS TELEGRAPHY
— **ra·dio·te·leg·ra·phy** \-tə-'le-grə-fē\ *noun*

**ra·dio·te·lem·e·try** \-tə-'le-mə-trē\ *noun* (1951)
**1** : TELEMETRY
**2** : BIOTELEMETRY
— **ra·dio·tele·met·ric** \-,te-lə-'me-trik\ *adjective*

**ra·dio·tele·phone** \-'te-lə-,fōn\ *noun* [International Scientific Vocabulary] (1904)
: an apparatus for carrying on wireless telephony by radio waves
— **ra·dio·te·le·pho·ny** \-tə-'le-fə-nē, -'te-lə-,fō-nē\ *noun*

**radio telescope** *noun* (1929)
: a radio receiver-antenna combination used for observation in radio astronomy

**ra·dio·ther·a·py** \,rā-dē-ō-'ther-ə-pē\ *noun* [International Scientific Vocabulary] (1903)
: the treatment of disease with radiation (as X rays)
— **ra·dio·ther·a·pist** \-pist\ *noun*

**ra·dio·tho·ri·um** \-'thōr-ē-əm, -'thȯr-\ *noun* [New Latin] (1905)
: a radioactive isotope of thorium with the mass number 228

**ra·dio·trac·er** \'rā-dē-ō-,trā-sər\ *noun* (1946)
: a radioactive tracer

**ra·dio–ul·na** \,rā-dē-ō-'əl-nə\ *noun* [New Latin] (1960)
: a single bone in the forelimb of an amphibian (as a frog) that represents fusion of the separate radius and ulna of higher vertebrate forms

**radio wave** *noun* (1916)
: an electromagnetic wave with radio frequency

**rad·ish** \'ra-dish *also* 're-\ *noun* [Middle English, alteration of Old English *rædic*, from Latin *radic-, radix* root, radish — more at ROOT] (15th century)
: the pungent fleshy root of a widely cultivated Eurasian plant (*Raphanus sativus*) of the mustard family usually eaten raw; *also* : a plant that produces radishes

**ra·di·um** \'rā-dē-əm\ *noun, often attributive* [New Latin, from Latin *radius* ray] (1899)
: an intensely radioactive brilliant white metallic element that resembles barium chemically, occurs in combination in minute quantities in minerals (as pitchblende or carnotite), emits alpha particles and gamma rays to form radon, and is used chiefly in luminous materials and in the treatment of cancer — see ELEMENT table

**radium therapy** *noun* (1904)
: RADIOTHERAPY

**ra·di·us** \'rā-dē-əs\ *noun, plural* **ra·dii** \-dē-,ī\ *also* **ra·di·us·es** [Latin, ray, radius] (circa 1611)
**1** : a line segment extending from the center of a circle or sphere to the circumference or bounding surface
**2 a** : the bone on the thumb side of the human forearm; *also* : a corresponding part of vertebrates above fishes **b** : the third and usually largest vein of an insect's wing
**3 a** : the length of a radius ⟨a truck with a short turning *radius*⟩ **b** : the circular area de-

fined by a stated radius **c :** a bounded or circumscribed area

**4 :** a radial part

**5 :** the distance from a center line or point to an axis of rotation

**radius of curvature** (circa 1753)
: the reciprocal of the curvature of a curve

**radius vector** *noun* (circa 1753)
**1 a :** the line segment or its length from a fixed point to a variable point **b :** the linear polar coordinate of a variable point
**2 :** a straight line joining the center of an attracting body (as the sun) with that of a body (as a planet) in orbit around it

**ra·dix** \'rā-diks\ *noun, plural* **ra·di·ces** \'rā-də-ˌsēz, 'ra-\ *or* **ra·dix·es** \'rā-dik-səz\ [Latin, root — more at ROOT] (1798)
**1 :** the base of a number system or of logarithms
**2 :** the primary source

**ra·dome** \'rā-ˌdōm\ *noun* [radar *dome*] (circa 1944)
: a plastic housing sheltering the antenna assembly of a radar set especially on an airplane

**ra·don** \'rā-ˌdän\ *noun* [International Scientific Vocabulary, from *radium*] (1918)
: a heavy radioactive gaseous element formed by the decay of radium — see ELEMENT table

**rad·u·la** \'ra-jə-lə\ *noun, plural* **-lae** \-ˌlē, -ˌlī\ *also* **-las** [New Latin, from Latin, scraper, from *radere* to scrape — more at RODENT] (circa 1859)
: a horny band or ribbon in mollusks other than bivalves that bears minute teeth on its dorsal surface and tears up food and draws it into the mouth
— **rad·u·lar** \-lər\ *adjective*

**rad·waste** \'rad-ˌwāst\ *noun, often attributive* [by shortening] (1973)
: radioactive waste

**raff** \'raf\ *noun* [Middle English *raf* rubbish] (14th century)
: RIFFRAFF

**raf·fia** \'ra-fē-ə\ *noun* [Malagasy *rafia*] (1882)
: the fiber of the raffia palm used especially for tying plants and making baskets and hats

**raffia palm** *noun* (1897)
: a pinnate-leaved palm (*Raphia farinifera* synonym *R. ruffia*) of Madagascar that is valued for the fiber from its leafstalks

**raf·fi·nose** \'ra-fə-ˌnōs, -ˌnōz\ *noun* [French, from *raffiner* to refine, from *re-* + *affiner* to make fine, from *a-* ad- (from Latin *ad-*) + *fin* fine] (1876)
: a crystalline slightly sweet sugar $C_{18}H_{32}O_{16}$ obtained commercially from cottonseed meal and present in many plant products

**raff·ish** \'ra-fish\ *adjective* (1801)
**1 :** marked by or suggestive of flashy vulgarity or crudeness
**2 :** marked by a careless unconventionality : RAKISH
— **raff·ish·ly** *adverb*
— **raff·ish·ness** *noun*

**¹raf·fle** \'ra-fəl\ *verb* **raf·fled; raf·fling** \'ra-f(ə-)liŋ\ (circa 1680)
*intransitive verb*
: to engage in a raffle
*transitive verb*
: to dispose of by means of a raffle ⟨*raffle* off a turkey⟩

**²raffle** *noun* [Middle English *rafle*, a dice game, from Middle French, dice game in which all the stakes can be won in a throw, literally, rake for a fire, from Middle High German *raffel* rake for a fire, from *raffen* to snatch, gather] (1766)
: a lottery in which the prize is won by one of numerous persons buying chances

**³raffle** *noun* [probably from French *rafle* act of snatching, sweeping, from Middle French, rake for a fire] (1881)
: RUBBISH; *especially* : a jumble or tangle of nautical equipment

**raf·fle·sia** \ra-'flē-zh(ē-)ə, ra-\ *noun* [New Latin, from Sir Stamford *Raffles* (died 1826)

English colonial administrator] (1830)
: any of a genus (*Rafflesia* of the family Rafflesiaceae) of Malaysian dicotyledonous plants that are parasitic in other plants and have fleshy usually foul-smelling apetalous flowers emerging from the host, imbricated scales in place of leaves, and no stems

**¹raft** \'raft\ *noun* [Middle English *rafte* rafter, raft, from Old Norse *raptr* rafter] (15th century)
**1 a :** a collection of logs or timber fastened together for conveyance by water **b :** a flat structure for support or transportation on water
**2 :** a floating cohesive mass
**3 :** an aggregation of animals (as waterfowl) resting on the water

**²raft** (1706)
*transitive verb*
**1 :** to transport in the form of or by means of a raft; *also* : to convey (as pebbles) in floating ice or masses of organic material
**2 :** to make into a raft
*intransitive verb*
: to travel by raft

**³raft** *noun* [alteration of *raff* jumble] (1830)
: a large collection or number

**¹raf·ter** \'raf-tər\ *noun* [Middle English, from Old English *ræfter*; akin to Old Norse *raptr* rafter] (before 12th century)
: any of the parallel beams that support a roof
— see RIDGEPOLE illustration
— **raf·tered** \-tərd\ *adjective*

**²rafter** \'raf-tər\ *noun* [²*raft*] (1809)
**1 :** one who maneuvers logs into position and binds them into rafts
**2 :** one who travels by raft

**rafts·man** \'raf(t)s-mən\ *noun* (1776)
: a man engaged in rafting

**¹rag** \'rag\ *noun* [Middle English *ragge*, from (assumed) Old English *ragg*, from Old Norse *rogg* tuft, shagginess] (14th century)
**1 a :** a waste piece of cloth **b** *plural* : clothes usually in poor or ragged condition **c :** CLOTHING ⟨the *rag* trade⟩
**2 :** something resembling a rag
**3 :** NEWSPAPER

**²rag** *noun* [Middle English *ragge*] (14th century)
**1 :** any of various hard rocks
**2 :** a large roofing slate that is rough on one side

**³rag** *transitive verb* **ragged** \'ragd\; **ragging** [origin unknown] (1739)
**1 :** to rail at : SCOLD
**2 :** TORMENT, TEASE

**⁴rag** *noun* (1864)
*chiefly British* : an outburst of boisterous fun; *also* : PRANK

**⁵rag** *noun* [short for *ragtime*] (1897)
: a composition in ragtime

**ra·ga** \'rä-gə\ *noun* [Sanskrit *rāga*, literally, color, tone; akin to Sanskrit *rajyati* it reddens, Greek *rhezein* to dye] (1788)
**1 :** one of the ancient traditional melodic patterns or modes in Indian music
**2 :** an improvisation based on a traditional raga — compare TALA

**rag·a·muf·fin** \'ra-gə-ˌmə-fən\ *noun* [Middle English *Ragamuffyn*, name for a ragged, oafish person] (1581)
: a ragged often disreputable person; *especially* : a poorly clothed often dirty child

**rag·bag** \'rag-ˌbag\ *noun* (1820)
**1 :** a bag for scraps
**2 :** a miscellaneous collection

**rag doll** *noun* (1853)
: a stuffed usually painted cloth doll

**¹rage** \'rāj\ *noun* [Middle English, from Old French, from Late Latin *rabia*, from Latin *rabies* rage, madness, from *rabere* to be mad; akin to Sanskrit *rabhas* violence] (14th century)
**1 a :** violent and uncontrolled anger **b :** a fit of violent wrath **c** *archaic* : INSANITY
**2 :** violent action (as of wind or sea)
**3 :** an intense feeling : PASSION

**4 :** a fad pursued with intense enthusiasm ⟨was all the *rage*⟩
*synonym* SEE ANGER, FASHION

**²rage** *intransitive verb* **raged; rag·ing** (14th century)
**1 :** to be in a rage
**2 :** to be in tumult
**3 :** to prevail uncontrollably

**rag·ged** \'ra-gəd\ *adjective* (14th century)
**1 :** roughly unkempt
**2 :** having an irregular edge or outline
**3 a :** torn or worn to tatters **b :** worn-out from stress and strain ⟨ran herself *ragged*⟩
**4 :** wearing tattered clothes
**5 a :** STRAGGLY **b :** executed in an irregular or uneven manner **c** *of a sound* : HARSH, DISSONANT
— **rag·ged·ly** *adverb*
— **rag·ged·ness** *noun*

**ragged robin** *noun* (1741)
: a perennial herb (*Lychnis flos-cuculi*) cultivated for its pink flowers with narrow-lobed petals

**rag·gedy** \'ra-gə-dē\ *adjective* (1890)
: RAGGED

**rag·gle–tag·gle** \'ra-gəl-ˌta-gəl\ *adjective* [irregular from *ragtag*] (1904)
: MOTLEY

**ra·gi** \'ra-gē, 'rä-\ *noun* [perhaps from Deccan Hindi *rāgī*] (1792)
: an Old World cereal grass (*Eleusine coracana*) yielding a staple food crop especially in India and Africa; *also* : the seeds of ragi used for food

**raging** *adjective* (15th century)
**1 :** causing great pain or distress
**2 :** VIOLENT, WILD
**3 :** EXTRAORDINARY, TREMENDOUS ⟨a *raging* success⟩

**rag·lan** \'ra-glən\ *noun* [F.J.H. Somerset, Baron *Raglan* (died 1855) British field marshal] (circa 1859)
: a loose overcoat with raglan sleeves

**raglan sleeve** *noun* (circa 1924)
: a sleeve that extends to the neckline with slanted seams from the underarm to the neck

**rag·man** \'rag-ˌman\ *noun* (1586)
: a man who collects or deals in rags

**Rag·na·rok** \'rag-nə-ˌräk, -ˌrök\ *noun* [Old Norse *Ragnarǫk*, literally, fate of the gods, from *ragna*, genitive plural of *regin* gods + *rǫk* fate, course (later rendered as *Ragnarǫkkr*, literally, twilight of the gods)]
: the final destruction of the world in the conflict between the Aesir and the powers of Hel led by Loki — called also *Twilight of the Gods*

**ra·gout** \ra-'gü\ *noun* [French *ragoût*, from *ragoûter* to revive the taste, from Middle French *ragouster*, from *re-* + *a-* ad- (from Latin *ad-*) + *goust* taste, from Latin *gustus*; akin to Latin *gustare* to taste — more at CHOOSE] (circa 1657)
**1 :** well-seasoned meat and vegetables cooked in a thick sauce
**2 :** MIXTURE, MÉLANGE

**rag·pick·er** \'rag-ˌpi-kər\ *noun* (1860)
: one who collects rags and refuse for a living

**rag·tag** \'rag-ˌtag\ *adjective* [*ragtag and bobtail*] (1882)
**1 :** RAGGED, UNKEMPT
**2 :** MOTLEY 2 ⟨a *ragtag* bunch of misfits⟩

**ragtag and bobtail** *noun* [¹*rag* + ¹*tag*] (1820)
: RABBLE

**rag·time** \'rag-ˌtīm\ *noun* [probably from *ragged* + *time*] (1897)
**1 :** rhythm characterized by strong syncopation in the melody with a regularly accented accompaniment

---

\ə\ abut \ᵊ\ kitten \ər\ further \a\ ash \ā\ ace
\ä\ mop, mar \aù\ out \ch\ chin \e\ bet \ē\ easy
\g\ go \i\ hit \ī\ ice \j\ job \ŋ\ sing \ō\ go
\ò\ law \òi\ boy \th\ thin \t̲h̲\ the \ü\ loot \ù\ foot
\y\ yet \zh\ vision    *see also* Guide to Pronunciation

**2 :** music having ragtime rhythm
**rag·top** \-,täp\ *noun* (1953)
**:** a convertible automobile
**rag·weed** \-,wēd\ *noun* (1790)
**:** any of various chiefly North American weedy composite herbs (genus *Ambrosia*) that produce highly allergenic pollen
**rag·wort** \-,wərt, -,wȯrt\ *noun* (14th century)
**:** any of several senecios; *especially* **:** TANSY RAGWORT
**rah** \'rä, 'rȯ\ *interjection* (1870)
**:** HURRAH — used especially to cheer on a team
**rah–rah** \'rä-(,)rä, 'rȯ-(,)rȯ\ *adjective* [reduplication of *rah*] (1911)
**:** marked by the enthusiastic expression of college spirit
**¹raid** \'rād\ *noun* [Middle English (Scots) *rade*, from Old English *rād* ride, raid — more at ROAD] (15th century)
**1 a :** a hostile or predatory incursion **b :** a surprise attack by a small force
**2 a :** a brief foray outside one's usual sphere **b :** a sudden invasion by officers of the law **c :** a daring operation against a competitor **d :** the recruiting of personnel (as faculty, executives, or athletes) from competing organizations
**3 :** the act of mulcting public money
**4 :** an attempt by professional operators to depress stock prices by concerted selling
**²raid** (1865)
*intransitive verb*
**:** to conduct or take part in a raid
*transitive verb*
**:** to make a raid on
**raid·er** \'rā-dər\ *noun* (1863)
**:** one that raids: as **a :** a fast lightly armed ship operating against merchant shipping **b :** a soldier specially trained for close-range fighting **c :** one that attempts a usually hostile takeover of a business corporation ⟨corporate *raiders*⟩
**¹rail** \'rā(ə)l\ *noun* [Middle English *raile*, from Middle French *reille* ruler, bar, from Latin *regula* ruler, from *regere* to keep straight, direct, rule — more at RIGHT] (14th century)
**1 a :** a bar extending from one post or support to another and serving as a guard or barrier **b :** a structural member or support
**2 a :** RAILING 1 **b :** a light structure serving as a guard at the outer edge of a ship's deck **c :** a fence bounding a racetrack
**3 a :** a bar of rolled steel forming a track for wheeled vehicles **b :** TRACK **c :** RAILROAD
**²rail** *transitive verb* (14th century)
**:** to provide with a railing **:** FENCE
**³rail** *noun, plural* **rail** *or* **rails** [Middle English *raile*, from Middle French *raale*] (15th century)
**:** any of numerous wading birds (family Rallidae, the rail family) that are of small or medium size and have short rounded wings, a short tail, and usually very long toes which enable them to run on the soft mud of marshes

rail

**⁴rail** *intransitive verb* [Middle English, from Middle French *railler* to mock, from Old Provençal *ralhar* to babble, joke, from (assumed) Vulgar Latin *ragulare* to bray, from Late Latin *ragere* to neigh] (15th century)
**:** to revile or scold in harsh, insolent, or abusive language
**synonym** see SCOLD
**— rail·er** *noun*
**rail·bird** \'rā(ə)l-,bərd\ *noun* (1892)
**:** a racing enthusiast who sits on or near the track rail to watch a race or workout
**rail·bus** \-,bəs\ *noun* (1933)
**:** a passenger car with an automotive engine for operation on rails
**rail·car** \-,kär\ *noun* (1834)
**1 :** a railroad car

**2 :** a self-propelled railroad car
**rail·head** \'rā(ə)l-,hed\ *noun* (1896)
**:** a point on a railroad at which traffic may originate or terminate
**rail·ing** \'rā-liŋ\ *noun* (15th century)
**1 :** a barrier consisting of a rail and supports
**2 :** RAILS; *also* **:** material for making rails
**rail·lery** \'rā-lə-rē\ *noun, plural* **-ler·ies** [French *raillerie*, from Middle French, from *railler* to mock] (1653)
**1 :** good-natured ridicule **:** BANTER
**2 :** JEST
**¹rail·road** \'rā(ə)l-,rōd, 're(ə)l-; 're-,rōd\ *noun* (1825)
**:** a permanent road having a line of rails fixed to ties and laid on a roadbed and providing a track for cars or equipment drawn by locomotives or propelled by self-contained motors; *also* **:** such a road and its assets constituting a single property
**²railroad** (1877)
*transitive verb*
**1 a :** to convict with undue haste and by means of false charges or insufficient evidence **b :** to push through hastily or without due consideration
**2 :** to transport by railroad
*intransitive verb*
**:** to work for a railroad company
**— rail·road·er** *noun*
**railroad flat** *noun* (1947)
**:** an apartment having a series of narrow rooms arranged in line
**rail·road·ing** *noun* (1870)
**:** construction or operation of a railroad
**railroad worm** *noun* (1909)
**1** [probably from its dissemination by railroad] **:** APPLE MAGGOT
**2** [from the rows of luminescent spots along its sides making it resemble a lighted train] **:** the larva or wingless female of any of several South American beetles (genus *Phrixothrix* of the family Cantharidae)
**rail–split·ter** \'rā(ə)l-,spli-tər\ *noun* (1860)
**:** one that makes logs into fence rails
**rail·way** \-,wā\ *noun* (1812)
**:** RAILROAD; *especially* **:** a railroad operating with light equipment or within a small area
**rai·ment** \'rā-mənt\ *noun* [Middle English *rayment*, short for *arrayment*, from *arrayen* to array] (15th century)
**:** CLOTHING, GARMENTS
**¹rain** \'rān\ *noun, often attributive* [Middle English *reyn*, from Old English *regn, rēn*; akin to Old High German *regan* rain] (before 12th century)
**1 a :** water falling in drops condensed from vapor in the atmosphere **b :** the descent of this water **c :** water that has fallen as rain **:** RAINWATER
**2 a :** a fall of rain **:** RAINSTORM **b** *plural* **:** the rainy season
**3 :** rainy weather
**4 :** a heavy fall of particles or bodies
**²rain** (before 12th century)
*intransitive verb*
**1 :** to send down rain
**2 :** to fall as water in drops from the clouds
**3 :** to fall like rain
*transitive verb*
**1 :** to pour down
**2 :** to bestow abundantly
**— rain cats and dogs :** to rain heavily
**rain·bird** \'rān-,bərd\ *noun* (1555)
**:** any of numerous birds (especially of the family Cuculidae) whose cries are popularly believed to augur rain
**rain·bow** \-,bō\ *noun* (before 12th century)
**1 :** an arc or circle that exhibits in concentric bands the colors of the spectrum and that is formed opposite the sun by the refraction and reflection of the sun's rays in raindrops, spray, or mist
**2 a :** a multicolored array **b :** a wide assortment or range

**3** [from the impossibility of reaching the rainbow, at whose foot a pot of gold is said to be buried] **:** an illusory goal or hope
**4 :** RAINBOW TROUT
**— rain·bow·like** *adjective*
**rainbow fish** *noun* (1888)
**:** any of numerous brilliantly colored fishes (as a wrasse, parrot fish, or guppy)
**rainbow runner** *noun* (1940)
**:** a large brilliantly marked blue and yellow carangid food and sport fish (*Elagatis bipinnulata*) common in warm seas
**rainbow trout** *noun* (1882)
**:** a large stout-bodied salmonid fish (*Oncorhynchus mykiss* synonym *Salmo gairdneri*) of western North America that is related to the Pacific salmon and is typically greenish above and white on the belly with a pink, red, or lavender stripe along each side of the body and with profuse black dots — compare STEELHEAD

rainbow trout

**rain check** *noun* (1884)
**1 :** a ticket stub good for a later performance when the scheduled one is rained out
**2 :** an assurance of a deferred extension of an offer; *especially* **:** an assurance that a customer can take advantage of a sale later if the item or service offered is not available (as by being sold out)
**rain·coat** \'rān-,kōt\ *noun* (1830)
**:** a waterproof or water-resistant coat
**rain·drop** \-,dräp\ *noun* (before 12th century)
**:** a drop of rain
**rain·fall** \-,fȯl\ *noun* (1854)
**1 :** the amount of precipitation usually measured by the depth in inches
**2 :** RAIN 2a
**rain forest** *noun* (1903)
**1 :** a tropical woodland with an annual rainfall of at least 100 inches (254 centimeters) and marked by lofty broad-leaved evergreen trees forming a continuous canopy — called also *tropical rain forest*
**2 :** TEMPERATE RAIN FOREST
**rain gauge** *noun* (1769)
**:** an instrument for measuring the quantity of precipitation
**rain·mak·er** \'rān-,mā-kər\ *noun* (1775)
**1 :** a person who produces or attempts to produce rain by artificial means
**2 :** a person (as a partner in a law firm) who brings in new business; *also* **:** a person whose influence can initiate progress or ensure success
**— rain·mak·ing** \-,mā-'kiŋ\ *noun*
**rain out** *transitive verb* (1928)
**:** to interrupt or prevent by rain
**rain·proof** \'rān-,prüf\ *adjective* (1831)
**:** impervious to rain
**rain·spout** \-,spau̇t\ *noun* (1922)
**:** GUTTER 1a; *also* **:** DOWNSPOUT
**rain·squall** \-,skwȯl\ *noun* (1849)
**:** a squall accompanied by rain
**rain·storm** \-,stȯrm\ *noun* (1816)
**:** a storm of or with rain
**rain tree** *noun* (circa 1890)
**:** MONKEYPOD
**rain·wash** \'rān-,wȯsh, -,wäsh\ *noun* (1876)
**:** the washing away of material by rain; *also* **:** the material so washed away
**rain·wa·ter** \-,wȯ-tər, -,wä-\ *noun* (before 12th century)
**:** water fallen as rain that has not collected soluble matter from the soil and is therefore soft
**rain·wear** \-,war, -,wer\ *noun* (1939)
**:** waterproof or water-resistant clothing

**rainy** \'rā-nē\ *adjective* **rain·i·er; -est** (before 12th century)
: marked by, abounding with, or bringing rain

**rainy day** *noun* (circa 1580)
: a period of want or need

**¹raise** \'rāz\ *verb* **raised; rais·ing** [Middle English, from Old Norse *reisa* — more at REAR] (13th century)
*transitive verb*
**1 :** to cause or help to rise to a standing position
**2 a :** AWAKEN, AROUSE **b :** to stir up : INCITE ⟨*raise* a rebellion⟩ **c :** to flush (game) from cover **d :** to recall from or as if from death **e :** to establish radio communication with
**3 a :** to set upright by lifting or building **b :** to lift higher **c :** to place higher in rank or dignity : ELEVATE **d :** HEIGHTEN, INVIGORATE ⟨*raise* the spirits⟩ **e :** to end or suspend the operation or validity of ⟨*raise* a siege⟩
**4 :** to get together for a purpose : COLLECT ⟨*raise* funds⟩
**5 a :** to breed and bring (an animal) to maturity **b :** GROW, CULTIVATE ⟨*raise* cotton⟩ **c :** to bring up (a child) : REAR
**6 a :** to give rise to : PROVOKE ⟨*raise* a commotion⟩ **b :** to give voice to ⟨*raise* a cheer⟩
**7 :** to bring up for consideration or debate ⟨*raise* an issue⟩
**8 a :** to increase the strength, intensity, or pitch of **b :** to increase the degree of **c :** to cause to rise in level or amount ⟨*raise* the rent⟩ **d** (1) : to increase the amount of (a poker bet) (2) : to bet more than (a previous bettor) **e** (1) : to make a higher bridge bid in (a partner's suit) (2) : to increase the bid of (one's partner)
**9 :** to make light and porous ⟨*raise* dough⟩
**10 :** to cause to ascend
**11 :** to multiply (a quantity) by itself a specified number of times
**12 :** to bring in sight on the horizon by approaching ⟨*raise* land⟩
**13 a :** to bring up the nap of (cloth) **b :** to cause (as a blister) to form on the skin
**14 :** to increase the nominal value of fraudulently ⟨*raise* a check⟩
**15 :** to articulate (a sound) with the tongue in a higher position
*intransitive verb*
**1** *dialect* : RISE
**2 :** to increase a bet or bid ◼
*synonym* see LIFT
— **rais·er** *noun*
— **raise Cain** *or* **raise hell** **1 :** to act wildly : create a disturbance **2 :** to scold or upbraid someone especially loudly
— **raise eyebrows :** to cause surprise or astonishment

**²raise** *noun* (1538)
**1 :** an act of raising or lifting
**2 :** a rising stretch of road : an upward grade : RISE
**3 :** an increase in amount: as **a :** an increase of a bet or bid **b :** an increase in wages or salary
**4 :** a vertical or inclined opening or passageway connecting one mine working area with another at a higher level

**raised** *adjective* (1599)
**1 a :** done in relief **b :** having a nap
**2 :** leavened with yeast rather than with baking powder or baking soda

**rai·sin** \'rā-zᵊn\ *noun* [Middle English, from Middle French, grape, from Latin *racemus* cluster of grapes or berries — more at RACEME] (14th century)
: a grape of any of several varieties that has been dried in the sun or by artificial heat

**rai·son d'être** *also* **rai·son d'etre** \ˌrā-ˌzōⁿ-'detrᵊ\ *noun* [French] (1864)
: reason or justification for existence

**raj** \'räj\ *noun* [Hindi *rāj*, from Sanskrit *rājya*; akin to Sanskrit *rājan* king] (1800)

: RULE; *especially, often* capitalized : the former British rule of the Indian subcontinent

**ra·ja** *or* **ra·jah** \'rä-jə, -(ˌ)jä, -zhə, -(ˌ)zhä\ *noun* [Hindi *rājā*, from Sanskrit *rājan* king — more at ROYAL] (1555)
**1 :** an Indian or Malay prince or chief
**2 :** the bearer of a title of nobility among the Hindus

**Ra·jab** \rə-'jab\ *noun* [Arabic] (circa 1771)
: the 7th month of the Islamic year — see MONTH table

**Ra·jas·tha·ni** \ˌrä-jə-'stä-nē, ˌrä-zhə-\ *noun* [Hindi *Rājasthānī*, from *Rājasthān* Rajasthan] (1901)
: the Indo-Aryan dialects of Rajasthan

**Raj·put** *or* **Raj·poot** \'räj-ˌpu̇t, 'räzh-\ *noun* [Hindi *rājpūt*, from Sanskrit *rājaputra* king's son, from *rājan* king + *putra* son — more at FEW] (1598)
: a member of a dominant military caste of northern India

**¹rake** \'rāk\ *noun* [Middle English, from Old English *racu*; akin to Old High German *rehho* rake] (before 12th century)
**1 a :** an implement equipped with projecting prongs to gather material (as leaves) or for loosening or smoothing the surface of the ground **b :** a machine for gathering hay
**2 :** an implement like a rake

**²rake** *transitive verb* **raked; rak·ing** (13th century)
**1 :** to gather, loosen, or smooth with or as if with a rake
**2 :** to gain rapidly or in abundance ⟨*rake* in a fortune⟩
**3 a :** to touch in passing over lightly **b :** SCRATCH
**4 :** to censure severely
**5 :** to search through : RANSACK
**6 :** to sweep the length of especially with gunfire : ENFILADE
**7 :** to glance over rapidly
— **rak·er** *noun*

**³rake** *noun* [origin unknown] (1626)
**1 :** inclination from the perpendicular; *especially* : the overhang of a ship's bow or stern
**2 :** inclination from the horizontal : SLOPE
**3 :** the angle between the top cutting surface of a tool and a plane perpendicular to the surface of the work
**4 :** the angle between a wing-tip edge that is sensibly straight in planform and the plane of symmetry of an airplane

**⁴rake** *intransitive verb* **raked; rak·ing** (1691)
: to incline from the perpendicular

**⁵rake** *noun* [short for *rakehell*] (1653)
: a dissolute person : LIBERTINE

**rake·hell** \'rāk-ˌhel\ *noun* (1554)
: LIBERTINE 2
— **rakehell** *or* **rake·helly** \-ˌhe-lē\ *adjective*

**rake–off** \'rāk-ˌȯf\ *noun* [*rake off*, verb; from the use of a rake by a croupier to collect the operator's profits in a gambling casino] (1888)
: a percentage or cut taken (as by an operator)

**rake up** *transitive verb* (1581)
: to make known or public : UNCOVER ⟨*rake up* a scandal⟩

**ra·ki** \rə-'kē; 'ra-kē, 'rä-\ *noun* [Turkish, from Arabic *'araqī*, literally, of liquor, from *'araq* liquor, arrack] (1675)
: a Turkish liqueur flavored with aniseed

**¹rak·ish** \'rā-kish\ *adjective* [⁵*rake*] (1706)
: of, relating to, or characteristic of a rake : DISSOLUTE

**²rakish** *adjective* [probably from ⁴*rake*; from the raking masts of pirate ships] (1824)
**1 :** having a trim or streamlined appearance suggestive of speed ⟨a *rakish* ship⟩
**2 :** dashingly or carelessly unconventional : JAUNTY ⟨*rakish* clothes⟩
— **rak·ish·ly** *adverb* (1838)
: in a rakish manner

**rak·ish·ness** *noun* (circa 1828)
: the quality or state of being rakish

**rale** \'ral, 'räl\ *noun* [French *râle*, from *râler* to make a rattling sound in the throat] (1828)
: an abnormal sound heard accompanying the normal respiratory sounds on auscultation of the chest

**ral·len·tan·do** \ˌrä-lən-'tän-(ˌ)dō\ *adverb or adjective* [Italian, literally, slowing down, verbal of *rallentare* to slow down again, from *re- + allentare* to slow down, from Late Latin, from Latin *al- ad- + lentus* slow, pliant — more at LITHE] (circa 1811)
: RITARDANDO

**¹ral·ly** \'ra-lē\ *verb* **ral·lied; ral·ly·ing** [French *rallier*, from Old French *ralier*, from *re- + alier* to unite — more at ALLY] (1603)
*transitive verb*
**1 a :** to muster for a common purpose **b :** to recall to order
**2 a :** to arouse for action **b :** to rouse from depression or weakness
*intransitive verb*
**1 :** to come together again to renew an effort
**2 :** to join in a common cause
**3 :** RECOVER, REBOUND
**4 :** to engage in a rally

**²rally** *noun, plural* **rallies** (1651)
**1 a :** a mustering of scattered forces to renew an effort **b :** a summoning up of strength or courage after weakness or dejection **c :** a recovery of price after a decline **d :** a renewed offensive
**2 :** a mass meeting intended to arouse group enthusiasm

□ **USAGE**
**raise** Some critics still offer the prescription "raise plants and animals and rear children." What is wrong with raising children? Actually, nothing. Sense 5c of *raise* dropped out of fashionable use in England around 1800 but continued in American use. Throughout the 19th century, English reviewers, who commonly found much to fault in the writing of American authors, seem to have included this use of *raise* among other objectionable usages. American literati appear to have been somewhat sensitive to the criticism, and *raise* came to be viewed as something less than elegant. In the opinion of some New Englanders, including Noah Webster, this use of *raise* was a Southernism. The two leading 19th century American dictionaries, Webster's and Worcester's, were both edited by New Englanders, and both labeled *raise* as a Southern usage. So when the question was picked up by handbooks, the dictionaries could be cited as evidence the usage was not standard, but regional. We now know that the description of *raise* as a Southernism was not quite accurate—John Adams had used it. The usage was simply American ⟨grew up, and married, and *raised* a large family —Mark Twain⟩ ⟨the small town in which I was *raised* —Sherwood Anderson⟩ ⟨a very great advantage to have been *raised* in an atmosphere of evangelical piety — Irving Howe⟩. We now know too that *raise* was used of humans in the English of Scotland, Ireland, and some northern and eastern counties of England. And it seems not to have died entirely in the mainstream even in England ⟨she had been *raised* in virtual seclusion —Lady Antonia Fraser⟩. This sense is standard and can be used without a second thought.

\ə\ **abut** \ᵊ\ **kitten** \ər\ **further** \a\ **ash** \ā\ **ace**
\ä\ **mop, mar** \au̇\ **out** \ch\ **chin** \e\ **bet** \ē\ **easy**
\g\ **go** \i\ **hit** \ī\ **ice** \j\ **job** \ŋ\ **sing** \ō\ **go**
\ȯ\ **law** \ȯi\ **boy** \th\ **thin** \th̷\ **the** \ü\ **loot** \u̇\ **foot**
\y\ **yet** \zh\ **vision** *see also* Guide to Pronunciation

**3 :** a series of shots interchanged between players (as in tennis) before a point is won
**4** *also* **ral·lye** [French *rallye,* from English ¹*rally*] **:** an automobile competition using public roads and ordinary traffic rules with the object of maintaining a specified average speed between checkpoints over a route unknown to the participants until the start of the event
³**rally** *transitive verb* **ral·lied; ral·ly·ing** [French *railler* to mock, rally — more at RAIL] (1668)
**:** to attack with raillery **:** BANTER
**ral·ly·ing** \'ra-lē-iŋ\ *noun* (1957)
**:** the sport of driving in automobile rallies
¹**ram** \'ram\ *noun* [Middle English, from Old English *ramm;* akin to Old High German *ram*] (before 12th century)
**1 a :** a male sheep **b** *capitalized* **:** ARIES
**2 a :** BATTERING RAM **b :** a warship with a heavy beak at the prow for piercing an enemy ship
**3 :** any of various guided pieces for exerting pressure or for driving or forcing something by impact: as **a :** the plunger of a hydrostatic press or force pump **b :** the weight that strikes the blow in a pile driver
²**ram** *verb* **rammed; ram·ming** [Middle English *rammen,* probably from *ram,* noun] (14th century)
*intransitive verb*
**1 :** to strike with violence **:** CRASH
**2 :** to move with extreme rapidity
*transitive verb*
**1 :** to force in by or as if by driving
**2 a :** to make compact (as by pounding) **b :** CRAM, CROWD
**3 :** to force passage or acceptance of ⟨*ram* home an idea⟩
**4 :** to strike against violently
— **ram·mer** *noun*
**RAM** \'ram\ *noun* (1957)
**:** RANDOM-ACCESS MEMORY
**Ra·ma** \'rä-mə\ *noun* [Sanskrit *Rāma*]
**:** a deity or deified hero of later Hinduism worshiped as an avatar of Vishnu
**Ram·a·dan** \'rä-mə-,dän, ,rä-mə-'-\ *noun* [Arabic *Ramaḍān*] (circa 1595)
**:** the 9th month of the Islamic year observed as sacred with fasting practiced daily from dawn to sunset — see MONTH table
**ra·mate** \'rä-,māt\ *adjective* [Latin *ramus* branch — more at RAMIFY] (1897)
**:** RAMOSE
¹**ram·ble** \'ram-bəl\ *verb* **ram·bled; rambling** \-b(ə-)liŋ\ [perhaps from Middle English *romblen,* frequentative of *romen* to roam] (1620)
*intransitive verb*
**1 a :** to move aimlessly from place to place **b :** to explore idly
**2 :** to talk or write in a desultory or long-winded wandering fashion
**3 :** to grow or extend irregularly
*transitive verb*
**:** to wander over **:** ROAM
**synonym** see WANDER
— **ram·bling·ly** \-b(ə-)liŋ-lē\ *adverb*
²**ramble** *noun* (1654)
**:** a leisurely excursion for pleasure; *especially* **:** an aimless walk
**ram·bler** \'ram-blər\ *noun* (1624)
**1 :** one that rambles
**2 :** any of various climbing roses with long flexible canes and rather small often double flowers in large clusters
**3 :** RANCH HOUSE
**ram·bouil·let** \,ram-bə-'lā, -bü-'yā\ *noun, often capitalized* [*Rambouillet,* France] (1906)
**:** any of a breed of large sturdy sheep developed in France
**ram·bunc·tious** \ram-'bəŋk-shəs\ *adjective* [probably alteration of *rumbustious*] (1830)
**:** marked by uncontrollable exuberance **:** UNRULY
— **ram·bunc·tious·ly** *adverb*
— **ram·bunc·tious·ness** *noun*

**ram·bu·tan** \ram-'bü-t°n\ *noun* [Malay] (1707)
**:** a bright red spiny Malayan fruit closely related to the litchi; *also* **:** a tree (*Nephelium lappaceum*) of the soapberry family that bears this fruit
**ram·e·kin** *also* **ram·e·quin** \'ram-kən, 'rami-\ *noun* [French *ramequin,* from Low German *ramken,* diminutive of *ram* cream] (circa 1706)
**1 :** a preparation of cheese especially with bread crumbs or eggs baked in a mold or shell
**2 :** an individual baking dish
**ra·met** \'rā-,met\ *noun* [Latin *ramus* branch] (1929)
**:** an independent member of a clone
**ra·mie** \'rā-mē, 'ra-\ *noun* [Malay *rami*] (1832)
**1 :** an Asian perennial plant (*Boehmeria nivea*) of the nettle family
**2 a :** the strong lustrous bast fiber of ramie capable of being spun or woven **b :** fabric made of ramie often resembling linen or silk
**ram·i·fi·ca·tion** \,ra-mə-fə-'kā-shən\ *noun* (1665)
**1 a :** BRANCH, OFFSHOOT **b :** a branched structure
**2 a :** the act or process of branching **b :** arrangement of branches (as on a plant)
**3 :** CONSEQUENCE, OUTGROWTH ⟨the *ramifications* of a problem⟩
**ram·i·fy** \'ra-mə-,fī\ *verb* **-fied; -fy·ing** [Middle English *ramifien,* from Middle French *ramifier,* from Medieval Latin *ramificare,* from Latin *ramus* branch; akin to Latin *radix* root — more at ROOT] (15th century)
*intransitive verb*
**1 :** to split up into branches or constituent parts
**2 :** to send forth branches or extensions
*transitive verb*
**1 :** to cause to branch
**2 :** to separate into divisions
**Ra·mism** \'rā-,mi-zəm\ *noun* [Petrus *Ramus* (died 1572) French philosopher] (1710)
**:** the doctrines of Ramus based on opposition to Aristotelianism and advocacy of a new logic blended with rhetoric
— **Ra·mist** \-mist\ *noun or adjective*
**ram·jet** \'ram-,jet\ *noun* (1942)
**:** a jet engine that consists essentially of a hollow tube without mechanical components and depends on the aircraft's speed of flight for the air compression necessary to produce the thrust obtained from the expansion of gases caused by the combustion of fuel
**ra·mose** \'rā-,mōs\ *adjective* [Latin *ramosus,* from *ramus* branch] (1689)
**:** consisting of or having branches ⟨a *ramose* sponge⟩
¹**ramp** \'ramp\ *verb* [Middle English, from Middle French *ramper* to crawl, rear, of Germanic origin; akin to Old High German *rimpfan* to wrinkle — more at RUMPLE] (14th century)
*intransitive verb*
**1 a :** to stand or advance menacingly with forelegs or with arms raised **b :** to move or act furiously
**2 :** to creep up — used especially of plants
*transitive verb*
[⁴*ramp* (electrical waveform)] **:** to increase or decrease especially at a constant rate — usually used with *up* or *down* ⟨*ramp* up production⟩
²**ramp** *noun* (1671)
**:** the act or an instance of ramping
³**ramp** *noun* [back-formation from *ramps,* alteration of *rams,* from Middle English, from Old English *hramsa;* akin to Old High German *ramusia* ramp, Greek *krommyon* onion] (1598)
**:** any of various alliums used for food

⁴**ramp** *noun* [French *rampe,* from *ramper,* from Middle French] (1778)
**1 :** a short bend, slope, or curve usually in the vertical plane where a handrail or coping changes its direction
**2 :** a sloping way: as **a :** a sloping floor, walk, or roadway leading from one level to another **b :** a stairway for entering or leaving an airplane **c :** a slope for launching boats
**3 :** APRON 2h
¹**ram·page** \'ram-,pāj, (,)ram-'\ *intransitive verb* **ram·paged; ram·pag·ing** [Scots] (1808)
**:** to rush wildly about
²**ram·page** \'ram-,pāj\ *noun* (1861)
**:** a course of violent, riotous, or reckless action or behavior
— **ram·pa·geous** \ram-'pā-jəs\ *adjective*
— **ram·pa·geous·ly** *adverb*
— **ram·pa·geous·ness** *noun*
**ram·pan·cy** \'ram-pən(t)-sē\ *noun* (1664)
**:** the quality or state of being rampant
**ram·pant** \'ram-pənt *also* -,pant\ *adjective* [Middle English, from Middle French, present participle of *ramper*] (14th century)
**1 a :** rearing upon the hind legs with forelegs extended **b :** standing on one hind foot with one foreleg raised above the other and the head in profile — used of a heraldic animal
**2 a :** marked by a menacing wildness, extravagance, or absence of restraint **b :** WIDESPREAD
**3 :** having one impost or abutment higher than the other ⟨a *rampant* arch⟩
— **ram·pant·ly** *adverb*
**ram·part** \'ram-,pärt, -pərt\ *noun* [Middle French, from *ramparer* to fortify, from *re-* + *emparer* to defend, from Old Provençal *antparar,* from (assumed) Vulgar Latin *anteparare,* from Latin *ante* before + *parare* to prepare — more at ANTE-, PARE] (1536)
**1 :** a protective barrier **:** BULWARK
**2 :** a broad embankment raised as a fortification and usually surmounted by a parapet
**3 :** a wall-like ridge (as of rock fragments, earth, or debris)
**ram·pike** \-,pīk\ *noun* [origin unknown] (1853)
**:** an erect broken or dead tree
¹**ram·rod** \'ram-,räd\ *noun* (1757)
**1 :** a rod for ramming home the charge in a muzzle-loading firearm
**2 :** a cleaning rod for small arms
**3 :** BOSS, OVERSEER
²**ramrod** *adjective* (1905)
**:** marked by rigidity, severity, or stiffness
³**ramrod** *transitive verb* (circa 1940)
**:** to direct, supervise, and control
**ram·shack·le** \'ram-,sha-kəl\ *adjective* [alteration of earlier *ransackled,* from past participle of obsolete *ransackle,* frequentative of *ransack*] (1830)
**1 :** appearing ready to collapse **:** RICKETY
**2 :** carelessly or loosely constructed
**rams·horn** \'ramz-,hòrn\ *noun* (1901)
**:** any of various snails (as genera *Planorbis, Helisoma,* and *Planorbarius*) often used as aquarium scavengers
**ra·mus** \'rā-məs\ *noun, plural* **ra·mi** \-,mī\ [New Latin, from Latin, branch — more at RAMIFY] (1803)
**:** a projecting part, elongated process, or branch: as **a :** the posterior more or less vertical part on each side of the lower jaw that articulates with the skull **b :** a branch of a nerve
**ran** *past of* RUN
¹**ranch** \'ranch\ *noun* [Mexican Spanish *rancho* small ranch, from Spanish, camp, hut & Spanish dialect, small farm, from Old Spanish *ranchearse* to take up quarters, from Middle French *se ranger* to take up a position, from *ranger* to set in a row — more at RANGE] (1831)
**1 :** a large farm for raising horses, beef cattle, or sheep
**2 :** a farm or area devoted to a particular specialty

**3 :** RANCH HOUSE ◆
**²ranch** (1866)
*intransitive verb*
**:** to live or work on a ranch
*transitive verb*
**1 :** to work as a rancher on
**2 :** to raise on a ranch
**ranch dressing** *noun* (1984)
**:** a creamy salad dressing usually containing milk or buttermilk and mayonnaise
**ranch·er** \'ran-chər\ *noun* (1836)
**:** one who owns or works on a ranch
**ran·che·ro** \ran-'cher-(ˌ)ō, rän-\ *noun, plural* **-ros** [Mexican Spanish, from *rancho*] (1826)
**:** RANCHER; *also* **:** RANCH 1
**ranch house** *noun* (1862)
**1 :** the main dwelling house on a ranch
**2 :** a one-story house typically with a low-pitched roof and an open plan
**word history** see RANCH
**ranch·man** \'ranch-mən\ *noun* (1856)
**:** RANCHER
**ran·cho** \'ran-(ˌ)chō, 'rän-\ *noun, plural* **ran·chos** [Mexican Spanish, small ranch] (1808)
**:** RANCH 1
**word history** see RANCH
**ran·cid** \'ran(t)-səd\ *adjective* [Latin *rancidus*, from *rancēre* to be rancid] (1646)
**1 :** having a rank smell or taste
**2 :** OFFENSIVE
— **ran·cid·i·ty** \ran-'si-də-tē\ *noun*
— **ran·cid·ness** \'ran(t)-səd-nəs\ *noun*
**ran·cor** \'ran-kər, -ˌkȯr\ *noun* [Middle English *rancour*, from Middle French *ranceur*, from Late Latin *rancor* rancidity, rancor, from Latin *rancēre*] (14th century)
**:** bitter deep-seated ill will
**synonym** see ENMITY
**ran·cor·ous** \'ran-k(ə-)rəs\ *adjective* (1590)
**:** marked by rancor
— **ran·cor·ous·ly** *adverb*
**ran·cour** *British variant of* RANCOR
**rand** \'rand, 'ränd, 'ränt\ *noun, plural* **rand** [the *Rand*, South Africa] (circa 1932)
**1 :** see MONEY table
**2 :** a former monetary unit of Botswana, Lesotho, and Swaziland
**R and D** *noun* (1966)
**:** research and development
**¹ran·dom** \'ran-dəm\ *noun* [Middle English, impetuosity, from Middle French *randon*, from Old French, from *randir* to run, of Germanic origin; akin to Old High German *rinnan* to run — more at RUN] (1561)
**:** a haphazard course
— **at random :** without definite aim, direction, rule, or method
**²random** *adjective* (1565)
**1 a :** lacking a definite plan, purpose, or pattern **b :** made, done, or chosen at random ⟨read *random* passages from the book⟩
**2 a :** relating to, having, or being elements or events with definite probability of occurrence ⟨*random* processes⟩ **b :** being or relating to a set or to an element of a set each of whose elements has equal probability of occurrence ⟨a *random* sample⟩; *also* **:** characterized by procedures designed to obtain such sets or elements ⟨*random* sampling⟩ ☆
— **ran·dom·ly** *adverb*
— **ran·dom·ness** *noun*
**³random** *adverb* (1618)
**:** in a random manner
**random–access** *adjective* (1953)
**:** permitting access to stored data in any order the user desires
**random–access memory** *noun* (1955)
**:** a computer memory that provides the main internal storage available to the user for programs and data — called also *RAM*; compare READ-ONLY MEMORY
**ran·dom·ize** \'ran-də-ˌmīz\ *transitive verb* **-ized; -iz·ing** (1926)
**:** to select, assign, or arrange in a random way
— **ran·dom·i·za·tion** \ˌran-də-mə-'zā-shən\ *noun*

— **ran·dom·iz·er** *noun*
**randomized block** *noun* (circa 1942)
**:** an experimental design (as in horticulture) in which different treatments are distributed in random order in a block or plot — called also *randomized block design*
**random variable** *noun* (1949)
**:** a variable that is itself a function of the result of a statistical experiment in which each outcome has a definite probability of occurrence — called also *variate*
**random walk** *noun* (1941)
**:** a process (as Brownian motion or genetic drift) consisting of a sequence of steps (as movements or changes in gene frequency) each of whose characteristics (as magnitude and direction) is determined by chance
**¹randy** \'ran-dē\ *adjective* [probably from obsolete *rand* to rant] (1698)
**1** *chiefly Scottish* **:** having a coarse manner
**2 :** LUSTFUL, LECHEROUS
**²randy** *noun, plural* **rand·ies** (1762)
*chiefly Scottish* **:** a scolding or dissolute woman
**rang** *past of* RING
**¹range** \'rānj\ *noun, often attributive* [Middle English, row of persons, from Middle French *renge*, from Old French *rengier* to range] (14th century)
**1 a** (1) **:** a series of things in a line **:** ROW (2) **:** a series of mountains (3) **:** one of the north-south rows of townships in a U.S. public-land survey that are numbered east and west from the principal meridian of the survey **b :** an aggregate of individuals in one order **c :** a direction line
**2 :** a cooking stove that has an oven and a flat top with burners or heating elements
**3 a :** a place that may be ranged over **b :** an open region over which animals (as livestock) may roam and feed **c :** the region throughout which a kind of organism or ecological community naturally lives or occurs
**4 :** the act of ranging about
**5 a** (1) **:** the horizontal distance to which a projectile can be propelled (2) **:** the horizontal distance between a weapon and target **b :** the maximum distance a vehicle or craft can travel without refueling **c** (1) **:** a place where shooting is practiced (2) **:** DRIVING RANGE
**6 a :** the space or extent included, covered, or used **:** SCOPE **b :** the extent of pitch covered by a melody or lying within the capacity of a voice or instrument
**7 a :** a sequence, series, or scale between limits ⟨a wide *range* of patterns⟩ **b :** the limits of a series **:** the distance or extent between possible extremes **c :** the difference between the least and greatest values of an attribute or of the variable of a frequency distribution
**8 a :** the set of values a function may take on **b :** the class of admissible values of a variable
**9 :** LINE 11 ☆
**²range** *verb* **ranged; rang·ing** [Middle English, from Middle French *ranger*, from Old French *rengier*, from *renc, reng* line, place, row — more at RANK] (14th century)
*transitive verb*
**1 a :** to set in a row or in the proper order **b :** to place among others in a position or situation **c :** to assign to a category **:** CLASSIFY
**2 a :** to rove over or through **b :** to sail or pass along
**3 :** to arrange (an anchor cable) on deck
**4 :** to graze (livestock) on a range
**5 :** to determine or give the elevation necessary for (a gun) to propel a projectile to a given distance
*intransitive verb*
**1 a :** to roam at large or freely **b :** to move over an area so as to explore it
**2 :** to take a position
**3 a :** to correspond in direction or line **:** ALIGN **b :** to extend in a particular direction
**4 :** to have range

**5 :** to change or differ within limits
**6** *of an organism* **:** to live or occur in or be native to a region
**7 :** to obtain the range of an object by instrument (as radar or laser)
**word history** see RANCH
**range finder** *noun* (1872)
**1 :** an instrument used in gunnery to determine the distance of a target

---

☆ **SYNONYMS**
**Random, haphazard, casual** mean determined by accident rather than design. RANDOM stresses lack of definite aim, fixed goal, or regular procedure ⟨a *random* selection of books⟩. HAPHAZARD applies to what is done without regard for regularity or fitness or ultimate consequence ⟨a *haphazard* collection of rocks⟩. CASUAL suggests working or acting without deliberation, intention, or purpose ⟨a *casual* collector⟩.

**Range, gamut, compass, sweep, scope, orbit** mean the extent that lies within the powers of something (as to cover or control). RANGE is a general term indicating the extent of one's perception or the extent of powers, capacities, or possibilities ⟨the entire *range* of human experience⟩. GAMUT suggests a graduated series running from one possible extreme to another ⟨a performance that ran the *gamut* of emotions⟩. COMPASS implies a sometimes limited extent of perception, knowledge, or activity ⟨your concerns lie beyond the narrow *compass* of this study⟩. SWEEP suggests extent, often circular or arc-shaped, of motion or activity ⟨the book covers the entire *sweep* of criminal activity⟩. SCOPE is applicable to an area of activity, predetermined and limited, but somewhat flexible ⟨as time went on, the *scope* of the investigation widened⟩. ORBIT suggests an often circumscribed range of activity or influence within which forces work toward accommodation ⟨within that restricted *orbit* they tried to effect social change⟩.

---

◇ **WORD HISTORY**
**ranch** Old French *renc* or *ranc* "row, line" (the source of English *rank*) gave rise to a verb *rengier* "to set in rows, place in proper order" (the source of English *range*). The reflexive form of this verb in Middle French, *se ranger,* meant "to line up, take a position." By the 16th century, *se ranger* had found its way into Spanish as *rancharse,* which meant in military contexts "to take up quarters, be billeted." The conquistadores who took this verb to the Americas were also familiar with a derivative noun *rancho,* denoting originally a camp or temporary dwelling such as a hut. The word *rancho* remains widely used in American Spanish, with much local variation in meaning. Both the general sense "habitation" and the specifically Mexican Spanish sense "small farm" were adopted into American English in the 19th century directly as *rancho* and in the Anglicized form *ranch*. By the late 19th century, *ranch* most often denoted not a small farm but a large tract of land devoted to livestock-raising—a meaning the word still maintains. The one-story, rambling dwelling typical of ranches was the prototype of that staple of American domestic architecture, the *ranch house*.

---

\ə\ abut \ˀ\ kitten \ər\ further \a\ ash \ā\ ace
\ä\ mop, mar \au̇\ out \ch\ chin \e\ bet \ē\ easy
\g\ go \i\ hit \ī\ ice \j\ job \ŋ\ sing \ō\ go
\ȯ\ law \ȯi\ boy \th\ thin \t̲h̲\ the \ü\ loot \u̇\ foot
\y\ yet \zh\ vision    *see also* Guide to Pronunciation

**2 :** a surveying instrument (as a transit) for determining quickly the distances, bearings, and elevations of distant objects

**3 :** a usually built-in adjustable optical device for focusing a camera that automatically indicates the correct focus (as when two parts of a split image are brought together)

**range·land** \'rānj-ˌland\ *noun* (1935)
**:** land used or suitable for range

**rang·er** \'rān-jər\ *noun* (14th century)
**1 a :** the keeper of a British royal park or forest **b :** FOREST RANGER
**2 :** one that ranges
**3 a :** one of a body of organized armed men who range over a region especially to enforce the law **b :** a soldier specially trained in close-range fighting and in raiding tactics

**rangy** \'rān-jē\ *adjective* **rang·i·er; -est** (1868)
**1 :** able to range for considerable distances
**2 a :** long-limbed and long-bodied ⟨*rangy* cattle⟩ **b :** being tall and slender
**3 :** having room for ranging
**4 :** having great scope
— **rang·i·ness** *noun*

**ra·ni** *or* **ra·nee** \rä-'nē, 'rä-ˌnē\ *noun* [Hindi *rānī*, from Sanskrit *rājñī*, feminine of *rājan* king — more at ROYAL] (1673)
**:** a Hindu queen : a rajah's wife

**ra·nid** \'ra-nəd, 'rā-\ *noun* [ultimately from Latin *rana* frog] (circa 1934)
**:** any of a large family (Ranidae) of frogs distinguished by slightly dilated transverse sacral processes

**¹rank** \'raŋk\ *adjective* [Middle English, from Old English *ranc* overbearing, strong; akin to Old Norse *rakkr* erect and perhaps to Old English *riht* right — more at RIGHT] (13th century)
**1 :** luxuriantly or excessively vigorous in growth
**2 :** offensively gross or coarse : FOUL
**3** *obsolete* **:** grown too large
**4 a :** shockingly conspicuous ⟨must lecture him on his *rank* disloyalty —David Walden⟩ **b :** OUTRIGHT — used as an intensive ⟨*rank* beginners⟩
**5** *archaic* **:** LUSTFUL, RUTTISH
**6 :** offensive in odor or flavor; *especially* **:** RANCID
**7 :** PUTRID, FESTERING
**8 :** high in amount or degree : FRAUGHT
**synonym** see MALODOROUS, FLAGRANT
— **rank·ly** *adverb*
— **rank·ness** *noun*

**²rank** *noun* [Middle English, from Middle French *renc, reng,* of Germanic origin; akin to Old High German *hring* ring — more at RING] (14th century)
**1 a :** ROW, SERIES **b :** a row of people **c** (1) **:** a line of soldiers ranged side by side in close order (2) *plural* **:** ARMED FORCES (3) *plural* **:** the body of enlisted personnel **d :** any of the rows of squares that extend across a chessboard perpendicular to the files **e** *British* **:** STAND 6
**2 a :** relative standing or position **b :** a degree or position of dignity, eminence, or excellence **:** DISTINCTION ⟨soon took *rank* as a leading attorney —J. D. Hicks⟩ **c :** high social position ⟨the privileges of *rank*⟩ **d :** a grade of official standing in a hierarchy
**3 :** an orderly arrangement : FORMATION
**4 :** an aggregate of individuals classed together — usually used in plural
**5 :** the order according to some statistical characteristic (as the score on a test)
**6 :** any of a series of classes of coal based on increasing alteration of the parent vegetable matter, increasing carbon content, and increasing fuel value
**7 :** the number of linearly independent rows or columns in a matrix
**word history** see RANCH

**³rank** (1573)
*transitive verb*
**1 :** to arrange in lines or in a regular formation

**2 :** to determine the relative position of **:** RATE
**3 :** to take precedence of
*intransitive verb*
**1 :** to form or move in ranks
**2 :** to take or have a position in relation to others

**rank and file** *noun* (1598)
**1 :** the enlisted personnel of an armed force
**2 :** the individuals who constitute the body of an organization, society, or nation as distinguished from the leaders
— **rank–and–file** \ˌraŋk-ᵊn-'fīl\ *adjective*
— **rank and fil·er** \-'fī-lər\ *noun*

**rank correlation** *noun* (1907)
**:** a measure of correlation depending on rank

**rank·er** \'raŋ-kər\ *noun* (1878)
**:** one who serves or has served in the ranks; *especially* **:** a commissioned officer promoted from the ranks

**Ran·kine** \'raŋ-kən\ *adjective* [William J. M. *Rankine* (died 1872) Scottish engineer & physicist] (circa 1926)
**:** being, according to, or relating to an absolute-temperature scale on which the unit of measurement equals a Fahrenheit degree and on which the freezing point of water is 491.67° and the boiling point 671.67°

**rank·ing** *adjective* (1862)
**:** having a high position: as **a :** FOREMOST ⟨*ranking* poet⟩ **b :** being next to the chairman in seniority ⟨*ranking* committee member⟩

**ran·kle** \'raŋ-kəl\ *verb* **ran·kled; ran·kling** \-k(ə-)liŋ\ [Middle English *ranclen* to fester, from Middle French *rancler*, from Old French *draoncler, raoncler*, from *draoncle, raoncle* festering sore, from Medieval Latin *dracunculus*, from Latin, diminutive of *draco* serpent — more at DRAGON] (1606)
*intransitive verb*
**1 :** to cause anger, irritation, or deep bitterness
**2 :** to feel anger and irritation
*transitive verb*
**:** to cause irritation or bitterness in ◆

**ran·sack** \'ran-ˌsak, (ˌ)ran-'\ *transitive verb* [Middle English *ransaken*, from Old Norse *rannsaka*, from *rann* house + *-saka* (akin to Old English *sēcan* to seek) — more at SEEK] (13th century)
**1 a :** to search thoroughly **b :** to examine closely and carefully
**2 :** to search through to commit robbery : PLUNDER
— **ran·sack·er** *noun*

**¹ran·som** \'ran(t)-səm\ *noun* [Middle English *ransoun*, from Old French *rançon*, from Latin *redemption-, redemptio* — more at REDEMPTION] (13th century)
**1 :** a consideration paid or demanded for the release of someone or something from captivity
**2 :** the act of ransoming

**²ransom** *transitive verb* (14th century)
**1 :** to deliver especially from sin or its penalty
**2 :** to free from captivity or punishment by paying a price
**synonym** see RESCUE
— **ran·som·er** *noun*

**¹rant** \'rant\ *verb* [obsolete Dutch *ranten, randen*] (1602)
*intransitive verb*
**1 :** to talk in a noisy, excited, or declamatory manner
**2 :** to scold vehemently
*transitive verb*
**:** to utter in a bombastic declamatory fashion
— **rant·er** *noun*
— **rant·ing·ly** \'ran-tiŋ-lē\ *adverb*

**²rant** *noun* (1649)
**1 a :** a bombastic extravagant speech **b :** bombastic extravagant language
**2** *dialect British* **:** a rousing good time

**ran·u·la** \'ran-yə-lə\ *noun* [New Latin, from Latin, swelling on the tongue of cattle, from diminutive of *rana* frog] (15th century)
**:** a cyst formed under the tongue by obstruction of a gland duct

**ra·nun·cu·lus** \rə-'nəŋ-kyə-ləs\ *noun, plural* **-lus·es** *or* **-li** \-ˌlī, -ˌlē\ [New Latin, from Latin, from diminutive of *rana* frog] (1543)
**:** BUTTERCUP

**¹rap** \'rap\ *noun* [Middle English *rappe*] (14th century)
**1 :** a sharp blow or knock
**2 a :** a sharp rebuke or criticism **b :** a negative and often undeserved reputation or charge — usually used with *bum* or *bad* ⟨given a bum *rap* by the press⟩
**3 a :** the responsibility for or adverse consequences of an action ⟨refused to take the *rap*⟩ **b :** a criminal charge **c :** a prison sentence

**²rap** *verb* **rapped; rap·ping** (14th century)
*transitive verb*
**1 :** to strike with a sharp blow
**2 :** to utter suddenly and forcibly
**3 :** to cause to be or come by raps ⟨*rap* the meeting to order⟩
**4 :** to criticize sharply
*intransitive verb*
**1 :** to strike a quick sharp blow
**2 :** to make a short sharp sound

**³rap** *transitive verb* **rapped** *also* **rapt** \'rapt\; **rap·ping** [back-formation from *rapt*] (1528)
**1 :** to snatch away or upward
**2 :** ENRAPTURE

**⁴rap** *noun* [perhaps from ¹*rap*] (1834)
**:** a minimum amount or degree (as of care or consideration) **:** the least bit ⟨doesn't care a *rap*⟩

**⁵rap** *intransitive verb* **rapped; rap·ping** [perhaps from ¹*rap*] (1929)
**1 :** to talk freely and frankly
**2 :** to perform rap music

**⁶rap** *noun* (1967)
**1 :** TALK, CONVERSATION; *also* **:** a line of talk **:** PATTER
**2 a :** a rhythmic chanting often in unison of usually rhymed couplets to a musical accompaniment **b :** a piece so performed

**ra·pa·cious** \rə-'pā-shəs\ *adjective* [Latin *rapac-, rapax*, from *rapere* to seize — more at RAPID] (1651)
**1 :** excessively grasping or covetous
**2 :** living on prey
**3 :** RAVENOUS
**synonym** see VORACIOUS
**word history** see RAPT
— **ra·pa·cious·ly** *adverb*
— **ra·pa·cious·ness** *noun*

**ra·pac·i·ty** \rə-'pa-sə-tē\ *noun* (1543)
**:** the quality of being rapacious

**¹rape** \'rāp\ *noun* [Middle English, from Latin *rapa, rapum* turnip, rape; akin to Old High German *rāba* turnip, rape, Lithuanian *ropė*] (14th century)
**:** a European herb (*Brassica napus*) of the mustard family grown as a forage crop for sheep and hogs and for its seeds which yield rapeseed oil and are a bird food — compare CANOLA

◇ **WORD HISTORY**
**rankle** The modern meaning of the verb *rankle* "to cause anger, irritation, or bitterness" is a figurative extension of the earlier meaning "to fester, swell," said of an ulcer or festering sore. The Middle English predecessor of this verb, *ranclen* or *ranklen*, was a loanword from Middle French *rancler*, contracted from Old French *draoncler* or *raoncler*, a derivative of *draoncle* "festering sore." *Draoncle* is descended from Latin *dracunculus*, which in classical Latin is a diminutive of *draco* "snake," though in spoken Latin, to judge by its offspring in Romance languages, it must also have had the meaning "festering sore." The comparison of something both painful and destructive of body tissue to a biting animal is not surprising; another example is the use of *cancer* "crab" in Latin to denote gangrene or a malignant tumor.

**word history** see RAPT

²**rape** *transitive verb* **raped; rap·ing** [Middle English, from Latin *rapere*] (14th century)
**1 a** *archaic* : to seize and take away by force **b** : DESPOIL
**2** : to commit rape on
— **rap·er** *noun*
— **rap·ist** \'rā-pist\ *noun*

³**rape** *noun* (14th century)
**1** : an act or instance of robbing or despoiling or carrying away a person by force
**2 a** : sexual intercourse with a woman by a man without her consent and chiefly by force or deception — compare STATUTORY RAPE **b** : unlawful sexual intercourse by force or threat other than by a man with a woman
**3** : an outrageous violation

⁴**rape** *noun* [French *râpe* grape stalk] (1657)
: grape pomace

**rape·seed** \'rāp-ˌsēd\ *noun* (1577)
: the seed of the rape plant

**rapeseed oil** *noun* (1816)
: a nondrying or semidrying oil obtained from rapeseed and turnip seed and used chiefly as a lubricant, illuminant, and food — called also *rape oil;* compare CANOLA OIL

**Ra·pha·el** \'ra-fē-əl, 'rā-, -ˌel\ *noun* [Late Latin, from Greek *Rhaphaēl,* from Hebrew *Rĕphāʾēl*]
: one of the four archangels named in Hebrew tradition

**ra·phe** \'rā-(ˌ)fē\ *noun* [New Latin, from Greek *rhaphē* seam, from *rhaptein* to sew] (circa 1753)
**1** : the seamlike union of the two lateral halves of a part or organ (as the tongue) having externally a ridge or furrow
**2 a** : the part of the stalk of an anatropous ovary that is united in growth to the outside covering and forms a ridge along the body of the ovule **b** : the median line or slit of a diatom's valve

**ra·phia** \'rā-fē-ə, 'ra-\ *noun* [New Latin, genus of palms, from Malagasy *rafia* raffia] (circa 1866)
: RAFFIA

**raph·ide** \'ra-ˌfīd\ *noun, plural* **raph·ides** \'ra-ˌfīdz, 'ra-fə-ˌdēz\ [French & New Latin; French *raphide,* from New Latin *raphides,* plural, from Greek *rhaphides,* plural of *rhaphid-, rhaphis* needle, from *rhaptein*] (circa 1842)
: any of the needle-shaped crystals usually of calcium oxalate that develop as metabolic by-products in plant cells

¹**rap·id** \'ra-pəd\ *adjective* [Latin *rapidus* seizing, sweeping, rapid, from *rapere* to seize, sweep away; akin to Lithuanian *aprėpti* to embrace] (1634)
: marked by a fast rate of motion, activity, succession, or occurrence
**synonym** see FAST
— **rap·id·ly** *adverb*
— **rap·id·ness** *noun*

²**rapid** *noun* (1765)
: a part of a river where the current is fast and the surface is usually broken by obstructions — usually used in plural but singular or plural in construction

**rapid eye movement** *noun* (1916)
: a rapid conjugate movement of the eyes associated especially with REM sleep

**rapid eye movement sleep** *noun* (1965)
: REM SLEEP

**rap·id-fire** \ˌra-pəd-'fīr\ *adjective* (1890)
**1** : firing or adapted for firing shots in rapid succession
**2** : marked by rapidity, liveliness, or sharpness

**ra·pid·i·ty** \rə-'pi-də-tē, ra-\ *noun* (1654)
: the quality or state of being rapid

**rapid transit** *noun* (1873)
: fast passenger transportation (as by subway) in urban areas

**ra·pi·er** \'rā-pē-ər\ *noun* [Middle French (*es-pee*) *rapiere*] (1553)
: a straight 2-edged sword with a narrow pointed blade

**rap·ine** \'ra-pən, -ˌpīn\ *noun* [Middle English *rapyne,* from Latin *rapina,* from *rapere* to seize, rob] (15th century)
: PILLAGE, PLUNDER

**ra·pi·ni** *also* **rap·pi·ni** \ra-'pē-nē\ *noun* [Italian *rapini,* plural of *rapino,* diminutive of *rapo* turnip, from Latin *rapum* — more at RAPE] (1942)
: BROCCOLI RABE

**rap·pa·ree** \ˌra-pə-'rē\ *noun* [Irish *rapaire, ropaire,* literally, thruster, stabber, from *rop* thrust, stab] (1690)
**1** : an Irish irregular soldier or bandit
**2** : VAGABOND, PLUNDERER

**rap·pee** \ra-'pā\ *noun* [French (*tabac*) *râpé,* literally, grated tobacco] (circa 1740)
: a pungent snuff made from dark tobacco leaves

**rap·pel** \rə-'pel, ra-\ *intransitive verb* **-pelled** *also* **-peled; -pel·ling** *also* **-pel·ing** [French, literally, recall, from Old French *rapel,* from *rapeler* to recall, from *re-* + *apeler* to appeal, call — more at APPEAL] (1944)
: to descend (as from a cliff) by sliding down a rope passed under one thigh, across the body, and over the opposite shoulder or through a special friction device
— **rappel** *noun*

**rap·pen** \'rä-pən\ *noun, plural* **rappen** [German, from German dialect, literally, raven] (1838)
: the centime of Switzerland

**rap·per** \'ra-pər\ *noun* (1640)
: one that raps or is used for rapping: as **a** : a door knocker **b** : a performer of rap music

**rap·port** \ra-'pōr, rə-, -'pȯr\ *noun* [French, from *rapporter* to bring back, refer, from Old French *raporter* to bring back, from *re-* + *aporter* to bring, from Latin *apportare,* from *ad-* ad- + *portare* to carry — more at FARE] (circa 1661)
: RELATION; *especially* : relation marked by harmony, conformity, accord, or affinity

**rap·por·teur** \ˌra-ˌpōr-'tər, -ˌpȯr-\ *noun* [Middle French, from *rapporter* to bring back, report] (circa 1500)
: a person who gives reports (as at a meeting of a learned society)

**rap·proche·ment** \ˌra-ˌprōsh-'mäⁿ, -ˌprȯsh-; ra-'prōsh-\ *noun* [French, from *rapprocher* to bring together, from Middle French, from *re-* + *approcher* to approach, from Old French *aprochier*] (1809)
: establishment of or state of having cordial relations

**rap·scal·lion** \rap-'skal-yən\ *noun* [alteration of earlier *rascallion,* irregular from *rascal*] (1699)
: RASCAL, NE'ER-DO-WELL

**rap sheet** *noun* (1960)
: a police arrest record especially for an individual

**rapt** \'rapt\ *adjective* [Middle English, from Latin *raptus,* past participle of *rapere* to seize — more at RAPID] (14th century)
**1** : lifted up and carried away
**2** : transported with emotion : ENRAPTURED
**3** : wholly absorbed : ENGROSSED ◆
— **rapt·ly** \'rap(t)-lē\ *adverb*
— **rapt·ness** \'rap(t)-nəs\ *noun*

**rap·tor** \'rap-tər, -ˌtȯr\ *noun* [New Latin *Raptores,* former order name, from Latin, plural of *raptor* plunderer, from *rapere*] (1873)
: BIRD OF PREY
**word history** see RAPT

**rap·to·ri·al** \rap-'tȯr-ē-əl, -'tȯr-\ *adjective* (1823)
**1** : PREDACEOUS 1
**2** : adapted to seize prey
**3** : of, relating to, or being a bird of prey

¹**rap·ture** \'rap-chər\ *noun* [Latin *raptus*] (1629)
**1 a** : a state or experience of being carried away by overwhelming emotion **b** : a mystical experience in which the spirit is exalted to a knowledge of divine things
**2** : an expression or manifestation of ecstasy or passion
**synonym** see ECSTASY
**word history** see RAPT
— **rap·tur·ous** \'rap-chə-rəs, 'rap-shrəs\ *adjective*
— **rap·tur·ous·ly** *adverb*
— **rap·tur·ous·ness** *noun*

²**rapture** *transitive verb* **rap·tured; rap·tur·ing** (1637)
: ENRAPTURE

**rapture of the deep** (1953)
: NITROGEN NARCOSIS

**ra·ra avis** \ˌrar-ə-'ā-vəs, ˌrer-; ˌrär-ə-'ä-wəs\ *noun, plural* **ra·ra avis·es** \-'ā-və-səz\ *or* **ra·rae aves** \ˌrär-ˌī-'ā-ˌwās\ [Latin, rare bird] (1607)
: RARITY 2

¹**rare** \'rar, 'rer\ *adjective* **rar·er; rar·est** [Middle English, from Latin *rarus*] (14th century)
**1** : marked by wide separation of component particles : THIN ⟨*rare* air⟩
**2 a** : marked by unusual quality, merit, or appeal : DISTINCTIVE **b** : superlative or extreme of its kind
**3** : seldom occurring or found : UNCOMMON
**synonym** see CHOICE, INFREQUENT
— **rare·ness** *noun*

²**rare** *adjective* **rar·er; rar·est** [alteration of earlier *rere,* from Middle English, from Old English *hrēre* boiled lightly; akin to Old English *hrēran* to stir, Old High German *hruoren*] (1784)
: cooked so that the inside is still red ⟨*rare* roast beef⟩

**rare bird** *noun* (1890)
: RARITY 2, RARA AVIS

**rare·bit** \'rar-bət, 'rer-\ *noun* [(*Welsh*) *rarebit*] (circa 1785)
: WELSH RABBIT

**rare earth** *noun* (1875)
**1** : any of a group of similar oxides of metals or a mixture of such oxides occurring together in widely distributed but relatively scarce minerals

◇ WORD HISTORY
**rapt** Current usage of the adjective *rapt* reflects its history only dimly. It is borrowed from Latin *raptus,* the past participle of *rapere* "to seize, carry off." This Latin verb is the ultimate source of a number of other English words, including *rapacious* and *raptor,* which still convey something of the idea of seizing, as well as *rapture,* now more usual in the figurative sense of being carried away with emotional ecstasy. In Middle English *rapt* simply functioned as the past participle of *rapen,* which meant both "to rape" or "to abduct (a woman) with the intent of raping her" and, with a wholly different connotation, "to carry off" or "to transport" by divine agency. Fifteenth century authors use the latter sense when they speak of a saint being "rapt in to paradys" or of someone whose body "was rapte up fro the erthe." In early Modern English *rape,* with its long vowel, and *rapt,* with its short vowel, went their own separate ways. While *rape* maintained its brutal literal sense, *rapt* came to mean solely "carried away in spirit" and hence "transported by emotion" or "wholly absorbed or engrossed," which are its usual modern senses.

\ə\ abut \ᵊ\ kitten \ər\ further \a\ ash \ā\ ace
\ä\ mop, mar \au̇\ out \ch\ chin \e\ bet \ē\ easy
\g\ go \i\ hit \ī\ ice \j\ job \ŋ\ sing \ō\ go
\ȯ\ law \ȯi\ boy \th\ thin \th̲\ the \ü\ loot \u̇\ foot
\y\ yet \zh\ vision    *see also* Guide to Pronunciation

**2 :** RARE EARTH ELEMENT
**rare earth element** *noun* (1942)
: any of a series of metallic elements of which the oxides are classed as rare earths and which include the elements of the lanthanide series and sometimes yttrium and scandium — called also *rare earth metal*

**rar·ee–show** \'rar-ē-ˌshō, 'rer-\ *noun* [alteration of *rare show*] (1684)
: a small display or scene viewed in a box
: PEEP SHOW; *broadly* : an unusual or amazing show or spectacle

**rar·e·fac·tion** \ˌrar-ə-'fak-shən, ˌrer-\ *noun* [French or Medieval Latin; French *raréfaction,* from Medieval Latin *rarefaction-, rarefactio,* from Latin *rarefacere* to rarefy] (1603)
**1 :** the action or process of rarefying
**2 :** the quality or state of being rarefied
**3 :** a state or region of minimum pressure in a medium traversed by compressional waves (as sound waves)
   — **rar·e·fac·tion·al** \-shnəl, -shə-n°l\ *adjective*

**rar·e·fied** *also* **rar·i·fied** \'rar-ə-ˌfīd, 'rer-\ *adjective* (1941)
**1 :** of, relating to, or interesting to a select group **:** ESOTERIC
**2 :** very high

**rar·e·fy** *also* **rar·i·fy** \-ə-ˌfī\ *verb* **-fied; -fy·ing** [Middle English *rarefien, rarifien,* from Middle French *rarefier,* modification of Latin *rarefacere,* from *rarus* rare + *facere* to make — more at DO] (14th century)
*transitive verb*
**1 :** to make rare, thin, porous, or less dense
: to expand without the addition of matter
**2 :** to make more spiritual, refined, or abstruse
*intransitive verb*
: to become less dense

**rare·ly** \'rar-lē, 'rer-\ *adverb* (1552)
**1 :** not often **:** SELDOM
**2 :** with rare skill **:** EXCELLENTLY
**3 :** in an extreme or exceptional manner

**rare·ripe** \'rar-ˌrīp, 'rer-\ *noun* [English dialect *rare* early + English *ripe*] (1722)
**1 :** an early ripening fruit or vegetable
**2** *dialect* **:** GREEN ONION

**rar·ing** \'rar-ən, 'rer-, -iŋ\ *adjective* [from present participle of English dialect *rare* to rear, alteration of English *rear*] (1909)
: full of enthusiasm or eagerness ⟨ready and *raring* to go⟩

**rar·i·ty** \'rar-ə-tē, 'rer-\ *noun, plural* **-ties** (1542)
**1 :** the quality, state, or fact of being rare
**2 :** one that is rare

**ras·bo·ra** \raz-'bōr-ə, -'bȯr-\ *noun* [New Latin] (1931)
: any of a genus (*Rasbora*) of tiny brilliantly colored cyprinid freshwater fishes often kept in tropical aquariums

**ras·cal** \'ras-kəl\ *noun* [Middle English *rascaile* rabble, one of the rabble] (15th century)
**1 :** a mean, unprincipled, or dishonest person
**2 :** a mischievous person or animal
   — **rascal** *adjective*

**ras·cal·i·ty** \ra-'ska-lə-tē\ *noun, plural* **-ties** (circa 1577)
**1 :** RABBLE
**2 a :** the character or actions of a rascal **:** KNAVERY **b :** a rascally act

**ras·cal·ly** \'ras-kə-lē\ *adjective* (1594)
: of or characteristic of a rascal
   — **rascally** *adverb*

**rase** \'rāz\ *transitive verb* **rased; ras·ing** [Middle English, from Middle French *raser,* from (assumed) Vulgar Latin *rasare,* frequentative of Latin *radere* to scrape, shave — more at RODENT] (14th century)
**1** *archaic* **:** ERASE
**2** *archaic* **:** RAZE 2

**¹rash** \'rash\ *adverb* [Middle English (northern dialect) *rasch* quickly; akin to Old High German *rasc* fast] (15th century)
*archaic* **:** in a rash manner

**²rash** *adjective* (1509)
**1 :** marked by or proceeding from undue haste or lack of deliberation or caution
**2** *obsolete* **:** quickly effective
**synonym** see ADVENTUROUS
   — **rash·ly** *adverb*
   — **rash·ness** *noun*

**³rash** *noun* [obsolete French *rache* scurf, from (assumed) Vulgar Latin *rasica,* from *rasicare* to scratch, from Latin *rasus,* past participle of *radere*] (1709)
**1 :** an eruption on the body
**2 :** a large number of instances in a short period ⟨a *rash* of complaints⟩

**rash·er** \'ra-shər\ *noun* [perhaps from obsolete *rash* to cut, from Middle English *rashen*] (1592)
: a thin slice of bacon or ham broiled or fried; *also* : a portion consisting of several such slices

**¹rasp** \'rasp\ *verb* [Middle English, from (assumed) Middle French *rasper,* of Germanic origin; akin to Old High German *raspōn* to scrape together] (14th century)
*transitive verb*
**1 :** to rub with something rough; *specifically* : to abrade with a rasp
**2 :** to grate upon **:** IRRITATE
**3 :** to utter in a raspy tone
*intransitive verb*
**1 :** SCRAPE
**2 :** to produce a grating sound
   — **rasp·er** *noun*
   — **rasp·ing·ly** \'ras-piŋ-lē\ *adverb*

**²rasp** *noun* (circa 1512)
**1 :** a coarse file with cutting points instead of lines
**2 :** something used for rasping
**3 a :** an act of rasping **b :** a rasping sound, sensation, or effect

**rasp·ber·ry** \'raz-ˌber-ē, -b(ə-)rē\ *noun* [English dialect *rasp* raspberry + English *berry*] (circa 1616)
**1 a :** any of various usually black or red edible berries that are aggregate fruits consisting of numerous small drupes on a fleshy receptacle and that are usually rounder and smaller than the closely related blackberries **b :** a plant (genus *Rubus*) of the rose family that bears raspberries
**2** [short for *raspberry tart,* rhyming slang for *fart*] : a sound of contempt made by protruding the tongue between the lips and expelling air forcibly to produce a vibration; *broadly* : an expression of disapproval or contempt

**raspy** \'ras-pē\ *adjective* (1838)
**1 :** HARSH, GRATING
**2 :** IRRITABLE

**Ras·ta** \'ras-tə, 'räs-\ *noun* (1955)
: RASTAFARIAN
   — **Rasta** *adjective*

**Ras·ta·far·i·an** \ˌras-tə-'far-ē-ən, ˌräs-tə-'fär-\ *noun* [*Ras Tafari,* precoronation name of Haile Selassie] (1955)
: an adherent of Rastafarianism
   — **Rastafarian** *adjective*

**Ras·ta·far·i·an·ism** \-ē-ə-ˌni-zəm\ *noun* (1968)
: a religious cult among black Jamaicans that teaches the eventual redemption of blacks and their return to Africa, employs the ritualistic use of marijuana, forbids the cutting of hair, and venerates Haile Selassie as a god

**ras·ter** \'ras-tər\ *noun* [German, from Latin *raster, rastrum* rake, from *radere* to scrape] (1934)
: a scan pattern (as of the electron beam in a cathode-ray tube) in which an area is scanned from side to side in lines from top to bottom; *also* : a pattern of closely spaced rows of dots that form the image on a cathode-ray tube (as of a television or computer display)

**ra·sure** \'rā-shər, -zhər\ *noun* [Middle French, from Latin *rasura,* from *rasus,* past participle of *radere*] (1508)
**:** ERASURE, OBLITERATION

**¹rat** \'rat\ *noun* [Middle English, from Old English *ræt;* akin to Old High German *ratta* rat and perhaps to Latin *rodere* to gnaw — more at RODENT] (before 12th century)
**1 a :** any of numerous rodents (*Rattus* and related genera) differing from the related mice by considerably larger size and by structural details (as of the teeth) **b :** any of various similar rodents
**2 :** a contemptible person: as **a :** one who betrays or deserts friends or associates **b :** SCAB 3b **c :** INFORMER 2
**3 :** a pad over which a woman's hair is arranged
**4 :** a person who spends much time especially idly in a specified place ⟨a mall *rat*⟩
   — **rat·like** \-ˌlīk\ *adjective*

**²rat** *verb* **rat·ted; rat·ting** (1812)
*intransitive verb*
**1 :** to betray, desert, or inform on one's associates — usually used with *on*
**2 :** to catch or hunt rats
**3 :** to work as a scab
*transitive verb*
: to give (hair) the effect of greater quantity by use of a rat

**rat·able** *or* **rate·able** \'rā-tə-bəl\ *adjective* (1503)
: capable of being rated, estimated, or apportioned
   — **rat·ably** \-blē\ *adverb*

**rat·a·fia** \ˌra-tə-'fē-ə\ *noun* [French] (1699)
**1 :** a liqueur made from an infusion of macerated fruit or fruit juice in a liquor (as brandy) and often flavored with almonds
**2 :** a sweet biscuit made of almond paste

**rat·a·plan** \'ra-tə-ˌplan\ *noun* [French, of imitative origin] (circa 1848)
: the iterative sound of beating ⟨a rolling *rataplan* of drums —*Time*⟩

**rat–a–tat** \'ra-tə-ˌtat\ *or* **rat–a–tat–tat** \ˌra-tə-ˌta(t)-'tat\ *noun* [imitative] (1681)
: a rapid succession of knocking, tapping, or cracking sounds

**ra·ta·tou·ille** \ˌra-tə-'twē, ˌrä-tä-, -'tü-ē\ *noun* [French, from blend of *ratouiller* to disturb, shake and *tatouiller* to stir] (circa 1877)
: a seasoned stew made of eggplant, tomatoes, green peppers, squash, and sometimes meat

**rat·bag** \'rat-ˌbag\ *noun* (1890)
*chiefly Australian* : a stupid, eccentric, or disagreeable person

**rat–bite fever** *noun* (1910)
: either of two febrile bacterial diseases of humans usually transmitted by the bite of a rat

**rat cheese** *noun* (1939)
**:** CHEDDAR

**¹ratch·et** \'ra-chət\ *noun* [alteration of earlier *rochet,* from French, alteration of Middle French *rocquet* ratchet, bobbin, of Germanic origin; akin to Old High German *rocko* distaff — more at ROCK] (1654)
**1 :** a mechanism that consists of a bar or wheel having inclined teeth into which a pawl drops so that motion can be imparted to the wheel or bar, governed, or prevented and that is used in a hand tool (as a wrench or screwdriver) to allow effective motion in one direction only
**2 :** a pawl or detent for holding or propelling a ratchet wheel

**²ratchet** (1973)
*transitive verb*
: to cause to move by steps or degrees — usually used with *up* or *down* ⟨tried to *ratchet* down the debt⟩
*intransitive verb*
: to proceed by steps or degrees

**ratchet wheel** *noun* (1777)
: a toothed wheel held in position or turned by an engaging pawl

ratchet wheel: *1* wheel, *2* reciprocating lever, *3* pawl for communicating motion, *4* pawl for preventing backward motion

**¹rate** \'rāt\ *verb* **rat·ed; rat·ing** [Middle English] (14th century)
*transitive verb*
**1 :** to rebuke angrily or violently
**2** *obsolete* **:** to drive away by scolding
*intransitive verb*
**:** to voice angry reprimands
**²rate** *noun* [Middle English, from Middle French, from Medieval Latin *rata*, from Latin (*pro*) *rata* (*parte*) according to a fixed proportion] (15th century)
**1 a :** reckoned value **:** VALUATION **b** *obsolete* **:** ESTIMATION
**2** *obsolete* **:** a fixed quantity
**3 a :** a fixed ratio between two things **b :** a charge, payment, or price fixed according to a ratio, scale, or standard: as (1) **:** a charge per unit of a public-service commodity (2) **:** a charge per unit of freight or passenger service (3) **:** a unit charge or ratio used by a government for assessing property taxes (4) *British* **:** a local tax
**4 a :** a quantity, amount, or degree of something measured per unit of something else **b :** an amount of payment or charge based on another amount; *specifically* **:** the amount of premium per unit of insurance
**5 :** relative condition or quality **:** CLASS
**— at any rate :** in any case **:** ANYWAY
**³rate** *verb* **rat·ed; rat·ing** (15th century)
*transitive verb*
**1** *obsolete* **:** ALLOT
**2 a :** to set an estimate on **:** VALUE, ESTEEM ⟨black is *rated* very high this season⟩ **b :** to determine or assign the relative rank or class of **:** GRADE ⟨*rate* a seaman⟩ **c :** to estimate the normal capacity or power of
**3 :** CONSIDER, REGARD ⟨was *rated* an excellent pianist⟩
**4 :** to fix the amount of premium to be charged per unit of insurance on
**5 :** to have a right to **:** DESERVE ⟨she *rated* special privileges⟩
*intransitive verb*
**:** to enjoy a status of special privilege ⟨really *rates* with the boss⟩
**synonym** see ESTIMATE
**ra·tel** \'rä-t°l, 'rā-\ *noun* [Afrikaans, literally, rattle, from Dutch, from Middle Dutch — more at RATTLE] (1777)
**:** an African or Asian nocturnal carnivorous mammal (*Mellivora capensis*) of the weasel family that resembles a badger
**rate·me·ter** \'rāt-,mē-tər\ *noun* (1949)
**:** an instrument that indicates the counting rate of an electronic counter
**rate of change** (circa 1939)
**:** a value that results from dividing the change in a function of a variable by the change in the variable ⟨velocity is the *rate of change* in distance with respect to time⟩
**rate of exchange** (circa 1741)
**:** the amount of one currency that will buy a given amount of another
**rate of interest** (1785)
**:** the percentage usually on an annual basis that is paid for the use of money borrowed from another
**rate·pay·er** \'rāt-,pā-ər\ *noun* (1845)
**1** *British* **:** TAXPAYER
**2 :** one who pays for the consumption of electricity according to established rates
**rat·er** \'rā-tər\ *noun* (1611)
**1 :** one that rates; *specifically* **:** a person who estimates or determines a rating
**2 :** one having a specified rating or class — usually used in combination ⟨first-*rater*⟩
**rat fink** *noun* (1964)
**:** FINK, INFORMER
**rat·fish** \'rat-,fish\ *noun* (1882)
**:** CHIMAERA; *especially* **:** a silvery iridescent white-spotted chimaera (*Hydrolagus colliei*) of cold deep waters of the Pacific coast of North America
**rathe** \'rāth, 'rath\ *adjective* [Middle English, quick, from Old English *hræth*, alteration of

*hræd;* akin to Old High German *hrad* quick] (14th century)
*archaic* **:** EARLY ⟨bring the *rathe* primrose that forsaken dies —John Milton⟩
**rath·er** \'ra-thər, 'rä-, 'rə- *also* 're-; *interjectionally* 'ra-'thər, 'rä-, 'rə-\ *adverb* [Middle English, from Old English *hrathor*, comparative of *hrathe* quickly; akin to Old High German *rado* quickly, Old English *hræd* quick] (before 12th century)
**1 :** with better reason or more propriety **:** more properly ⟨this you should pity *rather* than despise —Shakespeare⟩
**2 :** more readily or willingly **:** PREFERABLY ⟨I'd *rather* not go⟩ ⟨would *rather* read than watch television⟩ — often used interjectionally to express affirmation
**3 :** more correctly speaking ⟨my father, or *rather* my stepfather⟩
**4 :** to the contrary **:** INSTEAD ⟨was no better but *rather* grew worse —Mark 5:26 (Revised Standard Version)⟩
**5 :** in some degree **:** SOMEWHAT ⟨it's *rather* warm⟩ — often used as a mild intensive ⟨spent *rather* a lot of money⟩
**— the rather** *archaic* **:** the more quickly or readily
**rather than** *conjunction* (14th century)
**:** and not ⟨obscures *rather than* resolves the problem⟩ ⟨why do one thing *rather than* another?⟩
**raths·kel·ler** \'rät-,ske-lər, 'rat-, 'rath-\ *noun* [obsolete German (now *Ratskeller*), city-hall basement restaurant, from *Rat* council + *Keller* cellar] (1900)
**:** a usually basement tavern or restaurant
**rat·i·cide** \'ra-tə-,sīd\ *noun* (1908)
**:** a substance for killing rats
**rat·i·fy** \'ra-tə-,fī\ *transitive verb* **-fied; -fy·ing** [Middle English *ratifien*, from Middle French *ratifier*, from Medieval Latin *ratificare*, from Latin *ratus* determined, from past participle of *reri* to calculate — more at REASON] (14th century)
**:** to approve and sanction formally **:** CONFIRM ⟨*ratify* a treaty⟩
**— rat·i·fi·ca·tion** \,ra-tə-fə-'kā-shən\ *noun*
**— rat·i·fi·er** \'ra-tə-,fī(-ə)r\ *noun*
**ra·ti·né** \,ra-tə-'nā\ *or* **ra·tine** \,ra-tə-'nā, ra-'tēn\ *noun* [French *ratiné*] (circa 1914)
**1 :** a nubby ply yarn of various fibers made by twisting under tension a thick and a thin yarn
**2 :** a rough bulky fabric usually woven loosely in plain weave from ratiné yarns
**rat·ing** \'rā-tiŋ\ *noun* (1702)
**1 :** a classification according to grade; *specifically* **:** a military or naval specialist classification
**2** *chiefly British* **:** a naval enlisted man
**3 a :** relative estimate or evaluation **:** STANDING ⟨the school has a good academic *rating*⟩ **b :** an estimate of an individual's or business's credit and responsibility **c :** an estimate of the percentage of the public listening to or viewing a particular radio or television program
**4 :** a stated operating limit of a machine expressible in power units (as kilowatts of a direct-current generator) or in characteristics (as voltage)
**ra·tio** \'rā-(,)shō, -shē-,ō\ *noun, plural* **ra·tios** [Latin, computation, reason — more at REASON] (1660)
**1 a :** the indicated quotient of two mathematical expressions **b :** the relationship in quantity, amount, or size between two or more things **:** PROPORTION
**2 :** the expression of the relative values of gold and silver as determined by a country's currency laws
**ra·ti·o·ci·nate** \,ra-tē-'ō-s°n-,āt, ,ra-shē-, -'ä-\ *intransitive verb* **-nat·ed; -nat·ing** [Latin *ratiocinatus*, past participle of *ratiocinari* to reckon, from *ratio* + *-cinari* (as in *vaticinari* to prophesy) — more at VATICINATE] (1643)
**:** REASON
**— ra·ti·o·ci·na·tor** \-,ā-tər\ *noun*

**ra·ti·o·ci·na·tion** \-,ō-s°n-'ā-shən, -,ä-\ *noun* (circa 1530)
**1 :** the process of exact thinking **:** REASONING
**2 :** a reasoned train of thought
**— ra·ti·o·ci·na·tive** \-'ō-s°n-,ā-tiv, -'ä-\ *adjective*
**¹ra·tion** \'ra-shən, 'rā-\ *noun* [French, from Latin *ration-, ratio* computation, reason] (circa 1711)
**1 a :** a food allowance for one day **b** *plural* **:** FOOD, PROVISIONS
**2 :** a share especially as determined by supply
**²ration** *transitive verb* **ra·tioned; ra·tion·ing** \'ra-sh(ə-)niŋ, 'rā-\ (1859)
**1 :** to supply with or put on rations
**2 a :** to distribute as rations — often used with *out* **b :** to distribute equitably **c :** to use sparingly
**¹ra·tio·nal** \'rash-nəl, 'ra-shə-n°l\ *adjective* [Middle English *racional*, from Latin *rationalis*, from *ration-, ratio*] (14th century)
**1 a :** having reason or understanding **b :** relating to, based on, or agreeable to reason **:** REASONABLE ⟨a *rational* explanation⟩ ⟨*rational* behavior⟩
**2 :** involving only multiplication, division, addition, and subtraction and only a finite number of times
**3 :** relating to, consisting of, or being one or more rational numbers ⟨a *rational* root of an equation⟩
**— ra·tio·nal·ly** *adverb*
**— ra·tio·nal·ness** *noun*
**²rational** *noun* (1606)
**:** something rational; *specifically* **:** RATIONAL NUMBER
**ra·tio·nale** \,ra-shə-'nal\ *noun* [Latin, neuter of *rationalis*] (1657)
**1 :** an explanation of controlling principles of opinion, belief, practice, or phenomena
**2 :** an underlying reason **:** BASIS
**rational function** *noun* (1885)
**:** a function that is the quotient of two polynomials; *also* **:** POLYNOMIAL
**ra·tio·nal·ise** *British variant of* RATIONALIZE
**ra·tio·nal·ism** \'rash-nə-,li-zəm, 'ra-shə-n°l-,i-\ *noun* (1827)
**1 :** reliance on reason as the basis for establishment of religious truth
**2 a :** a theory that reason is in itself a source of knowledge superior to and independent of sense perceptions **b :** a view that reason and experience rather than the nonrational are the fundamental criteria in the solution of problems
**3 :** FUNCTIONALISM
**— ra·tio·nal·ist** \-nə-list, -n°l-ist\ *noun*
**— rationalist** *or* **ra·tio·nal·is·tic** \,rash-nə-'lis-tik, ,ra-shə-n°l-'is-\ *adjective*
**— ra·tio·nal·is·ti·cal·ly** \-ti-k(ə-)lē\ *adverb*
**ra·tio·nal·i·ty** \,ra-shə-'na-lə-tē\ *noun, plural* **-ties** (1628)
**1 :** the quality or state of being rational
**2 :** the quality or state of being agreeable to reason **:** REASONABLENESS
**3 :** a rational opinion, belief, or practice — usually used in plural
**ra·tio·nal·ize** \'rash-nə-,līz, 'ra-shə-n°l-,īz\ *verb* **-ized; -iz·ing** (1803)
*transitive verb*
**1 :** to free (a mathematical expression) from irrational parts ⟨*rationalize* a denominator⟩
**2 :** to bring into accord with reason or cause something to seem reasonable: as **a :** to substitute a natural for a supernatural explanation of

\ə\ **abut** \°\ **kitten** \ər\ **further** \a\ **ash** \ā\ **ace** \ä\ **mop, mar** \aù\ **out** \ch\ **chin** \e\ **bet** \ē\ **easy** \g\ **go** \i\ **hit** \ī\ **ice** \j\ **job** \ŋ\ **sing** \ō\ **go** \ò\ **law** \òi\ **boy** \th\ **thin** \ṯẖ\ **the** \ü\ **loot** \ù\ **foot** \y\ **yet** \zh\ **vision** *see also* Guide to Pronunciation

⟨*rationalize* a myth⟩ **b** : to attribute (one's actions) to rational and creditable motives without analysis of true and especially unconscious motives ⟨*rationalized* his dislike of his brother⟩
**3** : to apply the principles of scientific management to (as an industry or its operations) for a desired result (as increased efficiency)
*intransitive verb*
: to provide plausible but untrue reasons for conduct
— **ra·tio·nal·iz·able** \,rash-nə-'lī-zə-bəl, ,ra-shə-n°l-'ī-\ *adjective*
— **ra·tio·nal·i·za·tion** \,rash-nə-lə-'zā-shən, ,ra-shə-n°l-ə-\ *noun*
— **ra·tio·nal·iz·er** \'rash-nə-,lī-zər, 'ra-shə-n°l-,ī-\ *noun*
**rational number** *noun* (1904)
: an integer or the quotient of an integer divided by a nonzero integer
**rat·ite** \'ra-,tīt\ *noun* [ultimately from Latin *ratitus* marked with the figure of a raft, from *ratis* raft] (circa 1890)
: a bird with a flat breastbone; *especially* : any of various mostly flightless birds (as an ostrich, rhea, emu, moa, or kiwi) with small or rudimentary wings and no keel on the sternum that are probably of polyphyletic origin and are assigned to a number of different orders
— **ratite** *adjective*
**rat·line** \'rat-lən\ *noun* [Middle English *radelyng*] (15th century)
: any of the small transverse ropes attached to the shrouds of a ship so as to form the steps of a rope ladder

**ratline**

**¹ra·toon** \ra-'tün\ *noun* [Spanish *retoño*, from *retoñar* to sprout, from *re-* (from Latin) + *otoñar* to grow in autumn, from *otoño* autumn, from Latin *autumnus*] (1631)
**1** : a shoot of a perennial plant (as sugarcane)
**2** : a crop (as of bananas) produced on ratoons
**²ratoon** (1756)
*intransitive verb*
: to sprout or spring up from the root
*transitive verb*
: to grow or produce (a crop) from or on ratoons
**rat race** *noun* (1939)
: strenuous, wearisome, and usually competitive activity or rush
**rats** \'rats\ *interjection* (1890)
— used to express disappointment, frustration, or disgust
**rat snake** *noun* (1860)
: any of numerous large harmless rat-eating colubrid snakes (especially genus *Elaphe*) — called also *chicken snake*
**rat·tail** \'rat-,tāl\ *noun* (1705)
**1** : a horse's tail with little or no hair
**2** : GRENADIER 2
**rattail cactus** *noun* (1900)
: a commonly cultivated tropical American cactus (*Aporocactus flagelliformis*) with showy crimson flowers
**rat–tail file** *noun* (1744)
: a round slender tapered file
**rat·tan** \ra-'tan, rə-\ *noun* [Malay *rotan*] (1660)
**1** : a rattan cane or switch
**2 a** : a climbing palm (especially of the genera *Calamus* and *Daemonorops*) with very long tough stems **b** : a part of the stem of a rattan used especially for walking sticks and wickerwork
**rat·teen** \ra-'tēn\ *noun* [French *ratine*] (1685)
*archaic* : a coarse woolen fabric

**rat·ter** \'ra-tər\ *noun* (1857)
: one that catches rats; *specifically* : a rat-catching dog or cat
**¹rat·tle** \'ra-t°l\ *verb* **rat·tled; rat·tling** \'rat-liŋ, 'ra-t°l-iŋ\ [Middle English *ratelen*; akin to Middle Dutch *ratel* rattle] (14th century)
*intransitive verb*
**1** : to make a rapid succession of short sharp noises ⟨the windows *rattled* in the wind⟩
**2** : to chatter incessantly and aimlessly
**3** : to move with a clatter or rattle; *also* : to be or move about in a place or station too large or grand ⟨*rattled* around the big old house⟩
*transitive verb*
**1** : to say, perform, or affect in a brisk lively fashion ⟨*rattled* off four magnificent backhands —Kim Chapin⟩
**2** : to cause to make a rattling sound
**3** : ROUSE; *specifically* : to beat (a cover) for game
**4** : to upset to the point of loss of poise and composure
**synonym** see EMBARRASS
**²rattle** *noun* (1519)
**1 a** : a device that produces a rattle; *specifically* : a case containing pellets used as a baby's toy **b** : the sound-producing organ on a rattlesnake's tail
**2 a** : a rapid succession of sharp clattering sounds **b** : NOISE, RACKET
**3** : a throat noise caused by air passing through mucus and heard especially at the approach of death
**³rattle** *transitive verb* **rat·tled; rat·tling** \'rat-liŋ, 'ra-t°l-iŋ\ [irregular from *ratline*] (1729)
: to furnish with ratlines
**rat·tle·brain** \'ra-t°l-,brān\ *noun* (1709)
: a flighty or thoughtless person
— **rat·tle·brained** \-,brānd\ *adjective*
**rat·tler** \'rat-lər, 'ra-t°l-ər\ *noun* (15th century)
**1** : one that rattles
**2** : RATTLESNAKE
**rat·tle·snake** \'ra-t°l-,snāk\ *noun* (1630)
: any of the American pit vipers comprising two genera (*Crotalus* and *Sistrurus*) and having horny interlocking joints at the end of the tail that make a sharp rattling sound when shaken

**rattlesnake**

**rattlesnake plantain** *noun* (1778)
: an orchid (genus *Goodyera*) with checked or mottled leaves
**rattlesnake root** *noun* (1682)
: any of various plants formerly believed to be distasteful to rattlesnakes or effective against their venom: as **a** : any of a genus (*Prenanthes* and especially *P. altissima*) of composite plants that have lobed or pinnatifid leaves and small heads of drooping ligulate flowers **b** : SENECA SNAKEROOT
**rattlesnake weed** *noun* (1760)
: a hawkweed (*Hieracium venosum*) with purple-veined leaves
**rat·tle·trap** \'ra-t°l-,trap\ *noun* (1822)
: something rattly or rickety; *especially* : an old car
— **rattletrap** *adjective*
**¹rat·tling** \'rat-liŋ\ *adjective* (1560)
**1** : LIVELY, BRISK ⟨moved at a *rattling* pace⟩
**2** : extraordinarily good : SPLENDID
— **rat·tling·ly** \-liŋ-lē\ *adverb*
**²rattling** *adverb* (1829)
: to an extreme degree : VERY ⟨a *rattling* good argument —E. A. Betts⟩
**rat·tly** \'rat-lē, 'ra-t°l-ē\ *adjective* (1881)
: likely to rattle : making a rattle
**rat·ton** \'ra-t°n, 'rä-\ *noun* [Middle English *ratoun*, from Middle French *raton*, diminutive of

*rat*, probably of Germanic origin; akin to Old English *ræt* rat] (14th century)
*chiefly dialect* : RAT
**rat–trap** \'ra(t)-,trap\ *noun* (15th century)
**1** : a trap for rats
**2** : a dirty dilapidated structure
**3** : a hopeless situation
**rat trap cheese** *noun* (1927)
: CHEDDAR
**rat·ty** \'ra-tē\ *adjective* **rat·ti·er; -est** (1865)
**1 a** : infested with rats **b** : of, relating to, or suggestive of a rat
**2** : SHABBY, UNKEMPT ⟨a *ratty* brown overcoat —John Lardner⟩
**3 a** : DESPICABLE, TREACHEROUS **b** : IRRITABLE ⟨feeling *ratty* as hell —Richard Bissell⟩
**rau·cous** \'ro-kəs\ *adjective* [Latin *raucus* hoarse; akin to Latin *ravis* hoarseness] (1769)
**1** : disagreeably harsh or strident : HOARSE ⟨*raucous* voices⟩
**2** : boisterously disorderly ⟨a . . . *raucous* frontier town —Truman Capote⟩
**synonym** see LOUD
— **rau·cous·ly** *adverb*
— **rau·cous·ness** *noun*
**raunch** \'ronch, 'ränch\ *noun* [back-formation from *raunchy*] (1964)
: VULGARITY, LEWDNESS
**raun·chy** \'ron-chē, 'rän-\ *adjective* **raun·chi·er; -est** [origin unknown] (1939)
**1** : SLOVENLY, DIRTY ⟨a *raunchy* panhandler⟩; *also* : very smelly ⟨*raunchy* sneakers⟩
**2** : OBSCENE, SMUTTY ⟨*raunchy* jokes⟩
— **raun·chi·ly** \'ron-chə-lē, 'rän-\ *adverb*
— **raun·chi·ness** \-chē-nəs\ *noun*
**rau·wol·fia** \raú-'wúl-fē-ə, ro-\ *noun* [New Latin, from Leonhard *Rauwolf* (died 1596) German botanist] (1752)
**1** : any of a large pantropical genus (*Rauvolfia* synonym *Rauwolfia*) of somewhat poisonous trees and shrubs of the dogbane family that yield emetic and purgative substances
**2** : a medicinal extract from the root of an Asian rauwolfia (*Rauvolfia serpentina*) used in the treatment of hypertension and mental disorders
**¹rav·age** \'ra-vij\ *noun* [French, from Middle French, from *ravir* to ravish — more at RAVISH] (circa 1611)
**1** : an act or practice of ravaging
**2** : damage resulting from ravaging : violently destructive effect ⟨the *ravages* of time⟩
**²ravage** *verb* **rav·aged; rav·ag·ing** (circa 1611)
*transitive verb*
: to wreak havoc on : affect destructively
*intransitive verb*
: to commit destructive actions ☆
— **rav·age·ment** \-vij-mənt\ *noun*
— **rav·ag·er** *noun*
**¹rave** \'rāv\ *verb* **raved; rav·ing** [Middle English] (14th century)
*intransitive verb*

**1 a :** to talk irrationally in or as if in delirium **b :** to speak out wildly **c :** to talk with extreme enthusiasm ⟨*raved* about its beauty⟩ **2 :** to move or advance violently **:** STORM ⟨the iced gusts still *rave* and·beat —John Keats⟩
*transitive verb*
**:** to utter in madness or frenzy
— **rav·er** *noun*
**²rave** *noun* (1598)
**1 :** an act or instance of raving **2 :** an extravagantly favorable criticism ⟨the play received the critics' *raves*⟩
**¹rav·el** \'ra-vəl\ *verb* **-eled** *or* **-elled; -el·ing** *or* **-el·ling** \'rav-liŋ, 'ra-və-\ [Dutch *rafelen,* from *rafel* loose thread] (1582)
*transitive verb*
**1 a :** to separate or undo the texture of **:** UN-RAVEL **b :** to undo the intricacies of **:** DISEN-TANGLE
**2 :** ENTANGLE, CONFUSE
*intransitive verb*
**1** *obsolete* **:** to become entangled or confused **2 :** to become unwoven, untwisted, or un-wound **:** FRAY
**3 :** BREAK UP, CRUMBLE
— **rav·el·er** \'rav-lər, 'ra-və-\ *noun*
— **rav·el·ment** \'ra-vəl-mənt\ *noun*
**²ravel** *noun* (1634)
**:** an act or result of raveling: as **a :** something tangled **b :** something raveled out; *specifically* **:** a loose thread
**raveling** *or* **ravelling** *noun* (1658)
**:** RAVEL b
**¹ra·ven** \'rā-vən\ *noun* [Middle English, from Old English *hræfn;* akin to Old High German *hraban* raven, Latin *corvus,* Greek *korax*] (before 12th century)
**:** a large glossy black corvine bird (*Corvus corax*) of Europe, Asia, northern Africa, and America

raven

**²raven** *adjective* (1634)
**:** shiny and black like a raven's feathers ⟨*raven* hair⟩
**³rav·en** \'ra-vən\ *verb* **rav·ened; rav·en·ing** \'ra-və-niŋ, 'rav-niŋ\ [Middle French *raviner* to rush, take by force, from *ravine* rapine] (1530)
*transitive verb*
**1 :** to devour greedily **2 :** DESPOIL ⟨men . . . *raven* the earth, destroy-ing its resources —*New Yorker*⟩
*intransitive verb*
**1 :** to feed greedily **2 :** to prowl for food **:** PREY **3 :** PLUNDER
— **rav·en·er** \'ra-və-nər, 'rav-nər\ *noun*
**rav·en·ous** \'ra-və-nəs, 'rav-nəs\ *adjective* (15th century)
**1 :** RAPACIOUS ⟨*ravenous* wolves⟩ **2 :** very eager or greedy for food, satisfaction, or gratification ⟨a *ravenous* appetite⟩
**synonym** see VORACIOUS
— **rav·en·ous·ly** *adverb*
— **rav·en·ous·ness** *noun*
**rav·in** \'ra-vən\ *noun* [Middle English, from Middle French *ravine*] (14th century)
**1 :** PLUNDER, PILLAGE
**2 a :** an act or habit of preying **b :** something seized as prey
**ra·vine** \rə-'vēn\ *noun* [French, from Middle French, rapine, rush, from Latin *rapina* rap-ine] (1760)
**:** a small narrow steep-sided valley that is larg-er than a gully and smaller than a canyon and that is usually worn by running water
**rav·ined** \'ra-vənd\ *adjective* (1606)
*obsolete* **:** RAPACIOUS, RAVENOUS
**¹rav·ing** \'rā-viŋ\ *noun* (14th century)

**:** irrational, incoherent, wild, or extravagant utterance or declamation — usually used in plural
**²raving** *adjective* (15th century)
**1 :** talking wildly or irrationally ⟨a *raving* lu-natic⟩
**2 :** RAVISHING ⟨a *raving* beauty⟩
**rav·i·o·li** \ˌra-vē-'ō-lē, ˌrä-\ *noun, plural* **ra·violi** *also* **rav·i·o·lis** \-lēz\ [Italian, from Italian dialect, plural of *raviolo,* literally, little turnip, diminutive of *rava* turnip, from Latin *rapa* — more at RAPE] (circa 1611)
**:** pasta in the form of little cases of dough con-taining a savory filling (as of meat or cheese)
**rav·ish** \'ra-vish\ *transitive verb* [Middle En-glish *ravisshen,* from Middle French *raviss-,* stem of *ravir,* from (assumed) Vulgar Latin *rapire,* alteration of Latin *rapere* to seize, rob — more at RAPID] (14th century)
**1 a :** to seize and take away by violence **b :** to overcome with emotion (as joy or delight) ⟨*ravished* by the scenic beauty⟩ **c :** RAPE 2
**2 :** PLUNDER, ROB
— **rav·ish·er** *noun*
— **rav·ish·ment** \-mənt\ *noun*
**rav·ish·ing** \'ra-vi-shiŋ\ *adjective* (14th centu-ry)
**:** unusually attractive, pleasing, or striking
— **rav·ish·ing·ly** \-shiŋ-lē\ *adverb*
**¹raw** \'ro\ *adjective* **raw·er** \'ro-(ə)r\; **raw·est** \'ro-əst\ [Middle English, from Old En-glish *hrēaw;* akin to Old High German *hrō* raw, Latin *crudus* raw, *cruor* blood, Greek *kreas* flesh] (before 12th century)
**1 :** not cooked
**2 a (1) :** being in or nearly in the natural state **:** not processed or purified ⟨*raw* fibers⟩ ⟨*raw* sewage⟩ **(2) :** not diluted or blended ⟨*raw* spir-its⟩ **b :** unprepared or imperfectly prepared for use **c :** not being in polished, finished, or pro-cessed form ⟨*raw* data⟩ ⟨a *raw* draft of a the-sis⟩
**3 a (1) :** having the surface abraded or chafed **(2) :** very irritated ⟨a *raw* sore throat⟩ **b :** lack-ing covering **:** NAKED **c :** not protected **:** sus-ceptible to hurt ⟨*raw* emotions⟩
**4 a :** lacking experience or understanding **:** GREEN ⟨a *raw* recruit⟩ **b (1) :** marked by ab-sence of refinements **(2) :** VULGAR, COARSE **c :** not tempered **:** UNBRIDLED ⟨*raw* power⟩
**5 :** disagreeably damp or cold
**synonym** see RUDE
— **raw·ly** *adverb*
— **raw·ness** *noun*
**²raw** *noun* (1823)
**:** a raw place or state
— **in the raw 1 :** in a natural, unrefined, or crude state **2 :** NAKED ⟨slept *in the raw*⟩
**raw bar** *noun* (1943)
**:** a counter (as in a restaurant) that serves raw shellfish
**raw·boned** \'ro-ˌbōnd\ *adjective* (1591)
**:** relatively thin with prominent bone structure; *also* **:** heavy-framed and rugged but not attrac-tively built
**synonym** see LEAN
**raw deal** *noun* (circa 1912)
**:** an instance of unfair treatment
**¹raw·hide** \'ro-ˌhīd\ *noun* (1829)
**1 :** a whip of untanned hide **2 :** untanned cattle skin
**²rawhide** *transitive verb* **raw·hid·ed; raw·hid·ing** (1858)
**1 :** to whip or drive with or as if with a raw-hide
**2 :** CHASTISE 2
**ra·win·sonde** \'rā-wən-ˌsänd\ *noun* [*ra*dar + *win*d + radio*sonde*] (1946)
**:** a radiosonde tracked by a radio direction-finding device to determine the velocity of winds aloft
**raw material** *noun* (1796)
**:** crude or processed material that can be con-verted by manufacture, processing, or combi-nation into a new and useful product ⟨wheat . . . is *raw material* for the flour mill —C. A.

Koepke⟩; *broadly* **:** something with a potential for improvement, development, or elaboration ⟨perplexities are often the *raw material* of dis-coveries —Agnes M. Clerke⟩
**raw score** *noun* (1920)
**:** an individual's actual achievement score (as on a test) before being adjusted for relative position in the test group
**rax** \'raks\ *verb* [Middle English (northern dia-lect) *raxen,* from Old English *raxan;* akin to Old English *reccan* to stretch — more at RACK] (before 12th century)
*chiefly Scottish* **:** STRETCH
**¹ray** \'rā\ *noun* [Middle English *raye,* from Middle French *raie,* from Latin *raia*] (14th century)
**:** any of an order (Rajiformes) of cartilaginous fishes (as stingrays and skates) having the body flattened dorsoventrally, the eyes on the upper surface, and enlarged pectoral fins fused with the head
**²ray** *noun* [Middle English, from Middle French *rai,* from Latin *radius* rod, ray] (14th century)
**1 a :** any of the lines of light that appear to ra-diate from a bright object **b :** a beam of radi-ant energy (as light) of small cross section **c (1) :** a stream of material particles traveling in the same line (as in radioactive phenomena) **(2) :** a single particle of such a stream
**2 a :** light cast by rays **:** RADIANCE **b :** a moral or intellectual light
**3 :** a thin line suggesting a ray: as **a :** any of a group of lines diverging from a common cen-ter **b :** HALF LINE
**4 a :** one of the bony rods that extend and support the membrane in the fin of a fish **b :** one of the radiating divisions of the body of a radiate animal (as a starfish)
**5 a :** a branch or flower stalk of an umbel **b (1) :** MEDULLARY RAY **(2) :** VASCULAR RAY **c :** RAY FLOWER 1
**6 :** PARTICLE, TRACE ⟨*ray* of hope⟩
— **rayed** \'rād\ *adjective*
**³ray** (1598)
*intransitive verb*
**1 a :** to shine in or as if in rays **b :** to issue as rays
**2 :** to extend like the radii of a circle **:** RADIATE
*transitive verb*
**1 :** to emit in rays
**2 :** to furnish or mark with rays
**ray flower** *noun* (1842)
**1 :** one of the marginal flowers of the head in a composite plant (as the aster) that also has disk flowers
**2 :** the entire head in a plant (as chicory) that lacks disk flowers
**Ray·leigh scattering** \'rā-lē-\ *noun* [John W. S. *Rayleigh*] (1937)
**:** scattering of light by particles small enough to render the effect selective so that different colors are deflected through different angles
**ray·less** \'rā-ləs\ *adjective* (1747)
**:** having, admitting, or emitting no rays; *espe-cially* **:** DARK
— **ray·less·ness** *noun*
**rayless goldenrod** *noun* (1923)
**:** a shrubby to herbaceous composite plant (*Haplopappus heterophyllus* synonym *Iso-coma wrightii*) especially of open saline ground from Texas to Arizona and northern Mexico that lacks ray flowers and causes trembles in cattle
**ray·on** \'rā-ˌän\ *noun* [irregular from ²*ray*] (1924)
**1 :** any of a group of smooth textile fibers made from regenerated cellulose by extrusion through minute holes
**2 :** a rayon yarn, thread, or fabric

\ə\ **abut** \ᵊ\ **kitten** \ər\ **further** \a\ **ash** \ā\ **ace** \ä\ **mop, mar** \aú\ **out** \ch\ **chin** \e\ **bet** \ē\ **easy** \g\ **go** \i\ **hit** \ī\ **ice** \j\ **job** \ŋ\ **sing** \ō\ **go** \ò\ **law** \òi\ **boy** \th\ **thin** \t̷h\ **the** \ü\ **loot** \ù\ **foot** \y\ **yet** \zh\ **vision** *see also* Guide to Pronunciation

**raze** \'rāz\ *transitive verb* **razed; raz·ing** [alteration of *rase*] (1536)
**1 a** *archaic* **:** ERASE **b :** to scrape, cut, or shave off
**2 :** to destroy to the ground **:** DEMOLISH
— **raz·er** *noun*

**ra·zee** \rā-'zē\ *noun* [French (*vaisseau*) *rasé*, literally, cut-off ship] (1794)
**:** a wooden warship with the upper deck cut away

**ra·zor** \'rā-zər\ *noun* [Middle English *rasour*, from Old French *raseor*, from *raser* to raze, shave — more at RASE] (14th century)
**:** a keen-edged cutting instrument for shaving or cutting hair

**ra·zor·back** \'rā-zər-ˌbak\ *noun* (1849)
**:** a thin-bodied long-legged feral hog chiefly of the southeastern U.S.

**ra·zor-backed** \-ˌbakt\ *or* **ra·zor·back** \-ˌbak\ *adjective* (1829)
**:** having a sharp narrow back ⟨a *razor-backed* horse⟩

**ra·zor·bill** \-ˌbil\ *noun* (1674)
**:** a North Atlantic auk (*Alca torda*) with the plumage black above and white below and a compressed sharp-edged bill — called also *razor-billed auk*

**razor clam** *noun* (1882)
**:** any of a family (Solenidae) of marine bivalve mollusks having a long narrow thin shell

¹**razz** \'raz\ *noun* [short for *razzberry* sound of contempt, alteration of *raspberry*] (circa 1919)
**:** RASPBERRY 2

²**razz** *transitive verb* (1921)
**:** HECKLE, DERIDE ⟨the fans *razzed* the visiting players⟩

**razz·a·ma·tazz** \ˌra-zə-mə-'taz\ *chiefly British variant of* RAZZMATAZZ

**raz·zle–daz·zle** \ˌra-zəl-'da-zəl\ *noun* [reduplication of *dazzle*] (1889)
**1 :** a state of confusion or hilarity
**2 :** a complex maneuver (as in sports) designed to confuse an opponent
**3 :** a confusing or colorful often gaudy action or display
— **razzle–dazzle** *adjective*

**razz·ma·tazz** \ˌraz-mə-'taz\ *noun* [probably alteration of *razzle-dazzle*] (1942)
**1 :** RAZZLE-DAZZLE 3
**2 :** DOUBLE-TALK 2
**3 :** VIM, ZING

**RBI** \ˌär-(ˌ)bē-'ī, 'ri-bē\ *noun, plural* **RBIs** *or* **RBI** [*run batted in*] (1948)
**:** a run in baseball that is driven in by a batter; *also* **:** official credit to a batter for driving in a run ⟨led the league in *RBIs*⟩

**r color** *noun* (1937)
**:** an acoustic effect of a simultaneously articulated \r\ imparted to a vowel by retroflexion or constriction of the tongue
— **r–col·ored** \'är-ˌkə-lərd\ *adjective*

**-rd** *symbol*
— used after the figure 3 to indicate the ordinal number *third* ⟨3*rd*⟩ ⟨83*rd*⟩

¹**re** \'rā\ *noun* [Medieval Latin, from the syllable sung to this note in a medieval hymn to Saint John the Baptist] (14th century)
**:** the 2d tone of the diatonic scale in solmization

²**re** \'rā, 'rē\ *preposition* [Latin, ablative of *res* thing — more at REAL] (1707)
**:** with regard to **:** IN RE

**re-** *prefix* [Middle English, from Old French, from Latin *re-, red-* back, again, against]
**1 :** again **:** anew ⟨*retell*⟩
**2 :** back **:** backward ⟨*recall*⟩

| | |
|---|---|
| re·ac·cel·er·ate | re·ac·ti·vate |
| re·ac·cept | re·ac·ti·va·tion |
| re·ac·ces·sion | re·ad·dress |
| re·ac·cli·ma·tize | re·ad·just |
| re·ac·cred·it | re·ad·just·ment |
| re·ac·cred·i·ta·tion | re·ad·mis·sion |
| re·ac·quaint | re·ad·mit |
| re·ac·quire | re·adopt |
| re·ac·qui·si·tion | re·af·firm |

| | | | |
|---|---|---|---|
| re·af·fir·ma·tion | re·cir·cu·late | re·em·pha·size | re·im·plan·ta·tion |
| re·af·fix | re·cir·cu·la·tion | re·em·ploy | re·im·port |
| re·al·lo·cate | re·clad | re·em·ploy·ment | re·im·por·ta·tion |
| re·al·lo·ca·tion | re·clas·si·fi·ca·tion | re·en·coun·ter | re·im·pose |
| re·anal·y·sis | re·clas·si·fy | re·en·dow | re·im·po·si·tion |
| re·an·a·lyze | re·clothe | re·en·er·gize | re·in·cor·po·rate |
| re·an·i·mate | re·cock | re·en·gage | re·in·cor·po·ra·tion |
| re·an·i·ma·tion | re·cod·i·fi·ca·tion | re·en·gage·ment | re·in·dict |
| re·an·nex | re·cod·i·fy | re·en·gi·neer | re·in·dict·ment |
| re·an·nex·a·tion | re·col·o·ni·za·tion | re·en·grave | re·in·fes·ta·tion |
| re·ap·pear | re·col·o·nize | re·en·list | re·in·flate |
| re·ap·pear·ance | re·col·or | re·en·list·ment | re·in·fla·tion |
| re·ap·pli·ca·tion | re·com·bine | re·en·roll | re·in·hab·it |
| re·ap·ply | re·com·mence | re·en·throne | re·in·i·tiate |
| re·ap·point | re·com·mence·ment | re·equip | re·in·ject |
| re·ap·point·ment | re·com·mis·sion | re·equip·ment | re·in·jec·tion |
| re·ap·prais·al | re·com·pi·la·tion | re·erect | re·in·jure |
| re·ap·praise | re·com·pile | re·es·ca·late | re·in·ju·ry |
| re·ap·pro·pri·ate | re·com·pu·ta·tion | re·es·ca·la·tion | re·ink |
| re·ap·prove | re·com·pute | re·es·tab·lish | re·in·ner·vate |
| re·ar·gue | re·con·ceive | re·es·tab·lish·ment | re·in·ner·va·tion |
| re·ar·gu·ment | re·con·cen·trate | re·es·ti·mate | re·in·oc·u·late |
| re·arous·al | re·con·cen·tra·tion | re·eval·u·ate | re·in·oc·u·la·tion |
| re·arouse | re·con·cep·tion | re·eval·u·a·tion | re·in·sert |
| re·ar·range | re·con·cep·tu·al·i·za- | re·ex·am·i·na·tion | re·in·ser·tion |
| re·ar·range·ment | tion | re·ex·am·ine | re·in·spect |
| re·ar·rest | re·con·cep·tu·al·ize | re·ex·pe·ri·ence | re·in·spec·tion |
| re·ar·tic·u·late | re·con·dense | re·ex·plore | re·in·spire |
| re·as·cend | re·con·fig·u·ra·tion | re·ex·port | re·in·stall |
| re·as·cent | re·con·fig·ure | re·ex·por·ta·tion | re·in·stal·la·tion |
| re·as·sem·blage | re·con·nect | re·ex·pose | re·in·sti·tute |
| re·as·sem·ble | re·con·nec·tion | re·ex·po·sure | re·in·sti·tu·tion·al·i- |
| re·as·sem·bly | re·con·quer | re·ex·press | za·tion |
| re·as·sert | re·con·quest | re·face | re·in·ter |
| re·as·ser·tion | re·con·se·crate | re·feed | re·in·ter·view |
| re·as·sess | re·con·se·cra·tion | re·feel | re·in·tro·duce |
| re·as·sess·ment | re·con·sol·i·date | re·fence | re·in·tro·duc·tion |
| re·as·sign | re·con·tact | re·fight | re·in·vade |
| re·as·sign·ment | re·con·tam·i·nate | re·fig·ure | re·in·va·sion |
| re·as·sume | re·con·tam·i·na·tion | re·file | re·in·ves·ti·gate |
| re·at·tach | re·con·tex·tu·al·ize | re·find | re·in·ves·ti·ga·tion |
| re·at·tach·ment | re·con·tour | re·fire | re·in·vig·o·rate |
| re·at·tain | re·con·vene | re·fix | re·in·vig·o·ra·tion |
| re·at·tempt | re·con·ver·sion | re·float | re·in·vig·o·ra·tor |
| re·at·tri·bute | re·con·vert | re·fold | re·jack·et |
| re·at·tri·bu·tion | re·con·vict | re·forge | re·judge |
| re·au·tho·ri·za·tion | re·con·vic·tion | re·for·mat | re·jug·gle |
| re·au·tho·rize | re·con·vince | re·for·mu·late | re·key |
| re·awak·en | re·copy | re·for·mu·la·tion | re·key·board |
| re·bait | re·cork | re·for·ti·fi·ca·tion | re·kin·dle |
| re·bal·ance | re·cross | re·for·ti·fy | re·knit |
| re·bap·tism | re·cul·ti·vate | re·found | re·la·bel |
| re·bap·tize | re·date | re·foun·da·tion | re·lac·quer |
| re·be·gin | re·ded·i·cate | re·frame | re·land·scape |
| re·bid | re·ded·i·ca·tion | re·freeze | re·launch |
| re·bind | re·de·fect | re·fry | re·learn |
| re·blend | re·de·liv·er | re·fur·nish | re·lend |
| re·bloom | re·de·liv·ery | re·gain | re·li·cense |
| re·board | re·de·pos·it | re·gath·er | re·li·cen·sure |
| re·boil | re·de·ter·mi·na·tion | re·gear | re·light |
| re·book | re·de·ter·mine | re·gild | re·link |
| re·boot | re·di·ges·tion | re·give | re·liq·ue·fy |
| re·bore | re·dis·cov·er | re·glaze | re·load |
| re·bot·tle | re·dis·cov·ery | re·grade | re·lock |
| re·breed | re·dis·cuss | re·graft | re·look |
| re·buri·al | re·dis·play | re·grant | re·lu·bri·cate |
| re·bury | re·dis·pose | re·green | re·lu·bri·ca·tion |
| re·buy | re·dis·po·si·tion | re·grind | re·mar·ket |
| re·cal·cu·late | re·dis·solve | re·groom | re·mar·riage |
| re·cal·cu·la·tion | re·dis·till | re·groove | re·mar·ry |
| re·cal·i·brate | re·dis·til·la·tion | re·growth | re·mate |
| re·cal·i·bra·tion | re·di·vide | re·han·dle | re·ma·te·ri·al·ize |
| re·cen·tral·i·za·tion | re·di·vi·sion | re·hang | re·mea·sure |
| re·cen·tri·fuge | re·don | re·heat | re·mea·sure·ment |
| re·cer·ti·fi·ca·tion | re·draft | re·hinge | re·meet |
| re·cer·ti·fy | re·draw | re·hire | re·melt |
| re·chal·lenge | re·dream | re·hos·pi·tal·i·za·tion | re·merge |
| re·chan·nel | re·drill | re·hos·pi·tal·ize | re·mi·gra·tion |
| re·char·ter | re·dub | re·hu·man·ize | re·mil·i·ta·ri·za·tion |
| re·check | re·el·i·gi·bil·i·ty | re·hyp·no·tize | re·mil·i·ta·rize |
| re·cho·reo·graph | re·el·i·gi·ble | re·iden·ti·fy | re·mix |
| re·chris·ten | re·emerge | re·ig·nite | re·mo·bi·li·za·tion |
| re–Chris·tian·ize | re·emer·gence | re·ig·ni·tion | re·mo·bi·lize |
| re·chro·mato·graph | re·emis·sion | re·im·age | re·moist·en |
| re·chro·ma·tog·ra·phy | re·emit | re·im·merse | re·mold |
| | re·em·pha·sis | re·im·plant | re·mon·e·ti·za·tion |

re·mon·e·tize
re·mo·ti·vate
re·mo·ti·va·tion
re·my·thol·o·gize
re·nail
re·name
re·na·tion·al·i·za·tion
re·na·tion·al·ize
re·nest
re·num·ber
re·ob·serve
re·oc·cu·pa·tion
re·oc·cu·py
re·oc·cur
re·oc·cur·rence
re·oil
re·op·er·ate
re·op·er·a·tion
re·or·ches·trate
re·or·ches·tra·tion
re·ori·ent
re·ori·en·tate
re·ori·en·ta·tion
re·out·fit
re·ox·i·da·tion
re·ox·i·dize
re·pack
re·paint
re·park
re·patch
re·pat·tern
re·pave
re·peg
re·peo·ple
re·pho·to·graph
re·phrase
re·plan
re·plas·ter
re·plate
re·pledge
re·plot
re·plumb
re·pol·ish
re·poll
re·pop·u·lar·ize
re·pop·u·late
re·pop·u·la·tion
re·pot
re·pres·sur·ize
re·price
re·pri·vat·i·za·tion
re·pri·vat·ize
re·pro·vi·sion
re·pump
re·punc·tu·a·tion
re·pur·chase
re·pu·ri·fy
re·rack
re·raise
re·read
re·read·ing
re·re·cord
re·reg·is·ter
re·reg·is·tra·tion
re·reg·u·late
re·reg·u·la·tion
re·re·lease
re·re·mind
re·re·peat
re·re·view
re·rig
re·roof
re·route
re·sail
re·sam·ple
re·saw
re·school
re·score
re·screen
re·sculpt
re·seal
re·seal·able
re·sea·son
re·seat
re·se·cure
re·see

re·seg·re·gate
re·seg·re·ga·tion
re·sell
re·sell·er
re·sen·si·tize
re·sen·tence
re·ser·vice
re·set·tle
re·set·tle·ment
re·sew
re·shin·gle
re·shoe
re·shoot
re·show
re·sight
re·sil·ver
re·site
re·size
re·slate
re·soak
re·so·cial·i·za·tion
re·so·cial·ize
re·sod
re·sol·der
re·sole
re·so·lid·i·fi·ca·tion
re·so·lid·i·fy
re·sow
re·spir·i·tu·al·ize
re·spot
re·spray
re·sprout
re·sta·bi·lize
re·stack
re·stage
re·stamp
re·stim·u·late
re·stim·u·la·tion
re·stock
re·stoke
re·strength·en
re·stress
re·study
re·stuff
re·style
re·sub·mis·sion
re·sub·mit
re·sum·mon
re·sup·ply
re·sur·vey
re·syn·the·sis
re·syn·the·size
re·sys·tem·a·tize
re·tack·le
re·tag
re·tar·get
re·taste
re·teach
re·team
re·test
re·tex·ture
re·thread
re·tie
re·tight·en
re·tile
re·time
re·trace
re·trans·fer
re·trans·form
re·trans·for·ma·tion
re·trans·mis·sion
re·trans·mit
re·try
re·tune
re·type
re·uni·fy
re·uni·fi·ca·tion
re·up·hol·ster
re·uti·li·za·tion
re·uti·lize
re·vac·ci·nate
re·vac·ci·na·tion
re·val·i·date
re·val·i·da·tion
re·val·o·ri·za·tion
re·val·o·rize

re·vict·ual
re·vi·su·al·i·za·tion
re·vote
re·warm
re·wash
re·weave

re·weigh
re·wet
re·wire
re·wrap
re·zone

**¹re** \(ə)r\ *verb* (1591)
: ARE ⟨you*'re* right⟩

**re·ab·sorb** \ˌrē-əb-ˈsȯrb, -ˈzȯrb\ *transitive verb* (circa 1774)
: to take up (something previously secreted or emitted) ⟨sugars *reabsorbed* in the kidney⟩; *also* : RESORB 2

**¹reach** \ˈrēch\ *verb* [Middle English *rechen,* from Old English *rǣcan;* akin to Old High German *reichen* to reach, Lithuanian *raižytis* to stretch oneself] (before 12th century)
*transitive verb*
**1 a** : to stretch out : EXTEND **b** : THRUST
**2 a** : to touch or grasp by extending a part of the body (as a hand) or an object ⟨couldn't *reach* the apple⟩ **b** : to pick up and draw toward one : TAKE **c** (1) : to extend to ⟨the shadow *reached* the wall⟩ (2) : to get up to or as far as : come to ⟨your letter *reached* me yesterday⟩ ⟨his voice *reached* the last rows⟩ ⟨they hoped to *reach* an agreement⟩ **d** (1) : ENCOMPASS (2) : to make an impression on (3) : to communicate with
**3** : to hand over : PASS
*intransitive verb*
**1 a** : to make a stretch with or as if with one's hand **b** : to strain after something
**2 a** : PROJECT, EXTEND ⟨his land *reaches* to the river⟩ **b** : to arrive at or come to something ⟨as far as the eye could *reach*⟩
**3** : to sail on a reach
— **reach·able** \ˈrē-chə-bəl\ *adjective*
— **reach·er** *noun*

**²reach** *noun* (1536)
**1** : a continuous stretch or expanse; *especially* : a straight portion of a stream or river
**2 a** (1) : the action or an act of reaching (2) : an individual part of a progression or journey **b** (1) : a reachable distance ⟨within *reach*⟩ (2) : ability to reach ⟨had a long *reach*⟩ **c** : an extent or range especially of knowledge or comprehension
**3** : a bearing shaft or coupling pole; *especially* : the rod joining the hind axle to the forward bolster of a wagon
**4** : the tack sailed by a ship with the wind coming just forward of the beam or with the wind directly abeam or abaft the beam
**5** : ECHELON, LEVEL — usually used in plural ⟨the higher *reaches* of academic life⟩

**reach–me–down** \ˈrech-mē-ˌdaun\ *adjective or noun* (1862)
*chiefly British* : HAND-ME-DOWN

**re·act** \rē-ˈakt\ *verb* [New Latin *reactus,* past participle of *reagere,* from Latin *re-* + *agere* to act — more at AGENT] (1644)
*intransitive verb*
**1** : to exert a reciprocal or counteracting force or influence — often used with *on* or *upon*
**2** : to respond to a stimulus
**3** : to act in opposition to a force or influence — usually used with *against*
**4** : to move or tend in a reverse direction
**5** : to undergo chemical reaction
*transitive verb*
: to cause to react

**re·ac·tance** \rē-ˈak-tən(t)s\ *noun* (1893)
: the part of the impedance of an alternating-current circuit that is due to capacitance or inductance or both and that is expressed in ohms

**re·ac·tant** \-tənt\ *noun* (circa 1920)
: a substance that enters into and is altered in the course of a chemical reaction

**re·ac·tion** \rē-ˈak-shən\ *noun* (circa 1611)
**1 a** : the act or process or an instance of reacting **b** : resistance or opposition to a force, influence, or movement; *especially* : tendency toward a former and usually outmoded political or social order or policy

**2** : a response to some treatment, situation, or stimulus ⟨her stunned *reaction* to the news⟩; *also* : such a response expressed verbally ⟨critical *reaction* to the play⟩
**3** : bodily response to or activity aroused by a stimulus: **a** : an action induced by vital resistance to another action; *especially* : the response of tissues to a foreign substance (as an antigen or infective agent) **b** : depression or exhaustion due to excessive exertion or stimulation **c** : heightened activity and overaction succeeding depression or shock **d** : a mental or emotional disorder forming an individual's response to his or her life situation
**4** : the force that a body subjected to the action of a force from another body exerts in the opposite direction
**5 a** (1) : chemical transformation or change : the interaction of chemical entities (2) : the state resulting from such a reaction **b** : a process involving change in atomic nuclei

**re·ac·tion·ary** \rē-ˈak-shə-ˌner-ē\ *adjective* (1840)
: relating to, marked by, or favoring reaction; *especially* : ultraconservative in politics
— **reactionary** *noun*
— **re·ac·tion·ary·ism** \-ˌi-zəm\ *noun*

**re·ac·tive** \rē-ˈak-tiv\ *adjective* (1794)
**1** : of, relating to, or marked by reaction or reactance
**2 a** : readily responsive to a stimulus **b** : occurring as a result of stress or emotional upset ⟨*reactive* depression⟩
— **re·ac·tive·ly** *adverb*
— **re·ac·tive·ness** *noun*
— **re·ac·tiv·i·ty** \(ˌ)rē-ˌak-ˈti-və-tē\ *noun*

**re·ac·tor** \rē-ˈak-tər\ *noun* (circa 1904)
**1** : one that reacts
**2** : a device (as a coil, winding, or conductor of small resistance) used to introduce reactance into an alternating-current circuit
**3 a** : a vat for an industrial chemical reaction **b** : a device for the controlled release of nuclear energy (as for producing heat)

**¹read** \ˈrēd\ *verb* **read** \ˈred\; **read·ing** \ˈrē-diŋ\ [Middle English *reden* to advise, interpret, read, from Old English *rǣdan;* akin to Old High German *rātan* to advise, Sanskrit *rādhnoti* he achieves, prepares] (before 12th century)
*transitive verb*
**1 a** (1) : to receive or take in the sense of (as letters or symbols) especially by sight or touch (2) : to study the movements of (as lips) with mental formulation of the communication expressed (3) : to utter aloud the printed or written words of ⟨*read* them a story⟩ **b** : to learn from what one has seen or found in writing or printing **c** : to deliver aloud by or as if by reading; *specifically* : to utter interpretively **d** (1) : to become acquainted with or look over the contents of (as a book) (2) : to make a study of ⟨*read* law⟩ (3) : to read the works of **e** : to check (as copy or proof) for errors **f** (1) : to receive and understand (a voice message) by radio (2) : UNDERSTAND, COMPREHEND
**2 a** : to interpret the meaning or significance of ⟨*read* palms⟩ **b** : FORETELL, PREDICT ⟨able to *read* his fortune⟩
**3** : to recognize or interpret as if by reading: as **a** : to learn the nature of by observing outward expression or signs ⟨*reads* him like a book⟩ **b** : to note the action or characteristics of in order to anticipate what will happen ⟨a good canoeist *reads* the rapids⟩ ⟨a golfer *reading* a green⟩; *also* : to predict the movement of (a putt) by reading a green **c** : to anticipate by observation of an opponent's position or movement ⟨*read* a blitz⟩

\ə\ **abut** \ᵊ\ **kitten** \ər\ **further** \a\ **ash** \ā\ **ace**
\ä\ **mop, mar** \au\ **out** \ch\ **chin** \e\ **bet** \ē\ **easy**
\g\ **go** \i\ **hit** \ī\ **ice** \j\ **job** \ŋ\ **sing** \ō\ **go**
\ȯ\ **law** \ȯi\ **boy** \th\ **thin** \t͟h\ **the** \ü\ **loot** \u̇\ **foot**
\y\ **yet** \zh\ **vision** *see also* Guide to Pronunciation

**4 a :** to attribute a meaning to (as something read) **:** INTERPRET ⟨how do you *read* this passage⟩ **b :** to attribute (a meaning) to something read or considered ⟨*read* a nonexistent meaning into her words⟩
**5 :** to use as a substitute for or in preference to another word or phrase in a particular passage, text, or version ⟨*read* hurry for *harry*⟩ — often used to introduce a clarifying substitute for a euphemistic or misleading word or phrase ⟨a friendly, *read* nosy, coworker⟩
**6 :** INDICATE ⟨the thermometer *reads* zero⟩
**7 :** to interpret (a musical work) in performance
**8 a :** to acquire (information) from storage; *especially* **:** to sense the meaning of (data) in recorded and coded form — used of a computer or data processor **b :** to read the coded information on (as a floppy disk)
*intransitive verb*
**1 a :** to perform the act of reading words **:** read something **b (1) :** to learn something by reading **(2) :** to pursue a course of study
**2 a :** to yield a particular meaning or impression when read **b :** to be readable or read in a particular manner or to a particular degree ⟨this book *reads* smoothly⟩
**3 :** to consist of specific words, phrases, or other similar elements ⟨a passage that *reads* differently in older versions⟩
— **read between the lines :** to understand more than is directly stated
— **read the riot act 1 :** to order a mob to disperse **2 a :** to order or warn to cease something **b :** to protest vehemently **c :** to reprimand severely
²**read** \'red\ *adjective* (1586)
**:** instructed by or informed through reading
³**read** \'red\ *noun* (1825)
**1** *chiefly British* **:** a period of reading ⟨it was a night . . . for a *read* and a long sleep —William Sansom⟩
**2 :** something (as a book) that is read ⟨a novel that's a good *read*⟩
**3 :** the action or an instance of reading
**read·able** \'rē-də-bəl\ *adjective* (15th century)
**:** able to be read easily: as **a :** LEGIBLE **b :** interesting to read
— **read·abil·i·ty** \,rē-də-'bi-lə-tē\ *noun*
— **read·able·ness** \'rē-də-bəl-nəs\ *noun*
— **read·ably** \-blē\ *adverb*
**read·er** \'rē-dər\ *noun* (before 12th century)
**1 a :** one that reads **b :** one appointed to read to others: as **(1) :** LECTOR **(2) :** one chosen to read aloud selected material in a Christian Science church or society **c (1) :** PROOFREADER **(2)** **:** one who evaluates manuscripts **(3) :** one who reads periodical literature to discover items of special interest or value **d :** an employee who reads and records the indications of meters **e** **:** a teacher's assistant who reads and marks student papers
**2** *British* **:** one who reads lectures or expounds subjects to students
**3 a :** a device for projecting a readable image of a transparency **b :** a unit that scans material recorded (as on punched cards) for storage or computation
**4 a :** a book for instruction and practice especially in reading **b :** ANTHOLOGY
**read·er·ly** \-lē\ *adjective* (1959)
**:** of, relating to, or typical of a reader
**read·er·ship** \-,ship\ *noun* (1719)
**1 a :** the quality or state of being a reader **b :** the office or position of a reader
**2 :** the mass or a particular group of readers ⟨a magazine's *readership*⟩
**read·i·ly** \'re-d²l-ē\ *adverb* (14th century)
**:** in a ready manner: as **a :** without hesitating **:** WILLINGLY ⟨*readily* accepted advice⟩ **b :** without much difficulty **:** EASILY ⟨for reasons that anyone could *readily* understand⟩
**read·ing** \'rē-diŋ\ *noun* (before 12th century)
**1 :** the act of reading

**2 a :** material read or for reading **b :** extent of material read
**3 a :** a particular version **b :** data indicated by an instrument
**4 a :** a particular interpretation of something (as a law) **b :** a particular performance of something (as a musical work)
**5 :** an indication of a certain state of affairs ⟨a study to get some *reading* of shoppers' preferences⟩
**reading desk** *noun* (1703)
**:** LECTERN
**reading frame** *noun* (1965)
**:** any of the three possible ways of reading a sequence of nucleotides as a series of triplets
**read–only memory** *noun* (1961)
**:** a usually small computer memory that contains special-purpose information (as a program) which cannot be altered — called also *ROM*; compare RANDOM-ACCESS MEMORY
**read·out** \'rēd-,aut\ *noun* (1652)
**1 :** the process of reading
**2 a :** the process of removing information from an automatic device (as an electronic computer) and displaying it in an understandable form **b :** the information removed from such a device and displayed or recorded (as by magnetic tape or printing device) **c :** an electronic device that presents information in visual form
**3 :** the radio transmission of data or pictures from a space vehicle
**read out** *transitive verb* (1600)
**1 a :** to read aloud **b :** to produce a readout of
**2 :** to expel from an organization or group
¹**ready** \'re-dē\ *adjective* **read·i·er; -est** [Middle English *redy;* akin to Old English *gerǣde* ready, Gothic *garaiths* arranged] (13th century)
**1 a :** prepared mentally or physically for some experience or action **b :** prepared for immediate use ⟨dinner is *ready*⟩
**2 a :** willingly disposed **:** INCLINED ⟨*ready* to agree to his proposal⟩ **b :** likely to do something indicated ⟨a house that looks *ready* to collapse⟩
**3 :** displayed readily and spontaneously ⟨a *ready* wit⟩
**4 :** immediately available ⟨had little *ready* cash⟩
**synonym** see QUICK
— **read·i·ness** *noun*
— **at the ready :** ready for immediate use ⟨kept their guns *at the ready*⟩
²**ready** *transitive verb* **read·ied; ready·ing** (14th century)
**:** to make ready
**ready box** *noun* (1942)
**:** a box placed near a gun (as on a ship) to hold ammunition kept ready for immediate use
¹**ready–made** \,red-ē-'mād\ *adjective* (15th century)
**1 :** made beforehand especially for general sale ⟨*ready-made* suits⟩
**2 :** lacking originality or individuality
**3 :** readily available ⟨her illness provided a *ready-made* excuse⟩
²**ready–made** *noun* (1882)
**1 :** something (as a garment) that is ready-made
**2** *usually* **ready·made** [French *ready-made,* from English] **:** a commonplace artifact (as a comb or a pair of ice tongs) selected and displayed as a work of art
**ready room** *noun* (1941)
**:** a room in which pilots or astronauts are briefed and await orders
**ready–to–wear** *adjective* (1895)
**1** *of clothing* **:** READY-MADE
**2 :** dealing in ready-made clothes ⟨*ready-to-wear* stores⟩
— **ready–to–wear** *noun*

**ready–wit·ted** \,re-dē-'wi-təd\ *adjective* (1581)
**:** QUICK-WITTED
**re·af·for·es·ta·tion** \,rē-ə-,for-ə-'stā-shən, -,fär-\ *noun* (1884)
*chiefly British* **:** REFORESTATION
— **re·af·for·est** \-'for-əst, -'fär-\ *transitive verb, chiefly British*
**re·agent** \rē-'ā-jənt\ *noun* [New Latin *reagent, reagens,* present participle of *reagere* to react — more at REACT] (1797)
**:** a substance used (as in detecting or measuring a component, in preparing a product, or in developing photographs) because of its chemical or biological activity
**re·ag·gre·gate** \(,)rē-'a-gri-,gāt\ *transitive verb* (1849)
**:** to cause to re-form into an aggregate or a whole
— **re·ag·gre·gate** \-gət\ *noun*
— **re·ag·gre·ga·tion** \-,a-gri-'gā-shən\ *noun*
**re·agin** \rē-'ā-jən, -gən\ *noun* [International Scientific Vocabulary, from *reagent*] (circa 1911)
**1 :** a substance in the blood of persons with syphilis responsible for positive serological reactions for syphilis
**2 :** an antibody in the blood of individuals with some forms of allergy possessing the power of passively sensitizing the skin of normal individuals
— **re·agin·ic** \,rē-ə-'ji-nik, -'gi-\ *adjective*
¹**re·al** \'rē(-ə)l, 'ri(-ə)l\ *adjective* [Middle English, real, relating to things (in law), from Middle French, from Medieval Latin & Late Latin; Medieval Latin *realis* relating to things (in law), from Late Latin, real, from Latin *res* thing, fact; akin to Sanskrit *rayi* property] (14th century)
**1 :** of or relating to fixed, permanent, or immovable things (as lands or tenements)
**2 a :** not artificial, fraudulent, illusory, or apparent **:** GENUINE ⟨*real* gold⟩; *also* **:** being precisely what the name implies ⟨a *real* professional⟩ **b (1) :** occurring in fact ⟨a story of *real* life⟩ **(2) :** of or relating to practical or everyday concerns or activities ⟨left school to live in the *real* world⟩ **(3) :** existing as a physical entity and having properties that deviate from an ideal, law, or standard ⟨a *real* gas⟩ — compare IDEAL 3b **c :** having objective independent existence ⟨unable to believe that what he saw was *real*⟩ **d :** FUNDAMENTAL, ESSENTIAL **e (1) :** belonging to or having elements or components that belong to the set of real numbers ⟨the *real* roots of an equation⟩ ⟨a *real* matrix⟩ **(2) :** concerned with or containing real numbers ⟨*real* analysis⟩ **(3) :** REAL-VALUED ⟨*real* variable⟩ **f :** measured by purchasing power ⟨*real* income⟩ ⟨*real* dollars⟩ **g :** COMPLETE, UTTER ⟨a *real* fiasco⟩
**3** *of a particle* **:** capable of being detected — compare VIRTUAL 3
— **re·al·ness** *noun*
— **for real 1 :** in earnest **:** SERIOUSLY ⟨fighting *for real*⟩ **2 :** GENUINE ⟨couldn't believe the threats were *for real*⟩
²**real** *noun* (circa 1626)
**:** a real thing; *especially* **:** a mathematically real quantity
³**real** *adverb* (1718)
**:** VERY ⟨he was *real* cool —H. M. McLuhan⟩ ■

---

□ USAGE
**real** Most handbooks consider the adverb *real* to be informal and more suitable to speech than writing. Our evidence shows these observations to be true in the main, but *real* is becoming increasingly common in writing of an informal, conversational style. It is used as an intensifier only and is not interchangeable with *really* except in that use.

**⁴re·al** \rā-'äl\ *noun, plural* **reals** *or* **re·ales** \-'ä-(,)lās\ [Spanish, from *real* royal, from Latin *regalis* — more at ROYAL] (1555)
: a former monetary unit and coin of Spain and its possessions
**⁵re·al** \rā-'äl\ *noun, plural* **reals** *or* **reis** \'räsh, 'räs, 'räzh, 'räz\ [Portuguese, from *real* royal, from Latin *regalis*] (1951)
**1** : a former monetary unit and coin of Portugal
**2** — see MONEY table
**real estate** *noun* (1666)
: property in buildings and land
**real focus** *noun* (1909)
: a point at which rays (as of light) converge or from which they diverge
**re·al·gar** \rē-'al-gär, -gər\ *noun* [Middle English, from Medieval Latin, from Catalan, from Arabic *rahj al-ghār* powder of the mine] (15th century)
: an orange-red mineral consisting of arsenic sulfide and having a resinous luster
**re·a·lia** \rē-'a-lē-ə, -'ä-\ *noun plural* [Late Latin, neuter plural of *realis* real] (1937)
: objects or activities used to relate classroom teaching to the real life especially of peoples studied
**re·align** \,rē-ə-'līn\ *transitive verb* (1899)
: to align again; *especially* : to reorganize or make new groupings of
— **re·align·ment** \-mənt\ *noun*
**real image** *noun* (1899)
: an optical image formed of real foci
**re·al·ism** \'rē-ə-,li-zəm, 'ri-ə-\ *noun* (1817)
**1** : concern for fact or reality and rejection of the impractical and visionary
**2 a** : a doctrine that universals exist outside the mind; *specifically* : the conception that an abstract term names an independent and unitary reality **b** : the conception that objects of sense perception or cognition exist independently of the mind — compare NOMINALISM
**3** : fidelity in art and literature to nature or to real life and to accurate representation without idealization
— **re·al·ist** \-list\ *adjective or noun*
— **re·al·is·tic** \,rē-ə-'lis-tik, ,ri-ə-\ *adjective*
— **re·al·is·ti·cal·ly** \-ti-k(ə-)lē\ *adverb*
**re·al·i·ty** \rē-'a-lə-tē\ *noun, plural* **-ties** (1550)
**1** : the quality or state of being real
**2 a (1)** : a real event, entity, or state of affairs ⟨his dream became a *reality*⟩ **(2)** : the totality of real things and events ⟨trying to escape from *reality*⟩ **b** : something that is neither derivative nor dependent but exists necessarily
— **in reality** : in actual fact
**reality check** *noun* (1986)
: something that clarifies or serves as a reminder of reality often by correcting a misconception
**re·al·i·za·tion** \,rē-ə-lə-'zā-shən, ,ri-ə-\ *noun* (circa 1611)
**1** : the action of realizing : the state of being realized
**2** : something realized
**re·al·ize** \'rē-ə-,līz, 'ri-ə-\ *transitive verb* **-ized; -iz·ing** [French *réaliser*, from Middle French *realiser*, from *real* real] (circa 1611)
**1 a** : to bring into concrete existence : ACCOMPLISH ⟨finally *realized* her goal⟩ **b** : to cause to seem real : make appear real ⟨a book in which the characters are carefully *realized*⟩
**2 a** : to convert into actual money ⟨*realized* assets⟩ **b** : to bring or get by sale, investment, or effort : GAIN
**3** : to conceive vividly as real : be fully aware of ⟨did not *realize* the risk she was taking⟩
*synonym* see THINK
— **re·al·iz·able** \,rē-ə-'lī-zə-bəl, ,ri-\ *adjective*
— **re·al·iz·er** *noun*
**real–life** *adjective* (1938)

: existing or occurring in reality : drawn from or drawing on actual events or situations ⟨*real-life* problems⟩ ⟨*real-life* drama⟩
**re·al·ly** \'rē-(ə-)lē, 'ri-\ *adverb* (15th century)
**1 a** : in reality : ACTUALLY ⟨things as they *really* are⟩ ⟨there was nothing peculiar about her doing this, *really* —Peter Taylor⟩ **b** : TRULY, UNQUESTIONABLY — used as an intensifier ⟨a *really* beautiful day⟩
**2** — used to emphasize an assertion ⟨you *really* should read Yeats⟩ ⟨*really*, you're being ridiculous⟩
**realm** \'relm\ *noun* [Middle English *realme*, from Old French *reialme*, alteration of *reiame*, from Latin *regimen* rule — more at REGIMEN] (13th century)
**1** : KINGDOM 2
**2** : SPHERE, DOMAIN ⟨within the *realm* of possibility⟩
**3** : a primary marine or terrestrial biogeographic division of the earth's surface
**real number** *noun* (1909)
: one of the numbers that have no imaginary parts and comprise the rationals and the irrationals
**real part** *noun* (1949)
: the term in a complex number (as 2 in 2 + 3*i*) that does not contain the imaginary unit as a factor
**re·al·po·li·tik** \rā-'äl-,pō-li-,tēk\ *noun, often capitalized* [German, from *real* actual + *Politik* politics] (1914)
: politics based on practical and material factors rather than on theoretical or ethical objectives
**real presence** *noun, often R&P capitalized* (1559)
: the doctrine that Christ is actually present in the Eucharist
**real time** *noun* (1953)
: the actual time during which something takes place ⟨the computer may partly analyze the data in *real time* (as it comes in) —R. H. March⟩
— **real–time** *adjective*
**Re·al·tor** \'rē(-ə)l-tər, -,tȯr, ÷'rē-lə-tər *also* rē-'al-tər\ *collective mark*
— used for a real estate agent who is a member of the National Association of Realtors
**re·al·ty** \'rē-(ə)l-tē\ *noun* [*real* + *-ty* (as in *property*)] (1670)
: REAL ESTATE
**real–valued** *adjective* (1965)
: taking on only real numbers for values
**real–world** *adjective* (1963)
: REAL-LIFE
**¹ream** \'rēm\ *noun* [Middle English *reme*, from Middle French *raime*, from Arabic *rizmah*, literally, bundle] (14th century)
**1** : a quantity of paper being 20 quires or variously 480, 500, or 516 sheets
**2** : a great amount — usually used in plural
**²ream** *transitive verb* [perhaps from (assumed) Middle English *remen* to open up, from Old English *rēman*; akin to Old English *rȳman* to open up, *rūm* space — more at ROOM] (1815)
**1 a** : to widen the opening of (a hole) : COUNTERSINK **b (1)** : to enlarge or dress out (a hole) with a reamer **(2)** : to enlarge the bore of (as a gun) in this way **c** : to remove by reaming
**2 a** : to press out with a reamer **b** : to press out the juice of (as an orange) with a reamer
**3** : CHEAT, VICTIMIZE
**4** : REPRIMAND
**ream·er** \'rē-mər\ *noun* (1825)
: one that reams: as **a** : a rotating finishing tool with cutting edges used to enlarge or shape a hole **b** : a fruit juice extractor with a ridged and pointed center rising from a shallow dish
**reap** \'rēp\ *verb* [Middle English *repen*, from Old English *reopan*] (before 12th century)
*transitive verb*
**1 a (1)** : to cut with a sickle, scythe, or reaping

machine **(2)** : to clear of a crop by reaping **b** : to gather by reaping : HARVEST
**2** : OBTAIN, WIN
*intransitive verb*
: to reap something
**reap·er** \'rē-pər\ *noun* (before 12th century)
: one that reaps; *especially* : any of various machines for reaping grain
**reap·hook** \'rēp-,hŭk\ *noun* (1591)
: a hand implement with a hook-shaped blade used in reaping
**re·ap·por·tion** \,rē-ə-'pōr-shən, -'pȯr-\ (circa 1828)
*transitive verb*
: to apportion (as a house of representatives) anew
*intransitive verb*
: to make a new apportionment
— **re·ap·por·tion·ment** \-shən-mənt\ *noun*
**¹rear** \'rir, *transitive verb 4 & intransitive verb 2 are also* 'rar *or* 'rer\ *verb* [Middle English *reren*, from Old English *rǣran;* akin to Old Norse *reisa* to raise, Old English *rīsan* to rise] (before 12th century)
*transitive verb*
**1** : to erect by building : CONSTRUCT
**2** : to raise upright
**3 a (1)** : to breed and raise (an animal) for use or market **(2)** : BRING UP 1 **b** : to cause (as plants) to grow
**4** : to cause (a horse) to rise up on the hind legs
*intransitive verb*
**1** : to rise high
**2** *of a horse* : to rise up on the hind legs
*synonym* see LIFT
— **rear·er** *noun*
**²rear** \'rir\ *noun* [Middle English *rere*, short for *rerewarde* rearward] (14th century)
**1** : the back part of something: as **a** : the unit (as of an army) or area farthest from the enemy **b** : the part of something located opposite its front ⟨the *rear* of a house⟩ **c** : BUTTOCKS
**2** : the space or position at the back ⟨moved to the *rear*⟩
**³rear** \'rir\ *adjective* [Middle English *rere-*, from Middle French *rere* backward, behind, from Latin *retro-* — more at RETRO] (14th century)
: being at the back
**⁴rear** \'rir\ *adverb* (1855)
: toward or from the rear — usually used in combination ⟨a *rear*-driven car⟩
**rear admiral** *noun* (1589)
: a commissioned officer in the navy who ranks above a commodore and in the coast guard who ranks above a captain and whose insignia is two stars
**rear echelon** *noun* (circa 1934)
: an element of a military headquarters or unit located at a considerable distance from the front and concerned especially with administrative and supply duties
**rear–end** \'rir-'end, -,end\ *transitive verb* (1957)
: to crash into the back of (as an automobile)
**rear end** *noun* (circa 1930)
: BUTTOCKS
**rear·guard** \'rir-,gärd\ *adjective* (1898)
: of or relating to resistance especially to sweeping social forces ⟨fought a *rearguard* action against automation⟩
**rear guard** \-'gärd, -,gärd\ *noun* [Middle French *reregarde*, from Old French, from *rere* + *garde* guard] (1659)
: a military detachment detailed to bring up and protect the rear of a main body or force

**re·arm** \(ˌ)rē-'ärm\ (1871)
*transitive verb*
: to arm (as a nation or a military force) again with new or better weapons
*intransitive verb*
: to become armed again
— **re·ar·ma·ment** \-'är-mə-mənt\ *noun*
**rear·most** \'rir-ˌmōst\ *adjective* (1718)
: farthest in the rear : LAST
**rear·view mirror** \'rir-ˌvyü-\ *noun* (1926)
: a mirror (as in an automobile) that gives a view of the area behind a vehicle
¹**rear·ward** \'rir-ˌwòrd\ *noun* [Middle English *rerewarde*, from Anglo-French; akin to Old French *reregarde* rear guard] (14th century)
: REAR; *especially* : the rear division (as of an army)
²**rear·ward** \-wərd\ *adjective* [²*rear* + *-ward*] (1598)
**1** : located at, near, or toward the rear
**2** : directed toward the rear
³**rear·ward** \-wərd\ *also* **rear·wards** \-wərdz\ *adverb* (1625)
: at, near, or toward the rear : BACKWARD
¹**rea·son** \'rē-zᵊn\ *noun* [Middle English *resoun*, from Old French *raison*, from Latin *ration-, ratio* reason, computation, from *reri* to calculate, think; probably akin to Gothic *rathjo* account, explanation] (13th century)
**1 a** : a statement offered in explanation or justification ⟨gave *reasons* that were quite satisfactory⟩ **b** : a rational ground or motive ⟨a good *reason* to act soon⟩ **c** : a sufficient ground of explanation or of logical defense; *especially* : something (as a principle or law) that supports a conclusion or explains a fact ⟨the *reasons* behind her client's action⟩ **d** : the thing that makes some fact intelligible : CAUSE ⟨the *reason* for earthquakes⟩ ⟨the real *reason* why he wanted me to stay —Graham Greene⟩
**2 a** (1) : the power of comprehending, inferring, or thinking especially in orderly rational ways : INTELLIGENCE (2) : proper exercise of the mind (3) : SANITY **b** : the sum of the intellectual powers
**3** *archaic* : treatment that affords satisfaction ☐
— **in reason** : RIGHTLY, JUSTIFIABLY
— **within reason** : within reasonable limits
— **with reason** : with good cause
²**reason** *verb* **rea·soned; rea·son·ing** \'rēz-niŋ, 'rē-zᵊn-iŋ\ (15th century)
*intransitive verb*
**1 a** *obsolete* : to take part in conversation, discussion, or argument **b** : to talk with another so as to influence his actions or opinions ⟨can't *reason* with her⟩
**2** : to use the faculty of reason so as to arrive at conclusions
*transitive verb*
**1** *archaic* : to justify or support with reasons
**2** : to persuade or influence by the use of reason
**3** : to discover, formulate, or conclude by the use of reason ⟨a carefully *reasoned* analysis⟩
**synonym** see THINK
— **rea·son·er** \'rēz-nər, 'rē-zᵊn-ər\ *noun*
**rea·son·able** \'rēz-nə-bəl, 'rē-zᵊn-ə-bəl\ *adjective* (14th century)
**1 a** : being in accordance with reason ⟨a *reasonable* theory⟩ **b** : not extreme or excessive ⟨*reasonable* requests⟩ **c** : MODERATE, FAIR ⟨a *reasonable* chance⟩ ⟨a *reasonable* price⟩ **d** : INEXPENSIVE
**2 a** : having the faculty of reason **b** : possessing sound judgment
— **rea·son·abil·i·ty** \ˌrēz-nə-'bi-lə-tē, ˌrē-zᵊn-ə-\ *noun*
— **rea·son·able·ness** \'rēz-nə-bəl-nəs, 'rē-zᵊn-ə-\ *noun*
— **rea·son·ably** \-blē\ *adverb*
**reasoning** *noun* (14th century)
**1** : the use of reason; *especially* : the drawing of inferences or conclusions through the use of

**2** : an instance of the use of reason : ARGUMENT
**rea·son·less** \'rē-zᵊn-ləs\ *adjective* (14th century)
**1** : not having the faculty of reason ⟨a *reasonless* brute⟩
**2** : not reasoned : SENSELESS ⟨*reasonless* hostility⟩
**3** : not based on or supported by reasons ⟨a *reasonless* accusation⟩
— **rea·son·less·ly** *adverb*
**re·as·sur·ance** \ˌrē-ə-'shùr-ən(t)s\ *noun* (circa 1611)
**1** : the action of reassuring : the state of being reassured
**2** : REINSURANCE
**re·as·sure** \ˌrē-ə-'shùr\ *transitive verb* (1598)
**1** : to assure anew ⟨*reassured* him that the work was on schedule⟩
**2** : to restore to confidence ⟨felt *reassured* by their earnest promise to do better⟩
**3** : REINSURE
— **re·as·sur·ing·ly** \-'shùr-iŋ-lē\ *adverb*
**re·ata** \rē-'a-tə, -'ä-\ *noun* [American Spanish — more at LARIAT] (1846)
: LARIAT
**Re·au·mur** \ˌrā-ō-'myùr, 'rā-ō-ˌ\ *adjective* [René Antoine Ferchault de *Réaumur*] (1814)
: relating to or conforming to a thermometric scale on which the boiling point of water is at 80° above the zero of the scale and the freezing point is at zero
¹**reave** \'rēv\ *verb* **reaved** *or* **reft** \'reft\; **reav·ing** [Middle English *reven*, from Old English *rēafian*; akin to Old High German *roubōn* to rob, Latin *rumpere* to break] (before 12th century)
*intransitive verb*
: PLUNDER, ROB
*transitive verb*
**1** *archaic* **a** (1) : ROB, DESPOIL (2) : to deprive one of **b** : SEIZE
**2** *archaic* : to carry or tear away
— **reav·er** *noun*
²**reave** *transitive verb* **reaved** *or* **reft** \'reft\; **reav·ing** [Middle English *reven*, probably modification of Old Norse *rīfa* to rive] (13th century)
*archaic* : BURST
**reb** \'reb\ *noun* [short for *rebel*] (1862)
: JOHNNY REB
**Reb** \'reb\ *noun* [Yiddish, from Hebrew *rabbī* my master, rabbi] (1882)
: RABBI, MISTER — used as a title
**re·bar** \'rē-ˌbär\ *noun* [*reinforcing bar*] (1953)
: a steel rod with ridges for use in reinforced concrete
**re·bar·ba·tive** \ri-'bär-bə-tiv\ *adjective* [French *rébarbatif*, from Middle French, from *rebarber* to be repellent, from *re-* + *barbe* beard, from Latin *barba* — more at BEARD] (1892)
: REPELLENT, IRRITATING
— **re·bar·ba·tive·ly** *adverb*
¹**re·bate** \'rē-ˌbāt, ri-'bāt\ *verb* **re·bat·ed; re·bat·ing** [Middle English, from Middle French *rabattre* to beat down again, from Old French, from *re-* + *abattre* to beat down, from *a-* (from Latin *ad-*) + *battre* to beat, from Latin *battuere*] (14th century)
*transitive verb*
**1** : to reduce the force or activity of : DIMINISH
**2** : to reduce the sharpness of : BLUNT
**3 a** : to make a rebate of **b** : to give a rebate to
*intransitive verb*
: to give rebates
— **re·bat·er** *noun*
²**re·bate** \'rē-ˌbāt\ *noun* (1656)
: a return of a part of a payment
³**re·bate** \'ra-bət, 'rē-ˌbāt\ *chiefly British variant of* RABBET

**re·ba·to** \ri-'bä-(ˌ)tō\ *variant of* RABATO
**reb·be** \'re-bə\ *noun* [Yiddish *rebe*, from Hebrew *rabbī* rabbi] (1881)
: a Jewish spiritual leader or teacher : RABBI
**re·bec** *or* **re·beck** \'rē-ˌbek, 're-(ˌ)bek\ *noun* [Middle English *rebecke*, from Middle French *rebec*, alteration of Old French *rebebe*, from Old Provençal *rebeb*, from Arabic *rabāb*] (15th century)
: an ancient bowed usually 3-stringed musical instrument with a pear-shaped body and slender neck

rebec

**Re·bek·ah** \ri-'be-kə\ *noun* [Hebrew *Ribhqāh*]
: the wife of Isaac
¹**reb·el** \'re-bəl\ *adjective* [Middle English, from Old French *rebelle*, from Latin *rebellis*, from *re-* + *bellum* war, from Old Latin *duellum*] (14th century)
**1 a** : opposing or taking arms against a government or ruler **b** : of or relating to rebels ⟨the *rebel* camp⟩
**2** : DISOBEDIENT, REBELLIOUS
²**rebel** *noun* (14th century)
: one who rebels or participates in a rebellion
³**re·bel** \ri-'bel\ *intransitive verb* **re·belled; re·bel·ling** (14th century)
**1 a** : to oppose or disobey one in authority or control **b** : to renounce and resist by force the authority of one's government
**2 a** : to act in or show opposition or disobedience ⟨*rebelled* against the conventions of polite society⟩ **b** : to feel or exhibit anger or revulsion ⟨*rebelled* at the injustice of life⟩
**re·bel·lion** \ri-'bel-yən\ *noun* (14th century)
**1** : opposition to one in authority or dominance
**2 a** : open, armed, and usually unsuccessful defiance of or resistance to an established gov-

☐ USAGE
**reason** *The reason is because* is a short way of referring to a number of locutions in which a primary clause with *reason* as its subject is followed by a subordinate clause introduced by *because* ⟨the *reason* I didn't answer the other letter was because mine was already on the way to you —Ernest Hemingway⟩. This locution has been used in standard English since the 16th century at least, but it has been attacked since a commentator named Robert Baker decided it made no sense in 1770. Modern objections are that the expression is redundant or illogical (which follows Baker) or that it is ungrammatical (which is incorrect). The universal recommendation is to replace *the reason is because* with *the reason is that*. Our evidence shows that *the reason is that* is more often used in edited prose than *the reason is because*; the latter is the more common in speech. We find *because* quite common in informal prose ⟨the *reason* the story has never been made into a film is because I won't sign a contract —E. B. White⟩ ⟨the *reason* I had not seen the nomination in the Tazewell paper was . . . because I did not then, as I do not now, take that paper —Abraham Lincoln⟩ ⟨the only *reason* my appearances are rare . . . is because nobody asks me oftener —Groucho Marx⟩ ⟨now the *reason* hair falls off is because it hangs down —Lewis Carroll⟩. Although this locution is perfectly ordinary, perfectly understandable, and perfectly standard, the handbooks continue to advise against it. They omit, however, Baker's other observation, that "there are scarce any even of our greatest authors, that avoid this way of speaking."

ernment **b** : an instance of such defiance or resistance ☆

**re·bel·lious** \-yəs\ *adjective* (15th century)
**1 a** : given to or engaged in rebellion ⟨*rebellious* troops⟩ **b** : of, relating to, or characteristic of a rebel or rebellion ⟨a *rebellious* speech⟩
**2** : resisting treatment or management : REFRACTORY
— **re·bel·lious·ly** *adverb*
— **re·bel·lious·ness** *noun*
**rebel yell** *noun* (1863)
: a prolonged high-pitched yell often uttered by Confederate soldiers in the U.S. Civil War
**re·birth** \(ˌ)rē-ˈbərth, ˈrē-\ *noun* (1837)
**1 a** : a new or second birth : METEMPSYCHOSIS
**b** : spiritual regeneration
**2** : RENAISSANCE, REVIVAL ⟨a *rebirth* of nationalism⟩
**Re·blo·chon** \rə-blò-ˈshōⁿ\ *noun* [French *reblochon,* from French dialect (Savoy)] (1908)
: a semisoft creamy mild-flavored French cheese
**reb·o·ant** \ˈre-bə-wənt\ *adjective* [Latin *reboant-, reboans,* present participle of *reboare* to resound, from *re-* + *boare* to cry aloud, roar, from Greek *boan,* of imitative origin] (1830)
: marked by reverberation
**re·born** \(ˌ)rē-ˈbòrn\ *adjective* (1598)
: born again : REGENERATED, REVIVED
**¹re·bound** \ˈrē-ˌbaund, ri-\ *verb* [Middle English, from Middle French *rebondir,* from Old French, from *re-* + *bondir* to bound — more at BOUND] (14th century)
*intransitive verb*
**1 a** : to spring back on or as if on collision or impact with another body **b** : to recover from setback or frustration
**2** : REECHO
**3** : to gain possession of a rebound in basketball
*transitive verb*
: to cause to rebound
— **re·bound·er** \ˈrē-ˌbaun-dər, ri-\ *noun*
**²re·bound** \ˈrē-ˌbaund, ri-\ *noun* (1530)
**1 a** : the action of rebounding : RECOIL **b** : an upward leap or movement : RECOVERY ⟨a sharp *rebound* in prices⟩
**2 a** : a basketball or hockey puck that rebounds **b** : the act or an instance of gaining possession of a basketball rebound ⟨leads the league in *rebounds*⟩
**3** : a reaction to setback, frustration, or crisis ⟨on the *rebound* from an unhappy love affair⟩
**re·bo·zo** \ri-ˈbō-(ˌ)zō, -(ˌ)sō\ *noun, plural* **-zos** [Spanish, shawl, from *rebozar* to muffle, alteration of *embozar* to muffle, probably from (assumed) Vulgar Latin *imbucciare,* from Latin *in-* + *bucca* cheek] (1807)
: a long scarf worn chiefly by Mexican women
**re·branch** \(ˌ)rē-ˈbranch\ *intransitive verb* (1888)
: to form secondary branches
**re·broad·cast** \(ˌ)rē-ˈbròd-ˌkast\ *transitive verb* **-cast; -cast·ing** (1923)
**1** : to broadcast again ⟨a radio or television program being simultaneously received from another source⟩
**2** : to repeat (a broadcast) at a later time
— **rebroadcast** *noun*
**re·buff** \ri-ˈbəf\ *transitive verb* [Middle French *rebuffer,* from Old Italian *ribuffare* to reprimand, from *ribuffo* reprimand] (circa 1586)
: to reject or criticize sharply : SNUB
— **rebuff** *noun*
**re·build** \(ˌ)rē-ˈbild\ *verb* **-built** \-ˈbilt\; **-build·ing** (1537)
*transitive verb*
**1 a** : to make extensive repairs to : RECONSTRUCT ⟨*rebuild* a war-torn city⟩ **b** : to restore to a previous state ⟨*rebuild* inventories⟩
**2** : to make extensive changes in : REMODEL ⟨*rebuild* society⟩

*intransitive verb*
: to build again ⟨planned to *rebuild* after the fire⟩
**synonym** see MEND
**¹re·buke** \ri-ˈbyük\ *transitive verb* **re·buked; re·buk·ing** [Middle English, from Old North French *rebuker*] (14th century)
**1 a** : to criticize sharply : REPRIMAND **b** : to serve as a rebuke to
**2** : to turn back or keep down : CHECK
**synonym** see REPROVE
— **re·buk·er** *noun*
**²rebuke** *noun* (15th century)
: an expression of strong disapproval : REPRIMAND
**re·bus** \ˈrē-bəs\ *noun* [Latin, by things, ablative plural of *res* thing — more at REAL] (1605)
: a representation of words or syllables by pictures of objects or by symbols whose names resemble the intended words or syllables in sound; *also* : a riddle made up of such pictures or symbols

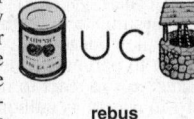

rebus

**re·but** \ri-ˈbət\ *verb* **re·but·ted; re·but·ting** [Middle English, from Middle French *reboter,* from *re-* + *boter* to butt — more at BUTT] (14th century)
*transitive verb*
**1** : to drive or beat back : REPEL
**2 a** : to contradict or oppose by formal legal argument, plea, or countervailing proof **b** : to expose the falsity of : REFUTE
*intransitive verb*
: to make or furnish an answer or counter proof
— **re·but·ta·ble** \-ˈbə-tə-bəl\ *adjective*
**re·but·tal** \ri-ˈbə-t°l\ *noun* (1830)
: the act of rebutting especially in a legal suit; *also* : argument or proof that rebuts
**¹re·but·ter** \-ˈbə-tər\ *noun* [Anglo-French *rebuter,* from Old French *reboter* to rebut] (1540)
: the answer of a defendant in matter of fact to a plaintiff's surrejoinder
**²rebutter** *noun* (1794)
: one that rebuts
**re·cal·ci·trance** \ri-ˈkal-sə-trən(t)s\ *noun* (1856)
: the state of being recalcitrant
**re·cal·ci·tran·cy** \-trən(t)-sē\ *noun* (1869)
: RECALCITRANCE
**re·cal·ci·trant** \-trənt\ *adjective* [Late Latin *recalcitrant-, recalcitrans,* present participle of *recalcitrare* to be stubbornly disobedient, from Latin, to kick back, from *re-* + *calcitrare* to kick, from *calc-, calx* heel] (1843)
**1** : obstinately defiant of authority or restraint
**2 a** : difficult to manage or operate **b** : not responsive to treatment **c** : RESISTANT ⟨this subject is *recalcitrant* both to observation and to experiment —G. G. Simpson⟩ ◆
**synonym** see UNRULY
— **recalcitrant** *noun*
**¹re·call** \ri-ˈkòl\ *transitive verb* (1582)
**1 a** : to call back ⟨was *recalled* to active duty⟩
**b** : to bring back to mind ⟨*recall* those early years⟩ **c** : to remind one of : RESEMBLE ⟨a playwright who *recalls* the Elizabethan dramatists⟩
**2** : CANCEL, REVOKE
**3** : RESTORE, REVIVE
**synonym** see REMEMBER
— **re·call·abil·i·ty** \-ˌkò-lə-ˈbi-lə-tē\ *noun*
— **re·call·able** \-ˈkò-lə-bəl\ *adjective*
— **re·call·er** *noun*
**²re·call** \ri-ˈkòl, ˈrē-ˌ\ *noun* (1611)
**1** : a call to return ⟨a *recall* of workers after a layoff⟩
**2** : the right or procedure by which an official may be removed by vote of the people
**3** : remembrance of what has been learned or experienced
**4** : the act of revoking

**5** : a public call by a manufacturer for the return of a product that may be defective or contaminated
**re·ca·mier** \ˌrā-käm-ˈyā\ *noun* [from its appearance in a portrait of Mme. Récamier by Jacques-Louis David] (1924)
: a sometimes backless couch with a high curved headrest and low footrest
**re·can·a·li·za·tion** \(ˌ)kā-nⁿl-ə-ˈzā-shən\ *noun* (1953)
: the process of restoring flow to or reuniting an interrupted channel of a bodily tube (as a blood vessel or vas deferens)

recamier

— **re·can·a·lize** \-kə-ˈna-ˌlīz, -ˈka-nⁿl-ˌīz\ *transitive verb*
**re·cant** \ri-ˈkant\ *verb* [Latin *recantare,* from *re-* + *cantare* to sing — more at CHANT] (1535)
*transitive verb*
**1** : to withdraw or repudiate (a statement or belief) formally and publicly : RENOUNCE
**2** : REVOKE
*intransitive verb*
: to make an open confession of error
**synonym** see ABJURE
— **re·can·ta·tion** \ˌrē-ˌkan-ˈtā-shən\ *noun*
**¹re·cap** \ˈrē-ˌkap\ *noun* [by shortening] (circa 1926)

☆ **SYNONYMS**
**Rebellion, revolution, uprising, revolt, insurrection, mutiny** mean an outbreak against authority. REBELLION implies an open formidable resistance that is often unsuccessful ⟨open *rebellion* against the officers⟩. REVOLUTION applies to a successful rebellion resulting in a major change (as in government) ⟨a political *revolution* that toppled the monarchy⟩. UPRISING implies a brief, limited and often immediately ineffective rebellion ⟨quickly put down the *uprising*⟩. REVOLT and INSURRECTION imply an armed uprising that quickly fails or succeeds ⟨a *revolt* by the Young Turks that surprised party leaders⟩ ⟨an *insurrection* of oppressed laborers⟩. MUTINY applies to group insubordination or insurrection especially against naval authority ⟨a *mutiny* led by the ship's cook⟩.

◇ **WORD HISTORY**
**recalcitrant** Underlying the word *recalcitrant* is the image of a stubborn beast of burden kicking back at its handlers. The rather uncommon Latin word *calcitrare* "to kick with the heels" was a derivative of an unattested noun *calcitrum,* which presumably meant "kick" and was itself formed from the well-attested *calx* "heel." The verb *recalcitrare* "to kick back," formed from *calcitrare* with the addition of the prefix *re-* "back," is known only once from classical Latin. But in the Latin of the church fathers the word occurs more frequently and in the figurative usage "to be disobedient, rebel," in part as a loan translation of the Greek verb *apolaktizein.* The now rare English word *recalcitrate* "to show opposition to" was borrowed from Latin *recalcitrare* in the 17th century, but much more common now is *recalcitrant* (based on the present participle of *recalcitrare*), which is not attested until the 19th century.

\ə\ **abut** \ᵊ\ **kitten** \ər\ **further** \a\ **ash** \ā\ **ace**
\ä\ **mop, mar** \au̇\ **out** \ch\ **chin** \e\ **bet** \ē\ **easy**
\g\ **go** \i\ **hit** \ī\ **ice** \j\ **job** \ŋ\ **sing** \ō\ **go**
\ò\ **law** \òi\ **boy** \th\ **thin** \t͟h\ **the** \ü\ **loot** \u̇\ **foot**
\y\ **yet** \zh\ **vision** *see also* Guide to Pronunciation

: RECAPITULATION

**²re·cap** \'rē-ˌkap, ri-'\ *verb* **re·capped; re-cap·ping** (1945)
: RECAPITULATE

**³re·cap** \'rē-ˌkap\ *noun* [⁴recap] (1940)
: RETREAD 1

**⁴re·cap** \(ˌ)rē-'kap\ *transitive verb* **re-capped; re·cap·ping** [re- + ¹cap] (1941)
: RETREAD
— **re·cap·pa·ble** \-'ka-pə-bəl\ *adjective*

**re·cap·i·tal·i·za·tion** \(ˌ)rē-ˌka-pə-t³l-ə-'zā-shən, -ˌkap-t³l-\ *noun* (1920)
: a revision of the capital structure of a corporation

**re·cap·i·tal·ize** \(ˌ)rē-'ka-pə-t³l-ˌīz, -'kap-t³l-\ *transitive verb* (1904)
: to change the capital structure of

**re·ca·pit·u·late** \ˌrē-kə-'pi-chə-ˌlāt\ *verb* **-lat·ed; -lat·ing** [Late Latin *recapitulatus*, past participle of *recapitulare* to restate by heads, sum up, from Latin *re-* + *capitulum* division of a book — more at CHAPTER] (1570)
*transitive verb*
: to repeat the principal points or stages of
: SUMMARIZE
*intransitive verb*
: SUM UP

**re·ca·pit·u·la·tion** \-ˌpi-chə-'lā-shən\ *noun* (14th century)
**1** : a concise summary
**2** : the hypothetical occurrence in an individual organism's development of successive stages resembling the series of ancestral types from which it has descended so that the ontogeny of the individual is a recapitulation of the phylogeny of its group
**3** : the third section of a sonata form

**¹re·cap·ture** \(ˌ)rē-'kap-chər\ *noun* (1752)
**1 a** : the act of retaking **b** : an instance of being retaken
**2** : the retaking of a prize or goods under international law
**3** : a government seizure under law of earnings or profits beyond a fixed amount

**²recapture** *transitive verb* (1799)
**1 a** : to capture again **b** : to experience again ⟨by no effort of the imagination could she *recapture* the ecstasy —Ellen Glasgow⟩
**2** : to take (as a portion of earnings or profits above a fixed amount) by law or through negotiations under law

**re·cast** \(ˌ)rē-'kast\ *transitive verb* **-cast; -cast·ing** (1603)
: to cast again ⟨*recast* a gun⟩ ⟨*recast* a play⟩; *also* : REMODEL, REFASHION ⟨*recasts* his political image to fit the times⟩
— **re·cast** \'rē-ˌkast, (ˌ)rē-'\ *noun*

**rec·ce** \'re-kē\ *noun, often attributive* [by shortening & alteration] (1941)
: RECONNAISSANCE

**¹re·cede** \ri-'sēd\ *intransitive verb* **re·ced·ed; re·ced·ing** [Middle English, from Latin *recedere* to go back, from *re-* + *cedere* to go] (15th century)
**1 a** : to move back or away : WITHDRAW **b** : to slant backward
**2** : to grow less or smaller : DIMINISH, DECREASE ☆

**²re·cede** \(ˌ)rē-'sēd\ *transitive verb* [re- + cede] (1771)
: to cede back to a former possessor

**¹re·ceipt** \ri-'sēt\ *noun* [Middle English *receite*, from Old North French, from Medieval Latin *recepta*, probably from Latin, neuter plural of *receptus*, past participle of *recipere* to receive] (14th century)
**1** : RECIPE
**2 a** *obsolete* : RECEPTACLE **b** *archaic* : a revenue office
**3** : the act or process of receiving
**4** : something received — usually used in plural
**5** : a writing acknowledging the receiving of goods or money

**²receipt** *transitive verb* (1787)

**1** : to give a receipt for or acknowledge the receipt of
**2** : to mark as paid

**re·ceiv·able** \ri-'sē-və-bəl\ *adjective* (14th century)
**1** : capable of being received
**2** : subject to call for payment ⟨notes *receivable*⟩

**re·ceiv·ables** \-bəlz\ *noun plural* (1863)
: amounts of money receivable

**re·ceive** \ri-'sēv\ *verb* **re·ceived; re·ceiv·ing** [Middle English, from Old North French *receivre*, from Latin *recipere*, from *re-* + *capere* to take — more at HEAVE] (14th century)
*transitive verb*
**1** : to come into possession of : ACQUIRE ⟨*receive* a gift⟩
**2 a** : to act as a receptacle or container for ⟨the cistern *receives* water from the roof⟩ **b** : to assimilate through the mind or senses ⟨*receive* new ideas⟩
**3 a** : to permit to enter : ADMIT **b** : WELCOME, GREET **c** : to react to in a specified manner
**4** : to accept as authoritative, true, or accurate : BELIEVE
**5 a** : to support the weight or pressure of : BEAR **b** : to take (a mark or impression) from the weight of something ⟨some clay *receives* clear impressions⟩ **c** : ACQUIRE, EXPERIENCE ⟨*received* his early schooling at home⟩ **d** : to suffer the hurt or injury of ⟨*received* a broken nose⟩
*intransitive verb*
**1** : to be a recipient
**2** : to be at home to visitors ⟨*receives* on Tuesdays⟩
**3** : to convert incoming radio waves into perceptible signals
**4** : to prepare to take possession of the ball from a kick in football

**received** *adjective* (15th century)
: generally accepted : COMMON ⟨a healthy skepticism about *received* explanations —B. K. Lewalski⟩

**Received Pronunciation** *noun* (1869)
: the pronunciation of Received Standard

**Received Standard** *noun* (1913)
: a traditionally prestigious form of English spoken at the English public schools, at the universities of Oxford and Cambridge, and by many educated British people elsewhere

**re·ceiv·er** \ri-'sē-vər\ *noun* (14th century)
: one that receives: as **a** : TREASURER **b** (1) : a person appointed to hold in trust and administer property under litigation (2) : a person appointed to settle the affairs of a business involving a public interest or to manage a corporation during reorganization **c** : one that receives stolen goods : FENCE **d** : a device for converting signals (as electromagnetic waves) into audio or visual form: as (1) : a device in a telephone for converting electric impulses or varying current into sound (2) : a radio receiver with a tuner and amplifier on one chassis **e** (1) : CATCHER (2) : a member of the offensive team in football eligible to catch a forward pass

**receiver general** *noun, plural* **receivers general** (15th century)
: a public officer in charge of the treasury (as of Massachusetts)

**re·ceiv·er·ship** \ri-'sē-vər-ˌship\ *noun* (15th century)
**1** : the office or function of a receiver
**2** : the state of being in the hands of a receiver

**receiving blanket** *noun* (1926)
: a small lightweight blanket used to wrap an infant (as after bathing)

**receiving end** *noun* (1937)
: the position of being a recipient or especially a victim — usually used in the phrase *on the receiving end*

**receiving line** *noun* (1933)
: a group of people who stand in a line and individually welcome guests (as at a wedding reception)

**re·cen·cy** \'rē-s³n(t)-sē\ *noun* (1612)
: the quality or state of being recent

**re·cen·sion** \ri-'sen(t)-shən\ *noun* [Latin *recension-, recensio* enumeration, from *recensēre* to review, from *re-* + *censēre* to assess, tax — more at CENSOR] (circa 1828)
**1** : a critical revision of a text
**2** : a text established by critical revision

**re·cent** \'rē-s³nt\ *adjective* [Middle English, from Middle French or Latin; Middle French, from Latin *recent-, recens;* perhaps akin to Greek *kainos* new] (15th century)
**1 a** : having lately come into existence : NEW, FRESH **b** : of or relating to a time not long past
**2** *capitalized* : HOLOCENE
— **re·cent·ness** *noun*

**re·cent·ly** *adverb* (1533)
: during a recent period of time : LATELY

**re·cep·ta·cle** \ri-'sep-ti-kəl\ *noun* [Middle English, from Latin *receptaculum*, from *receptare* to receive, frequentative of *recipere* to receive] (15th century)
**1** : one that receives and contains something : CONTAINER
**2** [New Latin *receptaculum*, from Latin] **a** : the end of the flower stalk upon which the floral organs are borne **b** : a modified branch bearing sporangia in a cryptogamous plant
**3** : a mounted female electrical fitting that contains the live parts of the circuit

**re·cep·tion** \ri-'sep-shən\ *noun* [Middle English *recepcion*, from Middle French or Latin; Middle French *reception*, from Latin *reception-, receptio*, from *recipere*] (15th century)
**1** : the act or action or an instance of receiving: as **a** : RECEIPT ⟨the *reception* and distribution of funds⟩ **b** : ADMISSION ⟨*reception* into the church⟩ **c** : RESPONSE, REACTION ⟨the play met with a mixed *reception*⟩ **d** : the receiving of a radio or television broadcast **e** : the catching of a forward pass by a receiver
**2** : a social gathering often for the purpose of extending a formal welcome

**re·cep·tion·ist** \-sh(ə-)nist\ *noun* (1901)
: a person employed to greet telephone callers, visitors, patients, or clients

**re·cep·tive** \ri-'sep-tiv\ *adjective* (15th century)
**1** : able or inclined to receive; *especially* : open and responsive to ideas, impressions, or suggestions
**2 a** *of a sensory end organ* : fit to receive and transmit stimuli **b** : SENSORY
— **re·cep·tive·ly** *adverb*
— **re·cep·tive·ness** *noun*
— **re·cep·tiv·i·ty** \ˌrē-ˌsep-'ti-və-tē, ri-\ *noun*

**re·cep·tor** \ri-'sep-tər\ *noun* (1898)
: RECEIVER: as **a** : a cell or group of cells that receives stimuli : SENSE ORGAN **b** : a chemical group or molecule (as a protein) on the cell surface or in the cell interior that has an affinity for a specific chemical group, molecule, or virus

**¹re·cess** \'rē-ˌses, ri-'\ *noun* [Latin *recessus*, from *recedere* to recede] (1531)
**1** : the action of receding : RECESSION
**2** : a hidden, secret, or secluded place or part
**3 a** : INDENTATION, CLEFT ⟨a deep *recess* in the hill⟩ **b** : ALCOVE ⟨a *recess* lined with books⟩

---

☆ **SYNONYMS**
**Recede, retreat, retract, back** mean to move backward. RECEDE implies a gradual withdrawing from a forward or high fixed point in time or space ⟨the flood waters gradually *receded*⟩. RETREAT implies withdrawal from a point or position reached ⟨*retreating* soldiers⟩. RETRACT implies drawing back from an extended position ⟨a cat *retracting* its claws⟩. BACK is used with *up, down, out,* or *off* to refer to any retrograde motion ⟨*backed* off on the throttle⟩.

**4 :** a suspension of business or procedure often for rest or relaxation ⟨children playing at *recess*⟩

²**recess** (1809)
*transitive verb*
**1 :** to put into a recess ⟨*recessed* lighting⟩
**2 :** to make a recess in
**3 :** to interrupt for a recess
*intransitive verb*
**:** to take a recess

¹**re·ces·sion** \ri-'se-shən\ *noun* (circa 1652)
**1 :** the act or action of receding **:** WITHDRAWAL
**2 :** a departing procession (as of clergy and choir at the end of a church service)
**3 :** a period of reduced economic activity
— **re·ces·sion·ary** \-shə-ˌner-ē\ *adjective*

²**re·ces·sion** \(ˌ)rē-'se-shən\ *noun* [*re-* + *cession*] (1828)
**:** the act of ceding back to a former possessor

¹**re·ces·sion·al** \ri-'sesh-nəl, -'se-shə-nᵊl\ *adjective* (1867)
**:** of or relating to a withdrawal

²**recessional** *noun* (1867)
**1 :** a hymn or musical piece at the conclusion of a service or program
**2 :** ¹RECESSION 2

¹**re·ces·sive** \ri-'se-siv\ *adjective* (circa 1673)
**1 a :** tending to recede **b :** WITHDRAWN 2
**2 a :** producing little or no phenotypic effect when occurring in heterozygous condition with a contrasting allele ⟨*recessive* genes⟩ **b :** expressed only when the determining gene is in the homozygous condition ⟨*recessive* traits⟩
— **re·ces·sive·ly** *adverb*
— **re·ces·sive·ness** *noun*

²**recessive** *noun* (1900)
**1 :** an organism possessing one or more recessive characters
**2 :** a recessive character or gene

**re·charge** \(ˌ)rē-'chärj\ (1598)
*intransitive verb*
**1 :** to make a new attack
**2 :** to regain energy or spirit
*transitive verb*
**1 :** to charge again; *especially* **:** to restore anew the active materials in (a storage battery)
**2 :** to inspire or invigorate afresh **:** RENEW
— **re·charge** \(ˌ)rē-'chärj, 'rē-ˌ\ *noun*
— **re·charge·able** \(ˌ)rē-'chär-jə-bəl\ *adjective*
— **re·charg·er** \-jər\ *noun*

**ré·chauf·fé** \ˌrā-shō-'fā, -'shō-ˌ\ *noun* [French, from *réchauffé* warmed-over, from past participle of *réchauffer* to warm over, from *ré-* re- + *chauffer* to warm, from Middle French *chaufer* — more at CHAFE] (1805)
**1 :** REHASH
**2 :** a warmed-over dish of food

**re·cheat** \ri-'chēt\ *noun* [Middle English *rechate,* from *rechaten* to blow the recheat, from Middle French *rachater* to assemble, rally, from *re-* + *achater* to acquire, from (assumed) Vulgar Latin *accaptare* — more at CATE] (15th century)
**:** a hunting call sounded on a horn to assemble the hounds

**re·cher·ché** \rə-ˌsher-'shā, -'sher-ˌ\ *adjective* [French, from past participle of *rechercher* to seek out, from Middle French *recherchier* — more at RESEARCH] (1722)
**1 a :** EXQUISITE, CHOICE **b :** EXOTIC, RARE
**2 :** excessively refined **:** AFFECTED
**3 :** PRETENTIOUS, OVERBLOWN

**re·cid·i·vism** \ri-'si-də-ˌvi-zəm\ *noun* (1886)
**:** a tendency to relapse into a previous condition or mode of behavior; *especially* **:** relapse into criminal behavior

**re·cid·i·vist** \-vist\ *noun* [French *récidiviste,* from *récidiver* to relapse, from Medieval Latin *recidivare,* from Latin *recidivus* recurring, from *recidere* to fall back, from *re-* + *cadere* to fall — more at CHANCE] (1880)
**:** one who relapses; *specifically* **:** an habitual criminal

— **recidivist** *adjective*
— **re·cid·i·vis·tic** \-ˌsi-də-'vis-tik\ *adjective*

**rec·i·pe** \'re-sə-(ˌ)pē\ *noun* [Latin, take, imperative of *recipere* to take, receive — more at RECEIVE] (1584)
**1 :** PRESCRIPTION 4a
**2 :** a set of instructions for making something from various ingredients
**3 :** a formula or procedure for doing or attaining something ⟨a *recipe* for success⟩

**re·cip·i·ent** \ri-'si-pē-ənt\ *noun* [Latin *recipient-, recipiens,* present participle of *recipere*] (1558)
**:** one that receives **:** RECEIVER
— **recipient** *adjective*

¹**re·cip·ro·cal** \ri-'si-prə-kəl\ *adjective* [Latin *reciprocus* returning the same way, alternating] (1570)
**1 a :** inversely related **:** OPPOSITE **b :** of, constituting, or resulting from paired crosses in which the kind that supplies the male parent of the first cross supplies the female parent of the second cross and vice versa
**2 :** shared, felt, or shown by both sides
**3 :** serving to reciprocate **:** consisting of or functioning as a return in kind ⟨the *reciprocal* devastation of nuclear war⟩
**4 a :** mutually corresponding ⟨agreed to extend *reciprocal* privileges to each other's citizens⟩ **b :** marked by or based on reciprocity ⟨*reciprocal* trade agreements⟩
— **re·cip·ro·cal·ly** \-k(ə-)lē\ *adverb*

²**reciprocal** *noun* (1570)
**1 :** something in a reciprocal relationship to another
**2 :** either of a pair of numbers (as ²⁄₃ and ³⁄₂ or 9 and ¹⁄₉) whose product is one; *broadly* **:** MULTIPLICATIVE INVERSE

**reciprocal pronoun** *noun* (1844)
**:** a pronoun (as *each other*) used when its referents are predicated to bear the same relationship to one another

**re·cip·ro·cate** \ri-'si-prə-ˌkāt\ *verb* **-cat·ed; -cat·ing** (1607)
*transitive verb*
**1 :** to give and take mutually
**2 :** to return in kind or degree ⟨*reciprocate* a compliment gracefully⟩
*intransitive verb*
**1 :** to make a return for something ⟨we hope to *reciprocate* for your kindness⟩
**2 :** to move forward and backward alternately ⟨a *reciprocating* valve⟩ ☆
— **re·cip·ro·ca·tor** \-ˌkā-tər\ *noun*

**reciprocating engine** *noun* (1822)
**:** an engine in which the to-and-fro motion of one or more pistons is transformed into the rotary motion of a crankshaft

**re·cip·ro·ca·tion** \ri-ˌsi-prə-'kā-shən\ *noun* (1561)
**1 a :** a mutual exchange **b :** a return in kind or of like value
**2 :** an alternating motion
— **re·cip·ro·ca·tive** \-'si-prə-ˌkā-tiv, -kə-\ *adjective*

**rec·i·proc·i·ty** \ˌre-sə-'prä-s(ə-)tē\ *noun, plural* **-ties** (1766)
**1 :** the quality or state of being reciprocal **:** mutual dependence, action, or influence
**2 :** a mutual exchange of privileges; *specifically* **:** a recognition by one of two countries or institutions of the validity of licenses or privileges granted by the other

**re·ci·sion** \ri-'si-zhən\ *noun* [Middle French, alteration of *rescision,* from Late Latin *rescission-, rescissio* rescission] (1611)
**:** an act of rescinding **:** CANCELLATION

**re·cit·al** \ri-'sī-tᵊl\ *noun* (1536)
**1 a :** a detailed account **:** ENUMERATION ⟨a *recital* of names and dates⟩ **b :** the act or process

or an instance of reciting **c :** DISCOURSE, NARRATION ⟨a colorful *recital* of a night on the town⟩
**2 a :** a concert given by an individual musician or dancer or by a dance troupe **b :** a public exhibition of skill given by music or dance pupils
— **re·cit·al·ist** \-tᵊl-ist\ *noun*

**rec·i·ta·tion** \ˌre-sə-'tā-shən\ *noun* (15th century)
**1 :** the act of enumerating ⟨a *recitation* of relevant details⟩
**2 :** the act or an instance of reading or repeating aloud especially publicly
**3 a :** a student's oral reply to questions **b :** a class period especially in association with and for review of a lecture

**rec·i·ta·tive** \ˌre-sə-tə-'tēv, ˌres-tə-\ *noun* [Italian *recitativo,* from *recitare* to recite, from Latin] (1656)
**1 :** a rhythmically free vocal style that imitates the natural inflections of speech and that is used for dialogue and narrative in operas and oratorios; *also* **:** a passage to be delivered in this style
**2 :** RECITATION 2
— **recitative** *adjective*

**rec·i·ta·ti·vo** \-tē-(ˌ)vō\ *noun, plural* **-vi** \-(ˌ)vē\ *or* **-vos** [Italian] (1645)
**:** RECITATIVE 1

**re·cite** \ri-'sīt\ *verb* **re·cit·ed; re·cit·ing** [Middle English, to state formally, from Middle French or Latin; Middle French *reciter* to recite, from Latin *recitare,* from *re-* + *citare* to summon — more at CITE] (15th century)
*transitive verb*
**1 :** to repeat from memory or read aloud publicly
**2 a :** to relate in full ⟨*recites* dull anecdotes⟩ **b :** to give a recital of **:** DETAIL ⟨*recited* a catalog of offenses⟩
**3 :** to repeat or answer questions about (a lesson)
*intransitive verb*
**1 :** to repeat or read aloud something memorized or prepared
**2 :** to reply to a teacher's question on a lesson
— **re·cit·er** *noun*

**reck** \'rek\ *verb* [Middle English, to take heed, from Old English *reccan;* akin to Old High German *ruohhen* to take heed] (before 12th century)
*intransitive verb*
**1 :** WORRY, CARE
**2** *archaic* **:** to be of account or interest **:** MATTER
*transitive verb*
**1** *archaic* **:** to care for **:** REGARD
**2** *archaic* **:** to matter to **:** CONCERN

**reck·less** \'re-kləs\ *adjective* (before 12th century)

---

☆ **SYNONYMS**
**Reciprocate, retaliate, requite, return** mean to give back usually in kind or in quantity. RECIPROCATE implies a mutual or equivalent exchange or a paying back of what one has received ⟨*reciprocated* their hospitality by inviting them for a visit⟩. RETALIATE usually implies a paying back of injury in exact kind, often vengefully ⟨the enemy *retaliated* by executing their prisoners⟩. REQUITE implies a paying back according to one's preference and often not equivalently ⟨*requited* her love with cold indifference⟩. RETURN implies a paying or giving back ⟨*returned* their call⟩ ⟨*return* good for evil⟩.

---

\ə\ **abut** \ᵊ\ **kitten** \ər\ **further** \a\ **ash** \ā\ **ace**
\ä\ **mop, mar** \au̇\ **out** \ch\ **chin** \e\ **bet** \ē\ **easy**
\g\ **go** \i\ **hit** \ī\ **ice** \j\ **job** \ŋ\ **sing** \ō\ **go**
\ȯ\ **law** \ȯi\ **boy** \th\ **thin** \t͟h\ **the** \ü\ **loot** \u̇\ **foot**
\y\ **yet** \zh\ **vision** *see also* Guide to Pronunciation

**1** : marked by lack of proper caution : careless of consequences
**2** : IRRESPONSIBLE ⟨*reckless* charges⟩
*synonym* see ADVENTUROUS
— **reck·less·ly** *adverb*
— **reck·less·ness** *noun*
**reck·on** \'re-kən\ *verb* **reck·oned; reck·on·ing** \'re-kə-niŋ, 'rek-niŋ\ [Middle English *rekenen*, from Old English *-recenian* (as in *gerecenian* to narrate); akin to Old English *reccan*] (13th century)
*transitive verb*
**1 a** : COUNT ⟨*reckon* the days till Christmas⟩ **b** : ESTIMATE, COMPUTE ⟨*reckon* the height of a building⟩ **c** : to determine by reference to a fixed basis ⟨the existence of the U.S. is *reck·oned* from the Declaration of Independence⟩
**2** : to regard or think of as : CONSIDER
**3** *chiefly dialect* : THINK, SUPPOSE ⟨I *reckon* I've outlived my time —Ellen Glasgow⟩
*intransitive verb*
**1** : to settle accounts
**2** : to make a calculation
**3 a** : JUDGE **b** *chiefly dialect* : SUPPOSE, THINK
**4** : to accept something as certain : place reliance ⟨I *reckon* on your promise to help⟩
— **reckon with** : to take into consideration
— **reckon without** : to fail to consider : IGNORE
**reckoning** *noun* (14th century)
**1** : the act or an instance of reckoning: as **a** : ACCOUNT, BILL **b** : COMPUTATION **c** : calculation of a ship's position
**2** : a settling of accounts ⟨day of *reckoning*⟩
**3** : a summing up
**re·claim** \ri-'klām\ *transitive verb* [Middle English *reclamen*, from Middle French *reclamer* to call back, from Latin *reclamare* to cry out against, from *re-* + *clamare* to cry out — more at CLAIM] (14th century)
**1 a** : to recall from wrong or improper conduct : REFORM **b** : TAME, SUBDUE
**2 a** : to rescue from an undesirable state **b** : to make available for human use by changing natural conditions ⟨*reclaim* swampland⟩
**3** : to obtain from a waste product or by-product : RECOVER
**4 a** : to demand or obtain the return of **b** : to regain possession of
*synonym* see RESCUE
— **re·claim·able** \-'klā-mə-bəl\ *adjective*
**rec·la·ma·tion** \,re-klə-'mā-shən\ *noun* [French *réclamation*, from Latin *reclamation-, reclamatio*, from *reclamare*] (1633)
: the act or process of reclaiming: as **a** : REFORMATION, REHABILITATION **b** : restoration to use : RECOVERY
**ré·clame** \rā-'kläm\ *noun* [French, advertising, from *réclamer* to appeal, from Middle French *reclamer*] (1883)
**1** : a gift for dramatization or publicity : SHOWMANSHIP
**2** : public acclaim : VOGUE
**re·cline** \ri-'klīn\ *verb* **re·clined; re·clin·ing** [Middle English, from Middle French or Latin; Middle French *recliner*, from Latin *reclinare*, from *re-* + *clinare* to bend — more at LEAN] (15th century)
*transitive verb*
: to cause or permit to incline backwards
*intransitive verb*
**1** : to lean or incline backwards
**2** : REPOSE, LIE
**re·clin·er** \-'klī-nər\ *noun* (1928)
: a chair with an adjustable back and footrest
**re·clos·able** \(,)rē-'klō-zə-bəl\ *adjective* (1965)
: capable of being tightly closed again after opening ⟨*reclosable* packages of bacon⟩
**¹re·cluse** \'re-klüs, ri-'klüs, 're-,klüz\ *adjective* [Middle English, from Old French *reclus*, literally, shut up, from Late Latin *reclusus*, past participle of *recludere* to shut up, from Latin *re-* + *claudere* to close — more at CLOSE] (13th century)

: marked by withdrawal from society : SOLITARY
— **re·clu·sive** \ri-'klü-siv, -ziv\ *adjective*
— **re·clu·sive·ly** *adverb*
— **re·clu·sive·ness** *noun*
**²recluse** *noun* (13th century)
: a person who leads a secluded or solitary life
**re·clu·sion** \ri-'klü-zhən\ *noun* (15th century)
: the state of being recluse
**rec·og·nise** *chiefly British variant of* RECOGNIZE
**rec·og·ni·tion** \,re-kig-'ni-shən, -kəg-\ *noun* [Middle English *recognicion*, from Latin *recognition-, recognitio*, from *recognoscere*] (15th century)
**1** : the action of recognizing : the state of being recognized: as **a** : ACKNOWLEDGMENT; *especially* : formal acknowledgment of the political existence of a government or nation **b** : knowledge or feeling that someone or something present has been encountered before
**2** : special notice or attention
**3** : the sensing and encoding of printed or written data by a machine ⟨optical character *recognition*⟩ ⟨magnetic ink character *recognition*⟩
**re·cog·ni·zance** \ri-'käg-nə-zən(t)s, -'kä-nə-\ *noun* [Middle English, alteration of *reconissaunce*, from Middle French *reconoissance* recognition, from *reconoistre* to recognize] (14th century)
**1 a** : an obligation of record entered into before a court or magistrate requiring the performance of an act (as appearance in court) usually under penalty of a money forfeiture ⟨released on his own *recognizance*⟩ **b** : the sum liable to forfeiture upon such an obligation
**2** *archaic* : TOKEN, PLEDGE
**rec·og·nize** \'re-kig-,nīz, -kəg-\ *transitive verb* **-nized; -niz·ing** [modification of Middle French *reconoiss-*, stem of *reconoistre*, from Latin *recognoscere*, from *re-* + *cognoscere* to know — more at COGNITION] (circa 1532)
**1** : to acknowledge formally: as **a** : to admit as being lord or sovereign **b** : to admit as being of a particular status **c** : to admit as being one entitled to be heard : give the floor to **d** : to acknowledge the de facto existence or the independence of
**2** : to acknowledge or take notice of in some definite way: as **a** : to acknowledge with a show of appreciation ⟨*recognize* an act of bravery with the award of a medal⟩ **b** : to acknowledge acquaintance with ⟨*recognize* a neighbor with a nod⟩
**3 a** : to perceive to be something or someone previously known ⟨*recognized* the word⟩ **b** : to perceive clearly : REALIZE
— **rec·og·niz·abil·i·ty** \,re-kig-,nī-zə-'bi-lə-tē, -kəg-\ *noun*
— **rec·og·niz·able** \'re-kəg-,nī-zə-bəl, -kig-\ *adjective*
— **rec·og·niz·ably** \-blē\ *adverb*
— **rec·og·niz·er** *noun*
**¹re·coil** \ri-'kói(ə)l\ *intransitive verb* [Middle English *reculen*, from Middle French *reculer*, from *re-* + *cul* backside — more at CULET] (14th century)
**1 a** : to fall back under pressure **b** : to shrink back physically or emotionally
**2** : to spring back to or as if to a starting point : REBOUND
**3** *obsolete* : DEGENERATE ☆
**²re·coil** \'rē-,kóil, ri-'kói(ə)l\ *noun* (14th century)
**1** : the act or action of recoiling; *especially* : the kickback of a gun upon firing
**2** : REACTION ⟨the *recoil* from the rigors of Calvinism —Edmund Wilson⟩
**re·coil·less** \-,kóil-ləs, -'kói(ə)l-\ *adjective* (1943)
: venting expanding propellant gas before recoil is produced ⟨*recoilless* rifle⟩ ⟨*recoilless* airgun⟩

**recoil-operated** *adjective* (1942)
*of a firearm* : utilizing the movement of parts in recoil to operate the action
**re·coin** \(,)rē-'kóin\ *transitive verb* (1685)
: to coin again or anew; *especially* : REMINT
— **re·coin·age** \-'kói-nij\ *noun*
**rec·ol·lect** \,re-kə-'lekt\ *verb* [Medieval Latin *recollectus*, past participle of *recolligere*, from Latin, to gather again] (1559)
*transitive verb*
**1** : to bring back to the level of conscious awareness : REMEMBER ⟨trying to *recollect* the name⟩
**2** : to remind (oneself) of something temporarily forgotten
*intransitive verb*
: to call something to mind
*synonym* see REMEMBER
**re·col·lect** \,rē-kə-'lekt\ *transitive verb* [partly from Latin *recollectus*, past participle of *recolligere*, from *re-* + *colligere* to collect; partly from *re-* + *collect*] (1604)
: to collect again; *especially* : RALLY, RECOVER
**re·col·lect·ed** \,rē-kə-'lek-təd\ *adjective* (1627)
: COMPOSED, CALM
**rec·ol·lec·tion** \,re-kə-'lek-shən\ *noun* (1624)
**1 a** : tranquillity of mind **b** : religious contemplation
**2 a** : the action or power of recalling to mind **b** : something recalled to the mind
*synonym* see MEMORY
**re·com·bi·nant** \(,)rē-'käm-bə-nənt\ *adjective* (1942)
**1** : relating to or exhibiting genetic recombination ⟨*recombinant* progeny⟩
**2** : relating to or containing recombinant DNA; *also* : produced by recombinant DNA technology
— **recombinant** *noun*
**recombinant DNA** *noun* (1975)
: genetically engineered DNA prepared in vitro by cutting up DNA molecules and splicing together specific DNA fragments usually from more than one species of organism
**re·com·bi·na·tion** \,rē-,käm-bə-'nā-shən\ *noun* (1903)
: the formation by the processes of crossing-over and independent assortment of new combinations of genes in progeny that did not occur in the parents
— **re·com·bi·na·tion·al** \-shnəl, -shə-nᵊl\ *adjective*
**rec·om·mend** \,re-kə-'mend\ *transitive verb* [Middle English, to praise, from Medieval Latin *recommendare*, from Latin *re-* + *commendare* to commend] (14th century)
**1 a** : to present as worthy of acceptance or trial ⟨*recommended* the medicine⟩ **b** : to endorse as fit, worthy, or competent ⟨*recommends* her for the position⟩
**2** : ENTRUST, COMMIT ⟨*recommended* his soul to God⟩

---

☆ **SYNONYMS**
**Recoil, shrink, flinch, wince, blench, quail** mean to draw back in fear or distaste. RECOIL implies a start or movement away through shock, fear, or disgust ⟨*recoiled* at the suggestion of stealing⟩. SHRINK suggests an instinctive recoil through sensitiveness, scrupulousness, or cowardice ⟨*shrank* from the unpleasant truth⟩. FLINCH implies a failure to endure pain or face something dangerous or frightening with resolution ⟨faced her accusers without *flinching*⟩. WINCE suggests a slight involuntary physical reaction (as a start or recoiling) ⟨*winced* in pain⟩. BLENCH implies fainthearted flinching ⟨stood their ground without *blenching*⟩. QUAIL suggests shrinking and cowering in fear ⟨*quailed* before the apparition⟩.

**3 :** to make acceptable ⟨has other points to *recommend* it⟩
**4 :** ADVISE ⟨*recommend* that the matter be dropped⟩
— **rec·om·mend·able** \-'men-də-bəl\ *adjective*
— **rec·om·men·da·to·ry** \-də-ˌtōr-ē, -ˌtòr-\ *adjective*
**rec·om·men·da·tion** \ˌre-kə-mən-'dā-shən, -ˌmen-\ *noun* (15th century)
**1 a :** the act of recommending **b :** something (as a procedure) recommended
**2 :** something that recommends or expresses commendation
**re·com·mit** \ˌrē-kə-'mit\ *transitive verb* (1621)
**1 :** to refer (as a bill) back to a committee
**2 :** to entrust or consign again
— **re·com·mit·ment** \-mənt\ *noun*
— **re·com·mit·tal** \-'mi-tᵊl\ *noun*
**¹rec·om·pense** \'re-kəm-ˌpen(t)s\ *transitive verb* **-pensed; -pens·ing** [Middle English, from Middle French *recompenser*, from Late Latin *recompensare*, from Latin *re- + compensare* to compensate] (15th century)
**1 a :** to give something to by way of compensation (as for a service rendered or damage incurred) **b :** to pay for
**2 :** to return in kind : REQUITE
*synonym* see PAY
**²recompense** *noun* (15th century)
**:** an equivalent or a return for something done, suffered, or given : COMPENSATION ⟨offered in *recompense* for injuries⟩
**re·com·pose** \ˌrē-kəm-'pōz\ *transitive verb* (1611)
**1 :** to compose again : REARRANGE
**2 :** to restore to composure
— **re·com·po·si·tion** \(ˌ)rē-ˌkäm-pə-'zi-shən\ *noun*
**re·con** \ri-'kän, 'rē-ˌkän\ *noun* (1918)
**:** RECONNAISSANCE
**rec·on·cile** \'re-kən-ˌsīl\ *verb* **-ciled; -cil·ing** [Middle English, from Middle French or Latin; Middle French *reconcilier*, from Latin *reconciliare*, from *re- + conciliare* to conciliate] (14th century)
*transitive verb*
**1 a :** to restore to friendship or harmony ⟨*reconciled* the factions⟩ **b :** SETTLE, RESOLVE ⟨*reconcile* differences⟩
**2 :** to make consistent or congruous ⟨*reconcile* an ideal with reality⟩
**3 :** to cause to submit to or accept something unpleasant ⟨was *reconciled* to hardship⟩
**4 a :** to check (a financial account) against another for accuracy **b :** to account for
*intransitive verb*
**:** to become reconciled
*synonym* see ADAPT
— **rec·on·cil·abil·i·ty** \ˌre-kən-ˌsī-lə-'bi-lə-tē\ *noun*
— **rec·on·cil·able** \ˌre-kən-'sī-lə-bəl, 're-kən-ˌ\ *adjective*
— **rec·on·cile·ment** \'re-kən-ˌsīl-mənt\ *noun*
— **rec·on·cil·er** *noun*
**rec·on·cil·i·a·tion** \ˌre-kən-ˌsi-lē-'ā-shən\ *noun* [Middle English, from Latin *reconciliation-, reconciliatio*, from *reconciliare*] (14th century)
**1 :** the action of reconciling : the state of being reconciled
**2 :** the Roman Catholic sacrament of penance
— **rec·on·cil·ia·to·ry** \-'sil-yə-ˌtōr-ē, -'si-lē-ə-, -ˌtòr-\ *adjective*
**re·con·dite** \'re-kən-ˌdīt, ri-'kän-\ *adjective* [Latin *reconditus*, past participle of *recondere* to conceal, from *re- + condere* to store up, from *com- + -dere* to put — more at COM-, DO] (1649)
**1 :** hidden from sight : CONCEALED

**2 :** difficult or impossible for one of ordinary understanding or knowledge to comprehend : DEEP ⟨a *recondite* subject⟩
**3 :** of, relating to, or dealing with something little known or obscure ⟨*recondite* fact about the origin of the holiday —Floyd Dell⟩
— **re·con·dite·ly** *adverb*
— **re·con·dite·ness** *noun*
**re·con·di·tion** \ˌrē-kən-'di-shən\ *transitive verb* (1920)
**1 :** to restore to good condition (as by replacing parts)
**2 :** to condition (as a person or a person's attitudes) anew; *also* **:** to reinstate (a response) in an organism
**re·con·firm** \ˌrē-kən-'fərm\ *transitive verb* (1611)
**:** to confirm again; *also* **:** to establish more strongly
— **re·con·fir·ma·tion** \(ˌ)rē-ˌkän-fər-'mā-shən\ *noun*
**re·con·nais·sance** \ri-'kä-nə-zən(t)s, -sən(t)s\ *noun* [French, literally, recognition, from Middle French *reconoissance* — more at RECOGNIZANCE] (1810)
**:** a preliminary survey to gain information; *especially* **:** an exploratory military survey of enemy territory
**re·con·noi·ter** *or* **re·con·noi·tre** \ˌrē-kə-'nòi-tər, ˌre-kə-\ *verb* **-noi·tered** *or* **-noi·tred; -noi·ter·ing** *or* **-noi·tring** \-'nòi-tə-riŋ, -'nòi-triŋ\ [obsolete French *reconnoître*, literally, to recognize, from Middle French *reconoistre* — more at RECOGNIZE] (1707)
*transitive verb*
**:** to make a reconnaissance of
*intransitive verb*
**:** to engage in reconnaissance
**re·con·sid·er** \ˌrē-kən-'si-dər\ (1571)
*transitive verb*
**:** to consider again especially with a view to changing or reversing
*intransitive verb*
**:** to consider something again
— **re·con·sid·er·a·tion** \-ˌsi-də-'rā-shən\ *noun*
**re·con·sti·tute** \(ˌ)rē-'kän(t)-stə-ˌtüt, -ˌtyüt\ *transitive verb* (1812)
**:** to constitute again or anew; *especially* **:** to restore to a former condition by adding water
— **re·con·sti·tu·tion** \(ˌ)rē-ˌkän(t)-stə-'tü-shən, -'tyü-\ *noun*
**re·con·struct** \ˌrē-kən-'strəkt\ *transitive verb* (1768)
**:** to construct again: as **a :** to establish or assemble again **b :** to build up again mentally : RE-CREATE ⟨*reconstructing* a lost civilization⟩
— **re·con·struct·ible** \-'strək-tə-bəl\ *adjective*
— **re·con·struc·tive** \-tiv\ *adjective*
— **re·con·struc·tor** \-tər\ *noun*
**re·con·struc·tion** \ˌrē-kən-'strək-shən\ *noun* (1791)
**1 a :** the action of reconstructing : the state of being reconstructed **b** *often capitalized* **:** the reorganization and reestablishment of the seceded states in the Union after the American Civil War
**2 :** something reconstructed
**re·con·struc·tion·ism** \-shə-ˌni-zəm\ *noun, often capitalized* (1942)
**1 :** a movement in 20th century American Judaism that advocates a creative adjustment to contemporary conditions through the cultivation of traditions and folkways shared by all Jews
**2 :** advocacy of post-Civil War reconstruction
— **re·con·struc·tion·ist** \-sh(ə-)nist\ *adjective or noun, often capitalized*
**reconstructive surgery** *noun* (1943)
**:** surgery to restore function or normal appearance by remaking defective organs or parts

**re·con·vey** \ˌrē-kən-'vā\ *transitive verb* (1506)
**:** to convey back to a previous position or owner
— **re·con·vey·ance** \-'vā-ən(t)s\ *noun*
**¹re·cord** \ri-'kòrd\ *verb* [Middle English, literally, to recall, from Old French *recorder*, from Latin *recordari*, from *re- + cord-, cor* heart — more at HEART] (14th century)
*transitive verb*
**1 a (1) :** to set down in writing : furnish written evidence of **(2) :** to deposit an authentic official copy of ⟨*record* a deed⟩ **b :** to state for or as if for the record ⟨voted in favor but *recorded* certain reservations⟩ **c (1) :** to register permanently by mechanical means ⟨earthquake shocks *recorded* by a seismograph⟩ **(2) :** INDICATE, READ ⟨the thermometer *recorded* 90°⟩
**2 :** to give evidence of
**3 :** to cause (as sound, visual images, or data) to be registered on something (as a disc or magnetic tape) in reproducible form
*intransitive verb*
**:** to record something
— **re·cord·able** \-'kòr-də-bəl\ *adjective*
**²rec·ord** \'re-kərd *also* -ˌkòrd\ *noun* (14th century)
**1 :** the state or fact of being recorded
**2 :** something that records: as **a :** something that recalls or relates past events **b :** an official document that records the acts of a public body or officer **c :** an authentic official copy of a document deposited with a legally designated officer **d :** the official copy of the papers used in a law case
**3 a (1) :** a body of known or recorded facts about something or someone especially with reference to a particular sphere of activity that often forms a discernible pattern ⟨a good academic *record*⟩ ⟨a liberal voting *record*⟩ **(2) :** a collection of related items of information (as in a database) treated as a unit **b (1) :** an attested top performance **(2) :** an unsurpassed statistic
**4 :** something on which sound or visual images have been recorded; *specifically* **:** a disc with a spiral groove carrying recorded sound for phonograph reproduction
— **for the record :** for public knowledge **:** on the record
— **off the record :** not for publication ⟨spoke *off the record*⟩ ⟨remarks that were *off the record*⟩
— **of record :** being documented or attested ⟨a partner *of record* in several firms⟩
— **on record 1 :** in the position of having publicly declared oneself ⟨went *on record* as opposed to higher taxes⟩ **2 :** being known, published, or documented ⟨the judge's opinion is *on record*⟩
— **on the record :** for publication
**³record** \*same as* ²\ *adjective* (1893)
**:** of, relating to, or being one that is extraordinary among or surpasses others of its kind
**re·cor·da·tion** \ˌre-ˌkòr-'dā-shən; ˌrē-, ri-\ *noun* (circa 1812)
**:** the action or process of recording
**record changer** *noun* (1931)
**:** a phonograph with a device that automatically positions and plays successively each of a stack of records; *also* **:** the automatic device on a record changer
**re·cord·er** \ri-'kòr-dər\ *noun* (15th century)
**1 a :** the chief judicial magistrate of some British cities and boroughs **b :** a municipal judge with criminal jurisdiction of first instance and sometimes limited civil jurisdiction
**2 :** one that records
**3 :** any of a group of wind instruments ranging from soprano to bass that are characterized by

---

\ə\ abut \ᵊ\ kitten \ər\ further \a\ ash \ā\ ace
\ä\ mop, mar \aù\ out \ch\ chin \e\ bet \ē\ easy
\g\ go \i\ hit \ī\ ice \j\ job \ŋ\ sing \ō\ go
\ò\ law \òi\ boy \th\ thin \t͟h\ the \ü\ loot \ù\ foot
\y\ yet \zh\ vision *see also* Guide to Pronunciation

a conical tube, a whistle mouthpiece, and eight finger holes ◆

**recorder 3**

**re·cord·ing** \ri-'kȯr-diŋ\ *noun* (1932)
: RECORD 4

**re·cord·ist** \ri-'kȯr-dist\ *noun* (circa 1930)
: one who records sound (as on magnetic tape)

**¹re·count** \ri-'kaúnt\ *transitive verb* [Middle English, from Middle French *reconter,* from *re-* + *conter* to count, relate — more at COUNT] (15th century)
: to relate in detail : NARRATE
— **re·count·er** *noun*

**²re·count** \(,)rē-'kaúnt\ *transitive verb* [*re-* + *count*] (1764)
: to count again

**³re·count** \'rē-,kaúnt, (,)rē-'\ *noun* (1884)
: a second or fresh count

**re·coup** \ri-'küp\ *verb* [French *recouper* to cut back, from Old French, from *re-* + *couper* to cut — more at COPE] (1628)
*transitive verb*
**1 a :** to get an equivalent for (as losses) : make up for **b :** REIMBURSE, COMPENSATE ⟨*recoup* a person for losses⟩
**2 :** REGAIN ⟨an attempt to *recoup* his fortune⟩
*intransitive verb*
: to make good or make up for something lost; *also :* RECUPERATE
— **re·coup·able** \-'kü-pə-bəl\ *adjective*
— **re·coup·ment** \-'küp-mənt\ *noun*

**re·course** \'rē-,kȯrs, ri-'\ *noun* [Middle English *recours,* from Middle French, from Late Latin *recursus,* from Latin, act of running back, from *recurrere* to run back — more at RECUR] (14th century)
**1 a :** a turning to someone or something for help or protection **b :** a source of help or strength : RESORT
**2 :** the right to demand payment from the maker or endorser of a negotiable instrument (as a check)

**re·cov·er** \ri-'kə-vər\ *verb* **re·cov·ered; re·cov·er·ing** \-'kə-və-riŋ, -'kəv-riŋ\ [Middle English, from Middle French *recoverer,* from Latin *recuperare,* from *re-* + (assumed) Latin *caperare,* from Latin *capere* to take — more at HEAVE] (14th century)
*transitive verb*
**1 :** to get back : REGAIN
**2 a :** to bring back to normal position or condition ⟨stumbled, then *recovered* himself⟩ **b** *archaic :* RESCUE
**3 a :** to make up for ⟨*recover* increased costs through higher prices⟩ **b :** to gain by legal process
**4** *archaic :* REACH
**5 :** to find or identify again ⟨*recover* a comet⟩
**6 a :** to obtain from an ore, a waste product, or a by-product **b :** to save from loss and restore to usefulness : RECLAIM
*intransitive verb*
**1 :** to regain a normal position or condition (as of health) ⟨*recovering* from a cold⟩
**2 :** to obtain a final legal judgment in one's favor
— **re·cov·er·abil·i·ty** \-,kə-və-rə-'bi-lə-tē, -,kəv-rə-\ *noun*
— **re·cov·er·able** \-'kə-və-rə-bəl, -'kəv-rə-\ *adjective*
— **re·cov·er·er** \-'kə-vər-ər\ *noun*

**re-cov-er** \(,)rē-'kə-vər\ *transitive verb* (15th century)
: to cover again or anew

**re·cov·ery** \ri-'kə-və-rē, -'kəv-rē\ *noun, plural* **-er·ies** (15th century)
: the act, process, or an instance of recovering; *especially :* an economic upturn (as after a depression)

**recovery room** *noun* (1916)

: a hospital room equipped for meeting post-operative emergencies

**¹rec·re·ant** \'re-krē-ənt\ *adjective* [Middle English, from Middle French, from present participle of *recroire* to renounce one's cause in a trial by battle, from *re-* + *croire* to believe, from Latin *credere* — more at CREED] (14th century)
**1 :** crying for mercy : COWARDLY
**2 :** unfaithful to duty or allegiance

**²recreant** *noun* (15th century)
**1 :** COWARD
**2 :** APOSTATE, DESERTER

**rec·re·ate** \'re-krē-,āt\ *verb* **-at·ed; -at·ing** [Latin *recreatus,* past participle of *recreare*] (1530)
*transitive verb*
: to give new life or freshness to : REFRESH
*intransitive verb*
: to take recreation
— **rec·re·a·tive** \-,ā-tiv\ *adjective*

**re-cre-ate** \,rē-krē-'āt\ *transitive verb* (1587)
: to create again; *especially :* to form anew in the imagination
— **re-cre·at·able** \-'ā-tə-bəl\ *adjective*
— **re-cre·a·tion** \-'ā-shən\ *noun*
— **re-cre·a·tive** \-'ā-tiv\ *adjective*
— **re-cre·a·tor** \-'ā-tər\ *noun*

**rec·re·a·tion** \,re-krē-'ā-shən\ *noun* [Middle English *recreacion,* from Middle French *recreation,* from Latin *recreation-, recreatio* restoration to health, from *recreare* to create anew, restore, refresh, from *re-* + *creare* to create] (15th century)
: refreshment of strength and spirits after work; *also :* a means of refreshment or diversion : HOBBY
— **rec·re·a·tion·al** \-shnəl, -shə-nᵊl\ *adjective*

**recreational vehicle** *noun* (1966)
: a vehicle designed for recreational use (as in camping); *especially :* MOTOR HOME

**rec·re·a·tion·ist** \-sh(ə-)nist\ *noun* (1904)
: a person who seeks recreation especially in the outdoors

**recreation room** *noun* (1854)
**1 :** a room (as a rumpus room) used for recreation and relaxation — called also *rec room*
**2 :** a public room (as in a hospital) for recreation and social activities

**re·crim·i·na·tion** \ri-,kri-mə-'nā-shən\ *noun* [Medieval Latin *recrimination-, recriminatio,* from *recriminare* to make a retaliatory charge, from Latin *re-* + *criminari* to accuse — more at CRIMINATE] (circa 1611)
: a retaliatory accusation; *also :* the making of such accusations ⟨endless *recrimination*⟩
— **re·crim·i·nate** \-'kri-mə-,nāt\ *intransitive verb*
— **re·crim·i·na·tive** \-,nā-tiv\ *adjective*
— **re·crim·i·na·to·ry** \-'kri-mə-nə-,tȯr-ē, -'krim-nə-, -,tȯr-\ *adjective*

**re·cru·desce** \,rē-krü-'des\ *intransitive verb* **-desced; -desc·ing** [Latin *recrudescere* to become raw again, from *re-* + *crudescere* to become raw, from *crudus* raw — more at RAW] (1884)
: to break out or become active again

**re·cru·des·cence** \-'de-sᵊn(t)s\ *noun* (circa 1721)
: a new outbreak after a period of abatement or inactivity : RENEWAL

**re·cru·des·cent** \-sᵊnt\ *adjective* (circa 1727)
: breaking out again : RENEWING

**¹re·cruit** \ri-'krüt\ *verb* (1643)
*transitive verb*
**1 a** (1) **:** to fill up the number of (as an army) with new members : REINFORCE (2) **:** to enlist as a member of an armed service **b :** to increase or maintain the number of ⟨America *recruited* her population from Europe⟩ **c :** to secure the services of : ENGAGE, HIRE **d :** to seek to enroll ⟨*recruit* students⟩
**2 :** REPLENISH
**3 :** to restore or increase the health, vigor, or intensity of

*intransitive verb*
: to enlist new members
— **re·cruit·er** *noun*

**²recruit** *noun* [French *recrute, recrue* fresh growth, new levy of soldiers, from Middle French, from *recroistre* to grow up again, from Latin *recrescere,* from *re-* + *crescere* to grow — more at CRESCENT] (circa 1645)
**1 :** a fresh or additional supply
**2 :** a newcomer to a field or activity; *specifically :* a newly enlisted or drafted member of the armed forces
**3 :** a former enlisted man of the lowest rank in the army

**re·cruit·ment** \ri-'krüt-mənt\ *noun* (circa 1828)
**1 :** the action or process of recruiting
**2 :** the process of adding new individuals to a population or subpopulation (as of breeding individuals) by growth, reproduction, immigration, and stocking; *also :* a measure (as in numbers or biomass) of recruitment

**re·crys·tal·ize** \(,)rē-'kris-tə-,līz\ *verb* (1797)
: to crystallize again or repeatedly
— **re·crys·tal·li·za·tion** \(,)rē-,kris-tə-lə-'zā-shən\ *noun*

**rec·tal** \'rek-tᵊl\ *adjective* (circa 1859)
: relating to, affecting, or being near the rectum
— **rec·tal·ly** *adverb*

**rect·an·gle** \'rek-,taŋ-gəl\ *noun* [Medieval Latin *rectangulus* having a right angle, from Latin *rectus* right + *angulus* angle — more at RIGHT, ANGLE] (1571)
: a parallelogram all of whose angles are right angles; *especially :* one with adjacent sides of unequal length

**rect·an·gu·lar** \rek-'taŋ-gyə-lər\ *adjective* (1624)
**1 :** shaped like a rectangle ⟨a *rectangular* area⟩
**2 a :** crossing, lying, or meeting at a right angle ⟨*rectangular* axes⟩ **b :** having edges, surfaces, or faces that meet at right angles : having faces or surfaces shaped like rectangles ⟨*rectangular* parallelepipeds⟩ ⟨a *rectangular* solid⟩
— **rect·an·gu·lar·i·ty** \(,)rek-,taŋ-gyə-'lar-ə-tē\ *noun*
— **rect·an·gu·lar·ly** \rek-'taŋ-gyə-lər-lē\ *adverb*

**rectangular coordinate** *noun* (circa 1864)
: a Cartesian coordinate of a Cartesian coordinate system whose straight-line axes or coordinate planes are perpendicular

◇ WORD HISTORY
**recorder** There is little obvious connection between the sweet-sounding wind instrument called the recorder and modern electronic devices that copy sound and image. In actuality, the origin of the woodwind's name is rather mysterious, and it has no relation to current senses of the verb *record.* The customary, though not totally satisfactory, solution is to see it as a derivative of Middle English *recorden* "to repeat, rehearse," one of several early senses that Modern English *record* has not retained. In Elizabethan English *record* could mean "to play (a tune)," but this more appropriate sense may come from the instrument's name. The oldest reference to the name appears to be a Latin notation in the household accounts of Henry, Earl of Derby, dated 1388, that mentions a *fistula nomine Ricordo* ("pipe called Ricordo"). If this is a hint of the word's origin, it sends us off in a quite different direction, for "Ricordo" appears to be Italian *ricordo* "remembrance, memento." Other languages offer no illumination, since their names for the instrument simply consist of the word for "flute" with some modifier, such as German *Blockflöte* ("fipple flute") or French *flûte à neuf trous* ("flute with nine holes").

**rec·ti·fi·able** \'rek-tə-ˌfī-ə-bəl\ *adjective* [*rectify* (to determine the length of an arc)] (1816)
: having finite length ⟨a *rectifiable* curve⟩
— **rec·ti·fi·abil·i·ty** \ˌrek-tə-ˌfī-ə-'bi-lə-tē\ *noun*
**rec·ti·fi·er** \'rek-tə-ˌfī(-ə)r\ *noun* (1611)
: one that rectifies; *specifically* : a device for converting alternating current into direct current
**rec·ti·fy** \'rek-tə-ˌfī\ *transitive verb* **-fied; -fy·ing** [Middle English *rectifien*, from Middle French *rectifier*, from Medieval Latin *rectificare*, from Latin *rectus* right — more at RIGHT] (14th century)
**1** : to set right : REMEDY
**2** : to purify (as alcohol) especially by repeated or fractional distillation
**3** : to correct by removing errors : ADJUST ⟨*rectify* the calendar⟩
**4** : to make (an alternating current) unidirectional
**synonym** see CORRECT
— **rec·ti·fi·ca·tion** \ˌrek-tə-fə-'kā-shən\ *noun*
**rec·ti·lin·e·ar** \ˌrek-tə-'li-nē-ər\ *adjective* [Late Latin *rectilineus*, from Latin *rectus* + *linea* line] (1659)
**1** : moving in or forming a straight line ⟨*rectilinear* motion⟩
**2** : characterized by straight lines
**3** : PERPENDICULAR 3
— **rec·ti·lin·e·ar·ly** *adverb*
**rec·ti·tude** \'rek-tə-ˌtüd, -ˌtyüd\ *noun* [Middle English, from Middle French, from Late Latin *rectitudo*, from Latin *rectus* straight, right] (15th century)
**1** : the quality or state of being straight
**2** : moral integrity : RIGHTEOUSNESS
**3** : the quality or state of being correct in judgment or procedure
**rec·ti·tu·di·nous** \ˌrek-tə-'tüd-nəs, -'tyüd-; -'tü-dᵊn-əs, -'tyü-\ *adjective* [Late Latin *rectitudin-, rectitudo* rectitude] (1897)
**1** : characterized by rectitude
**2** : piously self-righteous
**rec·to** \'rek-(ˌ)tō\ *noun, plural* **rectos** [New Latin *recto* (*folio*) on the right-hand leaf] (1824)
**1** : the side of a leaf (as of a manuscript) that is to be read first
**2** : a right-hand page — compare VERSO
**rec·tor** \'rek-tər\ *noun* [Middle English, from Latin, from *regere* to direct — more at RIGHT] (14th century)
**1** : one that directs : LEADER
**2 a** : a clergyman (as of the Protestant Episcopal Church) in charge of a parish **b** : an incumbent of a Church of England benefice in full possession of its rights **c** : a Roman Catholic priest directing a church with no pastor or one whose pastor has other duties
**3** : the head of a university or school
— **rec·tor·ate** \-t(ə-)rət\ *noun*
— **rec·to·ri·al** \rek-'tōr-ē-əl, -'tòr-\ *adjective*
— **rec·tor·ship** \'rek-tər-ˌship\ *noun*
**rec·to·ry** \'rek-t(ə-)rē\ *noun, plural* **-ries** (1594)
**1** : a benefice held by a rector
**2** : a residence of a rector or a parish priest
**rec·trix** \'rek-triks\ *noun, plural* **rec·tri·ces** \'rek-trə-ˌsēz, rek-'trī-(ˌ)sēz\ [New Latin, from Latin, feminine of *rector* one that directs] (1768)
: any of the quill feathers of a bird's tail that are important in controlling flight direction — see BIRD illustration
**rec·tum** \'rek-təm\ *noun, plural* **rectums** *or* **rec·ta** \-tə\ [Middle English, from Medieval Latin, from *rectum intestinum*, literally, straight intestine] (15th century)
: the terminal part of the intestine from the sigmoid flexure to the anus
**rec·tus** \'rek-təs\ *noun, plural* **rec·ti** \-ˌtī, -ˌtē\ [New Latin, from *rectus musculus* straight muscle] (circa 1704)

: any of several straight muscles (as of the abdomen)
**re·cum·ben·cy** \ri-'kəm-bən(t)-sē\ *noun, plural* **-cies** (1646)
: the state of leaning, resting, or reclining : REPOSE; *also* : a recumbent position
**re·cum·bent** \-bənt\ *adjective* [Latin *recumbent-, recumbens*, present participle of *recumbere* to lie down, from *re-* + *-cumbere* to lie down; akin to Latin *cubare* to lie] (1705)
**1 a** : suggestive of repose : LEANING, RESTING **b** : lying down
**2** : representing a person lying down ⟨a *recumbent* statue⟩
**synonym** see PRONE
**re·cu·per·ate** \ri-'kü-pə-ˌrāt, -'kyü-\ *verb* **-at·ed; -at·ing** [Latin *recuperatus*, past participle of *recuperare* — more at RECOVER] (1542)
*transitive verb*
: to get back : REGAIN
*intransitive verb*
: to regain a former state or condition; *especially* : to recover health or strength
— **re·cu·per·a·tion** \-ˌkü-pə-'rā-shən, -ˌkyü-\ *noun*
**re·cu·per·a·tive** \-'kü-pə-ˌrā-tiv, -'kyü-, -p(ə-)rə-tiv\ *adjective* (circa 1828)
**1** : of or relating to recuperation ⟨*recuperative* powers⟩
**2** : aiding in recuperation : RESTORATIVE
**re·cur** \ri-'kər\ *intransitive verb* **re·curred; re·cur·ring** [Middle English *recurren* to return, from Latin *recurrere*, literally, to run back, from *re-* + *currere* to run — more at CAR] (1529)
**1** : to have recourse : RESORT
**2** : to go back in thought or discourse
**3 a** : to come up again for consideration **b** : to come again to mind
**4** : to occur again after an interval : occur time after time
— **re·cur·rence** \-'kər-ən(t)s, -'kə-rən(t)s\ *noun*
**re·cur·rent** \-'kər-ənt, -'kə-rənt\ *adjective* [Latin *recurrent-, recurrens*, present participle of *recurrere*] (1611)
**1** : running or turning back in a direction opposite to a former course — used of various nerves and branches of vessels in the arms and legs
**2** : returning or happening time after time ⟨*recurrent* complaints⟩
— **re·cur·rent·ly** *adverb*
**recurring decimal** *noun* (1801)
: REPEATING DECIMAL
**re·cur·sion** \ri-'kər-zhən\ *noun* [Late Latin *recursion-, recursio*, from *recurrere*] (1616)
**1** : RETURN
**2** : the determination of a succession of elements (as numbers or functions) by operation on one or more preceding elements according to a rule or formula involving a finite number of steps
**3** : a computer programming technique involving the use of a procedure, subroutine, function, or algorithm that calls itself in a step having a termination condition so that successive repetitions are processed up to the critical step until the condition is met at which time the rest of each repetition is processed from the last one called to the first — compare ITERATION
**re·cur·sive** \ri-'kər-siv\ *adjective* (1934)
**1** : of, relating to, or involving recursion ⟨a *recursive* function in a computer program⟩
**2** : of, relating to, or constituting a procedure that can repeat itself indefinitely ⟨a *recursive* rule in a grammar⟩
— **re·cur·sive·ly** *adverb*
— **re·cur·sive·ness** *noun*
**re·curved** \(ˌ)rē-'kərvd\ *adjective* (1597)
: curved backward or inward
**re·cu·san·cy** \'re-kyə-zən(t)-sē, ri-'kyü-\ *noun* (circa 1600)
: the act or state of being a recusant

**re·cu·sant** \-zənt\ *noun* [Latin *recusant-, recusans*, present participle of *recusare* to refuse, from *re-* + *causari* to give a reason, from *causa* cause, reason] (1553)
**1** : an English Roman Catholic of the time from about 1570 to 1791 who refused to attend services of the Church of England and thereby committed a statutory offense
**2** : one who refuses to accept or obey established authority
— **recusant** *adjective*
**re·cuse** \ri-'kyüz\ *transitive verb* **re·cused; re·cus·ing** [Middle English, to refuse, from Middle French *recuser*, from Latin *recusare*] (1949)
: to disqualify (oneself) as judge in a particular case; *broadly* : to remove (oneself) from participation to avoid a conflict of interest
— **re·cus·al** \-'kyü-zəl\ *noun*
**re·cut** \(ˌ)rē-'kət, 'rē-\ *transitive verb* (1664)
**1** : to cut again
**2** : to edit (as a film) anew
¹**re·cy·cle** \(ˌ)rē-'sī-kəl\ (1926)
*transitive verb*
**1** : to pass again through a series of changes or treatments: as **a** : to process (as liquid body waste, glass, or cans) in order to regain material for human use **b** : RECOVER 6
**2** : to adapt to a new use : ALTER
**3** : to bring back : REUSE ⟨*recycles* a number of good anecdotes —Larry McMurtry⟩
**4** : to make ready for reuse ⟨a plan to *recycle* vacant tenements⟩
*intransitive verb*
**1** : to return to an earlier point in a countdown
**2** : to return to an original condition so that operation can begin again — used of an electronic device
— **re·cy·cla·ble** \-k(ə-)lə-bəl\ *adjective or noun*
— **re·cy·cler** \-k(ə-)lər\ *noun*
²**recycle** *noun* (1926)
: the process of recycling
¹**red** \'red\ *adjective* **red·der; red·dest** [Middle English, from Old English *rēad*; akin to Old High German *rōt* red, Latin *ruber* & *rufus*, Greek *erythros*] (before 12th century)
**1 a** : of the color red **b** : having red as a distinguishing color
**2 a** (1) : flushed especially with anger or embarrassment (2) : RUDDY, FLORID (3) : being or having skin of a coppery hue : BLOODSHOT ⟨eyes *red* from crying⟩ **c** : in the color range between a moderate orange and russet or bay **d** : tinged with red : REDDISH
**3** : heated to redness : GLOWING
**4 a** : inciting or endorsing radical social or political change especially by force **b** *often capitalized* : COMMUNIST **c** *often capitalized* : of or relating to a communist country and especially to the U.S.S.R.
²**red** *noun* (before 12th century)
**1** : a color whose hue resembles that of blood or of the ruby or is that of the long-wave extreme of the visible spectrum
**2** : red clothing ⟨the lady in *red*⟩
**3** : one that is of a red or reddish color: as **a** : RED WINE **b** : an animal with a red or reddish coat
**4 a** : a pigment or dye that colors red **b** : a shade or tint of red
**5 a** : one who advocates the violent overthrow of an existing social or political order **b** *capitalized* : COMMUNIST
**6** [from the bookkeeping practice of entering debit items in red ink] : the condition of showing a loss — usually used with *the* ⟨in the *red*⟩; compare BLACK

\ə\ **abut** \ᵊ\ **kitten** \ər\ **further** \a\ **ash** \ā\ **ace** \ä\ **mop, mar** \au̇\ **out** \ch\ **chin** \e\ **bet** \ē\ **easy** \g\ **go** \i\ **hit** \ī\ **ice** \j\ **job** \ŋ\ **sing** \ō\ **go** \ȯ\ **law** \ȯi\ **boy** \th\ **thin** \th̲\ **the** \ü\ **loot** \u̇\ **foot** \y\ **yet** \zh\ **vision** *see also* Guide to Pronunciation

**re·dact** \ri-'dakt\ *transitive verb* [Middle English, from Latin *redactus*, past participle of *redigere*] (15th century)
**1** : to put in writing : FRAME
**2** : to select or adapt for publication : EDIT
**re·dac·tion** \-'dak-shən\ *noun* [French *rédaction*, from Late Latin *redaction-*, *redactio* act of reducing, compressing, from Latin *redigere* to bring back, reduce, from *re-*, *red-* re- + *agere* to lead — more at AGENT] (1785)
**1** : an act or instance of redacting something
**2** : a work that has been redacted : EDITION, VERSION
— **re·dac·tion·al** \-shnəl, -shə-n°l\ *adjective*
**re·dac·tor** \-'dak-tər\ *noun* (1816)
: one who redacts a work; *especially* : EDITOR
**red admiral** *noun* (1840)
: a nymphalid butterfly (*Vanessa atalanta*) that is common in both Europe and America, has broad orange-red bands on the forewings, and feeds chiefly on nettles in the larval stage

**red admiral**

**red alert** *noun* (circa 1951)
: the final stage of alert in which enemy attack appears imminent; *broadly* : a state of alert brought on by impending danger
**red alga** *noun* (1852)
: any of a division (Rhodophyta) of chiefly marine algae that have predominantly red pigmentation
**red ant** *noun* (1667)
: any of various reddish ants (as the pharaoh ant)
**red·ar·gue** \ri-'där-(,)gyü\ *transitive verb* **-gued; -gu·ing** [Middle English, from Latin *redarguere*, from *red-* + *arguere* to demonstrate, prove — more at ARGUE] (1627)
*archaic* : CONFUTE, DISPROVE
**red-bait** \'red-,bāt\ *verb, often R capitalized* (1940)
*transitive verb*
: to subject (as a person or group) to red-baiting
*intransitive verb*
: to engage in red-baiting
— **red-bait·er** *noun, often R capitalized*
**red-bait·ing** *noun, often R capitalized* (1928)
: the act of attacking or persecuting as a Communist or as communistic
**red bay** *noun* (circa 1730)
: a small tree (*Persea borbonia*) of the southern U.S. that has dark red heartwood
**red·bel·ly dace** \'red-'be-lē-\ *noun* (1884)
: either of two small brightly marked North American cyprinid fishes (*Phoxinus eos* and *P. erythrogaster*) — called also *red-bel·lied dace* \-lēd-\
**red·bird** \'red-,bərd\ *noun* (1669)
: any of several birds (as a cardinal, several tanagers, or the bullfinch) with predominantly red plumage
**red blood cell** *noun* (1910)
: any of the hemoglobin-containing cells that carry oxygen to the tissues and are responsible for the red color of vertebrate blood — called also *erythrocyte, red blood corpuscle, red cell, red corpuscle*
**red-blood·ed** \'red-'blə-dəd\ *adjective* (1881)
: VIGOROUS, LUSTY
**red·bone** \'red-,bōn\ *noun* (1916)
: any of a breed of moderate-sized speedy dark red or red and tan coonhounds of American origin
**red·breast** \'red-,brest\ *noun* (15th century)
**1** : a bird (as a robin) with a reddish breast
**2** : a reddish-bellied sunfish (*Lepomis auritus*) of the eastern U.S. — called also *redbreasted bream*
**red-brick** \-,brik\ *adjective* (1943)
**1** : built of red brick

**2** *often capitalized* [from the common use of red brick in constructing the buildings of recently founded universities] : of, relating to, or being the British Universities founded in the 19th or early 20th century — compare OXBRIDGE, PLATEGLASS
**red-bud** \-,bəd\ *noun* (1705)
: any of several leguminous trees (genus *Cercis*) with usually pale rosy pink flowers
**red bug** *noun* (1804)
*Southern & Midland* : CHIGGER 2
**red-cap** \'red-,kap\ *noun* (1918)
: a baggage porter (as at a railroad station) — compare SKYCAP
**red-carpet** *adjective* [from the traditional laying down of a red carpet for important guests to walk on] (1952)
: marked by ceremonial courtesy ⟨*red-carpet* treatment⟩
**red carpet** *noun* (1951)
: a greeting or reception marked by ceremonial courtesy — usually used in the phrase *roll out the red carpet*
**red cedar** *noun* (1682)
**1** : a common juniper (*Juniperus virginiana*) chiefly of the eastern U.S. that has dark green closely imbricated scalelike leaves; *also* : a related tree (*J. silicicola*) of the southeastern U.S.
**2** : an arborvitae (*Thuja plicata*) of the Pacific Northwest
**3** : the red or reddish brown wood of a red cedar
**red cent** *noun* (circa 1839)
: PENNY — used for emphasis in negative constructions
**red clover** *noun* (before 12th century)
: a Eurasian clover (*Trifolium pratense*) that has globose heads of reddish purple flowers and is widely cultivated as a hay, forage, and cover crop
**red-coat** \'red-,kōt\ *noun* (1520)
: a British soldier especially in America during the Revolutionary War
**red coral** *noun* (circa 1864)
: a gorgonian (*Corallium nobile*) of the Mediterranean and adjacent parts of the Atlantic having a hard stony skeleton of a delicate red or pink color used for ornaments and jewelry
**Red Cross** *noun* (1863)
: a red Greek cross on a white background used as the emblem of the International Red Cross
**red currant** *noun* (1622)
: either of two currants (*Ribes sativum* and *R. rubrum*) often cultivated for their fruit; *also* : the fruit
**¹redd** \'red\ *verb* **redd·ed** *or* **redd; redd·ing** [Middle English (Scots), to clear, perhaps alteration of *ridden* — more at RID] (circa 1520)
*transitive verb*
*chiefly dialect* : to set in order — usually used with *up* or *out*
*intransitive verb*
*chiefly dialect* : to make things tidy — usually used with *up*
**²redd** *noun* [origin unknown] (1808)
: the spawning ground or nest of various fishes
**red deer** *noun* (15th century)
: ELK 1b — used for one of the Old World elk
**red-den** \'re-d°n\ *verb* **red·dened; red·den·ing** \'red-niŋ, 're-d°n-iŋ\ (circa 1611)
*transitive verb*
: to make red or reddish
*intransitive verb*
: to become red; *especially* : BLUSH
**red·dish** \'re-dish\ *adjective* (14th century)
: tinged with red
— **red·dish·ness** *noun*
**red dog** *noun* (1953)
: BLITZ 2b
— **red dog** *verb*
**red drum** *noun* (1709)
: CHANNEL BASS

**¹rede** \'rēd\ *transitive verb* [Middle English — more at READ] (before 12th century)
**1** *dialect* : to give counsel to : ADVISE
**2** *dialect* : INTERPRET, EXPLAIN
**²rede** *noun* (before 12th century)
**1** *chiefly dialect* : COUNSEL, ADVICE
**2** *archaic* : ACCOUNT, STORY
**red-ear** \'red-,ir\ *noun* (circa 1948)
: a common sunfish (*Lepomis microlophus*) of the southern and eastern U.S. resembling the bluegill but having the back part of the operculum bright orange-red — called also *red-ear sunfish, shellcracker*
**re·dec·o·rate** \(,)rē-'de-kə-,rāt\ (circa 1611) *transitive verb*
: to freshen or change in appearance : REFURBISH
*intransitive verb*
: to freshen or change a decorative scheme
— **re·dec·o·ra·tion** \(,)rē-,de-kə-'rā-shən\ *noun*
— **re·dec·o·ra·tor** \(,)rē-'de-kə-,rā-tər\ *noun*
**re·deem** \ri-'dēm\ *transitive verb* [Middle English *redemen*, modification of Middle French *redimer*, from Latin *redimere*, from *re-*, *red-* re- + *emere* to take, buy; akin to Lithuanian *imti* to take] (15th century)
**1 a** : to buy back : REPURCHASE **b** : to get or win back
**2** : to free from what distresses or harms: as **a** : to free from captivity by payment of ransom **b** : to extricate from or help to overcome something detrimental **c** : to release from blame or debt : CLEAR **d** : to free from the consequences of sin
**3** : to change for the better : REFORM
**4** : REPAIR, RESTORE
**5 a** : to free from a lien by payment of an amount secured thereby **b** (1) : to remove the obligation of by payment ⟨the U.S. Treasury *redeems* savings bonds on demand⟩ (2) : to exchange for something of value ⟨*redeem* trading stamps⟩ **c** : to make good : FULFILL
**6 a** : to atone for : EXPIATE **b** (1) : to offset the bad effect of (2) : to make worthwhile : RETRIEVE
**synonym** SEE RESCUE
— **re·deem·able** \-'dē-mə-bəl\ *adjective*
**re·deem·er** \-'dē-mər\ *noun* (15th century)
: a person who redeems; *especially, capitalized* : JESUS
**re·deem·ing** \-'dē-miŋ\ *adjective* (1631)
: serving to offset or compensate for a defect ⟨her performance is the film's *redeeming* feature⟩
**re·de·fine** \,rē-di-'fīn\ *transitive verb* (1872)
**1** : to define (as a concept) again : REFORMULATE ⟨had to *redefine* their terms⟩
**2 a** : to reexamine or reevaluate especially with a view to change **b** : TRANSFORM 1c
— **re·def·i·ni·tion** \(,)rē-,de-fə-'ni-shən\ *noun*
**re·demp·tion** \ri-'dem(p)-shən\ *noun* [Middle English *redempcioun*, from Middle French *redemption*, from Latin *redemption-*, *redemptio*, from *redimere* to redeem] (14th century)
: the act, process, or an instance of redeeming
**re·demp·tion·er** \-sh(ə-)nər\ *noun* (1771)
: an immigrant to America in the 18th and 19th centuries who obtained passage by becoming an indentured servant
**re·demp·tive** \-'dem(p)-tiv\ *adjective* (15th century)
: of, relating to, or bringing about redemption
**Re·demp·tor·ist** \ri-'dem(p)-t(ə-)rist\ *noun* [French *rédemptoriste*, from Late Latin *redemptor* redeemer, from Latin, contractor, from *redimere*] (circa 1842)
: a member of the Congregation of the Most Holy Redeemer founded by Saint Alphonsus Liguori in Scala, Italy, in 1732 and devoted to preaching
**re·demp·to·ry** \ri-'dem(p)-t(ə-)rē\ *adjective* (1602)
: serving to redeem

**re·de·ploy** \ˌrē-di-'plói\ (1945)
*transitive verb*
**:** to transfer from one area or activity to another
*intransitive verb*
**:** to relocate men or equipment
— **re·de·ploy·ment** \-mənt\ *noun*

**re·de·scribe** \ˌrē-di-'skrīb\ *transitive verb* (1871)
**:** to describe anew or again; *especially* **:** to give a new and more complete description to (a biological taxon)

**re·de·scrip·tion** \-'skrip-shən\ *noun* (1884)
**:** a new and more complete description especially of a biological taxon

**re·de·sign** \ˌrē-di-'zīn\ *transitive verb* (1891)
**:** to revise in appearance, function, or content
— **redesign** *noun*

**re·de·vel·op** \ˌrē-di-'ve-ləp\ *transitive verb* (1882)
**:** to develop again; *especially* **:** REDESIGN, REBUILD
— **re·de·vel·op·er** *noun*

**re·de·vel·op·ment** \-mənt\ *noun* (1873)
**:** the act or process of redeveloping; *especially* **:** renovation of a blighted area

**red–eye** \'red-ˌī\ *noun* (1819)
**1 :** cheap whiskey
**2 :** a late night or overnight flight

**red·eye gravy** \'red-ˌī-\ *noun* (1947)
**:** gravy made from the juices of ham and often flavored with coffee

**red fescue** *noun* (1900)
**:** a perennial pasture and turf grass (*Festuca rubra*) of Eurasia and North America with creeping rootstocks, erect culms, and reddish spikelets

**red·fish** \'red-ˌfish\ *noun* (15th century)
**:** any of various reddish fishes: as **a** (1) **:** a marine scorpaenid food fish (*Sebastes marinus*) of the northern coasts of Europe and North America that is usually bright rose-red when mature — called also *rosefish* (2) **:** a fish (*Sebastes mentella*) related to the redfish **b** **:** CHANNEL BASS

**red flag** *noun* (1777)
**1 :** a warning signal
**2 :** something that attracts usually irritated attention

**red flannel hash** *noun* (circa 1907)
**:** hash made especially from beef, potatoes, and beets

**red fox** *noun* (1778)
**:** a usually orange-red to reddish brown Holarctic fox (*Vulpes vulpes*) that has a white-tipped tail

**red  giant  noun** (1916)
**:** a star that has low surface temperature and a diameter that is large relative to the sun

red fox

**red–green blindness** *noun* (1888)
**:** dichromatism in which the spectrum is seen in tones of yellow and blue — called also *red-green color blindness*

**Red Guard** *noun* (1966)
**:** a member of a paramilitary youth organization in China in the 1960s

**red gum** *noun* (1788)
**1 a :** any of several Australian eucalyptus trees (especially *Eucalyptus camaldulensis, E. amygdalina,* and *E. calophylla*) **b :** eucalyptus gum
**2 :** SWEET GUM

**red–hand·ed** \'red-'han-dəd\ *adverb or adjective* (1819)
**:** in the act of committing a crime or misdeed ⟨caught *red-handed*⟩

**red·head** \'red-ˌhed\ *noun* (1664)
**1 :** a person having red hair
**2 :** a North American duck (*Aythya americana*) resembling the related canvasback but having a shorter bill with a black tip and in the male a brighter reddish head

**red·head·ed** \-ˌhe-dəd\ *adjective* (1565)
**:** having red hair or a red head

**red heat** *noun* (1686)
**:** the state of being red-hot; *also* **:** the temperature at which a substance is red-hot

**red herring** *noun* (15th century)
**1 :** a herring cured by salting and slow smoking to a dark brown color
**2** [from the practice of drawing a red herring across a trail to confuse hunting dogs] **:** something that distracts attention from the real issue

**red-horse** \'red-ˌhòrs\ *noun* (1796)
**:** any of numerous large suckers (genus *Moxostoma*) of North American rivers and lakes with the males having red fins especially in the breeding season

**red–hot** \'red-'hät\ *adjective* (14th century)
**:** extremely hot: as **a** **:** glowing with heat **b** **:** exhibiting or marked by intense emotion, enthusiasm, or violence ⟨a *red-hot* campaign⟩ **c** **:** FRESH, NEW ⟨*red-hot* news⟩ **d** **:** extremely popular

**red hot** *noun* (1835)
**1 :** one who shows intense emotion or partisanship
**2 :** HOT DOG 1
**3 :** a small red candy strongly flavored with cinnamon

**re·dia** \'rē-dē-ə\ *noun, plural* **re·di·ae** \-dē-ˌē\ *also* **re·di·as** [New Latin, from Francesco *Redi* (died 1698?) Italian naturalist] (1877)
**:** a larva produced within the sporocyst of many trematodes that produces another generation of rediae or develops into a cercaria
— **re·di·al** \-dē-əl\ *adjective*

**re·dial** \'rē-ˌdī(-ə)l, rē-'\ *noun* (1980)
**:** a function on a telephone that automatically repeats the dialing of the last number called; *also* **:** a button that invokes this function
— **re·dial** *verb*

**Red Indian** *noun* (1831)
*chiefly British* **:** AMERICAN INDIAN

**red·in·gote** \'re-diŋ-ˌgòt\ *noun* [French, modification of English *riding coat*] (1793)
**:** a fitted outer garment: as **a** **:** a double-breasted coat with wide flat cuffs and collar worn by men in the 18th century **b** **:** a woman's lightweight coat open at the front **c** **:** a dress with a front gore of contrasting material

**red ink** *noun* [from the use of red ink in financial statements to indicate a loss] (1926)
**1 :** a business loss **:** DEFICIT
**2 :** the condition of showing a business loss

**red·in·te·grate** \ri-'din-tə-ˌgrāt, re-\ *transitive verb* [Middle English, from Latin *redintegratus,* past participle of *redintegrare,* from *re-, red-* + *integrare* to make complete — more at INTEGRATE] (15th century)
*archaic* **:** to restore to a former and especially sound state

**red·in·te·gra·tion** \ri-ˌdin-tə-'grā-shən, re-\ *noun* (15th century)
**1** *archaic* **:** restoration to a former state
**2 a :** revival of the whole of a previous mental state when a phase of it recurs **b :** arousal of any response by a part of the complex of stimuli that originally aroused that response
— **red·in·te·gra·tive** \-'din-tə-ˌgrā-tiv\ *adjective*

**re·di·rect** \ˌrē-də-'rekt, ˌrē-(ˌ)dī-\ *transitive verb* (1844)
**:** to change the course or direction of
— **re·di·rec·tion** \-'rek-shən\ *noun*

**¹re·dis·count** \(ˌ)rē-'dis-ˌkaùnt, ˌrē-dis-'\ *transitive verb* (1866)
**:** to discount again (as commercial paper)
— **re·dis·count·able** \-ˌkaùn-tə-bəl, -'kaùn-\ *adjective*

**²re·dis·count** \(ˌ)rē-'dis-ˌkaùnt\ *noun* (1892)
**1 :** the act or process of rediscounting
**2 :** negotiable paper that is rediscounted

**re·dis·tri·bute** \ˌrē-də-'stri-byət\ *transitive verb* (1611)
**1 :** to alter the distribution of **:** REALLOCATE
**2 :** to spread to other areas
— **re·dis·tri·bu·tion** \(ˌ)rē-ˌdis-trə-'byü-shən\ *noun*
— **re·dis·tri·bu·tion·al** \-shnəl, -shə-nᵊl\ *adjective*
— **re·dis·trib·u·tive** \ˌrē-də-'stri-byə-tiv\ *adjective*

**re·dis·tri·bu·tion·ist** \(ˌ)rē-ˌdis-trə-'byü-sh(ə-)nist\ *noun* (1979)
**:** one that believes in or advocates a welfare state

**re·dis·trict** \(ˌ)rē-'dis-(ˌ)trikt\ (1850)
*transitive verb*
**:** to divide anew into districts; *specifically* **:** to revise the legislative districts of
*intransitive verb*
**:** to revise legislative districts

**red·i·vi·vus** \ˌre-də-'vī-vəs, -'vē-\ *adjective* [Late Latin, from Latin, reused] (1675)
**:** brought back to life **:** REBORN — used postpositively

**red lead** *noun* (15th century)
**:** an orange-red to brick-red lead oxide $Pb_3O_4$ used in storage-battery plates, in glass and ceramics, and as a paint pigment

**red leaf** *noun* (1909)
**:** any of several plant diseases characterized by reddening of the foliage

**red–leg** \'red-ˌleg, -ˌlāg\ *noun* (1900)
**:** ARTILLERYMAN

**red–legged grasshopper** *noun* (1867)
**:** a widely distributed and sometimes highly destructive small North American grasshopper (*Melanoplus femur-rubrum*) with red hind legs — called also *red-legged locust*

**red–let·ter** \'red-ˌle-tər\ *adjective* [from the practice of marking holy days in red letters in church calendars] (1704)
**:** of special significance
*word history* see RUBRIC

**red light** *noun* (1849)
**:** a warning signal; *especially* **:** a red traffic signal

**red–light district** *noun* (1900)
**:** a district in which houses of prostitution are numerous

**¹red·line** \'red-ˌlīn\ *noun* (1952)
**:** a recommended safety limit **:** the fastest, farthest, or highest point or degree considered safe; *also* **:** the red line which marks this point on a gauge

**²red·line** \'red-ˌlīn, -'līn\ (1968)
*intransitive verb*
**:** to withhold home-loan funds or insurance from neighborhoods considered poor economic risks
*transitive verb*
**:** to discriminate against in housing or insurance

**red·ly** \'red-lē\ *adverb* (1611)
**:** in a red manner **:** with red color

**red man** *noun* (1725)
**1 :** AMERICAN INDIAN
**2** *R&M capitalized* [Improved Order of *Red Men*] **:** a member of a major benevolent and fraternal order

**red maple** *noun* (1770)
**:** a common tree (*Acer rubrum*) of the eastern and central U.S. that grows chiefly on moist soils, has reddish twigs and flowers, and yields a lighter and softer wood than the sugar maple

**red marrow** *noun* (1900)

: reddish bone marrow that is the seat of blood-cell production

**red mass** *noun, often R&M capitalized* (1889)
: a votive mass of the Holy Spirit celebrated in red vestments especially at the opening of courts and congresses

**red mite** *noun* (1894)
: any of several mites having a red color: as **a** : EUROPEAN RED MITE **b** : CITRUS RED MITE

**red mulberry** *noun* (1717)
: a North American forest tree (*Morus rubra*) with toothed leaves and soft durable wood; *also* : its edible usually purple fruit

**red mullet** *noun* (1762)
: GOATFISH

**red·neck** \'red-ˌnek\ *noun* (1830)
**1** : a white member of the Southern rural laboring class — sometimes used disparagingly
**2** : a person whose behavior and opinions are similar to those attributed to rednecks — often used disparagingly
— **redneck** *also* **red·necked** \-ˌnekt\ *adjective*

**red·ness** \-nəs\ *noun* (before 12th century)
: the quality or state of being red or red-hot

**re·do** \(ˌ)rē-'dü\ *transitive verb* **-did** \-'did\; **-done** \-'dən\; **-do·ing** \-'dü-iŋ\; **-does** \-'dəz\ (1597)
**1** : to do over or again
**2** : REDECORATE
— **re·do** \'rē-ˌdü, ˌrē-'dü\ *noun*

**red oak** *noun* (1634)
**1** : any of numerous American oaks (as *Quercus rubra* and *Quercus falcata*) that have four stamens in each floret, acorns with the inner surface of the shell lined with woolly hairs, the acorn cap covered with thin scales, and leaf veins that usually run beyond the margin of the leaf to form bristles
**2** : the wood of red oak

**red ocher** *noun* (1572)
: a red earthy hematite used as a pigment

**red·o·lence** \'red-ᵊl-ən(t)s\ *noun* (15th century)
**1** : an often pungent or agreeable odor
**2** : the quality or state of being redolent
*synonym* see FRAGRANCE

**red·o·lent** \-ənt\ *adjective* [Middle English, from Middle French, from Latin *redolent-, redolens*, present participle of *redolēre* to emit a scent, from *re-, red- + olēre* to smell — more at ODOR] (15th century)
**1** : exuding fragrance : AROMATIC
**2 a** : full of a specified fragrance : SCENTED ⟨air *redolent* of seaweed⟩ **b** : EVOCATIVE, SUGGESTIVE ⟨a city *redolent* of antiquity⟩
*synonym* see ODOROUS
— **red·o·lent·ly** *adverb*

**red osier** *noun* (1807)
: a common shrubby North American dogwood (*Cornus sericea* synonym *C. stolonifera*) with reddish purple twigs, white flowers, and globose blue or whitish fruit

**re·dou·ble** \(ˌ)rē-'də-bəl\ (15th century)
*transitive verb*
**1** : to make twice as great in size or amount; *broadly* : INTENSIFY, STRENGTHEN
**2 a** *obsolete* : to echo back **b** *archaic* : REPEAT
*intransitive verb*
**1** : to become redoubled
**2** *archaic* : RESOUND
**3** : to double an opponent's double in bridge
— **redouble** *noun*

**re·doubt** \ri-'daut\ *noun* [French *redoute*, from Italian *ridotto*, from Medieval Latin *reductus* secret place, from Latin, withdrawn, from past participle of *reducere* to lead back — more at REDUCE] (circa 1608)
**1 a** : a small usually temporary enclosed defensive work **b** : a defended position : protective barrier
**2** : a secure retreat : STRONGHOLD

**re·doubt·able** \ri-'dau-tə-bəl\ *adjective* [Middle English *redoutable*, from Middle French,

from *redouter* to dread, from *re- + douter* to doubt] (15th century)
**1** : causing fear or alarm : FORMIDABLE
**2** : ILLUSTRIOUS, EMINENT; *broadly* : worthy of respect
— **re·doubt·ably** \-blē\ *adverb*

**re·dound** \ri-'daund\ *intransitive verb* [Middle English, from Middle French *redonder*, from Latin *redundare*, from *re-, red-* re- + *unda* wave — more at WATER] (14th century)
**1** *archaic* : to become swollen : OVERFLOW
**2** : to have an effect for good or ill ⟨new power alignments which may or may not *redound* to the faculty's benefit —G. W. Bonham⟩
**3** : to become transferred or added : ACCRUE
**4** : REBOUND, REFLECT

**red-out** \'red-ˌaut\ *noun* (1942)
: a condition in which centripetal acceleration (as that created when an aircraft abruptly enters a dive) drives blood to the head and causes reddening of the visual field and headache

**re·dox** \'rē-ˌdäks\ *adjective* [reduction + oxidation] (1928)
: of or relating to oxidation-reduction

**red panda** *noun* (1955)
: PANDA 1

**red-pen·cil** \'red-ˌpen(t)-səl\ *transitive verb* (1946)
**1** : CENSOR
**2** : CORRECT, REVISE

**red pepper** *noun* (circa 1591)
: CAYENNE PEPPER

**red pine** *noun* (1809)
**1** : a North American pine (*Pinus resinosa*) that has reddish bark and two long needles in each cluster
**2** : the relatively hard wood of the red pine that consists chiefly of sapwood

**red·poll** \'red-ˌpōl\ *noun* (1738)
: either of two small finches (genus *Carduelis* synonym *Acanthis*) having brownish streaked plumage and a red or rosy crown; *especially* : one (*C. flammea*) found in northern regions of both of the New and Old World

**red poll** *noun, often R&P capitalized* [alteration of *red polled*] (1891)
: any of a breed of large hornless red beef cattle of English origin

¹**re·dress** \ri-'dres\ *transitive verb* [Middle English, from Middle French *redresser*, from Old French *redrecier*, from *re- + drecier* to make straight — more at DRESS] (14th century)
**1 a** (1) : to set right : REMEDY (2) : to make up for : COMPENSATE **b** : to remove the cause of (a grievance or complaint) **c** : to exact reparation for : AVENGE
**2** *archaic* **a** : to requite (a person) for a wrong or loss **b** : HEAL
*synonym* see CORRECT
— **re·dress·er** *noun*

²**re·dress** \ri-'dres, 'rē-\ *noun* (14th century)
**1 a** : relief from distress **b** : means or possibility of seeking a remedy ⟨without *redress*⟩
**2** : compensation for wrong or loss : REPARATION
**3 a** : an act or instance of redressing **b** : RETRIBUTION, CORRECTION

**red ribbon** *noun* (1927)
: a red ribbon usually with appropriate words or markings awarded the second-place winner in a competition

**red-root** \'red-ˌrüt, -ˌrut\ *noun* (1709)
**1** : a perennial herb (*Lachnanthes caroliniana* synonym *L. tinctoria*) of the bloodwort family of the eastern U.S. whose red root is the source of a dye
**2** : NEW JERSEY TEA
**3** : BLOODROOT
**4** : a pigweed (*Amaranthus retroflexus*) that bears greenish flowers in dense spikes with bracts almost twice as long as the sepals

**red rust** *noun* (1846)
**1** : the uredinial stage of a rust
**2** : the diseased condition produced by red rust

**red salmon** *noun* (1881)

: SOCKEYE

**red–shaft·ed flicker** \'red-'shaf-təd-\ *noun* (1846)
: a flicker of western North America with light red on the underside of the tail and wings, a gray nape with no red, and in the male red on each cheek

**red·shank** \'red-ˌshaŋk\ *noun* (1525)
: a common Old World sandpiper (*Tringa totanus*) with pale red legs and feet

**red·shift** \'red-'shift\ *noun* (1923)
: a displacement of the spectrum of a celestial body toward longer wavelengths that is a consequence of the Doppler effect or the gravitational field of the source
— **red·shift·ed** *adjective*

**red·shirt** \'red-ˌshərt\ *noun* [from the red jersey commonly worn by such a player in practice scrimmages against the regulars] (1955)
: a college athlete who is kept out of varsity competition for a year in order to extend eligibility
— **redshirt** *verb*

**red–shoul·dered hawk** \-ˌshōl-dərd-\ *noun* (1812)
: a common North American hawk (*Buteo lineatus*) that has a banded tail and a light spot on the underside of the wings toward the tips

**red sin·dhi** \-'sin-dē\ *noun* [¹*red* + *sindhi* one belonging to Sind, Pakistan] (1946)
: any of a breed of humped rather small red dairy cattle developed in southwestern Asia and extensively used for crossbreeding with European stock in tropical areas

**red siskin** *noun* (1948)
: a finch (*Carduelis cucullata*) of northern South America that is scarlet with black head, wings, and tail

**red·skin** \'red-ˌskin\ *noun* (1699)
: AMERICAN INDIAN — usually taken to be offensive

**red snapper** *noun* (1755)
: any of various reddish fishes (as of the genera *Lutjanus* and *Sebastes*) including several food fishes

**red snow** *noun* (1678)
: snow colored by various airborne dusts or by a growth of algae (as of the genus *Chlamydomonas*) that contain red pigment and live in the upper layer of snow; *also* : an alga causing red snow

**red soil** *noun* (1889)
: any of a group of zonal soils that develop in a warm temperate moist climate under deciduous or mixed forests and that have thin organic and organic-mineral layers overlying a yellowish brown leached layer resting on an illuvial red horizon — called also *red podzolic soil*

**red spider** *noun* (1646)
: SPIDER MITE

**red spruce** *noun* (1777)
: a spruce (*Picea rubens*) of eastern North America that has pubescent twigs and yellowish green needles and is an important source of lumber and pulpwood

**red squill** *noun* (1738)
**1** : a red-bulbed form of squill (*Urginea maritima*)
**2** : a rat poison derived from the bulb of red squill

**red squirrel** *noun* (1682)
: a common and widely distributed North American squirrel (*Tamiasciurus hudsonicus*) that has reddish upper parts and is smaller than the gray squirrel

**red star** *noun* (1903)
: a star having a very low surface temperature and a red color

**red·start** \'red-ˌstärt\ *noun* [*red* + obsolete *start* handle, tail] (circa 1570)
**1** : a small Old World songbird (*Phoenicurus phoenicurus* of the family Turdidae) with the male having a white brow, black throat, and chestnut breast and tail

**2** : an American warbler (*Setophaga ruticilla* of the family Parulidae) with a black and orange male

**red-tailed hawk** \'red-ˌtāld-\ *noun* (1805)
: a widely distributed chiefly rodent-eating New World hawk (*Buteo jamaicensis*) that is usually mottled dusky above and white streaked dusky and tinged with buff below and has a rather short typically reddish tail — called also *redtail*

red-tailed hawk

**red tape** *noun* [from the red tape formerly used to bind legal documents in England] (1736)
: official routine or procedure marked by excessive complexity which results in delay or inaction

**red tide** *noun* (1904)
: seawater discolored by the presence of large numbers of dinoflagellates (especially of the genera *Gonyaulax* and *Gymnodinium*) which produce a toxin poisonous especially to many forms of marine vertebrate life and to humans who consume contaminated shellfish — compare SAXITOXIN

**red·top** \'red-ˌtäp\ *noun* (1790)
: any of various grasses (genus *Agrostis*) with usually reddish panicles; *especially* : an important forage and lawn grass (*A. alba* synonym *A. gigantea*) of eastern North America

**re·duce** \ri-'düs, -'dyüs\ *verb* **re·duced; re·duc·ing** [Middle English, to lead back, from Latin *reducere*, from *re-* + *ducere* to lead — more at TOW] (14th century)
*transitive verb*
**1 a** : to draw together or cause to converge : CONSOLIDATE ⟨*reduce* all the questions to one⟩ **b** (1) : to diminish in size, amount, extent, or number ⟨*reduce* taxes⟩ ⟨*reduce* the likelihood of war⟩ (2) : to decrease the volume and concentrate the flavor of by boiling ⟨add the wine and *reduce* the sauce for two minutes⟩ **c** : to narrow down : RESTRICT ⟨the Indians were *reduced* to small reservations⟩ **d** : to make shorter : ABRIDGE
**2** *archaic* : to restore to righteousness : SAVE
**3** : to bring to a specified state or condition ⟨the impact of the movie *reduced* them to tears⟩
**4 a** : to force to capitulate **b** : FORCE, COMPEL
**5 a** : to bring to a systematic form or character ⟨*reduce* natural events to laws⟩ **b** : to put down in written or printed form ⟨*reduce* an agreement to writing⟩
**6** : to correct (as a fracture) by bringing displaced or broken parts back into their normal positions
**7 a** : to lower in grade or rank : DEMOTE **b** : to lower in condition or status : DOWNGRADE
**8 a** : to diminish in strength or density **b** : to diminish in value
**9 a** (1) : to change the denominations or form of without changing the value (2) : to construct a geometrical figure similar to but smaller than (a given figure) **b** : to transpose from one form into another **c** : to change (an expression) to an equivalent but more fundamental expression ⟨*reduce* a fraction⟩
**10** : to break down (as by crushing or grinding) : PULVERIZE
**11 a** : to bring to the metallic state by removal of nonmetallic elements ⟨*reduce* an ore by heat⟩ **b** : DEOXIDIZE **c** : to combine with or subject to the action of hydrogen **d** (1) : to change (an element or ion) from a higher to a lower oxidation state (2) : to add one or more electrons to (an atom or ion or molecule)
**12** : to change (a stressed vowel) to an unstressed vowel
*intransitive verb*

**1 a** (1) : to become diminished or lessened; *especially* : to lose weight by dieting (2) : to become reduced ⟨ferrous iron *reduces* to ferric iron⟩ **b** : to become concentrated or consolidated **c** : to undergo meiosis
**2** : to become converted or equated
**synonym** see DECREASE, CONQUER
— **re·duc·er** *noun*
— **re·duc·ibil·i·ty** \-ˌdü-sə-'bi-lə-tē, -ˌdyü-\ *noun*
— **re·duc·ible** \-'dü-sə-bəl, -'dyü-\ *adjective*
— **re·duc·ibly** \-blē\ *adverb*

**reducing agent** *noun* (1885)
: a substance that reduces a chemical compound usually by donating electrons

**re·duc·tant** \ri-'dək-tənt\ *noun* (1925)
: REDUCING AGENT

**re·duc·tase** \-ˌtās, -ˌtāz\ *noun* (1902)
: an enzyme that catalyzes reduction

**re·duc·tio ad ab·sur·dum** \ri-'dək-tē-ˌō-ˌad-əb-'sər-dəm, -'dək-sē-ō-, -shē-, -'zər-\ *noun* [Late Latin, literally, reduction to the absurd] (1741)
**1** : disproof of a proposition by showing an absurdity to which it leads when carried to its logical conclusion
**2** : the carrying of something to an absurd extreme

**re·duc·tion** \ri-'dək-shən\ *noun* [Middle English *reduccion* restoration, from Middle French *reduction*, from Late Latin & Latin; Late Latin *reduction-, reductio* reduction (in a syllogism), from Latin, restoration, from *reducere*] (1546)
**1** : the act or process of reducing : the state of being reduced
**2 a** : something made by reducing **b** : the amount by which something is reduced
**3** [Spanish *reducción*, from Latin *reduction-, reductio*] : a South American Indian settlement directed by Jesuit missionaries
**4** : MEIOSIS 2; *specifically* : production of the gametic chromosome number in the first meiotic division
— **re·duc·tion·al** \-shnəl, -shə-nᵊl\ *adjective*

**reduction division** *noun* (1891)
: the usually first division of meiosis in which chromosome reduction occurs; *also* : MEIOSIS 2

**reduction gear** *noun* (1896)
: a combination of gears used to reduce the input speed (as of a marine turbine) to a lower output speed (as of a ship's propeller)

**re·duc·tion·ism** \ri-'dək-shə-ˌni-zəm\ *noun* (1943)
**1** : the attempt to explain all biological processes by the same explanations (as by physical laws) that chemists and physicists use to interpret inanimate matter; *also* : the theory that complete reductionism is possible
**2** : a procedure or theory that reduces complex data or phenomena to simpler terms; *especially* : OVERSIMPLIFICATION
— **re·duc·tion·ist** \-sh(ə-)nist\ *noun or adjective*
— **re·duc·tion·is·tic** \-ˌdək-shə-'nis-tik\ *adjective*

**re·duc·tive** \ri-'dək-tiv\ *adjective* (1633)
**1** : of, relating to, causing, or involving reduction
**2** : of or relating to reductionism : REDUCTIONISTIC
— **re·duc·tive·ly** *adverb*
— **re·duc·tive·ness** *noun*

**re·dun·dan·cy** \ri-'dən-dən(t)-sē\ *noun, plural* **-cies** (circa 1602)
**1 a** : the quality or state of being redundant : SUPERFLUITY **b** : the use of redundant components; *also* : such components **c** *chiefly British* : dismissal from a job especially by layoff
**2** : PROFUSION, ABUNDANCE
**3 a** : superfluous repetition : PROLIXITY **b** : an act or instance of needless repetition
**4** : the part of a message that can be eliminated without loss of essential information

**re·dun·dant** \-dənt\ *adjective* [Latin *redundant-, redundans*, present participle of *redundare* to overflow — more at REDOUND] (1594)
**1 a** : exceeding what is necessary or normal : SUPERFLUOUS **b** : characterized by or containing an excess; *specifically* : using more words than necessary **c** : characterized by similarity or repetition ⟨a group of particularly *redundant* brick buildings⟩ **d** *chiefly British* : no longer needed for a job and hence laid off
**2** : PROFUSE, LAVISH
**3** : serving as a duplicate for preventing failure of an entire system (as a spacecraft) upon failure of a single component
— **re·dun·dant·ly** *adverb*

**re·du·pli·cate** \ri-'dü-pli-ˌkāt, 'rē-, -'dyü-\ *transitive verb* [Late Latin *reduplicatus*, past participle of *reduplicare*, from Latin *re-* + *duplicare* to double — more at DUPLICATE] (circa 1570)
**1** : to make or perform again : COPY, REPEAT
**2** : to form (a word) by reduplication
— **re·du·pli·cate** \-kət\ *adjective*

**re·du·pli·ca·tion** \ri-ˌdü-pli-'kā-shən, ˌrē-, -'dyü-\ *noun* (1555)
**1** : an act or instance of doubling or reiterating
**2 a** : an often grammatically functional repetition of a radical element or a part of it occurring usually at the beginning of a word and often accompanied by change of the radical vowel **b** (1) : a word or form produced by reduplication (2) : the repeated element in such a word or form
**3** : ANADIPLOSIS
— **re·du·pli·ca·tive** \ri-'dü-pli-ˌkā-tiv, 'rē-, -'dyü-\ *adjective*
— **re·du·pli·ca·tive·ly** *adverb*

**re·du·vi·id** \ri-'dü-vē-əd, -'dyü-\ *noun* [ultimately from Latin *reduvia* hangnail] (1888)
: ASSASSIN BUG
— **reduviid** *adjective*

**re·dux** \(ˌ)rē-'dəks, 'rē-ˌ\ *adjective* [Latin, returning, from *reducere* to lead back] (1873)
: brought back — used postpositively

**red·ware** \'red-ˌwar, -ˌwer\ *noun* (circa 1797)
: earthenware pottery made of clay containing considerable iron oxide

**red water** *noun* (1594)
: any of several cattle diseases characterized by hematuria

**red wheat** *noun* (1523)
: a wheat that has red grains

**red wine** *noun* (circa 1754)
: a wine with a predominantly red color derived during fermentation from the natural pigment in the skins of dark-colored grapes

**red·wing** \'red-ˌwiŋ\ *noun* (1657)
**1** : a European thrush (*Turdus iliacus* synonym *T. musicus*) having the underwing coverts red
**2** : RED-WINGED BLACKBIRD

**red-winged blackbird** \'red-ˌwiŋd-\ *noun* (1797)
: a North American blackbird (*Agelaius phoeniceus*) of which the adult male is black with a patch of bright scarlet at the bend of the wings bordered behind with yellow or buff — called also *redwing blackbird*

**red wolf** *noun* (1840)
: a wolf (*Canis rufus* synonym *C. niger*) originally of the southeastern U.S.

**red·wood** \'red-ˌwu̇d\ *noun* (1634)
**1** : any of various woods yielding a red dye
**2** : a tree that yields a red dyewood or produces red or reddish wood
**3 a** : a commercially important coniferous timber tree (*Sequoia sempervirens*) of the bald cypress family that grows chiefly in coastal California and sometimes reaches a height of

\ə\ abut \ᵊ\ kitten \ər\ further \a\ ash \ā\ ace
\ä\ mop, mar \au̇\ out \ch\ chin \e\ bet \ē\ easy
\g\ go \i\ hit \ī\ ice \j\ job \ŋ\ sing \ō\ go
\ȯ\ law \ȯi\ boy \th\ thin \th̲\ the \ü\ loot \u̇\ foot
\y\ yet \zh\ vision     *see also* Guide to Pronunciation

360 feet (110 meters) — called also *coast redwood* **b :** its brownish red durable wood
**red worm** *noun* (1935)
**:** BLOODWORM
**re·echo** \\(,)rē-'e-(,)kō\ (1590)
*intransitive verb*
**:** to repeat or return an echo **:** echo again or repeatedly **:** REVERBERATE
*transitive verb*
**:** to echo back **:** REPEAT
**¹reed** \'rēd\ *noun* [Middle English *rede*, from Old English *hrēod*; akin to Old High German *hriot* reed] (before 12th century)
**1 a :** any of various tall grasses with slender often prominently jointed stems that grow especially in wet areas **b :** a stem of a reed **c :** a person or thing too weak to rely on **:** one easily swayed or overcome

reed 6a

**2 :** a growth or mass of reeds; *specifically* **:** reeds for thatching
**3 :** ARROW
**4 :** a wind instrument made from the hollow joint of a plant
**5 :** an ancient Hebrew unit of length equal to 6 cubits
**6 a :** a thin elastic tongue (as of cane, wood, metal, or plastic) fastened at one end over an air opening in a wind instrument (as a clarinet, organ pipe, or accordion) and set in vibration by an air current **b :** a woodwind instrument that produces sound by the vibrating of a reed against the mouthpiece ⟨the *reeds* of an orchestra⟩
**7 :** a device on a loom resembling a comb and used to space warp yarns evenly
**8 :** REEDING 1a
— **reed·like** \-,līk\ *adjective*
**²reed** *transitive verb* (1951)
**:** MILL 2
**reed·buck** \'rēd-,bək\ *noun, plural* **reed·buck** *also* **reedbucks** (1834)
**:** any of a genus (*Redunca*) of fawn-colored African antelopes in which the females are hornless
**reed·ed** \'rē-dəd\ *adjective* (1829)
**:** decorated with reeds or reeding ⟨a bed with *reeded* posts⟩
**re·ed·i·fy** \(,)rē-'e-də-,fī\ *transitive verb* **-fied; -fy·ing** [Middle English *reedifien*, from Middle French *reedifier*, from Late Latin *reaedificare*, from Latin *re-* + *aedificare* to build — more at EDIFY] (15th century)
*British* **:** REBUILD
**reed·ing** \'rē-diŋ\ *noun* (1815)
**1 a :** a small convex molding — see MOLDING illustration **b :** decoration by series of reedings
**2 :** MILLING
**re·edit** \(,)rē-'e-dət\ *transitive verb* (1797)
**:** to edit again **:** make a new edition of
— **re·edi·tion** \,rē-ə-'di-shən\ *noun*
**reed·man** \'rēd-,man\ *noun* (1938)
**:** one who plays a reed instrument
**reed organ** *noun* (1851)
**:** a keyboard wind instrument in which the wind acts on a set of free reeds
**reed pipe** *noun* (circa 1741)
**:** a pipe-organ pipe producing its tone by vibration of a beating reed in a current of air
**re·ed·u·cate** \(,)rē-'e-jə-,kāt\ *transitive verb* (1808)
**:** to train again; *especially* **:** to rehabilitate through education
— **re·ed·u·ca·tion** \(,)rē-,e-jə-'kā-shən\ *noun*
— **re·ed·u·ca·tive** \(,)rē-'e-jə-,kā-tiv\ *adjective*
**reedy** \'rē-dē\ *adjective* **reed·i·er; -est** (14th century)
**1 :** abounding in or covered with reeds

**2 :** made of or resembling reeds; *especially* **:** SLENDER, FRAIL
**3 :** having the tone quality of a reed instrument
— **reed·i·ness** \-nəs\ *noun*
**¹reef** \'rēf\ *noun* [Middle English *riff*, from Old Norse *rif*; akin to Old English *ribb* rib] (14th century)
**1 :** a part of a sail taken in or let out in regulating size
**2 :** reduction in sail area by reefing
**²reef** (1667)
*transitive verb*
**1 :** to reduce the area of (a sail) by rolling or folding a portion
**2 :** to lower or bring inboard (a spar) wholly or partially
*intransitive verb*
**:** to reduce a sail by taking in a reef
— **reef·able** \'rē-fə-bəl\ *adjective*
**³reef** *noun* [Dutch *rif*, probably of Scandinavian origin; akin to Old Norse *rif* reef of a sail] (1584)
**1 a :** a chain of rocks or coral or a ridge of sand at or near the surface of water **b :** a hazardous obstruction
**2 :** LODE, VEIN
— **reefy** \'rē-fē\ *adjective*
**¹reef·er** \'rē-fər\ *noun* (1818)
**1 :** one that reefs
**2 :** a close-fitting usually double-breasted jacket or coat of thick cloth
**²ree·fer** \'rē-fər\ *noun* [by shortening & alteration] (1914)
**1 :** REFRIGERATOR
**2 :** a refrigerator car, truck, trailer, or ship
**³ree·fer** *noun* [probably modification of Mexican Spanish *grifa*] (1931)
**:** a marijuana cigarette; *also* **:** MARIJUANA 2
**reef knot** *noun* (1841)
**:** a square knot used in reefing a sail
**¹reek** \'rēk\ *noun* [Middle English *rek*, from Old English *rēc*; akin to Old High German *rouh* smoke] (before 12th century)
**1** *chiefly dialect* **:** SMOKE
**2 :** VAPOR, FOG
**3 :** a strong or disagreeable fume or odor
**²reek** (before 12th century)
*intransitive verb*
**1 :** to emit smoke or vapor
**2 a :** to give off or become permeated with a strong or offensive odor **b :** to give a strong impression of some constituent quality or feature ⟨a neighborhood that *reeks* of poverty⟩
**3 :** EMANATE
*transitive verb*
**1 :** to subject to the action of smoke or vapor
**2 :** EXUDE, GIVE OFF ⟨a politician who *reeks* charm⟩
— **reek·er** *noun*
— **reeky** \'rē-kē\ *adjective*
**¹reel** \'rē(ə)l\ *noun* [Middle English, from Old English *hrēol*; akin to Old Norse *hrǽll* weaver's reed, Greek *krekein* to weave] (before 12th century)
**1 :** a revolvable device on which something flexible is wound: as **a :** a small windlass at the butt of a fishing rod for the line **b** *chiefly British* **:** a spool or bobbin for sewing thread **c :** a flanged spool for photographic film; *especially* **:** one for motion pictures
**2 :** a quantity of something wound on a reel
**²reel** (14th century)
*transitive verb*
**1 :** to wind on or as if on a reel
**2 :** to draw by reeling a line ⟨*reel* a fish in⟩
*intransitive verb*
**:** to turn a reel
— **reel·able** \'rē-lə-bəl\ *adjective*
**³reel** *verb* [Middle English *relen*, probably from *reel*, noun] (14th century)
*intransitive verb*
**1 a :** to turn or move round and round **b :** to be in a whirl
**2 :** to behave in a violent disorderly manner
**3 :** to waver or fall back (as from a blow)

**4 :** to walk or move unsteadily
*transitive verb*
**:** to cause to reel
**⁴reel** *noun* (1572)
**:** a reeling motion
**⁵reel** *noun* [probably from *⁴reel*] (circa 1585)
**1 :** a lively Scottish-Highland dance; *also* **:** the music for this dance
**2 :** VIRGINIA REEL
**re·elect** \,rē-ə-'lekt\ *transitive verb* (1601)
**:** to elect for another term in office
— **re·elec·tion** \-'lek-shən\ *noun*
**reel·er** \'rē-lər\ *noun* (circa 1598)
**1 :** one that reels
**2 :** a motion picture having a specified number of reels ⟨a two-*reeler*⟩
**reel off** *transitive verb* (1837)
**1 :** to tell or recite readily and usually at length ⟨*reel off* a few jokes to break the ice⟩
**2 :** to chalk up usually as a series
**reel–to–reel** *adjective* (1961)
**:** of, relating to, or utilizing magnetic tape that requires threading on a take-up reel ⟨a *reel-to-reel* tape recorder⟩
**re·em·broi·der** \,rē-əm-'broi-dər\ *transitive verb* (1927)
**:** to outline a design (as on lace) with embroidery stitching
**re·en·act** \,rē-ə-'nakt\ *transitive verb* (circa 1676)
**1 :** to enact (as a law) again
**2 :** to act or perform again
**3 :** to repeat the actions of (an earlier event or incident)
— **re·en·act·ment** \-'nak(t)-mənt\ *noun*
**re·en·force** \,rē-ən-'fōrs, -'fórs\ *variant of* REINFORCE
**re·en·ter** \(,)rē-'en-tər\ (15th century)
*transitive verb*
**1 :** to enter (something) again
**2 :** to return to and enter
*intransitive verb*
**:** to enter again
**re·en·trance** \(,)rē-'en-trən(t)s\ *noun* (1594)
**:** REENTRY
**¹re·en·trant** \-trənt\ *adjective* (1781)
**:** directed inward
**²reentrant** *noun* (1899)
**1 :** one that reenters
**2 :** one that is reentrant
**3 :** an indentation in a landform
**re·en·try** \(,)rē-'en-trē\ *noun* (15th century)
**1 :** a retaking possession; *especially* **:** entry by a lessor on leased premises on the tenant's failure to perform the conditions of the lease
**2 :** a second or new entry
**3 :** a playing card that will enable a player to regain the lead
**4 :** the action of reentering the earth's atmosphere after travel in space
**reest** \'rēst\ *intransitive verb* [probably short for Scots *arreest* to arrest, from Middle English (Scots) *arreisten*, from Middle French *arester* — more at ARREST] (1786)
*chiefly Scottish* **:** BALK
**¹reeve** \'rēv\ *noun* [Middle English *reve*, from Old English *gerēfa*, from *ge-* (associative prefix) + *-rēfa* (akin to Old English *-rōf* number, Old High German *ruova*) — more at CO-] (before 12th century)
**1 :** a local administrative agent of an Anglo-Saxon king
**2 :** a medieval English manor officer responsible chiefly for overseeing the discharge of feudal obligations
**3 a :** the council president in some Canadian municipalities **b :** a local official charged with enforcement of specific regulations ⟨deer *reeve*⟩
**²reeve** *verb* **rove** \'rōv\ *or* **reeved; reeving** [origin unknown] (1627)
*transitive verb*
**1 :** to pass (as a rope) through a hole or opening
**2 :** to fasten by passing through a hole or around something

**3 :** to pass a rope through
*intransitive verb*
*of a rope* **:** to pass through a block or similar device

³**reeve** *noun* [origin unknown] (1634)
**:** the female of the ruff (sandpiper)

**ref** \'ref\ *noun* (1899)
**:** a referee in a game or sport

**re·fash·ion** \(,)rē-'fa-shən\ *transitive verb* (1803)
**:** REMAKE, ALTER

**re·fect** \ri-'fekt\ *transitive verb* [Latin *refectus*, past participle of *reficere*] (14th century)
*archaic* **:** to refresh with food or drink

**re·fec·tion** \ri-'fek-shən\ *noun* [Middle English *refeccioun*, from Middle French *refection*, from Latin *refection-*, *refectio*, from *reficere* to restore, from *re-* + *facere* to make — more at DO] (14th century)
**1 :** refreshment of mind, spirit, or body; *especially* **:** NOURISHMENT
**2 a :** the taking of refreshment **b :** food and drink together **:** REPAST

**re·fec·to·ry** \ri-'fek-t(ə-)rē\ *noun, plural* **-ries** [Late Latin *refectorium*, from Latin *reficere*] (15th century)
**:** a dining hall (as in a monastery or college)

**refectory table** *noun* (1923)
**:** a long table with heavy legs

**re·fel** \ri-'fel\ *transitive verb* **re·felled; re·fel·ling** [Latin *refellere* to prove false, refute, from *re-* + *fallere* to deceive] (1530)
*obsolete* **:** REJECT, REPULSE

**re·fer** \ri-'fər\ *verb* **re·ferred; re·fer·ring** [Middle English *referren*, from Latin *referre* to bring back, report, refer, from *re-* + *ferre* to carry — more at BEAR] (14th century)
*transitive verb*
**1 a** (1) **:** to think of, regard, or classify within a general category or group (2) **:** to explain in terms of a general cause **b :** to allot to a particular place, stage, or period **c :** to regard as coming from or located in a specific area
**2 a :** to send or direct for treatment, aid, information, or decision ⟨*refer* a patient to a specialist⟩ ⟨*refer* a bill back to a committee⟩ **b :** to direct for testimony or guaranty as to character or ability
*intransitive verb*
**1 a :** to have relation or connection **:** RELATE **b :** to direct attention usually by clear and specific mention ⟨no one *referred* to yesterday's quarrel⟩
**2 :** to have recourse **:** glance briefly ⟨*referred* frequently to his notes while speaking⟩
— **re·fer·able** \'re-f(ə-)rə-bəl, ri-'fər-ə-\ *adjective*
— **re·fer·rer** \ri-'fər-ər\ *noun*

¹**ref·er·ee** \,re-fə-'rē\ *noun* (1621)
**1 :** one to whom a thing is referred: as **a :** a person to whom a legal matter if referred for investigation and report or for settlement **b :** a person who reviews a paper and especially a technical paper and recommends that it should or should not be published **c** *chiefly British* **:** REFERENCE 4a
**2 :** a sports official usually having final authority in administering a game

²**referee** *verb* **-eed; -ee·ing** (1889)
*transitive verb*
**1 :** to conduct (as a match or game) as referee
**2 a :** to arbitrate (as a legal matter) as a judge or third party **b :** to review (as a technical paper) before publication
*intransitive verb*
**:** to act as a referee

¹**ref·er·ence** \'re-fərn(t)s, 're-f(ə-)rən(t)s\ *noun* (1589)
**1 :** the act of referring or consulting
**2 :** a bearing on a matter **:** RELATION ⟨in *reference* to your recent letter⟩
**3 :** something that refers: as **a :** ALLUSION, MENTION **b :** something (as a sign or indication) that refers a reader or consulter to another source of information (as a book or pas-

sage) **c :** consultation of sources of information
**4 :** one referred to or consulted: as **a :** a person to whom inquiries as to character or ability can be made **b :** a statement of the qualifications of a person seeking employment or appointment given by someone familiar with the person **c** (1) **:** a source of information (as a book or passage) to which a reader or consulter is referred (2) **:** a work (as a dictionary or encyclopedia) containing useful facts or information **d :** DENOTATION, MEANING

²**reference** *adjective* (1856)
**:** used or usable for reference; *especially* **:** constituting a standard for measuring or constructing

³**reference** *transitive verb* **-enced; -enc·ing** (1891)
**1 a :** to supply with references **b :** to cite in or as a reference
**2 :** to put in a form (as a table) adapted to easy reference

**reference mark** *noun* (1856)
**:** a conventional mark (as *, †, or ‡) placed in written or printed text to direct the reader's attention especially to a footnote

**ref·er·en·dum** \,re-fə-'ren-dəm\ *noun, plural* **-da** \-də\ *or* **-dums** [New Latin, from Latin, neuter of *referendus*, gerundive of *referre* to refer] (1847)
**1 a :** the principle or practice of submitting to popular vote a measure passed on or proposed by a legislative body or by popular initiative **b :** a vote on a measure so submitted
**2 :** a diplomatic agent's note asking for government instructions

**ref·er·ent** \'re-f(ə-)rənt\ *noun* [Latin *referent-, referens*, present participle of *referre*] (1844)
**:** one that refers or is referred to; *especially* **:** the thing that a symbol (as a word or sign) stands for
— **referent** *adjective*

**ref·er·en·tial** \,re-fə-'ren(t)-shəl\ *adjective* (1660)
**:** of, containing, or constituting a reference
— **ref·er·en·tial·i·ty** \-,ren(t)-shē-'a-lə-tē\ *noun*
— **ref·er·en·tial·ly** \-'ren(t)-sh(ə-)lē\ *adverb*

**re·fer·ral** \ri-'fər-əl\ *noun* (1927)
**1 :** the act, action, or an instance of referring ⟨gave the patient a *referral* to a specialist⟩
**2 :** one that is referred

¹**re·fill** \(,)rē-'fil\ (1681)
*transitive verb*
**:** to fill again **:** REPLENISH
*intransitive verb*
**:** to become filled again
— **re·fill·able** \-'fi-lə-bəl\ *adjective*

²**re·fill** \'rē-,fil\ *noun* (1886)
**1 :** a product or a container and a product used to refill the exhausted supply of a device
**2 :** something provided again; *especially* **:** a second or later filling of a medical prescription

**re·fi·nance** \,rē-fə-'nan(t)s, (,)rē-'fī-, ,rē-(,)fī-'\ (1908)
*transitive verb*
**:** to renew or reorganize the financing of
*intransitive verb*
**:** to finance something anew

**re·fine** \ri-'fīn\ *verb* **re·fined; re·fin·ing** (1582)
*transitive verb*
**1 :** to free (as metal, sugar, or oil) from impurities or unwanted material
**2 :** to free from moral imperfection **:** ELEVATE
**3 :** to improve or perfect by pruning or polishing ⟨*refine* a poetic style⟩
**4 :** to reduce in vigor or intensity
**5 :** to free from what is coarse, vulgar, or uncouth
*intransitive verb*
**1 :** to become pure or perfected
**2 :** to make improvement by introducing subtleties or distinctions

— **re·fin·er** *noun*

**re·fined** \ri-'fīnd\ *adjective* (1588)
**1 :** FASTIDIOUS, CULTIVATED
**2 :** free from impurities
**3 :** PRECISE, EXACT ⟨a *refined* test for radioactivity⟩

**re·fine·ment** \ri-'fīn-mənt\ *noun* (circa 1611)
**1 :** the action or process of refining
**2 :** the quality or state of being refined **:** CULTIVATION
**3 a :** a refined feature or method **b :** a highly refined distinction **:** SUBTLETY **c :** a contrivance or device intended to improve or perfect

**re·fin·ery** \ri-'fī-nə-rē, -'fīn-rē\ *noun, plural* **-er·ies** (circa 1741)
**:** a building and equipment for refining or processing (as oil or sugar)

**re·fin·ish** \(,)rē-'fi-nish\ (1931)
*transitive verb*
**:** to give (as furniture) a new surface
*intransitive verb*
**:** to refinish furniture
— **re·fin·ish·er** *noun*

¹**re·fit** \(,)rē-'fit\ (1666)
*transitive verb*
**:** to fit out or supply again
*intransitive verb*
**:** to obtain repairs or fresh supplies or equipment

²**re·fit** \'rē-,fit, (,)rē-'\ *noun* (1799)
**:** the action of refitting; *especially* **:** a refitting and renovating of a ship

**re·fla·tion** \(,)rē-'flā-shən\ *noun* [*re-* + *-flation* (as in *deflation*)] (1932)
**:** restoration of deflated prices to a desirable level
— **re·flate** \(,)rē-'flāt\ *verb*
— **re·fla·tion·ary** \-shə-,ner-ē\ *adjective*

**re·flect** \ri-'flekt\ *verb* [Middle English, from Latin *reflectere* to bend back, from *re-* + *flectere* to bend] (15th century)
*transitive verb*
**1** *archaic* **:** to turn into or away from a course **:** DEFLECT
**2 :** to prevent passage of and cause to change direction ⟨a mirror *reflects* light⟩
**3 :** to bend or fold back
**4 :** to give back or exhibit as an image, likeness, or outline **:** MIRROR ⟨the clouds were *reflected* in the water⟩
**5 :** to bring or cast as a result ⟨his attitude *reflects* little credit on his judgment⟩
**6 :** to make manifest or apparent **:** SHOW ⟨the pulse *reflects* the condition of the heart⟩
**7 :** REALIZE, CONSIDER
*intransitive verb*
**1 :** to throw back light or sound
**2 a :** to think quietly and calmly **b :** to express a thought or opinion resulting from reflection
**3 a :** to tend to bring reproach or discredit ⟨an investigation that *reflects* on all the members of the department⟩ **b :** to bring about a specified appearance or characterization ⟨an act which *reflects* well on him⟩ **c :** to have a bearing or influence
*synonym* see THINK

**re·flec·tance** \ri-'flek-tən(t)s\ *noun* (1926)
**:** the fraction of the total radiant flux incident upon a surface that is reflected and that varies according to the wavelength distribution of the incident radiation — called also *re·flec·tiv·i·ty* \,rē-,flek-'ti-və-tē, ri-\

**reflecting telescope** *noun* (circa 1704)
**:** REFLECTOR 2

**re·flec·tion** \ri-'flek-shən\ *noun* [Middle English, alteration of *reflexion*, from Late Latin *reflexion-, reflexio* act of bending back, from Latin *reflectere*] (14th century)
**1 :** an instance of reflecting; *especially* **:** the return of light or sound waves from a surface

---

\ə\ abut \ᵊ\ kitten \ər\ further \a\ ash \ā\ ace
\ä\ mop, mar \aù\ out \ch\ chin \e\ bet \ē\ easy
\g\ go \i\ hit \ī\ ice \j\ job \ŋ\ sing \ō\ go
\ò\ law \òi\ boy \th\ thin \th\ the \ü\ loot \ù\ foot
\y\ yet \zh\ vision *see also* Guide to Pronunciation

**2 :** the production of an image by or as if by a mirror
**3 a :** the action of bending or folding back **b :** a reflected part **:** FOLD
**4 :** something produced by reflecting: as **a :** an image given back by a reflecting surface **b :** an effect produced by an influence ⟨the high crime rate is a *reflection* of our violent society⟩
**5 :** an often obscure or indirect criticism **:** REPROACH ⟨a *reflection* on his character⟩
**6 :** a thought, idea, or opinion formed or a remark made as a result of meditation
**7 :** consideration of some subject matter, idea, or purpose
**8** *obsolete* **:** turning back **:** RETURN
**9 a :** a transformation of a figure in which each point is replaced by a point symmetric with respect to a line or plane **b :** a transformation that involves reflection in more than one axis of a rectangular coordinate system
— **re·flec·tion·al** \-shnəl, -shə-nᵊl\ *adjective*

**re·flec·tive** \ri-'flek-tiv\ *adjective* (1627)
**1 :** capable of reflecting light, images, or sound waves
**2 :** marked by reflection **:** THOUGHTFUL, DELIBERATIVE
**3 :** of, relating to, or caused by reflection ⟨*reflective* glare⟩
**4 :** REFLEXIVE 3
— **re·flec·tive·ly** *adverb*
— **re·flec·tive·ness** *noun*

**re·flec·tom·e·ter** \ˌrē-ˌflek-'tä-mə-tər, ˌri-\ *noun* (1891)
**:** a device for measuring the reflectance of radiant energy (as light)
— **re·flec·tom·e·try** \-mə-trē\ *noun*

**re·flec·tor** \ri-'flek-tər\ *noun* (1665)
**1 :** one that reflects; *especially* **:** a polished surface for reflecting light or other radiation
**2 :** a telescope in which the principal focusing element is a mirror

**re·flec·tor·ize** \-tə-ˌrīz\ *transitive verb* **-ized; -iz·ing** (1940)
**1 :** to make reflecting
**2 :** to provide with reflectors

¹**re·flex** \'rē-ˌfleks\ *noun* [Latin *reflexus,* past participle of *reflectere* to reflect] (1508)
**1 a :** reflected heat, light, or color **b :** a mirrored image **c :** a copy exact in essential or peculiar features
**2 a :** an automatic and often inborn response to a stimulus that involves a nerve impulse passing inward from a receptor to a nerve center and thence outward to an effector (as a muscle or gland) without reaching the level of consciousness — compare HABIT **b :** the process that culminates in a reflex and comprises reception, transmission, and reaction — called also *reflex action* **c** *plural* **:** the power of acting or responding with adequate speed **d :** a way of thinking or behaving
**3 :** a linguistic element (as a word or sound) or system (as writing) that is derived from a prior and especially an older element or system ⟨*boat* is the *reflex* of Old English *bāt*⟩

²**reflex** *adjective* [Latin *reflexus*] (1649)
**1 :** directed back on the mind or its operations **:** INTROSPECTIVE
**2 :** bent, turned, or directed back **:** REFLECTED ⟨a stem with *reflex* leaves⟩
**3 :** produced or carried out in reaction, resistance, or return
**4** *of an angle* **:** being between 180° and 360°
**5 :** of, relating to, or produced by a reflex without intervention of consciousness
— **re·flex·ly** *adverb*

**reflex arc** *noun* (1882)
**:** the complete nervous path involved in a reflex

**re·flexed** \'rē-ˌflekst, ri-'\ *adjective* [Latin *reflexus* + English ¹*-ed*] (1733)
**:** bent or curved backward or downward ⟨*reflexed* petals⟩ ⟨*reflexed* leaves⟩

**re·flex·ion** *chiefly British variant of* REFLECTION

¹**re·flex·ive** \ri-'flek-siv\ *adjective* [Medieval Latin *reflexivus,* from Latin *reflexus*] (1640)
**1 a :** directed or turned back on itself **b :** marked by or capable of reflection **:** REFLECTIVE
**2 :** of, relating to, characterized by, or being a relation that exists between an entity and itself ⟨the relation "is equal to" is *reflexive* but the relation "is the father of" is not⟩
**3 :** of, relating to, or constituting an action (as in "he perjured himself") directed back on the agent or the grammatical subject
**4 :** characterized by habitual and unthinking behavior
— **re·flex·ive·ly** *adverb*
— **re·flex·ive·ness** *noun*
— **re·flex·iv·i·ty** \ˌrē-ˌflek-'si-və-tē, ri-\ *noun*

²**reflexive** *noun* (1866)
**:** REFLEXIVE PRONOUN

**reflexive pronoun** *noun* (1867)
**:** a pronoun referring to the subject of the sentence, clause, or verbal phrase in which it stands; *specifically* **:** a personal pronoun compounded with *-self*

**re·flex·ol·o·gy** \ˌrē-ˌflek-'sä-lə-jē\ *noun* [International Scientific Vocabulary] (1923)
**1 :** the study and interpretation of behavior in terms of simple and complex reflexes
**2 :** massage of the hands or feet based on the belief that pressure applied to specific points on these extremities benefits other parts of the body

**re·flow** \ˌ(ˌ)rē-'flō\ *intransitive verb* (14th century)
**1 :** to flow back **:** EBB
**2 :** to flow in again
— **re·flow** \'rē-ˌflō\ *noun*

**ref·lu·ence** \'re-ˌflü-ən(t)s, re-'flü-\ *noun* (15th century)
*archaic* **:** REFLUX 1

**ref·lu·ent** \-ənt\ *adjective* [Middle English, from Latin *refluent-, refluens,* present participle of *refluere* to flow back, from *re-* + *fluere* to flow — more at FLUID] (15th century)
**:** flowing back

¹**re·flux** \'rē-ˌfləks\ *noun* [Middle English, from Medieval Latin *refluxus,* from Latin *re-* + *fluxus* flow — more at FLUX] (15th century)
**1 :** a flowing back **:** EBB
**2 :** a process of refluxing or condition of being refluxed

²**reflux** \ri-'fləks, 'rē-\ *transitive verb* (1926)
**:** to cause to flow back or return; *especially* **:** to heat so that the vapors formed condense and return to be heated again

**re·fo·cus** \ˌ(ˌ)rē-'fō-kəs\ (circa 1865)
*transitive verb*
**1 :** to focus again
**2 :** to change the emphasis or direction of ⟨had *refocused* his life⟩
*intransitive verb*
**1 :** to focus something again
**2 :** to change emphasis or direction

**re·for·es·ta·tion** \ˌ(ˌ)rē-ˌfȯr-ə-'stā-shən, -ˌfär-\ *noun* (1887)
**:** the action of renewing forest cover by planting seeds or young trees
— **re·for·est** \ˌ(ˌ)rē-'fȯr-əst, -'fär-\ *transitive verb*

¹**re·form** \ri-'fȯrm\ *verb* [Middle English, from Middle French *reformer,* from Latin *reformare,* from *re-* + *formare* to form, from *forma* form] (14th century)
*transitive verb*
**1 a :** to put or change into an improved form or condition **b :** to amend or improve by change of form or removal of faults or abuses
**2 :** to put an end to (an evil) by enforcing or introducing a better method or course of action
**3 :** to induce or cause to abandon evil ways ⟨*reform* a drunkard⟩

**4 a :** to subject (hydrocarbons) to cracking **b :** to produce (as gasoline or gas) by cracking
*intransitive verb*
**:** to become changed for the better
**synonym** *see* CORRECT
— **re·form·abil·i·ty** \-ˌfȯr-mə-'bi-lə-tē\ *noun*
— **re·form·able** \-'fȯr-mə-bəl\ *adjective*

²**reform** *noun* (1663)
**1 :** amendment of what is defective, vicious, corrupt, or depraved
**2 :** a removal or correction of an abuse, a wrong, or errors
**3** *capitalized* **:** REFORM JUDAISM

³**reform** *adjective* (1819)
**:** relating to or favoring reform

**re–form** \ˌ(ˌ)rē-'fȯrm\ (14th century)
*transitive verb*
**:** to form again
*intransitive verb*
**:** to take form again ⟨the ice *re-formed* on the lake⟩

**re·for·mate** \ri-'fȯr-ˌmāt, -mət\ *noun* (1949)
**:** a product of hydrocarbon reforming

**ref·or·ma·tion** \ˌre-fər-'mā-shən\ *noun* (15th century)
**1 :** the act of reforming **:** the state of being reformed
**2** *capitalized* **:** a 16th century religious movement marked ultimately by rejection or modification of some Roman Catholic doctrine and practice and establishment of the Protestant churches
— **ref·or·ma·tion·al** \-shnəl, -shə-nᵊl\ *adjective*

**re·for·ma·tive** \ri-'fȯr-mə-tiv\ *adjective* (1593)
**:** intended or tending to reform

¹**re·for·ma·to·ry** \ri-'fȯr-mə-ˌtōr-ē, -ˌtȯr-\ *adjective* (1589)
**:** REFORMATIVE

²**reformatory** *noun, plural* **-ries** (1834)
**:** a penal institution to which especially young or first offenders are committed for training and reformation

**re·formed** *adjective* (1563)
**1 :** changed for the better
**2** *capitalized* **:** PROTESTANT; *specifically* **:** of or relating to the chiefly Calvinist Protestant churches formed in various continental European countries

**reformed spelling** *noun* (circa 1934)
**:** any of several methods of spelling English words that use letters with more phonetic consistency than conventional spelling and that usually discard some silent letters (as in *pedagog* for *pedagogue*)

**re·form·er** \ri-'fȯr-mər\ *noun* (1548)
**1 :** one that works for or urges reform
**2** *capitalized* **:** a leader of the Protestant Reformation
**3 :** an apparatus for cracking oils or gases to form specialized products

**re·form·ism** \ri-'fȯr-ˌmi-zəm\ *noun* (1904)
**:** a doctrine, policy, or movement of reform
— **re·form·ist** \-mist\ *noun or adjective*

**Reform Judaism** *noun* (circa 1905)
**:** Judaism marked by a liberal approach in nonobservance of much legal tradition regarded as irrelevant to the present and in shortening and simplification of traditional ritual — compare CONSERVATIVE JUDAISM, ORTHODOX JUDAISM

**reform school** *noun* (circa 1859)
**:** a reformatory for boys or girls

**re·fract** \ri-'frakt\ *transitive verb* [Latin *refractus,* past participle of *refringere* to break open, break up, from *re-* + *frangere* to break — more at BREAK] (1612)
**1 a :** to subject (as a ray of light) to refraction **b :** to alter or distort as if by refraction ⟨to *refract* that familiar world through the mind and heart of a romantic . . . woman —Anton Myrer⟩
**2 :** to determine the refracting power of

**re·frac·tile** \-'frak-t³l, -₁tīl\ *adjective* (circa 1849)
: capable of refracting : REFRACTIVE
**refracting telescope** *noun* (1764)
: REFRACTOR
**re·frac·tion** \ri-'frak-shən\ *noun* (1603)
**1** : deflection from a straight path undergone by a light ray or energy wave in passing obliquely from one medium (as air) into another (as glass) in which its velocity is different
**2** : the change in the apparent position of a celestial body due to bending of the light rays emanating from it as they pass through the atmosphere; *also*

refraction 1: *a* light ray, *b* reflected ray, *c* refracted ray

: the correction to be applied to the apparent position of a body because of this bending
**3** : the action of distorting an image by viewing through a medium; *also* : an instance of this
**re·frac·tive** \ri-'frak-tiv\ *adjective* (1673)
**1** : having power to refract
**2** : relating or due to refraction
— **re·frac·tive·ly** *adverb*
— **re·frac·tive·ness** *noun*
— **re·frac·tiv·i·ty** \₁rē-₁frak-'ti-və-tē, ri-\ *noun*
**refractive index** *noun* (1839)
: INDEX OF REFRACTION
**re·frac·tom·e·ter** \₁rē-₁frak-'tä-mə-tər, ri-\ *noun* [International Scientific Vocabulary] (circa 1859)
: an instrument for measuring indices of refraction
— **re·frac·to·met·ric** \ri-₁frak-tə-'me-trik\ *adjective*
— **re·frac·tom·e·try** \₁rē-₁frak-'tä-mə-trē, ri-\ *noun*
**re·frac·tor** \ri-'frak-tər\ *noun* (1769)
: a telescope whose principal focusing element is a lens
¹**re·frac·to·ry** \ri-'frak-t(ə-)rē\ *adjective* [alteration of *refractary,* from Latin *refractarius,* irregular from *refragari* to oppose, from *re-* + *-fragari* (as in *suffragari* to support with one's vote)] (1606)
**1** : resisting control or authority : STUBBORN, UNMANAGEABLE
**2 a** : resistant to treatment or cure ⟨a *refractory* lesion⟩ **b** : unresponsive to stimulus **c** : IMMUNE, INSUSCEPTIBLE ⟨after recovery they were *refractory* to infection⟩
**3** : difficult to fuse, corrode, or draw out; *especially* : capable of enduring high temperature
***synonym*** see UNRULY
— **re·frac·to·ri·ly** \-t(ə-)rə-lē; ₁rē-₁frak-'tōr-ə-lē, ri-, -'tòr-\ *adverb*
— **re·frac·to·ri·ness** \ri-'frak-t(ə-)rē-nəs\ *noun*
²**refractory** *noun, plural* **-ries** (1627)
: a refractory person or thing; *especially* : a heat-resisting ceramic material
**refractory period** *noun* (circa 1880)
: the brief period immediately following the response especially of a muscle or nerve before it recovers the capacity to make a second response — called also *refractory phase*
¹**re·frain** \ri-'frān\ *verb* [Middle English *refreynen,* from Middle French *refreiner, refrener,* from Latin *refrenare,* from *re-* + *frenum* bridle — more at FRENUM] (14th century)
*transitive verb*
*archaic* : CURB, RESTRAIN
*intransitive verb*
: to keep oneself from doing, feeling, or indulging in something and especially from following a passing impulse
— **re·frain·ment** \-mənt\ *noun*

²**refrain** *noun* [Middle English *refreyn,* from Middle French *refrain,* from *refraindre, refreindre* to resound, from Latin *refringere* to break up] (14th century)
: a regularly recurring phrase or verse especially at the end of each stanza or division of a poem or song : CHORUS; *also* : the musical setting of a refrain
**re·fran·gi·ble** \ri-'fran-jə-bəl\ *adjective* [irregular from Latin *refringere* to break up] (1673)
: capable of being refracted
— **re·fran·gi·bil·i·ty** \-₁fran-jə-'bi-lə-tē\ *noun*
— **re·fran·gi·ble·ness** \-'fran-jə-bəl-nəs\ *noun*
**re·fresh** \ri-'fresh\ *verb* [Middle English *refresshen,* from Middle French *refreschir,* from Old French, from *re-* + *freis* fresh — more at FRESH] (14th century)
*transitive verb*
**1** : to restore strength and animation to : REVIVE
**2** : to freshen up : RENOVATE
**3 a** : to restore or maintain by renewing supply : REPLENISH **b** : AROUSE, STIMULATE ⟨let me *refresh* your memory⟩
**4** : to run water over or restore water to
*intransitive verb*
**1** : to become refreshed
**2** : to take refreshment
**3** : to lay in fresh provisions
***synonym*** see RENEW
**re·fresh·en** \ri-'fre-shən, ₁rē-\ *transitive verb* [*re-* + *freshen*] (1782)
: REFRESH
**re·fresh·er** \ri-'fre-shər\ *noun* (15th century)
**1** : something (as a drink) that refreshes
**2** : REMINDER
**3** : review or instruction designed especially to keep one abreast of professional developments ⟨*refresher* course⟩
**re·fresh·ing** \-shiŋ\ *adjective* (circa 1580)
: serving to refresh; *especially* : agreeably stimulating because of freshness or newness
— **re·fresh·ing·ly** \-shiŋ-lē\ *adverb*
**re·fresh·ment** \ri-'fresh-mənt\ *noun* (14th century)
**1** : the act of refreshing : the state of being refreshed
**2 a** : something (as food or drink) that refreshes **b** *plural* (1) : a light meal (2) : assorted light foods
**re·fried beans** \'rē-₁frīd-\ *noun plural* (1957)
: beans cooked with seasonings, fried, then mashed and fried again
¹**re·frig·er·ant** \ri-'fri-jə-rənt, -'frij-rənt\ *adjective* (1599)
: allaying heat or fever
²**refrigerant** *noun* (1676)
: a refrigerant agent or agency: as **a** : a medication for reducing body heat **b** : a substance used in refrigeration
**re·frig·er·ate** \ri-'fri-jə-₁rāt\ *transitive verb* **-at·ed; -at·ing** [Latin *refrigeratus,* past participle of *refrigerare,* from *re-* + *frigerare* to cool, from *frigor-, frigus* cold — more at FRIGID] (1534)
: to make or keep cold or cool; *specifically* : to freeze or chill (as food) for preservation
— **re·frig·er·a·tion** \-₁fri-jə-'rā-shən\ *noun*
**re·frig·er·a·tor** \ri-'fri-jə-₁rā-tər\ *noun* (1803)
: something that refrigerates; *especially* : a room or appliance for keeping food or other items cool
**reft** *past of* REAVE
**re·fu·el** \(₁)rē-'fyü(-ə)l\ (1811)
*transitive verb*
: to provide with additional fuel
*intransitive verb*
: to take on additional fuel
¹**ref·uge** \'re-(₁)fyüj *also* -(₁)fyüzh\ *noun* [Middle English, from Middle French, from Latin *refugium,* from *refugere* to escape, from *re-* + *fugere* to flee — more at FUGITIVE] (14th century)

**1** : shelter or protection from danger or distress
**2** : a place that provides shelter or protection
**3** : something to which one has recourse in difficulty
²**refuge** *verb* **ref·uged; ref·ug·ing** (1594)
*transitive verb*
: to give refuge to
*intransitive verb*
: to seek or take refuge
**ref·u·gee** \₁re-fyu-'jē, 're-fyu-₁\ *noun* [French *réfugié,* past participle of (*se*) *réfugier* to take refuge, from Latin *refugium*] (1685)
: one that flees; *especially* : a person who flees to a foreign country or power to escape danger or persecution
— **ref·u·gee·ism** \-₁i-zəm\ *noun*
**re·fu·gi·um** \ri-'fyü-jē-əm\ *noun, plural* **-gia** \-jē-ə\ [New Latin, from Latin, refuge] (1943)
: an area of relatively unaltered climate that is inhabited by plants and animals during a period of continental climatic change (as a glaciation) and remains as a center of relict forms from which a new dispersion and speciation may take place after climatic readjustment
**re·ful·gence** \ri-'fùl-jən(t)s, -'fəl-\ *noun* [Latin *refulgentia,* from *refulgent-, refulgens,* present participle of *refulgēre* to shine brightly, from *re-* + *fulgēre* to shine — more at FULGENT] (1634)
: a radiant or resplendent quality or state : BRILLIANCE
— **re·ful·gent** \-jənt\ *adjective*
¹**re·fund** \ri-'fənd, 'rē-₁\ *transitive verb* [Middle English, from Middle French & Latin; Middle French *refonder,* from Latin *refundere,* literally, to pour back, from *re-* + *fundere* to pour — more at FOUND] (15th century)
**1** : to give or put back
**2** : to return (money) in restitution, repayment, or balancing of accounts
— **re·fund·abil·i·ty** \ri-₁fən-də-'bi-lə-tē, (₁)rē-\ *noun*
— **re·fund·able** \-'fən-də-bəl\ *adjective*
²**re·fund** \'rē-₁fənd\ *noun* (1866)
**1** : the act of refunding
**2** : a sum refunded
³**refund** \(₁)rē-'fənd\ *transitive verb* [*re-* + ²*fund*] (circa 1860)
: to fund again
**re·fur·bish** \ri-'fər-bish\ *transitive verb* (1611)
: to brighten or freshen up : RENOVATE
— **re·fur·bish·er** *noun*
— **re·fur·bish·ment** \-bish-mənt\ *noun*
**re·fus·al** \ri-'fyü-zəl\ *noun* (15th century)
**1** : the act of refusing or denying
**2** : the opportunity or right of refusing or taking before others
¹**re·fuse** \ri-'fyüz\ *verb* **re·fused; re·fus·ing** [Middle English, from Middle French *refuser,* from (assumed) Vulgar Latin *refusare,* perhaps blend of Latin *refutare* to refute and *recusare* to demur — more at RECUSE] (14th century)
*transitive verb*
**1** : to express oneself as unwilling to accept ⟨*refuse* a gift⟩ ⟨*refuse* a promotion⟩
**2 a** : to show or express unwillingness to do or comply with ⟨*refused* to answer the question⟩ **b** : DENY ⟨they were *refused* admittance to the game⟩
**3** *obsolete* : GIVE UP, RENOUNCE
**4** *of a horse* : to decline to jump or leap over
*intransitive verb*
: to withhold acceptance, compliance, or permission
***synonym*** see DECLINE
— **re·fus·er** *noun*

\ə\ abut \³\ kitten \ər\ further \a\ ash \ā\ ace \ä\ mop, mar \aú\ out \ch\ chin \e\ bet \ē\ easy \g\ go \i\ hit \ī\ ice \j\ job \ŋ\ sing \ō\ go \ò\ law \òi\ boy \th\ thin \t͟h\ the \ü\ loot \ú\ foot \y\ yet \zh\ vision *see also* Guide to Pronunciation

²**ref·use** \'re-ˌfyüs, -ˌfyüz\ noun [Middle English, from Middle French refus rejection, from Old French, from refuser] (14th century)
**1 :** the worthless or useless part of something **:** LEAVINGS
**2 :** TRASH, GARBAGE

³**ref·use** \'re-ˌfyüs, -ˌfyüz\ adjective (15th century)
**:** thrown aside or left as worthless

**re·fuse·nik** also **re·fus·nik** \ri-'fyüz-(ˌ)nik\ noun [part translation of Russian otkaznik, from otkaz refusal] (1974)
**:** a Soviet citizen and especially a Jew refused permission to emigrate

**ref·u·ta·tion** \ˌre-fyu̇-'tā-shən\ noun (circa 1548)
**:** the act or process of refuting

**re·fute** \ri-'fyüt\ transitive verb **re·fut·ed;** **re·fut·ing** [Latin refutare to check, suppress, refute] (1597)
**1 :** to prove wrong by argument or evidence **:** show to be false or erroneous
**2 :** to deny the truth or accuracy of ⟨refuted the allegations⟩
— **re·fut·able** \-'fyü-tə-bəl\ adjective
— **re·fut·ably** \-blē\ adverb
— **re·fut·er** noun

**reg** \'reg\ noun [by shortening] (circa 1925)
**:** REGULATION ⟨federal regs⟩

**re·gal** \'rē-gəl\ adjective [Middle English, from Middle French or Latin; Middle French, from Latin regalis — more at ROYAL] (14th century)
**1 :** of, relating to, or suitable for a king
**2 :** of notable excellence or magnificence **:** SPLENDID
— **re·gal·i·ty** \ri-'ga-lə-tē\ noun
— **re·gal·ly** \'rē-gə-lē\ adverb

¹**re·gale** \ri-'gā(ə)l\ verb **re·galed;** **re·gal·ing** [French régaler, from Middle French, from regale, noun] (circa 1656)
transitive verb
**1 :** to entertain sumptuously **:** feast with delicacies
**2 :** to give pleasure or amusement to ⟨regaled us with tall tales⟩
intransitive verb
**:** to feast oneself **:** FEED

²**regale** noun [French régal, from Middle French regale, from re- + galer to have a good time — more at GALLANT] (1670)
**1 :** a sumptuous feast
**2 :** a choice piece especially of food

**re·ga·lia** \ri-'gāl-yə\ noun plural [Medieval Latin, from Latin, neuter plural of regalis] (circa 1540)
**1 :** royal rights or prerogatives
**2 a :** the emblems, symbols, or paraphernalia indicative of royalty **b :** decorations or insignia indicative of an office or membership
**3 :** special dress; especially **:** FINERY

¹**re·gard** \ri-'gärd\ noun [Middle English, from Middle French, from Old French, from regarder] (14th century)
**1** archaic **:** APPEARANCE
**2 a :** ATTENTION, CONSIDERATION ⟨due regard should be given to all facets of the question⟩ **b :** a protective interest **:** CARE ⟨ought to have more regard for his health⟩
**3 :** LOOK, GAZE
**4 a :** the worth or estimation in which something or someone is held ⟨a man of small regard⟩ **b** (1) **:** a feeling of respect and affection **:** ESTEEM ⟨his hard work won him the regard of his colleagues⟩ (2) plural **:** friendly greetings implying such feeling ⟨give him my regards⟩
**5 :** a basis of action or opinion **:** MOTIVE
**6 :** an aspect to be taken into consideration **:** RESPECT ⟨is a small school, and is fortunate in this regard⟩
**7** obsolete **:** INTENTION
— **in regard to :** with respect to **:** CONCERNING
— **with regard to :** in regard to

²**regard** verb [Middle English, from Middle French regarder to look back at, regard, from Old French, from re- + garder to guard, look at — more at GUARD] (14th century)
transitive verb
**1 :** to consider and appraise usually from a particular point of view ⟨is highly regarded as a mechanic⟩
**2 :** to pay attention to **:** take into consideration or account
**3 a :** to show respect or consideration for **b :** to hold in high esteem
**4 :** to look at
**5** archaic **:** to relate to
intransitive verb
**1 :** to look attentively **:** GAZE
**2 :** to pay attention **:** HEED ☆
— **as regards :** with respect to **:** CONCERNING

**re·gar·dant** \ri-'gär-dᵊnt\ adjective [Middle English regardand, from Middle French regardant, present participle of regarder] (15th century)
**:** looking backward over the shoulder — used of a heraldic animal

**re·gard·ful** \ri-'gärd-fəl\ adjective (circa 1586)
**1 :** HEEDFUL, OBSERVANT
**2 :** full or expressive of regard or respect **:** RESPECTFUL
— **re·gard·ful·ly** \-fə-lē\ adverb
— **re·gard·ful·ness** noun

**re·gard·ing** preposition (1866)
**:** with respect to **:** CONCERNING

¹**re·gard·less** \ri-'gärd-ləs\ adjective (1591)
**:** HEEDLESS, CARELESS
— **re·gard·less·ly** adverb
— **re·gard·less·ness** noun

²**regardless** adverb (1872)
**:** despite everything ⟨went ahead with their plans regardless⟩
**usage** SEE IRREGARDLESS

**regardless of** preposition (1784)
**:** without taking into account ⟨accepts all regardless of age⟩; also **:** in spite of ⟨regardless of our mistakes⟩

**re·gat·ta** \ri-'gä-tə, -'ga-\ noun [Italian regata] (1652)
**:** a rowing, speedboat, or sailing race or a series of such races

**re·gen·cy** \'rē-jən(t)-sē\ noun, plural **-cies** (15th century)
**1 :** the office, jurisdiction, or government of a regent or body of regents
**2 :** a body of regents
**3 :** the period of rule of a regent or body of regents

**Regency** adjective (1880)
**:** of, relating to, or characteristic of the styles of George IV's regency as Prince of Wales during the period 1811–20

**re·gen·er·a·cy** \ri-'je-nə-rə-sē, -'jen-rə-\ noun (1626)
**:** the state of being regenerated

¹**re·gen·er·ate** \-rət\ adjective [Middle English regenerat, from Latin regeneratus, past participle of regenerare to regenerate, from re- + generare to beget — more at GENERATE] (15th century)
**1 :** formed or created again
**2 :** spiritually reborn or converted
**3 :** restored to a better, higher, or more worthy state
— **re·gen·er·ate·ly** adverb
— **re·gen·er·ate·ness** noun

²**re·gen·er·ate** \ri-'je-nə-ˌrāt\ (1541)
intransitive verb
**1 :** to become formed again
**2 :** to become regenerate **:** REFORM
**3 :** to undergo regeneration
transitive verb
**1 a :** to subject to spiritual regeneration **b :** to change radically and for the better
**2 a :** to generate or produce anew; especially **:** to replace (a body part) by a new growth of tissue **b :** to produce again chemically sometimes in a physically changed form
**3 :** to restore to original strength or properties

— **re·gen·er·a·ble** \-'je-nə-rə-bəl, -'jen-rə-\ adjective

³**re·gen·er·ate** \same as ¹\ noun (circa 1569)
**:** one that is regenerated: as **a :** an individual who is spiritually reborn **b** (1) **:** an organism that has undergone regeneration (2) **:** a regenerated body part

**regenerated cellulose** noun (1904)
**:** cellulose obtained in a changed form by chemical treatment (as of a cellulose solution or derivative)

**re·gen·er·a·tion** \ri-ˌje-nə-'rā-shən, ˌrē-\ noun (14th century)
**1 :** an act or the process of regenerating **:** the state of being regenerated
**2 :** spiritual renewal or revival
**3 :** renewal or restoration of a body or bodily part after injury or as a normal process
**4 :** utilization by special devices of heat or other products that would ordinarily be lost

**re·gen·er·a·tive** \ri-'je-nə-ˌrā-tiv, -'je-nə-rə-, -'jen-rə-\ adjective (14th century)
**1 :** of, relating to, or marked by regeneration
**2 :** tending to regenerate

**re·gen·er·a·tor** \ri-'je-nə-ˌrā-tər\ noun (circa 1550)
**1 :** one that regenerates
**2 :** a device used especially with hot-air engines or gas furnaces in which incoming air or gas is heated by contact with masses (as of brick) previously heated by outgoing hot air or gas

**re·gent** \'rē-jənt\ noun [Middle English, from Middle French or Medieval Latin; Middle French, from Medieval Latin regent-, regens, from present participle of regere to rule — more at RIGHT] (15th century)
**1 :** one who governs a kingdom in the minority, absence, or disability of the sovereign
**2 :** one who rules or reigns **:** GOVERNOR
**3 :** a member of a governing board (as of a state university)
— **regent** adjective
— **re·gent·al** \-jən-tᵊl\ adjective

**reg·gae** \'re-(ˌ)gā, 'rā-\ noun [origin unknown] (1968)
**:** popular music of Jamaican origin that combines native styles with elements of rock and soul music and is performed at moderate tempos with the accent on the offbeat

**reg·i·cide** \'re-jə-ˌsīd\ noun [Latin reg-, rex king + English -cide — more at ROYAL] (circa 1548)
**1 :** one who kills a king
**2 :** the killing of a king
— **reg·i·ci·dal** \ˌre-jə-'sī-dᵊl\ adjective

**re·gime** also **ré·gime** \rā-'zhēm, ri- also ri-'jēm\ noun [French régime, from Latin regimin-, regimen] (1776)
**1 a :** REGIMEN 1 **b :** a regular pattern of occurrence or action (as of seasonal rainfall) **c :** the characteristic behavior or orderly procedure of a natural phenomenon or process
**2 a :** mode of rule or management **b :** a form of government ⟨a socialist regime⟩ **c :** a government in power ⟨predicted that the new regime would fall⟩ **d :** a period of rule

---

☆ **SYNONYMS**
**Regard, respect, esteem, admire** mean to recognize the worth of a person or thing. REGARD is a general term that is usually qualified ⟨he is highly regarded in the profession⟩. RESPECT implies a considered evaluation or estimation ⟨after many years they came to respect her views⟩. ESTEEM implies greater warmth of feeling accompanying a high valuation ⟨no citizen of the town was more highly esteemed⟩. ADMIRE suggests usually enthusiastic appreciation and often deep affection ⟨a friend that I truly admire⟩.

**reg·i·men** \'re-jə-mən *also* 're-zhə-\ *noun* [Middle English, from Latin *regimin-*, *regimen* rule, from *regere* to rule] (14th century) **1 a :** a systematic plan (as of diet, therapy, or medication) especially when designed to improve and maintain the health of a patient **b :** a regular course of action and especially of strenuous training ⟨the daily *regimen* of a top ballet dancer⟩ **2 :** GOVERNMENT, RULE **3 :** REGIME 1c

**¹reg·i·ment** \'re-jə-mənt, 'rej-mənt\ *noun* [Middle English, from Middle French, from Late Latin *regimentum*, from Latin *regere*] (14th century) **1** *archaic* **:** governmental rule **2 :** a military unit consisting usually of a number of battalions

**²reg·i·ment** \'re-jə-,ment\ *transitive verb* (1617) **1 :** to form into or assign to a regiment **2 a :** to organize rigidly especially for the sake of regulation or control ⟨*regiment* an entire country⟩ **b :** to subject to order or uniformity — **reg·i·men·ta·tion** \,re-jə-mən-'tā-shən, -,men-\ *noun*

**reg·i·men·tal** \,re-jə-'men-tᵊl\ *adjective* (1659) **1 :** of or relating to a regiment **2 :** AUTHORITATIVE, DICTATORIAL

**reg·i·men·tals** \-tᵊlz\ *noun plural* (1742) **1 :** a regimental uniform **2 :** military dress

**re·gion** \'rē-jən\ *noun* [Middle English, from Middle French, from Latin *region-*, *regio*, from *regere* to rule] (14th century) **1 :** an administrative area, division, or district; *especially* **:** the basic administrative unit for local government in Scotland **2 a :** an indefinite area of the world or universe ⟨unknown *regions* left on earth⟩ **b :** a broad geographical area distinguished by similar features ⟨the Appalachian *region*⟩ **c** (1) **:** a major world area that supports a characteristic fauna (2) **:** an area characterized by the prevalence of one or more vegetational climax types **3 a :** any of the major subdivisions into which the body or one of its parts is divisible **b :** an indefinite area surrounding a specified body part ⟨a pain in the *region* of the heart⟩ **4 :** a sphere of activity or interest **:** FIELD **5 :** any of the zones into which the atmosphere is divided according to height or the sea according to depth **6 :** an open connected set together with none, some, or all of the points on its boundary ⟨a simple closed curve divides its plane into two *regions*⟩

**¹re·gion·al** \'rēj-nəl, 'rē-jə-nᵊl\ *adjective* (15th century) **1 :** affecting a particular region **:** LOCALIZED **2 :** of, relating to, characteristic of, or serving a region ⟨a *regional* high school⟩ **3 :** marked by regionalism ⟨*regional* art⟩

**²regional** *noun* (1936) **:** something (as a branch of an organization or an edition of a magazine) that serves a region

**re·gion·al·ism** \'rēj-nə-,li-zəm, 'rē-jə-nᵊl-,i-\ *noun* (1881) **1 a :** consciousness of and loyalty to a distinct region with a homogeneous population **b :** development of a political or social system based on one or more such areas **2 :** emphasis on regional locale and characteristics in art or literature **3 :** a characteristic feature (as of speech) of a geographic area — **re·gion·al·ist** \-list, -ist\ *noun or adjective* — **re·gion·al·is·tic** \,rēj-nə-'lis-tik, ,rē-jə-nᵊl-'is-\ *adjective*

**re·gion·al·ize** \'rēj-nə-,līz, 'rē-jə-nᵊl-,īz\ *transitive verb* **-ized; -iz·ing** (1921) **:** to divide into regions or administrative districts **:** arrange regionally

**— re·gion·al·i·za·tion** \,rēj-nə-lə-'zā-shən, ,rē-jə-nᵊl-ə-\ *noun*

**re·gion·al·ly** \'rēj-nə-lē, 'rē-jə-nᵊl-ē-\ *adverb* (1879) **:** on a regional basis

**re·gis·seur** *or* **ré·gis·seur** \,rā-zhi-'sər\ *noun* [French *régisseur*, from *régir* to direct, from Latin *regere* to rule] (1828) **:** a director responsible for staging a theatrical work (as a ballet)

**¹reg·is·ter** \'re-jə-stər\ *noun* [Middle English *registre*, from Middle French, from Medieval Latin *registrum*, alteration of Late Latin *regesta*, plural, register, from Latin, neuter plural of *regestus*, past participle of *regerere* to bring back, pile up, collect, from *re-* + *gerere* to bear] (14th century) **1 :** a written record containing regular entries of items or details **2 a :** a book or system of public records **b :** a roster of qualified or available individuals ⟨a civil service *register*⟩ **3 :** an entry in a register **4 a :** a set of organ pipes of like quality **:** STOP **b** (1) **:** the range of a human voice or a musical instrument (2) **:** a portion of such a range similarly produced or of the same quality **c :** any of the varieties of a language that a speaker uses in a particular social context **5 a :** a device regulating admission of air to fuel **b :** a grille often with shutters for admitting heated air or for ventilation **6 :** REGISTRATION, REGISTRY **7 a :** an automatic device registering a number or a quantity **b :** a number or quantity so registered **8 :** a condition of correct alignment or proper relative position **9 :** a device (as in a computer) for storing small amounts of data; *especially* **:** one in which data can be both stored and operated on

**²register** *verb* **reg·is·tered; reg·is·ter·ing** \-st(ə-)riŋ\ (14th century) *transitive verb* **1 a :** to make or secure official entry of in a register **b :** to enroll formally especially as a voter or student **c :** to record automatically **:** INDICATE **d :** to make a record of **:** NOTE **e :** PERCEIVE; *also* **:** COMPREHEND **2 :** to make or adjust so as to correspond exactly **3 :** to secure special protection for (a piece of mail) by prepayment of a fee **4 :** to convey an impression of **:** EXPRESS **5 :** ACHIEVE ⟨*registered* an impressive victory⟩ *intransitive verb* **1 a :** to enroll one's name in a register ⟨*registered* at the hotel⟩ **b :** to enroll one's name officially as a prerequisite for voting **c :** to enroll formally as a student **2 a :** to correspond exactly **b :** to be in correct alignment or register **3 :** to make or convey an impression

**³register** *noun* [probably alteration of Middle English *registrer*] (circa 1532) **:** REGISTRAR

**registered** *adjective* (1861) **1 a :** having the owner's name entered in a register ⟨*registered* security⟩ **b :** recorded as the owner of a security **2 :** recorded on the basis of pedigree or breed characteristics in the studbook of a breed association **3 :** qualified formally or officially

**registered mail** *noun* (1886) **:** mail recorded in the post office of mailing and at each successive point of transmission and guaranteed special care in delivery

**registered nurse** *noun* (1896) **:** a graduate trained nurse who has been licensed by a state authority after qualifying for registration

**register ton** *noun* (circa 1909) **:** TON 1a

**reg·is·tra·ble** \'re-jə-strə-bəl\ *also* **reg·is·ter·able** \-st(ə-)rə-bəl\ *adjective* (1765) **:** capable of being registered

**reg·is·trant** \'re-jə-strənt\ *noun* (circa 1890) **:** one that registers or is registered

**reg·is·trar** \'re-jə-,strär\ *noun* [alteration of Middle English *registrer*, from Middle French *registreur*, from *registrer* to register, from Medieval Latin *registrare*, from *registrum*] (1675) **:** an official recorder or keeper of records: as **a :** an officer of an educational institution responsible for registering students, keeping academic records, and corresponding with applicants and evaluating their credentials **b :** an admitting officer at a hospital **c** *chiefly British* **:** RESIDENT 3

**reg·is·tra·tion** \,re-jə-'strā-shən\ *noun* (circa 1566) **1 :** the act of registering **2 :** an entry in a register **3 :** the number of individuals registered **:** ENROLLMENT **4 a :** the art or act of selecting and adjusting pipe organ stops **b :** the combination of stops selected for performing a particular organ work **5 :** a document certifying an act of registering

**reg·is·try** \'re-jə-strē\ *noun, plural* **-tries** (1589) **1 :** REGISTRATION, ENROLLMENT **2 :** the nationality of a ship according to its entry in a register **:** FLAG **3 :** a place of registration **4 a :** an official record book **b :** an entry in a registry

**re·gius professor** \'rē-j(ē-)əs-\ *noun* [New Latin, royal professor] (1621) **:** a holder of a professorship founded by royal subsidy at a British university

**reg·let** \'re-glət\ *noun* [French *réglet*, from Middle French *reglet* straightedge, from *regle* rule, from Latin *regula* — more at RULE] (1664) **1 :** a flat narrow architectural molding **2 :** a strip of wood used like a lead between lines of type

**reg·nal** \'reg-nᵊl\ *adjective* [Medieval Latin *regnalis*, from Latin *regnum* reign — more at REIGN] (1612) **:** of or relating to a king or his reign; *specifically* **:** calculated from a monarch's accession to the throne ⟨in his eighth *regnal* year⟩

**reg·nant** \'reg-nənt\ *adjective* [Latin *regnant-*, *regnans*, present participle of *regnare* to reign, from *regnum*] (1600) **1 :** exercising rule **:** REIGNING **2 a :** having the chief power **:** DOMINANT **b :** of common or widespread occurrence

**reg·num** \'reg-nəm\ *noun, plural* **reg·na** \-nə\ [Latin] (circa 1890) **:** KINGDOM

**reg·o·lith** \'re-gə-,lith\ *noun* [Greek *rhēgós* blanket + English *-lith;* akin to Greek *rhezein* to dye — more at RAGA] (1897) **:** unconsolidated residual or transported material that overlies the solid rock on the earth, moon, or a planet

**reg·o·sol** \'re-gə-,säl, -,sòl\ *noun* [*rego-* (as in *regolith*) + Latin *solum* soil — more at SOLE] (1949) **:** any of a group of azonal soils consisting chiefly of imperfectly consolidated material and having no clear-cut and specific morphology

**re·greet** \(,)rē-'grēt\ *transitive verb* (1593) *archaic* **:** to greet in return

**regreets** *noun plural* (1596) *obsolete* **:** GREETINGS

**¹re·gress** \'rē-,gres\ *noun* [Middle English, from Latin *regressus*, from *regredi* to go back, from *re-* + *gradi* to go — more at GRADE] (14th century)

**1 a :** an act or the privilege of going or coming back **b :** REENTRY 1
**2 :** movement backward to a previous and especially worse or more primitive state or condition
**3 :** the act of reasoning backward
²**re·gress** \ri-'gres\ (1552)
*intransitive verb*
**1 a :** to make or undergo regress **:** RETROGRADE **b :** to be subject to or exhibit regression
**2 :** to tend to approach or revert to a mean
*transitive verb*
**:** to induce a state of psychological regression in
— **re·gres·sor** \-'gre-sər\ *noun*
**re·gres·sion** \ri-'gre-shən\ *noun* (1597)
**1 :** the act or an instance of regressing
**2 :** a trend or shift toward a lower or less perfect state: as **a :** progressive decline of a manifestation of disease **b** (1) **:** gradual loss of differentiation and function by a body part especially as a physiological change accompanying aging (2) **:** gradual loss of memories and acquired skills **c :** reversion to an earlier mental or behavioral level **d :** a functional relationship between two or more correlated variables that is often empirically determined from data and is used especially to predict values of one variable when given values of the others ⟨the *regression* of *y* on *x* is linear⟩; *specifically* **:** a function that yields the mean value of a random variable under the condition that one or more independent variables have specified values
**3 :** retrograde motion
**re·gres·sive** \ri-'gre-siv\ *adjective* (1634)
**1 :** tending to regress or produce regression
**2 :** being, characterized by, or developing in the course of an evolutionary process involving increasing simplification of bodily structure
**3 :** decreasing in rate as the base increases ⟨a *regressive* tax⟩
— **re·gres·sive·ly** *adverb*
— **re·gres·sive·ness** *noun*
— **re·gres·siv·i·ty** \,rē-,gre-'si-və-tē\ *noun*
¹**re·gret** \ri-'gret\ *verb* **re·gret·ted; re·gret·ting** [Middle English *regretten*, from Middle French *regreter*, from Old French, from *re-* + *-greter* (perhaps of Germanic origin; akin to Old Norse *grāta* to weep) — more at GREET] (14th century)
*transitive verb*
**1 a :** to mourn the loss or death of **b :** to miss very much
**2 :** to be very sorry for ⟨*regrets* his mistakes⟩
*intransitive verb*
**:** to experience regret
— **re·gret·ter** *noun*
²**regret** *noun* (1590)
**1 :** sorrow aroused by circumstances beyond one's control or power to repair
**2 a :** an expression of distressing emotion (as sorrow or disappointment) **b** *plural* **:** a note politely declining an invitation
*synonym* see SORROW
— **re·gret·ful** \-fəl\ *adjective*
— **re·gret·ful·ness** *noun*
**re·gret·ful·ly** \ri-'gret-fə-lē\ *adverb* (1682)
**1 :** with regret
**2 :** it is to be regretted
**re·gret·ta·ble** \ri-'gre-tə-bəl\ *adjective* (1603)
**:** deserving regret
**re·gret·ta·bly** \-blē\ *adverb* (1866)
**1 :** to a regrettable extent ⟨a *regrettably* steep decline in wages⟩
**2 :** it is to be regretted ⟨*regrettably*, they could not attend⟩
**re·group** \(,)rē-'grüp\ (1885)
*transitive verb*
**:** to form into a new grouping ⟨in order to subtract 129 from 531 *regroup* 531 into 5 hundreds, 2 tens, and 11 ones⟩ ⟨*regroup* military forces⟩
*intransitive verb*

**1 :** to reorganize (as after a setback) for renewed activity
**2 :** to alter the tactical formation of a military force
**re·grow** \(,)rē-'grō\ *verb* **-grew** \-'grü\; **-grown** \-'grōn\; **-grow·ing** (1872)
*transitive verb*
**:** to grow (as a missing part) anew
*intransitive verb*
**:** to continue growth after interruption or injury
¹**reg·u·lar** \'re-gyə-lər, 're-g(ə-)lər\ *adjective* [Middle English *reguler*, from Middle French, from Late Latin *regularis* regular, from Latin, of a bar, from *regula* rule — more at RULE] (14th century)
**1 :** belonging to a religious order
**2 a :** formed, built, arranged, or ordered according to some established rule, law, principle, or type **b** (1) **:** both equilateral and equiangular ⟨a *regular* polygon⟩ (2) **:** having faces that are congruent regular polygons and all the polyhedral angles congruent ⟨a *regular* polyhedron⟩ **c** *of a flower* **:** having the arrangement of floral parts exhibiting radial symmetry with members of the same whorl similar in form
**3 a :** ORDERLY, METHODICAL ⟨*regular* habits⟩ **b :** recurring, attending, or functioning at fixed or uniform intervals ⟨a *regular* income⟩ ⟨a *regular* churchgoer⟩
**4 a :** constituted, conducted, or done in conformity with established or prescribed usages, rules, or discipline **b :** NORMAL, STANDARD: as (1) **:** ABSOLUTE, COMPLETE ⟨a *regular* fool⟩ ⟨the office seemed like a *regular* madhouse⟩ (2) **:** thinking or behaving in an acceptable, normal, or agreeable manner ⟨was a *regular* guy⟩ **c** (1) **:** conforming to the normal or usual manner of inflection (2) **:** WEAK 7 **d** *of a postage stamp* **:** issued in large numbers over a long period for general use in prepayment of postage
**5 :** of, relating to, or constituting the permanent standing military force of a state ⟨*regular* army⟩ ⟨*regular* soldiers⟩ ☆
²**regular** *noun* (15th century)
**1 :** one who is regular: as **a :** one of the regular clergy **b :** a soldier in a regular army **c :** one who can be trusted or depended on ⟨a party *regular*⟩ **d :** a player on an athletic team who usually starts every game **e :** one who is usually present or participating; *especially* **:** a long-standing regular customer
**2 :** something of average or medium size; *especially* **:** a clothing size designed to fit a person of average height
**reg·u·lar·i·ty** \,re-gyə-'lar-ə-tē\ *noun, plural* **-ties** (1603)
**1 :** the quality or state of being regular
**2 :** something that is regular
**reg·u·lar·ize** \'re-gyə-lə-,rīz\ *transitive verb* **-ized; -iz·ing** (1833)
**:** to make regular by conformance to law, rules, or custom
— **reg·u·lar·i·za·tion** \,re-gyə-lə-rə-'zā-shən\ *noun*
**reg·u·lar·ly** \'re-gyə-lər-lē, 're-gyə(r)-lē\ *adverb* (14th century)
**1 :** in a regular manner
**2 :** on a regular basis **:** at regular intervals
**regular solid** *noun* (1841)
**:** any of the five possible regular polyhedrons that include the regular forms of the tetrahedron, hexahedron, octahedron, dodecahedron, and icosahedron
**reg·u·late** \'re-gyə-,lāt\ *transitive verb* **-lat·ed; -lat·ing** [Middle English, from Late Latin *regulatus*, past participle of *regulare*, from Latin *regula* rule] (15th century)
**1 a :** to govern or direct according to rule **b** (1) **:** to bring under the control of law or constituted authority (2) **:** to make regulations for or concerning ⟨*regulate* the industries of a country⟩

**2 :** to bring order, method, or uniformity to ⟨*regulate* one's habits⟩
**3 :** to fix or adjust the time, amount, degree, or rate of ⟨*regulate* the pressure of a tire⟩
— **reg·u·la·tive** \-,lā-tiv\ *adjective*
— **reg·u·la·to·ry** \-lə-,tōr-ē, -,tȯr-\ *adjective*
¹**reg·u·la·tion** \,re-gyə-'lā-shən, ,re-gə-\ *noun* (1665)
**1 :** the act of regulating **:** the state of being regulated
**2 a :** an authoritative rule dealing with details or procedure ⟨safety *regulations*⟩ **b :** a rule or order issued by an executive authority or regulatory agency of a government and having the force of law
**3 a :** the process of redistributing material (as in an embryo) to restore a damaged or lost part independent of new tissue growth **b :** the mechanism by which an early embryo maintains normal development
*synonym* see LAW
²**regulation** *adjective* (circa 1839)
**:** conforming to regulations **:** OFFICIAL
**reg·u·la·tor** \'re-gyə-,lā-tər\ *noun* (1655)
**1 :** one that regulates
**2 :** REGULATORY GENE
**regulatory gene** *or* **regulator gene** *noun* (1961)
**:** a gene that regulates the expression of one or more structural genes by controlling the production of a protein (as a genetic repressor) which regulates their rate of transcription
**reg·u·lus** \'re-gyə-ləs\ *noun* [New Latin, from Latin, petty king, from *reg-, rex* king — more at ROYAL]
**1** *capitalized* **:** a first-magnitude star in the constellation Leo
**2** [Medieval Latin, metallic antimony, from Latin] **:** the more or less impure mass of metal formed beneath the slag in smelting and reducing ores
**re·gur·gi·tate** \(,)rē-'gər-jə-,tāt\ *verb* **-tat·ed; -tat·ing** [Medieval Latin *regurgitatus*, past participle of *regurgitare*, from Latin *re-* + Late Latin *gurgitare* to engulf, from Latin *gurgit-, gurges* whirlpool — more at VORACIOUS] (1653)
*intransitive verb*
**:** to become thrown or poured back
*transitive verb*
**:** to throw or pour back or out from or as if from a cavity ⟨*regurgitate* food⟩ ⟨memorized facts to *regurgitate* on the exam⟩
**re·gur·gi·ta·tion** \(,)rē-,gər-jə-'tā-shən\ *noun* (1601)
**:** an act of regurgitating: as **a :** the casting up of incompletely digested food (as by some birds in feeding their young) **b :** the backward flow of blood through a defective heart valve
**re·hab** \'rē-,hab\ *noun, often attributive* [short for *rehabilitation* or *rehabilitate*] (1941)
**1 :** the action or process of rehabilitating **:** REHABILITATION
**2 :** a rehabilitated building or dwelling
— **rehab** *transitive verb*
— **re·hab·ber** \-,ha-bər\ *noun*

☆ **SYNONYMS**
**Regular, normal, typical, natural** mean being of the sort or kind that is expected as usual, ordinary, or average. REGULAR stresses conformity to a rule, standard, or pattern ⟨the club's *regular* monthly meeting⟩. NORMAL implies lack of deviation from what has been discovered or established as the most usual or expected ⟨*normal* behavior for a two-year-old⟩. TYPICAL implies showing all important traits of a type, class, or group and may suggest lack of strong individuality ⟨a *typical* small town⟩. NATURAL applies to what conforms to a thing's essential nature, function, or mode of being ⟨the *natural* love of a mother for her child⟩.

**re·ha·bil·i·tant** \ˌrē-ə-'bi-lə-tənt, ˌrē-hə-\ *noun* (1961)
**:** a disabled person undergoing rehabilitation
**re·ha·bil·i·tate** \ˌrē-ə-'bi-lə-ˌtāt, ˌrē-hə-\ *transitive verb* **-tat·ed; -tat·ing** [Medieval Latin *rehabilitatus*, past participle of *rehabilitare*, from Latin *re-* + Late Latin *habilitare* to habilitate] (circa 1581)
**1 a :** to restore to a former capacity **:** REINSTATE **b :** to restore to good repute **:** reestablish the good name of
**2 a :** to restore to a former state (as of efficiency, good management, or solvency) ⟨*rehabilitate* slum areas⟩ **b :** to restore or bring to a condition of health or useful and constructive activity
  **— re·ha·bil·i·ta·tion** \-ˌbi-lə-'tā-shən\ *noun*
  **— re·ha·bil·i·ta·tive** \-'bi-lə-ˌtā-tiv\ *adjective*
  **— re·ha·bil·i·ta·tor** \-ˌtā-tər\ *noun*
**¹re·hash** \(ˌ)rē-'hash\ *transitive verb* (circa 1822)
**1 :** to talk over or discuss again
**2 :** to present or use again in another form without substantial change or improvement
**²re·hash** \'rē-ˌhash\ *noun* (1849)
**1 :** something that is rehashed
**2 :** the action or process of rehashing
**re·hear** \(ˌ)rē-'hir\ *transitive verb* **-heard** \-'hərd\; **-hear·ing** \-'hir-iŋ\ (1756)
**:** to hear again or anew especially judicially
**rehearing** *noun* (1686)
**:** a second or new hearing by the same tribunal
**re·hears·al** \ri-'hər-səl\ *noun* (14th century)
**1 :** something recounted or told again **:** RECITAL
**2 a :** a private performance or practice session preparatory to a public appearance **b :** a practice exercise **:** TRIAL
**re·hearse** \ri-'hərs\ *verb* **re·hearsed; re·hears·ing** [Middle English *rehersen*, from Middle French *rehercier*, literally, to harrow again, from *re-* + *hercier* to harrow, from *herce* harrow — more at HEARSE] (14th century)
*transitive verb*
**1 a :** to say again **:** REPEAT **b :** to recite aloud in a formal manner
**2 :** to present an account of **:** RELATE ⟨*rehearse* a familiar story⟩
**3 :** to recount in order **:** ENUMERATE ⟨*rehearsed* their demands⟩
**4 a :** to give a rehearsal of **b :** to train or make proficient by rehearsal
**5 :** to perform or practice as if in a rehearsal
*intransitive verb*
**:** to engage in a rehearsal
  ***word history*** see HEARSE
  **— re·hears·er** *noun*
**re·house** \(ˌ)rē-'haüz\ *transitive verb* (1820)
**:** to house again or anew; *especially* **:** to establish in a new or different housing unit of a better quality
**re·hy·drate** \(ˌ)rē-'hī-ˌdrāt\ *transitive verb* (1943)
**:** to restore fluid to (something dehydrated)
  **— re·hy·drat·able** \-ˌdrā-tə-bəl\ *adjective*
  **— re·hy·dra·tion** \ˌrē-ˌhī-'drā-shən\ *noun*
**reichs·mark** \'rīks-ˌmärk\ *noun*, *plural* **reichsmarks** *also* **reichsmark** [German, from *Reich* empire, kingdom + *Mark* mark] (1924)
**:** the German mark from 1925 to 1948
**re·ifi·ca·tion** \ˌrā-ə-fə-'kā-shən, ˌrē-\ *noun* (1846)
**:** the process or result of reifying
**re·ify** \'rā-ə-ˌfī, 'rē-\ *transitive verb* **re·ified; re·ify·ing** [Latin *res* thing — more at REAL] (1854)
**:** to regard (something abstract) as a material or concrete thing
**¹reign** \'rān\ *noun* [Middle English *regne*, from Old French, from Latin *regnum*, from *reg-*, *rex* king — more at ROYAL] (13th century)
**1 a :** royal authority **:** SOVEREIGNTY ⟨under the

*reign* of the Stuart kings⟩ **b :** the dominion, sway, or influence of one resembling a monarch ⟨the *reign* of the Puritan ministers⟩
**2 :** the time during which one (as a sovereign) reigns
**²reign** *intransitive verb* (14th century)
**1 a :** to possess or exercise sovereign power **:** RULE **b :** to hold office as chief of state although possessing little governing power ⟨in England the sovereign *reigns* but does not rule⟩
**2 :** to exercise authority in the manner of a monarch
**3 :** to be predominant or prevalent ⟨chaos *reigned* in the classroom⟩
**reign of terror** [*Reign of Terror*, a period of the French Revolution that was conspicuous for mass executions of political suspects] (1801)
**:** a state or a period of time marked by violence often committed by those in power that produces widespread terror
**re·imag·ine** \ˌrē-i-'ma-jən\ *transitive verb* (circa 1934)
**:** to imagine again or anew; *especially* **:** to form a new conception of **:** RE-CREATE
**re·im·burse** \ˌrē-əm-'bərs\ *transitive verb* **-bursed; -burs·ing** [*re-* + obsolete English *imburse* to put in the pocket, pay, from Medieval Latin *imbursare*, from Latin *in-* in- + Medieval Latin *bursa* purse — more at PURSE] (1611)
**1 :** to pay back to someone **:** REPAY ⟨*reimburse* travel expenses⟩
**2 :** to make restoration or payment of an equivalent to ⟨*reimburse* him for his traveling expenses⟩
  ***synonym*** see PAY
  **— re·im·burs·able** \-'bər-sə-bəl\ *adjective*
  **— re·im·burse·ment** \-'bərs-mənt\ *noun*
**re·im·pres·sion** \ˌrē-əm-'pre-shən\ *noun* (1684)
**:** REPRINT a
**¹rein** \'rān\ *noun* [Middle English *reine*, from Middle French *rene*, from (assumed) Vulgar Latin *retina*, from Latin *retinēre* to restrain — more at RETAIN] (14th century)
**1 :** a strap fastened to a bit by which a rider or driver controls an animal — usually used in plural
**2 a :** a restraining influence **:** CHECK ⟨kept a tight *rein* on the proceedings⟩ **b :** controlling or guiding power — usually used in plural ⟨the *reins* of government⟩
**3 :** opportunity for unhampered activity or use ⟨gave full *rein* to her imagination⟩
**²rein** (15th century)
*transitive verb*
**1 :** to control or direct with or as if with reins
**2 :** to check or stop by or as if by a pull at the reins ⟨*reined* in her horse⟩ ⟨couldn't *rein* his impatience⟩
*intransitive verb*
**1** *archaic* **:** to submit to the use of reins
**2 :** to stop or slow up one's horse or oneself by or as if by pulling the reins
**re·in·car·nate** \ˌrē-ən-'kär-ˌnāt, (ˌ)rē-'in-ˌ\ *transitive verb* (1858)
**:** to incarnate again
**re·in·car·na·tion** \ˌrē-(ˌ)in-(ˌ)kär-'nā-shən\ *noun* (1858)
**1 a :** the action of reincarnating **:** the state of being reincarnated **b :** rebirth in new bodies or forms of life; *especially* **:** a rebirth of a soul in a new human body
**2 :** a fresh embodiment
**rein·deer** \'rān-ˌdir\ *noun* [Middle English *reindere*, from Old Norse *hreinn* reindeer + Middle English *deer* animal, deer] (14th century)
**:** CARIBOU — used especially for the Old World caribou
**reindeer moss** *noun* (circa 1753)
**:** a gray, erect, tufted, and much-branched lichen (*Cladonia rangiferina*) that forms extensive patches in arctic and north-temperate re-

gions, constitutes a large part of the food of caribou, and is sometimes eaten by humans — called also *reindeer lichen*
**re·in·dus·tri·al·i·za·tion** \ˌrē-in-ˌdəs-trē-ə-lə-'zā-shən\ *noun* (1979)
**:** a policy of stimulating economic growth especially through government aid to revitalize and modernize aging industries and encourage growth of new ones
  **— re·in·dus·tri·al·ize** \-'dəs-trē-ə-ˌlīz\ *verb*
**re·in·fec·tion** \ˌrē-ən-'fek-shən\ *noun* (1882)
**:** infection following recovery from or superimposed on infection of the same type
**re·in·force** \ˌrē-ən-'fōrs, -'fòrs\ *verb* [*re-* + *inforce*, alteration of *enforce*] (1600)
*transitive verb*
**1 :** to strengthen or increase by fresh additions ⟨*reinforce* our troops⟩ ⟨were *reinforcing* their pitching staff⟩
**2 :** to strengthen by additional assistance, material, or support **:** make stronger or more pronounced ⟨*reinforce* levees⟩ ⟨*reinforce* the elbows of a jacket⟩ ⟨*reinforce* ideas⟩
**3 :** to stimulate (as an experimental animal or a student) with a reinforcer; *also* **:** to encourage (a response) with a reinforcer
*intransitive verb*
**:** to seek or get reinforcements
  **— re·in·force·able** \-'fōr-sə-bəl, -'fòr-\ *adjective*
**reinforced concrete** *noun* (1902)
**:** concrete in which metal (as steel) is embedded so that the two materials act together in resisting forces
**re·in·force·ment** \ˌrē-ən-'fōrs-mənt, -'fòrs-\ *noun* (1617)
**1 :** the action of reinforcing **:** the state of being reinforced
**2 :** something that reinforces
**re·in·forc·er** \-'fōr-sər, -'fòr-\ *noun* (1955)
**:** a stimulus (as a reward or the removal of an electric shock) that increases the probability of a desired response in operant conditioning by being applied or effected following the desired response
**reins** \'rānz\ *noun plural* [Middle English, from Middle French & Latin; Middle French, from Latin *renes*] (14th century)
**1 a :** KIDNEYS **b :** the region of the kidneys **:** LOINS
**2 :** the seat of the feelings or passions
**reins·man** \'rānz-mən\ *noun* (1855)
**:** a skilled driver or rider of horses
**re·in·state** \ˌrē-ən-'stāt\ *transitive verb* **-stat·ed; -stat·ing** (1628)
**1 :** to place again (as in possession or in a former position)
**2 :** to restore to a previous effective state
  **— re·in·state·ment** \-'stāt-mənt\ *noun*
**re·in·sur·ance** \ˌrē-ən-'shur-ən(t)s *also* (ˌ)rē-'in-ˌ\ *noun* (1755)
**:** insurance by another insurer of all or a part of a risk previously assumed by an insurance company
**re·in·sure** \ˌrē-ən-'shur\ (1755)
*transitive verb*
**1 :** to insure again by transferring to another insurance company all or a part of a liability assumed
**2 :** to insure again by assuming all or a part of the liability of an insurance company already covering a risk
*intransitive verb*
**:** to provide increased insurance
  **— re·in·sur·er** *noun*
**re·in·te·grate** \(ˌ)rē-'in-tə-ˌgrāt\ *transitive verb* [Medieval Latin *reintegratus*, past participle of *reintegrare* to renew, reinstate, from Latin *re-* + *integrare* to integrate] (1626)

---

: to integrate again into an entity : restore to unity
— **re·in·te·gra·tion** \(ˌ)rē-ˌin-tə-'grā-shən\ noun
— **re·in·te·gra·tive** \(ˌ)rē-'in-tə-ˌgrā-tiv\ adjective
**re·in·ter·pret** \ˌrē-ən-'tər-prət, -pət\ transitive verb (1611)
: to interpret again; specifically : to give a new or different interpretation to
— **re·in·ter·pre·ta·tion** \-ˌtər-prə-'tā-shən, -pə-\ noun
**re·in·vent** \ˌrē-ən-'vent\ transitive verb (1686)
**1** : to make as if for the first time something already invented ⟨reinvent the wheel⟩
**2** : to remake or redo completely
**3** : to bring into use again
— **re·in·ven·tion** \-'ven(t)-shən\ noun
**re·in·vest** \ˌrē-ən-'vest\ transitive verb (1611)
**1** : to invest again or anew
**2 a** : to invest (as income from investments) in additional securities **b** : to invest (as earnings) in a business rather than distribute as dividends or profits
**re·in·vest·ment** \-'ves(t)-mənt\ noun (1611)
**1** : the action of reinvesting : the state of being reinvested
**2** : a second or repeated investment
**reis** plural of REAL
**re·is·sue** \(ˌ)rē-'i-(ˌ)shü, chiefly British -'is-(ˌ)yü\ (circa 1618)
intransitive verb
: to come forth again
transitive verb
: to issue again; especially : to cause to become available again
— **reissue** noun
**re·it·er·ate** \rē-'i-tə-ˌrāt\ transitive verb **-at·ed; -at·ing** [Middle English, from Latin reiteratus, past participle of reiterare to repeat, from re- + iterare to iterate] (15th century)
: to state or do over again or repeatedly sometimes with wearying effect
— **re·it·er·a·tion** \(ˌ)rē-ˌi-tə-'rā-shən\ noun
— **re·it·er·a·tive** \rē-'i-tə-ˌrā-tiv, -t(ə-)rə-tiv\ adjective
— **re·it·er·a·tive·ly** adverb
**Rei·ter's syndrome** \'rī-tərz-\ noun [Hans Reiter (died 1969) German physician] (circa 1947)
: a disease that is usually initiated by infection in genetically predisposed individuals and is characterized usually by recurrence of arthritis, conjunctivitis, and urethritis — called also Reiter's disease
**reive** \'rēv\ verb **reived; reiv·ing** [Middle English (Scots) reifen, from Old English rēafian to rob — more at REAVE] (before 12th century)
Scottish : RAID
— **reiv·er** noun, Scottish
**¹re·ject** \ri-'jekt\ transitive verb [Middle English, from Latin rejectus, past participle of reicere, from re- + jacere to throw — more at JET] (15th century)
**1 a** : to refuse to accept, consider, submit to, take for some purpose, or use ⟨rejected the suggestion⟩ ⟨reject a manuscript⟩ **b** : to refuse to hear, receive, or admit : REBUFF, REPEL ⟨parents who reject their children⟩ **c** : to refuse as lover or spouse
**2** obsolete : to cast off
**3** : THROW BACK, REPULSE
**4** : to spew out
**5** : to subject to immunological rejection
**synonym** see DECLINE
— **re·ject·er** or **re·jec·tor** \-'jek-tər\ noun
— **re·ject·ing·ly** \-tiŋ-lē\ adverb
— **re·jec·tive** \-'jek-tiv\ adjective
**²re·ject** \'rē-ˌjekt\ noun (circa 1555)
: a rejected person or thing; especially : one rejected as not wanted, unsatisfactory, or not fulfilling standard requirements
**re·ject·ee** \ri-ˌjek-'tē, ˌrē-\ noun (1941)
: one that is rejected; especially : a person rejected as unfit for military service

**re·jec·tion** \ri-'jek-shən\ noun (circa 1552)
**1 a** : the action of rejecting : the state of being rejected **b** : the immunological process of sloughing off foreign tissue or an organ (as a transplant) by the recipient organism
**2** : something rejected
**rejection slip** noun (1906)
: a printed slip enclosed with a rejected manuscript returned by an editor to an author
**re·jig·ger** \(ˌ)rē-'ji-gər\ transitive verb [re- + ³jigger] (1942)
: ALTER, REARRANGE
**re·joice** \ri-'jȯis\ verb **re·joiced; re·joic·ing** [Middle English, from Middle French rejoiss-, stem of rejoir, from re- + joir to rejoice, from Latin gaudēre — more at JOY] (14th century)
transitive verb
: to give joy to : GLADDEN
intransitive verb
: to feel joy or great delight
— **re·joic·er** noun
— **re·joic·ing·ly** \-'jȯi-siŋ-lē\ adverb
— **rejoice in** : HAVE, POSSESS
**rejoicing** noun (14th century)
**1** : the action of one that rejoices
**2** : an instance, occasion, or expression of joy : FESTIVITY
**re·join** \ri-'jȯin, transitive verb 1 is (ˌ)rē-\ verb [Middle English, from Middle French rejoin-, stem of rejoindre, from re- + Old French joindre to join — more at JOIN] (15th century)
intransitive verb
: to answer the replication of the plaintiff
transitive verb
**1** : to join again
**2** : to say often sharply or critically in response especially as a reply to a reply
**synonym** see ANSWER
**re·join·der** \ri-'jȯin-dər\ noun [Middle English rejoiner, from Middle French rejoindre to rejoin] (15th century)
**1** : the defendant's answer to the plaintiff's replication
**2** : REPLY; specifically : an answer to a reply
**re·ju·ve·nate** \ri-'jü-və-ˌnāt\ verb **-nat·ed; -nat·ing** [re- + Latin juvenis young — more at YOUNG] (1807)
transitive verb
**1 a** : to make young or youthful again : give new vigor to **b** : to restore to an original or new state ⟨rejuvenate old cars⟩
**2 a** : to stimulate (a stream) to renewed erosive activity especially by uplift **b** : to develop youthful features of topography in
intransitive verb
: to cause or undergo rejuvenescence
**synonym** see RENEW
— **re·ju·ve·na·tion** \ri-ˌjü-və-'nā-shən, ˌrē-\ noun
— **re·ju·ve·na·tor** \ri-'jü-və-ˌnā-tər\ noun
**re·ju·ve·nes·cence** \ri-ˌjü-və-'ne-sən(t)s, ˌrē-\ noun [Medieval Latin rejuvenescere to become young again, from Latin re- + juvenescere to become young, from juvenis] (circa 1631)
: a renewal of youthfulness or vigor : REJUVENATION
— **re·ju·ve·nes·cent** \-s°nt\ adjective
**¹re·lapse** \ri-'laps, 'rē-\ noun [Middle English, from Medieval Latin relapsus, from Latin relabi to slide back, from re- + labi to slide — more at SLEEP] (15th century)
**1** : the act or an instance of backsliding, worsening, or subsiding
**2** : a recurrence of symptoms of a disease after a period of improvement
**²re·lapse** \ri-'laps\ intransitive verb **re·lapsed; re·laps·ing** (1568)
**1** : to slip or fall back into a former worse state
**2** : SINK, SUBSIDE ⟨relapse into deep thought⟩
— **re·laps·er** noun
**relapsing fever** noun (1849)
: a variable acute epidemic disease that is marked by recurring high fever usually lasting

3 to 7 days and is caused by a spirochete (genus Borrelia) transmitted by the bites of lice and ticks
**re·late** \ri-'lāt\ verb **re·lat·ed; re·lat·ing** [Latin relatus (past participle of referre to carry back), from re- + latus, past participle of ferre to carry — more at TOLERATE, BEAR] (1530)
transitive verb
**1** : to give an account of : TELL
**2** : to show or establish logical or causal connection between ⟨seeks to relate crime to poverty⟩
intransitive verb
**1** : to apply or take effect retroactively
**2** : to have relationship or connection ⟨the readings relate to his lectures⟩
**3** : to have or establish a relationship : INTERACT ⟨the way a child relates to a teacher⟩
**4** : to respond especially favorably ⟨can't relate to that kind of music⟩
— **re·lat·able** \-'lā-tə-bəl\ adjective
— **re·lat·er** or **re·la·tor** \-'lā-tər\ noun
**related** adjective (circa 1663)
**1** : connected by reason of an established or discoverable relation
**2** : connected by common ancestry or sometimes by marriage
**3** : having close harmonic connection — used of tones, chords, or tonalities
— **re·lat·ed·ly** adverb
— **re·lat·ed·ness** noun
**re·la·tion** \ri-'lā-shən\ noun [Middle English relacioun, from Middle French relation, from Latin relation-, relatio, from referre (past participle relatus) to carry back] (14th century)
**1** : the act of telling or recounting : ACCOUNT
**2** : an aspect or quality (as resemblance) that connects two or more things or parts as being or belonging or working together or as being of the same kind ⟨the relation of time and space⟩; specifically : a property (as one expressed by is equal to, is less than, or is the brother of) that holds between an ordered pair of objects
**3** : the referring by a legal fiction of an act to a prior date as the time of its taking effect
**4 a** (1) : a person connected by consanguinity or affinity : RELATIVE (2) : a person legally entitled to a share of the property of an intestate **b** : relationship by consanguinity or affinity : KINSHIP
**5** : REFERENCE, RESPECT ⟨in relation to⟩
**6** : the attitude or stance which two or more persons or groups assume toward one another ⟨race relations⟩
**7 a** : the state of being mutually or reciprocally interested (as in social or commercial matters) **b** plural (1) : DEALINGS, AFFAIRS ⟨foreign relations⟩ (2) : INTERCOURSE (3) : SEXUAL INTERCOURSE
**re·la·tion·al** \-shnəl, -shə-n°l\ adjective (1662)
**1** : of or relating to kinship
**2** : characterized or constituted by relations
**3** : having the function chiefly of indicating a relation of syntax ⟨has is notional in he has luck, relational in he has gone⟩
**4** : relating to, using, or being a method of organizing data in a database so that it is perceived by the user as a set of tables
— **re·la·tion·al·ly** adverb
**relational grammar** noun (1982)
: a grammar based on a theory in which grammatical relations (as subject or object) are primitives in terms of which syntactic operations are defined
**re·la·tion·ship** \-shən-ˌship\ noun (circa 1744)
**1** : the state of being related or interrelated ⟨studied the relationship between the variables⟩
**2** : the relation connecting or binding participants in a relationship: as **a** : KINSHIP **b** : a specific instance or type of kinship

**3 a :** a state of affairs existing between those having relations or dealings ⟨had a good *relationship* with his family⟩ **b :** a romantic or passionate attachment

**¹rel·a·tive** \'re-lə-tiv\ *noun* (14th century)
**1 :** a word referring grammatically to an antecedent
**2 :** a thing having a relation to or connection with or necessary dependence on another thing
**3 a :** a person connected with another by blood or affinity **b :** an animal or plant related to another by common descent
**4 :** a relative term

**²relative** *adjective* (15th century)
**1 :** introducing a subordinate clause qualifying an expressed or implied antecedent ⟨*relative* pronoun⟩; *also* **:** introduced by such a connective ⟨*relative* clause⟩
**2 :** RELEVANT, PERTINENT ⟨matters *relative* to world peace⟩
**3 :** not absolute or independent **:** COMPARATIVE ⟨the *relative* isolation of life in the country⟩
**4 :** having the same key signature — used of major and minor keys and scales
**5 :** expressed as the ratio of the specified quantity (as an error in measuring) to the total magnitude (as the value of a measured quantity) or to the mean of all the quantities involved

**relative humidity** *noun* (1820)
**:** the ratio of the amount of water vapor actually present in the air to the greatest amount possible at the same temperature

**rel·a·tive·ly** *adverb* (1561)
**:** to a relative degree or extent **:** SOMEWHAT

**relatively prime** *adjective* (circa 1890)
*of integers* **:** having no common factors except +1 and −1 ⟨12 and 25 are *relatively prime*⟩

**relative to** *preposition* (1660)
**:** with regard to **:** in connection with

**relative wind** *noun* (circa 1918)
**:** the motion of the air relative to a body in it

**rel·a·tiv·ism** \'re-lə-ti-ˌvi-zəm\ *noun* (1865)
**1 a :** a theory that knowledge is relative to the limited nature of the mind and the conditions of knowing **b :** a view that ethical truths depend on the individuals and groups holding them
**2 :** RELATIVITY
— **rel·a·tiv·ist** \-vist\ *noun*

**rel·a·tiv·is·tic** \ˌre-lə-ti-'vis-tik\ *adjective* (1886)
**1 :** of, relating to, or characterized by relativity or relativism
**2 :** moving at a velocity such that there is a significant change in properties (as mass) in accordance with the theory of relativity ⟨a *relativistic* electron⟩
— **rel·a·tiv·is·ti·cal·ly** \-'vis-ti-k(ə-)lē\ *adverb*

**rel·a·tiv·i·ty** \ˌre-lə-'ti-və-tē\ *noun, plural* **-ties** (circa 1834)
**1 a :** the quality or state of being relative **b :** something that is relative
**2 :** the state of being dependent for existence on or determined in nature, value, or quality by relation to something else
**3 a :** a theory which is based on the two postulates (1) that the speed of light in a vacuum is constant and independent of the source or observer and (2) that the mathematical forms of the laws of physics are invariant in all inertial systems and which leads to the assertion of the equivalence of mass and energy and of change in mass, dimension, and time with increased velocity — called also *special relativity, special theory of relativity* **b :** an extension of the theory to include gravitation and related acceleration phenomena — called also *general relativity, general theory of relativity*
**4 :** RELATIVISM 1b

**rel·a·tiv·ize** \'re-lə-tə-ˌvīz\ *transitive verb* **-ized; -iz·ing** (1935)
**:** to treat or describe as relative

**re·lax** \ri-'laks\ *verb* [Middle English, from Latin *relaxare,* from *re-* + *laxare* to loosen, from *laxus* loose — more at SLACK] (15th century)
*transitive verb*
**1 :** to make less tense or rigid **:** SLACKEN ⟨*relaxed* his grip⟩
**2 :** to make less severe or stringent **:** MODIFY ⟨*relax* immigration laws⟩
**3 :** to make soft or enervated
**4 :** to relieve from nervous tension
*intransitive verb*
**1 :** to become lax, weak, or loose **:** REST
**2 :** to become less intense or severe ⟨hoped the committee would *relax* in its opposition⟩
**3** *of a muscle or muscle fiber* **:** to become inactive and lengthen
**4 :** to cast off social restraint, nervous tension, or anxiety ⟨couldn't *relax* in crowds⟩
**5 :** to seek rest or recreation ⟨*relax* at the seashore⟩
**6 :** to relieve constipation
**7 :** to attain equilibrium following the abrupt removal of some influence (as light, high temperature, or stress)
— **re·lax·er** *noun*

**¹re·lax·ant** \ri-'lak-sənt\ *adjective* (1771)
**:** of, relating to, or producing relaxation ⟨an anesthetic and *relaxant* agent⟩

**²relaxant** *noun* (circa 1847)
**:** a substance (as a drug) that relaxes; *specifically* **:** one that relieves muscular tension

**re·lax·a·tion** \ˌrē-ˌlak-'sā-shən, ri-ˌlak-, *especially British* ˌre-lək-\ *noun* (1548)
**1 :** the act of relaxing or state of being relaxed
**2 :** a relaxing or recreative state, activity, or pastime **:** DIVERSION
**3 :** the lengthening that characterizes inactive muscle fibers or muscles

**re·laxed** \ri-'lakst\ *adjective* (1623)
**1 :** freed from or lacking in precision or stringency
**2 :** set or being at rest or at ease
**3 :** easy of manner **:** INFORMAL
— **re·laxed·ly** \-'lak-səd-lē, -'lakst-lē\ *adverb*
— **re·laxed·ness** \-'lak-səd-nəs, -'laks(t)-nəs\ *noun*

**re·lax·in** \ri-'lak-sən\ *noun* (1930)
**:** a sex hormone of the corpus luteum that facilitates birth by causing relaxation of the pelvic ligaments

**¹re·lay** \'rē-ˌlā\ *noun* (1659)
**1 a :** a supply (as of horses) arranged beforehand for successive relief **b :** a number of persons who relieve others in some work ⟨worked in *relays* around the clock⟩
**2 a :** a race between teams in which each team member successively covers a specified portion of the course **b :** one of the divisions of a relay
**3 :** an electromagnetic device for remote or automatic control that is actuated by variation in conditions of an electric circuit and that operates in turn other devices (as switches) in the same or a different circuit
**4 :** SERVOMOTOR
**5 :** the act of passing along (as a message or ball) by stages; *also* **:** one of such stages

**²relay** \'rē-ˌlā, ri-'lā\ *transitive verb* **re·layed; re·lay·ing** [Middle English, to hunt with relays, from Middle French *relaier,* from Old French, from *re-* + *laier* to leave — more at DELAY] (1788)
**1 a :** to place or dispose in relays **b :** to provide with relays
**2 :** to pass along by relays ⟨news was *relayed* to distant points⟩
**3 :** to control or operate by a relay

**³re·lay** \(ˌ)rē-'lā\ *transitive verb* **-laid** \-'lād\; **-lay·ing** [*re-* + ¹*lay*] (1757)
**:** to lay again ⟨*relay* track⟩

**¹re·lease** \ri-'lēs\ *transitive verb* **re·leased; re·leas·ing** [Middle English *relesen,* from Middle French *relessier,* from Latin *relaxare* to relax] (14th century)

**1 :** to set free from restraint, confinement, or servitude ⟨*release* hostages⟩ ⟨*release* pent-up emotions⟩ ⟨*release* the brakes⟩; *also* **:** to let go **:** DISMISS ⟨*released* from her job⟩
**2 :** to relieve from something that confines, burdens, or oppresses ⟨was *released* from her promise⟩
**3 :** to give up in favor of another **:** RELINQUISH ⟨*release* a claim to property⟩
**4 :** to give permission for publication, performance, exhibition, or sale of; *also* **:** to make available to the public ⟨the commission *released* its findings⟩ ⟨*release* a new movie⟩
*synonym* see FREE
— **re·leas·able** \-'lē-sə-bəl\ *adjective*

**²release** *noun* (14th century)
**1 :** relief or deliverance from sorrow, suffering, or trouble
**2 a :** discharge from obligation or responsibility **b** (1) **:** relinquishment of a right or claim (2) **:** an act by which a legal right is discharged; *specifically* **:** a conveyance of a right in lands or tenements to another having an estate in possession
**3 a :** the act or an instance of liberating or freeing (as from restraint) **b :** the act or manner of concluding a musical tone or phrase **c :** the act or manner of ending a sound **:** the movement of one or more vocal organs in quitting the position for a speech sound
**4 :** an instrument effecting a legal release
**5 :** the state of being freed
**6 :** a device adapted to hold or release a mechanism as required
**7 a :** the act of permitting performance or publication; *also* **:** PERFORMANCE, PUBLICATION ⟨became a best-seller on its *release*⟩ **b :** the matter released; *especially* **:** a statement prepared for the press

**re·lease** \(ˌ)rē-'lēs\ *transitive verb* (1828)
**:** to lease again

**released time** *noun* (1941)
**:** time off from regularly scheduled activities (as school) given to take part in some other specified activity

**release print** *noun* (1937)
**:** a motion-picture film released for public showing

**re·leas·er** \ri-'lē-sər\ *noun* (15th century)
**:** one that releases; *specifically* **:** a stimulus that serves as the initiator of complex reflex behavior

**rel·e·gate** \'re-lə-ˌgāt\ *transitive verb* **-gat·ed; -gat·ing** [Latin *relegatus,* past participle of *relegare,* from *re-* + *legare* to send with a commission — more at LEGATE] (1599)
**1 :** to send into exile **:** BANISH
**2 :** ASSIGN: as **a :** to assign to a place of insignificance or of oblivion **:** put out of sight or mind **b :** to assign to an appropriate place or situation on the basis of classification or appraisal **c :** to submit to someone or something for appropriate action **:** DELEGATE
*synonym* see COMMIT
— **rel·e·ga·tion** \ˌre-lə-'gā-shən\ *noun*

**re·lent** \ri-'lent\ *verb* [Middle English, to melt, soften, from Anglo-French *relenter,* from *re-* + Latin *lentare* to bend, from *lentus* soft, pliant, slow — more at LITHE] (1526)
*intransitive verb*
**1 a :** to become less severe, harsh, or strict usually from reasons of humanity **b :** to cease resistance **:** GIVE IN
**2 :** LET UP, SLACKEN
*transitive verb*
*obsolete* **:** SOFTEN, MOLLIFY
*synonym* see YIELD

**re·lent·less** \-ləs\ *adjective* (1592)

| | | |
|---|---|---|
| \ə\ abut | \ᵊ\ kitten | \ər\ further |
| \a\ ash | \ā\ ace | |
| \ä\ mop, mar | \au̇\ out | \ch\ chin |
| \e\ bet | \ē\ easy | \g\ go |
| \i\ hit | \ī\ ice | \j\ job |
| \ŋ\ sing | \ō\ go | \ȯ\ law |
| \ȯi\ boy | \th\ thin | \th\ the |
| \ü\ loot | \u̇\ foot | \y\ yet |
| \zh\ vision | *see also* Guide to Pronunciation | |

: showing or promising no abatement of severity, intensity, strength, or pace : UNRELENTING ⟨*relentless* pressure⟩ ⟨a *relentless* campaign⟩
— **re·lent·less·ly** *adverb*
— **re·lent·less·ness** *noun*

**rel·e·vance** \'re-lə-vən(t)s\ *noun* (1733)
**1 a :** relation to the matter at hand **b :** practical and especially social applicability : PERTINENCE ⟨giving *relevance* to college courses⟩
**2 :** the ability (as of an information retrieval system) to retrieve material that satisfies the needs of the user

**rel·e·van·cy** \-vən(t)-sē\ *noun, plural* **-cies** (1561)
: RELEVANCE; *also* : something relevant

**rel·e·vant** \'re-lə-vənt\ *adjective* [Medieval Latin *relevant-, relevans,* from Latin, present participle of *relevare* to raise up — more at RELIEVE] (1560)
**1 a :** having significant and demonstrable bearing on the matter at hand **b :** affording evidence tending to prove or disprove the matter at issue or under discussion ⟨*relevant* testimony⟩ **c :** having social relevance
**2 :** PROPORTIONAL, RELATIVE ☆
— **rel·e·vant·ly** *adverb*

**re·li·abil·i·ty** \ri-ˌlī-ə-'bi-lə-tē\ *noun* (1816)
**1 :** the quality or state of being reliable
**2 :** the extent to which an experiment, test, or measuring procedure yields the same results on repeated trials

**¹re·li·able** \ri-'lī-ə-bəl\ *adjective* (1569)
**1 :** suitable or fit to be relied on : DEPENDABLE
**2 :** giving the same result on successive trials
— **re·li·able·ness** *noun*
— **re·li·ably** \-blē\ *adverb*

**²reliable** *noun* (1890)
: one that is reliable

**re·li·ance** \ri-'lī-ən(t)s\ *noun* (1607)
**1 :** the act of relying : the state of being reliant
**2 :** something or someone relied on

**re·li·ant** \-ənt\ *adjective* (1859)
: having reliance on something or someone : DEPENDENT
— **re·li·ant·ly** *adverb*

**rel·ic** \'re-lik\ *noun* [Middle English *relik,* from Old French *relique,* from Medieval Latin *reliquia,* from Late Latin *reliquiae,* plural, remains of a martyr, from Latin, remains, from *relinquere* to leave behind — more at RELINQUISH] (13th century)
**1 a :** an object esteemed and venerated because of association with a saint or martyr **b :** SOUVENIR, MEMENTO
**2** *plural* : REMAINS, CORPSE
**3 :** a survivor or remnant left after decay, disintegration, or disappearance
**4 :** a trace of some past or outmoded practice, custom, or belief

**¹rel·ict** \'re-likt\ *noun* [in sense 1, from Middle English *relicte,* from Late Latin *relicta,* from Latin, feminine of *relictus,* past participle of *relinquere;* in senses 2 & 3, from *relict* residual, adjective, from Latin *relictus*] (15th century)
**1 :** WIDOW
**2 :** a persistent remnant of an otherwise extinct flora or fauna or kind of organism
**3 a :** a relief feature or rock remaining after other parts have disappeared **b :** something left unchanged

**²relict** *adjective* (15th century)
: of, relating to, or being a relict ⟨*relict* populations⟩

**re·lic·tion** \ri-'lik-shən\ *noun* [Latin *reliction-, relictio* act of leaving behind, from *relinquere*] (circa 1676)
**1 :** the gradual recession of water leaving land permanently uncovered
**2 :** land uncovered by reliction

**¹re·lief** \ri-'lēf\ *noun* [Middle English, from Middle French, from Old French, from *relever* to relieve] (14th century)
**1 :** a payment made by a feudal tenant to a lord on succeeding to an inherited estate

**2 a :** removal or lightening of something oppressive, painful, or distressing **b :** WELFARE
**2a c :** military assistance to an endangered post or force **d :** means of breaking or avoiding monotony or boredom : DIVERSION
**3 :** release from a post or from the performance of duty
**4 :** one that takes the place of another on duty
**5 :** legal remedy or redress
**6** [French] **a :** a mode of sculpture in which forms and figures are distinguished from a surrounding plane surface **b :** sculpture or a sculptural form executed in this mode **c :** projecting detail, ornament, or figures
**7 :** sharpness of outline due to contrast ⟨a roof in bold *relief* against the sky⟩
**8 :** the elevations or inequalities of a land surface
**9 :** the pitching done by a relief pitcher ⟨two innings of hitless *relief*⟩

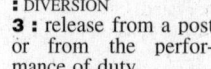
**relief 6b**

**²relief** *adjective* (1838)
**1 :** providing relief
**2 :** characterized by surface inequalities
**3 :** of or used in letterpress

**relief map** *noun* (1876)
: a map representing topographic relief

**relief pitcher** *noun* (circa 1949)
: a baseball pitcher who takes over for another during a game

**relief printing** *noun* (1875)
: LETTERPRESS 1

**re·lieve** \ri-'lēv\ *verb* **re·lieved; re·liev·ing** [Middle English *releven,* from Middle French *relever* to raise, relieve, from Latin *relevare,* from *re-* + *levare* to raise — more at LEVER] (14th century)
*transitive verb*
**1 a :** to free from a burden : give aid or help to **b :** to set free from an obligation, condition, or restriction **c :** to ease of a burden, wrong, or oppression by judicial or legislative interposition
**2 a :** to bring about the removal or alleviation of : MITIGATE **b :** ROB, DEPRIVE
**3 a :** to release from a post, station, or duty **b :** to take the place of
**4 :** to remove or lessen the monotony of
**5 a :** to set off by contrast **b :** to raise in relief
**6 :** to discharge the bladder or bowels of (oneself)
*intransitive verb*
**1 :** to bring or give relief
**2 :** to stand out in relief
**3 :** to serve as a relief pitcher ☆
— **re·liev·able** \-'lē-və-bəl\ *adjective*

**re·lieved** \ri-'lēvd\ *adjective* (1869)
: experiencing or showing relief especially from anxiety or pent-up emotions
— **re·liev·ed·ly** \-'lē-vəd-lē\ *adverb*

**re·liev·er** \ri-'lē-vər\ *noun* (15th century)
: one that relieves; *especially* : RELIEF PITCHER

**re·lie·vo** \ri-'lē-(ˌ)vō, rēl-'yā-(ˌ)vō\ *noun, plural* **-vos** [Italian *rilievo,* from *rilevare* to raise, from Latin *relevare*] (1625)
: RELIEF 6

**re·li·gio-** \ri-'li-j(ē-)ō\ *combining form*
: religion and ⟨*religio*-political⟩

**re·li·gion** \ri-'li-jən\ *noun* [Middle English *religioun,* from Latin *religion-, religio* supernatural constraint, sanction, religious practice, perhaps from *religare* to restrain, tie back — more at RELY] (13th century)
**1 a :** the state of a religious ⟨a nun in her 20th year of *religion*⟩ **b (1) :** the service and worship of God or the supernatural **(2) :** commitment or devotion to religious faith or observance
**2 :** a personal set or institutionalized system of religious attitudes, beliefs, and practices

**3** *archaic* **:** scrupulous conformity : CONSCIENTIOUSNESS
**4 :** a cause, principle, or system of beliefs held to with ardor and faith
— **re·li·gion·less** *adjective*

**re·li·gion·ist** \-'li-jə-nist, -'lij-nist\ *noun* (1653)
: a person adhering to a religion; *especially* : a religious zealot

**re·li·gi·ose** \ri-'li-jē-ˌōs\ *adjective* [*religi*on + *¹-ose*] (1853)
: RELIGIOUS; *especially* : excessively, obtrusively, or sentimentally religious
— **re·li·gi·os·i·ty** \-ˌli-jē-'ä-sə-tē\ *noun*

**¹re·li·gious** \ri-'li-jəs\ *adjective* [Middle English, from Old French *religieus,* from Latin *religiosus,* from *religio*] (13th century)
**1 :** relating to or manifesting faithful devotion to an acknowledged ultimate reality or deity ⟨a *religious* person⟩ ⟨*religious* attitudes⟩
**2 :** of, relating to, or devoted to religious beliefs or observances
**3 a :** scrupulously and consciensiously faithful **b :** FERVENT, ZEALOUS
— **re·li·gious·ly** *adverb*
— **re·li·gious·ness** *noun*

**²religious** *noun, plural* **religious** [Middle English, from Old French *religieus,* from *religieus,* adjective] (13th century)
: a member of a religious order under monastic vows

**re·line** \(ˌ)rē-'līn\ *transitive verb* (1851)
: to put new lines on or a new lining in

**re·lin·quish** \ri-'liŋ-kwish, -'lin-\ *transitive verb* [Middle English *relinquisshen,* from Middle French *relinquiss-,* stem of *relinquir,* from Latin *relinquere* to leave behind, from *re-* + *linquere* to leave — more at LOAN] (15th century)
**1 :** to withdraw or retreat from : leave behind
**2 :** GIVE UP ⟨*relinquish* a title⟩

---

☆ **SYNONYMS**
**Relevant, germane, material, pertinent, apposite, applicable, apropos** mean relating to or bearing upon the matter in hand. RELEVANT implies a traceable, significant, logical connection ⟨found material *relevant* to her case⟩. GERMANE may additionally imply a fitness for or appropriateness to the situation or occasion ⟨a point not *germane* to the discussion⟩. MATERIAL implies so close a relationship that it cannot be dispensed with without serious alteration of the case ⟨facts *material* to the investigation⟩. PERTINENT stresses a clear and decisive relevance ⟨a *pertinent* observation⟩. APPOSITE suggests a felicitous relevance ⟨add an *apposite* quotation to the definition⟩. APPLICABLE suggests the fitness of bringing a general rule or principle to bear upon a particular case ⟨the rule is not *applicable* in this case⟩. APROPOS suggests being both relevant and opportune ⟨the quip was *apropos*⟩.

**Relieve, alleviate, lighten, assuage, mitigate, allay** mean to make something less grievous. RELIEVE implies a lifting of enough of a burden to make it tolerable ⟨took an aspirin to *relieve* the pain⟩. ALLEVIATE implies temporary or partial lessening of pain or distress ⟨the lotion *alleviated* the itching⟩. LIGHTEN implies reducing a burdensome or depressing weight ⟨good news would *lighten* our worries⟩. ASSUAGE implies softening or sweetening what is harsh or disagreeable ⟨ocean breezes *assuaged* the intense heat⟩. MITIGATE suggests a moderating or countering of the effect of something violent or painful ⟨the need to *mitigate* barbaric laws⟩. ALLAY implies an effective calming or soothing of fears or alarms ⟨*allayed* their fears⟩.

**3 a :** to stop holding physically **:** RELEASE ⟨slowly *relinquished* his grip on the bar⟩ **b :** to give over possession or control of **:** YIELD ⟨few leaders willingly *relinquish* power⟩ ☆ — **re·lin·quish·ment** \-mənt\ *noun*

**rel·i·quary** \'re-lə-ˌkwer-ē\ *noun, plural* **-quar·ies** [French *reliquaire*, from Medieval Latin *reliquiarium*, from *reliquia* relic — more at RELIC] (circa 1656) **:** a container or shrine in which sacred relics are kept

**re·lique** \ri-'lēk, 're-lik\ *archaic variant of* RELIC

**re·liq·ui·ae** \ri-'li-kwē-ˌī, -kwē-ˌē\ *noun plural* [Latin — more at RELIC] (1654) **:** remains of the dead **:** RELICS

**¹rel·ish** \'re-lish\ *noun* [alteration of Middle English *reles* taste, from Old French, something left behind, release, from *relessier* to release] (1530)
**1 :** characteristic flavor; *especially* **:** pleasing or zestful flavor
**2 :** a quantity just sufficient to flavor or characterize **:** TRACE
**3 a :** enjoyment of or delight in something that satisfies one's tastes, inclinations, or desires ⟨eat with great *relish*⟩ **b :** a strong liking **:** INCLINATION ⟨has little *relish* for sports⟩
**4 a :** something adding a tasteful flavor; *especially* **:** a condiment (as of pickles or green tomatoes) eaten with other food to add flavor **b :** APPETIZER, HORS D'OEUVRE

**²relish** (1586)
*transitive verb*
**1 :** to add relish to
**2 :** to be pleased or gratified by **:** ENJOY
**3 :** to eat or drink with pleasure
**4 :** to appreciate with taste and discernment
*intransitive verb*
**:** to have a characteristic or pleasing taste — **rel·ish·able** \'re-li-shə-bəl\ *adjective*

**re·live** \(ˌ)rē-'liv\ (1548)
*intransitive verb*
**:** to live again
*transitive verb*
**:** to live over again; *especially* **:** to experience again in the imagination

**re·lo·cate** \(ˌ)rē-'lō-ˌkāt, ˌrē-lō-'\ (1834)
*transitive verb*
**:** to locate again **:** establish or lay out in a new place
*intransitive verb*
**:** to move to a new location — **re·lo·cat·able** \-'lō-ˌkā-tə-bəl, -ˌlō-'kā-\ *adjective* — **re·lo·ca·tion** \ˌrē-lō-'kā-shən\ *noun*

**re·lo·cat·ee** \ˌrē-lə-ˌkā-'tē, ˌrē-ˌlō-kə-'tē\ *noun* (1954)
**:** one who moves to a new location **:** one that is relocated

**re·lu·cent** \ri-'lü-s³nt\ *adjective* [Latin *relucent-, relucens*, past participle of *relucēre* to shine back, from *re-* + *lucēre* to shine — more at LIGHT] (15th century)
**:** reflecting light **:** SHINING

**re·luct** \ri-'lǝkt\ *intransitive verb* [Latin *reluctari*] (1547)
**:** to show reluctance

**re·luc·tance** \ri-'lǝk-tǝn(t)s\ *noun* (1710)
**1 :** the quality or state of being reluctant
**2 :** the opposition offered in a magnetic circuit to magnetic flux; *specifically* **:** the ratio of the magnetic potential difference to the corresponding flux

**re·luc·tan·cy** \-tǝn(t)-sē\ *noun* (1634)
**:** RELUCTANCE

**re·luc·tant** \ri-'lǝk-tǝnt\ *adjective* [Latin *reluctant-, reluctans*, present participle of *reluctari* to struggle against, from *re-* + *luctari* to struggle] (1667)
**:** feeling or showing aversion, hesitation, or unwillingness ⟨*reluctant* to get involved⟩; *also*
**:** having or assuming a specified role unwillingly ⟨a *reluctant* hero⟩
**synonym** see DISINCLINED — **re·luc·tant·ly** *adverb*

**re·luc·tate** \ri-'lǝk-ˌtāt\ *intransitive verb* **-tat·ed; -tat·ing** (1643)
**:** RELUCT — **re·luc·ta·tion** \ri-ˌlǝk-'tā-shən, ˌrē-\ *noun*

**re·lume** \(ˌ)rē-'lüm\ *transitive verb* **re·lumed; re·lum·ing** [irregular from Late Latin *reluminare*, from Latin *re-* + *luminare* to light up — more at ILLUMINATE] (1604)
*archaic* **:** to light or light up again **:** REKINDLE

**re·ly** \ri-'lī\ *intransitive verb* **re·lied; re·ly·ing** [Middle English *relien* to rally, from Middle French *relier* to connect, rally, from Latin *religare* to tie back, from *re-* + *ligare* to tie — more at LIGATURE] (1574)
**1 :** to be dependent ⟨the system on which we *rely* for water⟩
**2 :** to have confidence based on experience ⟨someone you can *rely* on⟩ — **re·li·er** \-'lī-(ə)r\ *noun*

**rem** \'rem\ *noun* [roentgen equivalent *man*] (1947)
**:** the dosage of an ionizing radiation that will cause the same biological effect as one roentgen of X-ray or gamma-ray exposure

**REM** \'rem\ *noun* (1957)
**:** RAPID EYE MOVEMENT

**¹re·main** \ri-'mān\ *intransitive verb* [Middle English, from Middle French *remaindre*, from Latin *remanēre*, from *re-* + *manēre* to remain — more at MANSION] (14th century)
**1 a :** to be a part not destroyed, taken, or used up ⟨only a few ruins *remain*⟩ **b :** to be something yet to be shown, done, or treated ⟨it *remains* to be seen⟩
**2 :** to stay in the same place or with the same person or group; *especially* **:** to stay behind
**3 :** to continue unchanged ⟨the fact *remains* that we can't go⟩

**²remain** *noun* (15th century)
**1** *obsolete* **:** STAY
**2 :** a remaining part or trace — usually used in plural
**3** *plural* **:** a dead body

**¹re·main·der** \ri-'mān-dər\ *noun* [Middle English, from Anglo-French, from Middle French *remaindre*] (14th century)
**1 :** an interest or estate in property that follows and is dependent on the termination of a prior intervening possessory estate created at the same time by the same instrument
**2 a :** a remaining group, part, or trace **b (1)** **:** the number left after a subtraction **(2) :** the final undivided part after division that is less or of lower degree than the divisor
**3 :** a book sold at a reduced price by the publisher after sales have slowed

**²remainder** *adjective* (1567)
**:** LEFTOVER, REMAINING

**³remainder** *transitive verb* **-dered; -der·ing** \-d(ə-)riŋ\ (1904)
**:** to dispose of as remainders

**remainder theorem** *noun* (1886)
**:** a theorem in algebra: if $f(x)$ is a polynomial in $x$ then the remainder on dividing $f(x)$ by $x - a$ is $f(a)$

**¹re·make** \(ˌ)rē-'māk\ *transitive verb* **-made** \-'mād\; **-mak·ing** (circa 1635)
**:** to make anew or in a different form — **re·mak·er** \-'mā-kər\ *noun*

**²re·make** \'rē-ˌmāk\ *noun* (1936)
**:** one that is remade; *especially* **:** a new version of a motion picture

**re·man** \(ˌ)rē-'man\ *transitive verb* (1666)
**1 :** to man again or anew
**2 :** to imbue with courage again

**re·mand** \ri-'mand\ *transitive verb* [Middle English *remaunden*, from Middle French *remander*, from Late Latin *remandare* to send back word, from Latin *re-* + *mandare* to order — more at MANDATE] (15th century)
**:** to order back: as **a :** to send back (a case) to another court or agency for further action **b :** to return to custody pending trial or for further detention — **remand** *noun*

**rem·a·nence** \'re-mə-nən(t)s, ri-'mā-\ *noun* (circa 1880)
**:** the magnetic induction remaining in a magnetized substance no longer under external magnetic influence

**rem·a·nent** \-nənt\ *adjective* [Middle English, from Latin *remanent-, remanens*, present participle of *remanēre* to remain] (15th century)
**1 :** RESIDUAL, REMAINING
**2 :** of, relating to, or characterized by remanence

**re·man·u·fac·ture** \(ˌ)rē-ˌma-nyə-'fak-chər, -ˌma-nə-\ *transitive verb* (1851)
**:** to manufacture into a new product — **remanufacture** *noun* — **re·man·u·fac·tur·er** \-chər-ər\ *noun*

**re·map** \(ˌ)rē-'map\ *transitive verb* (1931)
**:** to map again; *also* **:** to lay out in a new pattern

**¹re·mark** \ri-'märk\ *noun* [French *remarque*, from Middle French, from *remarquer* to remark, from *re-* *re-* + *marquer* to mark — more at MARQUE] (1660)
**1 :** the act of remarking **:** NOTICE
**2 :** an expression of opinion or judgment
**3 :** mention of that which deserves attention or notice

**²remark** (1675)
*transitive verb*
**1 :** to take notice of **:** OBSERVE
**2 :** to express as an observation or comment **:** SAY
*intransitive verb*
**:** to notice something and comment thereon — used with *on* or *upon*

**re·mark·able** \ri-'mär-kə-bəl\ *adjective* (circa 1604)
**:** worthy of being or likely to be noticed especially as being uncommon or extraordinary
**synonym** see NOTICEABLE — **re·mark·able·ness** *noun*

**re·mark·ably** \-blē\ *adverb* (1638)
**1 :** in a remarkable manner ⟨*remarkably* talented⟩
**2 :** as is remarkable ⟨*remarkably*, no one was hurt⟩

**re·marque** \ri-'märk\ *noun* [French *remarque* remark, note, from Middle French, from *remarquer*] (1882)
**1 :** a drawn, etched, or incised scribble or sketch done on the margin of a plate or stone and removed before the regular printing
**2 :** a proof taken before remarques have been removed

**re·mas·ter** \(ˌ)rē-'mas-tər\ *transitive verb* (1964)
**:** to create a new master of especially by altering or enhancing the sound quality of an older recording

**re·match** \(ˌ)rē-'mach, 'rē-ˌ\ *noun* (1941)

---

☆ **SYNONYMS**
**Relinquish, yield, resign, surrender, abandon, waive** mean to give up completely. RELINQUISH usually does not imply strong feeling but may suggest some regret, reluctance, or weakness ⟨*relinquished* her crown⟩. YIELD implies concession or compliance or submission to force ⟨the troops *yielded* ground grudgingly⟩. RESIGN emphasizes voluntary relinquishment or sacrifice without struggle ⟨*resigned* her position⟩. SURRENDER implies a giving up after a struggle to retain or resist ⟨*surrendered* their claims⟩. ABANDON stresses finality and completeness in giving up ⟨*abandoned* all hope⟩. WAIVE implies conceding or forgoing with little or no compulsion ⟨*waived* the right to a trial by jury⟩.

---

\ə\ abut \ᵊ\ kitten \ər\ further \a\ ash \ā\ ace
\ä\ mop, mar \au̇\ out \ch\ chin \e\ bet \ē\ easy
\g\ go \i\ hit \ī\ ice \j\ job \ŋ\ sing \ō\ go
\ȯ\ law \ȯi\ boy \th\ thin \t͟h\ the \ü\ loot \u̇\ foot
\y\ yet \zh\ vision *see also* Guide to Pronunciation

: a second match between the same contestants or teams

**re·me·di·a·ble** \ri-'mē-dē-ə-bəl\ *adjective* (15th century)
: capable of being remedied
— **re·me·di·abil·i·ty** \ri-,mē-dē-ə-'bi-lə-tē\ *noun*

**re·me·di·al** \ri-'mē-dē-əl\ *adjective* (1651)
**1** : intended as a remedy
**2** : concerned with the correction of faulty study habits and the raising of a pupil's general competence ⟨*remedial* reading courses⟩; *also* : receiving or requiring remedial instruction ⟨*remedial* students⟩
— **re·me·di·al·ly** \-ə-lē\ *adverb*

**re·me·di·ate** \ri-'mē-dē-ət\ *adjective* (1605)
*archaic* : REMEDIAL

**re·me·di·a·tion** \ri-,mē-dē-'ā-shən\ *noun* (1818)
: the act or process of remedying ⟨*remediation* of reading problems⟩
— **re·me·di·ate** \-'mē-dē-,āt\ *transitive verb*

**¹rem·e·dy** \'re-mə-dē\ *noun, plural* **-dies** [Middle English *remedie*, from Anglo-French, from Latin *remedium*, from *re-* + *mederi* to heal — more at MEDICAL] (13th century)
**1** : a medicine, application, or treatment that relieves or cures a disease
**2** : something that corrects or counteracts
**3** : the legal means to recover a right or to prevent or obtain redress for a wrong
— **rem·e·di·less** *adjective*

**²remedy** *transitive verb* **-died; -dy·ing** (15th century)
: to provide or serve as a remedy for : RELIEVE ⟨*remedy* a social evil⟩
*synonym* see CORRECT

**re·mem·ber** \ri-'mem-bər\ *verb* **-bered; -ber·ing** \-b(ə-)riŋ\ [Middle English *remembren*, from Middle French *remembrer*, from Late Latin *rememorari*, from Latin *re-* + Late Latin *memorari* to be mindful of, from Latin *memor* mindful — more at MEMORY] (14th century)
*transitive verb*
**1** : to bring to mind or think of again ⟨*remembers* the old days⟩
**2** *archaic* **a** : BETHINK 1b **b** : REMIND
**3 a** : to keep in mind for attention or consideration ⟨*remembers* friends at Christmas⟩ **b** : REWARD ⟨was *remembered* in the will⟩
**4** : to retain in the memory ⟨*remember* the facts until the test is over⟩
**5** : to convey greetings from ⟨*remember* me to her⟩
**6** : RECORD, COMMEMORATE
*intransitive verb*
**1** : to exercise or have the power of memory
**2** : to have a recollection or remembrance ☆
— **re·mem·ber·abil·i·ty** \-,mem-b(ə-)rə-'bi-lə-tē\ *noun*
— **re·mem·ber·able** \-'mem-b(ə-)rə-bəl\ *adjective*
— **re·mem·ber·er** \-bər-ər\ *noun*

**re·mem·brance** \ri-'mem-brən(t)s *also* -bə-rən(t)s\ *noun* (14th century)
**1** : the state of bearing in mind
**2 a** : the ability to remember : MEMORY **b** : the period over which one's memory extends
**3** : an act of recalling to mind
**4** : a memory of a person, thing, or event
**5 a** : something that serves to keep in or bring to mind : REMINDER **b** : COMMEMORATION, MEMORIAL **c** : a greeting or gift recalling or expressing friendship or affection
*synonym* see MEMORY

**Remembrance Day** *noun* (1918)
: November 11 set aside in commemoration of the end of hostilities in 1918 and 1945 and observed as a legal holiday in Canada; *also* : REMEMBRANCE SUNDAY

**re·mem·branc·er** \ri-'mem-brən(t)-sər\ *noun* (15th century)
**1** : any of several English officials
**2** : one that reminds

**Remembrance Sunday** *noun* (1942)
: a Sunday that is usually closest to November 11 and that in Great Britain is set aside in commemoration of the end of hostilities in 1918 and 1945

**re·mex** \'rē-,meks\ *noun, plural* **rem·i·ges** \'re-mə-,jēz\ [New Latin *remig-, remex,* from Latin, oarsman, from *remus* oar + *agere* to drive — more at ROW, AGENT] (1767)
: a primary or secondary quill feather of the wing of a bird

**re·mind** \ri-'mīnd\ *transitive verb* (1660)
: to put in mind of something : cause to remember
*synonym* see REMEMBER
— **re·mind·er** *noun*

**re·mind·ful** \-'mīn(d)-fəl\ *adjective* (1810)
**1** : MINDFUL
**2** : tending to remind : SUGGESTIVE, EVOCATIVE

**rem·i·nisce** \,re-mə-'nis\ *intransitive verb* **-nisced; -nisc·ing** [back-formation from *reminiscence*] (1829)
: to indulge in reminiscence
*synonym* see REMEMBER
— **rem·i·nis·cer** \-'ni-sər\ *noun*

**rem·i·nis·cence** \-'ni-s°n(t)s\ *noun* (1589)
**1** : apprehension of a Platonic idea as if it had been known in a previous existence
**2 a** : recall to mind of a long-forgotten experience or fact **b** : the process or practice of thinking or telling about past experiences
**3 a** : a remembered experience **b** : an account of a memorable experience — often used in plural
**4** : something so like another as to be regarded as an unconscious repetition, imitation, or survival
*synonym* see MEMORY

**rem·i·nis·cent** \-s°nt\ *adjective* [Latin *reminiscent-, reminiscens,* present participle of *reminisci* to remember, from *re-* + *-minisci* (akin to Latin *ment-, mens* mind) — more at MIND] (1765)
**1** : of the character of or relating to reminiscence
**2** : marked by or given to reminiscence
**3** : tending to remind : SUGGESTIVE
— **rem·i·nis·cent·ly** *adverb*

**rem·i·nis·cen·tial** \,re-mə-(,)ni-'sen(t)-shəl\ *adjective* (1646)
: REMINISCENT

**re·mint** \(,)rē-'mint\ *transitive verb* (1823)
: to melt down (old or worn coin) and make into new coin

**re·mise** \ri-'mīz\ *transitive verb* **re·mised; re·mis·ing** [Middle English, from Middle French *remis,* past participle of *remettre* to put back, from Latin *remittere* to send back] (15th century)
: to give, grant, or release a claim to : DEED

**re·miss** \ri-'mis\ *adjective* [Middle English, from Latin *remissus,* from past participle of *remittere* to send back, relax] (15th century)
**1** : negligent in the performance of work or duty : CARELESS
**2** : showing neglect or inattention : LAX
*synonym* see NEGLIGENT
— **re·miss·ly** *adverb*
— **re·miss·ness** *noun*

**re·mis·si·ble** \ri-'mi-sə-bəl\ *adjective* (1577)
: capable of being forgiven ⟨*remissible* sins⟩
— **re·mis·si·bly** \-blē\ *adverb*

**re·mis·sion** \ri-'mi-shən\ *noun* (13th century)
**1** : the act or process of remitting
**2** : a state or period during which something is remitted

**¹re·mit** \ri-'mit\ *verb* **re·mit·ted; re·mit·ting** [Middle English *remitten,* from Latin *remittere* to send back, from *re-* + *mittere* to send] (14th century)
*transitive verb*
**1 a** : to lay aside (a mood or disposition) partly or wholly **b** : to desist from (an activity) **c** : to let (as attention or diligence) slacken : RELAX

**2 a** : to release from the guilt or penalty of ⟨*remit* sins⟩ **b** : to refrain from exacting ⟨*remit* a tax⟩ **c** : to cancel or refrain from inflicting ⟨*remit* the penalty⟩ **d** : to give relief from (suffering)
**3** : to submit or refer for consideration, judgment, decision, or action; *specifically* : REMAND
**4** : to restore or consign to a former status or condition
**5** : POSTPONE, DEFER
**6** : to send (money) to a person or place especially in payment of a demand, account, or draft
*intransitive verb*
**1 a** : to abate in force or intensity : MODERATE **b** *of a disease or abnormality* : to abate symptoms for a period
**2** : to send money (as in payment)
— **re·mit·ment** \-'mit-mənt\ *noun*
— **re·mit·ta·ble** \-'mi-tə-bəl\ *adjective*
— **re·mit·ter** *noun*

**²re·mit** \ri-'mit, 'rē-\ *noun* (15th century)
**1** : an act of remitting
**2** : something remitted to another person or authority

**re·mit·tal** \ri-'mi-t°l\ *noun* (1596)
: REMISSION

**re·mit·tance** \ri-'mi-t°n(t)s\ *noun* (1705)
**1 a** : a sum of money remitted **b** : an instrument by which money is remitted
**2** : transmittal of money (as to a distant place)

**remittance man** *noun* (1886)
: one living abroad on remittances from home

**re·mit·tent** \ri-'mi-t°nt\ *adjective* [Latin *remittent-, remittens,* present participle of *remittere*] (1693)
*of a disease* : marked by alternating periods of abatement and increase of symptoms

**¹rem·nant** \'rem-nənt\ *noun* [Middle English, contraction of *remenant,* from Middle French, from present participle of *remenoir* to remain, from Latin *remanēre* — more at REMAIN] (14th century)
**1 a** : a usually small part, member, or trace remaining **b** : a small surviving group — often used in plural
**2** : an unsold or unused end of piece goods

**²remnant** *adjective* (1550)
: still remaining

**re·mod·el** \(,)rē-'mä-d°l\ *transitive verb* (1789)
: to alter the structure of : REMAKE

**re·mon·strance** \ri-'män(t)-strən(t)s\ *noun* (1585)
**1** : an earnest presentation of reasons for opposition or grievance; *especially* : a document formally stating such points
**2** : an act or instance of remonstrating

**re·mon·strant** \-strənt\ *adjective* (1641)
: vigorously objecting or opposing
— **remonstrant** *noun*
— **re·mon·strant·ly** *adverb*

**re·mon·strate** \'re-mən-,strāt, ri-'män-\ *verb* **-strat·ed; -strat·ing** [Medieval Latin *remonstratus,* past participle of *remonstrare* to

demonstrate, from Latin *re-* + *monstrare* to show — more at MUSTER] (1695)
*intransitive verb*
**:** to present and urge reasons in opposition **:** EXPOSTULATE — usually used with *with*
*transitive verb*
**:** to say or plead in protest, reproof, or opposition
— **re·mon·stra·tion** \ˌre-mən-'strā-shən, ri-'man-\ *noun*
— **re·mon·stra·tive** \ri-'män(t)-strə-tiv\ *adjective*
— **re·mon·stra·tive·ly** *adverb*
— **re·mon·stra·tor** \'re-mən-ˌstrā-tər, ri-'man-\ *noun*

**rem·o·ra** \'re-mə-rə *also* ri-'mȯr-ə *or* -'mȯr-\ *noun* [Late Latin, from Latin, delay, from *remorari* to delay, from *re-* + *morari* to delay — more at MORATORIUM] (1567)
**1 :** any of a family (Echeneididae) of marine bony fishes that have the anterior dorsal fin modified into a suctorial disk on the head by means of which they cling especially to other fishes
**2 :** HINDRANCE, DRAG

remoras on tiger shark

**re·morse** \ri-'mȯrs\ *noun* [Middle English, from Middle French *remors,* from Medieval Latin *remorsus,* from Late Latin, act of biting again, from Latin *remordēre* to bite again, from *re-* + *mordēre* to bite — more at MORDANT] (14th century)
**1 :** a gnawing distress arising from a sense of guilt for past wrongs **:** SELF-REPROACH
**2** *obsolete* **:** COMPASSION ◆
**synonym** see PENITENCE

**re·morse·ful** \-'mȯrs-fəl\ *adjective* (1592)
**:** motivated or marked by remorse
— **re·morse·ful·ly** \-fə-lē\ *adverb*
— **re·morse·ful·ness** *noun*

**re·morse·less** \-ləs\ *adjective* (1593)
**1 :** having no remorse **:** MERCILESS
**2 :** RELENTLESS
— **re·morse·less·ly** *adverb*
— **re·morse·less·ness** *noun*

**¹re·mote** \ri-'mōt\ *adjective* **re·mot·er; -est** [Middle English, from Latin *remotus,* from past participle of *removēre* to remove] (15th century)
**1 :** separated by an interval or space greater than usual ⟨an involucre *remote* from the flower⟩
**2 :** far removed in space, time, or relation **:** DIVERGENT ⟨the *remote* past⟩ ⟨comments *remote* from the truth⟩
**3 :** OUT-OF-THE-WAY, SECLUDED ⟨a *remote* cabin in the hills⟩
**4 :** acting, acted on, or controlled indirectly or from a distance ⟨*remote* computer operation⟩; *also* **:** relating to the acquisition of information about a distant object (as by radar or photography) without coming into physical contact with it ⟨*remote* sensing⟩
**5 :** not arising from a primary or proximate action
**6 :** small in degree **:** SLIGHT ⟨a *remote* possibility⟩
**7 :** distant in manner **:** ALOOF
— **re·mote·ly** *adverb*
— **re·mote·ness** *noun*

**²remote** *noun* (1937)
**1 :** a radio or television program or a portion of a program originating outside the studio
**2 :** REMOTE CONTROL 2

**remote control** *noun* (1904)
**1 :** control (as by radio signal) of operation from a point at some distance removed

**2 :** a device or mechanism for controlling something from a distance

**re·mo·tion** \ri-'mō-shən\ *noun* (15th century)
**1 :** the quality or state of being remote
**2 :** the act of removing **:** REMOVAL
**3** *obsolete* **:** DEPARTURE

**¹re·mount** \(ˌ)rē-'maunt\ *verb* [Middle English, partly from *re-* + *mounten* to mount, partly from Middle French *remonter,* from *re-* + *monter* to mount] (15th century)
*transitive verb*
**1 :** to mount (something) again ⟨*remount* a picture⟩
**2 :** to furnish remounts to
*intransitive verb*
**1 :** to mount again
**2 :** REVERT

**²re·mount** \'rē-ˌmaunt, (ˌ)rē-'\ *noun* (1781)
**:** a fresh horse to replace one no longer available

**re·mov·al** \ri-'mü-vəl\ *noun* (1597)
**:** the act or process of removing **:** the fact of being removed

**¹re·move** \ri-'müv\ *verb* **re·moved; re·mov·ing** [Middle English, from Old French *removoir,* from Latin *removēre,* from *re-* + *movēre* to move] (14th century)
*transitive verb*
**1 a :** to change the location, position, station, or residence of ⟨*remove* soldiers to the front⟩ **b :** to transfer (a legal proceeding) from one court to another
**2 :** to move by lifting, pushing aside, or taking away or off ⟨*remove* your hat⟩
**3 :** to dismiss from office
**4 :** to get rid of **:** ELIMINATE ⟨*remove* a tumor surgically⟩
*intransitive verb*
**1 :** to change location, station, or residence ⟨*removing* from the city to the suburbs⟩
**2 :** to go away
**3 :** to be capable of being removed
— **re·mov·abil·i·ty** \-ˌmü-və-'bi-lə-tē\ *noun*
— **re·mov·able** *also* **re·move·able** \ri-'mü-və-bəl\ *adjective*
— **re·mov·able·ness** \-'mü-və-bəl-nəs\ *noun*
— **re·mov·ably** \-blē\ *adverb*
— **re·mov·er** *noun*

**²remove** *noun* (1553)
**1 :** REMOVAL; *specifically* **:** MOVE 2c
**2 a :** a distance or interval separating one person or thing from another **b :** a degree or stage of separation

**removed** *adjective* (circa 1548)
**1 a :** distant in degree of relationship **b :** of a younger or older generation ⟨a second cousin's child is a second cousin once *removed*⟩
**2 :** separate or remote in space, time, or character

**REM sleep** *noun* (1965)
**:** a state of sleep that recurs cyclically several times during a normal period of sleep and that is characterized by increased neuronal activity of the forebrain and midbrain, by depressed muscle tone, and especially in humans by dreaming, rapid eye movements, and vascular congestion of the sex organs — called also *paradoxical sleep, rapid eye movement sleep*

**re·mu·da** \ri-'mü-də, -'myü-\ *noun* [American Spanish, relay of horses, from Spanish, exchange, from *remudar* to exchange, from *re-* + *mudar* to change, from Latin *mutare* — more at MUTABLE] (circa 1892)
**:** the herd of horses from which those to be used for the day are chosen

**re·mu·ner·ate** \ri-'myü-nə-ˌrāt\ *transitive verb* **-at·ed; -at·ing** [Latin *remuneratus,* past participle of *remunerare* to recompense, from *re-* + *munerare* to give, from *muner-, munus* gift — more at MEAN] (1523)
**1 :** to pay an equivalent for ⟨their services were generously *remunerated*⟩

**2 :** to pay an equivalent to for a service, loss, or expense **:** RECOMPENSE
**synonym** see PAY
— **re·mu·ner·a·tor** \-ˌrā-tər\ *noun*
— **re·mu·ner·a·to·ry** \-rə-ˌtōr-ē, -ˌtȯr-\ *adjective*

**re·mu·ner·a·tion** \ri-ˌmyü-nə-'rā-shən\ *noun* (15th century)
**1 :** something that remunerates **:** RECOMPENSE, PAY
**2 :** an act or fact of remunerating

**re·mu·ner·a·tive** \ri-'myü-nə-rə-tiv, -ˌrā-\ *adjective* (circa 1677)
**1 :** serving to remunerate
**2 :** providing remuneration **:** PROFITABLE
— **re·mu·ner·a·tive·ly** *adverb*
— **re·mu·ner·a·tive·ness** *noun*

**Re·mus** \'rē-məs\ *noun* [Latin]
**:** a son of Mars slain by his twin brother Romulus

**re·nais·sance** \ˌre-nə-'sän(t)s, -'zän(t)s, -'sän̄s, -'zän̄s, 're-nə-ˌ, *chiefly British* ri-'nā-s°n(t)s\ *noun, often attributive* [French, from Middle French, rebirth, from *renaistre* to be born again, from Latin *renasci,* from *re-* + *nasci* to be born — more at NATION] (1845)
**1** *capitalized* **a :** the transitional movement in Europe between medieval and modern times beginning in the 14th century in Italy, lasting into the 17th century, and marked by a humanistic revival of classical influence expressed in a flowering of the arts and literature and by the beginnings of modern science **b :** the period of the Renaissance **c :** the neoclassic style of architecture prevailing during the Renaissance
**2** *often capitalized* **:** a movement or period of vigorous artistic and intellectual activity
**3 :** REBIRTH, REVIVAL

**Renaissance man** *noun* (1906)
**:** a person who has wide interests and is expert in several areas

**re·nal** \'rē-n°l\ *adjective* [French or Late Latin; French *rénal,* from Late Latin *renalis,* from Latin *renes* kidneys] (circa 1656)
**:** relating to, involving, or located in the region of the kidneys **:** NEPHRITIC

**renal clearance** *noun* (1948)
**:** CLEARANCE 3

**re·na·scence** \ri-'na-s°n(t)s, -'nā-\ *noun, often capitalized* (1727)
**:** RENAISSANCE

**re·na·scent** \-s°nt\ *adjective* [Latin *renascent-, renascens,* present participle of *renasci*] (circa 1727)

\ə\ **abut** \ᵊ\ **kitten** \ər\ **further** \a\ **ash** \ā\ **ace**
\ä\ **mop, mar** \au̇\ **out** \ch\ **chin** \e\ **bet** \ē\ **easy**
\g\ **go** \i\ **hit** \ī\ **ice** \j\ **job** \ŋ\ **sing** \ō\ **go**
\ȯ\ **law** \ȯi\ **boy** \th\ **thin** \t̲h̲\ **the** \ü\ **loot** \u̇\ **foot**
\y\ **yet** \zh\ **vision** *see also* Guide to Pronunciation

: rising again into being or vigor

**re·na·ture** \(ˌ)rē-ˈnā-chər\ *transitive verb* **re·na·tured; re·na·tur·ing** \-ˈnā-chə-riŋ, -ˈnāch-riŋ\ [*re-* + de*nature*] (1926)
: to restore (as a denatured protein) to an original or normal condition
— **re·na·tur·ation** \(ˌ)rē-ˌnā-chə-ˈrā-shən\ *noun*

**ren·con·tre** \räⁿ-kōⁿtrᵊ, ren-ˈkän-tər\ *or* **ren·coun·ter** \ren-ˈkau̇n-tər\ *noun* [*rencounter* from Middle French *rencontre*, from *rencontrer; rencontre* from French] (1523)
**1** : a hostile meeting or a contest between forces or individuals : COMBAT
**2** : a casual meeting

**ren·coun·ter** \ren-ˈkau̇n-tər\ *transitive verb* [Middle French *rencontrer* to meet by chance or in hostility, from *re-* + *encontrer* to encounter] (1549)
*archaic* : to meet casually

**rend** \ˈrend\ *verb* **rent** \ˈrent\ *also* **rend·ed** \ˈren-dəd\; **rend·ing** [Middle English, from Old English *rendan;* akin to Old Frisian *renda* to tear and perhaps to Sanskrit *randhra* hole] (before 12th century)
*transitive verb*
**1** : to remove from place by violence : WREST
**2** : to split or tear apart or in pieces by violence
**3** : to tear (the hair or clothing) as a sign of anger, grief, or despair
**4 a** : to lacerate mentally or emotionally **b** : to pierce with sound **c** : to divide (as a nation) into contesting factions
*intransitive verb*
**1** : to perform an act of tearing or splitting
**2** : to become torn or split
**synonym** see TEAR

**¹ren·der** \ˈren-dər\ *verb* **ren·dered; ren·der·ing** \-d(ə-)riŋ\ [Middle English *rendren*, from Middle French *rendre* to give back, yield, from (assumed) Vulgar Latin *rendere*, alteration of Latin *reddere*, partly from *re-* + *dare* to give & partly from *re-* + *-dere* to put — more at DATE, DO] (14th century)
*transitive verb*
**1 a** : to melt down ⟨*render* suet⟩; *also* : to extract by melting ⟨*render* lard⟩ **b** : to treat so as to convert into industrial fats and oils or fertilizer
**2 a** : to transmit to another : DELIVER **b** : GIVE UP, YIELD **c** : to furnish for consideration, approval, or information: as (1) : to hand down (a legal judgment) (2) : to agree on and report (a verdict)
**3 a** : to give in return or retribution **b** (1) : GIVE BACK, RESTORE (2) : REFLECT, ECHO **c** : to give in acknowledgment of dependence or obligation : PAY **d** : to do (a service) for another
**4 a** (1) : to cause to be or become : MAKE ⟨enough rainfall . . . to *render* irrigation unnecessary —P. E. James⟩ ⟨*rendered* him helpless⟩ (2) : IMPART **b** (1) : to reproduce or represent by artistic or verbal means : DEPICT (2) : to give a performance of (3) : to produce a copy or version of ⟨the documents are *rendered* in the original French⟩ (4) : to execute the motions of ⟨*render* a salute⟩ **c** : TRANSLATE
**5** : to direct the execution of : ADMINISTER ⟨*render* justice⟩
**6** : to apply a coat of plaster or cement directly to
*intransitive verb*
: to give recompense
— **ren·der·able** \-d(ə-)rə-bəl\ *adjective*
— **ren·der·er** \-dər-ər\ *noun*

**²render** *noun* (1647)
: a return especially in goods or services due from a feudal tenant to his lord

**¹ren·dez·vous** \ˈrän-di-ˌvü, -dā-\ *noun, plural* **ren·dez·vous** \-ˌvüz\ [Middle French *rendez vous* present yourselves] (1591)
**1 a** : a place appointed for assembling or meeting **b** : a place of popular resort : HAUNT
**2** : a meeting at an appointed place and time

**3** : the process of bringing two spacecraft together

**²rendezvous** *verb* **-voused** \-ˌvüd\; **-vous·ing** \-ˌvü-iŋ\; **-vouses** \-ˌvüz\ (circa 1645)
*intransitive verb*
: to come together at a rendezvous
*transitive verb*
**1** : to bring together at a rendezvous
**2** : to meet at a rendezvous

**ren·di·tion** \ren-ˈdi-shən\ *noun* [obsolete French, from Middle French, alteration of *reddition*, from Late Latin *reddition-, redditio*, from Latin *reddere* to return] (1601)
: the act or result of rendering: as **a** : SURRENDER **b** : TRANSLATION **c** : PERFORMANCE, INTERPRETATION

**ren·dzi·na** \ren-ˈjē-nə\ *noun* [Polish *rędzina* rich limy soil] (1922)
: any of a group of dark grayish brown intrazonal soils developed in grassy regions of high to moderate humidity from soft calcareous marl or chalk

**¹ren·e·gade** \ˈre-ni-ˌgād\ *noun* [Spanish *renegado*, from Medieval Latin *renegatus*, from past participle of *renegare* to deny, from Latin *re-* + *negare* to deny — more at NEGATE] (1583)
**1** : a deserter from one faith, cause, or allegiance to another
**2** : an individual who rejects lawful or conventional behavior

**²renegade** *intransitive verb* **-gad·ed; -gad·ing** (circa 1611)
: to become a renegade

**³renegade** *adjective* (1705)
**1** : having deserted a faith, cause, or religion for a hostile one
**2** : having rejected tradition : UNCONVENTIONAL

**re·nege** \ri-ˈnig, -ˈneg, -ˈnēg, -ˈnāg\ *verb* **re·neged; re·neg·ing** [Medieval Latin *renegare*] (1548)
*transitive verb*
: DENY, RENOUNCE
*intransitive verb*
**1** *obsolete* : to make a denial
**2** : REVOKE
**3** : to go back on a promise or commitment
— **re·neg·er** *noun*

**re·ne·go·tia·ble** \ˌrē-ni-ˈgō-sh(ē-)ə-bəl\ *adjective* (1943)
: subject to renegotiation ⟨*renegotiable* mortgages⟩ ⟨*renegotiable* rates⟩

**re·ne·go·ti·ate** \ˌrē-ni-ˈgō-shē-ˌāt\ *transitive verb* (circa 1934)
: to negotiate again (as to adjust interest rates or repayments or to get more money) ⟨*renegotiate* a loan⟩ ⟨*renegotiate* a contract⟩
— **re·ne·go·ti·a·tion** \ˌrē-ni-ˌgō-shē-ˈā-shən, -sē-ˈā-\ *noun*

**re·new** \ri-ˈnü, -ˈnyü\ (14th century)
*transitive verb*
**1** : to make like new : restore to freshness, vigor, or perfection ⟨as we *renew* our strength in sleep⟩
**2** : to make new spiritually : REGENERATE
**3 a** : to restore to existence : REVIVE **b** : to make extensive changes in : REBUILD
**4** : to do again : REPEAT
**5** : to begin again : RESUME
**6** : REPLACE, REPLENISH ⟨*renew* water in a tank⟩
**7 a** : to grant or obtain an extension of or on ⟨*renew* a license⟩ **b** : to grant or obtain an extension on the loan of ⟨*renew* a library book⟩
*intransitive verb*
**1** : to become new or as new
**2** : to begin again : RESUME
**3** : to make a renewal (as of a lease) ☆
— **re·new·er** *noun*

**re·new·able** \-ˈnü-ə-bəl, -ˈnyü-\ *adjective* (1727)
**1** : capable of being renewed ⟨*renewable* contracts⟩
**2** : capable of being replaced by natural ecological cycles or sound management practices ⟨*renewable* resources⟩

— **re·new·abil·i·ty** \-ˌnü-ə-ˈbi-lə-tē, -ˌnyü-\ *noun*
— **re·new·ably** \-ˈnü-ə-blē, -ˈnyü-\ *adverb*

**re·new·al** \ri-ˈnü-əl, -ˈnyü-\ *noun* (circa 1686)
**1** : the act or process of renewing : REPETITION
**2** : the quality or state of being renewed
**3** : something (as a subscription to a magazine) renewed
**4** : something used for renewing; *specifically* : an expenditure that betters existing fixed assets
**5** : the rebuilding of a large area (as of a city) by a public authority

**reni-** *or* **reno-** *combining form* [Latin *renes* kidneys]
: kidney ⟨*reni*form⟩

**re·ni·form** \ˈrē-nə-ˌfȯrm, ˈre-\ *adjective* [New Latin *reniformis*, from *reni-* + *-formis* -form] (circa 1753)
: suggesting a kidney in outline

**re·nin** \ˈrē-nən, ˈre-\ *noun* [International Scientific Vocabulary, from Latin *renes*] (1906)
: a proteolytic enzyme of the kidney that plays a major role in the release of angiotensin

**re·ni·ten·cy** \ˈre-nə-tən(t)-sē, ri-ˈnī-tᵊn(t)-\ *noun* (1613)
: RESISTANCE, OPPOSITION

**re·ni·tent** \ˈre-nə-tənt, ri-ˈnī-tᵊnt\ *adjective* [French or Latin; French *rénitent*, from Latin *renitent-, renitens*, present participle of *reniti* to resist, from *re-* + *niti* to strive — more at NISUS] (1701)
**1** : resisting physical pressure
**2** : resisting constraint or compulsion : RECALCITRANT

**ren·min·bi** \ˈren-ˈmin-ˈbē\ *noun plural* [Chinese (Beijing) *rénmínbì*, from *rénmín* people + *bì* currency] (1957)
: the currency of the People's Republic of China consisting of yuan

**ren·net** \ˈre-nət\ *noun* [Middle English, from (assumed) Middle English *rennen* to cause to coagulate, from Old English *gerennan*, from *ge-* together + (assumed) Old English *rennan* to cause to run; akin to Old High German *rennen* to cause to run, Old English *rinnan* to run — more at CO-, RUN] (15th century)
**1 a** : the contents of the stomach of an unweaned animal and especially a calf **b** : the lining membrane of a stomach or one of its compartments (as the fourth of a ruminant) used for curdling milk; *also* : a preparation of the stomach of animals used for this purpose
**2 a** : RENNIN **b** : a substitute for rennin

**ren·nin** \ˈre-nən\ *noun* [*rennet* + ¹*-in*] (1897)
: an enzyme that coagulates milk and is used in making cheese and junkets; *especially* : one from the mucous membrane of the stomach of a calf

**re·no·gram** \ˈrē-nə-ˌgram\ *noun* (1952)
: a photographic depiction of the course of renal excretion of a radioactively labeled substance
— **re·no·graph·ic** \ˌrē-nə-ˈgra-fik\ *adjective*
— **re·nog·ra·phy** \rē-ˈnä-grə-fē\ *noun*

---

☆ **SYNONYMS**
**Renew, restore, refresh, renovate, rejuvenate** mean to make like new. RENEW implies a restoration of what had become faded or disintegrated so that it seems like new ⟨efforts to *renew* the splendor of the old castle⟩. RESTORE implies a return to an original state after depletion or loss ⟨*restored* a fine piece of furniture⟩. REFRESH implies the supplying of something necessary to restore lost strength, animation, or power ⟨a *refreshing* drink⟩. RENOVATE suggests a renewing by cleansing, repairing, or rebuilding ⟨the apartment has been entirely *renovated*⟩. REJUVENATE suggests the restoration of youthful vigor, powers, or appearance ⟨the change in jobs *rejuvenated* her spirits⟩.

**re·nom·i·nate** \(ˌ)rē-'nä-mə-ˌnāt\ *transitive verb* (1864)
: to nominate again especially for a succeeding term
— **re·nom·i·na·tion** \(ˌ)rē-ˌnä-mə-'nā-shən\ *noun*

**re·nounce** \ri-'naún(t)s\ *verb* **re·nounced; re·nounc·ing** [Middle English, from Middle French *renoncer*, from Latin *renuntiare*, from *re-* + *nuntiare* to report, from *nuntius* messenger] (14th century)
*transitive verb*
**1** : to give up, refuse, or resign usually by formal declaration ⟨*renounce* his errors⟩
**2** : to refuse to follow, obey, or recognize any further : REPUDIATE ⟨*renounce* the authority of the church⟩
*intransitive verb*
**1** : to make a renunciation
**2** : to fail to follow suit in a card game
**synonym** see ABDICATE, ABJURE
— **re·nounce·ment** \-'naún(t)s-mənt\ *noun*
— **re·nounc·er** *noun*

**re·no·vas·cu·lar** \ˌrē-nō-'vas-kyə-lər\ *adjective* (1961)
: of, relating to, or involving the blood vessels of the kidneys ⟨*renovascular* hypertension⟩

**ren·o·vate** \'re-nə-ˌvāt\ *transitive verb* **-vat·ed; -vat·ing** [Latin *renovatus*, past participle of *renovare*, from *re-* + *novare* to make new, from *novus* new — more at NEW] (circa 1522)
**1** : to restore to a former better state (as by cleaning, repairing, or rebuilding)
**2** : to restore to life, vigor, or activity : REVIVE ⟨the church was *renovated* by a new ecumenical spirit⟩
**synonym** see RENEW
— **ren·o·va·tion** \ˌre-nə-'vā-shən\ *noun*
— **ren·o·va·tive** \'re-nə-ˌvā-tiv\ *adjective*
— **ren·o·va·tor** \-ˌvā-tər\ *noun*

**¹re·nown** \ri-'naún\ *noun* [Middle English, from Middle French *renon*, from Old French, from *renomer* to celebrate, from *re-* + *nomer* to name, from Latin *nominare*, from *nomin-, nomen* name — more at NAME] (14th century)
**1** : a state of being widely acclaimed and highly honored : FAME
**2** *obsolete* : REPORT, RUMOR
**²renown** *transitive verb* (15th century)
: to give renown to

**re·nowned** *adjective* (14th century)
: having renown : CELEBRATED
**synonym** see FAMOUS

**¹rent** \'rent\ *noun* [Middle English *rente*, from Old French, income from a property, from (assumed) Vulgar Latin *rendita*, from feminine of *renditus*, past participle of *rendere* to yield — more at RENDER] (12th century)
**1** : property (as a house) rented or for rent
**2 a** : a usually fixed periodical return made by a tenant or occupant of property to the owner for the possession and use thereof; *especially* : an agreed sum paid at fixed intervals by a tenant to the landlord **b** : the amount paid by a hirer of personal property to the owner for the use thereof
**3 a** : the portion of the income of an economy (as of a nation) attributable to land as a factor of production in addition to capital and labor **b** : ECONOMIC RENT
— **for rent** : available for use or service in return for payment

**²rent** (15th century)
*transitive verb*
**1** : to grant the possession and enjoyment of in exchange for rent
**2** : to take and hold under an agreement to pay rent
*intransitive verb*
**1** : to be for rent

**2 a** : to obtain the possession and use of a place or article in exchange for rent **b** : to allow the possession and use of property in exchange for rent
**synonym** see HIRE
— **rent·abil·i·ty** \ˌren-tə-'bi-lə-tē\ *noun*
— **rent·able** \'ren-tə-bəl\ *adjective*

**³rent** *past and past participle of* REND

**⁴rent** *noun* [English dialect *rent* to rend, from Middle English, alteration of *renden* — more at REND] (1535)
**1** : an opening made by or as if by rending
**2** : a split in a party or organized group : SCHISM
**3** : an act or instance of rending

**rent-a-car** \'rent-ə-ˌkär\ *noun* (1935)
: a rented car

**¹rent·al** \'ren-tᵊl\ *noun* (14th century)
**1** : an amount paid or collected as rent
**2** : something that is rented
**3** : an act of renting
**4** : a business that rents something
**²rental** *adjective* (15th century)
**1 a** : of or relating to rent **b** : available for rent
**2** : dealing in rental property ⟨a *rental* agency⟩

**rental library** *noun* (1928)
: a commercially operated library (as in a store) that lends books at a fixed charge per book per day — called also *lending library*

**rent control** *noun* (1931)
: government regulation of the amount charged as rent for housing and often also of eviction
— **rent-controlled** *adjective*

**rente** \'rän(t)\ *noun* [French] (1873)
: a government security (as in France) paying interest; *also* : the interest paid

**rent·er** \'ren-tər\ *noun* (1655)
: one that rents; *specifically* : the lessee or tenant of property

**ren·tier** \rän-tyā\ *noun* [French, from Old French, from *rente*] (circa 1847)
: a person who lives on income from property or securities

**rent strike** *noun* (1964)
: a refusal by a group of tenants to pay rent (as in protest against high rates)

**re·nun·ci·a·tion** \ri-ˌnən(t)-sē-'ā-shən\ *noun* [Middle English, from Latin *renuntiation-, renuntiatio*, from *renuntiare* to renounce] (14th century)
: the act or practice of renouncing : REPUDIATION; *specifically* : ascetic self-denial
— **re·nun·ci·a·tive** \ri-'nən(t)-sē-ˌā-tiv\ *adjective*
— **re·nun·ci·a·to·ry** \-sē-ə-ˌtōr-ē, -ˌtór-\ *adjective*

**re·of·fer** \(ˌ)rē-'ó-fər, -'ä-\ *transitive verb* (1920)
: to offer (a security issue) for public sale

**re·open** \(ˌ)rē-'ō-pən, -'ō-pᵊm\ (1733)
*transitive verb*
**1** : to open again
**2 a** : to take up again : RESUME ⟨*reopen* discussion⟩ **b** : to resume discussion or consideration of ⟨*reopen* a contract⟩
**3** : to begin again
*intransitive verb*
: to open again ⟨school *reopens* in September⟩

**¹re·or·der** \(ˌ)rē-'ór-dər\ (1656)
*transitive verb*
**1** : to arrange in a different way
**2** : to give a reorder for
*intransitive verb*
: to place a reorder
**²reorder** *noun* (1901)
: an order like a previous order placed with the same supplier

**re·or·ga·ni·za·tion** \(ˌ)rē-ˌór-gə-nə-'zā-shən, -ˌórg-nə-\ *noun* (1813)
: the act or process of reorganizing : the state of being reorganized; *especially* : the financial reconstruction of a business concern
— **re·or·ga·ni·za·tion·al** \-shnəl, -shə-nᵊl\ *adjective*

**re·or·ga·nize** \(ˌ)rē-'ór-gə-ˌnīz\ (circa 1686)

*transitive verb*
: to organize again or anew
*intransitive verb*
: to reorganize something
— **re·or·ga·niz·er** *noun*

**reo·vi·rus** \ˌrē-ō-'vī-rəs\ *noun* [respiratory enteric orphan (i.e., unidentified) *virus*] (1959)
: any of a group of double-stranded RNA viruses lacking a lipoprotein envelope that includes many pathogens of plants or animals

**¹rep** \'rep\ *noun* (circa 1705)
*slang* : REPUTATION; *especially* : status in a group (as a gang)
**²rep** *noun* (1848)
: REPRESENTATIVE ⟨sales *reps*⟩
**³rep** *or* **repp** \'rep\ *noun* [French *reps*, modification of English *ribs*, plural of *rib*] (1860)
: a plain-weave fabric with prominent rounded crosswise ribs
**⁴rep** *noun* (1925)
: REPERTORY 2b, 3
**⁵rep** *noun* [*roentgen equivalent physical*] (1947)
: the dosage of an ionizing radiation that will develop the same amount of energy upon absorption in human tissue as one roentgen of X-ray or gamma-ray exposure
**⁶rep** *noun* [short for *repetition*] (1978)
: a repetition of a specified movement or exercise (as in weight lifting)

**re·pack·age** \(ˌ)rē-'pa-kij\ *transitive verb* (1946)
: to package again or anew; *specifically* : to put into a more efficient or attractive form
— **re·pack·ag·er** *noun*

**¹re·pair** \ri-'par, -'per\ *intransitive verb* [Middle English, from Middle French *repairier* to go back to one's country, from Late Latin *repatriare*, from Latin *re-* + *patria* native country — more at EXPATRIATE] (14th century)
**1 a** : to betake oneself : GO ⟨*repaired* to the judge's chambers⟩ **b** : to come together : RALLY
**2** *obsolete* : RETURN
**²repair** *noun* (14th century)
**1** : the act of repairing : RESORT
**2** : a popular gathering place
**³repair** *verb* [Middle English, from Middle French *reparer*, from Latin *reparare*, from *re-* + *parare* to prepare — more at PARE] (14th century)
*transitive verb*
**1 a** : to restore by replacing a part or putting together what is torn or broken : FIX ⟨*repair* a shoe⟩ **b** : to restore to a sound or healthy state : RENEW ⟨*repair* his strength⟩
**2** : to make good : compensate for : REMEDY ⟨*repair* a gap in my reading⟩
*intransitive verb*
: to make repairs
**synonym** see MEND
— **re·pair·abil·i·ty** \-ˌpar-ə-'bi-lə-tē, -ˌper-\ *noun*
— **re·pair·able** \-'par-ə-bəl, -'per-\ *adjective*
— **re·pair·er** \-'par-ər, -'per-\ *noun*
**⁴repair** *noun* (15th century)
**1 a** : an instance or result of repairing **b** : the act or process of repairing **c** : the replacement of destroyed cells or tissues by new formations
**2 a** : relative condition with respect to soundness or need of repairing **b** : the state of being in good or sound condition

**re·pair·man** \ri-'par-ˌman, -'per-, -mən\ *noun* (1871)
: one who repairs; *specifically* : one whose occupation is to make repairs in a mechanism

**re·pand** \ri-'pand\ *adjective* [Latin *repandus* spread out, from *repandere* to open wide, from *re-* + *pandere* to spread — more at FATHOM] (circa 1760)
: having a slightly undulating margin 〈a *repand* leaf〉 〈a *repand* colony of bacteria〉

**rep·a·ra·ble** \'re-p(ə-)rə-bəl\ *adjective* (1570)
: capable of being repaired

**rep·a·ra·tion** \,re-pə-'rā-shən\ *noun* [Middle English, from Middle French, from Late Latin *reparation-, reparatio*, from Latin *reparare*] (14th century)
**1 a** : a repairing or keeping in repair **b** *plural* : REPAIRS
**2 a** : the act of making amends, offering expiation, or giving satisfaction for a wrong or injury **b** : something done or given as amends or satisfaction
**3** : the payment of damages : INDEMNIFICATION; *specifically* : compensation in money or materials payable by a defeated nation for damages to or expenditures sustained by another nation as a result of hostilities with the defeated nation — usually used in plural

**re·par·a·tive** \ri-'par-ə-tiv\ *adjective* (1656)
**1** : of, relating to, or effecting repair
**2** : serving to make amends

**rep·ar·tee** \,re-pər-'tē, -,pär-, -'tā\ *noun* [French *repartie*, from *repartir* to retort, from Middle French, from *re-* + *partir* to divide — more at PART] (circa 1645)
**1 a** : a quick and witty reply **b** : a succession or interchange of clever retorts : amusing and usually light sparring with words
**2** : adroitness and cleverness in reply : skill in repartee
*synonym* see WIT

**¹re·par·ti·tion** \,re-,pär-'ti-shən, ,rē-\ *noun* [probably from Spanish *repartición*, from *repartir* to distribute, from *re-* + *partir* to divide, from Latin *partire* — more at PART] (1555)
: DISTRIBUTION

**²re·par·ti·tion** \,rē-,pär-'ti-shən\ *noun* [*re-* + *partition*] (1835)
: a second or additional dividing or distribution

**re·pass** \(,)rē-'pas\ *verb* [Middle English, from Middle French *repasser*, from Old French, from *re-* + *passer* to pass] (15th century)
*intransitive verb*
: to pass again especially in the opposite direction : RETURN
*transitive verb*
**1** : to pass through, over, or by again 〈*repass* the house〉
**2** : to cause to pass again
**3** : to adopt again 〈*repassed* the resolution〉
— **re·pas·sage** \-'pa-sij\ *noun*

**¹re·past** \ri-'past, 'rē-\ *noun* [Middle English, from Middle French, from Old French, from *repaistre* to feed, from *re-* + *paistre* to feed, from Latin *pascere* — more at FOOD] (14th century)
**1** : something taken as food : MEAL
**2** : the act or time of taking food

**²re·past** \ri-'past\ (15th century)
*transitive verb*
*obsolete* : FEED
*intransitive verb*
: to take food : FEAST

**re·pa·tri·ate** \(,)rē-'pā-trē-,āt, -'pa-\ *transitive verb* **-at·ed; -at·ing** [Late Latin *repatriatus*, past participle of *repatriare* to go back to one's country — more at REPAIR] (1611)
: to restore or return to the country of origin, allegiance, or citizenship 〈*repatriate* prisoners of war〉
— **re·pa·tri·ate** \-trē-ət, -trē-,āt\ *noun*
— **re·pa·tri·a·tion** \(,)rē-,pā-trē-'ā-shən, -,pa-\ *noun*

**re·pay** \(,)rē-'pā\ *verb* **-paid** \-'pād\; **-pay·ing** (15th century)
*transitive verb*
**1 a** : to pay back 〈*repay* a loan〉 **b** : to give or inflict in return or requital 〈*repay* evil for evil〉

**2** : to make a return payment to : COMPENSATE, REQUITE
**3** : to make requital for : RECOMPENSE 〈the success that *repays* hard work〉
*intransitive verb*
: to make return payment or requital
*synonym* see PAY
— **re·pay·able** \-'pā-ə-bəl\ *adjective*
— **re·pay·ment** \-'pā-mənt\ *noun*

**re·peal** \ri-'pē(ə)l\ *transitive verb* [Middle English *repelen*, from Middle French *repeler*, from Old French, from *re-* + *apeler* to appeal, call] (14th century)
**1** : to rescind or annul by authoritative act; *especially* : to revoke or abrogate by legislative enactment
**2** : ABANDON, RENOUNCE
**3** *obsolete* : to summon to return : RECALL
— **repeal** *noun*
— **re·peal·able** \-'pē-lə-bəl\ *adjective*

**re·peal·er** \ri-'pē-lər\ *noun* (1765)
: one that repeals; *specifically* : a legislative act that abrogates an earlier act

**¹re·peat** \ri-'pēt\ *verb* [Middle English *repeten*, from Middle French *repeter*, from Latin *repetere* to return to, repeat, from *re-* + *petere* to go to, seek — more at FEATHER] (14th century)
*transitive verb*
**1 a** : to say or state again **b** : to say over from memory : RECITE **c** : to say after another
**2 a** : to make, do, or perform again 〈*repeat* an experiment〉 **b** : to make appear again 〈the curtains *repeat* the wallpaper pattern〉 〈will *repeat* the program tomorrow〉 **c** : to go through or experience again 〈had to *repeat* third grade〉
**3** : to express or present (oneself) again in the same words, terms, or form
*intransitive verb*
: to say, do, or accomplish something again; *especially* : to win (as a sports championship) another time in succession
— **re·peat·abil·i·ty** \-,pē-tə-'bi-lə-tē\ *noun*
— **re·peat·able** \-'pē-tə-bəl\ *adjective*

**²re·peat** \ri-'pēt, 'rē-\ *noun* (15th century)
**1 a** : something repeated : REPETITION **b** : a musical passage to be repeated in performance; *also* : a sign placed before and after such a passage **c** : a usually transcribed repetition of a radio or television program **d** : a genetic duplication in which the duplicated parts are adjacent to each other along the chromosome
**2** : the act of repeating

**re·peat·ed** \ri-'pē-təd\ *adjective* (1611)
**1** : renewed or recurring again and again 〈*repeated* changes of plan〉
**2** : said, done, or presented again

**re·peat·ed·ly** *adverb* (circa 1718)
: AGAIN AND AGAIN

**re·peat·er** \ri-'pē-tər\ *noun* (1598)
: one that repeats: as **a** : one who relates or recites **b** : a watch or clock with a striking mechanism that upon pressure of a spring will indicate the time in hours or quarters and sometimes minutes **c** : a firearm having a magazine that holds a number of cartridges loaded one at a time into the chamber by the action of the piece **d** : an habitual violator of the laws **e** : one who votes illegally by casting more than one ballot in an election **f** : a student enrolled in a class or course for a second or subsequent time **g** : a device for receiving electronic communication signals and delivering corresponding amplified ones

**re·peat·ing** *adjective* (1824)
*of a firearm* : designed to load cartridges from a magazine

**repeating decimal** *noun* (1773)
: a decimal in which after a certain point a particular digit or sequence of digits repeats itself indefinitely — compare TERMINATING DECIMAL

**re·pe·chage** \,re-pə-'shäzh, 're-pə-,\ *noun* [French *repêchage* second chance, reexamination for a candidate who has failed, from *repêcher* to fish out, rescue, from *re-* + *pêcher* to fish, from Latin *piscari* — more at PISCATORY] (1928)
: a trial heat (as in rowing) in which first-round losers are given another chance to qualify for the semifinals

**re·pel** \ri-'pel\ *verb* **re·pelled; re·pel·ling** [Middle English *repellen*, from Latin *repellere*, from *re-* + *pellere* to drive — more at FELT] (15th century)
*transitive verb*
**1 a** : to drive back : REPULSE **b** : to fight against : RESIST
**2** : TURN AWAY, REJECT 〈*repelled* the insinuation〉
**3 a** : to drive away : DISCOURAGE 〈foul words and frowns must not *repel* a lover —Shakespeare〉 **b** : to be incapable of adhering to, mixing with, taking up, or holding **c** : to force away or apart or tend to do so by mutual action at a distance
**4** : to cause aversion in : DISGUST
*intransitive verb*
: to cause aversion
— **re·pel·ler** *noun*

**re·pel·len·cy** \ri-'pe-lən(t)-sē\ *noun* (1747)
: the quality or capacity of repelling

**¹re·pel·lent** *also* **re·pel·lant** \ri-'pe-lənt\ *adjective* [Latin *repellent-, repellens*, present participle of *repellere*] (1643)
**1** : serving or tending to drive away or ward off — often used in combination 〈a mosquito-*repellent* spray〉
**2** : arousing aversion or disgust : REPULSIVE
— **re·pel·lent·ly** *adverb*

**²repellent** *also* **repellant** *noun* (1661)
: something that repels; *especially* : a substance that repels insects

**¹re·pent** \ri-'pent\ *verb* [Middle English, from Old French *repentir*, from *re-* + *pentir* to be sorry, from Latin *paenitēre* — more at PENITENT] (14th century)
*intransitive verb*
**1** : to turn from sin and dedicate oneself to the amendment of one's life
**2 a** : to feel regret or contrition **b** : to change one's mind
*transitive verb*
**1** : to cause to feel regret or contrition
**2** : to feel sorrow, regret, or contrition for
— **re·pent·er** *noun*

**²re·pent** \'rē-pənt\ *adjective* [Latin *repent-, repens*, present participle of *repere* to creep — more at REPTILE] (1669)
: CREEPING, PROSTRATE 〈*repent* stems〉

**re·pen·tance** \ri-'pen-t²n(t)s\ *noun* (14th century)
: the action or process of repenting especially for misdeeds or moral shortcomings
*synonym* see PENITENCE

**re·pen·tant** \-t²nt\ *adjective* (13th century)
**1** : experiencing repentance : PENITENT
**2** : expressive of repentance
— **re·pen·tant·ly** *adverb*

**re·per·cus·sion** \,rē-pər-'kə-shən, ,re-\ *noun* [Latin *repercussion-, repercussio*, from *repercutere* to drive back, from *re-* + *percutere* to beat — more at PERCUSSION] (1536)
**1** : REFLECTION, REVERBERATION
**2 a** : an action or effect given or exerted in return : a reciprocal action or effect **b** : a widespread, indirect, or unforeseen effect of an act, action, or event — usually used in plural
— **re·per·cus·sive** \-'kə-siv\ *adjective*

**rep·er·toire** \'re-pə(r)-,twär\ *noun* [French *répertoire*, from Late Latin *repertorium*] (1847)
**1 a** : a list or supply of dramas, operas, pieces, or parts that a company or person is prepared to perform **b** : a supply of skills, devices, or expedients 〈part of the *repertoire* of a quarterback〉; *broadly* : AMOUNT, SUPPLY 〈an endless

**repeat 1b**

*repertoire* of summer clothes⟩ **c :** a list or supply of capabilities ⟨the instruction *repertoire* of a computer⟩
**2 a :** the complete list or supply of dramas, operas, or musical works available for performance ⟨our modern orchestral *repertoire*⟩ **b :** the complete list or supply of skills, devices, or ingredients used in a particular field, occupation, or practice ⟨the *repertoire* of literary criticism⟩

**rep·er·to·ry** \'re-pə(r)-ˌtōr-ē, -ˌtȯr-\ *noun, plural* **-ries** [Late Latin *repertorium* list, from Latin *reperire* to find, from *re-* + *parere* to produce — more at PARE] (1593)
**1 :** a place where something may be found **:** REPOSITORY
**2 a :** REPERTOIRE **b :** a company that presents several different plays, operas, or pieces usually alternately in the course of a season at one theater **c :** a theater housing such a company
**3 :** the production and presentation of plays by a repertory company ⟨acting in *repertory*⟩

**rep·e·tend** \'re-pə-ˌtend\ *noun* [Latin *repetendus* to be repeated, gerundive of *repetere* to repeat] (1874)
**:** a repeated sound, word, or phrase; *specifically* **:** REFRAIN

**rep·e·ti·tion** \ˌre-pə-'ti-shən\ *noun* [Middle English *repeticioun*, from Latin *repetition-*, *repetitio*, from *repetere* to repeat] (15th century)
**1 :** the act or an instance of repeating or being repeated
**2 :** MENTION, RECITAL
— **rep·e·ti·tion·al** \-'tish-nəl, -'ti-shə-n°l\ *adjective*

**rep·e·ti·tious** \-'ti-shəs\ *adjective* (1675)
**:** characterized or marked by repetition; *especially* **:** tediously repeating
— **rep·e·ti·tious·ly** *adverb*
— **rep·e·ti·tious·ness** *noun*

**re·pet·i·tive** \ri-'pe-tə-tiv\ *adjective* (1839)
**1 :** containing repetition
**2 :** REPETITIOUS
— **re·pet·i·tive·ly** *adverb*
— **re·pet·i·tive·ness** *noun*

**re·pine** \ri-'pīn\ *intransitive verb* (circa 1530)
**1 :** to feel or express dejection or discontent
**2 :** to long for something
— **re·pin·er** *noun*

**re·place** \ri-'plās\ *transitive verb* (1595)
**1 :** to restore to a former place or position ⟨*replace* cards in a file⟩
**2 :** to take the place of especially as a substitute or successor
**3 :** to put something new in the place of ⟨*replace* a worn carpet⟩ ☆
— **re·place·able** \-'plā-sə-bəl\ *adjective*
— **re·plac·er** *noun*

**re·place·ment** \ri-'plās-mənt\ *noun* (circa 1790)
**1 :** the action or process of replacing **:** the state of being replaced
**2 :** one that replaces another especially in a job or function

**replacement set** *noun* (1959)
**:** a set of elements any one of which may be used to replace a given variable or placeholder in a mathematical sentence or expression (as an equation)

**re·plant** \(ˌ)rē-'plant\ *transitive verb* (1575)
**1 :** to plant again or anew
**2 :** to provide with new plants
**3 :** to subject to replantation

**re·plan·ta·tion** \ˌrē-(ˌ)plan-'tā-shən\ *noun* (1870)
**:** reattachment or reinsertion of a bodily part (as a limb or tooth) after separation from the body

**¹re·play** \(ˌ)rē-'plā\ *transitive verb* (1884)
**:** to play again or over

**²re·play** \'rē-ˌplā\ *noun* (1895)
**1 a :** an act or instance of replaying **b :** the playing of a tape (as a videotape)
**2 :** REPETITION, REENACTMENT ⟨don't want a *replay* of our old mistakes⟩

**re·plead·er** \(ˌ)rē-'plē-dər\ *noun* [*replead* to plead again + *-er* (as in *misnomer*)] (1607)
**1 :** a second legal pleading
**2 :** the right of pleading again granted usually when the issue raised is immaterial or insufficient

**re·plen·ish** \ri-'ple-nish\ *verb* [Middle English *replenisshen*, from Middle French *repleniss-*, stem of *replenir* to fill, from Old French, from *re-* + *plein* full, from Latin *plenus* — more at FULL] (14th century)
*transitive verb*
**1 a :** to fill with persons or animals **:** STOCK **b** *archaic* **:** to supply fully **: PERFECT c :** to fill with inspiration or power **:** NOURISH
**2 a :** to fill or build up again ⟨*replenished* his glass⟩ **b :** to make good **:** REPLACE
*intransitive verb*
**:** to become full **:** fill up again
— **re·plen·ish·able** \-ni-shə-bəl\ *adjective*
— **re·plen·ish·er** *noun*
— **re·plen·ish·ment** \-nish-mənt\ *noun*

**re·plete** \ri-'plēt\ *adjective* [Middle English, from Middle French & Latin; Middle French *replet*, from Latin *repletus*, past participle of *replēre* to fill up, from *re-* + *plēre* to fill — more at FULL] (14th century)
**1 :** fully or abundantly provided or filled ⟨a book *replete* with . . . delicious details —William Safire⟩
**2 a :** abundantly fed **b :** FAT, STOUT
**3 :** COMPLETE
**synonym** *see* FULL
— **re·plete·ness** *noun*

**re·ple·tion** \ri-'plē-shən\ *noun* (14th century)
**1 :** the act of eating to excess **:** the state of being fed to excess **:** SURFEIT
**2 :** the condition of being filled up or overcrowded
**3 :** fulfillment of a need or desire **:** SATISFACTION

**¹re·plev·in** \ri-'ple-vən\ *noun* [Middle English, from Anglo-French *replevine*, from *replevir* to give security, from Old French, from *re-* + *plevir* to pledge, from (assumed) Late Latin *plebere* — more at PLEDGE] (15th century)
**1 :** the recovery by a person of goods or chattels claimed to be wrongfully taken or detained upon the person's giving security to try the matter in court and return the goods if defeated in the action
**2 :** the writ or the common-law action whereby goods and chattels are replevied

**²replevin** *transitive verb* (1678)
**:** REPLEVY

**¹re·plevy** \ri-'ple-vē\ *noun, plural* **re·plevies** [Middle English, from Anglo-French *replevir*, verb] (15th century)
**:** REPLEVIN

**²replevy** *transitive verb* **re·plev·ied; re·plevy·ing** (1596)
**:** to take or get back by a writ for replevin
— **re·plevi·able** \-vē-ə-bəl\ *adjective*

**rep·li·ca** \'re-pli-kə\ *noun* [Italian, repetition, from *replicare* to repeat, from Late Latin, from Latin, to fold back — more at REPLY] (1824)
**1 :** an exact reproduction (as of a painting) executed by the original artist ⟨a *replica* of this was painted . . . this year —Constance Strachey⟩
**2 :** a copy exact in all details ⟨DNA makes a *replica* of itself⟩ ⟨sailed a *replica* of the Viking ship⟩; *broadly* **:** COPY ⟨this faithful, pathetic *replica* of a Midwestern suburb —G. F. Kennan⟩ ◼
**synonym** *see* REPRODUCTION

**rep·li·ca·ble** \'re-plə-kə-bəl\ *adjective* (1950)
**:** capable of replication ⟨*replicable* experimental results⟩
— **rep·li·ca·bil·i·ty** \ˌre-plə-kə-'bi-lə-tē\ *noun*

**rep·li·case** \'re-pli-ˌkās, -ˌkāz\ *noun* [*replication* + *-ase*] (1963)

**:** a polymerase that promotes synthesis of a particular RNA in the presence of a template of RNA

**¹rep·li·cate** \'re-plə-ˌkāt\ *verb* **-cat·ed; -cat·ing** [Late Latin *replicatus*, past participle of *replicare*] (15th century)
*transitive verb*
**:** DUPLICATE, REPEAT ⟨*replicate* a statistical experiment⟩
*intransitive verb*
**:** to undergo replication **:** produce a replica of itself ⟨virus particles *replicating* in cells⟩

**²rep·li·cate** \-kət\ *adjective* (1922)
**:** MANIFOLD, REPEATED

**³rep·li·cate** \-kət\ *noun* (1929)
**:** one of several identical experiments, procedures, or samples

**rep·li·ca·tion** \ˌre-plə-'kā-shən\ *noun* (14th century)
**1 a :** ANSWER, REPLY **b** (1) **:** an answer to a reply **:** REJOINDER (2) **:** a plaintiff's reply to a defendant's plea, answer, or counterclaim
**2 :** ECHO, REVERBERATION
**3 a :** COPY, REPRODUCTION **b :** the action or process of reproducing
**4 :** performance of an experiment or procedure more than once; *especially* **:** systematic or random repetition of agricultural test rows or plats to reduce error

**rep·li·ca·tive** \'re-pli-ˌkā-tiv\ *adjective* (circa 1890)
**:** of, relating to, involved in, or characterized by replication ⟨the *replicative* form of tobacco mosaic virus⟩

**rep·li·con** \'re-pli-ˌkän\ *noun* [*replicate* + *²-on*] (1963)
**:** a linear or circular section of DNA or RNA which replicates sequentially as a unit

**¹re·ply** \ri-'plī\ *verb* **re·plied; re·ply·ing** [Middle English *replien*, from Middle French *replier* to fold again, from Latin *replicare* to fold back, from *re-* + *plicare* to fold — more at PLY] (14th century)
*intransitive verb*
**1 a :** to respond in words or writing **b :** ECHO, RESOUND **c :** to make a legal replication

---

☆ **SYNONYMS**
**Replace, displace, supplant, supersede** mean to put out of a usual or proper place or into the place of another. REPLACE implies a filling of a place once occupied by something lost, destroyed, or no longer usable or adequate ⟨*replaced* the broken window⟩. DISPLACE implies an ousting or dislodging ⟨war had *displaced* thousands⟩. SUPPLANT implies either a dispossessing or usurping of another's place, possessions, or privileges or an uprooting of something and its replacement with something else ⟨was abruptly *supplanted* in her affections by another⟩. SUPERSEDE implies replacing a person or thing that has become superannuated, obsolete, or otherwise inferior ⟨the new edition *supersedes* all previous ones⟩.

---

☐ **USAGE**
**replica** A number of language commentators would have us believe that sense 1 is the only proper meaning of the word. But their battle was lost more than a century ago; the word has been applied to various kinds of copies since the second half of the 19th century. Sense 1 is, in fact, the least common sense in current usage.

---

**2 :** to do something in response; *specifically* **:** to return gunfire or an attack
*transitive verb*
**:** to give as an answer
**synonym** see ANSWER
— **re·pli·er** \-'plī(-ə)r\ *noun*
²**reply** *noun, plural* **replies** (1560)
**1 :** something said, written, or done in answer or response
**2 :** REPLICATION 1b(2)
**re·po** \'rē-,pō\ *noun, plural* **repos** [by shortening & alteration] (1963)
**:** REPURCHASE AGREEMENT
**re·po·lar·i·za·tion** \,rē-,pō-lə-rə-'zā-shən\ *noun* (1922)
**:** polarization of a muscle fiber, cell, or membrane following depolarization
— **re·po·lar·ize** \(,)rē-'pō-lə-,rīz\ *verb*
¹**re·port** \ri-'pōrt, -'pȯrt\ *noun* [Middle English, from Middle French, from Old French, from *reporter* to report, from Latin *reportare*, from *re-* + *portare* to carry — more at FARE] (14th century)
**1 a :** common talk or an account spread by common talk **:** RUMOR **b :** quality of reputation ⟨a witness of good *report*⟩
**2 a :** a usually detailed account or statement ⟨a news *report*⟩ **b :** an account or statement of a judicial opinion or decision **c :** a usually formal record of the proceedings of a meeting or session
**3 :** an explosive noise
— **on report :** subject to disciplinary action
²**report** (14th century)
*transitive verb*
**1 a :** to give an account of **:** RELATE **b :** to describe as being in a specified state ⟨*reported* him much improved⟩
**2 a :** to serve as carrier of (a message) **b :** to relate the words or sense of (something said) **c :** to make a written record or summary of **d** (1) **:** to watch for and write about the newsworthy aspects or developments of **:** COVER (2) **:** to prepare or present an account of for broadcast
**3 a** (1) **:** to give a formal or official account or statement of ⟨the treasurer *reported* a balance of ten dollars⟩ (2) **:** to return or present (a matter referred for consideration) with conclusions or recommendations **b :** to announce or relate as the result of investigation ⟨*reported* no sign of disease⟩ **c :** to announce the presence, arrival, or sighting of **d :** to make known to the proper authorities ⟨*report* a fire⟩ **e :** to make a charge of misconduct against
*intransitive verb*
**1 a :** to give an account **:** TELL **b :** to present oneself **c :** to account for oneself ⟨*reported* sick on Friday⟩
**2 :** to make, issue, or submit a report
**3 :** to act in the capacity of a reporter
**re·port·able** \ri-'pōr-tə-bəl, -'pȯr-\ *adjective* (1858)
**1 :** worth reporting ⟨*reportable* news⟩
**2 :** required by law to be reported ⟨*reportable* income⟩ ⟨*reportable* diseases⟩
**re·port·age** \ri-'pōr-tij, -'pȯr-, *especially for* 2 ,re-pər-'täzh, ,re-,pȯr-'\ *noun* [French, from *reporter* to report] (circa 1864)
**1 a :** the act or process of reporting news **b :** something (as news) that is reported
**2 :** writing intended to give an account of observed or documented events
**report card** *noun* (1920)
**1 :** a report on a student that is periodically submitted by a school to the student's parents or guardian
**2 :** an evaluation of performance
**re·port·ed·ly** \ri-'pōr-təd-lē, -'pȯr-\ *adverb* (1901)
**:** according to report
**re·port·er** \ri-'pōr-tər, -'pȯr-\ *noun* (14th century)
**:** one that reports: as **a :** one who makes authorized statements of law decisions or legisla-

tive proceedings **b :** one who makes a shorthand record of a speech or proceeding **c** (1) **:** one employed by a newspaper, magazine, or television company to gather and report news (2) **:** one who broadcasts news
— **re·por·to·ri·al** \,re-pə(r)-'tōr-ē-əl, ,rē-, -'tȯr-\ *adjective*
— **re·por·to·ri·al·ly** \-ē-ə-lē\ *adverb*
**report out** *transitive verb* (1907)
**:** to return after consideration and often with revisions to a legislative body for action ⟨after much debate the committee *reported* the bill out⟩
**report stage** *noun* (circa 1906)
**:** the stage in the British legislative process preceding the third reading and concerned especially with amendments and details
**re·pos·al** \ri-'pō-zəl\ *noun* (1605)
*obsolete* **:** the act of reposing
¹**re·pose** \ri-'pōz\ *verb* **re·posed; re·pos·ing** [Middle English, from Middle French *reposer*, from Old French, from Late Latin *repausare*, from Latin *re-* + Late Latin *pausare* to stop, from Latin *pausa* pause] (15th century)
*transitive verb*
**:** to lay at rest
*intransitive verb*
**1 a :** to lie at rest **b :** to lie dead ⟨*reposing* in state⟩ **c :** to remain still or concealed
**2 :** to take a rest
**3** *archaic* **:** RELY
**4 :** to rest for support **:** LIE
²**repose** *noun* (1509)
**1 a :** a state of resting after exertion or strain; *especially* **:** rest in sleep **b :** eternal or heavenly rest ⟨pray for the *repose* of a soul⟩
**2 a :** a place of rest **b :** PEACE, TRANQUILLITY ⟨the *repose* of the bayous⟩ **c :** a harmony in the arrangement of parts and colors that is restful to the eye
**3 a :** lack of activity **:** QUIESCENCE **b :** cessation or absence of activity, movement, or animation ⟨the face in *repose* is grave and thoughtful⟩
**4 :** composure of manner **:** POISE
³**re·pose** *transitive verb* **re·posed; re·pos·ing** [Middle English, to replace, from Latin *reponere* (perfect indicative *reposui*)] (15th century)
**1** *archaic* **:** to put away or set down **:** DEPOSIT
**2 a :** to place (as confidence or trust) in someone or something **b :** to place for control, management, or use
**re·pose·ful** \ri-'pōz-fəl\ *adjective* (1852)
**:** of a kind to induce ease and relaxation
— **re·pose·ful·ly** \-fə-lē\ *adverb*
— **re·pose·ful·ness** *noun*
**re·pos·it** *transitive verb* **re·pos·it·ed** \-'pä-zə-təd, -'päz-təd\; **re·pos·it·ing** \-'pä-zə-tiŋ, -'päz-tiŋ\ [Latin *repositus*, past participle of *reponere* to replace, from *re-* + *ponere* to place — more at POSITION] (circa 1641)
**1** \ri-'pä-zət\ **:** DEPOSIT, STORE
**2** \(,)rē-\ **:** to put back in place **:** REPLACE
¹**re·po·si·tion** \,rē-pə-'zi-shən, ,re-\ *noun* (1588)
**:** the act of repositing **:** the state of being reposited
²**re·po·si·tion** \,rē-pə-'zi-shən\ *transitive verb* (circa 1859)
**1 :** to change the position of
**2 :** to revise the marketing strategy of (a product or a company) so as to increase sales
¹**re·pos·i·to·ry** \ri-'pä-zə-,tōr-ē, -,tȯr-\ *noun, plural* **-ries** (15th century)
**1 :** a place, room, or container where something is deposited or stored **:** DEPOSITORY
**2 :** a side altar in a Roman Catholic church where the consecrated Host is reserved from Maundy Thursday until Good Friday
**3 :** one that contains or stores something nonmaterial ⟨considered the book a *repository* of knowledge⟩
**4 :** a place or region richly supplied with a natural resource

**5 :** a person to whom something is confided or entrusted
²**repository** *adjective* (1950)
*of a drug* **:** designed to act over a prolonged period ⟨*repository* penicillin⟩
**re·pos·sess** \,rē-pə-'zes *also* -'ses\ *transitive verb* (15th century)
**1 a :** to regain possession of **b :** to resume possession of in default of the payment of installments due
**2 :** to restore to possession
— **re·pos·ses·sion** \-'ze-shən *also* -'se-\ *noun*
— **re·pos·ses·sor** \-'ze-sər *also* -'se-\ *noun*
¹**re·pous·sé** \rə-,pü-'sā, -'pü-,\ *adjective* [French, literally, pushed back] (1858)
**1 :** shaped or ornamented with patterns in relief made by hammering or pressing on the reverse side — used especially of metal
**2 :** formed in relief
²**repoussé** *noun* (1858)
**1 :** repoussé work
**2 :** repoussé decoration
**re·pow·er** \(,)rē-'paù(-ə)r\ *transitive verb* (1954)
**:** to provide again or anew with power; *especially* **:** to provide (as a boat) with a new engine
**repp** *variant of* REP
**rep·re·hend** \,re-pri-'hend\ *transitive verb* [Middle English, from Latin *reprehendere*, literally, to hold back, from *re-* + *prehendere* to grasp — more at GET] (14th century)
**:** to voice disapproval of **:** CENSURE
**synonym** see CRITICIZE
**rep·re·hen·si·ble** \,re-pri-'hen(t)-sə-bəl\ *adjective* (14th century)
**:** worthy of or deserving reprehension **:** CULPABLE
— **rep·re·hen·si·bil·i·ty** \-,hen(t)-sə-'bi-lə-tē\ *noun*
— **rep·re·hen·si·ble·ness** \-'hen(t)-sə-bəl-nəs\ *noun*
— **rep·re·hen·si·bly** \-blē\ *adverb*
**rep·re·hen·sion** \-'hen(t)-shən\ *noun* [Middle English *reprehensioun*, from Middle French or Latin; Middle French *reprehension*, from Latin *reprehension-, reprehensio*, from *reprehendere*] (14th century)
**:** the act of reprehending **:** CENSURE
**rep·re·hen·sive** \-'hen(t)-siv\ *adjective* (1589)
**:** serving to reprehend **:** conveying reprehension or reproof
**rep·re·sent** \,re-pri-'zent\ *verb* [Middle English, from Middle French *representer*, from Latin *repraesentare*, from *re-* + *praesentare* to present] (14th century)
*transitive verb*
**1 :** to bring clearly before the mind **:** PRESENT ⟨a book which *represents* the character of early America⟩
**2 :** to serve as a sign or symbol of ⟨the flag *represents* our country⟩
**3 :** to portray or exhibit in art **:** DEPICT
**4 :** to serve as the counterpart or image of **:** TYPIFY ⟨a movie hero who *represents* the ideals of the culture⟩
**5 a :** to produce on the stage **b :** to act the part or role of
**6 a** (1) **:** to take the place of in some respect (2) **:** to act in the place of or for usually by legal right **b :** to serve especially in a legislative body by delegated authority usually resulting from election
**7 :** to describe as having a specified character or quality ⟨*represents* himself as a friend⟩
**8 a :** to give one's impression and judgment of **:** state in a manner intended to affect action or judgment **b :** to point out in protest or remonstrance
**9 :** to serve as a specimen, example, or instance of

**10 a :** to form an image or representation of in the mind **b** (1) **:** to apprehend (an object) by means of an idea (2) **:** to recall in memory
**11 :** to correspond to in essence **:** CONSTITUTE
*intransitive verb*
**:** to make representations against something **:** PROTEST
— **rep·re·sent·able** \-'zen-tə-bəl\ *adjective*
— **rep·re·sent·er** *noun*
**re·pre·sent** \ˌrē-pri-'zent\ *transitive verb* (1564)
**:** to present again or anew
— **re·pre·sen·ta·tion** \ˌrē-ˌprē-ˌzen-'tā-shən, -ˌpre-zᵊn-, -ˌprē-zᵊn-\ *noun*
**rep·re·sen·ta·tion** \ˌre-pri-ˌzen-'tā-shən, -zən-\ *noun* (15th century)
**1 :** one that represents: as **a :** an artistic likeness or image **b** (1) **:** a statement or account made to influence opinion or action (2) **:** an incidental or collateral statement of fact on the faith of which a contract is entered into **c :** a dramatic production or performance **d** (1) **:** a usually formal statement made against something or to effect a change (2) **:** a usually formal protest
**2 :** the act or action of representing **:** the state of being represented: as **a :** REPRESENTATIONALISM 2 **b** (1) **:** the action or fact of one person standing for another so as to have the rights and obligations of the person represented (2) **:** the substitution of an individual or class in place of a person (as a child for a deceased parent) **c :** the action of representing or the fact of being represented especially in a legislative body
**3 :** the body of persons representing a constituency
— **rep·re·sen·ta·tion·al** \-shnəl, -shə-nᵊl\ *adjective*
— **rep·re·sen·ta·tion·al·ly** *adverb*
**rep·re·sen·ta·tion·al·ism** \-shnə-ˌli-zəm, -shə-nᵊl-ˌi-\ *noun* (1899)
**1 :** the doctrine that the immediate object of knowledge is an idea in the mind distinct from the external object which is the occasion of perception
**2 :** the theory or practice of realistic representation in art
— **rep·re·sen·ta·tion·al·ist** \-list, -ist\ *noun*
**¹rep·re·sen·ta·tive** \ˌre-pri-'zen-tə-tiv\ *adjective* (1532)
**1 :** serving to represent
**2 a :** standing or acting for another especially through delegated authority **b :** of, based on, or constituting a government in which the many are represented by persons chosen from among them usually by election
**3 :** serving as a typical or characteristic example ⟨a *representative* moviegoer⟩
**4 :** of or relating to representation or representationalism
— **rep·re·sen·ta·tive·ly** *adverb*
— **rep·re·sen·ta·tive·ness** *noun*
— **rep·re·sen·ta·tiv·i·ty** \-ˌzen-tə-'ti-və-tē\ *noun*
**²representative** *noun* (1647)
**1 :** a typical example of a group, class, or quality **:** SPECIMEN
**2 :** one that represents another or others: as **a** (1) **:** one that represents a constituency as a member of a legislative body (2) **:** a member of the house of representatives of the U.S. Congress or a state legislature **b :** one that represents another as agent, deputy, substitute, or delegate usually being invested with the authority of the principal **c :** one that represents a business organization **d :** one that represents another as successor or heir
**re·press** \ri-'pres\ *verb* [Middle English, from Latin *repressus*, past participle of *reprimere* to check, from *re-* + *premere* to press — more at PRESS] (14th century)
*transitive verb*

**1 a :** to check by or as if by pressure **:** CURB ⟨injustice was *repressed*⟩ **b :** to put down by force **:** SUBDUE ⟨*repress* a disturbance⟩
**2 a :** to hold in by self-control ⟨*repressed* a laugh⟩ **b :** to prevent the natural or normal expression, activity, or development of ⟨*repressed* her anger⟩
**3 :** to exclude from consciousness
**4 :** to inactivate (a gene or formation of a gene product) by allosteric combination at a DNA binding site
*intransitive verb*
**:** to take repressive action
— **re·press·ibil·i·ty** \-ˌpre-sə-'bi-lə-tē\ *noun*
— **re·press·ible** \-'pre-sə-bəl\ *adjective*
— **re·pres·sive** \-'pre-siv\ *adjective*
— **re·pres·sive·ly** *adverb*
— **re·pres·sive·ness** *noun*
**re·press** \ˌ(ˌ)rē-'pres\ *transitive verb* (14th century)
**:** to press again ⟨*re-press* a record⟩
**re·pressed** \ri-'prest\ *adjective* (1665)
**1 :** subjected to or marked by repression
**2 :** characterized by restraint
**re·pres·sion** \ri-'pre-shən\ *noun* (1533)
**1 a :** the action or process of repressing **:** the state of being repressed ⟨*repression* of unpopular opinions⟩ **b :** an instance of repressing ⟨racial *repressions*⟩
**2 a :** a process by which unacceptable desires or impulses are excluded from consciousness and left to operate in the unconscious **b :** an item so excluded
— **re·pres·sion·ist** \-sh(ə-)nist\ *adjective*
**re·pres·sor** \ri-'pre-sər\ *noun* [New Latin] (1611)
**:** one that represses; *especially* **:** a protein that is determined by a regulatory gene, binds to a genetic operator, and inhibits the initiation of transcription of messenger RNA
**re·priev·al** \ri-'prē-vəl\ *noun* (circa 1586)
*archaic* **:** REPRIEVE
**¹re·prieve** \ri-'prēv\ *transitive verb* **re·prieved; re·priev·ing** [alteration of earlier *repry*, perhaps from Middle French *repris*, past participle of *reprendre* to take back] (1596)
**1 :** to delay the punishment of (as a condemned prisoner)
**2 :** to give relief or deliverance to for a time
**²reprieve** *noun* (1592)
**1 a :** the act of reprieving **:** the state of being reprieved **b :** a formal temporary suspension of the execution of a sentence especially of death
**2 :** an order or warrant for a reprieve
**3 :** a temporary respite (as from pain or trouble)
**¹rep·ri·mand** \'re-prə-ˌmand\ *noun* [French *réprimande*, from Latin *reprimenda*, feminine of *reprimendus*, gerundive of *reprimere* to check — more at REPRESS] (1636)
**:** a severe or formal reproof
**²reprimand** *transitive verb* (1681)
**:** to reprove sharply or censure formally usually from a position of authority
**synonym** *see* REPROVE
**¹re·print** \ˌ(ˌ)rē-'print\ *transitive verb* (1551)
**:** to print again **:** make a reprint of
**²re·print** \'rē-ˌprint, ˌ(ˌ)rē-'\ *noun* (1611)
**:** a reproduction of printed matter: as **a :** a subsequent printing of a book already published that preserves the identical text of the previous printing **b :** OFFPRINT **c :** matter (as an article) that has appeared in print before
**re·print·er** \ˌ(ˌ)rē-'prin-tər\ *noun* (1689)
**:** one that publishes a reprint
**re·pri·sal** \ri-'prī-zəl\ *noun* [Middle English *reprisail*, from Middle French *reprisaille*, from Old Italian *ripresaglia*, from *ripreso*, past participle of *riprendere* to take back, from *ri-* re- (from Latin *re-*) + *prendere* to take, from Latin *prehendere* — more at GET] (15th century)
**1 a :** the act or practice in international law of resorting to force short of war in retaliation for

damage or loss suffered **b :** an instance of such action
**2** *obsolete* **:** PRIZE
**3 :** the regaining of something (as by recapture)
**4 :** something (as a sum of money) given or paid in restitution — usually used in plural
**5 :** a retaliatory act
**¹re·prise** \ri-'prēz, *1 is also* -'prīz\ *noun* [Middle English, from Middle French, literally, action of taking back, from Old French, from *reprendre* to take back, from *re-* + *prendre* to take, from Latin *prehendere*] (14th century)
**1 :** a deduction or charge made yearly out of a manor or estate — usually used in plural
**2 :** a recurrence, renewal, or resumption of an action
**3 a :** a musical repetition: (1) **:** the repetition of the exposition preceding the development (2) **:** RECAPITULATION **b :** a repeated performance **:** REPETITION
**²re·prise** \ri-'prīz, *3 is* -'prēz\ *transitive verb* **re·prised; re·pris·ing** [Middle French *reprise* action of taking back] (15th century)
**1** *archaic* **:** TAKE BACK; *especially* **:** to recover by force
**2** *archaic* **:** COMPENSATE
**3 a :** to repeat the performance of **b :** RECAPITULATE
**re·pris·ti·nate** \ˌ(ˌ)rē-'pris-tə-ˌnāt\ *transitive verb* **-nat·ed; -nat·ing** [*re-* + *pristine* + ⁴*-ate*] (1659)
**:** to restore to an original state or condition
— **re·pris·ti·na·tion** \ˌ(ˌ)rē-ˌpris-tə-'nā-shən\ *noun*
**re·pro** \'rē-ˌ(ˌ)prō\ *noun, plural* **repros** [short for *reproduction*] (1946)
**1 :** a clear sharp proof made especially from a letterpress printing surface to serve as photographic copy for a printing plate
**2 :** REPRODUCTION 2
**¹re·proach** \ri-'prōch\ *noun* [Middle English *reproche*, from Middle French, from Old French, from *reprochier* to reproach, from (assumed) Vulgar Latin *repropiare*, from Latin *re-* + *prope* near — more at APPROACH] (14th century)
**1 :** an expression of rebuke or disapproval
**2 :** the act or action of reproaching or disapproving ⟨was beyond *reproach*⟩
**3 a :** a cause or occasion of blame, discredit, or disgrace **b :** DISCREDIT, DISGRACE
**4** *obsolete* **:** one subjected to censure or scorn
— **re·proach·ful** \-fəl\ *adjective*
— **re·proach·ful·ly** \-fə-lē\ *adverb*
— **re·proach·ful·ness** *noun*
**²reproach** *transitive verb* (14th century)
**1 :** to express disappointment in or displeasure with (a person) for conduct that is blameworthy or in need of amendment
**2 :** to make (something) a matter of reproach
**3 :** to bring into discredit
**synonym** *see* REPROVE
— **re·proach·able** \-'prō-chə-bəl\ *adjective*
— **re·proach·er** *noun*
— **re·proach·ing·ly** \-'prō-chiŋ-lē\ *adverb*
**rep·ro·bance** \'re-prə-bən(t)s\ *noun* (1604)
*archaic* **:** REPROBATION
**¹rep·ro·bate** \'re-prə-ˌbāt\ *transitive verb* **-bat·ed; -bat·ing** [Middle English, from Late Latin *reprobatus*, past participle of *reprobare* — more at REPROVE] (15th century)
**1 :** to condemn strongly as unworthy, unacceptable, or evil ⟨*reprobating* the laxity of the age⟩
**2 :** to foreordain to damnation
**3 :** to refuse to accept **:** REJECT
**synonym** *see* CRITICIZE
— **rep·ro·ba·tive** \'re-prə-ˌbā-tiv\ *adjective*

— **re·pro·ba·to·ry** \-bə-ˌtōr-ē, -ˌtȯr-\ *adjective*

**²rep·ro·bate** *adjective* (15th century)
**1** *archaic* : rejected as worthless or not standing a test : CONDEMNED
**2 a** : foreordained to damnation **b** : morally corrupt : DEPRAVED
**3** : expressing or involving reprobation
**4** : of, relating to, or characteristic of a reprobate

**³rep·ro·bate** *noun* (1545)
: a reprobate person

**rep·ro·ba·tion** \ˌre-prə-'bā-shən\ *noun* (14th century)
: the act of reprobating or the state of being reprobated

**re·pro·cess** \(ˌ)rē-'prä-ˌses, -'prō-, -səs\ *transitive verb* (1921)
: to subject to a special process or treatment in preparation for reuse; *especially* : to extract uranium and plutonium from (the spent fuel rods of a nuclear reactor) for use again as fuel

**re·pro·duce** \ˌrē-prə-'düs, -'dyüs\ (1611)
*transitive verb*
: to produce again: as **a** : to produce (new individuals of the same kind) by a sexual or asexual process **b** : to cause to exist again or anew ⟨*reproduce* water from steam⟩ **c** : to imitate closely ⟨sound-effects can *reproduce* the sound of thunder⟩ **d** : to present again **e** : to make a representation (as an image or copy) of ⟨*reproduce* a face on canvas⟩ **f** : to revive mentally : RECALL **g** : to translate (a recording) into sound
*intransitive verb*
**1** : to undergo reproduction
**2** : to produce offspring
— **re·pro·duc·er** *noun*
— **re·pro·duc·ibil·i·ty** \-ˌdü-sə-'bi-lə-tē, -ˌdyü-\ *noun*
— **re·pro·duc·ible** \-'dü-sə-bəl, -'dyü-\ *adjective or noun*
— **re·pro·duc·ibly** \-blē\ *adverb*

**re·pro·duc·tion** \ˌrē-prə-'dək-shən\ *noun* (1659)
**1** : the act or process of reproducing; *specifically* : the process by which plants and animals give rise to offspring and which fundamentally consists of the segregation of a portion of the parental body by a sexual or an asexual process and its subsequent growth and differentiation into a new individual
**2** : something reproduced : COPY
**3** : young seedling trees in a forest ☆
**reproduction proof** *noun* (1945)
: REPRO 1

**¹re·pro·duc·tive** \ˌrē-prə-'dək-tiv\ *adjective* (1753)
: of, relating to, or capable of reproduction
— **re·pro·duc·tive·ly** *adverb*

**²reproductive** *noun* (1934)
: an actual or potential parent; *specifically* : a sexually functional social insect

**re·pro·gram** \(ˌ)rē-'prō-ˌgram, -grəm\ (1959)
*transitive verb*
: to program anew; *especially* : to write new programs for (as a computer)
*intransitive verb*
: to rewrite or revise a program especially of a computer
— **re·pro·gram·ma·ble** \-'prō-ˌgra-mə-bəl, -ˌprō-'gra-\ *adjective*

**re·prog·ra·phy** \ri-'prä-grə-fē\ *noun* [*reproduction* + *-graphy*] (1956)
: facsimile reproduction (as by photocopying) of graphic matter
— **re·prog·ra·pher** \-grə-fər\ *noun*
— **re·pro·graph·ic** \ˌrē-prə-'gra-fik, ˌre-\ *adjective*
— **re·pro·graph·ics** \-fiks\ *noun plural*

**re·proof** \ri-'prüf\ *noun* [Middle English *reprof*, from Middle French *reprove*, from Old French, from *reprover*] (14th century)
: criticism for a fault : REBUKE

**re·prove** \ri-'prüv\ *verb* **re·proved; re·prov·ing** [Middle English, from Middle

French *reprover*, from Late Latin *reprobare* to disapprove, condemn, from Latin *re-* + *probare* to test, approve — more at PROVE] (14th century)
*transitive verb*
**1** : to scold or correct usually gently or with kindly intent
**2** : to express disapproval of : CENSURE ⟨it is not for me to *reprove* popular taste —D. W. Brogan⟩
**3** *obsolete* : DISPROVE, REFUTE
**4** *obsolete* : CONVINCE, CONVICT
*intransitive verb*
: to express rebuke or reproof ☆
— **re·prov·er** *noun*
— **re·prov·ing·ly** \-'prü-viŋ-lē\ *adverb*

**¹rep·tile** \'rep-ˌtil, -t°l\ *noun* [Middle English *reptil*, from Middle French or Late Latin; Middle French *reptile* (feminine), from Late Latin *reptile* (neuter), from neuter of *reptilis* creeping, from Latin *reptus*, past participle of *repere* to crawl; akin to Lithuanian *rėplioti* to crawl] (14th century)
**1** : an animal that crawls or moves on its belly (as a snake) or on small short legs (as a lizard)
**2** : any of a class (Reptilia) of air-breathing vertebrates that include the alligators and crocodiles, lizards, snakes, turtles, and extinct related forms (as dinosaurs and pterosaurs) and are characterized by a completely ossified skeleton with a single occipital condyle, a distinct quadrate bone usually immovably articulated with the skull, ribs attached to the sternum, and a body usually covered with scales or bony plates
**3** : a groveling or despised person

**²reptile** *adjective* (1607)
: characteristic of a reptile : REPTILIAN

**¹rep·til·ian** \rep-'ti-lē-ən, -'til-yən\ *adjective* (circa 1846)
**1** : resembling or having the characteristics of the reptiles
**2** : of or relating to the reptiles
**3** : cold-bloodedly treacherous ⟨a *reptilian* villain —Theodore Dreiser⟩

**²reptilian** *noun* (circa 1847)
: REPTILE 2

**re·pub·lic** \ri-'pə-blik\ *noun* [French *république*, from Middle French *republique*, from Latin *respublica*, from *res* thing, wealth + *publica*, feminine of *publicus* public — more at REAL, PUBLIC] (1604)
**1 a** (1) : a government having a chief of state who is not a monarch and who in modern times is usually a president (2) : a political unit (as a nation) having such a form of government **b** (1) : a government in which supreme power resides in a body of citizens entitled to vote and is exercised by elected officers and representatives responsible to them and governing according to law (2) : a political unit (as a nation) having such a form of government **c** : a usually specified republican government of a political unit ⟨the French Fourth *Republic*⟩
**2** : a body of persons freely engaged in a specified activity ⟨the *republic* of letters⟩
**3** : a constituent political and territorial unit of the former nations of Czechoslovakia, the U.S.S.R., or Yugoslavia

**¹re·pub·li·can** \ri-'pə-bli-kən\ *noun* (1697)
**1** : one that favors or supports a republican form of government
**2** *capitalized* **a** : a member of a political party advocating republicanism **b** : a member of the Democratic-Republican party or of the Republican party of the U.S.

**²republican** *adjective* (1712)
**1 a** : of, relating to, or having the characteristics of a republic **b** : favoring, supporting, or advocating a republic **c** : belonging or appropriate to one living in or supporting a republic ⟨*republican* simplicity⟩
**2** *capitalized* **a** : DEMOCRATIC-REPUBLICAN **b** : of, relating to, or constituting the one of the

two major political parties evolving in the U.S. in the mid-19th century that is usually primarily associated with business, financial, and some agricultural interests and is held to favor a restricted governmental role in economic life

**re·pub·li·can·ism** \ri-'pə-bli-kə-ˌni-zəm\ *noun* (1689)
**1** : adherence to or sympathy for a republican form of government
**2** : the principles or theory of republican government
**3** *capitalized* **a** : the principles, policy, or practices of the Republican party of the U.S. **b** : the Republican party or its members

**re·pub·li·can·ize** \-kə-ˌnīz\ *transitive verb* **-ized; -iz·ing** (1797)
: to make republican in character, form, or principle

**re·pub·li·ca·tion** \(ˌ)rē-ˌpə-blə-'kā-shən\ *noun* (1730)
**1** : the act or action of republishing : the state of being republished
**2** : something that has been republished

**re·pub·lish** \(ˌ)rē-'pə-blish\ *transitive verb* (1592)
**1** : to publish again or anew
**2** : to execute (a will) anew
— **re·pub·lish·er** *noun*

**re·pu·di·ate** \ri-'pyü-dē-ˌāt\ *transitive verb* **-at·ed; -at·ing** [Latin *repudiatus*, past participle of *repudiare*, from *repudium* rejection of a prospective spouse, divorce, probably from *re-* + *pudēre* to shame] (1545)
**1** : to divorce or separate formally from (a woman)
**2** : to refuse to have anything to do with : DISOWN
**3 a** : to refuse to accept; *especially* : to reject as unauthorized or as having no binding force **b** : to reject as untrue or unjust ⟨*repudiate* a charge⟩
**4** : to refuse to acknowledge or pay
*synonym* see DECLINE
— **re·pu·di·a·tor** \-ˌā-tər\ *noun*

---

☆ **SYNONYMS**
**Reproduction, duplicate, copy, facsimile, replica** mean a thing made to closely resemble another. REPRODUCTION implies an exact or close imitation of an existing thing ⟨*reproductions* from the museum's furniture collection⟩. DUPLICATE implies a double or counterpart exactly corresponding to another thing ⟨a *duplicate* of a house key⟩. COPY applies especially to one of a number of things reproduced mechanically ⟨printed a thousand *copies* of the lithograph⟩. FACSIMILE suggests a close reproduction often of graphic matter that may differ in scale ⟨a *facsimile* of a rare book⟩. REPLICA implies the exact reproduction of a particular item in all details ⟨a *replica* of the Mayflower⟩ but not always in the same scale ⟨miniature *replicas* of classic cars⟩.

**Reprove, rebuke, reprimand, admonish, reproach, chide** mean to criticize adversely. REPROVE implies an often kindly intent to correct a fault ⟨gently *reproved* my table manners⟩. REBUKE suggests a sharp or stern reproof ⟨the papal letter *rebuked* dissenting clerics⟩. REPRIMAND implies a severe, formal, often public or official rebuke ⟨*reprimanded* by the ethics committee⟩. ADMONISH suggests earnest or friendly warning and counsel ⟨*admonished* by my parents to control expenses⟩. REPROACH and CHIDE suggest displeasure or disappointment expressed in mild reproof or scolding ⟨*reproached* him for tardiness⟩ ⟨*chided* by their mother for untidiness⟩.

**re·pu·di·a·tion** \ri-ˌpyü-dē-ˈā-shən\ *noun* (1545)
: the act of repudiating : the state of being repudiated; *especially* : the refusal of public authorities to acknowledge or pay a debt
— **re·pu·di·a·tion·ist** \-sh(ə-)nist\ *noun*

**re·pugn** \ri-ˈpyün\ *verb* [Middle English, from Middle French & Latin; Middle French *repugner*, from Latin *repugnare*] (14th century)
*intransitive verb*
*archaic* : to offer opposition, objection, or resistance
*transitive verb*
: to contend against : OPPOSE

**re·pug·nance** \ri-ˈpəg-nən(t)s\ *noun* (15th century)
**1 a** : the quality or fact of being contradictory or inconsistent **b** : an instance of such contradiction or inconsistency
**2** : strong dislike, distaste, or antagonism

**re·pug·nan·cy** \-nən(t)-sē\ *noun, plural* -**cies** (15th century)
: REPUGNANCE

**re·pug·nant** \-nənt\ *adjective* [Middle English, opposed, contradictory, incompatible, from Middle French, from Latin *repugnant-*, *repugnans*, present participle of *repugnare* to fight against, from *re-* + *pugnare* to fight — more at PUNGENT] (15th century)
**1** : INCOMPATIBLE, INCONSISTENT
**2** *archaic* : HOSTILE
**3** : exciting distaste or aversion
— **re·pug·nant·ly** *adverb*

**¹re·pulse** \ri-ˈpəls\ *transitive verb* **re·pulsed; re·puls·ing** [Latin *repulsus*, past participle of *repellere* to repel] (15th century)
**1** : to drive or beat back : REPEL
**2** : to repel by discourtesy, coldness, or denial
**3** : to cause repulsion in

**²repulse** *noun* (1533)
**1** : REBUFF, REJECTION
**2** : the action of repelling an attacker : the fact of being repelled

**re·pul·sion** \ri-ˈpəl-shən\ *noun* (15th century)
**1** : the action of repulsing : the state of being repulsed
**2** : the action of repelling : the force with which bodies, particles, or like forces repel one another
**3** : a feeling of aversion : REPUGNANCE

**re·pul·sive** \-siv\ *adjective* (1598)
**1** : tending to repel or reject : COLD, FORBIDDING
**2** : serving or able to repulse
**3** : arousing aversion or disgust
— **re·pul·sive·ly** *adverb*
— **re·pul·sive·ness** *noun*

**re·pur·chase agreement** \(ˌ)rē-ˈpər-chəs-\ *noun* (1952)
: a contract giving the seller of securities (as treasury bills) the right to repurchase after a stated period and the buyer the right to retain interest earnings

**rep·u·ta·ble** \ˈre-pyə-tə-bəl\ *adjective* (1674)
**1** : enjoying good repute : held in esteem
**2** : employed widely or sanctioned by good writers
— **rep·u·ta·bil·i·ty** \ˌre-pyə-tə-ˈbi-lə-tē\ *noun*
— **rep·u·ta·bly** \ˈre-pyə-tə-blē\ *adverb*

**rep·u·ta·tion** \ˌre-pyə-ˈtā-shən\ *noun* [Middle English *reputacioun*, from Latin *reputation-*, *reputatio* consideration, from *reputare*] (14th century)
**1 a** : overall quality or character as seen or judged by people in general **b** : recognition by other people of some characteristic or ability ⟨has the *reputation* of being clever⟩
**2** : a place in public esteem or regard : good name
— **rep·u·ta·tion·al** \-shnəl, -shə-nᵊl\ *adjective*

**¹re·pute** \ri-ˈpyüt\ *transitive verb* **re·put·ed; re·put·ing** [Middle English, from Middle French *reputer*, from Latin *reputare* to reckon

up, think over, from *re-* + *putare* to reckon] (15th century)
: BELIEVE, CONSIDER

**²repute** *noun* (1551)
**1** : the character or status commonly ascribed to one : REPUTATION
**2** : the state of being favorably known, spoken of, or esteemed

**reputed** *adjective* (1549)
**1** : having a good repute : REPUTABLE
**2** : being such according to reputation or popular belief

**re·put·ed·ly** *adverb* (1687)
: according to reputation or general belief

**¹re·quest** \ri-ˈkwest\ *noun* [Middle English *requeste*, from Middle French, from (assumed) Vulgar Latin *requaesta*, from feminine of *requaestus*, past participle of *requaerere* to require] (14th century)
**1** : the act or an instance of asking for something
**2** : something asked for
**3** : the condition or fact of being requested ⟨available on *request*⟩
**4** : the state of being sought after : DEMAND

**²request** *transitive verb* (1533)
**1** : to make a request to or of ⟨*requested* her to write a paper⟩
**2** : to ask as a favor or privilege ⟨*requests* to be excused⟩
**3** *obsolete* : to ask (a person) to come or go to a thing or place
**4** : to ask for ⟨*requested* a brief delay⟩
*synonym* see ASK
— **re·quest·er** *or* **re·quest·or** \-ˈkwes-tər\ *noun*

**re·qui·em** \ˈre-kwē-əm *also* ˈrā- *or* ˈrē-\ *noun* [Middle English, from Latin (first word of the introit of the requiem mass), accusative of *requies* rest, from *re-* + *quies* quiet, rest — more at WHILE] (14th century)
**1** : a mass for the dead
**2 a** : a solemn chant (as a dirge) for the repose of the dead **b** : something that resembles such a solemn chant
**3 a** : a musical setting of the mass for the dead **b** : a musical composition in honor of the dead

**requiem shark** *noun* [obsolete French *requiem shark*, alteration of French *requin*] (1900)
: any of a family (Carcharhinidae) of sharks (as the tiger shark) that includes some dangerous to humans

**re·qui·es·cat** \ˌre-kwē-ˈes-ˌkät, -ˌkat; ˌrā-kwē-ˈes-ˌkät\ *noun* [Latin, may he (or she) rest, from *requiescere* to rest, from *re-* + *quiescere* to be quiet, from *quies*] (1824)
: a prayer for the repose of a dead person

**re·quire** \ri-ˈkwīr\ *verb* **re·quired; re·quir·ing** [Middle English *requeren*, from Middle French *requerre*, from (assumed) Vulgar Latin *requaerere* to seek for, need, require, alteration of Latin *requirere*, from *re-* + *quaerere* to seek, ask] (14th century)
*transitive verb*
**1 a** : to claim or ask for by right and authority **b** *archaic* : REQUEST
**2 a** : to call for as suitable or appropriate ⟨the occasion *requires* formal dress⟩ **b** : to demand as necessary or essential : have a compelling need for ⟨all living beings *require* food⟩
**3** : to impose a compulsion or command on : COMPEL
**4** *chiefly British* : to feel or be obliged — used with a following infinitive ⟨one does not *require* to be a specialist —Elizabeth Bowen⟩
*intransitive verb*
*archaic* : ASK
*synonym* see DEMAND

**re·quire·ment** \-ˈkwīr-mənt\ *noun* (1662)
: something required: **a** : something wanted or needed : NECESSITY ⟨production was not sufficient to satisfy military *requirements*⟩ **b** : something essential to the existence or occurrence of something else : CONDITION ⟨failed to meet the school's *requirements* for graduation⟩

**req·ui·site** \ˈre-kwə-zət\ *adjective* [Middle English, from Latin *requisitus*, past participle of *requirere*] (15th century)
: ESSENTIAL, NECESSARY
— **requisite** *noun*
— **req·ui·site·ness** *noun*

**req·ui·si·tion** \ˌre-kwə-ˈzi-shən\ *noun* [Middle English *requisicion*, from Middle French or Medieval Latin; Middle French *requisition*, from Medieval Latin *requisition-*, *requisitio*, from Latin, act of searching, from *requirere*] (15th century)
**1 a** : the act of formally requiring or calling upon someone to perform an action **b** : a formal demand made by one nation upon another for the surrender or extradition of a fugitive from justice
**2 a** : the act of requiring something to be furnished **b** : a demand or application made usually with authority: as (1) : a demand made by military authorities upon civilians for supplies or other needs (2) : a written request for something authorized but not made available automatically
**3** : the state of being in demand or use
— **requisition** *transitive verb*

**re·quit·al** \ri-ˈkwī-tᵊl\ *noun* (1582)
**1** : something given in return, compensation, or retaliation
**2** : the act or action of requiting : the state of being requited

**re·quite** \ri-ˈkwīt\ *transitive verb* **re·quit·ed; re·quit·ing** [*re-* + obsolete *quite* to quit, pay, from Middle English *quiten* — more at QUIT] (1529)
**1 a** : to make return for : REPAY **b** : to make retaliation for : AVENGE
**2** : to make suitable return to for a benefit or service or for an injury
*synonym* see RECIPROCATE
— **re·quit·er** *noun*

**re·ra·di·ate** \(ˌ)rē-ˈrā-dē-ˌāt\ *transitive verb* (1913)
: to radiate again or anew; *especially* : to emit (energy) in the form of radiation after absorbing incident radiation
— **re·ra·di·a·tion** \(ˌ)rē-ˌrā-dē-ˈā-shən\ *noun*

**rere·dos** \ˈrer-ə-ˌdäs *also* ˈrir-ə-ˌdäs *or* ˈrir-ˌdäs\ *noun* [Middle English, from Anglo-French *areredos*, from Middle French *arrere* behind + *dos* back, from Latin *dorsum* — more at ARREAR] (14th century)
: a usually ornamental wood or stone screen or partition wall behind an altar

**rere·ward** *noun* [Middle English *rerewarde*, from Anglo-French, from Old French *rere* behind + Old North French *warde* guard; akin to Old French *garde* guard — more at REAR GUARD] (14th century)
*obsolete* : REAR GUARD

**¹re·run** \(ˌ)rē-ˈrən\ *transitive verb* **-ran** \-ˈran\; **-run; -run·ning** (1804)
: to run again or anew

**²re·run** \ˈrē-ˌrən, (ˌ)rē-ˈ\ *noun* (circa 1934)
: the act or action or an instance of rerunning : REPETITION; *especially* : a movie or television show that is rerun

**res** \ˈrās, ˈrēz\ *noun, plural* **res** [Latin — more at REAL] (1851)
: a particular thing : MATTER — used especially in legal phrases

**res ad·ju·di·ca·ta** \ˈrēz-ə-ˌjü-di-ˈkä-tə\ *noun* [Late Latin] (1902)
: RES JUDICATA

**re·sal·able** \(ˌ)rē-ˈsā-lə-bəl\ *adjective* (1866)
: fit for resale

**re·sale** \ˈrē-ˌsāl, (ˌ)rē-ˈsā(ə)l\ *noun* (1625)
**1** : the act of selling again usually to a new party

---

\ə\ abut \ᵊ\ kitten \ər\ further \a\ ash \ā\ ace
\ä\ mop, mar \aů\ out \ch\ chin \e\ bet \ē\ easy
\g\ go \i\ hit \ī\ ice \j\ job \ŋ\ sing \ō\ go
\ó\ law \ói\ boy \th\ thin \th\ the \ü\ loot \ů\ foot
\y\ yet \zh\ vision *see also* Guide to Pronunciation

a : a secondhand sale **b** : an additional sale o the same buyer

**e·scale** \(ˌ)rē-'skā(ə)l\ *transitive verb* (1944)
: to plan, establish, or formulate on a new and usually smaller scale

**re·sched·ule** \(ˌ)rē-'ske-(ˌ)jü(ə)l, -jəl, *Canadian also* -'she-, *British usually* -'she-(ˌ)dyü(ə)l\ *transitive verb* (1965)
: to schedule or plan again according to a different timetable; *especially* : to defer required payment of (a debt or loan)

**re·scind** \ri-'sind\ *transitive verb* [Latin *rescindere* to annul, from *re-* + *scindere* to cut — more at SHED] (1643)
**1** : to take away : REMOVE
**2 a** : TAKE BACK, CANCEL 〈refused to *rescind* the order〉 **b** : to abrogate (a contract) and restore the parties to the positions they would have occupied had there been no contract
**3** : to make void (as an act) by action of the enacting authority or a superior authority : REPEAL
— **re·scind·er** *noun*
— **re·scind·ment** \-'sin(d)-mənt\ *noun*

**re·scis·sion** \ri-'si-zhən\ *noun* [Late Latin *rescission-, rescissio*, from Latin *rescindere*] (1611)
: an act of rescinding

**re·scis·so·ry** \-'si-zə-rē, -'si-sə-\ *adjective* (1605)
: relating to or tending to or having the effect of rescission

**re·script** \'rē-ˌskript\ *noun* [Middle English *rescripte*, from Latin *rescriptum*, from neuter of *rescriptus*, past participle of *rescribere* to write in reply, from *re-* + *scribere* to write — more at SCRIBE] (15th century)
**1** : a written answer of a Roman emperor or of a pope to a legal inquiry or petition
**2** : an official or authoritative order, decree, edict, or announcement
**3** : an act or instance of rewriting

**res·cue** \'res-(ˌ)kyü\ *transitive verb* **res·cued; res·cu·ing** [Middle English, from Middle French *rescourre*, from Old French, from *re-* + *escourre* to shake out, from Latin *excutere*, from *ex-* + *quatere* to shake] (14th century)
: to free from confinement, danger, or evil : SAVE, DELIVER: as **a** : to take (as a prisoner) forcibly from custody **b** : to recover (as a prize) by force **c** : to deliver (as a place under siege) by armed force ☆
— **res·cu·able** \-ə-bəl\ *adjective*
— **rescue** *noun*
— **res·cu·er** *noun*

**rescue mission** *noun* (1902)
: a city religious mission seeking to convert and rehabilitate the down-and-out

**¹re·search** \ri-'sərch, 'rē-ˌ\ *noun* [Middle French *recerche*, from *recerchier* to investigate thoroughly, from Old French, from *re-* + *cerchier* to search — more at SEARCH] (1577)
**1** : careful or diligent search
**2** : studious inquiry or examination; *especially* : investigation or experimentation aimed at the discovery and interpretation of facts, revision of accepted theories or laws in the light of new facts, or practical application of such new or revised theories or laws
**3** : the collecting of information about a particular subject

**²research** (1593)
*transitive verb*
**1** : to search or investigate exhaustively 〈*research* a problem〉
**2** : to do research for 〈*research* a book〉
*intransitive verb*
: to engage in research
— **re·search·able** \ri-'sər-chə-bəl, 'rē-ˌ\ *adjective*
— **re·search·er** *noun*

**re·search·ist** \ri-'sər-chist, 'rē-ˌsər-\ *noun* (1921)
: one engaged in research

**re·seau** \rā-'zō, ri-\ *noun, plural* **re·seaux** \-'zōz\ [French *réseau*, from Old French *resel*, diminutive of *rais* net, from Latin *retis, rete*] (1578)
**1** : a net ground or foundation in lace
**2** : a grid photographed by a separate exposure onto a plate containing star images to facilitate astronomical measurements

**re·sect** \ri-'sekt\ *transitive verb* [Latin *resectus*, past participle of *resecare* to cut off, from *re-* + *secare* to cut — more at SAW] (1846)
: to perform resection on
— **re·sect·abil·i·ty** \-ˌsek-tə-'bi-lə-tē\ *noun*
— **re·sect·able** \-'sek-tə-bəl\ *adjective*

**re·sec·tion** \ri-'sek-shən\ *noun* (1775)
: the surgical removal of part of an organ or structure

**re·se·da** \'rā-zə-ˌdä\ *noun* [French *réséda*, from *réséda*, a mignonette] (1873)
: a grayish green color

**re·seed** \(ˌ)rē-'sēd\ (1888)
*transitive verb*
**1** : to sow seed on again or anew
**2** : to maintain (itself) by self-sown seed
*intransitive verb*
: to maintain itself by self-sown seed

**re·sem·blance** \ri-'zem-blən(t)s\ *noun* (14th century)
**1 a** : the quality or state of resembling; *especially* : correspondence in appearance or superficial qualities **b** : a point of likeness : SIMILARITY
**2** : REPRESENTATION, IMAGE
**3** *archaic* : characteristic appearance
**4** *obsolete* : PROBABILITY
*synonym see* LIKENESS

**re·sem·blant** \-blənt\ *adjective* (14th century)
: marked by or showing resemblance

**re·sem·ble** \ri-'zem-bəl\ *transitive verb* **re·sem·bled; re·sem·bling** \-b(ə-)liŋ\ [Middle English, from Middle French *resembler, ressembler*, from Old French, from *re-* + *sembler* to be like, seem, from Latin *similare* to copy, from *similis* like — more at SAME] (14th century)
**1** : to be like or similar to
**2** *archaic* : to represent as like

**re·send** \(ˌ)rē-'send\ *transitive verb* **-sent** \-'sent\; **-send·ing** (1554)
: to send again or back

**re·sent** \ri-'zent\ *transitive verb* [French *ressentir* to be emotionally sensible of, from Old French, from *re-* + *sentir* to feel, from Latin *sentire* — more at SENSE] (1628)
: to feel or express annoyance or ill will at

**re·sent·ful** \-fəl\ *adjective* (1656)
**1** : full of resentment : inclined to resent
**2** : caused or marked by resentment
— **re·sent·ful·ly** \-fə-lē\ *adverb*
— **re·sent·ful·ness** *noun*

**re·sent·ment** \ri-'zent-mənt\ *noun* (1619)
: a feeling of indignant displeasure or persistent ill will at something regarded as a wrong, insult, or injury
*synonym see* OFFENSE

**re·ser·pine** \ri-'sər-ˌpēn, -pən\ *noun* [German *Reserpin*, probably irregular from New Latin *Rauwolfia serpentina*, a species of rauwolfia] (1952)
: an alkaloid $C_{33}H_{40}N_2O_9$ extracted especially from the root of rauwolfias and used in the treatment of hypertension, mental disorders, and tension states

**res·er·va·tion** \ˌre-zər-'vā-shən\ *noun* (15th century)
**1** : an act of reserving something: as **a** (1) : the act or fact of a grantor's reserving some newly created thing out of the thing granted (2) : the right or interest so reserved **b** : the setting of limiting conditions or withholding from complete exposition 〈answered without *reservation*〉 **c** : an arrangement to have something (as a hotel room) held for one's use; *also* : a promise, guarantee, or record of such engagement

**2 a** : a limiting condition 〈agreed, but with *reservations*〉 **b** : DOUBT, MISGIVING 〈had serious *reservations* about marriage〉
**3** : something reserved: as **a** : a tract of public land set aside (as for use by American Indians) **b** : an area in which hunting is not permitted; *especially* : one set aside as a secure breeding place
— **res·er·va·tion·ist** \-sh(ə-)nist\ *noun*

**¹re·serve** \ri-'zərv\ *transitive verb* **re·served; re·serv·ing** [Middle English, from Middle French *reserver*, from Latin *reservare*, literally, to keep back, from *re-* + *servare* to keep — more at CONSERVE] (14th century)
**1 a** : to hold in reserve : keep back 〈*reserve* grain for seed〉 **b** : to set aside (part of the consecrated elements) at the Eucharist for future use **c** : to retain or hold over to a future time or place : DEFER 〈*reserve* one's judgment on a plan〉 **d** : to make legal reservation of
**2** : to set or have set aside or apart 〈*reserve* a hotel room〉
*synonym see* KEEP
— **re·serv·able** \-'zər-və-bəl\ *adjective*

**²reserve** *noun, often attributive* (1648)
**1** : something reserved or set aside for a particular purpose, use, or reason: as **a** (1) : a military force withheld from action for later decisive use — usually used in plural (2) : forces not in the field but available (3) : the military forces of a country not part of the regular services; *also* : RESERVIST **b** : a tract (as of public land) set apart : RESERVATION
**2** : something stored or kept available for future use or need : STOCK
**3** : an act of reserving : QUALIFICATION
**4 a** : restraint, closeness, or caution in one's words and actions **b** : forbearance from making a full explanation, complete disclosure, or free expression of one's mind
**5** *archaic* : SECRET
**6 a** : money or its equivalent kept in hand or set apart usually to meet liabilities **b** : the liquid resources of a nation for meeting international payments
**7** : SUBSTITUTE
**8** : RESERVE PRICE
**9** : a wine made from select grapes, bottled on the maker's premises, and aged specially and often longer
— **in reserve** : held back for future or special use

**reserve bank** *noun* (1905)
: a central bank holding reserves of other banks

**reserve clause** *noun* (1944)
: a clause formerly placed in a professional athlete's contract that reserved for the club the exclusive right automatically to renew the

☆ **SYNONYMS**
**Rescue, deliver, redeem, ransom, reclaim, save** mean to set free from confinement or danger. RESCUE implies freeing from imminent danger by prompt or vigorous action 〈*rescued* the crew of a sinking ship〉. DELIVER implies release usually of a person from confinement, temptation, slavery, or suffering 〈*delivered* his people from bondage〉. REDEEM implies releasing from bondage or penalties by giving what is demanded or necessary 〈job training designed to *redeem* school dropouts from chronic unemployment〉. RANSOM specifically applies to buying out of captivity 〈tried to *ransom* the kidnap victim〉. RECLAIM suggests a bringing back to a former state or condition of someone or something abandoned or debased 〈*reclaimed* long-abandoned farms〉. SAVE may replace any of the foregoing terms; it may further imply a preserving or maintaining for usefulness or continued existence 〈an operation that *saved* my life〉.

contract and that bound the athlete to the club until retirement or until the athlete was traded or released

**re·served** \ri-'zərvd\ *adjective* (1601)
**1 :** restrained in words and actions
**2 :** kept or set apart or aside for future or special use
**synonym** see SILENT
— **re·serv·ed·ly** \-'zər-vəd-lē\ *adverb*
— **re·serv·ed·ness** \-'zər-vəd-nəs\ *noun*

**reserved power** *noun* (1838)
**:** a political power reserved by a constitution to the exclusive jurisdiction of a specified political authority

**reserve price** *noun* (1919)
**:** a price announced at an auction as the lowest that will be considered

**re·serv·ist** \ri-'zər-vist\ *noun* (1876)
**:** a member of a military reserve

**res·er·voir** \'re-zə-ˌvwär, -zər-, -ˌvwȯr *also* -ˌvȯi\ *noun* [French *réservoir,* from Middle French, from *reserver*] (1690)
**1 :** a place where something is kept in store: as **a :** an artificial lake where water is collected and kept in quantity for use **b :** a part of an apparatus in which a liquid is held **c :** SUPPLY, STORE ⟨a large *reservoir* of educated people⟩
**2 :** an extra supply **:** RESERVE
**3 :** an organism in which a parasite that is pathogenic for some other species lives and multiplies without damaging its host; *also* **:** a noneconomic organism within which a pathogen of economic or medical importance flourishes

**re·set** \(ˌ)rē-'set\ *transitive verb* **-set; -set·ting** (1655)
**1 :** to set again or anew ⟨*reset* type⟩ ⟨*reset* a diamond⟩ ⟨*reset* a circuit breaker⟩
**2 :** to change the reading of often to zero ⟨*reset* an odometer⟩
— **re·set** \'rē-ˌset\ *noun*
— **re·set·table** \-'se-tə-bəl\ *adjective*

**res ges·tae** \'räs-'ges-ˌtī, 'rēz-'jes-(ˌ)tē\ *noun plural* [Latin] (1616)
**:** things done; *especially* **:** the facts that form the environment of a litigated issue and are admissible in evidence

**resh** \'räsh\ *noun* [Hebrew *rēsh*] (circa 1823)
**:** the 20th letter of the Hebrew alphabet — see ALPHABET table

**re·shape** \(ˌ)rē-'shāp\ *transitive verb* (1827)
**:** to give a new form or orientation to **:** REORGANIZE
— **re·shap·er** *noun*

**re·shuf·fle** \(ˌ)rē-'shə-fəl\ *transitive verb* (1830)
**1 :** to shuffle (as cards) again
**2 :** to reorganize usually by the redistribution of existing elements ⟨the cabinet was *reshuffled* by the prime minister⟩
— **reshuffle** *noun*

**re·sid** \ri-'zid\ *noun* (1967)
**:** RESIDUAL OIL

**re·side** \ri-'zīd\ *intransitive verb* **re·sid·ed; re·sid·ing** [Middle English, from Middle French or Latin; Middle French *resider,* from Latin *residēre* to sit back, remain, abide, from *re-* + *sedēre* to sit — more at SIT] (15th century)
**1 a :** to be in residence as the incumbent of a benefice or office **b :** to dwell permanently or continuously **:** occupy a place as one's legal domicile
**2 a :** to be present as an element or quality **b :** to be vested as a right
— **re·sid·er** *noun*

**res·i·dence** \'re-zə-dən(t)s, 'rez-dən(t)s, 're-zə-ˌden(t)s\ *noun* (14th century)
**1 a :** the act or fact of dwelling in a place for some time **b :** the act or fact of living or regularly staying at or in some place for the discharge of a duty or the enjoyment of a benefit
**2 a** (1) **:** the place where one actually lives as distinguished from one's domicile or a place of temporary sojourn (2) **:** DOMICILE 2a **b :** the place where a corporation is actually or officially established **c :** the status of a legal resident
**3 a :** a building used as a home **:** DWELLING **b :** housing or a unit of housing provided for students
**4 a :** the period or duration of abode in a place **b :** a period of active and especially full-time study, research, or teaching at a college or university
— **in residence :** engaged to live and work at a particular place often for a specified time ⟨poet *in residence* at a university⟩

**residence time** *noun* (1954)
**:** the duration of persistence of a mass or substance in a medium or place

**res·i·den·cy** \'re-zə-dən(t)-sē, 'rez-dən(t)-, 're-zə-ˌden(t)-\ *noun, plural* **-cies** (1579)
**1 :** a usually official place of residence
**2 :** a territory in a protected state in which the powers of the protecting state are executed by a resident agent
**3 :** a period of advanced training in a medical specialty after graduation from medical school and licensing to practice medicine

**¹res·i·dent** \'re-zə-dənt, 'rez-dənt, 're-zə-ˌdent\ *adjective* [Middle English, from Latin *resident-, residens,* present participle of *residēre*] (14th century)
**1 a :** living in a place for some length of time **:** RESIDING **b :** serving in a regular or full-time capacity ⟨the *resident* engineer for a highway department⟩; *also* **:** being in residence
**2 :** PRESENT, INHERENT
**3 :** not migratory

**²resident** *noun* (15th century)
**1 :** one who resides in a place
**2 :** a diplomatic agent residing at a foreign court or seat of government; *especially* **:** one exercising authority in a protected state as representative of the protecting power
**3 :** a physician serving a residency

**resident commissioner** *noun* (1902)
**1 :** a nonvoting representative of a dependency in the U.S. House of Representatives
**2 :** a resident administrator in a British colony or possession

**res·i·den·tial** \ˌre-zə-'den(t)-shəl, ˌrez-'den(t)-\ *adjective* (1654)
**1 a :** used as a residence or by residents **b :** providing living accommodations for students ⟨a *residential* college⟩
**2 :** restricted to or occupied by residences ⟨a *residential* neighborhood⟩
**3 :** of or relating to residence or residences
— **res·i·den·tial·ly** \-'den(t)-sh(ə-)lē\ *adverb*

**¹res·id·u·al** \ri-'zi-jə-wəl, -jəl; -'zij-wəl\ *noun* [Latin *residuum* residue] (1557)
**1 :** REMAINDER, RESIDUUM: as **a :** the difference between results obtained by observation and by computation from a formula or between the mean of several observations and any one of them **b :** a residual product or substance **c :** an internal aftereffect of experience or activity that influences later behavior; *especially* **:** a disability remaining from a disease or operation
**2 :** a payment (as to an actor or writer) for each rerun after an initial showing (as of a TV show)

**²residual** *adjective* (1570)
**1 :** of, relating to, or constituting a residue
**2 :** leaving a residue that remains effective for some time
— **re·sid·u·al·ly** *adverb*

**residual oil** *noun* (circa 1948)
**:** fuel oil that remains after the removal of valuable distillates (as gasoline) from petroleum and that is used especially by industry — called also *resid*

**residual power** *noun* (1919)
**:** power held to remain at the disposal of a governmental authority after an enumeration or delegation of specified powers to other authorities

**re·sid·u·ary** \ri-'zi-jə-ˌwer-ē\ *adjective* (1726)
**:** of, relating to, or constituting a residue ⟨*residuary* estate⟩

**res·i·due** \'re-zə-ˌdü, -ˌdyü\ *noun* [Middle English, from Middle French *residu,* from Latin *residuum,* from neuter of *residuus* left over, from *residēre* to remain] (14th century)
**:** something that remains after a part is taken, separated, or designated **:** REMNANT, REMAINDER: as **a :** the part of a testator's estate remaining after the satisfaction of all debts, charges, allowances, and previous devises and bequests **b :** the remainder after subtracting a multiple of a modulus from an integer or a power of the integer that can appear as the second of the two terms in an appropriate congruence ⟨2 and 7 are *residues* of 12 modulo 5⟩ **c :** a constituent structural unit (as a group or monomer) of a usually complex molecule ⟨amino acid *residues* from hydrolysis of protein⟩

**residue class** *noun* (1948)
**:** the set of elements (as integers) that leave the same remainder when divided by a given modulus

**re·sid·u·um** \ri-'zi-jə-wəm\ *noun, plural* **re·sid·ua** \-wə\ [Latin] (1672)
**:** something residual: as **a :** RESIDUE a **b :** a residual product (as from the distillation of petroleum)

**re·sign** \ri-'zīn\ *verb* [Middle English, from Middle French *resigner,* from Latin *resignare,* literally, to unseal, cancel, from *re-* + *signare* to sign, seal — more at SIGN] (14th century)
*transitive verb*
**1 :** RELEGATE, CONSIGN; *especially* **:** to give (oneself) over without resistance ⟨*resigned* herself to her fate⟩
**2 :** to give up deliberately; *especially* **:** to renounce (as a right or position) by a formal act
*intransitive verb*
**1 :** to give up one's office or position **:** QUIT
**2 :** to accept something as inevitable **:** SUBMIT
**synonym** see RELINQUISH, ABDICATE
— **re·sign·ed·ly** \-'zī-nəd-lē\ *adverb*
— **re·sign·ed·ness** \-'zī-nəd-nəs\ *noun*
— **re·sign·er** \-'zī-nər\ *noun*

**re–sign** \(ˌ)rē-'sīn\ (1805)
*transitive verb*
**:** to sign again
*intransitive verb*
**:** to sign up again

**res·ig·na·tion** \ˌre-zig-'nā-shən\ *noun* (14th century)
**1 a :** an act or instance of resigning something **:** SURRENDER **b :** a formal notification of resigning
**2 :** the quality or state of being resigned **:** SUBMISSIVENESS

**re·sile** \ri-'zī(ə)l\ *intransitive verb* **re·siled; re·sil·ing** [Late Latin & Latin; Late Latin *resilire* to withdraw, from Latin, to recoil] (1529)
**:** RECOIL, RETRACT; *especially* **:** to return to a prior position

**re·sil·ience** \ri-'zil-yən(t)s\ *noun* (1824)
**1 :** the capability of a strained body to recover its size and shape after deformation caused especially by compressive stress
**2 :** an ability to recover from or adjust easily to misfortune or change

**re·sil·ien·cy** \-yən(t)-sē\ *noun* (circa 1836)
**:** RESILIENCE

**re·sil·ient** \-yənt\ *adjective* [Latin *resilient-, resiliens,* present participle of *resilire* to jump back, recoil, from *re-* + *salire* to leap — more at SALLY] (1674)

: characterized or marked by resilience: as **a** : capable of withstanding shock without permanent deformation or rupture **b** : tending to recover from or adjust easily to misfortune or change

**synonym** see ELASTIC

— **re·sil·ient·ly** adverb

**¹res·in** \'re-z°n\ noun [Middle English, from Middle French resine, from Latin resina; akin to Greek rhētinē pine resin] (14th century) **1 a** : any of various solid or semisolid amorphous fusible flammable natural organic substances that are usually transparent or translucent and yellowish to brown, are formed especially in plant secretions, are soluble in organic solvents (as ether) but not in water, are electrical nonconductors, and are used chiefly in varnishes, printing inks, plastics, and sizes and in medicine **b** : ROSIN **2 a** : any of a large class of synthetic products that have some of the physical properties of natural resins but are different chemically and are used chiefly in plastics **b** : any various products made from a natural resin or a natural polymer

— **res·in·ous** \'re-z°n-əs, 'rez-nəs\ adjective

**²resin** transitive verb **res·ined; res·in·ing** \'re-z°n-iŋ, 'rez-niŋ\ (1865)
: to treat with resin

**res·in·ate** \'re-z°n-ˌāt\ transitive verb **-at·ed; -at·ing** (circa 1890)
: to impregnate or flavor with resin

**resin canal** noun (1884)
: a tubular intercellular space in gymnosperms and some angiosperms that is lined with epithelial cells which secrete resin — called also **resin duct**

**res·in·oid** \'re-z°n-ˌoid\ noun (1880)
: GUM RESIN

**¹re·sist** \ri-'zist\ verb [Middle English, from Middle French or Latin; Middle French resister, from Latin resistere, from re- + sistere to take a stand; akin to Latin stare to stand — more at STAND] (14th century)
intransitive verb
: to exert force in opposition
transitive verb
**1** : to exert oneself so as to counteract or defeat
**2** : to withstand the force or effect of
**synonym** see OPPOSE

**²resist** noun (1836)
: something (as a coating) that protects against a chemical, electrical, or physical action

**re·sis·tance** \ri-'zis-tən(t)s\ noun (14th century)
**1 a** : an act or instance of resisting : OPPOSITION **b** : a means of resisting
**2** : the ability to resist; especially : the inherent capacity of a living being to resist untoward circumstances (as disease, malnutrition, or toxic agents)
**3** : an opposing or retarding force
**4 a** : the opposition offered by a body or substance to the passage through it of a steady electric current **b** : a source of resistance
**5** often capitalized : an underground organization of a conquered or nearly conquered country engaging in sabotage and secret operations against occupation forces and collaborators

**¹re·sis·tant** \-tənt\ adjective (15th century)
: giving or capable of resistance — often used in combination ⟨wrinkle-resistant clothes⟩

**²resistant** noun (1600)
: one that resists : RESISTER

**re·sist·er** \ri-'zis-tər\ noun (14th century)
: one that resists; especially : one who actively opposes the policies of a government

**re·sist·ibil·i·ty** \ri-ˌzis-tə-'bi-lə-tē\ noun (1617)
**1** : the quality or state of being resistible
**2** : ability to resist

**re·sist·i·ble** \ri-'zis-tə-bəl\ adjective (1608)
: capable of being resisted

**re·sis·tive** \ri-'zis-tiv\ adjective (1603)

: marked by resistance — often used in combination ⟨fire-resistive material⟩
— **re·sis·tive·ly** adverb
— **re·sis·tive·ness** noun

**re·sis·tiv·i·ty** \ri-ˌzis-'ti-və-tē, ˌrē-\ noun, plural **-ties** (1885)
**1** : the longitudinal electrical resistance of a uniform rod of unit length and unit cross-sectional area : the reciprocal of conductivity
**2** : capacity for resisting : RESISTANCE

**re·sist·less** \ri-'zist-ləs\ adjective (1586)
**1** : IRRESISTIBLE
**2** : offering no resistance
— **re·sist·less·ly** adverb
— **re·sist·less·ness** noun

**re·sis·tor** \ri-'zis-tər\ noun (1905)
: a device that has electrical resistance and that is used in an electric circuit for protection, operation, or current control

**re·sit·ting** \(ˌ)rē-'si-tiŋ\ noun (1661)
: a sitting (as of a legislature) for a second time : another sitting

**res ju·di·ca·ta** \'rēz-ˌjü-di-'kä-tə\ noun [Latin, judged matter] (1693)
: a matter finally decided on its merits by a court having competent jurisdiction and not subject to litigation again between the same parties

**re·sol·u·ble** \ri-'zäl-yə-bəl\ adjective [Late Latin resolubilis, from Latin resolvere to resolve, unloose] (1602)
: capable of being resolved

**¹res·o·lute** \'re-zə-ˌlüt, -lət\ adjective [Latin resolutus, past participle of resolvere] (1533)
**1** : marked by firm determination : RESOLVED
**2** : BOLD, STEADY
**synonym** see FAITHFUL
— **res·o·lute·ly** \-ˌlüt-lē, -lət-; ˌre-zə-'lüt-\ adverb
— **res·o·lute·ness** \-ˌlüt-nəs, -lət-, -'lüt-\ noun

**²resolute** noun (1602)
: a resolute person

**res·o·lu·tion** \ˌre-zə-'lü-shən\ noun [Middle English, from Middle French or Latin; Middle French resolution, from Latin resolution-, resolutio, from resolvere] (14th century)
**1** : the act or process of reducing to simpler form: as **a** : the act of analyzing a complex notion into simpler ones **b** : the act of answering : SOLVING **c** : the act of determining **d** : the passing of a voice part from a dissonant to a consonant tone or the progression of a chord from dissonance to consonance **e** : the separating of a chemical compound or mixture into its constituents **f** (1) : the division of a prosodic element into its component parts (2) : the substitution in Greek or Latin prosody of two short syllables for a long syllable **g** : the analysis of a vector into two or more vectors of which it is the sum **h** : the process or capability of making distinguishable the individual parts of an object, closely adjacent optical images, or sources of light
**2** : the subsidence of a pathological state (as inflammation)
**3 a** : something that is resolved ⟨made a resolution to mend my ways⟩ **b** : firmness of resolve
**4** : a formal expression of opinion, will, or intent voted by an official body or assembled group
**5** : the point in a literary work at which the chief dramatic complication is worked out
**synonym** see COURAGE

**¹re·solve** \ri-'zälv, -'zolv also -'zäv or -'zov\ verb **re·solved; re·solv·ing** [Middle English, from Latin resolvere to unloose, dissolve, from re- + solvere to loosen, release — more at SOLVE] (14th century)
transitive verb
**1** obsolete : DISSOLVE, MELT
**2 a** : BREAK UP, SEPARATE ⟨the prism resolved the light into a play of color⟩; also : to change

by disintegration **b** : to reduce by analysis ⟨resolve the problem into simple elements⟩ **c** : to distinguish between or make independently visible adjacent parts of **d** : to separate (a racemic compound or mixture) into the two components
**3** : to cause resolution of (a pathological state)
**4 a** : to deal with successfully : clear up ⟨resolve doubts⟩ ⟨resolve a dispute⟩ **b** : to find an answer to **c** : to make clear or understandable **d** : to find a mathematical solution of **e** : to split up (as a vector) into two or more components especially in assigned directions
**5** : to reach a firm decision about ⟨resolve to get more sleep⟩ ⟨resolve disputed points in a text⟩
**6 a** : to declare or decide by a formal resolution and vote **b** : to change by resolution or formal vote ⟨the house resolved itself into a committee⟩
**7** : to make (as voice parts) progress from dissonance to consonance
**8** : to work out the resolution of (as a play)
intransitive verb
**1** : to become separated into component parts; also : to become reduced by dissolving or analysis
**2** : to form a resolution : DETERMINE
**3** : CONSULT, DELIBERATE
**4** : to progress from dissonance to consonance
**synonym** see DECIDE
— **re·solv·able** \-'zäl-və-bəl, -'zol- also -'zä-və- or -'zo-və-\ adjective
— **re·solv·er** noun

**²resolve** noun (1591)
**1** : fixity of purpose : RESOLUTENESS
**2** : something that is resolved
**3** : a legal or official determination; especially : a formal resolution

**re·sol·vent** \ri-'zäl-vənt, -'zol-\ noun (1851)
: a means of solving something (as an equation)
— **resolvent** adjective

**resolving power** noun (1879)
**1** : the ability of an optical system to form distinguishable images of objects separated by small angular distances
**2** : the ability of a photographic film or plate to reproduce the fine detail of an optical image

**res·o·nance** \'re-z°n-ən(t)s, 'rez-nən(t)s\ noun (15th century)
**1 a** : the quality or state of being resonant **b** (1) : a vibration of large amplitude in a mechanical or electrical system caused by a relatively small periodic stimulus of the same or nearly the same period as the natural vibration period of the system (2) : the state of adjustment that produces resonance in a mechanical or electrical system
**2 a** : the intensification and enriching of a musical tone by supplementary vibration **b** : a quality imparted to voiced sounds by vibration in anatomical resonating chambers or cavities (as the mouth or the nasal cavity) **c** : a quality of richness or variety **d** : a quality of evoking response ⟨how much resonance the scandal seems to be having —U.S. News & World Report⟩
**3** : the sound elicited on percussion of the chest
**4** : the conceptual alternation of a chemical species (as a molecule or ion) between two or more equivalent allowed structural representations differing only in the placement of electrons that aids in understanding the actual state of the species as an amalgamation of its possible structures and the usually higher-than-expected stability of the species
**5 a** : the enhancement of an atomic, nuclear, or particle reaction or a scattering event by excitation of internal motion in the system **b** : MAGNETIC RESONANCE
**6** : an extremely short-lived elementary particle
**7** : a synchronous gravitational relationship of two celestial bodies (as moons) that orbit a

third (as a planet) which can be expressed as a simple ratio of their orbital periods

**res·o·nant** \'re-z°n-ənt, 'rez-nənt\ *adjective* (1592)
**1 :** continuing to sound : ECHOING
**2 a :** capable of inducing resonance **b :** relating to or exhibiting resonance
**3 a :** intensified and enriched by or as if by resonance **b :** marked by grandiloquence
— **resonant** *noun*
— **res·o·nant·ly** *adverb*

**res·o·nate** \'re-z°n-‚āt\ *verb* **-nat·ed; -nat·ing** [Latin *resonatus,* past participle of *resonare* to resound — more at RESOUND] (1873)
*intransitive verb*
**1 :** to produce or exhibit resonance
**2 :** to respond as if by resonance ⟨*resonate* to the music⟩; *also* : to have a repetitive pattern that resembles resonance
**3 :** to relate harmoniously
*transitive verb*
: to subject to resonating

**res·o·na·tor** \-‚ā-tər\ *noun* (circa 1869)
: something that resounds or resonates: as **a** : a hollow metallic container for producing microwaves or a piezoelectric crystal put into oscillation by the oscillations of an outside source **b :** a device for increasing the resonance of a musical instrument

**re·sorb** \(‚)rē-'sòrb, -'zòrb\ *verb* [Latin *resorbēre,* from *re-* + *sorbēre* to suck up — more at ABSORB] (1640)
*transitive verb*
**1 :** to swallow or suck in again
**2 :** to break down and assimilate (something previously differentiated)
*intransitive verb*
: to undergo resorption

**res·or·cin** \rə-'zòr-s°n\ *noun* [International Scientific Vocabulary *res-* (from Latin *resina* resin) + *orcin,* a phenol ($C_7H_8O_2$)] (circa 1868)
: RESORCINOL

**res·or·cin·ol** \-‚òl, -‚ōl\ *noun* (1881)
: a crystalline phenol $C_6H_6O_2$ obtained from various resins or artificially and used especially in making dyes, pharmaceuticals, and resins

**re·sorp·tion** \(‚)rē-'sòrp-shən, -'zòrp-\ *noun* [Latin *resorbēre*] (circa 1820)
: the action or process of resorbing something
— **re·sorp·tive** \-tiv\ *adjective*

**¹re·sort** \ri-'zòrt\ *noun* [Middle English, from Middle French, resource, recourse, from *resortir* to rebound, resort, from Old French, from *re-* + *sortir* to escape, sally] (14th century)
**1 a :** one that affords aid or refuge : RESOURCE ⟨went to them as a last *resort*⟩ **b :** RECOURSE
**2 a :** frequent, habitual, or general visiting ⟨a place of popular *resort*⟩ **b :** persons who frequent a place : THRONG **c** (1) : a frequently visited place : HAUNT (2) : a place providing recreation and entertainment especially to vacationers
**synonym** see RESOURCE

**²resort** *intransitive verb* (15th century)
**1 :** to go especially frequently or habitually : REPAIR
**2 :** to have recourse ⟨*resort* to force⟩

**re–sort** \(‚)rē-'sòrt\ *transitive verb* (1889)
: to sort again

**re·sort·er** \ri-'zòr-tər\ *noun* (1917)
: a frequenter of resorts

**re·sound** \ri-'zaùnd *also* -'saùnd\ *verb* [Middle English *resounen,* from Middle French *resoner,* from Latin *resonare,* from *re-* + *sonare* to sound — more at SOUND] (14th century)
*intransitive verb*
**1 :** to become filled with sound : REVERBERATE
**2 a :** to sound loudly **b :** to produce a sonorous or echoing sound
**3 :** to become renowned
*transitive verb*
**1 :** to extol loudly or widely : CELEBRATE
**2 :** ECHO, REVERBERATE

**3 :** to sound or utter in full resonant tones

**re·sound·ing** *adjective* (15th century)
**1 :** producing or characterized by resonant sound : RESONATING
**2 a :** impressively sonorous **b :** EMPHATIC, UNEQUIVOCAL ⟨a *resounding* success⟩
— **re·sound·ing·ly** \-'zaùn-diŋ-lē *also* -'saùn-\ *adverb*

**re·source** \'rē-‚sòrs, -‚sòrs, -‚zòrs, -‚zòrs, ri-'\ *noun* [French *ressource,* from Old French *ressourse* relief, resource, from *resourdre* to relieve, literally, to rise again, from Latin *resurgere* — more at RESURRECTION] (1611)
**1 a :** a source of supply or support : an available means — usually used in plural **b :** a natural source of wealth or revenue — often used in plural **c :** computable wealth — usually used in plural **d :** a source of information or expertise
**2 :** something to which one has recourse in difficulty : EXPEDIENT
**3 :** a possibility of relief or recovery
**4 :** a means of spending one's leisure time
**5 :** an ability to meet and handle a situation : RESOURCEFULNESS ☆

**re·source·ful** \ri-'sòrs-fəl, -'sòrs-, -'zòrs-, -'zòrs-\ *adjective* (1851)
: able to meet situations : capable of devising ways and means
— **re·source·ful·ly** \-fə-lē\ *adverb*
— **re·source·ful·ness** *noun*

**¹re·spect** \ri-'spekt\ *noun* [Middle English, from Latin *respectus,* literally, act of looking back, from *respicere* to look back, regard, from *re-* + *specere* to look — more at SPY] (14th century)
**1 :** a relation or reference to a particular thing or situation ⟨remarks having *respect* to an earlier plan⟩
**2 :** an act of giving particular attention : CONSIDERATION
**3 a :** high or special regard : ESTEEM **b :** the quality or state of being esteemed **c** *plural* : expressions of respect or deference ⟨paid our *respects*⟩
**4 :** PARTICULAR, DETAIL ⟨a good plan in some *respects*⟩
— **in respect of** *chiefly British* : with respect to : CONCERNING
— **in respect to** : with respect to : CONCERNING
— **with respect to** : with reference to : in relation to

**²respect** *transitive verb* (1560)
**1 a :** to consider worthy of high regard : ESTEEM **b :** to refrain from interfering with
**2 :** to have reference to : CONCERN
**synonym** see REGARD
— **re·spect·er** *noun*

**¹re·spect·able** \ri-'spek-tə-bəl\ *adjective* (1599)
**1 :** worthy of respect : ESTIMABLE
**2 :** decent or correct in character or behavior : PROPER
**3 a :** fair in size or quantity ⟨*respectable* amount⟩ **b :** moderately good : TOLERABLE
**4 :** fit to be seen : PRESENTABLE ⟨*respectable* clothes⟩
— **re·spect·abil·i·ty** \-‚spek-tə-'bi-lə-tē\ *noun*
— **re·spect·able·ness** \-'spek-tə-bəl-nəs\ *noun*
— **re·spect·ably** \-blē\ *adverb*

**²respectable** *noun* (1814)
: a respectable person

**re·spect·ful** \ri-'spekt-fəl\ *adjective* (1687)
: marked by or showing respect or deference
— **re·spect·ful·ly** \-fə-lē\ *adverb*
— **re·spect·ful·ness** *noun*

**re·spect·ing** *preposition* (1611)
**1 :** in view of : CONSIDERING
**2 :** with respect to : CONCERNING

**re·spec·tive** \ri-'spek-tiv\ *adjective* (1592)
**1** *obsolete* : PARTIAL, DISCRIMINATIVE
**2 :** PARTICULAR, SEPARATE ⟨their *respective* homes⟩

— **re·spec·tive·ness** *noun*

**re·spec·tive·ly** *adverb* (1605)
**1 :** in particular : SEPARATELY ⟨could not recognize the solutions as salty or sour, *respectively*⟩
**2 :** in the order given ⟨Mary and Anne were *respectively* 12 and 16 years old⟩

**re·spell** \(‚)rē-'spel\ *transitive verb* (1806)
: to spell again or in another way; *especially*
: to spell out according to a phonetic system
— **re·spell·ing** \-'spe-liŋ\ *noun*

**re·spi·ra·ble** \'res-p(ə-)rə-bəl, ri-'spī-rə-\ *adjective* (1779)
: fit for breathing; *also* : capable of being taken in by breathing ⟨*respirable* particles of ash⟩

**res·pi·ra·tion** \‚res-pə-'rā-shən\ *noun* [Middle English *respiracioun,* from Latin *respiration-, respiratio,* from *respirare*] (15th century)
**1 a :** the placing of air or dissolved gases in intimate contact with the circulating medium of a multicellular organism (as by breathing) **b** : a single complete act of breathing
**2 :** the physical and chemical processes by which an organism supplies its cells and tissues with the oxygen needed for metabolism and relieves them of the carbon dioxide formed in energy-producing reactions
**3 :** any of various energy-yielding oxidative reactions in living matter
— **re·spi·ra·to·ry** \'res-p(ə-)rə-‚tōr-ē, ri-'spī-rə-, -‚tòr-\ *adjective*

**res·pi·ra·tor** \'res-pə-‚rā-tər\ *noun* (1836)
**1 :** a device worn over the mouth or nose for protecting the respiratory tract
**2 :** a device for maintaining artificial respiration

**respiratory pigment** *noun* (1896)
: any of various permanently or intermittently colored conjugated proteins and especially hemoglobin that function in the transfer of oxygen in cellular respiration

**respiratory quotient** *noun* (circa 1890)
: a ratio indicating the relation of the volume of carbon dioxide given off in respiration to that of the oxygen consumed

**respiratory system** *noun* (1940)
: a system of organs subserving the function of respiration and in air-breathing vertebrates consisting typically of the lungs and their nervous and circulatory supply and the channels by which these are continuous with the outer air

**re·spire** \ri-'spīr\ *verb* **re·spired; re·spir·ing** [Middle English, from Latin *respirare,* from *re-* + *spirare* to blow, breathe] (15th century)
*intransitive verb*

---

☆ SYNONYMS
**Resource, resort, expedient, shift, makeshift, stopgap** mean something one turns to in the absence of the usual means or source of supply. RESOURCE and RESORT apply to anything one falls back upon ⟨exhausted all of their *resources*⟩ ⟨a last *resort*⟩. EXPEDIENT may apply to any device or contrivance used when the usual one is not at hand or not possible ⟨a flimsy *expedient*⟩. SHIFT implies a tentative or temporary imperfect expedient ⟨desperate *shifts* to stave off foreclosure⟩. MAKESHIFT implies an inferior expedient adopted because of urgent need or countenanced through indifference ⟨old equipment employed as a *makeshift*⟩. STOPGAP applies to something used temporarily as an emergency measure ⟨a new law intended only as a *stopgap*⟩.

---

\ə\ abut \'ə\ kitten \ər\ further \a\ ash \ā\ ace
\ä\ mop, mar \aù\ out \ch\ chin \e\ bet \ē\ easy
\g\ go \i\ hit \ī\ ice \j\ job \ŋ\ sing \ō\ go
\ò\ law \òi\ boy \th\ thin \th\ the \ü\ loot \ù\ foot
\y\ yet \zh\ vision     *see also* Guide to Pronunciation

**1 :** BREATHE; *specifically* **:** to inhale and exhale air successively
**2** *of a cell or tissue* **:** to take up oxygen and produce carbon dioxide through oxidation ~ *transitive verb* **:** BREATHE

**res·pi·rom·e·ter** \ˌres-pə-ˈrä-mə-tər\ *noun* (circa 1883)
**:** an instrument for studying the character and extent of respiration
— **res·pi·ro·met·ric** \-rō-ˈme-trik\ *adjective*
— **res·pi·rom·e·try** \-ˈrä-mə-trē\ *noun*

**¹re·spite** \ˈres-pət *also* ri-ˈspīt, *British usually* ˈres-ˌpīt\ *noun* [Middle English *respit*, from Old French, from Medieval Latin *respectus*, from Latin, act of looking back — more at RESPECT] (13th century)
**1 ·:** a period of temporary delay; *especially* **:** REPRIEVE 1b
**2 :** an interval of rest or relief

**²respite** *transitive verb* **re·spit·ed; re·spit·ing** (14th century)
**1 :** to grant a respite to
**2 :** PUT OFF, DELAY

**re·splen·dence** \ri-ˈsplen-dən(t)s\ *noun* (15th century)
**:** the quality or state of being resplendent **:** SPLENDOR

**re·splen·den·cy** \-dən(t)-sē\ *noun* (1611)
**:** RESPLENDENCE

**re·splen·dent** \-dənt\ *adjective* [Latin *resplendent-, resplendens*, present participle of *resplendēre* to shine back, from *re-* + *splendēre* to shine — more at SPLENDID] (15th century)
**:** shining brilliantly **:** characterized by a glowing splendor ⟨meadows *resplendent* with wildflowers —*Outdoor World*⟩
**synonym** see SPLENDID
— **re·splen·dent·ly** *adverb*

**¹re·spond** \ri-ˈspänd\ *noun* (15th century)
**:** an engaged pillar supporting an arch or closing a colonnade or arcade

**²respond** *verb* [Middle French *respondre*, from Latin *respondēre* to promise in return, answer, from *re-* + *spondēre* to promise — more at SPOUSE] (1719)
*intransitive verb*
**1 :** to say something in return **:** make an answer ⟨*respond* to criticism⟩
**2 a :** to react in response ⟨*responded* to a call for help⟩ **b :** to show favorable reaction ⟨*respond* to surgery⟩
**3 :** to be answerable ⟨*respond* in damages⟩ ~ *transitive verb* **:** REPLY
**synonym** see ANSWER
— **re·spond·er** \-ˈspän-dər\ *noun*

**¹re·spon·dent** \ri-ˈspän-dənt\ *noun* [Latin *respondent-, respondens*, present participle of *respondēre*] (1528)
**1 :** one who responds: as **a :** one who maintains a thesis in reply **b** (1) **:** one who answers in various legal proceedings (as in equity cases) (2) **:** the prevailing party in the lower court **c :** a person who responds to a poll
**2 :** a reflex that occurs in response to a specific external stimulus — compare OPERANT

**²respondent** *adjective* (1726)
**1 :** making response **:** RESPONSIVE; *especially* **:** being a respondent at law
**2 :** relating to or being behavior or responses to a stimulus that are followed by a reward ⟨*respondent* conditioning⟩ — compare OPERANT 3

**re·sponse** \ri-ˈspän(t)s\ *noun* [Middle English & Latin; Middle English *respounse*, from Middle French *respons*, from Latin *responsum* reply, from neuter of *responsus*, past participle of *respondēre*] (14th century)
**1 :** an act of responding
**2 :** something constituting a reply or a reaction: as **a :** a verse, phrase, or word sung or said by the people or choir after or in reply to

the officiant in a liturgical service **b :** the activity or inhibition of previous activity of an organism or any of its parts resulting from stimulation **c :** the output of a transducer or detecting device resulting from a given input

**re·spon·si·bil·i·ty** \ri-ˌspän(t)-sə-ˈbi-lə-tē\ *noun, plural* **-ties** (1787)
**1 :** the quality or state of being responsible: as **a :** moral, legal, or mental accountability **b :** RELIABILITY, TRUSTWORTHINESS
**2 :** something for which one is responsible **:** BURDEN

**re·spon·si·ble** \ri-ˈspän(t)-sə-bəl\ *adjective* (1643)
**1 a :** liable to be called on to answer **b** (1) **:** liable to be called to account as the primary cause, motive, or agent ⟨a committee *responsible* for the job⟩ (2) **:** being the cause or explanation ⟨mechanical defects were *responsible* for the accident⟩ **c :** liable to legal review or in case of fault to penalties
**2 a :** able to answer for one's conduct and obligations **:** TRUSTWORTHY **b :** able to choose for oneself between right and wrong
**3 :** marked by or involving responsibility or accountability ⟨*responsible* financial policies⟩ ⟨a *responsible* job⟩
**4 :** politically answerable; *especially* **:** required to submit to the electorate if defeated by the legislature — used especially of the British cabinet ☆
— **re·spon·si·ble·ness** *noun*
— **re·spon·si·bly** \-blē\ *adverb*

**re·spon·sions** \ri-ˈspän(t)-shənz\ *noun plural* [Middle English *responcioun* response, sum to be paid, from Middle French or Medieval Latin; Middle French *responsion*, from Medieval Latin *responsion-, responsio*, from Latin, answer, from *respondēre*] (1813)
**:** an examination required for matriculation as an undergraduate at Oxford

**re·spon·sive** \ri-ˈspän(t)-siv\ *adjective* (15th century)
**1 :** giving response **:** constituting a response **:** ANSWERING ⟨a *responsive* glance⟩ ⟨responsive aggression⟩
**2 :** quick to respond or react appropriately or sympathetically **:** SENSITIVE
**3 :** using responses ⟨*responsive* worship⟩
— **re·spon·sive·ly** *adverb*
— **re·spon·sive·ness** *noun*

**re·spon·so·ry** \-ˈspän(t)s-(ə-)rē\ *noun, plural* **-ries** [Middle English, from Medieval Latin *responsorius*, from Latin *respondēre*] (15th century)
**:** a set of versicles and responses sung or said after or during a lection

**re·spon·sum** \ri-ˈspän(t)-səm\ *noun, plural* **-sa** \-sə\ [New Latin, from Latin, reply, response] (1896)
**:** a written decision from a rabbinic authority in response to a submitted question or problem

**res pu·bli·ca** \ˈräs-ˈpü-bli-ˌkä\ *noun* [Latin — more at REPUBLIC] (circa 1898)
**1 :** COMMONWEALTH, STATE, REPUBLIC
**2 :** COMMONWEAL

**res·sen·ti·ment** \rə-ˌsäⁿ-tē-ˈmäⁿ\ *noun* [French, resentment, from *ressentir* to resent — more at RESENT] (1941)
**:** deep-seated resentment, frustration, and hostility accompanied by a sense of being powerless to express these feelings directly

**¹rest** \ˈrest\ *noun* [Middle English, from Old English; akin to Old High German *rasta* rest and perhaps to Old High German *ruowa* calm] (before 12th century)
**1 :** REPOSE, SLEEP; *specifically* **:** a bodily state characterized by minimal functional and metabolic activities
**2 a :** freedom from activity or labor **b :** a state of motionlessness or inactivity **c :** the repose of death
**3 :** a place for resting or lodging
**4 :** peace of mind or spirit

**5 a** (1) **:** a rhythmic silence in music (2) **:** a character representing such a silence **b :** a brief pause in reading
**6 :** something used for support
— **at rest 1 :** resting or reposing especially in sleep or death **2 :** QUIESCENT, MOTIONLESS **3 :** free of anxieties

rest 5a(2): *1* whole, *2* half, *3* quarter, *4* eighth, *5* sixteenth

**²rest** (before 12th century)
*intransitive verb*
**1 a :** to get rest by lying down; *especially* **:** SLEEP **b :** to lie dead
**2 :** to cease from action or motion **:** refrain from labor or exertion
**3 :** to be free from anxiety or disturbance
**4 :** to sit or lie fixed or supported ⟨a column *rests* on its pedestal⟩
**5 a :** to remain confident **:** TRUST ⟨cannot *rest* on that assumption⟩ **b :** to be based or founded ⟨the verdict *rested* on several sound precedents⟩
**6 :** to remain for action or accomplishment ⟨the answer *rests* with you⟩
**7** *of farmland* **:** to remain idle or uncropped
**8 :** to bring to an end voluntarily the introduction of evidence in a law case ~ *transitive verb*
**1 :** to give rest to
**2 :** to set at rest
**3 :** to place on or against a support
**4 :** to cause to be firmly fixed ⟨*rested* all hope in his child⟩
**5 :** to stop voluntarily from presenting evidence pertinent to ⟨a case at law⟩
— **rest·er** *noun*

**³rest** *noun* [Middle English *reste*, literally, stoppage, short for *areste*, from Middle French, from Old French, from *arester* to arrest] (14th century)
**:** a projection or attachment on the side of the breastplate of medieval armor for supporting the butt of a lance

**⁴rest** *noun* [Middle English, from Middle French *reste*, from *rester* to remain, from Latin *restare*, from *re-* + *stare* to stand — more at STAND] (15th century)
**:** something that remains over **:** REMAINDER ⟨ate the *rest* of the candy⟩
— **for the rest :** with regard to remaining issues or needs

**re·start** \(ˌ)rē-ˈstärt\ (1845)
*transitive verb*
**1 :** to start anew
**2 :** to resume (as an activity) after interruption ~ *intransitive verb*
**:** to resume operation
— **re·start** \ˈrē-ˌstärt, (ˌ)rē-ˈ\ *noun*

☆ SYNONYMS
**Responsible, answerable, accountable, amenable, liable** mean subject to being held to account. RESPONSIBLE implies holding a specific office, duty, or trust ⟨the bureau *responsible* for revenue collection⟩. ANSWERABLE suggests a relation between one having a moral or legal obligation and a court or other authority charged with oversight of its observance ⟨an intelligence agency *answerable* to Congress⟩. ACCOUNTABLE suggests imminence of retribution for unfulfilled trust or violated obligation ⟨elected officials are *accountable* to the voters⟩. AMENABLE and LIABLE stress the fact of subjection to review, censure, or control by a designated authority under certain conditions ⟨laws are *amenable* to judicial review⟩ ⟨not *liable* for the debts of the former spouse⟩.

— **re·start·able** \-'stär-tə-bəl\ *adjective*

**re·state** \(ˌ)rē-'stāt\ *transitive verb* (circa 1713)
: to state again or in another way

**re·state·ment** \-mənt\ *noun* (1803)
**1** : something that is restated
**2** : the act of restating

**res·tau·rant** \'res-t(ə-)rənt, -tə-ˌränt, -ˌtränt, -ˌtȯrnt\ *noun* [French, from present participle of *restaurer* to restore, from Latin *restaurare*] (1827)
: a business establishment where meals or refreshments may be procured ◆

**res·tau·ra·teur** \ˌres-tə-rə-'tər\ *also* **res·tau·ran·teur** \-ˌrän-\ *noun* [French *restaurateur*, from Late Latin *restaurator* restorer, from Latin *restaurare*] (1796)
: the operator or proprietor of a restaurant

**rest·ful** \'rest-fəl\ *adjective* (14th century)
**1** : marked by, affording, or suggesting rest and repose ⟨a *restful* color scheme⟩
**2** : being at rest : QUIET
**synonym** see COMFORTABLE
— **rest·ful·ly** \-fə-lē\ *adverb*
— **rest·ful·ness** *noun*

**rest home** *noun* (1926)
: an establishment that provides housing and general care for the aged or the convalescent

**rest house** *noun* (1807)
: a building used for shelter by travelers

**rest·ing** *adjective* (14th century)
**1** : being or characterized by dormancy : QUIESCENT ⟨a *resting* spore⟩ ⟨bulbs in the *resting* state⟩
**2** : not undergoing or marked by division : VEGETATIVE ⟨a *resting* nucleus⟩

**res·ti·tute** \'res-tə-ˌtüt, -ˌtyüt\ *verb* **-tut·ed; -tut·ing** [Latin *restitutus,* past participle of *restituere*] (circa 1500)
*transitive verb*
**1** : to restore to a former state or position
**2** : GIVE BACK; *especially* : REFUND
*intransitive verb*
: to undergo restitution

**res·ti·tu·tion** \ˌres-tə-'tü-shən, -'tyü-\ *noun* [Middle English, from Middle French, from Latin *restitution-, restitutio,* from *restituere* to restore, from *re-* + *statuere* to set up — more at STATUTE] (14th century)
**1** : an act of restoring or a condition of being restored: as **a** : a restoration of something to its rightful owner **b** : a making good of or giving an equivalent for some injury
**2** : a legal action serving to cause restoration of a previous state

**res·tive** \'res-tiv\ *adjective* [Middle English *restyf,* from Middle French *restif,* from *rester* to stop behind, remain] (15th century)
**1** : stubbornly resisting control : BALKY
**2** : marked by impatience : FIDGETY
**synonym** see CONTRARY
— **res·tive·ly** *adverb*
— **res·tive·ness** *noun*

**rest·less** \'rest-ləs\ *adjective* (before 12th century)
**1** : lacking or denying rest : UNEASY ⟨a *restless* night⟩
**2** : continuously moving : UNQUIET ⟨the *restless* sea⟩
**3** : characterized by or manifesting unrest especially of mind ⟨*restless* pacing⟩; *also* : CHANGEFUL, DISCONTENTED
— **rest·less·ly** *adverb*
— **rest·less·ness** *noun*

**rest mass** *noun* (1914)
: the mass of a body exclusive of additional mass the body acquires by its motion according to the theory of relativity

**re·stor·able** \ri-'stōr-ə-bəl, -'stȯr-\ *adjective* (1611)
: fit for restoring or reclaiming

**re·stor·al** \-əl\ *noun* (1611)
: RESTORATION

**res·to·ra·tion** \ˌres-tə-'rā-shən\ *noun* (14th century)

**1** : an act of restoring or the condition of being restored: as **a** : a bringing back to a former position or condition : REINSTATEMENT ⟨the *restoration* of peace⟩ **b** : RESTITUTION **c** : a restoring to an unimpaired or improved condition ⟨the *restoration* of a painting⟩ **d** : the replacing of missing teeth or crowns
**2** : something that is restored; *especially* : a representation or reconstruction of the original form (as of a fossil or a building)
**3** *capitalized* **a** : the reestablishing of the monarchy in England in 1660 under Charles II **b** : the period in English history usually held to coincide with the reign of Charles II but sometimes to extend through the reign of James II

**¹re·stor·ative** \ri-'stōr-ə-tiv, -'stȯr-\ *adjective* (14th century)
: of or relating to restoration; *especially* : having power to restore

**²restorative** *noun* (15th century)
: something that serves to restore to consciousness, vigor, or health

**re·store** \ri-'stōr, -'stȯr\ *transitive verb* **restored; re·stor·ing** [Middle English, from Old French *restorer,* from Latin *restaurare* to renew, rebuild, alteration of *instaurare* to renew] (14th century)
**1** : GIVE BACK, RETURN
**2** : to put or bring back into existence or use
**3** : to bring back to or put back into a former or original state : RENEW
**4** : to put again in possession of something
**synonym** see RENEW
— **re·stor·er** *noun*

**re·strain** \ri-'strān\ *transitive verb* [Middle English *restraynen,* from Middle French *restraindre,* from Latin *restringere* to restrain, restrict, from *re-* + *stringere* to bind tight — more at STRAIN] (14th century)
**1 a** : to prevent from doing, exhibiting, or expressing something ⟨*restrained* the child from jumping⟩ **b** : to limit, restrict, or keep under control ⟨try to *restrain* your anger⟩
**2** : to moderate or limit the force, effect, development, or full exercise of ⟨*restrain* trade⟩
**3** : to deprive of liberty; *especially* : to place under arrest or restraint ☆
— **re·strain·able** \-'strā-nə-bəl\ *adjective*
— **re·strain·er** *noun*

**re·strained** \ri-'strānd\ *adjective* (14th century)
: marked by restraint : being without excess or extravagance
— **re·strain·ed·ly** \-'strā-nəd-lē\ *adverb*

**restraining order** *noun* (circa 1876)
**1** : a preliminary legal order sometimes issued to keep a situation unchanged pending decision upon an application for an injunction
**2** : a legal order issued against an individual to restrict or prohibit access or proximity to another specified individual

**re·straint** \ri-'strānt\ *noun* [Middle English, from Middle French *restrainte,* from *restraindre*] (15th century)
**1 a** : an act of restraining : the state of being restrained **b** (1) : a means of restraining : a restraining force or influence (2) : a device that restricts movement ⟨a *restraint* for children riding in cars⟩
**2** : a control over the expression of one's emotions or thoughts

**re·strict** \ri-'strikt\ *transitive verb* [Latin *restrictus,* past participle of *restringere*] (1535)
**1** : to confine within bounds : RESTRAIN
**2** : to place under restrictions as to use or distribution
**synonym** see LIMIT

**re·strict·ed** *adjective* (circa 1828)
: subject or subjected to restriction: as **a** : not general : LIMITED ⟨the decision had a *restricted* effect⟩ **b** : available to the use of particular groups or specifically excluding others ⟨a *restricted* country club⟩ **c** : not intended for general circulation or release ⟨a *restricted* document⟩

— **re·strict·ed·ly** *adverb*

**re·stric·tion** \ri-'strik-shən\ *noun* [Middle English *restriccioun,* from Late Latin *restriction-, restrictio,* from Latin *restringere*] (15th century)
**1** : something that restricts: as **a** : a regulation that restricts or restrains ⟨*restrictions* for hunters⟩ **b** : a limitation on the use or enjoyment of property or a facility
**2** : an act of restricting : the condition of being restricted

**restriction enzyme** *noun* (1965)
: any of various enzymes that break DNA into fragments at specific sites in the interior of the molecule — called also *restriction endonuclease*

**re·stric·tion·ism** \-shə-ˌni-zəm\ *noun* (1937)
: a policy or philosophy favoring restriction (as of trade or immigration)
— **re·stric·tion·ist** \-sh(ə-)nist\ *adjective or noun*

**re·stric·tive** \ri-'strik-tiv\ *adjective* (1579)
**1 a** : of or relating to restriction **b** : serving or tending to restrict ⟨*restrictive* regulations⟩
**2** : limiting the reference of a modified word or phrase
**3** : prohibiting further negotiation
— **restrictive** *noun*
— **re·stric·tive·ly** *adverb*
— **re·stric·tive·ness** *noun*

---

☆ SYNONYMS
**Restrain, check, curb, bridle** mean to hold back from or control in doing something. RESTRAIN suggests holding back by force or persuasion from acting or from going to extremes ⟨*restrained* themselves from laughing⟩. CHECK implies restraining or impeding a progress, activity, or impetus ⟨trying to *check* government spending⟩. CURB suggests an abrupt or drastic checking ⟨learn to *curb* your appetite⟩. BRIDLE implies keeping under control by subduing or holding in ⟨*bridle* an impulse to throw the book down⟩.

---

◇ WORD HISTORY
**restaurant** The *restaurant*—both word and institution—allegedly originated in Paris in the second half of the 18th century. According to an oft-repeated account first published in 1853, the first *restaurant* was opened in 1765 by a Parisian named Boulanger, though the word is not definitely attested in French before 1803. Boulanger's establishment offered to its customers *bouillons restaurants* ("restorative broths," from which the name *restaurant* supposedly derived), fowl, and eggs under the Latin motto *Venite ad me omnes qui stomacho laboratis et ego vos restaurabo* ("Come to me all who suffer from pain of the stomach and I will restore you"), which punningly alludes to both *restaurant* and the invitation of Matthew 11:28 (Revised Standard Version) "Come to me all who labor and are heavy-laden, and I will give you rest." Similar but more elaborate establishments soon opened, though cooked meat dishes (*ragoûts*) briefly remained the domain of someone called a *traiteur* "treater," a sort of caterer who had preceded the *restaurateur* in providing food to Frenchmen who did not have their own kitchens. (*Traiteur* was borrowed into Italian as *trattore,* the base of *trattoria,* a common Italian word for "restaurant" now familiar to many English-speaking diners.)

---

\ə\ abut \ᵊ\ kitten \ər\ further \a\ ash \ā\ ace
\ä\ mop, mar \au̇\ out \ch\ chin \e\ bet \ē\ easy
\g\ go \i\ hit \ī\ ice \j\ job \ŋ\ sing \ō\ go
\ȯ\ law \ȯi\ boy \th\ thin \ṯh\ the \ü\ loot \u̇\ foot
\y\ yet \zh\ vision *see also* Guide to Pronunciation

**restrictive clause** *noun* (circa 1895)
: a descriptive clause that is essential to the definiteness of the word it modifies (as *that you ordered* in "the book that you ordered is out of print")

**re·strike** \(ˌ)rē-ˈstrīk, ˈrē-\ *noun* (1899)
: a coin or medal struck from an original die at some time after the original issue

**rest room** *noun* (1899)
: a room or suite of rooms providing toilets and lavatories

**re·struc·ture** \(ˌ)rē-ˈstrək-chər\ (1942)
*transitive verb*
: to change the makeup, organization, or pattern of
*intransitive verb*
: to restructure something

¹**re·sult** \ri-ˈzəlt\ *intransitive verb* [Middle English, from Medieval Latin *resultare*, from Latin, to rebound, from *re-* + *saltare* to leap — more at SALTATION] (15th century)
**1 a :** to proceed or arise as a consequence, effect, or conclusion ⟨death *resulted* from the disease⟩ **b :** to have an issue or result ⟨the disease *resulted* in death⟩
**2 :** REVERT 2

²**result** *noun* (1647)
**1 :** something that results as a consequence, issue, or conclusion; *also* **:** beneficial or tangible effect **:** FRUIT
**2 :** something obtained by calculation or investigation
— **re·sult·ful** \-fəl\ *adjective*
— **re·sult·less** \-ləs\ *adjective*

¹**re·sul·tant** \ri-ˈzəl-tᵊnt\ *adjective* (1639)
: derived from or resulting from something else
— **re·sul·tant·ly** *adverb*

²**resultant** *noun* (1815)
: something that results **:** OUTCOME; *specifically* **:** the single vector that is the sum of a given set of vectors

**re·sume** \ri-ˈzüm\ *verb* **re·sumed; re·sum·ing** [Middle English, from Middle French or Latin; Middle French *resumer*, from Latin *resumere*, from *re-* + *sumere* to take up, take — more at CONSUME] (15th century)
*transitive verb*
**1 :** to assume or take again **:** REOCCUPY ⟨*resumed* his seat by the fire —Thomas Hardy⟩
**2 :** to return to or begin again after interruption ⟨*resumed* her work⟩
**3 :** to take back to oneself
**4 :** to pick up again
**5 :** REITERATE, SUMMARIZE
*intransitive verb*
: to begin again something interrupted

**ré·su·mé** *or* **re·su·me** *or* **re·su·mé** \ˈre-zə-ˌmā, ˌre-zə-ˈ *also* ˈrā- *or* ˌrā-\ *noun* [French *résumé*, from past participle of *résumer* to resume, summarize, from Middle French *resumer*] (1804)
**1 :** SUMMARY
**2 :** CURRICULUM VITAE

**re·sump·tion** \ri-ˈzəm(p)-shən\ *noun* [Middle English, from Middle French or Late Latin; Middle French *resomption,* from Late Latin *resumption-, resumptio,* from Latin *resumere*] (15th century)
**1 :** an act or instance of resuming **:** RECOMMENCEMENT
**2 :** a return to payment in specie

**re·su·pi·nate** \ri-ˈsü-pə-ˌnāt\ *adjective* [Latin *resupinatus,* past participle of *resupinare* to bend back to a supine position, from *re-* + *supinus* supine] (circa 1776)
**1 :** inverted in position ⟨*resupinate* orchid flowers⟩
**2 :** having or being a fruiting body lying flat on the substrate with the hymenium at the periphery or over the whole surface ⟨*resupinate* fungi⟩ ⟨*resupinate* sporophores⟩

**re·sur·face** \(ˌ)rē-ˈsər-fəs\ (1894)
*transitive verb*
: to provide with a new or fresh surface

*intransitive verb*
: to come again to the surface (as of the water); *broadly* **:** to appear or show up again
— **re·sur·fac·er** \-fə-sər\ *noun*

**re·surge** \ri-ˈsərj\ *intransitive verb* **re·surged; re·surg·ing** [Latin *resurgere*] (1575)
: to undergo a resurgence

**re·sur·gence** \ri-ˈsər-jən(t)s\ *noun* (circa 1834)
: a rising again into life, activity, or prominence **:** RENASCENCE

**re·sur·gent** \-jənt\ *adjective* [Latin *resurgent-, resurgens,* present participle of *resurgere*] (1808)
: undergoing or tending to produce resurgence

**res·ur·rect** \ˌre-zə-ˈrekt\ *transitive verb* [back-formation from *resurrection*] (1772)
**1 :** to raise from the dead
**2 :** to bring to view, attention, or use again

**res·ur·rec·tion** \ˌre-zə-ˈrek-shən\ *noun* [Middle English, from Late Latin *resurrection-, resurrectio* act of rising from the dead, from *resurgere* to rise from the dead, from Latin, to rise again, from *re-* + *surgere* to rise — more at SURGE] (14th century)
**1 a** *capitalized* **:** the rising of Christ from the dead **b** *often capitalized* **:** the rising again to life of all the human dead before the final judgment **c :** the state of one risen from the dead
**2 :** RESURGENCE, REVIVAL
**3** *Christian Science* **:** a spiritualization of thought **:** material belief that yields to spiritual understanding
— **res·ur·rec·tion·al** \-shnəl, -shə-nᵊl\ *adjective*

**res·ur·rec·tion·ist** \-sh(ə-)nist\ *noun* (1776)
**1 :** BODY SNATCHER
**2 :** one who resurrects

**re·sus·ci·tate** \ri-ˈsə-sə-ˌtāt\ *verb* **-tat·ed; -tat·ing** [Latin *resuscitatus,* past participle of *resuscitare* to reawaken, from *re-* + *suscitare* to rouse, from *sub-, sus-* up + *citare* to put in motion, stir — more at SUB-, CITE] (1532)
*transitive verb*
: to revive from apparent death or from unconsciousness; *also* **:** REVITALIZE
*intransitive verb*
: COME TO, REVIVE
— **re·sus·ci·ta·tion** \ri-ˌsə-sə-ˈtā-shən, ˌrē-\ *noun*
— **re·sus·ci·ta·tive** \ri-ˈsə-sə-ˌtā-tiv\ *adjective*

**re·sus·ci·ta·tor** \ri-ˈsə-sə-ˌtā-tər\ *noun* (circa 1843)
: one that resuscitates; *specifically* **:** an apparatus used to restore respiration (as to a partially asphyxiated person)

**ret** \ˈret\ *verb* **ret·ted; ret·ting** [Middle English, from Middle Dutch] (14th century)
*transitive verb*
: to soak (as flax) to loosen the fiber from the woody tissue
*intransitive verb*
: to become retted

**re·ta·ble** \ˈrē-ˌtā-bəl, rē-\ *noun* [French, from Middle French, modification of Old Provençal *retaule,* alteration of *reretaule,* ultimately from Latin *retro-* + *tabula* board, tablet] (circa 1823)
: a raised shelf above an altar for the altar cross, the altar lights, and flowers

¹**re·tail** \ˈrē-ˌtāl, *especially for 2 also* ri-ˈtā(ə)l\ *verb* [Middle English, from Middle French *retaillier* to cut back, divide into pieces, from Old French, from *re-* + *taillier* to cut — more at TAILOR] (15th century)
*transitive verb*
**1 :** to sell in small quantities directly to the ultimate consumer
**2 :** TELL, RETELL
*intransitive verb*
: to sell at retail
— **re·tail·er** *noun*

²**re·tail** \ˈrē-ˌtāl\ *noun* (15th century)

: the sale of commodities or goods in small quantities to ultimate consumers; *also* **:** the industry of such selling
— **at retail 1 :** at a retailer's price **2 :** ⁴RETAIL

³**re·tail** \ˈrē-ˌtāl\ *adjective* (1601)
: of, relating to, or engaged in the sale of commodities at retail ⟨*retail* trade⟩

⁴**re·tail** \ˈrē-ˌtāl\ *adverb* (1784)
: in small quantities **:** from a retailer

**re·tail·ing** \ˈrē-ˌtā-liŋ\ *noun* (14th century)
: the activities involved in the selling of goods to ultimate consumers for personal or household consumption

**re·tain** \ri-ˈtān\ *transitive verb* [Middle English *reteinen, retainen,* from Middle French *retenir,* from Latin *retinēre* to hold back, keep, restrain, from *re-* + *tenēre* to hold — more at THIN] (15th century)
**1 a :** to keep in possession or use **b :** to keep in one's pay or service; *specifically* **:** to employ by paying a retainer **c :** to keep in mind or memory **:** REMEMBER
**2 :** to hold secure or intact
*synonym* see KEEP

**retained object** *noun* (circa 1904)
: an object of a verb in the predicate of a passive construction (as *me* in "a book was given me" and *book* in "I was given a book")

¹**re·tain·er** \ri-ˈtā-nər\ *noun* (1540)
**1 a :** a person attached or owing service to a household; *especially* **:** SERVANT **b :** EMPLOYEE
**2 :** one that retains
**3 :** any of various devices used for holding something

²**retainer** *noun* [Middle English *reteiner* act of withholding, from *reteinen* + Anglo-French *-er* (as in *weyver* waiver)] (1775)
**1 :** the act of a client by which the services of a lawyer, counselor, or adviser are engaged
**2 :** a fee paid to a lawyer or professional adviser for advice or services or for a claim on services when needed

¹**re·take** \(ˌ)rē-ˈtāk\ *transitive verb* **-took** \-ˈtùk\; **-tak·en** \-ˈtā-kən\; **-tak·ing** (15th century)
**1 :** to take or receive again
**2 :** RECAPTURE
**3 :** to photograph again

²**re·take** \ˈrē-ˌtāk\ *noun* (1916)
: a subsequent filming, photographing, or recording undertaken to improve upon the first; *also* **:** an instance of this

**re·tal·i·ate** \ri-ˈta-lē-ˌāt\ *verb* **-at·ed; -at·ing** [Late Latin *retaliatus,* past participle of *retaliare,* from Latin *re-* + *talio* legal retaliation] (1611)
*transitive verb*
: to repay (as an injury) in kind
*intransitive verb*
: to return like for like; *especially* **:** to get revenge
*synonym* see RECIPROCATE
— **re·tal·i·a·tion** \ri-ˌta-lē-ˈā-shən, ˌrē-\ *noun*
— **re·tal·i·a·tive** \ri-ˈtal-yə-ˌā-tiv\ *adjective*
— **re·tal·ia·to·ry** \-ˈtal-yə-ˌtōr-ē, -ˈta-lē-ə-, -ˌtòr-\ *adjective*

¹**re·tard** \ri-ˈtärd\ *verb* [Middle English, from Middle French or Latin; Middle French *retarder,* from Latin *retardare,* from *re-* + *tardus* slow] (15th century)
*transitive verb*
**1 :** to slow up especially by preventing or hindering advance or accomplishment **:** IMPEDE
**2 :** to delay academic progress by failure to promote
*intransitive verb*
: to undergo retardation
*synonym* see DELAY
— **re·tard·er** *noun*

²**re·tard** *noun* (1788)
**1** \ri-ˈtärd\ **:** a holding back or slowing down **:** RETARDATION

**2** \'rē-ˌtärd\ : a retarded person; *also* : a person held to resemble a retarded person in behavior — often taken to be offensive

**re·tar·dant** \ri-'tär-dᵊnt\ *adjective* (1642) : serving or tending to retard ⟨a growth-*retardant* substance⟩
— **retardant** *noun*

**re·tar·date** \-'tär-ˌdāt, -dət\ *noun* (1915) : a mentally retarded person

**re·tar·da·tion** \ˌrē-ˌtär-'dā-shən, ri-\ *noun* (15th century)
**1** : an act or instance of retarding
**2** : the extent to which something is retarded
**3** : a musical suspension; *specifically* : one that resolves upward
**4 a** : an abnormal slowness of thought or action; *also* : less than normal intellectual competence usually characterized by an IQ of less than 70 **b** : slowness in development or progress

**re·tard·ed** \ri-'tär-dəd\ *adjective* (1895) : slow or limited in intellectual or emotional development or academic progress

**retch** \'rech, *especially British* 'rēch\ *verb* [(assumed) Middle English *rechen* to spit, retch, from Old English *hrǣcan* to spit, hawk; akin to Old Norse *hrækja* to spit] (circa 1798)
*transitive verb*
: VOMIT 1
*intransitive verb*
: to make an effort to vomit; *also* : VOMIT
— **retch** *noun*

**re·te** \'rē-tē, 'rā-\ *noun, plural* **re·tia** \'rē-tē-ə, 'rā-\ [New Latin, from Latin, net] (1541)
**1** : a network especially of blood vessels or nerves : PLEXUS
**2** : an anatomical part resembling or including a network

**re·tell** \(ˌ)rē-'tel\ *transitive verb* **-told** \-'tōld\; **-tell·ing** (1593)
**1** : to tell again or in another form
**2** : to count again

**re·tell·ing** *noun* (1883)
: a new version of a story ⟨a *retelling* of a Greek legend⟩

**re·ten·tion** \ri-'ten(t)-shən\ *noun* [Middle English *retencioun*, from Latin *retention-, retentio* to retain — more at RETAIN] (14th century)
**1 a** : the act of retaining : the state of being retained **b** : abnormal retaining of a fluid or secretion in a body cavity
**2 a** : power of retaining : RETENTIVENESS **b** : an ability to retain things in mind; *specifically* : a preservation of the aftereffects of experience and learning that makes recall or recognition possible
**3** : something retained

**re·ten·tive** \-'ten-tiv\ *adjective* [Middle English *retentif*, from Middle French & Medieval Latin; Middle French, from Medieval Latin *retentivus*, from Latin *retentus*, past participle of *retinēre*] (14th century)
: having the power, property, or capacity of retaining ⟨soils *retentive* of moisture⟩; *especially* : retaining knowledge easily
— **re·ten·tive·ly** *adverb*
— **re·ten·tive·ness** *noun*

**re·ten·tiv·i·ty** \ˌrē-ˌten-'ti-və-tē, ri-\ *noun* (1881)
: the power of retaining; *specifically* : the capacity for retaining magnetism after the action of the magnetizing force has ceased

**re·think** \(ˌ)rē-'thiŋk\ *verb* **-thought** \-'thȯt\; **-think·ing** (1700)
*transitive verb*
: to think about again : RECONSIDER
*intransitive verb*
: to engage in reconsideration
— **re·think** \'rē-ˌthiŋk, -'thiŋk\ *noun*
— **re·think·er** *noun*

**ret·i·cence** \'re-tə-sən(t)s\ *noun* (1603)
**1** : the quality or state of being reticent : RESERVE, RESTRAINT
**2** : an instance of being reticent
**3** : RELUCTANCE ]

**ret·i·cen·cy** \-sən(t)-sē\ *noun, plural* **-cies** (1617)
: RETICENCE

**ret·i·cent** \-sənt\ *adjective* [Latin *reticent-, reticens*, present participle of *reticēre* to keep silent, from *re-* + *tacēre* to be silent — more at TACIT] (circa 1834)
**1** : inclined to be silent or uncommunicative in speech : RESERVED
**2** : restrained in expression, presentation, or appearance ⟨the room has an aspect of *reticent* dignity —A. N. Whitehead⟩
**3** : RELUCTANT
*synonym* see SILENT
— **ret·i·cent·ly** *adverb*

**ret·i·cle** \'re-ti-kəl\ *noun* [Latin *reticulum* network] (circa 1731)
: a scale on transparent material (as in an optical instrument) used especially for measuring or aiming

**re·tic·u·lar** \ri-'ti-kyə-lər\ *adjective* (1597)
**1 a** : RETICULATE **b** : of, relating to, or forming a reticulum
**2** : INTRICATE

**reticular formation** *noun* (1887)
: a mass of nerve cells and fibers situated primarily in the brain stem and functioning upon stimulation especially in arousal of the organism

**¹re·tic·u·late** \-lət, -ˌlāt\ *adjective* [Latin *reticulatus*, from *reticulum*] (1658)
**1** : resembling a net; *especially* : having veins, fibers, or lines crossing ⟨a *reticulate* leaf⟩
**2** : being or involving evolutionary change dependent on genetic recombination involving diverse interbreeding populations
— **re·tic·u·late·ly** *adverb*

**²re·tic·u·late** \-ˌlāt\ *verb* **-lat·ed; -lat·ing** [back-formation from *reticulated*, adjective, reticulate] (1787)
*transitive verb*
: to divide, mark, or construct so as to form a network
*intransitive verb*
: to become reticulated

**re·tic·u·la·tion** \ri-ˌti-kyə-'lā-shən\ *noun* (1671)
: a reticulated formation : NETWORK; *also* : something reticulated

**ret·i·cule** \'re-ti-ˌkyü(ə)l\ *noun* [French *réticule*, from Latin *reticulum* network, network bag, from diminutive of *rete* net] (circa 1738)
**1** : RETICLE
**2** : a woman's drawstring bag used especially as a carryall

**re·tic·u·lo·cyte** \ri-'ti-kyə-lō-ˌsīt\ *noun* [New Latin *reticulum* + International Scientific Vocabulary *-cyte*] (1922)
: an immature red blood cell that appears especially during regeneration of lost blood and has a fine basophilic reticulum formed of ribosomal remains

**re·tic·u·lo·en·do·the·li·al** \ri-ˌti-kyə-lō-ˌen-də-'thē-lē-əl\ *adjective* [New Latin *reticulum* + *endothelium*] (circa 1923)
: of, relating to, or being the reticuloendothelial system

**reticuloendothelial system** *noun* (circa 1923)
: a diffuse system of cells arising from mesenchyme and comprising all the phagocytic cells of the body except the circulating white blood cells

**re·tic·u·lum** \ri-'ti-kyə-ləm\ *noun* [New Latin, from Latin, network] (circa 1658)
**1** : the second compartment of the stomach of a ruminant in which folds of the mucous membrane form hexagonal cells — compare ABOMASUM, OMASUM, RUMEN
**2** : a reticular structure : NETWORK; *especially* : interstitial tissue composed of reticulum cells

**reticulum cell** *noun* (1912)
: one of the branched anastomosing reticuloendothelial cells that form an intricate interstitial network ramifying through other tissues and organs

**retin-** *or* **retino-** *combining form* [retina]
**1** : retina ⟨*retinitis*⟩ ⟨*retinoscopy*⟩
**2** : retinol ⟨*retinoid*⟩

**ret·i·na** \'re-tᵊn-ə, 'ret-nə\ *noun, plural* **reti·nas** *or* **ret·i·nae** \-tᵊn-ˌē, -ˌī\ [Middle English *rethina*, from Medieval Latin *retina*, probably from Latin *rete* net] (14th century)
: the sensory membrane that lines the eye, is composed of several layers including one containing the rods and cones, and functions as the immediate instrument of vision by receiving the image formed by the lens and converting it into chemical and nervous signals which reach the brain by way of the optic nerve — see EYE illustration

**ret·i·nac·u·lum** \ˌre-tᵊn-'a-kyə-ləm\ *noun, plural* **-la** \-lə\ [New Latin, from Latin, halter, cable, from *retinēre* to hold back — more at RETAIN] (circa 1825)
: a small structure on the forewings of many lepidopterous insects (as a noctuid moth) that catches and holds the frenulum

**¹ret·i·nal** \'re-tᵊn-ᵊl, 'ret-nəl\ *adjective* (1838)
: of, relating to, involving, or being a retina

**²ret·i·nal** \'re-tᵊn-ˌal, -ˌȯl\ *noun* [retin- + ³-al] (1944)
: a yellowish to orange aldehyde $C_{20}H_{28}O$ derived from vitamin A that in combination with proteins forms the visual pigments of the retinal rods and cones

**ret·i·nene** \'re-tᵊn-ˌēn\ *noun* (1934)
: RETINAL

**ret·i·ni·tis** \ˌre-tᵊn-'ī-təs\ *noun* [New Latin] (1861)
: inflammation of the retina

**retinitis pig·men·to·sa** \-ˌpig-mən-'tō-sə, -(ˌ)men-, -zə\ *noun* [New Latin, pigmented retinitis] (1861)
: any of several hereditary progressive degenerative diseases of the eye marked by night blindness in the early stages, atrophy and pigment changes in the retina, constriction of the visual field, and eventual blindness

**ret·i·no·blas·to·ma** \ˌre-tᵊn-ō-ˌblas-'tō-mə\ *noun* [retin- + blast- + -oma] (1924)
: a malignant tumor of the retina that develops during childhood, is derived from retinal germ cells, and is associated with a chromosomal abnormality

**ret·i·no·ic acid** \ˌre-tᵊn-'ō-ik-\ *noun* (1965)
: an acid $C_{20}H_{28}O_2$ derived from vitamin A and used especially in the treatment of acne

**ret·i·noid** \'re-tᵊn-ˌȯid\ *noun* (1976)
: any of various synthetic or naturally occurring analogues of vitamin A

**ret·i·nol** \'re-tᵊn-ˌȯl, -ˌōl\ *noun* [retin- + ¹-ol; from its being the source of retinal] (1960)
: the chief and typical vitamin A

**ret·i·nop·a·thy** \ˌre-tᵊn-'ä-pə-thē\ *noun* (1932)
: any of various noninflammatory disorders of the retina including some that cause blindness

**ret·i·nos·co·py** \ˌre-tᵊn-'äs-kə-pē\ *noun* (1884)
: observation of the retina of the eye especially to determine the state of refraction

**ret·i·no·tec·tal** \ˌre-tᵊn-ō-'tek-təl\ *adjective* [retin- + tectum + ¹-al] (1951)
: of, relating to, or being the nerve fibers connecting the retina and the tectum of the midbrain ⟨*retinotectal* pathways⟩

**ret·i·nue** \'re-tᵊn-ˌü, -ˌyü\ *noun* [Middle English *retenue*, from Middle French, from feminine of *retenu*, past participle of *retenir* to retain] (14th century)
: a group of retainers or attendants

**re·tin·u·la** \re-'tin-yə-lə\ *noun, plural* **-lae** \-ˌlē, -ˌlī\ *also* **-las** [New Latin, diminutive of Medieval Latin *retina*] (1878)
: the neural receptor of a single facet of an arthropod compound eye

— **re·tin·u·lar** \-lər\ *adjective*
**re·tir·ant** \ri-'tī-rənt\ *noun* (1948)
: RETIREE
**re·tire** \ri-'tīr\ *verb* **re·tired; re·tir·ing**
[Middle French *retirer*, from *re-* + *tirer* to draw] (1533)
*intransitive verb*
**1** : to withdraw from action or danger : RE-TREAT
**2** : to withdraw especially for privacy
**3** : to move back : RECEDE
**4** : to withdraw from one's position or occupation : conclude one's working or professional career
**5** : to go to bed
*transitive verb*
**1** : WITHDRAW: as **a** : to march (a military force) away from the enemy **b** : to withdraw from circulation or from the market : RECALL **c** : to withdraw from usual use or service
**2** : to cause to retire from one's position or occupation
**3 a** : to put out (a batter or batsman) in baseball or cricket **b** : to cause (a side) to end a turn at bat in baseball
**4** : to win permanent possession of (as a trophy)
**re·tired** \ri-'tīrd\ *adjective* (1590)
**1** : SECLUDED ⟨*retired* village⟩
**2** : withdrawn from one's position or occupation : having concluded one's working or professional career
**3** : received by or due to one in retirement
— **re·tired·ly** \-'tī-rəd-lē, -'tīrd-\ *adverb*
— **re·tired·ness** \-'tīrd-nəs\ *noun*
**re·tir·ee** \ri-,tī-'rē\ *noun* (1945)
: a person who has retired from a working or professional career
¹**re·tire·ment** \ri-'tīr-mənt\ *noun* (1596)
**1 a** : an act of retiring : the state of being retired **b** : withdrawal from one's position or occupation or from active working life **c** : the age at which one normally retires ⟨reaches *retirement* in May⟩
**2** : a place of seclusion or privacy
²**retirement** *adjective* (1919)
: of, relating to, or designed for retired persons
**re·tir·ing** \ri-'tīr-iŋ\ *adjective* (1766)
: RESERVED, SHY
— **re·tir·ing·ly** \-iŋ-lē\ *adverb*
— **re·tir·ing·ness** *noun*
**re·tool** \(,)rē-'tül\ *transitive verb* (1927)
**1** : to reequip with tools
**2** : REORGANIZE
¹**re·tort** \ri-'tort\ *verb* [Latin *retortus*, past participle of *retorquēre*, literally, to twist back, hurl back, from *re-* + *torquēre* to twist — more at TORTURE] (circa 1557)
*transitive verb*
**1** : to pay or hurl back : RETURN ⟨*retort* an insult⟩
**2 a** : to make a reply to **b** : to say in reply
**3** : to answer (as an argument) by a counter argument
*intransitive verb*
**1** : to answer back usually sharply
**2** : to return an argument or charge
**3** : RETALIATE
**synonym** see ANSWER
²**retort** *noun* (1600)
: a quick, witty, or cutting reply; *especially* : one that turns back or counters the first speaker's words
³**re·tort** \ri-'tort, 'rē-,\ *noun* [Middle French *retorte*, from Medieval Latin *retorta*, from Latin, feminine of *retortus*; from its shape] (1605)
: a vessel or chamber in which substances are distilled or decomposed by heat
⁴**re·tort** \ri-'tort, 'rē-,\ *transitive verb* (1850)
: to treat (as oil shale) by heating in a retort

**retort**

**re·tort pouch** \ri-'tort-, 'rē-,\ *noun* (1977)
: a flexible package in which prepared food is hermetically sealed for long-term unrefrigerated storage
¹**re·touch** \(,)rē-'təch\ *verb* [French *retoucher*, from Middle French, from *re-* + *toucher* to touch] (1685)
*transitive verb*
**1** : to rework in order to improve : TOUCH UP
**2** : to alter (as a photographic negative) to produce a more desirable appearance
**3** : to color (new growth of hair) to match previously dyed, tinted, or bleached hair
*intransitive verb*
: to make or give retouches
— **re·touch·er** *noun*
²**re·touch** \'rē-,təch, (,)rē-'\ *noun* (1703)
: the act, process, or an instance of retouching; *especially* : the retouching of a new growth of hair
**re·tract** \ri-'trakt\ *verb* [Middle English, from Latin *retractus*, past participle of *retrahere* — more at RETREAT] (15th century)
*transitive verb*
**1** : to draw back or in ⟨cats *retract* their claws⟩
**2 a** : TAKE BACK, WITHDRAW ⟨*retract* a confession⟩ **b** : DISAVOW
*intransitive verb*
**1** : to draw or pull back
**2** : to recant or disavow something
**synonym** see ABJURE, RECEDE
— **re·tract·able** \-'trak-tə-bəl\ *adjective*
**re·trac·tile** \ri-'trak-t°l, -,tīl\ *adjective* (1777)
: capable of being drawn back or in ⟨*retractile* claws⟩
— **re·trac·til·i·ty** \,rē-,trak-'ti-lə-tē, ri-\ *noun*
**re·trac·tion** \ri-'trak-shən\ *noun* (14th century)
**1** : an act of recanting; *specifically* : a statement made by one retracting
**2** : an act of retracting : the state of being retracted
**3** : the ability to retract
**re·trac·tor** \ri-'trak-tər\ *noun* (1837)
: one that retracts: as **a** : a surgical instrument for holding open the edges of a wound **b** : a muscle that draws in an organ or part
**re·train** \(,)rē-'trān\ (1918)
*transitive verb*
: to train again or anew
*intransitive verb*
: to become trained again
— **re·train·able** \-'trā-nə-bəl\ *adjective*
**re·tral** \'rē-trəl, 're-\ *adjective* [Latin *retro* back — more at RETRO-] (1875)
**1** : situated at or toward the back : POSTERIOR
**2** : BACKWARD, RETROGRADE
— **re·tral·ly** \-trə-lē\ *adverb*
**re·trans·late** \,rē-tran(t)s-'lāt, -tranz-\ (1860)
*transitive verb*
: to translate (a translation) into another language; *also* : to give a new form to
*intransitive verb*
: to retranslate something
— **re·trans·la·tion** \-'lā-shən\ *noun*
¹**re·tread** \(,)rē-'tred\ *transitive verb* **re·tread·ed; re·tread·ing** (1907)
**1** : to bond or vulcanize a new tread to the prepared surface of (a worn tire)
**2** : to make over as if new ⟨*retread* an old plot⟩
²**re·tread** \'rē-,tred\ *noun* (1914)
**1** : a retreaded tire
**2** : something made or done again especially in slightly revised form : REMAKE
**3 a** : one (as a retired person) who is retrained for work **b** : one (as an athlete) who has previously held the same or a similar position
**re·tread** \(,)rē-'tred\ *transitive verb* **-trod** \-'träd\; **-trod·den** \-'trä-d°n\ *or* **-trod; -tread·ing** (1598)
: to tread again
¹**re·treat** \ri-'trēt\ *noun* [Middle English *retret*, from Middle French *retrait*, from past partici-

ple of *retraire* to withdraw, from Latin *retrahere*, from *re-* + *trahere* to draw] (14th century)
**1 a** (1) : an act or process of withdrawing especially from what is difficult, dangerous, or disagreeable (2) : the process of receding from a position or state attained ⟨the *retreat* of a glacier⟩ ⟨the slow *retreat* of an epidemic⟩ **b** (1) : the usually forced withdrawal of troops from an enemy or from an advanced position (2) : a signal for retreating **c** (1) : a signal given by bugle at the beginning of a military flag-lowering ceremony (2) : a military flag-lowering ceremony
**2** : a place of privacy or safety : REFUGE
**3** : a period of group withdrawal for prayer, meditation, study, and instruction under a director
²**retreat** (15th century)
*intransitive verb*
**1** : to make a retreat : WITHDRAW
**2** : to slope backward
*transitive verb*
: to draw or lead back : REMOVE; *specifically* : to move (a piece) back in chess
**synonym** see RECEDE
— **re·treat·er** *noun*
**re·treat·ant** \-'trē-t°nt\ *noun* (1880)
: a person on a religious retreat
**re·trench** \ri-'trench\ *verb* [obsolete French *retrencher* (now *retrancher*), from Middle French *retrenchier*, from *re-* + *trenchier* to cut] (1625)
*transitive verb*
**1 a** : CUT DOWN, REDUCE **b** : to cut out : EXCISE
**2** : to pare away : REMOVE
*intransitive verb*
: to make retrenchments; *specifically* : ECONO-MIZE
**synonym** see SHORTEN
**re·trench·ment** \-mənt\ *noun* (circa 1600)
: REDUCTION, CURTAILMENT; *specifically* : a cutting of expenses
**re·tri·al** \(,)rē-'trī(-ə)l\ *noun* (1875)
: a second trial, experiment, or test; *specifically* : a second judicial trial
**ret·ri·bu·tion** \,re-trə-'byü-shən\ *noun* [Middle English *retribucioun*, from Middle French *retribution*, from Late Latin *retribution-, retributio*, from Latin *retribuere* to pay back, from *re-* + *tribuere* to pay — more at TRIBUTE] (14th century)
**1** : RECOMPENSE, REWARD
**2** : the dispensing or receiving of reward or punishment especially in the hereafter
**3** : something given or exacted in recompense; *especially* : PUNISHMENT
**re·trib·u·tive** \ri-'tri-byə-tiv\ *adjective* (1678)
: of, relating to, or marked by retribution
— **re·trib·u·tive·ly** *adverb*
**re·trib·u·to·ry** \-byə-,tor-ē, -,tor-\ *adjective* (circa 1615)
: RETRIBUTIVE
**re·triev·al** \ri-'trē-vəl\ *noun* (circa 1643)
**1** : an act or process of retrieving
**2** : possibility of being retrieved or of recovering ⟨beyond *retrieval*⟩
¹**re·trieve** \ri-'trēv\ *verb* **re·trieved; re·triev·ing** [Middle English *retreven*, modification of Middle French *retrouver* to find again, from *re-* + *trouver* to find, from (assumed) Vulgar Latin *tropare* to find, compose — more at TROUBADOUR] (15th century)
*transitive verb*
**1** : to discover and bring in (killed or wounded game)
**2** : to call to mind again
**3** : to get back again : REGAIN
**4 a** : RESCUE, SALVAGE **b** : to return (as a ball or shuttlecock that is difficult to reach) successfully
**5** : RESTORE, REVIVE ⟨his writing *retrieves* the past⟩
**6** : to remedy the evil consequences of : COR-RECT

**7 :** to get and bring back; *especially* **:** to recover (as information) from storage
*intransitive verb*
**:** to bring in game ⟨a dog that *retrieves* well⟩; *also* **:** to bring back an object thrown by a person
— **re·triev·abil·i·ty** \-,trē-və-'bi-lə-tē\ *noun*
— **re·triev·able** \-'trē-və-bəl\ *adjective*
²**retrieve** *noun* (1575)
**1 :** RETRIEVAL
**2 :** the successful return of a ball that is difficult to reach or control (as in tennis)
**re·triev·er** \ri-'trē-vər\ *noun* (15th century)
**:** one that retrieves; *especially* **:** a dog of any of several breeds (as a golden retriever) having a heavy water-resistant coat and used especially for retrieving game
**ret·ro** \'re-(,)trō\ *adjective* [French *rétro*, short for *rétrospectif* retrospective] (1974)
**:** relating to, reviving, or being the styles or especially the fashions of the past **:** fashionably nostalgic or old-fashioned ⟨a *retro* look⟩
**retro-** *prefix* [Middle English, from Latin, from *retro*, from *re-* + *-tro* (as in *intro* within) — more at INTRO-]
**1 :** backward **:** back ⟨*retro*-rocket⟩
**2 :** situated behind ⟨*retro*peritoneal⟩
**ret·ro·ac·tion** \,re-trō-'ak-shən\ *noun* (circa 1738)
**1** [*retroactive*] **:** retroactive operation (as of a law or tax)
**2** [*retro-* + *action*] **:** a reciprocal action **:** REACTION
**ret·ro·ac·tive** \-'ak-tiv\ *adjective* [French *rétroactif*, from Latin *retroactus*, past participle of *retroagere* to drive back, reverse, from *retro-* + *agere* to drive — more at AGENT] (1611)
**:** extending in scope or effect to a prior time or to conditions that existed or originated in the past; *especially* **:** made effective as of a date prior to enactment, promulgation, or imposition ⟨*retroactive* tax⟩
— **ret·ro·ac·tive·ly** *adverb*
— **ret·ro·ac·tiv·i·ty** \-,ak-'ti-və-tē\ *noun*
**ret·ro·cede** \,re-trō-'sēd\ *verb* **-ced·ed; -ced·ing** [Latin *retrocedere*, from *retro-* + *cedere* to go, cede] (1654)
*intransitive verb*
**:** to go back **:** RECEDE
*transitive verb*
[French *rétrocéder*, from Medieval Latin *retrocedere*, from Latin *retro-* + *cedere* to cede]
**:** to cede back (as a territory)
— **ret·ro·ces·sion** \-'se-shən\ *noun*
**ret·ro·dict** \,re-trə-'dikt\ *transitive verb* [*retro-* + *predict*] (1949)
**:** to utilize present information or ideas to infer or explain (a past event or state of affairs) ⟨*retrodict* past eclipses⟩
— **ret·ro·dic·tion** \-'dik-shən\ *noun*
— **ret·ro·dic·tive** \-'dik-tiv\ *adjective*
**ret·ro·engine** \'re-trō-,en-jən\ *noun* (1965)
**:** RETRO-ROCKET
**ret·ro·fire** \-,fīr\ (1961)
*transitive verb*
**:** to cause (a retro-rocket) to become ignited
*intransitive verb*
*of a retro-rocket* **:** to become ignited
— **retrofire** *noun*
**ret·ro·fit** \,re-trə-'fit\ *transitive verb* (1953)
**1 :** to furnish (as a computer, airplane, or building) with new or modified parts or equipment not available or considered necessary at the time of manufacture
**2 :** to install (new or modified parts or equipment) in something previously manufactured or constructed
— **retrofit** *noun*
**ret·ro·flex** \'re-trə-,fleks\ *adjective* [New Latin *retroflexus*, from Latin *retro-* + *flexus*, past participle of *flectere* to bend] (1776)
**1 :** turned or bent abruptly backward

**2 :** articulated with the tongue tip turned up or curled back just under the hard palate ⟨*retroflex* vowel⟩
**ret·ro·flex·ion** *or* **ret·ro·flec·tion** \,re-trə-'flek-shən\ *noun* (1845)
**1 :** the state of being bent back; *especially* **:** the bending back of an organ (as a uterus) upon itself
**2 :** the act or process of bending back
**3 :** retroflex articulation
**ret·ro·gra·da·tion** \,re-trō-grā-'dā-shən, -grə-\ *noun* (circa 1545)
**:** the action or process of retrograding
¹**ret·ro·grade** \'re-trə-,grād\ *adjective* [Middle English, from Latin *retrogradus*, from *retrogradi*] (14th century)
**1 a** (1) *of a celestial body* **:** having a direction contrary to that of the general motion of similar bodies (2) **:** having or being a direction of rotation or revolution that is clockwise as viewed from the north pole of the sky or a planet **b :** moving, occurring, or performed in a backward direction or opposite to the usual direction ⟨a *retrograde* step⟩ ⟨*retrograde* peristalsis⟩ **c :** contrary to the normal order **:** INVERSE
**2 :** tending toward or resulting in a worse or previous state
**3** *archaic* **:** CONTRADICTORY, OPPOSED
**4 :** characterized by retrogression
**5 :** affecting a period prior to a precipitating cause ⟨*retrograde* amnesia⟩
**6 :** RETRO
— **ret·ro·grade·ly** *adverb*
²**retrograde** *adverb* (circa 1619)
**:** BACKWARD, REVERSELY
³**retrograde** *verb* [Latin *retrogradi*, from *retro-* + *gradi* to go — more at GRADE] (1582)
*transitive verb*
*archaic* **:** to turn back **:** REVERSE
*intransitive verb*
**1 a :** to go back **:** RETREAT **b :** to go back over or recapitulate something
**2 :** to decline to a worse condition
**ret·ro·gress** \,re-trə-'gres\ *intransitive verb* [Latin *retrogressus*, past participle of *retrogradi*] (1819)
**:** to move backward **:** REVERT
**ret·ro·gres·sion** \-'gre-shən\ *noun* (1646)
**1 :** REGRESSION 3
**2 :** return to a former and less complex level of development or organization
**ret·ro·gres·sive** \-'gre-siv\ *adjective* (1802)
**:** characterized by retrogression: as **a :** going or directed backward **b :** declining from a better to a worse state **c :** passing from a higher to a lower level of organization ⟨*retrogressive* evolution⟩
— **ret·ro·gres·sive·ly** *adverb*
**ret·ro·pack** \'re-trō-,pak\ *noun* (1962)
**:** a system of auxiliary rockets on a spacecraft that produces thrust in the direction opposite to the motion of the spacecraft and that is used to reduce speed
**ret·ro·per·i·to·ne·al** \,re-trō-,per-ə-t³n-'ē-əl\ *adjective* (1874)
**:** situated behind the peritoneum
— **ret·ro·per·i·to·ne·al·ly** \-ə-lē\ *adverb*
**ret·ro·re·flec·tion** \,re-trō-ri-'flek-shən\ *noun* (circa 1965)
**:** the action or use of a retroreflector
— **ret·ro·re·flec·tive** \-'flek-tiv\ *adjective*
**ret·ro·re·flec·tor** \-'flek-tər\ *noun* (1946)
**:** a device that reflects radiation (as light) so that the paths of the rays are parallel to those of the incident rays
**ret·ro·rock·et** \'re-trō-,rä-kət\ *noun* (1957)
**:** an auxiliary rocket engine (as on a spacecraft) used in decelerating
**re·trorse** \'rē-,trȯrs\ *adjective* [Latin *retrorsus*, contraction of *retroversus*] (circa 1825)
**:** bent backward or downward
¹**ret·ro·spect** \'re-trə-,spekt\ *noun* [probably from *retro-* + *prospect*] (1602)

**1** *archaic* **:** reference to or regard of a precedent or authority
**2 :** a review of or meditation on past events
— **in retrospect :** in considering the past or a past event
²**retrospect** *adjective* (1709)
**:** RETROSPECTIVE
³**retrospect** (1659)
*intransitive verb*
**1 :** to engage in retrospection
**2 :** to refer back **:** REFLECT
*transitive verb*
**:** to go back over in thought
**ret·ro·spec·tion** \,re-trə-'spek-shən\ *noun* (1674)
**:** the act or process or an instance of surveying the past
¹**ret·ro·spec·tive** \-'spek-tiv\ *adjective* (1664)
**1 a** (1) **:** of, relating to, or given to retrospection (2) **:** based on memory ⟨a *retrospective* report⟩ **b :** being a retrospective ⟨a *retrospective* exhibition⟩
**2 :** affecting things past **:** RETROACTIVE
— **ret·ro·spec·tive·ly** *adverb*
²**retrospective** *noun* (1932)
**:** a generally comprehensive exhibition or performance of the work of an artist over a span of years
**re·trous·sé** \rə-,trü-'sā, rə-'trü-,, ,re-trü-'\ *adjective* [French, from past participle of *retrousser* to tuck up, from Middle French, from *re-* + *trousser* to truss, tuck up — more at TRUSS] (1802)
**:** turned up ⟨*retroussé* nose⟩
**ret·ro·ver·sion** \,re-trō-'vər-zhən *also* -shən\ *noun* [Latin *retroversus* turned backward, from *retro-* + *versus*, past participle of *vertere* to turn — more at WORTH] (1776)
**1 :** the bending backward of the uterus and cervix
**2 :** the act or process of turning back or regressing
**ret·ro·vi·rus** \'re-trō-,vī-rəs\ *noun* (1975)
**:** any of a group of RNA-containing viruses (as HIV) that produce reverse transcriptase by means of which DNA is produced using their RNA as a template and incorporated into the genome of infected cells and that include numerous tumorigenic viruses
— **ret·ro·vi·ral** \-rəl\ *adjective*
**ret·si·na** \ret-'sē-nə\ *noun* [New Greek, perhaps from Italian *resina* resin, from Latin — more at RESIN] (1940)
**:** a resin-flavored Greek wine
¹**re·turn** \ri-'tərn\ *verb* [Middle English *retournen*, from Middle French *retourner*, from *re-* + *tourner* to turn — more at TURN] (14th century)
*intransitive verb*
**1 a :** to go back or come back again ⟨*return* home⟩ **b :** to go back in thought or practice **:** REVERT ⟨soon *returned* to her old habit⟩
**2 :** to pass back to an earlier possessor
**3 :** REPLY, RETORT
*transitive verb*
**1 a :** to give (as an official account) to a superior **b** *British* **:** to elect (a candidate) as attested by official report or returns **c :** to bring back (as a writ or verdict) to an office or tribunal
**2 a :** to bring, send, or put back to a former or proper place ⟨*return* the gun to its holster⟩ **b :** to restore to a former or to a normal state
**3 a :** to send back **:** VISIT — usually used with *on* or *upon* **b** *obsolete* **:** RETORT
**4 :** to bring in (as profit) **:** YIELD
**5 a :** to give or perform in return **:** REPAY ⟨*return* a compliment⟩ **b :** to give back to the owner **c :** REFLECT ⟨*return* an echo⟩

**6 :** to cause (as a wall) to continue in a different direction (as at a right angle)
**7 :** to lead (a specified suit or specified card of a suit) in response to a partner's earlier lead
**8 a :** to hit back (a ball or shuttlecock) **b :** to run with (a football) after a change of possession (as by a punt or a fumble)
**synonym** see RECIPROCATE
— **re·turn·er** *noun*

²**return** *noun* (14th century)
**1 a :** the act of coming back to or from a place or condition **b :** a regular or frequent returning **:** RECURRENCE
**2 a** (1) **:** the delivery of a legal order (as a writ) to the proper officer or court (2) **:** an endorsed certificate stating an official's action in the execution of such an order (3) **:** the sending back of a commission with the certificate of the commissioners **b :** an account or formal report **c** (1) **:** a report of the results of balloting — usually used in plural ⟨election *returns*⟩ (2) **:** an official declaration of the election of a candidate (3) *chiefly British* **:** ELECTION **d** (1) **:** a formal statement on a required legal form showing taxable income, allowable deductions and exemptions, and the computation of the tax due (2) **:** a list of taxable property
**3 a :** the continuation usually at a right angle of the face or of a member of a building or of a molding or group of moldings **b :** a turn, bend, or winding back (as in a rod, stream, or trench) **c :** a means for conveying something (as water) back to its starting point
**4 a :** a quantity of goods, consignment, or cargo coming back in exchange for goods sent out as a mercantile venture **b :** the value of or profit from such venture **c** (1) **:** the profit from labor, investment, or business **:** YIELD (2) *plural* **:** RESULTS **d :** the rate of profit in a process of production per unit of cost
**5 a :** the act of returning something to a former place, condition, or ownership **:** RESTITUTION **b :** something returned; *especially, plural* **:** unsold publications returned to the publisher for cash or credit
**6 a :** something given in repayment or reciprocation **b :** ANSWER, RETORT
**7 :** an answering play: as **a :** a lead in a suit previously led by one's partner in a card game **b :** the action or an instance of returning a ball (as in football or tennis)
— **in return :** in compensation or repayment

³**return** *adjective* (1676)
**1 a :** having or formed by a change of direction ⟨a *return* facade⟩ **b :** doubled on itself ⟨a *return* flue⟩
**2 :** played, delivered, or given in return **:** taking place for the second time ⟨a *return* meeting for the two champions⟩
**3 :** used or taken on returning ⟨the *return* road⟩
**4 :** returning or permitting return ⟨a *return* valve⟩
**5 :** of, relating to, or causing a return to a place or condition

¹**re·turn·able** \ri-'tər-nə-bəl\ *adjective* (15th century)
**1 :** legally required to be returned, delivered, or argued at a specified time or place ⟨a writ *returnable* on the date indicated⟩
**2 a :** capable of returning or of being returned (as for reuse) **b :** permitted to be returned

²**returnable** *noun* (1963)
**:** something designed to be returned (as for recycling); *especially* **:** a returnable beverage container

**re·turn·ee** \ri-ˌtər-'nē\ *noun* (1944)
**:** one who returns; *especially* **:** one returning to the U.S. after military service overseas

**re·tuse** \ri-'tüs, -'tyüs\ *adjective* [Latin *retusus* blunted, from past participle of *retundere* to pound back, blunt, from *re-* + *tundere* to beat, pound — more at CONTUSION] (circa 1753)

**:** having the apex rounded or obtuse with a slight notch

¹**Reu·ben** \'rü-bən\ *noun* [Hebrew *Rĕʾūbhēn*]
**:** a son of Jacob and the traditional eponymous ancestor of one of the tribes of Israel

²**Reuben** *noun* [probably from *Reuben* Kulakofsky (died 1960) American grocer] (1956)
**:** a grilled sandwich of corned beef, Swiss cheese, and sauerkraut usually on rye bread ◆

³**Reuben** *noun* [*Reuben* L. Goldberg (died 1970) American cartoonist] (1958)
**:** a statuette awarded annually by a professional organization for notable achievement in cartoon artistry

**re·union** \(ˌ)rē-'yün-yən\ *noun* (1610)
**1 :** an act of reuniting **:** the state of being reunited
**2 :** a reuniting of persons after separation

**re·union·ist** \-yə-nist\ *noun* (1866)
**:** an advocate of reunion (as of sects or parties)
— **re·union·is·tic** \(ˌ)rē-ˌyün-yə-'nis-tik\ *adjective*

**re·unite** \ˌrē-yù-'nīt\ *verb* [Medieval Latin *reunitus*, past participle of *reunire*, from Latin *re-* + Late Latin *unire* to unite — more at UNITE] (15th century)
*transitive verb*
**:** to bring together again
*intransitive verb*
**:** to come together again **:** REJOIN

**re–up** \(ˌ)rē-'əp\ *intransitive verb* [*re-* + sign *up*] (circa 1906)
**:** to enlist again

**re·us·able** \(ˌ)rē-'yü-zə-bəl\ *adjective* (1943)
**:** capable of being used again or repeatedly
— **re·us·abil·i·ty** \(ˌ)rē-ˌyü-zə-'bi-lə-tē\ *noun*

¹**re·use** \(ˌ)rē-'yüz\ *transitive verb* (1843)
**:** to use again especially after reclaiming or reprocessing ⟨the need to *reuse* scarce resources⟩

²**reuse** \-'yüs\ *noun* (1866)
**:** further or repeated use

¹**rev** \'rev\ *noun* [short for *revolution*] (circa 1890)
**:** a revolution of a motor

²**rev** *verb* **revved; rev·ving** (1920)
*transitive verb*
**1 a :** to step up the number of revolutions per minute of — often used with *up* ⟨*rev* up the engine⟩ **b :** INCREASE — used with *up* ⟨*rev* up production⟩
**2 :** to drive or operate especially at high speed — often used with *up*
**3 :** to make more active or effective — used with *up*
**4 :** to stir up **:** EXCITE — usually used with *up*
*intransitive verb*
**1 :** to operate at an increased speed of revolution — usually used with *up*
**2 :** to increase in amount or activity — used with *up*

**re·val·u·ate** \(ˌ)rē-'val-yə-ˌwāt\ *transitive verb* [back-formation from *revaluation*] (1921)
**:** REVALUE; *specifically* **:** to increase the value of (as currency)
— **re·val·u·a·tion** \(ˌ)rē-ˌval-yə-'wā-shən\ *noun*

**re·val·ue** \(ˌ)rē-'val-(ˌ)yü\ *transitive verb* (1592)
**1 :** to value (as currency) anew
**2 :** to make a new valuation of **:** REAPPRAISE

**re·vamp** \(ˌ)rē-'vamp\ *transitive verb* (1850)
**1 :** REMAKE, REVISE
**2 :** RENOVATE, RECONSTRUCT
— **re·vamp** \'rē-ˌ, ri-'\ *noun*

**re·vanche** \rə-'vän^sh\ *noun* [French, from Middle French, alteration of *revenche* — more at REVENGE] (1882)
**:** REVENGE; *especially* **:** a usually political policy designed to recover lost territory or status
— **re·vanch·ism** \-'vän^-shi-zəm\ *noun*

¹**re·vanch·ist** \-'vän^-shist\ *noun* (1926)
**:** one who advocates a policy of revanche

²**revanchist** *adjective* (1948)
**:** of or relating to a policy of revanche

**re·vas·cu·lar·i·za·tion** \ˌrē-ˌvas-kyə-lə-rə-'zā-shən\ *noun* (1951)
**:** a surgical procedure for the provision of a new, additional, or augmented blood supply to a body part or organ

¹**re·veal** \ri-'vē(ə)l\ *transitive verb* [Middle English *revelen*, from Middle French *reveler*, from Latin *revelare* to uncover, reveal, from *re-* + *velare* to cover, veil, from *velum* veil] (14th century)
**1 :** to make known through divine inspiration
**2 :** to make (something secret or hidden) publicly or generally known ⟨*reveal* a secret⟩
**3 :** to open up to view **:** DISPLAY ⟨the uncurtained window *revealed* a cluttered room⟩ ☆
— **re·veal·able** \-'vē-lə-bəl\ *adjective*
— **re·veal·er** *noun*

²**reveal** *noun* [alteration of earlier *revale*, from Middle English *revalen* to lower, from Middle French *revaler*, from *re-* + *val* valley — more at VALE] (1688)
**:** the side of an opening (as for a window) between a frame and the outer surface of a wall; *also* **:** JAMB

**re·veal·ing** *adjective* (circa 1925)
**:** allowing a look at or an understanding of something inner or hidden **:** INSIGHTFUL
— **re·veal·ing·ly** *adverb*

**re·veal·ment** \ri-'vē(ə)l-mənt\ *noun* (1584)

---

☆ SYNONYMS
**Reveal, disclose, divulge, tell, betray** mean to make known what has been or should be concealed. REVEAL may apply to supernatural or inspired revelation of truths beyond the range of ordinary human vision or reason ⟨divine will as *revealed* in sacred writings⟩. DISCLOSE may imply a discovering but more often an imparting of information previously kept secret ⟨candidates must *disclose* their financial assets⟩. DIVULGE implies a disclosure involving some impropriety or breach of confidence ⟨refused to *divulge* an anonymous source⟩. TELL implies an imparting of necessary or useful information ⟨*told* them what he had overheard⟩. BETRAY implies a divulging that represents a breach of faith or an involuntary or unconscious disclosure ⟨a blush that *betrayed* her embarrassment⟩.

---

◇ WORD HISTORY
**Reuben**   The history of American culinary items can be difficult to trace once we confront people's sometimes unconsciously embellished recollections with documentary evidence. One difficult item is the Reuben, winner of a national sandwich contest in 1956 after being submitted by Fern Snider, a waitress from Omaha, Nebraska. Ms. Snider had acquired the recipe from a former employer, the Schimmel family, who had for a number of years managed the Blackstone Hotel in downtown Omaha. According to local tradition, the combination of rye bread, corned beef, Swiss cheese, and sauerkraut had been dreamed up in the 1920's to feed participants in a late-night poker game at the hotel by Reuben Kulakofsky, an Omaha grocer. Charles Schimmel, the hotel's owner, was so taken with the sandwich that he then put it on their restaurant menu designated by its inventor's name. Is this tale fact or folklore? We can say for certain that there was a Reuben Kulakofsky—his 1960 obituary appeared in the *Omaha World-Herald*—and a sandwich called the "rueben" (not further described, hence presumably familiar to habitués) appears on a Blackstone Hotel menu datable to about 1944. The argument for the Reuben's Nebraskan origin is hence fairly convincing.

: an act of revealing

**re·veg·e·tate** \(ˌ)rē-'ve-jə-ˌtāt\ *transitive verb* (1804)
: to provide (barren or denuded land) with a new vegetative cover
— **re·veg·e·ta·tion** \(ˌ)rē-ˌve-jə-'tā-shən\ *noun*

**rev·eil·le** \'re-və-lē, *British* ri-'va-li *or* -'ve-\ *noun* [modification of French *réveillez,* imperative plural of *réveiller* to awaken, from Middle French *reveiller,* from *re-* + *eveiller* to awaken, from (assumed) Vulgar Latin *exvigilare,* from Latin *ex-* + *vigilare* to keep watch, stay awake — more at VIGILANT] (1644)
**1** : a signal to get up mornings
**2** : a bugle call at about sunrise signaling the first military formation of the day; *also* : the formation so signaled

**¹rev·el** \'re-vəl\ *intransitive verb* **-eled** *or* **-elled; -el·ing** *or* **-el·ling** \'re-və-liŋ, 're-vliŋ\ [Middle English, from Middle French *reveler,* literally, to rebel, from Latin *rebellare*] (14th century)
**1** : to take part in a revel : CAROUSE
**2** : to take intense pleasure or satisfaction

**²revel** *noun* (14th century)
: a usually wild party or celebration

**rev·e·la·tion** \ˌre-və-'lā-shən\ *noun* [Middle English, from Middle French, from Late Latin *revelation-, revelatio,* from Latin *revelare* to reveal] (14th century)
**1 a** : an act of revealing or communicating divine truth **b** : something that is revealed by God to humans
**2 a** : an act of revealing to view or making known **b** : something that is revealed; *especially* : an enlightening or astonishing disclosure ⟨shocking *revelations*⟩ **c** : a pleasant often enlightening surprise ⟨her talent was a *revelation*⟩
**3** *capitalized* : an apocalyptic writing addressed to early Christians of Asia Minor and included as a book in the New Testament — called also *Apocalypse;* see BIBLE table
**Rev·e·la·tions** \-shənz\ *noun plural but singular in construction*
: REVELATION 3

**rev·e·la·tor** \'re-və-ˌlā-tər\ *noun* (1801)
: one that reveals; *especially* : one that reveals the will of God

**re·ve·la·to·ry** \'re-və-lə-ˌtōr-ē, -ˌtȯr-, ri-'ve-lə-\ *adjective* (1882)
: of or relating to revelation : serving to reveal something

**rev·el·er** *or* **rev·el·ler** \'re-və-lər, 're-vlər\ *noun* (14th century)
: one who engages in revelry

**rev·el·ry** \'re-vəl-rē\ *noun* (15th century)
: noisy partying or merrymaking

**rev·e·nant** \'re-və-ˌnäⁿ, -nənt\ *noun* [French, from present participle of *revenir* to return] (1827)
: one that returns after death or a long absence
— **revenant** *adjective*

**¹re·venge** \ri-'venj\ *transitive verb* **revenged; re·veng·ing** [Middle English, from Middle French *revengier,* from Old French, from *re-* + *vengier* to avenge — more at VENGEANCE] (14th century)
**1** : to avenge (as oneself) usually by retaliating in kind or degree
**2** : to inflict injury in return for ⟨*revenge* an insult⟩
— **re·veng·er** *noun*

**²revenge** *noun* [Middle French *revenge, revenche,* from *revengier, revenchier* to revenge] (circa 1547)
**1** : a desire for revenge
**2** : an act or instance of retaliating in order to get even
**3** : an opportunity for getting satisfaction

**re·venge·ful** \ri-'venj-fəl\ *adjective* (circa 1586)
: full of or prone to revenge : determined to get even
— **re·venge·ful·ly** \-fə-lē\ *adverb*

— **re·venge·ful·ness** *noun*

**rev·e·nue** \'re-və-ˌnü, -ˌnyü\ *noun, often attributive* [Middle English, from Middle French, from *revenir* to return, from Latin *revenire,* from *re-* + *venire* to come — more at COME] (15th century)
**1** : the total income produced by a given source ⟨a property expected to yield a large annual *revenue*⟩
**2** : the gross income returned by an investment
**3** : the yield of sources of income (as taxes) that a political unit (as a nation or state) collects and receives into the treasury for public use
**4** : a government department concerned with the collection of the national revenue

**revenue bond** *noun* (1856)
: a bond issued by a public agency authorized to build, acquire, or improve a revenue-producing property (as a toll road) and payable out of revenue derived from such property

**rev·e·nu·er** \'re-və-ˌnü-ər, -ˌnyü-\ *noun* (1880)
: a revenue officer or boat

**revenue stamp** *noun* (1862)
: a stamp (as on a cigar box) for use as evidence of payment of a tax

**revenue tariff** *noun* (1820)
: a tariff intended wholly or primarily to produce public revenue — compare PROTECTIVE TARIFF

**re·verb** \ri-'vərb, 'rē-,\ *noun* [short for *reverberation*] (1953)
: an electronically produced echo effect in recorded music; *also* : a device for producing reverb

**re·ver·ber·ant** \ri-'vər-b(ə-)rənt\ *adjective* (circa 1798)
**1** : tending to reverberate
**2** : marked by reverberation : RESONANT
— **re·ver·ber·ant·ly** *adverb*

**¹re·ver·ber·ate** \-bə-ˌrāt\ *verb* **-at·ed; -at·ing** [Latin *reverberatus,* past participle of *reverberare,* from *re-* + *verberare* to lash, from *verber* rod — more at VERVAIN] (15th century)
*transitive verb*
**1** : REFLECT
**2** : REPEL
**3** : ECHO
*intransitive verb*
**1 a** : to become driven back **b** : to become reflected
**2** : to continue in or as if in a series of echoes : RESOUND

**²re·ver·ber·ate** \-b(ə-)rət\ *adjective* (1603)
: REVERBERANT

**re·ver·ber·a·tion** \ri-ˌvər-bə-'rā-shən\ *noun* (14th century)
**1** : an act of reverberating : the state of being reverberated
**2 a** : something that is reverberated **b** : an effect or impact that resembles an echo

**re·ver·ber·a·tive** \ri-'vər-bə-ˌrā-tiv, -b(ə-)rə-\ *adjective* (1716)
**1** : constituting reverberation
**2** : tending to reverberate : REVERBERANT

**re·ver·ber·a·to·ry** \ri-'vər-b(ə-)rə-ˌtōr-ē, -bə-ˌtȯr-, -ˌtȯr-\ *adjective* (1605)
: acting by reverberation

**reverberatory furnace** *noun* (1672)
: a furnace in which heat is radiated from the roof onto the material treated

**¹re·vere** \ri-'vir\ *transitive verb* **re·vered; re·ver·ing** [Latin *revereri,* from *re-* + *vereri* to fear, respect — more at WARY] (circa 1661)
: to show devoted deferential honor to : regard as worthy of great honor ⟨*revere* the aged⟩ ⟨*revere* tradition⟩ ☆

**²revere** *noun* [by alteration] (circa 1934)
: REVERS

**¹rev·er·ence** \'rev-rən(t)s, 're-və-; 're-vərn(t)s\ *noun* (14th century)

**1** : honor or respect felt or shown : DEFERENCE; *especially* : profound adoring awed respect
**2** : a gesture of respect (as a bow)
**3** : the state of being revered
**4** : one held in reverence — used as a title for a clergyman
*synonym* see HONOR

**²reverence** *transitive verb* **-enced; -enc·ing** (14th century)
: to regard or treat with reverence
*synonym* see REVERE
— **rev·er·enc·er** *noun*

**¹rev·er·end** \'rev-rənd, 're-və-; 're-vərnd\ *adjective* [Middle English, from Middle French, from Latin *reverendus,* gerundive of *revereri*] (15th century)
**1** : worthy of reverence : REVERED
**2 a** : of or relating to the clergy **b** : being a member of the clergy — used as a title ⟨the *Reverend* Mr. Doe⟩ ⟨the *Reverend* John Doe⟩ ⟨the *Reverend* Mrs. Jane Doe⟩

**²reverend** *noun* (1608)
: a member of the clergy — sometimes used in plural as a title

**rev·er·ent** \'rev-rənt, 're-və-; 're-vərnt\ *adjective* [Middle English, from Latin *reverent-, reverens,* present participle of *revereri*] (14th century)
: expressing or characterized by reverence : WORSHIPFUL
— **rev·er·ent·ly** *adverb*

**rev·er·en·tial** \ˌre-və-'ren(t)-shəl\ *adjective* (circa 1555)
**1** : expressing or having a quality of reverence ⟨*reverential* awe⟩
**2** : inspiring reverence
— **rev·er·en·tial·ly** \-'ren(t)-sh(ə-)lē\ *adverb*

**rev·er·ie** *also* **rev·ery** \'re-və-rē, 'rev-rē\ *noun, plural* **rev·er·ies** [French *rêverie,* from Middle French, delirium, from *resver, 'rever* to wander, be delirious] (1657)
**1** : DAYDREAM
**2** : the condition of being lost in thought

**re·vers** \ri-'vir, -'ver\ *noun, plural* **re·vers** \-'virz, -'verz\ [French, literally, reverse, from Middle French, from *revers,* adjective] (1869)
: a lapel especially on a woman's garment

**re·ver·sal** \ri-'vər-səl\ *noun* (15th century)
**1** : an act or the process of reversing
**2** : a conversion of a photographic positive into a negative or vice versa
**3** : a change of fortune usually for the worse

**¹re·verse** \ri-'vərs\ *adjective* [Middle English *revers,* from Middle French, from Latin *reversus,* past participle of *revertere* to turn back — more at REVERT] (14th century)

☆ **SYNONYMS**
**Revere, reverence, venerate, worship, adore** mean to honor and admire profoundly and respectfully. REVERE stresses deference and tenderness of feeling ⟨a professor *revered* by generations of students⟩. REVERENCE presupposes an intrinsic merit and inviolability in the one honored and a corresponding depth of feeling in the one honoring ⟨*reverenced* the academy's code of honor⟩. VENERATE implies a holding as holy or sacrosanct because of character, association, or age ⟨heroes still *venerated*⟩. WORSHIP implies homage usually expressed in words or ceremony ⟨*worships* their memory⟩. ADORE implies love and stresses the notion of an individual and personal attachment ⟨a doctor *adored* by her patients⟩.

\ə\ abut \ᵊ\ kitten \ər\ further \a\ ash \ā\ ace
\ä\ mop, mar \au̇\ out \ch\ chin \e\ bet \ē\ easy
\g\ go \i\ hit \ī\ ice \j\ job \ŋ\ sing \ō\ go
\ȯ\ law \ȯi\ boy \th\ thin \th\ the \ü\ loot \u̇\ foot
\y\ yet \zh\ vision    *see also* Guide to Pronunciation

**1 a :** opposite or contrary to a previous or normal condition ⟨*reverse* order⟩ **b :** having the back presented to the observer or opponent **2 :** coming from the rear of a military force **3 :** acting, operating, or arranged in a manner contrary to the usual **4 :** effecting reverse movement ⟨*reverse* gear⟩ **5 :** so made that the part which normally prints in color appears white against a colored background
— **re·verse·ly** *adverb*

²**reverse** *verb* **re·versed; re·vers·ing** (14th century)
*transitive verb*
**1 a :** to turn completely about in position or direction **b :** to turn upside down **:** INVERT **2 :** ANNUL: as **a :** to overthrow, set aside, or make void (a legal decision) by a contrary decision **b :** to cause to take an opposite point of view **c :** to change to the contrary ⟨*reverse* a policy⟩ **3 :** to cause to go in the opposite direction; *especially* **:** to cause (as an engine) to perform its action in the opposite direction
*intransitive verb*
**1 :** to turn or move in the opposite direction **2 :** to put a mechanism (as an engine) in reverse ☆
— **re·vers·er** *noun*
— **reverse field :** to make a sudden reversal in direction or opinion

³**reverse** *noun* (14th century)
**1 :** something directly contrary to something else **:** OPPOSITE **2 :** an act or instance of reversing; *especially* **:** DEFEAT, SETBACK **3 :** the back part of something **4 a** (1) **:** a gear that reverses something; *also* **:** the whole mechanism brought into play when such a gear is used (2) **:** movement in reverse **b :** an offensive play in football in which a back moving in one direction gives the ball to a player moving in the opposite direction
— **in reverse :** in an opposite manner or direction

**reverse discrimination** *noun* (1969)
**:** discrimination against whites or males (as in employment or education)

**reverse osmosis** *noun* (1955)
**:** the movement of fresh water through a semipermeable membrane when pressure is applied to a solution (as seawater) on one side of it

**reverse tran·scrip·tase** \-,tran-'skrip-(,)tās, -(,)tāz\ *noun* (1971)
**:** a polymerase that catalyzes the formation of DNA using RNA as a template and that is found especially in retroviruses

**reverse transcription** *noun* (1971)
**:** the process of synthesizing double-stranded DNA using RNA as a template and reverse transcriptase as a catalyst

¹**re·vers·ible** \ri-'vər-sə-bəl\ *adjective* (1648)
**:** capable of being reversed or of reversing: as **a :** capable of going through a series of actions (as changes) either backward or forward ⟨a *reversible* chemical reaction⟩ **b :** having two finished usable sides ⟨*reversible* fabric⟩ **c :** wearable with either side out ⟨a *reversible* coat⟩
— **re·vers·ibil·i·ty** \-,vər-sə-'bi-lə-tē\ *noun*
— **re·vers·ibly** \-'vər-sə-blē\ *adverb*

²**reversible** *noun* (1863)
**:** a reversible cloth or article of clothing

**re·ver·sion** \ri-'vər-zhən, -shən\ *noun* [Middle English, from Middle French, from Latin *reversion-, reversio* act of returning, from *revertere*] (15th century)
**1 a :** the part of a simple estate remaining in the control of its owner after the owner has granted therefrom a lesser particular estate **b :** a future interest in property left in the control of a grantor or the grantor's successor **2 :** the right of succession or future possession or enjoyment

**3 a :** an act or the process of returning (as to a former condition) **b :** a return toward an ancestral type or condition **:** reappearance of an ancestral character **4 :** an act or instance of turning the opposite way **:** the state of being so turned **5 :** a product of reversion; *specifically* **:** an organism with an atavistic character **:** THROWBACK

**re·ver·sion·al** \-'vərzh-nəl, -'vərsh-; -'vər-zhə-n°l, -shə-\ *adjective* (1675)
**:** REVERSIONARY

**re·ver·sion·ary** \-'vər-zhə-,ner-ē, -shə-\ *adjective* (1720)
**:** of, relating to, constituting, or involving especially a legal reversion

**re·ver·sion·er** \-'vərzh-nər, -'vərsh-; -'vər-zhə-nər, -shə-\ *noun* (1614)
**:** one that has or is entitled to a reversion; *broadly* **:** one having a vested right to a future estate

**re·vert** \ri-'vərt\ *intransitive verb* [Middle English, from Middle French *revertir,* transitive verb, to turn back & *reverti,* intransitive verb, to return, come back, from *re-* + *vertere, verti* to turn — more at WORTH] (15th century)
**1 :** to come or go back (as to a former condition, period, or subject) **2 :** to return to the proprietor or his heirs at the end of a reversion **3 :** to return to an ancestral type
— **re·vert·er** *noun*
— **re·vert·ible** \-'vər-tə-bəl\ *adjective*

**re·ver·tant** \ri-'vər-t°nt\ *noun* (1955)
**:** a mutant gene, individual, or strain that regains a former capability (as the production of a particular protein) by undergoing further mutation ⟨yeast *revertants*⟩
— **revertant** *adjective*

**re·vest** \(,)rē-'vest\ *transitive verb* (1561)
**:** REINSTATE, REINVEST

**re·vet** \ri-'vet\ *transitive verb* **re·vet·ted; re·vet·ting** [French *revêtir,* literally, to clothe again, dress up, from Latin *revestire,* from *re-* + *vestire* to clothe — more at VEST] (1812)
**:** to face (as an embankment) with a revetment

**re·vet·ment** \-'vet-mənt\ *noun* (1779)
**1 :** a facing (as of stone or concrete) to sustain an embankment **2 :** EMBANKMENT; *especially* **:** a barricade to provide shelter (as against bomb fragments or strafing)

¹**re·view** \ri-'vyü\ *noun* [Middle English, from Middle French *reveue,* from *revoir* to look over, from *re-* + *voir* to see — more at VIEW] (15th century)
**1 a :** a formal military inspection **b :** a military ceremony honoring a person or an event **2 :** REVISION 1a **3 :** a general survey (as of the events of a period) **4 :** an act or the process of reviewing **5 :** judicial reexamination (as of the proceedings of a lower tribunal by a higher) **6 a :** a critical evaluation (as of a book or play) **b :** a magazine devoted chiefly to reviews and essays **7 a :** a retrospective view or survey (as of one's life) **b** (1) **:** renewed study of material previously studied (2) **:** an exercise facilitating such study **8 :** REVUE

²**re·view** \ri-'vyü, *1 is also* 'rē-\ *verb* [in senses 1 & 2, from *re-* + *view;* in other senses, from ¹*review*] (1576)
*transitive verb*
**1 :** to view or see again **2 :** to examine or study again; *especially* **:** to reexamine judicially **3 :** to look back on **:** take a retrospective view of **4 a :** to go over or examine critically or deliberately ⟨*reviewed* the results of the study⟩ **b :** to give a critical evaluation of ⟨*review* a novel⟩

**5 :** to hold a review of ⟨*review* troops⟩
*intransitive verb*
**1 :** to study material again **:** make a review ⟨*review* for a test⟩ **2 :** to write reviews
— **re·view·able** \ri-'vyü-ə-bəl\ *adjective*

**re·view·er** \ri-'vyü-ər\ *noun* (1651)
**:** one that reviews; *especially* **:** a writer of critical reviews

**re·vile** \ri-'vī(ə)l\ *verb* **re·viled; re·vil·ing** [Middle English, from Middle French *reviler* to despise, from *re-* + *vil* vile] (14th century)
*transitive verb*
**:** to subject to verbal abuse **:** VITUPERATE
*intransitive verb*
**:** to use abusive language **:** RAIL
*synonym* see SCOLD
— **re·vile·ment** \-'vī(ə)l-mənt\ *noun*
— **re·vil·er** *noun*

**re·vis·al** \ri-'vī-zəl\ *noun* (1612)
**:** an act of revising **:** REVISION

¹**re·vise** \'rē-,vīz, ri-'\ *noun* (1591)
**1 :** an act of revising **:** REVISION **2 :** a printing proof that incorporates changes marked in a previous proof

²**re·vise** \ri-'vīz\ *verb* **re·vised; re·vis·ing** [Middle French *reviser,* from Latin *revisere* to look at again, frequentative of *revidēre* to see again, from *re-* + *vidēre* to see — more at WIT] (1596)
*transitive verb*
**1 a :** to look over again in order to correct or improve ⟨*revise* a manuscript⟩ **b** *British* **:** to study again **:** REVIEW **2 a :** to make a new, amended, improved, or up-to-date version of ⟨*revise* a dictionary⟩ **b :** to provide with a new taxonomic arrangement ⟨*revising* the alpine ferns⟩
*intransitive verb*
*British* **:** REVIEW 1
*synonym* see CORRECT
— **re·vis·able** \-'vī-zə-bəl\ *adjective*
— **re·vis·er** *or* **re·vi·sor** \-'vī-zər\ *noun*

**Revised Standard Version** *noun* (1946)
**:** a revision of the American Standard Version of the Bible published in 1946 and 1952

**Revised Version** *noun* (1880)
**:** a British revision of the Authorized Version of the Bible published in 1881 and 1885

**re·vi·sion** \ri-'vi-zhən\ *noun* (1611)
**1 a :** an act of revising **b :** a result of revising **:** ALTERATION **2 :** a revised version
— **re·vi·sion·ary** \-zhə-,ner-ē\ *adjective*

**re·vi·sion·ism** \ri-'vi-zhə-,ni-zəm\ *noun* (1903)
**1 :** a movement in revolutionary Marxian socialism favoring an evolutionary rather than a revolutionary spirit **2 :** advocacy of revision (as of a doctrine or policy or in historical analysis)
— **re·vi·sion·ist** \-nist\ *noun or adjective*

¹**re·vis·it** \(,)rē-'vi-zət\ *transitive verb* (15th century)
**:** to visit again **:** return to ⟨*revisit* the old neighborhood⟩; *also* **:** to consider or take up again ⟨reluctant to *revisit* past disputes⟩

²**revisit** *noun* (1623)
**:** a second or subsequent visit

**re·vi·so·ry** \ri-'vī-zə-rē, -'vīz-rē\ *adjective* (circa 1841)

---

☆ **SYNONYMS**
**Reverse, transpose, invert** mean to change to the opposite position. REVERSE is the most general term and may imply change in order, side, direction, meaning ⟨*reversed* his position on the trade agreement⟩. TRANSPOSE implies a change in order or relative position of units often through exchange of position ⟨*transposed* the letters to form an anagram⟩. INVERT applies chiefly to turning upside down or inside out ⟨a stamp with an *inverted* picture of an airplane⟩.

: having the power or purpose to revise ⟨a *revisory* committee⟩ ⟨a *revisory* function⟩

**re·vi·tal·ise** *British variant of* REVITALIZE

**re·vi·tal·ize** \(ˌ)rē-'vī-tᵊl-ˌīz\ *transitive verb* **-ized; -iz·ing** (1869)
: to give new life or vigor to
— **re·vi·tal·i·za·tion** \(ˌ)rē-ˌvī-tᵊl-ə-'zā-shən\ *noun*

**re·viv·al** \ri-'vī-vəl\ *noun* (1651)
**1** : an act or instance of reviving : the state of being revived: as **a** : renewed attention to or interest in something **b** : a new presentation or publication of something old **c** (1) : a period of renewed religious interest (2) : an often highly emotional evangelistic meeting or series of meetings
**2** : restoration of force, validity, or effect (as to a contract)

**re·viv·al·ism** \-'vī-və-ˌli-zəm\ *noun* (1815)
**1** : the spirit or methods characteristic of religious revivals
**2** : a tendency or desire to revive or restore

**re·viv·al·ist** \-'vī-və-list, -'vīv-list\ *noun* (1820)
**1** : one who conducts religious revivals; *specifically* : a clergyman who travels about to conduct revivals
**2** : one who revives or restores something disused
— **revivalist** *adjective*
— **re·viv·al·is·tic** \-ˌvī-və-'lis-tik\ *adjective*

**re·vive** \ri-'vīv\ *verb* **re·vived; re·viv·ing** [Middle English, from Middle French *revivre*, from Latin *revivere* to live again, from *re-* + *vivere* to live — more at QUICK] (15th century)
*intransitive verb*
: to return to consciousness or life : become active or flourishing again
*transitive verb*
**1** : to restore to consciousness or life
**2** : to restore from a depressed, inactive, or unused state : bring back
**3** : to renew in the mind or memory
— **re·viv·able** \-'vī-və-bəl\ *adjective*
— **re·viv·er** *noun*

**re·viv·i·fy** \rē-'vi-və-ˌfī\ *transitive verb* [French *révivifier*, from Late Latin *revivificare*, from Latin *re-* + Late Latin *vivificare* to vivify] (1675)
: to give new life to : REVIVE
— **re·viv·i·fi·ca·tion** \-ˌvi-və-fə-'kā-shən\ *noun*

**re·vi·vis·cence** \ˌrē-ˌvī-'vi-sᵊn(t)s, ri-\ *noun* [Latin *reviviscere* to come to life again, from *re-* + *viviscere* to come to life, from *vivus* alive, living — more at QUICK] (1626)
: an act of reviving : the state of being revived
— **re·vi·vis·cent** \-sᵊnt\ *adjective*

**rev·o·ca·ble** \'re-və-kə-bəl\ *also* ri-'vō-\ *also* **re·vok·able** \ri-'vō-kə-bəl\ *adjective* [Middle English, from Middle French, from Latin *revocabilis*, from *revocare*] (15th century)
: capable of being revoked

**rev·o·ca·tion** \ˌre-və-'kā-shən; ri-ˌvō-, ˌrē-\ *noun* [Middle English, from Middle French, from Latin *revocation-, revocatio*, from *revocare*] (15th century)
: an act or instance of revoking

**¹re·voke** \ri-'vōk\ *verb* **re·voked; re·vok·ing** [Middle English, from Middle French *revoquer*, from Latin *revocare*, from *re-* + *vocare* to call, from *voc-, vox* voice — more at VOICE] (14th century)
*transitive verb*
**1** : to annul by recalling or taking back : RESCIND ⟨*revoke* a will⟩
**2** : to bring or call back
*intransitive verb*
: to fail to follow suit when able in a card game in violation of the rules
— **re·vok·er** *noun*

**²revoke** *noun* (1709)
: an act or instance of revoking in a card game

**¹re·volt** \ri-'vōlt *also* -'völt\ *verb* [Middle French *revolter*, from Old Italian *rivoltare* to

overthrow, from (assumed) Vulgar Latin *revolvitare*, frequentative of Latin *revolvere* to revolve, roll back] (1539)
*intransitive verb*
**1** : to renounce allegiance or subjection (as to a government) : REBEL
**2 a** : to experience disgust or shock **b** : to turn away with disgust
*transitive verb*
: to cause to turn away or shrink with disgust or abhorrence
— **re·volt·er** *noun*

**²revolt** *noun* (1560)
**1** : a renouncing of allegiance (as to a government or party); *especially* : a determined armed uprising
**2** : a movement or expression of vigorous dissent
*synonym* see REBELLION

**re·volt·ing** *adjective* (1806)
: extremely offensive
— **re·volt·ing·ly** *adverb*

**rev·o·lute** \'re-və-ˌlüt\ *adjective* [Latin *revolutus*, past participle of *revolvere*] (circa 1753)
: rolled backward or downward ⟨a leaf with *revolute* margins⟩

**rev·o·lu·tion** \ˌre-və-'lü-shən\ *noun* [Middle English *revolucioun*, from Middle French *revolution*, from Late Latin *revolution-, revolutio*, from Latin *revolvere* to revolve] (14th century)
**1 a** (1) : the action by a celestial body of going round in an orbit or elliptical course; *also* : apparent movement of such a body round the earth (2) : the time taken by a celestial body to make a complete round in its orbit (3) : the rotation of a celestial body on its axis **b** : completion of a course (as of years); *also* : the period made by the regular succession of a measure of time or by a succession of similar events **c** (1) : a progressive motion of a body round an axis so that any line of the body parallel to the axis returns to its initial position while remaining parallel to the axis in transit and usually at a constant distance from it (2) : motion of any figure about a center or axis ⟨*revolution* of a right triangle about one of its legs generates a cone⟩ (3) : ROTATION 1b
**2 a** : a sudden, radical, or complete change **b** : a fundamental change in political organization; *especially* : the overthrow or renunciation of one government or ruler and the substitution of another by the governed **c** : activity or movement designed to effect fundamental changes in the socioeconomic situation **d** : a fundamental change in the way of thinking about or visualizing something : a change of paradigm ⟨the Copernican *revolution*⟩ **e** : a changeover in use or preference especially in technology ⟨the computer *revolution*⟩ ⟨the foreign car *revolution*⟩
*synonym* see REBELLION

**¹rev·o·lu·tion·ary** \-shə-ˌner-ē\ *adjective* (1774)
**1 a** : of, relating to, or constituting a revolution ⟨*revolutionary* war⟩ **b** : tending to or promoting revolution ⟨a *revolutionary* party⟩ **c** : constituting or bringing about a major or fundamental change ⟨*revolutionary* styling⟩ ⟨a *revolutionary* new product⟩
**2** *capitalized* : of or relating to the American Revolution or to the period in which it occurred
— **rev·o·lu·tion·ar·i·ly** \-ˌlü-shə-'ner-ə-lē\ *adverb*
— **rev·o·lu·tion·ar·i·ness** \-'lü-shə-ˌner-ē-nəs\ *noun*

**²revolutionary** *noun, plural* **-ar·ies** (1850)
**1** : one engaged in a revolution
**2** : an advocate or adherent of revolutionary doctrines

**rev·o·lu·tion·ise** *British variant of* REVOLUTIONIZE

**rev·o·lu·tion·ist** \ˌre-və-'lü-sh(ə-)nist\ *noun* (1710)
: REVOLUTIONARY

— **revolutionist** *adjective*

**rev·o·lu·tion·ize** \-shə-ˌnīz\ *verb* **-ized; -iz·ing** (1797)
*transitive verb*
**1** : to overthrow the established government of
**2** : to imbue with revolutionary doctrines
**3** : to change fundamentally or completely
*intransitive verb*
: to engage in revolution
— **rev·o·lu·tion·iz·er** *noun*

**re·volve** \ri-'välv, -'völv *also* -'väv *or* -'vòv\ *verb* **re·volved; re·volv·ing** [Middle English, from Latin *revolvere* to roll back, cause to return, from *re-* + *volvere* to roll — more at VOLUBLE] (15th century)
*transitive verb*
**1** : to turn over at length in the mind : PONDER ⟨*revolve* a scheme⟩
**2 a** *obsolete* : to cause to go round in an orbit **b** : ROTATE 1
*intransitive verb*
**1** : RECUR
**2 a** : to ponder something **b** : to remain under consideration ⟨ideas *revolved* in his mind⟩
**3 a** : to move in a curved path round a center or axis **b** : to turn or roll round on an axis
**4** : to come to a main or central point : CENTER ⟨the dispute *revolved* around wages⟩
— **re·volv·able** \-'väl-və-bəl, -'völ- *also* -'vä-və- *or* -'vò-və-\ *adjective*

**re·volv·er** \ri-'väl-vər, -'völ- *also* -'vä-vər *or* -'vò-vər\ *noun* (circa 1835)
**1** : one that revolves
**2** : a handgun with a cylinder of several chambers brought successively into line with the barrel and discharged with the same hammer

**revolving** *adjective* (1599)
**1** : tending to revolve or recur; *especially* : recurrently available
**2** : turning around on or as if on an axis ⟨a *revolving* platform⟩

**revolving charge account** *noun* (1967)
: a charge account under which payment is made in monthly installments and includes a carrying charge

**revolving credit** *noun* (1919)
: a credit which may be used repeatedly up to the limit specified after partial or total repayments have been made

**revolving–door** *adjective* (1973)
: characterized by a frequently repeated cycle of leaving and returning ⟨*revolving-door* governments⟩

**revolving fund** *noun* (1920)
: a fund set up for specified purposes with the proviso that repayments to the fund may be used again for these purposes

**re·vue** \ri-'vyü\ *noun* [French, from Middle French *reveue* review — more at REVIEW] (1872)
: a theatrical production consisting typically of brief loosely connected often satirical skits, songs, and dances

**re·vulsed** \ri-'vəlst\ *adjective* [Latin *revulsus*, past participle of *revellere* + English *-ed*] (circa 1934)
: affected with or having undergone revulsion

**re·vul·sion** \ri-'vəl-shən\ *noun* [Latin *revulsion-, revulsio* act of tearing away, from *revellere* to pluck away, from *re-* + *vellere* to pluck — more at VULNERABLE] (1609)
**1** : a strong pulling or drawing away : WITHDRAWAL
**2 a** : a sudden or strong reaction or change **b** : a sense of utter distaste or repugnance
— **re·vul·sive** \-'vəl-siv\ *adjective*

**revved** *past and past participle of* REV
**revving** *present participle of* REV

\ə\ **abut** \ᵊ\ **kitten** \ər\ **further** \a\ **ash** \ā\ **ace**
\ä\ **mop, mar** \au̇\ **out** \ch\ **chin** \e\ **bet** \ē\ **easy**
\g\ **go** \i\ **hit** \ī\ **ice** \j\ **job** \ŋ\ **sing** \ō\ **go**
\ȯ\ **law** \ȯi\ **boy** \th\ **thin** \th̲\ **the** \ü\ **loot** \u̇\ **foot**
\y\ **yet** \zh\ **vision** *see also* Guide to Pronunciation

**re·wake** \(ˌ)rē-ˈwāk\ *verb* **-waked** *or* **-woke** \-ˈwōk\; **-waked** *or* **-wo·ken** \-ˈwō-kən\ *or* **-woke**; **-wak·ing** (1593)
*transitive verb*
**:** to waken again or anew
*intransitive verb*
**:** to become awake again
**re·wak·en** \(ˌ)rē-ˈwā-kən\ *verb* (1638)
**:** REWAKE

**¹re·ward** \ri-ˈwȯrd\ *transitive verb* [Middle English, from Old North French *rewarder* to regard, reward, from *re-* + *warder* to watch, guard, of Germanic origin; akin to Old High German *wartēn* to watch — more at WARD] (14th century)
**1 :** to give a reward to or for
**2 :** RECOMPENSE
— **re·ward·able** \-ˈwȯr-də-bəl\ *adjective*
— **re·ward·er** *noun*

**²reward** *noun* (14th century)
**1 :** something that is given in return for good or evil done or received and especially that is offered or given for some service or attainment
**2 :** a stimulus administered to an organism following a correct or desired response that increases the probability of occurrence of the response

**re·ward·ing** *adjective* (1697)
**1 :** yielding or likely to yield a reward **:** VALUABLE, SATISFYING ⟨a *rewarding* experience⟩
**2 :** serving as a reward ⟨a *rewarding* smile of thanks⟩
— **re·ward·ing·ly** *adverb*

**¹re·wind** \(ˌ)rē-ˈwīnd\ *transitive verb* **-wound** \-ˈwaůnd\; **-wind·ing** (1717)
**:** to wind again; *especially* **:** to reverse the winding of (as film)

**²re·wind** \ˈrē-ˌwīnd, (ˌ)rē-ˈ\ *noun* (1926)
**1 :** something that rewinds or is rewound
**2 :** an act of rewinding

**re·word** \(ˌ)rē-ˈwərd\ *transitive verb* (1602)
**1 :** to repeat in the same words
**2 :** to alter the wording of; *also* **:** to restate in other words

**re·work** \(ˌ)rē-ˈwərk\ *transitive verb* (1842)
**:** to work again or anew: as **a :** REVISE **b :** to reprocess (as used material) for further use

**¹re·write** \(ˌ)rē-ˈrīt\ *verb* **-wrote** \-ˈrōt\; **-writ·ten** \-ˈri-tᵊn\; **-writ·ing** \-ˈrī-tiŋ\ (1567)
*transitive verb*
**1 :** to write in reply
**2 :** to make a revision of (as a story) **:** cause to be revised: as **a :** to put (contributed material) into form for publication **b :** to alter (previously published material) for use in another publication
*intransitive verb*
**:** to revise something previously written
— **re·writ·er** *noun*

**²re·write** \ˈrē-ˌrīt\ *noun* (1914)
**1 :** a piece of writing (as a news story) constructed by rewriting
**2 :** an act or instance of rewriting

**re·write man** \ˈrē-ˌrīt-ˌman\ *noun* (1901)
**:** a newspaperman who specializes in rewriting

**re·write rule** \ˈrē-ˌrīt-\ *noun* (1961)
**:** a rule in a grammar which specifies the constituents of a single symbol

**rex** \ˈreks\ *noun, plural* **rex·es** *or* **rex** [modification of French *rex·es, castorrex, castorex*, a variety of rabbit, perhaps from Latin *castor* beaver + *rex* king — more at CASTOR, ROYAL] (1920)
**:** an animal (as a domestic rabbit) showing a genetic recessive variation in which the guard hairs are very short or entirely lacking; *especially* **:** any of the slender domestic cats having a short

rex

curly undercoat and no guard hairs and belonging to either of two breeds

**Reye's syndrome** \ˈrīz-, ˈrāz-\ *noun* [R.D.K. *Reye* (died 1977) Australian pathologist] (1965)
**:** an often fatal encephalopathy especially of childhood characterized by fever, vomiting, fatty infiltration of the liver, and swelling of the kidneys and brain — called also *Reye syndrome*

**rey·nard** \ˈrā-nərd, ˈre-, -ˌnär(d)\ *noun, often capitalized* [Middle English *Renard*, name of the fox who is hero of the French beast epic *Roman de Renart*, from Middle French *Renart, Renard*] (14th century)
**:** FOX

**Rey·nolds number** \ˈre-nᵊldz-\ *noun* [Osborne *Reynolds* (died 1912) English physicist] (1910)
**:** a number characteristic of the flow of a fluid in a pipe or past an obstruction

**R factor** \ˈär-\ *noun* [resistance] (1962)
**:** a group of genes present in some bacteria that provide a basis for resistance to antibiotics and can be transferred from cell to cell by conjugation

**Rh** \ˌär-ˈāch\ *adjective* (1940)
**:** of, relating to, or being an Rh factor ⟨*Rh* antigens⟩ ⟨*Rh* sensitization in pregnancy⟩

**rhabdo-** *combining form* [Late Greek, from Greek *rhabdos* rod — more at VERVAIN]
**:** rodlike structure ⟨*rhabdo*virus⟩

**rhab·do·coele** \ˈrab-də-ˌsēl\ *noun* [New Latin *Rhabdocoela*, from *rhabdo-* + New Latin *-coela* -coele] (circa 1909)
**:** a turbellarian worm (order Rhabdocoela) with an unbranched intestine

**rhab·dom** \ˈrab-ˌdäm, -dəm\ *or* **rhab·dome** \-ˌdōm\ *noun* [New Latin, from Late Greek *rhabdōma* bundle of rods, from Greek *rhabdos* rod] (1878)
**:** one of the minute rodlike structures in the retinulae in the compound eyes of arthropods

**rhab·do·man·cy** \ˈrab-də-ˌman(t)-sē\ *noun* [Late Greek *rhabdomanteia*, from Greek *rhabdos* rod + *-manteia* -mancy] (1646)
**:** divination by rods or wands
— **rhab·do·man·cer** \-ˌman(t)-sər\ *noun*

**rhab·do·mere** \-ˌmir\ *noun* (circa 1884)
**:** a division of a rhabdom

**rhab·do·myo·sar·co·ma** \ˈrab-(ˌ)dō-ˌmī-ə-sär-ˈkō-mə\ *noun, plural* **-mas** *or* **-ma·ta** \-mə-tə\ [New Latin, from *rhabdo-* + *my-* + *sarcoma*] (1898)
**:** a malignant tumor composed of striated muscle fibers

**rhab·do·vi·rus** \-ˌvī-rəs\ *noun* [New Latin] (1966)
**:** any of a group of RNA-containing rod- or bullet-shaped viruses found in plants and animals and including the causative agents of rabies and vesicular stomatitis

**rhad·a·man·thine** \ˌra-də-ˈman(t)-thən, -ˈman-ˌthīn\ *adjective, often capitalized* [*Rhadamanthus*] (1840)
**:** rigorously strict or just

**Rhad·a·man·thus** \ˌra-də-ˈman(t)-thəs\ *noun*
**:** a judge of the underworld in Greek mythology

**Rhae·to-Ro·mance** \ˌrē-tō-rō-ˈman(t)s, -tō-rə-; -ˈrō-ˌman(t)s\ *also* **Rhae·to-Ro·man·ic** \-rō-ˈma-nik\ *noun* [Latin *Rhaetus* of Rhaetia, ancient Roman province] (1867)
**:** a group of Romance languages spoken in eastern Switzerland and northeastern Italy

**rham·nose** \ˈram-ˌnōs, -ˌnōz\ *noun* [International Scientific Vocabulary, from New Latin *Rhamnus*, genus of the buckthorn; from its being produced from a plant of this genus] (1888)
**:** a crystalline sugar $C_6H_{12}O_5$ that occurs usually in the form of a glycoside in many plants and is obtained in the common dextrorotatory L form

**rhap·sode** \ˈrap-ˌsōd\ *noun* [French, from Greek *rhapsōidos*] (1834)

**rhap·sod·ic** \rap-ˈsä-dik\ *also* **rhap·sod·i·cal** \-di-kəl\ *adjective* (1782)
**1 :** extravagantly emotional **:** RAPTUROUS
**2 :** resembling or characteristic of a rhapsody
— **rhap·sod·i·cal·ly** \-di-k(ə-)lē\ *adverb*

**rhap·so·dist** \ˈrap-sə-dist\ *noun* (circa 1656)
**1 :** a professional reciter of epic poems
**2 :** one who writes or speaks rhapsodically

**rhap·so·dize** \-sə-ˌdīz\ *intransitive verb* **-dized; -diz·ing** (1806)
**:** to speak or write in a rhapsodic manner ⟨*rhapsodize* about a new book⟩

**rhap·so·dy** \ˈrap-sə-dē\ *noun, plural* **-dies** [Latin *rhapsodia*, from Greek *rhapsōidia* recitation of selections from epic poetry, rhapsody, from *rhapsōidos* rhapsodist, from *rhaptein* to sew, stitch together + *aidein* to sing — more at ODE] (1542)
**1 :** a portion of an epic poem adapted for recitation
**2** *archaic* **:** a miscellaneous collection
**3 a** (1) **:** a highly emotional utterance (2) **:** a highly emotional literary work (3) **:** effusively rapturous or extravagant discourse **b :** RAPTURE, ECSTASY
**4 :** a musical composition of irregular form having an improvisatory character

**rhat·a·ny** \ˈra-tᵊn-ē\ *noun* [Spanish *ratania* & Portuguese *ratânhia*] (1808)
**1 :** the dried root of either of two South American shrubs (*Krameria triandra* and *K. argentea* of the family Krameriaceae) used as an astringent
**2 :** a plant yielding rhatany

**rhea** \ˈrē-ə\ *noun* [New Latin, genus of birds, probably from Latin *Rhea*, mother of Zeus, from Greek] (1797)
**:** either of two South American ratite birds (*Rhea americana* and *Pterocnemia pennata* of the family Rheidae) that resemble but are smaller than the African ostrich and that have three toes, a fully feathered head and neck, an undeveloped tail, and pale gray to brownish feathers that droop over the rump and back

rhea

**rhe·bok** \ˈrē-ˌbäk\ *noun* [Afrikaans *reebok*, from Dutch, male roe deer, from *ree* roe + *boc* buck] (1834)
**:** a brownish gray antelope (*Pelea capreolus*) of southern Africa

**rhe·ni·um** \ˈrē-nē-əm\ *noun* [New Latin, from Latin *Rhenus* Rhine River] (1925)
**:** a rare heavy metallic element that resembles manganese, is obtained either as a powder or as a silver-white hard metal, and is used in catalysts and thermocouples — see ELEMENT table

**rheo-** *combining form* [Greek *rhein* to flow — more at STREAM]
**:** flow **:** current ⟨*rheo*stat⟩

**rhe·ol·o·gy** \rē-ˈä-lə-jē\ *noun* [International Scientific Vocabulary] (1929)
**:** a science dealing with the deformation and flow of matter; *also* **:** the ability to flow or be deformed
— **rhe·o·log·i·cal** \ˌrē-ə-ˈlä-ji-kəl\ *adjective*
— **rhe·o·log·i·cal·ly** \-k(ə-)lē\ *adverb*
— **rhe·ol·o·gist** \rē-ˈä-lə-jist\ *noun*

**rhe·om·e·ter** \rē-ˈä-mə-tər\ *noun* [International Scientific Vocabulary] (circa 1859)
**:** an instrument for measuring flow (as of viscous substances)

**rheo·stat** \ˈrē-ə-ˌstat\ *noun* (1843)
**:** a resistor for regulating a current by means of variable resistances
— **rheo·stat·ic** \ˌrē-ə-ˈsta-tik\ *adjective*

**rhe·sus monkey** \'rē-səs-\ *noun* [New Latin *Rhesus,* genus of monkeys, from Latin, a mythical king of Thrace, from Greek *Rhēsos*] (1841)
: a pale brown Asian macaque (*Macaca mulatta*) often used in medical research

**rhe·tor** \'rē-,tor, 're-; 'rē-tər, 're-\ *noun* [Middle English *rethor,* from Latin *rhetor,* from Greek *rhētōr*] (14th century)
: RHETORICIAN 1

**rhet·o·ric** \'re-tə-rik\ *noun* [Middle English *rethorik,* from Middle French *rethorique,* from Latin *rhetorica,* from Greek *rhētorikē,* literally, art of oratory, from feminine of *rhētorikos* of an orator, from *rhētōr* orator, rhetorician, from *eirein* to say, speak — more at WORD] (14th century)
**1** : the art of speaking or writing effectively: as **a** : the study of principles and rules of composition formulated by critics of ancient times **b** : the study of writing or speaking as a means of communication or persuasion
**2 a** : skill in the effective use of speech **b** : a type or mode of language or speech; *also* : insincere or grandiloquent language
**3** : verbal communication : DISCOURSE

**rhe·tor·i·cal** \ri-'tor-i-kəl, -'tär-\ *also* **rhe·tor·ic** \ri-'tor-ik, -'tär-\ *adjective* (15th century)
**1 a** : of, relating to, or concerned with rhetoric **b** : employed for rhetorical effect; *especially* : asked merely for effect with no answer expected 〈a *rhetorical* question〉
**2 a** : given to rhetoric : GRANDILOQUENT **b** : VERBAL
— **rhe·tor·i·cal·ly** \-i-k(ə-)lē\ *adverb*

**rhet·o·ri·cian** \,re-tə-'ri-shən\ *noun* (15th century)
**1 a** : a master or teacher of rhetoric **b** : ORATOR
**2** : an eloquent or grandiloquent writer or speaker

**rheum** \'rüm\ *noun* [Middle English *reume,* from Middle French, from Latin *rheuma,* from Greek, literally, flow, flux, from *rhein* to flow — more at STREAM] (14th century)
**1** : a watery discharge from the mucous membranes especially of the eyes or nose
**2** *archaic* : TEARS
— **rheumy** \'rü-mē\ *adjective*

**¹rheu·mat·ic** \rü-'ma-tik\ *adjective* [Middle English *rewmatik* subject to rheum, from Latin *rheumaticus,* from Greek *rheumatikos,* from *rheumat-, rheuma*] (1711)
: of, relating to, characteristic of, or affected with rheumatism
— **rheu·mat·i·cal·ly** \-ti-k(ə-)lē\ *adverb*

**²rheumatic** *noun* (1884)
: one affected with rheumatism

**rheumatic fever** *noun* (1782)
: an acute disease that occurs chiefly in children and young adults and is characterized by fever, by inflammation and pain in and around the joints, and by inflammatory involvement of the pericardium and heart valves

**rheu·ma·tism** \'rü-mə-,ti-zəm, 'rù-\ *noun* [Latin *rheumatismus* flux, rheum, from Greek *rheumatismos,* from *rheumatizesthai* to suffer from a flux, from *rheumat-, rheuma* flux] (1677)
**1** : any of various conditions characterized by inflammation or pain in muscles, joints, or fibrous tissue 〈muscular *rheumatism*〉
**2** : RHEUMATOID ARTHRITIS

**rheu·ma·tiz** \-,tiz\ *noun* (1760)
*chiefly dialect* : RHEUMATISM

**rheu·ma·toid** \-,tóid\ *adjective* [International Scientific Vocabulary, from *rheumatism*] (1871)
: characteristic of or affected with rheumatoid arthritis

**rheumatoid arthritis** *noun* (1859)
: a usually chronic disease of unknown cause that is characterized especially by pain, stiffness, inflammation, swelling, and sometimes destruction of joints

**rheumatoid factor** *noun* (1960)
: an autoantibody of high molecular weight that is usually present in rheumatoid arthritis

**rheu·ma·tol·o·gy** \,rü-mə-'tä-lə-jē, ,rù-\ *noun* (circa 1941)
: a medical science dealing with rheumatic diseases
— **rheu·ma·tol·o·gist** \-jist\ *noun*

**Rh factor** \,är-'āch-\ *noun* [rhesus monkey (in which it was first detected)] (1942)
: any of one or more genetically determined antigens present in the red blood cells of most persons and of higher animals and capable of inducing intense immunogenic reactions

**rhin-** *or* **rhino-** *combining form* [New Latin, from Greek, from *rhin-, rhis*]
: nose 〈*rhino*plasty〉

**rhi·nal** \'rī-n°l\ *adjective* (circa 1859)
: of or relating to the nose : NASAL

**rhin·en·ceph·a·lon** \,rī-(,)nen-'se-fə-,län, -lən\ *noun* [New Latin] (1846)
: the chiefly olfactory part of the forebrain
— **rhin·en·ce·phal·ic** \,rī-,nen-sə-'fa-lik\ *adjective*

**rhine·stone** \'rīn-,stōn\ *noun* [Rhine River] (circa 1888)
: a colorless imitation stone of high luster made of glass, paste, or gem quartz
— **rhine·stoned** \-,stōnd\ *adjective*

**Rhine wine** \'rīn-\ *noun* (1843)
**1** : a usually white wine produced in the Rhine valley
**2** : a wine similar to Rhine wine produced elsewhere

**rhi·ni·tis** \rī-'nī-təs\ *noun* [New Latin] (circa 1884)
: inflammation of the mucous membrane of the nose

**¹rhi·no** \'rī-(,)nō\ *noun* [origin unknown] (1670)
: MONEY, CASH

**²rhino** *noun, plural* **rhino** *or* **rhinos** (1884)
: RHINOCEROS

**rhi·noc·er·os** \rī-'näs-rəs, rə-, -'nä-sə-\ *noun, plural* **-noc·er·os·es** *or* **-noc·er·os** *or* **-noc·eri** \-'nä-sə-,rī\ [Middle English *rinoceros,* from Latin *rhinocerot-, rhinoceros,* from Greek *rhinokerōt-, rhinokerōs,* from *rhin-* + *keras* horn — more at HORN] (14th century)
: any of a family (Rhinocerotidae) of large heavyset herbivorous perissodactyl mammals of Africa and Asia that have one or two upright keratinous horns on the snout and thick gray to brown skin with little hair

*word history* see UNICORN

**rhinoceros beetle** *noun* (1681)
: any of various large chiefly tropical scarab beetles (subfamily Dynastinae) having projecting horns on thorax and head

**rhinoceros beetle**

**rhi·no·plas·ty** \'rī-nō-,plas-tē\ *noun, plural* **-ties** (1842)
: plastic surgery on the nose usually for cosmetic purposes

**rhi·nos·co·py** \rī-'näs-kə-pē\ *noun* [International Scientific Vocabulary] (1861)
: examination of the nasal passages

**rhi·no·vi·rus** \,rī-nō-'vī-rəs\ *noun* [New Latin] (1961)
: any of a group of picornaviruses that are related to the enteroviruses and are associated with disorders of the upper respiratory tract (as the common cold)

**rhiz-** *or* **rhizo-** *combining form* [New Latin, from Greek, from *rhiza* — more at ROOT]
: root 〈*rhizo*plane〉

**-rhiza** *or* **-rrhiza** *noun combining form, plural* **-zae** *or* **-zas** [New Latin, from Greek *rhiza*]
: root : part resembling or connected with a root 〈coleo*rhiza*〉 〈mycor*rhiza*〉

**rhi·zo·bi·um** \rī-'zō-bē-əm\ *noun, plural* **-bia** \-bē-ə\ [New Latin, from *rhiz-* + Greek *bios* life — more at QUICK] (1921)
: any of a genus (*Rhizobium*) of small heterotrophic soil bacteria capable of forming symbiotic nodules on the roots of leguminous plants and of there becoming bacteroids that fix atmospheric nitrogen
— **rhi·zo·bi·al** \-bē-əl\ *adjective*

**rhi·zoc·to·nia** \,rī-,zäk-'tō-nē-ə\ *noun* [New Latin, from *rhiz-* + Greek *-ktonos* killing, from *kteinein* to kill; akin to Sanskrit *kṣaṇoti* he wounds] (1897)
: any of a form genus (*Rhizoctonia*) of imperfect fungi that includes major plant pathogens

**rhi·zoid** \'rī-,zóid\ *noun* (1875)
: a rootlike structure
— **rhi·zoi·dal** \rī-'zói-d°l\ *adjective*

**rhi·zo·ma·tous** \rī-'zō-mə-təs\ *adjective* [International Scientific Vocabulary, from New Latin *rhizomat-, rhizoma*] (1847)
: having, resembling, or being a rhizome 〈*rhizomatous* plants〉

**rhi·zome** \'rī-,zōm\ *noun* [New Latin *rhizomat-, rhizoma,* from Greek *rhizōmat-, rhizōma* mass of roots, from *rhizoun* to cause to take root, from *rhiza* root — more at ROOT] (1845)
: a somewhat elongate usually horizontal subterranean plant stem that is often thickened by deposits of reserve food material, produces shoots above and roots below, and is distinguished from a true root in possessing buds, nodes, and usually scalelike leaves
— **rhi·zo·mic** \rī-'zō-mik, -'zä-\ *adjective*

**rhi·zo·plane** \'rī-zə-,plān\ *noun* (1949)
: the external surface of roots together with closely adhering soil particles and debris

**rhi·zo·pod** \'rī-zə-,päd\ *noun* [New Latin *Rhizopoda,* from *rhiz-* + *-poda* -pod] (1851)
: any of a superclass (Rhizopoda) of usually creeping protozoans (as an amoeba or a foraminifer) having lobate or rootlike pseudopodia

**rhi·zo·pus** \'rī-zə-pəs, -,pùs\ *noun* [New Latin, from *rhiz-* + Greek *pous* foot — more at FOOT] (1887)
: any of a genus (*Rhizopus*) of mold fungi including some economically valuable forms and some plant or animal pathogens (as a bread mold)

**rhi·zo·sphere** \-,sfir\ *noun* [International Scientific Vocabulary] (1929)
: soil that surrounds and is influenced by the roots of a plant

**rhi·zot·o·my** \rī-'zä-tə-mē\ *noun, plural* **-mies** [International Scientific Vocabulary] (1911)
: the operation of cutting the anterior or posterior spinal nerve roots

**Rh-neg·a·tive** \,är-,āch-'ne-gə-tiv\ *adjective* (1945)
: lacking Rh factor in the blood

**rho** \'rō\ *noun* [Greek *rhō,* of Semitic origin; akin to Hebrew *rēsh* resh] (15th century)
: the 17th letter of the Greek alphabet — see ALPHABET table

**rhod-** *or* **rhodo-** *combining form* [New Latin, from Latin, from Greek, from *rhodon* rose — more at ROSE]
: rose : red 〈*rhodo*lite〉

**rho·da·mine** \'rō-də-,mēn\ *noun, often capitalized* [International Scientific Vocabulary] (1888)
: any of a group of yellowish red to blue fluorescent dyes; *especially* : a brilliant bluish red dye made by fusing an amino derivative of phenol with phthalic anhydride and used especially in coloring paper and as a biological stain

---

\ə\ abut   \°\ kitten   \ər\ further   \a\ ash   \ā\ ace
\ä\ mop, mar   \aù\ out   \ch\ chin   \e\ bet   \ē\ easy
\g\ go   \i\ hit   \ī\ ice   \j\ job   \ŋ\ sing   \ō\ go
\ò\ law   \òi\ boy   \th\ thin   \t̲h̲\ the   \ü\ loot   \ù\ foot
\y\ yet   \zh\ vision   *see also* Guide to Pronunciation

**Rhode Island Red** *noun* [*Rhode Island*, U.S. state] (1896)
: any of an American breed of general-purpose domestic fowls having a long heavy body, smooth yellow or reddish legs, and rich brownish red plumage

**Rhode Island White** *noun* (circa 1923)
: any of an American breed of domestic fowls resembling Rhode Island Reds but having pure white plumage

**Rhodes grass** \'rōdz-\ *noun* [Cecil J. *Rhodes*] (1915)
: an African perennial grass (*Chloris gayana*) widely cultivated as a forage grass especially in dry regions

**Rho·de·sian man** \rō-'dē-zh(ē-)ən-\ *noun* [Northern *Rhodesia*, Africa] (1921)
: an extinct African hominid (*Homo sapiens rhodesiensis*) having long bones of modern type, a skull with prominent brow ridges and large face but human palate and dentition, and a simple but relatively large brain

**Rhodesian Ridge·back** \-'rij-,bak\ *noun* (1925)
: any of an African breed of powerful long-bodied hunting dogs having a dense harsh short tan coat with a characteristic crest of reversed hair along the spine

**Rhodes scholar** \'rōd(z)-\ *noun* (1902)
: a holder of one of numerous scholarships founded under the will of Cecil J. Rhodes that can be used at Oxford University for two or three years and are open to candidates from the Commonwealth and the U.S.

**rho·di·um** \'rō-dē-əm\ *noun* [New Latin, from Greek *rhodon* rose] (1804)
: a white hard ductile metallic element that is resistant to acids, occurs in platinum ores, and is used in alloys with platinum — see ELEMENT table

**rho·do·chro·site** \,rō-də-'krō-,sīt\ *noun* [German *Rhodocrosit*, from Greek *rhodochrōs* rose-colored, from *rhod-* + *chrōs* color — more at CHROMATIC] (1836)
: a rose red mineral consisting essentially of manganese carbonate

**rho·do·den·dron** \,rō-də-'den-drən\ *noun* [New Latin, from Latin, oleander, from Greek, from *rhod-* + *dendron* tree — more at DENDR-] (1664)
: any of a genus (*Rhododendron*) of the heath family of widely cultivated shrubs and trees with alternate leaves and showy flowers; *especially* : one with leathery evergreen leaves as distinguished from a deciduous azalea

**rho·do·lite** \'rō-dᵊl-,īt\ *noun* (1897)
: a pink or purple garnet used as a gem

**rho·do·mon·tade** *variant of* RODOMONTADE

**rho·do·nite** \'rō-dᵊn-,īt\ *noun* [German *Rhodonit*, from Greek *rhodon* rose] (1823)
: a pale red triclinic mineral that consists essentially of manganese silicate and is used as an ornamental stone

**rho·dop·sin** \rō-'däp-sən\ *noun* [International Scientific Vocabulary *rhod-* + Greek *opsis* sight, vision + International Scientific Vocabulary [1]*-in* — more at OPTIC] (1886)
: a red photosensitive pigment in the retinal rods of marine fishes and most higher vertebrates that is important in vision in dim light — called also *visual purple*

**rho·do·ra** \rō-'dōr-ə, -'dȯr-ə\ *noun* [New Latin, alteration of Latin *rodarum*, a plant] (circa 1731)
: an azalea (*Rhododendron canadense*) of northeastern North America that has spring-flowering pink blossoms

**rhomb** \'räm(b)\ *noun, plural* **rhombs** \'rämz\ [Middle French *rhombe*, from Latin *rhombus*] (circa 1578)
**1** : RHOMBUS
**2** : RHOMBOHEDRON

**rhomb-** *or* **rhombo-** *combining form* [New Latin, from Greek *rhombos*]
: rhombus ⟨*rhomb*encephalon⟩

**rhomb·en·ceph·a·lon** \,räm-(,)ben-'se-fə-,län, -lən\ *noun* [New Latin] (1897)
: HINDBRAIN 1

**rhom·bic** \'räm-bik\ *adjective* (1701)
**1** : having the form of a rhombus
**2** : ORTHORHOMBIC

**rhom·bo·he·dron** \,räm-bō-'hē-drən\ *noun, plural* **-drons** *or* **-dra** \-drə\ [New Latin] (1836)
: a parallelepiped whose faces are rhombuses
— **rhom·bo·he·dral** \-drəl\ *adjective*

**¹rhom·boid** \'räm-,bȯid\ *noun* [Middle French *rhomboïde*, from Latin *rhomboides*, from Greek *rhomboeidēs* resembling a rhombus, from *rhombos*] (1570)
: a parallelogram with no right angles and with adjacent sides of unequal length

**²rhom·boid** \'räm-,bȯid\ *or* **rhom·boi·dal** \räm-'bȯi-dᵊl\ *adjective* (1693)
: shaped somewhat like a rhombus or rhomboid

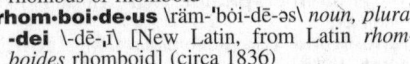
rhomboid

**rhom·boi·de·us** \räm-'bȯi-dē-əs\ *noun, plural* **-dei** \-dē-,ī\ [New Latin, from Latin *rhomboides* rhomboid] (circa 1836)
: either of two muscles that lie beneath the trapezius muscle and connect the spinous processes of various vertebrae with the medial border of the scapula

**rhom·bus** \'räm-bəs\ *noun, plural* **rhom·bus·es** *or* **rhom·bi** \-,bī, -,bē\ [Latin, from Greek *rhombos* piece of wood whirled on a string, lozenge, from *rhembein* to whirl] (circa 1567)
: a parallelogram with four equal sides and sometimes one with no right angles

**rhon·chus** \'rän-kəs\ *noun, plural* **rhon·chi** \'rän-,kī\ [Late Greek, from *rhenchein* to snore, wheeze; probably akin to Old Irish *sreinnid* he snores] (1829)
: a whistling or snoring sound heard on auscultation of the chest when the air channels are partly obstructed

**Rh–pos·i·tive** \,är-,āch-'pä-zə-tiv, -'päz-tiv\ *adjective* (1942)
: containing Rh factor in the red blood cells

**rhu·barb** \'rü-,bärb\ *noun* [Middle English *rubarbe*, from Middle French *reubarbe*, from Medieval Latin *reubarbarum*, alteration of *rha barbarum*, literally, barbarian rhubarb] (15th century)
**1** : any of a genus (*Rheum*) of Asian plants of the buckwheat family having large leaves with thick succulent petioles often used as food
**2** : the dried rhizome and roots of any of several rhubarbs grown in China and Tibet and used as a purgative and cathartic
**3** : a heated dispute or controversy

**rhumb** \'rəm(b)\ *noun, plural* **rhumbs** \'rəmz\ [Spanish *rumbo* rhumb, rhumb line] (1578)
**1** : a line or course on a single bearing
**2** : any of the points of the mariner's compass

**rhumba** *variant of* RUMBA

**rhumb line** *noun* [Spanish *rumbo*] (circa 1795)
: a line on the surface of the earth that follows a single compass bearing and makes equal oblique angles with all meridians — called also *loxodrome*

**rhus** \'rüs\ *noun, plural* **rhus·es** *or* **rhus** [New Latin, from Latin, sumac, from Greek *rhous*] (circa 1611)
: any of a genus (*Rhus*) of shrubs and trees (as sumac or poison ivy) of the cashew family that are native to temperate and warm regions, have compound trifoliolate or pinnate leaves, and sometimes produce substances causing dermatitis

**¹rhyme** \'rīm\ *noun* [Middle English *rime*, from Old French] (13th century)
**1 a** (1) : rhyming verse (2) : POETRY **b** : a composition in verse that rhymes
**2 a** : correspondence in terminal sounds of units of composition or utterance (as two or more words or lines of verse) **b** : one of two or more words thus corresponding in sound **c** : correspondence of other than terminal word sounds: as (1) : ALLITERATION (2) : INTERNAL RHYME
**3** : RHYTHM, MEASURE
— **rhyme·less** *adjective*

**²rhyme** *verb* **rhymed; rhym·ing** (14th century)
*transitive verb*
**1** : to relate or praise in rhyming verse
**2 a** : to put into rhyme **b** : to compose (verse) in rhyme **c** : to cause to rhyme : use as rhyme
*intransitive verb*
**1** : to make rhymes; *also* : to compose rhyming verse
**2** *of a word or verse* : to end in syllables that are rhymes
**3** : to be in accord : HARMONIZE
— **rhym·er** *noun*

**rhyme or reason** *noun* (15th century)
: good sense or reason

**rhyme royal** \-'rȯi(-ə)l\ *noun* (circa 1841)
: a stanza of seven lines in iambic pentameter with a rhyme scheme of *ababbcc*

**rhyme scheme** *noun* (1917)
: the arrangement of rhymes in a stanza or a poem

**rhyme·ster** \'rīm(p)-stər\ *noun* (1589)
: an inferior poet

**rhyming slang** *noun* (1859)
: slang in which the word intended is replaced by a word or phrase that rhymes with it (as *loaf of bread* for *head*) or the first part of the phrase (as *loaf* for *head*)

**rhyn·cho·ce·pha·lian** \,riŋ-kō-sə-'fāl-yən\ *noun* [ultimately from Greek *rhynchos* beak, snout + *kephalē* head — more at CEPHALIC] (1886)
: any of an order (Rhynchocephalia) of reptiles resembling lizards that includes the tuatara as the only living member
— **rhynchocephalian** *adjective*

**rhy·o·lite** \'rī-ə-,līt\ *noun* [German *Rhyolith*, from Greek *rhyax* stream, stream of lava (from *rhein*) + German *-lith* -lite] (1868)
: a very acid volcanic rock that is the lava form of granite
— **rhy·o·lit·ic** \,rī-ə-'li-tik\ *adjective*

**rhythm** \'ri-thəm\ *noun* [Middle French & Latin; Middle French *rhythme*, from Latin *rhythmus*, from Greek *rhythmos*, probably from *rhein* to flow — more at STREAM] (1560)
**1 a** : an ordered recurrent alternation of strong and weak elements in the flow of sound and silence in speech **b** : a particular example or form of rhythm ⟨iambic *rhythm*⟩
**2 a** : the aspect of music comprising all the elements (as accent, meter, and tempo) that relate to forward movement **b** : a characteristic rhythmic pattern ⟨rumba *rhythm*⟩; *also* : ¹METER 2 **c** : the group of instruments in a band supplying the rhythm — called also *rhythm section*
**3 a** : movement or fluctuation marked by the regular recurrence or natural flow of related elements **b** : the repetition in a literary work of phrase, incident, character type, or symbol
**4** : a regularly recurrent quantitative change in a variable biological process ⟨a circadian *rhythm*⟩ — compare BIORHYTHM
**5** : the effect created by the elements in a play, movie, or novel that relate to the temporal development of the action
**6** : RHYTHM METHOD

**rhythm and blues** *noun* (1949)
: popular music typically including elements of blues and black folk music and marked by a strong beat and simple chord structure

**rhythm band** *noun* (circa 1943)
: a band usually composed of schoolchildren who play simple percussion instruments (as rhythm sticks, sleigh bells, or tambourines) to learn fundamentals of coordination and music

**rhyth·mic** \'rith-mik\ *or* **rhyth·mi·cal** \-mi-kəl\ *adjective* (1589)

**1 :** marked by or moving in pronounced rhythm
**2 :** of, relating to, or involving rhythm
— **rhyth·mi·cal·ly** \-mi-k(ə-)lē\ adverb
**rhyth·mic·i·ty** \rith-'mi-sə-tē\ noun (1901)
**:** the state of being rhythmic or of responding rhythmically
**rhyth·mics** \'rith-miks\ noun plural but singular or plural in construction (circa 1859)
**:** the science or theory of rhythms
**rhyth·mist** \'ri-thə-mist, 'rith-mist\ noun (1864)
**:** one who studies or has a feeling for rhythm
**rhyth·mize** \-,mīz\ transitive verb **-mized; -miz·ing** (1885)
**:** to order or compose rhythmically
— **rhyth·mi·za·tion** \,ri-thə-mə-'zā-shən, ,rith-mə-\ noun
**rhythm method** noun (1940)
**:** a method of birth control involving continence during the period in which ovulation is most likely to occur
**rhythm stick** noun (1952)
**:** one of a pair of plain or notched wood sticks that are struck or rubbed together to produce various percussive sounds and are used especially by young children in rhythm bands
**rhyt·i·dome** \'ri-tə-,dōm, 'rī-\ noun [Greek rhytidōma wrinkle, from rhytidoun to wrinkle, from rhytid-, rhytis wrinkle] (1881)
**:** the bark external to the last formed periderm
**rhy·ton** \'rī-,tän\ noun [Greek, neuter of rhytos flowing, from rhein to flow — more at STREAM] (1850)
**:** any of various ornate drinking vessels of ancient times typically shaped in part like an animal or animal's head
**¹ri·al** \rē-'òl, -'äl\ noun [Persian, from Arabic riyāl riyal] (1932)
— see MONEY table
**²rial** variant of RIYAL
**ri·al·to** \rē-'al-(,)tō\ noun, plural **-tos** [Rialto, island and district in Venice] (1549)
**1 :** EXCHANGE, MARKETPLACE
**2 :** a theater district
**ri·ant** \'rī-ənt, 'rē-; rē-'äⁿ\ adjective [Middle French, present participle of rire to laugh, from Latin ridēre] (1567)
**:** GAY, MIRTHFUL
— **ri·ant·ly** \'rī-ənt-lē, 'rē-\ adverb
**ri·a·ta** \rē-'a-tə, -'ä-tə\ noun [modification of American Spanish reata] (1846)
**:** LARIAT
**¹rib** \'rib\ noun [Middle English, from Old English ribb; akin to Old High German rippi rib, Old Church Slavonic rebro, and probably to Greek erephein to roof over] (before 12th century)

**1 a :** any of the paired curved bony or partly cartilaginous rods that stiffen the walls of the body of most vertebrates and protect the viscera **b :** a cut of meat including a rib — see BEEF illustration **c** [from the account of Eve's creation from Adam's rib in Genesis 2:21–22] **:** WIFE
**2 :** something resembling a rib in shape or function: as **a** (1) **:** a traverse member of the frame of a ship that runs from keel to deck (2) **:** a light fore-and-aft member in an airplane's wing **b :** one of the stiff strips supporting an umbrella's fabric **c :** one of the arches in Romanesque and Gothic vaulting meeting and crossing one another and dividing the whole vaulted space into triangles
**3 :** an elongated ridge: as **a** (1) **:** a vein of an insect's wing (2) **:** one of the primary veins of a leaf **b :** one of the ridges in a knitted or woven fabric

rib 1a

**²rib** transitive verb **ribbed; rib·bing** (circa 1547)
**1 :** to furnish or enclose with ribs
**2 :** to form vertical ridges in in knitting
— **rib·ber** noun
**³rib** noun [⁴rib] (1929)
**1 :** JOKE
**2 :** PARODY
**⁴rib** transitive verb **ribbed; rib·bing** [probably from ¹rib; from the tickling of the ribs to cause laughter] (1930)
**:** to poke fun at **:** KID
— **rib·ber** noun
**¹rib·ald** \'ri-bəld also 'ri-,bòld, 'rī-,bòld\ noun [Middle English, from Middle French ribaut, ribauld wanton, rascal, from riber to be wanton, of Germanic origin; akin to Old High German rīban to be wanton, literally, to rub] (13th century)
**:** a ribald person
**²ribald** adjective (1508)
**1 :** CRUDE, OFFENSIVE ⟨ribald language⟩
**2 :** characterized by or using coarse indecent humor
**synonym** see COARSE
**rib·ald·ry** \'ri-bəl-drē also 'rī-\ noun, plural **-ries** (14th century)
**1 :** a ribald quality or element
**2 a :** ribald language or humor **b :** an instance of ribald language or humor
**rib·and** \'ri-bənd\ noun [Middle English, alteration of riban] (15th century)
**:** a ribbon used especially as a decoration
**ri·ba·vi·rin** \,rī-bə-'vī-rən\ noun [perhaps from ribonucleic acid + virus + ¹-in] (1976)
**:** a synthetic broad-spectrum antiviral nucleoside $C_8H_{12}N_4O_5$
**rib·band** \'ri(b)-,band, 'ri-bən(d)\ noun [¹rib + ¹band] (1711)
**:** a long narrow strip or bar used in shipbuilding; especially **:** one bent and bolted longitudinally to the frames to hold them in position during construction
**rib·bing** \'ri-biŋ\ noun (1564)
**:** an arrangement of ribs
**¹rib·bon** \'ri-bən\ noun [Middle English riban, from Middle French riban, ruban] (14th century)
**1 a :** a flat or tubular narrow closely woven fabric (as of silk or rayon) used for trimmings or knitting **b :** a narrow fabric used for tying packages **c :** a piece of usually multicolored ribbon worn as a military decoration or in place of a medal **d :** a strip of colored satin given for winning a place in a competition
**2 :** a strip of inked fabric (as in a typewriter)
**3** plural **:** reins for controlling an animal
**4 :** TATTER, SHRED — usually used in plural
**5 :** RIBBAND
— **rib·bon·like** \-,līk\ adjective
**²ribbon** transitive verb (1716)
**1 a :** to adorn with ribbons **b :** to divide into ribbons **c :** to cover with or as if with ribbons
**2 :** to rip to shreds
**ribbon development** noun (1927)
**:** a system of buildings built side by side along a road
**rib·bon·fish** \'ri-bən-,fish\ noun (circa 1798)
**:** any of a family (Trachipteridae) of elongate greatly compressed marine bony fishes (as a dealfish)
**ribbon worm** noun (1855)
**:** NEMERTEAN
**rib·by** \'ri-bē\ adjective (1849)
**:** showing or marked by ribs
**rib cage** noun (1909)
**:** the bony enclosing wall of the chest consisting chiefly of the ribs and the structures connecting them
**ri·bes** \'rī-(,)bēz\ noun, plural **ribes** [New Latin, from Medieval Latin, currant, from Arabic rībās rhubarb] (1543)

**:** any of a genus (Ribes) of shrubs (as a currant or a gooseberry) of the saxifrage family that have small racemose variously colored flowers and pulpy two-seeded to many-seeded berries
**rib eye** noun (1926)
**:** the large piece of meat that lies along the outer side of the rib (as of a steer)
**rib-grass** \'rib-,gras\ noun (circa 1500)
**:** ¹PLANTAIN; especially **:** an Old World plantain (Plantago lanceolata) with long narrow ribbed leaves
**rib·let** \'ri-blət\ noun (1943)
**:** one of the rib ends in the strip of breast of lamb or veal — see LAMB illustration
**ribo-** combining form [ribose]
**1 :** ribose ⟨riboflavin⟩
**2 :** ribonucleic acid ⟨ribosome⟩
**ri·bo·fla·vin** \,rī-bə-'flā-vən, 'rī-bə-,\ noun [International Scientific Vocabulary ribo- + Latin flavus yellow — more at BLUE] (1935)
**:** a yellow crystalline compound $C_{17}H_{20}N_4O_6$ that is a growth-promoting member of the vitamin B complex and occurs both free (as in milk) and combined (as in liver) — called also vitamin $B_2$, vitamin G
**ri·bo·nu·cle·ase** \,rī-bō-'nü-klē-,ās, -'nyü-, -,āz\ noun (1942)
**:** an enzyme that catalyzes the hydrolysis of RNA
**ri·bo·nu·cle·ic acid** \,rī-bō-nù-'klē-ik-, -nyü-, -,klā-\ noun (1931)
**:** RNA
**ri·bo·nu·cleo·pro·tein** \-,nü-klē-ō-'prō-,tēn, -'prō-tē-ən\ noun (1940)
**:** a nucleoprotein that contains RNA
**ri·bo·nu·cle·o·side** \-'nü-klē-ə-,sīd, -'nyü-\ noun (1931)
**:** a nucleoside that contains ribose
**ri·bo·nu·cle·o·tide** \-,tīd\ noun (1929)
**:** a nucleotide that contains ribose and occurs especially as a constituent of RNA
**ri·bose** \'rī-,bōs, -,bōz\ noun [International Scientific Vocabulary, from ribonic acid (an acid $C_5H_{10}O_6$ obtained by oxidation of ribose)] (1892)
**:** a pentose $C_5H_{10}O_5$ found especially in the dextrorotatory form and obtained especially from RNA
**ribosomal RNA** noun (1961)
**:** RNA that is a fundamental structural element of ribosomes
**ri·bo·some** \'rī-bə-,sōm\ noun (1958)
**:** any of the RNA-rich cytoplasmic granules that are sites of protein synthesis — see CELL illustration
— **ri·bo·som·al** \,rī-bə-'sō-məl\ adjective
**rib roast** noun (circa 1890)
**:** a cut of meat containing the large piece that lies along the outer side of the rib — see BEEF illustration
**rib·wort** \'rib-,wərt, -,wòrt\ noun (14th century)
**:** RIBGRASS
**rice** \'rīs\ noun [Middle English rys, from Old French ris, from Old Italian riso, from Greek oryza, oryzon, of Iranian origin; akin to Pashto wriže rice; akin to Sanskrit vrīhi rice] (13th century)
**:** the starchy seeds of an annual cereal grass (Oryza sativa) that are cooked and used for food; also **:** this cereal grass that occurs in southeastern Asia and is widely cultivated in warm climates for its seeds and by-products
**rice·bird** \'rīs-,bərd\ noun (1731)
**:** any of several small birds common in rice fields; especially **:** BOBOLINK
**rice paper** noun [from its resemblance to paper made from rice straw] (1822)

\ə\ abut \ᵊ\ kitten \ər\ further \a\ ash \ā\ ace
\ä\ mop, mar \aù\ out \ch\ chin \e\ bet \ē\ easy
\g\ go \i\ hit \ī\ ice \j\ job \ŋ\ sing \ō\ go
\ò\ law \òi\ boy \th\ thin \th\ the \ü\ loot \ù\ foot
\y\ yet \zh\ vision    see also Guide to Pronunciation

: a thin papery material made from the pith of a small Asian tree or shrub (*Tetrapanax papyriferum*) of the ginseng family

**rice polishings** *noun plural* (circa 1934)
: the inner bran layer of rice rubbed off in milling

**ric·er** \'rī-sər\ *noun* (1896)
: a kitchen utensil in which soft foods are pressed through a perforated container to produce strings

**ri·cer·car** \,rē-(,)chər-'kär\ *or* **ri·cer·ca·re** \-'kä-(,)rā\ *noun, plural* **ricercars** *or* **ri·cer·ca·ri** \-'kä-(,)rē\ [Italian, from *ricercare* to seek again, seek out, from *ri-* re- (from Latin *re-*) + *cercare* to seek, from Late Latin *circare* to go about — more at SEARCH] (1789)
: any of various usually keyboard musical forms especially of the 16th and 17th centuries in either quasi-improvisatory toccata style or strict polyphonic fugal style

**rich** \'rich\ *adjective* [Middle English *riche*, from Old English *rīce;* akin to Old High German *rīhhi* rich, Old English *rīce* kingdom, Old High German *rīhhi*, *noun;* all from prehistoric Germanic words borrowed from Celtic words akin to Old Irish *rí* (genitive *ríg*) king — more at ROYAL] (before 12th century)
**1** : having abundant possessions and especially material wealth
**2 a** : having high value or quality **b** : well supplied ⟨a city *rich* in traditions⟩
**3** : magnificently impressive : SUMPTUOUS
**4 a** : vivid and deep in color ⟨a *rich* red⟩ **b** : full and mellow in tone and quality ⟨a *rich* voice⟩ **c** : having a strong fragrance ⟨*rich* perfumes⟩
**5** : highly productive or remunerative ⟨a *rich* mine⟩
**6 a** : having abundant plant nutrients ⟨*rich* soil⟩ **b** : highly seasoned, fatty, oily, or sweet ⟨*rich* foods⟩ **c** : high in the combustible component ⟨a *rich* fuel mixture⟩ **d** : high in some component ⟨cholesterol-*rich* foods⟩
**7 a** : ENTERTAINING; *also* : LAUGHABLE **b** : MEANINGFUL, SIGNIFICANT ⟨*rich* allusions⟩ **c** : LUSH ⟨*rich* meadows⟩
**8** : pure or nearly pure ⟨*rich* lime⟩ ☆
— **rich·ness** *noun*

**Rich·ard Roe** \,rich-ərd-'rō\ *noun* (1768)
: a party to legal proceedings whose true name is unknown — compare JOHN DOE

**rich·en** \'ri-chən\ *transitive verb* **rich·ened; rich·en·ing** \'ri-chə-niŋ, 'rich-niŋ\ (1878)
: to make rich or richer

**rich·es** \'ri-chəz\ *noun plural* [Middle English, singular or plural, from *richesse*, literally, richness, from Old French, from *riche* rich, of Germanic origin; akin to Old English *rīce* rich] (13th century)
: things that make one rich : WEALTH

**rich·ly** \'rich-lē\ *adverb* [Middle English *richely*, from Old English *rīclīce*, from *rīce* rich] (before 12th century)
**1** : in a rich manner
**2** : in full measure : AMPLY ⟨praise *richly* deserved⟩

**Rich·ter scale** \'rik-tər-\ *noun* [Charles F. *Richter*] (1938)
: an open-ended logarithmic scale for expressing the magnitude of a seismic disturbance (as an earthquake) in terms of the energy dissipated in it with 1.5 indicating the smallest earthquake that can be felt, 4.5 an earthquake causing slight damage, and 8.5 a very devastating earthquake

**ri·cin** \'rī-sʳn, 'ri-\ *noun* [Latin *ricinus* castoroil plant] (1896)
: a poisonous protein in the castor bean

**ri·cin·ole·ic acid** \,rī-sʳn-ō-'lē-ik-, ,ri-, -'lā-\ *noun* [Latin *ricinus* + English *oleic acid*] (1848)
: an oily unsaturated hydroxy fatty acid

$C_{18}H_{34}O_3$ that occurs in castor oil as a glyceride and yields esters important as plasticizers

**¹rick** \'rik\ *noun* [Middle English *reek*, from Old English *hrēac;* akin to Old Norse *hraukr* rick] (before 12th century)
**1** : a stack (as of hay) in the open air
**2** : a pile of material (as cordwood) split from short logs

**²rick** *transitive verb* (1623)
: to pile (as hay) in ricks

**³rick** *transitive verb* [perhaps from Middle English *wrikken* to move unsteadily] (1798)
*chiefly British* : WRENCH, SPRAIN

**rick·ets** \'ri-kəts\ *noun plural but singular in construction* [origin unknown] (1634)
: a deficiency disease that affects the young during the period of skeletal growth, is characterized especially by soft and deformed bones, and is caused by failure to assimilate and use calcium and phosphorus normally due to inadequate sunlight or vitamin D

**rick·ett·sia** \ri-'ket-sē-ə\ *noun, plural* **-si·as** *or* **-si·ae** \-sē-,ē, -,ī\ *also* **-sia** [New Latin, genus name, from Howard T. *Ricketts* (died 1910) American pathologist] (1919)
: any of a family (Rickettsiaceae) of rodshaped, coccoid, or diplococcus-shaped, often pleomorphic bacteria that cause various diseases (as typhus)
— **rick·ett·si·al** \-sē-əl\ *adjective*

**rick·ety** \'ri-kə-tē\ *adjective* (1683)
**1** : affected with rickets
**2 a** : lacking stability or firmness : SHAKY 2a ⟨a *rickety* coalition⟩ **b** : in unsound physical condition ⟨*rickety* veterans⟩ ⟨*rickety* stairs⟩

**rick·ey** \'ri-kē\ *noun, plural* **rickeys** [probably from the name *Rickey*] (1895)
: a drink containing liquor, lime juice, sugar, and soda water; *also* : a similar drink without liquor

**rick·rack** *or* **ric·rac** \'rik-,rak\ *noun* [reduplication of ⁴*rack*] (1884)
: a flat braid woven to form zigzags and used especially as trimming on clothing

**rick·sha** *or* **rick·shaw** \'rik-,shò\ *noun* [alteration of *jinrikisha*] (1887)
: a small covered 2-wheeled vehicle usually for one passenger that is pulled by one man and that was used originally in Japan

**¹ric·o·chet** \'ri-kə-,shā, *British also* -,shet\ *noun* [French] (1769)
: a glancing rebound (as of a projectile off a flat surface); *also* : an object that ricochets

**²ricochet** *intransitive verb* **-cheted** \-,shād\ *or* **-chet·ted** \-,she-təd\; **-chet·ing** \-,shā-iŋ\ *or* **-chet·ting** \-,she-tiŋ\ (1828)
: to skip with or as if with glancing rebounds

**ri·cot·ta** \ri-'kä-tə, -'kò-\ *noun* [Italian, from feminine of past participle of *ricuocere* to cook again, from Latin *recoquere*, from *re-* + *coquere* to cook — more at COOK] (1877)
: a white unripened whey cheese of Italy that resembles cottage cheese; *also* : a similar cheese made in the U.S. from whole or skim milk

**ric·tal** \'rik-tʳl\ *adjective* (1825)
: of or relating to the rictus

**ric·tus** \'rik-təs\ *noun* [New Latin, from Latin, open mouth, from *ringi* to open the mouth; akin to Old Church Slavonic *rǫgǔ* mockery] (1827)
**1** : the gape of a bird's mouth
**2 a** : the mouth orifice **b** : a gaping grin or grimace

**rid** \'rid\ *transitive verb* **rid** *also* **rid·ded; rid·ding** [Middle English *ridden* to clear, from Old Norse *rythja;* akin to Old High German *riutan* to clear land] (13th century)
**1** *archaic* : SAVE, RESCUE
**2** : to make free : RELIEVE, DISENCUMBER ⟨*rid* the language of impropriety⟩ ⟨be *rid* of worries⟩ ⟨get *rid* of that junk⟩

**rid·dance** \'ri-dʳn(t)s\ *noun* (1533)
**1** : an act of ridding

**2** : DELIVERANCE, RELIEF — often used in the phrase *good riddance*

**rid·den** \'ri-dʳn\ *adjective* (1653)
**1** : harassed, oppressed, or obsessed by — usually used in combination ⟨guilt-*ridden*⟩ ⟨debt-*ridden*⟩
**2** : excessively full of or supplied with — usually used in combination ⟨slum-*ridden*⟩

**¹rid·dle** \'ri-dʳl\ *noun* [Middle English *redels, ridel*, from Old English *rædelse* opinion, conjecture, riddle; akin to Old English *rǣdan* to interpret — more at READ] (before 12th century)
**1** : a mystifying, misleading, or puzzling question posed as a problem to be solved or guessed : CONUNDRUM, ENIGMA
**2** : something or someone difficult to understand
*synonym* see MYSTERY

**²riddle** *verb* **rid·dled; rid·dling** \'rid-liŋ, 'ri-dʳl-iŋ\ (1571)
*intransitive verb*
: to speak in or propound riddles
*transitive verb*
**1** : to find the solution of : EXPLAIN
**2** : to set a riddle for : PUZZLE
— **rid·dler** \'rid-lər, 'ri-dʳl-ər\ *noun*

**³riddle** *noun* [Middle English *riddil*, from Old English *hriddel;* akin to Latin *cribrum* sieve, *cernere* to sift — more at CERTAIN] (before 12th century)
: a coarse sieve

**⁴riddle** *transitive verb* **rid·dled; rid·dling** \'rid-liŋ, 'ri-dʳl-iŋ\ (13th century)
**1** : to separate (as grain from chaff) with a riddle : SCREEN
**2** : to pierce with many holes ⟨*riddled* the car with bullets⟩
**3** : to spread through : PERMEATE ⟨a book *riddled* with errors⟩

**rid·dling** \'rid-liŋ, 'ri-dʳl-iŋ\ *adjective* (1591)
: containing or presenting riddles

**¹ride** \'rīd\ *verb* **rode** \'rōd\ *or chiefly dialect* **rid** \'rid\; **rid·den** \'ri-dʳn\ *or chiefly dialect* **rid** *or* **rode; rid·ing** \'rī-diŋ\ [Middle English, from Old English *rīdan;* akin to Old High German *rītan* to ride, Middle Irish *réidid* he rides] (before 12th century)
*intransitive verb*
**1 a** : to sit and travel on the back of an animal that one directs **b** : to travel in or on a conveyance
**2** : to travel as if on a conveyance : be borne ⟨*rode* on a wave of popularity⟩
**3 a** : to lie moored or anchored ⟨a ship *rides* at anchor⟩ **b** : SAIL **c** : to move like a floating object ⟨the moon *rode* in the sky⟩
**4** : to become supported on a point or surface
**5 a** : to travel over a surface ⟨the car *rides* well⟩ **b** : to move on the body ⟨shorts that *ride* up⟩
**6** : to continue without interference ⟨let it *ride*⟩
**7 a** : to be contingent : DEPEND ⟨plans on which the future *rides*⟩ **b** : to become bet ⟨a lot of money *riding* on the favorite⟩
*transitive verb*
**1 a** : to travel on ⟨*ride* a bike⟩ ⟨*ride* the bus⟩ **b** : to move with like a rider ⟨*ride* the waves⟩

**2 a :** to traverse by conveyance ⟨*rode* 500 miles⟩ **b :** to ride a horse in ⟨*ride* a race⟩ **3 :** SURVIVE, OUTLAST — usually used with *out* ⟨*rode* out the gale⟩ **4 :** to traverse on horseback to inspect or maintain ⟨*ride* fence⟩ **5 :** to mount in copulation **6 a :** OBSESS, OPPRESS ⟨*ridden* by anxiety⟩ **b :** to harass persistently ⟨NAG⟩ **c :** TEASE, RIB **7 :** CARRY, CONVEY **8 :** to project over **:** OVERLAP **9 :** to give with (a punch) to soften the impact **10 :** to keep in partial engagement by resting a foot continuously on the pedal ⟨*ride* the brakes⟩

— **rid·able** *or* **ride·able** \'rī-də-bəl\ *adjective*

— **ride circuit :** to hold court in the various towns of a judicial circuit

— **ride for a fall :** to court disaster

— **ride herd on :** to keep a check on

— **ride high :** to experience success

— **ride shotgun :** to ride in the front passenger seat of a motor vehicle

**²ride** *noun* (1759)
**1 :** an act of riding; *especially* **:** a trip on horseback or by vehicle **2 :** a way (as a road or path) suitable for riding **3 :** any of various mechanical devices (as at an amusement park) for riding on **4 a :** a trip on which gangsters take a victim to murder him **b :** something likened to such a trip ⟨take the taxpayers for a *ride*⟩ **5 :** a means of transportation **6 :** the qualities of travel comfort in a vehicle

**rid·er** \'rī-dər\ *noun* (14th century)
**1 :** one that rides **2 a :** an addition to a document often attached on a separate piece of paper **b :** a clause appended to a legislative bill to secure a usually distinct object **3 :** something used to overlie another or to move along on another piece

— **rid·er·less** \-ləs\ *adjective*

**rid·er·ship** \'rī-dər-,ship\ *noun* (1968)
**:** the number of persons who ride a system of public transportation

**¹ridge** \'rij\ *noun* [Middle English *rigge*, from Old English *hrycg*; akin to Old High German *hrukki* ridge, back] (before 12th century)
**1 :** an elevated body part (as along the backbone) **2 a :** a range of hills or mountains **b :** an elongate elevation on an ocean bottom **3 :** an elongate crest or a linear series of crests **4 :** a raised strip (as of plowed ground) **5 :** the line of intersection at the top between the opposite slopes or sides of a roof

— **ridged** \'rijd\ *adjective*

**²ridge** *verb* **ridged; ridg·ing** (1523)
*transitive verb*
**:** to form into a ridge
*intransitive verb*
**:** to extend in ridges

**ridge·line** \'rij-,līn\ *noun* (1833)
**:** a line marking or following a ridge top

**ridge·ling** *or* **ridg·ling** \'rij-liŋ\ *noun* [perhaps from ¹*ridge*; from the supposition that the undescended testis remains near the animal's back] (1555)
**1 :** a partially castrated male animal **2 :** a male animal having one or both testes retained in the inguinal canal

**ridge·pole** \'rij-,pōl\ *noun* (1788)
**1 :** the horizontal pole at the top of a tent **2 :** the highest horizontal timber in a roof against which the upper ends of the rafters are fixed

**ridgy** \'ri-jē\ *adjective* (1697)
**:** having or rising in ridges

*1 ridgepole, 2 rafters*

**¹rid·i·cule** \'ri-də-,kyü(ə)l\ *noun* [French or Latin; French, from Latin *ridiculum* jest] (1690)
**:** the act of exposing to laughter **:** DERISION, MOCKERY

**²ridicule** *transitive verb* **-culed; -cul·ing** (circa 1700)
**:** to make fun of ☆
— **rid·i·cul·er** *noun*

**ri·dic·u·lous** \rə-'di-kyə-ləs\ *adjective* [Latin *ridiculosus* (from *ridiculum* jest, from neuter of *ridiculus*) or *ridiculus*, literally, laughable, from *ridēre* to laugh] (1550)
**:** arousing or deserving ridicule **:** ABSURD, PREPOSTEROUS
**synonym** see LAUGHABLE
— **ri·dic·u·lous·ly** *adverb*
— **ri·dic·u·lous·ness** *noun*

**¹rid·ing** \'rī-diŋ\ *noun* (14th century)
**:** the action or state of one that rides

**²rid·ing** *adjective* (15th century)
**1 :** used for or when riding ⟨a *riding* horse⟩ ⟨*riding* boots⟩ **2 :** operated by a rider ⟨a *riding* mower⟩

**³rid·ing** \'rī-diŋ\ *noun* [Middle English -*redying* or *trithing*, alteration of (assumed) Old English *thriding*, from Old Norse *thrith-jungr* third part, from *thrithi* third; akin to Old English *thridda* third — more at THIRD] (15th century)
**1 :** one of the three administrative jurisdictions into which Yorkshire, England, was formerly divided **2 :** an administrative jurisdiction or electoral district in a British dominion (as Canada)

**rid·ley** \'rid-lē\ *noun* [origin unknown] (1926)
**:** either of two sea turtles: **a :** one (*Lepidochelys kempii*) of the Gulf of Mexico and the Atlantic coast of the U.S. — called also *Kemp's ridley* **b :** one (*L. olivacea*) of the Pacific, Atlantic, and Indian oceans

**ri·dot·to** \ri-'dä-(,)tō\ *noun, plural* **-tos** [Italian, retreat, place of entertainment, redoubt — more at REDOUBT] (1722)
**:** a public entertainment consisting of music and dancing often in masquerade popular in 18th century England

**ri·el** \rē-'el\ *noun* [origin unknown] (1956)
— see MONEY table

**Rie·mann·ian geometry** \rē-'mä-nē-ən-\ *noun* [G. F. B. *Riemann*] (1904)
**:** a non-Euclidean geometry in which straight lines are geodesics and in which the parallel postulate is replaced by the postulate that every pair of straight lines intersects

**Rie·mann integral** \'rē-,män-, -mən-\ *noun* (1914)
**:** a definite integral defined as the limit of sums found by partitioning the interval comprising the domain of definition into subintervals, by finding the sum of products each of which consists of the width of a subinterval multiplied by the value of the function at some point in it, and by letting the maximum width of the subintervals approach zero

**Ries·ling** \'rēz-liŋ, 'rēs-\ *noun* [German] (1833)
**:** a white wine that ranges from dry to very sweet and is made from a single variety of grape originally grown in Germany; *also* **:** the grape

**ri·fam·pin** \rī-'fam-pən\ *or* **ri·fam·pi·cin** \rī-'fam-pə-sən\ *noun* [International Scientific Vocabulary, alteration of *rifamycin*, antibiotic derived from *Streptomyces mediterranei*] (1966)
**:** a semisynthetic antibiotic $C_{43}H_{58}N_4O_{12}$ that acts against some viruses and bacteria especially by inhibiting RNA synthesis

**rife** \'rīf\ *adjective* [Middle English *ryfe*, from Old English *rȳfe*; akin to Old Norse *rīfr* abundant] (12th century)
**1 :** prevalent especially to an increasing degree ⟨fear was *rife* in the people⟩ **2 :** ABUNDANT, COMMON

**3 :** copiously supplied **:** ABOUNDING — usually used with *with* ⟨*rife* with rumors⟩
— **rife** *adverb*
— **rife·ly** *adverb*

**¹riff** \'rif\ *noun* [probably by shortening & alteration from *refrain*] (1935)
**1 :** an ostinato phrase (as in jazz) typically supporting a solo improvisation; *also* **:** a piece based on such a phrase **2 :** a short succinct usually witty comment; *also* **:** BIT, ROUTINE

**²riff** *intransitive verb* (1950)
**:** to perform a riff

**³riff** *verb* [short for *riffle*] (1952)
**:** RIFFLE, SKIM ⟨*riff* pages⟩

**Riff** \'rif\ *noun, plural* **Riffs** *or* **Riffi** \'ri-fē *or* **Riff** (1903)
**:** a Berber of the Rif Mountains in northern Morocco

**Riff·ian** \'ri-fē-ən\ *noun* (1867)
**:** RIFF

**¹rif·fle** \'ri-fəl\ *verb* **rif·fled; rif·fling** \'ri-f(ə-)liŋ\ [²*riffle*] (1752)
*intransitive verb*
**1 :** to form, flow over, or move in riffles **2 :** to flip cursorily **:** THUMB ⟨*riffle* through the catalog⟩
*transitive verb*
**1 :** to ruffle slightly **:** RIPPLE **2 a :** to leaf through hastily; *specifically* **:** to leaf (as a stack of paper) by sliding a thumb along the edge of the leaves **b :** to shuffle (playing cards) by separating the deck into two parts and riffling with the thumbs so the cards intermix **3 :** to manipulate (small objects) idly between the fingers

**²riffle** *noun* [perhaps alteration of *ruffle*] (1785)
**1 a :** a shallow extending across a streambed and causing broken water **b :** a stretch of water flowing over a riffle **2 :** a small wave or succession of small waves **:** RIPPLE **3 a :** any of various contrivances (as blocks or rails) laid on the bottom of a sluice or launder to make a series of grooves or interstices to catch and retain a mineral (as gold) **b :** a groove or interstice so formed **4 :** a cleat or bar fastened to an inclined surface in a gold-washing apparatus to catch and hold mineral grains **5** [¹*riffle*] **a :** the act or process of shuffling (as cards) **b :** the sound made while doing this

**rif·fler** \'ri-flər\ *noun* [French *rifloir*, from *rifler* to file, rifle] (circa 1797)
**:** a small filing or scraping tool

**riff·raff** \'rif-,raf\ *noun* [Middle English *ryffe raffe*, from *rif and raf* every single one, from Middle French *rif et raf* completely, from *rifler* to scratch, plunder + *raffe* act of sweeping] (15th century)
**1 a :** disreputable persons **b :** RABBLE **c :** one of the riffraff

---

☆ SYNONYMS

**Ridicule, deride, mock, taunt** mean to make an object of laughter of. RIDICULE implies a deliberate often malicious belittling ⟨consistently *ridiculed* everything she said⟩. DERIDE suggests contemptuous and often bitter ridicule ⟨*derided* their efforts to start their own business⟩. MOCK implies scorn often ironically expressed as by mimicry or sham deference ⟨youngsters began to *mock* the helpless wino⟩. TAUNT suggests jeeringly provoking insult or challenge ⟨hometown fans *taunted* the visiting team⟩.

---

\ə\ abut \ᵊ\ kitten \ər\ further \a\ ash \ā\ ace
\ä\ mop, mar \au̇\ out \ch\ chin \e\ bet \ē\ easy
\g\ go \i\ hit \ī\ ice \j\ job \ŋ\ sing \ō\ go
\ȯ\ law \ȯi\ boy \th\ thin \t̲h̲\ the \ü\ loot \u̇\ foot
\y\ yet \zh\ vision *see also* Guide to Pronunciation

**2 :** REFUSE, RUBBISH ◆
— **riffraff** *adjective*

**¹ri·fle** \'rī-fəl\ *verb* **ri·fled; ri·fling** \-f(ə-)liŋ\ [Middle English, from Middle French *rifler* to scratch, file, plunder, of Germanic origin; akin to Old High German *riffilōn* to saw, obsolete Dutch *riffelen* to scrape] (14th century)
*transitive verb*
**1 :** to ransack especially with the intent to steal
**2 :** to steal and carry away
*intransitive verb*
**:** to engage in ransacking and stealing
— **ri·fler** \-f(ə-)lər\ *noun*

**²rifle** *transitive verb* **ri·fled; ri·fling** \-f(ə-)liŋ\ [perhaps from French *rifler* to scratch, file] (1635)
**:** to cut spiral grooves into the bore of ⟨*rifled* arms⟩ ⟨*rifled* pipe⟩

**³rifle** *noun* (1770)
**1 a :** a shoulder weapon with a rifled bore **b :** a rifled artillery piece
**2** *plural* **:** soldiers armed with rifles
**word history** see MUSKET

**⁴rifle** *transitive verb* **ri·fled; ri·fling** \-f(ə-)liŋ\ [³*rifle*] (1937)
**:** to propel (as a ball) with great force or speed

**ri·fle·bird** \'rī-fəl-ˌbərd\ *noun* (1831)
**:** any of several birds of paradise (genus *Ptiloris*)

**ri·fle·man** \-mən\ *noun* (1775)
**1 :** a soldier armed with a rifle
**2 :** one skilled in shooting with a rifle

**ri·fle·ry** \'rī-fəl-rē\ *noun* (1935)
**:** the practice of shooting at targets with a rifle

**ri·fling** \'rī-f(ə-)liŋ\ *noun* (1797)
**1 :** the act or process of making spiral grooves
**2 :** a system of spiral grooves in the surface of the bore of a gun causing a projectile when fired to rotate about its longer axis

**¹rift** \'rift\ *noun* [Middle English, of Scandinavian origin; akin to Danish & Norwegian *rift* fissure, Old Norse *rīfa* to rive — more at RIVE] (14th century)
**1 a :** FISSURE, CREVASSE **b :** FAULT 5
**2 :** a clear space or interval
**3 :** BREACH, ESTRANGEMENT

**²rift** (14th century)
*intransitive verb*
**:** to burst open
*transitive verb*
**1 :** CLEAVE, DIVIDE ⟨hills were *rifted* by the earthquake⟩
**2 :** PENETRATE

**rift valley** *noun* (1894)
**:** an elongated valley formed by the depression of a block of the earth's crust between two faults or groups of faults of approximately parallel strike

**¹rig** \'rig\ *transitive verb* **rigged; rig·ging** [Middle English *riggen*] (15th century)
**1 :** to fit out (as a ship) with rigging
**2 :** CLOTHE, DRESS — usually used with *out*
**3 :** to furnish with special gear **:** EQUIP
**4 a :** to put in condition or position for use **:** ADJUST, ARRANGE ⟨a car *rigged* for manual control⟩ **b :** CONSTRUCT ⟨*rig* up a temporary shelter⟩

**²rig** *noun* (1822)
**1 :** the distinctive shape, number, and arrangement of sails and masts of a ship
**2 :** EQUIPAGE; *especially* **:** a carriage with its horse
**3 :** CLOTHING, DRESS
**4 :** tackle, equipment, or machinery fitted for a specified purpose ⟨an oil-drilling *rig*⟩
**5 :** a tractor-trailer combination

**³rig** *transitive verb* **rigged; rig·ging** [*rig*, noun, a swindle] (1851)
**1 :** to manipulate or control usually by deceptive or dishonest means ⟨*rig* an election⟩
**2 :** to fix in advance for a desired result ⟨*rig* a quiz program⟩

**rig·a·doon** \ˌri-gə-'dün\ *or* **ri·gau·don** \rē-gȯ-dōⁿ\ *noun* [French *rigaudon*] (1691)
**:** a lively dance of the 17th and 18th centuries; *also* **:** the music for a rigadoon

**rig·a·ma·role** *variant of* RIGMAROLE

**rig·a·to·ni** \ˌri-gə-'tō-nē\ *noun* [Italian, plural, from *rigato* furrowed, fluted, from past participle of *rigare* to furrow, flute, from *riga* line, of Germanic origin; akin to Old High German *rīga* line — more at ROW] (circa 1923)
**:** pasta made in short wide fluted tubes

**Ri·gel** \'rī-jəl, -gəl; 'ri-jəl\ *noun* [Arabic *Rijl*, literally, foot]
**:** a first-magnitude star in the left foot of the constellation Orion

**rig·ger** \'ri-gər\ *noun* (1611)
**1 :** one that rigs
**2 :** a long slender pointed sable paintbrush

**rig·ging** \'ri-giŋ, -gən\ *noun* (1594)
**1 a :** lines and chains used aboard a ship especially in working sail and supporting masts and spars **b :** a similar network (as in theater scenery) used for support and manipulation
**2 :** CLOTHING

**¹right** \'rīt\ *adjective* [Middle English, from Old English *riht;* akin to Old High German *reht* right, Latin *rectus* straight, right, *regere* to lead straight, direct, rule, *rogare* to ask, Greek *oregein* to stretch out] (before 12th century)
**1 :** RIGHTEOUS, UPRIGHT
**2 :** being in accordance with what is just, good, or proper ⟨*right* conduct⟩
**3 a :** agreeable to a standard **b :** conforming to facts or truth **:** CORRECT ⟨the *right* answer⟩
**4 :** SUITABLE, APPROPRIATE ⟨the *right* man for the job⟩
**5 :** STRAIGHT ⟨a *right* line⟩
**6 :** GENUINE, REAL
**7 a :** of, relating to, situated on, or being the side of the body which is away from the heart and on which the hand is stronger in most people **b :** located nearer to the right hand than to the left **c :** located to the right of an observer facing the object specified or directed as the right arm would point when raised out to the side **d** (1) **:** located on the right of an observer facing in the same direction as the object specified ⟨stage *right*⟩ (2) **:** located on the right when facing downstream ⟨the *right* bank of a river⟩
**8 :** having the axis perpendicular to the base ⟨*right* cone⟩
**9 :** of, relating to, or constituting the principal or more prominent side of an object ⟨made sure the socks were *right* side out⟩
**10 :** acting or judging in accordance with truth or fact ⟨time proved her *right*⟩
**11 a :** being in good physical or mental health or order ⟨not in his *right* mind⟩ **b :** being in a correct or proper state ⟨put things *right*⟩
**12 :** most favorable or desired **:** PREFERABLE; *also* **:** socially acceptable ⟨knew all the *right* people⟩
**13** *often capitalized* **:** of, adhering to, or constituted by the Right especially in politics
**synonym** see CORRECT
— **right·ness** *noun*

**²right** *noun* [Middle English, from Old English *riht,* from *riht,* adjective] (before 12th century)
**1 :** qualities (as adherence to duty or obedience to lawful authority) that together constitute the ideal of moral propriety or merit moral approval
**2 :** something to which one has a just claim: as **a :** the power or privilege to which one is justly entitled **b** (1) **:** the interest that one has in a piece of property — often used in plural ⟨mineral *rights*⟩ (2) *plural* **:** the property interest possessed under law or custom and agreement in an intangible thing especially of a literary and artistic nature ⟨film *rights* of the novel⟩
**3 :** something that one may properly claim as due
**4 :** the cause of truth or justice
**5 a :** RIGHT HAND 1a; *also* **:** a blow struck with this hand ⟨gave him a hard *right* on the jaw⟩ **b :** the location or direction of the right side

⟨woods on his *right*⟩ **c :** the part on the right side **d :** RIGHT FIELD
**6 a :** the true account or correct interpretation **b :** the quality or state of being factually correct
**7** *often capitalized* **a :** the part of a legislative chamber located to the right of the presiding officer **b :** the members of a continental European legislative body occupying the right as a result of holding more conservative political views than other members
**8 a** *often capitalized* **:** individuals sometimes professing opposition to change in the established order and favoring traditional attitudes and practices and sometimes advocating the forced establishment of an authoritarian order (as in government) **b** *often capitalized* **:** a conservative position
**9 a :** a privilege given stockholders to subscribe pro rata to a new issue of securities generally below market price **b :** the negotiable certificate evidencing such privilege — usually used in plural
— **right·most** \-ˌmōst\ *adjective*
— **by rights :** with reason or justice **:** PROPERLY
— **in one's own right :** by virtue of one's own qualifications or properties
— **of right 1 :** as an absolute right **2 :** legally or morally exactable
— **to rights :** into proper order

**³right** *adverb* (before 12th century)
**1 :** according to right ⟨live *right*⟩
**2 :** in the exact location, position, or moment **:** PRECISELY ⟨*right* at his fingertips⟩ ⟨quit *right* then and there⟩
**3 :** in a suitable, proper, or desired manner ⟨knew he wasn't doing it *right*⟩
**4 :** in a direct line, course, or manner **:** DIRECTLY, STRAIGHT ⟨go *right* home⟩ ⟨came *right* out and said it⟩
**5 :** according to fact or truth **:** TRULY ⟨guessed *right*⟩
**6 a :** all the way ⟨windows *right* to the floor⟩ **b :** in a complete manner ⟨felt *right* at home⟩
**7 :** without delay **:** IMMEDIATELY ⟨*right* after lunch⟩
**8 :** to a great degree **:** VERY ⟨a *right* pleasant day⟩
**9 :** on or to the right ⟨looked left and *right*⟩

**⁴right** (before 12th century)
*transitive verb*
**1 a :** to do justice to **:** redress the injuries of ⟨so just is God to *right* the innocent —Shakespeare⟩ **b :** JUSTIFY, VINDICATE ⟨felt the need to *right* himself in court⟩
**2 :** AVENGE ⟨vows to *right* the injustice done to his family⟩

◇ WORD HISTORY
**riffraff** The word *riffraff* seems to represent a triumph of sound over sense, for it is a compound of two quite different words that have little semantic connection. In Middle French the verb *rifler* meant "to scratch" or "to plunder" and the noun *rafle* or *raffe* meant "the act of sweeping or snatching." From these words about the late 13th century the French contrived the phrase *rif et raf*, used to mean "completely," "altogether." Later variants such as *rifle ou* [or] *rafle* and *rif ny* [nor] *raf* show that the phrase most likely also meant "anything" or with a negative adverb "nothing." Medieval French *rif et raf* was thus borrowed into Middle English as *rif and raf*, in the sense "one and all, every single one." No doubt it was the lack of exclusivity implied by "every single one" that led to *ryffe raffe* being used in early Modern English as a collective noun for the multitude of people of the lowest or most disreputable sort.

**3 a :** to adjust or restore to the proper state or condition ⟨*right* the economy⟩ **b :** to bring or restore to an upright position ⟨*right* a capsized boat⟩
*intransitive verb*
**:** to become upright
— **right·er** *noun*
**right and left** *adverb* (1829)
**:** on both or all sides **:** in every direction **:** EVERYWHERE
**right angle** *noun* (15th century)
**:** the angle bounded by two lines perpendicular to each other **:** an angle of 90° or ½ π radians
— **right–an·gled** \'rīt-'aŋ-gəld\ *or* **right–an·gle** \-gəl\ *adjective*
**right ascension** *noun* (15th century)
**:** the arc of the celestial equator between the vernal equinox and the point where the hour circle through the given body intersects the equator reckoned eastward commonly in terms of the corresponding interval of sidereal time in hours, minutes, and seconds
**right away** *adverb* (1818)
**:** without delay or hesitation **:** IMMEDIATELY
**right circular cone** *noun* (circa 1889)
**:** CONE 1a
**right circular cylinder** *noun* (1877)
**:** a cylinder with the bases circular and with the axis joining the two centers of the bases perpendicular to the planes of the two bases

right circular cylinder: *1* axis

**righ·teous** \'rī-chəs\ *adjective* [alteration of earlier *rightuous,* alteration of Middle English *rightwise, rightwos,* from Old English *rihtwīs,* from *riht,* noun, right + *wīs* wise] (1535)
**1 :** acting in accord with divine or moral law **:** free from guilt or sin
**2 a :** morally right or justifiable ⟨a *righteous* decision⟩ **b :** arising from an outraged sense of justice or morality ⟨*righteous* indignation⟩
**3** *slang* **:** GENUINE, GOOD
**synonym** see MORAL
— **righ·teous·ly** *adverb*
— **righ·teous·ness** *noun*
**right field** *noun* (1857)
**1 :** the part of the baseball outfield to the right looking out from home plate
**2 :** the position of the player defending right field
— **right fielder** *noun*
**right·ful** \'rīt-fəl\ *adjective* (14th century)
**1 :** JUST, EQUITABLE
**2 a :** having a just or legally established claim **:** LEGITIMATE ⟨the *rightful* owner⟩ **b :** held by right or just claim **:** LEGAL ⟨*rightful* authority⟩
**3 :** PROPER, FITTING ⟨assured of his *rightful* place in history —Brian Duff⟩
— **right·ful·ly** \-fə-lē\ *adverb*
— **right·ful·ness** *noun*
**right–hand** \'rīt-,hand\ *adjective* (1592)
**1 :** situated on the right
**2 :** RIGHT-HANDED
**3 :** chiefly relied on ⟨*right-hand* man⟩
**right hand** *noun* (before 12th century)
**1 a :** the hand on a person's right side **b :** an indispensable person
**2 a :** the right side **b :** a place of honor
**right–hand·ed** \-'han-dəd\ *adjective* (14th century)
**1 :** using the right hand habitually or more easily than the left; *also* **:** swinging from right to left ⟨a *right-handed* batter⟩
**2 :** relating to, designed for, or done with the right hand
**3 a :** having the same direction or course as the movement of the hands of a watch viewed from in front **:** CLOCKWISE **b :** having a spiral structure or form that ascends or advances to

the right ⟨a *right-handed* screw⟩ ⟨a *right-handed* double helix of DNA⟩
**4** *of a door* **:** opening to the right away from one
— **right–handed** *adverb*
— **right–hand·ed·ly** *adverb*
— **right–hand·ed·ness** *noun*
**right–hand·er** \-'han-dər\ *noun* (1857)
**1 :** a blow struck with the right hand
**2 :** a right-handed person; *especially* **:** a right-handed pitcher
**right·ism** \'rīt-,i-zəm\ *noun, often capitalized* (1939)
**1 :** the principles and views of the Right
**2 :** advocacy of or adherence to the doctrines of the Right
— **right·ist** \'rī-tist\ *noun or adjective, often capitalized*
**right·ly** \'rīt-lē\ *adverb* (before 12th century)
**1 :** in accordance with right conduct **:** FAIRLY, JUSTLY
**2 :** in the right or proper manner **:** PROPERLY, FITTINGLY
**3 :** according to truth or fact **:** CORRECTLY, EXACTLY
**right–mind·ed** \-'mīn-dəd\ *adjective* (circa 1586)
**:** having a right or honest mind ⟨a *right-minded* citizen⟩
— **right–mind·ed·ness** *noun*
**right now** *adverb* (14th century)
**1 :** RIGHT AWAY
**2 :** at present
**right·o** \,rīt-'ō, 'rī-(,)tō\ *interjection* (1896)
— used to express cheerful concurrence, assent, or understanding
**right off** *adverb* (1790)
**:** RIGHT AWAY **:** at once
— **right off the bat :** RIGHT OFF
**right–of–way** \,rīt-ə(v)-'wā\ *noun, plural* **rights–of–way** *also* **right–of–ways** (1768)
**1 :** a legal right of passage over another person's ground
**2 a :** the area over which a right-of-way exists **b :** the strip of land over which is built a public road **c :** the land occupied by a railroad especially for its main line **d :** the land used by a public utility (as for a transmission line)
**3 a :** a precedence in passing accorded to one vehicle over another by custom, decision, or statute **b :** the right of traffic to take precedence **c :** the right to take precedence over others ⟨gave the bill the *right-of-way* in the Senate⟩
**right on** *adjective* (1925)
**1 :** exactly correct — often used interjectionally to express agreement
**2** *usually* **right–on :** attuned to the spirit of the times
**Right Reverend** (15th century)
— used as a title for high ecclesiastical officials
**right shoulder arms** *noun* (1902)
**:** a position in the manual of arms in which the butt of the rifle is held in the right hand with the barrel resting on the right shoulder; *also* **:** a command to assume this position
**right–to–life** \'rīt-tə-'līf\ *adjective* (1973)
**:** opposed to abortion
— **right–to–lif·er** \-'lī-fər\ *noun*
**right–to–work** *adjective* (1949)
**:** opposing or banning the closed shop and the union shop
**right triangle** *noun* (1924)
**:** a triangle having a right angle — see TRIANGLE illustration
**right·ward** \'rīt-wərd\ *adjective* (1825)
**:** being toward or on the right
**right whale** *noun* (1725)
**:** any of a family (Balaenidae) of baleen whales having very long baleen, a large head on a stocky body, a smooth throat, and short broad rounded flippers
**right wing** *noun* (1905)
**1 :** the rightist division of a group or party

**2 :** RIGHT 8
— **right–wing** \'rīt-'wiŋ, -,wiŋ\ *adjective*
— **right–wing·er** \'rīt-'wiŋ-ər, ,rīt-\ *noun*
**righty** \'rī-tē\ *noun, plural* **right·ies** (1949)
**:** RIGHT-HANDER 2

right whale

**rig·id** \'ri-jəd\ *adjective* [Middle English *rigide,* from Middle French or Latin; Middle French, from Latin *rigidus,* from *rigēre* to be stiff] (15th century)
**1 a :** deficient in or devoid of flexibility ⟨*rigid* price controls⟩ ⟨a *rigid* bar of metal⟩ **b :** appearing stiff and unyielding ⟨his face *rigid* with pain⟩
**2 a :** inflexibly set in opinion **b :** strictly observed ⟨adheres to a *rigid* schedule⟩
**3 :** firmly inflexible rather than lax or indulgent ⟨a *rigid* disciplinarian⟩
**4 :** precise and accurate in procedure ⟨*rigid* control of the manufacturing process⟩
**5** *of an airship* **:** having the outer shape maintained by a fixed framework ☆
— **rig·id·ly** *adverb*
— **rig·id·ness** *noun*
**ri·gid·i·fy** \rə-'ji-də-,fī\ *verb* **-fied; -fy·ing** (1842)
*transitive verb*
**:** to make rigid
*intransitive verb*
**:** to become rigid
— **ri·gid·i·fi·ca·tion** \-,ji-də-fə-'kā-shən\ *noun*
**ri·gid·i·ty** \rə-'ji-də-tē\ *noun, plural* **-ties** (1624)
**1 :** the quality or state of being rigid
**2 :** one that is rigid (as in form or conduct)
**rig·ma·role** \'ri-gə-mə-,rōl, 'rig-mə-\ *noun* [alteration of obsolete *ragman roll* long list, catalog] (circa 1736)
**1 :** confused or meaningless talk
**2 :** a complex and ritualistic procedure
**rig·or** \'ri-gər\ *noun* [Middle English *rigour,* from Middle French *rigueur,* from Latin *rigor,* literally, stiffness, from *rigēre* to be stiff] (14th century)
**1 a** (1) **:** harsh inflexibility in opinion, temper, or judgment **:** SEVERITY (2) **:** the quality of being unyielding or inflexible **:** STRICTNESS (3) **:** severity of life **:** AUSTERITY **b :** an act or instance of strictness, severity, or cruelty
**2 :** a tremor caused by a chill
**3 :** a condition that makes life difficult, challenging, or uncomfortable; *especially* **:** extremity of cold
**4 :** strict precision **:** EXACTNESS ⟨logical *rigor*⟩
**5 a** *obsolete* **:** RIGIDITY, STIFFNESS **b :** rigidness or torpor of organs or tissue that prevents response to stimuli
**rig·or·ism** \'ri-gə-,ri-zəm\ *noun* (1704)
**:** rigidity in principle or practice

---

☆ **SYNONYMS**
**Rigid, rigorous, strict, stringent** mean extremely severe or stern. RIGID implies uncompromising inflexibility ⟨*rigid* rules of conduct⟩. RIGOROUS implies the imposition of hardship and difficulty ⟨the *rigorous* training of recruits⟩. STRICT emphasizes undeviating conformity to rules, standards, or requirements ⟨*strict* enforcement of the law⟩. STRINGENT suggests severe, tight restriction or limitation ⟨*stringent* standards of admission⟩. See in addition STIFF.

---

\ə\ abut \ᵊ\ kitten \ər\ further \a\ ash \ā\ ace \ä\ mop, mar \aü\ out \ch\ chin \e\ bet \ē\ easy \g\ go \i\ hit \ī\ ice \j\ job \ŋ\ sing \ō\ go \ò\ law \òi\ boy \th\ thin \th\ the \ü\ loot \ù\ foot \y\ yet \zh\ vision   *see also* Guide to Pronunciation

**— rig·or·ist** \-rist\ *noun or adjective*

**— rig·or·is·tic** \ˌri-gə-'ris-tik\ *adjective*

**rig·or mor·tis** \ˌri-gər-'mȯr-təs *also chiefly British* ˌrī-ˌgȯr-\ *noun* [New Latin, stiffness of death] (circa 1847)
: temporary rigidity of muscles occurring after death

**rig·or·ous** \'ri-g(ə-)rəs\ *adjective* (15th century)
**1** : manifesting, exercising, or favoring rigor : very strict
**2 a** : marked by extremes of temperature or climate **b** : HARSH, SEVERE
**3** : scrupulously accurate : PRECISE
*synonym* see RIGID
**— rig·or·ous·ly** *adverb*
**— rig·or·ous·ness** *noun*

**rig·our** *chiefly British variant of* RIGOR

**rijst·ta·fel** \'rīs-ˌtä-fəl\ *noun* [Dutch, from *rijst* rice + *tafel* table] (1889)
: an Indonesian meal consisting of rice and a variety of accompanying dishes (as meat, seafood, and vegetables)

**Riks·mål** *or* **Riks·maal** \'riks-ˌmȯl, 'rēks-\ *noun* [Norwegian, from *rik* kingdom + *mål* speech] (1913)
: BOKMÅL

**rile** \'rī(ə)l\ *transitive verb* **riled; ril·ing** [variant of *roil*] (1825)
**1** : to make agitated and angry : UPSET
**2** : ROIL 1 ◆
*synonym* see IRRITATE

**ril·ey** \'rī-lē\ *adjective* (1805)
**1** : TURBID
**2** : ANGRY

**¹rill** \'ril\ *noun* [Dutch *ril* or Low German *rille*; akin to Old English *rīth* rivulet] (1538)
: a very small brook

**²rill** *intransitive verb* (1610)
: to flow like a rill

**³rill** \'ril\ *or* **rille** \'ril, 'ri-lə\ *noun* [German *Rille*, literally, channel made by a small stream, from Low German, rill] (1868)
: any of several long narrow valleys on the moon's surface

**rill·et** \'ri-lət\ *noun* (1538)
: a little rill

**ril·lettes** \ri-'lets, -'yet\ *noun plural* [French, plural, diminutive of *rille*, singular, piece of pork, from Middle French, dialect variant of *reille* board, lath, from Latin *regula* straightedge — more at RULE] (1889)
: cooked shredded meat (as pork or duck) or fish preserved in fat

**¹rim** \'rim\ *noun* [Middle English, from Old English *rima*; akin to Old Norse *rimi* strip of land] (13th century)
**1 a** : BRINK **b** : the outer often curved or circular edge or border of something
**2 a** : the outer part of a wheel joined to the hub usually by spokes **b** : a removable outer metal band on an automobile wheel to which the tire is attached
**3** : FRAME 4c(1)
**— rim·less** \-ləs\ *adjective*

**²rim** *verb* **rimmed; rim·ming** (1794)
*transitive verb*
**1** : to serve as a rim for : BORDER ⟨cliffs *rimming* the camp⟩
**2** : to run around the rim of ⟨putts that *rim* the cup⟩
*intransitive verb*
: to form or show a rim

**¹rime** \'rīm\ *noun* [Middle English *rim*, from Old English *hrīm*; akin to Old Norse *hrīm* frost] (before 12th century)
**1** : FROST 1b
**2** : an accumulation of granular ice tufts on the windward sides of exposed objects that is formed from supercooled fog or cloud and built out directly against the wind
**3** : CRUST, INCRUSTATION ⟨a *rime* of snow⟩

**²rime** *transitive verb* **rimed; rim·ing** (circa 1755)
: to cover with or as if with rime

**³rime, rime·ster** *variant of* RHYME, RHYMESTER

**rim·fire** \'rim-ˌfīr\ *adjective* (1868)
*of a cartridge* : having the priming distributed in the rim of the shell
**— rimfire** *noun*

**rim·land** \'rim-ˌland\ *noun* (1944)
: a region on the periphery of the heartland

**rimmed** \'rimd\ *adjective* (1729)
: having a rim — usually used in combination ⟨dark-*rimmed* glasses⟩ ⟨red-*rimmed* eyes⟩

**rim·rock** \'rim-ˌräk\ *noun* (1860)
**1** : a top stratum or overlying strata of resistant rock of a plateau that outcrops to form a vertical face
**2** : the edge or face of a rimrock outcrop

**rimy** \'rī-mē\ *adjective* **rim·i·er; -est** [Old English *hrīmig*, from *hrīm*] (before 12th century)
: covered with rime : FROSTY

**rind** \'rīnd, *dialect* 'rīn\ *noun* [Middle English, from Old English; akin to Old High German *rinda* bark, and probably to Old English *rendan* to rend] (before 12th century)
**1** : the bark of a tree
**2** : a usually hard or tough outer layer : PEEL, CRUST ⟨grated lemon *rind*⟩
**— rind·ed** \'rīn-dəd\ *adjective*

**rin·der·pest** \'rin-dər-ˌpest\ *noun* [German, from *Rinder*, plural, cattle + *Pest* pestilence] (1865)
: an acute infectious febrile disease of ruminant mammals (as cattle) that is caused by a virus and is marked by diarrhea and inflammation of mucous membranes

**¹ring** \'riŋ\ *noun* [Middle English, from Old English *hring*; akin to Old High German *hring* ring, Old Church Slavonic *krǫgŭ* circle] (before 12th century)
**1** : a circular band for holding, connecting, hanging, pulling, packing, or sealing ⟨a key *ring*⟩ ⟨a towel *ring*⟩
**2** : a circlet usually of precious metal worn on the finger
**3 a** : a circular line, figure, or object ⟨smoke *ring*⟩ **b** : an encircling arrangement ⟨a *ring* of suburbs⟩ **c** : a circular or spiral course — often used in plural in the phrase *run rings around*
**4 (1)** : an often circular space especially for exhibitions or competitions; *especially* : such a space at a circus **(2)** : a structure containing such a ring **b** : a square enclosure in which boxers or wrestlers contest
**5** : a band believed to be composed of rocky fragments revolving around a planet (as Saturn)
**6** : ANNUAL RING
**7 a** : an exclusive combination of persons for a selfish and often corrupt purpose (as to control a market) ⟨a wheat *ring*⟩ **b** : GANG
**8** : the field of a political contest : RACE
**9** : food in the shape of a circle
**10** : an arrangement of atoms represented in formulas or models in a cyclic manner — called also *cycle*
**11** : a set of mathematical elements that is closed under two binary operations of which the first forms a commutative group with the set and the second is associative over the set and is distributive with respect to the first operation
**12** *plural* **a** : a pair of usually rubber-covered metal rings suspended from a ceiling or crossbar to a height of approximately eight feet above the floor and used for hanging, swinging, and balancing feats in gymnastics **b** : an event in gymnastics competition in which the rings are used
**13** : ²BOXING ⟨ended his *ring* career⟩
**— ring·like** \'riŋ-ˌlīk\ *adjective*

**²ring** *verb* **ringed; ring·ing** \'riŋ-iŋ\ (14th century)
*transitive verb*
**1** : to provide with a ring

**2** : to place or form a ring around : ENCIRCLE ⟨police *ringed* the building⟩
**3** : GIRDLE 2
**4** : to throw a ringer over (the peg) in a game (as horseshoes or quoits)
*intransitive verb*
**1 a** : to move in a ring **b** : to rise in the air spirally
**2** : to form or take the shape of a ring

**³ring** *verb* **rang** \'raŋ\; **rung** \'rəŋ\; **ring·ing** \'riŋ-iŋ\ [Middle English, from Old English *hringan*; akin to Old Norse *hringja* to ring] (before 12th century)
*intransitive verb*
**1** : to sound resonantly or sonorously ⟨the doorbell *rang*⟩ ⟨cheers *rang* out⟩
**2 a** : to be filled with a reverberating sound : RESOUND ⟨the halls *rang* with laughter⟩ **b** : to have the sensation of being filled with a humming sound ⟨his ears *rang*⟩
**3** : to cause something to ring ⟨*ring* for the butler⟩
**4 a** : to be filled with talk or report ⟨the whole land *rang* with her fame⟩ **b** : to have great renown **c** : to sound repetitiously ⟨their praise *rang* in his ears⟩
**5** : to have a sound or character expressive of some quality ⟨a story that *rings* true⟩
**6** *chiefly British* : to make a telephone call — usually used with *up*
*transitive verb*
**1** : to cause to sound especially by striking
**2** : to make (a sound) by or as if by ringing a bell
**3** : to announce by or as if by ringing
**4** : to repeat often, loudly, or earnestly
**5 a** : to summon especially by bell **b** *chiefly British* : TELEPHONE — usually used with *up*
**— ring a bell** : to arouse a response ⟨that name *rings a bell*⟩
**— ring down the curtain** : to conclude a performance or an action
**— ring off the hook** : to ring frequently or constantly with incoming calls ⟨the telephone was *ringing off the hook*⟩
**— ring the changes** *or* **ring changes** : to run through the range of possible variations
**— ring up the curtain** : to begin a performance or an action

**⁴ring** *noun* (1549)
**1** : a set of bells
**2** : a clear resonant sound made by or resembling that made by vibrating metal
**3** : resonant tone : SONORITY

◇ WORD HISTORY **rile** English words that now have the sound \ȯi\ such as *boil* and *voice* fall into two major groups of distinct historical origin. The diphthong (vowel combination) of the *voice* group had a sound in early modern English nearly the same as present-day \ȯi\; the *boil* group, on the other hand, had a sound close to \əi\. Because the \əi\ sound of the *boil* words was virtually identical to the sound that *i* had come to acquire in words such as *price* and *write*, the two merged, so that *boil* rhymed with *bile* and *toil* with *tile*. This pronunciation remained standard into the 18th century, though literate people, under the influence of English spelling, had begun to pronounce *boil* and *toil* with the diphthong of *toy* and *choice*. By the 19th century, standard pronunciation had shifted completely, and spellings such as *pizen* or *pison* for *poison* were used by Mark Twain and other American authors to characterize uneducated rural speech. The word *roil* underwent a unique development: in the sense "to make angry" it was disassociated from the spelling *roil* and written *rile*, becoming thereby a different word. Originally a colloquialism, it has since become standard written English.

**4 :** a loud sound continued, repeated, or reverberated
**5 :** a sound or character expressive of some particular quality ⟨the story had a familiar *ring*⟩
**6 a :** the act or an instance of ringing **b :** a telephone call ⟨give me a *ring* in the morning⟩

**ring-a-le-vio** \ˌriŋ-ə-ˈlē-vē-ˌō\ *or* **ring-a-lievo** \-ˈlē-(ˌ)vō\ *noun* [alteration of earlier *ring relievo*, from ¹*ring* + *relieve*] (circa 1901)
**:** a game in which players on one team are given time to hide and are then sought out by members of the other team who try to capture them, keep them in a place of confinement, and keep them from being released by their teammates

**ring–around–a–rosy** \ˌriŋ-ə-ˌraun-də-ˈrō-zē\ *or* **ring–around–the–rosy** \-ˌraun(d)-thə-\ *noun* (circa 1886)
**:** a children's singing game in which players dance around in a circle and at a given signal squat — called also *ring-a-rosy* \ˌriŋ-ə-ˈrō-zē\

**ring-bark** \ˈriŋ-ˌbärk\ *transitive verb* (1892)
**:** GIRDLE 2

**ring binder** *noun* (1929)
**:** a loose-leaf binder in which split metal rings attached to a metal back hold the perforated sheets of paper

**ring-bolt** \ˈriŋ-ˌbōlt\ *noun* (1599)
**:** an eyebolt with a ring through its eye

**ring-bone** \-ˌbōn\ *noun* (1523)
**:** a bony outgrowth on the pastern bones of the horse usually producing lameness

**ring dance** *noun* (1600)
**:** ROUND DANCE 1

**ring-dove** \-ˌdəv\ *noun* (1538)
**1 :** a chiefly European pigeon (*Columba palumbus*) with a whitish patch on each side of the neck and wings edged with white
**2 :** a small dove (*Streptopelia risoria*) of southeastern Europe and Asia — called also *ringed turtle dove*

**ringed** \ˈriŋd\ *adjective* (14th century)
**1 :** encircled or marked with or as if with rings
**2 :** composed or formed of rings

**¹ring-er** \ˈriŋ-ər\ *noun* (15th century)
**1 :** one that sounds especially by ringing
**2 a** (1) **:** one that enters a competition under false representations **:** IMPOSTER. FAKE **b** **:** one that strongly resembles another — often used with *dead* ⟨he's a dead *ringer* for the senator⟩

**²ringer** *noun* (1863)
**:** one that encircles or puts a ring around (as a quoit or horseshoe that lodges so as to surround the peg)

**Ring-er's solution** \ˈriŋ-ərz-\ *noun* [Sidney *Ringer* (died 1910) English physician] (1893)
**:** a balanced aqueous solution that contains chloride, sodium, potassium, calcium, bicarbonate, and phosphate ions and that is used in physiological experiments to provide a medium essentially isotonic to many animal tissues — called also *Ringer solution*

**ring finger** *noun* (before 12th century)
**:** the third finger especially of the left hand counting the forefinger as the first

**ring-git** \ˈriŋ-git\ *noun, plural* **ringgit** *or* **ringgits** [Malay, literally, toothed, serrated] (1967)
— see MONEY table

**ring-ing** \ˈriŋ-iŋ\ *adjective* (14th century)
**1 :** clear and full in tone **:** RESOUNDING ⟨a *ringing* baritone⟩
**2 :** vigorously unequivocal **:** DECISIVE ⟨a *ringing* condemnation of immorality⟩
— **ring-ing-ly** \-iŋ-lē\ *adverb*

**ring-lead-er** \ˈriŋ-ˌlē-dər\ *noun* (1503)
**:** a leader of a ring of individuals engaged especially in improper or unlawful activities

**ring-let** \ˈriŋ-lət\ *noun* (1555)
**1 :** a small ring or circle
**2 :** CURL; *especially* **:** a long curl of hair

**ring-mas-ter** \ˈriŋ-ˌmas-tər\ *noun* (1873)

**:** one in charge of performances in a ring (as of a circus); *broadly* **:** a supervisor or moderator especially of a performance or presentation

**ring-neck** \-ˌnek\ *noun* (1791)
**:** a ring-necked animal

**ring-necked** \ˈriŋ-ˌnekt\ *or* **ring-neck** \ˈriŋ-ˌnek\ *adjective* (1817)
**:** having a ring of color about the neck

**ring-necked duck** *noun* (1831)
**:** an American scaup duck (*Aythya collaris*) that has a white ring around the bill and in the male a faint narrow chestnut ring encircling the neck

**ring-necked pheasant** *noun* (1834)
**:** a Eurasian pheasant (*Phasianus colchicus*) that has been widely introduced as a game bird in North America and that has a white neck ring and an iridescent green and purplish head with red wattles around the eyes

**ring-necked pheasant**

**ring off** *intransitive verb* (1882)
*chiefly British* **:** HANG UP 1

**ring-po-rous** \ˈriŋ-ˌpōr-əs, -ˌpȯr-\ *adjective* (1902)
**:** having vessels more numerous and usually larger in cross section in the springwood with a resulting more or less distinct line between the springwood and the last season's wood — compare DIFFUSE-POROUS

**ring road** *noun* (1928)
*chiefly British* **:** a highway skirting an urban area

**¹ring-side** \ˈriŋ-ˌsīd\ *noun* (1866)
**1 :** the area just outside a ring especially in which a contest occurs
**2 :** a place from which one may have a close view

**²ringside** *adjective* (1896)
**:** being at the ringside ⟨a *ringside* seat⟩

**ring spot** *noun* (1923)
**1 :** a lesion of plant tissue consisting of yellowish, purplish, or necrotic, often concentric rings
**2 :** a viral disease of plants that is characterized by ring spots

**ring stand** *noun* (circa 1865)
**:** a metal stand consisting of a long upright rod attached to a heavy rectangular base that is used with rings and clamps for supporting laboratory apparatus

**ring-straked** \ˈriŋ-ˌstrākt\ *adjective* (1611)
*archaic* **:** marked with circular stripes

**ring-tail** \-ˌtāl\ *noun* (1844)
**1 :** RACCOON
**2 :** a carnivore (*Bassariscus astutus*) of the western U.S. and Mexico that is related to and resembles the raccoon — called also *cacomistle, civet cat, ringtail cat, ringtailed cat*
**3 :** CAPUCHIN 3

**ring-tailed** \-ˌtā(ə)ld\ *adjective* (1729)
**1 :** having a tail marked with rings of differing colors
**2 :** having a tail carried in a form approximating a circle ⟨a *ring-tailed* Afghan hound⟩

**ring-taw** \-ˌtȯ\ *noun* (1828)
**:** a game of marbles in which marbles are placed in a circle on the ground and shot at from the edge of the circle with the object being to knock them out of the circle

**ring-toss** \-ˌtȯs, -ˌtäs\ *noun* (1871)
**:** a game in which the object is to toss a ring so that it will fall over an upright stick

**ring up** *transitive verb* (1937)
**1 :** to total and record especially by means of a cash register
**2 :** ACHIEVE ⟨*rang up* many social triumphs⟩

**ring-worm** \ˈriŋ-ˌwərm\ *noun* (15th century)
**:** any of several contagious fungal diseases of the skin, hair, or nails of humans and domestic

animals that are characterized by ring-shaped discolored skin patches covered with vesicles and scales

**rink** \ˈriŋk\ *noun* [Middle English (Scots) *rinc* area in which a contest takes place, from Middle French *renc* place, row — more at RANK] (1787)
**1 a :** a smooth extent of ice marked off for curling or ice hockey **b :** a surface of ice for ice-skating; *also* **:** a building containing such a rink **c :** an enclosure for roller-skating
**2 :** an alley for lawn bowling
**3 :** a team in bowls or curling

**rinky-dink** \ˈriŋ-kē-ˌdiŋk\ *adjective* [origin unknown] (1913)
**1 :** SMALL-TIME
**2 :** OLD-FASHIONED

**¹rinse** \ˈrin(t)s, *especially dialect* ˈrench\ *transitive verb* **rinsed; rins-ing** [Middle English *rincen*, from Middle French *rincer*, from (assumed) Vulgar Latin *recentiare*, from Latin *recent-, recens* fresh, recent] (14th century)
**1 :** to cleanse by flushing with liquid (as water) — often used with *out* ⟨*rinse* out the mouth⟩
**2 a :** to cleanse (as of soap used in washing) by clear water **b :** to treat (hair) with a rinse
**3 :** to remove (dirt or impurities) by washing lightly or in water only
— **rins-er** *noun*

**²rinse** *noun* (1837)
**1 :** the act or process of rinsing
**2 a :** liquid used for rinsing **b :** a solution that temporarily tints hair

**rins-ing** *noun* (1818)
**1 :** DREGS, RESIDUE — usually used in plural
**2 :** water that has been used for rinsing — usually used in plural

**rio-ja** \rē-ˈō-(ˌ)hä\ *noun, often capitalized* (1907)
**:** a wine from the Rioja region of Spain; *especially* **:** a dry red wine from this region

**¹ri-ot** \ˈrī-ət\ *noun* [Middle English, from Old French, dispute, from *rioter* to quarrel] (13th century)
**1** *archaic* **a :** profligate behavior **:** DEBAUCHERY **b :** unrestrained revelry **c :** noise, uproar, or disturbance made by revelers
**2 a :** public violence, tumult, or disorder **b :** a violent public disorder; *specifically* **:** a tumultuous disturbance of the public peace by three or more persons assembled together and acting with a common intent
**3 :** a random or disorderly profusion ⟨the woods were a *riot* of color⟩
**4 :** one that is wildly amusing ⟨the new comedy is a *riot*⟩

**²riot** *intransitive verb* (14th century)
**1 :** to indulge in revelry or wantonness
**2 :** to create or engage in a riot
— **ri-ot-er** *noun*

**riot act** *noun* [the *Riot Act*, English law of 1715 providing for the dispersal of riots upon command of legal authority] (1819)
**:** a vigorous reprimand or warning — used in the phrase *read the riot act*

**riot gun** *noun* (1916)
**:** a small arm used to disperse rioters rather than to inflict serious injury or death; *especially* **:** a short-barreled shotgun

**ri-ot-ous** \ˈrī-ə-təs\ *adjective* (15th century)
**1 a :** of the nature of a riot **:** TURBULENT **b :** participating in riot
**2 :** ABUNDANT, EXUBERANT ⟨the garden was *riotous* with flowers⟩
— **ri-ot-ous-ly** *adverb*
— **ri-ot-ous-ness** *noun*

**¹rip** \ˈrip\ *verb* **ripped; rip-ping** [probably from Flemish *rippen* to strip off roughly] (15th century)

*transitive verb*
**1 a :** to tear or split apart or open **b :** to saw or split (wood) with the grain
**2 :** to slash or slit with or as if with a sharp blade
**3 :** to hit sharply ⟨*ripped* a double to left field⟩
**4 :** to utter violently : spit out ⟨*ripped* out an oath⟩
**5 :** CRITICIZE, PUT DOWN
*intransitive verb*
**1 :** to become ripped : REND
**2 :** to rush headlong ⟨*ripped* past second base⟩
**synonym** see TEAR
**— rip into :** to tear into : ATTACK
²**rip** *noun* (1711)
**1 :** a rent made by ripping : TEAR
**2 :** CUT 5b
³**rip** *noun* [perhaps from ²*rip*] (1775)
**1 :** a body of water made rough by the meeting of opposing tides, currents, or winds
**2 :** a current of water roughened by passing over an irregular bottom
**3 :** RIP CURRENT
⁴**rip** *noun* [perhaps by shortening & alteration from *reprobate*] (1797)
**:** a dissolute person : LIBERTINE
**ri·par·i·an** \rə-'per-ē-ən, rī-\ *adjective* [Latin *riparius* — more at RIVER] (circa 1841)
**:** relating to or living or located on the bank of a natural watercourse (as a river) or sometimes of a lake or a tidewater
**riparian right** *noun* (circa 1860)
**:** a right (as access to or use of the shore, bed, and water) of one owning riparian land
**rip cord** *noun* (1907)
**1 :** a cord by which the gasbag of a balloon may be ripped open for a limited distance to release the gas quickly and so cause immediate descent
**2 :** a cord or wire pulled in making a descent to release the pilot parachute which lifts the main parachute out of its container
**rip current** *noun* (1936)
**:** a strong usually narrow surface current flowing outward from a shore that results from the return flow of waves and wind-driven water
**ripe** \'rīp\ *adjective* **rip·er; rip·est** [Middle English, from Old English *rīpe;* akin to Old English *rīpan, reopan* to reap] (before 12th century)
**1 :** fully grown and developed : MATURE
**2 :** having mature knowledge, understanding, or judgment
**3 :** of advanced years : LATE ⟨lived to a *ripe* old age⟩
**4 a :** SUITABLE, APPROPRIATE ⟨the time seemed *ripe* for the experiment⟩ **b :** fully prepared : READY ⟨the colonies were *ripe* for revolution⟩
**5 a :** brought by aging to full flavor or the best state : MELLOW ⟨*ripe* cheese⟩ **b :** SMELLY, STINKING
**6 :** ruddy, plump, or full like ripened fruit
**7 :** INDECENT ⟨*ripe* language⟩
**— ripe·ly** *adverb*
**— ripe·ness** *noun*
**rip·en** \'rī-pən, 'rī-p°m\ *verb* **rip·ened; rip·en·ing** \'rī-pə-niŋ, 'rīp-niŋ\ (1561)
*intransitive verb*
**:** to grow or become ripe
*transitive verb*
**1 :** to make ripe
**2 a :** to bring to completeness or perfection **b :** to age or cure (cheese) to develop characteristic flavor, odor, body, texture, and color **c :** to improve flavor and tenderness of (beef or game) by aging under refrigeration
**— rip·en·er** \'rī-pə-nər, 'rīp-nər\ *noun*
**ri·pie·no** \ri-'pyā-(ˌ)nō, -'pye-\ *noun, plural* **-ni** \-(ˌ)nē\ *or* **-nos** [Italian, literally, filled up] (circa 1930)
**:** TUTTI
**rip-off** \'rip-ˌóf\ *noun* (1969)
**1 :** an act or instance of stealing : THEFT; *also* **:** a financial exploitation
**2 :** a usually cheap exploitive imitation
**rip off** *transitive verb* (1967)

**1 a :** ROB; *also* **:** CHEAT, DEFRAUD **b :** STEAL
**2 :** to copy or imitate blatantly or unscrupulously
**3 :** to perform, achieve, or score quickly or easily ⟨*ripped off* 10 straight points⟩
**ri·poste** \ri-'pōst\ *noun* [French, modification of Italian *risposta*, literally, answer, from *rispondere* to respond, from Latin *respondēre*] (1707)
**1 :** a fencer's quick return thrust following a parry
**2 :** a retaliatory verbal sally : RETORT
**3 :** a retaliatory maneuver or measure
**— riposte** *verb*
**ripped** \'ript\ *adjective* (1970)
*slang* **:** being under the influence of alcohol or drugs : HIGH, STONED
**rip·per** \'ri-pər\ *noun* (1611)
**1 :** one that rips; *especially* **:** a machine used to break up solid material (as rock or ore)
**2 :** an excellent example or instance of its kind
**rip·ping** \'ri-piŋ\ *adjective* [probably from present participle of ¹*rip*] (1846)
*chiefly British* **:** EXCELLENT, DELIGHTFUL ⟨wrote me some *ripping* letters⟩ ⟨had a *ripping* time⟩
¹**rip·ple** \'ri-pəl\ *verb* **rip·pled; rip·pling** \-p(ə-)liŋ\ [perhaps frequentative of ¹*rip*] (circa 1671)
*intransitive verb*
**1 a :** to become lightly ruffled or covered with small waves **b :** to flow in small waves **c :** to fall in soft undulating folds ⟨the scarf *rippled* to the floor⟩
**2 :** to flow with a light rise and fall of sound or inflection ⟨laughter *rippled* over the audience⟩
**3 :** to move with an undulating motion or so as to cause ripples ⟨the canoe *rippled* through the water⟩
**4 :** to have or produce a ripple effect : SPREAD ⟨the news *rippled* outwards⟩
*transitive verb*
**1 :** to stir up small waves on
**2 :** to impart a wavy motion or appearance to ⟨*rippling* his arm muscles⟩
**3 :** to utter or play with a slight rise and fall of sound
**— rip·pler** \-p(ə-)lər\ *noun*
²**ripple** *noun* (1755)
**1 a :** a shallow stretch of rough water in a stream **b** (1) **:** the ruffling of the surface of water (2) **:** a small wave
**2 a :** RIPPLE MARK **b :** a sound like that of rippling water ⟨a *ripple* of laughter⟩ **c :** a usually slight noticeable effect or reaction
**— rip·ply** \'ri-p(ə-)lē\ *adjective*
**ripple effect** *noun* (1966)
**:** a spreading, pervasive, and usually unintentional effect or influence ⟨the automotive industry has a *ripple effect* on many other industries⟩ — compare DOMINO EFFECT
**ripple mark** *noun* (1833)
**1 :** one of a series of small ridges produced especially on sand by the action of wind, a current of water, or waves
**2 :** a striation across the grain of wood especially on the tangential surface
**— rip·ple-marked** \'ri-pəl-ˌmärkt\ *adjective*
¹**rip·rap** \'rip-ˌrap\ *noun* [obsolete *riprap* sound of rapping] (1833)
**1 :** a foundation or sustaining wall of stones or chunks of concrete thrown together without order (as in deep water); *also* **:** a layer of this or similar material on an embankment slope to prevent erosion
**2 :** material used for riprap
²**riprap** *transitive verb* (1848)
**1 :** to form a riprap in or upon
**2 :** to strengthen or support with a riprap
**rip-roar·ing** \'rip-'rōr-iŋ, -'rȯr-\ *adjective* (1834)
**:** noisily excited or exciting
**rip·saw** \'rip-ˌsȯ\ *noun* (1846)

**:** a coarse-toothed saw used to cut wood in the direction of the grain — compare CROSSCUT SAW
**rip·snort·er** \'rip-'snȯr-tər\ *noun* (1840)
**:** something extraordinary : HUMDINGER ⟨the finale was a *ripsnorter*⟩
**— rip·snort·ing** \-tiŋ\ *adjective*
**rip·stop** \'rip-ˌstäp\ *adjective* (1949)
**:** of, relating to, or being a fabric woven with a double thread at regular intervals so that small tears do not spread ⟨*ripstop* nylon⟩
**— ripstop** *noun*
**rip·tide** \'rip-ˌtīd\ *noun* (1862)
**:** RIP CURRENT
**Rip·u·ar·i·an** \ˌri-pyə-'wer-ē-ən\ *adjective* [Medieval Latin *Ripuarius*] (1781)
**:** of, relating to, or constituting a group of Franks settling in the 4th century on the Rhine near Cologne
**Rip van Win·kle** \ˌrip-(ˌ)van-'wiŋ-kəl, -vən-\ *noun*
**:** a ne'er-do-well in a story in Washington Irving's *Sketch Book* who sleeps for 20 years
¹**rise** \'rīz\ *intransitive verb* **rose** \'rōz\; **ris·en** \'ri-z°n\; **ris·ing** \'rī-ziŋ\ [Middle English, from Old English *rīsan;* akin to Old High German *rīsan* to rise] (before 12th century)
**1 a :** to assume an upright position especially from lying, kneeling, or sitting **b :** to get up from sleep or from one's bed
**2 :** to return from death
**3 :** to take up arms ⟨*rise* in rebellion⟩
**4 :** to respond warmly : APPLAUD — usually used with *to* ⟨the audience *rose* to her verve and wit⟩
**5** *chiefly British* **:** to end a session : ADJOURN
**6 :** to appear above the horizon ⟨the sun *rises* at six⟩
**7 a :** to move upward : ASCEND **b :** to increase in height, size, or volume ⟨the river *rose* after the heavy rains⟩
**8 :** to extend above other objects ⟨mountain peaks *rose* to the west⟩
**9 a :** to become heartened or elated ⟨his spirits *rose*⟩ **b :** to increase in fervor or intensity ⟨my anger *rose* as I thought about the insult⟩
**10 a :** to attain a higher level or rank ⟨officers who *rose* from the ranks⟩ **b :** to increase in quantity or number
**11 a :** to take place : HAPPEN **b :** to come into being : ORIGINATE
**12 :** to follow as a consequence : RESULT
**13 :** to exert oneself to meet a challenge ⟨*rise* to the occasion⟩
**synonym** see SPRING
²**rise** \'rīz *also* 'rīs\ *noun* (15th century)
**1 a :** a spot higher than surrounding ground : HILLTOP **b :** an upward slope ⟨a *rise* in the road⟩
**2 :** an act of rising or a state of being risen: as **a :** a movement upward : ASCENT **b :** emergence (as of the sun) above the horizon **c :** the upward movement of a fish to seize food or bait
**3 :** BEGINNING, ORIGIN ⟨the river had its *rise* in the mountain⟩
**4 :** the distance or elevation of one point above another
**5 a :** an increase especially in amount, number, or volume **b** *chiefly British* **:** RAISE 3b **c :** an increase in price, value, rate, or sum ⟨a *rise* in the cost of living⟩
**6 :** an angry reaction ⟨got a *rise* out of him⟩
**7 :** the distance from the crotch to the waistline on pants
**ris·er** \'rī-zər\ *noun* (15th century)
**1 :** one that rises (as from sleep)
**2 :** the upright member between two stair treads
**3 :** a stage platform on which performers are placed for greater visibility
**4 :** a vertical pipe (as for water or gas) or a vertical portion of an electric wiring system
**5 :** one of the straps that connects a parachutist's harness with the shroud lines

**ris·i·bil·i·ty** \ˌri-zə-'bi-lə-tē\ *noun, plural* **-ties** (1620)
**1** : LAUGHTER
**2** : the ability or inclination to laugh — often used in plural ⟨our *risibilities* support us as we skim over the surface of a deep issue —J. A. Pike⟩

**ris·i·ble** \'ri-zə-bəl\ *adjective* [Late Latin *risibilis*, from Latin *risus*, past participle of *ridēre* to laugh] (1557)
**1 a** : capable of laughing **b** : disposed to laugh
**2** : arousing or provoking laughter; *especially* : LAUGHABLE
**3** : associated with, relating to, or used in laughter ⟨*risible* muscles⟩

**ris·i·bles** \-bəlz\ *noun plural* (1785)
: sense of the ridiculous : sense of humor

¹**ris·ing** \'rī-ziŋ\ *noun* (14th century)
: INSURRECTION, UPRISING

²**rising** *adverb* (circa 1772)
: approaching a stated age : NEARLY ⟨a red cow *rising* four years old —*Lancaster (Pennsylvania) Journal*⟩

**rising diphthong** *noun* (1888)
: a diphthong in which the second element is more sonorous than the first (as \wi\ in \'kwit\ *quit*)

**rising rhythm** *noun* (1881)
: rhythm with stress occurring regularly on the last syllable of each foot — compare FALLING RHYTHM

¹**risk** \'risk\ *noun* [French *risque*, from Italian *risco*] (circa 1661)
**1** : possibility of loss or injury : PERIL
**2** : someone or something that creates or suggests a hazard
**3 a** : the chance of loss or the perils to the subject matter of an insurance contract; *also* : the degree of probability of such loss **b** : a person or thing that is a specified hazard to an insurer ⟨a poor *risk* for insurance⟩ **c** : an insurance hazard from a specified cause or source ⟨war *risk*⟩
— **risk·less** \'ris-kləs\ *adjective*
— **at risk** : exposed to a usually specified danger or loss ⟨patients *at risk* of infection⟩

²**risk** *transitive verb* (circa 1687)
**1** : to expose to hazard or danger ⟨*risked* her life⟩
**2** : to incur the risk or danger of ⟨*risked* breaking his neck⟩
— **risk·er** *noun*

**risk capital** *noun* (1944)
: VENTURE CAPITAL

**risky** \'ris-kē\ *adjective* **risk·i·er; -est** (1827)
: attended with risk or danger : HAZARDOUS
**synonym** see DANGEROUS
— **risk·i·ness** *noun*

**ri·sor·gi·men·to** \(ˌ)rē-ˌzȯr-ji-'men-(ˌ)tō, -ˌsȯr-\ *noun, plural* **-tos** [Italian, literally, rising again, from *risorgere* to rise again, from Latin *resurgere* — more at RESURRECTION] (1902)
: a time of renewal or renaissance : REVIVAL; *specifically* : the 19th century movement for Italian political unity

**ri·sot·to** \ri-'sȯ-(ˌ)tō, -'zȯ-\ *noun, plural* **-tos** [Italian, from *riso* rice — more at RICE] (1855)
: rice cooked in meat stock and seasoned (as with Parmesan cheese or saffron)

**ris·qué** \ri-'skā\ *adjective* [French, from past participle of *risquer* to risk, from *risque*] (1867)
: verging on impropriety or indecency : OFF-COLOR

**Rit·a·lin** \'ri-tə-lən\ *trademark*
— used for methylphenidate

**ri·tard** \ri-'tärd\ *noun* (circa 1890)
: RITARDANDO

¹**ri·tar·dan·do** \ri-ˌtär-'dän-(ˌ)dō, ˌrē-\ *adverb or adjective* [Italian, from Latin *retardandum*, gerund of *retardare* to retard] (circa 1811)
: with a gradual slackening in tempo — used as a direction in music

²**ritardando** *noun, plural* **-dos** (1889)

: a ritardando passage

**rite** \'rīt\ *noun* [Middle English, from Latin *ritus*; akin to Greek *arithmos* number — more at ARITHMETIC] (14th century)
**1 a** : a prescribed form or manner governing the words or actions for a ceremony **b** : the liturgy of a church or group of churches
**2** : a ceremonial act or action ⟨initiation *rites*⟩
**3** : a division of the Christian church using a distinctive liturgy

**rite de pas·sage** \ˌrēt-də-pa-'säzh, -pä-\ *noun, plural* **rites de passage** \ˌrēt(s)-də-\ [French] (1911)
: RITE OF PASSAGE

**rite of passage** (1909)
: a ritual associated with a crisis or a change of status (as marriage, illness, or death) for an individual

**ri·tor·nel·lo** \ˌri-tər-'ne-(ˌ)lō, ˌri-ˌtȯr-\ *noun, plural* **-nel·li** \-'ne-(ˌ)lē\ *or* **-nellos** [Italian, diminutive of *ritorno* return, from *ritornare* to return, from *ri-* re- + *tornare* to turn, to turn on a lathe — more at TURN] (1675)
**1 a** : a short recurrent instrumental passage in a vocal composition **b** : an instrumental interlude in early opera
**2** : a tutti passage in a concerto or rondo refrain

¹**rit·u·al** \'ri-chə-wəl, -chəl; 'rich-wəl\ *adjective* [Latin *ritualis*, from *ritus* rite] (1570)
**1** : of or relating to rites or a ritual : CEREMONIAL ⟨a *ritual* dance⟩
**2** : according to religious law or social custom ⟨*ritual* purity⟩
— **rit·u·al·ly** *adverb*

²**ritual** *noun* (1649)
**1** : the established form for a ceremony; *specifically* : the order of words prescribed for a religious ceremony
**2 a** : ritual observance; *specifically* : a system of rites **b** : a ceremonial act or action **c** : a customarily repeated often formal act or series of acts

**rit·u·al·ism** \'ri-chə-wə-ˌli-zəm, -chə-ˌli-; 'rich-wə-\ *noun* (1843)
**1** : the use of ritual
**2** : excessive devotion to ritual
— **rit·u·al·ist** \-list\ *noun*
— **rit·u·al·is·tic** \ˌri-chə-wə-'lis-tik, -chə-'lis-; ˌrich-wə-\ *adjective*
— **rit·u·al·is·ti·cal·ly** \-ti-k(ə-)lē\ *adverb*

**rit·u·al·ize** \-ˌlīz\ *verb* **-ized; -iz·ing** (1842)
*intransitive verb*
: to practice ritualism
*transitive verb*
**1** : to make a ritual of
**2** : to impose a ritual on
— **rit·u·al·i·za·tion** \ˌri-chə-wə-lə-'zā-shən, -chə-lə-; ˌrich-wə-\ *noun*

**ritzy** \'rit-sē\ *adjective* **ritz·i·er; -est** [*Ritz* hotels, noted for their opulence] (1920)
**1** : SNOBBISH
**2** : ostentatiously smart : FASHIONABLE, POSH
— **ritz·i·ness** *noun*

¹**ri·val** \'rī-vəl\ *noun* [Middle French or Latin; Middle French, from Latin *rivalis* one using the same stream as another, rival in love, from *rivalis* of a stream, from *rivus* stream — more at RUN] (1577)
**1 a** : one of two or more striving to reach or obtain something that only one can possess **b** : one striving for competitive advantage
**2** *obsolete* : COMPANION, ASSOCIATE
**3** : one that equals another in desired qualities : PEER ◆

²**rival** *adjective* (1590)
: having the same pretensions or claims : COMPETING

³**rival** *verb* **ri·valed** *or* **ri·valled; ri·val·ing** *or* **ri·val·ling** \'rīv-(ə-)liŋ\ (1605)
*intransitive verb*
: to act as a rival : COMPETE
*transitive verb*
**1** : to be in competition with
**2** : to strive to equal or excel : EMULATE

**3** : to possess qualities or aptitudes that approach or equal (those of another)

**ri·val·rous** \'rī-vəl-rəs\ *adjective* (1812)
: given to rivalry : COMPETITIVE

**ri·val·ry** \'rī-vəl-rē\ *noun, plural* **-ries** (1598)
: the act of rivaling : the state of being a rival : COMPETITION

**rive** \'rīv\ *verb* **rived** \'rīvd\; **riv·en** \'ri-vən\ *also* **rived; riv·ing** \'rī-viŋ\ [Middle English, from Old Norse *rīfa*; akin to Greek *ereipein* to tear down] (14th century)
*transitive verb*
**1 a** : to wrench open or tear apart or to pieces : REND **b** : to split with force or violence ⟨lightning *rived* the tree⟩
**2 a** : to divide into pieces : SHATTER **b** : FRACTURE
*intransitive verb*
: to become split : CRACK
**synonym** see TEAR

**riv·er** \'ri-vər\ *noun, often attributive* [Middle English *rivere*, from Old French, from (assumed) Vulgar Latin *riparia*, from Latin, feminine of *riparius* riparian, from *ripa* bank, shore; perhaps akin to Greek *ereipein* to tear down] (14th century)
**1 a** : a natural stream of water of usually considerable volume **b** : WATERCOURSE
**2 a** : something resembling a river ⟨a *river* of lava⟩ **b** *plural* : large or overwhelming quantities ⟨drank *rivers* of coffee⟩
**word history** see RIVAL
— **up the river** : to or in prison ⟨takes the rap and goes *up the river* —Nigel Balchin⟩

**riv·er·bank** \'ri-vər-ˌbaŋk\ *noun* (1565)
: the bank of a river

**riv·er·bed** \-ˌbed\ *noun* (1833)
: the channel occupied by a river

**river blindness** *noun* (1953)
: ONCHOCERCIASIS

**riv·er·boat** \-ˌbōt\ *noun* (1565)
: a boat for use on a river

**river duck** *noun* (1837)
: DABBLER b

**riv·er·front** \-ˌfrənt\ *noun* (1855)
: the land or area along a river

**river horse** *noun* (1601)
: HIPPOPOTAMUS

**riv·er·ine** \'ri-və-ˌrīn, -ˌrēn\ *adjective* (1860)
**1** : relating to, formed by, or resembling a river
**2** : living or situated on the banks of a river

**riv·er·side** \'ri-vər-ˌsīd\ *noun* (14th century)

◇ WORD HISTORY
**rival** *Rival* is borrowed, directly or indirectly through French, from Latin *rivalis*, which, as an adjective derivative of *rivus* "brook or stream," meant "of a brook or stream." As a noun, *rivalis* occurs only in its plural forms in Latin texts, referring literally to those who used the same stream as a source of water. Just as neighbors are likely to dispute each other's rights to a common source of water, so too contention is inevitable when two or more persons strive to obtain something that only one can possess. Thus Latin *rivalis* also developed a sense relating to competition in other areas, especially love, and in this sense it came into French and English. Despite its aquatic background, *rival* is unrelated to *river*, which descends ultimately not from Latin *rivus*, but rather from an unrelated word *ripa* "bank, shore." The Old French word *rivere* or *riviere* (from an unattested spoken Latin word *riparia*) meant "riverbank" or "land along a river" as well as "watercourse, stream."

: the side or bank of a river

**riv·er·ward** \-wərd\ *or* **riv·er·wards** \-wərdz\ *adverb or adjective* (1833)
: toward a river

**¹riv·et** \'ri-vət\ *noun* [Middle English *ryvette*, from Middle French *rivet*, from *river* to attach] (15th century)
: a headed pin or bolt of metal used for uniting two or more pieces by passing the shank through a hole in each piece and then beating or pressing down the plain end so as to make a second head

**²rivet** *transitive verb* (15th century)
**1 :** to fasten with or as if with rivets
**2 :** to upset the end or point of (as a metallic pin, rod, or bolt) by beating or pressing so as to form a head
**3 :** to fasten firmly ⟨they *rivet* these feelings . . . tightly together —Michael Novak⟩
**4 :** to attract and hold (as the attention) completely
— **riv·et·er** *noun*

**riv·et·ing** \'ri-və-tiŋ\ *adjective* (1677)
: having the power to fix the attention **:** ENGROSSING, FASCINATING
— **riv·et·ing·ly** \-lē\ *adverb*

**ri·vi·era** \,ri-vē-'er-ə, ri-'vyer-\ *noun, often capitalized* [from the *Riviera*, region in southeastern France and northwestern Italy] (1766)
: a coastal region frequented as a resort area and usually marked by a mild climate

**ri·vi·ère** \,ri-vē-'er, ri-'vyer\ *noun* [French, literally, river, from Old French *rivere*] (1879)
: a necklace of precious stones (as diamonds)

**riv·u·let** \'ri-vyə-lət, -və-\ *noun* [Italian *rivoletto*, diminutive of *rivolo*, from Latin *rivulus*, diminutive of *rivus* stream — more at RUN] (1587)
: a small stream

**¹ri·yal** \rē-'yäl, -'yal\ *noun* [Arabic *riyāl*, from Spanish *real* real] (1928)
— see MONEY table

**²riyal** *variant of* RIAL

**RN** \,är-'en\ *noun* (1903)
: REGISTERED NURSE

**RNA** \,är-(,)en-'ā\ *noun* [*ribonucleic acid*] (1948)
: any of various nucleic acids that contain ribose and uracil as structural components and are associated with the control of cellular chemical activities — compare MESSENGER RNA, RIBOSOMAL RNA, TRANSFER RNA

**RNA polymerase** *noun* (circa 1962)
: any of a group of enzymes that promote the synthesis of RNA using DNA or RNA as a template

**RN·ase** \,är-'en-,ās, -,āz\ *or* **RNA·ase** \,är-(,)en-'ā-,ās, -'ā-,āz\ *noun* [*RNA + -ase*] (1957)
: RIBONUCLEASE

**¹roach** \'rōch\ *noun, plural* **roach** *also* **roach·es** [Middle English *roche*, from Middle French] (13th century)
**1 :** a silver-green European freshwater cyprinid fish (*Rutilus rutilus*); *also* **:** any of various related fishes (as some shiners)
**2 :** any of several American freshwater sunfishes (family Centrarchidae)

**²roach** *noun* [origin unknown] (1794)
**1 :** a curved cut in the edge of a sail to prevent chafing or to secure a better fit
**2 :** a roll of hair brushed straight back from the forehead or side of the head

**³roach** *transitive verb* (1818)
**1 :** to cut (as a horse's mane) so that the remainder stands upright
**2 :** to cause to arch; *specifically* **:** to brush (the hair) in a roach — often used with *up*

**⁴roach** *noun* [by shortening] (circa 1848)
**1 :** COCKROACH
**2 :** the butt of a marijuana cigarette

**roach back** *noun* (1874)
: an arched back (as of a dog)

**roach clip** *noun* (1968)
: a metal clip that resembles tweezers and is used by marijuana smokers to hold a roach — called also *roach holder*

**road** \'rōd\ *noun* [Middle English *rode*, from Old English *rād* ride, journey; akin to Old English *rīdan* to ride] (14th century)
**1 :** ROADSTEAD — often used in plural
**2 a :** an open way for vehicles, persons, and animals; *especially* **:** one lying outside of an urban district **:** HIGHWAY **b** **:** ROADBED 2b
**3 :** ROUTE, PATH
**4 :** RAILWAY
**5 :** a series of scheduled visits or appearances (as games or performances) in several locations or the travel necessary to make these visits ⟨the team is on the *road*⟩ ⟨on tour with the musical's *road* company⟩
— **road·less** \'rōd-ləs\ *adjective*
— **down the road :** in or into the future

**road·abil·i·ty** \,rō-də-'bi-lə-tē\ *noun* (circa 1914)
: the qualities (as steadiness and balance) desirable in an automobile on the road

**road agent** *noun* (1863)
: a highwayman who formerly operated especially on stage routes in unsettled districts

**road·bed** \'rōd-,bed\ *noun* (circa 1840)
**1 a :** the bed on which the ties, rails, and ballast of a railroad rest **b** **:** the ballast or the upper surface of the ballast on which the ties rest
**2 a :** the earth foundation of a road prepared for surfacing **b** **:** the part of the surface of a road traveled by vehicles

**road·block** \-,bläk\ *noun* (1940)
**1 a :** a barricade often with traps or mines for holding up an enemy at a point on a road covered by fire **b** **:** a road barricade set up especially by law enforcement officers
**2 :** an obstruction in a road
**3 :** something (as a fact, condition, or countermeasure) that blocks progress or prevents accomplishment of an objective
— **roadblock** *transitive verb*

**road hog** *noun* (1891)
: a driver of an automotive vehicle who obstructs others especially by occupying part of another's traffic lane

**road·hold·ing** \'rōd-,hōl-diŋ\ *noun* (1932)
*chiefly British* **:** the qualities of an automobile that tend to make it respond precisely to the driver's steering

**road·house** \'rōd-,haus\ *noun* (1857)
: an inn or tavern usually outside city limits providing liquor and usually meals, dancing, and often gambling

**road·ie** \'rō-dē\ *noun* [*road + -ie*] (1969)
: one who works (as by moving heavy equipment) for traveling entertainers

**road·kill** \'rōd-,kil\ *noun* (1979)
: an animal that has been killed on a road by a motor vehicle
— **road–killed** \-,kild\ *adjective*

**road map** *noun* (1883)
**1 :** a map showing roads especially for automobile travel
**2 a :** a detailed plan to guide progress toward a goal **b** **:** a detailed explanation

**road metal** *noun* (1818)
: broken stone or cinders used in making and repairing roads or ballasting railroads

**road racing** *noun* (1828)
: racing over public roads; *especially* **:** automobile racing over roads or over a closed course designed to simulate public roads
— **road race** *noun*

**road roller** *noun* (circa 1876)
: one that rolls roadways; *specifically* **:** a machine with heavy wide smooth rollers for compacting roadbeds

**road·run·ner** \'rōd-,rə-nər\ *noun* (1856)

**roadrunner**

: a largely terrestrial bird (*Geococcyx californianus*) of the cuckoo family that has a long tail and a crest, is a speedy runner, and ranges from the southwestern U.S. to Mexico; *also* **:** a closely related bird (*G. velox*) of Mexico and Central America

**road show** *noun* (1908)
**1 :** a theatrical performance given by a troupe on tour
**2 :** a special engagement of a new motion picture usually at increased prices
**3 :** a promotional presentation or meeting conducted in a series of locations

**road·side** \'rōd-,sīd\ *noun* (1744)
: the strip of land along a road **:** the side of a road
— **roadside** *adjective*

**road·stead** \'rōd-,sted\ *noun* (1556)
: a place less enclosed than a harbor where ships may ride at anchor

**road·ster** \'rōd-stər\ *noun* (1818)
**1 a :** a horse for riding or driving on roads **b** **:** a utility saddle horse of the hackney type
**2 a :** a light carriage **:** BUGGY **b** **:** an automobile with an open body that seats two and has a folding fabric top and a luggage compartment in the rear

**road test** *noun* (1906)
**1 :** a test of a vehicle under practical operating conditions on the road
**2 :** a test on the road of a person's driving ability as a requirement for a driver's license
— **road test** *transitive verb*

**road·way** \'rōd-,wā\ *noun* (1600)
**1 a :** the strip of land over which a road passes **b** **:** ROAD; *specifically* **:** ROADBED 2b
**2 :** the part of a bridge used by vehicles

**road·work** \-,wərk\ *noun* (1869)
**1 :** work done in constructing or repairing roads
**2 :** conditioning for an athletic contest (as a boxing match) consisting mainly of long runs

**road·wor·thy** \-,wər-the\ *adjective* (1819)
: fit for use on the road
— **road·wor·thi·ness** *noun*

**roam** \'rōm\ *verb* [Middle English *romen*] (14th century)
*intransitive verb*
**1 :** to go from place to place without purpose or direction **:** WANDER
**2 :** to travel purposefully unhindered through a wide area ⟨cattle *roaming* in search of water⟩
*transitive verb*
: to range or wander over
*synonym* see WANDER
— **roam** *noun*
— **roam·er** *noun*

**¹roan** \'rōn *also* 'rō-ən\ *adjective* [Middle French, from Old Spanish *roano*] (1530)
: having the base color (as red, black, or brown) muted and lightened by admixture of white hairs ⟨a *roan* horse⟩ ⟨a *roan* calf⟩

**²roan** *noun* (1580)
**1 :** an animal (as a horse) with a roan coat — usually used of a red roan when unqualified
**2 :** the color of a roan horse — used especially when the base color is red

**³roan** *noun* [origin unknown] (1818)
: sheepskin tanned with sumac and colored and finished to imitate morocco

**¹roar** \'rōr, 'ror\ *verb* [Middle English *roren*, from Old English *rārian*; akin to Old High German *rērēn* to bleat] (before 12th century)
*intransitive verb*
**1 a :** to utter or emit a full loud prolonged sound **b** **:** to sing or shout with full force
**2 a :** to make or emit a loud confused sound (as background reverberation or rumbling) **b** **:** to laugh loudly

**3 a :** to be boisterous or disorderly **b :** to proceed or rush with great noise or commotion
**4 :** to make a loud noise during inhalation (as that of a horse affected with roaring)
*transitive verb*
**1 :** to utter or proclaim with a roar
**2 :** to cause to roar
²**roar** *noun* (14th century)
**1 :** the deep cry of a wild animal
**2 :** a loud deep cry (as of pain or anger)
**3 :** a loud continuous confused sound ⟨the *roar* of the crowd⟩
**4 :** a boisterous outcry
**roar·er** \'rōr-ər, 'ror-\ *noun* (14th century)
**1 :** one that roars
**2 :** a horse subject to roaring
¹**roar·ing** \'rōr-iŋ, 'ror-\ *adjective* (14th century)
**1 :** making or characterized by a sound resembling a roar **:** LOUD ⟨*roaring* applause⟩
**2 :** marked by prosperity especially of a temporary nature **:** BOOMING
**3 :** INTENSE, UTTER ⟨in the *roaring* heat⟩ ⟨a *roaring* success⟩
**— roar·ing·ly** *adverb*
²**roaring** *adverb* (1697)
**:** EXTREMELY ⟨was *roaring* hungry —Herman Wouk⟩
³**roaring** *noun* (1823)
**:** noisy inhalation in a horse caused by nerve paralysis and muscular atrophy and constituting an unsoundness
**roaring boy** *noun* (circa 1590)
**:** a noisy street bully especially of Elizabethan and Jacobean England who intimidated passersby
¹**roast** \'rōst\ *verb* [Middle English *rosten*, from Old French *rostir*, of Germanic origin; akin to Old High German *rōsten* to roast] (13th century)
*transitive verb*
**1 a :** to cook by exposing to dry heat (as in an oven or before a fire) or by surrounding with hot embers, sand, or stones ⟨*roast* a potato in ashes⟩ **b :** to dry and parch by exposure to heat ⟨*roast* coffee⟩
**2 :** to heat (inorganic material) with access of air and without fusing to effect change (as expulsion of volatile matter, oxidation, or removal of sulfur from sulfide ores)
**3 :** to heat to excess ⟨*roasted* by the summer sun⟩
**4 :** to subject to severe criticism or ridicule ⟨films have been *roasted* by most critics —H. J. Seldes⟩
**5 :** to honor (a person) at a roast
*intransitive verb*
**1 :** to cook food by heat
**2 :** to undergo being roasted
²**roast** *noun* (14th century)
**1 :** a piece of meat suitable for roasting
**2 :** a gathering at which food is roasted before an open fire or in hot ashes or sand
**3 :** an act or process of roasting; *specifically* **:** severe banter or criticism
**4 :** a banquet honoring a person (as a celebrity) who is subjected to humorous tongue-in-cheek ridicule by friends
³**roast** *adjective* (14th century)
**:** that has been roasted ⟨*roast* beef⟩
**roast·er** \'rōs-tər\ *noun* (15th century)
**1 :** one that roasts
**2 :** a device for roasting
**3 :** something adapted to roasting: as **a :** a suckling pig **b :** a bird fit for roasting; *especially* **:** a young chicken of more than four pounds (1.8 kilograms) dressed weight
**roast·ing ear** \'rōs-tiŋ-,ir, *sense 2 usually* 'rō-sᵉn-,ir *or* 'rōs-,nir\ *noun* (1650)
**1 :** an ear of young corn roasted or suitable for roasting usually in the husk
**2** *chiefly Southern & Midland* **:** an ear of corn suitable for boiling or steaming
**rob** \'räb\ *verb* **robbed; rob·bing** [Middle English *robben*, from Old French *rober*, of

Germanic origin; akin to Old High German *roubōn* to rob — more at REAVE] (13th century)
*transitive verb*
**1 a** (1) **:** to take something away from by force **:** steal from (2) **:** to take personal property from by violence or threat **b** (1) **:** to remove valuables without right from (a place) (2) **:** to take the contents of (a receptacle) **c :** to take away as loot **:** STEAL ⟨*rob* jewelry⟩
**2 a :** to deprive of something due, expected, or desired **b :** to withhold unjustly or injuriously
*intransitive verb*
**:** to commit robbery ☐
**— rob·ber** *noun*
**ro·ba·lo** \rō-'bä-(,)lō\ *noun, plural* **-los** *or* **-lo** [Spanish] (circa 1890)
**:** SNOOK 1
**ro·band** \'rō-,band, -bənd\ *noun* [probably from Middle Dutch *rabant*] (1762)
**:** a piece of spun yarn or marline used to fasten the head of a sail to a spar
**robber baron** *noun* (1878)
**:** an American capitalist of the latter part of the 19th century who became wealthy through exploitation (as of natural resources, governmental influence, or low wage scales)
**robber fly** *noun* (1871)
**:** any of a family (Asilidae) of predaceous flies including some closely resembling bumblebees
**rob·bery** \'rä-b(ə-)rē\ *noun, plural* **-ber·ies** (13th century)
**:** the act or practice of robbing; *specifically* **:** larceny from the person or presence of another by violence or threat
¹**robe** \'rōb\ *noun* [Middle English, from Old French, robe, booty, of Germanic origin; akin to Old High German *roubōn* to rob] (13th century)
**1 a :** a long flowing outer garment; *especially* **:** one used for ceremonial occasions or as a symbol of office or profession **b :** a loose garment (as a bathrobe) for informal wear especially at home
**2 :** COVERING, MANTLE ⟨peaks on the axis of the range in their *robes* of snow and light —John Muir (died 1914)⟩
**3 :** a covering of pelts or fabric for the lower body used while driving or at outdoor events
²**robe** *verb* **robed; rob·ing** (14th century)
*transitive verb*
**:** to clothe or cover with or as if with a robe
*intransitive verb*
**1 :** to put on a robe
**2 :** DRESS
**robe de cham·bre** \,rōb-də-'shäⁿbrᵊ, -'shämbrə\ *noun, plural* **robes de chambre** \,rōb(z)-\ [French] (1731)
**:** DRESSING GOWN
**rob·in** \'rä-bən\ *noun* [short for *robin redbreast*] (1549)
**1 a :** a small chiefly European thrush (*Erithacus rubecula*) resembling a warbler and having a brownish olive back and orangish face and breast **b :** any of various Old World songbirds that are related to or resemble the European robin
**2 :** a large North American thrush (*Turdus migratorius*) with olivaceous to slate gray upperparts, blackish head and tail, black and whitish streaked throat, and dull reddish breast and underparts
**Rob·in Good·fel·low** \'rä-bən-'gùd-,fe-(,)lō\ *noun*
**:** a mischievous sprite in English folklore
**Robin Hood** \-,hùd\ *noun* [*Robin Hood*, legendary English outlaw who gave to the poor what he stole from the rich] (1597)
**:** a person or group likened to a heroic outlaw; *especially* **:** one that robs the rich and gives to the poor
**robin red·breast** \-'red-,brest\ *noun* [Middle English, from *Robin*, nickname for *Robert*] (15th century)

**:** ROBIN
**Rob·in·son Cru·soe** \'rä-bə(n)-sən-'krü-(,)sō\ *noun*
**:** a shipwrecked sailor in Defoe's *Robinson Crusoe* who lives for many years on a desert island
**Rob·in·son projection** \'rä-bən-sən-\ *noun* [Arthur H. *Robinson* (born 1915) American geographer] (1978)
**:** a compromise map projection showing the poles as lines rather than points and more accurately portraying high latitutude lands and water to land ratio
**ro·ble** \'rō-(,)blā\ *noun* [American Spanish, from Spanish, oak, from Latin *robur*] (1864)
**:** any of several oaks of California and Mexico
**ro·bot** \'rō-,bät, -bət\ *noun* [Czech, from *robota* compulsory labor; akin to Old High German *arabeit* trouble, Latin *orbus* orphaned — more at ORPHAN] (1923)
**1 a :** a machine that looks like a human being and performs various complex acts (as walking or talking) of a human being; *also* **:** a similar but fictional machine whose lack of capacity for human emotions is often emphasized **b :** an efficient insensitive person who functions automatically
**2 :** a device that automatically performs complicated often repetitive tasks
**3 :** a mechanism guided by automatic controls ◆
**— ro·bot·ism** \'rō-,bä-,ti-zəm, -bə-\ *noun*
**ro·bot·ic** \rō-'bä-tik, rə-\ *adjective* (1941)
**1 :** of or relating to mechanical robots
**2 :** having the characteristics of a robot ⟨performs with *robotic* consistency⟩
**— ro·bot·i·cal·ly** \-ti-k(ə-)lē\ *adverb*

---

**☐ USAGE**
**rob** Sense *transitive verb* 1c, in which the direct object is the thing stolen, is sometimes considered to be wrong, or perhaps archaic. The sense has been in use since the 13th century and is found in earlier literature ⟨contrive to *rob* the honey and subvert the hive —John Dryden⟩. It is still in use though not as common as other senses ⟨then *robbed* $100 after the clerk fled —*Springfield (Massachusetts) Morning Union*⟩.

---

**◇ WORD HISTORY**
**robot** In 1923 the play *R.U.R.*, by Czech author Karel Čapek, opened in London and New York. The title in the Czech version as well as its English translation stands for "Rossum's Universal Robots." In Čapek's drama this is the name of a company formed by Rossum, an English scientist, to manufacture "robots," humanlike machines that do manual labor. Another scientist decides to make the machines more human, which he does by gradually adding such traits as the capacity to feel pain. Eventually the robots, created to serve humans, come to dominate them completely. Čapek based his coinage *robot* on the Czech word *robota* "compulsory labor." Highly successful in its day, his play caught the imagination of the public. *Robot* was soon used generically for a humanoid machine but then also for a human who has become machinelike and stolid as a result of performing mindless tasks. Appropriately, given the origin of *robot*, the word *robotics* was also first used in a work of fiction, by the American writer Isaac Asimov.

---

\ə\ abut \ᵊ\ kitten \ər\ further \a\ ash \ā\ ace
\ä\ mop, mar \aù\ out \ch\ chin \e\ bet \ē\ easy
\g\ go \i\ hit \ī\ ice \j\ job \ŋ\ sing \ō\ go
\ò\ law \òi\ boy \th\ thin \ṯh\ the \ü\ loot \ù\ foot
\y\ yet \zh\ vision *see also* Guide to Pronunciation

**ro·bot·ics** \rō-'bä-tiks\ *noun plural but singular in construction* (1941)
: technology dealing with the design, construction, and operation of robots in automation
*word history* see ROBOT

**ro·bot·i·za·tion** \,rō-,bä-tə-'zā-shən, -bə-\ *noun* (circa 1927)
**1** : AUTOMATION
**2** : the process of turning a human being into a robot

**ro·bot·ize** \'rō-,bä-,tīz, -bə-\ *transitive verb* **-ized; -iz·ing** (1927)
**1** : to make automatic : equip with robots
**2** : to turn (a human being) into a robot

**Rob Roy** \'räb-'rȯi\ *noun* [*Rob Roy*, nickname of Robert McGregor (died 1734) Scottish freebooter] (1919)
: a manhattan made with Scotch whisky

**ro·bust** \rō-'bəst, 'rō-(,)bəst\ *adjective* [Latin *robustus* oaken, strong, from *robor-, robur* oak, strength] (1549)
**1 a** : having or exhibiting strength or vigorous health **b** : having or showing vigor, strength, or firmness ⟨a *robust* debate⟩ ⟨a *robust* faith⟩ **c** : strongly formed or constructed : STURDY ⟨a *robust* plastic⟩
**2** : ROUGH, RUDE ⟨stories . . . laden with *robust*, down-home imagery —*Playboy*⟩
**3** : requiring strength or vigor ⟨*robust* work⟩
**4** : FULL-BODIED ⟨*robust* coffee⟩; *also* : HEARTY ⟨a *robust* dinner⟩
**5** : relating to, resembling, or being any of the primitive, relatively large, heavyset hominids (genus *Australopithecus* and especially *A. robustus* and *A. boisei*) characterized especially by heavy molars and small incisors adapted to a vegetarian diet — compare GRACILE 3
*synonym* see HEALTHY
— **ro·bust·ly** *adverb*
— **ro·bust·ness** \-'bəs(t)-nəs, -(,)bəs(t)-\ *noun*

**ro·bus·ta** \rō-'bəs-tə\ *noun, often attributive* [New Latin *robusta*, specific epithet of *Coffea robusta*, synonym of *Coffea canephora*] (1909)
**1** : a coffee (*Coffea canephora*) that is indigenous to central Africa but has been introduced elsewhere (as in Java)
**2 a** : the seed of robusta coffee **b** : coffee brewed from the seed of robusta coffee

**ro·bus·tious** \rō-'bəs-chəs\ *adjective* (circa 1548)
**1** : ROBUST
**2** : vigorous in a rough or unrefined way : BOISTEROUS
— **ro·bus·tious·ly** *adverb*
— **ro·bus·tious·ness** *noun*

**roc** \'räk\ *noun* [Arabic *rukhkh*]
: a legendary bird of great size and strength believed to inhabit the Indian Ocean area

**ro·caille** \rō-'kī, rä-\ *noun* [French, literally, stone debris, from Middle French *roquailles*, plural, rocky terrain, from *roc* rock, alteration of *roche*, from (assumed) Vulgar Latin *rocca*] (1856)
**1** : a style of ornament developed in the 18th century and characterized by sinuous foliate forms
**2** : ROCOCO

**Roche limit** \'rȯsh-, 'rōsh-\ *noun* [E. A. *Roche* (died 1883) French mathematician] (1889)
: the distance between a planet's center and its satellite within which the satellite cannot approach without becoming disrupted

**Ro·chelle salt** \rō-'shel-\ *noun* [La *Rochelle*, France] (1753)
: a crystalline salt $KNaC_4H_4O_6 \cdot 4H_2O$ that is a mild purgative

**roche mou·ton·née** \'rȯsh-,mü-t³n-'ā, 'rōsh-\ *noun, plural* **roches mou·ton·nées** \*same or* -'āz\ [French, literally, fleecy rock] (1843)
: an elongate rounded ice-sculptured hillock of bedrock

**roch·et** \'rä-chət\ *noun* [Middle English, from Middle French, from Old French, from (as-

sumed) Old French *roc* coat, of Germanic origin; akin to Old High German *roc* coat] (13th century)
: a white linen vestment resembling a surplice with close-fitting sleeves worn especially by bishops and privileged prelates

**¹rock** \'räk\ *verb* [Middle English *rokken*, from Old English *roccian*; akin to Old High German *rucken* to cause to move] (12th century)
*transitive verb*
**1 a** : to move back and forth in or as if in a cradle **b** : to wash (placer gravel) in a cradle
**2 a** : to cause to sway back and forth ⟨a boat *rocked* by the waves⟩ **b** (1) : to cause to shake violently (2) : to daze with or as if with a vigorous blow ⟨a hard right *rocked* the contender⟩ (3) : to astonish or disturb greatly ⟨the scandal *rocked* the community⟩
*intransitive verb*
**1** : to become moved backward and forward under often violent impact; *also* : to move gently back and forth
**2** : to move forward at a steady pace; *also* : to move forward at a high speed ⟨the train *rocked* through the countryside⟩
**3** : to sing, dance to, or play rock music
*synonym* see SHAKE
— **rock the boat** : to do something that disturbs the equilibrium of a situation

**²rock** *noun, often attributive* (1823)
**1** : a rocking movement
**2** : popular music usually played on electronically amplified instruments and characterized by a persistent heavily accented beat, much repetition of simple phrases, and often country, folk, and blues elements

**³rock** *noun* [Middle English *roc*, from Middle Dutch *rocke*; akin to Old High German *rocko* distaff] (14th century)
**1** : DISTAFF
**2** : the wool or flax on a distaff

**⁴rock** *noun* [Middle English *rokke*, from Old North French *roque*, from (assumed) Vulgar Latin *rocca*] (14th century)
**1** : a large mass of stone forming a cliff, promontory, or peak
**2** : a concreted mass of stony material; *also* : broken pieces of such masses
**3** : consolidated or unconsolidated solid mineral matter; *also* : a particular mass of it
**4 a** : something like a rock in firmness: (1) : FOUNDATION, SUPPORT (2) : REFUGE ⟨a *rock* of independent thought . . . in an ocean of parochialism —Thomas Molnar⟩ **b** : something that threatens or causes disaster — often used in plural
**5 a** : a flavored stick candy with color running through **b** : ROCK CANDY
**6** *slang* **a** : GEM **b** : DIAMOND
**7 a** : a small crystallized mass of crack cocaine **b** : CRACK 9
— **rock** *adjective*
— **rock·like** \'räk-,līk\ *adjective*
— **between a rock and a hard place** *also* **between the rock and the hard place** : in a difficult or uncomfortable position with no attractive way out
— **on the rocks 1** : in or into a state of destruction or wreckage ⟨their marriage went *on the rocks*⟩ **2** : on ice cubes ⟨bourbon *on the rocks*⟩

**rock·a·bil·ly** \'rä-kə-,bi-lē\ *noun* [²*rock* + -a- (as in *rock-a-bye*, phrase used to put a child to sleep) + hill*billy*] (1956)
: pop music marked by features of rock and country music

**rock and roll** *noun* (1954)
: ²ROCK 2

**rock and roller** *noun* (1956)
: ROCKER 3

**rock·a·way** \'rä-kə-,wā\ *noun* [perhaps from *Rockaway*, New Jersey] (1846)
: a light low four-wheel carriage with a fixed top and open sides

**rock bass** *noun* (1811)

: a brown spotted sunfish (*Ambloplites rupestris*) found especially in the upper Mississippi valley and Great Lakes region

**rock–bottom** *adjective* (1884)
: being the very lowest ⟨*rock-bottom* off-season rates⟩; *also* : FUNDAMENTAL ⟨the *rock-bottom* question⟩

**rock bottom** *noun* (1890)
: the lowest or most fundamental part or level

**rock·bound** \'räk-,baund\ *adjective* (1840)
: fringed, surrounded, or covered with rocks : ROCKY

**rock brake** *noun* (circa 1850)
: any of several ferns that grow chiefly on or among rocks

**rock candy** *noun* (1723)
**1** : boiled sugar crystallized in large masses on string
**2** : ⁴ROCK 5a

**rock climbing** *noun* (1892)
: mountain climbing on rocky cliffs
— **rock climb** *intransitive verb*
— **rock climber** *noun*

**Rock Cornish** *noun* (1956)
: a crossbred domestic fowl produced by interbreeding Cornish and white Plymouth Rock fowls and used especially for small roasters

**rock crystal** *noun* (1666)
: CRYSTAL 1

**rock dove** *noun* (1655)
: a bluish gray dove (*Columba livia*) of Europe and Asia that is the ancestor of many domesticated pigeons and of the feral pigeons found in cities and towns throughout most of the world — called also *rock pigeon*

**rock·er** \'rä-kər\ *noun* (1760)
**1 a** : either of two curving pieces of wood or metal on which an object (as a cradle) rocks **b** : any of various objects (as a rocking chair or an infant's toy having a seat placed between side pieces) that rock on rockers **c** : any of various objects in the form of a rocker or with parts resembling a rocker (as a skate with a curved blade) **d** (1) : any of the curved stripes at the lower part of a chevron worn by a non-commissioned officer above the rank of sergeant (2) : the curved stripe at the upper part of a chevron worn by a chief petty officer
**2** : any of various devices that work with a rocking motion
**3** : a rock performer, song, or enthusiast
— **off one's rocker** : in a state of extreme confusion or insanity ⟨went *off her rocker*, and had to be put away —Mervyn Wall⟩

**rocker arm** *noun* (1860)
: a center-pivoted lever to push an automotive engine valve down

**rock·ery** \'rä-k(ə-)rē\ *noun, plural* **-er·ies** [⁴*rock* + -*ery*] (1845)
*chiefly British* : ROCK GARDEN

**¹rock·et** \'rä-kət, rä-'ket\ *noun* [Middle French *roquette*, from Old Italian *rochetta*, diminutive of *ruca* arugula, from Latin *eruca*] (1530)
: any of several plants of the mustard family: as **a** : ARUGULA **b** : DAME'S ROCKET

**²rock·et** \'rä-kət\ *noun, often attributive* [Italian *rocchetta*, literally, small distaff, from diminutive of *rocca* distaff, of Germanic origin; akin to Old High German *rocko* distaff] (1611)
**1 a** : a firework consisting of a case partly filled with a combustible composition fastened to a guiding stick and propelled through the air by the rearward discharge of the gases liberated by combustion **b** : a similar device used as an incendiary weapon or as a propelling unit (as for a lifesaving line)
**2** : a jet engine that operates on the same principle as the firework rocket, consists essentially of a combustion chamber and an exhaust nozzle, carries either liquid or solid propellants which provide the fuel and oxygen needed for combustion and thus make the engine independent of the oxygen of the air, and is used especially for the propulsion of a missile (as a bomb or shell) or a vehicle (as an airplane)

**3 :** a rocket-propelled bomb, missile, or projectile

³**rock·et** \'rä-kət\ (1837)
*transitive verb*
**:** to convey or propel by means of or as if by a rocket
*intransitive verb*
**1 :** to rise up swiftly, spectacularly, and with force
**2 :** to travel rapidly in or as if in a rocket

**rock·e·teer** \,rä-kə-'tir\ *noun* (1832)
**1 :** one who fires, pilots, or rides in a rocket
**2 :** a scientist who specializes in rocketry

**rocket plane** *noun* (1928)
**:** an airplane propelled by rockets

**rock·et·ry** \'rä-kə-trē\ *noun* (1930)
**:** the study of, experimentation with, or use of rockets

**rocket ship** *noun* (1927)
**:** a rocket-propelled spaceship

**rocket sled** *noun* (1954)
**:** a rocket-propelled vehicle that runs usually on a single rail and that is used especially in aeronautical experimentation

**rock·fall** \'räk-,fȯl\ *noun* (1924)
**:** a mass of falling or fallen rocks

**rock·fish** \-,fish\ *noun* (1598)
**:** any of various important market fishes that live among rocks or on rocky bottoms: as **a :** any of numerous scorpaenid fishes (especially genus *Sebastes*) **b :** STRIPED BASS **c :** any of several groupers

**rock garden** *noun* (1836)
**:** a garden laid out among rocks or decorated with rocks and adapted for the growth of particular kinds of plants (as alpines)

**rock hind** *noun* (circa 1867)
**:** a red-spotted tan to olive brown grouper (*Epinephelus adscensionis*) of the Atlantic especially from Massachusetts to southeastern Brazil

**rock·hop·per** \'räk-,hä-pər\ *noun* (1875)
**:** a small penguin (*Eudyptes crestatus*) with a short thick bill and a yellow crest

**rock hound** *noun* (1915)
**1 :** a specialist in geology
**2 :** an amateur rock and mineral collector
**— rock·hound·ing** \'räk-,haun-diŋ\ *noun*

**rock·i·ness** \'rä-kē-nəs\ *noun* (1611)
**:** the quality or state of being rocky

**rocking chair** *noun* (1766)
**:** a chair mounted on rockers

**rocking horse** *noun* (1724)
**:** a toy horse mounted on rockers — called also *hobbyhorse*

**rock·ling** \'rä-kliŋ\ *noun* (1602)
**:** any of several small rather elongate marine bony fishes (especially genera *Enchelyopus* and *Gaidropsarus*) of the cod family

**rock lobster** *noun* (1884)
**1 :** SPINY LOBSTER
**2 :** the flesh of a spiny lobster especially when canned or frozen for use as food

**rock maple** *noun* (1775)
**:** SUGAR MAPLE 1

**rock 'n' roll, rock 'n' roller** *variant of* ROCK AND ROLL, ROCK AND ROLLER

**rock oil** *noun* (1668)
**:** PETROLEUM

**rock pigeon** *noun* (1611)
**:** ROCK DOVE

**rock rabbit** *noun* (1840)
**1 :** HYRAX
**2 :** PIKA

**rock–ribbed** \'räk-'ribd\ *adjective* (1776)
**1 :** ¹ROCKY 1
**2 :** firm and inflexible in doctrine or integrity ⟨a *rock-ribbed* conservative community —John Hale⟩

**rock·rose** \'räk-,rōz\ *noun* (1731)
**:** any of various shrubs or woody herbs (family Cistaceae, the rockrose family) with simple entire leaves and a capsular fruit

**rock salt** *noun* (1707)

**:** common salt occurring in solid form as a mineral; *also* **:** salt artificially prepared in large crystals or masses

**rock·shaft** \'räk-,shaft\ *noun* (circa 1864)
**:** a shaft that oscillates on its journals instead of revolving

**rock tripe** *noun* (1854)
**:** any of various dark leathery umbilicate foliose lichens (as of the genus *Umbilicaria*) that are widely distributed on rocks in boreal and alpine areas and are sometimes used as food

**rock wallaby** *noun* (1841)
**:** any of various medium-sized kangaroos (genus *Petrogale*)

**rock·weed** \'räk-,wēd\ *noun* (1626)
**:** any of various coarse brown algae (family Fucaceae, especially genera *Fucus* and *Ascophyllum*) growing in marine environments attached to rocks

**rock wool** *noun* (circa 1909)
**:** mineral wool made by blowing a jet of steam through molten rock (as limestone or siliceous rock) or through slag and used chiefly for heat and sound insulation

¹**rocky** \'rä-kē\ *adjective* **rock·i·er; -est** [Middle English *rokky,* from *rokke* rock] (15th century)
**1 :** abounding in or consisting of rocks
**2 :** difficult to impress or affect **:** INSENSITIVE
**3 :** firmly held **:** STEADFAST

²**rocky** *adjective* **rock·i·er; -est** [¹*rock*] (1737)
**1 :** UNSTABLE, WOBBLY
**2 :** physically upset or mentally confused (as from drinking excessively)
**3 :** marked by obstacles **:** DIFFICULT ⟨a financially *rocky* year —Michael Murray⟩

**Rocky Mountain sheep** *noun* [*Rocky Mountains,* North America] (1817)
**:** BIGHORN

**Rocky Mountain spotted fever** *noun* (1905)
**:** an acute disease that is characterized by chills, fever, prostration, pains in muscles and joints, and a red to purple eruption and that is caused by a rickettsia (*Rickettsia rickettii*) usually transmitted by an ixodid tick and especially either the American dog tick or a wood tick (*Dermacentor andersoni*)

¹**ro·co·co** \rə-'kō-(,)kō, rō-kə-'kō\ *noun* (1840)
**:** rococo work or style

²**rococo** *adjective* [French, irregular from *rocaille* rocaille] (1841)
**1 a :** of or relating to an artistic style especially of the 18th century characterized by fanciful curved asymmetrical forms and elaborate ornamentation **b :** of or relating to an 18th century musical style marked by light gay ornamentation and departure from thorough-bass and polyphony
**2 :** excessively ornate or intricate

**rod** \'räd\ *noun* [Middle English, from Old English *rodd;* akin to Old Norse *rudda* club] (before 12th century)
**1 a** (1) **:** a straight slender stick growing on or cut from a tree or bush (2) **:** OSIER (3) **:** a stick or bundle of twigs used to punish; *also* **:** PUNISHMENT (4) **:** a shepherd's cudgel (5) **:** a pole with a line and usually a reel attached for fishing **b** (1) **:** a slender bar (as of wood or metal) (2) **:** a bar or staff for measuring (3) **:** SCEPTER; *also* **:** a wand or staff carried as a badge of office (as of marshal)
**2 a :** a unit of length — see WEIGHT table **b :** a square rod
**3 :** any of the long rod-shaped photosensitive receptors in the retina responsive to faint light — compare CONE 3a
**4 :** a rod-shaped bacterium
**5** *slang* **:** HANDGUN
**— rod·less** \-ləs\ *adjective*
**— rod·like** \-,līk\ *adjective*

**rode** *past and chiefly dialect past participle of* RIDE

**ro·dent** \'rō-dᵊnt\ *noun* [ultimately from Latin *rodent-, rodens,* present participle of *rodere* to

gnaw; akin to Latin *radere* to scrape, scratch, Sanskrit *radati* he gnaws] (1859)
**1 :** any of an order (Rodentia) of relatively small gnawing mammals (as a mouse, a squirrel, or a beaver) that have in both jaws a single pair of incisors with a chisel-shaped edge
**2 :** a small mammal (as a rabbit or a shrew) other than a true rodent
**— rodent** *adjective*

**ro·den·ti·cide** \rō-'den-tə-,sīd\ *noun* (circa 1935)
**:** an agent that kills, repels, or controls rodents

**rodent ulcer** *noun* [Latin *rodent-, rodens* gnawing] (1853)
**:** a chronic persisting ulcer of the exposed skin and especially of the face that is destructive locally, spreads slowly, and is usually a carcinoma derived from basal cells — called also *rodent cancer*

¹**ro·deo** \'rō-dē-,ō, rə-'dā-(,)ō\ *noun, plural* **ro·de·os** [Spanish, from *rodear* to surround, from *rueda* wheel, from Latin *rota* — more at ROLL] (1834)
**1 :** ROUNDUP
**2 a :** a public performance featuring bronco riding, calf roping, steer wrestling, and Brahma bull riding **b :** a contest resembling a rodeo

²**rodeo** *intransitive verb* (1951)
**:** to participate in a rodeo

**rod·man** \'räd-mən, -,man\ *noun* (1853)
**:** a surveyor's assistant who holds the leveling rod

**ro·do·mon·tade** \,rä-də-mən-'tād, ,rō-, -'täd\ *noun* [Middle French, from Italian *Rodomonte,* character in *Orlando Innamorato* by Matteo M. Boiardo] (1612)
**1 :** a bragging speech
**2 :** vain boasting or bluster **:** RANT
**— rodomontade** *adjective*

¹**roe** \'rō\ *noun, plural* **roe** *or* **roes** [Middle English *ro,* from Old English *rā;* akin to Old High German *rēh* roe] (before 12th century)
**:** DOE

²**roe** *noun* [Middle English *roof, roughe, row;* akin to Old Norse *hrogn* roe and probably to Lithuanian *kurkulai* frog's eggs] (15th century)
**1 :** the eggs of a fish especially when still enclosed in the ovarian membrane
**2 :** the eggs or ovaries of an invertebrate (as the coral of a lobster)

**roe·buck** \'rō-,bək\ *noun, plural* **roebuck** *or* **roebucks** (14th century)
**:** ROE DEER; *especially* **:** the male roe deer

**roe deer** *noun* (1575)
**:** either of two small European or Asian deer (*Capreolus capreolus* and *C. pygarus*) that have erect cylindrical antlers forked at the summit, are reddish brown in summer and grayish in winter, have a white rump patch, and are noted for their nimbleness and grace

roe deer

¹**roent·gen** \'rent-gən, 'rənt-, -jən, -shən\ *adjective* [International Scientific Vocabulary, from Wilhelm *Röntgen*] (1896)
**:** of or relating to X rays ⟨*roentgen* examinations⟩

²**roentgen** *noun* (1922)
**:** the international unit of x-radiation or gamma radiation equal to the amount of radiation that produces in one cubic centimeter of dry air at 0°C and standard atmospheric pressure

\ə\ **abut** \ᵊ\ **kitten** \ər\ **further** \a\ **ash** \ā\ **ace**
\ä\ **mop, mar** \aú\ **out** \ch\ **chin** \e\ **bet** \ē\ **easy**
\g\ **go** \i\ **hit** \ī\ **ice** \j\ **job** \ŋ\ **sing** \ō\ **go**
\ȯ\ **law** \ȯi\ **boy** \th\ **thin** \th\ **the** \ü\ **loot** \ú\ **foot**
\y\ **yet** \zh\ **vision** *see also* Guide to Pronunciation

ionization of either sign equal to one electro-static unit of charge

**roent·gen·o·gram** \-gə-nə-ˌgram, -jə-, -shə-\ *noun* [International Scientific Vocabulary] (circa 1904)
: a photograph made with X rays

**roent·gen·og·ra·phy** \ˌrent-gə-ˈnä-grə-fē, ˌrənt-, -jə-, -shə-\ *noun* [International Scientific Vocabulary] (1905)
: photography by means of X rays
— **roent·gen·o·graph·ic** \-nə-ˈgra-fik\ *adjective*
— **roent·gen·o·graph·i·cal·ly** \-fi-k(ə-)lē\ *adverb*

**roent·gen·ol·o·gy** \-ˈnä-lə-jē\ *noun* [International Scientific Vocabulary] (1905)
: a branch of radiology that deals with the use of X rays for diagnosis or treatment of disease
— **roent·gen·o·log·ic** \-nə-ˈlä-jik\ *or*
**roent·gen·o·log·i·cal** \-ji-kəl\ *adjective*
— **roent·gen·o·log·i·cal·ly** \-ji-k(ə-)lē\ *adverb*
— **roent·gen·ol·o·gist** \-ˈnä-lə-jist\ *noun*

**roentgen ray** *noun, often 1st R capitalized* (circa 1890)
: X RAY

**ro·ga·tion** \rō-ˈgā-shən\ *noun* [Middle English *rogacion*, from Late Latin *rogation-, rogatio*, from Latin, questioning, from *rogare* to ask — more at RIGHT] (14th century)
**1** : LITANY, SUPPLICATION
**2** : the religious observance of the Rogation Days — often used in plural

**Rogation Day** *noun* (15th century)
: any of the days of prayer especially for the harvest observed on the three days before Ascension Day and by Roman Catholics also on April 25

**rog·er** \ˈrä-jər\ *interjection* [from *Roger*, former communications code word for the letter *r*] (circa 1941)
— used especially in radio and signaling to indicate that a message has been received and understood

**¹rogue** \ˈrōg\ *noun* [origin unknown] (1561)
**1** : VAGRANT, TRAMP
**2** : a dishonest or worthless person : SCOUNDREL
**3** : a mischievous person : SCAMP
**4** : a horse inclined to shirk or misbehave
**5** : an individual exhibiting a chance and usually inferior biological variation
— **rogu·ish** \ˈrō-gish\ *adjective*
— **rogu·ish·ly** *adverb*
— **rogu·ish·ness** *noun*

**²rogue** *intransitive verb* **rogued; rogu·ing** *or* **rogue·ing** (1766)
: to weed out inferior, diseased, or nontypical individuals from a crop plant or a field

**³rogue** *adjective* (1872)
**1** *of an animal* : being vicious and destructive
**2** : resembling or suggesting a rogue elephant especially in being isolated and dangerous or uncontrollable ⟨capsized by a *rogue* wave⟩

**rogue elephant** *noun* (1859)
: a vicious elephant that separates from the herd and roams alone

**rogu·ery** \ˈrō-g(ə-)rē\ *noun, plural* **-er·ies** (1592)
**1** : an act or behavior characteristic of a rogue
**2** : mischievous play

**rogues' gallery** *noun* (1859)
: a collection of pictures of persons arrested as criminals; *also* : a collection or list likened to a rogues' gallery ⟨a *rogues' gallery* of infectious diseases⟩

**roil** \ˈrȯi(ə)l, *verb transitive 2 is also* ˈrī(ə)l\ *verb* [origin unknown] (1590)
*transitive verb*
**1 a** : to make turbid by stirring up the sediment or dregs of **b** : to stir up : DISTURB, DISORDER
**2** : RILE 1
*intransitive verb*
: to move turbulently : be in a state of turbulence or agitation

**word history** see RILE

**roily** \ˈrȯi-lē\ *adjective* (1823)
**1** : full of sediment or dregs : MUDDY
**2** : TURBULENT ⟨*roily* waters⟩

**¹rois·ter** \ˈrȯi-stər\ *noun* [Middle French *rustre* lout, alteration of *ruste*, from *ruste*, adjective, rude, rough, from Latin *rusticus* rural — more at RUSTIC] (1551)
*archaic* : one that roisters : ROISTERER

**²roister** *intransitive verb* **rois·tered; rois·ter·ing** \-st(ə-)riŋ\ (1582)
: to engage in noisy revelry : CAROUSE
— **rois·ter·er** \-stər-ər\ *noun*
— **rois·ter·ous** \-st(ə-)rəs\ *adjective*
— **rois·ter·ous·ly** *adverb*

**Ro·land** \ˈrō-lənd\ *noun* [French]
: a stalwart defender of the Christians against the Saracens in the Charlemagne legends who is killed at Roncesvalles

**role** *also* **rôle** \ˈrōl\ *noun* [French *rôle*, literally, roll, from Old French *rolle*] (1606)
**1 a** : a character assigned or assumed (2) : a socially expected behavior pattern usually determined by an individual's status in a particular society **b** : a part played by an actor or singer
**2** : a function or part performed especially in a particular operation or process ⟨played a major *role* in the negotiations⟩
**3** : an identifier attached to an index term to show functional relationships between terms

**role model** *noun* (1957)
: a person whose behavior in a particular role is imitated by others

**role–play** \ˈrōl-ˌplā, -ˈplā\ (1949)
*transitive verb*
: ACT OUT ⟨students were asked to *role-play* the thoughts and feelings of each character —R. G. Lambert⟩
*intransitive verb*
: to play a role

**rolf** \ˈrȯlf *also* ˈrȯf\ *transitive verb, often capitalized* (1970)
: to practice Rolfing on
— **rolf·er** \ˈrȯl-fər *also* ˈrȯ-\ *noun, often capitalized*

**Rolf·ing** \ˈrȯl-fiŋ *also* ˈrȯ-\ *service mark*
— used for a system of muscle massage intended to serve as both physical and emotional therapy

**¹roll** \ˈrōl\ *noun* [Middle English *rolle*, from Old French, from Latin *rotulus*, diminutive of *rota* wheel; akin to Old High German *rad* wheel, Welsh *rhod*, Sanskrit *ratha* wagon] (13th century)
**1 a** (1) : a written document that may be rolled up : SCROLL; *specifically* : a document containing an official or formal record ⟨the *rolls* of parliament⟩ (2) : a manuscript book **b** : a list of names or related items : CATALOG **c** : an official list: as (1) : MUSTER ROLL (2) : a list of members of a school or class or of members of a legislative body
**2** : something that is rolled up into a cylinder or ball or rounded as if rolled: as **a** : a quantity (as of fabric or paper) rolled up to form a single package **b** : a hairdo in which some or all of the hair is rolled or curled up or under ⟨a pageboy *roll*⟩ **c** : any of various food preparations rolled up for cooking or serving; *especially* : a small piece of baked yeast dough **d** : a cylindrical twist of tobacco **e** : a flexible case (as of leather) in which articles may be rolled and fastened by straps or clasps **f** (1) : paper money folded or rolled into a wad (2) *slang* : BANKROLL
**3** : something that performs a rolling action or movement : ROLLER: as **a** : a wheel for making decorative lines on book covers; *also* : a design impressed by such a tool **b** : a typewriter platen

**²roll** *verb* [Middle English, from Middle French *roller*, from (assumed) Vulgar Latin *rotulare*, from Latin *rotulus*] (14th century)
*transitive verb*

**1 a** : to impel forward by causing to turn over and over on a surface **b** : to cause to revolve by turning over and over on or as if on an axis **c** : to cause to move in a circular manner **d** : to form into a mass by turning over and over **e** : to impel forward with an easy continuous motion
**2 a** : to put a wrapping around : ENFOLD, ENVELOP **b** : to wrap round on itself : shape into a ball or roll; *also* : to produce by such shaping ⟨*rolled* his own cigarettes⟩
**3 a** : to press, spread, or level with a roller : make smooth, even, or compact ⟨hulled and *rolled* oats⟩ **b** : to spread out : EXTEND ⟨*roll* out the red carpet⟩
**4 a** : to move on rollers or wheels **b** : to cause to begin operating or moving ⟨*roll* the cameras⟩
**5 a** : to sound with a full reverberating tone ⟨*rolled* out the words⟩ **b** : to make a continuous beating sound upon : sound a roll upon ⟨*rolled* their drums⟩ **c** : to utter with a trill ⟨*rolled* his r's⟩ **d** : to play (a chord) in arpeggio style
**6** : to rob (a drunk, sleeping, or unconscious person) usually by going through the pockets
*intransitive verb*
**1 a** : to move along a surface by rotation without sliding **b** (1) : to turn over and over ⟨the children *rolled* in the grass⟩ (2) : to luxuriate in an abundant supply : WALLOW ⟨fairly *rolling* in money⟩
**2 a** : to move onward or around as if by completing a revolution : ELAPSE, PASS ⟨the months *roll* on⟩ **b** : to shift the gaze continually ⟨eyes *rolling* in terror⟩ **c** : to revolve on an axis
**3** : to move about : ROAM, WANDER
**4 a** : to go forward in an easy, gentle, or undulating manner ⟨the waves *rolled* in⟩ **b** : to flow in a continuous stream : POUR ⟨money was *rolling* in⟩ **c** : to flow as part of a stream of words **d** : to have an undulating contour ⟨*rolling* prairie⟩ **e** : to lie extended : STRETCH
**5 a** : to travel in a vehicle **b** : to become carried on a stream **c** : to move on wheels
**6 a** : to make a deep reverberating sound ⟨the thunder *rolls*⟩ **b** : TRILL
**7 a** : to swing from side to side ⟨the ship heaved and *rolled*⟩ **b** : to walk with a swinging gait : SWAY **c** : to move so as to lessen the impact of a blow — used with *with* ⟨*rolled* with the punch⟩
**8 a** : to take the form of a cylinder or ball **b** : to respond to rolling in a specified way
**9 a** : to get under way : begin to move or operate **b** : to move forward : develop and maintain impetus; *especially* : to proceed or progress with notable ease or success ⟨the team was *rolling*⟩
**10 a** : BOWL **b** : to execute a somersault
**11** *of a football quarterback* : to run toward one flank usually parallel to the line of scrimmage especially before throwing a pass — often used with *out*
— **roll the bones** : to shoot craps

**³roll** *noun* (1688)
**1 a** : a sound produced by rapid strokes on a drum **b** : a sonorous and often rhythmical flow of speech **c** : a heavy reverberatory sound ⟨the *roll* of cannon⟩ **d** : a chord in arpeggio style **e** : a trill of some birds (as a canary)
**2** : a rolling movement or an action or process involving such movement ⟨a *roll* of the dice⟩ ⟨an airplane's takeoff *roll*⟩: as **a** : a swaying movement of the body **b** : a side-to-side movement (as of a ship or train) **c** (1) : a flight maneuver in which a complete revolution about the longitudinal axis of an airplane is made with the horizontal direction of flight being approximately maintained (2) : the motion of an aircraft or spacecraft about its longitudinal axis **d** : SOMERSAULT **e** : the movement of a curling stone after impact with another stone

**— on a roll** : in the midst of a series of successes : on a hot streak — sometimes used with a modifier ⟨has been *on a* brilliant *roll*⟩

**roll·back** \'rōl-ˌbak\ *noun* (1942)
: the act or an instance of rolling back ⟨a government-ordered *rollback* of gasoline prices⟩

**roll back** *transitive verb* (1942)
**1** : to reduce (as a commodity price) to or toward a previous level on a national scale
**2** : to cause to retreat or withdraw : push back
**3** : RESCIND ⟨attempted to *roll back* antipollution standards⟩

**roll bar** *noun* (circa 1952)
: an overhead metal bar on an automobile that is designed to protect the occupant in case of a rollover

**roll cage** *noun* (1966)
: a protective framework of metal bars encasing the driver of a vehicle (as a racing car)

**roll call** *noun* (1775)
**1** : the act or an instance of calling off a list of names (as for checking attendance); *also* : a time for a roll call
**2** : ⁶LIST 1

¹**roll·er** \'rō-lər\ *noun* (13th century)
**1 a** : a revolving cylinder over or on which something is moved or which is used to press, shape, spread, or smooth something **b** : a cylinder or rod on which something (as a shade) is rolled up
**2 a** : a long heavy ocean wave **b** : a tumbler pigeon
**3** : one that rolls or performs a rolling operation
**4** : a slowly rolling ground ball

²**rol·ler** \'rō-lər\ *noun* [German, from *rollen* to roll, reverberate, from Middle French *roller* — more at ROLL] (1678)
**1** : any of numerous mostly brightly colored nonpasserine Old World birds (family Coraciidae) that perform rolling aerial dives during courtship displays
**2** : a canary having a song in which the notes are soft and run together

**roller bearing** *noun* (1857)
: a bearing in which the journal rotates in peripheral contact with a number of rollers usually contained in a cage

**roll·er–coast·er** \'rō-lər-ˌkō-stər, 'rō-lə-ˌkō-\ *adjective* (1940)
: marked by numerous ups and downs ⟨an entertainer's *roller-coaster* career⟩

**roll·er coast·er** \'rō-lər-ˌkō-stər, 'rō-lē-ˌkō-\ *noun* (1888)
**1** : an elevated railway (as in an amusement park) constructed with sharp curves and steep inclines on which cars roll
**2** : something resembling a roller coaster; *especially* : behavior, events, or experiences characterized by sudden and extreme changes ⟨an emotional *roller coaster*⟩

**Roller Derby** *service mark*
— used for an entertainment involving two roller-skating teams on an oval track in which each team attempts to maneuver a skater into position to score points by circling the track and lapping opponents within a given time period

**roller rink** *noun* (1885)
: RINK 1c

**roller skate** *noun* (1863)
: a shoe with a set of wheels attached for skating over a flat surface; *also* : a metal frame with wheels attached that can be fitted to the sole of a shoe
**— roller–skate** *intransitive verb*
**— roller skater** *noun*

**roller towel** *noun* (1845)
: an endless towel hung from a roller

---

**Rolle's theorem** \'rōlz-, 'rōlz-\ *noun* [Michel *Rolle* (died 1719) French mathematician] (circa 1891)
: a theorem in mathematics: if a curve is continuous, crosses the x-axis at two points, and has a tangent at every point between the two intercepts, its tangent is parallel to the x-axis at some point between the intercepts

**roll film** *noun* (1895)
: a strip of film for still camera use wound on a spool

**rol·lick** \'rä-lik\ *intransitive verb* [origin unknown] (1826)
: to move or behave in a carefree joyous manner : FROLIC
**— rollick** *noun*

**rol·lick·ing** \'rä-li-kiŋ\ *adjective* (1811)
: boisterously carefree, joyful, or high-spirited ⟨a *rollicking* adventure film⟩

**rolling hitch** *noun* (circa 1769)
: a hitch for fastening a line to a spar or to the standing part of another line that will not slip when the pull is parallel to the spar or line — see KNOT illustration

**rolling mill** *noun* (1787)
: an establishment where metal is rolled into plates and bars

**rolling pin** *noun* (circa 1589)
: a long cylinder for rolling out dough

**rolling stock** *noun* (1853)
: the wheeled vehicles owned and used by a railroad or motor carrier

**roll–neck** \'rōl-ˌnek\ *noun, often attributive* (1943)
*British* : TURTLENECK
**— roll–necked** \-ˌnekt\ *adjective*

**roll–off** \'rōl-ˌóf\ *noun* (1947)
: a play-off match in bowling

**roll–out** \'rō-ˌlaút\ *noun* (1952)
**1** : the public introduction of a new aircraft; *broadly* : the widespread public introduction of a new product
**2** : a football play in which the quarterback rolls to the left or right

**roll out** (1884)
*intransitive verb*
: to get out of bed
*transitive verb*
: to introduce (as a new product) especially for widespread sale to the public

**roll·over** \'rō-ˌlō-vər\ *noun* (1945)
**1** : the act or process of rolling over
**2** : a motor vehicle accident in which the vehicle overturns

**roll over** *transitive verb* (1949)
**1 a** : to defer payment of (an obligation) **b** : to renegotiate the terms of (a financial agreement)
**2** : to place (invested funds) in a new investment of the same kind : REINVEST ⟨*roll over* IRA funds⟩

**roll–over arm** *noun* (circa 1925)
: a fully upholstered chair or sofa arm curving outward from the seat

**roll·top desk** \'rōl-ˌtäp-\ *noun* (1887)
: a writing desk with a sliding cover often of parallel slats fastened to a flexible backing

**roll up** (1859)
*transitive verb*
: to increase or acquire by successive accumulations : ACCUMULATE ⟨*rolled up* a large majority⟩
*intransitive verb*
**1** : to become larger by successive accumulations
**2** : to arrive in a vehicle

**rolltop desk**

¹**ro·ly–po·ly** \ˌrō-lē-'pō-lē\ *adjective* [reduplication of *roly,* from ²*roll*] (1820)
: being short and pudgy : ROTUND

²**roly–poly** *noun, plural* **-lies** (1836)
**1** : a roly-poly person or thing

---

**2** *British* : a sweet dough spread with a filling, rolled, and baked or steamed — called also *roly-poly pudding*

**Rom** \'rōm\ *noun, plural* **Rom** *also* **Roma** \'rō-mə\ [Romany, married man, husband, male Gypsy, from Sanskrit *ḍomba, ḍoma* low caste male musician] (1841)
: GYPSY 1

**ROM** \'räm\ *noun* (1966)
: READ-ONLY MEMORY

**Ro·ma·ic** \rō-'mā-ik\ *noun* [New Greek *Rhōmaiikos,* from Greek *Rhōmaïkos* Roman, from *Rhōmē* Rome] (1810)
: the modern Greek vernacular
**— Romaic** *adjective*

**ro·maine** \rō-'mān, 'rō-\ *noun* [French, from feminine of *romain* Roman, from Latin *Romanus*] (1907)
: a lettuce that belongs to a cultivar of garden lettuce (*Lactuca sativa*) and has long crisp leaves and columnar heads — called also *cos lettuce*

**ro·man** \rō-'mäⁿ\ *noun* [French, from Old French *romans* romance] (1765)
: a metrical romance

¹**Ro·man** \'rō-mən\ *noun* [partly from Middle English, from Old English, from Latin *Romanus,* adjective & noun, from *Roma* Rome; partly from Middle English *Romain,* from Old French, from Latin *Romanus*] (before 12th century)
**1** : a native or resident of Rome
**2** : ROMAN CATHOLIC — often taken to be offensive
**3** *not capitalized* : roman letters or type

²**Roman** *adjective* (14th century)
**1** : of or relating to Rome or the people of Rome; *specifically* : characteristic of the ancient Romans ⟨*Roman* fortitude⟩
**2 a** : LATIN 1a **b** : of or relating to the Latin alphabet
**3** *not capitalized* : of or relating to a type style with upright characters — compare ITALIC
**4** : of or relating to the see of Rome or the Roman Catholic Church
**5** : having a semicircular intrados ⟨*Roman* arch⟩
**6** : having a prominent slightly aquiline bridge ⟨*Roman* nose⟩

**ro·man à clef** \rō-ˌmä(ⁿ)n-(ˌ)ä-'klä\ *noun, plural* **romans à clef** \-ˌmäⁿ-(ˌ)zä-\ [French, literally, novel with a key] (1893)
: a novel in which real persons or actual events figure under disguise

**Roman candle** *noun* (1834)
: a cylindrical firework that discharges at intervals balls or stars of fire

¹**Roman Catholic** *noun* (1605)
: a member of the Roman Catholic Church

²**Roman Catholic** *adjective* (1614)
: of, relating to, or being a Christian church having a hierarchy of priests and bishops under the pope, a liturgy centered in the Mass, veneration of the Virgin Mary and saints, clerical celibacy, and a body of dogma including transubstantiation and papal infallibility

**Roman Catholicism** *noun* (circa 1823)
: the faith, doctrine, or polity of the Roman Catholic Church

¹**ro·mance** \rō-'man(t)s, rə-; 'rō-ˌ\ *noun* [Middle English *romauns,* from Old French *romans* French, something written in French, from Latin *romanice* in the Roman manner, from *romanicus* Roman, from *Romanus*] (14th century)
**1 a** (1) : a medieval tale based on legend, chivalric love and adventure, or the supernatural (2) : a prose narrative treating imaginary characters involved in events remote in time or place and usually heroic, adventurous, or

---

roller bearing: *1* outer race, *2* cage, *3* roller, *4* inner race

mysterious (3) **:** a love story **b :** a class of such literature
**2 :** something (as an extravagant story or account) that lacks basis in fact
**3 :** an emotional attraction or aura belonging to an especially heroic era, adventure, or activity
**4 :** LOVE AFFAIR
**5** *capitalized* **:** the Romance languages ◆
**²romance** *verb* **ro·manced; ro·manc·ing** (1671)
*intransitive verb*
**1 :** to exaggerate or invent detail or incident
**2 :** to entertain romantic thoughts or ideas
*transitive verb*
**1 :** to try to influence or curry favor with especially by lavishing personal attention, gifts, or flattery
**2 :** to carry on a love affair with
**³romance** *noun* (circa 1854)
**:** a short instrumental piece in ballad style
**Ro·mance** \rō-ˈman(t)s, rə-; ˈrō-,\ *adjective* (1690)
**:** of, relating to, or being any of several languages developed from Latin (as Italian, French, and Spanish)
**ro·manc·er** \rō-ˈman(t)-sər, rə-; ˈrō-,\ *noun* (1654)
**1 :** a writer of romance
**2 :** one that romances
**Roman collar** *noun* (circa 1890)
**:** CLERICAL COLLAR
**Ro·man·esque** \,rō-mə-ˈnesk\ *adjective* (1819)
**:** of or relating to a style of architecture developed in Italy and western Europe between the Roman and the Gothic styles and characterized in its development after 1000 by the use of the round arch and vault, substitution of piers for columns, decorative use of arcades, and profuse ornament
**— Romanesque** *noun*
**ro·man–fleuve** \rō-,mäⁿ-ˈflœv, -ˈflə(r)v\ *noun,* *plural* **ro·mans–fleuves** \-,mäⁿ-ˈflœv, ˈflə(r)v(z)\ [French, literally, river novel] (1935)
**:** a novel in the form of a long usually easygoing chronicle of a social group (as a family or a community)
**Roman holiday** *noun* (1886)
**1 :** a time of debauchery or of sadistic enjoyment
**2 :** a destructive or tumultuous disturbance **:** RIOT
**Ro·ma·nian** \ru̇-ˈmā-nē-ən, rō-, -nyən\ *noun* (1868)
**1 :** a native or inhabitant of Romania
**2 :** the Romance language of the Romanians
**Ro·man·ic** \rō-ˈma-nik\ *adjective* (1708)
**:** ROMANCE
**— Romanic** *noun*
**ro·man·ise** *British variant of* ROMANIZE
**Ro·man·ism** \ˈrō-mə-,ni-zəm\ *noun* (1674)
**:** ROMAN CATHOLICISM — often taken to be offensive
**Ro·man·ist** \-nist\ *noun* (1523)
**1 :** ROMAN CATHOLIC — often taken to be offensive
**2 :** a specialist in the language, culture, or law of ancient Rome
**— Romanist** *or* **Ro·man·is·tic** \,rō-mə-ˈnis-tik\ *adjective*
**ro·man·ize** \ˈrō-mə-,nīz\ *transitive verb* **-ized; -iz·ing** (1607)
**1** *often capitalized* **:** to make Roman in character
**2 :** to write or print (as a language) in the Latin alphabet ⟨*romanize* Chinese⟩
**3** *capitalized* **a :** to convert to Roman Catholicism **b :** to give a Roman Catholic character to
**— ro·man·i·za·tion** \,rō-mə-nə-ˈzā-shən\ *noun, often capitalized*
**roman law** *noun, often R capitalized* (1660)
**:** the legal system of the ancient Romans that includes written and unwritten law, is based

on the traditional law and the legislation of the city of Rome, and in form comprises legislation of the assemblies, resolves of the senate, enactments of the emperors, edicts of the praetors, writings of the jurisconsults, and the codes of the later emperors
**Roman numeral** *noun* (1735)
**:** a numeral in a system of notation that is based on the ancient Roman system — see NUMBER table
**Ro·ma·no** \rə-ˈmä-(,)nō, rō-\ *noun* [Italian, Roman, from Latin *Romanus*] (1908)
**:** a hard sharp cheese of Italian origin that is often served grated
**Ro·mans** \ˈrō-mənz\ *noun plural but singular in construction*
**:** a letter on doctrine written by Saint Paul to the Christians of Rome and included as a book in the New Testament — see BIBLE table
**Ro·mansh** *or* **Ro·mansch** \rō-ˈmänch, -ˈmanch\ *noun* [Romansh *romonsch*] (1663)
**:** the Rhaeto-Romance dialects spoken in the Grisons, Switzerland
**¹ro·man·tic** \rō-ˈman-tik, rə-\ *adjective* [French *romantique,* from obsolete *romant* romance, from Old French *romans*] (1650)
**1 :** consisting of or resembling a romance
**2 :** having no basis in fact **:** IMAGINARY
**3 :** impractical in conception or plan **:** VISIONARY
**4 a :** marked by the imaginative or emotional appeal of what is heroic, adventurous, remote, mysterious, or idealized **b** *often capitalized* **:** of, relating to, or having the characteristics of romanticism **c :** of or relating to music of the 19th century characterized by an emphasis on subjective emotional qualities and freedom of form; *also* **:** of or relating to a composer of this music
**5 a :** having an inclination for romance **:** responsive to the appeal of what is idealized, heroic, or adventurous **b :** marked by expressions of love or affection **c :** conducive to or suitable for lovemaking
**6 :** of, relating to, or constituting the part of the hero especially in a light comedy
**— ro·man·ti·cal·ly** \-ti-k(ə-)lē\ *adverb*
**²romantic** *noun* (1679)
**1 :** a romantic person, trait, or component
**2** *capitalized* **:** a romantic writer, artist, or composer
**ro·man·ti·cise** *British variant of* ROMANTICIZE
**ro·man·ti·cism** \rō-ˈman-tə-,si-zəm, rə-\ *noun* (1823)
**1** *often capitalized* **a** (1) **:** a literary, artistic, and philosophical movement originating in the 18th century, characterized chiefly by a reaction against neoclassicism and an emphasis on the imagination and emotions, and marked especially in English literature by sensibility and the use of autobiographical material, an exaltation of the primitive and the common man, an appreciation of external nature, an interest in the remote, a predilection for melancholy, and the use in poetry of older verse forms (2) **:** an aspect of romanticism **b :** adherence to a romantic attitude or style
**2 :** the quality or state of being romantic
**— ro·man·ti·cist** \-sist\ *noun, often capitalized*
**ro·man·ti·cize** \-ˈman-tə-,sīz\ *verb* **-cized; -ciz·ing** (1818)
*transitive verb*
**:** to make romantic **:** treat as idealized or heroic
*intransitive verb*
**1 :** to hold romantic ideas
**2 :** to present details, incidents, or people in a romantic way
**— ro·man·ti·ci·za·tion** \-,man-tə-sə-ˈzā-shən\ *noun*
**Ro·ma·ny** \ˈrä-mə-nē, ˈrō-\ *noun, plural* **Ro·manies** [Romany *romani,* feminine of *romano,* adjective, Gypsy, from *rom* Gypsy man — more at ROM] (circa 1812)

**1 :** GYPSY 1
**2 :** the Indo-Aryan language of the Gypsies
**— Romany** *adjective*
**ro·maunt** \rō-ˈmȯnt, -ˈmänt\ *noun* [Middle English, from Middle French *romant*] (1530)
*archaic* **:** ROMANCE 1a(1)
**rom·el·dale** \ˈrä-məl-,dāl\ *noun, often capitalized* [blend of *Romney* (Marsh), *Rambouillet,* and *Corriedale*] (circa 1948)
**:** any of an American breed of utility sheep yielding a heavy fleece of fine wool and producing a quickly maturing high-grade market lamb
**¹Ro·meo** \ˈrō-mē-,ō, *in Shakespeare also* ˈrōm-(,)yō\ *noun, plural* **Ro·me·os**
**1 :** the hero of Shakespeare's *Romeo and Juliet* who dies for love of Juliet
**2 :** a male lover
**²Romeo** (1952)
**—** a communications code word for the letter *r*
**Rom·ish** \ˈrō-mish\ *adjective* (1531)
**:** ROMAN CATHOLIC — usually used disparagingly
**— Rom·ish·ly** *adverb*
**— Rom·ish·ness** *noun*
**Rom·ney Marsh** \ˈräm-nē-, ˈrəm-\ *noun* [*Romney Marsh,* pasture tract in England] (1832)
**:** any of a British breed of hardy long-wooled mutton-type sheep especially adapted to damp or marshy regions — called also *Romney*
**¹romp** \ˈrämp, ˈrȯmp\ *noun* [partly alteration of ²*ramp;* partly alteration of *ramp* bold woman] (1706)
**1 :** one that romps; *especially* **:** a romping girl or woman
**2 a :** high-spirited, carefree, and boisterous play **b :** something suggestive of such play: as (1) **:** a light fast-paced narrative, dramatic, or musical work usually in a comic mood (2) **:** an episode of lovemaking
**3 :** an easy winning pace; *also* **:** RUNAWAY
**²romp** *intransitive verb* [alteration of ¹*ramp*] (1709)
**1 :** to run or play in a lively, carefree, or boisterous manner
**2 :** to move or proceed in a brisk, easy, or playful manner
**3 :** to win a contest easily
**romp·er** \ˈräm-pər, ˈrȯm-\ *noun* (1842)
**1 :** one that romps
**2 :** a one-piece garment especially for children with the lower part shaped like bloomers — usually used in plural

◇ **WORD HISTORY**
**romance** The Latin word *Romanus* "of Rome, Roman" was used by the inhabitants of Gaul in the declining years of the Roman Empire to refer to their own Latin-derived speech, Gallo-Romance, as opposed to the language of the Franks and other Germanic peoples who had overwhelmed Gaul by the end of the 5th century. In the Middle Ages, the Latin adverb *Romanice,* a derivative of *Romanus,* meant "in the vernacular," alluding to the languages that had developed out of Gallo-Romance (namely Old French in the north of what had been Gaul and Old Occitan in the south), as opposed to Latin, the language of the church and of most formal writing. The Old French outcome of *Romanice* was *romans* or *romanz,* which was used as a noun referring not only to Old French, but to works composed in it, and then specifically to a verse narrative in the vernacular, typically one dealing with chivalric love and adventure. Middle English *romaunce* was borrowed from Old French with all these senses. The close association of the word with tales of love has led to the use of Modern English *romance* for both love stories in fiction and real love affairs.

**Rom·u·lus** \'räm-yə-ləs\ *noun* [Latin]
: a son of Mars and legendary founder of Rome

**ron·deau** \'rän-(,)dō, rän-'dō\ *noun, plural* **ron·deaux** \-(,)dōz, -'dōz\ [Middle French *rondel, rondeau*] (1525)
**1 a :** a fixed form of verse based on two rhyme sounds and consisting usually of 13 lines in three stanzas with the opening words of the first line of the first stanza used as an independent refrain after the second and third stanzas **b :** a poem in this form
**2 :** a monophonic trouvère song with a 2-part refrain

**ron·del** \'rän-dᵊl, rän-'del\ *or* **ron·delle** \rän-'del\ *noun* [Middle English, from Old French, literally, small circle — more at ROUNDEL] (14th century)
**1** *usually* **rondelle :** a circular object; *especially* **:** a circular jewel or jeweled ring
**2 a** *usually* **rondel :** a fixed form of verse based on two rhyme sounds and consisting usually of 14 lines in three stanzas in which the first two lines of the first stanza are repeated as the refrain of the second and third stanzas **b :** a poem in this form **c :** RONDEAU 1

**ron·de·let** \,rän-də-'let, -'lā\ *noun* (15th century)
: a modified rondeau consisting usually of seven lines in which the first line of four syllables is repeated as the third line and as the final line or refrain and the remaining lines are made up of eight syllables each

**ron·do** \'rän-(,)dō, rän-'dō\ *noun, plural* **ron·dos** [Italian *rondò*, from Middle French *rondeau*] (1797)
**1 :** an instrumental composition typically with a refrain recurring four times in the tonic and with three couplets in contrasting keys
**2 :** the musical form of a rondo used especially for a movement in a concerto or sonata

**ron·dure** \'rän-jər, -(,)dyùr, -(,)dùr\ *noun* [French *rondeur* roundness, from Middle French, from *rond* round, from Old French *roont* — more at ROUND] (circa 1600)
**1 :** ROUND 1a
**2 :** gracefully rounded curvature

**ron·yon** \'rən-yən, 'rän-\ *noun* [perhaps modification of Middle French *rogne* scab] (1598)
*obsolete* **:** a mangy or scabby creature

**rood** \'rüd\ *noun* [Middle English, from Old English *rōd* rod, rood; akin to Old High German *ruota* rod and perhaps to Old Russian *ratište* lance] (before 12th century)
**1 :** a cross or crucifix symbolizing the cross on which Jesus Christ died; *specifically* **:** a large crucifix on a beam or screen at the entrance of the chancel of a medieval church
**2 a :** any of various units of land area; *especially* **:** a British unit equal to ¼ acre **b :** any of various units of length; *especially* **:** a British unit equal to seven or eight yards or sometimes a rod

**¹roof** \'rüf, 'rùf\ *noun, plural* **roofs** \'rüfs, 'rùfs *also* 'rüvz, 'rùvz\ [Middle English, from Old English *hrōf*; akin to Old Norse *hrōf* roof of a boathouse and perhaps to Old Church Slavonic *stropŭ* roof] (before 12th century)
**1 a** (1) **:** the cover of a building (2) **:** material used for a roof **:** ROOFING **b :** the roof of a dwelling conventionally designating the home itself ⟨didn't have a *roof* over my head⟩ ⟨they share the same *roof*⟩
**2 a :** the highest point **:** SUMMIT **b :** an upper limit **:** CEILING
**3 a :** the vaulted upper boundary of the mouth **b :** a covering structure of any of various parts of the body ⟨*roof* of the skull⟩
**4 :** something suggesting a roof: as **a :** a canopy of leaves and branches **b :** the top over the passenger section of a vehicle
— **roofed** \'rüft, 'rùft\ *adjective*
— **roof·less** \'rü-fləs, 'rù-\ *adjective*
— **roof·like** \-,līk\ *adjective*

**²roof** *transitive verb* (15th century)

roof 1a(1): *1* gambrel, *2* mansard, *3* hip, *4* lean-to

**1 a :** to cover with or as if with a roof **b :** to provide with a particular kind of roof or roofing — often used in combination ⟨slate-*roofed* houses⟩
**2 :** to constitute a roof over
— **roof·er** *noun*

**roof garden** *noun* (1893)
: a restaurant or nightclub at the top of a building often in connection with or decorated to suggest an outdoor garden

**roof·ing** *noun* (15th century)
: material for a roof

**roof·line** \'rüf-,līn, 'rùf-\ *noun* (1857)
: the profile of a roof (as of a house)

**¹roof·top** \-,täp\ *noun* (1611)
: ROOF; *especially* **:** the outer surface of a usually flat roof ⟨sunning themselves on the *rooftop*⟩

**²rooftop** *adjective* (1935)
: situated or taking place on a rooftop

**roof·tree** \'rüf-,trē, 'rùf-\ *noun* (14th century)
: RIDGEPOLE

**¹rook** \'rùk\ *noun* [Middle English, from Old English *hrōc*; akin to Old High German *hruoch* rook] (before 12th century)
: a common Old World gregarious bird (*Corvus frugilegus*) about the size and color of the related American crow but having a bare patch of skin at the base of the bill

**²rook** *transitive verb* (circa 1590)
: to defraud by cheating or swindling

**³rook** *noun* [Middle English *rok*, from Middle French *roc*, from Arabic *rukhkh*, from Persian *rukh*] (14th century)
: either of two pieces of the same color in a set of chessmen having the power to move along the ranks or files across any number of unoccupied squares — called also *castle*

**rook**

**rook·ery** \'rùk-ə-rē\ *noun, plural* **-er·ies** (1725)
**1 a :** the nests or breeding place of a colony of rooks; *also* **:** a colony of rooks **b :** a breeding ground or haunt especially of gregarious birds or mammals; *also* **:** a colony of such birds or mammals
**2 :** a crowded dilapidated tenement or group of dwellings
**3 :** a place teeming with like individuals

**rook·ie** \'rùk-ē\ *noun* [perhaps alteration of *recruit*] (1892)
**1 :** RECRUIT; *also* **:** NOVICE
**2 :** a first-year participant in a major professional sport

**rooky** \'rùk-ē\ *adjective* (1605)
: full of or containing rooks

**¹room** \'rüm, 'rùm\ *noun* [Middle English, from Old English *rūm*; akin to Old High German *rūm* room, Latin *rur-, rus* open land] (before 12th century)
**1 :** an extent of space occupied by or sufficient or available for something ⟨in the country where there is *room* to run and play⟩

**2 a** *obsolete* **:** an appropriate or designated position, post, or station **b :** PLACE, STEAD ⟨in whose *room* I am now assuming the pen —Sir Walter Scott⟩
**3 a :** a partitioned part of the inside of a building; *especially* **:** such a part used as a lodging **b :** the people in a room
**4 :** a suitable or fit occasion or opportunity **:** CHANCE ⟨left no *room* for doubt⟩
— **roomed** \'rümd, 'rùmd\ *adjective*

**²room** (1817)
*intransitive verb*
: to occupy a room especially as a lodger
*transitive verb*
: to accommodate with lodgings

**room and board** *noun* (1955)
: lodging and food usually furnished for a set price or as part of wages

**room·er** \'rü-mər, 'rù-\ *noun* (circa 1871)
: one who occupies a rented room in another's house

**room·ette** \rü-'met, rù-\ *noun* (1937)
: a small private single room on a railroad sleeping car

**room·ful** \'rüm-,fùl, 'rùm-\ *noun* (1710)
: as much or as many as a room will hold; *also* **:** the persons or objects in a room

**rooming house** *noun* (1893)
: a house where lodgings are provided for rent

**rooming-in** \'rü-miŋ-'in, 'rù-\ *noun* (1943)
: an arrangement in a hospital whereby a newborn infant is kept in a crib at the mother's bedside instead of in a nursery

**room·mate** \'rüm-,māt, 'rùm-\ *noun* (1789)
: one of two or more persons sharing the same room or living quarters — called also *room·ie* \'rü-mē, 'rù-\

**room service** *noun* (1930)
: service provided to hotel guests in their rooms; *also* **:** the hotel department responsible for such service ⟨ordered a meal from *room service*⟩

**roomy** \'rü-mē, 'rù-\ *adjective* **room·i·er; -est** (1627)
**1 :** having ample room **:** SPACIOUS
**2** *of a female mammal* **:** having a large or well-proportioned body suited for breeding
— **room·i·ness** *noun*

**roor·back** \'rùr-,bak\ *noun* [from an attack on James K. Polk in 1844 purporting to quote from an invented book by a Baron von *Roorback*] (1855)
: a defamatory falsehood published for political effect

**roose** \'rüz\ *transitive verb* [Middle English *rusen*, from Old Norse *hrōsa*] (14th century)
*chiefly dialect* **:** PRAISE

**¹roost** \'rüst\ *noun* [Middle English, from Old English *hrōst*; akin to Old Saxon *hrōst* attic] (before 12th century)
**1 a :** a support on which birds rest **b :** a place where winged animals and especially birds customarily roost
**2 :** a group of birds (as fowl) roosting together

**²roost** (1530)
*intransitive verb*
**1 :** to settle down for rest or sleep **:** PERCH
**2 :** to settle oneself as if on a roost
*transitive verb*
: to supply a roost for or put to roost

**roost·er** \'rüs-tər *also* 'rùs-\ *noun* (1772)
**1 a :** an adult male domestic fowl **:** COCK **b :** an adult male of various birds other than the domestic fowl
**2 :** a cocky or vain man

**rooster tail** *noun* (1946)
: a high arching spray of water thrown up behind a fast-moving motorboat

**¹root** \'rüt, 'rùt\ *noun, often attributive* [Middle English, from Old English *rōt*, from Old

\ə\ abut \ᵊ\ kitten \ər\ further \a\ ash \ā\ ace
\ä\ mop, mar \aù\ out \ch\ chin \e\ bet \ē\ easy
\g\ go \i\ hit \ī\ ice \j\ job \ŋ\ sing \ō\ go
\ò\ law \òi\ boy \th\ thin \th\ the \ü\ loot \ù\ foot
\y\ yet \zh\ vision *see also* Guide to Pronunciation

Norse; akin to Old English *wyrt* root, Latin *radix*, Greek *rhiza*] (12th century)
**1 a :** the usually underground part of a seed plant body that originates usually from the hypocotyl, functions as an organ of absorption, aeration, and food storage or as a means of anchorage and support, and differs from a stem especially in lacking nodes, buds, and leaves **b :** any subterranean plant part (as a true root or a bulb, tuber, rootstock, or other modified stem) especially when fleshy and edible
**2 a :** the part of a tooth within the socket; *also* **:** any of the processes into which this part is often divided — see TOOTH illustration **b :** the enlarged basal part of a hair within the skin **c :** the proximal end of a nerve **d :** the part of an organ or physical structure by which it is attached to the body ⟨the *root* of the tongue⟩
**3 a :** something that is an origin or source (as of a condition or quality) ⟨the love of money is the *root* of all evil —1 Timothy 6:10 (Authorized Version)⟩ **b :** one or more progenitors of a group of descendants — usually used in plural **c :** an underlying support **:** BASIS **d :** the essential core **:** HEART — often used in the phrase *at root* **e :** close relationship with an environment **:** TIE — usually used in plural
**4 a :** a quantity taken an indicated number of times as an equal factor ⟨2 is a fourth *root* of 16⟩ **b :** a number that reduces an equation to an identity when it is substituted for one variable
**5 a :** the lower part **:** BASE **b :** the part by which an object is attached to something else
**6 :** the simple element inferred as the basis from which a word is derived by phonetic change or by extension (as composition or the addition of an affix or inflectional ending)
**7 :** the tone from whose overtones a chord is composed **:** the lowest tone of a chord in normal position
**synonym** see ORIGIN
**— root·ed** \'rü-təd, 'rú-\ *adjective*
**— root·less** \'rüt-ləs, 'rút-\ *adjective*
**— root·less·ness** *noun*
**— root·like** \-,līk\ *adjective*
**²root** (14th century)
*transitive verb*
**1 a :** to furnish with or enable to develop roots **b :** to fix or implant by or as if by roots
**2 :** to remove altogether by or as if by pulling out by the roots — usually used with *out* ⟨*root* out dissenters⟩
*intransitive verb*
**1 :** to grow roots or take root
**2 :** to have an origin or base
**³root** *verb* [alteration of *wroot,* from Middle English *wroten,* from Old English *wrōtan;* akin to Old High German *ruozzan* to root] (1532)
*intransitive verb*
**1 :** to turn up or dig in the earth with the snout **:** GRUB
**2 :** to poke or dig about
*transitive verb*
**:** to turn over, dig up, or discover and bring to light — usually used with *out* ⟨*root* out the cause of the problem⟩
**⁴root** \'rüt *also* 'rút\ *intransitive verb* [perhaps alteration of *²rout*] (1889)
**1 :** to noisily applaud or encourage a contestant or team **:** CHEER
**2 :** to wish the success of or lend support to someone or something
**— root·er** *noun*
**root·age** \'rü-tij, 'rú-\ *noun* (circa 1895)
**1 :** a developed system of roots
**2 :** ROOT 3a
**root beer** *noun* (1843)
**:** a sweetened carbonated beverage flavored with extracts of roots (as sarsaparilla) and herbs
**root canal** *noun* (1893)
**:** the part of the pulp cavity lying in the root of a tooth; *also* **:** a dental operation to save a

tooth by removing the contents of its root canal and filling the cavity with a protective substance
**root cap** *noun* (1875)
**:** a protective cap of parenchyma cells that covers the terminal meristem in most root tips
**root cellar** *noun* (1822)
**:** a pit used for the storage especially of root crops
**root crop** *noun* (1834)
**:** a crop (as turnips) grown for its enlarged roots
**root·ed·ness** \'rü-təd-nəs, 'rú-\ *noun* (1642)
**:** the quality or state of having roots
**root hair** *noun* (1857)
**:** a filamentous extension of an epidermal cell near the tip of a rootlet that functions in absorption of water and minerals
**root·hold** \'rüt-,hōld, 'rút-\ *noun* (1864)
**1 :** the anchorage of a plant to soil through the growing and spreading of roots
**2 :** a place where plants may obtain a roothold
**root knot** *noun* (1889)
**:** a plant disease caused by nematodes that produce characteristic enlargements on the roots and stunt the growth of the plant
**root–knot nematode** *noun* (1922)
**:** any of several small plant-parasitic nematodes (genus *Meloidogyne*) that cause root knot
**root·let** \'rüt-lət, 'rút-\ *noun* (circa 1793)
**:** a small root
**root–mean–square** *noun* (1895)
**:** the square root of the arithmetic mean of the squares of a set of numbers
**root pressure** *noun* (1875)
**:** the chiefly osmotic pressure by which water rises into the stems of plants from the roots
**root rot** *noun* (1883)
**:** any of various plant diseases characterized by decay of the roots and caused especially by fungi
**root·stock** \'rüt-,stäk, 'rút-\ *noun* (1832)
**1 :** a rhizomatous underground part of a plant
**2 :** a stock for grafting consisting of a root or a piece of root; *broadly* **:** STOCK 3b
**rooty** \'rü-tē, 'rú-\ *adjective* (15th century)
**:** full or consisting of roots ⟨*rooty* soil⟩
**¹rope** \'rōp\ *noun* [Middle English, from Old English *rāp;* akin to Old High German *reif* hoop] (before 12th century)
**1 a :** a large stout cord of strands of fibers or wire twisted or braided together **b :** a long slender strip of material used as rope ⟨rawhide *rope*⟩ **c :** a hangman's noose **d :** LARIAT
**2 :** a row or string consisting of things united by or as if by braiding, twining, or threading
**3** *plural* **:** special or basic techniques or procedures ⟨show him the *ropes*⟩
**4 :** LINE DRIVE
**— rope·like** \-,līk\ *adjective*
**— on the ropes :** in a defensive and often helpless position
**²rope** *verb* **roped; rop·ing** (14th century)
*transitive verb*
**1 a :** to bind, fasten, or tie with a rope or cord **b :** to partition, separate, or divide by a rope ⟨*rope* off the street⟩ **c :** LASSO
**2 :** to draw as if with a rope **:** LURE
*intransitive verb*
**:** to take the form of or twist in the manner of rope
**— rop·er** *noun*
**rope·danc·er** \'rōp-,dan(t)-sər\ *noun* (1648)
**:** one that dances, walks, or performs acrobatic feats on a rope high in the air
**— rope·danc·ing** \-,siŋ\ *noun*
**rop·ery** \'rō-p(ə-)rē\ *noun* [probably from the thought that the perpetrator deserved the gallows] (1592)
*archaic* **:** roguish tricks or banter
**rope tow** *noun* (1948)
**:** SKI TOW 1
**rope·walk** \'rōp-,wȯk\ *noun* (1672)
**:** a long covered walk, building, or room where ropes are manufactured

**rope·walk·er** \-,wȯ-kər\ *noun* (1615)
**:** an acrobat who walks on a rope high in the air
**rope·way** \-,wā\ *noun* (1889)
**1 :** an endless aerial cable moved by a stationary engine and used to transport freight (as logs and ore)
**2 :** a fixed cable or a pair of fixed cables between supporting towers serving as a track for suspended passenger or freight carriers
**ropy** *also* **rop·ey** \'rō-pē\ *adjective* **rop·i·er; -est** (15th century)
**1 a :** capable of being drawn into a thread **:** VISCOUS; *also* **:** tending to adhere in stringy masses **b :** having a gelatinous or slimy quality from bacterial or fungal contamination ⟨*ropy* milk⟩ ⟨*ropy* flour⟩
**2 a :** resembling rope **b :** MUSCULAR, SINEWY
**3** *usually* **ropey,** *slang* **:** extremely unsatisfactory **:** LOUSY
**— rop·i·ness** *noun*
**roque** \'rōk\ *noun* [alteration of *croquet*] (1899)
**:** croquet played on a hard-surfaced court with a raised border
**Roque·fort** \'rōk-fərt\ *trademark*
— used for a pungent French blue cheese made from sheep's milk
**ro·que·laure** \,rō-kə-'lōr, ,rä-, -'lȯr\ *noun* [French, from the Duc de *Roquelaure* (died 1738) French marshal] (1716)
**:** a knee-length cloak worn especially in the 18th and 19th centuries
**ror·qual** \'rȯr-kwəl, -,kwȯl\ *noun* [French, from Norwegian *rørhval,* from Old Norse *reytharhvalr,* from *reythr* rorqual + *hvalr* whale] (1827)
**:** any of a family (Balaenopteridae) of large baleen whales (as a blue whale or humpback whale) having the skin of the throat marked with deep longitudinal furrows
**Ror·schach** \'rȯr-,shäk\ *adjective* (1927)
**:** of, relating to, used in connection with, or resulting from the Rorschach test
**Rorschach test** *noun* [Hermann *Rorschach* (died 1922) Swiss psychiatrist] (1927)
**:** a personality and intelligence test in which a subject interprets inkblot designs in terms that reveal intellectual and emotional factors — called also *Rorschach, Rorschach inkblot test*
**ro·sa·ceous** \rō-'zā-shəs\ *adjective* [ultimately from Latin *rosa*] (1731)
**1 :** of or relating to the rose family
**2 :** of, relating to, or resembling a rose especially in having a 5-petaled regular corolla
**ro·sar·i·an** \rō-'zar-ē-ən, -'zer-\ *noun* (1864)
**:** a cultivator of roses
**ro·sa·ry** \'rō-zə-rē, 'rōz-rē\ *noun, plural* **-ries** [Medieval Latin *rosarium,* from Latin, rose garden, from neuter of *rosarius* of roses, from *rosa* rose] (1547)
**1** *often capitalized* **:** a Roman Catholic devotion consisting of meditation on usually five sacred mysteries during recitation of five decades of Hail Marys of which each begins with an Our Father and ends with a Gloria Patri
**2 :** a string of beads used in counting prayers especially of the Roman Catholic rosary
**rosary pea** *noun* (circa 1866)
**1 :** a tropical leguminous twining herb (*Abrus precatorius*) that bears jequirity beans and has a root used as a substitute for licorice — called also *Indian licorice, jequirity bean*
**2 :** JEQUIRITY BEAN 1
**ros·coe** \'räs-(,)kō\ *noun* [probably from the name *Roscoe*] (circa 1914)
*slang* **:** HANDGUN
**¹rose** *past of* RISE
**²rose** \'rōz\ *noun* [Middle English, from Old English, from Latin *rosa;* akin to Greek *rhodon* rose, Persian *gul*] (before 12th century)
**1 a :** any of a genus (*Rosa* of the family Rosaceae, the rose family) of usually prickly shrubs with pinnate leaves and showy flowers

having five petals in the wild state but being often double or partly double under cultivation **b** : the flower of a rose
**2** : something resembling a rose in form: as **a** (1) : COMPASS CARD (2) : a circular card with radiating lines used in other instruments **b** : a rosette especially on a shoe **c** : ROSE CUT
**3** *plural* : a comfortable situation or an easily accomplished task ⟨it was not all sunshine and *roses* —Anthony Lewis⟩
**4** : a moderate purplish red
**5** : a plane curve which consists of three or more loops meeting at the origin and whose equation is in polar coordinates is of the form $\rho = a \sin n\theta$ or $\rho = a \cos n\theta$ where $n$ is an integer greater than zero
— **rose·like** \-,līk\ *adjective*
— **under the rose** : SUB ROSA

**³rose** *adjective* (14th century)
**1 a** : containing or used for roses **b** : of or relating to a rose **c** : flavored, scented, or colored with or like roses
**2** : of the color rose

**ro·sé** \rō-'zā\ *noun* [French] (1897)
: a light pink table wine made from red grapes by removing the skins after fermentation has begun

**ro·se·ate** \'rō-zē-ət, -zē-,āt\ *adjective* [Latin *roseus* rosy, from *rosa*] (1589)
**1** : resembling a rose especially in color
**2** : overly optimistic : viewed favorably
— **ro·se·ate·ly** *adverb*

**roseate spoonbill** *noun* (circa 1785)
: a spoonbill (*Ajaia ajaja*) that is found from the southern U.S. to Patagonia and has chiefly pink plumage

**rose·bay** \'rōz-,bā\ *noun* (1760)
**1** : RHODODENDRON; *especially* : GREAT LAUREL
**2** : FIREWEED b

**rosebay rhododendron** *noun* (circa 1949)
: GREAT LAUREL

**rose–breast·ed grosbeak** \'rōz-,bres-təd-\ *noun* (1810)
: a grosbeak (*Pheucticus ludovicianus*) chiefly of eastern North America that in the male is chiefly black and white with a rose-red breast and in the female is grayish brown with a streaked breast

**rose·bud** \'rōz-,bəd\ *noun* (15th century)
: the bud of a rose

**rose·bush** \-,bùsh\ *noun* (1587)
: a shrub that produces roses

**rose chafer** *noun* (1704)
: a common North American beetle (*Macrodactylus subspinosus*) that feeds on plant roots as a larva and on leaves and flowers (as of rose or grapevines) as an adult — called also *rose bug*

**rose–col·ored** \'rōz-,kə-lərd\ *adjective* (1526)
**1** : having a rose color
**2** : seeing or seen in a promising light : OPTIMISTIC

**rose–colored glasses** *noun plural* (1950)
: favorably disposed opinions : optimistic eyes ⟨views the world through *rose-colored glasses*⟩

**rose cut** *noun* (circa 1842)
: a form in which gems (as diamonds) are cut that usually has a flat circular base and facets in two ranges rising to a point
— **rose–cut** *adjective*

**rose fever** *noun* (1851)
: hay fever occurring in the spring or early summer — called also *rose cold*

**rose·fish** \'rōz-,fish\ *noun* (1731)
: REDFISH

**rose geranium** *noun* (1832)
: any of several pelargoniums grown for their fragrant 3- to 5-lobed leaves and small pink flowers

**rose hip** *noun* (1857)
: the ripened accessory fruit of a rose that consists of a fleshy receptacle enclosing numerous achenes

**ro·se·ma·ling** \'rō-zə-,mä-liŋ, -sə-\ *noun* [Norwegian, from *rose* rose + *maling* painting] (1942)
: painted or sometimes carved decoration (as on furniture, walls, or wooden dinnerware) in Scandinavian peasant style that consists especially of floral designs and inscriptions

**rose mallow** *noun* (1857)
: any of several hibiscuses with large rose-colored flowers; *especially* : a showy plant (*Hibiscus moscheutos*) of the salt marshes of the eastern U.S.

**rose·mary** \'rōz-,mer-ē\ *noun, plural* **-maries** [Middle English *rosmarine*, from Latin *rosmarinus*, from *ror-, ros* dew + *marinus* of the sea; akin to Sanskrit *rasa* sap, juice — more at MARINE] (14th century)
: a fragrant shrubby mint (*Rosmarinus officinalis*) of southern Europe and Asia Minor; *also* : its leaves used as a seasoning

**rose of Jer·i·cho** \-'jer-i-,kō\ [Middle English, from *Jericho,* ancient city in Palestine] (15th century)
: an Asian plant (*Anastatica hierochuntica*) of the mustard family that rolls up when dry and expands when moistened

**rose of Shar·on** \-'shar-ən, -'sher-\ [Plain of *Sharon,* Palestine] (circa 1847)
: a commonly cultivated Asian shrub or small tree (*Hibiscus syriacus*) having showy bell-shaped rose, purple, or white flowers

**rose oil** *noun* (1552)
: a fragrant essential oil obtained from roses and used chiefly in perfumery and in flavoring

**ro·se·o·la** \rō-zē-'ō-lə, rō-'zē-ə-lə\ *noun* [New Latin, from Latin *roseus* rosy, from *rosa* rose] (circa 1818)
: a rose-colored eruption in spots or a disease marked by such an eruption; *especially* : ROSEOLA INFANTUM
— **ro·se·o·lar** \-lər\ *adjective*

**roseola in·fan·tum** \-in-'fan-təm\ *noun* [Latin, infant roseola] (circa 1935)
: a mild disease of infants and children characterized by fever lasting usually three days followed by an eruption of rose-colored spots

**rose pink** *noun* (circa 1859)
: a moderate pink

**rose slug** *noun* (1877)
: the slimy green larva of either of two sawflies (*Claudius isomerus* and *Endelomyia aethiops*) that feed on the parenchyma of and skeletonize the leaves of roses

**ro·set** \'rō-zət\ *noun* [alteration of Middle English *rosin*] (14th century)
*chiefly Scottish* : RESIN

**Ro·set·ta stone** \rō-'ze-tə-\ *noun* [*Rosetta,* Egypt] (circa 1859)
**1** : a black basalt stone found in 1799 that bears an inscription in hieroglyphics, demotic characters, and Greek and is celebrated for having given the first clue to the decipherment of Egyptian hieroglyphics
**2** : one that gives a clue to understanding

**ro·sette** \rō-'zet\ *noun* [French, literally, small rose, from Old French, from *rose,* from Latin *rosa*] (1790)
**1** : an ornament usually made of material gathered or pleated so as to resemble a rose and worn as a badge of office, as evidence of having won a decoration (as the Medal of Honor), or as trimming
**2** : a disk of foliage or a floral design usually in relief used as a decorative motif
**3** : a structure or color marking on an animal suggestive of a rosette; *especially* : one of the groups of spots on a leopard
**4** : a cluster of leaves in crowded circles or spirals arising basally from a crown (as in the

rosette 2

dandelion) or apically from an axis with greatly shortened internodes (as in many tropical palms)
**5** : a food decoration or garnish in the shape of a rose ⟨icing *rosettes*⟩ ⟨carrot *rosettes*⟩

**rose-wa·ter** \'rōz-,wò-tər, -,wä-\ *adjective* (1840)
**1** : affectedly nice or delicate
**2** : having the odor of rose water

**rose water** *noun* (14th century)
: a watery solution of the odoriferous constituents of the rose used as a perfume or a flavoring

**rose window** *noun* (1773)
: a circular window filled with tracery

rose window

**rose·wood** \'rōz-,wùd\ *noun* (1660)
: any of various tropical trees (especially genus *Dalbergia*) yielding valuable cabinet woods of a dark red or purplish color or streaked and variegated with black; *also* : the wood

**Rosh Ha·sha·nah** \,räsh-(h)ə-'shä-nə, ,rōsh-, -'shò-\ *noun* [Late Hebrew *rōsh hashshānāh,* literally, beginning of the year] (1846)
: the Jewish New Year observed on the first and by Orthodox and Conservative Jews also on the second of Tishri

**Ro·si·cru·cian** \,rō-zə-'krü-shən, ,rä-\ *noun* [Christian *Rosenkreutz* (New Latin *Rosae Crucis*) reputed 15th century founder of the movement] (1624)
**1** : an adherent of a 17th and 18th century movement devoted to esoteric wisdom with emphasis on psychic and spiritual enlightenment
**2** : a member of one of several organizations held to be descended from the Rosicrucians
— **Rosicrucian** *adjective*
— **Ro·si·cru·cian·ism** \-shə-,ni-zəm\ *noun*

**ros·i·ly** \'rō-zə-lē\ *adverb* (1809)
**1** : in an optimistic manner
**2** : with a rosy color or tinge

**¹ros·in** \'räz-ºn, 'rò-, *dialect* 'rò-zəm\ *noun* [Middle English, modification of Middle French *resine* resin] (13th century)
: a translucent amber-colored to almost black brittle friable resin that is obtained by chemical means from the oleoresin or deadwood of pine trees or from tall oil and used especially in making varnish, paper size, soap, and soldering flux and in rosining violin bows

**²rosin** *transitive verb* **ros·ined; ros·in·ing** \'räz-niŋ, 'ròz-; 'rä-z°n-iŋ, 'rò-\ (15th century)
: to rub or treat (as the bow of a violin) with rosin

**ros·in·weed** \'rä-z°n-,wēd, 'rò-\ *noun* (1831)
: any of several American plants (as the compass plant) having resinous foliage or a resinous odor

**ros·tel·lum** \rä-'ste-ləm\ *noun* [New Latin, from Latin, diminutive of *rostrum* beak] (circa 1826)
: a small process resembling a beak : a diminutive rostrum: as **a** : an extension of the stigma of an orchid flower **b** : an anterior prolongation of the head of a tapeworm bearing hooks
— **ros·tel·lar** \rä-'ste-lər\ *adjective*

**ros·ter** \'räs-tər *also* 'ròs- *or* 'rōs-\ *noun* [Dutch *rooster,* literally, gridiron; from the parallel lines] (1727)

---

**1 a :** a roll or list of personnel **b :** such a list giving the order in which a duty is to be performed ⟨duty *roster*⟩ **c :** the persons listed on a roster
**2 :** an itemized list

**ros·tral** \'räs-trəl *also* 'ròs-\ *adjective* [New Latin *rostralis*, from Latin *rostrum*] (1709)
**1 :** of or relating to a rostrum
**2 :** situated toward the oral or nasal region: as **a** of a part of the spinal cord **:** SUPERIOR 6a **b** of a part of the brain **:** ANTERIOR, VENTRAL
— **ros·tral·ly** \-trə-lē\ *adverb*

**ros·trate** \'räs-,trāt, -trət *also* 'ròs-\ *adjective* (circa 1819)
**:** having a rostrum

**ros·trum** \'räs-trəm *also* 'ròs-\ *noun, plural* **ros·tra** \-trə\ *or* **rostrums** [Latin, beak, ship's beak, from *rodere* to gnaw — more at RODENT] (1542)
**1** [Latin *Rostra,* plural, a platform for speakers in the Roman Forum decorated with the beaks of captured ships, from plural of *rostrum*] **a :** an ancient Roman platform for public orators **b :** a stage for public speaking **c :** a raised platform on a stage
**2 :** the curved end of a ship's prow; *especially* **:** the beak of a war galley
**3 :** a bodily part or process suggesting a bird's bill: as **a :** the beak, snout, or proboscis of any of various insects or arachnids **b :** the often spinelike anterior median prolongation of the carapace of a crustacean (as a crayfish or lobster) ◆

**rosy** \'rō-zē\ *adjective* **ros·i·er; -est** (14th century)
**1 a :** of the color rose **b :** having a pinkish usually healthy-looking complexion **:** BLOOMING **c :** marked by blushes
**2 :** characterized by or tending to promote optimism
— **ros·i·ness** *noun*

**¹rot** \'rät\ *verb* **rot·ted; rot·ting** [Middle English *roten,* from Old English *rotian;* akin to Old High German *rōzzēn* to rot] (before 12th century)
*intransitive verb*
**1 a :** to undergo decomposition from the action of bacteria or fungi **b :** to become unsound or weak (as from use or chemical action)
**2 a :** to go to ruin **:** DETERIORATE **b :** to become morally corrupt **:** DEGENERATE
*transitive verb*
**:** to cause to decompose or deteriorate with or as if with rot
**synonym** see DECAY

**²rot** *noun* (14th century)
**1 a :** the process of rotting **:** the state of being rotten **:** DECAY **b :** something rotten or rotting
**2 a** *archaic* **:** a wasting putrescent disease **b :** any of several parasitic diseases especially of sheep marked by necrosis and wasting **c :** plant disease marked by breakdown of tissues and caused especially by fungi or bacteria
**3 :** NONSENSE — often used interjectionally

**ro·ta** \'rō-tə\ *noun* [Latin, wheel — more at ROLL] (1673)
**1** *chiefly British* **a :** a fixed order of rotation (as of persons or duties) **b :** a roll or list of persons **:** ROSTER
**2** *capitalized* [Medieval Latin, from Latin] **:** a tribunal of the papal curia exercising jurisdiction especially in matrimonial cases appealed from diocesan courts

**ro·ta·me·ter** \'rō-tə-,mē-tər, rō-'ta-mə-tər\ *noun* [Latin *rota* + English *-meter*] (1907)
**:** a gauge that consists of a graduated glass tube containing a free float for measuring the flow of a fluid

**Ro·tar·i·an** \rō-'ter-ē-ən\ *noun* [*Rotary (club)*] (1911)
**:** a member of a major national and international service club

**¹ro·ta·ry** \'rō-tə-rē\ *adjective* [Medieval Latin *rotarius,* from Latin *rota* wheel] (circa 1731)

**1 a :** turning on an axis like a wheel **b :** taking place about an axis ⟨*rotary* motion⟩
**2 :** having an important part that turns on an axis ⟨*rotary* cutter⟩
**3 :** characterized by rotation
**4 :** of, relating to, or being a press in which paper is printed by rotation in contact with a curved printing surface attached to a cylinder

**²rotary** *noun, plural* **-ries** (circa 1888)
**1 :** a rotary machine
**2 :** a road junction formed around a central circle about which traffic moves in one direction only — called also *circle, traffic circle*

**rotary cultivator** *noun* (1926)
**:** ROTOTILLER

**rotary engine** *noun* (1837)
**1 :** any of various engines (as a turbine) in which power is applied to vanes or similar parts constrained to move in a circular path
**2 :** a radial engine in which the cylinders revolve about a stationary crankshaft

**rotary–wing aircraft** *noun* (1935)
**:** ROTORCRAFT; *specifically* **:** HELICOPTER — usually used in plural

**¹ro·tate** \'rō-,tāt\ *adjective* [Latin *rota*] (1785)
**:** having the parts flat and spreading or radiating like the spokes of a wheel ⟨*rotate* blue flowers⟩

**²ro·tate** \'rō-,tāt, *especially British* rō-'\ *verb* **ro·tat·ed; ro·tat·ing** [Latin *rotatus,* past participle of *rotare,* from *rota* wheel — more at ROLL] (1808)
*intransitive verb*
**1 :** to turn about an axis or a center **:** REVOLVE; *especially* **:** to move in such a way that all particles follow circles with a common angular velocity about a common axis
**2 a :** to perform an act, function, or operation in turn **b :** to pass or alternate in a series
*transitive verb*
**1 a :** to cause to turn or move about an axis or a center **b :** to cause (a plane region or line) to sweep out a volume or surface by moving around an axis so that each of its points remains at a constant distance from the axis ⟨generate a torus by *rotating* a circle about an external line⟩
**2 :** to cause to grow in rotation ⟨*rotate* crops⟩
**3 :** to cause to pass or act in a series **:** ALTERNATE
**4 :** to exchange (individuals or units) with others
— **ro·tat·able** \'rō-,tā-tə-bəl *also* rō-'\ *adjective*

**ro·ta·tion** \rō-'tā-shən\ *noun* (1555)
**1 a** (1) **:** the action or process of rotating on or as if on an axis or center (2) **:** the act or an instance of rotating something **b :** one complete turn **:** the angular displacement required to return a rotating body or figure to its original orientation
**2 a :** return or succession in a series ⟨*rotation* of the seasons⟩ **b :** the growing of different crops in succession in one field usually in a regular sequence
**3 :** the turning of a body part about its long axis as if on a pivot
**4 :** a game of pool in which all 15 object balls are shot in numerical order
**5 :** the series of pitchers on a baseball team who regularly start successive games in turn
— **ro·ta·tion·al** \-shnəl, -shə-nᵊl\ *adjective*

**ro·ta·tive** \'rō-,tā-tiv *also* rō-'\ *adjective* (1778)
**1 :** turning like a wheel **:** ROTARY
**2 :** relating to, occurring in, or characterized by rotation
— **ro·ta·tive·ly** *adverb*

**ro·ta·tor** \'rō-,tā-tər *also* rō-'\ *noun* (1676)
**:** one that rotates or causes rotation; *especially, plural* **-tors** *or* **-tor·es** \,rō-tə-'tōr-,ēz, -'tòr-\ **:** a muscle that partially rotates a part on its axis

**rotator cuff** *noun* (1961)
**:** a supporting and strengthening structure of the shoulder joint that is made up of the cap-

sule of the shoulder joint blended with tendons and muscles as they pass to the capsule or across it to insert on the head of the humerus

**ro·ta·to·ry** \'rō-tə-,tōr-ē, -,tòr-, *British* -t(ə-)ri *also* rō-'tā-tə-ri\ *adjective* (1755)
**1 :** of, relating to, or producing rotation
**2 :** occurring in rotation

**ro·ta·vi·rus** \'rō-tə-,vī-rəs\ *noun* [New Latin, from Latin *rota* wheel + New Latin *virus*] (1974)
**:** a reovirus that has a double-layered capsid and that causes diarrhea especially in infants

**¹rote** \'rōt\ *noun* [Middle English, from Middle French, of Germanic origin; akin to Old High German *hruozza* crowd] (14th century)
**:** ³CROWD 1

**²rote** *noun* [Middle English] (14th century)
**1 :** the use of memory usually with little intelligence ⟨learn by *rote*⟩
**2 :** routine or repetition carried out mechanically or unthinkingly ⟨a joyless sense of order, *rote,* and commercial hustle —L. L. King⟩

**³rote** *adjective* (1641)
**1 :** learned or memorized by rote
**2 :** MECHANICAL 3a

**⁴rote** *noun* [perhaps of Scandinavian origin; akin to Old Norse *rauta* to roar — more at ROUT] (1610)
**:** the noise of surf on the shore

**ro·te·none** \'rō-tᵊn-,ōn\ *noun* [International Scientific Vocabulary, from Japanese *roten* derris plant] (1924)
**:** a crystalline insecticide $C_{23}H_{22}O_6$ that is obtained from the roots of several tropical plants (as a derris) and is of low toxicity for warm-blooded animals and is used especially in home gardens

**rot·gut** \'rät-,gət\ *noun* (1633)
**:** cheap or inferior liquor

**ro·ti** \'rō-tē\ *noun* [Hindi *roṭī* bread; akin to Sanskrit *roṭika,* kind of bread] (1920)
**:** a round soft flat unleavened bread; *also* **:** such a bread wrapped around a filling and eaten as a sandwich

**ro·ti·fer** \'rō-tə-fər\ *noun* [ultimately from Latin *rota* + *-fer*] (1793)
**:** any of a class (Rotifera of the phylum Aschelminthes) of minute usually microscopic but many-celled chiefly freshwater aquatic invertebrates having the anterior end modified into a retractile disk bearing circles of strong cilia that often give the appearance of rapidly revolving wheels

**ro·tis·ser·ie** \rō-'tis-rē, -'ti-sə-\ *noun* [French *rôtisserie,* from Middle French *rostisserie,* from *rostir* to roast — more at ROAST] (circa 1920)
**1 :** a restaurant specializing in broiled and barbecued meats
**2 :** an appliance fitted with a spit on which food is rotated before or over a source of heat

**ro·to** \'rō-(,)tō\ *noun, plural* **rotos** (1926)
**:** ROTOGRAVURE

**ro·to·gra·vure** \ˌrō-tə-grə-'vyu̇r\ *noun* [German *Rotogravur*, blend of Latin *rota* wheel and German *Photogravur* photogravure] (1913)
**1** : PHOTOGRAVURE
**2** : a section of a newspaper devoted to rotogravure pictures
**ro·tor** \'rō-tər\ *noun* [contraction of *rotator*] (1903)
**1** : a part that revolves in a stationary part; *especially* : the rotating member of an electrical machine
**2** : a complete system of horizontal rotating blades that supplies lift for a rotorcraft
**ro·tor·craft** \-ˌkraft\ *noun, plural* **rotorcraft** (1940)
: an aircraft (as a helicopter) whose lift is derived principally from rotating airfoils
**ro·to·till** \'rō-tə-ˌtil\ *transitive verb* [backformation from *rototiller*] (1939)
: to till or plow (soil) with a rototiller
**ro·to·till·er** \-ˌti-lər\ *noun* [from *Rototiller*, a trademark] (1923)
: a landscaping implement with engine-powered rotating blades used to lift and turn over soil
**¹rot·ten** \'rä-tᵊn\ *adjective* [Middle English *roten*, from Old Norse *rotinn;* akin to Old English *rotian* to rot] (13th century)
**1** : having rotted : PUTRID
**2** : morally corrupt
**3** : extremely unpleasant or inferior ⟨a *rotten* day⟩ ⟨a *rotten* job⟩
**4** : very uncomfortable ⟨feeling *rotten*⟩
**5** : of very poor quality : LOUSY, ABOMINABLE ⟨a *rotten* show⟩ ⟨what *rotten* luck⟩
— **rot·ten·ly** *adverb*
— **rot·ten·ness** \-tᵊn-(n)əs\ *noun*
**²rotten** *adverb* (1880)
: to an extreme degree ⟨spoiled *rotten*⟩
**rotten borough** *noun* (1812)
: an election district that has many fewer inhabitants than other election districts with the same voting power
**rot·ten·stone** \'rä-tᵊn-ˌstōn\ *noun* (1677)
: a decomposed siliceous limestone used for polishing
**rot·ter** \'rä-tər\ *noun* (1894)
: a thoroughly objectionable person
**rott·wei·ler** \'rät-ˌwī-lər, 'ròt-ˌvī-\ *noun, often capitalized* [German, from *Rottweil*, city in Germany] (1907)
: any of a breed of tall powerful black-and-tan short-haired dogs of German origin that are commonly used as guard dogs

**rottweiler**

**ro·tund** \rō-'tənd, 'rō-ˌ\ *adjective* [Latin *rotundus*, probably alteration of (assumed) Old Latin *retundus;* akin to Latin *rota* wheel — more at ROLL] (1705)
**1** : marked by roundness : ROUNDED
**2** : marked by fullness of sound or cadence : OROTUND, SONOROUS ⟨a master of *rotund* phrase⟩
**3** : notably plump : CHUBBY
— **ro·tun·di·ty** \rō-'tən-də-tē\ *noun*
— **ro·tund·ly** \-'tənd-lē, 'rō-ˌ\ *adverb*
— **ro·tund·ness** \rō-'tən(d)-nəs, 'rō-ˌ\ *noun*
**ro·tun·da** \rō-'tən-də\ *noun* [Italian *rotonda*, from Latin *rotunda*, feminine of *rotundus*] (circa 1700)
**1** : a round building; *especially* : one covered by a dome
**2 a** : a large round room **b** : a large central area (as in a hotel)
**ro·tu·ri·er** \rō-'tür-ē-ˌā, -'tyu̇r-\ *noun* [Middle French] (1586)
: a person not of noble birth
**rou·ble** *variant of* RUBLE

**roué** \rü-'ā\ *noun* [French, literally, broken on the wheel, from past participle of *rouer* to break on the wheel, from Medieval Latin *rotare*, from Latin, to rotate; from the feeling that such a person deserves this punishment] (1800)
: a man devoted to a life of sensual pleasure : RAKE ◆
**¹rouge** \'rüzh, *especially Southern* 'rüj\ *noun* [French, from Middle French, from *rouge* red, from Latin *rubeus* reddish — more at RUBY] (1753)
**1** : any of various cosmetics for coloring the cheeks or lips red
**2** : a red powder consisting essentially of ferric oxide used in polishing glass, metal, or gems and as a pigment
**²rouge** *verb* **rouged; roug·ing** (1777)
*transitive verb*
**1** : to apply rouge to
**2** : to cause to redden
*intransitive verb*
: to use rouge
**¹rough** \'rəf\ *adjective* **rough·er; rough·est** [Middle English, from Old English *rūh;* akin to Old High German *rūh* rough, Lithuanian *raukas* wrinkle] (before 12th century)
**1 a** : marked by inequalities, ridges, or projections on the surface : COARSE **b** : covered with or made up of coarse and often shaggy hair ⟨*rough*-coated collie⟩ — compare SMOOTH, WIREHAIRED **c** (1) : having a broken, uneven, or bumpy surface ⟨*rough* terrain⟩ (2) : difficult to travel through or penetrate : WILD ⟨into the *rough* woods —P. B. Shelley⟩
**2 a** : TURBULENT, TEMPESTUOUS ⟨*rough* seas⟩ **b** (1) : characterized by harshness, violence, or force (2) : presenting a challenge : DIFFICULT ⟨*rough* to deal with —R. M. McAlmon⟩
**3** : coarse or rugged in character or appearance: as **a** : harsh to the ear **b** : crude in style or expression **c** : INDELICATE **d** : marked by a lack of refinement or grace : UNCOUTH
**4 a** : CRUDE, UNFINISHED ⟨*rough* carpentry⟩ **b** : executed or ventured hastily, tentatively, or imperfectly ⟨a *rough* draft⟩ ⟨*rough* estimate⟩; *also* : APPROXIMATE ⟨this gives a *rough* idea⟩ ☆
— **rough·ish** \'rə-fish\ *adjective*
— **rough·ness** \'rəf-nəs\ *noun*
**²rough** *adverb* (14th century)
: ROUGHLY 1
**³rough** *noun* (15th century)
**1** : uneven ground covered with high grass, brush, and stones; *specifically* : such ground bordering a golf fairway
**2** : the rugged or disagreeable side or aspect ⟨hiking-camping admirers of nature in the *rough* —Eleanor Stirling⟩
**3 a** : something in a crude, unfinished, or preliminary state **b** : broad outline : general terms ⟨the question . . . has been discussed in *rough* —*Manchester Guardian Weekly*⟩ **c** : a hasty preliminary drawing or layout
**4** : ROWDY
**⁴rough** *transitive verb* (1763)
**1** : ROUGHEN
**2 a** : to subject to abuse : MANHANDLE, BEAT — usually used with *up* **b** : to subject to unnecessary and intentional violence in a sport
**3** : to calk or otherwise roughen ⟨a horse's shoes⟩ to prevent slipping
**4 a** : to shape, make, or dress in a rough or preliminary way **b** : to indicate the chief lines of ⟨*rough* out the structure of a building⟩
— **rough·er** *noun*
— **rough it** : to live under harsh or primitive conditions
**rough·age** \'rə-fij\ *noun* (circa 1900)
: FIBER 1d; *also* : food containing much indigestible material acting as fiber
**rough–and–ready** \ˌrə-fən-'re-dē\ *adjective* (1810)
: crude in nature, method, or manner but effective in action or use

**¹rough–and–tum·ble** \-'təm-bəl\ *noun* (1792)
: rough disorderly unrestrained fighting or struggling; *also* : INFIGHTING
**²rough–and–tumble** *adjective* (1832)
**1** : marked by rough-and-tumble ⟨grew up in a *rough-and-tumble* atmosphere —E. J. Kahn⟩; *also* : ROUGH-AND-READY
**2** : put together haphazardly : MAKESHIFT ⟨a *rough-and-tumble* fence⟩
**rough bluegrass** *noun* (circa 1925)
: a forage grass (*Poa trivialis*) of Eurasia and northern Africa that is naturalized in North America
**rough breathing** *noun* (1899)
**1** : a mark ʽ used in Greek over some initial vowels to show that they are aspirated or over ρ to show that it is voiceless
**2** : the sound indicated by a mark ʽ over a Greek vowel or ρ
**¹rough·cast** \'rəf-ˌkast, *for 2 also* -'kast\ *transitive verb* **-cast; -cast·ing** (1565)
**1** : to plaster (as a wall) with roughcast
**2** : to shape or form roughly
**²rough·cast** \-ˌkast\ *noun* (1579)
**1** : a rough model
**2** : a plaster of lime mixed with shells or pebbles used for covering buildings
**3** : a rough surface finish (as of a plaster wall)
**rough cut** *noun* (1937)

---

☆ **SYNONYMS**
**Rough, harsh, uneven, rugged, scabrous** mean not smooth or even. ROUGH implies points, bristles, ridges, or projections on the surface ⟨a *rough* wooden board⟩. HARSH implies a surface or texture distinctly unpleasant to the touch ⟨a *harsh* fabric that chafes the skin⟩. UNEVEN implies a lack of uniformity in height, breadth, or quality ⟨an old house with *uneven* floors⟩. RUGGED implies irregularity or roughness of land surface and connotes difficulty of travel ⟨a *rugged* landscape⟩. SCABROUS implies scaliness or prickliness of surface ⟨a *scabrous* leaf⟩. See in addition RUDE.

---

◇ **WORD HISTORY**
**roué** In ancient and medieval times wheels were used as instruments of torture and execution, employed in devices that in one way or another disjointed or mutilated the victim. In 16th century France the use of the wheel in a somewhat more symbolic way was introduced as a means of capital punishment: a criminal would have his limbs and chest crushed by iron bars, after which he would be tied onto a carriage wheel placed upright on a post and exposed until he died. The French verb denoting this means of execution was *rouer*, a derivative of *roue* "wheel," corresponding to Medieval Latin *rotare* "to break on the wheel," a derivative of Latin *rota* "wheel." About the year 1720 Philippe II, the Duke of Orleans and Regent of France, who was himself a libertine, allegedly called his debauched companions *roués*, meaning literally "those executed on the wheel." The customary interpretation is that this epithet was a wry acknowledgment, or even boast, that they all deserved to be so killed for their wicked ways. *Roué* became a generic word in French for someone devoted to a life of sensual pleasure and by 1800 had been borrowed into English.

---

\ə\ abut \ᵊ\ kitten \ər\ further \a\ ash \ā\ ace
\ä\ mop, mar \au̇\ out \ch\ chin \e\ bet \ē\ easy
\g\ go \i\ hit \ī\ ice \j\ job \ŋ\ sing \ō\ go
\ò\ law \òi\ boy \th\ thin \th̲\ the \ü\ loot \u̇\ foot
\y\ yet \zh\ vision *see also* Guide to Pronunciation

: a print of an incompletely edited motion picture

**¹rough–dry** \'rəf-'drī\ *transitive verb* (1837)
: to dry (laundry) without smoothing or ironing

**²rough–dry** *adjective* (1856)
: being dry after laundering but not ironed or smoothed over ⟨*rough-dry* clothes⟩

**rough·en** \'rə-fən\ *verb* **rough·ened; rough·en·ing** \'rə-fə-niŋ, 'rəf-niŋ\ (1582)
*transitive verb*
: to make rough or rougher ⟨her hands were *roughened* by work —Ellen Glasgow⟩
*intransitive verb*
: to become rough

**rough fish** *noun* (1843)
: a fish that is neither a sport fish nor an important food for sport fishes

**rough–hew** \'rəf-'hyü\ *transitive verb* **-hewed; -hewn** \-'hyün\; **-hew·ing** (1530)
**1** : to hew (as timber) coarsely without smoothing or finishing
**2** : to form crudely

**rough–hewn** \-'hyün\ *adjective* (1530)
**1** : being in a rough, unsmoothed, or unfinished state : crudely formed ⟨*rough-hewn* beams⟩
**2** : lacking refinement ⟨he was rather attractive, in a *rough-hewn* kind of way —Jan Speas⟩

**¹rough·house** \'rəf-ˌhaůs\ *noun* (1887)
: violence or rough boisterous play

**²rough·house** \-ˌhaůs, -ˌhaůz\ *verb* **rough·housed; rough·hous·ing** (1902)
*transitive verb*
: to treat in a boisterously rough manner
*intransitive verb*
: to engage in roughhouse

**rough·leg** \'rəf-ˌleg, -ˌläg\ *noun* (1895)
: ROUGH-LEGGED HAWK

**rough–legged hawk** *noun* (1811)
: a large circumpolar arctic hawk (*Buteo lagopus*) that winters southward and typically has a white tail with a wide black band or bands at the tip

**rough lemon** *noun* (1900)
**1** : a hybrid lemon that forms a large spreading thorny tree, bears rough-skinned nearly globular acid fruit, and is important chiefly as a rootstock for other citrus trees
**2** : the fruit of a rough lemon

**rough·ly** \'rə-flē\ *adverb* (14th century)
**1** : in a rough manner: as **a** : with harshness or violence ⟨treated the prisoner *roughly*⟩ **b** : in crude fashion : IMPERFECTLY ⟨*roughly* dressed lumber⟩
**2** : without completeness or exactness : APPROXIMATELY ⟨*roughly* 20 percent⟩

**¹rough·neck** \'rəf-ˌnek\ *noun* (1836)
**1 a** : a rough or uncouth person **b** : ROWDY, TOUGH
**2** : a worker of an oil-well-drilling crew other than the driller

**²roughneck** *adjective* (1916)
: having the characteristics of or suitable for a roughneck

**rough·ri·der** \'rəf-ˌrī-dər\ *noun* (1733)
**1** : one who is accustomed to riding unbroken or little-trained horses
**2** *usually* **Rough Rider** : a member of the 1st U.S. Volunteer Cavalry regiment in the Spanish-American War commanded by Theodore Roosevelt

**¹rough·shod** \-ˌshäd\ *adjective* (circa 1688)
**1** : shod with calked shoes
**2** : marked by tyrannical force ⟨*roughshod* rule⟩

**²roughshod** *adverb* (1813)
: in a roughshod manner ⟨rode *roughshod* over the opposition⟩

**rough trade** *noun* (circa 1935)
: male homosexuals who are or affect to be rugged and potentially violent; *also* : such a homosexual

**rouille** \'rü-ē, rüy\ *noun* [French, literally, rust; from its color] (1951)

: a peppery garlic sauce

**rou·lade** \rü-'läd\ *noun* [French, literally, act of rolling] (circa 1706)
**1** : a florid vocal embellishment sung to one syllable
**2** : a slice of usually stuffed meat that is rolled, browned, and steamed or braised

**rou·leau** \rü-'lō\ *noun, plural* **rou·leaux** \-'lōz\ [French] (1693)
: a little roll; *especially* : a roll of coins put up in paper

**¹rou·lette** \rü-'let\ *noun* [French, literally, small wheel, from Old French *roelete*, diminutive of *roele* small wheel, from Late Latin *rotella*, diminutive of Latin *rota* wheel — more at ROLL] (1745)
**1** : a gambling game in which players bet on which compartment of a revolving wheel a small ball will come to rest in
**2 a** : any of various toothed wheels or disks (as for producing rows of dots on engraved plates or for making short consecutive incisions in paper to facilitate subsequent division) **b** : tiny slits between rows of stamps in a sheet that are made by a roulette and serve as an aid in separation — compare PERFORATION

**²roulette** *transitive verb* **rou·lett·ed; rou·lett·ing** (1867)
: to make roulettes in

**Rou·ma·nian** \rü-'mā-nē-ən, -nyən\ *variant of* RUMANIAN

**¹round** \'raůnd\ *adjective* [Middle English, from Old French *roont*, from Latin *rotundus* — more at ROTUND] (14th century)
**1 a** (1) : having every part of the surface or circumference equidistant from the center (2) : CYLINDRICAL ⟨a *round* peg⟩ **b** : approximately round ⟨a *round* face⟩
**2** : well filled out : PLUMP, SHAPELY
**3 a** : COMPLETE, FULL ⟨a *round* dozen⟩ ⟨a *round* ton⟩ **b** : approximately correct; *especially* : exact only to a specific decimal or place ⟨use the *round* number 1400 for the exact figure 1411⟩ **c** : substantial in amount : AMPLE ⟨a good *round* price —T. B. Costain⟩
**4** : direct in utterance : OUTSPOKEN ⟨a *round* oath⟩
**5** : moving in or forming a circle
**6 a** : brought to completion or perfection : FINISHED **b** : presented with lifelike fullness or vividness
**7** : delivered with a swing of the arm ⟨a *round* blow⟩
**8 a** : having full or unimpeded resonance or tone : SONOROUS **b** : pronounced with rounded lips : LABIALIZED
**9** : of or relating to handwriting predominantly curved rather than angular
— **round·ness** \'raůn(d)-nəs\ *noun*

**²round** *adverb* (14th century)
: AROUND 1, 2b, 3, 4, 5

**³round** *noun* (14th century)
**1 a** : something (as a circle, globe, or ring) that is round **b** (1) : a knot of people (2) : a circle of things
**2** : ROUND DANCE 1
**3** : a musical canon sung in unison in which each part is continuously repeated
**4 a** : a rung of a ladder or a chair **b** : a rounded molding
**5 a** : a circling or circuitous path or course **b** : motion in a circle or a curving path
**6 a** : a route or circuit habitually covered (as by a security guard or police officer) **b** : a series of similar or customary calls or stops ⟨making the *rounds* of his friends —*Current Biography*⟩; *especially* : a series of regularly scheduled professional calls on hospital patients made by a doctor or nurse — usually used in plural
**7** : a drink of liquor apiece served at one time to each person in a group ⟨I'll buy the next *round*⟩
**8** : a sequence of recurring routine or repetitive actions or events ⟨went about my *round* of chores⟩ ⟨the newest *round* of talks⟩

**9** : a period of time that recurs in a fixed pattern ⟨the daily *round*⟩
**10 a** : one shot fired by a weapon or by each man in a military unit **b** : a unit of ammunition consisting of the parts necessary to fire one shot
**11 a** : a unit of action in a contest or game which comprises a stated period, covers a prescribed distance, includes a specified number of plays, or gives each player one turn **b** : a division of a tournament in which each contestant plays an opponent
**12** : a prolonged burst (as of applause)
**13 a** : a cut of meat (as beef) especially between the rump and the lower leg — see BEEF illustration **b** : a slice of food ⟨a *round* of bread⟩
**14** : a rounded or curved part
— **in the round 1** : in full sculptured form unattached to a background **2** : with an inclusive or comprehensive view or representation **3** : with a center stage surrounded by an audience ⟨theater *in the round*⟩

**⁴round** (14th century)
*transitive verb*
**1 a** : to make round **b** (1) : to make (the lips) round and protruded (as in the pronunciation of \ü\) (2) : to pronounce with lip rounding : LABIALIZE
**2 a** : GO AROUND **b** : to pass part of the way around
**3** : ENCIRCLE, ENCOMPASS
**4** : to bring to completion or perfection — often used with *off* or *out*
**5** : to express as a round number — often used with *off* ⟨11.3572 *rounded* off to two decimal places becomes 11.36⟩
*intransitive verb*
**1 a** : to become round, plump, or shapely **b** : to reach fullness or completion
**2** : to follow a winding course : BEND
— **round on** : to turn against : ASSAIL

**⁵round** *preposition* (1602)
**1** : AROUND
**2** : all during : THROUGHOUT ⟨*round* the year⟩

**⁶round** *transitive verb* [alteration of Middle English *rounen*, from Old English *rūnian*; akin to Old English *rūn* mystery — more at RUNE] (circa 1529)
**1** *archaic* : WHISPER
**2** *archaic* : to speak to in a whisper

**¹round·about** \'raůn-də-ˌbaůt\ *adjective* (1608)
: CIRCUITOUS, INDIRECT ⟨had to take a *roundabout* course⟩
— **round·about·ness** *noun*

**²roundabout** *noun* (1755)
**1** : a circuitous route : DETOUR
**2** *British* : MERRY-GO-ROUND
**3** : a short close-fitting jacket worn by men and boys especially in the 19th century
**4** *British* : ROTARY 2

**round angle** *noun* (circa 1934)
: an angle of 360° or 2 π radians

**round clam** *noun* (circa 1843)
: QUAHOG

**round dance** *noun* (1683)
**1** : a folk dance in which participants form a ring and move in a prescribed direction
**2** : a ballroom dance in which couples progress around the room
**3** : a series of movements performed by a bee to indicate that a source of food is nearby

**round·ed** \'raůn-dəd\ *adjective* (1712)
**1** : made round : flowing rather than jagged or angular
**2** : fully developed
— **round·ed·ness** *noun*

**roun·del** \'raůn-d°l\ *noun* [Middle English, from Old French *rondel*, from *roont* round — more at ROUND] (14th century)
**1** : a round figure or object (as a circular panel, window, or niche)
**2 a** : RONDEL 2a **b** : an English modified rondeau

**roun·de·lay** \'raùn-də-ˌlā\ *noun* [Middle English, modification of Middle French *rondelet*, diminutive of *rondel*] (15th century)
**1 :** a simple song with a refrain
**2 :** a poem with a refrain recurring frequently or at fixed intervals as in a rondel

**round·er** \'raùn-dər\ *noun* (1828)
**1** *plural but singular in construction* **:** a game of English origin that is played with ball and bat and that somewhat resembles baseball
**2 :** a dissolute person **:** WASTREL
**3 :** one that rounds by hand or by machine
**4 :** a boxing match lasting a specified number of rounds — usually used in combination ⟨a 10-*rounder*⟩

**Round·head** \'raùnd-ˌhed\ *noun* [from the Puritans' cropping their hair short in contrast to the Cavaliers] (1642)
**1 :** a member of the parliamentary party in England at the time of Charles I and Oliver Cromwell
**2 :** PURITAN 1

**round·head·ed** \-'he-dəd\ *adjective* (1729)
**:** having a round head; *specifically* **:** BRACHYCEPHALIC
— **round·head·ed·ness** *noun*

**round·house** \'raùnd-ˌhaùs\ *noun* (1589)
**1** *archaic* **:** LOCKUP
**2 :** a circular building for housing and repairing locomotives
**3 :** a blow delivered with a wide swing

**round·ish** \'raùn-dish\ *adjective* (1545)
**:** somewhat round

**round lot** *noun* (circa 1902)
**:** the standard unit of trading in a security market usually amounting to 100 shares of stock

**round·ly** \'raùn(d)-lē\ *adverb* (15th century)
**1 a :** in a complete or thorough manner **:** THOROUGHLY ⟨*roundly* disliked⟩ ⟨*roundly* satisfying⟩ **b :** by nearly everyone **:** WIDELY ⟨*roundly* praised⟩
**2 :** in a plainspoken manner **:** BLUNTLY ⟨told them *roundly* they would get no help⟩
**3 :** with vigor or asperity ⟨*roundly* attacked the plan⟩

**round–rob·in** \'raùnd-ˌrä-bən\ *noun* [from the name *Robin*] (1730)
**1 a :** a written petition, memorial, or protest to which the signatures are affixed in a circle so as not to indicate who signed first **b :** a statement signed by several persons **c :** something (as a letter) sent in turn to the members of a group each of whom signs and forwards it sometimes after adding comment
**2 :** ROUND TABLE 2
**3 :** a tournament in which every contestant meets every other contestant in turn
**4 :** SERIES, ROUND

**round–shoul·dered** \'raùn(d)-ˌshōl-dərd\ *adjective* (1586)
**:** having the shoulders stooping or rounded

**rounds·man** \'raùn(d)z-mən\ *noun* (1795)
**1 :** one that makes rounds
**2 :** a supervisory police officer of the grade of sergeant or just below

**round steak** *noun* (1876)
**:** a steak cut from the round of beef — see BEEF illustration

**round ta·ble** \'raùn(d)-ˌtā-bəl\ *noun* (14th century)
**1 a** *R&T capitalized* **:** the large circular table of King Arthur and his knights **b :** the knights of King Arthur
**2** *usually* **round·ta·ble :** a conference for discussion or deliberation by several participants; *also* **:** the participants in such a conference

**round–the–clock** *adjective* (1937)
**:** AROUND-THE-CLOCK

**round–trip** \'raùn(d)-ˌtrip\ *noun, often attributive* (1860)
**:** a trip to a place and back usually over the same route

**round·up** \'raùn-ˌdəp\ *noun* (1873)
**1 a** (1) **:** the act or process of collecting animals (as cattle) by riding around them and

driving them in (2) **:** the cowboys and ranch personnel engaged in a cattle roundup **b :** a gathering in of scattered persons or things ⟨a *roundup* of all suspects⟩
**2 :** a summary of information ⟨a *roundup* of the news⟩

**round up** *transitive verb* (1844)
**1 :** to collect (as cattle) by means of a roundup
**2 :** to gather in or bring together from various quarters

**round window** *noun* (circa 1903)
**:** FENESTRA 1b

**round·wood** \'raùnd-ˌwùd\ *noun* (1910)
**:** timber used (as for poles) without being squared by sawing or hewing

**round·worm** \'raùnd-ˌwərm\ *noun* (1565)
**:** NEMATODE; *also* **:** a related round-bodied unsegmented worm (as a spiny-headed worm) as distinguished from a flatworm

**roup** \'rüp, 'raùp\ *noun* [origin unknown] (circa 1808)
**:** TRICHOMONIASIS c

**¹rouse** \'raùz\ *verb* **roused; rous·ing** [Middle English, to shake the feathers] (1531)
*transitive verb*
**1** *archaic* **:** to cause to break from cover
**2 a :** to stir up **:** EXCITE ⟨was *roused* to fury⟩ **b :** to arouse from or as if from sleep or repose **:** AWAKEN
*intransitive verb*
**1 :** to become aroused **:** AWAKEN
**2 :** to become stirred
— **rouse·ment** \'raùz-mənt\ *noun*
— **rous·er** *noun*

**²rouse** *noun* (circa 1802)
**:** an act or instance of rousing; *especially* **:** an excited stir

**³rouse** *noun* [alteration (from misdivision of *to drink carouse*) of *carouse*] (1602)
**1** *obsolete* **:** DRINK, TOAST
**2** *archaic* **:** CAROUSAL

**rouse·about** \'raù-zə-ˌbaùt\ *noun* (1861)
*Australian* **:** an unskilled worker

**rous·ing** \'raù-ziŋ\ *adjective* (1641)
**1 a :** giving rise to excitement **:** STIRRING **b :** BRISK, LIVELY
**2 :** EXCEPTIONAL, SUPERLATIVE
— **rous·ing·ly** *adverb*

**Rous sarcoma** \'raùs-\ *noun* [F. Peyton *Rous* (died 1970) American physician] (circa 1925)
**:** a readily transplantable malignant fibrosarcoma of chickens that is caused by a specific carcinogenic virus

**Rous·seau·ism** \rü-'sō-ˌi-zəm\ *noun* (1865)
**1 :** the philosophical, educational, and political doctrines of Jean Jacques Rousseau
**2 :** the return to or glorification of a simpler and more primitive way of life
— **Rous·seau·ist** \-ist\ *noun*
— **Rous·seau·is·tic** \ˌrü-ˌsō-'is-tik, rü-\ *adjective*

**roust** \'raùst\ *transitive verb* [alteration of ¹*rouse*] (1658)
**:** to drive (as from bed) roughly or unceremoniously

**roust·about** \'raù-stə-ˌbaùt\ *noun* (1868)
**1 a :** DECKHAND **b :** LONGSHOREMAN
**2 :** an unskilled or semiskilled laborer especially in an oil field or refinery
**3 :** a circus worker who erects and dismantles tents, cares for the grounds, and handles animals and equipment

**roust·er** \'raù-stər\ *noun* (1883)
**1 :** DECKHAND
**2 :** LONGSHOREMAN

**¹rout** \'raùt\ *noun* [Middle English *route*, from Middle French, troop, defeat, from (assumed) Vulgar Latin *rupta*, from Latin, feminine of *ruptus*, past participle of *rumpere* to break — more at REAVE] (13th century)
**1 :** a crowd of people **:** THRONG; *specifically* **:** RABBLE 2b
**2 a :** DISTURBANCE **b** *archaic* **:** FUSS
**3 :** a fashionable gathering

**²rout** \'rōt, 'rüt\ *intransitive verb* [Middle English *rowten*, from Old Norse *rauta*; akin to

Old English *rēotan* to weep, Latin *rudere* to roar] (14th century)
*dialect chiefly British* **:** to low loudly **:** BELLOW — used of cattle

**³rout** \'raùt\ *verb* [alteration of ³*root*] (circa 1564)
*intransitive verb*
**1 :** to poke around with the snout **:** ROOT ⟨pigs *routing* in the earth⟩
**2 :** to search haphazardly
*transitive verb*
**1 a** *archaic* **:** to dig up with the snout **b :** to gouge out or make a furrow in (as wood or metal)
**2 a :** to force out as if by digging — usually used with *out* **b :** to cause to emerge especially from bed
**3 :** to come up with **:** UNCOVER

**⁴rout** \'raùt\ *noun* [Middle French *route* troop, defeat] (1598)
**1 :** a state of wild confusion or disorderly retreat
**2 a :** a disastrous defeat **:** DEBACLE **b :** a precipitate flight

**⁵rout** \'raùt\ *transitive verb* (1600)
**1 a :** to disorganize completely **:** DEMORALIZE **b :** to put to precipitate flight **c :** to defeat decisively or disastrously ⟨the discomfiture of seeing their party *routed* at the polls —A. N. Holcombe⟩
**2 :** to drive out **:** DISPEL

**¹route** \'rüt, 'raùt\ *noun* [Middle English, from Old French, from (assumed) Vulgar Latin *rupta* (*via*), literally, broken way, from Latin *rupta*, feminine of *ruptus*, past participle] (13th century)
**1 a :** a traveled way **:** HIGHWAY ⟨the main *route* north⟩ **b :** a means of access **:** CHANNEL ⟨the *route* to social mobility —T. F. O'Dea⟩
**2 :** a line of travel **:** COURSE
**3 a :** an established or selected course of travel or action **b :** an assigned territory to be systematically covered ⟨a newspaper *route*⟩

**²route** *transitive verb* **rout·ed; rout·ing** (1832)
**1 :** to send by a selected route **:** DIRECT ⟨was *routed* along the scenic shore road⟩
**2 :** to divert in a specified direction

**route·man** \'rüt-mən, 'raùt-ˌman\ *noun* (1918)
**:** one who is responsible for making sales or deliveries on an assigned route

**¹rout·er** \'raù-tər\ *noun* (1846)
**:** one that routs: as **a :** a routing plane **b :** a machine with a revolving vertical spindle and cutter for milling out the surface of wood or metal

**²rout·er** \'rü-tər, 'raù-\ *noun* (1903)
**:** one that routes

**³rout·er** \'rü-tər, 'raù-\ *noun* [*route* (race of a mile or more)] (circa 1951)
**:** a horse trained for distance races

**route step** *noun* (1867)
**:** a style of marching in which troops maintain prescribed intervals but are not required to keep in step or to maintain silence — called also *route march*

**route·way** \'rüt-ˌwā, 'raùt-\ *noun* (1946)
*chiefly British* **:** ROUTE 3a

**routh** \'raùth, 'rüth\ *noun* [origin unknown] (circa 1689)
*chiefly Scottish* **:** PLENTY

**¹rou·tine** \rü-'tēn\ *noun* [French, from Middle French, from *route* traveled way] (1676)
**1 a :** a regular course of procedure ⟨if resort to legal action becomes a campus *routine* —J. A. Perkins⟩ **b :** habitual or mechanical performance of an established procedure ⟨the *routine* of factory work⟩
**2 :** a reiterated speech or formula ⟨the old "After you" *routine* —Ray Russell⟩

**3 :** a worked-out part (as of an entertainment or sports contest) that may be often repeated ⟨a dance *routine*⟩ ⟨a gymnastic *routine*⟩; *especially* **:** a theatrical number

**4 :** a sequence of computer instructions for performing a particular task

²**rou·tine** \rü-'tēn, 'rü-,\ *adjective* (1817)
**1 :** of a commonplace or repetitious character **:** ORDINARY
**2 :** of, relating to, or being in accordance with established procedure ⟨*routine* business⟩
— **rou·tine·ly** *adverb*

**rou·tin·ize** \rü-'tē-,nīz, 'rü-t°n-,īz\ *transitive verb* **-ized; -iz·ing** (1921)
**:** to discipline in or reduce to a routine
— **rou·tin·i·za·tion** \(,)rü-,tē-nə-'zā-shən, ,rü-t°n-ə-\ *noun*

**roux** \'rü\ *noun, plural* **roux** \'rüz\ [French, from *beurre roux* brown butter] (1813)
**:** a cooked mixture of flour and fat used as a thickening agent in a soup or a sauce

¹**rove** \'rōv\ *verb* **roved; rov·ing** [Middle English *roven* to shoot at random, wander] (1536)
*intransitive verb*
**:** to move aimlessly **:** ROAM
*transitive verb*
**:** to wander through or over
**synonym** see WANDER

²**rove** *noun* (1606)
**:** an act or instance of wandering

³**rove** *past and past participle of* REEVE

⁴**rove** *transitive verb* **roved; rov·ing** [origin unknown] (1789)
**:** to join (textile fibers) with a slight twist and draw out into roving

⁵**rove** *noun* (1789)
**:** ROVING

**rove beetle** *noun* [perhaps from ¹*rove*] (circa 1771)
**:** any of a family (Staphylinidae) of often predatory active beetles having a long body and very short wing covers beneath which the wings are folded transversely — called also *staphylinid*

¹**ro·ver** \'rō-vər\ *noun* [Middle English, from Middle Dutch, from *roven* to rob; akin to Old English *rēafian* to reave — more at REAVE] (14th century)
**:** PIRATE

²**rov·er** \'rō-vər\ *noun* [Middle English, from *roven*] (15th century)
**1 :** a random or long-distance mark in archery — usually used in plural
**2 :** WANDERER, ROAMER
**3 :** a player who is not assigned to a specific position on a team and who plays wherever needed
**4 :** a vehicle for exploring the surface of an extraterrestrial body (as the moon or Mars)

¹**rov·ing** \'rō-vin\ *adjective* [¹*rove*] (1596)
**1 a :** capable of being shifted from place to place **:** MOBILE **b :** not restricted as to location or area of concern
**2 :** inclined to ramble or stray ⟨a *roving* fancy⟩

²**roving** *noun* [⁴*rove*] (1802)
**:** a slightly twisted roll or strand of usually textile fibers

¹**row** \'rō\ *verb* [Middle English, from Old English *rōwan*; akin to Middle High German *rüejen* to row, Latin *remus* oar] (before 12th century)
*intransitive verb*
**1 :** to propel a boat by means of oars
**2 :** to move by or as if by the propulsion of oars
*transitive verb*
**1 a :** to propel with or as if with oars **b :** to be equipped with (a specified number of oars) **c** (1) **:** to participate in (a rowing match) (2) **:** to compete against in rowing (3) **:** to pull (an oar) in a crew
**2 :** to transport in an oar-propelled boat
— **row·er** \'rō-(ə)r\ *noun*

²**row** *noun* (1832)
**:** an act or instance of rowing

³**row** *noun* [Middle English *rawe;* akin to Old English *rǣw* row, Old High German *rīga* line, and perhaps to Sanskrit *rikhati* he scratches] (13th century)
**1 :** a number of objects arranged in a usually straight line ⟨a *row* of bottles⟩; *also* **:** the line along which such objects are arranged ⟨planted the corn in parallel *rows*⟩
**2 a :** WAY, STREET **b :** a street or area dominated by a specific kind of enterprise or occupancy ⟨doctors' *row*⟩
**3 :** TWELVE-TONE ROW
**4 a :** a continuous strip usually running horizontally or parallel to a base line **b :** a horizontal arrangement of items
— **in a row :** one after another **:** SUCCESSIVELY

⁴**row** *transitive verb* (1657)
**:** to form into rows

⁵**row** \'raü\ *noun* [origin unknown] (1746)
**:** a noisy disturbance or quarrel

⁶**row** \'raü\ *intransitive verb* (1797)
**:** to engage in a row **:** have a quarrel

**row·an** \'raü-ən, 'rō-ən\ *noun* [of Scandinavian origin; akin to Old Norse *reynir* rowan; akin to Old English *rēad* red — more at RED] (1804)
**1 a :** a Eurasian mountain ash (*Sorbus aucuparia*) with flat corymbs of white flowers followed by small red pomes **b :** an American mountain ash (*Sorbus americana*) with flat corymbs of white flowers followed by small orange red pomes
**2 :** the fruit of a rowan

rowan 1b: leaves and fruit

**row·an·ber·ry** \-,ber-ē\ *noun* (1814)
**:** ROWAN 2

**row·boat** \'rō-,bōt\ *noun* (1538)
**:** a small boat designed to be rowed

¹**row·dy** \'raü-dē\ *adjective* **row·di·er; -est** [perhaps irregular from ⁵*row*] (1819)
**:** coarse or boisterous in behavior **:** ROUGH; *also* **:** characterized by such behavior ⟨*rowdy* local bars⟩
— **row·di·ly** \'raü-d°l-ē\ *adverb*
— **row·di·ness** \'raü-dē-nəs\ *noun*
— **row·dy·ish** \-ish\ *adjective*

²**rowdy** *noun, plural* **rowdies** (1819)
**:** a rowdy person **:** TOUGH

**row·dy·ism** \'raü-dē-,i-zəm\ *noun* (1842)
**:** rowdy character or behavior

¹**row·el** \'raü(-ə)l\ *noun* [Middle English *rowelle*, from Middle French *rouelle* small wheel, from Old French *roele* — more at ROULETTE] (15th century)
**:** a revolving disk with sharp marginal points at the end of a spur

²**rowel** *transitive verb* **-eled** *or* **-elled; -el·ing** *or* **-el·ling** (1599)
**1 :** to goad with or as if with a rowel
**2 :** VEX, TROUBLE

**row·en** \'raü-ən\ *noun* [Middle English *rowein*, from (assumed) Old North French *rewain;* akin to Old French *regaïn* aftermath, from *re- + gaïn* aftermath, of Germanic origin; akin to Old High German *weida* pasture, *weidanōn* to hunt for food — more at GAIN] (15th century)
**:** AFTERMATH 1

**row house** \'rō-\ *noun* (1936)
**:** one of a series of houses connected by common sidewalls and forming a continuous group

**row·ing** \'rō-in\ *noun* (before 12th century)
**1 :** the propelling of a boat by means of oars **:** the action of one that rows
**2 :** the sport of racing in shells

**rowing boat** *noun* (1820)
*chiefly British* **:** ROWBOAT

**rowing machine** *noun* (1848)

**:** an exercise machine that simulates the action of rowing

**row·lock** \'rä-lək, 'rə-; 'rō-,läk\ *noun* [probably by alteration] (circa 1750)
*chiefly British* **:** OARLOCK

¹**roy·al** \'rȯi(-ə)l\ *adjective* [Middle English *roial*, from Middle French, from Latin *regalis*, from *reg-, rex* king; akin to Old Irish *rī* (genitive *rīg*) king, Sanskrit *rājan*, Latin *regere* to rule — more at RIGHT] (14th century)
**1 a :** of kingly ancestry ⟨the *royal* family⟩ **b :** of, relating to, or subject to the crown ⟨the *royal* estates⟩ **c :** being in the crown's service ⟨*Royal* Air Force⟩
**2 a :** suitable for royalty **:** MAGNIFICENT **b :** requiring no exertion **:** EASY ⟨there is no *royal* road to logic —Justus Buchler⟩
**3 a :** of superior size, magnitude, or quality ⟨a patronage of *royal* dimensions —J. H. Plumb⟩ — often used as an intensive ⟨a *royal* pain⟩ **b :** established or chartered by the crown
**4 :** of, relating to, or being a part (as a mast, sail, or yard) next above the topgallant
— **roy·al·ly** \'rȯi-ə-lē\ *adverb*

²**royal** *noun* (14th century)
**1 :** a person of royal blood
**2 :** a small sail on the royal mast immediately above the topgallant sail
**3 :** a stag of 8 years or more having antlers with at least 12 points

**royal blue** *noun* (1789)
**:** a vivid purplish blue

**royal flush** *noun* (circa 1868)
**:** a straight flush having an ace as the highest card — see POKER illustration

**roy·al·ism** \'rȯi-ə-,li-zəm\ *noun* (1793)
**:** MONARCHISM

**roy·al·ist** \-list\ *noun* (1643)
**1** *often capitalized* **:** an adherent of a king or of monarchical government: as **a :** CAVALIER 3 **b :** TORY 4
**2 :** a reactionary business tycoon
— **royalist** *adjective*

**royal jelly** *noun* (1817)
**:** a highly nutritious secretion of the pharyngeal glands of the honeybee that is fed to the very young larvae in a colony and to all queen larvae

**royal palm** *noun* (1861)
**:** any of a genus (*Roystonea*) of palms chiefly of the Caribbean region; *especially* **:** a tall graceful pinnate-leaved palm (*R. regia*) native to Cuba that is widely planted for ornament

**royal poinciana** *noun* (circa 1900)
**:** a showy tropical tree (*Delonix regia* synonym *Poinciana regia*) widely planted for its immense racemes of scarlet and orange flowers — called also *flamboyant, peacock flower*

**royal purple** *noun* (1661)
**:** a dark reddish purple

**roy·al·ty** \'rȯi(-ə)l-tē\ *noun, plural* **-ties** [Middle English *roialte*, from Middle French *roialté*, from Old French, from *roial*] (14th century)
**1 a :** royal status or power **:** SOVEREIGNTY **b :** a right or perquisite of a sovereign (as a percentage paid to the crown of gold or silver taken from mines)
**2 :** regal character or bearing **:** NOBILITY
**3 a :** persons of royal lineage **b :** a person of royal rank ⟨how to address *royalties* —George Santayana⟩ **c :** a privileged class
**4 :** a right of jurisdiction granted to an individual or corporation by a sovereign
**5 a :** a share of the product or profit reserved by the grantor especially of an oil or mining lease **b :** a payment made to an author or composer for each copy of a work sold or to an inventor for each article sold under a patent

**royster** *variant of* ROISTER

**roz·zer** \'rä-zər\ *noun* [origin unknown] (1893)
*slang British* **:** POLICE OFFICER

**RPG** \,är-(,)pē-'jē\ *noun* [report program generator] (1966)

: a computer language that generates programs from the user's specifications especially to produce business reports

**RPV** \ˌär-(ˌ)pē-'vē\ *noun* [remotely *p*iloted vehicle] (1970)
: an unmanned aircraft flown by remote control and used especially for reconnaissance

**-rrhagia** *noun combining form* [New Latin, from Greek, from *rhēgnynai* to break, burst; probably akin to Lithuanian *rėžti* to cut]
: abnormal or excessive discharge or flow ⟨metro*rrhagia*⟩

**-rrhea** *noun combining form* [Middle English *-ria*, from Late Latin *-rrhoea*, from Greek *-rrhoia*, from *rhoia*, from *rhein* to flow — more at STREAM]
: flow : discharge ⟨logo*rrhea*⟩ ⟨leuko*rrhea*⟩

**-rrhiza** — see -RHIZA

**-rrhoea** *chiefly British variant of* -RRHEA

**rRNA** \ˌär-(ˌ)är-(ˌ)en-'ā\ *noun* (circa 1965)
: RIBOSOMAL RNA

**ru·a·na** \rü-'ä-nə\ *noun* [American Spanish, from Spanish, woolen fabric] (1903)
: a woolen covering resembling a poncho

**¹rub** \'rəb\ *verb* **rubbed; rub·bing** [Middle English *rubben;* akin to Icelandic *rubba* to scrape] (14th century)
*intransitive verb*
**1 a :** to move along the surface of a body with pressure : GRATE **b** (1) : to fret or chafe with or as if with friction (2) : to cause discontent, irritation, or anger
**2 :** to continue in a situation usually with slight difficulty ⟨in spite of financial difficulties, he is *rubbing* along⟩
**3 :** to admit of being rubbed (as for erasure or obliteration)
*transitive verb*
**1 a :** to subject to or as if to the action of something moving especially back and forth with pressure and friction **b** (1) : to cause (a body) to move with pressure and friction along a surface (2) : to treat in any of various ways by rubbing **c :** to bring into reciprocal back-and-forth or rotary contact
**2 :** ANNOY, IRRITATE
**— rub elbows** *or* **rub shoulders :** to associate closely : MINGLE
**— rub one's nose in :** to bring forcefully or repeatedly to one's attention
**— rub the wrong way :** to arouse the antagonism or displeasure of : IRRITATE

**²rub** *noun* (1586)
**1 a :** an unevenness of surface (as of the ground in lawn bowling) **b :** OBSTRUCTION, DIFFICULTY ⟨the *rub* is that so few of the scholars have any sense of this truth themselves —Benjamin Farrington⟩ **c :** something grating to the feelings (as a gibe or harsh criticism) **d :** something that mars serenity
**2 :** the application of friction with pressure ⟨an alcohol *rub*⟩

**Ru·bai·yat stanza** \'rü-bē-ˌät-, -ˌbī-, -ˌat-\ *noun* [*The Rubáiyát of Omar Khayyám,* quatrains translated by Edward FitzGerald (1859)] (1940)
: an iambic pentameter quatrain with a rhyme scheme *aaba*

**ru·basse** \rü-'bas, 'rü-ˌ\ *noun* [French *rubace,* irregular from *rubis* ruby — more at RUBY] (circa 1890)
: a quartz stained a ruby red

**ru·ba·to** \rü-'bä-(ˌ)tō\ *noun, plural* **-tos** [Italian, literally, robbed] (circa 1883)
: a fluctuation of tempo within a musical phrase often against a rhythmically steady accompaniment

**¹rub·ber** \'rə-bər\ *noun* (1536)
**1 a :** one that rubs **b :** an instrument or object (as a rubber eraser) used in rubbing, polishing, scraping, or cleaning **c :** something that prevents rubbing or chafing
**2** [from its use in erasers] **a :** an elastic substance that is obtained by coagulating the milky juice of any of various tropical plants (as of the genera *Hevea* and *Ficus*), is essen-

tially a polymer of isoprene, and is prepared as sheets and then dried — called also *caoutchouc, india rubber* **b :** any of various synthetic rubberlike substances **c :** natural or synthetic rubber modified by chemical treatment to increase its useful properties (as toughness and resistance to wear) and used especially in tires, electrical insulation, and waterproof materials
**3 :** something made of or resembling rubber: as **a :** a rubber overshoe **b** (1) : a rubber tire (2) : the set of tires on a vehicle **c :** a rectangular slab of white rubber in the middle of a baseball infield on which a pitcher stands while pitching **d :** CONDOM
**— rubber** *adjective*

**²rubber** *noun* [origin unknown] (1599)
**1 :** a contest consisting of an odd number of games won by the side that takes a majority (as two out of three)
**2 :** an odd game played to determine the winner of a tie

**rubber band** *noun* (1886)
: a continuous band of rubber used in various ways (as for holding together a sheaf of papers)

**rubber bridge** *noun* (1936)
: a form of contract bridge in which settlement is made at the end of each rubber

**rubber cement** *noun* (1886)
: an adhesive consisting typically of a dispersion of vulcanized rubber in an organic solvent

**rubber check** *noun* [from its coming back like a bouncing rubber ball] (1926)
: a check returned by a bank because of insufficient funds in the payer's account

**rub·ber·ized** \'rə-bə-ˌrīzd\ *adjective* (1908)
: coated or saturated with rubber or a rubber solution

**rub·ber·like** \'rə-bər-ˌlīk\ *adjective* (1922)
: resembling rubber especially in physical properties (as elasticity and toughness)

**¹rub·ber·neck** \-ˌnek\ *noun* (circa 1896)
**1 :** an overly inquisitive person
**2 :** TOURIST; *especially* : one on a guided tour

**²rubberneck** *intransitive verb* (1896)
**1 :** to look about, stare, or listen with exaggerated curiosity
**2 :** to go on a tour : SIGHTSEE
**— rub·ber·neck·er** \-ne-kər\ *noun*

**rubber plant** *noun* (1888)
: a plant that yields rubber; *especially* : a tall tropical Asian tree (*Ficus elastica*) of the mulberry family that is frequently dwarfed as an ornamental

**rubber-stamp** *transitive verb* (1918)
**1 :** to approve, endorse, or dispose of as a matter of routine or at the command of another
**2 :** to mark with a rubber stamp

**rubber stamp** *noun* (1881)
**1 :** a stamp of rubber for making imprints
**2 a :** a person who echoes or imitates others **b :** a body or person that approves or endorses a program or policy with little or no dissent or discussion
**3 a :** a stereotyped copy or expression ⟨the usual *rubber stamps* of criticism —H. L. Mencken⟩ **b :** a routine endorsement or approval
**— rubber-stamp** *adjective*

**rubber tree** *noun* (1847)
: a tree that yields rubber; *especially* : a South American tree (*Hevea brasiliensis*) of the spurge family that is cultivated in plantations and is a chief source of rubber

**rub·bery** \'rə-b(ə-)rē\ *adjective* (1907)
: resembling rubber (as in elasticity, consistency, or texture) ⟨*rubbery* legs⟩

rubber tree

**rub·bing** \'rə-biŋ\ *noun* (1845)
: an image of a raised, incised, or textured surface obtained by placing paper over it and rubbing the paper with a colored substance

**rubbing alcohol** *noun* (circa 1931)
: a cooling and soothing liquid for external application that contains approximately 70 percent denatured ethyl alcohol or isopropanol

**rub·bish** \'rə-bish, *dialect* -bij\ *noun* [Middle English *robys*] (15th century)
**1 :** useless waste or rejected matter : TRASH
**2 :** something that is worthless or nonsensical ⟨few real masterpieces are forgotten and not much *rubbish* survives —William Bridges-Adams⟩
**— rub·bishy** \-bə-shē\ *adjective*

**¹rub·ble** \'rə-bəl\ *noun* [Middle English *robyl*] (14th century)
**1 a :** broken fragments (as of rock) resulting from the decay or destruction of a building ⟨fortifications knocked into *rubble* —C. S. Forester⟩ **b :** a miscellaneous confused mass or group of usually broken or worthless things ⟨lay in a pile of *rubble*, only this time there was more of it, additional gear having hit the deck —K. M. Dodson⟩
**2 :** waterworn or rough broken stones or bricks used in coarse masonry or in filling courses of walls
**3 :** rough stone as it comes from the quarry

**²rubble** *transitive verb* **rub·bled; rub·bling** \-b(ə-)liŋ\ (1926)
: to reduce to rubble

**rub·down** \'rab-ˌdaún\ *noun* (1896)
: a brisk rubbing of the body

**rube** \'rüb\ *noun* [*Rube,* nickname for *Reuben*] (1896)
: an awkward unsophisticated person : RUSTIC

**¹ru·be·fa·cient** \ˌrü-bə-'fā-shənt\ *adjective* [Latin *rubefacient-, rubefaciens,* present participle of *rubefacere* to make red, from *rubeus* reddish + *facere* to make — more at RUBY, DO] (1804)
: causing redness (as of the skin)

**²rubefacient** *noun* (1805)
: a substance for external application that produces redness of the skin

**Rube Gold·berg** \'rüb-'gōl(d)-ˌbərg\ *also* **Rube Gold·berg·i·an** \-ˌbər-gē-ən, -ˌbərg-yən\\ *adjective* [Reuben (*Rube*) L. *Goldberg* (died 1970) American cartoonist] (1931)
: accomplishing by complex means what seemingly could be done simply ⟨a kind of *Rube Goldberg* contraption . . . with five hundred moving parts —L. T. Grant⟩; *also* : characterized by such complex means

**ru·bel·la** \rü-'be-lə\ *noun* [New Latin, from Latin, feminine of *rubellus* reddish, from *ruber* red — more at RED] (1883)
: GERMAN MEASLES

**ru·bel·lite** \rü-'be-ˌlīt, 'rü-bə-ˌlīt\ *noun* [Latin *rubellus*] (circa 1796)
: a red tourmaline used as a gem

**Ru·ben·esque** \ˌrü-bə-'nesk\ *adjective* (1925)
: of, relating to, or suggestive of the painter Rubens or his works; *especially* : plump or rounded usually in a pleasing or attractive way ⟨a *Rubenesque* figure⟩

**ru·be·o·la** \ˌrü-bē-'ō-lə, rü-'bē-ə-lə\ *noun* [New Latin, from neuter plural of (assumed) New Latin *rubeolus* reddish, from Latin *rubeus*] (1803)
: MEASLES

**Ru·bi·con** \'rü-bi-ˌkän\ *noun* [Latin *Rubicon-, Rubico,* river of northern Italy forming part of the boundary between Cisalpine Gaul and Italy whose crossing by Julius Caesar in 49 B.C. was regarded by the Senate as an act of war] (1626)

\ə\ abut \ᵊ\ kitten \ər\ further \a\ ash \ā\ ace
\ä\ mop, mar \aú\ out \ch\ chin \e\ bet \ē\ easy
\g\ go \i\ hit \ī\ ice \j\ job \ŋ\ sing \ō\ go
\ȯ\ law \ȯi\ boy \th\ thin \th\ the \ü\ loot \ú\ foot
\y\ yet \zh\ vision    *see also* Guide to Pronunciation

: a bounding or limiting line; *especially* : one that when crossed commits a person irrevocably

**ru·bi·cund** \'rü-bi-(,)kənd\ *adjective* [Middle English *rubicunde*, from Latin *rubicundus*, from *rubēre* to be red; akin to Latin *rubeus*] (15th century)
: RUDDY
— **ru·bi·cun·di·ty** \,rü-bi-'kən-də-tē\ *noun*

**ru·bid·i·um** \rü-'bi-dē-əm\ *noun* [New Latin, from Latin *rubidus* red, from *rubēre*] (1861)
: a soft silvery metallic element of the alkali metal group that reacts violently with water and bursts into flame spontaneously in air — see ELEMENT table

**rub in** *transitive verb* (1851)
: to harp on (as something unpleasant) : EMPHASIZE

**ru·bi·ous** \'rü-bē-əs\ *adjective* (1601)
: RED, RUBY

**ru·ble** \'rü-bəl\ *noun* [Russian *rubl'*] (1554)
— see MONEY table

**rub off** *intransitive verb* (1950)
: to become transferred 〈bad habits *rubbed off* on them〉 〈carbon *rubs off* on your hands〉
— **rub–off** \'rəb-,óf\ *noun*

**rub out** *transitive verb* (14th century)
**1** : to obliterate or extinguish by or as if by rubbing
**2** : to destroy completely; *specifically* : KILL, MURDER 〈somebody *rubbed* him *out* . . . with a twenty-two —Raymond Chandler〉
— **rub·out** \'rəb-,aůt\ *noun*

**ru·bric** \'rü-brik, -,brik\ *noun* [Middle English *rubrike* red ocher, heading in red letters of part of a book, from Middle French *rubrique*, from Latin *rubrica*, from *rubr-, ruber* red] (14th century)
**1 a** : an authoritative rule; *especially* : a rule for conduct of a liturgical service **b** (1) : NAME, TITLE; *specifically* : the title of a statute (2) : something under which a thing is classed : CATEGORY 〈the sensations falling under the general *rubric*, "pressure" —F. A. Geldard〉 **c** : an explanatory or introductory commentary : GLOSS; *specifically* : an editorial interpolation
**2** : a heading of a part of a book or manuscript done or underlined in a color (as red) different from the rest
**3** : an established rule, tradition, or custom ◆
— **rubric** *or* **ru·bri·cal** \-bri-kəl\ *adjective*
— **ru·bri·cal·ly** \-bri-k(ə-)lē\ *adverb*

**ru·bri·cate** \'rü-bri-,kāt\ *transitive verb* **-cat·ed; -cat·ing** (1570)
**1** : to write or print as a rubric
**2** : to provide with a rubric
— **ru·bri·ca·tion** \,rü-bri-'kā-shən\ *noun*
— **ru·bri·ca·tor** \'rü-bri-,kā-tər\ *noun*

**rub up** *transitive verb* (1572)
**1** : to revive or refresh knowledge of : RECALL
**2** : to improve the keenness of (a mental faculty)

**ru·bus** \'rü-bəs\ *noun, plural* **rubus** [New Latin, from Latin, blackberry] (circa 1921)
: any of a genus (*Rubus*) of plants (as a blackberry or a raspberry) of the rose family having 3- to 7-foliolate or simple lobed leaves, white or pink flowers, and a mass of carpels ripening into an aggregate fruit composed of many drupelets

**¹ru·by** \'rü-bē\ *noun, plural* **rubies** [Middle English, from Middle French *rubis, rubi*, alteration of *robin*, from Medieval Latin *rubinus*, from Latin *rubeus* reddish; akin to Latin *ruber* red — more at RED] (14th century)
**1 a** : a precious stone that is a red corundum **b** : something (as a watch bearing) made of ruby
**2 a** : the dark red color of the ruby **b** : something resembling a ruby in color

**²ruby** *adjective* (1508)
: of the color ruby

**ruby glass** *noun* (1797)
: glass of a deep red color containing selenium, an oxide of copper, or a chloride of gold

**ruby spinel** *noun* (1839)
: a usually red spinel used as a gem

**ru·by-throat** \'rü-bē-,thrōt\ *noun* (circa 1783)
: RUBY-THROATED HUMMINGBIRD

**ru·by-throat·ed hummingbird** \'rü-bē-,thrō-təd-\ *noun* (circa 1782)
: a hummingbird (*Archilochus colubris*) of eastern North America having a bright green back, whitish underparts, and in the adult male a red throat with metallic reflections

**ruche** \'rüsh\ *or* **ruch·ing** \'rü-shiŋ\ *noun* [French *ruche* literally, beehive, from Medieval Latin *rusca* bark] (1827)
: a pleated, fluted, or gathered strip of fabric used for trimming
— **ruched** \'rüsht\ *adjective*

**¹ruck** \'rək\ *noun* [Middle English, of Scandinavian origin; akin to Old Norse *hraukr* rick — more at RICK] (15th century)
**1 a** : the usual run of persons or things : GENERALITY 〈trying to rise above the *ruck* —Richard Holt〉 **b** : an indistinguishable gathering : JUMBLE
**2** : the persons or things following the vanguard 〈finished the race in the *ruck*〉

**²ruck** *verb* [*ruck*, noun, wrinkle] (1812)
: PUCKER, WRINKLE

**ruck·sack** \'rək-,sak, 'růk-\ *noun* [German, from German dialect, from *Rucken* back + *Sack* sack] (1866)
: KNAPSACK

**ruck·us** \'rə-kəs *also* 'rü- *or* 'rů-\ *noun* [probably blend of *ruction* and *rumpus*] (circa 1890)
: ROW, DISTURBANCE 〈raise a *ruckus*〉

**ruc·tion** \'rək-shən\ *noun* [perhaps by shortening & alteration from *insurrection*] (circa 1825)
**1** : a noisy fight
**2** : DISTURBANCE, UPROAR

**rud·beck·ia** \,rəd-'be-kē-ə, rüd-\ *noun* [New Latin, from Olof *Rudbeck* (died 1702) Swedish scientist] (circa 1759)
: any of a genus (*Rudbeckia*) of North American perennial composite herbs having showy flower heads with mostly yellow ray flowers and a conical chaffy receptacle

**rudd** \'rəd, 'růd\ *noun* [probably from *rud* redness, red ocher, from Middle English *rude*, from Old English *rudu* — more at RUDDY] (1526)
: a freshwater European cyprinid fish (*Scardinius erythrophthalmus*) resembling the roach

**rud·der** \'rə-dər\ *noun* [Middle English *rother*, from Old English *rōther* paddle; akin to Old English *rōwan* to row] (14th century)
**1** : a flat piece or structure of wood or metal attached upright to the stern of a boat or ship so that it can be turned causing the vessel's head to turn in the same direction
**2** : a movable auxiliary airfoil on an airplane usually attached at the rear end that serves to control direction of flight in the horizontal plane — see AIRPLANE illustration
**3** : a guiding force or strategy
— **rud·der·less** \-ləs\ *adjective*

**rud·der·post** \-,pōst\ *noun* (1691)
**1** : the shaft of a rudder
**2** : an additional sternpost in a ship with a single screw propeller to which the rudder is attached

**¹rud·dle** \'rə-d°l\ *noun* [diminutive of *rud* red ocher] (1538)
: RED OCHER

**²ruddle** *transitive verb* **rud·dled; rud·dling** \'rəd-liŋ, 'rə-d°l-iŋ\ (1718)
: to color with or as if with red ocher : REDDEN

**rud·dock** \'rə-dək, 'rů-\ *noun* [Middle English *ruddok*, from Old English *rudduc*; akin to Old English *rudu*] (before 12th century)
*archaic* : ROBIN 1a

**rud·dy** \'rə-dē\ *adjective* **rud·di·er; -est** [Middle English *rudi*, from Old English *rudig*, from *rudu* redness; akin to Old English *rēad* red — more at RED] (before 12th century)
**1** : having a healthy reddish color
**2** : RED, REDDISH

**3** *British* — used as an intensive 〈bellowed like a *ruddy* bull when she wanted food —Doreen Tovey〉
— **rud·di·ly** \'rə-d°l-ē\ *adverb*
— **rud·di·ness** \'rə-dē-nəs\ *noun*

**ruddy duck** *noun* (1814)
: an American duck (*Oxyura jamaicensis*) which has a wedge-shaped tail of stiff sharp feathers, a broad bill, and white cheeks and the adult male of which has rich brownish red on the upper side and a blue bill during breeding season

**rude** \'rüd\ *adjective* **rud·er; rud·est** [Middle English, from Middle French, from Latin *rudis;* probably akin to Latin *rudus* rubble] (14th century)
**1 a** : being in a rough or unfinished state : CRUDE 〈*rude* line illustrations〉 **b** : NATURAL, RAW 〈*rude* cotton〉 **c** : PRIMITIVE, UNDEVELOPED 〈peasants use *rude* wooden plows —Jack Raymond〉 **d** : SIMPLE, ELEMENTAL 〈landscape done in *rude* whites, blacks, deep browns —Richard Harris〉
**2** : lacking refinement or delicacy: **a** : IGNORANT, UNLEARNED **b** : INELEGANT, UNCOUTH **c** : offensive in manner or action : DISCOURTEOUS **d** : UNCIVILIZED, SAVAGE **e** : COARSE, VULGAR
**3** : marked by or suggestive of lack of training or skill : INEXPERIENCED 〈*rude* workmanship〉
**4** : ROBUST, STURDY 〈in *rude* health〉
**5** : occurring abruptly and disconcertingly 〈a *rude* awakening〉 ☆
— **rude·ly** *adverb*

**rude·ness** *noun* (14th century)
**1** : the quality or state of being rude
**2** : a rude action

**¹ru·der·al** \'rü-də-rəl\ *adjective* [New Latin *ruderalis*, from Latin *ruder-, rudus* rubble] (circa 1858)
: growing where the natural vegetational cover has been disturbed by humans 〈*ruderal* weeds of old fields and roadsides〉

**²ruderal** *noun* (circa 1928)
: a weedy and commonly introduced plant growing where the vegetational cover has been interrupted

**ru·di·ment** \'rü-də-mənt\ *noun* [Latin *rudimentum* beginning, from *rudis* raw, rude] (1548)

---

---

**1** : a basic principle or element or a fundamental skill — usually used in plural ⟨teaching themselves the *rudiments* of rational government —G. B. Galanti⟩ **2 a** : something unformed or undeveloped : BEGINNING — usually used in plural ⟨the *rudiments* of a plan⟩ **b** (1) : a body part so deficient in size or structure as to be entirely unable to perform its normal function (2) : an organ just beginning to develop : ANLAGE
— **ru·di·men·tal** \ˌrü-də-'men-tʳl\ *adjective*
**ru·di·men·ta·ry** \ˌrü-də-'men-tə-rē, -'men-trē\ *adjective* (1839)
**1** : consisting in first principles : FUNDAMENTAL ⟨had only a *rudimentary* formal education —D. J. Boorstin⟩ **2** : of a primitive kind ⟨the equipment of these past empire-builders was *rudimentary* —A. J. Toynbee⟩ **3** : very imperfectly developed or represented only by a vestige ⟨the *rudimentary* tail of a hyrax⟩
— **ru·di·men·tar·i·ly** \-ˌmen-'ter-ə-lē, -'men-trə-lē\ *adverb*
— **ru·di·men·ta·ri·ness** \-'men-tə-rē-nəs, -'men-trē-\ *noun*
**¹rue** \'rü\ *noun* [Middle English *rewe,* from Old English *hrēow;* akin to Old High German *hriuwa* sorrow] (before 12th century) : REGRET, SORROW
**²rue** *verb* **rued; ru·ing** (12th century) *transitive verb* : to feel penitence, remorse, or regret for *intransitive verb* : to feel sorrow, remorse, or regret
**³rue** *noun* [Middle English, from Middle French, from Latin *ruta,* from Greek *rhytē*] (13th century) : a European strong-scented perennial woody herb (*Ruta graveolens* of the family Rutaceae, the rue family) that has bitter leaves used medicinally
**rue anemone** *noun* (circa 1818) : a delicate vernal North American herb (*Anemonella thalictroides*) of the buttercup family with white flowers resembling those of the wood anemone
**rue·ful** \'rü-fəl\ *adjective* (13th century) **1** : exciting pity or sympathy : PITIABLE ⟨*rueful* squalid poverty . . . by every wayside —John Morley⟩ **2** : MOURNFUL, REGRETFUL ⟨troubled her with a *rueful* disquiet —W. M. Thackeray⟩
— **rue·ful·ly** \-fə-lē\ *adverb*
— **rue·ful·ness** *noun*
**ru·fes·cent** \rü-'fe-sᵊnt\ *adjective* [Latin *rufescent-, rufescens,* present participle of *rufescere* to become reddish, from *rufus* red — more at RED] (1817) : REDDISH
**¹ruff** *also* **ruffe** \'rəf\ *noun* [Middle English *ruf*] (15th century) : a small freshwater European perch (*Acerina cernua*)
**²ruff** *noun* [probably back-formation from *ruffle*] (1555) **1** : a large round collar of pleated muslin or linen worn by men and women of the late 16th and early 17th centuries **2** : a fringe or frill of long hairs or feathers growing around or on the neck **3** : a common Eurasian sandpiper (*Philomachus pugnax*) whose male during the breeding season has a large ruff of erectile feathers on the neck
— **ruffed** \'rəft\ *adjective*

**ruff 1**

**³ruff** *verb* [Middle French *roffler*] (1598) *intransitive verb* : to take a trick with a trump

*transitive verb* : to play a trump on (a card previously led or played)
**⁴ruff** *noun* (circa 1828) : the act of trumping
**ruffed grouse** *noun* (circa 1782) : a North American grouse (*Bonasa umbellus*) of heavy forests that has a ruff of erectile black feathers in the male that is lighter and less conspicuous in the female
**ruf·fi·an** \'rə-fē-ən\ *noun* [Middle French *rufian*] (1531) : a brutal person : BULLY
— **ruffian** *adjective*
— **ruf·fi·an·ism** \-ə-ˌni-zəm\ *noun*
— **ruf·fi·an·ly** *adjective*
**¹ruf·fle** \'rə-fəl\ *verb* **ruf·fled; ruf·fling** \-f(ə-)liŋ\ [Middle English *ruffelen;* akin to Low German *ruffelen* to crumple] (14th century) *transitive verb* **1 a** : ROUGHEN, ABRADE **b** : TROUBLE, VEX ⟨is not *ruffled* by such barbs —Bruce Anderson⟩ **2** : to erect (as feathers) in or like a ruff **3 a** : to flip through (as pages) **b** : SHUFFLE **4** : to make into a ruffle *intransitive verb* : to become ruffled ⟨their dispositions *ruffle* perceptibly —*Life*⟩
**²ruffle** *noun* (1534) **1** : COMMOTION, BRAWL **2** : a state or cause of irritation **3 a** : a strip of fabric gathered or pleated on one edge **b** : ²RUFF 2 **4** : an unevenness or disturbance of surface : RIPPLE
— **ruf·fly** \'rə-f(ə-)lē\ *adjective*
**³ruffle** *noun* [*ruff* a drumbeat] (circa 1802) : a low vibrating drumbeat less loud than a roll
**ru·fi·yaa** \'rü-fē-ˌyä\ *noun, plural* **rufiyaa** [probably from Divehi (Indo-Aryan language of the Maldive Islands), from Hindi *rupīyā, rūpaiyā* rupee] (1982) — see MONEY table
**RU 486** \ˌär-ˌyü-ˌfōr-ˌā-tē-'siks, -ˌfor-\ *noun* [*Roussel-UCLAF,* the drug's French manufacturer + *486,* laboratory serial number] (1983) : a drug $C_{29}H_{35}NO_2$ taken orally to induce abortion especially early in pregnancy by blocking the body's use of progesterone
**ru·fous** \'rü-fəs\ *adjective* [Latin *rufus* red — more at RED] (1782) : REDDISH
**rug** \'rəg\ *noun* [(assumed) Middle English, *rag, tuft,* of Scandinavian origin; akin to Old Norse *rǫgg* tuft] (1591) **1** : LAP ROBE **2** : a piece of thick heavy fabric that usually has a nap or pile and is used as a floor covering **3** : a floor mat of an animal pelt ⟨a bearskin *rug*⟩ **4** *slang* : TOUPEE 2 **5** *British* : a blanket for an animal (as a horse or dog)
**ru·ga** \'rü-gə\ *noun, plural* **ru·gae** \-ˌgī, -ˌgē, -ˌjē\ [New Latin, from Latin, wrinkle — more at CORRUGATE] (1775) : an anatomical fold or wrinkle especially of the viscera — usually used in plural
**rug·by** \'rəg-bē\ *noun, often capitalized* [*Rugby* School, Rugby, England] (1864) : a football game in which play is continuous without time-outs or substitutions, interference and forward passing are not permitted, and kicking, dribbling, lateral passing, and tackling are featured
**rug·ged** \'rə-gəd\ *adjective* [Middle English, from (assumed) Middle English *rug*] (14th century) **1** *obsolete* : SHAGGY, HAIRY **2** : having a rough uneven surface : JAGGED ⟨*rugged* mountains⟩ **3** : TURBULENT, STORMY ⟨*rugged* weather⟩

**4 a** : seamed with wrinkles and furrows : WEATHERED — used of a human face **b** : showing facial signs of strength ⟨*rugged* good looks⟩ **5 a** : AUSTERE, STERN **b** : COARSE, RUDE **c** : rough and strong in character **6 a** : presenting a severe test of ability, stamina, or resolution **b** : strongly built or constituted : ROBUST ⟨those that survive are stalwart, *rugged* men —L. D. Stamp⟩
**synonym** see ROUGH
— **rug·ged·ly** *adverb*
— **rug·ged·ness** *noun*
**rug·ged·ize** \'rə-gə-ˌdīz\ *transitive verb* **-ized; -iz·ing** (1950) : to strengthen (as a machine) for better resistance to wear, stress, and abuse ⟨a *ruggedized* camera⟩
— **rug·ged·i·za·tion** \ˌrə-gə-də-'zā-shən\ *noun*
**rug·ger** \'rə-gər\ *noun* [by alteration] (1893) *British* : RUGBY; *also* : a rugby player
**ru·go·la** \'rü-gə-lə\ *noun* [probably from Italian dialect; akin to Italian dialect *ruga* arugula, Italian *ruca* — more at ROCKET] (1973) : ARUGULA
**ru·go·sa rose** \rü-'gō-sə-, -zə-\ *noun* [New Latin *rugosa,* specific epithet of *Rosa rugosa* rugose rose] (1892) : any of various garden roses descended from a rose (*Rosa rugosa*) introduced from China and Japan — called also *rugosa*
**ru·gose** \'rü-ˌgōs\ *adjective* [Latin *rugosus,* from *ruga*] (1676) **1** : full of wrinkles ⟨*rugose* cheeks⟩ **2** : having the veinlets sunken and the spaces between elevated ⟨*rugose* leaves of the sage⟩
— **ru·gos·i·ty** \rü-'gä-sə-tē\ *noun*
**ru·gu·lose** \'rü-gyə-ˌlōs\ *adjective* [New Latin *rugula,* diminutive of Latin *ruga*] (circa 1819) : having small rugae : finely wrinkled
**¹ru·in** \'rü-ən, -ˌin; 'rün\ *noun* [Middle English *ruine,* from Middle French, from Latin *ruina,* from *ruere* to rush headlong, fall, collapse] (12th century) **1 a** *archaic* : a falling down : COLLAPSE ⟨from age to age . . . the crash of *ruin* fitfully resounds —William Wordsworth⟩ **b** : physical, moral, economic, or social collapse **2 a** : the state of being ruined — archaic except in plural ⟨the city lay in *ruins*⟩ **b** : the remains of something destroyed — usually used in plural ⟨the *ruins* of an ancient temple⟩ ⟨the *ruins* of his life⟩ **3** : a cause of destruction **4 a** : the action of destroying, laying waste, or wrecking **b** : DAMAGE, INJURY **5** : a ruined building, person, or object
— **ru·in·ate** \'rü-ə-ˌnāt, -nət\ *adjective*
— **ruinate** \-ˌnāt\ *transitive verb*
**²ruin** (1585) *transitive verb* **1** : to reduce to ruins : DEVASTATE **2 a** : to damage irreparably **b** : BANKRUPT, IMPOVERISH ⟨*ruined* by stock speculation⟩ **3** : to subject to frustration, failure, or disaster ⟨will *ruin* your chances of promotion⟩ *intransitive verb* : to become ruined
— **ru·in·er** *noun*
**ru·in·a·tion** \ˌrü-ə-'nā-shən\ *noun* (1664) : RUIN, DESTRUCTION
**ru·in·ous** \'rü-ə-nəs\ *adjective* (14th century) **1** : DILAPIDATED, RUINED **2** : causing or tending to cause ruin
— **ru·in·ous·ly** *adverb*
— **ru·in·ous·ness** *noun*
**¹rule** \'rül\ *noun* [Middle English *reule,* from Old French, from Latin *regula* straightedge,

rule, from *regere* to direct — more at RIGHT] (13th century)
**1 a :** a prescribed guide for conduct or action **b :** the laws or regulations prescribed by the founder of a religious order for observance by its members **c :** an accepted procedure, custom, or habit **d** (1) **:** a usually written order or direction made by a court regulating court practice or the action of parties (2) **:** a legal precept or doctrine **e :** a regulation or bylaw governing procedure or controlling conduct **2 a** (1) **:** a usually valid generalization (2) **:** a generally prevailing quality, state, or mode ⟨fair weather was the *rule* yesterday —*N.Y. Times*⟩ **b :** a standard of judgment **:** CRITERION **c :** a regulating principle **d :** a determinate method for performing a mathematical operation and obtaining a certain result **3 a :** the exercise of authority or control **:** DOMINION **b :** a period during which a specified ruler or government exercises control **4 a :** a strip of material marked off in units used especially for measuring **:** RULER 3, TAPE MEASURE **b :** a metal strip with a type-high face that prints a linear design; *also* **:** a linear design produced by or as if by such a strip
**synonym** see LAW
— **as a rule :** for the most part **:** GENERALLY
**²rule** *verb* **ruled; rul·ing** (13th century)
*transitive verb*
**1 a :** to exert control, direction, or influence on ⟨the passions that *rule* our minds⟩ **b :** to exercise control over especially by curbing or restraining ⟨*rule* a fractious horse⟩ ⟨*ruled* his appetites firmly⟩
**2 a :** to exercise authority or power over often harshly or arbitrarily ⟨the speaker *ruled* the legislature with an iron hand⟩ **b :** to be preeminent in **:** DOMINATE
**3 :** to determine and declare authoritatively; *especially* **:** to command or determine judicially
**4 a** (1) **:** to mark with lines drawn along or as if along the straight edge of a ruler (2) **:** to mark (a line) on a paper with a ruler **b :** to arrange in a line
*intransitive verb*
**1 a :** to exercise supreme authority **b :** to be first in importance or prominence **:** PREDOMINATE ⟨the physical did not *rule* in her nature —Sherwood Anderson⟩
**2 :** to exist in a specified state or condition
**3 :** to lay down a legal rule
**synonym** see DECIDE
**ruled surface** *noun* (1862)
**:** a surface generated by a moving straight line with the result that through every point on the surface a line can be drawn lying wholly in the surface
**rule·less** \'rül-ləs\ *adjective* (15th century)
**:** not restrained or regulated by law
**rule of the road** (1871)
**:** a customary practice (as driving always on a particular side of the road or yielding the right of way) developed in the interest of safety and often subsequently reinforced by law; *especially* **:** any of the rules making up a code governing ships in matters relating to mutual safety
**rule of thumb** (1692)
**1 :** a method of procedure based on experience and common sense
**2 :** a general principle regarded as roughly correct but not intended to be scientifically accurate
**rule out** *transitive verb* (1869)
**1 :** EXCLUDE, ELIMINATE
**2 :** to make impossible **:** PREVENT ⟨heavy rain *ruled out* the picnic⟩
**rul·er** \'rü-lər\ *noun* (14th century)
**1 :** one that rules; *specifically* **:** SOVEREIGN
**2 :** a worker or a machine that rules paper
**3 :** a smooth-edged strip (as of wood or metal) that is usually marked off in units (as inches) and is used as a straightedge or for measuring
— **rul·er·ship** \-,ship\ *noun*

**¹rul·ing** \'rü-liŋ\ *noun* (15th century)
**:** an official or authoritative decision, decree, statement, or interpretation (as by a judge on a point of law)
**²ruling** *adjective* (1593)
**1 a :** exerting power or authority ⟨the *ruling* party⟩ **b :** CHIEF, PREDOMINATING ⟨a *ruling* passion⟩
**2 :** generally prevailing
**ruly** \'rü-lē\ *adjective* [back-formation from *unruly*] (15th century)
**:** OBEDIENT, ORDERLY ⟨a *ruly* crowd⟩
**¹rum** \'rəm\ *noun* [probably short for obsolete *rumbullion* rum] (1654)
**1 :** an alcoholic beverage distilled from a fermented cane product (as molasses)
**2 :** alcoholic liquor ⟨the demon *rum*⟩
**²rum** *adjective* **rum·mer; rum·mest** [origin unknown] (1752)
**1** *chiefly British* **:** QUEER, ODD ⟨writing is a *rum* trade . . . and what is all right one day is all wrong the next —Angela Thirkell⟩
**2** *chiefly British* **:** DIFFICULT, DANGEROUS
**ru·ma·ki** \rə-'mä-kē\ *noun* [perhaps modification of Japanese *harumaki*, translation of Chinese (Beijing) *chūnjuǎn* spring roll] (1961)
**:** a cooked appetizer made of pieces of usually marinated chicken liver wrapped together with sliced water chestnuts in bacon slices
**Ru·ma·nian** \rü-'mā-nē-ən, -nyən\ *noun* (1878)
**:** ROMANIAN
— **Rumanian** *adjective*
**rum·ba** \'rəm-bə, 'rüm-, 'rüm-\ *noun* [American Spanish] (1922)
**:** a ballroom dance of Cuban origin in ²⁄₄ or ⁴⁄₄ time with a basic pattern of step-close-step and marked by a delayed transfer of weight and pronounced hip movements; *also* **:** the music for this dance
**¹rum·ble** \'rəm-bəl\ *verb* **rum·bled; rum·bling** \-b(ə-)liŋ\ [Middle English; akin to Middle High German *rummeln* to rumble] (14th century)
*intransitive verb*
**1 :** to make a low heavy rolling sound ⟨thunder *rumbling* in the distance⟩
**2 :** to travel with a low reverberating sound ⟨wagons *rumbled* into town⟩
**3 :** to speak in a low rolling tone
**4 :** to engage in a rumble
*transitive verb*
**1 :** to utter or emit in a low rolling voice
**2** *British* **:** to reveal or discover the true character of
— **rum·bler** \-b(ə-)lər\ *noun*
**²rumble** *noun* (14th century)
**1 a :** a low heavy continuous reverberating often muffled sound (as of thunder) **b :** low frequency noise in phonographic playback caused by the transmission of mechanical vibrations by the turntable to the pickup
**2 :** a seat for servants behind the body of a carriage
**3 a :** widespread expression of dissatisfaction or unrest **b :** a street fight especially among gangs
**rumble seat** *noun* (1912)
**:** a folding seat in the back of an automobile (as a coupe or roadster) not covered by the top
**rum·bling** \'rəm-bliŋ\ *noun* (14th century)
**1 :** RUMBLE
**2 :** general but unofficial talk or opinion often of dissatisfaction — usually used in plural ⟨*rumblings* of political trouble —Anthony Burgess⟩
**rum·bly** \'rəm-b(ə-)lē\ *adjective* (1874)
**:** tending to rumble or rattle
**rum·bus·tious** \,rəm-'bəs-chəs\ *adjective* [alteration of *robustious*] (1778)
*chiefly British* **:** RAMBUNCTIOUS
— **rum·bus·tious·ly** *adverb*, *chiefly British*
— **rum·bus·tious·ness** *noun*, *chiefly British*

**ru·men** \'rü-mən\ *noun, plural* **ru·mi·na** \-mə-nə\ *or* **rumens** [New Latin *rumin-, rumen*, from Latin] (circa 1728)
**:** the large first compartment of the stomach of a ruminant in which cellulose is broken down by the action of symbiotic microorganisms — compare ABOMASUM, OMASUM, RETICULUM
— **ru·mi·nal** \-mə-nᵊl\ *adjective*
**¹ru·mi·nant** \'rü-mə-nənt\ *noun* (1661)
**:** a ruminant mammal
**²ruminant** *adjective* (1691)
**1 a** (1) **:** chewing the cud (2) **:** characterized by chewing again what has been swallowed **b :** of or relating to a suborder (Ruminantia) of even-toed hoofed mammals (as sheep, giraffes, deer, and camels) that chew the cud and have a complex usually 4-chambered stomach
**2 :** given to or engaged in contemplation **:** MEDITATIVE ⟨stood there with her hands clasped in this attitude of *ruminant* relish —Thomas Wolfe⟩
— **ru·mi·nant·ly** *adverb*
**ru·mi·nate** \'rü-mə-,nāt\ *verb* **-nat·ed; -nat·ing** [Latin *ruminatus*, past participle of *ruminari* to chew the cud, muse upon, from *rumin-, rumen* rumen; perhaps akin to Sanskrit *romantha* act of chewing the cud] (1533)
*transitive verb*
**1 :** to go over in the mind repeatedly and often casually or slowly
**2 :** to chew repeatedly for an extended period
*intransitive verb*
**1 :** to chew again what has been chewed slightly and swallowed **:** chew the cud
**2 :** to engage in contemplation **:** REFLECT ◆
**synonym** see PONDER
— **ru·mi·na·tion** \,rü-mə-'nā-shən\ *noun*
— **ru·mi·na·tive** \'rü-mə-,nā-tiv\ *adjective*
— **ru·mi·na·tive·ly** *adverb*
— **ru·mi·na·tor** \-,nā-tər\ *noun*
**¹rum·mage** \'rə-mij\ *verb* **rum·maged; rum·mag·ing** [²*rummage*] (circa 1595)
*intransitive verb*
**1 :** to make a thorough search or investigation
**2 :** to engage in an undirected or haphazard search
*transitive verb*
**1 :** to make a thorough search through **:** RANSACK ⟨*rummaged* the attic⟩
**2 :** to examine minutely and completely
**3 :** to discover by searching
— **rum·mag·er** *noun*
**²rummage** *noun* [obsolete English *rummage* act of packing cargo, modification of Middle French *arrimage*] (1598)
**1 a :** a confused miscellaneous collection **b :** items for sale at a rummage sale
**2 :** a thorough search especially among a confusion of objects
**rummage sale** *noun* (circa 1858)

---

◇ WORD HISTORY
**ruminate** Hoofed animals such as deer, sheep, and domestic cattle digest their food in stages, first swallowing the vegetation that they crop into a special stomach, where it is partially digested, then bringing it back up for some further leisurely chewing. This process is known as chewing the cud, and the animals that engage in it are called *ruminants*, from the present participle of the Latin verb *ruminari* "to chew the cud," a derivative of *rumen*, the Latin name for a ruminant's first stomach. The similarity between recalling food to the mouth for further chewing and recalling an idea to the mind for further thought—as well, perhaps, as the contemplative expression characteristic of a cow in mid-chew—led the Romans to use *ruminari* in an extended sense "to think over, meditate on." The English verb *ruminate*, from the past participle of *ruminari*, retains both the literal and figurative applications of its Latin source.

: a usually informal sale of miscellaneous goods; *especially* : a sale of donated articles conducted by a nonprofit organization (as a church or charity) to help support its programs

**rum·mer** \'rə-mər\ *noun* [German or Dutch; German *Römer*, from Dutch *roemer*] (1654) : a large-bowled footed drinking glass often elaborately etched or engraved

**¹rum·my** \'rə-mē\ *adjective* **rum·mi·er; -est** [²*rum*] (1828) : QUEER, ODD ⟨were still feeling a little *rummy* from our trip up the escalator —*New Yorker*⟩

**²rummy** *noun, plural* **rummies** [¹*rum*] (1851) : DRUNKARD

**³rummy** *noun* [perhaps from ¹*rummy*] (1915) : any of several card games for two or more players in which each player tries to assemble groups of three or more cards of the same rank or suit and to be the first to meld them all

**¹ru·mor** \'rü-mər\ *noun* [Middle English *rumour*, from Middle French, from Latin *rumor* clamor, gossip; akin to Old English *rēon* to lament, Sanskrit *rauti* he roars] (14th century)
**1** : talk or opinion widely disseminated with no discernible source
**2** : a statement or report current without known authority for its truth
**3** *archaic* : talk or report of a notable person or event
**4** : a soft low indistinct sound : MURMUR

**²rumor** *transitive verb* **ru·mored; ru·mor·ing** (1594) : to tell or spread by rumor

**ru·mor·mon·ger** \-ˌməŋ-gər, -ˌmäŋ-\ *noun* (1884) : a person who spreads rumors
— **ru·mor·mon·ger·ing** \-gər-iŋ\ *noun*

**ru·mour** \'rü-mər\ *chiefly British variant of* RU-MOR

**rump** \'rəmp\ *noun* [Middle English, of Scandinavian origin; akin to Icelandic *rumpr* rump; akin to Middle High German *rumph* torso] (15th century)
**1 a** : the upper rounded part of the hindquarters of a quadruped mammal **b** : BUTTOCKS **c** : the sacral or dorsal part of the posterior end of a bird
**2** : a cut of meat (as beef) between the loin and round — see BEEF illustration
**3** : a small or inferior remnant or offshoot; *especially* : a group (as a parliament) carrying on in the name of the original body after the departure or expulsion of a large number of its members

**¹rum·ple** \'rəm-pəl\ *noun* (circa 1520) : FOLD, WRINKLE

**²rumple** *verb* **rum·pled; rum·pling** \-p(ə-)liŋ\ [Dutch *rompelen*; akin to Old High German *rimpfan* to wrinkle] (1603)
*transitive verb*
**1** : WRINKLE, CRUMPLE
**2** : to make unkempt : TOUSLE
*intransitive verb*
: to become rumpled

**rum·ply** \'rəm-p(ə-)lē\ *adjective* **rum·pli·er; -est** (1833) : having rumples

**rum·pus** \'rəm-pəs\ *noun* [origin unknown] (1764) : a usually noisy commotion

**rumpus room** *noun* (1939) : a room usually in the basement of a home that is used for games, parties, and recreation

**rum·run·ner** \'rəm-ˌrə-nər\ *noun* (1920) : a person or ship engaged in bringing prohibited liquor ashore or across a border
— **rum–run·ning** \-ˌrə-niŋ\ *adjective or noun*

**¹run** \'rən\ *verb* **ran** \'ran\ *also chiefly dialect* **run; run; run·ning** [Middle English *ronnen*, alteration of *rinnen*, intransitive verb (from Old English *iernan, rinnan* & Old Norse *rinna*) & of *rennen*, transitive verb, from Old Norse *renna*; akin to Old High German *rinnan*, intransitive verb, to run, Sanskrit *riṇāti*

he causes to flow, and probably to Latin *rivus* stream] (before 12th century)
*intransitive verb*
**1 a** : to go faster than a walk; *specifically* : to go steadily by springing steps so that both feet leave the ground for an instant in each step **b** *of a horse* : to move at a fast gallop **c** : FLEE, RETREAT, ESCAPE ⟨dropped the gun and *ran*⟩ **d** : to utilize a running play on offense — used of a football team
**2 a** : to go without restraint : move freely about at will ⟨let chickens *run* loose⟩ **b** : to keep company : CONSORT ⟨a ram *running* with ewes⟩ ⟨*ran* with a wild crowd when he was young⟩ **c** : to sail before the wind in distinction from reaching or sailing close-hauled **d** : ROAM, ROVE ⟨*running* about with no overcoat⟩
**3 a** : to go rapidly or hurriedly : HASTEN ⟨*run* and fetch the doctor⟩ **b** : to go in urgency or distress : RESORT ⟨*runs* to mother at every little difficulty⟩ **c** : to make a quick, easy, or casual trip or visit ⟨*ran* over to borrow some sugar⟩
**4 a** : to contend in a race **b** : to enter into an election contest
**5 a** : to move on or as if on wheels : GLIDE ⟨file drawers *running* on ball bearings⟩ **b** : to roll forward rapidly or freely **c** : to pass or slide freely ⟨a rope *runs* through the pulley⟩ **d** : to ravel lengthwise ⟨stockings guaranteed not to *run*⟩
**6** : to sing or play a musical passage quickly ⟨*run* up the scale⟩
**7 a** : to go back and forth : PLY ⟨the train *runs* between New York and Washington⟩ **b** *of fish* : to migrate or move in considerable numbers; *especially* : to move up or down a river to spawn
**8 a** : TURN, ROTATE ⟨a swiftly *running* grindstone⟩ **b** : FUNCTION, OPERATE ⟨the engine *runs* on gasoline⟩
**9 a** (1) : to continue in force, operation, or production ⟨the contract has two more years to *run*⟩ ⟨the play *ran* for six months⟩ (2) : to have a specified duration, extent, or length ⟨the manuscript *runs* nearly 500 pages⟩ **b** : to accompany as a valid obligation or right ⟨a right-of-way that *runs* with the land⟩ **c** : to continue to accrue or become payable ⟨interest on the loan *runs* from July 1st⟩
**10** : to pass from one state to another ⟨*run* into debt⟩
**11 a** : to flow rapidly or under pressure **b** : MELT, FUSE **c** : SPREAD, DISSOLVE ⟨colors guaranteed not to *run*⟩ **d** : to discharge pus or serum ⟨a *running* sore⟩
**12 a** : to develop rapidly in some specific direction; *especially* : to throw out an elongated shoot of growth **b** : to tend to produce or develop a specified quality or feature ⟨they *run* to big noses in that family⟩
**13 a** : to lie in or take a certain direction ⟨the boundary line *runs* east⟩ **b** : to lie or extend in relation to something **c** : to go back : REACH **d** (1) : to be in a certain form or expression ⟨the letter *runs* as follows⟩ (2) : to be in a certain order of succession
**14 a** : to occur persistently ⟨musical talent *runs* in the family⟩ **b** (1) : to remain of a specified size, amount, character, or quality ⟨profits were *running* high⟩ (2) : to have or maintain a relative position or condition (as in a race) ⟨*ran* third⟩ ⟨*running* late⟩ **c** : to exist or occur in a continuous range of variation ⟨shades *run* from white to dark gray⟩
**15 a** : to spread or pass quickly from point to point ⟨chills *ran* up her spine⟩ **b** : to be current : CIRCULATE ⟨speculation *ran* rife⟩
*transitive verb*
**1 a** : to cause (an animal) to go rapidly : ride or drive fast **b** : to bring to a specified condition by or as if by running ⟨*ran* himself to death⟩ **c** : to go in pursuit of : HUNT, CHASE ⟨dogs that *run* deer⟩ **d** : to follow the trail of backward : TRACE ⟨*ran* the rumor to its source⟩

**e** : to enter, register, or enroll as a contestant in a race **f** : to put forward as a candidate for office
**2 a** : to drive (livestock) especially to a grazing place **b** : to provide pasturage for (livestock) **c** : to keep or maintain (livestock) on or as if on pasturage
**3 a** : to pass over or traverse with speed **b** : to accomplish or perform by or as if by running ⟨*ran* a great race⟩ ⟨*running* errands for a bank⟩ **c** : to slip or go through or past ⟨*run* a blockade⟩ ⟨*run* a red light⟩
**4 a** : to cause to penetrate or enter : THRUST ⟨*ran* a splinter into her toe⟩ **b** : STITCH **c** : to cause to pass : LEAD ⟨*run* a wire in from the antenna⟩ **d** : to cause to collide ⟨*ran* his head into a post⟩ **e** : SMUGGLE ⟨*run* guns⟩
**5** : to cause to pass lightly or quickly over, along, or into something ⟨*ran* her eye down the list⟩
**6 a** : to cause or allow (as a vehicle or a vessel) to go in a specified manner or direction ⟨*ran* the car off the road⟩ **b** : OPERATE ⟨*run* a lathe⟩ **c** : to direct the business or activities of : MANAGE, CONDUCT ⟨*run* a factory⟩
**7 a** : to be full of or drenched with ⟨streets *ran* blood⟩ **b** : CONTAIN, ASSAY
**8 a** : to cause to move or flow in a specified way or into a specified position ⟨*run* cards into a file⟩ **b** : to cause to produce a flow (as of water) ⟨*run* the faucet⟩; *also* : to prepare by running a faucet ⟨*run* a hot bath⟩
**9 a** : to melt and cast in a mold ⟨*run* bullets⟩ **b** : TREAT, PROCESS, REFINE ⟨*run* oil in a still⟩ ⟨*run* a problem through a computer⟩
**10** : to make oneself liable to : INCUR ⟨*ran* the risk of discovery⟩
**11** : to mark out : DRAW ⟨*run* a contour line on a map⟩
**12 a** : to permit (as charges) to accumulate before settling ⟨*run* an account at the grocery⟩ — often used with *up* ⟨*ran* up a large phone bill⟩ **b** : COST 1 ⟨rooms that *run* $50 a night⟩
**13 a** : to produce by or as if by printing — usually used with *off* ⟨*ran* off 10,000 copies of the first edition⟩ **b** : to carry in a printed medium : PRINT ⟨every newspaper *ran* the story⟩
**14 a** : to make (a series of counts) without a miss ⟨*run* 19 in an inning in billiards⟩ **b** : to lead winning cards of (a suit) successively **c** : to alter by addition ⟨*ran* his record to six wins and four losses⟩
**15** : to make (a golf ball) roll forward after alighting ▪
— **run across** : to meet with or discover by chance
— **run a fever** *or* **run a temperature** : to have a fever
— **run after 1** : PURSUE, CHASE; *especially* : to seek the company of **2** : to take up with : FOLLOW ⟨*run after* new theories⟩
— **run against 1** : to meet suddenly or unexpectedly **2** : to work or take effect unfavorably to : DISFAVOR, OPPOSE
— **run foul of 1** : to collide with ⟨*ran* foul *of* a hidden reef⟩ **2** : to come into conflict with ⟨*run* foul *of* the law⟩

□ USAGE
**run** The past tense *run* still survives in speech in southern England and in the speech especially of older people in some parts of the U.S. It was formerly used in literature, and was a standard variant in our dictionaries from 1828 until 1934. Grammarians have generally opposed it, and many people consider it nonstandard. Just about everybody uses *ran* in writing now.

\ə\ abut \ᵊ\ kitten \ər\ further \a\ ash \ā\ ace
\ä\ mop, mar \au̇\ out \ch\ chin \e\ bet \ē\ easy
\g\ go \i\ hit \ī\ ice \j\ job \ŋ\ sing \ō\ go
\ȯ\ law \ȯi\ boy \th\ thin \th\ the \ü\ loot \u̇\ foot
\y\ yet \zh\ vision *see also* Guide to Pronunciation

— **run into 1 a :** to change or transform into **:** BECOME **b :** to merge with **c :** to mount up to ⟨their yearly income often *runs into* six figures⟩ **2 a :** to collide with **b :** to meet by chance ⟨*ran into* an old classmate the other day⟩

— **run low on :** to approach running out of ⟨*running low on* options⟩

— **run rings around :** to show marked superiority over **:** defeat decisively or overwhelmingly

— **run riot 1 :** to act wildly or without restraint **2 :** to occur in profusion ⟨daffodils *running riot*⟩

— **run short :** to become insufficient

— **run short of :** to use up **:** run low on

— **run to :** to mount up to ⟨the book *runs to* 500 pages⟩

— **run upon :** to run across **:** meet with

²**run** *noun* (14th century)
**1 a :** an act or the action of running **:** continued rapid movement **b :** a quickened gallop **c :** a migration of fish (as up or down a river) especially to spawn; *also* **:** such fish in the process of migration **d :** a running race ⟨a mile *run*⟩ **e :** a score made in baseball by a runner reaching home plate safely **f :** strength or ability to run **g :** a gain of a usually specified distance made on a running play in football ⟨scored on a 25-yard *run*⟩; *also* **:** a running play **h :** a sustained usually aggressive effort (as to win or obtain something) ⟨making a *run* at the championship⟩
**2 a** *chiefly Midland* **:** CREEK 2 **b :** something that flows in the course of an operation or during a particular time ⟨the first *run* of sap in sugar maples⟩
**3 a :** the stern of the underwater body of a ship from where it begins to curve or slope upward and inward **b :** the direction in which a vein of ore lies **c :** a direction of secondary or minor cleavage **:** GRAIN ⟨the *run* of a mass of granite⟩ **d :** a horizontal distance (as that covered by a flight of steps) **e :** general tendency or direction
**4 :** a continuous period or series especially of things of identical or similar sort ⟨a *run* of bad luck⟩: as **a :** a rapid passage up or down a scale in vocal or instrumental music **b :** a number of rapid small dance steps executed in even tempo **c :** the act of making successively a number of successful shots or strokes; *also* **:** the score thus made ⟨a *run* of 20 in billiards⟩ **d :** an unbroken course of performances or showings **e :** a set of consecutive measurements, readings, or observations **f :** persistent and heavy demands from depositors, creditors, or customers ⟨a *run* on a bank⟩ **g :** SEQUENCE 2b
**5 :** the quantity of work turned out in a continuous operation ⟨a press *run* of 10,000 copies⟩
**6 :** the usual or normal kind, character, type, or group ⟨the average *run* of students⟩
**7 a :** the distance covered in a period of continuous traveling or sailing **b :** a course or trip especially if mapped out and traveled with regularity **c :** a news reporter's regular territory **:** BEAT **d :** freedom of movement in or access to a place or area ⟨has the *run* of the house⟩
**8 a :** the period during which a machine or plant is in continuous operation **b :** the use of machinery for a single set of processing procedures ⟨a computer *run*⟩
**9 a :** a way, track, or path frequented by animals **b :** an enclosure for domestic animals where they may feed or exercise **c** *Australian* (1) **:** a large area of land used for grazing ⟨a sheep *run*⟩ (2) **:** RANCH, STATION ⟨*run*-holder⟩ **d :** an inclined passageway
**10 a :** an inclined course (as for skiing or bobsledding) **b :** a support (as a track, pipe, or trough) on which something runs
**11 a :** a ravel in a knitted fabric (as in hosiery) caused by the breaking of stitches **b :** a paint defect caused by excessive flow

**12** *plural but singular or plural in construction* **:** DIARRHEA — used with *the*

— **on the run 1 :** in haste **:** without pausing ⟨ate lunch *on the run*⟩ **2 :** in retreat **:** in flight (as from the law) ⟨an escaped convict *on the run*⟩

³**run** *adjective* (1774)
**1 a :** being in a melted state ⟨*run* butter⟩ **b :** made from molten material **:** cast in a mold ⟨*run* metal⟩
**2** *of fish* **:** having made a migration or spawning run ⟨a fresh *run* salmon⟩
**3 :** exhausted or winded from running

**run·about** \'rə-nə-ˌbaut\ *noun* (1549)
**1 :** one who wanders about **:** STRAY
**2 :** a light usually open wagon, car, or motorboat

**run·a·gate** \'rə-nə-ˌgāt\ *noun* [alteration of *renegate*, from Medieval Latin *renegatus* — more at RENEGADE] (1547)
**1 :** VAGABOND
**2 :** FUGITIVE, RUNAWAY

**run along** *intransitive verb* (1902)
**:** to go away **:** be on one's way **:** DEPART

**run·around** \'rə-nə-ˌraund\ *noun* (1915)
**1 :** deceptive or delaying action especially in response to a request ⟨tired of getting the *run-around*⟩
**2 :** matter typeset in shortened measure to run around something (as a cut)

¹**run·away** \'rə-nə-ˌwā\ *noun* (1547)
**1 :** one that runs away from danger, duty, or restraint **:** FUGITIVE
**2 :** the act of running away out of control; *also* **:** something (as a horse) that is running out of control
**3 :** a one-sided or overwhelming victory

²**runaway** *adjective* (1548)
**1 a :** running away **:** FUGITIVE **b :** leaving to gain special advantages (as lower wages) or avoid disadvantages (as governmental or union restrictions) ⟨*runaway* shipping firms⟩ ⟨a *runaway* shop⟩
**2 :** accomplished by elopement or during flight
**3 :** won by or having a long lead ⟨a *runaway* success⟩; *also* **:** extremely successful ⟨a *runaway* best-seller⟩
**4 :** subject to uncontrolled changes ⟨*runaway* inflation⟩
**5 :** being or operating out of control ⟨a *runaway* oil well⟩ ⟨a *runaway* nuclear reactor⟩

**run away** *intransitive verb* (13th century)
**1 a :** to leave quickly in order to avoid or escape something **b :** to leave home; *especially* **:** ELOPE
**2 :** to run out of control **:** STAMPEDE, BOLT
**3 :** to gain a substantial lead **:** win by a large margin

— **run away with 1 :** to take away in haste or secretly; *especially* **:** STEAL **2 :** to outshine the others in (a theatrical performance) **3 :** to carry or drive beyond prudent or reasonable limits ⟨your imagination *ran away with* you⟩

**run·back** \'rən-ˌbak\ *noun* (1929)
**:** a run made in football after catching an opponent's kick or intercepting a pass

**run·ci·ble spoon** \'rən(t)-sə-bəl-\ *noun* [coined with an obscure meaning by Edward Lear] (1871)
**:** a sharp-edged fork with three broad curved prongs

**run·ci·nate** \'rən(t)-sə-ˌnāt\ *adjective* [Latin *runcinatus*, past participle of *runcinare* to plane off, from *runcina* plane] (1776)
**:** pinnately cut with the lobes pointing downward ⟨*runcinate* leaves of the dandelion⟩ — see LEAF illustration

**run·dle** \'rən-d°l\ *noun* [Middle English *roundel* circle — more at ROUNDEL] (1565)
**1 :** a step of a ladder **:** RUNG
**2 :** the drum of a windlass or capstan

**rund·let** *or* **run·let** \'rən(d)-lət\ *noun* [Middle English *roundelet*, from Middle French *rondelet* — more at ROUNDELAY] (14th century)
**:** a small barrel **:** KEG

**run·down** \'rən-ˌdaun\ *noun* (1908)
**1 :** a play in baseball in which a base runner who is caught off base is chased by two or more opposing players who throw the ball from one to another in an attempt to tag the runner out
**2 :** a item-by-item report or review **:** SUMMARY

**run–down** \'rən-'daun\ *adjective* (1866)
**1 :** WORN-OUT, EXHAUSTED
**2 :** completely unwound
**3 :** being in poor repair **:** DILAPIDATED

**run down** (circa 1578)
*transitive verb*
**1 a :** to collide with and knock down **b :** to run against and cause to sink
**2 a :** to chase to exhaustion or until captured **b :** to trace the source of **c :** to tag out (a base runner) between bases on a rundown
**3 :** DISPARAGE
*intransitive verb*
**1 :** to cease to operate because of the exhaustion of motive power ⟨the clock *ran down*⟩
**2 :** to decline in physical condition or vigor

**rune** \'rün\ *noun* [Old Norse & Old English *rūn* mystery, runic character, writing; akin to Old High German *rūna* secret discussion, Old Irish *rún* mystery] (1690)
**1 :** any of the characters of any of several alphabets used by the Germanic peoples from about the 3d to the 13th centuries
**2 :** MYSTERY, MAGIC
**3** [Finnish *runo*, of Germanic origin; akin to Old Norse *rūn*] **a :** a Finnish or Old Norse poem **b :** POEM, SONG

— **ru·nic** \'rü-nik\ *adjective*

rune 1: Anglo-Saxon runic alphabet

¹**rung** *past participle of* RING

²**rung** \'rəŋ\ *noun* [Middle English, from Old English *hrung* crossbar; akin to Gothic *hrunga* staff and perhaps to Old English *hring* ring — more at RING] (14th century)
**1 a :** a rounded part placed as a crosspiece between the legs of a chair **b :** one of the crosspieces of a ladder
**2** *Scottish* **:** a heavy staff or cudgel
**3 :** a spoke of a wheel
**4 :** a level in a hierarchy ⟨rise a few *rungs* on the social scale —H. W. Van Loon⟩

**run–in** \'rən-ˌin\ *noun* (1857)
**1** *British* **:** the final part of a race or racetrack
**2 :** ALTERCATION, QUARREL
**3 :** something inserted as a substantial addition in copy or typeset matter

**run in** (1817)
*transitive verb*
**1 a :** to insert as additional matter **b :** to make (typeset matter) continuous without a paragraph or other break
**2 :** to arrest for a usually minor offense
**3** *chiefly British* **:** to operate (a new machine) carefully until there is efficient running
*intransitive verb*
**:** to pay a casual visit

**run·less** \'rən-ləs\ *adjective* (1921)
**:** scoring or allowing no runs

**run·let** \'rən-lət\ *noun* (circa 1755)
**:** RIVULET, STREAMLET

**run·nel** \'rə-n°l\ *noun* [alteration of Middle English *rinel*, from Old English *rynel;* akin to Old English *rinnan* to run — more at RUN] (before 12th century)
**:** RIVULET, STREAMLET

**run·ner** \'rə-nər\ *noun* (14th century)
**1 a :** one that runs **:** RACER **b :** BASE RUNNER **c :** BALLCARRIER
**2 a :** MESSENGER **b :** one that smuggles or distributes illicit or contraband goods (as drugs, liquor, or guns)
**3 :** any of several large active carangid fishes

**4 a :** either of the longitudinal pieces on which a sled or sleigh slides **b :** the part of a skate that slides on the ice **:** BLADE **c :** the support of a drawer or a sliding door
**5 a :** a growth produced by a plant in running; *especially* **:** STOLON 1a **b :** a plant that forms or spreads by means of runners **c :** a twining vine (as a scarlet runner)
**6 a :** a long narrow carpet for a hall or staircase **b :** a narrow decorative cloth cover for a table or dresser top

**runner bean** *noun* (1882)
*chiefly British* **:** SCARLET RUNNER

**run·ner-up** \'rə-nə-,rəp, ,rə-nə-'\ *noun, plural* **run·ners-up** \-nər-,zəp, -'zəp\ *also* **runner-ups** (1842)
**:** the competitor that does not win first place in a contest; *especially* **:** one that finishes in second place

**¹run·ning** \'rə-niŋ\ *noun* (before 12th century)
**1 a :** the action of running **b :** RACE
**2 :** physical condition for running
**3 :** MANAGEMENT, CARE
**— in the running 1 :** competing in a contest **2 :** having a chance to win a contest
**— out of the running 1 :** not competing in a contest **2 :** having no chance of winning a contest

**²running** *adjective* (14th century)
**1 :** CURSIVE, FLOWING
**2 :** FLUID, RUNNY
**3 a :** INCESSANT, CONTINUOUS (a *running* battle) **b :** made during the course of a process or activity (a *running* commentary on the game)
**4 :** measured in a straight line (cost of lumber per *running* foot)
**5 a :** initiated or performed while running or with a running start (*running* catch) **b :** of, relating to, or being a football play in which the ball is advanced by running rather than by passing (their *running* game was off) **c :** designed for use by runners (a *running* track) (*running* shoes)
**6 :** fitted or trained for running rather than walking, trotting, or jumping (a *running* horse)

**³running** *adverb* (1719)
**:** in succession **:** CONSECUTIVELY (three days *running*)

**running back** *noun* (1924)
**:** a football back (as a halfback or fullback) who carries the ball on running plays

**running board** *noun* (1817)
**:** a footboard especially at the side of an automobile

running board

**running dog** *noun* (1927)
**:** one who does someone else's bidding **:** LACKEY

**running gear** *noun* (1662)
**1 :** the working and carrying parts of a machine (as a locomotive)
**2 :** the parts of an automobile chassis not used in developing, transmitting, and controlling power

**running hand** *noun* (1648)
**:** handwriting in which the letters are usually slanted and the words formed without lifting the pen

**running head** *noun* (1839)
**:** a headline repeated on consecutive pages (as of a book) — called also *running headline*

**running knot** *noun* (1648)
**:** a knot that slips along the rope or line round which it is tied; *especially* **:** an overhand slipknot

**running light** *noun* (1881)
**:** any of the lights carried by a vehicle (as a ship) under way at night that indicate size, position, and course

**running mate** *noun* (1868)
**1 :** a horse entered in a race to set the pace for a horse of the same owner or stable

**2 :** a candidate running for a subordinate place on a ticket; *especially* **:** the candidate for vice-president
**3 :** COMPANION

**running start** *noun* (1926)
**:** FLYING START 1

**running stitch** *noun* (1848)
**:** a small even stitch run in and out in cloth

**running title** *noun* (1668)
**:** the title or short title of a volume printed at the top of left-hand text pages or sometimes of all text pages

**running water** *noun* (1912)
**:** water distributed through pipes and fixtures (a cabin with hot and cold *running water*)

**run·ny** \'rə-nē\ *adjective* (1817)
**:** having a tendency to run: as **a :** extremely or excessively soft and liquid (a *runny* dough) **b :** secreting a thin flow of mucus (a *runny* nose)

**run-off** \'rən-,ȯf\ *noun* (1873)
**1 :** a final race, contest, or election to decide an earlier one that has not resulted in a decision in favor of any one competitor
**2 :** the portion of precipitation on land that ultimately reaches streams often with dissolved or suspended material

**run off** (1683)
*transitive verb*
**1 a :** to recite, compose, or produce rapidly **b :** to cause to be run or played to a finish **c :** to decide (as a race) by a runoff **d :** CARRY OUT
**2 :** to drain off **:** DRAW OFF
**3 a :** to drive off (as trespassers) **b :** to steal (as cattle) by driving away
*intransitive verb*
**:** RUN AWAY 1
**— run off with :** to carry off **:** STEAL

**run-of-paper** \,rən-əv-'pā-pər\ *adjective* (circa 1923)
**:** to be placed anywhere in a newspaper at the option of the editor (*run-of-paper* advertisement)

**run-of-the-mill** \,rən-ə(v)-thə-'mil\ *adjective* (1930)
**:** not outstanding in quality or rarity **:** AVERAGE, ORDINARY

**run-of-the-mine** \-'mīn\ *or* **run-of-mine** \-əv-'mīn\ *adjective* (1903)
**1 :** not graded (*run-of-the-mine* coal)
**2 :** RUN-OF-THE-MILL

**¹run-on** \'rən-,ȯn, -,än\ *adjective* (1877)
**:** continuing without rhetorical pause from one line of verse into another

**²run-on** \-,ȯn, -,än\ *noun* (circa 1909)
**:** something (as a dictionary entry) that is run on

**run on** (15th century)
*intransitive verb*
**1 :** to talk or narrate at length
**2 :** to keep going **:** CONTINUE
*transitive verb*
**1 :** to continue (matter in type) without a break or a new paragraph **:** RUN IN
**2 :** to place or add (as an entry in a dictionary) at the end of a paragraphed item

**run-on sentence** *noun* (1914)
**:** a sentence containing a comma splice

**run out** (14th century)
*intransitive verb*
**1 a :** to come to an end **:** EXPIRE (time *ran out*) **b :** to become exhausted or used up (the gasoline *ran out*)
**2 :** to jut out
*transitive verb*
**1 :** to finish out (as a course, series, or contest) **:** COMPLETE
**2 a :** to fill out (a typeset line) with quads, leaders, or ornaments **b :** to set (as the first line of a paragraph) with a hanging indention
**3 :** to exhaust (oneself) in running
**4 :** to cause to leave by force or coercion **:** EXPEL
**— run out of :** to use up the available supply of
**— run out on :** DESERT

**run·over** \'rən-,ō-vər\ *noun* (1927)

**:** matter for publication that exceeds the space allotted

**run-over** \'rən-,ō-vər\ *adjective* (circa 1934)
**:** extending beyond the allotted space

**run over** (15th century)
*intransitive verb*
**1 :** to exceed a limit
**2 :** OVERFLOW
*transitive verb*
**1 :** to go over, examine, repeat, or rehearse quickly
**2 :** to collide with, knock down, and often drive over (*ran over* a dog)

**runt** \'rənt\ *noun* [origin unknown] (1501)
**1** *chiefly Scottish* **:** a hardened stalk or stem of a plant
**2 :** an animal unusually small of its kind; *especially* **:** the smallest of a litter of pigs
**3 :** a person of small stature
**— runt·i·ness** \'rən-tē-nəs\ *noun*
**— runt·ish** \-tish\ *adjective*
**— runty** \-tē\ *adjective*

**run-through** \'rən-,thrü\ *noun* (1923)
**:** a usually cursory reading, summary, or rehearsal

**run through** *transitive verb* (15th century)
**1 :** PIERCE
**2 :** to spend or consume wastefully and rapidly
**3 :** to read or rehearse without pausing
**4 a :** CARRY OUT, DO **b :** to subject to a process

**run-up** \'rən-,əp\ *noun* (1834)
**1 :** the act of running up something
**2 :** a usually sudden increase in volume or price
**3** *chiefly British* **:** a period immediately preceding an action or event

**run up** (1664)
*intransitive verb*
**:** to grow rapidly **:** shoot up
*transitive verb*
**1 :** to increase by bidding **:** bid up
**2 :** to stitch together quickly
**3 :** to erect hastily
**4 :** to achieve by accumulating (*ran up* a big lead)

**run·way** \'rən-,wā\ *noun* (1833)
**1 a :** a beaten path made by animals **b :** a passageway for animals
**2 :** a paved strip of ground on a landing field for the landing and takeoff of airplanes
**3 a :** a narrow platform from a stage into an auditorium **b :** a platform along which models walk in a fashion show
**4 :** RUN 10b
**5 :** the area or path along which a jumper, pole vaulter, or javelin thrower runs

**ru·pee** \rü-'pē, 'rü-,pē\ *noun* [Hindi *rūpaiyā*, from Sanskrit *rūpya* coined silver] (1610)
**—** see MONEY table

**ru·pi·ah** \rü-'pē-ə\ *noun, plural* **rupiah** *or* **ru·piahs** [Malay, from Hindi *rūpaiyā* rupee] (1947)
**—** see MONEY table

**¹rup·ture** \'rəp(t)-shər\ *noun* [Middle English *ruptur*, from Middle French or Latin; Middle French *rupture*, from Latin *ruptura* fracture, from *ruptus*, past participle of *rumpere* to break — more at REAVE] (15th century)
**1 :** breach of peace or concord; *specifically* **:** open hostility or war between nations
**2 a :** the tearing apart of a tissue (*rupture* of the heart muscle) (*rupture* of an intervertebral disk) **b :** HERNIA
**3 :** a breaking apart or the state of being broken apart

**²rupture** *verb* **rup·tured; rup·tur·ing** \-sh(ə-)riŋ\ (1739)
*transitive verb*

\ə\ abut \ᵊ\ kitten \ər\ further \a\ ash \ā\ ace
\ä\ mop, mar \au̇\ out \ch\ chin \e\ bet \ē\ easy
\g\ go \i\ hit \ī\ ice \j\ job \ŋ\ sing \ō\ go
\ȯ\ law \ȯi\ boy \th\ thin \t͟h\ the \ü\ loot \u̇\ foot
\y\ yet \zh\ vision    *see also* Guide to Pronunciation

**1 a :** to part by violence **:** BREAK, BURST **b :** to create or induce a breach of
**2 :** to produce a rupture in
*intransitive verb*
**:** to have or undergo a rupture

**ru·ral** \'rùr-əl\ *adjective* [Middle English, from Middle French, from Latin *ruralis,* from *rur-, rus* open land — more at ROOM] (15th century)
**:** of or relating to the country, country people or life, or agriculture
— **ru·ral·i·ty** \rù-'ra-lə-tē\ *noun*
— **ru·ral·ly** \'rùr-ə-lē\ *adverb*
**rural dean** *noun* (circa 1628)
**:** DEAN 1b
**rural free delivery** *noun* (1892)
**:** free delivery of mail to a rural area — called also *rural delivery*
**ru·ral·ist** \'rùr-ə-list\ *noun* (1739)
**:** one who lives in a rural area
**rural route** *noun* (1898)
**:** a mail-delivery route in a rural free delivery area
**rur·ban** \'rər-bən, 'rùr-\ *adjective* [blend of *rural* and *urban*] (1918)
**:** of, relating to, or constituting an area which is chiefly residential but where some farming is carried on
**Ru·ri·tan** \'rùr-ə-tən\ *noun* [*Ruritan National,* a service club] (1968)
**:** a member of a major national service club
**Ru·ri·ta·ni·an** \'rùr-ə-,tā-nē-ən, ,rùr-ə-\ *adjective* [*Ruritania,* fictional kingdom in the novel *Prisoner of Zenda* (1894) by Anthony Hope] (1896)
**:** of, relating to, or having the characteristics of an imaginary place of high romance
**ruse** \'rüs, 'rüz\ *noun* [French, from Middle French, from *ruser* to dodge, deceive] (1625)
**:** a wily subterfuge
*synonym* see TRICK
**¹rush** \'rəsh\ *noun* [Middle English, from Old English *rysc;* akin to Middle High German *rusch* rush, Lithuanian *regzti* to knit] (before 12th century)
**:** any of various monocotyledonous often tufted marsh plants (as of the genera *Juncus* and *Scirpus* of the family Juncaceae, the rush family) with cylindrical often hollow stems which are used in bottoming chairs and plaiting mats
— **rushy** \'rə-shē\ *adjective*
**²rush** *verb* [Middle English *russhen,* from Middle French *ruser* to put to flight, repel, deceive, from Latin *recusare* to refuse — more at RECUSANT] (14th century)
*intransitive verb*
**1 :** to move forward, progress, or act with haste or eagerness or without preparation
**2 :** to advance a football by running plays ⟨*rushed* for a total of 150 yards⟩
*transitive verb*
**1 :** to push or impel on or forward with speed, impetuosity, or violence
**2 :** to perform in a short time or at high speed
**3 :** to urge to an unnatural or extreme speed ⟨don't *rush* me⟩
**4 :** to run toward or against in attack **:** CHARGE
**5 a :** to carry (a ball) forward in a running play **b :** to move in quickly on (a kicker or passer) to hinder, prevent, or block a kick or pass — used especially of defensive linemen
**6 a :** to lavish attention on **:** COURT **b :** to try to secure a pledge of membership (as in a fraternity) from
**³rush** *noun* (14th century)
**1 a :** a violent forward motion **b :** ATTACK, ON-SET **c :** a surging of emotion
**2 a :** a burst of activity, productivity, or speed **b :** a sudden insistent demand
**3 :** a thronging of people usually to a new place in search of wealth ⟨gold *rush*⟩
**4 a :** the act of carrying a football during a game **:** running play **b :** the action or an instance of rushing a passer or kicker in football ⟨pass *rush*⟩

**5 a :** a round of attention usually involving extensive social activity **b :** a drive by a fraternity or sorority to recruit new members
**6 :** a print of a motion-picture scene processed directly after the shooting for review by the director or producer — usually used in plural
**7 a :** the immediate pleasurable feeling produced by a drug (as heroin or amphetamine) — called also *flash* **b :** a sudden feeling of intense pleasure or euphoria **:** THRILL
**⁴rush** *adjective* (1887)
**:** requiring or marked by special speed or urgency ⟨*rush* orders⟩ ⟨the *rush* season⟩ ⟨a *rush* job⟩
**rush candle** *noun* (1591)
**:** RUSHLIGHT
**rush·ee** \,rə-'shē\ *noun* (circa 1916)
**:** a college or university student who is being rushed by a fraternity or sorority
**rush·er** \'rə-shər\ *noun* (1654)
**:** one that rushes; *especially* **:** BALLCARRIER
**rush hour** *noun* (1898)
**:** a period of the day when the demands especially of traffic or business are at a peak
**rush·ing** *noun* (1883)
**:** the act of advancing a football by running plays **:** the use of running plays; *also* **:** yardage gained by running plays
**rush·light** \'rəsh-,līt\ *noun* (1710)
**:** a candle that consists of the pith of a rush dipped in grease
**rusk** \'rəsk\ *noun* [modification of Spanish & Portuguese *rosca* coil, twisted roll] (1595)
**1 :** hard crisp bread originally used as ship's stores
**2 :** a sweet or plain bread baked, sliced, and baked again until dry and crisp
**Russ** \'rəs, 'rüs, 'rùs\ *noun, plural* **Russian** or **Russ·es** [ultimately from Old Russian *Rus'* the East Slavic-speaking lands] (1537)
**:** RUSSIAN
— **Russ** *adjective*
**¹rus·set** \'rə-sət\ *noun* [Middle English, from Old French *rousset,* from *rousset,* adjective, russet, from *rous* russet, from Latin *russus* red; akin to Latin *ruber* red — more at RED] (13th century)
**1 :** coarse homespun usually reddish brown cloth
**2 :** a strong brown
**3 :** any of various winter apples having russet rough skins
**4 :** IDAHO
**²russet** *adjective* (15th century)
**:** of the color russet
**rus·set·ing** *also* **rus·set·ting** \'rə-sə-tiŋ\ *noun* (1912)
**:** a brownish roughened area on the skin of fruit (as apples) caused by injury
**Rus·sia leather** \'rə-shə-\ *noun* [*Russia,* Europe] (1658)
**:** leather made by tanning various skins with willow, birch, or oak and then rubbing the flesh side with a phenolic oil distilled from a European birch — called also *Russia calf*
**Rus·sian** \'rə-shən\ *noun* (1538)
**1 a :** a native or inhabitant of Russia **b :** a member of the dominant Slavic-speaking ethnic group of Russia **c :** a person of Russian descent
**2 :** a Slavic language of the Russian people spoken as a second language by many non-Russian ethnic groups of the Soviet Union and its successor states
— **Russian** *adjective*
— **Rus·sian·ness** \-nəs\ *noun*
**Russian blue** *noun, often B capitalized* (1889)
**:** any of a breed of slender long-bodied large-eared domestic cats with short silky bluish gray fur
**Russian dressing** *noun* (1922)
**:** a dressing (as of mayonnaise or oil and vinegar) with added chili sauce, chopped pickles, or pimientos

**Rus·sian·ize** \'rə-shə-,nīz\ *transitive verb* **-ized; -iz·ing** (1831)
**:** to make Russian
— **Rus·sian·i·za·tion** \,rə-shə-nə-'zā-shən\ *noun*
**Russian olive** *noun* (1913)
**:** a chiefly silvery Eurasian large shrub or small tree (*Elaeagnus angustifolia* of the family Elaeagnaceae) cultivated especially as a shelterbelt plant
**Russian roulette** *noun* (1937)
**1 :** an act of bravado consisting of spinning the cylinder of a revolver loaded with one cartridge, pointing the muzzle at one's own head, and pulling the trigger
**2 :** something resembling Russian roulette in its potential for disaster ⟨taking cocaine is playing *Russian roulette* —Jonathan Nicholas⟩
**Russian thistle** *noun* (1894)
**:** a prickly European saltwort (*Salsola kali*) that is a serious pest in North America — called also *Russian tumbleweed*
**Russian wolfhound** *noun* (1872)
**:** BORZOI
**Rus·si·fy** \'rə-sə-,fī\ *transitive verb* **-fied; -fy·ing** (1865)
**:** RUSSIANIZE
— **Rus·si·fi·ca·tion** \,rə-sə-fə-'kā-shən\ *noun*
**Russ·ki** *or* **Russ·ky** *or* **Russ·kie** \'rəs-kē, 'rùs-\ *noun, plural* **Russkies** *or* **Russkis** [Russian *russkiĭ,* adjective & noun, Russian, from Old Russian, from *Rus'*] (1858)
**:** RUSSIAN 1
**Rus·so-** \'rə-(,)sō, ,rə-, -(,)shō\ *combining form* [*Russia & Russian*]
**:** Russian and ⟨the *Russo*-Japanese war⟩
**¹rust** \'rəst\ *noun* [Middle English, from Old English *rūst;* akin to Old English *rēad* red — more at RED] (before 12th century)
**1 a :** the reddish brittle coating formed on iron especially when chemically attacked by moist air and composed essentially of hydrated ferric oxide **b :** a comparable coating produced on a metal other than iron by corrosion **c :** something resembling rust **:** ACCRETION
**2 :** corrosive or injurious influence or effect
**3 :** any of numerous destructive diseases of plants produced by fungi (order Uredinales) and characterized by usually reddish brown pustular lesions; *also* **:** a fungus causing this
**4 :** a strong reddish brown
**²rust** (13th century)
*intransitive verb*
**1 :** to form rust **:** become oxidized ⟨iron *rusts*⟩
**2 :** to degenerate especially from inaction, lack of use, or passage of time ⟨most men would . . . have allowed their faculties to *rust* —T. B. Macaulay⟩
**3 :** to become reddish brown as if with rust ⟨the leaves slowly *rusted*⟩
**4 :** to be affected with a rust fungus
*transitive verb*
**1 :** to cause (a metal) to form rust ⟨keep up your bright swords, for the dew will *rust* them —Shakespeare⟩
**2 :** to impair or corrode by or as if by time, inactivity, or deleterious use
**3 :** to cause to become reddish brown **:** turn the color of rust
**rust belt** *noun, often R&B capitalized* (1983)
**:** the northeastern and midwestern states of the U.S. in which heavy industry has declined
**rust bucket** *noun* (1945)
**:** an old and dilapidated ship
**¹rus·tic** \'rəs-tik\ *also* **rus·ti·cal** \-ti-kəl\ *adjective* [Middle English *rustik,* from Middle French *rustique,* from Latin *rusticus,* from *rus* open land — more at ROOM] (15th century)
**1 :** of, relating to, or suitable for the country **:** RURAL
**2 a :** made of the rough limbs of trees ⟨*rustic* furniture⟩ **b :** finished by rusticating ⟨a *rustic* joint in masonry⟩

**3 a :** characteristic of or resembling country people **b :** lacking in social graces or polish
**4 :** appropriate to the country (as in plainness or sturdiness) ⟨heavy *rustic* boots⟩
— **rus·ti·cal·ly** \-ti-k(ə-)lē\ *adverb*
— **rus·tic·i·ty** \ˌrəs-ˈti-sə-tē\ *noun*
²**rustic** *noun* (circa 1550)
**1 :** an inhabitant of a rural area
**2 a :** an awkward coarse person **b :** an unsophisticated rural person
**rus·ti·cate** \ˈrəs-ti-ˌkāt\ *verb* **-cat·ed; -cat·ing** (1660)
*intransitive verb*
**:** to go into or reside in the country **:** follow a rustic life
*transitive verb*
**1** *chiefly British* **:** to suspend from school or college
**2 :** to build or face with usually rough-surfaced masonry blocks having beveled or rebated edges producing pronounced joints ⟨a *rusticated* facade⟩
**3 a :** to compel to reside in the country **b :** to cause to become rustic **:** implant rustic mannerisms in
— **rus·ti·ca·tion** \ˌrəs-ti-ˈkā-shən\ *noun*
— **rus·ti·ca·tor** \ˈrəs-ti-ˌkā-tər\ *noun*
¹**rus·tle** \ˈrə-səl\ *verb* **rus·tled; rus·tling** \ˈrə-s(ə-)liŋ\ [Middle English *rustelen*] (14th century)
*intransitive verb*
**1 :** to make or cause a rustle
**2 a :** to act or move with energy or speed **b :** to forage food
**3 :** to steal cattle
*transitive verb*
**1 :** to cause to rustle
**2 a :** to obtain by one's own exertions — often used with *up* ⟨able to *rustle* up $5,000 bail —Jack McCallum⟩ **b :** FORAGE
**3 :** to steal (as livestock) especially from a farm or ranch
— **rus·tler** \-s(ə-)lər\ *noun*
²**rustle** *noun* (1759)
**:** a quick succession or confusion of small sounds
**rust mite** *noun* (1884)
**:** any of various small gall mites that burrow in the surface of leaves or fruits usually producing brown or reddish patches
**rust·proof** \ˈrəst-ˌprüf\ *adjective* (1691)
**:** incapable of rusting
¹**rusty** \ˈrəs-tē\ *adjective* **rust·i·er; -est** (before 12th century)
**1 :** affected by or as if by rust; *especially* **:** stiff with or as if with rust
**2 :** inept and slow through lack of practice or old age
**3 a :** of the color rust **b :** dulled in color or appearance by age and use ⟨a *rusty* old suit of clothes⟩
**4 :** OUTMODED
**5 :** HOARSE, GRATING
— **rust·i·ly** \-tə-lē\ *adverb*

— **rust·i·ness** \-tē-nəs\ *noun*
²**rus·ty** \ˈrəs-tē\ *adjective* **rus·ti·er; -est** [alteration of *restive*] (1625)
*chiefly dialect* **:** ILL-NATURED, SURLY
¹**rut** \ˈrət\ *noun* [Middle English *rutte*, from Middle French *rut* roar, from Late Latin *rugitus*, from Latin *rugire* to roar; akin to Middle Irish *rucht* roar, Old-Church Slavonic *ružati* to neigh] (15th century)
**1 :** an annually recurrent state of sexual excitement in the male deer; *broadly* **:** sexual excitement in a mammal (as estrus in the female) especially when periodic
**2 :** the period during which rut normally occurs — often used with *the*
²**rut** *intransitive verb* **rut·ted; rut·ting** (1625)
**:** to be in or enter into a state of rut
³**rut** *noun* [perhaps modification of Middle French *route* way, route] (1580)
**1 a :** a track worn by a wheel or by habitual passage **b :** a groove in which something runs **c :** CHANNEL, FURROW
**2 :** a usual or fixed practice; *especially* **:** a monotonous routine ⟨fall easily into a conversational *rut*⟩
⁴**rut** *transitive verb* **rut·ted; rut·ting** (1607)
**:** to make a rut in **:** FURROW
**ru·ta·ba·ga** \ˌrü-tə-ˈbā-gə, ˌrü-, -ˈbe-; ˈrü-tə-ˌ, ˈrü-\ *noun* [Swedish dialect *rotabagge*, from *rot* root + *bagge* bag] (1799)
**:** a turnip (*Brassica napus napobrassica*) that usually produces a large yellowish root
**ruth** \ˈrüth\ *noun* [Middle English *ruthe*, from *ruen* to rue] (13th century)
**1 :** compassion for the misery of another
**2 :** sorrow for one's own faults **:** REMORSE
**Ruth** \ˈrüth\ *noun* [Hebrew *Rūth*]
**1 :** a Moabite woman who accompanied Naomi to Bethlehem and became the ancestress of David
**2 :** a short narrative book of canonical Jewish and Christian Scriptures — see BIBLE table
**ru·the·ni·um** \rü-ˈthē-nē-əm\ *noun* [New Latin, from Medieval Latin *Ruthenia* Ruthenia] (1848)
**:** a hard brittle grayish polyvalent rare metallic element occurring in platinum ores and used in hardening platinum alloys — see ELEMENT table
**ruth·er·ford·ium** \ˌrə-thə(r)-ˈfȯr-dē-əm\ *noun* [New Latin, from Ernest *Rutherford*] (1969)
**:** UNNILQUADIUM
**ruth·ful** \ˈrüth-fəl\ *adjective* (13th century)
**1 :** full of ruth **:** TENDER
**2 :** full of sorrow **:** WOEFUL
**3 :** causing sorrow
— **ruth·ful·ly** \-fə-lē\ *adverb*
— **ruth·ful·ness** *noun*
**ruth·less** \ˈrüth-ləs *also* ˈrüth-\ *adjective* (14th century)
**:** having no ruth **:** MERCILESS, CRUEL
— **ruth·less·ly** *adverb*
— **ruth·less·ness** *noun*

**ru·ti·lant** \ˈrü-tᵊl-ənt\ *adjective* [Middle English *rutilaunt*, from Latin *rutilant-, rutilans*, past participle of *rutilare* to glow reddish, from *rutilus* ruddy; probably akin to Latin *ruber* red — more at RED] (15th century)
**:** having a reddish glow
**ru·tile** \ˈrü-ˌtēl\ *noun* [German *Rutil*, from Latin *rutilus*] (1803)
**:** a mineral that consists of titanium dioxide usually with a little iron, is typically of a reddish brown color but sometimes deep red or black, and has a brilliant metallic or adamantine luster
**rut·tish** \ˈrə-tish\ *adjective* (1601)
**:** inclined to rut **:** LUSTFUL
— **rut·tish·ly** *adverb*
— **rut·tish·ness** *noun*
**rut·ty** \ˈrə-tē\ *adjective* **rut·ti·er; -est** (1596)
**:** full of ruts
**RV** \ˌär-ˈvē\ *noun* (1967)
**:** RECREATIONAL VEHICLE
**R-value** \ˈär-ˌval-(ˌ)yü\ *noun* [probably from thermal *resistance*] (1948)
**:** a measure of resistance to the flow of heat through a given thickness of a material (as insulation) with higher numbers indicating better insulating properties — compare U-VALUE
**Rx** \ˌär-ˈeks\ *noun* [alteration of ℞, symbol used at the beginning of a prescription, abbreviation for Latin *recipe*, literally, take — more at RECIPE] (1926)
**:** a medical prescription
**-ry** *noun suffix* [Middle English *-rie*, from Old French, short for *-erie -ery*]
**:** -ERY ⟨wizard*ry*⟩ ⟨citizen*ry*⟩ ⟨ancient*ry*⟩
**rya** \ˈrē-ə\ *noun* [*Rya*, village in southwest Sweden] (1945)
**:** a Scandinavian handwoven rug with a deep resilient comparatively flat pile; *also* **:** the weave typical of this rug
¹**rye** \ˈrī\ *noun* [Middle English, from Old English *ryge*; akin to Old High German *rocko* rye, Lithuanian *rugys*] (before 12th century)
**1 :** a hardy annual grass (*Secale cereale*) that is widely grown for grain and as a cover crop
**2 :** the seeds of rye
**3 :** RYE BREAD
**4 :** RYE WHISKEY
²**rye** *noun* [Romany *rai* gentleman, master, from Sanskrit *rājan* king — more at ROYAL] (1851)
**:** a male Gypsy
**rye bread** *noun* (1579)
**:** bread made wholly or in part of rye flour; *especially* **:** a light bread often with caraway seeds
**rye·grass** \ˈrī-ˌgras\ *noun* (1747)
**:** any of several grasses (genus *Lolium*); *especially* **:** either of two grasses (Latin *perenne* and Latin *multiflorum*) that are used especially for pasture, a cover crop, or lawn grass
**rye whiskey** *noun* (1785)
**:** a whiskey distilled from rye or from rye and malt

# S

*S is the nineteenth letter of the English alphabet. It came through Latin via Etruscan from Greek* sigma, *which borrowed the character from the Phoenician* šîn, *pronounced "sh." In English,* s *usually represents the sibilant sound in* soon, hates, *and* hats. *In certain positions, however,* s *may represent the sound of* z *(as in* deserve; loves; heads*), and it sometimes has the value of* sh *or* zh, *as in* sure *and* measure. *In a few words it is silent (as* isle *and* debris*). With the letter* h *it forms the digraph* sh, *as in* ship. *In related languages, English* s *corresponds to German* s, *Latin* s *or* r, *Greek* s *or* h *(rough breathing), and Sanskrit* s *or* ṣ. *For example, English* sit *is historically related to German* sitzen, *Latin* sedere, *Greek* hezesthai, *and Sanskrit* sadas *("a seat"). The small form of* s *began as a simple reduction in size of the capital form. In printing, the "long* s*" (ſ), formerly much used, now appears only rarely, usually joined with a following consonant such as* s *or* t.

---

**s** \'es\ *noun, plural* **s's** *or* **ss** \'e-səz\ *often capitalized, often attributive* (before 12th century)
**1 a :** the 19th letter of the English alphabet **b :** a graphic representation of this letter **c :** a speech counterpart of orthographic *s*
**2 :** a graphic device for reproducing the letter *s*
**3 :** one designated *s* especially as the 19th in order or class
**4** [abbreviation for *satisfactory*] **a :** a grade rating a student's work as satisfactory **b :** one graded or rated with an S
**5 :** something shaped like the letter S
**¹-s** \s *after a voiceless consonant,* z *after a voiced consonant or a vowel*\ *noun plural suffix* [Middle English *-es, -s,* from Old English *-as,* nominative & accusative plural ending of some masculine nouns; akin to Old Saxon *-os*]
— used to form the plural of most nouns that do not end in *s, z, sh, ch,* or postconsonantal *y* ⟨heads⟩ ⟨books⟩ ⟨boys⟩ ⟨beliefs⟩, to form the plural of proper nouns that end in postconsonantal *y* ⟨Marys⟩, and with or without a preceding apostrophe to form the plural of abbreviations, numbers, letters, and symbols used as nouns ⟨MCs⟩ ⟨PhD's⟩ ⟨4s⟩ ⟨the 1940's⟩ ⟨$s⟩ ⟨B's⟩; compare ¹-ES
**²-s** *adverb suffix* [Middle English *-es, -s,* plural ending of nouns, from *-es,* genitive singular ending of nouns (functioning adverbially), from Old English *-es*]
— used to form adverbs denoting usual or repeated action or state ⟨always at home Sundays⟩ ⟨mornings he stops by the newsstand⟩
**³-s** *verb suffix* [Middle English (Northern & North Midland dialect) *-es,* from Old English (Northumbrian dialect) *-es, -as,* probably from Old English *-es, -as,* 2d singular present indicative ending — more at *-EST*]
— used to form the third person singular present of most verbs that do not end in *s, z, sh, ch,* or postconsonantal *y* ⟨falls⟩ ⟨takes⟩ ⟨plays⟩; compare ²-ES
**¹'s** \same *as* -'s\ *verb* [contraction of *is, has, does*] (1584)
**1 a :** IS ⟨she's here⟩ **b :** WAS ⟨when's the last time you ate⟩
**2 :** HAS ⟨he's seen them⟩
**3 :** DOES ⟨what's he want⟩
**²'s** \s\ *pronoun* [by contraction] (1588)
**:** US — used with *let* ⟨let's⟩
**-'s** \s *after voiceless consonants other than s, sh, ch;* z *after vowels and voiced consonants other than z, zh, j;* əz *after s, sh, ch, z, zh, j*\ *noun suffix or pronoun suffix* [Middle English *-es, -s,* genitive singular ending, from Old English *-es;* akin to Old High German *-es,* genitive singular ending, Greek *-oio, -ou,* Sanskrit *-asya*]
— used to form the possessive of singular nouns ⟨boy's⟩, of plural nouns not ending in *s* ⟨children's⟩, of some pronouns ⟨anyone's⟩, and of word groups functioning as nouns ⟨the man in the corner's hat⟩ or pronouns ⟨someone else's⟩

**Saa·nen** \'sä-nən, 'zä-\ *noun* [*Saanen,* locality in southwest Switzerland] (1906)
**:** any of a Swiss breed of usually white and hornless short-haired dairy goats
**sab·a·dil·la** \,sa-bə-'di-lə, -'dē-yə\ *noun* [Spanish *cebadilla*] (1812)
**:** a Mexican plant (*Schoenocaulon officinalis*) of the lily family; *also* : its seeds that are used as a source of veratrine and in insecticides
**sa·ba·yon** \sà-bà-yō\ⁿ\ *noun* [French, modification of Italian *zabaione*] (1906)
**:** ZABAGLIONE
**sab·bat** \'sa-bət\ *noun, often capitalized* [French, literally, sabbath, from Latin *sabbatum*] (1652)
**:** a midnight assembly of diabolists (as witches and sorcerers) held especially in medieval and Renaissance times to renew allegiance to the devil through mystic rites and orgies
**¹Sab·ba·tar·i·an** \,sa-bə-'ter-ē-ən\ *noun* [Latin *sabbatarius,* from *sabbatum* sabbath] (1613)
**1 :** one who observes the Sabbath on Saturday in conformity with the letter of the fourth commandment
**2 :** an adherent of Sabbatarianism
**²Sabbatarian** *adjective* (circa 1631)
**1 :** of or relating to the Sabbath
**2 :** of or relating to the Sabbatarians or Sabbatarianism
**Sab·ba·tar·i·an·ism** \,sa-bə-'ter-ē-ə-,ni-zəm\ *noun* (circa 1674)
**:** strict and often rigorous observance of the Sabbath
**Sab·bath** \'sa-bəth\ *noun* [Middle English *sabat,* from Old French & Old English, from Latin *sabbatum,* from Greek *sabbaton,* from Hebrew *shabbāth,* literally, rest] (before 12th century)
**1 a :** the seventh day of the week observed from Friday evening to Saturday evening as a day of rest and worship by Jews and some Christians **b :** Sunday observed among Christians as a day of rest and worship
**2 :** a time of rest
**¹sab·bat·i·cal** \sə-'ba-ti-kəl\ *or* **sab·bat·ic** \-tik\ *adjective* [Late Latin *sabbaticus,* from Greek *sabbatikos,* from *sabbaton*] (1645)
**1 :** of or relating to the sabbath ⟨*sabbatical* laws⟩
**2 :** of or relating to a sabbatical year
**²sabbatical** *noun* (1903)
**1 :** SABBATICAL YEAR 2
**2 :** LEAVE 1b
**3 :** a break or change from a normal routine (as of employment)
**sabbatical year** *noun* (1599)

**1** *often S capitalized* **:** a year of rest for the land observed every seventh year in ancient Judea
**2 :** a leave often with pay granted usually every seventh year (as to a college professor) for rest, travel, or research — called also *sabbatical leave*
**Sa·bel·li·an** \sə-'be-lē-ən\ *noun* [Latin *Sabellus* Sabine] (1601)
**1 :** a member of one of a group of early Italian peoples including Sabines and Samnites
**2 :** one or all of several little known languages or dialects of ancient Italy presumably closely related to Oscan and Umbrian
— **Sabellian** *adjective*
**¹sa·ber** *or* **sa·bre** \'sā-bər\ *noun* [French *sabre,* modification of German dialect *Sabel,* from Middle High German, probably of Slavic origin; akin to Russian *sablya* saber] (1680)
**1 :** a cavalry sword with a curved blade, thick back, and guard
**2 a :** a light fencing or dueling sword having an arched guard that covers the back of the hand and a tapering flexible blade with a full cutting edge along one side and a partial cutting edge on the back at the tip — compare ÉPÉE, FOIL **b :** the sport of fencing with the saber

saber 1

**²saber** *or* **sabre** *transitive verb* **sa·bered** *or* **sa·bred; sa·ber·ing** *or* **sa·bring** \-b(ə-)riŋ\ (1790)
**:** to strike, cut, or kill with a saber
**sa·ber·met·rics** \,sā-bər-'me-triks\ *noun plural but singular in construction* [*saber-* (from Society for American Baseball Research) + *-metrics* (as in *econometrics*)] (1982)
**:** the statistical analysis of baseball data
— **sa·ber·me·tri·cian** \,sā-bər-mə-'tri-shən\ *noun*
**saber rattling** *noun* (1922)
**:** ostentatious display of military power
**saber saw** *noun* (1953)
**:** a light portable electric saw with a pointed reciprocating blade
**sa·ber–toothed** \'sā-bər-,tütht\ *adjective* (1849)
**:** having long sharp canine teeth
**saber–toothed tiger** *noun* (1849)
**:** any of numerous extinct cats (as genus *Smilodon*) widely distributed from the Oligocene through the Pleistocene and characterized by long curving upper canines — called also *saber-toothed cat*
**sa·bin** \'sā-bən\ *noun* [Wallace C. W. *Sabine* (died 1919) American physicist] (1934)
**:** a unit of acoustic absorption equivalent to the absorption by one square foot of a perfect absorber
**Sa·bine** \'sā-,bīn, *especially British* 'sa-\ *noun* [Middle English *Sabin,* from Latin *Sabinus*] (14th century)
**1 :** a member of an ancient people of the Apennines northeast of Latium
**2 :** the Italic language of the Sabine people
— **Sabine** *adjective*
**¹sa·ble** \'sā-bəl\ *noun, plural* **sables** [Middle English, sable or its fur, the heraldic color black, black, from Middle French, sable or its fur, the heraldic color black from Middle Low German *sabel* sable or its fur, from Middle High German *zobel,* of Slavic origin; akin to Russian *sobol'* sable or its fur] (14th century)
**1 a :** the color black **b :** black clothing worn in mourning — usually used in plural
**2 a** *or plural* **sable** (1) **:** a carnivorous mammal (*Martes zibellina*) of the weasel family that occurs chiefly in northern Asia (2) **:** any of various animals related to the sable **b :** the fur or pelt of a sable

**3 a :** the usually dark brown color of the fur of the sable **b :** a grayish yellowish brown

**²sable** *adjective* (15th century)
**1 :** of the color black
**2 :** DARK, GLOOMY

**sa·ble·fish** \'sā-bəl-ˌfish\ *noun* (1917)
**:** a large spiny-finned gray to blackish bony fish (*Anoplopoma fimbria* of the family Anoplomatidae) of the Pacific coast that is an important food fish and has a liver rich in vitamins

**sa·bot** \sa-'bō, 'sa-(ˌ)bō, *for 1b also* 'sa-bət\ *noun* [French] (1607)
**1 a :** a wooden shoe worn in various European countries **b** (1) **:** a strap across the instep in a shoe especially of the sandal type (2) **:** a shoe having a sabot strap
**2 :** a thrust-transmitting carrier that positions a missile in a gun barrel or launching tube and that prevents the escape of gas ahead of the missile
**3 :** SHOE 6

**¹sab·o·tage** \'sa-bə-ˌtäzh\ *noun* [French, from *saboter* to clatter with sabots, botch, sabotage, from *sabot*] (1910)
**1 :** destruction of an employer's property (as tools or materials) or the hindering of manufacturing by discontented workers
**2 :** destructive or obstructive action carried on by a civilian or enemy agent to hinder a nation's war effort
**3 a :** an act or process tending to hamper or hurt **b :** deliberate subversion ◆

**²sabotage** *transitive verb* **-taged; -tag·ing** (1913)
**:** to practice sabotage on

**sab·o·teur** \ˌsa-bə-'tər, -'tùr, -'tyùr\ *noun* [French, from *saboter*] (1921)
**:** one that practices sabotage

**sa·bra** \'sä-brə\ *noun, often capitalized* [New Hebrew *ṣabhār*, literally, prickly pear] (1945)
**:** a native-born Israeli

**sac** \'sak\ *noun* [French, literally, bag, from Latin *saccus* — more at SACK] (1741)
**:** a pouch within an animal or plant often containing a fluid ⟨a synovial *sac*⟩
**— sac·like** \-ˌlīk\ *adjective*

**Sac** \'sak, 'sök\ *variant of* SAUK

**sa·ca·huis·te** \ˌsa-kə-'wis-tə, ˌsä-, -tē\ *or* **sa·ca·huis·ta** \-tə\ *noun* [Mexican Spanish *zacahuiscle*, from (assumed) Nahuatl *zacahuitztli*, from Nahuatl *zacatl* grass, hay + *huitztli* thorn] (1896)
**:** a bear grass (*Nolina texana*) that may cause poisoning in livestock

**sac·a·ton** \'sa-kə-ˌtōn\ *noun* [American Spanish *zacatón*, from *zacate* coarse grass, from Nahuatl *zacatl*] (1846)
**:** a coarse perennial grass (*Sporobolus wrightii*) of the southwestern U.S. that is used for hay in alkaline regions

**sac·cade** \sa-'käd\ *noun* [French, twitch, jerk, from Middle French, from *saquer* to pull, draw] (1938)
**:** a small rapid jerky movement of the eye especially as it jumps from fixation on one point to another (as in reading)
**— sac·cad·ic** \-'kä-dik\ *adjective*

**sac·cate** \'sa-ˌkāt\ *adjective* [New Latin *saccatus,* from Latin *saccus*] (1830)
**:** having the form of a sac or pouch ⟨*saccate* pollen grains⟩

**sacchar-** *or* **sacchari-** *or* **saccharo-** *combining form* [Latin *saccharum,* from Greek *sakcharon,* from Prakrit *sakkharā,* from Sanskrit *śarkarā* gravel, sugar]
**:** sugar ⟨*sacchari*fy⟩ ⟨*saccharo*meter⟩

**sac·cha·rase** \'sa-kə-ˌrās, -ˌrāz\ *noun* [International Scientific Vocabulary] (1920)
**:** INVERTASE

**sac·cha·ride** \'sa-kə-ˌrīd\ *noun* (1895)
**:** a simple sugar, combination of sugars, or polymerized sugar **:** CARBOHYDRATE

**sac·char·i·fi·ca·tion** \sə-ˌkar-ə-fə-'kā-shən\ *noun* (1839)

**:** the process of breaking a complex carbohydrate (as starch or cellulose) into simple sugars

**— sac·char·i·fy** \sə-'kar-ə-ˌfī, sa-\ *transitive verb*

**sac·cha·rim·e·ter** \ˌsa-kə-'ri-mə-tər\ *noun* [International Scientific Vocabulary] (1874)
**:** a device for measuring the amount of sugar in a solution; *specifically* **:** a polarimeter so used

**sac·cha·rin** \'sa-k(ə-)rən\ *noun* [International Scientific Vocabulary] (1885)
**:** a crystalline compound $C_7H_5NO_3S$ that is unrelated to the carbohydrates, is several hundred times sweeter than cane sugar, and is used as a calorie-free sweetener

**sac·cha·rine** \'sa-k(ə-)rən, -kə-ˌrēn, -kə-ˌrīn\ *adjective* [Latin *saccharum*] (circa 1674)
**1 a :** of, relating to, or resembling that of sugar ⟨*saccharine* taste⟩ **b :** yielding or containing sugar ⟨*saccharine* vegetables⟩
**2 :** overly or sickishly sweet ⟨*saccharine* flavor⟩
**3 :** ingratiatingly or affectedly agreeable or friendly
**4 :** overly sentimental **:** MAWKISH
**— sac·cha·rin·i·ty** \ˌsa-kə-'ri-nə-tē\ *noun*

**sac·cha·roi·dal** \ˌsa-kə-'rói-d°l\ *adjective* (1838)
**:** having or being a fine granular texture like that of loaf sugar ⟨*saccharoidal* marble⟩

**sac·cha·rom·e·ter** \-'rä-mə-tər\ *noun* (1784)
**:** SACCHARIMETER; *especially* **:** a hydrometer with a special scale

**sac·cha·ro·my·ces** \-rō-'mī-(ˌ)sēz\ *noun* [New Latin, from *sacchar-* + *-myces* fungus, from Greek *mykēs* — more at MYC-] (1873)
**:** any of a genus (*Saccharomyces* of the family Saccharomycetaceae) of usually unicellular yeasts (as a brewer's yeast) that are distinguished by their sparse or absent mycelium and by their facility in reproducing asexually by budding

**sac·cu·lar** \'sa-kyə-lər\ *adjective* (circa 1859)
**:** resembling a sac ⟨a *saccular* aneurysm⟩

**sac·cu·lat·ed** \-ˌlā-təd\ *also* **sac·cu·late** \-ˌlāt, -lət\ *adjective* (circa 1836)
**:** having or formed of a series of saccular expansions
**— sac·cu·la·tion** \ˌsa-kyə-'lā-shən\ *noun*

**sac·cule** \'sa-(ˌ)kyü(ə)l\ *noun* [New Latin *sacculus,* from Latin, diminutive of *saccus* bag — more at SACK] (1839)
**:** a little sac; *specifically* **:** the smaller chamber of the membranous labyrinth of the ear

**sac·cu·lus** \'sa-kyə-ləs\ *noun, plural* **-li** \-ˌlī, -ˌlē\ [New Latin] (1748)
**:** SACCULE

**sac·er·do·tal** \ˌsa-sər-'dō-t°l, ˌsa-kər-\ *adjective* [Middle English, from Middle French, from Latin *sacerdotalis,* from *sacerdot-, sacerdos* priest, from *sacer* sacred + *-dot-, -dos* (akin to *facere* to make) — more at SACRED, DO] (15th century)
**1 :** of or relating to priests or a priesthood **:** PRIESTLY
**2 :** of, relating to, or suggesting sacerdotalism
**— sac·er·do·tal·ly** \-t°l-ē\ *adverb*

**sac·er·do·tal·ism** \-t°l-ˌi-zəm\ *noun* (1856)
**:** religious belief emphasizing the powers of priests as essential mediators between God and mankind
**— sac·er·do·tal·ist** \-t°l-ist\ *noun*

**sac fungus** *noun* (circa 1929)
**:** ASCOMYCETE

**sa·chem** \'sā-chəm, 'sa-\ *noun* [Narraganset *sâchim*] (1622)
**1 :** a North American Indian chief; *especially* **:** the chief of a confederation of the Algonquian tribes of the North Atlantic coast
**2 :** a Tammany leader
**— sa·chem·ic** \sā-'che-mik, sa-\ *adjective*

**Sa·cher torte** \'sä-kər-, 'zä-\ *noun* [German *Sachertorte,* from *Sacher* (name of a family of 19th and 20th century Austrian restaurant proprietors) + German *Torte* torte] (1906)

**:** a rich chocolate torte with an apricot jam filling

**sa·chet** \sa-'shā\ *noun* [Middle French, from Old French, diminutive of *sac* bag — more at SAC] (15th century)
**1 :** a small bag or packet
**2 :** a small bag containing a perfumed powder or potpourri used to scent clothes and linens
**— sa·cheted** \-'shād\ *adjective*

**¹sack** \'sak\ *noun* [Middle English *sak* bag, sackcloth, from Old English *sacc,* from Latin *saccus* bag & Late Latin *saccus* sackcloth, both from Greek *sakkos* bag, sackcloth, of Semitic origin; akin to Hebrew *śaq* bag, sackcloth] (before 12th century)
**1 :** a usually rectangular-shaped bag (as of paper, burlap, or canvas)
**2 :** the amount contained in a sack; *especially* **:** a fixed amount of a commodity used as a unit of measure
**3 a :** a woman's loose-fitting dress **b :** a short usually loose-fitting coat for women and children **c :** SACQUE 2
**4 :** DISMISSAL
**5 a :** HAMMOCK, BUNK **b :** BED
**6 :** a base in baseball
**7 :** an instance of sacking the quarterback in football
**— sack·ful** \-ˌfùl\ *noun*

**²sack** *transitive verb* (14th century)
**1 :** to put in or as if in a sack
**2 :** to dismiss especially summarily
**3 :** to tackle (the quarterback) behind the line of scrimmage in football
**— sack·er** *noun*

**³sack** *noun* [modification of Middle French *sec* dry, from Latin *siccus;* probably akin to Old High German *sīhan* to filter, Sanskrit *siñcati* he pours] (circa 1532)
**:** any of several white wines imported to England from Spain and the Canary Islands during the 16th and 17th centuries

**⁴sack** *transitive verb* [⁵*sack*] (circa 1547)
**1 :** to plunder (as a town) especially after capture
**2 :** to strip of valuables **:** LOOT
*synonym* see RAVAGE
**— sack·er** *noun*

---

◇ WORD HISTORY
**sabotage** Because the word *sabotage* appears to have some relation to French *sabot* "wooden shoe," the suggestion has often been made that *sabotage* in France originally alluded to disgruntled industrial workers throwing their sabots into machinery in order to damage it. In fact, there is no evidence to support such an etymology. The meaning "to damage an employer's property" of the French verb *saboter,* attested in the first decade of our century, is clearly built on an older sense "to perform haphazardly, botch, bungle," first attested in 1808. This meaning is in turn usually explained as proceeding from a yet older sense, "to make a clattering noise with sabots," on the premise that walking with wooden shoes suggests clumsy performance. Though the hypothesis is not implausible, *saboter* is attested in the 17th century with the sense "to torment," and as early as the 14th century in the meaning "to shake, knock." It is difficult to determine if these diverse meanings constitute a single line of development, or if the many associations evoked in Frenchmen by this piece of peasant footwear caused repeated episodes of verb creation from the same noun.

---

\ə\ abut \ᵊ\ kitten \ər\ further \a\ ash \ā\ ace \ä\ mop, mar \aù\ out \ch\ chin \e\ bet \ē\ easy \g\ go \i\ hit \ī\ ice \j\ job \ŋ\ sing \ō\ go \ò\ law \òi\ boy \th\ thin \th\ the \ü\ loot \ù\ foot \y\ yet \zh\ vision *see also* Guide to Pronunciation

**⁵sack** noun [Middle French sac, from Old Italian sacco, literally, bag, from Latin saccus] (1549)
: the plundering of a captured town

**sack·but** \'sak-(,)bət\ noun [Middle French saqueboute, literally, hooked lance, from Old French, from saquer to pull + boter to push — more at BUTT] (1533)
: the medieval and Renaissance trombone

**sack·cloth** \'sa(k)-,klȯth\ noun [¹sack] (13th century)
**1** : a coarse cloth of goat or camel's hair or of flax, hemp, or cotton
**2** : a garment of sackcloth worn as a sign of mourning or penitence

**sack coat** noun (1847)
: a man's jacket with a straight back

**sack·ing** \'sa-kiŋ\ noun (1707)
: material for sacks; especially : a coarse fabric (as burlap)

**sack out** intransitive verb [¹sack] (1946)
: to go to bed : go to sleep

**sack race** noun (1859)
: a jumping race in which each contestant's legs are enclosed in a sack

**sacque** \'sak\ noun [alteration of ¹sack] (1846)
**1** : SACK 3a, b
**2** : an infant's usually short jacket that fastens at the neck

**¹sa·cral** \'sa-krəl, 'sā-\ adjective (1767)
: of, relating to, or lying near the sacrum

**²sa·cral** \'sā-krəl, 'sa-\ adjective [Latin sacr-, sacer — more at SACRED] (1882)
: HOLY, SACRED

**sac·ra·ment** \'sa-krə-mənt\ noun [Middle English sacrement, sacrament, from Old French & Late Latin; Old French, from Late Latin sacramentum, from Latin, oath of allegiance, obligation, from sacrare to consecrate] (13th century)
**1 a** : a Christian rite (as baptism or the Eucharist) that is believed to have been ordained by Christ and that is held to be a means of divine grace or to be a sign or symbol of a spiritual reality **b** : a religious rite or observance comparable to a Christian sacrament
**2** capitalized **a** : COMMUNION 2a **b** : BLESSED SACRAMENT
**3** : something likened to a religious sacrament ⟨saw voting as a sacrament of democracy⟩

**¹sac·ra·men·tal** \,sa-krə-'men-t°l\ adjective (15th century)
**1** : of, relating to, or having the character of a sacrament
**2** : suggesting a sacrament (as in sacredness)
— **sac·ra·men·tal·ly** \-t°l-ē\ adverb

**²sacramental** noun (15th century)
: an action or object (as the rosary) of ecclesiastical origin that serves to express or increase devotion

**sac·ra·men·tal·ism** \-t°l-,i-zəm\ noun (1861)
: belief in or use of sacramental rites, acts, or objects; specifically : belief that the sacraments are inherently efficacious and necessary for salvation

**sac·ra·men·tal·ist** \-t°l-ist\ noun (1840)
**1** : SACRAMENTARIAN
**2** : an adherent of sacramentalism

**Sac·ra·men·tar·i·an** \,sa-krə-,men-'ter-ē-ən, -mən-\ noun (1535)
**1** : one who interprets sacraments as merely visible symbols
**2** : SACRAMENTALIST
— **Sacramentarian** adjective
— **Sac·ra·men·tar·i·an·ism** \-ē-ə-,ni-zəm\ noun

**sa·crar·i·um** \sə-'krer-ē-əm, sa-, sā-\ noun, plural **-ia** \-ē-ə\ [Medieval Latin, from Latin, shrine, from sacr-, sacer sacred] (1727)
**1 a** : SANCTUARY 1b **b** : SACRISTY **c** : PISCINA
**2** : an ancient Roman shrine or sanctuary in a temple or a home holding sacred objects

**sa·cred** \'sā-krəd\ adjective [Middle English, from past participle of sacren to consecrate,

from Old French sacrer, from Latin sacrare, from sacr-, sacer sacred; akin to Latin sancire to make sacred, Hittite šaklāi- rite] (14th century)
**1 a** : dedicated or set apart for the service or worship of a deity ⟨a tree sacred to the gods⟩ **b** : devoted exclusively to one service or use (as of a person or purpose) ⟨a fund sacred to charity⟩
**2 a** : worthy of religious veneration : HOLY **b** : entitled to reverence and respect
**3** : of or relating to religion : not secular or profane ⟨sacred music⟩
**4** archaic : ACCURSED
**5 a** : UNASSAILABLE, INVIOLABLE **b** : highly valued and important ⟨a sacred responsibility⟩
— **sa·cred·ly** adverb
— **sa·cred·ness** noun

**sacred baboon** noun [from its veneration by the ancient Egyptians] (circa 1890)
: HAMADRYAS BABOON

**sacred cow** noun [from the veneration of the cow by Hindus] (1910)
: one that is often unreasonably immune from criticism or opposition

**sacred mushroom** noun (1930)
**1** : any of various New World hallucinogenic fungi (genus Psilocybe) used especially in some Indian ceremonies
**2** : MESCAL BUTTON

**¹sac·ri·fice** \'sa-krə-,fīs, also -fəs or -,fīz\ noun [Middle English, from Old French, from Latin sacrificium, from sacr-, sacer + facere to make — more at DO] (13th century)
**1** : an act of offering to a deity something precious; especially : the killing of a victim on an altar
**2** : something offered in sacrifice
**3 a** : destruction or surrender of something for the sake of something else **b** : something given up or lost ⟨the sacrifices made by parents⟩
**4** : LOSS ⟨goods sold at a sacrifice⟩
**5** : SACRIFICE HIT

**²sacrifice** verb **-ficed; -fic·ing** (14th century)
transitive verb
**1** : to offer as a sacrifice
**2** : to suffer loss of, give up, renounce, injure, or destroy especially for an ideal, belief, or end
**3** : to sell at a loss
intransitive verb
**1** : to make or perform the rites of a sacrifice
**2** : to make a sacrifice hit in baseball
— **sac·ri·fic·er** noun

**sacrifice fly** noun (1944)
: an outfield fly in baseball caught by a fielder after which a runner scores

**sacrifice hit** noun (1880)
: a bunt in baseball that allows a runner to advance one base while the batter is put out

**sac·ri·fi·cial** \,sa-krə-'fi-shəl\ adjective (1607)
**1** : of, relating to, of the nature of, or involving sacrifice
**2** : of or relating to a metal that serves as the anode and is electrolytically consumed instead of another metal that is present
— **sac·ri·fi·cial·ly** \-shə-lē\ adverb

**sac·ri·lege** \'sa-krə-lij\ noun [Middle English, from Middle French, from Latin sacrilegium, from sacrilegus one who steals sacred things, from sacr-, sacer + legere to gather, steal — more at LEGEND] (14th century)
**1** : a technical and not necessarily intrinsically outrageous violation (as improper reception of a sacrament) of what is sacred because consecrated to God
**2** : gross irreverence toward a hallowed person, place, or thing
— **sac·ri·le·gious** \÷,sa-krə-'li-jəs also -'lē-\ adjective
— **sac·ri·le·gious·ly** adverb
— **sac·ri·le·gious·ness** noun

**sac·ris·tan** \'sa-krə-stən\ noun [Middle English, from Medieval Latin sacristanus, from Latin sacr-, sacer] (14th century)

: a person in charge of the sacristy and ceremonial equipment; also : SEXTON

**sac·ris·ty** \'sa-krə-stē\ noun, plural **-ties** [Middle English sacristie, from Medieval Latin sacristia, from sacrista sacristan, from Latin sacr-, sacer] (15th century)
: a room in a church where sacred vessels and vestments are kept and where the clergy vests

**¹sa·cro·il·i·ac** \,sa-krō-'i-lē-,ak, ,sā-\ adjective [probably from French sacro-iliaque, from New Latin sacrum + French iliaque iliac] (1831)
: of, relating to, or being the region of juncture of the sacrum and ilium

**²sacroiliac** noun (1936)
: the sacroiliac region; also : its firm fibrous cartilage

**sac·ro·sanct** \'sa-krō-,saŋ(k)t\ adjective [Latin sacrosanctus, probably from sacro sanctus hallowed by a sacred rite] (1601)
**1** : most sacred or holy : INVIOLABLE
**2** : treated as if holy : immune from criticism or violation ⟨politically sacrosanct programs⟩
— **sac·ro·sanc·ti·ty** \,sa-krō-'saŋ(k)-tə-tē\ noun

**sa·crum** \'sa-krəm, 'sā-\ noun, plural **sa·cra** \'sa-krə, 'sā-\ [New Latin, from Late Latin os sacrum last bone of the spine, literally, holy bone, translation of Greek hieron osteon] (1753)
: the part of the vertebral column that is directly connected with or forms a part of the pelvis and in humans consists of five fused vertebrae

**sad** \'sad\ adjective **sad·der; sad·dest** [Middle English, from Old English sæd sated; akin to Old High German sat sated, Latin satis enough] (13th century)
**1 a** : affected with or expressive of grief or unhappiness : DOWNCAST **b** (1) : causing or associated with grief or unhappiness : DEPRESSING ⟨sad news⟩ (2) : REGRETTABLE, DEPLORABLE ⟨a sad relaxation of morals —C. W. Cunnington⟩ **c** : of little worth
**2** : of a dull somber color ◆
— **sad·ly** adverb
— **sad·ness** noun

**sad·den** \'sa-d°n\ verb **sad·dened; sad·den·ing** \'sad-niŋ, 'sa-d°n-iŋ\ (1628)
transitive verb
: to make sad
intransitive verb
: to become sad

◇ WORD HISTORY
**sad** The word sad goes back to the remote Germanic past of the English language, though the ordinary modern meanings of the word, such as "downcast," "depressing," or "deplorable," give little hint of its history. Its Old English ancestor sæd meant "filled, full, satiated," a meaning matched by cognate words in other early Germanic languages, and continued by Modern German satt "full, having had enough to eat." In Middle English, though sad continued to have the Old English sense "full, sated," it underwent a great burst of semantic diversification. Common senses were "firmly established, fixed," "solid, weighty," "sober, serious," "powerful, strong," "hard, stout (of a blow)," "true, real," "deep, intense (of a color)." The meaning "sorrowful" was in use fairly early, by about 1300, though peculiarly it alone has been retained, as virtually all the other senses developed in Middle English gradually fell from use in early Modern English. The sense "sober, serious" occurs notably in Samuel Taylor Coleridge's poem "The Rime of the Ancient Mariner" ("A sadder and a wiser man,/He rose the following morn"), though Coleridge may have already been employing it as a conscious archaism.

¹**sad·dle** \'sa-d°l\ *noun, often attributive* [Middle English *sadel*, from Old English *sadol*; akin to Old High German *satul* saddle] (before 12th century)

**1 a** (1) **:** a girthed usually padded and leather-covered seat for the rider of an animal (as a horse) (2) **:** a part of a driving harness comparable to a saddle that is used to keep the breeching

saddle 1a(1): *1* western, *2* English

in place **b :** a seat to be straddled by the rider of a vehicle (as a bicycle) **2 :** a device mounted as a support and often shaped to fit the object held **3 a :** a ridge connecting two higher elevations **b :** a pass in a mountain range **4 a :** both sides of the unsplit back of a carcass including both loins **b :** a colored marking on the back of an animal **c :** the rear part of a male fowl's back extending to the tail — see DUCK illustration **5 :** the central part of the backbone of the binding of a book **6 :** a piece of leather across the instep of a shoe
— **sad·dle·less** \-d°l-(l)əs\ *adjective*
— **in the saddle :** in control

²**saddle** *verb* **sad·dled; sad·dling** \'sad-liŋ, 'sa-d°l-iŋ\ (before 12th century)
*transitive verb*
**1 :** to put a saddle on **2 a :** to place under a burden or encumbrance **b :** to place (an onerous responsibility) on a person or group
*intransitive verb*
**:** to mount a saddled horse

**sad·dle·bag** \'sa-d°l-,bag\ *noun* (1773)
**:** one of a pair of covered pouches laid across the back of a horse behind the saddle or hanging over the rear wheel of a bicycle or motorcycle

**saddle blanket** *noun* (1737)
**:** a folded blanket or pad under a saddle to prevent galling the horse

**sad·dle·bow** \'sa-d°l-,bō\ *noun* (before 12th century)
**:** the arch in or the pieces forming the front of a saddle

**sad·dle·bred** \-,bred\ *noun* (1948)
**:** AMERICAN SADDLEBRED

**sad·dle·cloth** \-,klȯth\ *noun* (15th century)
**:** a cloth placed under or over a saddle

**sad·dled prominent** \'sa-d°ld-\ *noun* [from the hump or prominence on the back of the larva] (1910)
**:** a moth (*Heterocampa guttivitta*) whose larva is a serious defoliator of hardwood trees in the eastern and midwestern U.S.

**saddle horn** *noun* (1856)
**:** a hornlike prolongation of the pommel of a stock saddle

**saddle horse** *noun* (1662)
**:** a horse suited for or trained for riding

**saddle leather** *noun* (1832)
**:** leather made of cowhide that is vegetable tanned and used especially for saddlery; *also* **:** smooth polished leather simulating this

**sad·dler** \'sad-lər\ *noun* (14th century)
**:** one that makes, repairs, or sells saddles and other furnishings for horses

**sad·dlery** \'sad-lə-rē, 'sa-d°l-rē\ *noun, plural* **-dler·ies** (15th century)
**:** the trade, articles of trade, or shop of a saddler

**saddle seat** *noun* (1895)
**:** a slightly concave chair seat (as of a Windsor chair) with sometimes a thickened ridge at the center front

**saddle shoe** *noun* (1939)

**:** an oxford-style shoe having a saddle of contrasting color or leather — called also *saddle oxford*

**saddle soap** *noun* (1889)
**:** a mild soap used for cleansing and conditioning leather

**saddle sore** *noun* (1946)
**1 :** a gall or open sore developing on the back of a horse at points of pressure from an ill-fitting or ill-adjusted saddle **2 :** an irritation or sore on parts of the rider chafed by the saddle

**sad·dle·tree** \'sa-d°l-,trē\ *noun* (15th century)
**:** the frame of a saddle

**Sad·du·ce·an** \,sa-jə-'sē-ən, ,sa-dyə-\ *adjective* (1593)
**:** of or relating to the Sadducees

**Sad·du·cee** \'sa-jə-,sē, 'sa-dyə-\ *noun* [Middle English *saducee*, from Old English *sadduce*, from Late Latin *sadducaeus*, from Greek *saddoukaios*, from Late Hebrew *ṣaddūqī*] (before 12th century)
**:** a member of a Jewish party of the intertestamental period consisting of a traditional ruling class of priests and rejecting doctrines not in the Law (as resurrection, retribution in a future life, and the existence of angels)
— **Sad·du·cee·ism** \-,i-zəm\ *noun*

**sa·dhe** \'(t)sä-də, -dē\ *noun* [Hebrew *ṣādhē*] (circa 1899)
**:** the 18th letter of the Hebrew alphabet — see ALPHABET table

**sa·dhu** *also* **sad·dhu** \'sä-(,)dü\ *noun* [Sanskrit *sādhu*] (1845)
**:** a usually Hindu mendicant ascetic

**sad·iron** \'sad-,ī(-ə)rn\ *noun* [*sad* (compact, heavy) + *iron*] (1761)
**:** a flatiron pointed at both ends and having a removable handle

**sa·dism** \'sā-,di-zəm, 'sa-\ *noun* [International Scientific Vocabulary, from Marquis de *Sade*] (1888)
**1 :** a sexual perversion in which gratification is obtained by the infliction of physical or mental pain on others (as on a love object) — compare MASOCHISM **2 a :** delight in cruelty **b :** excessive cruelty
— **sa·dist** \'sā-dist, 'sa-\ *noun*
— **sa·dis·tic** \sə-'dis-tik *also* sā- *or* sa-\ *adjective*
— **sa·dis·ti·cal·ly** \-ti-k(ə-)lē\ *adverb*

**sa·do·mas·och·ism** \sā-(,)dō-'ma-sə-,ki-zəm, ,sa-, -'ma-zə-\ *noun* [International Scientific Vocabulary *sadism* + *-o-* + *masochism*] (1922)
**:** the derivation of pleasure from the infliction of physical or mental pain either on others or on oneself
— **sa·do·mas·och·ist** \-kist\ *noun or adjective*
— **sa·do·mas·och·is·tic** \-,ma-sə-'kis-tik, -,ma-zə-\ *adjective*

**sad sack** *noun* (1943)
**:** an inept person; *especially* **:** an inept soldier
— **sad–sack** *adjective*

**Sa·far** \sə-'fär\ *noun* [Arabic *ṣafar*] (circa 1771)
**:** the 2d month of the Islamic year — see MONTH table

**sa·fa·ri** \sə-'fär-ē, -'far-\ *noun* [Arabic *safarīy* of a trip] (1896)
**1 :** the caravan and equipment of a hunting expedition especially in eastern Africa; *also* **:** such a hunting expedition **2 :** JOURNEY, EXPEDITION ⟨an arctic *safari*⟩
— **safari** *intransitive verb*

**safari jacket** *noun* (1951)
**:** a usually belted shirt jacket with pleated expansible pockets

**safari suit** *noun* (1967)
**:** a safari jacket with matching pants

¹**safe** \'sāf\ *adjective* **saf·er; saf·est** [Middle English *sauf*, from Old French, from Latin *salvus* safe, healthy; akin to Latin *solidus* solid, Greek *holos* whole, safe, Sanskrit *sarva* entire] (14th century)

**1 :** free from harm or risk **:** UNHURT **2 a :** secure from threat of danger, harm, or loss **b :** successful at getting to a base in baseball without being put out **3 :** affording safety or security from danger, risk, or difficulty **4** *obsolete, of mental or moral faculties* **:** HEALTHY, SOUND **5 a :** not threatening danger **:** HARMLESS **b :** unlikely to produce controversy or contradiction **6 a :** not likely to take risks **:** CAUTIOUS **b :** TRUSTWORTHY, RELIABLE
— **safe** *or* **safe·ly** *adverb*
— **safe·ness** *noun*

²**safe** *noun* (15th century)
**1 :** a place or receptacle to keep articles (as valuables) safe **2 :** CONDOM

**safe–con·duct** \'sāf-'kän-(,)dəkt\ *noun* [Middle English *sauf conduit*, from Old French, *safe conduct*] (14th century)
**1 :** protection given a person passing through a military zone or occupied area **2 :** a document authorizing safe-conduct

**safe·crack·er** \'sāf-,kra-kər\ *noun* (circa 1825)
**:** one that breaks open safes to steal
— **safe·crack·ing** \-kiŋ\ *noun*

**safe–deposit box** *noun* (1882)
**:** a box (as in the vault of a bank) for safe storage of valuables — called also *safety-deposit box*

¹**safe·guard** \'sāf-,gärd\ *noun* [Middle English *saufgarde*, from Middle French *saufegarde*, from Old French, from *sauve* safe + *garde* guard] (14th century)
**1 a :** PASS, SAFE-CONDUCT **b :** CONVOY, ESCORT **2 a :** a precautionary measure, stipulation, or device **b :** a technical contrivance to prevent accident

²**safeguard** *transitive verb* (15th century)
**1 :** to provide a safeguard for **2 :** to make safe **:** PROTECT
**synonym** see DEFEND

**safe house** *noun* (1946)
**:** a place where one may engage in secret activities or take refuge

**safe·keep·ing** \'sāf-'kē-piŋ\ *noun* (15th century)
**1 :** the act or process of preserving in safety **2 :** the state of being preserved in safety

**safe·light** \'sāf-,līt\ *noun* (1903)
**:** a darkroom lamp with a filter to screen out rays that are harmful to sensitive film or paper

**safe sex** *noun* (1985)
**:** sexual activity and especially sexual intercourse in which various measures (as the use of latex condoms or the practice of monogamy) are taken to avoid disease (as AIDS) transmitted by sexual contact

¹**safe·ty** \'sāf-tē\ *noun, plural* **safeties** [Middle English *saufte*, from Middle French *sauveté*, from Old French, from *sauve*, feminine of *sauf* safe] (14th century)
**1 :** the condition of being safe from undergoing or causing hurt, injury, or loss **2 :** a device (as on a weapon or a machine) designed to prevent inadvertent or hazardous operation **3 a** (1) **:** a situation in football in which a member of the offensive team is tackled behind its own goal line that counts two points for the defensive team — compare TOUCHBACK (2) **:** a member of a defensive backfield in football who occupies the deepest position in order to receive a kick, defend against a forward pass, or stop a ballcarrier **b :** a billiard shot made with no attempt to score or so as to

leave the balls in an unfavorable position for the opponent **c :** BASE HIT

**²safety** *transitive verb* **safe·tied; safe·ty·ing** (1940)
**:** to protect against failure, breakage, or accident ⟨*safety* a rifle⟩

**safety belt** *noun* (circa 1858)
**:** a belt fastening a person to an object (as a car seat) to prevent falling or injury

**safety glass** *noun* (1919)
**:** transparent material that is made by laminating a sheet of transparent plastic between sheets of clear glass and is used especially for windows (as of automobiles) likely to be subjected to shock or impact

**safety lamp** *noun* (1816)
**:** a miner's lamp constructed to avoid explosion in an atmosphere containing flammable gas usually by enclosing the flame in fine wire gauze

**safe·ty·man** \'saf-tē-ˌman\ *noun* (1927)
**:** SAFETY 3a(2)

**safety match** *noun* (1863)
**:** a match capable of being struck and ignited only on a specially prepared friction surface

**safety net** *noun* (1950)
**:** something that provides security against misfortune or difficulty

**safety pin** *noun* (1857)
**:** a pin in the form of a clasp with a guard covering its point when fastened

**safety razor** *noun* (circa 1875)
**:** a razor provided with a guard for the blade to prevent deep cuts in the skin

**safety valve** *noun* (1813)
**1 :** an automatic escape or relief valve (as for a steam boiler)
**2 :** an outlet for pent-up energy or emotion
**3 :** something that relieves the pressure of overcrowding

**saf·flow·er** \'sa-ˌflau̇(-ə)r\ *noun* [Middle French *saffleur,* from Old Italian *saffiore,* from Arabic *aṣfar,* a yellow plant] (1642)
**:** a widely cultivated Old World composite herb (*Carthamus tinctorius*) with large orange or red flower heads and seeds rich in oil; *also*
**:** a red dyestuff prepared from the flower heads

**safflower oil** *noun* (circa 1857)
**:** an edible drying oil obtained from the seeds of the safflower

**saf·fron** \'sa-frən\ *noun* [Middle English, from Old French *safran,* from Medieval Latin *safranum,* from Arabic *za'farān*] (13th century)
**1 a :** the deep orange aromatic pungent dried stigmas of a purple-flowered crocus (*Crocus sativus*) used to color and flavor foods and formerly as a dyestuff and in medicine **b :** the crocus supplying saffron
**2 :** a moderate orange to orange yellow

**saf·ra·nine** \'saf-rə-ˌnēn, -nən\ *or* **saf·ra·nin** \-nən\ *noun* [International Scientific Vocabulary, from French or German *safran* saffron] (1868)
**1 :** any of various usually red synthetic dyes that are amino derivatives of bases
**2 :** any of various mixtures of safranine salts used in dyeing and as biological stains

**saf·role** \'saf-ˌrōl\ *noun* [International Scientific Vocabulary, from sass*afras* + -*ole*] (1869)
**:** a poisonous oily cyclic ether $C_{10}H_{10}O_2$ that is the principal component of sassafras oil and is used chiefly in perfumery

**¹sag** \'sag\ *verb* **sagged; sag·ging** [Middle English *saggen,* probably of Scandinavian origin; akin to Swedish *sacka* to sag] (14th century)
*intransitive verb*
**1 :** to droop, sink, or settle from or as if from pressure or loss of tautness
**2 a :** to lose firmness, resiliency, or vigor ⟨spirits *sagging* from overwork⟩ **b :** to decline especially from a thriving state
**3 :** DRIFT
**4 :** to fail to stimulate or retain interest

*transitive verb*
**:** to cause to sag **:** leave slack in

**²sag** *noun* (1580)
**1 :** a tendency to drift (as of a ship to leeward)
**2 a :** a sagging part ⟨the *sag* in a rope⟩ **b :** a drop or depression below the surrounding area **c :** an instance or amount of sagging
**3 :** a temporary decline (as in the price of a commodity)

**sa·ga** \'sä-gə *also* 'sa-\ *noun* [Old Norse — more at SAW] (1709)
**1 :** a prose narrative recorded in Iceland in the 12th and 13th centuries of historic or legendary figures and events of the heroic age of Norway and Iceland
**2 :** a modern heroic narrative resembling the Icelandic saga
**3 :** a long detailed account ⟨a *saga* of the Old South⟩

**sa·ga·cious** \sə-'gā-shəs, si-\ *adjective* [Latin *sagac-, sagax,* from *sagire* to perceive keenly; akin to Latin *sagus* prophetic — more at SEEK] (1607)
**1** *obsolete* **:** keen in sense perception
**2 a :** of keen and farsighted penetration and judgment **:** DISCERNING ⟨*sagacious* judge of character⟩ **b :** caused by or indicating acute discernment ⟨*sagacious* purchase of stock⟩
**synonym** see SHREWD
— **sa·ga·cious·ly** *adverb*
— **sa·ga·cious·ness** *noun*

**sa·gac·i·ty** \sə-'ga-sə-tē, si-\ *noun* (15th century)
**:** the quality of being sagacious

**sag·a·more** \'sa-gə-ˌmōr, -ˌmȯr\ *noun* [Eastern Abenaki *sàkəma*] (1613)
**1 :** a subordinate chief of the Algonquian Indians of the North Atlantic coast
**2 :** SACHEM 1

**saga novel** *noun* (circa 1938)
**:** ROMAN-FLEUVE

**¹sage** \'sāj\ *adjective* **sag·er; sag·est** [Middle English, from Old French, from (assumed) Vulgar Latin *sapius,* from Latin *sapere* to taste, have good taste, be wise; akin to Oscan *sipus* knowing, Old Saxon an*sebbian* to perceive] (14th century)
**1 a :** wise through reflection and experience **b** *archaic* **:** GRAVE, SOLEMN
**2 :** proceeding from or characterized by wisdom, prudence, and good judgment ⟨*sage* advice⟩
**synonym** see WISE
— **sage·ly** *adverb*
— **sage·ness** *noun*

**²sage** *noun* (14th century)
**1 :** one (as a profound philosopher) distinguished for wisdom
**2 :** a mature or venerable man of sound judgment

**³sage** *noun* [Middle English, from Middle French *sauge,* from Latin *salvia,* from *salvus* healthy; from its use as a medicinal herb — more at SAFE] (14th century)
**1 :** a mint (*Salvia officinalis*) with grayish green aromatic leaves used especially in flavoring meats; *broadly* **:** SALVIA
**2 :** SAGEBRUSH

**sage·brush** \'sāj-ˌbrəsh\ *noun* (1850)
**:** any of several North American hoary composite subshrubs (genus *Artemisia*); *especially* **:** one (*A. tridentata*) having a bitter juice and an odor resembling sage and often covering vast tracts of alkaline plains in the western U.S.

**sage cheese** *noun* (1699)
**:** a cheese similar to mild cheddar flecked with green and flavored with sage

**sage grouse** *noun* (1876)
**:** a large grouse (*Centrocercus urophasianus*) of the dry sagebrush plains of western North America that has mottled gray and buff plumage with a contrasting black belly

**sag·er** *or* **sag·gar** \'sa-gər\ *noun* [probably alteration of *safeguard*] (1752)

**:** a box made of fireclay in which delicate ceramic pieces are fired

**sag·it·tal** \'sa-jə-t°l\ *adjective* [Middle English *sagittale,* from Medieval Latin *sagittalis,* from Latin *sagitta* arrow] (14th century)
**1 :** of or relating to the suture between the parietal bones of the skull
**2 :** of, relating to, situated in, or being the median plane of the body or any plane parallel thereto
— **sag·it·tal·ly** \-t°l-ē\ *adverb*

**Sag·it·tar·i·an** \ˌsa-jə-'ter-ē-ən\ *noun* (1911)
**:** SAGITTARIUS 2b

**Sag·it·tar·i·us** \-ē-əs\ *noun* [Latin (genitive *Sagittarii*), literally, archer, from *sagitta*]
**1 :** a southern zodiacal constellation pictured as a centaur shooting an arrow and containing the point in the sky where the center of the Milky Way galaxy is located
**2 a :** the 9th sign of the zodiac in astrology — see ZODIAC table **b :** one born under the sign of Sagittarius

**sag·it·tate** \'sa-jə-ˌtāt\ *adjective* [Latin *sagitta*] (1760)
**:** shaped like an arrowhead; *specifically* **:** elongated, triangular, and having the two basal lobes prolonged downward ⟨*sagittate* leaf⟩ — see LEAF illustration

**sa·go** \'sā-(ˌ)gō\ *noun, plural* **sagos** [Malay *sagu* sago palm] (circa 1580)
**:** a dry granulated or powdered starch prepared from the pith of a sago palm and used in foods and as textile stiffening

**sago palm** *noun* (1769)
**:** a plant that yields sago; *especially* **:** any of various lofty pinnate-leaved Indian and Malaysian palms (genus *Metroxylon*)

**sa·gua·ro** \sə-'wär-ə, -'gwär-, -ō\ *noun, plural* **-ros** [Mexican Spanish] (1856)
**:** an arborescent cactus (*Carnegiea gigantea*) of desert regions of the southwestern U.S. and Mexico that has a tall columnar simple or sparsely branched trunk of up to 60 feet (18 meters) and bears white flowers and edible fruit

**Sa·hap·ti·an** \sə-'hap-tē-ən\ *variant of* SHAHAPTIAN

**sa·hib** \'sä-ˌ(h)ib, -ˌ(h)ēb, ˌsä-'\ *noun* [Hindi *sāheb,* from Arabic *ṣāḥib*] (1673)
**:** SIR, MASTER — used especially among the native inhabitants of colonial India when addressing or speaking of a European of some social or official status

**¹said** *past and past participle of* SAY

**²said** \'sed\ *adjective* [past participle of *say*] (14th century)
**:** AFOREMENTIONED

**¹sail** \'sā(ə)l, *as last element in compounds often* səl\ *noun* [Middle English, from Old English *segl;* akin to Old High German *segal* sail] (before 12th century)
**1 a** (1) **:** an extent of fabric (as canvas) by means of which wind is used to propel a ship through water (2) **:** the sails of a ship **b** *plural usually* **sail :** a ship equipped with sails
**2 :** an extent of fabric used in propelling a wind-driven vehicle (as an iceboat)

saguaro

sail 1a (of a schooner):
*1 flying jib, 2 jib, 3 forestaysail, 4 foresail, 5 fore gafftopsail, 6 main-topmast staysail, 7 mainsail,*
*8 main gaff-topsail*

**3 :** something that resembles a sail; *especially*
**:** a streamlined conning tower on a submarine
**4 :** a passage by a sailing craft **:** CRUISE
— **sailed** \'sā(ə)ld\ *adjective*
— **under sail :** in motion with sails set

**²sail** (before 12th century)
*intransitive verb*
**1 a :** to travel on water in a ship **b :** YACHT
**2 a :** to travel on water by the action of wind upon sails or by other means **b :** to move or proceed easily, gracefully, nonchalantly, or without resistance ⟨*sails* through all sorts of contradictions —Vicki Hearne⟩ ⟨the bill *sailed* through the legislature⟩
**3 :** to begin a water voyage ⟨*sail* with the tide⟩
*transitive verb*
**1 a :** to travel on (water) by means of motive power (as sail) **b :** to glide through
**2 :** to direct or manage the motion of (as a ship)
— **sail·able** \'sā-lə-bəl\ *adjective*
— **sail into :** to attack vigorously or sharply ⟨*sailed into* me for being late⟩

**sail·board** \'sā(ə)l-ˌbōrd, -ˌbȯrd\ *noun* (1962)
**:** a modified surfboard having a mast mounted on a universal joint and sailed by one person standing up
— **sail·board·ing** *noun*

**sail·boat** \'sā(ə)l-ˌbōt\ *noun* (1798)
**:** a boat usually propelled by sail
— **sail·boat·er** \-ˌbō-tər\ *noun*
— **sail·boat·ing** *noun*

**sail·cloth** \-ˌklȯth\ *noun* (13th century)
**:** a heavy canvas used for sails, tents, or upholstery; *also* **:** a lightweight canvas used for clothing

**sail·er** \'sā-lər\ *noun* (15th century)
**:** a ship or boat especially having specified sailing qualities

**sail·fish** \'sā(ə)l-ˌfish\ *noun* (1879)
**:** any of a genus (*Istiophorus* and especially *I. platypterus*) of billfishes having a very large dorsal fin

**sail·ing** \'sā-liŋ\ *noun* (before 12th century)
**1 a :** the technical skill of managing a ship **:** NAVIGATION **b :** the method of determining the course to be followed to reach a given point
**2 a :** the sport of handling or riding in a sailboat **b :** a departure from a port

**sail·or** \'sā-lər\ *noun* [alteration of *sailer*] (circa 1642)
**1 a :** one that sails; *especially* **:** MARINER **b** (1) **:** a member of a ship's crew (2) **:** SEAMAN 2b
**2 :** a traveler by water
**3 :** a stiff straw hat with a low flat crown and straight circular brim

**sailor collar** *noun* (1895)
**:** a broad collar having a square flap across the back and tapering to a V in the front

**sail·or's-choice** \ˌsā-lərz-'chȯis\ *noun* (1850)
**:** any of several small grunts of the Western Atlantic: as **a :** PINFISH **b :** PIGFISH

**sail·plane** \'sā(ə)l-ˌplān\ *noun* (1922)
**:** a glider of such design that it is able to rise in an upward air current
— **sailplane** *intransitive verb*
— **sail·plan·er** *noun*

**sai·min** \'sī-ˌmin\ *noun* [probably from Chinese (Guangdong) *sai mihn* fine noodles] (1949)
**:** a Hawaiian noodle soup

**sain** \'sān\ *transitive verb* [Middle English, from Old English *segnian*, from Late Latin *signare*, from Latin, to mark — more at SIGN] (before 12th century)
**1** *dialect British* **:** to make the sign of the cross on (oneself)
**2** *dialect British* **:** BLESS

**sain·foin** \'sān-ˌfȯin, 'san-\ *noun* [French, from Middle French, from *sain* healthy (from Latin *sanus*) + *foin* hay, from Latin *fenum*] (1626)
**:** a pink-flowered Eurasian perennial leguminous herb (*Onobrychis viciaefolia* synonym *O. viciifolia*) grown for forage

**¹saint** \'sānt, *before a name* (ˌ)sānt *or* sənt\ *noun* [Middle English, from Old French, from Late Latin *sanctus*, from Latin, sacred, from past participle of *sancire* to make sacred — more at SACRED] (13th century)
**1 :** one officially recognized especially through canonization as preeminent for holiness
**2 a :** one of the spirits of the departed in heaven **b :** ANGEL 1a
**3 a :** one of God's chosen and usually Christian people **b** *capitalized* **:** a member of any of various Christian bodies; *specifically* **:** LATTER-DAY SAINT
**4 :** one eminent for piety or virtue
**5 :** an illustrious predecessor
— **saint·dom** \'sānt-dəm\ *noun*
— **saint·like** \'sānt-ˌlīk\ *adjective*

**²saint** \'sānt\ *transitive verb* (13th century)
**:** to recognize or designate as a saint; *specifically* **:** CANONIZE

**Saint Ag·nes' Eve** \-'ag-nə-səz-, -'ag-nəs-\ *noun* [*Saint Agnes*] (1820)
**:** the night of January 20 when a woman is traditionally held to have a revelation of her future husband

**Saint An·drew's cross** \-'an-ˌdrüz-\ *noun* [*Saint Andrew* (died about A.D. 60), apostle who, according to tradition, was crucified on a cross of this type] (1615)
**:** a figure of a cross that has the form of two intersecting oblique bars — see CROSS illustration

**Saint An·tho·ny's cross** \-'an(t)-thə-nēz-, *chiefly British* -'an-tə-\ *noun* [*Saint Anthony*] (1885)
**:** TAU CROSS

**Saint Anthony's fire** *noun* (14th century)
**:** any of several inflammations or gangrenous conditions (as erysipelas or ergotism) of the skin

**saint au·gus·tine grass** \-'ȯ-gə-ˌstēn-\ *noun, often S&A capitalized* [probably from *Saint Augustine*, Fla.] (1900)
**:** a perennial much-branched creeping grass (*Stenotaphrum secundatum*) of the southern U.S. that is valuable as a sand binder and as sod grass

**Saint Ber·nard** \-bər-'närd\ *noun* [the hospice of Grand *Saint Bernard*, where such dogs were first bred] (1839)
**:** any of a Swiss alpine breed of tall powerful working dogs used especially formerly in aiding lost travelers

**Saint Bernard**

**saint·ed** \'sān-təd\ *adjective* (1598)
**1 :** befitting or relating to a saint
**2 :** SAINTLY, PIOUS
**3 :** entered into heaven **:** DEAD
**4 :** much admired **:** IDOLIZED

**Saint El·mo's fire** \'sānt-'el-(ˌ)mōz-\ *noun* [*Saint Elmo* (*Erasmus*) (died 303) Italian bishop & patron saint of sailors] (1814)
**:** a flaming phenomenon sometimes seen in stormy weather at prominent points on an airplane or ship and on land that is of the nature of a brush discharge of electricity — called also *Saint Elmo's light*

**Saint Emi·lion** \ˌsaⁿ-tā-mēl-'yōⁿ\ *noun* [*Saint-Émilion*, village in SW France] (1833)
**:** a red Bordeaux wine

**saint·hood** \'sānt-ˌhůd\ *noun* (1550)
**1 :** the quality or state of being a saint
**2 :** saints as a group

**Saint John's bread** \-'jänz-ˌbred\ *noun* (1591)
**:** CAROB 2

**Saint-John's-wort** \-ˌwərt, -ˌwȯrt\ *noun* [*Saint John* the Baptist] (15th century)
**:** any of a genus (*Hypericum* of the family Guttiferae, the Saint-John's-wort family) of herbs and shrubs with showy pentamerous yellow flowers

**Saint Lou·is encephalitis** \-'lü-əs-\ *noun* [*Saint Louis*, Mo.] (1934)
**:** a North American viral encephalitis that is transmitted by several culex mosquitoes

**saint·ly** \'sānt-lē\ *adjective* **saint·li·er; -est** (1534)
**:** relating to, resembling, or befitting a saint **:** HOLY
— **saint·li·ness** *noun*

**Saint Mar·tin's summer** \-'mär-tⁿnz-\ *noun* [*Saint Martin's* Day, November 11] (1591)
**:** Indian summer when occurring in November

**Saint Pat·rick's Day** \-'pa-triks-\ *noun* (1844)
**:** March 17 observed by the Roman Catholic Church in honor of Saint Patrick and celebrated in Ireland in commemoration of his death

**saint's day** *noun* (15th century)
**:** a day in a church calendar on which a saint is commemorated

**saint·ship** \'sānt-ˌship\ *noun* (1631)
**:** SAINTHOOD 1

**Saint Val·en·tine's Day** \-'va-lən-ˌtīnz-\ *noun* [*Saint Valentine* (died about 270) Italian priest] (14th century)
**:** February 14 observed in honor of Saint Valentine and as a time for sending valentines

**Saint Vi·tus' dance** \-'vī-təs-, -'vī-tə-səz-\ *noun* [*Saint Vitus*, 3d century Christian child martyr] (1621)
**:** CHOREA — called also *Saint Vitus's dance* \same\

**saith** \'seth, 'sā-əth\ *archaic present 3d singular of* SAY

**saithe** \'sāth, 'sāth\ *noun, plural* **saithe** [of Scandinavian origin; akin to Old Norse *seithr* coalfish] (1632)
**:** POLLACK

**Sai·va** \'sī-və, 'shī-\ *noun* [Sanskrit *Śaiva*, from *Śiva* Siva] (1810)
**:** a member of a major Hindu sect devoted to the cult of Siva
— **Sai·vism** \-ˌvi-zəm\ *noun*

**¹sake** \'sāk\ *noun* [Middle English, dispute, guilt, purpose, from Old English *sacu* guilt, action at law; akin to Old High German *sahha* action at law, cause, Old English *sēcan* to seek — more at SEEK] (13th century)
**1 :** END, PURPOSE ⟨for the *sake* of argument⟩
**2 a :** the good, advantage, or enhancement of some entity (as an ideal) ⟨free to pursue learning for its own *sake* —M. S. Eisenhower⟩ **b :** personal or social welfare, safety, or benefit

**²sa·ke** *or* **sa·ki** \'sä-kē\ *noun* [Japanese *sake*] (1687)
**:** a Japanese alcoholic beverage of fermented rice usually served hot

**sa·ker** \'sā-kər\ *noun* [Middle English *sagre*, from Middle French *sacre*, from Arabic *ṣaqr*] (15th century)
**:** an Old World falcon (*Falco cherrug*) used in falconry

**Sak·ti** \'säk-tē, 'shäk-\, **Sak·tism** *variant of* SHAKTI, SHAKTISM

**sal** \'sal\ *noun* [Middle English, from Latin — more at SALT] (14th century)
**:** SALT

**¹sa·laam** \sə-'läm\ *noun* [Arabic *salām*, literally, peace] (1613)
**1 :** a salutation or ceremonial greeting in the East
**2 :** an obeisance performed by bowing very low and placing the right palm on the forehead

**²salaam** (1693)
*transitive verb*
**:** to greet or pay homage to with a salaam

\ə\ abut \ᵊ\ kitten \ər\ further \a\ ash \ā\ ace
\ä\ mop, mar \aů\ out \ch\ chin \e\ bet \ē\ easy
\g\ go \i\ hit \ī\ ice \j\ job \ŋ\ sing \ō\ go
\ȯ\ law \ȯi\ boy \th\ thin \t͟h\ the \ü\ loot \ů\ foot
\y\ yet \zh\ vision *see also* Guide to Pronunciation

*intransitive verb*
: to perform a salaam

**sal·able** *or* **sale·able** \'sā-lə-bəl\ *adjective* (1530)
: capable of being or fit to be sold : MARKETABLE
— **sal·abil·i·ty** \ˌsā-lə-'bi-lə-tē\ *noun*

**sa·la·cious** \sə-'lā-shəs\ *adjective* [Latin *salac-, salax,* from *salire* to move spasmodically, leap — more at SALLY] (circa 1645)
1 : arousing or appealing to sexual desire or imagination : LASCIVIOUS
2 : LECHEROUS, LUSTFUL
— **sa·la·cious·ly** *adverb*
— **sa·la·cious·ness** *noun*

**sal·ad** \'sa-ləd\ *noun* [Middle English *salade,* from Middle French, from Old Provençal *salada,* from *salar* to salt, from *sal* salt, from Latin] (14th century)
1 a : green vegetables (as lettuce, endive, or romaine) and often tomatoes, cucumbers, or radishes served with dressing **b** : a dish of meat, fish, shellfish, eggs, fruits, or vegetables singly or in combination usually served cold with a dressing
2 : a green vegetable or herb grown for salad; *especially* : LETTUCE
3 : a usually incongruous mixture : HODGEPODGE

**salad bar** *noun* (1973)
: a self-service counter (as in a restaurant) featuring an array of salad makings and dressings

**salad days** *noun plural* (1606)
: time of youthful inexperience or indiscretion ⟨my *salad days* when I was green in judgment —Shakespeare⟩; *also* : an early flourishing period : HEYDAY

**salad dressing** *noun* (circa 1839)
: a dressing either uncooked (as French dressing) or cooked (as a boiled dressing) that is used for salad

**salad oil** *noun* (1537)
: an edible vegetable oil suitable for use in salad dressings

**sa·lal** \sə-'lal, sa-\ *noun* [Chinook Jargon, from Lower Chinook *sálal*] (1825)
: a small shrub (*Gaultheria shallon*) of the heath family found on the Pacific coast of North America and bearing edible grape-sized dark purple berries

**sal·a·man·der** \'sa-lə-ˌman-dər *also* ˌsa-lə-'\ *noun* [Middle English *salamandre,* from Middle French, from Latin *salamandra,* from Greek] (14th century)
1 : a mythical animal having the power to endure fire without harm
2 : an elemental being in the theory of Paracelsus inhabiting fire
3 : any of numerous amphibians (order Caudata) superficially resembling lizards but scaleless and covered with a soft moist skin and breathing by gills in the larval stage
4 : an article used in connection with fire: as **a** : a cooking utensil for browning a food (as pastry or pudding) **b** : a portable stove **c** : a cooking device with an overhead heat source like a broiler
— **sal·a·man·drine** \ˌsa-lə-'man-drən\ *adjective*

**sa·la·mi** \sə-'lä-mē\ *noun* [Italian, plural of *salame* salami, from *salare* to salt, from *sale* salt, from Latin *sal* — more at SALT] (1852)
: a highly seasoned sausage of pork and beef either dried or fresh

**sal ammoniac** *noun* [Middle English *sal armoniak,* from Latin *sal ammoniacus,* literally, salt of Ammon] (14th century)
: AMMONIUM CHLORIDE

**sa·lar·i·at** \sə-'lar-ē-ət, -'ler-\ *noun* [French, from *salaire* salary (from Latin *salarium*) + *-ariat* (as in *prolétariat* proletariat)] (1917)
: the class or body of salaried persons usually as distinguished from wage earners

**sal·a·ry** \'sal-rē, 'sa-lə-\ *noun, plural* **-ries** [Middle English *salarie,* from Latin *salarium*

pension, salary, from neuter of *salarius* of salt, from *sal* salt — more at SALT] (13th century)
: fixed compensation paid regularly for services ◆
— **sal·a·ried** \-rēd\ *adjective*

**sal·a·ry·man** \-ˌman\ *noun* [Japanese *sararīman,* from English *salary* + *man*] (1962)
: a Japanese white-collar businessman

**sal·chow** \'sal-ˌkaù, -ˌkȯv, -ˌ(ˌ)kō\ *noun* [Ulrich Salchow (died 1949) Swedish figure skater] (1940)
: a figure-skating jump with a takeoff from the back inside edge of one skate followed by a full turn in the air and a landing on the back outside edge of the opposite skate

**sale** \'sā(ə)l\ *noun* [Middle English, from Old English *sala,* from Old Norse — more at SELL] (before 12th century)
1 : the act of selling; *specifically* : the transfer of ownership of and title to property from one person to another for a price
2 a : opportunity of selling or being sold : DEMAND **b** : distribution by selling
3 : public disposal to the highest bidder : AUCTION
4 : a selling of goods at bargain prices
5 *plural* a : operations and activities involved in promoting and selling goods or services ⟨vice-president in charge of *sales*⟩ **b** : gross receipts
— **for sale** : available for purchase
— **on sale** 1 : for sale 2 : available for purchase at a reduced price

**sa·lep** \'sa-ləp, sə-'lep\ *noun* [French or Spanish, both from Arabic dialect *sahlab,* perhaps alteration of Arabic (*khusy ath-*)*tha'lab,* literally, testicles of the fox] (1736)
: the starchy or mucilaginous dried tubers of various Old World orchids (especially genus *Orchis*) used for food or in medicine

**sal·e·ra·tus** \ˌsa-lə-'rā-təs\ *noun* [New Latin *sal aeratus* aerated salt] (1837)
: a leavening agent consisting of potassium or sodium bicarbonate

**sale·room** \'sā(ə)l-ˌrüm, -ˌrùm\ *noun chiefly British variant of* SALESROOM

**sales** \'sā(ə)lz\ *adjective* (1913)
: of, relating to, or used in selling

**sales·clerk** \'sā(ə)lz-ˌklərk\ *noun* (1926)
: a salesperson in a store

**sales·girl** \-ˌgər(-ə)l\ *noun* (1887)
: SALESWOMAN

**Sa·le·sian** \sə-'lē-zhən, sā-\ *noun* (1884)
: a member of the Society of Saint Francis de Sales founded by Saint John Bosco in Turin, Italy in the 19th century and devoted chiefly to education

**sales·la·dy** \'sā(ə)lz-ˌlā-dē\ *noun* (1856)
: SALESWOMAN

**sales·man** \'sā(ə)lz-mən\ *noun* (1523)
: one who sells in a given territory, in a store, or by telephone

**sales·man·ship** \-ˌship\ *noun* (1880)
1 : the skill or art of selling
2 : ability or effectiveness in selling or in presenting persuasively ⟨political *salesmanship*⟩

**sales·peo·ple** \-ˌpē-pəl\ *noun plural* (1876)
: persons employed to sell goods or services

**sales·per·son** \-ˌpər-s°n\ *noun* (1901)
: a salesman or saleswoman

**sales·room** \'sā(ə)lz-ˌrüm, -ˌrùm\ *noun* (1840)
: a place where goods are displayed for sale; *especially* : an auction room

**sales slip** *noun* (1926)
: a receipt for a purchase

**sales tax** *noun* (1921)
: a tax levied on the sale of goods and services that is usually calculated as a percentage of the purchase price and collected by the seller

**sales·wom·an** \'sā(ə)lz-ˌwù-mən\ *noun* (1704)
: a woman who sells in a given territory, in a store, or by telephone

**sal·ic** \'sa-lik\ *adjective* [by alteration] (1902)
: SIALIC

**Sal·ic** \'sā-lik, 'sa-\ *adjective* [Middle French or Medieval Latin; Middle French *salique,* from Medieval Latin *Salicus,* from Late Latin *Salii* Salic Franks] (circa 1548)
: of, relating to, or being a Frankish people that settled on the IJssel river early in the 4th century

**sal·i·cin** \'sa-lə-sən\ *noun* [French *salicine,* from Latin *salic-, salix* willow — more at SALLOW] (1830)
: a bitter white crystalline glucoside $C_{13}H_{18}O_7$ found in the bark and leaves of several willows and poplars and used in medicine like salicylic acid

**Salic law** *noun* (1599)
1 : a rule held to derive from the legal code of the Salic Franks excluding females from the line of succession to a throne
2 : the legal code of the Salic Franks

**sal·ic·y·late** \sə-'li-sə-ˌlāt\ *noun* (1842)
: a salt or ester of salicylic acid

**sal·i·cyl·ic acid** \ˌsa-lə-ˌsi-lik-\ *noun* [International Scientific Vocabulary, from *salicyl* (the group $HOC_6H_4CO$)] (1840)
: a crystalline phenolic acid $C_7H_6O_3$ used especially in the form of salts and other derivatives as an analgesic and antipyretic

**sa·lience** \'sā-lyən(t)s, -lē-ən(t)s\ *noun* (1836)
1 : the quality or state of being salient
2 : a striking point or feature : HIGHLIGHT

**sa·lien·cy** \-lyən(t)-sē, -lē-ən(t)-\ *noun, plural* **-cies** (1664)
: SALIENCE

¹**sa·lient** \'sā-lyənt, -lē-ənt\ *adjective* [Latin *salient-, saliens,* present participle of *salire* to leap — more at SALLY] (1646)
1 : moving by leaps or springs : JUMPING
2 : jetting upward ⟨a *salient* fountain⟩
3 a : projecting beyond a line, surface, or level **b** : standing out conspicuously : PROMINENT; *especially* : of notable significance ⟨similar to . . . Prohibition, but there are a couple of *salient* differences —Tony Gibbs⟩
*synonym* see NOTICEABLE
— **sa·lient·ly** *adverb*

²**salient** *noun* (1828)
: something (as a promontory) that projects outward or upward from its surroundings; *especially* : an outwardly projecting part of a fortification, trench system, or line of defense

¹**sa·line** \'sā-ˌlēn, -ˌlīn\ *adjective* [Middle English, from Latin *salinus,* from *sal* salt — more at SALT] (15th century)
1 : consisting of or containing salt ⟨a *saline* solution⟩
2 : of, relating to, or resembling salt : SALTY ⟨a *saline* taste⟩

◇ WORD HISTORY

**salary** The word *salary* is a loan from Latin *salarium,* a derivative of *sal* "salt," and perhaps originally short for *salarium argentum* "salt money." According to a customary explanation, it was originally money paid to Roman soldiers with which they were supposed to buy salt, but nothing in the attested history of the Latin word supports this. From the evidence of extant documents and inscriptions, the *salarium* was a fixed payment, introduced under the rule of Augustus, that was made to officials of a certain rank. The word was also applied to fees given to scholars and physicians by the Roman state or a community, as well as a payment to army officers. Presumably *salarium* was a kind of euphemism, since the sums involved in such payments were in excess of what would have been needed just to buy salt. Our modern idea of providing public office holders with a fixed income was not well developed in ancient Rome, where personal relations rather than bureaucratic rules determined much behavior and the lines between bribe, gift, and payment were often fuzzy.

**3** : consisting of or relating to the salts of the alkali metals or of magnesium ⟨a *saline* cathartic⟩
— **sa·lin·i·ty** \sā-'li-nə-tē, sə-\ *noun*
**²saline** *noun* (1662)
**1** : a metallic salt; *especially* : a salt of potassium, sodium, or magnesium with a cathartic action
**2** : a saline solution; *especially* : one isotonic with body fluids
**sa·li·nize** \'sa-lə-ˌnīz *also* 'sā-\ *transitive verb* **-nized; -niz·ing** (1926)
: to treat or impregnate with salt
— **sa·li·ni·za·tion** \ˌsa-lə-nə-'zā-shən *also* ˌsā-\ *noun*
**sa·li·nom·e·ter** \ˌsa-lə-'nä-mə-tər, ˌsā-\ *noun* [International Scientific Vocabulary *saline* + *-o-* + *-meter*] (1844)
: an instrument (as a hydrometer) for measuring the amount of salt in a solution
**Sa·lique** \'sā-lik, 'sa-; sə-'lēk, sā-\ *variant of* SALIC
**Salis·bury steak** \'sȯlz-ˌber-ē-, 'salz-, -b(ə-)rē-\ *noun* [J. H. *Salisbury*, 19th century English physician] (1897)
: ground beef mixed with egg, milk, bread crumbs, and seasonings and formed into a large patty and cooked
**Sa·lish** \'sā-lish\ *noun* (1831)
**1** : a group of American Indian peoples of British Columbia and the northwestern U.S.
**2** : the family of languages spoken by the Salish peoples
— **Sa·lish·an** \-li-shən\ *adjective or noun*
**sa·li·va** \sə-'lī-və\ *noun* [Latin] (15th century)
: a slightly alkaline secretion of water, mucin, protein, salts, and often a starch-splitting enzyme (as ptyalin) that is secreted into the mouth by salivary glands, lubricates ingested food, and often begins the breakdown of starches
**sal·i·vary** \'sa-lə-ˌver-ē\ *adjective* (1709)
: of or relating to saliva or the glands that secrete it; *especially* : producing or carrying saliva
**sal·i·vate** \'sa-lə-ˌvāt\ *intransitive verb* **-vat·ed; -vat·ing** (circa 1706)
**1** : to have a flow of saliva especially in excess
**2** : DROOL 2
— **sal·i·va·tion** \ˌsa-lə-'vā-shən\ *noun*
— **sal·i·va·tor** \'sa-lə-ˌvā-tər\ *noun*
**Salk vaccine** \'sȯk-, 'sȯlk-\ *noun* [Jonas *Salk*] (1954)
: a vaccine consisting of poliomyelitis virus inactivated with formaldehyde
**sal·let** \'sa-lət\ *noun* [Middle English, from Middle French *sallade*] (15th century)
: a light 15th century helmet with or without a visor and with a projection over the neck
**¹sal·low** \'sa-(ˌ)lō\ *noun* [Middle English, from Old English *sealh*; akin to Old High German *salha* sallow, Latin *salix* willow] (before 12th century)
: any of several Old World broad-leaved willows (as *Salix caprea*) including important sources of charcoal and tanbark
**²sallow** *adjective* [Middle English *salowe*, from Old English *salu*; akin to Old High German *salo* murky, Russian *solovyĭ* yellowish gray] (before 12th century)
: of a grayish greenish yellow color
— **sal·low·ish** \'sa-lə-wish\ *adjective*
— **sal·low·ness** \'sa-lō-nəs, -lə-\ *noun*
**¹sal·ly** \'sa-lē\ *noun, plural* **sallies** [Middle French *saillie*, from Old French, from *saillir* to rush forward, from Latin *salire* to leap; akin to Greek *hallesthai* to leap] (1560)
**1** : an action of rushing or bursting forth; *especially* : a sortie of troops from a defensive position to attack the enemy
**2 a** : a brief outburst : OUTBURST **b** : a witty or imaginative saying : QUIP
**3** : a venture or excursion usually off the beaten track : JAUNT

**²sally** *intransitive verb* **sal·lied; sal·ly·ing** (1560)
**1** : to leap out or burst forth suddenly
**2** : SET OUT, DEPART — often used with *forth*
**Sal·ly Lunn** \ˌsa-lē-'lən\ *noun* [*Sally Lunn*, 18th century English baker] (1780)
: a slightly sweetened yeast-leavened bread
**sally port** *noun* (1649)
: a gate or passage in a fortified place for use by troops making a sortie
**sal·ma·gun·di** \ˌsal-mə-'gən-dē\ *noun* [French *salmigondis*] (circa 1674)
**1** : a salad plate of chopped meats, anchovies, eggs, and vegetables arranged in rows for contrast and dressed with a salad dressing
**2** : a heterogeneous mixture : POTPOURRI
**sal·mi** \'sal-mē\ *noun* [French *salmis*, short for *salmigondis*] (1759)
: a ragout of partly roasted game stewed in a rich sauce
**salm·on** \'sa-mən\ *noun, plural* **salmon** *also* **salmons** [Middle English *samon*, from Middle French, from Latin *salmon-, salmo*] (13th century)
**1 a** : a large anadromous salmonid fish (*Salmo salar*) of the North Atlantic noted as a game and food fish — called also *Atlantic salmon* **b** : any of various anadromous salmonid fishes other than the salmon; *especially* : PACIFIC SALMON **c** : a fish (as a barramunda) resembling a salmon
**2** : the variable color of salmon's flesh averaging a strong yellowish pink
**salm·on·ber·ry** \-ˌber-ē\ *noun* (1844)
: a showy red-flowered raspberry (*Rubus spectabilis*) of the Pacific coast; *also* : its edible salmon-colored fruit
**sal·mo·nel·la** \ˌsal-mə-'ne-lə\ *noun, plural* **-nel·lae** \-'ne-(ˌ)lē, -ˌlī\ *or* **-nellas** *or* **-nella** [New Latin, from Daniel E. *Salmon* (died 1914) American veterinarian] (1913)
: any of a genus (*Salmonella*) of usually motile enterobacteria that are pathogenic for humans and other warm-blooded animals and cause food poisoning, gastrointestinal inflammation, typhoid fever, or septicemia
**sal·mo·nel·lo·sis** \ˌsal-mə-(ˌ)ne-'lō-səs\ *noun, plural* **-lo·ses** \-ˌsēz\ [New Latin] (circa 1913)
: infection with or disease caused by salmonellae
**sal·mo·nid** \'sa-mə-nid, 'sal-\ *noun* [New Latin *Salmonidae*, from *Salmon-, Salmo*, genus name, from Latin *salmo* salmon] (1868)
: any of a family (Salmonidae) of elongate bony fishes (as a salmon or trout) that have the last three vertebrae upturned
— **salmonid** *adjective*
**salm·on·oid** \'sa-mə-ˌnȯid\ *noun* (circa 1842)
: SALMONID; *also* : a related fish
— **salmonoid** *adjective*
**salmon pink** *noun* (1882)
: a strong yellowish pink
**Sa·lo·me** \sə-'lō-mē, 'sa-lə-(ˌ)mā\ *noun* [Late Latin, from Greek *Salōmē*]
: a niece of Herod Antipas given the head of John the Baptist as a reward for her dancing
**sa·lom·e·ter** \sā-'lä-mə-tər, sə-\ *noun* [Latin *sal* salt + English *-o-* + *-meter*] (1860)
: a hydrometer for indicating the percentage of salt in a solution
**sa·lon** \sə-'län, 'sa-ˌlän, sa-'lōⁿ\ *noun* [French] (1699)
**1** : an elegant apartment or living room (as in a fashionable home)
**2** : a fashionable assemblage of notables (as literary figures, artists, or statesmen) held by custom at the home of a prominent person
**3 a** : a hall for exhibition of art **b** *capitalized* : an annual exhibition of works of art
**4** : a stylish business establishment or shop ⟨a beauty *salon*⟩
**sa·loon** \sə-'lün\ *noun* [French *salon*, from Italian *salone*, augmentative of *sala* hall, of Germanic origin; akin to Old High German *sal* hall; akin to Lithuanian *sala* village] (1728)

**1 a** *chiefly British* : SALON 1 **b** *chiefly British* : an often elaborately decorated public hall **c** (1) : a usually large public cabin on a ship (as for dining) (2) : the living area on a yacht **d** *chiefly British* : SALON 4 **e** : BARROOM
**2** : SALON 2
**3** *British* **a** : PARLOR CAR **b** : SEDAN 2a — called also *saloon car*
**salp** \'salp\ *also* **sal·pa** \'sal-pə\ *noun* [New Latin, from Latin, a kind of deep-sea fish, from Greek *salpē*] (1835)
: any of various transparent barrel-shaped or fusiform free-swimming tunicates (class Thaliacea) abundant in warm seas
**sal·pi·glos·sis** \ˌsal-pə-'glä-səs\ *noun* [New Latin, irregular from Greek *salpinx* trumpet + *glōssa* tongue — more at GLOSS] (1827)
: any of a small genus (*Salpiglossis*) of Chilean herbs of the nightshade family with large funnel-shaped varicolored flowers often strikingly marked
**sal·pin·gi·tis** \ˌsal-pən-'jī-təs\ *noun* [New Latin, from *salping-, salpinx* fallopian or eustachian tube, from Greek, trumpet] (1860)
: inflammation of a fallopian or eustachian tube
**sal·sa** \'sȯl-sə, 'säl-\ *noun* [Spanish, literally, sauce, from Latin, feminine of *salsus* salted — more at SAUCE] (circa 1962)
**1** : a spicy sauce of tomatoes, onions, and hot peppers
**2** : popular music of Latin American origin that has absorbed characteristics of rhythm and blues, jazz, and rock
**sal·si·fy** \'sal-sə-fē, -ˌfī\ *noun* [French *salsifis*, from Italian *salsefica, sassefrica*] (circa 1706)
: a European biennial composite herb (*Tragopogon porrifolius*) with a long fusiform edible root — called also *oyster plant, vegetable oyster*
**sal soda** *noun* (15th century)
: WASHING SODA
**¹salt** \'sȯlt\ *noun* [Middle English, from Old English *sealt*; akin to Old High German *salz* salt, Lithuanian *saldus* sweet, Latin *sal* salt, Greek *hals* salt, sea] (before 12th century)
**1 a** : a crystalline compound NaCl that consists of sodium chloride, is abundant in nature, and is used especially to season or preserve food or in industry — called also *common salt* **b** : a substance (as washing soda) resembling common salt **c** *plural* (1) : a mineral or saline mixture (as Epsom salts) used as an aperient or cathartic (2) : SMELLING SALTS **d** : any of numerous compounds that result from replacement of part or all of the acid hydrogen of an acid by a metal or a group acting like a metal : an ionic crystalline compound
**2** : a container for salt at table — often used in the phrases *above the salt* and *below the salt* alluding to the former custom of seating persons of higher rank above and those of lower rank below a saltcellar placed in the middle of a long table
**3 a** : an ingredient that gives savor, piquancy, or zest : FLAVOR ⟨a people . . . full of life, vigor, and the *salt* of personality —Clifton Fadiman⟩ **b** : sharpness of wit : PUNGENCY **c** : COMMON SENSE **d** : RESERVE, SKEPTICISM — usually used in the phrases *with a grain of salt* and *with a pinch of salt* **e** : a dependable steadfast person or group of people — usually used in the phrase *salt of the earth*
**4** : SAILOR ⟨a tale worthy of an old *salt*⟩
**5** : KEEP 3 — usually used in the phrase *worth one's salt*
— **salt·like** \-ˌlīk\ *adjective*
**²salt** *transitive verb* (before 12th century)

\ə\ abut \ᵊ\ kitten \ər\ further \a\ ash \ā\ ace
\ä\ mop, mar \aú\ out \ch\ chin \e\ bet \ē\ easy
\g\ go \i\ hit \ī\ ice \j\ job \ŋ\ sing \ō\ go
\ȯ\ law \ȯi\ boy \th\ thin \tẖ\ the \ü\ loot \ú\ foot
\y\ yet \zh\ vision    *see also* Guide to Pronunciation

**1 a :** to treat, provide, or season with common salt **b :** to preserve (food) with salt or in brine **c :** to supply (as an animal) with salt **2 a :** to give flavor or piquancy to (as a story) **3 :** to enrich (as a mine) artificially by secretly placing valuable mineral in some of the working places **4 :** to sprinkle with or as if with a salt — **salt·er** \'sòl-tər\ *noun*

³**salt** *adjective* (before 12th century)
**1 a :** SALINE, SALTY **b :** being or inducing the one of the four basic taste sensations that is suggestive of seawater — compare BITTER, SOUR, SWEET
**2 :** cured or seasoned with salt **:** SALTED
**3 :** overflowed with salt water ⟨a *salt* pond⟩
**4 :** SHARP, PUNGENT
— **salt·ness** *noun*

⁴**salt** *adjective* [by shortening & alteration from *assaut,* from Middle English *a sawt,* from Middle French *a saut,* literally, on the jump] (1598)
*obsolete* **:** LUSTFUL, LASCIVIOUS

**salt–and–pepper** *adjective* (1915)
**:** having black-and-white or dark and light color or intermingled in small flecks ⟨a *salt-and-pepper* suit⟩

**sal·ta·rel·lo** \,sal-tə-'re-(,)lō, ,säl-\ *noun, plural* **-los** [Italian, from *saltare* to jump, from Latin] (circa 1724)
**:** an Italian dance with a lively hop step beginning each measure

**sal·ta·tion** \sal-'tā-shən, sòl-\ *noun* [Latin *saltation-, saltatio,* from *saltare* to leap, dance, frequentative of *salire* to leap — more at SALLY] (1646)
**1 a :** the action or process of leaping or jumping **b :** DANCE
**2 a :** the origin of a new species or a higher taxon in essentially a single evolutionary step that in some especially former theories is held to be due to a major mutation or to unknown causes — compare DARWINISM, NEO-DARWINISM, PUNCTUATED EQUILIBRIUM **b :** MUTATION — used especially of bacteria and fungi

**sal·ta·to·ri·al** \,sal-tə-'tòr-ē-əl, ,sòl-, -'tòr-\ *adjective* (1789)
**:** relating to, marked by, or adapted for leaping ⟨*saltatorial* legs of a grasshopper⟩

**sal·ta·to·ry** \'sal-tə-,tòr-ē, 'sòl-, -,tòr-\ *adjective* (1656)
**1** *archaic* **:** of or relating to dancing
**2 :** proceeding by leaps rather than by gradual transitions **:** DISCONTINUOUS

**salt away** *transitive verb* (circa 1890)
**:** to lay away (as money) safely **:** SAVE

**salt–box** \'sòlt-,bäks\ *noun* (1876)
**:** a frame dwelling with two stories in front and one behind and a roof with a long rear slope

**salt–bush** \-,bùsh\ *noun* (1863)
**:** any of various shrubby plants of the goosefoot family that thrive in dry alkaline soil; *especially* **:** any of numerous oraches that are important browse plants in dry regions

saltbox

**salt·cel·lar** \'sòlt-,se-lər\ *noun* [Middle English *salt saler,* from *salt* + *saler* saltcellar, from Middle French, from Latin *salarius* of salt — more at SALARY] (14th century)
**:** a small container for holding salt at the table

**salt dome** *noun* (1908)
**:** a domical anticline in sedimentary rock that has a mass of rock salt as its core

**salt flat** *noun* (1816)
**:** a salt-encrusted flat area resulting from evaporation of a former body of water

**salt gland** *noun* (1950)
**:** a gland (as of a marine bird) capable of excreting a concentrated salt solution

**salt grass** *noun* (1704)

**:** a grass (especially *Distichlis spicata*) native to an alkaline habitat (as a salt marsh)

**sal·tim·boc·ca** \,sòl-təm-'bä-kə\ *noun* [Italian, from *saltare* to jump + *in* in + *bocca* mouth] (1937)
**:** scallops of veal prepared with sage, slices of ham, and sometimes cheese and served with a wine sauce

**sal·tine** \sòl-'tēn\ *noun* (1907)
**:** a thin crisp cracker usually sprinkled with salt

**salt·ing** \'sòl-tiŋ\ *noun* (1712)
*chiefly British* **:** land flooded regularly by tides — usually used in plural

**sal·tire** \'sòl-,tīr, 'sal-\ *noun* [Middle English *sautire,* from Middle French *saultoir* X-shaped animal barricade that can be jumped over by people, saltire, from *saulter* to jump, from Latin *saltare* — more at SALTATION] (14th century)
**:** a heraldic charge consisting of a cross formed by a bend and a bend sinister crossing in the center

**salt lake** *noun* (1763)
**:** a landlocked body of water that has become salty through evaporation

**salt·less** \'sòlt-ləs\ *adjective* (14th century)
**1 :** having no salt
**2 :** INSIPID

**salt lick** *noun* (1751)
**:** LICK 3

**salt marsh** *noun* (before 12th century)
**:** flat land subject to overflow by salt water

**salt out** (1939)
*transitive verb*
**:** to precipitate, coagulate, or separate (as a dissolved substance or lyophilic sol) especially from a solution by the addition of salt
*intransitive verb*
**:** to become salted out

**salt pan** *noun* (15th century)
**:** an undrained natural depression in which water gathers and leaves a deposit of salt on evaporation

**salt·pe·ter** \'sòlt-'pē-tər\ *noun* [Middle English *salt petre,* alteration of *salpetre,* from Middle French, from Medieval Latin *sal petrae,* literally, salt of the rock] (14th century)
**1 :** POTASSIUM NITRATE
**2 :** SODIUM NITRATE

**salt pork** *noun* (1723)
**:** fat pork cured in salt or brine

**salt·shak·er** \'sòlt-,shā-kər\ *noun* (1895)
**:** a container with a perforated top for sprinkling salt

**salt·wa·ter** \'sòlt-,wò-tər, -,wä-\ *adjective* (before 12th century)
**:** relating to, living in, located near, or consisting of salt water

**salt·works** \'sòlt-,wərks\ *noun plural but singular or plural in construction* (1565)
**:** a plant where salt is prepared commercially

**salt·wort** \-,wərt, -,wòrt\ *noun* (1568)
**1 :** any of a genus (*Salsola*) of plants (as the Russian thistle) of the goosefoot family of which some have been used in making soda ash
**2 :** a low-growing strong-smelling coastal shrub (*Batis maritima* of the family Bataceae) of warm parts of the New World

**salty** \'sòl-tē\ *adjective* **salt·i·er; -est** (15th century)
**1 :** of, seasoned with, or containing salt
**2 :** smacking of the sea or nautical life
**3 a :** PIQUANT **b :** EARTHY, CRUDE ⟨*salty* language⟩
— **salt·i·ly** \-tə-lē\ *adverb*
— **salt·i·ness** \-tē-nəs\ *noun*

**sa·lu·bri·ous** \sə-'lü-brē-əs\ *adjective* [Latin *salubris;* akin to *salvus* safe, healthy — more at SAFE] (1547)
**:** favorable to or promoting health or well-being
*synonym* SEE HEALTHFUL
— **sa·lu·bri·ous·ly** *adverb*
— **sa·lu·bri·ous·ness** *noun*

— **sa·lu·bri·ty** \-brə-tē\ *noun*
**sa·lu·ki** \sə-'lü-kē\ *noun* [Arabic *salūqīy* of Saluq, from *Salūq* Saluq, ancient city in Arabia] (1809)
**:** any of an ancient northern African and Asian breed of tall swift slender hunting dogs having long narrow heads, long silky ears, and a smooth silky coat

saluki

**sal·u·tary** \'sal-yə-,ter-ē\ *adjective* [Middle French *salutaire,* from Latin *salutaris,* from *salut-, salus* health] (15th century)
**1 :** producing a beneficial effect **:** REMEDIAL ⟨*salutary* influences⟩
**2 :** promoting health **:** CURATIVE
*synonym* SEE HEALTHFUL
— **sal·u·tar·i·ly** \,sal-yə-'ter-ə-lē\ *adverb*
— **sal·u·tar·i·ness** \'sal-yə-,ter-ē-nəs\ *noun*

**sal·u·ta·tion** \,sal-yə-'tā-shən\ *noun* (14th century)
**1 a :** an expression of greeting, goodwill, or courtesy by word, gesture, or ceremony **b** *plural* **:** REGARDS
**2 :** the word or phrase of greeting (as *Gentlemen* or *Dear Sir* or *Madam*) that conventionally comes immediately before the body of a letter
— **sal·u·ta·tion·al** \-shnəl, -shə-nᵊl\ *adjective*

**sa·lu·ta·to·ri·an** \sə-,lü-tə-'tōr-ē-ən, -'tòr-\ *noun* (circa 1847)
**:** the student usually having the second highest rank in a graduating class who delivers the salutatory address at the commencement exercises

¹**sa·lu·ta·to·ry** \sə-'lü-tə-,tōr-ē, -,tòr-\ *adjective* (1702)
**:** of or relating to a salutation **:** expressing or containing a welcome or greeting

²**salutatory** *noun, plural* **-ries** (1779)
**:** an address or statement of welcome or greeting

¹**sa·lute** \sə-'lüt\ *verb* **sa·lut·ed; sa·lut·ing** [Middle English, from Latin *salutare,* from *salut-, salus* health, safety, greeting, from *salvus* safe, healthy — more at SAFE] (14th century)
*transitive verb*
**1 a :** to address with expressions of kind wishes, courtesy, or honor **b :** to give a sign of respect, courtesy, or goodwill to **:** GREET
**2 :** to become apparent to (one of the senses)
**3 a :** to honor (as a person, nation, or event) by a conventional military or naval ceremony **b :** to show respect and recognition to (a military superior) by assuming a prescribed position **c :** to express commendation of **:** PRAISE
*intransitive verb*
**:** to make a salute
— **sa·lut·er** *noun*

²**salute** *noun* (14th century)
**1 :** GREETING, SALUTATION
**2 a :** a sign, token, or ceremony expressing goodwill, compliment, or respect ⟨the festival was a *salute* to the arts⟩ **b :** the position (as of the hand) or the entire attitude of a person saluting a superior
**3 :** FIRECRACKER

**sal·u·tif·er·ous** \,sal-yə-'ti-f(ə-)rəs\ *adjective* [Latin *salutifer,* from *salut-, salus* + *-i-* + *-fer* -ferous] (circa 1540)
**:** SALUTARY

**salv·able** \'sal-və-bəl\ *adjective* [Late Latin *salvare* to save — more at SAVE] (1667)
**:** capable of being saved or salvaged

¹**sal·vage** \'sal-vij\ *noun* [French, from Middle French, from *salver* to save — more at SAVE] (1645)
**1 a :** compensation paid for saving a ship or its cargo from the perils of the sea or for the

lives and property rescued in a wreck **b** : the act of saving or rescuing a ship or its cargo **c** : the act of saving or rescuing property in danger (as from fire)

**2 a** : property saved from destruction in a calamity (as a wreck or fire) **b** : something extracted (as from rubbish) as valuable or useful

²**salvage** *transitive verb* **sal·vaged; sal·vag·ing** (1889)
: to rescue or save especially from wreckage or ruin
— **sal·vage·abil·i·ty** \ˌsal-vi-jə-ˈbi-lə-tē\ *noun*
— **sal·vage·able** \ˈsal-vi-jə-bəl\ *adjective*
— **sal·vag·er** *noun*

**sal·var·san** \ˈsal-vər-ˌsan\ *noun* [from *Salvarsan*, a trademark] (1909)
: ARSPHENAMINE

**sal·va·tion** \sal-ˈvā-shən\ *noun* [Middle English, from Old French, from Late Latin *salvation-, salvatio,* from *salvare* to save — more at SAVE] (13th century)
**1 a** : deliverance from the power and effects of sin **b** : the agent or means that effects salvation **c** *Christian Science* : the realization of the supremacy of infinite Mind over all bringing with it the destruction of the illusion of sin, sickness, and death
**2** : liberation from ignorance or illusion
**3 a** : preservation from destruction or failure **b** : deliverance from danger or difficulty
— **sal·va·tion·al** \-shnəl, -shə-nᵊl\ *adjective*

**Salvation Army** *noun* (1878)
: an international religious and charitable group organized on military lines and founded in 1865 by William Booth for evangelizing and social betterment (as of the poor)

**sal·va·tion·ism** \sal-ˈvā-shə-ˌni-zəm\ *noun* (1883)
: religious teaching emphasizing the saving of the soul

**Sal·va·tion·ist** \-sh(ə-)nist\ *noun* (1882)
**1** : a soldier or officer of the Salvation Army
**2** *often not capitalized* : EVANGELIST
— **salvationist** *adjective, often capitalized*

¹**salve** \ˈsav, ˈsäv, ˈsȧv, ˈsalv, ˈsälv\ *noun* [Middle English, from Old English *sealf;* akin to Old High German *salba* salve, Greek *olpē* oil flask] (before 12th century)
**1** : an unctuous adhesive substance for application to wounds or sores
**2** : a remedial or soothing influence or agency ⟨a *salve* to their hurt feelings⟩

²**salve** *transitive verb* **salved; salv·ing** (before 12th century)
**1** : to remedy (as disease) with or as if with a salve
**2** : QUIET, ASSUAGE ⟨give him a raise in salary to *salve* his feelings —Upton Sinclair⟩

³**salve** \ˈsalv\ *transitive verb* **salved; salv·ing** [back-formation from *salvage*] (circa 1706)
: SALVAGE
— **sal·vor** \ˈsal-vər, -ˌvȯr\ *noun*

**sal·ver** \ˈsal-vər\ *noun* [modification of French *salve,* from Spanish *salva* sampling of food to detect poison, tray, from *salvar* to save, sample food to detect poison, from Late Latin *salvare* to save — more at SAVE] (circa 1661)
: a tray especially for serving food or beverages

**sal·ver·form** \ˈsal-vər-ˌfȯrm\ *adjective* (1821)
: tubular with a spreading limb — used of a gamopetalous corolla

**sal·via** \ˈsal-vē-ə\ *noun* [New Latin, from Latin, sage — more at SAGE] (1601)
: any of a large and widely distributed genus (*Salvia*) of herbs and shrubs of the mint family having a 2-lipped open calyx and two anthers; *especially* : one (*S. splendens*) with scarlet flowers

**sal·vif·ic** \sal-ˈvi-fik\ *adjective* [Late Latin *salvificus,* from Latin *salvus* safe + *-ficus* -fic] (1591)

: having the intent or power to save or redeem ⟨the *salvific* life and death of Christ —E. A. Walsh⟩

¹**sal·vo** \ˈsal-(ˌ)vō\ *noun, plural* **salvos** *or* **salvoes** [Italian *salva,* from French *salve,* from Latin, hail!, from *salvus* healthy — more at SAFE] (1591)
**1 a** : a simultaneous discharge of two or more guns in military action or as a salute **b** : the release all at one time of a rack of bombs or rockets (as from an airplane) **c** : a series of shots by an artillery battery with each gun firing one round in turn after a prescribed interval **d** : the bombs or projectiles released in a salvo
**2** : something suggestive of a salvo: as **a** : a sudden burst ⟨a *salvo* of cheers⟩ **b** : a spirited attack ⟨the first *salvo* of a political campaign⟩

²**salvo** (1839)
*transitive verb*
: to release a salvo of
*intransitive verb*
: to fire a salvo

³**salvo** *noun, plural* **salvos** [Medieval Latin *salvo jure* with the right reserved] (1621)
**1** : a mental reservation : PROVISO
**2** : a means of safeguarding one's name or honor or allaying one's conscience : SALVE

**sal vo·la·ti·le** \ˌsal-və-ˈla-tᵊl-ē\ *noun* [New Latin, literally, volatile salt] (1654)
: SMELLING SALTS

**SAM** \ˈsam, ˌes-(ˌ)ā-ˈem\ *noun* (1950)
: a surface-to-air missile

**sa·ma·ra** \ˈsa-mə-rə, sə-ˈmar-ə, -ˈmär-\ *noun* [New Latin, from Latin, seed of the elm] (1577)
: a dry indehiscent usually one-seeded winged fruit (as of an ash or elm tree) — called also *key*

**Sa·mar·i·tan** \sə-ˈmar-ə-tᵊn, -ˈmer-\ *noun* [Middle English, from Old English, from Late Latin *samaritanus,* noun & adjective, from Greek *samaritēs* inhabitant of Samaria, from *Samaria*] (before 12th century)
**1** : a native or inhabitant of Samaria
**2** [from the parable of the good Samaritan in Luke 10:30–37] : one ready and generous in helping those in distress
— **samaritan** *adjective, often capitalized*

**sa·mar·i·um** \sə-ˈmer-ē-əm, -ˈmar-\ *noun* [New Latin, from French *samarskite*] (1879)
: a pale gray lustrous metallic element used especially in alloys that form permanent magnets — see ELEMENT table

**sa·mar·skite** \sə-ˈmär-ˌskīt, ˈsa-mər-\ *noun* [German *Samarskit,* from V. E. *Samarskiĭ*-Bykhovets (died 1870) Russian mining engineer] (1849)
: a black or brownish black orthorhombic mineral that is a complex oxide of rare earths, uranium, iron, lead, thorium, niobium, tantalum, titanium, and tin

**sam·ba** \ˈsam-bə, ˈsäm-\ *noun* [Portuguese] (1885)
: a Brazilian dance of African origin with a basic pattern of step-close-step-close and characterized by a dip and spring upward at each beat of the music; *also* : the music for this dance
— **samba** *intransitive verb*

**sam·bar** *or* **sam·bur** \ˈsäm-bər, ˈsam-\ *noun* [Hindi *sābar,* from Sanskrit *śambara*] (1698)
: a large Asian deer (*Cervus unicolor*) with the male having strong 3-pointed antlers and long coarse hair on the throat

**sam·bo** \ˈsam-(ˌ)bō, ˈsäm-\ *noun* [Russian, from *samozashchita bez oruzhiya* self-defense without weapons] (1972)
: an international style of wrestling employing judo techniques

**Sam Browne** \ˈsam-ˈbraŭn\ *noun* [Sir *Samuel* James *Browne* (died 1901) British army officer] (1915)
: a leather belt for a dress uniform supported by a light strap passing over the right shoulder

¹**same** \ˈsām\ *adjective* [Middle English, from Old Norse *samr;* akin to Old High German *sama* same, Latin *simulis* like, *simul* together, at the same time, *similis* like, *sem-* one, Greek *homos* same, *hama* together, *hen-, heis* one] (13th century)
**1 a** : resembling in every relevant respect **b** : conforming in every respect — used with *as*
**2 a** : being one without addition, change, or discontinuance : IDENTICAL **b** : being the one under discussion or already referred to
**3** : corresponding so closely as to be indistinguishable
**4** : equal in size, shape, value, or importance — usually used with *the* or a demonstrative (as *that, those*) in all senses ☆

²**same** *pronoun* (14th century)
**1** : something identical with or similar to another
**2** : something or someone previously mentioned or described — often used with *the* or a demonstrative (as *that, those*) in both senses
— **all the same** *or* **just the same** : despite everything : NEVERTHELESS

³**same** *adverb* (1766)
: in the same manner — used with *the* or a demonstrative (as *that, those*)

**sa·mekh** \ˈsä-ˌmek\ *noun* [Hebrew *sāmekh*] (1823)
: the 15th letter of the Hebrew alphabet — see ALPHABET table

**same·ness** \ˈsām-nəs\ *noun* (1581)
**1** : the quality or state of being the same : IDENTITY, SIMILARITY
**2** : MONOTONY, UNIFORMITY

**sam·i·sen** \ˈsa-mə-ˌsen\ *noun* [Japanese] (1864)
: a 3-stringed Japanese musical instrument resembling a banjo

**sa·mite** \ˈsa-ˌmīt, ˈsā-\ *noun* [Middle English *samit,* from Middle French, from Medieval Latin *examitum, samitum,* from Middle Greek *hexamiton,* from Greek, neuter of *hexamitos* of six threads, from *hexa-* + *mitos* thread of the warp] (13th century)
: a rich medieval silk fabric interwoven with gold or silver

**sa·miz·dat** \ˈsä-mēz-ˌdät\ *noun* [Russian, from *sam-* self- + *izdatel'stvo* publishing house] (1967)
: a system in the U.S.S.R. and countries within its orbit by which government-suppressed literature was clandestinely printed and distributed; *also* : such literature

**sam·let** \ˈsam-lət\ *noun* [irregular from *salmon* + *-let*] (1655)
: PARR

---

☆ **SYNONYMS**
**Same, selfsame, very, identical, equivalent, equal** mean not different or not differing from one another. SAME may imply and SELFSAME always implies that the things under consideration are one thing and not two or more things ⟨took the *same* route⟩ ⟨derived from the *selfsame* source⟩. VERY, like SELFSAME, may imply identity, or, like SAME, may imply likeness in kind ⟨the *very* point I was trying to make⟩. IDENTICAL may imply selfsameness or suggest absolute agreement in all details ⟨their test answers were *identical*⟩. EQUIVALENT implies amounting to the same thing in worth or significance ⟨two houses *equivalent* in market value⟩. EQUAL implies being identical in value, magnitude, or some specified quality ⟨*equal* shares in the business⟩.

---

**Sam·ma·ri·nese** \(,)sa(m)-,mar-ə-'nēz, -'nēs\ *noun, plural* **-ne·si** \-'nä-zē\ [Italian *sammarinese*, from *San Marino*] (1938)
**:** a native or inhabitant of San Marino
**Sam·nite** \'sam-,nīt\ *noun* [*Samnium*, Italy] (14th century)
**:** a member of an ancient people of central Italy
**Sa·mo·an** \sə-'mō-ən\ *noun* (1846)
**1 :** the Polynesian language of the Samoans
**2 :** a native or inhabitant of Samoa
**— Samoan** *adjective*
**Samoa time** *noun* (1983)
**:** the time of the 11th time zone west of Greenwich that includes American Samoa
**sam·o·var** \'sa-mə-,vär\ *noun* [Russian, from *samo-* self + *varit'* to boil] (1830)
**1 :** an urn with a spigot at its base used especially in Russia to boil water for tea
**2 :** an urn similar to a Russian samovar with a device for heating the contents
**Sam·o·yed** *also* **Sam·o·yede** \'sa-mə-,yed, -,mòi-\ *noun* [Russian *samoed*] (1589)
**1 :** a member of any of a group of peoples inhabiting the far north of European Russia and parts of northwestern Siberia
**2 :** the family of Uralic languages spoken by the Samoyed people
**3 :** any of a Siberian breed of medium-sized white or cream-colored sled dogs
**— Samoyed** *adjective*
**— Sam·o·yed·ic** \,sa-mə-'ye-dik, -,mòi-\ *adjective*

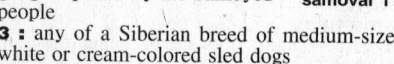
**samovar 1**

**samp** \'samp\ *noun* [modification of Narraganset *nasàump* corn mush] (1643)
**:** coarse hominy or a boiled cereal made from it
**sam·pan** \'sam-,pan\ *noun* [Chinese (Guangdong) *sàambáan*, from *sàam* three + *báan* board, plank] (1620)
**:** a flat-bottomed Chinese skiff usually propelled by two short oars
**sam·phire** \'sam-,fīr\ *noun* [alteration of earlier *sampiere*, from Middle French (*herbe de*) *Saint Pierre*, literally, Saint Peter's herb] (1545)
**1 :** a fleshy European seacoast plant (*Crithmum maritimum*) of the carrot family that is sometimes pickled
**2 :** a common glasswort (*Salicornia europaea*) that is sometimes pickled
**¹sam·ple** \'sam-pəl\ *noun* [Middle English, from Middle French *essample*, from Latin *exemplum* — more at EXAMPLE] (15th century)
**1 :** a representative part or a single item from a larger whole or group especially when presented for inspection or shown as evidence of quality **:** SPECIMEN
**2 :** a finite part of a statistical population whose properties are studied to gain information about the whole
**synonym** see INSTANCE
**²sample** *transitive verb* **sam·pled; sam·pling** \-p(ə-)liŋ\ (1767)
**:** to take a sample of or from; *especially* **:** to judge the quality of by a sample **:** TEST ⟨*sampled* his output for defects⟩ ⟨*sample* a wine⟩
**³sample** *adjective* (1820)
**:** serving as an illustration or example ⟨*sample* questions⟩
**¹sam·pler** \'sam-plər\ *noun* (1523)
**:** a decorative piece of needlework typically having letters or verses embroidered on it in various stitches as an example of skill
**²sam·pler** \-p(ə-)lər\ *noun* (1778)
**1 :** one that collects, prepares, or examines samples
**2 :** something containing representative specimens or selections ⟨a *sampler* of nineteen poets —K. E. Judd⟩; *also* **:** ASSORTMENT
**sample space** *noun* (1951)

**:** a set in which all of the possible outcomes of a statistical experiment are represented as points
**sam·pling** \'sam-pliŋ, *for 1 & 3* -p(ə-)liŋ\ *noun* (1778)
**1 :** the act, process, or technique of selecting a suitable sample; *specifically* **:** the act, process, or technique of selecting a representative part of a population for the purpose of determining parameters or characteristics of the whole population
**2 :** a small part selected as a sample for inspection or analysis ⟨ask a *sampling* of people which candidate they favor⟩
**3 :** the introduction or promotion of a product by distributing trial packages of it
**sam·sa·ra** \səm-'sär-ə\ *noun* [Sanskrit *saṁsāra*, literally, passing through] (1886)
**:** the indefinitely repeated cycles of birth, misery, and death caused by karma
**Sam·son** \'sam(p)-sən\ *noun* [Late Latin, from Greek *Sampsōn*, from Hebrew *Shimshōn*]
**:** a Hebrew hero who wreaked havoc among the Philistines by means of his great strength
**Sam·so·ni·an** \sam(p)-'sō-nē-ən\ *adjective* [*Samson*] (circa 1623)
**:** of heroic strength or proportions **:** MIGHTY
**Sam·u·el** \'sam-yə-wəl, -yəl\ *noun* [Late Latin, from Greek *Samouel*, from Hebrew *Shĕmū'ēl*]
**1 :** the early Hebrew judge who successively anointed Saul and David king
**2 :** either of two narrative and historical books of canonical Jewish and Christian Scriptures — see BIBLE table
**sam·u·rai** \'sa-mə-,rī, 'sam-yə-\ *noun, plural* **samurai** [Japanese] (1727)
**1 :** a military retainer of a Japanese daimyo practicing the code of conduct of Bushido
**2 :** the warrior aristocracy of Japan
**San** \'sän\ *noun* (1876)
**1** *plural in construction* **:** BUSHMEN
**2 :** BUSHMAN 2
**san·a·tive** \'sa-nə-tiv\ *adjective* [Middle English *sanatif*, from Middle French, from Late Latin *sanativus*, from Latin *sanatus*, past participle of *sanare* to cure, from *sanus* healthy] (15th century)
**:** having the power to cure or heal **:** CURATIVE, RESTORATIVE
**san·a·to·ri·um** \,sa-nə-'tōr-ē-əm, -'tòr-\ *noun, plural* **-riums** *or* **-ria** \-ē-ə\ [New Latin, from Late Latin, neuter of *sanatorius* curative, from *sanare*] (1839)
**1 :** an establishment that provides therapy combined with a regimen (as of diet and exercise) for treatment or rehabilitation
**2 a :** an institution for rest and recuperation (as of convalescents) **b :** an establishment for the treatment of the chronically ill
**san·be·ni·to** \,san-bə-'nē-(,)tō, ,sam-\ *noun, plural* **-tos** [Spanish *sambenito*, from *San Benito* Saint Benedict of Nursia] (circa 1560)
**1 :** a sackcloth coat worn by penitents on being reconciled to the church
**2 :** a Spanish Inquisition garment resembling a scapular and being either yellow with red crosses for the penitent or black with painted devils and flames for the impenitent condemned to an auto-da-fé
**San·cerre** \sä<sup>n</sup>-ser\ *noun* [*Sancerre*, village in France] (circa 1946)
**:** a dry white wine from the Loire valley of France
**San·cho Pan·za** \,san-chō-'pan-zə, ,sän-chō-'pän-\ *noun* [Spanish]
**:** the squire of Don Quixote in Cervantes' *Don Quixote*
**sanc·ti·fi·ca·tion** \,saŋ(k)-tə-fə-'kā-shən\ *noun* (14th century)
**1 :** an act of sanctifying
**2 a :** the state of being sanctified **b :** the state of growing in divine grace as a result of Christian commitment after baptism or conversion
**sanc·ti·fi·er** \'saŋ(k)-tə-,fī(-ə)r\ *noun* (1548)

**:** one that sanctifies; *specifically, capitalized* **:** HOLY SPIRIT
**sanc·ti·fy** \-,fī\ *transitive verb* **-fied; -fy·ing** [Middle English *sanctifien*, from Middle French *sanctifier*, from Late Latin *sanctificare*, from Latin *sanctus* sacred — more at SAINT] (14th century)
**1 :** to set apart to a sacred purpose or to religious use **:** CONSECRATE
**2 :** to free from sin **:** PURIFY
**3 a :** to impart or impute sacredness, inviolability, or respect to **b :** to give moral or social sanction to
**4 :** to make productive of holiness or piety ⟨observe the day of the sabbath, to *sanctify* it —Deuteronomy 5:12 (Douay Version)⟩
**sanc·ti·mo·nious** \,saŋ(k)-tə-'mō-nē-əs, -nyəs\ *adjective* (1603)
**1 :** affecting piousness **:** hypocritically devout; *also* **:** indicative of affected piousness ⟨the king's *sanctimonious* rebuke —G. B. Shaw⟩
**2** *obsolete* **:** possessing sanctity **:** HOLY
**— sanc·ti·mo·nious·ly** *adverb*
**— sanc·ti·mo·nious·ness** *noun*
**sanc·ti·mo·ny** \'saŋ(k)-tə-,mō-nē\ *noun, plural* **-nies** [Middle French *sanctimonie*, from Latin *sanctimonia*, from *sanctus*] (circa 1541)
**1** *obsolete* **:** HOLINESS
**2 :** affected or hypocritical holiness
**¹sanc·tion** \'saŋ(k)-shən\ *noun* [Middle French or Latin; Middle French, from Latin *sanction-, sanctio*, from *sancire* to make holy — more at SACRED] (15th century)
**1 :** a formal decree; *especially* **:** an ecclesiastical decree
**2 a** *obsolete* **:** a solemn agreement **:** OATH **b :** something that makes an oath binding
**3 :** the detriment, loss of reward, or coercive intervention annexed to a violation of a law as a means of enforcing the law
**4 a :** a consideration, principle, or influence (as of conscience) that impels to moral action or determines moral judgment **b :** a mechanism of social control for enforcing a society's standards **c :** explicit or official approval, permission, or ratification **:** APPROBATION
**5 :** an economic or military coercive measure adopted usually by several nations in concert for forcing a nation violating international law to desist or yield to adjudication
**²sanction** *transitive verb* **sanc·tioned; sanc·tion·ing** \-sh(ə-)niŋ\ (1778)
**1 :** to make valid or binding usually by a formal procedure (as ratification)
**2 :** to give effective or authoritative approval or consent to
**synonym** see APPROVE
**— sanc·tion·able** \-sh(ə-)nə-bəl\ *adjective*
**sanc·ti·ty** \'saŋ(k)-tə-tē\ *noun, plural* **-ties** [Middle English *saunctite*, from Middle French *saincteté*, from Latin *sanctitat-, sanctitas*, from *sanctus* sacred] (14th century)
**1 :** holiness of life and character **:** GODLINESS
**2 a :** the quality or state of being holy or sacred **:** INVIOLABILITY **b** *plural* **:** sacred objects, obligations, or rights
**sanc·tu·ary** \'saŋ(k)-chə-,wer-ē\ *noun, plural* **-ar·ies** [Middle English *sanctuarie*, from Middle French *sainctuarie*, from Late Latin *sanctuarium*, from Latin *sanctus*] (14th century)
**1 :** a consecrated place: as **a :** the ancient Hebrew temple at Jerusalem or its holy of holies **b** (1) **:** the most sacred part of a religious building (as the part of a Christian church in which the altar is placed) (2) **:** the room in which general worship services are held (3) **:** a place (as a church or a temple) for worship
**2 a** (1) **:** a place of refuge and protection (2) **:** a refuge for wildlife where predators are controlled and hunting is illegal **b :** the immunity from law attached to a sanctuary
**sanc·tum** \'saŋ(k)-təm\ *noun, plural* **sanc·tums** *also* **sanc·ta** \-tə\ [Late Latin, from Latin, neuter of *sanctus* sacred] (1577)
**1 :** a sacred place

**2 :** a place where one is free from intrusion ⟨an editor's *sanctum*⟩ ⟨the inner *sanctums* of research⟩

**sanc·tum sanc·to·rum** \ˌsaŋ(k)-təm-ˌsäŋ(k)-ˈtōr-əm, -ˈtȯr-\ *noun* [Late Latin] (1558)
**1 :** HOLY OF HOLIES
**2 :** SANCTUM 2

**Sanc·tus** \ˈsaŋ(k)-təs; ˈsäŋ(k)-təs, -ˌtüs\ *noun* [Middle English, from Late Latin *Sanctus, sanctus, sanctus* Holy, holy, holy, opening of a hymn sung by the angels in Isaiah 6:3] (15th century)
**:** an ancient Christian hymn of adoration sung or said immediately before the prayer of consecration in traditional liturgies

**Sanctus bell** *noun* (15th century)
**:** a bell rung by the server at several points (as at the Sanctus) during the mass

**¹sand** \ˈsand\ *noun* [Middle English, from Old English; akin to Old High German *sant* sand, Latin *sabulum,* Greek *psammos*] (before 12th century)
**1 a :** a loose granular material that results from the disintegration of rocks, consists of particles smaller than gravel but coarser than silt, and is used in mortar, glass, abrasives, and foundry molds **b :** soil containing 85 percent or more of sand and a maximum of 10 percent of clay; *broadly :* sandy soil
**2 a :** a tract of sand **:** BEACH **b :** a sandbank or sandbar
**3 :** the sand in an hourglass; *also :* the moments of a lifetime — usually used in plural ⟨the *sands* of this government run out very rapidly —H. J. Laski⟩
**4 :** an oil-producing formation of sandstone or unconsolidated sand
**5 :** firm resolution
**6 :** a yellowish gray color

**²sand** *transitive verb* (14th century)
**1 :** to sprinkle or dust with or as if with sand
**2 :** to cover or fill with sand
**3 :** to smooth or dress by grinding or rubbing with an abrasive (as sandpaper)

**san·dal** \ˈsan-dᵊl\ *noun* [Middle English *sandalie,* from Latin *sandalium,* from Greek *sandalion,* diminutive of *sandalon* sandal] (14th century)
**1 :** a shoe consisting of a sole strapped to the foot
**2 :** a low-cut shoe that fastens by an ankle strap
**3 :** a strap to hold on a slipper or low shoe
**4 :** a rubber overshoe cut very low
— **san·daled** \ˈsan-dᵊld\ *adjective*

**san·dal·wood** \-ˌwu̇d\ *noun* [*sandal* sandalwood (from Middle English, from Middle French, from Medieval Latin *sandalum,* from Late Greek *santalon,* ultimately from Sanskrit *cāntana,* of Dravidian origin; akin to Tamil *cāntu* sandalwood tree) + ²*wood*] (circa 1511)
**1 :** the compact close-grained fragrant yellowish heartwood of a parasitic tree (*Santalum album* of the family Santalaceae, the sandalwood family) of southern Asia much used in ornamental carving and cabinetwork; *also* **:** the tree that yields this wood
**2 :** any of various trees other than the sandalwood some of which yield dyewoods; *also* **:** the fragrant wood of such a tree

**sandalwood oil** *noun* (1851)
**:** an essential oil obtained from sandalwood: as **a :** a pale yellow somewhat viscous aromatic liquid obtained from a sandalwood (*Santalum album*) and used chiefly in perfumes and soaps **b :** an oil obtained from a sandalwood (*Eucarya spicata*) of Australia

**san·da·rac** \ˈsan-də-ˌrak\ *noun* [Latin *sandaraca* red coloring, from Greek *sandarakē* realgar, red pigment from realgar] (1543)
**:** a brittle faintly aromatic translucent resin obtained from a northern African tree (*Tetraclinis articulata*) of the cypress family and used chiefly in making varnish and as incense; *also*

**:** a similar resin obtained from any of several Australian trees (genus *Callitris*) of the same family

**¹sand·bag** \ˈsan(d)-ˌbag\ *noun* (1590)
**:** a bag filled with sand and used in fortifications, as ballast, or as a weapon

**²sandbag** *transitive verb* (1860)
**1 :** to bank, stop up, or weight with sandbags
**2 a :** to hit or stun with or as if with a sandbag **b :** to treat unfairly or harshly **c :** to coerce by crude means ⟨are raiding the Treasury and *sandbagging* the government —C. W. Ferguson⟩ **d :** to conceal or misrepresent one's true position, potential, or intent especially in order to take advantage of
— **sand·bag·ger** *noun*

**sand·bank** \ˈsan(d)-ˌbaŋk\ *noun* (15th century)
**:** a large deposit of sand forming a mound, hillside, bar, or shoal

**sand·bar** \-ˌbär\ *noun* (1766)
**:** a ridge of sand built up by currents especially in a river or in coastal waters

**¹sand·blast** \-ˌblast\ *noun* (1871)
**:** a stream of sand projected by compressed air (as for engraving, cutting, or cleaning glass or stone)

**²sandblast** *transitive verb* (1888)
**:** to affect or treat with or as if with a sandblast
— **sand·blast·er** *noun*

**sand-blind** \ˈsan(d)-ˌblīnd\ *adjective* [Middle English, probably from (assumed) Middle English *samblind,* from Old English *sam-* half (akin to Old High German *sāmi-* half) + *blind* — more at SEMI-] (15th century)
**:** having poor eyesight **:** PURBLIND

**sand bluestem** *noun* (circa 1946)
**:** a tall rhizomatous grass (*Andropogon hallii*) of the western U.S. used for forage and as a soil binder

**sand·box** \ˈsan(d)-ˌbäks\ *noun* (1688)
**:** a box or receptacle containing loose sand: as **a :** a shaker for sprinkling sand on wet ink **b :** a box that contains sand for children to play in

**sand·bur** \ˈsan(d)-ˌbər\ *noun* (1830)
**:** any of a genus (*Cenchrus*) of grasses producing spikelets enclosed in ovoid spiny involucres that form burs; *also* **:** one of these burs

**sand–cast** \-ˌkast\ *transitive verb* **-cast; -cast·ing** (1928)
**:** to make (a casting) by pouring metal in a sand mold

**sand casting** *noun* (1926)
**:** a casting made in a mold of sand

**sand crack** *noun* (1754)
**:** a fissure in the wall of a horse's hoof often causing lameness

**sand dab** *noun* (1946)
**:** any of several Pacific flounders (genus *Citharichthys* of the family Bothidae); *especially* **:** a common food fish (*C. sordidus*)

**sand dollar** *noun* (1884)
**:** any of numerous flat circular sea urchins (order Clypeasteroida) that live chiefly in shallow water on sandy bottoms

**sand·er** \ˈsan-dər\ *noun* (1627)
**:** one that sands: as **a :** a device for spreading sand on newly surfaced or icy roads; *also* **:** the device together with the truck that bears it **b :** a machine or device that smooths, polishes, or scours by means of abrasive material usually in the form of a disk or belt — called also *sanding machine*

**sand·er·ling** \ˈsan-dər-liŋ\ *noun* [*sand* + *-erling,* perhaps from Old English *yrthling,* kind of bird found in fields, literally, plowman, from *yrth, earth* plowing, from *erian* to plow — more at ARABLE] (1602)
**:** a small widely distributed sandpiper (*Calidris alba*) with pale gray and white plumage in winter

**sand flea** *noun* (1796)
**1 :** a flea (as a chigoe) found in sandy places
**2 :** BEACH FLEA

**sand fly** *noun* (1736)
**:** any of various small biting dipteran flies (families Psychodidae, Simuliidae, and Ceratopogonidae)

**sand·fly fever** \ˈsan(d)-ˌflī-\ *noun* (1910)
**:** a virus disease of brief duration that is characterized by fever, headache, pain in the eyes, malaise, and leukopenia and is transmitted by the bite of a sand fly (*Phlebotomus papatasii*) — called also *phlebotomus fever*

**sand·glass** \ˈsan(d)-ˌglas\ *noun* (1556)
**:** an instrument (as an hourglass) for measuring time by the running of sand

**sand·grouse** \-ˌgrau̇s\ *noun* (1783)
**:** any of numerous birds (family Pteroclidae) of arid parts of southern Europe, Asia, and Africa that are closely related to the pigeons but have precocial downy young

**san·dhi** \ˈsan-dē, ˈsän-, ˈsən-\ *noun* [Sanskrit *saṃdhi,* literally, placing together] (1806)
**:** modification of the sound of a morpheme (as a word or affix) conditioned by syntactic context in which it is uttered (as pronunciation of *-ed* as \d\ in *glazed* and as \t\ in *paced* or occurrence of *a* in *a cow* and of *an* in *an old cow*)

**sand–hill crane** \ˈsand-ˌhil-\ *noun* (1805)
**:** a crane (*Grus canadensis*) of North America and Siberia that has a red crown and is chiefly bluish gray tinged with a sandy yellow

**sand·hog** \ˈsand-ˌhȯg, -ˌhäg\ *noun* (1903)
**:** a laborer who works in a caisson in driving underwater tunnels

**San·di·nis·ta** \ˌsan-də-ˈnēs-tə, ˌsän-\ *noun* [American Spanish, from Augusto César Sandino (died 1933) Nicaraguan rebel leader] (1974)
**:** a member of a military and political coalition taking power in Nicaragua in 1979

**S and L** *noun* (1951)
**:** SAVINGS AND LOAN ASSOCIATION

**sand lance** *noun* (1776)
**:** any of several small elongate marine bony fishes (genus *Ammodytes* of the family Ammodytidae) that associate in large schools and remain buried in sandy beaches at ebb tide — called also *sand eel, sand launce*

**sand lily** *noun* (circa 1900)
**:** a western North American spring herb (*Leucocrinum montanum*) of the lily family with narrow linear leaves and fragrant salverform flowers

**sand·lot** \ˈsan(d)-ˌlät\ *noun* (1878)
**:** a vacant lot especially when used (as by children) for usually unorganized sports
— **sandlot** *adjective*
— **sand·lot·ter** \-ˌlä-tər\ *noun*

**sand·man** \ˈsan(d)-ˌman\ *noun*
**:** a genie in folklore who makes children sleepy by sprinkling sand in their eyes

**sand myrtle** *noun* (1814)
**:** a variable low-branching evergreen upland shrub (*Leiophyllum buxifolium*) of the heath family found in the southeastern U.S.

**sand·paint·ing** \ˈsan(d)-ˌpān-tiŋ\ *noun* (1900)
**:** a Navajo and Pueblo Indian ceremonial design made of various materials (as colored sands) on a flat surface of sand or buckskin

**¹sand·pa·per** \-ˌpā-pər\ *noun* (1825)
**:** paper covered on one side with abrasive material (as sand) glued fast and used for smoothing and polishing
— **sand·pa·pery** \-p(ə-)rē\ *adjective*

**²sandpaper** *transitive verb* (1846)
**:** to rub with or as if with sandpaper

**sand·pile** \ˈsan(d)-ˌpīl\ *noun* (1901)
**:** a pile of sand; *especially* **:** sand for children to play in

**sand·pip·er** \-ˌpī-pər\ *noun* (1674)
: any of numerous small shorebirds (family Scolopacidae) distinguished from the related plovers chiefly by the longer and soft-tipped bill

**sandpiper**

**sand·pit** \-ˌpit\ *noun* (1898)
*British* : SANDBOX b

**sand·shoe** \-ˌshü\ *noun* (1855)
*chiefly Australian & New Zealand* : TENNIS SHOE

**sand·soap** \ˈsan(d)-ˌsōp\ *noun* (1854)
: a gritty soap for all-purpose cleaning

**sand·spur** \-ˌspər\ *noun* (circa 1898)
: SANDBUR

**sand·stone** \-ˌstōn\ *noun* (1668)
: a sedimentary rock consisting of usually quartz sand united by some cement (as silica or calcium carbonate)

**sand·storm** \-ˌstorm\ *noun* (1774)
: a windstorm (as in a desert) driving clouds of sand before it

**sand table** *noun* (1812)
**1** : a table holding sand for children to mold
**2** : a table bearing a relief model of a terrain built to scale for study or demonstration especially of military tactics

**sand trap** *noun* (1922)
: an artificial hazard on a golf course consisting of a depression containing sand

**sand verbena** *noun* (1898)
: any of several western North American herbs (genus *Abronia*) of the four-o'clock family with flowers like the verbena; *especially* : either of two plants (*A. latifolia* and *A. umbellata*) of the Pacific coast

**¹sand·wich** \ˈsan(d)-ˌwich, ˈsam-\ *noun* [John Montagu, 4th Earl of *Sandwich* (died 1792) English diplomat] (1762)
**1 a** : two or more slices of bread or a split roll having a filling in between **b** : one slice of bread covered with food
**2** : something resembling a sandwich; *especially* : composite structural material consisting of layers often of high-strength facings bonded to a low strength central core ◆

**²sandwich** *transitive verb* (1861)
**1** : to make into or as if into a sandwich; *especially* : to insert or enclose between usually two things of another quality or character
**2** : to make a place for — often used with *in* or *between*

**sandwich board** *noun* (1897)
: two usually hinged boards designed for hanging from the shoulders with one board before and one behind and used especially for advertising or picketing

**sandwich coin** *noun* (1965)
: a clad coin

**sandwich man** *noun* (1864)
: one who wears a sandwich board

**sand·worm** \ˈsan(d)-ˌwərm\ *noun* (1776)
: any of various sand-dwelling polychaete worms: as **a** : any of several large burrowing worms (especially genus *Nereis*) often used as bait b : LUGWORM

**sand·wort** \ˈsan(d)-ˌwərt, -ˌwort\ *noun* (1597)
: any of a genus (*Arenaria*) of low tufted herbs of the pink family growing usually in dry sandy regions

**sandy** \ˈsan-dē\ *adjective* **sand·i·er; -est** (before 12th century)
**1 a** : consisting of or containing sand : full of sand **b** : sprinkled with sand
**2** : of the color sand
— **sand·i·ness** *noun*

**sane** \ˈsān\ *adjective* **san·er; san·est** [Latin *sanus* healthy, sane] (1628)
**1** : proceeding from a sound mind : RATIONAL
**2** : mentally sound; *especially* : able to anticipate and appraise the effect of one's actions

**3** : healthy in body
*synonym* see WISE
— **sane·ly** *adverb*
— **sane·ness** \ˈsān-nəs\ *noun*

**San·for·ized** \ˈsan-fə-ˌrīzd\ *trademark*
— used for fabrics that are shrunk by a mechanical process before being manufactured into articles (as clothing)

**sang** *past of* SING

**san·ga·ree** \ˌsaŋ-gə-ˈrē\ *noun* [Spanish *sangría*, literally, act of bleeding, from *sangre* blood, from Latin *sanguin-, sanguis*] (1736)
**1** : a sweetened iced drink of wine or sometimes of ale, beer, or liquor garnished with nutmeg
**2** : SANGRIA

**sang·froid** \ˈsän-ˈf(r)wä\ *noun* [French *sang-froid*, literally, cold blood] (1750)
: self-possession or imperturbability especially under strain
*synonym* see EQUANIMITY

**San·greal** \ˈsan-ˈgrā(ə)l, ˈsaŋ-\ *noun* [Middle English *Sangrayll*, from Middle French *Saint Graal* Holy Grail]
: GRAIL

**san·gria** \saŋ-ˈgrē-ə, san-\ *noun* [Spanish] (1736)
: a usually iced punch made of red wine, fruit juice, and soda water

**san·gui·nar·ia** \ˌsaŋ-gwə-ˈner-ē-ə, -ˈnar-\ *noun* [New Latin, from Latin, an herb that stanches blood, from feminine of *sanguinarius* sanguinary] (1808)
**1** : BLOODROOT
**2** : the rhizome and roots of a bloodroot used as an expectorant and emetic

**san·gui·nary** \ˈsaŋ-gwə-ˌner-ē\ *adjective* [Latin *sanguinarius*, from *sanguin-, sanguis* blood] (1623)
**1** : BLOODTHIRSTY, MURDEROUS ⟨*sanguinary* hatred⟩
**2** : attended by bloodshed : BLOODY ⟨this bitter and *sanguinary* war —T. H. D. Mahoney⟩
**3** : consisting of blood ⟨a *sanguinary* stream⟩
*synonym* see BLOODY
— **san·gui·nar·i·ly** \ˌsaŋ-gwə-ˈner-ə-lē\ *adverb*

**¹san·guine** \ˈsaŋ-gwən\ *adjective* [Middle English *sanguin*, from Middle French, from Latin *sanguineus*, from *sanguin-, sanguis*] (14th century)
**1** : BLOODRED
**2 a** : consisting of or relating to blood **b** : BLOODTHIRSTY, SANGUINARY **c** *of the complexion* : RUDDY
**3** : having blood as the predominating bodily humor; *also* : having the bodily conformation and temperament held characteristic of such predominance and marked by sturdiness, high color, and cheerfulness
**4** : CONFIDENT, OPTIMISTIC
— **san·guine·ly** *adverb*
— **san·guine·ness** \-gwən-nəs\ *noun*
— **san·guin·i·ty** \saŋ-ˈgwi-nə-tē, san-\ *noun*

**²sanguine** *noun* (1500)
: a moderate to strong red

**san·guin·e·ous** \saŋ-ˈgwi-nē-əs, saŋ-\ *adjective* [Latin *sanguineus*] (circa 1520)
**1** : BLOODRED
**2** : of, relating to, or involving bloodshed : BLOODTHIRSTY
**3** : of, relating to, or containing blood

**San·he·drin** \san-ˈhe-drən, sän-; san-ˈhē-, sa-nə-\ *noun* [Late Hebrew *sanhedhrīn* (*gĕdhōlāh*) (great) *Sanhedrin*, from Greek *synedrion* council, from *synedros* sitting in council, from *syn-* + *hedra* seat — more at SIT] (1588)
: the supreme council and tribunal of the Jews during postexilic times headed by a High Priest and having religious, civil, and criminal jurisdiction

**san·i·cle** \ˈsa-ni-kəl\ *noun* [Middle English, from Middle French, from Medieval Latin *sanicula*] (14th century)

: any of several plants sometimes held to have healing powers; *especially* : a plant (genus *Sanicula*) of the carrot family with a root used in folk medicine as an anodyne or astringent

**san·i·tar·i·an** \ˌsa-nə-ˈter-ē-ən\ *noun* (1859)
: a specialist in sanitary science and public health ⟨milk *sanitarian*⟩

**san·i·tar·i·um** \ˌsa-nə-ˈter-ē-əm\ *noun, plural* **-i·ums** *or* **-ia** \-ē-ə\ [New Latin, from Latin *sanitat-, sanitas* health] (1851)
: SANATORIUM

**san·i·tary** \ˈsa-nə-ˌter-ē\ *adjective* [French *sanitaire*, from Latin *sanitas*] (1842)
**1** : of or relating to health ⟨*sanitary* measures⟩
**2** : of, relating to, or used in the disposal especially of domestic waterborne waste ⟨*sanitary* sewage⟩
**3** : characterized by or readily kept in cleanliness ⟨*sanitary* packages⟩
— **san·i·tar·i·ly** \ˌsa-nə-ˈter-ə-lē\ *adverb*

**sanitary landfill** *noun* (1968)
: LANDFILL

**sanitary napkin** *noun* (1917)
: a disposable absorbent pad used postpartum or during menstruation to absorb the uterine flow

**sanitary ware** *noun* (1872)
: ceramic plumbing fixtures (as sinks, lavatories, or toilet bowls)

**san·i·tate** \ˈsa-nə-ˌtāt\ *transitive verb* **-tat·ed; -tat·ing** [back-formation from *sanitation*] (1882)
: to make sanitary especially by providing with sanitary appliances or facilities

**san·i·ta·tion** \ˌsa-nə-ˈtā-shən\ *noun* (1848)
**1** : the act or process of making sanitary
**2** : the promotion of hygiene and prevention of disease by maintenance of sanitary conditions

**san·i·tize** \ˈsa-nə-ˌtīz\ *transitive verb* **-tized; -tiz·ing** [Latin *sanitas*] (1836)
**1** : to make sanitary (as by cleaning or sterilizing)
**2** : to make more acceptable by removing unpleasant or undesired features ⟨*sanitize* a document⟩
— **san·i·ti·za·tion** \ˌsa-nə-tə-ˈzā-shən\ *noun*

**san·i·to·ri·um** \ˌsa-nə-ˈtōr-ē-əm, -ˈtor-\ *noun, plural* **-ri·ums** *or* **-ria** \-ē-ə\ [by alteration (influenced by *sanitarium*)] (1917)
: SANATORIUM

**san·i·ty** \ˈsa-nə-tē\ *noun* [Middle English *sanite*, from Latin *sanitat-, sanitas* health, sanity, from *sanus* healthy, sane] (15th century)

◇ WORD HISTORY
**sandwich** John Montagu, the 4th Earl of Sandwich (1718–1792), was not the most distinguished figure in 18th century British politics, and his maladministration of the Royal Navy as First Lord of the Admiralty had a role in the American colonies winning their war for independence from Britain. Among his few positive deeds was the funding of Captain James Cook's third and last expedition to the Pacific, as a result of which Cook named a newly discovered Polynesian archipelago the Sandwich Islands. Unfortunately for the perpetuation of the Earl's memory, the archipelago has since become much better known as the Hawaiian Islands. The Earl's chief claim to fame lies elsewhere, however. According to the French historian and memoirist Pierre-Jean Grosley, who lived in London in the 1760s, the Earl once spent 24 hours at the gaming tables without eating anything but slices of cold beef between pieces of toast. Thus, allegedly, was born the *sandwich*, the archetypal convenience food. The word as well as the item have since been borrowed into most languages of Europe, from Portuguese *sanduíche* to Serbo-Croatian *sandvič*.

**:** the quality or state of being sane; *especially*
**:** soundness or health of mind

**San Ja·cin·to Day** \ˌsan-jə-'sin-tə-, -hə-ˌsin-\ *noun* (1907)
**:** April 21 observed as a legal holiday in Texas in commemoration of the battle of San Jacinto in 1836 by which independence from Mexico was won

**sank** *past of* SINK

**San Jo·se scale** \ˌsa-nə-'zā-, ˌsan-(h)ō-\ *noun* [*San Jose,* Calif.] (1887)
**:** a scale insect (*Quadraspidiotus perniciosus*) probably of Asian origin that is naturalized in the U.S. and is destructive to fruit trees

**San·khya** \'säŋ-kyə\ *noun* [Sanskrit *sāṁkhya,* literally, based on calculation] (1788)
**:** an orthodox Hindu philosophy teaching salvation through knowledge of the dualism of matter and souls

**sann hemp** \'sən-, 'sän-\ *noun* [Hindi *san*] (1939)
**:** SUNN

**san·nup** \'sa-nəp\ *noun* [Eastern Abenaki *sénǫpe* man, male human] (1628)
**:** a married male American Indian

**sann·ya·si** \ˌsən-'yä-sē\ *or* **sann·ya·sin** \-'yä-s°n\ *noun* [Hindi *sannyāsī,* from Sanskrit *sannyāsin*] (1613)
**:** a Hindu mendicant ascetic

**¹sans** \'sanz\ *preposition* [Middle English *saun, sans,* from Middle French *san, sans,* modification of Latin *sine* without — more at SUNDER] (14th century)
**:** WITHOUT ⟨my love to thee is sound, *sans* crack or flaw —Shakespeare⟩

**²sans** \'sanz\ *noun, plural* **sans** (circa 1909)
**:** SANS SERIF

**sans·cu·lotte** \ˌsanz-kü-'lät, -kyü-\ *noun* [French *sans-culotte,* literally, without breeches] (1790)
**1 :** an extreme radical republican in France at the time of the Revolution
**2 :** a radical or violent extremist in politics
— **sans·cu·lott·ic** \-'lä-tik\ *adjective*
— **sans·cu·lott·ish** \-tish\ *adjective*
— **sans·cu·lott·ism** \-ˌti-zəm\ *noun*

**san·sei** \ˌsän-'sā, 'sän-\ *noun, plural* **sansei** *often capitalized* [Japanese *san* third + *sei* generation] (1940)
**:** a son or daughter of nisei parents who is born and educated in America and especially in the U.S.

**san·se·vie·ria** \ˌsan(t)-sə-'vir-ē-ə\ *noun* [New Latin, from Raimondo di Sangro, prince of *San Severo* (died 1774) Italian scholar] (1804)
**:** any of a genus (*Sansevieria*) of tropical herbs of the agave family with showy mottled sword-shaped leaves usually yielding a strong fiber

**San·skrit** \'san-ˌskrit, 'san(t)-skrət\ *noun* [Sanskrit *saṁskṛta,* literally, perfected, from *sam* together + *karoti* he makes] (1696)
**1 :** an ancient Indo-Aryan language that is the classical language of India and of Hinduism
**2 :** classical Sanskrit together with the older Vedic and various later modifications of classical Sanskrit — see INDO-EUROPEAN LANGUAGES table
— **Sanskrit** *adjective*
— **San·skrit·ic** \san-'skri-tik\ *adjective*
— **San·skrit·ist** \-ˌskri-tist\ *noun*

**sans ser·if** *or* **san·ser·if** \san-'ser-əf, 'sanz-\ *noun* [probably from *sans* + modification of Dutch *schreef* stroke — more at SERIF] (1830)
**:** a letter or typeface with no serifs

**San·ta Ana** \ˌsan-tə-'a-nə\ *noun* [*Santa Ana* Mountains in southern Calif.] (1880)

**:** a strong hot dry foehn wind from the north, northeast, or east in southern California

**San·ta Claus** \'san-tə-ˌklȯz *also* 'san-tē-\ *noun* [modification of Dutch *Sinterklaas,* alteration of *Sint Nikolaas* Saint Nicholas]
**:** a plump white-bearded and red-suited old man in modern folklore who delivers presents to good children at Christmastime — called also *Santa*

**San·ta Ger·tru·dis** \ˌsan-tə-(ˌ)gər-'trü-dəs\ *noun* [*Santa Gertrudis,* section of the King Ranch, Kingsville, Texas] (1942)
**:** any of a breed of red beef cattle developed from a Brahman-shorthorn cross and valued for their hardiness in hot climates

Santa Gertrudis

**San·te·ria** *also* **San·te·ría** \ˌsan-tə-'rē-ə, ˌsän-\ *noun* [American Spanish *santería,* from *santero* practitioner of Santeria, from *santo* Yoruba deity, literally, saint's image, saint, from Spanish] (1950)
**:** a religion practiced originally in Cuba in which Yoruba deities are identified with Roman Catholic saints

**san·tir** \san-'tir\ *or* **san·tour** \-'tur\ *noun* [Arabic *sanṭīr, sanṭūr,* from Greek *psaltērion* psaltery] (1853)
**:** a Persian dulcimer

**san·to** \'sän-(ˌ)tō\ *noun, plural* **santos** [Spanish, literally, saint, from Late Latin *sanctus* — more at SAINT] (1834)
**:** a painted or carved wooden image of a saint common especially in Mexico and the southwestern U.S.

**san·to·li·na** \ˌsan-t°l-'ē-nə\ *noun* [New Latin, alteration of Latin *santonica,* an herb, feminine of *santonicus* of the Santoni, from *Santoni,* a people of Aquitania] (1578)
**:** any of a genus (*Santolina*) of Mediterranean composite subshrubs that have dissected leaves and clustered flower heads lacking ray flowers

**san·to·nin** \'san-t°n-ən, san-'tä-nən\ *noun* [International Scientific Vocabulary, from New Latin *santonica,* from Latin] (1838)
**:** a poisonous slightly bitter crystalline compound $C_{15}H_{18}O_3$ found especially in the unopened flower heads of several artemisias (especially *Artemisia maritima*) and used as an anthelmintic

**¹sap** \'sap\ *noun* [Middle English, from Old English *sæp;* akin to Old High German *saf* sap] (before 12th century)
**1 a :** the fluid part of a plant; *specifically* **:** a watery solution that circulates through a plant's vascular system **b** (1) **:** a body fluid (as blood) essential to life, health, or vigor (2) **:** bodily health and vigor
**2 :** a foolish gullible person
**3 :** BLACKJACK, BLUDGEON
— **sap·less** \'sa-pləs\ *adjective*
— **sap·less·ness** \-nəs\ *noun*

**²sap** *transitive verb* **sapped; sap·ping** (1725)
**1 :** to drain or deprive of sap
**2 :** to knock out with a sap

**³sap** *verb* **sapped; sap·ping** [Middle French *sapper,* from Old Italian *zappare,* from *zappa* hoe] (1598)
*intransitive verb*
**:** to proceed by digging a sap
*transitive verb*
**1 :** to subvert by digging or eroding the substratum or foundation **:** UNDERMINE
**2 a :** to gradually diminish the supply or intensity of ⟨*sapped* her strength⟩ **b :** to weaken or exhaust the energy or vitality of
**3 :** to operate against or pierce by a sap
**synonym** see WEAKEN

**⁴sap** *noun* [Middle French *sape,* from *saper*] (1642)
**:** the extension of a trench to a point beneath an enemy's fortifications

**sap green** *noun* (1578)
**:** a strong yellow green

**sap·head** \'sap-ˌhed\ *noun* (1798)
**:** a weak-minded stupid person **:** SAP
— **sap·head·ed** \-'he-dəd\ *adjective*

**sa·phe·nous** \sə-'fē-nəs, 'sa-fə-nəs\ *adjective* [*saphena* saphenous vein, from Middle English, from Medieval Latin, from Arabic *ṣāfin*] (1840)
**:** of, relating to, associated with, or being either of the two chief superficial veins of the leg ⟨*saphenous* nerve⟩

**sap·id** \'sa-pəd\ *adjective* [Latin *sapidus* tasty, from *sapere* to taste — more at SAGE] (1623)
**1 :** having flavor **:** FLAVORFUL
**2** *archaic* **:** agreeable to the mind
— **sa·pid·i·ty** \sa-'pi-də-tē\ *noun, archaic*

**sa·pi·ence** \'sā-pē-ən(t)s, 'sa-\ *noun* [Middle English, from Middle French, from Latin *sapientia,* from *sapient-, sapiens,* present participle] (14th century)
**:** WISDOM, SAGACITY

**sa·pi·ens** \'sā-pē-ənz, 'sā-, -ˌenz\ *adjective* [New Latin (specific epithet of *Homo sapiens*), from Latin, present participle of *sapere*] (1939)
**:** of, relating to, or being recent humans (*Homo sapiens*) as distinguished from various fossil hominids

**sa·pi·ent** \'sā-pē-ənt, 'sa-\ *adjective* [Middle English, from Middle French, from Latin *sapient-, sapiens,* from present participle of *sapere* to taste, be wise — more at SAGE] (15th century)
**:** possessing or expressing great sagacity
**synonym** see WISE
— **sa·pi·ent·ly** *adverb*

**sap·ling** \'sa-pliŋ, -plən\ *noun* (14th century)
**1 :** a young tree; *specifically* **:** one not over four inches in diameter at breast height
**2 :** YOUTH 2a

**sap·o·dil·la** \ˌsa-pə-'di-lə, -'dē-yə\ *noun* [Spanish *zapotillo,* diminutive of *zapote* sapodilla, from Nahuatl *tzapotl*] (1697)
**:** a tropical evergreen tree (*Manilkara zapota* synonym *Achras zapota* of the family Sapotaceae, the sapodilla family) with hard reddish wood, a latex that yields chicle, and a rough-skinned brownish edible fruit; *also* **:** its fruit

**sap·o·ge·nin** \ˌsa-pə-'je-nən, sə-'pä-jə-nən\ *noun* [International Scientific Vocabulary *saponin* + *-genin* (compound formed from another compound)] (circa 1862)
**:** a nonsugar portion of a saponin that is typically obtained by hydrolysis, has either a complex terpenoid or a steroidal structure, and in the latter case forms a practicable starting point in the synthesis of steroid hormones

**sap·o·na·ceous** \ˌsa-pə-'nā-shəs\ *adjective* [New Latin *saponaceus,* from Latin *sapon-, sapo* soap, of Germanic origin; akin to Old English *sāpe* soap] (1710)
**:** resembling or having the qualities of soap
— **sap·o·na·ceous·ness** *noun*

**sa·pon·i·fy** \sə-'pä-nə-ˌfī\ *verb* **-fied; -fy·ing** [French *saponifier,* from Latin *sapon-, sapo*] (1821)
*transitive verb*
**:** to convert (as fat) into soap; *specifically* **:** to hydrolyze (a fat) with alkali to form a soap and glycerol
*intransitive verb*
**:** to undergo saponifying
— **sa·pon·i·fi·able** \-ˌfī-ə-bəl\ *adjective*
— **sa·pon·i·fi·ca·tion** \-ˌpä-nə-fə-'kā-shən\ *noun*

---

\ə\ abut \ᵊ\ kitten \ər\ further \a\ ash \ā\ ace
\ä\ mop, mar \au̇\ out \ch\ chin \e\ bet \ē\ easy
\g\ go \i\ hit \ī\ ice \j\ job \ŋ\ sing \ō\ go
\ȯ\ law \ȯi\ boy \th\ thin \t͟h\ the \ü\ loot \u̇\ foot
\y\ yet \zh\ vision *see also* Guide to Pronunciation

— **sa·pon·i·fi·er** \-'pä-nə-,fī(-ə)r\ *noun*

**sa·po·nin** \'sa-pə-nən, sə-'pō-\ *noun* [French *saponine*, from Latin *sapon-, sapo*] (1831)
: any of various mostly toxic glucosides that occur in plants (as soapwort or soapbark) and are characterized by the property of producing a soapy lather; *especially* : a hygroscopic amorphous saponin mixture used especially as a foaming and emulsifying agent and detergent

**sap·o·nite** \'sa-pə-,nīt\ *noun* [Swedish *saponit*, from Latin *sapon-, sapo* soap] (circa 1849)
: a hydrous magnesium aluminum silicate occurring in soft soapy amorphous masses and filling veins and cavities (as in serpentine)

**sap·per** \'sa-pər\ *noun* (1626)
**1** : a military specialist in field fortification work (as sapping)
**2** : a military demolitions specialist

¹**sap·phic** \'sa-fik\ *adjective* (1501)
**1** *capitalized* : of or relating to the Greek lyric poet Sappho
**2** : of, relating to, or consisting of a 4-line strophe made up of chiefly trochaic and dactylic feet
**3** : LESBIAN 2

²**sapphic** *noun* (1586)
**1** : a verse having the metrical pattern of one of the first three lines of a sapphic strophe
**2** : a sapphic strophe

**sap·phire** \'sa-,fīr\ *noun* [Middle English *safir*, from Old French, from Latin *sapphirus*, from Greek *sappheiros*, perhaps of Semitic origin; akin to Hebrew *sappīr* sapphire] (13th century)
**1 a** : a gem variety of corundum in transparent or translucent crystals of a color other than red; *especially* : one of a transparent rich blue **b** : a gem of such corundum
**2** : a deep purplish blue color
— **sapphire** *adjective*

**sap·phi·rine** \'sa-fə-,rīn, 'sa-,fīr-,ēn, sa-'fī-rən\ *adjective* (15th century)
**1** : made of sapphire
**2** : resembling sapphire especially in color

**sap·phism** \'sa-,fi-zəm\ *noun* [*Sappho* + *-ism*; from the belief that Sappho was homosexual] (circa 1890)
: LESBIANISM

**sap·pi·ness** \'sa-pē-nəs\ *noun* (1552)
**1** : the state of being full of or smelling of sap
**2** : the quality or state of being sappy : FOOLISHNESS

**sap·py** \'sa-pē\ *adjective* **sap·pi·er; -est** (12th century)
**1** : abounding with sap
**2** : resembling or consisting largely of sapwood
**3 a** : overly sweet or sentimental **b** : lacking in good sense : SILLY

**sapr-** *or* **sapro-** *combining form* [New Latin, from Greek *sapros* rotten]
**1** : dead or decaying organic matter ⟨*sapro*phyte⟩
**2** : decay : putrefaction ⟨*sapro*genic⟩

**sap·ro·gen·ic** \,sa-prə-'je-nik\ *adjective* (1876)
: of, causing, or resulting from putrefaction
— **sap·ro·ge·nic·i·ty** \-jə-'ni-sə-tē\ *noun*

**sap·ro·lite** \'sa-prə-,līt\ *noun* (1894)
: disintegrated rock that lies in its original place

**sa·proph·a·gous** \sa-'prä-fə-gəs\ *adjective* [New Latin *saprophagus*, from *sapr-* + *-phagus* -phagous] (1819)
: feeding on decaying matter

**sap·ro·phyte** \'sa-prə-,fīt\ *noun* [International Scientific Vocabulary] (1875)
: a saprophytic organism; *especially* : a plant living on dead or decaying organic matter

**sap·ro·phyt·ic** \,sa-prə-'fi-tik\ *adjective* (1882)
: obtaining food by absorbing dissolved organic material; *especially* : obtaining nourishment

osmotically from the products of organic breakdown and decay
— **sap·ro·phyt·i·cal·ly** \-ti-k(ə-)lē\ *adverb*

**sap·ro·zo·ic** \,sa-prə-'zō-ik\ *adjective* (circa 1920)
: SAPROPHYTIC — used of animals (as protozoans)

**sap·sa·go** \sap-'sä-(,)gō, 'sap-sə-,gō\ *noun* [modification of German *Schabzieger*] (circa 1846)
: a very hard green skim-milk cheese flavored with the powdered leaves of an aromatic legume (*Trigonella coerulea*)

**sap·suck·er** \'sap-,sə-kər\ *noun* (1805)
: any of a genus (*Sphyrapicus*) of small North American woodpeckers that drill holes in trees in order to obtain sap and insects for food

**sap·wood** \-,wùd\ *noun* (1791)
: the younger softer living or physiologically active outer portion of wood that lies between the cambium and the heartwood and is more permeable, less durable, and usually lighter in color than the heartwood

**sar·a·band** *or* **sar·a·bande** \'sar-ə-,band\ *noun* [French *sarabande*, from Spanish *zarabanda*] (1616)
**1** : a stately court dance of the 17th and 18th centuries resembling the minuet
**2** : the music for the saraband in slow triple time with accent on the second beat

**Sar·a·cen** \'sar-ə-sən\ *noun* [Middle English, from Old English, from Late Latin *Saracenus*, from Late Greek *Sarakēnos*] (before 12th century)
: a member of a nomadic people of the deserts between Syria and Arabia; *broadly* : ARAB
— **Saracen** *adjective*
— **Sar·a·cen·ic** \,sar-ə-'se-nik\ *adjective*

**Sa·rah** \'ser-ə, 'sar-ə, 'sā-rə\ *noun* [Hebrew *Śārāh*]
**1** : the wife of Abraham and mother of Isaac
**2** : a kinswoman of Tobias married to him

**sa·ran** \sə-'ran\ *noun* [from *Saran*, a trademark] (1940)
: a tough flexible thermoplastic resin

**sarape** \sə-'rä-pē\ *variant of* SERAPE

**Sar·a·to·ga trunk** \,sar-ə-'tō-gə-\ *noun* [*Saratoga* Springs, N.Y.] (1858)
: a large traveling trunk usually with a rounded top

**sarc-** *or* **sarco-** *combining form* [Greek *sark-, sarko-,* from *sark-, sarx*]
**1** : flesh ⟨*sarc*oid⟩
**2** : striated muscle ⟨*sarco*lemma⟩

**sar·casm** \'sär-,ka-zəm\ *noun* [French or Late Latin; French *sarcasme*, from Late Latin *sarcasmos*, from Greek *sarkasmos*, from *sarkazein* to tear flesh, bite the lips in rage, sneer, from *sark-, sarx* flesh; probably akin to Avestan *thwarəs-* to cut] (1550)
**1** : a sharp and often satirical or ironic utterance designed to cut or give pain ⟨tired of continual *sarcasms*⟩
**2 a** : a mode of satirical wit depending for its effect on bitter, caustic, and often ironic language that is usually directed against an individual **b** : the use or language of sarcasm ⟨this is no time to indulge in *sarcasm*⟩
**synonym** see WIT

**sar·cas·tic** \sär-'kas-tik\ *adjective* (1695)
**1** : having the character of sarcasm ⟨*sarcastic* criticism⟩
**2** : given to the use of sarcasm : CAUSTIC ⟨a *sarcastic* critic⟩ ☆
— **sar·cas·ti·cal·ly** \-ti-k(ə-)lē\ *adverb*

¹**sarce·net** \'sär-snət\ *noun* [Middle English, from Anglo-French *sarzinett*] (15th century)
: a soft thin silk in plain or twill weaves; *also* : a garment made of this

²**sarcenet** *adjective* (1521)
**1** *archaic* : made of sarcenet
**2** *archaic* : soft like sarcenet

**sar·coid** \'sär-,kòid\ *noun* (1899)
**1** : any of various diseases characterized especially by the formation of nodules in the skin

**2** : a nodule characteristic of sarcoid or of sarcoidosis

**sar·coid·o·sis** \,sär-,kòi-'dō-səs\ *noun, plural* **-o·ses** \-,sēz\ [New Latin] (1936)
: a chronic disease of unknown cause that is characterized by the formation of nodules especially in the lymph nodes, lungs, bones, and skin

**sar·co·lem·ma** \,sär-kə-'le-mə\ *noun* [New Latin, from *sarc-* + Greek *lemma* husk — more at LEMMA] (1840)
: the thin transparent homogeneous sheath enclosing a striated muscle fiber
— **sar·co·lem·mal** \-məl\ *adjective*

**sar·co·ma** \sär-'kō-mə\ *noun, plural* **-mas** *also* **-ma·ta** \-mə-tə\ [New Latin, from Greek *sarkōmat-, sarkōma* fleshy growth, from *sarkoun* to grow flesh, from *sark-, sarx*] (1804)
: a malignant neoplasm arising in tissue of mesodermal origin (as connective tissue, bone, cartilage, or striated muscle)
— **sar·co·ma·tous** \sär-'kō-mə-təs\ *adjective*

**sar·co·ma·to·sis** \(,)sär-,kō-mə-'tō-səs\ *noun, plural* **-to·ses** \-,sēz\ [New Latin] (circa 1890)
: a disease characterized by the presence and spread of sarcomas

**sar·co·mere** \'sär-kə-,mir\ *noun* (1891)
: any of the repeating structural units of striated muscle fibrils

**sar·coph·a·gus** \sär-'kä-fə-gəs\ *noun, plural* **-gi** \-,gī, -,jī, -,gē\ *also* **-gus·es** [Latin *sarcophagus* (lapis) limestone used for coffins, from Greek (*lithos*) *sarkophagos*, literally, flesh-eating stone, from *sark-* sarc- + *phagein* to eat — more at BAKSHEESH] (1619)
: a stone coffin; *broadly* : COFFIN

**sar·co·plasm** \'sär-kə-,pla-zəm\ *noun* [New Latin *sarcoplasma*] (1899)
: the cytoplasm of a striated muscle fiber
— **sar·co·plas·mic** \'plaz-mik\ *adjective*

**sarcoplasmic reticulum** *noun* (1953)
: the specialized endoplasmic reticulum of cardiac muscle and skeletal striated muscle that functions especially as a storage and release area for calcium

**sar·cop·tic mange** \(,)sär-'käp-tik-\ *noun* [New Latin *Sarcoptes*, from *sarc-* + Greek *koptein* to cut — more at CAPON] (1886)
: mange caused by mites (genus *Sarcoptes*) burrowing in the skin especially of the head and face

**sar·co·some** \'sär-kə-,sōm\ *noun* [New Latin *sarcosoma*, from *sarc-* + *-soma* -some] (1899)
: a mitochondrion of a striated muscle fiber
— **sar·co·som·al** \,sär-kə-'sō-məl\ *adjective*

**sard** \'särd\ *noun* [French *sarde*, from Latin *sarda*] (14th century)
: a reddish brown variety of chalcedony sometimes classified as a variety of carnelian

**sardar** *variant of* SIRDAR

**sar·dine** \sär-'dēn\ *noun, plural* **sardines** *also* **sardine** [Middle English *sardeine*, from

Middle French *sardine,* from Latin *sardina*] (14th century)
**1 :** any of several small or immature clupeid fishes; *especially* **:** the young of the European pilchard (*Sardina pilchardus*) when of a size suitable for preserving for food
**2 :** any of various small fishes (as an anchovy) resembling the true sardines or similarly preserved for food
**Sar·din·ian** \sär-'di-nē-ən, -'din-yən\ *noun* (1598)
**1 :** a native or inhabitant of Sardinia
**2 :** the Romance language of central and southern Sardinia
— **Sardinian** *adjective*
**sar·don·ic** \sär-'dä-nik\ *adjective* [French *sardonique,* from Greek *sardonios*] (1638)
**:** disdainfully or skeptically humorous **:** derisively mocking 〈a *sardonic* comment〉 〈his *sardonic* expression〉
**synonym** see SARCASTIC
— **sar·don·i·cal·ly** \-ni-k(ə-)lē\ *adverb*
**sar·don·i·cism** \sär-'dä-nə-,si-zəm\ *noun* (1926)
**:** sardonic quality or humor
**sar·don·yx** \sär-'dä-niks *also* 'sär-d°n-iks\ *noun* [Middle English *sardonix,* from Latin *sardonyx,* from Greek] (14th century)
**:** an onyx having parallel layers of sard
**sar·gas·so** \sär-'ga-(,)sō\ *noun, plural* **-sos** [Portuguese *sargaço*] (1598)
**1 :** GULFWEED, SARGASSUM
**2 :** a mass of floating vegetation and especially sargassums
**sar·gas·sum** \sär-'ga-səm\ *noun* [New Latin, genus name, from International Scientific Vocabulary *sargasso*] (circa 1890)
**:** any of a genus (*Sargassum*) of brown algae that have a branching thallus with lateral outgrowths differentiated as leafy segments, air bladders, or spore-bearing structures **:** GULFWEED
**sarge** \'särj\ *noun* [by shortening & alteration] (1867)
**:** SERGEANT
**sa·ri** *also* **sa·ree** \'sär-ē\ *noun* [Hindi *sārī,* from Sanskrit *śāṭī* strip of cloth] (1785)
**:** a garment of southern Asian women that consists of several yards of lightweight cloth draped so that one end forms a skirt and the other a head or shoulder covering
**sa·rin** \'sär-ən, zä-'rēn\ *noun* [German] (1951)
**:** an extremely toxic chemical warfare agent $C_4H_{10}FO_2P$ that is a powerful cholinesterase inhibitor
**sark** \'särk\ *noun* [Middle English (Scots) *serk,* from Old English *serc;* akin to Old Norse *serkr* shirt] (before 12th century)
*dialect chiefly British* **:** SHIRT
**sa·rod** *also* **sa·rode** \sə-'rōd\ *noun* [Hindi *sarod,* from Persian] (1865)
**:** a lute of northern India
— **sa·rod·ist** \-'rō-dist\ *noun*
**sa·rong** \sə-'rȯŋ, -'räŋ\ *noun* [Malay] (1830)
**:** a loose garment made of a long strip of cloth wrapped around the body that is worn as a skirt or dress by men and women chiefly of the Malay Archipelago and the Pacific islands
**Sar·pe·don** \sär-'pē-d°n\ *noun* [Latin, from Greek *Sarpēdōn*]
**:** a son of Zeus and Europa and king of Lycia killed in the Trojan War
**sar·ra·ce·nia** \,sar-ə-'sē-nē-ə, -'se-\ *noun* [New Latin, from Michel *Sarrazin* (died 1734) French physician & naturalist] (1884)
**:** any of a genus (*Sarracenia* of the family Sarraceniaceae) that includes the insectivorous bog pitcher plants of eastern North America
**sar·sa·pa·ril·la** \,sas-pə-'ri-lə, ,särs-, -'re-; ,sa-sə-, ,sär-sə-\ *noun* [Spanish *zarzaparrilla,*

from *zarza* bush + *parrilla,* diminutive of *parra* vine] (1577)
**1 a :** any of various tropical American greenbriers **b :** the dried roots of a sarsaparilla used especially as a flavoring
**2 :** any of various plants (as wild sarsaparilla) that resemble or are used as a substitute for sarsaparilla
**3 :** a sweetened carbonated beverage flavored with sassafras and oil distilled from a European birch
**sarsenet** *variant of* SARCENET
**sar·to·ri·al** \sär-'tȯr-ē-əl, -'tȯr-\ *adjective* [Medieval Latin *sartor*] (1823)
**:** of or relating to a tailor or tailored clothes; *broadly* **:** of or relating to clothes
— **sar·to·ri·al·ly** \-ē-ə-lē\ *adverb*
**sar·to·ri·us** \sär-'tȯr-ē-əs, -'tȯr-\ *noun, plural* **-rii** \-ē-,ī, -ē-,ē\ [New Latin, from Medieval Latin *sartor* tailor, from Latin *sarcire* to mend] (1704)
**:** a muscle that crosses the front of the thigh obliquely, assists in rotating the leg to the cross-legged position in which the knees are spread wide apart, and in humans is the longest muscle
**Sar·um** \'sar-əm, 'ser-\ *adjective* [Sarum, old borough near Salisbury, England] (1570)
**:** of or relating to the Roman rite as modified in Salisbury and used in England, Wales, and Ireland before the Reformation
**¹sash** \'sash\ *noun* [Arabic *shāsh* muslin] (1681)
**:** a band worn about the waist or over one shoulder and used as a dress accessory or the emblem of an honorary or military order
— **sashed** \'sasht\ *adjective*
**²sash** *noun, plural* **sash** *also* **sash·es** [probably modification of French *châssis* chassis (taken as plural)] (1681)
**:** the framework in which panes of glass are set in a window or door; *also* **:** such a framework together with its panes forming a usually movable part of a window
**¹sa·shay** \sa-'shā *also* sī-\ *intransitive verb* [alteration of *chassé*] (1836)
**1 :** to make a chassé
**2 a :** WALK, GLIDE, GO **b :** to strut or move about in an ostentatious or conspicuous manner **c :** to proceed or move in a diagonal or sideways manner
**²sashay** *noun* [by alteration] (1900)
**1 :** TRIP, EXCURSION
**2 :** a square-dance figure in which partners sidestep in a circle around each other with the man moving behind the woman
**3 :** CHASSÉ
**sa·shi·mi** \'sä-shə-mē\ *noun* [Japanese] (1880)
**:** a Japanese dish consisting of thinly sliced raw fish served with a sauce for dipping
**sas·ka·toon** \,sas-kə-'tün\ *noun* [modification of Cree *misa'skwato'min* serviceberry fruit] (1810)
**:** SERVICEBERRY
**Sas·quatch** \'sas-,kwach, -,kwäch\ *noun* [Halkomelem (Salishan language of southwestern British Columbia) *sésq̓əc*] (1929)
**:** a hairy creature like a human being reported to exist in the northwestern U.S. and western Canada and said to be a primate between 6 and 15 feet (1.8 and 4.6 meters) tall — called *also* bigfoot
**¹sass** \'sas\ *noun* [alteration of ¹*sauce*] (1835)
**:** impudent speech ◆
**²sass** *transitive verb* (1856)
**:** to talk impudently or disrespectfully to
**sas·sa·fras** \'sa-sə-,fras\ *noun* [Spanish *sasafrás*] (1577)
**1 :** an eastern North American tree (*Sassafras albidum*) of the laurel family having both ovate and lobed aromatic leaves
**2 :** the carcinogenic dried root bark of the sassafras used formerly as a diaphoretic or flavoring agent
**¹Sas·sa·ni·an** *or* **Sa·sa·ni·an** \sə-'sā-nē-ən, sa-'sā-\ *adjective* (1788)

**:** of, relating to, or having the characteristics of the Sassanid dynasty of ancient Persia or its art or architecture
**²Sassanian** *or* **Sasanian** *noun* (1855)
**:** SASSANID
**Sas·sa·nid** *or* **Sa·sa·nid** \sə-'sä-nəd, -'sa-; 'sa-s°n-əd\ *noun* [New Latin *Sassanidae* Sassanids, from *Sassan,* founder of the dynasty] (1776)
**:** a member of a dynasty of Persian kings of the 3d to 7th centuries
— **Sassanid** *or* **Sasanid** *adjective*
**sassy** \'sa-sē\ *adjective* **sass·i·er; -est** [alteration of *saucy*] (1833)
**1 :** IMPUDENT, SAUCY
**2 :** VIGOROUS, LIVELY
**3 :** distinctively smart and stylish 〈a *sassy* black-and-white bow tie —Jean Stafford〉
**sat** *past and past participle of* SIT
**Sa·tan** \'sā-t°n\ *noun* [Middle English, from Old English, from Late Latin, from Greek, from Hebrew *śāṭān* adversary] (before 12th century)
**:** the adversary of God and lord of evil in Judaism and Christianity
**sa·tang** \sə-'täŋ\ *noun, plural* **satang** *or* **satangs** [Thai *sataŋ*] (circa 1915)
— see *baht* at MONEY table
**sa·tan·ic** \sə-'ta-nik, sā-\ *adjective* (1667)
**1 :** of, relating to, or characteristic of Satan or satanism 〈*satanic* pride〉 〈*satanic* rites〉
**2 :** characterized by extreme cruelty or viciousness
— **sa·tan·i·cal·ly** \-ni-k(ə-)lē\ *adverb*
**sa·tan·ism** \'sā-t°n-,i-zəm\ *noun, often capitalized* (1565)
**1 :** innate wickedness **:** DIABOLISM
**2 :** obsession with or affinity for evil; *specifically* **:** the worship of Satan marked by the travesty of Christian rites
— **sa·tan·ist** \-ist\ *noun, often capitalized*
**satch·el** \'sa-chəl\ *noun* [Middle English *sachel,* from Middle French, from Late Latin *saccellum,* diminutive of Latin *sacculus,* diminutive of *saccus* bag — more at SACK] (14th century)
**:** a small bag often with a shoulder strap
— **satch·el·ful** \-,fül\ *noun*
**¹sate** \'sāt, 'sat\ *archaic past of* SIT

\ə\ abut \°\ kitten \ər\ further \a\ ash \ā\ ace \ä\ mop, mar \au\ out \ch\ chin \e\ bet \ē\ easy \g\ go \i\ hit \ī\ ice \j\ job \ŋ\ sing \ō\ go \ȯ\ law \ȯi\ boy \th\ thin \th\ the \ü\ loot \u\ foot \y\ yet \zh\ vision *see also* Guide to Pronunciation

**²sate** \'sāt\ *transitive verb* **sat·ed; sat·ing**
[probably by shortening & alteration from *satiate*] (1602)
**1** : to cloy with overabundance : GLUT
**2** : to appease (as a thirst) by indulging to the full
**synonym** see SATIATE

**sa·teen** \sa-'tēn, sə-\ *noun* [alteration of *satin*] (circa 1878)
: a smooth durable lustrous fabric usually made of cotton in satin weave

**sat·el·lite** \'sa-t°l-,īt\ *noun* [Middle French, from Latin *satellit-, satelles* attendant] (circa 1548)
**1** : a hired agent or obsequious follower : MINION, SYCOPHANT
**2 a** : a celestial body orbiting another of larger size **b** : a manufactured object or vehicle intended to orbit the earth, the moon, or another celestial body
**3** : someone or something attendant, subordinate, or dependent; *especially* : a country politically and economically dominated or controlled by another more powerful country
**4** : a usually independent urban community situated near but not immediately adjacent to a large city
— **satellite** *adjective*

**satellite DNA** *noun* (1969)
: a fraction of a eukaryotic organism's DNA that differs in density from most of its DNA as determined by centrifugation, that apparently consists of short repetitive nucleotide sequences, that does not undergo transcription, and that in some organisms (as the mouse) is found especially in centromeric regions

**sa·tem** \'sä-təm\ *adjective* [Avestan *satəm* hundred; from the fact that its initial sound (derived from an alveolar fricative) is the representative of an Indo-European palatal stop — more at HUNDRED] (1901)
: of, relating to, or constituting an Indo-European language group in which the palatal stops became in prehistoric times palatal or alveolar fricatives — compare CENTUM

**sa·ti** \(,)sə-'tē, 'sə-,tē\ *variant of* SUTTEE

**sa·tia·ble** \'sā-shə-bəl\ *adjective* (1570)
: capable of being appeased or satisfied

**¹sa·tiate** \'sā-sh(ē-)ət\ *adjective* (15th century)
: filled to satiety

**²sa·ti·ate** \'sā-shē-,āt\ *transitive verb* **-at·ed; -at·ing** [Latin *satiatus*, past participle of *satiare*, from *satis* enough — more at SAD] (15th century)
: to satisfy (as a need or desire) fully or to excess ☆
— **sa·ti·a·tion** \,sā-shē-'ā-shən, ,sā-sē-\ *noun*

**sa·ti·ety** \sə-'tī-ə-tē *also* 'sā-sh(ē-)ə-\ *noun* [Middle French *satieté*, from Latin *satietat-, satietas*, from *satis*] (1533)
**1** : the quality or state of being fed or gratified to or beyond capacity : SURFEIT, FULLNESS
**2** : the revulsion or disgust caused by overindulgence or excess

**¹sat·in** \'sa-t°n\ *noun* [Middle English, from Middle French, probably from Arabic *zaytūnī*, literally, of Zaytūn, seaport in China during the Middle Ages] (14th century)
: a fabric (as of silk) in satin weave with lustrous face and dull back

**²satin** *adjective* (1521)
**1** : made of or covered with satin
**2** : suggestive of satin especially in smooth lustrous appearance or sleekness to touch

**sat·in·et** \,sa-t°n-'et\ *noun* (1703)
**1** : a thin silk satin or imitation satin
**2** : a variation of satin weave used in making satinet

**satin stitch** *noun* (1684)
: an embroidery stitch nearly alike on both sides and worked so closely as to resemble satin

**satin weave** *noun* (circa 1883)

: a weave in which warp threads interlace with filling threads to produce a smooth-faced fabric

**satin stitch**

**sat·in·wood** \'sa-t°n-,wud\ *noun* (1792)
**1 a** : an East Indian tree (*Chloroxylon swietenia*) of the rue family that yields a lustrous yellowish brown wood **b** : a tree (as *Zanthoxylum flavum* of the rue family) with wood resembling true satinwood
**2** : the wood of a satinwood

**sat·iny** \'sat-nē, 'sa-t°n-ē\ *adjective* (1786)
: having or resembling the soft usually lustrous smoothness of satin

**sat·ire** \'sa-,tīr\ *noun* [Middle French or Latin; Middle French, from Latin *satura, satira*, perhaps from (*lanx*) *satura* dish of mixed ingredients, from feminine of *satur* well-fed; akin to Latin *satis* enough — more at SAD] (1501)
**1** : a literary work holding up human vices and follies to ridicule or scorn
**2** : trenchant wit, irony, or sarcasm used to expose and discredit vice or folly
**synonym** see WIT

**sa·tir·ic** \sə-'tir-ik\ *or* **sa·tir·i·cal** \-i-kəl\ *adjective* (1509)
**1** : of, relating to, or constituting satire ⟨*satiric* writers⟩
**2** : manifesting or given to satire
**synonym** see SARCASTIC
— **sa·tir·i·cal·ly** \-i-k(ə-)lē\ *adverb*

**sat·i·rise** *British variant of* SATIRIZE

**sat·i·rist** \'sa-tə-rist\ *noun* (1589)
: one that satirizes; *especially* : a writer of satire

**sat·i·rize** \-,rīz\ *verb* **-rized; -riz·ing** (1601)
*intransitive verb*
: to utter or write satire
*transitive verb*
: to censure or ridicule by means of satire
— **sat·i·riz·a·ble** \,sa-tə-'rī-zə-bəl\ *adjective*

**sat·is·fac·tion** \,sa-təs-'fak-shən\ *noun* [Middle English, from Middle French, from Late Latin *satisfaction-, satisfactio*, from Latin, reparation, amends, from *satisfacere* to satisfy] (14th century)
**1 a** : the payment through penance of the temporal punishment incurred by a sin **b** : reparation for sin that meets the demands of divine justice
**2 a** : fulfillment of a need or want **b** : the quality or state of being satisfied : CONTENTMENT **c** : a source or means of enjoyment : GRATIFICATION
**3 a** : compensation for a loss or injury : ATONEMENT, RESTITUTION **b** : the discharge of a legal obligation or claim **c** : VINDICATION
**4** : convinced assurance or certainty ⟨proved to the *satisfaction* of the court⟩

**sat·is·fac·to·ry** \,sa-təs-'fak-t(ə-)rē\ *adjective* (15th century)
: giving satisfaction : ADEQUATE
— **sat·is·fac·to·ri·ly** \-t(ə-)rə-lē\ *adverb*
— **sat·is·fac·to·ri·ness** *noun*

**sat·is·fi·able** \'sa-təs-,fī-ə-bəl\ *adjective* (1609)
: capable of being satisfied

**sat·is·fy** \'sa-təs-,fī\ *verb* **-fied; -fy·ing** [Middle English *satisfien*, from Middle French *satisfier*, modification of Latin *satisfacere*, from *satis* enough + *facere* to do, make — more at SAD, DO] (15th century)
*transitive verb*
**1 a** : to carry out the terms of (as a contract) : DISCHARGE **b** : to meet a financial obligation to
**2** : to make reparation to (an injured party) : INDEMNIFY
**3 a** : to make happy : PLEASE **b** : to gratify to the full : APPEASE
**4 a** : CONVINCE **b** : to put an end to (doubt or uncertainty) : DISPEL

**5 a** : to conform to (as specifications) : be adequate to (an end in view) **b** : to make true by fulfilling a condition ⟨values that *satisfy* an equation⟩ ⟨*satisfy* a hypothesis⟩
*intransitive verb*
: to be adequate : SUFFICE; *also* : PLEASE
**synonym** see PAY
— **sat·is·fy·ing·ly** \-iŋ-lē\ *adverb*

**sa·to·ri** \sə-'tōr-ē, sä-, -'tór-\ *noun* [Japanese] (1727)
: a state of intuitive illumination sought in Zen Buddhism

**sa·trap** \'sā-,trap *also* 'sa-,trap *or* 'sa-trəp\ *noun* [Middle English, from Latin *satrapes*, from Greek *satrapēs*, from Old Persian *khshathrapāvan*, literally, protector of the dominion] (14th century)
**1** : the governor of a province in ancient Persia
**2 a** : RULER **b** : a subordinate official : HENCHMAN

**sa·tra·py** \'sā-trə-pē, 'sa-, -,tra-pē\ *noun, plural* **-pies** (1603)
: the territory or jurisdiction of a satrap

**sat·su·ma** \sat-'sü-mə, 'sat-sə-\ *noun* [*Satsuma*, former province in Kyushu, Japan] (1882)
**1** : any of several cultivated mandarin trees that bear medium-sized largely seedless fruits with thin smooth skin
**2** : the fruit of a satsuma

**sat·u·ra·ble** \'sach-rə-bəl, 'sa-chə-\ *adjective* (1570)
: capable of being saturated

**sat·u·rant** \-rənt\ *noun* (circa 1775)
: something that saturates

**¹sat·u·rate** \'sa-chə-,rāt\ *transitive verb* **-rat·ed; -rat·ing** [Latin *saturatus*, past participle of *saturare*, from *satur* well-fed — more at SATIRE] (1538)
**1** : to satisfy fully : SATIATE
**2** : to treat, furnish, or charge with something to the point where no more can be absorbed, dissolved, or retained ⟨water *saturated* with salt⟩
**3 a** : to fill completely with something that permeates or pervades ⟨book is *saturated* with Hollywood, old and new —Newgate Callendar⟩ **b** : to load to capacity
**4** : to cause to combine till there is no further tendency to combine
**synonym** see SOAK
— **sat·u·ra·tor** \-,rā-tər\ *noun*

**²sat·u·rate** \'sach-rət, 'sa-chə-\ *adjective* (1782)
: SATURATED

**sat·u·rat·ed** \'sa-chə-,rā-təd\ *adjective* (1728)
**1** : full of moisture : made thoroughly wet
**2 a** : being a solution that is unable to absorb or dissolve any more of a solute at a given temperature and pressure **b** : being an organic compound having no double or triple bonds between carbon atoms
**3** *of a color* : having high saturation : PURE

---

☆ **SYNONYMS**
**Satiate, sate, surfeit, cloy, pall, glut, gorge** mean to fill to repletion. SATIATE and SATE may sometimes imply only complete satisfaction but more often suggest repletion that has destroyed interest or desire ⟨years of globe-trotting had *satiated* their interest in travel⟩ ⟨readers were *sated* with sensationalistic stories⟩. SURFEIT implies a nauseating repletion ⟨*surfeited* themselves with junk food⟩. CLOY stresses the disgust or boredom resulting from such surfeiting ⟨sentimental pictures that *cloy* after a while⟩. PALL emphasizes the loss of ability to stimulate interest or appetite ⟨a life of leisure eventually begins to *pall*⟩. GLUT implies excess in feeding or supplying ⟨a market *glutted* with diet books⟩. GORGE suggests glutting to the point of bursting or choking ⟨*gorged* themselves with chocolate⟩.

**sat·u·ra·tion** \,sa-chə-'rā-shən\ *noun* (circa 1554)
**1 a :** the act of saturating **:** the state of being saturated **b :** SATIETY, SURFEIT
**2 :** conversion of an unsaturated to a saturated chemical compound (as by hydrogenation)
**3 :** a state of maximum impregnation: as **a :** complete infiltration **:** PERMEATION **b :** the presence in air of the most water possible under existent pressure and temperature **c :** magnetization to the point beyond which a further increase in the intensity of the magnetizing force will produce no further magnetization
**4 a :** chromatic purity **:** freedom from dilution with white **b** (1) **:** degree of difference from the gray having the same lightness — used of an object color (2) **:** degree of difference from the achromatic light-source color of the same brightness — used of a light-source color; compare HUE 2c
**5 :** the supplying of a market with as much of a product as it will absorb
**6 :** an overwhelming concentration of military forces or firepower

**Sat·ur·day** \'sa-tər-dē, -(,)dā\ *noun* [Middle English *saterday*, from Old English *sæterndæg* (akin to Old Frisian *sāterdei*), from Latin *Saturnus* Saturn + Old English *dæg* day] (before 12th century)
**:** the seventh day of the week
— **Sat·ur·days** \-dēz, -(,)dāz\ *adverb*

**Saturday night special** *noun* (1968)
**:** a cheap easily concealed handgun

**Sat·urn** \'sa-tərn\ *noun* [Latin *Saturnus*]
**1 :** a Roman god of agriculture and father by Ops of Jupiter
**2 :** the planet 6th in order from the sun — see PLANET table

**sat·ur·na·lia** \,sa-tər-'nāl-yə, -'nā-lē-ə\ *noun plural but singular or plural in construction* [Latin, from neuter plural of *saturnalis* of Saturn, from *Saturnus*] (1591)
**1** *capitalized* **:** the festival of Saturn in ancient Rome beginning on Dec. 17
**2** *singular, plural* **saturnalias** *also* **saturnalia a :** an unrestrained often licentious celebration **:** ORGY **b :** EXCESS, EXTRAVAGANCE
— **sat·ur·na·lian** \-'nāl-yən, -'nā-lē-ən\ *adjective*
— **sat·ur·na·lian·ly** *adverb*

**Sa·tur·ni·an** \sa-'tər-nē-ən, sə-\ *adjective* (1557)
**1 :** of, relating to, or influenced by the planet Saturn
**2** *archaic* **:** of or relating to the god Saturn or the golden age of his reign

**sa·tur·ni·id** \-nē-əd\ *noun* [New Latin *Saturniidae*, from *Saturnia*, genus of moths, from Latin, daughter of the god Saturn] (circa 1909)
**:** any of a family (Saturniidae) of usually large stout strong-winged moths (as a luna moth or a cecropia moth) with hairy bodies
— **saturniid** *adjective*

**sat·ur·nine** \'sa-tər-,nīn\ *adjective* (15th century)
**1 :** born under or influenced astrologically by the planet Saturn
**2 a :** cold and steady in mood **:** slow to act or change **b :** of a gloomy or surly disposition **c :** having a sardonic aspect ⟨a *saturnine* smile⟩
*synonym* see SULLEN

**sat·urn·ism** \'sa-tər-,ni-zəm\ *noun* [*saturn* lead] (1855)
**:** LEAD POISONING

**sa·tya·gra·ha** \(,)sə-'tyä-grə-hə, 'sə-tyə-\ *noun* [New Sanskrit *satyāgraha*, from Sanskrit *satya* truth + *āgraha* persistence] (1920)
**:** pressure for social and political reform through friendly passive resistance practiced by M. K. Gandhi and his followers in India

**sa·tyr** \'sā-tər, *chiefly British* 'sa-\ *noun* [Middle English, from Latin *satyrus*, from Greek *satyros*]
**1** *often capitalized* **:** a sylvan deity in Greek mythology having certain characteristics of a horse or goat and fond of Dionysian revelry

**2 a :** a lecherous man **b :** one having satyriasis
**3 :** any of various usually brown and gray satyrid butterflies
— **sa·tyr·ic** \sa-'tir-ik, sə-, -sä-\ *adjective*

**sa·ty·ri·a·sis** \,sā-tə-'rī-ə-səs, ,sa-\ *noun* [Late Latin, from Greek, from *satyros*] (15th century)
**:** excessive or abnormal sexual craving in the male

**sa·tyr·id** \sə-'tī-rəd\ *noun* [New Latin *Satyridae*, ultimately from Greek *satyros*] (1901)
**:** any of a family (Satyridae) of usually brownish butterflies that feed on grasses as larvae and have one or more forewing veins swollen basally
— **satyrid** *adjective*

**satyr play** *noun* (1929)
**:** a comic play of ancient Greece burlesquing a mythological subject and having a chorus representing satyrs

**¹sauce** \'sos, *usually* 'sas *for 4*\ *noun* [Middle English, from Middle French, from Latin *salsa*, feminine of *salsus* salted, from past participle of *sallere* to salt, from *sal* salt — more at SALT] (14th century)
**1 :** a condiment or relish for food; *especially* **:** a fluid dressing or topping
**2 :** something that adds zest or piquancy
**3 :** stewed fruit eaten with other food or as a dessert
**4 :** pert or impudent language or actions
**5** *slang* **:** LIQUOR — used with *the*

**²sauce** \'sos, *usually* 'sas *for 3*\ *transitive verb* **sauced; sauc·ing** (15th century)
**1 a :** to dress with relish or seasoning **b :** to cover or serve with a sauce
**2 a** *archaic* **:** to modify the harsh or unpleasant characteristics of **b :** to give zest or piquancy to
**3 :** to be rude or impudent to

**sauce-boat** \'sos-,bōt\ *noun* (1747)
**:** a low boat-shaped pitcher for serving sauces and gravies

**sauce-box** \'sos-,bäks, 'sas-\ *noun* (1588)
**:** a saucy impudent person

**sauce-pan** \'sos-,pan, *especially British* -pən\ *noun* (1686)
**:** a small deep cooking pan with a handle

**sau·cer** \'so-sər\ *noun* [Middle English, plate containing sauce, from Middle French *saussier*, from *sausse*, sauce] (1607)
**1 :** a small shallow dish in which a cup is set at table
**2 :** something resembling a saucer especially in shape; *especially* **:** FLYING SAUCER
— **sau·cer·like** \-,līk\ *adjective*

**saucy** \'so-sē, 'sa-\ *adjective* **sauc·i·er; -est** (1508)
**1 :** served with or having the consistency of sauce
**2 a :** impertinently bold and impudent **b :** amusingly forward and flippant **:** IRREPRESSIBLE
**3 :** SMART, TRIM ⟨a *saucy* little hat⟩
— **sauc·i·ly** \-sə-lē\ *adverb*
— **sauc·i·ness** \-sē-nəs\ *noun*

**sau·er·bra·ten** \'saù-(ə)r-,brä-t³n\ *noun* [German, from *sauer* sour + *Braten* roast meat] (1889)
**:** oven-roasted or pot-roasted beef marinated before cooking in vinegar with peppercorns, garlic, onions, and bay leaves

**sau·er·kraut** \'saù(-ə)r-,kraùt\ *noun* [German, from *sauer* sour + *Kraut* greens] (1617)
**:** cabbage cut fine and fermented in a brine made of its own juice with salt

**sau·ger** \'so-gər\ *noun* [origin unknown] (1882)
**:** a pike perch (*Stizostedion canadense*) similar to but smaller than the walleye

**saugh** *or* **sauch** \'säk, 'sòk\ *noun* [Middle English (Scots) *sauch*, from Old English *salh*, alteration of *sealh* — more at SALLOW] (before 12th century)
*chiefly Scottish* **:** SALLOW

**Sauk** \'sok\ *noun, plural* **Sauk** *or* **Sauks** (1762)
**:** a member of an American Indian people formerly living in what is now Wisconsin

**Saul** \'sol\ *noun* [Late Latin *Saulus*, from Greek *Saulos*, from Hebrew *Shā'ūl*]
**1 :** the first king of Israel
**2 :** the apostle Paul — called also *Saul of Tarsus*

**sau·na** \'sò-nə, 'saù-nə\ *noun* [Finnish] (1891)
**1 :** a Finnish steam bath in which the steam is provided by water thrown on hot stones; *also* **:** a bathhouse or room used for such a bath
**2 :** a dry heat bath; *also* **:** a room or cabinet used for such a bath

**saun·ter** \'sòn-tər, 'sän-\ *intransitive verb* [probably from Middle English *santren* to muse] (circa 1667)
**:** to walk about in an idle or leisurely manner **:** STROLL
— **saunter** *noun*
— **saun·ter·er** \-tər-ər\ *noun*

**sau·rel** \sò-'rel\ *noun* [French, from Late Latin *saurus* horse mackerel, from Greek *sauros* horse mackerel, lizard] (1882)
**:** JACK MACKEREL

**sau·ri·an** \'sor-ē-ən\ *noun* [New Latin *Sauria*, from New Latin *saurus* lizard, from Greek *sauros*] (circa 1829)
**:** any of a suborder (Sauria) of reptiles including the lizards and in older classifications the crocodiles and various extinct forms (as the dinosaurs and ichthyosaurs) that resemble lizards
— **saurian** *adjective*

**sau·ris·chi·an** \(,)sò-'ris-kē-ən\ *noun* [New Latin *Saurischia*, from Greek *sauros* lizard + New Latin *ischium* ischium] (circa 1891)
**:** any of an order (Saurischia) of herbivorous or carnivorous dinosaurs (as a brontosaurus) that have a triradiate pelvis with the pubis typically pointed forward — compare ORNITHISCHIAN
— **saurischian** *adjective*

**sau·ro·pod** \'sor-ə-,päd\ *noun* [New Latin *Sauropoda*, from Greek *sauros* lizard + New Latin *-poda*] (circa 1891)
**:** any of a suborder (Sauropoda) of quadrupedal saurischian dinosaurs comprising herbivorous forms with a long neck and tail, small head, and more or less plantigrade 5-toed limbs
— **sauropod** *adjective*

**sau·ry** \'sor-ē\ *noun, plural* **sauries** [New Latin *saurus* lizard] (circa 1771)
**1 :** a slender long-beaked fish (*Scombresox saurus*) related to the needlefishes and found in temperate parts of the Atlantic
**2 :** a widely distributed fish (*Cololabris saira*) of the Pacific similar to the related Atlantic saury

**sau·sage** \'so-sij\ *noun* [Middle English *sausige*, from Old North French *saussiche*, from Late Latin *salsicia*, from Latin *salsus* salted — more at SAUCE] (15th century)
**:** a highly seasoned minced meat (as pork) usually stuffed in casings of prepared animal intestine; *also* **:** a link or patty of sausage

**¹sau·té** *also* **sau·te** \sò-'tā, sō-\ *noun* [French, from past participle of *sauter* to jump, from Latin *saltare* — more at SALTATION] (1813)
**:** a sautéed dish
— **sauté** *adjective*

**²sauté** *also* **saute** *transitive verb* **sau·téed** *or* **sau·téd; sau·té·ing** (1859)
**:** to fry in a small amount of fat

**sau·ternes** \sō-'tərn, sò-, -'tern\ *noun, often capitalized* [French, from *Sauternes*, commune in France] (1711)

\ə\ abut \ə\ kitten \ər\ further \a\ ash \ā\ ace
\ä\ mop, mar \aù\ out \ch\ chin \e\ bet \ē\ easy
\g\ go \i\ hit \ī\ ice \j\ job \ŋ\ sing \ō\ go
\o\ law \oi\ boy \th\ thin \th\ the \ü\ loot \ù\ foot
\y\ yet \zh\ vision *see also* Guide to Pronunciation

**1 :** a full-bodied sweet white wine from the Bordeaux region of France
**2** *usually* **sauterne :** a semidry to semisweet American white wine that is a blend of several grapes

**sau·vi·gnon blanc** \ˌsō-vēn-ˈyōⁿ-ˈblä''\ *noun* [French, white sauvignon (variety of grape)] (1941)
**:** a dry white wine made from a grape original-ly grown in Bordeaux and the Loire valley

**¹sav·age** \ˈsa-vij\ *adjective* [Middle English *sauvage*, from Middle French, from Medieval Latin *salvaticus*, alteration of Latin *silvaticus* of the woods, wild, from *silva* wood, forest] (13th century)
**1 a :** not domesticated or under human control **:** UNTAMED ⟨*savage* beasts⟩ **b :** lacking the re-straints normal to civilized human beings **:** FIERCE, FEROCIOUS
**2 :** WILD, UNCULTIVATED ⟨seldom have I seen such *savage* scenery —Douglas Carruthers⟩
**3 a :** BOORISH, RUDE ⟨the *savage* bad manners of most motorists —M. P. O'Connor⟩ **b :** MA-LICIOUS
**4 :** lacking complex or advanced culture **:** UN-CIVILIZED ◆
*synonym* see FIERCE
— **sav·age·ly** *adverb*
— **sav·age·ness** *noun*

**²savage** *noun* (15th century)
**1 :** a person belonging to a primitive society
**2 :** a brutal person
**3 :** a rude or unmannerly person

**³savage** *transitive verb* **sav·aged; sav·ag·ing** (1880)
**:** to attack or treat brutally

**sav·age·ry** \ˈsa-vij-rē, -vi-jə-\ *noun, plural* **-ries** (1595)
**1 a :** the quality of being savage **b :** an act of cruelty or violence
**2 :** an uncivilized state

**sav·ag·ism** \ˈsa-vi-ˌji-zəm\ *noun* (1796)
**:** SAVAGERY

**sa·van·na** *also* **sa·van·nah** \sə-ˈva-nə\ *noun* [Spanish *zavana*, from Taino *zabana*] (1555)
**1 :** a treeless plain especially in Florida
**2 :** a tropical or subtropical grassland contain-ing scattered trees and drought-resistant under-growth

**sa·vant** \sa-ˈvänt, sə-, -ˈväⁿ; sə-ˈvant, ˈsa-vənt\ *noun* [French, from Middle French, from present participle of *savoir* to know, from Lat-in *sapere* to be wise — more at SAGE] (1719)
**1 :** a person of learning; *especially* **:** one with detailed knowledge in some specialized field (as of science or literature)
**2 :** IDIOT SAVANT 1

**sav·a·rin** \ˈsa-və-rən\ *noun* [French, from An-thelme Brillat-*Savarin* (died 1826) French pol-itician, writer, and gourmet] (1877)
**:** a rich yeast cake baked in a ring mold and soaked in a rum or kirsch syrup

**sa·vate** \sə-ˈvät, sa-, -ˈvat\ *noun* [French, liter-ally, old shoe] (1862)
**:** a form of boxing in which blows are deliv-ered with either the hands or the feet

**¹save** \ˈsāv\ *verb* **saved; sav·ing** [Middle English, from Old French *salver*, from Late Latin *salvare*, from Latin *salvus* safe — more at SAFE] (13th century)
*transitive verb*
**1 a :** to deliver from sin **b :** to rescue or deliv-er from danger or harm **c :** to preserve or guard from injury, destruction, or loss
**2 a :** to put aside as a store or reserve **:** ACCU-MULATE **b :** to spend less by ⟨*save* 25%⟩
**3 a :** to make unnecessary **:** AVOID ⟨it *saves* an hour's driving⟩ **b** (1) **:** to keep from being lost to an opponent (2) **:** to prevent an opponent from scoring or winning
**4 :** MAINTAIN, PRESERVE ⟨*save* appearances⟩
*intransitive verb*
**1 :** to rescue or deliver someone
**2 a :** to put aside money **b :** to avoid unnec-essary waste or expense **:** ECONOMIZE **c :** to spend less money ⟨buy now and *save*⟩

**3 :** to make save
*synonym* see RESCUE
— **sav·able** *or* **save·able** \ˈsā-və-bəl\ *ad-jective*
— **sav·er** *noun*

**²save** *noun* (1890)
**1 :** a play that prevents an opponent from scoring or winning
**2 :** the action of a relief pitcher in baseball in successfully protecting a team's lead

**³save** *preposition* [Middle English *sauf*, from Middle French, from *sauf*, adjective, safe — more at SAFE] (14th century)
**:** other than **:** BUT, EXCEPT ⟨no hope *save* one⟩

**⁴save** *conjunction* (14th century)
**1 :** except for the fact that **:** ONLY — used with *that* ⟨of his earlier years little is known, *save* that he studied violin —J. N. Burk⟩
**2 :** BUT, EXCEPT — used before a word often taken to be the subject of a clause ⟨no one knows about it *save* she⟩

**save–all** \ˈsā-ˌvȯl\ *noun* (circa 1645)
**:** something that prevents waste, loss, or dam-age (as a receptacle for catching waste prod-ucts for further utilization)

**sav·e·loy** \ˈsa-və-ˌlȯi\ *noun* [modification of French *cervelas*, from Middle French, from Old Italian *cervellata*, literally, pig's brains, from *cervello* brain, from Latin *cerebellum* — more at CEREBELLUM] (1837)
*British* **:** a ready-cooked highly seasoned dry sausage

**sav·in** \ˈsa-vən\ *noun* [Middle English, from Middle French *savine*, from Latin (*herba*) sa-*bina*, literally, Sabine plant] (14th century)
**1 :** a Eurasian juniper (*Juniperus sabina*) with dark foliage and small yellowish green berries
**2 :** RED CEDAR 1

**¹sav·ing** \ˈsā-viŋ\ *noun* [Middle English, from gerund of *saven* to save] (14th century)
**1 :** preservation from danger or destruction **:** DELIVERANCE
**2 :** the act or an instance of economizing
**3 a** *plural* **:** money put by **b :** the excess of in-come over consumption expenditures — of-ten used in plural **c :** a usually specified lower cost — often used in plural ⟨a *savings* of 50%⟩

**²saving** *preposition* [Middle English, from present participle of *saven*] (14th century)
**1 :** EXCEPT, SAVE
**2 :** without disrespect to

**³saving** *conjunction* (15th century)
**:** EXCEPT, SAVE

**saving grace** *noun* (1597)
**:** a redeeming quality or factor

**savings account** *noun* (1911)
**:** an account (as in a bank) on which interest is usually paid and from which withdrawals can be made usually only by presentation of a passbook or by written authorization on a pre-scribed form

**savings and loan association** *noun* (circa 1924)
**:** a cooperative association organized to hold savings of members in the form of dividend-bearing shares and to invest chiefly in home mortgage loans

**savings bank** *noun* (1817)
**:** a bank organized to hold funds of individual depositors in interest-bearing accounts and to make long-term investments (as in home mort-gage loans)

**savings bond** *noun* (1948)
**:** a nontransferable registered U.S. bond issued in denominations of $50 to $10,000

**sav·ior** *or* **sav·iour** \ˈsāv-yər *also* -ˌyȯr\ *noun* [Middle English *saveour*, from Middle French, from Late Latin *salvator*, from *salvare* to save] (14th century)
**1 :** one that saves from danger or destruction
**2 :** one who brings salvation; *specifically, cap-italized* **:** JESUS 1

**sa·voir faire** \ˌsav-ˌwär-ˈfar, -ˈfer\ *noun* [French *savoir-faire*, literally, knowing how to do] (1815)

**:** capacity for appropriate action; *especially* **:** a polished sureness in social behavior
*synonym* see TACT

**¹sa·vor** *also* **sa·vour** \ˈsā-vər\ *noun* [Middle English, from Old French, from Latin *sapor*, from *sapere* to taste — more at SAGE] (13th century)
**1 :** the taste or smell of something
**2 :** a particular flavor or smell
**3 :** a distinctive quality
— **sa·vor·less** \-ləs\ *adjective*
— **sa·vor·ous** \ˈsā-vər-əs, ˈsāv-rəs\ *adjec-tive*

**²savor** *also* **savour** *verb* **sa·vored; sa·vor·ing** \ˈsā-vər-iŋ, ˈsāv-riŋ\ (14th century)
*intransitive verb*
**:** to have a specified smell or quality **:** SMACK
*transitive verb*
**1 :** to give flavor to **:** SEASON
**2 a :** to have experience of **:** TASTE **b :** to taste or smell with pleasure **:** RELISH **c :** to delight in **:** ENJOY
— **sa·vor·er** \ˈsā-vər-ər\ *noun*

**¹sa·vory** *also* **sa·voury** \ˈsā-və-rē, ˈsāv-rē\ *adjective* (13th century)
**:** having savor: as **a :** piquantly pleasant to the mind ⟨a *savory* collection of essays⟩ **b :** moral-ly exemplary **:** EDIFYING ⟨his reputation was anything but *savory*⟩ **c :** pleasing to the sense of taste especially by reason of effective sea-soning
*synonym* see PALATABLE
— **sa·vor·i·ly** \-rə-lē\ *adverb*
— **sa·vor·i·ness** \-rē-nəs\ *noun*

**²savory** *also* **savoury** *noun, plural* **sa·vor·ies** (1661)
*British* **:** a dish of stimulating flavor served usually at the end of dinner but sometimes as an appetizer

**³sa·vo·ry** \ˈsā-və-rē, ˈsāv-rē\ *noun, plural* **-ries** [Middle English *saverey*] (14th century)
**:** either of two aromatic mints: **a :** SUMMER SA-VORY **b :** WINTER SAVORY

**Sa·voy·ard** \sə-ˈvȯi-ˌärd, ˌsa-ˌvȯi-ˈärd, ˌsav-ˌwä-ˈyär(d)\ *noun* [*Savoy* Theater, London, built for the presentation of Gilbert and Sulli-van operas] (1890)
**:** a devotee, performer, or producer of the comic operas of W. S. Gilbert and A. S. Sulli-van

**sa·voy cabbage** \sə-ˈvȯi-, ˈsa-ˌvȯi-\ *noun, of-ten S capitalized* [translation of French *chou de Savoie* cabbage of Savoy] (1707)
**:** a cabbage with compact heads of wrinkled and curled leaves

**¹sav·vy** \ˈsa-vē\ *verb* **sav·vied; sav·vy·ing** [alteration of *sabi* know (in English-based cre-oles and pidgins), from Portuguese *sabe* he knows, from *saber* to know, from Latin *sapere* to be wise — more at SAGE] (1785)

---

◇ WORD HISTORY

**savage**   In Latin the adjective *silvaticus*, a derivative of *silva* "forest," meant, when ap-plied to animals or plants, "growing or living in the forest." Because forest life is wild rath-er than domesticated, the adjective easily acquired the meaning "wild, uncultivated" in literary Late Latin as well as the spoken Latin of the declining Roman Empire. Old French inherited Late Latin *silvaticus*, altered to *sal-vaticus*, as *salvage*. In later medieval French this became *sauvage*, which was borrowed into Middle English in the 13th century. The Old French adjective retained the source meanings "wild, uncultivated (of fruit)" and "untamed (of animals)." But *sauvage* could also be applied to humans, in which case its meanings could range from "lacking civiliza-tion, barbarous" to "fierce, cruel." English *savage* has had all these meanings at some point in its history, though the "fierce" sense is the one we now perhaps associate most closely with the word.

: UNDERSTAND

**²savvy** *noun* (circa 1785)
: practical know-how ⟨political *savvy*⟩
— **savvy** *adjective*

**¹saw** *past of* SEE

**²saw** \'sȯ\ *noun* [Middle English *sawe,* from Old English *sagu;* akin to Old High German *sega* saw, Latin *secare* to cut] (before 12th century)
: a hand or power tool or a machine used to cut hard material (as wood, metal, or bone) and equipped usually with a toothed blade or disk
— **saw·like** \-ˌlīk\ *adjective*

**³saw** *verb* **sawed** \'sȯd\; **sawed** *or* **sawn** \'sȯn\; **saw·ing** \'sȯ(-)iŋ\ (13th century)
*transitive verb*
**1** : to cut with a saw
**2** : to produce or form by cutting with a saw
**3** : to slash as though with a saw
*intransitive verb*
**1 a** : to use a saw **b** : to cut with or as if with a saw
**2** : to undergo cutting with a saw
**3** : to make motions as though using a saw ⟨*sawed* at the reins⟩
— **saw·er** \'sȯ(-ə)r\ *noun*

**⁴saw** *noun* [Middle English *sawe,* from Old English *sagu* discourse; akin to Old High German & Old Norse *saga* tale, Old English *secgan* to say — more at SAY] (before 12th century)
: MAXIM, PROVERB

**saw·bones** \'sȯ-ˌbōnz\ *noun, plural* **saw·bones** *or* **saw·bones·es** (1837)
*slang* : PHYSICIAN, SURGEON

**saw·buck** \'sȯ-ˌbək\ *noun* (1850)
**1** *slang* : a 10-dollar bill
**2** : SAWHORSE; *especially* : one with X-shaped ends

**saw·dust** \'sȯ-(ˌ)dəst\ *noun* (1530)
: fine particles (as of wood) made by a saw in cutting

**sawed–off** \'sȯ-ˌdȯf\ *adjective* (1869)
**1** : having an end sawed off ⟨a *sawed-off* shotgun⟩
**2** : of less than average height

**saw·fish** \'sȯ-ˌfish\ *noun* (1664)
: any of a family (Pristidae) of large elongate rays that resemble sharks but have a long flattened snout with a row of serrate structures along each edge and that live in tropical and subtropical shallow seas and in or near the mouths of rivers

**saw·fly** \-ˌflī\ *noun* (1773)
: any of numerous hymenopterous insects (superfamily Tenthredinoidea) with the female usually having a sawlike ovipositor and with the larva resembling a plant-feeding caterpillar

**saw grass** *noun* (1822)
: any of various sedges (as of the genus *Cladium*) having the edges of the leaves set with minute sharp teeth

**saw·horse** \'sȯ-ˌhȯrs\ *noun* (1778)
: a frame on which wood is laid for sawing by hand; *especially*
: HORSE 2b

**word history**
see EASEL

**saw·log** \-ˌlȯg, -ˌläg\ *noun* (1756)
: a log of suitable size for sawing into lumber

**saw·mill** \-ˌmil\ *noun* (1553)
: a mill or machine for sawing logs

**saw·ney** \'sȯ-nē\ *noun* [perhaps from *sawney* Scotsman, from Scots, alteration of *Sandy,* short for *Alexander*] (circa 1700)
*chiefly British* : FOOL, SIMPLETON
— **sawney** *adjective*

**saw palmetto** *noun* (1797)
: any of several shrubby palms chiefly of the southern U.S. and West Indies that have spiny-toothed petioles; *especially* : a common palm

(*Serenoa repens*) of the southeastern U.S. with a usually creeping stem

**saw set** *noun* (1846)
: an instrument used to set the teeth of saws

**saw·tim·ber** \'sȯ-ˌtim-bər\ *noun* (1901)
: timber suitable for sawing into lumber

**saw·tooth** \-ˌtüth\ *adjective* (circa 1859)
: having serrations : arranged or having parts arranged like the teeth of a saw ⟨a *sawtooth* roof⟩

**saw–toothed** \-'tütht\ *adjective* (circa 1857)
**1** : having teeth like those of a saw ⟨a *saw-toothed* shark⟩
**2** : SAWTOOTH

**saw–whet owl** \'sȯ-ˌhwet-, -ˌwet-\ *noun* [from the supposed resemblance of its cry to the sound made in filing a saw] (1834)
: a very small harsh-voiced North American owl (*Aegolius acadicus*) that is largely dark brown above and chestnut streaked with white beneath — called also *saw-whet*

**saw·yer** \'sȯ-yər, 'sȯi-ər\ *noun* (13th century)
**1** : one that saws
**2** : any of several large longicorn beetles whose larvae bore large holes in timber or dead wood
**3** : a tree fast in the bed of a stream with its branches projecting to the surface

**sax** \'saks\ *noun* (circa 1923)
: SAXOPHONE

**sax·horn** \'saks-ˌhȯrn\ *noun* [Antoine *Sax* (died 1894) Belgian instrument maker + English *horn*] (1844)
: any of a group of valved brass instruments ranging from soprano to bass and characterized by a conical tube, oval shape, and cup-shaped mouthpiece

**sax·ic·o·lous** \sak-'si-kə-ləs\ *adjective* [Latin *saxum* rock (akin to Latin *secare* to cut) + English *-colous* — more at SAW] (1856)
: inhabiting or growing among rocks ⟨*saxicolous* lichens⟩

**sax·i·frage** \'sak-sə-frij, -ˌfrāj\ *noun* [Middle English, from Middle French, from Late Latin *saxifraga,* from Latin, feminine of *saxifragus* breaking rocks, from *saxum* rock + *frangere* to break — more at BREAK] (14th century)
: any of a genus (*Saxifraga* of the family Saxifragaceae, the saxifrage family) of chiefly perennial herbs with showy pentamerous flowers and often with basal tufted leaves

**sax·i·tox·in** \ˌsak-sə-'täk-sən\ *noun* [*saxi-* (from New Latin *Saxidomus giganteus,* species of butter clam from which it is isolated) + *toxin*] (1962)
: a potent nonprotein neurotoxin $C_{10}H_{17}N_7O_4$·2HCl that originates in dinoflagellates (genus *Gonyaulax*) found in red tides and that sometimes occurs in and renders toxic normally edible mollusks which feed on them

**Sax·on** \'sak-sən\ *noun* [Middle English, from Late Latin *Saxones* Saxons, of Germanic origin; akin to Old English *Seaxan* Saxons] (13th century)
**1 a** (1) : a member of a Germanic people that entered and conquered England with the Angles and Jutes in the 5th century A.D. and merged with them to form the Anglo-Saxon people (2) : an Englishman or lowlander as distinguished from a Welshman, Irishman, or Highlander **b** : a native or inhabitant of Saxony
**2 a** : the Germanic language or dialect of any of the Saxon peoples **b** : the Germanic element in the English language especially as distinguished from the French and Latin
— **Saxon** *adjective*

**sax·o·ny** \'sak-s(ə-)nē\ *noun, plural* **-nies** *often capitalized* [*Saxony,* Germany] (1842)
**1 a** : a fine soft woolen fabric **b** : a fine closely twisted knitting yarn
**2** : a Wilton jacquard carpet

**sax·o·phone** \'sak-sə-ˌfōn\ *noun* [French, from Antoine *Sax* (died 1894) Belgian instrument maker + French *-phone*] (1851)

: one of a group of single-reed woodwind instruments ranging from soprano to bass and characterized by a conical metal tube and finger keys
— **sax·o·phon·ic** \ˌsak-sə-'fä-nik, -'fä-\ *adjective*
— **sax·o·phon·ist** \'sak-sə-ˌfō-nist, *especially British* sak-'sä-fə-\ *noun*

**sax·tu·ba** \'saks-ˌtü-bə, -ˌtyü-\ *noun* [Antoine *Sax* + English *tuba*] (1856)
: a bass saxhorn

saxophone

**¹say** \'sā, *Southern also* 'se\ *verb* **said** \'sed, *especially when subject follows* səd\; **say·ing** \'sā-iŋ\ **says** \'sez, *sometimes* 'sāz, *especially when subject follows* səz\ [Middle English, from Old English *secgan;* akin to Old High German *sagēn* to say, Lithuanian *sakyti,* Greek *en-nepein* to speak, tell] (before 12th century)
*transitive verb*
**1 a** : to express in words : STATE **b** : to state as opinion or belief : DECLARE
**2 a** : UTTER, PRONOUNCE **b** : RECITE, REPEAT ⟨*say* your prayers⟩
**3 a** : INDICATE, SHOW ⟨the clock *says* five minutes after twelve⟩ **b** : to give expression to : COMMUNICATE ⟨a glance that *said* all that was necessary⟩
*intransitive verb*
: to express oneself : SPEAK
— **say·er** \'sā-ər, 'se(-ə)r\ *noun*
— **say uncle** : to admit defeat
— **that is to say** : in other words : in effect

**²say** *noun, plural* **says** \'sāz, *Southern also* 'sez\ (1571)
**1** *archaic* : something that is said : STATEMENT
**2** : an expression of opinion ⟨had my *say*⟩
**3** : a right or power to influence action or decision; *especially* : the authority to make final decisions

**³say** *adverb* [from imperative of ¹*say*] (1596)
**1** : ABOUT, APPROXIMATELY ⟨the property is worth, *say,* four million dollars⟩
**2** : for example : AS ⟨if we compress any gas, *say* oxygen⟩

**say·able** \'sā-ə-bəl, 'se-\ *adjective* (1856)
**1** : capable of being said
**2** : capable of being spoken effectively or easily ⟨readings in sayable Chinese —*Linguistic Reporter*⟩

**say·est** \'sā-əst\ *archaic 2d person singular of* SAY

**say·ing** \'sā-iŋ, 'se-\ *noun* (14th century)
: something said; *especially* : ADAGE

**say–so** \'sā-(ˌ)sō, 'se-\ *noun* (1637)
**1 a** : one's unsupported assertion or assurance **b** : an authoritative pronouncement ⟨left the hospital on the *say-so* of his doctor⟩
**2** : a right of final decision ⟨has the ultimate *say-so* on what will be taught⟩

**say·yid** \'sī-yəd, 'sā-; 'sīd, 'säd\ *noun* [Arabic] (1788)
**1** : an Islamic chief or leader
**2** : LORD, SIR — used as a courtesy title for a Muslim of rank or lineage

**Saz·e·rac** \'sa-zə-ˌrak\ *trademark*
— used for a cocktail with a whiskey base

**¹scab** \'skab\ *noun* [Middle English, of Scandinavian origin; akin to Old Swedish *skabbr* scab; akin to Old English *sceabb* scab, Latin *scabere* to scratch — more at SHAVE] (13th century)
**1** : scabies of domestic animals
**2** : a crust of hardened blood and serum over a wound

sawhorses

**3 a :** a contemptible person **b** (1) **:** a worker who refuses to join a labor union (2) **:** a union member who refuses to strike or returns to work before a strike has ended (3) **:** a worker who accepts employment or replaces a union worker during a strike (4) **:** one who works for less than union wages or on nonunion terms
**4 :** any of various bacterial or fungus diseases of plants characterized by crustaceous spots; *also* **:** one of the spots
**²scab** *intransitive verb* **scabbed; scab·bing** (1683)
**1 :** to become covered with a scab
**2 :** to act as a scab
**scab·bard** \'ska-bərd\ *noun* [Middle English *scaubert*, from Anglo-French *escaubers*] (13th century)
**:** a sheath for a sword, dagger, or bayonet
— **scabbard** *transitive verb*
**scab·by** \'ska-bē\ *adjective* **scab·bi·er; -est** (15th century)
**1 a :** covered with or full of scabs ⟨*scabby* skin⟩ **b :** diseased with scab ⟨a *scabby* animal⟩ ⟨*scabby* potatoes⟩
**2 :** MEAN, CONTEMPTIBLE ⟨a *scabby* trick⟩
**sca·bies** \'skā-bēz\ *noun, plural* **scabies** [Latin; from *scabere* to scratch] (1814)
**:** contagious itch or mange especially with exudative crusts that is caused by parasitic mites (especially *Sarcoptes scabiei*)
— **sca·bi·et·ic** \ˌskā-bē-'e-tik\ *adjective*
**¹sca·bi·ous** \'skā-bē-əs, 'ska-\ *noun* [Middle English *scabiose*, from Medieval Latin *scabiosa*, from Latin, feminine of *scabiosus*, adjective] (14th century)
**:** any of a genus (*Scabiosa*) of Old World herbs of the teasel family with terminal flower heads subtended by a leafy involucre
**²scabious** *adjective* [Latin *scabiosus*, from *scabies*] (1603)
**1 :** SCABBY
**2 :** of, relating to, or resembling scabies ⟨*scabious* eruptions⟩
**scab·land** \'skab-ˌland\ *noun* (1904)
**:** a region characterized by elevated tracts of rocky land with little or no soil cover and traversed or isolated by postglacial dry stream channels — usually used in plural
**sca·brous** \'ska-brəs *also* 'skā-\ *adjective* [Latin *scabr-, scaber* rough, scurfy; akin to Latin *scabere* to scratch — more at SCAB] (1646)
**1 :** DIFFICULT, KNOTTY ⟨a *scabrous* problem⟩
**2 :** rough to the touch: as **a :** having small raised dots, scales, or points ⟨a *scabrous* leaf⟩ **b :** covered with raised, roughened, or unwholesome patches ⟨*scabrous* paint⟩ ⟨yellowed *scabrous* skin⟩
**3 :** dealing with suggestive, indecent, or scandalous themes **:** SALACIOUS; *also* **:** SQUALID
**synonym** see ROUGH
— **sca·brous·ly** *adverb*
— **sca·brous·ness** *noun*
**¹scad** \'skad\ *noun, plural* **scad** *also* **scads** [origin unknown] (1602)
**:** any of several carangid fishes (especially of the genus *Decapterus*)
**²scad** *noun* [probably alteration of English dialect *scald* a multitude] (1869)
**:** a large number or quantity — usually used in plural ⟨*scads* of money⟩
**scaf·fold** \'ska-fəld *also* -ˌfōld\ *noun* [Middle English, from Old North French *escafaut*, modification of (assumed) Vulgar Latin *catafalicum*, from Greek *kata-* cata- + Latin *fala* siege tower] (14th century)
**1 a :** a temporary or movable platform for workers (as bricklayers, painters, or miners) to stand or sit on when working at a height above the floor or ground **b :** a platform on which a criminal is executed (as by hanging or beheading) **c :** a platform at a height above ground or floor level
**2 :** a supporting framework
**scaf·fold·ing** \-fəl-diŋ, -ˌfōl-\ *noun* (14th century)

**:** a system of scaffolds; *also* **:** material for scaffolds
**scag** \'skag\ *noun* [origin unknown] (1967)
*slang* **:** HEROIN
**sca·glio·la** \skal-'yō-lə, -'yò-\ *noun, often attributive* [Italian, literally, little chip] (1747)
**:** an imitation marble used for floors, columns, and ornamental interior work
**scal·able** \'skā-lə-bəl\ *adjective* (circa 1580)
**:** capable of being scaled
**sca·lade** \skə-'lād, -'läd\ *or* **sca·la·do** \-'lā-ˌdō, -'lä-\ *noun, plural* **-lades** *or* **-lados** [obsolete Italian *scalada*, from *scalare* to scale, from *scala* ladder, staircase, from Late Latin — more at SCALE] (1591)
*archaic* **:** ESCALADE
**¹sca·lar** \'skā-lər, -ˌlär\ *adjective* [Latin *scalaris*, from *scalae* stairs, ladder — more at SCALE] (circa 1656)
**1 :** having an uninterrupted series of steps **:** GRADUATED ⟨*scalar* chain of authority⟩ ⟨*scalar* cells⟩
**2 a :** capable of being represented by a point on a scale ⟨*scalar* quantity⟩ **b :** of or relating to a scalar or scalar product ⟨*scalar* multiplication⟩
**²scalar** *noun* (1846)
**1 :** a real number rather than a vector
**2 :** a quantity (as mass or time) that has a magnitude describable by a real number and no direction
**sca·la·re** \skə-'lar-ē, -'ler-, -'lär-\ *noun* [New Latin, specific epithet, from Latin, neuter of *scalaris*; from the barred pattern on its body] (1928)
**:** a black and silver laterally compressed South American cichlid fish (*Pterophyllum scalare*) popular in aquariums
**sca·lar·i·form** \skə-'lar-ə-ˌfòrm\ *adjective* [New Latin *scalariformis*, from Latin *scalaris* + *-iformis* -iform] (1836)
**:** resembling a ladder especially in having transverse bars or markings like the rungs of a ladder ⟨*scalariform* cells in plants⟩
— **sca·lar·i·form·ly** *adverb*
**scalar product** *noun* (1878)
**:** a real number that is the product of the lengths of two vectors and the cosine of the angle between them — called also *dot product, inner product*
**scal·a·wag** \'ska-li-ˌwag\ *noun* [origin unknown] (circa 1848)
**1 :** SCAMP, REPROBATE
**2 :** a white Southerner acting in support of the reconstruction governments after the American Civil War often for private gain
**¹scald** \'skòld\ *verb* [Middle English, from Old North French *escalder*, from Late Latin *excaldare* to wash in warm water, from Latin *ex-* + *calida, calda* warm water, from feminine of *calidus* warm, from *calēre* to be warm — more at LEE] (13th century)
*transitive verb*
**1 :** to burn with or as if with hot liquid or steam
**2 a :** to subject to the action of boiling water or steam **b :** to bring to a temperature just below the boiling point ⟨*scald* milk⟩
**3 :** SCORCH
*intransitive verb*
**1 :** to scald something
**2 :** to become scalded
**²scald** *noun* (1601)
**1 :** an injury to the body caused by scalding
**2 :** an act or process of scalding
**3 :** any of various conditions or diseases of plants or fruits marked especially by a usually brownish discoloration of tissue
**³scald** *adjective* [*scall* + *¹-ed*] (1561)
**1** *archaic* **:** SCABBY, SCURFY
**2** *archaic* **:** SHABBY, CONTEMPTIBLE
**⁴scald** \'skòld, 'skäld\ *variant of* SKALD
**⁵scald** \'skòld\ *adjective* [alteration of *scalded*] (1791)
**:** subjected to scalding ⟨coffee . . . with *scald* cream —Charles Kingsley⟩

**scald·ing** \'skòl-diŋ\ *adjective* (13th century)
**1 :** hot enough to scald ⟨*scalding* water⟩
**2 a :** having or producing the feeling of being burned ⟨*scalding* sun⟩ ⟨*scalding* sand⟩ **b :** SCATHING ⟨*scalding* criticism⟩
**¹scale** \'skā(ə)l\ *noun* [Middle English, bowl, scale of a balance, from Old Norse *skál*; akin to Old Norse *skel* shell — more at SHELL] (14th century)
**1 a :** either pan or tray of a balance **b :** a beam that is supported freely in the center and has two pans of equal weight suspended from its ends — usually used in plural
**2 :** an instrument or machine for weighing
**²scale** *verb* **scaled; scal·ing** (1603)
*transitive verb*
**:** to weigh in scales
*intransitive verb*
**:** to have a specified weight on scales
**³scale** *noun* [Middle English, from Middle French *escale*, of Germanic origin; akin to Old English *scealu* shell, husk — more at SHELL] (14th century)
**1 a :** a small, flattened, rigid, and definitely circumscribed plate forming part of the external body covering especially of a fish **b :** a small thin plate suggesting a fish scale ⟨*scales* of mica⟩ ⟨the *scales* on a moth's wing⟩ **c :** the scaly covering of a scaled animal
**2 :** a small thin dry lamina shed (as in many skin diseases) from the skin
**3 :** a thin coating, layer, or incrustation: **a :** a usually black scaly coating of oxide forming on the surface of a metal (as iron) when it is heated for processing **b :** a hard incrustation usually rich in sulfate of calcium that is deposited on the inside of a vessel (as a boiler) in which water is heated
**4 a :** a modified leaf protecting a seed plant bud before expansion **b :** a thin, membranous, chaffy, or woody bract
**5 a :** any of the small overlapping usually metal pieces forming the outer surface of scale armor **b :** SCALE ARMOR
**6 a :** SCALE INSECT **b :** infestation with or disease caused by scale insects
— **scaled** \'skā(ə)ld\ *adjective*
— **scale·less** \'skā(ə)l-ləs\ *adjective*
**⁴scale** *verb* **scaled; scal·ing** (15th century)
*transitive verb*
**1 :** to remove the scale or scales from (as by scraping) ⟨*scale* a fish⟩
**2 :** to take off in thin layers or scales
**3 :** to form scale on ⟨hard water *scales* a boiler⟩
**4 :** to throw (as a thin flat stone) so that the edge cuts the air or so that it skips on water **:** SKIM
*intransitive verb*
**1 :** to separate and come off in scales **:** FLAKE
**2 :** to shed scales ⟨*scaling* skin⟩
**3 :** to become encrusted with scale
**⁵scale** *verb* **scaled; scal·ing** [Middle English, from *⁶scale*] (14th century)
*transitive verb*
**1 a :** to attack with or take by means of scaling ladders ⟨*scale* a castle wall⟩ **b :** to climb up or reach by means of a ladder **c :** to reach the highest point of **:** SURMOUNT
**2 a :** to arrange in a graduated series ⟨*scale* a test⟩ **b** (1) **:** to measure by or as if by a scale (2) **:** to measure or estimate the sound content of (as logs) **c :** to pattern, make, regulate, set, or estimate according to some rate or standard **:** ADJUST ⟨a production schedule *scaled* to actual need⟩ — often used with *down* or *up* ⟨*scale* down imports⟩
*intransitive verb*
**1 :** to climb by or as if by a ladder
**2 :** to rise in a graduated series
**3 :** MEASURE
**⁶scale** *noun* [Middle English, from Late Latin *scala* ladder, staircase, from Latin *scalae*, plural, stairs, rungs, ladder; akin to Latin *scandere* to climb — more at SCAN] (15th century)

**1 a** *obsolete* **:** LADDER **b** *archaic* **:** a means of ascent
**2 :** a graduated series of musical tones ascending or descending in order of pitch according to a specified scheme of their intervals
**3 :** something graduated especially when used as a measure or rule: as **a :** a series of marks or points at known intervals used to measure distances (as the height of the mercury in a thermometer) **b :** an indication of the relationship between the distances on a map and the corresponding actual distances **c :** RULER 3
**4 a :** a graduated series or scheme of rank or order ⟨a *scale* of taxation⟩ **b :** MINIMUM WAGE 2
**5 a :** a proportion between two sets of dimensions (as between those of a drawing and its original) **b :** a distinctive relative size, extent, or degree ⟨projects done on a large *scale*⟩
**6 :** a graded series of tests or of performances used in rating individual intelligence or achievement
— **scale** *adjective*
— **to scale :** according to the proportions of an established scale of measurement ⟨floor plans drawn *to scale*⟩
⁷**scale** *noun* [⁵*scale*] (circa 1587)
**1** *obsolete* **:** ESCALADE
**2 :** an estimate of the amount of sound lumber in logs or standing timber
**scale armor** *noun* (1842)
**:** armor of small metallic scales on leather or cloth
**scale–down** \'skā(ə)l-ˌdaùn\ *noun* (1931)
**:** a reduction according to a fixed ratio ⟨a *scale-down* of debts⟩
**scale insect** *noun* (1840)
**:** any of numerous small but very prolific homopterous insects (superfamily Coccoidea) that have winged males, wingless scale-covered females attached to the host plant, and young that suck the juices of plants and some of which are economic pests — compare LAC
**scale·like** \'skā(ə)l-ˌlīk\ *adjective* (1883)
**:** resembling a scale ⟨*scalelike* design⟩; *specifically* **:** reduced to a minute appressed element resembling a scale
**sca·lene** \'skā-ˌlēn, skā-'\ *adjective* [Late Latin *scalenus*, from Greek *skalēnos*, literally, uneven; perhaps akin to Greek *skolios* crooked, *skelos* leg — more at ISOSCELES] (1734)
*of a triangle* **:** having the three sides of unequal length — see TRIANGLE illustration
**scal·er** \'skā-lər\ *noun* (1568)
**1 :** one that scales
**2 :** a dental instrument for removing tartar from teeth
**3 :** an electronic device that operates a recorder or produces an output pulse after a specified number of input impulses
**scale–up** \'skā-ˌləp\ *noun* (1945)
**:** an increase according to a fixed ratio
**scall** \'skòl\ *noun* [Middle English, from Old Norse *skalli* bald head; akin to Swedish *skulle* skull] (14th century)
**:** a scurf or scabby disorder (as of the scalp)
**scal·lion** \'skal-yən\ *noun* [Middle English *scaloun*, from Anglo-French *scalun*, from (assumed) Vulgar Latin *escalonia*, from Latin *ascalonia* (*caepa*) onion of Ascalon, from feminine of *ascalonius* of Ascalon, from *Ascalon-*, *Ascalo* Ascalon, seaport in southern Palestine] (14th century)
**1 :** SHALLOT
**2 :** LEEK
**3 :** an onion forming a thick basal portion without a bulb; *also* **:** GREEN ONION
¹**scal·lop** \'skä-ləp, 'ska-, 'skò-\ *noun* [Middle English *scalop*, from Middle French *escalope* shell, of Germanic origin; akin to Middle Dutch *schelpe* shell] (15th century)
**1 a :** any of numerous marine bivalve lamellibranch mollusks (family Pectinidae) that have a radially ribbed shell with the edge undulated and that swim by opening and closing the valves **b :** the adductor muscle of a scallop as an article of food

**2 a :** a valve or shell of a scallop **b :** a baking dish shaped like a valve of a scallop
**3 :** one of a continuous series of circle segments or angular projections forming a border
**4 :** PATTYPAN
**5** [French *escalope*, probably from Middle French, shell] **:** a thin slice of boneless meat (as veal)
²**scallop** (1737)
*transitive verb*
**1** [from the use of a scallop shell as a baking dish] **:** to bake in a sauce usually covered with seasoned bread or cracker crumbs ⟨*scalloped* potatoes⟩
**2 a :** to shape, cut, or finish in scallops **b :** to form scallops in
*intransitive verb*
**:** to gather or dredge scallops
**scal·lop·er** \-lə-pər\ *noun* (circa 1881)
**1 :** a person who dredges for or gathers scallops
**2 :** a boat equipped and used to dredge for scallops
**scal·lo·pi·ni** *or* **sca·lop·pi·ne** \ˌskä-lə-'pē-nē, ˌska-\ *noun* [Italian *scaloppine*, ultimately from French *escalope* thin slice of meat, probably from Middle French, shell] (1946)
**:** thin slices of meat (as veal) sautéed or coated with flour and fried
**scal·ly·wag** variant of SCALAWAG
**sca·lo·gram** \'skā-lə-ˌgram\ *noun* [⁶*scale* + *-o-* + *-gram*] (1944)
**:** an arrangement of items (as problems on a test or features of speech) in ascending order so that the presence or accomplishment of an item at one level implies the presence of or the capability to accomplish items at all lower levels
¹**scalp** \'skalp\ *noun* [Middle English, of Scandinavian origin; akin to Old Norse *skālpr* sheath; akin to Middle Dutch *schelpe* shell] (14th century)
**1 a :** the part of the integument of the human head usually covered with hair in both sexes **b :** the part of an animal (as a wolf or fox) corresponding to the human scalp
**2 a :** a part of the human scalp with attached hair cut or torn from an enemy as a token of victory (as by Indian warriors of North America) **b :** a trophy of victory or accomplishment
**3** *chiefly Scottish* **:** a projecting mass of bare ground or rock
²**scalp** (1676)
*transitive verb*
**1 a :** to deprive of the scalp **b :** to remove an upper part from
**2 :** to remove a desired constituent from and discard the rest
**3 :** to buy and sell so as to make small quick profits ⟨*scalp* stocks⟩ ⟨*scalp* grain⟩; *especially* **:** to resell at greatly increased prices ⟨*scalp* theater tickets⟩
*intransitive verb*
**1 :** to take scalps
**2 :** to profit by slight market fluctuations
— **scalp·er** *noun*
**scal·pel** \'skal-pəl *also* skal-'pel\ *noun* [Latin *scalpellus*, *scalpellum*, diminutive of *scalper*, *scalprum* chisel, knife, from *scalpere* to scratch, carve] (1742)
**:** a small straight thin-bladed knife used especially in surgery
**scalp lock** *noun* (1826)
**:** a long tuft of hair on the crown of the otherwise shaved head especially of a warrior of some American Indian tribes
**scaly** \'skā-lē\ *adjective* **scal·i·er; -est** (14th century)
**1 a :** covered with, composed of, or rich in scale or scales **b :** FLAKY
**2 :** of or relating to scaly animals
**3 :** DESPICABLE, POOR
**4 :** infested with scale insects ⟨*scaly* fruit⟩
— **scal·i·ness** *noun*
**scaly anteater** *noun* (1840)

**:** PANGOLIN
**scam** \'skam\ *noun* [origin unknown] (1963)
**:** a fraudulent or deceptive act or operation ⟨an insurance *scam*⟩
**scam·mo·ny** \'ska-mə-nē\ *noun, plural* **-nies** [Middle English *scamonie*, from Old English *scammoniam*, from Latin *scammonia*, from Greek *skammōnia*] (before 12th century)
**1 :** a twining convolvulus (*Convolvulus scammonia*) of Asia Minor with a large thick root
**2 a :** the dried root of scammony **b :** a cathartic resin obtained from scammony
¹**scamp** \'skamp\ *noun* [obsolete *scamp* to roam about idly] (1808)
**1 :** RASCAL, ROGUE
**2 :** an impish or playful young person
— **scamp·ish** \'skam-pish\ *adjective*
²**scamp** *transitive verb* [origin unknown] (1837)
**:** to perform or deal with in a hasty, neglectful, or imperfect manner
¹**scam·per** \'skam-pər\ *intransitive verb* **scam·pered; scam·per·ing** \-p(ə-)riŋ\ [probably from obsolete Dutch *schampen* to flee, from Middle French *escamper*, from Italian *scampare*, from (assumed) Vulgar Latin *excampare* to decamp, from Latin *ex-* + *campus* field] (1691)
**:** to run nimbly and usually playfully about
²**scamper** *noun* (1697)
**:** a playful or hurried run or movement
**scam·pi** \'skam-pē, 'skäm-\ *noun, plural* **scampi** [Italian, plural of *scampo*, a European lobster] (1925)
**:** SHRIMP; *especially* **:** large shrimp prepared with a garlic-flavored sauce
¹**scan** \'skan\ *verb* **scanned; scan·ning** [Middle English *scannen*, from Late Latin *scandere*, from Latin, to climb; akin to Middle Irish *sceinnid* he springs, Sanskrit *skandati* he leaps] (14th century)
*transitive verb*
**1 :** to read or mark so as to show metrical structure
**2 :** to examine by point-by-point observation or checking: **a :** to investigate thoroughly by checking point by point and often repeatedly ⟨a fire lookout *scanning* the hills with binoculars⟩ **b :** to glance from point to point of often hastily, casually, or in search of a particular item ⟨*scan* the want ads looking for a job⟩
**3 a :** to examine especially systematically with a sensing device (as a photometer or a beam of radiation) usually to obtain information **b :** to pass an electron beam over and convert (an image) into variations of electrical properties (as voltage) that convey information electronically **c :** to pass over in the formation of an image ⟨the electron beam *scans* the picture tube⟩
*intransitive verb*
**1 :** to scan verse
**2 :** to conform to a metrical pattern
**synonym** see SCRUTINIZE
— **scan·na·ble** \'ska-nə-bəl\ *adjective*
²**scan** *noun* (1706)
**1 :** the act or process of scanning
**2 :** a radar or television trace
**3 a :** a depiction (as a photograph) of the distribution of a radioactive material in something (as a bodily organ) **b :** an image of a bodily part produced (as by computer) by combining radiographic data obtained from several angles or sections
¹**scan·dal** \'skan-d³l\ *noun* [Middle English, from Late Latin *scandalum* stumbling block, offense, from Greek *skandalon* trap, stumbling block, offense; akin to Latin *scandere* to climb] (13th century)

\ə\ **abut** \ᵊ\ **kitten** \ər\ **further** \a\ **ash** \ā\ **ace**
\ä\ **mop, mar** \aù\ **out** \ch\ **chin** \e\ **bet** \ē\ **easy**
\g\ **go** \i\ **hit** \ī\ **ice** \j\ **job** \ŋ\ **sing** \ō\ **go**
\ò\ **law** \òi\ **boy** \th\ **thin** \t̷h\ **the** \ü\ **loot** \ù\ **foot**
\y\ **yet** \zh\ **vision** *see also* Guide to Pronunciation

**1 a :** discredit brought upon religion by unseemly conduct in a religious person **b :** conduct that causes or encourages a lapse of faith or of religious obedience in another
**2 :** loss of or damage to reputation caused by actual or apparent violation of morality or propriety **:** DISGRACE
**3 a :** a circumstance or action that offends propriety or established moral conceptions or disgraces those associated with it **b :** a person whose conduct offends propriety or morality
**4 :** malicious or defamatory gossip
**5 :** indignation, chagrin, or bewilderment brought about by a flagrant violation of morality, propriety, or religious opinion
***synonym*** see OFFENSE
²**scandal** *transitive verb* (1592)
**1** *obsolete* **:** DISGRACE
**2** *chiefly dialect* **:** DEFAME, SLANDER
**scan·dal·ise** *chiefly British variant of* SCANDALIZE
**scan·dal·ize** \'skan-də-ˌlīz\ *transitive verb* **-ized; -iz·ing** (1566)
**1 :** to speak falsely or maliciously of
**2** *archaic* **:** to bring into reproach
**3 :** to offend the moral sense of **:** SHOCK
**scan·dal·mon·ger** \'skan-dᵊl-ˌməŋ-gər, -ˌmän-\ *noun* (1721)
**:** a person who circulates scandal
— **scan·dal·mon·ger·ing** \-g(ə-)riŋ\ *noun*
**scan·dal·ous** \'skan-dᵊl-əs\ *adjective* (1603)
**1 :** LIBELOUS, DEFAMATORY
**2 :** offensive to propriety or morality **:** SHOCKING
— **scan·dal·ous·ly** *adverb*
— **scan·dal·ous·ness** *noun*
**scandal sheet** *noun* (1904)
**:** a newspaper or periodical dealing to a large extent in scandal and gossip
**scan·dent** \'skan-dənt\ *adjective* [Latin *scandent-, scandens,* present participle of *scandere* to climb — more at SCAN] (circa 1682)
**:** characterized by a climbing mode of growth ⟨*scandent* stems⟩ ⟨*scandent* vines⟩
**Scan·di·an** \'skan-dē-ən\ *adjective* [Latin *Scandia*] (1668)
**1 :** SCANDINAVIAN
**2 :** of or relating to the languages of Scandinavia
— **Scandian** *noun*
**Scan·di·na·vian** \ˌskan-də-'nā-vē-ən, -vyən\ *noun* (1766)
**1 :** the North Germanic languages
**2 a :** a native or inhabitant of Scandinavia **b :** a person of Scandinavian descent
— **Scandinavian** *adjective*
**scan·di·um** \'skan-dē-əm\ *noun* [New Latin, from Latin *Scandia,* ancient name of southern Scandinavian peninsula] (1879)
**:** a white metallic element found in association with rare earth elements — see ELEMENT table
**scan·ner** \'ska-nər\ *noun* (1557)
**:** one that scans: as **a :** a device for sensing recorded data **b :** a device (as a CAT scanner) used for scanning something (as the human body)
**scanning electron microscope** *noun* (1953)
**:** an electron microscope in which a beam of focused electrons moves across the object with the secondary electrons produced by the object and the electrons scattered by the object being collected to form a three-dimensional image on a cathode-ray tube — called also *scanning microscope*
— **scanning electron microscopy** *noun*
**scanning tunneling microscope** *noun* (1983)
**:** a microscope that makes use of the phenomenon of electron tunneling to map the positions of individual atoms in a surface or to move atoms around on a surface
— **scanning tunneling microscopy** *noun*

**scan·sion** \'skan(t)-shən\ *noun* [Late Latin *scansion-, scansio,* from Latin, act of climbing, from *scandere*] (1671)
**:** the analysis of verse to show its meter
¹**scant** \'skant\ *adjective* [Middle English, from Old Norse *skamt,* neuter of *skammr* short] (14th century)
**1** *dialect* **a :** excessively frugal **b :** not prodigal **:** CHARY
**2 a :** barely or scarcely sufficient; *especially* **:** not quite coming up to a stated measure **b :** lacking in amplitude or quantity
**3 :** having a small or insufficient supply ⟨he's fat, and *scant* of breath —Shakespeare⟩
***synonym*** see MEAGER
— **scant·ly** *adverb*
— **scant·ness** *noun*
²**scant** *adverb* (15th century)
*dialect* **:** SCARCELY, HARDLY
³**scant** *transitive verb* (circa 1580)
**1 :** to provide an incomplete supply of
**2 :** to make small, narrow, or meager
**3 :** to give scant attention to **:** SLIGHT
**4 :** to provide with a meager or inadequate portion or supply **:** STINT
**scant·ies** \'skan-tēz\ *noun plural* [blend of ¹*scant* and *panties*] (1929)
**:** abbreviated panties for women
**scant·ling** \'skant-liŋ, -lən\ *noun* [alteration of Middle English *scantilon,* literally, mason's or carpenter's gauge, from Old North French *escantillon*] (1555)
**1 a :** the dimensions of timber and stone used in building **b :** the dimensions of a frame or strake used in shipbuilding
**2 :** a small quantity, amount, or proportion **:** MODICUM
**3 :** a small piece of lumber (as an upright piece in house framing)
**scanty** \'skan-tē\ *adjective* **scant·i·er; -est** [English dialect *scant* scanty supply, from Middle English, from Old Norse *skamt,* from neuter of *skammr* short] (1660)
**:** limited or less than sufficient in degree, quantity, or extent
***synonym*** see MEAGER
— **scant·i·ly** \'skan-tᵊl-ē\ *adverb*
— **scant·i·ness** \'skan-tē-nəs\ *noun*
¹**scape** \'skāp\ *verb* **scaped; scap·ing** [Middle English, short for *escapen*] (13th century)
**:** ESCAPE
²**scape** *noun* [Latin *scapus* shaft, stalk — more at SHAFT] (1601)
**1 :** a peduncle arising at or beneath the surface of the ground in an acaulescent plant (as the tulip); *broadly* **:** a flower stalk
**2 :** the shaft of an animal part (as an antenna or feather)
³**scape** *noun* [*landscape*] (1773)
**:** a view or picture of a scene — usually used in combination ⟨city*scape*⟩
***word history*** see LANDSCAPE
¹**scape·goat** \'skāp-ˌgōt\ *noun* [¹*scape;* intended as translation of Hebrew *'azāzēl* (probably name of a demon), as if *'ēz 'ōzēl* goat that departs—Leviticus 16:8 (Authorized Version)] (1530)
**1 :** a goat upon whose head are symbolically placed the sins of the people after which he is sent into the wilderness in the biblical ceremony for Yom Kippur
**2 a :** one that bears the blame for others **b :** one that is the object of irrational hostility ◆
²**scapegoat** *transitive verb* (1943)
**:** to make a scapegoat of
— **scape·goat·ism** \-ˌgō-ˌti-zəm\ *noun*
**scape·grace** \'skāp-ˌgrās\ *noun* [¹*scape*] (1809)
**:** an incorrigible rascal
**scaph·oid** \'ska-ˌfȯid\ *noun* [New Latin *scaphoides,* from Greek *skaphoeidēs,* from *skaphos* boat] (1846)
**:** the bone of the thumb side of the carpus that is the largest in the proximal row; *also* **:** the navicular bone of the tarsus

— **scaphoid** *adjective*
**scap·o·lite** \'ska-pə-ˌlīt\ *noun* [French, from Latin *scapus* shaft + French *-o-* + *-lite;* from the prismatic shape of its crystals] (1802)
**:** any of a group of minerals that are essentially complex silicates of aluminum, calcium, and sodium and that include some used as semiprecious stones
**sca·pose** \'skā-ˌpōs\ *adjective* (circa 1903)
**:** bearing, resembling, or consisting of a scape ⟨the terminal *scapose* flowers of a pyrola⟩
**scap·u·la** \'ska-pyə-lə\ *noun, plural* **-lae** \-ˌlē, -ˌlī\ *or* **-las** [New Latin, from Latin, shoulder blade, shoulder] (1578)
**:** either of a pair of large triangular bones lying one in each dorsal lateral part of the thorax, being the principal bone of the corresponding half of the shoulder girdle, and articulating with the corresponding clavicle or coracoid — called also *shoulder blade*
¹**scap·u·lar** \-lər\ *noun* [Middle English *scapulare,* from Late Latin, from Latin *scapula* shoulder] (15th century)
**1 a :** a long wide band of cloth with an opening for the head worn front and back over the shoulders as part of a monastic habit **b :** a pair of small cloth squares joined by shoulder tapes and worn under the clothing on the breast and back as a sacramental and often also as a badge of a third order or confraternity
**2 a :** SCAPULA **b :** one of the feathers covering the base of a bird's wing — see BIRD illustration
²**scapular** *adjective* [New Latin *scapularis,* from *scapula*] (1713)
**:** of or relating to the shoulder, the scapula, or scapulars
**scapular medal** *noun* (1912)
**:** a medal worn in place of a sacramental scapular
¹**scar** \'skär\ *noun* [Middle English *skere,* from Old Norse *sker* skerry; probably akin to Old Norse *skera* to cut — more at SHEAR] (14th century)
**1 :** an isolated or protruding rock
**2 :** a steep rocky eminence **:** a bare place on the side of a mountain
²**scar** *noun* [Middle English *escare, scar,* from Middle French *escare* scab, from Late Latin *eschara,* from Greek, hearth, brazier, scab] (14th century)
**1 :** a mark left (as in the skin) by the healing of injured tissue

◇ **WORD HISTORY**
**scapegoat** An ancient Hebrew custom called for the high priest on Yom Kippur, the Jewish Day of Atonement, to take two goats, one to be sacrificed to the Lord, the other to carry the sins of the people away into the desert. After the Lord's goat had been sacrificed, the priest confessed the sins of the people over the head of the live goat, which was then released "to Azazel." Modern commentators have usually interpreted Azazel as the name of a demon living in the desert, but the name was interpreted by ancient Biblical translators as referring to the goat itself, and hence being a form of the Hebrew phrase *'ez 'ōzēl,* which means "goat that departs." In the Greek translation of the passage referring to Azazel's goat, the goat became *tragos apopompaios* "goat sent out," and in the Latin Vulgate the animal became *caper emissarius* "emissary goat." Perpetuating the tradition, William Tyndale in his 1530 English translation of the Pentateuch rendered the Latin as *scapegoat,* that is, "escape goat." Although the goat for Azazel did in fact escape sacrifice, he bore the heavy burden of the people's sins. It is for this reason that we call anyone who bears the blame for others' transgressions or mistakes a *scapegoat.*

**2 a :** a mark left on a stem or branch by a fallen leaf or harvested fruit **b :** CICATRIX 2
**3 :** a mark or indentation resulting from damage or wear
**4 :** a lasting moral or emotional injury ⟨one of his men had been killed . . . in a manner that left a *scar* upon his mind —H. G. Wells⟩
— **scar·less** \-ləs\ *adjective*
³**scar** *verb* **scarred; scar·ring** (1555)
*transitive verb*
**1 :** to mark with a scar
**2 :** to do lasting injury to
*intransitive verb*
**1 :** to form a scar
**2 :** to become scarred
**scar·ab** \'skar-əb\ *noun* [Middle French *scarabee*, from Latin *scarabaeus*] (1579)
**1 :** any of a family (Scarabaeidae) of stout-bodied beetles (as a dung beetle) with lamellate or flabellate antennae
**2 :** a stone or faience beetle used in ancient Egypt as a talisman, ornament, and a symbol of resurrection
**scar·a·bae·us** \,skar-ə-'bē-əs\ *noun* [Latin] (1664)
**:** SCARAB 2
**scar·a·mouch** *or* **scar·a·mouche** \'skar-ə-,müsh, -,müch, -,maůch\ *noun* [French *Scaramouche*, from Italian *Scaramuccia*, from *scaramuccia* skirmish] (1662)
**1** *capitalized* **:** a stock character in the Italian commedia dell'arte that burlesques the Spanish don and is characterized by boastfulness and cowardliness
**2 a :** a cowardly buffoon **b :** RASCAL, SCAMP
¹**scarce** \'skers, 'skars\ *adjective* **scarc·er; scarc·est** [Middle English *scars*, from Old North French *escars*, from (assumed) Vulgar Latin *excarpsus*, literally, plucked out, past participle of Latin *excerpere* to pluck out — more at EXCERPT] (14th century)
**1 :** deficient in quantity or number compared with the demand **:** not plentiful or abundant
**2 :** intentionally absent ⟨made himself *scarce* at inspection time⟩
*synonym* see INFREQUENT
— **scarce·ness** *noun*
²**scarce** *adverb* (15th century)
**:** SCARCELY, HARDLY
**scarce·ly** *adverb* (14th century)
**1 a :** by a narrow margin **:** only just ⟨had *scarcely* rung the bell when the door flew open —Agnes S. Turnbull⟩ **b :** almost not ⟨could *scarcely* see for the fog⟩
**2 a :** certainly not ⟨could *scarcely* interfere⟩ **b :** probably not ⟨there could *scarcely* have been found a leader better equipped —V. L. Parrington⟩
**scar·ci·ty** \'sker-sə-tē, 'skar-, -stē\ *noun, plural* **-ties** (14th century)
**:** the quality or state of being scarce; *especially* **:** want of provisions for the support of life
¹**scare** \'sker, 'skar\ *verb* **scared; scar·ing** [Middle English *skerren*, from Old Norse *skirra*, from *skjarr* shy, timid] (13th century)
*transitive verb*
**:** to frighten especially suddenly **:** ALARM
*intransitive verb*
**:** to become scared
— **scar·er** *noun*
²**scare** *noun* (circa 1548)
**1 :** a sudden fright
**2 :** a widespread state of alarm **:** PANIC
— **scare** *adjective*
**scare·crow** \'sker-,krō, 'skar-\ *noun* (1573)
**1 a :** an object usually suggesting a human figure that is set up to frighten birds away from crops **b :** something frightening but harmless
**2 :** a skinny or ragged person
**scared** *adjective* (1590)
**:** thrown into or being in a state of fear, fright, or panic ⟨*scared* of snakes⟩ ⟨*scared* to go out⟩
**scaredy–cat** \'sker-dē-,kat, 'skar-\ *noun* [*scared* (past participle of *scare*) + ¹*-y* + *cat*] (1948)

**:** an unduly fearful person
**scare·head** \'sker-,hed, 'skar-\ *noun* (1887)
**:** a big, sensational, or alarming newspaper headline
**scare·mon·ger** \-,məŋ-gər, -,mäŋ-\ *noun* (1888)
**:** one inclined to raise or excite alarms especially needlessly
**scare up** *transitive verb* (1841)
**:** to find or get together with considerable labor or difficulty **:** scrape up ⟨managed to *scare up* the money⟩
¹**scarf** \'skärf\ *noun, plural* **scarfs** [Middle English *skarf*, probably of Scandinavian origin; akin to Old Norse *skarfr* scarf] (15th century)
**1 :** either of the chamfered or cutaway ends that fit together to form a scarf joint
**2 :** a joint made by chamfering, halving, or notching two pieces to correspond and lapping and bolting them — called also *scarf joint*

¹**scarf 2**

²**scarf** *also* **scarph** \'skärf\ *transitive verb* (1627)
**1 :** to unite by a scarf joint
**2 :** to form a scarf on
³**scarf** *noun, plural* **scarves** \'skärvz\ *or* **scarfs** [Old North French *escarpe* sash, sling] (1555)
**1 a :** a military or official sash usually indicative of rank **b** *archaic* **:** TIPPET 3
**2 :** a broad band of cloth worn about the shoulders, around the neck, or over the head
**3 :** RUNNER 6b
⁴**scarf** *transitive verb* (1598)
**1 :** to wrap, cover, or adorn with or as if with a scarf
**2 :** to wrap or throw on (a scarf or mantle) loosely
⁵**scarf** *transitive verb* [by alteration] (circa 1960)
**:** ³SCOFF 1 ⟨*scarfed* down my sandwich⟩
**scarf·pin** \'skärf-,pin\ *noun* (1859)
**:** TIEPIN
**scarf·skin** \'skärf-,skin\ *noun* [³*scarf*] (1615)
**:** EPIDERMIS; *especially* **:** that forming the cuticle of a nail
**scar·i·fi·ca·tion** \,skar-ə-fə-'kā-shən, ,sker-\ *noun* (14th century)
**1 :** the act or process of scarifying
**2 :** a mark or marks made by scarifying
¹**scar·i·fy** \'skar-ə-,fī, 'sker-\ *transitive verb* **-fied; -fy·ing** [Middle English *scarifien*, from Middle French *scarifier*, from Late Latin *scarificare*, alteration of Latin *scarifare*, from Greek *skariphasthai* to scratch an outline, sketch — more at SCRIBE] (14th century)
**1 :** to make scratches or small cuts in (as the skin) ⟨*scarify* an area for vaccination⟩
**2 :** to lacerate the feelings of
**3 :** to break up and loosen the surface of (as a field or road)
**4 :** to cut or soften the wall of (a hard seed) to hasten germination
— **scar·i·fi·er** \-,fī(-ə)r\ *noun*
²**scarify** *transitive verb* **-fied; -fy·ing** (1794)
**:** SCARE, FRIGHTEN
— **scar·i·fy·ing·ly** \-,fī-iŋ-lē\ *adverb*
**scar·i·ous** \'sker-ē-əs, 'skar-\ *adjective* [New Latin *scariosus*] (circa 1806)
**:** dry and membranous in texture ⟨a *scarious* bract⟩
**scar·la·ti·na** \,skär-lə-'tē-nə\ *noun* [New Latin, from Medieval Latin *scarlata* scarlet] (1803)
**:** SCARLET FEVER
— **scar·la·ti·nal** \-'tē-nᵊl\ *adjective*
¹**scar·let** \'skär-lət\ *noun* [Middle English *scarlat, scarlet*, from Old French or Medieval Latin; Old French *escarlate*, from Medieval

Latin *scarlata*, from Persian *saqalāt*, a kind of rich cloth] (13th century)
**1 :** scarlet cloth or clothes
**2 :** any of various bright reds
²**scarlet** *adjective* (14th century)
**1 :** of the color scarlet
**2 a :** grossly and glaringly offensive ⟨sinning in flagrant and *scarlet* fashion —G. W. Johnson⟩ **b** [from the use of the word in Isaiah 1:18 & Revelation 17:1–6 (Authorized Version)] **:** of, characterized by, or associated with sexual immorality ⟨a *scarlet* woman⟩
**scarlet fever** *noun* (1676)
**:** an acute contagious febrile disease caused by hemolytic streptococci (especially various strains of *Streptococcus pyogenes*) and characterized by inflammation of the nose, throat, and mouth, generalized toxemia, and a red rash
**scarlet letter** *noun* [from such a letter in the novel *The Scarlet Letter* (1850) by Nathaniel Hawthorne] (1850)
**:** a scarlet A worn as a punitive mark of adultery
**scarlet pimpernel** *noun* (1855)
**1 :** a common pimpernel (*Anagallis arvensis*) having scarlet, white, or purplish flowers that close in cloudy weather
**2** [*Scarlet Pimpernel*, assumed name of the hero of *The Scarlet Pimpernel* (1905), novel by Baroness Orczy] **:** a person who rescues others from mortal danger by smuggling them across a border
**scarlet runner** *noun* (1806)
**:** a tropical American high-climbing bean (*Phaseolus coccineus*) that has large bright red flowers and red-and-black seeds and is grown widely as an ornamental and as a food bean — called also *scarlet runner bean*
**scarlet sage** *noun* (circa 1890)
**:** a garden salvia (*Salvia splendens*) of Brazil with long racemes of intense typically scarlet flowers
**scarlet tanager** *noun* (1810)
**:** a common American tanager (*Piranga olivacea*) with the male having scarlet plumage and black wings during the breeding season and the female having chiefly olive plumage
**scarp** \'skärp\ *noun* [Italian *scarpa*] (1589)
**1 :** the inner side of a ditch below the parapet of a fortification
**2 a :** a line of cliffs produced by faulting or erosion — see FAULT illustration **b :** a low steep slope along a beach caused by wave erosion
— **scarped** *adjective*
**scar·per** \'skär-pər\ *intransitive verb* [probably ultimately from Italian *scappare*, from (assumed) Vulgar Latin *excappare* — more at ESCAPE] (circa 1846)
*British* **:** FLEE, RUN AWAY; *broadly* **:** LEAVE, DEPART
**scar·ry** \'skär-ē\ *adjective* [²*scar*] (1653)
**:** bearing marks of wounds **:** SCARRED
¹**scart** \'skärt\ *verb* [Middle English, alteration of *scratten* to scratch] (14th century)
*chiefly Scottish* **:** SCRATCH, SCRAPE
²**scart** *noun* (circa 1585)
*chiefly Scottish* **:** SCRATCH, MARK; *especially* **:** one made in writing
**scar tissue** *noun* (1875)
**:** the connective tissue forming a scar and composed chiefly of fibroblasts in recent scars and largely of dense collagenous fibers in old scars
**scary** \'sker-ē, 'skar-\ *adjective* **scar·i·er; -est** (1582)
**1 :** causing fright **:** ALARMING ⟨a *scary* story⟩
**2 :** easily scared **:** TIMID
**3 :** feeling alarm or fright **:** FRIGHTENED

— **scar·i·ly** \'sker-ə-lē, 'skar-\ *adverb*

**¹scat** \'skat\ *intransitive verb* **scat·ted; scat·ting** [*scat,* interjection used to drive away a cat] (1838)
**1 :** to go away quickly
**2 :** to move fast **:** SCOOT

**²scat** *noun* [perhaps from Greek *skat-, skōr* excrement — more at SCATOLOGY] (1927)
**:** an animal fecal dropping

**³scat** *noun* [origin unknown] (1929)
**:** jazz singing with nonsense syllables

**⁴scat** *intransitive verb* **scat·ted; scat·ting** (1935)
**:** to improvise nonsense syllables usually to an instrumental accompaniment **:** sing scat

**scat·back** \'skat-,bak\ *noun* [¹*scat* + *back*] (1945)
**:** an offensive back in football who is an especially fast and elusive ballcarrier

**¹scathe** \'skāth, 'skäth\ *noun* [Middle English *skathe,* from Old Norse *skathi;* akin to Old English *sceatha* injury, Greek *askēthēs* unharmed] (13th century)
**:** HARM, INJURY
— **scathe·less** \-ləs\ *adjective*

**²scathe** \'skäth\ *transitive verb* **scathed; scath·ing** (13th century)
**1 :** to do harm to; *specifically* **:** SCORCH, SEAR
**2 :** to assail with withering denunciation

**scath·ing** \'skā-thiŋ\ *adjective* (1794)
**:** bitterly severe ⟨a *scathing* condemnation⟩
*synonym* see CAUSTIC
— **scath·ing·ly** \-thiŋ-lē\ *adverb*

**sca·tol·o·gy** \ska-'tä-lə-jē, skə-\ *noun* [Greek *skat-, skōr* excrement; akin to Old English *scearn* dung, Latin mu*scerdae* mouse droppings] (1876)
**1 :** interest in or treatment of obscene matters especially in literature
**2 :** the biologically oriented study of excrement (as for taxonomic purposes or for the determination of diet)
— **scat·o·log·i·cal** \,ska-tᵊl-'ä-ji-kəl\ *adjective*

**scatt** \'skat\ *noun* [Middle English *scat,* from Old Norse *skattr;* akin to Old English *sceat* property, money, a small coin, Old Church Slavonic *skotŭ* domestic animal] (13th century)
*archaic* **:** TAX, TRIBUTE

**¹scat·ter** \'ska-tər\ *verb* [Middle English *scateren*] (14th century)
*transitive verb*
**1 a :** to cause to separate widely **b :** to cause to vanish
**2** *archaic* **:** to fling away heedlessly **:** SQUANDER
**3 :** to distribute irregularly
**4 :** to sow by casting in all directions **:** STREW
**5 a :** to reflect irregularly and diffusely **b :** to cause (a beam of radiation) to diffuse or disperse
**6 :** to divide into ineffectual small portions
*intransitive verb*
**1 :** to separate and go in various directions **:** DISPERSE
**2 :** to occur or fall irregularly or at random ☆
— **scat·ter·er** \-tər-ər\ *noun*

**²scatter** *noun* (1642)
**1 :** the act of scattering
**2 :** a small quantity or number irregularly distributed or strewn about **:** SCATTERING
**3 :** the state or extent of being scattered; *especially* **:** DISPERSION

**scat·ter·a·tion** \,ska-tə-'rā-shən\ *noun* (1776)
**1 :** the act or process of scattering **:** the state of being scattered
**2 :** the movement of people and industry away from the city; *also* **:** the resulting regional urbanization
**3 :** a policy of distributing funds and energies in too many ineffectively small units

**scat·ter·brain** \'ska-tər-,brān\ *noun* (1790)
**:** a giddy heedless person

**scat·ter·brained** \-,brānd\ *adjective* (1747)
**:** having the characteristics of a scatterbrain

**scatter diagram** *noun* (1925)
**:** a two-dimensional graph in rectangular coordinates consisting of points whose coordinates represent values of two variables under study

**scat·ter·good** \'ska-tər-,gùd\ *noun* (1577)
**:** a wasteful person **:** SPENDTHRIFT

**scat·ter·gram** \-,gram\ *noun* (1938)
**:** SCATTER DIAGRAM

**scat·ter·gun** \-,gən\ *noun or adjective* (1836)
**:** SHOTGUN

**¹scat·ter·ing** *noun* (14th century)
**1 :** an act or process in which something scatters or is scattered
**2 :** something scattered: as **a :** a small number or quantity interspersed here and there ⟨a *scattering* of visitors⟩ **b :** the random change in direction of the particles constituting a beam or wave front due to collision with particles of the medium traversed

**²scattering** *adjective* (15th century)
**1 :** going in various directions
**2 :** found or placed far apart and in no order
**3 :** divided among many or several ⟨*scattering* votes⟩
— **scat·ter·ing·ly** \'ska-tə-riŋ-lē\ *adverb*

**scatter rug** *noun* (1926)
**:** a rug of such a size that several can be used in a room

**scat·ter·shot** \'ska-tər-,shät\ *adjective* (1951)
**:** broadly and often randomly inclusive **:** SHOTGUN

**scat·ty** \'ska-tē\ *adjective* **scat·ti·er; -est** [probably from *scatter*brain + ¹-y] (1911)
*chiefly British* **:** CRAZY

**scaup** \'skȯp\ *noun, plural* **scaup** *or* **scaups** [short for *scaup duck; scaup* probably alteration of *scalp* bed of shellfish] (1797)
**:** either of two diving ducks (*Aythya affinis* or *A. marila*) with the male having a glossy purplish or greenish head and a black breast and tail

**scav·enge** \'ska-vənj, -vinj\ *verb* **scav·enged; scav·eng·ing** [back-formation from *scavenger*] (circa 1644)
*transitive verb*
**1 a** (1) **:** to remove (as dirt or refuse) from an area (2) **:** to clean away dirt or refuse from **:** CLEANSE ⟨*scavenge* a street⟩ **b :** to feed on (carrion or refuse)
**2 a :** to remove (burned gases) from the cylinder of an internal combustion engine after a working stroke **b :** to remove (as an undesirable constituent) from a substance or region by chemical or physical means **c :** to clean and purify (molten metal) by taking up foreign elements in chemical union
**3 :** to salvage from discarded or refuse material; *also* **:** to salvage usable material from
*intransitive verb*
**:** to work or act as a scavenger

**scav·en·ger** \'ska-vən-jər\ *noun* [alteration of earlier *scavager,* from Middle English *skawager* customs collector, from *skawage* customs, from Old North French *escauwage* inspection, from *escauwer* to inspect, of Germanic origin; akin to Old English *scēawian* to look at — more at SHOW] (1530)
**1** *chiefly British* **:** a person employed to remove dirt and refuse from streets
**2 :** one that scavenges: as **a :** a garbage collector **b :** a junk collector **c :** a chemically active substance acting to make innocuous or remove an undesirable substance
**3 :** an organism that feeds habitually on refuse or carrion

**scavenger hunt** *noun* (1936)
**:** a game in which players try to acquire without buying specified items within a time limit

**sce·na** \'shā-(,)nä\ *noun* [Italian, literally, scene, from Latin] (1819)

**:** an elaborate solo vocal composition that consists of a recitative usually followed by one or more aria sections

**sce·nar·io** \sə-'nar-ē-,ō, -'ner-\ *noun, plural* **-i·os** [Italian, from Latin *scaenarium* place for erecting stages, from *scaena* stage] (1878)
**1 a :** an outline or synopsis of a play; *especially* **:** a plot outline used by actors of the commedia dell'arte **b :** the libretto of an opera
**2 a :** SCREENPLAY **b :** SHOOTING SCRIPT
**3 :** a sequence of events especially when imagined; *especially* **:** an account or synopsis of a possible course of action or events ⟨his *scenario* for a settlement envisages . . . reunification —Selig Harrison⟩

**sce·nar·ist** \-'nar-ist, -'ner-\ *noun* (1920)
**:** a writer of scenarios

**scend** \'send\ *noun* [perhaps short for *ascend*] (circa 1883)
**1 :** the lift of a wave **:** SEND
**2 :** the upward movement of a pitching ship

**scene** \'sēn\ *noun* [Middle French, stage, from Latin *scena, scaena* stage, scene, probably from Etruscan, from Greek *skēnē* shelter, tent, building forming the background for a dramatic performance, stage; perhaps akin to Greek *skia* shadow — more at SHINE] (1540)
**1 :** one of the subdivisions of a play; as **a :** a division of an act presenting continuous action in one place **b :** a single situation or unit of dialogue in a play ⟨the love *scene*⟩ **c :** a motion-picture or television episode or sequence
**2 a :** a stage setting **b :** a real or imaginary prospect suggesting a stage setting ⟨a sylvan *scene*⟩
**3 :** the place of an occurrence or action **:** LOCALE ⟨*scene* of the crime⟩
**4 :** an exhibition of anger or indecorous behavior ⟨make a *scene*⟩
**5 a :** sphere of activity ⟨the drug *scene*⟩ **b :** SITUATION ⟨a bad *scene*⟩
— **behind the scenes 1 :** out of public view; *also* **:** in secret **2 :** in a position to see the hidden workings ⟨taken *behind the scenes* and told just how in fact the actual government . . . has operated —William Clark⟩

**scen·ery** \'sē-nə-rē, 'sēn-rē\ *noun, plural* **-er·ies** (1770)
**1 :** the painted scenes or hangings and accessories used on a theater stage
**2 :** a picturesque view or landscape

**scene·shift·er** \'sēn-,shif-tər\ *noun* (1752)
**:** a worker who moves the scenes in a theater

**scene–steal·er** \-,stē-lər\ *noun* (1949)
**:** an actor who attracts attention when another is intended to be the center of attention

**sce·nic** \'sē-nik *also* 'se-\ *also* **sce·ni·cal** \-ni-kəl\ *adjective* (1623)
**1 :** of or relating to the stage, a stage setting, or stage representation
**2 :** of or relating to natural scenery ⟨a *scenic* view⟩
**3 :** representing graphically an action, event, or episode ⟨a *scenic* bas-relief⟩
— **sce·ni·cal·ly** \-ni-k(ə-)lē\ *adverb*

**scenic railway** *noun* (1894)
*chiefly British* **:** a miniature railway (as in an amusement park) with artificial scenery along the way

---

☆ **SYNONYMS**
**Scatter, disperse, dissipate, dispel** mean to cause to separate or break up. SCATTER implies a force that drives parts or units irregularly in many directions (the bowling ball *scattered* the pins). DISPERSE implies a wider separation and a complete breaking up of a mass or group ⟨police *dispersed* the crowd⟩. DISSIPATE stresses complete disintegration or dissolution and final disappearance (the fog was *dissipated* by the morning sun). DISPEL stresses a driving away or getting rid of as if by scattering ⟨an authoritative statement that *dispelled* all doubt⟩.

**sce·nog·ra·phy** \sē-'nä-grə-fē\ *noun* [Greek *skēnographia* painting of scenery, from *skēnē* + *-graphia* -graphy] (1645)
: the art of perspective representation especially as applied to the painting of stage scenery (as by the ancient Greeks)
— **sce·nog·ra·pher** \-grə-fər\ *noun*
— **sce·no·graph·ic** \ˌsē-nə-'gra-fik\ *adjective*

**¹scent** \'sent\ *noun* [Middle English *sent*, from *senten*] (14th century)
**1** : effluvia from a substance that affect the sense of smell: as **a** : an odor left by an animal on a surface passed over **b** : a characteristic or particular odor; *especially* : one that is agreeable
**2 a** : power of smelling : sense of smell ⟨a keen *scent*⟩ **b** : power of detection : NOSE ⟨a *scent* for heresy⟩
**3** : a course of pursuit or discovery ⟨throw one off the *scent*⟩
**4** : INKLING, INTIMATION ⟨a *scent* of trouble⟩
**5** : PERFUME 2
**6** : bits of paper dropped in the game of hare and hounds
**7** : a mixture prepared for use as a lure in hunting or fishing
**synonym** see FRAGRANCE, SMELL
— **scent·less** \'sent-ləs\ *adjective*

**²scent** *verb* [Middle English *senten*, from Middle French *sentir* to feel, smell, from Latin *sentire* to perceive, feel — more at SENSE] (15th century)
*transitive verb*
**1 a** : to perceive by the olfactory organs : SMELL **b** : to get or have an inkling of ⟨*scent* trouble⟩
**2** : to imbue or fill with odor ⟨*scented* the air with perfume⟩
*intransitive verb*
**1** : to yield an odor of some specified kind ⟨this *scents* of sulfur⟩; *also* : to bear indication or suggestions
**2** : to use the nose in seeking or tracking prey

**scent·ed** *adjective* (1666)
: having scent: as **a** : having the sense of smell **b** : having a perfumed smell **c** : having or exhaling an odor

**¹scep·ter** \'sep-tər\ *noun* [Middle English *sceptre*, from Middle French *ceptre*, from Latin *sceptrum*, from Greek *skēptron* staff, scepter, from *skēptesthai* to prop oneself — more at SHAFT] (14th century)
**1** : a staff or baton borne by a sovereign as an emblem of authority
**2** : royal or imperial authority : SOVEREIGNTY

**²scepter** *transitive verb* **scep·tered; scep·ter·ing** \-t(ə-)riŋ\ (1526)
: to invest with the scepter in token of royal authority

**scep·tered** \'sep-tərd\ *adjective* (1513)
**1** : invested with a scepter or sovereign authority
**2** : of or relating to a sovereign or to royalty

**scep·tic, scep·ti·cal, scep·ti·cism** *variant of* SKEPTIC, SKEPTICAL, SKEPTICISM

**sceptre** *British variant of* SCEPTER

**scha·den·freu·de** \'shä-d°n-ˌfrȯi-də\ *noun*, *often capitalized* [German, from *Schaden* damage + *Freude* joy] (1895)
: enjoyment obtained from the troubles of others

**¹sched·ule** \'ske-(ˌ)jü(ə)l, -jəl, *Canadian also* 'she-, *British usually* 'she-(ˌ)dyü(ə)l\ *noun* [alteration of Middle English *cedule*, from Middle French, slip of paper, note, from Late Latin *schedula* slip of paper, diminutive of (assumed) Latin *scheda* strip of papyrus, probably back-formation from Latin *schedium* impromptu speech, from Greek *schedion*, from neuter of *schedios* casual; akin to Greek *schedon* near at hand, *echein* to seize, have] (1560)

**1 a** *obsolete* : a written document **b** : a statement of supplementary details appended to a legal or legislative document
**2** : a written or printed list, catalog, or inventory; *also* : TIMETABLE 1
**3** : PROGRAM; *especially* : a procedural plan that indicates the time and sequence of each operation ⟨finished on *schedule*⟩
**4** : a body of items to be dealt with : AGENDA
**5** : a governmental list of drugs all subject to the same legal restrictions and controls ◼

**²schedule** *transitive verb* **sched·uled; sched·ul·ing** (1862)
**1 a** : to place in a schedule **b** : to make a schedule of
**2** : to appoint, assign, or designate for a fixed time
— **sched·ul·er** *noun*

**schee·lite** \'shā-ˌlīt\ *noun* [German *Scheelit*, from Karl W. *Scheele* (died 1786) Swedish chemist] (circa 1837)
: a mineral consisting of the tungstate of calcium that is a source of tungsten and its compounds

**Sche·her·a·zade** \shə-ˌher-ə-'zäd; -'zä-də, -dē\ *noun* [German *Scheherazade*, from Persian *Shīrazād*]
: the fictional wife of an oriental king and the narrator of the tales in the *Arabian Nights' Entertainments*

**sche·ma** \'skē-mə\ *noun*, *plural* **sche·ma·ta** \-mə-tə\ *also* **schemas** [Greek *schēmat-*, *schēma*] (circa 1890)
**1** : a diagrammatic presentation; *broadly* : a structured framework or plan : OUTLINE
**2** : a mental codification of experience that includes a particular organized way of perceiving cognitively and responding to a complex situation or set of stimuli

**¹sche·mat·ic** \ski-'ma-tik\ *adjective* [New Latin *schematicus*, from Greek *schēmat-*, *schēma*] (1701)
: of or relating to a scheme or schema
— **sche·mat·i·cal·ly** \-ti-k(ə-)lē\ *adverb*

**²schematic** *noun* (1929)
: a schematic drawing or diagram

**sche·ma·tism** \'skē-mə-ˌti-zəm\ *noun* (1660)
: the disposition of constituents in a pattern or according to a scheme : DESIGN; *also* : a particular systematic disposition of parts

**sche·ma·tize** \'skē-mə-ˌtīz\ *transitive verb* **-tized; -tiz·ing** [Greek *schēmatizein*, from *schēmat-*, *schēma*] (1828)
**1** : to form or to form into a scheme or systematic arrangement
**2** : to express or depict schematically
— **sche·ma·ti·za·tion** \ˌskē-mə-tə-'zā-shən\ *noun*

**¹scheme** \'skēm\ *noun* [Latin *schemat-*, *schema* arrangement, figure, from Greek *schēmat-*, *schēma*, from *echein* to have, hold, be in (such) a condition; akin to Old English *sige* victory, Sanskrit *sahate* he prevails] (1610)
**1 a** *archaic* (1) : a mathematical or astronomical diagram (2) : a representation of the astrological aspects of the planets at a particular time **b** : a graphic sketch or outline
**2** : a concise statement or table : EPITOME
**3** : a plan or program of action; *especially* : a crafty or secret one
**4** : a systematic or organized framework : DESIGN
**synonym** see PLAN

**²scheme** *verb* **schemed; schem·ing** (1767)
*transitive verb*
: to form a scheme for
*intransitive verb*
: to form plans; *also* : PLOT, INTRIGUE
— **schem·er** *noun*

**schem·ing** *adjective* (circa 1828)
: given to forming schemes; *especially* : shrewdly devious and intriguing

**¹scher·zan·do** \skert-'sän-(ˌ)dō\ *adverb or*
*adjective* [Italian, from verbal of *scherzare* to joke, of Germanic origin; akin to Middle High German *scherzen* to leap for joy, joke; perhaps akin to Greek *skairein* to gambol] (circa 1811)
: in sportive manner : PLAYFULLY — used as a direction in music indicating style and tempo ⟨allegretto *scherzando*⟩

**²scherzando** *noun*, *plural* **-dos** (circa 1876)
: a passage or movement in scherzando style

**scher·zo** \'skert-(ˌ)sō\ *noun*, *plural* **scher·zos** *or* **scher·zi** \-(ˌ)sē\ [Italian, literally, joke, from *scherzare*] (1852)
: a sprightly humorous instrumental musical composition or movement commonly in quick triple time

**Schick test** \'shik-\ *noun* [Béla *Schick*] (1916)
: a serological test for susceptibility to diphtheria by cutaneous injection of a diluted diphtheria toxin that causes an area of reddening and induration in susceptible individuals

**Schiff's reagent** \'shifs-\ *noun* [Hugo *Schiff* (died 1915) German chemist] (1897)
: a solution of fuchsine decolorized by treatment with sulfur dioxide that gives a useful test for aldehydes because they restore the dye's color — called also *Schiff reagent* \'shif-\; compare FEULGEN REACTION

**schil·ler** \'shi-lər\ *noun* [German] (1885)
: a bronzy iridescent luster (as of a mineral)

**schil·ling** \'shi-liŋ\ *noun* [German, from Old High German *skilling*, a gold coin — more at SHILLING] (1753)
— see MONEY table

**schip·per·ke** \'ski-pər-kē, 'shi-, -kə; -pərk\ *noun* [Flemish, diminutive of *schipper* skipper; from its use as a watchdog on boats — more at SKIPPER] (1887)
: any of a Belgian breed of small stocky black dogs with foxy head and heavy coat

**schism** \'si-zəm, 'ski- *also* 'shi-; *among clergy usually* 'si-\ *noun* [Middle English *scisme*, from Middle French *cisme*, from Late Latin *schismat-*, *schisma*, from Greek, cleft, division, from *schizein* to split — more at SHED] (14th century)
**1** : DIVISION, SEPARATION; *also* : DISCORD, DISHARMONY

schipperke

---

□ USAGE
**schedule** British pronunciation maintains an aura of prestige in American ears, and thus some critics insist that the American habit of saying *sch* like \sk\ and not \sh\ in *schedule* is incorrect. In Middle English the word began with a simple \s\, spelled *c*. Both the \sk\ and \sh\ sounds in *schedule* are innovations. In eighteenth-century Britain the *sch* was pronounced either as \s\ or \sk\; the \sh\ variant is a later development modeled along the lines of French pronunciation. Noah Webster advised Americans to pronounced the *sch* as \sk\ in his 1828 dictionary. The \sk\ variant is closer in spirit to the Latin and Greek ancestors of *schedule*, and though it does not have the allure of the distinctive but quirky Received Pronunciation, it is universal in educated American speech.

---

\ə\ **abut** \ə\ **kitten** \ər\ **further** \a\ **ash** \ā\ **ace**
\ä\ **mop, mar** \aȯ\ **out** \ch\ **chin** \e\ **bet** \ē\ **easy**
\g\ **go** \i\ **hit** \ī\ **ice** \j\ **job** \ŋ\ **sing** \ō\ **go**
\ȯ\ **law** \ȯi\ **boy** \th\ **thin** \t͟h\ **the** \ü\ **loot** \u̇\ **foot**
\y\ **yet** \zh\ **vision** *see also* Guide to Pronunciation

**2 a :** formal division in or separation from a church or religious body **b :** the offense of promoting schism ◻

¹**schis·mat·ic** \siz-'ma-tik, ski-\ *noun* (14th century)

**:** one who creates or takes part in schism

²**schismatic** *also* **schis·mat·i·cal** \-ti-kəl\ *adjective* (15th century)

**:** of, relating to, or guilty of schism

— **schis·mat·i·cal·ly** \-ti-k(ə-)lē\ *adverb*

**schis·ma·tize** \'siz-mə-ˌtīz, 'skiz-\ *verb* **-tized; -tiz·ing** (1601)
*intransitive verb*

**:** to take part in schism; *especially* **:** to make a breach of union (as in the church)
*transitive verb*

**:** to induce into schism

**schist** \'shist\ *noun* [French *schiste,* from Latin *schistos* (*lapis*), literally, fissile stone, from Greek *schistos* that may be split, from *schizein*] (circa 1782)

**:** a metamorphic crystalline rock that has a closely foliated structure and can be split along approximately parallel planes

**schis·tose** \'shis-ˌtōs\ *adjective* (1794)

**:** of or relating to schist **:** having the character or structure of a schist

— **schis·tos·i·ty** \shis-'tä-sə-tē\ *noun*

**schis·to·some** \'shis-tə-ˌsōm\ *noun* [New Latin *Schistosoma,* from Greek *schistos* + *sōma* body] (1905)

**:** any of a genus (*Schistosoma*) of elongated trematode worms with the sexes separate that parasitize the blood vessels of birds and mammals and cause a destructive human schistosomiasis; *broadly* **:** a worm of the family (Schistosomatidae) that includes this genus

— **schis·to·som·al** \ˌshis-tə-'sō-məl\ *adjective*

— **schistosome** *adjective*

**schis·to·so·mi·a·sis** \ˌshis-tə-sō-'mī-ə-səs\ *noun, plural* **-a·ses** \-ˌsēz\ [New Latin, from *Schistosoma*] (1906)

**:** infestation with or disease caused by schistosomes; *specifically* **:** a severe endemic disease of humans in much of Asia, Africa, and South America marked especially by blood loss and tissue damage

**schiz-** *or* **schizo-** *combining form* [New Latin, from Greek *schizo-,* from *schizein* to split — more at SHED]

**1 :** split **:** cleft ⟨*schizo*carp⟩

**2 :** characterized by or involving cleavage ⟨*schizo*gony⟩

**3 :** schizophrenia ⟨*schiz*oid⟩

**schizo** \'skit-(ˌ)sō\ *noun, plural* **schiz·os** (1945)

**:** a schizophrenic individual

**schizo·carp** \'ski-zə-ˌkärp, 'skit-sə-\ *noun* [International Scientific Vocabulary] (1870)

**:** a dry compound fruit that splits at maturity into several indehiscent one-seeded carpels

**schi·zog·o·ny** \ski-'zä-gə-nē, skit-'sä-\ *noun* [New Latin *schizogonia,* from *schiz-* + Latin *-gonia* -gony] (1887)

**:** asexual reproduction by multiple segmentation characteristic of sporozoans (as the malaria parasite)

— **schizo·gon·ic** \ˌski-zə-'gä-nik, ˌskit-sə-\ *or* **schi·zog·o·nous** \ski-'zä-gə-nəs, skit-'sä-gə-\ *adjective*

**schiz·oid** \'skit-ˌsȯid\ *adjective* [International Scientific Vocabulary] (1924)

**:** characterized by, resulting from, tending toward, or suggestive of schizophrenia

— **schizoid** *noun*

**schiz·ont** \'ski-ˌzänt, 'skit-ˌsänt\ *noun* [International Scientific Vocabulary] (1900)

**:** a multinucleate sporozoan that reproduces by schizogony

**schizo·phrene** \'skit-sə-ˌfrēn\ *noun* [International Scientific Vocabulary, probably back-formation from New Latin *schizophrenia*] (1925)

**:** one affected with schizophrenia **:** SCHIZO-PHRENIC

**schizo·phre·nia** \ˌskit-sə-'frē-nē-ə\ *noun* [New Latin] (1912)

**1 :** a psychotic disorder characterized by loss of contact with the environment, by noticeable deterioration in the level of functioning in everyday life, and by disintegration of personality expressed as disorder of feeling, thought (as in hallucinations and delusions), and conduct — called also *dementia praecox*

**2 :** contradictory or antagonistic qualities or attitudes ⟨both parties . . . have exhibited *schizophrenia* over the desired outcome —Elizabeth Drew⟩

— **schizo·phren·ic** \-'fre-nik\ *adjective or noun*

— **schizo·phren·i·cal·ly** \-ni-k(ə-)lē\ *adverb*

**schizy** *or* **schiz·zy** \'skit-sē\ *adjective* [by shortening & alteration] (1927)

**:** SCHIZOID

**schle·miel** \shlə-'mē(ə)l\ *noun* [Yiddish *shlemil*] (1892)

**:** an unlucky bungler **:** CHUMP

**schlepp** *or* **schlep** \'shlep\ *verb* [Yiddish *shlepn,* from Middle High German *sleppen,* from Middle Low German *slēpen*] (1922)
*transitive verb*

**:** DRAG, HAUL
*intransitive verb*

**:** to proceed or move slowly, tediously, or awkwardly

**schlie·ren** \'shlir-ən\ *noun plural* [German] (1898)

**1 :** small masses or streaks in an igneous rock that differ in composition from the main body

**2 :** regions of varying refraction in a transparent medium often caused by pressure or temperature differences and detectable especially by photographing the passage of a beam of light

— **schlie·ric** \'shlir-ik\ *adjective*

**schlock** \'shläk\ *also* **schlocky** \'shlä-kē\ *adjective* [perhaps from Yiddish *shlak* evil, nuisance, literally, blow, from Middle High German *slag, slac,* from Old High German *slag,* from *slahan* to strike — more at SLAY] (1915)

**:** of low quality or value

— **schlock** *noun*

**schm-** *or* **shm-** \shm\ *prefix* [Yiddish *shm-*]

— used to form a rhyming term of derision by replacing the initial consonant or consonant cluster of a word or by preceding the initial vowel ⟨fancy, *schm*ancy, I prefer plain⟩ ⟨Godfather-*shm*odfather—enough already —Judith Crist⟩

**schmaltz** *also* **schmalz** \'shmȯlts, 'shmälts\ *noun* [Yiddish *shmalts,* literally, rendered fat, from Middle High German *smalz;* akin to Old High German *smelzan* to melt — more at SMELT] (1935)

**1 :** sentimental or florid music or art

**2 :** SENTIMENTALITY

— **schmaltzy** \'shmȯlt-sē, 'shmält-\ *adjective*

**schmear** *or* **schmeer** \'shmir\ *noun* [Yiddish *shmir* smear; akin to Old High German *smero* grease — more at SMEAR] (1965)

**:** an aggregate of related things ⟨the whole *schmear*⟩

**Schmidt camera** \'shmit-\ *noun* [B. *Schmidt* (died 1935) German optical scientist] (1936)

**:** a photographic telescope with specialized optics that correct for spherical aberration and coma — called also *Schmidt telescope*

**schmo** *or* **schmoe** \'shmō\ *noun, plural* **schmoes** [origin unknown] (1947)

*slang* **:** JERK 4

**schmooze** *or* **shmooze** \'shmüz\ *intransitive verb* [Yiddish *shmuesn,* from *schmues* talk, from Hebrew *shĕmu'ōth* news, rumor] (1897)

**:** to converse informally **:** CHAT

**schmuck** \'shmək\ *noun* [Yiddish *shmok,* literally, penis] (1892)

*slang* **:** JERK 4

**schnapps** \'shnaps\ *noun, plural* **schnapps** [German *Schnaps,* literally, dram of liquor, from Low German *snaps* dram, mouthful, from *snappen* to snap] (1818)

**:** any of various liquors of high alcoholic content; *especially* **:** strong Holland gin

**schnau·zer** \'shnaut-sər, 'shnau-zər\ *noun* [German, from *Schnauze* snout — more at SNOUT] (1923)

**:** a dog of any of three breeds that originated in Germany and are characterized by a wiry coat, long head, small ears, heavy eyebrows, and long hair on the muzzle: **a :** STANDARD SCHNAUZER **b :** GIANT SCHNAUZER **c :** MINIATURE SCHNAUZER

**schnit·zel** \'shnit-səl\ *noun* [German, literally, shaving, chip, diminutive of *Schnitz* slice, from Middle High German *snitz;* akin to Old High German *snīdan* to cut, Old English *snīthan,* and perhaps to Czech *snět* bough] (1854)

**:** a seasoned and garnished veal cutlet

**schnook** \'shnuk\ *noun* [origin unknown] (1940)

*slang* **:** a stupid or unimportant person **:** DOLT

**schnor·kel** \'shnȯr-kəl\ *variant of* SNORKEL

**schnor·rer** \'shnȯr-ər, 'shnȯr-\ *noun* [Yiddish *shnorer*] (1892)

**:** BEGGAR; *especially* **:** one who wheedles others into supplying his wants

**schnoz·zle** \'shnä-zəl\ *noun* [probably modification of Yiddish *shnoitsl,* diminutive of *shnoits* snout; akin to German *Schnauze* snout, muzzle — more at SNOUT] (1937)

*slang* **:** NOSE

**scho·la can·to·rum** \ˌskō-lə-kan-'tȯr-əm, -'tȯr-\ *noun, plural* **scho·lae can·torum** \-ˌlē-, -ˌlä-, -ˌlī-\ [Medieval Latin, school of singers] (1782)

**1 :** a singing school especially for church choristers; *specifically* **:** the choir or choir school of a monastery or of a cathedral

**2 :** an enclosure designed for a choir and located in the center of the nave in early church buildings

**schol·ar** \'skä-lər\ *noun* [Middle English *scoler,* from Old English *scolere* & Old French *escoler,* from Medieval Latin *scholaris,* from Late Latin, of a school, from Latin *schola* school] (before 12th century)

**1 :** one who attends a school or studies under a teacher **:** PUPIL

**2 a :** one who has done advanced study in a special field **b :** a learned person

**3 :** a holder of a scholarship

**schol·ar·ly** \-lē\ *adjective* (1638)

**:** of, characteristic of, or suitable to learned persons **:** LEARNED, ACADEMIC

---

◻ USAGE

**schism** With the rebirth of classical learning in the Renaissance came a "silent" revolution in English spelling, whereby words formerly spelled as they were pronounced (like *onur, douten, indite,* and *receite*) were given extra letters to match their ancestral forms in Latin and Greek (yielding *honor, doubt, indict,* and *receipt*). The modern spelling of Middle English *scisme* is a product of this reform, as is the modern confusion over its pronunciation. The \'ski-zəm\ variant is a spelling pronunciation, the \'shi-zəm\ variant is another spelling pronunciation following the conventions of modern French or German, and the \'si-zəm\ variant retains the original Middle English and Middle French sound. Some insist the original \'si-zəm\ alone is correct, but these critics are not similarly exercised by the modern spelling pronunciations of *hermit* and *hostage,* which like *schism* originally had no *h* in spelling or pronunciation. Many educated speakers today use the fully acceptable spelling pronunciation \'ski-zəm\.

**schol·ar·ship** \-ˌship\ *noun* (circa 1536)
**1 :** a grant-in-aid to a student (as by a college or foundation)
**2 :** the character, qualities, activity, or attainments of a scholar **:** LEARNING
**3 :** a fund of knowledge and learning ⟨drawing on the *scholarship* of the ancients⟩
*synonym* see KNOWLEDGE
**Scholarship level** *noun* (1947)
**:** S LEVEL

**¹scho·las·tic** \skə-ˈlas-tik\ *adjective* [Medieval Latin & Latin; Medieval Latin *scholasticus* of the schoolmen, from Latin, of a school, from Greek *scholastikos*, from *scholazein* to keep a school, from *scholē* school] (1596)
**1 a :** *often capitalized* **:** of or relating to Scholasticism ⟨*scholastic* theology⟩ ⟨*scholastic* philosophy⟩ **b :** suggestive or characteristic of a scholastic especially in subtlety or aridity **:** PEDANTIC ⟨dull *scholastic* reports⟩
**2 :** of or relating to schools or scholars; *especially* **:** of or relating to high school or secondary school
— **scho·las·ti·cal·ly** \-ti-k(ə-)lē\ *adverb*
**²scholastic** *noun* (1644)
**1 a :** *capitalized* **:** a Scholastic philosopher **b :** PEDANT, FORMALIST
**2** [New Latin *scholasticus*, from Latin *scholasticus*, adjective] **:** a student in a scholasticate
**3 :** one who adopts academic or traditional methods in art

**scho·las·ti·cate** \skə-ˈlas-tə-ˌkāt, -ti-kət\ *noun* [New Latin *scholasticatus*, from *scholasticus* student in a scholasticate] (1875)
**:** a college-level school of general study for those preparing for membership in a Roman Catholic religious order

**scho·las·ti·cism** \skə-ˈlas-tə-ˌsi-zəm\ *noun* (circa 1782)
**1** *capitalized* **a :** a philosophical movement dominant in western Christian civilization from the 9th until the 17th century and combining religious dogma with the mystical and intuitional tradition of patristic philosophy especially of Saint Augustine and later with Aristotelianism **b :** NEO-SCHOLASTICISM
**2 a :** close adherence to the traditional teachings or methods of a school or sect **b :** pedantic adherence to scholarly methods

**scho·li·ast** \ˈskō-lē-ˌast, -lē-əst\ *noun* [Middle Greek *scholiastēs*, from *scholiazein* to write scholia on, from Greek *scholion*] (1583)
**:** a maker of scholia **:** COMMENTATOR, ANNOTATOR
— **scho·li·as·tic** \ˌskō-lē-ˈas-tik\ *adjective*

**scho·li·um** \ˈskō-lē-əm\ *noun, plural* **-lia** \-lē-ə\ *or* **-li·ums** [New Latin, from Greek *scholion* comment, scholium, from diminutive of *scholē* lecture] (1535)
**1 :** a marginal annotation or comment (as on the text of a classic) by an early grammarian
**2 :** a remark or observation subjoined but not essential to a demonstration or a train of reasoning

**¹school** \ˈskül\ *noun* [Middle English *scole*, from Old English *scōl*, from Latin *schola*, from Greek *scholē* leisure, discussion, lecture, school; perhaps akin to Greek *echein* to hold — more at SCHEME] (before 12th century)
**1 :** an organization that provides instruction: as **a :** an institution for the teaching of children **b :** COLLEGE, UNIVERSITY **c** (1) **:** a group of scholars and teachers pursuing knowledge together that with similar groups constituted a medieval university (2) **:** one of the four faculties of a medieval university (3) **:** an institution for specialized higher education often associated with a university ⟨the *school* of engineering⟩ **d :** an establishment offering specialized instruction ⟨a secretarial *school*⟩ ⟨driving *schools*⟩

**2 a** (1) **:** the process of teaching or learning especially at a school (2) **:** attendance at a school (3) **:** a session of a school **b :** a school building **c :** the students attending a school; *also* **:** its teachers and students
**3 :** a source of knowledge ⟨experience was his *school*⟩
**4 a :** persons who hold a common doctrine or follow the same teacher (as in philosophy, theology, or medicine) ⟨the Aristotelian *school*⟩ **b :** a group of artists under a common influence **c :** persons of similar opinions or behavior ⟨other *schools* of thought⟩
**5 :** the regulations governing military drill of individuals or units; *also* **:** the exercises carried out ⟨the *school* of the soldier⟩ ◆

**²school** *transitive verb* (15th century)
**1 a :** to teach or drill in a specific knowledge or skill ⟨well *schooled* in languages⟩ **b :** to discipline or habituate to something ⟨*school* oneself in patience⟩
**2 :** to educate in an institution of learning
*synonym* see TEACH

**³school** *noun* [Middle English *scole*, from Middle Dutch *schole*; akin to Old English *scolu* multitude and probably to Old English *scylian* to separate — more at SKILL] (15th century)
**:** a large number of fish or aquatic animals of one kind swimming together

**⁴school** *intransitive verb* (1597)
**:** to swim or feed in a school ⟨bluefish are *schooling*⟩

**school–age** *adjective* (1741)
**:** old enough to go to school ⟨*school-age* children⟩

**school·bag** \ˈskül-ˌbag\ *noun* (1895)
**:** a bag for carrying schoolbooks and school supplies

**school board** *noun* (1836)
**:** a board in charge of local public schools

**school·book** \-ˌbùk\ *noun* (1745)
**:** a school textbook

**¹school·boy** \-ˌbȯi\ *noun* (1588)
**:** a boy attending school

**²schoolboy** *adjective* (1687)
**1 :** of, relating to, or characteristic of a schoolboy ⟨*schoolboy* pranks⟩
**2 :** of, relating to, or being a sport for high school or prep school boys; *also* **:** being one who participates in such sports ⟨a former *schoolboy* and collegiate goalie —D. J. Barr⟩

**school·boy·ish** \-ˌbȯi-ish\ *adjective* (1831)
**:** SCHOOLBOY 1

**school bus** *noun* (1908)
**:** a vehicle used for transporting children to or from school or on activities connected with school

**school·child** \ˈskül-ˌchīld\ *noun* (1840)
**:** a child attending school

**school committee** *noun* (1787)
**:** SCHOOL BOARD

**school district** *noun* (1809)
**:** a unit for administration of a public-school system often comprising several towns within a state

**school·fel·low** \ˈskül-ˌfe-(ˌ)lō\ *noun* (15th century)
**:** SCHOOLMATE

**school·girl** \-ˌgər(-)l\ *noun* (1777)
**:** a girl attending school

**school·house** \-ˌhaús\ *noun* (14th century)
**:** a building used as a school and especially as an elementary school

**school·ing** *noun* (15th century)
**1 a :** instruction in school **:** EDUCATION **b :** training, guidance, or discipline derived from experience
**2** *archaic* **:** REPROOF
**3 :** the cost of instruction and maintenance at school
**4 :** the training of a horse to service; *especially* **:** the teaching and exercising of horse and rider in the formal techniques of equitation

**school·kid** \ˈskül-ˌkid\ *noun* (1938)
**:** a child or teenager attending school

**school–leav·er** \ˈskül-ˌlē-vər\ *noun* (1925)
*British* **:** one who has left school usually after completing a course of study

**school·man** \ˈskül-mən, -ˌman\ *noun* (circa 1540)
**1 a :** one skilled in academic disputation **b** *capitalized* **:** SCHOLASTIC 1a
**2 :** EDUCATOR 1, 2b

**school·marm** \-ˌmä(r)m\ *or* **school·ma'am** \-ˌmäm, -ˌmam\ *noun* [*school* + *marm*, alteration of *ma'am*] (1831)
**1 :** a woman schoolteacher especially in a rural or small-town school
**2 :** a person who exhibits characteristics attributed to schoolteachers (as strict adherence to arbitrary rules)
— **school·marm·ish** \-ˌmä(r)-mish\ *adjective*

**school·mas·ter** \-ˌmas-tər\ *noun* (13th century)
**1 :** a man who teaches school
**2 :** one that disciplines or directs
**3 :** a reddish brown edible snapper (*Lutjanus apodus*) of the tropical Atlantic and the Gulf of Mexico
— **school·mas·ter·ish** \-tə-rish\ *adjective*
— **school·mas·ter·ly** *adjective*

**school·mate** \-ˌmāt\ *noun* (1563)
**:** a companion at school

**school·mis·tress** \-ˌmis-trəs\ *noun* (15th century)
**:** a woman who teaches school

**school·room** \-ˌrüm, -ˌrùm\ *noun* (1773)
**:** CLASSROOM

**school·teach·er** \-ˌtē-chər\ *noun* (circa 1847)
**:** one who teaches school

**school·time** \-ˌtīm\ *noun* (1740)
**1 :** the time for beginning a session of school or during which school is held
**2 :** the period of life spent in school or in study

**school·work** \-ˌwərk\ *noun* (1857)
**:** lessons done in class or assigned to be done at home

---

◇ WORD HISTORY

**school** The work we associate with elementary education today may make it hard to believe that the Greek ancestor of the word *school* meant "leisure," but such is the case. Ancient Greek *scholē* "rest, leisure" came to be applied to the learned discussions and philosophical disputations in which the cream of Greek society spent their free time (of which they had much). Its use was then extended to groups who listened to the lectures of a particular philosopher, and finally, in Hellenistic and later Greek, to the set of beliefs held by a particular philosophical group. When Latin *schola* was borrowed from Greek, the emphasis fell more on the place where a particular teacher expounded his views. The Romans later generalized *schola* to "place of instruction" and applied it to an establishment where a scholar tutored young students in the basics of writing and rhetoric. (The earlier Latin word for "place of instruction" was usually *ludus*, which had originally meant, ironically, "play, sport.") *Schola* also was applied in Latin to assembly places for fraternities of priests or other groups; a distant reflection of this sense, filtered through centuries of Jewish history, is the use of *shul* in Yiddish to mean "synagogue."

---

\ə\ abut \ᵊ\ kitten \ər\ further \a\ ash \ā\ ace
\ä\ mop, mar \aú\ out \ch\ chin \e\ bet \ē\ easy
\g\ go \i\ hit \ī\ ice \j\ job \ŋ\ sing \ō\ go
\ȯ\ law \ȯi\ boy \th\ thin \th\ the \ü\ loot \ù\ foot
\y\ yet \zh\ vision    *see also* Guide to Pronunciation

**schoo·ner** \'skü-nər\ *noun* [origin unknown] (1716)
**1 :** a typically 2-masted fore-and-aft rigged vessel with a foremast and a mainmast stepped nearly amidships
**2 :** a larger-than-usual drinking glass (as for beer)
**3 :** PRAIRIE SCHOONER

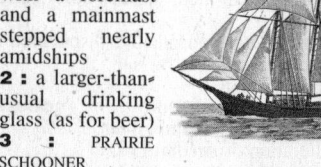
schooner 1

**schooner rig** *noun* (1866)
**:** FORE-AND-AFT RIG
**— schoo·ner–rigged** \'skü-nə(r)-'rigd\ *adjective*

**schorl** \'shȯr(ə)l\ *noun* [German *Schörl*] (1779)
**:** TOURMALINE; *especially* **:** tourmaline of the black variety

**schot·tische** \'shä-tish, shä-'tēsh\ *noun* [German, from *schottisch* Scottish, from *Schotte* Scotsman; akin to Old English *Scottas* Scots] (1849)
**1 :** a round dance resembling a slow polka
**2 :** music for the schottische

**schrod** *variant of* SCROD

**Schrö·ding·er equation** \'shrā-diŋ-ər, 'shrœ-, 'shrə(r)-\ *noun* [Erwin *Schrödinger*] (1936)
**:** an equation that describes the wave nature of elementary particles and is fundamental to the description of the properties of all matter

**schtick** *variant of* SHTICK

**schuss** \'shu̇s, 'shüs\ *intransitive verb* [*schuss*, noun, from German *Schuss*, literally, shot, from Old High German *scuz* — more at SHOT] (1940)
**:** to ski directly down a slope at high speed
**— schuss** *noun*

**schuss·boom·er** \-ˌbü-mər\ *noun* (1953)
**:** a skier who schusses

**schwa** \'shwä\ *noun* [German, from Hebrew *schĕwā'*] (1895)
**1 :** an unstressed mid-central vowel (as the usual sound of the first and last vowels of the English word *America*)
**2 :** the symbol ə used for the schwa sound and less widely for a similarly articulated stressed vowel (as in *cut*)

**Schwann cell** \'shwän-\ *noun* [Theodor *Schwann* (died 1882) German naturalist] (circa 1909)
**:** the myelin-secreting cell surrounding a myelinated nerve fiber between two nodes of Ranvier

**schwar·me·rei** \ˌshver-mə-'rī\ *noun* [German *Schwärmerei*, from *schwärmen* to be enthusiastic, literally, to swarm] (1845)
**:** excessive or unwholesome sentiment

**sci·at·ic** \sī-'a-tik\ *adjective* [Middle French *sciatique*, from Late Latin *sciaticus*, alteration of Latin *ischiadicus* of sciatica, from Greek *ischiadikos*, from *ischiad-, ischias* sciatica, from *ischion* ischium] (1586)
**1 :** of, relating to, or situated near the hip
**2 :** of, relating to, or caused by sciatica 〈*sciatic* pains〉

**sci·at·i·ca** \sī-'a-ti-kə\ *noun* [Middle English, from Medieval Latin, from Late Latin, feminine of *sciaticus*] (14th century)
**:** pain along the course of a sciatic nerve especially in the back of the thigh; *broadly* **:** pain in the lower back, buttocks, hips, or adjacent parts

**sciatic nerve** *noun* (1741)
**:** either of the pair of largest nerves in the body that arise one on each side from the nerve plexus supplying the posterior limb and pelvic region and that pass out of the pelvis and down the back of the thigh

**sci·ence** \'sī-ən(t)s\ *noun* [Middle English, from Middle French, from Latin *scientia*, from

*scient-, sciens* having knowledge, from present participle of *scire* to know; probably akin to Sanskrit *chyati* he cuts off, Latin *scindere* to split — more at SHED] (14th century)
**1 :** the state of knowing **:** knowledge as distinguished from ignorance or misunderstanding
**2 a :** a department of systematized knowledge as an object of study 〈the *science* of theology〉
**b :** something (as a sport or technique) that may be studied or learned like systematized knowledge 〈have it down to a *science*〉
**3 a :** knowledge or a system of knowledge covering general truths or the operation of general laws especially as obtained and tested through scientific method **b :** such knowledge or such a system of knowledge concerned with the physical world and its phenomena **:** NATURAL SCIENCE
**4 :** a system or method reconciling practical ends with scientific laws 〈culinary *science*〉
**5** *capitalized* **:** CHRISTIAN SCIENCE

**science fiction** *noun* (1851)
**:** fiction dealing principally with the impact of actual or imagined science on society or individuals or having a scientific factor as an essential orienting component

**sci·en·tial** \sī-'en(t)-shəl\ *adjective* (15th century)
**1 :** relating to or producing knowledge or science
**2 :** having efficient knowledge **:** CAPABLE

**sci·en·tif·ic** \ˌsī-ən-'ti-fik\ *adjective* [Medieval Latin *scientificus* producing knowledge, from Latin *scient-, sciens* + *-i-* + *-ficus* -fic] (1589)
**:** of, relating to, or exhibiting the methods or principles of science
**— sci·en·tif·i·cal·ly** \-fi-k(ə-)lē\ *adverb*

**scientific method** *noun* (1854)
**:** principles and procedures for the systematic pursuit of knowledge involving the recognition and formulation of a problem, the collection of data through observation and experiment, and the formulation and testing of hypotheses

**scientific notation** *noun* (circa 1934)
**:** a widely used floating-point system in which numbers are expressed as products consisting of a number between 1 and 10 multiplied by an appropriate power of 10

**sci·en·tism** \'sī-ən-ˌti-zəm\ *noun* (1877)
**1 :** methods and attitudes typical of or attributed to the natural scientist
**2 :** an exaggerated trust in the efficacy of the methods of natural science applied to all areas of investigation (as in philosophy, the social sciences, and the humanities)

**sci·en·tist** \'sī-ən-tist\ *noun* [Latin *scientia*] (1834)
**1 :** a person learned in science and especially natural science **:** a scientific investigator
**2** *capitalized* **:** CHRISTIAN SCIENTIST

**sci·en·tize** \'sī-ən-ˌtīz\ *transitive verb* **-tized; -tiz·ing** (1917)
**:** to treat with a scientific approach 〈the attempt to *scientize* reality, to name it and classify it —John Fowles〉

**sci–fi** \'sī-'fī\ *adjective* [*science fiction*] (1955)
**:** of, relating to, or being science fiction 〈a *sci-fi* film〉
**— sci–fi** *noun*

**sci·li·cet** \'ske-li-ˌket; 'sī-lə-ˌset, 'si-\ *adverb* [Middle English, from Latin, surely, to wit, from *scire* to know + *licet* it is permitted, from *licēre* to be permitted — more at LICENSE] (14th century)
**:** TO WIT, NAMELY

**scil·la** \'si-lə, 'ski-\ *noun* [New Latin, from Latin, squill — more at SQUILL] (1824)
**:** any of a genus (*Scilla*) of Old World bulbous herbs of the lily family with narrow basal leaves and pink, blue, or white racemose flowers

**scim·i·tar** \'si-mə-tər, -ˌtär\ *noun* [Italian *scimitarra*] (circa 1548)

**:** a saber having a curved blade with the edge on the convex side and used chiefly by Arabs and Turks

**scin·tig·ra·phy** \sin-'ti-grə-fē\ *noun* [*scintillation* + *-graphy;* from the scintillation counter used to record radiation on the picture] (1958)
**:** a diagnostic technique in which a two-dimensional picture of a bodily radiation source is obtained by the use of radioisotopes
**— scin·ti·graph·ic** \ˌsin-tə-'gra-fik\ *adjective*

**scin·til·la** \sin-'ti-lə\ *noun* [Latin] (1692)
**:** SPARK, TRACE

**scin·til·lant** \'sin-t°l-ənt\ *adjective* (1737)
**:** that scintillates **:** SPARKLING
**— scin·til·lant·ly** *adverb*

**scin·til·late** \'sin-t°l-ˌāt\ *verb* **-lat·ed; -lat·ing** [Latin *scintillatus*, past participle of *scintillare* to sparkle, from *scintilla* spark] (circa 1623)
*intransitive verb*
**1 :** to emit sparks **:** SPARK
**2 :** to emit quick flashes as if throwing off sparks **:** SPARKLE
*transitive verb*
**:** to throw off as a spark or as sparkling flashes 〈*scintillate* witticisms〉
**— scin·til·la·tor** \-ˌā-tər\ *noun*

**scin·til·lat·ing** *adjective* (1883)
**:** brilliantly lively, stimulating, or witty 〈*scintillating* conversation〉

**scin·til·la·tion** \ˌsin-t°l-'ā-shən\ *noun* (circa 1623)
**1 :** an act or instance of scintillating; *especially* **:** rapid changes in the brightness of a celestial body
**2 a :** a spark or flash emitted in scintillating **b :** a flash of light produced in a phosphor by an ionizing event
**3 :** a brilliant outburst (as of wit)
**4 :** a flash of the eye

**scintillation counter** *noun* (1948)
**:** a device for detecting and registering individual scintillations (as in radioactive emission)

**scin·til·lom·e·ter** \ˌsin-t°l-'ä-mə-tər\ *noun* [Latin *scintilla* + International Scientific Vocabulary *-o-* + *-meter*] (1877)
**:** SCINTILLATION COUNTER

**sci·o·lism** \'sī-ə-ˌli-zəm\ *noun* [Late Latin *sciolus* smatterer, from diminutive of Latin *scius* knowing, from *scire* to know — more at SCIENCE] (1816)
**:** a superficial show of learning
**— sci·o·list** \-list\ *noun*
**— sci·o·lis·tic** \ˌsī-ə-'lis-tik\ *adjective*

**sci·on** \'sī-ən\ *noun* [Middle English, from Middle French *cion*, of Germanic origin; akin to Old High German *chīnan* to sprout, split open, Old English *cīnan* to gape] (13th century)
**1 :** a detached living portion of a plant joined to a stock in grafting and usually supplying solely aerial parts to a graft
**2 :** DESCENDANT, CHILD

**sci·re fa·cias** \ˌsī-rē-'fā-sh(ē-)əs\ *noun* [Middle English, from Medieval Latin, you should cause to know] (15th century)
**1 :** a judicial writ founded on some matter of record and requiring the party proceeded against to show cause why the record should not be enforced, annulled, or vacated
**2 :** a legal proceeding instituted by a scire facias

**sci·roc·co** \shi-'rä-(ˌ)kō, sə-\ *variant of* SIROCCO

**scir·rhous** \'sir-əs, 'skir-\ *adjective* [New Latin *scirrhosus*, from *scirrhus* scirrhous tumor, from Greek *skiros, skirrhos* overgrown land, hardened tumor] (1563)
**:** of, relating to, or being a hard slow-growing malignant tumor having a preponderance of fibrous tissue

**scis·sile** \'si-səl, -ˌsīl\ *adjective* [French, from Latin *scissilis*, from *scissus*, past participle of *scindere* to split — more at SHED] (1621)

: capable of being cut smoothly or split easily ⟨a *scissile* peptide bond⟩

**scis·sion** \'si-zhən\ *noun* [Middle English *scissione,* from Middle French *scission,* from Late Latin *scission-, scissio,* from Latin *scindere*] (15th century)
**1** : a division or split in a group or union : SCHISM
**2** : an action or process of cutting, dividing, or splitting : the state of being cut, divided, or split

¹**scis·sor** \'si-zər\ *noun* [Middle English *sisoure,* from Middle French *cisoire,* from Late Latin *cisorium* cutting instrument, irregular from Latin *caedere* to cut] (15th century)
: SCISSORS

²**scissor** *transitive verb* **scis·sored; scis·sor·ing** \'si-zə-riŋ, 'siz-riŋ\ (1612)
: to cut, cut up, or cut off with scissors or shears

**scis·sors** \'si-zərz\ *noun plural but singular or plural in construction* (14th century)
**1** : a cutting instrument having two blades whose cutting edges slide past each other
**2 a** : a gymnastic feat in which the leg movements suggest the opening and closing of scissors **b** : SCISSORS HOLD

**scissors–and–paste** *adjective* (1902)
: being a compilation rather than an effort of original and independent investigation

**scissors hold** *noun* (1909)
: a wrestling hold in which the legs are locked around the head or body of an opponent

**scissors kick** *noun* (circa 1930)
: a swimming kick used especially in sidestrokes in which the legs move like scissors

**scis·sor–tailed flycatcher** \'si-zər-ˌtāld-\ *noun* (circa 1909)
: a flycatcher (*Muscivora forficata*) of the southern U.S., Mexico, and Central America that has a deeply forked tail — called also *scissortail*

**sclaff** \'sklaf\ *intransitive verb* [Scots, from *sclaff,* noun, literally, blow with the palm; probably of imitative origin] (1893)
: to scrape the ground instead of hitting the ball cleanly on a golf stroke
— **sclaff** *noun*
— **sclaff·er** *noun*

**scler-** *or* **sclero-** *combining form* [New Latin, from Greek *sklēr-, sklēro-,* from *sklēros* — more at SKELETON]
**1** : hard ⟨*scler*ite⟩ ⟨*sclero*derma⟩
**2** : hardness ⟨*sclero*meter⟩

**scle·ra** \'skler-ə\ *noun* [New Latin, from Greek *sklēros*] (1888)
: the dense fibrous opaque white outer coat enclosing the eyeball except the part covered by the cornea — see EYE illustration
— **scler·al** \-əl\ *adjective*

**scler·e·id** \'skler-ē-əd\ *noun* [International Scientific Vocabulary, irregular from Greek *sklēros*] (circa 1900)
: a variably shaped sclerenchymatous cell of a higher plant that is often nearly isodiametric

**scle·ren·chy·ma** \sklə-'reŋ-kə-mə\ *noun* [New Latin] (1875)
: a protective or supporting tissue in higher plants composed of cells with walls thickened and often lignified
— **scler·en·chy·ma·tous** \ˌskler-ən-'ki-mə-təs, -'kī-\ *adjective*

**scler·ite** \'skler-ˌīt\ *noun* [International Scientific Vocabulary] (1861)
: a hard chitinous or calcareous plate, piece, or spicule (as of the arthropod integument)

**scle·ro·der·ma** \ˌskler-ə-'dər-mə\ *noun* [New Latin] (circa 1860)
: a usually slowly progressive disease marked by the deposition of fibrous connective tissue in the skin and often in internal organs

**scle·rom·e·ter** \sklə-'rä-mə-tər\ *noun* [International Scientific Vocabulary] (circa 1879)
: an instrument for determining the relative hardness of materials

**sclero·pro·tein** \ˌskler-ō-'prō-ˌtēn, -'prōtē-ən\ *noun* [International Scientific Vocabulary] (1907)
: any of various fibrous proteins especially from connective and skeletal tissues

**scle·ros·ing** \sklə-'rō-siŋ, -ziŋ\ *adjective* [New Latin *sclerosis* + English ¹-*ing*] (1885)
: causing or characterized by sclerosis ⟨*sclerosing* agents⟩

**scle·ro·sis** \sklə-'rō-səs\ *noun* [Middle English *sclirosis* tumor, from Medieval Latin, from Greek *sklērōsis* hardening, from *sklēroun* to harden, from *sklēros*] (1846)
: pathological hardening of tissue especially from overgrowth of fibrous tissue or increase in interstitial tissue; *also* : a disease characterized by sclerosis

¹**scle·rot·ic** \sklə-'rä-tik\ *adjective* (1543)
**1** : being or relating to the sclera
**2** : of, relating to, or affected with sclerosis
**3** : grown rigid or unresponsive especially with age ⟨*sclerotic* institutions⟩

²**sclerotic** *noun* [Medieval Latin *sclerotica,* from (assumed) Greek *sklērōtos,* verbal of Greek *sklēroun* to harden] (1690)
: SCLERA

**sclerotic coat** *noun* (1741)
: SCLERA

**scle·ro·tin** \'skler-ə-tən, sklə-'rō-tᵊn\ *noun* [probably *scler-* + -*tin* (as in *chitin*)] (1940)
: an insoluble tanned protein permeating and stiffening the chitin of the cuticle of arthropods

**scle·ro·tium** \sklə-'rō-sh(ē-)əm\ *noun, plural* -**tia** \-sh(ē-)ə\ [New Latin, from (assumed) Greek *sklērōtos*] (1871)
: a compact mass of hardened mycelium stored with reserve food material that in some higher fungi becomes detached and remains dormant until a favorable opportunity for growth occurs
— **scle·ro·tial** \-'rō-shəl\ *adjective*

**scle·ro·tized** \'skler-ə-ˌtīzd\ *adjective* [¹*sclerotic* + -*ize* + ¹-*ed*] (circa 1890)
: hardened especially by the formation of sclerotin ⟨*sclerotized* insect cuticle⟩
— **scle·ro·ti·za·tion** \ˌskler-ə-tə-'zā-shən\ *noun*

¹**scoff** \'skäf, 'skof\ *noun* [Middle English *scof,* probably of Scandinavian origin; akin to obsolete Danish *skof* jest; akin to Old Frisian *skof* mockery] (14th century)
**1** : an expression of scorn, derision, or contempt : GIBE
**2** : an object of scorn, mockery, or derision

²**scoff** (14th century)
*intransitive verb*
: to show contempt by derisive acts or language
*transitive verb*
: to treat or address with derision : MOCK ☆
— **scoff·er** *noun*

³**scoff** *verb* [alteration of dialect *scaff* to eat greedily] (1846)
*transitive verb*
**1** : to eat greedily
**2** : SEIZE — often used with *up*
*intransitive verb*
: to eat something greedily

**scoff·law** \-ˌlo\ *noun* (1924)
: a contemptuous law violator

¹**scold** \'skōld\ *noun* [Middle English *scald, scold,* perhaps of Scandinavian origin; akin to Old Norse *skāld* poet, skald, Icelandic *skālda* to make scurrilous verse] (12th century)
**1 a** : one who scolds habitually or persistently **b** : a woman who disturbs the public peace by noisy and quarrelsome or abusive behavior
**2** : SCOLDING

²**scold** (14th century)
*intransitive verb*
**1** *obsolete* : to quarrel noisily
**2** : to find fault noisily or angrily
*transitive verb*
: to censure severely or angrily : REBUKE ☆
— **scold·er** *noun*

**scold·ing** *noun* (1547)
**1** : the action of one who scolds
**2** : a harsh reproof

**sco·le·cite** \'skä-lə-ˌsīt, 'skō-\ *noun* [German *Skolezit,* from Greek *skōlēk-, skōlēx* worm; from the motion of some forms when heated] (circa 1823)
: a zeolite mineral that is a hydrous calcium aluminum silicate and occurs in radiating groups of crystals, in fibrous masses, and in nodules

**sco·lex** \'skō-ˌleks\ *noun, plural* **sco·li·ces** \-lə-ˌsēz\ *also* **sco·le·ces** \'skō-lə-ˌsēz, 'skä-\ [New Latin *scolic-, scolex,* from Greek *skōlēk-, skōlēx* worm; akin to Greek *skolios* crooked, *skelos* leg — more at ISOSCELES] (1855)
: the head of a tapeworm either in the larva or adult stage

**sco·li·o·sis** \ˌskō-lē-'ō-səs\ *noun, plural* -**o·ses** \-ˌsēz\ [New Latin, from Greek *skoliōsis* crookedness of a bodily part, from *skolios*] (circa 1706)
: a lateral curvature of the spine
— **sco·li·ot·ic** \-'ä-tik\ *adjective*

**scol·lop** \'skä-ləp, 'skō-\ *variant of* SCALLOP

**scol·o·pen·dra** \ˌskä-lə-'pen-drə\ *noun* [New Latin, genus of centipedes, from Latin, a kind of millipede, from Greek *skolopendra*] (1608)
: CENTIPEDE

**scom·broid** \'skäm-ˌbroid\ *noun* [ultimately from Greek *skombros* mackerel] (circa 1842)
: any of a suborder (Scombroidei) of marine bony fishes (as mackerels, tunas, albacores, bonitos, and swordfishes) of great economic importance as food fishes
— **scombroid** *adjective*

¹**sconce** \'skän(t)s\ *noun* [Middle English, from Middle French *esconse* screened lantern, from Old French, from feminine of *escons,*

\ə\ abut \ᵊ\ kitten \ər\ further \a\ ash \ā\ ace
\ä\ mop, mar \au̇\ out \ch\ chin \e\ bet \ē\ easy
\g\ go \i\ hit \ī\ ice \j\ job \ŋ\ sing \ō\ go
\ȯ\ law \ȯi\ boy \th\ thin \t̲h̲\ the \ü\ loot \u̇\ foot
\y\ yet \zh\ vision *see also* Guide to Pronunciation

past participle of *escondre* to hide, from Latin *abscondere* — more at ABSCOND] (15th century)
**1 :** a bracket candlestick or group of candlesticks; *also* **:** an electric light fixture patterned on a candle sconce
**2 :** HEAD, SKULL

²**sconce** *noun* [Dutch *schans*, from German *Schanze*] (1571)
**:** a detached defensive work

**scone** \'skōn, 'skän\ *noun* [perhaps from Dutch *schoonbrood* fine white bread, from *schoon* pure, clean + *brood* bread] (1513)
**:** a rich quick bread cut into usually triangular shapes and cooked on a griddle or baked on a sheet

¹**scoop** \'sküp\ *noun* [Middle English *scope*, from Middle Dutch *schope*; akin to Old High German *skepfen* to shape — more at SHAPE] (14th century)
**1 a :** a large ladle **b :** a deep shovel or similar implement for digging, dipping, or shoveling **c :** a usually hemispherical utensil for dipping food **d :** a small spoon-shaped utensil or instrument for cutting or gouging
**2 :** the action of scooping
**3 a :** a hollow place **:** CAVITY **b :** a part forming or surrounding an opening for channeling a fluid (as air) into a desired path
**4 a :** information especially of immediate interest **b :** BEAT 5b
**5 :** a rounded and usually low-cut neckline on a woman's garment — called also *scoop neck*
— **scoop·ful** \-,fül\ *noun*

²**scoop** *transitive verb* (14th century)
**1 a :** to take out or up with or as if with a scoop **:** DIP **b :** to pick up quickly or surreptitiously with or as if with a sweep of the hand — often used with *up*
**2 :** to empty by ladling out the contents
**3 :** to make hollow **:** DIG OUT
**4 :** BEAT 5a(2)
— **scoop·er** *noun*

**scoot** \'sküt\ *intransitive verb* [perhaps of Scandinavian origin; akin to Old Norse *skjōta* to shoot — more at SHOOT] (1758)
**1 :** to move swiftly
**2 :** to slide especially while seated ⟨*scoot* over and let me sit down⟩
— **scoot** *noun*

**scoot·er** \'skü-tər\ *noun* (1916)
**1 :** a child's foot-operated vehicle consisting of a narrow footboard mounted between two wheels tandem with an upright steering handle attached to the front wheel
**2 :** MOTOR SCOOTER

**scop** \'shōp, 'skōp, 'skäp\ *noun* [Old English; akin to Old High German *schof* poet] (before 12th century)
**:** an Old English bard or poet

¹**scope** \'skōp\ *noun* [Italian *scopo* purpose, goal, from Greek *skopos*; akin to Greek *skeptesthai* to watch, look at — more at SPY] (circa 1555)
**1 :** INTENTION, OBJECT
**2 :** space or opportunity for unhampered motion, activity, or thought
**3 :** extent of treatment, activity, or influence
**4 :** range of operation: as **a :** the range of a logical operator **:** a string in predicate calculus that is governed by a quantifier **b :** a grammatical constituent that determines the interpretation of a predicate or quantifier
**synonym** see RANGE

²**scope** *noun* [-*scope*] (1872)
**1 :** an instrument (as a telescope or radarscope) for viewing
**2 :** HOROSCOPE

³**scope** *transitive verb* **scoped; scop·ing** [perhaps from ²*scope*] (1974)
**:** to look at especially for the purpose of evaluation — often used with *out* ⟨*scoped* her out from across the room —Tim Allis⟩

-**scope** *noun combining form* [New Latin -*scopium*, from Greek -*skopion*; akin to Greek *skeptesthai*]
**:** means (as an instrument) for viewing or observing ⟨endo*scope*⟩ ⟨spectro*scope*⟩

**sco·pol·a·mine** \skō-'pä-lə-,mēn, -mən\ *noun* [German *Scopolamin*, from New Latin *Scopolia*, genus of plants + German *Amin* amine] (1892)
**:** a poisonous alkaloid $C_{17}H_{21}NO_4$ found in various plants (as jimsonweed) of the nightshade family and used especially as a truth serum or usually with morphine as a sedative in surgery and obstetrics — called also *hyoscine*

-**scopy** *noun combining form* [Greek -*skopia*, from *skeptesthai*]
**:** viewing **:** observation ⟨spectro*scopy*⟩

**scor·bu·tic** \skōr-'byü-tik\ *adjective* [New Latin *scorbuticus*, from *scorbutus* scurvy, probably of Germanic origin; akin to Old English *scurf* scurf] (1655)
**:** of, relating to, producing, or affected with scurvy

¹**scorch** \'skōrch\ *verb* [Middle English; akin to Middle English *scorcnen*, probably of Scandinavian origin; akin to Old Norse *skorpna* to shrivel up — more at SHRIMP] (14th century)
*transitive verb*
**1 :** to burn a surface of so as to change its color and texture
**2 a :** to dry or shrivel with or as if with intense heat **:** PARCH **b :** to afflict painfully with censure or sarcasm
**3 :** DEVASTATE; *especially* **:** to destroy (as property of possible use to an advancing enemy) before abandoning — used in the phrase *scorched earth*
*intransitive verb*
**1 :** to become scorched
**2 :** to travel at great and usually excessive speed
**3 :** to cause intense heat or mental anguish ⟨*scorching* sun⟩ ⟨*scorching* fury⟩
— **scorch·ing·ly** \'skōr-chin-lē\ *adverb*

²**scorch** *noun* (15th century)
**1 :** a result of scorching
**2 :** a browning of plant tissues usually from disease or heat

³**scorch** *transitive verb* [Middle English, perhaps blend of *scoren* to score and *scocchen* to scotch] (14th century)
*dialect British* **:** CUT, SLASH

**scorched** *adjective* (1590)
**:** parched or discolored by scorching

**scorch·er** \'skòr-chər\ *noun* (1842)
**:** one that scorches; *especially* **:** a very hot day

¹**score** \'skōr, 'skòr\ *noun, plural* **scores** [Middle English *scor*, from Old Norse *skor* notch, tally, twenty; akin to Old English *sciveran* to cut — more at SHEAR] (14th century)
**1** *or plural* **score a :** TWENTY **b :** a group of 20 things — often used in combination with a cardinal number ⟨four*score*⟩ **c :** an indefinitely large number
**2 a :** a line (as a scratch or incision) made with or as if with a sharp instrument **b** (1) **:** a mark used as a starting point or goal (2) **:** a mark used for keeping account
**3 a :** an account or reckoning originally kept by making marks on a tally **b :** amount due **:** INDEBTEDNESS
**4 :** GRUDGE ⟨a *score* to settle⟩
**5 a :** REASON, GROUND **b :** SUBJECT, TOPIC
**6 a :** the copy of a musical composition in written or printed notation **b :** a musical composition; *specifically* **:** the music for a movie or theatrical production **c :** a complete description of a dance composition in choreographic notation
**7 a :** a number that expresses accomplishment (as in a game or test) or excellence (as in quality) either absolutely in points gained or by comparison to a standard **b :** an act (as a goal, run, or touchdown) in any of various games or contests that gains points

**8 :** success in obtaining something (as money or drugs) especially through illegal or irregular means
**9 :** the stark inescapable facts of a situation ⟨knows the *score*⟩

²**score** *verb* **scored; scor·ing** (14th century)
*transitive verb*
**1 a :** to keep a record or account of by or as if by notches on a tally **:** RECORD **b :** to enter in a record **c :** to mark with significant lines or notches (as in keeping account)
**2 :** to mark with lines, grooves, scratches, or notches
**3 :** BERATE, SCOLD; *also* **:** DENOUNCE
**4 a** (1) **:** to make (a score) in a game or contest ⟨*scored* a touchdown⟩ ⟨*scored* three points⟩ (2) **:** to enable (a base runner) to make a score (3) **:** to have as a value in a game or contest **:** COUNT ⟨a touchdown *scores* six points⟩ **b** (1) **:** ACHIEVE, WIN ⟨*scored* a dazzling success⟩ (2) **:** ACQUIRE ⟨help a traveler *score* local drugs —Poitor Koper⟩
**5 :** to determine the merit of **:** GRADE
**6 a :** to write or arrange (music) for a specific performance medium **b :** to make an orchestration of **c :** to compose a score for (a movie)
*intransitive verb*
**1 :** to keep score in a game or contest
**2 :** to make a score in a game or contest
**3 a :** to gain or have the advantage **b :** to be successful: as (1) **:** to succeed in having sexual intercourse (2) **:** to manage to obtain illicit drugs **c :** ³RATE
— **scor·er** *noun*
— **score points :** to gain favor, status, or advantage

**score·board** \'skōr-,bōrd, 'skòr-,bòrd\ *noun* (1826)
**:** a large board for displaying the score of a game or match

**score·card** \-,kärd\ *noun* (circa 1877)
**:** a card for recording the score of a game

**score·keep·er** \-,kē-pər\ *noun* (1880)
**:** one that keeps score; *specifically* **:** an official who records the score during a game or contest

**score·less** \-ləs\ *adjective* (1885)
**:** having no score

**sco·ria** \'skōr-ē-ə, 'skòr-\ *noun, plural* **-ri·ae** \-ē-,ē, -ē-,ī\ [Middle English, from Latin, from Greek *skōria*, from *skōr* excrement — more at SCATOLOGY] (14th century)
**1 :** the refuse from melting of metals or reduction of ores **:** SLAG
**2 :** rough vesicular cindery lava
— **sco·ri·a·ceous** \,skōr-ē-'ā-shəs, ,skòr-\ *adjective*

¹**scorn** \'skòrn\ *noun* [Middle English, from Old French *escarn*, of Germanic origin; akin to Old High German *scern* jest] (13th century)
**1 :** open dislike and disrespect or derision often mixed with indignation
**2 :** an expression of contempt or derision
**3 :** an object of extreme disdain, contempt, or derision **:** something contemptible

²**scorn** (13th century)
*transitive verb*
**:** to treat with scorn **:** reject or dismiss as contemptible or unworthy ⟨*scorned* the traditions of their ancestors⟩ ⟨*scorned* to reply to the charge⟩
*intransitive verb*
**:** to show disdain or derision **:** SCOFF
**synonym** see DESPISE
— **scorn·er** *noun*

**scorn·ful** \'skòrn-fəl\ *adjective* (14th century)
**:** full of scorn **:** CONTEMPTUOUS
— **scorn·ful·ly** \-fə-lē\ *adverb*
— **scorn·ful·ness** *noun*

**scor·pae·nid** \skòr-'pē-nəd\ *noun* [ultimately from Greek *skorpaina*, a kind of fish] (1885)
**:** any of a family (Scorpaenidae) of marine spiny-finned fishes that includes the scorpion fishes

— **scorpaenid** *adjective*

**Scor·pio** \'skȯr-pē-ˌō\ *noun* [Latin (genitive *Scorpionis*), from Greek *Skorpios,* literally, scorpion]
**1 :** SCORPIUS
**2 a :** the 8th sign of the zodiac in astrology — see ZODIAC table **b :** one born under this sign

**scor·pi·on** \'skȯr-pē-ən\ *noun* [Middle English, from Old French, from Latin *scorpion-, scorpio,* from Greek *skorpios*] (12th century)
**1 a :** any of an order (Scorpionida) of nocturnal arachnids that have an elongated body and a narrow segmented tail bearing a venomous stinger at the tip **b** *capitalized* **:** SCORPIO
**2 :** a scourge probably studded with metal
**3 :** something that incites to action like the sting of an insect

scorpion 1a

**scorpion fish** *noun* (1661)
**:** any of various scorpaenid fishes; *especially* **:** one (as genus *Scorpaena*) with a venomous spine on the dorsal fin

**scorpion fly** *noun* (1668)
**:** any of a family (Panorpidae) of insects that have cylindrical bodies, a long beak with biting mouthparts, and the male genitalia enlarged into a swollen bulb; *broadly* **:** an insect of the order (Mecoptera) that includes this family

**Scor·pi·us** \'skȯr-pē-əs\ *noun* [Latin (genitive *Scorpii*), from Greek *Skorpios,* literally, scorpion]
**:** a southern zodiacal constellation partly in the Milky Way and between Libra and Sagittarius

**scot** \'skät\ *noun* [Middle English, from Old Norse *skot* shot, contribution — more at SHOT] (14th century)
**:** money assessed or paid

**Scot** \'skät\ *noun* [Middle English *Scottes* Scots, from Old English *Scottas* from Late Latin *Scotus*] (before 12th century)
**1 :** a member of a Celtic people of northern Ireland settling in Scotland about A.D. 500
**2 a :** a native or inhabitant of Scotland **b :** a person of Scottish descent

**scot and lot** *noun* (15th century)
**1 :** a parish assessment formerly laid on subjects in Great Britain according to their ability to pay
**2 :** obligations of all kinds taken as a whole

**¹scotch** \'skäch\ *transitive verb* [Middle English *scocchen* to gash] (15th century)
**1** *archaic* **:** CUT, GASH, SCORE; *also* **:** WOUND ⟨we have *scotched* the snake, not killed it —Shakespeare⟩
**2 :** to put an end to ⟨*scotched* rumors of a military takeover⟩

**²scotch** *noun* (15th century)
**:** a superficial cut **:** SCORE

**³scotch** *noun* [origin unknown] (1639)
**:** a chock to prevent rolling or slipping

**⁴scotch** *transitive verb* (1642)
**1 :** to block with a chock
**2 :** HINDER, THWART

**¹Scotch** \'skäch\ *adjective* [contraction of *Scottish*] (1591)
**1 :** SCOTTISH
**2 :** inclined to frugality ▯

**²Scotch** *noun* (circa 1700)
**1 :** SCOTS
**2** *plural in construction* **:** the people of Scotland
**3** *often not capitalized* **:** whiskey distilled in Scotland especially from malted barley — called also *Scotch whisky*

**³Scotch** *trademark*
— used for any of numerous adhesive tapes

**Scotch broom** *noun* (circa 1818)
**:** a deciduous broom (*Cytisus scoparius*) of western Europe that is widely cultivated for its

bright yellow or partly red flowers and that has become a pest in some areas (as California)

**Scotch broth** *noun* (1834)
**:** a soup made from beef or mutton and vegetables and thickened with barley

**Scotch egg** *noun* (1809)
**:** a hard-boiled egg wrapped in sausage meat, covered with bread crumbs, and fried

**Scotch–Irish** *adjective* (1744)
**:** of, relating to, or descended from Scottish settlers in northern Ireland

**Scotch·man** \'skäch-mən\ *noun* (15th century)
**:** SCOTSMAN

**Scotch pine** *noun* (1731)
**:** a pine (*Pinus sylvestris*) of northern Europe and Asia with spreading or pendulous branches, short rigid twisted needles, and hard yellow wood that provides valuable timber

**Scotch terrier** *noun* (1810)
**:** SCOTTISH TERRIER

**Scotch verdict** *noun* (1912)
**1 :** a verdict of not proven that is allowed by Scottish criminal law in some cases instead of a verdict of not guilty
**2 :** an inconclusive decision or pronouncement

**Scotch·wom·an** \'skäch-ˌwu̇-mən\ *noun* (1818)
**:** SCOTSWOMAN

**Scotch woodcock** *noun* (1879)
**:** buttered toast spread with anchovy paste and scrambled egg

**sco·ter** \'skō-tər\ *noun, plural* **scoters** *or* **scoter** [origin unknown] (circa 1674)
**:** any of a genus (*Melanitta*) of sea ducks especially of northern coasts of Europe and North America that have males with chiefly black plumage

**scot–free** \'skät-'frē\ *adjective* [*scot*] (1528)
**:** completely free from obligation, harm, or penalty

**sco·tia** \'skō-sh(ē-)ə, -tē-ə\ *noun* [Latin, from Greek *skotia,* from feminine of *skotios* dark, shadowy, from *skotos* darkness — more at SHADE] (1563)
**:** a concave molding used especially in classical architecture in the bases of columns — see BASE illustration

**Scot·ic** \'skä-tik\ *adjective* (1796)
**:** of or relating to the ancient Scots

**Sco·tism** \'skō-ˌti-zəm\ *noun* (circa 1871)
**:** the doctrines of Duns Scotus
— **Sco·tist** \'skō-tist\ *noun*

**Scot·land Yard** \ˌskät-lən(d)-'yärd\ *noun* [*Scotland Yard,* street in London, formerly the headquarters of the metropolitan police] (1864)
**:** the detective department of the London metropolitan police

**sco·to·ma** \skə-'tō-mə\ *noun, plural* **-mas** *or* **-ma·ta** \-mə-tə\ [New Latin, from Medieval Latin, dimness of vision, from Greek *skotōmat-, skotōma,* from *skotoun* to darken, from *skotos*] (1875)
**:** a blind or dark spot in the visual field

**sco·top·ic** \skə-'tō-pik, -'tä-\ *adjective* [New Latin *scotopia* scotopic vision, from Greek *skotos* darkness + New Latin *-opia*] (1915)
**:** relating to or being vision in dim light with dark-adapted eyes which involves only the retinal rods as light receptors

**¹Scots** \'skäts\ *adjective* [Middle English *Scottis,* alteration of *Scottish*] (14th century)
**:** SCOTTISH — used especially of the people and language and in legal context
*usage* see SCOTCH

**²Scots** *noun* (1542)
**:** the English language of Scotland

**Scots·man** \'skäts-mən\ *noun* (14th century)
**:** a native or inhabitant of Scotland

**Scots pine** *noun* (1797)
*chiefly British* **:** SCOTCH PINE

**Scots·wom·an** \'skäts-ˌwu̇-mən\ *noun* (1820)
**:** a woman who is a native or inhabitant of Scotland

**Scot·ti·cism** \'skä-tə-ˌsi-zəm\ *noun* [Late Latin *scotticus* of the ancient Scots, from *Scotus* Scot] (1706)
**:** a word, phrase, or expression characteristic of Scottish English

**Scot·tie** \'skä-tē\ *noun* (circa 1896)
**1 :** SCOTSMAN
**2 :** SCOTTISH TERRIER

**¹Scot·tish** \'skä-tish\ *adjective* [Middle English, from *Scottes* Scotsmen] (13th century)
**:** of, relating to, or characteristic of Scotland, Scots, or the Scots
*usage* see SCOTCH
— **Scot·tish·ness** \-nəs\ *noun*

**²Scottish** *noun* (1759)
**:** SCOTS

**Scottish deerhound** *noun* (1891)
**:** any of an old breed of dogs of Scottish origin that have the general form of a greyhound but are larger and taller with a rough coat

**Scottish Gaelic** *noun* (1956)
**:** the Gaelic language of Scotland

**Scottish rite** *noun* (1903)
**1 :** a ceremonial observed by one of the Masonic systems
**2 :** a system or organization that observes the Scottish rite and confers the 4th through the 33d degrees

**Scottish terrier** *noun* (1837)
**:** any of an old Scottish breed of terrier that has short legs, a large head with small erect ears and a powerful muzzle, a broad deep chest, and a very hard coat of wiry hair

Scottish terrier

**scoun·drel** \'skau̇n-drəl\ *noun* [origin unknown] (1589)
**:** a disreputable person **:** RASCAL
— **scoundrel** *adjective*
— **scoun·drel·ly** \-drə-lē\ *adjective*

**¹scour** \'skau̇(-ə)r\ *verb* [Middle English, probably from Middle Dutch *schuren,* from Old French *escurer,* from Late Latin *excurare* to clean off, from Latin, to take good care of, from *ex-* + *curare* to care for, from *cura* care] (13th century)
*transitive verb*
**1 a :** to rub hard especially with a rough material for cleansing **b :** to remove by rubbing hard and washing
**2** *archaic* **:** to clear (a region) of enemies or outlaws
**3 :** to clean by purging **:** PURGE
**4 :** to remove dirt and debris from (as a pipe or ditch)
**5 :** to free from foreign matter or impurities by or as if by washing ⟨*scour* wool⟩

\ə\ abut \ᵊ\ kitten \ər\ further \a\ ash \ā\ ace \ä\ mop, mar \au̇\ out \ch\ chin \e\ bet \ē\ easy \g\ go \i\ hit \ī\ ice \j\ job \ŋ\ sing \ō\ go \ȯ\ law \ȯi\ boy \th\ thin \tẖ\ the \ü\ loot \u̇\ foot \y\ yet \zh\ vision    *see also* Guide to Pronunciation

**6 :** to clear, dig, or remove by or as if by a powerful current of water
*intransitive verb*
**1 :** to perform a process of scouring
**2 :** to suffer from diarrhea or dysentery
**3 :** to become clean and bright by rubbing
— **scour·er** *noun*
²**scour** *noun* (1681)
**1 :** a place scoured by running water
**2 :** scouring action (as of a glacier)
**3 :** DIARRHEA, DYSENTERY — usually used in plural but singular or plural in construction
**4 :** SCOURING 1; *also* **:** damage done by scouring action
³**scour** *verb* [Middle English *scuren*, probably of Scandinavian origin; akin to Swedish *skura* to rush] (14th century)
*intransitive verb*
**:** to move about quickly especially in search
*transitive verb*
**:** to go through or range over in or as if in a search
¹**scourge** \'skərj *also* 'skōrj, 'skòrj, 'skürj\ *noun* [Middle English, from Anglo-French *escorge*, from (assumed) Old French *escorgier* to whip, from Old French *es-* ex- + Latin *corrigia* whip] (13th century)
**1 :** WHIP; *especially* **:** one used to inflict pain or punishment
**2 :** an instrument of punishment or criticism
**3 :** a cause of widespread or great affliction
²**scourge** *transitive verb* **scourged; scourg·ing** (13th century)
**1 :** FLOG, WHIP
**2 a :** to punish severely **b :** AFFLICT **c :** to drive as if by blows of a whip **d :** CHASTISE
— **scourg·er** *noun*
**scour·ing** \'skaùr-iŋ\ *noun* (1588)
**1 :** material removed by scouring or cleaning
**2 :** the lowest rank of society — usually used in plural
**scouring rush** *noun* (circa 1818)
**:** EQUISETUM; *especially* **:** one (*Equisetum hyemale*) with strongly siliceous stems formerly used for scouring
**scouse** \'skaùs\ *noun* (1840)
**1 :** LOBSCOUSE
**2** *capitalized* **a :** SCOUSER **b :** a dialect of English spoken in Liverpool
**Scous·er** \'skaù-sər\ *noun* (1959)
**:** a native or inhabitant of Liverpool, England
¹**scout** \'skaùt\ *verb* [Middle English, from Middle French *escouter* to listen, from Latin *auscultare* — more at AUSCULTATION] (14th century)
*intransitive verb*
**1 :** to explore an area to obtain information (as about an enemy)
**2 a :** to make a search **b :** to work as a talent scout
*transitive verb*
**1 :** to observe in order to obtain information or evaluate
**2 :** to explore in order to obtain information
**3 :** to find by making a search — often used with *up*
²**scout** *noun* (1534)
**1 a :** one sent to obtain information; *especially* **:** a soldier, ship, or plane sent out in war to reconnoiter **b :** WATCHMAN, LOOKOUT **c :** TALENT SCOUT
**2 a :** the act of scouting **b :** a scouting expedition **:** RECONNAISSANCE
**3** *often capitalized* **:** a member of any of various scouting movements: as **a :** BOY SCOUT **b :** GIRL SCOUT
**4 :** INDIVIDUAL, PERSON — used chiefly in the phrase *good scout*
³**scout** *verb* [probably of Scandinavian origin; akin to Old Norse *skūti* taunt; akin to Old English *scēotan* to shoot — more at SHOOT] (1605)
*transitive verb*
**1 :** MOCK
**2 :** to reject scornfully

*intransitive verb*
**:** SCOFF
**scout car** *noun* (1933)
**1 :** a military reconnaissance vehicle
**2 :** SQUAD CAR
**scout·craft** \'skaùt-,kraft\ *noun* (1908)
**:** the craft, skill, or practice of a scout
**scout·er** \'skaù-tər\ *noun* (1642)
**1 :** one that scouts
**2** *often capitalized* **:** an adult leader in the Boy Scouts of America
**scouth** \'sküth, 'skaùth\ *noun* [origin unknown] (1591)
*Scottish* **:** PLENTY
**scout·ing** \'skaù-tiŋ\ *noun* (1644)
**1 :** the action of one that scouts
**2** *often capitalized* **:** the activities of various national and worldwide organizations for youth directed to developing character, citizenship, and individual skills
**scout·mas·ter** \'skaùt-,mas-tər\ *noun* (1579)
**:** the leader of a band of scouts; *specifically* **:** the adult leader of a troop of Boy Scouts
**scow** \'skaù\ *noun* [Dutch *schouw*; akin to Old High German *scalta* punt pole] (1669)
**:** a large flat-bottomed boat with broad square ends used chiefly for transporting bulk material (as ore, sand, or refuse)
¹**scowl** \'skaù(ə)l\ *verb* [Middle English *skoulen*, probably of Scandinavian origin; akin to Danish *skule* to scowl] (14th century)
*intransitive verb*
**1 :** to contract the brow in an expression of displeasure
**2 :** to exhibit a threatening aspect
*transitive verb*
**:** to express with a scowl
— **scowl·er** *noun*
— **scowl·ing·ly** \'skaù-liŋ-lē\ *adverb*
²**scowl** *noun* (1500)
**:** a facial expression of displeasure **:** FROWN
¹**scrab·ble** \'skra-bəl\ *verb* **scrab·bled; scrab·bling** \-b(ə-)liŋ\ [Dutch *schrabbelen* to scratch] (1537)
*intransitive verb*
**1 :** SCRAWL, SCRIBBLE
**2 :** to scratch, claw, or grope about clumsily or frantically
**3 a :** SCRAMBLE, CLAMBER **b :** to struggle by or as if by scraping or scratching ⟨*scrabble* for survival⟩
*transitive verb*
**1 :** SCRAMBLE
**2 :** SCRIBBLE
— **scrab·bler** \-b(ə-)lər\ *noun*
²**scrabble** *noun* (1842)
**1 :** SCRIBBLE
**2 :** a repeated scratching or clawing
**3 :** SCRAMBLE
**scrab·bly** \'skra-b(ə-)lē\ *adjective* (1945)
**1 :** SCRATCHY, RASPY
**2 :** SPARSE, SCRUBBY
¹**scrag** \'skrag\ *noun* [perhaps alteration of ²*crag*] (1542)
**1 :** a rawboned or scrawny person or animal
**2 :** the lean end of a neck of mutton or veal; *broadly* **:** NECK — called also *scrag end*
²**scrag** *transitive verb* **scragged; scrag·ging** (1756)
**1 a :** to execute by hanging or garroting **b :** to wring the neck of
**2 a :** CHOKE **b :** MANHANDLE 1 **c :** KILL, MURDER
**scrag·gly** \'skra-g(ə-)lē\ *adjective* (1869)
**:** irregular in form or growth ⟨*scraggly* hills⟩ ⟨a *scraggly* beard⟩; *also* **:** UNKEMPT
¹**scrag·gy** \'skra-gē\ *adjective* **scrag·gi·er; -est** [Middle English *scraggi*; akin to English dialect *scrag* tree stump, uneven ground, Middle English *scrogge* bush] (13th century)
**:** ROUGH, JAGGED; *also* **:** SCRAGGLY
²**scraggy** *adjective* **scrag·gi·er; -est** [¹*scrag*] (1611)
**:** being lean and long **:** SCRAWNY
¹**scram** \'skram\ *intransitive verb* **scrammed; scram·ming** [short for *scramble*] (circa 1928)

**:** to go away at once ⟨*scram*, you're not wanted⟩
²**scram** *noun* (1953)
**:** a rapid emergency shutdown of a nuclear reactor
¹**scram·ble** \'skram-bəl\ *verb* **scram·bled; scram·bling** \-b(ə-)liŋ\ [perhaps alteration of ¹*scrabble*] (circa 1586)
*intransitive verb*
**1 a :** to move or climb hastily on all fours **b :** to move with urgency or panic
**2 a :** to struggle eagerly or unceremoniously for possession of something ⟨*scramble* for front seats⟩ **b :** to get or gather something with difficulty or in irregular ways ⟨*scramble* for a living⟩
**3 :** to spread or grow irregularly **:** SPRAWL, STRAGGLE
**4 :** to take off quickly in response to an alert
**5** *of a football quarterback* **:** to run with the ball after the pass protection breaks down
*transitive verb*
**1 :** to collect by scrambling
**2 a :** to toss or mix together **:** JUMBLE **b :** to prepare (eggs) by stirring during frying
**3 :** to cause or order (a fighter-interceptor group) to scramble
**4 :** to disarrange the elements of a transmission (as a telephone or television signal) in order to make unintelligible to interception
— **scram·bler** \-b(ə-)lər\ *noun*
²**scramble** *noun* (1674)
**1 :** the act or an instance of scrambling
**2 :** a disordered mass **:** JUMBLE ⟨a . . . *scramble* of patterns and textures —*Vogue*⟩
**3 :** a rapid emergency takeoff of fighter-interceptor planes
**scran·nel** \'skra-n°l\ *adjective* [origin unknown] (1637)
**:** HARSH, UNMELODIOUS
¹**scrap** \'skrap\ *noun, often attributive* [Middle English, from Old Norse *skrap* scraps; akin to Old Norse *skrapa* to scrape] (14th century)
**1** *plural* **:** fragments of discarded or leftover food
**2 a :** a small detached piece ⟨a *scrap* of paper⟩ **b :** a fragment of something written, printed, or spoken ⟨*scraps* of conversation⟩ **c :** the least bit ⟨not a *scrap* of evidence⟩
**3** *plural* **:** CRACKLINGS
**4 a :** fragments of stock removed in manufacturing **b :** manufactured articles or parts rejected or discarded and useful only as material for reprocessing; *especially* **:** waste and discarded metal
²**scrap** *transitive verb* **scrapped; scrapping** (circa 1891)
**1 :** to convert into scrap
**2 :** to abandon or get rid of as no longer of enough worth or effectiveness to retain ⟨*scrap* outworn methods⟩
*synonym* see DISCARD
³**scrap** *noun* [origin unknown] (circa 1889)
**:** FIGHT
⁴**scrap** *intransitive verb* **scrapped; scrapping** (circa 1895)
**:** QUARREL, FIGHT
**scrap·book** \'skrap-,bùk\ *noun* (1825)
**:** a blank book in which miscellaneous items (as newspaper clippings or pictures) are collected and preserved
¹**scrape** \'skrāp\ *verb* **scraped; scrap·ing** [Middle English, from Old Norse *skrapa*; akin to Old English *scrapian* to scrape, Latin *scrobis* ditch, Russian *skresti* to scrape] (14th century)
*transitive verb*
**1 a :** to remove from a surface by usually repeated strokes of an edged instrument **b :** to make (a surface) smooth or clean with strokes of an edged instrument or an abrasive
**2 a :** to grate harshly over or against **b :** to damage or injure the surface of by contact with a rough surface **c :** to draw roughly or noisily over a surface

**3 :** to collect by or as if by scraping — often used with *up* or *together* ⟨*scrape* up the price of a ticket⟩
*intransitive verb*
**1 :** to move in sliding contact with a rough surface
**2 :** to accumulate money by small economies
**3 :** to draw back the foot along the ground in making a bow
**4 :** to make one's way with difficulty or succeed by a narrow margin ⟨just *scraped* by at school⟩
— **scrap·er** *noun*
— **scrape a leg :** to make a low bow
²**scrape** *noun* (15th century)
**1 a :** the act or process of scraping **b :** a sound made by scraping **c :** damage or injury caused by scraping **:** ABRASION ⟨bumps and *scrapes*⟩
**2 :** a bow made with a drawing back of the foot along the ground
**3 a :** a distressing encounter ⟨a *scrape* with death⟩ **b :** QUARREL, FIGHT
**scrap heap** *noun* (circa 1902)
**1 :** a pile of discarded metal
**2 :** the place where useless things are discarded
**scra·pie** \'skrā-pē\ *noun* [¹*scrape*] (1910)
**:** a usually fatal disease of the nervous system especially of sheep that is characterized by twitching, intense itching, excessive thirst, emaciation, weakness, and finally paralysis
**scrap·page** \'skra-pij\ *noun* (circa 1909)
**1 :** the scrapping of discarded objects (as automobiles)
**2 :** the rate at which objects are scrapped
**scrap·per** \'skra-pər\ *noun* (1874)
**:** FIGHTER, QUARRELER
**scrap·pi·ly** \'skra-pə-lē\ *adverb* (1886)
**:** in a scrappy manner
**scrap·pi·ness** \'skra-pē-nəs\ *noun* (1867)
**:** the quality or state of being scrappy
**scrap·ple** \'skra-pəl\ *noun* [diminutive of ¹*scrap*] (1855)
**:** a seasoned mixture of ground meat (as pork) and cornmeal set in a mold and served sliced and fried
¹**scrap·py** \'skra-pē\ *adjective* **scrap·pi·er; -est** [¹*scrap*] (1837)
**:** consisting of scraps ⟨*scrappy* meals⟩
²**scrappy** *adjective* **scrap·pi·er; -est** [³*scrap*] (circa 1896)
**1 :** QUARRELSOME
**2 :** having an aggressive and determined spirit **:** FEISTY
¹**scratch** \'skrach\ *verb* [Middle English *scracchen,* probably blend of *scratten* to scratch and *cracchen* to scratch] (15th century)
*transitive verb*
**1 :** to scrape or dig with the claws or nails
**2 :** to rub and tear or mark the surface of with something sharp or jagged
**3 :** to scrape or rub lightly (as to relieve itching)
**4 :** to scrape together **:** collect with difficulty or by effort
**5 :** to write or draw on a surface
**6 a :** to cancel or erase by or as if by drawing a line through **b :** to withdraw (an entry) from competition
**7 :** SCRIBBLE, SCRAWL
**8 :** to scrape along a rough surface ⟨*scratch* a match⟩
*intransitive verb*
**1 :** to use the claws or nails in digging, tearing, or wounding
**2 :** to scrape or rub oneself lightly (as to relieve itching)
**3 :** to gather money or get a living by hard work and especially through irregular means and sacrifice
**4 :** to make a thin grating sound
**5 :** to withdraw from a contest or engagement
**6 :** to make a scratch in billiards or pool
— **scratch·er** *noun*

— **scratch one's back :** to accommodate with a favor especially in expectation of like return
— **scratch the surface :** to make a superficial effort or modest start
²**scratch** *noun* (circa 1586)
**1 :** a mark or injury produced by scratching; *also* **:** a slight wound
**2 :** SCRAWL, SCRIBBLE
**3 :** the sound made by scratching
**4 a :** the starting line in a race **b :** a point at the beginning of a project at which nothing has been done ahead of time ⟨build a school system from *scratch*⟩
**5 a :** a test of courage **b :** satisfactory condition, level, or performance ⟨not up to *scratch*⟩
**6 :** a contestant whose name is withdrawn
**7 :** poultry feed (as mixed grains) scattered on the litter or ground especially to induce birds to exercise — called also *scratch feed*
**8 a :** a shot in billiards or pool that ends a player's turn; *specifically* **:** a shot in pool in which the cue ball falls into the pocket **b :** a shot that scores by chance **:** FLUKE
**9** *slang* **:** MONEY, FUNDS
³**scratch** *adjective* (1897)
**1 :** made as or used for a tentative effort
**2 :** made or done by chance and not as intended ⟨a *scratch* shot⟩
**3 :** arranged or put together with little selection **:** HAPHAZARD ⟨a *scratch* team⟩
**4 :** having no handicap or allowance ⟨a *scratch* golfer⟩
**5 :** made from scratch **:** made with basic ingredients ⟨a *scratch* cake⟩
**scratch-board** \'skrach-ˌbōrd, -ˌbȯrd\ *noun* (circa 1908)
**:** a black-surfaced cardboard having an undercoat of white clay on which an effect resembling engraving is achieved by scratching away portions of the surface to produce white lines
**scratch hit** *noun* (1903)
**:** a batted ball not solidly hit yet credited to the batter as a base hit
**scratch pad** *noun* (1895)
**:** a pad of scratch paper
**scratch paper** *noun* (1899)
**:** paper that may be used for casual writing
**scratch sheet** *noun* (1939)
**:** a racing publication listing competitors scratched from races and giving odds
**scratch test** *noun* (1937)
**:** a test for allergic susceptibility made by rubbing an extract of an allergy-producing substance into small breaks or scratches in the skin
**scratchy** \'skra-chē\ *adjective* **scratch·i·er; -est** (1827)
**1 :** marked or made with scratches ⟨*scratchy* drawing⟩ ⟨*scratchy* handwriting⟩
**2 :** likely to scratch **:** PRICKLY ⟨*scratchy* undergrowth⟩
**3 :** making a scratching noise
**4 :** uneven in quality **:** RAGGED
**5 :** causing tingling or itching **:** IRRITATING ⟨*scratchy* wool⟩
— **scratch·i·ly** \-chə-lē\ *adverb*
— **scratch·i·ness** \-chē-nəs\ *noun*
**scrawl** \'skrȯl\ *verb* [origin unknown] (1612)
*transitive verb*
**:** to write or draw awkwardly, hastily, or carelessly
*intransitive verb*
**:** to write awkwardly or carelessly
— **scrawl** *noun*
— **scrawl·er** *noun*
— **scrawly** \'skrȯ-lē\ *adjective*
**scraw·ny** \'skrȯ-nē\ *adjective* **scraw·ni·er; -est** [origin unknown] (1833)
**:** exceptionally thin and slight or meager in body ⟨*scrawny* scrub cattle⟩
**synonym** see LEAN
— **scraw·ni·ness** *noun*

**screak** \'skrēk\ *intransitive verb* [of Scandinavian origin; akin to Old Norse *skrækja* to screech] (circa 1500)
**:** to make a harsh shrill noise **:** SCREECH
— **screak** *noun*
— **screaky** \'skrē-kē\ *adjective*
¹**scream** \'skrēm\ *verb* [Middle English *scremen;* akin to Middle Dutch *schreem* scream] (12th century)
*intransitive verb*
**1 a** (1) **:** to voice a sudden sharp loud cry (2) **:** to produce harsh high tones **b :** to make a noise resembling a scream ⟨a *screaming* siren⟩ **c :** to move with great rapidity
**2 a :** to speak or write with intense or hysterical emotion **b :** to protest or complain vehemently **c :** to laugh hysterically
**3 :** to produce a vivid startling effect
*transitive verb*
**:** to utter with or as if with a scream
²**scream** *noun* (1605)
**1 :** a loud sharp penetrating cry or noise
**2 :** one that is very funny
**scream·er** \'skrē-mər\ *noun* (1712)
**1 :** one that screams
**2 :** any of a small family (Anhimidae) of South American wetland birds having a large body, long legs, and spurred wings
**3 :** a sensationally startling headline
**scream·ing** *adjective* (1848)
**1 :** so striking or conspicuous as to attract notice as if by screaming ⟨*screaming* headlines⟩ ⟨a *screaming* need for reform⟩ ⟨dressed in *screaming* red⟩
**2 :** so funny as to provoke screams of laughter ⟨a *screaming* farce⟩
— **scream·ing·ly** *adverb*
**screaming mee·mies** \-'mē-mēz\ *noun plural but singular in construction* [origin unknown] (1942)
**:** nervous hysteria **:** JITTERS
**scree** \'skrē\ *noun* [of Scandinavian origin; akin to Old Norse *skritha* landslide, from *skrītha* to creep; akin to Old High German *scrītan* to go, Lithuanian *skriesti* to turn] (circa 1781)
**:** an accumulation of loose stones or rocky debris lying on a slope or at the base of a hill or cliff **:** TALUS
¹**screech** \'skrēch\ *noun* (1560)
**1 :** a high shrill piercing cry usually expressing pain or terror
**2 :** a sound resembling a screech
²**screech** *verb* [alteration of earlier *scritch,* from Middle English *scrichen;* akin to Old Norse *skrækja* to screech] (1577)
*intransitive verb*
**1 :** to utter a high shrill piercing cry **:** make an outcry usually in terror or pain
**2 :** to make a shrill high-pitched sound resembling a screech; *also* **:** to move with such a sound ⟨the car *screeched* to a stop⟩
*transitive verb*
**:** to utter with or as if with a screech
— **screech·er** *noun*
**screech owl** *noun* (1593)
**1 :** BARN OWL
**2 :** any of numerous New World owls (genus *Otus*); *especially* **:** a small North American owl (*O. asio*) with a pair of tufts of lengthened feathers on the head resembling ears
**screechy** \'skrē-chē\ *adjective* (circa 1830)
**:** producing a screech
**screed** \'skrēd\ *noun* [Middle English *screde* fragment, alteration of Old English *scrēade* — more at SHRED] (circa 1789)
**1 a :** a lengthy discourse **b :** an informal piece of writing
**2 :** a strip (as of plaster of the thickness planned for the coat) laid on as a guide

\ə\ abut \ᵊ\ kitten \ər\ further \a\ ash \ā\ ace
\ä\ mop, mar \au̇\ out \ch\ chin \e\ bet \ē\ easy
\g\ go \i\ hit \ī\ ice \j\ job \ŋ\ sing \ō\ go
\ȯ\ law \ȯi\ boy \th\ thin \th\ the \ü\ loot \u̇\ foot
\y\ yet \zh\ vision    *see also* Guide to Pronunciation

**3 :** a leveling device drawn over freshly poured concrete

**¹screen** \'skrēn\ *noun* [Middle English *screne,* from Middle French *escren,* from Middle Dutch *scherm;* akin to Old High German *skirm* shield; probably akin to Sanskrit *carman* skin, *kṛnāti* he injures — more at SHEAR] (14th century)
**1 :** a protective or ornamental device (as a movable partition) shielding an area from heat or drafts or from view
**2 :** something that shelters, protects, or hides: as **a :** a growth or stand of trees, shrubs, or plants **b :** a protective formation of troops, ships, or planes **c :** something that covers or disguises the true nature (as of an activity or feeling) ⟨greets strangers with a *screen* of excessive friendliness —Tony Schwartz⟩ **d** (1) **:** a maneuver in various sports (as basketball or ice hockey) whereby an opponent is legally impeded or his view of the play is momentarily blocked (2) **:** SCREEN PASS
**3 a :** a perforated plate or cylinder or a meshed wire or cloth fabric usually mounted and used to separate coarser from finer parts **b :** a system for examining and separating into different groups **c :** a piece of apparatus designed to prevent agencies in one part from affecting other parts ⟨an optical *screen*⟩ ⟨an electric *screen*⟩ ⟨a magnetic *screen*⟩ **d :** a frame holding a usually metallic netting used especially in a window or door to exclude pests (as insects)
**4 a :** a flat surface on which a picture or series of pictures is projected or reflected **b :** the surface on which the image appears in an electronic display (as in a television set, radar receiver, or computer terminal)
**5 :** a glass plate ruled with crossing opaque lines through which an image is photographed in making a halftone
**6 :** the motion-picture medium or industry

**²screen** (15th century)
*transitive verb*
**1 :** to guard from injury or danger
**2 a :** to give shelter or protection to with or as if with a screen **b :** to separate with or as if with a screen; *also* **:** to shield (an opponent) from a play or from view of a play
**3 a :** to pass (as coal, gravel, or ashes) through a screen to separate the fine part from the coarse; *also* **:** to remove by a screen **b** (1) **:** to examine usually methodically in order to make a separation into different groups (2) **:** to select or eliminate by a screening process
**4 :** to provide with a screen to keep out pests (as insects)
**5 a** (1) **:** to present (as a motion picture) for viewing on a screen (2) **:** to view the presentation of (as a motion picture) **b :** to present in a motion picture
*intransitive verb*
**1 :** to appear on a motion-picture screen
**2 :** to provide a screen in a game or sport
**synonym** see HIDE
— **screen·able** \'skrē-nə-bəl\ *adjective*
— **screen·er** *noun*

**screen·ing** \'skrē-niŋ\ *noun* (1725)
**1 :** the act or process of one that screens
**2** *plural but singular or plural in construction* **:** material (as waste or fine coal) separated out by means of a screen
**3 :** metal or plastic mesh (as for window screens)
**4 :** a showing of a motion picture

**screen·land** \'skrēn-ˌland\ *noun* (1925)
**:** FILMDOM

**screen memory** *noun* (1923)
**:** a recollection of early childhood that may be falsely recalled or magnified in importance and that masks another memory of deep emotional significance

**screen pass** *noun* (circa 1949)
**:** a forward pass in football to a receiver at or behind the line of scrimmage who is protected by a screen of blockers

**screen·play** \'skrēn-ˌplā\ *noun* (1916)
**:** the script and often shooting directions of a story prepared for motion-picture production

**screen test** *noun* (1927)
**:** a short film sequence for assessing the ability or suitability of a person for a motion-picture role
— **screen–test** *transitive verb*

**screen·writ·er** \'skrēn-ˌrī-tər\ *noun* (1921)
**:** a writer of screenplays

**¹screw** \'skrü\ *noun* [Middle English, from Middle French *escroe* female screw, nut, from Medieval Latin *scrofa,* from Latin, sow] (15th century)
**1 a :** a simple machine of the inclined plane type consisting of a spirally grooved solid cylinder and a correspondingly grooved hollow cylinder into which it fits **b :** a nail-shaped or rod-shaped piece with a spiral groove and a slotted or recessed head designed to be inserted into material by rotating (as with a screwdriver) and used for fastening pieces of solid material together
**2 a :** a screwlike form **:** SPIRAL **b :** a turn of a screw; *also* **:** a twist like the turn of a screw **c :** a screwlike device (as a corkscrew)
**3 :** a worn-out horse
**4** *chiefly British* **:** a small packet (as of tobacco)
**5 :** a prison guard
**6 :** one who bargains shrewdly; *also* **:** SKINFLINT
**7 :** a propeller especially of a ship
**8 a :** THUMBSCREW **2 b :** pressure or punitive measures intended to coerce — used chiefly in the phrase *put the screws on* or *put the screws to*
**9 a :** an act of sexual intercourse — usually considered vulgar **b :** a partner in sexual intercourse — usually considered vulgar
— **screw·like** \-ˌlīk\ *adjective*
— **have a screw loose :** to be mentally unbalanced

**²screw** (1605)
*transitive verb*
**1 a** (1) **:** to attach, fasten, or close by means of a screw (2) **:** to unite or separate by means of a screw or a twisting motion ⟨*screw* the two pieces together⟩ (3) **:** to press tightly in a device (as a vise) operated by a screw (4) **:** to operate, tighten, or adjust by means of a screw (5) **:** to torture by means of a thumbscrew **b :** to cause to rotate spirally about an axis
**2 a** (1) **:** to twist into strained configurations **:** CONTORT ⟨*screw* up his face⟩ (2) **:** SQUINT (3) **:** CRUMPLE **b :** to furnish with a spiral groove or ridge **:** THREAD
**3 :** to increase the intensity, quantity, or capability of ⟨trying to *screw* up courage to confess —Will Scott⟩
**4 a** (1) **:** to mistreat or exploit through extortion, trickery, or unfair actions; *especially* **:** to deprive of or cheat out of something due or expected ⟨*screwed* out of a job⟩ (2) **:** to treat so as to bring about injury or loss (as to a person's reputation) ⟨use the available Federal machinery to *screw* our political enemies —J. W. Dean III⟩ — often used as a generalized curse ⟨*screw* you!⟩ **b :** to extract by pressure or threat
**5 :** to copulate with — usually considered vulgar
*intransitive verb*
**1 :** to rotate like or as a screw
**2 :** to turn or move with a twisting or writhing motion
**3 :** COPULATE — usually considered vulgar
— **screw·er** *noun*

**screw around** *intransitive verb* (1939)
**1 :** to waste time with unproductive activity **:** DALLY
**2 :** to have sexual relations with someone outside of a marriage or steady relationship **:** be sexually promiscuous

**¹screw·ball** \'skrü-ˌböl\ *noun* (1928)

**1 :** a baseball pitch that spins and breaks in the opposite direction to a curve
**2 :** a whimsical, eccentric, or crazy person **:** ZANY

**²screwball** *adjective* (circa 1936)
**:** crazily eccentric or whimsical **:** ZANY

**screw·bean** \'skrü-ˌbēn\ *noun* (1866)
**1 :** a leguminous shrub or small tree (*Prosopis pubescens*) of the southwestern U.S. and northern Mexico — called also *screwbean mesquite*
**2 :** a spirally twisted sweet pod that is the fruit of the screwbean

**screw·driv·er** \'skrü-ˌdrī-vər\ *noun* (1779)
**1 :** a tool for turning screws
**2 :** vodka and orange juice served with ice

**screw eye** *noun* (1873)
**:** a wood screw with a head in the form of a loop

**screw jack** *noun* (1719)
**:** a screw-operated jack for lifting, exerting pressure, or adjusting position (as of a machine part)

**screw pine** *noun* (1836)
**:** any of a genus (*Pandanus* of the family Pandanaceae, the screw-pine family) of tropical monocotyledonous Old World plants with slender palmlike stems, often huge prop roots, and terminal crowns of swordlike leaves

**screw propeller** *noun* (1839)
**:** PROPELLER

**screw thread** *noun* (circa 1812)
**1 :** the projecting helical rib of a screw
**2 :** one complete turn of a screw thread

**screw·up** \'skrü-ˌəp\ *noun* (circa 1960)
**1 :** one who screws up
**2 :** BOTCH, BLUNDER

**screw up** (1680)
*transitive verb*
**1 :** to tighten, fasten, or lock by or as if by a screw
**2 a :** BUNGLE, BOTCH **b :** to cause to act or function in a crazy or confused way **:** CONFOUND, DISTURB
*intransitive verb*
**:** to botch an activity or undertaking

**screw·worm** \'skrü-ˌwərm\ *noun* (1879)
**1 :** a blowfly (*Cochliomyia hominivorax*) of the warmer parts of America whose larva develops in sores or wounds or in the nostrils of mammals including humans with serious or sometimes fatal results; *especially* **:** its larva
**2 :** any of several flies other than the screwworm and especially their larvae which parasitize the flesh of mammals

**screwy** \'skrü-ē\ *adjective* **screw·i·er; -est** (1887)
**1 :** crazily absurd, eccentric, or unusual
**2 :** CRAZY, INSANE
— **screw·i·ness** *noun*

**scrib·al** \'skrī-bəl\ *adjective* (1857)
**:** of, relating to, or due to a scribe

**scrib·ble** \'skri-bəl\ *verb* **scrib·bled; scrib·bling** \-b(ə-)liŋ\ [Middle English *scriblen,* from Medieval Latin *scribillare,* from Latin *scribere* to write] (15th century)
*transitive verb*
**1 :** to write hastily or carelessly without regard to legibility or form
**2 :** to cover with careless or worthless writings or drawings
*intransitive verb*
**:** to write or draw hastily and carelessly
— **scribble** *noun*

**scrib·bler** \'skri-b(ə-)lər\ *noun* (circa 1553)
**1 :** one that scribbles
**2 :** a minor or insignificant author

**¹scribe** \'skrīb\ *noun* [Middle English, from Latin *scriba* official writer, from *scribere* to write; akin to Greek *skariphasthai* to scratch an outline] (14th century)
**1 :** one of a learned class in ancient Israel through New Testament times studying the Scriptures and serving as copyists, editors, teachers, and jurists

**2 a :** an official or public secretary or clerk **b** : a copier of manuscripts
**3 :** WRITER; *specifically* : JOURNALIST
**²scribe** *intransitive verb* **scribed; scribing** (1782)
: to work as a scribe : WRITE
**³scribe** *transitive verb* **scribed; scrib·ing** [probably short for *describe*] (1678)
**1 :** to mark a line on by cutting or scratching with a pointed instrument
**2 :** to make by cutting or scratching
**⁴scribe** *noun* (1812)
: SCRIBER
**scrib·er** \'skrī-bər\ *noun* (circa 1836)
: a sharp-pointed tool for making marks and especially for marking off material (as wood or metal) to be cut
**scrieve** \'skrēv\ *intransitive verb* [of Scandinavian origin; akin to Old Norse *skrefa* to stride] (1785)
*Scottish* : to move along swiftly and smoothly
**scrim** \'skrim\ *noun* [origin unknown] (1792)
**1 :** a durable plain-woven usually cotton fabric for use in clothing, curtains, building, and industry
**2 :** a theater drop that appears opaque when a scene in front is lighted and transparent or translucent when a scene in back is lighted
**3 :** something likened to a theater scrim
**¹scrim·mage** \'skri-mij\ *noun* [Middle English *scrymmage*, alteration of *skyrmissh* skirmish] (15th century)
**1 a :** a minor battle : SKIRMISH **b :** a confused fight : SCUFFLE
**2 a :** the interplay between two football teams that begins with the snap of the ball and continues until the ball is dead **b :** practice play (as in football or basketball) between two squads
**²scrimmage** *verb* **scrim·maged; scrim·mag·ing** (circa 1825)
*intransitive verb*
: to take part in a scrimmage
*transitive verb*
: to play a scrimmage against
— **scrim·mag·er** *noun*
**scrimmage line** *noun* (circa 1909)
: LINE OF SCRIMMAGE
**scrimp** \'skrimp\ *verb* [perhaps of Scandinavian origin; akin to Swedish *skrympa* to shrink, Middle Low German *schrempen* to contract — more at SHRIMP] (circa 1774)
*transitive verb*
**1 :** to be stingy in providing for
**2 :** to make too small, short, or scanty
*intransitive verb*
: to be frugal or stingy
— **scrimpy** \'skrim-pē\ *adjective*
**scrim·shan·der** \'skrim-,shan-dər\ *noun* [origin unknown] (1851)
: a person who creates scrimshaw
**¹scrim·shaw** \'skrim-,shȯ\ *verb* [origin unknown] (circa 1826)
*transitive verb*
: to carve or engrave into scrimshaw
*intransitive verb*
: to produce scrimshaw
**²scrimshaw** *noun* (circa 1864)
**1 :** any of various carved or engraved articles made originally by American whalers usually from baleen or whale ivory
**2 :** scrimshawed work
**3 :** the art, practice, or technique of producing scrimshaw
**¹scrip** \'skrip\ *noun* [Middle English *scrippe*, from Medieval Latin *scrippum* pilgrim's knapsack] (13th century)
*archaic* : a small bag or wallet
**²scrip** *noun* [alteration of *script*] (1590)
**1 :** a short writing (as a certificate, schedule, or list)
**2 :** a small piece
**3 a :** any of various documents used as evidence that the holder or bearer is entitled to receive something (as a fractional share of

stock or an allotment of land) **b :** paper currency or a token issued for temporary use in an emergency
**¹script** \'skript\ *noun* [Middle English, from Latin *scriptum* thing written, from neuter of *scriptus*, past participle of *scribere* to write — more at SCRIBE] (14th century)
**1 a :** something written : TEXT **b :** an original or principal instrument or document **c** (1) : MANUSCRIPT 1 (2) : the written text of a stage play, screenplay, or broadcast; *specifically* : the one used in production or performance
**2 a :** a style of printed letters that resembles handwriting **b :** written characters : HANDWRITING **c :** ALPHABET
**3 :** a plan of action
**²script** *transitive verb* (1935)
**1 :** to prepare a script for or from
**2 :** to provide carefully considered details for (as a plan of action)
**script·er** \'skrip-tər\ *noun* (1939)
: SCRIPTWRITER
**scrip·to·ri·um** \skrip-'tōr-ē-əm, -'tȯr-\ *noun, plural* **-ria** \-ē-ə\ [Medieval Latin, from Latin *scribere*] (1774)
: a copying room for the scribes in a medieval monastery
**scrip·tur·al** \'skrip(t)-sh(ə-)rəl\ *adjective* (1641)
: of, relating to, contained in, or according to a sacred writing; *especially* : BIBLICAL
— **scrip·tur·al·ly** *adverb*
**scrip·ture** \'skrip(t)-shər\ *noun* [Middle English, from Late Latin *scriptura*, from Latin, act or product of writing, from *scriptus*] (14th century)
**1 a** (1) *capitalized* : the books of the Bible — often used in plural (2) *often capitalized* : a passage from the Bible **b :** a body of writings considered sacred or authoritative
**2 :** something written ⟨the primitive man's awe for any *scripture* —George Santayana⟩
**script·writ·er** \'skrip(t)-,rī-tər\ *noun* (1935)
: a person who writes scripts
**scriv·en·er** \'skriv-nər, 'skri-və-\ *noun* [Middle English *scriveiner*, alteration of *scrivein*, from Middle French *escrivein*, from (assumed) Vulgar Latin *scriban-, scriba*, alteration of Latin *scriba* scribe] (14th century)
**1 :** a professional or public copyist or writer : SCRIBE
**2 :** NOTARY PUBLIC
**scrod** \'skräd\ *noun* [origin unknown] (1841)
: a young fish (as a cod or haddock); *especially* : one split and boned for cooking
**scrof·u·la** \'skrȯ-fyə-lə, 'skrä-\ *noun* [New Latin, back-formation from Late Latin *scrofulae*, plural, swellings of the lymph nodes of the neck, from plural of *scrofula*, diminutive of Latin *scrofa* breeding sow] (1791)
: tuberculosis of lymph nodes especially in the neck
**scrof·u·lous** \-ləs\ *adjective* (1612)
**1 :** of, relating to, or affected with scrofula
**2 a :** having a diseased run-down appearance **b :** morally contaminated
**¹scroll** \'skrōl\ *noun* [Middle English *scrowle*, blend of *rolle* roll and *scrowe* scrap, scroll (from Middle French *escroue*, of Germanic origin; akin to Old English *scrēade* shred)] (15th century)
**1 a :** a roll (as of papyrus, leather, or parchment) for writing a document **b** *archaic* : a written message **c :** ROSTER, LIST **d :** a riband with rolled ends often inscribed with a motto
**2 a :** something resembling a scroll in shape; *especially* : a spiral or convoluted form in ornamental design derived from the curves of a loosely or partly rolled parchment scroll **b :** the curved head of a bowed stringed musical instrument — see VIOLIN illustration
**²scroll** (1973)

scroll 1

*intransitive verb*
: to move text or graphics up or down or across a display screen as if by unrolling a scroll
*transitive verb*
: to cause (text or graphics on a display screen) to move in scrolling
**scroll saw** *noun* (1851)
**1 :** FRETSAW
**2 :** JIGSAW 1
**scroll·work** \'skrōl-,wərk\ *noun* (1739)
: ornamentation characterized by scrolls; *especially* : fancy designs in wood often made with a scroll saw
**scrooge** \'skrüj\ *noun, often capitalized* [Ebenezer *Scrooge*, character in the story *A Christmas Carol* (1843) by Charles Dickens] (1899)
: a miserly person
**scro·tum** \'skrō-təm\ *noun, plural* **scro·ta** \-tə\ *or* **scrotums** [Latin; akin to Latin *scrautum* quiver] (1597)
: the external pouch that in most mammals contains the testes
— **scro·tal** \'skrō-t³l\ *adjective*
**scrouge** \'skraůj, 'skrüj\ *verb* **scrouged; scroug·ing** [alteration of English dialect *scruze* to squeeze] (1755)
*chiefly dialect* : CROWD, PRESS
**scrounge** \'skraůnj\ *verb* **scrounged; scroung·ing** [alteration of English dialect *scrunge* to wander about idly] (circa 1909)
*transitive verb*
**1 :** STEAL, SWIPE
**2 a :** to get as needed by or as if by foraging, scavenging, or borrowing **b :** FINAGLE, WHEEDLE — often used with *up*
*intransitive verb*
: to search about and turn up something needed from whatever source is available; *also* : to actively seek money, work, or sustenance from any available source
— **scroung·er** *noun*
**scroungy** \'skraůn-jē\ *adjective* **scroung·i·er; -est** (circa 1960)
: being shabby, dirty, or unkempt
**¹scrub** \'skrəb\ *noun, often attributive* [Middle English, alteration of *schrobbe* shrub — more at SHRUB] (14th century)
**1 a :** a stunted tree or shrub **b :** vegetation consisting chiefly of scrubs **c :** a tract covered with scrub
**2 :** a domestic animal of mixed or unknown parentage and usually inferior conformation : MONGREL
**3 :** a person of insignificant size or standing
**4 :** a player not belonging to the first string
**²scrub** *verb* **scrubbed; scrub·bing** [of Low German or Scandinavian origin; akin to Middle Low German & Middle Dutch *schrubben* to scrub, Swedish *skrubba*] (circa 1595)
*transitive verb*
**1 a** (1) : to clean with hard rubbing : SCOUR (2) : to remove by scrubbing **b :** to subject to friction : RUB
**2 :** WASH 6c(2)
**3 :** CANCEL, ELIMINATE
*intransitive verb*
**1 :** to use hard rubbing in cleaning
**2 :** to prepare for surgery by scrubbing oneself
— **scrub·ba·ble** \'skrə-bə-bəl\ *adjective*
**³scrub** *noun* (1621)
**1 :** an act or instance of scrubbing; *especially* : CANCELLATION
**2 :** one that scrubs
**¹scrubbed** \'skrə-bəd\ *adjective* [¹*scrub*] (1596)
*archaic* : SCRUBBY 1

**²scrubbed** \'skrəbd\ *adjective* [from past participle of ²*scrub*] (1948)
: giving the impression of being clean or wholesome as if from scrubbing ⟨days when studios manufactured *scrubbed* public images for their stars —Sally Helgesen⟩

**scrub·ber** \'skrə-bər\ *noun* (1839)
: one that scrubs; *especially* : an apparatus for removing impurities especially from gases

**scrub brush** *noun* (1897)
: a brush with hard bristles for heavy cleaning — called also *scrubbing brush*

**scrub·by** \'skrə-bē\ *adjective* **scrub·bi·er; -est** [¹*scrub*] (1591)
1 : inferior in size or quality : STUNTED ⟨*scrubby* cattle⟩
2 : covered with or consisting of scrub
3 : SHABBY, PALTRY

**scrub·land** \'skrəb-,land\ *noun* (1779)
: land covered with scrub

**scrub nurse** *noun* (1905)
: a nurse who assists the surgeon in an operating room

**scrub oak** *noun* (1766)
: any of various chiefly American oaks (as *Quercus ilicifolia* of the northeastern U.S.) of small size and usually shrubby habit

**scrub pine** *noun* (1791)
: a pine of dwarf, straggly, or scrubby growth usually by reason of environmental conditions; *specifically* : a pine tree unsuitable for lumber by reason of inferior or defective growth

**scrub typhus** *noun* (1929)
: TSUTSUGAMUSHI DISEASE

**scrub·wom·an** \'skrəb-,wu̇-mən\ *noun* (1873)
: CHARWOMAN

**scruff** \'skrəf\ *noun* [alteration of earlier *scuff*, of unknown origin] (1790)
: the back of the neck : NAPE

**scruffy** \'skrə-fē\ *adjective* **scruff·i·er; -est** [English dialect *scruff* something worthless] (1871)
: UNKEMPT, SLOVENLY, SHAGGY
— **scruff·i·ly** \-fə-lē\ *adverb*
— **scruff·i·ness** \-fē-nəs\ *noun*

**scrum** \'skrəm\ *noun* [short for *scrummage*, alteration of *scrimmage*] (1857)
1 *or* **scrum·mage** \'skrə-mij\ : a rugby play in which the forwards of each side come together in a tight formation and struggle to gain possession of the ball when it is tossed in among them
2 *British* : MADHOUSE 2
— **scrummage** *intransitive verb*

**scrump·tious** \'skrəm(p)-shəs\ *adjective* [perhaps alteration of *sumptuous*] (1830)
: DELIGHTFUL, EXCELLENT; *especially* : DELICIOUS
— **scrump·tious·ly** *adverb*

**¹scrunch** \'skrənch, 'skrunch\ *verb* [alteration of ¹*crunch*] (circa 1790)
*transitive verb*
1 : CRUNCH, CRUSH
2 a : to draw or squeeze together tightly **b** : CRUMPLE — often used with *up* **c** : to cause (as one's features) to draw together — usually used with *up*
*intransitive verb*
1 : to move with or make a crunching sound
2 : CROUCH, HUNCH; *also* : SQUEEZE

**²scrunch** *noun* (1857)
: a crunching sound

**¹scru·ple** \'skrü-pəl\ *noun* [Middle English *scriple*, from Latin *scrupulus* a unit of weight, diminutive of *scrupus* sharp stone] (14th century)
1 — see WEIGHT table
2 : a minute part or quantity : IOTA

**²scruple** *noun* [Middle English *scrupul*, from Middle French *scrupule*, from Latin *scrupulus*, diminutive of *scrupus* source of uneasiness, literally, sharp stone] (15th century)
1 : an ethical consideration or principle that inhibits action
2 : the quality or state of being scrupulous

3 : mental reservation ◆
*synonym* see QUALM

**³scruple** *intransitive verb* **scru·pled; scru·pling** \-p(ə-)liŋ\ (1627)
1 : to have scruples
2 : to show reluctance on grounds of conscience : HESITATE

**scru·pu·los·i·ty** \,skrü-pyə-'lä-sə-tē\ *noun* (1526)
1 : the quality or state of being scrupulous
2 : ²SCRUPLE 1

**scru·pu·lous** \'skrü-pyə-ləs\ *adjective* [Middle English, from Latin *scrupulosus*, from *scrupulus*] (15th century)
1 : having moral integrity : acting in strict regard for what is considered right or proper
2 : punctiliously exact : PAINSTAKING ⟨working with *scrupulous* care⟩
*synonym* see UPRIGHT, CAREFUL
*word history* see SCRUPLE
— **scru·pu·lous·ly** *adverb*
— **scru·pu·lous·ness** *noun*

**scru·ta·ble** \'skrü-tə-bəl\ *adjective* [Late Latin *scrutabilis* searchable, from Latin *scrutari*] (circa 1600)
: capable of being deciphered : COMPREHENSIBLE

**scru·ti·neer** \,skrü-t³n-'ir\ *noun* (1557)
1 : one that examines
2 *British* : one who takes or counts votes

**scru·ti·nise** *British variant of* SCRUTINIZE

**scru·ti·nize** \'skrü-t³n-,īz\ *verb* **-nized; -nizing** (1671)
*transitive verb*
: to examine closely and minutely
*intransitive verb*
: to make a scrutiny ☆
— **scru·ti·niz·er** *noun*

**scru·ti·ny** \'skrü-t³n-ē, 'skrüt-nē\ *noun, plural* **-nies** [Latin *scrutinium*, from *scrutari* to search, examine, probably from *scruta* trash] (1604)
1 : a searching study, inquiry, or inspection : EXAMINATION
2 : a searching look
3 : close watch : SURVEILLANCE

**scu·ba** \'skü-bə\ *noun, often attributive* [*self-contained underwater breathing apparatus*] (1952)
: an apparatus utilizing a portable supply of compressed gas (as air) supplied at a regulated pressure and used for breathing while swimming underwater

**scuba diver** *noun* (1958)
: one who swims underwater with the aid of scuba gear
— **scuba dive** *intransitive verb*

**¹scud** \'skəd\ *intransitive verb* **scud·ded; scud·ding** [probably of Scandinavian origin; akin to Norwegian *skudda* to push] (1532)
1 : to move or run swiftly especially as if driven forward
2 : to run before a gale

**²scud** *noun* (1609)
1 : the action of scudding : RUSH
2 a : loose vapory clouds driven swiftly by the wind **b** (1) : a slight sudden shower (2) : mist, rain, snow, or spray driven by the wind **c** : a gust of wind

**scu·do** \'skü-(,)dō\ *noun, plural* **scu·di** \-(,)dē\ [Italian, literally, shield, from Latin *scutum* — more at ESQUIRE] (1644)
1 : a gold or silver coin formerly used in Italy
2 : a unit of value equivalent to a scudo

**¹scuff** \'skəf\ *verb* [probably of Scandinavian origin; akin to Swedish *skuffa* to push] (1768)
*intransitive verb*
1 a : to walk without lifting the feet : SHUFFLE
**b** : to poke or shuffle a foot in exploration or embarrassment
2 : to become scratched, chipped, or roughened by wear

*transitive verb*
1 : ³CUFF
2 a : to scrape (the feet) along a surface while walking or back and forth while standing **b** : to poke at with the toe
3 : to scratch, gouge, or wear away the surface of

**²scuff** *noun* (1899)
1 a : a noise of or as if of scuffing **b** : the act or an instance of scuffing **c** : a mark or injury caused by scuffing
2 : a flat-soled slipper without quarter or heel strap — compare MULE

**scuf·fle** \'skə-fəl\ *intransitive verb* **scuf·fled; scuf·fling** \-f(ə-)liŋ\ [probably of Scandinavian origin; akin to Swedish *skuffa* to push] (1590)
1 a : to struggle at close quarters with disorder and confusion **b** : to struggle (as by working odd jobs) to get by
2 a : to move with a quick shuffling gait : SCURRY **b** : SHUFFLE
— **scuffle** *noun*

**scuffle hoe** *noun* (1856)
: a garden hoe that has both edges sharpened and can be pushed forward or drawn back

**¹scull** \'skəl\ *noun* [Middle English *sculle*] (14th century)
1 a : an oar used at the stern of a boat to propel it forward with a thwartwise motion **b** : either of a pair of oars usually less than 10 feet (3 meters) in length and operated by one person
2 : a racing shell propelled by one or two persons using sculls

**²scull** (1624)
*transitive verb*
: to propel (a boat) by sculls or by a large oar worked thwartwise
*intransitive verb*
: to scull a boat
— **scull·er** *noun*

**scul·lery** \'skə-lə-rē, 'skəl-rē\ *noun, plural* **-ler·ies** [Middle English, department of household in charge of dishes, from Middle French *escuelerie*, from *escuelle* bowl, from Latin *scutella* drinking bowl — more at SCUTTLE] (15th century)

---

☆ **SYNONYMS**
**Scrutinize, scan, inspect, examine** mean to look at or over. SCRUTINIZE stresses close attention to minute detail ⟨*scrutinized* the hospital bill⟩. SCAN implies a surveying from point to point often suggesting a cursory overall observation ⟨*scanned* the wine list⟩. INSPECT implies scrutinizing for errors or defects ⟨*inspected* my credentials⟩. EXAMINE suggests a scrutiny in order to determine the nature, condition, or quality of a thing ⟨*examined* the specimens⟩.

---

◇ **WORD HISTORY**
**scruple** In Latin *scrupus* meant literally "sharp stone" and metaphorically "source of uneasiness," alluding to the way a sharp pebble that has worked its way into one's shoe becomes a nagging cause of discomfort. The much more commonly used diminutive form *scrupulus* had the same metaphorical meaning "source of anxiety." The derived adjective *scrupulosus* had likewise both a concrete meaning, "full of sharp rocks, jagged," and a metaphorical one—not "full of sources of anxiety," as one might expect, but "marked by careful attention to detail, taking precautions." Thus it denoted the attitude of someone following a rocky path and trying to avoid a spill. Both *scrupulus* and *scrupulosus* found their way into English in their metaphorical senses, respectively as *scruple* "an ethical consideration" and *scrupulous*.

: a room for cleaning and storing dishes and cooking utensils and for doing messy kitchen work

**scul·lion** \'skəl-yən\ *noun* [Middle English *sculion*, from Middle French *escouillon* dish-cloth, alteration of *escouve*, from *escouve* broom, from Latin *scopae*, literally, twigs bound together] (15th century)
: a kitchen helper

**scul·pin** \'skəl-pən\ *noun, plural* **sculpins** *also* **sculpin** [origin unknown] (1672)
**1** : any of a family (Cottidae) of spiny large-headed broad-mouthed often scale-less bony fishes
**2** : a scorpion fish (*Scorpaena guttata*) of the southern California coast caught for food and sport

sculpin 1

**sculpt** \'skəlpt\ *verb* [French *sculpter*, alteration of obsolete *sculper*, from Latin *sculpere*] (1864)
: CARVE, SCULPTURE

**sculp·tor** \'skəlp-tər\ *noun* [Latin, from *sculpere*] (1634)
: an artist who makes sculptures

**sculp·tress** \-trəs\ *noun* (1662)
: a woman artist who makes sculptures

**sculp·tur·al** \'skəlp-chə-rəl, 'skəlp-shrəl\ *adjective* (1819)
**1** : of or relating to sculpture
**2** : resembling sculpture : SCULPTURESQUE
— **sculp·tur·al·ly** *adverb*

**¹sculp·ture** \'skəlp-chər\ *noun* [Middle English, from Latin *sculptura*, from *sculptus*, past participle of *sculpere* to carve, alteration of *scalpere* to scratch, carve] (14th century)
**1 a** : the action or art of processing (as by carving, modeling, or welding) plastic or hard materials into works of art **b** (1) : work produced by sculpture (2) : a three-dimensional work of art (as a statue)
**2** : impressed or raised markings or a pattern of such especially on a plant or animal part

**²sculpture** *verb* **sculp·tured; sculp·tur·ing** \'skəlp-chə-riŋ, 'skəlp-shriŋ\ (1645)
*transitive verb*
**1 a** : to form an image or representation of from solid material (as wood or stone) **b** : to form into a three-dimensional work of art
**2** : to change (the form of the earth's surface) by natural processes (as erosion and deposition)
**3** : to shape by or as if by carving or molding
*intransitive verb*
: to work as a sculptor

**sculp·tur·esque** \,skəlp-chə-'resk\ *adjective* (1835)
: done in the manner of or resembling sculpture
— **sculp·tur·esque·ly** *adverb*

**¹scum** \'skəm\ *noun* [Middle English, from Middle Dutch *schum*; akin to Old High German *scūm* foam] (14th century)
**1 a** : extraneous matter or impurities risen to or formed on the surface of a liquid often as a foul filmy covering **b** : the scoria of metals in a molten state : DROSS **c** : a slimy film on a solid or gelatinous object
**2 a** : REFUSE **b** : a low, vile, or worthless person or group of people
— **scum·my** \'skə-mē\ *adjective*

**²scum** *intransitive verb* **scummed; scum·ming** (1661)
: to become covered with or as if with scum

**scum·bag** \'skəm-,bag *also* -,bāg\ *noun* (1967)
*slang* : a dirty or despicable person

**¹scum·ble** \'skəm-bəl\ *transitive verb* **scum·bled; scum·bling** \-b(ə-)liŋ\ [perhaps frequentative of ²*scum*] (1798)
**1 a** : to make (as color or a painting) less brilliant by covering with a thin coat of opaque or semiopaque color **b** : to apply (a color) in this manner

**2** : to soften the lines or colors of (a drawing) by rubbing lightly

**²scumble** *noun* (1834)
**1** : the act or effect of scumbling
**2** : a material used for scumbling

**scun·gil·li** \skün-'jē-lē, -'gē-, -'ji-\ *noun* [Italian dialect (Neapolitan) *scuncigli*, plural of *scunciglio* conch] (1945)
: conch used as food

**¹scun·ner** \'skə-nər\ *intransitive verb* [Middle English (Scots) *skunniren*] (14th century)
*chiefly Scottish* : to be in a state of disgusted irritation

**²scunner** *noun* (circa 1520)
: an unreasonable or extreme dislike or prejudice

**scup** \'skəp\ *noun, plural* **scup** *also* **scups** [short for *scuppaug*, modification of Narraganset *mishcuppaûog*] (circa 1848)
: a porgy (*Stenotomus chrysops*) occurring along the Atlantic coast of the U.S. chiefly from North Carolina to Maine and used as a panfish

**¹scup·per** \'skə-pər\ *noun* [Middle English *skopper*] (15th century)
**1** : an opening cut through the bulwarks of a ship so that water falling on deck may flow overboard
**2** : an opening in the wall of a building through which water can drain from a floor or flat roof

**²scupper** *transitive verb* [origin unknown] (1899)
*British* : to defeat or put an end to : DO IN 1a

**scup·per·nong** \-,nòŋ, -,näŋ\ *noun* [*Scuppernong*, river and lake in North Carolina] (1811)
**1** : MUSCADINE; *especially* : a cultivated muscadine with yellowish green plum-flavored fruits
**2** : a sweet aromatic amber-colored wine made from scuppernongs

**scurf** \'skərf\ *noun* [Middle English, from Old English, of Scandinavian origin; akin to Icelandic *skurfa* scurf, Old High German *scorf* scurf, Old English *sceorfan* to scarify] (before 12th century)
**1** : thin dry scales detached from the epidermis especially in an abnormal skin condition; *specifically* : DANDRUFF
**2 a** : something like flakes or scales adhering to a surface **b** : the foul remains of something adherent
**3 a** : a scaly deposit or covering on some plant parts; *also* : a localized or general darkening and roughening of a plant surface usually more pronounced than russeting **b** : a plant disease characterized by scurf
— **scurfy** \'skər-fē\ *adjective*

**scur·rile** *or* **scur·ril** \'skər-əl, 'skə-rəl\ *adjective* [Middle French *scurrile*, from Latin *scurrilis*, from *scurra* buffoon] (1567)
: SCURRILOUS

**scur·ril·i·ty** \skə-'ri-lə-tē\ *noun, plural* **-ties** (1508)
**1** : the quality or state of being scurrilous
**2 a** : scurrilous or abusive language **b** : an offensively rude or abusive remark

**scur·ri·lous** \'skər-ə-ləs, 'skə-rə-\ *adjective* (1576)
**1 a** : using or given to coarse language **b** : being vulgar and evil 〈*scurrilous* imposters who used a religious exterior to rob poor people —Edwin Benson〉
**2** : containing obscenities, abuse, or slander 〈a . . . campaign filled with *scurrilous* charges and countercharges —A. D. Graeff〉
— **scur·ri·lous·ly** *adverb*
— **scur·ri·lous·ness** *noun*

**scur·ry** \'skər-ē, 'skə-rē\ *intransitive verb* **scur·ried; scur·ry·ing** [short for *hurry-scurry*, reduplication of *hurry*] (1810)
**1** : to move in or as if in a brisk pace : SCAMPER
**2** : to move around in an agitated, confused, or fluttering manner
— **scurry** *noun*

**¹scur·vy** \'skər-vē\ *noun* [²*scurvy*] (circa 1565)
: a disease marked by spongy gums, loosening of the teeth, and a bleeding into the skin and mucous membranes and caused by a lack of vitamin C

**²scurvy** *adjective* [*scurf*] (1579)
: disgustingly mean or contemptible : DESPICABLE 〈a *scurvy* trick〉
**synonym** see CONTEMPTIBLE
— **scur·vi·ly** \-və-lē\ *adverb*
— **scur·vi·ness** \-vē-nəs\ *noun*

**scurvy grass** *noun* (1597)
: a cruciferous herb (as *Cochlearia officinalis*) formerly believed useful in preventing or treating scurvy

**scut** \'skət\ *noun* [origin unknown] (circa 1530)
: a short erect tail (as of a hare)

**scu·tage** \'skü-tij, 'skyü-\ *noun* [Middle English, from Medieval Latin *scutagium*, from Latin *scutum* shield — more at ESQUIRE] (15th century)
: a tax levied on a vassal or a knight in lieu of military service

**¹scutch** \'skəch\ *transitive verb* [obsolete French *escoucher*, from (assumed) Vulgar Latin *excuticare* to beat out, from Latin *excutere*, from *ex-* + *quatere* to shake, strike] (1733)
: to separate the woody fiber from (flax or hemp) by beating

**²scutch** *noun* (circa 1791)
**1** : SCUTCHER
**2** : a bricklayer's hammer for cutting, trimming, and dressing bricks

**scutch·eon** \'skə-chən\ *noun* [Middle English *scochon*, from Middle French *escuchon*] (14th century)
: ESCUTCHEON

**scutch·er** \'skə-chər\ *noun* (1776)
: an implement or machine for scutching flax or cotton

**scute** \'sküt, 'skyüt\ *noun* [New Latin *scutum*, from Latin, shield — more at ESQUIRE] (1898)
: an external bony or horny plate or large scale

**scu·tel·late** \skü-'te-lət, skyü-; 'sk(y)ü-t°l-,āt\ *or* **scu·tel·lat·ed** \'sk(y)ü-t°l-,ā-təd\ *adjective* (1785)
: having or covered with scutella

**scu·tel·lum** \skü-'te-ləm, skyü-\ *noun, plural* **-la** \-lə\ [New Latin, diminutive of Latin *scutum* shield] (circa 1760)
**1** : a hard plate or scale (as on the thorax of an insect or the tarsus of a bird)
**2** : the shield-shaped cotyledon of a monocotyledon (as a grass)
— **scu·tel·lar** \-lər\ *adjective*

**scut·ter** \'skə-tər\ *intransitive verb* [alteration of ⁵*scuttle*] (1781)
: SCURRY, SCAMPER

**¹scut·tle** \'skə-t°l\ *noun* [Middle English *scutel*, from Latin *scutella* drinking bowl, tray, diminutive of *scutra* platter] (15th century)
**1** : a shallow open basket for carrying something (as grain or garden produce)
**2** : a metal pail that usually has a bail and a sloped lip and is used especially for carrying coal

**²scuttle** *noun* [Middle English *skottell*] (15th century)
**1** : a small opening in a wall or roof furnished with a lid: as **a** : a small opening or hatchway in the deck of a ship large enough to admit a person and with a lid for covering it **b** : a small hole in the side or bottom of a ship fitted with a covering or glazed
**2** : a covering that closes a scuttle

**³scuttle** *transitive verb* **scut·tled; scut·tling** \'skət-liŋ, 'skə-t°l-iŋ\ (1642)

**1 :** to cut a hole through the bottom, deck, or side of (a ship); *specifically* **:** to sink or attempt to sink by making holes through the bottom **2 :** DESTROY, WRECK; *also* **:** SCRAP 2

⁴**scuttle** *noun* [perhaps blend of *scud* and *shuttle*] (1623)
**1 :** a quick shuffling pace **2 :** a short swift run

⁵**scuttle** *intransitive verb* **scut·tled; scut·tling** \'skət-liŋ, 'skə-t°l-iŋ\ (1657)
**:** SCURRY

**scut·tle·butt** \'skə-t°l-,bət\ *noun* [²*scuttle* + ³*butt*] (1805)
**1 a :** a cask on shipboard to contain fresh water for a day's use **b :** a drinking fountain on a ship or at a naval or marine installation **2 :** RUMOR, GOSSIP

**scu·tum** \'skü-təm, 'skyü-\ *noun, plural* **scu·ta** \-tə\ [New Latin, from Latin, shield — more at ESQUIRE] (1771)
**:** a bony, horny, or chitinous plate **:** SCUTE

**scut work** \'skət-\ *noun* [probably from medical argot *scut* junior intern] (circa 1962)
**:** routine and often menial labor

**scuz·zy** \'skə-zē\ *adjective* **scuz·zi·er; -est** [origin unknown] (1969)
*slang* **:** dirty, shabby, or foul in condition or character

**Scyl·la** \'si-lə\ *noun* [Latin, from Greek *Skyllē*]
**:** a nymph changed into a monster in Greek mythology who terrorizes mariners in the Strait of Messina
**— between Scylla and Charybdis**
**:** between two equally hazardous alternatives

**scy·phis·to·ma** \sī-'fis-tə-mə\ *noun, plural* **-mae** \-(,)mē\ *also* **-mas** [New Latin, from Latin *scyphus* cup + Greek *stoma* mouth — more at STOMACH] (1878)
**:** a sexually produced scyphozoan larva that ultimately repeatedly constricts transversely to form free-swimming medusae

**scy·pho·zo·an** \,sī-fə-'zō-ən\ *noun* [New Latin *Scyphozoa*, from Latin *scyphus* + New Latin *-zoa*] (circa 1909)
**:** any of a class (Scyphozoa) of coelenterates that comprise jellyfishes lacking a true polyp and usually a velum
**— scyphozoan** *adjective*

¹**scythe** \'sīth, 'sī\ *noun* [Middle English *sithe*, from Old English *sīthe*; akin to Old English *sagu* saw — more at SAW] (before 12th century)
**:** an implement used for mowing (as grass) and composed of a long curving blade fastened at an angle to a long handle

²**scythe** *verb* **scythed; scyth·ing** (circa 1580)
*intransitive verb*
**:** to use a scythe
*transitive verb*
**:** to cut with or as if with a scythe

scythe

**Scyth·i·an** \'si-thē-ən, -thē-\ *noun* [Latin *Scytha*, from Greek *Skythēs*] (15th century)
**1 :** a member of an ancient nomadic people inhabiting Scythia **2 :** the Iranian language of the Scythians
**— Scythian** *adjective*

**sea** \'sē\ *noun* [Middle English *see*, from Old English *sǣ*; akin to Old High German *sē* sea, Gothic *saiws*] (before 12th century)
**1 a :** a great body of salty water that covers much of the earth; *broadly* **:** the waters of the earth as distinguished from the land and air **b :** a body of salt water of second rank more or less landlocked ⟨the Mediterranean *sea*⟩ **c :** OCEAN **d :** an inland body of water — used especially for names of such bodies ⟨the Caspian *Sea*⟩ ⟨the *Sea* of Galilee⟩ **2 a :** surface motion on a large body of water or its direction; *also* **:** a large swell or wave

— often used in plural ⟨heavy *seas*⟩ **b :** the disturbance of the ocean or other body of water due to the wind **3 :** something likened to the sea especially in vastness ⟨the crowd was a *sea* of faces⟩ **4 :** the seafaring life **5 :** ³MARE
**— sea** *adjective*
**— at sea 1 :** on the sea; *specifically* **:** on a sea voyage **2 :** LOST, BEWILDERED
**— to sea :** to or on the open waters of the sea

**sea anchor** *noun* (1769)
**:** a drag typically of canvas thrown overboard to retard the drifting of a ship or seaplane and to keep its head to the wind

**sea anemone** *noun* (1742)
**:** any of numerous usually solitary anthozoan polyps (order Actiniaria) whose form, bright and varied colors, and cluster of tentacles superficially resemble a flower

**sea·bag** \'sē-,bag\ *noun* (1919)
**:** a cylindrical canvas bag used especially by a sailor for clothes and other gear

**sea bass** *noun* (1765)
**1 :** any of numerous marine bony fishes (family Serranidae) that are usually smaller and more active than the groupers; *especially* **:** a food and sport fish (*Centropristis striata*) of the Atlantic coast of the U.S. **2 :** any of numerous croakers or drums including noted sport and food fishes

**sea·bed** \-,bed\ *noun* (1838)
**:** the floor of a sea or ocean

**Sea·bee** \'sē-(,)bē\ *noun* [alteration of *cee* + *bee*; from the initials of *construction battalion*] (1942)
**:** a member of one of the U.S. Navy construction battalions for building naval shore facilities in combat zones

**sea·bird** \'sē-,bərd\ *noun* (1589)
**:** a bird (as a gull or albatross) frequenting the open ocean

**sea biscuit** *noun* (circa 1690)
**:** HARDTACK 1

**sea·board** \'sē-,bōrd, -,bȯrd\ *noun* (1788)
**:** SEACOAST; *also* **:** the country bordering a seacoast
**— seaboard** *adjective*

**sea·boot** \-,büt\ *noun* (1851)
**:** a very high waterproof boot used especially by sailors and fishermen

**sea·borg·i·um** \sē-'bȯr-gē-əm\ *noun* [New Latin, from Glenn T. *Seaborg*] (1994)
**:** UNNILHEXIUM

**sea·borne** \-,bōrn, -,bȯrn\ *adjective* (1823)
**1 :** borne over or on the sea ⟨a *seaborne* invasion⟩ **2 :** carried on by oversea shipping ⟨*seaborne* trade⟩

**sea bream** *noun* (circa 1530)
**:** any of numerous marine bony fishes (as of the family Sparidae)

**sea breeze** *noun* (1697)
**:** a cooling breeze blowing generally in the daytime inland from the sea

**sea captain** *noun* (1612)
**:** the master especially of a merchant vessel

**sea change** *noun* (1610)
**1** *archaic* **:** a change brought about by the sea **2 :** a marked change **:** TRANSFORMATION

**sea chest** *noun* (1669)
**:** a sailor's storage chest for personal property

**sea·coast** \'sē-,kōst\ *noun* (14th century)
**:** the shore or border of the land adjacent to the sea

**sea cow** *noun* (1613)
**:** SIRENIAN

**sea·craft** \'sē-,kraft\ *noun* (1727)
**1 :** skill in navigation **2 :** seagoing ships

**sea crayfish** *noun* (1601)
**:** SPINY LOBSTER

**sea cucumber** *noun* (1601)
**:** any of a class (Holothurioidea) of echinoderms having a tough muscular elongate body

with tentacles surrounding the mouth — called also *holothurian*

**sea devil** *noun* (1634)
**:** DEVILFISH 1

**sea dog** *noun* (1823)
**:** a veteran sailor

**sea duck** *noun* (1753)
**:** a diving duck (as a scoter, merganser, or eider) that frequents the sea

**sea duty** *noun* (1946)
**:** duty in the U.S. Navy performed with a deployable unit (as a ship or aircraft squadron)

**sea eagle** *noun* (1668)
**:** any of various fish-eating eagles (especially genus *Haliaeetus*)

**Sea Explorer** *noun* (1948)
**:** an Explorer in a scouting program that teaches seamanship

**sea fan** *noun* (1633)
**:** a gorgonian with a fan-shaped skeleton; *especially* **:** one (*Gorgonia flabellum*) of Florida and the West Indies

**sea·far·er** \'sē-,far-ər, -,fer-\ *noun* [*sea* + ¹*fare* + ²*-er*] (1513)
**:** MARINER

**sea·far·ing** \-,far-iŋ, -,fer-\ *noun* (1592)
**:** the use of the sea for travel or transportation
**— seafaring** *adjective*

**sea fire** *noun* (1814)
**:** marine bioluminescence

**sea·floor** \'sē-,flōr, -,flȯr\ *noun* (1855)
**:** SEABED

**sea·food** \-,füd\ *noun* (1836)
**:** edible marine fish and shellfish

**sea·fowl** \-,faul\ *noun* (14th century)
**:** SEABIRD

**sea·front** \-,frənt\ *noun* (1879)
**:** the waterfront of a seaside place

**sea·girt** \'sē-,gərt\ *adjective* (1616)
**:** surrounded by the sea

**sea·go·ing** \-,gō-iŋ, -,gȯ(-)iŋ\ *adjective* (1828)
**:** OCEANGOING

**sea grape** *noun* (1806)
**:** a tree (*Coccoloba uvifera*) of the buckwheat family that inhabits sandy shores from Florida to South America, has rounded leaves, and bears clusters of purple to whitish edible berries

**sea grass** *noun* (1578)
**:** any of various grasslike plants that inhabit coastal areas; *especially* **:** EELGRASS 1

**sea green** *noun* (1598)
**1 :** a moderate green or bluish green **2 :** a moderate yellow green

**sea·gull** \'sē-,gəl\ *noun* (1542)
**:** a gull frequenting the sea; *broadly* **:** GULL

**sea hare** *noun* (1593)
**:** any of various large opisthobranch mollusks (especially genus *Aplysia*) that have an arched back and two anterior tentacles and have the shell much reduced or missing

**sea holly** *noun* (1548)
**:** a European coastal herb (*Eryngium maritimum*) of the carrot family with spiny leaves and pale blue flowers

**sea horse** *noun* (circa 1500)
**1 :** WALRUS **2 :** a mythical creature half horse and half fish **3 :** any of a genus (*Hippocampus* of the family Syngnathidae) of small bony fishes that have the head angled downward toward the body which is carried vertically and are equipped with a prehensile tail

sea horse 3

**sea island cotton** *noun, often* S&I *capitalized* [*Sea Islands*, chain of islands off the southeastern U.S. coast] (1805)
**:** a cotton (*Gossypium barbadense*) with especially long silky fiber — called also *sea island*

**sea kale** *noun* (1699)
: a succulent Eurasian perennial herb (*Crambe maritima*) of the mustard family used as a potherb

**sea king** *noun* (1819)
: a Norse pirate chief

**¹seal** \'sē(ə)l\ *noun, plural* **seals** *also* **seal** [Middle English *sele,* from Old English *seolh;* akin to Old High German *selah* seal] (before 12th century)
**1** : any of numerous carnivorous marine mammals (families Phocidae and Otariidae) that live chiefly in cold regions and have limbs modified into webbed flippers adapted primarily to swimming; *especially* : a fur seal or hair seal as opposed to a sea lion
**2 a** : the pelt of a fur seal **b** : leather made from the skin of a seal
**3** : a dark brown

**²seal** *intransitive verb* (1828)
: to hunt seals

**³seal** *noun* [Middle English *seel,* from Old French, from Latin *sigillum* seal, from diminutive of *signum* sign, seal — more at SIGN] (13th century)
**1 a** : something that confirms, ratifies, or makes secure : GUARANTEE, ASSURANCE **b** (1) : a device with a cut or raised emblem, symbol, or word used especially to certify a signature or authenticate a document (2) : a medallion or ring face bearing such a device incised so that it can be impressed on wax or moist clay; *also* : a piece of wax or a wafer bearing such an impression **c** : an impression, device, or mark given the effect of a common-law seal by statute law or by American local custom recognized by judicial decision **d** : a usually ornamental adhesive stamp that may be used to close a letter or package; *especially* : one given in a fund-raising campaign
**2 a** : something that secures (as a wax seal on a document) **b** : a closure that must be broken to be opened and that thus reveals tampering **c** (1) : a tight and perfect closure (as against the passage of gas or water) (2) : a device to prevent the passage or return of gas or air into a pipe or container
**3** : a seal that is a symbol or mark of office
— **under seal** : with an authenticating seal affixed

**⁴seal** *transitive verb* (14th century)
**1 a** : to confirm or make secure by or as if by a seal **b** : to solemnize for eternity (as a marriage) by a Mormon rite
**2 a** : to set or affix an authenticating seal to; *also* : AUTHENTICATE, RATIFY **b** : to mark with a stamp or seal usually as an evidence of standard exactness, legal size, weight, or capacity, or merchantable quality
**3 a** : to fasten with or as if with a seal to prevent tampering **b** : to close or make secure against access, leakage, or passage by a fastening or coating **c** : to fix in position or close breaks in with a filling (as of plaster)
**4** : to determine irrevocably or indisputably ⟨that answer *sealed* our fate⟩

**sea lamprey** *noun* (1879)
: a large anadromous lamprey (*Petromyzon marinus*) that has a mottled upper surface, is an ectoparasite of fish, and is sometimes used as food

**sea–lane** \'sē-ˌlān\ *noun* (1927)
: an established sea route

**seal·ant** \'sē-lənt\ *noun* (1944)
: a sealing agent ⟨radiator *sealant*⟩

**sea lavender** *noun* (1597)
: any of a genus (*Limonium*) of chiefly perennial herbs of the plumbago family with small flowers and basal leaves

**sea lawyer** *noun* (1848)
: an argumentative captious sailor

**sealed–beam** \'sē(ə)l(d)-ˌbēm\ *adjective* (1939)
: being an electric lamp with a prefocused reflector and lens sealed in the lamp vacuum

**sea legs** *noun plural* (1712)
: bodily adjustment to the motion of a ship indicated especially by ability to walk steadily and by freedom from seasickness

**¹seal·er** \'sē-lər\ *noun* (15th century)
**1** : an official who attests or certifies conformity to a standard of correctness
**2** : a coat (as of size) applied to prevent subsequent coats of paint or varnish from sinking in

**²sealer** *noun* (1842)
: a person or a ship engaged in hunting seals

**sea lettuce** *noun* (1668)
: any of a genus (*Ulva*) of seaweeds with green fronds sometimes eaten as salad

**sea level** *noun* (1806)
: the level of the surface of the sea especially at its mean position midway between mean high and low water

**sea lily** *noun* (1876)
: CRINOID; *especially* : a stalked crinoid

**sealing wax** *noun* (14th century)
: a resinous composition that is plastic when warm and is used for sealing (as letters, dry cells, or cans)

**sea lion** *noun* (1697)
: any of several Pacific eared seals (as genera *Eumetopius* and *Zalophus*) that are usually larger than the related fur seals and lack a thick underfur

**seal off** *transitive verb* (1931)
: to close tightly

**seal point** *noun* [¹seal (the color)] (1939)
: a coat color of cats characterized by a cream or fawn body with dark brown points; *also* : a Siamese cat with such coloring

**seal ring** *noun* (1608)
: a finger ring engraved with a seal : SIGNET RING

**seal·skin** \'sē(ə)l-ˌskin\ *noun* (14th century)
**1** : the fur or pelt of a fur seal
**2** : a garment (as a jacket, coat, or cape) of sealskin
— **sealskin** *adjective*

**Sea·ly·ham terrier** \'sē-lē-ˌham-, *especially British* -lē-əm-\ *noun* [*Sealyham,* Pembrokeshire, Wales] (1907)
: any of a breed of short-legged long-headed strong-jawed heavy-boned chiefly white terriers developed in Wales

**¹seam** \'sēm\ *noun* [Middle English *seem,* from Old English *sēam;* akin to Old English *sīwian* to sew — more at SEW] (before 12th century)
**1 a** : the joining of two pieces (as of cloth or leather) by sewing usually near the edge **b** : the stitching used in such a joining
**2** : the space between adjacent planks or strakes of a ship
**3 a** : a line, groove, or ridge formed by the abutment of edges **b** : a thin layer or stratum (as of rock) between distinctive layers; *also* : a bed of valuable mineral and especially coal irrespective of thickness **c** : a line left by a cut or wound; *also* : WRINKLE
**4** : a weak or vulnerable area or gap ⟨found a *seam* in the zone defense⟩
— **seam·like** \-ˌlīk\ *adjective*
— **at the seams** : ENTIRELY, COMPLETELY ⟨falling apart *at the seams*⟩

**²seam** (1582)
*transitive verb*
**1 a** : to join by sewing **b** : to join as if by sewing (as by welding, riveting, or heat-sealing)
**2** : to mark with lines suggesting seams
*intransitive verb*
: to become fissured or ridgy
— **seam·er** *noun*

**sea–maid** \'sē-ˌmād\ *or* **sea–maid·en** \-ˌmā-dᵊn\ *noun* (1590)
: MERMAID; *also* : a goddess or nymph of the sea

**sea·man** \'sē-mən\ *noun* (before 12th century)
**1** : SAILOR, MARINER
**2 a** : any of the three ranks below petty officer in the navy or coast guard **b** : an enlisted man in the navy or coast guard ranking above a seaman apprentice and below a petty officer

**seaman apprentice** *noun* (1947)
: an enlisted man in the navy or coast guard ranking above a seaman recruit and below a seaman

**sea·man·like** \'sē-mən-ˌlīk\ *adjective* (1796)
: characteristic of or befitting a competent seaman

**sea·man·ly** \-lē\ *adjective* (1798)
: SEAMANLIKE

**seaman recruit** *noun* (1947)
: an enlisted man of the lowest rank in the navy or coast guard

**sea·man·ship** \'sē-mən-ˌship\ *noun* (1766)
: the art or skill of handling, working, and navigating a ship

**sea·mark** \-ˌmärk\ *noun* (15th century)
**1** : a line on a coast marking the tidal limit
**2** : an elevated object serving as a beacon to mariners

**sea mew** *noun* (15th century)
: SEAGULL; *especially* : a common gull (*Larus canus*) chiefly of Europe and northwestern North America

**sea mile** *noun* (1796)
: NAUTICAL MILE

**seam·less** \'sēm-ləs\ *adjective* (15th century)
**1** : having no seams
**2** : having no awkward transitions or indications of disparity : perfectly smooth ⟨a *seamless* fusion of beauty and intelligence —Jack Kroll *et al.*⟩
— **seam·less·ly** \-lē\ *adverb*
— **seam·less·ness** \-nəs\ *noun*

**sea·mount** \'sē-ˌmaůnt\ *noun* (1941)
: a submarine mountain rising above the deep-sea floor

**sea mouse** *noun* (circa 1520)
: any of various large broad marine polychaete worms (especially genus *Aphrodite*) covered with hairlike setae

**seam·ster** \'sēm(p)-stər *also* 'sem(p)-\ *noun* [Middle English *semester, semster,* from Old English *sēamestre* seamstress, tailor, from *sēam* seam] (before 12th century)
: a person employed at sewing; *especially* : TAILOR

**seam·stress** \-strəs\ *noun* (1644)
: a woman whose occupation is sewing

**seamy** \'sē-mē\ *adjective* **seam·i·er; -est** (1604)
**1** *archaic* : having the rough side of the seam showing
**2 a** : UNPLEASANT **b** : DEGRADED, SORDID
— **seam·i·ness** *noun*

**sé·ance** \'sā-ˌän(t)s, -ˌäⁿs, sā-\ *noun* [French, from *seoir* to sit, from Latin *sedēre* — more at SIT] (1803)
**1** : SESSION, SITTING
**2** : a spiritualist meeting to receive spirit communications

**sea nettle** *noun* (1601)
: a stinging jellyfish; *especially* : one (*Chrysaora quinquecirrha*) occurring especially in Atlantic estuaries from Cape Cod to the West Indies

**sea oats** *noun plural but singular or plural in construction* (1894)
: a tall grass (*Uniola panicolata*) that has panicles resembling those of the oat, grows chiefly on the coast of the southern U.S., and is useful as a sand binder

**sea onion** *noun* (14th century)
: SQUILL 1a

**sea otter** *noun* (1664)
: a rare marine otter (*Enhydra lutris*) of the northern Pacific coasts that may attain a length of six feet (two meters), is chiefly brown but with lighter coloration on the back of the head and neck, and feeds largely on shellfish

**sea pen** *noun* (1763)

---

: any of numerous anthozoans (order Pennatulacea) growing in colonies with a feathery form

**sea·piece** \'sē-ˌpēs\ *noun* (1656)
: SEASCAPE 2

**sea pink** (1731)
**1** : THRIFT 4
**2** : any of a genus (*Sabatia*) of smooth slender North American herbs of the gentian family typically having pink or white cymose flowers

**sea·plane** \'sē-ˌplān\ *noun* (1913)
: an airplane designed to take off from and land on the water

**sea·port** \'sē-ˌpōrt, -ˌpȯrt\ *noun* (1596)
: a port, harbor, or town accessible to seagoing ships

**sea power** *noun* (1849)
**1** : a nation having formidable naval strength
**2** : naval strength

**sea puss** \-ˌpu̇s\ *noun* [alteration of dialect *seapoose* tidal stream, from Unquachog (Algonquian language of Long Island) *seépus* river] (circa 1891)
: a swirling or along shore undertow

**sea·quake** \'sē-ˌkwāk\ *noun* [*sea* + *earthquake*] (1680)
: a submarine earthquake

**¹sear** *variant of* SERE

**²sear** \'sir\ *verb* [Middle English *seren,* from Old English *sēarian* to become sere, from *sēar* sere] (before 12th century)
*intransitive verb*
: to cause withering or drying
*transitive verb*
**1** : to make withered and dry : PARCH
**2** : to burn, scorch, or injure with or as if with sudden application of intense heat
— **sear·ing·ly** \-iŋ-lē\ *adverb*

**³sear** *noun* (1874)
: a mark or scar left by searing

**⁴sear** *noun* [probably from Middle French *serre* grasp, from *serrer* to press, grasp, from Late Latin *serare* to bolt, latch, from Latin *sera* bar for fastening a door] (1596)
: the catch that holds the hammer of a gun's lock at cock or half cock

**¹search** \'sərch\ *verb* [Middle English *cerchen,* from Middle French *cerchier* to go about, survey, search, from Late Latin *circare* to go about, from Latin *circum* round about — more at CIRCUM-] (14th century)
*transitive verb*
**1** : to look into or over carefully or thoroughly in an effort to find or discover something: as **a** : to examine in seeking something ⟨*searched* the north field⟩ **b** : to look through or explore by inspecting possible places of concealment or investigating suspicious circumstances **c** : to read thoroughly : CHECK; *especially* : to examine a public record or register for information about ⟨*search* land titles⟩ **d** : to examine for articles concealed on the person **e** : to look at as if to discover or penetrate intention or nature
**2** : to uncover, find, or come to know by inquiry or scrutiny — usually used with *out*
*intransitive verb*
**1** : to look or inquire carefully ⟨*searched* for the papers⟩
**2** : to make painstaking investigation or examination
— **search·able** \'sər-chə-bəl\ *adjective*
— **search·er** *noun*
— **search·ing·ly** \-chiŋ-lē\ *adverb*

**²search** *noun* (15th century)
**1 a** : an act of searching ⟨a *search* for food⟩ ⟨go in *search* of help⟩ **b** : an act of boarding and inspecting a ship on the high seas in exercise of right of search
**2** *obsolete* : a party that searches
**3** : power or range of penetrating; *also* : a penetrating effect

**search·less** \'sərch-ləs\ *adjective* (1605)
: INSCRUTABLE, IMPENETRABLE

**search·light** \-ˌlīt\ *noun* (1883)

: an apparatus for projecting a powerful beam of light; *also* : a beam of light projected by it

**search warrant** *noun* (1818)
: a warrant authorizing a search (as of a house) for stolen goods or unlawful possessions

**sea robin** *noun* (1814)
: any of a family (Triglidae) of marine bony fishes typically having a spiny armored head and the bottom three rays of the pectoral fin on each side free of membrane and modified for use as feelers or in crawling — called also *gurnard*

**sea room** *noun* (circa 1554)
: room for maneuver at sea

**sea rover** *noun* (circa 1580)
: one that roves the sea; *specifically* : PIRATE

**sea-run** \'sē-ˌrən\ *adjective* (1885)
: ANADROMOUS ⟨a *sea-run* salmon⟩

**sea·scape** \'sē-ˌskāp\ *noun* (1799)
**1** : a view of the sea
**2** : a picture representing a scene at sea
*word history* see LANDSCAPE

**sea scorpion** *noun* (1896)
**1** : SCULPIN 1
**2** : EURYPTERID

**Sea Scout** *noun* (1911)
: SEA EXPLORER

**sea serpent** *noun* (1774)
: a large marine animal resembling a serpent often reported to have been seen but never proved to exist

**sea·shell** \'sē-ˌshel\ *noun* (before 12th century)
: the shell of a marine animal and especially a mollusk

**sea·shore** \-ˌshōr, -ˌshȯr\ *noun* (1526)
**1 a** : land adjacent to the sea : SEACOAST **b** : NATIONAL SEASHORE
**2** : all the ground between the ordinary high-water and low-water marks : FORESHORE

**sea·sick** \-ˌsik\ *adjective* (circa 1566)
: affected with or suggestive of seasickness

**sea·sick·ness** \-nəs\ *noun* (1625)
: motion sickness experienced on the water

**sea·side** \'sē-ˌsīd\ *noun* (13th century)
: the district or land bordering the sea : country adjacent to the sea : SEASHORE
— **seaside** *adjective*

**sea slug** *noun* (1779)
**1** : HOLOTHURIAN
**2** : a naked marine gastropod; *specifically* : NUDIBRANCH

**sea snake** *noun* (1755)
**1** : SEA SERPENT
**2** : any of numerous venomous aquatic chiefly viviparous elapid snakes of warm seas

**¹sea·son** \'sē-z°n\ *noun* [Middle English, from Middle French *saison,* from Old French, from Latin *sation-, satio* action of sowing, from *serere* to sow — more at SOW] (14th century)
**1 a** : a time characterized by a particular circumstance or feature ⟨in a *season* of religious awakening —F. A. Christie⟩ **b** : a suitable or natural time or occasion ⟨when my *season* comes to sit on David's throne —John Milton⟩ **c** : an indefinite period of time : WHILE ⟨sent home again to her father for a *season* —Francis Hackett⟩
**2 a** : a period of the year characterized by or associated with a particular activity or phenomenon ⟨hay fever *season*⟩: as (1) : a period associated with some phase or activity of agriculture (as growth or harvesting) (2) : a period in which an animal engages in some activity (as migrating or mating); *also* : ESTRUS, HEAT (3) : the period normally characterized by a particular kind of weather ⟨a long rainy *season*⟩ (4) : a period marked by special activity especially in some field ⟨the theatrical *season*⟩ ⟨tourist *season*⟩ (5) : a period in which a place is most frequented **b** : one of the four quarters into which the year is commonly divided **c** : the time of a major holiday
**3** : YEAR ⟨a boy of seven *seasons*⟩
**4** [Middle English *sesoun,* from *sesounen* to season] : SEASONING

**5** : the schedule of official games played or to be played by a sports team during a playing season ⟨try to get through the *season* undefeated⟩
**6** : OFF-SEASON ⟨closed for the *season*⟩
— **in season 1** : at the right time **2** : at the stage of greatest fitness (as for eating) ⟨peaches are *in season*⟩ **3** : legally available to be hunted or caught
— **out of season** : not in season

**²season** *verb* **sea·soned; sea·son·ing** \'sēz-niŋ, 'sē-z°n-iŋ\ [Middle English *sesounen,* from Middle French *assaisoner* to ripen, season, from Old French, from *a-* (from Latin *ad-*) + *saison* season] (14th century)
*transitive verb*
**1 a** : to give (food) more flavor or zest by adding seasoning or savory ingredients **b** : to give a distinctive quality to as if by seasoning; *especially* : to make more agreeable ⟨advice *seasoned* with wit⟩ **c** *archaic* : to qualify by admixture : TEMPER
**2 a** : to treat (as wood or a skillet) so as to prepare for use **b** : to make fit by experience ⟨a *seasoned* veteran⟩
*intransitive verb*
: to become seasoned

**sea·son·able** \'sēz-nə-bəl, 'sē-z°n-ə-bəl\ *adjective* (14th century)
**1** : suitable to the season or circumstances : TIMELY ⟨a *seasonable* frost⟩
**2** : occurring in good or proper time : OPPORTUNE ⟨a *seasonable* time for discussion⟩
— **sea·son·able·ness** *noun*
— **sea·son·ably** \-blē\ *adverb*

**sea·son·al** \'sēz-nəl, 'sē-z°n-əl\ *adjective* (1838)
**1** : of, relating to, or varying in occurrence according to the season ⟨*seasonal* storms⟩ ⟨*seasonal* fruits⟩
**2** : affected or caused by seasonal need or availability ⟨*seasonal* unemployment⟩ ⟨*seasonal* industries⟩
— **sea·son·al·i·ty** \ˌsē-z°n-'a-lə-tē\ *noun*
— **sea·son·al·ly** \'sēz-nə-lē, 'sē-z°n-ə-lē\ *adverb*

**seasonal affective disorder** *noun* (1985)
: depression that tends to recur as the days grow shorter during the fall and winter

**sea·son·er** \'sēz-nər, 'sē-z°n-ər\ *noun* (1598)
: one that seasons: as **a** : a user of seasonings ⟨a heavy *seasoner*⟩ **b** : SEASONING

**sea·son·ing** \'sēz-niŋ, 'sē-z°n-iŋ\ *noun* (1580)
: something that serves to season; *especially* : an ingredient (as a condiment, spice, or herb) added to food primarily for the savor that it imparts

**sea·son·less** \'sē-z°n-ləs\ *adjective* (1816)
**1** : exhibiting no seasonal changes
**2** : not restricted to a particular season; *especially* : suitable for wearing in any season ⟨*seasonless* fabrics⟩

**season ticket** *noun* (1820)
: a ticket (as to all of a club's home games or for specified daily transportation) valid during a specified time

**sea spider** *noun* (1666)
: any of various small long-legged marine arthropods (class Pycnogonida) that superficially resemble spiders

**sea squirt** *noun* (1850)
: ASCIDIAN

**sea star** *noun* (1569)
: STARFISH

**sea stores** *noun plural* (1659)
: supplies (as of foodstuffs) laid in before starting on a sea voyage

**sea·strand** \'sē-ˌstrand\ *noun* (before 12th century)
: SEASHORE

**¹seat** \'sēt\ *noun* [Middle English *sete,* from Old Norse *sæti;* akin to Old English *gesete* seat, *sittan* to sit] (13th century)

**1 a :** a special chair of one in eminence; *also* **:** the status represented by it **b :** a chair, stool, or bench intended to be sat in or on **c :** the particular part of something on which one rests in sitting ⟨the *seat* of a chair⟩ ⟨trouser *seat*⟩ **d :** BUTTOCKS

**2 a :** a seating accommodation ⟨a *seat* for the game⟩ ⟨a 200-*seat* restaurant⟩ **b :** a right of sitting ⟨lost his *seat* in Congress⟩ **c :** membership on an exchange

**3 a :** a place where something specified is prevalent **:** CENTER ⟨a *seat* of learning⟩ **b :** a place from which authority is exercised ⟨the county *seat*⟩ **c :** a bodily part in which some function or condition is centered ⟨the brain as the *seat* of the mind⟩

**4 :** posture in or way of sitting on horseback

**5 a :** a part at or forming the base of something **b :** a part (as a socket) or surface on or in which another part or surface rests

**— by the seat of one's pants :** using experience and intuition rather than mechanical aids or formal theory

**²seat** (1593)
*transitive verb*

**1 a :** to install in a seat of dignity or office **b** (1) **:** to cause to sit or assist in finding a seat (2) **:** to provide seats for ⟨a theater *seating* 1000 persons⟩ **c :** to put in a sitting position

**2 :** to repair the seat of or provide a new seat for

**3 :** to fit to or with a seat ⟨*seat* a valve⟩
*intransitive verb*

**1** *archaic* **:** to take one's seat or place

**2 :** to fit correctly on a seat

**seat belt** *noun* (1932)
**:** an arrangement of straps designed to hold a person steady in a seat (as in an airplane or automobile)

**seat·er** \'sē-tər\ *noun* (1693)
**1 :** one that seats
**2 :** one that has a specified number of seats — used in combination ⟨a two-*seater* jet⟩

**seat·ing** \'sē-tiŋ\ *noun* (circa 1859)
**1 :** the act of providing with seats
**2 a :** material for covering or upholstering seats **b :** a seat on or in which something rests ⟨a valve *seating*⟩

**seat·mate** \'sēt-ˌmāt\ *noun* (1859)
**:** one with whom one shares a seat (as in a vehicle with double or paired seats)

**seat–of–the–pants** *adjective* (1942)
**:** employing or based on personal experience, judgment, and effort rather than technological aids or formal theory ⟨*seat-of-the-pants* navigation⟩ ⟨a *seat-of-the-pants* decision⟩

**sea·train** \'sē-ˌtrān\ *noun* (1932)
**:** a seagoing ship equipped for carrying a train of railroad cars

**sea trout** *noun* (1745)
**1 :** any of various trouts or chars that as adults inhabit the sea but ascend rivers to spawn
**2 :** any of various marine fishes resembling trouts: as **a :** WEAKFISH 1 **b :** SPOTTED SEA TROUT

**sea turtle** *noun* (1612)
**:** any of two families (Cheloniidae and Dermochelyidae) of widely distributed marine turtles with the feet modified into paddles that include the green turtle, leatherback, hawksbill, loggerhead, and ridley

**sea urchin** *noun* (1591)
**:** any of numerous echinoderms (class Echinoidea) that are usually enclosed in thin brittle globular tests covered with movable spines

**sea·wall** \'sē-ˌwȯl\ *noun* (15th century)
**:** a wall or embankment to protect the shore from erosion or to act as a breakwater

**¹sea·ward** \'sē-wərd\ *noun* (14th century)
**:** the direction or side away from land and toward the open sea

**²seaward** *also* **sea·wards** \-wərdz\ *adverb* (1517)
**:** toward the sea

**³seaward** *adjective* (circa 1621)
**1 :** directed or situated toward the sea

**2 :** coming from the sea ⟨a *seaward* wind⟩

**sea wasp** *noun* (1910)
**:** any of various scyphozoan jellyfishes (order or suborder Cubomedusae) that sting virulently and sometimes fatally

**sea·wa·ter** \'sē-ˌwȯ-tər, -ˌwä-\ *noun* (before 12th century)
**:** water in or from the sea

**sea·way** \-ˌwā\ *noun* (before 12th century)
**1 :** the sea as a route for travel; *also* **:** an ocean traffic lane
**2 :** a moderate or rough sea
**3 :** a deep inland waterway that admits ocean shipping

**sea·weed** \-ˌwēd\ *noun* (1577)
**1 :** a mass or growth of marine plants
**2 :** a plant growing in the sea; *especially* **:** a marine alga (as a kelp)

**sea whip** *noun* (1775)
**:** any of various gorgonian corals with elongated flexible unbranched or little-branched skeletons

**sea·wor·thy** \'sē-ˌwər-thē\ *adjective* (1807)
**:** fit or safe for a sea voyage ⟨a *seaworthy* ship⟩

**— sea·wor·thi·ness** \-thē-nəs\ *noun*

**sea wrack** *noun* (1551)
**:** SEAWEED; *especially* **:** seaweed cast ashore in masses

**se·ba·ceous** \si-'bā-shəs\ *adjective* [Latin *sebaceus* made of tallow, from *sebum* tallow] (1728)
**1 :** secreting sebum ⟨*sebaceous* glands⟩
**2 :** of, relating to, or being fatty material **:** FATTY ⟨a *sebaceous* exudate⟩

**se·ba·cic acid** \si-'ba-sik-, -ˌsē-, -'bā-\ *noun* [International Scientific Vocabulary, from Latin *sebaceus*] (1790)
**:** a crystalline dicarboxylic acid $C_{10}H_{18}O_4$ used especially in the manufacture of synthetic resins

**seb·or·rhea** \ˌse-bə-'rē-ə\ *noun* [New Latin, from Latin *sebum* + New Latin *-rrhea*] (circa 1860)
**:** abnormally increased secretion and discharge of sebum

**— seb·or·rhe·ic** \-'rē-ik\ *adjective*

**se·bum** \'sē-bəm\ *noun* [Latin, tallow, grease] (circa 1860)
**:** fatty lubricant matter secreted by sebaceous glands of the skin

**sec** \'sek\ *adjective* [French, literally, dry — more at SACK] (1863)
*of champagne* **:** moderately dry

**se·cant** \'sē-ˌkant, -kənt\ *noun* [New Latin *secant-, secans,* from Latin, present participle of *secare* to cut — more at SAW] (1593)
**1 :** a straight line cutting a curve at two or more points — see CIRCLE illustration
**2 :** a straight line drawn from the center of a circle through one end of a circular arc to a tangent drawn from the other end of the arc
**3 a :** a trigonometric function that for an acute angle is the ratio of the hypotenuse of a right triangle of which the angle is considered part and the leg adjacent to the angle **b :** a trigonometric function sec θ that is the reciprocal of the cosine for all real numbers θ for which the cosine is not zero and that is exactly equal to the secant of an angle of measure θ in radians

**sec·a·teur** \ˌse-kə-'tər, 'se-kə-ˌ\ *noun* [French *sécateur,* from Latin *secare* to cut] (1881)
*chiefly British* **:** pruning shears — usually used in plural

**¹sec·co** \'se-(ˌ)kō\ *noun* [Italian, from *secco* dry, from Latin *siccus* — more at SACK] (1852)
**:** the art of painting on dry plaster

**²secco** *adjective or adverb* [Italian, literally, dry] (circa 1854)
**1 :** short and very staccato — used as a direction in music
**2** *of a recitative* **:** accompanied only by the instruments playing the continuo

**se·cede** \si-'sēd\ *intransitive verb* **se·ced·ed; se·ced·ing** [Latin *secedere,* from *sed-,*

*se-* apart (from *sed, se* without) + *cedere* to go — more at SUICIDE] (circa 1755)
**:** to withdraw from an organization (as a religious communion or political party or federation)

**— se·ced·er** *noun*

**se·cern** \si-'sərn\ *transitive verb* [Latin *secernere* to separate — more at SECRET] (circa 1656)
**:** to discriminate in thought **:** DISTINGUISH

**se·ces·sion** \si-'se-shən\ *noun* [Latin *secession-, secessio,* from *secedere*] (1604)
**1 :** withdrawal into privacy or solitude **:** RETIREMENT
**2 :** formal withdrawal from an organization

**se·ces·sion·ist** \-'se-sh(ə-)nist\ *noun* (circa 1860)
**:** one who joins in a secession or maintains that secession is a right

**— se·ces·sion·ism** \-shə-ˌni-zəm\ *noun*
**— secessionist** *adjective*

**se·clude** \si-'klüd\ *transitive verb* **se·clud·ed; se·clud·ing** [Middle English, to keep away, from Latin *secludere* to separate, seclude, from *se-* apart + *claudere* to close — more at SECEDE, CLOSE] (circa 1533)
**1** *obsolete* **:** to exclude from a privilege, rank, or dignity **:** DEBAR
**2 :** to remove or separate from intercourse or outside influence **:** ISOLATE
**3 :** SHUT OFF, SCREEN

**secluded** *adjective* (1604)
**1 :** screened or hidden from view **:** SEQUESTERED ⟨a *secluded* valley⟩
**2 :** living in seclusion **:** SOLITARY ⟨*secluded* monks⟩

**— se·clud·ed·ly** *adverb*
**— se·clud·ed·ness** *noun*

**se·clu·sion** \si-'klü-zhən\ *noun* [Medieval Latin *seclusion-, seclusio,* from Latin *secludere*] (circa 1616)
**1 :** the act of secluding **:** the condition of being secluded
**2 :** a secluded or isolated place

**synonym** see SOLITUDE

**— se·clu·sive** \-'klü-siv, -ziv\ *adjective*
**— se·clu·sive·ly** *adverb*
**— se·clu·sive·ness** *noun*

**seco·bar·bi·tal** \ˌse-kō-'bär-bə-ˌtȯl\ *noun* [from *Seco*nal, a trademark + *barbital*] (1951)
**:** a barbiturate $C_{12}H_{18}N_2O_3$ that is used chiefly in the form of its bitter hygroscopic sodium salt as a hypnotic and sedative

**Sec·o·nal** \'se-kə-ˌnȯl, -ˌnal, -n°l\ *trademark*
**— used for a preparation of secobarbital

**¹sec·ond** \'se-kənd *also* -kənt, *especially before a consonant* -kən, -k°ŋ\ *adjective* [Middle English, from Old French, from Latin *secundus* second, following, favorable, from *sequi* to follow — more at SUE] (13th century)
**1 a :** next to the first in place or time ⟨*second* in line⟩ **b** (1) **:** next to the first in value, excellence, or degree ⟨his *second* choice of schools⟩ (2) **:** INFERIOR, SUBORDINATE ⟨was *second* to none⟩ **c :** ranking next below the top of a grade or degree in authority or precedence ⟨*second* mate⟩ **d :** ALTERNATE, OTHER ⟨elects a mayor every *second* year⟩ **e :** resembling or suggesting a prototype **:** ANOTHER ⟨a *second* Thoreau⟩ **f :** ingrained by discipline, training, or effort **:** ACQUIRED ⟨*second* nature⟩ **g :** being the forward gear or speed next higher than first in a motor vehicle
**2 :** relating to or having a part typically subordinate to and lower in pitch than the first part in concerted or ensemble music

**— second** *or* **sec·ond·ly** *adverb*
**²second** *noun* (14th century)

**1 a** — see NUMBER table **b :** one that is next after the first in rank, position, authority, or precedence ⟨the *second* in line⟩
**2 :** one that assists or supports another; *especially* **:** the assistant of a duelist or boxer
**3 a :** the musical interval embracing two diatonic degrees **b :** a tone at this interval; *specifically* **:** SUPERTONIC **c :** the harmonic combination of two tones a second apart
**4 a** *plural* **:** merchandise that is usually slightly flawed and does not meet the manufacturer's standard for firsts or irregulars **b :** an article of such merchandise
**5 :** the act or declaration by which a parliamentary motion is seconded
**6 :** a place next below the first in a competition, examination, or contest
**7 :** SECOND BASE
**8 :** the second forward gear or speed of a motor vehicle
**9** *plural* **:** a second helping of food
³**second** *noun* [Middle English *secunde,* from Medieval Latin *secunda,* from Latin, feminine of *secundus* second; from its being the second sexagesimal division of a unit, as a minute is the first] (14th century)
**1 a :** the 60th part of a minute of angular measure **b :** the 60th part of a minute of time **:** 1/86,400 part of the mean solar day; *specifically* **:** the base unit of time in the International System of Units that is equal to the duration of 9,192,631,770 periods of the radiation corresponding to the transition between the two hyperfine levels of the ground state of the cesium-133 atom
**2 :** an instant of time **:** MOMENT
⁴**second** *transitive verb* [Latin *secundare,* from *secundus* second, favorable] (circa 1586)
**1 a :** to give support or encouragement to **:** ASSIST **b :** to support (a fighting person or group) in combat **:** bring up reinforcements for
**2 a :** to support or assist in contention or debate **b :** to endorse (a motion or a nomination) so that debate or voting may begin
**3** \si-ˈkänd\ *chiefly British* **:** to release (as a military officer) from a regularly assigned position for temporary duty with another unit or organization
— **sec·ond·er** *noun*
¹**sec·ond·ary** \ˈse-kən-ˌder-ē\ *adjective* (14th century)
**1 a :** of second rank, importance, or value **b :** of, relating to, or constituting the second strongest of the three or four degrees of stress recognized by most linguists ⟨the fourth syllable of *basketball team* carries *secondary* stress⟩ **c** *of a tense* **:** expressive of past time
**2 a :** immediately derived from something original, primary, or basic **b :** of, relating to, or being the induced current or its circuit in an induction coil or transformer ⟨*secondary* voltage⟩ **c :** characterized by or resulting from the substitution of two atoms or groups in a molecule ⟨a *secondary* salt⟩; *especially* **:** being, characterized by, or attached to a carbon atom having bonds to two other carbon atoms **d** (1) **:** not first in order of occurrence or development (2) **:** produced by activity of formative tissue and especially cambium other than that at a growing point ⟨*secondary* growth⟩ ⟨*secondary* phloem⟩
**3 a :** of, relating to, or being the second order or stage in a series **b :** of, relating to, or being the second segment of the wing of a bird or the quills of this segment **c :** of or relating to a secondary school ⟨*secondary* education⟩
— **sec·ond·ar·i·ly** \ˌse-kən-ˈder-ə-lē\ *adverb*
— **sec·ond·ar·i·ness** \ˈse-kən-ˌder-ē-nəs\ *noun*
²**secondary** *noun, plural* **-ar·ies** (15th century)
**1 :** one occupying a subordinate or auxiliary position rather than that of a principal
**2 :** a defensive football backfield

**3 :** the coil through which the secondary current passes in an induction coil or transformer — called also *secondary coil*
**4 :** any of the quill feathers of the forearm of a bird — see WING illustration
**secondary cell** *noun* (circa 1909)
**:** STORAGE BATTERY
**secondary color** *noun* (1831)
**:** a color formed by mixing primary colors in equal or equivalent quantities
**secondary emission** *noun* (1931)
**:** the emission of electrons from a surface that is bombarded by particles (as electrons or ions) from a primary source
**secondary radiation** *noun* (1900)
**:** radiation emitted by molecules or atoms after bombardment by a primary radiation
**secondary road** *noun* (1903)
**1 :** a road not of primary importance
**2 :** a feeder road
**secondary root** *noun* (1861)
**:** one of the branches of a primary root
**secondary school** *noun* (1835)
**:** a school intermediate between elementary school and college and usually offering general, technical, vocational, or college-preparatory courses
**secondary sex characteristic** *noun* (1927)
**:** a physical characteristic (as the breasts of a female mammal or the breeding plumage of a male bird) that appears in members of one sex at puberty or in seasonal breeders at the breeding season and is not directly concerned with reproduction — called also *secondary sexual characteristic*
**secondary syphilis** *noun* (1885)
**:** the second stage of syphilis that appears from 2 to 6 months after primary infection, that is marked by lesions especially in the skin but also in organs and tissues, and that lasts from 3 to 12 weeks
**second banana** *noun* (1953)
**:** a comedian who plays a supporting role to a top banana; *broadly* **:** a person in a subservient position
**second base** *noun* (1845)
**1 :** the base that must be touched second by a base runner in baseball
**2 :** the player position for defending the area on the first-base side of second base
— **second baseman** *noun*
**sec·ond–best** \ˌse-kən(d)-ˈbest, -kᵊŋ-\ *adjective* (14th century)
**:** next to the best
¹**second best** *noun* (1708)
**:** one that is below or after the best
²**second best** *adverb* (1777)
**:** in second place
**second blessing** *noun* (1891)
**:** sanctification as a second gift of the Holy Spirit that follows an initial experience of conversion
**second childhood** *noun* (1641)
**:** DOTAGE
**second–class** *adjective* (circa 1838)
**1 :** of or relating to a second class
**2 :** MEDIOCRE; *also* **:** socially, politically, or economically deprived
**second class** *noun* (1810)
**1 :** the second and usually next to highest group in a classification
**2 :** CABIN CLASS
**3 :** a class of U.S. or Canadian mail comprising periodicals sent to regular subscribers
**Second Coming** *noun* (1644)
**:** the coming of Christ as judge on the last day
**second–degree burn** *noun* (1937)
**:** a burn marked by pain, blistering, and superficial destruction of dermis with edema and hyperemia of the tissues beneath the burn
**Second Empire** *adjective* (1873)
**:** of, relating to, or characteristic of a style (as of furniture) developed in France under Napoleon III and marked by heavy ornate modification of Empire styles

**second estate** *noun, often S&E capitalized* (circa 1935)
**:** the second of the traditional political classes; *specifically* **:** NOBILITY
**second fiddle** *noun* (1809)
**:** one that plays a supporting or subservient role
**second growth** *noun* (1829)
**:** forest trees that come up naturally after removal of the first growth by cutting or by fire
**sec·ond–guess** \ˌse-kᵊŋ-ˈges, -kən(d)-\ *transitive verb* (1941)
**1 :** to criticize or question actions or decisions of (someone) often after the results of those actions or decisions are known ⟨meet almost every morning and, over coffee, *second-guess* the local coach —Bruce Newman⟩; *also* **:** to engage in such criticism of (an action or decision) ⟨*second-guess* the general's strategy⟩
**2 :** to seek to anticipate or predict ⟨lived royally by his ability to *second-guess* the stock market —*Time*⟩
— **sec·ond–guess·er** *noun*
¹**sec·ond·hand** \ˈse-kən(d)-ˈhand\ *adjective* (1654)
**1 a :** received from or through an intermediary **:** BORROWED **b :** DERIVATIVE ⟨*secondhand* ideas⟩
**2 a :** acquired after being used by another **:** not new ⟨*secondhand* books⟩ **b :** dealing in secondhand merchandise ⟨a *secondhand* bookstore⟩
²**secondhand** *adverb* (1849)
**:** at second hand **:** INDIRECTLY
¹**second hand** \ˌse-kən(d)-ˈhand\ *noun* (1588)
**:** an intermediate person or means **:** INTERMEDIARY — usually used in the phrase *at second hand*
²**second hand** \ˈsek-ən(d)-\ *noun* (1759)
**:** the hand marking seconds on a timepiece
**secondhand smoke** *noun* (1976)
**:** tobacco smoke that is exhaled by smokers and inhaled by persons nearby
**second lieutenant** *noun* (1702)
**:** a commissioned officer of the lowest rank in the army, air force, or marine corps
**second mortgage** *noun* (1912)
**:** a mortgage the lien of which is subordinate to that of a first mortgage
**se·con·do** \si-ˈkōn-(ˌ)dō, -ˈkän-\ *noun, plural* **-di** \-(ˌ)dē\ [Italian, from *secondo,* adjective, second, from Latin *secundus*] (1792)
**:** the second part in a concerted piece; *especially* **:** the lower part (as in a piano duet)
**second person** *noun* (1672)
**1 a :** a set of linguistic forms (as verb forms, pronouns, and inflectional affixes) referring to the person or thing addressed in the utterance in which they occur **b :** a linguistic form belonging to such a set
**2 :** reference of a linguistic form to the person or thing addressed in the utterance in which it occurs
**sec·ond–rate** \ˌse-kən(d)-ˈrāt\ *adjective* (1669)
**:** of second or inferior quality or value **:** MEDIOCRE
— **sec·ond–rate·ness** *noun*
— **sec·ond–rat·er** \-ˈrā-tər\ *noun*
**Second Reader** *noun* (1895)
**:** a member of a Christian Science church or society chosen for a term of office to assist the First Reader in conducting services by reading aloud selections from the Bible
**second reading** *noun* (1647)
**1 :** the stage in the British legislative process following the first reading and usually providing for debate on the principal features of a bill before its submission to a committee for consideration of details
**2 :** the stage in the U.S. legislative process that occurs when a bill has been reported back from committee and that provides an opportunity for full debate and amendment before a vote is taken on the question of a third reading
**second sight** *noun* (1616)

: the capacity to see remote or future objects or events : CLAIRVOYANCE, PRECOGNITION

**second–story man** *noun* (1886)
: a burglar who enters a house by an upstairs window

**sec·ond–string** \,se-kən(d)-'striŋ, ,se-k°ŋ-\ *adjective* [from the reserve bowstring carried by an archer in case the first breaks] (1922)
: being a substitute as distinguished from a regular (as on a ball team)

**second thought** *noun* (1633)
: reconsideration or a revised opinion of a previous often hurried decision (began to have *second thoughts*)

**second wind** *noun* (1824)
: renewed energy or endurance

**second world** *noun, often S&W capitalized* [after *third world*] (1973)
: the Communist nations as a political and economic bloc

**se·cre·cy** \'sē-krə-sē\ *noun, plural* **-cies** [alteration of earlier *secretie,* from Middle English *secretee,* from *secre* secret, from Middle French *secré,* from Latin *secretus*] (1575)
**1** : the condition of being hidden or concealed
**2** : the habit or practice of keeping secrets or maintaining privacy or concealment

¹**se·cret** \'sē-krət\ *adjective* [Middle English, from Middle French, from Latin *secretus,* from past participle of *secernere* to separate, distinguish, from *se-* apart + *cernere* to sift — more at SECEDE, CERTAIN] (14th century)
**1 a** : kept from knowledge or view : HIDDEN **b** : marked by the habit of discretion : CLOSE-MOUTHED **c** : working with hidden aims or methods ⟨UNDERCOVER ⟨a *secret* agent⟩ **d** : not acknowledged : UNAVOWED ⟨a *secret* bride⟩ **e** : conducted in secret ⟨a *secret* trial⟩
**2** : remote from human frequentation or notice : SECLUDED
**3** : revealed only to the initiated : ESOTERIC
**4** : constructed so as to elude observation or detection ⟨a *secret* panel⟩
**5** : containing information whose unauthorized disclosure could endanger national security — compare CONFIDENTIAL, TOP SECRET ☆
— **se·cret·ly** *adverb*

²**secret** *noun* (14th century)
**1 a** : something kept hidden or unexplained : MYSTERY **b** : something kept from the knowledge of others or shared only confidentially with a few **c** : a method, formula, or process used in an art or a manufacturing operation and divulged only to those of one's own company or craft **d** *plural* : the practices or knowledge making up the shared discipline or culture of an esoteric society
**2** : a prayer traditionally said inaudibly by the celebrant just before the preface of the mass
**3** : something taken to be a specific or key to a desired end ⟨the *secret* of longevity⟩
— **in secret** : in a private place or manner

**se·cre·ta·gogue** \si-'krē-tə-,gäg\ *noun* [*secretion* + *-agogue*] (1919)
: a substance stimulating secretion (as by the stomach or pancreas)

**sec·re·tar·i·at** \,se-krə-'ter-ē-ət, -ē-,at\ *noun* [French *secrétariat,* from Medieval Latin *secretariatus,* from *secretarius*] (1811)
**1** : the office of secretary
**2** : a secretarial corps; *specifically* : the clerical staff of an organization
**3** : the administrative department of a governmental organization

**sec·re·tary** \'se-krə-,ter-ē, 'se-kə-,ter-, *in rapid speech also* 'sek-,ter-, *especially British* 'se-k(r)ə-trē\ *noun, plural* **-tar·ies** [Middle English *secretarie,* from Medieval Latin *secretarius,* confidential employee, secretary, from Latin *secretum* secret, from neuter of *secretus*] (15th century)
**1** : one employed to handle correspondence and manage routine and detail work for a superior
**2 a** : an officer of a business concern who may keep records of directors' and stockhold-

ers' meetings and of stock ownership and transfer and help supervise the company's legal interests **b** : an officer of an organization or society responsible for its records and correspondence
**3** : an officer of state who superintends a government administrative department
**4 a** : WRITING DESK, ESCRITOIRE **b** : a writing desk with a top section for books
— **sec·re·tar·i·al** \,se-krə-'ter-ē-əl\ *adjective*
— **sec·re·tary·ship** \'se-krə-,ter-ē-,ship\ *noun*

**secretary bird** *noun* [probably from the resemblance of its crest to a bunch of quill pens stuck behind the ear] (1824)
: a large long-legged African bird of prey (*Sagittarius serpentarius* of the family Sagittariidae) that feeds largely on reptiles

**secretary–general** *noun, plural* **secretaries-general** (1701)
: a principal administrative officer

secretary 4b

secretary bird

**secret ballot** *noun* (1917)
: AUSTRALIAN BALLOT

¹**se·crete** \si-'krēt\ *transitive verb* **se·cret·ed; se·cret·ing** [back-formation from *secretion*] (1707)
: to form and give off (a secretion)

²**se·crete** \si-'krēt, 'sē-krət\ *transitive verb* **se·cret·ed; se·cret·ing** [alteration of obsolete *secret,* from ¹*secret*] (1741)
**1** : to deposit or conceal in a hiding place
**2** : to appropriate secretly : ABSTRACT
*synonym* see HIDE

**se·cre·tin** \si-'krē-t°n\ *noun* [*secretion* + ¹*-in*] (1902)
: an intestinal proteinaceous hormone capable of stimulating secretion by the pancreas and liver

**se·cre·tion** \si-'krē-shən\ *noun* [French *sécrétion,* from Latin *secretion-, secretio* separation, from *secernere* to separate — more at SECRET] (1646)
**1 a** : the process of segregating, elaborating, and releasing some material either functionally specialized (as saliva) or isolated for excretion (as urine) **b** : a product of secretion formed by an animal or plant; *especially* : one performing a specific useful function in the organism
**2** [²*secrete*] : the act of hiding something : CONCEALMENT
— **se·cre·tion·ary** \-shə-,ner-ē\ *adjective*

**se·cre·tive** \'sē-krə-tiv, si-'krē-\ *adjective* [back-formation from *secretiveness,* part translation of French *secrétivité*] (1853)
: disposed to secrecy : not open or outgoing in speech, activity, or purposes
*synonym* see SILENT
— **se·cre·tive·ly** *adverb*
— **se·cre·tive·ness** *noun*

**se·cre·tor** \si-'krē-tər\ *noun* (1941)
: an individual of blood group A, B, or AB who secretes the antigens characteristic of these blood groups in bodily fluids (as saliva)

**se·cre·to·ry** \'sē-krə-,tòr-ē, *especially British* si-'krē-t(ə-)rē\ *adjective* (1692)
: of, relating to, or promoting secretion; *also* : produced by secretion

**secret partner** *noun* (circa 1909)

: a partner whose membership in a partnership is kept secret from the public

**secret police** *noun* (1823)
: a police organization operating for the most part in secrecy and especially for the political purposes of its government often with terroristic methods

**secret service** *noun* (1737)
**1** : a governmental service of a secret nature
**2** *both Ss capitalized* : a division of the U.S. Treasury Department charged chiefly with the suppression of counterfeiting and the protection of the president

**secret society** *noun* (1829)
: any of various oath-bound societies often devoted to brotherhood, moral discipline, and mutual assistance

**sect** \'sekt\ *noun* [Middle English *secte,* from Middle French & Late Latin & Latin; Middle French, group, sect, from Late Latin *secta* organized ecclesiastical body, from Latin, course of action, way of life, probably from *sectari* to pursue, frequentative of *sequi* to follow — more at SUE] (14th century)
**1 a** : a dissenting or schismatic religious body; *especially* : one regarded as extreme or heretical **b** : a religious denomination
**2** *archaic* : SEX 1 ⟨so is all her *sect* —Shakespeare⟩
**3 a** : a group adhering to a distinctive doctrine or to a leader **b** : PARTY **c** : FACTION

¹**sec·tar·i·an** \sek-'ter-ē-ən\ *adjective* (1649)
**1** : of, relating to, or characteristic of a sect or sectarian
**2** : limited in character or scope : PAROCHIAL
— **sec·tar·i·an·ism** \-ē-ə-,ni-zəm\ *noun*

²**sectarian** *noun* (1819)
**1** : an adherent of a sect
**2** : a narrow or bigoted person

**sec·tar·i·an·ize** \sek-'ter-ē-ə-,nīz\ *verb* **-ized; -iz·ing** (1842)
*intransitive verb*
: to act as sectarians
*transitive verb*
: to make sectarian

**sec·ta·ry** \'sek-tə-rē\ *noun, plural* **-ries** (1556)
: a member of a sect

**sec·tile** \'sek-t°l, -,tīl\ *adjective* [Latin *sectilis,* from *sectus,* past participle of *secare*] (1805)
: capable of being severed by a knife with a smooth cut
— **sec·til·i·ty** \sek-'ti-lə-tē\ *noun*

---

☆ SYNONYMS
**Secret, covert, stealthy, furtive, clandestine, surreptitious, underhanded** mean done without attracting observation. SECRET implies concealment on any grounds for any motive ⟨met at a *secret* location⟩. COVERT stresses the fact of not being open or declared ⟨*covert* intelligence operations⟩. STEALTHY suggests taking pains to avoid being seen or heard especially in some misdoing ⟨the *stealthy* step of a burglar⟩. FURTIVE implies a sly or cautious stealthiness ⟨lovers exchanging *furtive* glances⟩. CLANDESTINE implies secrecy usually for an evil, illicit, or unauthorized purpose and often emphasizes the fear of being discovered ⟨a *clandestine* meeting of conspirators⟩. SURREPTITIOUS applies to action or behavior done secretly often with skillful avoidance of detection and in violation of custom, law, or authority ⟨the *surreptitious* stockpiling of weapons⟩. UNDERHANDED stresses fraud or deception ⟨an *underhanded* trick⟩.

---

\ə\ **abut** \°\ **kitten** \ər\ **further** \a\ **ash** \ā\ **ace**
\ä\ **mop, mar** \aú\ **out** \ch\ **chin** \e\ **bet** \ē\ **easy**
\g\ **go** \i\ **hit** \ī\ **ice** \j\ **job** \ŋ\ **sing** \ō\ **go**
\ò\ **law** \òi\ **boy** \th\ **thin** \t͟h\ **the** \ü\ **loot** \ú\ **foot**
\y\ **yet** \zh\ **vision**    *see also* Guide to Pronunciation

**¹sec·tion** \'sek-shən\ *noun* [Latin *section-, sectio,* from *secare* to cut — more at SAW] (1559)
**1 a** : the action or an instance of cutting or separating by cutting **b** : a part set off by or as if by cutting
**2** : a distinct part or portion of something written (as a chapter, law, or newspaper)
**3 a** : the profile of something as it would appear if cut through by an intersecting plane **b** : the plane figure resulting from the cutting of a solid by a plane
**4** : a natural subdivision of a taxonomic group
**5** : a character § used as a mark for the beginning of a section and as a reference mark
**6** : a piece of land one square mile in area forming one of the 36 subdivisions of a township
**7** : a distinct part of a territorial or political area, community, or group of people
**8 a** : a part that may be, is, or is viewed as separated ⟨chop the stalks into *sections*⟩ ⟨the northern *section* of the route⟩ **b** : one segment of a fruit : CARPEL
**9** : a basic military unit usually having a special function
**10** : a very thin slice (as of tissue) suitable for microscopic examination
**11 a** : one of the classes formed by dividing the students taking a course **b** : one of the discussion groups into which a conference or organization is divided
**12 a** : a part of a permanent railroad way under the care of a particular crew **b** : one of two or more vehicles or trains which run on the same schedule
**13** : one of several component parts that may be assembled or reassembled ⟨a bookcase in *sections*⟩
**14** : a division of an orchestra composed of one class of instruments
**15** : SIGNATURE 3b
**synonym** see PART
**²section** *verb* **sec·tioned; sec·tion·ing** \-sh(ə-)niŋ\ (1819)
*transitive verb*
**1** : to cut or separate into sections
**2** : to represent in sections
*intransitive verb*
: to become cut or separated into parts
**¹sec·tion·al** \'sek-shnəl, -shə-n°l\ *adjective* (1806)
**1 a** : of or relating to a section **b** : local or regional rather than general in character ⟨*sectional* interests⟩
**2** : consisting of or divided into sections ⟨*sectional* furniture⟩
— **sec·tion·al·ly** *adverb*
**²sectional** *noun* (1901)
: a piece of furniture made up of modular units capable of use separately or in various combinations
**sec·tion·al·ism** \'sek-shnə-₁li-zəm, -shə-n°l-₁i-\ *noun* (1855)
: an exaggerated devotion to the interests of a region
**Section Eight** *noun* [*Section VIII,* Army Regulation 615-360, in effect from December 1922 to July 1944] (1943)
: a discharge from the U.S. Army for military inaptitude or undesirable habits or traits of character; *also* : a soldier receiving such a discharge
**section gang** *noun* (1890)
: a crew of track workers employed to maintain a railroad section
**section hand** *noun* (1873)
: a laborer belonging to a section gang
**¹sec·tor** \'sek-tər, -₁tȯr\ *noun* [Late Latin, from Latin, cutter, from *secare* to cut — more at SAW] (1570)
**1 a** : a geometric figure bounded by two radii and the included arc of a circle **b** (1) : a subdivision of a defensive military position (2) : a portion of a military front or area of operation

**c** : an area or portion resembling a sector ⟨bilingual *sector* of town —David Kleinberg⟩ **d** : a sociological, economic, or political subdivision of society ⟨greater cooperation between the public and private *sectors* —Peter Chapman⟩
**2** : a mathematical instrument consisting of two rulers connected at one end by a joint and marked with several scales
**3** : a subdivision of a track on a computer disk
**²sec·tor** \-tər\ *transitive verb* **sec·tored; sec·tor·ing** \-t(ə-)riŋ\ (1884)
: to divide into or furnish with sectors
**sec·to·ri·al** \sek-'tȯr-ē-əl, -'tȯr-\ *adjective* (1803)
**1** : of, relating to, or having the shape of a sector of a circle
**2** *of a chimera* : having a sector of variant growth interposed in an otherwise normal body of tissue
**¹sec·u·lar** \'se-kyə-lər\ *adjective* [Middle English, from Old French *seculer,* from Late Latin *saecularis,* from *saeculum* the present world, from Latin, generation, age, century, world; akin to Welsh *hoedl* lifetime] (14th century)
**1 a** : of or relating to the worldly or temporal ⟨*secular* concerns⟩ **b** : not overtly or specifically religious ⟨*secular* music⟩ **c** : not ecclesiastical or clerical ⟨*secular* courts⟩ ⟨*secular* landowners⟩
**2** : not bound by monastic vows or rules; *specifically* : of, relating to, or forming clergy not belonging to a religious order or congregation ⟨a *secular* priest⟩
**3 a** : occurring once in an age or a century **b** : existing or continuing through ages or centuries **c** : of or relating to a long term of indefinite duration
— **sec·u·lar·i·ty** \₁se-kyə-'lar-ə-tē\ *noun*
— **sec·u·lar·ly** \'se-kyə-lər-lē\ *adverb*
**²secular** *noun, plural* **seculars** *or* **secular** (14th century)
**1** : a secular ecclesiastic (as a diocesan priest)
**2** : LAYMAN
**secular humanism** *noun* (1933)
: HUMANISM 3; *especially* : humanistic philosophy viewed as a nontheistic religion antagonistic to traditional religion
— **secular humanist** *noun or adjective*
**sec·u·lar·ise** *British variant of* SECULARIZE
**sec·u·lar·ism** \'se-kyə-lə-₁ri-zəm\ *noun* (1851)
: indifference to or rejection or exclusion of religion and religious considerations
— **sec·u·lar·ist** \-rist\ *noun*
— **secularist** *or* **sec·u·lar·is·tic** \₁se-kyə-lə-'ris-tik\ *adjective*
**sec·u·lar·ize** \'se-kyə-lə-₁rīz\ *transitive verb* **-ized; -iz·ing** (1611)
**1** : to make secular
**2** : to transfer from ecclesiastical to civil or lay use, possession, or control
**3** : to convert to or imbue with secularism
— **sec·u·lar·i·za·tion** \₁se-kyə-lə-rə-'zā-shən\ *noun*
— **sec·u·lar·iz·er** *noun*
**se·cund** \si-'kənd, 'sē-₁\ *adjective* [Latin *secundus* following — more at SECOND] (circa 1777)
: having some part or element arranged on one side only
**¹se·cure** \si-'kyu̇r\ *adjective* **se·cur·er; -est** [Latin *securus* safe, secure, from *se* without + *cura* care — more at SUICIDE] (circa 1533)
**1 a** *archaic* : unwisely free from fear or distrust : OVERCONFIDENT **b** : easy in mind : CONFIDENT **c** : assured in opinion or expectation : having no doubt
**2 a** : free from danger **b** : free from risk of loss **c** : affording safety ⟨a *secure* hideaway⟩ **d** : TRUSTWORTHY, DEPENDABLE ⟨*secure* foundation⟩
**3** : ASSURED 1 ⟨*secure* victory⟩
— **se·cure·ly** *adverb*
— **se·cure·ness** *noun*

**²secure** *verb* **se·cured; se·cur·ing** (1593)
*transitive verb*
**1 a** : to relieve from exposure to danger : act to make safe against adverse contingencies ⟨*secure* a supply line from enemy raids⟩ **b** : to put beyond hazard of losing or of not receiving : GUARANTEE ⟨*secure* the blessings of liberty —U.S. *Constitution*⟩ **c** : to give pledge of payment to (a creditor) or of (an obligation) ⟨*secure* a note by a pledge of collateral⟩
**2 a** : to take (a person) into custody : hold fast : PINION **b** : to make fast : SEAL ⟨*secure* a door⟩
**3 a** : to get secure usually lasting possession or control of ⟨*secure* a job⟩ **b** : BRING ABOUT, EFFECT
**4** : to release (naval personnel) from work or duty
*intransitive verb*
**1** *of naval personnel* : to stop work : go off duty
**2** *of a ship* : to tie up : BERTH
**synonym** see ENSURE
— **se·cur·er** *noun*
**se·cure·ment** \si-'kyu̇r-mənt\ *noun* (1622)
**1** *obsolete* : PROTECTION
**2** : the act or process of securing
**se·cu·ri·tize** \si-'kyu̇r-ə-₁tīz\ *transitive verb* **-tized; -tiz·ing** (1981)
: to consolidate (as mortgage loans) and sell to other investors for resale to the public in the form of securities
— **se·cu·ri·ti·za·tion** \-₁kyu̇r-ə-tə-'zà-shən\ *noun*
**se·cu·ri·ty** \si-'kyu̇r-ə-tē\ *noun, plural* **-ties** (15th century)
**1** : the quality or state of being secure: **as a** : freedom from danger : SAFETY **b** : freedom from fear or anxiety **c** : freedom from the prospect of being laid off ⟨job *security*⟩
**2 a** : something given, deposited, or pledged to make certain the fulfillment of an obligation **b** : SURETY
**3** : an evidence of debt or of ownership (as a stock certificate or bond)
**4 a** : something that secures : PROTECTION **b** (1) : measures taken to guard against espionage or sabotage, crime, attack, or escape (2) : an organization or department whose task is security
**security blanket** *noun* (1968)
**1** : a blanket carried by a child as a protection against anxiety
**2** : a usually familiar object whose presence dispels anxiety
**Security Council** *noun* (1944)
: a permanent council of the United Nations with primary responsibility for maintaining peace and security
**security interest** *noun* (1951)
: the rights that a creditor has in the personal property of a debtor that secures an obligation : LIEN
**security police** *noun* (1920)
**1** : police engaged in counterespionage
**2** : AIR POLICE
**se·dan** \si-'dan\ *noun* [origin unknown] (1635)
**1** : a portable often covered chair that is designed to carry one person and that is borne on poles by two men
**2 a** : a 2- or 4-door automobile seating 4 or more persons and usually having a permanent top — compare COUPE **b** : a motorboat having one passenger compartment
**¹se·date** \si-'dāt\ *adjective* [Latin *sedatus,* from past participle of *sedare* to calm; akin to *sedēre* to sit — more at SIT] (1663)
: keeping a quiet steady attitude or pace : UNRUFFLED
**synonym** see SERIOUS
— **se·date·ly** *adverb*
— **se·date·ness** *noun*
**²sedate** *transitive verb* **se·dat·ed; se·dat·ing** [back-formation from *sedative*] (1945)
: to dose with sedatives
**se·da·tion** \si-'dā-shən\ *noun* (1543)

**1 :** the inducing of a relaxed easy state especially by the use of sedatives
**2 :** a state resulting from or as if from sedation
**¹sed·a·tive** \'se-də-tiv\ *adjective* [Middle English, alleviating pain, from Middle French *sedatif*, from Medieval Latin *sedativus*, from Latin *sedatus*] (1795)
: tending to calm, moderate, or tranquilize nervousness or excitement
**²sedative** *noun* (1797)
: a sedative agent or drug
**sed·en·tary** \'se-d°n-ter-ē\ *adjective* [Middle French *sedentaire*, from Latin *sedentarius*, from *sedent-, sedens*, present participle of *sedēre* to sit — more at SIT] (1598)
**1 :** not migratory : SETTLED ⟨*sedentary* birds⟩
**2 :** doing or requiring much sitting
**3 :** permanently attached ⟨*sedentary* barnacles⟩
**se·der** \'sā-dər\ *noun, often capitalized* [Hebrew *sēdher* order] (1865)
: a Jewish home or community service including a ceremonial dinner held on the first or first and second evenings of the Passover in commemoration of the exodus from Egypt
**se·de·runt** \sə-'dir-ənt, -'der-\ *noun* [Latin, there (they) sat (from *sedēre* to sit), word used to introduce list of those attending a session — more at SIT] (1825)
: a prolonged sitting (as for discussion)
**sedge** \'sej\ *noun* [Middle English *segge*, from Old English *secg*; akin to Middle High German *segge* sedge, Old English *sagu* saw — more at SAW] (before 12th century)
: any of a family (Cyperaceae, the sedge family) of usually tufted marsh plants differing from the related grasses in having achenes and solid stems; *especially* : any of a cosmopolitan genus (*Carex*)
— **sedgy** \'se-jē\ *adjective*
**se·di·lia** \sə-'dēl-yə, -'dil-, *especially British* -'dīl-\ *noun plural* [Latin, plural of *sedile* seat, from *sedēre*] (1793)
: seats on the south side of the chancel for the celebrant, deacon, and subdeacon
**¹sed·i·ment** \'se-də-mənt\ *noun* [Middle French, from Latin *sedimentum* settling, from *sedēre* to sit, sink down] (1547)
**1 :** the matter that settles to the bottom of a liquid
**2 :** material deposited by water, wind, or glaciers
**²sed·i·ment** \-ˌment\ (1859)
*transitive verb*
: to deposit as sediment
*intransitive verb*
**1 :** to settle to the bottom in a liquid
**2 :** to deposit sediment
**sed·i·ment·able** \ˌse-də-'men-tə-bəl\ *adjective* (1943)
: capable of being sedimented by centrifugation ⟨*sedimentable* ribosomal particles⟩
**sed·i·men·ta·ry** \ˌse-də-'men-tə-rē, -'men-trē\ *adjective* (1830)
**1 :** of, relating to, or containing sediment ⟨*sedimentary* deposits⟩
**2 :** formed by or from deposits of sediment ⟨*sedimentary* rock⟩
**sed·i·men·ta·tion** \ˌse-də-mən-'tā-shən, -ˌmen-\ *noun* (1874)
: the action or process of forming or depositing sediment : SETTLING
**sed·i·men·tol·o·gy** \ˌse-də-mən-'tä-lə-jē, -ˌmen-\ *noun* (1932)
: a branch of science that deals with sedimentary rocks and their inclusions
— **sed·i·men·to·log·ic** \-ˌmen-t°l-'ä-jik\ *or* **sed·i·men·to·log·i·cal** \-ji-kəl\ *adjective*
— **sed·i·men·to·log·i·cal·ly** \-ji-k(ə-)lē\ *adverb*
— **sed·i·men·tol·o·gist** \-mən-'tä-lə-jist, -ˌmen-\ *noun*
**se·di·tion** \si-'di-shən\ *noun* [Middle English, from Middle French, from Latin *sedition-, seditio*, literally, separation, from *se-* apart +

*ition-, itio* act of going, from *ire* to go — more at SECEDE, ISSUE] (14th century)
: incitement of resistance to or insurrection against lawful authority
**se·di·tious** \si-'di-shəs\ *adjective* (15th century)
**1 :** disposed to arouse or take part in or guilty of sedition
**2 :** of, relating to, or tending toward sedition
— **se·di·tious·ly** *adverb*
— **se·di·tious·ness** *noun*
**se·duce** \si-'düs, -'dyüs\ *transitive verb* **se·duced; se·duc·ing** [Middle English, from Late Latin *seducere*, from Latin, to lead away, from *se-* apart + *ducere* to lead — more at TOW] (15th century)
**1 :** to persuade to disobedience or disloyalty
**2 :** to lead astray usually by persuasion or false promises
**3 :** to carry out the physical seduction of : entice to sexual intercourse
**4 :** ATTRACT
**synonym** see LURE
— **se·duc·er** *noun*
**se·duce·ment** \-mənt\ *noun* (1586)
**1 :** SEDUCTION
**2 :** something that serves to seduce
**se·duc·tion** \si-'dək-shən\ *noun* [Middle French, from Late Latin *seduction-, seductio*, from Latin, act of leading aside, from *seducere*] (1526)
**1 :** the act of seducing to wrong; *especially* : the often unlawful enticement of a female to sexual intercourse
**2 :** something that seduces : TEMPTATION
**3 :** something that attracts or charms
**se·duc·tive** \-'dək-tiv\ *adjective* (1771)
: tending to seduce : having alluring or tempting qualities ⟨a *seductive*, sometimes disingenuous man —Thatcher Freund⟩ ⟨a *seductive* spring morning⟩
— **se·duc·tive·ly** *adverb*
— **se·duc·tive·ness** *noun*
**se·duc·tress** \-'dək-trəs\ *noun* [obsolete *seductor* male seducer, from Late Latin, from *seducere* to seduce] (1803)
: a woman who seduces
**se·du·li·ty** \si-'dü-lə-tē, -'dyü-\ *noun* (1542)
: sedulous activity : DILIGENCE
**sed·u·lous** \'se-jə-ləs\ *adjective* [Latin *sedulus*, from *sedulo* sincerely, diligently, from *se* without + *dolus* guile — more at SUICIDE] (1540)
**1 :** involving or accomplished with careful perseverance ⟨*sedulous* craftsmanship⟩
**2 :** diligent in application or pursuit ⟨a *sedulous* student⟩
**synonym** see BUSY
— **sed·u·lous·ly** *adverb*
— **sed·u·lous·ness** *noun*
**se·dum** \'sē-dəm\ *noun* [New Latin, from Latin, houseleek] (1760)
: any of a genus (*Sedum*) of fleshy widely distributed herbs of the orpine family — compare STONECROP
**¹see** \'sē\ *verb* **saw** \'sȯ\; **seen** \'sēn\; **see·ing** \'sē-iŋ\ [Middle English, from Old English *sēon*; akin to Old High German *sehan* to see and perhaps to Latin *sequi* to follow — more at SUE] (before 12th century)
*transitive verb*
**1 a :** to perceive by the eye **b :** to perceive or detect as if by sight
**2 a :** to have experience of : UNDERGO ⟨*see* army service⟩ **b :** to come to know : DISCOVER **c :** to be the setting or time of ⟨the last fifty years have *seen* a sweeping revolution in science —Barry Commoner⟩
**3 a :** to form a mental picture of : VISUALIZE ⟨can still *see* her as she was years ago⟩ **b :** to perceive the meaning or importance of : UNDERSTAND **c :** to be aware of : RECOGNIZE ⟨*sees* only our faults⟩ **d :** to imagine as a possibility : SUPPOSE ⟨couldn't *see* him as a crook⟩

**4 a :** EXAMINE, WATCH ⟨want to *see* how she handles the problem⟩ **b** (1) **:** READ (2) **:** to read of **c :** to attend as a spectator ⟨*see* a play⟩
**5 a :** to take care of : provide for ⟨had enough money to *see* us through⟩ **b :** to make sure ⟨*see* that order is kept⟩
**6 a :** to regard as : JUDGE **b :** to prefer to have ⟨I'll *see* him hanged first⟩ ⟨I'll *see* you dead before I accept your terms⟩ **c :** to find acceptable or attractive ⟨can't understand what he *sees* in her⟩
**7 a :** to call on : VISIT **b** (1) **:** to keep company with especially in courtship or dating ⟨had been *seeing* each other for a year⟩ (2) **:** to grant an interview to : RECEIVE ⟨the president will *see* you now⟩
**8 :** ACCOMPANY, ESCORT ⟨*see* the guests to the door⟩
**9 :** to meet (a bet) in poker or to equal the bet of (a player) : CALL
*intransitive verb*
**1 a :** to give or pay attention **b :** to look about
**2 a :** to have the power of sight **b :** to apprehend objects by sight **c :** to perceive objects as if by sight
**3 :** to grasp something mentally
**4 :** to make investigation or inquiry
— **see·able** \-ə-bəl\ *adjective*
— **see after :** to attend to : care for
— **see eye to eye :** to have a common viewpoint : AGREE
— **see things :** HALLUCINATE
— **see through :** to grasp the true nature of ⟨*saw through* the scheme⟩
— **see to :** to attend to : care for
**²see** *noun* [Middle English *se*, from Old French, from Latin *sedes* seat; akin to Latin *sedēre* to sit — more at SIT] (14th century)
**1 a** *archaic* **:** CATHEDRA **b :** a cathedral town **c :** a seat of a bishop's office, power, or authority
**2 :** the authority or jurisdiction of a bishop
**¹seed** \'sēd\ *noun, plural* **seed** *or* **seeds** [Middle English, from Old English *sǣd*; akin to Old High German *sāt* seed, Old English *sāwan* to sow — more at SOW] (before 12th century)
**1 a** (1) **:** the grains or ripened ovules of plants used for sowing (2) **:** the fertilized ripened ovule of a flowering plant containing an embryo and capable normally of germination to produce a new plant; *broadly* **:** a propagative plant structure (as a spore or small dry fruit) **b :** a propagative animal structure: (1) **:** MILT, SEMEN (2) **:** a small egg (as of an insect) (3) **:** a developmental form of a lower animal suitable for transplanting; *specifically* **:** SPAT **c :** the condition or stage of bearing seed ⟨in *seed*⟩
**2 :** PROGENY
**3 :** a source of development or growth : GERM ⟨sowed the *seeds* of discord⟩
**4 :** something (as a tiny particle or a bubble in glass) that resembles a seed in shape or size
**5 :** a competitor who has been seeded in a tournament
— **seed** *adjective*
— **seed·ed** \'sē-dəd\ *adjective*
— **seed·less** \'sēd-ləs\ *adjective*
— **seed·like** \-ˌlīk\ *adjective*
— **go to seed** *or* **run to seed 1 :** to develop seed **2 :** DECAY
**²seed** (14th century)
*intransitive verb*
**1 :** to bear or shed seed
**2 :** to sow seed : PLANT
*transitive verb*

**1 a :** to plant seeds in **:** SOW ⟨*seed* land to grass⟩ **b :** to furnish with something that causes or stimulates growth or development **c :** IN-OCULATE **d :** to supply with nuclei (as of crystallization or condensation); *especially* **:** to treat (a cloud) with solid particles to convert water droplets into ice crystals in an attempt to produce precipitation **e :** to cover or permeate by or as if by scattering something ⟨*seeded* [the] sea-lanes with thousands of magnetic mines —Otto Friedrich⟩
**2 :** PLANT 1a
**3 :** to extract the seeds from (as raisins)
**4 a :** to schedule (tournament players or teams) so that superior ones will not meet in early rounds **b :** to rank (a contestant) relative to others in a tournament on the basis of previous record ⟨the top-*seeded* tennis star⟩
**seed·bed** \'sēd-,bed\ *noun* (1660)
**1 :** soil or a bed of soil prepared for planting seed
**2 :** a place or source of growth or development
**seed·cake** \-,kāk\ *noun* (1573)
**1 :** a cake or cookie containing aromatic seeds (as sesame or caraway)
**2 :** OIL CAKE
**seed coat** *noun* (1796)
**:** an outer protective covering of a seed
**seed·eat·er** \'sēd-,ē-tər\ *noun* (circa 1879)
**:** a bird (as a finch) whose diet consists basically of seeds
**seed·er** \'sē-dər\ *noun* (1868)
**1 :** an implement for planting or sowing seeds
**2 :** a device for seeding fruit
**3 :** one that seeds clouds
**seed fern** *noun* (1927)
**:** any of an order (Pteridospermales) of extinct cycadophytes with foliage like that of ferns and with naked seeds
**seed leaf** *noun* (circa 1693)
**:** COTYLEDON 2
**seed·ling** \'sēd-liŋ\ *noun* (1660)
**1 :** a young plant grown from seed
**2 a :** a young tree before it becomes a sapling **b :** a nursery plant not yet transplanted
**— seedling** *adjective*
**seed money** *noun* (1943)
**:** money used for setting up a new enterprise
**seed oyster** *noun* (1885)
**:** a young oyster especially of a size for transplantation
**seed pearl** *noun* (1553)
**1 :** a very small and often irregular pearl
**2 :** minute pearls imbedded in some binding material
**seed plant** *noun* (1707)
**:** a plant that bears seeds; *specifically* **:** SPER-MATOPHYTE
**seed·pod** \'sēd-,päd\ *noun* (1718)
**:** ²POD 1
**seeds·man** \'sēdz-mən\ *noun* (1601)
**1 :** one who sows seeds
**2 :** a dealer in seeds
**seed stock** *noun* (1926)
**:** a supply (as of seed) for planting; *broadly* **:** a source of new individuals ⟨a *seed stock* of trout in the streams⟩
**seed tick** *noun* (1705)
**:** the 6-legged larva of a tick
**seed·time** \'sēd-,tīm\ *noun* (before 12th century)
**1 :** the season of sowing
**2 :** a period of original development
**seedy** \'sē-dē\ *adjective* **seed·i·er; -est** (1574)
**1 :** containing or full of seeds ⟨a *seedy* fruit⟩
**2 :** inferior in condition or quality: as **a :** SHABBY, RUN-DOWN ⟨*seedy* clothes⟩ **b :** somewhat disreputable **:** SQUALID ⟨a *seedy* district⟩ ⟨*seedy* entertainment⟩ **c :** slightly unwell **:** DE-BILITATED ⟨felt *seedy* and went home early⟩
**— seed·i·ly** \'sē-d°l-ē\ *adverb*
**— seed·i·ness** \'sē-dē-nəs\ *noun*
**¹see·ing** \'sē-iŋ\ *conjunction* (1503)
**:** INASMUCH AS — often used with *as* or *that*

**²seeing** *noun* (1903)
**:** the quality of the images of celestial bodies observed telescopically
**Seeing Eye** *trademark*
— used for a guide dog trained to lead the blind
**seek** \'sēk\ *verb* **sought** \'sȯt\; **seek·ing** [Middle English *seken,* from Old English *sēcan;* akin to Old High German *suohhen* to seek, Latin *sagus* prophetic, Greek *hēgeisthai* to lead] (before 12th century)
*transitive verb*
**1 :** to resort to **:** go to
**2 a :** to go in search of **:** look for **b :** to try to discover
**3 :** to ask for **:** REQUEST ⟨*seeks* advice⟩
**4 :** to try to acquire or gain **:** aim at ⟨*seek* fame⟩
**5 :** to make an attempt **:** TRY — used with *to* and an infinitive ⟨governments . . . *seek* to keep the bulk of their people contented —D. M. Potter⟩
*intransitive verb*
**1 :** to make a search or inquiry
**2 a :** to be sought **b :** to be lacking ⟨in critical judgment . . . they were sadly to *seek* —*Times Literary Supplement*⟩
**— seek·er** *noun*
**seel** \'sē(ə)l\ *transitive verb* [Middle English *selen,* alteration of *silen,* from Middle French *siller,* from Medieval Latin *ciliare,* from Latin *cilium* eyelid] (15th century)
**1 :** to close the eyes of (as a hawk) by drawing threads through the eyelids
**2** *archaic* **:** to close up (one's eyes)
**see·ly** \'sē-lē\ *adjective* [Middle English *sely* — more at SILLY] (14th century)
*archaic* **:** pitiable especially because of weak physical or mental condition **:** FRAIL
**seem** \'sēm\ *intransitive verb* [Middle English *semen,* of Scandinavian origin; akin to Old Norse *sœma* to honor, *sœmr* fitting, *samr* same — more at SAME] (13th century)
**1 :** to appear to the observation or understanding
**2 :** to give the impression of being
**¹seem·ing** *noun* (15th century)
**:** external appearance as distinguished from true character **:** LOOK
**²seeming** *adjective* (circa 1557)
**:** having an often deceptive or delusive appearance on superficial examination ⟨their wealth gave them a *seeming* security⟩
**synonym** see APPARENT
**— seem·ing·ly** \'sē-miŋ-lē\ *adverb*
**seem·ly** \'sēm-lē\ *adjective* **seem·li·er; -est** [Middle English *semely,* from Old Norse *sœmiligr,* from *sœmr* fitting] (13th century)
**1 a :** GOOD-LOOKING, HANDSOME **b :** agreeably fashioned **:** ATTRACTIVE
**2 :** conventionally proper **:** DECOROUS
**3 :** suited to the occasion, purpose, or person **:** FIT
**— seem·li·ness** *noun*
**— seemly** *adverb*
**seen** *past participle of* SEE
**¹seep** \'sēp\ *intransitive verb* [alteration of earlier *sipe,* from Middle English *sipen,* from Old English *sipian;* akin to Middle Low German *sipen* to seep] (1790)
**1 :** to flow or pass slowly through fine pores or small openings **:** OOZE ⟨water *seeped* in through a crack⟩
**2 a :** to enter or penetrate slowly ⟨fear of nuclear war had *seeped* into the national consciousness —Tip O'Neill⟩ **b :** to become diffused or spread ⟨a sadness *seeped* through his being —Agnes S. Turnbull⟩
**²seep** *noun* (circa 1825)
**1 a :** a spot where a fluid (as water, oil, or gas) contained in the ground oozes slowly to the surface and often forms a pool **b :** a small spring
**2 :** SEEPAGE
**— seepy** \'sē-pē\ *adjective*
**seep·age** \'sē-pij\ *noun* (circa 1825)

**1 :** the process of seeping **:** OOZING
**2 :** a quantity of fluid that has seeped (as through porous material)
**¹seer** \'sir, 'sē-ər\ *noun* (14th century)
**1 :** one that sees
**2 a :** one that predicts events or developments **b :** a person credited with extraordinary moral and spiritual insight
**3 :** one that practices divination especially by concentrating on a glass or crystal globe
**²seer** *noun, plural* **seers** *or* **seer** [Hindi *ser*] (1618)
**:** an Indian unit of weight equal to 2.057 pounds (0.9330 kilograms)
**seer·ess** \'sir-əs, 'sē-ər-əs\ *noun* (1845)
**:** a woman who predicts events or developments **:** PROPHETESS
**seer·suck·er** \'sir-,sə-kər\ *noun* [Hindi *śīr-śaker,* from Persian *shīr-o-shakar,* literally, milk and sugar] (1722)
**:** a light fabric of linen, cotton, or rayon usually striped and slightly puckered
**¹see–saw** \'sē-,sȯ\ *noun* [probably from reduplication of ³*saw*] (1704)
**1 :** an alternating up-and-down or backward-and-forward motion or movement; *also* **:** a contest or struggle in which now one side now the other has the lead
**2 a :** a pastime in which two children or groups of children ride on opposite ends of a plank balanced in the middle so that one end goes up as the other goes down **b :** the plank or apparatus so used
**— seesaw** *adjective*
**²seesaw** (1712)
*intransitive verb*
**1 a :** to move backward and forward or up and down **b :** to play at seesaw
**2 :** ALTERNATE
*transitive verb*
**:** to cause to move in seesaw fashion
**¹seethe** \'sēth\ *verb* **seethed; seeth·ing** [Middle English *sethen,* from Old English *sēothan;* akin to Old High German *siodan* to seethe] (before 12th century)
*transitive verb*
**1** *archaic* **:** BOIL, STEW
**2 :** to soak or saturate in a liquid
*intransitive verb*
**1** *archaic* **:** BOIL
**2 a :** to be in a state of rapid agitated movement **b :** to churn or foam as if boiling
**3 :** to suffer violent internal excitement
**²seethe** *noun* (1816)
**:** a state of seething **:** EBULLITION
**seething** *adjective* (14th century)
**1 :** intensely hot **:** BOILING ⟨a *seething* inferno⟩
**2 :** constantly moving or active **:** AGITATED
**see–through** \'sē-,thrü\ *adjective* (1945)
**:** TRANSPARENT 1
**¹seg·ment** \'seg-mənt\ *noun* [Latin *segmentum,* from *secare* to cut — more at SAW] (1570)
**1 a :** a separate piece of something **:** BIT, FRAG-MENT ⟨chop the stalks into short *segments*⟩ **b :** one of the constituent parts into which a body, entity, or quantity is divided or marked off by or as if by natural boundaries ⟨all *segments* of the population agree⟩
**2 :** a portion cut off from a geometric figure by one or more points, lines, or planes: as **a :** the part of a circular area bounded by a chord and an arc of that circle or so much of the area as is cut off by the chord **b :** the part of a sphere cut off by a plane or included between two parallel planes **c :** the finite part of a line between two points in the line
**synonym** see PART
**— seg·men·tary** \-mən-,ter-ē\ *adjective*
**²seg·ment** \'seg-,ment\ *transitive verb* (1859)
**:** to separate into segments **:** give off as segments
**seg·men·tal** \seg-'men-t°l\ *adjective* (1816)
**1 :** of, relating to, or having the form of a segment and especially the sector of a circle ⟨*segmental* fanlight⟩

**2 :** of, relating to, or composed of somites or metameres **:** METAMERIC
**3 a :** divided into segments ⟨*segmental* knowledge⟩ **b :** PARTIAL, INCOMPLETE **c :** resulting from segmentation
— **seg·men·tal·ly** \-t⁰l-ē\ *adverb*
**seg·men·ta·tion** \ˌseg-mən-'tā-shən, -ˌmen-\ *noun* (1851)
**:** the process of dividing into segments; *especially* **:** the formation of many cells from a single cell (as in a developing egg)
**segmentation cavity** *noun* (1888)
**:** BLASTOCOEL
**seg·ment·ed** \'seg-ˌmen-təd, seg-\ *adjective* (1854)
**:** divided into or composed of segments or sections ⟨*segmented* worms⟩
**se·gno** \'sān-(ˌ)yō\ *noun, plural* **segnos** [Italian, sign, from Latin *signum* — more at SIGN] (1908)
**:** a notational sign; *specifically* **:** the sign that marks the beginning or end of a musical repeat
**se·go lily** \'sē-(ˌ)gō-\ *noun* [*sego* the bulb of the sego lily, from Southern Paiute *siɣoʔo*] (1913)
**:** a mariposa lily (*Calochortus nuttallii*) of western North America having mostly white or in some areas mostly yellow flowers mottled with a darker color

sego lily

**seg·re·gant** \'se-gri-gənt\ *noun* (1926)
**:** a genetic segregate
**¹seg·re·gate** \'se-gri-ˌgāt\ *verb* **-gat·ed; -gat·ing** [Latin *segregatus*, past participle of *segregare*, from *se-* apart + *greg-, grex* herd — more at SECEDE] (1542)
*transitive verb*
**1 :** to separate or set apart from others or from the general mass **:** ISOLATE
**2 :** to cause or force the separation of (as from the rest of society)
*intransitive verb*
**1 :** SEPARATE, WITHDRAW
**2 :** to practice or enforce a policy of segregation
**3 :** to undergo genetic segregation
— **seg·re·ga·tive** \-ˌgā-tiv\ *adjective*
**²seg·re·gate** \'se-gri-gət, -ˌgāt\ *noun* (1871)
**:** one that is in some respect segregated; *especially* **:** one that differs genetically from the parental line because of genetic segregation
**segregated** *adjective* (1652)
**1 a :** set apart or separated from others of the same kind or group ⟨a *segregated* account in a bank⟩ **b :** divided in facilities or administered separately for members of different groups or races ⟨*segregated* education⟩ **c :** restricted to members of one group or one race by a policy of segregation ⟨*segregated* schools⟩
**2 :** practicing or maintaining segregation especially of races ⟨*segregated* states⟩
**seg·re·ga·tion** \ˌse-gri-'gā-shən\ *noun* (1555)
**1 :** the act or process of segregating **:** the state of being segregated
**2 a :** the separation or isolation of a race, class, or ethnic group by enforced or voluntary residence in a restricted area, by barriers to social intercourse, by separate educational facilities, or by other discriminatory means **b :** the separation for special treatment or observation of individuals or items from a larger group ⟨*segregation* of gifted children into accelerated classes⟩
**3 :** the separation of allelic genes that occurs typically during meiosis
**seg·re·ga·tion·ist** \-sh(ə-)nist\ *noun* (1913)
**:** a person who believes in or practices segregation especially of races
— **segregationist** *adjective*

**¹se·gue** \'se-(ˌ)gwā, 'sā-\ *imperative verb* [Italian, there follows, from *seguire* to follow, from Latin *sequi* — more at SUE] (circa 1740)
**1 :** proceed to what follows without pause — used as a direction in music
**2 :** perform the music that follows like that which has preceded — used as a direction in music
**²segue** *intransitive verb* **se·gued; se·gue·ing** (circa 1913)
**1 :** to proceed without pause from one musical number or theme to another
**2 :** to make a transition without interruption from one activity, topic, scene, or part to another
**³segue** *noun* (circa 1937)
**:** the act or an instance of segueing
**se·gui·dil·la** \ˌse-gə-'dē-yə, -'dēl-yə\ *noun* [Spanish, diminutive of *seguida*, a dance, literally, sequence, from *seguido*, past participle of *seguir* to follow, from Latin *sequi*] (1763)
**1 a :** a Spanish dance with many regional variations **b :** the music for such a dance
**2 :** a Spanish stanza of four or seven short partly assonant verses
**sei·cen·to** \sā-'chen-(ˌ)tō\ *noun* [Italian, literally, six-hundred, from *sei* six (from Latin *sex*) + *cento* hundred — more at SIX, CINQUE-CENTO] (circa 1902)
**:** the 17th century; *specifically* **:** the 17th century period in Italian literature and art
**seiche** \'sāsh, 'sēch\ *noun* [French] (circa 1839)
**:** an oscillation of the surface of a landlocked body of water (as a lake) that varies in period from a few minutes to several hours
**sei·del** \'sī-d⁰l, 'zī-\ *noun* [German, from Middle High German *sīdel*, from Latin *situla* bucket] (1908)
**:** a large glass for beer
**Seid·litz powders** \'sed-ləts-\ *noun plural* [*Sedlitz*, (Sedlčany), village in Bohemia; from the similarity of their effect to that of the water of the village] (1815)
**:** effervescing salts consisting of one powder of sodium bicarbonate and Rochelle salt and another of tartaric acid that are mixed in water and drunk as a mild cathartic
**sei·gneur** \sān-'yər\ *noun, often capitalized* [Middle French, from Medieval Latin *senior*, from Latin, adjective, elder — more at SENIOR] (1592)
**1 :** a man of rank or authority; *especially* **:** the feudal lord of a manor
**2 :** a member of the landed gentry of Canada
**sei·gneur·ial** \-'yúr-ē-əl, -'yər-\ *adjective* (1656)
**:** of, relating to, or befitting a seigneur
**sei·gneury** \'sān-yə-rē\ *noun, plural* **-gneur·ies** (1683)
**1 a :** the territory under the government of a feudal lord **b :** a landed estate held in Canada by feudal tenure until 1854
**2 :** the manor house of a Canadian seigneur
**sei·gnior** \sān-'yȯr, 'sān-ˌ\ *noun* [Middle English *seigniour*, from Middle French *seigneur*] (15th century)
**:** SEIGNEUR 1
**sei·gnior·age** *or* **sei·gnor·age** \'sān-yə-rij\ *noun* [Middle English *seigneurage*, from Middle French, right of the lord (especially to coin money), from *seigneur*] (15th century)
**:** a government revenue from the manufacture of coins calculated as the difference between the face value and the metal value of the coins
**sei·gniory** *or* **sei·gnory** \'sān-yə-rē\ *noun, plural* **-gnior·ies** *or* **-gnor·ies** (14th century)
**1 :** LORDSHIP, DOMINION; *specifically* **:** the power or authority of a feudal lord
**2 :** the territory over which a lord holds jurisdiction
**sei·gno·ri·al** \sān-'yȯr-ē-əl, -'yȯr-\ *adjective* (1818)

**:** of, relating to, or befitting a seignior **:** MANORIAL
**¹seine** \'sān\ *noun* [Middle English, from Old English *segne*, from Latin *sagena*, from Greek *sagēnē*] (before 12th century)
**:** a large net with sinkers on one edge and floats on the other that hangs vertically in the water and is used to enclose fish when its ends are pulled together or are drawn ashore
**²seine** *verb* **seined; sein·ing** (1836)
*intransitive verb*
**:** to fish with or catch fish with a seine
*transitive verb*
**:** to fish for or in with a seine
**sein·er** \'sā-nər\ *noun* (1602)
**1 :** one who fishes with a seine
**2 :** a boat used for seining
**sei·sin** *or* **sei·zin** \'sē-z⁰n\ *noun* [Middle English *seisine*, from Old French *saisine*, from *saisir* to seize — more at SEIZE] (14th century)
**1 :** the possession of land or chattels
**2 :** the possession of a freehold estate in land by one having title thereto
**seis·mic** \'sīz-mik, 'sīs-\ *adjective* [Greek *seismos* shock, earthquake, from *seiein* to shake; probably akin to Avestan *thwaēshō* fear] (1858)
**1 :** of, subject to, or caused by an earthquake; *also* **:** of or relating to an earth vibration caused by something else (as an explosion or the impact of a meteorite)
**2 :** of or relating to a vibration on a celestial body (as the moon) comparable to a seismic event on earth
**3 :** having a strong or widespread impact **:** EARTHSHAKING ⟨*seismic* social changes⟩
— **seis·mi·cal·ly** \-mi-k(ə-)lē\ *adverb*
**seis·mic·i·ty** \sīz-'mi-sə-tē, sīs-\ *noun* (1902)
**:** the relative frequency and distribution of earthquakes
**seismo-** *combining form* [Greek, from *seismos*]
**:** earthquake **:** vibration ⟨*seismo*meter⟩
**seis·mo·gram** \'sīz-mə-ˌgram, 'sīs-\ *noun* [International Scientific Vocabulary] (circa 1891)
**:** the record of an earth tremor by a seismograph
**seis·mo·graph** \-ˌgraf\ *noun* [International Scientific Vocabulary] (1858)
**:** an apparatus to measure and record vibrations within the earth and of the ground
— **seis·mog·ra·pher** \sīz-'mä-grə-fər, sīs-\ *noun*
— **seis·mo·graph·ic** \ˌsīz-mə-'gra-fik, ˌsīs-\ *adjective*
— **seis·mog·ra·phy** \sīz-'mä-grə-fē, sīs-\ *noun*
**seis·mol·o·gy** \sīz-'mä-lə-jē, sīs-\ *noun* [International Scientific Vocabulary] (1858)
**:** a science that deals with earthquakes and with artificially produced vibrations of the earth
— **seis·mo·log·i·cal** \ˌsīz-mə-'lä-ji-kəl, sīs-\ *adjective*
— **seis·mol·o·gist** \sīz-'mä-lə-jist, sīs-\ *noun*
**seis·mom·e·ter** \sīz-'mä-mə-tər, sīs-\ *noun* (1841)
**:** a seismograph measuring the actual movements of the ground (as on the earth or the moon)
— **seis·mo·met·ric** \ˌsīz-mə-'me-trik, ˌsīs-\ *adjective*
— **seis·mom·e·try** \sīz-'mä-mə-trē, sīs-\ *noun* [International Scientific Vocabulary] (1858)
**:** the scientific study of earthquakes
**sei whale** \'sā-, 'sī-\ *noun* [part translation of Norwegian *seihval*, from *sei* coalfish + *hval* whale] (1912)

\ə\ abut  \⁰\ kitten  \ər\ further  \a\ ash  \ā\ ace
\ä\ mop, mar  \aú\ out  \ch\ chin  \e\ bet  \ē\ easy
\g\ go  \i\ hit  \ī\ ice  \j\ job  \ŋ\ sing  \ō\ go
\ȯ\ law  \ȯi\ boy  \th\ thin  \th\ the  \ü\ loot  \ú\ foot
\y\ yet  \zh\ vision  *see also* Guide to Pronunciation

: a common and widely distributed dark gray rorqual (*Balaenoptera borealis*) that has a ridge on the top of the head and grows to a length of nearly 60 feet (18 meters) — called also *sei*

**seize** \'sēz\ *verb* **seized; seiz·ing** [Middle English *saisen*, from Old French *saisir* to put in possession of, from Medieval Latin *sacire*, of Germanic origin; perhaps akin to Old High German *sezzen* to set — more at SET] (14th century)
*transitive verb*
**1 a** *usually* **seise** \'sēz\ : to vest ownership of a freehold estate in **b** *often* **seise** : to put in possession of something ⟨the biographer will be *seized* of all pertinent papers⟩
**2 a** : to take possession of : CONFISCATE **b** : to take possession of by legal process
**3 a** : to possess or take by force : CAPTURE **b** : to take prisoner : ARREST
**4 a** : to take hold of : CLUTCH **b** : to possess oneself of : GRASP **c** : to understand fully and distinctly : APPREHEND
**5 a** : to attack or overwhelm physically : AFFLICT ⟨suddenly *seized* with an acute illness —H. G. Armstrong⟩ **b** : to possess (as one's mind) completely or overwhelmingly ⟨*seized* the popular imagination —Basil Davenport⟩
**6** : to bind or fasten together with a lashing of small stuff (as yarn, marline, or fine wire)
*intransitive verb*
**1** : to take or lay hold suddenly or forcibly
**2 a** : to cohere to a relatively moving part through excessive pressure, temperature, or friction — used especially of machine parts (as bearings, brakes, or pistons) **b** : to fail to operate due to the seizing of a part — used of an engine
**synonym** see TAKE
— **seiz·er** *noun*

**seizing** *noun* (14th century)
**1 a** : the cord or lashing used in binding or fastening **b** : the fastening so made — see KNOT illustration
**2** : the operation of fastening together or lashing with tarred small stuff

**sei·zure** \'sē-zhər\ *noun* (15th century)
**1 a** : the act, action, or process of seizing : the state of being seized **b** : the taking possession of person or property by legal process
**2** : a sudden attack (as of disease) ⟨an epileptic *seizure*⟩

**se·jant** \'sē-jənt\ *adjective* [modification of Middle French *seant*, present participle of *seoir* to sit, from Latin *sedēre* — more at SIT] (circa 1500)
: SITTING — used of a heraldic animal

**sel** \'sel\ *chiefly Scottish variant of* SELF

**se·la·chi·an** \sə-'lā-kē-ən\ *noun* [ultimately from Greek *selachos* cartilaginous phosphorescent fish; akin to Greek *selas* brightness] (1835)
: any of a variously defined group (Selachii) of cartilaginous fishes that includes all the elasmobranchs or all elasmobranchs except the chimaeras, the existing sharks and rays or in its most restricted use the existing sharks as distinguished from the rays
— **selachian** *adjective*

**se·lag·i·nel·la** \sə-ˌla-jə-'ne-lə\ *noun* [New Latin, from Latin *selagin-*, *selago*, a plant resembling the savin] (1835)
: any of a genus (Selaginella) of mossy lower tracheophytes that are related to or grouped with the club mosses and have branching stems and scalelike leaves and produce one-celled sporangia containing both megaspores and microspores

**se·lah** \'sē-lə, -ˌlä\ *interjection* [Hebrew *selāh*] (1530)
— a term of uncertain meaning found in the Hebrew text of the Psalms and Habakkuk carried over untranslated into some English versions

**sel·couth** \'sel-ˌküth\ *adjective* [Middle English, from Old English *seldcūth*, from *seldan*

*seldom* + *cūth* known — more at UNCOUTH] (before 12th century)
*archaic* : UNUSUAL, STRANGE

**¹sel·dom** \'sel-dəm\ *adverb* [Middle English, from Old English *seldan*; akin to Old High German *seltan* seldom] (before 12th century)
: in few instances : RARELY, INFREQUENTLY

**²seldom** *adjective* (13th century)
: RARE, INFREQUENT

**¹se·lect** \sə-'lekt\ *adjective* [Latin *selectus*, past participle of *seligere* to select, from *se-* apart (from *sed*, *se* without) + *legere* to gather, select — more at SUICIDE, LEGEND] (1565)
**1** : chosen from a number or group by fitness or preference
**2 a** : of special value or excellence : SUPERIOR, CHOICE **b** : exclusively or fastidiously chosen often with regard to social, economic, or cultural characteristics
**3** : judicious or restrictive in choice : DISCRIMINATING ⟨pleased with the *select* appreciation of his books —Osbert Sitwell⟩
— **se·lect·able** \sə-'lek-tə-bəl\ *adjective*
— **se·lect·ness** \sə-'lek(t)-nəs\ *noun*
— **se·lec·tor** \sə-'lek-tər\ *noun*

**²select** (1567)
*transitive verb*
: to choose (as by fitness or excellence) from a number or group : pick out
*intransitive verb*
: to make a choice

**³select** *noun* (1610)
: one that is select — often used in plural

**se·lect·ed** *adjective* (1590)
: SELECT; *specifically* : of a higher grade or quality than the ordinary

**se·lect·ee** \sə-ˌlek-'tē\ *noun* (1940)
**1** : one inducted into military service under selective service
**2** : one who is chosen from a group by fitness or preference

**se·lec·tion** \sə-'lek-shən\ *noun* (circa 1623)
**1** : the act or process of selecting : the state of being selected
**2** : one that is selected : CHOICE; *also* : a collection of selected things
**3** : a natural or artificial process that results in or tends to result in the survival and propagation of some individuals or organisms but not of others with the result that the inherited traits of the survivors are perpetuated — compare DARWINISM, NATURAL SELECTION
**synonym** see CHOICE

**se·lec·tion·ist** \-sh(ə-)nist\ *noun* (1892)
: one who considers natural selection a fundamental factor in evolution
— **selectionist** *adjective*

**se·lec·tive** \sə-'lek-tiv\ *adjective* (1625)
**1** : of, relating to, or characterized by selection : selecting or tending to select
**2** : highly specific in activity or effect ⟨*selective* pesticides⟩ ⟨*selective* absorption⟩
— **se·lec·tive·ly** *adverb*
— **se·lec·tive·ness** *noun*
— **se·lec·tiv·i·ty** \sə-ˌlek-'ti-və-tē, ˌsē-\ *noun*

**selective service** *noun* (1917)
: a system under which men are called up for military service : DRAFT

**se·lect·man** \si-'lek(t)-ˌman, -ˌlek(t)-'man, -'lek(t)-mən; 'sē-ˌlek(t)-ˌman\ *noun* (1635)
: one of a board of officials elected in towns of all New England states except Rhode Island to serve as the chief administrative authority of the town

**¹selen-** *or* **seleno-** *combining form* [Latin *selen-*, from Greek *selēn-*, from *selēnē* — more at SELENIUM]
: moon ⟨*selenium*⟩ ⟨*selenology*⟩

**²selen-** *or* **seleni-** *combining form* [Swedish, from New Latin *selenium*]
: selenium ⟨*seleniferous*⟩

**se·le·nate** \'se-lə-ˌnāt\ *noun* [Swedish *selenat*, from *selen* of or containing selenium, from New Latin *selenium*] (1818)
: a salt containing the anion SeO₄²⁻

**Se·le·ne** \sə-'lē-nē\ *noun*
: the Greek goddess of the moon

**sel·e·nide** \'se-lə-ˌnīd\ *noun* (1849)
: a binary compound of selenium with a more electropositive element or group

**sel·e·nif·er·ous** \ˌse-lə-'ni-f(ə-)rəs\ *adjective* (1823)
: containing or yielding selenium ⟨*seleniferous* vegetation⟩ ⟨*seleniferous* soils⟩

**sel·e·nite** \'se-lə-ˌnīt\ *noun* [Middle English *selinete*, from Latin *selenites*, from Greek *selēnītēs* (*lithos*), literally, stone of the moon, from *selēnē*; from the belief that it waxed and waned with the moon] (15th century)
: a variety of gypsum occurring in transparent crystals or crystalline masses

**se·le·ni·um** \sə-'lē-nē-əm\ *noun* [New Latin, from Greek *selēnē* moon, from *selas* brightness] (1818)
: a nonmetallic element that resembles sulfur and tellurium chemically, is obtained chiefly as a by-product in copper refining, and is a photoconductive semiconductor in its crystalline form — see ELEMENT table

**selenium cell** *noun* (1880)
: an insulated strip of selenium mounted with electrodes and used as a photoconductive element

**se·le·no·cen·tric** \sə-ˌlē-nə-'sen-trik\ *adjective* [International Scientific Vocabulary] (circa 1852)
: of or relating to the center of the moon; *also* : referred to or involving the moon as a center

**sel·e·nol·o·gy** \ˌse-lə-'nä-lə-jē\ *noun* (1821)
: a branch of astronomy that deals with the moon
— **se·le·no·log·i·cal** \ˌse-lə-nō-'lä-ji-kəl, sə-ˌlē-nᵊl-'ä-\ *adjective*
— **se·le·nol·o·gist** \ˌse-lə-'nä-lə-jist\ *noun*

**Se·leu·cid** \sə-'lü-səd, səl-'yü-\ *noun* [New Latin *seleucides*, from *Seleucus I*] (1851)
: a member of a Greek dynasty ruling Syria and at various times other Asian territories from 312 B.C. to 64 B.C.
— **Seleucid** *adjective*

**¹self** \'self, *Southern also* 'sef\ *pronoun* [Middle English (intensive pronoun), from Old English; akin to Old High German *selb*, intensive pronoun, and probably to Latin *suus* one's own — more at SUICIDE] (before 12th century)
: MYSELF, HIMSELF, HERSELF ⟨check payable to *self*⟩

**²self** *adjective* (before 12th century)
**1** *obsolete* : IDENTICAL, SAME
**2** *obsolete* : belonging to oneself : OWN
**3 a** : having a single character or quality throughout; *specifically* : having one color only ⟨a *self* flower⟩ **b** : of the same kind (as in color, material, or pattern) as something with which it is used ⟨*self* trimming⟩

**³self** *noun, plural* **selves** \'selvz, *Southern also* 'sevz\ (13th century)
**1 a** : the entire person of an individual **b** : the realization or embodiment of an abstraction
**2 a** (1) : an individual's typical character or behavior ⟨her true *self* was revealed⟩ (2) : an individual's temporary behavior or character ⟨his better *self*⟩ **b** : a person in prime condition ⟨feel like my old *self* today⟩
**3** : the union of elements (as body, emotions, thoughts, and sensations) that constitute the individuality and identity of a person
**4** : personal interest or advantage
**5** : material that is part of an individual organism ⟨ability of the immune system to distinguish *self* from nonself⟩

**⁴self** (1914)
*transitive verb*
**1** : INBREED
**2** : to pollinate with pollen from the same flower or plant
*intransitive verb*
: to undergo self-pollination

**self-** *combining form* [Middle English, from Old English, from *self*]

**1 a :** oneself or itself ⟨*self*-supporting⟩ **b :** of oneself or itself ⟨*self*-abasement⟩ **c :** by oneself or itself ⟨*self*-propelled⟩ ⟨*self*-acting⟩
**2 a :** to, with, for, or toward oneself or itself ⟨*self*-consistent⟩ ⟨*self*-addressed⟩ ⟨*self*-love⟩ **b :** of or in oneself or itself inherently ⟨*self*-evident⟩ **c :** from or by means of oneself or itself ⟨*self*-fertile⟩

self-abase-ment
self-ab-ne-gat-ing
self-ab-ne-ga-tion
self-ac-cel-er-at-ing
self-ac-cep-tance
self-ac-cu-sa-tion
self-ac-cu-sa-to-ry
self-ac-cus-ing
self-ac-knowl-edged
self-ad-just-ing
self-ad-min-is-ter
self-ad-min-is-tra-tion
self-ad-mit-ted
self-ad-mit-ted-ly
self-ad-u-la-to-ry
self-ad-vance-ment
self-ad-ver-tise-ment
self-ad-ver-tis-er
self-af-fir-ma-tion
self-ag-gran-dize-ment
self-ag-gran-diz-ing
self-alien-ation
self-anoint-ed
self-ap-prais-al
self-ap-pro-ba-tion
self-as-sess-ment
self-as-sign-ment
self-au-then-ti-cat-ing
self-avowed
self-bet-ter-ment
self-can-cel
self-care
self-car-i-ca-ture
self-cas-ti-gate
self-cas-ti-ga-tion
self-cen-sor-ship
self-char-ac-ter-i-za-tion
self-clas-si-fi-ca-tion
self-clean-ing
self-com-mand
self-com-mun-ing
self-com-mu-nion
self-com-pla-cen-cy
self-com-pla-cent
self-con-dem-na-tion
self-con-demned
self-con-firm-ing
self-con-se-cra-tion
self-con-sti-tut-ed
self-con-sum-ing
self-con-tempt
self-cre-at-ed
self-cre-a-tion
self-crit-i-cal
self-crit-i-cism
self-cri-tique
self-cul-ti-va-tion
self-cul-ture
self-damn-ing
self-de-base-ment
self-de-ceit
self-de-ceive
self-de-cep-tion
self-de-feat-ing
self-de-lud-ed
self-de-lud-ing
self-de-lu-sion
self-den-i-grat-ing
self-den-i-gra-tion
self-de-pen-dence
self-de-pen-dent

self-dep-re-cat-ing
self-dep-re-cat-ing-ly
self-dep-re-ca-tion
self-dep-re-ca-to-ry
self-de-pre-ci-a-tion
self-de-scribed
self-de-scrip-tion
self-de-scrip-tive
self-de-vel-op-ment
self-de-vour-ing
self-dif-fer-en-ti-a-tion
self-di-rect-ed
self-di-rect-ing
self-di-rec-tion
self-di-rec-tive
self-dis-gust
self-dis-play
self-dis-sat-is-fac-tion
self-doubt
self-ed-u-cat-ed
self-ed-u-cat-ing
self-ed-u-ca-tion
self-ef-face-ment
self-ef-fac-ing
self-eman-ci-pa-tion
self-emas-cu-la-tion
self-en-closed
self-en-grossed
self-en-hance-ment
self-eval-u-ate
self-eval-u-a-tion
self-ex-clu-sion
self-ex-cul-pa-tion
self-ex-hi-bi-tion
self-ex-is-tence
self-ex-is-tent
self-ex-plain-ing
self-ex-tinc-tion
self-fi-nance
self-formed
self-gen-er-ate
self-giv-ing
self-guid-ed
self-hate
self-hat-ing
self-ha-tred
self-heal-ing
self-help
self-hum-bling
self-hu-mil-i-a-tion
self-hyp-no-sis
self-idol-a-try
self-im-posed
self-im-prove-ment
self-im-prov-er
self-in-duced
self-in-fat-u-at-ed
self-in-fla-tion
self-in-flict-ed
self-ini-ti-at-ed
self-in-struct-ed
self-in-struc-tion
self-in-struc-tion-al
self-in-ter-view
self-in-vent-ed
self-in-ven-tion
self-iso-la-tion
self-la-beled
self-lac-er-at-ing
self-lac-er-a-tion
self-loath-ing
self-lock-ing
self-lu-bri-cat-ing
self-lu-mi-nous

self-main-te-nance
self-man-age-ment
self-mas-tery
self-med-i-ca-tion
self-mock-ery
self-mock-ing
self-mor-ti-fi-ca-tion
self-mo-ti-vat-ed
self-mu-ti-lat-ing
self-mu-ti-la-tion
self-ne-gat-ing
self-ob-sessed
self-op-er-at-ing
self-or-dained
self-ori-ent-ed
self-par-o-dist
self-par-o-dy
self-penned
self-per-pet-u-at-ing
self-per-pet-u-a-tion
self-pla-gia-rism
self-pleas-ing
self-po-lic-ing
self-praise
self-pre-oc-cu-pa-tion
self-pre-oc-cu-pied
self-pre-serv-ing
self-pro-claimed
self-pro-duced
self-pro-fessed
self-pro-mot-er
self-pro-mot-ing
self-pro-mo-tion
self-pro-tec-tion
self-pro-tec-tive
self-pro-tec-tive-ness
self-pun-ish-ing

self-pun-ish-ment
self-raised
self-re-crim-i-na-tion
self-ref-er-en-tial
self-re-fer-ring
self-re-flex-ive
self-ref-or-ma-tion
self-reg-u-la-tion
self-reg-u-la-tive
self-reg-u-la-to-ry
self-re-in-forc-ing
self-re-new-al
self-re-new-ing
self-re-nounc-ing
self-re-nun-ci-a-tion
self-re-proach
self-re-proach-ful
self-re-proof
self-re-prov-ing
self-re-straint
self-rid-i-cule
self-sat-i-riz-ing
self-se-lect-ed
self-se-lec-tion
self-set
self-sur-ren-der
self-sus-tained
self-ther-a-py
self-tor-ment
self-tor-men-tor
self-tor-ture
self-tran-scen-dence
self-trans-for-ma-tion
self-un-der-stand-ing
self-val-i-dat-ing
self-wor-ship
self-wor-ship-er

**self–aban-doned** \,self-ə-'ban-dənd\ *adjective* (1791)
**:** abandoned by oneself; *especially* **:** given up to one's impulses
**self–aban-don-ment** \-dən-mənt\ *noun* (1818)
**1 :** a surrender of one's selfish interests or desires
**2 :** a lack of self-restraint
**self–ab-sorbed** \-əb-'sòrbd, -'zòrbd\ *adjective* (1847)
**:** absorbed in one's own thoughts, activities, or interests
**self–ab-sorp-tion** \-'sòrp-shən, -'zòrp-\ *noun* (1862)
**:** preoccupation with oneself
**self–abuse** \-ə-'byüs\ *noun* (1605)
**1 :** reproach of oneself
**2 :** MASTURBATION
**3 :** abuse of one's body or health
**self–act-ing** \-'ak-tiŋ\ *adjective* (circa 1680)
**:** acting or capable of acting of or by itself
**:** AUTOMATIC
**self–ac-tiv-i-ty** \-,ak-'ti-və-tē\ *noun* (1644)
**:** independent and especially self-determined activity
**self–ac-tu-al-ize** \-'ak-ch(ə-w)ə-,līz, -sh(ə-w)ə-,līz\ *intransitive verb* (1874)
**:** to realize fully one's potential
— **self–ac-tu-al-i-za-tion** \-,ak-ch(ə-w)ə-lə-'zā-shən, -sh(ə-w)ə-lə-\ *noun*
**self–ad-dressed** \-ə-'drest, -'a-,drest\ *adjective* (1904)
**:** addressed for return to the sender ⟨a *self-addressed* envelope⟩
**self–ad-he-sive** \-əd-'hē-siv, -ziv\ *adjective* (1958)
**:** having a side coated with an adhesive that sticks without wetting ⟨*self-adhesive* labels⟩
**self–ad-just-ment** \-ə-'jəs(t)-mənt\ *noun* (1848)
**:** adjustment to oneself or one's environment
**self–ad-mi-ra-tion** \-,ad-mə-'rā-shən\ *noun* (1661)
**:** SELF-CONCEIT
**self–af-fect-ed** \-ə-'fek-təd\ *adjective* (1606)

**:** CONCEITED, SELF-LOVING
**self–anal-y-sis** \-ə-'na-lə-səs\ *noun* (1860)
**:** a systematic attempt by an individual to understand his or her own personality without the aid of another person
**self–an-a-lyt-i-cal** \-,a-nᵊl-'i-ti-kəl\ *also* **self–an-a-lyt-ic** *adjective* (1943)
**:** using self-analysis
**self–an-ni-hi-la-tion** \-ə-,nī-ə-'lā-shən\ *noun* (1647)
**:** annihilation of the self (as in mystical contemplation of God)
**self–ap-plaud-ing** \-ə-'plò-diŋ\ *adjective* (1654)
**:** marked by self-applause
**self–ap-plause** \-'plòz\ *noun* (1678)
**:** an expression or feeling of approval of oneself
**self–ap-point-ed** \-ə-'pòin-təd\ *adjective* (1799)
**:** appointed by oneself **:** SELF-STYLED
**self–as-sem-bly** \-ə-'sem-blē\ *noun* (1966)
**:** the process by which a complex macromolecule (as collagen) or a supramolecular system (as a virus) spontaneously assembles itself from its components
— **self–as-sem-ble** \-ə-'sem-bəl\ *intransitive verb*
**self–as-sert-ing** \-ə-'sər-tiŋ\ *adjective* (1837)
**1 :** asserting oneself or one's own rights, claims, or opinions
**2 a :** SELF-ASSURED, CONFIDENT **b :** ARROGANT
— **self–as-sert-ing-ly** \-tiŋ-lē\ *adverb*
**self–as-ser-tion** \-ə-'sər-shən\ *noun* (1806)
**1 :** the act of asserting oneself or one's own rights, claims, or opinions
**2 :** the act of asserting one's superiority over others
**self–as-ser-tive** \-'sər-tiv\ *adjective* (1865)
**:** given to or characterized by self-assertion
**synonym** see AGGRESSIVE
— **self–as-ser-tive-ly** *adverb*
— **self–as-ser-tive-ness** *noun*
**self–as-sump-tion** \-ə-'səm(p)-shən\ *noun* (1606)
**:** SELF-CONCEIT
**self–as-sur-ance** \-ə-'shùr-ən(t)s\ *noun* (1594)
**:** SELF-CONFIDENCE
**self–as-sured** \-'shùrd\ *adjective* (1711)
**:** sure of oneself **:** SELF-CONFIDENT
— **self–as-sured-ly** \-'shùr-əd-lē, -'shùrd-\ *adverb*
— **self–as-sured-ness** \-'shùr-əd-nəs, -'shùrd-\ *noun*
**self–aware** \-ə-'war, -'wer\ *adjective* (circa 1934)
**:** characterized by self-awareness
**self–aware-ness** *noun* (1880)
**:** an awareness of one's own personality or individuality
**self–belt** \'self-'belt\ *noun* (1965)
**:** a belt made of the same material as the garment with which it is worn
— **self–belt-ed** \-'bel-təd\ *adjective*
**self–be-tray-al** \,self-bi-'trā-(ə)l\ *noun* (1857)
**:** SELF-REVELATION
**self–born** \-'bòrn\ *adjective* (1587)
**1 :** arising within the self ⟨*self-born* sorrows⟩
**2 :** springing from a prior self ⟨phoenix rising *self-born* from the fire⟩
**self–ca-ter-ing** \-'kā-tər-iŋ\ *adjective* (1970)
*British* **:** provided with lodging and cooking facilities but not meals ⟨*self-catering* holiday cottages⟩
**self–cen-tered** \-'sen-tərd\ *adjective* (circa 1764)
**1 :** independent of outside force or influence
**:** SELF-SUFFICIENT

\ə\ abut \ᵊ\ kitten \ər\ further \a\ ash \ā\ ace \ä\ mop, mar \aů\ out \ch\ chin \e\ bet \ē\ easy \g\ go \i\ hit \ī\ ice \j\ job \ŋ\ sing \ō\ go \ò\ law \òi\ boy \th\ thin \th̲\ the \ü\ loot \ů\ foot \y\ yet \zh\ vision *see also* Guide to Pronunciation

**2 :** concerned solely with one's own desires, needs, or interests
— **self·cen·tered·ly** *adverb*
— **self·cen·tered·ness** *noun*
**self·clos·ing** \-'klō-ziŋ\ *adjective* (circa 1875)
**:** closing or shutting automatically after being opened
**self·cock·ing** \-'kä-kiŋ\ *adjective* (1862)
*of a firearm* **:** cocked by the operation of some part of the action ⟨*self-cocking* on pushing the bolt forward⟩
**self·col·lect·ed** \-kə-'lek-təd\ *adjective* (circa 1711)
**:** SELF-POSSESSED
**self·col·ored** \-'kə-lərd\ *adjective* (1759)
**:** of a single color ⟨a *self-colored* flower⟩
**self·com·pat·i·ble** \-kəm-'pa-tə-bəl\ *adjective* (1922)
**:** capable of effective self-pollination that results in the production of seeds and fruits
— **self·com·pat·i·bil·i·ty** \-,pa-tə-'bi-lə-tē\ *noun*
**self·com·posed** \-kəm-'pōzd\ *adjective* (circa 1934)
**:** having control over one's emotions **:** CALM
— **self·com·pos·ed·ly** \-'pō-zəd-lē\ *adverb*
— **self·com·posed·ness** \-'pō-zəd-nəs, -'pōz(d)-nəs\ *noun*
**self·con·ceit** \-kən-'sēt\ *noun* (circa 1589)
**:** an exaggerated opinion of one's own qualities or abilities **:** VANITY
— **self·con·ceit·ed** \-'sē-təd\ *adjective*
**self·con·cept** \'self-'kän-,sept\ *noun* (1925)
**:** the mental image one has of oneself
**self·con·cep·tion** \,self-kən-'sep-shən\ *noun* (1950)
**:** SELF-CONCEPT
**self·con·cern** \-'sərn\ *noun* (1681)
**:** a selfish or morbid concern for oneself
— **self·con·cerned** \-'sərnd\ *adjective*
**self·con·fessed** \-'fest\ *adjective* (circa 1900)
**:** openly acknowledged by oneself **:** AVOWED
— **self·con·fess·ed·ly** \-'fe-səd-lē, -'fest-lē\ *adverb*
**self·con·fes·sion** \-'fe-shən\ *noun* (circa 1961)
**:** open acknowledgment **:** AVOWAL
**self·con·fi·dence** \-'kän-fə-dən(t)s, -,den(t)s\ *noun* (1637)
**:** confidence in oneself and in one's powers and abilities
— **self·con·fi·dent** \-fə-dənt, -,dent\ *adjective*
— **self·con·fi·dent·ly** *adverb*
**self·con·fron·ta·tion** \-,kän-(,)frən-'tā-shən\ *noun* (1961)
**:** SELF-ANALYSIS
**self·con·grat·u·la·tion** \-kən-,gra-chə-'lā-shən, -,gra-jə-\ *noun* (1712)
**:** congratulation of oneself; *especially* **:** a complacent acknowledgment of one's own superiority or good fortune
**self·con·grat·u·la·to·ry** \-'gra-chə-lə-,tōr-ē, -,gra-jə-, -,tòr-\ *adjective* (1877)
**:** expressive of self-congratulation ⟨*self-congratulatory* memoirs⟩
**self·con·scious** \-'kän(t)-shəs\ *adjective* (circa 1680)
**1 a :** conscious of one's own acts or states as belonging to or originating in oneself **:** aware of oneself as an individual **b :** intensely aware of oneself **:** CONSCIOUS ⟨a rising and *self-conscious* social class⟩; *also* **:** produced or done with such awareness ⟨*self-conscious* art⟩
**2 :** uncomfortably conscious of oneself as an object of the observation of others **:** ILL AT EASE
— **self·con·scious·ly** *adverb*
— **self·con·scious·ness** *noun*
**self·con·se·quence** \-'kän(t)-sə-,kwen(t)s, -si-kwən(t)s\ *noun* (1778)
**:** SELF-IMPORTANCE

**self·con·sis·ten·cy** \-kən-'sis-tən(t)-sē\ *noun* (1692)
**:** the quality or state of being self-consistent
**self·con·sis·tent** \-tənt\ *adjective* (1683)
**:** having each part logically consistent with the rest
**self·con·tained** \-kən-'tānd\ *adjective* (1591)
**1 a :** complete in itself **:** INDEPENDENT ⟨a *self-contained* machine⟩ ⟨a *self-contained* program of study⟩ **b :** BUILT-IN ⟨a lectern with a *self-contained* light fixture⟩
**2 a :** showing self-control **b :** formal and reserved in manner
— **self·con·tained·ly** \-'tā-nəd-lē, -'tānd-lē\ *adverb*
— **self·con·tained·ness** \-'tā-nəd-nəs, -'tān(d)-nəs\ *noun*
— **self·con·tain·ment** \-'tān-mənt\ *noun*
**self·con·tam·i·na·tion** \-kən-,ta-mə-'nā-shən\ *noun* (1955)
**1 :** contamination by oneself
**2 :** contamination from within
**self·con·tent** \-kən-'tent\ *noun* (1654)
**:** SELF-SATISFACTION
**self·con·tent·ed** \-'ten-təd\ *adjective* (1818)
**:** SELF-SATISFIED
— **self·con·tent·ed·ly** *adverb*
— **self·con·tent·ed·ness** *noun*
**self·con·tent·ment** \-'tent-mənt\ *noun* (1815)
**:** SELF-SATISFACTION
**self·con·tra·dic·tion** \-,kän-trə-'dik-shən\ *noun* (1658)
**1 :** contradiction of oneself
**2 :** a self-contradictory statement or proposition
**self·con·tra·dic·to·ry** \-'dik-t(ə-)rē\ *adjective* (1657)
**:** consisting of two contradictory members or parts
**self·con·trol** \-kən-'trōl\ *noun* (1711)
**:** restraint exercised over one's own impulses, emotions, or desires
— **self·con·trolled** \-'trōld\ *adjective*
**self·cor·rect·ing** \-kə-'rek-tiŋ\ *adjective* (1939)
**:** correcting or compensating for one's own errors or weaknesses
**self·cor·rec·tive** \-'rek-tiv\ *adjective* (circa 1925)
**:** SELF-CORRECTING
**self·deal·ing** \'self-'dē-liŋ\ *noun* (1940)
**:** financial dealing that is not at arm's length; *especially* **:** borrowing from or lending to a company by a controlling individual primarily to the individual's own advantage
**self·de·fense** \-di-'fen(t)s\ *noun* (1651)
**1 :** a plea of justification for the use of force or for homicide
**2 :** the act of defending oneself, one's property, or a close relative
**self·de·fen·sive** \-'fen(t)-siv\ *adjective* (1828)
**:** of, relating to, or given to self-defense ⟨a *self-defensive* person⟩ ⟨a *self-defensive* attitude⟩
**self·def·i·ni·tion** \-,de-fə-'ni-shən\ *noun* (1957)
**:** the evaluation by oneself of one's worth as an individual in distinction from one's interpersonal or social roles
**self·de·ni·al** \-di-'nī(-ə)l\ *noun* (1642)
**:** a restraint or limitation of one's own desires or interests
**self·de·ny·ing** \-'nī-iŋ\ *adjective* (1632)
**:** showing self-denial
— **self·de·ny·ing·ly** \-iŋ-lē\ *adverb*
**self·de·spair** \-di-'spar, -'sper\ *noun* (1677)
**:** despair of oneself **:** HOPELESSNESS
**self·de·stroy·er** \-di-'stròi(-ə)r\ *noun* (1654)
**:** one who destroys oneself
**self·de·stroy·ing** \-'stròi-iŋ\ *adjective* (1645)
**:** SELF-DESTRUCTIVE
**self·de·struct** \-di-'strəkt\ *intransitive verb* (1968)
**:** to destroy oneself or itself

— **self·de·struct** *adjective*
**self·de·struc·tion** \-'strək-shən\ *noun* (circa 1586)
**:** destruction of oneself; *especially* **:** SUICIDE
**self·de·struc·tive** \-'strək-tiv\ *adjective* (1654)
**:** acting or tending to harm or destroy oneself; *also* **:** SUICIDAL
— **self·de·struc·tive·ness** *noun*
**self·de·ter·mi·na·tion** \-di-,tər-mə-'nā-shən\ *noun* (circa 1670)
**1 :** free choice of one's own acts or states without external compulsion
**2 :** determination by the people of a territorial unit of their own future political status
**self·de·ter·mined** \-'tər-mənd\ *adjective* (circa 1670)
**:** determined by oneself
**self·de·ter·min·ing** \-'tər-mə-niŋ, -'tərm-niŋ\ *adjective* (1662)
**:** capable of determining one's or its own acts
**self·de·ter·min·ism** \-'tər-mə-,ni-zəm\ *noun* (1936)
**:** a doctrine that the actions of a self are determined by itself
**self·de·vot·ed** \-di-'vō-təd\ *adjective* (1713)
**:** characterized by total devotion of oneself (as to a cause)
— **self·de·vot·ed·ness** *noun*
**self·dis·ci·pline** \-'di-sə-plən\ *noun* (1838)
**:** correction or regulation of oneself for the sake of improvement
**self·dis·ci·plined** \-plənd\ *adjective* (1932)
**:** capable of or subject to self-discipline
**self·dis·cov·ery** \-dis-'kə-v(ə-)rē\ *noun* (1924)
**:** the act or process of achieving self-knowledge
**self·dis·trust** \-'trəst\ *noun* (1789)
**:** a lack of confidence in oneself **:** DIFFIDENCE
— **self·dis·trust·ful** \-fəl\ *adjective*
**self·dra·ma·ti·za·tion** \,self-,dra-mə-tə-'zā-shən, -,drä-\ *noun* (1937)
**:** the act or an instance of dramatizing oneself
**self·dra·ma·tiz·ing** \-'dra-mə-,tī-ziŋ, -'drä-\ *adjective* (1938)
**:** seeing and presenting oneself as an important or dramatic figure
**self·drive** \'self-'drīv\ *adjective* (1929)
*chiefly British* **:** being a rental car
**self·elect·ed** \,self-ə-'lek-təd\ *adjective* (1818)
**:** SELF-APPOINTED
**self·em·ployed** \-im-'plóid\ *adjective* (1946)
**:** earning income directly from one's own business, trade, or profession rather than as a specified salary or wages from an employer
— **self·em·ployed** *noun*
**self·em·ploy·ment** \-'plói-mənt\ *noun* (1745)
**:** the state of being self-employed
**self·en·er·giz·ing** \-'e-nər-,jī-ziŋ\ *adjective* (1931)
**:** containing means for augmentation of power within itself ⟨a *self-energizing* brake⟩
**self·en·forc·ing** \-in-'fōr-siŋ, -'fòr-\ *adjective* (1952)
**:** containing in itself the authority or means that provide for its enforcement
**self·en·rich·ment** \-in-'rich-mənt\ *noun* (1920)
**:** the act or process of increasing one's intellectual or spiritual resources
**self·es·teem** \-ə-'stēm\ *noun* (1657)
**1 :** a confidence and satisfaction in oneself **:** SELF-RESPECT
**2 :** SELF-CONCEIT
**self·ev·i·dence** \-'e-və-dən(t)s, -,den(t)s\ *noun* (1671)
**:** the quality or state of being self-evident
**self·ev·i·dent** \-dənt, -,dent\ *adjective* (1671)
**:** evident without proof or reasoning
— **self·ev·i·dent·ly** *adverb*
**self·ex·am·i·na·tion** \-ig-,za-mə-'nā-shən\ *noun* (1647)

**1** : a reflective examination (as of one's beliefs or motives) : INTROSPECTION
**2** : examination of one's body especially for evidence of disease

**self-ex·cit·ed** \-ik-'sī-təd\ *adjective* (circa 1896)
: excited by a current produced by the generator itself ⟨*self-excited* generators⟩

**self-ex·e·cut·ing** \-'ek-sə-ˌkyü-tiŋ\ *adjective* (1868)
: taking effect immediately without implementing legislation ⟨a *self-executing* treaty⟩

**self-ex·iled** \-'eg-ˌzīld, -'ek-ˌsīld\ *adjective* (1737)
: exiled by one's own wish or decision

**self-ex·plan·a·to·ry** \ik-'spla-nə-ˌtȯr-ē, -ˌtȯr-\ *adjective* (1898)
: explaining itself : capable of being understood without explanation

**self-ex·plo·ra·tion** \-ˌek-splə-'rā-shən, -ˌsplȯ-\ *noun* (1959)
: the examination and analysis of one's own unrealized spiritual or intellectual capacities

**self-ex·pres·sion** \-ik-'spre-shən\ *noun* (1892)
: the expression of one's own personality : assertion of one's individual traits
— **self-ex·pres·sive** \-'spre-siv\ *adjective*

**self-feed** \'self-'fēd\ *transitive verb* **-fed** \-'fed\ **-feed·ing** (circa 1924)
: to provide rations to (animals) in bulk so as to permit feeding as wanted

**self-feed·er** \-'fē-dər\ *noun* (1924)
: a device for providing feed to livestock that is equipped with a feed hopper that automatically supplies a trough below

**self-feel·ing** \'self-'fē-liŋ\ *noun* (1879)
: self-centered emotion

**self-fer·tile** \'self-'fər-t°l\ *adjective* (1865)
: fertile by means of its own pollen or sperm
— **self-fer·til·i·ty** \-(ˌ)fər-'ti-lə-tē\ *noun*

**self-fer·til·i·za·tion** \-ˌfər-t°l-ə-'zā-shən\ *noun* (1859)
: fertilization effected by union of ova with pollen or sperm from the same individual

**self-fer·til·ized** \-'fər-t°l-ˌīzd\ *adjective* (1871)
: fertilized by one's own pollen or sperm

**self-fer·til·iz·ing** \-ˌī-ziŋ\ *adjective* (1859)
: SELF-FERTILIZED

**self-flag·el·la·tion** \-ˌfla-jə-'lā-shən\ *noun* (1845)
: extreme criticism of oneself

**self-flat·ter·ing** \-'fla-tə-riŋ\ *adjective* (circa 1586)
: given to self-flattery

**self-flat·tery** \-tə-rē\ *noun* (1680)
: the glossing over of one's own weaknesses or mistakes and the exaggeration of one's own good qualities and achievements

**self-for·get·ful** \-fər-'get-fəl\ *adjective* (1848)
: having or showing no thought of self or selfish interests
— **self-for·get·ful·ly** \-fə-lē\ *adverb*
— **self-for·get·ful·ness** *noun*

**self-for·get·ting** \-'ge-tiŋ\ *adjective* (1847)
: SELF-FORGETFUL
— **self-for·get·ting·ly** \-tiŋ-lē\ *adverb*

**self-fruit·ful** \'self-'früt-fəl\ *adjective* (1940)
: capable of setting a crop of self-pollinated fruit
— **self-fruit·ful·ness** *noun*

**self-ful·fill·ing** \ˌself-fül-'fi-liŋ\ *adjective* (1949)
**1** : marked by or achieving self-fulfillment
**2** : becoming real or true by virtue of having been predicted or expected ⟨a *self-fulfilling* prophecy⟩

**self-ful·fill·ment** \-'fil-mənt\ *noun* (circa 1864)
: fulfillment of oneself

**self-giv·en** \-'gi-vən\ *adjective* (1742)
**1** : derived from itself ⟨a *self-given* entity⟩
**2** : given by oneself ⟨*self-given* authority⟩

**self-glo·ri·fi·ca·tion** \-ˌglȯr-ə-fə-'kā-shən, -ˌglȯr-\ *noun* (1838)
: a feeling or expression of one's own superiority

**self-glo·ri·fy·ing** \-'glȯr-ə-ˌfī-iŋ, -'glȯr-\ *adjective* (1860)
: given to or marked by boasting : BOASTFUL

**self-glo·ry** \-'glȯr-ē, -'glȯr-ē\ *noun* (1647)
: personal vanity : PRIDE

**self-gov·er·nance** \-'gə-vər-nən(t)s\ *noun* (1964)
: SELF-GOVERNMENT 2

**self-gov·erned** \-'gə-vərnd\ *adjective* (1709)
**1** : not influenced or controlled by others
**2** : exercising self-control

**self-gov·ern·ing** \-'gə-vər-niŋ\ *adjective* (1845)
: having control or rule over oneself; *specifically* : having self-government : AUTONOMOUS

**self-gov·ern·ment** \-'gə-vər(n)-mənt, -'gəv°m-ənt\ *noun* (1734)
**1** : SELF-COMMAND, SELF-CONTROL
**2** : government under the control and direction of the inhabitants of a political unit rather than by an outside authority; *broadly* : control of one's own affairs

**self-grat·i·fi·ca·tion** \-ˌgra-tə-fə-'kā-shən\ *noun* (1677)
: the act of pleasing oneself or of satisfying one's desires; *especially* : the satisfying of one's own sexual urges

**self-grat·u·la·tion** \-ˌgra-chə-'lā-shən\ *noun* (1802)
: SELF-CONGRATULATION

**self-grat·u·la·to·ry** \-'gra-chə-lə-ˌtȯr-ē, -ˌtȯr-\ *adjective* (1859)
: SELF-CONGRATULATORY

**self-heal** \'self-ˌhēl\ *noun* (14th century)
: a blue-flowered Eurasian mint (*Prunella vulgaris*) naturalized throughout North America and formerly considered to have medicinal properties

**self-hood** \-ˌhud\ *noun* (1649)
**1** : INDIVIDUALITY
**2** : the quality or state of being selfish

**self-iden·ti·cal** \ˌself-ī-'den-ti-kəl, -ə-'den-\ *adjective* (1877)
: having self-identity

**self-iden·ti·fi·ca·tion** \-ˌden-tə-fə-'kā-shən\ *noun* (1941)
: identification with someone or something outside oneself

**self-iden·ti·ty** \-'den-tə-tē, -'de-nə-tē\ *noun* (1866)
**1** : sameness of a thing with itself
**2** : INDIVIDUALITY ⟨*self*-understanding is the necessary condition of a sense of *self-identity* —J. C. Murray⟩

**self-ig·nite** \-ig-'nīt\ *intransitive verb* (1943)
: to become ignited without flame or spark (as under high compression)

**self-ig·ni·tion** \-'ni-shən\ *noun* (1903)
: ignition without flame or spark

**self-im·age** \'self-'i-mij\ *noun* (1939)
: one's conception of oneself or of one's role

**self-im·mo·la·tion** \ˌself-ˌi-mə-'lā-shən\ *noun* (1817)
: a deliberate and willing sacrifice of oneself often by fire
— **self-im·mo·late** \-'i-mə-ˌlāt\ *verb*

**self-im·por·tance** \-im-'pȯr-t°n(t)s, -tən(t)s\ *noun* (circa 1775)
**1** : an exaggerated estimate of one's own importance : SELF-CONCEIT
**2** : arrogant or pompous behavior

**self-important** \-t°nt, -tənt\ *adjective* (circa 1775)
: having or showing self-importance
— **self-im·por·tant·ly** *adverb*

**self-in·clu·sive** \-in-'klü-siv, -ziv\ *adjective* (circa 1909)
**1** : enclosing itself
**2** : complete in itself

**self-in·com·pat·i·ble** \-ˌin-kəm-'pa-tə-bəl\ *adjective* (1922)
: incapable of effective self-pollination

**self-in·com·pat·i·bil·i·ty** \-ˌpa-tə-'bi-lə-tē\ *noun*

**self-in·crim·i·nat·ing** \-in-'kri-mə-ˌnā-tiŋ\ *adjective* (1931)
: serving or tending to incriminate oneself

**self-in·crim·i·na·tion** \-ˌkri-mə-'nā-shən\ *noun* (1911)
: incrimination of oneself; *specifically* : the giving of testimony which will likely subject one to criminal prosecution

**self-in·duc·tance** \-'dək-tən(t)s\ *noun* (1865)
: inductance in which an electromotive force is produced by self-induction

**self-in·duc·tion** \-'dək-shən\ *noun* (1873)
: induction of an electromotive force in a circuit by a varying current in the same circuit

**self-in·dul·gence** \-'dəl-jən(t)s\ *noun* (1753)
: excessive or unrestrained gratification of one's own appetites, desires, or whims
— **self-in·dul·gent** \-jənt\ *adjective*
— **self-in·dul·gent·ly** *adverb*

**self-in·sur·ance** \in-'shúr-ən(t)s, -'in-ˌ\ *noun* (circa 1897)
: insurance of oneself or of one's own interests by the setting aside of money at regular intervals to provide a fund to cover possible losses

**self-insure** \-in-'shúr\ *verb* (1932)
: to insure oneself; *especially* : to practice self-insurance
— **self-insurer** \-'shúr-ər\ *noun*

**self-in·ter·est** \-'in-t(ə-)rəst; -'in-tə-ˌrest, -ˌtrest; -'in-tərst\ *noun* (1649)
**1** : a concern for one's own advantage and well-being ⟨acted out of *self-interest* and fear⟩
**2** : one's own interest or advantage ⟨*self-interest* requires that we be generous in foreign aid⟩
— **self-in·ter·est·ed** *adjective*
— **self-in·ter·est·ed·ness** *noun*

**self-in·volved** \-in-'välvd, -'vȯlvd also -'vävd or 'vȯvd\ *adjective* (1842)
: SELF-ABSORBED

**self-ish** \'sel-fish\ *adjective* (1640)
**1** : concerned excessively or exclusively with oneself : seeking or concentrating on one's own advantage, pleasure, or well-being without regard for others
**2** : arising from concern with one's own welfare or advantage in disregard of others ⟨a *selfish* act⟩
— **self-ish·ly** *adverb*
— **self-ish·ness** *noun*

**self-jus·ti·fi·ca·tion** \ˌself-ˌjəs-tə-fə-'kā-shən\ *noun* (circa 1775)
: the act or an instance of making excuses for oneself

**self-jus·ti·fy·ing** \-'jəs-tə-ˌfī-iŋ\ *adjective* (1740)
: seeking to justify oneself

**self-know·ing** \-'nō-iŋ\ *adjective* (1667)
: having self-knowledge

**self-knowl·edge** \-'nä-lij\ *noun* (circa 1613)
: knowledge or understanding of one's own capabilities, character, feelings, or motivations

**self-less** \'sel-fləs\ *adjective* (1825)
: having no concern for self : UNSELFISH
— **self-less·ly** *adverb*
— **self-less·ness** *noun*

**self-lim·it·ed** \ˌself-'li-mə-təd\ *adjective* (1845)
: limited by one's or its own nature; *specifically* : running a definite and limited course ⟨a *self-limited* disease⟩

**self-lim·it·ing** \-tiŋ\ *adjective* (1863)
: limiting oneself or itself; *especially, of a disease* : SELF-LIMITED

**self-liq·ui·dat·ing** \-'li-kwə-ˌdā-tiŋ\ *adjective* (1915)

**1 :** of or relating to a commercial transaction in which goods are converted into cash in a short time
**2 :** generating funds from its own operations to repay the investment made to create it ⟨a *self-liquidating* housing project⟩
**self-load·er** \-'lō-dər\ *noun* (circa 1936)
**:** a semiautomatic firearm
**self-load·ing** \-diŋ\ *adjective* (1899)
*of a firearm* : SEMIAUTOMATIC
**self-love** \'self-'ləv\ *noun* (1563)
**:** love of self: **a :** CONCEIT **b :** regard for one's own happiness or advantage
— **self-lov·ing** \-'lə-viŋ\ *adjective*
**self-made** \'self-'mād\ *adjective* (1615)
**:** made such by one's own actions; *especially* : having achieved success or prominence by one's own efforts ⟨a *self-made* man⟩
**self-mail·er** \-'mā-lər\ *noun* (circa 1942)
**:** a folder that can be sent by mail without enclosure in an envelope by use of a gummed sticker or a precanceled stamp to hold the leaves together
**self-mail·ing** \-liŋ\ *adjective* (circa 1948)
**:** capable of being mailed without being enclosed in an envelope
**self-moved** \'self-'müvd\ *adjective* (circa 1670)
**:** moved by inherent power
**self-mur·der** \-'mər-dər\ *noun* (1563)
**:** SELF-DESTRUCTION, SUICIDE
**self-ness** \'self-nəs\ *noun* (circa 1586)
**1 :** EGOISM, SELFISHNESS
**2 :** PERSONALITY, SELFHOOD
**self-ob·ser·va·tion** \,self-,äb-sər-'vā-shən, -zər-\ *noun* (1832)
**1 :** INTROSPECTION
**2 :** observation of one's own appearance
**self-opin·ion** \-ə-'pin-yən\ *noun* (circa 1580)
**:** high or exaggerated opinion of oneself **:** SELF-CONCEIT
**self-opin·ion·at·ed** \-yə-,nā-təd\ *adjective* (1671)
**1 :** CONCEITED
**2 :** stubbornly holding to one's own opinion **:** OPINIONATED
— **self-opin·ion·at·ed·ness** *noun*
**self-or·ga·ni·za·tion** \-,ȯr-gə-nə-'zā-shən, -,ȯrg-nə-\ *noun* (1898)
**:** organization of oneself or itself; *specifically* **:** the act or process of forming or joining a labor union
**self-paced** \'self-'pāst\ *adjective* (1962)
**:** designed to permit learning at the student's own pace ⟨*self-paced* mathematical course⟩
**self-par·ti·al·i·ty** \,self-,pär-shē-'a-lə-tē, -,pär-'sha-\ *noun* (1628)
**1 :** an excessive estimate of oneself as compared with others
**2 :** a prejudice in favor of one's own claims or interests
**self-per·cep·tion** \-pər-'sep-shən\ *noun* (1678)
**:** perception of oneself; *especially* **:** SELF-CONCEPT
**self-pity** \'self-'pi-tē\ *noun* (1621)
**:** pity for oneself; *especially* **:** a self-indulgent dwelling on one's own sorrows or misfortunes
— **self-pity·ing** \-tē-iŋ\ *adjective*
— **self-pity·ing·ly** \-iŋ-lē\ *adverb*
**self-pleased** \-'plēzd\ *adjective* (1748)
**:** SELF-SATISFIED
**self-poise** \-'pȯiz\ *noun* (1854)
**:** the quality or state of being self-poised
**self-poised** \-'pȯizd\ *adjective* (1621)
**:** having poise through self-command
**self-pol·li·nate** \'self-'pä-lə-,nāt\ (1890) *transitive verb*
**:** SELF 2
*intransitive verb*
**:** to undergo self-pollination
**self-pol·li·na·tion** \,self-,pä-lə-'nā-shən\ *noun* (1872)
**:** the transfer of pollen from the anther of a flower to the stigma of the same flower or

sometimes to that of a genetically identical flower (as of the same plant or clone)
**self-por·trait** \-'pȯr-trət, -'pȯr-, -,trāt\ *noun* (1831)
**:** a portrait of oneself done by oneself
**self-pos·sessed** \-pə-'zest *also* -'sest\ *adjective* (1818)
**:** having or showing self-possession **:** composed in mind or manner **:** CALM
— **self-pos·sessed·ly** \-'ze-səd-lē, -'se-; -'zest-lē, -'sest-\ *adverb*
**self-pos·ses·sion** \-pə-'ze-shən *also* -'se-\ *noun* (1745)
**:** control of one's emotions or reactions especially when under stress **:** PRESENCE OF MIND, COMPOSURE
**synonym** see CONFIDENCE
**self-pres·er·va·tion** \-,pre-zər-'vā-shən\ *noun* (circa 1614)
**1 :** preservation of oneself from destruction or harm
**2 :** a natural or instinctive tendency to act so as to preserve one's own existence
**self-pride** \'self-'prīd\ *noun* (circa 1586)
**:** pride in oneself or in that which relates to oneself
**self-pro·pelled** \,self-prə-'peld\ *adjective* (1899)
**1 :** containing within itself the means for its own propulsion ⟨a *self-propelled* vehicle⟩
**2 :** mounted on or fired from a moving vehicle ⟨a *self-propelled* gun⟩
**self-pro·pel·ling** \-'pe-liŋ\ *adjective* (1862)
**:** SELF-PROPELLED 1
**self-pro·pul·sion** \-'pəl-shən\ *noun* (circa 1934)
**:** propulsion by one's own power
**self-pub·lished** \-'pə-blisht\ *adjective* (1975)
**:** published by the author ⟨*self-published* book⟩
**self-pu·ri·fi·ca·tion** \-,pyu̇r-ə-fə-'kā-shən\ *noun* (1919)
**1 :** purification by natural process ⟨*self-purification* of water⟩
**2 :** purification of oneself
**self-ques·tion** \'self-'kwes-chən, -'kwesh-\ *noun* (1917)
**:** a question asked of oneself by oneself
**self-ques·tion·ing** \-chə-niŋ\ *noun* (1856)
**:** examination of one's own actions and motives
**self-rat·ing** \-'rā-tiŋ\ *noun* (1925)
**:** determination of one's own rating with reference to a standard scale
**self-re·al·i·za·tion** \-,rē-ə-lə-'zā-shən, -,ri-ə-\ *noun* (1874)
**:** fulfillment by oneself of the possibilities of one's character or personality
**self-re·al·i·za·tion·ism** \-shə-,ni-zəm\ *noun* (circa 1874)
**:** the ethical theory that the highest good for a person consists in realizing or fulfilling oneself usually on the assumption that one has certain inborn abilities constituting one's real or ideal self
— **self-re·al·i·za·tion·ist** \-sh(ə-)nist\ *noun*
**self-rec·og·ni·tion** \-,re-kig-'ni-shən, -kəg-\ *noun* (1946)
**1 :** recognition of one's own self
**2 :** the process by which the immune system of an organism distinguishes between the body's own chemicals, cells, and tissues and those of foreign organisms and agents
**self-re·cord·ing** \-ri-'kȯr-diŋ\ *adjective* (1875)
**:** making an automatic record ⟨*self-recording* instruments⟩
**self-re·flec·tion** \-ri-'flek-shən\ *noun* (1652)
**:** SELF-EXAMINATION 1
**self-re·flec·tive** \-ri-'flek-tiv\ *adjective* (1875)
**:** marked by or engaging in self-reflection
**self-re·gard** \-ri-'gärd\ *noun* (1595)
**:** regard for or consideration of oneself or one's own interests

**self-re·gard·ing** \-ri-'gär-diŋ\ *adjective* (1789)
**:** concerned with oneself or one's own interests
**self-reg·u·lat·ing** \-'re-gyə-,lā-tiŋ\ *adjective* (1837)
**:** regulating oneself or itself; *especially* **:** AUTOMATIC ⟨a *self-regulating* mechanism⟩
**self-re·li·ance** \-ri-'lī-ənts\ *noun* (1833)
**:** reliance on one's own efforts and abilities
**self-re·li·ant** \-ənt\ *adjective* (1848)
**:** having confidence in and exercising one's own powers or judgment
**self-rep·li·cat·ing** \-'re-plə-,kā-tiŋ\ *adjective* (1946)
**:** reproducing itself autonomously ⟨DNA is a *self-replicating* molecule⟩
— **self-rep·li·ca·tion** \-,re-plə-'kā-shən\ *noun*
**self-re·spect** \-ri-'spekt\ *noun* (circa 1814)
**1 :** a proper respect for oneself as a human being
**2 :** regard for one's own standing or position
**self-re·spect·ing** \-ri-'spek-tiŋ\ *adjective* (1786)
**:** having or characterized by self-respect
**self-re·veal·ing** \-ri-'vē-liŋ\ *adjective* (1839)
**:** marked by self-revelation
**self-rev·e·la·tion** \-,re-və-'lā-shən\ *noun* (1852)
**:** revelation of one's own thoughts, feelings, and attitudes especially without deliberate intent
**self-re·ward·ing** \-ri-'wȯr-diŋ\ *adjective* (1740)
**:** containing or producing its own reward ⟨virtue is *self-rewarding*⟩
**self-righ·teous** \-'rī-chəs\ *adjective* (circa 1680)
**:** convinced of one's own righteousness especially in contrast with the actions and beliefs of others **:** narrow-mindedly moralistic
— **self-righ·teous·ly** *adverb*
— **self-righ·teous·ness** *noun*
**self-ris·ing flour** \'self-'rī-ziŋ-\ *noun* (1854)
**:** a commercially prepared mixture of flour, salt, and a leavening agent
**self-rule** \'self-'rül\ *noun* (circa 1855)
**:** SELF-GOVERNMENT
**self-rul·ing** \-'rü-liŋ\ *adjective* (circa 1680)
**:** SELF-GOVERNING
**self-sac·ri·fice** \'self-'sa-krə-,fīs *also* -fəs *or* -,fīz\ *noun* (1805)
**:** sacrifice of oneself or one's interest for others or for a cause or ideal
**self-sac·ri·fic·er** \-,fī-sər *also* -fə- *or* -,fī-\ *noun* (1668)
**:** one that practices self-sacrifice
**self-sa·cri·fic·ing** \-,fīs-iŋ *also* -fə- *or* -,fī-\ *adjective* (1817)
**:** sacrificing oneself for others
— **self-sac·ri·fic·ing·ly** \-siŋ-lē\ *adverb*
**self·same** \'self-,sām\ *adjective* (15th century)
**:** being the one mentioned or in question **:** IDENTICAL ⟨left the *selfsame* day⟩
**synonym** see SAME
— **self·same·ness** \-,sām-nəs, -'sām-\ *noun*
**self-sat·is·fac·tion** \,self-,sa-təs-'fak-shən\ *noun* (1739)
**:** a usually smug satisfaction with oneself or one's position or achievements
**self-sat·is·fied** \'self-'sa-təs-,fīd\ *adjective* (1734)
**:** feeling or showing self-satisfaction
**self-scru·ti·ny** \'self-'skrü-t°n-ē, -'skrüt-nē\ *noun* (circa 1711)
**:** SELF-EXAMINATION
**self-seal·ing** \'self-'sē-liŋ\ *adjective* (1924)
**1 :** capable of sealing itself (as after puncture) ⟨a *self-sealing* tire⟩
**2 :** capable of being sealed by pressure without the addition of moisture ⟨*self-sealing* envelopes⟩
**self-search·ing** \-'sər-chiŋ\ *noun* (1687)

: SELF-QUESTIONING

**self-seek·er** \-'sē-kər\ *noun* (1632)
: a self-seeking person

¹**self-seek·ing** \-kiŋ\ *noun* (circa 1586)
: the act or practice of selfishly advancing one's own ends

²**self-seeking** *adjective* (circa 1628)
: seeking only to further one's own interests

**self-serve** \'self-'sərv\ *adjective* (1926)
: permitting self-service

**self-ser·vice** \'self-'sər-vəs\ *noun* (1919)
: the serving of oneself (as in a restaurant or service station) with goods or services to be paid for at a cashier's desk or by means of a coin-operated mechanism
— **self-service** *adjective*

**self-serv·ing** \-'sər-viŋ\ *adjective* (1827)
: serving one's own interests often in disregard of the truth or the interests of others
— **self-serv·ing·ly** *adverb*

**self-slaugh·ter** \-'slô-tər\ *noun* (1602)
: SUICIDE 1a

**self-slaugh·tered** \-tərd\ *adjective* (1593)
: killed by oneself

**self-sow** \'self-'sō\ *intransitive verb* **-sowed** \-'sōd\; **-sown** \-'sōn\ *or* **-sowed; -sow·ing** (1608)
: to sow itself by dropping seeds or by natural action (as of wind or water)

**self-start·er** \,self-'stär-tər\ *noun* (1894)
**1** : STARTER 3a
**2** : a person who has initiative

**self-start·ing** \-'stär-tiŋ\ *adjective* (1866)
: capable of starting by oneself or itself

**self-ster·ile** \-'ster-əl\ *adjective* (1876)
: sterile to its own pollen or sperm
— **self-ste·ril·i·ty** \-stə-'ri-lə-tē\ *noun*

**self-stick** \'self-'stik\ *adjective* (1947)
: capable of adhering to a surface by application of pressure without the addition of moisture

**self-stim·u·la·tion** \,self-,stim-yə-'lā-shən\ *noun* (1947)
: stimulation of oneself as a result of one's own activity or behavior (electrical *self-stimulation* of the brain); *especially* : MASTURBATION
— **self-stim·u·la·to·ry** \-'stim-yə-lə-,tōr-ē, -,tòr-\ *adjective*

**self-study** \'self-'stə-dē\ *noun* (1683)
: study of oneself; *also* : a record of observations from such study

**self-styled** \-'stī(ə)ld\ *adjective* (1823)
: called by oneself (*self-styled* experts)

**self-sub·sis·tent** \,self-səb-'sis-tənt\ *adjective* (1647)
: subsisting independently of anything external to itself
— **self-sub·sis·tence** \-tən(t)s\ *noun*

**self-sub·sist·ing** \-'sis-tiŋ\ *adjective* (1654)
: SELF-SUBSISTENT

**self-suf·fi·cien·cy** \-sə-'fi-shən(t)-sē\ *noun* (1623)
: the quality or state of being self-sufficient

**self-suf·fi·cient** \-'fi-shənt\ *adjective* (1589)
**1** : able to maintain oneself or itself without outside aid : capable of providing for one's own needs
**2** : having an extreme confidence in one's own ability or worth : HAUGHTY, OVERBEARING

**self-suf·fic·ing** \-'fī-siŋ *also* -ziŋ\ *adjective* (1687)
: SELF-SUFFICIENT
— **self-suf·fic·ing·ly** *adverb*
— **self-suf·fic·ing·ness** *noun*

**self-sug·ges·tion** \-səg-'jes-chən, -sə-, -'jesh-\ *noun* (1892)
: AUTOSUGGESTION

**self-sup·port** \,self-sə-'pōrt, -'pòrt\ *noun* (1774)
: independent support of oneself or itself
— **self-sup·port·ed** *adjective*

**self-supporting** *adjective* (1829)

: characterized by self-support: as **a** : meeting one's needs by one's own efforts or output **b** : supporting itself or its own weight (a *self-supporting* wall)

**self-sus·tain·ing** \-sə-'stā-niŋ\ *adjective* (1844)
**1** : maintaining or able to maintain oneself or itself by independent effort
**2** : maintaining or able to maintain itself once commenced (a *self-sustaining* nuclear reaction)

**self-taught** \'self-'tòt\ *adjective* (1725)
**1** : having knowledge or skills acquired by one's own efforts without formal instruction (a *self-taught* musician)
**2** : learned by oneself (*self-taught* knowledge)

**self-tol·er·ance** \-'tä-lə-rən(t)s, -'tál-rən(t)s\ *noun* (1964)
: the physiological state that exists in an organism when its immune system has proceeded far enough in the process of self-recognition to lose the capacity to attack and destroy its own bodily constituents

**self-treat·ment** \-'trēt-mənt\ *noun* (1886)
: medication of oneself or treatment of one's own disease or condition without medical supervision or prescription

**self-trust** \-'trəst\ *noun* (1583)
: SELF-CONFIDENCE

**self-will** \-'wil\ *noun* (14th century)
: stubborn or willful adherence to one's own desires or ideas : OBSTINACY

**self-willed** \-'wild\ *adjective* (14th century)
: governed by one's own will : not yielding to the wishes of others : OBSTINATE
— **self-willed·ly** \-'wild-lē\ *adverb*
— **self-willed·ness** \-'wild-nəs\ *noun*

**self-wind·ing** \-'wīn-diŋ\ *adjective* (1825)
: not needing to be wound by hand (a *self-winding* watch)

**self-worth** \-'wərth\ *noun* (1944)
: SELF-ESTEEM

**Sel·juk** \'sel-,jük, sel-\ *or* **Sel·ju·ki·an** \sel-'jü-kē-ən\ *adjective* [Turkish *Selçuk*, eponymous ancestor of the dynasties] (1855)
**1** : of or relating to any of several Turkish dynasties ruling over a great part of western Asia in the 11th, 12th, and 13th centuries
**2** : of, relating to, or characteristic of a Turkish people ruled over by a Seljuk dynasty
— **Seljuk** *or* **Seljukian** *noun*

¹**sell** \'sel\ *verb* **sold** \'sōld\; **sell·ing** [Middle English, from Old English *sellan*; akin to Old High German *sellen* to sell, Old Norse *sala* sale, Greek *helein* to take] (before 12th century)
*transitive verb*
**1** : to deliver or give up in violation of duty, trust, or loyalty : BETRAY — often used with *out*
**2 a** (1) : to give up (property) to another for something of value (as money) (2) : to offer for sale **b** : to give up in return for something else especially foolishly or dishonorably (*sold* his birthright for a mess of pottage) **c** : to exact a price for (*sold* their lives dearly)
**3 a** : to deliver into slavery for money **b** : to give into the power of another (*sold* his soul to the devil) **c** : to deliver the personal services of for money
**4** : to dispose of or manage for profit instead of in accordance with conscience, justice, or duty (*sold* their votes)
**5 a** : to develop a belief in the truth, value, or desirability of : gain acceptance for (trying to *sell* a program to the Congress) **b** : to persuade or influence to a course of action or to the acceptance of something (*sell* children on reading)
**6** : to impose on : CHEAT
**7 a** : to cause or promote the sale of (using television advertising to *sell* cereal) **b** : to make or attempt to make sales to **c** : to influence or induce to make a purchase
**8** : to achieve a sale of (*sold* a million copies)
*intransitive verb*

**1** : to dispose of something by sale
**2** : to achieve a sale; *also* : to achieve satisfactory sales (hoped that the new line would *sell*)
**3** : to have a specified price
— **sell·able** \'se-lə-bəl\ *adjective*
— **sell down the river** : to betray the faith of
— **sell short 1** : to make a short sale **2** : to fail to value properly : UNDERESTIMATE

²**sell** *noun* (1838)
**1** : a deliberate deception : HOAX
**2** : the act or an instance of selling

³**sell** *or* **selle** \'sel\ *noun* [Middle English *selle*, from Middle French, from Latin *sella* — more at SETTLE] (15th century)
*archaic* : SADDLE

⁴**sell** *chiefly Scottish variant of* SELF

**sell·er** \'se-lər\ *noun* (13th century)
**1** : one that offers for sale
**2** : a product offered for sale and selling well, to a specified extent, or in a specified manner (a million-copy *seller*) (a poor *seller*)

**seller's market** *noun* (1932)
: a market in which goods are scarce, buyers have a limited range of choice, and prices are high — compare BUYER'S MARKET

**selling climax** *noun* (circa 1949)
: a sharp decline in stock prices for a short time on very heavy trading volume followed by a rally

**sell·ing-plat·er** \'se-liŋ-,plā-tər\ *noun* (1886)
: a horse that runs in selling races

**selling point** *noun* (1923)
: an aspect or detail of something that is emphasized (as in selling or promoting)

**selling race** *noun* (1898)
: a claiming race in which the winning horse is put up for auction

**sell-off** \'sel-,òf\ *noun* (1937)
: a usually sudden sharp decline in security prices accompanied by increased volume of trading

**sell off** *intransitive verb* (circa 1700)
: to suffer a drop in prices

**sell·out** \'sel-,aùt\ *noun* (1859)
**1** : the act or an instance of selling out
**2** : something sold out; *especially* : something (as a concert or contest) for which all tickets are sold
**3** : one who sells out

**sell out** (1796)
*transitive verb*
**1** : to sell the goods of (a debtor) in order to satisfy creditors
**2** : to sell security or commodity holdings of usually to satisfy an uncovered margin
**3 a** : to sell all the available tickets for **b** : to sell all of (the merchandise was quickly *sold out*)
*intransitive verb*
**1** : to dispose of one's goods by sale; *especially* : to sell one's business
**2** : to betray one's cause or associates
**3** : to be or achieve a sellout

**sel·syn** \'sel-,sin\ *noun* [*self-synchronizing*] (1926)
: a system comprising a generator and a motor so connected by wire that angular rotation or position in the generator is reproduced simultaneously in the motor — called also *synchro*

**selt·zer** \'selt-sər\ *noun* [modification of German *Selterser* (*Wasser*) water of Selters, from Nieder *Selters*, Germany] (1775)
: artificially carbonated water

**sel·vage** *or* **sel·vedge** \'sel-vij\ *noun* [Middle English *selvage*, probably from Middle Dutch *selvegge*, *selvage*, from *selv* self + *egge* edge; akin to Old English *self* and to Old English *ecg* edge — more at EDGE] (15th century)

**1 a :** the edge on either side of a woven or flat-knitted fabric so finished as to prevent raveling; *specifically* **:** a narrow border often of different or heavier threads than the fabric and sometimes in a different weave **b :** an edge (as of fabric or paper) meant to be cut off and discarded
**2 :** an outer or peripheral part **:** BORDER, EDGE
— **sel·vaged** *or* **sel·vedged** \-vijd\ *adjective*

**selves** *plural of* SELF

**se·man·tic** \si-'man-tik\ *also* **se·man·ti·cal** \-ti-kəl\ *adjective* [Greek *sēmantikos* significant, from *sēmainein* to signify, mean, from *sēma* sign, token] (1894)
**1 :** of or relating to meaning in language
**2 :** of or relating to semantics
— **se·man·ti·cal·ly** \-ti-k(ə-)lē\ *adverb*

**se·man·ti·cist** \-'man-tə-sist\ *noun* (1902)
**:** a specialist in semantics

**se·man·tics** \si-'man-tiks\ *noun plural but singular or plural in construction* (1893)
**1 :** the study of meanings: **a :** the historical and psychological study and the classification of changes in the signification of words or forms viewed as factors in linguistic development **b** (1) **:** SEMIOTIC (2) **:** a branch of semiotic dealing with the relations between signs and what they refer to and including theories of denotation, extension, naming, and truth
**2 :** GENERAL SEMANTICS
**3 a :** the meaning or relationship of meanings of a sign or set of signs; *especially* **:** connotative meaning **b :** the language used (as in advertising or political propaganda) to achieve a desired effect on an audience especially through the use of words with novel or dual meanings

**¹sem·a·phore** \'se-mə-,fōr, -,fȯr\ *noun* [Greek *sēma* sign, signal + International Scientific Vocabulary *-phore*] (1816)
**1 :** an apparatus for visual signaling (as by the position of one or more movable arms)
**2 :** a system of visual signaling by two flags held one in each hand

**semaphore 2: alphabet; 3 positions following Z: error, end of word, numerals follow; numerals 1, 2, 3, 4, 5, 6, 7, 8, 9, 0 same as A through J**

**²semaphore** *verb* **-phored; -phor·ing** (1893)
*transitive verb*
**:** to convey (information) by or as if by semaphore
*intransitive verb*
**:** to send signals by or as if by semaphore

**se·ma·si·ol·o·gy** \si-,mā-sē-'ä-lə-jē, -,mā-zē-\ *noun* [International Scientific Vocabulary, from Greek *sēmasia* meaning, from *sēmainein* to mean] (1857)
**:** SEMANTICS 1
— **se·ma·si·o·log·i·cal** \-sē-ə-'lä-ji-kəl, -zē-\ *adjective*

**¹sem·bla·ble** \'sem-blə-bəl\ *adjective* [Middle English, from Middle French, from Old French, from *sembler* to be like, seem] (14th century)
**1 :** SIMILAR
**2 :** SUITABLE
**3 :** APPARENT, SEEMING
— **sem·bla·bly** \-blə-blē\ *adverb*

**²semblable** *noun* (15th century)
**1** *archaic* **:** something similar **:** LIKE
**2 :** one that is like oneself **:** one's fellow

**sem·blance** \'sem-blən(t)s\ *noun* [Middle English, from Middle French, from Old French *sembler* to be like, seem — more at RESEMBLE] (14th century)
**1 a :** outward and often specious appearance or show **:** FORM ⟨wrapped in a *semblance* of composure —Harry Hervey⟩ **b :** MODICUM ⟨has been struggling to get some *semblance* of justice for his people —Bayard Rustin⟩
**2 :** ASPECT, COUNTENANCE
**3 a :** a phantasmal form **:** APPARITION **b :** IMAGE, LIKENESS
**4 :** actual or apparent resemblance

**seme** \'sēm\ *noun* [Greek *sēma* sign] (circa 1866)
**1 :** a linguistic sign
**2 :** any of the basic components of the meaning of a morpheme

**se·mei·ol·o·gy** *variant of* SEMIOLOGY
**se·mei·ot·ic** *variant of* SEMIOTIC

**Sem·e·le** \'se-mə-,lē\ *noun* [Latin, from Greek *Semelē*]
**:** a daughter of Cadmus consumed by flames when visited by Zeus in his divine splendor

**sem·eme** \'se-,mēm\ *noun* [International Scientific Vocabulary, from Greek *sēma* + International Scientific Vocabulary *-eme*] (1913)
**1 :** the meaning of a morpheme
**2 a :** SEME 2 **b :** a class of related semes
— **se·me·mic** \sə-'mē-mik\ *adjective*

**se·men** \'sē-mən\ *noun* [Middle English, from Latin, seed, semen; akin to Old High German *sāmo* seed, Latin *serere* to sow — more at SOW] (14th century)
**:** a viscid whitish fluid of the male reproductive tract consisting of spermatozoa suspended in secretions of accessory glands

**se·mes·ter** \sə-'mes-tər\ *noun* [German, from Latin *semestris* half-yearly, from *sex* six + *mensis* month — more at SIX, MOON] (1827)
**1 :** either of the two usually 18-week periods of instruction into which an academic year is often divided
**2 :** a period of six months
— **se·mes·tral** \-trəl\ *or* **se·mes·tri·al** \-trē-əl\ *adjective*

**semester hour** *noun* (1922)
**:** a unit of academic credit representing an hour of class (as lecture class) or three hours of laboratory work each week for an academic semester

**¹semi** \'se-mē *also* -,mī\ *noun, plural* **sem·is** [short for *semidetached*] (1912)
*chiefly British* **:** a semidetached house

**²semi** \'se-,mī *also* -mē\ *noun, plural* **sem·is** (1942)
**:** SEMITRAILER

**³semi** \*same as* ² *noun, plural* **sem·is** (1942)
**:** SEMIFINAL — often used in plural

**semi-** \,se-mē, -,mī, -mi\ *prefix* [Middle English, from Latin; akin to Old High German *sāmi-* half, Greek *hēmi-*]
**1 a :** precisely half of: (1) **:** forming a bisection of ⟨*semi*diameter⟩ (2) **:** being a usually vertically bisected form of (a specified architectural feature) ⟨*semi*dome⟩ **b :** half in quantity or value **:** half of or occurring halfway through a specified period of time ⟨*semi*annual⟩ ⟨*semi*monthly⟩ — compare BI-
**2 :** to some extent **:** partly **:** incompletely ⟨*semi*civilized⟩ ⟨*semi*-independent⟩ ⟨*semi*dry⟩ — compare DEMI-, HEMI-

**3 a :** partial **:** incomplete ⟨*semi*consciousness⟩ ⟨*semi*darkness⟩ **b :** having some of the characteristics of ⟨*semi*porcelain⟩ **c :** QUASI- ⟨*semi*governmental⟩ ⟨*semi*monastic⟩

**semi·ab·stract** \-ab-'strakt, -'ab-,\ *adjective* (1871)
**:** having subject matter that is easily recognizable although the form is stylized ⟨*semi*abstract art⟩
— **semi·ab·strac·tion** \-ab-'strak-shən\ *noun*

**semi·an·nu·al** \-'an-yə(-wə)l\ *adjective* (1794)
**:** occurring every six months or twice a year
— **semi·an·nu·al·ly** *adverb*

**semi·an·tique** \-an-'tēk\ *adjective* (circa 1930)
**:** being approximately 50 to 100 years old ⟨a *semi*-antique carpet⟩
— **semi·antique** *noun*

**semi·aquat·ic** \-ə-'kwä-tik, -'kwa-\ *adjective* (1833)
**:** growing equally well in or adjacent to water; *also* **:** frequenting but not living wholly in water

**semi·ar·bo·re·al** \-är-'bōr-ē-əl, -'bȯr-\ *adjective* (1938)
**:** often inhabiting and frequenting trees but not completely arboreal

**semi·ar·id** \-'ar-əd\ *adjective* (1898)
**:** characterized by light rainfall; *especially* **:** having from about 10 to 20 inches (25 to 51 centimeters) of annual precipitation
— **semi·arid·i·ty** \-ə-'ri-də-tē, -a-'ri-\ *noun*

**semi·au·to·bio·graph·i·cal** \-,ȯ-tə-,bī-ə-'gra-fi-kəl\ *adjective* (1939)
**:** partly autobiographical ⟨a *semi*autobiographical comedy⟩

**semi·au·to·mat·ic** \-,ȯ-tə-'ma-tik\ *adjective* (1890)
**:** not fully automatic: as **a :** operated partly automatically and partly by hand **b** *of a firearm* **:** employing gas pressure or force of recoil and mechanical spring action to eject the empty cartridge case after the first shot and load the next cartridge from the magazine but requiring release and another pressure of the trigger for each successive shot
— **semiautomatic** *noun*
— **semi·au·to·mat·i·cal·ly** \-ti-k(ə-)lē\ *adverb*

**semi·au·ton·o·mous** \-ȯ-'tä-nə-məs\ *adjective* (1915)
**:** largely self-governing within a larger political or organizational entity

**semi·breve** \'se-mē-,brēv, 'se-,mī-, -mi-, -,brev\ *noun* (15th century)
**:** WHOLE NOTE

**semi·cen·ten·ni·al** \-sen-'te-nē-əl\ *noun* (1859)
**:** a 50th anniversary or its celebration
— **semicentennial** *adjective*

**semi·cir·cle** \'se-mē-,sər-kəl, 'se-,mī-, -mi-\ *noun* [Latin *semicirculus*, from *semi-* + *circulus* circle] (1526)
**1 :** a half of a circle
**2 :** an object or arrangement of objects in the form of a half circle
— **semi·cir·cu·lar** \,se-mē-'sər-kyə-lər\ *adjective*

**semicircular canal** *noun* (1748)
**:** any of the loop-shaped tubular parts of the labyrinth of the ear that together constitute a sensory organ associated with the maintenance of bodily equilibrium — see EAR illustration

**semi·civ·i·lized** \,se-mē-'si-və-,līzd, ,se-,mī-, -mi-\ *adjective* (1836)
**:** partly civilized

**semi·clas·sic** \-'kla-sik\ *noun* (1843)
**:** a semiclassical work (as of music)

**semi·clas·si·cal** \-si-kəl\ *adjective* (1904)
**:** having some of the characteristics of the classical: as **a :** of, relating to, or being a musical composition that acts as a bridge between

classical and popular music **b :** of, relating to, or being a classical composition that has developed popular appeal

**semi·co·lon** \'se-mē-ˌkō-lən, 'se-ˌmī-, -mi-\ *noun* (1644)
: a punctuation mark ; used chiefly in a coordinating function between major sentence elements (as independent clauses of a compound sentence)

**semi·co·lo·nial** \ˌse-mē-kə-'lō-nyəl, ˌse-ˌmī-, -mi-, -nē-əl\ *adjective* (1932)
**1 :** nominally independent but actually under foreign domination
**2 :** dependent on foreign nations as suppliers of manufactured goods and as purchasers of raw materials
— **semi·co·lo·nial·ism** \-nyə-ˌli-zəm, -nē-ə-\ *noun*

**semi·col·o·ny** \-'kä-lə-nē\ *noun* (1945)
: a semicolonial state

**semi·com·mer·cial** \-kə-'mər-shəl\ *adjective* (1926)
: of, relating to, adapted to, or characterized by limited marketing of an experimental product

**semi·con·duct·ing** \ˌse-mē-kən-'dək-tiŋ, ˌse-ˌmī-, -mi-\ *adjective* (1782)
: of, relating to, or having the characteristics of a semiconductor

**semi·con·duc·tor** \-'dək-tər\ *noun* (1838)
: any of a class of solids (as germanium or silicon) whose electrical conductivity is between that of a conductor and that of an insulator in being nearly as great as that of a metal at high temperatures and nearly absent at low temperatures

**semi·con·scious** \-'kän(t)-shəs\ *adjective* (1839)
: incompletely conscious : imperfectly aware or responsive
— **semi·con·scious·ness** *noun*

**semi·con·ser·va·tive** \-kən-'sər-və-tiv\ *adjective* (1957)
: relating to or being genetic replication in which a double-stranded molecule of nucleic acid separates into two single strands each of which serves as a template for the formation of a complementary strand that together with the template forms a complete molecule
— **semi·con·ser·va·tive·ly** *adverb*

**semi·crys·tal·line** \-'kris-tə-lən\ *adjective* (1816)
: incompletely or imperfectly crystalline

**semi·cy·lin·dri·cal** \-sə-'lin-dri-kəl\ *adjective* (circa 1731)
: having the shape of a longitudinal half of a cylinder

**semi·dark·ness** \-'därk-nəs\ *noun* (1849)
: partial darkness

**semi·de·ify** \-'dē-ə-ˌfī, -'dā-\ *transitive verb* (1953)
: to regard as somewhat godlike

**semi·des·ert** \-'de-zərt\ *noun* (1849)
: an arid area that has some of the characteristics of a desert but has greater annual precipitation

**semi·de·tached** \-di-'tacht\ *adjective* (1859)
: forming one of a pair of residences joined into one building by a common sidewall

**semi·di·am·e·ter** \-dī-'a-mə-tər\ *noun* (14th century)
: RADIUS; *specifically* : the apparent radius of a generally spherical celestial body

**semi·di·ur·nal** \-dī-'ər-n°l\ *adjective* (1594)
**1 :** relating to or accomplished in half a day
**2 :** occurring twice a day
**3 :** occurring approximately every half day ⟨the *semidiurnal* tides⟩

**semi·di·vine** \-də-'vīn\ *adjective* (1600)
: more than mortal but not fully divine

**semi·doc·u·men·ta·ry** \-ˌdä-kyə-'men-tə-rē, -'men-trē\ *noun* (1939)
: a motion picture that uses many details taken from actual events or situations in presenting a fictional story
— **semidocumentary** *adjective*

**semi·dome** \'se-mē-ˌdōm, 'se-ˌmī-, -mi-\ *noun* (1788)
: a roof or ceiling covering a semicircular or nearly semicircular room or recess
— **semi·domed** \-ˌdōmd\ *adjective*

**semi·do·mes·ti·ca·tion** \ˌse-mē-də-ˌmes-ti-'kā-shən, ˌse-ˌmī-, -mi-\ *noun* (circa 1835)
: a captive state of a wild animal in which its living conditions and often its breeding are controlled by humans
— **semi·do·mes·ti·cat·ed** \-də-'mes-ti-ˌkā-təd\ *adjective*

**semi·dom·i·nant** \-'dä-mə-nənt, -'däm-nənt\ *adjective* (1942)
: producing an intermediate phenotype in the heterozygous condition ⟨a *semidominant* mutant gene⟩

**semi·dry** \-'drī\ *adjective* (1878)
: moderately dry

**semi·dry·ing** \-'drī-iŋ\ *adjective* (1905)
: that dries imperfectly or slowly — used of some oils (as cottonseed oil)

**semi·dwarf** \-'dwórf\ *adjective* (1959)
: of or being a plant of a variety that is undersized but larger than a dwarf ⟨*semidwarf* wheats⟩
— **semidwarf** *noun*

**semi·em·pir·i·cal** \-im-'pir-ə-kəl, -em-\ *adjective* (1935)
: partly empirical; *especially* : involving assumptions, approximations, or generalizations designed to simplify calculation or to yield a result in accord with observation

**semi·erect** \-ə-'rekt\ *adjective* (1822)
**1 :** incompletely upright in bodily posture ⟨*semierect* primates⟩
**2 :** erect for half the length ⟨*semierect* stems⟩

**semi·ev·er·green** \-'e-vər-ˌgrēn\ *adjective* (1901)
**1 :** having functional and persistent foliage during part of the winter or dry season
**2 :** tending to be evergreen in a mild climate but deciduous in a rigorous climate

**semi·feu·dal** \-'fyü-d°l\ *adjective* (1898)
: having some characteristics of feudalism

¹**semi·fi·nal** \-'fī-n°l\ *adjective* (1884)
**1 :** being next to the last in an elimination tournament
**2 :** of or participating in a semifinal

²**semi·fi·nal** \'se-mē-ˌfī-n°l, 'se-ˌmī-, -mi-\ *noun* (1895)
**1 :** a semifinal match
**2 :** a semifinal round
— **semi·fi·nal·ist** \ˌse-mē-'fī-n°l-ist, ˌse-ˌmī-, -mi-\ *noun*

**semi·fin·ished** \ˌse-mē-'fi-nisht, ˌse-ˌmī-, -mi-\ *adjective* (1902)
: partially finished or processed; *especially, of steel* : rolled from raw ingots into shapes (as bars, billets, or plates) suitable for further processing

**semi·fit·ted** \-'fi-təd\ *adjective* (circa 1950)
: conforming somewhat to the lines of the body

**semi·flex·i·ble** \-'flek-sə-bəl\ *adjective* (1925)
**1 :** somewhat flexible
**2** *of a book cover* : having a thin board stiffener under the covering material

**semi·flu·id** \-'flü-əd\ *adjective* (circa 1735)
: having the qualities of both a fluid and a solid : VISCOUS ⟨fluid and *semifluid* lubricants⟩
— **semifluid** *noun*

**semi·for·mal** \-'fòr-məl\ *adjective* (1906)
: being or suitable for an occasion of moderate formality ⟨a *semiformal* dinner⟩ ⟨*semiformal* gowns⟩

**semi·gloss** \'se-mē-ˌgläs, 'se-ˌmī-, -mi-, -ˌglós\ *adjective* (1937)
: having a low luster; *specifically* : producing a finish midway between gloss and flat

**semi·gov·ern·men·tal** \ˌse-mē-ˌgəv-ər(n)-'men-t°l, ˌse-ˌmī-, -mi-, -ˌgə-v°m-'en-\ *adjective* (1919)
: having some governmental functions and powers

**semi·group** \'se-mē-ˌgrüp, 'se-ˌmī-, -mi-\ *noun* (1904)
: a mathematical set that is closed under an associative binary operation

**semi·in·de·pen·dent** \-ˌin-də-'pen-dənt\ *adjective* (1860)
: partially independent; *specifically* : SEMIAUTONOMOUS

**semi·leg·end·ary** \-'le-jən-ˌder-ē\ *adjective* (1878)
: having historical foundation but elaborated in legend

**semi·le·thal** \-'lē-thəl\ *noun* (1919)
: a mutation that in the homozygous condition produces more than 50 percent mortality but not complete mortality
— **semilethal** *adjective*

**semi·liq·uid** \-'li-kwəd\ *adjective* (1684)
: having the qualities of both a liquid and a solid : SEMIFLUID ⟨*semiliquid* manure⟩
— **semiliquid** *noun*

**semi·lit·er·ate** \-'li-tə-rət *also* -'li-trət\ *adjective* (1927)
**1 a :** able to read and write on an elementary level **b :** able to read but unable to write
**2 :** having limited knowledge or understanding : not well-versed
— **semiliterate** *noun*

**semi·log** \-'lóg, -'läg\ *adjective* (1921)
: SEMILOGARITHMIC

**semi·log·a·rith·mic** \-ˌlò-gə-'rith-mik, -ˌlä-\ *adjective* (1919)
: having one scale logarithmic and the other arithmetic — used of graph paper or of a graph on such paper

**semi·lu·nar** \-'lü-nər\ *adjective* [New Latin *semilunaris*, from Latin *semi-* + *lunaris* lunar] (1597)
: shaped like a crescent

**semilunar valve** *noun* (circa 1719)
: any of the crescent-shaped cusps that occur as a set of three between the heart and the aorta and another of three between the heart and the pulmonary artery, are forced apart by pressure in the ventricles during systole and pushed together by pressure in the arteries during diastole, and prevent regurgitation of blood into the ventricles; *also* : either set of three cusps

**semi·lus·trous** \-'ləs-trəs\ *adjective* (1953)
: slightly lustrous

**semi·ma·jor axis** \-'mā-jər\ *noun* (1899)
: one half of the major axis of an ellipse (as that formed by the orbit of a planet)

**semi·matte** *also* **semi·mat** *or* **semi·matt** \-'mat\ *adjective* [*semi-* + ²*matte*] (1937)
: having a slight luster

**semi·met·al** \-'me-t°l\ *noun* (1661)
: an element (as arsenic) possessing metallic properties in an inferior degree and not malleable
— **semi·me·tal·lic** \-mə-'ta-lik\ *adjective*

**semi·mi·cro** \-'mī-(ˌ)krō\ *adjective* (1935)
: of, relating to, or dealing with quantities intermediate between those treated as micro and macro ⟨*semimicro* analysis for chlorine⟩ ⟨a *semimicro* balance⟩

**semi·mi·nor axis** \-'mī-nər-\ *noun* (1909)
: one half of the minor axis of an ellipse (as that formed by the orbit of a planet)

**semi·moist** \-'móist\ *adjective* (1903)
: slightly moist

**semi·mo·nas·tic** \-mə-'nas-tik\ *adjective* (1911)
: having some features characteristic of a monastic order

¹**semi·month·ly** \-'mən(t)th-lē\ *noun* (1851)
: a semimonthly publication

²**semimonthly** *adjective* (1860)
: occurring twice a month

---

³**semi·month·ly** *adverb* (circa 1890)
: twice a month

**semi·mys·ti·cal** \-'mis-ti-kəl\ *adjective* (1890)
: having some of the qualities of mysticism

**sem·i·nal** \'se-mə-n°l\ *adjective* [Middle English, from Middle French, from Latin *seminalis*, from *semin-*, *semen* seed — more at SEMEN] (14th century)
**1** : of, relating to, or consisting of seed or semen
**2** : containing or contributing the seeds of later development : CREATIVE, ORIGINAL ⟨a *seminal* book⟩ ⟨one of the most *seminal* of the great poets⟩
— **sem·i·nal·ly** \-n°l-ē\ *adverb*

**seminal duct** *noun* (circa 1909)
: a tube or passage serving especially or exclusively as an efferent duct of the testis and in the human male being made up of the tubules of the epididymis, the vas deferens, and the ejaculatory duct

**seminal fluid** *noun* (circa 1929)
**1** : SEMEN
**2** : the part of the semen that is produced by various accessory glands : semen excepting the spermatozoa

**seminal vesicle** *noun* (circa 1890)
: either of a pair of glandular pouches that lie one on either side of the male reproductive tract and in the human male secrete a sugar- and protein-containing fluid into the ejaculatory duct

**sem·i·nar** \'se-mə-ˌnär\ *noun* [German, from Latin *seminarium* nursery] (1889)
**1** : a group of advanced students studying under a professor with each doing original research and all exchanging results through reports and discussions
**2 a** (1) : a course of study pursued by a seminar (2) : an advanced or graduate course often featuring informality and discussion **b** : a scheduled meeting of a seminar or a room for such meetings
**3** : a meeting for giving and discussing information

**sem·i·nar·i·an** \ˌse-mə-'ner-ē-ən\ *noun* (1794)
: a student in a seminary especially of the Roman Catholic Church

**sem·i·na·rist** \'se-mə-nə-rist\ *noun* (1835)
: SEMINARIAN

**sem·i·nary** \'se-mə-ˌner-ē\ *noun, plural* **-nar·ies** [Middle English, seedbed, nursery, from Latin *seminarium*, from *semin-*, *semen* seed] (1542)
**1** : an environment in which something originates and from which it is propagated ⟨a *seminary* of vice and crime⟩
**2 a** : an institution of secondary or higher education **b** : an institution for the training of candidates for the priesthood, ministry, or rabbinate ◆

**semi·nat·u·ral** \ˌse-mē-'na-chə-rəl, ˌse-ˌmī-, -mi-, -'nach-rəl\ *adjective* (circa 1962)
: modified by human influence but retaining many natural features ⟨a *seminatural* park⟩

**sem·i·nif·er·ous** \ˌse-mə-'ni-f(ə-)rəs\ *adjective* [Latin *semin-*, *semen* seed + English *-iferous*] (1692)
: producing or bearing seed or semen

**seminiferous tubule** *noun* (1860)
: any of the coiled threadlike tubules that make up the bulk of the testis and are lined with a layer of epithelial cells from which the spermatozoa are produced

**Sem·i·nole** \'se-mə-ˌnōl\ *noun, plural* **Seminoles** *or* **Seminole** [Creek *simanó'li* fugitive, wild, alteration of *simaló'ni*, from American Spanish *cimarrón* wild] (1771)
: a member of any of the groups of American Indians that emigrated to Florida from Georgia and Alabama in the 18th century and that are now located in southern Florida and Oklahoma

**semi·no·mad** \ˌse-mē-'nō-ˌmad, ˌse-ˌmī-, -mi-\ *noun* (circa 1934)
: a member of a people living usually in portable or temporary dwellings and practicing seasonal migration but having a base camp at which some crops are cultivated
— **semi·no·mad·ic** \-nō-'ma-dik\ *adjective*

**semi·nude** \-'nüd, -'nyüd\ *adjective* (1849)
: partially nude
— **semi·nu·di·ty** \-'nü-də-tē, -'nyü-\ *noun*

**semi·of·fi·cial** \-ə-'fi-shəl\ *adjective* (1806)
: having some official authority or standing
— **semi·of·fi·cial·ly** \-'fi-sh(ə-)lē\ *adverb*

**se·mi·ol·o·gy** \ˌsē-mē-'ä-lə-jē, ˌse-mē-, ˌsē-ˌmī-\ *noun* [Greek *sēmeion* sign] (circa 1890)
: the study of signs; *especially* : SEMIOTIC
— **se·mi·o·log·i·cal** \(ˌ)sē-ˌmī-ə-'lä-ji-kəl, ˌse-mē-ə-\ *adjective*
— **se·mi·o·log·i·cal·ly** \-ə-'lä-ji-k(ə-)lē\ *adverb*
— **se·mi·ol·o·gist** \-'ä-lə-jist\ *noun*

**semi·opaque** \ˌse-mē-ō-'pāk, ˌse-ˌmī-, -mi-\ *adjective* (1691)
: nearly opaque

**se·mi·o·sis** \ˌsē-mē-'ō-səs, ˌse-mē-, ˌsē-ˌmī-\ *noun* [New Latin, from Greek *sēmeiōsis* observation of signs, from *sēmeioun* to observe signs, from *sēmeion*] (circa 1907)
: a process in which something functions as a sign to an organism

**se·mi·ot·ic** \-'ä-tik\ *or* **se·mi·ot·ics** \-tiks\ *noun, plural* **semiotics** [Greek *sēmeiōtikos* observant of signs, from *sēmeiousthai* to interpret signs, from *sēmeion* sign, from *sēma* sign] (1880)
: a general philosophical theory of signs and symbols that deals especially with their function in both artificially constructed and natural languages and comprises syntactics, semantics, and pragmatics
— **semiotic** *adjective*
— **se·mi·o·ti·cian** \-ə-'ti-shən\ *noun*
— **se·mi·ot·i·cist** \-'ä-tə-sist\ *noun*

**semi·pal·mat·ed** \ˌse-mē-'pal-ˌmā-təd, ˌse-ˌmī-, -mi-, -'päl-\ *adjective* (1785)
: having the toes joined only part way down with a web ⟨a plover with *semipalmated* feet⟩

**semi·par·a·sit·ic** \-ˌpar-ə-'si-tik\ *adjective* (circa 1880)
: of, relating to, or being a parasitic plant that contains some chlorophyll and is capable of photosynthesis
— **semi·par·a·site** \-'par-ə-ˌsīt\ *noun*

**semi·per·ma·nent** \-'pər-mə-nənt, -'pərm-nənt\ *adjective* (circa 1890)
: lasting or intended to last for a long time but not permanent

**semi·per·me·able** \-'pər-mē-ə-bəl\ *adjective* (1888)
: partially but not freely or wholly permeable; *specifically* : permeable to some usually small molecules but not to other usually larger particles ⟨a *semipermeable* membrane⟩
— **semi·per·me·abil·i·ty** \-ˌpər-mē-ə-'bi-lə-tē\ *noun*

**semi·po·lit·i·cal** \-pə-'li-ti-kəl\ *adjective* (1857)
: of, relating to, or involving some political features or activity

**semi·pop·u·lar** \-'pä-pyə-lər\ *adjective* (1860)
: somewhat popular

**semi·por·ce·lain** \-'pōr-s(ə-)lən, -'pȯr-\ *noun* (1880)
: any of several ceramic wares resembling or imitative of porcelain; *especially* : a relatively high-fired and hard-glazed white earthenware widely used for tableware

**semi·por·no·graph·ic** \-ˌpȯr-nə-'gra-fik\ *adjective* (1964)
: somewhat pornographic
— **semi·por·nog·ra·phy** \-pȯr-'nä-grə-fē\ *noun*

**semi·post·al** \-'pōs-t°l\ *noun* (1927)
: a postage stamp sold at a premium over its postal value especially for a humanitarian purpose

**semi·pre·cious** \-'pre-shəs\ *adjective* (circa 1890)
*of a gemstone* : of less commercial value than a precious stone

**semi·pri·vate** \-'prī-vət\ *adjective* (1876)
: of, receiving, or associated with hospital service giving a patient more privileges than a ward patient but fewer than a private patient

**semi·pro** \'se-mē-ˌprō, 'se-ˌmī-, -mi-\ *adjective or noun* (1908)
: SEMIPROFESSIONAL

¹**semi·pro·fes·sion·al** \ˌse-mē-prə-'fesh-nəl, ˌse-ˌmī-, -mi-, -'fe-shə-n°l\ *noun* (1897)
: one who engages in an activity (as a sport) semiprofessionally

²**semiprofessional** *adjective* (1900)
**1** : engaging in an activity for pay or gain but not as a full-time occupation
**2** : engaged in by semiprofessional players ⟨*semiprofessional* baseball⟩
— **semi·pro·fes·sion·al·ly** *adverb*

**semi·pub·lic** \-'pə-blik\ *adjective* (1804)
**1** : open to some persons outside the regular constituency
**2** : having some features of a public institution; *specifically* : maintained as a public service by a private nonprofit organization

**semi·quan·ti·ta·tive** \-'kwän-tə-ˌtā-tiv\ *adjective* (1927)
: constituting or involving less than quantitative precision
— **semi·quan·ti·ta·tive·ly** *adverb*

**semi·qua·ver** \'se-mē-ˌkwā-vər, 'se-ˌmī-, -mi-\ *noun* (1576)
: SIXTEENTH NOTE

**semi·re·li·gious** \ˌse-mē-ri-'li-jəs, ˌse-ˌmī-, -mi-\ *adjective* (1864)
: somewhat religious

**semi·re·tired** \-ri-'tīrd\ *adjective* (1937)
: working only part-time especially because of age or ill health

**semi·re·tire·ment** \-'tīr-mənt\ *noun* (1923)
: the state or condition of being semiretired

**semi·rig·id** \-'ri-jəd\ *adjective* (1908)
**1** : rigid to some degree or in some parts
**2** *of an airship* : having a flexible cylindrical gas container with an attached stiffening keel that carries the load

**semi·ru·ral** \-'rur-əl\ *adjective* (1835)
: somewhat rural

**semi·sa·cred** \-'sā-krəd\ *adjective* (1898)
: SEMIRELIGIOUS

**semi·se·cret** \-'sē-krət\ *adjective* (1917)
: not publicly announced but widely known nevertheless

◇ WORD HISTORY
**seminary** The English word *seminary* and its Latin source *seminarium*, a derivative of *semen* "seed," both originally denoted a nursery for young plants. Though the classical Latin word was sometimes used figuratively, English has gone much further in metaphorical extensions of the word, while the old sense "nursery" is now long obsolete. The use of *seminary* in reference to training schools for the clergy was an outgrowth of 16th century reforms in the Roman Catholic Church: decrees of the Council of Trent (1545–63) applied the Latin word *seminarium* to newly established institutes for educating priests, which were meant to raise the educational level of the clergy as well as train missionaries to non-Catholic countries. In application to such schools, English *seminary* long retained a strong association with Roman Catholicism; now the word refers equally to Catholic, Protestant, or Jewish colleges for training priests, ministers, or rabbis. *Seminary* has also been applied to other kinds of schools since the 16th century. When they were first formed in the 19th century, women's colleges were called "female seminaries" or "seminaries for young ladies."

**semi·sed·en·tary** \-'se-d°n-ˌter-ē\ *adjective* (circa 1930)
: sedentary during part of the year and nomadic otherwise ⟨*semisedentary* tribes⟩

**semi·shrub·by** \'se-mē-ˌshrə-bē, 'se-ˌmī-, -mi-, *especially Southern* -ˌsrə-\ *adjective* (1930)
: resembling or being a subshrub

**semi·skilled** \ˌse-mē-'skild, ˌse-ˌmī-, -mi-\ *adjective* (1916)
: having or requiring less training than skilled labor and more than unskilled labor

**semi·soft** \-'soft\ *adjective* (circa 1903)
: moderately soft; *specifically* : firm but easily cut ⟨*semisoft* cheese⟩

**semi·sol·id** \-'sä-ləd\ *adjective* (1834)
: having the qualities of both a solid and a liquid : highly viscous
— **semisolid** *noun*

**semi·sub·mers·ible** \-səb-'mər-sə-bəl\ *adjective* (1962)
: being a floating deepwater drilling platform that is towed to a desired location and then partially flooded for stabilization and usually anchored
— **semisubmersible** *noun*

**semi·sweet** \-'swēt\ *adjective* (1943)
: slightly sweetened ⟨*semisweet* chocolate⟩

**semi·syn·thet·ic** \-sin-'the-tik\ *adjective* (1937)
**1** : produced by chemical alteration of a natural starting material ⟨*semisynthetic* penicillins⟩
**2** : containing both chemically identified and complex natural ingredients ⟨a *semisynthetic* diet⟩

**Sem·ite** \'se-ˌmīt, *especially British* 'sē-ˌmīt\ *noun* [French *sémite*, from *Semitic* Shem, from Late Latin, from Greek *Sēm*, from Hebrew *Shēm*] (1848)
**1 a** : a member of any of a number of peoples of ancient southwestern Asia including the Akkadians, Phoenicians, Hebrews, and Arabs **b** : a descendant of these peoples
**2** : a member of a modern people speaking a Semitic language

**semi·ter·res·tri·al** \ˌse-mē-tə-'res-trē-əl, ˌse-ˌmī-, -mi-, -'res-chəl, -'resh-\ *adjective* (1919)
**1** : growing on boggy ground
**2** : frequenting but not living wholly on land

**¹Se·mit·ic** \sə-'mi-tik *also* -'me-\ *adjective* [German *semitisch*, from *Semit, Semite* Semite, probably from New Latin *Semita*, from Late Latin *Semitic* Shem] (1813)
**1** : of, relating to, or constituting a subfamily of the Afro-Asiatic language family that includes Hebrew, Aramaic, Arabic, and Amharic
**2** : of, relating to, or characteristic of the Semites
**3** : JEWISH

**²Semitic** *noun* (1875)
: any or all of the Semitic languages

**Se·mit·i·cist** \sə-'mi-tə-sist\ *noun* (1956)
: SEMITIST

**Se·mit·ics** \-'mi-tiks\ *noun plural but singular in construction* (1895)
: the study of the language, literature, and history of Semitic peoples; *specifically* : Semitic philology

**Sem·i·tism** \'se-mə-ˌti-zəm\ *noun* (1851)
**1 a** : Semitic character or qualities **b** : a characteristic feature of a Semitic language occurring in another language
**2** : policy favorable to Jews : predisposition in favor of Jews

**Sem·i·tist** \-tist\ *noun* (1885)
**1** : a scholar of the Semitic languages, cultures, or histories
**2** *often not capitalized* : a person favoring or disposed to favor the Jews

**semi·ton·al** \ˌse-mē-'tō-n°l, ˌse-ˌmī-, -mi-\ *adjective* (1863)
: CHROMATIC 3a, SEMITONIC
— **semi·ton·al·ly** *adverb*

**semi·tone** \'se-mē-ˌtōn, 'se-ˌmī-, -mi-\ *noun* (15th century)

: the tone at a half step; *also* : HALF STEP
— **semi·ton·ic** \ˌse-mē-'tä-nik, ˌse-ˌmī-, -mi-\ *adjective*
— **semi·ton·i·cal·ly** \-ni-k(ə-)lē\ *adverb*

**semi·trail·er** \'se-ˌmī-ˌtrā-lər, 'se-mē-, -mi-\ *noun* (1919)
**1** : a freight trailer that when attached is supported at its forward end by the fifth wheel device of the truck tractor
**2** : a trucking rig made up of a tractor and a semitrailer

**semi·trans·lu·cent** \ˌse-mē-ˌtran(t)s-'lü-s°nt, ˌse-ˌmī-, -mi-, -ˌtranz-\ *adjective* (1832)
: somewhat translucent

**semi·trans·par·ent** \-ˌtran(t)s-'par-ənt, -'per-\ *adjective* (circa 1793)
: imperfectly transparent

**semi·trop·i·cal** \-'trä-pi-kəl\ *also* **semi·trop·ic** \-pik\ *adjective* (1853)
: SUBTROPICAL

**semi·trop·ics** \-piks\ *noun plural* (1908)
: SUBTROPICS

**semi·vow·el** \'se-mē-ˌvau̇(-ə)l, 'se-ˌmī-, -mi-\ *noun* (1530)
**1** : a speech sound (as \y\, \w\, or \r\) that has the articulation of a vowel but that is shorter in duration and is treated as a consonant in syllabication
**2** : a letter representing a semivowel

**¹semi·week·ly** \ˌse-mē-'wē-klē, ˌse-ˌmī-, -mi-\ *adjective* (1791)
: occurring twice a week
— **semiweekly** *adverb*

**²semiweekly** *noun* (1833)
: a semiweekly publication

**semi·works** \'se-mē-ˌwərks, 'se-ˌmī-, -mi-\ *noun plural, often attributive* (1926)
: a manufacturing plant operating on a limited commercial scale to provide final tests of a new product or process

**semi·year·ly** \ˌse-mē-'yir-lē, ˌse-ˌmī-, -mi-\ *adjective* (circa 1928)
: occurring twice a year

**sem·o·li·na** \ˌse-mə-'lē-nə\ *noun* [Italian *semolino*, diminutive of *semola* bran, from Latin *simila* wheat flour] (1797)
: the purified middlings of hard wheat (as durum) used especially for pasta (as macaroni or spaghetti)

**sem·per·vi·vum** \ˌsem-pər-'vī-vəm\ *noun* [New Latin, from Latin, neuter of *sempervivus* ever-living, from *semper* ever + *vivus* living — more at QUICK] (1591)
: any of a large genus (*Sempervivum*) of Old World fleshy herbs of the orpine family often grown as ornamentals

**sem·pi·ter·nal** \ˌsem-pi-'tər-n°l\ *adjective* [Middle English, from Late Latin *sempiternalis*, from Latin *sempiternus*, from *semper* ever, always, from *sem-* one, same (akin to Old Norse *samr* same) + *per* through — more at SAME, FOR] (15th century)
: of never-ending duration : ETERNAL
— **sem·pi·ter·nal·ly** *adverb*

**sem·pi·ter·ni·ty** \-'tər-nə-tē\ *noun* (1599)
: ETERNITY

**sem·ple** \'sem-pəl\ *adjective* [alteration of *simple*] (1759)
*Scottish* : of humble birth

**sem·pli·ce** \'sem-pli-ˌchā\ *adjective or adverb* [Italian, from Latin *simplic-, simplex* — more at SIMPLE] (circa 1740)
: SIMPLE — used as a direction in music

**sem·pre** \'sem-(ˌ)prā\ *adverb* [Italian, from Latin *semper*] (circa 1801)
: ALWAYS — used in music directions ⟨*sempre* legato⟩

**semp·stress** \'sem(p)-strəs\ *variant of* SEAMSTRESS

**¹sen** \'sen\ *noun, plural* **sen** [Japanese] (1875)
— see *yen* at MONEY table

**²sen** *noun, plural* **sen** [Malay, probably from English *century*] (1952)
— see *dollar, ringgit, rupiah* at MONEY table

**³sen** *noun, plural* **sen** [Khmer *sein*, probably from French *century*, abbreviation of *centime* centime] (1964)
— see *riel* at MONEY table

**se·nar·i·us** \si-'nar-ē-əs, -'ner-\ *noun, plural* **se·nar·ii** \-ē-ˌī, -ē-ˌē\ [Latin, from *senarius* consisting of six each, from *seni* six each, from *sex* six — more at SIX] (1540)
: a verse consisting of six feet especially in Latin prosody

**se·na·ry** \'se-nə-rē, 'sē-\ *adjective* [Latin *senarius* consisting of six] (1661)
: of, based on, or characterized by six : compounded of six things or six parts ⟨*senary* scale⟩ ⟨*senary* division⟩

**sen·ate** \'se-nət\ *noun* [Middle English *senat*, from Old French, from Latin *senatus*, from *sen-, senex* old, old man — more at SENIOR] (13th century)
**1** : an assembly or council usually possessing high deliberative and legislative functions: as
**a** : the supreme council of the ancient Roman republic and empire **b** : the second chamber in the bicameral legislature of a major political unit (as a nation, state, or province)
**2** : the hall or chamber in which a senate meets
**3** : a governing body of some universities charged with maintaining academic standards and regulations and usually composed of the principal or representative members of the faculty

**sen·a·tor** \'se-nə-tər\ *noun* [Middle English *senatour*, from Old French *senateur*, from Latin *senator*, from *senatus*] (13th century)
: a member of a senate
— **sen·a·tor·ship** \-ˌship\ *noun*

**sen·a·to·ri·al** \ˌse-nə-'tōr-ē-əl, -'tor-\ *adjective* (1740)
: of, relating to, or befitting a senator or a senate ⟨*senatorial* office⟩ ⟨*senatorial* rank⟩

**senatorial courtesy** *noun* (1884)
: a custom of the U.S. Senate of refusing to confirm a presidential appointment of an official in or from a state when the appointment is opposed by the senators or senior senator of the president's party from that state

**senatorial district** *noun* (1785)
: a territorial division from which a senator is elected — compare CONGRESSIONAL DISTRICT

**sen·a·to·ri·an** \ˌse-nə-'tōr-ē-ən, -'tor-\ *adjective* (1614)
: SENATORIAL; *specifically* : of or relating to the ancient Roman senate

**se·na·tus con·sul·tum** \sə-ˌnä-təs-kən-'səl-təm, -'sul-\ *noun, plural* **senatus con·sul·ta** \-tə\ [Latin, decree of the senate] (1696)
: a decree of the ancient Roman senate

**¹send** \'send\ *verb* **sent** \'sent\; **send·ing** [Middle English, from Old English *sendan*; akin to Old High German *sendan* to send, Old English *sith* road, journey, Old Irish *sét* path, way] (before 12th century)
*transitive verb*
**1** : to cause to go: as **a** : to propel or throw in a particular direction **b** : DELIVER ⟨*sent* a blow to the chin⟩ **c** : DRIVE ⟨*sent* the ball between the goalposts⟩
**2** : to cause to happen ⟨whatever fate may *send*⟩
**3** : to dispatch by a means of communication
**4 a** : to direct, order, or request to go **b** : to permit or enable to attend a term or session ⟨*send* a daughter to college⟩ **c** : to direct by advice or reference **d** : to cause or order to depart : DISMISS
**5 a** : to force to go : drive away **b** : to cause to assume a specified state ⟨*sent* them into a rage⟩

\ə\ abut \ᵊ\ kitten \ər\ further \a\ ash \ā\ ace
\ä\ mop, mar \au̇\ out \ch\ chin \e\ bet \ē\ easy
\g\ go \i\ hit \ī\ ice \j\ job \ŋ\ sing \ō\ go
\ȯ\ law \oi\ boy \th\ thin \t͟h\ the \ü\ loot \u̇\ foot
\y\ yet \zh\ vision *see also* Guide to Pronunciation

**6 :** to cause to issue: as **a :** to pour out **:** DIS-CHARGE ⟨clouds *sending* forth rain⟩ **b :** UTTER ⟨*send* forth a cry⟩ **c :** EMIT ⟨*sent* out waves of perfume⟩ **d :** to grow out (parts) in the course of development ⟨a plant *sending* forth shoots⟩
**7 :** to cause to be carried to a destination; *especially* **:** to consign to death or a place of punishment
**8 :** to convey or cause to be conveyed or transmitted by an agent ⟨*send* a package by mail⟩ ⟨*sent* out invitations⟩
**9 :** to strike or thrust so as to impel violently ⟨*sent* him sprawling⟩
**10 :** DELIGHT, THRILL
*intransitive verb*
**1 a :** to dispatch someone to convey a message or do an errand — often used with *out* ⟨*send* out for pizza⟩ **b :** to dispatch a request or order — often used with *away*
**2 :** SCEND
**3 :** TRANSMIT
— **send·er** *noun*
— **send for :** to request by message to come **:** SUMMON
— **send packing :** to send off or dismiss roughly or in disgrace
**²send** *noun* (1726)
**:** the lift of a wave
**send down** *transitive verb* (1853)
*British* **:** to suspend or expel from a university
**send in** (1715)
*transitive verb*
**1 :** to cause to be delivered ⟨*send in* a letter of complaint⟩
**2 :** to give (one's name or card) to a servant when making a call
**3 :** to send (a player) into an athletic contest
**send–off** \'send-ˌȯf\ *noun* (1872)
**:** a demonstration of goodwill and enthusiasm for the beginning of a new venture (as a trip)
**send–up** \-ˌəp\ *noun* (1958)
**:** PARODY, TAKEOFF
**send up** *transitive verb* (1852)
**1 :** to sentence to imprisonment **:** send to jail
**2 :** to make fun of **:** SATIRIZE, PARODY
**se·ne** \'sā-ˌnā\ *noun, plural* **sene** [Samoan, from English *century*] (1967)
— see *tala* at MONEY table
**Sen·e·ca** \'se-ni-kə\ *noun, plural* **Seneca** *or* **Senecas** [Dutch *Sennecaas*, plural, the Iroquois living west of the Mohawks] (circa 1616)
**1 :** a member of an American Indian people of what is now western New York
**2 :** the Iroquoian language of the Seneca people

**seneca snakeroot** *noun* (1789)
**:** a milkwort (*Polygala senega*) of eastern North America having racemes of small white flowers — called also *rattlesnake root, senega root;* compare SENEGA
**se·ne·cio** \si-'nē-sh(ē-ˌ)ō\ *noun, plural* **-cios** [New Latin, from Latin, old man, groundsel (from its hoary pappus), from *sen-, senic-, senex* old man] (circa 1890)
**:** any of a genus (*Senecio*) of widely distributed composite plants that have alternate or basal leaves and flower heads usually with yellow ray flowers
**se·nec·ti·tude** \si-'nek-tə-ˌtüd, -ˌtyüd\ *noun* [Medieval Latin *senectitudo,* alteration of Latin *senectus* old age, from *sen-, senic-, senex* old, old man — more at SENIOR] (1796)
**:** the final stage of the normal life span
**sen·e·ga** \'se-ni-gə\ *noun* (1748)
**:** the dried root of seneca snakeroot that contains an irritating saponin and is used medicinally
**senega root** *noun* [alteration of *Seneca* root; from its use by the Seneca as a remedy for snakebite] (circa 1846)

seneca snakeroot

**1 :** SENECA SNAKEROOT
**2 :** SENEGA
**se·nes·cence** \si-'ne-sᵊn(t)s\ *noun* [*senescent,* from Latin *senescent-, senescens,* present participle of *senescere* to grow old, from *sen-, senex* old] (1695)
**1 :** the state of being old **:** the process of becoming old
**2 :** the growth phase in a plant or plant part (as a leaf) from full maturity to death
— **se·nes·cent** \-sᵊnt\ *adjective*
**sen·e·schal** \'se-nə-shəl\ *noun* [Middle English, from Middle French, of Germanic origin; akin to Gothic *sineigs* old and to Old High German *scalc* servant — more at SENIOR] (14th century)
**:** an agent or steward in charge of a lord's estate in feudal times
**se·nhor** \si-'nyȯr, -'nyȯr\ *noun, plural* **senhors** *or* **se·nho·res** \-'nyȯr-ēsh, -'nyȯr-, -ēzh, -ēs, -ēz\ [Portuguese, from Medieval Latin *senior* superior, lord, from Latin, adjective, elder] (1795)
**:** a Portuguese or Brazilian man — used as a title equivalent to *Mr.*
**se·nho·ra** \-'nyȯr-ə, -'nyȯr-\ *noun* [Portuguese, feminine of *senhor*] (1802)
**:** a married Portuguese or Brazilian woman — used as a title equivalent to *Mrs.*
**se·nho·ri·ta** \ˌsē-nyə-'rē-tə\ *noun* [Portuguese, from diminutive of *senhora*] (1874)
**:** an unmarried Portuguese or Brazilian girl or woman — used as a title equivalent to *Miss*
**se·nile** \'sē-ˌnīl *also* 'se-\ *adjective* [Latin *senilis,* from *sen-, senex* old, old man] (1661)
**1 :** of, relating to, exhibiting, or characteristic of old age ⟨*senile* weakness⟩; *especially* **:** exhibiting a loss of mental faculties associated with old age
**2 :** approaching the end of a geological cycle of erosion
— **se·nile·ly** \-ˌnīl-lē\ *adverb*
**senile dementia** *noun* (circa 1851)
**:** a mental disorder of old age especially of the degenerative type associated with Alzheimer's disease
**se·nil·i·ty** \si-'ni-lə-tē *also* se-\ *noun* (1791)
**:** the quality or state of being senile; *specifically* **:** the physical and mental infirmity of old age
**¹se·nior** \'sē-nyər\ *noun* [Middle English, from Latin, from *senior,* adjective] (14th century)
**1 :** a person older than another ⟨five years my *senior*⟩
**2 a :** a person with higher standing or rank **b :** a senior fellow of a college at an English university **c :** a student in the year preceding graduation from a school of secondary or higher level
**3** *capitalized* **:** a member of a program of the Girl Scouts for girls in the ninth through twelfth grades in school
**4 :** SENIOR CITIZEN
**²senior** *adjective* [Middle English, from Latin, older, elder, comparative of *sen-, senex* old; akin to Gothic *sineigs* old, Greek *henos*] (14th century)
**1 :** of prior birth, establishment, or enrollment — often used to distinguish a father with the same given name as his son
**2 :** higher ranking **:** SUPERIOR ⟨*senior* officers⟩
**3 :** of or relating to seniors ⟨the *senior* class⟩
**4 :** having a claim on corporate assets and income prior to other securities
**senior airman** *noun* (circa 1977)
**:** an enlisted man in the air force who ranks above an airman first class but who has not been made sergeant
**senior chief petty officer** *noun* (circa 1960)
**:** an enlisted man in the navy or coast guard ranking above a chief petty officer and below a master chief petty officer
**senior citizen** *noun* (1938)

**:** an elderly person; *especially* **:** one who has retired
**senior high school** *noun* (1909)
**:** a school usually including grades 10 to 12
**se·nior·i·ty** \sēn-'yȯr-ə-tē, -'yär-\ *noun* (15th century)
**1 :** the quality or state of being senior **:** PRIORITY
**2 :** a privileged status attained by length of continuous service (as in a company)
**senior master sergeant** *noun* (circa 1962)
**:** a noncommissioned officer in the air force ranking above a master sergeant and below a chief master sergeant
**sen·i·ti** \'se-nə-tē\ *noun, plural* **seniti** [Tongan, modification of English *century*] (1967)
— see *pa'anga* at MONEY table
**sen·na** \'se-nə\ *noun* [New Latin, from Arabic *sanā*] (1543)
**1 :** any of a genus (*Cassia*) of leguminous herbs, shrubs, and trees native to warm regions; *especially* **:** one used medicinally
**2 :** the dried leaflets or pods of various sennas (especially *Cassia acutifolia* and *C. angustifolia*) used as a purgative
**sen·net** \'se-nət\ *noun* [probably alteration of obsolete *signet* signal] (circa 1590)
**:** a signal call on a trumpet or cornet for entrance or exit on the stage
**sen·night** *also* **se'n·night** \'se-ˌnīt\ *noun* [Middle English, from Old English *seofon nihta* seven nights] (15th century)
*archaic* **:** the space of seven nights and days **:** WEEK
**sen·nit** \'se-nət\ *noun* [origin unknown] (circa 1769)
**1 :** a braided cord or fabric (as of plaited rope yarns)
**2 :** a straw or grass braid for hats
**se·nor** *or* **se·ñor** \sān-'yȯr\ *noun, plural* **senors** *or* **se·ño·res** \-'yȯr-(ˌ)ās, -'yȯr-\ [Spanish *señor,* from Medieval Latin *senior* superior, lord, from Latin, adjective, elder] (1622)
**:** a Spanish or Spanish-speaking man — used as a title equivalent to *Mr.*
**se·no·ra** *or* **se·ño·ra** \sān-'yȯr-ə, -'yȯr-\ *noun* [Spanish *señora,* feminine of *señor*] (1579)
**:** a married Spanish or Spanish-speaking woman — used as a title equivalent to *Mrs.*
**se·no·ri·ta** *or* **se·ño·ri·ta** \ˌsān-yə-'rē-tə\ *noun* [Spanish *señorita,* from diminutive of *señora*] (1823)
**:** an unmarried Spanish or Spanish-speaking girl or woman — used as a title equivalent to *Miss*
**sen·ryu** \'sen-rē-(ˌ)ü\ *noun, plural* **senryu** [Japanese] (1938)
**:** a 3-line unrhymed Japanese poem structurally similar to haiku but treating human nature usually in an ironic or satiric vein
**sensa** *plural of* SENSUM
**sen·sate** \'sen-ˌsāt\ *adjective* [Middle English *sensat,* from Medieval Latin *sensatus,* from Late Latin, endowed with sense, from Latin *sensus* sense] (15th century)
**1 :** relating to or apprehending or apprehended through the senses
**2 :** preoccupied with things that can be experienced through a sense modality
— **sen·sate·ly** *adverb*
**sen·sa·tion** \sen-'sā-shən, sən-\ *noun* [Medieval Latin *sensation-, sensatio,* from Late Latin, understanding, idea, from Latin *sensus*] (1615)
**1 a :** a mental process (as seeing, hearing, or smelling) due to immediate bodily stimulation often as distinguished from awareness of the process — compare PERCEPTION **b :** awareness (as of heat or pain) due to stimulation of a sense organ **c :** a state of consciousness of a kind usually due to physical objects or internal bodily changes ⟨a burning *sensation* in his chest⟩ **d :** an indefinite bodily feeling ⟨a *sensation* of buoyancy⟩

**2 :** something (as a physical object, sense-datum, pain, or afterimage) that causes or is the object of sensation
**3 a :** a state of excited interest or feeling ⟨their elopement caused a *sensation*⟩ **b :** a cause of such excitement ⟨the show was the musical *sensation* of the season⟩; *especially* **:** one (as a person) in some respect exceptional or outstanding ⟨the rookie hitting *sensation* of the American League⟩

**sen·sa·tion·al** \-shnəl, -shə-nᵊl\ *adjective* (1840)
**1 :** of or relating to sensation or the senses
**2 :** arousing or tending to arouse (as by lurid details) a quick, intense, and usually superficial interest, curiosity, or emotional reaction
**3 :** exceedingly or unexpectedly excellent or great
— **sen·sa·tion·al·ly** *adverb*

**sen·sa·tion·al·ise** *British variant of* SENSATIONALIZE

**sen·sa·tion·al·ism** \-shnə,li-zəm, -shə-nᵊl-,i-zəm\ *noun* (1846)
**1 :** empiricism that limits experience as a source of knowledge to sensation or sense perceptions
**2 :** the use or effect of sensational subject matter or treatment
— **sen·sa·tion·al·ist** \-list, -ist\ *adjective or noun*
— **sen·sa·tion·al·is·tic** \-,sā-shnə-'lis-tik, -shən-ᵊl-'is-tik\ *adjective*

**sen·sa·tion·al·ize** \-,līz, -,ĭz\ *transitive verb* **-ized; -iz·ing** (1869)
**:** to present in a sensational manner

**¹sense** \'sen(t)s\ *noun* [Middle English, from Middle French or Latin; Middle French *sens* sensation, feeling, mechanism of perception, meaning, from Latin *sensus*, from *sentire* to perceive, feel; perhaps akin to Old High German *sinnan* to go, strive, Old English *sith* journey — more at SEND] (14th century)
**1 :** a meaning conveyed or intended **:** IMPORT, SIGNIFICATION; *especially* **:** one of a set of meanings a word or phrase may bear especially as segregated in a dictionary entry
**2 a :** the faculty of perceiving by means of sense organs **b :** a specialized animal function or mechanism (as sight, hearing, smell, taste, or touch) basically involving a stimulus and a sense organ **c :** the sensory mechanisms constituting a unit distinct from other functions (as movement or thought)
**3 :** conscious awareness or rationality — usually used in plural ⟨finally came to his *senses*⟩
**4 a :** a particular sensation or kind or quality of sensation ⟨a good *sense* of balance⟩ **b :** a definite but often vague awareness or impression ⟨felt a *sense* of insecurity⟩ ⟨a *sense* of danger⟩ **c :** a motivating awareness ⟨a *sense* of shame⟩ **d :** a discerning awareness and appreciation ⟨her *sense* of humor⟩
**5 :** CONSENSUS ⟨the *sense* of the meeting⟩
**6 a :** capacity for effective application of the powers of the mind as a basis for action or response **:** INTELLIGENCE **b :** sound mental capacity and understanding typically marked by shrewdness and practicality; *also* **:** agreement with or satisfaction of such power ⟨this decision makes *sense*⟩
**7 :** one of two opposite directions especially of motion (as of a point, line, or surface) ☆

**²sense** *transitive verb* **sensed; sens·ing** (circa 1531)
**1 a :** to perceive by the senses **b :** to be or become conscious of ⟨*sense* danger⟩
**2 :** GRASP, COMPREHEND
**3 :** to detect automatically especially in response to a physical stimulus (as light or movement)

**sense–datum** *noun, plural* **sense-data** (1882)
**:** an immediate unanalyzable private object of sensation

**sense·ful** \'sen(t)s-fəl\ *adjective* (1591)

**:** REASONABLE, JUDICIOUS

**sense·less** \'sen(t)s-ləs\ *adjective* (1557)
**:** destitute of, deficient in, or contrary to sense: as **a :** UNCONSCIOUS ⟨knocked *senseless*⟩ **b :** FOOLISH, STUPID ⟨it was some *senseless* practical joke —A. Conan Doyle⟩ **c :** MEANINGLESS, PURPOSELESS ⟨a *senseless* murder⟩
— **sense·less·ly** *adverb*
— **sense·less·ness** *noun*

**sense organ** *noun* (1854)
**:** a bodily structure that receives a stimulus (as heat or sound waves) and is affected in such a manner as to initiate a wave of excitation in associated sensory nerve fibers which convey specific impulses to the central nervous system where they are interpreted as corresponding sensations **:** RECEPTOR

**sen·si·bil·ia** \,sen(t)-sə-'bi-lē-ə, -'bil-yə\ *noun plural* [Late Latin, from neuter plural of Latin *sensibilis* sensible] (1856)
**:** what may be sensed

**sen·si·bil·i·ty** \,sen(t)-sə-'bi-lə-tē\ *noun, plural* **-ties** (15th century)
**1 :** ability to receive sensations **:** SENSITIVENESS ⟨tactile *sensibility*⟩
**2 :** peculiar susceptibility to a pleasurable or painful impression (as from praise or a slight) — often used in plural
**3 :** awareness of and responsiveness toward something (as emotion in another)
**4 :** refined or excessive sensitiveness in emotion and taste with especial responsiveness to the pathetic

**¹sen·si·ble** \'sen(t)-sə-bəl\ *adjective* [Middle English, from Middle French, from Latin *sensibilis*, from *sensus*, past participle of *sentire* to feel] (14th century)
**1 :** of a kind to be felt or perceived: as **a :** perceptible to the senses or to reason or understanding ⟨felt a *sensible* chill⟩ ⟨her distress was *sensible* from her manner⟩ **b** *archaic* **:** perceptibly large **:** CONSIDERABLE **c** (1) **:** perceptible as real or material **:** SUBSTANTIAL ⟨the *sensible* world in which we live⟩ (2) **:** of a kind to arouse emotional response ⟨his whipping was a *sensible* expression of his father's anger⟩
**2 a :** capable of receiving sensory impressions ⟨*sensible* to pain⟩ **b :** receptive to external influences **:** SENSITIVE ⟨the most *sensible* reaches of the spirit⟩
**3 a :** perceiving through the senses or mind **:** COGNIZANT ⟨*sensible* of the increasing heat⟩; *also* **:** convinced by perceived evidence **:** SATISFIED ⟨*sensible* of my error⟩ **b :** emotionally aware and responsive ⟨we are *sensible* of your problems⟩ **c :** CONSCIOUS
**4 :** having, containing, or indicative of good sense or reason **:** RATIONAL, REASONABLE ⟨*sensible* people⟩ ⟨made a *sensible* answer⟩
**synonym** see MATERIAL, PERCEPTIBLE, AWARE, WISE
— **sen·si·ble·ness** *noun*
— **sen·si·bly** \-blē\ *adverb*

**²sensible** *noun* (1589)
**:** something that can be sensed

**sen·sil·lum** \sen-'si-ləm\ *also* **sen·sil·la** \-'si-lə\ *noun, plural* **-sil·la** \-'si-lə\ *also* **-sil·lae** \-'si-(,)lē\ [New Latin *sensillum*, diminutive of Medieval Latin *sensus* sense organ, from Latin, sense] (1925)
**:** a simple epithelial sense organ of an invertebrate (as an insect) usually in the form of a spine, plate, rod, cone, or peg that is composed of one or a few cells with a nerve connection

**sen·si·ti·sa·tion, sen·si·tise** *British variant of* SENSITIZATION, SENSITIZE

**¹sen·si·tive** \'sen(t)-sə-tiv, 'sen(t)s-təv\ *adjective* [Middle English, from Middle French *sensitif*, from Medieval Latin *sensitivus*, probably alteration of *sensativus*, from *sensatus* sensate] (15th century)
**1 :** SENSORY 2
**2 a :** receptive to sense impressions **b :** capable of being stimulated or excited by external agents (as light, gravity, or contact) ⟨a photo-graphic emulsion *sensitive* to red light⟩ ⟨*sensitive* protoplasm⟩
**3 :** highly responsive or susceptible: as **a** (1) **:** easily hurt or damaged; *especially* **:** easily hurt emotionally (2) **:** delicately aware of the attitudes and feelings of others **b :** excessively or abnormally susceptible **:** HYPERSENSITIVE ⟨*sensitive* to egg protein⟩ **c :** readily fluctuating in price or demand ⟨*sensitive* commodities⟩ **d :** capable of indicating minute differences **:** DELICATE ⟨*sensitive* scales⟩ **e :** readily affected or changed by various agents (as light or mechanical shock) **f :** highly radiosensitive
**4 a :** concerned with highly classified government information or involving discretionary authority over important policy matters ⟨*sensitive* documents⟩ **b :** calling for tact, care, or caution in treatment **:** TOUCHY ⟨a *sensitive* issue like race relations⟩
**synonym** see LIABLE
— **sen·si·tive·ly** *adverb*
— **sen·si·tive·ness** *noun*

**²sensitive** *noun* (1850)
**1 :** a person having occult or psychical abilities
**2 :** a sensitive person

**sensitive plant** *noun* (1659)
**:** any of several mimosas (especially *Mimosa pudica*) with leaves that fold or droop when touched; *broadly* **:** a plant responding to touch with movement

**sen·si·tiv·i·ty** \,sen(t)-sə-'ti-və-tē\ *noun, plural* **-ties** (1803)
**:** the quality or state of being sensitive: as **a :** the capacity of an organism or sense organ to respond to stimulation **:** IRRITABILITY **b :** the quality or state of being hypersensitive **c :** the degree to which a radio receiving set responds to incoming waves **d :** the capacity of being easily hurt **e :** awareness of the needs and emotions of others ⟨a book written with just the right mix of empathy and *sensitivity* —L.C. Brown⟩

**sen·si·ti·za·tion** \,sen(t)-sə-tə-'zā-shən, ,sen(t)s-tə-'zā-\ *noun* (1887)
**1 :** the action or process of sensitizing
**2 :** the quality or state of being sensitized (as to an antigen)

**sen·si·tize** \'sen(t)-sə-,tīz\ *verb* **-tized; -tiz·ing** [*sensitive* + *-ize*] (circa 1859)
*transitive verb*
**:** to make sensitive or hypersensitive
*intransitive verb*
**:** to become sensitive
— **sen·si·tiz·er** *noun*

**sen·si·tom·e·ter** \,sen(t)-sə-'tä-mə-tər\ *noun* [International Scientific Vocabulary *sensitive* + *-o-* + *-meter*] (1880)
**:** an instrument for measuring sensitivity of photographic material
— **sen·si·to·met·ric** \,sen(t)-sə-tə-'me-trik\ *adjective*

---

☆ **SYNONYMS**
**Sense, common sense, judgment, wisdom** mean ability to reach intelligent conclusions. SENSE implies a reliable ability to judge and decide with soundness, prudence, and intelligence ⟨a choice showing good *sense*⟩. COMMON SENSE suggests an average degree of such ability without sophistication or special knowledge ⟨*common sense* tells me it's wrong⟩. JUDGMENT implies sense tempered and refined by experience, training, and maturity ⟨they relied on her *judgment* for guidance⟩. WISDOM implies sense and judgment far above average ⟨a leader of rare *wisdom*⟩.

---

\ə\ abut \ᵊ\ kitten \ər\ further \a\ ash \ā\ ace \ä\ mop, mar \au̇\ out \ch\ chin \e\ bet \ē\ easy \g\ go \i\ hit \ī\ ice \j\ job \ŋ\ sing \ō\ go \ȯ\ law \ȯi\ boy \th\ thin \th̶\ the \ü\ loot \u̇\ foot \y\ yet \zh\ vision *see also* Guide to Pronunciation

— **sen·si·tom·e·try** \-sə-'tä-mə-trē\ *noun*

**sen·sor** \'sen-,sȯr, 'sen(t)-sər\ *noun* [Latin *sentire* to perceive + English ¹*-or* — more at SENSE] (circa 1928)
: a device that responds to a physical stimulus (as heat, light, sound, pressure, magnetism, or a particular motion) and transmits a resulting impulse (as for measurement or operating a control); *also* : SENSE ORGAN

**sen·so·ri·al** \sen-'sȯr-ē-əl, -'sȯr-\ *adjective* (1768)
: SENSORY
— **sen·so·ri·al·ly** \-ə-lē\ *adverb*

**sen·so·ri·mo·tor** \,sen(t)s-rē-'mō-tər, ,sen(t)-sə-\ *adjective* [*sensory* + *motor*] (1855)
: of, relating to, or functioning in both sensory and motor aspects of bodily activity

**sen·so·ri·neu·ral** \-'nùr-əl, -'nyùr-\ *adjective* (circa 1977)
: of, relating to, or involving the aspects of sense perception mediated by nerves ⟨*sensorineural* hearing loss⟩

**sen·so·ri·um** \sen-'sōr-ē-əm, -'sȯr-\ *noun, plural* **-ri·ums** *or* **-ria** \-ē-ə\ [Late Latin, sense organ, from Latin *sentire*] (1647)
: the parts of the brain or the mind concerned with the reception and interpretation of sensory stimuli; *broadly* : the entire sensory apparatus

**sen·so·ry** \'sen(t)s-rē, 'sen(t)-sə-rē\ *adjective* (1749)
**1** : of or relating to sensation or to the senses
**2** : conveying nerve impulses from the sense organs to the nerve centers : AFFERENT

**sensory area** *noun* (1896)
: an area of the cerebral cortex that receives afferent nerve fibers from lower sensory or motor areas

**sen·su·al** \'sen(t)-sh(ə-)wəl, -shəl\ *adjective* [Middle English, from Late Latin *sensualis*, from Latin *sensus* sense] (15th century)
**1** : relating to or consisting in the gratification of the senses or the indulgence of appetite : FLESHLY
**2** : SENSORY
**3 a** : devoted to or preoccupied with the senses or appetites **b** : VOLUPTUOUS **c** : deficient in moral, spiritual, or intellectual interests : WORLDLY; *especially* : IRRELIGIOUS
**synonym** see CARNAL, SENSUOUS
— **sen·su·al·i·ty** \,sen(t)-shə-'wa-lə-tē\ *noun*
— **sen·su·al·ly** \'sen(t)-sh(ə-)wə-lē, 'sen-shə-lē\ *adverb*

**sen·su·al·ism** \'sen(t)-sh(ə-)wə-,li-zəm, 'sen-shə-,li-\ *noun* (1813)
: persistent or excessive pursuit of sensual pleasures and interests
— **sen·su·al·ist** \-list\ *noun*
— **sen·su·al·is·tic** \,sen(t)-sh(ə-)wə-'lis-tik, ,sen-shə-'lis-\ *adjective*

**sen·su·al·ize** \'sen(t)-sh(ə-)wə-,līz, 'sen-shə-,līz\ *transitive verb* **-ized; -iz·ing** (circa 1687)
: to make sensual
— **sen·su·al·i·za·tion** \,sen(t)-sh(ə-)wə-lə-'zā-shən, ,sen-shə-lə-\ *noun*

**sen·sum** \'sen(t)-səm\ *noun, plural* **sen·sa** \-sə\ [Medieval Latin, from Latin, neuter of *sensus*, past participle of *sentire* to feel — more at SENSE] (1868)
: SENSE-DATUM

**sen·su·ous** \'sen(t)-sh(ə-)wəs\ *adjective* [Latin *sensus* sense + English *-ous*] (1640)
**1 a** : of or relating to the senses or sensible objects **b** : producing or characterized by gratification of the senses : having strong sensory appeal ⟨*sensuous* pleasure⟩
**2** : characterized by sense impressions or imagery aimed at the senses ⟨*sensuous* verse⟩
**3** : highly susceptible to influence through the senses ☆
— **sen·su·os·i·ty** \,sen(t)-shə-'wä-sə-tē\ *noun*
— **sen·su·ous·ly** \'sen(t)-sh(ə-)wəs-lē\ *adverb*

— **sen·su·ous·ness** *noun*

**sen·su stric·to** \'sen-(,)sü-'strik-(,)tō\ *adverb* [New Latin] (1902)
: in a narrow or strict sense

**sent** *past and past participle of* SEND

**sen·te** \'sen-tē\ *noun, plural* **li·cen·te** *or* **li·sen·te** \li-'sen-tē\ [Sesotho, from English *century*] (1966)
— see *loti* at MONEY table

¹**sen·tence** \'sen-t°n(t)s, -t°nz\ *noun* [Middle English, from Middle French, from Latin *sententia* feeling, opinion, from (assumed) *sentent-, sentens,* irregular present participle of *sentire* to feel — more at SENSE] (14th century)
**1** *obsolete* : OPINION; *especially* : a conclusion given on request or reached after deliberation
**2 a** : JUDGMENT 2a; *specifically* : one formally pronounced by a court or judge in a criminal proceeding and specifying the punishment to be inflicted upon the convict **b** : the punishment so imposed ⟨serve out a *sentence*⟩
**3** *archaic* : MAXIM, SAW
**4 a** : a word, clause, or phrase or a group of clauses or phrases forming a syntactic unit which expresses an assertion, a question, a command, a wish, an exclamation, or the performance of an action, that in writing usually begins with a capital letter and concludes with appropriate end punctuation, and that in speaking is distinguished by characteristic patterns of stress, pitch, and pauses **b** : a mathematical or logical statement (as an equation or a proposition) in words or symbols
**5** : PERIOD 2b

²**sentence** *transitive verb* **sen·tenced; sen·tenc·ing** (1592)
**1** : to impose a sentence on
**2** : to cause to suffer something ⟨*sentenced* these most primitive cultures to extinction —E. W. Count⟩

**sentence fragment** *noun* (1947)
: a word, phrase, or clause that usually has in speech the intonation of a sentence but lacks the grammatical structure usually found in the sentences of formal and especially written composition

**sentence stress** *noun* (1884)
: the manner in which stresses are distributed on the syllables of words assembled into sentences — called also *sentence accent*

**sen·ten·tia** \sen-'ten(t)-sh(ē-)ə\ *noun, plural* **-ti·ae** \-shē-,ē\ [Latin, literally, feeling, opinion] (1917)
: APHORISM — usually used in plural

**sen·ten·tial** \sen-'ten(t)-shəl\ *adjective* (1646)
**1** : of or relating to a sentence ⟨a relative clause with a *sentential* antecedent⟩
**2** : of, relating to, or involving a proposition in logic ⟨*sentential* connective⟩

**sentential calculus** *noun* (1937)
: PROPOSITIONAL CALCULUS

**sentential function** *noun* (1937)
: an expression that contains one or more variables and becomes a declarative sentence when constants are substituted for the variables

**sen·ten·tious** \sen-'ten(t)-shəs\ *adjective* [Middle English, full of meaning, from Latin *sententiosus,* from *sententia* sentence, maxim] (1509)
**1 a** : given to or abounding in aphoristic expression **b** : given to or abounding in excessive moralizing
**2** : terse, aphoristic, or moralistic in expression : PITHY, EPIGRAMMATIC
— **sen·ten·tious·ly** *adverb*
— **sen·ten·tious·ness** *noun*

**sen·tience** \'sen(t)-sh(ē-)ən(t)s, 'sen-tē-ən(t)s\ *noun* (1839)
**1** : a sentient quality or state
**2** : feeling or sensation as distinguished from perception and thought

**sen·tient** \'sen(t)-sh(ē-)ənt, 'sen-tē-ənt\ *adjective* [Latin *sentient-, sentiens,* present participle of *sentire* to perceive, feel] (1632)

**1** : responsive to or conscious of sense impressions
**2** : AWARE
**3** : finely sensitive in perception or feeling
— **sen·tient·ly** *adverb*

**sen·ti·ment** \'sen-tə-mənt\ *noun* [French or Medieval Latin; French, from Medieval Latin *sentimentum,* from Latin *sentire*] (1639)
**1 a** : an attitude, thought, or judgment prompted by feeling : PREDILECTION **b** : a specific view or notion : OPINION
**2 a** : EMOTION **b** : refined feeling : delicate sensibility especially as expressed in a work of art **c** : emotional idealism **d** : a romantic or nostalgic feeling verging on sentimentality
**3 a** : an idea colored by emotion **b** : the emotional significance of a passage or expression as distinguished from its verbal context
**synonym** see FEELING, OPINION

**sen·ti·men·tal** \,sen-tə-'men-t°l\ *adjective* (1749)
**1 a** : marked or governed by feeling, sensibility, or emotional idealism **b** : resulting from feeling rather than reason or thought
**2** : having an excess of sentiment or sensibility
— **sen·ti·men·tal·ly** *adverb*

**sen·ti·men·tal·ise** *British variant of* SENTIMENTALIZE

**sen·ti·men·tal·ism** \,sen-tə-'men-t°l-,i-zəm\ *noun* (1817)
**1** : the disposition to favor or indulge in sentimentality
**2** : an excessively sentimental conception or statement
— **sen·ti·men·tal·ist** \-t°l-ist\ *noun*

**sen·ti·men·tal·i·ty** \,sen-tə-,men-'ta-lə-tē, -mən-\ *noun, plural* **-ties** (1770)
**1** : the quality or state of being sentimental especially to excess or in affectation
**2** : a sentimental idea or its expression

**sen·ti·men·tal·ize** \-'men-t°l-,īz\ *verb* **-ized; -iz·ing** (1788)
*intransitive verb*
: to indulge in sentiment
*transitive verb*
: to look upon or imbue with sentiment
— **sen·ti·men·tal·i·za·tion** \-,men-t°l-ə-'zā-shən\ *noun*

**sen·ti·mo** \sen-'tē-(,)mō\ *noun, plural* **-mos** [Tagalog, from Spanish *céntimo*] (1968)
— see *peso* at MONEY table

¹**sen·ti·nel** \'sent-nəl, 'sen-t°n-əl\ *noun* [Middle French *sentinelle,* from Old Italian *sentinella,* from *sentina* vigilance, from *sentire* to perceive, from Latin] (1579)
: SENTRY

²**sentinel** *transitive verb* **-neled** *or* **-nelled; -nel·ing** *or* **-nel·ling** (1593)
**1** : to watch over as a sentinel
**2** : to furnish with a sentinel
**3** : to post as sentinel

**sen·try** \'sen-trē\ *noun, plural* **sentries** [perhaps from obsolete *sentry* sanctuary, watch-tower] (1632)
: GUARD, WATCH; *especially* : a soldier standing guard at a point of passage (as a gate)

---

☆ SYNONYMS
**Sensuous, sensual, luxurious, voluptuous** mean relating to or providing pleasure through gratification of the senses. SENSUOUS implies gratification of the senses for the sake of aesthetic pleasure (the *sensuous* delights of great music). SENSUAL tends to imply the gratification of the senses or the indulgence of the physical appetites as ends in themselves (a life devoted to *sensual* pleasures). LUXURIOUS suggests the providing of or indulgence of a sensuous pleasure inducing bodily ease and languor (a *luxurious* hotel). VOLUPTUOUS implies more strongly an abandonment especially to sensual pleasure (a *voluptuous* feast).

**sentry box** *noun* (circa 1728)
: a shelter for a sentry on his post

**se·pal** \'sē-pəl, 'se-\ *noun* [New Latin *sepalum*, from *sep-* (irregular from Greek *skepē* covering) + *-alum* (as in *petalum* petal)] (1821)
: one of the modified leaves comprising a calyx — see FLOWER illustration

**se·pal·oid** \-pə-‚lȯid\ *adjective* (1830)
: resembling or functioning as a sepal

**sep·a·ra·ble** \'se-p(ə-)rə-bəl\ *adjective* [Middle English, from Latin *separabilis*, from *separare*] (14th century)
**1** : capable of being separated or dissociated
**2** *obsolete* : causing separation
— **sep·a·ra·bil·i·ty** \‚se-p(ə-)rə-'bi-lə-tē\ *noun*
— **sep·a·ra·ble·ness** *noun*

¹**sep·a·rate** \'se-p(ə-)‚rāt\ *verb* **-rat·ed; -rat·ing** [Middle English, from Latin *separatus*, past participle of *separare*, from *se-* apart + *parare* to prepare, procure — more at SE-CEDE, PARE] (15th century)
*transitive verb*
**1 a** : to set or keep apart : DISCONNECT, SEVER **b** : to make a distinction between : DISCRIMINATE, DISTINGUISH ⟨*separate* religion from magic⟩ **c** : SORT ⟨*separate* mail⟩ **d** : to disperse in space or time : SCATTER ⟨widely *separated* homesteads⟩
**2** *archaic* : to set aside for a special purpose : CHOOSE, DEDICATE
**3** : to part by a legal separation: **a** : to sever conjugal ties with **b** : to sever contractual relations with : DISCHARGE ⟨*separated* from the army⟩
**4** : to block off : SEGREGATE
**5 a** : to isolate from a mixture : EXTRACT ⟨*separate* cream from milk⟩ **b** : to divide into constituent parts
**6** : to dislocate (as a shoulder) especially in sports
*intransitive verb*
**1** : to become divided or detached
**2 a** : to sever an association : WITHDRAW **b** : to cease to live together as a married couple
**3** : to go in different directions
**4** : to become isolated from a mixture ☆

²**sep·a·rate** \'se-p(ə-)rət\ *adjective* (15th century)
**1 a** : set or kept apart : DETACHED **b** *archaic* : SOLITARY, SECLUDED **c** : IMMATERIAL, DISEMBODIED
**2 a** : not shared with another : INDIVIDUAL ⟨*separate* rooms⟩ **b** *often capitalized* : estranged from a parent body ⟨*separate* churches⟩
**3 a** : existing by itself : AUTONOMOUS **b** : dissimilar in nature or identity
*synonym* see DISTINCT
— **sep·a·rate·ly** \-p(ə-)rət-lē, 'se-pərt-lē\ *adverb*
— **sep·a·rate·ness** \-nəs\ *noun*

³**sep·a·rate** \'se-p(ə-)rət\ *noun* (1886)
**1** : OFFPRINT
**2** : an article of dress designed to be worn interchangeably with others to form various costume combinations — usually used in plural

**sep·a·ra·tion** \‚se-pə-'rā-shən\ *noun* (14th century)
**1** : the act or process of separating : the state of being separated
**2 a** : a point, line, or means of division **b** : an intervening space : GAP
**3 a** : cessation of cohabitation between a married couple by mutual agreement or judicial decree **b** : termination of a contractual relationship (as employment or military service)

**sep·a·ra·tion·ist** \-sh(ə-)nist\ *noun* (1831)
: SEPARATIST

**sep·a·rat·ism** \'se-p(ə-)rə-‚ti-zəm\ *noun* (1628)
: a belief in, movement for, or state of separation (as schism, secession, or segregation)

**sep·a·rat·ist** \'se-p(ə-)rə-tist, 'se-pə-‚rā-\ *noun* (1608)

: one that favors separatism: as **a** *capitalized* : one of a group of 16th and 17th century English Protestants preferring to separate from rather than to reform the Church of England **b** : an advocate of independence or autonomy for a part of a political unit (as a nation) **c** : an advocate of racial or cultural separation
— **separatist** *adjective*
— **sep·a·ra·tis·tic** \‚se-p(ə-)rə-'tis-tik\ *adjective*

**sep·a·ra·tive** \'se-pə-‚rā-tiv, 'se-p(ə-)rə-\ *adjective* (1592)
: tending toward, causing, or expressing separation

**sep·a·ra·tor** \'se-p(ə-)‚rā-tər\ *noun* (1607)
: one that separates; *especially* : a device for separating liquids of different specific gravities (as cream from milk) or liquids from solids

**Se·phar·di** \sə-'fär-dē\ *noun, plural* **Se·phar·dim** \-'fär-dəm\ [Late Hebrew *sĕphāradhī*, from *sĕphāradh* Spain, from Hebrew, region where Jews were once exiled (Obadiah 1:20)] (1851)
: a member of the occidental branch of European Jews settling in Spain and Portugal and later in the Balkans, the Levant, England, the Netherlands, and the Americas; *also* : one of their descendants — compare ASHKENAZI
— **Se·phar·dic** \-'fär-dik\ *adjective*

¹**se·pia** \'sē-pē-ə\ *noun* [Latin, cuttlefish, ink, from Greek *sēpia*] (1821)
**1 a** : the inky secretion of a cuttlefish **b** : a brown melanin-containing pigment from the ink of cuttlefishes
**2** : a print or photograph of a brown color resembling sepia
**3** : a brownish gray to dark olive brown color

²**sepia** *adjective* (1827)
**1** : made of or done in sepia
**2** : of the color sepia

**se·pi·o·lite** \'sē-pē-ə-‚līt\ *noun* [German *Sepiolith*, from Greek *sēpion* cuttlebone (from *sēpia*) + German *-lith* -lite] (1854)
: MEERSCHAUM 1

**se·poy** \'sē-‚pȯi\ *noun* [Portuguese *sipai*, from Hindi *sipāhī*, from Persian, cavalryman] (circa 1718)
: a native of India employed as a soldier by a European power

**sep·pu·ku** \se-'pü-(‚)kü, 'se-pə-‚kü\ *noun* [Japanese] (1871)
: HARA-KIRI 1

**sep·sis** \'sep-səs\ *noun, plural* **sep·ses** \'sep-‚sēz\ [New Latin, from Greek *sēpsis* decay, from *sēpein* to putrefy] (1876)
: a toxic condition resulting from the spread of bacteria or their products from a focus of infection; *especially* : SEPTICEMIA

**sept** \'sept\ *noun* [perhaps from Latin *septum*, *saeptum* enclosure, fold — more at SEPTUM] (1517)
: a branch of a family; *especially* : CLAN

**sep·tal** \'sep-t³l\ *adjective* (circa 1847)
: of or relating to a septum

**sep·tate** \'sep-‚tāt\ *adjective* (1846)
: divided by or having a septum

**Sep·tem·ber** \sep-'tem-bər, səp-\ *noun* [Middle English *Septembre*, from Old French & Old English, both from Latin *September* (seventh month), from *septem* seven — more at SEVEN] (before 12th century)
: the 9th month of the Gregorian calendar ◆

**sep·te·nar·i·us** \‚sep-tə-'nar-ē-əs, -'ner-\ *noun, plural* **-nar·ii** \-ē-‚ī, -ē-‚ē\ [Latin, from *septenarius* of seven, from *septeni* seven each, from *septem* seven] (1819)
: a verse consisting of seven feet especially in Latin prosody

**sep·ten·de·cil·lion** \‚(‚)sep-‚ten-di-'sil-yən\ *noun, often attributive* [Latin *septendecim* seventeen (from *septem* seven + *decem* ten) + English *-illion* (as in *million*) — more at TEN] (circa 1938)
— see NUMBER table

**sep·ten·ni·al** \sep-'te-nē-əl\ *adjective* [Late Latin *septennium* period of seven years, from Latin *septem* + *-ennium* (as in *biennium*)] (1640)
**1** : occurring or being done every seven years
**2** : consisting of or lasting for seven years
— **sep·ten·ni·al·ly** \-ə-lē\ *adverb*

**sep·ten·tri·on** \sep-'ten-trē-‚än, -trē-ən\ *noun* [Middle English, from Middle French, from Latin *septentriones*, plural, the seven stars of Ursa Major or Ursa Minor, from *septem* seven + *triones* plowing oxen] (14th century)
*obsolete* : the northern regions : NORTH

**sep·ten·tri·o·nal** \-trē-ə-n³l\ *adjective* (14th century)
: NORTHERN

**sep·tet** \sep-'tet\ *noun* [German, from Latin *septem*] (1828)
**1** : a musical composition for seven instruments or voices
**2** : a group or set of seven; *especially* : the performers of a septet

---

☆ **SYNONYMS**
**Separate, part, divide, sever, sunder, divorce** mean to become or cause to become disunited or disjointed. SEPARATE may imply any of several causes such as dispersion, removal of one from others, or presence of an intervening thing ⟨*separated* her personal life from her career⟩. PART implies the separating of things or persons in close union or association ⟨vowed never to *part*⟩. DIVIDE implies separating into pieces or sections by cutting or breaking ⟨civil war *divided* the nation⟩. SEVER implies violence especially in the removal of a part or member ⟨a *severed* limb⟩. SUNDER suggests violent rending or wrenching apart ⟨a city *sundered* by racial conflict⟩. DIVORCE implies separating two things that commonly interact and belong together ⟨cannot *divorce* scientific research from moral responsibility⟩.

---

◇ **WORD HISTORY**
**September** The earliest Roman calendar appears to have had just ten lunar months, March to December, with an uncounted intervening gap in the winter. The names of the last four months, in Latin *September*, *October*, *November*, and *December*, were formed, appropriately enough, from the numerals *septem* "seven," *octo* "eight," *novem* "nine," and *decem* "ten." The original names of *September*, *November*, and *December* were presumably compounds made up with the aid of an unattested element *mensri-*, itself derived from *mensis* "month" and a suffix *ri-*. Through a series of sound changes, *mensri-* became *membri-*. The resulting words should have been *Septemmember*, *Novemmember*, and *Decemmember*, but these likewise unattested forms appear to have undergone contraction by dropping one pair of the identical sounds found next to each other (a process called haplology) to give *September*, *November*, and *December*. October was simply formed by analogy to fit the shape of the other three words; its earlier name in Latin is unknown. The subsequent changes in the calendar that added two months, January and February, and made January rather than March the beginning of the year rendered the numerical sequence incorrect, but the Romans retained the old names, which we have inherited.

---

**sep·tic** \'sep-tik\ *adjective* [Latin *septicus,* from Greek *sēptikos,* from *sēpein* to putrefy] (1605)
**1** : of, relating to, or causing putrefaction
**2** : relating to, involving, or characteristic of sepsis

**sep·ti·ce·mia** \,sep-tə-'sē-mē-ə\ *noun* [New Latin, from Latin *septicus* + New Latin *-emia*] (circa 1860)
: invasion of the bloodstream by virulent microorganisms from a local seat of infection accompanied especially by chills, fever, and prostration — called also *blood poisoning;* compare SEPSIS
— **sep·ti·ce·mic** \-'sē-mik\ *adjective*

**sep·ti·ci·dal** \,sep-tə-'sī-d²l\ *adjective* [New Latin *septum* + Latin *-cidere* to cut, from *caedere*] (1819)
: dehiscent longitudinally at or along a septum ⟨a *septicidal* fruit⟩

**septic sore throat** *noun* (1924)
: STREP THROAT

**septic tank** *noun* (circa 1902)
: a tank in which the solid matter of continuously flowing sewage is disintegrated by bacteria

**sep·til·lion** \sep-'til-yən\ *noun, often attributive* [French, from Latin *septem* + French *-illion* (as in *million*) — more at SEVEN] (1690)
— see NUMBER table

**sep·tu·a·ge·nar·i·an** \(,)sep-,tü-ə-jə-'ner-ē-ən, -,tyü-, -,chü-\ *noun* [Late Latin *septuagenarius* seventy years old, from Latin, of or containing seventy, from *septuageni* seventy each, from *septuaginta*] (1805)
: a person whose age is in the seventies
— **septuagenarian** *adjective*

**Sep·tu·a·ge·si·ma** \,sep-tə-wə-'je-sə-mə, -'jā-zə-\ *noun* [Middle English, from Late Latin, from Latin, feminine of *septuagesimus* seventieth, from *septuaginta* seventy; from its being approximately seventy days before Easter] (14th century)
: the third Sunday before Lent

**Sep·tu·a·gint** \sep-'tü-ə-jənt, -'tyü-; 'sep-tə-wə-,jint\ *noun* [Late Latin *Septuaginta,* from Latin, seventy, irregular from *septem* seven + *-ginta* (akin to Latin *viginti* twenty); from the approximate number of its translators — more at SEVEN, VIGESIMAL] (1633)
: a Greek version of the Jewish Scriptures redacted in the 3d and 2d centuries B.C. by Jewish scholars and adopted by Greek-speaking Christians
— **Sep·tu·a·gin·tal** \(,)sep-,tü-ə-'jin-t²l, -,tyü-; ,sep-tə-wə-\ *adjective*

**sep·tum** \'sep-təm\ *noun, plural* **sep·ta** \-tə\ [New Latin, from Latin *saeptum* enclosure, fence, wall, from *saepire* to fence in, from *saepes* fence, hedge] (1698)
: a dividing wall or membrane especially between bodily spaces or masses of soft tissue — compare DISSEPIMENT

**se·pul·chral** \sə-'pəl-krəl *also* -'púl-\ *adjective* (1615)
: suited to or suggestive of a sepulchre : FUNEREAL, MORTUARY
— **se·pul·chral·ly** \-krə-lē\ *adverb*

**¹sep·ul·chre** *or* **sep·ul·cher** \'se-pəl-kər\ *noun* [Middle English *sepulcre,* from Old French, from Latin *sepulcrum, sepulchrum,* from *sepelire* to bury; akin to Greek *hepein* to care for, Sanskrit *saparyati* he honors] (13th century)
**1** : a place of burial : TOMB
**2** : a receptacle for religious relics especially in an altar

**²sepulchre** *or* **sepulcher** *transitive verb* **-chred** *or* **-chered; -chring** *or* **-chering** \-k(ə-)rin\ (1591)
**1** *archaic* : to place in or as if in a sepulchre : BURY

**2** *archaic* : to serve as a sepulchre for

**sep·ul·ture** \'se-pəl-,chúr\ *noun* [Middle English, from Old French, from Latin *sepultura,* from *sepultus,* past participle of *sepelire*] (14th century)
**1** : BURIAL
**2** : SEPULCHRE

**se·qua·cious** \si-'kwā-shəs\ *adjective* [Latin *sequac-, sequax* inclined to follow, from *sequi*] (1643)
**1** *archaic* : SUBSERVIENT, TRACTABLE
**2** : intellectually servile
— **se·qua·cious·ly** *adverb*
— **se·quac·i·ty** \-'kwa-sə-tē\ *noun*

**se·quel** \'sē-kwəl *also* -,kwel\ *noun* [Middle English, from Middle French *sequelle,* from Latin *sequela,* from *sequi* to follow — more at SUE] (15th century)
**1** : CONSEQUENCE, RESULT
**2 a** : subsequent development **b** : the next installment (as of a speech or story); *especially* : a literary or cinematic work continuing the course of a story begun in a preceding one

**se·quela** \si-'kwe-lə\ *noun, plural* **se·quel·ae** \-'kwe-(,)lē\ [New Latin, from Latin, sequel] (circa 1793)
**1** : an aftereffect of disease or injury
**2** : a secondary result

**¹se·quence** \'sē-kwən(t)s, -,kwen(t)s\ *noun* [Middle English, from Medieval Latin *sequentia,* from Late Latin, sequel, literally, act of following, from Latin *sequent-, sequens,* present participle of *sequi*] (14th century)
**1** : a hymn in irregular meter between the gradual and Gospel in masses for special occasions (as Easter)
**2** : a continuous or connected series: as **a** : an extended series of poems united by a single theme ⟨a sonnet *sequence*⟩ **b** : three or more playing cards usually of the same suit in consecutive order of rank **c** : a succession of repetitions of a melodic phrase or harmonic pattern each in a new position **d** : a set of elements ordered so that they can be labeled with the positive integers **e** (1) : a succession of related shots or scenes developing a single subject or phase of a film story (2) : EPISODE
**3 a** : order of succession **b** : an arrangement of the tenses of successive verbs in a sentence designed to express a coherent relationship especially between main and subordinate parts
**4 a** : CONSEQUENCE, RESULT **b** : a subsequent development
**5** : continuity of progression

**²sequence** *transitive verb* **se·quenced; se·quenc·ing** (1941)
**1** : to arrange in a sequence
**2** : to determine the sequence of chemical constituents (as amino-acid residues) in ⟨*sequenced* biological macromolecules⟩

**se·quenc·er** \'sē-kwən(t)-sər, -,kwen(t)-\ *noun* (1949)
: one that sequences: as **a** : a device for arranging (as events in the ignition of a rocket) in a sequence **b** : a device for determining the order of occurrence of amino acids in a protein

**se·quen·cy** \'sē-kwən(t)-sē\ *noun* [Late Latin *sequentia*] (1818)
: SEQUENCE 3a, 5

**se·quent** \'sē-kwənt\ *adjective* [Latin *sequent-, sequens,* present participle] (1601)
**1** : CONSECUTIVE, SUCCEEDING
**2** : CONSEQUENT, RESULTANT

**se·quen·tial** \si-'kwen(t)-shəl\ *adjective* (1854)
**1** : of, relating to, or arranged in a sequence : SERIAL ⟨*sequential* file systems⟩
**2** : following in sequence
**3** : relating to or based on a method of testing a statistical hypothesis that involves examination of a sequence of samples for each of which the decision is made to accept or reject the hypothesis or to continue sampling

— **se·quen·tial·ly** \-'kwen(t)-sh(ə-)lē\ *adverb*

**¹se·ques·ter** \si-'kwes-tər\ *transitive verb* **-tered; -ter·ing** \-t(ə-)rin\ [Middle English *sequestren,* from Middle French *sequestrer,* from Latin *sequestrare* to hand over to a trustee, from *sequester* third party to whom disputed property is entrusted, agent, from *secus* beside, otherwise; akin to Latin *sequi* to follow] (14th century)
**1 a** : to set apart : SEGREGATE **b** : SECLUDE, WITHDRAW
**2 a** : to seize especially by a writ of sequestration **b** : to place (property) in custody especially in sequestration
**3** : to hold (as a metallic ion) in solution usually by inclusion in an appropriate coordination complex

**²sequester** *noun* (1604)
*obsolete* : SEPARATION, ISOLATION

**se·ques·trate** \'sē-kwəs-,trāt, 'se-; si-'kwes-\ *transitive verb* **-trat·ed; -trat·ing** [Latin *sequestratus,* past participle of *sequestrare*] (15th century)
: SEQUESTER

**se·ques·tra·tion** \,sē-kwəs-'trā-shən, ,se-; (,)sē-,kwes-\ *noun* (15th century)
**1** : the act of sequestering : the state of being sequestered
**2 a** : a legal writ authorizing a sheriff or commissioner to take into custody the property of a defendant who is in contempt until the orders of a court are complied with **b** : a deposit whereby a neutral depositary agrees to hold property in litigation and to restore it to the party to whom it is adjudged to belong

**se·ques·trum** \si-'kwes-trəm\ *noun, plural* **-trums** *also* **-tra** \-trə\ [New Latin, from Latin, legal sequestration, from *sequester*] (1831)
: a fragment of dead bone detached from adjoining sound bone

**se·quin** \'sē-kwən\ *noun* [French, from Italian *zecchino,* from *zecca* mint, from Arabic *sikkah* die, coin] (1617)
**1** : an old gold coin of Italy and Turkey
**2** : a small plate of shining metal or plastic used for ornamentation especially on clothing

**se·quined** *or* **se·quinned** \-kwənd\ *adjective* (1894)
: ornamented with or as if with sequins

**se·qui·tur** \'se-kwə-tər, -,túr\ *noun* [Latin, it follows, 3d person singular present indicative of *sequi* to follow — more at SUE] (1836)
: the conclusion of an inference : CONSEQUENCE

**se·quoia** \si-'kwói-ə\ *noun* [New Latin, genus name, from *Sequoya* (George Guess)] (circa 1866)
: either of two huge coniferous California trees of the bald cypress family that may reach a height of over 300 feet (90 meters): **a** : BIG TREE **b** : REDWOOD 3a

**sera** *plural of* SERUM

**se·rac** \sə-'rak, sā-\ *noun* [French *sérac,* literally, a kind of white cheese, from Medieval Latin *seracium* whey, from Latin *serum* whey — more at SERUM] (1860)
: a pinnacle, sharp ridge, or block of ice among the crevasses of a glacier

**se·raglio** \sə-'ral-(,)yō, -'räl-\ *noun, plural* **-glios** [Italian *serraglio,* modification of Turkish *saray* palace] (1581)
**1** : HAREM 1a
**2** : a palace of a sultan

**se·rai** \sə-'rī\ *noun* [Turkish & Persian; Turkish *saray* mansion, palace, from Persian *sarāī* mansion, inn] (1609)
**1** : CARAVANSARY
**2** : SERAGLIO 2

**ser·al** \'sir-əl\ *adjective* (1916)
: of, relating to, or constituting an ecological sere

**se·ra·pe** \sə-'rä-pē, -'ra-\ *noun* [Mexican Spanish *sarape*] (1834)

: a colorful woolen shawl worn over the shoulders especially by Mexican men

**ser·aph** \'ser-əf\ *noun, plural* **ser·a·phim** \-ə-,fim, -,fēm\ *or* **seraphs** [assumed singular of Hebrew *śĕrāphīm*] (1667)
: SERAPHIM 2

**ser·a·phim** \'ser-ə-,fim, -,fēm\ *noun plural* [Late Latin *seraphim,* plural, seraphs, from Hebrew *śĕrāphīm*] (12th century)
**1** : an order of angels — see CELESTIAL HIERARCHY
**2** *singular, plural* **seraphim** : one of the 6-winged angels standing in the presence of God
— **se·raph·ic** \sə-'ra-fik\ *adjective*
— **se·raph·i·cal·ly** \-fi-k(ə-)lē\ *adverb*

**Se·ra·pis** \sə-'rā-pəs\ *noun* [Latin, from Greek *Sarapis*]
: an Egyptian god combining attributes of Osiris and Apis and having a widespread cult in Ptolemaic Egypt and ancient Greece

**Serb** \'sərb\ *noun* [ultimately from Serbo-Croatian *srb*] (1860)
**1** : a native or inhabitant of Serbia
**2** : SERBIAN 2
— **Serb** *adjective*

**Ser·bi·an** \'sər-bē-ən\ *noun* (1848)
**1** : SERB 1
**2 a** : the Serbo-Croatian language as spoken in Serbia **b** : a literary form of Serbo-Croatian using the Cyrillic alphabet
— **Serbian** *adjective*

**Ser·bo–Cro·a·tian** \,sər-(,)bō-krō-'ā-shən\ *noun* (1883)
**1** : a Slavic language spoken in Croatia, Bosnia and Herzegovina, Serbia, and Montenegro
**2** : a person whose native language is Serbo-Croatian
— **Serbo–Croatian** *adjective*

**¹sere** \'sir\ *adjective* [Middle English, from Old English *sēar* dry; akin to Old High German *sōrēn* to wither, Greek *hauos* dry, Lithuanian *sausas*] (before 12th century)
**1** : being dried and withered
**2** *archaic* : THREADBARE

**²sere** *noun* [Latin *series* series] (1916)
: a series of ecological communities formed in ecological succession

**¹ser·e·nade** \,ser-ə-'nād\ *noun* [French *sérénade,* from Italian *serenata,* from *sereno* clear, calm (of weather), from Latin *serenus* serene] (1649)
**1 a** : a complimentary vocal or instrumental performance; *especially* : one given outdoors at night for a woman being courted **b** : a work so performed
**2** : an instrumental composition in several movements, written for a small ensemble, and midway between the suite and the symphony in style

**²serenade** *verb* **-nad·ed; -nad·ing** (1668)
*intransitive verb*
: to play a serenade
*transitive verb*
: to perform a serenade in honor of
— **ser·e·nad·er** *noun*

**ser·e·na·ta** \,ser-ə-'nä-tə\ *noun* [Italian, serenade] (circa 1724)
: an 18th century secular cantata of a dramatic character usually composed in honor of an individual or event

**ser·en·dip·i·tous** \,ser-ən-'di-pə-təs\ *adjective* (1943)
: obtained or characterized by serendipity ⟨*serendipitous* discoveries⟩
— **ser·en·dip·i·tous·ly** *adverb*

**ser·en·dip·i·ty** \-'di-pə-tē\ *noun* [from its possession by the heroes of the Persian fairy tale *The Three Princes of Serendip*] (1754)
: the faculty or phenomenon of finding valuable or agreeable things not sought for

**¹se·rene** \sə-'rēn\ *adjective* [Latin *serenus* clear, cloudless, untroubled] (15th century)
**1 a** : clear and free of storms or unpleasant change ⟨*serene* skies⟩ **b** : shining bright and steady (the moon, *serene* in glory —Alexander Pope)
**2** : AUGUST — used as part of a title ⟨His *Serene* Highness⟩
**3** : marked by or suggestive of utter calm and unruffled repose or quietude ⟨a *serene* smile⟩
*synonym* see CALM
— **se·rene·ly** *adverb*
— **se·rene·ness** \-'rēn-nəs\ *noun*

**²serene** *noun* (1644)
**1** *archaic* : a serene condition or expanse (as of sky, sea, or light)
**2** *archaic* : SERENITY, TRANQUILLITY

**se·ren·i·ty** \sə-'re-nə-tē\ *noun* (15th century)
: the quality or state of being serene

**serf** \'sərf\ *noun* [French, from Old French, from Latin *servus* slave] (1611)
: a member of a servile feudal class bound to the soil and subject to the will of his lord
— **serf·age** \'sər-fij\ *noun*
— **serf·dom** \'sərf-dəm, -təm\ *noun*

**serge** \'sərj\ *noun* [Middle English *sarge,* from Middle French, from (assumed) Vulgar Latin *sarica,* alteration of Latin *serica,* feminine of *sericus* silken — more at SERICEOUS] (14th century)
: a durable twilled fabric having a smooth clear face and a pronounced diagonal rib on the front and the back

**ser·gean·cy** \'sär-jən(t)-sē\ *noun* (circa 1670)
: the function, office, or rank of a sergeant

**ser·geant** \'sär-jənt\ *noun* [Middle English, servant, attendant, sergeant, from Middle French *sergent, serjant,* from Latin *servient-, serviens,* present participle of *servire* to serve] (13th century)
**1** : SERGEANT AT ARMS
**2** *obsolete* : an officer who enforces the judgments of a court or the commands of one in authority
**3** : a noncommissioned officer ranking in the army and marine corps above a corporal and below a staff sergeant and in the air force above an airman first class or senior airman and below a staff sergeant; *broadly* : NONCOMMISSIONED OFFICER
**4** : an officer in a police force ranking in the U.S. just below captain or sometimes lieutenant and in England just below inspector

**sergeant at arms** (14th century)
: an officer of an organization (as a legislative body or court of law) who preserves order and executes commands

**sergeant first class** *noun* (1948)
: a noncommissioned officer in the army ranking above a staff sergeant and below a master sergeant

**sergeant fish** *noun* (1873)
**1** : COBIA
**2** : SNOOK 1

**sergeant major** *noun, plural* **sergeants major** *or* **sergeant majors** (1802)
**1** : a noncommissioned officer in the army, air force, or marine corps serving as chief administrative assistant in a headquarters
**2** : a noncommissioned officer in the marine corps ranking above a first sergeant
**3** : a bluish green to yellow bony fish (*Abudefduf saxatilis* of the family Pomacentridae) with black vertical stripes on the sides that is widely distributed in the western tropical Atlantic Ocean

**sergeant major of the army** (1966)
: the ranking noncommissioned officer of the army serving as adviser to the chief of staff

**sergeant major of the marine corps** (circa 1971)
: the ranking noncommissioned officer of the marine corps serving as adviser to the commandant

**ser·geant·y** \'sär-jən-tē\ *noun, plural* **-geant·ies** [Middle English *sergeantie,* from Middle French *sergentie,* from *sergent* sergeant] (15th century)
: any of numerous feudal services of a personal nature by which an estate is held of the king or other lord distinct from military tenure and from socage tenure

**serg·ing** \'sər-jiŋ\ *noun* [*serge*] (circa 1909)
: the process of overcasting the raw edges of a piece of fabric (as a carpet) to prevent raveling

**¹se·ri·al** \'sir-ē-əl\ *adjective* (1840)
**1** : of, relating to, consisting of, or arranged in a series, rank, or row ⟨*serial* order⟩
**2** : appearing in successive parts or numbers ⟨a *serial* story⟩
**3** : belonging to a series maturing periodically rather than on a single date ⟨*serial* bonds⟩
**4** : of, relating to, or being music based on a series of tones in a chosen pattern without regard for traditional tonality
**5 a** : effecting a series of similar acts over a period of time ⟨a *serial* killer⟩ **b** : occurring in such a series ⟨a *serial* murder⟩
**6** : relating to or being a connection in a computer system in which the bits of a byte are transmitted sequentially over a single wire — compare PARALLEL
— **se·ri·al·ly** \-ə-lē\ *adverb*

**²serial** *noun* (1846)
**1 a** : a work appearing (as in a magazine or on television) in parts at intervals **b** : one part of a serial work : INSTALLMENT
**2** : a publication (as a newspaper or journal) issued as one of a consecutively numbered and indefinitely continued series

**se·ri·al·ise** *British variant of* SERIALIZE

**se·ri·al·ism** \'sir-ē-ə-,li-zəm\ *noun* (1958)
: serial music; *also* : the theory or practice of composing serial music

**se·ri·al·ist** \-list\ *noun* (1846)
**1** : a writer of serials
**2** : a composer of serial music

**se·ri·al·ize** \-,līz\ *transitive verb* **-ized; -iz·ing** (1857)
: to arrange or publish in serial form
— **se·ri·al·i·za·tion** \,sir-ē-ə-lə-'zā-shən\ *noun*

**serial number** *noun* (1896)
: a number indicating place in a series and used as a means of identification

**¹se·ri·ate** \'sir-ē-,āt, -ē-ət\ *adjective* [Latin *series*] (1846)
: arranged in a series or succession
— **se·ri·ate·ly** *adverb*

**²se·ri·ate** \'sir-ē-,āt\ *transitive verb* **-at·ed; -at·ing** (circa 1899)
: to arrange in a series

**¹se·ri·a·tim** \,sir-ē-'ā-təm, -'a-\ *adverb* [Medieval Latin, from Latin *series*] (1680)
: in a series

**²seriatim** *adjective* (1871)
: following seriatim

**se·ri·ceous** \sə-'ri-shəs\ *adjective* [Late Latin *sericeus* silken, from Latin *sericum* silk garment, silk, from neuter of *sericus* silken, from Greek *sērikos,* from *Sēres,* an eastern Asian people, probably the Chinese] (circa 1777)
: covered with fine silky hair ⟨*sericeous* leaf⟩

**ser·i·cin** \'ser-ə-sən\ *noun* [International Scientific Vocabulary, from Latin *sericum* silk] (circa 1868)
: a gelatinous protein that cements the two fibroin filaments in a silk fiber

**seri·cul·ture** \'ser-ə-,kəl-chər\ *noun* [Latin *sericum* silk + English *culture*] (circa 1854)
: the production of raw silk by raising silkworms
— **seri·cul·tur·al** \-'kəl-chə-rəl, -'kəlch-rəl\ *adjective*

---

\ə\ abut \ˀ\ kitten \ər\ further \a\ ash \ā\ ace
\ä\ mop, mar \au̇\ out \ch\ chin \e\ bet \ē\ easy
\g\ go \i\ hit \ī\ ice \j\ job \ŋ\ sing \ō\ go
\ȯ\ law \ȯi\ boy \th\ thin \t͟h\ the \ü\ loot \u̇\ foot
\y\ yet \zh\ vision *see also* Guide to Pronunciation

— **se·ri·cul·tur·ist** \-rist\ *noun*

**se·ries** \'sir-(ˌ)ēz\ *noun, plural* **series** *often attributive* [Latin, from *serere* to join, link together; akin to Greek *eirein* to string together, *hormos* chain, necklace, and perhaps to Latin *sort-, sors* lot] (1611)
**1 a** : a number of things or events of the same class coming one after another in spatial or temporal succession ⟨a concert *series*⟩ ⟨the hall opened into a *series* of small rooms⟩ **b** : a set of regularly presented television programs each of which is complete in itself
**2** : the indicated sum of a usually infinite sequence of numbers
**3 a** : the coins or currency of a particular country and period **b** : a group of postage stamps in different denominations
**4** : a succession of volumes or issues published with related subjects or authors, similar format and price, or continuous numbering
**5** : a division of rock formations that is smaller than a system and comprises rocks deposited during an epoch
**6** : a group of chemical compounds related in composition and structure
**7** : an arrangement of the parts of or elements in an electric circuit whereby the whole current passes through each part or element without branching — compare PARALLEL
**8** : a set of vowels connected by ablaut (as *i, a, u* in *ring, rang, rung*)
**9** : a number of games (as of baseball) played usually on consecutive days between two teams ⟨in town for a 3-game *series*⟩
**10** : a group of successive coordinate sentence elements joined together
**11** : SOIL SERIES
**12** : three consecutive games in bowling
— **in series** : in a serial arrangement

**ser·if** \'ser-əf\ *noun* [probably from Dutch *schreef* stroke, line, from Middle Dutch, from *schriven* to write, from Latin *scribere* — more at SCRIBE] (1841)
: any of the short lines stemming from and at an angle to the upper and lower ends of the strokes of a letter
— **ser·ifed** *or* **ser·iffed** \-əft\ *adjective*

**seri·graph** \'ser-ə-ˌgraf\ *noun* [Latin *sericum* silk + Greek *graphein* to write, draw — more at CARVE] (1940)
: an original silk-screen color print
— **se·rig·ra·pher** \sə-'ri-grə-fər\ *noun*
— **se·rig·ra·phy** \-fē\ *noun*

**se·rin** \sə-'raⁿ\ *noun* [French] (1530)
: a small yellow and grayish Old World finch (*Serinus serinus*) that is related to the canary

**ser·ine** \'ser-ˌēn\ *noun* [International Scientific Vocabulary *sericin* + $^2$-*ine*] (1880)
: a crystalline nonessential amino acid $C_3H_7NO_3$ that occurs especially as a structural part of many proteins

**se·rio·com·ic** \ˌsir-ē-ō-'kä-mik\ *adjective* [*serious* + -*o*- + *comic*] (1783)
: having a mixture of the serious and the comic ⟨a *seriocomic* novel⟩
— **se·rio·com·i·cal·ly** \-mi-k(ə-)lē\ *adverb*

**se·ri·ous** \'sir-ē-əs\ *adjective* [Middle English *seryows*, from Middle French or Late Latin; Middle French *serieux*, from Late Latin *seriosus*, alteration of Latin *serius* weighty, serious; probably akin to Old English *swǣr* heavy, sad] (15th century)
**1** : thoughtful or subdued in appearance or manner : SOBER
**2 a** : requiring much thought or work ⟨*serious* study⟩ **b** : of or relating to a matter of importance ⟨a *serious* play⟩
**3 a** : not joking or trifling : being in earnest **b** *archaic* : PIOUS **c** : deeply interested : DEVOTED ⟨a *serious* musician⟩

**4 a** : not easily answered or solved ⟨*serious* objections⟩ **b** : having important or dangerous possible consequences ⟨a *serious* injury⟩
**5** : excessive or impressive in quantity, extent, or degree : CONSIDERABLE ⟨making *serious* money⟩ ⟨*serious* drinking⟩ ☆
— **se·ri·ous·ness** *noun*

**se·ri·ous·ly** *adverb* (1509)
**1** : in a sincere manner : EARNESTLY
**2** : to a serious extent : SEVERELY

**se·ri·ous–mind·ed** \ˌsir-ē-əs-'mīn-dəd\ *adjective* (1845)
: having a serious disposition or trend of thought
— **se·ri·ous–mind·ed·ly** *adverb*
— **se·ri·ous–mind·ed·ness** *noun*

**ser·jeant, ser·jeanty** *variant of* SERGEANT, SERGEANTY

**ser·jeant–at–law** \ˌsär-jənt-ət-'lȯ\ *noun, plural* **ser·jeants–at–law** (1503)
: a member of a former class of barristers of the highest rank

**ser·mon** \'sər-mən\ *noun* [Middle English, from Old French, from Medieval Latin *sermon-, sermo*, from Latin, speech, conversation, from *serere* to link together — more at SERIES] (13th century)
**1** : a religious discourse delivered in public usually by a clergyman as a part of a worship service
**2** : a speech on conduct or duty
— **ser·mon·ic** \ˌsər-'mä-nik\ *adjective*

**ser·mon·ette** \ˌsər-mə-'net\ *noun* (1814)
: a short sermon

**ser·mon·ize** \'sər-mə-ˌnīz\ *verb* **-ized; -iz·ing** (1635)
*intransitive verb*
**1** : to compose or deliver a sermon
**2** : to speak didactically or dogmatically
*transitive verb*
: to preach to or on at length
— **ser·mon·iz·er** *noun*

**Sermon on the Mount**
: an ethical discourse delivered by Jesus and recorded in Matthew 5–7 and paralleled briefly in Luke 6:20–49

**sero-** *combining form* [Latin *serum*]
: serum ⟨*serology*⟩

**se·ro·con·ver·sion** \ˌsir-ō-kən-'vər-zhən, -shən\ *noun* (1963)
: the production of antibodies in response to an antigen

**se·ro·di·ag·no·sis** \-ˌdī-ig-'nō-səs\ *noun* [New Latin] (1896)
: diagnosis by the use of serum (as in the Wassermann test)
— **se·ro·di·ag·nos·tic** \-'näs-tik\ *adjective*

**se·rol·o·gy** \sə-'rä-lə-jē, si-\ *noun* [International Scientific Vocabulary] (1909)
: a science dealing with serums and especially their reactions and properties
— **se·ro·log·i·cal** \ˌsir-ə-'lä-ji-kəl\ *or* **se·ro·log·ic** \-jik\ *adjective*
— **se·ro·log·i·cal·ly** \-ji-k(ə-)lē\ *adverb*
— **se·rol·o·gist** \sə-'rä-lə-jist, si-\ *noun*

**se·ro·neg·a·tive** \ˌsir-ō-'ne-gə-tiv\ *adjective* (1927)
: having or being a negative serum reaction especially in a test for the presence of an antibody
— **se·ro·neg·a·tiv·i·ty** \-ˌne-gə-'ti-və-tē\ *noun*

**se·ro·pos·i·tive** \-'pä-zə-tiv, -'päz-tiv\ *adjective* (circa 1930)
: having or being a positive serum reaction especially in a test for the presence of an antibody
— **se·ro·pos·i·tiv·i·ty** \-ˌpä-zə-'ti-və-tē\ *noun*

**se·ro·pu·ru·lent** \-'pyur-ə-lənt, ˌser-, -'pyur-yə-\ *adjective* (circa 1836)
: consisting of a mixture of serum and pus ⟨a *seropurulent* exudate⟩

**se·ro·sa** \sə-'rō-zə\ *noun* [New Latin, from feminine of *serosus* serous, from Latin *serum*] (circa 1890)

: a usually enclosing serous membrane
— **se·ro·sal** \-zəl\ *adjective*

**se·ro·ti·nal** \sə-'rät-nəl, -ˌrä-t°n-əl; ˌser-ə-'tī-n°l\ *adjective* [Latin *serotinus* coming late] (1898)
: of or relating to the latter and usually drier part of summer

**se·rot·i·nous** \sə-'rät-nəs, -'rä-t°n-əs; ˌser-ə-'tī-nəs\ *adjective* [Latin *serotinus* coming late, from *sero* late — more at SOIREE] (circa 1656)
: remaining closed on the tree with seed dissemination delayed or occurring gradually ⟨*serotinous* cones⟩

**se·ro·to·ner·gic** \ˌsir-ə-tə-'nər-jik\ *also* **se·ro·to·nin·er·gic** \ˌsir-ə-ˌtō-nə-'nər-jik\ *adjective* [*serotonin* + -*ergic*] (1957)
: liberating, activated by, or involving serotonin in the transmission of nerve impulses ⟨*serotonergic* pathways⟩

**se·ro·to·nin** \ˌsir-ə-'tō-nən, ˌser-\ *noun* [*sero-* + *tonic* + $^1$-*in*] (1948)
: a phenolic amine neurotransmitter $C_{10}H_{12}N_2O$ that is a powerful vasoconstrictor and is found especially in the brain, blood serum, and gastric mucosa of mammals

**se·ro·type** \'sir-ə-ˌtīp, 'ser-\ *noun* (1946)
: a group of intimately related microorganisms distinguished by a common set of antigens; *also* : the set of antigens characteristic of such a group

**se·rous** \'sir-əs\ *adjective* [Middle English, from Medieval Latin *serosus*, from Latin *serum*] (15th century)
: of, relating to, or resembling serum; *especially* : of thin watery constitution ⟨a *serous* exudate⟩

**serous membrane** *noun* (circa 1852)
: a thin membrane (as the peritoneum) with cells that secrete a serous fluid; *especially* : SEROSA

**se·row** \sə-'rō\ *noun* [Lepcha *să-ro* long-haired Tibetan goat] (1847)
: any of several artiodactyl mammals (genus *Capricornis*) of eastern Asia that are usually rather dark and heavily built and some of which have distinct manes

**ser·pent** \'sər-pənt\ *noun* [Middle English, from Middle French, from Latin *serpent-, serpens*, from present participle of *serpere* to creep; akin to Greek *herpein* to creep, Sanskrit *sarpati* he creeps] (13th century)
**1 a** *archaic* : a noxious creature that creeps, hisses, or stings **b** : SNAKE
**2** : DEVIL 1
**3** : a treacherous person

$^1$**ser·pen·tine** \'sər-pən-ˌtēn, -ˌtīn\ *adjective* [Middle English, from Middle French *serpentin*, from Late Latin *serpentinus*, from Latin *serpent-, serpens*] (15th century)
**1** : of or resembling a serpent (as in form or movement)
**2** : subtly wily or tempting

---

☆ **SYNONYMS**
**Serious, grave, solemn, sedate, staid, sober, earnest** mean not light or frivolous. SERIOUS implies a concern for what really matters ⟨a *serious* play about social injustice⟩. GRAVE implies both seriousness and dignity in expression or attitude ⟨read the proclamation in a *grave* voice⟩. SOLEMN suggests an impressive gravity utterly free from levity ⟨a sad and *solemn* occasion⟩. SEDATE implies a composed and decorous seriousness ⟨remained *sedate* amid the commotion⟩. STAID suggests a settled, accustomed sedateness and prim self-restraint ⟨a quiet and *staid* community⟩. SOBER stresses seriousness of purpose and absence of levity or frivolity ⟨a *sober* look at the state of our schools⟩. EARNEST suggests sincerity or often zealousness of purpose ⟨an *earnest* reformer⟩.

---

ABC
1 serif

**3 a :** winding or turning one way and another **b :** having a compound curve whose central curve is convex
— **ser·pen·tine·ly** *adverb*

²**serpentine** *noun* (1519)
**:** something that winds sinuously

³**ser·pen·tine** \-,tēn\ *noun* [Middle English, from Medieval Latin *serpentina, serpentinum,* from Late Latin, feminine & neuter of *serpentinus* resembling a serpent] (15th century)
**:** a mineral or rock consisting essentially of a hydrous magnesium silicate usually having a dull green color and often a mottled appearance

**ser·pig·i·nous** \(,)sər-'pi-jə-nəs\ *adjective* [Middle English *serpiginose,* from Medieval Latin *serpiginosus,* from *serpigin-, serpigo* creeping skin disease, from Latin *serpere* to creep] (15th century)
**:** CREEPING, SPREADING; *especially* **:** healing over in one portion while continuing to advance in another 〈*serpiginous* ulcer〉
— **ser·pig·i·nous·ly** *adverb*

**ser·ra·nid** \sə-'ra-nəd, 'ser-ə-nəd\ *noun* [ultimately from Latin *serra* saw] (circa 1900)
**:** any of a large family (Serranidae) of carnivorous marine bony fishes which have an oblong compressed body covered with usually ctenoid scales and many of which are important food and sport fishes (as the sea basses) especially of warm seas
— **serranid** *adjective*

**ser·ra·no** \sə-'rä-(,)nō, si-\ *noun, plural* **-nos** [probably from Mexican Spanish, from Spanish *serrano,* adjective, montane, highland, from *sierra* mountain range — more at SIERRA] (circa 1972)
**:** a small Mexican hot pepper

¹**ser·rate** \'ser-,āt, sə-'rāt\ *adjective* [Latin *serratus,* from *serra* saw] (1668)
**:** notched or toothed on the edge; *specifically* **:** having marginal teeth pointing forward or toward the apex 〈a *serrate* leaf〉

²**ser·rate** \sə-'rāt, 'ser-,āt\ *transitive verb* **ser·rat·ed; ser·rat·ing** [Late Latin *serratus,* past participle of *serrare* to saw, from Latin *serra*] (1750)
**:** to mark or make with serrations 〈a *serrated* knife〉

**ser·ra·tion** \sə-'rā-shən, se-\ *noun* (1842)
**1 :** the condition of being serrate
**2 :** a formation resembling the toothed edge of a saw
**3 :** one of the teeth in a serrate margin

**ser·ried** \'ser-ēd\ *adjective* (1667)
**1 :** crowded or pressed together **:** COMPACT 〈the crowd collected in a *serried* mass —W. S. Maugham〉
**2** [by alteration] **:** marked by ridges **:** SERRATE 〈the *serried* contours of the . . . mountains —*American Guide Series: Oregon*〉
— **ser·ried·ly** *adverb*
— **ser·ried·ness** *noun*

**ser·ry** \'ser-ē\ *verb* **ser·ried; ser·ry·ing** [Middle French *serré,* past participle of *serrer* to press, crowd — more at SEAR] (1581)
*intransitive verb*
*archaic* **:** to press together especially in ranks
*transitive verb*
**:** to crowd together

**Ser·to·li cell** \,sər-'tō-lē-\ *noun* [Enrico *Sertoli* (died 1910) Italian histologist] (1888)
**:** one of the elongated striated cells lining the seminiferous tubules that support and apparently nourish the spermatids

**Ser·to·man** \(,)sər-'tō-mən\ *noun* [*Sertoma* (Club)] (1956)
**:** a member of a major international service club

**se·rum** \'sir-əm\ *noun, plural* **serums** *or* **se·ra** \-ə\ [Latin, whey, wheylike fluid; akin to Greek *oros* whey] (1665)
**1 :** the watery portion of an animal fluid remaining after coagulation: **a** (1) **:** BLOOD SERUM (2) **:** ANTISERUM **b :** WHEY **c :** a normal or pathological serous fluid (as in a blister)

**2 :** the watery part of a plant fluid
**serum albumin** *noun* (1879)
**:** a crystallizable albumin or mixture of albumins that normally constitutes more than half of the protein in blood serum and serves to maintain the osmotic pressure of the blood

**serum globulin** *noun* (circa 1890)
**:** a globulin or mixture of globulins occurring in blood serum and containing most of the antibodies of the blood

**serum hepatitis** *noun* (1932)
**:** HEPATITIS B

**serum sickness** *noun* (circa 1913)
**:** an allergic reaction to the injection of foreign serum manifested by urticaria, swelling, eruption, arthritis, and fever

**ser·val** \'sər-vəl, (,)sər-'val\ *noun* [French, from Portuguese *lobo cerval* lynx, from Medieval Latin *lupus cervalis,* literally, deerlike wolf] (1771)
**:** a long-legged African wildcat (*Felis serval*) having large ears and a tawny black-spotted coat

**ser·vant** \'sər-vənt\ *noun* [Middle English, from Old French, from present participle of *servir*] (13th century)
**:** one that serves others 〈a public *servant*〉; *especially* **:** one that performs duties about the person or home of a master or personal employer

serval

— **ser·vant·hood** \-,hud\ *noun*
— **ser·vant·less** *adjective*

¹**serve** \'sərv\ *verb* **served; serv·ing** [Middle English, from Middle French *servir,* from Old French, from Latin *servire* to be a slave, serve, from *servus* slave, servant] (13th century)
*intransitive verb*
**1 a :** to be a servant **b :** to do military or naval service
**2 :** to assist a celebrant as server at mass
**3 a :** to be of use 〈in a day when few people could write, seals *served* as signatures —Elizabeth W. King〉 **b :** to be favorable, opportune, or convenient **c :** to be worthy of reliance or trust 〈if memory *serves*〉 **d :** to hold an office **:** discharge a duty or function 〈*serve* on a jury〉
**4 :** to prove adequate or satisfactory **:** SUFFICE
**5 :** to help persons to food: as **a :** to wait at table **b :** to set out portions of food or drink
**6 :** to wait on customers
**7 :** to put the ball or shuttlecock in play in various games (as tennis, volleyball, or badminton)
*transitive verb*
**1 a :** to be a servant to **:** ATTEND **b :** to give the service and respect due to (a superior) **c :** to comply with the commands or demands of **:** GRATIFY **d :** to give military or naval service to **e :** to perform the duties of (an office or post)
**2 :** to act as server at (mass)
**3** *archaic* **:** to pay a lover's or suitor's court to (a lady) 〈that gentle lady, whom I love and *serve* —Edmund Spenser〉
**4 a :** to work through (a term of service) **b :** to put in (a term of imprisonment)
**5 a :** to wait on at table **b :** to bring (food) to a diner **c :** PRESENT, PROVIDE — usually used with *up* 〈the novel *served* up many laughs〉
**6 a :** to furnish or supply with something needed or desired **b :** to wait on (a customer) in a store **c :** to furnish professional service to
**7 a :** to answer the needs of **b :** to be enough for **:** SUFFICE **c :** to contribute or conduce to **:** PROMOTE
**8 :** to treat or act toward in a specified way 〈he *served* me ill〉

**9 a :** to bring to notice, deliver, or execute as required by law **b :** to make legal service upon (a person named in a process)
**10** *of a male animal* **:** to copulate with
**11 :** to wind yarn or wire tightly around (a rope or stay) for protection
**12 :** to provide services that benefit or help
**13 :** to put (the ball or shuttlecock) in play (as in tennis or badminton)
— **serve one right :** to be deserved

²**serve** *noun* (1688)
**:** the act or action of putting the ball or shuttlecock in play in various games (as volleyball, badminton, or tennis); *also* **:** a turn to serve

**serv·er** \'sər-vər\ *noun* (15th century)
**1 :** one that serves food or drink
**2 :** the player who serves (as in tennis)
**3 :** something used in serving food or drink
**4 :** one that serves legal processes upon another
**5 :** the celebrant's assistant at low mass
**6 :** a computer in a network that is used to provide services (as access to files or shared peripherals or the routing of electronic mail) to other computers in the network

¹**ser·vice** \'sər-vəs\ *noun* [Middle English, from Middle French, from Latin *servitium* condition of a slave, body of slaves, from *servus* slave] (13th century)
**1 a :** the occupation or function of serving 〈in active *service*〉 **b :** employment as a servant 〈entered his *service*〉
**2 a :** the work performed by one that serves 〈good *service*〉 **b :** HELP, USE, BENEFIT 〈glad to be of *service*〉 **c :** contribution to the welfare of others **d :** disposal for use 〈I'm entirely at your *service*〉
**3 a :** a form followed in worship or in a religious ceremony 〈the burial *service*〉 **b :** a meeting for worship — often used in plural 〈held evening *services*〉
**4 :** the act of serving: as **a :** a helpful act 〈did him a *service*〉 **b :** useful labor that does not produce a tangible commodity — usually used in plural 〈charge for professional *services*〉 **c :** SERVE
**5 :** a set of articles for a particular use 〈a silver tea *service*〉
**6 a :** an administrative division (as of a government or business) 〈the consular *service*〉 **b :** one of a nation's military forces (as the army or navy)
**7 a :** a facility supplying some public demand 〈telephone *service*〉 〈bus *service*〉 **b :** a facility providing maintenance and repair 〈television *service*〉
**8 :** the materials (as spun yarn, small lines, or canvas) used for serving a rope
**9 :** the act of bringing a legal writ, process, or summons to notice as prescribed by law
**10 :** the act of copulating with a female animal
**11 :** a branch of a hospital medical staff devoted to a particular specialty 〈obstetrical *service*〉

²**service** *transitive verb* **ser·viced; ser·vic·ing** (1528)
**:** to perform services for: as **a :** to repair or provide maintenance for **b :** to meet interest and sinking fund payments on (as government debt) **c :** to perform any of the business functions auxiliary to production or distribution of **d** *of a male animal* **:** SERVE 10
— **ser·vic·er** *noun*

³**service** *adjective* (1837)
**1 :** of or relating to the armed services
**2 :** used in serving or supplying 〈delivery men use the *service* entrance〉
**3 :** intended for hard or everyday use

---

**4 a :** providing services ⟨the *service* trades—from filling stations to universities —John Fischer⟩ **b :** offering repair, maintenance, or incidental services

**⁴ser·vice** \'sər-vəs\ *noun* [Middle English *serves,* plural of *serve* fruit of the service tree, service tree, from Old English *syrfe,* from (assumed) Vulgar Latin *sorbea,* from Latin *sorbus* service tree] (1530)
**:** an Old World tree (*Sorbus domestica*) resembling the related mountain ashes but having larger flowers and larger edible fruit; *also* **:** a related Old World tree (*S. torminalis*) with bitter fruits

**ser·vice·able** \'sər-və-sə-bəl\ *adjective* (14th century)
**1 :** HELPFUL, USEFUL
**2 :** fit for use ⟨her *serviceable* but not exceptional voice —Irving Kolodin⟩
— **ser·vice·abil·i·ty** \,sər-və-sə-'bi-lə-tē\ *noun*
— **ser·vice·able·ness** \'sər-və-sə-bəl-nəs\ *noun*
— **ser·vice·ably** \-blē\ *adverb*

**ser·vice·ber·ry** \'sər-vəs-,ber-ē *also* 'sär-\ *noun* (⁴*service*) (1784)
**1 :** the edible purple or red fruit of any of various North American trees or shrubs (genus *Amelanchier*) of the rose family
**2 :** a tree or shrub that produces serviceberries and has showy white flowers in the spring — called also *Juneberry, shadblow, shadbush*

**service book** *noun* (1580)
**:** a book setting forth forms of worship used in religious services

**service box** *noun* (circa 1898)
**:** the area in which a player stands while serving in various court games (as squash or handball)

**service cap** *noun* (circa 1908)
**:** a flat-topped visor cap worn as part of a military uniform — compare GARRISON CAP

**service ceiling** *noun* (1920)
**:** the altitude at which under standard air conditions a particular airplane can no longer rise at a rate greater than a small designated rate (as 100 feet per minute)

**service charge** *noun* (1917)
**:** a fee charged for a particular service often in addition to a standard or basic fee — called also *service fee*

**service club** *noun* (1926)
**1 :** a club of business or professional men or women organized for their common benefit and active in community service
**2 :** a recreation center for enlisted personnel provided by one of the armed services

**service court** *noun* (circa 1878)
**:** a part of the court into which the ball or shuttlecock must be served

**service line** *noun* (1875)
**:** a line marked on a court in various games (as handball or tennis) parallel to the front wall or to the net to mark a boundary of the service area or service court

**ser·vice·man** \'sər-vəs-,man, -mən\ *noun* (1899)
**1 :** a male member of the armed forces
**2 :** a man employed to repair or maintain equipment
**3 :** a service station attendant

**service mark** *noun* (1945)
**:** a mark or device used to identify a service (as transportation or insurance) offered to customers

**service medal** *noun* (circa 1934)
**:** a medal awarded to an individual for military service in a specified war or campaign

**service module** *noun* (1961)
**:** a space vehicle module that contains oxygen, water, fuel cells, propellant tanks, and the main rocket engine

**service road** *noun* (1921)
**:** FRONTAGE ROAD

**service station** *noun* (1916)

**1 :** a retail station for servicing motor vehicles especially with gasoline and oil
**2 :** a place at which some service is offered

**service stripe** *noun* (circa 1920)
**:** a stripe worn on an enlisted man's left sleeve to indicate three years of service in the army or four years in the navy

**service tree** *noun* (1600)
**:** ⁴SERVICE

**ser·vice·wom·an** \'sər-vəs-,wu̇-mən\ *noun* (1943)
**:** a female member of the armed forces

**ser·vi·ette** \,sər-vē-'et\ *noun* [French, from Middle French, from *servir* to serve] (1818) *chiefly British* **:** a table napkin

**ser·vile** \'sər-vəl, -,vīl\ *adjective* [Middle English, from Latin *servilis,* from *servus* slave] (15th century)
**1 :** of or befitting a slave or a menial position
**2 :** meanly or cravenly submissive **:** ABJECT
*synonym* see SUBSERVIENT
— **ser·vile·ly** \-və(l)-lē, -,vīl-lē\ *adverb*
— **ser·vile·ness** \-vəl-nəs, -,vīl-\ *noun*
— **ser·vil·i·ty** \(,)sər-'vi-lə-tē\ *noun*

**serv·ing** \'sər-viŋ\ *noun* (1864)
**:** a helping of food or drink

**Ser·vite** \'sər-,vīt\ *noun* [Medieval Latin *Servitae,* plural, Servites, from Latin *servus*] (circa 1550)
**:** a member of the mendicant Order of Servants of Mary founded in Florence, Italy, in 1233
— **Servite** *adjective*

**ser·vi·tor** \'sər-və-tər, -,tȯr\ *noun* [Middle English *servitour,* from Middle French, from Late Latin *servitor,* from Latin *servire* to serve] (14th century)
**:** a male servant

**ser·vi·tude** \'sər-və-,tüd, -,tyüd\ *noun* [Middle English, from Middle French, from Latin *servitudo* slavery, from *servus* slave] (15th century)
**1 :** a condition in which one lacks liberty especially to determine one's course of action or way of life
**2 :** a right by which something (as a piece of land) owned by one person is subject to a specified use or enjoyment by another

**ser·vo** \'sər-(,)vō\ *noun, plural* **servos** (1947)
**1 :** SERVOMOTOR
**2 :** SERVOMECHANISM

**ser·vo·mech·a·nism** \'sər-vō-,me-kə-,ni-zəm\ *noun* [*servo-* (as in *servomotor*) + *mechanism*] (1926)
**:** an automatic device for controlling large amounts of power by means of very small amounts of power and automatically correcting the performance of a mechanism

**ser·vo·mo·tor** \'sər-vō-,mō-tər\ *noun* [French *servo-moteur,* from Latin *servus* slave, servant + French *-o-* + *moteur* motor, from Latin *motor* one that moves — more at MOTOR] (1889)
**:** a power-driven mechanism that supplements a primary control operated by a comparatively feeble force (as in a servomechanism)

**-ses** *plural of* -SIS

**ses·a·me** \'se-sə-mē *also* 'se-zə-\ *noun* [alteration of earlier *sesam, sesama,* from Latin *sesamum, sesama,* from Greek *sēsamon, sēsamē,* of Semitic origin; akin to Akkadian *šamaššamu* sesame] (1682)
**1 :** a widely cultivated chiefly tropical or subtropical annual erect herb (*Sesamum indicum* of the family Pedaliaceae); *also* **:** its small seeds used especially as a source of oil and a flavoring agent
**2 :** OPEN SESAME

**sesame oil** *noun* (1870)
**:** a pale yellow bland semi-drying fatty oil obtained from sesame seeds and used chiefly as an edible

**sesame 1**

oil, as a vehicle for various pharmaceuticals, and in cosmetics and soaps

**ses·a·moid** \'se-sə-,mȯid\ *noun* [Greek *sēsamoeidēs,* literally, resembling sesame seed, from *sēsamon*] (circa 1696)
**:** a nodular mass of bone (as the patella) or cartilage in a tendon especially at a joint or bony prominence
— **sesamoid** *adjective*

**Se·so·tho** \se-'sō-(,)thō, -(,)tō\ *noun* [Sesotho] (1846)
**:** the Bantu language of the Basotho people

**sesqui-** *combining form* [Latin, one and a half, half again, literally, and a half, from *semis* half of an *as,* one half (probably from *semi-* + *as* as) + *-que* (enclitic) and; akin to Greek *te* and, Sanskrit *ca,* Gothic *-h, -uh*]
**1 :** one and a half times ⟨*sesqui*centennial⟩
**2 :** containing half again as many atoms ⟨*sesqui*terpene⟩
**3 :** intermediate **:** combination ⟨*sesqui*carbonate⟩

**ses·qui·car·bon·ate** \,ses-kwi-'kär-bə-,nāt, -nət\ *noun* (1825)
**:** a salt that is neither a simple normal carbonate nor a simple bicarbonate but often (as $Na_2CO_3 \cdot NaHCO_3 \cdot 2H_2O$) a combination of the two

**ses·qui·cen·te·na·ry** \-kwi-sen-'te-nə-rē, -'sen-t°n-,er-ē, -sen-'tē-nə-rē\ *noun* (1954)
**:** SESQUICENTENNIAL

**ses·qui·cen·ten·ni·al** \-sen-'te-nē-əl\ *noun* (1880)
**:** a 150th anniversary or its celebration
— **sesquicentennial** *adjective*

**ses·qui·pe·da·lian** \,ses-kwə-pə-'dāl-yən\ *adjective* [Latin *sesquipedalis,* literally, a foot and a half long, from *sesqui-* + *ped-, pes* foot — more at FOOT] (1656)
**1 :** having many syllables **:** LONG ⟨*sesquipedalian* terms⟩
**2 :** given to or characterized by the use of long words ⟨a *sesquipedalian* television commentator⟩

**ses·qui·ter·pene** \,ses-kwə-'tər-,pēn\ *noun* (circa 1888)
**:** any of a class of terpenes $C_{15}H_{24}$; *also* **:** a derivative of such a terpene

**ses·sile** \'se-,sīl, -səl\ *adjective* [Latin *sessilis* of or fit for sitting, low, dwarf (of plants), from *sessus,* past participle of *sedēre*] (1753)
**1 :** attached directly by the base **:** not raised upon a stalk or peduncle ⟨a *sessile* leaf⟩ ⟨*sessile* bubbles⟩
**2 :** permanently attached or established **:** not free to move about ⟨*sessile* polyps⟩

**ses·sion** \'se-shən\ *noun* [Middle English, from Middle French, from Latin *session-, sessio,* literally, act of sitting, from *sedēre* to sit — more at SIT] (14th century)
**1 :** a meeting or series of meetings of a body (as a court or legislature) for the transaction of business ⟨morning *session*⟩
**2** *plural* **a** (1) **:** a sitting of English justices of peace in execution of the powers conferred by their commissions (2) **:** an English court holding such sessions **b :** any of various courts similar to the English sessions
**3 :** the period between the first meeting of a legislative or judicial body and the prorogation or final adjournment
**4 :** the ruling body of a Presbyterian congregation consisting of the elders in active service
**5 :** the period during the year or day in which a school conducts classes
**6 :** a meeting or period devoted to a particular activity ⟨a recording *session*⟩
— **ses·sion·al** \'sesh-nəl, 'se-shə-n°l\ *adjective*

**session man** *noun* (1958)
**:** a studio musician who backs up a performer at a recording session

**ses·terce** \'ses-,tərs\ *noun* [Latin *sestertius,* from *sestertius* two and a half times as great (from its being equal originally to two and a

half asses), from *semis* half of an as, one half + *tertius* third — more at SESQUI-, THIRD] (1598)
: an ancient Roman coin equal to ¼ denarius

**ses·ter·tium** \se-'stər-sh(ē-)əm\ *noun, plural* **-tia** \-sh(ē-)ə\ [Latin, from genitive plural of *sestertius* (in the phrase *milia sestertium* thousands of sesterces)] (circa 1541)
: a unit of value in ancient Rome equal to 1000 sesterces

**ses·tet** \ses-'tet\ *noun* [Italian *sestetto*, from *sesto* sixth, from Latin *sextus* — more at SEXT] (1859)
: a stanza or a poem of six lines; *specifically* : the last six lines of an Italian sonnet

**ses·ti·na** \se-'stē-nə\ *noun* [Italian, from *sesto* sixth] (circa 1586)
: a lyrical fixed form consisting of six 6-line usually unrhymed stanzas in which the end words of the first stanza recur as end words of the following five stanzas in a successively rotating order and as the middle and end words of the three verses of the concluding tercet

**¹set** \'set\ *verb* **set; set·ting** [Middle English *setten*, from Old English *settan;* akin to Old High German *sezzen* to set, Old English *sittan* to sit] (before 12th century)
*transitive verb*
**1** : to cause to sit : place in or on a seat
**2 a** : to put (a fowl) on eggs to hatch them **b** : to put (eggs) for hatching under a fowl or into an incubator
**3** : to place (oneself) in position to start running in a race
**4 a** : to place with care or deliberate purpose and with relative stability ⟨*set* a ladder against the wall⟩ ⟨*set* a stone on the grave⟩ **b** : TRANSPLANT 1 ⟨*set* seedlings⟩ **c** (1) : to make (as a trap) ready to catch prey (2) : to fix (a hook) firmly into the jaw of a fish **d** : to put aside (as dough containing yeast) for fermenting
**5** : to direct with fixed attention ⟨*set* your mind to it⟩
**6 a** : to cause to assume a specified condition, relation, or occupation ⟨slaves were *set* free⟩ ⟨*set* the house on fire⟩ **b** : to cause the start of ⟨*set* a fire⟩
**7 a** : to appoint or assign to an office or duty **b** : POST, STATION
**8** : to cause to assume a specified posture or position ⟨*set* the door ajar⟩
**9 a** : to fix as a distinguishing imprint, sign, or appearance ⟨the years have *set* their mark on him⟩ **b** : AFFIX **c** : APPLY ⟨*set* a match to kindling⟩
**10** : to fix or decide on as a time, limit, or regulation : PRESCRIBE ⟨*set* a wedding day⟩ ⟨*set* the rules for the game⟩
**11 a** : to establish as the highest level or best performance ⟨*set* a record for the half mile⟩ **b** : to furnish as a pattern or model ⟨*set* an example of generosity⟩ **c** : to allot as a task ⟨*setting* lessons for the children to work upon at home —*Manchester Examiner*⟩
**12 a** : to adjust (a device and especially a measuring device) to a desired position ⟨*set* the alarm for 7:00⟩ ⟨*set* a thermostat at 68⟩; *also* : to adjust (as a clock) in conformity with a standard **b** : to restore to normal position or connection when dislocated or fractured ⟨*set* a broken bone⟩ **c** : to spread to the wind ⟨*set* the sails⟩
**13 a** : to put in order for use ⟨*set* a place for a guest⟩ **b** : to make scenically ready for a performance ⟨*set* the stage⟩ **c** (1) : to arrange (type) for printing ⟨*set* type by hand⟩ (2) : to put into type or its equivalent (as on film) ⟨*set* the first word in italic⟩
**14 a** : to put a fine edge on by grinding or honing ⟨*set* a razor⟩ **b** : to bend slightly the tooth points of (a saw) alternately in opposite directions **c** : to sink (the head of a nail) below the surface
**15** : to fix in a desired position (as by heating or stretching)

**16** : to arrange (hair) in a desired style by using implements (as curlers, rollers, or clips) and gels or lotions
**17 a** : to adorn with something affixed or infixed : STUD, DOT ⟨clear sky *set* with stars⟩ **b** : to fix (as a precious stone) in a border of metal : place in a setting
**18 a** : to hold something in regard or esteem at the rate of ⟨*sets* a great deal by daily exercise⟩ **b** : to place in a relative rank or category ⟨*set* duty before pleasure⟩ **c** : to fix at a certain amount ⟨*set* bail at $500⟩ **d** : VALUE, RATE ⟨their promises were *set* at naught⟩ **e** : to place as an estimate of worth ⟨*set* a high value on life⟩
**19** : to place in relation for comparison or balance ⟨theory *set* against practice⟩
**20 a** : to direct to action **b** : to incite to attack or antagonism ⟨war *sets* brother against brother⟩
**21 a** : to place by transporting ⟨was *set* ashore on the island⟩ **b** : to put in motion **c** : to put and fix in a direction ⟨*set* our faces toward home once more⟩ **d** *of a dog* : to point out the position of (game) by holding a fixed attitude
**22** : to defeat (an opponent or a contract) in bridge
**23 a** : to fix firmly : make immobile : give rigid form or condition to ⟨*set* her jaw in determination⟩ **b** : to make unyielding or obstinate
**24** : to cause to become firm or solid ⟨*set* milk for cheese⟩
**25** : to cause (as fruit) to develop
*intransitive verb*
**1** *chiefly dialect* : SIT
**2** : to be becoming : be suitable : FIT ⟨the coat *sets* well⟩
**3** : to cover and warm eggs to hatch them
**4 a** : to become lodged or fixed ⟨the pudding *set* heavily on my stomach⟩ **b** : to place oneself in position in preparation for an action (as running)
**5** *of a plant part* : to undergo development usually as a result of pollination
**6 a** : to pass below the horizon : go down ⟨the sun *sets*⟩ **b** : to come to an end ⟨this century *sets* with little mirth —Thomas Fuller⟩
**7** : to apply oneself to some activity ⟨*set* to work⟩
**8** : to have a specified direction in motion : FLOW, TEND ⟨the wind was *setting* from Pine Hill to the farm —Esther Forbes⟩
**9** *of a dog* : to indicate the position of game by crouching or pointing
**10** : to dance face to face with another in a square dance ⟨*set* to your partner and turn⟩
**11 a** : to become solid or thickened by chemical or physical alteration ⟨the cement *sets* rapidly⟩ **b** *of a dye or color* : to become permanent **c** *of a bone* : to become whole by knitting **d** *of metal* : to acquire a permanent twist or bend from strain ■
— **set about** : to begin to do
— **set apart 1** : to reserve to a particular use **2** : to make noticeable or outstanding
— **set aside 1** : to put to one side : DISCARD **2** : to reserve for a purpose : SAVE **3** : DISMISS **4** : ANNUL, OVERRULE
— **set at** : to mount an attack on : ASSAIL ⟨would go although . . . devils should *set at* me —Charlotte Yonge⟩
— **set eyes on** : to catch sight of
— **set foot in** : ENTER
— **set foot on** : to step onto
— **set forth 1** : to give an account or statement of **2** : to start out on a journey
— **set forward 1** : FURTHER **2** : to start out on a journey
— **set in motion** : to give impulse to ⟨*sets* the story *in motion* vividly —Howard Thompson⟩
— **set one's hand to** : to become engaged in
— **set one's heart on** : RESOLVE *verb transitive* 5 ⟨she *set her heart on* going to medical school⟩

— **set one's house in order** : to organize one's affairs
— **set one's sights on** : to determine to pursue
— **set one's teeth on edge** : IRRITATE, ANNOY
— **set one straight** : to correct someone by providing accurate information
— **set sail** : to start out on a course; *especially* : to begin a voyage ⟨*set sail* for Bermuda⟩
— **set store by** *or* **set store on** : to consider valuable, trustworthy, or worthwhile
— **set the stage** : to provide the basis or background ⟨this trend will *set the stage* for higher earnings⟩
— **set to music** : to provide music or instrumental accompaniment for (a text)
— **set upon** : to attack usually with violence ⟨the dogs *set upon* the trespassers⟩

**²set** *noun* (14th century)
**1 a** : the act or action of setting **b** : the condition of being set
**2** : a number of things of the same kind that belong or are used together ⟨an electric train *set*⟩
**3 a** : mental inclination, tendency, or habit : BENT ⟨a *set* toward mathematics⟩ **b** : a state of psychological preparedness usually of limited duration for action in response to an anticipated stimulus or situation ⟨the influence of mental *set* on the effect experienced with marijuana⟩
**4** : direction of flow ⟨the *set* of the wind⟩
**5** : form or carriage of the body or of its parts ⟨her face took on a cynical *set* —Raymond Kennedy⟩
**6** : the manner of fitting or of being placed or suspended ⟨in order to give the skirt a pretty *set* —Mary J. Howell⟩
**7** : amount of deflection from a straight line ⟨*set* of a saw's teeth⟩

□ USAGE
**set** *Set* has been used intransitively in the sense of "sit" since about the 14th century. The practice went unnoticed until Samuel Johnson observed in his 1755 dictionary that is was "commonly used in conversation" and "though undoubtedly barbarous" was "sometimes found in authors." Attempts to correct the usage have been a fixture of schoolbooks ever since. Noah Webster did not include Johnson's definition in his 1828 dictionary probably because he had earlier disapproved the use in one of his school grammars. Generations of teachers and critics have succeeded in chastening the use of most literary and learned writers; these writers have, however, used it freely to establish a character whose language use is not especially fastidious ⟨he never done nothing for three months but *set* in his back yard and learn that frog to jump —Mark Twain⟩. It turns up occasionally in general prose, but not as often as intransitive *lay* does. It still is used in familiar speech, but appears to be somewhat more marked socially than *lay* is. There is apparently a folk belief that *sit* is for people and *set* for things; such a belief may account for the "ore *setting* on the docks at Chicago" from a steel company spokesman in one of our citations. You should remember that the basic objection to intransitive *set* is in its literal meaning; it shares with *sit* some figurative meanings that draw no criticism ⟨grammatically, the first example does not *set* well —Morton S. Freeman⟩.

\ə\ abut \ᵊ\ kitten \ər\ further \a\ ash \ā\ ace \ä\ mop, mar \aù\ out \ch\ chin \e\ bet \ē\ easy \g\ go \i\ hit \ī\ ice \j\ job \ŋ\ sing \ō\ go \ò\ law \òi\ boy \th\ thin \th\ the \ü\ loot \ù\ foot \y\ yet \zh\ vision *see also* Guide to Pronunciation

**8 :** permanent change of form (as of metal) due to repeated or excessive stress
**9 :** the act or result of arranging hair by curling or waving
**10** *also* **sett** \'set\ **a :** a young plant or rooted cutting ready for transplanting **b :** a small bulb, corm, or tuber or a piece of tuber used for propagation ⟨onion *sets*⟩
**11** *or* **sett :** the burrow of a badger
**12 :** the width of the body of a piece of type
**13 :** an artificial setting for a scene of a theatrical or film production
**14** *also* **sett :** a rectangular paving stone of sandstone or granite
**15 :** a division of a tennis match won by the side that wins at least six games beating the opponent by two games or by winning a tie-breaker
**16 :** a collection of books or periodicals forming a unit
**17 :** a clutch of eggs
**18 :** the basic formation in a country-dance or square dance
**19 :** a session of music (as jazz or dance music) usually followed by an intermission; *also* **:** the music played at one session
**20 :** a group of persons associated by common interests
**21 :** a collection of elements and especially mathematical ones (as numbers or points) — called also *class*
**22 :** an apparatus of electronic components assembled so as to function as a unit ⟨a television *set*⟩
**23 :** a usually offensive formation in football or basketball
**24 :** a group of a specific number of repetitions of a particular exercise

³**set** *adjective* [Middle English *sett*, from Old English *gesett*, past participle of *settan*] (14th century)
**1 :** INTENT, DETERMINED ⟨*set* upon going⟩
**2 :** INTENTIONAL, PREMEDITATED ⟨did it of *set* purpose⟩
**3 :** fixed by authority or appointment **:** PRESCRIBED, SPECIFIED ⟨*set* hours of study⟩
**4 :** reluctant to change ⟨*set* in their ways⟩
**5 a :** IMMOVABLE, RIGID ⟨*set* frown⟩ **b :** BUILT-IN ⟨a *set* tub⟩
**6 :** SETTLED, PERSISTENT ⟨*set* defiance⟩
**7 :** being in readiness **:** PREPARED ⟨*set* for an early morning start⟩

**se·ta** \'sē-tə\ *noun, plural* **se·tae** \'sē-ˌtē\ [New Latin, from Latin *saeta, seta* bristle] (circa 1793)
**:** a slender usually rigid or bristly and springy organ or part of an animal or plant
— **se·tal** \'sē-t²l\ *adjective*

**se·ta·ceous** \si-'tā-shəs\ *adjective* [Latin *saeta, seta*] (1664)
**1 :** set with or consisting of bristles
**2 :** resembling a bristle in form or texture

**set–aside** \'set-ə-ˌsīd\ *noun* (1943)
**:** something (as a portion of receipts or production) that is set aside for a specified purpose

**set·back** \'set-ˌbak\ *noun* (1674)
**1 :** a checking of progress
**2 :** DEFEAT, REVERSE
**3 :** ⁴PITCH 7
**4 :** a placing of the face of a building on a line some distance to the rear of the building line or of the wall below; *also* **:** the rooftop area produced by a setback
**5 :** automatic scheduled adjustment to a lower temperature setting of a thermostat

**set back** *transitive verb* (1600)
**1 :** to slow the progress of **:** HINDER, DELAY
**2 :** COST ⟨a new suit will *set* you *back* $200⟩

**set by** *transitive verb* (1595)
**:** to set apart for future use

**set down** *transitive verb* (15th century)
**1 :** to cause to sit down **:** SEAT
**2 :** to place at rest on a surface or on the ground
**3 :** to suspend (a jockey) from racing

**4 :** to cause or allow to get off a vehicle **:** DELIVER
**5 :** to land (an airplane) on the ground or water
**6 a :** ORDAIN, ESTABLISH **b :** to put in writing
**7 a :** REGARD, CONSIDER ⟨*set* him *down* as a liar⟩ **b :** ATTRIBUTE

**se te·nant** \sə-'te-nənt, sē-; ˌse-tə-'nän\ *adjective* [French, literally, holding one another] (circa 1911)
*of postage stamps* **:** joined together as in the original sheet but differing in design, overprint, color, or perforation

**Seth** \'seth\ *noun* [Hebrew *Shēth*]
**:** a son of Adam and Eve

¹**set–in** \'set-'in\ *adjective* (1534)
**1 :** placed, located, or built as a part of some other construction ⟨a *set-in* bookcase⟩ ⟨a *set-in* washbasin⟩
**2 :** cut separately and stitched in ⟨*set-in* sleeves⟩

²**set–in** \'set-ˌin\ *noun* (1953)
**:** INSERT

**set in** (15th century)
*transitive verb*
**:** INSERT; *especially* **:** to stitch (a small part) within a large article ⟨*set in* a sleeve of a dress⟩
*intransitive verb*
**:** to become established

**set·line** \'set-ˌlīn\ *noun* (1865)
**:** a long heavy fishing line to which several hooks are attached in series

**set·off** \'set-ˌof\ *noun* (1621)
**1 :** something that is set off against another thing: **a :** DECORATION, ORNAMENT **b :** COMPENSATION, COUNTERBALANCE
**2 :** the discharge of a debt by setting against it a distinct claim in favor of the debtor; *also* **:** the claim itself
**3 :** OFFSET 7a

**set off** (1596)
*transitive verb*
**1 a :** to put in relief **:** show up by contrast **b :** ADORN, EMBELLISH **c :** to set apart **:** make distinct or outstanding
**2 a :** OFFSET, COMPENSATE ⟨more variety in the Lancashire weather to *set off* its most disagreeable phases —*Geographical Journal*⟩ **b :** to make a setoff of ⟨the respective totals shall be *set off* against one another —O. R. Hobson⟩
**3 a :** to set in motion **:** cause to begin **b :** to cause to explode
**4 :** to measure off on a surface
*intransitive verb*
**:** to start out on a course or a journey ⟨*set off* for home⟩

**set on** (14th century)
*transitive verb*
**1 :** ATTACK
**2 a** *obsolete* **:** PROMOTE **b :** to urge (as a dog) to attack or pursue **c :** to incite to action **:** INSTIGATE **d :** to set to work
*intransitive verb*
**:** GO ON, ADVANCE

**se·tose** \'sē-ˌtōs\ *adjective* [Latin *saetosus*, from *saeta*] (1661)
**:** SETACEOUS, BRISTLY

**set·out** \'set-ˌaůt\ *noun* (1537)
**1 a** (1) **:** ARRAY, DISPLAY (2) **:** ARRANGEMENT, LAYOUT **b :** BUFFET, SPREAD **c :** TURNOUT 5
**2 :** PARTY, ENTERTAINMENT
**3 :** BEGINNING, OUTSET

**set out** (14th century)
*transitive verb*
**1 a :** to arrange and present graphically or systematically **b :** to mark out (as a design) **:** lay out the plan of
**2 :** to state, describe, or recite at length ⟨distributed copies of a pamphlet *setting out* his ideas in full —S. F. Mason⟩
**3 :** to begin with a definite purpose **:** INTEND, UNDERTAKE
*intransitive verb*
**:** to start out on a course, a journey, or a career

**set piece** *noun* (circa 1909)

**1 :** a realistic piece of stage scenery standing by itself
**2 a :** a composition (as in literature, art, or music) executed in a fixed or ideal form often with studied artistry and brilliant effect **b :** a scene, depiction, speech, or event that is obviously designed to have an imposing effect
**3 :** a precisely planned and conducted military operation
— **set–piece** *adjective*

**set point** *noun* (1928)
**:** a situation (as in tennis) in which one player will win the set by winning the next point; *also* **:** the point won

**set·screw** \'set-ˌskrü\ *noun* (circa 1855)
**1 :** a screw screwed through one part tightly upon or into another part to prevent relative movement
**2 :** a screw for regulating a valve opening or a spring tension

**set shot** *noun* (1937)
**:** a two-handed shot in basketball taken from a stationary position

**sett** *variant of* SET

**set·tee** \se-'tē\ *noun* [alteration of *settle*] (1716)
**1 :** a long seat with a back
**2 :** a medium-sized sofa with arms and a back

**set·ter** \'se-tər\ *noun* (15th century)
**1 :** one that sets
**2 :** a large bird dog of a type trained to point on finding game

**set theory** *noun* (1936)
**:** a branch of mathematics or of symbolic logic that deals with the nature and relations of sets
— **set theoretic** *adjective*

**set·ting** \'se-tiŋ\ *noun* (14th century)
**1 :** the manner, position, or direction in which something is set
**2 :** the frame or bed in which a gem is set; *also* **:** style of mounting
**3 a :** the time, place, and circumstances in which something occurs or develops **b :** the time and place of the action of a literary, dramatic, or cinematic work **c :** the scenery used in a theatrical or film production
**4 :** the music composed for a text (as a poem)
**5 :** the articles of tableware for setting a place at table ⟨two *settings* of sterling silver⟩
**6 :** a batch of eggs for incubation
*synonym* see BACKGROUND

**setting circle** *noun* (circa 1891)
**:** a graduated scale or wheel on the mounting of an equatorial telescope for indicating right ascension or declination

**setting–up exercise** *noun* (circa 1900)
**:** any of a series of gymnastic exercises used to give an erect carriage, supple muscles, and easy control of the limbs

¹**set·tle** \'se-t²l\ *verb* **set·tled; set·tling** \'set-liŋ, 'se-t²l-iŋ\ [Middle English, to seat, bring to rest, come to rest, from Old English *setlan*, from *setl* seat] (1515)
*transitive verb*
**1 :** to place so as to stay
**2 a :** to establish in residence **b :** to furnish with inhabitants **:** COLONIZE
**3 a :** to cause to pack down **b :** to clarify by causing dregs or impurities to sink
**4 :** to make quiet or orderly
**5 a :** to fix or resolve conclusively ⟨*settle* the question⟩ **b :** to establish or secure permanently ⟨*settle* the order of royal succession⟩ **c :** to conclude (a lawsuit) by agreement between parties usually out of court **d :** to close (as an account) by payment often of less than is due
**6 :** to arrange in a desired position
**7 :** to make or arrange for final disposition of ⟨*settled* his affairs⟩
**8** *of an animal* **:** IMPREGNATE
*intransitive verb*
**1 :** to come to rest
**2 a :** to sink gradually or to the bottom **b :** to become clear by the deposit of sediment or scum **c :** to become compact by sinking

**3 a :** to become fixed, resolved, or established ⟨a cold *settled* in his chest⟩ **b :** to establish a residence or colony ⟨*settled* in Wisconsin⟩ — often used with *down*
**4 a :** to become quiet or orderly **b :** to take up an ordered or stable life — often used with *down* ⟨marry and *settle* down⟩
**5 a :** to adjust differences or accounts **b :** to come to a decision — used with *on* or *upon* ⟨*settleed* on a new plan⟩ **c :** to conclude a lawsuit by agreement out of court
**6** *of an animal* **:** CONCEIVE
**synonym** see DECIDE
— **set·tle·able** \'se-t°l-ə-bəl, 'set-lə-bəl\ *adjective*
— **settle for :** to be content with
— **settle one's hash :** to silence or subdue someone by decisive action
— **settle the stomach :** to remove or relieve the distress or nausea of indigestion

²**set·tle** *noun* [Middle English, place for sitting, seat, chair, from Old English *setl*; akin to Old High German *sezzal* seat, Latin *sella* seat, chair, Old English *sittan* to sit] (1553)
**:** a wooden bench with arms, a high solid back, and an enclosed foundation which can be used as a chest

**settle**

**set·tle·ment** \'se-t°l-mənt\ *noun* (1648)
**1 :** the act or process of settling
**2 a :** an act of bestowing or giving possession under legal sanction **b :** the sum, estate, or income secured to one by such a settlement
**3 a :** occupation by settlers **b :** a place or region newly settled **c :** a small village
**4 :** SETTLEMENT HOUSE
**5 :** an agreement composing differences
**6 :** payment or adjustment of an account
**settlement house** *noun* (1907)
**:** an institution providing various community services especially to large city populations
**set·tler** \'set-lər, 'se-t°l-ər\ *noun* (1696)
**:** one that settles (as a new region)
**set·tling** \'set-liŋ, 'se-t°l-iŋ\ *noun* (1594)
**:** SEDIMENT, DREGS — usually used in plural
**set·tlor** \'set-ˌlȯr, 'se-t°l-ˌȯr\ *noun* (1818)
**:** one that makes a settlement or creates a trust of property
**set–to** \'set-ˌtü\ *noun, plural* **set–tos** (1743)
**:** a usually brief and vigorous fight or debate
**set to** *intransitive verb* (circa 1525)
**1 :** to begin actively and earnestly
**2 :** to begin fighting
**set·up** \'set-ˌəp\ *noun* (1890)
**1 a :** carriage of the body; *especially* **:** erect and soldierly bearing **b :** CONSTITUTION, MAKE-UP
**2 a :** the assembly and arrangement of the tools and apparatus required for the performance of an operation **b :** the preparation and adjustment of machines for an assigned task
**3 a :** a table setting **:** glass, ice, and mixer served to patrons who supply their own liquor
**4 a :** a camera position from which a scene is filmed; *also* **:** the footage taken from one camera position **b :** the final arrangement of the scenery and properties for a scene of a theatrical or cinematic production
**5 a :** a position of the balls in billiards or pool from which it is easy to score **b :** a task or contest purposely made easy **c :** something easy to get or accomplish **d :** something (as a plot) that has been constructed or contrived **e :** the execution of a planned scoring play in sports
**6 a :** the manner in which the elements or components of a machine, apparatus, or mechanical, electrical, or hydraulic system are arranged, designed, or assembled **b :** the patterns within which political, social, or administrative forces operate **:** customary or established practice

**7 :** PROJECT, PLAN
**8 :** something done by deceit or trickery in order to compromise or frame someone
**set up** (13th century)
*transitive verb*
**1 a :** to raise to and place in a high position **b :** to place in view **:** POST **c :** to put forward (as a plan) for acceptance
**2 a :** to place upright **:** ERECT ⟨*set up* a statue⟩ **b :** to assemble the parts of and erect in position ⟨*set up* a printing press⟩ **c :** to put (a machine) in readiness or adjustment for a tooling operation
**3 a :** CAUSE, CREATE ⟨*set up* a clamor⟩ **b :** BRING ABOUT
**4 :** to place in power or in office ⟨*set up* the general as dictator⟩
**5 a :** to raise from depression **:** ELATE, GRATIFY **b :** to make proud or vain
**6 a :** to put forward or extol as a model **b :** to claim oneself to be ⟨*sets* himself *up* as an authority⟩
**7 :** FOUND, INAUGURATE ⟨*set up* a home for orphans⟩
**8 a :** to provide with means of making a living ⟨*set* him *up* in business⟩ **b :** to bring or restore to normal health **c :** to cause (one) to take on a soldierly or athletic appearance especially through drill
**9 :** to erect (a perpendicular or a figure) on a base in a drawing
**10 a :** to make taut (a stay or hawser) **b :** to tighten firmly
**11 :** to make carefully worked out plans for ⟨*set up* a bank robbery⟩
**12 a :** to pay for (drinks) **b :** to treat (someone) to something
**13 a :** to put in a compromising or dangerous position usually by trickery or deceit **b :** FRAME 3
**14 :** to execute one or more plays in preparation for scoring
*intransitive verb*
**1 :** to come into active operation or use
**2 :** to begin business
**3 :** to make pretensions ⟨has never *set up* to be a wise man —Thomas Rogers⟩
**4 :** to become firm or consolidated **:** HARDEN
— **set up housekeeping :** to establish one's living quarters
— **set up shop :** to establish one's business
**sev·en** \'se-vən, 'se-b°m\ *noun* [Middle English, from *seven*, adjective, from Old English *seofon*; akin to Old High German *sibun* seven, Latin *septem*, Greek *hepta*] (before 12th century)
**1** — see NUMBER table
**2 :** the seventh in a set or series ⟨the *seven* of diamonds⟩
**3 :** something having seven units or members
— **seven** *adjective*
— **seven** *pronoun, plural in construction*
**sev·en·fold** \-ˌfōld\ *adjective* (before 12th century)
**1 :** having seven units or members
**2 :** being seven times as great or as many
— **sevenfold** *adverb*
**seven seas** *noun plural* (1872)
**:** all the waters or oceans of the world
**sev·en·teen** \ˌse-vən-'tēn, ˌse-b°m-\ *noun* [*seventeen*, adjective, from Middle English *seventene*, from Old English *seofontēne*; akin to Old English *tīen* ten] (14th century)
— see NUMBER table
— **seventeen** *adjective*
— **seventeen** *pronoun, plural in construction*
— **sev·en·teenth** \-'tēn(t)th\ *adjective or noun*
**seventeen–year locust** *noun* (1817)
**:** a cicada (*Magicicada septendecim*) of the U.S. that has in the North a life of seventeen years and in the South of thirteen years of which most is spent underground as a nymph and only a few weeks as a winged adult

**sev·enth** \'se-vən(t)th, 'se-b°m(t)th\ *noun, plural* **sevenths** \'se-vən(t)s, -vən(t)ths; 'se-b°m(t)s, -b°m(t)ths\ (12th century)
**1** — see NUMBER table
**2 a :** a musical interval embracing seven diatonic degrees **b :** a tone at this interval; *specifically* **:** LEADING TONE **c :** the harmonic combination of two tones a seventh apart
— **seventh** *adjective or adverb*
**seventh chord** *noun* (circa 1909)
**:** a chord comprising a fundamental tone with its third, fifth, and seventh
**Seventh–Day** *adjective* (1684)
**:** advocating or practicing observance of Saturday as the Sabbath
**seventh heaven** *noun* [from the seventh being the highest of the seven heavens of Islamic and cabalist doctrine] (1818)
**:** a state of extreme joy
**sev·en·ty** \'se-vən-tē, 'se-b°m-, -dē\ *noun, plural* **-ties** [*seventy*, adjective, from Middle English, from Old English *seofontig*, short for *hundseofontig*, from *hundseofontig*, noun, group of seventy, from *hund* hundred + *seofon* seven + -*tig* group of ten; akin to Old English *tīen* ten] (13th century)
**1** — see NUMBER table
**2** *plural* **:** the numbers 70 to 79; *specifically* **:** the years 70 to 79 in a lifetime or century
**3** *capitalized* **:** a Mormon elder ordained for missionary work under the apostles
— **sev·en·ti·eth** \-tē-əth, -dē-\ *adjective or noun*
— **seventy** *adjective*
— **seventy** *pronoun, plural in construction*
**sev·en·ty–eight** \ˌse-vən-tē-'āt, ˌse-b°m-, -dē-'āt\ *noun* (circa 1934)
**1** — see NUMBER table
**2 :** a phonograph record designed to be played at 78 revolutions per minute — usually written 78
— **seventy–eight** *adjective*
— **seventy–eight** *pronoun, plural in construction*
**sev·en–up** \ˌse-və-'nəp, ˌse-b°m-'əp\ *noun* (1830)
**:** an American variety of all fours in which a total of seven points constitutes game
**sev·er** \'se-vər\ *verb* **sev·ered; sev·er·ing** \'sev-riŋ, 'se-və-\ [Middle English, from Middle French *severer*, from Latin *separare* — more at SEPARATE] (14th century)
*transitive verb*
**:** to put or keep apart **:** DIVIDE; *especially* **:** to remove (as a part) by or as if by cutting
*intransitive verb*
**:** to become separated
**synonym** see SEPARATE
**sev·er·able** \'sev-rə-bəl, 'se-və-\ *adjective* (1548)
**:** capable of being severed; *especially* **:** capable of being divided into legally independent rights or obligations
— **sev·er·abil·i·ty** \ˌsev-rə-'bi-lə-tē, ˌse-və-\ *noun*
¹**sev·er·al** \'sev-rəl, 'se-və-\ *adjective* [Middle English, from Anglo-French, from Medieval Latin *separalis*, from Latin *separ* separate, back-formation from *separare* to separate] (15th century)
**1 a :** separate or distinct from one another ⟨federal union of the *several* states⟩ **b** (1) **:** individually owned or controlled **:** EXCLUSIVE ⟨a *several* fishery⟩ — compare COMMON (2) **:** of or relating separately to each individual involved ⟨a *several* judgment⟩ **c :** being separate and distinctive **:** RESPECTIVE ⟨specialists in their *several* fields⟩
**2 a :** more than one ⟨*several* pleas⟩ **b :** more than two but fewer than many ⟨moved *several*

inches⟩ **c** *chiefly dialect* **:** being a great many

²**sev·er·al** *pronoun, plural in construction* (1686)

**:** an indefinite number more than two and fewer than many ⟨*several* of the guests⟩

**sev·er·al·fold** \,sev-rəl-'fōld, -se-və-\ *adjective* (1738)

**1 :** having several parts or aspects

**2 :** being several times as large, as great, or as many as some understood size, degree, or amount

— **severalfold** *adverb*

**sev·er·al·ly** \'sev-rə-lē, 'se-və-\ *adverb* (14th century)

**1 :** one at a time **:** each by itself **:** SEPARATELY

**2 :** apart from others **:** INDEPENDENTLY

**sev·er·al·ty** \'sev-rəl-tē, 'se-və-\ *noun* [Middle English *severalte*, from Anglo-French *severalté*, from *several*] (15th century)

**1 :** the quality or state of being several **:** DISTINCTNESS, SEPARATENESS

**2 a :** a sole, separate, and exclusive possession, dominion, or ownership **:** one's own right without a joint interest in any other person ⟨tenants in *severalty*⟩ **b :** the quality or state of being individual or particular

**3 a :** land owned in severalty **b :** the quality or state of being held in severalty

**sev·er·ance** \'sev-rən(t)s, 'se-və-\ *noun* (15th century)

**:** the act or process of severing **:** the state of being severed

**severance pay** *noun* (1943)

**:** an allowance usually based on length of service that is payable to an employee on termination of employment

**severance tax** *noun* (1928)

**:** a tax levied by a state on the extractor of oil, gas, or minerals intended for consumption in other states — compare ROYALTY 5a

**se·vere** \sə-'vir\ *adjective* **se·ver·er; -est** [Middle French or Latin; Middle French, from Latin *severus*] (1548)

**1 a :** strict in judgment, discipline, or government **b :** of a strict or stern bearing or manner **:** AUSTERE

**2 :** rigorous in restraint, punishment, or requirement **:** STRINGENT, RESTRICTIVE

**3 :** strongly critical or condemnatory **:** CENSORIOUS ⟨a *severe* critic⟩

**4 a :** maintaining a scrupulously exacting standard of behavior or self-discipline **b :** establishing exacting standards of accuracy and integrity in intellectual processes ⟨a *severe* logician⟩

**5 :** sober or restrained in decoration or manner **:** PLAIN

**6 a :** inflicting physical discomfort or hardship **:** HARSH ⟨*severe* winters⟩ **b :** inflicting pain or distress **:** GRIEVOUS ⟨a *severe* wound⟩

**7 :** requiring great effort **:** ARDUOUS ⟨a *severe* test⟩

**8 :** of a great degree **:** SERIOUS ⟨*severe* depression⟩ ☆

— **se·vere·ly** *adverb*

— **se·vere·ness** *noun*

— **se·ver·i·ty** \sə-'ver-ə-tē\ *noun*

**severe combined immunodeficiency** *noun* (1974)

**:** a rare congenital disorder of the immune system that is characterized by inability to produce a normal complement of antibodies and T cells and that usually results in early death — called also *severe combined immune deficiency*

**se·vi·che** \sə-'vē-(,)chā, -chē\ *noun* [American Spanish] (1952)

**:** a dish of raw fish marinated in lime or lemon juice often with oil, onions, peppers, and seasonings and served especially as an appetizer

**Sevres** *or* **Sèvres** \'sev-rə, 'sev(r³)\ *noun* [*Sèvres*, France] (1786)

**:** an often elaborately decorated French porcelain

**sev·ru·ga** \sə-'vrü-gə, se-\ *noun* [Russian *sevryuga*, a species of sturgeon] (1591)

**:** a light to dark gray caviar from a sturgeon (*Acipenser sevru*) of the Caspian Sea that has very small roe; *also* **:** the fish

**sew** \'sō\ *verb* **sewed; sewn** \'sōn\ *or* **sewed; sew·ing** [Middle English, from Old English *sīwian*; akin to Old High German *siuwen* to sew, Latin *suere*] (before 12th century) *transitive verb*

**1 :** to unite or fasten by stitches

**2 :** to close or enclose by sewing ⟨*sew* the money in a bag⟩ *intransitive verb*

**:** to practice or engage in sewing

— **sew·abil·i·ty** \,sō-ə-'bi-lə-tē\ *noun*

— **sew·able** \'sō-ə-bəl\ *adjective*

**sew·age** \'sü-ij\ *noun* [¹*sewer*] (1834)

**:** refuse liquids or waste matter carried off by sewers

¹**sew·er** \'sü-ər, 'sü(-ə)r\ *noun* [Middle English, from Anglo-French *asseour*, literally, seater, from Old French *asseoir* to seat — more at ASSIZE] (14th century)

**:** a medieval household officer often of high rank in charge of serving the dishes at table and sometimes of seating and tasting

²**sew·er** \'sō(-ə)r\ *noun* (14th century)

**:** one that sews

³**sew·er** \'sü-ər, 'sü(-ə)r\ *noun* [Middle English, from Middle French *esseweur, seweur*, from *essewer* to drain, from (assumed) Vulgar Latin *exaquare*, from Latin *ex-* + *aqua* water — more at ISLAND] (15th century)

**:** an artificial usually subterranean conduit to carry off sewage and sometimes surface water (as from rainfall)

**sew·er·age** \'sü-ə-rij, 'sü(-ə)r-ij\ *noun* (1834)

**1 :** the removal and disposal of sewage and surface water by sewers

**2 :** a system of sewers

**3 :** SEWAGE

**sew·ing** \'sō-iŋ\ *noun* (14th century)

**1 :** the act, method, or occupation of one that sews

**2 :** material that has been or is to be sewed

**sew up** *transitive verb* (15th century)

**1 :** to mend completely by sewing

**2 :** to get exclusive use or control of

**3 :** to make certain of **:** ASSURE

¹**sex** \'seks\ *noun* [Middle English, from Latin *sexus*] (14th century)

**1 :** either of the two major forms of individuals that occur in many species and that are distinguished respectively as female or male

**2 :** the sum of the structural, functional, and behavioral characteristics of living things that are involved in reproduction by two interacting parents and that distinguish males and females

**3 a :** sexually motivated phenomena or behavior **b :** SEXUAL INTERCOURSE

**4 :** GENITALIA

²**sex** *transitive verb* (1884)

**1 :** to identify the sex of ⟨*sex* chicks⟩

**2 a :** to increase the sexual appeal of — often used with *up* **b :** to arouse the sexual desires of

**sex·a·ge·nar·i·an** \,sek-sə-jə-'ner-ē-ən\ *noun* [Latin *sexagenarius* of or containing sixty, sixty years old, from *sexageni* sixty each, from *sexaginta* sixty, from *sex* six + *-ginta* (akin to Latin *viginti* twenty) — more at SIX, VIGESIMAL] (1738)

**:** a person whose age is in the sixties

— **sexagenarian** *adjective*

¹**sex·a·ges·i·mal** \-'je-sə-məl\ *adjective* [Latin *sexagesimus* sixtieth, from *sexaginta* sixty] (1685)

**:** of, relating to, or based on the number 60

²**sexagesimal** *noun* (1685)

**:** a sexagesimal fraction

**sex appeal** *noun* (1924)

**1 :** personal appeal or physical attractiveness for members of the opposite sex

**2 :** general attractiveness

**sex cell** *noun* (1889)

**:** GAMETE; *also* **:** its cellular precursor

**sex chromatin** *noun* (1952)

**:** BARR BODY

**sex chromosome** *noun* (1906)

**:** a chromosome that is inherited differently in the two sexes, that is concerned directly with the inheritance of sex, and that is the seat of factors governing the inheritance of various sex-linked and sex-limited characters

**sex·de·cil·lion** \,seks-di-'sil-yən\ *noun, often attributive* [Latin *sedecim, sexdecim* sixteen (from *sex* six + *decem* ten) + English *-illion* (as in *million*) — more at TEN] (circa 1934)

— see NUMBER table

**sexed** \'sekst\ *adjective* (circa 1891)

**1 :** having sex or sexual instincts

**2 :** having sex appeal

**sex gland** *noun* (1935)

**:** GONAD

**sex hormone** *noun* (1917)

**:** a hormone (as from the gonads or adrenal cortex) that affects the growth or function of the reproductive organs or the development of secondary sex characteristics

**sex·ism** \'sek-,si-zəm\ *noun* [¹*sex* + *-ism* (as in *racism*)] (1968)

**1 :** prejudice or discrimination based on sex; *especially* **:** discrimination against women

**2 :** behavior, conditions, or attitudes that foster stereotypes of social roles based on sex

— **sex·ist** \'sek-sist\ *adjective or noun*

**sex kitten** *noun* (1958)

**:** a young woman with conspicuous sex appeal

**sex·less** \'seks-ləs\ *adjective* (1598)

**1 :** lacking sex **:** NEUTER

**2 :** devoid of sexual interest or activity ⟨a *sexless* relationship⟩

— **sex·less·ly** *adverb*

— **sex·less·ness** *noun*

**sex–lim·it·ed** \'seks-'li-mə-təd\ *adjective* (1923)

**:** expressed in the phenotype of only one sex

**sex–link·age** \-,liŋ-kij\ *noun* (1912)

**:** the quality or state of being sex-linked

**sex–linked** \-,liŋ(k)t\ *adjective* (1912)

**1 :** located on a sex chromosome ⟨a *sex-linked* gene⟩

**2 :** mediated by a sex-linked gene ⟨a *sex-linked* character⟩

**sex object** *noun* (1911)

**:** a person regarded especially exclusively as an object of sexual interest

**sex·ol·o·gy** \sek-'sä-lə-jē\ *noun* (1902)

**:** the study of sex or of the interaction of the sexes especially among human beings

— **sex·ol·o·gist** \-jist\ *noun*

**sex·ploi·ta·tion** \,seks-,plȯi-'tā-shən\ *noun* [blend of *sex* and *exploitation*] (circa 1942)

**:** the exploitation of sex in the media and especially in film

**sex·pot** \'seks-,pät\ *noun* (1948)

**:** a conspicuously sexy woman

**sex symbol** *noun* (circa 1911)

**:** a usually renowned person (as an entertainer) noted and admired for conspicuous sex appeal

**sext** \'sekst\ *noun, often capitalized* [Middle English *sexte*, from Late Latin *sexta*, from

---

☆ **SYNONYMS**

**Severe, stern, austere, ascetic** mean given to or marked by strict discipline and firm restraint. SEVERE implies standards enforced without indulgence or laxity and may suggest harshness ⟨*severe* military discipline⟩. STERN stresses inflexibility and inexorability of temper or character ⟨*stern* arbiters of public morality⟩. AUSTERE stresses absence of warmth, color, or feeling and may apply to rigorous restraint, simplicity, or self-denial ⟨living an *austere* life in the country⟩. ASCETIC implies abstention from pleasure and comfort or self-indulgence as spiritual discipline ⟨the *ascetic* life of the monastic orders⟩.

Latin, sixth hour of the day, from feminine of *sextus* sixth, from *sex* six] (15th century)
: the fourth of the canonical hours

**Sex·tans** \'seks-ˌtanz\ *noun* [New Latin (genitive *Sextantis*), literally, sextant]
: a constellation on the equator south of Leo

**sex·tant** \'seks-tənt\ *noun* [New Latin *sextant-, sextans* sixth part of a circle, from Latin, sixth part, from *sextus* sixth] (1628)
: an instrument for measuring angular distances used especially in navigation to observe altitudes of celestial bodies (as in ascertaining latitude and longitude)

**sextant**

**sex·tet** \seks-'tet\ *noun* [alteration of *sestet*] (1841)
**1** : a musical composition for six instruments or voices
**2** : a group or set of six: as **a** : the performers of a sextet **b** : a hockey team

**sex·til·lion** \seks-'til-yən\ *noun, often attributive* [French, irregular from *sex-* (from Latin *sex*) + *-illion* (as in *million*)] (1690)
— see NUMBER table

**sex·to** \'seks-(ˌ)tō\ *noun, plural* **sextos** [Latin *sexto*, ablative of *sextus* sixth] (1847)
: SIXMO

**sex·to·dec·i·mo** \ˌseks-tə-'de-sə-ˌmō\ *noun, plural* **-mos** [Latin, ablative of *sextus decimus* sixteenth, from *sextus* sixth + *decimus* tenth — more at DIME] (1688)
: SIXTEENMO

**sex·ton** \'seks-tən\ *noun* [Middle English *secresteyn, sexteyn*, from Middle French *secrestain*, from Medieval Latin *sacristan* — more at SACRISTAN] (14th century)
: a church officer or employee who takes care of the church property and performs related minor duties (as ringing the bell for services and digging graves)

**¹sex·tu·ple** \seks-'tü-pəl, -'tyü-, -'tə-; 'seks-tə-\ *adjective* [probably from Medieval Latin *sextuplus*, from Latin *sextus* sixth + *-plus* multiplied by; akin to Latin *-plex -plex* — more at -FOLD] (1626)
**1** : having six units or members
**2** : being six times as great or as many
**3** : marked by six beats per measure of music ⟨*sextuple* time⟩
— **sextuple** *noun*

**²sextuple** *verb* **sex·tu·pled; sex·tu·pling** \-p(ə-)liŋ\ (1632)
*transitive verb*
: to make six times as much or as many
*intransitive verb*
: to become six times as much or as numerous

**sex·tu·plet** \seks-'tə-plət, -'tü-; -'tyü-; 'seks-t(y)ə-\ *noun* (1852)
**1** : a combination of six of a kind
**2** : one of six offspring born at one birth
**3** : a group of six equal musical notes performed in the time ordinarily given to four of the same value

**¹sex·tu·pli·cate** \seks-'tü-pli-kət, -'tyü-\ *adjective* [blend of *sextuple* and *-plicate* (as in *duplicate*)] (1657)
**1** : repeated six times
**2** : SIXTH ⟨file the *sextuplicate* copy⟩
— **sextuplicate** *noun*

**²sex·tu·pli·cate** \-plə-ˌkāt\ *transitive verb* **-cat·ed; -cat·ing** (circa 1934)
**1** : SEXTUPLE
**2** : to provide in sextuplicate

**sex·u·al** \'sek-sh(ə-)wəl, 'sek-shəl\ *adjective* [Late Latin *sexualis*, from Latin *sexus* sex] (1651)
**1** : of, relating to, or associated with sex or the sexes ⟨*sexual* differentiation⟩ ⟨*sexual* conflict⟩
**2** : having or involving sex ⟨*sexual* reproduction⟩

— **sex·u·al·ly** \'sek-sh(ə-)wə-lē, 'sek-sh(ə-)lē\ *adverb*

**sexual generation** *noun* (1880)
: the generation of an organism with alternation of generations that reproduces sexually

**sexual harassment** *noun* (1975)
: uninvited and unwelcome verbal or physical conduct directed at an employee because of his or her sex

**sexual intercourse** *noun* (1799)
**1** : heterosexual intercourse involving penetration of the vagina by the penis : COITUS
**2** : intercourse involving genital contact between individuals other than penetration of the vagina by the penis

**sex·u·al·i·ty** \ˌsek-shə-'wa-lə-tē\ *noun* (circa 1800)
: the quality or state of being sexual: **a** : the condition of having sex **b** : sexual activity **c** : expression of sexual receptivity or interest especially when excessive

**sex·u·al·ize** \'sek-sh(ə-)wə-ˌlīz, 'sek-shə-ˌlīz\ *transitive verb* **-ized; -iz·ing** (1839)
: to make sexual : endow with a sexual character or cast

**sexual relations** *noun plural* (1950)
: COITUS

**sexual selection** *noun* (1859)
: natural selection for characters that confer success in competition for a mate as distinguished from competition with other species; *also* : the choice of a mate based on a preference for certain characteristics (as color or bird song)

**sexy** \'sek-sē\ *adjective* **sex·i·er; -est** (1925)
**1** : sexually suggestive or stimulating : EROTIC
**2** : generally attractive or interesting : APPEALING ⟨a *sexy* stock⟩
— **sex·i·ly** \-sə-lē\ *adverb*
— **sex·i·ness** \-sē-nəs\ *noun*

**Sey·fert galaxy** \'sē-fərt- *also* 'sī-\ *noun* [Carl K. *Seyfert* (died 1960) American astronomer] (1959)
: any of a class of spiral galaxies that have small compact bright nuclei characterized by variability in light intensity, emission of radio waves, and spectra which indicate hot gases in rapid motion — called also *Seyfert*

**sfer·ics** \'sfir-iks, 'sfer-\ *noun plural* [by shortening & alteration] (1945)
: ATMOSPHERICS

**¹sfor·zan·do** \sfȯrt-'sän-(ˌ)dō, -'san-\ *adjective or adverb* [Italian, verbal of *sforzare* to force] (circa 1801)
: played with prominent stress or accent — used as a direction in music

**²sforzando** *noun, plural* **-dos** *or* **-di** \-(ˌ)dē\ (1890)
: an accented tone or chord

**sfu·ma·to** \sfü-'mä-(ˌ)tō\ *noun* [Italian, from past participle of *sfumare* to evaporate] (1909)
: the definition of form in painting without abrupt outline by the blending of one tone into another

**sgraf·fi·to** \zgra-'fē-(ˌ)tō, skra-\ *noun, plural* **-ti** \-(ˌ)tē\ [Italian, from past participle of *sgraffire* to scratch, produce sgraffito] (circa 1730)
**1** : decoration by cutting away parts of a surface layer (as of plaster or clay) to expose a different colored ground — compare GRAFFITO
**2** : something (as traditional Pennsylvania Dutch pottery) decorated with sgraffito

**sh** \sh *often prolonged*\ *interjection* (1847)
— used often in prolonged or rapidly repeated form to urge or command silence or less noise

**Sha·'ban** \shə-'bän\ *noun* [Arabic *sha'bān*] (circa 1771)
: the 8th month of the Islamic year — see MONTH table

**Shab·bat** \shə-'bät, 'shä-bəs\ *noun* [Hebrew *shabbāth*] (circa 1905)
: the Jewish Sabbath

**shab·by** \'sha-bē\ *adjective* **shab·bi·er; -est** [obsolete English *shab* a low fellow] (1669)

**1** : clothed with worn or seedy garments ⟨a *shabby* hobo⟩
**2 a** : threadbare and faded from wear ⟨a *shabby* sofa⟩ **b** : ill-kept : DILAPIDATED ⟨a *shabby* neighborhood⟩
**3 a** : MEAN, DESPICABLE, CONTEMPTIBLE ⟨must feel *shabby* . . . because of his compromises —Nat Hentoff⟩ **b** : UNGENEROUS, UNFAIR ⟨laments the *shabby* way in which this country often treated a poet —Paul Engle⟩ **c** : inferior in quality ⟨*shabby* reasoning⟩
— **shab·bi·ly** \'sha-bə-lē\ *adverb*
— **shab·bi·ness** \'sha-bē-nəs\ *noun*

**Sha·bu·oth** \shä-'vü-ˌȯt, -ˌōth, -ˌōs, -əs\ *noun* [Hebrew *shābhū'ōth*, literally, weeks] (circa 1903)
: a Jewish holiday observed on the 6th and 7th of Sivan in commemoration of the revelation of the Ten Commandments at Mount Sinai — called also *Pentecost*

**shack** \'shak\ *noun* [probably back-formation from English dialect *shackly* rickety] (1878)
**1** : HUT, SHANTY
**2** : a room or similar enclosed structure for a particular person or use ⟨a guard *shack*⟩

**¹shack·le** \'sha-kəl\ *noun* [Middle English *schakel*, from Old English *sceacul*; akin to Old Norse *skǫkull* pole of a cart] (before 12th century)
**1** : something (as a manacle or fetter) that confines the legs or arms
**2** : something that checks or prevents free action as if by fetters — usually used in plural
**3** : a usually U-shaped fastening device secured by a bolt or pin through holes in the end of the two arms
**4** : a length of cable or anchor chain of usually 15 fathoms

**²shackle** *transitive verb* **shack·led; shack·ling** \-k(ə-)liŋ\ (15th century)
**1 a** : to bind with shackles : FETTER **b** : to make fast with or as if with a shackle
**2** : to deprive of freedom especially of action by means of restrictions or handicaps : IMPEDE
*synonym* see HAMPER
— **shack·ler** \-k(ə-)lər\ *noun*

**shack·le·bone** \'sha-kəl-ˌbōn, 'shä-\ *noun* (1571)
*Scottish* : WRIST

**shack up** *intransitive verb* (1935)
: to sleep or live together as unmarried sexual partners

**shad** \'shad\ *noun, plural* **shad** [(assumed) Middle English, from Old English *sceadd*] (before 12th century)
: any of several clupeid fishes (especially genus *Alosa*) that differ from the typical herrings in having a relatively deep body and in being anadromous and that include some important food fishes of Europe and North America

**shad·ber·ry** \-ˌber-ē\ *noun* (1847)
: SERVICEBERRY

**shad·blow** \'shad-ˌblō\ *noun* (1846)
: SERVICEBERRY 2

**shad·bush** \-ˌbush\ *noun* (circa 1818)
: SERVICEBERRY 2

**shad·dock** \'sha-dək\ *noun* [Captain *Shaddock*, 17th century English ship commander] (1696)
: a very large thick-rinded usually pear-shaped citrus fruit differing from the closely related grapefruit especially in its loose rind and often coarse dry pulp; *also* : the tree (*Citrus maxima* synonym *C. grandis*) that bears it

**¹shade** \'shād\ *noun* [Middle English, from Old English *sceadu*; akin to Old High German *scato* shadow, Greek *skotos* darkness] (before 12th century)

**1 a :** comparative darkness or obscurity owing to interception of the rays of light **b :** relative obscurity or retirement
**2 a :** shelter (as by foliage) from the heat and glare of sunlight **b :** a place sheltered from the sun
**3 :** an evanescent or unreal appearance
**4** *plural* **a :** the shadows that gather as darkness comes on **b :** NETHERWORLD, HADES
**5 a :** a disembodied spirit **:** GHOST **b** — used to signal the similarity between a previously encountered person or situation and one at hand; usually used in plural ⟨*shades* of my childhood⟩
**6 :** something that intercepts or shelters from light, sun, or heat: as **a :** a device partially covering a lamp so as to reduce glare **b :** a flexible screen usually mounted on a roller for regulating the light or the view through a window **c** *plural* **:** SUNGLASSES
**7 a :** the reproduction of the effect of shade in painting or drawing **b :** a subdued or somber feature
**8 a :** a color produced by a pigment or dye mixture having some black in it **b :** a color slightly different from the one under consideration
**9 a :** a minute difference or variation **:** NUANCE **b :** a minute degree or quantity
**10 :** a facial expression of sadness or displeasure
— **shade·less** \-ləs\ *adjective*
**²shade** *verb* **shad·ed; shad·ing** (14th century)
*transitive verb*
**1 a :** to shelter or screen by intercepting radiated light or heat **b :** to cover with a shade
**2 :** to hide partly by or as if by a shadow
**3 :** to darken with or as if with a shadow
**4 :** to better or exceed by a shade **:** SURPASS, ECLIPSE
**5 a :** to represent the effect of shade or shadow on **b :** to add shading to **c :** to color so that the shades pass gradually from one to another
**6 :** to change by gradual transition or qualification
**7 :** to reduce slightly (as a price)
**8 :** SLANT, BIAS
*intransitive verb*
**1 :** to pass by slight changes or imperceptible degrees
**2 :** to undergo or exhibit minute difference or variation
— **shad·er** *noun*
**shade–grown** \'shād-ˌgrōn\ *adjective* (1922)
**:** grown in the shade; *specifically* **:** grown under cloth ⟨*shade-grown* tobacco⟩
**shade tree** *noun* (1806)
**:** a tree grown primarily to produce shade
**shad·ing** \'shā-diŋ\ *noun* (1663)
**1 :** the use of marking made within outlines to suggest three-dimensionality, shadow, or degrees of light and dark in a picture or drawing
**2 :** an interpretative effect in music gained especially by subtle changes in dynamics
**sha·doof** *also* **sha·duf** \shə-'düf, sha-\ *noun* [Arabic *shādūf*] (1836)
**:** a counterbalanced sweep used since ancient times especially in Egypt for raising water (as for irrigation)
**¹shad·ow** \'sha-(ˌ)dō\ *noun* [Middle English *shadwe*, from Old English *sceaduw-, sceadu* shade] (before 12th century)
**1 :** partial darkness or obscurity within a part of space from which rays from a source of light are cut off by an interposed opaque body
**2 :** a reflected image
**3 :** shelter from danger or observation
**4 a :** an imperfect and faint representation **b :** an imitation of something **:** COPY
**5 :** the dark figure cast upon a surface by a body intercepting the rays from a source of light
**6 :** PHANTOM
**7** *plural* **:** DARK 1a
**8 :** a shaded or darker portion of a picture

**9 :** an attenuated form or a vestigial remnant
**10 a :** an inseparable companion or follower **b :** one (as a spy or detective) that shadows
**11 :** a small degree or portion **:** TRACE
**12 :** a source of gloom or unhappiness
**13 a :** an area near an object **:** VICINITY **b :** pervasive and dominant influence
**14 :** a state of ignominy or obscurity
— **shad·ow·less** \'sha-dō-ləs, -də-ləs\ *adjective*
— **shad·ow·like** \-ˌlīk\ *adjective*
**²shadow** (before 12th century)
*transitive verb*
**1** *archaic* **:** SHELTER, PROTECT
**2 :** to cast a shadow upon **:** CLOUD
**3** *obsolete* **:** to shelter from the sun
**4** *obsolete* **:** CONCEAL
**5 :** to represent or indicate obscurely or faintly — often used with *forth* or *out*
**6 :** to follow especially secretly **:** TRAIL
**7** *archaic* **:** SHADE 5
*intransitive verb*
**1 :** to pass gradually or by degrees
**2 :** to become overcast with or as if with shadows
— **shad·ow·er** \-dō-ər, -də-wər\ *noun*
**³shadow** *adjective* (1906)
**1 :** of, relating to, or resembling a shadow cabinet ⟨*shadow* minister of defense⟩
**2 a :** having an indistinct pattern ⟨*shadow* plaid⟩ **b :** having darker sections of design ⟨*shadow* lace⟩
**shadow band** *noun* (1900)
**:** one of a series of dark narrow parallel bands that appear to rush swiftly across the landscape just before or after totality in a solar eclipse
**shad·ow·box** \'sha-dō-ˌbäks, -də-ˌbäks\ *intransitive verb* (1919)
**:** to box with an imaginary opponent especially as a form of training
**shadow box** *noun* (circa 1909)
**:** a shallow enclosing case usually with a glass front in which something is set for protection and display
**shadow cabinet** *noun* (1906)
**:** a group of leaders of a parliamentary opposition who constitute the probable membership of the cabinet when their party is returned to power
**shadow dance** *noun* (circa 1909)
**:** a dance shown by throwing the shadows of dancers on a screen
**shad·ow·graph** \'sha-dō-ˌgraf, -də-ˌgraf\ *noun* (1888)
**1 :** SHADOW PLAY
**2 :** a photographic image resembling a shadow
— **shad·ow·graphy** \-ˌgra-fē\ *noun*
**shadow mask** *noun* (1951)
**:** a metal plate in a color television tube that contains minute apertures permitting passage of electron beams to specific phosphors on the screen during a scan
**shadow play** *noun* (1895)
**:** a drama exhibited by throwing shadows of puppets or actors on a screen — called also *shadow show*
**shad·owy** \'sha-dō-ē, -də-wē\ *adjective* (14th century)
**1 a :** of the nature of or resembling a shadow **:** UNSUBSTANTIAL **b :** faintly perceptible **:** INDISTINCT, VAGUE
**2 :** being in or obscured by shadow ⟨deep *shadowy* interiors⟩
**3 :** SHADY 1, 3
— **shad·ow·i·ly** \-wə-lē\ *adverb*
— **shad·ow·i·ness** \-wē-nəs\ *noun*
**shady** \'shā-dē\ *adjective* **shad·i·er; -est** (1579)
**1 :** producing or affording shade
**2 :** sheltered from the sun's rays
**3 a :** of questionable merit **:** UNCERTAIN, UNRELIABLE **b :** DISREPUTABLE
— **shad·i·ly** \'shā-dᵊl-ē\ *adverb*
— **shad·i·ness** \'shā-dē-nəs\ *noun*

**¹shaft** \'shaft\ *noun, plural* **shafts** \'shaf(t)s\, *for 1b usually* 'shavz\ [Middle English, from Old English *sceaft;* akin to Old High German *scaft* shaft, Latin *scapus* shaft, stalk, Greek *skēptesthai* to prop oneself, lean] (before 12th century)
**1 a** (1) **:** the long handle of a spear or similar weapon (2) **:** SPEAR, LANCE **b** *or plural* **shaves** \'shavz\ **:** POLE; *specifically* **:** either of two long pieces of wood between which a horse is hitched to a vehicle **c** (1) **:** an arrow especially for a longbow (2) **:** the body or stem of an arrow extending from the nock to the head
**2 :** a sharply delineated beam of light shining through an opening
**3 :** something suggestive of the shaft of a spear or arrow especially in long slender cylindrical form: as **a :** the trunk of a tree **b :** the cylindrical pillar between the capital and the base **c :** the handle of a tool or instrument (as a golf club) **d :** a commonly cylindrical bar used to support rotating pieces or to transmit power or motion by rotation **e :** the stem or central axis of a feather **f :** the upright member of a cross especially below the arms **g :** a small architectural column (as at each side of a doorway) **h :** a column, obelisk, or other spire-shaped or columnar monument **i :** a vertical or inclined opening of uniform and limited cross section made for finding or mining ore, raising water, or ventilating underground workings (as in a cave) **j :** a vertical opening or passage through the floors of a building
**4 a :** a projectile thrown like a spear or shot like an arrow **b :** a scornful, satirical, or pithily critical remark or attack **c :** harsh or unfair treatment — usually used with *the*
**²shaft** *transitive verb* (1611)
**1 :** to fit with a shaft
**2 :** to treat unfairly or harshly
**shaft horsepower** *noun* (1908)
**:** horsepower transmitted by an engine shaft
**shaft·ing** \'shaf-tiŋ\ *noun* (1825)
**:** shafts or material for shafts
**¹shag** \'shag\ *noun* [(assumed) Middle English *shagge*, from Old English *sceacga;* akin to Old Norse *skegg* beard, *skaga* to project] (before 12th century)
**1 a :** a shaggy tangled mass or covering (as of hair) **b :** long coarse or matted fiber, nap, or pile
**2 :** tobacco cut into fine shreds
**3 :** CORMORANT 1
**²shag** *adjective* (1592)
**:** SHAGGY
**³shag** *verb* **shagged; shag·ging** (1596)
*intransitive verb*
**:** to fall or hang in shaggy masses
*transitive verb*
**:** to make rough or shaggy
**⁴shag** *transitive verb* **shagged; shag·ging** [origin unknown] (1904)
**1 a :** to chase after; *especially* **:** to chase after and return (a ball) hit usually out of play **b :** to catch (a fly) in baseball practice
**2 :** to chase away
**⁵shag** *intransitive verb* **shagged; shag·ging** [perhaps alteration of *shack* to lumber along] (1914)
**1 :** to move or lope along
**2 :** to dance the shag
**⁶shag** *noun* (1932)
**:** a dance step executed by hopping livelily on each foot in turn
**shag·bark** \'shag-ˌbärk\ *noun* (1777)
**:** SHAGBARK HICKORY
**shagbark hickory** *noun* (1751)
**:** a hickory (*Carya ovata*) with sweet edible nuts and a gray shaggy outer bark that peels off in long strips; *also* **:** its wood
**shag·gy** \'sha-gē\ *adjective* **shag·gi·er; -est** (circa 1590)

**1 a :** covered with or consisting of long, coarse, or matted hair **b :** covered with or consisting of thick, tangled, or unkempt vegetation **c :** having a rough nap, texture, or surface **d :** having hairlike processes
**2 a :** UNKEMPT **b :** confused or unclear in conception or thinking
— **shag·gi·ly** \'sha-gə-lē\ *adverb*
— **shag·gi·ness** \'sha-gē-nəs\ *noun*
**shag·gy-dog story** \,sha-gē-'dȯg-\ *noun* (1946)
**:** a long-drawn-out circumstantial story concerning an inconsequential happening that impresses the teller as humorous but the hearer as boring and pointless; *also* : a similar humorous story whose humor lies in the pointlessness or irrelevance of the punch line
**shag·gy·mane** \'sha-gē-,mān\ *noun* (circa 1909)
**:** a common edible mushroom (*Coprinus comatus*) having an elongated shaggy white pileus with deliquescing gills and black spores — called also *shaggy cap*
**sha·green** \sha-'grēn, shə-\ *noun* [by folk etymology from French *chagrin*, modification of Turkish *saǧrı*] (1677)
**1 :** an untanned leather covered with small round granulations and usually dyed green
**2 :** the rough skin of various sharks and rays when covered with small close-set tubercles
— **shagreen** *adjective*

**shaggymane**

**shah** \'shä, 'shȯ\ *noun, often capitalized* [Persian *shāh* king — more at CHECK] (1566)
**:** a sovereign of Iran
— **shah·dom** \'shä-dəm, 'shȯ-\ *noun*
**Sha·hap·ti·an** \shə-'hap-tē-ən\ *noun, plural* **Shahaptian** *or* **Shahaptians** (1836)
**1 :** a member of a group of American Indian peoples who formerly inhabited a large territory along the Columbia River and its tributaries
**2 :** the language of the Shahaptian people including Nez Percé and Yakima
**shai·tan** \shā-'tän, shī-\ *noun* [Arabic *shayṭān*] (1638)
**:** an evil spirit; *specifically* : an evil jinni
¹**shake** \'shāk\ *verb* **shook** \'shu̇k\; **shak·en** \'shā-kən\; **shak·ing** [Middle English, from Old English *sceacan;* akin to Old Norse *skaka* to shake] (before 12th century)
*intransitive verb*
**1 :** to move irregularly to and fro
**2 :** to vibrate especially as the result of a blow or shock
**3 :** to tremble as a result of physical or emotional disturbance
**4 :** to experience a state of instability : TOTTER
**5 :** to briskly move something to and fro or up and down especially in order to mix
**6 :** to clasp hands
**7 :** ³TRILL
*transitive verb*
**1 :** to brandish, wave, or flourish often in a threatening manner
**2 :** to cause to move in a usually quick jerky manner
**3 :** to cause to quake, quiver, or tremble
**4 a :** to free oneself from ⟨*shake* a habit⟩ ⟨*shake* off a cold⟩ **b :** to get away from : get rid of ⟨can you *shake* your friend? I want to talk to you alone —Elmer Davis⟩
**5 :** to lessen the stability of : WEAKEN ⟨*shake* one's faith⟩
**6 :** to bring to a specified condition by or as if by repeated quick jerky movements ⟨*shook* himself loose from the man's grasp⟩
**7 :** to dislodge or eject by quick jerky movements ⟨*shook* the dust from the cloth⟩
**8 :** to clasp (hands) in greeting or farewell or as a sign of goodwill or agreement
**9 :** to stir the feelings of : UPSET ⟨*shook* her up⟩

**10 :** ³TRILL ☆
— **shak·able** *or* **shake·able** \'shā-kə-bəl\ *adjective*
— **shake a leg 1 :** DANCE **2 :** to hurry up
²**shake** *noun* (1581)
**1 :** an act of shaking: as **a :** an act of shaking hands **b :** an act of shaking oneself
**2 a :** a blow or shock that upsets the equilibrium or disturbs the balance of something **b :** EARTHQUAKE
**3** *plural* **a :** a condition of trembling or nervousness; *specifically* : DELIRIUM TREMENS **b :** MALARIA 2a
**4 :** something produced by shaking: as **a :** a fissure separating annual rings of growth in timber **b** (1) : MILK SHAKE (2) : a beverage resembling a milk shake but made without milk
**5 :** a wavering, quivering, or alternating motion caused by a blow or shock
**6 :** TRILL
**7 :** a very brief period of time
**8** *plural* **:** one that is exceptional especially in importance, ability, or merit — usually used in the phrase *no great shakes*
**9 :** a shingle split from a piece of log usually three or four feet (about one meter) long
**10 :** ³DEAL 3 ⟨a fair *shake*⟩
**shake·down** \'shāk-,dau̇n\ *noun* (circa 1730)
**1 :** an improvised bed (as one made up on the floor)
**2 :** a boisterous dance
**3 :** an act or instance of shaking someone down; *especially* : EXTORTION
**4 :** a thorough search
**5 :** a process or period of adjustment
**6 :** a testing under operating conditions of something new (as a ship) for possible faults and defects and for familiarizing the operators with it
**shake down** (circa 1859)
*intransitive verb*
**1 a :** to take up temporary quarters **b :** to occupy an improvised or makeshift bed
**2 a :** to become accustomed especially to new surroundings or duties **b :** to settle down
*transitive verb*
**1 :** to obtain money from in a deceitful or illegal manner
**2 :** to make a thorough search of
**3 :** to bring about a reduction of
**4 :** to give a shakedown test to
**shake·out** \'shā-,kau̇t\ *noun* (1895)
**1 :** the failure or retrenchment of a significant number of firms in the economy or a sector or an industry that usually results in a depressed market
**2 :** a period or process in which the relatively weak or unessential are eliminated
**shak·er** \'shā-kər\ *noun* (15th century)
**1 :** one that shakes: as **a :** a utensil or machine used in shaking ⟨cocktail *shaker*⟩ **b :** one that incites, promotes, or directs action ⟨a mover and *shaker*⟩
**2** *capitalized* [from a dance with shaking movements performed as part of worship] **:** a member of a millenarian sect originating in England in 1747 and practicing celibacy and an ascetic communal life
— **Shaker** *adjective*
— **Shak·er·ism** \-kə-,ri-zəm\ *noun*
¹**Shake·spear·ean** *or* **Shake·spear·ian** *also* **Shak·sper·ean** *or* **Shak·sper·ian** \shāk-'spir-ē-ən\ *adjective* (1755)
**1 :** of, relating to, or having the characteristics of Shakespeare or his writings
**2 :** evocative of a theme, setting, or event from a work of Shakespeare ⟨*Shakespearean* pageantry⟩
²**Shakespearean** *or* **Shakespearian** *also* **Shaksperean** *or* **Shaksperian** *noun* (1837)
**:** an authority on or devotee of Shakespeare
**Shake·spear·eana** *or* **Shake·spear·iana** \(,)shāk-,spir-ē-'a-nə, -'ä-, -'ā-\ *noun plural* (1718)

**:** collected items by, about, or relating to Shakespeare
**Shakespearean sonnet** *noun* (1903)
**:** ENGLISH SONNET
**shake-up** \'shā-,kəp\ *noun* (1847)
**:** an act or instance of shaking up; *specifically* : an extensive and often drastic reorganization
**shake up** *transitive verb* (1538)
**1** *obsolete* **:** CHIDE, SCOLD
**2 :** to jar by or as if by a physical shock ⟨the collision *shook up* both drivers⟩
**3 :** to effect an extensive and often drastic reorganization of
**shaking palsy** *noun* (1615)
**:** PARKINSON'S DISEASE
**sha·ko** \'sha-(,)kō, 'shā-, 'shä-\ *noun, plural* **shakos** *or* **shakoes** [French, from Hungarian *csákó*] (1815)
**:** a stiff military hat with a high crown and plume
**Shak·ta** \'shäk-tə, 'säk-\ *noun or adjective* [Sanskrit *śākta*, from *Śakti*] (1810)
**:** an adherent of Shaktism
**Shak·ti** \-tē\ *noun* [Sanskrit *Śakti*] (1810)
**:** the dynamic energy of a Hindu god personified as his female consort; *broadly* : cosmic energy as conceived in Hindu thought
**Shak·tism** \-,ti-zəm\ *noun* (1877)
**:** a Hindu sect worshiping Shakti under various names (as Kali or Durga) in a cult of devotion to the female principle often with magical or orgiastic rites
**shaky** \'shā-kē\ *adjective* **shak·i·er; -est** (1703)
**1 :** characterized by shakes ⟨*shaky* timber⟩
**2 a :** lacking stability : PRECARIOUS **b :** lacking in firmness (as of beliefs or principles) **c :** lacking in authority or reliability : QUESTIONABLE
**3 a :** somewhat unsound in health **b :** characterized by shaking
**4 :** likely to give way or break down
— **shak·i·ly** \-kə-lē\ *adverb*
— **shak·i·ness** \-kē-nəs\ *noun*
**shale** \'shā(ə)l\ *noun* [probably from obsolete or dialect *shale* scale, shell, from Middle English, from Old English *scealu* — more at SHELL] (1747)
**:** a fissile rock that is formed by the consolidation of clay, mud, or silt, has a finely stratified or laminated structure, and is composed of minerals essentially unaltered since deposition
— **shal·ey** \'shā-lē\ *adjective*
**shale oil** *noun* (1857)
**:** a crude dark oil obtained from oil shale by heating
**shall** \shəl, 'shal\ *verb, past* **should** \shəd, 'shu̇d\; *present singular & plural* **shall** [Middle English *shal* (1st & 3d singular present indicative), from Old English *sceal;* akin to Old High German *scal* (1st & 3d singular present indicative) ought to, must, Lithuanian *skola* debt] (before 12th century)

---

☆ **SYNONYMS**
**Shake, agitate, rock, convulse** mean to move up and down or to and fro with some violence. SHAKE often carries a further implication of a particular purpose ⟨*shake* well before using⟩. AGITATE suggests a violent and prolonged tossing or stirring ⟨an ocean *agitated* by storms⟩. ROCK suggests a swinging or swaying motion resulting from violent impact or upheaval ⟨the whole city was *rocked* by the explosion⟩. CONVULSE suggests a violent pulling or wrenching as of a body in a paroxysm ⟨spectators were *convulsed* with laughter⟩.

---

\ə\ abut \ᵊ\ kitten \ər\ further \a\ ash \ā\ ace
\ä\ mop, mar \au̇\ out \ch\ chin \e\ bet \ē\ easy
\g\ go \i\ hit \ī\ ice \j\ job \ŋ\ sing \ō\ go
\ȯ\ law \ȯi\ boy \th\ thin \t͟h\ the \ü\ loot \u̇\ foot
\y\ yet \zh\ vision    *see also* Guide to Pronunciation

*verbal auxiliary*
**1** *archaic* **a :** will have to **:** MUST **b :** will be able to **:** CAN
**2 a** — used to express a command or exhortation ⟨you *shall* go⟩ **b** — used in laws, regulations, or directives to express what is mandatory ⟨it *shall* be unlawful to carry firearms⟩
**3 a** — used to express what is inevitable or seems likely to happen in the future ⟨we *shall* have to be ready⟩ ⟨we *shall* see⟩ **b** — used to express simple futurity ⟨when *shall* we expect you⟩
**4** — used to express determination ⟨they *shall* not pass⟩
*intransitive verb*
*archaic* **:** will go ⟨he to England *shall* along with you —Shakespeare⟩ ■
**shal·loon** \shə-'lün, sha-\ *noun* [*Châlons*-sur-Marne, France] (1678)
**:** a lightweight twilled fabric of wool or worsted used chiefly for the linings of coats and uniforms
**shal·lop** \'sha-ləp\ *noun* [Middle French *chaloupe*] (circa 1578)
**1 :** a usually 2-masted ship with lugsails
**2 :** a small open boat propelled by oars or sails and used chiefly in shallow waters
**shal·lot** \shə-'lät *also* 'sha-lət\ *noun* [modification of French *échalote*, from Middle French *eschalotte*, alteration of *eschaloigne*, from (assumed) Vulgar Latin *escalonia* — more at SCALLION] (1664)
**1 :** a bulbous perennial herb (*Allium cepa aggregatum*) that resembles an onion and produces small clustered bulbs used in seasoning
**2 :** GREEN ONION
**¹shal·low** \'sha-(ˌ)lō\ *adjective* [Middle English *schalowe*; probably akin to Old English *sceald* shallow — more at SKELETON] (14th century)
**1 :** having little depth ⟨*shallow* water⟩
**2 :** having little extension inward or backward ⟨office buildings have taken the form of *shallow* slabs —Lewis Mumford⟩
**3 a :** penetrating only the easily or quickly perceived ⟨*shallow* generalizations⟩ **b :** lacking in depth of knowledge, thought, or feeling ⟨a *shallow* demagogue⟩
**4 :** displacing comparatively little air **:** WEAK ⟨*shallow* breathing⟩
*synonym* see SUPERFICIAL
— **shal·low·ly** \-lō-lē, -lə-lē\ *adverb*
— **shal·low·ness** *noun*
**²shallow** (1510)
*transitive verb*
**:** to make shallow
*intransitive verb*
**:** to become shallow
**³shallow** *noun* (1571)
**:** a shallow place or area in a body of water — usually used in plural but singular or plural in construction
**sha·lom** \shä-'lōm, shə-\ *interjection* [Hebrew *shālōm* peace] (1904)
— used as a Jewish greeting and farewell
**sha·lom alei·chem** \-ˌshó-ləm-ə-'lā-kəm, ˌshō-, -ˌkəm\ *interjection* [Hebrew *shālōm 'alēkhem* peace unto you] (1881)
— used as a traditional Jewish greeting
**shalt** \shəlt, 'shalt\ *archaic present 2d singular of* SHALL
**¹sham** \'sham\ *noun* [perhaps from English dialect *sham* shame, alteration of English *shame*] (1677)
**1 :** a trick that deludes **:** HOAX
**2 :** cheap falseness **:** HYPOCRISY
**3 :** an ornamental covering for a pillow
**4 :** an imitation or counterfeit purporting to be genuine
**5 :** a person who shams
*synonym* see IMPOSTURE
**²sham** *adjective* (1681)
**1 :** not genuine **:** FALSE, FEIGNED
**2 :** having such poor quality as to seem false

**³sham** *verb* **shammed; sham·ming** (1755)
*transitive verb*
**:** to go through the external motions necessary to counterfeit
*intransitive verb*
**:** to act intentionally so as to give a false impression **:** FEIGN
— **sham·mer** \'sha-mər\ *noun*
*synonym* see ASSUME
**sha·man** \'shä-mən, 'shā- *also* shə-'män\ *noun, plural* **shamans** [ultimately from Evenki (Tungusic language of Siberia) *šamān*] (1698)
**1 :** a priest or priestess who uses magic for the purpose of curing the sick, divining the hidden, and controlling events
**2 :** one who resembles a shaman; *especially* **:** HIGH PRIEST 3
— **sha·man·ic** \shə-'ma-nik, -'mä-\ *adjective*
**sha·man·ism** \-ˌni-zəm\ *noun* (1780)
**:** a religion practiced by indigenous peoples of far northern Europe and Siberia that is characterized by belief in an unseen world of gods, demons, and ancestral spirits responsive only to the shamans; *also* **:** any similar religion
— **sha·man·ist** \-nist\ *noun*
— **sha·man·is·tic** \ˌshä-mə-'nis-tik, ˌshä-mə-\ *adjective*
**sham·ble** \'sham-bəl\ *intransitive verb* **sham·bled; sham·bling** \-b(ə-)liŋ\ [*shamble* bowed, malformed] (1681)
**:** to walk awkwardly with dragging feet **:** SHUFFLE
— **shamble** *noun*
**sham·bles** \'sham-bəlz\ *noun plural but singular or plural in construction* [Middle English *shameles*, plural of *schamel* vendor's table, footstool, from Old English *sceamol* stool, from Latin *scamillum*, diminutive of *scamnum* stool, bench; perhaps akin to Sanskrit *skambha* pillar] (15th century)
**1** *archaic* **:** a meat market
**2 :** SLAUGHTERHOUSE
**3 a :** a place of mass slaughter or bloodshed **b :** a scene or a state of great destruction **:** WRECKAGE **c** (1) **:** a scene or a state of great disorder or confusion (2) **:** great confusion **:** MESS
**sham·bling** *adjective* (1592)
**:** characterized by slow awkward movement
**sham·bol·ic** \sham-'bä-lik\ *adjective* [probably from *shambles*] (1970)
*chiefly British* **:** obviously disorganized or confused
**¹shame** \'shām\ *noun* [Middle English, from Old English *scamu*; akin to Old High German *scama* shame] (before 12th century)
**1 a :** a painful emotion caused by consciousness of guilt, shortcoming, or impropriety **b :** the susceptibility to such emotion
**2 :** a condition of humiliating disgrace or disrepute **:** IGNOMINY
**3 :** something that brings censure or reproach; *also* **:** something to be regretted **:** PITY ⟨it's a *shame* you can't go⟩ **b :** a cause of feeling shame
**²shame** *transitive verb* **shamed; sham·ing** (13th century)
**1 :** to bring shame to **:** DISGRACE
**2 :** to put to shame by outdoing
**3 :** to cause to feel shame
**4 :** to force by causing to feel guilty ⟨*shamed* into confessing⟩
**shame·faced** \'shām-ˌfāst\ *adjective* [alteration of *shamefast*] (1593)
**1 :** showing modesty **:** BASHFUL
**2 :** showing shame **:** ASHAMED ◆
— **shame·faced·ly** \-ˌfā-səd-lē, -ˌfāst-lē\ *adverb*
— **shame·faced·ness** \-ˌfā-səd-nəs, -ˌfās(t)-nəs\ *noun*
**shame·fast** \'shām-ˌfast\ *adjective* [Middle English, from Old English *scamfæst*, from *scamu* + *fæst* fixed, fast] (before 12th century)

*archaic* **:** SHAMEFACED
**shame·ful** \'shām-fəl\ *adjective* (13th century)
**1 a :** bringing shame **:** DISGRACEFUL **b :** arousing the feeling of shame
**2** *archaic* **:** full of the feeling of shame **:** ASHAMED
— **shame·ful·ly** \-fə-lē\ *adverb*
— **shame·ful·ness** *noun*
**shame·less** \'shām-ləs\ *adjective* (before 12th century)
**1 :** having no shame **:** insensible to disgrace
**2 :** showing lack of shame **:** DISGRACEFUL
— **shame·less·ly** *adverb*
— **shame·less·ness** *noun*
**sham·mes** \'shä-məs\ *noun, plural* **sham·mo·sim** \shä-'mó-səm\ [Yiddish *shames*, from Late Hebrew *shammāsh*] (1650)
**1 :** the sexton of a synagogue
**2 :** the candle or taper used to light the other candles in a Hanukkah menorah
**sham·my** \'sha-mē\ *variant of* CHAMOIS
**¹sham·poo** \sham-'pü\ *transitive verb* [Hindi *cāpo*, imperative of *cāpnā* to press, shampoo] (1762)
**1** *archaic* **:** MASSAGE
**2 a :** to wash (as the hair) with soap and water or with a special preparation **b :** to wash the hair of
— **sham·poo·er** *noun*
**²shampoo** *noun, plural* **shampoos** (1838)
**1 :** an act or instance of shampooing
**2 :** a preparation used in shampooing
**sham·rock** \'sham-ˌräk\ *noun* [Irish *seamróg*, diminutive of *seamar* clover] (1577)
**:** a trifoliolate plant used as a floral emblem by the Irish: as **a :** a yellow-flowered clover (*Trifolium dubium*) often regarded as the true shamrock **b :** WOOD SORREL **c :** WHITE CLOVER
**sha·mus** \'shä-məs, 'shā-\ *noun* [perhaps from Yiddish *shames* shammes; from a jocular comparison of the duties of a sexton and those of a store detective] (1925)

□ USAGE
**shall** From the reams of pronouncements written about the distinction between *shall* and *will*—dating back as far as the 17th century—it is clear that the rules laid down have never very accurately reflected actual usage. The nationalistic statements of 18th and 19th century British grammarians, who commonly cited the misuses of the Irish, the Scots, and occasionally the Americans, suggest that the traditional rules may have come closest to the usage of southern England. Some modern commentators believe that English usage is still the closest to the traditionally prescribed norms. Most modern commentators allow that *will* is more common in nearly all uses. The entries for *shall* and *will* in this dictionary show current usage.

◇ WORD HISTORY
**shamefaced** Old English *scamfæst* meant "bashful" or "modest" or, more literally, "held fast by shame." The second element of *shamefaced* was thus originally the same as that of *steadfast*, meaning "fixed in place." While we can be sure that the similarity of consonant sounds between *-fast* and *-faced* contributed to the alteration of *shamefast* to *shamefaced*, the belief that modesty or bashfulness is reflected in a person's face probably had some influence too. For instance, we find this sentence in a 15th century English translation from a Latin text: "Tho that haue the face sumwhate ruddy bene schamefast." (Those who have a somewhat ruddy face are shamefast.) Around the middle of the 16th century the alteration to *shamefaced* began to appear in print, and since then the folk etymology has been firmly established.

**1** *slang* : POLICE OFFICER

**2** *slang* : PRIVATE INVESTIGATOR

**Shan** \'shän, 'shan\ *noun, plural* **Shan** *or* **Shans** (1795)
**1** : a member of a people living primarily in Myanmar and southern China
**2** : the Thai language of the Shan

**shan·dy** \'shan-dē\ *noun, plural* **shandies** (1888)
**1** : SHANDYGAFF
**2** : a drink consisting of beer and lemonade

**shan·dy·gaff** \'shan-dē-,gaf\ *noun* [origin unknown] (1853)
: beer diluted with a nonalcoholic drink (as ginger beer)

**Shang** \'shäŋ\ *noun* [Chinese (Beijing) *Shāng*] (1669)
: a Chinese dynasty traditionally dated 1766–1122 B.C. and known especially for bronze work

**shang·hai** \shaŋ-'hī\ *transitive verb* **shang·haied; shang·hai·ing** [*Shanghai*, China; from the formerly widespread use of this method to secure sailors for voyages to the Orient] (1871)
**1 a** : to put aboard a ship by force often with the help of liquor or a drug **b** : to put by force or threat of force into or as if into a place of detention
**2** : to put by trickery into an undesirable position
— **shang·hai·er** \-'hī(-ə)r\ *noun*

**Shan·gri-la** \,shaŋ-gri-'lä\ *noun* [*Shangri-La*, imaginary land depicted in the novel *Lost Horizon* (1933) by James Hilton] (1940)
**1** : a remote beautiful imaginary place where life approaches perfection : UTOPIA
**2** : a remote usually idyllic hideaway

¹**shank** \'shaŋk\ *noun* [Middle English *shanke*, from Old English *scanca*; akin to Old Norse *skakkr* crooked, Greek *skazein* to limp] (before 12th century)
**1 a** : the part of the leg between the knee and the ankle in humans or the corresponding part in various other vertebrates **b** : LEG **c** : a cut of beef, veal, mutton, or lamb from the upper or the lower part of the leg : SHIN — see BEEF illustration
**2** : a straight narrow usually essential part of an object: as **a** : the straight part of a nail or pin **b** : a straight part of a plant : STEM, STALK **c** : the part of an anchor between the ring and the crown — see ANCHOR illustration **d** : the part of a fishhook between the eye and the bend **e** : the part of a key between the handle and the bit **f** : the stem of a tobacco pipe or the part between the stem and the bowl **g** : TANG 1 **h** (1) : the narrow part of the sole of a shoe beneath the instep (2) : SHANKPIECE
**3** : a part of an object by which it can be attached: as **a** (1) : a projection on the back of a solid button (2) : a short stem of thread that holds a sewn button away from the cloth **b** : the end (as of a drill bit) that is gripped in a chuck
**4 a** : the latter part of a period of time **b** : the early or main part of a period of time
**5** *slang* : an often homemade knife
— **shanked** \'shaŋ(k)t\ *adjective*

²**shank** *transitive verb* (1927)
: to hit (a golf ball or shot) with the extreme heel of the club so that the ball goes off in an unintended direction; *also* : to kick (a football) in an unintended direction

**shank·piece** \'shaŋk-,pēs\ *noun* (1885)
: a support for the arch of the foot inserted in the shank of a shoe

**shank's mare** *noun* (circa 1795)
: one's own legs ⟨traveling by *shank's mare*⟩

**shan't** \'shant, 'shȧnt\ (1664)
: shall not

**shan·tung** \(,)shan-'təŋ\ *noun* [*Shantung* (Shandong), China] (circa 1882)
: a fabric in plain weave having a slightly irregular surface due to uneven slubbed filling yarns

¹**shan·ty** \'shan-tē\ *variant of* CHANTEY

²**shanty** *noun, plural* **shanties** [probably from Canadian French *chantier* lumber camp, hut, from French, gantry, from Latin *cantherius* rafter, trellis] (1820)
: a small crudely built dwelling or shelter usually of wood

**shan·ty·man** \-mən, -,man\ *noun* (circa 1858)
: one who lives in a shanty

**shan·ty·town** \-,taùn\ *noun* (1876)
: a usually poor town or section of a town consisting mostly of shanties

**shap·able** *or* **shape·able** \'shā-pə-bəl\ *adjective* (1647)
**1** : capable of being shaped
**2** : SHAPELY

¹**shape** \'shāp\ *verb* **shaped; shap·ing** [Middle English, alteration of Old English *scieppan;* akin to Old High German *skepfen* to shape] (before 12th century)
*transitive verb*
**1** : FORM, CREATE; *especially* : to give a particular form or shape to
**2** *obsolete* : ORDAIN, DECREE
**3** : to adapt in shape so as to fit neatly and closely ⟨a dress *shaped* to her figure⟩
**4 a** : DEVISE, PLAN **b** : to embody in definite form ⟨*shaping* a folktale into an epic⟩
**5 a** : to make fit for (as a particular use or purpose) : ADAPT **b** : to determine or direct the course or character of (as life) **c** : to modify (behavior) by rewarding changes that tend toward a desired response
*intransitive verb*
**1** : HAPPEN, BEFALL
**2** : to take on or approach a mature or definite form — often used with *up*
— **shap·er** *noun*

²**shape** *noun* (before 12th century)
**1 a** : the visible makeup characteristic of a particular item or kind of item **b** (1) : spatial form or contour (2) : a standard or universally recognized spatial form
**2** : the appearance of the body as distinguished from that of the face : FIGURE
**3 a** : PHANTOM, APPARITION **b** : assumed appearance : GUISE
**4** : form of embodiment
**5** : a mode of existence or form of being having identifying features
**6** : something having a particular form
**7** : the condition in which someone or something exists at a particular time ⟨the car was in fine *shape*⟩
— **shaped** \,shāpt\ *adjective*
— **in shape** : in an original, normal, or fit condition ⟨exercises to keep *in shape*⟩

**shape·less** \'shā-pləs\ *adjective* (14th century)
**1** : having no definite shape
**2 a** : deprived of usual or normal shape : MISSHAPEN ⟨a *shapeless* old hat⟩ **b** : not shapely
— **shape·less·ly** *adverb*
— **shape·less·ness** *noun*

**shape·ly** \'shā-plē\ *adjective* **shape·li·er; -est** (14th century)
**1** : having a regular or pleasing shape
**2** : orderly and consistent in arrangement or plan
— **shape·li·ness** *noun*

**shap·en** \'shā-pən\ *adjective* [Middle English, from past participle of *shapen* to shape] (14th century)
: fashioned in or provided with a definite shape — usually used in combination ⟨an ill-*shapen* body⟩

**shape note** *noun* (1932)
: one of a system of seven notes showing the musical scale degree by the shape of the note head

**shape–shift·er** \'shāp-,shif-tər\ *noun* (1887)
: one that seems able to change form at will

**shape–up** \'shāp-,əp\ *noun* (1940)
: a system of hiring workers and especially longshoremen by the day or shift by having

applicants gather for each day's selection; *also* : an instance of such hiring practice

**shape up** (circa 1920)
*intransitive verb*
: to improve to a good or acceptable condition or standard of behavior
*transitive verb*
: to bring to a good or acceptable condition or standard of behavior

**shard** \'shärd\ *also* **sherd** \'shərd\ *noun* [Middle English, from Old English *sceard;* akin to Old English *scieran* to cut — more at SHEAR] (before 12th century)
**1 a** : a piece or fragment of a brittle substance; *broadly* : a small piece or part **b** : SHELL, SCALE; *especially* : ELYTRON
**2** *usually* **sherd** : fragments of pottery vessels found on sites and in refuse deposits where pottery-making peoples have lived
**3** : highly angular curved glass fragments of tuffaceous sediments

¹**share** \'shar, 'sher\ *noun* [Middle English *schare*, from Old English *scear;* akin to Old High German *scaro* plowshare, Old English *scieran* to cut — more at SHEAR] (before 12th century)
: PLOWSHARE

²**share** *noun* [Middle English, from Old English *scearu* cutting, tonsure; akin to Old English *scieran* to cut] (14th century)
**1 a** : a portion belonging to, due to, or contributed by an individual or group **b** : one's full or fair portion
**2 a** : the part allotted or belonging to one of a number owning together property or interest **b** : any of the equal portions into which property or invested capital is divided; *specifically* : any of the equal interests or rights into which the entire capital stock of a corporation is divided and ownership of which is regularly evidenced by one or more certificates **c** *plural, chiefly British* : STOCK 7c(1)

³**share** *verb* **shared; shar·ing** (1590)
*transitive verb*
**1** : to divide and distribute in shares : APPORTION — usually used with *out* or *with*
**2 a** : to partake of, use, experience, occupy, or enjoy with others **b** : to have in common
**3** : to grant or give a share in
*intransitive verb*
**1** : to have a share — used with *in*
**2** : to apportion and take shares of something ☆
— **shar·er** *noun*

**share·able** *or* **shar·able** \'sher-ə-bəl, 'shar-\ *adjective* (1920)
: capable of being shared
— **share·abil·i·ty** \,sher-ə-'bi-lə-tē, ,shar-\ *noun*

**share·crop** \'sher-,kräp, 'shar-\ *verb* [back-formation from *sharecropper*] (circa 1930)
*intransitive verb*
: to farm as a sharecropper

---

☆ SYNONYMS
**Share, participate, partake** mean to have, get, or use in common with another or others. SHARE usually implies that one as the original holder grants to another the partial use, enjoyment, or possession of a thing ⟨*shared* my toys with the others⟩. PARTICIPATE implies a having or taking part in an undertaking, activity, or discussion ⟨*participated* in sports⟩. PARTAKE implies accepting or acquiring a share especially of food or drink ⟨*partook* freely of the refreshments⟩.

---

\ə\ abut  \ᵊ\ kitten  \ər\ further  \a\ ash  \ā\ ace
\ä\ mop, mar  \aù\ out  \ch\ chin  \e\ bet  \ē\ easy
\g\ go  \i\ hit  \ī\ ice  \j\ job  \ŋ\ sing  \ō\ go
\ò\ law  \òi\ boy  \th\ thin  \th\ the  \ü\ loot  \ù\ foot
\y\ yet  \zh\ vision   *see also* Guide to Pronunciation

*transitive verb*
**:** to farm (land) or produce (a crop) as a share-cropper
**share·crop·per** \-ˌkrä-pər\ *noun* (1923)
**:** a tenant farmer especially in the southern U.S. who is provided with credit for seed, tools, living quarters, and food, who works the land, and who receives an agreed share of the value of the crop minus charges
**share·hold·er** \-ˌhōl-dər\ *noun* (circa 1828)
**:** one that holds or owns a share in property; *especially* **:** STOCKHOLDER
**share·ware** \-ˌwar, -ˌwer\ *noun* (1983)
**:** software with usually limited capability or incomplete documentation which is available for trial use at little or no cost but which can be upgraded upon payment of a fee to the author
**sha·rif** \shə-ˈrēf\ *noun* [Arabic *sharīf*, literally, illustrious] (1599)
**:** a descendant of the prophet Muhammad through his daughter Fatima; *broadly* **:** one of noble ancestry or political preeminence in predominantly Islamic countries
— **sha·rif·ian** \-ˈrē-fē-ən\ *adjective*
¹**shark** \ˈshärk\ *noun* [Middle English] (15th century)
**:** any of numerous mostly marine cartilaginous fishes of medium to large size that have a fusiform body, lateral branchial clefts, and a tough usually dull gray skin roughened by minute tubercles and are typically active predators sometimes dangerous to humans
— **shark·like** \ˈshärk-ˌlīk\ *adjective*

shark: *1* mako, *2* tiger, *3* thresher, *4* hammerhead, *5* great white

²**shark** *noun* [probably modification of German *Schurke* scoundrel] (1599)
**1 :** a rapacious crafty person who preys upon others through usury, extortion, or trickery
**2 :** one who excels greatly especially in a particular field
³**shark** (1602)
*transitive verb*
**1** *archaic* **:** to gather hastily
**2** *archaic* **:** to obtain by some irregular means
*intransitive verb*
**1** *archaic* **:** to practice fraud or trickery
**2** *archaic* **:** SNEAK
**shark·skin** \ˈshärk-ˌskin\ *noun* (1851)
**1 :** the hide of a shark or leather made from it
**2 a :** a smooth durable woolen or worsted suiting in twill or basket weave with small woven designs **b :** a smooth crisp fabric with a dull finish made usually of rayon in basket weave
**shark sucker** *noun* (circa 1850)
**:** REMORA 1
¹**sharp** \ˈshärp\ *adjective* [Middle English, from Old English *scearp;* akin to Old High German *scarf* sharp and perhaps to Old English *scrapian* to scrape — more at SCRAPE] (before 12th century)

**1 :** adapted to cutting or piercing: as **a :** having a thin keen edge or fine point **b :** briskly or bitingly cold **:** NIPPING ⟨a *sharp* wind⟩
**2 a :** keen in intellect **:** QUICK-WITTED **b :** keen in perception **:** ACUTE ⟨*sharp* sight⟩ **c :** keen in attention **:** VIGILANT ⟨keep a *sharp* lookout⟩ **d :** keen in attention to one's own interest sometimes to the point of being unethical ⟨a *sharp* trader⟩
**3 :** keen in spirit or action: as **a :** full of activity or energy **:** BRISK ⟨*sharp* blows⟩ **b :** capable of acting or reacting strongly; *especially* **:** CAUSTIC
**4 :** SEVERE, HARSH: as **a :** inclined to or marked by irritability or anger ⟨a *sharp* temper⟩ **b :** causing intense mental or physical distress ⟨a *sharp* pain⟩ **c :** cutting in language or import ⟨a *sharp* rebuke⟩
**5 :** affecting the senses or sense organs intensely: as **a** (1) **:** having a strong odor or flavor ⟨*sharp* cheese⟩ (2) **:** ACRID **b :** having a strong piercing sound **c :** having the effect of or involving a sudden brilliant display of light ⟨a *sharp* flash⟩
**6 a :** terminating in a point or edge ⟨*sharp* features⟩ **b :** involving an abrupt or marked change especially in direction ⟨a *sharp* turn⟩ **c :** clear in outline or detail **:** DISTINCT ⟨a *sharp* image⟩ **d :** set forth with clarity and distinctness ⟨*sharp* contrast⟩
**7 a** *of a tone* **:** raised a half step in pitch **b :** higher than the proper pitch **c :** MAJOR, AUGMENTED — used of an interval in music
**8 :** STYLISH, DRESSY ☆
— **sharp·ly** *adverb*
— **sharp·ness** *noun*
²**sharp** *adverb* (before 12th century)
**1 :** in a sharp manner
**2 :** EXACTLY ⟨1:15 *sharp*⟩
³**sharp** *noun* (14th century)
**:** one that is sharp: as **a :** a sharp edge or point **b** (1) **:** a musical note or tone one half step higher than a note or tone named (2) **:** a character ♯ on a line or space of the musical staff indicating a pitch a half step higher than the degree would indicate without it **c :** a needle with a small eye for sewing by hand **d :** a real or self-styled expert; *also* **:** SHARPER
⁴**sharp** (1662)
*transitive verb*
**:** to raise (as a musical tone) in pitch; *especially* **:** to raise in pitch by a half step
*intransitive verb*
**:** to sing or play above the proper pitch
**shar-pei** \ˌshä-ˈpā, ˌshär-\ *noun, plural* **shar-peis** [Chinese (Guangdong) *sà* sand + *péi* fur] (1975)
**:** any of an ancient breed of dogs originating in China that have loose wrinkled skin especially when young, a short bristly coat, blue-black tongue, and wide blunt muzzle
**sharp·en** \ˈshär-pən\ *verb* **sharp·ened; sharp·en·ing** \ˈshärp-niŋ, ˈshär-pə-\ (15th century)
*transitive verb*
**:** to make sharp or sharper; *especially* **:** HONE
*intransitive verb*
**:** to become sharp or sharper
— **sharp·en·er** \ˈshärp-nər, ˈshär-pə-\ *noun*
**sharp·er** \ˈshär-pər\ *noun* (1681)
**:** CHEAT, SWINDLER; *especially* **:** a cheating gambler
**sharp–eyed** \ˈshärp-ˈīd\ *adjective* (1670)
**:** having keen sight; *also* **:** keen in observing or penetrating
**sharp·ie** *or* **sharpy** \ˈshär-pē\ *noun, plural* **sharp·ies** (circa 1859)
**1 :** a long narrow shallow-draft boat with flat or slightly V-shaped bottom and one or two masts each carrying a triangular sail
**2 a :** SHARPER **b :** an exceptionally keen or alert person
**sharp–nosed** \ˈshärp-ˈnōzd\ *adjective* (1561)
**1 :** keen in smelling
**2 :** having a pointed nose or snout
**sharp practice** *noun* (1845)

**:** the act of dealing in which advantage is taken or sought unscrupulously
**sharp–set** \ˈshärp-ˈset\ *adjective* (1540)
**:** eager in appetite or desire
**sharp–shinned hawk** \ˈshärp-ˈshind-\ *noun* (circa 1812)
**:** a common widely distributed American accipiter (*Accipiter striatus*) that is grayish above, has a chestnut breast, short rounded wings, and a tail with a notched or square tip when folded — called also *sharp-shin*
**sharp·shoot·er** \ˈshärp-ˌshü-tər\ *noun* (1802)
**:** a good marksman
**sharp·shoot·ing** \-ˌshü-tiŋ\ *noun* (1806)
**1 :** shooting with great precision
**2 :** accurate and usually unexpected attack (as in words)
**sharp–sight·ed** \-ˈsī-təd\ *adjective* (1571)
**1 :** having acute sight
**2 :** mentally keen or alert
— **sharp–sight·ed·ly** *adverb*
— **sharp–sight·ed·ness** *noun*
**sharp–tongued** \-ˈtəŋd\ *adjective* (1837)
**:** having a sharp tongue **:** harsh or bitter in speech or language
**sharp–wit·ted** \-ˈwi-təd\ *adjective* (circa 1586)
**:** having an acute mind
**shash·lick** *also* **shash·lik** *or* **shas·lik** \shäsh-ˈlik, ˈshäsh-lik\ *noun* [Russian *shashlyk*, probably modification of Crimean Tatar *šišlik*, from *šiš* skewer] (1926)
**:** KABOB
**Shas·ta daisy** \ˈshas-tə-\ *noun* [Mount *Shasta*, California] (circa 1893)
**:** a large-flowered garden daisy (*Chrysanthemum superbum* synonym *C. maximum*) that resembles the oxeye daisy
**shat** *past and past participle of* SHIT
¹**shat·ter** \ˈsha-tər\ *verb* [Middle English *schateren*] (14th century)
*transitive verb*
**1 :** to cause to drop or be dispersed
**2 a :** to break at once into pieces **b :** to damage badly **:** RUIN
**3 :** to cause the disruption or annihilation of **:** DEMOLISH
*intransitive verb*
**1 :** to break apart **:** DISINTEGRATE
**2 :** to drop off parts (as leaves, petals, or fruit)
— **shat·ter·ing·ly** \-tə-riŋ-lē\ *adverb*
²**shatter** *noun* (circa 1640)
**1 :** FRAGMENT, SHRED — usually used in plural ⟨the broken vase lay in *shatters*⟩
**2 :** an act of shattering **:** the state of being shattered
**3 :** a result of shattering **:** SHOWER
**shatter cone** *noun* (1933)
**:** a conical fragment of rock that has striations radiating from the apex and that is formed by high pressure (as from volcanism or meteorite impact)
**shat·ter·proof** \ˈsha-tər-ˌprüf\ *adjective* (1930)
**:** proof against shattering
¹**shave** \ˈshāv\ *verb* **shaved; shaved** *or* **shav·en** \ˈshā-vən\; **shav·ing** [Middle English, from Old English *scafan;* akin to Lithuanian *skobti* to pluck, Latin *scabere* to scratch, and perhaps to Greek *koptein* to cut — more at CAPON] (before 12th century)

*transitive verb*
**1 a :** to remove a thin layer from **b :** to cut off in thin layers or shreds **:** SLICE **c :** to cut off closely
**2 a :** to sever the hair from (the head or another part of the body) close to the roots **b :** to cut off (hair or beard) close to the skin
**3 a :** to discount (a note) at an exorbitant rate **b :** DEDUCT, REDUCE
**4 :** to come close to or touch lightly in passing
*intransitive verb*
**1 :** to cut off hair or beard close to the skin
**2 :** to proceed with difficulty **:** SCRAPE
**²shave** *noun* (before 12th century)
**1 :** SHAVER 3
**2 :** a thin slice **:** SHAVING
**3 :** an act or the process of shaving
**shave·ling** \'shāv-liŋ\ *noun* (1529)
**1 :** a tonsured clergyman **:** PRIEST — usually used disparagingly
**2 :** YOUTH, STRIPLING
**shav·er** \'shā-vər\ *noun* (15th century)
**1 :** a person who shaves
**2** *archaic* **:** one who swindles
**3 :** a tool or machine for shaving; *especially* **:** an electric razor
**4 :** BOY, YOUNGSTER
**shaves** *plural of* SHAFT
**shave·tail** \'shāv-ˌtāl\ *noun* [from the practice of shaving the tails of newly broken mules to distinguish them from seasoned ones] (1846)
**1 :** a pack mule especially when newly broken in
**2 :** SECOND LIEUTENANT — usually used disparagingly
**Sha·vi·an** \'shā-vē-ən\ *noun* [New Latin *Shavius*, Latinized form of George Bernard *Shaw*] (1905)
**:** an admirer or devotee of G. B. Shaw, his writings, or his social and political theories
**— Shavian** *adjective*
**shav·ie** \'shā-vē\ *noun* [*shave* (swindle) + *-ie*] (1737)
*Scottish* **:** PRANK
**shav·ing** \'shā-viŋ\ *noun* (14th century)
**1 :** the act of one that shaves
**2 :** something shaved off ⟨wood *shavings*⟩
**¹shaw** \'shȯ\ *noun* [Middle English, from Old English *sceaga*; akin to Old Norse *skegg* beard — more at SHAG] (before 12th century)
*dialect* **:** COPPICE, THICKET
**²shaw** *noun* [probably alteration of *show*] (1726)
*chiefly British* **:** the tops and stalks of a cultivated crop (as potatoes or turnips)
**¹shawl** \'shȯl\ *noun* [Persian *shāl*] (1662)
**:** a square or oblong usually fabric garment or wrapper used especially as a covering for the head or shoulders
**²shawl** *transitive verb* (1812)
**:** to wrap in or as if in a shawl
**shawl collar** *noun* (circa 1908)
**:** a turned-over collar of a garment that combines with lapels forming an unbroken curving line
**shawm** \'shȯm\ *noun* [Middle English *schalme*, from Middle French *chalemie*, from Old French, alteration of *chalemel*, from Late Latin *calamellus*, diminutive of Latin *calamus* reed — more at CALAMUS] (14th century)
**:** an early double-reed woodwind instrument

**shawl collar**

**Shaw·nee** \shȯ-'nē, shä-\ *noun, plural* **Shawnee** *or* **Shawnees** [back-formation from obsolete English *Shawnese*, ultimately from Shawnee *šaˀwanoˀki*, literally, southerners] (1769)
**1 :** a member of an American Indian people originally of the central Ohio valley
**2 :** the Algonquian language of the Shawnee people

**Shaw·wal** \shə-'wäl\ *noun* [Arabic *shawwāl*] (circa 1771)
**:** the 10th month of the Islamic year — see MONTH table
**shay** \'shā\ *noun* [back-formation from *chaise*, taken as plural] (1717)
*chiefly dialect* **:** CHAISE 1
**¹she** \'shē\ *pronoun* [Middle English, probably alteration of *hye*, alteration of Old English *hēo* she — more at HE] (12th century)
**1 :** that female one who is neither speaker nor the one addressed ⟨*she* is my wife⟩ — compare HE, HER, HERS, IT, THEY
**2 :** — used to refer to one regarded as feminine (as by personification) ⟨*she* was a fine ship⟩
**usage** see HE
**²she** *noun* (14th century)
**:** a female person or animal — often used in combination ⟨*she*-cat⟩ ⟨*she*-cousin⟩
**s/he** \'shē-'hē; 'shē-ər-'hē; 'shē-ˌslash-'hē\ *pronoun* (1973)
**:** she or he — used in writing as a pronoun of common gender
**shea butter** \'shē-, 'shā-\ *noun* (1847)
**:** a pale solid fat from the seeds of the shea tree used in food, soap, and candles
**sheaf** \'shēf\ *noun, plural* **sheaves** \'shēvz\ [Middle English *sheef*, from Old English *scēaf*; akin to Old High German *scoub* sheaf, Russian *chub* forelock] (before 12th century)
**1 :** a quantity of the stalks and ears of a cereal grass or sometimes other plant material bound together
**2 :** something resembling a sheaf of grain ⟨a *sheaf* of papers⟩
**— sheaf·like** \'shēf-ˌlīk\ *adjective*
**shea nut** *noun* (1919)
**:** the seed of the shea tree
**¹shear** \'shir\ *verb* **sheared; sheared** *or* **shorn** \'shōrn, 'shȯrn\; **shear·ing** [Middle English *sheren*, from Old English *scieran*; akin to Old Norse *skera* to cut, Latin *curtus* shortened, Greek *keirein* to cut, shear, Sanskrit *kṛṇāti* he injures] (before 12th century)
*transitive verb*
**1 a :** to cut off the hair from ⟨with crown *shorn*⟩ **b :** to cut or clip (as hair or wool) from someone or something; *also* **:** to cut something from ⟨*shear* a lawn⟩ **c** *chiefly Scottish* **:** to reap with a sickle **d :** to cut or trim with shears or a similar instrument
**2 :** to cut with something sharp
**3 :** to deprive of something as if by cutting
**4 a :** to subject to a shear force **b :** to cause (as a rock mass) to move along the plane of contact
*intransitive verb*
**1 :** to cut through something with or as if with a sharp instrument
**2** *chiefly Scottish* **:** to reap crops with a sickle
**3 :** to become divided under the action of a shear ⟨the bolt may *shear* off⟩
**— shear·er** *noun*
**²shear** *noun* (before 12th century)
**1 a** (1) **:** a cutting implement similar or identical to a pair of scissors but typically larger — usually used in plural (2) **:** one blade of a pair of shears **b :** any of various cutting tools or machines operating by the action of opposed cutting edges of metal — usually used in plural **c** (1) **:** something resembling a shear or a pair of shears (2) **:** a hoisting apparatus consisting of two or sometimes more upright spars fastened together at their upper ends and having tackle for masting or dismasting ships or lifting heavy loads (as guns) — usually used in plural but singular or plural in construction
**2** *chiefly British* **:** the action or process or an instance of shearing — used in combination to indicate the approximate age of sheep in terms of shearings undergone
**3 a :** internal force tangential to the section on which it acts — called also *shearing force* **b :** an action or stress resulting from applied forces that causes or tends to cause two con-

tiguous parts of a body to slide relatively to each other in a direction parallel to their plane of contact
**sheared** *adjective* (1616)
**:** formed or finished by shearing; *especially* **:** cut to uniform length ⟨a *sheared* rug⟩
**shear·ling** \'shir-liŋ\ *noun* (14th century)
**:** skin from a recently sheared sheep or lamb that has been tanned and dressed with the wool left on
**shear pin** *noun* (circa 1931)
**:** an easily replaceable pin inserted at a critical point in a machine and designed to break when subjected to excess stress
**shear·wa·ter** \'shir-ˌwȯ-tər, -ˌwä-\ *noun* (circa 1671)
**:** any of numerous oceanic birds (especially genus *Puffinus*) that are related to the petrels and usually skim close to the waves in flight
**sheath** \'shēth\ *noun, plural* **sheaths** \'shēthz, 'shēths\ [Middle English *shethe*, from Old English *scēath*; akin to Old High German *sceida* sheath and perhaps to Latin *scindere* to split — more at SHED] (before 12th century)
**1 :** a case for a blade (as of a knife)
**2 :** an investing cover or case of a plant or animal body or body part: as **a :** the tubular fold of skin into which the penis of many mammals is retracted **b** (1) **:** the lower part of a leaf (as of a grass) when surrounding the stem (2) **:** an ensheathing spathe
**3 :** any of various covering or supporting structures that are applied like or resemble in appearance or function the sheath of a blade: as **a :** SHEATHING 2 **b :** a woman's close-fitting dress usually worn without a belt **c** *British* **:** CONDOM
**sheath·bill** \'shēth-ˌbil\ *noun* (circa 1781)
**:** either of two white shorebirds (*Chionis alba* and *C. minor* of the family Chionididae) of colder parts of the southern hemisphere that have a horny sheath over the base of the upper mandible and suggest the pigeons in general appearance
**sheathe** \'shēth\ *also* **sheath** \'shēth\ *transitive verb* **sheathed; sheath·ing** [Middle English *shethen*, from *shethe* sheath] (15th century)
**1 :** to put into or furnish with a sheath
**2 :** to plunge or bury (as a sword) in flesh
**3 :** to withdraw (a claw) into a sheath
**4 :** to case or cover with something (as sheets of metal) that protects
**— sheath·er** \'shē-thər, -thər\ *noun*
**sheath·ing** \'shē-thiŋ, -thiŋ\ *noun* (15th century)
**1 :** the action of one that sheathes something
**2 :** material used to sheathe something; *especially* **:** the first covering of boards or of waterproof material on the outside wall of a frame house or on a timber roof
**sheath knife** *noun* (1837)
**:** a knife having a fixed blade and designed to be carried in a sheath
**shea tree** \'shē-, 'shā-\ *noun* [Bambara *si*] (1799)
**:** a tropical African tree (*Vitellaria paradoxa* synonym *Butyrospermum parkii*) of the sapodilla family with fatty nuts that yield shea butter
**¹sheave** \'shiv, 'shēv\ *noun* [Middle English *sheve*; akin to Old High German *scība* disk] (14th century)
**:** a grooved wheel or pulley (as of a pulley block)
**²sheave** \'shēv\ *transitive verb* **sheaved; sheav·ing** [*sheaf*] (1598)
**:** to gather and bind into a sheaf
**she·bang** \shi-'baŋ\ *noun* [origin unknown] (1869)

: everything involved in what is under consideration — usually used in the phrase *the whole shebang*

**She·bat** \shə-'bät, -'vät\ *noun* [Hebrew *shĕbhāṭ*] (1535)
: the 5th month of the civil year or the 11th month of the ecclesiastical year in the Jewish calendar — see MONTH table

**she·been** \shə-'bēn\ *noun* [Irish *síbín* illicit whiskey, shebeen] (circa 1787)
*chiefly Irish* : an unlicensed or illegally operated drinking establishment

**She·chi·nah** \shə-'kē-nə, -'kē-nə, -'kī-nə\ *noun* [Hebrew *shĕkhīnāh*] (1663)
: the presence of God in the world as conceived in Jewish theology

**¹shed** \'shed\ *verb* **shed; shed·ding** [Middle English, to divide, separate, from Old English *scēadan;* akin to Old High German *skeidan* to separate, Latin *scindere* to split, cleave, Greek *schizein* to split] (before 12th century)
*transitive verb*
**1** *chiefly dialect* : to set apart : SEGREGATE
**2** : to cause to be dispersed without penetrating ⟨duck's plumage *sheds* water⟩
**3 a** : to cause (blood) to flow by cutting or wounding **b** : to pour forth in drops ⟨*shed* tears⟩ **c** : to give off in a stream ⟨fish *shedding* their eggs in spawning⟩ **d** : to give off or out ⟨*sheds* some light on the subject⟩
**4 a** (1) : to cast off (as a body covering) : MOLT (2) : to let fall (as leaves) (3) : to eject (as seed or spores) from a natural receptacle **b** : to rid oneself of temporarily or permanently as superfluous or unwanted ⟨*shed* her inhibitions⟩ ⟨the company *shed* 100 jobs⟩
*intransitive verb*
**1** : to pour out : SPILL
**2** : to become dispersed : SCATTER
**3** : to cast off some natural covering (as fur or skin) ⟨the cat is *shedding*⟩
*synonym* see DISCARD
— **shed blood** : to cause death by violence

**²shed** *noun* (12th century)
**1** *obsolete* : DISTINCTION, DIFFERENCE
**2** : something (as the skin of a snake) that is discarded in shedding
**3** : a divide of land

**³shed** *noun* [alteration of earlier *shadde*, probably from Middle English *shade* shade] (1557)
**1 a** : a slight structure built for shelter or storage; *especially* : a single-storied building with one or more sides unenclosed **b** : a building that resembles a shed
**2** *archaic* : HUT
— **shed·like** \-,līk\ *adjective*

**⁴shed** *transitive verb* **shed·ded; shed·ding** (1850)
: to put or house in a shed

**she'd** \'shēd\ (1609)
: she had : she would

**shed·der** \'she-dər\ *noun* (14th century)
: one that sheds something: as **a** : a crab or lobster about to molt **b** : a newly molted crab

**shed dormer** *noun* (1948)
: a dormer with a roof sloping in the same direction as the roof from which the dormer projects

**¹sheen** \'shēn\ *adjective* [Middle English *shene,* from Old English *scīene;* akin to Old English *scēawian* to look — more at SHOW] (before 12th century)
**1** *archaic* : BEAUTIFUL
**2** *archaic* : SHINING, RESPLENDENT

**²sheen** *intransitive verb* (14th century)
: to be bright : show a sheen

**³sheen** *noun* (1602)
**1 a** : a bright or shining condition : BRIGHTNESS **b** : a subdued glitter approaching but short of optical reflection **c** : a lustrous surface imparted to textiles through finishing processes or use of shiny yarns
**2** : a textile exhibiting notable sheen
— **sheeny** \'shē-nē\ *adjective*

**sheep** \'shēp\ *noun, plural* **sheep** *often attributive* [Middle English, from Old English *scēap;* akin to Old High German *scāf* sheep] (before 12th century)
**1** : any of various ruminant mammals (genus *Ovis*) related to the goats but stockier and lacking a beard in the male; *specifically* : one (*O. aries*) long domesticated especially for its flesh and wool
**2 a** : a timid defenseless creature **b** : a timid docile person; *especially* : one easily influenced or led
**3** : leather prepared from the skins of sheep : SHEEPSKIN

**sheep·ber·ry** \-,ber-ē\ *noun* (circa 1818)
: an often shrubby North American viburnum (*Viburnum lentago*) with white flowers in flat cymes

**sheep·cote** \-,kōt, -,kät\ *noun* (15th century)
*chiefly British* : SHEEPFOLD

**sheep–dip** \-,dip\ *noun* (1865)
: a liquid preparation of usually toxic chemicals into which sheep are plunged especially to destroy parasitic arthropods

**sheep–dog** \-,dȯg\ *noun* (circa 1774)
: a dog (as a Border collie) used to tend, drive, or guard sheep

**sheep fescue** *noun* (1945)
: a hardy fine-foliaged perennial grass (*Festuca ovina*) widely used as a pasture grass — called also *sheep's fescue*

**sheep·fold** \'shēp-,fōld\ *noun* (15th century)
: a pen or shelter for sheep

**sheep·herd·er** \'shēp-,hər-dər\ *noun* (1871)
: a worker in charge of sheep especially on open range

**sheep·herd·ing** \-,hər-diŋ\ *noun* (1891)
: the activities of a worker engaged in tending sheep

**sheep·ish** \'shē-pish\ *adjective* (13th century)
**1** : resembling a sheep in meekness, stupidity, or timidity
**2** : affected by or showing embarrassment caused by consciousness of a fault ⟨a *sheepish* grin⟩
— **sheep·ish·ly** *adverb*
— **sheep·ish·ness** *noun*

**sheep ked** \'shēp-,ked\ *noun* [sheep + ked sheep ked, of unknown origin] (1925)
: a wingless bloodsucking dipteran fly (*Melophagus ovinus*) that feeds chiefly on sheep and is a vector of sheep trypanosomiasis — called also *sheep tick*

**sheep laurel** *noun* (1810)
: a dwarf shrub (*Kalmia angustifolia*) of the eastern U.S. that is poisonous to young stock and resembles mountain laurel but has narrower leaves and smaller bright red flowers — called also *lambkill*

**sheep's eye** *noun* (circa 1529)
: a shy longing usually amorous glance — usually used in plural

**sheep·shank** \'shēp-,shaŋk\ *noun* (1627)
**1** : a knot for shortening a line — see KNOT illustration
**2** *Scottish* : something of no worth or importance

**sheeps·head** \'shēps-,hed\ *noun* (1643)
**1** : a marine bony fish (*Archosargus probatocephalus* of the family Sparidae) of the Atlantic and Gulf coasts of the U.S. that has broad incisor teeth and is used for food
**2** : FRESHWATER DRUM
**3** : a largely red or rose California wrasse (*Semicossyphus pulcher*)

**sheep·shear·er** \'shēp-,shir-ər\ *noun* (1539)
: one that shears sheep

**sheep·shear·ing** \'shēp-,shir-iŋ\ *noun* (1586)
**1** : the act of shearing sheep
**2** : the time or season for shearing sheep

**sheep·skin** \-,skin\ *noun* (13th century)
**1 a** : the skin of a sheep; *also* : leather prepared from it **b** : PARCHMENT **c** : a garment made of or lined with sheepskin
**2** : DIPLOMA

**sheep sorrel** *noun* (1806)

: a small dock (*Rumex acetosella*) of acidic soils

**sheep walk** *noun* (1586)
*chiefly British* : a pasture or range for sheep

**¹sheer** \'shir\ *verb* [perhaps alteration of ¹*shear*] (1539)
*intransitive verb*
: to deviate from a course : SWERVE
*transitive verb*
: to cause to sheer

**²sheer** *noun* (1670)
**1** : a turn, deviation, or change in a course (as of a ship)
**2** : the position of a ship riding to a single anchor and heading toward it

**³sheer** *adjective* [Middle English *schere* freed from guilt, probably alteration of *skere,* from Old Norse *skærr* pure; akin to Old English *scīnan* to shine] (circa 1568)
**1** *obsolete* : BRIGHT, SHINING
**2** : of very thin or transparent texture : DIAPHANOUS
**3 a** : UNQUALIFIED, UTTER ⟨*sheer* folly⟩ ⟨*sheer* ignorance⟩ **b** : being free from an adulterant : PURE, UNMIXED **c** : viewed or acting in dissociation from all else ⟨in terms of *sheer* numbers⟩
**4** : marked by great and continuous steepness
*synonym* see STEEP
— **sheer·ly** *adverb*
— **sheer·ness** *noun*

**⁴sheer** *adverb* (circa 1600)
**1** : in a complete manner : ALTOGETHER
**2** : straight up or down without a break : PERPENDICULARLY

**⁵sheer** *noun* (circa 1920)
: a sheer fabric; *also* : an article of such a fabric

**⁶sheer** *noun* [perhaps alteration of ²*shear*] (1691)
: the fore-and-aft curvature from bow to stern of a ship's deck as shown in side elevation

**sheer·legs** \'shir-,legz, -,lāgz\ *noun plural but singular or plural in construction* (circa 1860)
: SHEAR 1c(2)

**¹sheet** \'shēt\ *noun* [Middle English *shete,* from Old English *scȳte;* akin to Old English *scēat* edge, Old High German *scōz* flap, skirt] (before 12th century)
**1 a** : a broad piece of cloth; *especially* : BEDSHEET **b** : SAIL 1a(1)
**2 a** : a usually rectangular piece of paper; *especially* : one manufactured for printing (2) : a rectangular piece of heavy paper with a plant specimen mounted on it ⟨an herbarium of 100,000 *sheets*⟩ **b** : a printed signature for a book especially before it has been folded, cut, or bound — usually used in plural **c** : a newspaper, periodical, or occasional publication ⟨a gossip *sheet*⟩ **d** : the unseparated postage stamps printed by one impression of a plate on a single piece of paper; *also* : a pane of stamps
**3** : a broad stretch or surface of something ⟨a *sheet* of ice⟩
**4** : a suspended or moving expanse (as of fire or rain)
**5 a** : a portion of something that is thin in comparison to its length and breadth **b** : a flat baking pan of tinned metal ⟨a cookie *sheet*⟩
**6** : a surface or part of a surface in which it is possible to pass from any one point of it to any other without leaving the surface ⟨a hyperboloid of two *sheets*⟩
— **sheet·like** \-,līk\ *adjective*

**²sheet** *adjective* (1582)
**1** : rolled or spread out in a sheet
**2** : of, relating to, or concerned with the making of sheet metal

**³sheet** (1606)
*transitive verb*
**1** : to cover with a sheet : SHROUD
**2** : to furnish with sheets
**3** : to form into sheets

*intransitive verb*
**:** to fall, spread, or flow in a sheet ⟨the rain *sheeted* against the windows⟩
— **sheet·er** *noun*
— **sheet home 1 :** to extend (a sail) and set as flat as possible by hauling upon the sheets **2 :** to fix the responsibility for **:** bring home to one
**⁴sheet** *noun* [Middle English *shete,* from Old English *scēata* lower corner of a sail; akin to Old English *scȳte* sheet] (13th century)
**1 :** a rope or chain that regulates the angle at which a sail is set in relation to the wind
**2** *plural* **:** the spaces at either end of an open boat not occupied by thwarts **:** foresheets and stern sheets together
— **three sheets in the wind** *or* **three sheets to the wind :** DRUNK 1a
**sheet anchor** *noun* (15th century)
**1 :** a large strong anchor formerly carried in the waist of a ship and used as a spare in an emergency
**2 :** something that constitutes a main support or dependence especially in danger
**sheet bend** *noun* (circa 1823)
**:** a bend or hitch used for temporarily fastening a rope to the bight of another rope or to an eye — see KNOT illustration
**sheet·fed** \'shēt-ˌfed\ *adjective* (1926)
**:** of, relating to, being, or printed by a press that prints on paper in sheet form
**sheet glass** *noun* (1805)
**:** glass made in large sheets directly from the furnace or by making a cylinder and then flattening it
**sheet·ing** \'shē-tiŋ\ *noun* (1711)
**1 :** material in the form of sheets or suitable for forming into sheets
**2 :** a lining (as wood or steel) used to support an embankment or the walls of an excavation
**sheet lightning** *noun* (1794)
**:** lightning in diffused or sheet form due to reflection and diffusion by the clouds and sky
**sheet metal** *noun* (circa 1909)
**:** metal in the form of a sheet
**sheet music** *noun* (1857)
**:** music printed on large unbound sheets of paper
**Sheet·rock** \'shēt-ˌräk\ *trademark*
— used for plasterboard
**sheikh** *or* **sheik** \'shēk, *also* 'shāk *for 1*\ *noun* [Arabic *shaykh*] (1577)
**1 :** an Arab chief
**2** *usually* **sheik :** a man held to be irresistibly attractive to romantic young women
**sheikh·dom** *or* **sheik·dom** \-dəm, -ˌtəm\ *noun* (1860)
**:** a region under the rule of a sheikh
**shei·la** \'shē-lə\ *noun* [probably from *Sheila,* female given name] (circa 1919)
*Australian & New Zealand* **:** a girl or young woman
**shek·el** \'she-kəl\ *noun* [Hebrew *sheqel*] (15th century)
**1 a :** any of various ancient units of weight; *especially* **:** a Hebrew unit equal to about 252 grains troy **b :** a unit of value based on a shekel weight of gold or silver
**2 :** a coin weighing one shekel
**3** *plural* **:** MONEY
**4** — see MONEY table
**Shekinah** *variant of* SHECHINAH
**shel·drake** \'shel-ˌdrāk\ *noun* [Middle English, from *sheld-* (akin to Middle Dutch *schillede* parti-colored) + *drake*] (14th century)
**1 :** SHELDUCK
**2 :** MERGANSER
**shel·duck** \-ˌdək\ *noun* [*shel-* (as in *sheldrake*) + *duck*] (1707)
**:** any of various Old World ducks (genus *Tadorna*); *especially* **:** a common mostly black-and-white duck (*T. tadorna*) slightly larger than the mallard
**shelf** \'shelf\ *noun, plural* **shelves** \'shelvz\ [Middle English, probably from Old English

*scylfe;* akin to Old Norse *hlīthskjalf* Odin's seat] (14th century)
**1 a :** a thin flat usually long and narrow piece of material (as wood) fastened horizontally (as on a wall) at a distance from the floor to hold objects **b :** one of several similar pieces in a closet, bookcase, or similar structure **c :** the contents of a shelf
**2 :** something resembling a shelf in form or position: as **a :** a sandbank or ledge of rocks usually partially submerged **b :** a flat projecting layer of rock **c :** the submerged gradually sloping border of a continent or island **:** CONTINENTAL SHELF
— **shelf·ful** \'shelf-ˌfu̇l\ *noun*
— **shelf·like** \'shelf-ˌlīk\ *adjective*
— **off the shelf :** available from stock **:** not made to order ⟨*off the shelf* equipment⟩
— **on the shelf :** in a state of inactivity or uselessness
**shelf fungus** *noun* (circa 1903)
**:** BRACKET FUNGUS
**shelf ice** *noun* (1910)
**:** an extensive ice sheet originating on land but continuing out to sea beyond the depths at which it rests on the sea bottom
**shelf life** *noun* (1927)
**:** the period of time during which a material may be stored and remain suitable for use; *broadly* **:** the period of time during which something lasts or remains popular
**¹shell** \'shel\ *noun* [Middle English, from Old English *sciell;* akin to Old English *scealu* shell, Old Norse *skel,* Lithuanian *skelti* to split, Greek *skallein* to hoe] (before 12th century)
**1 a :** a hard rigid usually largely calcareous covering or support of an animal **b :** the hard or tough often thin outer covering of an egg (as of a bird or reptile) — see EGG illustration
**2 :** the covering or outside part of a fruit or seed especially when hard or fibrous
**3 :** shell material (as of mollusks or turtles) or their substance
**4 :** something that resembles a shell: as **a :** a framework or exterior structure; *especially* **:** a building with an unfinished interior **b** (1) **:** an external case or outside covering ⟨the *shell* of a ship⟩ (2) **:** a thin usually spherical layer or surface enclosing a space or surrounding an object ⟨an expanding *shell* of gas around a neutron star⟩ **c :** a casing without substance ⟨mere effigies and *shells* of men —Thomas Carlyle⟩ **d :** an edible crust for holding a filling ⟨a pastry *shell*⟩ **e :** BAND SHELL **f :** a small beer glass **g :** an unlined article of outerwear
**5 :** a shell-bearing mollusk
**6 :** an impersonal attitude or manner that conceals the presence or absence of feeling ⟨he retreated into his *shell*⟩
**7 :** a narrow light racing boat propelled by one or more persons pulling oars or sculls
**8 :** any of the spaces occupied by the orbits of a group of electrons of approximately equal energy surrounding the nucleus of an atom
**9 a :** a projectile for cannon containing an explosive bursting charge **b :** a metal or paper case which holds the charge of powder and shot or bullet used with breech-loading small arms
**10 :** a plain usually sleeveless blouse or sweater
**11 :** a company or corporation that exists without assets or independent operations as a legal entity through which another company or corporation can conduct various dealings
— **shell** *adjective*
**²shell** (1562)

**shelduck**

*transitive verb*
**1 a :** to take out of a natural enclosing cover (as a shell, husk, pod, or capsule) ⟨*shell* peanuts⟩ **b :** to separate the kernels of (as an ear of Indian corn, wheat, or oats) from the cob, ear, or husk
**2 :** to throw shells at, upon, or into **:** BOMBARD
**3 :** to score heavily against (as an opposing pitcher in baseball)
*intransitive verb*
**1 :** to fall or scale off in thin pieces
**2 :** to cast the shell or exterior covering **:** fall out of the pod or husk ⟨nuts which *shell* in falling⟩
**3 :** to gather shells (as from a beach) **:** collect shells
**she'll** \'shē(ə)l, shil\ (circa 1590)
**:** she will **:** she shall
**¹shel·lac** \shə-'lak\ *noun* [¹*shell* + *lac*] (1713)
**1 :** purified lac usually prepared in thin orange or yellow flakes by heating and filtering and often bleached white
**2 :** a preparation of lac dissolved usually in alcohol and used chiefly as a wood filler and finish
**3 a :** a composition containing shellac formerly used for making phonograph records **b :** an old 78 rpm phonograph record
**²shellac** *transitive verb* **shel·lacked; shel·lack·ing** (1876)
**1 :** to coat or otherwise treat with shellac or a shellac varnish
**2 :** to defeat decisively
**shellacking** *noun* (1931)
**:** a decisive defeat **:** DRUBBING
**shell·back** \'shel-ˌbak\ *noun* (1853)
**1 :** an old or veteran sailor
**2 :** a person who has crossed the equator and been initiated in the traditional ceremony
**shell bean** *noun* (1868)
**1 :** a bean grown primarily for its edible seeds — compare SNAP BEAN
**2 :** the edible seed of a bean
**shell·crack·er** \'shel-ˌkra-kər\ *noun* (circa 1890)
**:** REDEAR
**shelled** \'sheld\ *adjective* (15th century)
**1 :** having a shell especially of a specified kind — often used in combination ⟨pink-*shelled*⟩ ⟨thick-*shelled*⟩
**2 a :** having the shell removed ⟨*shelled* oysters⟩ ⟨*shelled* nuts⟩ **b :** removed from the cob ⟨*shelled* corn⟩
**shell·er** \'she-lər\ *noun* (1694)
**1 :** one that shells ⟨a peanut *sheller*⟩
**2 :** a person who collects seashells
**shell·fish** \-ˌfish\ *noun* (before 12th century)
**:** an aquatic invertebrate animal with a shell; *especially* **:** an edible mollusk or crustacean
**shell·fish·ery** \-ˌfi-shə-rē, -ˌfish-rē\ *noun* (1885)
**:** a commercially exploited population of shellfish
**shell game** *noun* (1890)
**1 :** thimblerig played especially with three walnut shells
**2 :** FRAUD; *especially* **:** a swindle involving the substitution of something of little or no value for a valuable one
**shell jacket** *noun* (1840)
**1 :** a short tight military jacket worn buttoned up the front
**2 :** MESS JACKET
**shell out** *verb* (1801)
**:** PAY
**shell pink** *noun* (1887)
**:** a light yellowish pink
**shell·proof** \'shel-ˌprüf\ *adjective* (circa 1859)
**:** capable of resisting shells or bombs
**shell shock** *noun* (1915)

\ə\ abut \ᵊ\ kitten \ər\ further \a\ ash \ā\ ace \ä\ mop, mar \au̇\ out \ch\ chin \e\ bet \ē\ easy \g\ go \i\ hit \ī\ ice \j\ job \ŋ\ sing \ō\ go \ȯ\ law \ȯi\ boy \th\ thin \ th\ the \ü\ loot \u̇\ foot \y\ yet \zh\ vision *see also* Guide to Pronunciation

: post-traumatic stress disorder in soldiers as a result of combat experience

**shell–shocked** *adjective* (1918)
**1** : affected with shell shock
**2** : mentally confused, upset, or exhausted as a result of excessive stress

**shell steak** *noun* (circa 1968)
: the part of a short loin of beef that contains no tenderloin

**shell·work** \'shel-,wərk\ *noun* (1611)
: work adorned with shells or composed of a pattern of shells

**shelly** \'she-lē\ *adjective* **shell·i·er; -est** (1555)
**1** : abounding in or covered with shells ⟨a *shelly* shore⟩
**2** : of, relating to, or resembling a shell

**¹shel·ter** \'shel-tər\ *noun* [origin unknown] (1585)
**1 a** : something that covers or affords protection ⟨a bomb *shelter*⟩ **b** : an establishment providing food and shelter (as to the homeless) **c** : an establishment that houses and feeds stray animals
**2** : a position or the state of being covered and protected ⟨took *shelter*⟩
— **shel·ter·less** \-ləs\ *adjective*

**²shelter** *verb* **shel·tered; shel·ter·ing** \-t(ə-)riŋ\ (1590)
*transitive verb*
**1** : to constitute or provide a shelter for : PROTECT ⟨has led a *sheltered* life⟩
**2** : to place under shelter or protection ⟨*sheltered* himself in a mountain cave⟩
**3** : to protect (income) from taxation
*intransitive verb*
: to take shelter
— **shel·ter·er** \-tər-ər\ *noun*

**shel·ter·belt** \'shel-tər-,belt\ *noun* (1868)
: a barrier of trees and shrubs that protects (as crops) from wind and storm and lessens erosion

**shelter half** *noun* (1911)
: one of the halves of a shelter tent

**shelter tent** *noun* (1862)
: a small tent usually consisting of two interchangeable pieces : PUP TENT

**shel·tie** *or* **shel·ty** \'shel-tē\ *noun, plural* **shelties** [probably from Old Norse *Hjalti* Shetlander] (1650)
**1** : SHETLAND PONY
**2** : SHETLAND SHEEPDOG

**shelve** \'shelv\ *verb* **shelved; shelv·ing** [*shelf*] (1598)
*transitive verb*
**1** : to furnish with shelves
**2** : to place on a shelf
**3 a** : to remove from active service **b** : to put off or aside ⟨*shelve* a project⟩
*intransitive verb*
: to slope in a formation like a shelf
— **shelv·er** *noun*

**¹shelv·ing** \'shel-viŋ\ *noun* (1687)
**1** : the state or degree of sloping
**2** : a sloping surface or place

**²shelving** *noun* (1817)
**1** : material for shelves
**2** : SHELVES

**Shem** \'shem\ *noun* [Hebrew *Shēm*]
: the eldest son of Noah held to be the progenitor of the Semitic peoples

**She·ma** \shə-'mä\ *noun* [Hebrew *shĕma'* hear, first word of Deuteronomy 6:4] (1706)
: the Jewish confession of faith made up of Deuteronomy 6:4–9 and 11:13–21 and Numbers 15:37–41

**She·mi·ni Atze·reth** \shə-'mē-nē-ät-'ser-ət, -əth, -əs\ *noun* [Late Hebrew *shĕmīnī 'ăşereth*, from Hebrew *shĕmīnī* eighth + *'ăşereth* assembly] (circa 1905)
: a Jewish festival following the seventh day of Sukkoth and marked by a special prayer for seasonal rain

**Shem·ite** \'she-,mīt\ *noun* [*Shem*] (1659)
*archaic* : SEMITE

— **She·mit·ic** \shə-'mi-tik\ *or* **Shem·it·ish** \'she-,mi-tish\ *adjective, archaic*

**she·nan·i·gan** \shə-'na-ni-gən\ *noun* [origin unknown] (1855)
**1** : a devious trick used especially for an underhand purpose
**2 a** : tricky or questionable practices or conduct — usually used in plural **b** : high-spirited or mischievous activity — usually used in plural

**shend** \'shend\ *transitive verb* **shent** \'shent\; **shend·ing** [Middle English, from Old English *scendan;* akin to Old English *scamu* shame — more at SHAME] (before 12th century)
**1** *archaic* : to put to shame or confusion
**2** *archaic* : REPROVE, REVILE
**3** *chiefly dialect* **a** : INJURE, MAR **b** : RUIN, DESTROY

**she–oak** \'shē-,ōk\ *noun* (1792)
: any of several casuarinas

**She·ol** \shē-'ōl, 'shē-,\ *noun* [Hebrew *Shĕ'ōl*] (1599)
: the abode of the dead in early Hebrew thought

**¹shep·herd** \'she-pərd\ *noun* [Middle English *sheepherde,* from Old English *scēaphyrde,* from *scēap* sheep + *hierde* herdsman; akin to Old English *heord* herd] (before 12th century)
**1** : one who tends sheep
**2** : PASTOR
**3** : GERMAN SHEPHERD

**²shepherd** *transitive verb* (1790)
**1** : to tend as a shepherd
**2** : to guide or guard in the manner of a shepherd ⟨*shepherded* the bill through Congress⟩

**shepherd dog** *noun* (15th century)
: SHEEPDOG

**shep·herd·ess** \'she-pər-dəs\ *noun* (14th century)
: a woman or girl who tends sheep; *also* : a rural girl or woman

**shepherd's check** *noun* (1896)
: a pattern of small even black-and-white checks; *also* : a fabric woven in this pattern — called also *shepherd's plaid*

**shepherd's pie** *noun* (1877)
: a meat pie with a mashed potato crust

**shepherd's purse** *noun* (15th century)
: a white-flowered weedy annual herb (*Capsella bursa-pastoris*) of the mustard family with flat heart-shaped pods

**sheq·el** \'she-kəl\ *noun, plural* **sheq·a·lim** \she-'kä-lim\ *variant of* SHEKEL

**Sher·a·ton** \'sher-ə-t'n\ *adjective* [Thomas Sheraton] (1883)
: of, relating to, or being a style of furniture that originated in England around 1800 and is characterized by straight lines and graceful proportions

**sher·bet** \'shər-bət\ *also* **sher·bert** \-bərt\ *noun* [Turkish & Persian; Turkish *şerbet,* from Persian *sharbat,* from Arabic *sharbah* drink] (1603)
**1** : a cold drink of sweetened and diluted fruit juice
**2** : an ice with milk, egg white, or gelatin added

**sherd** *variant of* SHARD

**sher·got·tite** \'shər-gə-,tīt\ *noun* [Shergotty (Sherghati), town in India] (circa 1911)
: any of a class of rare achondritic geologically young meteorites that are apparently composed of solidified lava from celestial bodies other than earth

**she·rif** \shə-'rēf\ *variant of* SHARIF

**sher·iff** \'sher-əf\ *noun* [Middle English *shirreve,* from Old English *scīrgerēfa,* from *scīr* shire + *gerēfa* reeve — more at SHIRE, REEVE] (before 12th century)

*shepherd's check*

: an important official of a shire or county charged primarily with judicial duties (as executing the processes and orders of courts and judges)
— **sher·iff·dom** \-əf-dəm, -,təm\ *noun*

**sher·lock** \'shər-,läk, -lək\ *noun, often capitalized* [*Sherlock* Holmes, detective in stories by Sir Arthur Conan Doyle] (1903)
: DETECTIVE

**Sher·pa** \'sher-pə, 'shər-\ *noun* (1847)
: a member of a Tibetan people living on the high southern slopes of the Himalayas in eastern Nepal who provide support for foreign trekkers and mountain climbers

**sher·ris** \'sher-is\ *archaic variant of* SHERRY

**sher·ry** \'sher-ē\ *noun, plural* **sherries** [alteration of earlier *sherris* (taken as plural), from *Xeres* (now *Jerez*), Spain] (1597)
: a Spanish fortified wine with a distinctive nutty flavor; *also* : a similar wine produced elsewhere ◆

**she's** \'shēz\ (circa 1592)
: she is : she has

**Shet·land** \'shet-lənd\ *noun* (1836)
**1 a** : SHETLAND PONY **b** : SHETLAND SHEEPDOG
**2** *often not capitalized* **a** : a lightweight loosely twisted yarn of Shetland wool used for knitting and weaving **b** : a fabric or a garment made from Shetland wool

**Shetland pony** *noun* (1801)
: any of a breed of small stocky hardy ponies that originated in the Shetland Islands

**Shetland sheepdog** *noun* (1909)
: any of a breed of small heavy-coated dogs developed in the Shetland Islands that resemble miniature collies

**Shetland wool** *noun* (1790)
: fine wool from sheep raised in the Shetland Islands; *also* : yarn spun from this

**sheugh** \'shük\ *noun* [Middle English *sogh* swamp; akin to Middle Low German *sō* gutter] (1501)
*chiefly Scottish* : DITCH, TRENCH

**shew** \'shō\ *British variant of* SHOW

**shew·bread** \'shō-,bred\ *noun* [translation of German *Schaubrot*] (1530)
: consecrated unleavened bread ritually placed by the Jewish priests of ancient Israel on a table in the sanctuary of the Tabernacle on the Sabbath

**Shia** \'shē-(,)ä\ *noun* [Arabic *shī'ah* sect] (1626)
**1** : the Muslims of the branch of Islam comprising sects believing in Ali and the Imams as the only rightful successors of Muhammad and in the concealment and messianic return of the last recognized Imam — compare SUNNI
**2** : SHIITE
**3** : the branch of Islam formed by the Shia

---

◇ WORD HISTORY

**sherry**   Wines and distilled spirits are often named after the places where they are made. The region around the town of Jerez (formerly Xeres) in southern Spain produced a type of fortified wine with a rather nutty flavor that was introduced into England in the 16th century. The name *Xeres* was rendered *Sherries* or *Sherris* in English—the initial *sh* was a good approximation of the contemporary pronunciation of the Spanish sound represented by *x* (which has since changed to a \k\ or \h\ sound). Consequently, the wine from Xeres was sold under the name *sherris.* Some English speakers, however, believing that *sherris* was a plural noun, created a singular form *sherry,* which has since become standard. Other English words created by this process of back-formation from a presumed plural form are *pea* from *pease* and *cherry* from *cherise,* a northern dialectal form of Old French *cerise* "cherry."

**shi·at·su** *also* **shi·at·zu** \shē-'ät-(ˌ)sü\ *noun, often capitalized* [short for Japanese *shiatsuryōhō*, from *shi-* finger + *-atsu* pressure + *ryōhō* treatment] (1967)
: a massage with the fingers applied to those specific areas of the body used in acupuncture

**shib·bo·leth** \'shi-bə-ləth *also* -ˌleth\ *noun* [Hebrew *shibbōleth* stream; from the use of this word in Judges 12:6 as a test to distinguish Gileadites from Ephraimites, who pronounced it *sibbōleth*] (1638)
**1 a :** a word or saying used by adherents of a party, sect, or belief and usually regarded by others as empty of real meaning ⟨the old *shibboleths* come rolling off their lips —Joseph Epstein⟩ **b :** a widely held belief ⟨today this book publishing *shibboleth* is a myth —L. A. Wood⟩ **c :** TRUISM, PLATITUDE ⟨some truth in the *shibboleth* that crime does not pay —Lee Rogow⟩
**2 a :** a use of language regarded as distinctive of a particular group ⟨accent was . . . a *shibboleth* of social class —Vivian Ducat⟩ **b :** a custom or usage regarded as distinguishing one group from others ⟨for most of the well-to-do in the town, dinner was a *shibboleth*, its hour dividing mankind —Osbert Sitwell⟩ ◆

**shiel** \'shē(ə)l\ *noun* [Middle English (northern dialect) *schele*] (13th century)
*chiefly Scottish* **:** SHIELING

**¹shield** \'shē(ə)ld\ *noun* [Middle English *sheld*, from Old English *scield*; akin to Old High German *scilt* shield and probably to Old English *sciell* shell] (before 12th century)
**1 :** a broad piece of defensive armor carried on the arm
**2 :** one that protects or defends **:** DEFENSE
**3 :** DRESS SHIELD
**4 a :** a device or part that serves as a protective cover or barrier **b :** a protective structure (as a carapace, scale, or plate) of some animals
**5 :** ESCUTCHEON; *especially* **:** one that is wide at the top and rounds to a point at the bottom
**6 :** the Precambrian nuclear mass of a continent that is surrounded and sometimes covered by sedimentary rocks
**7 :** something resembling a shield: as **a** **:** APOTHECIUM **b :** a police officer's badge **c :** a decorative or identifying emblem

**²shield** *transitive verb* (before 12th century)
**1 a :** to protect with or as if with a shield **:** provide with a protective cover or shelter **b :** to cut off from observation **:** HIDE
**2** *obsolete* **:** FORBID
*synonym* see DEFEND
— **shield·er** *noun*

**shield law** *noun* (1971)
: a law that protects journalists from forced disclosure of confidential news sources

**shield volcano** *noun* (1911)
: a broad rounded volcano that is built up by successive outpourings of very fluid lava

**shiel·ing** \'shē-lən, -liŋ\ *noun* (1568)
**1** *British* **:** a mountain hut used as a shelter by shepherds
**2** *dialect British* **:** a summer pasture in the mountains

**shier** *comparative of* SHY
**shiest** *superlative of* SHY

**¹shift** \'shift\ *verb* [Middle English, from Old English *sciftan* to divide, arrange; akin to Old Norse *skipa* to arrange, assign] (13th century)
*transitive verb*
**1 :** to exchange for or replace by another **:** CHANGE
**2 a :** to change the place, position, or direction of **:** MOVE **b :** to make a change in (place)
**3 :** to change phonetically
*intransitive verb*
**1 a :** to change place or position **b :** to change direction ⟨the wind *shifted*⟩ **c :** to change gears **d :** to depress the shift key (as on a typewriter)
**2 a :** to assume responsibility ⟨had to *shift* for themselves⟩ **b :** to resort to expedients

**3 a :** to go through a change **b :** to change one's clothes **c :** to become changed phonetically
— **shift·able** \'shif-tə-bəl\ *adjective*
— **shift·er** *noun*
— **shift gears :** to make a change

**²shift** *noun* (1523)
**1 a :** a means or device for effecting an end **b** (1) **:** a deceitful or underhand scheme **:** DODGE (2) **:** an expedient tried in difficult circumstances **:** EXTREMITY
**2 a** *chiefly dialect* **:** a change of clothes **b** (1) *chiefly dialect* **:** SHIRT (2) **:** a woman's slip or chemise (3) **:** a usually loose-fitting or semifitted dress
**3 a :** a change in direction ⟨a *shift* in the wind⟩ **b :** a change in emphasis, judgment, or attitude
**4 a :** a group of people who work or occupy themselves in turn with other groups **b** (1) **:** a change of one group of people (as workers) for another in regular alternation (2) **:** a scheduled period of work or duty
**5 :** a change in place or position: as **a :** a change in the position of the hand on a fingerboard (as of a violin) **b** (1) **:** FAULT 5 (2) **:** the relative displacement of rock masses on opposite sides of a fault or fault zone **c** (1) **:** a simultaneous change of position in football by two or more players from one side of the line to the other (2) **:** a change of positions made by one or more players in baseball to provide better defense against a particular hitter **d :** a change in frequency resulting in a change in position of a spectral line or band — compare DOPPLER EFFECT **e :** a movement of bits in a computer register a specified number of places to the right or left
**6 :** a removal from one person or thing to another **:** TRANSFER
**7 :** CONSONANT SHIFT
**8 :** a bid in bridge in a suit other than the suit one's partner has bid — compare JUMP
**9 :** GEARSHIFT
*synonym* see RESOURCE

**shift key** *noun* (1893)
: a key on a keyboard (as of a typewriter) that when pressed enables an alternate set of characters to be printed

**shift·less** \'shif(t)-ləs\ *adjective* [*shift* (resourcefulness)] (1584)
**1 :** lacking in resourcefulness **:** INEFFICIENT
**2 :** lacking in ambition or incentive **:** LAZY
— **shift·less·ly** *adverb*
— **shift·less·ness** *noun*

**shifty** \'shif-tē\ *adjective* **shift·i·er; -est** (circa 1570)
**1 :** full of or ready with expedients **:** RESOURCEFUL
**2 a :** given to deception, evasion, or fraud **:** TRICKY **b :** capable of evasive movement **:** ELUSIVE ⟨a *shifty* boxer⟩
**3 :** indicative of a tricky nature ⟨*shifty* eyes⟩
— **shift·i·ly** \-tə-lē\ *adverb*
— **shift·i·ness** \-tē-nəs\ *noun*

**shi·gel·la** \shi-'ge-lə\ *noun, plural* **-gel·lae** \-'ge-(ˌ)lē, -(ˌ)lī\ *also* **-gellas** [New Latin, from Kiyoshi *Shiga* (died 1957) Japanese bacteriologist] (1937)
: any of a genus (*Shigella*) of nonmotile rod-shaped bacteria that cause dysenteries in animals and especially humans

**shig·el·lo·sis** \ˌshi-gə-'lō-səs\ *noun, plural* **-lo·ses** \-'lō-ˌsēz\ [New Latin] (1944)
: dysentery caused by shigellae

**shih tzu** \'shēd-'zü, 'shēt-'sü\ *noun, plural* **shih tzus** *also* **shih tzu** *often S&T capitalized* [Chinese (Beijing) *shīzi* (*gǒu*), from *shīzi* lion + *gǒu* dog] (1921)
: any of a breed of small short-legged dogs of Chinese origin that have a short muzzle and a long dense coat

**Shi·ism** \'shē-ˌi-zəm\ *noun* (circa 1883)
: Islam as taught by the Shia

**shii·ta·ke** \shē-'tä-kē\ *noun* [Japanese, from *shii*, the Japanese chinquapin + *take* mushroom] (1877)
: a dark Oriental mushroom (*Lentinus edodes* of the family Agaricaceae) widely cultivated especially on woods of the beech family for its edible flavorful cap

**Shi·ite** \'shē-ˌīt\ *noun* (1728)
: a Muslim of the Shia branch of Islam

**¹shi·kar** \shi-'kär\ *noun* [Hindi *shikār*, from Persian] (circa 1610)
*India* **:** HUNTING

**²shikar** *verb* **shi·karred; shi·kar·ring** (1872)
*India* **:** HUNT

**shi·ka·ri** \shi-'kär-ē, -'kar-\ *noun* [Hindi *shikārī*, from Persian, from *shikār*] (1827)
*India* **:** a big game hunter; *especially* **:** a professional hunter or guide

**shik·sa** *or* **shik·se** \'shik-sə\ *noun* [Yiddish *shikse*, feminine of *sheygets* non-Jewish boy, from Hebrew *sheqes* blemish, abomination] (1892)
**1 :** a non-Jewish girl or woman — often used disparagingly
**2 :** a Jewish girl or woman who does not observe Jewish precepts — used especially by Orthodox Jews

**¹shill** \'shil\ *intransitive verb* [²*shill*] (circa 1914)
**1 :** to act as a shill
**2 :** to act as a spokesperson or promoter ⟨the eminent Shakespearean producer, director, actor and star . . . is now *shilling* for a brokerage house —Andy Rooney⟩

**²shill** *noun* [perhaps short for *shillaber*, of unknown origin] (circa 1916)
**1 :** one who acts as a decoy (as for a pitchman or gambler); *also* **:** one who makes a sales pitch
**2 :** PITCH 8a

**shil·le·lagh** *also* **shil·la·lah** \shə-'lā-lē\ *noun* [*Shillelagh*, town in Ireland] (1772)
: CUDGEL

**shil·ling** \'shi-liŋ\ *noun* [Middle English, from Old English *scilling*; akin to Old High German *skilling*, a gold coin] (before 12th century)
**1 a :** a former monetary unit of the United Kingdom equal to 12 pence or 1/20 pound **b :** a former monetary unit equal to 1/20 pound of any of various countries in or formerly in the Commonwealth
**2 :** a coin representing one shilling
**3 :** any of several early American coins

\ə\ abut \ᵊ\ kitten \ər\ further \a\ ash \ā\ ace
\ä\ mop, mar \aů\ out \ch\ chin \e\ bet \ē\ easy
\g\ go \i\ hit \ī\ ice \j\ job \ŋ\ sing \ō\ go
\ȯ\ law \ȯi\ boy \th\ thin \th\ the \ü\ loot \ů\ foot
\y\ yet \zh\ vision    *see also* Guide to Pronunciation

**4** — see MONEY table

**Shil·luk** \shi-'lük\ *noun, plural* **Shilluk** *or* **Shilluks** (1790)
**1 :** a member of a Nilotic people of the Sudan dwelling mainly on the west bank of the White Nile
**2 :** the language of the Shilluk people

**¹shilly–shally** \'shi-lē-,sha-lē\ *adverb* [irregular reduplication of *shall I*] (1700)
**:** in an irresolute, undecided, or hesitating manner

**²shilly–shally** *adjective* (1734)
**:** IRRESOLUTE, VACILLATING

**³shilly–shally** *noun* (1755)
**:** INDECISION, IRRESOLUTION

**⁴shilly–shally** *intransitive verb* **shilly–shall·ied; shilly–shally·ing** (1782)
**1 :** to show hesitation or lack of decisiveness or resolution
**2 :** DAWDLE

**shil·pit** \'shil-pət\ *adjective* [origin unknown] (1812)
**1** *Scottish* **:** pinched and starved in appearance
**2** *Scottish* **:** WEAK, INSIPID — used of drink

**¹shim** \'shim\ *noun* [origin unknown] (1860)
**:** a thin often tapered piece of material (as wood, metal, or stone) used to fill in space between things (as for support, leveling, or adjustment of fit)

**²shim** *transitive verb* **shimmed; shim·ming** (circa 1890)
**:** to fill out or level up by the use of a shim

**¹shim·mer** \'shi-mər\ *verb* **shim·mered; shim·mer·ing** \'shi-mə-riŋ, 'shim-riŋ\ [Middle English *schimeren*, from Old English *scimerian*; akin to Old English *scīnan* to shine — more at SHINE] (before 12th century)
*intransitive verb*
**1 :** to shine with a soft tremulous or fitful light **:** GLIMMER
**2 :** to reflect a wavering sometimes distorted visual image
*transitive verb*
**:** to cause to shimmer
*synonym* see FLASH

**²shimmer** *noun* (1821)
**1 :** a light that shimmers **:** subdued sparkle or sheen **:** GLIMMER
**2 :** a wavering sometimes distorted visual image usually resulting from heat-induced changes in atmospheric refraction
— **shim·mery** \'shi-mə-rē, 'shim-rē\ *adjective*

**¹shim·my** \'shi-mē\ *noun, plural* **shimmies** (1837)
**1** [by alteration] **:** CHEMISE
**2** [short for *shimmy-shake*] **:** a jazz dance characterized by a shaking of the body from the shoulders down
**3 :** an abnormal vibration especially in the front wheels of a motor vehicle

**²shimmy** *intransitive verb* **shim·mied; shim·my·ing** (1919)
**1 :** to shake, quiver, or tremble in or as if in dancing a shimmy
**2 :** to vibrate abnormally — used especially of automobiles

**¹shin** \'shin\ *noun* [Middle English *shine*, from Old English *scinu*; akin to Old High German *scina* shin, Old English *scīa* shin, leg] (before 12th century)
**:** the front part of the vertebrate leg below the knee

**²shin** *verb* **shinned; shin·ning** (1829)
*intransitive verb*
**1 :** to move oneself up or down something vertical (as a pole) especially by alternately hugging it with the arms or hands and the legs
**2 :** to move forward rapidly on foot
*transitive verb*
**1 :** to kick or strike on the shins
**2 :** to climb by shinning

**³shin** \'shēn, 'shin\ *noun* [Hebrew *shīn*] (circa 1823)
**:** the 22d letter of the Hebrew alphabet — see ALPHABET table

**Shin** \'shin, 'shēn\ *noun* [Japanese, literally, truth] (1877)
**:** a major Japanese Buddhist sect that emphasizes salvation by faith in exclusive worship of Amida Buddha

**Shi·na** \'shē-nə\ *noun* (1854)
**:** an Indo-Aryan language spoken in Gilgit in northern Kashmir

**shin·bone** \'shin-,bōn\ *noun* (before 12th century)
**:** TIBIA 1

**shin·dig** \'shin-,dig\ *noun* [probably alteration of *shindy*] (1871)
**1 a :** a social gathering with dancing **b :** a usually large or lavish party
**2 :** SHINDY 2

**shin·dy** \'shin-dē\ *noun, plural* **shindys** *or* **shindies** [probably alteration of ¹*shinny*] (1821)
**1 :** SHINDIG 1
**2 :** FRACAS, UPROAR

**¹shine** \'shīn\ *verb* **shone** \'shōn, *especially Canadian & British* 'shän\ *or* **shined; shin·ing** [Middle English, from Old English *scīnan*; akin to Old High German *skīnan* to shine and perhaps to Greek *skia* shadow] (before 12th century)
*intransitive verb*
**1 :** to emit rays of light
**2 :** to be bright by reflection of light
**3 :** to be eminent, conspicuous, or distinguished ⟨*shines* in math⟩
**4 :** to have a bright glowing appearance ⟨his face *shone* with enthusiasm⟩
**5 :** to be conspicuously evident or clear
*transitive verb*
**1 a :** to cause to emit light **b :** to throw or direct the light of
**2** *past & past part* **shined :** to make bright by polishing ⟨*shined* his shoes⟩

**²shine** *noun* (15th century)
**1 :** brightness caused by the emission of light
**2 :** brightness caused by the reflection of light **:** LUSTER
**3 :** BRILLIANCE, SPLENDOR
**4 :** fair weather **:** SUNSHINE ⟨rain or *shine*⟩
**5 :** TRICK, CAPER — usually used in plural
**6 :** LIKING, FANCY ⟨took a *shine* to him⟩
**7 a :** a polish or gloss given to shoes **b :** a single polishing of a pair of shoes

**shin·er** \'shī-nər\ *noun* (14th century)
**1 :** one that shines
**2 :** a silvery fish; *especially* **:** any of numerous small freshwater American cyprinid fishes (especially genus *Notropis*) — compare GOLDEN SHINER
**3 :** BLACK EYE 1

**¹shin·gle** \'shiŋ-gəl\ *noun* [Middle English *schingel*] (13th century)
**1 :** a small thin piece of building material often with one end thicker than the other for laying in overlapping rows as a covering for the roof or sides of a building
**2 :** a small signboard especially designating a professional office — used chiefly in the phrase *hang out one's shingle*
**3 :** a woman's haircut with the hair trimmed short from the back of the head to the nape

**²shingle** *transitive verb* **shin·gled; shin·gling** \-g(ə-)liŋ\ (1562)
**1 :** to cover with or as if with shingles
**2 :** to bob and shape (the hair) in a shingle
**3 :** to lay out or arrange so as to overlap
— **shin·gler** \-g(ə-)lər\ *noun*

**³shingle** *noun* [probably of Scandinavian origin; akin to Norwegian *singel* coarse gravel] (15th century)
**1 :** coarse rounded detritus or alluvial material especially on the seashore that differs from ordinary gravel only in the larger size of the stones
**2 :** a place strewn with shingle
— **shin·gly** \-g(ə-)lē\ *adjective*

**shin·gles** \'shiŋ-gəlz\ *noun plural but singular in construction* [Middle English *schingles*, by folk etymology from Medieval Latin *cingulus*,

from Latin *cingulum* girdle — more at CINGULUM] (14th century)
**:** HERPES ZOSTER

**Shin·gon** \'shin-,gän, 'shēn-\ *noun* [Japanese] (1727)
**:** an esoteric Japanese Buddhist sect claiming the achievement of Buddhahood in this life through prescribed rituals

**shin·ing** \'shī-niŋ\ *adjective* (before 12th century)
**1 :** emitting or reflecting light
**2 :** bright and often splendid in appearance **:** RESPLENDENT
**3 :** possessing a distinguished quality **:** ILLUSTRIOUS
**4 :** full of sunshine

**shin·leaf** \'shin-,lēf\ *noun, plural* **shinleafs** (circa 1818)
**:** any of several wintergreens (especially *Pyrola elliptica*) with lustrous evergreen basal leaves and racemose white or pinkish flowers

**shin·nery** \'shi-nə-rē\ *noun, plural* **-ner·ies** [modification of Louisiana French *chênière*, from French *chêne* oak] (1901)
**:** a dense growth of small trees or an area of such growth; *especially* **:** one of scrub oak in the West and Southwest

**¹shin·ny** *also* **shin·ney** \'shi-nē\ *noun* [perhaps from ¹*shin*] (1672)
**:** a variation of hockey played by children with a curved stick and a ball or block of wood; *also* **:** the stick used

**²shinny** *intransitive verb* **shin·nied; shin·ny·ing** [alteration of ²*shin*] (1851)
**:** SHIN 1

**shin·plas·ter** \'shin-,plas-tər\ *noun* (1824)
**1 :** a piece of privately-issued paper currency; *especially* **:** one poorly secured and depreciated in value
**2 :** a piece of fractional currency

**shin·splints** \'shin-,splin(t)s\ *noun plural but singular or plural in construction* (circa 1930)
**:** injury to and inflammation of the tibial and toe extensor muscles or their fasciae caused by repeated minimal traumas (as by running)

**Shin·to** \'shin-(,)tō\ *noun* [Japanese *shintō*] (1727)
**:** the indigenous religion of Japan consisting chiefly in the cultic devotion to deities of natural forces and veneration of the Emperor as a descendant of the sun goddess
— **Shinto** *adjective*
— **Shin·to·ism** \-(,)tō-,i-zəm\ *noun*
— **Shin·to·ist** \-,tō-ist\ *noun or adjective*
— **Shin·to·is·tic** \,shin-tō-'is-tik\ *adjective*

**shiny** \'shī-nē\ *adjective* **shin·i·er; -est** (1590)
**1 a :** bright with the rays of the sun **:** SUNSHINY **b :** filled with light
**2 :** bright in appearance **:** POLISHED ⟨*shiny* new shoes⟩
**3 :** rubbed or worn smooth
**4 :** lustrous with natural secretions ⟨a *shiny* nose⟩
— **shin·i·ness** *noun*

**¹ship** \'ship\ *noun, often attributive* [Middle English, from Old English *scip*; akin to Old High German *skif* ship] (before 12th century)
**1 a :** a large seagoing vessel **b :** a sailing vessel having a bowsprit and usually three masts each composed of a lower mast, a topmast, and a topgallant mast
**2 :** BOAT; *especially* **:** one propelled by power or sail
**3 :** a ship's crew
**4 :** FORTUNE 3 ⟨when their *ship* comes in they'll be able to live in better style⟩
**5 :** AIRSHIP, AIRPLANE, SPACECRAFT

**²ship** *verb* **shipped; ship·ping** (14th century)
*transitive verb*
**1 a :** to place or receive on board a ship for transportation by water **b :** to cause to be transported ⟨*shipped* him off to prep school⟩
**2** *obsolete* **:** to provide with a ship

**3 :** to put in place for use ⟨*ship* the tiller⟩
**4 :** to take into a ship or boat ⟨*ship* the gang-plank⟩
**5 :** to engage for service on a ship
**6 :** to take (as water) over the side — used of a boat or a ship
*intransitive verb*
**1 :** to embark on a ship
**2 a :** to go or travel by ship — often used with *out* **b :** to proceed by ship or other means under military orders — often used with *out*
**3 :** to engage to serve on shipboard
— **ship·pa·ble** \'shi-pə-bəl\ *adjective*
**-ship** *noun suffix* [Middle English, from Old English *-scipe;* akin to Old High German *-scaft* -ship, Old English *scieppan* to shape — more at SHAPE]
**1 :** state : condition : quality ⟨friend*ship*⟩
**2 :** office : dignity : profession ⟨clerk*ship*⟩
**3 :** art : skill ⟨horseman*ship*⟩
**4 :** something showing, exhibiting, or embodying a quality or state ⟨town*ship*⟩
**5 :** one entitled to a (specified) rank, title, or appellation ⟨his Lord*ship*⟩
**6 :** the body of persons participating in a specified activity ⟨reader*ship*⟩ ⟨listener*ship*⟩
**ship biscuit** *noun* (1799)
**:** HARDTACK — called also *ship bread*
**¹ship·board** \'ship-ˌbōrd, -ˌbȯrd\ *noun* (13th century)
**1 :** the side of a ship
**2 :** SHIP ⟨met on *shipboard*⟩
**²shipboard** *adjective* (1857)
**:** existing or taking place on board a ship
**ship·borne** \'ship-ˌbōrn, -ˌbȯrn\ *adjective* (circa 1835)
**:** transported or designed to be transported by ship ⟨*shipborne* aircraft⟩
**ship·build·er** \'ship-ˌbil-dər\ *noun* (circa 1700)
**:** one who designs or constructs ships
— **ship·build·ing** \-diŋ\ *noun*
**ship·fit·ter** \'ship-ˌfi-tər\ *noun* (1941)
**1 :** one that fits together the structural members of ships and puts them into position for riveting or welding
**2 :** a naval enlisted man who works in sheet metal and performs the work of a plumber aboard ship
**ship·lap** \-ˌlap\ *noun* (1895)
**:** wooden sheathing in which the boards are rabbeted so that the edges of each board lap over the edges of adjacent boards to make a flush joint
**ship·load** \-ˈlōd, -ˌlōd\ *noun* (1639)
**1 :** as much or as many as will fill or load a ship
**2 :** an indefinitely large amount or number
**ship·man** \-mən\ *noun* (before 12th century)
**1 :** SAILOR, SEAMAN
**2 :** SHIPMASTER
**ship·mas·ter** \-ˌmas-tər\ *noun* (14th century)
**:** the master or commander of a ship other than a warship
**ship·mate** \-ˌmāt\ *noun* (1748)
**:** a fellow sailor
**ship·ment** \-mənt\ *noun* (1802)
**1 :** the act or process of shipping
**2 :** the goods shipped
**ship of state** *noun* (1847)
**:** the affairs of a state symbolized as a ship on a course
**ship of the line** (1706)
**:** a warship large enough to have a place in the line of battle
**ship·own·er** \'ship-ˌō-nər\ *noun* (circa 1530)
**:** the owner of a ship or of a share in a ship
**ship·per** \'shi-pər\ *noun* (1755)
**:** one that sends goods by any form of conveyance
**ship·ping** \'shi-piŋ\ *noun* (14th century)
**1 a :** passage on a ship **b :** SHIPS **c :** the body of ships in one place or belonging to one port or country
**2 :** the act or business of one that ships
**shipping clerk** *noun* (circa 1858)

**:** one who is employed in a shipping room to assemble, pack, and send out or receive goods
**ship·shape** \ˌship-ˈshāp, 'ship-ˌ\ *adjective* [short for earlier *shipshapen,* from *ship* + *shapen,* archaic past participle of *shape*] (1644)
**:** TRIM, TIDY
**ship·side** \'ship-ˌsīd\ *noun* (15th century)
**:** the area adjacent to a ship; *specifically* **:** a dock at which a ship loads or unloads passengers and freight
**ship's papers** *noun plural*
**:** the papers a ship is legally required to carry for due inspection to show the character of the ship and cargo
**ship·way** \'ship-ˌwā\ *noun* (1834)
**:** the ways on which a ship is built
**ship·worm** \-ˌwərm\ *noun* (circa 1778)
**:** any of various elongated marine clams (especially family Teredinidae) that resemble worms, burrow in submerged wood, and damage wharf piles and wooden ships
**¹ship·wreck** \-ˌrek\ *noun* [alteration of earlier *shipwrack,* from Middle English *schipwrak,* from Old English *scipwræc,* from *scip* ship + *wræc* something driven by the sea — more at WRACK] (12th century)
**1 :** a wrecked ship or its parts
**2 :** the destruction or loss of a ship
**3 :** an irretrievable loss or failure
**²shipwreck** *transitive verb* (1589)
**1 a :** to cause to experience shipwreck **b :** RUIN
**2 :** to destroy (a ship) by grounding or foundering
**ship·wright** \'ship-ˌrīt\ *noun* (before 12th century)
**:** a carpenter skilled in ship construction and repair
**ship·yard** \-ˌyärd\ *noun* (circa 1700)
**:** a yard, place, or enclosure where ships are built or repaired
**shire** \'shīr, *in place-name compounds* ˌshir, shər\ *noun* [Middle English, from Old English *scīr* office, shire; akin to Old High German *scīra* care] (before 12th century)
**1 :** an administrative subdivision; *especially* **:** a county in England
**2 :** any of a breed of large heavy draft horses of British origin that have heavily feathered legs
**shire town** *noun* (15th century)
**1** *British* **:** a town that is the seat of the government of a shire
**2** *New England* **:** a town where a court of superior jurisdiction (as a circuit court or a court with a jury) sits
**shirk** \'shərk\ *verb* [origin unknown] (1681)
*intransitive verb*
**1 :** to go stealthily : SNEAK
**2 :** to evade the performance of an obligation
*transitive verb*
**:** AVOID, EVADE ⟨*shirk* one's duty⟩
— **shirk·er** *noun*
**shirr** \'shər\ *transitive verb* [origin unknown] (1891)
**1 :** to draw (as cloth) together in a shirring
**2 :** to bake (eggs removed from the shell) until set
**shirr·ing** \'shər-iŋ\ *noun* (circa 1882)
**:** a decorative gathering (as of cloth) made by drawing up the material along two or more parallel lines of stitching

shire 2

shirring

**shirt** \'shərt\ *noun* [Middle

English *shirte,* from Old English *scyrte;* akin to Old Norse *skyrta* shirt, Old English *scort* short] (before 12th century)
**1 :** a garment for the upper part of the body: as **a :** a cloth garment usually having a collar, sleeves, a front opening, and a tail long enough to be tucked inside trousers or a skirt **b :** UNDERSHIRT
**2 :** all or a large part of one's money or resources ⟨lost his *shirt* on that business deal⟩
— **shirt·less** \-ləs\ *adjective*
**shirt·dress** \-ˌdres\ *noun* (1943)
**:** a tailored dress patterned after a shirt and having buttons down the front
**shirt·front** \-ˌfrənt\ *noun* (1838)
**:** the front of a shirt; *also* **:** the part of a man's shirt not covered by coat or vest
**shirt·ing** \'shər-tiŋ\ *noun* (1604)
**:** fabric suitable for shirts
**shirt jacket** *noun* (1879)
**:** a jacket designed in the style of a shirt — called also *shirt-jac*
**shirt·mak·er** \'shərt-ˌmā-kər\ *noun* (circa 1858)
**:** one that makes shirts
**¹shirt·sleeve** \-ˌslēv\ *noun* (circa 1566)
**:** the sleeve of a shirt
— **in shirtsleeves :** wearing a shirt but no coat
**²shirtsleeve** *also* **shirt·sleeves** \-ˌslēvz\ *or* **shirt·sleeved** \-ˌslēvd\ *adjective* (1864)
**1 a :** being without a coat ⟨a *shirtsleeve* spectator⟩ **b :** calling for the removal of coats for the sake of comfort or efficiency ⟨*shirtsleeve* weather⟩
**2 :** marked by informality and directness ⟨*shirtsleeve* diplomacy⟩
**¹shirt·tail** \'shərt-ˌtāl\ *adjective* (1845)
**1 :** very young : IMMATURE ⟨*shirttail* boys fishing in the creek⟩
**2 :** distantly and indefinitely related ⟨a *shirttail* cousin on her father's side⟩
**3 :** small, trivial, or short typically to the point of inadequacy ⟨has a gullied *shirttail* ranch in the hills⟩
**²shirttail** *noun* (1873)
**1 :** the part of a shirt that reaches below the waist especially in the back
**2 :** something small or inadequate
**shirt·waist** \'shərt-ˌwāst\ *noun* (1879)
**:** a woman's tailored garment (as a blouse or dress) with details copied from men's shirts
**shirty** \'shər-tē\ *adjective* (1846)
*chiefly British* **:** ANGRY, IRRITATED
**shish ke·bab** \'shish-kə-ˌbäb\ *noun* [Turkish *şişkebabı,* from *şiş* spit + *kebap* roast meat] (1914)
**:** kabob cooked on skewers
**¹shit** \'shit, *interjectionally also* 'shē-ət\ *noun* [(assumed) Middle English, from Old English *scite;* akin to Old English *-scītan* to defecate] (circa 1585)
**1 :** EXCREMENT — usually considered vulgar
**2 :** an act of defecation — usually considered vulgar
**3 :** NONSENSE, CRAP — usually considered vulgar
**4 :** any of several intoxicating or narcotic drugs; *especially* **:** HEROIN — usually considered vulgar
**5 :** DAMN 2 — usually considered vulgar
**6 :** a worthless, offensive, or detestable person — usually considered vulgar
— **shit·ty** \'shi-tē\ *adjective*
**²shit** \'shit\ *verb* **shit** *or* **shat** \'shat\; **shit·ting** [alteration of earlier *shite,* from Middle English *shiten,* from Old English *-scītan;* akin to Old High German *scīzan* to defecate and probably to Old English *scēadan* to separate — more at SHED] (circa 1720)

\ə\ abut  \ᵊ\ kitten  \ər\ further  \a\ ash  \ā\ ace
\ä\ mop, mar  \au̇\ out  \ch\ chin  \e\ bet  \ē\ easy
\g\ go  \i\ hit  \ī\ ice  \j\ job  \ŋ\ sing  \ō\ go
\ȯ\ law  \ȯi\ boy  \th\ thin  \th\ the  \ü\ loot  \u̇\ foot
\y\ yet  \zh\ vision    *see also* Guide to Pronunciation

*intransitive verb*
**:** DEFECATE — usually considered vulgar
*transitive verb*
**1 :** to defecate in — usually considered vulgar
**2 :** to attempt to deceive **:** BULLSHIT — usually considered vulgar
**shi·ta·ke** *variant of* SHIITAKE
**shit·tah** \'shi-tə\ *noun, plural* **shittahs** *or* **shit·tim** \'shi-təm\ [Hebrew *shiṭṭāh*] (1611)
**:** a tree of uncertain identity but probably an acacia (as *Acacia seyal*) from the wood of which the ark and fittings of the Hebrew tabernacle were made
**shit·tim·wood** \'shi-təm-ˌwud\ *noun* [Hebrew *shiṭṭīm* (plural of *shiṭṭāh*) + English *wood*] (1588)
**1 :** the wood of the shittah tree
**2 :** any of several trees (genus *Bumelia*, especially *B. lanuginosa*) of the sapodilla family of the southern U.S.; *also* **:** their hard heavy dense wood
**shiv** \'shiv\ *noun* [alteration of *chiv*, of unknown origin] (1674)
*slang* **:** KNIFE
**Shi·va** \'shi-və, 'shē-\ *variant of* SIVA
**shi·vah** *or* **shi·va** *also* **shi·ve** \'shi-və\ *noun* [Hebrew *shibh'āh* seven (days)] (1892)
**:** a traditional seven-day period of mourning the dead that is observed in Jewish homes — often used in the phrase *sit shivah*
**shiv·a·ree** \ˌshi-və-'rē, 'shi-və-ˌ\ *noun* [modification of French *charivari* — more at CHARIVARI] (1843)
**:** a noisy mock serenade to a newly married couple ◆
— **shivaree** *transitive verb*
**¹shiv·er** \'shi-vər\ *noun* [Middle English; akin to Old High German *scivaro* splinter] (13th century)
**:** one of the small pieces into which a brittle thing is broken by sudden violence
**²shiver** *verb* **shiv·ered; shiv·er·ing** \'shi-və-riŋ, 'shiv-riŋ\ (13th century)
**:** to break into many small pieces **:** SHATTER
**³shiver** *verb* **shiv·ered; shiv·er·ing** \'shi-və-riŋ, 'shiv-riŋ\ [Middle English, alteration of *chiveren*] (15th century)
*intransitive verb*
**1 :** to undergo trembling **:** QUIVER
**2 :** to tremble in the wind as it strikes first one and then the other side (of a sail)
*transitive verb*
**:** to cause (a sail) to shiver by steering close to the wind
**⁴shiver** *noun* (1727)
**1 :** an instance of shivering **:** TREMBLE
**2 :** an intense shivery sensation especially of fear — often used in plural with *the* ⟨horror movies give him the *shivers*⟩
**¹shiv·ery** \'shi-və-rē, 'shiv-rē\ *adjective* (1683)
**:** easily broken into shivers
**²shivery** *adjective* (1747)
**1 :** characterized by shivers
**2 :** causing shivers
**shle·miehl** *variant of* SCHLEMIEL
**shlep, shlepp** *variant of* SCHLEPP
**shlock** *variant of* SCHLOCK
**shm-** — see SCHM-
**¹shoal** \'shōl\ *adjective* [alteration of Middle English *shold*, from Old English *sceald* — more at SKELETON] (1554)
**:** SHALLOW
**²shoal** *noun* (1555)
**1 :** SHALLOW
**2 :** a sandbank or sandbar that makes the water shallow; *specifically* **:** an elevation which is not rocky and on which there is a depth of water of six fathoms (11 meters) or less
**³shoal** (1574)
*intransitive verb*
**:** to become shallow
*transitive verb*
**1 :** to come to a shallow or less deep part of
**2 :** to cause to become shallow or less deep

**⁴shoal** *noun* [(assumed) Middle English *shole*, from Old English *scolu* multitude — more at SCHOOL] (1579)
**:** a large group or number **:** CROWD ⟨a *shoal* of fish⟩
**⁵shoal** (1610)
*intransitive verb*
**:** THRONG, SCHOOL
**shoat** \'shōt\ *noun* [Middle English *shote*; akin to Flemish *schote* shoat] (15th century)
**:** a young hog usually less than one year old
**¹shock** \'shäk\ *noun* [Middle English; akin to Middle High German *schoc* heap] (14th century)
**:** a pile of sheaves of grain or stalks of Indian corn set up in a field with the butt ends down
**²shock** *transitive verb* (15th century)
**:** to collect into shocks
**³shock** *noun, often attributive* [Middle French *choc*, from *choquer* to strike against, from Old French *choquier*, probably of Germanic origin; akin to Middle Dutch *schocken* to jolt] (1565)
**1 :** the impact or encounter of individuals or groups in combat
**2 a :** a violent shake or jar **:** CONCUSSION **b :** an effect of such violence
**3 a** (1) **:** a disturbance in the equilibrium or permanence of something (2) **:** a sudden or violent mental or emotional disturbance **b :** something that causes such disturbance **c :** a state of being so disturbed
**4 :** a state of profound depression of the vital processes associated with reduced blood volume and pressure and caused usually by severe especially crushing injuries, hemorrhage, or burns
**5 :** sudden stimulation of the nerves and convulsive contraction of the muscles caused by the discharge of electricity through the animal body
**6 a :** STROKE 5 **b :** CORONARY THROMBOSIS
**7 :** SHOCK ABSORBER
**⁴shock** (1576)
*transitive verb*
**1 a :** to strike with surprise, terror, horror, or disgust **b :** to cause to undergo a physical or nervous shock **c :** to subject to the action of an electrical discharge
**2 :** to drive by or as if by a shock
*intransitive verb*
**1 :** to meet with a shock **:** COLLIDE
**2 :** to cause surprise or shock
— **shock·able** \'shä-kə-bəl\ *adjective*
**⁵shock** *adjective* [perhaps from ¹*shock*] (1681)
**:** BUSHY, SHAGGY
**⁶shock** *noun* (1819)
**:** a thick bushy mass (as of hair)
**shock absorber** *noun* (1906)
**:** any of several devices for absorbing the energy of sudden impulses or shocks in machinery or structures
**shock·er** \'shä-kər\ *noun* (circa 1824)
**:** one that shocks; *especially* **:** something horrifying or offensive (as a sensational film or work of fiction)
**shock front** *noun* (1949)
**:** the advancing edge of a shock wave
**shock·ing** \'shä-kiŋ\ *adjective* (1703)
**:** extremely startling, distressing, or offensive
— **shock·ing·ly** \-kiŋ-lē\ *adverb*
**shocking pink** *noun* (1938)
**:** a striking, vivid, bright, or intense pink
**shock·proof** \'shäk-ˌprüf\ *adjective* (1911)
**1 :** incapable of being shocked
**2 a :** resistant to damage by shock **b :** unlikely to cause shock **:** protectively insulated ⟨a *shockproof* switch⟩
**shock therapy** *noun* (1917)
**:** the treatment of mental disorder by the artificial induction of coma or convulsions through use of drugs or electric current — called also *shock treatment*
**shock troops** *noun plural* (1917)
**1 :** troops especially suited and chosen for offensive work because of their high morale, training, and discipline

**2 :** a group of people militant in pressing for a cause
**shock tube** *noun* (1949)
**:** a usually enclosed tube in which experimental shock waves are produced as a result of the rupturing of a diaphragm separating two chambers containing a gas or gases at differential pressure
**shock wave** *noun* (1907)
**1 :** a compressional wave of high amplitude caused by a shock (as from an earthquake or explosion) to the medium through which the wave travels
**2 :** a violent often pulsating disturbance or reaction ⟨*shock waves* of rebellion⟩
**shod** \'shäd\ *adjective* [Middle English, from past participle of *shoen* to shoe, from Old English *scōgan*, from *scōh* shoe — more at SHOE] (13th century)
**1 a :** wearing footgear (as shoes) **b :** equipped with tires
**2 :** furnished or equipped with a shoe
**¹shod·dy** \'shä-dē\ *noun* [origin unknown] (1832)
**1 a :** a reclaimed wool from materials that are not felted that is of better quality and longer staple than mungo **b :** a fabric often of inferior quality manufactured wholly or partly from reclaimed wool
**2 a :** inferior, imitative, or pretentious articles or matter **b :** pretentious vulgarity
**²shoddy** *adjective* **shod·di·er; -est** (1847)
**1 :** made wholly or partly of shoddy
**2 a :** cheaply imitative **:** vulgarly pretentious **b :** hastily or poorly done **:** INFERIOR **c :** SHABBY
— **shod·di·ly** \'shä-dᵊl-ē\ *adverb*
— **shod·di·ness** \'shä-dē-nəs\ *noun*
**¹shoe** \'shü\ *noun* [Middle English *shoo*, from Old English *scōh*; akin to Old High German *scuoh* shoe] (before 12th century)
**1 a :** an outer covering for the human foot typically having a thick or stiff sole with an attached heel and an upper part of lighter material (as leather) **b :** a metal plate or rim for the hoof of an animal
**2 :** something resembling a shoe in function or placement
**3** *plural* **:** another's place, function, or viewpoint ⟨steps from assistant stage manager into the star's *shoes* —Steven Fuller⟩

◇ WORD HISTORY
**shivaree**  In 19th century rural America, a newly wed couple—often one whose marriage was because of discrepancy in age or some other cause considered incongruous by the local community—might have their wedding night interrupted by an unwanted disturbance. A motley band of revelers outside the windows of their home would treat them to a cacophonous serenade, delivered in derision on a battery of pots, pans, cowbells, and other ersatz musical instruments. In the eastern U.S. this custom, imported from rural England, was simply called a *serenade* or known under a variety of colorful local names. In much of the central U.S. and Canada, however, it was called a *shivaree*, a loan from French *charivari*, a word that denotes the same folk custom in France. American English *shivaree* is part of our small linguistic heritage from Mississippi Valley French, the language of French pioneers who explored and settled the Mississippi and its tributaries. The greater part of this heritage consists of place names, from the obvious (*St. Louis* and *New Orleans*) to the buried (*Ozark*, a phonetic rendering of French *Aux Arcs* "At the Arcs," *Arcs* being a French name for several tribes of Indians living in that area).

**4 :** a device that retards, stops, or controls the motion of an object; *especially* **:** the part of a brake that presses on the brake drum
**5 a :** any of various devices that are inserted in or run along a track or groove to guide a movement, provide a contact or friction grip, or protect against wear, damage, or slipping **b :** a device (as a clip or track) on a camera that permits attachment of an accessory item (as a flash unit)
**6 :** a dealing box designed to hold several decks of playing cards
— **shoe·less** *adjective*

**²shoe** *transitive verb* **shod** \'shäd\ *also* **shoed** \'shüd\; **shoe·ing** \'shü-iŋ\ (before 12th century)
**1 :** to furnish with a shoe
**2 :** to cover for protection, strength, or ornament

**shoe·bill** \'shü-ˌbil\ *noun* (1874)
**:** a large broad-billed wading bird (*Balaeniceps rex*) of the valley of the White Nile that is related to the storks and herons

**shoe·black** \-ˌblak\ *noun* (1778)
**:** BOOTBLACK

**¹shoe·horn** \-ˌhȯrn\ *noun* (1589)
**:** a curved piece (as of horn, wood, or metal) used in putting on a shoe

**²shoehorn** *transitive verb* (1926)
**:** to force into a small, narrow, or insufficient space **:** SQUEEZE ⟨*shoehorn* the past, present, and future into about 500 pages —Otis Port⟩

**shoe·lace** \'shü-ˌlās\ *noun* (circa 1647)
**:** a lace or string for fastening a shoe

**shoe·mak·er** \-ˌmā-kər\ *noun* (14th century)
**:** one whose occupation is making or repairing shoes

**shoe·pac** *or* **shoe·pack** \'shü-ˌpak\ *noun* [by folk etymology from Delaware Jargon (Delaware-based pidgin) *seppock* shoe, from Delaware (Unami dialect) *čípahkə* shoes] (1755)
**:** a waterproof laced boot worn especially over heavy socks in cold weather

**¹shoe·string** \'shü-ˌstriŋ\ *noun* (1616)
**1 :** SHOELACE
**2** [from shoestrings being a typical item sold by itinerant vendors] **:** a small sum of money **:** capital inadequate or barely adequate to the needs of a transaction ⟨started the business on a *shoestring*⟩

**²shoestring** *adjective* (1878)
**1 :** narrow and long like a shoestring ⟨a *shoestring* tie⟩
**2 :** operating on, accomplished by, or consisting of a small amount of money or capital ⟨a *shoestring* budget⟩

**shoestring catch** *noun* (1926)
**:** a catch (as in baseball) made very close to the feet

**shoe tree** *noun* (1827)
**:** a foot-shaped device for inserting in a shoe to preserve its shape

**sho·far** \'shō-ˌfär, -fər\ *noun, plural* **sho·froth** \shō-ˈfrōt, -'frōth, -'frōs\ [Hebrew *shōphār*] (1833)
**:** a ram's-horn trumpet blown by the ancient Hebrews in battle and high religious observances and used in synagogues before and during Rosh Hashanah and at the conclusion of Yom Kippur

**shofar**

**¹shog** \'shäg\ *intransitive verb* **shogged; shog·ging** [Middle English *shoggen*] (15th century)
*chiefly dialect* **:** to move along

**²shog** *noun* (1611)
*chiefly dialect* **:** SHAKE, JOLT

**sho·gun** \'shō-gən\ *noun* [Japanese *shōgun* general] (1727)
**:** one of a line of military governors ruling Japan until the revolution of 1867–68
— **sho·gun·al** \'shō-gə-nəl\ *adjective*
— **sho·gun·ate** \'shō-gə-nət, -ˌnāt\ *noun*

**sho·ji** \'shō-(ˌ)jē\ *noun, plural* **shoji** *also* **shojis** [Japanese *shōji*] (1880)
**:** a paper screen serving as a wall, partition, or sliding door

**sho·lom** \shä-'lōm, shə-\ *variant of* SHALOM

**Sho·na** \'shō-nə\ *noun, plural* **Shona** *or* **Shonas** (circa 1895)
**1 :** a member of any of a group of Bantu peoples of Zimbabwe and southern Mozambique
**2 :** the group of languages spoken by the Shona

**shone** *past and past participle of* SHINE

**¹shoo** \'shü\ *interjection* [Middle English *schowe*] (15th century)
— used especially in driving away an unwanted animal

**²shoo** *transitive verb* (circa 1798)
**:** to scare, drive, or send away by or as if by crying *shoo*

**shoo·fly** \'shü-ˌflī\ *noun* [¹*shoo* + *fly*] (1887)
**1 :** a child's rocker having the seat built on or usually between supports representing an animal figure
**2 :** any of several plants held to repel flies

**shoofly pie** *noun* (1926)
**:** a rich pie of Pennsylvania-Dutch origin made of molasses or brown sugar sprinkled with a crumbly mixture of flour, sugar, and butter

**shoo–in** \'shü-ˌin\ *noun* (1937)
**:** one that is a certain and easy winner

**¹shook** *past or chiefly dialect past participle of* SHAKE

**²shook** \'shuk\ *noun* [origin unknown] (1796)
**1 a :** a set of staves and headings for one hogshead, cask, or barrel **b :** a bundle of parts (as of boxes) ready to be put together
**2 :** ¹SHOCK

**shook–up** \ˌshuk-'əp\ *adjective* (1897)
**:** nervously upset **:** AGITATED

**shoon** \'shün, 'shōn\ *chiefly dialect plural of* SHOE

**¹shoot** \'shüt\ *verb* **shot** \'shät\; **shoot·ing** [Middle English *sheten, shuten,* from Old English *scēotan;* akin to Old Norse *skjōta* to shoot] (before 12th century)
*transitive verb*
**1 a (1) :** to eject or impel or cause to be ejected or impelled by a sudden release of tension (as of a bowstring or slingshot or by a flick of a finger) ⟨*shoot* an arrow⟩ ⟨*shoot* a spitball⟩ ⟨*shoot* a marble⟩ **(2) :** to drive forth or cause to be driven forth by an explosion (as of a powder charge in a firearm or of ignited fuel in a rocket) **(3) :** to drive forth or cause to be driven forth by a sudden release of gas or air ⟨*shoot* darts from a blowgun⟩ ⟨a steam catapult *shoots* planes from a carrier⟩ **(4) :** to propel (as a ball or puck) toward a goal by striking or pushing with part of the body (as the hand or foot) or with an implement; *also* **:** to score by so doing ⟨*shoot* the winning goal⟩ ⟨*shoot* a basket⟩ **(5) :** to throw or cast off or out often with force ⟨*shoot* dice⟩ ⟨the horse *shot* his rider out of the saddle⟩ **b :** to cause (as a gun or bow) to propel a missile **c (1) :** to utter (as words or sounds) rapidly or suddenly or with force ⟨*shoot* out a stream of invective⟩ **(2) :** to emit (as light, flame, or fumes) suddenly and rapidly **(3) :** to send forth with suddenness or intensity ⟨*shot* a look of anger at them⟩ **d :** to discharge, dump, or empty especially by overturning, upending, or directing into a slide
**2 :** to affect by shooting: as **a :** to strike with a missile especially from a bow or gun; *especially* **:** to wound or kill with a missile discharged from a bow or firearm **b :** to remove or destroy by use of firearms ⟨*shot* out the light⟩; *also* **:** WRECK, EXPLODE
**3 a :** to push or slide (as the bolt of a door or lock) into or out of a fastening **b :** to push or thrust forward **:** stick out ⟨toads *shooting* out

their tongues⟩ **c :** to put forth in growing **:** to place, send, or bring into position abruptly
**4 a :** to engage in (a sport or game or a portion of a game that involves shooting) **:** PLAY ⟨*shoot* pool⟩ ⟨*shoot* a round of golf⟩ ⟨*shoot* craps⟩ **b (1) :** to place or offer (a bet) on the result of casting dice ⟨*shoot* $5⟩ **(2) :** to use up by or as if by betting **:** EXHAUST ⟨*shot* his whole wad on a shady deal⟩
**5 a :** to engage in the hunting and killing of (as game) with firearms especially as a sport ⟨*shoot* woodcock⟩ **b :** to hunt over ⟨*shoot* a tract of woodland⟩
**6 a :** to cause to move suddenly or swiftly forward ⟨*shot* the car onto the highway⟩ **b :** to send or carry quickly **:** DISPATCH ⟨*shoot* the letter on to me as soon as you receive it⟩
**7 :** to variegate as if by sprinkling color in streaks, flecks, or patches
**8 :** to pass swiftly by, past, or along ⟨*shooting* rapids⟩
**9 :** to plane (as the edge of a board) straight or true
**10 a :** SET OFF, DETONATE, IGNITE ⟨*shoot* a charge of dynamite⟩ **b :** to effect by blasting
**11 :** to determine the altitude of
**12 :** to take a picture or series of pictures or television images of **:** PHOTOGRAPH, FILM
**13 a :** to give an injection to **b :** to inject (an illicit drug) especially into the bloodstream
*intransitive verb*
**1 a :** to go or pass rapidly and precipitately ⟨sparks *shooting* all over⟩ ⟨his feet *shot* out from under him⟩ **b :** to move ahead by force of momentum **c :** to stream out suddenly **:** SPURT **d :** to dart in or as if in rays from a source of light **e :** to dart with a piercing sensation ⟨pain *shot* up my arm⟩
**2 a :** to cause an engine or weapon to discharge a missile **b :** to use a firearm or bow especially for sport (as in hunting)
**3 :** to propel a missile ⟨guns that *shoot* many miles⟩
**4 :** PROTRUDE, PROJECT
**5 a :** to grow or sprout by or as if by putting forth shoots **b :** DEVELOP, MATURE **c :** to spring or rise rapidly or suddenly — often used with *up* ⟨in a burst of growth he *shot* up to six feet tall⟩ ⟨prices *shot* up⟩
**6 a :** to propel an object (as a ball) in a particular way **b :** to drive the ball or puck toward a goal
**7 :** to cast dice
**8 :** to slide into or out of a fastening ⟨a bolt that *shoots* in either direction⟩
**9 :** to record something (as on film or videotape) with a camera
**10 :** to begin to speak — usually used as an imperative ⟨OK, *shoot,* what do you have to say⟩
— **shoot at** *or* **shoot for :** to aim at **:** strive for
— **shoot from the hip :** to act or speak hastily without consideration of the consequences
— **shoot one's bolt :** to exhaust one's capabilities and resources
— **shoot oneself in the foot :** to act against one's own best interests
— **shoot the breeze :** to converse idly **:** GOSSIP
— **shoot the works 1 :** to venture all one's capital on one play **2 :** to put forth all one's efforts

**²shoot** *noun* (15th century)
**1 :** a sending out of new growth or the growth sent out: as **a :** a stem or branch with its leaves and appendages especially when not yet mature **b :** OFFSHOOT

---

\ə\ abut  \ᵊ\ kitten  \ər\ further  \a\ ash  \ā\ ace
\ä\ mop, mar  \aú\ out  \ch\ chin  \e\ bet  \ē\ easy
\g\ go  \i\ hit  \ī\ ice  \j\ job  \ŋ\ sing  \ō\ go
\ȯ\ law  \ȯi\ boy  \th\ thin  \t͟h\ the  \ü\ loot  \ú\ foot
\y\ yet  \zh\ vision    *see also* Guide to Pronunciation

**2 a :** an act of shooting (as with a bow or a firearm): (1) : SHOT (2) : the firing of a missile especially by artillery **b** (1) : a hunting trip or party (2) : the right to shoot game in a particular area or land over which it is held **c** (1) : a shooting match ⟨skeet *shoot*⟩ (2) : a round of shots in a shooting match **d** : the action or an instance of shooting with a camera : a session or a series of sessions of photographing or filming ⟨a movie *shoot*⟩
**3 a :** a motion or movement of rapid thrusting: as (1) : a sudden or rapid advance (2) : a momentary darting sensation : TWINGE (3) : THRUST 2b (4) : the pace between strokes in rowing **b** : a bar of rays : BEAM ⟨a *shoot* of sunlight⟩
**4** [probably by folk etymology from French *chute* — more at CHUTE] **a** : a rush of water down a steep or rapid **b** : a place where a stream runs or descends swiftly
**³shoot** *interjection* [euphemism for *shit*] (1876)
— used to express annoyance or surprise
**shoot down** *transitive verb* (1845)
**1 :** to cause to fall by shooting ⟨enemy aircraft *shot down* the helicopter⟩; *especially* : to kill in this way ⟨was *shot down* in cold blood⟩
**2 :** to put an end to : DEFEAT
**3 :** DEFLATE, RIDICULE
**4 :** DISCREDIT 2 ⟨*shoot down* a theory⟩
**shoot–'em–up** \'shüt-əm-ˌəp\ *noun* (1947)
: a movie or television show with much shooting and bloodshed
**shoot·er** \'shü-tər\ *noun* (13th century)
**1 :** one that shoots: as **a** : a person who fires a missile-discharging device (as a rifle or bow) **b** : the person who is shooting or whose turn it is to shoot
**2 :** something that is used in shooting: as **a** : a marble shot from the hand **b** : REVOLVER — usually used in combination ⟨six-*shooter*⟩
**3 :** a shot of whiskey or whiskey diluted with something (as soda); *also* : a shot glass containing a bit of food (as a raw oyster)
**shooting gallery** *noun* (1836)
**1 :** a usually covered range equipped with targets for practice with firearms
**2** *slang* : a place where one can obtain narcotics and shoot up
**shooting iron** *noun* (1775)
: FIREARM
**shooting script** *noun* (1929)
**1 :** the final completely detailed version of a motion-picture script in which scenes are grouped in the order most convenient for shooting
**2 :** the final version of a television script used in the production of a program
**shooting star** *noun* (1593)
**1 :** a visual meteor appearing as a temporary streak of light in the night sky
**2 :** any of several North American perennial herbs (genus *Dodecatheon*, especially *D. meadia*) of the primrose family that have entire oblong leaves and showy flowers with reflexed petals
**shooting stick** *noun* (1926)
: a spiked stick with a top that opens into a seat
**shoot–out** \'shüt-ˌaut\ *noun* (1948)
**1 :** a battle fought with handguns or rifles
**2 :** something resembling a shoot-out; *broadly* : SHOWDOWN
**shoot–the–chutes** \ˌshüt-thə-'shüts\ *noun plural but singular in construction* (1920)
: an amusement ride consisting of a steep incline down which boats slide into a pool at the bottom
**shoot up** (1890)
*transitive verb*
**1 :** to shoot or shoot at especially indiscriminately or recklessly ⟨cowboys *shooting up* the town⟩
**2 :** to inject (a narcotic drug) into a vein
*intransitive verb*
: to inject a narcotic into a vein

— **shoot–up** \'shüt-ˌəp\ *noun*
**¹shop** \'shäp\ *noun, often attributive* [Middle English *shoppe*, from Old English *sceoppa* booth; akin to Old High German *scopf* shed] (14th century)
**1 :** a handicraft establishment : ATELIER
**2 a :** a building or room stocked with merchandise for sale : STORE **b** *or* **shoppe** \'shäp\ : a small retail establishment or a department in a large one offering a specified line of goods or services ⟨a millinery *shop*⟩ ⟨a sandwich *shop*⟩
**3 :** a commercial establishment for the making or repair of goods or machinery ⟨machine *shop*⟩ ⟨repair *shop*⟩
**4 a :** a school laboratory equipped for manual training **b** : the art or science of working with tools and machinery
**5 a :** a business establishment : OFFICE **b** : SHOPTALK
**²shop** *verb* **shopped; shop·ping** (1764)
*intransitive verb*
**1 a :** to examine goods or services with intent to buy **b** : to hunt through a market in search of the best buy
**2 :** to make a search : HUNT
*transitive verb*
: to examine the stock or offerings of ⟨*shop* the stores for Christmas gift ideas⟩
**shop·keep·er** \'shäp-ˌkē-pər\ *noun* (1530)
: STOREKEEPER 2
**shop·lift** \-ˌlift\ *verb* [back-formation from *shoplifter*] (1820)
*intransitive verb*
: to steal displayed goods from a store
*transitive verb*
: to steal (displayed goods) from a store
**shop·lift·er** \-ˌlif-tər\ *noun* (1680)
: one who shoplifts
**shop·per** \'shä-pər\ *noun* (1860)
**1 :** one that shops
**2 :** one whose occupation is shopping as an agent for customers or for an employer
**3 :** a usually free paper carrying advertising and sometimes local news
**shopping bag** *noun* (1886)
: a bag (as of strong paper) that has handles and is intended for carrying purchases
**shopping center** *noun* (1898)
: a group of retail stores and service establishments usually with ample parking facilities and usually designed to serve a community or neighborhood — called also *shopping plaza*
**shopping list** *noun* (1913)
: a list of items to be purchased; *broadly* : a list of related items ⟨the biggest possible *shopping list* of budget cuts —Leonard Silk⟩
**shopping mall** *noun* (1959)
: MALL 3
**shop steward** *noun* (1904)
: a union member elected as the union representative of a shop or department in dealings with the management
**shop·talk** \'shäp-ˌtòk\ *noun* (1881)
: the jargon or subject matter peculiar to an occupation or a special area of interest
**shop·win·dow** \-ˌwin-(ˌ)dō\ *noun* (15th century)
: a display window of a store
**shop·worn** \-ˌwōrn, -ˌwòrn\ *adjective* (1838)
**1 :** faded, soiled, or otherwise impaired by remaining too long in a store
**2 :** stale from excessive use or familiarity ⟨*shopworn* clichés⟩
**3 :** WORN-OUT ⟨think of himself as a *shopworn* Hollywood cynic —A. H. Johnston⟩
**¹shore** \'shōr, 'shòr\ *noun, often attributive* [Middle English, from (assumed) Old English *scor*; akin to Middle Low German *schōr* foreland and perhaps to Old English *scieran* to cut — more at SHEAR] (14th century)
**1 :** the land bordering a usually large body of water; *specifically* : COAST
**2 :** a boundary or the country or place that it bounds ⟨hold him accountable for difficulties

beyond our *shores* that he could do nothing about —Dorothy Fosdick⟩
**3 :** land as distinguished from the sea ⟨shipboard and *shore* duty⟩
**²shore** *transitive verb* **shored; shor·ing** [Middle English; akin to Old Norse *skortha* to prop] (14th century)
**1 :** to support by a shore : PROP
**2 :** to give support to : BRACE — usually used with *up*
**³shore** *noun* (14th century)
: a prop for preventing sinking or sagging
**shore·bird** \'shōr-ˌbərd, 'shòr-\ *noun* (circa 1672)
: any of a suborder (Charadrii) of birds (as a plover or snipe) that frequent the seashore
**shore dinner** *noun* (1892)
: a dinner consisting chiefly of seafoods
**shore·front** \-ˌfrənt\ *noun* (1919)
: land along a shore; *specifically* : BEACHFRONT
**shore leave** *noun* (1888)
: a leave of absence to go on shore granted to a sailor or naval officer
**shore·line** \-ˌlīn\ *noun* (1852)
**1 :** the line where a body of water and the shore meet
**2 :** the strip of land along the shoreline
**shore patrol** *noun* (1917)
**1 :** a branch of a navy that exercises guard and police functions — compare MILITARY POLICE
**2 :** petty officers detailed to perform police duty while a ship is in port
**shore·side** \-ˌsīd\ *adjective* (1883)
: situated at or near a shore
**shore·ward** \-wərd\ *or* **shore·wards** \-wərdz\ *adverb* (circa 1691)
: toward the shore
**shor·ing** \'shōr-iŋ, 'shòr-\ *noun* (15th century)
**1 :** the act of supporting with or as if with a prop
**2 :** a system or group of shores
**shorn** *past participle of* SHEAR
**¹short** \'shòrt\ *adjective* [Middle English, from Old English *sceort*; akin to Old High German *scurz* short, Old Norse *skortr* lack] (before 12th century)
**1 a :** having little length **b** : not tall or high : LOW
**2 a :** not extended in time : BRIEF ⟨a *short* vacation⟩ **b** : not retentive ⟨a *short* memory⟩ **c** : EXPEDITIOUS, QUICK ⟨made *short* work of the problem⟩ **d** : seeming to pass quickly ⟨made great progress in just a few *short* years⟩
**3 a :** *of a speech sound* : having a relatively short duration **b** : being the member of a pair of similarly spelled vowel or vowel-containing sounds that is descended from a vowel that was short in duration but is no longer so and that does not necessarily have duration as its chief distinguishing feature ⟨*short i* in *sin*⟩ **c** *of a syllable in prosody* (1) : of relatively brief duration (2) : UNSTRESSED
**4 :** limited in distance ⟨a *short* trip⟩
**5 a :** not coming up to a measure or requirement : INSUFFICIENT ⟨in *short* supply⟩ **b** : not reaching far enough ⟨the throw to first was *short*⟩ **c** : enduring privation **d** : insufficiently supplied ⟨*short* of cash⟩ ⟨*short* on brains⟩
**6 a :** ABRUPT, CURT **b** : quickly provoked
**7 :** CHOPPY 2
**8 :** payable at an early date
**9 a :** containing or cooked with shortening; *also* : FLAKY ⟨*short* pastry⟩ **b** *of metal* : brittle under certain conditions
**10 a :** not lengthy or drawn out **b** : made briefer : ABBREVIATED
**11 a :** not having goods or property that one has sold in anticipation of a fall in prices **b** : consisting of or relating to a sale of securities or commodities that the seller does not possess or has not contracted for at the time of the sale ⟨*short* sale⟩
**12 :** near the end of a tour of duty
— **short·ish** \'shòr-tish\ *adjective*
— **in short order :** with dispatch : QUICKLY
**²short** *adverb* (14th century)

**1 :** in a curt manner
**2 :** for or during a brief time ⟨*short*-lasting⟩
**3 :** at a disadvantage **:** UNAWARES ⟨caught *short*⟩
**4 :** in an abrupt manner **:** SUDDENLY ⟨the car stopped *short*⟩
**5 :** at some point or degree before a goal or limit aimed at or under consideration ⟨the shells fell *short*⟩ ⟨quit a month *short* of graduation⟩
**6 :** clean across ⟨the axle was snapped *short*⟩
**7 :** by or as if by a short sale
³**short** *noun* (circa 1586)
**1 :** the sum and substance **:** UPSHOT
**2 a :** a short syllable **b :** a short sound or signal
**3** *plural* **a :** a by-product of wheat milling that includes the germ, fine bran, and some flour **b :** refuse, clippings, or trimmings discarded in various manufacturing processes
**4 a :** knee-length or less than knee-length trousers — usually used in plural **b** *plural* **:** short drawers **c :** a size in clothing for short men
**5 a :** one who operates on the short side of the market **b** *plural* **:** short-term bonds
**6** *plural* **:** DEFICIENCIES
**7 :** SHORT CIRCUIT
**8 :** SHORTSTOP
**9 a :** SHORT SUBJECT **b :** a brief story or article (as in a newspaper)
**— for short :** as an abbreviation ⟨named Katherine or Kate *for short*⟩
**— in short :** by way of summary **:** BRIEFLY
⁴**short** *transitive verb* (1904)
**1 :** SHORT-CIRCUIT
**2 :** SHORTCHANGE, CHEAT
**short account** *noun* (circa 1902)
**:** the total of open short sales in a given subject of trade or in the market as a whole
**short·age** \ˈshȯr-tij\ *noun* (1868)
**:** LACK, DEFICIT
**short ballot** *noun* (1909)
**:** a ballot limiting the number of elective offices to the most important legislative and executive posts and leaving minor positions to be filled by appointment
**short·bread** \ˈshȯrt-ˌbred\ *noun* (1801)
**:** a thick cookie made of flour, sugar, and a large amount of shortening
**short·cake** \-ˌkāk\ *noun* (1594)
**1 :** a crisp and often unsweetened biscuit or cookie
**2 a :** a dessert made typically of very short baking-powder-biscuit dough spread with sweetened fruit **b :** a dish consisting of a rich biscuit split and covered with a meat mixture
**short·change** \-ˈchānj\ *transitive verb* (1903)
**1 :** to give less than the correct amount of change to
**2 :** to deprive of or give less than something due **:** CHEAT
**— short·chang·er** *noun*
**short·cir·cuit** *transitive verb* (1867)
**1 :** to apply a short circuit to or establish a short circuit in
**2 :** BYPASS
**3 :** FRUSTRATE, IMPEDE
**short circuit** *noun* (1854)
**:** a connection of comparatively low resistance accidentally or intentionally made between points on a circuit between which the resistance is normally much greater
**short·com·ing** \ˈshȯrt-ˌkə-miŋ, ˌshȯrt-ˈ\ *noun* (15th century)
**:** DEFICIENCY, DEFECT
¹**short·cut** \ˈshȯrt-ˌkət *also* -ˈkət\ *noun* (1637)
**1 :** a route more direct than the one ordinarily taken
**2 :** a method of doing something more directly and quickly than and often not so thoroughly as by ordinary procedure
²**shortcut** *verb* **-cut; -cut·ting** (1915)
*transitive verb*
**:** to shorten (as a route or procedure) by use of a shortcut; *also* **:** CIRCUMVENT

*intransitive verb*
**:** to take or use a shortcut
**short–day** \ˈshȯrt-ˌdā\ *adjective* (1920)
**:** responding to or relating to a short photoperiod — used especially of a plant; compare DAY-NEUTRAL, LONG-DAY
**short division** *noun* (circa 1890)
**:** mathematical division in which the successive steps are performed without writing out the remainders
**short–eared owl** \ˈshȯrt-ˌird-\ *noun* (1766)
**:** a medium-sized nearly cosmopolitan owl (*Asio flammeus*) that has very short ear tufts and usually nests on the ground
**short·en** \ˈshȯr-t°n\ *verb* **short·ened; short·en·ing** \ˈshȯrt-niŋ, ˈshȯr-t°n-iŋ\ (14th century)
*transitive verb*
**1 a :** to reduce the length or duration of **b :** to cause to seem short
**2 a :** to reduce in power or efficiency ⟨is my hand *shortened*, that it cannot redeem —Isaiah 50:2 (Revised Standard Version)⟩ **b** *obsolete* **:** to deprive of effect
**3 :** to add fat to (as pastry dough) in order to make tender and flaky
*intransitive verb*
**:** to become short or shorter ☆
**— short·en·er** \ˈshȯrt-nər, ˈshȯr-t°n-ər\ *noun*
**short·en·ing** \ˈshȯrt-niŋ, ˈshȯr-t°n-iŋ\ *noun* (1538)
**1 :** the action or process of making or becoming short; *specifically* **:** the dropping of the latter part of a word so as to produce a new and shorter word of the same meaning
**2 :** an edible fat used to shorten baked goods
**short·fall** \ˈshȯrt-ˌfȯl\ *noun* (1895)
**:** a failure to come up to expectation or need; *also* **:** the amount of such failure
**short–grass prairie** \ˈshȯrt-ˌgras-\ *noun* (1844)
**:** PRAIRIE 2b
**short·hair** \-ˌhar, -ˌher\ *noun* (1903)
**:** a domestic cat with a short thick coat; *especially* **:** a member of any of several breeds of muscular medium- to large-sized cats with a short plushy coat
**— short·haired** *adjective*
**short·hand** \-ˌhand\ *noun* (1636)
**1 :** a method of writing rapidly by substituting characters, abbreviations, or symbols for letters, sounds, words, or phrases **:** STENOGRAPHY
**2 :** a system or instance of rapid or abbreviated communication or representation
**— shorthand** *adjective*
**short·hand·ed** \ˌshȯrt-ˈhan-dəd\ *adjective* (1794)
**:** having, working with, or done with fewer than the regular or necessary number of people
**short–haul** \ˈshȯrt-ˌhȯl\ *adjective* (1895)
**:** traveling or involving a short distance ⟨*short-haul* flights⟩
**short·horn** \-ˌhȯrn\ *noun, often capitalized* (1847)
**:** any of a breed of red, roan, or white beef cattle originating in the north of England and including good milk-producing strains — called also *Durham*

shorthorn

**short–horned grasshopper** \ˈshȯrt-ˌhȯrn(d)-\ *noun* (circa 1890)
**:** any of a family (Acrididae) of grasshoppers with short antennae
**short hundredweight** *noun* (1924)
**:** HUNDREDWEIGHT 1
**short–leaf pine** \ˈshȯrt-ˌlēf-\ *noun* (1796)
**:** a pine (*Pinus echinata*) of the southeastern U.S. that has short flexible needles usually in

clusters of two and reddish brown bark; *also* **:** its yellow wood
**short line** *noun* (circa 1917)
**:** a transportation system (as a railroad) operating over a relatively short distance
**short·list** \ˈshȯrt-ˌlist\ *noun* (1927)
**:** a list of candidates for final consideration (as for a position or a prize)
**— short–list** *transitive verb, chiefly British*
**short–lived** \ˈshȯrt-ˈlivd *also* -ˈlīvd\ *adjective* (1588)
**:** not living or lasting long ⟨*short-lived* insects⟩ ⟨*short-lived* joy⟩
*usage* see LONG–LIVED
**short loin** *noun* (circa 1923)
**:** a portion of the hindquarter of beef immediately behind the ribs that is usually cut into steaks — see BEEF illustration
**short·ly** \ˈshȯrt-lē\ *adverb* (before 12th century)
**1 a :** in a few words **:** BRIEFLY **b :** in an abrupt manner
**2 a :** in a short time ⟨we will be there *shortly*⟩ **b :** at a short interval ⟨*shortly* after sunset⟩
**short·ness** \-nəs\ *noun* (before 12th century)
**:** the quality or state of being short
**short–nosed cattle louse** \ˈshȯrt-ˌnōz(d)-\ *noun* (1942)
**:** a large bluish sucking louse (*Haematopinus eurysternus*) that attacks domestic cattle
**short–order** \ˈshȯrt-ˌȯr-dər, -ˈȯr-\ *adjective* (1920)
**:** preparing or serving food that can be cooked quickly to a customer's order ⟨a *short-order* cook⟩
**short–range** \ˈshȯrt-ˈrānj\ *adjective* (1869)
**1 :** involving or taking into account a short period of time ⟨*short-range* plans⟩
**2 :** relating to or fit for short distances
**short ribs** *noun plural* (1912)
**:** a cut of beef consisting of rib ends between the rib roast and the plate — see BEEF illustration
**short run** *noun* (1879)
**:** a relatively brief period of time — often used in the phrase *in the short run*
**— short–run** *adjective*
**short shrift** *noun* (1594)
**1 :** barely adequate time for confession before execution
**2 a :** little or no attention or consideration **b :** quick work — usually used in the phrase *make short shrift of*
**short sight** *noun* (circa 1829)
**:** MYOPIA
**short·sight·ed** \ˈshȯrt-ˌsī-təd\ *adjective* (circa 1649)
**1 :** NEARSIGHTED
**2 :** lacking foresight
**— short·sight·ed·ly** *adverb*

---

☆ **SYNONYMS**
**Shorten, curtail, abbreviate, abridge, retrench** mean to reduce in extent. SHORTEN implies reduction in length or duration ⟨*shorten* a speech⟩. CURTAIL adds an implication of cutting that in some way deprives of completeness or adequacy ⟨ceremonies *curtailed* because of rain⟩. ABBREVIATE implies a making shorter usually by omitting some part ⟨using an *abbreviated* title⟩. ABRIDGE implies a reduction in compass or scope with retention of essential elements and a relative completeness in the result ⟨the *abridged* version of the novel⟩. RETRENCH suggests a reduction in extent or costs of something felt to be excessive ⟨declining business forced the company to *retrench*⟩.

---

\ə\ abut  \°\ kitten  \ər\ further  \a\ ash  \ā\ ace
\ä\ mop, mar  \au̇\ out  \ch\ chin  \e\ bet  \ē\ easy
\g\ go  \i\ hit  \ī\ ice  \j\ job  \ŋ\ sing  \ō\ go
\ȯ\ law  \ȯi\ boy  \th\ thin  \th\ the  \ü\ loot  \u̇\ foot
\y\ yet  \zh\ vision      *see also* Guide to Pronunciation

— **short·sight·ed·ness** *noun*

**short–spo·ken** \-ˌspō-kən\ *adjective* (1865)
: CURT

**short·stop** \-ˌstäp\ *noun* (1857)
**1** : the player position in baseball for defending the infield area on the third-base side of second base
**2** : the player stationed in the shortstop position

**short–stop** \-ˌstäp\ *noun* (1936)
: STOP BATH

**short story** *noun* (1877)
: an invented prose narrative shorter than a novel usually dealing with a few characters and aiming at unity of effect and often concentrating on the creation of mood rather than plot

**short subject** *noun* (1944)
: a brief often documentary or educational film

**short–tem·pered** \ˌshort-'tem-pərd\ *adjective* (1900)
: having a quick temper

**short–term** \'short-ˌtərm\ *adjective* (1901)
**1** : occurring over or involving a relatively short period of time
**2 a** : of, relating to, or constituting a financial operation or obligation based on a brief term and especially one of less than a year **b** : generated by assets held for less than six months

**short ton** *noun* (1881)
— see WEIGHT table

**short·wave** \'short-ˌwāv\ *noun, often attributive* (1902)
**1** : a radio wave having a wavelength between 10 and 100 meters
**2** : a radio transmitter using shortwaves
**3** : electromagnetic radiation having a wavelength equal to or less than that of visible light

**short–weight** \'short-'wāt\ *transitive verb* (1926)
: to defraud with short weight

**short weight** \'short-'wāt\ *noun* (1789)
: weight less than the stated weight or less than one is charged for

**short–wind·ed** \ˌshort-'win-dəd\ *adjective* (15th century)
**1** : affected with or characterized by shortness of breath
**2 a** : BRIEF **b** : broken up into short units

**shorty** *or* **short·ie** \'shor-tē\ *noun, plural* **short·ies** (1888)
: one that is short

**Sho·shone** \shə-'shōn, -'shō-nē; 'shō-ˌshōn\ *or* **Sho·sho·ni** \shə-'shō-nē\ *noun, plural* **Shoshones** *or* **Shoshoni** *also* **Shoshone** *or* **Shoshonis** (1805)
**1** : a member of a group of American Indian peoples originally ranging through California, Idaho, Nevada, Utah, and Wyoming
**2** : the Uto-Aztecan language of the Shoshones

¹**shot** \'shät\ *noun* [Middle English, from Old English *scot;* akin to Old Norse *skot* shot, Old High German *scuz,* Old English *scēotan* to shoot — more at SHOOT] (before 12th century)
**1 a** : an action of shooting **b** : a directed propelling of a missile; *specifically* : a directed discharge of a firearm **c** : a stroke or throw in an attempt to score points in a game (as tennis, pool, or basketball); *also* : HOME RUN **d** : BLAST **e** : a metal or narcotics injection
**2 a** *plural* **shot** : something propelled by shooting; *especially* : small lead or steel pellets especially forming a charge for a shotgun **b** : a metal sphere of iron or brass that is heaved in the shot put
**3 a** : the distance that a missile is or can be thrown **b** : RANGE, REACH
**4** : a charge to be paid : SCOT
**5** : one that shoots; *especially* : MARKSMAN
**6 a** : ATTEMPT, TRY **b** : GUESS, CONJECTURE **c** : CHANCE **d** : a single appearance as an entertainer ⟨did a guest *shot* for the program⟩
**7** : an effective remark

**8 a** : a single photographic exposure; *especially* : SNAPSHOT **b** : a single sequence of a motion picture or a television program shot by one camera without interruption
**9** : a charge of explosives
**10 a** : a small measure or serving (as one ounce) of undiluted liquor **b** : a small amount applied at one time : DOSE
**11 shot** *plural* : SPRINKLES, JIMMIES
— **a shot** : for each one : APIECE
— **like a shot** : very rapidly
— **shot in the arm** : STIMULUS, BOOST
— **shot in the dark 1** : a wild guess **2** : an attempt that has little chance of success

²**shot** *past and past participle of* SHOOT

³**shot** *adjective* (1763)
**1 a** *of a fabric* : having contrasting and changeable color effects : IRIDESCENT **b** : suffused or streaked with a color ⟨hair *shot* with gray⟩ **c** : infused or permeated with a quality or element ⟨*shot* through with wit⟩
**2** : having the form of pellets resembling shot
**3** : reduced to a state of ruin, prostration, or uselessness ⟨his nerves are *shot*⟩

¹**shot·gun** \'shät-ˌgən\ *noun* (1776)
**1** : a smoothbore shoulder weapon for firing shot at short ranges
**2** : an offensive football formation in which the quarterback plays a few yards behind the line of scrimmage and the other backs are scattered as flankers or slotbacks
— **shotgun** *transitive verb*
— **shot·gun·ner** \-ˌgə-nər\ *noun*

²**shotgun** *adjective* (1892)
**1** : of, relating to, or using a shotgun
**2** : involving coercion
**3** : covering a wide field with hit-or-miss effectiveness

**shotgun house** *noun* (1940)
: a house in which all the rooms are in direct line with each other usually front to back — called also *shotgun cottage;* compare RAILROAD FLAT

**shotgun marriage** *noun* (1929)
**1** : a marriage forced or required because of pregnancy — called also *shotgun wedding*
**2** : a forced union ⟨a spate of brokerage mergers . . . hastily arranged *shotgun marriages* —John Brooks⟩

**shot hole** *noun* (1875)
**1** : a drilled hole in which a charge of dynamite is exploded
**2** : the dropping out of small rounded fragments of leaves that produces a shot-riddled appearance and is caused especially by parasitic action

**shot put** *noun* (1894)
: a field event in which a shot is heaved for distance
— **shot–put·ter** \'shät-ˌpu̇-tər\ *noun*

**shot·ten** \'shä-t°n\ *adjective* [Middle English *shotyn,* from past participle of *shuten* to shoot] (15th century)
: having ejected the spawn and so of inferior food value ⟨*shotten* herring⟩

**should** \shəd, 'shu̇d\ [Middle English *sholde,* from Old English *sceolde* owed, was obliged to, ought to] *past of* SHALL (before 12th century)
**1** — used in auxiliary function to express condition ⟨if he *should* leave his father, his father would die —Genesis 44:22 (Revised Standard Version)⟩
**2** — used in auxiliary function to express obligation, propriety, or expediency ⟨'tis commanded I *should* do so —Shakespeare⟩ ⟨this is as it *should* be —H. L. Savage⟩ ⟨you *should* brush your teeth after each meal⟩
**3** — used in auxiliary function to express futurity from a point of view in the past ⟨realized that she *should* have to do most of her farm work before sunrise —Ellen Glasgow⟩
**4** — used in auxiliary function to express what is probable or expected ⟨with an early start, they *should* be here by noon⟩

**5** — used in auxiliary function to express a request in a polite manner or to soften direct statement ⟨I *should* suggest that a guide . . . is the first essential —L. D. Reddick⟩

¹**shoul·der** \'shōl-dər\ *noun* [Middle English *sholder,* from Old English *sculdor;* akin to Old High German *scultra* shoulder] (before 12th century)
**1 a** : the laterally projecting part of the human body formed of the bones and joints with their covering tissue by which the arm is connected with the trunk **b** : the region of the body of nonhuman vertebrates that corresponds to the shoulder but is less projecting
**2 a** : the two shoulders and the upper part of the back — usually used in plural **b** *plural* : capacity for bearing a task or blame ⟨placed the guilt squarely on his *shoulders*⟩
**3** : a cut of meat including the upper joint of the foreleg and adjacent parts — see LAMB illustration
**4** : the part of a garment at the wearer's shoulder
**5** : an area adjacent to or along the edge of a higher, more prominent, or more important part: as **a** (1) : the part of a hill or mountain near the top (2) : a lateral protrusion or extension of a hill or mountain **b** : either edge of a roadway; *specifically* : the part of a roadway outside of the traveled way
**6** : a rounded or sloping part (as of a stringed instrument or a bottle) where the neck joins the body
— **shoul·dered** \-dərd\ *adjective*

²**shoulder** *verb* **shoul·dered; shoul·der·ing** \-d(ə-)riŋ\ (14th century)
*transitive verb*
**1** : to push or thrust with or as if with the shoulder : JOSTLE ⟨*shouldered* his way through the crowd⟩
**2 a** : to place or bear on the shoulder ⟨*shouldered* her knapsack and took off⟩ **b** : to assume the burden or responsibility of ⟨*shoulder* the blame⟩
*intransitive verb*
: to push with or as if with the shoulders aggressively

**shoulder bag** *noun* (1912)
: a handbag looped over the shoulder by a strap

**shoulder belt** *noun* (1967)
: an automobile safety belt worn across the torso and over the shoulder — called also *shoulder harness*

**shoulder blade** *noun* (14th century)
: SCAPULA

**shoulder board** *noun* (1945)
: one of a pair of broad pieces of stiffened cloth worn on the shoulders of a military uniform and carrying insignia

**shoulder girdle** *noun* (1868)
: PECTORAL GIRDLE

**shoulder knot** *noun* (1676)
**1** : an ornamental knot of ribbon or lace worn on the shoulder in the 17th and 18th centuries
**2** : a detachable ornament of braided wire cord worn on ceremonial occasions on the shoulders of a uniform by a commissioned officer

**shoulder patch** *noun* (1945)
: a cloth patch bearing an identifying mark and worn on one sleeve of a uniform below the shoulder

**shoulder strap** *noun* (1688)
: a strap that passes across the shoulder and holds up an article or garment

**should·est** \'shu̇-dəst\ *archaic past 2d singular of* SHALL

**shouldn't** \'shu̇-d°nt, -d°n, *dialect also* 'shu̇-t°n(t) *or* 'shu̇nt\ (1848)
: should not

**shouldst** \shədst, 'shu̇dst, shətst, 'shu̇tst\ *archaic past 2d singular of* SHALL

¹**shout** \'shau̇t\ *verb* [Middle English] (14th century)
*intransitive verb*
**1** : to utter a sudden loud cry

**2** : to command attention as if by shouting ⟨a quality that *shouts* from good novels —John Gardner⟩
*transitive verb*
**1** : to utter in a loud voice
**2** : to cause to be, come, or stop by or as if by shouting ⟨*shouted* himself hoarse⟩ ⟨the proponents *shouted* down the opposition⟩
— **shout·er** *noun*
**²shout** *noun* (14th century)
: a loud cry or call
**shouting distance** *noun* (1930)
: a short distance : easy reach — usually used with *within* ⟨lived within *shouting distance* of her cousins⟩
**shout song** *noun* (1925)
: a rhythmic song sung at religious services especially by black Americans and characterized by responsive singing or shouting between leader and congregation
**¹shove** \'shəv\ *verb* **shoved; shov·ing** [Middle English, from Old English *scūfan* to thrust away; akin to Old High German *scioban* to push and probably to Lithuanian *skubti* to hurry] (before 12th century)
*transitive verb*
**1** : to push along
**2** : to push or put in a rough, careless, or hasty manner : THRUST
**3** : to force by other than physical means : COMPEL ⟨*shove* a bill through the legislature⟩
*intransitive verb*
**1** : to move by forcing a way ⟨bargain hunters *shoving* up to the counter⟩
**2 a** : to move something by exerting force **b** : LEAVE — usually used with *off* ⟨*shoved* off for home⟩
— **shov·er** *noun*
**²shove** *noun* (14th century)
: an act or instance of shoving : a forcible push
**¹shov·el** \'shə-vəl\ *noun* [Middle English, from Old English *scofl*; akin to Old High German *scūfla* shovel, Old English *scūfan* to thrust away] (before 12th century)
**1 a** : a hand implement consisting of a broad scoop or a more or less hollowed out blade with a handle used to lift and throw material **b** : something that resembles a shovel **c** : an excavating machine; *especially* : an hydraulic diesel-engine driven power shovel
**2** : SHOVELFUL
**²shovel** *verb* **-eled** *or* **-elled; -el·ing** *or* **-el·ling** \'shə-və-liŋ, 'shəv-liŋ\ (15th century)
*transitive verb*
**1** : to take up and throw with a shovel
**2** : to dig or clean out with a shovel
**3** : to throw or convey roughly or in a mass as if with a shovel ⟨*shoveled* his food into his mouth⟩
*intransitive verb*
: to use a shovel
**shov·el·er** *or* **shov·el·ler** \'shə-və-lər, 'shəv-lər\ *noun* (15th century)
**1** : one that shovels
**2** : any of several river ducks (genus *Anas*) having a large and very broad bill
**shov·el·ful** \'shə-vəl-,fůl\ *noun, plural* **shov·elfuls** \-,fůlz\ *also* **shov·els·ful** \-vəlz-,fůl\ (1533)
: as much as a shovel will hold
**shovel hat** *noun* (1829)
: a shallow-crowned hat with a wide brim curved up at the sides that is worn by some clergymen
**shov·el·nose** \-,nōz\ *noun* (1709)
: a shovel-nosed animal and especially a fish
**shov·el-nosed** \'shə-vəl-,nōzd\ *adjective* (1707)
: having a broad flat head, nose, or beak
**¹show** \'shō\ *verb* **showed** \'shōd\; **shown** \'shōn\ *or* **showed; show·ing** [Middle English *shewen, showen*, from Old English *scēawian* to look, look at, see; akin to Old High German *scouwōn* to look, look at, and

probably to Latin *cavēre* to be on one's guard] (12th century)
*transitive verb*
**1** : to cause or permit to be seen : EXHIBIT ⟨*showed* pictures of the baby⟩
**2** : to offer for sale ⟨stores were *showing* new spring suits⟩
**3** : to present as a public spectacle : PERFORM
**4** : to reveal by one's condition, nature, or behavior ⟨*showed* themselves to be cowards⟩
**5** : to give indication or record of ⟨an anemometer *shows* wind speed⟩
**6 a** : to point out : direct attention to ⟨*showed* the view from the terrace⟩ **b** : CONDUCT, USHER ⟨*showed* me to an aisle seat⟩
**7** : ACCORD, BESTOW ⟨*shows* them no mercy⟩
**8 a** : to set forth : DECLARE **b** : ALLEGE, PLEAD — used especially in law ⟨*show* cause⟩
**9 a** : to demonstrate or establish by argument or reasoning ⟨*show* a plan to be faulty⟩ **b** : INFORM, INSTRUCT ⟨*showed* me how to solve the problem⟩
**10** : to present (an animal) for judging in a show
*intransitive verb*
**1 a** : to be or come in view ⟨3:15 *showed* on the clock⟩ **b** : to put in an appearance ⟨failed to *show*⟩
**2 a** : to appear in a particular way ⟨anger *showed* in their faces⟩ **b** : SEEM, APPEAR
**3 a** : to give a theatrical performance **b** : to be staged or presented
**4 a** : to appear as a contestant **b** : to present an animal in a show
**5** : to finish third or at least third (as in a horse race)
**6** : to exhibit one's artistic work ☆ ☆
— **show·able** \'shō-ə-bəl\ *adjective*
— **show one's hand 1** : to display one's cards faceup **2** : to declare one's intentions or reveal one's resources
— **show one the door** : to tell someone to get out
**²show** *noun, often attributive* (13th century)
**1** : a demonstrative display ⟨a *show* of strength⟩
**2 a** *archaic* : outward appearance **b** : a false semblance : PRETENSE ⟨made a *show* of friendship⟩ **c** : a more or less true appearance of something : SIGN **d** : an impressive display ⟨his role as househusband . . . was purely for *show* —John Lahr⟩ **e** : OSTENTATION
**3** : CHANCE ⟨gave him a *show* in spite of his background⟩
**4** : something exhibited especially for wonder or ridicule : SPECTACLE
**5 a** : a large display or exhibition arranged to arouse interest or stimulate sales ⟨the national auto *show*⟩ **b** : a competitive exhibition of animals (as dogs) to demonstrate quality in breeding
**6 a** : a theatrical presentation **b** : a radio or television program **c** : ENTERTAINMENT 3a
**7** : ENTERPRISE, AFFAIR ⟨they ran the whole *show*⟩
**8** : an indication of metal in a mine or of gas or oil in a well
**9** : third place at the finish (as of a horse race)
**show–and–tell** \'shō-ən(d)-'tel\ *noun* (1950)
**1** : a classroom exercise in which children display an item and talk about it
**2** : a public display or demonstration
**show bill** *noun* (1801)
: an advertising poster
**show·biz** \'shō-,biz\ *noun, often attributive* [by shortening & alteration] (1945)
: SHOW BUSINESS; *also* : RAZZLE-DAZZLE 3
— **show·biz·zy** \-,bi-zē\ *adjective*
**¹show·boat** \'shō-,bōt\ *noun* (1869)
**1** : a river steamship containing a theater and carrying a troupe of actors to give plays at river communities
**2** : one who tries to attract attention by conspicuous behavior
**²showboat** *intransitive verb* (1951)

: to behave in a conspicuous or ostentatious manner : SHOW OFF
**showbread** *variant of* SHEWBREAD
**show business** *noun* (1850)
: the arts, occupations, and businesses (as theater, motion pictures, and television) that comprise the entertainment industry
**¹show·case** \'shō-,kās\ *noun* (1835)
**1** : a glazed case, box, or cabinet for displaying and protecting wares in a store or articles in a museum
**2** : a setting, occasion, or medium for exhibiting something or someone especially in an attractive or favorable aspect
**²showcase** *transitive verb* **show·cased; show·cas·ing** (1945)
: to exhibit especially in an attractive or favorable aspect ⟨*showcase* new talent⟩
**show·down** \'shō-,daůn\ *noun* (1884)
**1** : the placing of poker hands faceup on the table to determine the winner of a pot
**2** : a decisive confrontation or contest
**¹show·er** \'shaů-(ə)r\ *noun* [Middle English *shour*, from Old English *scūr*; akin to Old High German *scūr* shower, storm, Latin *caurus* northwest wind] (before 12th century)
**1 a** : a fall of rain of short duration **b** : a similar fall of sleet, hail, or snow
**2** : something resembling a rain shower ⟨*shower* of statistics⟩; *especially* : a fall of meteors which belong to a single group and whose trails appear to originate at the same point in space
**3** : a party given by friends who bring gifts often of a particular kind
**4** : a bath in which water is showered on the body; *also* : the apparatus that provides a shower
— **show·er·less** \-ləs\ *adjective*
— **show·ery** \'shaů(-ə)-rē\ *adjective*

☆ SYNONYMS
**Show, exhibit, display, expose, parade, flaunt** mean to present so as to invite notice or attention. SHOW implies no more than enabling another to see or examine ⟨*showed* her snapshots to the whole group⟩. EXHIBIT stresses putting forward prominently or openly ⟨*exhibit* paintings at a gallery⟩. DISPLAY emphasizes putting in a position where others may see to advantage ⟨*display* sale items⟩. EXPOSE suggests bringing forth from concealment and displaying ⟨sought to *expose* the hypocrisy of the town fathers⟩. PARADE implies an ostentatious or arrogant displaying ⟨*parading* their piety for all to see⟩. FLAUNT suggests a shameless, boastful, often offensive parading ⟨nouveaux riches *flaunting* their wealth⟩.

**Show, manifest, evidence, evince, demonstrate** mean to reveal outwardly or make apparent. SHOW is the general term but sometimes implies that what is revealed must be gained by inference from acts, looks, or words ⟨careful not to *show* his true feelings⟩. MANIFEST implies a plainer, more immediate revelation ⟨*manifested* musical ability at an early age⟩. EVIDENCE suggests serving as proof of the actuality or existence of something ⟨a commitment *evidenced* by years of loyal service⟩. EVINCE implies a showing by outward marks or signs ⟨*evinced* not the slightest fear⟩. DEMONSTRATE implies showing by action or by display of feeling ⟨*demonstrated* their approval by loud applause⟩.

\ə\ **abut** \ᵊ\ **kitten** \ər\ **further** \a\ **ash** \ā\ **ace**
\ä\ **mop, mar** \aů\ **out** \ch\ **chin** \e\ **bet** \ē\ **easy**
\g\ **go** \i\ **hit** \ī\ **ice** \j\ **job** \ŋ\ **sing** \ō\ **go**
\ȯ\ **law** \ȯi\ **boy** \th\ **thin** \t͟h\ **the** \ü\ **loot** \ů\ **foot**
\y\ **yet** \zh\ **vision** *see also* Guide to Pronunciation

**— to the showers :** out of the ball game

**²shower** (15th century)
*intransitive verb*
**1 :** to rain or fall in or as if in a shower ⟨letters *showered* on him in praise and protest⟩
**2 :** to bathe in a shower
*transitive verb*
**1 a :** to wet (as with water) in a spray, fine stream, or drops **b** (1) : to cause to fall in a shower ⟨factory chimneys *showered* soot on the district⟩ (2) : to cause a shower to fall on ⟨*showered* the newlyweds with rice⟩
**2 :** to give in abundance ⟨*showered* the writer with honors⟩
**— show·er·er** \'shaú(-ə)r-ər\ *noun*

**³show·er** \'shō(-ə)r\ *noun* (14th century)
**:** one that shows **:** EXHIBITOR

**shower bath** *noun* (1785)
**:** SHOWER 4

**show·er·head** \'shaú(-ə)r-,hed\ *noun* (1925)
**:** a fixture for directing the spray of water in a bathroom shower

**show·girl** \'shō-,gər(-ə)l\ *noun* (1836)
**:** a chorus girl in a musical comedy or night-club show

**show·ing** \'shō-iŋ\ *noun* (before 12th century)
**1 :** an act or an instance of putting something (as an artist's work) on view **:** DISPLAY
**2 :** PERFORMANCE, RECORD ⟨made a good *showing* in competition⟩
**3 a :** a statement or presentation of a case **b** **:** APPEARANCE, EVIDENCE

**show jumping** *noun* (1929)
**:** the competitive riding of horses one at a time over a set course of obstacles in which the winner is judged according to ability and speed
**— show jumper** *noun*

**show·man** \'shō-mən\ *noun* (circa 1734)
**1 :** the producer of a play or theatrical show
**2 :** an individual having a sense or knack for dramatically effective presentation
**— show·man·ship** \-,ship\ *noun*

**show–me** \'shō-mē\ *adjective* (1909)
**:** insistent on proof or evidence

**show–off** \'shō-,òf\ *noun, often attributive* (1843)
**1 :** the act of showing off
**2 :** one that shows off **:** EXHIBITIONIST
**— show–offy** \-,ò-fē\ *adjective*

**show off** (circa 1793)
*transitive verb*
**:** to display proudly ⟨wanted to *show* our new car *off*⟩
*intransitive verb*
**:** to seek to attract attention by conspicuous behavior ⟨boys *showing off* for the girls⟩

**show·piece** \'shō-,pēs\ *noun* (1885)
**:** a prime or outstanding example used for exhibition

**show·place** \-,plās\ *noun* (1794)
**:** a place (as an estate or building) that is regarded as an example of beauty or excellence

**show·ring** \-,riŋ\ *noun* (1926)
**:** a ring (as at a cattle show) where animals are displayed

**show·room** \-,rüm, -,rúm\ *noun* (1616)
**:** a room where merchandise is exhibited for sale or where samples are displayed

**show·stop·per** \-,stä-pər\ *noun* (1926)
**1 :** an act, song, or performer that wins applause so prolonged as to interrupt a performance
**2 :** something or someone exceptionally arresting or attractive ⟨the gold crown was the *showstopper* of the exhibition⟩
**— show·stop·ping** \-,stä-piŋ\ *adjective*

**show trial** *noun* (1937)
**:** a trial (as of political opponents) in which the verdict is rigged and a public confession is often extracted

**show up** (1826)
*transitive verb*
**1 :** to expose or discredit especially by revealing faults ⟨*showed* them *up* as frauds⟩

**2 :** to embarrass or cause to look bad especially by comparison ⟨trying to *show up* the boss⟩
**3 :** REVEAL ⟨*showed up* my ignorance⟩
*intransitive verb*
**1 :** ARRIVE, APPEAR ⟨*showed up* late for his own wedding⟩
**2 :** to be plainly evident

**show window** *noun* (1826)
**1 :** an outside display window in which a store exhibits merchandise
**2 :** a sample or setting used to exhibit or illustrate something at its best

**showy** \'shō-ē\ *adjective* **show·i·er; -est** (1712)
**1 :** making an attractive show **:** STRIKING ⟨a *showy* orchid⟩
**2 :** given to or marked by a flashy often tasteless display ☆
**— show·i·ly** \'shō-ə-lē\ *adverb*
**— show·i·ness** \'shō-ē-nəs\ *noun*

**sho·yu** \'shō-(,)yü\ *noun* [Japanese *shōyu*] (1727)
**:** SOY 1

**shrank** *past of* SHRINK

**shrap·nel** \'shrap-n°l, *especially Southern* 'srap-\ *noun, plural* **shrapnel** [Henry *Shrapnel* (died 1842) English artillery officer] (1806)
**1 :** a projectile that consists of a case provided with a powder charge and a large number of usually lead balls and that is exploded in flight
**2 :** bomb, mine, or shell fragments

**¹shred** \'shred, *especially Southern* 'sred\ *noun* [Middle English *shrede*, from Old English *scrēade;* akin to Old High German *scrōt* piece cut off] (before 12th century)
**1 a :** a long narrow strip cut or torn off **b** *plural* **:** a shredded, damaged, disrupted, or ruined condition ⟨torn to *shreds* by an air attack⟩
**2 :** PARTICLE, SCRAP ⟨not a *shred* of evidence⟩

**²shred** *verb* **shred·ded; shred·ding** (before 12th century)
*transitive verb*
**1** *archaic* **:** to cut off
**2 :** to cut or tear into shreds ⟨*shredded* the documents⟩
**3 :** DEMOLISH 2 ⟨sharp lawyers *shredding* hapless witnesses —Charles Krauthammer⟩
*intransitive verb*
**:** to come apart or break up into shreds
**— shred·der** *noun*

**shredded wheat** *noun* (1898)
**:** a breakfast cereal made from cooked partially dried wheat that is shredded and molded into biscuits which are then oven-baked and toasted

**¹shrew** \'shrü, *especially Southern* 'srü\ *noun* [Middle English *shrewe* evil or scolding person, from Old English *scrēawa* shrew (animal)] (before 12th century)
**1 :** any of a family (Soricidae) of small chiefly nocturnal insectivores related to the moles and distinguished by a long pointed snout, very small eyes, and velvety fur
**2 :** an ill-tempered scolding woman
**— shrew·like** \-,līk\ *adjective*

**²shrew** *transitive verb* (14th century)
*obsolete* **:** CURSE

**shrewd** \'shrüd, *especially Southern* 'srüd\ *adjective* [Middle English *shrewed*, from *shrewe* + ¹*-ed*] (13th century)
**1** *archaic* **:** MISCHIEVOUS
**2** *obsolete* **:** ABUSIVE, SHREWISH
**3** *obsolete* **:** OMINOUS, DANGEROUS
**4 a :** SEVERE, HARD ⟨a *shrewd* knock⟩ **b :** SHARP, PIERCING ⟨a *shrewd* wind⟩
**5 a :** marked by clever discerning awareness and hardheaded acumen ⟨*shrewd* common sense⟩ **b :** given to wily and artful ways or dealing ⟨a *shrewd* operator⟩ ☆
**— shrewd·ly** *adverb*
**— shrewd·ness** *noun*

**shrew·ish** \'shrü-ish, *especially Southern* 'srü-\ *adjective* (1565)
**:** ILL-NATURED, INTRACTABLE
**— shrew·ish·ly** *adverb*

**— shrew·ish·ness** *noun*

**shri** \'shrē, 'srē\ *variant of* SRI

**¹shriek** \'shrēk, *especially Southern* 'srēk\ *verb* [Middle English *shreken*, probably irregular from *shriken* to shriek; akin to Old Norse *skrækja* to shriek] (15th century)
*intransitive verb*
**1 :** to utter a sharp shrill sound
**2 a :** to cry out in a high-pitched voice **:** SCREECH **b :** to suggest such a cry (as by vividness of expression) ⟨neon colors *shrieked* for attention —Calvin Tomkins⟩
*transitive verb*
**1 :** to utter with a shriek or sharply and shrilly ⟨*shriek* an alarm⟩
**2 :** to express in a manner suggestive of a shriek

**²shriek** *noun* (1590)
**1 :** a shrill usually wild or involuntary cry
**2 :** a sound resembling a shriek ⟨the *shriek* of chalk on the blackboard⟩

**shrie·val** \'shrē-vəl, *especially Southern* 'srē-\ *adjective* [obsolete *shrieve* sheriff, from Middle English *shirreve* — more at SHERIFF] (1681)
*chiefly British* **:** of or relating to a sheriff

**shrie·val·ty** \-vəl-tē\ *noun* (1502)
*chiefly British* **:** the office, term of office, or jurisdiction of a sheriff

**shrieve** \'shrēv, *especially Southern* 'srēv\ *archaic variant of* SHRIVE

**shrift** \'shrift, *especially Southern* 'srift\ *noun* [Middle English, from Old English *scrift*, from *scrīfan* to shrive — more at SHRIVE] (before 12th century)
**1** *archaic* **a :** a remission of sins pronounced by a priest in the sacrament of reconciliation **b :** the act of shriving **:** CONFESSION
**2** *obsolete* **:** CONFESSIONAL

**shrike** \'shrīk, *especially Southern* 'srīk\ *noun* [perhaps from (assumed) Middle English *shrik*, from Old English *scrīc* thrush; akin to Middle English *shriken* to shriek] (1544)
**:** any of numerous usually largely gray or brownish oscine birds (family Laniidae) that have a hooked bill, feed chiefly on insects, and often impale their prey on thorns

**¹shrill** \'shril, *especially Southern* 'sril\ *verb* [Middle English; probably akin to Old English *scrallettan* to resound loudly — more at SKIRL] (13th century)
*transitive verb*
**:** SCREAM

---

☆ **SYNONYMS**
**Showy, pretentious, ostentatious** mean given to excessive outward display. SHOWY implies an imposing or striking appearance but usually suggests cheapness or poor taste ⟨the performers' *showy* costumes⟩. PRETENTIOUS implies an appearance of importance not justified by the thing's value or the person's standing ⟨a *pretentious* parade of hard words⟩. OSTENTATIOUS stresses vainglorious display or parade ⟨the *ostentatious* summer homes of the rich⟩.

**Shrewd, sagacious, perspicacious, astute** mean acute in perception and sound in judgment. SHREWD stresses practical, hardheaded cleverness and judgment ⟨a *shrewd* judge of character⟩. SAGACIOUS suggests wisdom, penetration, and farsightedness ⟨*sagacious* investors got in on the ground floor⟩. PERSPICACIOUS implies unusual power to see through and understand what is puzzling or hidden ⟨a *perspicacious* counselor saw through the child's facade⟩. ASTUTE suggests shrewdness, perspicacity, and diplomatic skill ⟨an *astute* player of party politics⟩.

*intransitive verb*
**:** to utter or emit an acute piercing sound
**²shrill** *adjective* (14th century)
**1 a :** having or emitting a sharp high-pitched tone or sound **:** PIERCING **b :** accompanied by sharp high-pitched sounds or cries ⟨*shrill* gaiety⟩
**2 :** having a sharp or vivid effect on the senses ⟨*shrill* light⟩
**3 :** STRIDENT, INTEMPERATE ⟨*shrill* anger⟩ ⟨*shrill* criticism⟩
— **shrill** *adverb*
— **shrill·ness** *noun*
— **shril·ly** \'shril-lē, *especially Southern* 'sril-\ *adverb*
**³shrill** *noun* (1591)
**:** a shrill sound ⟨the *shrill* of the ship's whistle⟩
**¹shrimp** \'shrimp, *especially Southern* 'srimp\ *noun, plural* **shrimps** *or* **shrimp** [Middle English *shrimpe;* akin to Middle Low German *schrempen* to contract, wrinkle, Old Norse *skorpna* to shrivel up] (14th century)
**1 :** any of numerous mostly small and marine decapod crustaceans (suborders Dendrobranchiata and Pleocyemata) having a slender elongated body, a compressed abdomen, and a long spiny rostrum; *also* **:** a small crustacean (as an amphipod or a branchiopod) resembling the true shrimps
**2 :** a very small or puny person or thing
— **shrimp·like** \-ˌlīk\ *adjective*
— **shrimpy** \'shrim-pē, 'srim-\ *adjective*
**²shrimp** *intransitive verb* (circa 1859)
**:** to fish for or catch shrimps
**shrimp·er** \'shrim-pər, *especially Southern* 'srim-\ *noun* (1851)
**1 :** a shrimp fisherman
**2 :** a boat engaged in shrimping
**shrimp pink** *noun* (1882)
**:** a deep pink
**¹shrine** \'shrīn, *especially Southern* 'srīn\ *noun* [Middle English, from Old English *scrīn,* from Latin *scrinium* case, chest] (before 12th century)
**1 a :** a case, box, or receptacle; *especially* **:** one in which sacred relics (as the bones of a saint) are deposited **b :** a place in which devotion is paid to a saint or deity **:** SANCTUARY **c :** a niche containing a religious image
**2 :** a receptacle (as a tomb) for the dead
**3 :** a place or object hallowed by its associations
**²shrine** *transitive verb* **shrined; shrin·ing** (14th century)
**:** ENSHRINE
**Shrin·er** \'shrī-nər, *especially Southern* 'srī-\ *noun* [Ancient Arabic Order of Nobles of the Mystic *Shrine*] (1886)
**:** a member of a secret fraternal society that is non-Masonic but admits only Knights Templars and 32d-degree Masons to membership
**¹shrink** \'shriŋk, *especially Southern* 'sriŋk\ *verb* **shrank** \'shraŋk, 'sraŋk\ *also* **shrunk** \'shrəŋk, 'srəŋk\; **shrunk** *or* **shrunk·en** \'shrəŋ-kən, 'srəŋ-\; **shrink·ing** [Middle English, from Old English *scrincan;* akin to Middle Dutch *schrinken* to draw back] (before 12th century)
*intransitive verb*
**1 :** to contract or curl up the body or part of it **:** HUDDLE, COWER
**2 a :** to contract to less extent or compass **b :** to become smaller or more compacted **c :** to lose substance or weight **d :** to lessen in value **:** DWINDLE
**3 :** to recoil instinctively (as from something painful or horrible) ⟨*shrank* from the challenge⟩
*transitive verb*
**:** to cause to contract or shrink; *specifically* **:** to compact (cloth) by causing to contract when subjected to washing, boiling, steaming, or other processes ∎
**synonym** *see* CONTRACT, RECOIL

— **shrink·able** \'shriŋ-kə-bəl, 'sriŋ-\ *adjective*
— **shrink·er** *noun*
**²shrink** *noun* (1590)
**1 :** the act of shrinking
**2 :** SHRINKAGE
**3** [short for *headshrinker*] **:** a clinical psychiatrist or psychologist ⟨regaling us with all the stories he never told his *shrink* —*Rolling Stone*⟩
**shrink·age** \'shriŋ-kij, *especially Southern* 'sriŋ-\ *noun* (1800)
**1 :** the act or process of shrinking
**2 :** the loss in weight of livestock during shipment and in the process of preparing the meat for consumption
**3 :** the amount lost by shrinkage
**shrinking violet** *noun* (1915)
**:** a bashful or retiring person
**shrink–wrap** \'shriŋk-ˌrap, *especially Southern* 'sriŋk-\ *transitive verb* (1966)
**:** to wrap (as a book or meat) in tough clear plastic film that is then shrunk (as by heating) to form a tightly fitting package
— **shrink–wrap** *noun*
**shrive** \'shrīv, *especially Southern* 'srīv\ *verb* **shrived** *or* **shrove** \'shrōv, 'srōv\; **shriv·en** \'shri-vən, 'sri-\ *or* **shrived; shriv·ing** [Middle English, from Old English *scrīfan* to shrive, prescribe (akin to Old High German *scrīban* to write), from Latin *scribere* to write — more at SCRIBE] (before 12th century)
*transitive verb*
**1 :** to administer the sacrament of reconciliation to
**2 :** to free from guilt
*intransitive verb*
*archaic* **:** to confess one's sins especially to a priest
**shriv·el** \'shri-vəl, *especially Southern* 'sri-\ *verb* **-eled** *or* **-elled; -el·ing** *or* **-el·ling** \'shri-vəl-iŋ, 'sri-; 'shriv-liŋ, 'sriv-\ [origin unknown] (1588)
*intransitive verb*
**1 :** to draw into wrinkles especially with a loss of moisture
**2 a :** to become reduced to inanition, helplessness, or inefficiency **b :** DWINDLE
*transitive verb*
**:** to cause to shrivel
**shroff** \'shräf, 'shróf, *especially Southern* 'sräf, 'sróf\ *noun* [Hindi *śaraf,* from Arabic *ṣarrāf*] (1618)
**:** a banker or money changer in the Far East; *especially* **:** one who tests and evaluates coin
**Shrop·shire** \'shräp-ˌshir, -shər, *especially US* -ˌshīr, *especially Southern* 'sräp-\ *noun* [*Shropshire,* England] (1803)
**:** any of a breed of dark-faced hornless sheep of English origin that are raised for both mutton and wool
**¹shroud** \'shraúd, *especially Southern* 'sraúd\ *noun* [Middle English, garment, from Old English *scrūd;* akin to Old English *scrēade* shred — more at SHRED] (14th century)
**1** *obsolete* **:** SHELTER, PROTECTION
**2 :** something that covers, screens, or guards: as **a :** one of two flanges that give peripheral support to turbine or fan bedding **b :** a usually fiberglass guard that protects a spacecraft from the heat of launching
**3 :** burial garment **:** WINDING-SHEET, CEREMENT
**4 a :** one of the ropes leading usually in pairs from a ship's mastheads to give lateral support to the masts **b :** one of the cords that suspend the harness of a parachute from the canopy
**²shroud** (14th century)
*transitive verb*

*1 shroud 4a*

**1 a** *archaic* **:** to cover for protection **b** *obsolete* **:** CONCEAL
**2 a :** to cut off from view **:** OBSCURE ⟨trees *shrouded* by a heavy fog⟩ **b :** to veil under another appearance (as by obscuring or disguising) ⟨*shrouded* the decision in a series of formalities⟩
**3 :** to dress for burial
*intransitive verb*
*archaic* **:** to seek shelter
**Shrove·tide** \'shrōv-ˌtīd, *especially Southern* 'srōv-\ *noun* [Middle English *schroftide,* from *schrof-* (from *shriven* to shrive) + *tide*] (15th century)
**:** the period usually of three days immediately preceding Ash Wednesday
**Shrove Tuesday** \'shrōv-, *especially Southern* 'srōv-\ *noun* [Middle English *schroftewesday,* from *schrof-* (as in *schroftide*) + *tewesday* Tuesday] (15th century)
**:** the Tuesday before Ash Wednesday
**¹shrub** \'shrəb, *especially Southern* 'srəb\ *noun* [Middle English *schrobbe,* from Old English *scrybb* brushwood; akin to Norwegian *skrubbebær* a cornel of a dwarf species] (before 12th century)
**:** a low usually several-stemmed woody plant
**²shrub** *noun* [Arabic *sharāb* beverage] (1747)
**1 :** an aged blend of fruit juice, sugar, and spirits served chilled and diluted with water
**2 :** a beverage made by adding acidulated fruit juice to iced water
**shrub·bery** \'shrə-b(ə-)rē, *especially Southern* 'srə-\ *noun, plural* **-ber·ies** (1748)
**:** a planting or growth of shrubs
**shrub·by** \'shrə-bē, *especially Southern* 'srə-\ *adjective* **shrub·bi·er; -est** (1540)
**1 :** consisting of or covered with shrubs
**2 :** resembling a shrub
**¹shrug** \'shrəg, *especially Southern* 'srəg\ *verb* **shrugged; shrug·ging** [Middle English *schruggen*] (14th century)
*intransitive verb*
**:** to raise or draw in the shoulders especially to express aloofness, indifference, or uncertainty
*transitive verb*
**:** to lift or contract (the shoulders) especially to express aloofness, indifference, or uncertainty
**²shrug** *noun* (1594)
**1 :** an act of shrugging
**2 :** a woman's small waist-length or shorter jacket
**shrug off** *transitive verb* (1904)
**1 :** to brush aside **:** MINIMIZE ⟨*shrugs off* the problem⟩
**2 :** to shake off ⟨*shrugging off* sleep⟩
**3 :** to remove (a garment) by wriggling out
**shtetl** *also* **shte·tel** \'shte-t°l, 'shtā-\ *noun, plural* **shtet·lach** \'shtet-ˌläk, 'shtāt-\ *also* **shtetels** [Yiddish *shtetl,* from Middle High German *stetel,* diminutive of *stat* place, town, city, from Old High German, place — more at STEAD] (1949)
**:** a small Jewish town or village formerly found in Eastern Europe

\ə\ **abut** \ᵊ\ **kitten** \ər\ **further** \a\ **ash** \ā\ **ace**
\ä\ **mop, mar** \aú\ **out** \ch\ **chin** \e\ **bet** \ē\ **easy**
\g\ **go** \i\ **hit** \ī\ **ice** \j\ **job** \ŋ\ **sing** \ō\ **go**
\ó\ **law** \ói\ **boy** \th\ **thin** \t͟h\ **the** \ü\ **loot** \ú\ **foot**
\y\ **yet** \zh\ **vision** *see also* Guide to Pronunciation

**shtick** *also* **shtik** \'shtik\ *noun* [Yiddish *shtik* pranks, literally, piece, from Middle High German *stücke,* from Old High German *stucki;* akin to Old English *stycce* piece, Old High German *stoc* stick — more at STOCK] (1959)
**1 :** a show-business routine, gimmick, or gag **:** BIT
**2 :** one's special trait, interest, or activity **:** BAG ⟨he's alive and well and now doing his *shtick* out in Hollywood —Robert Daley⟩

¹**shuck** \'shək\ *noun* [origin unknown] (circa 1674)
**1 :** SHELL, HUSK: as **a :** the outer covering of a nut or of Indian corn **b :** the shell of an oyster or clam
**2 :** something of little value — usually used in plural often interjectionally ⟨not worth *shucks*⟩ ⟨*shucks,* it was nothing⟩

²**shuck** *transitive verb* (1772)
**1 :** to strip of shucks
**2 a :** to peel off (as clothing) — often used with *off* **b :** to lay aside — often used with *off* ⟨bad habits are being *shucked* off —A. W. Smith⟩
— **shuck·er** *noun*

¹**shud·der** \'shə-dər\ *intransitive verb* **shud-dered; shud·der·ing** \-d(ə-)riŋ\ [Middle English *shoddren;* akin to Old High German *skutten* to shake and perhaps to Lithuanian *kutéti* to shake up] (13th century)
**1 :** to tremble convulsively **:** SHIVER
**2 :** QUIVER

²**shudder** *noun* (1607)
**:** an act of shuddering
— **shud·dery** \-d(ə-)rē\ *adjective*

¹**shuf·fle** \'shə-fəl\ *verb* **shuf·fled; shuf-fling** \-f(ə-)liŋ\ [perhaps irregular from ¹*shove*] (1570)
*transitive verb*
**1 :** to mix in a mass confusedly **:** JUMBLE
**2 :** to put or thrust aside or under cover ⟨*shuffled* the whole matter out of his mind⟩
**3 a :** to rearrange (as playing cards, dominoes, or tiles) to produce a random order **b :** to move about, back and forth, or from one place to another **:** SHIFT ⟨*shuffle* funds among various accounts⟩
**4 a :** to move (as the feet) by sliding along or back and forth without lifting **b :** to perform (as a dance) with a dragging, sliding step
*intransitive verb*
**1 :** to work into or out of trickily ⟨*shuffled* out of the difficulty⟩
**2 :** to act or speak in a shifty or evasive manner
**3 a :** to move or walk in a sliding dragging manner without lifting the feet **b :** to dance in a lazy nonchalant manner with sliding and tapping motions of the feet **c :** to execute in a perfunctory or clumsy manner
**4 :** to mix playing cards or counters by shuffling
— **shuf·fler** \-f(ə-)lər\ *noun*

²**shuffle** *noun* (1628)
**1 :** an evasion of the issue **:** EQUIVOCATION
**2 a :** an act of shuffling (as of cards) **b :** a right or turn to shuffle ⟨was reminded that it was his *shuffle*⟩ **c :** JUMBLE ⟨lost in the *shuffle* of papers⟩
**3 a :** a dragging sliding movement; *specifically* **:** a sliding or scraping step in dancing **b :** a dance characterized by such a step

**shuf·fle·board** \'shə-fəl-ˌbȯrd, -ˌbȯrd\ *noun* [alteration of obsolete English *shove-board*] (1836)
**1 :** a game in which players use long-handled cues to shove disks into scoring areas of a diagram marked on a smooth surface
**2 :** a diagram on which shuffleboard is played

**shul** \'shu̇l\ *noun* [Yiddish, school, synagogue, from Middle High German *schuol* school] (circa 1874)
**:** SYNAGOGUE

**shun** \'shən\ *transitive verb* **shunned; shun-ning** [Middle English *shunnen,* from Old English *scunian*] (before 12th century)

**:** to avoid deliberately and especially habitually
**synonym** see ESCAPE
— **shun·ner** *noun*

**shun·pike** \'shən-ˌpīk\ *noun* (1862)
**:** a side road used to avoid the toll on or the speed and traffic of a superhighway
— **shun·pik·er** \-ˌpī-kər\ *noun*
— **shun·pik·ing** \-kiŋ\ *noun*

¹**shunt** \'shənt\ *verb* [Middle English, to flinch] (13th century)
*transitive verb*
**1 a :** to turn off to one side **:** SHIFT ⟨was *shunted* aside⟩ **b :** to switch (as a train) from one track to another
**2 :** to provide with or divert by means of an electrical shunt
**3 :** to divert (blood) from one part to another by a surgical shunt
**4 :** SHUTTLE ⟨*shunted* the missiles from shelter to shelter⟩
*intransitive verb*
**1 :** to move to the side
**2 :** to travel back and forth ⟨*shunted* between the two towns⟩
— **shunt·er** *noun*

²**shunt** *noun* (circa 1859)
**1 :** a means or mechanism for turning or thrusting aside: as **a** *chiefly British* **:** a railroad switch **b :** a conductor joining two points in an electrical circuit so as to form a parallel or alternative path through which a portion of the current may pass (as for regulating the amount passing in the main circuit) **c :** a surgical passage created between two blood vessels to divert blood from one part to another
**2 :** an accident (as a collision between two cars) especially in auto racing

**shush** \'shəsh, 'shu̇sh\ *transitive verb* [imitative] (1925)
**:** to urge to be quiet **:** HUSH
— **shush** *noun*

¹**shut** \'shət\ *verb* **shut; shut·ting** [Middle English *shutten,* from Old English *scyttan;* akin to Middle Dutch *schutten* to shut in, Old English *scēotan* to shoot — more at SHOOT] (before 12th century)
*transitive verb*
**1 a :** to move into position to close an opening ⟨*shut* the lid⟩ **b :** to prevent entrance to or passage to or from
**2 :** to confine by or as if by enclosure ⟨*shut* herself in her study⟩
**3 :** to fasten with a lock or bolt
**4 :** to close by bringing enclosing or covering parts together ⟨*shut* the eyes⟩
**5 :** to cause to cease or suspend an operation or activity — often used with *down*
*intransitive verb*
**1 :** to close itself or become closed ⟨flowers that *shut* at night⟩
**2 :** to cease or suspend an operation or activity — often used with *down*

²**shut** *adjective* (15th century)
**1 :** closed, fastened, or folded together
**2 :** RID, CLEAR, FREE — usually used with *of*

³**shut** *noun* (1667)
**:** the act of shutting

**shut·down** \'shət-ˌdau̇n\ *noun* (1888)
**:** the cessation or suspension of an operation or activity

**shut down** *intransitive verb* (1779)
**:** to settle so as to obscure vision **:** CLOSE IN ⟨the night *shut down* early⟩

**shute** *variant of* CHUTE

**shut-eye** \'shət-ˌī\ *noun* (1899)
**:** SLEEP ⟨get some *shut-eye*⟩

¹**shut-in** \'shət-ˌin\ *noun* (1903)
**1 :** an invalid confined to home, a room, or bed
**2 :** a narrow gorge-shaped part of an otherwise wide valley
**3 :** available oil or gas which is not being produced from an existing well

²**shut-in** \'shət-'in\ *adjective* (1909)
**1 :** confined to one's home or an institution by illness or incapacity

**2 a :** SECRETIVE, BROODING ⟨a bitter, *shut-in* face —Claudia Cassidy⟩ **b :** tending to avoid social contact **:** WITHDRAWN ⟨the *shut-in* personality type —S. K. Weinberg⟩

**shut in** *transitive verb* (14th century)
**1 :** CONFINE, ENCLOSE
**2 :** to prevent production of (oil or gas) by closing down a well

**shut·off** \'shət-ˌȯf\ *noun* (1869)
**1 :** something (as a valve) that shuts off
**2 :** STOPPAGE, INTERRUPTION

**shut off** (1824)
*transitive verb*
**1 a :** to cut off (as flow or passage) **:** STOP ⟨*shuts off* the oxygen supply⟩ **b :** to stop the operation of (as a machine) ⟨*shut* the motor *off*⟩
**2 :** to close off **:** SEPARATE — usually used with *from* ⟨*shut off* from the rest of the world⟩
*intransitive verb*
**:** to cease operating **:** STOP ⟨*shuts off* automatically⟩

**shut·out** \'shət-ˌau̇t\ *noun* (1889)
**1 :** a game or contest in which one side fails to score
**2 :** a preemptive bid in bridge

**shut out** *transitive verb* (14th century)
**1 :** EXCLUDE
**2 :** to prevent (an opponent) from scoring in a game or contest
**3 :** to forestall the bidding of (bridge opponents) by making a high or preemptive bid

¹**shut·ter** \'shə-tər\ *noun* (1542)
**1 :** one that shuts
**2 :** a usually movable cover or screen for a window or door
**3 :** a mechanical device that limits the passage of light; *especially* **:** a camera attachment that exposes the film or plate by opening and closing an aperture
**4 :** the movable louvers in a pipe organ by which the swell box is opened
— **shut·ter·less** \-ləs\ *adjective*

²**shutter** *transitive verb* (1826)
**1 :** to close by or as if by shutters
**2 :** to furnish with shutters

**shut·ter·bug** \'shə-tər-ˌbəg\ *noun* (1940)
**:** a photography enthusiast

¹**shut·tle** \'shə-t°l\ *noun* [Middle English *shittle,* probably from Old English *scytel* bar, bolt; akin to Old Norse *skutill* bolt, Old English *scēotan* to shoot — more at SHOOT] (14th century)
**1 a :** a device used in weaving for passing the thread of the weft between the threads of the warp **b :** a spindle-shaped device holding the thread in tatting, knotting, or netting **c :** a sliding thread holder for the lower thread of a sewing machine that carries the lower thread through a loop of the upper thread to make a stitch
**2 :** SHUTTLECOCK
**3 a :** a going back and forth regularly over an often short route by a vehicle **b :** an established route used in a shuttle; *also* **:** a vehicle used in a shuttle **c :** SPACE SHUTTLE
— **shut·tle·less** *adjective*

²**shuttle** *verb* **shut·tled; shut·tling** \'shət-liŋ, 'shə-t°l-iŋ\ (1550)
*transitive verb*
**1 :** to cause to move or travel back and forth frequently
**2 :** to transport in, by, or as if by a shuttle
*intransitive verb*
**1 :** to move or travel back and forth frequently
**2 :** to move by or as if by a shuttle

¹**shut·tle·cock** \'shə-t°l-ˌkäk\ *noun* (1522)
**:** a lightweight conical object with a rounded often rubber-covered nose that is used in badminton

²**shuttlecock** *transitive verb* (1687)
**:** to send or toss to and fro **:** BANDY

**shuttlecock**

**shuttle diplomacy** *noun* (1974)
: negotiations especially between nations carried on by an intermediary who shuttles back and forth between the disputants

**shut up** (1814)
*transitive verb*
: to cause (a person) to stop talking
*intransitive verb*
: to cease writing or speaking

¹**shy** \'shī\ *adjective* **shi·er** *or* **shy·er** \'shī(-ə)r\; **shi·est** *or* **shy·est** \'shī-əst\ [Middle English *schey,* from Old English *scēoh;* akin to Old High German *sciuhen* to frighten off] (before 12th century)
**1** : easily frightened : TIMID
**2** : disposed to avoid a person or thing ⟨publicity *shy*⟩ ⟨book-*shy* children⟩
**3** : hesitant in committing oneself : CIRCUMSPECT
**4** : sensitively diffident or retiring : RESERVED ⟨a *shy* seclusive person⟩; *also* : expressive of such a state or nature ⟨spoke in a *shy* voice⟩
**5** : SECLUDED, HIDDEN
**6** : having less than the full or specified amount or number : SHORT ⟨just *shy* of six feet tall⟩ ⟨the stew is a little *shy* of seasoning⟩
**7** : DISREPUTABLE ⟨gambling hells and *shy* saloons —*Blackwood's*⟩ ☆
— **shy·ly** *adverb*
— **shy·ness** *noun*

²**shy** *intransitive verb* **shied; shy·ing** (1650)
**1** : to develop or show a dislike or distaste — usually used with *from* or *away from* ⟨an author who *shies* away from publicity⟩
**2** : to start suddenly aside through fright or alarm

³**shy** *noun, plural* **shies** (1791)
: a sudden start aside (as from fright)

⁴**shy** *verb* **shied; shy·ing** [perhaps from ¹*shy*] (1787)
*intransitive verb*
: to make a sudden throw
*transitive verb*
: to throw (an object) with a jerk : FLING

⁵**shy** *noun, plural* **shies** (1791)
**1** : the act of shying : TOSS, THROW
**2** : a verbal fling or attack
**3** : COCKSHY

¹**shy·lock** \'shī-,läk\ *noun*
**1** *capitalized* : the Jewish usurer and antagonist of Antonio in Shakespeare's *The Merchant of Venice*
**2** : an extortionate creditor : LOAN SHARK

²**shylock** *intransitive verb* (circa 1934)
: to lend money at high rates of interest ⟨exposé of systematic thievery . . . *shylocking,* and murder —*Current Biography*⟩

**shy·ster** \'shīs-tər\ *noun* [probably from German *Scheisser,* literally, defecator] (1844)
: one who is professionally unscrupulous especially in the practice of law or politics : PETTIFOGGER ◆

**si** \'sē\ *noun* [Italian] (1728)
: ²TI

**si·al·a·gogue** \sī-'a-lə-,gäg\ *noun* [New Latin *sialagogus* promoting the expulsion of saliva, from Greek *sialon* saliva + New Latin *-agogus* -agogue] (circa 1783)
: an agent that promotes the flow of saliva

**si·al·ic** \sī-'a-lik\ *adjective* [International Scientific Vocabulary *si*licon + *al*uminum] (1924)
: of, relating to, or being relatively light rock that is rich in silica and alumina and is typical of the outer layers of the earth

**sialic acid** *noun* [Greek *sialon* saliva] (1952)
: any of a group of reducing amido acids that are essentially carbohydrates and are found especially as components of blood glycoproteins and mucoproteins

**si·a·mang** \'sē-ə-,maŋ, 'sī-\ *noun* [Malay] (1822)
: a black gibbon (*Hylobates syndactylus*) of Sumatra and the Malay Peninsula that is the largest of the gibbons

¹**Si·a·mese** \,sī-ə-'mēz, -'mēs\ *adjective* [*Siam* (Thailand); in senses 2 & 3, from *Siamese twin*] (1693)
**1** : of, relating to, or characteristic of Thailand, the Thais, or their language
**2** : exhibiting great resemblance : very like
**3** *not capitalized* : connecting two or more pipes or hoses so as to permit discharge in a single stream

²**Siamese** *noun, plural* **Siamese** (1693)
**1** : THAI 2
**2** : THAI 3
**3** : SIAMESE CAT

**Siamese cat** *noun* (1871)
: any of a breed of slender blue-eyed shorthaired domestic cats of oriental origin with pale fawn or gray body and darker ears, paws, tail, and face

**Siamese fighting fish** *noun* (1933)
: a brightly colored betta (*Betta splendens*) that has highly aggressive males and is a popular aquarium fish

**Siamese fighting fish**

**Siamese twin** *noun* [from Chang (died 1874) and Eng (died 1874) congenitally united twins born in Siam] (1829)
: one of a pair of congenitally united twins in humans or other vertebrates

¹**sib** \'sib\ *adjective* [Middle English, from Old English *sibb,* from *sibb* kinship; akin to Old High German *sippa* kinship, family, Latin *sodalis* comrade, Greek *ēthos* custom, character, Latin *suus* one's own — more at SUICIDE] (before 12th century)
: related by blood : AKIN

²**sib** *noun* (before 12th century)
**1 a** : KINDRED, RELATIVES **b** : a blood relation : KINSMAN
**2** : a brother or sister considered irrespective of sex; *broadly* : any plant or animal of a group sharing a degree of genetic relationship corresponding to that of human sibs
**3** : a group of persons unilaterally descended from a real or supposed ancestor

**Si·be·ri·an husky** \sī-'bir-ē-ən-\ *noun* (1930)
: any of a breed of medium-sized thick-coated compact dogs that were developed in Siberia for use as sled dogs and that have erect ears and a bushy tail

**Siberian husky**

**sib·i·lance** \'si-bə-lən(t)s\ *noun* (1823)
: a sibilant quality or sound

¹**sib·i·lant** \'si-bə-lənt\ *adjective* [Latin *sibilant-, sibilans,* present participle of *sibilare* to hiss, whistle, of imitative origin] (1669)
: having, containing, or producing the sound of or a sound resembling that of the *s* or the *sh* in *sash* ⟨a *sibilant* affricate⟩ ⟨a *sibilant* snake⟩
— **sib·i·lant·ly** *adverb*

²**sibilant** *noun* (1788)
: a sibilant speech sound (as English \s\, \z\, \sh\, \zh\, \ch(=tsh)\, or \j(=dzh)\)

**sib·i·late** \'si-bə-,lāt\ *verb* **-lat·ed; -lat·ing** [Latin *sibilatus,* past participle of *sibilare*] (circa 1656)
*intransitive verb*
**1** : HISS
**2** : to utter an initial sibilant : prefix an \s\ sound
*transitive verb*
**1** : HISS
**2** : to pronounce with an initial sibilant : prefix an \s\-sound to
— **sib·i·la·tion** \,si-bə-'lā-shən\ *noun*

**sib·ling** \'si-bliŋ\ *noun* (before 12th century)

**1** : SIB 2; *also* : one of two or more individuals having one common parent
**2** : one of two or more things related by a common tie or characteristic

**sibling species** *noun* (1940)
: one of two or more species that are nearly indistinguishable morphologically

**sib·yl** \'si-bəl\ *noun, often capitalized* [Middle English *sibile, sybylle,* from Middle French & Latin; Middle French *sibile,* from Latin *sibylla,* from Greek] (14th century)
**1** : any of several prophetesses usually accepted as 10 in number and credited to widely separate parts of the ancient world (as Babylonia, Egypt, Greece, and Italy)
**2 a** : a female prophet **b** : FORTUNE-TELLER
— **si·byl·ic** *or* **si·byl·lic** \sə-'bi-lik\ *adjective*
— **sib·yl·line** \'si-bə-,līn, -,lēn\ *adjective*

¹**sic** \'sik\ *chiefly Scottish variant of* SUCH

²**sic** *also* **sick** \'sik\ *transitive verb* **sicced** *also* **sicked** \'sikt\; **sic·cing** *also* **sick·ing** [alteration of *seek*] (1845)
**1** : CHASE, ATTACK — usually used as a command especially to a dog ⟨*sic* 'em⟩
**2** : to incite or urge to an attack, pursuit, or harassment : SET

³**sic** \'sik, 'sēk\ *adverb* [Latin, so, thus — more at SO] (circa 1859)

---

---

\ə\ **abut** \ᵊ\ **kitten** \ər\ **further** \a\ **ash** \ā\ **ace**
\ä\ **mop, mar** \aů\ **out** \ch\ **chin** \e\ **bet** \ē\ **easy**
\g\ **go** \i\ **hit** \ī\ **ice** \j\ **job** \ŋ\ **sing** \ō\ **go**
\ȯ\ **law** \ȯi\ **boy** \th\ **thin** \th\ **the** \ü\ **loot** \ů\ **foot**
\y\ **yet** \zh\ **vision**    *see also* Guide to Pronunciation

: intentionally so written — used after a printed word or passage to indicate that it is intended exactly as printed or to indicate that it exactly reproduces an original ⟨said he seed [*sic*] it all⟩

**Sichuan** *variant of* SZECHUAN

**sick** \'sik\ *adjective* [Middle English *sek, sik*, from Old English *sēoc*; akin to Old High German *sioh* sick] (before 12th century) **1 a** (1) **:** affected with disease or ill health **:** AILING (2) **:** of, relating to, or intended for use in sickness ⟨*sick* pay⟩ ⟨a *sick* ward⟩ **b :** QUEASY, NAUSEATED ⟨*sick* to one's stomach⟩ ⟨was *sick* in the car⟩ **c :** undergoing menstruation **2 :** spiritually or morally unsound or corrupt **3 a :** sickened by strong emotion ⟨*sick* with fear⟩ ⟨worried *sick*⟩ **b :** having a strong distaste from surfeit **:** SATIATED ⟨*sick* of flattery⟩ **c :** filled with disgust or chagrin ⟨gossip makes me *sick*⟩ **d :** depressed and longing for something ⟨*sick* for one's home⟩ **4 a :** mentally or emotionally unsound or disordered **:** MORBID ⟨*sick* thoughts⟩ **b :** MACABRE, SADISTIC ⟨*sick* jokes⟩ **5 :** lacking vigor **:** SICKLY: as **a :** badly outclassed ⟨looked *sick* in the contest⟩ **b :** incapable of yielding a profitable crop especially because of buildup of disease organisms ⟨clover*sick* soils⟩

**sick and tired** *adjective* (1783)
**:** thoroughly fatigued or bored; *also* **:** FED UP

**sick bay** *noun* (1813)
**:** a compartment in a ship used as a dispensary and hospital; *broadly* **:** a place for the care of the sick or injured

**sick·bed** \'sik-,bed\ *noun* (14th century)
**:** the bed on which one lies sick

**sick call** *noun* (1836)
**:** a scheduled time at which individuals (as soldiers) may report as sick to the medical officer

**sick day** *noun* (1968)
**:** a paid day of sick leave

**sick·en** \'si-kən\ *verb* **sick·ened; sick·en·ing** \'si-kə-niŋ, 'sik-niŋ\ (13th century) *intransitive verb* **1 :** to become sick **2 :** to become weary or satiated *transitive verb* **1 :** to make sick **2 :** to cause revulsion in as a result of weariness or satiety — **sick·en·er** \'si-kə-nər, 'sik-nər\ *noun*

**sick·en·ing** \-niŋ\ *adjective* (1789)
**:** causing sickness or disgust ⟨a *sickening* odor⟩ ⟨a *sickening* display⟩ — **sick·en·ing·ly** \-niŋ-lē\ *adverb*

**sick·er** \'si-kər\ *adjective* [Middle English *siker*, from Old English *sicor*, from Latin *securus* secure] (before 12th century) *chiefly Scottish* **:** SECURE, SAFE; *also* **:** DEPENDABLE — **sicker** *adverb, chiefly Scottish* — **sick·er·ly** *adverb, chiefly Scottish*

**sick headache** *noun* (1778)
**:** MIGRAINE

**sick·ie** \'si-kē\ *noun* (1967)
**:** a person who is mentally or morally sick

**sick·ish** \'si-kish\ *adjective* (1581) **1** *archaic* **:** somewhat ill **:** SICKLY **2 :** somewhat nauseated **:** QUEASY **3 :** somewhat sickening ⟨a *sickish* odor⟩ — **sick·ish·ly** *adverb* — **sick·ish·ness** *noun*

**¹sick·le** \'si-kəl\ *noun* [Middle English *sikel*, from Old English *sicol*, from Latin *secula* sickle, from *secare* to cut — more at SAW] (before 12th century) **1 :** an agricultural implement consisting of a curved metal blade with a short handle fitted on a tang

**¹sickle 1**

**2 :** the cutting mechanism (as of a reaper, combine, or mower) consisting of a bar with a series of cutting elements

**²sickle** *adjective* (1688)
**:** having the form of a sickle blade **:** having a curve similar to that of a sickle blade ⟨the *sickle* moon⟩

**³sickle** *verb* **sick·led; sick·ling** \'si-k(ə-)liŋ\ (1922) *transitive verb* **1 :** to mow or reap with a sickle **2 :** to change (a red blood cell) into a sickle cell *intransitive verb* **:** to change into a sickle cell ⟨the ability of red blood cells to *sickle*⟩

**sick leave** *noun* (1840)
**1 :** an absence from work permitted because of illness **2 :** the number of days per year for which an employer agrees to pay employees who are sick

**sickle cell** *noun* (1923)
**:** an abnormal red blood cell of crescent shape

**sickle–cell anemia** *noun* (1922)
**:** a chronic inherited anemia in which a large proportion or the majority of the red blood cells tend to sickle, which occurs primarily in individuals of African, Mediterranean, or southwest Asian ancestry, and which results from homozygosity for a semidominant gene — called also *sickle-cell disease*

**sickle–cell trait** *noun* (1928)
**:** an inherited blood condition in which some red blood cells tend to sickle but usually not enough to produce anemia, which occurs primarily in individuals of African, Mediterranean, or southwest Asian ancestry, and which results from heterozygosity for a semidominant gene

**sick·le·mia** \,si-kə-'lē-mē-ə\ *noun* [New Latin, from English *sickle* (cell) + New Latin *-emia*] (1932)
**:** SICKLE-CELL TRAIT

**¹sick·ly** \'si-klē\ *adjective* (14th century) **1 :** somewhat unwell; *also* **:** habitually ailing **2 :** produced by or associated with sickness ⟨a *sickly* complexion⟩ ⟨a *sickly* appetite⟩ **3 :** producing or tending to produce disease **:** UNWHOLESOME ⟨a *sickly* climate⟩ **4 a :** appearing as if sick **b :** lacking in vigor **:** WEAK ⟨a *sickly* plant⟩ **5 :** SICKENING ⟨a *sickly* odor⟩ ⟨a *sickly* green⟩ — **sick·li·ness** *noun* — **sickly** *adverb*

**²sickly** *transitive verb* **sick·lied; sick·ly·ing** (1763)
**:** to make sick or sickly

**sick·ness** \'sik-nəs\ *noun* (before 12th century) **1 a :** ill health **:** ILLNESS **b :** a disordered, weakened, or unsound condition **2 :** a specific disease **3 :** NAUSEA, QUEASINESS

**sicko** \'si-(,)kō\ *noun, plural* **sick·os** (1963)
**:** SICKIE

**sick–out** \'sik-,aut\ *noun* (1951)
**:** an organized absence from work by workers on the pretext of sickness

**sick pay** *noun* (1887)
**:** salary or wages paid to an employee while on sick leave

**sick·room** \'sik-,rüm, -,rum\ *noun* (1749)
**:** a room in which a person is confined by sickness

**sic pas·sim** \'sik-'pa-səm, 'sēk-'pä-sim\ *adverb* [Latin] (1921)
**:** so throughout — used of a word or idea to be found throughout a book or a writer's work

**sid·dur** \'si-dər, -,dùr\ *noun, plural* **sid·du·rim** \sə-'dür-əm\ [Late Hebrew *siddûr*, literally, order, arrangement] (1864)
**:** a Jewish prayer book containing liturgies for daily, Sabbath, and holiday observances

**¹side** \'sīd\ *noun* [Middle English, from Old English *sīde*; akin to Old High German *sīta* side, Old English *sīd* ample, wide] (before 12th century) **1 a :** the right or left part of the wall or trunk of the body ⟨a pain in the *side*⟩ **b** (1) **:** one of the halves of the animal body on either side of the mesial plane (2) **:** a cut of meat including that the ribs of one half of the body — used chiefly of smoked pork products **c :** one longitudinal half of a hide **2 :** a place, space, or direction with respect to a center or to a line of division (as of an aisle, river, or street) **3 a :** one of the longer bounding surfaces or lines of an object especially contrasted with the ends ⟨the *side* of a barn⟩ **b :** a line or surface forming a border or face of an object ⟨a die has six *sides*⟩ ⟨the back *side* of the moon⟩ **c :** either surface of a thin object ⟨one *side* of a record⟩ ⟨right *side* of the cloth⟩ **d :** a bounding line of a geometric figure ⟨*side* of a triangle⟩ **4 a :** the space beside one ⟨stood by my *side*⟩ **b :** an area next to something — usually used in combination ⟨a pool*side* interview⟩ **5 :** a slope (as of a hill) considered as opposed to another slope ⟨the far *side* of the hill⟩ **6 a :** the attitude or activity of one person or group with respect to another **:** PART ⟨there was no malice on my *side*⟩ **b :** a position that is opposite to or contrasted with another ⟨two *sides* to every question⟩ ⟨came down on the *side* of law and order⟩ **c :** a body of partisans or contestants ⟨victory for neither *side*⟩ **d :** TEAM ⟨11 players on each *side*⟩ **7 :** a line of descent traced through one's parent ⟨grandfather on his mother's *side*⟩ **8 :** an aspect or part of something contrasted with some other real or implied aspect or part ⟨the better *side* of his nature⟩ ⟨the sales *side* of the business⟩ ⟨the seasoning is a bit on the heavy *side*⟩ **9** *British* **:** sideways spin imparted to a billiard or snooker ball **10 :** a sheet containing the lines and cues for a single theatrical role **11 :** a recording of music **12 :** a side order or dish ⟨a *side* of fries⟩ — **on the side 1 :** in addition to the main portion **2 :** in addition to a principal occupation — **this side of :** short of **:** ALMOST ⟨an attitude just *this side of* scandalous⟩

**²side** *adjective* (14th century) **1 a :** situated on the side ⟨*side* window⟩ **b :** of or relating to the side **2 a :** directed toward or from the side ⟨*side* thrust⟩ ⟨*side* wind⟩ **b :** INCIDENTAL, INDIRECT ⟨*side* issue⟩ ⟨*side* remark⟩ **c :** made on the side ⟨*side* payment⟩ **d :** additional to the main portion ⟨*side* order of french fries⟩

**³side** *verb* **sid·ed; sid·ing** (1591) *transitive verb* **1 :** to agree with **:** SUPPORT **2 :** to be side by side with **3 :** to set or put aside **:** clear away ⟨*side* the dishes⟩ **4 :** to furnish with sides or siding ⟨*side* a house⟩ *intransitive verb* **:** to take sides **:** join or form sides ⟨*sided* with the rebels⟩

**⁴side** *noun* [obsolete English *side* proud, boastful] (1878) *chiefly British* **:** swaggering or arrogant manner **:** PRETENTIOUSNESS

**side·arm** \'sīd-,ärm\ *adjective* (1908)
**:** of, relating to, using, or being a baseball pitching style in which the arm is not raised above the shoulder and the ball is thrown with a sideways sweep of the arm between shoulder and hip ⟨*sidearm* delivery⟩ — **sidearm** *adverb*

**side arm** *noun* (1689)

: a weapon (as a sword, revolver, or bayonet) worn at the side or in the belt

**side·band** \-ˌband\ *noun* (1922)
: the band of frequencies (as of radio waves) on either side of the carrier frequency produced by modulation

**side·bar** \-ˌbär\ *noun* (1945)
: a short news story accompanying and presenting sidelights of a major story

**side bearing** *noun* (circa 1894)
: the space provided at each side of a typeset letter to prevent its touching adjoining letters

**side·board** \'sīd-ˌbōrd, -ˌbord\ *noun* (1671)
: a piece of dining-room furniture having compartments and shelves for holding articles of table service

sideboard

**side·burns** \-ˌbərnz\ *noun plural* [anagram of *burnsides*] (1887)
**1** : SIDE-WHISKERS
**2** : continuations of the hairline in front of the ears ◆
— **side·burned** \-ˌbərnd\ *adjective*

**side by side** *adverb* (13th century)
**1** : beside one another
**2** : in the same place, time, or circumstance ⟨lived peacefully *side by side* for many years⟩
— **side–by–side** *adjective*

**side·car** \'sīd-ˌkär\ *noun* (1904)
**1** : a car attached to the side of a motorcycle for a passenger
**2** : a cocktail consisting of a liqueur with lemon juice and brandy

**side chain** *noun* (1886)
: a shorter chain or group of atoms attached to a principal chain or to a ring in a molecule

**side chair** *noun* (1925)
: a chair without arms used usually in a dining room

**sid·ed** \'sī-dəd\ *adjective* (15th century)
: having sides often of a specified number or kind ⟨one-*sided*⟩ ⟨glass-*sided*⟩
— **sid·ed·ness** *noun*

**side dish** *noun* (1725)
: a food served separately along with the main course

**side·dress** \'sīd-ˌdres\ *noun* (1966)
: SIDE-DRESSING
— **side–dress** \'sīd-ˌdres\ *transitive verb*

**side–dress·ing** \-ˌdre-siŋ\ *noun* (1935)
**1** : plant nutrients placed on or in the soil near the roots of a growing crop often by means of a cultivator having a fertilizer-distributing attachment
**2** : the act or process of applying side-dressing to a crop

**side drum** *noun* (circa 1800)
: SNARE DRUM

**side effect** *noun* (1884)
: a secondary and usually adverse effect (as of a drug) ⟨toxic *side effects*⟩ — called also *side reaction*

**side–glance** \'sīd-ˌglan(t)s\ *noun* (1611)
**1** : a glance directed to the side
**2** : a passing allusion : an indirect or slight reference

**side·hill** \-ˌhil\ *noun* (1674)
: HILLSIDE
— **sidehill** *adjective*

**side horse** *noun* (circa 1934)
: POMMEL HORSE

**side·kick** \'sīd-ˌkik\ *noun* (1906)
: a person closely associated with another as subordinate or partner

**side·light** \-ˌlīt\ *noun* (1610)
**1 a** : light coming or produced from the side **b** : incidental light or information
**2** : the red light on the port bow or the green light on the starboard bow carried by ships under way at night

**¹side·line** \-ˌlīn\ *noun* (1862)

**1** : a line at right angles to a goal line or end line and marking a side of a court or field of play for athletic games
**2 a** : a line of goods sold in addition to one's principal line **b** : a business or activity pursued in addition to one's regular occupation
**3 a** : the space immediately outside the lines along either side of an athletic field or court **b** : a sphere of little or no participation or activity — usually used in plural

**²sideline** *transitive verb* (1943)
: to put out of action : to put on the sidelines

**side·lin·er** \'sīd-ˌlī-nər\ *noun* (1947)
: one that remains on the sidelines during an activity : one that does not participate

**¹side·ling** \'sīd-liŋ\ *adverb* [Middle English *sidling*, from ¹*side* + ²*-ling*] (14th century)
*archaic* : in a sidelong direction : SIDEWAYS

**²sideling** *adjective* (1611)
**1** *archaic* : directed toward one side : OBLIQUE
**2** *archaic* : having an inclination : SLOPING ⟨*sideling* ground⟩

**¹side·long** \'sīd-ˌloŋ\ *adverb* [alteration of ¹*sideling*] (14th century)
**1** : SIDEWAYS, OBLIQUELY
**2** *archaic* : on the side

**²sidelong** *adjective* (1597)
**1** : lying or inclining to one side : SLANTING
**2 a** : directed to one side ⟨*sidelong* looks⟩ **b** : indirect rather than straightforward

**side·man** \'sīd-ˌman\ *noun* (1936)
: a member of a band or orchestra and especially of a jazz or swing orchestra

**side·piece** \-ˌpēs\ *noun* (1802)
: a piece forming or contained in the side of something ⟨the *sidepiece* of a carriage⟩

**sider-** *or* **sidero-** *combining form* [Middle French, from Latin, from Greek *sidēr-*, *sidēro-*, from *sidēros*]
: iron ⟨*sidero*lite⟩ ⟨hemo*siderin*⟩

**-sid·er** \'sīd-ər\ *combining form*
: one placed or living in a usually specified side (as a section of the city) ⟨an east-*sider*⟩

**si·de·re·al** \sī-'dir-ē-əl, sə-\ *adjective* [Latin *sidereus*, from *sider-, sidus* star, constellation] (1647)
**1** : of, relating to, or expressed in relation to stars or constellations : ASTRAL

**sidereal day** *noun* (1794)
: the interval between two successive transits of a point on the celestial sphere (as the vernal equinox) over the upper meridian of a place : 23 hours, 56 minutes, 4.1 seconds of mean time

**sidereal hour** *noun* (circa 1891)
: the 24th part of a sidereal day

**sidereal minute** *noun* (circa 1909)
: the 60th part of a sidereal hour

**sidereal month** *noun* (1868)
: the mean time of the moon's revolution in its orbit with reference to a star's position : 27 days, 7 hours, 43 minutes, 11.5 seconds of mean time

**sidereal second** *noun* (circa 1909)
: the 60th part of a sidereal minute

**sidereal time** *noun* (1812)
**1** : time based on the sidereal day
**2** : the hour angle of the vernal equinox at a place

**sidereal year** *noun* (1681)
: the time in which the earth completes one revolution in its orbit around the sun measured with respect to the fixed stars : 365 days, 6 hours, 9 minutes, and 9.5 seconds of mean time

**¹sid·er·ite** \'si-də-ˌrīt\ *noun* [German *Siderit*, from Greek *sidēros* iron] (1850)
: a native ferrous carbonate $FeCO_3$ that is a valuable iron ore

**²siderite** *noun* (1875)
: a nickel-iron meteorite

**side road** *noun* (1854)
: a smaller road off a main road

**si·de·ro·lite** \sī-'dir-ə-ˌlīt, 'si-də-rə-\ *noun* (1863)
: a stony iron meteorite

**side·sad·dle** \'sīd-ˌsa-dᵊl\ *noun* (15th century)
: a saddle for women in which the rider sits with both legs on the same side of the horse
— **sidesaddle** *adverb*

**side–scan sonar** \-ˌskan-\ *noun* (1967)
: a sonar that scans the ocean floor to the side of a ship's track and is used especially for mapping the ocean bottom

**side·show** \-ˌshō\ *noun* (1846)
**1** : a minor show offered in addition to a main exhibition (as of a circus)
**2** : an incidental diversion or spectacle

**side·slip** \-ˌslip\ *intransitive verb* (1887)
**1** : to skid or slide sideways
**2** : to slide sideways through the air in a downward direction in an airplane along an inclined lateral axis
— **sideslip** *noun*

**side·spin** \-ˌspin\ *noun* (1926)
: a rotary motion that causes a ball to revolve horizontally

**side·split·ting** \-ˌspli-tiŋ\ *adjective* (1856)
: extremely funny
— **side·split·ting·ly** *adverb*

**side·step** \'sīd-ˌstep\ (1901)
*intransitive verb*
**1** : to take a side step
**2** : to avoid an issue or decision
*transitive verb*
**1** : to move out of the way of : AVOID ⟨*sidestep* a blow⟩
**2** : BYPASS, EVADE ⟨*sidestep* a question⟩
— **side·step·per** *noun*

**side step** *noun* (1789)
**1** : a step aside (as in boxing to avoid a blow)
**2** : a step taken sideways (as when climbing on skis)

**side–strad·dle hop** \'sīd-ˌstra-dᵊl-\ *noun* (1952)
: JUMPING JACK 2

**side·stream** \-ˌstrēm\ *adjective* (1951)
: relating to or being tobacco smoke that is emitted from the lighted end of a cigarette or cigar

**side street** *noun* (1617)
: a street joining and often terminated by a main thoroughfare

**side·stroke** \'sīd-ˌstrōk\ *noun* (1867)
: a swimming stroke which is executed on the side and in which the arms are swept in separate strokes towards the feet and downward and the legs do a scissors kick

**¹side·swipe** \-ˌswīp\ *transitive verb* (1904)
: to strike with a glancing blow along the side ⟨*sideswiped* a parked car⟩

**²sideswipe** *noun* (1917)
**1 a** : the action of sideswiping **b** : an instance of sideswiping : a glancing blow

◇ WORD HISTORY
**sideburns** During the American Civil War, Union general Ambrose Everett Burnside (1824–1881) cultivated long bushy side-whiskers. His appearance first struck the fancy of Washingtonians as he conducted parades and maneuvers with his regiment of Rhode Island volunteers in the early days of the war. Despite a later military career that had its ups and downs, this early popularity fostered the fashion for such whiskers in 19th century America, which originally were called *burnsides*. By the 1880s the order of the two words comprising *burnsides* was reversed to give *sideburns*, most likely by analogy with *side-whiskers*. And whereas the general's whiskers were flamboyantly bushy, today sideburns can be of any length or fullness.

\ə\ abut \ᵊ\ kitten \ər\ further \a\ ash \ā\ ace
\ä\ mop, mar \aú\ out \ch\ chin \e\ bet \ē\ easy
\g\ go \i\ hit \ī\ ice \j\ job \ŋ\ sing \ō\ go
\ó\ law \ói\ boy \th\ thin \t͟h\ the \ü\ loot \ú\ foot
\y\ yet \zh\ vision *see also* Guide to Pronunciation

**2** : an incidental deprecatory remark, allusion, or reference

**side table** *noun* (14th century)
: a table designed to be placed against a wall

**¹side·track** \'sīd-ˌtrak\ *noun* (1835)
**1** : SIDING 2
**2** : a position or condition of secondary importance to which one may be diverted

**²sidetrack** *transitive verb* (1880)
**1** : to shunt aside (as to a railroad siding)
**2 a** : to turn aside from a purpose : DEFLECT **b** : to prevent action on by diversionary tactics ⟨*sidetrack* an issue⟩

**side·walk** \'sīd-ˌwȯk\ *noun* (1739)
: a usually paved walk for pedestrians at the side of a street

**sidewalk superintendent** *noun* (1940)
: a spectator at a building or demolition job

**side·wall** \'sīd-ˌwȯl\ *noun* (14th century)
**1** : a wall forming the side of something
**2** : the side of an automotive tire between the tread shoulder and the rim bead

**side·ward** \'sīd-wərd\ *or* **side·wards** \-wərdz\ *adverb* (15th century)
: toward a side

**side·way** \'sīd-ˌwā\ *adverb or adjective* (1612)
: SIDEWAYS

**side·ways** \-ˌwāz\ *adverb or adjective* (1577)
**1** : from one side
**2** : with one side forward ⟨turn *sideways*⟩
**3 a** : in a lateral direction or downward to one side ⟨hopped *sideways*⟩ ⟨slump *sideways*⟩ **b** : ASKANCE ⟨look *sideways* at someone⟩

**side–wheel** \'sīd-ˌhwēl, -ˌwēl\ *adjective* (1857)
: of or being a steamer having a paddle wheel on each side

— **side–wheel·er** \-ˌhwē-lər, -ˌwē-\ *noun*

**side–whis·kers** \'sīd-ˌhwis-kərz, -ˌwis-\ *noun plural* (1888)
: whiskers on the side of the face usually worn long

— **side–whis·kered** \-kərd\ *adjective*

**side·wind·er** \'sīd-ˌwīn-dər\ *noun* (1840)
**1** : a heavy swinging blow from the side
**2** : a small pale-colored desert rattlesnake (*Crotalus cerastes*) of the southwestern U.S. that moves by thrusting its body diagonally forward in a series of flat S-shaped curves

sidewinder 2

**side·wise** \'sīd-ˌwīz\ *adverb* (1571)
: SIDEWAYS

**sid·ing** \'sī-diŋ\ *noun* (1603)
**1** *archaic* : the taking of sides : PARTISANSHIP
**2** : a short railroad track connected with the main track
**3** : material (as boards or metal pieces) forming the exposed surface of outside walls of frame buildings

**si·dle** \'sī-d°l\ *verb* **si·dled**; **si·dling** \'sīd-liŋ, 'sī-d°l-iŋ\ [probably back-formation from ²*sideling*] (1697)
*intransitive verb*
: to go or move with one side foremost especially in a furtive advance
*transitive verb*
: to cause to move or turn sideways
— **sidle** *noun*

**siege** \'sēj *also* 'sēzh\ *noun* [Middle English *sege*, from Old French, seat, blockade, from *siegier* to seat, settle, from (assumed) Vulgar Latin *sedicare*, from Latin *sedēre* to sit — more at SIT] (13th century)
**1** *obsolete* : a seat of distinction : THRONE
**2 a** : military blockade of a city or fortified place to compel it to surrender **b** : a persistent or serious attack (as of illness)

— **siege** *transitive verb*
— **lay siege to 1** : to besiege militarily **2** : to pursue diligently or persistently

**siege mentality** *noun* (1953)
: a defensive or overly fearful attitude

**Siege Perilous** *noun*
: a seat at King Arthur's Round Table reserved for the knight destined to achieve the quest of the Holy Grail and fatal to any other occupying it

**Sieg·fried** \'sig-ˌfrēd, 'sēg-\ *noun* [German]
: a hero in Germanic legend who slays a dragon guarding a gold hoard and wakes Brunhild from her enchanted sleep

**Siegfried line** *noun* [*Siegfried*] (1918)
: a line of German defensive fortifications facing the Maginot Line

**sie·mens** \'sē-mənz, 'zē-\ *noun, plural* **siemens** [Werner von *Siemens* (died 1892) German electrical engineer] (circa 1933)
: a unit of conductance in the meter-kilogram-second system equivalent to one ampere per volt

**si·en·na** \sē-'e-nə\ *noun* [Italian *terra di Siena*, literally, Siena earth, from *Siena*, Italy] (1787)
: an earthy substance containing oxides of iron and usually of manganese that is brownish yellow when raw and orange red or reddish brown when burnt and is used as a pigment

**si·er·o·zem** \ˌsē-ər-ə-ˌzem, sē-ˌer-ə-'zyȯm\ *noun* [Russian *serozem*, from *seryĭ* gray + *zemlya* earth; akin to Latin *humus* earth — more at HUMBLE] (1934)
: any of a group of zonal soils brownish gray at the surface and lighter below, based in a carbonate or hardpan layer, and characteristic of temperate to cool arid regions

**si·er·ra** \sē-'er-ə\ *noun* [Spanish, literally, saw, from Latin *serra*] (1600)
**1 a** : a range of mountains especially with a serrated or irregular outline **b** : the country about a sierra
**2** : any of several large fishes (genus *Scomberomorus*) related to the mackerel

**Sierra** (1952)
— a communications code word for the letter s

**si·er·ran** \sē-'er-ən\ *adjective* (1873)
**1** : of or relating to a sierra ⟨*sierran* foothills⟩
**2** *capitalized* : of or relating to the Sierra Nevada Mountains of the western U.S.

**Sierran** *noun* (1906)
: a native or inhabitant of the region around the Sierra Nevada Mountains

**si·es·ta** \sē-'es-tə\ *noun* [Spanish, from Latin *sexta* (*hora*) noon, literally, sixth hour — more at SEXT] (1655)
: an afternoon nap or rest

**sie·va bean** \'sē-və-, 'si-vē-\ *noun* [origin unknown] (1888)
: a bean plant (*Phaseolus lunatus*) of tropical America that is closely related to and sometimes classified with the lima bean; *also* : its flat edible seed

**¹sieve** \'siv\ *noun* [Middle English *sive*, from Old English *sife*; akin to Old High German *sib* sieve] (before 12th century)
: a device with meshes or perforations through which finer particles of a mixture (as of ashes, flour, or sand) of various sizes may be passed to separate them from coarser ones, through which the liquid may be drained from liquid-containing material, or through which soft materials may be forced for reduction to fine particles

**²sieve** *verb* **sieved**; **siev·ing** (15th century)
: SIFT

**sieve of Er·a·tos·the·nes** \-ˌer-ə-'täs-thə-ˌnēz\ (1803)
: a procedure for finding prime numbers that involves writing down the odd numbers from 2 up in succession and lining out every third number after 3, every fifth after 5 including those already lined out, every seventh after 7, and so on with each successive number which

has not been lined out with every number that is not lined out being prime

**sieve plate** *noun* (1875)
: a perforated wall or part of a wall at the end of one of the individual cells making up a sieve tube

**sieve tube** *noun* (1875)
: a tube consisting of an end-to-end series of thin-walled living plant cells characteristic of the phloem and held to function chiefly in translocation of organic solutes

**si·faka** \sə-'fä-kə\ *noun* [Malagasy] (1845)
: any of several diurnal mostly black and white lemurs (genus *Propithecus*) with a long tail and silky fur

**sift** \'sift\ *verb* [Middle English, from Old English *siftan*; akin to Old English *sife* sieve] (before 12th century)
*transitive verb*
**1 a** : to put through a sieve ⟨*sift* flour⟩ **b** : to separate or separate out by or as if by putting through a sieve
**2** : to go through especially to sort out what is useful or valuable ⟨*sifted* the evidence⟩ — often used with *through* ⟨*sift* through a pile of old letters⟩
**3** : to scatter by or as if by sifting ⟨*sift* sugar on a cake⟩
*intransitive verb*
**1** : to use a sieve
**2** : to pass or fall as if through a sieve
— **sift·er** *noun*

**sift·ing** *noun* (15th century)
**1** : the act or process of sifting
**2** *plural* : sifted material

**¹sigh** \'sī\ *verb* [Middle English *sihen*, alteration of *sichen*, from Old English *sīcan*; akin to Middle Dutch ver*siken* to sigh] (13th century)
*intransitive verb*
**1** : to take a deep audible breath (as in weariness or relief)
**2** : to make a sound like sighing ⟨wind *sighing* in the branches⟩
**3** : GRIEVE, YEARN ⟨*sighing* for days gone by⟩
*transitive verb*
**1** : to express by sighs
**2** *archaic* : to utter sighs over : MOURN
— **sigh·er** \'sī(-ə)r\ *noun*

**²sigh** *noun* (14th century)
**1** : an often involuntary act of sighing especially when expressing an emotion or feeling (as weariness or relief)
**2** : the sound of gently moving or escaping air ⟨*sighs* of the summer breeze⟩

**¹sight** \'sīt\ *noun* [Middle English, from Old English *gesiht* faculty or act of sight, thing seen; akin to Old High German *gisiht* sight, Old English *sēon* to see] (before 12th century)
**1** : something that is seen : SPECTACLE
**2 a** : a thing regarded as worth seeing — usually used in plural ⟨the *sights* of the city⟩ **b** : something ludicrous or disorderly in appearance ⟨you look a *sight*⟩
**3 a** *chiefly dialect* : a great number or quantity **b** : a good deal : LOT ⟨a far *sight* better⟩ ⟨not by a damn *sight*⟩
**4 a** : the process, power, or function of seeing; *specifically* : the animal sense of which the end organ is the eye and by which the position, shape, and color of objects are perceived **b** : mental or spiritual perception **c** : mental view; *specifically* : JUDGMENT
**5 a** : the act of looking at or beholding **b** : INSPECTION, PERUSAL **c** : VIEW, GLIMPSE **d** : an observation to determine direction or position (as by a navigator)
**6 a** : a perception of an object by or as if by the eye ⟨never lost *sight* of the objective⟩ **b** : the range of vision ⟨was nowhere in *sight*⟩
**7** : presentation of a note or draft to the maker or draftee : DEMAND
**8 a** : a device that aids the eye in aiming or in finding the direction of an object **b** *plural* : ASPIRATION ⟨set her *sights* on a medical career⟩

**— in sight :** at or within a reasonable distance or time

**— on sight :** as soon as seen ⟨ordered to shoot *on sight*⟩

**— out of sight 1 :** beyond comparison **2 :** beyond all expectation or reason **3** — used as a generalized expression of approval

**— sight for sore eyes :** one whose appearance or arrival is an occasion for joy or relief

²**sight** (1602)
*transitive verb*
**1 :** to get or catch sight of ⟨several whales were *sighted*⟩
**2 :** to look at through or as if through a sight; *especially* **:** to test for straightness
**3 :** to aim by means of sights
**4 a :** to equip with sights **b :** to adjust the sights of
*intransitive verb*
**1 :** to take aim
**2 :** to look carefully in a particular direction

³**sight** *adjective* (1801)
**1 :** based on recognition or comprehension without previous study ⟨*sight* translation⟩
**2 :** payable on presentation ⟨a *sight* draft⟩

**sight·ed** \'sī-təd\ *adjective* (1552)
**:** having sight ⟨clear-*sighted*⟩ ⟨a *sighted* person⟩

**sight gag** *noun* (1949)
**:** a comic bit or episode whose effect is produced by pantomime or camera shot rather than by words

**sight·less** \'sīt-ləs\ *adjective* (13th century)
**1 :** lacking sight **:** BLIND
**2 :** INVISIBLE l
**— sight·less·ly** *adverb*
**— sight·less·ness** *noun*

**sight line** *noun* (1859)
**:** a line extending from an observer's eye to a viewed object or area (as a stage) ⟨a theater with excellent *sight lines*⟩

**sight·ly** \-lē\ *adjective* (1534)
**1 :** pleasing to the sight **:** ATTRACTIVE
**2 :** affording a fine view
**— sight·li·ness** *noun*
**— sightly** *adverb*

**sight–read** \-,rēd\ *verb* **-read** \-,red\; **-read·ing** \-,rē-diŋ\ [back-formation from *sight reader*] (1903)
*transitive verb*
**:** to read (as a foreign language) or perform (music) without previous preparation or study
*intransitive verb*
**:** to read at sight; *especially* **:** to perform music at sight
**— sight reader** *noun*

**sight rhyme** *noun* (circa 1936)
**:** EYE RHYME

**sight·see** \'sīt-,sē\ *intransitive verb, past* **-saw** *present participle* **-see·ing** [back-formation from *sight-seeing*] (1824)
**:** to go about seeing sights of interest
**— sight·seer** \-,sē-ər, -,sir\ *noun*

**sight–see·ing** \'sīt-,sē-iŋ\ *adjective* (1827)
**:** devoted to or used for seeing sights
**— sight-seeing** *noun*

**sight unseen** *adverb* (1892)
**:** without inspection or appraisal

**sig·il** \'si-jil\ *noun* [Middle English *sigulle*, from Latin *sigillum* — more at SEAL] (15th century)
**1 :** SEAL, SIGNET
**2 :** a sign, word, or device held to have occult power in astrology or magic

**sig·ma** \'sig-mə\ *noun* [Greek] (1607)
**1 :** the 18th letter of the Greek alphabet — see ALPHABET table
**2 :** STANDARD DEVIATION

**sig·moid** \'sig-,mȯid\ *also* **sig·moi·dal** \sig-'mȯi-d°l\ *adjective* [Greek *sigmoeidēs*, from *sigma;* from a common form of sigma shaped like the Roman letter C] (1670)
**1 a :** curved like the letter C **b :** curved in two directions like the letter S

**2 :** of, relating to, or being the sigmoid flexure of the intestine
**— sig·moi·dal·ly** \sig-'mȯi-d°l-ē\ *adverb*

**sigmoid flexure** *noun* (1786)
**:** the contracted and crooked part of the colon immediately above the rectum — called also *sigmoid colon*

**sig·moid·os·co·py** \,sig-,mȯi-'däs-kə-pē\ *noun* (circa 1900)
**:** the process of using a long hollow tubular instrument passed through the anus for inspection, diagnosis, treatment, and photography especially of the sigmoid flexure

¹**sign** \'sīn\ *noun* [Middle English *signe*, from Old French, from Latin *signum* mark, token, sign, image, seal; perhaps akin to Latin *secare* to cut — more at SAW] (13th century)
**1 a :** a motion or gesture by which a thought is expressed or a command or wish made known **b :** SIGNAL 2a **c :** a fundamental linguistic unit that designates an object or relation or has a purely syntactic function **d :** one of a set of gestures used to represent language; *also* **:** SIGN LANGUAGE
**2 :** a mark having a conventional meaning and used in place of words or to represent a complex notion
**3 :** one of the 12 divisions of the zodiac
**4 a** (1) **:** a character (as a flat or sharp) used in musical notation (2) **:** SEGNO **b :** a character (as ÷) indicating a mathematical operation; *also* **:** one of two characters + and − that form part of the symbol of a number and characterize it as positive or negative
**5 a :** a display (as a lettered board or a configuration of neon tubing) used to identify or advertise a place of business or a product **b :** a posted command, warning, or direction **c :** SIGNBOARD
**6 a :** something material or external that stands for or signifies something spiritual **b :** something indicating the presence or existence of something else ⟨*signs* of success⟩ ⟨a *sign* of the times⟩ **c :** PRESAGE, PORTENT ⟨*signs* of an early spring⟩ **d :** an objective evidence of plant or animal disease
**7** *plural usually* **sign :** traces of a usually wild animal ⟨red fox *sign*⟩ ☆
**— signed** *adjective*

²**sign** *verb* [Middle English, from Middle French *signer*, from Latin *signare* to mark, sign, seal, from *signum*] (13th century)
*transitive verb*
**1 a :** CROSS 2 **b :** to place a sign on **c :** to represent or indicate by a sign
**2 a :** to affix a signature to **:** ratify or attest by hand or seal ⟨*sign* a bill into law⟩ ⟨the prisoner *signed* a confession⟩ **b :** to assign or convey formally ⟨*signed* over his property to his brother⟩ **c :** to write down (one's name)
**3 :** to communicate by making a sign or by sign language
**4 :** to engage or hire by securing the signature of on a contract of employment — often used with *up* or *on*
*intransitive verb*
**1 :** to write one's name in token of assent, responsibility, or obligation
**2 a :** to make a sign or signal **b :** to use sign language
**— sign·ee** \,sī-'nē\ *noun*
**— sign·er** \'sī-nər\ *noun*

**sign·age** \'sī-nij\ *noun* (1976)
**:** signs (as of identification, warning, or direction) or a system of such signs

¹**sig·nal** \'sig-n°l\ *noun* [Middle English, from Middle French, from Medieval Latin *signale*, from Late Latin, neuter of *signalis* of a sign, from Latin *signum*] (14th century)
**1 :** SIGN, INDICATION
**2 a :** an act, event, or watchword that has been agreed on as the occasion of concerted action **b :** something that incites to action
**3 :** something (as a sound, gesture, or object) that conveys notice or warning

**4 a :** an object used to transmit or convey information beyond the range of human voice **b :** the sound or image conveyed in telegraphy, telephony, radio, radar, or television **c :** a detectable physical quantity or impulse (as a voltage, current, or magnetic field strength) by which messages or information can be transmitted

²**signal** *verb* **sig·naled** *or* **sig·nalled; sig·nal·ing** *or* **sig·nal·ling** \-nə-liŋ\ (1805)
*transitive verb*
**1 :** to notify by a signal ⟨*signal* the fleet to turn back⟩
**2 a :** to communicate or indicate by or as if by signals ⟨*signaled* the end of an era⟩ **b :** to constitute a characteristic feature of (a meaningful linguistic form)
*intransitive verb*
**:** to make or send a signal
**— sig·nal·er** *or* **sig·nal·ler** *noun*

³**signal** *adjective* [modification of French *signalé*, past participle of *signaler* to distinguish, from Old Italian *segnalare* to signal, distinguish, from *segnale* signal, from Medieval Latin *signale*] (1641)
**:** distinguished from the ordinary ⟨*signal* achievement⟩

**sig·nal·ise** *British variant of* SIGNALIZE

**sig·nal·ize** \'sig-nə-,līz\ *transitive verb* **-ized; -iz·ing** (1654)
**1 :** to make conspicuous **:** DISTINGUISH
**2 :** to point out carefully or distinctly
**3 :** to make signals to **:** SIGNAL; *also* **:** INDICATE
**4 :** to place traffic signals at or on
**— sig·nal·i·za·tion** \,sig-nə-lə-'zā-shən\ *noun*

**sig·nal·ly** \'sig-nə-lē\ *adverb* (1641)
**:** in a signal manner **:** NOTABLY

**sig·nal·man** \'sig-n°l-mən, -,man\ *noun* (1737)
**:** a person who signals or works with signals (as on a railway)

**sig·nal·ment** \-mənt\ *noun* [French *signalement*, from *signaler*] (1778)
**:** description by peculiar, appropriate, or characteristic marks; *specifically* **:** the systematic description of a person for purposes of identification

**sig·na·to·ry** \'sig-nə-,tōr-ē, -,tȯr-\ *noun, plural* **-ries** [Latin *signatorius* of sealing, from *signare*] (1866)
**:** a signer with another or others ⟨*signatories* to a petition⟩; *especially* **:** a government bound with others by a signed convention
**— signatory** *adjective*

**sig·na·ture** \'sig-nə-,chür, -chər, -,tyür, -,tür\ *noun* [Middle French or Medieval Latin; Middle French, from Medieval Latin *signatura*, from Latin *signatus*, past participle of *signare* to sign, seal] (1536)

---

☆ **SYNONYMS**
**Sign, mark, token, note, symptom** mean a discernible indication of what is not itself directly perceptible. SIGN applies to any indication to be perceived by the senses or the reason ⟨encouraging *signs* for the economy⟩. MARK suggests something impressed on or inherently characteristic of a thing often in contrast to general outward appearance ⟨a *mark* of a good upbringing⟩. TOKEN applies to something that serves as a proof of something intangible ⟨this gift is a *token* of our esteem⟩. NOTE suggests a distinguishing mark or characteristic ⟨a *note* of irony in her writing⟩. SYMPTOM suggests an outward indication of an internal change or condition ⟨rampant crime is a *symptom* of that city's decay⟩.

---

\ə\ **abut** \°\ **kitten** \ər\ **further** \a\ **ash** \ā\ **ace**
\ä\ **mop, mar** \aú\ **out** \ch\ **chin** \e\ **bet** \ē\ **easy**
\g\ **go** \i\ **hit** \ī\ **ice** \j\ **job** \ŋ\ **sing** \ō\ **go**
\ȯ\ **law** \ȯi\ **boy** \th\ **thin** \ṯh\ **the** \ü\ **loot** \ú\ **foot**
\y\ **yet** \zh\ **vision**   *see also* Guide to Pronunciation

**1 a :** the act of signing one's name **b :** the name of a person written with his or her own hand
**2 :** a feature in the appearance or qualities of a natural object formerly held to indicate its utility in medicine
**3 a :** a letter or figure placed usually at the bottom of the first page on each sheet of printed pages (as of a book) as a direction to the binder in arranging and gathering the sheets **b :** a folded sheet that is one unit of a book
**4 a :** KEY SIGNATURE **b :** TIME SIGNATURE
**5 :** the part of a medical prescription that contains the directions to the patient
**6 :** something (as a tune, style, or logo) that serves to identify; *also :* a characteristic mark
**sign·board** \'sīn-,bōrd, -,bȯrd\ *noun* (1632)
**:** a board bearing a notice or sign
**signed** \'sīnd\ *adjective* (1873)
**:** having a sign and especially a plus or minus sign ⟨*signed* numbers like +6 and −4⟩
**¹sig·net** \'sig-nət\ *noun* [Middle English, from Middle French, diminutive of *signe* sign, seal] (14th century)
**1 :** a seal used officially to give personal authority to a document in lieu of signature
**2 :** the impression made by or as if by a signet
**3 :** a small intaglio seal (as in a finger ring)
**²signet** *transitive verb* (15th century)
**:** to stamp or authenticate with a signet
**signet ring** *noun* (1681)
**:** a finger ring engraved with a signet, seal, or monogram **:** SEAL RING
**sig·nif·i·cance** \sig-'ni-fi-kən(t)s\ *noun* (13th century)
**1 a :** something that is conveyed as a meaning often obscurely or indirectly **b :** the quality of conveying or implying
**2 a :** the quality of being important **:** MOMENT **b :** the quality of being statistically significant
**synonym** see IMPORTANCE
**significance level** *noun* (1947)
**:** LEVEL OF SIGNIFICANCE
**sig·nif·i·can·cy** \sig-'ni-fi-kən(t)-sē\ *noun* (circa 1595)
**:** SIGNIFICANCE
**sig·nif·i·cant** \-kənt\ *adjective* [Latin *significant-, significans*, present participle of *significare* to signify] (1579)
**1 :** having meaning; *especially :* SUGGESTIVE ⟨a *significant* glance⟩
**2 a :** having or likely to have influence or effect **:** IMPORTANT ⟨a *significant* piece of legislation⟩; *also :* of a noticeably or measurably large amount ⟨a *significant* number of layoffs⟩ ⟨producing *significant* profits⟩ **b :** probably caused by something other than mere chance ⟨statistically *significant* correlation between vitamin deficiency and disease⟩
**significant digit** *noun* (1923)
**:** one of the digits of a number beginning with the digit farthest to the left that is not zero and ending with the last digit farthest to the right that is not zero or is a zero considered to be exact — called also *significant figure*
**sig·nif·i·cant·ly** \sig-'ni-fi-kənt-lē\ *adverb* (1577)
**1 :** in a significant manner **:** to a significant degree
**2 :** it is significant
**significant other** *noun* (1953)
**:** a person who is important to one's well-being; *especially :* a spouse or one in a similar relationship
**sig·ni·fi·ca·tion** \,sig-nə-fə-'kā-shən\ *noun* (14th century)
**1 a :** the act or process of signifying by signs or other symbolic means **b :** a formal notification
**2 :** PURPORT; *especially :* the meaning that a term, symbol, or character regularly conveys or is intended to convey
**3** *chiefly dialect :* IMPORTANCE, CONSEQUENCE
**sig·nif·i·ca·tive** \sig-'ni-fə-,kā-tiv\ *adjective* (15th century)
**1 :** SIGNIFICANT, SUGGESTIVE

**2 :** INDICATIVE ⟨symptoms *significative* of malaria⟩
**sig·nif·ics** \sig-'ni-fiks\ *noun plural but singular or plural in construction* [*signify*] (1896)
**:** SEMIOTIC, SEMANTICS
**signified** *noun* (1939)
**:** a concept or meaning as distinguished from the sign through which it is communicated — compare SIGNIFIER 2
**sig·ni·fi·er** \'sig-nə-,fī(-ə)r\ *noun* (1532)
**1 :** one that signifies
**2 :** a symbol, sound, or image (as a word) that represents an underlying concept or meaning — compare SIGNIFIED
**sig·ni·fy** \'sig-nə-,fī\ *verb* **-fied; -fy·ing** [Middle English *signifien*, from Old French *signifier*, from Latin *significare* to indicate, signify, from *signum* sign] (13th century)
*transitive verb*
**1 a :** to be a sign of **:** MEAN **b :** IMPLY
**2 :** to show especially by a conventional token (as word, signal, or gesture)
*intransitive verb*
**1 :** to have significance **:** MATTER
**2 :** to engage in signifying
**sig·ni·fy·ing** \'sig-nə-,fī-iŋ\ *noun* (1959)
**:** a good-natured needling or goading especially among urban blacks by means of indirect gibes and clever often preposterous put-downs; *also :* DOZENS
**sign in** (1930)
*intransitive verb*
**:** to make a record of arrival by signing a register or punching a time clock
*transitive verb*
**:** to record arrival of (a person) or receipt of (an article) by signing
**sign language** *noun* (1847)
**1 :** a formal language employing a system of hand gestures for communication (as by the deaf)
**2 :** an unsystematic method of communicating chiefly by manual gestures used by people speaking different languages
**sign of aggregation** (circa 1942)
**:** any of various conventional devices (as braces, brackets, parentheses, or vinculums) used in mathematics to indicate that two or more terms are to be treated as one quantity
**sign off** *intransitive verb* (1926)
**1 :** to announce the end of something (as a message or broadcast)
**2 :** to approve or acknowledge something by or as if by a signature ⟨*sign off* on a memo⟩
— **sign–off** \'sī-,nȯf\ *noun*
**sign of the cross** (14th century)
**:** a gesture of the hand forming a cross especially on forehead, breast, and shoulders to profess Christian faith or invoke divine protection or blessing
**sign on** *intransitive verb* (1885)
**1 :** to engage oneself by or as if by a signature
**2 :** to announce the start of broadcasting for the day
— **sign–on** \'sī-,nȯn, -,nän\ *noun*
**si·gnor** *also* **si·gnior** \'sēn-'yȯr, -'yōr\ *noun*, *plural* **signors** *or* **si·gno·ri** \sēn-'yȯr-(,)ē, -'yȯr-\ *also* **signiors** [Italian *signore, signor*, from Medieval Latin *senior* superior, lord — more at SENOR] (circa 1580)
**:** an Italian man usually of rank or gentility — used as a title equivalent to *Mister*
**si·gno·ra** \sēn-'yȯr-ə, -'yȯr-\ *noun*, *plural* **si·gno·ras** *or* **si·gno·re** \-'yȯr-(,)ā, -'yȯr-\ [Italian, feminine of *signore, signor*] (1763)
**:** a married Italian woman usually of rank or gentility — used as a title equivalent to *Mrs.*
**si·gno·re** \sēn-'yȯr-(,)ā, -'yȯr-\ *noun*, *plural* **si·gno·ri** \-'yȯr-(,)ē, -'yȯr-\ [Italian] (1594)
**:** SIGNOR
**si·gno·ri·na** \,sē-nyə-'rē-nə\ *noun*, *plural* **-nas** *or* **-ne** \-(,)nā\ [Italian, from diminutive of *signora*] (1820)
**:** an unmarried Italian woman — used as a title equivalent to *Miss*

**si·gno·ry** *or* **si·gniory** \'sē-nyə-rē\ *noun*, *plural* **si·gnor·ies** *or* **si·gnior·ies** [Middle English *signorie*, from Middle French *seigneurie*] (14th century)
**:** SEIGNIORY
**sign out** (1948)
*intransitive verb*
**:** to indicate departure by signing a register
*transitive verb*
**:** to record or approve the release or departure of
— **sign–out** \'sī-,naút\ *noun or adjective*
**¹sign-post** \'sīn-,pōst\ *noun* (1620)
**1 :** a post (as at the fork of a road) with signs on it to direct travelers
**2 :** GUIDE, BEACON
**²signpost** *transitive verb* (1895)
**:** to provide with signposts or guides
**sign up** *intransitive verb* (1903)
**:** to sign one's name (as to a contract) in order to obtain, do, or join something ⟨*sign up* for insurance⟩ ⟨*sign up* for classes⟩
— **sign–up** \'sī-,nəp\ *noun or adjective*
**Sig·urd** \'si-gúrd, -gərd\ *noun* [Old Norse *Sigurthr*]
**:** a hero in Norse mythology who slays the dragon Fafnir
**sike** \'sīk\ *noun* [Middle English, from Old English *sīc*; akin to Old Norse *sīk* slow stream, Old English *sicerian* to trickle] (before 12th century)
**1** *dialect chiefly British :* a small stream; *especially :* one that dries up in summer
**2** *dialect chiefly British :* DITCH
**¹Sikh** \'sēk\ *noun* [Hindi, literally, disciple] (1756)
**:** an adherent of a monotheistic religion of India founded about 1500 by Guru Nānak and marked by rejection of idolatry and caste
— **Sikh·ism** \'sē-,ki-zəm\ *noun*
**²Sikh** *adjective* (1845)
**:** of or relating to Sikhs or Sikhism
**si·lage** \'sī-lij\ *noun* [short for *ensilage*] (1884)
**:** fodder converted into succulent feed for livestock through processes of anaerobic acid fermentation (as in a silo)
**si·lane** \'si-,lān, 'sī-\ *noun* [International Scientific Vocabulary *silicon* + *methane*] (1916)
**:** any of various compounds of hydrogen and silicon that have the general formula $Si_nH_{2n+2}$ and are analogous to alkanes
**Si·las·tic** \sə-'las-tik, sī-\ *trademark*
— used for a soft pliable plastic
**sild** \'sil(d)\ *noun*, *plural* **sild** *or* **silds** [Norwegian] (1921)
**:** a young herring other than a brisling that is canned as a sardine in Norway
**¹si·lence** \'sī-lən(t)s\ *noun* [Middle English, from Old French, from Latin *silentium*, from *silent-, silens*] (13th century)
**1 :** forbearance from speech or noise **:** MUTENESS — often used interjectionally
**2 :** absence of sound or noise **:** STILLNESS
**3 :** absence of mention: **a :** OBLIVION, OBSCURITY **b :** SECRECY ⟨weapons research was conducted in *silence*⟩
**²silence** *transitive verb* **si·lenced; si·lenc·ing** (1597)
**1 :** to compel or reduce to silence **:** STILL
**2 :** to restrain from expression **:** SUPPRESS
**3 :** to cause to cease hostile firing or criticism
**si·lenc·er** \'sī-lən(t)-sər\ *noun* (1600)
**:** one that silences: as **a** *chiefly British :* the muffler of an internal combustion engine **b :** a silencing device for small arms
**¹si·lent** \'sī-lənt\ *adjective* [Middle English *sylent*, from Latin *silent-, silens*, from present participle of *silēre* to be silent; akin to Gothic *anasilan* to cease, grow calm] (15th century)
**1 a :** making no utterance **:** MUTE, SPEECHLESS **b :** indisposed to speak **:** not loquacious
**2 :** free from sound or noise **:** STILL
**3 :** performed or borne without utterance **:** UNSPOKEN ⟨*silent* prayer⟩ ⟨*silent* grief⟩

**4 a :** making no mention ⟨history is *silent* about this person⟩ **b :** not widely or generally known or appreciated ⟨the *silent* pressures on a person in public office⟩ **c :** making no protest or outcry ⟨the *silent* majority⟩
**5 :** UNPRONOUNCED ⟨*silent* b in *doubt*⟩
**6 :** not exhibiting the usual signs or symptoms of presence ⟨a *silent* infection⟩
**7 a :** made without spoken dialogue ⟨*silent* movies⟩ **b :** of or relating to silent movies ☆
— **si·lent·ly** *adverb*
— **si·lent·ness** *noun*

**²silent** *noun* (1929)
**:** a motion picture made without spoken dialogue — usually used in plural

**silent auction** *noun* (1952)
**:** an auction in which sealed bids are submitted beforehand

**silent butler** *noun* (1937)
**:** a receptacle with hinged lid for collecting table crumbs and the contents of ashtrays

**silent partner** *noun* (1828)
**1 :** a partner who is known to the public but has no voice in the conduct of a firm's business
**2 :** SECRET PARTNER

**silent service** *noun* (circa 1929)
**1 :** NAVY — used with *the*
**2 :** the submarine service — used with *the*

**silent treatment** *noun* (1947)
**:** an act of completely ignoring a person or thing by resort to silence especially as a means of expressing contempt or disapproval

**si·le·nus** \sī-'lē-nəs\ *noun, plural* **-ni** \-,nī\ *often capitalized* [Latin, from Greek *silēnos,* from *Silēnos* foster father of Dionysus]
**:** a minor woodland deity and companion of Dionysus in Greek mythology with a horse's ears and tail

**si·lex** \'sī-,leks\ *noun* [Latin *silic-, silex* hard stone, flint] (circa 1592)
**:** silica or a siliceous material (as powdered tripoli) especially for use as a filler in paints or wood

**¹sil·hou·ette** \,si-lə-'wet\ *noun* [French, from Étienne de *Silhouette* (died 1767) French controller general of finances; perhaps from his ephemeral tenure] (1783)
**1 :** a likeness cut from dark material and mounted on a light ground or one sketched in outline and solidly colored in
**2 :** the outline of a body viewed as circumscribing a mass ⟨the *silhouette* of a bird⟩
*synonym* see OUTLINE

**²silhouette** *transitive verb* **-ett·ed; -ett·ing** (1876)
**:** to represent by a silhouette; *also* **:** to project on a background like a silhouette
— **sil·hou·et·tist** \-'we-tist\ *noun*

**sil·i·ca** \'si-li-kə\ *noun* [New Latin, from Latin *silic-, silex* hard stone, flint] (circa 1801)
**:** silicon dioxide $SiO_2$ occurring in crystalline, amorphous, and impure forms (as in quartz, opal, and sand respectively)

**silica gel** *noun* (1919)
**:** colloidal silica resembling coarse white sand in appearance but possessing many fine pores and therefore extremely adsorbent

**sil·i·cate** \'si-lə-,kāt, -kət\ *noun* [*silicic (acid)*] (1811)
**:** a salt or ester derived from a silicic acid; *especially* **:** any of numerous insoluble often complex metal salts that contain silicon and oxygen in the anion, constitute the largest class of minerals, and are used in building materials (as cement, bricks, and glass)

**si·li·ceous** *or* **si·li·cious** \sə-'li-shəs\ *adjective* [Latin *siliceus* of flint, from *silic-, silex* hard stone, flint] (circa 1656)
**:** of, relating to, or containing silica or a silicate ⟨*siliceous* limestone⟩

**si·lic·ic** \sə-'li-sik\ *adjective* [New Latin *silica* & New Latin *silicium* silicon (from *silica*)] (1817)
**:** of, relating to, or derived from silica or silicon

**silicic acid** *noun* (1817)
**:** any of various weakly acid substances obtained as gelatinous masses by treating silicates with acids

**sil·i·cide** \'si-lə-,sīd\ *noun* [International Scientific Vocabulary *silic*on + *-ide*] (circa 1868)
**:** a binary compound of silicon with a more electropositive element or group

**si·lic·i·fi·ca·tion** \sə-,li-sə-fə-'kā-shən\ *noun* (1830)
**:** the action or process of silicifying **:** the state of being silicified

**si·lic·i·fy** \sə-'li-sə-,fī\ *verb* **-fied; -fy·ing** (circa 1828)
*transitive verb*
**:** to convert into or impregnate with silica
*intransitive verb*
**:** to become silicified

**sil·i·con** \'si-li-kən, 'si-lə-,kän\ *noun* [New Latin *silica* + English *-on* (as in *carbon*)] (1817)
**:** a tetravalent nonmetallic element that occurs combined as the most abundant element next to oxygen in the earth's crust and is used especially in alloys and electronic devices — see ELEMENT table

**silicon carbide** *noun* (1893)
**:** a very hard dark crystalline compound SiC of silicon and carbon that is used as an abrasive and as a refractory and in electric resistors

**sil·i·cone** \'si-lə-,kōn\ *noun* [*silic*on + *-one*] (1943)
**:** any of various polymeric organic silicon compounds obtained as oils, greases, or plastics and used especially for water-resistant and heat-resistant lubricants, varnishes, binders, and electric insulators

**silicone rubber** *noun* (1944)
**:** rubber made from silicone elastomers and noted for its retention of flexibility, resilience, and tensile strength over a wide temperature range

**sil·i·con·ized** \'si-lə-kə-,nīzd, -,kō-\ *adjective* (1949)
**:** treated or coated with a silicone ⟨*siliconized* glassware⟩

**silicon nitride** *noun* (1903)
**:** any of several compounds of silicon and nitrogen; *specifically* **:** a compound $Si_3N_4$ that is a hard ceramic used in high-temperature applications and in composites

**sil·i·co·sis** \,si-lə-'kō-səs\ *noun* [New Latin, from *silica* + *-osis*] (1881)
**:** pneumoconiosis characterized by massive fibrosis of the lungs resulting in shortness of breath and caused by prolonged inhalation of silica dusts
— **sil·i·cot·ic** \-'kä-tik\ *adjective or noun*

**si·lique** \sə-'lēk\ *noun* [French, from New Latin *siliqua,* from Latin, pod, husk] (1785)
**:** a narrow elongated two-valved usually many-seeded capsule that is characteristic of the mustard family, opens by sutures at either margin, and has two parietal placentas

**¹silk** \'silk\ *noun, often attributive* [Middle English, from Old English *seolc,* probably ultimately from Greek *sērikos* silken — more at SERICEOUS] (before 12th century)
**1 :** a fine continuous protein fiber produced by various insect larvae usually for cocoons; *especially* **:** a lustrous tough elastic fiber produced by silkworms and used for textiles
**2 :** thread, yarn, or fabric made from silk filaments
**3 a :** a garment of silk **b** (1) **:** a distinctive silk gown worn by a King's or Queen's Counsel (2) **:** a King's or Queen's Counsel **c** *plural* **:** the colored cap and blouse of a jockey or harness horse driver made in the registered racing color of the employing stable
**4 a :** a filament resembling silk; *especially* **:** one produced by a spider **b :** silky material ⟨milkweed *silk*⟩; *especially* **:** the styles of an ear of Indian corn
**5 :** PARACHUTE

— **silk·like** \-,līk\ *adjective*

**²silk** *intransitive verb* (1783)
*of corn* **:** to develop the silk

**silk·a·line** *or* **silk·o·line** \,sil-kə-'lēn\ *noun* [¹*silk* + *-oline* (as in *crinoline*)] (1896)
**:** a soft light cotton fabric with a smooth lustrous finish like that of silk

**silk cotton** *noun* (1697)
**:** the silky or cottony covering of seeds of various silk-cotton trees; *especially* **:** KAPOK

**silk–cotton tree** *noun* (1712)
**:** any of various tropical trees (family Bombacaceae, the silk-cotton family) with palmate leaves and large fruits with the seeds enveloped by silk cotton; *especially* **:** CEIBA 1

**silk·en** \'sil-kən\ *adjective* (before 12th century)
**1 :** made or consisting of silk
**2 :** resembling silk: as **a :** SOFT, LUSTROUS **b** (1) **:** agreeably smooth **:** HARMONIOUS (2) **:** SUAVE, INGRATIATING
**3 a :** dressed in silk ⟨*silken* ankles⟩ **b :** LUXURIOUS 2, 3

**silk gland** *noun* (1870)
**:** a gland that produces a viscid fluid which is extruded in filaments and hardens into silk on exposure to air: as **a :** either of a pair of greatly enlarged and modified salivary glands of an insect larva that produce a compound filament from which a larval or pupal cover (as a cocoon) is spun **b :** any of two or more abdominal glands of a spider that open through spinnerets and produce a filament used chiefly in the spinning of webs

**silk hat** *noun* (1834)
**:** a hat with a tall cylindrical crown and a silk-plush finish worn by men as a dress hat

**silk oak** *noun* (1866)
**:** any of various Australian timber trees (especially genus *Grevillea*) of the protea family that have mottled wood used in cabinetmaking and veneering — called also *silky oak*

**silk screen** *noun* (1930)
**:** a stencil process in which coloring matter is forced onto the material to be printed through the meshes of a silk or organdy screen so prepared as to have pervious printing areas and impervious nonprinting areas; *also* **:** a print made by this process
— **silk–screen** *transitive verb*

**silk-stock·ing** \'silk-'stä-kiŋ\ *adjective* (1798)
**1 :** ARISTOCRATIC, WEALTHY ⟨a *silk-stocking* district⟩
**2 :** fashionably dressed ⟨a *silk-stocking* audience⟩
**3 :** of or relating to the American Federalist party

---

☆ **SYNONYMS**
**Silent, taciturn, reticent, reserved, secretive** mean showing restraint in speaking. SILENT implies a habit of saying no more than is needed ⟨the strong, *silent* type⟩. TACITURN implies a temperamental disinclination to speech and usually connotes unsociability ⟨*taciturn* villagers⟩. RETICENT implies a reluctance to speak out or at length, especially about one's own affairs ⟨was *reticent* about his plans⟩. RESERVED implies reticence and suggests the restraining influence of caution or formality in checking easy informal conversational exchange ⟨greetings were brief, formal, and *reserved*⟩. SECRETIVE, too, implies reticence but usually carries a suggestion of deviousness and lack of frankness or of an often ostentatious will to conceal ⟨the *secretive* research and development division⟩.

---

\ə\ abut \ᵊ\ kitten \ər\ further \a\ ash \ā\ ace
\ä\ mop, mar \au̇\ out \ch\ chin \e\ bet \ē\ easy
\g\ go \i\ hit \ī\ ice \j\ job \ŋ\ sing \ō\ go
\ȯ\ law \ȯi\ boy \th\ thin \th\ the \ü\ loot \u̇\ foot
\y\ yet \zh\ vision *see also* Guide to Pronunciation

**silk stocking** *noun* (1891)
**1** : an aristocratic or wealthy person
**2** : a fashionably dressed person
**3** : FEDERALIST 2

**silk tree** *noun* (circa 1852)
: a leguminous Asian tree (*Albizia julibrissin*) having pink flowers with long silky stamens — called also *mimosa*

**silk·weed** \'silk-ˌwēd\ *noun* (1784)
: MILKWEED

**silk·worm** \-ˌwərm\ *noun* (before 12th century)
: a moth whose larva spins a large amount of strong silk in constructing its cocoon; *especially* : an Asian moth (*Bombyx mori* of the family Bombycidae) whose rough wrinkled hairless yellowish caterpillar produces the silk of commerce

**silky** \'sil-kē\ *adjective* **silk·i·er; -est** (1611)
**1** : SILKEN 1, 2
**2** : having or covered with fine soft hairs, plumes, or scales
— **silk·i·ly** \-kə-lē\ *adverb*
— **silk·i·ness** \-kē-nəs\ *noun*

**silky terrier** *noun* (1959)
: any of a breed of low-set toy terriers of Australian origin that have a flat silky glossy coat colored blue with tan on the head, chest, and legs — called also *silky*

silky terrier

**sill** \'sil\ *noun* [Middle English *sille*, from Old English *syll*; akin to Old High German *swelli* beam, threshold] (before 12th century)
**1** : a horizontal piece (as a timber) that forms the lowest member or one of the lowest members of a framework or supporting structure: as **a** : the horizontal member at the base of a window **b** : the threshold of a door
**2** : a tabular body of igneous rock injected while molten between sedimentary or volcanic beds or along foliation planes of metamorphic rocks
**3** : a submerged ridge at relatively shallow depth separating the basins of two bodies of water

**sillabub** *variant of* SYLLABUB

**sil·li·man·ite** \'si-lə-mə-ˌnīt\ *noun* [Benjamin Silliman (died 1864) American geologist] (circa 1830)
: a brown, grayish, or pale green mineral that consists of an aluminum silicate in orthorhombic crystals often occurring in fibrous or columnar forms

**sil·ly** \'si-lē\ *adjective* **sil·li·er; -est** [Middle English *sely, silly* happy, innocent, pitiable, feeble, from Old English *sǣlig*, from Old English *sǣl* happiness; akin to Old High German *sālig* happy] (14th century)
**1** *archaic* : HELPLESS, WEAK
**2 a** : RUSTIC, PLAIN **b** *obsolete* : lowly in station : HUMBLE
**3 a** : weak in intellect : FOOLISH **b** : exhibiting or indicative of a lack of common sense or sound judgment ⟨a very *silly* mistake⟩ **c** : TRIFLING, FRIVOLOUS
**4** : being stunned or dazed ⟨scared *silly*⟩ ⟨knocked me *silly*⟩ ◆
*synonym* see SIMPLE
— **sil·li·ly** \'si-lə-lē\ *adverb*
— **sil·li·ness** \'si-lē-nəs\ *noun*
— **silly** *noun or adverb*

**silly season** *noun* (1861)
**1** : a period (as late summer) when newspapers often resort to trivial or frivolous matters for lack of major news stories
**2** : a period marked by frivolous, outlandish, or illogical activity or behavior

**si·lo** \'sī-(ˌ)lō\ *noun, plural* **silos** [Spanish] (1881)
**1** : a trench, pit, or especially a tall cylinder (as of wood or concrete) usually sealed to exclude air and used for making and storing silage
**2 a** : a deep bin for storing material (as cement or coal) **b** : an underground structure for housing a guided missile

silo 1

**si·lox·ane** \sə-'läk-ˌsān, sī-\ *noun* [*silicon* + *oxygen* + meth*ane*] (1917)
: any of various compounds containing alternate silicon and oxygen atoms in either a linear or cyclic arrangement usually with one or two organic groups attached to each silicon atom

**¹silt** \'silt\ *noun* [Middle English *cylte*, probably of Scandinavian origin; akin to Danish *sylt* salt marsh; akin to Old High German *sulza* salt marsh, Old English *sealt* salt] (15th century)
**1** : loose sedimentary material with rock particles usually ¹/₂₀ millimeter or less in diameter; *also* : soil containing 80 percent or more of such silt and less than 12 percent of clay
**2** : a deposit of sediment (as by a river)
— **silty** \'sil-tē\ *adjective*

**²silt** (1799)
*intransitive verb*
: to become choked or obstructed with silt — often used with *up* ⟨the channel *silted* up⟩
*transitive verb*
: to choke, fill, cover, or obstruct with silt or mud ⟨the beaver had *silted* the creek —Hugh Fosburgh⟩
— **silt·a·tion** \sil-'tā-shən\ *noun*

**silt·stone** \'silt-ˌstōn\ *noun* (circa 1920)
: a rock composed chiefly of indurated silt

**Sil·u·res** \'sil-yə-ˌrēz\ *noun* [Latin] (circa 1895)
: a people of ancient Britain described by Tacitus as occupying chiefly southern Wales

**Si·lu·ri·an** \sī-'lùr-ē-ən, sə-\ *adjective* [Latin *Silures*] (1708)
**1** : of or relating to the Silures or their place of habitation
**2** : of, relating to, or being a period of the Paleozoic era between the Ordovician and Devonian or the corresponding system of rocks marked by numerous eurypterid crustaceans and the appearance of the first land plants — see GEOLOGIC TIME table
— **Silurian** *noun*

**sil·va** \'sil-və\ *noun* [New Latin, from Latin *silva*, *sylva* wood, forest] (circa 1848)
: the forest trees of a region or country

**silvan** *variant of* SYLVAN

**¹sil·ver** \'sil-vər\ *noun* [Middle English, from Old English *seolfor*; akin to Old High German *silbar* silver, Lithuanian *sidabras*] (before 12th century)
**1** : a white metallic element that is sonorous, ductile, very malleable, capable of a high degree of polish, and chiefly univalent in compounds, and that has the highest thermal and electric conductivity of any substance — see ELEMENT table
**2** : silver as a commodity ⟨the value of *silver* has risen⟩
**3** : coin made of silver
**4** : articles (as hollowware or table flatware) made of or plated with silver; *also* : similar articles and especially flatware of other metals (as stainless steel)
**5** : a nearly neutral slightly brownish medium gray

**²silver** *adjective* (before 12th century)
**1** : made of silver

**2** : resembling silver: as **a** : having a white lustrous sheen **b** : giving a soft resonant sound : dulcet in tone **c** : eloquently persuasive
**3** : consisting of or yielding silver
**4** : of, relating to, or characteristic of silver
**5** : advocating the use of silver as a standard of currency
**6** : of, relating to, or being a 25th anniversary or its celebration

**³silver** *transitive verb* **sil·vered; sil·ver·ing** \'sil-v(ə-)riŋ\ (14th century)
**1 a** : to cover with silver (as by electroplating) **b** : to coat with a substance (as a metal) resembling silver
**2 a** : to give a silvery luster to **b** : to make white like silver
— **sil·ver·er** \'sil-vər-ər\ *noun*

**silver age** *noun* (1565)
: an historical period of achievement secondary to that of a golden age

**sil·ver·back** \'sil-vər-ˌbak\ *noun* (1963)
: an older adult usually dominant male gorilla having gray or whitish hair on the back

**silver bell** *noun* (1785)
: any of a genus (*Halesia*) of trees and shrubs of the storax family; *especially* : one (*H. carolina*) of the southeastern U.S. cultivated for its bell-shaped white flowers

**sil·ver·ber·ry** \'sil-vər-ˌber-ē\ *noun* (1856)
: a silvery North American shrub (*Elaeagnus commutata*) of the oleaster family

**silver bromide** *noun* (1885)
: a compound AgBr that is extremely sensitive to light and is much used in the preparation of sensitive emulsion coatings for photographic materials

**silver bullet** *noun* (1935)
: something that acts as a magical weapon; *especially* : one that instantly solves a long-standing problem

**silver certificate** *noun* (1882)
: a certificate formerly issued against the deposit of silver coin as legal tender in the U.S. and its possessions

**silver chloride** *noun* (1885)
: a compound AgCl sensitive to light and used especially for photographic materials

**silver cord** *noun* [*The Silver Cord* (1926), play by Sidney Howard] (1942)
: the emotional tie between mother and child and especially son

**silver fir** *noun* (1707)
: any of various firs (genus *Abies*) with leaves that are white or silvery white beneath; *especially* : a valuable European timber tree (*A. alba*)

**sil·ver·fish** \'sil-vər-ˌfish\ *noun* (1703)

◇ WORD HISTORY
**silly** *Silly* in the now common senses "foolish" or "lacking in sound judgment" is the product of a remarkable string of sense shifts. The Anglian dialect variant *sēlig* of Old English *sǣlig* "happy, blessed, fortunate" was continued by Middle English *sely*, which developed from the Old English sense several new ones, including "innocent, harmless," then "pitiable, helpless" and finally "miserable, unfortunate"—the complete opposite of its original meaning. The "innocent, harmless" sense developed in another direction, to "simple, gullible," and finally, in early Modern English, "lacking in sound judgment." By the late 15th century, Middle English *sely* began to turn up in spellings such as *syly* and *silly*, the original vowel having turned into \i\ for most speakers. Without the change the result would have been *seely* (rhyming with *freely*), a pronunciation which some speakers seem to have retained into the 17th century. The same sound change is evident in the word *breeches* "pants," usually pronounced \'bri-chəz\ in spite of its spelling.

**1 :** any of various silvery fishes (as a tarpon or silversides)
**2 :** any of various small wingless insects (order Thysanura); *especially* **:** one (*Lepisma saccharina*) found in houses and sometimes injurious especially to sized papers or starched clothes
**silver fox** *noun* (circa 1792)
**:** a genetically determined color phase of the common red fox in which the fur is black tipped with white
**silver hake** *noun* (1884)
**:** a common hake (*Merluccius bilinearis*) of the northern Atlantic coast of the U.S. that is an important food fish
**silver iodide** *noun* (1885)
**:** a compound AgI that darkens on exposure to light and is used in photography, rainmaking, and medicine
**silver lining** *noun* [from the phrase "every cloud has a *silver lining*"] (1871)
**:** a consoling or hopeful prospect
**sil·ver·ly** \'sil-vər-lē\ *adverb* (1595)
**:** with silvery appearance or sound
**silver maple** *noun* (1765)
**1 :** a common maple (*Acer saccharinum*) of eastern North America with deeply cut leaves that are light green above and silvery white below
**2 :** the hard close-grained but brittle light brown wood of the silver maple
**sil·vern** \'sil-vərn\ *adjective* (before 12th century)
**1 :** made of silver
**2 :** resembling or characteristic of silver **:** SILVERY
**silver nitrate** *noun* (1885)
**:** an irritant compound AgNO$_3$ that in contact with organic matter turns black and is used as a chemical reagent, in photography, and in medicine especially as an antiseptic and caustic
**silver paper** *noun* (circa 1875)
**:** TIN FOIL
**silver perch** *noun* (1820)
**:** any of various somewhat silvery fishes that resemble perch: as **a :** a drum (*Bairdiella chrysoura*) that occurs especially along the more southern Atlantic coast of the U.S. — called also *mademoiselle, yellowtail* **b :** WHITE PERCH 1
**silver plate** *noun* (1610)
**1 :** domestic flatware and hollowware of silver or of a silver-plated base metal
**2 :** a plating of silver
**sil·ver·point** \'sil-vər-ˌpȯint\ *noun* (1882)
**:** a drawing technique utilizing a pencil of silver usually on specially prepared paper or parchment
**silver protein** *noun* (1928)
**:** any of several colloidal light-sensitive preparations of silver and protein used in aqueous solution on mucous membranes as antiseptics
**silver salmon** *noun* (1878)
**:** COHO
**silver screen** *noun* (1918)
**1 :** a motion-picture screen
**2 :** MOTION PICTURES
**sil·ver·side** \'sil-vər-ˌsīd\ *noun* (1820)
**:** SILVERSIDES
**sil·ver·sides** \'sil-vər-ˌsīdz\ *noun plural but singular or plural in construction* (1851)
**:** any of various small bony fishes (family Atherinidae) with a silvery stripe along each side of the body
**sil·ver·smith** \-ˌsmith\ *noun* (before 12th century)
**:** an artisan who makes articles of silverware
**— sil·ver·smith·ing** *noun*
**silver spoon** *noun* [from the phrase "born with a *silver spoon* in one's mouth" (born wealthy)] (1801)
**:** WEALTH; *especially* **:** inherited wealth
**silver standard** *noun* (1860)
**:** a monetary standard under which the currency unit is defined by a stated quantity of silver

**Silver Star Medal** *noun* (1932)
**:** a U.S. military decoration awarded for gallantry in action
**silver–tongued** \'sil-vər-ˌtəŋd\ *adjective* (1592)
**:** marked by convincing and eloquent expression
**sil·ver·ware** \'sil-vər-ˌwar, -ˌwer\ *noun* (1860)
**1 :** SILVER PLATE 1
**2 :** FLATWARE
**sil·ver·weed** \-ˌwēd\ *noun* (1578)
**:** any of several cinquefoils with leaves silvery or white-tomentose beneath; *especially* **:** one (*Potentilla anserina*) with silky hairs over the entire plant
**sil·very** \'sil-v(ə-)rē\ *adjective* (14th century)
**1 :** having the luster of silver
**2 :** having a soft clear musical tone **:** RESONANT ⟨a *silvery* voice⟩
**3 :** containing or consisting of silver
**— sil·ver·i·ness** *noun*
**sil·vex** \'sil-ˌveks\ *noun* [probably from Latin *silva* wood + English *exterminator*] (1961)
**:** a selective herbicide C$_9$H$_7$Cl$_3$O$_3$ especially effective in controlling woody plants but toxic to animals
**sil·vi·cul·ture** \'sil-və-ˌkəl-chər\ *noun* [French, from Latin *silva* + *cultura* culture] (1880)
**:** a branch of forestry dealing with the development and care of forests
**— sil·vi·cul·tur·al** \ˌsil-və-'kəlch-rəl, -'kəlchə-\ *adjective*
**— sil·vi·cul·tur·al·ly** \-rə-lē\ *adverb*
**— sil·vi·cul·tur·ist** \ˌsil-və-'kəlch-rist, -'kəl-chə-\ *noun*
**si·ma·zine** \'sī-mə-ˌzēn\ *noun* [*sim-* (probably alteration of *sym-* symmetrical, prefix used in names of organic compounds) + tri*azine*] (1956)
**:** a selective herbicide C$_7$H$_{12}$N$_5$Cl used to control weeds especially among crop plants
**Sim·chas To·rah** \ˌsim-kəs-'tōr-ə, -'tȯr-\ *noun* [Hebrew *śimḥath tōrāh* rejoicing of the Torah] (1891)
**:** a Jewish holiday observed on the 23d of Tishri in celebration of the completion of the annual reading of the Torah
**Sim·e·on** \'si-mē-ən\ *noun* [Late Latin, from Greek *Symeōn*, from Hebrew *Shim'ōn*]
**1 :** a son of Jacob and the traditional eponymous ancestor of one of the tribes of Israel
**2 :** a devout man of Jerusalem held to have uttered the Nunc Dimittis on seeing the infant Jesus in the temple
**¹sim·i·an** \'si-mē-ən\ *adjective* [Latin *simia* ape, from *simus* snub-nosed, from Greek *simos*] (1607)
**:** of, relating to, or resembling monkeys or apes
**²simian** *noun* (1880)
**:** MONKEY, APE
**sim·i·lar** \'si-mə-lər, 'sim-lər\ *adjective* [French *similaire*, from Latin *similis* like, similar — more at SAME] (1611)
**1 :** having characteristics in common **:** strictly comparable
**2 :** alike in substance or essentials **:** CORRESPONDING ⟨no two animal habitats are exactly *similar* —W. H. Dowdeswell⟩
**3 :** not differing in shape but only in size or position ⟨*similar* triangles⟩ ⟨*similar* polygons⟩ ☆
**— sim·i·lar·ly** *adverb*
**sim·i·lar·i·ty** \ˌsi-mə-'lar-ə-tē\ *noun, plural* **-ties** (1664)
**1 :** the quality or state of being similar **:** RESEMBLANCE
**2 :** a comparable aspect **:** CORRESPONDENCE
**synonym** see LIKENESS
**sim·i·le** \'si-mə-(ˌ)lē\ *noun* [Middle English, from Latin, comparison, from neuter of *similis*] (14th century)
**:** a figure of speech comparing two unlike things that is often introduced by *like* or *as* (as in *cheeks like roses*) — compare METAPHOR

**si·mil·i·tude** \sə-'mi-lə-ˌtüd, -ˌtyüd\ *noun* [Middle English, from Middle French, resemblance, likeness, from Latin *similitudo*, from *similis*] (14th century)
**1 a :** COUNTERPART, DOUBLE **b :** a visible likeness **:** IMAGE
**2 :** an imaginative comparison **:** SIMILE
**3 a :** correspondence in kind or quality **b :** a point of comparison
**synonym** see LIKENESS
**Sim·men·tal** *also* **Sim·men·thal** \'zi-mən-ˌtäl\ *noun* [Simmental, valley of the Simme River in Switzerland] (1906)
**:** any of a breed of large buff or dull red and white cattle of Swiss origin that are used widely throughout the world for meat and milk
**¹sim·mer** \'si-mər\ *verb* **sim·mered; sim·mer·ing** \'si-mə-riŋ, 'sim-riŋ\ [alteration of English dialect *simper*, from Middle English *simperen*, of imitative origin] (1653)
*intransitive verb*
**1 :** to stew gently below or just at the boiling point
**2 a :** to be in a state of incipient development **:** FERMENT ⟨ideas *simmering* in the back of my mind⟩ **b :** to be in inward turmoil **:** SEETHE
*transitive verb*
**:** to cook slowly in a liquid just below the boiling point
**²simmer** *noun* (1809)
**:** the state of simmering
**simmer down** *intransitive verb* (1871)
**1 :** to become calm or peaceful
**2 :** to become reduced by or as if by simmering
**sim·nel** \'sim-n°l\ *noun* [Middle English *simenel*, from Middle French, ultimately from Latin *simila* wheat flour] (13th century)
**1 :** a bun or bread of fine wheat flour
**2** *British* **:** a rich fruitcake sometimes coated with almond paste and baked for mid-Lent, Easter, and Christmas
**si·mo·le·on** \sə-'mō-lē-ən\ *noun* [origin unknown] (1896)
*slang* **:** DOLLAR
**Si·mon** \'sī-mən\ *noun* [Greek *Simōn*, from Hebrew *Shim'ōn*]
**1 :** PETER — called also *Simon Peter*
**2 :** one of the twelve disciples of Jesus — called also *Simon the Zealot*
**3 :** a kinsman of Jesus
**4 :** a Cyrenian constrained to help Jesus bear his cross to his place of crucifixion — called also *Simon the Cyrenian*
**5 :** SIMON MAGUS
**si·mo·ni·ac** \sī-'mō-nē-ˌak, sə-\ *noun* [Middle English, from Middle French or Medieval Latin; Middle French *simoniaque*, from Medieval Latin *simoniacus*, from Late Latin *simonia* simony] (14th century)
**:** one who practices simony
**— simoniac** *or* **si·mo·ni·a·cal** \ˌsī-mə-'nī-ə-kəl, ˌsi-\ *adjective*
**— si·mo·ni·a·cal·ly** \-k(ə-)lē\ *adverb*

☆ **SYNONYMS**
**Similar, analogous, parallel** mean closely resembling each other. SIMILAR implies the possibility of being mistaken for each other ⟨all the houses in the development are *similar*⟩. ANALOGOUS applies to things belonging in essentially different categories but nevertheless having many similarities ⟨*analogous* political systems⟩. PARALLEL suggests a marked likeness in the development of two things ⟨the *parallel* careers of two movie stars⟩.

\ə\ abut \ᵊ\ kitten \ər\ further \a\ ash \ā\ ace
\ä\ mop, mar \aů\ out \ch\ chin \e\ bet \ē\ easy
\g\ go \i\ hit \ī\ ice \j\ job \ŋ\ sing \ō\ go
\ȯ\ law \ȯi\ boy \th\ thin \th\ the \ü\ loot \ů\ foot
\y\ yet \zh\ vision *see also* Guide to Pronunciation

**si·mo·nize** \'sī-mə-ˌnīz\ *transitive verb* **-nized; -niz·ing** [from *Simoniz*, a trademark] (1934)
: to polish with or as if with wax

**Si·mon Le·gree** \ˌsī-mən-lə-'grē\ *noun*
: a slave owner who has Tom flogged to death in Harriet B. Stowe's novel *Uncle Tom's Cabin*

**Simon Ma·gus** \-'mā-gəs\ *noun*
: a Samaritan sorcerer converted by the apostle Philip and severely rebuked by Peter for offering money for the gifts of the Holy Ghost

**si·mon–pure** \ˌsī-mən-'pyúr\ *adjective* [from *the real Simon Pure*, alluding to a character impersonated by another in the play *A Bold Stroke for a Wife* (1718) by Susannah Centlivre (died 1723) English dramatist and actress] (1840)
: of untainted purity or integrity; *also* : pretentiously or hypocritically pure

**si·mo·ny** \'sī-mə-nē, 'si-\ *noun* [Middle English *symonie*, from Late Latin *simonia*, from *Simon* Magus, Samaritan sorcerer in Acts 8: 9–24] (13th century)
: the buying or selling of a church office or ecclesiastical preferment

**si·moom** \sə-'müm, sī-\ *or* **si·moon** \-'mün\ *noun* [Arabic *samūm*] (1790)
: a hot dry violent dust-laden wind from Asian and African deserts

**simp** \'simp\ *noun* (1903)
: SIMPLETON

**sim·pa·ti·co** \sim-'pä-ti-ˌkō, -'pa-\ *adjective* [Italian *simpatico* & Spanish *simpático*, ultimately from Latin *sympathia* sympathy] (1864)
**1** : AGREEABLE, LIKABLE
**2** : being on the same wavelength : CONGENIAL, SYMPATHETIC

**¹sim·per** \'sim-pər\ *verb* **sim·pered; sim·per·ing** \-p(ə-)riŋ\ [perhaps of Scandinavian origin; akin to Danish dialect *simper* affected, coy] (circa 1563)
*intransitive verb*
: to smile in a silly manner
*transitive verb*
: to say with a simper ⟨*simpered* an apology⟩
— **sim·per·er** \-pər-ər\ *noun*

**²simper** *noun* (1599)
: a silly smile : SMIRK

**¹sim·ple** \'sim-pəl\ *adjective* **sim·pler** \-p(ə-)lər\; **sim·plest** \-p(ə-)ləst\ [Middle English, from Old French, plain, uncomplicated, artless, from Latin *simplus, simplex*, literally, single; Latin *simplus* from *sem-*, one + *-plus* multiplied by; Latin *simplic-, simplex* from *sem-, sim-* + *-plic-, -plex* -fold — more at SAME, -FOLD] (13th century)
**1** : free from guile : INNOCENT
**2 a** : free from vanity : MODEST **b** : free from ostentation or display
**3** : of humble origin or modest position ⟨a *simple* farmer⟩
**4 a** : lacking in knowledge or expertise ⟨a *simple* amateur of the arts⟩ **b** : STUPID; *especially* : mentally retarded **c** : not socially or culturally sophisticated : NAIVE; *also* : CREDULOUS
**5 a** : SHEER, UNMIXED ⟨*simple* honesty⟩ **b** : free of secondary complications ⟨a *simple* vitamin deficiency⟩ **c** (1) : having only one main clause and no subordinate clauses ⟨a *simple* sentence⟩ (2) *of a subject or predicate* : having no modifiers, complements, or objects **d** : constituting a basic element : FUNDAMENTAL **e** : not made up of many like units ⟨a *simple* eye⟩
**6** : free from elaboration or figuration ⟨*simple* harmony⟩
**7 a** (1) : not subdivided into branches or leaflets ⟨a *simple* stem⟩ ⟨a *simple* leaf⟩ (2) : consisting of a single carpel (3) : developing from a single ovary ⟨a *simple* fruit⟩ **b** : controlled by a single gene ⟨*simple* inherited characters⟩
**8** : not limited or restricted : UNCONDITIONAL ⟨a *simple* obligation⟩

**9** : readily understood or performed ⟨*simple* directions⟩ ⟨the adjustment was *simple* to make⟩
**10** *of a statistical hypothesis* : specifying exact values for one or more statistical parameters — compare COMPOSITE 3 ☆
— **sim·ple·ness** \-pəl-nəs\ *noun*

**²simple** *noun* (14th century)
**1 a** : a person of humble birth : COMMONER ⟨thought very little of anybody, *simples* or gentry —Virginia Woolf⟩ **b** (1) : a rude or credulous person : IGNORAMUS (2) : a mentally retarded person
**2 a** : a medicinal plant **b** : a vegetable drug having only one ingredient
**3** : one component of a complex; *specifically* : an unanalyzable constituent

**simple closed curve** *noun* (1919)
: a closed plane curve (as a circle or an ellipse) that does not intersect itself — called also *Jordan curve*

**simple equation** *noun* (1798)
: a linear equation

**simple fraction** *noun* (1910)
: a fraction having whole numbers for the numerator and denominator — compare COMPLEX FRACTION

**simple fracture** *noun* (1685)
: a bone fracture that does not form an open wound in the skin — compare COMPOUND FRACTURE

**simple interest** *noun* (1798)
: interest paid or computed on the original principal only of a loan or on the amount of an account

**simple machine** *noun* (1704)
: any of various elementary mechanisms formerly considered as the elements of which all machines are composed and including the lever, the wheel and axle, the pulley, the inclined plane, the wedge, and the screw

**sim·ple-mind·ed** \ˌsim-pəl-'mīn-dəd, 'sim-pəl-\ *adjective* (1744)
: devoid of subtlety : UNSOPHISTICATED; *also* : FOOLISH
— **sim·ple-mind·ed·ly** *adverb*
— **sim·ple-mind·ed·ness** *noun*

**simple protein** *noun* (circa 1909)
: a protein (as a globulin) that yields amino acids as the chief or only products of complete hydrolysis — compare CONJUGATED PROTEIN

**simple sugar** *noun* (1942)
: MONOSACCHARIDE

**sim·ple·ton** \'sim-pəl-tən\ *noun* [¹*simple* + *-ton* (as in surnames such as *Washington*)] (1650)
: a person lacking in common sense

**simple vow** *noun* (1759)
: a public vow taken by a religious in the Roman Catholic Church under which retention of property by the individual is permitted and marriage though illicit is valid under canon law

**¹sim·plex** \'sim-ˌpleks\ *adjective* [Latin *simplic-, simplex* — more at SIMPLE] (1594)
**1** : SIMPLE, SINGLE
**2** : allowing telecommunication in only one direction at a time ⟨*simplex* system⟩

**²simplex** *noun, plural* **sim·plex·es** (1892)
**1** *or plural* **sim·pli·ces** \-plə-ˌsēz\ *or* **sim·pli·cia** \sim-'pli-sh(ē-)ə\ : a simple word
**2** : a spatial configuration of *n* dimensions determined by *n* + 1 points in a space of dimension equal to or greater than *n* ⟨a triangle together with its interior determined by its three vertices is a two-dimensional *simplex* in the plane or any space of higher dimension⟩

**sim·pli·cial** \sim-'pli-shəl\ *adjective* (1926)
: of or relating to simplexes
— **sim·pli·cial·ly** \-shə-lē\ *adverb*

**sim·plic·i·ty** \sim-'pli-sə-tē, -'plis-tē\ *noun* [Middle English *simplicite*, from Middle French *simplicité*, from Latin *simplicitat-, simplicitas*, from *simplic-, simplex*] (14th century)
**1** : the state of being simple, uncomplicated, or uncompounded

**2 a** : lack of subtlety or penetration : INNOCENCE, NAIVETÉ **b** : FOLLY, SILLINESS
**3** : freedom from pretense or guile : CANDOR
**4 a** : directness of expression : CLARITY **b** : restraint in ornamentation : AUSTERITY

**sim·pli·fy** \'sim-plə-ˌfī\ *transitive verb* **-fied; -fy·ing** [French *simplifier*, from Medieval Latin *simplificare*, from Latin *simplus* simple] (1759)
: to make simple or simpler: as **a** : to reduce to basic essentials **b** : to diminish in scope or complexity : STREAMLINE ⟨was urged to *simplify* management procedures⟩ **c** : to make more intelligible : CLARIFY
— **sim·pli·fi·ca·tion** \ˌsim-plə-fə-'kā-shən\ *noun*
— **sim·pli·fi·er** \'sim-plə-ˌfī(-ə)r\ *noun*

**sim·plism** \'sim-ˌpli-zəm\ *noun* (circa 1882)
: the act or an instance of oversimplifying; *especially* : the reduction of a problem to a false simplicity by ignoring complicating factors

**sim·plis·tic** \sim-'plis-tik\ *adjective* (circa 1881)
**1** : SIMPLE
**2** : of, relating to, or characterized by simplism : OVERSIMPLE ⟨adequate, if occasionally *simplistic*, historical background —Harlow Robinson⟩
— **sim·plis·ti·cal·ly** \-ti-k(ə-)lē\ *adverb*

**sim·ply** \'sim-plē, *for 1 also* -pə-lē\ *adverb* (14th century)
**1 a** : without ambiguity : CLEARLY **b** : without embellishment : PLAINLY **c** : DIRECTLY, CANDIDLY
**2 a** : SOLELY, MERELY ⟨eats *simply* to keep alive⟩ ⟨*simply* cleaned it up and went to bed —Garrison Keillor⟩ **b** : REALLY, LITERALLY ⟨the concert was *simply* marvelous⟩ — often used as an intensive ⟨*simply* crawling with geniuses —F. Scott Fitzgerald⟩

**simply connected** *adjective* (1893)
: being or characterized by a surface that is divided into two separate parts by every closed curve it contains

**simply ordered** *adjective* (circa 1909)
: having any two elements connected by a relationship that is reflexive, antisymmetric, and transitive

**Simp·son's rule** \'sim(p)-sənz-\ *noun* [Thomas *Simpson* (died 1761) English mathematician] (1875)
: a method for approximating the area under a curve over a given interval that involves partitioning the interval by an odd number *n* + 1 of equally spaced ordinates and adding the areas of the *n*/2 figures formed by pairs of successive odd-numbered ordinates and the parabolas which they determine with their included even-numbered ordinates

**sim·u·la·cre** \'sim-yə-ˌlā-kər, -ˌla-\ *noun* [Middle English, from Middle French, from Latin *simulacrum*] (14th century)
*archaic* : SIMULACRUM

---

☆ **SYNONYMS**
**Simple, foolish, silly, fatuous, asinine** mean actually or apparently deficient in intelligence. SIMPLE implies a degree of intelligence inadequate to cope with anything complex or involving mental effort ⟨considered people *simple* who had trouble with computers⟩. FOOLISH implies the character of being or seeming unable to use judgment, discretion, or good sense ⟨*foolish* stunts⟩. SILLY suggests failure to act as a rational being especially by ridiculous behavior ⟨the *silly* antics of revelers⟩. FATUOUS implies foolishness, inanity, and disregard of reality ⟨*fatuous* conspiracy theories⟩. ASININE suggests utter and contemptible failure to use normal rationality or perception ⟨an *asinine* plot⟩. See in addition EASY.

**sim·u·la·crum** \ˌsim-yə-'la-krəm, -'lā-\ *noun, plural* **-cra** \-krə\ *also* **-crums** [Middle English, from Latin, from *simulare*] (15th century)
**1** : IMAGE, REPRESENTATION ⟨a reasonable *simulacrum* of reality —Martin Mayer⟩
**2** : an insubstantial form or semblance of something : TRACE

**¹sim·u·lar** \'sim-yə-lər, -ˌlär\ *noun* [irregular from Latin *simulare* to simulate] (1526)
*archaic* : one that simulates : DISSEMBLER

**²simular** *adjective* (1611)
*archaic* : COUNTERFEIT, PRETENDED

**sim·u·late** \'sim-yə-ˌlāt\ *transitive verb* **-lat·ed; -lat·ing** [Latin *simulatus*, past participle of *simulare* to copy, represent, feign, from *similis* like — more at SAME] (1652)
**1** : to give or assume the appearance or effect of often with the intent to deceive : IMITATE
**2** : to make a simulation of (as a physical system)
*synonym* see ASSUME
**— sim·u·la·tive** \-ˌlā-tiv\ *adjective*

**simulated** *adjective* (1622)
: made to look genuine : FAKE ⟨*simulated* pearls⟩

**sim·u·la·tion** \ˌsim-yə-'lā-shən\ *noun* [Middle English *simulacion*, from Middle French, from Latin *simulation-, simulatio*, from *simulare*] (14th century)
**1** : the act or process of simulating
**2** : a sham object : COUNTERFEIT
**3 a** : the imitative representation of the functioning of one system or process by means of the functioning of another ⟨a computer *simulation* of an industrial process⟩ **b** : examination of a problem often not subject to direct experimentation by means of a simulating device

**sim·u·la·tor** \'sim-yə-ˌlā-tər\ *noun* (1835)
: one that simulates; *especially* : a device that enables the operator to reproduce or represent under test conditions phenomena likely to occur in actual performance

**si·mul·cast** \'sī-məl-ˌkast *also* 'si-\ *verb* [*simul*taneous broad*cast*] (1948)
*intransitive verb*
: to broadcast simultaneously (as by radio and television)
*transitive verb*
: to broadcast (a program) by simulcasting
**— simulcast** *noun*

**si·mul·ta·ne·ous** \ˌsī-məl-'tā-nē-əs, -nyəs *also* ˌsi-\ *adjective* [Latin *simul* at the same time + English *-taneous* (as in *instantaneous*) — more at SAME] (circa 1660)
**1** : existing or occurring at the same time : exactly coincident
**2** : satisfied by the same values of the variables ⟨*simultaneous* equations⟩
*synonym* see CONTEMPORARY
**— si·mul·ta·ne·ity** \-tə-'nē-ə-tē, -'nā-\ *noun*
**— si·mul·ta·neous·ly** \-'tā-nē-əs-lē, -nyəs-\ *adverb*
**— si·mul·ta·neous·ness** *noun*

**¹sin** \'sin\ *noun* [Middle English *sinne*, from Old English *synn;* akin to Old High German *sunta* sin; probably akin to Latin *sont-, sons* guilty, *est* is — more at IS] (before 12th century)
**1 a** : an offense against religious or moral law **b** : an action that is or is felt to be highly reprehensible ⟨it's a *sin* to waste food⟩ **c** : an often serious shortcoming : FAULT
**2 a** : transgression of the law of God **b** : a vitiated state of human nature in which the self is estranged from God
*synonym* see OFFENSE

**²sin** *intransitive verb* **sinned; sin·ning** (before 12th century)
**1** : to commit a sin
**2** : to commit an offense or fault

**³sin** \'sēn, 'sin\ *noun* [Hebrew *śin*] (circa 1823)
: the 21st letter of the Hebrew alphabet — see ALPHABET table

**Sin·an·thro·pus** \sī-'nan(t)-thrə-pəs, sə-; ˌsī-ˌnan-'thrō-, ˌsi-\ *noun* [New Latin, from Late Latin *Sinae*, plural, Chinese + Greek *anthrōpos* man — more at SINO-] (1928)
: PEKING MAN

**Sin·bad** *or* **Sind·bad** \'sin-ˌbad\ *noun*
: a citizen of Baghdad whose adventures at sea are told in the *Arabian Nights' Entertainments*

**¹since** \'sin(t)s\ *adverb* [Middle English *sins*, contraction of *sithens*, from *sithen*, from Old English *siththan*, from *sīth tham* after that, from *sīth* after, late + *tham*, dative of *thæt* that; akin to Old High German *sīd* later and perhaps to Latin *setius* to a lesser degree] (before 12th century)
**1** : from a definite past time until now ⟨has stayed there ever *since*⟩
**2** : before the present time : AGO ⟨long *since* dead⟩
**3** : after a time in the past : SUBSEQUENTLY ⟨has *since* become rich⟩

**²since** *conjunction* (15th century)
**1** : at a time in the past after or later than ⟨has held two jobs *since* he graduated⟩ : from the time in the past when ⟨ever *since* I was a child⟩
**2** *obsolete* : WHEN
**3** : in view of the fact that : BECAUSE ⟨*since* it was raining she took an umbrella⟩

**³since** *preposition* (circa 1530)
: in the period after a specified time in the past : from a specified time in the past

**sin·cere** \sin-'sir, sən-\ **sin·cer·er; sin·cer·est** *adjective* [Middle French, from Latin *sincerus* whole, pure, genuine, probably from *sem-* one + *-cerus* (akin to Latin *crescere* to grow) — more at SAME, CRESCENT] (1533)
**1 a** : free of dissimulation : HONEST ⟨*sincere* interest⟩ **b** : free from adulteration : PURE ⟨a *sincere* doctrine⟩ ⟨*sincere* wine⟩
**2** : marked by genuineness : TRUE ☆
**— sin·cere·ly** *adverb*
**— sin·cere·ness** *noun*

**sin·cer·i·ty** \-'ser-ə-tē, -'sir-\ *noun* (15th century)
: the quality or state of being sincere : honesty of mind : freedom from hypocrisy

**sin·cip·i·tal** \sin-'sip-ə-t'l\ *adjective* (1653)
: of or relating to the sinciput

**sin·ci·put** \'sin(t)-sə-(ˌ)pət\ *noun, plural* **sin·ciputs** *or* **sin·cip·i·ta** \sin-'si-pə-tə\ [Latin *sincipit-, sinciput*, from *semi-* + *caput* head — more at HEAD] (1578)
**1** : FOREHEAD
**2** : the upper half of the skull

**Sind·hi** \'sin-dē\ *noun, plural* **Sindhi** *or* **Sindhis** [Arabic *Sindī*] (1815)
**1** : a member of a mostly Muslim people of Sind
**2** : the Indo-Aryan language of the Sindhi people

**sine** \'sīn\ *noun* [Medieval Latin *sinus*, from Latin, curve] (1593)
**1** : the trigonometric function that for an acute angle is the ratio between the leg opposite the angle when it is considered part of a right triangle and the hypotenuse
**2** : a trigonometric function sin $\theta$ that for all real numbers $\theta$ is exactly equal to the sine of an angle of measure $\theta$ in radians and that is given by the sum of the alternating series

$$\sin \theta = \theta - \frac{\theta^3}{3!} + \frac{\theta^5}{5!} - \frac{\theta^7}{7!} + \frac{\theta^9}{9!} - \cdots$$

**si·ne·cure** \'sī-ni-ˌkyu̇r, 'si-\ *noun* [Medieval Latin *sine cura* without cure (of souls)] (1662)
**1** *archaic* : an ecclesiastical benefice without cure of souls
**2** : an office or position that requires little or no work and that usually provides an income

**sine curve** *noun* (1902)
: the graph in rectangular coordinates of the equation $y=a \sin bx$ where $a$ and $b$ are constants

sine curve: graph of
$y = a \sin bx$ where
$a=1, b=1$

**si·ne die** \ˌsī-ni-'dī(-ˌē), ˌsi-nā-'dē-ˌā\ *adverb* [Latin, without day] (1607)
: without any future date being designated (as for resumption) : INDEFINITELY ⟨the meeting adjourned *sine die*⟩

**si·ne qua non** \ˌsi-ni-ˌkwä-'nän, -'nōn *also* ˌsē-, *also* ˌsī-ni-ˌkwä-'nän\ *noun, plural* **sine qua nons** *also* **sine qui·bus non** \-ˌkwi-(ˌ)bu̇s- *also* -ˌkwī-\ [Late Latin, without which not] (1602)
: something absolutely indispensable or essential

**¹sin·ew** \'sin-(ˌ)yü *also* 'si-(ˌ)nü\ *noun* [Middle English *sinewe*, from Old English *seono;* akin to Old High German *senawa* sinew, Sanskrit *syati* he binds] (before 12th century)
**1** : TENDON; *especially* : one dressed for use as a cord or thread
**2** *obsolete* : NERVE
**3 a** : solid resilient strength : POWER ⟨astonishing intellectual *sinew* and clarity —Reynolds Price⟩ **b** : the chief supporting force : MAINSTAY — usually used in plural ⟨providing the *sinews* of better living —Sam Pollock⟩

**²sinew** *transitive verb* (circa 1614)
: to strengthen as if with sinews

**sine wave** *noun* (1893)
: a waveform that represents periodic oscillations in which the amplitude of displacement at each point is proportional to the sine of the phase angle of the displacement and that is visualized as a sine curve : SINE CURVE; *also* : a wave so represented

**sin·ewy** \'sin-yə-wē *also* 'si-nə-\ *adjective* (14th century)
**1** : full of sinews: as **a** : TOUGH, STRINGY ⟨*sinewy* meat⟩ **b** : STRONG ⟨*sinewy* arms⟩
**2** : marked by the strength of sinews ⟨a demanding *sinewy* intelligence —Helen Dudar⟩

**sin·fo·nia** \ˌsin-fə-'nē-ə\ *noun, plural* **-nie** \-'nē-ˌā\ [Italian, from Latin *symphonia* symphony] (1773)
**1** : an orchestral musical composition serving as an introduction to choral works (as opera) especially in the 18th century : OVERTURE
**2** : RITORNELLO 1, SYMPHONY 2c

**sinfonia con·cer·tante** \-ˌkän(t)-sər-'tän-tē, -shər-, -ˌtā\ *noun* [Italian, literally, symphony in concerto style] (circa 1903)
: a concerto for more than one solo instrument

---

☆ **SYNONYMS**
**Sincere, wholehearted, heartfelt, hearty, unfeigned** mean genuine in feeling. SINCERE stresses absence of hypocrisy, feigning, or any falsifying embellishment or exaggeration ⟨a *sincere* apology⟩. WHOLEHEARTED suggests sincerity and earnest devotion without reservation or misgiving ⟨promised our *wholehearted* support⟩. HEARTFELT suggests depth of genuine feeling outwardly expressed ⟨expresses our *heartfelt* gratitude⟩. HEARTY suggests honesty, warmth, and exuberance in displaying feeling ⟨received a *hearty* welcome⟩. UNFEIGNED stresses spontaneity and absence of pretense ⟨her *unfeigned* delight at receiving the award⟩.

---

\ə\ abut \ᵊ\ kitten \ər\ further \a\ ash \ā\ ace
\ä\ mop, mar \au̇\ out \ch\ chin \e\ bet \ē\ easy
\g\ go \i\ hit \ī\ ice \j\ job \ŋ\ sing \ō\ go
\ȯ\ law \ȯi\ boy \th\ thin \th\ the \ü\ loot \u̇\ foot
\y\ yet \zh\ vision    *see also* Guide to Pronunciation

**sin·fo·niet·ta** \ˌsin-fən-'ye-tə, -ˌfōn-\ *noun* [Italian, diminutive of *sinfonia*] (circa 1907)
**1** : a symphony of less than standard length or for fewer instruments
**2** : a small symphony orchestra; *especially* : an orchestra of strings only

**sin·ful** \'sin-fəl\ *adjective* (before 12th century)
**1** : tainted with, marked by, or full of sin : WICKED
**2** : such as to make one feel guilty ⟨a *sinful* chocolate cake⟩
— **sin·ful·ly** \-fə-lē\ *adverb*
— **sin·ful·ness** *noun*

**¹sing** \'siŋ\ *verb* **sang** \'saŋ\ *or* **sung** \'səŋ\; **sung; sing·ing** \'siŋ-iŋ\ [Middle English, from Old English *singan;* akin to Old High German *singan* to sing, Greek *omphē* voice] (before 12th century)
*intransitive verb*
**1 a** : to produce musical tones by means of the voice **b** : to utter words in musical tones and with musical inflections and modulations **c** : to deliver songs as a trained or professional singer
**2** : to make a shrill whining or whistling sound
**3 a** : to relate or celebrate something in verse **b** : to compose poetry **c** : to create in or through words a feeling or sense of song ⟨prose that *sings*⟩
**4** : to produce musical or harmonious sounds
**5** : BUZZ, RING
**6** : to make a cry : CALL
**7** : to give information or evidence
*transitive verb*
**1** : to utter with musical inflections; *especially* : to interpret in musical tones produced by the voice
**2** : to relate or celebrate in verse
**3** : CHANT, INTONE
**4** : to bring or accompany to a place or state by singing ⟨*sings* the child to sleep⟩
— **sing·able** \'siŋ-ə-bəl\ *adjective*

**²sing** *noun* (1850)
: a session of group singing

**sing–along** \'siŋ-ə-ˌlȯŋ\ *noun* (1966)
: SONGFEST; *also* : a song appropriate for a sing-along

**¹singe** \'sinj\ *transitive verb* **singed; singe·ing** \'sin-jiŋ\ [Middle English *sengen,* from Old English *sengan;* akin to Old High German *bisengan* to singe, Old Church Slavonic *isęknǫti* to dry up] (before 12th century)
: to burn superficially or lightly : SCORCH; *especially* : to remove the hair, down, or fuzz from usually by passing rapidly over a flame

**²singe** *noun* (1658)
: a slight burn : SCORCH

**¹sing·er** \'siŋ-ər\ *noun* (14th century)
: one that sings

**²sing·er** \'sin-jər\ *noun* (circa 1875)
: one that singes

**singing game** *noun* (1881)
: a children's game in which the players accompany their actions with the singing of a narrative song

**¹sin·gle** \'siŋ-gəl\ *adjective* [Middle English, from Middle French, from Latin *singulus* one only; akin to Latin *sem-* one — more at SAME] (14th century)
**1 a** : not married **b** : of or relating to celibacy
**2** : unaccompanied by others : LONE, SOLE ⟨the *single* survivor of the disaster⟩
**3 a** (1) : consisting of or having only one part, feature, or portion ⟨*single* consonants⟩ (2) : consisting of one as opposed to or in contrast with many : UNIFORM ⟨a *single* standard for men and women⟩ (3) : consisting of only one in number ⟨holds to a *single* ideal⟩ **b** : having but one whorl of petals or ray flowers ⟨a *single* rose⟩
**4 a** : consisting of a separate unique whole : INDIVIDUAL ⟨every *single* citizen⟩ **b** : of, relating to, or involving only one person
**5 a** : FRANK, HONEST ⟨a *single* devotion⟩ **b** : exclusively attentive ⟨an eye *single* to the truth⟩

**6** : UNBROKEN, UNDIVIDED
**7** : having no equal or like : SINGULAR
**8** : designed for the use of one person only ⟨a *single* room⟩ ⟨*single* bed⟩

**²single** *verb* **sin·gled; sin·gling** \-g(ə-)liŋ\ (1628)
*transitive verb*
**1** : to select or distinguish from a number or group — usually used with *out*
**2 a** : to advance or score (a base runner) by a single **b** : to bring about the scoring of (a run) by a single
*intransitive verb*
: to make a single in baseball

**³single** *noun* (1646)
**1 a** : a separate individual person or thing **b** : an unmarried person and especially one young and socially active — usually used in plural **c** : a recording having one short tune on each side
**2** : a base hit that allows the batter to reach first base
**3 a** *plural* : a tennis match or similar game with one player on each side **b** : a golf match between two players — usually used in plural
**4** : a room (as in a hotel) for one guest — compare DOUBLE 7

**sin·gle–ac·tion** \ˌsiŋ-gəl-'ak-shən\ *adjective* (1900)
*of a revolver* : that can be cocked only by manually retracting the hammer

**sin·gle–blind** \ˌsiŋ-gəl-ˌblīnd\ *adjective* (1963)
: of, relating to, or being an experimental procedure in which the experimenters but not the subjects know the makeup of the test and control groups during the actual course of the experiments — compare DOUBLE-BLIND

**single bond** *noun* (1903)
: a chemical bond in which one pair of electrons is shared by two atoms in a molecule especially when the atoms can share more than one pair of electrons — compare DOUBLE BOND, TRIPLE BOND

**sin·gle–breast·ed** \ˌsiŋ-gəl-'bres-təd\ *adjective* (1796)
: having a center closing with one row of buttons and no lap ⟨a *single-breasted* coat⟩

**single combat** *noun* (1610)
: combat between two persons

**single cross** *noun* (1940)
: a first-generation hybrid between two selected and usually inbred lines — compare DOUBLE CROSS 2

**single entry** *noun* (1826)
: a method of bookkeeping that recognizes only one side of a business transaction and usually consists only of a record of cash and personal accounts with debtors and creditors

**single file** *noun* (1670)
: ⁶FILE 1
— **single file** *adverb*

**¹sin·gle–foot** \'siŋ-gəl-ˌfu̇t\ *noun, plural* **single–foots** (1867)
: ⁷RACK b

**²single–foot** *intransitive verb* (1890)
*of a horse* : to go at a rack
— **sin·gle–foot·er** *noun*

**¹sin·gle–hand·ed** \ˌsiŋ-gəl-'han-dəd\ *adjective* (1709)
**1** : managed or done by one person or with one on a side
**2** : working alone or unassisted by others
— **sin·gle–hand·ed·ly** *adverb*

**²single–handed** *adverb* (1815)
: in a single-handed manner

**sin·gle–hand·er** \-'han-dər\ *noun* (1946)
: a person who sails single-handed

**sin·gle–heart·ed** \ˌsiŋ-gəl-'här-təd\ *adjective* (1577)
: characterized by sincerity and unity of purpose or dedication
— **sin·gle–heart·ed·ly** *adverb*
— **sin·gle–heart·ed·ness** *noun*

**single knot** *noun* (circa 1930)

: OVERHAND KNOT

**single–lens reflex** \'siŋ-gəl-'lenz-\ *noun* (1940)
: a camera having a single lens that forms an image which is reflected to the viewfinder or recorded on film

**sin·gle–mind·ed** \ˌsiŋ-gəl-'mīn-dəd, 'siŋ-gəl-\ *adjective* (1860)
: having one driving purpose or resolve : DETERMINED, DEDICATED
— **sin·gle–mind·ed·ly** *adverb*
— **sin·gle–mind·ed·ness** *noun*

**sin·gle·ness** \'siŋ-gəl-nəs\ *noun* (1560)
: the quality or state of being single

**sin·gle–phase** \'siŋ-gəl-'fāz\ *adjective* (1900)
: of or relating to a circuit energized by a single alternating electromotive force

**sin·gle–space** \-'spās\ *transitive verb* (1928)
: to type or print with no blank lines between lines of text

**sin·gle·stick** \-ˌstik\ *noun* (1771)
: fighting or fencing with a wooden stick or sword held in one hand; *also* : the weapon used

**sin·glet** \'siŋ-glət\ *noun* (circa 1746)
**1** [from its having only one thickness of cloth] *chiefly British* : an athletic jersey : UNDERSHIRT
**2** : an atom or molecule that has no net electronic magnetic moment; *also* : an excited state of an atom or molecule that is a singlet

**single tax** *noun* (1853)
: a tax to be levied on a single item (as real estate) as the sole source of public revenue

**sin·gle·ton** \'siŋ-gəl-tən\ *noun* [French, from English *single*] (1876)
**1** : a card that is the only one of its suit originally dealt to a player
**2 a** : an individual member or thing distinct from others grouped with it **b** : an offspring born singly ⟨*singletons* are more common than twins⟩

**sin·gle–track** \'siŋ-gəl-'trak\ *adjective* (1849)
**1** : having only one track
**2** : lacking intellectual range, receptiveness, or flexibility : ONE-TRACK

**sin·gle·tree** \'siŋ-gəl-(ˌ)trē\ *noun* (circa 1841)
: WHIFFLETREE

**sin·gle–val·ued** \ˌsiŋ-gəl-'val-(ˌ)yüd\ *adjective* (1879)
: having one and only one value of the range associated with each value of the domain ⟨a *single-valued* function⟩ — compare MULTIPLE-VALUED

**single wing** *noun* (1945)
: an offensive football formation in which one back plays as a flanker and two backs line up four or five yards behind the line in position to receive a direct snap from center

**sin·gly** \'siŋ-g(ə-)lē\ *adverb* (14th century)
**1** : without the company of others : INDIVIDUALLY
**2** : SINGLE-HANDED

**¹sing·song** \'siŋ-ˌsȯŋ\ *noun* (1609)
**1** : verse with marked and regular rhythm and rhyme
**2** : a voice delivery marked by a narrow range or monotonous pattern of pitch
**3** *British* : SONGFEST
— **sing·songy** \-ˌsȯŋ-ē\ *adjective*

**²singsong** *adjective* (1734)
: having a monotonous cadence or rhythm

**sing·spiel** \'siŋ-ˌspēl, 'ziŋ-ˌshpēl\ *noun* [German, from *singen* to sing + *Spiel* play] (1876)
: a musical work popular in Germany especially in the latter part of the 18th century characterized by spoken dialogue interspersed with popular or folk songs

**¹sin·gu·lar** \'siŋ-gyə-lər\ *adjective* [Middle English *singuler,* from Middle French, from Latin *singularis,* from *singulus* only one — more at SINGLE] (14th century)
**1 a** : of or relating to a separate person or thing : INDIVIDUAL **b** : of, relating to, or being a word form denoting one person, thing, or instance **c** : of or relating to a single instance or to something considered by itself

**2 :** distinguished by superiority **:** EXCEPTIONAL ⟨an artist of *singular* attainments⟩

**3 :** being out of the ordinary **:** UNUSUAL ⟨on the way home we had a *singular* adventure⟩

**4 :** departing from general usage or expectation **:** PECULIAR, ODD ⟨the air had a *singular* chill⟩

**5 a** *of a matrix* **:** having a determinant equal to zero **b** *of a linear transformation* **:** having the property that the matrix of coefficients of the new variables has a determinant equal to zero

*synonym* see STRANGE

— **sin·gu·lar·ly** *adverb*

**²singular** *noun* (14th century)

**1 :** the singular number, the inflectional form denoting it, or a word in that form

**2 :** a singular term

**sin·gu·lar·i·ty** \ˌsiŋ-gyə-'lar-ə-tē\ *noun, plural* **-ties** (14th century)

**1 :** something that is singular: as **a :** a separate unit **b :** unusual or distinctive manner or behavior **:** PECULIARITY

**2 :** the quality or state of being singular

**3 :** a point at which the derivative of a given function of a complex variable does not exist but every neighborhood of which contains points for which the derivative exists

**4 :** a point or region of infinite mass density at which space and time are infinitely distorted by gravitational forces and which is held to be the final state of matter falling into a black hole

**sin·gu·lar·ize** \'siŋ-gyə-lə-ˌrīz\ *transitive verb* **-ized; -iz·ing** (1589)

**:** to make singular

**singular point** *noun* (circa 1856)

**:** SINGULARITY 3

**Sin·ha·la** \sin-'hä-lä, siŋ-\ *noun* [Sanskrit *Siṁhala* Sri Lanka] (circa 1954)

**:** SINHALESE 2

**Sin·ha·lese** *or* **Sin·gha·lese** \ˌsiŋ-gə-'lēz, ˌsin-(h)ə-, -'lēs\ *noun, plural* **Sinhalese** *or* **Singhalese** (1598)

**1 :** a member of a people that inhabit Sri Lanka and form a major part of its population

**2 :** the Indo-Aryan language of the Sinhalese people

— **Sinhalese** *or* **Sin·ghalese** *adjective*

**si·ni·cize** \'sī-nə-ˌsīz, 'si-\ *transitive verb* **-cized; -ciz·ing** *often capitalized* [Medieval Latin *sinicus* Chinese, from Late Latin *Sinae*, plural, Chinese — more at SINO-] (1889)

**:** to modify by Chinese influence

**sin·is·ter** \'si-nəs-tər, *archaic* sə-'nis-\ *adjective* [Middle English *sinistre*, from Latin *sinistr-, sinister* on the left side, unlucky, inauspicious] (15th century)

**1** *archaic* **:** UNFAVORABLE, UNLUCKY

**2** *archaic* **:** FRAUDULENT

**3 :** singularly evil or productive of evil

**4 a :** of, relating to, or situated to the left or on the left side of something; *especially* **:** being or relating to the side of a heraldic shield at the left of the person bearing it **b :** of ill omen by reason of being on the left

**5 :** presaging ill fortune or trouble

**6 :** accompanied by or leading to disaster ☆ ◆

— **sin·is·ter·ly** *adverb*

— **sin·is·ter·ness** *noun*

**si·nis·tral** \'si-nəs-trəl, sə-'nis-\ *adjective* (1803)

**:** of, relating to, or inclined to the left: as **a :** LEFT-HANDED **b** *of a gastropod shell* **:** having the whorls coiling counterclockwise down the spire when viewed with the apex toward the observer and having the aperture situated on the left of the axis when held with the spire uppermost and with the aperture opening toward the observer — compare DEXTRAL b

**si·nis·trous** \'si-nəs-trəs, sə-'nis-\ *adjective* (circa 1575)

*archaic* **:** SINISTER

**Si·nit·ic** \sə-'ni-tik, sī-\ *adjective* [Late Latin *Sinae*, plural, Chinese + English *-itic* (as in *Semitic*) — more at SINO-] (circa 1895)

**:** of or relating to the Chinese, their language, or their culture

**¹sink** \'siŋk\ *verb* **sank** \'saŋk\ *or* **sunk** \'səŋk\; **sunk; sink·ing** [Middle English, from Old English *sincan*; akin to Old High German *sinkan* to sink] (before 12th century)

*intransitive verb*

**1 a :** to go to the bottom **:** SUBMERGE **b :** to become partly buried (as in mud) **c :** to become engulfed

**2 a (1) :** to fall or drop to a lower place or level **(2) :** to flow at a lower depth or level **(3) :** to burn with lower intensity **(4) :** to fall to a lower pitch or volume ⟨his voice *sank* to a whisper⟩ **b :** to subside gradually **:** SETTLE **c :** to disappear from view **d :** to slope gradually **:** DIP

**3 a :** to soak or become absorbed **:** PENETRATE **b :** to become impressively known or felt ⟨the lesson had *sunk* in⟩

**4 :** to become deeply absorbed ⟨*sank* into reverie⟩

**5 a :** to go downward in quality, state, or condition **b :** to grow less in amount or worth

**6 a :** to fall or drop slowly for lack of strength **b :** to become depressed **c :** to fail in health or strength

*transitive verb*

**1 a :** to cause to sink ⟨*sink* a battleship⟩ **b :** to force down especially below the earth's surface **c :** to cause (something) to penetrate

**2 :** to engage deeply the attention of **:** IMMERSE

**3 a :** to dig or bore (a well or shaft) in the earth **:** EXCAVATE **b :** to form by cutting or excising ⟨*sink* words in stone⟩

**4 :** to cast down or bring to a low condition or state **:** OVERWHELM, DEFEAT

**5 :** to lower in standing or reputation **:** ABASE

**6 a :** to lessen in value or amount **b :** to lower or soften (the voice) in speaking

**7 :** RESTRAIN, SUPPRESS ⟨*sinks* her pride and approaches the despised neighbor —Richard Harrison⟩

**8 :** to pay off (as a debt) **:** LIQUIDATE

**9 :** INVEST

**10 :** DROP 7c ⟨*sink* a putt⟩

— **sink·able** \'siŋ-kə-bəl\ *adjective*

**²sink** *noun* (15th century)

**1 a :** a pool or pit for the deposit of waste or sewage **:** CESSPOOL **b :** a ditch or tunnel for carrying off sewage **:** SEWER **c :** a stationary basin connected with a drain and usually a water supply for washing and drainage

**2 :** a place where vice, corruption, or evil collects

**3 :** SUMP 3

**4 a :** a depression in the land surface; *especially* **:** one having a saline lake with no outlet **b :** SINKHOLE

**5 :** a body or process that acts as a storage device or disposal mechanism: as **a :** HEAT SINK; *broadly* **:** a device that collects or dissipates energy (as radiation) **b :** a reactant with or absorber of a substance

**sink·age** \'siŋ-kij\ *noun* (1883)

**1 :** the process or degree of sinking

**2 :** DEPRESSION, INDENTATION

**3 :** the distance from the top line of a full page to the first line of sunk matter

**sink·er** \'siŋ-kər\ *noun* (1708)

**1 :** one that sinks; *specifically* **:** a weight for sinking a fishing line, seine, or sounding line

**2 :** DOUGHNUT

**3 :** a fastball that sinks as it reaches the plate — called also *sinker ball*

**sink·hole** \'siŋk-ˌhōl\ *noun* (15th century)

**1 :** a hollow place or depression in which drainage collects

**2 :** a hollow in a limestone region that communicates with a cavern or passage

**3 :** SINK 2

**sinking fund** *noun* (1724)

**:** a fund set up and accumulated by usually regular deposits for paying off the principal of a debt when it falls due

**sin·less** \'sin-ləs\ *adjective* (before 12th century)

**:** free from sin **:** IMPECCABLE

— **sin·less·ly** *adverb*

— **sin·less·ness** *noun*

**sin·ner** \'si-nər\ *noun* (14th century)

**1 :** one that sins

**2 :** REPROBATE, SCAMP

**Si·no-** \ˌsī-(ˌ)nō, 'sī-, -nə\ *combining form* [French, from Late Latin *Sinae*, plural, Chinese, from Greek *Sinai*, probably of Indo-Aryan origin; akin to Sanskrit *Cīnā*, plural, Chinese]

**1 :** Chinese ⟨*sinology*⟩

**2 :** Chinese and ⟨*Sino*-Tibetan⟩

**si·no·atri·al** \ˌsī-nō-'ā-trē-əl\ *adjective* [New Latin *sinus* + *atrium*] (1913)

**:** of, involving, or being the sinoatrial node ⟨*sinoatrial* block⟩

**sinoatrial node** *noun* (1913)

**:** a small mass of tissue that is embedded in the musculature of the right atrium of higher vertebrates and that originates the impulses stimulating the heartbeat

**si·no·logue** \'sī-nᵊl-ˌȯg, 'si-, -ˌäg\ *noun* [French, from Late Latin *Sinae* + French *-logue*] (1853)

**:** a specialist in sinology

**si·nol·o·gy** \sī-'nä-lə-jē, sə-\ *noun* [probably from French *sinologie*, from *sino-* + *-logie* *-logy*] (circa 1882)

**:** the study of the Chinese and especially their language, literature, history, and culture

— **si·no·log·i·cal** \ˌsī-nᵊl-'ä-ji-kəl, ˌsi-\ *adjective*

---

☆ **SYNONYMS**

**Sinister, baleful, malign** mean seriously threatening evil or disaster. SINISTER suggests a general or vague feeling of fear or apprehension on the part of the observer ⟨a *sinister* aura haunts the place⟩. BALEFUL imputes perniciousness or destructiveness to something whether working openly or covertly ⟨exerting a corrupt and *baleful* influence⟩. MALIGN applies to what is inherently evil or harmful ⟨the *malign* effects of racism⟩.

---

◇ **WORD HISTORY**

**sinister** Words for "left" and "right" in a wide variety of languages betray an ancient prejudice toward left-handers. Because most people are right-handed and use their left hand much less deftly, the left side is typically associated with clumsiness or weakness; and in the primitive, male-dominated world of farmers, warriors, and hunters from which we all ultimately descend, an attack by a wild animal or another warrior on one's weaker left side could be fatal, so that left-handedness was also associated with evil and ill fortune. The "right" word, on the other hand, is often, as in English, associated with correctness and moral rectitude. The Latin words *sinister, scaevus,* and *laevus* all had both the literal meaning "on the left" and various negative meanings: "unlucky," "harmful," or "perverted." Idiosyncratically, Latin *sinister* could also mean "favorable" in reference to an omen, because a Roman augur, when following the Etruscan method of doing divinations, faced the south as he stood in a ritually prescribed space, and favorable omens, such as the flight of a bird, were thought to appear from the east, the augur's left side.

---

\ə\ **abut** \ᵊ\ **kitten** \ər\ **further** \a\ **ash** \ā\ **ace**
\ä\ **mop, mar** \aů\ **out** \ch\ **chin** \e\ **bet** \ē\ **easy**
\g\ **go** \i\ **hit** \ī\ **ice** \j\ **job** \ŋ\ **sing** \ō\ **go**
\ȯ\ **law** \ȯi\ **boy** \th\ **thin** \ṯẖ\ **the** \ü\ **loot** \ů\ **foot**
\y\ **yet** \zh\ **vision**    *see also* Guide to Pronunciation

— **si·nol·o·gist** \sī-'nä-lə-jist, sə-\ *noun*

**si·no·pia** \sə-'nō-pē-ə\ *noun, plural* **-pi·as** *or* **-pie** \-pē-,ā\ [Italian, from Latin *sinopis,* from Greek *sinōpis,* from *Sinōpē* Sinop, ancient seaport in Asia Minor] (1844)
**1** : a red to reddish brown earth pigment used by the ancients that depends for its color on its content of red ferric oxide
**2** : a preliminary drawing for a fresco done in sinopia

**Si·no-Ti·bet·an** \,sī-nō-tə-'be-t°n, 'sī-\ *noun* (1920)
: a language family comprising Tibeto-Burman and Chinese

**sin·se·mil·la** \,sin-sə-'mē-lə, -'mi-; -'mē-yə, -'mēl-\ *noun* [American Spanish, from *sin* without + *semilla* seed] (1975)
: highly potent marijuana from female plants that are specially tended and kept seedless by preventing pollination in order to induce a high resin content; *also* : a female hemp plant grown to produce sinsemilla

**sin·syne** \'sin-,sīn\ *adverb* [Middle English (Scots) *sensyne,* from *sen* since (contraction of Middle English *sithen*) + *syne* since — more at SINCE, SYNE] (14th century)
*chiefly Scottish* : since that time

**sin tax** *noun* (1964)
: a tax on substances or activities considered sinful or harmful (as tobacco, alcohol, or gambling)

**sin·ter** \'sin-tər\ *verb* [German *Sinter* slag, cinder, from Old High German *sintar* — more at CINDER] (1871)
*transitive verb*
: to cause to become a coherent mass by heating without melting
*intransitive verb*
: to undergo sintering
— **sinter** *noun*
— **sin·ter·abil·i·ty** \,sin-tə-rə-'bi-lə-tē\ *noun*

**sin·u·ate** \'sin-yə-wət, -,wāt\ *adjective* [Latin *sinuatus,* past participle of *sinuare* to bend, from *sinus* curve] (1688)
: having the margin wavy with strong indentations ⟨*sinuate* leaves⟩

**sin·u·os·i·ty** \,sin-yə-'wä-sə-tē\ *noun, plural* **-ties** (1598)
**1** : the quality or state of being sinuous
**2** : something that is sinuous

**sin·u·ous** \'sin-yə-wəs\ *adjective* [Latin *sinuosus,* from *sinus*] (1578)
**1 a** : of a serpentine or wavy form : WINDING **b** : marked by strong lithe movements
**2** : INTRICATE, COMPLEX
— **sin·u·ous·ly** *adverb*
— **sin·u·ous·ness** *noun*

**si·nus** \'sī-nəs\ *noun* [Middle English, from Medieval Latin, from Latin, curve, fold, hollow] (15th century)
: CAVITY, HOLLOW: as **a** : a narrow elongated tract extending from a focus of suppuration and serving for the discharge of pus **b** (1) : a cavity in the substance of a bone of the skull that usually communicates with the nostrils and contains air (2) : a channel for venous blood (3) : a dilatation in a bodily canal or vessel **c** : a cleft or indentation between adjoining lobes (as of a leaf or corolla)

**si·nus·i·tis** \,sīn-yə-'sī-təs, ,sī-nə-\ *noun* (1896)
: inflammation of a sinus of the skull

**si·nu·soid** \'sīn-yə-,sóid, 'sī-nə-\ *noun* [Medieval Latin *sinus* sine] (1823)
**1** : SINE CURVE, SINE WAVE
**2** [New Latin *sinus*] : a minute endothelium-lined space or passage for blood in the tissues of an organ (as the liver)

**si·nu·soi·dal** \,sīn-yə-'sói-d°l, ,sī-nə-\ *adjective* (1878)
: of, relating to, shaped like, or varying according to a sine curve or sine wave ⟨*sinusoidal* motion⟩ ⟨*sinusoidal* alternating current⟩ ⟨*sinusoidal* grooves⟩
— **si·nu·soi·dal·ly** \-d°l-ē\ *adverb*

**sinusoidal projection** *noun* (1944)
: an equal-area map projection capable of showing the entire surface of the earth with all parallels as straight lines evenly spaced, the central meridian as one half the length of the equator, and all other meridians as curved lines

**si·nus ve·no·sus** \'sī-nəs-vi-'nō-səs\ *noun* [New Latin, venous sinus] (circa 1839)
: an enlarged pouch that adjoins the heart, is formed by the union of the large systemic veins, and is the passage through which venous blood enters the heart in lower vertebrates and in embryos of higher forms

**Si·on** \'sī-ən\ *variant of* ZION

**Siou·an** \'sü-ən\ *noun* (1889)
**1** : an American Indian language family of central and southeastern North America
**2** : a member of any of the peoples speaking Siouan languages

**Sioux** \'sü\ *noun, plural* **Sioux** \'sü, 'süz\ [French, short for *Nadouessioux,* from Ojibwa *na·towe·ssiw-*] (1712)
**1** : DAKOTA
**2** : SIOUAN

**¹sip** \'sip\ *verb* **sipped; sip·ping** [Middle English *sippen;* akin to Low German *sippen* to sip] (14th century)
*intransitive verb*
: to take a sip of something especially repeatedly
*transitive verb*
**1** : to drink in small quantities
**2** : to take sips from
— **sip·per** *noun*

**²sip** *noun* (15th century)
**1** : a small draft taken with the lips
**2** : the act of sipping

**¹si·phon** \'sī-fən\ *noun* [French *siphon,* from Latin *siphon-, sipho* tube, pipe, siphon, from Greek *siphōn*] (1659)
**1 a** : a tube bent to form two legs of unequal length by which a liquid can be transferred to a lower level over an intermediate elevation by the pressure of the

siphon 1a

atmosphere in forcing the liquid up the shorter branch of the tube immersed in it while the excess of weight of the liquid in the longer branch when once filled causes a continuous flow **b** *usually* **syphon** : a bottle for holding aerated water that is driven out through a bent tube in its neck by the pressure of the gas when a valve in the tube is opened
**2** : any of various tubular organs in animals and especially mollusks or arthropods that are used for drawing in or ejecting fluids — see CLAM illustration

**²siphon** *verb* **si·phoned; si·phon·ing** \'sī-fə-niŋ, 'sīf-niŋ\ (1859)
*transitive verb*
: to convey, draw off, or empty by or as if by a siphon — often used with *off*
*intransitive verb*
: to pass by or as if by a siphon

**si·pho·no·phore** \sī-'fä-nə-,fōr, 'sī-fə-nə-, -,fôr\ *noun* [ultimately from Greek *siphōn* + *pherein* to carry — more at BEAR] (1883)
: any of an order (Siphonophora) of compound free-swimming or floating pelagic hydrozoans that are mostly delicate, transparent, and colored and have specialized zooids

**si·pho·no·stele** \sī-'fä-nə-,stēl, ,sī-fə-nə-'stē-lē\ *noun* [Greek *siphōn* tube, siphon] (1902)
: a stele consisting of vascular tissue surrounding a central core of pith parenchyma

**sip·pet** \'si-pət\ *noun* [alteration of *sop*] (1530)
*chiefly British* : a small bit of toast or fried bread especially for garnishing

**sir** \'sər\ *noun* [Middle English, from *sire*] (13th century)
**1 a** : a man entitled to be addressed as *sir* — used as a title before the given name of a knight or baronet and formerly sometimes before the given name of a priest **b** : a man of rank or position
**2 a** — used as a usually respectful form of address **b** *capitalized* — used as a conventional form of address in the salutation of a letter

**Si·rach** \'sī-rak *also* sə-'räk\ *noun* [Greek *Seirach*]
: a didactic book of the Roman Catholic canon of the Old Testament

**sir·dar** \'sər-,där, sər-'\ *noun* [Hindi *sardār,* from Persian] (1595)
**1 a** : a person of high rank (as an hereditary noble) especially in India **b** : the commander of the Anglo-Egyptian army
**2** : one (as a foreman) holding a responsible position especially in India

**¹sire** \'sīr\ *noun* [Middle English, from Old French, from Latin *senior* older — more at SENIOR] (13th century)
**1 a** : FATHER **b** *archaic* : male ancestor : FOREFATHER **c** : AUTHOR, ORIGINATOR
**2 a** *archaic* : a man of rank or authority; *especially* : LORD — used formerly as a form of address and as a title **b** *obsolete* : an elderly man : SENIOR
**3** : the male parent of an animal and especially of a domestic animal

**²sire** *transitive verb* **sired; sir·ing** (1611)
**1** : BEGET — used especially of male domestic animals
**2** : to bring into being : ORIGINATE

**¹si·ren** \'sī-rən, *for 3 also* sī-'rēn\ *noun* [Middle English, from Middle French & Latin; Middle French *sereine,* from Late Latin *sirena,* from Latin *siren,* from Greek *seirēn*] (14th century)
**1** *often capitalized* : any of a group of female and partly human creatures in Greek mythology that lured mariners to destruction by their singing
**2 a** : a woman who sings with bewitching sweetness **b** : TEMPTRESS
**3 a** : an apparatus producing musical tones especially in acoustical studies by the rapid interruption of a current of air, steam, or fluid by a perforated rotating disk **b** : a device often electrically operated for producing a penetrating warning sound ⟨ambulance *siren*⟩ ⟨air-raid *siren*⟩
**4** [New Latin, from Latin] : either of two North American eel-shaped amphibians that constitute a genus (*Siren*) and have small forelimbs but neither hind legs nor pelvis and have permanent external gills as well as lungs

**²si·ren** \'sī-rən\ *adjective* (1568)
: resembling that of a siren : ENTICING

**si·re·ni·an** \sī-'rē-nē-ən\ *noun* [New Latin *Sirenia,* from Latin *siren*] (1883)
: any of an order (Sirenia) of aquatic herbivorous mammals including the manatee, dugong, and Steller's sea cow

**siren song** *noun* (1568)
: an alluring utterance or appeal; *especially* : one that is seductive or deceptive

**Sir·i·us** \'sir-ē-əs\ *noun* [Middle English, from Latin, from Greek *Seirios*]
: a star of the constellation Canis Major that is the brightest star in the heavens — called also *Dog Star*

**sir·loin** \'sər-,lóin\ *noun* [alteration of earlier *surloin,* modification of Middle French *surlonge,* from *sur* over (from Latin *super*) + *loigne, longe* loin — more at OVER, LOIN] (1554)
: a cut of meat and especially of beef from the part of the hindquarter just in front of the round — see BEEF illustration

**si·roc·co** \sə-'rä-(,)kō, shə-\ *noun, plural* **-cos** [Italian *scirocco, sirocco,* from Arabic *sharq* east] (1617)

**1 a :** a hot dust-laden wind from the Libyan deserts that blows on the northern Mediterranean coast chiefly in Italy, Malta, and Sicily **b :** a warm moist oppressive southeast wind in the same regions
**2 :** a hot or warm wind of cyclonic origin from an arid or heated region

**sir·rah** *also* **sir·ra** \'sir-ə\ *noun* [alteration of *sir*] (1526)
*obsolete* — used as a form of address implying inferiority in the person addressed

**sir·ree** *also* **sir·ee** \(,)sər-'ē\ *noun* [by alteration] (1823)
**:** SIR — used as an emphatic form usually after *yes* or *no*

**sir-reverence** *noun* [probably alteration of *save-reverence*, translation of Medieval Latin *salva reverentia* saving (your) reverence] (1575)
**1** *obsolete* — used as an expression of apology before a statement that might be taken as offensive
**2** *obsolete* **:** human feces; *also* **:** a lump of human feces

**Sir Rog·er de Cov·er·ley** \sə(r)-,rä-jər-di-'kə-vər-lē\ *noun* [alteration of *roger of coverley*, probably from *Roger*, male given name + *of* + *Coverley*, a fictitious place name] (1804)
**:** an English country-dance that resembles the Virginia reel

**sirup** *variant of* SYRUP

**sir·vente** \sir-'vänt\ *or* **sir·ven·tes** \-'ven-təs\ *noun, plural* **sir·ventes** \-'vänt, -'vän(t)s, -'ven-təs\ [French, from Provençal *sirventes*, literally, servant's song, from *sirvent* servant, from Latin *servient-, serviens*, present participle of *servire* to serve] (1819)
**:** a usually moral or religious song of the Provençal troubadours satirizing social vices

**sis** \'sis\ *noun* (1656)
**:** SISTER — usually used in direct address

**-sis** *noun suffix, plural* **-ses** [Latin, from Greek, feminine suffix of action]
**:** process **:** action ⟨peristal*sis*⟩

**si·sal** \'sī-səl, -zəl\ *noun* [*Sisal*, port in Yucatán, Mexico] (1843)
**1 a :** a strong durable white fiber used especially for hard fiber cordage and twine — called also *sisal hemp* **b :** a widely cultivated Mexican agave (*Agave sisalana*) whose leaves yield sisal
**2 :** any of several fibers similar to true sisal

**sis·kin** \'sis-kən\ *noun* [German dialect *Sisschen*, diminutive of Middle High German *zīse* siskin, of Slavic origin; akin to Czech *čížek* siskin] (1562)
**:** a small chiefly greenish and yellowish finch (*Carduelis spinus*) of Europe, Asia, and northern Africa that is related to the goldfinch — compare PINE SISKIN, RED SISKIN

**sis·si·fied** \'si-si-,fīd\ *adjective* (circa 1903)
**:** of, relating to, or having the characteristics of a sissy

**sis·sy** \'si-sē\ *noun, plural* **sissies** [*sis*] (1891)
**:** an effeminate man or boy; *also* **:** a timid or cowardly person
**— sissy** *adjective*

**sis·ter** \'sis-tər\ *noun* [Middle English *suster, sister*, partly from Old English *sweostor* and partly of Scandinavian origin; akin to Old Norse *systir* sister; akin to Latin *soror* sister, Sanskrit *svasṛ*] (before 12th century)
**1 :** a female who has one or both parents in common with another
**2** *often capitalized* **a :** a member of a women's religious order (as of nuns or deaconesses); *especially* **:** one of a Roman Catholic congregation under simple vows **b :** a woman or girl who is a member of a Christian church
**3 :** a woman regarded as a comrade ⟨my Korean *sisters* —Alice Walker⟩
**4 :** one that is closely similar to or associated with another ⟨*sister* schools⟩ ⟨*sister* cities⟩
**5** *chiefly British* **:** NURSE

**6 a :** GIRL, WOMAN; *especially* **:** a girl or woman who is black **b :** PERSON — usually used in the phrase *weak sister*
**7 :** a member of a sorority

**sis·ter·hood** \-,hud\ *noun* (1609)
**1 a :** the state of being a sister **b :** sisterly relationship
**2 :** a community or society of sisters; *especially* **:** a society of women religious
**3 :** the solidarity of women based on shared conditions, experiences, or concerns

**sis·ter–in–law** \'sis-t(ə-)rən-,lo, -tərn-,lo\ *noun, plural* **sis·ters–in–law** \-tər-zən-\ (15th century)
**1 :** the sister of one's spouse
**2 a :** the wife of one's brother **b :** the wife of one's spouse's brother

**sis·ter·ly** \'sis-tər-lē\ *adjective* (circa 1570)
**:** of, relating to, or having the characteristics of a sister
**— sisterly** *adverb*

**Sis·tine** \'sis-,tēn, sis-'\ *adjective* [Italian *sistino*, from New Latin *sixtinus*, from *Sixtus*, name of some popes] (circa 1864)
**1 :** of or relating to any of the popes named Sixtus
**2** [from Pope *Sixtus* IV (died 1484)] **:** of or relating to the Sistine chapel in the Vatican

**Sis·y·phe·an** \,si-sə-'fē-ən\ *or* **Si·syph·i·an** \si-'si-fē-ən\ *adjective* (1635)
**:** of, relating to, or suggestive of the labors of Sisyphus

**Sis·y·phus** \'si-sə-fəs\ *noun* [Latin, from Greek *Sisyphos*]
**:** a legendary king of Corinth condemned eternally to repeat the cycle of rolling a heavy rock up a hill in Hades only to have it roll down again as it nears the top

**¹sit** \'sit\ *verb* **sat** \'sat\; **sit·ting** [Middle English *sitten*, from Old English *sittan*; akin to Old High German *sizzen* to sit, Latin *sedēre*, Greek *hezesthai* to sit, *hedra* seat] (before 12th century)
*intransitive verb*
**1 a :** to rest on the buttocks or haunches ⟨*sit* in a chair⟩ — often used with *down* **b :** PERCH, ROOST
**2 :** to occupy a place as a member of an official body ⟨*sit* in Congress⟩
**3 :** to hold a session **:** be in session for official business
**4 :** to cover eggs for hatching **:** BROOD
**5 a :** to take a position for having one's portrait painted or for being photographed **b :** to serve as a model
**6** *archaic* **:** to have one's dwelling place **:** DWELL
**7 a :** to lie or hang relative to a wearer ⟨the collar *sits* awkwardly⟩ **b :** to affect one with or as if with weight ⟨the food *sat* heavily on his stomach⟩
**8 :** LIE, REST ⟨a kettle *sitting* on the stove⟩
**9 a :** to have a location ⟨the house *sits* well back from the road⟩ **b** *of wind* **:** to blow from a certain direction
**10 :** to remain inactive or quiescent ⟨the car *sits* in the garage⟩
**11 :** to take an examination
**12 :** BABY-SIT
**13 :** to please or agree with one — used with *with* and an adverb ⟨the decision did not *sit* well with me⟩
*transitive verb*
**1 :** to cause to be seated **:** place on or in a seat — often used with *down*
**2 :** to sit on ⟨eggs⟩
**3 :** to keep one's seat on ⟨*sit* a horse⟩
**4 :** to provide seats or seating room for ⟨the car will *sit* six people⟩
*usage* see SET
**— sit on 1 :** to hold deliberations concerning **2 :** REPRESS, SQUELCH **3 :** to delay action or decision concerning
**— sit pretty :** to be in a highly favorable situation

**— sit tight 1 :** to maintain one's position without change **2 :** to remain quiet in or as if in hiding
**— sit under :** to attend religious service under the instruction or ministrations of; *also* **:** to attend the classes or lectures of

**²sit** *noun* (1776)
**1 :** the manner in which a garment fits
**2 :** an act or period of sitting

**si·tar** \si-'tär, 'si-,\ *noun* [Hindi *sitār*, from Persian, a three-stringed lute, from *sih* three + *tār* string, thread] (1845)
**:** an Indian lute with a long neck and a varying number of strings
**— si·tar·ist** \-ist\ *noun*

sitar

**sit·com** \'sit-,käm\ *noun* [*sit*uation *com*edy] (1964)
**:** SITUATION COMEDY

**¹sit–down** \'sit-,daun\ *adjective* (circa 1837)
**:** served to seated diners ⟨a *sit-down* dinner⟩; *also* **:** of, relating to, or serving sit-down meals ⟨a *sit-down* restaurant⟩

**²sit–down** \'sit-,daun\ *noun* (1936)
**1 :** a cessation of work by employees while maintaining continuous occupation of their place of employment as a protest and means toward forcing compliance with demands
**2 :** a mass obstruction of an activity by sitting down to demonstrate a grievance or to get the activity modified or halted

**¹site** \'sīt\ *noun* [Middle English, place, position, from Middle French or Latin; Middle French, from Latin *situs*, from *sinere* to leave, allow] (14th century)
**1 a :** the spatial location of an actual or planned structure or set of structures (as a building, town, or monuments) **b :** a space of ground occupied or to be occupied by a building
**2 :** the place, scene, or point of something

**²site** *transitive verb* **sit·ed; sit·ing** (15th century)
**:** to place on a site or in position **:** LOCATE

**sith** \'sith\ *or* **sith·ence** \'si-thən(t)s\ *or* **sithens** \'si-thənz\ *archaic variant of* SINCE

**sit–in** \'sit-,in\ *noun* (1937)
**1 :** SIT-DOWN 1
**2 a :** an act of occupying seats in a racially segregated establishment in organized protest against discrimination **b :** an act of sitting in the seats or on the floor of an establishment as a means of organized protest

**sit in** *intransitive verb* (1868)
**1 :** to take part in or be present at a session of music or discussion as a visitor
**2 :** to participate in a sit-in

**Sit·ka spruce** \'sit-kə-\ *noun* [*Sitka*, Alaska] (1895)
**:** a tall spruce (*Picea sitchensis*) of the northern Pacific coast that has thin reddish brown bark, flat needles, and cones with slightly toothed scales

**si·tos·ter·ol** \sī-'täs-tə-,rol, sə-, -,rōl\ *noun* [Greek *sitos* grain + English *sterol*] (1898)
**:** any of several sterols that are widespread especially in plant products (as wheat germ or soy bean oil) and are used as starting materials for the synthesis of steroid hormones

**sit out** *transitive verb* (1659)
**:** to refrain from participating in ⟨*sit out* the next dance⟩

**sit·ter** \'si-tər\ *noun* (14th century)
**:** one that sits; *especially* **:** one who baby-sits children

**¹sit·ting** \'si-tiŋ\ *noun* (13th century)
**1 a :** the act of one that sits **b :** a single occasion of continuous sitting (as for a portrait or meal)
**2 a :** a brooding over eggs for hatching **b** : SETTING 6
**3 :** SESSION ⟨a *sitting* of the legislature⟩
**²sitting** *adjective* (15th century)
**1 :** that is setting ⟨a *sitting* hen⟩
**2 :** occupying a judicial, legislative, or executive seat : being in office
**3 :** easily hit or played ⟨a *sitting* target⟩
**4 a :** used in or for sitting ⟨a *sitting* position⟩ **b** : performed while sitting ⟨a *sitting* shot⟩
**sitting duck** *noun* (1942)
**:** an easy or defenseless target for attack or criticism or unscrupulous dealings
**sitting room** *noun* (1771)
: LIVING ROOM 1
**¹sit·u·ate** \'si-chə-wət, -ˌwāt; 'sich-wət\ *adjective* [Middle English, from Late Latin *situatus*, from Latin *situs*] (15th century)
: having a site : LOCATED
**²sit·u·ate** \'si-chə-ˌwāt\ *transitive verb* **-at·ed; -at·ing** (circa 1532)
: to place in a site, situation, context, or category : LOCATE
**situated** *adjective* (15th century)
**1 :** having a site, situation, or location : LOCATED
**2 :** provided with money or possessions ⟨comfortably *situated*⟩
**sit·u·a·tion** \ˌsi-chə-'wā-shən\ *noun* (15th century)
**1 a :** the way in which something is placed in relation to its surroundings **b** : SITE **c** *archaic* : LOCALITY
**2** *archaic* : state of health
**3 a :** position or place of employment : POST, JOB **b** : position in life : STATUS
**4 :** position with respect to conditions and circumstances ⟨the military *situation* remains obscure⟩
**5 a :** relative position or combination of circumstances at a certain moment in a critical, trying, or unusual state of affairs : PROBLEM **c** : a particular or striking complex of affairs at a stage in the action of a narrative or drama
**sit·u·a·tion·al** \-shnəl, -shə-n°l\ *adjective* (1903)
**1 :** of, relating to, or appropriate to a situation
**2 :** of or relating to situation ethics
— **sit·u·a·tion·al·ly** *adverb*
**situation comedy** *noun* (1946)
: a radio or television comedy series that involves a continuing cast of characters in a succession of episodes
**situation ethics** *noun* (1955)
: a system of ethics by which acts are judged within their contexts instead of by categorical principles
**sit–up** \'sit-ˌəp\ *noun* (1938)
: a conditioning exercise performed from a supine position by raising the trunk to a sitting position without lifting the feet and returning to the original position
**sit up** *intransitive verb* (13th century)
**1 a :** to rise from a lying to a sitting position **b** : to sit with the back erect
**2 :** to show interest, alertness, or surprise ⟨*sit up* and take notice⟩
**3 :** to stay up after the usual time for going to bed ⟨*sat up* late to watch the movie⟩
**si·tus** \'sī-təs\ *noun* [Latin — more at SITE] (1701)
: the place where something exists or originates; *specifically* : the place where something (as a right) is held to be located in law
**sitz bath** \'sits-\ *noun* [part translation of German *Sitzbad*, from *Sitz* act of sitting + *Bad* bath] (1849)
: a tub in which one bathes in a sitting posture; *also* : a bath so taken especially therapeutically

**sitz·mark** \'sits-ˌmärk, 'zits-\ *noun* [part translation of German *Sitzmarke*, from *Sitz* + *Marke* mark] (1935)
: a depression left in the snow by a skier falling backward
**Si·va** \'si-və, 'shi-, 'sē-, 'shē-\ *noun* [Sanskrit *Śiva*] (1788)
: the god of destruction and regeneration in the Hindu sacred triad — compare BRAHMA, VISHNU
**Si·van** \'si-vən\ *noun* [Hebrew *Sīwān*] (1535)
: the 9th month of the civil year or the 3d month of the ecclesiastical year in the Jewish calendar — see MONTH table
**Si·wash** \'sī-ˌwȯsh, -ˌwäsh\ *noun* [*Siwash*, fictional college in stories by George Fitch (died 1915) American author] (1936)
: a small usually inland college that is notably provincial in outlook ⟨cheer for dear old *Siwash*⟩
**six** \'siks\ *noun* [Middle English, from *six*, adjective, from Old English *siex*; akin to Old High German *sehs* six, Latin *sex*, Greek *hex*] (before 12th century)
**1** — see NUMBER table
**2 :** the sixth in a set or series ⟨the *six* of spades⟩
**3 :** something having six units or members: as **a :** an ice-hockey team **b :** a 6-cylinder engine or automobile
— **six** *adjective*
— **six** *pronoun, plural in construction*
— **at sixes and sevens :** being in disorder
**six·fold** \'siks-ˌfōld, -'fōld\ *adjective* (before 12th century)
**1 :** having six units or members
**2 :** being six times as great or as many
— **six·fold** \-'fōld\ *adverb*
**six–gun** \'siks-ˌgən\ *noun* (1912)
: a 6-chambered revolver
**six·mo** \'siks-(ˌ)mō\ *noun, plural* **sixmos** (1924)
: the size of a piece of paper cut six from a sheet; *also* : a book, a page, or paper of this size
**six–o–six** *or* **606** \ˌsiks-ˌō-'siks\ *noun* [from its having been the 606th compound tested and introduced by Paul Ehrlich (died 1915)] (1910)
: ARSPHENAMINE
**six–pack** \'siks-ˌpak\ *noun* (1952)
**1 :** six bottles or cans (as of beer) packaged and purchased as a unit
**2 :** the contents of a six-pack
**six·pence** \'siks-pən(t)s, *US also* -ˌpen(t)s\ *noun* (14th century)
**1 :** a former British monetary unit equal to six pennies
**2** *plural* **sixpence** *or* **six·penc·es :** a coin worth sixpence
**six·pen·ny** \'siks-pə-nē, *US also* -ˌpe-nē\ *adjective* (15th century)
: costing or worth sixpence
**sixpenny bit** *noun* (circa 1887)
: SIXPENCE 2
**six·pen·ny nail** \'siks-ˌpe-nē-\ *noun* (15th century)
: a nail about two inches long
**six–shoot·er** \'sik(s)-ˌshü-tər\ *noun* (1844)
: SIX-GUN
**six·teen** \ˌsik-'stēn, 'siks-ˌtēn\ *noun* [Middle English *sixtene*, from Old English *sixtȳne*, adjective, from *six* six + *-tȳne* (akin to Old English *tīen* ten) — more at TEN] (before 12th century)
— see NUMBER table
— **sixteen** *adjective*
— **sixteen** *pronoun, plural in construction*
— **six·teenth** \-'stēn(t)th, -ˌtēn(t)th\ *adjective or noun*
**six·teen–mo** \sik-'stēn-(ˌ)mō\ *noun, plural* **-mos** (1847)
: the size of a piece of paper cut 16 from a sheet; *also* : a book, a page, or paper of this size

**sixteenth note** *noun* (circa 1861)
: a musical note with the time value of $1/16$ of a whole note — see NOTE illustration
**sixteenth rest** *noun* (circa 1890)
: a musical rest corresponding in time value to a sixteenth note — see REST illustration
**sixth** \'siks(t)th, 'siks(t)\ *noun, plural* **sixths** \'siks(t)ths, 'siks(t)s\ (12th century)
**1** — see NUMBER table
**2 a :** a musical interval embracing six diatonic degrees **b :** a tone at this interval; *specifically* : SUBMEDIANT **c :** the harmonic combination of two tones a sixth apart
— **sixth** *adjective or adverb*
— **sixth·ly** \'siksth-lē, 'sikst-\ *adverb*
**sixth chord** *noun* (circa 1903)
: a musical chord consisting of a tone with its third and its sixth above and usually being the first inversion of a triad
**sixth sense** *noun* (1761)
: a power of perception like but not one of the five senses : a keen intuitive power
**Six·tine** \'sik-ˌstīn, -ˌstēn\ *variant of* SISTINE
**six·ty** \'siks-tē\ *noun, plural* **sixties** [Middle English, from *sixty*, adjective, from Old English *siextig*, noun, group of sixty, from *siex* six + *-tig* group of ten; akin to Old English *tīen* ten] (14th century)
**1** — see NUMBER table
**2** *plural* : the numbers 60 to 69; *specifically* : the years 60 to 69 in a lifetime or century
— **six·ti·eth** \'siks-tē-əth\ *adjective or noun*
— **sixty** *adjective*
— **sixty** *pronoun, plural in construction*
— **six·ty·ish** \'siks-tē-ish\ *adjective*
**sixty–fourth note** \ˌsiks-tē-'fȯrth-, -'fȯrth-\ *noun* (circa 1890)
: a musical note with the time value of $1/64$ of a whole note — see NOTE illustration
**sixty–fourth rest** *noun* (circa 1903)
: a musical rest corresponding in time value to a sixty-fourth note
**six·ty–nine** \ˌsiks-tē-'nīn\ *noun* (1924)
**1** — see NUMBER table
**2 :** mutual cunnilingus and fellatio : mutual fellatio : mutual cunnilingus
**siz·able** *or* **size·able** \'sī-zə-bəl\ *adjective* (1613)
: fairly large : CONSIDERABLE
— **siz·able·ness** *noun*
— **siz·ably** \-blē\ *adverb*
**siz·ar** *also* **siz·er** \'sī-zər\ *noun* [*sizar* alteration of *sizer*, from ¹*size*] (1588)
: a student (as in the university of Cambridge) who receives an allowance toward college expenses and who originally acted as a servant to other students in return for this allowance
**¹size** \'sīz\ *noun* [Middle English *sise* assize, from Middle French, from Old French, short for *assise* — more at ASSIZE] (13th century)
**1** *dialect British* : ASSIZE 2a — usually used in plural
**2** *obsolete* : a fixed portion of food or drink
**3 a :** physical magnitude, extent, or bulk : relative or proportionate dimensions **b :** relative aggregate amount or number **c :** considerable proportions : BIGNESS
**4 :** one of a series of graduated measures especially of manufactured articles (as of clothing) conventionally identified by numbers or letters ⟨a *size* 7 hat⟩
**5 :** character, quality, or status of a person or thing especially with reference to importance, relative merit, or correspondence to needs ⟨try this idea on for *size*⟩
**6 :** actual state of affairs ⟨that's about the *size* of it⟩
**²size** *verb* **sized; siz·ing** (1609)
*transitive verb*
**1 :** to make a particular size : bring to proper or suitable size
**2 :** to arrange, grade, or classify according to size or bulk

*intransitive verb*
: to equal in size or other particular characteristic : COMPARE — usually used with *up* and often with *to* or *with*

³**size** \'sīz, ˌsīz\ *adjective* (1924)
: SIZED — usually used in combination ⟨bite-size⟩

⁴**size** \'sīz\ *noun* [Middle English *sise*] (15th century)
: any of various glutinous materials (as preparations of glue, flour, varnish, or resins) used for filling the pores in surfaces (as of paper, textiles, leather, or plaster) or for applying color or metal leaf (as to book edges or covers)

⁵**size** *transitive verb* **sized; siz·ing** (1667)
: to cover, stiffen, or glaze with or as if with size

**sized** \'sīzd, ˌsīzd\ *adjective* (1582)
**1** : having a specified size or bulk — usually used in combination ⟨a small-*sized* house⟩
**2** : arranged or adjusted according to size

**size up** *transitive verb* (1884)
: to form a judgment of

**siz·ing** \'sī-ziŋ\ *noun* (1825)
: ⁴SIZE

¹**siz·zle** \'si-zəl\ *verb* **siz·zled; siz·zling** \'si-zə-liŋ, 'siz-liŋ\ [perhaps frequentative of *siss* to hiss] (1603)
*transitive verb*
: to burn up or sear with or as if with a hissing sound
*intransitive verb*
**1** : to make a hissing sound in or as if in burning or frying
**2** : to seethe with deep anger or resentment

²**sizzle** *noun* (circa 1823)
: a hissing sound (as of something frying over a fire)

**siz·zler** \'si-zə-lər, 'siz-lər\ *noun* (1848)
: one that sizzles; *especially* : SCORCHER

**ska** \'skä\ *noun* [origin unknown] (1969)
: popular music of Jamaican origin that combines elements of traditional Caribbean rhythms and jazz

**skag** *variant of* SCAG

**skald** \'skóld, 'skäld\ *noun* [Old Norse *skáld*] (1780)
: an ancient Scandinavian poet; *broadly* : BARD
— **skald·ic** \'skól-dik, 'skäl-\ *adjective*

**skat** \'skät, 'skat\ *noun* [German, modification of Italian *scarto* discard, from *scartare* to discard, from *s-* (from Latin *ex-*) + *carta* card — more at CARD] (1864)
**1** : a three-handed card game played with 32 cards in which players bid for the privilege of attempting any of several contracts
**2** : a widow of two cards in skat that may be used by the winner of the bid

¹**skate** \'skāt\ *noun, plural* **skates** *also* **skate** [Middle English *scate*, from Old Norse *skata*] (14th century)
: any of a family (Rajidae, especially genus *Raja*) of rays with the pectoral fins greatly developed giving the fish a flat diamond shape

²**skate** *noun* [modification of Dutch *schaats* stilt, skate, from Old North French *escache* stilt, probably of Germanic origin; akin to Old English *sceacan* to shake — more at SHAKE] (1684)
**1 a** : a metal frame that can be fitted to the sole of a shoe and to which is attached a runner or a set of wheels for gliding over ice or a surface other than ice **b** : ROLLER SKATE **c** : ICE SKATE
**2** : a period of skating

**skate**

³**skate** *verb* **skat·ed; skat·ing** (1696)

*intransitive verb*
**1** : to glide along on skates propelled by the alternate action of the legs
**2** : to slip or glide as if on skates
**3** : to proceed in a superficial or blithe manner
*transitive verb*
: to go along or through by skating

⁴**skate** *noun* [probably alteration of English dialect *skite* an offensive person] (1894)
**1** : a thin awkward-looking or decrepit horse : NAG
**2** : FELLOW 4c

**skate·board** \'skāt-ˌbōrd, -ˌbórd\ *noun* (1964)
: a short board mounted on small wheels that is used for coasting and often for performing athletic stunts
— **skate·board·er** \-ˌbōr-dər, -ˌbór-\ *noun*
— **skate·board·ing** \-diŋ\ *noun*

**skat·er** \'skā-tər\ *noun* (1700)
**1** : one that skates
**2** : WATER STRIDER

**skat·ing** \'skā-tiŋ\ *noun* (1723)
: the act, art, or sport of gliding on skates

**ska·tole** \'ska-ˌtōl, 'skā-\ *also* **ska·tol** \-ˌtól, -ˌtōl\ *noun* [International Scientific Vocabulary, from Greek *skat-, skōr* excrement — more at SCATOLOGY] (1879)
: a foul-smelling compound $C_9H_9N$ found in the intestines and feces, in civet, and in several plants or made synthetically and used in perfumes as a fixative

¹**skean** *or* **skeane** *variant of* SKEIN

²**skean** *or* **skene** \'skē(-ə)n\ *noun* [Middle English *skene*, from Irish *scian* & Scottish Gaelic *sgian*, from Old Irish *scían;* probably akin to Sanskrit *chyati* he cuts off — more at SCIENCE] (15th century)
: DAGGER, DIRK

**ske·dad·dle** \ski-'da-dᵊl\ *intransitive verb* **ske·dad·dled; ske·dad·dling** \-'dad-liŋ, -'da-dᵊl-iŋ\ [origin unknown] (1861)
: RUN AWAY, SCRAM; *especially* : to flee in a panic
— **ske·dad·dler** \-'dad-lər, -'da-dᵊl-ər\ *noun*

**skeet** \'skēt\ *noun* [perhaps from Norwegian *skyte* to shoot] (1926)
: trapshooting in which clay targets are thrown in such a way as to simulate the angles of flight of birds

¹**skee·ter** \'skē-tər\ *noun* [by shortening & alteration] (1839)
**1** : MOSQUITO
**2** : an iceboat 16 feet (5 meters) or more in length equipped with a single sail

²**skeet·er** \'skē-tər\ *noun* (1926)
: a skeet shooter

**skeg** \'skeg\ *also* **skag** \'skag\ *noun* [Middle English *skegge*, from Old Norse *skegg* cutwater, literally, beard — more at SHAG] (13th century)
**1** : the stern of the keel of a ship near the sternpost; *especially* : the part connecting the keel with the bottom of the rudderpost in a single-screw ship
**2** : a fin situated on the rear bottom of a surfboard that is used for steering and stability

**skeigh** \'skēk\ *adjective* [perhaps of Scandinavian origin; akin to Swedish *skygg* shy; akin to Old English *scēoh* shy — more at SHY] (1508)
*chiefly Scottish* : proudly spirited : SKITTISH

¹**skein** \'skān\ *noun* [Middle English *skeyne*, from Middle French *escaigne*] (14th century)
**1** *or* **skean** *or* **skeane** \'skān\ : a loosely coiled length of yarn or thread wound on a reel
**2** : something suggesting the twists or coils of a skein : TANGLE
**3** : a flock of wildfowl (as geese or ducks) in flight

²**skein** *transitive verb* (circa 1775)
: to wind into skeins ⟨*skein* yarn⟩

**skel·e·tal** \'ske-lə-tᵊl\ *adjective* (1854)
: of, relating to, forming, attached to, or resembling a skeleton

— **skel·e·tal·ly** \-tᵊl-ē\ *adverb*

**skeletal muscle** *noun* (1877)
: striated muscle that is usually attached to the skeleton and is usually under voluntary control

¹**skel·e·ton** \'ske-lə-tᵊn\ *noun* [New Latin, from Greek, neuter of *skeletos* dried up; akin to Greek *skellein* to dry up, *sklēros* hard and perhaps to Old English *sceald* shallow] (1578)
**1** : a usually rigid supportive or protective structure or framework of an organism; *especially* : the bony or more or less cartilaginous framework supporting the soft tissues and protecting the internal organs of a vertebrate
**2** : something reduced to its minimum form or essential parts
**3** : an emaciated person or animal
**4 a** : something forming a structural framework **b** : the straight or branched chain or ring of atoms that forms the basic structure of an organic molecule
**5** : something shameful and kept secret (as in a family) — often used in the phrase *skeleton in the closet*
— **skel·e·ton·ic** \ˌske-lə-'tä-nik\ *adjective*

skeleton 1: *1* skull, *2* clavicle, *3* scapula, *4* sternum, *5* humerus, *6* rib, *7* pelvis, *8* radius, *9* ulna, *10* carpus, *11* metacarpal bones, *12* phalanges (fingers), *13* femur, *14* patella, *15* tibia, *16* fibula, *17* tarsus, *18* metatarsal bones, *19* phalanges (toes), *20* spinal column

²**skeleton** *adjective* (1778)
: of, consisting of, or resembling a skeleton

**skel·e·ton·ise** *British variant of* SKELETONIZE

**skel·e·ton·ize** \-ˌīz\ *transitive verb* **-ized; -iz·ing** (1644)
: to produce in or reduce to skeleton form ⟨*skeletonize* a leaf⟩ ⟨*skeletonize* a news story⟩ ⟨*skeletonize* a regiment⟩

**skel·e·ton·iz·er** \-ˌī-zər\ *noun* (circa 1891)
: any of various lepidopterous larvae that eat the parenchyma of leaves reducing them to a skeleton of veins

**skeleton key** *noun* (1810)
: a key with a large part of the bit filed away to enable it to open low quality locks as a master key

**skel·lum** \'ske-ləm\ *noun* [Dutch *schelm*, from Low German; akin to Old High German *skelmo* person deserving death] (1611)
*chiefly Scottish* : SCOUNDREL, RASCAL

¹**skelp** \'skelp\ *verb* **skelped** \'skelpt\ *also* **skel·pit** \'skel-pət\; **skelp·ing** [Middle English] (15th century)
*transitive verb*
*dialect British* : STRIKE, SLAP, BEAT
*intransitive verb*
: to step lively : HUSTLE

²**skelp** *noun* (15th century)
*dialect British* : a smart blow : SLAP

**skel·ter** \'skel-tər\ *intransitive verb* **skeltered; skel·ter·ing** \-t(ə-)riŋ\ [from *-skelter* (in *helter-skelter*)] (1852)

: SCURRY

**Skel·ton·ics** \skel-'tä-niks\ *noun plural* [John *Skelton*] (1898)
: short verses of an irregular meter with two or three stresses sometimes in falling and sometimes in rising rhythm and usually with rhymed couplets

**skep** \'skep\ *noun* [Middle English *skeppe* basket, beehive, from Old English *sceppe* basket, from Old Norse *skeppa* bushel; akin to Old High German *sceffil* bushel, *scaf* tub] (15th century)
: BEEHIVE; *especially* : a domed hive made of twisted straw

**skep·sis** \'skep-səs\ *noun* [New Latin, from Greek *skepsis* examination, doubt, skeptical philosophy, from *skeptesthai*] (circa 1864)
: philosophic doubt as to the objective reality of phenomena; *broadly* : a skeptical outlook or attitude

**skep·tic** \'skep-tik\ *noun* [Latin or Greek; Latin *scepticus*, from Greek *skeptikos*, from *skeptikos* thoughtful, from *skeptesthai* to look, consider — more at SPY] (1587)
**1** : an adherent or advocate of skepticism
**2** : a person disposed to skepticism especially regarding religion or religious principles

**skep·ti·cal** \-ti-kəl\ *adjective* (1639)
: relating to, characteristic of, or marked by skepticism ⟨a *skeptical* listener⟩
— **skep·ti·cal·ly** \-k(ə-)lē\ *adverb*

**skep·ti·cism** \'skep-tə-ˌsi-zəm\ *noun* (1646)
**1** : an attitude of doubt or a disposition to incredulity either in general or toward a particular object
**2 a** : the doctrine that true knowledge or knowledge in a particular area is uncertain **b** : the method of suspended judgment, systematic doubt, or criticism characteristic of skeptics
**3** : doubt concerning basic religious principles (as immortality, providence, and revelation)
**synonym** see UNCERTAINTY

**sker·ry** \'sker-ē\ *noun, plural* **skerries** [of Scandinavian origin; akin to Old Norse *sker* skerry and to Old Norse *ey* island; akin to Latin *aqua* water — more at SCAR, ISLAND] (1612)
: a rocky isle : REEF

**¹sketch** \'skech\ *noun* [Dutch *schets*, from Italian *schizzo*, literally, splash, from *schizzare* to splash, of imitative origin] (1668)
**1 a** : a rough drawing representing the chief features of an object or scene and often made as a preliminary study **b** : a tentative draft (as for a literary work)
**2** : a brief description (as of a person) or outline
**3 a** : a short literary composition somewhat resembling the short story and the essay but intentionally slight in treatment, discursive in style, and familiar in tone **b** : a short instrumental composition usually for piano **c** : a slight theatrical piece having a single scene; *especially* : a comic variety act

**²sketch** (1694)
*transitive verb*
: to make a sketch, rough draft, or outline of
*intransitive verb*
: to draw or paint a sketch
— **sketch·er** *noun*

**sketch·book** \'skech-ˌbuk\ *noun* (1820)
: a book of or for sketches

**sketchy** \'ske-chē\ *adjective* **sketch·i·er; -est** (1805)
**1** : of the nature of a sketch : roughly outlined
**2** : wanting in completeness, clearness, or substance : SLIGHT, SUPERFICIAL
— **sketch·i·ly** \'ske-chə-lē\ *adverb*
— **sketch·i·ness** \'ske-chē-nəs\ *noun*

**¹skew** \'skyü\ *verb* [Middle English, to escape, skew, from Old North French *escuer* to shun, of Germanic origin; akin to Old High German *sciuhen* to frighten off — more at SHY] (15th century)
*intransitive verb*

**1** : to take an oblique course
**2** : to look askance
*transitive verb*
**1** : to make, set, or cut on the skew
**2** : to distort especially from a true value or symmetrical form ⟨*skewed* statistical data⟩

**²skew** *adjective* (1609)
**1** : set, placed, or running obliquely : SLANTING
**2** : more developed on one side or in one direction than another : not symmetrical

**³skew** *noun* (1688)
: a deviation from a straight line : SLANT

**skew·back** \'skyü-ˌbak\ *noun* (1703)
: a course of masonry, a stone, or an iron plate having an inclined face against which the voussoirs of an arch abut

**¹skew·bald** \-ˌbóld\ *adjective* [*skewed* (skewbald) + *bald*] (1654)
*of an animal* : marked with patches of white and any other color but black

**²skewbald** *noun* (1863)
: a skewbald horse

**skew curve** *noun* (circa 1889)
: a curve in three-dimensional space that does not lie in a single plane

**skew distribution** *noun* (circa 1931)
: an unsymmetrical frequency distribution having the mode at a different value from the mean

**¹skew·er** \'skyü-ər, 'skyu(-ə)r\ *noun* [Middle English *skeuier*] (15th century)
**1** : a pin of wood or metal for fastening meat to keep it in form while roasting or to hold small pieces of meat or vegetables for broiling
**2** : any of various things shaped or used like a meat skewer

**²skewer** *transitive verb* (1701)
**1** : to fasten or pierce with or as if with a skewer
**2** : to criticize or ridicule sharply and effectively

**skew lines** *noun plural* (1952)
: straight lines that do not intersect and are not in the same plane

**skew·ness** \'skyü-nəs\ *noun* (1894)
: lack of straightness or symmetry : DISTORTION; *especially* : lack of symmetry in a frequency distribution

**¹ski** \'skē, *British sometimes* 'shē\ *noun, plural* **skis** *also* **ski** [Norwegian, from Old Norse *skīth* stick of wood, ski; akin to Old English *scīd* board, *scēadan* to divide — more at SHED] (1755)
**1 a** : one of a pair of narrow strips of wood, metal, or plastic curving upward in front that are used especially for gliding over snow **b** : WATER SKI
**2** : a piece of material that resembles a ski and is used as a runner on a vehicle

**²ski** *verb* **skied** \'skēd, 'shēd\; **ski·ing** (circa 1890)
*intransitive verb*
: to glide on skis in travel or as a sport
*transitive verb*
: to travel or pass over on skis
— **ski·able** \'skē-ə-bəl\ *adjective*
— **ski·er** *noun*

**skia·gram** \'skī-ə-ˌgram\ *noun* [International Scientific Vocabulary, from Greek *skia* shadow + International Scientific Vocabulary -*gram* — more at SCENE] (1801)
**1** : a figure formed by shading in the outline of a shadow
**2** : RADIOGRAPH

**ski·bob** \'skē-ˌbäb\ *noun* [¹*ski* + ⁷*bob*] (1966)
: a vehicle that resembles a bicycle with two short skis in place of wheels and that is used for gliding downhill over snow by a rider wearing miniature skis for balance
— **ski·bob·ber** \-ˌbä-bər\ *noun*
— **ski·bob·bing** \-ˌbä-biŋ\ *noun*

**ski boot** *noun* (1907)
: a rigid padded shoe that extends just above the ankle, is securely fastened to the foot (as

with laces, buckles, or clasps), and is locked into position in a ski binding

**¹skid** \'skid\ *noun* [perhaps of Scandinavian origin; akin to Old Norse *skīth* stick of wood — more at SKI] (circa 1610)
**1** : one of a group of objects (as planks or logs) used to support or elevate a structure or object
**2** : a wooden fender hung over a ship's side to protect it in handling cargo
**3** : a usually iron shoe or clog attached to a chain and placed under a wheel to prevent its turning when descending a steep hill : DRAG
**4** : a timber, bar, rail, pole, or log used in pairs or sets to form a slideway (as for an incline from a truck to the sidewalk)
**5** : the act of skidding : SLIP, SIDESLIP
**6** : a runner used as a member of the landing gear of an airplane or helicopter
**7 a** *plural* : a route to defeat or downfall ⟨on the *skids*⟩ ⟨his career hit the *skids*⟩ **b** : a losing streak ⟨a five-game *skid*⟩
**8** : a low platform mounted (as on wheels) on which material is set for handling and moving; *also* : PALLET 3
— **skidproof** *adjective*

**²skid** *verb* **skid·ded; skid·ding** (1674)
*transitive verb*
**1** : to apply a brake or skid to : slow or halt by a skid
**2 a** : to haul (as logs) by dragging ⟨cutting and *skidding* firewood⟩ **b** : to haul along, slide, hoist, or store on skids
*intransitive verb*
**1** : to slide without rotating (as a wheel held from turning while a vehicle moves onward)
**2 a** : to fail to grip the roadway; *especially* : to slip sideways on the road **b** *of an airplane* : to slide sideways away from the center of curvature when turning **c** : SLIDE, SLIP
**3** : to fall rapidly, steeply, or far

**skid·der** \'ski-dər\ *noun* (1870)
**1** : one that skids or uses a skid
**2** : a tractor used especially for hauling logs

**skid·doo** *or* **ski·doo** \ski-'dü, skē-\ *intransitive verb* [probably alteration of *skedaddle*] (1903)
: to go away : DEPART

**skid·dy** \'ski-dē\ *adjective* **skid·di·er; -est** (1902)
: likely to skid or cause skidding ⟨a wet *skiddy* road⟩

**skid road** *noun* (1880)
**1** : a road along which logs are skidded
**2 a** *West* : the part of a town frequented by loggers **b** : SKID ROW

**skid row** \-'rō\ *noun* [alteration of *skid road*] (circa 1931)
: a district of cheap saloons and flophouses frequented by vagrants and alcoholics

**ski·ey** *variant of* SKYEY

**skiff** \'skif\ *noun* [Middle English *skif*, from Middle French or Old Italian; Middle French *esquif*, from Old Italian *schifo*, of Germanic origin; akin to Old English *scip* ship] (15th century)
: any of various small boats; *especially* : a flat-bottomed rowboat

**skif·fle** \'ski-fəl\ *noun* [origin unknown] (1926)
: American jazz or folk music played entirely or in part on nonstandard instruments (as jugs, washboards, or Jew's harps); *also* : a derivative form of music formerly popular in Great Britain featuring vocals with a simple instrumental accompaniment

**ski·ing** *noun* (1893)
: the art or sport of sliding and jumping on skis

**ski·jor·ing** \'skē-ˌjōr-iŋ, -ˌjor-, (ˌ)skē-'\ *noun* [modification of Norwegian *skikjøring*, from *ski* + *kjøring* driving] (1910)
: a winter sport in which a person wearing skis is drawn over snow or ice (as by a horse or vehicle)

**ski jump** *noun* (1907)

: a jump made by a person wearing skis; *also*
: a course or track especially prepared for such jumping
— **ski jump** *intransitive verb*
— **ski jumper** *noun*
**skil·ful** *chiefly British variant of* SKILLFUL
**ski lift** *noun* (1939)
: a motor-driven conveyor consisting usually of a series of bars or seats suspended from an overhead moving cable and used for transporting skiers or sightseers up a long slope
¹**skill** \'skil\ *intransitive verb* [Middle English *skilen,* from Old Norse *skilja* to separate, divide; akin to Old Norse *skil* distinction] (13th century)
*archaic* : to make a difference : MATTER, AVAIL
²**skill** *noun* [Middle English *skil,* from Old Norse, distinction, knowledge; probably akin to Old English *scylian* to separate, *sciell* shell — more at SHELL] (13th century)
**1** *obsolete* : CAUSE, REASON
**2 a** : the ability to use one's knowledge effectively and readily in execution or performance **b** : dexterity or coordination especially in the execution of learned physical tasks
**3** : a learned power of doing something competently : a developed aptitude or ability ⟨language *skills*⟩
*synonym* see ART
— **skill–less** *or* **skil·less** \'skil-ləs\ *adjective*
— **skill–less·ness** *or* **skil·less·ness** *noun*
**skilled** \'skild\ *adjective* (1552)
**1** : having acquired mastery of or skill in something (as a technique or a trade)
**2** : of, relating to, or requiring workers or labor with skill and training in a particular occupation, craft, or trade
*synonym* see PROFICIENT
**skil·let** \'ski-lət\ *noun* [Middle English *skelet*] (15th century)
**1** *chiefly British* : a small kettle or pot usually having three or four often long feet and used for cooking on the hearth
**2** : FRYING PAN
**skill·ful** \'skil-fəl\ *adjective* (14th century)
**1** : possessed of or displaying skill : EXPERT
**2** : accomplished with skill
*synonym* see PROFICIENT
— **skill·ful·ly** \-fə-lē\ *adverb*
— **skill·ful·ness** *noun*
**skil·ling** \'ski-liŋ, 'shi-\ *noun* [Swedish, Norwegian, & Danish, from Old Norse *skillingr,* a gold coin; akin to Old English *scilling* shilling] (1793)
: any of various old Scandinavian units of value or the coins representing them
¹**skim** \'skim\ *verb* **skimmed; skim·ming** [Middle English *skymmen*] (14th century)
*transitive verb*
**1 a** : to clear (a liquid) of scum or floating substance ⟨*skim* boiling syrup⟩ **b** : to remove (as film or scum) from the surface of a liquid **c** : to remove cream from by skimming **d** : to remove the best or most easily obtainable contents from
**2** : to read, study, or examine superficially and rapidly; *especially* : to glance through (as a book) for the chief ideas or the plot
**3** : to throw in a gliding path; *especially* : to throw so as to ricochet along the surface of water
**4** : to cover with or as if with a film, scum, or coat
**5** : to pass swiftly or lightly over
**6** : to remove or conceal (as a portion of casino profits) to avoid payment of taxes
*intransitive verb*
**1 a** : to pass lightly or hastily : glide or skip along, above, or near a surface **b** : to give a cursory glance, consideration, or reading
**2** : to become coated with a thin layer of film or scum
**3** : to put on a finishing coat of plaster
²**skim** *noun* (14th century)

**1** : a thin layer, coating, or film
**2** : the act of skimming
**3** : something skimmed; *specifically* : SKIM MILK
³**skim** *adjective* (1794)
**1** : having the cream removed by skimming
**2** : made of skim milk ⟨*skim* cheese⟩
**ski mask** *noun* (1966)
: a knit fabric mask that covers the head, has openings for the eyes, mouth, and sometimes the nose, and is worn especially by skiers for protection from the cold
**skim·ble–skam·ble** \,skim-bəl-'skam-bəl\ *adjective* [reduplication of English dialect *scamble* to stumble along] (1596)
: rambling and confused : SENSELESS
**skim·mer** \'ski-mər\ *noun* (14th century)
**1** : one that skims; *specifically* : a flat perforated scoop or spoon used for skimming
**2** : any of a small genus (*Rynchops*) of long-winged marine birds that have the lower mandible longer than the upper
**3** : a usually straw flat-crowned hat with a wide straight brim
**4** : a fitted sleeveless dress with a usually flaring skirt
**skim milk** *noun* (1596)
: milk from which the cream has been taken — called also *skimmed milk*
**skimming** *noun* (15th century)
: that which is skimmed from a liquid
**ski·mo·bile** \'skē-mō-,bēl\ *noun* (1944)
: SNOWMOBILE
¹**skimp** \'skimp\ *adjective* [perhaps alteration of *scrimp*] (1775)
: SKIMPY
²**skimp** (circa 1879)
*transitive verb*
: to give insufficient or barely sufficient attention or effort to or funds for
*intransitive verb*
: to save by or as if by skimping
**skimpy** \'skim-pē\ *adjective* **skimp·i·er; -est** (1842)
: deficient in supply or execution especially through skimping : SCANTY
*synonym* see MEAGER
— **skimp·i·ly** \-pə-lē\ *adverb*
— **skimp·i·ness** \-pē-nəs\ *noun*
¹**skin** \'skin\ *noun, often attributive* [Middle English, from Old Norse *skinn;* akin to Old English *scinn* skin, Middle High German *schint* fruit peel] (13th century)
**1 a** (1) : the integument of an animal (as a fur-bearing mammal or a bird) separated from the body usually with its hair or feathers (2) : a usually unmounted specimen of a vertebrate (as in a museum) **b** : the hide or pelt of a game or domestic animal **c** (1) : the pelt of an animal prepared for use as a trimming or in a garment — compare ⁴HIDE (2) : a sheet of parchment or vellum made from a hide (3) : BOTTLE 1b
**2 a** : the external limiting tissue layer of an animal body especially when forming a tough but flexible cover relatively impermeable from without while intact **b** : any of various outer or surface layers (as a rind, husk, or pellicle)
**3** : the life or physical well-being of a person ⟨saved his own *skin*⟩
**4** : a sheathing or casing forming the outside surface of a structure (as a ship or airplane)
— **skin·less** \-ləs\ *adjective*
— **by the skin of one's teeth** : by a very narrow margin
— **under one's skin** : so deeply penetrative as to irritate, stimulate, provoke thought, or otherwise excite
— **under the skin** : beneath apparent or surface differences : at heart
²**skin** *verb* **skinned; skin·ning** (14th century)
*transitive verb*

**1 a** : to strip, scrape, or rub off an outer covering (as the skin or rind) of **b** : to strip or peel off **c** : to cut, chip, or damage the surface of ⟨fell and *skinned* my knee⟩
**2 a** : to cover with or as if with skin **b** : to heal over with skin
**3 a** : to strip of money or property : FLEECE **b** : to defeat badly **c** : CENSURE, CASTIGATE
**4** : to urge on and direct the course of (as a draft animal)
*intransitive verb*
**1** : to become covered with or as if with skin
**2 a** : SHIN 1 **b** : to pass or get by with scant room to spare
³**skin** *adjective* (circa 1935)
: involving subjects who are nude ⟨expected to conduct *skin* searches for weapons —Diane K. Shah⟩; *especially* : devoted to showing nudes ⟨*skin* magazines⟩
**skin–deep** \'skin-'dēp\ *adjective* (1613)
**1** : as deep as the skin
**2** : not thorough or lasting in impression : SUPERFICIAL
**skin diving** *noun* (1938)
: the sport of swimming under water with a face mask and flippers and especially without a portable breathing device
— **skin–dive** *intransitive verb*
— **skin diver** *noun*
**skin effect** *noun* (1891)
: an effect characteristic of current distribution in a conductor at high frequencies by virtue of which the current density is greater near the surface of the conductor than in its interior
**skin·flint** \'skin-,flint\ *noun* (circa 1700)
: a person who would save, gain, or extort money by any means : MISER, NIGGARD
**skin·ful** \-,fùl\ *noun* (1788)
**1** : a large or satisfying quantity especially of liquor
**2** : the contents of a skin bottle
**skin game** *noun* (1868)
: a swindling game or trick
**skin graft** *noun* (1871)
: a piece of skin that is taken from a donor area to replace skin in a defective or denuded area (as one that has been burned)
— **skin grafting** *noun*
**skin·head** \'skin-,hed\ *noun* (circa 1953)
**1** : a person whose hair is cut very short
**2** : a usually white male belonging to any of various sometimes violent youth gangs whose members have close-shaven hair and often espouse white-supremacist beliefs
¹**skink** \'skiŋk\ *transitive verb* [Middle English, from Middle Dutch *schenken;* akin to Old English *scencan* to pour out drink and probably to *scanca* shank] (15th century)
*chiefly dialect* : to draw, pour out, or serve (drink)
²**skink** *noun* [Latin *scincus,* from Greek *skinkos*] (1590)
: any of a family (Scincidae) of typically small insectivorous lizards with long tapering bodies
**skink·er** \'skiŋ-kər\ *noun* (1586)
: one that serves liquor : BARTENDER
**skinned** \'skind\ *adjective* (15th century)
: having skin especially of a specified kind — usually used in combination ⟨dark-*skinned*⟩
**skin·ner** \'ski-nər\ *noun* (14th century)
**1 a** : one that deals in skins, pelts, or hides **b** : one that removes, cures, or dresses skins
**2** : SHARPER
**3** : a driver of draft animals : TEAMSTER
**Skin·ner box** \'ski-nər-,bäks\ *noun* [B. F. *Skinner*] (1940)
: a laboratory apparatus in which an animal is caged for experiments in operant conditioning and which typically contains a lever that must

---

\ə\ abut \ᵊ\ kitten \ər\ further \a\ ash \ā\ ace
\ä\ mop, mar \aù\ out \ch\ chin \e\ bet \ē\ easy
\g\ go \i\ hit \ī\ ice \j\ job \ŋ\ sing \ō\ go
\ò\ law \òi\ boy \th\ thin \t̲h̲\ the \ü\ loot \ù\ foot
\y\ yet \zh\ vision    *see also* Guide to Pronunciation

be pressed by the animal to gain reward or avoid punishment

**¹skin·ny** \'ski-nē\ *adjective* **skin·ni·er; -est** (1573)
**1 :** resembling skin **:** MEMBRANOUS
**2 a :** lacking sufficient flesh **:** very thin **:** EMACIATED **b :** lacking usual or desirable bulk, quantity, qualities, or significance
*synonym* see LEAN
— **skin·ni·ness** *noun*

**²skinny** *noun* [perhaps from ¹*skin* + ⁴-y] (1938)
*slang* **:** inside information **:** DOPE 〈the straight *skinny* on what's going on —John Geary〉

**skin·ny–dip** \'ski-nē-ˌdip\ *intransitive verb* (1964)
**:** to swim in the nude
— **skinny–dip** *noun*
— **skin·ny–dip·per** \-ˌdi-pər\ *noun*

**skin–pop** \'skin-ˌpäp\ (circa 1952)
*intransitive verb*
**:** to inject a drug subcutaneously rather than into a vein
*transitive verb*
**:** to inject (a drug) by skin-popping
— **skin–pop·per** \-ˌpä-pər\ *noun*

**skint** \'skint\ *adjective* [alteration of *skinned*, past participle of ²*skin*] (circa 1925)
*chiefly British* **:** PENNILESS

**skin test** *noun* (1925)
**:** a test (as a scratch test) performed on the skin and used in detecting allergic hypersensitivity

**skin·tight** \'skin-ˈtīt\ *adjective* (1885)
**:** closely fitted to the figure

**¹skip** \'skip\ *verb* **skipped; skip·ping** [Middle English *skippen*, perhaps of Scandinavian origin; akin to Swedish dialect *skopa* to hop] (14th century)
*intransitive verb*
**1 a :** to move or proceed with leaps and bounds or with a skip **b :** to bound off one point after another **:** RICOCHET
**2 :** to leave hurriedly or secretly 〈*skipped* out without paying their bill〉
**3 a :** to pass over or omit an interval, item, or step **b :** to omit a grade in school in advancing to the next **c :** MISFIRE 1
*transitive verb*
**1 a :** to pass over without notice or mention **:** OMIT **b :** to pass by or leave out (a step in a progression or series)
**2 a :** to cause to skip (a grade in school) **b :** to cause to bound or skim over a surface 〈*skip* a stone across a pond〉
**3 :** to leap over lightly and nimbly
**4 a :** to depart from quickly and secretly 〈*skipped* town〉 **b :** to fail to attend or participate in 〈*skip* the tournament〉 〈*skip* the meeting〉
— **skip·pa·ble** \'ski-pə-bəl\ *adjective*
— **skip bail :** to jump bail
— **skip rope :** to use a jump rope (as for exercise or a game)

**²skip** *noun* (15th century)
**1 a :** a light bounding step **b :** a gait composed of alternating hops and steps
**2 :** an act of omission or the thing omitted

**³skip** *noun* [short for ²*skipper*] (1830)
**1 :** the captain of a side in a game (as curling or lawn bowling) who advises the team as to the play and controls the action
**2 :** ²SKIPPER

**⁴skip** *transitive verb* **skipped; skip·ping** (1900)
**:** to act as skipper of

**skip bomb** *transitive verb* (1943)
**:** to attack by releasing delayed-action bombs from a low-flying airplane so that they skip along a land or water surface and strike a target

**skip·jack** \'skip-ˌjak\ *noun, plural* **skip·jacks** *or* **skipjack** (1703)
**1 :** any of various fishes (as a ladyfish or bluefish) that jump above or are active at the surface of the water; *especially* **:** SKIPJACK TUNA

**2 :** a sailboat with vertical sides and a bottom similar to a flat V

**skipjack tuna** *noun* (1950)
**:** a relatively small scombroid food and sport fish (*Katsuwonus pelamis* synonym *Euthynnus pelamis*) that is bluish above and silvery below with oblique dark stripes on the sides and belly

**ski pole** *noun* (1920)
**:** one of a pair of lightweight poles used in skiing that have a handgrip and usually a wrist strap at one end and an encircling disk set above the point at the other end

**¹skip·per** \'ski-pər\ *noun* (13th century)
**1 :** any of various erratically active insects (as a click beetle or a water strider)
**2 :** one that skips
**3 :** SAURY
**4 :** any of a superfamily (Hesperioidea, especially family Hesperiidae) of stout-bodied lepidopterous insects that differ from the typical butterflies especially in wing venation and the form of the antennae

**²skipper** *noun* [Middle English, from Middle Dutch *schipper*, from *schip* ship; akin to Old English *scip* ship — more at SHIP] (14th century)
**1 :** the master of a ship; *especially* **:** the master of a fishing, small trading, or pleasure boat
**2 :** the captain or first pilot of an airplane
**3 :** a person in a position of leadership; *especially* **:** a baseball team's manager

**³skip·per** *transitive verb* **skip·pered; skip·per·ing** \'ski-p(ə-)riŋ\ (1893)
**1 :** to act as skipper of (as a boat)
**2 :** to act as coach of (as a team)

**¹skirl** \'skər(-ə)l, 'skir(-ə)l\ *verb* [Middle English (Scots) *skrillen, skirlen* to scream, shriek, of Scandinavian origin; akin to Old Swedish *skrælla* to rattle; akin to Old English *scrallettan* to resound loudly] (circa 1665)
*intransitive verb*
*of a bagpipe* **:** to emit the high shrill tone of the chanter; *also* **:** to give forth music
*transitive verb*
**:** to play (music) on the bagpipe

**²skirl** *noun* (1856)
**:** a high shrill sound produced by the chanter of a bagpipe

**¹skir·mish** \'skər-mish\ *noun* [Middle English *skyrmissh*, alteration of *skarmish*, from Middle French *escarmouche*, from Old Italian *scaramuccia*] (14th century)
**1 :** a minor fight in war usually incidental to larger movements
**2 a :** a brisk preliminary verbal conflict **b :** a minor dispute or contest between opposing parties

**²skirmish** *intransitive verb* (14th century)
**1 :** to engage in a skirmish
**2 :** to search about (as for supplies) **:** scout around
— **skir·mish·er** *noun*

**¹skirr** \'skər, 'skir\ *verb* [perhaps alteration of ³*scour*] (circa 1548)
*intransitive verb*
**1 :** to leave hastily **:** FLEE 〈birds *skirred* off from the bushes —D. H. Lawrence〉
**2 :** to run, fly, sail, or move along rapidly
*transitive verb*
**1 :** to search about in 〈*skirr* the country round —Shakespeare〉
**2 a :** to pass rapidly over **:** SKIM **b** *dialect* **:** to cause to skim

**²skirr** *noun* [probably imitative] (circa 1870)
**:** WHIR, ROAR

**¹skirt** \'skərt\ *noun* [Middle English, from Old Norse *skyrta* shirt, kirtle — more at SHIRT] (14th century)
**1 a** (1) **:** a free-hanging part of an outer garment or undergarment extending from the waist down (2) **:** a separate free-hanging outer garment or undergarment usually worn by women and girls covering some or all of the

body from the waist down **b :** either of two usually leather flaps on a saddle covering the bars on which the stirrups are hung **c :** a cloth facing that hangs loosely and usually in folds or pleats from the bottom edge or across the front of a piece of furniture **d :** the lower branches of a tree when near the ground
**2 a :** the rim, periphery, or environs of an area **b** *plural* **:** outlying parts (as of a town or city)
**3 :** a part or attachment serving as a rim, border, or edging
**4 :** a girl or woman
— **skirt·ed** *adjective*

**²skirt** (1602)
*transitive verb*
**1 :** to form or run along the border or edge of **:** BORDER
**2 a :** to provide a skirt for **b :** to furnish a border or shield for
**3 a :** to go or pass around or about; *specifically* **:** to go around or keep away from in order to avoid danger or discovery **b :** to avoid especially because of difficulty or fear of controversy 〈*skirted* the issue〉 **c :** to evade or miss by a narrow margin 〈having *skirted* disaster —Edith Wharton〉
*intransitive verb*
**:** to be, lie, or move along an edge or border
— **skirt·er** *noun*

**skirt·ing** \'skər-tiŋ\ *noun* (1764)
**1 :** something that skirts: as **a :** BORDER, EDGING **b** *chiefly British* **:** BASEBOARD
**2 :** fabric suitable for skirts

**skirt steak** *noun* (circa 1909)
**:** a boneless strip of beef cut from the plate

**ski run** *noun* (1924)
**:** a slope or trail suitable for skiing

**skit** \'skit\ *noun* [origin unknown] (circa 1727)
**1 :** a jeering or satirical remark **:** TAUNT
**2 a :** a satirical or humorous story or sketch **b** (1) **:** a brief burlesque or comic sketch included in a dramatic performance (as a revue) (2) **:** a short serious dramatic piece; *especially* **:** one done by amateurs

**ski touring** *noun* (1935)
**:** cross-country skiing for pleasure

**ski tow** *noun* (1935)
**1 :** a motor-driven conveyor that is used for pulling skiers up a slope and that consists usually of an endless moving rope which a skier grasps
**2 :** SKI LIFT

**skit·ter** \'ski-tər\ *verb* [probably frequentative of English dialect *skite* to move quickly] (1845)
*intransitive verb*
**1 :** to glide or skip lightly or quickly
**2 :** to twitch the hook of a fishing line through or along the surface of water
*transitive verb*
**:** to cause to skitter

**skit·tery** \'ski-tə-rē\ *adjective* (1941)
**:** SKITTISH

**skit·tish** \'ski-tish\ *adjective* [Middle English] (15th century)
**1 a :** lively or frisky in action **:** CAPRICIOUS **b :** VARIABLE, FLUCTUATING
**2 :** easily frightened **:** RESTIVE 〈a *skittish* horse〉
**3 a :** COY, BASHFUL **b :** marked by extreme caution **:** WARY
— **skit·tish·ly** *adverb*
— **skit·tish·ness** *noun*

**skit·tle** \'ski-t°l\ *noun* [perhaps of Scandinavian origin; akin to Old Norse *skutill* bolt — more at SHUTTLE] (1634)
**1** *plural but singular in construction* **:** English ninepins played with a wooden disk or ball
**2 :** one of the pins used in skittles

**skive** \'skīv\ *transitive verb* **skived; skiv·ing** [probably of Scandinavian origin; akin to Old Norse *skīfa* to slice] (circa 1825)
**:** to cut off (as leather or rubber) in thin layers or pieces **:** PARE

**skiv·er** \'skī-vər\ *noun* (1800)

**1 :** a thin soft leather made of the grain side of a split sheepskin, usually tanned in sumac and dyed
**2 :** one that skives something (as leather)
**Skiv·vies** \'ski-vēz\ *trademark*
— used for men's underwear
**skiv·vy** \'ski-vē\ *noun, plural* **skivvies** [origin unknown] (circa 1902)
*British* **:** a female domestic servant
**ski·wear** \'skē-ˌwar, -ˌwer\ *noun* (1961)
**·** clothing suitable for wear while skiing
**sklent** \'sklent\ *verb* [Middle English *sclenten* to strike obliquely, alteration of *slenten* — more at SLANT] (1805)
*intransitive verb*
**1** *chiefly Scottish* **:** to look askance
**2** *chiefly Scottish* **:** to cast aspersions
*transitive verb*
*Scottish* **:** to direct sideways **:** SLANT
**skoal** \'skōl\ *noun* [Danish *skaal,* literally, cup; akin to Old Norse *skāl* bowl — more at SCALE] (1600)
**:** TOAST, HEALTH — often used interjectionally
**skosh** \'skōsh\ *noun* [Japanese *sukoshi*] (1952)
**:** a small amount **:** BIT, SMIDGEN — used adverbially with *a* ⟨just a *skosh* bit shook —Josiah Bunting⟩
**skua** \'skyü-ə\ *noun* [New Latin, from Faeroese *skúgvur;* akin to Old Norse *skūfr* tassel, skua, Old English *scēaf* sheaf — more at SHEAF] (1678)
**:** either of two seabirds related to the jaegers:
**a :** GREAT SKUA **b :** a bird (*Catharacta maccormicki*) that resembles but is slightly smaller than the great skua and that breeds in the Antarctic
**skul·dug·gery** *or* **skull·dug·gery** \ˌskəl-'də-g(ə-)rē, 'skəl-ˌ\ *noun, plural* **-ger·ies** [origin unknown] (1867)
**:** a devious device or trick; *also* **:** underhanded or unscrupulous behavior
**¹skulk** \'skəlk\ *intransitive verb* [Middle English, of Scandinavian origin; akin to Danish *skulke* to shirk, play truant] (13th century)
**1 :** to move in a stealthy or furtive manner
**2 a :** to hide or conceal something (as oneself) often out of cowardice or fear or with sinister intent **b** *chiefly British* **:** MALINGER
**synonym** see LURK
— **skulk·er** *noun*
**²skulk** *noun* (14th century)
**1 :** one that skulks
**2 :** a group of foxes
**skull** \'skəl\ *noun* [Middle English *skulle,* of Scandinavian origin; akin to Swedish *skulle* skull] (13th century)
**1 :** the skeleton of the head of a vertebrate forming a bony or cartilaginous case that encloses and protects the brain and chief sense organs and supports the jaws
**2 :** the seat of understanding or intelligence **:** MIND
— **skulled** \'skəld\ *adjective*
**skull and cross·bones** \-'kròs-ˌbōnz\ *noun, plural* **skulls and crossbones** (1826)
**:** a representation of a human skull over crossbones usually used as a warning of danger to life
**skull·cap** \'skəl-ˌkap\ *noun* (1682)
**1 :** a close-fitting cap; *especially* **:** a light cap without brim for indoor wear
**2 :** any of various mints (genus *Scutellaria*) having a calyx that when inverted resembles a helmet
**3 :** the upper portion of the skull **:** CALVARIUM
**skull session** *noun* (1937)
**1 :** a strategy class for an athletic team
**2 :** a meeting for consultation, discussion, or the interchange of ideas or information — called also *skull practice*
**¹skunk** \'skəŋk\ *noun, plural* **skunks** *also* **skunk** [of Algonquian origin; akin to Eastern Abenaki *seganḱ8* skunk] (1634)
**1 a :** any of various common omnivorous black-and-white New World mammals (especially genus *Mephitis*) of the weasel family

that have a pair of perineal glands from which a secretion of pungent and offensive odor is ejected **b :** the fur of a skunk
**2 :** an obnoxious or disliked person
**²skunk** *transitive verb* (1843)
**1 a :** DEFEAT **b :** to shut out in a game
**2 :** to fail to pay; *also* **:** CHEAT
**skunk cabbage** *noun* (1751)
**:** either of two North American perennial herbs of the arum family that occur in shaded wet to swampy areas and have a fetid odor suggestive of a skunk: **a :** one (*Symplocarpus foetidus*) of eastern North America that sends up in spring a cowl-shaped brownish purple spathe **b :** one (*Lysichitum*

skunk cabbage

*americana*) chiefly of the Pacific coast region that has a large yellow spathe
**skunk works** *noun plural but singular or plural in construction* [from the *Skonk Works,* illicit distillery in the comic strip *Li'l Abner* by Al Capp] (circa 1974)
**:** a usually small and often isolated department or facility (as for engineering research and development) that functions with minimal supervision within a company or corporation
**¹sky** \'skī\ *noun, plural* **skies** [Middle English, cloud, sky, from Old Norse *skȳ* cloud; akin to Old English *scēo* cloud] (13th century)
**1 :** the upper atmosphere or expanse of space that constitutes an apparent great vault or arch over the earth
**2 :** HEAVEN 2
**3 a :** weather in the upper atmosphere **b :** CLIMATE ⟨temperate English *skies* —G. G. Coulton⟩
**²sky** *transitive verb* **skied** *or* **skyed; sky·ing** (1802)
**1** *chiefly British* **:** to throw or toss up **:** FLIP
**2 :** to hang (as a painting) above the line of vision
**3 :** to hit (a ball) high into the air
**sky blue** *noun* (1738)
**:** a pale to light blue color
**sky·borne** \'skī-ˌbōrn, -ˌbòrn\ *adjective* (1589)
**:** AIRBORNE ⟨*skyborne* troops⟩
**sky·box** \-ˌbäks\ *noun* (1974)
**:** a roofed enclosure of private seats situated high in a sports stadium and typically featuring luxurious amenities
**sky·cap** \-ˌkap\ *noun* [¹*sky* + *-cap* (as in *redcap*)] (1941)
**:** one employed to carry hand luggage at an airport — compare REDCAP
**sky·div·ing** \-ˌdī-viŋ\ *noun* (1957)
**:** the sport of jumping from an airplane at a moderate altitude (as 6000 feet) and executing various body maneuvers before pulling the rip cord of a parachute
— **sky diver** *noun*
**Skye terrier** \'skī-\ *noun* [*Skye,* Scotland] (1847)
**:** any of a Scottish breed of terriers with a long low body and long straight coat
**sky·ey** \'skī-ē\ *adjective* (1603)
**:** of or resembling the sky **:** ETHEREAL
**¹sky–high** \'skī-'hī\ *adverb* (1818)
**1 a :** high into the air **b :** to a high or exorbitant level or degree
**2 :** in an enthusiastic manner
**3 :** to bits **:** APART ⟨blown *sky-high*⟩
**²sky–high** *adjective* (1945)
**:** excessively expensive **:** EXORBITANT
**sky·hook** \-ˌhùk\ *noun* (1915)
**:** a hook conceived as being suspended from the sky
**sky·jack** \'skī-ˌjak\ *transitive verb* [¹*sky* + *-jack* (as in *hijack*)] (1961)

**:** to commandeer (an airplane in flight) by the threat of violence
— **sky·jack·er** \-ˌja-kər\ *noun*
— **sky·jack·ing** \-kiŋ\ *noun*
**¹sky·lark** \'skī-ˌlärk\ *noun* (1686)
**1 :** a common largely brown Old World lark (*Alauda arvensis*) noted for its song especially as uttered in flight
**2 :** any of various birds resembling the skylark
**²skylark** *intransitive verb* (1809)
**1 :** to run up and down the rigging of a ship in sport
**2 :** FROLIC, SPORT
— **sky·lark·er** *noun*
**sky·light** \'skī-ˌlīt\ *noun* (1679)
**1 :** the diffused and reflected light of the sky
**2 :** an opening in a house roof or ship's deck that is covered with translucent or transparent material and that is designed to admit light
**sky·light·ed** \-ˌlī-təd\ *also* **sky·lit** \-ˌlit\ *adjective* (1849)
**:** having a skylight
**sky·line** \-ˌlīn\ *noun* (1824)
**1 :** the apparent juncture of earth and sky **:** HORIZON
**2 :** an outline (as of buildings or a mountain range) against the background of the sky
**sky marshal** *noun* (1968)
**:** an armed federal plainclothesman assigned to prevent skyjackings
**sky pilot** *noun* (1883)
**:** CLERGYMAN; *specifically* **:** CHAPLAIN
**¹sky·rock·et** \'skī-ˌrä-kət\ *noun* (1688)
**:** ²ROCKET 1a
**²skyrocket** (1851)
*transitive verb*
**1 :** to cause to rise or increase abruptly and rapidly
**2 :** CATAPULT
*intransitive verb*
**:** to shoot up abruptly ⟨prices are *skyrocketing*⟩
**sky·sail** \'skī-ˌsāl, -səl\ *noun* (1829)
**:** the sail above the royal
**sky·scrap·er** \-ˌskrā-pər\ *noun* (1883)
**:** a very tall building
**sky·walk** \-ˌwók\ *noun* (1953)
**:** a usually enclosed aerial walkway connecting two buildings
**sky·ward** \-wərd\ *adverb* (1582)
**1 :** toward the sky
**2 :** UPWARD
**sky wave** *noun* (1928)
**:** a radio wave that is propagated by means of the ionosphere
**sky·way** \'skī-ˌwā\ *noun* (1919)
**1 :** a route used by airplanes **:** AIR LANE
**2 :** an elevated highway
**3 :** SKYWALK
**sky·write** \-ˌrīt\ *verb* **-wrote** \-ˌrōt\; **-written** \-ˌri-t²n\; **-writ·ing** \-ˌrī-tiŋ\ [back-formation from *skywriting*] (1926)
*transitive verb*
**:** to letter by skywriting
*intransitive verb*
**:** to do skywriting
— **sky·writ·er** *noun*
**sky·writ·ing** \-ˌrī-tiŋ\ *noun* (1922)
**:** writing formed in the sky by means of a visible substance (as smoke) emitted from an airplane
**¹slab** \'slab\ *noun* [Middle English *slabbe*] (14th century)
**1 :** a thick plate or slice (as of stone, wood, or bread): as **a :** the outside piece cut from a log in squaring it **b :** concrete pavement (as of a road); *specifically* **:** a strip of concrete pavement laid as a single unjointed piece **c** (1) **:** a flat rectangular architectural element that is usually formed of a single piece or mass ⟨a

concrete foundation *slab*⟩ (2) **:** a rectangular building having little width with respect to its length and usually height **2 :** something that resembles a slab (as in size) ⟨backed up by a solid *slab* of reference material —*Times Literary Supplement*⟩ — **slab·like** \-ₗlīk\ *adjective*

²**slab** *transitive verb* **slabbed; slab·bing** (1703) **1 a :** to remove an outer slab from (as a log) **b :** to divide or form into slabs **2 :** to cover or support (as a roadbed or roof) with slabs **3 :** to put on thickly

³**slab** *adjective* [probably of Scandinavian origin; akin to obsolete Danish *slab* slippery] (1605) *dialect chiefly English* **:** THICK, VISCOUS

¹**slab·ber** \'sla-bər\ *verb* **slab·bered; slab·ber·ing** \-b(ə-)riŋ\ [probably from Dutch *slabberen*, frequentative of *slabben* to slaver — more at SLAVER] (1542) **:** SLOBBER, DROOL

²**slabber** *noun* (1718) **:** SLOBBER, SLAVER

**slab–sid·ed** \'slab-'sī-dəd\ *adjective* (1817) **:** having flat sides; *also* **:** being tall or long and lank

¹**slack** \'slak\ *adjective* [Middle English *slak*, from Old English *sleac;* akin to Old High German *slah* slack, Latin *laxus* slack, loose, *languēre* to languish, Greek *lagnos* lustful and perhaps to Greek *lēgein* to stop] (before 12th century) **1 :** not using due diligence, care, or dispatch **:** NEGLIGENT **2 a :** characterized by slowness, sluggishness, or lack of energy ⟨a *slack* pace⟩ **b :** moderate in some quality; *especially* **:** moderately warm ⟨a *slack* oven⟩ **c :** blowing or flowing at low speed ⟨the tide was *slack*⟩ **3 a :** not tight or taut ⟨a *slack* rope⟩ **b :** lacking in usual or normal firmness and steadiness **:** WEAK ⟨*slack* muscles⟩ ⟨*slack* supervision⟩ **4 :** wanting in activity **:** DULL ⟨a *slack* market⟩ **5 :** lacking in completeness, finish, or perfection ⟨a very *slack* piece of work⟩ *synonym* see NEGLIGENT — **slack·ly** *adverb* — **slack·ness** *noun*

²**slack** (13th century) *intransitive verb* **1 :** to be or become slack **2 :** to shirk or evade work or duty *transitive verb* **1 a :** to be slack or negligent in performing or doing **b :** LESSEN, MODERATE **2 :** to release tension on **:** LOOSEN **3 a :** to cause to abate **b :** SLAKE 3

³**slack** *noun* (1756) **1 :** cessation in movement or flow **2 :** a part of something that hangs loose without strain ⟨take up the *slack* of a rope⟩ **3 :** trousers especially for casual wear — usually used in plural **4 :** a dull season or period **5 a :** a part that is available but not used ⟨some *slack* in the budget⟩ **b :** a part that is wanted but not supplied **:** SHORTFALL ⟨take up the *slack* in supplying oil⟩

⁴**slack** *noun* [Middle English *slak*, from Old Norse *slakki*] (14th century) *dialect English* **:** a pass between hills

⁵**slack** *noun* [Middle English *sleck*] (15th century) **:** the finest screenings of coal produced at a mine unusable as fuel unless cleaned

**slack·en** \'sla-kən\ *verb* **slack·ened; slack·en·ing** \'sla-kᵊn-iŋ\ (15th century) *transitive verb* **1 :** to make less active **:** slow up ⟨*slacken* speed at a crossing⟩ **2 :** to make slack (as by lessening tension or firmness) ⟨*slacken* sail⟩ *intransitive verb*

**1 :** to become slack or slow or negligent **:** slow down **2 :** to become less active **:** SLACK *synonym* see DELAY

**slack·er** \'sla-kər\ *noun* (1898) **:** a person who shirks work or obligation; *especially* **:** one who evades military service in time of war

**slack water** *noun* (circa 1769) **:** the period at the turn of the tide when there is little or no horizontal motion of tidal water — called also *slack tide*

**slag** \'slag\ *noun* [Middle Low German *slagge*] (1552) **:** the dross or scoria of a metal

**slain** *past participle of* SLAY

**slake** \'slāk, *intransitive verb* 2 & *transitive verb* 3 are also* 'slak\ *verb* **slaked; slak·ing** [Middle English, from Old English *slacian*, from *sleac* slack] (14th century) *intransitive verb* **1** *archaic* **:** SUBSIDE, ABATE **2 :** to become slaked **:** CRUMBLE ⟨lime may *slake* spontaneously in moist air⟩ *transitive verb* **1** *archaic* **:** to lessen the force of **:** MODERATE **2 :** SATISFY, QUENCH ⟨*slake* your thirst⟩ ⟨will *slake* your curiosity⟩ **3 :** to cause (as lime) to heat and crumble by treatment with water **:** HYDRATE

¹**sla·lom** \'slä-ləm\ *noun, often attributive* [Norwegian *slalåm*, literally, sloping track] (1921) **1 :** skiing in a zigzag or wavy course between upright obstacles (as flags) **2 :** a timed race (as on skis or in an automobile or kayak) over a winding or zigzag course past a series of flags or markers; *broadly* **:** movement over a zigzag route

²**slalom** *intransitive verb* (1932) **:** to move over a zigzag course in or as if in a slalom

¹**slam** \'slam\ *noun* [origin unknown] (1660) **1 :** GRAND SLAM **2 :** LITTLE SLAM

²**slam** *noun* [probably of Scandinavian origin; akin to Icelandic *slæma* to slam] (1672) **1 :** a heavy blow or impact **2 a :** a noisy violent closing **b :** a banging noise; *especially* **:** one made by the slam of a door **3 :** a cutting or violent criticism **4 :** SLAMMER

³**slam** *verb* **slammed; slam·ming** (circa 1691) *transitive verb* **1 :** to strike or beat hard **:** KNOCK **2 :** to shut forcibly and noisily **:** BANG **3 a :** to set or slap down violently or noisily ⟨*slammed* down the phone⟩ **b :** to propel, thrust, or produce by or as if by striking hard ⟨*slam* on the brakes⟩ ⟨*slammed* the car into a wall⟩ **4 :** to criticize harshly *intransitive verb* **1 :** to make a banging noise **2 :** to function (as in moving) with emphatic and usually noisy vigor ⟨the hurricane *slammed* into the coast⟩ ⟨*slammed* out of the room⟩ **3 :** to utter verbal abuse or harsh criticism

**slam–bang** \'slam-'baŋ\ *adjective* (circa 1823) **1 :** unduly loud or violent ⟨a *slam-bang* clatter⟩ **2 :** having fast-paced often nonstop action ⟨a *slam-bang* adventure novel⟩ **3 :** vigorously enthusiastic ⟨made a *slam-bang* effort to win⟩

**slam dunk** *noun* (1972) **:** DUNK SHOT — **slam–dunk** *verb*

**slam·mer** \'sla-mər\ *noun* (1952) **:** JAIL, PRISON

¹**slan·der** \'slan-dər\ *transitive verb* **slandered; slan·der·ing** \-d(ə-)riŋ\ (13th century)

**:** to utter slander against **:** DEFAME *synonym* see MALIGN — **slan·der·er** \-dər-ər\ *noun*

²**slander** *noun* [Middle English *sclaundre, slaundre*, from Old French *esclandre*, from Late Latin *scandalum* stumbling block, offense — more at SCANDAL] (14th century) **1 :** the utterance of false charges or misrepresentations which defame and damage another's reputation **2 :** a false and defamatory oral statement about a person — compare LIBEL — **slan·der·ous** \-d(ə-)rəs\ *adjective* — **slan·der·ous·ly** *adverb* — **slan·der·ous·ness** *noun*

¹**slang** \'slaŋ\ *noun* [origin unknown] (1756) **1 :** language peculiar to a particular group: as **a :** ARGOT **b :** JARGON 2 **2 :** an informal nonstandard vocabulary composed typically of coinages, arbitrarily changed words, and extravagant, forced, or facetious figures of speech — **slang** *adjective* — **slang·i·ly** \'slaŋ-ə-lē\ *adverb* — **slang·i·ness** \'slaŋ-ē-nəs\ *noun* — **slangy** \'slaŋ-ē\ *adjective*

²**slang** (1828) *intransitive verb* **:** to use slang or vulgar abuse *transitive verb* **:** to abuse with harsh or coarse language

**slanging match** *noun* (1896) *chiefly British* **:** a heated exchange of abuse

**slan·guage** \'slaŋ-gwij\ *noun* [blend of *slang* and *language*] (1879) **:** slangy speech or writing

¹**slant** \'slant\ *noun* (1655) **1 :** a slanting direction, line, or plane **:** SLOPE **2 a :** something that slants **b :** DIAGONAL **3 c :** a football running play in which the ballcarrier runs obliquely toward the line of scrimmage **3 a :** a peculiar or personal point of view, attitude, or opinion **b :** a slanting view **:** GLANCE — **slant** *adjective* — **slant·ways** \-ₗwāz\ *adverb* — **slant·wise** \-ₗwīz\ *adverb or adjective* — **slanty** \'slan-tē\ *adjective*

²**slant** *verb* [Middle English *slenten* to fall obliquely, of Scandinavian origin; akin to Swedish *slinta* to slide] (1692) *intransitive verb* **1 :** to take a diagonal course, direction, or path **2 :** to turn or incline from a right line or a level **:** SLOPE *transitive verb* **1 :** to give an oblique or sloping direction to **2 :** to interpret or present in line with a special interest **:** ANGLE ⟨stories *slanted* toward youth⟩; *especially* **:** to maliciously or dishonestly distort or falsify — **slant·ing·ly** \'slan-tiŋ-lē\ *adverb*

**slant height** *noun* (1798) **1 :** the length of an element of a right circular cone **2 :** the altitude of a side of a regular pyramid

¹**slap** \'slap\ *noun* [Middle English *slop*, from Middle Dutch; akin to Middle Dutch *slippen* to slip] (14th century) *dialect British* **:** OPENING, BREACH

²**slap** *transitive verb* **slapped; slap·ping** [akin to Low German *slapp*, noun blow] (15th century) **1 a :** to strike sharply with or as if with the open hand **b :** to cause to strike with a motion or sound like that of a blow with the open hand **2 :** to put, place, or throw with careless haste or force ⟨*slapped* on a coat of paint⟩ **3 :** to assail verbally **:** INSULT **4 :** to subject to a penalty — usually used with *with* ⟨*slapped* him with a $10 fine⟩

³**slap** *noun* (1648) **1 a :** a blow with the open hand **b :** a quick sharp blow **2 :** a noise like that of a slap

**3** : REBUFF, INSULT
— **slap on the wrist** : a gentle usually ineffectual reprimand

**⁴slap** adverb [probably from Low German slapp, from slapp, noun] (1672)
: DIRECTLY, SMACK

**slap·dash** \'slap-'dash, -,dash\ adjective (circa 1792)
: HAPHAZARD, SLIPSHOD

**slap down** transitive verb (1842)
**1** : to prohibit or restrain usually abruptly and with censure from acting in a specified way : SQUELCH
**2** : to put an abrupt stop to : SUPPRESS

**slap-hap·py** \'slap-,ha-pē\ adjective (1936)
**1** : PUNCH-DRUNK
**2** : buoyantly or recklessly carefree or foolish : HAPPY-GO-LUCKY

**slap·jack** \-,jak\ noun [²slap + -jack (as in flapjack)] (1796)
**1** : PANCAKE
**2** : a card game in which each player tries to be the first to slap a hand on any jack that appears faceup

**slap shot** noun (1942)
: a shot in ice hockey made with a swinging stroke

**slap·stick** \'slap-,stik\ noun (1896)
**1** : a device made of two flat pieces of wood fastened at one end so as to make a loud noise when used by an actor to strike a person
**2** : comedy stressing farce and horseplay; also : activity resembling slapstick
— **slapstick** adjective

**slap–up** \'slap-,əp\ adjective (circa 1823)
chiefly British : FIRST-RATE, BANG-UP

**¹slash** \'slash\ verb [origin unknown] (1548)
intransitive verb
: to lash out, cut, or thrash about with or as if with an edged blade
transitive verb
**1** : to cut with or as if with rough sweeping strokes
**2** : CANE, LASH
**3** : to cut slits in (as a garment) so as to reveal a color beneath
**4** : to criticize cuttingly
**5** : to reduce sharply : CUT
— **slash·er** noun

**²slash** noun (1576)
**1** : the act of slashing; also : a long cut or stroke made by or as if by slashing
**2** : an ornamental slit in a garment
**3 a** : an open tract in a forest strewn with debris (as from logging) **b** : the debris in such a tract
**4** : DIAGONAL 3 — called also slash mark

**³slash** noun [origin unknown] (1652)
: a low swampy area often overgrown with brush

**slash–and–burn** adjective (1939)
: characterized or developed by felling and burning trees to clear land especially for temporary agriculture

**¹slash·ing** \'sla-shiŋ\ adjective (1593)
**1** : incisively satiric or critical
**2** : DRIVING, PELTING
**3** : VIVID, BRILLIANT
— **slash·ing·ly** \-shiŋ-lē\ adverb

**²slashing** noun (1596)
**1** : the act or process of slashing
**2** : an insert or layer of contrasting color revealed by a slash (as in a garment)
**3** : SLASH 3

**slash pine** noun [³slash] (1882)
: a pine (Pinus elliottii) of the southeastern U.S. that has two or three needles in a cluster and is a source of turpentine and lumber

**slash pocket** noun (1799)
: a pocket suspended on the wrong side of a garment from a finished slit on the right side that serves as its opening

**¹slat** \'slat\ transitive verb **slat·ted; slat·ting** [probably of Scandinavian origin; akin to Old Norse sletta to slap, throw] (1611)
: to hurl or throw smartly

**2** : STRIKE, PUMMEL

**²slat** noun [Middle English, slate, from Middle French esclat splinter, from Old French, from esclater to burst, splinter] (1764)
**1** : a thin narrow flat strip especially of wood or metal
**2** plural, slang : RIBS
**3** : an auxiliary airfoil at the leading edge of the wing of an airplane
— **slat** adjective
— **slat·ted** \'sla-təd\ adjective

**³slat** transitive verb **slat·ted; slat·ting** (1886)
: to make or equip with slats

**¹slate** \'slāt\ noun [Middle English, from Middle French esclat splinter] (14th century)
**1** : a piece of construction material (as laminated rock) prepared as a shingle for roofing and siding
**2** : a dense fine-grained metamorphic rock produced by the compression of various sediments (as clay or shale) so as to develop a characteristic cleavage
**3** : a tablet (as of slate) used for writing on
**4 a** : a written or unwritten record (as of deeds) ⟨started with a clean slate⟩ **b** : a list of candidates for nomination or election
**5 a** : a dark purplish gray **b** : any of various grays similar in color to common roofing slates
— **slate** adjective
— **slate·like** \-,līk\ adjective

**²slate** transitive verb **slat·ed; slat·ing** (15th century)
**1** : to cover with slate or a slatelike substance ⟨slate a roof⟩
**2** : to designate for a specified purpose or action : SCHEDULE ⟨was slated to direct the play⟩

**³slate** transitive verb **slat·ed; slat·ing** [probably alteration of ¹slat] (1825)
**1** : to thrash or pummel severely
**2** chiefly British : to criticize or censure severely

**slate black** noun (circa 1890)
: a nearly neutral slightly purplish black

**slate blue** noun (1796)
: a grayish blue color

**slat·er** \'slā-tər\ noun (14th century)
**1** : one that slates
**2** [¹slate; from its color] **a** : WOOD LOUSE **b** : any of various marine isopods

**¹slath·er** \'sla-thər\ noun [origin unknown] (1857)
: a great quantity — often used in plural

**²slather** transitive verb **slath·ered; slath·er·ing** \'sla-thə-riŋ, 'slath-riŋ\ (1866)
**1** : to use or spend in a wasteful or lavish manner : SQUANDER
**2 a** : to spread thickly or lavishly **b** : to spread something thickly or lavishly on

**slat·ing** \'slā-tiŋ\ noun (15th century)
: the work of a slater

**¹slat·tern** \'sla-tərn\ noun [probably from German schlottern to hang loosely, slouch; akin to Dutch slodderen to hang loosely, slodder slut] (circa 1639)
: an untidy slovenly woman; also : SLUT, PROSTITUTE

**²slattern** adjective (1716)
: SLATTERNLY

**slat·tern·ly** \'sla-tərn-lē\ adjective (circa 1680)
**1** : untidy and dirty through habitual neglect; also : CARELESS, DISORDERLY
**2** : of, relating to, or characteristic of a slut or prostitute
— **slat·tern·li·ness** noun

**slaty** also **slat·ey** \'slā-tē\ adjective (circa 1529)
: of, containing, or characteristic of slate; also : gray like slate

**¹slaugh·ter** \'slȯ-tər\ noun [Middle English, of Scandinavian origin; akin to Old Norse slātra to slaughter; akin to Old English sleaht slaughter, slēan to slay — more at SLAY] (14th century)

**1** : the act of killing; specifically : the butchering of livestock for market
**2** : killing of great numbers of human beings (as in battle or a massacre) : CARNAGE

**²slaughter** transitive verb (1535)
**1** : to kill (animals) for food : BUTCHER
**2 a** : to kill in a bloody or violent manner : SLAY **b** : to kill in large numbers : MASSACRE
**3** : to discredit or demolish completely
— **slaugh·ter·er** \-tər-ər\ noun

**slaugh·ter·house** \'slȯ-tər-,haus\ noun (14th century)
: an establishment where animals are butchered

**slaugh·ter·ous** \'slȯ-tə-rəs\ adjective (1582)
: of or relating to slaughter : MURDEROUS
— **slaugh·ter·ous·ly** adverb

**Slav** \'släv, 'slav\ noun [Middle English Sclav, from Medieval Latin Sclavus, from Late Greek Sklabos, from Sklabēnoi Slavs, of Slavic origin; akin to Old Russian Slověne, an East Slavic tribe] (14th century)
: a person whose native tongue is a Slavic language
word history see SLAVE
— **Slav** adjective

**¹slave** \'slāv\ noun [Middle English sclave, from Old French or Medieval Latin; Old French esclave, from Medieval Latin sclavus, from Sclavus Slav; from the frequent enslavement of Slavs in central Europe] (14th century)
**1** : a person held in servitude as the chattel of another
**2** : one that is completely subservient to a dominating influence
**3** : a device (as the printer of a computer) that is directly responsive to another
**4** : DRUDGE, TOILER ◆
— **slave** adjective

**²slave** verb **slaved; slav·ing** (1602)
transitive verb
**1** archaic : ENSLAVE
**2** : to make directly responsive to another mechanism
intransitive verb
**1** : to work like a slave : DRUDGE

◇ WORD HISTORY
**slave** The words Slav and slave both come ultimately from a Slavic word that variously groups of early medieval Slavs used in order to distinguish themselves from their neighbors. An early form of this word was Slověne, applied to 9th century Slavs living outside the Greek city of Thessaloniki in South Slavic versions of the life of St. Cyril, the missionary who introduced Christianity and literacy to Slavic lands. Slověne is the likely source of Medieval Greek Sklabēnoi, from which shortened Medieval Latin Sclavus and hence the word for "Slav" in Western European languages derive. In Medieval Latin Sclavus shifted in sense from "Slav" to "Slav in servitude" to "slave" in the 10th century, when German princes in central Europe were expanding their territories eastward at the expense of West Slavic tribes too decentralized to resist invasion. Many Slavic prisoners of war were sold into slavery, often ending up in Muslim Spain, then the wealthiest part of western Europe. Captives were also taken from among Balkan Slavs by the Byzantine Greeks, especially after the fall of the first Bulgarian Empire in 1018, and were sold throughout the Mediterranean. Such traffic probably led to the adoption of Medieval Latin sclavus into Romance languages.

**2** : to traffic in slaves
**slave driver** *noun* (1807)
**1** : a supervisor of slaves at work
**2** : a harsh taskmaster
**slave·hold·er** \'slāv-,hōl-dər\ *noun* (1776)
: an owner of slaves
— **slave·hold·ing** \-diŋ\ *adjective or noun*
**slave–mak·ing ant** \'slāv-,mā-kiŋ-\ *noun* (1817)
: an ant that attacks the colonies of ants of other species and carries off the larvae and pupae to be reared in its own nest as slaves
¹**sla·ver** \'sla-vər, 'slā-, 'slä-\ *verb* **sla·vered; sla·ver·ing** \-v(ə-)riŋ\ [Middle English, of Scandinavian origin; akin to Old Norse *slafra* to slaver; akin to Middle Dutch *slabben* to slaver] (14th century)
*intransitive verb*
: DROOL, SLOBBER
*transitive verb*
*archaic* : to smear with or as if with saliva
²**slaver** *noun* (14th century)
: saliva dribbling from the mouth
³**slav·er** \'slā-vər\ *noun* [¹*slave*] (1827)
**1 a** : a person engaged in the slave trade **b** : a ship used in the slave trade
**2** : WHITE SLAVER
**slav·ery** \'slā-v(ə-)rē\ *noun* (1551)
**1** : DRUDGERY, TOIL
**2** : submission to a dominating influence
**3 a** : the state of a person who is a chattel of another **b** : the practice of slaveholding
**slave state** *noun* (1809)
**1** : a state of the U.S. in which slavery was legal until the Civil War
**2** : a nation subjected to totalitarian rule
**slave trade** *noun* (1734)
: traffic in slaves; *especially* : the buying and selling of blacks for profit prior to the American Civil War
**slav·ey** \'slā-vē\ *noun, plural* **slaveys** (circa 1812)
: DRUDGE; *especially* : a household servant who does general housework
¹**Slav·ic** \'slä-vik, 'sla-\ *noun* (1812)
: a branch of the Indo-European language family containing Belorussian, Bulgarian, Czech, Polish, Serbo-Croatian, Slovene, Russian, and Ukrainian — see INDO-EUROPEAN LANGUAGES table
²**Slavic** *adjective* (1813)
: of, relating to, or characteristic of the Slavs or their languages
**Slav·i·cist** \'slä-və-sist, 'sla-\ *noun* (1930)
: a specialist in the Slavic languages or literatures
**slav·ish** \'slā-vish *sometimes* 'sla-\ *adjective* (1565)
**1 a** : of or characteristic of a slave; *especially* : basely or abjectly servile **b** *archaic* : DESPICABLE, LOW
**2** *archaic* : OPPRESSIVE, TYRANNICAL
**3** : copying obsequiously or without originality : IMITATIVE
**synonym** see SUBSERVIENT
— **slav·ish·ly** *adverb*
— **slav·ish·ness** *noun*
**Slav·ist** \'slä-vist, 'sla-\ *noun* (1863)
: SLAVICIST
**slav·oc·ra·cy** \slä-'vä-krə-sē\ *noun* (1840)
: a faction of slaveholders and advocates of slavery in the South before the Civil War
¹**Sla·von·ic** \slə-'vä-nik\ *adjective* [New Latin *slavonicus*, from Medieval Latin *Sclavonia, Slavonia,* the Slavic-speaking countries, from *Sclavus* Slav] (circa 1645)
: SLAVIC
²**Slavonic** *noun* (1668)
**1** : SLAVIC
**2** : OLD CHURCH SLAVONIC
**Slav·o·phile** \'slä-və-,fīl, 'sla-\ *or* **Slav·o·phil** \-,fil\ *noun* (1877)
: an admirer of the Slavs : an advocate of Slavophilism
**Slav·oph·i·lism** \slä-'vä-fə-,li-zəm; 'sla-və-,fī-,li-, 'slä-\ *noun* (1877)

: advocacy of Slavic and specifically Russian culture over western European culture especially as practiced among some members of the Russian intelligentsia in the middle 19th century
**slaw** \'slò\ *noun* (1861)
: COLESLAW
**slay** \'slā\ *verb* **slew** \'slü\ *also especially in sense 2* **slayed; slain** \'slān\; **slay·ing** [Middle English *slen,* from Old English *slēan* to strike, slay; akin to Old High German *slahan* to strike, Middle Irish *slachta* stricken] (before 12th century)
*transitive verb*
**1** : to kill violently, wantonly, or in great numbers; *broadly* : to strike down : KILL
**2** : to delight or amuse immensely ⟨*slayed* the audience⟩
*intransitive verb*
: KILL, MURDER
**synonym** see KILL
— **slay·er** *noun*
¹**sleave** \'slēv\ *noun* [²*sleave*] (1591)
*archaic* : SKEIN ⟨sleep that knits up the raveled *sleave* of care —Shakespeare⟩
²**sleave** *transitive verb* [(assumed) Middle English *sleven,* from Old English *-slæfan* to cut] (circa 1628)
*obsolete* : to separate (silk thread) into filaments
**sleave silk** *noun* (1588)
*obsolete* : floss silk that is easily separated into filaments for embroidery
**sleaze** \'slēz *also* 'slāz\ *noun* [back-formation from *sleazy*] (1954)
**1** : sleazy quality, appearance, or behavior; *also* : sleazy material
**2** : a sleazy person
**sleaze·bag** \-,bag *also* -,bȧg\ *noun* (1983)
*slang* : a sleazy person
**sleaze·ball** \-,bòl\ *noun* (1981)
*slang* : a sleazy person
**sleazo** \'slē-(,)zō\ *adjective* (1972)
*slang* : SLEAZY
**slea·zy** \'slē-zē *also* 'slā-\ *adjective* **slea·zi·er; -est** [origin unknown] (circa 1645)
**1 a** : lacking firmness of texture : FLIMSY **b** : carelessly made of inferior materials : SHODDY
**2 a** : marked by low character or quality ⟨*sleazy* tabloids⟩ **b** : SQUALID, DILAPIDATED ⟨*sleazy* bars⟩
— **slea·zi·ly** \-zə-lē\ *adverb*
— **slea·zi·ness** \-zē-nəs\ *noun*
¹**sled** \'sled\ *noun* [Middle English *sledde,* from Middle Dutch; akin to Old English *slīdan* to slide] (14th century)
**1** : a vehicle on runners for transportation especially on snow or ice; *especially* : a small steerable one used especially by children for coasting down snow-covered hills
**2** : ROCKET SLED
²**sled** *verb* **sled·ded; sled·ding** (1706)
*transitive verb*
: SLEDGE
*intransitive verb*
: to ride on a sled or sleigh
— **sled·der** *noun*
**sledding** *noun* (15th century)
**1 a** : the use of a sled **b** : the conditions under which one may use a sled
**2** : GOING 4 ⟨tough *sledding*⟩
**sled dog** *noun* (1692)
: a dog trained to draw a sledge especially in the Arctic regions — called also *sledge dog*
¹**sledge** \'slej\ *noun* [Middle English *slegge,* from Old English *slecg;* akin to Old Norse *sleggja* sledgehammer, Old English *slēan* to strike — more at SLAY] (before 12th century)
: SLEDGEHAMMER
²**sledge** *verb* **sledged; sledg·ing** (1654)
: SLEDGEHAMMER
³**sledge** *noun* [Dutch dialect *sleedse;* akin to Middle Dutch *sledde* sled] (1617)
**1** *British* : SLEIGH
**2** : a strong heavy sled

⁴**sledge** *verb* **sledged; sledg·ing** (1853)
*intransitive verb*
**1** : to travel with a sledge
**2** *British* : to ride in a sleigh
*transitive verb*
: to transport on a sledge
¹**sledge·ham·mer** \'slej-,ha-mər\ *noun* (15th century)
: a large heavy hammer that is wielded with both hands; *also* : something that resembles a sledgehammer in action
²**sledgehammer** (1834)
*transitive verb*
: to strike with or as if with a sledgehammer
*intransitive verb*
: to strike blows with or as if with a sledgehammer
³**sledgehammer** *adjective* (1843)
: marked by heavy-handed directness or hard-hitting force ⟨trusting in *sledgehammer* warfare —C. J. Rolo⟩
¹**sleek** \'slēk\ *verb* [Middle English *sleken,* alteration of *sliken* — more at SLICK] (15th century)
*transitive verb*
**1** : SLICK ⟨grooms *sleeking* cooled horses —Sunset⟩
**2** : to cover up : gloss over
*intransitive verb*
: SLICK
²**sleek** *adjective* [alteration of ²*slick*] (1589)
**1 a** : smooth and glossy as if polished ⟨*sleek* dark hair⟩ **b** : having a smooth well-groomed look ⟨*sleek* cattle⟩ **c** : healthy-looking
**2** : smooth in speech or manner; *also* : UNCTUOUS
**3 a** : having a prosperous air ⟨a *sleek* apartment building with a pool on the roof⟩ **b** : having trim graceful lines ⟨a *sleek* car⟩ **c** : ELEGANT, STYLISH ⟨*sleek* restaurants⟩ ☆
— **sleek·ly** *adverb*
— **sleek·ness** *noun*
**sleek·en** \'slē-kən\ *transitive verb* **sleekened; sleek·en·ing** \'slē-kə-niŋ, 'slēk-niŋ\ (1621)
: to make sleek
**sleek·it** \'slē-kət\ *adjective* [Scots, from past participle of ¹*sleek*] (1513)
**1** *chiefly Scottish* : SLEEK, SMOOTH
**2** *chiefly Scottish* : CRAFTY, DECEITFUL
¹**sleep** \'slēp\ *noun* [Middle English *slepe,* from Old English *slǣp;* akin to Old High German *slāf* sleep and perhaps to Latin *labi* to slip, slide] (before 12th century)
**1** : the natural periodic suspension of consciousness during which the powers of the body are restored
**2** : a state resembling sleep: as **a** : a state of torpid inactivity **b** : DEATH ⟨put a pet cat to *sleep*⟩; *also* : TRANCE, COMA **c** : the closing of leaves or petals especially at night **d** : a state marked by a diminution of feeling followed by tingling ⟨my foot's gone to *sleep*⟩ **e** : the state of an animal during hibernation
**3 a** : a period spent sleeping **b** : NIGHT **c** : a day's journey
— **sleep·like** \-,līk\ *adjective*
²**sleep** *verb* **slept** \'slept\; **sleep·ing** (before 12th century)
*intransitive verb*
**1** : to rest in a state of sleep
**2** : to be in a state (as of quiescence or death) resembling sleep

---

☆ **SYNONYMS**
**Sleek, slick, glossy** mean having a smooth bright surface or appearance. SLEEK suggests a smoothness or brightness resulting from attentive grooming or physical conditioning ⟨a *sleek* racehorse⟩. SLICK suggests extreme smoothness that results in a slippery surface ⟨slipped and fell on the *slick* floor⟩. GLOSSY suggests a highly reflective surface ⟨photographs having a *glossy* finish⟩.

**3 :** to have sexual relations — usually used with *with*
*transitive verb*
**1 :** to be slumbering in ⟨*slept* the sleep of the dead⟩
**2 :** to get rid of or spend in or by sleep ⟨*sleep* away the hours⟩ ⟨*sleep* off a drunk⟩
**3 :** to provide sleeping accommodations for ⟨the boat *sleeps* six⟩

**sleep around** *intransitive verb* (1928)
**:** to engage in sex promiscuously

**sleep·er** \'slē-pər\ *noun* (12th century)
**1 :** one that sleeps
**2 :** a piece of timber, stone, or steel on or near the ground to support a superstructure, keep railroad rails in place, or receive floor joists **:** STRINGPIECE
**3 :** SLEEPING CAR
**4 :** someone or something unpromising or un-noticed that suddenly attains prominence or value ⟨the low-budget film became the sum-mer's *sleeper*⟩
**5 :** children's pajamas usually with feet — usually used in plural
**6** *chiefly British* **:** a small earring or stud worn to keep the hole of a pierced ear from closing
**7 :** MOLE 4

**sleep–in** \'slēp-'in\ *adjective* (1951)
**:** that lives at the place of employment ⟨a *sleep-in* maid⟩

**sleep in** *intransitive verb* (1827)
**1 :** to sleep where one is employed
**2 a :** OVERSLEEP **b :** to sleep late intentionally

**sleeping bag** *noun* (1850)
**:** a bag that is warmly lined or padded for sleeping outdoors or in a camp or tent

**Sleeping Beauty** *noun*
**:** a princess of a fairy tale who is wakened from an enchanted sleep by the kiss of a prince

**sleeping car** *noun* (1839)
**:** a railroad passenger car having berths for sleeping

**sleeping partner** *noun* (circa 1785)
*chiefly British* **:** SILENT PARTNER

**sleeping pill** *noun* (1664)
**:** a drug and especially a barbiturate that is taken as a tablet or capsule to induce sleep — called also *sleeping tablet*

**sleeping porch** *noun* (1915)
**:** a porch or room having open sides or many windows arranged to permit sleeping in the open air

**sleeping sickness** *noun* (1875)
**1 :** a serious disease that is prevalent in much of tropical Africa, is marked by fever, protract-ed lethargy, tremors, and loss of weight, is caused by either of two trypanosomes (*Trypa-nosoma brucei gambiense* and *T. b. rhodesiense*), and is transmitted by tsetse flies
**2 :** any of various viral encephalitides or en-cephalomyelitides of which lethargy or som-nolence is a prominent feature

**sleep·less** \'slēp-ləs\ *adjective* (15th century)
**1 :** not able to sleep ⟨lay *sleepless* with fever⟩
**2 :** affording no sleep ⟨*sleepless* nights⟩
**3 :** unceasingly active or operative ⟨*sleepless* casinos⟩
— **sleep·less·ly** *adverb*
— **sleep·less·ness** *noun*

**sleep out** *intransitive verb* (1908)
**:** to sleep outdoors

**sleep·over** \'slēp-ō-vər\ *noun* (1965)
**1 :** an overnight stay (as at another's home)
**2 :** an instance of hosting a sleepover in one's home

**sleep·walk·er** \'slēp-,wȯ-kər\ *noun* (1747)
**:** one that walks while or as if while asleep **:** SOMNAMBULIST
— **sleep·walk** \-,wȯk\ *intransitive verb or noun*

**sleep·wear** \-,war, -,wer\ *noun* (1935)
**:** NIGHTCLOTHES

**sleepy** \'slē-pē\ *adjective* **sleep·i·er; -est** (13th century)

**1 a :** ready to fall asleep **b :** of, relating to, or characteristic of sleep
**2 :** sluggish as if from sleep **:** LETHARGIC; *also* **:** having little activity ⟨a *sleepy* coastal village⟩
**3 :** sleep-inducing
— **sleep·i·ly** \-pə-lē\ *adverb*
— **sleep·i·ness** \-pē-nəs\ *noun*

**sleepy·head** \'slē-pē-,hed\ *noun* (1577)
**:** a sleepy person

¹**sleet** \'slēt\ *noun* [Middle English *slete*; akin to Middle High German *slōz* hailstone] (13th century)
**:** frozen or partly frozen rain
— **sleety** \'slē-tē\ *adjective*

²**sleet** *intransitive verb* (14th century)
**:** to shower sleet

**sleeve** \'slēv\ *noun* [Middle English *sleve*, from Old English *slīefe*; perhaps akin to Old English *slēfan* to slip (clothes) on, *slūpan* to slip, Old High German *sliofan*, Latin *lubricus* slippery] (before 12th century)
**1 a :** a part of a garment covering an arm **b** **:** SLEEVELET
**2 a :** a tubular part (as a hollow axle or a bushing) designed to fit over another part **b** **:** an open-ended flat or tubular packaging or cover; *especially* **:** JACKET 3c(2)
— **sleeved** \'slēvd\ *adjective*
— **sleeve·less** \'slēv-ləs\ *adjective*
— **up one's sleeve :** held secretly in re-serve

**sleeve·let** \'slēv-lət\ *noun* (1889)
**:** a covering for the forearm to protect clothing from wear or dirt

¹**sleigh** \'slā\ *noun* [Dutch *slee*, alteration of *slede*; akin to Middle Dutch *sledde* sled] (1703)
**:** an open usually horse-drawn vehi-cle with runners for use on snow or ice

sleigh

²**sleigh** *intransitive verb* (circa 1729)
**:** to drive or travel in a sleigh

**sleigh bed** *noun* (1902)
**:** a bed common especially in the first half of the 19th century having a solid headboard and footboard that roll outward at the top

**sleigh bell** *noun* (1772)
**:** any of various bells commonly attached to a sleigh or to the harness of a horse drawing a sleigh: as **a :** CASCABEL 2 **b :** a hemispherical bell with an attached clapper

**sleight** \'slīt\ *noun* [Middle English, from Old Norse *slægth*, from *slægr* sly — more at SLY] (14th century)
**1 :** deceitful craftiness; *also* **:** STRATAGEM
**2 :** DEXTERITY, SKILL

**sleight of hand** (circa 1605)
**1 a :** a conjuring trick requiring manual dex-terity **b :** a cleverly executed trick or decep-tion
**2 a :** skill and dexterity in conjuring tricks **b** **:** adroitness in deception

**slen·der** \'slen-dər\ *adjective* [Middle English *sclendre, slendre*] (14th century)
**1 a :** spare in frame or flesh; *especially* **:** gracefully slight **b :** small or narrow in cir-cumference or width in proportion to length or height
**2 :** limited or inadequate in amount or scope **:** MEAGER ⟨people of *slender* means⟩
*synonym* see THIN
— **slen·der·ly** *adverb*
— **slen·der·ness** *noun*

**slen·der·ize** \-də-,rīz\ *transitive verb* **-ized; -iz·ing** (1923)
**:** to make slender

¹**sleuth** \'slüth\ *noun* [short for *sleuthhound*] (1872)
**:** DETECTIVE ◆

²**sleuth** (1900)
*intransitive verb*

**:** to act as a detective **:** search for information
*transitive verb*
**:** to search for and discover

**sleuth·hound** \'slüth-,haůnd\ *noun* [Middle English *sleuth hund*, a kind of bloodhound, from *sleuth* track of an animal or person (from Old Norse *slōth*) + *hund* hound] (1856)
**:** DETECTIVE

**S level** *noun* (1951)
**1 :** the highest of three standardized British examinations in a secondary school subject used as a qualification for university entrance; *also* **:** successful completion of an S-level ex-amination in a particular subject — called also *Scholarship level*; compare A LEVEL, O LEVEL
**2 a :** the level of education required to pass an S-level examination **b :** a course leading to an S-level examination

¹**slew** \'slü\ *past of* SLAY

²**slew** *variant of* SLOUGH

³**slew** *verb* [origin unknown] (circa 1769)
*transitive verb*
**1 :** to turn (as a telescope or a ship's spar) about a fixed point that is usually the axis
**2 :** to cause to skid **:** VEER ⟨*slew* a car around a turn⟩
*intransitive verb*
**1 :** to turn, twist, or swing about **:** PIVOT
**2 :** SKID

⁴**slew** *noun* [perhaps from Irish *slua* army, host, throng, from Old Irish *slúag*; akin to Lithuanian *slaugyti* to tend] (1839)
**:** a large number ⟨a *slew* of books⟩

¹**slice** \'slīs\ *verb* **sliced; slic·ing** [Middle English *sklicen*, from Middle French *esclicier* to splinter, from Old French, of Germanic ori-gin; akin to Old High German *slīzan* to tear apart — more at SLIT] (1551)
*transitive verb*
**1 :** to cut with or as if with a knife
**2 :** to stir or spread with a slice
**3 :** to hit (a ball) so that a slice results
*intransitive verb*
**1 :** to slice something
**2 :** to move with a cutting action ⟨the ship *sliced* through the waves⟩
— **slice·able** \'slī-sə-bəl\ *adjective*
— **slic·er** *noun*

²**slice** *noun* [Middle English *sklice*, from Mid-dle French *esclice* splinter, from Old French, from *esclicier*] (1613)
**1 a :** a thin flat piece cut from something **b :** a wedge-shaped piece (as of pie or cake)
**2 :** a spatula for spreading paint or ink

**3 :** a serving knife with wedge-shaped blade ⟨a fish *slice*⟩
**4 :** a flight of a ball that deviates from a straight course in the direction of the dominant hand of the player propelling it; *also* : a ball following such a course — compare HOOK
**5 :** PORTION, SHARE ⟨a *slice* of the profits⟩

**slice–of–life** *adjective* (1895)
**:** of, relating to, or marked by the accurate transcription (as into drama) of a segment of actual life experience

**¹slick** \'slik\ *verb* [Middle English *sliken*; akin to Old High German *slīhhan* to glide] (14th century)
*transitive verb*
**:** to make sleek or smooth
*intransitive verb*
**:** SPRUCE — usually used with *up*

**²slick** *adjective* (14th century)
**1 a :** having a smooth surface : SLIPPERY ⟨*slick* wet leaves⟩ **b :** having surface plausibility or appeal : GLIB, GLOSSY ⟨*slick* advertising⟩ **c :** based on stereotype : TRITE ⟨*slick* stories soon forgotten⟩
**2** *archaic* : SLEEK 1
**3 a :** characterized by subtlety or nimble wit : CLEVER; *especially* : WILY ⟨a reputation as a *slick* operator⟩ **b :** DEFT, SKILLFUL ⟨a *slick* ball-player⟩
**4 :** extremely good : FIRST-RATE
*synonym* see SLEEK, SLY
— **slick** *adverb*
— **slick·ly** *adverb*
— **slick·ness** *noun*

**³slick** *noun* (1849)
**1 a :** something that is smooth or slippery; *especially* : a smooth patch of water covered with a film of oil **b :** a film of oil
**2 :** an implement for producing a slick surface: as **a :** a flat paddle usually of steel for smoothing a sample of flour **b :** a foundry tool for smoothing the surface of a sand mold or unbaked core
**3 :** a shrewd untrustworthy person
**4 :** a popular magazine printed on coated stock and intended to appeal to sophisticated readers
**5 :** an automobile tire made without a tread for maximum traction (as in drag racing)

**slick–ear** \'slik-,ir\ *noun* (1914)
**:** a range animal lacking an earmark

**slick·en·side** \'sli-kən-,sīd\ *noun* [English dialect *slicken* smooth (alteration of English ²*slick*) + English *side*] (1822)
**:** a smooth often striated surface produced on rock by movement along a fault or a subsidiary fracture — usually used in plural

**slick·er** \'sli-kər\ *noun* (1881)
**1** [²*slick*] : OILSKIN; *broadly* : RAINCOAT
**2** [*slick* to defraud cleverly] **a :** a clever crook : SWINDLER **b :** a city dweller especially of natty appearance or sophisticated mannerisms

**slick·rock** \'slik-,räk\ *noun* (1925)
**:** smooth wind-polished rock

**¹slide** \'slīd\ *verb* **slid** \'slid\; **slid·ing** \'slī-diŋ\ [Middle English, from Old English *slīdan*; akin to Middle High German *slīten* to slide] (before 12th century)
*intransitive verb*
**1 a :** to move smoothly along a surface : SLIP **b :** to coast over snow or ice ⟨*of a base runner in baseball*⟩ **c :** to fall or dive feetfirst or headfirst when approaching a base
**2 a :** to slip or fall by loss of footing **b :** to change position or become dislocated : SHIFT
**3 a :** to slither along the ground : CRAWL **b :** to stream along : FLOW
**4 a :** to move or pass smoothly or easily ⟨*slid* into the prepared speech⟩ **b :** to pass unnoticed or unremarked ⟨could have responded but let it *slide*⟩
**5 a :** to pass unobtrusively : STEAL **b :** to pass by gradations especially downward ⟨the economy *slid* from recession to depression⟩
*transitive verb*
**1 a :** to cause to glide or slip **b :** to traverse in a sliding manner

**2 :** to put unobtrusively or stealthily ⟨*slid* the bill into his hand⟩

**²slide** *noun* (1570)
**1 a :** an act or instance of sliding **b** (1) **:** a musical grace of two or more small notes (2) **:** PORTAMENTO
**2 :** a sliding part or mechanism: as **a** (1) **:** a U-shaped section of tube in the trombone that is pushed out and in to produce the tones between the fundamental and its harmonics (2) **:** a short U-shaped section of tube in a brass instrument that is used to adjust the pitch of the instrument or of individual valves **b** (1) **:** a moving piece (as the ram of a punch press) that is guided by a part along which it slides (2) **:** a guiding surface (as a feeding mechanism) along which something slides **c :** SLIDING SEAT
**3 a :** the descent of a mass of earth, rock, or snow down a hill or mountainside **b :** a dislocation in which one rock mass in a mining lode has slid on another : FAULT
**4 a** (1) **:** a slippery surface for coasting (2) **:** a chute with a slippery bed down which children slide in play **b :** a channel or track on which something is slid **c :** a sloping trough down which objects are carried by gravity ⟨a log *slide*⟩
**5 a :** a flat piece of glass on which an object is mounted for microscopic examination **b :** a photographic transparency on a small plate or film mounted for projection
**6 :** BOTTLENECK 3

**slide fastener** *noun* (1934)
**:** ZIPPER

**slid·er** \'slī-dər\ *noun* (1530)
**1 :** one that slides
**2 :** a fast baseball pitch that breaks slightly in the same direction as a curve

**slide rule** *noun* (1663)
**:** a manual device used for calculation that consists in its simple form of a ruler and a movable middle piece which are graduated with similar logarithmic scales

**slide valve** *noun* (1802)
**:** a valve that opens and closes a passageway by sliding over a port; *specifically* : such a valve often used in steam engines for admitting steam to the piston and releasing it

**slide·way** \'slīd-,wā\ *noun* (1856)
**:** a way along which something slides

**sliding scale** *noun* (1842)
**1 :** a wage scale geared to the selling price of the product or to the consumer price index but usually guaranteeing a minimum below which the wage will not fall
**2 a :** a system for raising or lowering tariffs in accord with price changes **b :** a flexible scale (as of fees or subsidies) adjusted to the needs or income of individuals ⟨the *sliding scale* of medical fees⟩

**sliding seat** *noun* (1874)
**:** a rower's seat (as in a racing shell) that slides fore and aft — called also *slide*

**slier** *comparative of* SLY
**sliest** *superlative of* SLY

**¹slight** \'slīt\ *adjective* [Middle English, smooth, slight, probably from Middle Dutch *slicht*; akin to Old High German *slīhhan* to glide — more at SLICK] (14th century)
**1 a :** having a slim or delicate build : not stout or massive in body **b :** lacking in strength or substance : FLIMSY, FRAIL **c :** deficient in weight, solidity, or importance : TRIVIAL
**2 :** small of its kind or in amount : SCANTY, MEAGER
*synonym* see THIN
— **slight·ly** *adverb*
— **slight·ness** *noun*

**²slight** *transitive verb* (1597)
**1 :** to treat as slight or unimportant : make light of
**2 :** to treat with disdain or indifference
**3 :** to perform or attend to carelessly and inadequately

**4 :** ³SLUR 3
*synonym* see NEGLECT

**³slight** *noun* (1701)
**1 :** an act or an instance of slighting
**2 :** an instance of being slighted : a humiliating discourtesy

**slight·ing** *adjective* (1632)
**:** characterized by disregard or disrespect : DISPARAGING ⟨a *slighting* remark⟩
— **slight·ing·ly** \'slī-tiŋ-lē\ *adverb*

**sli·ly** *variant of* SLYLY

**¹slim** \'slim\ *adjective* **slim·mer; slim·mest** [Dutch, bad, inferior, from Middle Dutch *slimp* crooked, bad; akin to Middle High German *slimp* awry] (1657)
**1 :** of small diameter or thickness in proportion to the height or length : SLENDER
**2 a :** MEAN, WORTHLESS **b :** ADROIT, CRAFTY
**3 a :** inferior in quality or amount : SLIGHT **b :** SCANTY, SMALL ⟨a *slim* chance⟩
*synonym* see THIN
— **slim·ly** *adverb*
— **slim·ness** *noun*

**²slim** *verb* **slimmed; slim·ming** (1862)
*transitive verb*
**:** to make slender : decrease the size of
*intransitive verb*
**:** to become slender

**¹slime** \'slīm\ *noun* [Middle English, from Old English *slīm*; akin to Middle High German *slīm* slime, Latin *limus* mud — more at LIME] (before 12th century)
**1 :** soft moist earth or clay; *especially* : viscous mud
**2 :** a viscous or glutinous substance: as **a :** a mucous or mucoid secretion of various animals (as slugs and catfishes) **b :** a product of wet crushing consisting of ore ground so fine as to pass a 200-mesh screen
**3 :** a repulsive or odious person

**²slime** *verb* **slimed; slim·ing** (1628)
*transitive verb*
**1 :** to smear or cover with slime
**2 :** to remove slime from (as fish for canning)
*intransitive verb*
**:** to become slimy

**slime·ball** \'slīm-,bȯl\ *noun* (1986)
*slang* : SLIME 3

**slime mold** *noun* (1880)
**:** any of a group (Myxomycetes or Mycetozoa) of organisms usually held to be lower fungi but sometimes considered protozoans that exist vegetatively as mobile plasmodia and reproduce by spores

**slim–jim** \'slim-'jim, -,jim\ *adjective* [¹*slim* + *Jim*, nickname for *James*] (1889)
**:** notably slender

**slim·mer** \'sli-mər\ *noun* (1967)
*chiefly British* : a person dieting to lose weight : DIETER

**slim·nas·tics** \,slim-'nas-tiks\ *noun plural but singular in construction* [¹*slim* + *gymnastics*] (1967)
**:** exercises designed to reduce one's weight

**slim·sy** *or* **slimp·sy** \'slim-zē, 'slim(p)-sē\ *adjective* [blend of *slim* and *flimsy*] (1845)
**:** FLIMSY, FRAIL

**slimy** \'slī-mē\ *adjective* **slim·i·er; -est** (14th century)
**1 :** of, relating to, or resembling slime : VISCOUS; *also* : covered with or yielding slime
**2 :** VILE, OFFENSIVE
— **slim·i·ly** \-mə-lē\ *adverb*
— **slim·i·ness** \-mē-nəs\ *noun*

**¹sling** \'sliŋ\ *transitive verb* **slung** \'sləŋ\; **sling·ing** \'sliŋ-iŋ\ [Middle English, probably from Old Norse *slyngva* to hurl; akin to Old English & Old High German *slingan* to worm, twist, Lithuanian *slinkti*] (14th century)
**1 :** to cast with a sudden and usually sweeping or swirling motion ⟨*slung* the sack over my shoulder⟩
**2 :** to throw with or as if with a sling ⟨*slinging* punches⟩ ⟨*sling* mud⟩
*synonym* see THROW
— **sling·er** \'sliŋ-ər\ *noun*

**²sling** *noun* (14th century)
**1 a :** an instrument for throwing stones that usually consists of a short strap with strings fastened to its ends and is whirled round to discharge its missile by centrifugal force **b :** SLINGSHOT 1
**2 a :** a usually looped line (as of strap, chain, or rope) used to hoist, lower, or carry something; *especially* **:** a hanging bandage suspended from the neck to support an arm or hand **b :** a chain or rope attached to a lower yard at the middle and passing around a mast near the masthead to support a yard **c :** a chain hooked at the bow and stern of a boat for lowering or hoisting **d :** a device (as a rope net) for enclosing material to be hoisted by a tackle or crane
**3 :** a slinging or hurling of or as if of a missile
**³sling** *transitive verb* **slung** \'sləŋ\; **sling·ing** \'sliŋ-iŋ\ (1522)
**1 :** to place in a sling for hoisting or lowering
**2 :** to suspend by or as if by a sling
**⁴sling** *noun* [origin unknown] (1768)
**:** an alcoholic drink that is served hot or cold and that usually consists of liquor, sugar, lemon juice, and plain or carbonated water ⟨gin *sling*⟩ ⟨rum *sling*⟩
**slings and arrows** *noun plural* [from the phrase "the slings and arrows of outrageous fortune" in Shakespeare's *Hamlet*] (1963)
**:** pointed often acerbic critical attacks ⟨has suffered the *slings and arrows* of detractors —Roland Gelatt⟩
**sling·shot** \'sliŋ-ˌshät\ *noun* (1849)
**1 :** a forked stick with an elastic band attached for shooting small stones
**2 a :** a maneuver in auto racing in which a drafting car accelerates past the car in front by taking advantage of reserve power **b :** a dragster in which the driver sits behind the rear wheels
**¹slink** \'sliŋk\ *verb* **slunk** \'sləŋk\ *also* **slinked** \'sliŋ(k)t\; **slink·ing** [Middle English, from Old English *slincan* to creep; akin to Old English *slingan* to worm, twist] (14th century)
*intransitive verb*
**1 :** to go or move stealthily or furtively (as in fear or shame) **:** STEAL
**2 :** to move in a sinuous provocative manner
*transitive verb*
**:** to give premature birth to — used especially of a domestic animal ⟨a cow that *slinks* her calf⟩
*synonym* see LURK
**²slink** *noun* (1607)
**:** the young of an animal (as a calf) brought forth prematurely; *also* **:** the flesh or skin of such an animal
**³slink** *adjective* (1750)
**:** born prematurely or abortively ⟨a *slink* calf⟩
**slinky** \'sliŋ-kē\ *adjective* **slink·i·er; -est** (1918)
**1 :** characterized by slinking **:** stealthily quiet ⟨*slinky* movements⟩
**2 :** sleek and sinuous in movement or outline; *especially* **:** following the lines of the figure in a gracefully flowing manner ⟨a *slinky* evening gown⟩
— **slink·i·ly** \-kə-lē\ *adverb*
— **slink·i·ness** \-kē-nəs\ *noun*
**¹slip** \'slip\ *verb* **slipped; slip·ping** [Middle English *slippen*, from Middle Dutch or Middle Low German; akin to Middle High German *slipfen* to slide, Old High German *slīfan* to smooth, and perhaps to Greek *olibros* slippery] (14th century)
*intransitive verb*
**1 :** to move with a smooth sliding motion **b :** to move quietly and cautiously **:** STEAL **c :** ELAPSE, PASS
**2 a** (1) **:** to escape from memory or consciousness (2) **:** to become uttered through inadvertence **b :** to pass quickly or easily away **:** become lost ⟨let an opportunity *slip*⟩
**3 :** to fall into error or fault **:** LAPSE

**4 a :** to slide out of place or away from a support or one's grasp **b :** to slide on or down a slippery surface ⟨*slip* on the stairs⟩ **c :** to flow smoothly
**5 :** to get speedily into or out of clothing ⟨*slipped* into his coat⟩
**6 :** to fall off from a standard or accustomed level by degrees **:** DECLINE
**7 :** SIDESLIP
*transitive verb*
**1 :** to cause to move easily and smoothly **:** SLIDE
**2 a :** to get away from **:** ELUDE, EVADE ⟨*slipped* his pursuers⟩ **b :** to free oneself from ⟨the dog *slipped* its collar⟩ **c :** to escape from ⟨one's memory or notice⟩ ⟨their names *slip* my mind⟩
**3 :** SHED, CAST ⟨the snake *slipped* its skin⟩
**4 :** to put on (a garment) quickly — usually used with *on* ⟨*slip* on a coat⟩
**5 a :** to let loose from a restraining leash or grasp **b :** to cause to slip open **:** RELEASE, UNDO ⟨*slip* a lock⟩ **c :** to let go of **d :** to disengage from (an anchor) instead of hauling
**6 a :** to insert, place, or pass quietly or secretly **b :** to give or pay on the sly
**7 :** SLINK, ABORT
**8 :** DISLOCATE ⟨*slipped* his shoulder⟩
**9 :** to transfer (a stitch) from one needle to another without working a stitch
**10 :** to avoid (a punch) by moving the body or head quickly to one side
**²slip** *noun* (15th century)
**1 a :** a sloping ramp extending out into the water to serve as a place for landing or repairing ships **b :** a ship's or boat's berth between two piers
**2 :** the act or an instance of departing secretly or hurriedly ⟨gave his pursuer the *slip*⟩
**3 a :** a mistake in judgment, policy, or procedure **b :** an unintentional and trivial mistake or fault **:** LAPSE ⟨a *slip* of the tongue⟩
**4 :** a leash so made that it can be quickly slipped
**5 a :** the act or an instance of slipping down or out of a place ⟨a *slip* on the ice⟩; *also* **:** a sudden mishap **b :** a movement dislocating parts (as of a rock or soil mass); *also* **:** the result of such movement **c :** a fall from some level or standard **:** DECLINE ⟨a *slip* in stock prices⟩
**6 a :** an undergarment made in dress length with shoulder straps; *also* **:** HALF-SLIP **b :** a case into which something is slipped; *specifically* **:** PILLOWCASE
**7 a :** the motion of the center of resistance of the float of a paddle wheel or the blade of an oar through the water horizontally **b :** retrograde movement of a belt on a pulley **c :** the amount of leakage past the piston of a pump or the impellers of a blower
**8 :** a disposition or tendency to slip easily
**9 :** the action of sideslipping **:** an instance of sideslipping
*synonym* see ERROR
**³slip** *noun* [Middle English *slippe*, probably from Middle Dutch or Middle Low German, split, slit, flap] (15th century)
**1 a :** a small shoot or twig cut for planting or grafting **:** SCION **b :** DESCENDANT, OFFSPRING
**2 a :** a long narrow strip of material **b :** a small piece of paper
**3 :** a young and slender person ⟨a *slip* of a girl⟩
**4 :** a long seat or narrow pew
**⁴slip** *transitive verb* **slipped; slip·ping** (1530)
**:** to take cuttings from (a plant) **:** divide into slips ⟨*slip* a geranium⟩
**⁵slip** *noun* [Middle English *slyp* slime, from Old English *slypa* slime, paste; akin to Old English *slūpan* to slip — more at SLEEVE] (1640)
**:** a mixture of finely divided clay and water used by potters (as for casting or decorating wares or in cementing separately formed parts)

**slip·case** \'slip-ˌkās\ *noun* (circa 1925)
**:** a protective container with one open end for books
— **slip·cased** \-ˌkāst\ *adjective*
**slip·cov·er** \'slip-ˌkə-vər\ *noun* (1886)
**:** a cover that may be slipped off and on; *specifically* **:** a removable covering for an article of furniture
**slip-form** \'slip-ˌfȯrm\ *transitive verb* (1962)
**:** to construct with the use of a slip form
**slip form** *noun* (1949)
**:** a form that is moved slowly as concrete is placed during construction (as of a building or pavement)
**slip·knot** \'slip-ˌnät\ *noun* (1659)
**:** a knot that slips along the rope or line around which it is made; *especially* **:** one made by tying an overhand knot around the standing part of a rope — see KNOT illustration
**slip noose** *noun* (1847)
**:** a noose with a slipknot
**slip-on** \'slip-ˌȯn, -ˌän\ *noun* (1815)
**:** an article of clothing that is easily slipped on or off: as **a :** a glove or shoe without fastenings **b :** a garment (as a girdle) that one steps into and pulls up **c :** PULLOVER
**slip·over** \-ˌō-vər\ *noun* (1917)
**:** a garment or cover that slips on and off easily; *specifically* **:** a pullover sweater
**slip·page** \'sli-pij\ *noun* (1850)
**1 :** an act, instance, or process of slipping
**2 :** a loss in transmission of power; *also* **:** the difference between theoretical and actual output (as of power)
**slipped disk** *noun* (1942)
**:** a protrusion of one of the cartilage disks between vertebrae with pressure on spinal nerves resulting in low back pain or sciatic pain
**¹slip·per** \'sli-pər\ *adjective* [Middle English, from Old English *slipor*; akin to Middle Low German *slipper* slippery, *slippen* to slip] (before 12th century)
*chiefly dialect* **:** SLIPPERY
**²slipper** *noun* [Middle English, from *slippen* to slip] (15th century)
**:** a light low-cut shoe that is easily slipped on the foot
— **slip·pered** \-pərd\ *adjective*
**slip·pery** \'sli-p(ə-)rē\ *adjective* **slip·per·i·er; -est** [alteration of Middle English *slipper*] (circa 1500)
**1 a :** causing or tending to cause something to slide or fall ⟨*slippery* roads⟩ **b :** tending to slip from the grasp
**2 :** not firmly fixed **:** UNSTABLE
**3 :** not to be trusted **:** TRICKY
— **slip·per·i·ness** *noun*
**slippery elm** *noun* (1748)
**:** a large-leaved elm (*Ulmus rubra* synonym *U. fulva*) of eastern North America that has hard wood and fragrant mucilaginous inner bark; *also* **:** the bark
**slip·py** \'sli-pē\ *adjective* **slip·pi·er; -est** (1548)
**:** SLIPPERY
**slip ring** *noun* [²slip] (1898)
**:** one of two or more continuous conducting rings from which the brushes take or to which they deliver current in a generator or motor
**slip–sheet** \'slip-ˌshēt\ *transitive verb* (circa 1909)
**:** to insert slip sheets between (newly printed sheets)
**slip sheet** *noun* [¹slip] (1903)
**:** a sheet of paper placed between newly printed sheets to prevent offsetting
**slip·shod** \'slip-'shäd\ *adjective* [¹slip] (1580)
**1 a :** wearing loose shoes or slippers **b :** down at the heel **:** SHABBY
**2 :** CARELESS, SLOVENLY

**slip·slop** \-,släp\ *noun* [reduplication of ²*slop*] (1675)
**1** *archaic* **:** watery food **:** SLOPS
**2** *archaic* **:** shallow talk or writing
— **slip–slop** *adjective*
**slip·sole** \-,sōl\ *noun* (circa 1908)
**1 :** a thin insole
**2 :** a half sole inserted between the insole or welt and the outsole of a shoe to give additional height — called also *slip tap*
**slip stitch** *noun* (circa 1882)
**1 :** a concealed stitch for sewing folded edges (as hems) made by alternately running the needle inside the fold and picking up a thread or two from the body of the article
**2 :** an unworked stitch; *especially* **:** a knitting stitch that is shifted from one needle to another without knitting it
**¹slip·stream** \'slip-,strēm\ *noun* (1913)
**1 :** a stream of fluid (as air or water) driven aft by a propeller
**2 :** an area of reduced air pressure and forward suction immediately behind a rapidly moving vehicle
**²slipstream** *intransitive verb* (1957)
**:** to drive in the slipstream of a vehicle
**slip–up** \'slip-,əp\ *noun* (1854)
**1 :** MISTAKE
**2 :** MISCHANCE
**slip up** *intransitive verb* (1909)
**:** to make a mistake **:** BLUNDER
**slip·ware** \'slip-,war, -,wer\ *noun* (1883)
**:** pottery coated with slip to improve or decorate the surface
**slip·way** \-,wā\ *noun* (1840)
**:** an inclined usually concrete surface for a ship being built or repaired
**¹slit** \'slit\ *noun* [Middle English, from *slitten*] (12th century)
**:** a long narrow cut or opening
— **slit** *adjective*
— **slit·less** \'slit-ləs\ *adjective*
**²slit** *transitive verb* **slit; slit·ting** [Middle English *slitten*; akin to Middle High German *slitzen* to slit, Old High German *slīzan* to tear apart, Old English *sciell* shell — more at SHELL] (14th century)
**1 a :** to make a slit in **b :** to cut off or away **:** SEVER **c :** to form into a slit
**2 :** to cut into long narrow strips
— **slit·ter** *noun*
**slith·er** \'sli-<u>th</u>ər\ *verb* [Middle English *slideren*, from Old English *slidrian*, frequentative of *slīdan* to slide] (before 12th century)
*intransitive verb*
**1 :** to slide on or as if on a loose gravelly surface
**2 :** to slip or slide like a snake
*transitive verb*
**:** to cause to slide
**slith·ery** \'sli-<u>th</u>ə-rē\ *adjective* (circa 1825)
**:** having a slippery surface, texture, or quality
**slit trench** *noun* (1942)
**:** a narrow trench especially for shelter in battle from bomb and shell fragments
**¹sliv·er** \'sli-vər, 2 is usually 'slī-\ *noun* [Middle English *slivere*, from *sliven* to slice off, from Old English -*slīfan*; akin to Old English -*slǣfan* to cut] (14th century)
**1 a :** a long slender piece cut or torn off **:** SPLINTER **b :** a small and narrow portion ⟨a *sliver* of land⟩ **c :** PARTICLE, SCRAP ⟨not a *sliver* of evidence⟩
**2 :** an untwisted strand or rope of textile fiber produced by a carding or combing machine and ready for drawing, roving, or spinning
**²sliv·er** \'sli-vər\ *verb* **sliv·ered; sliv·er·ing** \'sli-və-riŋ, 'sliv-riŋ\ (1605)
*transitive verb*
**:** to cut into slivers **:** SPLINTER
*intransitive verb*
**:** to become split into slivers
**sliv·o·vitz** \'sli-və-,vits, 'slē-, -,wits\ *noun* [Serbo-Croatian *šljivovica*, from *šljiva, sliva* plum; akin to Russian *sliva* plum — more at LIVID] (1885)

**:** a dry usually colorless plum brandy made especially in the Balkan countries
**slob** \'släb\ *noun* [Irish *slab* mud, ooze, slovenly person] (1861)
**:** a slovenly or boorish person
— **slob·bish** \'slä-bish\ *adjective*
— **slob·by** \-bē\ *adjective*
**¹slob·ber** \'slä-bər\ *verb* **slob·bered; slob·ber·ing** \-b(ə-)riŋ\ [Middle English *sloberen* to eat in a slovenly manner; akin to Low German *slubberen* to sip] (1733)
*intransitive verb*
**1 :** to let saliva dribble from the mouth **:** DROOL
**2 :** to indulge the feelings effusively and without restraint
*transitive verb*
**:** to smear with or as if with dribbling saliva or food
— **slob·ber·er** \-bər-ər\ *noun*
**²slobber** *noun* (circa 1755)
**1 :** saliva drooled from the mouth
**2 :** driveling, sloppy, or incoherent utterance
— **slob·bery** \'slä-b(ə-)rē\ *adjective*
**sloe** \'slō\ *noun* [Middle English *slo*, from Old English *slāh*; akin to Old High German *slēha* sloe and probably to Russian *sliva* plum — more at LIVID] (before 12th century)
**:** the small dark globose astringent fruit of the blackthorn; *also* **:** BLACKTHORN
**sloe–eyed** \'slō-,īd\ *adjective* (1867)
**1 :** having soft dark bluish or purplish black eyes
**2 :** having slanted eyes
**sloe gin** *noun* (1895)
**:** a sweet reddish liqueur consisting of grain spirits flavored chiefly with sloes
**¹slog** \'släg\ *verb* **slogged; slog·ging** [origin unknown] (1824)
*transitive verb*
**1 :** to hit hard **:** BEAT
**2 :** to plod (one's way) perseveringly especially against difficulty
*intransitive verb*
**1 :** to plod heavily **:** TRAMP ⟨*slogged* through the snow⟩
**2 :** to work hard and steadily **:** PLUG
— **slog·ger** *noun*
**²slog** *noun* (1888)
**1 :** hard persistent work
**2 :** a hard dogged march or tramp
**slo·gan** \'slō-gən\ *noun* [alteration of earlier *slogorn*, from Scottish Gaelic *sluagh-ghairm*, from *sluagh* army, host + *gairm* cry] (1513)
**1 a :** a war cry or rallying cry especially of a Scottish clan **b :** a word or phrase used to express a characteristic position or stand or a goal to be achieved
**2 :** a brief attention-getting phrase used in advertising or promotion ◆
**slo·gan·eer** \,slō-gə-'nir\ *noun* (1922)
**:** a maker or user of slogans
— **sloganeer** *intransitive verb*
**slo·gan·ize** \'slō-gə-,nīz\ *transitive verb* **-ized; -iz·ing** (1926)
**:** to express as a slogan
**sloop** \'slüp\ *noun* [Dutch *sloep*] (1629)
**:** a fore-and-aft rigged boat with one mast and a single jib
**sloop of war** (1704)
**:** a small warship with guns on only one deck
**¹slop** \'släp\ *noun* [Middle English *sloppe*, probably from Middle Dutch *slop*; akin to Old English ofer*slop* surplice] (14th century)
**1 :** a loose smock or overall

**sloop**

**2** *plural* **:** short full breeches worn by men in the 16th century
**3** *plural* **:** articles (as clothing) sold to sailors
**²slop** *noun* [Middle English *sloppe*] (15th century)
**1 :** soft mud **:** SLUSH
**2 :** thin tasteless drink or liquid food — usually used in plural
**3 :** liquid spilled or splashed
**4 a :** food waste (as garbage) fed to animals **:** SWILL 2a **b :** excreted body waste — usually used in plural
**5 :** sentimental effusiveness in speech or writing **:** GUSH
**³slop** *verb* **slopped; slop·ping** (1557)
*transitive verb*
**1 a :** to spill from a container **b :** to splash or spill liquid on **c :** to cause (a liquid) to splash
**2 :** to dish out messily
**3 :** to eat or drink greedily or noisily
**4 :** to feed slop to ⟨*slop* the hogs⟩
*intransitive verb*
**1 :** to tramp in mud or slush
**2 :** to become spilled or splashed
**3 :** to be effusive **:** GUSH
**4 :** to pass beyond or exceed a boundary or limit
**slop basin** *noun* (1731)
*British* **:** SLOP BOWL
**slop bowl** *noun* (1810)
**:** a bowl for receiving the leavings of tea or coffee cups at table
**slop chest** *noun* [¹*slop*] (1840)
**:** a store of clothing and personal requisites (as tobacco) carried on merchant ships for issue to the crew usually as a charge against their wages
**¹slope** \'slōp\ *adjective* [Middle English *slope*, adverb, obliquely] (1502)
**:** that slants **:** SLOPING — often used in combination ⟨*slope*-sided⟩
**²slope** *verb* **sloped; slop·ing** (1591)
*intransitive verb*
**1 :** to take an oblique course
**2 :** to lie or fall in a slant **:** INCLINE
**3 :** GO, TRAVEL ⟨*slopes* off into the night —Wolcott Gibbs⟩
*transitive verb*
**:** to cause to incline or slant
— **slop·er** *noun*
**³slope** *noun* (circa 1611)
**1 :** upward or downward slant or inclination or degree of slant
**2 :** ground that forms a natural or artificial incline
**3 :** the part of a continent draining to a particular ocean ⟨Alaska's North *Slope*⟩
**4 a :** the tangent of the angle made by a straight line with the x-axis **b :** the slope of the line tangent to a plane curve at a point

◇ **WORD HISTORY**
**slogan** The Scottish Gaelic word *sluagh-ghairm* "battle cry," a compound of *sluagh* "army, host" and *gairm* "cry," was borrowed into Scots, the English of lowland Scotland, as *slogorn, slughorne,* or, with loss of the *r, slogan*. A slogan in the Highlands and the Borders region was typically the name of a clan chief or rendezvous point, used originally as a summons to arms or a password. Made familiar to a wider English-speaking public in Walter Scott's poems *The Lay of the Last Minstrel* and *Marmion, slogan* was taken up outside of Scotland in the extended sense "word or phrase used to express a characteristic position." Irish and Scottish Gaelic *sluagh* (spelled *slua* in contemporary Irish) both go back to Old Irish *slóg* or *slúag,* which denoted the body of men who owed military service to their clan chief or king and took up arms at his call.

**slope–intercept form** *noun* (circa 1942)
: the equation of a straight line in the form $y = mx + b$ where $m$ is the slope of the line and $b$ is the point on the y-axis through which the line passes

**slo–pitch** \'slō-'pich, -,pich\ *noun* [alteration of *slow pitch*] (1967)
: SLOW-PITCH

**slop jar** *noun* (1855)
: a large pail used as a chamber pot or to receive waste water from a washbowl or the contents of chamber pots

**slop pail** *noun* (1864)
: a pail for toilet or household slops

**slop·py** \'slä-pē\ *adjective* **slop·pi·er; -est** (1707)
**1 a :** wet so as to spatter easily : SLUSHY ⟨a *sloppy* racetrack⟩ **b :** wet or smeared with or as if with something slopped over
**2 :** SLOVENLY, CARELESS ⟨a *sloppy* dresser⟩ ⟨did *sloppy* work⟩
**3 :** disagreeably effusive ⟨*sloppy* sentimentalism⟩
— **slop·pi·ly** \'slä-pə-lē\ *adverb*
— **slop·pi·ness** *noun*

**sloppy joe** \-'jō\ *noun* [probably from the name *Joe*, nickname for *Joseph*] (1961)
: ground beef cooked in a thick spicy sauce and usually served on a bun

**slop·work** \'släp-,wərk\ *noun* (1849)
**1 :** the manufacture of cheap ready-made clothing
**2 :** hasty slovenly work

**¹slosh** \'släsh, 'slòsh\ *noun* [probably blend of *slop* and *slush*] (1814)
**1 :** SLUSH
**2 :** the slap or splash of liquid

**²slosh** (1844)
*intransitive verb*
**1 :** to flounder or splash through water, mud, or slush
**2 :** to move with a splashing motion ⟨the water *sloshed* around him —Bill Alcine⟩
*transitive verb*
**1 :** to splash about in liquid
**2 :** to splash (a liquid) about or on something
**3 :** to splash with liquid

**sloshed** \'släsht, 'slòsht\ *adjective* (circa 1946)
*slang* : DRUNK, INTOXICATED

**¹slot** \'slät\ *noun* [Middle English, the hollow running down the middle of the breast, from Middle French *esclot*] (1523)
**1 a :** a narrow opening or groove : SLIT, NOTCH ⟨a mail *slot* in a door⟩ **b :** a narrow passage or enclosure **c :** a passage through the wing of an airplane or of a missile that is located usually near the leading edge and formed between a main and an auxiliary airfoil for improving flow conditions over the wing so as to increase lift and delay stalling of the wing
**2 :** a place or position in an organization or sequence : NICHE
**3 :** SLOT MACHINE
**4 :** a gap between an end and a tackle in an offensive football line

**²slot** *transitive verb* **slot·ted; slot·ting** (1747)
**1 :** to cut a slot in
**2 :** to place in or assign to a slot

**³slot** *noun, plural* **slot** [Middle French *esclot* track] (1575)
: the track of an animal (as a deer)

**slot·back** \'slät-,bak\ *noun* (1959)
: an offensive football halfback who lines up just behind the slot between an offensive end and tackle

**slot car** *noun* (1966)
: an electric toy racing car with a pin underneath that fits into a groove on a track for guidance

**sloth** \'slòth, 'släth *also* 'slōth\ *noun, plural* **sloths** \with ths *or* thz\ [Middle English *slouthe*, from *slow* slow] (12th century)
**1 a :** disinclination to action or labor : INDOLENCE **b :** spiritual apathy and inactivity ⟨the deadly sin of *sloth*⟩

**2 :** any of the slow-moving arboreal edentate mammals that comprise two genera (*Bradypus* and *Choloepus*), inhabit tropical forests of South and Central America, hang from the branches back downward, and feed on leaves, shoots, and fruits — compare THREE-TOED SLOTH, TWO-TOED SLOTH

sloth 2

**sloth·ful** \'slòth-fəl, 'släth- *also* 'slōth-\ *adjective* (15th century)
: inclined to sloth : INDOLENT
*synonym* see LAZY
— **sloth·ful·ly** \-fə-lē\ *adverb*
— **sloth·ful·ness** *noun*

**slot machine** *noun* (1891)
**1 :** a machine whose operation is begun by dropping a coin into a slot
**2 :** a coin-operated gambling machine that pays off according to the matching of symbols on wheels spun by a handle — called also *one-armed bandit*

**slot racing** *noun* (1965)
: the racing of slot cars
— **slot racer** *noun*

**¹slouch** \'slauch\ *noun* [origin unknown] (1515)
**1 a :** an awkward fellow : LOUT **b :** one that is unimpressive; *especially* : a lazy or incompetent person — used in negative constructions ⟨was no *slouch* at cooking⟩
**2 :** a gait or posture characterized by an ungainly stooping of the head and shoulders or excessive relaxation of body muscles

**²slouch** (1754)
*intransitive verb*
**1 :** to walk, stand, or sit with a slouch : assume a slouch
**2 :** DROOP
*transitive verb*
: to cause to droop ⟨*slouched* his shoulders⟩
— **slouch·er** *noun*

**slouch hat** *noun* (1837)
: a soft usually felt hat with a wide flexible brim

**slouchy** \'slau-chē\ *adjective* **slouch·i·er; -est** (circa 1693)
: lacking erectness or stiffness (as in form or posture) ⟨a *slouchy* sweater⟩ ⟨*slouchy* figures waiting in line⟩
— **slouch·i·ly** \-chə-lē\ *adverb*
— **slouch·i·ness** \-chē-nəs\ *noun*

**¹slough** \'slü, 'slau; *in the US* (*except New England*) 'slü *is usual for sense 1 with those to whom the sense is familiar; British usually* 'slau *for both senses*\ *noun* [Middle English *slogh*, from Old English *slōh*; akin to Middle High German *slouche* ditch] (before 12th century)
**1 a :** a place of deep mud or mire **b :** (1) : SWAMP (2) : an inlet on a river; *also* : BACKWATER (3) : a creek in a marsh or tide flat
**2 :** a state of moral degradation or spiritual dejection
— **sloughy** \-ē\ *adjective*

**²slough** (1846)
*transitive verb*
: to engulf in a slough
*intransitive verb*
: to plod through or as if through mud : SLOG

**³slough** \'sləf\ *also* **sluff** *noun* [Middle English *slughe*; akin to Middle High German *slūch* snakeskin] (14th century)
**1 :** the cast-off skin of a snake
**2 :** a mass of dead tissue separating from an ulcer
**3 :** something that may be shed or cast off

**⁴slough** \'sləf\ *also* **sluff** (1720)
*intransitive verb*
**1 a :** to become shed or cast off **b :** to cast off one's skin **c :** to separate in the form of dead tissue from living tissue
**2 :** to crumble slowly and fall away
*transitive verb*
**1 :** to cast off
**2 a :** to get rid of or discard as irksome, objectionable, or disadvantageous — usually used with *off* **b :** to dispose of (a losing card in bridge) by discarding
*synonym* see DISCARD

**slough of de·spond** \,slau-əv-di-'spänd, ,slü-\ [from the *Slough of Despond*, deep bog into which Christian falls on the way from the City of Destruction and from which Help saves him in the allegory *Pilgrim's Progress* (1678) by John Bunyan] (1776)
: a state of extreme depression

**Slo·vak** \'slō-,väk, -,vak\ *noun* [Slovak *slovák*] (1829)
**1 :** a member of a Slavic people of Slovakia
**2 :** the Slavic language of the Slovak people
— **Slovak** *adjective*
— **Slo·va·ki·an** \slō-'vä-kē-ən, -'va-\ *adjective or noun*

**¹slov·en** \'slə-vən\ *noun* [Middle English *sloveyn* rascal, perhaps from Flemish *sloovin* woman of low character] (15th century)
: one habitually negligent of neatness or cleanliness especially in personal appearance

**²sloven** *adjective* (1815)
: SLOVENLY

**Slo·vene** \'slō-,vēn\ *noun* [German *Slowene* from Slovene *Slovenec*] (1883)
**1 :** a member of a Slavic people living largely in Slovenia
**2 :** the language of the Slovenes
— **Slovene** *adjective*
— **Slo·ve·nian** \slō-'vē-nē-ən, -nyən\ *adjective or noun*

**slov·en·ly** \'slə-vən-lē *also* 'slä-\ *adjective* (circa 1568)
**1 a :** untidy especially in personal appearance **b :** lazily slipshod ⟨*slovenly* in thought⟩
**2 :** characteristic of a sloven ⟨*slovenly* habits⟩
— **slo·ven·li·ness** *noun*
— **slovenly** *adverb*

**¹slow** \'slō\ *adjective* [Middle English, from Old English *slāw*; akin to Old High German *slēo* dull] (before 12th century)
**1 a :** mentally dull : STUPID ⟨a *slow* student⟩ **b :** naturally inert or sluggish
**2 a :** lacking in readiness, promptness, or willingness **b :** not hasty or precipitate ⟨was *slow* to anger⟩
**3 a :** moving, flowing, or proceeding without speed or at less than usual speed ⟨traffic was *slow*⟩ **b :** exhibiting or marked by low speed ⟨he moved with *slow* deliberation⟩ **c :** not acute ⟨a *slow* disease⟩ **d :** LOW, GENTLE ⟨*slow* fire⟩
**4 :** requiring a long time : GRADUAL ⟨a *slow* recovery⟩
**5 :** having qualities that hinder rapid progress or action ⟨a *slow* track⟩
**6 a :** registering behind or below what is correct ⟨the clock is *slow*⟩ **b :** less than the time indicated by another method of reckoning **c :** that is behind the time at a specified time or place
**7 a :** lacking in life, animation, or gaiety : BORING **b :** marked by reduced sales or patronage ⟨business was *slow*⟩
— **slow·ish** \'slō-ish\ *adjective*
— **slow·ness** *noun*

**²slow** *adverb* (15th century)

: SLOWLY ▪

**³slow** (1557)
*transitive verb*
: to make slow or slower : slacken the speed of ⟨*slow* a car⟩ — often used with *down* or *up*
*intransitive verb*
: to go or become slower ⟨production of new cars *slowed* sharply⟩
**synonym** see DELAY

**slow·down** \'slō-,daůn\ *noun* (1897)
: a slowing down ⟨a business *slowdown*⟩

**slow–foot·ed** \-'fů-təd\ *adjective* (1642)
: moving at a very slow pace : PLODDING ⟨a *slow-footed* novel⟩ ⟨a *slow-footed* ship⟩
— **slow–foot·ed·ness** *noun*

**slow·ly** \-lē\ *adverb* (13th century)
: in a slow manner : not quickly, fast, early, rashly, or readily
*usage* see SLOW

**slow match** *noun* (circa 1802)
: a match or fuse made so as to burn slowly and evenly and used for firing (as of blasting charges)

**slow–motion** \'slō-'mō-shən\ *adjective* (1923)
: of, relating to, or being motion-picture or video photography in which the action that has been photographed is made to appear to occur slower than it actually occurred ⟨a *slow-motion* replay⟩; *also* : slowly moving ⟨a *slow-motion* dance⟩

**slow motion** *noun* (1924)
: slow-motion photography

**slow–pitch** \'slō-,pich\ *noun* (1967)
: softball which is played with 10 players on each side and in which each pitch must have an arc 3 to 10 feet high and base stealing is not allowed

**slow·poke** \'slō-,pōk\ *noun* [¹*slow* + *poke* annoyingly stupid person] (1848)
: a very slow person

**slow–twitch** \'slō-,twich\ *adjective* (1971)
: of, relating to, or being muscle fiber that contracts slowly especially during sustained physical activity requiring endurance — compare FAST-TWITCH

**slow virus** *noun* (1954)
: any of various viruses with a long incubation period between infection and development of a degenerative disease (as kuru or Creutzfeldt-Jakob disease)

**slow–wit·ted** \-'wi-təd\ *adjective* (1571)
: mentally slow : DULL

**slow·worm** \-,wərm\ *noun* [Middle English *sloworm,* from Old English *slāwyrm,* from *slā-* (akin to Swedish *slå* earthworm) + *wyrm* worm] (before 12th century)
: a burrowing limbless European lizard (*Anguis fragilis*) with small eyes — called also *blindworm*

**¹slub** \'sləb\ *transitive verb* **slubbed; slubbing** [back-formation from *slubbing*] (1834)
: to draw out and twist (as slivers of wool) slightly

**²slub** *noun* (1851)
: a soft thick uneven section in a yarn or thread

**slub·ber** \'slə-bər\ *transitive verb* **slubbered; slub·ber·ing** \-b(ə-)riŋ\ [probably from obsolete Dutch *slubberen*] (1530)
**1** *dialect chiefly English* : STAIN, SULLY
**2** : to perform in a slipshod fashion

**slub·bing** \'slə-biŋ\ *noun* [origin unknown] (1786)
: ROVING

**sludge** \'sləj\ *noun* [Middle English *slugge,* perhaps alteration of *slicche* mud, slush; akin to Old High German *slīh* mire] (15th century)
**1** : MUD, MIRE; *especially* : a muddy deposit (as on a riverbed) : OOZE
**2** : a muddy or slushy mass, deposit, or sediment: as **a** : precipitated solid matter produced by water and sewage treatment processes **b** : muddy sediment in a steam boiler **c** : a precipitate or settling (as a mixture of impurities and acid) from a mineral oil
**3** : SLUSH 5

— **sludgy** \'slə-jē\ *adjective*

**¹slue** \'slü\ *variant of* ¹SLOUGH

**²slue** *variant of* ³SLEW

**³slue** *noun* [²*slue*] (circa 1860)
**1** : position or inclination after slewing
**2** : SKID 5

**¹slug** \'sləg\ *noun* [Middle English *slugge,* of Scandinavian origin; akin to Norwegian dialect *slugga* to walk sluggishly] (15th century)
**1** : SLUGGARD
**2** : a lump, disk, or cylinder of material (as plastic or metal): as **a** (1) : a musket ball (2) : BULLET **b** : a piece of metal roughly shaped for subsequent processing **c** : a $50 gold piece **d** : a disk for insertion in a slot machine; *especially* : one used illegally instead of a coin

**slug 3**

**3** : any of numerous chiefly terrestrial pulmonate gastropods (order Stylommatophora) that are found in most parts of the world where there is a reasonable supply of moisture and are closely related to the land snails but are long and wormlike and have only a rudimentary shell often buried in the mantle or entirely absent
**4** : a smooth soft larva of a sawfly or moth that creeps like a mollusk
**5 a** : a quantity of liquor drunk in one swallow **b** : a detached mass of fluid (as water vapor or oil) that causes impact (as in a circulating system)
**6 a** : a strip of metal thicker than a printer's lead **b** : a line of type cast as one piece **c** : a usually temporary type line serving to instruct or identify
**7** : the gravitational unit of mass in the foot-pound-second system to which a pound force can impart an acceleration of one foot per second per second and which is equal to the mass of an object weighing 32 pounds

**²slug** *transitive verb* **slugged; slug·ging** (1912)
**1** : to add a printer's slug to
**2** : to drink in gulps — often used with *down*

**³slug** *noun* [perhaps from *slug* to load with slugs] (1830)
: a heavy blow especially with the fist

**⁴slug** *transitive verb* **slugged; slug·ging** (circa 1861)
**1** : to strike heavily with or as if with the fist or a bat
**2** : FIGHT 4b — usually used in the phrase *slug it out*

**slug·abed** \'slə-gə-,bed\ *noun* (1592)
: a person who stays in bed after the usual or proper time to get up; *broadly* : SLUGGARD

**slug·fest** \'sləg-,fest\ *noun* (1916)
: a fight marked by the exchange of heavy blows; *also* : a heated dispute ⟨a vocal *slugfest*⟩

**¹slug·gard** \'slə-gərd\ *noun* [Middle English *sluggart*] (14th century)
: an habitually lazy person

**²sluggard** *adjective* (1593)
: SLUGGARDLY
— **slug·gard·ness** *noun*

**slug·gard·ly** \'slə-gərd-lē\ *adjective* (1865)
: lazily inactive

**slug·ger** \'slə-gər\ *noun* (1877)
: one that strikes hard or with heavy blows: as **a** : a prizefighter who punches hard but has usually little defensive skill **b** : a hard-hitting batter in baseball

**slugging percentage** *noun* (circa 1949)
: the ratio (as a rate per thousand) of the total number of bases reached on base hits to official times at bat for a baseball player — called also *slugging average*

**slug·gish** \'slə-gish\ *adjective* (15th century)
**1** : averse to activity or exertion : INDOLENT; *also* : TORPID

**2** : slow to respond (as to stimulation or treatment)
**3 a** : markedly slow in movement, flow, or growth **b** : economically inactive or slow
— **slug·gish·ly** *adverb*
— **slug·gish·ness** *noun*

**¹sluice** \'slüs\ *noun* [Middle English *sluse,* alteration of *scluse,* from Middle French *escluse,* from Late Latin *exclusa,* from Latin, feminine of *exclusus,* past participle of *excludere* to exclude] (15th century)
**1 a** : an artificial passage for water (as in a millstream) fitted with a valve or gate for stopping or regulating flow **b** : a body of water pent up behind a floodgate
**2** : a dock gate : FLOODGATE
**3 a** : a stream flowing through a floodgate **b** : a channel to drain or carry off surplus water
**4** : a long inclined trough usually on the ground; *especially* : such a contrivance paved usually with riffles to hold quicksilver for catching gold

**²sluice** *verb* **sluiced; sluic·ing** (1593)
*transitive verb*
**1** : to draw off by or through a sluice
**2 a** : to wash with or in water running through or from a sluice **b** : to drench with a sudden flow : FLUSH
**3** : to transport (as logs) in a sluice
*intransitive verb*
: to pour as if from a sluice

**sluice·way** \'slüs-,wā\ *noun* (1779)
: an artificial channel into which water is let by a sluice

**sluicy** \'slü-sē\ *adjective* (1697)
: falling copiously or in streams : STREAMING

**¹slum** \'sləm\ *noun, often attributive* [origin unknown] (1825)
: a densely populated usually urban area marked by crowding, dirty run-down housing, poverty, and social disorganization

**²slum** *intransitive verb* **slummed; slumming** (1884)
: to visit slums especially out of curiosity; *broadly* : to go somewhere or do something that might be considered beneath one's station — sometimes used with *it* ⟨*slumming* it in a cabin without plumbing⟩
— **slum·mer** *noun*

**¹slum·ber** \'sləm-bər\ *intransitive verb* **slumbered; slum·ber·ing** \-b(ə-)riŋ\ [Middle English, frequentative of *slumen* to doze, probably from *slume* slumber, from Old English *slūma;* akin to Middle High German *slumen* to slumber] (13th century)
**1 a** : to sleep lightly : DOZE **b** : SLEEP
**2 a** : to be in a torpid, slothful, or negligent state **b** : to lie dormant or latent
— **slum·ber·er** \-bər-ər\ *noun*

**²slumber** *noun* (14th century)
**1 a** : SLEEP **b** : a light sleep

**2 :** LETHARGY, TORPOR
**slum·ber·ous** or **slum·brous** \'sləm-b(ə-)rəs\ *adjective* (15th century)
**1 :** heavy with sleep **:** SLEEPY
**2 :** inducing slumber **:** SOPORIFIC
**3 :** marked by or suggestive of a state of sleep or lethargy ⟨a *slumberous* state of peace⟩
**slumber party** *noun* (1925)
**:** an overnight gathering especially of teenage girls usually at one of their homes
**slum·bery** \'sləm-b(ə-)rē\ *adjective* (14th century)
*archaic* **:** SLUMBEROUS
**slum·gul·lion** \'sləm-,gəl-yən, ,sləm-'\ *noun* [perhaps from *slum* slime + English dialect *gullion* mud, cesspool] (1902)
**:** a meat stew
**slum·lord** \'sləm-,lòrd\ *noun* [¹*slum* + *landlord*] (1953)
**:** a landlord who receives unusually large profits from substandard properties
**slum·my** \'slə-mē\ *adjective* **slum·mi·er; -est** (1873)
**:** of, relating to, or suggestive of a slum ⟨*slummy* streets⟩
¹**slump** \'sləmp\ *intransitive verb* [probably of Scandinavian origin; akin to Norwegian *slumpa* to fall] (circa 1677)
**1 a :** to fall or sink suddenly **b :** to drop or slide down suddenly **:** COLLAPSE ⟨*slumped* to the floor⟩
**2 :** to assume a drooping posture or carriage **:** SLOUCH
**3 :** to go into a slump ⟨sales *slumped*⟩
²**slump** *noun* (1887)
**1 a :** a marked or sustained decline especially in economic activity or prices ⟨a post-election *slump*⟩ **b :** a period of poor or losing play by a team or individual ⟨one spring I was in a batting *slump* —Ted Williams⟩
**2 :** a downward slide of a mass of rock or land
**slump·fla·tion** \,sləmp-'flā-shən\ *noun* [²*slump* + in*flation*] (1974)
**:** a state or period of combined economic decline and rising inflation
**slung** *past and past participle of* SLING
**slung-shot** \'sləŋ-,shät\ *noun* (1842)
**:** a striking weapon consisting of a small mass of metal or stone fixed on a flexible handle or strap
**slunk** *past and past participle of* SLINK
¹**slur** \'slər\ *noun* [obsolete English dialect *slur* thin mud, from Middle English *sloor;* akin to Middle High German *slier* mud] (1609)
**1 a :** an insulting or disparaging remark or innuendo **:** ASPERSION **b :** a shaming or degrading effect **:** STAIN, STIGMA
**2 :** a blurred spot in printed matter **:** SMUDGE
²**slur** *verb* **slurred; slur·ring** (1660)
*transitive verb*
**1 :** to cast aspersions on **:** DISPARAGE
**2 :** to make indistinct **:** OBSCURE
*intransitive verb*
**:** to slip so as to cause a slur — used of a sheet being printed
³**slur** *verb* **slurred; slur·ring** [probably from Low German *slurrn* to shuffle; akin to Middle English *sloor* mud] (1660)
*transitive verb*
**1 a :** to slide or slip over without due mention, consideration, or emphasis ⟨*slurred* over certain facts⟩ **b :** to perform hurriedly **:** SKIMP ⟨let him not *slur* his lesson —R. W. Emerson⟩
**2 :** to perform (successive tones of different pitch) in a smooth or connected manner
**3 a :** to reduce, make a substitution for, or omit (sounds that would normally occur in an utterance) **b :** to utter with such reduction, substitution, or omission of sounds ⟨his speech was *slurred*⟩
*intransitive verb*
**1** *dialect chiefly English* **:** SLIP, SLIDE
**2 :** DRAG, SHUFFLE
⁴**slur** *noun* (circa 1801)
**1 a :** a curved line connecting notes to be sung to the same syllable or performed without a

break **b :** the combination of two or more slurred tones
**2 :** a slurring manner of speech
**slurp** \'slərp\ *verb* [Dutch *slurpen;* akin to Middle Low German *slorpen* to slurp] (1648)
*intransitive verb*
**:** to make a sucking noise while eating or drinking
*transitive verb*
**:** to eat or drink noisily or with a sucking sound
— **slurp** *noun*
¹**slur·ry** \'slər-ē, 'slə-rē\ *noun, plural* **slur·ries** [Middle English *slory*] (15th century)
**:** a watery mixture of insoluble matter (as mud, lime, or plaster of paris)
²**slurry** *transitive verb* **slur·ried; slur·ry·ing** (1947)
**:** to convert into a slurry
¹**slush** \'sləsh\ *noun* [perhaps of Scandinavian origin; akin to Norwegian *slusk* slush] (1641)
**1 a :** partly melted or watery snow **b :** loose ice crystals formed during the early stages of freezing of salt water
**2 :** soft mud **:** MIRE
**3 :** refuse grease and fat from cooking especially on shipboard
**4 :** paper pulp in water suspension
**5 :** trashy and usually cheaply sentimental material
**6 :** unsolicited writings submitted (as to a magazine) for publication
²**slush** (1807)
*transitive verb*
**:** to wet, splash, or paint with slush
*intransitive verb*
**1 :** to make one's way through slush
**2 :** to make a splashing sound
**slush fund** *noun* (1864)
**1 :** a fund raised from the sale of refuse to obtain small luxuries or pleasures for a warship's crew
**2 :** a fund for bribing public officials or carrying on corruptive propaganda
**slushy** \'slə-shē\ *adjective* **slush·i·er; -est** (1791)
**1 :** being, involving, or resembling slush: as **a :** full of or covered with slush ⟨*slushy* streets⟩ **b :** made up of or having the consistency of slush ⟨*slushy* snow⟩ ⟨a *slushy* mixture⟩ **c :** having a cheaply sentimental quality **:** TRASHY ⟨a *slushy* novel⟩
— **slush·i·ness** *noun*
**slut** \'slət\ *noun* [Middle English *slutte*] (15th century)
**1** *chiefly British* **:** a slovenly woman
**2 a :** a promiscuous woman; *especially* **:** PROSTITUTE **b :** a saucy girl **:** MINX
— **slut·tish** \'slə-tish\ *adjective*
— **slut·tish·ly** *adverb*
— **slut·tish·ness** *noun*
— **slut·ty** \'slə-tē\ *adjective*
**sly** \'slī\ *adjective* **sli·er** or **sly·er** \'slī(-ə)r\; **sli·est** or **sly·est** \'slī-əst\ [Middle English *sli,* from Old Norse *slœgr;* akin to Old English *slēan* to strike — more at SLAY] (13th century)
**1** *chiefly dialect* **a :** wise in practical affairs **b :** displaying cleverness **:** INGENIOUS
**2 a :** clever in concealing one's aims or ends **:** FURTIVE ⟨the *sly* fox⟩ **b :** lacking in straightforwardness and candor **:** DISSEMBLING ⟨a *sly* scheme⟩
**3 :** lightly mischievous **:** ROGUISH ⟨a *sly* jest⟩ ⟨a *sly* smile⟩ ☆
— **sly·ly** *adverb*
— **sly·ness** *noun*
— **on the sly :** in a manner intended to avoid notice
**sly·boots** \'slī-,büts\ *noun plural but singular in construction* (circa 1700)
**:** a sly tricky person; *especially* **:** one who is cunning or mischievous in an engaging way
¹**smack** \'smak\ *noun* [Middle English, from Old English *smæc;* akin to Old High German

*smac* taste and probably to Lithuanian *smaguris* sweet tooth] (before 12th century)
**1 :** characteristic taste or flavor; *also* **:** a perceptible taste or tincture
**2 :** a small quantity
²**smack** *intransitive verb* (13th century)
**1 :** to have a taste or flavor
**2 :** to have a trace, vestige, or suggestion ⟨a proposal that *smacks* of treason⟩
³**smack** *noun* [Dutch *smak* or Low German *smack*] (1533)
**:** a sailing ship (as a sloop or cutter) used chiefly in coasting and fishing
⁴**smack** *verb* [akin to Middle Dutch *smacken* to strike] (1557)
*transitive verb*
**1 :** to close and open (lips) noisily and in rapid succession especially in eating
**2 a :** to kiss with or as if with a smack **b :** to strike so as to produce a smack
*intransitive verb*
**:** to make or give a smack
⁵**smack** *noun* (1570)
**1 :** a quick sharp noise made by rapidly compressing and opening the lips
**2 :** a loud kiss
**3 :** a sharp slap or blow
⁶**smack** *adverb* (1782)
**:** squarely and sharply **:** DIRECTLY ⟨*smack* in the middle⟩
⁷**smack** *noun* [perhaps from Yiddish *shmek* sniff, whiff, pinch (of snuff)] (circa 1960)
*slang* **:** HEROIN
**smack–dab** \'smak-'dab\ *adverb* (1892)
**:** EXACTLY, SQUARELY
**smack·er** \'sma-kər\ *noun* (1611)
**1 :** one that smacks
**2** *slang* **:** DOLLAR
**smack·ing** \'sma-kiŋ\ *adjective* (1820)
**:** BRISK, LIVELY ⟨a *smacking* breeze⟩
¹**small** \'smól\ *adjective* [Middle English *smal,* from Old English *smæl;* akin to Old High German *smal* small, Greek *mēlon* small domestic animal] (before 12th century)
**1 a :** having comparatively little size or slight dimensions **b :** LOWERCASE
**2 a :** minor in influence, power, or rank **b :** operating on a limited scale
**3 :** lacking in strength ⟨a *small* voice⟩
**4 a :** little or close to zero in an objectively measurable aspect (as quantity, amount, or value) **b :** made up of few or little units

---

☆ **SYNONYMS**
**Sly, cunning, crafty, wily, tricky, foxy, artful, slick** mean attaining or seeking to attain one's ends by guileful or devious means. SLY implies furtiveness, lack of candor, and skill in concealing one's aims and methods ⟨a *sly* corporate raider⟩. CUNNING suggests the inventive use of sometimes limited intelligence in overreaching or circumventing ⟨the *cunning* fox avoided the trap⟩. CRAFTY implies cleverness and subtlety of method ⟨a *crafty* lefthander⟩. WILY implies skill and deception in maneuvering ⟨the *wily* fugitive escaped the posse⟩. TRICKY is more likely to suggest shiftiness and unreliability than skill in deception and maneuvering ⟨a *tricky* political operative⟩. FOXY implies a shrewd and wary craftiness usually involving devious dealing ⟨a *foxy* publicity man planting stories⟩. ARTFUL implies indirectness in dealing and often connotes sophistication or cleverness ⟨elicited the information by *artful* questioning⟩. SLICK emphasizes smoothness and guile ⟨*slick* operators selling timesharing⟩.

---

\ə\ abut \ᵊ\ kitten \ər\ further \a\ ash \ā\ ace
\ä\ mop, mar \aù\ out \ch\ chin \e\ bet \ē\ easy
\g\ go \i\ hit \ī\ ice \j\ job \ŋ\ sing \ō\ go
\ò\ law \òi\ boy \th\ thin \t͟h\ the \ü\ loot \ù\ foot
\y\ yet \zh\ vision *see also* Guide to Pronunciation

**5 a :** of little consequence **:** TRIVIAL, INSIGNIFI-
CANT **b :** HUMBLE, MODEST ⟨a *small* beginning⟩
**6 :** limited in degree
**7 a :** MEAN, PETTY **b :** reduced to a humiliating
position ☆
— **small·ish** \'smȯ-lish\ *adjective*
— **small·ness** \'smȯl-nəs\ *noun*
²**small** *adverb* (before 12th century)
**1 :** in or into small pieces
**2 :** without force or loudness ⟨speak as *small*
as you will —Shakespeare⟩
**3 :** in a small manner
³**small** *noun* (14th century)
**1 :** a part smaller and especially narrower than
the remainder ⟨the *small* of the back⟩
**2 a** *plural* **:** small-sized products **b** *plural,
chiefly British* **:** SMALLCLOTHES; *especially*
**:** UNDERWEAR
**small arm** *noun* (1689)
**:** a handheld firearm (as a handgun or shoulder
arm) — usually used in plural
**small beer** *noun* (1568)
**1 :** weak or inferior beer
**2 :** something of small importance **:** TRIVIA
— **small–beer** *adjective*
**small calorie** *noun* (circa 1889)
**:** CALORIE 1a
**small capital** *noun* (1770)
**:** a letter having the form of but smaller than a
capital letter (as in THESE WORDS) — called
also *small cap*
**small change** *noun* (1819)
**1 :** coins of low denomination
**2 :** something trifling or petty
**small–claims court** *noun* (1925)
**:** a special court intended to simplify and expedite the handling of small claims on debts
— called also *small-debts court*
**small·clothes** \'smȯl-ˌklō(th)z\ *noun plural*
(1796)
**1 :** close-fitting knee breeches worn in the
18th century
**2 :** small articles of clothing (as underclothing
or handkerchiefs)
**smaller European elm bark beetle** *noun*
(circa 1945)
**:** ELM BARK BEETLE b
**small–fry** \'smȯl-ˌfrī\ *adjective* (1817)
**1 :** MINOR, UNIMPORTANT ⟨a *small-fry* politician⟩
**2 :** of, relating to, or intended for children
**:** CHILDISH
**small·hold·ing** \-ˌhōl-diŋ\ *noun* (1892)
*chiefly British* **:** a small farm
— **small·hold·er** \-dər\ *noun*
**small hours** *noun plural* (circa 1837)
**:** the early morning hours
**small intestine** *noun* (1767)
**:** the part of the intestine that lies between the
stomach and colon, consists of duodenum, jejunum, and ileum, secretes digestive enzymes,
and is the chief site of the absorption of digested nutrients
**small–mind·ed** \'smȯl-'mīn-dəd\ *adjective*
(1847)
**1 :** having narrow interests, sympathies, or
outlook
**2 :** typical of a small-minded person **:** marked
by pettiness, narrowness, or meanness ⟨*small-
minded* conduct⟩
— **small–mind·ed·ly** *adverb*
— **small–mind·ed·ness** *noun*
**small·mouth bass** \'smȯl-ˌmau̇th-\ *noun*
(1938)
**:** a black bass
(*Micropterus do-
lomieu*) of clear
rivers and lakes
that is bronzy
green above and
lighter below
and has the ver-

**smallmouth bass**

tex of the angle of the jaw falling below the
eye — called also *smallmouth, smallmouth
black bass*
**small octave** *noun* (circa 1890)

**:** the musical octave that begins on the first C
below middle C — see PITCH illustration
**small potato** *noun* (1831)
**:** one that is of trivial importance or worth —
usually used in plural but singular or plural in
construction
**small·pox** \'smȯl-ˌpäks\ *noun* (1518)
**:** an acute contagious febrile disease caused by
a poxvirus and characterized by skin eruption
with pustules, sloughing, and scar formation
**small–scale** \-'skā(ə)l\ *adjective* (1852)
**1 :** small in scope; *especially* **:** small in output
or operation
**2** *of a map* **:** having a scale (as one inch to 25
miles) that permits plotting of comparatively
little detail and shows mainly large features
**small screen** *noun* (1956)
**:** TELEVISION
**small stuff** *noun* (circa 1857)
**:** small rope (as spun yarn or marline) usually
identified by the number of threads or yarns
which it contains
**small·sword** \'smȯl-ˌsȯrd, -ˌsȯrd\ *noun*
(1687)
**:** a light tapering sword for thrusting used
chiefly in dueling and fencing
**small talk** *noun* (1751)
**:** light or casual conversation **:** CHITCHAT
**small–time** \'smȯl-'tīm\ *adjective* (1910)
**:** insignificant in performance, scope, or standing ⟨*small-time* thieves⟩
— **small–tim·er** \-'tī-mər\ *noun*
**smalt** \'smȯlt\ *noun* [Middle French, from Old
Italian *smalto*, of Germanic origin; akin to Old
High German *smelzan* to melt — more at
SMELT] (1558)
**:** a deep blue pigment used especially as a ceramic color and prepared by fusing together
silica, potash, and oxide of cobalt and grinding
to powder the resultant glass
**smalt·ite** \'smȯl-ˌtīt\ *noun* [alteration of *smal-
tine*, from French, from *smalt*, from Middle
French] (1868)
**:** a bluish white or gray isometric mineral of
metallic luster that is essentially an arsenide of
cobalt and nickel
**smal·to** \'smäl-(ˌ)tō, 'smȯl-\ *noun, plural*
**smal·ti** \-(ˌ)tē\ [Italian, smalt, smalto] (1705)
**:** colored glass or enamel or a piece of either
used in mosaic work
**sma·ragd** \smə-'ragd, 'smar-ˌagd\ *noun* [Mid-
dle English *smaragde*, from Latin *smaragdus*]
(13th century)
**:** EMERALD
— **sma·rag·dine** \smə-'rag-dən, 'smar-əg-
ˌdīn\ *adjective*
**sma·rag·dite** \smə-'rag-ˌdīt, 'smar-əg-ˌdīt\
*noun* [French, from Latin *smaragdus* emerald
— more at EMERALD] (1804)
**:** a green foliated amphibole
**smarm** \'smärm\ *noun* [back-formation from
*smarmy*] (1937)
**:** smarmy language or behavior
**smarmy** \'smär-mē\ *adjective* [*smarm* to gush,
slobber] (1924)
**1 :** revealing or marked by a smug, ingratiating, or false earnestness ⟨a tone of *smarmy*
self-satisfaction —*New Yorker*⟩
**2 :** of low sleazy taste or quality ⟨*smarmy*
eroticism⟩
— **smarm·i·ly** \-mə-lē\ *adverb*
— **smarm·i·ness** \-mē-nəs\ *noun*
¹**smart** \'smärt\ *adjective* (before 12th century)
**1 :** making one smart **:** causing a sharp stinging
**2 :** marked by often sharp forceful activity or
vigorous strength ⟨a *smart* pull of the starter
cord⟩
**3 :** BRISK, SPIRITED
**4 a :** mentally alert **:** BRIGHT **b :** KNOWLEDGE-
ABLE **c :** SHREWD ⟨a *smart* investment⟩
**5 a :** WITTY, CLEVER **b :** PERT, SAUCY ⟨don't get
*smart* with me⟩

**6 a :** NEAT, TRIM **b :** stylish or elegant in dress
or appearance **c** (1) **:** SOPHISTICATED (2) **:** characteristic of or patronized by fashionable society
**7 a :** being a guided missile ⟨a laser-guided
*smart* bomb⟩ **b :** operating by automation ⟨a
*smart* machine tool⟩ **c :** INTELLIGENT 3
— **smart·ly** *adverb*
— **smart·ness** *noun*
²**smart** *intransitive verb* [Middle English
*smerten*, from Old English *smeortan*; akin to
Old High German *smerzan* to pain] (13th century)
**1 :** to cause or be the cause or seat of a sharp
poignant pain; *also* **:** to feel or have such a
pain
**2 a :** to feel or endure distress, remorse, or
embarrassment ⟨*smarting* from wounded vanity —W. L. Shirer⟩ **b :** to pay a heavy or stinging penalty ⟨would have to *smart* for this fool-
ishness⟩
³**smart** *noun* (13th century)
**1 :** a smarting pain; *especially* **:** a stinging local pain
**2 :** poignant grief or remorse ⟨was not the sort
to get over *smarts* —Sir Winston Churchill⟩
**3 :** an affectedly witty or fashionable person
**4** *plural, slang* **:** INTELLIGENCE, KNOW-HOW
⁴**smart** *adverb* (13th century)
**:** in a smart manner **:** SMARTLY
**smart al·eck** *also* **smart al·ec** \'smärt-ˌa-
lik, -ˌe-\ *noun* [*Aleck*, nickname for *Alexander*]
(1865)
**:** an obnoxiously conceited and self-assertive
person with pretensions to smartness or cleverness
— **smart–aleck** *adjective*
— **smart–al·ecky** \-ˌa-lə-kē, -ˌe-\ *adjective*
**smart–ass** \-ˌas\ *noun* (1964)
**:** SMART ALECK
— **smart–ass** *adjective*
— **smart–assed** \-ˌast\ *adjective*
**smart card** *noun* (1980)
**:** a small plastic card that has a built-in microprocessor to store and process data and
records
**smart·en** \'smär-tən\ *verb* **smart·ened;**
**smart·en·ing** \'smärt-niŋ, 'smär-tən-iŋ\
(1815)
*transitive verb*
**:** to make smart or smarter; *especially* **:** SPRUCE
— usually used with *up*
*intransitive verb*
**:** to smarten oneself — used with *up*
¹**smart money** \'smärt-ˌmə-nē\ *noun* [³*smart*]
(1693)
**:** PUNITIVE DAMAGES
²**smart money** \-'mə-nē, -ˌmə-nē\ *noun*
[¹*smart*] (1926)
**1 :** money ventured by one having inside information or much experience
**2 :** well-informed bettors or speculators
**smart·weed** \'smärt-ˌwēd\ *noun* (circa 1787)

---

☆ SYNONYMS
**Small, little, diminutive, minute, tiny,
miniature** mean noticeably below average
in size. SMALL and LITTLE are often interchangeable, but SMALL applies more to relative size determined by capacity, value, number ⟨a relatively *small* backyard⟩. LITTLE is
more absolute in implication often carrying
the idea of petiteness, pettiness, insignificance, or immaturity ⟨your pathetic *little*
smile⟩. DIMINUTIVE implies abnormal smallness ⟨*diminutive* bonsai plants⟩. MINUTE implies extreme smallness ⟨a *minute* amount of
caffeine in the soda⟩. TINY is an informal
equivalent to MINUTE ⟨*tiny* cracks formed in
the painting⟩. MINIATURE applies to an exactly
proportioned reproduction on a very small
scale ⟨a dollhouse complete with *miniature*
furnishings⟩.

: any of various polygonums with strong acid juice

**smarty** or **smart·ie** \'smär-tē\ *noun, plural* **smart·ies** (1861)
: SMART ALECK

**smarty–pants** \-ˌpan(t)s\ *noun plural but singular in construction* (1941)
: SMART ALECK
— **smarty–pants** *adjective*

¹**smash** \'smash\ *noun* [perhaps blend of ⁴*smack* and ²*mash*] (1725)
**1 a** : a smashing blow or attack **b** : a hard overhand stroke (as in tennis or badminton)
**2 a** : the action or sound of smashing; *especially* : a wreck due to collision : CRASH **b** : utter collapse : RUIN
**3** : a striking success

²**smash** (1778)
*transitive verb*
**1** : to break or crush by violence
**2 a** : to drive or throw violently especially with a shattering or battering effect; *also* : to effect in this way **b** : to hit violently : BATTER **c** (1) : to hit (as a tennis ball) with a hard overhand stroke (2) : to drive (a ball) with a forceful stroke
**3** : to destroy utterly : WRECK
*intransitive verb*
**1** : to move or become propelled with violence or crashing effect ⟨*smashed* into a tree⟩
**2** : to become wrecked
**3** : to go to pieces suddenly under collision or pressure
— **smash·er** *noun*

³**smash** *adjective* (1923)
: being a smash : OUTSTANDING ⟨a *smash* hit⟩

**smashed** \'smasht\ *adjective* (circa 1959)
*slang* : DRUNK, INTOXICATED

**smash·ing** \'sma-shiŋ\ *adjective* (1833)
**1** : that smashes : CRUSHING ⟨a *smashing* defeat⟩
**2** : extraordinarily impressive or effective ⟨a *smashing* performance⟩
— **smash·ing·ly** \-shiŋ-lē\ *adverb*

**smash·up** \'smash-ˌəp\ *noun* (1856)
**1** : a collision between vehicles
**2** : a complete collapse

¹**smat·ter** \'sma-tər\ *verb* [Middle English *smateren*] (15th century)
*intransitive verb*
: to talk superficially : BABBLE
*transitive verb*
**1** : to speak with spotty or superficial knowledge ⟨*smatters* French⟩
**2** : to dabble in
— **smat·ter·er** \-tər-ər\ *noun*

²**smatter** *noun* (1668)
: SMATTERING

**smat·ter·ing** \'sma-tə-riŋ\ *noun* (1538)
**1** : superficial piecemeal knowledge ⟨a *smattering* of carpentry, house painting, bricklaying —Alva Johnston⟩
**2** : a small scattered number or amount ⟨a *smattering* of spectators⟩

¹**smear** \'smir\ *noun* [Middle English *smere*, from Old English *smeoru*; akin to Old High German *smero* grease and probably to Old Irish *smiur* marrow] (before 12th century)
**1 a** : a viscous or sticky substance **b** : a spot made by or as if by an unctuous or adhesive substance
**2** : material smeared on a surface (as of a microscopic slide); *also* : a preparation made by smearing material on a surface ⟨a vaginal *smear*⟩
**3** : a usually unsubstantiated charge or accusation against a person or organization

²**smear** *transitive verb* (before 12th century)
**1 a** : to overspread with something unctuous, viscous, or adhesive **b** : to spread over a surface
**2 a** : to stain, smudge, or dirty by or as if by smearing **b** : SULLY, BESMIRCH; *specifically* : to vilify especially by secretly and maliciously spreading grave charges and imputations

**3** : to obliterate, obscure, blur, blend, wipe out, or defeat by or as if by smearing
— **smear·er** *noun*

**smear·case** *also* **smier·case** \'smir-ˌkäs\ *noun* [modification of German *Schmierkäse*, from *schmieren* to smear + *Käse* cheese] (1829)
*chiefly Midland* : COTTAGE CHEESE

**smeary** \'smir-ē\ *adjective* (circa 1529)
**1** : marked by or covered with smears
**2** : liable to cause smears ⟨*smeary* lipstick⟩

**smec·tic** \'smek-tik\ *adjective* [Latin *smecticus* cleansing, having the properties of soap, from Greek *smēktikos*, from *smēchein* to clean] (1923)
: of, relating to, or being the phase of a liquid crystal characterized by arrangement of molecules in layers with the long molecular axes in a given layer being parallel to one another and those of other layers and perpendicular or slightly inclined to the plane of the layer — compare CHOLESTERIC, NEMATIC

**smec·tite** \'smek-ˌtīt\ *noun* [*smectis* fuller's earth, modification of Greek *smēktris* kind of fuller's earth, from *smēchein* to clean] (1811)
: MONTMORILLONITE
— **smec·tit·ic** \(ˌ)smek-'ti-tik\ *adjective*

**smeg·ma** \'smeg-mə\ *noun* [New Latin, from Latin, detergent, soap, from Greek *smēgma*, from *smēchein* to wash off, clean] (circa 1819)
: the secretion of a sebaceous gland; *specifically* : the cheesy sebaceous matter that collects between the glans penis and the foreskin or around the clitoris and labia minora

¹**smell** \'smel\ *verb* **smelled** \'smeld\ *or* **smelt** \'smelt\; **smell·ing** [Middle English] (12th century)
*transitive verb*
**1** : to perceive the odor or scent of through stimuli affecting the olfactory nerves : get the odor or scent of with the nose
**2** : to detect or become aware of as if by the sense of smell
**3** : to emit the odor of
*intransitive verb*
**1** : to exercise the sense of smell
**2 a** (1) : to have an odor or scent (2) : to have a characteristic aura or atmosphere : SMACK ⟨the accounts . . . seemed to me to *smell* of truth —R. S. Bourne⟩; *also* : SEEM, APPEAR ⟨the story didn't *smell* right⟩ **b** (1) : to have an offensive odor : STINK (2) : to be of bad or questionable quality ⟨all this from the moral point of view *smells* —A. F. Wills⟩
— **smell·er** *noun*
— **smell a rat** : to have a suspicion of something wrong

²**smell** *noun* (12th century)
**1** : the property of a thing that affects the olfactory organs : ODOR
**2 a** : the process, function, or power of smelling **b** : the special sense concerned with the perception of odor
**3 a** : a very small amount : TRACE ⟨add only a *smell* of garlic⟩ **b** : a pervading or characteristic quality : AURA ⟨the *smell* of affluence, of power —Harry Hervey⟩
**4** : an act or instance of smelling ☆

**smelling salts** *noun plural but singular or plural in construction* (1840)
: a usually scented aromatic preparation of ammonium carbonate and ammonia water used as a stimulant and restorative

**smelly** \'sme-lē\ *adjective* **smell·i·er; -est** (1862)
: having a smell; *especially* : MALODOROUS

¹**smelt** \'smelt\ *noun, plural* **smelts** *or* **smelt** [Middle English, from Old English; akin to Norwegian *smelte* whiting] (before 12th century)
: any of a family (Osmeridae) of small salmonoid fishes that closely resemble the trouts in general structure, live along coasts and ascend rivers to spawn or are landlocked, and have delicate oily flesh with a distinctive odor and taste

²**smelt** *transitive verb* [Dutch or Low German *smelten*; akin to Old High German *smelzan* to melt, Old English *meltan* — more at MELT] (1543)
**1** : to melt or fuse (as ore) often with an accompanying chemical change usually to separate the metal
**2** : REFINE, REDUCE

**smelt·er** \'smel-tər\ *noun* (15th century)
: one that smelts: **a** : a worker who smelts ore **b** : an owner or operator of a smeltery **c** *or* **smelt·ery** \-t(ə-)rē\ : an establishment for smelting

**smew** \'smyü\ *noun* [akin to Middle High German *smiehe* smew] (1674)
: a small Eurasian merganser (*Mergus albellus*) with the male being white, gray, and black and the female chiefly gray but with a chestnut and white head

**smid·gen** *also* **smid·geon** *or* **smid·gin** \'smi-jən\ *or* **smidge** \'smij\ *noun* [probably alteration of English dialect *smitch* soiling mark] (1845)
: a small amount : BIT

**smi·lax** \'smī-ˌlaks\ *noun* [Latin, bindweed, yew, from Greek] (1601)
**1** : GREENBRIER
**2** : a tender twining plant (*Asparagus asparagoides*) of the lily family that has ovate bright green cladophylls and is often grown in greenhouses

¹**smile** \'smī(ə)l\ *verb* **smiled; smil·ing** [Middle English; akin to Old English *smerian* to laugh, Sanskrit *smayate* he smiles] (14th century)
*intransitive verb*
**1** : to have, produce, or exhibit a smile
**2 a** : to look or regard with amusement or ridicule ⟨*smiled* at his own folly —Martin Gardner⟩ **b** : to bestow approval ⟨feeling that Heaven *smiled* on his labors —Sheila Rowlands⟩ **c** : to appear pleasant or agreeable
*transitive verb*
**1** : to affect with or by smiling
**2** : to express by a smile
— **smil·er** *noun*
— **smil·ey** \'smī-lē\ *adjective*
— **smil·ing·ly** \'smī-liŋ-lē\ *adverb*

²**smile** *noun* (15th century)
**1** : a facial expression in which the eyes brighten and the corners of the mouth curve slightly upward and which expresses especially amusement, pleasure, approval, or sometimes scorn
**2** : a pleasant or encouraging appearance
— **smile·less** \'smī(ə)l-ləs\ *adjective*

**smirch** \'smərch\ *transitive verb* [Middle English *smorchen*] (15th century)
**1 a** : to make dirty, stained, or discolored : SULLY **b** : to smear with something that stains or dirties
**2** : to bring discredit or disgrace on
— **smirch** *noun*

---

☆ **SYNONYMS**
**Smell, scent, odor, aroma** mean the quality that makes a thing perceptible to the olfactory sense. SMELL implies solely the sensation without suggestion of quality or character ⟨an odd *smell* permeated the room⟩. SCENT applies to the characteristic smell given off by a substance, an animal, or a plant ⟨the *scent* of lilacs⟩. ODOR may imply a stronger or more readily distinguished scent or it may be equivalent to SMELL ⟨a cheese with a strong *odor*⟩. AROMA suggests a somewhat penetrating usually pleasant odor ⟨the *aroma* of freshly ground coffee⟩.

---

\ə\ abut \ᵊ\ kitten \ər\ further \a\ ash \ā\ ace
\ä\ mop, mar \aů\ out \ch\ chin \e\ bet \ē\ easy
\g\ go \i\ hit \ī\ ice \j\ job \ŋ\ sing \ō\ go
\ô\ law \ói\ boy \th\ thin \th̠\ the \ü\ loot \ů\ foot
\y\ yet \zh\ vision *see also* Guide to Pronunciation

**smirk** \'smərk\ *intransitive verb* [Middle English, from Old English *smearcian* to smile; akin to Old English *smerian* to laugh] (before 12th century)
: to smile in an affected or smug manner : SIMPER
— **smirk** *noun*
**smirky** \'smər-kē\ *adjective* (1728)
: that smirks : SMIRKING
**smite** \'smīt\ *verb* **smote** \'smōt\; **smit·ten** \'smi-t°n\ *or* **smote; smit·ing** \'smī-tiŋ\ [Middle English, from Old English *smītan* to smear, defile; akin to Old High German bi*smīzan* to defile] (12th century)
*transitive verb*
**1** : to strike sharply or heavily especially with the hand or an implement held in the hand
**2 a** : to kill or severely injure by smiting **b** : to attack or afflict suddenly and injuriously ⟨*smitten* by disease⟩
**3** : to cause to strike
**4** : to affect as if by striking ⟨children *smitten* with the fear of hell —V. L. Parrington⟩
**5** : CAPTIVATE, TAKE ⟨*smitten* with her beauty⟩
*intransitive verb*
: to deliver or deal a blow with or as if with the hand or something held
— **smit·er** \'smī-tər\ *noun*
**smith** \'smith\ *noun* [Middle English, from Old English; akin to Old High German *smid* smith and probably to Greek *smilē* wood-carving knife] (before 12th century)
**1** : a worker in metals : BLACKSMITH
**2** : MAKER — often used in combination ⟨gun*smith*⟩ ⟨tune*smith*⟩
**smith·er·eens** \ˌsmi-thə-'rēnz\ *noun plural* [perhaps from Irish *smidiríní*] (1829)
: FRAGMENTS, BITS ⟨the house was blown to *smithereens* by the explosion⟩
**smith·ery** \'smi-thə-rē\ *noun, plural* **-er·ies** (1625)
**1** : the work, art, or trade of a smith
**2** : SMITHY 1
**Smith·field ham** \'smith-ˌfēld-\ *noun* (1908)
: a Virginia ham produced in or near Smithfield, Va.
**smith·son·ite** \'smith-sə-ˌnīt\ *noun* [James *Smithson*] (1856)
: a mineral that is a carbonate of zinc and constitutes an important ore of zinc
**smithy** \'smi-thē *also* -t͟hē\ *noun, plural* **smith·ies** (13th century)
**1** : the workshop of a smith
**2** : BLACKSMITH
**¹smock** \'smäk\ *noun* [Middle English *smok*, from Old English *smoc;* akin to Old High German *smocco* adornment] (before 12th century)
**1** *archaic* : a woman's undergarment; *especially* : CHEMISE
**2** : a light loose garment worn especially for protection of clothing while working
**²smock** *transitive verb* (1888)
: to embroider or shirr with smocking
**smock frock** *noun* (circa 1800)
: a loose outer garment worn by workmen especially in Europe
**smock·ing** \'smä-kiŋ\ *noun* (1888)
: a decorative embroidery or shirring made by gathering cloth in regularly spaced round tucks
**smog** \'smäg, 'smȯg\ *noun* [*smo*ke + f*og*] (1905)
: a fog made heavier and darker by smoke and chemical fumes; *also* : a photochemical haze caused by the action of solar ultraviolet radiation on atmosphere polluted with hydrocarbons and oxides of nitrogen from automobile exhaust
— **smog·less** \'smäg-ləs, 'smȯ-\ *adjective*
**smog·gy** \'smä-gē, 'smȯ-\ *adjective* **smog·gi·er; -est** (1905)
: characterized by or abounding in smog
**smok·able** *or* **smoke·able** \'smō-kə-bəl\ *adjective* (1839)
: fit for smoking

**¹smoke** \'smōk\ *noun* [Middle English, from Old English *smoca;* akin to Old English *smēocan* to emit smoke, Middle High German *smouch* smoke, and probably to Greek *smychein* to smolder] (before 12th century)
**1 a** : the gaseous products of burning materials especially of organic origin made visible by the presence of small particles of carbon **b** : a suspension of particles in a gas
**2 a** : a mass or column of smoke **b** : SMUDGE
**3** : fume or vapor often resulting from the action of heat on moisture
**4** : something of little substance, permanence, or value
**5** : something that obscures
**6 a** (1) : something (as a cigarette) to smoke (2) : MARIJUANA 2 **b** : an act or spell of smoking tobacco
**7 a** : a pale blue **b** : any of the colors of smoke
**8** : pitches that are fastballs ⟨if a guy's going to hit you . . . he certainly isn't going to throw a spitter—he gives you *smoke* —Tony Conigliaro⟩
— **smoke·less** \'smō-kləs\ *adjective*
— **smoke·like** \'smōk-ˌlīk\ *adjective*
**²smoke** *verb* **smoked; smok·ing** (before 12th century)
*intransitive verb*
**1 a** : to emit or exhale smoke **b** : to emit excessive smoke
**2** *archaic* : to undergo punishment : SUFFER
**3** : to spread or rise like smoke
**4** : to inhale and exhale the fumes of burning plant material and especially tobacco; *especially* : to smoke tobacco habitually
*transitive verb*
**1 a** : FUMIGATE **b** : to drive (as mosquitoes) away by smoke **c** : to blacken or discolor with smoke ⟨*smoked* glasses⟩ **d** : to cure by exposure to smoke **e** : to stupefy (as bees) by smoke
**2** *archaic* : SUSPECT
**3** : to inhale and exhale the smoke of
**4** *archaic* : RIDICULE
**smoke and mirrors** *noun plural* (1982)
: something intended to disguise or draw attention away especially from an embarrassing or unpleasant issue — usually hyphenated when used attributively
**smoke detector** *noun* (circa 1927)
: an alarm that activates automatically when it detects smoke
**smoke–filled room** \'smōk-'fild-\ *noun* (1920)
: a room (as in a hotel) in which a small group of politicians carry on negotiations
**smoke·house** \'smōk-ˌhau̇s\ *noun* (1746)
: a building where meat or fish is cured by means of dense smoke
**smoke·jack** \-ˌjak\ *noun* (1675)
: a device for turning a spit by a fly or wheel moved by rising gases in a chimney
**smoke jumper** *noun* (1927)
: a forest firefighter who parachutes to locations otherwise difficult to reach
**smokeless powder** *noun* (1890)
: any of a class of explosive propellants that produce comparatively little smoke on explosion and consist mostly of gelatinized nitrocellulose
**smokeless tobacco** *noun* (1981)
: pulverized or shredded tobacco chewed or placed between cheek and gum
**smoke out** *transitive verb* (1593)
**1** : to drive out by or as if by smoke
**2** : to cause to be made public
**smok·er** \'smō-kər\ *noun* (1599)
**1** : one that smokes
**2** : a railroad car or compartment in which smoking is allowed
**3** : an informal social gathering for men
**smoke screen** *noun* (1915)
**1** : a screen of smoke to hinder enemy observation of a military force, area, or activity

**2** : something designed to obscure, confuse, or mislead
**¹smoke·stack** \'smōk-ˌstak\ *noun* (1859)
: a pipe or funnel through which smoke and gases are discharged
**²smokestack** *adjective* (1926)
: of, relating to, being, or characterized by manufacturing and especially heavy industry ⟨*smokestack* industries⟩
**smoke tree** *noun* (1846)
: either of two small shrubby trees (genus *Cotinus*) of the cashew family with large panicles of minute flowers that suggest a cloud of smoke: **a** : one (*C. coggygria*) of the Old World that is widely planted in the eastern U.S. **b** : one (*C. obovatus*) of the southeastern U.S. and Texas
**smoking gun** *noun* (1974)
: something that serves as conclusive evidence or proof especially of a crime
**smoking jacket** *noun* (1878)
: a loose-fitting jacket or short robe for wear at home
**smoking lamp** *noun* (circa 1881)
: a lamp on a ship kept lighted during the hours when smoking is allowed
**smoking room** *noun* (1689)
: a room (as in a hotel or club) set apart for smokers
**smoky** *also* **smok·ey** \'smō-kē\ *adjective* **smok·i·er; -est** (14th century)
**1** : emitting smoke especially in large quantities
**2 a** : having the characteristics of or resembling smoke **b** : suggestive of smoke especially in flavor or odor
**3 a** : filled with smoke **b** : made dark or black by or as if by smoke
— **smok·i·ly** \-kə-lē\ *adverb*
— **smok·i·ness** \-kē-nəs\ *noun*
**smoky quartz** *noun* (1837)
: CAIRNGORM
**smoky topaz** *noun* (1797)
: CAIRNGORM
**smol·der** *or* **smoul·der** \'smōl-dər\ *intransitive verb* **smol·dered** *or* **smoul·dered; smol·der·ing** *or* **smoul·der·ing** \-d(ə-)riŋ\ [Middle English *smolderen* to smother, from *smolder* smoke, smudge; akin to Middle Dutch *smōlen* to smolder] (1529)
**1 a** : to burn sluggishly, without flame, and often with much smoke **b** : to be consumed by smoldering — often used with *out*
**2** : to exist in a state of suppressed activity ⟨hostilities *smoldered* for years⟩
**3** : to show suppressed anger, hate, or jealousy ⟨eyes *smoldering* with hate⟩
**smolt** \'smōlt\ *noun* [Middle English (Scots)] (15th century)
: a young salmon or sea trout about two years old that is at the stage of development when it assumes the silvery color of the adult and is ready to migrate to the sea
**¹smooch** \'smüch\ *noun* (1578)
: KISS
**²smooch** *intransitive verb* [alteration of *smouch* to kiss loudly] (1588)
: KISS, PET
**³smooch** *transitive verb* [probably alteration of *smutch*, verb] (1631)
: SMUDGE, SMEAR
**⁴smooch** *noun* (1825)
: SMUDGE, SMEAR
— **smoochy** \'smü-chē\ *adjective*
**¹smooth** \'smü͟th\ *adjective* [Middle English *smothe*, from Old English *smōth;* akin to Old Saxon *smōthi* smooth] (before 12th century)
**1 a** (1) : having a continuous even surface (2) *of a curve* : being the representation of a function with a continuous first derivative (3) : having or being a short even coat of hair ⟨a *smooth* collie⟩ — compare ROUGH, WIREHAIRED **b** : being without hair **c** : GLABROUS ⟨a *smooth* leaf⟩ **d** : causing no resistance to sliding

**2 :** free from difficulties or impediments ⟨the *smooth* course of his life⟩
**3 :** even and uninterrupted in flow or flight
**4 :** excessively and often artfully suave : IN-GRATIATING ⟨a *smooth* operator⟩
**5 a :** SERENE, EQUABLE ⟨a *smooth* disposition⟩ **b** : AMIABLE, COURTEOUS
**6 a :** not sharp or harsh ⟨a *smooth* sherry⟩ **b** : free from lumps
***synonym*** see LEVEL, EASY, SUAVE
— **smooth** *adverb*
— **smooth·ly** *adverb*
— **smooth·ness** *noun*

**²smooth** *verb* **smoothed; smooth·ing; smooths** *also* **smoothes** (15th century)
*transitive verb*
**1 :** to make smooth
**2 a :** to free from what is harsh or disagreeable : POLISH ⟨*smoothed* out his style⟩ **b** : SOOTHE
**3 :** to minimize (as a fault) especially in order to allay anger or ill will ⟨his main job is to *smooth* over the friction that so often arises —Brian Crozier⟩
**4 :** to free from obstruction or difficulty
**5 a :** to press flat **b** : to remove expression from (one's face) : COMPOSE
**6 :** to cause to lie evenly and in order : PREEN
**7 :** to free (as a graph or data) from irregularities
*intransitive verb*
**:** to become smooth
— **smooth·er** *noun*

**³smooth** *noun* (15th century)
**1 :** a smooth part
**2 :** the act of smoothing
**3 :** a smoothing implement

**smooth·bore** \'smüth-ˌbōr, -ˌbȯr\ *adjective* (1799)
*of a firearm* : having a barrel with an unrifled bore
— **smoothbore** \-ˌbōr, -ˌbȯr\ *noun*

**smooth breathing** *noun* (circa 1888)
**1 :** a mark ' placed over some initial vowels in Greek to show that they are not aspirated (as in ἐκεῖ pronounced \e-ˈkā\)
**2 :** the absence of aspiration indicated by a mark '

**smooth·en** \'smü-thən\ *verb* **smooth·ened; smooth·en·ing** \'smü-thə-niŋ, 'smüth-niŋ\ (1635)
*transitive verb*
**:** to make smooth
*intransitive verb*
**:** to become smooth

**smooth hound** *noun* [from the absence of a spine in front of the dorsal fin] (1603)
**:** any of several dogfishes (genus *Mustelus*) closely related to or included with the requiem sharks

**smooth muscle** *noun* (circa 1890)
**:** muscle tissue that lacks cross striations, that is made up of elongated spindle-shaped cells having a central nucleus, and that is found in vertebrate visceral structures (as the stomach and bladder) as thin sheets performing functions not subject to conscious control by the mind and in all or most of the musculature of invertebrates other than arthropods — compare STRIATED MUSCLE

**smooth–tongued** \'smüth-ˈtəŋd\ *adjective* (1592)
**:** ingratiating in speech

**smoothy** *or* **smooth·ie** \'smü-thē\ *noun, plural* **smooth·ies** (1904)
**1 :** a smooth-tongued person
**2 a :** a person with polished manners **b** : one who behaves or performs with deftness, assurance, and easy competence; *especially* : a man with an ingratiating manner toward women

**smor·gas·bord** \'smȯr-gəs-ˌbȯrd, -ˌbȯrd\ *noun* [Swedish *smörgåsbord*, from *smörgås* open sandwich + *bord* table] (1893)
**1 :** a luncheon or supper buffet offering a variety of foods and dishes (as hors d'oeuvres, hot

and cold meats, smoked and pickled fish, cheeses, salads, and relishes)
**2 :** a heterogeneous mixture : MÉLANGE ◆

**smote** *past of* SMITE

**¹smoth·er** \'smə-thər\ *noun* [Middle English, alteration of *smorther*, from *smoren* to smother, from Old English *smorian* to suffocate; akin to Middle Dutch *smoren* to suffocate] (13th century)
**1 a :** thick stifling smoke or smudge **b :** a state of being stifled or suppressed
**2 :** a dense cloud (as of fog, spray, or dust)
**3 :** a confused multitude of things : WELTER
— **smoth·ery** \'smə-thə-rē, 'sməth-rē\ *adjective*

**²smother** *verb* **smoth·ered; smoth·er·ing** \'smə-thə-riŋ, 'sməth-riŋ\ (circa 1520)
*intransitive verb*
**:** to be overcome or killed through or as if through lack of air
*transitive verb*
**1 :** to overcome or kill with smoke or fumes
**2 a :** to destroy the life of by depriving of air **b :** to overcome or discomfit through or as if through lack of air **c :** to suppress (a fire) by excluding oxygen
**3 a :** to cause to smolder **b :** to suppress expression or knowledge of ⟨*smothered* his rage⟩ **c :** to stop or prevent the growth or activity of ⟨*smother* a child with too much care⟩; *also* : OVERWHELM **d :** to cover thickly : BLANKET ⟨snow *smothered* the trails⟩ **e :** to overcome or vanquish quickly or decisively
**4 :** to cook in a covered pan or pot with little liquid over low heat

**¹smudge** \'sməj\ *verb* **smudged; smudg·ing** [Middle English *smogen*] (15th century)
*transitive verb*
**1 a :** to make a smudge on **b :** to soil as if by smudging
**2 a :** to rub, daub, or wipe in a smeary manner **b :** to make indistinct : BLUR
**3 :** to smoke or protect by means of a smudge
*intransitive verb*
**1 :** to make a smudge
**2 :** to become smudged

**²smudge** *noun* (circa 1774)
**1 a :** a blurry spot or streak **b :** an immaterial stain ⟨cleanse him of every last *smudge* of impropriety —Richard Hanser⟩ **c :** an indistinct mass : BLUR
**2 :** a smoldering mass placed on the windward side (as to protect from frost)
**3 :** a bid of 4 in pitch that if made wins the game
— **smudg·i·ly** \'smə-jə-lē\ *adverb*
— **smudg·i·ness** \'smə-jē-nəs\ *noun*
— **smudgy** \-jē\ *adjective*

**smug** \'sməg\ *adjective* **smug·ger; smug·gest** [probably modification of Low German *smuck* neat, from Middle Low German, from *smucken* to dress; akin to Old English *smoc* smock] (1551)
**1 :** trim or smart in dress : SPRUCE
**2 :** scrupulously clean, neat, or correct : TIDY
**3 :** highly self-satisfied
— **smug·ly** *adverb*
— **smug·ness** *noun*

**smug·gle** \'smə-gəl\ *verb* **smug·gled; smug·gling** \-g(ə-)liŋ\ [Low German *smuggeln* & Dutch *smokkelen*] (1687)
*transitive verb*
**1 :** to import or export secretly contrary to the law and especially without paying duties imposed by law
**2 :** to convey or introduce surreptitiously
*intransitive verb*
**:** to import or export something in violation of the customs laws
— **smug·gler** \'smə-glər\ *noun*

**¹smut** \'smət\ *verb* **smut·ted; smut·ting** [probably alteration of earlier *smot* to stain, from Middle English *smotten;* akin to Middle High German *smutzen* to stain] (1587)
*transitive verb*
**1 :** to stain or taint with smut

**2 :** to affect (a crop or plant) with smut
*intransitive verb*
**:** to become affected by smut

**²smut** *noun* (1664)
**1 :** matter that soils or blackens; *specifically* : a particle of soot
**2 :** any of various destructive diseases especially of cereal grasses caused by parasitic fungi (order Ustilaginales) and marked by transformation of plant organs into dark masses of spores; *also* : a fungus causing a smut
**3 :** obscene language or matter

**smutch** \'sməch\ *noun* [akin to Middle English *smogen* to smudge] (1530)
**:** a dark stain : SMUDGE
— **smutch** *transitive verb*
— **smutchy** \'smə-chē\ *adjective*

**smut·ty** \'smə-tē\ *adjective* **smut·ti·er; -est** (1597)
**1 :** soiled or tainted with smut; *especially* : affected with smut fungus
**2 :** OBSCENE, INDECENT
**3 :** resembling smut in appearance : SOOTY
— **smut·ti·ly** \'smə-tᵊl-ē\ *adverb*
— **smut·ti·ness** \'smə-tē-nəs\ *noun*

**¹snack** \'snak\ *noun* [Middle English *snak* bite, from *snaken* to bite, perhaps from Middle Dutch *snacken* to snap at — more at SNATCH] (1757)
**:** a light meal : food eaten between regular meals; *also* : food suitable for snacking

**²snack** *intransitive verb* (1807)
**:** to eat a snack

**snack bar** *noun* (1930)
**:** a public eating place where snacks are served usually at a counter

**¹snaf·fle** \'sna-fəl\ *noun* [origin unknown] (1533)
**:** a simple usually jointed bit for a bridle

**²snaffle** *transitive verb* **snaf·fled; snaf·fling** \'sna-f(ə-)liŋ\ [origin unknown] (1724)
**:** to obtain especially by devious or irregular means

**¹sna·fu** \sna-ˈfü, ˈsna-ˌfü\ *noun* [*situation normal all fucked up (fouled up)*] (circa 1941)
**:** CONFUSION, MUDDLE

**²snafu** *adjective* (1943)
**:** snarled or stalled in confusion : AWRY

**³snafu** *transitive verb* (1943)
**:** to bring into a state of confusion

**¹snag** \'snag\ *noun* [of Scandinavian origin; akin to Old Norse *snagi* clothes peg] (circa 1587)

---

◇ **WORD HISTORY**

**smorgasbord**   In Swedish the word *smörgås* literally means "butter goose." *Smör* simply means "butter," and *gås* has the literal meaning "goose" and the figurative sense "a lump of butter," the result of a fancied resemblance between a buttery lump and a goose. In Swedish *smörgås* also has the extended senses "bread and butter" and "open-faced sandwich." It is in the latter sense that *smörgås* forms part of *smörgåsbord,* the name for the traditional Swedish buffet of delicacies, which are typically assembled by diners into open-faced sandwiches. (The *bord* of *smörgåsbord* is related to English *board* and simply means "table.") Swedish-style buffets first gained popularity among American diners in the early decades of the 20th century. By the 1940s *smorgasbord,* stripped of its Swedish diacritics, was sufficiently established in English to have given rise to the figurative sense "a heterogeneous mixture."

---

\ə\ abut  \ᵊ\ kitten  \ər\ further  \a\ ash  \ā\ ace
\ä\ mop, mar  \au̇\ out  \ch\ chin  \e\ bet  \ē\ easy
\g\ go  \i\ hit  \ī\ ice  \j\ job  \ŋ\ sing  \ō\ go
\ȯ\ law  \ȯi\ boy  \th\ thin  \t̶h\ the  \ü\ loot  \u̇\ foot
\y\ yet  \zh\ vision  *see also* Guide to Pronunciation

**1 a :** a tree or branch embedded in a lake or stream bed and constituting a hazard to navigation **b :** a standing dead tree
**2 :** a rough sharp or jagged projecting part **:** PROTUBERANCE: as **a :** a projecting tooth; *also* **:** a stump of a tooth **b :** one of the secondary branches of an antler
**3 :** a concealed or unexpected difficulty or obstacle
**4 :** a jagged tear made by or as if by catching on a snag ⟨a *snag* in her stocking⟩
— **snag·gy** \'sna-gē\ *adjective*
²**snag** *transitive verb* **snagged; snag·ging** (1807)
**1 a :** to catch and usually damage on or as if on a snag **b :** to halt or impede as if by catching on a snag
**2 :** to hew, trim, or cut roughly or jaggedly
**3 :** to clear (as a river) of snags
**4 :** to catch or obtain by quick action or good fortune
**snag·gle·tooth** \'sna-gəl-ˌtüth\ *noun* [English dialect *snaggle* irregularly shaped tooth + English *tooth*] (circa 1825)
**:** an irregular, broken, or projecting tooth
— **snag·gle·toothed** \-ˌtütht\ *adjective*
¹**snail** \'snā(ə)l\ *noun* [Middle English, from Old English *snægl;* akin to Old High German *snecko* snail, *snahhan* to creep] (before 12th century)
**1 :** a gastropod mollusk especially when having an external enclosing spiral shell
**2 :** a slow-moving or sluggish person or thing
— **snail·like** \'snā(ə)l-ˌlīk\ *adjective*
²**snail** *intransitive verb* (1582)
**:** to move, act, or go slowly or lazily
**snail darter** *noun* (1975)
**:** a darter (*Percina tanasi*) of the Tennessee River drainage system of eastern Tennessee and northern Georgia
**snail fever** *noun* [from the snails which serve as intermediate hosts to the schistosomes causing the disease] (1947)
**:** SCHISTOSOMIASIS
**snail-paced** \'snā(ə)l-ˌpāst\ *adjective* (1594)
**:** moving very slowly
**snail's pace** *noun* (15th century)
**:** an extremely slow pace
¹**snake** \'snāk\ *noun* [Middle English, from Old English *snaca;* akin to Old Norse *snakr* snake, Old High German *snahhan* to crawl] (before 12th century)
**1 :** any of numerous limbless scaled reptiles (suborder Serpentes synonym Ophidia) with a long tapering body and with salivary glands often modified to produce venom which is injected through grooved or tubular fangs
**2 :** a worthless or treacherous fellow
**3 :** something (as a plumber's snake) resembling a snake
— **snake·like** \-ˌlīk\ *adjective*
²**snake** *verb* **snaked; snak·ing** (1653)
*transitive verb*
**1 :** to wind (as one's way) in the manner of a snake
**2 :** to move (as logs) by dragging
*intransitive verb*
**:** to crawl, move, or extend silently, secretly, or sinuously
**snake·bird** \'snāk-ˌbərd\ *noun* (1791)
**:** ANHINGA
**snake-bit** \-ˌbit\ *or* **snake-bit·ten** \-ˌbi-tᵊn\ *adjective* (1957)
**:** UNLUCKY 1, 3
**snake·bite** \-ˌbīt\ *noun* (1839)
**:** the bite of a snake and especially a venomous snake
**snake charmer** *noun* (1836)
**:** an entertainer who exhibits a professed power to charm or fascinate venomous snakes
**snake–dance** *intransitive verb* (1922)
**:** to engage in a snake dance
**snake dance** *noun* (1772)
**1 :** a ceremonial dance in which snakes or their images are handled, invoked, or symbolically imitated by individual sinuous actions

**2 :** a group progression in a single-file serpentine path (as in celebration of an athletic victory)
**snake doctor** *noun* (1862)
**1 :** DRAGONFLY
**2 :** HELLGRAMMITE
**snake fence** *noun* (1805)
**:** WORM FENCE
**snake in the grass** (1696)
**:** a secretly faithless friend
**snake oil** *noun* (1927)
**1 :** any of various substances or mixtures sold (as by a traveling medicine show) as medicine usually without regard to their medical worth or properties
**2 :** POPPYCOCK, BUNKUM
**snake pit** *noun* (1946)
**1 :** a hospital for mental diseases
**2 :** a place or state of chaotic disorder and distress
**snake·root** \'snāk-ˌrüt, -ˌrȯt\ *noun* (1635)
**:** any of numerous plants (as seneca snakeroot) most of which have roots sometimes believed to cure snakebites; *also* **:** the root of such a plant
**snake·skin** \'snāk-ˌskin\ *noun* (1825)
**:** leather prepared from the skin of a snake
**snake·weed** \-ˌwēd\ *noun* (1597)
**:** any of various plants popularly associated with snakes (as in appearance, habitat, or the treatment of snakebite); *especially* **:** any of an American genus (*Gutierrezia*) of composite herbs or low shrubs with clustered yellow flower heads
**snaky** *also* **snak·ey** \'snā-kē\ *adjective* (1567)
**1 :** of, formed of, or entwined with snakes ⟨the Gorgon with *snaky* hair —Joseph Addison⟩
**2 :** SERPENTINE, SNAKELIKE ⟨*snaky* coils⟩
**3 :** suggestive of a snake (the oiliness and *snaky* insinuation of his demeanor —Thomas DeQuincy)
**4 :** abounding in snakes
— **snak·i·ly** \-kə-lē\ *adverb*
¹**snap** \'snap\ *verb* **snapped; snap·ping** [Dutch or Low German *snappen;* akin to Middle High German *snappen* to snap] (1530)
*intransitive verb*
**1 a :** to make a sudden closing of the jaws **:** seize something sharply with the mouth ⟨fish *snapping* at the bait⟩ **b :** to grasp at something eagerly **:** make a pounce or snatch ⟨*snap* at any chance⟩
**2 :** to utter sharp biting words **:** bark out irritable or peevish retorts
**3 a :** to break suddenly with a sharp sound ⟨the twig *snapped*⟩ **b :** to give way suddenly under strain
**4 :** to make a sharp or crackling sound
**5 :** to close or fit in place with an abrupt movement or sharp sound ⟨the lock *snapped* shut⟩
**6 a :** to move briskly or sharply ⟨*snaps* to attention⟩ **b :** to undergo a sudden and rapid change (as from one condition to another) ⟨*snap* out of it⟩ ⟨*snapped* awake⟩
**7 :** SPARKLE, FLASH ⟨eyes *snapping* with fury⟩
*transitive verb*
**1 :** to seize with or as if with a snap of the jaws
**2 :** to take possession or advantage of suddenly or eagerly — usually used with *up* ⟨shoppers *snapping* up bargains⟩
**3 a :** to retort to or interrupt curtly and irritably **b :** to utter curtly or abruptly
**4 :** to break suddenly **:** break short or in two
**5 a :** to cause to make a snapping sound ⟨*snap* a whip⟩ **b :** to put into or remove from a particular position by a sudden movement or with a sharp sound ⟨*snap* the lock shut⟩
**6 a :** to project with a snap **b :** to put (a football) in play with a snap **c** (1) **:** to take photographically ⟨*snapping* exclusive news pictures —*Current Biography*⟩ (2) **:** to take a snapshot of
²**snap** *noun* (1555)

**1 :** an abrupt closing (as of the mouth in biting or of scissors in cutting)
**2 a** *archaic* **:** a share of profits or booty **b :** something that brings quick and easy profit or advantage **c :** something that is easy and presents no problems **:** CINCH
**3 :** a small amount **:** BIT
**4 a :** an act or instance of seizing abruptly **:** a sudden snatching at something **b :** a quick short movement ⟨lithe *snaps* of its body —Barbara Taylor⟩ **c :** a sudden sharp breaking
**5 a :** a sound made by snapping something ⟨shut the book with a *snap*⟩ **b :** a brief sharp and usually irritable speech or retort
**6 :** a sudden spell of weather ⟨a cold *snap*⟩
**7 :** a catch or fastening that closes or locks with a click ⟨the *snap* of a bracelet⟩
**8 :** a flat brittle cookie — compare GINGER-SNAP
**9 :** SNAPSHOT
**10 a :** the condition of being vigorous in body, mind, or spirit **:** ALERTNESS, ENERGY **b :** a pleasing vigorous quality
**11 :** the act of a center's putting the football in play from its position on the ground by quickly passing it between his legs to a teammate (as a quarterback) standing behind him
³**snap** *adverb* (1583)
**:** with a snap
⁴**snap** *adjective* (1739)
**1 :** done, made, or carried through suddenly or without deliberation ⟨a *snap* judgment⟩
**2 :** called or taken without prior warning ⟨a *snap* election⟩
**3 :** fastening with a snap ⟨a *snap* lock⟩
**4 :** unusually easy or simple ⟨a *snap* course⟩
**snap-back** \'snap-ˌbak\ *noun* (1887)
**1 :** a football snap
**2 :** a sudden rebound or recovery ⟨a *snapback* of prices on the stock exchange⟩
**snap back** *intransitive verb* (1945)
**:** to make a quick or vigorous recovery
**snap bean** *noun* (1770)
**:** a bean grown primarily for its pods that are usually broken in pieces and cooked as a vegetable while young and tender and before the seeds have become enlarged — compare SHELL BEAN
**snap–brim** \'snap-ˌbrim\ *noun, often attributive* (circa 1908)
**:** a usually felt hat with brim turned up in back and down in front and with a dented crown
**snap·drag·on** \'snap-ˌdra-gən\ *noun* [from the fancied resemblance of the flowers to the face of a dragon] (1593)
**:** any of a genus (*Antirrhinum* and especially the widely cultivated *A. majus* of the family Scrophulariaceae, the snapdragon family) of herbs having showy white, crimson, or yellow bilabiate flowers
**snap-on** \'snap-ˌȯn, -ˌän\ *adjective* (1925)
**:** designed to snap into position and fit tightly ⟨*snap-on* cuffs⟩
**snap pea** *noun* (1980)
**:** a cultivated pea that has edible usually round pods easily snapped like beans and that is classified with the snow pea as a variety (*Pisum sativum macrocarpon*) — called also *sugar snap pea*

snapdragon

**snap·per** \'sna-pər\ *noun, plural* **snappers** (circa 1587)
**1 :** one that snaps: as **a :** something (as a remark) that gives new orientation to a situation or utterance **b** (1) **:** SNAPPING TURTLE (2) **:** CLICK BEETLE
**2** *plural also* **snapper a :** any of numerous active carnivorous fishes (family Lutjanidae) of warm seas important as food and often as sport fishes **b :** any of several immature fishes (as the young of the bluefish) that resemble a snapper
**snap·per–back** \-ˌbak\ *noun* (1887)

: a football center
**snapping turtle** *noun* (1784)
: either of two
large Ameri-
can aquatic
turtles (family
Chelydridae)
with powerful
jaws and a
strong musky
odor: **a** : one

**snapping turtle**

(*Chelydra serpentina*) that has the head covered with smooth skin, has large plates in a
double row on the underside of the tail, and is
distributed from eastern Canada to Central
America **b** : ALLIGATOR SNAPPER
**snap·pish** \'sna-pish\ *adjective* (1542)
**1 a** : given to curt irritable speech **b** : arising
from annoyance or irascibility
**2** : inclined to bite ⟨a *snappish* dog⟩
— **snap·pish·ly** *adverb*
— **snap·pish·ness** *noun*
**snap·py** \'sna-pē\ *adjective* **snap·pi·er; -est**
(1746)
**1** : SNAPPISH 1
**2 a** : quickly made or done **b** : marked by vig-
or or liveliness **c** : briskly cold **d** : STYLISH,
SMART ⟨a *snappy* dresser⟩
— **snap·pi·ly** \'sna-pə-lē\ *adverb*
— **snap·pi·ness** \'sna-pē-nəs\ *noun*
**snap roll** *noun* (circa 1934)
: an airplane maneuver in which a rapid full
revolution is completed about the plane's longitudinal axis while an approximately level
line of flight is maintained
**snap·shoot·er** \'snap-ˌshü-tər\ *noun* (1896)
: a person who takes snapshots
**snap·shot** \'snap-ˌshät\ *noun* (1890)
**1** : a casual photograph made typically by an
amateur with a small handheld camera
**2** : an impression or view of something brief
or transitory
**¹snare** \'snar, 'sner\ *noun* [Middle English,
from Old English *sneare*, from Old Norse
*snara*; akin to Old High German *snuor* cord
and perhaps to Greek *narkē* numbness] (before
12th century)
**1 a** (1) : a contrivance often consisting of a
noose for entangling birds or mammals (2)
: TRAP, GIN **b** (1) : something by which one is
entangled, involved in difficulties, or impeded
(2) : something deceptively attractive
**2** [probably from Dutch *snaar*, literally, cord;
akin to Old High German *snuor*] **a** : one of the
catgut strings or metal spirals of a snare drum
**b** : SNARE DRUM
**3** : a surgical instrument consisting usually of
a wire loop constricted by a mechanism in the
handle and used for removing tissue masses
(as tonsils)
**²snare** *transitive verb* **snared; snar·ing**
(14th century)
**1 a** : to capture by or as if by use of a snare **b**
: to win or attain by artful or skillful maneuvers
**2** : to entangle or hold as if in a snare ⟨any object that *snared* his eye —*Current Biography*⟩
**synonym** see CATCH
— **snar·er** *noun*
**snare drum** *noun* (circa 1859)
: a small double-headed drum with one or
more snares stretched across its lower head —
see DRUM illustration
**snarky** \'snär-kē\ *adjective* [dialect *snark* to
annoy, perhaps alteration of *nark* to irritate]
(1906)
: CROTCHETY, SNAPPISH
**¹snarl** \'snär(-ə)l\ *verb* [²*snarl*] (14th century)
*transitive verb*
**1** : to cause to become knotted and intertwined
: TANGLE
**2** : to make excessively complicated
*intransitive verb*
: to become snarled
— **snarl·er** *noun*

**²snarl** *noun* [Middle English *snarle*, probably
diminutive of *snare*] (1609)
**1** : a tangle especially of hairs or thread : KNOT
**2** : a tangled situation ⟨traffic *snarls*⟩
— **snarly** \'snär-lē\ *adjective*
**³snarl** *verb* [frequentative of obsolete English
*snar* to growl] (1589)
*intransitive verb*
**1** : to growl with a snapping or gnashing of
teeth
**2** : to give vent to anger in surly language
*transitive verb*
: to utter or express with a snarl or by snarling
— **snarl·er** *noun*
**⁴snarl** *noun* (1613)
: a surly angry growl
— **snarly** \'snär-lē\ *adjective*
**¹snatch** \'snach\ *verb* [Middle English *snac-
chen* to give a sudden snap, seize; akin to
Middle Dutch *snacken* to snap at] (13th century)
*intransitive verb*
: to attempt to seize something suddenly
*transitive verb*
: to take or grasp abruptly or hastily; *also* : to
seize or grab suddenly without permission,
ceremony, or right
**synonym** see TAKE
— **snatch·er** *noun*
**²snatch** *noun* (1563)
**1 a** : a brief period ⟨caught *snatches* of sleep⟩
**b** : a brief, fragmentary, or hurried part : BIT
⟨caught *snatches* of the conversation⟩
**2 a** : a snatching at or of something **b** *slang*
: an act or instance of kidnapping
**3** : a lift in weight lifting in which the weight
is raised from the floor directly to an overhead
position in a single motion — compare
CLEAN AND JERK, PRESS
**4** : the female pudenda — usually considered
vulgar
**snatch block** *noun* (circa 1625)
: a block that can be opened on one side to receive the bight of a rope
**snath** \'snath, 'sneth\ *or* **snathe** \'snāth,
'snäth\ *noun* [Middle English *snede*, from Old
English *snæd*] (1574)
: the handle of a scythe
**snaz·zy** \'sna-zē\ *adjective* **snaz·zi·er; -est**
[origin unknown] (1932)
: conspicuously or flashily attractive : FANCY
**¹sneak** \'snēk\ *verb* **sneaked** \'snēkt\ *or*
**snuck** \'snək\; **sneak·ing** [akin to Old English *snīcan* to sneak along, Old Norse *snīkja*]
(1596)
*intransitive verb*
**1** : to go stealthily or furtively : SLINK
**2** : to act in or as if in a furtive manner
**3** : to carry the football on a quarterback sneak
*transitive verb*
: to put, bring, or take in a furtive or artful
manner ⟨*sneak* a smoke⟩ ▪
**synonym** see LURK
— **sneak up on** : to approach or act on
stealthily
**²sneak** *noun* (circa 1643)
**1** : a person who acts in a stealthy, furtive, or
shifty manner
**2 a** : a stealthy or furtive move **b** : an unobserved departure or escape
**3** : SNEAKER 2
**4** : QUARTERBACK SNEAK
**³sneak** *adjective* (circa 1859)
**1** : carried on secretly : CLANDESTINE
**2** : occurring without warning : SURPRISE ⟨a
*sneak* attack⟩
**sneak·er** \'snē-kər\ *noun* (1598)
**1** : one that sneaks
**2** : a usually canvas sports shoe with a pliable
rubber sole
— **sneak·ered** \-kərd\ *adjective*
**sneak·ing** \'snē-kiŋ\ *adjective* (1582)
**1** : MEAN, CONTEMPTIBLE
**2** : characteristic of a sneak : FURTIVE, UNDER-
HANDED

**3 a** : not openly expressed or acknowledged
⟨he has a *sneaking* respect for culture —H. A.
Burton⟩ **b** : that is a persistent conjecture ⟨a
*sneaking* suspicion⟩
— **sneak·ing·ly** \-kiŋ-lē\ *adverb*
**sneak preview** *noun* (circa 1937)
: a special advance showing of a motion picture usually announced but not named
**sneak thief** *noun* (circa 1859)
: a thief who steals whatever is readily available without using violence or forcibly breaking into buildings
**sneaky** \'snē-kē\ *adjective* **sneak·i·er; -est**
(1833)
: marked by stealth, furtiveness, or shiftiness
— **sneak·i·ly** \-kə-lē\ *adverb*
— **sneak·i·ness** \-kē-nəs\ *noun*
**¹sneap** \'snēp\ *transitive verb* [Middle English
*snaipen*, probably of Scandinavian origin; akin
to Icelandic *sneypa* to scold — more at SNUB]
(14th century)
**1** *archaic* : to blast or blight with cold : NIP
**2** *dialect English* : CHIDE
**²sneap** *noun* (1597)
*archaic* : REBUKE, SNUB
**sneck** \'snek\ *noun* [Middle English *snekke*]
(14th century)
*chiefly dialect* : LATCH
**¹sneer** \'snir\ *verb* [probably akin to Middle
High German *snerren* to chatter, gossip —
more at SNORE] (1680)
*intransitive verb*
**1** : to smile or laugh with facial contortions
that express scorn or contempt
**2** : to speak or write in a scornfully jeering
manner
*transitive verb*
: to utter with a sneer
**synonym** see SCOFF
— **sneer·er** *noun*
**²sneer** *noun* (1707)
: the act of sneering; *also* : a sneering expression or remark
**¹sneeze** \'snēz\ *intransitive verb* **sneezed;
sneez·ing** [Middle English *snesen*, alteration
of *fnesen*, from Old English *fnēosan*; akin to
Middle High German *pfnūsen* to snort, sneeze,
Greek *pnein* to breathe] (14th century)
: to make a sudden violent spasmodic audible
expiration of breath through the nose and
mouth especially as a reflex act
— **sneez·er** *noun*
— **sneeze at** : to make light of
**²sneeze** *noun* (1646)
: an act or instance of sneezing
**sneeze·weed** \'snēz-ˌwēd\ *noun* (circa 1837)
: any of several composite plants; *especially*
: a North American perennial herb (*Helenium
autumnale*) with yellow ray flowers and a
darker globose disk
**sneezy** \'snē-zē\ *adjective* (1839)
: given to or causing sneezing
**¹snell** \'snel\ *adjective* [Middle English, from
Old English; akin to Old High German *snel*
bold, agile] (before 12th century)
**1** *chiefly Scottish* : QUICK, ACUTE

□ USAGE
**sneak**  From its earliest appearance in
print in the late 19th century as a dialectal
and probably uneducated form, the past and
past participle *snuck* has risen to the status
of standard and to approximate equality with
*sneaked*. Indications are that it is continuing
to grow in frequency. It is most common in
the U.S. and Canada, but has also been
spotted in British and Australian English.

\ə\ **abut** \ᵊ\ **kitten** \ər\ **further** \a\ **ash** \ā\ **ace**
\ä\ **mop, mar** \aů\ **out** \ch\ **chin** \e\ **bet** \ē\ **easy**
\g\ **go** \i\ **hit** \ī\ **ice** \j\ **job** \ŋ\ **sing** \ō\ **go**
\ȯ\ **law** \ȯi\ **boy** \th\ **thin** \ṯẖ\ **the** \ü\ **loot** \ů\ **foot**
\y\ **yet** \zh\ **vision** *see also* Guide to Pronunciation

**2** *chiefly Scottish* : KEEN, PIERCING ⟨a *snell* wind smote us —*Scotsman*⟩
**3** *chiefly Scottish* : GRIEVOUS, SEVERE
**²snell** *noun* [origin unknown] (1846)
: a short line (as of gut) by which a fishhook is attached to a longer line
**¹snick** \'snik\ *verb* [probably from obsolete *snick* or *snee* to engage in cut-and-thrust fighting — more at SNICKERSNEE] (circa 1700)
*transitive verb*
**1** *archaic* : to cut through
**2** : to cut slightly : NICK
*intransitive verb*
: to perform a light cutting action
**²snick** *noun* (circa 1775)
: a small cut : NICK
**³snick** *verb* [imitative] (1828)
: CLICK
**⁴snick** *noun* (circa 1886)
: a slight often metallic sound : CLICK
**¹snick·er** \'sni-kər\ *intransitive verb* **snick·ered; snick·er·ing** \-k(ə-)riŋ\ [origin unknown] (1694)
: to laugh in a covert or partly suppressed manner : TITTER
— **snick·er·er** \-kər-ər\ *noun*
— **snick·ery** \-k(ə-)rē\ *adjective*
**²snicker** *noun* (1835)
: an act or sound of snickering
**snick·er·snee** \'sni-kə(r)-ˌsnē\ *noun* [obsolete *snick or snee* to engage in cut-and-thrust fighting, alteration of earlier *steake or snye*, from Dutch *steken of snijden* to thrust or cut] (circa 1775)
: a large knife
**snide** \'snīd\ *adjective* [origin unknown] (circa 1859)
**1 a** : FALSE, COUNTERFEIT **b** : practicing deception : DISHONEST ⟨a *snide* merchant⟩
**2** : unworthy of esteem : LOW ⟨a *snide* trick⟩
**3** : slyly disparaging : INSINUATING ⟨*snide* remarks⟩
— **snide·ly** *adverb*
— **snide·ness** *noun*
**¹sniff** \'snif\ *verb* [Middle English] (14th century)
*intransitive verb*
**1** : to draw air audibly up the nose especially for smelling ⟨*sniffed* at the flowers⟩
**2** : to show or express disdain or scorn
*transitive verb*
**1** : to smell or take by inhalation through the nose
**2** : to utter contemptuously
**3** : to recognize or detect by or as if by smelling ⟨*sniff* out trouble⟩
**²sniff** *noun* (1767)
**1** : an act or sound of sniffing
**2** : a quantity that is sniffed
**sniff·er** *noun* (1864)
: one that sniffs; *especially* : one who takes drugs illicitly by sniffing
**sniff·ish** \'sni-fish\ *adjective* (1923)
: having or expressing a haughty attitude : DISDAINFUL, SUPERCILIOUS
— **sniff·ish·ly** *adverb*
— **sniff·ish·ness** *noun*
**¹snif·fle** \'sni-fəl\ *intransitive verb* **snif·fled; snif·fling** \-f(ə-)liŋ\ [frequentative of *sniff*] (1632)
**1** : to sniff repeatedly : SNUFFLE
**2** : to speak with or as if with sniffling
— **snif·fler** \-f(ə-)lər\ *noun*
**²sniffle** *noun* (circa 1825)
**1** *plural* : a head cold marked by nasal discharge
**2** : an act or sound of sniffling
**sniffy** \'sni-fē\ *adjective* **sniff·i·er; -est** (1871)
: SNIFFISH, SUPERCILIOUS
— **sniff·i·ly** \'sni-fə-lē\ *adverb*
— **sniff·i·ness** \'sni-fē-nəs\ *noun*
**snif·ter** \'snif-tər\ *noun* [English dialect, sniff, snort, from Middle English, to sniff, snort] (1844)
**1** : a small drink of distilled liquor

**2** : a short-stemmed goblet with a bowl narrowing toward the top
**¹snig·ger** \'sni-gər\ *intransitive verb* **snig·gered; snig·ger·ing** \-g(ə-)riŋ\ [by alteration] (circa 1706)
: SNICKER
— **snig·ger·er** \-gər-ər\ *noun*
**²snigger** *noun* (circa 1823)
: SNICKER
**snig·gle** \'sni-gəl\ *verb* **snig·gled; snig·gling** \-g(ə-)liŋ\ [English dialect *snig* small eel, from Middle English *snygge*] (1653)
*intransitive verb*
: to fish for eels by thrusting a baited hook or needle into their hiding places
*transitive verb*
: to catch (an eel) by sniggling
**¹snip** \'snip\ *noun* [from or akin to Dutch & Low German *snip*; akin to Middle High German *snipfen* to snap the fingers] (1558)
**1 a** : a small piece that is snipped off; *also* : FRAGMENT, BIT **b** : a cut or notch made by snipping **c** : an act or sound of snipping
**2 a** : a white or light mark; *especially* : a white spot between the nostrils of a horse
**3** : a presumptuous or impertinent person; *especially* : an impertinent or saucy girl
**4** *British* : BARGAIN, BUY
**²snip** *verb* **snipped; snip·ping** (1586)
*transitive verb*
: to cut or cut off with or as if with shears or scissors; *specifically* : to clip suddenly or by bits
*intransitive verb*
: to make a short quick cut with or as if with shears or scissors
— **snip·per** *noun*
**¹snipe** \'snīp\ *noun, plural* **snipes** [Middle English, of Scandinavian origin; akin to Old Norse *snīpa* snipe; akin to Old High German *snepfa* snipe] (14th century)
**1** *or plural* **snipe** : any of various usually slender-billed birds of the same family as the sandpipers; *especially* : any of several game birds (especially genus *Gallinago*) especially of marshy areas
**2** : a contemptible person
**²snipe** *intransitive verb* **sniped; snip·ing** (1832)
**1** : to shoot at exposed individuals (as of an enemy's forces) from a usually concealed point of vantage
**2** : to aim a carping or snide attack
— **snip·er** *noun*
**snip·er·scope** \'snī-pər-ˌskōp\ *noun* (1941)
: an optical device for use especially with a rifle that allows a person to see targets better in the dark
**snip·per·snap·per** \'sni-pər-ˌsna-pər\ *noun* [origin unknown] (circa 1590)
: WHIPPERSNAPPER
**snip·pet** \'sni-pət\ *noun* [¹*snip*] (1664)
: a small part, piece, or thing; *especially* : a brief quotable passage
**snip·pety** \-pə-tē\ *adjective* (1864)
**1** : made up of snippets
**2** [probably from ²*snip* + *-ety* (as in *pernickety*)] : SNIPPY
**snip·py** \'sni-pē\ *adjective* **snip·pi·er; -est** [²*snip*] (circa 1848)
**1** : SHORT-TEMPERED, SNAPPISH
**2** : unduly brief or curt
**3** : putting on airs : SNIFFY
— **snip·pi·ly** \'sni-pə-lē\ *adverb*
**snips** \'snips\ *noun plural but singular or plural in construction* (circa 1846)
: hand shears used especially for cutting sheet metal
**snit** \'snit\ *noun* [origin unknown] (1939)
: a state of agitation
**¹snitch** \'snich\ *noun* [origin unknown] (circa 1785)
: one that snitches : TATTLETALE
**²snitch** *intransitive verb* (1801)
: INFORM, TATTLE
— **snitch·er** *noun*

**³snitch** *transitive verb* [probably alteration of *snatch*] (1904)
: to take by stealth : PILFER
**¹sniv·el** \'sni-vəl\ *intransitive verb* **-eled** *or* **-elled; -el·ing** *or* **-el·ling** \'sni-və-liŋ, 'sniv-liŋ\ [Middle English, from (assumed) Old English *snyflan*; akin to Dutch *snuffelen* to snuffle, *snuffen* to sniff] (14th century)
**1** : to run at the nose
**2** : to snuff mucus up the nose audibly : SNUFFLE
**3** : to cry or whine with snuffling
**4** : to speak or act in a whining, sniffling, tearful, or weakly emotional manner
— **sniv·el·er** \'sni-və-lər, 'sniv-lər\ *noun*
**²snivel** *noun* (1600)
**1** *plural, dialect* : HEAD COLD
**2** : an act or instance of sniveling
**snob** \'snäb\ *noun* [origin unknown] (1781)
**1** *British* : COBBLER
**2** : one who blatantly imitates, fawningly admires, or vulgarly seeks association with those regarded as social superiors
**3 a** : one who tends to rebuff, avoid, or ignore those regarded as inferior **b** : one who has an offensive air of superiority in matters of knowledge or taste
**snob appeal** *noun* (1933)
: qualities in a product that appeal to the snobbery in a purchaser
**snob·bery** \'snä-b(ə-)rē\ *noun, plural* **-ber·ies** (1843)
**1** : snobbish conduct or character : SNOBBISHNESS
**2** : an instance of snobbery
**snob·bish** \'snä-bish\ *adjective* (1840)
: being, characteristic of, or befitting a snob
— **snob·bish·ly** *adverb*
— **snob·bish·ness** *noun*
**snob·bism** \'snä-ˌbi-zəm\ *noun* (1845)
: SNOBBERY
**snob·by** \'snä-bē\ *adjective* **snob·bi·er; -est** (1846)
: characterized by snobbery
**sno—cone** *variant of* SNOW CONE
**snol·ly·gos·ter** \'snä-lē-ˌgäs-tər\ *noun* [probably alteration of *snallygaster* a mythical creature that preys on poultry and children] (circa 1860)
: a shrewd unprincipled person
**¹snood** \'snüd\ *noun* [(assumed) Middle English, from Old English *snōd*] (before 12th century)
**1 a** *Scottish* : a fillet or band for a woman's hair **b** : a net or fabric bag pinned or tied on at the back of a woman's head for holding the hair
**2** : SNELL
**²snood** *transitive verb* (1714)
: to secure with a snood
**¹snook** \'snuk, 'snük\ *noun, plural* **snook** *or* **snooks** [Dutch *snoek* pike, snook] (1697)
**1** : a large vigorous bony fish (*Centropomus undecimalis* of the family Centropomidae) of warm seas and rivers that is a prized food and sport fish
**2** : any of various marine fishes of the same family as the snook
**²snook** *noun* [origin unknown] (1879)
: a gesture of derision made by thumbing the nose
**¹snook·er** \'snu-kər\ *noun* [origin unknown] (1889)
: a variation of pool played with 15 red balls and 6 variously colored balls
**²snooker** *transitive verb* (1925)
: to make a dupe of : HOODWINK
**¹snoop** \'snüp\ *intransitive verb* [Dutch *snoepen* to buy or eat on the sly; akin to Dutch *snappen* to snap] (1832)
: to look or pry especially in a sneaking or meddlesome manner
— **snoop·er** *noun*

snood 1b

**²snoop** *noun* (circa 1890)
: one that snoops
**snoopy** \'snü-pē\ *adjective* (circa 1895)
: given to snooping especially for personal information about others
— **snoop·i·ly** \-pə-lē\ *adverb*
**¹snoot** \'snüt\ *noun* [Middle English *snute*] (1861)
**1 a :** SNOUT **b :** NOSE
**2 :** a grimace expressive of contempt
**3 :** a snooty person : SNOB
**²snoot** *transitive verb* (1928)
: to treat with disdain : look down one's nose at
**snooty** \'snü-tē\ *adjective* **snoot·i·er; -est** (1919)
**1 :** looking down the nose : showing disdain ⟨*snooty* people who won't speak to their neighbors⟩
**2 :** characterized by snobbery ⟨a *snooty* store⟩
— **snoot·i·ly** \'snü-t°l-ē\ *adverb*
— **snoot·i·ness** \'snü-tē-nəs\ *noun*
**¹snooze** \'snüz\ *intransitive verb* **snoozed; snooz·ing** [origin unknown] (1788)
: to take a nap : DOZE
— **snooz·er** *noun*
**²snooze** *noun* (1793)
: NAP
**snoo·zle** \'snü-zəl\ *verb* **snoo·zled; snoo·zling** \'snü-zə-liŋ, 'snüz-liŋ\ [perhaps blend of *snooze* and *nuzzle*] (1831)
*chiefly dialect* : NUZZLE
**¹snore** \'snōr, 'snȯr\ *verb* **snored; snor·ing** [Middle English; akin to Middle Low German *snorren* to drone, Middle High German *snerren* to chatter] (15th century)
*intransitive verb*
: to breathe during sleep with a rough hoarse noise due to vibration of the soft palate
*transitive verb*
: to spend (time) in snoring or sleeping
— **snor·er** *noun*
**²snore** *noun* (1605)
**1 :** an act of snoring
**2 :** a noise of or as if of snoring
**¹snor·kel** \'snȯr-kəl\ *noun* [German *Schnorchel*] (1944)
**1 :** a tube housing air intake and exhaust pipes for a submarine's diesel engine that can be extended above the water's surface so that the engines can be operated while the submarine is submerged
**2 :** any of various devices (as for an underwater swimmer) resembling a snorkel in function
**²snorkel** *intransitive verb* **snor·keled; snor·kel·ing** \-k(ə-)liŋ\ (1949)
: to operate or swim submerged with only a snorkel above water
— **snor·kel·er** \-k(ə-)lər\ *noun*
**¹snort** \'snȯrt\ *verb* [Middle English] (14th century)
*intransitive verb*
**1 a :** to force air violently through the nose with a rough harsh sound **b :** to express scorn, anger, indignation, or surprise by a snort
**2 :** to emit explosive sounds resembling snorts
**3 :** to take in a drug by inhalation
*transitive verb*
**1 :** to utter with or express by a snort
**2 :** to expel or emit with or as if with snorts
**3 :** to take in (a drug) by inhalation
**²snort** *noun* (1808)
**1 :** an act or sound of snorting
**2 :** a drink of usually straight liquor taken in one draft
**snort·er** \'snȯr-tər\ *noun* (1601)
**1 :** one that snorts
**2 :** something that is extraordinary or prominent : HUMDINGER
**3 :** SNORT 2
**snot** \'snät\ *noun* [Middle English, from Old English *gesnot*; akin to Old High German *snuzza* nasal mucus] (15th century)
**1 :** nasal mucus
**2 :** a snotty person

**snot·ty** \'snä-tē\ *adjective* **snot·ti·er; -est** (circa 1570)
**1 :** foul with nasal mucus
**2 :** annoyingly or spitefully unpleasant
— **snot·ti·ly** \'snä-t°l-ē\ *adverb*
— **snot·ti·ness** \'snä-tē-nəs\ *noun*
**snout** \'snaut\ *noun* [Middle English *snute*; akin to Middle Dutch *snūt* snout, German *Schnauze*] (13th century)
**1 a** (1) **:** a long projecting nose (as of a swine) (2) **:** an anterior prolongation of the head of various animals (as a weevil) : ROSTRUM **b** : the human nose especially when large or grotesque
**2 :** something resembling an animal's snout in position, function, or shape: as **a :** PROW **b** : NOZZLE **c :** the terminal face of a glacier
— **snout·ed** \'snau-təd\ *adjective*
— **snout·ish** \-tish\ *adjective*
— **snouty** \-tē\ *adjective*
**snout beetle** *noun* (1862)
: WEEVIL
**¹snow** \'snō\ *noun, often attributive* [Middle English, from Old English *snāw*; akin to Old High German *snēo* snow, Latin *niv-, nix*, Greek *nipha* (accusative)] (before 12th century)
**1 a :** precipitation in the form of small white ice crystals formed directly from the water vapor of the air at a temperature of less than 32°F (0°C) **b** (1) **:** a descent or shower of snow crystals (2) **:** a mass of fallen snow crystals
**2 :** something resembling snow: as **a :** a dessert made of stiffly beaten whites of eggs, sugar, and fruit pulp ⟨apple *snow*⟩ **b :** a usually white crystalline substance that condenses from a fluid phase as snow does ⟨ammonia *snow*⟩ **c** *slang* (1) **:** COCAINE (2) **:** HEROIN **d** : small transient light or dark spots on a television screen
— **snow·less** \-ləs\ *adjective*
**²snow** (14th century)
*intransitive verb*
: to fall in or as snow
*transitive verb*
**1 :** to cause to fall like or as snow
**2 a :** to cover, shut in, or imprison with or as if with snow **b :** to deceive, persuade, or charm glibly
**3 :** to whiten like snow
**¹snow·ball** \'snō-ˌbȯl\ *noun* (15th century)
**1 a :** a round mass of snow pressed or rolled together **b :** shaved ice molded into a ball and flavored with a syrup
**2 :** any of several cultivated shrubs (genus *Viburnum*) with clusters of white sterile flowers — called also *snowball bush*
**²snowball** (1854)
*transitive verb*
**1 :** to throw snowballs at
**2 :** to cause to increase or multiply at a rapidly accelerating rate
*intransitive verb*
**1 :** to engage in throwing snowballs
**2 :** to increase, accumulate, expand, or multiply at a rapidly accelerating rate
**snow·bank** \'snō-ˌbaŋk\ *noun* (1779)
: a mound or slope of snow
**snow·belt** \-ˌbelt\ *noun, often capitalized* (1874)
: a region that receives an appreciable amount of annual snowfall
**snow·ber·ry** \-ˌber-ē\ *noun* (1760)
: any of several white-berried shrubs (especially genus *Symphoricarpos* of the honeysuckle family); *especially* : a low-growing North American shrub (*S. albus*) with pink flowers in small axillary clusters
**snow·bird** \-ˌbərd\ *noun* (1674)
**1 :** any of several birds (as a junco or fieldfare) seen chiefly in winter
**2 :** one who travels to warm climes for the winter
**snow blindness** *noun* (1748)

: inflammation and photophobia caused by exposure of the eyes to ultraviolet rays reflected from snow or ice
— **snow–blind** \'snō-ˌblīnd\ *or* **snow–blind·ed** \-ˌblīn-dəd\ *adjective*
**snow-blow·er** \'snō-ˌblō(-ə)r\ *noun* (1950)
: SNOW THROWER
**snow·board** \-ˌbōrd, -ˌbȯrd\ *noun* (1981)
: a board like a wide ski ridden in a surfing position downhill over snow
— **snow·board·er** *noun*
— **snow·board·ing** *noun*
**snow·bound** \-'baund\ *adjective* (1814)
: shut in or blockaded by snow
**snow·brush** \-ˌbrəsh\ *noun* (circa 1923)
: a spreading white-flowered western North American shrub (*Ceanothus velutinus*) of the buckthorn family with scented leaves and panicles of small flowers
**snow·cap** \-ˌkap\ *noun* (1871)
: a covering cap of snow (as on a mountain peak)
— **snow·capped** \-ˌkapt\ *adjective*
**snow cone** *noun* (1964)
: SNOWBALL 1b
**snow crab** *noun* (1974)
: either of two crabs (*Chionoecetes opilio* and *C. bairdi*) of the northern Pacific Ocean and especially Alaska marketed for food
**snow·drift** \'snō-ˌdrift\ *noun* (14th century)
: a bank of drifted snow
**snow·drop** \-ˌdräp\ *noun* (1664)
: a bulbous European herb (*Galanthus nivalis*) of the amaryllis family bearing nodding white flowers that often appear while the snow is on the ground
**snow·fall** \-ˌfȯl\ *noun* (1821)
: a fall of snow; *specifically* : the amount of snow that falls in a single storm or in a given period
**snow fence** *noun* (1872)
: a usually slatted fence placed across the path of prevailing winds to protect (as a building, road, or railroad track) from drifting snow by disrupting the flow of wind and causing the snow to be deposited on the lee side of the fence
**snow·field** \'snō-ˌfēld\ *noun* (1845)
: a broad level expanse of snow; *especially* : a mass of perennial snow at the head of a glacier
**snow·flake** \-ˌflāk\ *noun* (1734)
**1 :** a flake or crystal of snow
**2 :** any of a genus (*Leucojum*) of bulbous plants of the amaryllis family; *especially* : one (*L. vernum*) resembling the snowdrop
**snow goose** *noun* (1771)
: a wild goose (*Anser caerulescens* synonym *Chen caerulescens*) that has a pinkish bill and exists either as a white form with black primaries or as a grayish black form with a white head
**snow job** *noun* (1943)
: an intensive effort at persuasion or deception
**snow leopard** *noun* (1866)
: a large cat (*Panthera uncia*) of upland central Asia with long heavy grayish white fur irregularly marked with brownish black spots, rosettes, and rings

**snow leopard**

**snow line** *noun* (circa 1835)
: the lower margin of a perennial snowfield
**snow·mak·er** \'snō-ˌmā-kər\ *noun* (1954)
: a device for making snow artificially
**snow·mak·ing** \-ˌmā-kiŋ\ *adjective* (1953)

: used for the production of artificial snow usually for ski slopes ⟨*snowmaking* machines⟩

**snow·man** \-,man\ *noun* (1827)
: snow shaped to resemble a human figure

**snow·melt** \-,melt\ *noun* (circa 1946)
: runoff produced by the melting of snow

**snow·mo·bile** \'snō-mō-,bēl\ *noun* (1923)
: any of various automotive vehicles for travel on snow; *specifically* : an open vehicle for usually one or two persons with steerable skis on the front and an endless belt at the rear

**snow·mo·bil·ing** \-,bē-liŋ\ *noun* (1964)
: the sport of driving a snowmobile
— **snow·mo·bil·er** \-lər\ *also* **snow·mo·bil·ist** \-list\ *noun*

**snow–on–the–mountain** *noun* (1873)
: a spurge (*Euphorbia marginata*) of the central and western U.S. that has showy white-bracted flower clusters and is grown as an ornamental

**snow·pack** \'snō-,pak\ *noun* (circa 1946)
: a seasonal accumulation of slow-melting packed snow

**snow pea** *noun* (1949)
: a cultivated pea with flat edible pods that is classified with the snap pea as a variety (*Pisum sativum macrocarpon*)

**snow plant** *noun* (1846)
: a fleshy bright-red saprophytic chiefly California herb (*Sarcodes sanguinea*) of the wintergreen family that grows in high-altitude coniferous woods and often appears before the snow melts

**¹snow·plow** \'snō-,plaù\ *noun* (1792)
**1** : any of various devices used for clearing away snow
**2** : a stemming with both skis used for coming to a stop, slowing down, or descending slowly

**²snowplow** *intransitive verb* (1904)
: to execute a snowplow ⟨*snowplowed* to a stop⟩

**snow pudding** *noun* (1876)
: a pudding made very fluffy and light by the addition of whipped egg whites and gelatin

**snow·scape** \'snō-,skāp\ *noun* (1886)
: a landscape covered with snow

**snow·shed** \-,shed\ *noun* (1868)
: a shelter against snowslides

**¹snow·shoe** \-,shü\ *noun* (1666)
: a light oval frame that is strengthened by two crosspieces, strung with thongs, and attached to the foot and that is used to enable a person to walk on soft snow without sinking

**²snowshoe** *intransitive verb* **snow·shoed; snow·shoe·ing** (1880)
: to travel on snowshoes
— **snow·sho·er** \-,shü-ər\ *noun*

**snowshoe hare** *noun* (circa 1890)
: a hare (*Lepus americanus*) of northern North America with heavy fur on the hind feet and a coat that in most populations is brown in the summer but usually white in the winter — called also *snowshoe rabbit, varying hare*

**snow·slide** \'snō-,slīd\ *noun* (1841)
: an avalanche of snow

**snow·storm** \-,stòrm\ *noun* (1771)
**1** : a storm of or with snow
**2** : something that resembles a snowstorm

**snow·suit** \-,süt\ *noun* (1937)
: a one-piece or two-piece lined garment for winter wear by children

**snow thrower** *noun* (1954)
: a machine for removing snow (as from a driveway or sidewalk) in which a rotating spiral blade picks up and propels the snow aside

**snow tire** *noun* (1943)

snowshoe hare

: an automotive tire with a tread designed to give added traction on snow

**snow under** *transitive verb* (1880)
**1** : to overwhelm especially in excess of capacity to absorb or deal with something
**2** : to defeat by a large margin

**snow–white** \'snō-'hwīt, -'wīt\ *adjective* (before 12th century)
: white as snow

**snowy** \'snō-ē\ *adjective* **snow·i·er; -est** (before 12th century)
**1 a** : composed of snow or melted snow **b** : marked by or covered with snow
**2 a** : whitened by snow **b** : SNOW-WHITE
— **snow·i·ly** \'snō-ə-lē\ *adverb*
— **snow·i·ness** \'snō-ē-nəs\ *noun*

**snowy egret** *noun* (1869)
: a white American egret (*Egretta thula*) having a slender black bill, black legs, and yellow feet

**snowy owl** *noun* (1781)
: a large ground-nesting diurnal arctic owl (*Nyctea scandiaca*) that enters the chiefly northern parts of the U.S. in winter and has plumage that is sometimes nearly pure white but usually with brownish spots or bars

snowy owl

**¹snub** \'snəb\ *transitive verb* **snubbed; snub·bing** [Middle English *snubben*, of Scandinavian origin; akin to Old Norse *snubba* to scold; akin to Icelandic *sneypa* to scold] (13th century)
**1** : to check or stop with a cutting retort : REBUKE
**2 a** : to check (as a line) suddenly while running out especially by turning around a fixed object (as a post); *also* : to check the motion of by snubbing a line ⟨*snub* a horse to a tree⟩ **b** : to restrain the action of : SUPPRESS ⟨*snub* a vibration⟩
**3** : to treat with contempt or neglect
**4** : to extinguish by stubbing ⟨*snub* out a cigarette⟩

**²snub** *noun* (14th century)
: an act or an instance of snubbing; *especially* : SLIGHT

**³snub** *adjective* (1724)
**1** *or* **snubbed** \'snəbd\ : BLUNT, STUBBY ⟨a *snub* nose⟩
**2** : used in snubbing ⟨*snub* line⟩
— **snub·ness** *noun*

**snub·ber** \'snə-bər\ *noun* (1853)
**1** : one that snubs
**2** : SHOCK ABSORBER

**snub·by** \'snə-bē\ *adjective* (1828)
**1** : SNUB
**2** : SNUB-NOSED
— **snub·bi·ness** *noun*

**snub–nosed** \'snəb-,nōzd\ *adjective* (1725)
**1** : having a stubby and usually slightly turned-up nose
**2** : having a very short barrel ⟨a *snub-nosed* revolver⟩

**snuck** *past and past participle of* SNEAK

**¹snuff** \'snəf\ *noun* [Middle English *snoffe*] (14th century)
**1** : the charred part of a candlewick
**2 a** *obsolete* : UMBRAGE, OFFENSE **b** *chiefly Scottish* : HUFF

**²snuff** *transitive verb* (15th century)
**1** : to crop the snuff of (a candle) by pinching or by the use of snuffers so as to brighten the light
**2 a** : to extinguish by or as if by the use of a snuffer — often used with *out* **b** : to make extinct : put an end to — usually used with *out* ⟨an accident that *snuffed* out a life⟩

**³snuff** *adjective* (1975)
: characterized by the sensationalistic depiction of violence; *especially* : featuring a real rather than a staged murder ⟨*snuff* movies⟩

**⁴snuff** *verb* [akin to Dutch *snuffen* to sniff, snuff — more at SNIVEL] (1527)
*transitive verb*
**1** : to draw forcibly through or into the nostrils
**2** : SCENT, SMELL
**3** : to sniff at in order to examine — used of an animal
*intransitive verb*
**1** : to inhale through the nose noisily and forcibly; *also* : to sniff or smell inquiringly
**2** *obsolete* : to sniff loudly in or as if in disgust
**3** : to take snuff

**⁵snuff** *noun* (1570)
: the act of snuffing : SNIFF

**⁶snuff** *noun* [Dutch *snuf*, short for *snuftabak*, from *snuffen* to snuff + *tabak* tobacco] (1683)
**1** : a preparation of pulverized tobacco to be inhaled through the nostrils, chewed, or placed against the gums
**2** : the amount of snuff taken at one time
— **up to snuff** : of sufficient quality : meeting an applicable standard

**snuff·box** \'snəf-,bäks\ *noun* (circa 1687)
: a small box for holding snuff usually carried about the person

**¹snuff·er** \'snə-fər\ *noun* (15th century)
**1** : a device similar to a pair of scissors for cropping and holding the snuff of a candle — usually used in plural but singular or plural in construction
**2** : a device for extinguishing candles

**²snuffer** *noun* (circa 1610)
: one that snuffs or sniffs

**¹snuf·fle** \'snə-fəl\ *verb* **snuf·fled; snuf·fling** \-f(ə-)liŋ\ [akin to Dutch *snuffelen* to snuffle — more at SNIVEL] (circa 1600)
*intransitive verb*
**1** : to snuff or sniff usually audibly and repeatedly
**2** : to breathe through an obstructed nose with a sniffing sound
**3** : to speak through or as if through the nose : WHINE
*transitive verb*
: to seek or test by or as if by repeated sniffs
— **snuf·fler** \-f(ə-)lər\ *noun*

**²snuffle** *noun* (circa 1764)
**1** : the act or sound of snuffling
**2** : a nasal twang
**3** *plural* : SNIFFLES

**¹snuffy** \'snə-fē\ *adjective* [⁴*snuff*] (1678)
**1** : quick to become annoyed or take offense
**2** : marked by snobbery

**²snuffy** *adjective* [⁶*snuff*] (1787)
**1** : resembling snuff
**2 a** : addicted to the use of snuff **b** : having unpleasant habits
**3** : soiled with snuff

**¹snug** \'snəg\ *verb* **snugged; snug·ging** [²*snug*] (1583)
*intransitive verb*
: SNUGGLE
*transitive verb*
**1** : to cause to fit closely
**2** : to make snug
**3** : HIDE
**4** : to secure by fastening or lashing down

**²snug** *adjective* **snug·ger; snug·gest** [perhaps of Scandinavian origin; akin to Swedish *snygg* tidy] (circa 1595)
**1 a** *of a ship* : manifesting seaworthiness : TAUT **b** : TRIM, NEAT **c** : fitting closely and comfortably ⟨a *snug* coat⟩
**2 a** : enjoying or affording warm secure shelter or cover and opportunity for ease and contentment **b** : marked by cordiality and secure privacy
**3** : affording a degree of comfort and ease
**4** : offering safe concealment ⟨a *snug* hideout⟩
*synonym* SEE COMFORTABLE
— **snug** *adverb*
— **snug·ly** *adverb*
— **snug·ness** *noun*

**³snug** *noun* [short for *snuggery*] (1860)

*British* : a small private room or compartment in a pub

**snug·gery** \'snə-g(ə-)rē\ *noun, plural* **-ger·ies** (1812)
*chiefly British* : a snug cozy place; *especially* : a small room

**snug·gle** \'snə-gəl\ *verb* **snug·gled; snug·gling** \-g(ə-)liŋ\ [frequentative of ¹*snug*] (1687)
*intransitive verb*
: to curl up comfortably or cozily
*transitive verb*
**1** : to draw close especially for comfort or in affection
**2** : to make snug
— **snuggle** *noun*

¹**so** \'sō, *especially before adjective or adverb followed by "that"* sə\ *adverb* [Middle English, from Old English *swā;* akin to Old High German *sō* so, Latin *sīc* so, thus, *sī* if, Greek *hōs* so, thus, Latin *suus* one's own — more at SUICIDE] (before 12th century)
**1 a** : in a manner or way indicated or suggested ⟨do you really think *so*⟩ — often used as a substitute for a preceding clause ⟨are you ready? I think *so*⟩ ⟨I didn't like it and I told her *so*⟩ **b** : in the same manner or way : ALSO ⟨worked hard and *so* did she⟩ **c** : THUS ⟨for *so* the Lord said —Isaiah 18:4 (Authorized Version)⟩ **d** : THEN, SUBSEQUENTLY ⟨and *so* home and to bed⟩
**2 a** : to an indicated or suggested extent or degree ⟨had never been *so* happy⟩ **b** : to a great extent or degree : VERY, EXTREMELY ⟨loves her *so*⟩ **c** : to a definite but unspecified extent or degree ⟨can only do *so* much in a day⟩ **d** : most certainly : INDEED ⟨you did *so* do it⟩
**3** : THEREFORE, CONSEQUENTLY ⟨the witness is biased and *so* unreliable⟩ □

²**so** *conjunction* (before 12th century)
**1 a** : with the result that ⟨the acoustics are good, *so* every note is clear⟩ **b** : in order that ⟨be quiet *so* he can sleep⟩
**2** *archaic* : provided that
**3 a** : for that reason : THEREFORE ⟨don't want to go, *so* I won't⟩ **b** (1) — used as an introductory particle ⟨*so* here we are⟩ often to belittle a point under discussion ⟨*so* what?⟩ (2) — used interjectionally to indicate awareness of a discovery ⟨*so,* that's who did it⟩ or surprised dissent □

³**so** *adjective* (before 12th century)
**1** : conforming with actual facts : TRUE ⟨said things that were not *so*⟩
**2** : marked by a desired order ⟨his books are always just *so*⟩
**3** — used to replace a preceding adjective ⟨was witty by adult standards and of course doubly *so* by mine —Sally Kempton⟩

⁴**so** *pronoun* (before 12th century)
**1** : such as has been specified or suggested : the same ⟨if you have to file a claim, do *so* as soon as possible⟩
**2** — used in the phrase *or so* to indicate an estimate, approximation, or conjecture ⟨stayed a week or *so*⟩ ⟨cost $15 or *so*⟩

⁵**so** *variant of* SOL

¹**soak** \'sōk\ *verb* [Middle English *soken,* from Old English *socian;* akin to Old English *sūcan* to suck] (before 12th century)
*intransitive verb*
**1** : to lie immersed in liquid (as water) : become saturated by or as if by immersion
**2 a** : to enter or pass through something by or as if by pores or interstices : PERMEATE **b** : to penetrate or affect the mind or feelings — usually used with *in* or *into*
**3** : to drink alcoholic beverages intemperately
*transitive verb*
**1** : to permeate so as to wet, soften, or fill thoroughly
**2** : to place in a surrounding element (as liquid) to wet or permeate thoroughly
**3** : to extract by or as if by steeping ⟨*soak* the dirt out⟩

**4 a** : to draw in by or as if by suction or absorption ⟨*soaked* up the sunshine⟩ **b** : to intoxicate (oneself) by drinking alcoholic beverages
**5** : to cause to pay an exorbitant amount ☆
— **soak·er** *noun*

²**soak** *noun* (15th century)
**1 a** : the act or process of soaking : the state of being soaked **b** : that (as liquid) in which something is soaked
**2** : DRUNKARD
**3** *slang* : ²PAWN 2

¹**so-and-so** \'sō-ən-,sō\ *noun, plural* **so-and-sos** *or* **so-and-so's** \-,sōz\ (1596)
**1** : an unnamed or unspecified person, thing, or action
**2** : BASTARD 3

²**so-and-so** *adverb* (1631)
**1** : to an unspecified amount or degree
**2** : in an unspecified manner or fashion

¹**soap** \'sōp\ *noun* [Middle English *sope,* from Old English *sāpe;* akin to Old High German *seifa* soap] (before 12th century)
**1 a** : a cleansing and emulsifying agent made usually by action of alkali on fat or fatty acids and consisting essentially of sodium or potassium salts of such acids **b** : a salt of a fatty acid and a metal
**2** : SOAP OPERA

²**soap** *transitive verb* (1585)
**1** : to rub soap over or into
**2** : FLATTER

**soap·bark** \'sōp-,bärk\ *noun* (1861)
: a Chilean tree (*Quillaja saponaria*) of the rose family with glossy leaves and terminal white flowers; *also* : its saponin-rich bark used in cleaning and in emulsifying oils

**soap·ber·ry** \-,ber-ē\ *noun* (1693)
: any of a genus (*Sapindus* of the family Sapindaceae, the soapberry family) of chiefly tropical woody plants; *also* : the fruit of a soapberry and especially of a tree (*S. saponaria*) that is saponin-rich and used as a soap substitute

**soap·box** \-,bäks\ *noun* (1907)
: an improvised platform used by a self-appointed, spontaneous, or informal orator; *broadly* : something that provides an outlet for delivering opinions
— **soapbox** *adjective*

**soap bubble** *noun* (1800)
: a hollow iridescent globe formed by blowing a film of soapsuds (as from a pipe)

**soap·er** \'sō-pər\ *noun* (1946)
: SOAP OPERA

**soap opera** *noun* [from its sponsorship by soap manufacturers] (1939)
**1 a** : a serial drama performed originally on a daytime radio or television program and chiefly characterized by tangled interpersonal situations and melodramatic or sentimental treatment **b** : a series of real-life events resembling a soap opera
**2** : the melodrama and sentimentality characteristic of a soap opera ⟨even cops need a little *soap opera* in their lives —Joseph Wambaugh⟩; *also* : something (as a novel) having such qualities

**soap plant** *noun* (1844)
: a plant having a part (as a root or fruit) that may be used in place of soap; *especially* : a California plant (*Chlorogalum pomeridianum*) of the lily family

**soap·stone** \'sōp-,stōn\ *noun* (circa 1681)
: a soft stone having a soapy feel and composed essentially of talc, chlorite, and often some magnetite

**soap·suds** \-,sədz\ *noun plural* (1611)
: SUDS 1

**soap·wort** \-,wərt, -,wórt\ *noun* (1548)
: BOUNCING BET

**soapy** \'sō-pē\ *adjective* **soap·i·er; -est** (1610)
**1** : smeared with soap : LATHERED
**2** : containing or combined with soap or saponin

**3 a** : resembling or having the qualities of soap; *especially* : being smooth and slippery **b** : UNCTUOUS, SUAVE
**4** : of, relating to, or having the characteristics of soap opera
— **soap·i·ly** \-pə-lē\ *adverb*
— **soap·i·ness** \-pē-nəs\ *noun*

¹**soar** \'sōr, 'sor\ *intransitive verb* [Middle English *soren,* from Middle French *essorer,* from (assumed) Vulgar Latin *exaurare,* from Latin *ex- + aura* air — more at AURA] (14th century)
**1 a** : to fly aloft or about **b** (1) : to sail or hover in the air often at a great height : GLIDE (2) *of a glider* : to fly without engine power and without loss of altitude
**2** : to rise or increase dramatically (as in position, value, or price)
**3** : to ascend to a higher or more exalted level
**4** : to rise to majestic stature
— **soar·er** *noun*

²**soar** *noun* (1596)
**1** : the range, distance, or height attained in soaring
**2** : the act of soaring : upward flight

**soar·ing** *noun* (15th century)
: the act or process of soaring; *specifically* : the act or sport of flying a heavier-than-air craft without power by utilizing ascending air currents

**Soa·ve** \'swä-(,)vā\ *noun* [*Soave,* village near Verona, Italy] (1935)

---

☆ **SYNONYMS**
**Soak, saturate, drench, steep, impregnate** mean to permeate or be permeated with a liquid. SOAK implies usually prolonged immersion as for softening or cleansing ⟨*soak* the garment in soapy water⟩. SATURATE implies a resulting effect of complete absorption until no more liquid can be held ⟨a *saturated* sponge⟩. DRENCH implies a thorough wetting by something that pours down or is poured ⟨clothes *drenched* by a cloudburst⟩. STEEP suggests either the extraction of an essence (as of tea leaves) by the liquid or the imparting of a quality (as a color) to the thing immersed ⟨*steep* the tea for five minutes⟩. IMPREGNATE implies a thorough interpenetration of one thing by another ⟨a cake strongly *impregnated* with brandy⟩.

---

□ **USAGE**
¹**so** The intensive use of the adverb *so* (sense 2b) is widely condemned in college handbooks but is nonetheless standard ⟨why is American television *so* shallow? —Anthony Lewis⟩ ⟨the cephalopod eye is an example of a remarkable evolutionary parallel because it is *so* like the eye of a vertebrate —Sarah F. Robbins⟩ ⟨the kind of sterile over-ingenuity which afflicts *so* many academic efforts —*Times Literary Supplement*⟩. There is no stigma attached to its use in negative contexts and when qualified by a dependent clause ⟨not *so* long ago⟩ ⟨was *so* good in mathematics that he began to consider engineering —*Current Biography*⟩. The denotation in these uses is, of course, slightly different (see sense 2a).

²**so** Although occasionally condemned, use of the conjunction *so* to introduce clauses of result (sense 1a) and purpose (sense 1b) is standard. In sense 1b *so that* is more common in formal contexts than *so* alone.

---

\ə\ **abut** \ᵊ\ **kitten** \ər\ **further** \a\ **ash** \ā\ **ace**
\ä\ **mop, mar** \au̇\ **out** \ch\ **chin** \e\ **bet** \ē\ **easy**
\g\ **go** \i\ **hit** \ī\ **ice** \j\ **job** \ŋ\ **sing** \ō\ **go**
\ȯ\ **law** \ȯi\ **boy** \th\ **thin** \t͟h\ **the** \ü\ **loot** \u̇\ **foot**
\y\ **yet** \zh\ **vision** *see also* Guide to Pronunciation

: a dry white Italian wine

**¹sob** \'säb\ *verb* **sobbed; sob·bing** [Middle English *sobben*] (13th century)
*intransitive verb*
**1 a :** to catch the breath audibly in a spasmodic contraction of the throat **b :** to cry or weep with convulsive catching of the breath
**2 :** to make a sound like that of a sob or sobbing
*transitive verb*
**1 :** to bring (as oneself) to a specified state by sobbing ⟨*sobbed* himself to sleep⟩
**2 :** to utter with sobs ⟨*sobbed* out her grief⟩

**²sob** *noun* (14th century)
**1 :** an act of sobbing
**2 :** a sound like that of a sob

**SOB** \,es-,ō-'bē\ *noun* [*son of a bitch*] (1918)
: BASTARD 3, SON OF A BITCH

**¹so·ber** \'sō-bər\ *adjective* **so·ber·er** \-bər-ər\; **so·ber·est** \-b(ə-)rəst\ [Middle English *sobre*, from Middle French, from Latin *sobrius*; akin to Latin *ebrius* drunk] (14th century)
**1 a :** sparing in the use of food and drink : ABSTEMIOUS **b :** not addicted to intoxicating drink **c :** not drunk
**2 :** marked by sedate or gravely or earnestly thoughtful character or demeanor
**3 :** UNHURRIED, CALM
**4 :** marked by temperance, moderation, or seriousness
**5 :** subdued in tone or color
**6 :** showing no excessive or extreme qualities of fancy, emotion, or prejudice
*synonym* see SERIOUS
— **so·ber·ly** \-bər-lē\ *adverb*
— **so·ber·ness** *noun*

**²sober** *verb* **so·bered; so·ber·ing** \-b(ə-)riŋ\ (14th century)
*transitive verb*
: to make sober
*intransitive verb*
: to become sober — usually used with *up*

**so·ber·ing** *adjective* (1816)
: tending to make one thoughtful or sober

**so·ber·ize** \'sō-bə-,rīz\ *transitive verb* **-ized; -iz·ing** (1706)
*archaic* : to make sober

**so·ber·sid·ed** \,sō-bər-'sī-dəd\ *adjective* (1847)
: solemn or serious in nature or appearance
— **so·ber·sid·ed·ness** \-nəs\ *noun*

**so·ber·sides** \'sō-bər-,sīdz\ *noun plural but singular or plural in construction* (1705)
: a sobersided person

**so·bri·ety** \sə-'brī-ə-tē, sō-\ *noun* [Middle English *sobrietie*, from Middle French *sobrieté*, from Latin *sobrietat-, sobrietas*, from *sobrius*] (15th century)
: the quality or state of being sober

**so·bri·quet** \'sō-bri-,kā, -,ket, ,sō-bri-'\ *noun* [French] (1646)
: a descriptive name or epithet : NICKNAME

**sob sister** *noun* (1912)
**1 :** a journalist who specializes in writing or editing sob stories or other material of a sentimental type
**2 :** a sentimental and often impractical person usually engaged in good works

**sob story** *noun* (1913)
: a sentimental story or account intended chiefly to evoke sympathy or sadness

**so·cage** \'sä-kij, 'sō-\ *also* **soc·cage** \'sä-\ *noun* [Middle English, from *soc* soke] (14th century)
: a tenure of land by agricultural service fixed in amount and kind or by payment of money rent only and not burdened with any military service
— **so·cag·er** \-ki-jər\ *noun*

**so–called** \'sō-'köld\ *adjective* (15th century)
**1 :** commonly named : popularly so termed ⟨the *so-called* pocket veto⟩
**2 :** falsely or improperly so named ⟨deceived by a *so-called* friend⟩

**soc·cer** \'sä-kər\ *noun* [by shortening & alteration from *association football*] (1889)
: a game played on a field between two teams of 11 players each with the object to propel a round ball into the opponent's goal by kicking or by hitting it with any part of the body except the hands and arms — called also *association football* ◆

**so·cia·bil·i·ty** \,sō-shə-'bi-lə-tē\ *noun, plural* **-ties** (15th century)
: the quality or state of being sociable; *also* : the act or an instance of being sociable

**¹so·cia·ble** \'sō-shə-bəl\ *adjective* [Middle French or Latin; Middle French, from Latin *sociabilis*, from *sociare* to join, associate, from *socius*] (1553)
**1 :** inclined by nature to companionship with others of the same species : SOCIAL
**2 a :** inclined to seek or enjoy companionship **b :** marked by or conducive to friendliness or pleasant social relations
*synonym* see GRACIOUS
— **so·cia·ble·ness** *noun*
— **so·cia·bly** \-blē\ *adverb*

**²sociable** *noun* (1750)
: an informal social gathering frequently involving a special activity or interest

**¹so·cial** \'sō-shəl\ *adjective* [Middle English, from Latin *socialis*, from *socius* companion, ally, associate; akin to Old English *secg* man, companion, Latin *sequi* to follow — more at SUE] (14th century)
**1 :** involving allies or confederates ⟨the *Social* War between the Athenians and their allies⟩
**2 a :** marked by or passed in pleasant companionship with one's friends or associates ⟨leads a very full *social* life⟩ **b :** SOCIABLE **c :** of, relating to, or designed for sociability ⟨a *social* club⟩
**3 :** of or relating to human society, the interaction of the individual and the group, or the welfare of human beings as members of society ⟨*social* institutions⟩
**4 a :** tending to form cooperative and interdependent relationships with others of one's kind : GREGARIOUS **b :** living and breeding in more or less organized communities ⟨*social* insects⟩ **c** *of a plant* : tending to grow in groups or masses so as to form a pure stand
**5 a :** of, relating to, or based on rank or status in a particular society ⟨a member of our *social* set⟩ **b :** of, relating to, or characteristic of the upper classes **c :** FORMAL

**²social** *noun* (1870)
: SOCIABLE

**social climber** *noun* (1924)
: one who attempts to gain a higher social position or acceptance in fashionable society
— **social climbing** *noun*

**social contract** *noun* (circa 1850)
: an actual or hypothetical agreement among individuals forming an organized society or between the community and the ruler that defines and limits the rights and duties of each

**social Darwinism** *noun* (1887)
: an extension of Darwinism to social phenomena; *specifically* : a theory in sociology: sociocultural advance is the product of intergroup conflict and competition and the socially elite classes (as those possessing wealth and power) possess biological superiority in the struggle for existence
— **social Darwinist** *noun or adjective*

**social democracy** *noun* (1888)
: a political movement advocating a gradual and peaceful transition from capitalism to socialism by democratic means
— **social democrat** *noun*
— **social democratic** *adjective*

**social disease** *noun* (1891)
**1 :** VENEREAL DISEASE
**2 :** a disease (as tuberculosis) whose incidence is directly related to social and economic factors

**social drinker** *noun* (circa 1949)

: a person who drinks alcoholic beverages in moderation at social gatherings especially as distinguished from one who drinks habitually or to excess

**social engineering** *noun* (1925)
: management of human beings in accordance with their place and function in society : applied social science
— **social engineer** *noun*

**social gospel** *noun* (1890)
**1 :** the application of Christian principles to social problems
**2** *S&G capitalized* : a movement in American Protestant Christianity especially in the first part of the 20th century to bring the social order into conformity with Christian principles

**social insurance** *noun* (1909)
: protection of the individual against economic hazards (as unemployment, old age, or disability) in which the government participates or enforces the participation of employers and affected individuals

**so·cial·ise** *British variant of* SOCIALIZE

**so·cial·ism** \'sō-shə-,li-zəm\ *noun* (1837)
**1 :** any of various economic and political theories advocating collective or governmental ownership and administration of the means of production and distribution of goods
**2 a :** a system of society or group living in which there is no private property **b :** a system or condition of society in which the means of production are owned and controlled by the state
**3 :** a stage of society in Marxist theory transitional between capitalism and communism and distinguished by unequal distribution of goods and pay according to work done

**so·cial·ist** \'sō-sh(ə-)list\ *noun* (1827)
**1 :** one who advocates or practices socialism
**2** *capitalized* : a member of a party or political group advocating socialism
— **socialist** *adjective, often capitalized*
— **so·cial·is·tic** \,sō-shə-'lis-tik\ *adjective*
— **so·cial·is·ti·cal·ly** \-ti-k(ə-)lē\ *adverb*

**socialist realism** *noun* (1934)
: a Marxist aesthetic theory calling for the didactic use of literature, art, and music to develop social consciousness in an evolving socialist state
— **socialist realist** *noun or adjective*

**so·cial·ite** \'sō-shə-,līt\ *noun* (1928)
: a socially prominent person

◇ WORD HISTORY
**soccer** At University College, Oxford, in 1875, it became fashionable among students to create slang versions of everyday words or phrases by clipping them to a single syllable and adding the empty suffix *-er*. Allegedly this linguistic fad originated at Rugby, one of England's exclusive private boys schools (called by tradition "public schools"). Whether this is true or not, *footer* for *football* is attested at Harrow, another private school, in 1863—the earliest of these clipped words to see print. Most examples, such as *fresher* "freshman," *brekker* "breakfast," *tosher* "student unattached to a college," and *ekker* "exercise" are unfamiliar to North Americans, and many more have proved ephemeral even in Britain. However, one *-er* coinage has become extraordinarily successful in the U.S.: the word *soccer*, clipped from *association* (or *assoc.*) *football*, the game played according to the rules of the Football Association founded in England in 1863. *Football* now denotes only the game of soccer in most of the English-speaking world and has been borrowed into many other languages around the world. But in the U.S. a different kind of kicking game claimed the word, and *soccer* has been adopted as the name for what Americans still tend to think of as an imported sport.

**so·ci·al·i·ty** \ˌsō-shē-ˈa-lə-tē\ *noun, plural* **-ties** (circa 1649)
**1 a :** SOCIABILITY **b :** an instance of social intercourse or sociability
**2 :** the tendency to associate in or form social groups

**so·cial·ize** \ˈsō-shə-ˌlīz\ *verb* **-ized; -iz·ing** (1828)
*transitive verb*
**1 :** to make social; *especially* **:** to fit or train for a social environment
**2 a :** to constitute on a socialistic basis ⟨*socialize* industry⟩ **b :** to adapt to social needs or uses ⟨*socialize* science⟩
**3 :** to organize group participation in ⟨*socialize* a recitation⟩
*intransitive verb*
**:** to participate actively in a social group
— **so·cial·i·za·tion** \ˌsō-sh(ə-)lə-ˈzā-shən\ *noun*
— **so·cial·iz·er** \ˈsō-shə-ˌlī-zər\ *noun*

**socialized medicine** *noun* (1938)
**:** medical and hospital services for the members of a class or population administered by an organized group (as a state agency) and paid for from funds obtained usually by assessments, philanthropy, or taxation

**so·cial·ly** \ˈsō-sh(ə-)lē\ *adverb* (circa 1763)
**1 :** in a social manner
**2 :** with respect to society
**3 :** by or through society

**so·cial–mind·ed** \ˌsō-shəl-ˈmīn-dəd\ *adjective* (1927)
**:** having an interest in society; *specifically* **:** actively interested in social welfare or the well-being of society as a whole

**social psychology** *noun* (1891)
**:** the study of the manner in which the personality, attitudes, motivations, and behavior of the individual influence and are influenced by social groups
— **social psychologist** *noun*

**social science** *noun* (1811)
**1 :** a branch of science that deals with the institutions and functioning of human society and with the interpersonal relationships of individuals as members of society
**2 :** a science (as economics or political science) dealing with a particular phase or aspect of human society
— **social scientist** *noun*

**social secretary** *noun* (1903)
**:** a personal secretary employed to handle social correspondence and appointments

**social security** *noun* (1908)
**1 :** the principle or practice or a program of public provision (as through social insurance or assistance) for the economic security and social welfare of the individual and his or her family; *especially, often both Ss capitalized* **:** a U.S. government program established in 1935 to include old-age and survivors insurance, contributions to state unemployment insurance, and old-age assistance
**2 :** money paid out through a social security program ⟨began collecting *social security*⟩

**social service** *noun* (1851)
**:** an activity designed to promote social well-being; *specifically* **:** organized philanthropic assistance of the sick, destitute, or unfortunate **:** WELFARE WORK

**social studies** *noun plural* (1926)
**:** a part of a school or college curriculum concerned with the study of social relationships and the functioning of society and usually made up of courses in history, government, economics, civics, sociology, geography, and anthropology

**social welfare** *noun* (1917)
**:** organized public or private social services for the assistance of disadvantaged groups; *specifically* **:** SOCIAL WORK

**social work** *noun* (1890)
**:** any of various professional activities or methods concretely concerned with providing social services and especially with the investi-gation, treatment, and material aid of the economically underprivileged and socially maladjusted
— **social worker** *noun*

**so·ci·e·tal** \sə-ˈsī-ə-t°l\ *adjective* (1898)
**:** of or relating to society **:** SOCIAL ⟨*societal* forces⟩
— **so·ci·e·tal·ly** \-t°l-ē\ *adverb*

**¹so·ci·e·ty** \sə-ˈsī-ə-tē\ *noun, plural* **-ties** [Middle French *societé,* from Latin *societat-, societas,* from *socius* companion — more at SOCIAL] (1531)
**1 :** companionship or association with one's fellows **:** friendly or intimate intercourse **:** COMPANY
**2 :** a voluntary association of individuals for common ends; *especially* **:** an organized group working together or periodically meeting because of common interests, beliefs, or profession
**3 a :** an enduring and cooperating social group whose members have developed organized patterns of relationships through interaction with one another **b :** a community, nation, or broad grouping of people having common traditions, institutions, and collective activities and interests
**4 a :** a part of a community that is a unit distinguishable by particular aims or standards of living or conduct **:** a social circle or a group of social circles having a clearly marked identity ⟨move in polite *society*⟩ ⟨literary *society*⟩ **b :** a part of the community that sets itself apart as a leisure class and that regards itself as the arbiter of fashion and manners
**5 a :** a natural group of plants usually of a single species or habit within an association **b :** the progeny of a pair of insects when constituting a social unit (as a hive of bees); *broadly* **:** an interdependent system of organisms or biological units

**²society** *adjective* (1693)
**:** of, relating to, or characteristic of fashionable society

**So·cin·i·an** \sə-ˈsi-nē-ən, sō-\ *noun* [New Latin *socinianus,* from Faustus *Socinus*] (1645)
**:** an adherent of a 16th and 17th century theological movement professing belief in God and adherence to the Christian Scriptures but denying the divinity of Christ and consequently denying the Trinity
— **Socinian** *adjective*
— **So·cin·i·an·ism** \-nē-ə-ˌni-zəm\ *noun*

**socio-** *combining form* [French, from Latin *socius* companion]
**1 :** society **:** social ⟨*socio*gram⟩
**2 :** social and ⟨*socio*political⟩

**so·cio·bi·ol·o·gy** \ˌsō-sē-ō-bī-ˈä-lə-jē, ˌsō-shē-\ *noun* (1946)
**:** the comparative study of social organization in animals including humans especially with regard to its genetic basis and evolutionary history
— **so·cio·bio·log·i·cal** \-ˌbī-ə-ˈlä-ji-kəl\ *adjective*
— **so·cio·bi·ol·o·gist** \-bī-ˈä-lə-jist\ *noun*

**so·cio·cul·tur·al** \-ˈkəlch-rəl, -ˈkəl-chə-\ *adjective* (1928)
**:** of, relating to, or involving a combination of social and cultural factors
— **so·cio·cul·tur·al·ly** \-rə-lē\ *adverb*

**so·cio·eco·nom·ic** \-ˌe-kə-ˈnä-mik, -ˌē-kə-\ *adjective* (1883)
**:** of, relating to, or involving a combination of social and economic factors
— **so·cio·eco·nom·i·cal·ly** \-mi-k(ə-)lē\ *adverb*

**so·cio·gram** \ˈsō-sē-ə-ˌgram, ˈsō-shē-\ *noun* (1933)
**:** a sociometric chart plotting the structure of interpersonal relations in a group situation

**so·cio·his·tor·i·cal** \ˌsō-sē-ō-his-ˈtȯr-i-kəl, ˌsō-shē-, -ˈtär-\ *adjective* (1949)
**:** of, relating to, or involving social history or a combination of social and historical factors

**so·cio·lin·guist** \-ˈliŋ-gwist\ *noun* (1960)

**:** a linguist specializing in sociolinguistics

**so·cio·lin·guis·tic** \-liŋ-ˈgwis-tik\ *adjective* (1949)
**1 :** of or relating to the social aspects of language
**2 :** of or relating to sociolinguistics

**so·cio·lin·guis·tics** \-tiks\ *noun plural but singular in construction* (1938)
**:** the study of linguistic behavior as determined by sociocultural factors

**so·ci·ol·o·gese** \ˌsō-sē-ä-lə-ˈjēz, ˌsō-shē-, -ˈjēs\ *noun* [*sociology* + *²-ese*] (1952)
**:** a style of writing held to be characteristic of sociologists

**so·cio·log·i·cal** \ˌsō-sē-ə-ˈlä-ji-kəl, ˌsō-sh(ē-)ə-\ *also* **so·cio·log·ic** \-jik\ *adjective* (1843)
**1 :** of or relating to sociology or to the methodological approach of sociology
**2 :** oriented or directed toward social needs and problems
— **so·cio·log·i·cal·ly** \-ji-k(ə-)lē\ *adverb*

**so·ci·ol·o·gy** \ˌsō-sē-ä-lə-jē, ˌsō-shē-\ *noun* [French *sociologie,* from *socio-* + *-logie -logy*] (1843)
**1 :** the science of society, social institutions, and social relationships; *specifically* **:** the systematic study of the development, structure, interaction, and collective behavior of organized groups of human beings
**2 :** the scientific analysis of a social institution as a functioning whole and as it relates to the rest of society
**3 :** SYNECOLOGY
— **so·ci·ol·o·gist** \-jist\ *noun*

**so·ci·om·e·try** \-ˈä-mə-trē\ *noun* [International Scientific Vocabulary] (1908)
**:** the study and measurement of interpersonal relationships in a group of people
— **so·cio·met·ric** \ˌsō-sē-ə-ˈme-trik, ˌsō-shē-\ *adjective*

**so·cio·path** \ˈsō-sē-ə-ˌpath, ˈsō-sh(ē-)ə-\ *noun* (1930)
**:** PSYCHOPATH

**so·cio·path·ic** \ˌsō-sē-ə-ˈpa-thik, ˌsō-sh(ē-)ə-\ *adjective* (1930)
**:** of, relating to, or characterized by asocial or antisocial behavior or a psychopathic personality

**so·cio·po·lit·i·cal** \ˌsō-sē-ō-pə-ˈli-ti-kəl, ˌsō-shē-\ *adjective* (1884)
**:** of, relating to, or involving a combination of social and political factors

**so·cio·psy·cho·log·i·cal** \-ˌsī-kə-ˈlä-ji-kəl\ *adjective* (1899)
**1 :** of, relating to, or involving a combination of social and psychological factors
**2 :** of or relating to social psychology

**so·cio·re·li·gious** \-ri-ˈli-jəs\ *adjective* (1871)
**:** involving a combination of social and religious factors

**so·cio·sex·u·al** \-ˈsek-sh(ə-)wəl, -ˈsek-shəl\ *adjective* (1932)
**:** of or relating to the interpersonal aspects of sexuality

**¹sock** \ˈsäk\ *noun, plural* **socks** [Middle English *socke,* from Old English *socc,* from Latin *soccus*] (before 12th century)
**1** *archaic* **:** a low shoe or slipper
**2** *also plural* **sox** \ˈsäks\ **:** a knitted or woven covering for the foot usually extending above the ankle and sometimes to the knee
**3 a :** a shoe worn by actors in Greek and Roman comedy **b :** comic drama
— **sock·less** *adjective*

**²sock** *verb* [origin unknown] (circa 1700)
*transitive verb*
**:** to hit, strike, or apply forcefully ⟨*sock* a home run⟩ ⟨an area *socked* by a blizzard⟩

---

\ə\ abut \ᵊ\ kitten \ər\ further \a\ ash \ā\ ace
\ä\ mop, mar \au̇\ out \ch\ chin \e\ bet \ē\ easy
\g\ go \i\ hit \ī\ ice \j\ job \ŋ\ sing \ō\ go
\ȯ\ law \ȯi\ boy \th\ thin \t̲h̲\ the \ü\ loot \u̇\ foot
\y\ yet \zh\ vision   *see also* Guide to Pronunciation

*intransitive verb*
: to deliver a blow : HIT
— **sock it to** *slang* : to subject to or as if to a vigorous assault ⟨they may let you off the first time . . . but the second time they'll *sock it to* you —James Jones⟩

³**sock** *noun* (circa 1700)
: a vigorous or violent blow; *also* : ²PUNCH 3

**sock away** *transitive verb* [from the practice of concealing savings in the toe of a sock] (circa 1942)
: to put away (money) as savings or investment

**sock·dol·a·ger** *or* **sock·dol·o·ger** \säk-ˈdä-li-jər\ *noun* [origin unknown] (circa 1830)
**1** : something that settles a matter : a decisive blow or answer : FINISHER
**2** : something outstanding or exceptional

¹**sock·et** \ˈsä-kət\ *noun* [Middle English *soket*, from Anglo-French, diminutive of Old French *soc* plowshare, of Celtic origin; akin to Middle Irish *soc* plowshare, snout; akin to Old English *sugu* sow — more at SOW] (15th century)
: an opening or hollow that forms a holder for something ⟨an electric bulb *socket*⟩ ⟨the eye *socket*⟩

²**socket** *transitive verb* (1533)
: to provide with or support in or by a socket

**socket wrench** *noun* (circa 1890)
: a wrench usually in the form of a bar and removable socket made to fit a bolt or nut

**sock·eye** \ˈsäk-ˌī\ *noun* [by folk etymology from Northern Straits (Salishan language of southern Vancouver Island and nearby islands) *sə́qəy̓*] (1869)
: a small but commercially important Pacific salmon (*Oncorhynchus nerka*) that ascends rivers chiefly from the Columbia northward to spawn in late summer or fall — called also *red salmon*

**socket wrenches**

**sock in** *transitive verb* [(wind) *sock*] (1944)
**1** : to close to takeoffs or landings by aircraft ⟨an airport *socked in* by fog⟩
**2** : to restrict from flying

**socko** \ˈsä-(ˌ)kō\ *adjective* [²*sock*] (1938)
: strikingly impressive, effective, or successful : OUTSTANDING

**so·cle** \ˈsō-kəl, ˈsä-\ *noun* [French, from Italian *zoccolo* sock, socle, from Latin *socculus*, diminutive of *soccus* sock] (circa 1704)
: a projecting usually molded member at the foot of a wall or pier or beneath the base of a column, pedestal, or superstructure

¹**So·crat·ic** \sə-ˈkra-tik, sō-\ *adjective* (1628)
: of or relating to Socrates, his followers, or his philosophical method of systematic doubt and questioning of another to elicit a clear expression of a truth supposed to be implicitly known by all rational beings
— **So·crat·i·cal·ly** \-ti-k(ə-)lē\ *adverb*

²**Socratic** *noun* (1678)
: a follower of Socrates

**Socratic irony** *noun* (circa 1871)
: IRONY 1

¹**sod** \ˈsäd\ *noun* [Middle English, from Middle Dutch or Middle Low German *sode*; akin to Old Frisian *sātha* sod] (15th century)
**1** : TURF 1; *also* : the grass- and forb-covered surface of the ground
**2** : one's native land

²**sod** *transitive verb* **sod·ded; sod·ding** (1653)
: to cover with sod or turfs

³**sod** *noun* [short for *sodomite*] (1818)
*chiefly British* : BUGGER ⟨if I ever find the *sod* I'll kill him —John Le Carré⟩ ⟨he's not a bad little *sod* taken by and large —Noel Coward⟩

⁴**sod** *transitive verb* (1904)
*chiefly British* : DAMN 2

**so·da** \ˈsō-də\ *noun* [Italian, from Arabic *suwwād*, any of several saltworts from the ashes of which sodium carbonate is obtained] (1558)
**1 a** : SODIUM CARBONATE **b** : SODIUM BICARBONATE **c** : SODIUM — used in combination ⟨*soda* alum⟩
**2 a** : SODA WATER 2a **b** : SODA POP **c** : a sweet drink consisting of soda water, flavoring, and often ice cream
**3** : the faro card that shows faceup in the dealing box before play begins

**soda ash** *noun* (1839)
: commercial anhydrous sodium carbonate

**soda biscuit** *noun* (1830)
**1** : a biscuit leavened with baking soda and sour milk or buttermilk
**2** : SODA CRACKER

**soda bread** *noun* (1850)
: a quick bread made especially with buttermilk and leavened with baking soda

**soda cracker** *noun* (1830)
: a cracker leavened with bicarbonate of soda and cream of tartar

**soda fountain** *noun* (1824)
**1** : an apparatus with delivery tube and faucets for drawing soda water
**2** : the equipment and counter for the preparation and serving of sodas, sundaes, and ice cream

**soda jerk** \-ˌjərk\ *noun* (1922)
: a person who dispenses carbonated drinks and ice cream at a soda fountain — called also *soda jerker*

**soda lime** *noun* (1862)
: a mixture of sodium hydroxide and slaked lime used especially to absorb moisture and gases

**so·da·list** \ˈsō-dᵊl-ist, sō-ˈda-list\ *noun* (1794)
: a member of a sodality

**so·da·lite** \ˈsō-dᵊl-ˌīt\ *noun* [*soda*] (1810)
: a transparent to translucent mineral that consists of a silicate of sodium and aluminum with some chlorine, has a vitreous or greasy luster, and is found in various igneous rocks

**so·dal·i·ty** \sō-ˈda-lə-tē\ *noun, plural* **-ties** [Latin *sodalitat-, sodalitas* comradeship, club, from *sodalis* comrade — more at SIB] (1600)
**1** : BROTHERHOOD, COMMUNITY
**2** : an organized society or fellowship; *specifically* : a devotional or charitable association of Roman Catholic laity

**soda pop** *noun* (1863)
: a beverage consisting of soda water, flavoring, and a sweet syrup

**soda water** *noun* (1802)
**1** : a weak solution of sodium bicarbonate with some acid added to cause effervescence
**2 a** : a beverage consisting of water highly charged with carbon dioxide **b** : SODA POP

**sod·bust·er** \ˈsäd-ˌbəs-tər\ *noun* (circa 1918)
: one (as a farmer or a plow) that breaks the sod

¹**sod·den** \ˈsä-dᵊn\ *adjective* [Middle English *soden*, from past participle of *sethen* to seethe] (1589)
**1 a** : dull or expressionless especially from continued indulgence in alcoholic beverages ⟨*sodden* features⟩ **b** : TORPID, SLUGGISH ⟨*sodden* minds⟩
**2 a** : heavy with or as if with moisture or water ⟨the *sodden* ground⟩ **b** : heavy or doughy because of imperfect cooking ⟨*sodden* biscuits⟩
— **sod·den·ly** *adverb*
— **sod·den·ness** \-dᵊn-(n)əs\ *noun*

²**sodden** *verb* **sod·dened; sod·den·ing** \ˈsäd-niŋ, ˈsä-dᵊn-iŋ\ (1812)
*transitive verb*
: to make sodden
*intransitive verb*
: to become soaked or saturated

**so·dic** \ˈsō-dik\ *adjective* (1859)
: of, relating to, or containing sodium

**so·di·um** \ˈsō-dē-əm\ *noun* [New Latin, from English *soda*] (1807)

: a silver white soft waxy ductile element of the alkali metal group that occurs abundantly in nature in combined form and is very active chemically — see ELEMENT table

**sodium azide** *noun* (circa 1937)
: a poisonous crystalline salt $NaN_3$ used especially to make lead azide

**sodium benzoate** *noun* (circa 1900)
: a crystalline or granular salt $C_7H_5O_2Na$ used chiefly as a food preservative

**sodium bicarbonate** *noun* (1885)
: a white crystalline weakly alkaline salt $NaHCO_3$ used especially in baking powders, fire extinguishers, and medicine — called also *baking soda, bicarbonate of soda*

**sodium bo·ro·hy·dride** \-ˌbōr-ə-ˈhī-ˌdrīd, -ˌbȯr-\ *noun* [*sodium* + *boron* + *hydride*] (1946)
: a crystalline compound $NaBH_4$ used in various industrial applications and as a reducing agent in organic chemistry

**sodium carbonate** *noun* (1868)
: a sodium salt of carbonic acid used especially in making soaps and chemicals, in water softening, in cleaning and bleaching, and in photography: as **a** : a hygroscopic crystalline anhydrous strongly alkaline salt $Na_2CO_3$ **b** : WASHING SODA

**sodium chlorate** *noun* (1885)
: a colorless crystalline salt $NaClO_3$ used especially as an oxidizing agent and weed killer

**sodium chloride** *noun* (1868)
: an ionic crystalline chemical compound consisting of equal numbers of sodium and chlorine atoms : SALT 1a

**sodium citrate** *noun* (1919)
: a crystalline salt $Na_3C_6H_5O_7$ used chiefly as a buffering agent, as an emulsifier, as an alkalizer and cathartic in pharmaceuticals, and as a blood anticoagulant

**sodium cyanide** *noun* (1885)
: a white deliquescent poisonous salt $NaCN$ used especially in electroplating, in fumigating, and in treating steel

**sodium dichromate** *noun* (circa 1903)
: a red crystalline salt $Na_2Cr_2O_7$ used especially in tanning leather, in cleaning metals, and as an oxidizing agent

**sodium fluoride** *noun* (circa 1903)
: a poisonous crystalline salt $NaF$ that is used in trace amounts in the fluoridation of water, in metallurgy, as a flux, and as a pesticide

**sodium fluo·ro·ac·e·tate** \-ˌflu̇r-ō-ˈa-sə-ˌtāt, -ˌflȯr-, -ˌflȯr-\ *noun* (1945)
: a poisonous powdery compound $C_2H_2FNaO_2$ — compare 1080

**sodium hydroxide** *noun* (1885)
: a white brittle solid $NaOH$ that is a strong caustic base used especially in making soap, rayon, and paper

**sodium hypochlorite** *noun* (1885)
: an unstable salt $NaOCl$ produced usually in aqueous solution and used as a bleaching and disinfecting agent

**sodium meta·sil·i·cate** \-ˌme-tə-ˈsi-lə-ˌkāt, -ˈsi-li-kət\ *noun* (circa 1926)
: a toxic corrosive crystalline salt $Na_2SiO_3$ used especially as a detergent or as a substitute for phosphates in detergent formulations

**sodium nitrate** *noun* (1885)
: a deliquescent crystalline salt $NaNO_3$ used as a fertilizer and an oxidizing agent and in curing meat

**sodium nitrite** *noun* (circa 1903)
: a salt $NaNO_2$ used especially in dye manufacture and as a meat preservative

**sodium pump** *noun* (1951)
: a molecular mechanism by which sodium ions are actively transported across a cell membrane; *especially* : the one by which the appropriate internal and external concentrations of sodium and potassium ions are maintained in a nerve fiber and which involves the active transport of sodium ions outward with movement of potassium ions to the interior

**sodium salicylate** *noun* (circa 1904)

: a crystalline salt $NaC_7H_5O_3$ that has a sweetish saline taste and is used chiefly as an analgesic, antipyretic, and antirheumatic

**sodium sulfate** noun (1885)
: a bitter salt $Na_2SO_4$ used especially in detergents, in the manufacture of wood pulp and rayon, in dyeing and finishing textiles, and in its hydrated form as a cathartic — compare GLAUBER'S SALT

**sodium thiosulfate** noun (1885)
: a hygroscopic crystalline salt $Na_2S_2O_3$ used especially as a photographic fixing agent and a reducing or bleaching agent — called also *hypo*

**sodium tri·poly·phos·phate** \-,trī-,pä-li-'fās-,fāt\ noun (1945)
: a crystalline salt $Na_5P_3O_{10}$ that is used as a food additive and as a component in some detergents and is suspected of contributing to water pollution

**sodium–vapor lamp** noun (1936)
: an electric lamp that contains sodium vapor and electrodes between which a luminous discharge takes place and that is used especially for lighting highways

**sod off** intransitive verb [⁴sod] (1960)
*British* : SCRAM — usually used as a command

**Sod·om** \'sä-dəm\ noun [*Sodom*, ancient city destroyed by God for its wickedness in Genesis 19] (1598)
: a place notorious for vice or corruption

**sod·om·ist** \'sä-də-mist\ noun (1891)
: SODOMITE

**sod·om·ite** \-,mīt\ noun (14th century)
: one who practices sodomy

**sod·om·ize** \-,mīz\ transitive verb **-ized; -iz·ing** (1868)
: to perform sodomy on

**sod·omy** \'sä-də-mē\ noun [Middle English, from Old French *sodomie*, from Late Latin *Sodoma* Sodom; from the homosexual proclivities of the men of the city in Genesis 19:1–11] (13th century)
**1** : copulation with a member of the same sex or with an animal
**2** : noncoital and especially anal or oral copulation with a member of the opposite sex
— **sod·om·it·ic** \,sä-də-'mi-tik\ *or* **sod·om·it·i·cal** \-ti-kəl\ adjective

**so·ev·er** \sō-'e-vər\ adverb [-*soever* (as in *howsoever*)] (12th century)
**1** : to any possible or known extent — used after an adjective preceded by *how* or a superlative preceded by *the* ⟨how fair *soever* she may be⟩ ⟨the most selfish *soever* in this world⟩
**2** : of any or every kind that may be specified — used after a noun modified especially by *any, no,* or *what* ⟨gives no information *soever*⟩

**so·fa** \'sō-fə\ noun [Arabic *ṣuffah* long bench] (1717)
: a long upholstered seat usually with arms and a back and often convertible into a bed

**sofa bed** noun (1816)
: a sofa that can be made to serve as a bed by lowering its hinged upholstered back to horizontal position or by pulling out a concealed mattress

**so·far** \'sō-,fär\ noun [*so*und *f*ixing *a*nd *r*anging] (1946)
: a system for locating an underwater explosion at sea by triangulation based on the reception of the sound by three widely separated stations

**so far as** conjunction (1565)
: INSOFAR AS

**sof·fit** \'sä-fət\ noun [French *soffite*, from Italian *soffitto*, from (assumed) Vulgar Latin *suffictus*, past participle of Latin *suffigere* to fasten underneath — more at SUFFIX] (1592)
: the underside of a part or member of a building (as of an overhang or staircase); *especially*
: the intrados of an arch

¹**soft** \'sȯft\ adjective [Middle English, from Old English *sōfte*, alteration of *sēfte;* akin to Old High German *semfti* soft] (before 12th century)
**1 a** : pleasing or agreeable to the senses : bringing ease, comfort, or quiet ⟨the *soft* influences of home⟩ **b** : having a bland or mellow rather than a sharp or acid taste **c** (1) : not bright or glaring : SUBDUED (2) : having or producing little contrast or a relatively short range of tones ⟨a *soft* photographic print⟩ **d** : quiet in pitch or volume **e** *of the eyes* : having a liquid or gentle appearance **f** : smooth or delicate in texture, grain, or fiber ⟨*soft* cashmere⟩ ⟨*soft* fur⟩ **g** (1) : balmy, mild, or clement in weather or temperature (2) : moving or falling with slight force or impact : not violent ⟨*soft* breezes⟩
**2** : demanding little work or effort : EASY ⟨a *soft* job⟩
**3 a** : sounding as in *ace* and *gem* respectively — used of *c* and *g* or their sound **b** *of a consonant* : VOICED **c** : constituting a vowel before which there is a \y\ sound or a \y\-like modification of a consonant or constituting a consonant in whose articulation there is a \y\-like modification or which is followed by a \y\ sound (as in Russian)
**4** *archaic* : moving in a leisurely manner
**5** : rising gradually ⟨a *soft* slope⟩
**6** : having curved or rounded outline : not harsh or jagged ⟨*soft* hills against the horizon⟩
**7** : marked by a gentleness, kindness, or tenderness: as **a** (1) : not harsh or onerous in character ⟨a policy of *soft* competition⟩ (2) : based on negotiation, conciliation, or flexibility rather than on force, threats, or intransigence ⟨took a *soft* line during the crisis⟩ (3) : tending to take a soft line — usually used with *on* ⟨*soft* on dictators⟩ ⟨*soft* on law and order⟩ **b** : tending to ingratiate or disarm : ENGAGING, KIND ⟨a *soft* answer turns away wrath —Proverbs 15:1 (Revised Standard Version)⟩ **c** : marked by mildness : UNASSUMING, LOW-KEY
**8 a** : emotionally suggestible or responsive : IMPRESSIONABLE **b** : unduly susceptible to influence : COMPLIANT **c** : lacking firmness or strength of character : FEEBLE, UNMANLY **d** : amorously attracted or emotionally involved — used with *on* ⟨has been *soft* on her for years⟩
**9 a** : lacking robust strength, stamina, or endurance especially because of living in ease or luxury ⟨grown *soft* and indolent⟩ **b** : weak or deficient mentally ⟨*soft* in the head⟩
**10 a** : yielding to physical pressure **b** : permitting someone or something to sink in — used of wet ground **c** (1) : of a consistency that may be shaped or molded (2) : capable of being spread **d** : easily magnetized and demagnetized **e** : lacking relatively or comparatively in hardness ⟨*soft* iron⟩
**11** : deficient in or free from substances (as calcium and magnesium salts) that prevent lathering of soap ⟨*soft* water⟩
**12** : having relatively low energy ⟨*soft* X rays⟩
**13** *of news* : relatively less serious or significant
**14** : occurring at such a speed and under such circumstances as to avoid destructive impact ⟨*soft* landing of a spacecraft on the moon⟩
**15** : not protected against enemy attack ⟨a *soft* aboveground launching site⟩ ⟨*soft* targets⟩
**16** : BIODEGRADABLE ⟨a *soft* detergent⟩ ⟨*soft* pesticides⟩
**17** *of a drug* : considered less detrimental than a hard narcotic
**18** : easily polarized — used of acids and bases
**19 a** *of currency* : not readily convertible **b** *of a loan* : not secured by collateral
**20 a** : being low due to sluggish market conditions ⟨*soft* prices⟩ **b** : SLUGGISH, SLOW ⟨a *soft* market⟩

**21** : not firmly committed ⟨*soft* unreliable political support⟩
**22** : SOFT-CORE ⟨*soft* porn⟩
**23 a** : being or based on interpretive or speculative data ⟨*soft* evidence⟩ **b** : utilizing or based on soft data ⟨*soft* science⟩
**24** : being or using renewable sources of energy (as solar radiation, wind, or tides) ⟨*soft* technologies⟩
— **soft·ish** \'sȯf-tish\ adjective
— **soft·ly** \'sȯf(t)-lē\ adverb
— **soft·ness** \'sȯf(t)-nəs\ noun
²**soft** adverb (before 12th century)
: in a soft or gentle manner : SOFTLY
³**soft** noun (15th century)
: a soft object, material, or part ⟨the *soft* of the thumb⟩

**soft·back** \'sȯf(t)-,bak\ adjective (1958)
: SOFTCOVER
— **softback** noun

**soft·ball** \-,bȯl\ noun (1926)
: baseball played on a small diamond with a ball that is larger than a baseball and that is pitched underhand; *also* : the ball used in this game
— **soft·ball·er** \-,bȯ-lər\ noun

**soft–boiled** \-'bȯi(ə)ld\ adjective (circa 1902)
**1** *of an egg* : boiled to a soft consistency
**2** : SENTIMENTAL

**soft·bound** \-,baȯnd\ adjective (1953)
: SOFTCOVER

**soft chancre** noun (1859)
: CHANCROID

**soft coal** noun (1789)
: BITUMINOUS COAL

**soft–coated wheaten terrier** noun (1948)
: any of a breed of compact medium-sized terriers developed in Ireland and having a soft abundant light fawn coat

**soft–core** \'sȯf(t)-'kȯr, -'kȯr\ adjective [¹*soft* + hard-*core*] (1966)
*of pornography* : containing descriptions or scenes of sex acts that are less explicit than hard-core material

**soft·cov·er** \-,kə-vər\ adjective (1952)
: bound in flexible covers : not bound in hard covers; *specifically* : PAPERBACK ⟨*softcover* books⟩
— **softcover** noun

**soft drink** noun (1880)
: a usually carbonated nonalcoholic beverage; *especially* : SODA POP

**soft·en** \'sȯ-fən\ verb **soft·ened; soft·en·ing** \'sȯ-fə-niŋ, 'sȯf-niŋ\ (14th century)
*transitive verb*
**1** : to make soft or softer
**2 a** : to weaken the military resistance or the morale of especially by harassment (as preliminary bombardment) — often used with *up* **b** : to impair the strength or resistance of — often used with *up* ⟨*soften* up a sales prospect⟩
*intransitive verb*
: to become soft or softer
— **soft·en·er** \'sȯ-fə-nər, 'sȯf-nər\ noun

**soft–fo·cus** \'sȯf(t)-'fō-kəs\ adjective (1916)
**1** *of a photographic image* : having unsharp outlines
**2** *of a lens* : producing an image having unsharp outlines

**soft goods** noun plural (1894)
: goods that are not durable — used especially of textile products

**soft hail** noun (1894)
: GRAUPEL

**soft·head** \'sȯft-,hed\ noun (1650)
: a silly or feebleminded person

**soft·head·ed** \-,he-dəd\ adjective (1667)
: having or indicative of a weak, unrealistic, or uncritical mind
— **soft·head·ed·ly** adverb

---

\ə\ abut  \ᵊ\ kitten  \ər\ further  \a\ ash  \ā\ ace
\ä\ mop, mar  \aȯ\ out  \ch\ chin  \e\ bet  \ē\ easy
\g\ go  \i\ hit  \ī\ ice  \j\ job  \ŋ\ sing  \ō\ go
\ȯ\ law  \ȯi\ boy  \th\ thin  \ṯẖ\ the  \ü\ loot  \ȯ\ foot
\y\ yet  \zh\ vision  *see also* Guide to Pronunciation

— **soft·head·ed·ness** *noun*

**soft·heart·ed** \-ˌhär-təd\ *adjective* (1593)
: emotionally responsive : SYMPATHETIC
— **soft·heart·ed·ly** *adverb*
— **soft·heart·ed·ness** *noun*

**soft–land** \-ˈland\ *verb* [back-formation from *soft landing*] (1960)
*transitive verb*
: to cause to make a soft landing on a celestial body (as the moon)
*intransitive verb*
: to make a soft landing
— **soft–lander** *noun*

**soft–line** \-ˈlīn\ *adjective* (1949)
: advocating or involving a conciliatory or flexible course of action
— **soft–lin·er** \-ˈlī-nər\ *noun*

**soft palate** *noun* (circa 1811)
: the fold at the back of the hard palate that partially separates the mouth and pharynx

**soft–ped·al** \ˈsȯf(t)-ˈpe-dᵊl\ *transitive verb* (1925)
**1 :** PLAY DOWN, DE-EMPHASIZE ⟨*soft-pedal* the issue⟩
**2 :** to use the soft pedal in playing

**soft pedal** *noun* (1854)
**1 :** a foot pedal on a piano that reduces the volume of sound
**2 :** something that muffles, deadens, or reduces effect

**soft rock** *noun* (1967)
: rock music that is less driving and gentler sounding than hard rock

**soft rot** *noun* (1901)
: a mushy, watery, or slimy decay of plants or their parts caused by bacteria or fungi

**soft sell** *noun* (1954)
: the use of suggestion or gentle persuasion in selling rather than aggressive pressure — compare HARD SELL

**soft·shell** \ˈsȯf(t)-ˌshel\ *noun* (1771)
: any of a family (Trionychidae) of aquatic turtles that have sharp claws and mandibles and a flat shell covered with soft leathery skin instead of with horny plates — called also *soft-shelled turtle*

**softshell**

**soft–shell** \ˈsȯf(t)-ˌshel\ *or* **soft–shelled** \-ˈsheld\ *adjective* (1805)
: having a soft or fragile shell especially as a result of recent shedding ⟨*soft-shell* crabs⟩

**soft–shell clam** *noun* (1796)
: an elongated clam (*Mya arenaria*) of the east coast of North America that has a thin friable shell and long siphons and is used especially for steaming — called also *soft-shelled clam, steamer*

**soft–shoe** \ˈsȯf(t)-ˈshü\ *adjective* (1920)
: of or relating to tap dancing done in soft-soled shoes without metal taps

**soft–soap** \ˈsȯf(t)-ˈsōp\ *transitive verb* (1840)
: to soothe or persuade with flattery or blarney
— **soft–soap·er** \-ˌsō-pər\ *noun*

**soft soap** *noun* (1634)
**1 :** a semifluid soap made especially from potassium hydroxide
**2 :** FLATTERY

**soft–spo·ken** \-ˈspō-kən\ *adjective* (1609)
: having a mild or gentle voice; *also* : SUAVE

**soft spot** *noun* (1845)
**1 :** a sentimental weakness ⟨has a *soft spot* for him⟩
**2 :** a vulnerable point ⟨a *soft spot* in the defense system⟩

**soft touch** *noun* (1939)
: one who is easily imposed on or taken advantage of

**soft·ware** \ˈsȯft-ˌwar, -ˌwer\ *noun* (1960)

: something used or associated with and usually contrasted with hardware: as **a :** the entire set of programs, procedures, and related documentation associated with a system and especially a computer system; *specifically* : computer programs **b :** materials for use with audiovisual equipment

**soft wheat** *noun* (1812)
: a wheat with soft starchy kernels high in starch but usually low in gluten

**¹soft·wood** \ˈsȯft-ˌwud\ *noun* (1832)
**1 :** the wood of a coniferous tree (as a fir or pine) whether hard or soft as distinguished from that of an angiospermous tree
**2 :** a tree that yields softwood

**²softwood** *adjective* (1905)
: having or made of softwood

**soft–wood·ed** \ˈsȯft-ˌwu-dəd\ *adjective* (1827)
**1 :** having soft wood that is easy to work or finish
**2 :** SOFTWOOD

**softy** *or* **soft·ie** \ˈsȯf-tē\ *noun, plural* **soft·ies** [¹*soft*] (1863)
**1 :** a weak or foolish person
**2 :** a softhearted or sentimental person

**Sog·di·an** \ˈsäg-dē-ən\ *noun* [Latin *Sogdiani,* plural, from Greek *Sogdianoi,* from Old Persian *Suguda* Sogdiana] (1553)
**1 :** a native or inhabitant of Sogdiana
**2 :** an Iranian language of the Sogdians — see INDO-EUROPEAN LANGUAGES table
— **Sogdian** *adjective*

**sog·gy** \ˈsä-gē, ˈsȯ-\ *adjective* **sog·gi·er; -est** [English dialect *sog* to soak] (1599)
**1 :** saturated or heavy with water or moisture: as **a :** WATERLOGGED, SOAKED ⟨a *soggy* lawn⟩ **b :** heavy or doughy because of imperfect cooking ⟨*soggy* bread⟩
**2 :** heavily dull : SPIRITLESS ⟨*soggy* prose⟩
— **sog·gi·ly** \ˈsä-gə-lē, ˈsȯ-\ *adverb*
— **sog·gi·ness** \ˈsä-gē-nəs, ˈsȯ-\ *noun*

**soi–di·sant** \ˌswä-dē-ˈzäⁿ\ *adjective* [French, literally, saying oneself] (1752)
: SELF-STYLED, SO-CALLED — usually used disparagingly ⟨a *soi-disant* artist⟩

**soi·gné** *or* **soi·gnée** \swän-ˈyā\ *adjective* [French, from past participle of *soigner* to take care of] (1821)
**1 :** WELL-GROOMED, SLEEK
**2 :** elegantly maintained or designed ⟨a *soigné* restaurant⟩ ⟨a *soigné* black dress⟩

**¹soil** \ˈsȯi(ə)l\ *verb* [Middle English, from Old French *souillier* to wallow, soil, from *soil* abyss, pigpen, probably from Latin *solium* chair, bathtub; akin to Latin *sedēre* to sit — more at SIT] (13th century)
*transitive verb*
**1 :** to stain or defile morally : CORRUPT, POLLUTE
**2 :** to make unclean especially superficially : DIRTY
**3 :** to blacken or besmirch (as a person's reputation) by word or deed
*intransitive verb*
: to become soiled or dirty

**²soil** *noun* (1501)
**1 a :** SOILAGE, STAIN ⟨protect a dress from *soil*⟩ **b :** moral defilement : CORRUPTION
**2 :** something that spoils or pollutes: as **a :** REFUSE **b :** SEWAGE **c :** DUNG, EXCREMENT

**³soil** *noun* [Middle English, from Anglo-French, probably from Latin *solium* chair] (14th century)
**1 :** firm land : EARTH
**2 a :** the upper layer of earth that may be dug or plowed and in which plants grow **b :** the superficial unconsolidated and usually weathered part of the mantle of a planet and especially of the earth
**3 :** COUNTRY, LAND ⟨our native *soil*⟩
**4 :** the agricultural life or calling
**5 :** a medium in which something takes hold and develops

**⁴soil** *transitive verb* [origin unknown] (1605)

: to feed (livestock) in the barn or an enclosure with fresh grass or green food; *also* : to purge (livestock) by feeding on green food

**¹soil·age** \ˈsȯi-lij\ *noun* [¹*soil*] (1926)
: the act of soiling : the condition of being soiled

**²soilage** *noun* [⁴*soil*] (1928)
: green crops for feeding confined animals

**soil bank** *noun* (1955)
: acreage retired from crop cultivation and planted with soil-building crops under a plan sponsored by the U.S. government that provides subsidies to farmers for the retired land

**soil·borne** \ˈsȯil-ˌbōrn, -ˌbȯrn\ *adjective* (1944)
: transmitted by or in soil ⟨*soilborne* fungi⟩ ⟨*soilborne* diseases⟩

**soil·less** \ˈsȯi(ə)l-ləs\ *adjective* (1938)
: having, containing, or utilizing no soil ⟨*soilless* agriculture⟩

**soil pipe** *noun* (1833)
: a pipe for carrying off wastes from toilets

**soil science** *noun* (1915)
: a science dealing with soils — called also *pedology*
— **soil scientist** *noun*

**soil series** *noun* (1905)
: a group of soils with similar profiles developed from similar parent materials under comparable climatic and vegetational conditions

**soil·ure** \ˈsȯil-yər\ *noun* [Middle English, from Old French *soilleure,* from *souillier* to soil] (13th century)
**1 :** the act of soiling : the condition of being soiled
**2 :** STAIN, SMUDGE

**soi·ree** *or* **soi·rée** \swä-ˈrā\ *noun* [French *soirée* evening period, evening party, from Middle French, from *soir* evening, from Latin *sero* at a late hour, from *serus* late; akin to Old Irish *sír* long, lasting and perhaps to Old English *sīth* late — more at SINCE] (1802)
: a party or reception held in the evening

**soi·xante–neuf** \swä-säⁿt-nœf\ *noun* [French] (1888)
: SIXTY-NINE 2

**¹so·journ** \ˈsō-ˌjərn, sō-ˈ\ *noun* [Middle English *sojorn,* from Old French, from *sojorner*] (13th century)
: a temporary stay ⟨a *sojourn* in the country⟩

**²sojourn** *intransitive verb* [Middle English *sojornen,* from Old French *sojorner,* from (assumed) Vulgar Latin *subdiurnare,* from Latin *sub* under, during + Late Latin *diurnum* day — more at UP, JOURNEY] (14th century)
: to stay as a temporary resident : STOP ⟨*sojourned* for a month at a resort⟩
— **so·journ·er** *noun*

**soke** \ˈsōk\ *noun* [Middle English *soc, soke,* from Old English *soca,* from Medieval Latin *soca,* from Old English *sōcn* inquiry, jurisdiction; akin to Old English *sēcan* to seek] (12th century)
**1 :** the right in Anglo-Saxon and early English law to hold court and administer justice with the franchise to receive certain fees or fines arising from it : jurisdiction over a territory or over people
**2 :** the district included in a soke jurisdiction or franchise

**soke·man** \ˈsōk-mən\ *noun* (1579)
: a man who is under the soke of another

**¹sol** \ˈsōl\ *also* **so** \ˈsō\ *noun* [Medieval Latin *sol;* from the syllable sung to this note in a medieval hymn to Saint John the Baptist] (14th century)
: the 5th tone of the diatonic scale in solmization

**²sol** \ˈsäl, ˈsȯl\ *noun* [Middle French — more at SOU] (1583)
: an old French coin equal to 12 deniers; *also* : a corresponding unit of value

**³sol** \ˈsäl, ˈsȯl\ *noun, plural* **so·les** \ˈsō-(ˌ)lās\ [American Spanish, from Spanish, sun, from Latin] (circa 1883)

: the basic monetary unit of Peru before 1985 and since 1990 — see MONEY table

**⁴sol** \'säl, 'sȯl\ *noun* [*-sol* (as in *hydrosol*), from *solution*] (1899)

: a fluid colloidal system; *especially* : one in which the continuous phase is a liquid

**Sol** \'säl\ *noun* [Middle English, from Latin]
**1** : the Roman god of the sun — compare HELIOS
**2** : SUN

**sola** *plural of* SOLUM

**¹so·lace** \'sä-ləs *also* 'sō-\ *transitive verb* **so·laced; so·lac·ing** (13th century)
**1** : to give solace to : CONSOLE
**2 a** : to make cheerful **b** : AMUSE
**3** : ALLAY, SOOTHE ⟨*solace* grief⟩
— **so·lace·ment** \-mənt\ *noun*
— **so·lac·er** *noun*

**²solace** *noun* [Middle English *solas*, from Old French, from Latin *solacium*, from *solari* to console] (14th century)
**1** : alleviation of grief or anxiety
**2** : a source of relief or consolation

**so·la·na·ceous** \ˌsō-lə-'nā-shəs\ *adjective* [New Latin *Solanaceae*, family name, from *Solanum*] (1804)
: of or relating to the nightshade family of plants

**so·la·nine** *also* **so·la·nin** \'sō-lə-ˌnēn, -nən\ *noun* [French *solanine*, from Latin *solanum*] (1838)
: a bitter poisonous crystalline alkaloid $C_{45}H_{73}NO_{15}$ from several plants (as some potatoes or tomatoes) of the nightshade family

**so·la·num** \sə-'lā-nəm, -'lä-, -'lā-\ *noun* [New Latin, from Latin, nightshade] (circa 1652)
: any of a genus (*Solanum*) chiefly of herbs and shrubs of the nightshade family that have often prickly-veined leaves, cymose white, purple, or yellow flowers, and a fruit that is a berry

**so·lar** \'sō-lər, -ˌlär\ *adjective* [Middle English, from Latin *solaris*, from *sol* sun; akin to Old English & Old Norse *sōl* sun, Lithuanian *saulė*, Greek *hēlios*] (15th century)
**1** : of, derived from, or relating to the sun especially as affecting the earth
**2** : measured by the earth's course in relation to the sun ⟨*solar* time⟩ ⟨*solar* year⟩; *also* : relating to or reckoned by solar time
**3 a** : produced or operated by the action of the sun's light or heat ⟨*solar* energy⟩ ⟨*solar* cooker⟩ **b** : utilizing the sun's rays especially to produce heat or electricity ⟨a *solar* house⟩; *also* : of or relating to such utilization ⟨*solar* design⟩ ⟨*solar* subsidies⟩

**solar battery** *noun* (1954)
: an array of solar cells

**solar cell** *noun* (1955)
: a photovoltaic cell (as one including a junction between two types of silicon semiconductors) that is able to convert light into electrical energy and is used as a power source

**solar collector** *noun* (1955)
: any of various devices for the absorption of solar radiation for the heating of water or buildings or the production of electricity

**solar constant** *noun* (1869)
: the quantity of radiant solar energy received at the outer layer of the earth's atmosphere that has a mean value of 1370 watts per square meter

**solar day** *noun* (1764)
: the interval between transits of the apparent or mean sun across the meridian at any place

**solar eclipse** *noun* (circa 1890)
: an eclipse of the sun by the moon — see ECLIPSE illustration

**solar flare** *noun* (1938)
: a sudden temporary outburst of energy from a small area of the sun's surface — called also *flare*

**so·lar·i·um** \sō-'lar-ē-əm, sə-, -'ler-\ *noun*, *plural* **-ia** \-ē-ə\ *also* **-ums** [Latin, porch exposed to the sun, from *sol*] (circa 1823)

: a glass-enclosed porch or room; *also* : a room (as in a hospital) used especially for sunbathing or therapeutic exposure to light

**so·lar·i·za·tion** \ˌsō-lə-rə-'zā-shən\ *noun* (1853)
**1** : a reversal of gradation in a photographic image obtained by intense or continued exposure
**2** : an act or process of solarizing

**so·lar·ize** \'sō-lə-ˌrīz\ *transitive verb* **-ized; -iz·ing** (1853)
**1 a** : to affect by the action of the sun's rays **b** : to expose to sunlight
**2** : to subject (photographic materials) to solarization

**solar panel** *noun* (1961)
: a battery of solar cells (as in a spacecraft)

**so·lar plexus** \'sō-lər-\ *noun* [from the radiating nerve fibers] (1771)
**1** : a nerve plexus in the abdomen that is situated behind the stomach and in front of the aorta and the crura of the diaphragm and contains several ganglia distributing nerve fibers to the viscera
**2** : the pit of the stomach

**solar pond** *noun* (1961)
: a pool of salt water heated by the sun and used either as a direct source of heat or to provide power for an electric generator

**solar sail** *noun* (1958)
: a propulsive device for a spacecraft that consists of a flat material (as aluminized plastic) designed to receive thrust from solar radiation pressure

**solar system** *noun* (circa 1704)
: the sun together with the group of celestial bodies that are held by its attraction and revolve around it; *also* : a similar system centered on another star

**solar wind** *noun* (1958)
: plasma continuously ejected from the sun's surface into and through interplanetary space

**sol·ation** \sä-'lā-shən, sȯ-\ *noun* (1915)
: the process of changing to a sol

**so·la·ti·um** \sō-'lā-shē-əm\ *noun*, *plural* **-tia** \-shē-ə\ [Late Latin *solacium, solatium*, from Latin, solace] (1817)
: a compensation (as money) given as solace for suffering, loss, or injured feelings

**sold** *past and past participle of* SELL

**sol·dan** \'säl-dən, 'sȯl-\ *noun* [Middle English, from Old French, from Arabic *sulṭān*] (14th century)
*archaic* : SULTAN; *especially* : the sultan of Egypt

**¹sol·der** \'sä-dər, 'sȯ-, *British also* 'säl-dər, 'sȯl-\ *noun* [Middle English *soudure*, from Middle French, from *souder* to solder, from Latin *solidare* to make solid, from *solidus* solid] (14th century)
**1** : a metal or metallic alloy used when melted to join metallic surfaces; *especially* : an alloy of lead and tin so used
**2** : something that unites

**²solder** *verb* **sol·dered; sol·der·ing** \-d(ə-)riŋ\ (15th century)
*transitive verb*
**1** : to unite or make whole by solder
**2** : to bring into or restore to firm union ⟨a friendship *soldered* by common interests⟩
*intransitive verb*
**1** : to use solder
**2** : to become united or repaired by or as if by solder
— **sol·der·abil·i·ty** \ˌsä-də-rə-'bi-lə-tē, ˌsȯ-\ *noun*
— **sol·der·er** \'sä-dər-ər, 'sȯ-\ *noun*

**soldering iron** *noun* (1688)
: a pointed or wedge-shaped device that is usually electrically heated and that is used for soldering

**¹sol·dier** \'sōl-jər\ *noun* [Middle English *soudier*, from Middle French, from *soulde* pay, from Late Latin *solidus* solidus] (14th century)

**1 a** : one engaged in military service and especially in the army **b** : an enlisted man or woman **c** : a skilled warrior
**2** : a militant leader, follower, or worker
**3 a** : one of a caste of wingless sterile termites usually differing from workers in larger size and head and long jaws **b** : one of a type of worker ants distinguished by exceptionally large head and jaws
**4** \'sō-jər, 'sōl-\ : one who shirks work
— **sol·dier·ly** \-lē\ *adjective or adverb*
— **sol·dier·ship** \-ˌship\ *noun*

**²soldier** *intransitive verb* **soldiered; sol·dier·ing** \'sōl-jə-riŋ, 'sōlj-riŋ\ (1647)
**1 a** : to serve as a soldier **b** : to behave in a soldierly manner **c** : to push doggedly forward — usually used with *on* ⟨*soldiered* on to the end⟩
**2** : to make a pretense of working while really loafing

**soldiering** *noun* (1643)
: the life, service, or practice of one who soldiers

**soldier of fortune** (1661)
: one who follows a military career wherever there is promise of profit, adventure, or pleasure

**soldiers' home** *noun* (1860)
: an institution maintained (as by the federal or a state government) for the care and relief of military veterans

**soldier's medal** *noun* (circa 1930)
: a U.S. military decoration awarded for heroism not involving combat

**sol·diery** \'sōl-jə-rē, 'sōlj-rē\ *noun* (circa 1570)
**1 a** : a body of soldiers **b** : SOLDIERS, MILITARY
**2** : the profession or technique of soldiering

**sol·do** \'sȯl-(ˌ)dō\ *noun*, *plural* **sol·di** \-(ˌ)dē\ [Italian, from Late Latin *solidus* solidus] (1599)
: an old Italian coin worth five centesimi

**sold–out** \'sōld-'aut\ *adjective* (1907)
: having all available tickets or accommodations sold completely and especially in advance

**¹sole** \'sōl\ *noun* [Middle English, from Middle French, from Latin *solea* sandal, a flatfish] (13th century)
: any of various flatfishes (family Soleidae) having a small mouth, small or rudimentary fins, and small eyes placed close together and including superior food fishes (as the European Dover sole); *also* : any of various mostly market flatfishes (as lemon sole) of other families (as Pleuronectidae)

**²sole** *noun* [Middle English, from Middle French, from Latin *solea* sandal; akin to Latin *solum* base, ground, soil] (14th century)
**1 a** : the undersurface of a foot **b** : the part of an item of footwear on which the sole rests and upon which the wearer treads
**2** : the usually flat or flattened bottom or lower part of something or the base on which something rests
— **soled** \'sōld\ *adjective*

**³sole** *transitive verb* **soled; sol·ing** (1570)
**1** : to furnish with a sole ⟨*sole* a shoe⟩
**2** : to place the sole of (a golf club) on the ground

**⁴sole** *adjective* [Middle English, alone, from Middle French *seul*, from Latin *solus*] (14th century)
**1** : not married — used chiefly of women
**2** *archaic* : having no companion : SOLITARY
**3 a** : having no sharer **b** : being the only one ⟨she was her mother's *sole* support⟩
**4** : functioning independently and without assistance or interference ⟨let conscience be the *sole* judge⟩

---

\ə\ abut \ᵊ\ kitten \ər\ further \a\ ash \ā\ ace
\ä\ mop, mar \au̇\ out \ch\ chin \e\ bet \ē\ easy
\g\ go \i\ hit \ī\ ice \j\ job \ŋ\ sing \ō\ go
\ȯ\ law \ȯi\ boy \th\ thin \th̲\ the \ü\ loot \u̇\ foot
\y\ yet \zh\ vision   *see also* Guide to Pronunciation

**5 :** belonging exclusively or otherwise limited to one usually specified individual, unit, or group
— **sole·ness** \'sōl-nəs\ *noun*
**so·le·cism** \'sä-lə-ˌsi-zəm, 'sō-\ *noun* [Latin *soloecismus*, from Greek *soloikismos*, from *soloikos* speaking incorrectly, literally, inhabitant of Soloi, from *Soloi*, city in ancient Cilicia where a substandard form of Attic was spoken] (circa 1555)
**1 :** an ungrammatical combination of words in a sentence; *also :* a minor blunder in speech
**2 :** something deviating from the proper, normal, or accepted order
**3 :** a breach of etiquette or decorum
— **so·le·cis·tic** \ˌsä-lə-'sis-tik, ˌsō-\ *adjective*
**sole·ly** \'sō(l)-lē\ *adverb* (15th century)
**1 :** without another **:** SINGLY ⟨went *solely* on her way⟩
**2 :** to the exclusion of all else ⟨done *solely* for money⟩
**sol·emn** \'sä-ləm\ *adjective* [Middle English *solemne*, from Middle French, from Latin *sollemnis* regularly appointed, solemn] (14th century)
**1 :** marked by the invocation of a religious sanction ⟨a *solemn* oath⟩
**2 :** marked by the observance of established form or ceremony; *specifically :* celebrated with full liturgical ceremony
**3 a :** awe-inspiring **:** SUBLIME **b :** marked by grave sedateness and earnest sobriety **c :** SOMBER, GLOOMY
*synonym* see SERIOUS
— **sol·emn·ly** *adverb*
— **sol·emn·ness** *noun*
**so·lem·ni·fy** \sə-'lem-nə-ˌfī\ *transitive verb* **-fied; -fy·ing** (1780)
**:** to make solemn
**so·lem·ni·ty** \sə-'lem-nə-tē\ *noun, plural* **-ties** (14th century)
**1 :** formal or ceremonious observance of an occasion or event
**2 :** a solemn event or occasion
**3 :** a solemn condition or quality ⟨the *solemnity* of his words⟩
**sol·em·nize** \'sä-ləm-ˌnīz\ *verb* **-nized; -niz·ing** (14th century)
*transitive verb*
**1 :** to observe or honor with solemnity
**2 :** to perform with pomp or ceremony; *especially :* to celebrate (a marriage) with religious rites
**3 :** to make solemn **:** DIGNIFY
*intransitive verb*
**:** to speak or act with solemnity
— **sol·em·ni·za·tion** \ˌsä-ləm-nə-'zā-shən\ *noun*
**solemn mass** *noun* (15th century)
**:** a mass marked by the use of incense and by the presence of a deacon and a subdeacon in attendance on the celebrant
**solemn vow** *noun* (14th century)
**:** an absolute and irrevocable public vow taken by a religious in the Roman Catholic Church under which ownership of property by the individual is prohibited and marriage is invalid under canon law
**so·le·noid** \'sō-lə-ˌnoid, 'sä-\ *noun* [French *solénoïde*, from Greek *sōlēnoeidēs* pipe-shaped, from Greek *sōlēn* pipe] (1827)
**:** a coil of wire usually in cylindrical form that when carrying a current acts like a magnet so that a movable core is drawn into the coil when a current flows and that is used especially as a switch or control for a mechanical device (as a valve)
— **so·le·noi·dal** \ˌsō-lə-'noi-dᵊl, ˌsä-\ *adjective*
**sole·plate** \'sōl-ˌplāt\ *noun* (1741)
**1 :** the lower plate of a studded partition on which the bases of the studs butt
**2 :** the undersurface of a flatiron
**soles** *plural of* SOL

**so·le·us** \'sō-lē-əs\ *noun, plural* **so·lei** \-lē-ˌī\ [New Latin, from Latin *solea* sandal — more at SOLE] (1676)
**:** a broad flat muscle of the calf of the leg lying immediately below the gastrocnemius
¹**sol–fa** \ˌsōl-'fä, 'sōl-ˌ\ (circa 1529)
*intransitive verb*
**:** to sing the sol-fa syllables
*transitive verb*
**:** to sing (as a melody) to sol-fa syllables
²**sol–fa** *noun* (1548)
**1 :** SOL-FA SYLLABLES
**2 :** SOLMIZATION; *also :* an exercise thus sung
**3 :** TONIC SOL-FA
— **sol–fa·ist** \-'fä(-i)st, -'fä-ˌist\ *noun*
**sol–fa syllables** *noun plural* (1913)
**:** the syllables *do, re, mi, fa, sol, la, ti,* used in singing the tones of the scale
**sol·fa·ta·ra** \ˌsōl-fə-'tär-ə\ *noun* [Italian, sulfur mine, from *solfo* sulfur, from Latin *sulfur*] (1777)
**:** a volcanic area or vent that yields only hot vapors and sulfurous gases
**sol·fège** \säl-'fezh\ *noun* [French, from Italian *solfeggio*] (circa 1903)
**1 :** the application of the sol-fa syllables to a musical scale or to a melody
**2 :** a singing exercise especially using sol-fa syllables; *also :* practice in sight-reading vocal music using the sol-fa syllables
**sol·feg·gio** \säl-'fe-j(ē-ˌ)ō\ *noun* [Italian, from *sol-fa*] (1774)
**:** SOLFÈGE
**sol–gel** \'säl-ˌjel, 'sȯl-\ *adjective* (1915)
**:** involving alternation between sol and gel states
**soli** *plural of* SOLO
**so·lic·it** \sə-'li-sət\ *verb* [Middle English, to disturb, take charge of, from Middle French *solliciter*, from Latin *sollicitare* to disturb, from *sollicitus* anxious, from *sollus* whole (from Oscan; akin to Greek *holos* whole) + *citus*, past participle of *ciēre* to move — more at SAFE, -KINESIS] (15th century)
*transitive verb*
**1 a :** to make petition to **:** ENTREAT **b :** to approach with a request or plea
**2 :** to urge (as one's cause) strongly
**3 a :** to entice or lure especially into evil **b :** to proposition (someone) especially as or in the character of a prostitute
**4 :** to try to obtain by usually urgent requests or pleas
*intransitive verb*
**1 :** to make solicitation **:** IMPORTUNE
**2** *of a prostitute* **:** to offer to have sexual relations with someone for money
*synonym* see ASK
**so·lic·i·tant** \sə-'li-sə-tənt\ *noun* (circa 1812)
**:** one who solicits
**so·lic·i·ta·tion** \sə-ˌli-sə-'tā-shən\ *noun* (circa 1520)
**1 :** the practice or act or an instance of soliciting; *especially :* ENTREATY, IMPORTUNITY
**2 :** a moving or drawing force **:** INCITEMENT, ALLUREMENT
**so·lic·i·tor** \sə-'li-sə-tər, -'lis-tər\ *noun* (15th century)
**1 :** one that solicits; *especially :* an agent that solicits (as contributions to charity)
**2 :** a British lawyer who advises clients, represents them in the lower courts, and prepares cases for barristers to try in higher courts
**3 :** the chief law officer of a municipality, county, or government department
— **so·lic·i·tor·ship** \-ˌship\ *noun*
**solicitor general** *noun, plural* **solicitors general** (1647)
**:** a law officer appointed primarily to assist an attorney general
**so·lic·i·tous** \sə-'li-sə-təs, -'lis-təs\ *adjective* [Latin *sollicitus*] (1563)
**1 :** manifesting or expressing solicitude ⟨a *solicitous* inquiry about his health⟩
**2 :** full of concern or fears **:** APPREHENSIVE ⟨*solicitous* about the future⟩

**3 :** meticulously careful ⟨*solicitous* in matters of dress⟩
**4 :** full of desire **:** EAGER
— **so·lic·i·tous·ly** *adverb*
— **so·lic·i·tous·ness** *noun*
**so·lic·i·tude** \sə-'li-sə-ˌtüd, -ˌtyüd\ *noun* (15th century)
**1 a :** the state of being solicitous **:** ANXIETY **b :** attentive care and protectiveness; *also :* an attitude of solicitous concern or attention
**2 :** a cause of care or concern — usually used in plural
¹**sol·id** \'sä-ləd\ *adjective* [Middle English *solide*, from Middle French, from Latin *solidus*; akin to Greek *holos* whole — more at SAFE] (14th century)
**1 a :** being without an internal cavity ⟨a *solid* ball of rubber⟩ **b** (1) **:** printed with minimum space between lines (2) **:** joined without a hyphen ⟨a *solid* compound⟩ **c :** not interrupted by a break or opening ⟨a *solid* wall⟩
**2 :** having, involving, or dealing with three dimensions or with solids ⟨*solid* configuration⟩
**3 a :** of uniformly close and coherent texture **:** not loose or spongy **:** COMPACT **b :** possessing or characterized by the properties of a solid **:** neither gaseous nor liquid
**4 :** of good substantial quality or kind ⟨*solid* comfort⟩: as **a :** SOUND ⟨*solid* reasons⟩ **b :** made firmly and well ⟨*solid* furniture⟩
**5 a :** having no break or interruption ⟨waited three *solid* hours⟩ **b :** UNANIMOUS ⟨had the *solid* support of the party⟩ **c :** intimately friendly or associated ⟨*solid* with the boss⟩
**6 a :** PRUDENT; *also :* well-established financially **b :** serious in purpose or character
**7 :** of one substance or character: as **a :** entirely of one metal or containing the minimum of alloy necessary to impart hardness ⟨*solid* gold⟩ **b :** of a single color
— **sol·id·ly** *adverb*
— **sol·id·ness** *noun*
²**solid** *noun* (15th century)
**1 :** a geometrical figure or element (as a cube or sphere) having three dimensions — see VOLUME table
**2 a :** a substance that does not flow perceptibly under moderate stress, has a definite capacity for resisting forces (as compression or tension) which tend to deform it, and under ordinary conditions retains a definite size and shape **b :** the part of a solution or suspension that when freed from solvent or suspending medium has the qualities of a solid — usually used in plural ⟨milk *solids*⟩
**3 :** something that is solid: as **a :** a solid color **b :** a compound word whose members are joined together without a hyphen
³**solid** *adverb* (1651)
**:** in a solid manner; *also :* UNANIMOUSLY
**sol·i·da·go** \ˌsä-lə-'dā-(ˌ)gō, -'dä-\ *noun, plural* **-gos** [New Latin, from Medieval Latin *soldago*, an herb reputed to heal wounds, from *soldare* to make whole, from Latin *solidare*, from *solidus* solid] (circa 1771)
**:** any of a genus (*Solidago*) of chiefly North American composite herbs including the typical goldenrods
**solid angle** *noun* (circa 1704)
**:** the three-dimensional angular spread at the vertex of a cone measured by the area intercepted by the cone on a unit sphere whose center is the vertex of the cone
**sol·i·da·rism** \'sä-lə-də-ˌri-zəm\ *noun* (1906)
**:** SOLIDARITY
— **sol·i·da·rist** \-rist\ *noun*
— **sol·i·da·ris·tic** \ˌsä-lə-də-'ris-tik\ *adjective*
**sol·i·dar·i·ty** \ˌsä-lə-'dar-ə-tē\ *noun* [French *solidarité*, from *solidaire* characterized by solidarity, from Latin *solidum* whole sum, from neuter of *solidus* solid] (1841)
**:** unity (as of a group or class) that produces or is based on community of interests, objectives, and standards
**solid geometry** *noun* (1733)

: a branch of geometry that deals with figures of three-dimensional space

**so·lid·i·fy** \sə-'li-də-ˌfī\ *verb* **-fied; -fy·ing** (1799)
*transitive verb*
**1 :** to make solid, compact, or hard
**2 :** to make secure, substantial, or firmly fixed ⟨factors that *solidify* public opinion⟩
*intransitive verb*
: to become solid, compact, or hard
— **so·lid·i·fi·ca·tion** \-ˌli-də-fə-'kā-shən\ *noun*

**so·lid·i·ty** \sə-'li-də-tē\ *noun, plural* **-ties** (14th century)
**1 :** the quality or state of being solid
**2 :** something solid

**sol·id–look·ing** \ˌsä-ləd-'lük-iŋ\ *adjective* (1840)
: giving an impression of solid worth or substance ⟨*solid-looking* citizens⟩

**solid of revolution** (1816)
: a mathematical solid conceived as formed by the revolution of a plane figure about an axis in its plane

**solid–state** *adjective* (circa 1951)
**1 :** relating to the properties, structure, or reactivity of solid material; *especially* **:** relating to the arrangement or behavior of ions, molecules, nucleons, electrons, and holes in the crystals of a substance (as a semiconductor) or to the effect of crystal imperfections on the properties of a solid substance ⟨*solid-state* physics⟩
**2 a :** utilizing the electric, magnetic, or optical properties of solid materials ⟨*solid-state* circuitry⟩ **b :** using semiconductor devices rather than electron tubes ⟨a *solid-state* stereo system⟩

**sol·i·dus** \'sä-lə-dəs\ *noun, plural* **-i·di** \-lə-ˌdī, -ˌdē\ [Middle English, from Late Latin, from Latin, solid] (14th century)
**1 :** an ancient Roman gold coin introduced by Constantine and used to the fall of the Byzantine Empire
**2** [Medieval Latin, shilling, from Late Latin; from its use as a symbol for shillings] **:** DIAGONAL 3

**so·li·fluc·tion** \'sō-lə-ˌflək-shən\ *noun* [Latin *solum* soil + *-i-* + *fluction-, fluctio* act of flowing, from *fluere* to flow — more at FLUID] (1906)
: the slow creeping of saturated fragmental material (as soil) down a slope that usually occurs in regions of perennial frost

**so·lil·o·quist** \sə-'li-lə-kwist\ *noun* (1804)
: one who soliloquizes

**so·lil·o·quise** *British variant of* SOLILOQUIZE

**so·lil·o·quize** \-ˌkwīz\ *intransitive verb* **-quized; -quiz·ing** (1759)
: to utter a soliloquy : talk to oneself
— **so·lil·o·quiz·er** *noun*

**so·lil·o·quy** \sə-'li-lə-kwē\ *noun, plural* **-quies** [Late Latin *soliloquium*, from Latin *solus* alone + *loqui* to speak] (circa 1613)
**1 :** the act of talking to oneself
**2 :** a dramatic monologue that gives the illusion of being a series of unspoken reflections

**so·lip·sism** \'sō-ləp-ˌsi-zəm, 'sä-\ *noun* [Latin *solus* alone + *ipse* self] (1874)
: a theory holding that the self can know nothing but its own modifications and that the self is the only existent thing
— **so·lip·sist** \'sō-ləp-sist, 'sä-ləp-, sə-'lip-\ *noun*
— **so·lip·sis·tic** \ˌsō-ləp-'sis-tik, ˌsä-\ *adjective*
— **so·lip·sis·ti·cal·ly** \-ti-k(ə-)lē\ *adverb*

**sol·i·taire** \'sä-lə-ˌtar, -ˌter\ *noun* [French, from *solitaire*, adjective, solitary, from Latin *solitarius*] (circa 1727)
**1 :** a single gem (as a diamond) set alone
**2 :** any of various card games that can be played by one person

**¹sol·i·tary** \'sä-lə-ˌter-ē\ *adjective* [Middle English, from Latin *solitarius*, from *solitas* aloneness, from *solus* alone] (14th century)

**1 a :** being, living, or going alone or without companions **b :** saddened by isolation
**2 :** UNFREQUENTED, DESOLATE
**3 a :** taken, passed, or performed without companions ⟨a *solitary* ramble⟩ **b :** keeping a prisoner apart from others ⟨*solitary* confinement⟩
**4 :** being at once single and isolated ⟨a *solitary* example⟩
**5 a :** occurring singly and not as part of a group or cluster ⟨flowers terminal and *solitary*⟩ **b :** not gregarious, colonial, social, or compound ⟨*solitary* bees⟩
*synonym* see ALONE
— **sol·i·tar·i·ly** \ˌsä-lə-'ter-ə-lē\ *adverb*
— **sol·i·tar·i·ness** \'sä-lə-ˌter-ē-nəs\ *noun*

**²solitary** *noun, plural* **-tar·ies** (15th century)
**1 :** one who lives or seeks to live a solitary life **:** RECLUSE
**2 :** solitary confinement in prison

**sol·i·ton** \'sä-lə-ˌtän\ *noun* [*solit*ary + ²*-on*] (1965)
: a solitary wave (as in a gaseous plasma) that propagates with little loss of energy and retains its shape and speed after colliding with another such wave

**sol·i·tude** \'sä-lə-ˌtüd, -ˌtyüd\ *noun* [Middle English, from Middle French, from Latin *solitudin-, solitudo*, from *solus*] (14th century)
**1 :** the quality or state of being alone or remote from society **:** SECLUSION
**2 :** a lonely place (as a desert) ☆

**sol·i·tu·di·nar·i·an** \ˌsä-lə-ˌtü-d°n-'er-ē-ən, -ˌtyü-\ *noun* [Latin *solitudin-, solitudo* + English *-arian*] (1691)
**:** RECLUSE

**sol·ler·et** \ˌsä-lə-'ret\ *noun* [French] (1826)
: a flexible steel shoe forming part of a medieval suit of armor — see ARMOR illustration

**sol·mi·za·tion** \ˌsäl-mə-'zā-shən\ *noun* [French *solmisation*, from *solmiser* to sol-fa, from *sol* (from Medieval Latin) + *mi* (from Medieval Latin) + *-iser* -ize] (1730)
: the act, practice, or system of using syllables to denote the tones of a musical scale

**¹so·lo** \'sō-(ˌ)lō\ *noun, plural* **solos** [Italian, from *solo* alone, from Latin *solus*] (1695)
**1** *or plural* **so·li** \'sō-(ˌ)lē\ **a :** a musical composition for a single voice or instrument with or without accompaniment **b :** the featured part of a concerto or similar work
**2 :** a performance in which the performer has no partner or associate
**3 :** any of several card games in which a player elects to play without a partner against the other players

**²solo** *adverb* (1712)
: without a companion **:** ALONE ⟨fly *solo*⟩

**³solo** *adjective* (1774)
: of, relating to, or being a solo ⟨a *solo* performance⟩

**⁴solo** *intransitive verb* **so·loed; so·lo·ing** \-(ˌ)lō-iŋ, -lə-wiŋ\ (1886)
: to perform by oneself; *especially* **:** to fly an airplane without one's instructor on board

**so·lo·ist** \'sō-lə-wist, -(ˌ)lō-ist\ *noun* (1864)
: one who performs a solo

**Sol·o·mon** \'sä-lə-mən\ *noun* [Late Latin, from Hebrew *Shĕlōmōh*]
: a son of David and 10th century B.C. king of Israel proverbial for his wisdom

**Sol·o·mon·ic** \ˌsä-lə-'mä-nik\ *adjective* (1857)
: marked by notable wisdom, reasonableness, or discretion especially under trying circumstances

**Solomon's seal** *noun* (1543)
**1 :** any of a genus (*Polygonatum*) of perennial herbs of the lily family with tubular flowers and gnarled rhizomes — called also *Solomonseal*
**2 :** an emblem consisting of two interlaced triangles forming a 6-pointed star and formerly used as an amulet especially against fever — compare HEXAGRAM

**so·lon** \'sō-lən, -ˌlän\ *noun* [*Solon*] (1625)
**1 :** a wise and skillful lawgiver

**2 :** a member of a legislative body

**sol·on·chak** \ˌsä-lən-'chak\ *noun* [Russian, salt marsh] (1925)
: any of a group of intrazonal strongly saline usually pale soils found especially in poorly drained arid or semiarid areas

**sol·o·netz** \ˌsä-lə-'nets\ *noun* [Russian *solonets* salt not extracted by decoction] (1924)
: any of a group of intrazonal dark hard alkaline soils evolved by leaching and alkalizing from solonchak
— **sol·o·netz·ic** \-'net-sik\ *adjective*

**so long** \sō-'loŋ, sə-\ *interjection* [origin unknown] (circa 1861)
— used to express farewell

**so long as** *conjunction* (14th century)
**1 :** during and up to the end of the time that **:** WHILE
**2 :** provided that

**sol·stice** \'säl-stəs, 'sōl-, 'sȯl-\ *noun* [Middle English, from Old French, from Latin *solstitium*, from *sol* sun + *-stit-, -stes* standing; akin to Latin *stare* to stand — more at SOLAR, STAND] (13th century)
**1 :** either of the two points on the ecliptic at which its distance from the celestial equator is greatest and which is reached by the sun each year about June 22d and December 22d
**2 :** the time of the sun's passing a solstice which occurs about June 22d to begin summer in the northern hemisphere and about December 22d to begin winter in the northern hemisphere

**sol·sti·tial** \säl-'sti-shəl, sōl-, sȯl-\ *adjective* [Middle English *solsticial*, from Old French & Latin; Old French, from Latin *solstitialis*, from *solstitium*] (14th century)
**1 :** of, relating to, or characteristic of a solstice and especially the summer solstice
**2 :** happening or appearing at or associated with a solstice

**sol·u·bi·lise** *British variant of* SOLUBILIZE

**sol·u·bil·i·ty** \ˌsäl-yə-'bi-lə-tē\ *noun* (1661)
**1 :** the quality or state of being soluble
**2 :** the amount of a substance that will dissolve in a given amount of another substance

**sol·u·bi·lize** \'säl-yə-bə-ˌlīz\ *transitive verb* **-lized; -liz·ing** (circa 1926)
: to make soluble or increase the solubility of
— **sol·u·bi·li·za·tion** \ˌsäl-yə-bə-lə-'zā-shən\ *noun*

**sol·u·ble** \'säl-yə-bəl\ *adjective* [Middle English, from Middle French, capable of being loosened or dissolved, from Late Latin *solubilis*, from Latin *solvere* to loosen, dissolve — more at SOLVE] (15th century)
**1 :** susceptible of being dissolved in or as if in a liquid and especially water
**2 :** subject to being solved or explained ⟨*soluble* questions⟩

**so·lum** \'sō-ləm\ *noun, plural* **so·la** \-lə\ *or* **solums** [New Latin, from Latin, ground, soil] (1928)

---

---

\ə\ abut  \ᵊ\ kitten  \ər\ further  \a\ ash  \ā\ ace
\ä\ mop, mar  \aú\ out  \ch\ chin  \e\ bet  \ē\ easy
\g\ go  \i\ hit  \ī\ ice  \j\ job  \ŋ\ sing  \ō\ go
\ȯ\ law  \ȯi\ boy  \th\ thin  \th\ the  \ü\ loot  \ù\ foot
\y\ yet  \zh\ vision  *see also* Guide to Pronunciation

: the altered layer of soil above the parent material that includes the A and B horizons

**so·lus** \'sō-ləs\ *adverb or adjective* [Latin] (1599)
: ALONE — often used in stage directions

**sol·ute** \'säl-,yüt\ *noun* [Latin *solutus,* past participle of *solvere*] (1893)
: a dissolved substance

**so·lu·tion** \sə-'lü-shən\ *noun* [Middle English, from Middle French, from Latin *solution-, solutio,* from *solvere* to loosen, solve] (14th century)
**1 a :** an action or process of solving a problem **b :** an answer to a problem **:** EXPLANATION; *specifically* **:** a set of values of the variables that satisfies an equation
**2 a :** an act or the process by which a solid, liquid, or gaseous substance is homogeneously mixed with a liquid or sometimes a gas or solid **b :** a homogeneous mixture formed by this process; *especially* **:** a single-phase liquid system **c :** the condition of being dissolved
**3 :** a bringing or coming to an end or into a state of discontinuity

**solution set** *noun* (1959)
: the set of values that satisfy an equation; *also* **:** TRUTH SET

**So·lu·tre·an** \sə-'lü-trē-ən\ *adjective* [Solutré, village in France] (1888)
: of or relating to an upper Paleolithic culture characterized by leaf-shaped finely flaked stone implements

**solv·able** \'säl-və-bəl, 'sȯl-\ *adjective* (circa 1676)
: susceptible of solution or of being solved, resolved, or explained
— **solv·abil·i·ty** \,säl-və-'bi-lə-tē, ,sȯl-\ *noun*

**¹sol·vate** \'säl-,vāt, 'sȯl-\ *noun* [solvent + ¹-ate] (1904)
: an aggregate that consists of a solute ion or molecule with one or more solvent molecules; *also* **:** a substance (as a hydrate) containing such ions

**²solvate** *transitive verb* **sol·vat·ed; sol·vat·ing** (1909)
: to make part of a solvate
— **sol·va·tion** \säl-'vā-shən, sȯl-\ *noun*

**Sol·vay process** \'säl-,vā-\ *noun* [Ernest Solvay (died 1922) Belgian chemist] (1884)
: a process for making soda from common salt by passing carbon dioxide into ammoniacal brine resulting in precipitation of sodium bicarbonate which is then calcined to carbonate

**solve** \'sälv, 'sȯlv\ *verb* **solved; solv·ing** [Middle English, to loosen, from Latin *solvere* to loosen, solve, dissolve, from *sed-, se-* apart + *luere* to release — more at SECEDE, LOSE] (circa 1533)
*transitive verb*
**1 :** to find a solution, explanation, or answer for ⟨*solve* a problem⟩ ⟨*solved* the crime⟩
**2 :** to pay (as a debt) in full
*intransitive verb*
: to solve something ⟨substitute the known values of the constants and *solve* for *x*⟩
— **solv·er** *noun*

**sol·ven·cy** \'säl-vən(t)-sē, 'sȯl-\ *noun* (circa 1727)
: the quality or state of being solvent

**¹sol·vent** \-vənt\ *adjective* [Latin *solvent-, solvens,* present participle of *solvere* to dissolve, pay] (1630)
**1 :** able to pay all legal debts
**2 :** that dissolves or can dissolve ⟨*solvent* action of water⟩
— **sol·vent·ly** *adverb*

**²solvent** *noun* (1671)
**1 :** a usually liquid substance capable of dissolving or dispersing one or more other substances
**2 :** something that provides a solution
**3 :** something that eliminates or attenuates something especially unwanted
— **sol·vent·less** *adjective*

**sol·vol·y·sis** \säl-'vä-lə-səs, sȯl-\ *noun* [New Latin, from English *solvent* + New Latin *-o-* + *-lysis*] (1916)
: a chemical reaction (as hydrolysis) of a solvent and solute that results in the formation of new compounds
— **sol·vo·lyt·ic** \,säl-və-'li-tik, ,sȯl-\ *adjective*

**¹so·ma** \'sō-mə\ *noun* [Sanskrit; akin to Avestan *haoma,* a Zoroastrian ritual drink, Sanskrit *sunoti* he presses out] (1827)
: an intoxicating plant juice probably from a leafless vine (*Sarcostemma intermedium*) of the milkweed family used in ancient India as an offering to the gods and as a drink of immortality by worshipers in Vedic ritual and worshiped as a Vedic god

**²soma** *noun, plural* **so·ma·ta** \'sō-mə-tə\ *or* **somas** [New Latin *somat-, soma,* from Greek *sōmat-, sōma* body] (circa 1885)
**1 :** the body of an organism
**2 :** all of an organism except the germ cells
**3 :** CELL BODY

**So·ma·li** \sō-'mä-lē, sə-\ *noun, plural* **Somali** *or* **Somalis** (1814)
**1 :** a member of a people of Somaliland
**2 :** the Cushitic language of the Somali

**so many** *adjective* (1533)
**1 :** constituting an unspecified number ⟨read *so many* chapters each night⟩
**2 :** constituting a group or pack ⟨behaved like *so many* animals⟩

**somat-** *or* **somato-** *combining form* [New Latin, from Greek *sōmat-, sōmato-,* from *sōmat-, sōma* body]
: body ⟨*somatology*⟩

**so·mat·ic** \sō-'ma-tik, sə-\ *adjective* [Greek *sōmatikos,* from *sōmat-, sōma* body] (circa 1775)
**1 :** of, relating to, or affecting the body especially as distinguished from the germ plasm or the psyche
**2 :** of or relating to the wall of the body **:** PARIETAL
— **so·mat·i·cal·ly** \-ti-k(ə-)lē\ *adverb*

**somatic cell** *noun* (1888)
: one of the cells of the body that compose the tissues, organs, and parts of that individual other than the germ cells

**so·ma·tol·o·gy** \,sō-mə-'tä-lə-jē\ *noun* [New Latin *somatologia,* from *somat-* + *-logia* *-logy*] (circa 1878)
: a branch of anthropology primarily concerned with the comparative study of human evolution, variation, and classification especially through measurement and observation
— **so·ma·to·log·i·cal** \,sō-mə-t°l-'ä-ji-kəl, sō-,ma-\ *adjective*

**so·mato·me·din** \,sō-mə-tō-'mē-d°n, sō-,ma-tə-\ *noun* [*somat-* + *intermed*iary + ¹-*in*] (1971)
: any of several endogenous peptides produced especially in the liver that are dependent on and probably mediate growth hormone activity (as in sulfate uptake by epiphyseal cartilage)

**so·mato·pleure** \sō-'ma-tə-,plu̇r\ *noun* [New Latin *somatopleura,* from *somat-* + Greek *pleura* side] (1874)
: a complex fold of tissue in the embryo of a craniate vertebrate consisting of an outer layer of mesoderm together with the ectoderm that sheathes it and giving rise to the amnion and chorion

**so·mato·sen·so·ry** \sō-,ma-tə-'sen(t)s-rē, -'sen(t)-sə-rē\ *adjective* (1952)
: of, relating to, or being sensory activity having its origin elsewhere than in the special sense organs (as eyes and ears) and conveying information about the state of the body proper and its immediate environment

**so·mato·stat·in** \sō-,ma-tə-'sta-t°n\ *noun* [*somat-* + Latin *status* (past participle of *sistere* to halt, cause to stand) + English ¹-*in*; akin to Latin *stare* to stand — more at STAND] (1973)

: a polypeptide neurohormone that is found especially in the hypothalamus and inhibits the secretion of several other hormones (as growth hormone, insulin, and gastrin)

**so·mato·tro·pic hormone** \-'trō-pik-\ *noun* [*somat-* + *-tropic*] (1938)
: GROWTH HORMONE 1

**so·mato·tro·pin** \-'trō-pən\ *also* **so·mato·tro·phin** \-fən\ *noun* [*somatotropic* + ¹-*in*] (1941)
: GROWTH HORMONE 1

**so·mato·type** \sō-'ma-tə-,tīp\ *noun* (1940)
: body type **:** PHYSIQUE

**som·ber** *or* **som·bre** \'säm-bər\ *adjective* [French *sombre*] (1760)
**1 :** so shaded as to be dark and gloomy
**2 a :** of a serious mien **:** GRAVE **b :** of a dismal or depressing character **:** MELANCHOLY **c :** conveying gloomy suggestions or ideas
**3 :** of a dull or heavy cast or shade **:** dark colored
— **som·ber·ly** *adverb*
— **som·ber·ness** *noun*

**som·bre·ro** \səm-'brer-(,)ō, säm-\ *noun, plural* **-ros** [Spanish, from *sombra* shade] (1599)
: a high-crowned hat of felt or straw with a very wide brim worn especially in the Southwest and Mexico

**som·brous** \'säm-brəs\ *adjective* [French *sombre*] (1730)
*archaic* **:** SOMBER

sombrero

**¹some** \'səm, *for* 2 *without stress*\ *adjective* [Middle English *som,* adjective & pronoun, from Old English *sum;* akin to Old High German *sum* some, Greek *hamē* somehow, *homos* same — more at SAME] (before 12th century)
**1 :** being an unknown, undetermined, or unspecified unit or thing ⟨*some* person knocked⟩
**2 a :** being one, a part, or an unspecified number of something (as a class or group) named or implied ⟨*some* gems are hard⟩ **b :** being of an unspecified amount or number ⟨give me *some* water⟩ ⟨have *some* apples⟩
**3 :** REMARKABLE, STRIKING ⟨that was *some* party⟩
**4 :** being at least one — used to indicate that a logical proposition is asserted only of a subclass or certain members of the class denoted by the term which it modifies

**²some** \'səm\ *pronoun, singular or plural in construction* (before 12th century)
**1 :** one indeterminate quantity, portion, or number as distinguished from the rest
**2 :** an indefinite additional amount ⟨ran a mile and then *some*⟩

**³some** \'səm, ,səm\ *adverb* (before 12th century)
**1 :** ABOUT ⟨*some* 80 houses⟩ ⟨twenty-*some* people⟩
**2 a :** in some degree **:** SOMEWHAT ⟨felt *some* better⟩ **b :** to some degree or extent **:** a little ⟨the cut bled *some*⟩ ⟨I need to work on it *some* more⟩ — used as a mild intensive ⟨that's going *some*⟩ ◼

**¹-some** *adjective suffix* [Middle English *-som,* from Old English *-sum;* akin to Old High German *-sam* -some, Old English *sum* some]
: characterized by a (specified) thing, quality, state, or action ⟨awe*some*⟩ ⟨burden*some*⟩ ⟨cuddle*some*⟩

**²-some** *noun suffix* [Middle English (northern dialect) *-sum,* from Middle English *sum,* pronoun, one, some]
: group of (so many) members and especially persons ⟨four*some*⟩

**³-some** *noun combining form* [New Latin *-somat-, -soma,* from Greek *sōmat-, sōma*]
**1 :** body ⟨chromo*some*⟩
**2 :** chromosome ⟨mono*some*⟩

**¹some·body** \'səm-(,)bə-dē, -,bä-\ *pronoun* (14th century)

: one or some person of unspecified or indefinite identity ⟨*somebody* will come in⟩ ▢

²**somebody** *noun* (circa 1566)
: a person of position or importance

**some·day** \'səm-ˌdā\ *adverb* (14th century)
: at some future time

**some·deal** \'səm-ˌdēl\ *adverb* (before 12th century)
*archaic* : SOMEWHAT

**some·how** \'səm-ˌhau̇\ *adverb* (1664)
: in one way or another not known or designated : by some means

**some·one** \-(ˌ)wən\ *pronoun* (14th century)
: some person : SOMEBODY
*usage* see SOMEBODY

**some·place** \'səm-ˌplās\ *adverb* (1880)
: SOMEWHERE

**som·er·sault** \'sə-mər-ˌsȯlt\ *noun* [Middle French *sombresaut* leap, ultimately from Latin *super* over + *saltus* leap, from *salire* to jump — more at OVER, SALLY] (circa 1530)
: a leap or roll in which a person turns forward or backward in a complete revolution bringing the feet over the head and finally landing on the feet; *also* : a falling or tumbling head over heels
— **somersault** *intransitive verb*

**som·er·set** \-ˌset\ *noun or intransitive verb* [by alteration] (1591)
: SOMERSAULT

¹**some·thing** \'səm(p)-thiŋ, *especially in rapid speech or for 2* 'səm-pᵊm\ *pronoun* (before 12th century)
**1** : some indeterminate or unspecified thing
**2** : a person or thing of consequence
**3** : one having more or less the character, qualities, or nature of something different ⟨is *something* of a bore⟩
— **something else** : something or someone special or extraordinary

²**something** *adverb* (13th century)
**1** : in some degree : SOMEWHAT
**2** — used as an intensive giving adverbial force to an adjective ⟨swears *something* awful⟩

¹**some·time** \'səm-ˌtīm\ *adverb* (14th century)
**1** *archaic* : in the past : FORMERLY
**2** *archaic* : once in a while : OCCASIONALLY
**3** : at some time in the future ⟨I'll do it *sometime*⟩
**4** : at some not specified or definitely known point of time ⟨*sometime* last night⟩

²**sometime** *adjective* (14th century)
**1** : having been formerly : FORMER, LATE
**2** : being so occasionally or in only some respects ⟨a *sometime* . . . father who appears and disappears —Evelyn Shelby⟩

¹**some·times** \'səm-ˌtīmz *also* (ˌ)səm-'\ *adverb* (14th century)
: at times : now and then : OCCASIONALLY

²**sometimes** *adjective* (1593)
: SOMETIME

**some·way** \'səm-ˌwā\ *also* **some·ways** \-ˌwāz\ *adverb* (15th century)
: SOMEHOW

¹**some·what** \-(ˌ)hwät, -(ˌ)hwət, (ˌ)səm-'\ *pronoun* (13th century)
: SOMETHING

²**somewhat** *adverb* (13th century)
: in some degree or measure : SLIGHTLY

**some·when** \'səm-ˌ(h)wen\ *adverb* (1833)
: SOMETIME

¹**some·where** \-ˌ(h)wer, -ˌ(h)war, -(ˌ)(h)wər\ *adverb* (13th century)
**1** : in, at, from, or to a place unknown or unspecified ⟨mentions it *somewhere*⟩
**2** : to a place symbolizing positive accomplishment or progress ⟨now we're getting *somewhere*⟩
**3** : in the vicinity of : APPROXIMATELY ⟨*somewhere* about nine o'clock⟩

²**somewhere** *noun* (1647)
: an undetermined or unnamed place

**some·wheres** \-ˌ(h)werz, -ˌ(h)warz, -(ˌ)(h)wərz\ *adverb* (1815)
: SOMEWHERE

**some·whith·er** \-ˌ(h)wi-t͟hər\ *adverb* (1530)

*archaic* : to some place : SOMEWHERE

**-somic** *adjective combining form* [International Scientific Vocabulary ³-*some* + -*ic*]
: having or being a chromosome complement of which one or more but not all members exhibit (such) a degree of reduplication of chromosomes or genomes ⟨mono*somic*⟩

**so·mite** \'sō-ˌmīt\ *noun* [International Scientific Vocabulary, from Greek *sōma* body] (1869)
: one of the longitudinal series of segments into which the body of many animals (as articulate animals and vertebrates) is divided : METAMERE

**som·me·lier** \ˌsə-məl-'yā\ *noun, plural* **som·meliers** \-'yā(z)\ [French, from Middle French, court official charged with transportation of supplies, pack animal driver, from Old Provençal *saumalier* pack animal driver, from *sauma* pack animal, load of a pack animal, from Late Latin *sagma* packsaddle — more at SUMPTER] (1829)
: a waiter in a restaurant who has charge of wines and their service : a wine steward

**somnambul-** *combining form* [New Latin, from *somnambulus* somnambulist, from Latin *somnus* sleep + -*ambulus* (as in *funambulus* funambulist) — more at SOMNOLENT]
: somnambulism : somnambulist ⟨*somnambulant*⟩

**som·nam·bu·lant** \säm-'nam-byə-lənt\ *adjective* (1866)
: walking or addicted to walking while asleep

**som·nam·bu·late** \-ˌlāt\ *intransitive verb* **-lat·ed; -lat·ing** (1833)
: to walk when asleep
— **som·nam·bu·la·tion** \(ˌ)säm-ˌnam-byə-'lā-shən\ *noun*

**som·nam·bu·lism** \säm-'nam-byə-ˌli-zəm\ *noun* (1797)
**1** : an abnormal condition of sleep in which motor acts (as walking) are performed
**2** : actions characteristic of somnambulism
— **som·nam·bu·list** \-list\ *noun*
— **som·nam·bu·lis·tic** \(ˌ)säm-ˌnam-byə-'lis-tik\ *adjective*
— **som·nam·bu·lis·ti·cal·ly** \-ti-k(ə-)lē\ *adverb*

**som·ni·fa·cient** \ˌsäm-nə-'fā-shənt\ *adjective* [Latin *somnus* sleep + English -*facient*] (circa 1890)
: HYPNOTIC 1
— **somnifacient** *noun*

**som·nif·er·ous** \säm-'ni-f(ə-)rəs\ *adjective* [Latin *somnifer* somniferous, from *somnus* + -*fer* -ferous] (1602)
: SOPORIFIC

**som·no·lence** \'säm-nə-lən(t)s\ *noun* (14th century)
: the quality or state of being drowsy : SLEEPINESS

**som·no·lent** \-lənt\ *adjective* [Middle English *sompnolent*, from Middle French, from Latin *somnolentus*, from *somnus* sleep; akin to Old English *swefn* sleep, Greek *hypnos*] (15th century)
**1** : of a kind likely to induce sleep ⟨a *somnolent* sermon⟩
**2 a** : inclined to or heavy with sleep : DROWSY
**b** : SLEEPY 2 ⟨*somnolent* rivers⟩
— **som·no·lent·ly** *adverb*

¹**so much** *adverb* (13th century)
: by the amount indicated or suggested ⟨if they lose their way, *so much* the better for us⟩

²**so much** *pronoun* (14th century)
**1** : something (as an amount or price) unspecified or undetermined ⟨charge *so much* a mile⟩
**2** : all that can be or is to be said or done ⟨*so much* for the history of the case⟩

³**so much** *adjective* (1557)
— used as an intensive ⟨the house burned like *so much* paper⟩ ⟨sounded like *so much* nonsense⟩

**so much as** *adverb* (15th century)
: EVEN 3d

**son** \'sən\ *noun* [Middle English *sone*, from Old English *sunu*; akin to Old High German *sun* son, Greek *hyios*] (before 12th century)
**1 a** : a male offspring especially of human beings **b** : a male adopted child **c** : a male descendant
**2** *capitalized* : the second person of the Trinity
**3** : a person closely associated with or deriving from a formative agent (as a nation, school, or race)
— **son·hood** \-ˌhu̇d\ *noun*

**son-** *or* **sono-** *combining form* [Latin *sonus* sound]
: sound ⟨*sonic*⟩ ⟨*sonogram*⟩

**so·nant** \'sō-nənt\ *adjective* [Latin *sonant-, sonans*, present participle of *sonare* to sound — more at SOUND] (1846)
**1** : VOICED 2
**2** : SYLLABIC 1a
— **sonant** *noun*

**so·nar** \'sō-ˌnär\ *noun* [*so*und *na*vigation *r*anging] (1945)

\ə\ abut \ᵊ\ kitten \ər\ further \a\ ash \ā\ ace \ä\ mop, mar \au̇\ out \ch\ chin \e\ bet \ē\ easy \g\ go \i\ hit \ī\ ice \j\ job \ŋ\ sing \ō\ go \ȯ\ law \ȯi\ boy \th\ thin \t͟h\ the \ü\ loot \u̇\ foot \y\ yet \zh\ vision *see also* Guide to Pronunciation

: a method or device for detecting and locating objects especially underwater by means of sound waves sent out to be reflected by the objects; *also* : a device for detecting the presence of a vessel (as a submarine) by the sound it emits in water ◆

**so·na·ta** \sə-ˈnä-tə\ *noun* [Italian, from *sonare* to sound, from Latin] (1694)
: an instrumental musical composition typically of three or four movements in contrasting forms and keys

**sonata form** *noun* (1873)
: a musical form that consists basically of an exposition, a development, and a recapitulation and that is used especially for the first movement of a sonata

**son·a·ti·na** \ˌsä-nə-ˈtē-nə\ *noun* [Italian, diminutive of *sonata*] (circa 1801)
: a short usually simplified sonata

**sonde** \ˈsänd\ *noun* [French, literally, sounding line — more at SOUND] (1901)
: any of various devices for testing physical conditions (as at high altitudes, below the earth's surface, or inside the body)

**sone** \ˈsōn\ *noun* [International Scientific Vocabulary, from Latin *sonus* sound — more at SOUND] (1948)
: a subjective unit of loudness for an average listener equal to the loudness of a 1000-hertz sound that has an intensity 40 decibels above the listener's own threshold of hearing

**son et lu·mière** \ˌsōⁿ-(n)ā-lüm-ˈyer\ *noun* [French, literally, sound and light] (1957)
: an outdoor spectacle at an historic site consisting of recorded narration with light and sound effects

**song** \ˈsȯŋ\ *noun* [Middle English, from Old English *sang*; akin to Old English *singan* to sing] (before 12th century)
**1** : the act or art of singing
**2** : poetical composition
**3 a** : a short musical composition of words and music **b** : a collection of such compositions
**4** : a distinctive or characteristic sound or series of sounds (as of a bird or insect)
**5 a** : a melody for a lyric poem or ballad **b** : a poem easily set to music
**6 a** : a habitual or characteristic manner **b** : a violent, abusive, or noisy reaction ⟨put up quite a *song*⟩
**7** : a small amount ⟨sold for a *song*⟩
— **song·like** \-ˌlīk\ *adjective*

**song and dance** *noun* (1872)
**1** : a theatrical performance (as a vaudeville performance) combining singing and dancing
**2** : a long and often familiar statement or explanation that is usually not true or pertinent

**song·bird** \ˈsȯŋ-ˌbərd\ *noun* (1774)
**1 a** : a bird that utters a succession of musical tones **b** : an oscine bird
**2** : a female singer

**song·book** \-ˌbu̇k\ *noun* (before 12th century)
: a collection of songs; *specifically* : a book containing vocal music (as hymns)

**song cycle** *noun* (1899)
: a group of related songs designed to form a musical entity

**song·fest** \ˈsȯŋ-fest\ *noun* (circa 1912)
: an informal session of group singing of popular or folk songs

**song·ful** \-fəl\ *adjective* (14th century)
: given to or suggestive of singing : MELODIOUS
— **song·ful·ly** \-fə-lē\ *adverb*
— **song·ful·ness** *noun*

**song·less** \-ləs\ *adjective* (circa 1805)
: lacking in, incapable of, or not given to song
— **song·less·ly** *adverb*

**Song of Sol·o·mon** \-ˈsä-lə-mən\ [from the opening verse: "The song of songs, which is Solomon's"]
: a collection of love poems forming a book in the Protestant canon of the Old Testament — see BIBLE table

**Song of Songs** [translation of Hebrew *shīr hashshīrīm*]
: a collection of love poems forming a book in the canonical Jewish Scriptures and in the Roman Catholic canon of the Old Testament and corresponding to the Song of Solomon in the Protestant canon of the Old Testament — see BIBLE table

**song·smith** \ˈsȯŋ-ˌsmith\ *noun* (1795)
: a composer of songs

**song sparrow** *noun* (1810)
: a common North American sparrow (*Melospiza melodia*) that is brownish above and white below with brownish streaks on the breast and that is noted for it melodious song

**song·ster** \ˈsȯŋ(k)-stər\ *noun* (14th century)
**1** : one that sings with skill
**2** : SONGBOOK

**song·stress** \ˈsȯŋ(k)-strəs\ *noun* (1703)
: a female singer

**song thrush** *noun* (1668)
: an Old World thrush (*Turdus philomelos*) that is largely brown above with brown-spotted white underparts — called also *mavis, throstle*

**song·writ·er** \ˈsȯŋ-ˌrī-tər\ *noun* (1821)
: a person who composes words or music or both especially for popular songs
— **song·writ·ing** \-ˌrī-tiŋ\ *noun*

**son·ic** \ˈsä-nik\ *adjective* (1923)
**1** : utilizing, produced by, or relating to sound waves ⟨*sonic* altimeter⟩; *broadly* : of or involving sound ⟨*sonic* pollution⟩
**2** : having a frequency within the audibility range of the human ear — used of waves and vibrations
**3** : of, relating to, or being the speed of sound in air or about 761 miles per hour (1224 kilometers per hour) at sea level at 59°F (15°C)
**4** : capable of uttering sounds
— **son·i·cal·ly** \-ni-k(ə-)lē\ *adverb*

**son·i·cate** \ˈsä-nə-ˌkāt\ *transitive verb* **-cat·ed; -cat·ing** [*sonic* + -*ate*] (1960)
: to disrupt (as bacteria) by treatment with high-frequency sound waves
— **son·i·ca·tion** \ˌsä-nə-ˈkā-shən\ *noun*

**sonic barrier** *noun* (1946)
: SOUND BARRIER

**sonic boom** *noun* (1952)
: a sound resembling an explosion produced when a shock wave formed at the nose of an aircraft traveling at supersonic speed reaches the ground — called also *sonic bang*

**son–in–law** \ˈsən-ən-ˌlȯ\ *noun, plural* **sons–in–law** (14th century)
: the husband of one's daughter

**son·less** \ˈsən-ləs\ *adjective* (14th century)
: not possessing or never having had a son

**son·ly** \-lē\ *adjective* (15th century)
: FILIAL

**son·net** \ˈsä-nət\ *noun* [Italian *sonetto*, from Old Provençal *sonet* little song, from *son* sound, song, from Latin *sonus* sound] (1557)
: a fixed verse form of Italian origin consisting of fourteen lines that are typically five-foot iambics rhyming according to a prescribed scheme; *also* : a poem in this pattern

**son·ne·teer** \ˌsä-nə-ˈtir\ *noun* (1665)
**1** : a composer of sonnets
**2** : a minor or insignificant poet
— **son·ne·teer·ing** \-iŋ\ *noun*

**sonnet sequence** *noun* (1881)
: a series of sonnets often having a unifying theme

**son·ny** \ˈsə-nē\ *noun* (1850)
: a young boy — usually used in address

**so·no·buoy** \ˈsä-nə-ˌbȯi, -ˌbü-ē\ *noun* (1945)
: a buoy equipped for detecting underwater sounds and transmitting them by radio

**son of a bitch** \ˈsən-ə-və-ˌbich *also* ˈsəm-ˌbich; *as an interjection* ˌsən-ə-və-ˈbich\ *noun, plural* **sons of bitch·es** \ˌsən-zə-ˈbi-chəz\ (1671)
: BASTARD 3 — sometimes considered vulgar; sometimes used interjectionally to express surprise or disappointment

**son of a gun** \ˈsən-ə-və-ˌgən; *as an interjection* ˌsən-ə-və-ˈgən\ *noun, plural* **sons of guns** (1708)
— usually used as a mild or euphemistic alternative to *son of a bitch;* sometimes used interjectionally to express surprise or disappointment

**son of God** (14th century)
**1** *often S capitalized* : a superhuman or divine being (as an angel)
**2** *S capitalized* : MESSIAH 1
**3** : a person established in the love of God by divine promise

**son of man** (14th century)
**1** : a human being
**2** *often S capitalized* : God's messiah destined to preside over the final judgment of mankind

**sono·gram** \ˈsä-nə-ˌgram\ *noun* (1956)
: an image produced by ultrasound

**so·nog·ra·phy** \sō-ˈnä-grə-fē\ *noun* (1977)
: ULTRASOUND 2

**so·nor·i·ty** \sə-ˈnȯr-ə-tē, -ˈnär-\ *noun, plural* **-ties** (circa 1623)
**1** : the quality or state of being sonorous : RESONANCE
**2** : a sonorous tone or speech

**so·no·rous** \sə-ˈnȯr-əs, -ˈnȯr-; ˈsä-nə-rəs\ *adjective* [Latin *sonorus;* akin to Latin *sonus* sound] (1611)
**1** : producing sound (as when struck)
**2** : full or loud in sound
**3** : imposing or impressive in effect or style
**4** : having a high or an indicated degree of sonority ⟨*sonorous* sounds such as \ä\ and \ȯ\⟩
— **so·no·rous·ly** *adverb*
— **so·no·rous·ness** *noun*

**son·ship** \ˈsən-ˌship\ *noun* (1587)
: the relationship of son to father

**sonsy** *or* **sons·ie** \ˈsän(t)-sē\ *adjective* [Scots *sons* health] (1725)
*chiefly dialect* : BUXOM, COMELY

**soon** \ˈsün, *especially New England* ˈsu̇n\ *adverb* [Middle English *soone*, from Old English *sōna;* akin to Old High German *sān* immediately] (before 12th century)
**1 a** *obsolete* : at once : IMMEDIATELY **b** : before long : without undue time lapse ⟨*soon* after sunrise⟩
**2** : in a prompt manner : SPEEDILY ⟨as *soon* as possible⟩ ⟨the *sooner* the better⟩
**3** *archaic* : before the usual time

◇ **WORD HISTORY**
**sonar** The shadowy history of acronymic words such as *sonar* that have grown out of secret government projects sets many pitfalls for the etymologist. When F.V. ("Ted") Hunt, the director of the Harvard Underwater Sound Laboratory, coined *sonar*, most likely in 1942, he applied it to a specific piece of scanning equipment rather than the general technique of active echolocation, perhaps having in mind the words *sonic, azimuth,* and *range.* Years later Hunt recalled that he intended it as a phonetic analogue to *radar* (*radio detection and ranging*), and that *sonar* had a more pleasing sound than *sodar.* The interpretation of *sonar* as *sound navigation and ranging* was promulgated by the U.S. Navy only after the fact. *Asdic,* the British counterpart to *sonar* but developed decades earlier, also has an involved history. After Winston Churchill uttered what had long been a top secret term in the House of Commons in 1939, the British Admiralty said that *asdic* stood for *Allied Submarine Detection Investigation Committee,* allegedly formed during World War I. But no such committee ever existed. First noted as *asdics* in a now declassified report of 1918, the word appears to have been coined from *Anti-Submarine Division,* an Admiralty department, with *-ics* extracted from *supersonics.*

**4 :** in agreement with one's choice or preference **:** WILLINGLY ⟨I'd just as *soon* walk as drive⟩

**soon·er** \'sü-nər\ *noun* [*sooner,* comparative of *soon*] (1890)
**1 :** a person settling on land in the early West before its official opening to settlement in order to gain the prior claim allowed by law to the first settler after official opening
**2** *capitalized* **:** a native or resident of Oklahoma — used as a nickname

**sooner or later** *adverb* (1577)
**:** at some uncertain future time **:** SOMETIME

**¹soot** \'sút, 'sət, 'süt\ *noun* [Middle English, from Old English *sōt;* akin to Old Irish *suide* soot, Old English *sittan* to sit] (before 12th century)
**:** a black substance formed by combustion or separated from fuel during combustion, rising in fine particles, and adhering to the sides of the chimney or pipe conveying the smoke; *especially* **:** the fine powder consisting chiefly of carbon that colors smoke

**²soot** *transitive verb* (1602)
**:** to coat or cover with soot

**¹sooth** \'süth\ *adjective* [Middle English, from Old English *sōth;* akin to Old High German *sand* true, Latin *esse* to be] (before 12th century)
**1** *archaic* **:** TRUE
**2** *archaic* **:** SOFT, SWEET

**²sooth** *noun* (before 12th century)
**1 :** TRUTH, REALITY
**2** *obsolete* **:** BLANDISHMENT

**soothe** \'süth\ *verb* **soothed; sooth·ing** [Middle English *sothen* to verify, from Old English *sōthian,* from *sōth*] (1697)
*transitive verb*
**1 :** to please by or as if by attention or concern **:** PLACATE
**2 :** RELIEVE, ALLEVIATE
**3 :** to bring comfort, solace, or reassurance to
*intransitive verb*
**:** to bring peace, composure, or quietude
**— sooth·er** *noun*

**sooth·fast** \'süth-ˌfast\ *adjective* (before 12th century)
**1** *archaic* **:** TRUE
**2** *archaic* **:** TRUTHFUL

**sooth·ing** \'sü-thiŋ\ *adjective* (1749)
**:** tending to soothe; *also* **:** having a sedative effect ⟨*soothing* syrup⟩
**— sooth·ing·ly** \-thiŋ-lē\ *adverb*
**— sooth·ing·ness** *noun*

**sooth·ly** \'süth-lē\ *adverb* (before 12th century)
*archaic* **:** in truth **:** TRULY

**sooth·say·er** \-ˌsā-ər, -ˌse(-ə)r\ *noun* (14th century)
**:** a person who predicts the future by magical, intuitive, or more rational means **:** PROGNOSTICATOR

**sooth·say·ing** \-ˌsā-iŋ\ *noun* (15th century)
**1 :** the act of foretelling events
**2 :** PREDICTION, PROPHECY
**— sooth·say** \-ˌsā\ *intransitive verb*

**sooty** \'sú-tē, 'sə-, 'sü-\ *adjective* **soot·i·er; -est** (13th century)
**1 a :** of, relating to, or producing soot **b :** soiled with soot
**2 :** of the color of soot
**— soot·i·ly** \-tᵊl-ē\ *adverb*
**— soot·i·ness** \-tē-nəs\ *noun*

**sooty mold** *noun* (1901)
**:** a dark growth of fungus mycelium growing in insect honeydew on plants; *also* **:** a fungus producing such growth

**sooty tern** *noun* (1785)
**:** a widely distributed tern (*Sterna fuscata*) of tropical oceans that is blackish above and white below — called also *wideawake*

**¹sop** \'säp\ *noun* [Middle English *soppe,* from Old English *sopp;* akin to Old English *sūpan* to swallow — more at SUP] (before 12th century)

**1** *chiefly dialect* **:** a piece of food dipped or steeped in a liquid
**2 :** a conciliatory or propitiatory bribe, gift, or gesture

**²sop** *transitive verb* **sopped; sop·ping** (circa 1529)
**1 a :** to steep or dip in or as if in liquid **b :** to wet thoroughly **:** SOAK
**2 :** MOP a
**3 :** to give a bribe or conciliatory gift to

**so·pai·pil·la** \ˌsō-pī-'pē-yə, -'pēl-yə\ *or* **so·pa·pil·la** \ˌsō-pə-\ *noun* [American Spanish *sopaipilla,* diminutive of Spanish *sopaipa* fritter soaked in honey, from *sopa* food soaked in milk, of Germanic origin; akin to Old English *sūpan* to swallow] (circa 1940)
**:** a square of deep-fried dough often sweetened and eaten as dessert

**soph·ism** \'sä-ˌfi-zəm\ *noun* (15th century)
**1 :** an argument apparently correct in form but actually invalid; *especially* **:** such an argument used to deceive
**2 :** SOPHISTRY 1

**soph·ist** \'sä-fist\ *noun* [Latin *sophista,* from Greek *sophistēs,* literally, expert, wise man, from *sophizesthai* to become wise, deceive, from *sophos* clever, wise] (1542)
**1** *capitalized* **:** any of a class of ancient Greek teachers of rhetoric, philosophy, and the art of successful living prominent about the middle of the 5th century B.C. for their adroit subtle and allegedly often specious reasoning
**2 :** PHILOSOPHER, THINKER
**3 :** a captious or fallacious reasoner

**so·phis·tic** \sä-'fis-tik, sə-\ *or* **so·phis·ti·cal** \-ti-kəl\ *adjective* (15th century)
**1 :** of or relating to sophists, sophistry, or the ancient Sophists ⟨*sophistic* rhetoric⟩ ⟨*sophistic* subtleties⟩
**2 :** plausible but fallacious ⟨*sophistic* reasoning⟩
**— so·phis·ti·cal·ly** \-ti-k(ə-)lē\ *adverb*

**¹so·phis·ti·cate** \sə-'fis-tə-ˌkāt\ *transitive verb* **-cat·ed; -cat·ing** [Middle English, from Medieval Latin *sophisticatus,* past participle of *sophisticare,* from Latin *sophisticus* sophistic, from Greek *sophistikos,* from *sophistēs* sophist] (15th century)
**1 :** to alter deceptively; *especially* **:** ADULTERATE
**2 :** to deprive of genuineness, naturalness, or simplicity; *especially* **:** to deprive of naïveté and make worldly-wise **:** DISILLUSION
**3 :** to make complicated or complex

**²so·phis·ti·cate** \-ti-kət, -tə-ˌkāt\ *noun* (1923)
**:** a sophisticated person

**so·phis·ti·cat·ed** \-tə-ˌkā-təd\ *adjective* [Medieval Latin *sophisticatus*] (1601)
**1 :** not in a natural, pure, or original state **:** ADULTERATED ⟨a *sophisticated* oil⟩
**2 :** deprived of native or original simplicity: as **a :** highly complicated or developed **:** COMPLEX ⟨*sophisticated* electronic devices⟩ **b :** having a refined knowledge of the ways of the world cultivated especially through wide experience ⟨a *sophisticated* lady⟩
**3 :** devoid of grossness: as **a :** finely experienced and aware ⟨a *sophisticated* columnist⟩ **b :** intellectually appealing ⟨a *sophisticated* novel⟩ ☆
**— so·phis·ti·cat·ed·ly** *adverb*

**so·phis·ti·ca·tion** \sə-ˌfis-tə-'kā-shən\ *noun* (15th century)
**1 a :** the use of sophistry **:** sophistic reasoning **b :** SOPHISM, QUIBBLE
**2 :** the process of making impure or weak **:** ADULTERATION
**3 :** the process or result of becoming cultured, knowledgeable, or disillusioned; *especially* **:** CULTIVATION, URBANITY
**4 :** the process or result of becoming more complex, developed, or subtle

**soph·ist·ry** \'sä-fə-strē\ *noun* (14th century)
**1 :** subtly deceptive reasoning or argumentation

**2 :** SOPHISM 1

**soph·o·more** \'säf-ˌmōr, -ˌmor *also* 'sof- *or* 'sä-fə- *or* 'sò-fə-\ *noun* [perhaps from Greek *sophos* wise + *mōros* foolish] (1688)
**:** a student in the second year at college or a 4-year secondary school

**soph·o·mor·ic** \ˌsäf-'mōr-ik, -'mòr-, -'mär- *also* ˌsof- *or* ˌsä-fə- *or* ˌsò-fə-\ *adjective* (1813)
**1 :** conceited and overconfident of knowledge but poorly informed and immature
**2 :** of, relating to, or characteristic of a sophomore ⟨a *sophomoric* prank⟩

**So·pho·ni·as** \ˌsä-fə-'nī-əs, ˌsō-\ *noun* [Late Latin, from Greek, from Hebrew *Sĕphanyāh*] **:** ZEPHANIAH

**so·phy** \'sō-fē\ *noun* [Persian *Safī*] (1534)
*archaic* **:** a sovereign of Persia

**-sophy** *noun combining form* [Middle English *-sophie,* from Old French, from Latin *-sophia,* from Greek, from *sophia* wisdom, from *sophos*]
**:** knowledge **:** wisdom **:** science ⟨anthropo*sophy*⟩

**so·pite** \sō-'pīt\ *transitive verb* **so·pit·ed; so·pit·ing** [Latin *sopitus,* past participle of *sopire* to put to sleep; akin to Latin *sopor* deep sleep] (1542)
**1** *archaic* **:** to put to sleep **:** LULL
**2** *archaic* **:** to put an end to (as a claim) **:** SETTLE

**sop·o·rif·er·ous** \ˌsä-pə-'ri-f(ə-)rəs\ *adjective* [Latin *soporifer* soporiferous, from *sopor* + *-fer* -ferous] (1590)
**:** SOPORIFIC
**— sop·o·rif·er·ous·ness** *noun*

**¹sop·o·rif·ic** \-'ri-fik\ *adjective* [probably from French *soporifique,* from Latin *sopor* deep sleep; akin to Latin *somnus* sleep — more at SOMNOLENT] (1665)
**1 a :** causing or tending to cause sleep **b :** tending to dull awareness or alertness
**2 :** of, relating to, or marked by sleepiness or lethargy

**²soporific** *noun* (circa 1727)
**:** a soporific agent; *specifically* **:** HYPNOTIC 1

**sop·ping** \'sä-piŋ\ *adjective* (1877)
**:** wet through **:** SOAKING

**sop·py** \'sä-pē\ *adjective* **sop·pi·er; -est** (1823)
**1 a :** soaked through **:** SATURATED **b :** very wet
**2 :** SENTIMENTAL, MAWKISH
**— sop·pi·ness** \-nəs\ *noun*

**so·pra·ni·no** \ˌsō-prə-'nē-(ˌ)nō, ˌsä-\ *noun, plural* **-nos** [Italian, diminutive of *soprano*] (1905)
**:** a musical instrument (as a recorder or saxophone) higher in pitch than the soprano

**¹so·pra·no** \sə-'pra-(ˌ)nō, -'prä-\ *adjective* [Italian, adjective & noun, from *sopra* above, from Latin *supra* — more at SUPRA-] (1730)
**:** relating to or having the range or part of a soprano

---

☆ **SYNONYMS**
**Sophisticated, worldly-wise, blasé** mean experienced in the ways of the world. SOPHISTICATED often implies refinement, urbanity, cleverness, and cultivation ⟨guests at her salon were usually rich and *sophisticated*⟩. WORLDLY-WISE suggests a close and practical knowledge of the affairs and manners of society and an inclination toward materialism ⟨a *worldly-wise* woman with a philosophy of personal independence⟩. BLASÉ implies a lack of responsiveness to common joys as a result of a real or affected surfeit of experience and cultivation ⟨*blasé* travelers who claimed to have been everywhere⟩.

---

**²soprano** *noun, plural* **-nos** (1738)
**1 :** the highest singing voice of women, boys, or castrati; *also* **:** a person having this voice
**2 :** the highest voice part in a 4-part chorus
**3 :** a member of a family of instruments having the highest range

**so·ra** \'sōr-ə, 'sȯr-\ *noun* [origin unknown] (1705)
**:** a small short-billed North American rail (*Porzana carolina*) common in marshes

**sorb** \'sȯrb\ *transitive verb* [back-formation from *absorb* & *adsorb*] (1909)
**:** to take up and hold by either adsorption or absorption
— **sorb·abil·i·ty** \,sȯr-bə-'bi-lə-tē\ *noun*
— **sorb·able** \'sȯr-bə-bəl\ *adjective*

**Sorb** \'sȯrb\ *noun* [German *Sorbe,* from Sorbian *serbje*] (1843)
**1 :** WEND
**2 :** WENDISH
— **Sor·bi·an** \'sȯr-bē-ən\ *adjective or noun*

**sor·bate** \'sȯr-,bāt, 'sȯr-bət\ *noun* (circa 1823)
**:** a salt or ester of sorbic acid — compare POTASSIUM SORBATE

**sor·bent** \'sȯr-bənt\ *noun* [Latin *sorbent-, sorbens,* present participle of *sorbēre* to suck up — more at ABSORB] (circa 1856)
**:** a substance that sorbs

**sor·bet** \sȯr-'bā *also* 'sȯr-bət\ *noun* [Middle French, from Old Italian *sorbetto,* from Turkish *şerbet* — more at SHERBET] (1864)
**:** a fruit-flavored ice served as a dessert or between courses as a palate refresher

**sor·bic acid** \'sȯr-bik-\ *noun* [*sorb* fruit of the service or related trees, from French *sorbe,* from Latin *sorbum*] (1815)
**:** a crystalline acid $C_6H_8O_2$ obtained from the unripe fruits of the mountain ash or synthesized and used especially as a fungicide and food preservative

**sor·bi·tol** \'sȯr-bə-,tȯl, -,tōl\ *noun* [*sorb* fruit of the service or related trees + *-itol*] (1895)
**:** a faintly sweet alcohol $C_6H_{14}O_6$ that occurs in some fruits, is made synthetically, and is used especially as a humectant and softener and in making ascorbic acid

**sor·cer·er** \'sȯr-sə-rər, 'sȯrs-rər\ *noun* (15th century)
**:** a person who practices sorcery **:** WIZARD

**sor·cer·ess** \-rəs\ *noun* (14th century)
**:** a woman who is a sorcerer

**sor·cer·ous** \-rəs\ *adjective* (1546)
**:** of or relating to sorcery **:** MAGICAL

**sor·cery** \-rē\ *noun* [Middle English *sorcerie,* from Middle French, from *sorcier* sorcerer, from (assumed) Vulgar Latin *sortiarius,* from Latin *sort-, sors* chance, lot — more at SERIES] (14th century)
**1 :** the use of power gained from the assistance or control of evil spirits especially for divining **:** NECROMANCY
**2 :** MAGIC 2a

**sor·did** \'sȯr-dəd\ *adjective* [Latin *sordidus,* from *sordes* dirt — more at SWART] (1609)
**1 :** marked by baseness or grossness **:** VILE ⟨*sordid* motives⟩
**2 a :** DIRTY, FILTHY **b :** WRETCHED, SQUALID
**3 :** meanly avaricious **:** COVETOUS
**4 :** of a dull or muddy color
***synonym*** see MEAN
— **sor·did·ly** *adverb*
— **sor·did·ness** *noun*

**sor·di·no** \sȯr-'dē-(,)nō\ *noun, plural* **-di·ni** \-(,)nē\ [Italian, from *sordo* silent, from Latin *surdus*] (circa 1801)
**:** MUTE 3

**¹sore** \'sōr, 'sȯr\ *adjective* **sor·er; sor·est** [Middle English *sor,* from Old English *sār;* akin to Old High German *sēr* sore and probably to Old Irish *saeth* distress] (before 12th century)
**1 a :** causing pain or distress **b :** painfully sensitive **:** TENDER ⟨*sore* muscles⟩ **c :** hurt or inflamed so as to be or seem painful ⟨*sore* runny eyes⟩ ⟨a dog limping on a *sore* leg⟩

**2 :** attended by difficulties, hardship, or exertion
**3 :** ANGRY, IRKED ⟨a *sore* loser⟩
— **sore·ness** *noun*

**²sore** *noun* (before 12th century)
**1 :** a localized sore spot on the body; *especially* **:** one (as an ulcer) with the tissues ruptured or abraded and usually with infection
**2 :** a source of pain or vexation **:** AFFLICTION

**³sore** *adverb* (before 12th century)
**:** SORELY

**sore·head** \'sōr-,hed, 'sȯr-\ *noun* (1848)
**:** a person easily angered or disgruntled
— **sorehead** *or* **sore·head·ed** \-'he-dəd\ *adjective*

**sore·ly** \'sōr-lē, 'sȯr-\ *adverb* (before 12th century)
**1 :** in a sore manner **:** PAINFULLY
**2 :** VERY, EXTREMELY ⟨*sorely* needed changes⟩

**sore throat** *noun* (1686)
**:** pain in the throat due to inflammation of the fauces and pharynx

**sor·ghum** \'sȯr-gəm\ *noun* [New Latin, from Italian *sorgo,* from (assumed) Vulgar Latin *Syricum* (*granum*), literally, Syrian grain] (1597)
**1 :** any of an economically important genus (*Sorghum*) of Old World tropical grasses similar to Indian corn in habit but with the spikelets in pairs on a hairy rachis; *especially* **:** any of various cultivars (as grain sorghum or sorgo) derived from a wild form (*S. bicolor* synonym *S. vulgare*)
**2 :** syrup from the juice of a sorgo that resembles cane syrup
**3 :** something cloyingly sentimental

**sor·go** \'sȯr-(,)gō\ *noun* [Italian] (circa 1760)
**:** a sorghum cultivated primarily for the sweet juice in its stems from which sugar and syrup are made but also used for fodder and silage — called also *sweet sorghum*

**sorghum 1**

**so·ri·tes** \sə-'rī-(,)tēz\ *noun, plural* **sorites** [Latin, from Greek *sōritēs,* from *sōros* heap] (1551)
**:** an argument consisting of propositions so arranged that the predicate of any one forms the subject of the next and the conclusion unites the subject of the first proposition with the predicate of the last

**So·rop·ti·mist** \sə-'räp-tə-mist, sō-\ *noun* [*Soroptimist* (Club)] (1924)
**:** a member of a service club composed of professional women and women business executives

**so·ro·ral** \sə-'rōr-əl, -'rȯr-\ *adjective* [Latin *soror* sister — more at SISTER] (1858)
**:** of, relating to, or characteristic of a sister **:** SISTERLY

**so·ro·rate** \sə-'rōr-ət, -'rȯr-\ *noun* [Latin *soror*] (1910)
**:** the marriage of one man to two or more sisters usually successively and after the first wife has been found to be barren or after her death

**so·ror·i·ty** \sə-'rȯr-ə-tē, -'rär-\ *noun, plural* **-ties** [Medieval Latin *sororitas* sisterhood, from Latin *soror* sister] (1900)
**:** a club of women; *specifically* **:** a women's student organization (as at a college) that is formed chiefly for social purposes and has a name consisting of Greek letters

**sorp·tion** \'sȯrp-shən\ *noun* [back-formation from *absorption* & *adsorption*] (1909)
**:** the process of sorbing **:** the state of being sorbed
— **sorp·tive** \'sȯrp-tiv\ *adjective*

**¹sor·rel** \'sȯr-əl, 'sär-\ *noun* [Middle English *sorelle,* from Middle French *sorel,* noun & adjective, from *sor* reddish brown] (15th century)

**1 :** a sorrel-colored animal; *especially* **:** a light bright chestnut horse often with white mane and tail — compare ¹CHESTNUT 4, ²BAY 1
**2 :** a brownish orange to light brown

**²sorrel** *noun* [Middle English *sorel,* from Middle French *surele,* from Old French *sur* sour, of Germanic origin; akin to Old High German *sūr* sour — more at SOUR] (15th century)
**:** any of various plants or plant parts with sour juice: as **a :** any of various docks (as *Rumex acetosa* and *R. acetosella*); *also* **:** the leaves used as a potherb **b :** WOOD SORREL

**sorrel tree** *noun* (1687)
**:** SOURWOOD

**¹sor·row** \'sär-(,)ō, 'sȯr-\ *noun* [Middle English *sorow,* from Old English *sorg;* akin to Old High German *sorga* sorrow] (before 12th century)
**1 a :** deep distress, sadness, or regret especially for the loss of someone or something loved **b :** resultant unhappy or unpleasant state ⟨to his *sorrow* he lost his temper⟩
**2 :** a cause of grief or sadness
**3 :** a display of grief or sadness ☆

**²sorrow** *intransitive verb* (before 12th century)
**:** to feel or express sorrow
— **sor·row·er** \'sär-ə-wər, 'sȯr-\ *noun*

**sor·row·ful** \-ō-fəl, -ə-fəl\ *adjective* (before 12th century)
**1 :** full of or marked by sorrow
**2 :** expressive of or inducing sorrow
— **sor·row·ful·ly** \-f(ə-)lē\ *adverb*
— **sor·row·ful·ness** \-fəl-nəs\ *noun*

**sor·ry** \'sär-ē, 'sȯr-\ *adjective* **sor·ri·er; -est** [Middle English *sory,* from Old English *sārig,* from *sār* sore] (before 12th century)
**1 :** feeling sorrow, regret, or penitence
**2 :** MOURNFUL, SAD
**3 :** inspiring sorrow, pity, scorn, or ridicule
***synonym*** see CONTEMPTIBLE
— **sor·ri·ly** \-ə-lē\ *adverb*
— **sor·ri·ness** \-ē-nəs\ *noun*

**¹sort** \'sȯrt\ *noun* [Middle English, from Middle French *sorte,* probably from Medieval Latin *sort-, sors,* from Latin, chance, lot — more at SERIES] (14th century)
**1 a :** a group set up on the basis of any characteristic in common **:** CLASS, KIND **b :** an instance of a kind ⟨a *sort* of black Paul Bunyan, towering 6′10″ —Jack Olsen⟩ **c :** PERSON, INDIVIDUAL ⟨he's not a bad *sort*⟩
**2** *archaic* **:** GROUP, COMPANY
**3 a :** method or manner of acting **:** WAY, MANNER **b :** CHARACTER, NATURE ⟨people of an evil *sort*⟩
**4 a :** a letter or character that is one element of a font **b :** a character or piece of type that is not part of a regular font
**5 :** an instance of sorting ⟨a numeric *sort* of a data file⟩
***synonym*** see TYPE
— **after a sort :** in a rough or haphazard way
— **of sorts** *or* **of a sort :** of an inconsequential or mediocre quality ⟨a poet *of sorts*⟩

---

☆ **SYNONYMS**
**Sorrow, grief, anguish, woe, regret** mean distress of mind. SORROW implies a sense of loss or a sense of guilt and remorse ⟨a family united in *sorrow* upon the patriarch's death⟩. GRIEF implies poignant sorrow for an immediate cause ⟨the inexpressible *grief* of the bereaved parents⟩. ANGUISH suggests torturing grief or dread ⟨the *anguish* felt by the parents of the kidnapped child⟩. WOE is deep or inconsolable grief or misery ⟨cries of *woe* echoed throughout the bombed city⟩. REGRET implies pain caused by deep disappointment, fruitless longing, or unavailing remorse ⟨nagging *regret* for missed opportunities⟩.

**— out of sorts 1 :** somewhat ill **2 :** GROUCHY, IRRITABLE

**²sort** (14th century)
*transitive verb*
**1 a :** to put in a certain place or rank according to kind, class, or nature ⟨*sort* apples⟩ ⟨*sort* mail⟩ **b :** to arrange according to characteristics **:** CLASSIFY ⟨*sort* out colors⟩
**2** *chiefly Scottish* **:** to put to rights **:** put in order
**3 a :** to examine in order to clarify ⟨*sorting* out his problems⟩ **b :** to free of confusion **:** CLARIFY ⟨waited until things *sorted* themselves out⟩
*intransitive verb*
**1 :** to join or associate with others especially of the same kind ⟨*sort* with thieves⟩
**2 :** SUIT, AGREE
**— sort·able** \ˈsȯr-tə-bəl\ *adjective*
**— sort·er** *noun*

**sor·tie** \ˈsȯr-tē, sȯr-ˈtē\ *noun* [French, from Middle French, from *sortir* to escape] (1778)
**1 :** a sudden issuing of troops from a defensive position against the enemy
**2 :** one mission or attack by a single plane
**3 :** FORAY, RAID
**— sortie** *intransitive verb*

**sor·ti·lege** \ˈsȯr-tᵊl-ij, -ˌej\ *noun* [Middle English, from Medieval Latin *sortilegium*, from Latin *sortilegus* foretelling, from *sort-, sors* lot + *-i- + legere* to gather — more at LEGEND] (14th century)
**1 :** divination by lots
**2 :** SORCERY

**sor·ti·tion** \sȯr-ˈti-shən\ *noun* [Latin *sortition-, sortitio*, from *sortiri* to cast or draw lots, from *sort-, sors* lot] (1597)
**:** the act or an instance of casting lots

**sort of** \ˈsȯr-dəv, -dər\ *adverb* (1790)
**:** to a moderate degree **:** RATHER

**so·rus** \ˈsōr-əs, ˈsȯr-\ *noun, plural* **so·ri** \ˈsōr-ˌī, ˈsȯr-, -ˌē\ [New Latin, from Greek *sōros* heap] (1832)
**:** a cluster of plant reproductive bodies: as **a :** one of the dots on the underside of a fertile fern frond consisting of a cluster of sporangia **b :** a mass of spores bursting through the epidermis of the host plant of a parasitic fungus **c :** a cluster of gemmae on the thallus of a lichen

**SOS** \ˌes-(ˌ)ō-ˈes\ *noun* (1910)
**1 :** an internationally recognized signal of distress in radio code ··· ——— ··· used especially by ships calling for help
**2 :** a call or request for help or rescue

**¹so–so** \ˈsō-ˈsō\ *adverb* (circa 1530)
**:** moderately well **:** TOLERABLY, PASSABLY

**²so–so** *adjective* (1542)
**:** neither very good nor very bad **:** MIDDLING

**¹so·ste·nu·to** \ˌsōs-tə-ˈnü-(ˌ)tō, ˌsȯs-\ *adjective or adverb* [Italian, from past participle of *sostenere* to sustain, from Latin *sustinēre*] (circa 1724)
**:** sustained to or beyond the note's full value — used as a direction in music

**²sostenuto** *noun* (1757)
**:** a movement or passage whose notes are markedly prolonged

**sot** \ˈsät\ *noun* [Middle English, fool, from Old English *sott*] (1592)
**:** a habitual drunkard

**so·te·ri·ol·o·gy** \sō-ˌtir-ē-ˈä-lə-jē\ *noun* [Greek *sōtērion* salvation (from *sōtēr* savior, preserver) + English *-logy* — more at CREOSOTE] (circa 1774)
**:** theology dealing with salvation especially as effected by Jesus Christ
**— so·te·ri·o·log·i·cal** \-ē-ə-ˈlä-ji-kəl\ *adjective*

**so that** *conjunction* (before 12th century)
**:** THAT 2a(1)

**So·tho** \ˈsō-(ˌ)tō\ *noun* (1928)
**1 :** any one of the Sotho languages and especially Sesotho

**2 :** a group of closely related Bantu languages of Lesotho, Botswana, and northern South Africa

**so·tol** \ˈsō-ˌtōl\ *noun* [American Spanish, from Nahuatl *zōtōlin* palm tree] (1881)
**:** any of several plants (genus *Dasylirion*) of the agave family of the southwestern U.S. and Mexico that resemble a yucca

**sot·tish** \ˈsä-tish\ *adjective* (1583)
**:** resembling a sot **:** DRUNKEN; *also* **:** DOLTISH, STUPID
**— sot·tish·ly** *adverb*
**— sot·tish·ness** *noun*

**sot·to vo·ce** \ˌsä-tō-ˈvō-chē\ *adverb or adjective* [Italian *sottovoce*, literally, under the voice] (1737)
**1 :** under the breath **:** in an undertone; *also* **:** in a private manner
**2 :** very softly — used as a direction in music

**sou** \ˈsü\ *noun, plural* **sous** \ˈsüz\ [French, from Old French *sol*, from Late Latin *solidus* solidus] (1814)
**1 :** ²SOL
**2 :** a 5-centime piece

**sou·bise** \sü-ˈbēz\ *noun* [French, from Charles de Rohan, Prince de *Soubise* (died 1787) French nobleman] (1822)
**:** a garnish or white sauce containing onions or onion purée

**sou·brette** \sü-ˈbret\ *noun* [French, from Provençal *soubreto*, feminine of *soubret* coy, from *soubra* to surmount, exceed, from Latin *superare* — more at INSUPERABLE] (1753)
**1 a :** a coquettish maid or frivolous young woman in comedies **b :** an actress who plays such a part
**2 :** a soprano who sings supporting roles in comic opera

**sou·bri·quet** \ˈsō-, ˌsō-, ˈsü-, ˌsü-\ *variant of* SOBRIQUET

**sou·chong** \ˈsü-ˌchȯŋ, -ˌshȯŋ\ *noun* [of Chinese origin; akin to Chinese (Beijing) *xiǎozhǒng*, literally, small sort] (1760)
**:** a tea made from the larger leaves of the shoot

**¹souf·flé** \sü-ˈflā, ˈsü-ˌ\ *noun* [French, from *soufflé*, past participle of *souffler* to blow, puff up, from Latin *sufflare*, from *sub- + flare* to blow — more at BLOW] (1813)
**:** a dish that is made from a sauce, egg yolks, beaten egg whites, and a flavoring or purée (as of seafood, fruit, or vegetables) and baked until puffed up

**²soufflé** *or* **souf·fléed** \-ˈflād, -ˌflād\ *adjective* (1888)
**:** puffed up by or in cooking

**sough** \ˈsaủ, ˈsəf\ *intransitive verb* [Middle English *swoughen*, from Old English *swōgan*; akin to Gothic *gaswogjan* to groan, Lithuanian *svagėti* to sound] (before 12th century)
**:** to make a moaning or sighing sound
**— sough** *noun*

**sought** *past and past participle of* SEEK

**souk** \ˈsük\ *noun* [Arabic *sūq* market] (1826)
**:** a marketplace in northern Africa or the Middle East; *also* **:** a stall in such a marketplace

**¹soul** \ˈsōl\ *noun* [Middle English *soule*, from Old English *sāwol*; akin to Old High German *sēula* soul] (before 12th century)
**1 :** the immaterial essence, animating principle, or actuating cause of an individual life
**2 a :** the spiritual principle embodied in human beings, all rational and spiritual beings, or the universe **b** *capitalized, Christian Science* **:** GOD 1b
**3 :** a person's total self
**4 a :** an active or essential part **b :** a moving spirit **:** LEADER
**5 a :** the moral and emotional nature of human beings **b :** the quality that arouses emotion and sentiment **c :** spiritual or moral force **:** FERVOR
**6 :** PERSON
**7 :** EXEMPLIFICATION, PERSONIFICATION ⟨she is the *soul* of integrity⟩
**8 a :** a strong positive feeling (as of intense sensitivity and emotional fervor) conveyed es-

pecially by black American performers **b :** NEGRITUDE **c :** SOUL MUSIC **d :** SOUL FOOD **e :** SOUL BROTHER

**²soul** *adjective* (1958)
**1 :** of, relating to, or characteristic of black Americans or their culture
**2 :** designed for or controlled by blacks ⟨*soul* radio stations⟩

**soul brother** *noun* (1959)
**:** a black male

**souled** \ˈsōld\ *adjective* (15th century)
**:** having a soul **:** possessing soul and feeling — usually used in combination ⟨whole-*souled* repentance⟩

**soul food** *noun* (1964)
**:** food (as chitterlings, ham hocks, and collard greens) traditionally eaten by southern black Americans

**soul·ful** \ˈsōl-fəl\ *adjective* (1860)
**:** full of or expressing feeling or emotion
**— soul·ful·ly** \-fə-lē\ *adverb*
**— soul·ful·ness** *noun*

**soul kiss** *noun* (circa 1948)
**:** FRENCH KISS

**soul·less** \ˈsōl-ləs\ *adjective* (15th century)
**:** having no soul or no greatness or warmth of mind or feeling
**— soul·less·ly** *adverb*
**— soul·less·ness** *noun*

**soul mate** *noun* (1822)
**:** a person temperamentally suited to another

**soul music** *noun* (1961)
**:** music that originated in black American gospel singing, is closely related to rhythm and blues, and is characterized by intensity of feeling and earthiness

**soul–search·ing** \ˈsōl-ˌsər-chiŋ\ *noun* (1924)
**:** examination of one's conscience especially with regard to motives and values

**¹sound** \ˈsaủnd\ *adjective* [Middle English, from Old English *gesund*; akin to Old High German *gisunt* healthy] (13th century)
**1 a :** free from injury or disease **:** exhibiting normal health **b :** free from flaw, defect, or decay ⟨*sound* timber⟩
**2 :** SOLID, FIRM; *also* **:** STABLE
**3 a :** free from error, fallacy, or misapprehension ⟨*sound* reasoning⟩ **b :** exhibiting or based on thorough knowledge and experience ⟨*sound* scholarship⟩ **c :** legally valid ⟨a *sound* title⟩ **d :** logically valid and having true premises **e :** agreeing with accepted views **:** ORTHODOX
**4 a :** THOROUGH **b :** deep and undisturbed ⟨a *sound* sleep⟩ **c :** HARD, SEVERE ⟨a *sound* whipping⟩
**5 :** showing good judgment or sense
*synonym* see HEALTHY, VALID
**— sound·ly** \ˈsaủn(d)-lē\ *adverb*
**— sound·ness** \ˈsaủn(d)-nəs\ *noun*

**²sound** *adverb* (14th century)
**:** to the full extent **:** THOROUGHLY ⟨*sound* asleep⟩

**³sound** *noun* [Middle English *soun*, from Old French *son*, from Latin *sonus*, from *sonare* to sound; akin to Old English *swinn* melody, Sanskrit *svanati* it sounds] (13th century)
**1 a :** a particular auditory impression **:** TONE **b :** the sensation perceived by the sense of hearing **c :** mechanical radiant energy that is transmitted by longitudinal pressure waves in a material medium (as air) and is the objective cause of hearing
**2 a :** a speech sound ⟨a peculiar *r-sound*⟩ **b :** value in terms of speech sounds ⟨*-cher* of *teacher* and *-ture* of *creature* have the same *sound*⟩
**3** *archaic* **:** RUMOR, FAME
**4 a :** meaningless noise **b** *obsolete* **:** MEANING **c :** the impression conveyed **:** IMPORT
**5 :** hearing distance **:** EARSHOT

---

\ə\ abut \ᵊ\ kitten \ər\ further \a\ ash \ā\ ace
\ä\ mop, mar \aủ\ out \ch\ chin \e\ bet \ē\ easy
\g\ go \i\ hit \ī\ ice \j\ job \ŋ\ sing \ō\ go
\ȯ\ law \ȯi\ boy \th\ thin \t̲h̲\ the \ü\ loot \ủ\ foot
\y\ yet \zh\ vision *see also* Guide to Pronunciation

**6 :** recorded auditory material

**7 :** a particular musical style characteristic of an individual, a group, or an area ⟨the Nashville *sound*⟩

⁴**sound** (13th century)
*transitive verb*
**1 a :** to cause to sound ⟨*sound* a trumpet⟩ **b :** PRONOUNCE 3a
**2 :** to put into words **:** VOICE
**3 a :** to make known **:** PROCLAIM **b :** to order, signal, or indicate by a sound ⟨*sound* the alarm⟩
**4 :** to examine by causing to emit sounds ⟨*sound* the lungs⟩
**5** *chiefly British* **:** to convey the impression of **:** sound like ⟨that *sounds* a logical use of resources —*Economist*⟩
*intransitive verb*
**1 a :** to make a sound **b :** RESOUND **c :** to give a summons by sound ⟨the bugle *sounds* to battle⟩
**2 :** to make or convey an impression especially when heard ⟨it *sounds* good to me⟩ ⟨you *sound* just like your mother⟩
— **sound·able** \'saun-də-bəl\ *adjective*

⁵**sound** *noun* [Middle English, from Old English *sund* swimming, sea & Old Norse *sund* swimming, strait; akin to Old English *swimman* to swim] (14th century)
**1 a :** a long broad inlet of the ocean generally parallel to the coast **b :** a long passage of water connecting two larger bodies (as a sea with the ocean) or separating a mainland and an island
**2 :** the air bladder of a fish

⁶**sound** *verb* [Middle English, from Middle French *sonder*, from *sonde* sounding line, probably of Germanic origin; akin to Old English *sundlīne* sounding line, *sund* sea] (15th century)
*transitive verb*
**1 :** to measure the depth of **:** FATHOM
**2 :** to try to find out the views or intentions of **:** PROBE — often used with *out*
**3 :** to explore or examine ⟨a body cavity⟩ with a sound
*intransitive verb*
**1 a :** to ascertain the depth of water especially with a sounding line **b :** to look into or investigate the possibility ⟨sent commissioners . . . to *sound* for peace —Thomas Jefferson⟩
**2 :** to dive down suddenly — used of a fish or whale

⁷**sound** *noun* [French *sonde*, from Middle French, literally, sounding line] (1739)
**:** an elongated instrument for exploring or sounding body cavities

**sound·alike** \'saun-də-,līk\ *noun* (1970)
**:** one that sounds like another

**sound–and–light show** *noun* (1967)
**:** SON ET LUMIÈRE

**sound barrier** *noun* (1939)
**:** a sudden large increase in aerodynamic drag that occurs as the speed of an aircraft approaches the speed of sound

**sound bite** *noun* (1972)
**:** a brief recorded statement (as by a public figure) broadcast especially on a television news program; *also* **:** a brief catchy comment suitable for use as a sound bite

**sound·board** \'saun(d)-,bōrd, -,bord\ *noun* (1504)
**1 :** a thin resonant board (as the belly of a violin) so placed in an instrument as to reinforce its tones by sympathetic vibration — see VIOLIN illustration
**2 :** SOUNDING BOARD 1a

**sound bow** *noun* (1688)
**:** the thick part of a bell against which the clapper strikes

**sound box** *noun* (circa 1875)
**1 :** a device in an early phonograph for producing sound from a record by using the vibration of a needle to move a diaphragm

**2 :** a hollow chamber in a musical instrument for increasing its sonority

**sound effects** *noun plural* (1909)
**:** effects that are imitative of sounds called for in the script of a dramatic production (as a radio show) and that enhance the production's illusion of reality

**sound·er** \'saun-dər\ *noun* (1575)
**:** one that sounds; *specifically* **:** a device for making soundings

**sound hole** *noun* (1611)
**:** an opening in the top surface of a stringed instrument (as a violin) to enhance vibration and resonance — see VIOLIN illustration

¹**sound·ing** \'saun-diŋ\ *adjective* (14th century)
**1 :** RESONANT, SONOROUS
**2 a :** POMPOUS **b :** IMPOSING
— **sound·ing·ly** \-diŋ-lē\ *adverb*

²**sounding** *noun* (15th century)
**1 a :** measurement of depth especially with a sounding line **b :** the depth so ascertained **c** *plural* **:** a place or part of a body of water where a hand sounding line will reach bottom
**2 :** measurement of atmospheric conditions at various heights
**3 :** a probe, test, or sampling of opinion or intention

**sounding board** *noun* (1729)
**1 a :** a structure behind or over a pulpit, rostrum, or platform to give distinctness and sonority to sound **b :** a device or agency that helps propagate opinions or utterances **c :** a person or group on whom one tries out an idea or opinion as a means of evaluating it
**2 :** SOUNDBOARD 1

**sounding line** *noun* (14th century)
**:** a line or wire weighted at one end for sounding

**sounding rocket** *noun* (circa 1945)
**:** a rocket used to obtain information concerning atmospheric conditions at various altitudes

¹**sound·less** \'saun(d)-ləs\ *adjective* [⁶sound] (1586)
**:** incapable of being sounded **:** UNFATHOMABLE

²**soundless** *adjective* [³sound] (1601)
**:** making no sound **:** SILENT
— **sound·less·ly** *adverb*

**sound·man** \'saun(d)-,man\ *noun* (1929)
**:** a person who controls the volume and tone of sound picked up by a microphone (as in a recording studio or on a motion-picture set) for recording

**sound off** *intransitive verb* (1909)
**1 :** to play three chords before and after marching up and down a line of troops during a ceremonial parade or formal guard mount
**2 :** to count cadence while marching
**3 a :** to speak up in a loud voice **b :** to voice one's opinions freely and vigorously

**sound pressure** *noun* (1893)
**:** the difference between the actual pressure at any point in the field of a sound wave at any instant and the average pressure at that point

¹**sound·proof** \'saun(d)-,prüf\ *adjective* (circa 1878)
**:** impervious to sound

²**soundproof** *transitive verb* (1919)
**:** to insulate so as to obstruct the passage of sound

**sound·stage** \'saun(d)-,stāj\ *noun* (1931)
**:** the part of a motion-picture studio in which a production is filmed

**sound track** *noun* (circa 1929)
**1 :** the area on a motion-picture film or television videotape that carries the sound record
**2 :** the sound recorded on a sound track; *especially* **:** the music on a sound track

**sound truck** *noun* (1936)
**:** a truck equipped with a loudspeaker

**sound wave** *noun* (1848)
**1 :** ¹SOUND 1a
**2** *plural* **:** longitudinal pressure waves in any material medium regardless of whether they

constitute audible sound ⟨earthquake waves and ultrasonic waves are sometimes called *sound waves*⟩

**soup** \'süp\ *noun* [Middle English *soupe*, from Middle French, sop, soup, of Germanic origin; akin to Old Norse *soppa* soup, Old English *sopp* sop — more at SUP] (14th century)
**1 :** a liquid food especially with a meat, fish, or vegetable stock as a base and often containing pieces of solid food
**2 :** something (as a heavy fog or nitroglycerine) having or suggesting the consistency or nutrient qualities of soup
**3 :** an unfortunate predicament

**soup·çon** \süp-'sōⁿ, 'süp-,sän\ *noun* [French, literally, suspicion, from (assumed) Vulgar Latin *suspection-, suspectio*, from Latin *suspicere* to suspect — more at SUSPECT] (1766)
**:** a little bit **:** TRACE

**soup du jour** \,süp-də-'zhür\ *noun* [part translation of French *soupe du jour* soup of the day] (circa 1945)
**:** a soup that is offered by a restaurant on a particular day

**soup kitchen** *noun* (1839)
**:** an establishment dispensing minimum dietary essentials (as soup and bread) to the needy

**soup·spoon** \'süp-,spün\ *noun* (1705)
**:** a spoon with a large or rounded bowl for eating soup

**soup up** *transitive verb* [*soup* (drug injected into a racehorse to improve its performance)] (circa 1933)
**:** to increase the power or efficiency of ⟨*soup up* an engine⟩

**soupy** \'sü-pē\ *adjective* **soup·i·er; -est** (1869)
**1 :** having the consistency of soup
**2 :** densely foggy or cloudy
**3 :** overly sentimental

¹**sour** \'sau̇(-ə)r\ *adjective* [Middle English, from Old English *sūr;* akin to Old High German *sūr* sour, Lithuanian *sūrus* salty] (before 12th century)
**1 :** causing or characterized by the one of the four basic taste sensations that is produced chiefly by acids ⟨*sour* pickles⟩ — compare BITTER, SALT, SWEET
**2 a** (1) **:** having the acid taste or smell of or as if of fermentation **:** TURNED ⟨*sour* milk⟩ (2) **:** of or relating to fermentation **b :** smelling or tasting of decay **:** RANCID, ROTTEN ⟨*sour* breath⟩ **c** (1) **:** BAD, WRONG ⟨a project gone *sour*⟩ (2) **:** HOSTILE, DISENCHANTED ⟨went *sour* on Marxism⟩
**3 a :** UNPLEASANT, DISTASTEFUL **b :** CROSS, SULLEN **c :** not up to the usual, expected, or standard quality or pitch
**4 :** acid in reaction — used especially of soil
**5 :** containing malodorous sulfur compounds — used especially of petroleum products
— **sour·ish** \'sau̇(-ə)r-ish\ *adjective*
— **sour·ly** *adverb*
— **sour·ness** *noun*

²**sour** *noun* (before 12th century)
**1 a :** something sour **b :** the primary taste sensation produced by acid stimuli
**2 :** a cocktail consisting of a liquor (as whiskey), lemon or lime juice, sugar, and sometimes ice

³**sour** (14th century)
*intransitive verb*
**:** to become sour
*transitive verb*
**:** to make sour

**sour ball** *noun* (circa 1909)
**:** a spherical hard candy having a tart flavor

¹**source** \'sōrs, 'sors\ *noun* [Middle English *sours*, from Middle French *sors, sourse*, from Old French, from past participle of *sourdre* to rise, spring forth, from Latin *surgere* — more at SURGE] (14th century)

**1 a** : a generative force : CAUSE **b** (1) : a point of origin or procurement : BEGINNING (2) : one that initiates : AUTHOR; *also* : PROTOTYPE, MODEL (3) : one that supplies information
**2 a** : the point of origin of a stream of water : FOUNTAINHEAD **b** *archaic* : SPRING, FOUNT
**3** : a firsthand document or primary reference work
**4** : an electrode in a field-effect transistor that supplies the charge carriers for current flow — compare DRAIN, GATE
**synonym** see ORIGIN
— **source·less** \-ləs\ *adjective*
²**source** *transitive verb* **sourced; sourc·ing** (1957)
**1** : to specify the source of (as quoted material)
**2** : to obtain from a source ⟨metals *sourced* from abroad⟩
³**source** *adjective* (1959)
: of, relating to, or being a computer program in its original programming language ⟨*source* listing⟩ ⟨*source* code⟩
**source·book** \-,bùk\ *noun* (1899)
: a fundamental document or record (as of history, literature, art, or religion) on which subsequent writings, compositions, opinions, beliefs, or practices are based; *also* : a collection of such documents
**source language** *noun* (1953)
: a language which is to be translated into another language — compare TARGET LANGUAGE
**sour cherry** *noun* (circa 1884)
: a widely cultivated cherry (*Prunus cerasus*) that has a round crown and bright red to almost black soft-fleshed acid fruits; *also* : the fruit
**sour cream** *noun* (1855)
: a soured cream product produced by the action of lactobacilli
**sour·dough** \'saù(-ə)r-,dō, *1 is also* -'dō\ *noun* (14th century)
**1** : a leaven consisting of dough in which fermentation is active
**2** [from the use of sourdough for making bread in prospectors' camps] : a veteran inhabitant and especially an old-time prospector of Alaska or northwestern Canada
**sour grapes** *noun plural* [from the fable ascribed to Aesop of the fox who after finding himself unable to reach some grapes he had desired disparaged them as sour] (1760)
: disparagement of something that has proven unattainable
**sour gum** *noun* (1785)
: BLACK GUM
**sour mash** *noun* (1885)
: grain mash for brewing or distilling whose initial acidity has been adjusted to optimum condition for yeast fermentation by mash from a previous run
**sour orange** *noun* (1748)
: a citrus tree (*Citrus aurantium*) that is used especially as a stock in grafting citrus; *also* : its bitter fruit
**sour·puss** \'saù(-ə)r-,pùs\ *noun* [²*puss*] (1937)
: GROUCH, KILLJOY
**sour·sop** \'saù(-ə)r-,säp\ *noun* (1667)
: a small tropical American tree (*Annona muricata*) of the custard-apple family that has spicy odoriferous leaves; *also* : its large edible fruit that has fleshy spines and a slightly acid fibrous pulp
**sour·wood** \-,wùd\ *noun* (1709)
: a small U.S. tree (*Oxydendrum arboreum*) of the heath family with white flowers and sour-tasting leaves
**sous** \'sü\ *adjective* [French, preposition, literally, under, from Latin *subtus*, adverb, below, under; akin to Latin *sub* under — more at UP] (1687)
: being an assistant — used chiefly in titles ⟨a *sous*-chef⟩

**sou·sa·phone** \'sü-zə-,fōn, -sə-\ *noun* [John Philip *Sousa*] (1925)
: a large circular tuba that has a flared adjustable bell — compare HELICON
¹**souse** \'saùs\ *verb* **soused; sous·ing** [Middle English, from Middle French *souz, souce* pickling solution, of Germanic origin; akin to Old High German *sulza* brine, Old English *sealt* salt] (14th century)
*transitive verb*
**1** : PICKLE
**2 a** : to plunge in liquid : IMMERSE **b** : DRENCH, SATURATE
**3** : to make drunk : INEBRIATE
*intransitive verb*
: to become immersed or drenched
²**souse** *noun* (14th century)
**1** : something pickled; *especially* : seasoned and chopped pork trimmings, fish, or shellfish
**2** : an act of sousing : WETTING
**3 a** : a habitual drunkard **b** : a drinking spree : BINGE
³**souse** *verb* **soused; sous·ing** [Middle English *souce*, noun, start of a bird's flight, alteration of *sours*, from Middle French *sourse* source — more at SOURCE] (1583)
*intransitive verb*
*archaic* : to swoop down : PLUNGE
*transitive verb*
*archaic* : to swoop down on
**sou·tache** \sü-'tash\ *noun* [French, from Hungarian *sujtás*] (circa 1856)
: a narrow braid with herringbone pattern used as trimming
**sou·tane** \sü-'tän, -'tan\ *noun* [French, from Italian *sottana*, literally, undergarment, from feminine of *sottano* being underneath, from Medieval Latin *subtanus*, from Latin *subtus* underneath — more at SOUS] (1838)
: CASSOCK
**sou·ter** \'sü-tər\ *noun* [Middle English, from Old English *sūtere*, from Latin *sutor*, from *suere* to sew — more at SEW] (before 12th century)
*chiefly Scottish* : SHOEMAKER
¹**south** \'saùth\ *adverb* [Middle English, from Old English *sūth*; akin to Old High German *sund-* south and probably to Old English *sunne* sun] (before 12th century)
**1** : to, toward, or in the south
**2** : into a state of decline or ruin ⟨causes the sluggish economy to go *south* —G. F. Will⟩
²**south** *adjective* (12th century)
**1** : situated toward or at the south ⟨the *south* entrance⟩
**2** : coming from the south ⟨a *south* wind⟩
³**south** *noun* (13th century)
**1 a** : the direction of the south terrestrial pole : the direction to the right of one facing east **b** : the compass point directly opposite to north
**2** *capitalized* : regions or countries lying to the south of a specified or implied point of orientation; *especially* : the southeastern part of the U.S.
**3** : the right side of a church looking toward the altar from the nave
**4** *often capitalized* **a** : the one of four positions at 90-degree intervals that lies to the south or at the bottom of a diagram **b** : a person (as a bridge player) occupying this position in the course of a specified activity; *specifically* : the declarer in bridge
**5** *often capitalized* : the developing nations of the world : THIRD WORLD 3 — compare NORTH 2b
**South African** *noun* (1806)

: a native or inhabitant of the Republic of South Africa; *especially* : AFRIKANER
— **South African** *adjective*
**south·bound** \'saùth-,baùnd\ *adjective* (1885)
: traveling or heading south
**south by east** (circa 1771)
: a compass point that is one point east of due south : S11°15′E
**south by west** (circa 1743)
: a compass point that is one point west of due south : S11°15′W
**South Dev·on** \-'de-vən\ *noun* [*Devon*, England] (1897)
: any of a breed of large red dual-purpose cattle of English origin
**South·down** \'saùth-,daùn\ *noun* [*South Downs*, England] (1787)
: any of a breed of small medium-wooled hornless sheep of English origin
¹**south·east** \saù-'thēst, *nautical* saù-'ēst\ *adverb* (before 12th century)
: to, toward, or in the southeast
²**southeast** *noun* (14th century)
**1 a** : the general direction between south and east **b** : the point midway between the south and east compass points
**2** *capitalized* : regions or countries lying to the southeast of a specified or implied point of orientation
³**southeast** *adjective* (14th century)
**1** : coming from the southeast ⟨a *southeast* wind⟩
**2** : situated toward or at the southeast ⟨the *southeast* corner⟩
**southeast by east** (circa 1771)
: a compass point that is one point east of due southeast : S56°15′E
**southeast by south** (1682)
: a compass point that is one point south of due southeast : S33°45′E
**south·east·er** \saù-'thē-stər, saù-'ē-\ *noun* (1797)
**1** : a strong southeast wind
**2** : a storm with southeast winds
**south·east·er·ly** \-stər-lē\ *adverb or adjective* [²*southeast* + -*erly* (as in *easterly*)] (1708)
**1** : from the southeast
**2** : toward the southeast
**south·east·ern** \-stərn\ *adjective* [²*southeast* + -*ern* (as in *eastern*)] (1577)
**1** *often capitalized* : of, relating to, or characteristic of a region conventionally designated southeast
**2** : lying toward or coming from the southeast
— **south·east·ern·most** \-,mōst\ *adjective*
**South·east·ern·er** \-stə(r)-nər\ *noun* (1919)
: a native or inhabitant of the Southeast; *especially* : a native or resident of the southeastern part of the U.S.
¹**south·east·ward** \saù-'thēs-twərd, saù-'ēs-\ *adverb or adjective* (1528)
: toward the southeast
— **south·east·wards** \-twərdz\ *adverb*
²**southeastward** *noun* (1555)
: SOUTHEAST
¹**south·er·ly** \'sə-thər-lē\ *adjective or adverb* [³*south* + -*erly* (as in *easterly*)] (1551)
**1** : situated toward or belonging to the south ⟨the *southerly* shore of the lake⟩
**2** : coming from the south ⟨a *southerly* wind⟩
²**southerly** *noun, plural* -**lies** (1943)
: a wind from the south
**south·ern** \'sə-thərn\ *adjective* [Middle English *southern, southren*, from Old English *sūtherne*; akin to Old High German *sundrōni* southern, Old English *sūth* south] (before 12th century)
**1** *capitalized* : of, relating to, or characteristic of a region conventionally designated South

**2 a :** lying toward the south **b :** coming from the south ⟨a *southern* breeze⟩
— **south·ern·most** \-,mōst\ *adjective*
— **south·ern·ness** \-thərn-nəs\ *noun, often capitalized*
**Southern** *noun* (1935)
**:** the dialect of English spoken in most of the Chesapeake Bay area, the coastal plain and the greater part of the upland plateau in Virginia, North Carolina, South Carolina, and Georgia, and the Gulf states at least as far west as the valley of the Brazos in Texas and sometimes taken to include the south Midland area
**Southern blot** *noun* [Edwin M. *Southern* 20th century British biologist] (1981)
**:** a blot consisting of a nitrocellulose sheet containing spots of DNA for identification by a suitable molecular probe — compare WEST-ERN BLOT
— **Southern blotting** *noun*
**southern corn rootworm** *noun* (1918)
**:** SPOTTED CUCUMBER BEETLE
**Southern Cross** *noun*
**:** four bright stars in the southern hemisphere, situated as if at the extremities of a Latin cross; *also* **:** the constellation of which these four stars are the brightest
**Southern Crown** *noun*
**:** CORONA AUSTRALIS
**Southern English** *noun* (14th century)
**1 :** the English spoken especially by cultivated people native to or educated in the South of England
**2 :** SOUTHERN
**South·ern·er** \'sə-thə(r)-nər\ *noun* (1828)
**:** a native or inhabitant of the South; *especially* **:** a native or resident of the southern part of the U.S.
**southern hemisphere** *noun, often S&H capitalized* (circa 1771)
**:** the part of the earth that lies south of the equator
**South·ern·ism** \'sə-thər,ni-zəm\ *noun* (1861)
**1 :** an attitude or trait characteristic of the South or Southerners especially in the U.S.
**2 :** a locution or pronunciation characteristic of the southern U.S.
**southern lights** *noun plural* (1775)
**:** AURORA AUSTRALIS
**south·ern·wood** \'sə-thərn-,wůd\ *noun* (before 12th century)
**:** a shrubby fragrant European wormwood (*Artemisia abrotanum*) with bitter foliage
**south·ing** \'saů-thiŋ, -thin\ *noun* (1669)
**1 :** difference in latitude to the south from the last preceding point of reckoning
**2 :** southerly progress
**south·land** \'saůth-,land, -lənd\ *noun, often capitalized* (before 12th century)
**:** land in the south of a country
**south·paw** \-,pȯ\ *noun* (1891)
**:** LEFT-HANDER; *especially* **:** a left-handed baseball pitcher ◆
— **southpaw** *adjective*
**south pole** *noun* (14th century)
**1 a** *often S&P capitalized* **:** the southernmost point of the earth **b :** the zenith of the heavens as viewed from the south terrestrial pole
**2** *of a magnet* **:** the pole that points toward the south
**¹South·ron** \'səth-rən\ *adjective* [Middle English (Scots)] (15th century)
*chiefly Scottish* **:** SOUTHERN; *specifically* **:** ENGLISH
**²Southron** *noun* (15th century)
**:** SOUTHERNER: as **a** *chiefly Scottish* **:** ENGLISH-MAN **b** *chiefly Southern* **:** a native or inhabitant of the southern U.S.
**south–seek·ing pole** *noun* (circa 1922)
**:** SOUTH POLE 2
**south–southeast** *noun* (15th century)
**:** a compass point that is two points east of due south **:** S22°30′E
**south–southwest** *noun* (1513)
**:** a compass point that is two points west of due south **:** S22°30′W

**¹south·ward** \'saůth-wərd\ *adverb or adjective* (before 12th century)
**:** toward the south
— **south·wards** \-wərdz\ *adverb*
**²southward** *noun* (14th century)
**:** southward direction or part ⟨sail to the *southward*⟩
**¹south·west** \saůth-'west, *nautical* saů-'west\ *adverb* (before 12th century)
**:** to, toward, or in the southwest
**²southwest** *noun* (12th century)
**1 a :** the general direction between south and west **b :** the point midway between the south and west compass points
**2** *capitalized* **:** regions or countries lying to the southwest of a specified or implied point of orientation
**³southwest** *adjective* (14th century)
**1 :** coming from the southwest ⟨a *southwest* wind⟩
**2 :** situated toward or at the southwest ⟨the *southwest* corner⟩
**southwest by south** (1725)
**:** a compass point that is one point south of due southwest **:** S33°45′W
**southwest by west** (circa 1771)
**:** a compass point that is one point west of due southwest **:** S56°15′W
**south·west·er** \saů(th)-'wes-tər\ *noun* (1833)
**1 :** a strong southwest wind
**2 :** a storm with southwest winds
**south·west·er·ly** \-tər-lē\ *adverb or adjective* [²*southwest* + -*erly* (as in *westerly*)] (1708)
**1 :** from the southwest
**2 :** toward the southwest
**south·west·ern** \-tərn\ *adjective* [Middle English, from Old English *sūth-westerne*, from *sūth* south + *westerne* western] (before 12th century)
**1 :** lying toward or coming from the southwest
**2** *often capitalized* **:** of, relating to, or characteristic of a region conventionally designated Southwest
— **south·west·ern·most** \-,mōst\ *adjective*
**southwestern corn borer** *noun* (1943)
**:** a pyralid moth (*Diatraea grandiosella*) whose larva causes serious damage especially to corn crops by boring in the stalks
**South·west·ern·er** \saů(th)-'wes-tə(r)-nər\ *noun* (1860)
**:** a native or inhabitant of the Southwest; *especially* **:** a native or resident of the southwestern U.S.
**¹south·west·ward** \saů(th)-'wes-twərd\ *adverb or adjective* (1548)
**:** toward the southwest
— **south·west·wards** \-twərdz\ *adverb*
**²southwestward** *noun* (1775)
**:** SOUTHWEST
**sou·ve·nir** \'sü-və-,nir, ,sü-və-'\ *noun* [French, literally, act of remembering, from Middle French, from (*se*) *souvenir* to remember, from Latin *subvenire* to come up, come to mind — more at SUBVENTION] (1782)
**:** something that serves as a reminder **:** MEMEN-TO
**souvenir sheet** *noun* (1940)
**:** a block or set of postage stamps or a single stamp printed on a single sheet of paper often without gum or perforations and with margins containing lettering or design that identifies some notable event being commemorated
**sou·vla·kia** \süv-'lä-kē-ə\ *or* **sou·vla·ki** \-'lä-kē\ *noun* [New Greek *soublakia*, plural of *soublaki*, from diminutive of *soubla* skewer, from Middle Greek, from Latin *subula* awl, from *suere* to sew — more at SEW] (1950)
**:** SHISH KEBAB
**sou'·west·er** \saů-'wes-tər\ *noun* (1837)
**1 :** a long oilskin coat worn especially at sea during stormy weather
**2 :** a waterproof hat with wide slanting brim longer in back than in front

**¹sov·er·eign** *also* **sov·ran** \'sä-v(ə-)rən, -vərn\ *also* 'sə-\ *noun* [Middle English *soverain*, from Old French, from *soverain*, adjective] (13th century)
**1 a :** one possessing or held to possess sovereignty **b :** one that exercises supreme authority within a limited sphere **c :** an acknowledged leader **:** ARBITER
**2 :** any of various gold coins of the United Kingdom
**²sovereign** *also* **sovran** *adjective* [Middle English *soverain*, from Middle French, from Old French, from (assumed) Vulgar Latin *superanus*, from Latin *super* over, above — more at OVER] (14th century)
**1 a :** superlative in quality **:** EXCELLENT **b :** of the most exalted kind **:** SUPREME ⟨*sovereign* virtue⟩ **c :** having generalized curative powers ⟨a *sovereign* remedy⟩ **d :** of an unqualified nature **:** UNMITIGATED ⟨*sovereign* contempt⟩ **e :** having undisputed ascendancy **:** PARAMOUNT
**2 a :** possessed of supreme power ⟨*sovereign* ruler⟩ **b :** unlimited in extent **:** ABSOLUTE **c :** enjoying autonomy **:** INDEPENDENT ⟨*sovereign* state⟩
**3 :** relating to, characteristic of, or befitting a sovereign
*synonym* see FREE
— **sov·er·eign·ly** *adverb*
**sov·er·eign·ty** *also* **sov·ran·ty** \-tē\ *noun, plural* **-ties** [Middle English *soverainte*, from Middle French *soveraineté*, from Old French, from *soverain*] (14th century)
**1** *obsolete* **:** supreme excellence or an example of it
**2 a :** supreme power especially over a body politic **b :** freedom from external control **:** AU-TONOMY **c :** controlling influence
**3 :** one that is sovereign; *especially* **:** an autonomous state
**so·vi·et** \'sō-vē-,et, 'sä-, -vē-ət\ *noun* [Russian *sovet* council, soviet] (1917)
**1 :** an elected governmental council in a Communist country
**2** *plural, capitalized* **a :** BOLSHEVIKS **b :** the people and especially the political and military leaders of the U.S.S.R.
— **soviet** *adjective, often capitalized*
— **so·vi·et·ism** \-vē-ə-,ti-zəm\ *noun, often capitalized*
**so·vi·et·ize** \'sō-vē-,e-,tīz, 'sä-, -vē-ə-\ *transitive verb* **-ized; -iz·ing** *often capitalized* (1919)
**1 :** to bring under Soviet control

**2 :** to force into conformity with Soviet cultural patterns or governmental policies
— **so·vi·et·i·za·tion** \ˌsō-vē-ˌe-tə-'zā-shən, -vē-ə-\ *noun, often capitalized*
**So·vi·et·ol·o·gist** \ˌsō-vē-ˌe-'tä-lə-jist, ˌsä-, -vē-ə-\ *noun* (1955)
**:** one who studies or is knowledgeable about the policies and practices of the Soviet government **:** KREMLINOLOGIST
**sov·khoz** \säf-'kȯz, -'kós\ *noun, plural* **sov·kho·zy** \-'kȯ-zē\ *or* **sov·khoz·es** [Russian, short for *sovetskoe khozyaĭstvo* soviet farm] (1921)
**:** a state-owned farm of the U.S.S.R. paying wages to the workers
**¹sow** \'saú\ *noun* [Middle English *sowe,* from Old English *sugu;* akin to Old English & Old High German *sū* sow, Latin *sus* pig, swine, hog, Greek *hys*] (before 12th century)
**1 :** an adult female swine; *also* **:** the adult female of various other animals (as a bear)
**2 a :** a channel that conducts molten metal to molds **b :** a mass of metal solidified in such a mold **:** INGOT
**²sow** \'sō\ *verb* **sowed; sown** \'sōn\ *or* **sowed; sow·ing** [Middle English, from Old English *sāwan;* akin to Old High German *sā·wen* to sow, Latin *serere,* Lithuanian *sėti*] (before 12th century)
*intransitive verb*
**1 :** to plant seed for growth especially by scattering
**2 :** to set something in motion **:** begin an enterprise
*transitive verb*
**1 a :** to scatter (as seed) upon the earth for growth; *broadly* **:** PLANT 1a **b :** to strew with or as if with seed **c :** to introduce into a selected environment **:** IMPLANT
**2 :** to set in motion **:** FOMENT ⟨*sow* suspicion⟩
**3 :** to spread abroad **:** DISPERSE
— **sow·er** \'sō(-ə)r\ *noun*
**sow·bel·ly** \'saú-ˌbe-lē\ *noun* (1867)
**:** fat salt pork or bacon
**sow bug** \'saú-\ *noun* (1750)
**:** WOOD LOUSE
**sow·ens** \'sü-ənz, 'sō-\ *noun plural but singular or plural in construction* [Scottish Gaelic *sùghan*] (1582)
**:** porridge from oat husks and siftings
**sow thistle** \'saú-\ *noun* (13th century)
**:** any of a genus (*Sonchus*) of spiny weedy European composite herbs widely naturalized in North America
**sox** *plural of* SOCK
**soy** \'sói\ *noun* [Japanese *shōyu*] (1679)
**1 :** a brown liquid sauce made by subjecting beans (as soybeans) to long fermentation and to digestion in brine
**2** *also* **soya** \'sói-ə\ **:** SOYBEAN
**soy·bean** \'sói-ˌbēn\ *also* **soya bean** \'sói-ə-\ *noun* (1802)
**:** a hairy annual Asian legume (*Glycine max*) widely grown for its oil-rich proteinaceous seeds and for forage and soil improvement; *also* **:** its seed

**soybean**

**soybean oil** *noun* (circa 1916)
**:** a pale yellow drying or semidrying oil that is obtained from soybeans and is used chiefly as a food, in paints, varnishes, linoleum, printing ink, and soap, and as a source of phospholipids, fatty acids, and sterols — called also *soya oil*
**soz·zled** \'sä-zəld\ *adjective* [*sozzle* to splash, intoxicate, alteration of *sossle,* probably frequentative of British dialect *soss* to mess] (circa 1880)

**:** DRUNK, INTOXICATED
**spa** \'spä, 'spó\ *noun* [*Spa,* watering place in Belgium] (1610)
**1 a :** a mineral spring **b :** a resort with mineral springs
**2 :** a fashionable resort or hotel
**3** *New England* **:** SODA FOUNTAIN
**4 :** HEALTH SPA
**5 :** a hot tub with a whirlpool device
**¹space** \'spās\ *noun, often attributive* [Middle English, from Old French *espace,* from Latin *spatium* area, room, interval of space or time] (14th century)
**1 :** a period of time; *also* **:** its duration
**2 a :** a limited extent in one, two, or three dimensions **:** DISTANCE, AREA, VOLUME **b :** an extent set apart or available ⟨parking *space*⟩ ⟨floor *space*⟩
**3 :** one of the degrees between or above or below the lines of a musical staff — compare LINE
**4 a :** a boundless three-dimensional extent in which objects and events occur and have relative position and direction **b :** physical space independent of what occupies it — called also *absolute space*
**5 :** the region beyond the earth's atmosphere or beyond the solar system
**6 a :** a blank area separating words or lines **b :** material used to produce such blank area; *especially* **:** a piece of type less than one en in width
**7 :** a set of mathematical elements and especially of abstractions of all the points on a line, in a plane, or in physical space; *especially* **:** a set of mathematical entities with a set of axioms of geometric character — compare METRIC SPACE, TOPOLOGICAL SPACE, VECTOR SPACE
**8 :** an interval in operation during which a telegraph key is not in contact
**9 a :** LINAGE **b :** broadcast time available especially to advertisers
**10 :** accommodations on a public vehicle
**11 :** the opportunity to assert or experience one's identity or needs freely
**²space** *verb* **spaced; spac·ing** (1703)
*transitive verb*
**:** to place at intervals or arrange with space between — often used with *out*
*intransitive verb*
**:** to leave one or more blank spaces (as in a line of typing)
— **spac·er** *noun*
**space-age** \'spās-'āj\ *adjective* (1946)
**:** of, relating to, or befitting the age of space exploration; *especially* **:** MODERN ⟨*space-age* technology⟩
**space·band** \-ˌband\ *noun* (1904)
**:** a device on a linecaster that provides variable but even spacing between words in a justified line
**space cadet** *noun* (1979)
**:** a flaky, lightheaded, or forgetful person
**space charge** *noun* (1913)
**:** an electric charge distributed throughout a three-dimensional region
**space·craft** \'spās-ˌkraft\ *noun* (1930)
**:** a vehicle or device designed for travel or operation outside the earth's atmosphere
**spaced-out** \ˌspāst-'aút\ *adjective* (1937)
**1** *or* **spaced** \'spāst\ **:** dazed or stupefied by or as if by a narcotic substance **:** HIGH
**2 :** of very strange character **:** WEIRD ⟨a *spaced-out* fantasy⟩
**space-flight** \'spās-ˌflīt\ *noun* (1931)
**:** flight beyond the earth's atmosphere
**space frame** *noun* (1912)
**:** a usually open three-dimensional framework of struts and braces (as in buildings and racing cars) which defines a structure and in which the weight of the structure is evenly distributed in all directions

**space heater** *noun* (1925)
**:** a usually portable appliance for heating a relatively small area
**space heating** *noun* (1934)
**:** heating of spaces especially for human comfort by any means (as fuel, electricity, or solar radiation) with the heater either within the space or external to it
**space lattice** *noun* (1895)
**:** LATTICE 2
**space·less** \'spās-ləs\ *adjective* (1606)
**1 :** having no limits **:** BOUNDLESS
**2 :** occupying no space
**space·man** \'spās-ˌman, -mən\ *noun* (1938)
**1 :** one who travels outside the earth's atmosphere
**2 :** a visitor to earth from outer space
**space mark** *noun* (circa 1890)
**:** the symbol #
**space medicine** *noun* (1949)
**:** a branch of medicine that deals with the physiological and biological effects on the human body of rocket or jet flight beyond the earth's atmosphere
**space opera** *noun* (1949)
**:** a futuristic melodramatic fantasy involving space travelers and extraterrestrial beings
**space·port** \'spās-ˌpōrt, -ˌpȯrt\ *noun* (1935)
**:** an installation for testing and launching spacecraft
**space·ship** \-ˌship\ *noun* (1894)
**:** a vehicle used for space travel
**space shuttle** *noun* (1969)
**:** a reusable spacecraft designed to transport people and cargo between earth and space
**space station** *noun* (1936)
**:** a large artificial satellite designed to be occupied for long periods and to serve as a base (as for scientific observation) — called also *space platform*
**space suit** *noun* (1929)
**1 :** a suit equipped with life supporting provisions to make life in space possible for its wearer
**2 :** G SUIT
**space-time** \'spās-'tīm, 'spās-ˌ\ *noun* (1915)
**1 :** a system of one temporal and three spatial coordinates by which any physical object or event can be located — called also *space-time continuum*
**2 :** the whole or a portion of physical reality determinable by a usually four-dimensional coordinate system; *also* **:** the properties characteristic of such an order
**space walk** *noun* (1965)
**:** a period of activity spent outside a spacecraft by an astronaut in space
— **space·walk** \'spās-ˌwȯk\ *intransitive verb*
— **space·walk·er** \-ˌwȯ-kər\ *noun*
**space·ward** \'spās-wərd\ *adverb* (1958)
**:** toward space
**spac·ey** *also* **spacy** \'spā-sē\ *adjective* **spac·i·er; -est** (1970)
**:** SPACED-OUT
**spa·cial** *variant of* SPATIAL
**spac·ing** \'spā-siŋ\ *noun* (1683)
**1 a :** the act of providing with spaces or placing at intervals **b :** an arrangement in space
**2 a :** a limited extent **:** SPACE **b :** the distance between any two objects in a usually regularly arranged series
**spa·cious** \'spā-shəs\ *adjective* [Middle English, from Middle French *spacieux,* from Latin *spatiosus,* from *spatium* space, room] (14th century)
**1 :** vast or ample in extent **:** ROOMY ⟨a *spacious* residence⟩

**2** : large or magnificent in scale : EXPANSIVE ⟨a more *spacious* and stimulating existence than the farm could offer —H. L. Mencken⟩ ☆
— **spa·cious·ly** *adverb*
— **spa·cious·ness** *noun*
**spack·le** \'spa-kəl\ *transitive verb* **spack·led; spack·ling** \-k(ə-)liŋ\ [*Spackle*] (1940)
: to apply Spackle paste to
**Spackle** *trademark*
— used for a powder mixed with water to form a paste and used as a filler for cracks in a surface before painting
**¹spade** \'spād\ *noun* [Middle English, from Old English *spadu*; akin to Greek *spathē* blade of a sword or oar] (before 12th century)
**1** : a digging implement adapted for being pushed into the ground with the foot
**2** : a spade-shaped instrument
— **spade·ful** \-,fůl\ *noun*
— **call a spade a spade 1** : to call a thing by its right name however coarse **2** : to speak frankly
**²spade** *verb* **spad·ed; spad·ing** (1647)
*transitive verb*
: to dig up or out or shape with or as if with a spade
*intransitive verb*
: to use a spade
— **spad·er** *noun*
**³spade** *noun* [Italian *spada* or Spanish *espada* broadsword; both from Latin *spatha*, from Greek *spathē* blade] (1598)
**1 a** : a black figure that resembles a stylized spearhead on each playing card of one of the four suits; *also* : a card marked with this figure **b** *plural but singular or plural in construction* : the suit comprising cards marked spades
**2** : BLACK 4 — usually taken to be offensive
— **in spades** : to an unusually great degree : in the extreme
**spade beard** *noun* [¹*spade*] (1598)
**1** : an oblong beard with square ends
**2** : a beard rounded off at the top and pointed at the bottom
— **spade–beard·ed** \'spād-'bir-dəd\ *adjective*
**spade·fish** \'spād-,fish\ *noun* (1704)
: a deep-bodied bony fish (*Chaetodipterus faber* of the family Ephippidae) that resembles the angelfishes and is found in the warmer parts of the western Atlantic
**spade·foot toad** \'spād-,fůt-\ *noun* (1867)
: any of a family (Pelobatidae) of burrowing toads having the inner bone of the tarsus edged with a strong horny sheath with which they dig
**spade·work** \-,wərk\ *noun* (1778)
**1** : work done with a spade
**2** : the hard plain preliminary drudgery in an undertaking
**spa·dille** \spə-'dil, -'dē\ *noun* [French, from Spanish *espadilla*, diminutive of *espada* broadsword, spade (in cards) — more at SPADE] (1728)
: the highest trump in various card games (as ombre)
**spa·dix** \'spā-diks\ *noun, plural* **spa·di·ces** \'spā-də-,sēz\ [New Latin *spadic-, spadix*, from Latin, frond torn from a palm tree, from Greek *spadik-, spadix*, from *span* to draw, pull] (circa 1760)
: a floral spike with a fleshy or succulent axis usually enclosed in a spathe
**spae** \'spā\ *transitive verb* **spaed; spae·ing** [Middle English *span*, from Old Norse *spā*; akin to Old High German *spehōn* to watch, spy — more at SPY] (14th century)
*chiefly Scottish* : FORETELL

*1 spadix*

**spaetz·le** \'shpet-slə, -s°l, -slē *also* 'shpāt-\ *noun, plural* **spaetzle** *or* **spaetzles** [German *Spätzle*, from German dialect, diminutive of *Spatz* sparrow, dumpling] (1933)
: a small dumpling cooked by running batter through a colander into boiling water
**spa·ghet·ti** \spə-'ge-tē\ *noun* [Italian, from plural of *spaghetto*, diminutive of *spago* cord, string, from Late Latin *spacus*] (1888)
**1** : pasta made in thin solid strings
**2** : insulating tubing typically of varnished cloth or of plastic for covering bare wire or holding insulated wires together
— **spa·ghet·ti·like** \-,līk\ *adjective*
**spa·ghet·ti·ni** \spə-,ge-'tē-nē\ *noun* [Italian, diminutive of *spaghetti*] (1923)
: a pasta thinner than spaghetti but thicker than vermicelli
**spaghetti squash** *noun* (1975)
: an oval winter squash with flesh that once cooked is similar in texture to spaghetti
**spaghetti western** *noun, often W capitalized* (1969)
: a western motion picture produced in Italy
**spa·hi** \'spä-,hē\ *noun* [Middle French, from Turkish *sipahi*, from Persian *sipāhī* cavalryman] (1562)
**1** : one of a former corps of irregular Turkish cavalry
**2** : one of a former corps of Algerian native cavalry in the French army
**spake** \'spāk\ *archaic past of* SPEAK
**¹spall** \'spól\ *noun* [Middle English *spalle*] (15th century)
: a small fragment or chip especially of stone
**²spall** (1758)
*transitive verb*
: to break up or reduce by or as if by chipping with a hammer
*intransitive verb*
**1** : to break off chips, scales, or slabs : EXFOLIATE
**2** : to undergo spallation
— **spall·able** \'spó-lə-bəl\ *adjective*
**spall·ation** \spó-'lā-shən\ *noun* (1947)
**1** : a nuclear reaction in which light particles are ejected as the result of bombardment (as by high-energy protons)
**2** : the process of spalling
**spal·peen** \spal-'pēn, spól-\ *noun* [Irish *spailpín* seasonal laborer, rascal] (1815)
*chiefly Irish* : RASCAL
**¹span** \'span\ *archaic past of* SPIN
**²span** *noun* [Middle English, from Old English *spann;* akin to Old High German *spanna* span, Middle Dutch *spannen* to stretch, hitch up] (before 12th century)
**1** : the distance from the end of the thumb to the end of the little finger of a spread hand; *also* : an English unit of length equal to 9 inches (22.9 centimeters)
**2** : an extent, stretch, reach, or spread between two limits: as **a** : a limited space (as of time); *especially* : an individual's lifetime **b** : the spread or extent between abutments or supports (as of a bridge); *also* : a portion thus supported **c** : the maximum distance laterally from tip to tip of an airplane
**³span** *transitive verb* **spanned; span·ning** (1560)
**1 a** : to measure by or as if by the hand with fingers and thumb extended **b** : MEASURE
**2 a** : to extend across ⟨a career that *spanned* four decades⟩ **b** : to form an arch over ⟨a small bridge *spanned* the pond⟩ **c** : to place or construct a span over
**3** : to be capable of expressing any element of under given operations ⟨a set of vectors that *spans* a vector space⟩
**⁴span** *noun* [Dutch, from Middle Dutch, from *spannen* to hitch up] (1769)
: a pair of animals (as mules) usually matched in appearance and action and driven together
**spa·na·ko·pi·ta** *also* **spa·no·ko·pi·ta** \,spä-nə-'kō-pē-tə, -pi-tə\ *noun* [New Greek

*spanakopēta*, from *spanaki* spinach + *pēta, pita* pie] (1950)
: a traditional Greek pie of spinach, feta cheese, and seasonings baked in phyllo
**span·dex** \'span-,deks\ *noun* [anagram of *expands*] (1959)
: any of various elastic textile fibers made chiefly of polyurethane; *also* : clothing made of this material
**span·drel** *also* **span·dril** \'span-drəl\ *noun* [Middle English *spandrell*, from Anglo-French *spaundre*, from Old French *espandre* to spread out — more at SPAWN] (15th century)
**1** : the sometimes ornamented space between the right or left exterior curve of an arch and an enclosing right angle
**2** : the triangular space beneath the string of a stair
**spang** \'span\ *adverb* [Scots *spang* to leap, cast, bang] (1843)
**1** : to a complete degree
**2** : in an exact or direct manner : SQUARELY
**¹span·gle** \'span-gəl\ *noun* [Middle English *spangel*, diminutive of *spang* shiny ornament, probably of Scandinavian origin; akin to Old Norse *spǫng* spangle; akin to Old English *spang* buckle, Middle Dutch *spannen* to stretch] (15th century)
**1** : a small plate of shining metal or plastic used for ornamentation especially on clothing
**2** : a small glittering object or particle
**²spangle** *verb* **span·gled; span·gling** \'span-g(ə-)liŋ\ (1598)
*transitive verb*
: to set or sprinkle with or as if with spangles
*intransitive verb*
: to glitter as if covered with spangles : SPARKLE
**Span·glish** \'span-glish, -lish\ *noun* [blend of *Spanish* and *English*] (1965)
: Spanish marked by numerous borrowings from English; *broadly* : any of various combinations of Spanish and English
**Span·iard** \'span-yərd\ *noun* [Middle English *Spaignard*, from Middle French *Espaignart*, from *Espaigne* Spain, from Latin *Hispania*] (15th century)
: a native or inhabitant of Spain
**span·iel** \'span-yəl *also* 'spa-n°l\ *noun* [Middle English *spaniell*, from Middle French *espaignol*, literally, Spaniard, from (assumed) Vulgar Latin *Hispaniolus*, from Latin *Hispania* Spain] (14th century)
**1** : a member of any of several breeds of small or medium-sized mostly short-legged dogs usually having long wavy hair, feathered legs and tail, and large drooping ears
**2** : a fawning servile person
**Span·ish** \'spa-nish\ *noun* [Spanish, adjective, from Middle English *Spainish*, from *Spain*] (15th century)
**1** : the Romance language of the largest part of Spain and of the countries colonized by Spaniards
**2** *plural in construction* : the people of Spain
— **Spanish** *adjective*
— **Span·ish·ness** *noun*
**Spanish American** *noun* (1811)

**1 :** a resident of the U.S. whose native language is Spanish and whose culture is of Spanish origin
**2 :** a native or inhabitant of one of the countries of America in which Spanish is the national language
— **Spanish–American** *adjective*
**Spanish bayonet** *noun* (1843)
**:** any of several yuccas; *especially* **:** one (*Yucca aloifolia*) with a short trunk and rigid spine-tipped leaves
**Spanish chestnut** *noun* (1699)
**:** MARRON
**Spanish fly** *noun* (1634)
**1 :** a green blister beetle (*Lytta vesicatoria*) of southern Europe
**2 :** CANTHARIS 2
**Spanish mackerel** *noun* (1666)
**:** a large scombroid food and game fish (*Scomberomorus maculatus*) that is bluish above with oval brown spots on the sides and is found off the American Atlantic coast from Cape Ann to Brazil
**Spanish moss** *noun* (1823)
**:** an epiphytic plant (*Tillandsia usneoides*) of the pineapple family forming pendent tufts of grayish green filaments on trees from the southern U.S. to Argentina

**Spanish moss**

**Spanish needles** *noun plural but singular or plural in construction* (1743)
**:** any of several bur marigolds; *especially* **:** an annual (*Bidens bipinnata*) of North America and Asia having yellow flowers and dissected leaves
**Spanish omelet** *noun* (circa 1886)
**:** an omelet served with a sauce containing chopped green pepper, onion, and tomato
**Spanish rice** *noun* (1928)
**:** rice cooked with onions, green pepper, and tomatoes
¹**spank** \'spaŋk\ *transitive verb* [imitative] (circa 1727)
**:** to strike especially on the buttocks with the open hand
— **spank** *noun*
²**spank** *intransitive verb* [back-formation from *spanking*] (circa 1810)
**:** to move quickly, dashingly, or spiritedly ⟨*spanking* along in his new car⟩
**span·ker** \'spaŋ-kər\ *noun* [origin unknown] (1794)
**1 :** the fore-and-aft sail on the mast nearest the stern of a square-rigged ship
**2 :** the sail on the sternmost mast in a schooner of four or more masts
¹**spank·ing** \'spaŋ-kiŋ\ *adjective* [origin unknown] (1666)
**1 :** remarkable of its kind
**2 :** being fresh and strong **:** BRISK
²**spanking** *adverb* (1886)
**:** VERY ⟨a *spanking* clean floor⟩ ⟨*spanking* new⟩
**span·ner** \'spa-nər\ *noun* [German, instrument for winding springs, from *spannen* to stretch; akin to Middle Dutch *spannen* to stretch — more at SPAN] (circa 1790)
**1** *chiefly British*
**:** WRENCH
**2 :** a wrench that has a hole, projection, or hook at one or both ends of the head for engaging with a corresponding device on the object that is to be turned
**span–new** \'span-'nü, -'nyü\ *adjective* [Middle English, part translation of Old Norse *spānnȳr*, from *spānn* chip of wood + *nȳr* new] (14th century)

**spanner 2**

**:** BRAND-NEW
**span·worm** \'span-,wərm\ *noun* [³*span*] (1820)
**:** LOOPER 1
¹**spar** \'spär\ *noun* [Middle English *sparre;* akin to Old English *spere* spear — more at SPEAR] (14th century)
**1 :** a stout pole
**2 a :** a stout rounded wood or metal piece (as a mast, boom, gaff, or yard) used to support rigging **b :** any of the main longitudinal members of the wing of an airplane that carry the ribs
²**spar** *intransitive verb* **sparred; spar·ring** [probably alteration of ²*spur*] (1537)
**1 a :** BOX; *especially* **:** to gesture without landing a blow to draw one's opponent or create an opening **b :** to engage in a practice or exhibition bout of boxing
**2 :** SKIRMISH, WRANGLE
**3 :** to strike or fight with feet or spurs in the manner of a gamecock
³**spar** *noun* (1814)
**1 :** a movement of offense or defense in boxing
**2 :** a sparring match or session
⁴**spar** *noun* [Low German; akin to Old English *spærstān* gypsum, *spæren* of plaster] (1581)
**:** any of various nonmetallic usually cleavable and lustrous minerals
**SPAR** \'spär\ *noun* [*Semper Paratus*, motto of the U.S. Coast Guard, from New Latin, always ready] (1942)
**:** a member of the women's reserve of the U.S. Coast Guard
¹**spare** \'spar, 'sper\ *verb* **spared; spar·ing** [Middle English, from Old English *sparian;* akin to Old High German *sparōn* to spare, Old English *spær,* adjective, scant] (before 12th century)
*transitive verb*
**1 :** to forbear to destroy, punish, or harm
**2 :** to refrain from attacking or reprimanding with necessary or salutary severity
**3 :** to relieve of the necessity of doing or undergoing something ⟨*spare* yourself the trouble⟩
**4 :** to refrain from **:** AVOID ⟨*spared* no expense⟩
**5 :** to use or dispense frugally — used chiefly in the negative ⟨don't *spare* the syrup⟩
**6 a :** to give up as not strictly needed ⟨do you have any cash to *spare*⟩ **b :** to have left over or as margin ⟨time to *spare*⟩
*intransitive verb*
**1 :** to be frugal
**2 :** to refrain from doing harm **:** be lenient
— **spare·able** \-ə-bəl\ *adjective*
— **spar·er** *noun*
²**spare** *adjective* **spar·er; spar·est** [Middle English, from Old English *spær* sparing, scant; akin to Old High German *spar* spare] (14th century)
**1 :** not being used; *especially* **:** held for emergency use ⟨a *spare* tire⟩
**2 :** being over and above what is needed **:** SUPERFLUOUS ⟨*spare* time⟩
**3 :** not liberal or profuse **:** SPARING ⟨a *spare* prose style⟩
**4 :** healthily lean
**5 :** not abundant or plentiful
*synonym* see LEAN, MEAGER
— **spare·ly** *adverb*
— **spare·ness** *noun*
³**spare** *noun* (1642)
**1 a :** a spare tire **b :** a duplicate (as a key or a machine part) kept in reserve
**2 :** the knocking down of all 10 pins with the first 2 balls in a frame in bowling
**spare·ribs** \'spar-,(r)ibz, 'sper-, -əbz\ *noun plural* [by folk etymology from Low German *ribbesper* pickled pork ribs roasted on a spit, from Middle Low German, from *ribbe* rib + *sper* spear, spit] (1596)
**:** a cut of pork ribs separated from the bacon strip

**sparge** \'spärj\ *transitive verb* **sparged; sparg·ing** [probably from Middle French *espargier,* from Latin *spargere* to scatter] (1785)
**1 :** SPRINKLE, BESPATTER; *especially* **:** SPRAY
**2 :** to agitate (a liquid) by means of compressed air or gas entering through a pipe
— **sparge** *noun*
— **sparg·er** *noun*
**spar·ing** \'spar-iŋ, 'sper-\ *adjective* (14th century)
**1 :** marked by or practicing careful restraint (as in the use of resources)
**2 :** MEAGER, BARE ⟨the map is *sparing* of information⟩ ☆
— **spar·ing·ly** \-iŋ-lē\ *adverb*
¹**spark** \'spärk\ *noun* [Middle English *sparke,* from Old English *spearca;* akin to Middle Dutch *sparke* spark and perhaps to Latin *spargere* to scatter] (before 12th century)
**1 a :** a small particle of a burning substance thrown out by a body in combustion or remaining when combustion is nearly completed **b :** a hot glowing particle struck from a larger mass; *especially* **:** one heated by friction
**2 a :** a luminous disruptive electrical discharge of very short duration between two conductors separated by a gas (as air) **b :** the discharge in a spark plug **c :** the mechanism controlling the discharge in a spark plug
**3 :** SPARKLE, FLASH
**4 :** something that sets off a sudden force ⟨provided the *spark* that helped the team to rally⟩
**5 :** a latent particle capable of growth or developing **:** GERM ⟨still retains a *spark* of decency⟩
**6** *plural but singular in construction* **:** a radio operator on a ship
²**spark** (13th century)
*intransitive verb*
**1 a :** to throw out sparks **b :** to flash or fall like sparks
**2 :** to produce sparks; *specifically* **:** to have the electric ignition working
**3 :** to respond with enthusiasm
*transitive verb*
**1 :** to set off in a burst of activity **:** ACTIVATE ⟨the question *sparked* a lively discussion⟩ — often used with *off*
**2 :** to stir to activity **:** INCITE ⟨*sparked* her team to victory⟩
— **spark·er** *noun*
³**spark** *noun* [perhaps of Scandinavian origin; akin to Old Norse *sparkr* sprightly] (circa 1600)
**1 :** a foppish young man
**2 :** LOVER, BEAU
— **spark·ish** \'spär-kish\ *adjective*
⁴**spark** *verb* (1787)
**:** WOO, COURT
— **spark·er** *noun*
**spark chamber** *noun* (1961)
**:** a device usually used to detect the path of a high-energy particle that consists of a series of

---

☆ **SYNONYMS**
**Sparing, frugal, thrifty, economical**
mean careful in the use of one's money or resources. SPARING stresses abstention and restraint ⟨*sparing* in the offering of advice⟩. FRUGAL implies absence of luxury and simplicity of lifestyle ⟨ran a *frugal* household⟩. THRIFTY stresses good management and industry ⟨*thrifty* use of nonrenewable resources⟩. ECONOMICAL stresses prudent management, lack of wastefulness, and use of things to their best advantage ⟨an *economical* health care plan⟩.

---

\ə\ **abut** \ᵊ\ **kitten** \ər\ **further** \a\ **ash** \ā\ **ace**
\ä\ **mop, mar** \aú\ **out** \ch\ **chin** \e\ **bet** \ē\ **easy**
\g\ **go** \i\ **hit** \ī\ **ice** \j\ **job** \ŋ\ **sing** \ō\ **go**
\ò\ **law** \ói\ **boy** \th\ **thin** \th\ **the** \ü\ **loot** \ú\ **foot**
\y\ **yet** \zh\ **vision** *see also* Guide to Pronunciation

charged metal plates or wires separated by a gas (as neon) in which observable electric discharges follow the path of the particle

**spark coil** *noun* (1896)
: an induction coil for producing the spark for an internal combustion engine

**spark gap** *noun* (1889)
: a space between two high-potential terminals (as of an induction coil) through which pass discharges of electricity; *also* : a device having a spark gap

**sparking plug** *noun* (1902)
*British* : SPARK PLUG

¹**spar·kle** \'spär-kəl\ *verb* **spar·kled; spar·kling** \-k(ə-)liŋ\ [Middle English, frequentative of *sparken* to spark] (13th century)
*intransitive verb*
**1 a** : to throw out sparks **b** : to give off or reflect bright moving points of light **c** : to perform brilliantly
**2** : EFFERVESCE ⟨wine that *sparkles*⟩
**3** : to become lively or animated ⟨the dialogue *sparkles* with wit⟩ ⟨eyes *sparkling* with anger⟩
*transitive verb*
: to cause to glitter or shine
**synonym** see FLASH
— **spar·kly** \-k(ə-)lē\ *adjective*

²**sparkle** *noun* [Middle English, diminutive of *sparke*] (14th century)
**1** : a little spark : SCINTILLATION
**2** : the quality of sparkling
**3 a** : ANIMATION, LIVELINESS **b** : the quality or state of being effervescent

**spar·kler** \'spär-klər\ *noun* (1713)
: one that sparkles: as **a** : DIAMOND **b** : a firework that throws off brilliant sparks on burning **c** : SPARKLING WINE

**sparkling wine** *noun* (1697)
: an effervescent table wine

**spark plug** *noun* (1903)
**1** : a part that fits into the cylinder head of an internal combustion engine and carries two electrodes separated by an air gap across which the current from the ignition system discharges to form the spark for combustion
**2** : one that initiates or gives impetus to an undertaking
— **spark·plug** \'spärk-,pləg\ *transitive verb*

**sparky** \'spär-kē\ *adjective* **spark·i·er; -est** (circa 1865)
: marked by animation : LIVELY
— **spark·i·ly** \-kə-lē\ *adverb*

**spar·row** \'spar-(,)ō\ *noun* [Middle English *sparow*, from Old English *spearwa;* akin to Old High German *sparo* sparrow] (before 12th century)
**1** : any of a genus (*Passer* of the family Ploceidae) of small chiefly brownish or grayish Old World oscine songbirds that include some which have been widely introduced; *especially* : HOUSE SPARROW
**2** : any of various finches (as the song sparrow or tree sparrow) resembling the true sparrows
— **spar·row·like** \-ō-,līk, -ə-,līk\ *adjective*

**sparrow hawk** *noun* (15th century)
: any of various small hawks: as **a** : an Old World accipiter (*Accipiter nisus*) that is dark gray to blackish above with the female having a grayish brown barred underside and the male having a chestnut barred underside **b** : KESTREL b

sparrow hawk

**sparse** \'spärs\ *adjective* **spars·er; spars·est** [Latin *sparsus* spread out, from past participle of *spargere* to scatter — more at SPARK] (1753)
: of few and scattered elements; *especially* : not thickly grown or settled
**synonym** see MEAGER

— **sparse·ly** *adverb*
— **sparse·ness** *noun*
— **spar·si·ty** \'spär-sə-tē, -stē\ *noun*

**Spar·ta·cist** \'spär-tə-sist\ *noun* [German *Spartakist*, from *Spartakusbund*, literally, league of Spartakus, a revolutionary organization, from *Spartakus*, pen name of Karl Liebknecht, its cofounder] (1919)
: a member of a revolutionary political group organized in Germany in 1918 and advocating extreme socialistic doctrines

¹**Spar·tan** \'spär-t�ᵊn\ *noun* (15th century)
**1** : a native or inhabitant of ancient Sparta
**2** : a person of great courage and self-discipline
— **Spar·tan·ism** \-,i-zəm\ *noun*

²**Spartan** *adjective* (1582)
**1** : of or relating to Sparta in ancient Greece
**2 a** *often not capitalized* : marked by strict self-discipline or self-denial ⟨a *Spartan* athlete⟩ **b** *often not capitalized* : marked by simplicity, frugality, or avoidance of luxury and comfort ⟨a *Spartan* room⟩ **c** : LACONIC **d** : undaunted by pain or danger
— **Spar·tan·ly** *adverb*

**spar·te·ine** \'spär-tē-ən, 'spär-,tēn\ *noun* [Latin *spartum* esparto, broom + International Scientific Vocabulary *-eine* — more at ESPARTO] (1851)
: a liquid alkaloid $C_{15}H_{26}N_2$ extracted from the Scotch broom and used in medicine in the form of its sulfate

**spar varnish** *noun* [¹*spar*] (circa 1909)
: an exterior waterproof varnish

**spasm** \'spa-zəm\ *noun* [Middle English *spasme*, from Middle French, from Latin *spasmus*, from Greek *spasmos*, from *span* to draw, pull] (14th century)
**1** : an involuntary and abnormal muscular contraction
**2** : a sudden violent and temporary effort or emotion ⟨a *spasm* of creativity⟩

**spas·mod·ic** \spaz-'mä-dik\ *adjective* [New Latin *spasmodicus*, from Greek *spasmōdēs*, from *spasmos*] (circa 1681)
**1 a** : relating to or affected or characterized by spasm **b** : resembling a spasm especially in sudden violence ⟨a *spasmodic* jerk⟩
**2** : acting or proceeding fitfully : INTERMITTENT
**3** : subject to outbursts of emotional excitement : EXCITABLE
**synonym** see FITFUL
— **spas·mod·i·cal·ly** \-di-k(ə-)lē\ *adverb*

**spas·mo·lyt·ic** \,spaz-mə-'li-tik\ *adjective* [International Scientific Vocabulary *spasmo-* (from Greek *spasmos* spasm) + *-lytic*] (circa 1935)
: tending or having the power to relieve spasms or convulsions
— **spasmolytic** *noun*

¹**spas·tic** \'spas-tik\ *adjective* [Latin *spasticus*, from Greek *spastikos* drawing in, from *span*] (1753)
**1** : of, relating to, characterized by, or affected with spasm ⟨a *spastic* colon⟩ ⟨a *spastic* patient⟩
**2** : SPASMODIC 2 ⟨a *spastic* influx of data⟩
— **spas·ti·cal·ly** \-ti-k(ə-)lē\ *adverb*

²**spastic** *noun* (1896)
: one suffering from spastic paralysis

**spas·tic·i·ty** \spa-'sti-sə-tē\ *noun* (circa 1827)
: a spastic state or condition; *especially* : muscular hypertonicity with increased tendon reflexes

**spastic paralysis** *noun* (1879)
: paralysis with tonic spasm of the affected muscles and with increased tendon reflexes
— compare CEREBRAL PALSY

¹**spat** \'spat\ *past and past participle of* SPIT

²**spat** *noun, plural* **spat** *or* **spats** [origin unknown] (1667)
: a young bivalve (as an oyster)

³**spat** *noun* [short for *spatterdash* legging] (circa 1802)
: a cloth or leather gaiter covering the instep and ankle

⁴**spat** *noun* [origin unknown] (1804)
**1** : a brief petty quarrel or angry outburst
**2** *chiefly dialect* : SLAP
**3** : a sound like that of rain falling in large drops

⁵**spat** *verb* **spat·ted; spat·ting** (circa 1832)
*transitive verb*
*chiefly dialect* : SLAP
*intransitive verb*
**1** : to quarrel pettily or briefly
**2** : to strike with a sound like that of rain falling in large drops

**spate** \'spāt\ *noun* [Middle English] (15th century)
**1** : FRESHET, FLOOD
**2 a** : a large number or amount ⟨a *spate* of books on gardening⟩ **b** : a sudden or strong outburst : RUSH ⟨a *spate* of anger⟩

**spathe** \'spāth\ *noun* [New Latin *spatha*, from Latin, broadsword — more at SPADE] (1785)
: a sheathing bract or pair of bracts partly enclosing an inflorescence and especially a spadix on the same axis ⟨the *spathe* of the calla lily⟩

**spath·u·late** \'spath-yə-lət\ *adjective* [Late Latin *spathula, spatula* spatula] (1821)
: SPATULATE ⟨*spathulate* petals of a flower⟩

**spa·tial** \'spā-shəl\ *adjective* [Latin *spatium* space] (1847)
: relating to, occupying, or having the character of space
— **spa·ti·al·i·ty** \,spā-shē-'a-lə-tē\ *noun*
— **spa·tial·ly** \'spā-sh(ə-)lē\ *adverb*

**spatial summation** *noun* (1968)
: sensory summation that involves stimulation of several spatially separated neurons at the same time

**spa·tio·tem·po·ral** \,spā-shē-ō-'tem-p(ə-)rəl\ *adjective* [Latin *spatium* + *tempor-, tempus* time] (1900)
**1** : having both spatial and temporal qualities
**2** : of or relating to space-time
— **spa·tio·tem·po·ral·ly** \-p(ə-)rə-lē\ *adverb*

¹**spat·ter** \'spa-tər\ *verb* [akin to Flemish *spetteren* to spatter] (1600)
*intransitive verb*
: to spurt forth in scattered drops ⟨blood *spattering* everywhere⟩
*transitive verb*
**1** : to splash with or as if with a liquid; *also* : to soil in this way ⟨his coat was *spattered* with mud⟩
**2** : to scatter by or as if by splashing ⟨*spatter* water⟩
**3** : to cover with or as if with splashes or spots
**4** : to injure by aspersion : DEFAME ⟨*spattered* my reputation⟩

²**spatter** *noun* (1797)
**1 a** : the act or process of spattering : the state of being spattered **b** : the noise of spattering
**2 a** : a drop or splash spattered on something or a spot or stain due to spattering **b** : a small amount or number : SPRINKLE ⟨a *spatter* of applause⟩

**spat·ter·dock** \'spa-tər-,däk\ *noun* (1813)
: a common yellow North American water lily (*Nuphar advena*); *also* : a congeneric plant

**spat·u·la** \'spa-chə-lə, 'spach-lə\ *noun* [Late Latin, spoon, spatula — more at EPAULET] (1525)
: a flat thin usually metal implement used especially for spreading or mixing soft substances, scooping, or lifting

**spat·u·late** \'spa-chə-lət\ *adjective* (1760)
: shaped like a spatula ⟨a *spatulate* leaf⟩ ⟨*spatulate* spines of a caterpillar⟩ ⟨a *spatulate* tool⟩
— see LEAF illustration

**spätz·le** \'shpet-slə\ *variant of* SPAETZLE

**spav·in** \'spa-vən\ *noun* [Middle English *spavayne*, from Middle French *espavain*] (15th century)
: SWELLING; *especially* : a bony enlargement of the hock of a horse associated with strain

**spav·ined** \-vənd\ *adjective* (15th century)
**1** : affected with spavin

**2 :** old and decrepit **:** OVER-THE-HILL

**¹spawn** \'spón, 'spän\ *verb* [Middle English, from Anglo-French *espaundre*, from Old French *espandre* to spread out, expand, from Latin *expandere*] (15th century)
*intransitive verb*
**1 :** to deposit spawn
**2 :** to produce young especially in large numbers
*transitive verb*
**1 a :** to produce or deposit (eggs) — used of an aquatic animal **b :** to induce (fish) to spawn **c :** to plant with mushroom spawn
**2 :** BRING FORTH, GENERATE
— **spawn·er** *noun*

**²spawn** *noun* (15th century)
**1 :** the eggs of aquatic animals (as fishes or oysters) that lay many small eggs
**2 :** PRODUCT, OFFSPRING; *also* **:** numerous issue
**3 :** the seed, germ, or source of something
**4 :** mycelium especially prepared (as in bricks) for propagating mushrooms

**spay** \'spā, *nonstandard* 'spād\ *transitive verb*
**spayed** \'spād, *nonstandard* 'spā-dəd\; **spay·ing** \'spā-iŋ, *nonstandard* 'spā-diŋ\ [Middle English, from Middle French *espeer* to cut with a sword, from Old French, from *espee* sword, from Latin *spatha* sword — more at SPADE] (15th century)
**:** to remove the ovaries of (a female animal)

**spaz** \'spaz\ *noun, plural* **spaz·zes** [by shortening & alteration from *spastic*] (1965)
*slang* **:** one who is inept **:** KLUTZ

**speak** \'spēk\ *verb* **spoke** \'spōk\; **spo·ken** \'spō-kən\; **speak·ing** [Middle English *speken*, from Old English *sprecan, specan*; akin to Old High German *sprehhan* to speak, Greek *spharageisthai* to crackle] (before 12th century)
*intransitive verb*
**1 a :** to utter words or articulate sounds with the ordinary voice **:** TALK **b** (1) **:** to express thoughts, opinions, or feelings orally (2) **:** to extend a greeting (3) **:** to be on speaking terms ⟨still were not *speaking* after the dispute⟩ **c** (1) **:** to express oneself before a group (2) **:** to address one's remarks ⟨*speak* to the issue⟩
**2 a :** to make a written statement ⟨his diaries . . . *spoke* . . . of his entrancement with death —Sy Kahn⟩ **b :** to use such an expression — often used in the phrase *so to speak* ⟨was at the enemy's gates, so to *speak* —C. S. Forester⟩ **c :** to serve as spokesman ⟨*spoke* for the whole group⟩
**3 a :** to express feelings by other than verbal means ⟨actions *speak* louder than words⟩ **b :** SIGNAL **c :** to be interesting or attractive **:** APPEAL ⟨great music . . . *speaks* directly to the emotions —A. N. Whitehead⟩
**4 :** to make a request **:** ASK ⟨*spoke* for the remaining piece of pie⟩
**5 :** to make a characteristic or natural sound ⟨all at once the thunder *spoke* —George Meredith⟩
**6 a :** TESTIFY **b :** to be indicative or suggestive ⟨his gold . . . *spoke* of riches in the land —Julian Dana⟩
*transitive verb*
**1 a** (1) **:** to utter with the speaking voice **:** PRONOUNCE (2) **:** to give a recitation of **:** DECLAIM **b :** to express orally **:** DECLARE ⟨free to *speak* their minds⟩ **c :** ADDRESS, ACCOST; *especially* **:** HAIL
**2 :** to make known in writing **:** STATE
**3 :** to use or be able to use in speaking ⟨*speaks* Spanish⟩
**4 :** to indicate by other than verbal means
**5** *archaic* **:** DESCRIBE, DEPICT
— **speak·able** \'spē-kə-bəl\ *adjective*
— **to speak of :** worthy of mention or notice — usually used in negative constructions
**-speak** \-ˌspēk\ *noun combining form* [*newspeak*]
— used to form especially nonce words denoting a particular kind of jargon ⟨architect*speak*⟩ ⟨California*speak*⟩

**speak·easy** \'spēk-ˌē-zē\ *noun, plural* **-eas·ies** (1889)
**:** a place where alcoholic beverages are illegally sold; *specifically* **:** such a place during the period of prohibition in the U.S.

**speak·er** \'spē-kər\ *noun* (14th century)
**1 a :** one that speaks; *especially* **:** one who uses a language ⟨native *speakers* of French⟩ **b :** one who makes a public speech **c :** one who acts as a spokesman
**2 :** the presiding officer of a deliberative assembly ⟨*Speaker* of the House of Representatives⟩
**3 :** LOUDSPEAKER
— **speak·er·ship** \-ˌship\ *noun*

**speak·er·phone** \'spē-kər-ˌfōn\ *noun* (1955)
**:** a combination microphone and loudspeaker device for two-way communication by telephone lines

**speak·ing** \'spē-kiŋ\ *adjective* (13th century)
**1 a :** that speaks **:** capable of speech **b :** having a population that speaks a specified language — usually used in combination ⟨English-*speaking* countries⟩ **c :** that involves talking or giving speeches ⟨a *speaking* role⟩ ⟨a *speaking* tour⟩
**2 :** highly significant or expressive **:** ELOQUENT
**3 :** resembling a living being or a real object

**speaking tube** *noun* (1833)
**:** a pipe through which conversation may be conducted (as between different parts of a building)

**speak–out** \'spēk-ˌaůt\ *noun* (1968)
**:** an event in which people publicly share their experiences of or views on an issue

**speak out** *intransitive verb* (1530)
**1 :** to speak loud enough to be heard
**2 :** to speak boldly **:** express an opinion frankly ⟨*spoke out* on the issues⟩

**speak up** *intransitive verb* (1705)
**1 :** to express an opinion freely ⟨*speak up* for truth and justice —Clive Bell⟩
**2 :** to speak loudly and distinctly

**spean** \'spēn\ *transitive verb* [Middle Dutch *spenen*] (1595)
*chiefly Scottish* **:** WEAN

**¹spear** \'spir\ *noun* [Middle English *spere*, from Old English; akin to Old High German *sper* spear, Latin *sparus* hunting spear] (before 12th century)
**1 :** a thrusting or throwing weapon with long shaft and sharp head or blade
**2 :** a sharp-pointed instrument with barbs used in spearing fish
**3 :** SPEARMAN

**²spear** (15th century)
*transitive verb*
**1 :** to pierce, strike, or take with or as if with a spear ⟨*spear* salmon⟩ ⟨*speared* a chop from the platter⟩
**2 :** to catch (as a baseball) with a sudden thrust of the arm
*intransitive verb*
**:** to thrust at or wound something with or as if with a spear
— **spear·er** *noun*

**³spear** *adjective* (1861)
**:** PATERNAL, MALE ⟨the *spear* side of the family⟩ — compare DISTAFF

**⁴spear** *intransitive verb* [⁵*spear*] (1573)
*of a plant* **:** to thrust a spear upward

**⁵spear** *noun* [alteration of ¹*spire*] (1647)
**:** a usually young blade, shoot, or sprout (as of grass)

**spear–car·ri·er** \'spir-ˌkar-ē-ər\ *noun* (1953)
**1 a :** a member of an opera chorus **b :** a bit actor in a play
**2 :** a person whose actions are of little significance or value in an event or organization

**¹spear·fish** \-ˌfish\ *noun* (circa 1882)
**:** any of several billfishes (genus *Tetrapturus*) having the anterior part of the first dorsal fin about as high as the body is deep

**²spearfish** *intransitive verb* (circa 1949)
**:** to fish with a spear

**spear·gun** \'spir-ˌgən\ *noun* (1951)

**:** a gun that shoots a spear and is used in spearfishing

**¹spear·head** \-ˌhed\ *noun* (14th century)
**1 :** the sharp-pointed head of a spear
**2 :** a leading element, force, or influence in an undertaking or development

**²spearhead** *transitive verb* (1937)
**:** to serve as leader or leading element of

**spear·man** \'spir-mən\ *noun* (14th century)
**:** one armed with a spear

**spear·mint** \-ˌmint, -mənt\ *noun* (1562)
**:** a common mint (*Mentha spicata*) grown for flavoring and especially for its aromatic oil

**spear–throw·er** \-ˌthrō(-ə)r\ *noun* (1871)
**:** ATLATL

**spear·wort** \-ˌwərt, -ˌwórt\ *noun* (14th century)
**:** any of several buttercups (especially *Ranunculus flammula*) with spear-shaped leaves

**spec** \'spek\ *transitive verb* **specced** *or* **spec'd** \'spekt\; **spec·cing** [²*specs*] (1965)
**:** to write specifications for

**¹spe·cial** \'spe-shəl\ *adjective* [Middle English, from Old French or Latin; Old French *especial*, from Latin *specialis* individual, particular, from *species* species] (13th century)
**1 :** distinguished by some unusual quality; *especially* **:** being in some way superior ⟨our *special* blend⟩
**2 :** held in particular esteem ⟨a *special* friend⟩
**3 a :** readily distinguishable from others of the same category **:** UNIQUE ⟨they set it apart as a *special* day of thanksgiving⟩ **b :** of, relating to, or constituting a species **:** SPECIFIC
**4 :** being other than the usual **:** ADDITIONAL, EXTRA
**5 :** designed for a particular purpose or occasion ☆
— **spe·cial·ness** *noun*

**²special** *noun* (1866)
**1 :** one that is used for a special service or occasion ⟨caught the commuter *special* to work⟩
**2 :** something (as a television program) that is not part of a regular series

**special assessment** *noun* (1875)
**:** a specific tax levied on private property to meet the cost of public improvements that enhance the value of the property

**special delivery** *noun* (1886)
**:** expedited messenger delivery of mail matter for an extra fee

**special district** *noun* (1950)
**:** a political subdivision of a state established to provide a single public service (as water supply or sanitation) within a specific geographical area

spearmint

---

☆ **SYNONYMS**
**Special, especial, specific, particular, individual** mean of or relating to one thing or class. SPECIAL stresses having a quality, character, identity, or use of its own ⟨*special* ingredients⟩. ESPECIAL may add implications of preeminence or preference ⟨a matter of *especial* importance⟩. SPECIFIC implies a quality or character distinguishing a kind or a species ⟨children with *specific* nutritional needs⟩. PARTICULAR stresses the distinctness of something as an individual ⟨a ballet step of *particular* difficulty⟩. INDIVIDUAL implies unequivocal reference to one of a class or group ⟨valued each *individual* opinion⟩.

---

**special drawing rights** *noun* (1967)
: a means of exchange used by governments to settle their international indebtedness

**special education** *noun* (1921)
: classes for students (as the handicapped) with special educational needs

**special effects** *noun plural* (1937)
: visual or sound effects introduced into a motion picture or a taped television production

**Special Forces** *noun plural* (1962)
: a branch of the army composed of soldiers specially trained in guerrilla warfare

**special handling** *noun* (1928)
: the handling of parcel-post or fourth-class mail as first-class but not as special-delivery matter for an extra fee

**special interest** *noun* (1910)
: a person or group seeking to influence legislative or government policy to further often narrowly defined interests; *especially* : LOBBY

**spe·cial·i·sa·tion, spe·cial·ise, special·ised** *British variant of* SPECIALIZATION, SPECIALIZE, SPECIALIZED

**spe·cial·ism** \'spe-shə-ˌli-zəm\ *noun* (1856)
**1** : specialization in an occupation or branch of learning
**2** : a field of specialization : SPECIALTY

**spe·cial·ist** \'spe-sh(ə-)list\ *noun* (1856)
**1** : one who specializes in a particular occupation, practice, or branch of learning
**2** : any of four enlisted ranks in the army corresponding to the grades of corporal through sergeant first class
— **specialist** *or* **spe·cial·is·tic** \ˌspe-shə-'lis-tik\ *adjective*

**spe·ci·al·i·ty** \ˌspe-shē-'a-lə-tē\ *noun, plural* **-ties** (15th century)
**1** : a special mark or quality
**2** : a special object or class of objects
**3 a** : a special aptitude or skill **b** : SPECIALTY 3

**spe·cial·i·za·tion** \ˌspe-sh(ə-)lə-'zā-shən\ *noun* (1843)
**1** : a making or becoming specialized
**2 a** : structural adaptation of a body part to a particular function or of an organism for life in a particular environment **b** : a body part or an organism adapted by specialization

**spe·cial·ize** \'spe-shə-ˌlīz\ *verb* **-ized; -iz·ing** (1613)
*transitive verb*
**1** : to make particular mention of : PARTICULARIZE
**2** : to apply or direct to a specific end or use ⟨*specialized* their study⟩
*intransitive verb*
**1** : to concentrate one's efforts in a special activity, field, or practice
**2** : to undergo specialization; *especially* : to change adaptively

**specialized** *adjective* (1853)
**1** : characterized by or exhibiting biological specialization; *especially* : highly differentiated especially in a particular direction or for a particular end
**2** : designed or fitted for one particular purpose or occupation ⟨*specialized* personnel⟩

**spe·cial·ly** \'spe-sh(ə-)lē\ *adverb* (14th century)
**1** : in a special manner ⟨treated her friends *specially*⟩
**2 a** : for a special purpose ⟨dresses made *specially* for the occasion⟩ ⟨wines *specially* selected to match each course⟩ **b** : in particular : SPECIFICALLY ⟨made *specially* for you⟩
**3** : ESPECIALLY 2 ⟨makes a *specially* fine curry⟩ ⟨was *specially* pleased with the gift⟩

**special pleading** *noun* (1684)
**1** : the allegation of special or new matter to offset the effect of matter pleaded by the opposite side and admitted, as distinguished from a direct denial of the matter pleaded
**2** : misleading argument that presents one point or phase as if it covered the entire question at issue

**special relativity** *noun* (1941)
: RELATIVITY 3a

**special theory of relativity** (1920)
: RELATIVITY 3a

**spe·cial·ty** \'spe-shəl-tē\ *noun, plural* **-ties** [Middle English *specialte*, from Middle French *especialté*, from Late Latin *specialitat-, specialitas*, from Latin *specialis* special] (15th century)
**1** : a distinctive mark or quality
**2 a** : a special object or class of objects: as (1) : a legal agreement embodied in a sealed instrument (2) : a product of a special kind or of special excellence ⟨fried chicken is my *specialty*⟩ **b** : the state of being special, distinctive, or peculiar
**3** : something in which one specializes

**spe·ci·a·tion** \ˌspē-shē-'ā-shən, -sē-\ *noun* (1906)
: the process of biological species formation
— **spe·ci·ate** \'spē-shē-ˌāt, -sē-\ *intransitive verb*
— **spe·ci·a·tion·al** \ˌspē-shē-'ā-shnəl, -shə-nᵊl\ *adjective*

**¹spe·cie** \'spē-shē, -sē\ *noun* [from *in specie*, from Latin, in kind] (1617)
: money in coin
— **in specie** : in the same or like form or kind ⟨ready to return insult *in specie*⟩; *also* : in coin

**²specie** *noun* [back-formation from *species* (taken as a plural)] (1711)
*nonstandard* : SPECIES

**¹spe·cies** \'spē-(ˌ)shēz, -(ˌ)sēz\ *noun, plural* **species** [Middle English, from Latin, appearance, kind, species, from *specere* to look — more at SPY] (14th century)
**1 a** : KIND, SORT **b** : a class of individuals having common attributes and designated by a common name; *specifically* : a logical division of a genus or more comprehensive class **c** : the human race : human beings — often used with *the* ⟨survival of the *species* in the nuclear age⟩ **d** (1) : a category of biological classification ranking immediately below the genus or subgenus, comprising related organisms or populations potentially capable of interbreeding, and being designated by a binomial that consists of the name of a genus followed by a Latin or latinized uncapitalized noun or adjective agreeing grammatically with the genus name (2) : an individual or kind belonging to a biological species **e** : a particular kind of atomic nucleus, atom, molecule, or ion
**2** : the consecrated eucharistic elements of the Roman Catholic or Eastern Orthodox Eucharist
**3 a** : a mental image; *also* : a sensible object **b** : an object of thought correlative with a natural object
**word history** see SPICE

**²species** *adjective* (1899)
: belonging to a biological species as distinguished from a horticultural variety ⟨a *species* rose⟩

**spe·cies·ism** \'spē-shē-ˌzi-zəm, -sē-\ *noun* (1973)
**1** : prejudice or discrimination based on species; *especially* : discrimination against animals
**2** : the assumption of human superiority on which speciesism is based

**¹spe·cif·ic** \spi-'si-fik\ *adjective* [Late Latin *specificus*, from Latin *species*] (circa 1631)
**1 a** : constituting or falling into a specifiable category **b** : sharing or being those properties of something that allow it to be referred to a particular category
**2 a** : restricted to a particular individual, situation, relation, or effect ⟨a disease *specific* to horses⟩ **b** : exerting a distinctive influence (as on a body part or a disease) ⟨*specific* antibodies⟩
**3** : free from ambiguity : ACCURATE ⟨a *specific* statement of faith⟩
**4** : of, relating to, or constituting a species and especially a biologic species

**5 a** : being any of various arbitrary physical constants and especially one relating a quantitative attribute to unit mass, volume, or area **b** : imposed at a fixed rate per unit (as of weight or count) ⟨*specific* import duties⟩ — compare AD VALOREM
**synonym** see SPECIAL, EXPLICIT
— **spe·cif·i·cal·ly** \-fi-k(ə-)lē\ *adverb*

**²specific** *noun* (1661)
**1 a** : something peculiarly adapted to a purpose or use **b** : a drug or remedy having a specific mitigating effect on a disease
**2 a** : a characteristic quality or trait **b** : DETAILS, PARTICULARS — usually used in plural ⟨haggling over the legal and financial *specifics* of independence —*Time*⟩ **c** *plural* : SPECIFICATION 2a

**spec·i·fi·ca·tion** \ˌspe-sə-fə-'kā-shən, ˌspes-fə-\ *noun* (1633)
**1** : the act or process of specifying
**2 a** : a detailed precise presentation of something or of a plan or proposal for something — usually used in plural **b** : a statement of legal particulars (as of charges or of contract terms); *also* : a single item of such statement **c** : a written description of an invention for which a patent is sought

**specific epithet** *noun* (1906)
: the Latin or latinized noun or adjective that follows the genus name in a taxonomic binomial

**specific gravity** *noun* (1666)
: the ratio of the density of a substance to the density of some substance (as pure water) taken as a standard when both densities are obtained by weighing in air

**specific heat** *noun* (1832)
: the heat in calories required to raise the temperature of one gram of a substance one degree Celsius

**specific impulse** *noun* (1947)
: the thrust produced per unit rate of consumption of the propellant that is usually expressed in pounds of thrust per pound of propellant used per second and that is a measure of the efficiency of a rocket engine

**spec·i·fic·i·ty** \ˌspe-sə-'fi-sə-tē\ *noun* (1876)
: the quality or condition of being specific: as **a** : the condition of being peculiar to a particular individual or group of organisms ⟨host *specificity* of a parasite⟩ **b** : the condition of participating in or catalyzing only one or a few chemical reactions ⟨the *specificity* of an enzyme⟩

**specific performance** *noun* (circa 1876)
**1** : the performance of a legal contract strictly or substantially according to its terms
**2** : an equitable remedy enjoining specific performance

**spec·i·fy** \'spe-sə-ˌfī\ *transitive verb* **-fied; -fy·ing** [Middle English *specifien*, from Middle French *specifier*, from Late Latin *specificare*, from *specificus*] (14th century)
**1** : to name or state explicitly or in detail
**2** : to include as an item in a specification
— **spec·i·fi·able** \ˌspe-sə-'fī-ə-bəl\ *adjective*
— **spec·i·fi·er** \'spe-sə-ˌfī-(ə)r\ *noun*

**spec·i·men** \'spes-mən, 'spe-sə-\ *noun* [Latin, from *specere* to look at, look — more at SPY] (1610)
**1 a** : an individual, item, or part considered typical of a group, class, or whole **b** : a portion or quantity of material for use in testing, examination, or study ⟨a urine *specimen*⟩
**2 a** : something that obviously belongs to a particular category but is noticed by reason of an individual distinguishing characteristic **b** : PERSON, INDIVIDUAL ⟨he's a tough *specimen*⟩
**3** : a plant grown for exhibition or in the open to display its full development ⟨*specimen* trees⟩ ⟨*specimen* plantings⟩
**synonym** see INSTANCE

**spe·ci·os·i·ty** \ˌspē-shē-'ä-sə-tē\ *noun* (1608)
: the quality or state of being specious : SPECIOUSNESS

**spe·cious** \'spē-shəs\ *adjective* [Middle English, visually pleasing, from Latin *speciosus* beautiful, plausible, from *species*] (1513)
**1** *obsolete* **:** SHOWY
**2 :** having deceptive attraction or allure
**3 :** having a false look of truth or genuineness **:** SOPHISTIC
— **spe·cious·ly** *adverb*
— **spe·cious·ness** *noun*

**¹speck** \'spek\ *noun* [Middle English *specke*, from Old English *specca*] (before 12th century)
**1 :** a small discoloration or spot especially from stain or decay
**2 :** a very small amount **:** BIT
**3 :** something marked or marred with specks
— **specked** \'spekt\ *adjective*

**²speck** *transitive verb* (1580)
**:** to produce specks on or in

**¹speck·le** \'spe-kəl\ *noun* [Middle English; akin to Old English *specca*] (15th century)
**:** a little speck (as of color)

**²speckle** *transitive verb* **speck·led; speck·ling** \-k(ə-)liŋ\ (circa 1570)
**1 :** to mark with speckles
**2 :** to be distributed in or on like speckles

**speckled perch** *noun* (1877)
**:** BLACK CRAPPIE

**speckled trout** *noun* (1805)
**1 :** BROOK TROUT
**2 :** SPOTTED SEA TROUT

**speckle interferometry** *noun* (1970)
**:** a technique for generating a clear composite image of a celestial object blurred by atmospheric turbulence in which a large number of short-exposure photographs are mathematically correlated by a computer

**¹specs** \'speks\ *noun plural* [contraction of *spectacles*] (1807)
**:** GLASSES

**²specs** *noun plural* [by contraction] (1942)
**:** SPECIFICATIONS

**spec·ta·cle** \'spek-ti-kəl *also* -ˌti-kəl\ *noun* [Middle English, from Middle French, from Latin *spectaculum*, from *spectare* to watch, frequentative of *specere* to look, look at — more at SPY] (14th century)
**1 a :** something exhibited to view as unusual, notable, or entertaining; *especially* **:** an eye-catching or dramatic public display **b :** an object of curiosity or contempt ⟨made a *spectacle* of herself⟩
**2** *plural* **:** GLASSES
**3 :** something (as natural markings on an animal) suggesting a pair of glasses

**spec·ta·cled** \-kəld\ *adjective* (1607)
**1 :** having or wearing spectacles
**2 :** having markings suggesting a pair of spectacles ⟨a *spectacled* alligator⟩

**¹spec·tac·u·lar** \spek-'ta-kyə-lər, spək-\ *adjective* [Latin *spectaculum*] (1682)
**:** of, relating to, or being a spectacle **:** STRIKING, SENSATIONAL ⟨a *spectacular* display of fireworks⟩
— **spec·tac·u·lar·ly** *adverb*

**²spectacular** *noun* (1890)
**:** something that is spectacular; *especially* **:** an elaborate film, television, or theatrical production

**spec·tate** \'spek-ˌtāt\ *intransitive verb* **spec·tat·ed; spec·tat·ing** [back-formation from *spectator*] (1858)
**:** to be present as a spectator (as at a sports event)

**spec·ta·tor** \'spek-ˌtā-tər, spek-'\ *noun* [Latin, from *spectare* to watch] (circa 1586)
**1 :** one who looks on or watches
**2 :** a woman's pump usually having contrasting colors with a perforated design at the toe and sometimes heel
— **spectator** *adjective*
— **spec·ta·tor·i·al** \ˌspek-tə-'tōr-ē-əl, -'tȯr-\ *adjective*
— **spec·ta·tor·ship** \'spek-ˌtā-tər-ˌship, spek-'\ *noun*

**spec·ter** *or* **spec·tre** \'spek-tər\ *noun* [French *spectre*, from Latin *spectrum* appearance, specter, from *specere* to look, look at — more at SPY] (1605)
**1 :** a visible disembodied spirit **:** GHOST
**2 :** something that haunts or perturbs the mind **:** PHANTASM ⟨the *specter* of hunger⟩

**spec·ti·no·my·cin** \ˌspek-tə-nō-'mī-sⁿn\ *noun* [*spect*- (from New Latin *spectabilis*, specific epithet of *Streptomyces spectabilis*) + *actinomycin*] (1964)
**:** a white crystalline broad-spectrum antibiotic $C_{14}H_{24}N_2O_7$ produced by a bacterium (*Streptomyces spectabilis*) that is used clinically especially in the form of its hydrochloride to treat gonorrhea

**spec·tral** \'spek-trəl\ *adjective* (1815)
**1 :** of, relating to, or suggesting a specter **:** GHOSTLY
**2 :** of, relating to, or made by a spectrum
— **spec·tral·ly** \'spek-trə-lē\ *adverb*

**spectral line** *noun* (1866)
**:** one of a series of linear images of the narrow slit of a spectrograph or similar instrument corresponding to a component of the spectrum of the radiation emitted by a particular source

**spectro-** *combining form* [New Latin *spectrum*]
**:** spectrum ⟨*spectro*scope⟩

**spec·tro·flu·o·rom·e·ter** \'spek-(ˌ)trō-ˌflü-'rä-mə-tər, -flō-, -flō-\ *also* **spec·tro·flu·o·rim·e·ter** \-'ri-\ *noun* (1957)
**:** a device for measuring and recording fluorescence spectra
— **spec·tro·flu·o·ro·met·ric** \-ˌflür-ə-'me-trik, -ˌflō-, -ˌflō-\ *adjective*
— **spec·tro·flu·o·rom·e·try** \-flü-'rä-mə-trē, -ˌflō-, -ˌflō-\ *noun*

**spec·tro·gram** \'spek-t(r)ə-ˌgram\ *noun* [International Scientific Vocabulary] (1892)
**:** a photograph or diagram of a spectrum

**spec·tro·graph** \-ˌgraf\ *noun* [International Scientific Vocabulary] (1884)
**:** an instrument for dispersing radiation (as electromagnetic radiation or sound waves) into a spectrum and photographing or mapping the spectrum
— **spec·tro·graph·ic** \ˌspek-t(r)ə-'gra-fik\ *adjective*
— **spec·tro·graph·i·cal·ly** \-fi-k(ə-)lē\ *adverb*
— **spec·trog·ra·phy** \spek-'trä-grə-fē\ *noun*

**spec·tro·he·lio·gram** \ˌspek-trō-'hē-lē-ə-ˌgram\ *noun* (1905)
**:** a photograph of the sun that is made by monochromatic light and shows the sun's faculae and prominences

**spec·tro·he·lio·graph** \-ˌgraf\ *noun* [International Scientific Vocabulary] (1892)
**:** an apparatus for making spectroheliograms
— **spec·tro·he·li·og·ra·phy** \-ˌhē-lē-'ä-grə-fē\ *noun*

**spec·tro·he·lio·scope** \-'hē-lē-ə-ˌskōp\ *noun* [International Scientific Vocabulary] (1906)
**1 :** SPECTROHELIOGRAPH
**2 :** an instrument similar to a spectroheliograph used for visual as distinguished from photographic observations

**spec·trom·e·ter** \spek-'trä-mə-tər\ *noun* [International Scientific Vocabulary] (1874)
**1 :** an instrument used for measuring wavelengths of light spectra
**2 :** any of various analytical instruments in which an emission (as of particles or radiation) is dispersed according to some property (as mass or energy) of the emission and the amount of dispersion is measured ⟨nuclear magnetic resonance *spectrometer*⟩
— **spec·tro·met·ric** \ˌspek-trə-'me-trik\ *adjective*
— **spec·trom·e·try** \spek-'trä-mə-trē\ *noun*

**spec·tro·pho·tom·e·ter** \ˌspek-trō-fə-'tä-mə-tər\ *noun* [International Scientific Vocabulary] (1881)
**:** a photometer for measuring the relative intensities of the light in different parts of a spectrum
— **spec·tro·pho·to·met·ric** \-trə-ˌfō-tə-'me-trik\ *also* **spec·tro·pho·to·met·ri·cal** \-tri-kəl\ *adjective*
— **spec·tro·pho·to·met·ri·cal·ly** \-tri-k(ə-)lē\ *adverb*
— **spec·tro·pho·tom·e·try** \ˌspek-(ˌ)trō-fə-'tä-mə-trē\ *noun*

**spec·tro·scope** \'spek-trə-ˌskōp\ *noun* [International Scientific Vocabulary] (1861)
**:** an instrument for forming and examining spectra especially in the visible region of the electromagnetic spectrum
— **spec·tro·scop·ic** \ˌspek-trə-'skä-pik\ *adjective*
— **spec·tro·scop·i·cal·ly** \-pi-k(ə-)lē\ *adverb*
— **spec·tros·co·pist** \spek-'träs-kə-pist\ *noun*

**spec·tros·co·py** \spek-'träs-kə-pē\ *noun* (1870)
**1 :** the production and investigation of spectra
**2 :** the process or technique of using a spectroscope or spectrometer

**spec·trum** \'spek-trəm\ *noun, plural* **spec·tra** \-trə\ *or* **spectrums** [New Latin, from Latin, appearance — more at SPECTER] (1671)
**1 a :** a continuum of color formed when a beam of white light is dispersed (as by passage through a prism) so that its component wavelengths are arranged in order **b :** any of various continua that resemble a spectrum in consisting of an ordered arrangement by a particular characteristic (as frequency or energy): as **(1)** **:** ELECTROMAGNETIC SPECTRUM **(2)** **:** RADIO SPECTRUM **(3)** **:** the range of frequencies of sound waves **(4)** **:** MASS SPECTRUM **c :** the representation (as a plot) of a spectrum
**2 a :** a continuous sequence or range ⟨a wide *spectrum* of interests⟩ **b :** kinds of organisms associated with a particular situation (as an environment) or susceptible to an agent (as an antibiotic)

**spec·u·lar** \'spe-kyə-lər\ *adjective* [Latin *specularis* of a mirror, from *speculum*] (1661)
**:** of, relating to, or having the qualities of a mirror
— **spec·u·lar·i·ty** \ˌspe-kyə-'lar-ə-tē\ *noun*
— **spec·u·lar·ly** \'spe-kyə-lər-lē\ *adverb*

**spec·u·late** \'spe-kyə-ˌlāt\ *verb* **-lat·ed; -lat·ing** [Latin *speculatus*, past participle of *speculari* to spy out, examine, from *specula* watchtower, from *specere* to look, look at — more at SPY] (1599)
*intransitive verb*
**1 a :** to meditate on or ponder a subject **:** REFLECT **b :** to review something idly or casually and often inconclusively
**2 :** to assume a business risk in hope of gain; *especially* **:** to buy or sell in expectation of profiting from market fluctuations
*transitive verb*
**1 :** to take to be true on the basis of insufficient evidence **:** THEORIZE ⟨*speculated* that a virus caused the disease⟩
**2 :** to be curious or doubtful about **:** WONDER ⟨*speculates* whether it will rain all vacation⟩
**synonym** see THINK
— **spec·u·la·tor** \-ˌlā-tər\ *noun*

**spec·u·la·tion** \ˌspe-kyə-'lā-shən\ *noun* (14th century)
**:** an act or instance of speculating: as **a :** assumption of unusual business risk in hopes of

\ə\ abut \ᵊ\ kitten \ər\ further \a\ ash \ā\ ace \ä\ mop, mar \au̇\ out \ch\ chin \e\ bet \ē\ easy \g\ go \i\ hit \ī\ ice \j\ job \ŋ\ sing \ō\ go \ȯ\ law \ȯi\ boy \th\ thin \ṯẖ\ the \ü\ loot \u̇\ foot \y\ yet \zh\ vision *see also* Guide to Pronunciation obtaining commensurate gain **b** : a transaction involving such speculation

**spec·u·la·tive** \'spe-kyə-lə-tiv, -ˌlā-\ *adjective* (14th century)
**1** : involving, based on, or constituting intellectual speculation; *also* : theoretical rather than demonstrable ⟨*speculative* knowledge⟩
**2** : marked by questioning curiosity ⟨gave him a *speculative* glance⟩
**3** : of, relating to, or being a financial speculation ⟨*speculative* stocks⟩ ⟨*speculative* venture⟩
— **spec·u·la·tive·ly** *adverb*

**spec·u·lum** \'spe-kyə-ləm\ *noun*, *plural* **-la** \-lə\ *also* **-lums** [Middle English, from Latin, mirror, from *specere*] (15th century)
**1** : an instrument inserted into a body passage for inspection or medication
**2** : a drawing or table showing the relative positions of all the planets (as in an astrological nativity)
**3** : a patch of color on the secondaries of most ducks and some other birds

**speech** \'spēch\ *noun* [Middle English *speche*, from Old English *sprǣc*, *spǣc*; akin to Old English *sprecan* to speak — more at SPEAK] (before 12th century)
**1 a** : the communication or expression of thoughts in spoken words **b** : exchange of spoken words : CONVERSATION
**2 a** : something that is spoken : UTTERANCE **b** : a usually public discourse : ADDRESS
**3 a** : LANGUAGE, DIALECT **b** : an individual manner or style of speaking
**4** : the power of expressing or communicating thoughts by speaking

**speech community** *noun* (1894)
: a group of people sharing characteristic patterns of vocabulary, grammar, and pronunciation

**speech form** *noun* (1863)
: LINGUISTIC FORM

**speech·ify** \'spē-chə-ˌfī\ *intransitive verb* **-ified; -ify·ing** (1723)
: to make a speech

**speech·less** \'spēch-ləs\ *adjective* (before 12th century)
**1** : unable to speak : DUMB
**2** : not speaking : SILENT
**3** : not capable of being expressed in words
— **speech·less·ly** *adverb*
— **speech·less·ness** *noun*

**speech·writ·er** \-ˌrī-tər\ *noun* (1834)
: a person who writes speeches (as for a politician)

¹**speed** \'spēd\ *noun* [Middle English *spede*, from Old English *spēd;* akin to Old High German *spuot* prosperity, speed, Old English *spōwan* to succeed, Latin *spes* hope, Latin *spēti* to be in time] (before 12th century)
**1** *archaic* : prosperity in an undertaking : SUCCESS
**2 a** : the act or state of moving swiftly : SWIFTNESS **b** : rate of motion: as (1) : VELOCITY 1, 3a (2) : the magnitude of a velocity irrespective of direction **c** : IMPETUS
**3** : swiftness or rate of performance or action
**4 a** : the sensitivity of a photographic film, plate, or paper expressed numerically **b** : the light-gathering power of a lens or optical system **c** : the time during which a camera shutter is open
**5** : a transmission gear in automotive vehicles or bicycles — usually used in combination ⟨a ten-*speed* bicycle⟩
**6** : someone or something that appeals to one's taste
**7** : METHAMPHETAMINE; *also* : a related stimulant drug and especially an amphetamine
**synonym** see HASTE
— **speed·ster** \'spēd-stər\ *noun*
— **at speed** *chiefly British* : FAST, RAPIDLY
— **up to speed** : operating at full effectiveness or potential

²**speed** *verb* **sped** \'sped\ *or* **speed·ed; speed·ing** (before 12th century)
*intransitive verb*
**1 a** *archaic* : to prosper in an undertaking **b** *archaic* : GET ALONG, FARE
**2 a** : to make haste ⟨*sped* to her bedside⟩ **b** : to go or drive at excessive or illegal speed
**3** : to move, work, or take place faster : ACCELERATE ⟨the heart *speeds* up⟩
*transitive verb*
**1 a** *archaic* : to cause or help to prosper : AID **b** : to further the success of
**2 a** : to cause to move quickly : HASTEN **b** : to wish Godspeed to **c** : to increase the speed of : ACCELERATE
**3** : to send out ⟨*speed* an arrow⟩
— **speed·er** *noun*

¹**speed·ball** \'sped-ˌbol\ *noun* (1905)
**1** *slang* : a dose of cocaine mixed with heroin or morphine or an amphetamine and usually taken by injection
**2** : a game which resembles soccer but in which a ball caught in the air may be passed with the hands and in which a score is made by kicking or heading the ball between the goalposts or by a successful forward pass over the goal line
**3** : one that is outstandingly fast

²**speedball** *intransitive verb* (1970)
*slang* : to take a speedball especially by injection

**speed·boat** \-ˌbōt\ *noun* (1911)
: a fast launch or motorboat
— **speed·boat·ing** \-ˌbō-tiŋ\ *noun*

**speed bump** *noun* (1972)
: a low raised ridge across a roadway (as in a parking lot) to limit vehicle speed

**speed freak** *noun* (1967)
: one who habitually misuses amphetamines and especially methamphetamine

**speed limit** *noun* (1902)
: the maximum or minimum speed permitted by law in a given area under specified circumstances

**speedo** \'spē-(ˌ)dō\ *noun*, *plural* **speed·os** [by shortening] (1934)
*chiefly British* : SPEEDOMETER

**speed of light** (1823)
: a fundamental physical constant that is the speed at which electromagnetic radiation propagates in a vacuum and that has a value fixed by international convention of 299,792,458 meters per second — symbol *c*

**speed·om·e·ter** \spi-'dä-mə-tər\ *noun* (1903)
**1** : an instrument for indicating speed : TACHOMETER
**2** : an instrument for indicating distance traversed as well as speed of travel; *also* : ODOMETER

**speed–read·ing** \'spēd-ˌrē-diŋ\ *noun* (1962)
: a method of reading rapidly by skimming
— **speed–read** *transitive verb*

**speed shop** *noun* (1953)
: a shop that sells custom automotive equipment especially to hot-rodders

**speed skating** *noun* (1885)
: the sport of racing on skates
— **speed skater** *noun*

**speed trap** *noun* (1925)
: a stretch of road policed by often concealed officers or devices (as radar) so as to catch speeders

**speed·up** \'spēd-ˌəp\ *noun* (1921)
**1** : ACCELERATION
**2** : an employer's demand for accelerated output without increased pay

**speed·way** \'spēd-ˌwā\ *noun* (1894)
**1** : a public road on which fast driving is allowed; *specifically* : EXPRESSWAY
**2** : a racecourse for automobiles or motorcycles
**3** : a sprint race for motorcycles

**speed·well** \'spēd-ˌwel\ *noun* (1578)
: a perennial European herb (*Veronica officinalis*) of the snapdragon family that is naturalized in North America and has small bluish flowers in axillary racemes; *also* : any plant of the same genus

**speedy** \'spē-dē\ *adjective* **speed·i·er; -est** (14th century)
: marked by swiftness of motion or action; *also* : PROMPT 2
**synonym** see FAST
— **speed·i·ly** \'spē-dᵊl-ē\ *adverb*
— **speed·i·ness** \'spē-dē-nəs\ *noun*

**speel** \'spē(ə)l\ *verb* [origin unknown] (1513)
*chiefly Scottish* : CLIMB

**speer** *or* **speir** \'spir\ *verb* [Middle English (Scots) *speren*, from Old English *spyrian* to seek after; akin to Old English *spor* spoor] (before 12th century)
*chiefly Scottish* : ASK, INQUIRE

**spe·le·ol·o·gy** \ˌspē-lē-'ä-lə-jē, ˌspe-\ *noun* [Latin *speleum* cave (from Greek *spēlaion*) + International Scientific Vocabulary *-o- + -logy* — more at SPELUNKER] (1895)
: the scientific study or exploration of caves
— **spe·le·o·log·i·cal** \ˌspē-lē-ə-'lä-ji-kəl, ˌspe-\ *adjective*
— **spe·le·ol·o·gist** \ˌspē-lē-'ä-lə-jist, ˌspe-\ *noun*

¹**spell** \'spel\ *verb* **spelled** \'speld, 'spelt\; **spell·ing** [Middle English, from Middle French *espeller*, of Germanic origin; akin to Old English *spell* talk] (14th century)
*transitive verb*
**1** : to read slowly and with difficulty — often used with *out*
**2** : to find out by study : come to understand — often used with *out* ⟨it requires some pains to *spell* out those decorations —F. J. Mather⟩
**3 a** (1) : to name the letters of in order; *also* : to write or print the letters of in order (2) : to write or print the letters of in a particular way ⟨you can *spell* it either way⟩ ⟨I *spelled* it wrong⟩ **b** : to make up (a word) ⟨what word do these letters *spell*⟩ **c** : WRITE 1b ⟨*catnip* is *spelled* as one word⟩
**4** : to add up to : MEAN ⟨crop failure was likely to *spell* stark famine —Stringfellow Barr⟩
*intransitive verb*
: to form words with letters ⟨teach children to *spell*⟩; *also* : to spell words in a certain way ⟨*spells* the way he speaks⟩

²**spell** *noun* [Middle English, talk, tale, from Old English; akin to Old High German *spel* talk, tale] (1579)
**1 a** : a spoken word or form of words held to have magic power : INCANTATION **b** : a state of enchantment
**2** : a strong compelling influence or attraction

³**spell** \'spel\ *transitive verb* **spelled** \'speld\; **spell·ing** (circa 1623)
: to put under a spell

⁴**spell** *noun* [probably alteration of Middle English *spale* substitute, from Old English *spala*] (1593)
**1 a** *archaic* : a shift of workers **b** : one's turn at work
**2 a** : a period spent in a job or occupation **b** *chiefly Australian* : a period of rest from work, activity, or use
**3 a** : an indeterminate period of time ⟨waited a *spell* before advancing⟩; *also* : a continuous period of time ⟨did a *spell* in prison⟩ **b** : a stretch of a specified type of weather
**4** : a period of bodily or mental distress or disorder ⟨a *spell* of coughing⟩ ⟨fainting *spells*⟩

⁵**spell** *verb* **spelled** \'speld\; **spell·ing** [Middle English *spelen*, from Old English *spelian;* akin to Old English *spala* substitute] (1595)
*transitive verb*
**1** : to take the place of for a time : RELIEVE ⟨he and the other assistant . . . *spelled* each other —Mary McCarthy⟩
**2** : REST
*intransitive verb*
**1** : to work in turns
**2** *chiefly Australian* : to rest from work or activity for a time

**spell·bind** \'spel-ˌbīnd\ *transitive verb* **-bound** \-ˌbaúnd\; **-bind·ing** [back-formation from spellbound] (1808)

: to bind or hold by or as if by a spell or charm : FASCINATE

**spell·bind·er** \-ˌbīn-dər\ *noun* (1888)
: a speaker of compelling eloquence; *also* : one that compels attention

**spell·bind·ing** \-ˌbīn-diŋ\ *adjective* (circa 1934)
: holding the attention as if by a spell
— **spell·bind·ing·ly** \-diŋ-lē\ *adverb*

**spell·bound** \-ˌbaund\ *adjective* (1799)
: held by or as if by a spell

**spell·er** \ˈspe-lər\ *noun* (15th century)
**1** : a person who spells words especially in a certain way ⟨a poor *speller*⟩
**2** : a book with exercises for teaching spelling

**spell·ing** \ˈspe-liŋ\ *noun* (15th century)
**1** : the forming of words from letters according to accepted usage : ORTHOGRAPHY
**2 a** : a sequence of letters composing a word **b** : the way in which a word is spelled

**spelling bee** *noun* (1872)
: a spelling contest in which contestants are eliminated as soon as they misspell a word

**spelling pronunciation** *noun* (1901)
: a pronunciation of a word based on its spelling alone

**spell out** *transitive verb* (1940)
**1** : to make plain ⟨*spelled out* the orders in detail⟩
**2** : to write or print in letters and in full ⟨numbers are to be *spelled out*⟩

**¹spelt** \ˈspelt\ *noun* [Middle English, from Old English, from Late Latin *spelta*, of Germanic origin; perhaps akin to Middle High German *spelte* split piece of wood, Old High German *spaltan* to split — more at SPLIT] (before 12th century)
: a wheat (*Triticum aestivum spelta*) with lax spikes and spikelets containing two light red kernels

**²spelt** \ˈspelt\ *chiefly British past and past participle of* SPELL

**spel·ter** \ˈspel-tər\ *noun* [probably alteration of Middle Dutch *speauter*] (1661)
: ZINC; *especially* : zinc cast in slabs for commercial use

**spe·lunk·er** \spi-ˈləŋ-kər, ˈspē-ˌ\ *noun* [Latin *spelunca* cave, from Greek *spēlynx*; akin to Greek *spēlaion* cave] (1944)
: one who makes a hobby of exploring and studying caves

**spe·lunk·ing** \-kiŋ\ *noun* (1944)
: the hobby or practice of exploring caves

**spence** \ˈspen(t)s\ *noun* [Middle English, from Middle French *despense*, from Medieval Latin *dispensa*, from Latin, feminine of *dispensus*, past participle of *dispendere* to weigh out — more at DISPENSE] (14th century)
*chiefly dialect British* : PANTRY

**¹spen·cer** \ˈspen(t)-sər\ *noun* [George John, 2d earl *Spencer* (died 1834) English politician] (1795)
: a short waist-length jacket

**²spencer** *noun* [probably from the name *Spencer*] (1840)
: a trysail abaft the foremast or mainmast

**Spen·ce·ri·an** \spen-ˈsir-ē-ən\ *adjective* [Platt R. *Spencer* (died 1864) American calligrapher] (1863)
: of or relating to a form of slanting handwriting

**Spen·ce·ri·an·ism** \spen-ˈsir-ē-ə-ˌni-zəm\ *noun* (1881)
: the synthetic philosophy of Herbert Spencer that has as its central idea the mechanistic evolution of the cosmos from relative simplicity to relative complexity

**spend** \ˈspend\ *verb* **spent** \ˈspent\; **spending** [Middle English, from Old English & Old French; Old English *spendan*, from Latin *expendere* to expend; Old French *despendre*, from Latin *dispendere* to weigh out — more at DISPENSE] (13th century)
*transitive verb*
**1** : to use up or pay out : EXPEND

**2 a** : EXHAUST, WEAR OUT ⟨the hurricane gradually *spent* itself⟩ **b** : to consume wastefully : SQUANDER ⟨the waters are not ours to *spend* —J. R. Ellis⟩
**3** : to cause or permit to elapse : PASS ⟨*spend* the night⟩
**4** : GIVE UP, SACRIFICE
*intransitive verb*
**1** : to expend or waste wealth or strength
**2** : to become expended or consumed
**3** : to have an orgasm
— **spend·able** \ˈspen-də-bəl\ *adjective*
— **spend·er** *noun*

**spending money** *noun* (15th century)
: POCKET MONEY

**spend·thrift** \ˈspen(d)-ˌthrift\ *noun* (1601)
: a person who spends improvidently or wastefully
— **spendthrift** *adjective*

**Spen·gle·ri·an** \ˌshpeŋ-ˈglir-ē-ən, ˌspeŋ-, -ˈlir-\ *adjective* (1922)
: of or relating to the theory of world history developed by Oswald Spengler which holds that all major cultures undergo similar cyclical developments from birth to maturity to decay
— **Spenglerian** *noun*

**Spen·se·ri·an stanza** \spen-ˈsir-ē-ən-\ *noun* [Edmund *Spenser*] (1817)
: a stanza consisting of eight verses of iambic pentameter and an alexandrine with a rhyme scheme *ababbcbcc*

**spent** \ˈspent\ *adjective* [Middle English, from past participle of *spenden* to spend] (15th century)
**1 a** : used up : CONSUMED **b** : exhausted of active or required components or qualities often for a particular purpose ⟨*spent* nuclear fuel⟩
**2** : drained of energy or effectiveness : EXHAUSTED
**3** : exhausted of spawn or sperm ⟨a *spent* salmon⟩

**sperm** \ˈspərm\ *noun, plural* **sperm** *or* **sperms** [Middle English, from Middle French *esperme*, from Late Latin *spermat-, sperma*, from Greek, literally, seed, from *speirein* to sow; probably akin to Armenian *p'aratem* I dispense] (14th century)
**1 a** : the male fecundating fluid : SEMEN **b** : a male gamete
**2** : a product (as spermaceti or oil) of the sperm whale

**sperm-** *or* **spermo-** *or* **sperma-** *or* **spermi-** *combining form* [Greek *sperm-, spermo-*, from *sperma*]
: seed : germ : sperm ⟨*sperm*atheca⟩ ⟨*spermi*cide⟩

**sper·ma·ce·ti** \ˌspər-mə-ˈsē-tē, -ˈse-\ *noun* [Middle English *sperma cete*, from Medieval Latin *sperma ceti* whale sperm] (15th century)
: a waxy solid obtained from the oil of cetaceans and especially sperm whales and used in ointments, cosmetics, and candles

**sper·ma·go·ni·um** \ˌspər-mə-ˈgō-nē-əm\ *noun, plural* **-nia** \-nē-ə\ [New Latin] (1861)
: a flask-shaped or depressed receptacle in which spermatia are produced in some fungi and lichens

**sper·ma·ry** \ˈspər-mə-rē, ˈspərm-rē\ *noun, plural* **-ries** [New Latin *spermarium*, from Greek *sperma*] (circa 1859)
: an organ in which male gametes are developed

**spermat-** *or* **spermato-** *combining form* [Middle French, from Late Latin, from Greek, from *spermat-, sperma*]
: seed : spermatozoon ⟨*spermat*id⟩ ⟨*spermato*cyte⟩

**sper·ma·the·ca** \ˌspər-mə-ˈthē-kə\ *noun* [New Latin] (1826)
: a sac for sperm storage in the female reproductive tract of various lower animals and especially insects

**sper·mat·ic** \(ˌ)spər-ˈma-tik\ *adjective* (15th century)
**1** : relating to sperm or a spermary
**2** : resembling, carrying, or full of sperm

**spermatic cord** *noun* (1797)
: a cord that suspends the testis within the scrotum and contains the vas deferens and vessels and nerves of the testis

**sper·ma·tid** \ˈspər-mə-təd\ *noun* (1889)
: one of the haploid cells that are formed by division of the secondary spermatocytes and that differentiate into spermatozoa

**sper·ma·ti·um** \(ˌ)spər-ˈmā-sh(ē-)əm\ *noun, plural* **-tia** \-sh(ē-)ə\ [New Latin, from Greek *spermation*, diminutive of *spermat-, sperma*] (1856)
: a nonmotile cell functioning as a male gamete in some lower plants (as red algae)
— **sper·ma·tial** \-sh(ē-)əl\ *adjective*

**sper·mato·cyte** \(ˌ)spər-ˈma-tə-ˌsīt\ *noun* (1886)
: a cell giving rise to sperm cells; *especially* : a cell that is derived from a spermatogonium and ultimately gives rise to four haploid spermatids

**sper·mato·gen·e·sis** \(ˌ)spər-ˌma-tə-ˈje-nə-səs\ *noun* [New Latin] (1881)
: the process of male gamete formation including formation of a primary spermatocyte from a spermatogonium, meiotic division of the spermatocyte, and transformation of the four resulting spermatids into spermatozoa
— **sper·mato·gen·ic** \-ˈje-nik\ *adjective*

**sper·mato·go·ni·um** \-ˈgō-nē-əm\ *noun, plural* **-nia** \-nē-ə\ [New Latin] (1861)
: a primitive male germ cell
— **sper·mato·go·ni·al** \-nē-əl\ *adjective*

**sper·mato·phore** \(ˌ)spər-ˈma-tə-ˌfōr, -ˌfȯr\ *noun* [International Scientific Vocabulary] (circa 1849)
: a capsule, packet, or mass enclosing spermatozoa extruded by the male and conveyed to the female in the insemination of various lower animals (as insects)

**sper·mato·phyte** \-ˌfīt\ *noun* [ultimately from New Latin *spermat-* + Greek *phyton* plant — more at PHYT-] (1897)
: any of a group (Spermatophyta) of higher plants comprising those that produce seeds and including the gymnosperms and angiosperms
— **sper·mato·phyt·ic** \-ˌma-tə-ˈfi-tik\ *adjective*

**sper·ma·to·zo·an** \(ˌ)spər-ˌma-tə-ˈzō-ən, ˌspər-mə-tə-\ *noun* (circa 1900)
: SPERMATOZOON
— **spermatozoan** *adjective*

**sper·ma·to·zo·id** \-ˈzō-əd\ *noun* [International Scientific Vocabulary, from New Latin *spermatozoon*] (1857)
: a male gamete of a plant motile by anterior cilia and usually produced in an antheridium

**sper·ma·to·zo·on** \-ˈzō-ˌän, -ˈzō-ən\ *noun, plural* **-zoa** \-ˈzō-ə\ [New Latin] (circa 1839)
**1** : a motile male gamete of an animal usually with rounded or elongate head and a long posterior flagellum
**2** : SPERMATOZOID
— **sper·ma·to·zo·al** \-ˈzō-əl\ *adjective*

**sperm cell** *noun* (1851)
: a male gamete : a male germ cell

**sper·mi·cide** \ˈspər-mə-ˌsīd\ *noun* (1929)
: a preparation or substance (as nonoxynol-9) used to kill sperm
— **sper·mi·cid·al** \ˌspər-mə-ˈsī-dəl\ *adjective*

**sper·mio·gen·e·sis** \ˌspər-mē-ō-ˈje-nə-səs\ *noun* [New Latin, from *spermium* spermatozoon + -*o*- + Latin *genesis*] (1916)
: SPERMATOGENESIS; *specifically* : transformation of a spermatid into a spermatozoon

**sperm nucleus** *noun* (1887)

---

\ə\ abut \ᵊ\ kitten \ər\ further \a\ ash \ā\ ace
\ä\ mop, mar \au̇\ out \ch\ chin \e\ bet \ē\ easy
\g\ go \i\ hit \ī\ ice \j\ job \ŋ\ sing \ō\ go
\ȯ\ law \ȯi\ boy \th\ thin \th\ the \ü\ loot \u̇\ foot
\y\ yet \zh\ vision    *see also* Guide to Pronunciation

: either of two nuclei that derive from the generative nucleus of a pollen grain and function in the fertilization of a seed plant

**sperm oil** *noun* (1839)
: a pale yellow oil from the sperm whale

**sper·mo·phile** \'spər-mə-ˌfīl\ *noun* [ultimately from Greek *sperma* seed + *philos* loving] (1824)
: GROUND SQUIRREL

**sperm whale** \'spərm-\ *noun* [short for *spermaceti whale*] (1834)
: a large toothed whale (*Physeter macrocephalus* synonym *P. catodon*) with a large closed cavity in the head containing a fluid mixture of spermaceti and oil

sperm whale

**-spermy** *noun combining form* [Greek *sperma* seed, sperm]
: state of exhibiting or resulting from (such) a fertilization ⟨agamo*spermy*⟩

**sper·ry·lite** \'sper-i-ˌlīt\ *noun* [Francis L. *Sperry,* 19th century Canadian chemist + English *-lite*] (1889)
: a mineral consisting of an arsenide of platinum that is found near Sudbury, Ontario, and occurs in grains and minute isometric crystals of a bluish white color

**spes·sar·tite** \'spes-sər-ˌtīt\ *or* **spes·sar·tine** \-ˌtēn\ *noun* [French, from *Spessart* mountain range, Germany] (1868)
: a manganese aluminum garnet usually containing other elements (as iron and magnesium) in minor amounts

**¹spew** \'spyü\ *verb* [Middle English, from Old English *spīwan;* akin to Old High German *spīwan* to spit, Latin *spuere,* Greek *ptyein*] (before 12th century)
*intransitive verb*
**1** : VOMIT
**2** : to come forth in a flood or gush
**3** : to ooze out as if under pressure : EXUDE
*transitive verb*
**1** : VOMIT
**2** : to send or cast forth with vigor or violence or in great quantity — often used with *out*
— **spew·er** *noun*

**²spew** *noun* (15th century)
**1** : matter that is vomited : VOMIT
**2** : material that exudes or is extruded

**sphag·nous** \'sfag-nəs\ *adjective* (circa 1828)
: of, relating to, or abounding in sphagnum

**sphag·num** \'sfag-nəm\ *noun* [New Latin, from Latin *sphagnos,* a moss, from Greek] (1741)
**1** : any of an order (Sphagnales, containing a single genus *Sphagnum*) of atypical mosses that grow only in wet acid areas where their remains become compacted with other plant debris to form peat
**2** : a mass of sphagnum plants

**sphal·er·ite** \'sfa-lə-ˌrīt\ *noun* [German *Sphalerit,* from Greek *sphaleros* deceitful, from *sphallein* to cause to fall; from its often being mistaken for galena — more at SPILL] (circa 1868)
: a widely distributed ore of zinc composed essentially of zinc sulfide

**S phase** *noun* [*synthesis*] (1945)
: the period in the cell cycle during which DNA replication takes place — compare $G_1$ PHASE, $G_2$ PHASE, M PHASE

**sphene** \'sfēn\ *noun* [French *sphène,* from Greek *sphēn* wedge] (1815)
: a mineral that is a silicate of calcium and titanium and often contains other elements

**sphen·odon** \'sfē-nə-ˌdän, 'sfe-\ *noun* [New Latin, genus name, from Greek *sphēn* wedge + *odōn, odous* tooth — more at TOOTH] (1878)
: TUATARA
— **sphen·odont** \-ˌdänt\ *adjective*

**¹sphe·noid** \'sfē-ˌnȯid\ *or* **sphe·noi·dal** \sfi-'nȯi-dᵊl\ *adjective* [New Latin *sphenoides,* from Greek *sphēnoeidēs* wedge-shaped, from *sphēn* wedge] (1732)
**1** : of, relating to, or being a winged compound bone of the base of the cranium
**2** *usually* sphenoidal : having a wedged shape

**²sphenoid** *noun* (1828)
: a sphenoid bone

**sphe·nop·sid** \sfi-'näp-səd\ *noun* [ultimately from Greek *sphēn* wedge + New Latin *-opsis*] (1957)
: any of a class (Sphenopsida or Sphenophyta) of the tracheophytes characterized by jointed ribbed stems, small leaves usually in whorls at distinct stem nodes, and sporangia in sporangiophores and made up of the equisetums and extinct related forms

**spher-** *or* **sphero-** *also* **sphaer-** *or* **sphaero-** *combining form* [Latin *sphaer-,* from Greek *sphair-, sphairo-,* from *sphaira* sphere]
: sphere ⟨*spher*ule⟩ ⟨*sphero*meter⟩

**spher·al** \'sfir-əl\ *adjective* (1545)
**1** : SPHERICAL
**2** : of or relating to the spheres of ancient astronomy

**¹sphere** \'sfir\ *noun* [Middle English *spere* globe, celestial sphere, from Middle French *espere,* from Latin *sphaera,* from Greek *sphaira,* literally, ball; perhaps akin to Greek *spairein* to quiver — more at SPURN] (14th century)
**1 a** (1) : the apparent surface of the heavens of which half forms the dome of the visible sky (2) : any of the concentric and eccentric revolving spherical transparent shells in which according to ancient astronomy stars, sun, planets, and moon are set **b** : a globe depicting such a sphere; *broadly* : GLOBE a
**2 a** : a globular body : BALL **b** : PLANET, STAR **c** (1) : a solid that is bounded by a surface consisting of all points at a given distance from a point constituting its center — see VOLUME table (2) : the bounding surface of a sphere
**3** : natural, normal, or proper place; *especially* : social order or rank
**4 a** *obsolete* : ORBIT **b** : an area or range over or within which someone or something acts, exists, or has influence or significance
— **spher·ic** \'sfir-ik, 'sfer-\ *adjective, archaic*
— **sphe·ric·i·ty** \sfir-'i-sə-tē\ *noun*

**²sphere** *transitive verb* **sphered; spher·ing** (1607)
**1** : to place in a sphere or among the spheres : ENSPHERE
**2** : to form into a sphere

**sphere of influence** (1885)
: a territorial area within which the political influence or the interests of one nation are held to be more or less paramount

**spher·i·cal** \'sfir-i-kəl, 'sfer-\ *adjective* (15th century)
**1** : having the form of a sphere or of one of its segments
**2** : relating to or dealing with a sphere or its properties
— **spher·i·cal·ly** \-k(ə-)lē\ *adverb*

**spherical aberration** *noun* (1868)
: aberration that is caused by the spherical form of a lens or mirror and that gives different foci for central and marginal rays

**spherical angle** *noun* (1678)
: the angle between two intersecting arcs of great circles of a sphere measured by the plane angle formed by the tangents to the arcs at the point of intersection

**spherical coordinate** *noun* (circa 1864)

: one of three coordinates that are used to locate a point in space and that comprise the radius of the sphere on which the point lies in a system of concentric spheres, the angle formed by the point, the center, and a given axis of the sphere, and the angle between the plane of the first angle and a reference plane through the given axis of the sphere

**spherical geometry** *noun* (1728)
: the geometry of figures on a sphere

**spherical polygon** *noun* (circa 1825)
: a figure analogous to a plane polygon that is formed on a sphere by arcs of great circles

**spherical triangle** *noun* (1585)
: a spherical polygon of three sides

**spherical trigonometry** *noun* (1728)
: trigonometry applied to spherical triangles and polygons

**spher·oid** \'sfir-ˌȯid, 'sfer-\ *noun* (1570)
: a figure resembling a sphere; *also* : an object of approximately spherical shape
— **sphe·roi·dal** \sfi-'rȯi-dᵊl\ *also* **spheroid** *adjective*
— **sphe·roi·dal·ly** \-dᵊl-ē\ *adverb*

**sphe·rom·e·ter** \sfir-'ä-mə-tər\ *noun* [International Scientific Vocabulary] (circa 1828)
: an instrument for measuring the curvature of a surface

**sphe·ro·plast** \'sfir-ə-ˌplast, 'sfer-\ *noun* (circa 1920)
: a bacterium or yeast cell that is modified by nutritional or environmental factors or by artificial means (as the use of a lysozyme) and that is characterized by partial loss of the cell wall and by increased osmotic sensitivity

**spher·ule** \'sfir-ü(ə)l, 'sfer-, -ˌyü(ə)l\ *noun* (1665)
: a little sphere or spherical body

**spher·u·lite** \'sfir-yə-ˌlīt, 'sfer-, -ə-ˌlīt\ *noun* (1823)
: a usually spherical crystalline body of radiating crystal fibers often found in vitreous volcanic rocks
— **spher·u·lit·ic** \ˌsfir-yə-'li-tik, ˌsfer-, -ə-ˌli-\ *adjective*

**sphery** \'sfir-ē\ *adjective* (1590)
**1** : of, relating to, or suggestive of the celestial bodies
**2** : ROUND, SPHERICAL

**sphinc·ter** \'sfiŋ(k)-tər\ *noun* [Late Latin, from Greek *sphinktēr,* literally, band, from *sphingein* to bind tight] (1578)
: an annular muscle surrounding and able to contract or close a bodily opening
— **sphinc·ter·ic** \sfiŋ(k)-'ter-ik\ *adjective*

**sphin·gid** \'sfin-jəd\ *noun* [ultimately from Greek *sphing-, sphinx* sphinx] (circa 1909)
: HAWKMOTH

**sphin·go·sine** \'sfiŋ-gə-ˌsēn\ *noun* [Greek *sphingos* (genitive of *sphinx*) + English *²-ine;* from riddles it posed to its first investigators] (1884)
: a long-chain unsaturated amino alcohol $C_{18}H_{37}O_2N$ found especially in nervous tissue and cell membranes

**sphinx** \'sfiŋ(k)s\ *noun, plural* **sphinx·es** *or* **sphin·ges** \'sfin-ˌjēz\ [Latin, from Greek *Sphinx, Sphix*]
**1 a** *capitalized* : a winged female monster in Greek mythology having a woman's head and a lion's body and noted for killing anyone unable to answer its riddle **b** : an enigmatic or mysterious person
**2** : an ancient Egyptian image in the form of a recumbent lion having a man's head, a ram's head, or a hawk's head
**3** : HAWKMOTH
— **sphinx·like** \-ˌlīk\ *adjective*

**sphyg·mo·graph** \'sfig-mə-ˌgraf\ *noun* [Greek *sphygmos* pulse + International Scientific Vocabulary *-graph*] (circa 1859)
: an instrument that records graphically the movements or character of the pulse

**sphyg·mo·ma·nom·e·ter** \ˌsfig-mō-mə-'nä-mə-tər\ *noun* [Greek *sphygmos* pulse (from

*sphyzein* to throb) + International Scientific Vocabulary *manometer*] (circa 1891)
: an instrument for measuring blood pressure and especially arterial blood pressure
— **sphyg·mo·ma·nom·e·try** \-mə-'nä-mə-ˌtrē\ *noun*

**spi·ca** \'spī-kə\ *noun, plural* **spi·cae** \-ˌkē\ *or* **spicas** [Latin, ear of grain — more at SPINE] (circa 1731)
: a bandage that is applied in successive V-shaped crossings and is used to immobilize a limb especially at a joint

**Spi·ca** \'spī-kə\ *noun* [Latin, literally, ear of grain]
: a star of the first magnitude in the constellation Virgo

**spi·cate** \'spī-ˌkāt\ *adjective* [Latin *spicatus*, past participle of *spicare* to arrange in the shape of heads of grain, from *spica*] (1668)
: arranged in the form of a spike ⟨a *spicate* inflorescence⟩

**¹spic·ca·to** \spi-'kä-(ˌ)tō\ *adjective* [Italian, past participle of *spiccare* to detach, pick off] (circa 1724)
: performed with a slight lifting of the bow after each note — used as a direction in music

**²spiccato** *noun, plural* **-tos** (circa 1903)
: a spiccato technique, performance, or passage

**¹spice** \'spīs\ *noun* [Middle English, from Old French *espice*, from Late Latin *species* spices, from Latin, species, from *specere* to look — more at SPY] (13th century)
**1** : any of various aromatic vegetable products (as pepper or nutmeg) used to season or flavor foods
**2 a** *archaic* : a small portion, quantity, or admixture : DASH **b** : something that gives zest or relish ⟨variety's the very *spice* of life —William Cowper⟩
**3** : a pungent or fragrant odor : PERFUME ◆
— **spice·less** \-ləs\ *adjective*

**²spice** *transitive verb* **spiced; spic·ing** (14th century)
**1** : to season with spices
**2** : to add zest or relish to ⟨cynicism *spiced* with humor —J. W. Dawson⟩ — often used with *up*

**spice·bush** \'spīs-ˌbush\ *noun* (1770)
: an aromatic shrub (*Lindera benzoin*) of the laurel family that bears dense clusters of small yellow flowers followed by scarlet or yellow berries

**spic·ery** \'spī-sə-rē, 'spīs-rē\ *noun, plural* **-er·ies** (13th century)
**1** : SPICES
**2** *archaic* : a repository of spices
**3** : a spicy quality

**spick** *or* **spic** *or* **spik** \'spik\ *noun* [by shortening & alteration from *spiggoty*, of unknown origin] (1916)
: SPANISH AMERICAN — usually taken to be offensive

**spick–and–span** *or* **spic–and–span** \ˌspik-ən(d)-'span, ˌspik-ˀŋ-\ *adjective* [short for *spick-and-span-new*, from obsolete English *spick* spike + English *and* + *span-new* brand-new] (1665)
**1** : FRESH, BRAND-NEW
**2** : spotlessly clean

**spic·ule** \'spi-(ˌ)kyü(ə)l\ *noun* [New Latin *spicula* & Latin *spiculum*; New Latin *spicula*, alteration of Latin *spiculum* head of a spear or arrow, diminutive of *spicum, spica* ear of grain] (1785)
**1** : a slender pointed usually hard body; *especially* : one of the minute calcareous or siliceous bodies that support the tissue of various invertebrates (as a sponge)
**2** : a spikelike short-lived prominence appearing close to the chromosphere of the solar atmosphere
— **spic·u·lar** \'spi-kyə-lər\ *adjective*
— **spic·u·la·tion** \ˌspi-kyə-'lā-shən\ *noun*

**spicy** \'spī-sē\ *adjective* **spic·i·er; -est** (1562)

**1** : having the quality, flavor, or fragrance of spice
**2** : producing or abounding in spices
**3** : LIVELY, SPIRITED
**4** : PIQUANT, RACY; *especially* : somewhat scandalous or salacious ⟨*spicy* gossip⟩
— **spic·i·ly** \-sə-lē\ *adverb*
— **spic·i·ness** \-sē-nəs\ *noun*

**spi·der** \'spī-dər\ *noun* [Middle English *spyder*, alteration of *spithre*; akin to Old English *spinnan* to spin] (15th century)
**1** : any of an order (Araneae synonym Araneida) of arachnids having the abdomen usually unsegmented and constricted at the base, chelicerae modified into poison fangs, and two or more pairs of abdominal spinnerets for spinning threads of silk used in making cocoons for their eggs, nests for themselves, or webs to catch prey
**2** : a cast-iron frying pan originally made with short feet to stand among coals on the hearth
**3** : any of various devices consisting of a frame or skeleton with radiating arms or members
— **spi·der·ish** \-də-rish\ *adjective*
— **spi·der·like** \-dər-ˌlīk\ *adjective*

**spider crab** *noun* (circa 1710)
: any of a family (Majidae) of crabs with extremely long legs and nearly triangular bodies which they often cover with kelp

**spider mite** *noun* (1870)
: any of several small web-spinning mites (family Tetranychidae) that attack forage and crop plants — called also *red spider*

**spider monkey** *noun* (1764)
: any of a genus (*Ateles*) of New World monkeys with long slender limbs, the thumb absent or rudimentary, and a very long prehensile tail

**spider plant** *noun* (1944)
: a widely grown houseplant (*Chlorophytum comosum* variety *variegatum*) of the lily family having long narrow green leaves usually striped with white or ivory and producing white flowers and tufts of plantlets on long hanging stems

**spi·der·web** \'spī-dər-ˌweb\ *noun* (circa 1649)
**1** : the network of silken thread spun by most spiders and used as a resting place and as a trap for small prey
**2** : something that resembles or suggests a spiderweb

**spi·der·wort** \-ˌwərt, -ˌwȯrt\ *noun* (1629)
: any of a genus (*Tradescantia* of the family Commelinaceae, the spiderwort family) of American monocotyledonous plants with ephemeral often blue or violet flowers

**spi·dery** \'spī-də-rē\ *adjective* (1837)
**1 a** : resembling a spider in form or manner **b** : resembling a spiderweb; *especially* : composed of fine threads or lines in a weblike arrangement ⟨*spidery* lace⟩
**2** : infested with spiders

**spie·gel·ei·sen** \'spē-gə-ˌlī-z°n\ *also* **spiegel** \'spē-gəl\ *noun* [German *Spiegeleisen*, from *Spiegel* mirror + *Eisen* iron] (1868)
: a composition of iron that contains 15 to 30 percent manganese and 4.5 to 6.5 percent carbon

**¹spiel** \'spē(ə)l\ *verb* [German *spielen* to play, from Old High German *spilōn*; akin to Old English *spilian* to revel] (1870)
*intransitive verb*
**1** : to play music
**2** : to talk volubly or extravagantly
*transitive verb*
: to utter, express, or describe volubly or extravagantly
— **spiel·er** \'spē-lər\ *noun*

**²spiel** *noun* (1896)
: a voluble line of often extravagant talk : PITCH

**¹spi·er** \'spī-(ə)r\ *noun* (13th century)
: SPY

**²spier** \'spir\ *chiefly Scottish variant of* SPEER

**spiff** \'spif\ *verb* [English dialect spiff *dandified*] (1877)
: SPRUCE — usually used with *up* ⟨*spiff* up your wardrobe⟩
— **spiffed–up** \'spift-'əp\ *adjective*

**spiffy** \'spi-fē\ *adjective* **spiff·i·er; -est** (1853)
: fine looking : SMART ⟨a *spiffy* sports jacket⟩
— **spiff·i·ly** \-fə-lē\ *adverb*
— **spiff·i·ness** \-fē-nəs\ *noun*

**spig·ot** \'spi-gət, -kət\ *noun* [Middle English] (14th century)
**1 a** : SPILE 2 **b** : the plug of a faucet or cock **c** : FAUCET
**2** : something resembling a spigot especially in regulating availability or flow (as of money)

**¹spike** \'spīk\ *noun* [Middle English, probably from Middle Dutch; akin to Middle High German *spīcher* spike] (13th century)
**1** : a very large nail
**2 a** : one of a row of pointed irons placed (as on the top of a wall) to prevent passage **b** (1) : one of several metal projections set in the sole and heel of a shoe to improve traction (2) *plural* : a pair of shoes having spikes attached to the soles or soles and heels : SPINDLE 1e
**3** : something resembling a spike: as **a** : a young mackerel not over six inches (15.2 centimeters) long **b** : an unbranched antler of a young deer
**4** *plural* : shoes with spike heels
**5** : the act or an instance of spiking (as in volleyball)
**6 a** : a pointed element in a graph or tracing **b** : an unusually high and sharply defined maximum (as of amplitude in a wave train)
**7** *slang* : HYPODERMIC NEEDLE
**8** : a momentary sharp increase and fall in the record of an electric potential; *also* : ACTION POTENTIAL
**9** : an abrupt sharp increase in prices or rates
— **spike·like** \-ˌlīk\ *adjective*

**²spike** *transitive verb* **spiked; spik·ing** (1624)
**1** : to fasten or furnish with spikes

◇ **WORD HISTORY**
**spice** The Latin word *species* originally meant "appearance," but it developed a distinctive range of secondary meanings. In philosophers' parlance *species* referred to a division of a larger class, called a *genus*: a *species* was a particular "appearance" that a member of a *genus* might take, and hence one kind or sort of something. These meanings are the basis of English *species* and *genus* in modern biological classification. They did not arise within Latin, however, but rather are exact translations of the Greek philosophical use of *eidos* "kind, sort" (literally, "form, appearance") and *genos* "class" (literally, "race, kin"). Imperial legal Latin of the 2d century A.D. reflects another Greek philosophical distinction, between "form, appearance" (*eidos*) and "matter" (*hylē*): again translating *eidos* as *species*, jurists used the word to refer to agricultural products, the "form" taken by grain, oil, and wine after their conversion from "matter," that is, unprocessed plants. On this basis Late Latin *species* began to denote any taxed commodity, especially those imported from the East, such as drugs and aromatic seasonings. *Species* in the sense "seasoning" developed via the spoken Latin of Gaul into Old French *espice*, borrowed into Middle English as *spice* by the 13th century.

**2 a :** to disable (a muzzle-loading cannon) temporarily by driving a spike into the vent **b :** to suppress or block completely ⟨*spiked* the rumor⟩
**3 a :** to pierce or impale with or on a spike **b :** to reject (as a story) for publication or broadcast for editorial reasons
**4 a :** to add an alcoholic beverage to (a drink) **b :** to add something highly reactive (as a radioactive tracer) to **c :** to add vitality, zest, or spice to : LIVEN ⟨*spiked* the speech with humor⟩ ⟨*spike* the broth with peppers⟩
**5 :** to drive (as a volleyball) sharply downward with a hard blow; *also* **:** to throw down sharply ⟨*spiked* the ball in the end zone⟩
**6 :** to undergo a sudden sharp increase in (temperature or fever) ⟨the patient *spiked* a fever of 103°⟩
— **spik·er** *noun*
**³spike** *noun* [Middle English *spik*, from Latin *spica* — more at SPINE] (14th century)
**1 :** an ear of grain
**2 :** an elongated inflorescence similar to a raceme but having the flowers sessile on the main axis — see INFLORESCENCE illustration
**spiked** \'spīkt, 'spī-kəd\ *adjective* (1601)
**1 :** having an inflorescence that is a spike
**2 :** having a sharp projecting point
**spike heel** *noun* (1926)
**:** a very high tapering heel used on women's shoes
**spike lavender** \'spīk-\ *noun* [alteration of English dialect *spick* lavender] (1607)
**:** a European mint (*Lavandula latifolia*) related to true lavender
**spike·let** \'spī-klət\ *noun* (1851)
**:** a small or secondary spike; *specifically* **:** one of the small few-flowered bracted spikes that make up the compound inflorescence of a grass or sedge
**spike·nard** \'spīk-ˌnärd\ *noun* [Middle English, from Middle French or Medieval Latin; Middle French *spicanarde*, from Medieval Latin *spica nardi*, literally, spike of nard] (14th century)
**1 a :** a fragrant ointment of the ancients **b :** a Himalayan aromatic plant (*Nardostachys jatamansi*) of the valerian family from which spikenard is believed to have been derived
**2 :** an American herb (*Aralia racemosa*) of the ginseng family with aromatic root and panicled umbels
**spike–tooth harrow** \'spīk-'tüth-\ *noun* (1926)
**:** a harrow with straight steel teeth set in horizontal bars
**spiky** *also* **spikey** \'spī-kē\ *adjective* **spik·i·er; -est** (1720)
**1 :** of, relating to, or characterized by spikes
**2 :** sharply irritating or acerbic (as in temper or manner)
**3** [from the alleged harshness of such views] *British* **:** strongly favoring Anglo-Catholic teaching or practice
— **spik·i·ly** \-kə-lē\ *adverb*
— **spik·i·ness** \-kē-nəs\ *noun*
**¹spile** \'spī(ə)l\ *noun* [probably from Dutch *spijl* stake] (1513)
**1 :** ¹PILE 1
**2 :** a small plug used to stop the vent of a cask **:** BUNG
**3 :** a spout inserted in a tree to draw off sap
**²spile** *transitive verb* **spiled; spil·ing** (1691)
**1 :** to plug with a spile
**2 :** to supply with a spile
**¹spill** \'spil\ *verb* **spilled** \'spild, 'spilt\ *also* **spilt** \'spilt\; **spill·ing** [Middle English, from Old English *spillan;* akin to Old English *spildan* to destroy and perhaps to Latin *spolium* animal skin, Greek *sphallein* to cause to fall] (before 12th century)
*transitive verb*
**1 a** *archaic* **:** KILL, DESTROY **b :** to cause (blood) to flow

**2 :** to cause or allow especially accidentally or unintentionally to fall, flow, or run out so as to be lost or wasted
**3 a :** to relieve (a sail) from the pressure of the wind so as to reef or furl it **b :** to relieve the pressure of (wind) on a sail by coming about or by adjusting the sail with lines
**4 :** to throw off or out ⟨a horse *spilled* him⟩
**5 :** to let out **:** DIVULGE ⟨*spill* a secret⟩
*intransitive verb*
**1 a :** to flow, run, or fall out, over, or off and become wasted, scattered, or lost **b :** to cause or allow something to spill
**2 :** to spread profusely or beyond bounds ⟨crowds *spilled* into the streets⟩
**3 :** to fall from one's place (as on a horse)
— **spill·able** \'spi-lə-bəl\ *adjective*
— **spill·er** *noun*
— **spill the beans :** to divulge secret or hidden information
**²spill** *noun* (circa 1845)
**1 :** the act or an instance of spilling; *especially* **:** a fall from a horse or vehicle or an erect position
**2 :** something spilled
**³spill** *noun* [Middle English *spille*] (14th century)
**1 :** a wooden splinter
**2 :** a slender piece: **as a :** a metallic rod or pin **b** (1) **:** a small roll or twist of paper or slip of wood for lighting a fire (2) **:** a roll or cone of paper serving as a container **c :** a peg or pin for plugging a hole **:** SPILE
**spill·age** \'spi-lij\ *noun* (1924)
**1 :** the act or process of spilling
**2 :** the quantity that spills **:** material lost or scattered by spilling
**spil·li·kin** \'spi-li-kən\ *noun* [probably alteration of obsolete Dutch *spelleken* small peg] (1734)
**1 :** JACKSTRAW 2
**2** *plural* **:** JACKSTRAW 1
**spill·over** \'spil-ˌō-vər\ *noun, often attributive* (1920)
**1 :** the act or an instance of spilling over
**2 :** a quantity that spills over
**3 :** an extension of something especially when due to an excess
**spill·way** \-ˌwā\ *noun* (1889)
**:** a passage for surplus water to run over or around an obstruction (as a dam)
**spilth** \'spilth\ *noun* (1607)
**1 :** the act or an instance of spilling
**2 a :** something spilled **b :** REFUSE, RUBBISH
**¹spin** \'spin\ *verb* **spun** \'spən\; **spin·ning** [Middle English *spinnen*, from Old English *spinnan;* akin to Old High German *spinnan* to spin and perhaps to Lithuanian *spęsti* to set (a trap)] (before 12th century)
*intransitive verb*
**1 :** to draw out and twist fiber into yarn or thread
**2 :** to form a thread by extruding a viscous rapidly hardening fluid — used especially of a spider or insect
**3 a :** to revolve rapidly **:** GYRATE **b :** to feel as if in a whirl **:** REEL ⟨my head is *spinning*⟩
**4 :** to move swiftly especially on or as if on wheels or in a vehicle
**5 :** to fish with spinning bait **:** TROLL
**6 a** *of an airplane* **:** to fall in a spin **b :** to plunge helplessly and out of control
*transitive verb*
**1 a :** to draw out and twist into yarns or threads **b :** to produce by drawing out and twisting a fibrous material
**2 :** to form (as a web or cocoon) by spinning
**3 a :** to stretch out or extend (as a story) lengthily **:** PROTRACT — usually used with *out* **b :** to evolve, express, or fabricate by processes of mind or imagination ⟨*spin* a yarn⟩
**4 :** to cause to whirl **:** impart spin to ⟨*spin* a top⟩
**5 :** to shape into threadlike form in manufacture; *also* **:** to manufacture by a whirling process

**²spin** *noun* (1831)
**1 a :** the act of spinning or twirling something; *also* **:** an instance of spinning or of spinning something ⟨doing axels and *spins*⟩ ⟨an assortment of *spins* and lobs⟩ **b :** the whirling motion imparted (as to a ball or top) by spinning **c :** an excursion or ride in a vehicle especially on wheels ⟨go for a *spin*⟩
**2 a :** an aerial maneuver or flight condition consisting of a combination of roll and yaw with the longitudinal axis of the airplane inclined steeply downward **b :** a plunging descent or downward spiral **c :** a state of mental confusion ⟨in a *spin*⟩
**3 a :** a quantum characteristic of an elementary particle that is visualized as the rotation of the particle on its axis and that is responsible for measurable angular momentum and magnetic moment **b :** the angular momentum associated with such rotation whose magnitude is quantized and which may assume either of two possible directions; *also* **:** the angular momentum of a system of such particles derived from the spins and orbital motions of the particles
**4 :** a special point of view, emphasis, or interpretation ⟨put the most favorable *spin* on the findings⟩
— **spin·less** \'spin-ləs\ *adjective*
**spi·na bi·fi·da** \ˌspī-nə-'bi-fə-də\ *noun* [New Latin, literally, spine split in two] (1720)
**:** a congenital cleft of the vertebral column with hernial protrusion of the meninges and sometimes the spinal cord
**spin·ach** \'spi-nich\ *noun* [Middle English *spynache*, from Middle French *espinache, espinage*, from Old Spanish *espinaca*, from Arabic *isfānākh*, from Persian] (15th century)
**1 :** an Asian herb (*Spinacia oleracea*) of the goosefoot family cultivated for its edible leaves which form in a dense basal rosette
**2 a :** something unwanted, pretentious, or spurious **b :** an untidy overgrowth
— **spin·ach·like** \-nich-ˌlīk\ *adjective*
— **spin·achy** \-ni-chē\ *adjective*
**¹spi·nal** \'spī-nᵊl\ *adjective* (1578)
**1 :** of, relating to, or situated near the backbone
**2 a :** of, relating to, or affecting the spinal cord ⟨*spinal* reflexes⟩ **b :** having the spinal cord functionally isolated (as by surgical section) from the brain ⟨experiments on *spinal* animals⟩
**3 :** of, relating to, or resembling a spine
**²spinal** *noun* (1944)
**:** a spinal anesthetic
**spinal canal** *noun* (1845)
**:** VERTEBRAL CANAL
**spinal column** *noun* (1836)
**:** the axial skeleton of the trunk and tail of a vertebrate consisting of an articulated series of vertebrae and protecting the spinal cord — called also *backbone*
**spinal cord** *noun* (1836)
**:** the cord of nervous tissue that extends from the brain lengthwise along the back in the vertebral canal, gives off the pairs of spinal nerves, carries impulses to and from the brain, and serves as a center for initiating and coordinating many reflex acts — see BRAIN illustration
**spinal ganglion** *noun* (circa 1860)
**:** a ganglion on the dorsal root of each spinal nerve that is one of a series of ganglia lodging cell bodies of sensory neurons
**spi·nal·ly** \'spī-nᵊl-ē\ *adverb* (1885)
**:** with respect to or along the spine
**spinal nerve** *noun* (circa 1793)
**:** any of the paired nerves which leave the spinal cord of a craniate vertebrate, supply muscles of the trunk and limbs, and connect with the nerves of the sympathetic nervous system, which arise by a short motor ventral root and a short sensory dorsal root, and of which there are 31 pairs in humans classified according to the part of the spinal cord from which they

arise into 8 cervical pairs, 12 thoracic pairs, 5 lumbar pairs, 5 sacral pairs, and one coccygeal pair

¹**spin·dle** \'spin-d³l\ *noun* [Middle English *spindel*, from Old English *spinel;* akin to Old English *spinnan* to spin] (12th century)
**1 a :** a round stick with tapered ends used to form and twist the yarn in hand spinning **b :** the long slender pin by which the thread is twisted in a spinning wheel **c :** any of various rods or pins holding a bobbin in a textile machine (as a spinning frame) **d :** the pin in a loom shuttle **e :** a device usually consisting of a long upright pin in a base on which papers can be stuck for filing — called also *spindle file*
**2 :** something shaped like a spindle: as **a :** a spindle-shaped network of chiefly microtubular fibers along which the chromosomes are distributed during mitosis and meiosis **b :** MUSCLE SPINDLE
**3 a :** the bar or shaft usually of square section that carries the knobs and actuates the latch or bolt of a lock **b** (1) **:** a turned often decorative piece (as in a baluster) (2) **:** NEWEL **c** (1) **:** a revolving piece especially when thinner than a shaft (2) **:** a horizontal or vertical axle revolving on pin or pivot ends **d :** the part of an axle on which a vehicle wheel turns

²**spindle** *verb* **spin·dled; spin·dling** \'spin(d)-liŋ, 'spin-d³l-iŋ\ (1577)
*intransitive verb*
**1 :** to shoot or grow into a long slender stalk
**2 :** to grow to stalk or stem rather than to flower or fruit
*transitive verb*
**1 :** to impale, thrust, or perforate on the spike of a spindle file
**2 :** to make or equip (as a piece of furniture) with spindles
— **spin·dler** \'spin(d)-lər, 'spin-d³l-ər\ *noun*

**spindle cell** *noun* (1878)
**:** a fusiform cell (as in some tumors)

**spin·dle–legged** \'spin-d³l-,(l)e-gəd *also* -,(l)ā- *or* -,(l)egd\ *adjective* (1710)
**:** having long slender legs

**spin·dle–shanked** \-,shaŋ(k)t\ *adjective* (circa 1600)
**:** SPINDLE-LEGGED

**spindle tree** *noun* (1548)
**:** any of various often evergreen shrubs, small trees, or vines (genus *Euonymus*) of the staff-tree family

**spin·dling** \'spin(d)-liŋ, -lən; 'spin-d³l-iŋ, -ən\ *adjective* (1750)
**:** SPINDLY

**spin·dly** \'spin(d)-lē, 'spin-d³l-ē\ *adjective* **spin·dli·er; -est** (1651)
**1 :** of a disproportionately tall or long and thin appearance that often suggests physical weakness ⟨*spindly* legs⟩
**2 :** frail or flimsy in appearance or structure

**spin doctor** *noun* (1984)
**:** a person (as a political aide) responsible for ensuring that others interpret an event from a particular point of view

**spin·drift** \'spin-,drift\ *noun* [alteration of Scots *speendrift,* from *speen* to drive before a strong wind + English *drift*] (1823)
**1 :** sea spray; *especially* **:** spray blown from waves during a gale
**2 :** fine wind-borne snow or sand

**spine** \'spīn\ *noun* [Middle English, thorn, spinal column, from Latin *spina;* perhaps akin to Latin *spica* ear of grain] (15th century)
**1 a :** SPINAL COLUMN **b :** something resembling a spinal column or constituting a central axis or chief support **c :** the part of a book to which the pages are attached and on the cover of which usually appear the title and author's and publisher's names
**2 :** a stiff pointed plant process; *especially* **:** one that is a modified leaf or leaf part
**3 :** a sharp rigid process on an animal: as **a :** SPICULE **b :** a stiff unsegmented fin ray of a fish **c :** a pointed prominence on a bone

— **spined** \'spīnd\ *adjective*
— **spine–like** \-,līk\ *adjective*

**spine–chill·ing** \-,chi-liŋ\ *adjective* (1946)
**:** alarmingly or eerily frightening

**spi·nel** *or* **spi·nelle** \spə-'nel\ *noun* [Italian *spinella,* diminutive of *spina* thorn, from Latin] (1528)
**1 :** a hard crystalline mineral consisting of an oxide of magnesium and aluminum that varies from colorless to ruby-red to black and is used as a gem
**2 :** any of a group of minerals that are essentially oxides of magnesium, ferrous iron, zinc, or manganese

**spine·less** \'spīn-ləs\ *adjective* (1827)
**1 :** free from spines, thorns, or prickles
**2 a :** having no spinal column **:** INVERTEBRATE **b :** lacking strength of character
— **spine·less·ly** *adverb*
— **spine·less·ness** *noun*

**spin·et** \'spi-nət *also* spi-'net\ *noun* [Italian *spinetta,* from diminutive of *spina* thorn, from Latin; from the manner of plucking its strings] (1664)
**1 :** an early harpsichord having a single keyboard and only one string for each note
**2 a :** a compactly built small upright piano **b :** a small electronic organ

**spin fishing** *noun* (1950)
**:** SPINNING

**spi·ni·fex** \'spī-nə-,feks\ *noun* [New Latin, from Latin *spina* + *facere* to make — more at DO] (1846)
**:** any of several Australian grasses (genera *Spinifex* and *Triodia*) with spiny seeds or stiff sharp leaves

**spin·na·ker** \'spi-ni-kər\ *noun* [origin unknown] (1866)
**:** a large triangular sail set on a long light pole and used when running before the wind

**spin·ner** \'spi-nər\ *noun* (13th century)
**1 :** one that spins
**2 :** a fisherman's lure consisting of a spoon, blade, or set of wings that revolves when drawn through the water
**3 :** a conical sheet metal fairing that is attached to an airplane propeller boss and revolves with it
**4 :** a movable arrow that is spun on its dial to indicate the number or kind of moves a player may make in a board game

**spin·ner·et** \,spi-nə-'ret\ *noun* (1826)
**1 :** an organ (as of a spider or caterpillar) for producing threads of silk from the secretion of silk glands
**2 *or* spin·ner·ette :** a small metal plate, thimble, or cap with fine holes through which a chemical solution (as of cellulose) is forced in the spinning of man-made filaments (as of rayon or nylon)

**spin·ney** \'spi-nē\ *noun, plural* **spinneys** [Middle French *espinaye* thorny thicket, from *espine* thorn, from Latin *spina*] (1597)
*chiefly British* **:** a small wood with undergrowth

**spin·ning** \'spi-niŋ\ *noun* (1855)
**:** a method of fishing in which a lure is cast by use of a light flexible rod, a spinning reel, and a light line

**spinning frame** *noun* (1825)
**:** a machine that draws, twists, and winds yarn

**spinning jen·ny** \-,je-nē\ *noun* [*Jenny,* nickname for *Jane*] (1783)
**:** an early multiple-spindle machine for spinning wool or cotton

**spinning reel** *noun* (1950)
**:** a fishing reel with a nonmoving spool on which the line is wound by means of a revolving arm which can be disengaged to allow the line to spiral freely off the spool during casting

**spinning rod** *noun* (1870)
**:** a light flexible fishing rod used with a spinning reel

**spinning wheel** *noun* (15th century)

**:** a small domestic hand-driven or foot-driven machine for spinning yarn or thread

**spin–off** \'spin-,óf\ *noun* (1950)
**1 :** the distribution by a business to its stockholders of particular assets and especially of stock of another company; *also* **:** the new company created by such a distribution
**2 :** a collateral or derived product or effect **:** BY-PRODUCT; *also* **:** a number of such products ⟨the *spin-off* from the space program⟩
**3 :** something that is imitative or derivative of an earlier work; *especially* **:** a television show starring a character popular in a secondary role of an earlier show

**spin off** (1950)
*transitive verb*
**:** to establish or produce as a spin-off ⟨the company *spun off* its computer division⟩ ⟨*spin off* a new TV series⟩
*intransitive verb*
**:** to establish or become a spin-off

**spin·or** \'spin-ər, -,nór\ *noun* [International Scientific Vocabulary *spin* + *-or* (as in *vector*)] (1931)
**:** a vector whose components are complex numbers in a two-dimensional or four-dimensional space and which is used especially in the mathematics of the theory of relativity

**spi·nose** \'spī-,nōs\ *adjective* (1660)
**:** SPINY ⟨a fly with black *spinose* legs⟩
— **spi·nos·i·ty** \spī-'nä-sə-tē\ *noun*

**spi·nous** \'spī-nəs\ *adjective* (15th century)
**1 :** SPINY 1, 3 ⟨*spinous* appendages⟩ ⟨a *spinous* larva⟩
**2 :** difficult or unpleasant to handle or meet **:** THORNY

**spin·out** \'spin-,aút\ *noun* (1955)
**:** a rotational skid by an automobile that usually causes it to leave the roadway

**spin out** *intransitive verb* (1951)
**:** to make a rotational skid in an automobile

**Spi·no·zism** \spi-'nō-,zi-zəm\ *noun* (1728)
**:** the philosophy of Baruch Spinoza who taught that reality is one substance with an infinite number of attributes of which only thought and extension are capable of being apprehended by the human mind
— **Spi·no·zist** \-zist\ *noun*
— **Spi·no·zis·tic** \,spi-nō-'zis-tik\ *adjective*

**spin·ster** \'spin(t)-stər\ *noun* (14th century)
**1 :** a woman whose occupation is spinning
**2 a** *archaic* **:** an unmarried woman of gentle family **b :** an unmarried woman and especially one past the common age for marrying
**3 :** a woman who seems unlikely to marry ◆
— **spin·ster·hood** \-,húd\ *noun*
— **spin·ster·ish** \-st(ə-)rish\ *adjective*
— **spin·ster·ly** *adjective*

◇ WORD HISTORY
**spinster** Before the industrial revolution spinning was a humble but all-important task generally carried out in the home. When the word *spinster* appeared in 14th century English, it meant a person of either sex who spun, especially as a regular occupation. Since spinning was traditionally regarded as women's work, *spinster* gradually came to be applied exclusively to women spinners. By the 17th century the word had also become an established legal designation for an unmarried woman. Not until the 18th century did *spinster* refer to a single woman who, according to the mores of her time, is regarded as having passed the usual or desirable age for marrying.

**spin·thar·i·scope** \spin-'thar-ə-ˌskōp\ *noun* [Greek *spintharis* spark + English *-scope*] (1903)
: an instrument for visual detection of alpha particles that consists of a fluorescent screen and a magnifying lens system

**spin the bottle** *noun* (1955)
: a kissing game in which one has as a partner the person a bottle points to when it stops spinning

**spin·to** \'spēn-(ˌ)tō, 'spin-\ *noun, plural* **spin·tos** [Italian, literally, pushed, from past participle of *spingere* to push, from (assumed) Vulgar Latin *expingere*, from Latin *ex-* + *pangere* to fasten — more at PACT] (1944)
: a singing voice having both lyric and dramatic qualities
— **spinto** *adjective*

**spi·nule** \'spī-(ˌ)nyü(ə)l\ *noun* [Latin *spinula*, diminutive of *spina* thorn — more at SPINE] (1752)
: a minute spine
— **spi·nu·lose** \'spī-nyə-ˌlōs\ *adjective*

**spiny** \'spī-nē\ *adjective* **spin·i·er; -est** (1586)
**1** : covered or armed with spines; *broadly* : bearing spines, prickles, or thorns
**2** : abounding with difficulties, obstacles, or annoyances : THORNY ⟨*spiny* problems⟩
**3** : slender and pointed like a spine
— **spin·i·ness** *noun*

**spiny anteater** *noun* (1827)
: ECHIDNA

**spiny–head·ed worm** \'spī-nē-ˌhe-dəd-\ *noun* (1946)
: any of a small phylum (Acanthocephala) of unsegmented parasitic worms that have a proboscis bearing hooks by which attachment is made to the intestinal wall of the host

**spiny lobster** *noun* (1819)
: any of several edible crustaceans (family Palinuridae and especially genus *Panulirus*) distinguished from the true lobsters by the simple unenlarged first pair of legs and claws and the spiny carapace

**spi·ra·cle** \'spir-i-kəl, 'spī-ri-\ *noun* [Middle English, from Latin *spiraculum*, from *spirare* to breathe] (15th century)
**1** : a breathing hole : VENT
**2** : a breathing orifice: as **a** : BLOWHOLE 2 **b** : an external tracheal aperture of a terrestrial arthropod that in an insect is usually one of a series of small apertures located along each side of the thorax and abdomen — see INSECT illustration
— **spi·rac·u·lar** \spə-'ra-kyə-lər, spī-\ *adjective*

**¹spi·ral** \'spī-rəl\ *adjective* [Medieval Latin *spiralis*, from Latin *spira* coil — more at SPIRE] (1551)
**1 a** : winding around a center or pole and gradually receding from or approaching it ⟨the *spiral* curve of a watch spring⟩ **b** : HELICAL **c** : SPIRAL-BOUND ⟨a *spiral* notebook⟩
**2** : of or relating to the advancement to higher levels through a series of cyclical movements
— **spi·ral·ly** \-rə-lē\ *adverb*

**²spiral** *noun* (1656)
**1 a** : the path of a point in a plane moving around a central point while continuously receding from or approaching it **b** : a three-dimensional curve (as a helix) with one or more turns about an axis
**2** : a single turn or coil in a spiral object
**3 a** : something having a spiral form **b** (1) : a spiral flight (2) : a kick or pass in which a football rotates on its long axis while moving through the air
**4** : a continuously spreading and accelerating increase or decrease ⟨wage *spirals*⟩

**³spiral** *verb* **-raled** *or* **-ralled; -ral·ing** *or* **-ral·ling** (1834)
*intransitive verb*
: to go and especially to rise or fall in a spiral course ⟨costs *spiraled* upward⟩
*transitive verb*

**1** : to form into a spiral
**2** : to cause to spiral

**spiral binding** *noun* (1944)
: a book or notebook binding in which a continuous spiral wire or plastic strip is passed through holes along one edge

**spi·ral–bound** \'spī-rəl-ˌbau̇nd\ *adjective* (1941)
: having a spiral binding

**spiral cleavage** *noun* (1892)
: holoblastic cleavage that is typical of protostomes and that is characterized by arrangement of the blastomeres of each upper tier over the cell junctions of the next lower tier so that the blastomeres spiral around the pole to pole axis of the embryo — compare RADIAL CLEAVAGE

**spiral galaxy** *noun* (1913)
: a galaxy exhibiting a central nucleus or barred structure from which extend concentrations of matter forming curved arms — called also *spiral nebula*

**spiral of Ar·chi·me·des** \-ˌär-kə-'mē-dēz\ [*Archimedes*] (circa 1856)
: a plane curve that is generated by a point moving away from or toward a fixed point at a constant rate while the radius vector from the fixed point rotates at a constant rate and that has the equation $\rho = a\,\theta$ in polar coordinates

**spiral spring** *noun* (1690)
: a spring consisting of a wire coiled usually in a flat spiral or in a helix

**spi·rant** \'spī-rənt\ *noun* [International Scientific Vocabulary, from Latin *spirant-, spirans*, present participle of *spirare* to breathe] (1862)
: a consonant (as \f\, \s\, \sh\) uttered with friction of the breath against some part of the oral passage : FRICATIVE
— **spirant** *adjective*

**¹spire** \'spīr\ *noun* [Middle English, from Old English *spīr;* akin to Middle Dutch *spier* blade of grass] (before 12th century)
**1** : a slender tapering blade or stalk (as of grass)
**2** : the upper tapering part of something (as a tree or antler) : PINNACLE
**3 a** : a tapering roof or analogous pyramidal construction surmounting a tower **b** : STEEPLE

**²spire** *intransitive verb* **spired; spir·ing** (14th century)
: to rise like a spire

**³spire** *noun* [Latin *spira* coil, from Greek *speira;* perhaps akin to Greek *sparton* rope, esparto] (1545)
**1 a** : SPIRAL **b** : COIL
**2** : the inner or upper part of a spiral gastropod shell consisting of all the whorls except the whorl in contact with the body

**⁴spire** *intransitive verb* **spired; spir·ing** (1591)
: to rise in or as if in a spiral

**spi·rea** *or* **spi·raea** \spī-'rē-ə\ *noun* [New Latin *Spiraea*, from Latin, a plant, from Greek *speiraia*] (1669)
**1** : any of a genus (*Spiraea*) of shrubs of the rose family with small perfect usually white or pink flowers in dense racemes, corymbs, cymes, or panicles
**2** : any of several garden plants resembling spireas; *especially* : a shrub (*Astilbe japonica*) of the saxifrage family

**spired** \'spīrd\ *adjective* (1610)
**1** : having a spire ⟨a *spired* church⟩
**2** : tapering usually to a sharp point ⟨*spired* cedars⟩

**spi·ril·lum** \spī-'ri-ləm\ *noun, plural* **-ril·la** \-'ri-lə\ [New Latin, from diminutive of Latin *spira* coil] (circa 1875)
: any of a genus (*Spirillum*) of long curved bacteria having tufts of flagella; *broadly* : a spiral filamentous bacterium (as a spirochete)

**¹spir·it** \'spir-ət\ *noun* [Middle English, from Old French or Latin; Old French, from Latin *spiritus*, literally, breath, from *spirare* to blow, breathe] (13th century)

**1** : an animating or vital principle held to give life to physical organisms
**2** : a supernatural being or essence: as **a** *capitalized* : HOLY SPIRIT **b** : SOUL 2a **c** : an often malevolent being that is bodiless but can become visible; *specifically* : GHOST 2 **d** : a malevolent being that enters and possesses a human being
**3** : temper or disposition of mind or outlook especially when vigorous or animated ⟨in high *spirits*⟩
**4** : the immaterial intelligent or sentient part of a person
**5 a** : the activating or essential principle influencing a person ⟨acted in a *spirit* of helpfulness⟩ **b** : an inclination, impulse, or tendency of a specified kind : MOOD
**6 a** : a special attitude or frame of mind ⟨the money-making *spirit* was for a time driven back —J. A. Froude⟩ **b** : the feeling, quality, or disposition characterizing something ⟨undertaken in a *spirit* of fun⟩
**7** : a lively or brisk quality in a person or a person's actions
**8** : a person having a character or disposition of a specified nature
**9** : a mental disposition characterized by firmness or assertiveness ⟨denied the charge with *spirit*⟩
**10 a** : DISTILLATE 1: as (1) : the liquid containing ethyl alcohol and water that is distilled from an alcoholic liquid or mash — often used in plural (2) : any of various volatile liquids obtained by distillation or cracking (as of petroleum, shale, or wood) — often used in plural **b** : a usually volatile organic solvent (as an alcohol, ester, or hydrocarbon)
**11 a** : prevailing tone or tendency ⟨*spirit* of the age⟩ **b** : general intent or real meaning ⟨*spirit* of the law⟩
**12** : an alcoholic solution of a volatile substance ⟨*spirit* of camphor⟩
**13** : enthusiastic loyalty ⟨school *spirit*⟩
**14** *capitalized, Christian Science* : GOD 1b
**synonym** see COURAGE

**²spirit** *transitive verb* (1608)
**1** : to infuse with spirit; *especially* : ANIMATE ⟨hope and apprehension of feasibleness *spirits* all industry —John Goodman⟩
**2** : to carry off usually secretly or mysteriously ⟨was hustled into a . . . motorcar and *spirited* off to the country —W. L. Shirer⟩

**spir·it·ed** \'spir-ə-təd\ *adjective* (1592)
: full of energy, animation, or courage ⟨a *spirited* discussion⟩
— **spir·it·ed·ly** *adverb*
— **spir·it·ed·ness** *noun*

**spirit gum** *noun* (1886)
: a solution (as of gum arabic in ether) used especially for attaching false hair to the skin

**spir·it·ism** \'spir-ə-ˌti-zəm\ *noun* (1856)
: SPIRITUALISM 2a
— **spir·it·ist** \-tist\ *noun*
— **spir·it·is·tic** \ˌspir-ə-'tis-tik\ *adjective*

**spir·it·less** \'spir-ət-ləs\ *adjective* (1597)
: lacking animation, cheerfulness, or courage
— **spir·it·less·ly** *adverb*
— **spir·it·less·ness** *noun*

**spirit level** *noun* (1768)
: LEVEL 1

**spirit of hartshorn** (circa 1684)
: AMMONIA WATER

**spirit of wine** (1753)
: ALCOHOL 1c

**spir·i·to·so** \ˌspir-ə-'tō-(ˌ)sō, -(ˌ)zō\ *adjective* [Italian, from *spirito* spirit, from Latin *spiritus*] (circa 1724)
: ANIMATED — used as a direction in music

**spir·it·ous** \'spir-ə-təs\ *adjective* (1605)
**1** *archaic* : PURE, REFINED
**2** : SPIRITUOUS

**spirit rapping** *noun* (1852)
: communication by raps held to be from the spirits of the dead

**spirits of hartshorn** (circa 1909)
: AMMONIA WATER

**spirits of turpentine** (circa 1792)
: TURPENTINE 2a

**spirits of wine** (1710)
: rectified spirit : ALCOHOL 1c

¹**spir·i·tu·al** \'spir-i-chə-wəl, -i-chəl, -ich-wəl\ *adjective* [Middle English, from Middle French & Late Latin; Middle French *spirituel*, from Late Latin *spiritualis*, from Latin, of breathing, of wind, from *spiritus*] (14th century)
**1** : of, relating to, consisting of, or affecting the spirit : INCORPOREAL ⟨man's *spiritual* needs⟩
**2 a** : of or relating to sacred matters ⟨*spiritual* songs⟩ **b** : ecclesiastical rather than lay or temporal ⟨*spiritual* authority⟩ ⟨lords *spiritual*⟩
**3** : concerned with religious values
**4** : related or joined in spirit ⟨our *spiritual* home⟩ ⟨his *spiritual* heir⟩
**5 a** : of or relating to supernatural beings or phenomena **b** : of, relating to, or involving spiritualism : SPIRITUALISTIC
— **spir·i·tu·al·ly** *adverb*
— **spir·i·tu·al·ness** *noun*

²**spiritual** *noun* (1582)
**1** *plural* : things of a spiritual, ecclesiastical, or religious nature
**2** : a religious song usually of a deeply emotional character that was developed especially among blacks in the southern U.S.
**3** *capitalized* : any of a party of 13th and 14th century Franciscans advocating strict observance of a rule of poverty for their order

**spiritual bouquet** *noun* (1926)
: a card notifying the recipient of a number of devotional acts performed by a Roman Catholic on behalf of a person on special occasions (as name days or anniversaries) or for the soul of someone recently deceased especially as an expression of sympathy

**spir·i·tu·al·ism** \'spir-i-chə-wə-,li-zəm, -i-chə-,li-, -ich-wə-,li-\ *noun* (1796)
**1** : the view that spirit is a prime element of reality
**2 a** : a belief that spirits of the dead communicate with the living usually through a medium **b** *capitalized* : a movement comprising religious organizations emphasizing spiritualism
— **spir·i·tu·al·ist** \-list\ *noun, often capitalized*
— **spir·i·tu·al·is·tic** \,spir-i-chə-wə-'lis-tik, -i-chə-'lis-, -ich-wə-'lis-\ *adjective*

**spir·i·tu·al·i·ty** \,spir-i-chə-'wa-lə-tē\ *noun, plural* **-ties** (15th century)
**1** : something that in ecclesiastical law belongs to the church or to a cleric as such
**2** : CLERGY
**3** : sensitivity or attachment to religious values
**4** : the quality or state of being spiritual

**spir·i·tu·al·ize** \'spir-i-chə-wə-,līz, -i-chə-,līz, -ich-wə-,līz\ *transitive verb* **-ized; -iz·ing** (1631)
**1** : to make spiritual; *especially* : to purify from the corrupting influences of the world
**2** : to give a spiritual meaning to or understand in a spiritual sense
— **spir·i·tu·al·i·za·tion** \,spir-i-chə-wə-lə-'zā-shən, -i-chə-lə-, -ich-wə-lə-\ *noun*

**spir·i·tu·al·ty** \'spir-i-chə-wəl-tē, -i-chəl-tē, -ich-wəl-tē\ *noun* [Middle English *spiritualte*, from Middle French *spiritualté*, from Medieval Latin *spiritualitat-, spiritualitas*, from Late Latin *spiritualis* spiritual] (14th century)
**1** : SPIRITUALITY 1
**2** : CLERGY

**spi·ri·tu·el** *or* **spi·ri·tu·elle** \,spir-i-chə-'wel, spē-rē-ē-tw⁽ʸ⁾el\ *adjective* [*spirituel* from French, literally, spiritual; *spirituelle* from French, feminine of *spirituel*] (1673)
: having or marked by a refined and especially sprightly or witty nature

**spir·i·tu·ous** \'spir-i-chə-wəs, -ich-wəs\ *adjective* [probably from French *spiritueux*, from Latin *spiritus* spirit] (1681)
: containing or impregnated with alcohol obtained by distillation ⟨*spirituous* liquors⟩

**spirit varnish** *noun* (1850)
: a varnish in which a volatile liquid (as alcohol) is the solvent

**spirit writing** *noun* (1864)
: automatic writing held to be produced under the influence of spirits

**spi·ro·chet·al** \,spī-rə-'kē-t⁰l\ *adjective* (1915)
: caused by spirochetes

**spi·ro·chete** *also* **spi·ro·chaete** \'spī-rə-,kēt\ *noun* [New Latin *Spirochaeta*, genus of bacteria, from Latin *spira* coil + Greek *chaitē* long hair — more at SPIRE] (circa 1877)
: any of an order (Spirochaetales) of slender spirally undulating bacteria including those causing syphilis and relapsing fever

**spi·ro·chet·osis** \,spī-rə-,kē-'tō-səs\ *noun, plural* **-oses** \-,sēz\ [New Latin] (1906)
: infection with or a disease caused by spirochetes

**spi·ro·gy·ra** \,spī-rə-'jī-rə\ *noun* [New Latin, from Latin *spira* + Greek *gyros* ring, circle] (1875)
: any of a genus (*Spirogyra*) of freshwater green algae with spiral chloroplasts

**spi·rom·e·ter** \spī-'rä-mə-tər\ *noun* [International Scientific Vocabulary *spiro-* (from Latin *spirare* to breathe) + *-meter*] (1846)
: an instrument for measuring the air entering and leaving the lungs
— **spi·ro·met·ric** \,spī-rə-'me-trik\ *adjective*
— **spi·rom·e·try** \spī-'rä-mə-trē\ *noun*

**spirt** *variant of* SPURT

**spiry** \'spīr-ē\ *adjective* (1602)
: resembling a spire; *especially* : being tall, slender, and tapering ⟨*spiry* trees⟩

¹**spit** \'spit\ *noun* [Middle English, from Old English *spitu*; akin to Old High German *spiz* spit, *spizzi* pointed] (before 12th century)
**1** : a slender pointed rod for holding meat over a fire
**2** : a small point of land especially of sand or gravel running into a body of water

²**spit** *transitive verb* **spit·ted; spit·ting** (13th century)
: to fix on or as if on a spit : IMPALE

³**spit** *verb* **spit** *or* **spat** \'spat\; **spit·ting** [Middle English *spitten*, from Old English *spittan*; akin to Middle High German *spiutzen* to spit] (before 12th century)
*transitive verb*
**1 a** : to eject (as saliva) from the mouth : EXPECTORATE **b** (1) : to express (unpleasant or malicious feelings) by or as if by spitting (2) : to utter with a spitting sound or scornful expression ⟨*spat* out his words⟩ **c** : to emit as if by spitting; *especially* : to emit (precipitation) in driving particles or in flurries ⟨*spit* rain⟩
**2** : to set to burning ⟨*spit* a fuse⟩
*intransitive verb*
**1 a** (1) : to eject saliva as an expression of aversion or contempt (2) : to exhibit contempt **b** : to eject matter (as saliva) from the mouth : EXPECTORATE
**2** : to rain or snow slightly or in flurries
**3** : to make a noise suggesting expectoration : SPUTTER
— **spit it out** : to say what is in the mind without further delay

⁴**spit** *noun* (14th century)
**1 a** (1) : SPITTLE, SALIVA (2) : the act or an instance of spitting **b** (1) : a frothy secretion exuded by spittlebugs (2) : SPITTLEBUG
**2** : perfect likeness
**3** : a sprinkle of rain or flurry of snow

**spit·al** \'spi-t⁰l\ *noun* [Middle English *spitel*, modification of Medieval Latin *hospitale* — more at HOSPITAL] (14th century)
*archaic* : LAZARETTO, HOSPITAL

**spit and polish** *noun* [from the practice of polishing objects such as shoes by spitting on them and then rubbing them with a cloth] (1895)
: extreme attention to cleanliness, orderliness, smartness of appearance, and ceremony often at the expense of operational efficiency
— **spit-and–polish** *adjective*

**spit·ball** \'spit-,bȯl\ *noun* (1846)
**1** : paper chewed and rolled into a ball to be thrown or shot as a missile
**2** : a baseball pitch delivered after the ball has been moistened with saliva or sweat

**spit curl** *noun* [probably from its being sometimes plastered down with saliva] (1831)
: a spiral curl that is usually plastered on the forehead, temple, or cheek

¹**spite** \'spīt\ *noun* [Middle English, short for *despite*] (14th century)
**1** : petty ill will or hatred with the disposition to irritate, annoy, or thwart
**2** : an instance of spite
*synonym* see MALICE
— **in spite of** : in defiance or contempt of : without being prevented by

²**spite** *transitive verb* **spit·ed; spit·ing** (circa 1555)
**1 a** : ANNOY, OFFEND **b** : to fill with spite
**2** : to treat maliciously (as by shaming or thwarting)

**spite·ful** \'spīt-fəl\ *adjective* (15th century)
: filled with or showing spite : MALICIOUS
— **spite·ful·ly** \-fə-lē\ *adverb*
— **spite·ful·ness** *noun*

**spit·fire** \'spit-,fīr\ *noun* (1680)
: a quick-tempered or highly emotional person

¹**spit·ter** \'spi-tər\ *noun* (14th century)
: one that spits

²**spitter** *noun* (1908)
: SPITBALL 2

**spitting cobra** *noun* (1910)
: either of two African cobras (*Naja nigricollis* and *Hemachatus haemachatus*) that in defense typically eject their venom toward the victim without striking

**spitting image** *noun* [alteration of *spit and image*] (1901)
: IMAGE 3b

**spit·tle** \'spi-t⁰l\ *noun* [Middle English *spetil*, from Old English *spætl*; akin to Old English *spittan* to spit] (before 12th century)
**1** : SALIVA
**2** : ⁴SPIT 1b(1)

**spit·tle·bug** \-,bəg\ *noun* (1882)
: any of a family (Cercopidae) of leaping homopterous insects whose larvae secrete froth — called also *froghopper*

**spittle insect** *noun* (1891)
: SPITTLEBUG

**spit·toon** \spi-'tün, spə-\ *noun* [⁴*spit* + *-oon* (as in *balloon*)] (1823)
: a receptacle for spit — called also *cuspidor*

**spit up** *verb* (1779)
: REGURGITATE, VOMIT

**spitz** \'spits\ *noun* [German, from *spitz* pointed, from Old High German *spizzi*; from the shape of its ears and muzzle — more at SPIT] (1842)
: a member of any of several breeds of stocky heavy-coated dogs of northern origin with erect ears and usually a heavily furred tail carried over the back

spitz

**spiv** \'spiv\ *noun* [alteration of English dialect *spiff* flashy dresser, from *spiff* dandified] (circa 1934)
**1** *British* : one who lives by his wits without regular employment

**2** *British* : SLACKER

**splanch·nic** \'splaŋk-nik\ *adjective* [New Latin *splanchnicus,* from Greek *splanchnikos,* from *splanchna,* plural, viscera; akin to Greek *splēn* spleen] (1681)
: of or relating to the viscera : VISCERAL

¹**splash** \'splash\ *verb* [alteration of *plash*] (circa 1727)
*transitive verb*
**1 a** (1) : to dash a liquid or thinly viscous substance upon or against (2) : to soil or stain with splashed liquid **b** : to mark or overlay with patches of contrasting color or texture **c** : to display prominently
**2 a** : to cause (a liquid or thinly viscous substance) to spatter about especially with force **b** : to scatter in the manner of a splashed liquid
*intransitive verb*
**1 a** : to strike and dash about a liquid or semiliquid substance **b** : to move in or into a liquid or semiliquid substance and cause it to spatter
**2 a** (1) : to become spattered about (2) : to spread or scatter in the manner of splashed liquid **b** : to fall, strike, or move with a splashing sound ⟨a brook *splashing* over rocks⟩
— **splash·er** *noun*

²**splash** *noun* (1736)
**1 a** (1) : splashed liquid or semiliquid substance; *also* : impounded water released suddenly (2) : a spot or daub from or as if from splashed liquid ⟨a mud *splash* on the fender⟩ **b** : a colored patch
**2 a** : the action of splashing **b** : a short plunge
**3** : a sound produced by or as if by a liquid falling, moving, being hurled, or oscillating
**4 a** : a vivid impression created especially by ostentatious activity or appearance **b** : ostentatious display
**5** : a small amount : SPRINKLING

**splash·board** \'splash-ˌbōrd, -ˌbȯrd\ *noun* (1826)
**1** : DASHBOARD 1
**2** : a panel to protect against splashes

**splash·down** \'splash-ˌdau̇n\ *noun* (1959)
: the landing of a manned spacecraft in the ocean
— **splash down** *intransitive verb*

**splash guard** *noun* (1926)
: a flap suspended behind a rear wheel to prevent tire splash from muddying windshields of following vehicles

**splashy** \'spla-shē\ *adjective* **splash·i·er; -est** (1856)
**1** : that can be easily splashed about
**2** : moving or being moved with a splash or splashing sounds
**3** : tending to or exhibiting ostentatious display
**4** : consisting of, being, or covered with colored splashes
— **splash·i·ly** \'spla-shə-lē\ *adverb*
— **splash·i·ness** \'spla-shē-nəs\ *noun*

¹**splat** \'splat\ *noun* [obsolete *splat* to spread flat] (1833)
: a single flat thin often ornamental member of a back of a chair

²**splat** *noun* [imitative] (1897)
: a splattering or slapping sound

¹**splat·ter** \'spla-tər\ *verb* [probably blend of *splash* and *spatter*] (1785)
*transitive verb*
: SPATTER
*intransitive verb*
: to scatter or fall in or as if in drops

²**splatter** *noun* (1819)
: SPATTER, SPLASH

¹**splay** \'splā\ *verb* [Middle English, short for *displayen* — more at DISPLAY] (15th century)
*transitive verb*
**1** : to cause to spread outward
**2** : to make oblique : BEVEL
*intransitive verb*
**1** : to extend apart or outward especially in an awkward manner
**2** : SLOPE, SLANT

²**splay** *noun* (circa 1508)

**1** : a slope or bevel especially of the sides of a door or window
**2** : SPREAD, EXPANSION

³**splay** *adjective* (1767)
**1** : turned outward ⟨*splay* knees⟩
**2** : AWKWARD, UNGAINLY

**splay·foot** \'splā-ˌfu̇t\ *noun* (1548)
: a foot abnormally flattened and spread out; *specifically* : FLATFOOT
— **splay·foot·ed** \-ˌfu̇-təd\ *adjective*

**spleen** \'splēn\ *noun* [Middle English *splen,* from Middle French or Latin; Middle French *esplen,* from Latin *splen,* from Greek *splēn;* akin to Latin *lien* spleen, Sanskrit *plīhan*] (14th century)
**1** : a highly vascular ductless organ that is located in the left abdominal region near the stomach or intestine of most vertebrates and is concerned with final destruction of red blood cells, filtration and storage of blood, and production of lymphocytes
**2** *obsolete* : the seat of emotions or passions
**3** *archaic* : MELANCHOLY
**4** : feelings of anger or ill will often suppressed
**5** *obsolete* : a sudden impulse or whim : CAPRICE
*synonym* see MALICE

**spleen·ful** \-fəl\ *adjective* (1588)
: full of or affected with spleen : SPLENETIC

**spleen·wort** \-ˌwərt, -ˌwȯrt\ *noun* [from the belief in its power to cure disorders of the spleen] (1578)
: any of a large genus (*Asplenium*) of chiefly evergreen ferns having linear or oblong sori

**spleeny** \'splē-nē\ *adjective* (1604)
**1** : full of or displaying spleen
**2** *New England* : peevish and irritable with hypochondriac inclinations

**splen-** *or* **spleno-** *combining form* [Latin, from Greek *splēn-, splēno-,* from *splēn*]
: spleen ⟨*splen*ectomy⟩ ⟨*spleno*megaly⟩

**splen·dent** \'splen-dənt\ *adjective* [Middle English, from Late Latin *splendent-, splendens,* from Latin, present participle of *splendēre*] (15th century)
**1** : SHINING, GLOSSY ⟨*splendent* luster⟩
**2** : ILLUSTRIOUS, BRILLIANT ⟨*splendent* genius⟩

**splen·did** \'splen-dəd\ *adjective* [Latin *splendidus,* from *splendēre* to shine; perhaps akin to Middle Irish *lainn* bright] (1634)
**1** : possessing or displaying splendor: as **a** : SHINING, BRILLIANT **b** : marked by showy magnificence
**2** : ILLUSTRIOUS, GRAND
**3 a** : EXCELLENT ⟨a *splendid* opportunity⟩ **b** : being out of the ordinary : SINGULAR ☆
— **splen·did·ly** *adverb*
— **splen·did·ness** *noun*

**splen·dif·er·ous** \splen-'di-f(ə-)rəs\ *adjective* [*splendor* + *-i-* + *-ferous*] (1843)
: extraordinarily or showily impressive
— **splen·dif·er·ous·ly** *adverb*
— **splen·dif·er·ous·ness** *noun*

**splen·dor** \'splen-dər\ *noun* [Middle English *splendure,* from Anglo-French *splendur,* from Latin *splendor,* from *splendēre*] (15th century)
**1 a** : great brightness or luster : BRILLIANCY **b** : MAGNIFICENCE, POMP
**2** : something splendid
— **splen·dor·ous** *also* **splen·drous** \-d(ə-)rəs\ *adjective*

**splen·dour** \-dər\ *chiefly British variant of* SPLENDOR

**sple·nec·to·my** \spli-'nek-tə-mē\ *noun, plural* **-mies** [International Scientific Vocabulary] (circa 1859)
: surgical removal of the spleen
— **sple·nec·to·mize** \-ˌmīz\ *transitive verb*

**sple·net·ic** \spli-'ne-tik, *archaic* 'sple-nə-ˌtik\ *adjective* [Late Latin *spleneticus,* from Latin *splen* spleen] (1697)
**1** *archaic* : given to melancholy
**2** : marked by bad temper, malevolence, or spite

— **splenetic** *noun*
— **sple·net·i·cal·ly** \spli-'ne-ti-k(ə-)lē\ *adverb*

**splen·ic** \'sple-nik\ *adjective* [Latin *splenicus,* from Greek *splēnikos,* from *splēn* spleen] (1619)
: of, relating to, or located in the spleen ⟨*splenic* blood flow⟩

**sple·ni·us** \'splē-nē-əs\ *noun, plural* **-nii** \-nē-ˌī\ [New Latin, from Latin *splenium* plaster, compress, from Greek *splēnion,* from *splēn*] (1732)
: either of two flat oblique muscles on each side of the back of the neck and upper thoracic region

**spleno·meg·a·ly** \ˌsple-nō-'me-gə-lē\ *noun, plural* **-lies** [International Scientific Vocabulary] (circa 1900)
: enlargement of the spleen

**spleu·chan** \'splü-kən, 'splyü-\ *noun* [Scottish Gaelic *spliùcan* & Irish *spliúchán*] (1785)
*Scottish & Irish* : a pouch especially for tobacco or money

¹**splice** \'splīs\ *transitive verb* **spliced; splic·ing** [obsolete Dutch *splissen;* akin to Middle Dutch *splitten* to split] (circa 1525)
**1 a** : to unite (as two ropes) by interweaving the strands **b** : to unite (as lengths of magnetic tape) by lapping two ends together or by applying a piece that laps upon two ends and making fast
**2** : to unite, link, or insert as if by splicing
**3** : to combine (genetic material) from either the same organism or different organisms ⟨use enzymes to cut and *splice* genes⟩
— **splic·er** *noun*

²**splice** *noun* (1627)
**1** : a joining or joint made by splicing something
**2** : MARRIAGE, WEDDING

splice 1

**spliff** \'splif\ *noun* [origin unknown] (1936)
: JOINT 4

**spline** \'splīn\ *noun* [origin unknown] (1756)
**1** : a thin wood or metal strip used in building construction
**2** : a key that is fixed to one of two connected mechanical parts and fits into a keyway in the other; *also* : a keyway for such a key
**3** : a function that is defined on an interval, is used to approximate a given function, and is composed of pieces of simple functions defined on subintervals and joined at their endpoints with a suitable degree of smoothness

¹**splint** \'splint\ *also* **splent** \'splent\ *noun* [Middle English, from Middle Low German *splinte, splente;* probably akin to Middle Dutch *splitten* to split] (14th century)
**1** : a small plate or strip of metal used in making armor

☆ **SYNONYMS**
**Splendid, resplendent, gorgeous, glorious, sublime, superb** mean extraordinarily or transcendently impressive. SPLENDID implies outshining the usual or customary ⟨the wedding was a *splendid* occasion⟩. RESPLENDENT suggests a glowing or blazing splendor ⟨*resplendent* in her jewelry⟩. GORGEOUS implies a rich splendor especially in display of color ⟨a *gorgeous* red dress⟩. GLORIOUS suggests radiance that heightens beauty or distinction ⟨a *glorious* sunset⟩. SUBLIME implies an exaltation or elevation almost beyond human comprehension ⟨a vision of *sublime* beauty⟩. SUPERB suggests a magnificence or excellence reaching the highest conceivable degree ⟨her singing was *superb*⟩.

**2 a :** a thin strip of wood suitable for interweaving (as into baskets) **b :** SPLINTER **c :** material or a device used to protect and immobilize a body part (as a broken arm)
**3 :** a bony enlargement on the upper part of the cannon bone of a horse usually on the inside of the leg
**²splint** *transitive verb* (15th century)
**1 :** to support and immobilize (as a broken bone) with a splint
**2 :** to brace with or as if with splints
**splint bone** *noun* (1704)
**:** one of the slender rudimentary metacarpal or metatarsal bones on either side of the cannon bone in the limbs of the horse and related animals
**¹splin·ter** \'splin-tər\ *noun* [Middle English, from Middle Dutch; akin to Middle Low German *splinte* splint] (14th century)
**1 a :** a thin piece split or broken off lengthwise : SLIVER **b :** a small needlelike particle
**2 :** a group or faction broken away from a parent body
**— splinter** *adjective*
**— splin·tery** \'splin-tə-rē, -trē\ *adjective*
**²splinter** *verb* **splin·tered; splin·ter·ing** \'splin-tə-riŋ, -triŋ\ (1582)
*transitive verb*
**1 :** to split or rend into long thin pieces : SHIVER
**2 :** to split into fragments, parts, or factions
*intransitive verb*
**:** to become splintered
**¹split** \'split\ *verb* **split; split·ting** [Dutch *splitten*, from Middle Dutch; akin to Middle High German *splīzen* to split and probably to Old High German *spaltan* to split] (1593)
*transitive verb*
**1 a :** to divide lengthwise usually along a grain or seam or by layers **b :** to affect as if by cleaving or forcing apart ⟨the river *splits* the town in two⟩
**2 a** (1) **:** to tear or rend apart : BURST (2) **:** to subject (an atom or atomic nucleus) to artificial disintegration by fission **b :** to affect as if by breaking up or tearing apart : SHATTER ⟨a roar that *split* the air⟩
**3 :** to divide into parts or portions: as **a :** to divide between persons : SHARE **b :** to divide into factions, parties, or groups **c :** to mark (a ballot) or cast or register (a vote) so as to vote for candidates of different parties **d** (1) **:** to divide or break down (a chemical compound) into constituents ⟨*split* a fat into glycerol and fatty acids⟩ (2) **:** to remove by such separation ⟨*split* off carbon dioxide⟩ **e :** to divide (stock) by issuing a larger number of shares to existing shareholders usually without increase in total par value
**4 :** to separate (the parts of a whole) by interposing something ⟨*split* an infinitive⟩
**5 :** LEAVE ⟨*split* the party⟩ ⟨*split* town⟩
*intransitive verb*
**1 a :** to become split lengthwise or into layers **b :** to break apart : BURST
**2 a :** to become divided up or separated off ⟨*split* into factions⟩ **b :** to sever relations or connections **c :** LEAVE; *especially* **:** to leave without delay
**3** *British* **:** to betray confidence : act as an informer — usually used with *on*
**4 :** to apportion shares
**synonym** see TEAR
**— split hairs :** to make oversubtle or trivial distinctions
**— split one's sides :** to laugh heartily
**²split** *noun* (1597)
**1 a :** a narrow break made by or as if by splitting **b :** an arrangement of bowling pins left standing with space for pins between them
**2 :** a piece split off or made thin by splitting
**3 a :** a division into or between divergent or antagonistic elements or forces **b :** a faction formed in this way

**4 a :** the act or process of splitting (as the stock of a corporation) **b :** the act of lowering oneself to the floor or leaping into the air with legs extended at right angles to the trunk
**5 :** a product of division by or as if by splitting
**6 :** a wine bottle holding one quarter the usual amount or about .1875 liters (6 to 6.5 ounces); *also* **:** the quantity held by a split
**7 :** an ice cream sundae served over slices of fruit (as banana)
**8 :** the recorded time at or for a specific part of a race
**³split** *adjective* (1648)
**1 :** DIVIDED, FRACTURED
**2 :** prepared for use by splitting ⟨*split* bamboo⟩ ⟨*split* hides⟩
**3 :** HETEROZYGOUS — used especially by breeders of cage birds sometimes with *for*
**4 :** widely spaced
**split–brain** \'split-'brān\ *adjective* (1958)
**:** having the optic chiasma and corpus callosum severed ⟨behavior in *split-brain* animals⟩
**split decision** *noun* (1952)
**:** a decision in a boxing match reflecting a division of opinion among the referee and judges
**split end** *noun* (1955)
**:** an offensive football end who lines up usually several yards to the side of the formation
**split–fingered fastball** \'split-'fiŋ-gərd-\ *noun* (1979)
**:** a fast baseball pitch thrown with the ball gripped as for a forkball
**split infinitive** *noun* (1897)
**:** an infinitive with *to* having a modifier between the *to* and the verbal (as in "to really start") □
**split–lev·el** \'split-'le-vəl\ *adjective* (1946)
**:** divided vertically so that the floor level of rooms in one part is approximately midway between the levels of two successive stories in an adjoining part ⟨a *split-level* house⟩
**— split–lev·el** \-,le-vəl\ *noun*
**split pea** *noun* (1736)
**:** a dried hulled pea in which the cotyledons usually split apart
**split personality** *noun* (1927)
**:** SCHIZOPHRENIA; *also* **:** MULTIPLE PERSONALITY
**split rail** *noun* (1826)
**:** a fence rail split from a log
**split screen** *noun* (1944)
**:** a film or video technique in which the frame is divided into discrete nonoverlapping images; *also* **:** the visual composition based on this technique
**split second** *noun* (1912)
**:** a fractional part of a second : FLASH
**split shift** *noun* (1943)
**:** a shift of working hours divided into two or more working periods at times (as morning and evening) separated by more than normal periods of time off (as for lunch or rest)
**split·ter** \'spli-tər\ *noun* (1648)
**1 :** one that splits
**2 :** one who classifies organisms into numerous named groups based on relatively minor variations or characters — compare LUMPER
**3 :** SPLIT-FINGERED FASTBALL
**split ticket** *noun* (1836)
**:** a ballot cast by a voter who votes for candidates of more than one party
**split·ting** \'spli-tiŋ\ *adjective* (1593)
**:** that splits or causes to split: as **a :** causing a piercing sensation ⟨a *splitting* headache⟩ **b :** very fast or quick **c :** SIDESPLITTING ⟨a *splitting* laugh⟩
**splore** \'splōr, 'splȯr\ *noun* [origin unknown] (1785)
**1** *Scottish* **:** FROLIC, CAROUSAL
**2** *Scottish* **:** COMMOTION
**¹splotch** \'spläch\ *noun* [perhaps blend of *spot* and *blotch*] (1601)
**:** SPOT, BLOTCH
**— splotchy** \'splä-chē\ *adjective*
**²splotch** *transitive verb* (1654)

**:** to mark with a splotch : cover with splotches
**¹splurge** \'splərj\ *noun* [perhaps blend of *splash* and *surge*] (1830)
**:** an ostentatious effort, display, or expenditure
**²splurge** *verb* **splurged; splurg·ing** (1843)
*intransitive verb*
**1 :** to make a splurge
**2 :** to indulge oneself extravagantly — often used with *on* ⟨*splurge* on a new dress⟩
*transitive verb*
**:** to spend extravagantly or ostentatiously
**¹splut·ter** \'splə-tər\ *noun* [probably alteration of *sputter*] (1677)
**1 :** a confused noise (as of hasty speaking)
**2 :** a splashing or sputtering sound
**²splutter** (1818)
*intransitive verb*
**1 :** to make a noise as if spitting
**2 :** to speak hastily and confusedly
*transitive verb*
**:** to utter hastily or confusedly : STAMMER
**— splut·ter·er** \'splə-tər-ər\ *noun*
**splut·tery** \'splə-tə-rē\ *adjective* (1866)
**:** marked by spluttering
**Spode** \'spōd\ *noun* (1869)
**:** ceramic ware (as bone china, stone china, or Parian ware) made at the works established by Josiah Spode in 1770 at Stoke in Staffordshire, England
**spod·u·mene** \'spä-jə-,mēn\ *noun* [probably from French *spodumène*, from German *Spodumen*, from Greek *spodoumenos*, present participle of *spodousthai* to be burnt to ashes, from *spodos* ashes] (1893)
**:** a white to yellowish, purplish, or emerald-green monoclinic mineral that is a silicate of lithium and aluminum and occurs in prismatic crystals often of great size
**¹spoil** \'spȯi(ə)l\ *noun* [Middle English *spoile*, from Middle French *espoille*, from Latin *spolia*, plural of *spolium* animal skin — more at SPILL] (14th century)
**1 a :** plunder taken from an enemy in war or a victim in robbery : LOOT **b :** public offices made the property of a successful party — usually used in plural **c :** something valuable or desirable gained through special effort or opportunism or in return for a favor — usually used in plural
**2 a :** SPOLIATION, PLUNDERING **b :** the act of damaging : HARM, IMPAIRMENT
**3 :** an object of plundering : PREY
**4 :** earth and rock excavated or dredged

---

□ USAGE
**split infinitive** The split infinitive was discovered and named in the 19th century. 19th century writers seem to have made greater use of this construction than earlier writers; the frequency of occurrence attracted the disapproving attention of grammarians, many of whom thought it to be a modern corruption. The construction had in fact been in occasional use since the 14th century; only its frequency had changed. Even though there has never been a rational basis for objecting to the split infinitive, the subject has become a fixture of folk belief about grammar. You can hardly publish a sentence containing one without hearing about it from somebody. Modern commentators know the split infinitive is not a vice, but they are loath to drop such a popular subject. They usually say it's all right to split an infinitive in the interest of clarity. Since clarity is the usual reason for splitting, this advice means merely that you can split them whenever you need to.

---

\ə\ abut \ᵊ\ kitten \ər\ further \a\ ash \ā\ ace
\ä\ mop, mar \au̇\ out \ch\ chin \e\ bet \ē\ easy
\g\ go \i\ hit \ī\ ice \j\ job \ŋ\ sing \ō\ go
\ȯ\ law \ȯi\ boy \th\ thin \t͟h\ the \ü\ loot \u̇\ foot
\y\ yet \zh\ vision *see also* Guide to Pronunciation

**5 :** an object damaged or flawed in the making
☆
²**spoil** *verb* **spoiled** \'spȯi(ə)ld, 'spȯi(ə)lt\ *also* **spoilt** \'spȯi(ə)lt\; **spoil·ing** [Middle English, from Middle French *espoillier*, from Latin *spoliare*, from *spolium*] (14th century) *transitive verb*
**1 a** *archaic* **:** DESPOIL, STRIP **b :** PILLAGE, ROB
**2** *archaic* **:** to seize by force
**3 a :** to damage seriously **:** RUIN **b :** to impair the quality or effect of ⟨a quarrel *spoiled* the celebration⟩
**4 a :** to impair the disposition or character of by overindulgence or excessive praise **b :** to pamper excessively **:** CODDLE
*intransitive verb*
**1 :** to practice plunder and robbery
**2 :** to lose valuable or useful qualities usually as a result of decay
**3 :** to have an eager desire ⟨*spoiling* for a fight⟩
***synonym*** see DECAY, INDULGE
— **spoil·able** \'spȯi-lə-bəl\ *adjective*
**spoil·age** \'spȯi-lij\ *noun* (1597)
**1 :** the act or process of spoiling; *especially* **:** the process of decay in foodstuffs
**2 :** something spoiled or wasted
**3 :** loss by spoilage
**spoil·er** \'spȯi-lər\ *noun* (15th century)
**1 a :** one that spoils **b :** one (as a political candidate) having little or no chance of winning but capable of depriving a rival of success
**2 a :** a long narrow plate along the upper surface of an airplane wing that may be raised for reducing lift and increasing drag — see AIRPLANE illustration **b :** an air deflector on an automobile to reduce the tendency to lift off the road at high speeds
**spoils·man** \'spȯi(ə)lz-mən\ *noun* (1846)
**:** one who serves a party for a share of the spoils; *also* **:** one who sanctions such practice
**spoil·sport** \'spȯi(ə)l-ˌspōrt, -ˌspȯrt\ *noun* (1821)
**:** one who spoils the sport or pleasure of others
**spoils system** *noun* (1838)
**:** a practice of regarding public offices and their emoluments as plunder to be distributed to members of the victorious party
¹**spoke** \'spōk\ *past & archaic past participle of* SPEAK
²**spoke** *noun* [Middle English, from Old English *spāca*; akin to Middle Dutch *spike* spike — more at SPIKE] (before 12th century)
**1 a :** any of the small radiating bars inserted in the hub of a wheel to support the rim **b :** something resembling the spoke of a wheel
**2 :** any of the projecting handles of a steering wheel of a boat
³**spoke** *transitive verb* **spoked; spok·ing** (before 12th century)
**:** to furnish with or as if with spokes
**spo·ken** \'spō-kən\ *adjective* [past participle of *speak*] (1595)
**1 :** delivered by word of mouth **:** ORAL
**2 :** characterized by speaking in (such) a manner — used in combination ⟨soft-*spoken*⟩ ⟨plain*spoken*⟩
**spoke·shave** \'spōk-ˌshāv\ *noun* [²*spoke*] (1510)
**:** a drawknife or small transverse plane with end handles for planing convex or concave surfaces
**spokes·man** \'spōks-mən\ *noun* [probably irregular from *spoke*, obsolete past participle of *speak*] (1537)
**:** a person who speaks as the representative of another or others often in a professional capacity
— **spokes·man·ship** \-ˌship\ *noun*
**spokes·peo·ple** \-ˌpē-pəl\ *noun plural* (1972)
**:** people serving as spokesmen or spokeswomen
**spokes·per·son** \-ˌpər-s³n\ *noun* (1972)
**:** SPOKESMAN
**spokes·wom·an** \-ˌwu̇-mən\ *noun* (1654)

**:** a woman who speaks as the representative of another or others often in a professional capacity
**spo·li·ate** \'spō-lē-ˌāt\ *transitive verb* **-at·ed; -at·ing** [Latin *spoliatus*, past participle of *spoliare*] (circa 1727)
**:** DESPOIL
— **spo·li·a·tor** \-ˌā-tər\ *noun*
**spo·li·a·tion** \ˌspō-lē-'ā-shən\ *noun* [Middle English, from Latin *spoliation-, spoliatio*, from *spoliare* to plunder — more at SPOIL] (15th century)
**1 a :** the act of plundering **b :** the state of having been plundered especially in war
**2 :** the act of injuring especially beyond reclaim
**spon·dee** \'spän-ˌdē\ *noun* [Middle English *sponde*, from Middle French or Latin; Middle French *spondee*, from Latin *spondeum*, from Greek *spondeios*, from *spondeios* of a libation, from *spondē* libation, from *spendein* to make a libation; from its use in music accompanying libations — more at SPOUSE] (14th century)
**:** a metrical foot consisting of two long or stressed syllables
— **spon·da·ic** \spän-'dā-ik\ *adjective or noun*
**spon·dy·li·tis** \ˌspän-də-'lī-təs\ *noun* [New Latin, from Greek *sphondylos, spondylos* vertebra] (circa 1849)
**:** inflammation of the vertebrae
¹**sponge** \'spənj\ *noun* [Middle English, from Old English, from Latin *spongia*, from Greek] (before 12th century)
**1 a** (1) **:** an elastic porous mass of interlacing horny fibers that forms the internal skeleton of various marine animals (phylum Porifera) and is able when wetted to absorb water (2) **:** a piece of sponge (as for scrubbing and cleaning) (3) **:** a porous rubber or cellulose product used similarly to a sponge **b :** any of a phylum (Porifera) of aquatic chiefly marine lower invertebrate animals that are essentially double-walled cell colonies that are permanently attached as adults
**2 :** a pad (as of folded gauze) used in surgery and medicine (as to remove discharge or apply medication)
**3 :** one who lives on others **:** SPONGER
**4 a :** raised dough (as for yeast bread) **b :** a whipped dessert usually containing whites of eggs or gelatin **c :** a metal (as platinum) obtained in porous form usually by reduction without fusion ⟨titanium *sponge*⟩ **d :** the egg mass of a crab
**5 :** an absorbent contraceptive device that is impregnated with spermicide and inserted into the vagina before sexual intercourse to cover the cervix
***synonym*** see PARASITE
²**sponge** *verb* **sponged; spong·ing** (14th century)
*transitive verb*
**1 :** to cleanse, wipe, or moisten with or as if with a sponge
**2 :** to erase or destroy with or as if with a sponge — often used with *out*
**3 :** to get by sponging on another
**4 :** to absorb with or as if with or in the manner of a sponge
*intransitive verb*
**1 :** to absorb, soak up, or imbibe like a sponge
**2 :** to get something from or live on another by imposing on hospitality or good nature
**3 :** to dive or dredge for sponges
— **spong·er** *noun*
**sponge cake** *noun* (1805)
**:** a light cake made without shortening
**sponge cloth** *noun* (1862)
**:** any of various soft porous fabrics especially in a loose honeycomb weave
**sponge rubber** *noun* (1886)
**:** cellular rubber resembling a natural sponge in structure used especially for cushions, vibration dampeners, weather stripping, and gaskets

**sponge·ware** \'spənj-ˌwar, -ˌwer\ *noun* (1943)
**:** a typically 19th century earthenware with background color spattered or dabbed (as with a sponge) and usually a freehand central design
**spon·gin** \'spən-jən\ *noun* [German, from Latin *spongia* sponge] (circa 1868)
**:** a scleroprotein that is the chief constituent of flexible fibers in sponge skeletons
**spongy** \'spən-jē\ *adjective* **spong·i·er; -est** (14th century)
**1 :** resembling a sponge: **a :** soft and full of cavities ⟨*spongy* ice⟩ **b :** elastic, porous, and absorbent
**2 a :** not firm or solid **b :** being in the form of a metallic sponge ⟨*spongy* iron⟩
**3 :** moist and soft like a sponge full of water ⟨a *spongy* moor⟩
— **spong·i·ness** *noun*
**spongy parenchyma** *noun* (1884)
**:** a spongy layer of irregular chlorophyll-bearing cells interspersed with air spaces that fills the interior part of a leaf below the palisade layer — called also *spongy layer, spongy tissue*
**spon·son** \'spän(t)-sən\ *noun* [perhaps by shortening & alteration from *expansion*] (1835)
**1 a :** a projection (as a gun platform) from the side of a ship or a tank **b :** an air chamber along a canoe to increase stability and buoyancy
**2 :** a light air-filled structure or a winglike part protruding from the hull of a seaplane to steady it on water
¹**spon·sor** \'spän(t)-sər\ *noun* [Late Latin, from Latin, guarantor, surety, from *spondēre* to promise — more at SPOUSE] (1651)
**1 :** one who presents a candidate for baptism or confirmation and undertakes responsibility for the person's religious education or spiritual welfare
**2 :** one who assumes responsibility for some other person or thing
**3 :** a person or an organization that pays for or plans and carries out a project or activity; *especially* **:** one that pays the cost of a radio or television program usually in return for advertising time during its course
— **spon·so·ri·al** \spän-'sōr-ē-əl, -'sȯr-\ *adjective*
— **spon·sor·ship** \'spän(t)-sər-ˌship\ *noun*
²**sponsor** *transitive verb* **spon·sored; spon·sor·ing** \'spän(t)s-(ə-)riŋ\ (1884)
**:** to be or stand sponsor for
**spon·ta·ne·i·ty** \ˌspän-tə-'nē-ə-tē, -'nā-; -t³n-'ē-, -'ā-\ *noun* (1651)
**1 :** the quality or state of being spontaneous
**2 :** voluntary or undetermined action or movement; *also* **:** its source
**spon·ta·ne·ous** \spän-'tā-nē-əs\ *adjective* [Late Latin *spontaneus*, from Latin *sponte* of one's free will, voluntarily] (1656)
**1 :** proceeding from natural feeling or native tendency without external constraint

---

☆ SYNONYMS
**Spoil, plunder, booty, prize, loot** mean something taken from another by force or craft. SPOIL, more commonly SPOILS, applies to what belongs by right or custom to the victor in war or political contest ⟨the *spoils* of political victory⟩. PLUNDER applies to what is taken not only in war but in robbery, banditry, grafting, or swindling ⟨a bootlegger's *plunder*⟩. BOOTY implies plunder to be shared among confederates ⟨thieves dividing up their *booty*⟩. PRIZE applies to spoils captured on the high seas or territorial waters of the enemy ⟨the wartime right of seizing *prizes* at sea⟩. LOOT applies especially to what is taken from victims of a catastrophe ⟨picked through the ruins for *loot*⟩.

**2 :** arising from a momentary impulse
**3 :** controlled and directed internally **:** SELF-ACTING ⟨*spontaneous* movement characteristic of living things⟩
**4 :** produced without being planted or without human labor **:** INDIGENOUS
**5 :** developing without apparent external influence, force, cause, or treatment
**6 :** not apparently contrived or manipulated **:** NATURAL ☆
— **spon·ta·ne·ous·ly** *adverb*
— **spon·ta·ne·ous·ness** *noun*
**spontaneous combustion** *noun* (1795)
**:** self-ignition of combustible material through chemical action (as oxidation) of its constituents — called also *spontaneous ignition*
**spontaneous generation** *noun* (1665)
**:** ABIOGENESIS
**spontaneous recovery** *noun* (1943)
**:** reappearance of an extinguished conditioned response without positive reinforcement
**spon·toon** \spän-'tün\ *noun* [French *sponton*, from Italian *spuntone*, from *punta* sharp point, from (assumed) Vulgar Latin *puncta* — more at POINT] (1598)
**:** a short pike formerly borne by subordinate officers of infantry
**¹spoof** \'spüf\ *transitive verb* [*Spoof*, a hoaxing game invented by Arthur Roberts (died 1933) English comedian] (1889)
**1 :** DECEIVE, HOAX
**2 :** to make good-natured fun of
**²spoof** *noun* (1889)
**1 :** HOAX, DECEPTION
**2 :** a light humorous parody
— **spoof·ery** \'spü-f(ə-)rē\ *noun*
— **spoofy** \'spü-fē\ *adjective*
**¹spook** \'spük\ *noun* [Dutch; akin to Middle Low German *spōk* ghost] (1801)
**1 :** GHOST, SPECTER
**2 :** an undercover agent **:** SPY
— **spook·ish** \'spü-kish\ *adjective*
**²spook** (1883)
*transitive verb*
**1 :** HAUNT 3
**2 :** to make frightened or frantic **:** SCARE; *especially* **:** to startle into violent activity (as stampeding)
*intransitive verb*
**:** to become spooked ⟨cattle *spooking* at shadows⟩
**spook·ery** \'spü-k(ə-)rē\ *noun, plural* **-er·ies** (1893)
**:** the quality of being spooky; *also* **:** something (as a story) that involves spooks
**spooky** \'spü-kē\ *adjective* **spook·i·er; -est** (1854)
**1 :** relating to, resembling, or suggesting spooks
**2 :** NERVOUS, SKITTISH ⟨a *spooky* horse⟩
— **spook·i·ly** \-kə-lē\ *adverb*
— **spook·i·ness** \-kē-nəs\ *noun*
**¹spool** \'spül\ *noun* [Middle English *spole*, from Middle French or Middle Dutch; Middle French *espole*, from Middle Dutch *spoele*; akin to Old High German *spuola* spool] (14th century)
**1 :** a cylindrical device which has a rim or ridge at each end and an axial hole for a pin or spindle and on which material (as thread, wire, or tape) is wound
**2 :** material or the amount of material wound on a spool
**²spool** (1603)
*transitive verb*
**1 :** to wind on a spool
**2 :** WIND ⟨*spool* the thread off the bobbin⟩
*intransitive verb*
**1 :** to wind itself on a spool
**2 :** WIND
**¹spoon** \'spün\ *noun* [Middle English, from Old English *spōn* splinter, chip; akin to Old High German *spān* splinter, chip] (14th century)

**1 :** an eating or cooking implement consisting of a small shallow bowl with a relatively long handle
**2 :** something (as a tool or fishing lure) that resembles a spoon in shape
**²spoon** (1715)
*transitive verb*
**:** to take up and usually transfer in a spoon
*intransitive verb*
[perhaps from the Welsh custom of an engaged man's presenting his fiancée with an elaborately carved wooden spoon] **:** to make love by caressing, kissing, and talking amorously **:** NECK
**spoon·bill** \'spün-ˌbil\ *noun* (circa 1678)
**1 :** any of several wading birds (family Threskiornithidae) related to the ibises that have an expanded bill that is flattened and rounded at the tip
**2 :** any of several broad-billed ducks (as the shoveler)
**spoonbill cat** *noun* (circa 1882)
**:** a paddlefish (*Polyodon spathula*)
**spoon–billed** \'spün-ˌbild\ *adjective* (1668)
**:** having the bill or snout expanded and spatulate at the end
**spoon bread** *noun* (1916)
**:** soft bread made of cornmeal mixed with milk, eggs, and shortening and served with a spoon
**spoo·ner·ism** \'spü-nə-ˌri-zəm\ *noun* [William A. *Spooner* (died 1930) English clergyman & educator] (1900)
**:** a transposition of usually initial sounds of two or more words (as in *tons of soil* for *sons of toil*) ◆
**spoon–feed** \'spün-ˌfēd\ *transitive verb* **-fed** \-ˌfed\; **-feed·ing** (1615)
**1 :** to feed by means of a spoon
**2 a :** to present (information) so completely as to preclude independent thought ⟨*spoon-feed* material to students⟩ **b :** to present information to in this manner
**spoon·ful** \'spün-ˌfül\ *noun, plural* **spoon·fuls** \-ˌfülz\ *also* **spoons·ful** \'spünz-ˌfül\ (14th century)
**:** as much as a spoon will hold; *specifically* **:** TEASPOONFUL
*usage* see ²-FUL
**spoony** *or* **spoon·ey** \'spü-nē\ *adjective* **spoon·i·er; -est** [English slang *spoon* simpleton] (circa 1812)
**1 :** SILLY, FOOLISH; *especially* **:** unduly sentimental
**2 :** being sentimentally in love
**¹spoor** \'spur, 'spōr, 'spȯr\ *noun, plural* **spoor** *or* **spoors** [Afrikaans, from Dutch; akin to Old English *spor* footprint, spoor, *spurnan* to kick — more at SPURN] (1823)
**1 :** a track, a trail, a scent, or droppings especially of a wild animal
**2 :** a trace by which the progress of someone or something may be followed
**²spoor** (1850)
*transitive verb*
**:** to track by a spoor
*intransitive verb*
**:** to track something by its spoor
**spor-** *or* **spori-** *or* **sporo-** *combining form* [New Latin *spora*]
**:** seed **:** spore ⟨*sporo*cyst⟩ ⟨*spor*angium⟩ ⟨*spori*cidal⟩
**spo·rad·ic** \spə-'ra-dik\ *adjective* [Medieval Latin *sporadicus*, from Greek *sporadikos*, from *sporadēn* here and there, from *sporad-*, *sporas* scattered; akin to Greek *speirein* to sow — more at SPERM] (circa 1689)
**:** occurring occasionally, singly, or in scattered instances
*synonym* see INFREQUENT
— **spo·rad·i·cal·ly** \-di-k(ə-)lē\ *adverb*
**sporadic E layer** *noun* (1949)
**:** a layer of ionization occurring irregularly within the E region of the ionosphere
**spo·ran·gio·phore** \spə-'ran-jē-ə-ˌfōr, -ˌfȯr\ *noun* (1875)

**:** a stalk or similar structure bearing sporangia
**spo·ran·gi·um** \spə-'ran-jē-əm\ *noun, plural* **-gia** \-jē-ə\ [New Latin, from *spor-* + Greek *angeion* vessel — more at ANGI-] (1821)
**:** a structure within which spores are produced
— **spo·ran·gial** \-j(ē-)əl\ *adjective*
**¹spore** \'spōr, 'spȯr\ *noun* [New Latin *spora* seed, spore, from Greek, act of sowing, seed, from *speirein* to sow — more at SPERM] (1836)
**:** a primitive usually unicellular often environmentally resistant dormant or reproductive body produced by plants and some microorganisms and capable of development into a new individual either directly or after fusion with another spore
— **spored** \'spōrd, 'spȯrd\ *adjective*
**²spore** *intransitive verb* **spored; spor·ing** (1903)
**:** to produce or reproduce by spores
**spore case** *noun* (1836)
**:** a case containing spores **:** SPORANGIUM
**spo·ri·cid·al** \ˌspōr-ə-'sī-dᵊl, ˌspȯr-\ *adjective* (1939)
**:** tending to kill spores
— **spo·ri·cide** \'spōr-ə-ˌsīd, 'spȯr-\ *noun*
**spo·ro·carp** \'spōr-ə-ˌkärp, 'spȯr-\ *noun* [International Scientific Vocabulary] (1849)
**:** a structure (as in red algae, fungi, or mosses) in or on which spores are produced
**spo·ro·cyst** \-ˌsist\ *noun* [International Scientific Vocabulary] (1861)
**1 :** a case or cyst secreted by some sporozoans preliminary to sporogony; *also* **:** a sporozoan encysted in such a case

---

☆ **SYNONYMS**
**Spontaneous, impulsive, instinctive, automatic, mechanical** mean acting or activated without deliberation. SPONTANEOUS implies lack of prompting and connotes naturalness ⟨a *spontaneous* burst of applause⟩. IMPULSIVE implies acting under stress of emotion or spirit of the moment ⟨*impulsive* acts of violence⟩. INSTINCTIVE stresses spontaneous action involving neither judgment nor will ⟨blinking is an *instinctive* reaction⟩. AUTOMATIC implies action engaging neither the mind nor the emotions and connotes a predictable response ⟨his denial was *automatic*⟩. MECHANICAL stresses the lifeless, often perfunctory character of the response ⟨a *mechanical* teaching method⟩.

◇ **WORD HISTORY**
**spoonerism** William Archibald Spooner (1844–1930) was an English clergyman and scholar who served as warden of New College at Oxford. Known for his wit, humor and devotion to Oxford University, Spooner had a tendency while delivering sermons to transpose the initial letters or syllables of adjoining words. He once announced that "Kinquering Kongs their titles take" would be the theme for that day's sermon. On another occasion he assured his flock that "Yes, indeed; the Lord is a shoving leopard." Even more puzzling to his parishioners was his observation that "We all know what it is to have a half-warmed fish within us." Spooner's actual, unintentional lapses so amused his listeners that they were inspired to devise their own transpositions and to attribute them to the minister. Toward the end of the 19th century *spoonerism* became a general term for such verbal slips.

---

\ə\ **abut** \ᵊ\ **kitten** \ər\ **further** \a\ **ash** \ā\ **ace**
\ä\ **mop, mar** \au̇\ **out** \ch\ **chin** \e\ **bet** \ē\ **easy**
\g\ **go** \i\ **hit** \ī\ **ice** \j\ **job** \ŋ\ **sing** \ō\ **go**
\ȯ\ **law** \ȯi\ **boy** \th\ **thin** \t̲h̲\ **the** \ü\ **loot** \u̇\ **foot**
\y\ **yet** \zh\ **vision**    *see also* Guide to Pronunciation

**2** : a saccular body that is the first asexual reproductive form of a digenetic trematode, develops from a miracidium, and buds off cells from its inner surface which develop into rediae

**spo·ro·gen·e·sis** \ˌspȯr-ə-ˈje-nə-səs, ˌspȯr-\ *noun* [New Latin] (circa 1890)
**1** : reproduction by spores
**2** : spore formation
— **spo·rog·e·nous** \spə-ˈrä-jə-nəs, spȯ-\ *also* **spo·ro·gen·ic** \ˌspȯr-ə-ˈje-nik, ˌspȯr-\ *adjective*

**spo·ro·go·ni·um** \ˌspȯr-ə-ˈgō-nē-əm, ˌspȯr-\ *noun, plural* **-nia** \-nē-ə\ [New Latin, from *spor-* + *-gonium* (as in *archegonium*)] (1875)
: the sporophyte of a moss or liverwort consisting typically of a stalk bearing a spore-producing capsule which remains permanently attached to the gametophyte

**spo·rog·o·ny** \spə-ˈrä-gə-nē, spȯ-\ *noun* [International Scientific Vocabulary] (1888)
: reproduction by spores; *specifically* : formation of spores typically containing sporozoites that is characteristic of some sporozoans and that results from the encystment and subsequent division of a zygote
— **spo·ro·gon·ic** \ˌspȯr-ə-ˈgä-nik, ˌspȯr-\ *adjective*

**spo·ro·phore** \ˈspȯr-ə-ˌfōr, ˈspȯr-ə-ˌfȯr\ *noun* [International Scientific Vocabulary] (1849)
: the spore-producing organ of a fungus or slime mold

**spo·ro·phyll** \-ˌfil\ *noun* [International Scientific Vocabulary] (1888)
: a spore-bearing and usually greatly modified leaf

**spo·ro·phyte** \-ˌfīt\ *noun* [International Scientific Vocabulary] (1886)
: the individual or generation of a plant exhibiting alternation of generations that bears asexual spores — compare GAMETOPHYTE
— **spo·ro·phyt·ic** \ˌspȯr-ə-ˈfi-tik, ˌspȯr-\ *adjective*

**spo·ro·pol·len·in** \ˌspȯr-ə-ˈpä-lə-nən, ˌspȯr-\ *noun* [International Scientific Vocabulary *spor-* + *pollen* + [1]*-in*] (1931)
: a relatively chemically inert polymer that makes up the outer layer of pollen grains and some spores

**spo·ro·tri·cho·sis** \spə-ˌrä-tri-ˈkō-səs; ˌspȯr-ə-tri-, ˌspȯr-\ *noun* [New Latin, from *Sporotrich-, Sporothrix,* genus name, from *spor-* + Greek *trich-, thrix* hair] (1908)
: infection with or disease caused by a fungus (*Sporothrix schenckii*) that is characterized by nodules and abscesses in the superficial lymph nodes, skin, and subcutaneous tissues and that is usually transmitted by entry of the fungus through a skin abrasion or wound

**-sporous** *adjective combining form* [New Latin *spora* spore]
: having (such or so many) spores ⟨homo*sporous*⟩

**spo·ro·zo·an** \ˌspȯr-ə-ˈzō-ən, ˌspȯr-\ *noun* [New Latin *Sporozoa,* from *spor-* + *-zoa*] (1888)
: any of a large class (Sporozoa) of strictly parasitic protozoans that have a complicated life cycle usually involving both asexual and sexual generations often in different hosts and include important pathogens (as malaria parasites and babesias)
— **sporozoan** *adjective*

**spo·ro·zo·ite** \-ˈzō-ˌīt\ *noun* [New Latin *Sporozoa* + International Scientific Vocabulary *-ite*] (1888)
: a usually motile infective form of some sporozoans that is a product of sporogony and initiates an asexual cycle in the new host

**spor·ran** \ˈspȯr-ən, ˈspär-\ *noun* [Scottish Gaelic *sporan* purse] (1752)
: a pouch usually of skin with the hair or fur on that is worn in front of the kilt with Scots Highland dress

---

[1]**sport** \ˈspōrt, ˈspȯrt\ *verb* [Middle English, to divert, disport, short for *disporten*] (15th century)
*intransitive verb*
**1 a** : to amuse oneself : FROLIC ⟨lambs *sporting* in the meadow⟩ **b** : to engage in a sport
**2 a** : to mock or ridicule something **b** : to speak or act in jest : TRIFLE
**3** [[2]*sport*] : to deviate or vary abruptly from type (as by bud variation) : MUTATE
*transitive verb*
**1** : to display or wear usually ostentatiously : BOAST
**2** [[2]*sport*] : to put forth as a sport or bud variation

[2]**sport** *noun* (15th century)
**1 a** : a source of diversion : RECREATION **b** : sexual play **c** (1) : physical activity engaged in for pleasure (2) : a particular activity (as an athletic game) so engaged in
**2 a** : PLEASANTRY, JEST **b** : often mean-spirited jesting : MOCKERY, DERISION
**3 a** : something tossed or driven about in or as if in play **b** : LAUGHINGSTOCK
**4 a** : SPORTSMAN **b** : a person considered with respect to living up to the ideals of sportsmanship ⟨a good *sport*⟩ ⟨a poor *sport*⟩ **c** : a companionable person
**5** : an individual exhibiting a sudden deviation from type beyond the normal limits of individual variation usually as a result of mutation especially of somatic tissue
*synonym* see FUN

[3]**sport** *or* **sports** *adjective* (1582)
: of, relating to, or suitable for sports; *especially* : styled in a manner suitable for casual or informal wear ⟨*sport* coats⟩

**sport fish** *noun* (1944)
: a fish important for the sport it affords anglers

**sport·fish·er·man** \ˈspȯrt-ˌfi-shər-mən, ˈspȯrt-\ *noun* (1954)
: a motorboat equipped for sportfishing

**sport·fish·ing** \-ˌfi-shiŋ\ *noun* (1910)
: fishing done with a rod and reel for sport or recreation

**sport·ful** \-fəl\ *adjective* (15th century)
**1 a** : productive of sport or amusement : ENTERTAINING, DIVERTING **b** : PLAYFUL, FROLICSOME
**2** : done in sport
— **sport·ful·ly** \-fə-lē\ *adverb*
— **sport·ful·ness** *noun*

**spor·tif** \ˈspȯr-tif, ˈspȯr-\ *adjective* [French, sporting, of sports, from *sport* sport, from English] (1920)
: SPORTY

**sport·ing** \ˈspȯr-tiŋ, ˈspȯr-\ *adjective* (1799)
**1 a** : of, relating to, used, or suitable for sport **b** : marked by or calling for sportsmanship **c** : involving such risk as a sports contender may expect to take or encounter ⟨a *sporting* chance⟩
**2** : of or relating to dissipation and especially gambling
**3** : tending to mutate freely
— **sport·ing·ly** \-tiŋ-lē\ *adverb*

**sporting house** *noun* (1894)
: BORDELLO

**sport·ive** \ˈspȯr-tiv, ˈspȯr-\ *adjective* (1590)
**1 a** : FROLICSOME, PLAYFUL **b** : ARDENT, WANTON
**2** : of or relating to sports and especially field sports
— **sport·ive·ly** *adverb*
— **sport·ive·ness** *noun*

**sports car** *noun* (1928)
: a low small usually 2-passenger automobile designed for quick response, easy maneuverability, and high-speed driving

---

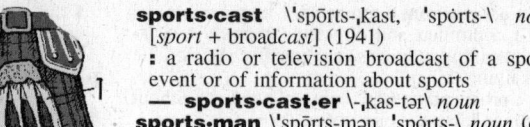

*1 sporran*

**sports·cast** \ˈspōrts-ˌkast, ˈspȯrts-\ *noun* [*sport* + broad*cast*] (1941)
: a radio or television broadcast of a sports event or of information about sports
— **sports·cast·er** \-ˌkas-tər\ *noun*

**sports·man** \ˈspōrts-mən, ˈspȯrts-\ *noun* (circa 1707)
**1** : a person who engages in sports (as in hunting or fishing)
**2** : a person who shows sportsmanship
— **sports·man·like** \-ˌlīk\ *adjective*
— **sports·man·ly** \-lē\ *adjective*

**sports·man·ship** \-ˌship\ *noun* (1745)
: conduct (as fairness, respect for one's opponent, and graciousness in winning or losing) becoming to one participating in a sport

**sports·wear** \ˈspōrts-ˌwar, ˈspȯrts-, -ˌwer\ *noun* (1912)
: clothing suitable for recreation; *broadly* : clothing designed for casual or informal wear

**sports·wom·an** \-ˌwu̇-mən\ *noun* (1754)
: a woman who engages in sports

**sports·writ·er** \ˈspōrts-ˌrī-tər, ˈspȯrts-\ *noun* (1927)
: one who writes about sports especially for a newspaper
— **sports·writ·ing** \-tiŋ\ *noun*

**sporty** \ˈspōr-tē, ˈspȯr-\ *adjective* **sport·i·er; -est** (1889)
**1** : of, relating to, or typical of sports, sportsmen, sportswomen, or sportswear ⟨a *sporty* life⟩ ⟨clothes of a *sporty* cut⟩
**2** *of an automobile* : resembling a sports car in styling or performance
— **sport·i·ly** \ˈspōr-t°l-ē, ˈspȯr-\ *adverb*
— **sport·i·ness** \ˈspōr-tē-nəs, ˈspȯr-\ *noun*

**spor·u·late** \ˈspōr-yə-ˌlāt, ˈspȯr-, -ə-ˌlāt\ *intransitive verb* **-lat·ed; -lat·ing** [back-formation from *sporulation*] (circa 1891)
: to undergo sporulation

**spor·u·la·tion** \ˌspōr-yə-ˈlā-shən, ˌspȯr-, -ə-ˈlā-\ *noun* [International Scientific Vocabulary, from New Latin *sporula,* diminutive of *spora* spore] (1876)
: the formation of spores; *especially* : division into many small spores (as after encystment)
— **spor·u·la·tive** \ˈspōr-yə-ˌlā-tiv, ˈspȯr-, -ə-ˌlā-\ *adjective*

**-spory** *noun combining form* [*-sporous* + [2]*-y*]
: quality or state of having (such) spores ⟨homo*spory*⟩

[1]**spot** \ˈspät\ *noun* [Middle English; akin to Middle Dutch *spotte* stain, speck, Old Norse *spotti* small piece] (13th century)
**1** : a taint on character or reputation : FAULT ⟨the only *spot* on the family name⟩
**2 a** : a small area visibly different (as in color, finish, or material) from the surrounding area **b** (1) : an area marred or marked (as by dirt) (2) : a circumscribed surface lesion of disease (as measles) or decay ⟨*spots* of rot⟩ ⟨rust *spots* on a leaf⟩ **c** : a conventionalized design used on playing cards to distinguish the suits and indicate values
**3** : an object having a specified number of spots or a specified numeral on its surface
**4** : a small quantity or amount : BIT
**5 a** : a particular place, area, or part **b** : a small extent of space
**6** *plural usually* **spot** : a small croaker (*Leiostomus xanthurus*) of the Atlantic coast with a black spot behind the opercula
**7 a** : a particular position (as in an organization or a hierarchy) **b** : a place or appearance on an entertainment program
**8** : SPOTLIGHT
**9** : a position usually of difficulty or embarrassment
**10** : a brief announcement or advertisement broadcast between scheduled radio or television programs
**11** : a brief segment or report on a broadcast especially of news

**— on the spot 1 :** at once **: IMMEDIATELY 2 :** at the place of action **3 a :** in a responsible or accountable position **b :** in a difficult or trying situation

²**spot** *verb* **spot·ted; spot·ting** (14th century)
*transitive verb*
**1 :** to stain the character or reputation of **: DISGRACE**
**2 :** to mark in or with a spot **: STAIN**
**3 :** to locate or identify by a spot
**4 a :** to single out **: IDENTIFY;** *especially* **:** to note as a known criminal or a suspicious person **b : DETECT, NOTICE** ⟨*spot* a mistake⟩ **c** (1) **:** to locate accurately ⟨*spot* an enemy position⟩ (2) **:** to cause to strike accurately ⟨*spot* the battery's fire⟩
**5 a :** to lie at intervals in or over **: STUD b :** to place at intervals or in a desired spot ⟨*spot* field telephones⟩ **c :** to fix in or as if in the beam of a spotlight **d :** to schedule in a particular spot or at a particular time
**6 :** to remove a spot from
**7 :** to allow as a handicap
*intransitive verb*
**1 :** to become stained or discolored in spots
**2 :** to cause a spot
**3 :** to act as a spotter; *especially* **:** to locate targets
**4 :** to experience abnormal and sporadic bleeding in small amounts from the uterus
**— spot·ta·ble** \'spä-tə-bəl\ *adjective*
³**spot** *adjective* (1881)
**1 a :** being, originating, or done on the spot or in or for a particular spot ⟨*spot* coverage of the news⟩ **b :** available for immediate delivery after sale ⟨*spot* commodities⟩ **c** (1) **:** paid out upon delivery ⟨*spot* cash⟩ (2) **:** involving immediate cash payment ⟨*spot* transaction⟩ **d** (1) **:** broadcast between scheduled programs ⟨*spot* announcements⟩ (2) **:** originating in a local station for a national advertiser **e :** performing occasionally when needed ⟨chance of making the . . . varsity as a *spot* starter and relief pitcher —*N. Y. Times*⟩
**2 :** made at random or restricted to a few places or instances ⟨a *spot* check⟩; *also* **:** selected at random or as a sample
**spot–check** \'spät-,chek\ (1943)
*transitive verb*
**:** to sample or investigate quickly or at random
*intransitive verb*
**:** to make a spot check
**spot·less** \'spät-ləs\ *adjective* (14th century)
**:** having no spot: **a :** free from impurity **: IMMACULATE** ⟨*spotless* kitchens⟩ **b : PURE, UNBLEMISHED** ⟨*spotless* reputation⟩
**— spot·less·ly** *adverb*
**— spot·less·ness** *noun*
¹**spot·light** \'spät-,līt\ *noun* (1904)
**1 a :** a projected spot of light used to illuminate brilliantly a person, object, or group on a stage **b :** conspicuous public notice ⟨held the political *spotlight*⟩
**2 a :** a light designed to direct a narrow intense beam of light on a small area **b :** something that illuminates brilliantly
²**spotlight** *transitive verb* **-light·ed** *or* **-lit; -light·ing** (1922)
**:** to illuminate with or as if with a spotlight
**spot pass** *noun* (1948)
**:** a pass (as in football or basketball) made to a predetermined spot on the field or court rather than directly to a player
**spot·ted** \'spä-təd\ *adjective* (13th century)
**1 :** marked with spots
**2 :** being sullied **: TARNISHED**
**3 :** characterized by the appearance of spots
**spotted alfalfa aphid** *noun* (1958)
**:** a highly destructive Old World aphid (*Therioaphis maculata*) that is established in the U.S. in warmer areas and causes yellowing and stunting of affected plants
**spotted cucumber beetle** *noun* (1923)
**:** a rather slender greenish yellow beetle (*Diabrotica undecimpunctata howardi*) that feeds

as an adult on various ornamental and crop plants and is a vector of wilt disease especially of cucumbers and melons
**spotted fever** *noun* (1650)
**:** any of various eruptive fevers: as **a : TYPHUS b :** ROCKY MOUNTAIN SPOTTED FEVER
**spotted owl** *noun* (1910)
**:** a rare large dark brown dark-eyed owl (*Strix occidentalis*) that has barred and spotted underparts and is found in humid old growth forests and thickly wooded canyons from British Columbia to southern California and central Mexico
**spotted salamander** *noun* (1922)
**:** a common salamander (*Ambystoma maculatum*) of eastern North America with glossy black skin spotted with yellow or orange on the back
**spotted sea trout** *noun* (1902)
**:** a weakfish (*Cynoscion nebulosus*) that is a valuable food and sport fish of the southern Atlantic and Gulf coasts of the U.S. — called also *sea trout, speckled trout, spotted weakfish*
**spotted turtle** *noun* (circa 1909)
**:** a freshwater turtle (*Clemmys guttata*) of the eastern U.S. that has a blackish carapace with round yellow spots
**spot·ter** \'spä-tər\ *noun* (1611)
**1 :** one that makes or applies a spot (as for identification)
**2 :** one that looks or keeps watch: as **a :** one that locates enemy targets **b :** a civilian who watches for approaching airplanes
**3 :** one that removes spots
**4 :** one that places something on or in a desired spot
**spot test** *noun* (1922)
**1 :** a test limited to a few key or sample points or a relatively small percentage of random spots
**2 :** a test conducted on the spot to yield immediate results
**spot·ty** \'spä-tē\ *adjective* **spot·ti·er; -est** (14th century)
**1 :** marked with spots **: SPOTTED**
**2 :** lacking uniformity especially in quality ⟨the performance was *spotty*⟩; *also* **:** irregularly or sparsely distributed ⟨*spotty* attendance⟩ ⟨*spotty* data⟩
**— spot·ti·ly** \'spä-t°l-ē\ *adverb*
**— spot·ti·ness** \'spä-tē-nəs\ *noun*
**spou·sal** \'spaù-zəl, -səl\ *noun* [Middle English *spousaille*, from Middle French *espousailles* espousal] (14th century)
**: NUPTIALS** — usually used in plural
¹**spouse** \'spaùs *also* 'spaùz\ *noun* [Middle English, from Old French *espous* (masculine) & *espouse* (feminine), from Latin *sponsus* betrothed man, groom & *sponsa* betrothed woman, bride, both from *sponsus*, past participle of *spondēre* to promise, betroth; akin to Greek *spendein* to pour a libation, Hittite *šipant-*] (13th century)
**:** married person **: HUSBAND, WIFE**
**— spou·sal** \'spaù-zəl, -səl\ *adjective*
²**spouse** \'spaùz, 'spaùs\ *transitive verb* **spoused; spous·ing** (13th century)
*archaic* **: WED**
¹**spout** \'spaùt\ *verb* [Middle English; akin to Middle Dutch *spoiten* to spout, Old English *spīwan* to spew] (14th century)
*transitive verb*
**1 :** to eject (as liquid) in a stream ⟨wells *spouting* oil⟩
**2 a :** to speak or utter readily, volubly, and at length **b :** to speak or utter in a pompous or oratorical manner **: DECLAIM**
*intransitive verb*
**1 :** to issue with force or in a jet **: SPURT**
**2 :** to eject material (as liquid) in a jet
**3 : DECLAIM**
**— spout·er** *noun*
²**spout** *noun* (14th century)

**1 :** a pipe or conductor through which a liquid is discharged or conveyed in a stream: as **a :** a pipe for carrying rainwater from a roof **b :** a projecting tube or lip from which a liquid (as water) issues
**2 :** a discharge or jet of liquid from or as if from a pipe; *especially* **: WATERSPOUT**
**3** *archaic* **: PAWNSHOP**
**— spout·ed** \'spaù-təd\ *adjective*
**sprach·ge·fühl** \'shpräk-gə-,fuel\ *noun* [German, from *Sprache* language + *Gefühl* feeling] (1894)
**1 :** the character of a language
**2 :** an intuitive sense of what is linguistically appropriate
**sprad·dle** \'spra-d°l\ *verb* **sprad·dled; sprad·dling** \'sprad-liŋ, 'spra-d°l-iŋ\ [perhaps blend of *straddle* and *sprawl*] (1632)
*intransitive verb*
**1 : SPRAWL**
**2 :** to go or walk with a straddling gait **: STRADDLE**
*transitive verb*
**1 : SPRAWL**
**2 :** to spread (the legs) in walking **: STRADDLE**
**sprag** \'sprag\ *noun* [origin unknown] (1878)
**:** a pointed stake or steel bar let down from a halted vehicle (as a wagon) to prevent it from rolling
¹**sprain** \'sprān\ *noun* [origin unknown] (1601)
**1 :** a sudden or violent twist or wrench of a joint with stretching or tearing of ligaments
**2 :** a sprained condition
²**sprain** *transitive verb* (1622)
**:** to injure by a sudden or severe twist
¹**sprang** \'spraŋ\ *past of* SPRING
²**sprang** *noun* [probably from Norwegian, a kind of embroidery] (1951)
**:** a weaving technique in which threads or cords are intertwined and twisted over one another to form an openwork mesh
**sprat** \'sprat\ *noun* [alteration of Middle English *sprot*, from Old English *sprott*] (1537)
**1 a :** a small European herring (*Sprattus sprattus*) related to the common herring — called also *brisling* **b :** a small or young herring or similar fish (as an anchovy)
**2 :** a young, small, or insignificant person
**sprawl** \'sprol\ *verb* [Middle English, from Old English *sprēawlian*] (before 12th century)
*intransitive verb*
**1 a** *archaic* **:** to lie thrashing or tossing about **b :** to creep or clamber awkwardly
**2 :** to lie or sit with arms and legs spread out
**3 :** to spread or develop irregularly
*transitive verb*
**:** to cause to spread out carelessly or awkwardly
**— sprawl** *noun*
¹**spray** \'sprā\ *noun* [Middle English] (13th century)
**1 :** a usually flowering branch or shoot
**2 :** a decorative flat arrangement of flowers and foliage (as on a coffin)
**3 :** something (as a jeweled pin) resembling a spray
²**spray** *noun* [obsolete English *spray* to sprinkle, from Middle Dutch *sprayen*] (1621)
**1 :** water flying in small drops or particles blown from waves or thrown up by a waterfall
**2 a :** a jet of vapor or finely divided liquid **b :** a device (as an atomizer or sprayer) by which a spray is dispersed or applied **c** (1) **:** an application of a spray or by spraying (2) **:** a substance (as paint) so applied
³**spray** (1829)
*transitive verb*
**1 :** to disperse or apply as a spray
**2 :** to project spray on or into
*intransitive verb*

| | | |
|---|---|---|
| \ə\ abut | \°\ kitten | \ər\ **further** \a\ ash \ā\ ace |
| \ä\ mop, mar | \aù\ out | \ch\ chin \e\ bet \ē\ easy |
| \g\ go | \i\ hit | \ī\ ice \j\ job \ŋ\ sing \ō\ go |
| \ò\ law | \òi\ boy | \th\ thin \th\ the \ü\ loot \ù\ foot |
| \y\ yet | \zh\ vision | *see also* Guide to Pronunciation |

**1 :** to break up into spray
**2 :** to disperse or apply a spray
**3 :** to emit a stream or spray of urine ⟨a cat may *spray* to mark its territory⟩
— **spray·er** *noun*
**spray can** *noun* (1958)
**:** a pressurized container from which aerosols are dispensed
**spray gun** *noun* (1920)
**:** an apparatus resembling a gun for applying a substance (as paint or insecticide) in the form of a spray
¹**spread** \'spred\ *verb* **spread; spread·ing** [Middle English *spreden,* from Old English *-sprædan;* akin to Old High German *spreiten* to spread] (13th century)
*transitive verb*
**1 a :** to open or expand over a larger area ⟨*spread* out the map⟩ **b :** to stretch out **:** EXTEND ⟨*spread* its wings for flight⟩
**2 a :** to distribute over an area ⟨*spread* fertilizer⟩ **b :** to distribute over a period or among a group ⟨*spread* the work over a few weeks⟩ **c :** to apply on a surface ⟨*spread* butter on bread⟩ **d** (1) **:** to cover or overlay something with ⟨*spread* the cloth on the table⟩ (2) *archaic* **:** to cover completely **e** (1) **:** to prepare or furnish for dining **:** SET ⟨*spread* the table⟩ (2) **:** SERVE ⟨*spread* the afternoon tea⟩
**3 a :** to make widely known ⟨*spread* the news⟩ **b :** to extend the range or incidence of ⟨*spread* a disease⟩ **c :** DIFFUSE, EMIT ⟨flowers *spreading* their fragrance⟩
**4 :** to push apart by weight or force
*intransitive verb*
**1 a :** to become dispersed, distributed, or scattered **b :** to become known or disseminated ⟨panic *spread* rapidly⟩
**2 :** to grow in length or breadth **:** EXPAND
**3 :** to move apart (as from pressure or weight) **:** SEPARATE
— **spread·abil·i·ty** \,spre-də-'bi-lə-tē\ *noun*
— **spread·able** \'spre-də-bəl\ *adjective*
²**spread** *noun* (1626)
**1 a :** the act or process of spreading **b :** extent of spreading
**2 :** something spread out: as **a :** a surface area **:** EXPANSE **b** *West* (1) **:** RANCH (2) **:** a herd of animals **c** (1) **:** a prominent display in a periodical (2) **:** two facing pages (as of a newspaper) usually with matter running across the fold; *also* **:** the matter occupying these pages
**3 :** something spread on or over a surface: as **a :** a food to be spread (as on bread or crackers) ⟨a cheese *spread*⟩ **b :** a sumptuous meal **:** FEAST **c :** a cloth cover for a table or bed
**4 :** distance between two points **:** GAP
**5 :** a commodities market transaction in which a participant hedges with simultaneous long and short options in different commodities or different delivery dates in the same commodity
¹**spread–ea·gle** \'spred-,ē-gəl\ *verb* **-ea·gled; -ea·gling** \-,ē-g(ə-)liŋ\ (1826)
*intransitive verb*
**1 :** to execute a spread eagle (as in skating)
**2 :** to stand or move with arms and legs stretched out **:** SPRAWL
*transitive verb*
**1 :** to stretch out into the position of a spread eagle
**2 :** to spread over
²**spread–eagle** *adjective* [from the spread eagle on the Great Seal of the U.S.] (1858)
**:** marked by bombast and boastful exaggeration especially of the greatness of the U.S. ⟨*spread-eagle* oratory⟩
**spread eagle** *noun* (1570)
**1 :** a representation of an eagle with wings raised and legs extended
**2 :** something resembling or suggestive of a spread eagle; *specifically* **:** a skating figure executed with the skates heel to heel in a straight line
**spread·er** \'spre-dər\ *noun* (15th century)

**:** one that spreads: as **a :** an implement for scattering material **b :** a small knife for spreading butter **c :** a device (as a bar) holding two linear elements (as lines, guys, rails) apart and usually taut
**spread formation** *noun* (circa 1949)
**:** an offensive football formation in which the pass receivers are spread out across the field
**spreading factor** *noun* (1932)
**:** HYALURONIDASE
**spread·sheet** \'spred-,shēt\ *noun* (1982)
**:** an accounting program for a computer; *also* **:** the ledger layout modeled by such a program
**spree** \'sprē\ *noun* [origin unknown] (1804)
**:** an unrestrained indulgence in or outburst of an activity ⟨went on a buying *spree*⟩; *especially* **:** BINGE, CAROUSAL
**sprent** \'sprent\ *adjective* [Middle English *spreynt,* from past participle of *sprengen* to sprinkle] (14th century)
*archaic* **:** sprinkled over
**sprier** *comparative of* SPRY
**spriest** *superlative of* SPRY
¹**sprig** \'sprig\ *noun* [Middle English *sprigge*] (14th century)
**1 a :** a small shoot **:** TWIG ⟨a *sprig* of parsley⟩ **b :** a small division of grass used for propagation
**2 a :** HEIR **b :** YOUTH **c :** a small specimen
**3 :** an ornament resembling a sprig, stemmed flower, or leaf
**4 :** a small headless nail **:** BRAD
²**sprig** *transitive verb* **sprigged; sprig·ging** (1713)
**1 :** to drive sprigs or brads into
**2 :** to mark or adorn with the representation of plant sprigs
**3 :** to propagate (a grass) by means of stolons or small divisions
**spright·ful** \'sprīt-fəl\ *adjective* [obsolete *spright*] (1595)
*archaic* **:** full of life or spirit **:** SPRIGHTLY
— **spright·ful·ly** \-fə-lē\ *adverb*
— **spright·ful·ness** *noun*
**spright·ly** \-lē\ *adjective* **spright·li·er; -est** [obsolete *spright* (sprite), alteration of *sprite*] (1596)
**:** marked by a gay lightness and vivacity **:** SPIRITED
**synonym** see LIVELY
— **spright·li·ness** *noun*
— **sprightly** *adverb*
¹**spring** \'spriŋ\ *verb* **sprang** \'spraŋ\ *or* **sprung** \'sprəŋ\; **sprung; spring·ing** \'spriŋ-iŋ\ [Middle English, from Old English *springan;* akin to Old High German *springan* to jump and perhaps to Greek *sperchesthai* to hasten] (before 12th century)
*intransitive verb*
**1 a** (1) **:** DART, SHOOT (2) **:** to be resilient or elastic; *also* **:** to move by elastic force ⟨the lid *sprang* shut⟩ **b :** to become warped
**2 :** to issue with speed and force or as a stream
**3 a :** to grow as a plant **b :** to issue by birth or descent **c :** to come into being **:** ARISE ⟨towns *sprang* up across the plains⟩ **d** *archaic* **:** DAWN **e :** to begin to blow — used with *up* ⟨a breeze quickly *sprang*⟩
**4 a :** to make a leap or series of leaps **b :** to leap or jump up suddenly
**5 :** to stretch out in height **:** RISE
**6 :** PAY — used with *for* ⟨I'll *spring* for the drinks⟩
*transitive verb*
**1 :** to cause to spring
**2 a :** to undergo or bring about the splitting or cracking of ⟨wind *sprang* the mast⟩ **b :** to undergo the opening of (a leak)
**3 a :** to cause to operate suddenly ⟨*spring* a trap⟩ **b :** to apply or insert by bending **c :** to bend by force
**4 :** to leap over
**5 :** to produce or disclose suddenly or unexpectedly
**6 :** to make lame

**7 :** to release or cause to be released from confinement or custody ☆
²**spring** *noun, often attributive* (before 12th century)
**1 a :** a source of supply; *especially* **:** a source of water issuing from the ground **b :** an ultimate source especially of action or motion
**2 :** SPRING TIDE
**3 :** a time or season of growth or development; *specifically* **:** the season between winter and summer comprising in the northern hemisphere usually the months of March, April, and May or as reckoned astronomically extending from the March equinox to the June solstice
**4 :** an elastic body or device that recovers its original shape when released after being distorted
**5 a :** the act or an instance of leaping up or forward **:** BOUND **b** (1) **:** capacity for springing **:** RESILIENCE (2) **:** ENERGY, BOUNCE
**6 :** the point or plane at which an arch or vault curve springs from its impost
— **spring·like** \-,līk\ *adjective*
³**spring** *transitive verb* **sprung** \'sprəŋ\; **spring·ing** \'spriŋ-iŋ\ (1884)
**:** to fit with springs
**spring·ald** \'spriŋ-əld\ *or* **spring·al** \-əl\ *noun* [probably from Middle English, a kind of catapult, from Middle French *espringale*] (1501)
**:** a young man **:** STRIPLING
**spring beauty** *noun* (1821)
**:** any of a genus (*Claytonia*) of herbs of the purslane family; *especially* **:** one (*C. virginica*) that sends up in early spring a 2-leaved stem bearing delicate pink flowers
**spring·board** \'spriŋ-,bōrd, -,bȯrd\ *noun* (1799)
**1 :** a flexible board usually secured at one end and used for gymnastic stunts or diving
**2 :** a point of departure **:** JUMPING-OFF PLACE
**spring·bok** \'spriŋ-,bäk\ *noun, plural* **spring·bok** *or* **springboks** [Afrikaans, from *spring* to jump + *bok* male goat] (1775)
**:** a swift and graceful southern African gazelle (*Antidorcas marsupialis*) noted for its habit of springing lightly and suddenly into the air
**spring bolt** *noun* (1634)
**:** a bolt retracted by pressure and shot by a spring when the pressure is released
**spring chicken** *noun* (1879)
**:** a young person ⟨is no *spring chicken*⟩

---

☆ **SYNONYMS**
**Spring, arise, rise, originate, derive, flow, issue, emanate, proceed, stem** mean to come up or out of something into existence. SPRING implies rapid or sudden emerging ⟨an idea that *springs* to mind⟩. ARISE and RISE may both convey the fact of coming into existence or notice but RISE often stresses gradual growth or ascent ⟨new questions have *arisen*⟩ ⟨slowly *rose* to prominence⟩. ORIGINATE implies a definite source or starting point ⟨the fire *originated* in the basement⟩. DERIVE implies a prior existence in another form ⟨the holiday *derives* from an ancient Roman feast⟩. FLOW adds to SPRING a suggestion of abundance or ease of inception ⟨words *flowed* easily from her pen⟩. ISSUE suggests emerging from confinement through an outlet ⟨blood *issued* from the cut⟩. EMANATE applies to the coming of something immaterial (as a thought) from a source ⟨reports *emanating* from the capital⟩. PROCEED stresses place of origin, derivation, parentage, or logical cause ⟨advice that *proceeds* from the best of intentions⟩. STEM implies originating by dividing or branching off from something as an outgrowth or subordinate development ⟨industries *stemming* from space research⟩.

**spring–clean·ing**
\'spriŋ-'klē-niŋ\ noun
[²spring] (1857)
: the act or process of doing a thorough cleaning of a place

**springe** \'sprinj\ noun [Middle English sprenge, springe; akin to Old English springan to spring] (13th century)
**1 :** a noose fastened to an elastic body to catch small game
**2 :** SNARE, TRAP

springbok

**spring·er** \'spriŋ-ər\ noun (1611)
**1 :** a stone or other solid laid at the impost of an arch — see ARCH illustration
**2 :** one that springs
**3 :** SPRINGER SPANIEL
**4 :** a cow nearly ready to calve

**springer spaniel** noun (1885)
: a medium-sized sporting dog of either of two breeds that is often used for finding and flushing small game: **a :** ENGLISH SPRINGER SPANIEL **b :** WELSH SPRINGER SPANIEL

**spring fever** noun (1843)
: a lazy or restless feeling often associated with the onset of spring

**Spring·field rifle** \'spriŋ-,fēld-\ noun [Springfield, Mass.] (1888)
: a .30 caliber bolt-action rifle used by U.S. troops especially in World War I

**spring–form pan** \'spriŋ-,fòrm-\ noun (1927)
: a pan or mold with an upright detachable rim fastened to the bottom of the pan with a clamp or spring

**spring·head** \'spriŋ-,hed\ noun (1561)
: FOUNTAINHEAD

**spring·house** \-,haùs\ noun (1755)
: a small building situated over a spring and used for cool storage (as of dairy products or meat)

**spring·ing** \'spriŋ-iŋ\ noun (1590)
**1 :** SPRING 5
**2 :** a point where an arch rises from its support

**spring–load** \'spriŋ-'lōd\ transitive verb (1944)
: to load or secure by means of spring tension or compression

**spring peeper** noun (1906)
: a small brown tree frog (Hyla crucifer) of the eastern U.S. and Canada that has a shrill piping call and breeds in ponds and streams in the spring

**spring roll** noun (1943)
: EGG ROLL; also : any of various similar appetizers in oriental cuisine

spring peeper

**spring·tail** \'spriŋ-,tāl\ noun (circa 1797)
: any of an order (Collembola) of small primitive wingless insects usually with a forked structure on the fourth or fifth abdominal segment that is used for jumping — called also collembolan

**spring·tide** \-,tīd\ noun (1530)
: SPRINGTIME

**spring tide** noun (1548)
: a tide of greater-than-average range around the times of new and full moon

**spring·time** \'spriŋ-,tīm\ noun (15th century)
**1 :** the season of spring
**2 :** YOUTH 1a
**3 :** an early or flourishing stage of development

**spring wagon** noun (1794)
: a light farm wagon equipped with springs

**spring·wa·ter** \'spriŋ-,wò-tər, -,wä-\ noun (15th century)
: water from a spring

**spring·wood** \-,wùd\ noun (1884)
: the softer more porous portion of an annual ring of wood that develops early in the growing season — compare SUMMERWOOD

**springy** \'spriŋ-ē\ adjective **spring·i·er; -est** (1641)
**1 :** having an elastic quality : RESILIENT
**2 :** having or showing a lively and energetic movement ⟨walks with a springy step⟩
**synonym** see ELASTIC
— **spring·i·ly** \'spriŋ-ə-lē\ adverb
— **spring·i·ness** \'spriŋ-ē-nəs\ noun

**¹sprin·kle** \'spriŋ-kəl\ verb **sprin·kled; sprin·kling** \-k(ə-)liŋ\ [Middle English sprenklen, sprinclen; akin to Middle High German spreckel, sprenkel spot] (14th century)
transitive verb
**1 :** to scatter in drops or particles
**2 a :** to scatter over **b :** to scatter at intervals in or among : DOT ⟨sprinkled the speech with quips⟩ **c :** to wet lightly
intransitive verb
**1 :** to scatter a liquid in fine drops
**2 :** to rain lightly in scattered drops
— **sprin·kler** \-k(ə-)lər\ noun

**²sprinkle** noun (1641)
**1 :** the act or an instance of sprinkling; especially : a light rain
**2 :** SPRINKLING
**3** plural : small particles of candy used as a topping (as on ice cream) : JIMMIES

**sprin·klered** \'spriŋ-klərd\ adjective (1927)
: having a sprinkler system

**sprinkler system** noun (circa 1909)
: a system for protecting a building against fire by means of overhead pipes which convey an extinguishing fluid (as water) to heat-activated outlets

**sprin·kling** \'spriŋ-kliŋ\ noun (1594)
**1 :** a limited quantity or amount : MODICUM
**2 :** a small quantity falling in scattered drops or particles
**3 :** a small number distributed at random : SCATTERING

**¹sprint** \'sprint\ intransitive verb [of Scandinavian origin; akin to Swedish dialect sprinta to jump, hop; akin to Old High German sprinzan to jump up] (circa 1864)
: to run or go at top speed especially for a short distance
— **sprint·er** noun

**²sprint** noun (circa 1865)
**1 :** the act or an instance of sprinting
**2 a :** DASH 6b **b :** a burst of speed

**sprint car** noun (circa 1965)
: a rugged racing automobile that is midway in size between midget racers and ordinary racers, has about the same horsepower as the larger racers, and is usually raced on a dirt track

**sprit** \'sprit\ noun [Middle English spret, sprit, from Old English sprēot pole, spear; akin to Old English -sprūtan to sprout] (14th century)
: a spar that crosses a fore-and-aft sail diagonally

**sprite** \'sprīt\ noun [Middle English sprit, from Middle French esprit, from Latin spiritus spirit — more at SPIRIT] (14th century)
**1 a** archaic : SOUL **b :** a disembodied spirit : GHOST
**2 a :** ELF, FAIRY **b :** an elfish person

**sprit·sail** \'sprit-,sāl, -səl\ noun (15th century)
**1 :** a sail extended by a sprit
**2 :** a sail formerly set on a yard beneath the bowsprit

**spritz** \'sprits, 'shprits\ verb [German spritzen to squirt, spray] (1902)
transitive verb
: SPRAY
intransitive verb
: to disperse or apply a spray
— **spritz** noun

**spritz·er** \'sprit-sər, 'shprit-\ noun [German, from spritzen] (1945)
: a beverage of usually white wine and soda water

**sprock·et** \'sprä-kət\ noun [origin unknown] (1750)
**1 :** a toothed wheel whose teeth engage the links of a chain
**2 :** a cylinder with teeth around the circumference at either end that project through perforations in something (as motion-picture film) to move it through a mechanism (as a projector)

**¹sprout** \'spraùt\ verb [Middle English spruten, from Old English -sprūtan; akin to Old High German spriozan to sprout, Lithuanian sprausti to squeeze, thrust] (13th century)
intransitive verb
**1 :** to grow, spring up, or come forth as or as if a sprout
**2 :** to send out new growth
transitive verb
: to send forth or up : cause to develop : GROW

**²sprout** noun (13th century)
**1 a :** SHOOT 1a; especially : a young shoot (as from a seed or root) **b** plural (1) chiefly British : BRUSSELS SPROUT 2 (2) : edible sprouts especially from recently germinated seeds (as of alfalfa or mung beans)
**2 :** something resembling a sprout: as **a :** a young person **b :** SCION

**sprouting broccoli** noun (1852)
: BROCCOLI 2a(2)

**¹spruce** \'sprüs\ verb **spruced; spruc·ing** (1594)
transitive verb
: to make spruce — often used with up
intransitive verb
: to make oneself spruce ⟨spruce up a bit⟩

**²spruce** adjective **spruc·er; spruc·est** [perhaps from obsolete English Spruce leather leather imported from Prussia] (1599)
: neat or smart in appearance : TRIM
— **spruce·ly** adverb
— **spruce·ness** noun

**³spruce** noun [obsolete Spruce Prussia, from Middle English, alteration of Pruce, from Old French] (1670)
**1 a :** any of a genus (Picea) of evergreen trees of the pine family with a conical head of dense foliage and soft light wood **b :** any of several coniferous trees (as Douglas fir) of similar habit
**2 :** the wood of a spruce ◆

**spruce beer** noun (1500)

◇ WORD HISTORY
**spruce** Between the 14th and 17th centuries Prussia was called Pruce or Spruce in English, and hence Spruce was used attributively to characterize goods imported from Prussia, as spruce canvas, spruce iron, and spruce leather. Perhaps the most important of these Prussian products was a tall, straight conifer, called the spruce tree or spruce, that was especially desirable for use as the mast of a ship. By the middle of the 17th century Spruce as a name for the country had largely been supplanted by Prussia. By that time, however, spruce had become well established as the name for the tree. The particular species (Picea abies) that was originally called spruce is not limited to Prussia. Another of its native countries gave it its present common name, Norway spruce, which is something of an etymological paradox. Spruce is now the common name applied to any member of the genus Picea.

\ə\ abut  \ᵊ\ kitten  \ər\ further  \a\ ash  \ā\ ace
\ä\ mop, mar  \aù\ out  \ch\ chin  \e\ bet  \ē\ easy
\g\ go  \i\ hit  \ī\ ice  \j\ job  \ŋ\ sing  \ō\ go
\ò\ law  \òi\ boy  \th\ thin  \th\ the  \ü\ loot  \ù\ foot
\y\ yet  \zh\ vision  see also Guide to Pronunciation

**:** a beverage flavored with spruce; *especially* **:** one made from spruce twigs and leaves boiled with molasses or sugar and fermented with yeast

**spruce budworm** *noun* (1884)
**:** a tortricid moth (*Choristoneura fumiferana*) whose larva feeds on evergreen trees (as spruce and balsam fir) in the northern U.S. and Canada

**spruce pine** *noun* (1684)
**:** an American tree (as some pines and spruces or the common eastern hemlock) of the pine family with light, soft, or weak wood

**sprucy** \'sprü-sē\ *adjective* **spruc·i·er; -est** (1774)
**:** SPRUCE

¹**sprue** \'sprü\ *noun* [origin unknown] (1880)
**1 :** the hole through which metal or plastic is poured into the gate and thence into a mold
**2 :** the waste piece cast in a sprue

²**sprue** *noun* [Dutch *spruw;* akin to Middle Low German *sprūwe,* a kind of tumor] (1888)
**1 :** CELIAC DISEASE
**2 :** a disease of tropical regions that is of unknown cause and is characterized by fatty diarrhea and malabsorption of nutrients — called also *tropical sprue*

**sprung** *past and past participle of* SPRING

**sprung rhythm** *noun* (1877)
**:** a poetic rhythm designed to approximate the natural rhythm of speech and characterized by the frequent juxtaposition of single accented syllables and the occurrence of mixed types of feet

**spry** \'sprī\ *adjective* **spri·er** *or* **spry·er** \'sprī(-ə)r\; **spri·est** *or* **spry·est** \'sprī-əst\ [perhaps of Scandinavian origin; akin to Swedish dialect *sprygg* spry] (1746)
**:** NIMBLE 1 ⟨a *spry* 75-year-old⟩
— **spry·ly** *adverb*
— **spry·ness** *noun*

¹**spud** \'spəd\ *verb* **spud·ded; spud·ding** (1652)
*transitive verb*
**1 :** to dig with a spud
**2 :** to begin to drill (an oil well)
*intransitive verb*
**:** to use a spud

²**spud** *noun* [Middle English *spudde* dagger] (1667)
**1 :** a tool or device (as for digging, lifting, or cutting) having the characteristics of a spade and a chisel
**2 :** POTATO

¹**spume** \'spyüm\ *noun* [Middle English, from Middle French, from Latin *spuma* — more at FOAM] (14th century)
**:** frothy matter on liquids **:** FOAM, SCUM
— **spu·mous** \'spyü-məs\ *adjective*
— **spumy** \-mē\ *adjective*

²**spume** *intransitive verb* **spumed; spum·ing** (14th century)
**:** FROTH, FOAM

**spu·mo·ni** *or* **spu·mo·ne** \spü-'mō-nē\ *noun* [Italian *spumone,* augmentative of *spuma* foam, from Latin] (1924)
**:** ice cream in layers of different colors, flavors, and textures often with candied fruits and nuts

**spun** *past and past participle of* SPIN

**spun·bond·ed** \'spən-,bän-dəd\ *adjective* (1961)
**:** of or relating to a nonwoven polymeric material that resembles cloth or fabric

**spun glass** *noun* (1779)
**1 :** blown glass that has slender threads of glass incorporated in it
**2 :** FIBERGLASS

¹**spunk** \'spəŋk\ *noun* [Scottish Gaelic *spong* sponge, tinder, from Latin *spongia* sponge] (1582)
**1 a :** a woody tinder **:** PUNK **b :** any of various fungi used to make tinder
**2 :** METTLE, PLUCK
**3 :** SPIRIT, LIVELINESS

²**spunk** *intransitive verb* (1840)

**dialect :** to show spirit — usually used with *up*

**spunk·ie** \'spəŋ-kē\ *noun* (1727)
*Scottish* **:** IGNIS FATUUS 1

**spunky** \'spəŋ-kē\ *adjective* **spunk·i·er; -est** (1786)
**:** full of spunk **:** SPIRITED
— **spunk·i·ly** \-kə-lē\ *adverb*
— **spunk·i·ness** \-kē-nəs\ *noun*

**spun sugar** *noun* (1846)
**:** sugar boiled to long threads and gathered up and shaped or heaped on a stick as a candy

**spun yarn** *noun* (14th century)
**1 :** a textile yarn spun from staple-length fiber
**2 :** a small rope or stuff formed of two or more rope yarns loosely twisted and used for seizings especially on board ship

¹**spur** \'spər\ *noun* [Middle English *spure,* from Old English *spura;* akin to Old English *spurnan* to kick — more at SPURN] (before 12th century)
**1 a :** a pointed device secured to a rider's heel and used to urge on the horse **b** *plural* [from the acquisition of spurs by a person achieving knighthood] **:** recognition and reward for achievement ⟨won his academic *spurs* as the holder of a chair in a university —James Mountford⟩
**2 :** a goad to action **:** STIMULUS
**3 :** something projecting like or suggesting a spur: as **a :** a projecting root or branch of a tree, shrub, or vine **b** (1) **:** a stiff sharp spine (as on the wings or legs of a bird or insect); *especially* **:** one on a cock's leg (2) **:** a gaff for a gamecock **c :** a hollow projecting appendage of a corolla or calyx (as in larkspur or columbine) **d :** a bony outgrowth (as on the heel of the foot) **e :** CLIMBING IRON
**4 a :** an angular projection, offshoot, or branch extending out beyond or away from a main body or formation; *especially* **:** a ridge or lesser elevation that extends laterally from a mountain or mountain range **b :** a railroad track that branches off from a main line
**5 :** a reinforcing buttress of masonry in a fortification
**synonym** see MOTIVE
— **on the spur of the moment :** on impulse **:** SUDDENLY

²**spur** *verb* **spurred; spur·ring** (13th century)
*transitive verb*
**1 :** to urge (a horse) on with spurs
**2 :** to incite to action or accelerated growth or development **:** STIMULATE
**3 :** to put spurs on
*intransitive verb*
**:** to spur one's horse on

**spurge** \'spərj\ *noun* [Middle English, from Middle French, purge, spurge, from *espurgier* to purge, from Latin *expurgare* — more at EXPURGATE] (14th century)
**:** any of a genus (*Euphorbia* of the family Euphorbiaceae, the spurge family) of chiefly herbs and shrubs with a bitter milky juice

**spur gear** *noun* (1823)
**:** a gear wheel with radial teeth parallel to its axis — called also *spur wheel*

**spurge laurel** *noun* (1597)
**:** a low Eurasian shrub (*Daphne laureola*) with oblong evergreen leaves and axillary racemes of yellowish flowers

**spur·ri·ous** \'spyùr-ē-əs\ *adjective* [Late Latin & Latin; Late Latin *spurius* false, from Latin, of illegitimate birth, from *spurius,* noun, bastard] (1598)
**1 :** of illegitimate birth **:** BASTARD
**2 :** outwardly similar or corresponding to something without having its genuine qualities **:** FALSE
**3 a :** of falsified or erroneously attributed origin **:** FORGED **b :** of a deceitful nature or quality
— **spu·ri·ous·ly** *adverb*
— **spu·ri·ous·ness** *noun*

*spur gear*

¹**spurn** \'spərn\ *verb* [Middle English, from Old English *spurnan;* akin to Old High German *spurnan* to spurn, Latin *spernere* to spurn, Greek *spairein* to quiver] (before 12th century)
*intransitive verb*
**1** *obsolete* **a :** STUMBLE **b :** KICK
**2** *archaic* **:** to reject something disdainfully
*transitive verb*
**1 :** to tread sharply or heavily upon **:** TRAMPLE
**2 :** to reject with disdain or contempt **:** SCORN
**synonym** see DECLINE
— **spurn·er** *noun*

²**spurn** *noun* (14th century)
**1 a :** KICK **b** *obsolete* **:** STUMBLE
**2 a :** disdainful rejection **b :** contemptuous treatment

**spur–of–the–moment** *adjective* (1948)
**:** occurring or developing without premeditation **:** hastily extemporized ⟨a *spur-of-the-moment* decision⟩

**spurred** \'spərd\ *adjective* (15th century)
**1 :** wearing spurs
**2 :** having one or more spurs ⟨a *spurred* violet⟩

**spur·rey** *or* **spur·ry** \'spər-ē, 'spə-rē\ *noun,* *plural* **spurreys** *or* **spurries** [Dutch *spurrie,* from Medieval Latin *spergula*] (1577)
**:** a small white-flowered European weed (*Spergula arvensis*) of the pink family with whorled filiform leaves; *also* **:** any of several related and similar herbs

¹**spurt** \'spərt\ *verb* [perhaps akin to Middle High German *spürzen* to spit, Old English *-sprūtan* to sprout — more at SPROUT] (1570)
*intransitive verb*
**:** to gush forth **:** SPOUT
*transitive verb*
**:** to expel in a stream or jet **:** SQUIRT

²**spurt** *noun* (circa 1775)
**:** a sudden gush **:** JET

³**spurt** *noun* [origin unknown] (circa 1591)
**1 :** a short period of time **:** MOMENT
**2 a :** a sudden brief burst of effort or activity **b :** a sharp or sudden increase in business activity

⁴**spurt** *intransitive verb* (1664)
**:** to make a spurt

**spur·tle** \'spər-t°l\ *noun* [origin unknown] (1756)
*chiefly Scottish* **:** a wooden stick for stirring porridge

**sput·nik** \'spùt-nik, 'spət-, 'spüt-\ *noun* [Russian, literally, traveling companion, from *s, so* with + *put'* path] (1957)
**:** SATELLITE 2b

¹**sput·ter** \'spə-tər\ *verb* [akin to Dutch *sputteren* to sputter] (1598)
*transitive verb*
**1 :** to spit or squirt from the mouth with explosive sounds
**2 :** to utter hastily or explosively in confusion or excitement
**3 :** to dislodge (atoms) from the surface of a material by collision with high energy particles; *also* **:** to deposit (a metallic film) by such a process
*intransitive verb*
**1 :** to spit or squirt particles of food or saliva noisily from the mouth
**2 :** to speak explosively or confusedly in anger or excitement
**3 :** to make explosive popping sounds
— **sput·ter·er** *noun*

²**sputter** *noun* (1673)
**1 :** confused and excited speech or discussion
**2 :** the act or sound of sputtering

**spu·tum** \'spyü-təm, 'spü-\ *noun,* *plural* **spu·ta** \-tə\ [Latin, from neuter of *sputus,* past participle of *spuere* to spit — more at SPEW] (circa 1693)
**:** expectorated matter made up of saliva and often discharges from the respiratory passages

**¹spy** \'spī\ *verb* **spied; spy·ing** [Middle English *spien*, from Old French *espier*, of Germanic origin; akin to Old High German *spehōn* to spy; akin to Latin *specere* to look, look at, Greek *skeptesthai* & *skopein* to watch, look at, consider] (13th century)
*transitive verb*
**1 :** to watch secretly usually for hostile purposes
**2 :** to catch sight of **:** SEE
**3 :** to search or look for intensively
*intransitive verb*
**1 :** to observe or search for something **:** LOOK
**2 :** to watch secretly as a spy
**²spy** *noun, plural* **spies** (13th century)
**1 :** one that spies: **a :** one who keeps secret watch on a person or thing to obtain information **b :** a person employed by one nation to secretly convey classified information of strategic importance to another nation; *also* **:** a person who conveys the trade secrets of one company to another
**2 :** an act of spying
**spy·glass** \'spī-,glas\ *noun* (1706)
**:** a small telescope
**spy·mas·ter** \'spī-,mas-tər\ *noun* (1938)
**:** the head of a ring of spies **:** a director of intelligence
**squab** \'skwäb\ *noun, plural* **squabs** [probably of Scandinavian origin; akin to Swedish dialect *skvabb* anything soft and thick] (1664)
**1 a :** COUCH **b :** a cushion for a chair or couch
**2 or plural squab :** a fledgling bird; *specifically* **:** a fledgling pigeon about four weeks old
**3 :** a short fat person
**— squab** *adjective*
**¹squab·ble** \'skwä-bəl\ *noun* [probably of Scandinavian origin; akin to Swedish dialect *skvabbel* dispute] (1602)
**:** a noisy altercation or quarrel usually over trifles
**²squabble** *intransitive verb* **squab·bled; squab·bling** \-b(ə-)liŋ\ (1604)
**:** to quarrel noisily and usually over trifles
**— squab·bler** \-b(ə-)lər\ *noun*
**¹squad** \'skwäd\ *noun* [Middle French *esquade*, from Old Spanish & Old Italian; Old Spanish *escuadra* & Old Italian *squadra*, ultimately from (assumed) Vulgar Latin *exquadrare* to make square — more at SQUARE] (1649)
**1 :** a small organized group of military personnel; *especially* **:** a tactical unit that can be easily directed in the field
**2 :** a small group engaged in a common effort or occupation
**²squad** *transitive verb* **squad·ded; squad·ding** (circa 1802)
**:** to arrange in squads
**squad car** *noun* (1938)
**:** a police automobile connected by a two-way radio with headquarters — called also *cruiser, prowl car*
**squad·ron** \'skwä-drən\ *noun* [Italian *squadrone*, augmentative of *squadra* squad, from Old Italian] (1562)
**:** a unit of military organization: **a :** a cavalry unit higher than a troop and lower than a regiment **b :** a naval unit consisting of two or more divisions and sometimes additional vessels **c** (1) **:** a unit of the U.S. Air Force higher than a flight and lower than a group (2) **:** a military flight formation
**squadron leader** *noun* (1919)
**:** a commissioned officer in the British air force who ranks with a major in the army
**squad room** *noun* (1943)
**1 :** a room in a barracks used to billet soldiers
**2 :** a room in a police station where members of the force assemble
**squa·lene** \'skwä-,lēn\ *noun* [International Scientific Vocabulary, from Latin *squalus*, a sea fish — more at WHALE] (1916)
**:** an acyclic hydrocarbon $C_{30}H_{50}$ that is widely distributed in nature (as a major component of

sebum and in shark-liver oils) and is a precursor of sterols (as cholesterol)
**squal·id** \'skwä-ləd\ *adjective* [Latin *squalidus* rough, dirty, from *squalēre* to be covered with scales or dirt, from *squalus* dirty; perhaps akin to *squama* scale] (1596)
**1 :** marked by filthiness and degradation from neglect or poverty
**2 :** SORDID
**synonym** see DIRTY
**— squal·id·ly** *adverb*
**— squal·id·ness** *noun*
**¹squall** \'skwȯl\ *verb* [probably of Scandinavian origin; akin to Old Norse *skval* useless chatter] (circa 1631)
*intransitive verb*
**:** to cry out raucously **:** SCREAM
*transitive verb*
**:** to utter in a strident voice
**— squall·er** *noun*
**²squall** *noun* (1709)
**:** a raucous cry
**³squall** *noun* [probably of Scandinavian origin; akin to Swedish *skval* rushing water] (1699)
**1 :** a sudden violent wind often with rain or snow
**2 :** a short-lived commotion
**⁴squall** *intransitive verb* (circa 1890)
**:** to blow a squall
**squally** \'skwȯ-lē\ *adjective* **squall·i·er; -est** (1719)
**1 :** marked by squalls
**2 :** GUSTY
**squa·lor** \'skwä-lər *also* 'skwā- *or* 'skwȯ-\ *noun* [Latin, from *squalēre*] (1621)
**:** the quality or state of being squalid
**squa·ma** \'skwā-mə, 'skwä-\ *noun, plural* **squa·mae** \'skwā-,mē, 'skwä-,mī\ {Latin} (circa 1706)
**:** SCALE; *also* **:** a structure resembling a scale
**squa·mate** \-,māt\ *adjective* (1826)
**:** SCALY ⟨*squamate* reptiles⟩
**squa·ma·tion** \skwə-'mā-shən\ *noun* (1881)
**1 :** the state of being scaly
**2 :** the arrangement of scales on an animal
**¹squa·mo·sal** \skwə-'mō-səl, -zəl\ *noun* (1848)
**:** a squamosal bone
**²squamosal** *adjective* (circa 1852)
**1 :** SQUAMOUS
**2 :** of, relating to, or being a bone of the skull of many vertebrates corresponding to the squamous portion of the temporal bone of most mammals including humans
**squa·mous** \'skwā-məs *also* 'skwä-\ *adjective* [Middle English, from Latin *squamosus*, from *squama* scale] (15th century)
**1 a :** covered with or consisting of scales **:** SCALY **b :** of, relating to, or being a stratified epithelium that consists at least in its outer layers of small scalelike cells
**2 :** of, relating to, or being the anterior upper portion of the temporal bone of most mammals including humans
**squamous cell** *noun* (circa 1947)
**:** a cell of or derived from squamous epithelium
**squa·mu·lose** \'skwä-myə-,lōs, 'skwä-\ *adjective* [Latin *squamula*, diminutive of *squama*] (1846)
**:** being or having a thallus made up of small leafy lobes ⟨a *squamulose* lichen⟩
**¹squan·der** \'skwän-dər\ *verb* **squan·dered; squan·der·ing** \-d(ə-)riŋ\ [origin unknown] (1536)
*transitive verb*
**1 :** to spend extravagantly or foolishly **:** DISSIPATE
**2 :** to cause to disperse **:** SCATTER
**3 :** to lose (as an advantage or opportunity) through negligence or inaction
*intransitive verb*
**:** DISPERSE, SCATTER
**— squan·der·er** \-dər-ər\ *noun*
**²squander** *noun* (1709)

**:** an act of squandering
**¹square** \'skwar, 'skwer\ *noun* [Middle English, from Middle French *esquarre*, from (assumed) Vulgar Latin *exquadra*, from *exquadrare* to square, from Latin *ex-* + *quadrare* to square — more at QUADRATE] (13th century)
**1 :** an instrument having at least one right angle and two straight edges used especially to lay out or test right angles
**2 :** a rectangle with all four sides equal
**3 :** any of the quadrilateral spaces marked out on a board for playing games
**4 :** the product of a number multiplied by itself
**5 a :** an open place or area formed at the meeting of two or more streets **b :** BLOCK 6a
**6 :** a solid object or piece approximating a cube or having a square as its largest face
**7 :** an unopened cotton flower with its enclosing bracts
**8 :** a person who is conventional or conservative in taste or way of life
**— on the square 1 :** at right angles **2 :** in a fair open manner **:** HONESTLY
**— out of square :** not at an exact right angle
**²square** *adjective* **squar·er; squar·est** (14th century)
**1 a :** having four equal sides and four right angles **b :** forming a right angle ⟨*square* corner⟩ **c :** having a square base ⟨a *square* pyramid⟩
**2 :** raised to the second power
**3 a :** being approximately a cube ⟨*square* cabinet⟩ **b :** having a shape that is broad for the height and rectangular rather than curving in outline ⟨*square* shoulders⟩ ⟨a *square*, thick, hard-working man —Maria Edgeworth⟩ **c :** rectangular and equilateral in section ⟨*square* tower⟩
**4 a :** being or converted to a unit of area equal in measure to a square each side of which measures one unit of a specified unit of length ⟨a *square* foot⟩ — see METRIC SYSTEM table, WEIGHT table **b :** being of a specified length in each of two equal dimensions ⟨10 feet *square*⟩
**5 a :** exactly adjusted **:** precisely constructed or aligned **b :** JUST, FAIR ⟨a *square* deal⟩ ⟨*square* in all his dealings⟩ **c :** leaving no balance **:** SETTLED **d :** EVEN, TIED **e :** SUBSTANTIAL, SATISFYING ⟨*square* meal⟩ **f :** being unsophisticated, conservative, or conventional
**6 :** set at right angles with the mast and keel — used of the yards of a square-rigged ship
**— square·ness** *noun*
**³square** *verb* **squared; squar·ing** (14th century)
*transitive verb*
**1 a :** to make square or rectangular ⟨*square* a building stone⟩ **b :** to test for deviation from a right angle, straight line, or plane surface
**2 :** to bring approximately to a right angle ⟨*squared* his shoulders⟩
**3 a :** to multiply (a number) by itself **:** raise to the second power **b :** to find a square equal in area to ⟨*square* a circle⟩
**4 :** to regulate or adjust by or to some standard or principle ⟨*square* our actions by the opinions of others —John Milton⟩
**5 a :** BALANCE, SETTLE ⟨*square* an account⟩ **b :** to even the score of
**6 :** to mark off into squares
**7 a :** to set right **:** bring into agreement **b :** BRIBE, FIX
*intransitive verb*
**1 :** to agree precisely **:** CORRESPOND ⟨your actions should *square* with your words⟩
**2 :** to settle matters; *especially* **:** to pay the bill
**— squar·er** *noun*
**⁴square** *adverb* (circa 1582)

**1 :** in a straightforward or honest manner
**2 a :** so as to face or be face to face **b :** at right angles
**3 :** with nothing intervening **:** DIRECTLY ⟨ran *square* into it⟩
**4 :** in a firm manner ⟨looked her *square* in the eye⟩
**5 :** in a square shape
**square away** (1849)
*intransitive verb*
**1 :** to square the yards so as to sail before the wind
**2 :** to put everything in order or in readiness
**3 :** to take up a fighting stance
*transitive verb*
**:** to put in order or in readiness
**square bracket** *noun* (circa 1888)
**:** BRACKET 3a
**square dance** *noun* (1870)
**:** a dance for four couples who form the sides of a square
— **square–dance** *intransitive verb*
— **square dancer** *noun*
— **square dancing** *noun*
**square knot** *noun* (circa 1867)
**:** a knot made of two reverse half-knots and typically used to join the ends of two cords — see KNOT illustration
**square·ly** \'skwar-lē, 'skwer-\ *adverb* (1564)
**1 :** in a straightforward or honest manner ⟨we must *squarely* face the issue⟩
**2 a :** EXACTLY, PRECISELY ⟨*squarely* in the middle⟩ **b :** so as to make solid contact ⟨hit the ball *squarely*⟩ ⟨feet *squarely* planted⟩
**3 :** in a square form or manner ; so as to be square ⟨a *squarely* cut dress⟩
**4 :** in a plain or unequivocal manner ⟨the responsibility lies *squarely* with us⟩ ⟨align ourselves *squarely* with our allies⟩
**square matrix** *noun* (1858)
**:** a mathematical matrix with the same number of rows and columns
**square measure** *noun* (1728)
**:** a unit or system of units for measuring area — see METRIC SYSTEM table, WEIGHT table
**square off** *intransitive verb* (1837)
**:** to take a fighting stance ; prepare to fight; *also* **:** FIGHT
**square of opposition** (1864)
**:** a square figure on which may be demonstrated the logical relationships of contraries, contradictories, subcontraries, and subalterns and superalterns
**square one** *noun* [from the use of numbered squares in some board games] (1960)
**:** the initial stage or starting point ⟨the failure set us back to *square one*⟩
**square rig** *noun* (circa 1875)
**:** a sailing-ship rig in which the principal sails are extended on yards fastened to the masts horizontally and at their center
**square–rigged** \'skwar-'rigd, 'skwer-\ *adjective* (1769)
**:** having or equipped with a square rig
**square–rig·ger** \-,ri-gər\ *noun* (1855)
**:** a square-rigged craft

**square root**
*noun* (1557)
**:** a factor of a number that when squared gives the number ⟨the *square root* of 9 is ±3⟩

**square sail**     square-rigger
\'skwar-,sāl,
'skwer-, -səl\ *noun* (1600)
**:** a 4-sided sail extended on a yard suspended at the middle from a mast
**square shooter** *noun* (circa 1914)
**:** a just or honest person
**square–shoul·dered** \'skwar-'shōl-dərd, 'skwer-\ *adjective* (1825)
**:** having shoulders of a rectangular outline that are straight across the back

**square–toed** \-'tōd\ *adjective* (1785)
**1 :** having a toe that is square
**2 :** OLD-FASHIONED, CONSERVATIVE
**square wave** *noun* (1932)
**:** the rectangular waveform of a quantity that varies periodically and abruptly from one to the other of two uniform values
**squar·ish** \'skwar-ish, 'skwer-\ *adjective* (1742)
**:** somewhat square in form or appearance
— **squar·ish·ly** *adverb*
— **squar·ish·ness** *noun*
**¹squash** \'skwäsh, 'skwȯsh\ *verb* [Middle French *esquasser,* from (assumed) Vulgar Latin *exquassare,* from Latin *ex-* + *quassare* to shake — more at QUASH] (1565)
*transitive verb*
**1 :** to press or beat into a pulp or a flat mass **:** CRUSH
**2 :** PUT DOWN, SUPPRESS ⟨*squash* a revolt⟩
*intransitive verb*
**1 :** to flatten out under pressure or impact
**2 :** to proceed with a splashing or squelching sound
**3 :** SQUEEZE, PRESS
— **squash·er** *noun*
**²squash** *noun* (1590)
**1** *obsolete* **:** something soft and easily crushed; *specifically* **:** an unripe pod of peas
**2 :** the sudden fall of a heavy soft body or the sound of such a fall
**3 :** a squelching sound made by walking on oozy ground or in water-soaked boots
**4 :** a crushed mass
**5** *British* **:** sweetened citrus fruit juice often served with added soda water
**6 :** a singles or doubles game played in a 4-wall court with a long-handled racket and a rubber ball that can be hit off any number of walls
**³squash** *adverb* (1766)
**:** with a squash or a squashing sound
**⁴squash** *noun,* *plural* **squash·es** *or* **squash** [by shortening & alteration from earlier *isquoutersquash,* from Narraganset *askútasquash*] (1634)
**:** any of various fruits of plants (genus *Cucurbita*) of the gourd family widely cultivated as vegetables; *also* **:** a plant and especially a vine that bears squashes — compare SUMMER SQUASH, WINTER SQUASH
**squash bug** *noun* (circa 1846)
**:** a large black American bug (*Anasa tristis* of the family Coreidae) injurious to plants of the gourd family
**squash racquets** *noun plural but singular in construction* (1886)
**:** SQUASH 6
**squash tennis** *noun* (1901)
**:** a singles racket game resembling squash played with an inflated ball the size of a tennis ball
**squashy** \'skwä-shē, 'skwȯ-\ *adjective*
**squash·i·er; -est** (1698)
**1 :** easily squashed **:** very soft ⟨*squashy* cushions⟩
**2 :** softly wet **:** BOGGY
**3 :** soft because overripe ⟨*squashy* melons⟩
— **squash·i·ly** \-shə-lē\ *adverb*
— **squash·i·ness** \-shē-nəs\ *noun*
**¹squat** \'skwät\ *verb* **squat·ted; squat·ting** [Middle English *squatten,* from Middle French *esquatir,* from *es-* ex- (from Latin *ex-*) + *quatir* to press, from (assumed) Vulgar Latin *coactire* to press together, from Latin *coactus,* past participle of *cogere* to drive together — more at COGENT] (15th century)
*transitive verb*
**1 :** to cause (oneself) to crouch or sit on the ground
**2 :** to occupy as a squatter
*intransitive verb*
**1 :** to crouch close to the ground as if to escape observation ⟨a hare *squatting* in the grass⟩

**2 :** to assume or maintain a position in which the body is supported on the feet and the knees are bent so that the buttocks rest on or near the heels
**3 :** to be or become a squatter
**²squat** *adjective* **squat·ter; squat·test** (15th century)
**1 :** sitting with the haunches close above the heels
**2 a :** low to the ground **b :** marked by disproportionate shortness or thickness
— **squat·ly** *adverb*
— **squat·ness** *noun*
**³squat** *noun* (1580)
**1 a :** the act of squatting **b :** the posture of one that squats
**2 a :** a place where one squats **b :** the lair of a small animal ⟨*squat* of a hare⟩
**3 :** a lift in weight lifting in which the lifter performs a knee bend while holding a barbell on the shoulders; *also* **:** a competitive event involving this lift
**4** *chiefly British* **:** an empty house or building that is occupied by squatters
**5** *slang* **:** DIDDLY-SQUAT
**¹squat·ter** \'skwä-tər\ *intransitive verb* [imitative] (1785)
**:** to go along through or as if through water
**²squatter** *noun* (1788)
**:** one that squats: as **a :** one that settles on property without right or title or payment of rent **b :** one that settles on public land under government regulation with the purpose of acquiring title
**squatter sovereignty** *noun* (1854)
**:** POPULAR SOVEREIGNTY 2
**squat·ty** \'skwä-tē\ *adjective* **squat·ti·er; -est** (1881)
**1 :** low to the ground
**2 :** DUMPY, THICKSET
**squaw** \'skwȯ\ *noun* [Massachuset *squa, ussqua* woman] (1634)
**1 :** an American Indian woman
**2 :** WOMAN, WIFE — usually used disparagingly
**squaw·fish** \-,fish\ *noun* (1881)
**:** any of several large cyprinid fishes (genus *Ptychocheilus*) of western North America
**¹squawk** \'skwȯk\ *intransitive verb* [probably blend of *squall* and *squeak*] (1821)
**1 :** to utter a harsh abrupt scream
**2 :** to complain or protest loudly or vehemently
— **squawk·er** *noun*
**²squawk** *noun* (1850)
**1 :** a harsh abrupt scream
**2 :** a noisy complaint
**squawk box** *noun* (1945)
**:** an intercom speaker
**squaw man** *noun* (1866)
**:** a white man married to an Indian woman and usually living as one of her tribe
**squaw·root** \'skwȯ-,rüt, -,rut\ *noun* (circa 1848)
**:** a North American scaly herb (*Conopholis americana*) of the broomrape family parasitic on oak and hemlock roots
**¹squeak** \'skwēk\ *verb* [Middle English *squeken*] (14th century)
*intransitive verb*
**1 :** to utter or make a short shrill cry or noise
**2 :** SQUEAL 2a
**3 :** to pass, succeed, or win by a narrow margin ⟨just *squeaked* by in the election⟩
*transitive verb*
**:** to utter in a shrill piping tone
**²squeak** *noun* (1700)
**1 :** a sharp shrill cry or sound
**2 :** ESCAPE ⟨a close *squeak*⟩
— **squeaky** \'skwē-kē\ *adjective*
**squeak·er** \'skwē-kər\ *noun* (1671)
**1 :** one that squeaks
**2 :** a contest (as a game or an election) won by a small margin
**squeaky–clean** *adjective* (1968)
**1 :** completely clean ⟨*squeaky-clean* hair⟩

**2 :** completely free from moral taint of any kind ⟨a *squeaky-clean* reputation⟩

**¹squeal** \'skwē(ə)l\ *verb* [Middle English *squelen*] (14th century)
*intransitive verb*
**1 :** to make a shrill cry or noise
**2 a :** to turn informer **b :** COMPLAIN, PROTEST
*transitive verb*
**1 :** to utter or express with or as if with a squeal
**2 :** to cause to make a loud shrill noise ⟨*squealing* the tires⟩
— **squeal·er** *noun*

**²squeal** *noun* (1747)
**:** a shrill sharp cry or noise

**squea·mish** \'skwē-mish\ *adjective* [Middle English *squaymisch*, modification of Anglo-French *escoymous*] (15th century)
**1 a :** easily nauseated : QUEASY **b :** affected with nausea
**2 a :** excessively fastidious or scrupulous in conduct or belief **b :** easily offended or disgusted
— **squea·mish·ly** *adverb*
— **squea·mish·ness** *noun*

**¹squee·gee** \'skwē-ˌjē\ *noun* [origin unknown] (1844)
**:** a blade of leather or rubber set on a handle and used for spreading, pushing, or wiping liquid material on, across, or off a surface (as a window); *also* **:** a smaller similar device or a small rubber roller with handle used by a photographer or lithographer

**²squeegee** *transitive verb* **squee·geed; squee·gee·ing** (1883)
**:** to smooth, wipe, or treat with a squeegee

**¹squeeze** \'skwēz\ *verb* **squeezed; squeez·ing** [alteration of obsolete English *quease*, from Middle English *queysen*, from Old English *cwȳsan;* akin to Icelandic *kveisa* stomach cramps] (circa 1601)
*transitive verb*
**1 a :** to exert pressure especially on opposite sides of **:** COMPRESS **b :** to extract or emit under pressure **c :** to force or thrust by compression
**2 a** (1) **:** to get by extortion (2) **:** to deprive by extortion **b :** to cause economic hardship to **c :** to reduce the amount of ⟨*squeezes* profits⟩
**3 :** to crowd into a limited area
**4 :** to gain or win by a narrow margin
**5 :** to force (another player) to discard in bridge so as to unguard a suit
**6 :** to score by means of a squeeze play
*intransitive verb*
**1 :** to give way before pressure
**2 :** to exert pressure; *also* **:** to practice extortion or oppression
**3 :** to force one's way ⟨*squeeze* through a door⟩
**4 :** to pass, win, or get by narrowly
— **squeez·abil·i·ty** \ˌskwē-zə-'bi-lə-tē\ *noun*
— **squeez·able** \'skwē-zə-bəl\ *adjective*
— **squeez·er** *noun*

**²squeeze** *noun* (1611)
**1 a :** an act or instance of squeezing **:** COMPRESSION **b :** HANDCLASP; *also* **:** EMBRACE
**2 a :** a quantity squeezed out from something ⟨a *squeeze* of lemon⟩ **b :** a group crowded together **:** CROWD
**3 :** a profit taken by a middleman on goods or transactions
**4 :** a financial pressure caused by narrowing margins or by shortages
**5 :** a forced discard in bridge
**6 :** SQUEEZE PLAY
**7** *slang* **:** MAIN SQUEEZE

**squeeze bottle** *noun* (1950)
**:** a bottle of flexible plastic that dispenses its contents when it is squeezed

**squeeze off** (circa 1949)
*transitive verb*
**:** to fire (a round) by squeezing the trigger
*intransitive verb*
**:** to fire a weapon by squeezing the trigger

**squeeze play** *noun* (1905)

**1 :** a baseball play in which a runner on third base starts for home plate as the ball is being pitched and the batter attempts to bunt to give the runner a chance to score
**2 :** the exertion of pressure in order to extort a concession or gain a goal

**¹squelch** \'skwelch\ *verb* [origin unknown] (1624)
*transitive verb*
**1 a :** to fall or stamp on so as to crush **b** (1) **:** to completely suppress **:** QUELL (2) **:** SILENCE
**2 :** to emit or move with a sucking sound
*intransitive verb*
**1 :** to emit a sucking sound
**2 :** to splash through water, slush, or mire
— **squelch·er** *noun*

**²squelch** *noun* (1895)
**1 :** a sound of or as if of semiliquid matter under suction ⟨the *squelch* of mud⟩
**2 :** the act of suppressing; *especially* **:** a retort that silences an opponent
— **squelchy** *adjective*

**sque·teague** \skwi-'tēg\ *noun, plural* **squeteague** [of Algonquian origin; akin to Mohegan *cheegut* weakfish] (1803)
**:** any of several weakfishes (especially *Cynoscion regalis*)

**¹squib** \'skwib\ *noun* [origin unknown] (circa 1525)
**1 a :** a short humorous or satiric writing or speech **b :** a short news item; *especially* **:** FILLER
**2 a :** a small firecracker **b :** a broken firecracker in which the powder burns with a fizz
**3 :** a small electric or pyrotechnic device used to ignite a charge

**²squib** *verb* **squibbed; squib·bing** (circa 1580)
*intransitive verb*
**1 :** to speak, write, or publish squibs
**2 :** to fire a squib
*transitive verb*
**1 a :** to utter in an offhand manner **b :** to make squibs against **:** LAMPOON
**2 :** to shoot off **:** FIRE
**3 :** to kick (a football) just far enough on a kickoff to be legally recoverable by the kicking team

**squib kick** *noun* (circa 1956)
**:** ONSIDE KICK

**¹squid** \'skwid\ *noun, plural* **squid** *or* **squids** [origin unknown] (1613)
**:** any of an order (Teuthoidea) of cephalopods having eight short arms and two usually longer tentacles, a long tapered body, a caudal fin on each side, and usually a slender internal chitinous support

**²squid** *intransitive verb* **squid·ded; squid·ding** (circa 1859)
**:** to fish with or for squid

**SQUID** \'skwid\ *noun* [*s*uperconducting *qu*antum *i*nterference *d*evice] (1967)
**:** an instrument for detecting and measuring very weak magnetic fields

**squiffed** \'skwift\ *or* **squif·fy** \'skwi-fē\ *adjective* [origin unknown] (circa 1855)
**:** INTOXICATED, DRUNK

**¹squig·gle** \'skwi-gəl\ *verb* **squig·gled; squig·gling** \-g(ə-)liŋ\ [blend of *squirm* and *wriggle*] (circa 1816)
*intransitive verb*
**1 :** SQUIRM, WRIGGLE
**2 :** to write or paint hastily **:** SCRIBBLE
*transitive verb*
**1 :** SCRIBBLE
**2 :** to form or cause to form in squiggles

**²squiggle** *noun* (1900)
**:** a short wavy twist or line **:** CURLICUE; *especially* **:** an illegible scrawl
— **squig·gly** \-g(ə-)lē\ *adjective*

**squil·gee** \'skwē-ˌjē, 'skwil-ˌjē\ *variant of* SQUEEGEE

**squill** \'skwil\ *noun* [Middle English, from Latin *squilla, scilla*, from Greek *skilla*] (14th century)

**1 a :** a Mediterranean bulbous herb (*Urginea maritima*) of the lily family — called also *sea onion*; compare RED SQUILL 1 **b** (1) **:** the dried sliced bulb scales of a squill used as an expectorant, cardiac stimulant, and diuretic (2) **:** RED SQUILL 2
**2 :** SCILLA

**squil·la** \'skwi-lə\ *noun, plural* **squillas** *or* **squil·lae** \'skwi-ˌlē, -ˌlī\ [New Latin, from Latin, shrimp, crayfish] (1658)
**:** any of various stomatopod crustaceans (especially genus *Squilla*) that burrow in mud or beneath stones in shallow water along the seashore

**¹squinch** \'skwinch\ *verb* [probably blend of *squint* and *pinch*] (1835)
*transitive verb*
**1 :** to screw up (the eyes or face) **:** SQUINT
**2 a :** to make more compact **b :** to cause to crouch down or draw together
*intransitive verb*
**1 :** FLINCH
**2 :** to crouch down or draw together
**3 :** SQUINT

**²squinch** *noun* [alteration of earlier *scunch* back part of the side of an opening] (circa 1840)
**:** a support (as an arch, lintel, or corbeling) carried across the corner of a room under a superimposed mass

**¹squin·ny** \'skwi-nē\ *verb* **squin·nied; squin·ny·ing** [probably from obsolete English *squin* asquint, from Middle English *skuin*] (1605)
**:** SQUINT

**²squinny** *noun* (circa 1881)
**:** SQUINT
— **squinny** *adjective*

**¹squint** \'skwint\ *adjective* [Middle English *asquint*] (1579)
**1** *of an eye* **:** looking or tending to look obliquely or askance (as with envy or disdain)
**2** *of the eyes* **:** not having the visual axes parallel **:** CROSSED

**²squint** (1599)
*intransitive verb*
**1 a :** to have an indirect bearing, reference, or aim **b :** to deviate from a true line
**2 a :** to look in a squint-eyed manner **b :** to be cross-eyed **c :** to look or peer with eyes partly closed
*transitive verb*
**:** to cause (an eye) to squint
— **squint·er** *noun*
— **squint·ing·ly** \'skwin-tiŋ-lē\ *adverb*

**³squint** *noun* (circa 1652)
**1 :** STRABISMUS
**2 :** an instance of squinting
**3 :** HAGIOSCOPE
— **squinty** \'skwin-tē\ *adjective*

**squint–eyed** \'skwint-ˌīd\ *adjective* (1589)
**1 :** having eyes that squint; *specifically* **:** affected with cross-eye
**2 :** looking askance (as in envy)

**squinting modifier** *noun* (1924)
**:** a modifier (as *often* in "getting dressed often is a nuisance") so placed in a sentence that it can be interpreted as modifying either what precedes or what follows

**¹squire** \'skwīr\ *noun* [Middle English *squier*, from Old French *esquier* — more at ESQUIRE] (13th century)
**1 :** a shield bearer or armor bearer of a knight
**2 a :** a male attendant especially on a great personage **b :** a man who devotedly attends a lady **:** GALLANT
**3 a :** a member of the British gentry ranking below a knight and above a gentleman **b :** an owner of a country estate; *especially* **:** the

---

\ə\ abut   \ᵊ\ kitten   \ər\ further   \a\ ash   \ā\ ace
\ä\ mop, mar   \au̇\ out   \ch\ chin   \e\ bet   \ē\ easy
\g\ go   \i\ hit   \ī\ ice   \j\ job   \ŋ\ sing   \ō\ go
\ȯ\ law   \ȯi\ boy   \th\ thin   \th̲\ the   \ü\ loot   \u̇\ foot
\y\ yet   \zh\ vision   *see also* Guide to Pronunciation

principal landowner in a village or district **c** (1) **:** JUSTICE OF THE PEACE (2) **:** LAWYER (3) **:** JUDGE
— **squir·ish** \'skwīr-ish\ *adjective*
²**squire** *transitive verb* **squired; squir·ing** (14th century)
**:** to attend as a squire **:** ESCORT
**squire·ar·chy** *also* **squir·ar·chy** \'skwīr-,är-kē\ *noun, plural* **-chies** (1796)
**:** the class of landed gentry or landed proprietors
**squirm** \'skwərm\ *intransitive verb* [origin unknown] (circa 1691)
**:** to twist about like a worm **:** FIDGET
— **squirm** *noun*
— **squirmy** \'skwər-mē\ *adjective*
¹**squir·rel** \'skwər(-ə)l, 'skwə-rəl, *chiefly British* 'skwir-əl\ *noun, plural* **squirrels** *also* **squirrel** [Middle English *squirel*, from Middle French *esquireul*, from (assumed) Vulgar Latin *scuriolus*, diminutive of *scurius*, alteration of Latin *sciurus*, from Greek *skiouros*, probably from *skia* shadow + *oura* tail — more at SHINE, ASS] (14th century)
**1 :** any of various small or medium-sized rodents (family Sciuridae, the squirrel family): as **a :** any of numerous New or Old World arboreal forms having a long bushy tail and strong hind legs **b :** GROUND SQUIRREL
**2 :** the fur of a squirrel ◆
²**squirrel** *transitive verb* **-reled** *or* **-relled; -rel·ing** *or* **-rel·ling** [from the squirrel's habit of storing up gathered nuts and seeds for winter use] (1925)
**:** to store up for future use — often used with *away*
**squirrel cage** *noun* (1821)
**1 :** a cage for a small animal (as a squirrel) that contains a rotatable cylinder for exercising
**2 :** something resembling the working of a squirrel cage in repetitiveness or endlessness
**squirrel corn** *noun* (1843)
**:** a North American herb (*Dicentra canadensis*) of the fumitory family with much-divided leaves and a scapose raceme of cream-colored flowers
**squir·rel·ly** \'skwər(-ə)-lē, 'skwə-rə-\ *adjective* (1928)
**:** NUTTY 3
**squirrel monkey** *noun* (1773)
**:** a small soft-haired South American monkey (*Saimiri sciureus*) that has a long tail not used for grasping and is colored chiefly yellowish gray with a white face and black muzzle
**squirrel rifle** *noun* [from its being suitable only for small game] (1834)
**:** a small-caliber rifle — called also *squirrel gun*
¹**squirt** \'skwərt\ *verb* [Middle English; akin to Low German *swirtjen* to squirt] (15th century)
*intransitive verb*
**:** to come forth in a sudden rapid stream from a narrow opening **:** SPURT
*transitive verb*
**:** to cause to squirt
— **squirt·er** *noun*
²**squirt** *noun* (15th century)
**1 a :** an instrument (as a syringe) for squirting a liquid **b :** a small quick stream **:** JET **c :** the action or an instance of squirting
**2 a :** an impudent youngster **b :** KID
**squirt gun** *noun* (1803)
**:** WATER PISTOL
**squirting cucumber** *noun* (1802)
**:** a Mediterranean plant (*Ecballium elaterium*) of the gourd family with oblong fruit that bursts from the peduncle when ripe and forcibly ejects the seeds
**squish** \'skwish\ *verb* [alteration of *squash*] (circa 1647)
*transitive verb*
**1 :** SQUASH
**2 :** SQUELCH, SUCK

*intransitive verb*
**:** SQUELCH, SUCK ⟨their wet tennis shoes squished —Frank Noel⟩
— **squish** *noun*
**squishy** \'skwi-shē\ *adjective* **squish·i·er; -est** (circa 1847)
**:** being soft, yielding, and damp
— **squish·i·ness** *noun*
**squoosh** \'skwüsh, 'skwush\ *verb* [by alteration] (1942)
**:** SQUASH
**squush** \'skwəsh\ *verb* [by alteration] (1837)
**:** SQUASH
**Sra·nan** \'srä-nən\ *noun* [Sranan, short for *Sranan Tongo*, literally, Suriname tongue] (1953)
**:** an English-based creole widely spoken in Suriname
**sri** \'srē, 'shrē\ *noun* [Sanskrit *śrī*, literally, beauty, majesty; akin to Greek *kreiōn* ruler, master] (1799)
**:** — used as a conventional title of respect when addressing or speaking of a distinguished Indian
**sRNA** \'es-,är-,en-'ā\ *noun* [soluble *RNA*] (1957)
**:** TRANSFER RNA
**SRO** \,es-(,)är-'ō\ *noun* [single-room occupancy] (1941)
**:** a house, apartment building, or residential hotel in which low-income or welfare tenants live in single rooms
**SS** \,es-'es\ *noun* [German, abbreviation for *Schutzstaffel*, literally, protection echelon] (1932)
**:** a unit of Nazis created to serve as bodyguard to Hitler and later expanded to take charge of intelligence, central security, policing action, and the mass extermination of those they considered inferior or undesirable
**SST** \,es-,es-'tē\ *noun* [*supersonic transport*] (1961)
**:** SUPERSONIC TRANSPORT
¹**-st** — see -EST
²**-st** *symbol*
— used after the figure 1 to indicate the ordinal number *first* ⟨1st⟩ ⟨91st⟩
¹**stab** \'stab\ *noun* [Middle English *stabbe*] (15th century)
**1 :** a wound produced by a pointed weapon
**2 a :** a thrust of a pointed weapon **b :** a jerky thrust
**3 :** EFFORT, TRY
²**stab** *verb* **stabbed; stab·bing** (1530)
*transitive verb*
**1 :** to wound or pierce by the thrust of a pointed weapon
**2 :** THRUST, DRIVE
*intransitive verb*
**:** to thrust or give a wound with or as if with a pointed weapon
— **stab·ber** *noun*
¹**sta·bile** \'stā-,bīl, -,bil\ *adjective* [Latin *stabilis* — more at STABLE] (1896)
**:** STATIONARY, STABLE
²**sta·bile** \-,bēl\ *noun* [probably from French, from Latin *stabilis*, adjective] (1937)
**:** an abstract sculpture or construction similar in appearance to a mobile but made to be stationary
**sta·bil·i·ty** \stə-'bi-lə-tē\ *noun, plural* **-ties** (14th century)
**1 :** the quality, state, or degree of being stable: as **a :** the strength to stand or endure **:** FIRMNESS **b :** the property of a body that causes it when disturbed from a condition of equilibrium or steady motion to develop forces or moments that restore the original condition **c :** resistance to chemical change or to physical disintegration
**2 :** residence for life in one monastery
**sta·bi·lize** \'stā-bə-,līz\ *verb* **-lized; -liz·ing** (1861)
*transitive verb*
**1 :** to make stable, steadfast, or firm

**2 :** to hold steady: as **a :** to maintain the stability of (as an airplane) by means of a stabilizer **b :** to limit fluctuations of (as prices) **:** to establish a minimum price for
*intransitive verb*
**:** to become stable, firm, or steadfast
— **sta·bi·li·za·tion** \,stā-bə-lə-'zā-shən\ *noun*
**sta·bi·liz·er** \'stā-bə-,lī-zər\ *noun* (circa 1909)
**:** one that stabilizes something: as **a :** a substance added to another substance (as an explosive or plastic) or to a system (as an emulsion) to prevent or retard an unwanted alteration of physical state **b :** a gyroscope device to keep ships steady in a heavy sea **c :** an airfoil providing stability for an airplane; *specifically* **:** the fixed horizontal member of the tail assembly — see AIRPLANE illustration
¹**sta·ble** \'stā-bəl\ *noun* [Middle English, from Old French *estable*, from Latin *stabulum*, from *stare* to stand — more at STAND] (13th century)
**1 :** a building in which domestic animals are sheltered and fed; *especially* **:** such a building having stalls or compartments ⟨horse *stable*⟩
**2 a :** the racehorses of one owner **b :** a group of athletes (as boxers) or performers under one management **c :** the racing cars of one owner **d :** GROUP, COLLECTION
— **sta·ble·man** \-mən, -,man\ *noun*
²**stable** *verb* **sta·bled; sta·bling** \-b(ə-)liŋ\ (14th century)
*transitive verb*
**:** to put or keep in a stable
*intransitive verb*
**:** to dwell in or as if in a stable
³**stable** *adjective* **sta·bler** \-b(ə-)lər\; **sta·blest** \-b(ə-)ləst\ [Middle English, from Middle French *estable*, from Latin *stabilis*, from *stare* to stand] (13th century)
**1 a :** firmly established **:** FIXED, STEADFAST **b :** not changing or fluctuating **:** UNVARYING **c :** PERMANENT, ENDURING
**2 a :** steady in purpose **:** firm in resolution **b :** not subject to insecurity or emotional illness **:** SANE, RATIONAL ⟨a *stable* personality⟩
**3 a** (1) **:** placed so as to resist forces tending to cause motion or change of motion (2) **:** designed so as to develop forces that restore the original condition when disturbed from a condition of equilibrium or steady motion **b** (1) **:** not readily altering in chemical makeup or physical state ⟨*stable* emulsions⟩ (2) **:** not spontaneously radioactive
**synonym** see LASTING
— **sta·ble·ness** \-bəl-nəs\ *noun*
— **sta·bly** \-b(ə-)lē\ *adverb*
**stable fly** *noun* (1862)
**:** a biting dipteran fly (*Stomoxys calcitrans*) that resembles the common housefly and is abundant about stables

---

◇ WORD HISTORY
**squirrel** The ultimate source of English *squirrel* is Greek *skiouros*, a word first attested in the early centuries A.D. whose literal meaning is probably "shadow-tailed." This name would appear to come from the Greeks' observation that when the animal sits upright with its bushy tail behind its back, it looks as if it could be shading itself from the sun. The Greek word entered Latin as *sciurus*, which underwent a variety of permutations in the spoken Latin of the Roman provinces. One outcome is presumed to be a diminutive form *scuriolus*, which developed into Old French *escuiruel*. This was eventually borrowed into Middle English as *squirel* or *squerel*. The Old English word for "squirrel" was *ācwern*, with a Germanic and Indo-European pedigree; *ācwern* passed as *ocquerne* or *aquerne* into early Middle English, but no trace of the word is found after the 13th century.

**sta·ble·mate** \'stā-bəl-ˌmāt\ *noun* (1926)
**1** : an animal stabled with another
**2** : a member of a stable

**sta·bler** \-b(ə-)lər\ *noun* (15th century)
: one who keeps a stable

**sta·bling** \-b(ə-)liŋ\ *noun* (15th century)
: accommodation for animals in a building;
*also* : the building for this

**stab·lish** \'sta-blish\ *verb* [Middle English, short for *establissen*] (14th century)
*archaic* : ESTABLISH
— **stab·lish·ment** \-mənt\ *noun, archaic*

**stac·ca·to** \stə-'kä-(ˌ)tō\ *adjective* [Italian, from past participle of *staccare* to detach, from *s-* ex- (from Latin *ex-*) + at*taccare* to attack, attach, perhaps from Old French *estachier* — more at ATTACH] (circa 1724)
**1 a** : cut short or apart in performing : DISCONNECTED ⟨*staccato* notes⟩ **b** : marked by short clear-cut playing or singing of tones or chords ⟨a *staccato* style⟩
**2** : ABRUPT, DISJOINTED
— **staccato** *adverb*
— **staccato** *noun*

**staccato mark** *noun* (circa 1903)
: a pointed vertical stroke or a dot placed over or under a musical note to be produced staccato

**¹stack** \'stak\ *noun* [Middle English *stak*, from Old Norse *stakkr*; akin to Russian *stog* stack and probably to Old English *staca* stake] (14th century)
**1** : a large usually conical pile (as of hay, straw, or grain in the sheaf) left standing in the field for storage
**2 a** : an orderly pile or heap **b** : a large quantity or number
**3** : an English unit of measure especially for firewood that is equal to 108 cubic feet
**4 a** : a number of flues embodied in one structure rising above a roof **b** : a vertical pipe (as to carry off smoke) **c** : the exhaust pipe of an internal combustion engine
**5** : a structure of bookshelves for compact storage of books — usually used in plural
**6** : a pile of chips sold to or won by a poker player
**7 a** : a memory or a section of memory in a computer for temporary storage in which the last item stored is the first retrieved; *also* : a data structure that simulates a stack ⟨a pushdown *stack*⟩ **b** : a computer memory consisting of arrays of memory elements stacked one on top of another

**²stack** (14th century)
*transitive verb*
**1 a** : to arrange in a stack : PILE **b** : to pile in or on ⟨*stacked* the table with books⟩ ⟨*stack* the dishwasher⟩
**2 a** : to arrange secretly for cheating ⟨*stack* a deck of cards⟩ **b** : to arrange or fix so as to make a particular result likely ⟨the odds are *stacked* against us⟩ ⟨will *stack* juries to suit themselves —Patrice Horn⟩
**3 a** : to assign (an airplane) by radio to a particular altitude and position within a group circling before landing **b** : to put into a waiting line ⟨another dozen rigs are *stacked* up and waiting —P. H. Hutchins, Jr.⟩
**4** : COMPARE — used with *against* ⟨such a crime is nothing when *stacked* against a murder —Pete Censky⟩
*intransitive verb*
: to form a stack
— **stack·er** *noun*

**stack·able** \'sta-kə-bəl\ *adjective* (1958)
: easily arranged in a stack

**stacked** \'stakt\ *adjective* (1942)
*of a woman* : being shapely and having large breasts

**stack up** *intransitive verb* (1896)
**1** : to add up : TOTAL
**2** : MEASURE UP, COMPARE — usually used with *against*

**stac·te** \'stak-tē\ *noun* [Middle English *stacten*, from Latin *stacte*, from Greek *staktē*,

from feminine of *staktos* oozing out in drops, from *stazein* to drip] (1535)
: a sweet spice used by the ancient Jews in preparing incense

**stad·dle** \'sta-dᵊl\ *noun* [Middle English *stathel* base, support, bottom of a stack, from Old English *statho* base; akin to Old High German *stān* to stand — more at STAND] (15th century)
: a base (as of piling) for a stack of hay or straw

**stade** \'stād\ *noun* [Middle French *estade*, from Latin *stadium*] (1537)
: STADIUM 1a

**sta·dia** \'stā-dē-ə\ *noun* [Italian, probably from Latin, plural of *stadium*] (1865)
: a surveying method for determination of distances and differences of elevation by means of a telescopic instrument having two horizontal lines through which the marks on a graduated rod are observed; *also* : the instrument or rod

**sta·di·um** \'stā-dē-əm\ *noun, plural* **-dia** \-dē-ə\ *or* **-di·ums** [Middle English, from Latin, from Greek *stadion*] (14th century)
**1 a** : any of various ancient Greek units of length ranging in value from 607 to 738 feet (about 185 to 225 meters) **b** : an ancient Roman unit of length equal to 607 feet (185 meters)
**2 a** : a course for footraces in ancient Greece originally one stadium in length **b** : a tiered structure with seats for spectators surrounding an ancient Greek running track **c** : a large usually unroofed building with tiers of seats for spectators at sports events
**3** [New Latin, from Latin] : a stage in a life history; *especially* : one between successive molts ◆

**stadt·hold·er** \'stat-ˌhōl-dər\ *noun* [part translation of Dutch *stadhouder*, from *stad* place + *houder* holder] (1668)
**1** : a viceroy in a province of the Netherlands
**2** : a chief executive officer of the provinces that formed a union leading to establishment of the Netherlands
— **stadt·hold·er·ate** \-də-rət\ *noun*
— **stadt·hold·er·ship** \-dər-ˌship\ *noun*

**¹staff** \'staf\ *noun, plural* **staffs** \'stafs, 'stavz\ *or* **staves** \'stavz, 'stāvz\ [Middle English *staf*, from Old English *stæf*; akin to Old High German *stab* staff, Sanskrit *stabhnāti* he supports] (before 12th century)
**1 a** : a long stick carried in the hand for support in walking **b** : a supporting rod: as (1) *archaic* : SHAFT 1a(1) (2) : a crosspiece in a ladder or chair : RUNG (3) : FLAGSTAFF (4) : a pivoted arbor **c** : CLUB, CUDGEL
**2 a** : CROSIER **b** : a rod carried as a symbol of office or authority
**3** : the horizontal lines with their spaces on which music is written — called also *stave*
**4** : any of various graduated sticks or rules used for measuring : ROD
**5** *plural* **staffs a** : the officers chiefly responsible for the internal operations of an institution or business **b** : a group of officers appointed to assist a civil executive or commanding officer **c** : military or naval officers not eligible for operational command **d** : the personnel who assist a director in carrying out an assigned task **e** *plural* **staff** : a member of a staff
— **staff** *adjective*

**²staff** *transitive verb* (1859)
**1** : to supply with a staff or with workers
**2** : to serve as a staff member of

**³staff** *noun* [probably from German *staffieren* to trim] (1892)
: a building material having a plaster of Paris base and used in exterior wall coverings of temporary buildings

**staff·er** \'sta-fər\ *noun* (1941)
: a member of a staff (as of a newspaper)

**staff officer** *noun* (1777)
: a commissioned officer assigned to a military commander's staff — compare LINE OFFICER

**staff of life** (1638)
: a staple of diet; *especially* : BREAD

**Staf·ford·shire bull terrier** \'sta-fərd-ˌshir-, -shər-\ *noun* [*Staffordshire*, England] (1901)
: any of a breed of compact muscular terriers that have a short stiff glossy coat

**Staffordshire bull terrier**

**staff sergeant** *noun* (1851)
: a noncommissioned officer ranking in the army above a sergeant and below a platoon sergeant or sergeant first class, in the air force above a sergeant and below a technical sergeant, and in the marine corps above a sergeant and below a gunnery sergeant

**staff sergeant major** *noun* (1967)
: a noncommissioned officer in the army ranking above a master sergeant

**staff tree** *noun* (circa 1633)
: any of a genus (*Celastrus* of the family Celastraceae, the staff-tree family) of mostly twining shrubby plants including the common bittersweet

**¹stag** \'stag\ *noun, plural* **stags** [Middle English *stagge*, from Old English *stagga*; akin to Old Norse andar*steggi* drake] (12th century)
**1** *or plural* **stag** : an adult male red deer; *also* : the male of various other deer (especially genus *Cervus*)
**2** *chiefly Scottish* : a young horse; *especially* : a young unbroken stallion
**3** : a male animal castrated after maturity — compare STEER 1
**4** : a young adult male domestic fowl
**5 a** : a social gathering of men only **b** : one who attends a dance or party without a companion

**²stag** *verb* **stagged; stag·ging** [*stag* (informer)] (circa 1823)
*transitive verb*
*British* : to spy on
*intransitive verb*
: to attend a dance or party without a companion

**³stag** *adjective* (1843)
**1 a** : restricted to men ⟨a *stag* party⟩ **b** : intended or suitable for a gathering of men only; *especially* : PORNOGRAPHIC ⟨*stag* movies⟩
**2** : unaccompanied by someone of the opposite sex ⟨*stag* women⟩
— **stag** *adverb*

---

◇ **WORD HISTORY**
**stadium** In ancient Greece a *stadion* was a unit of measurement equal to about 185 meters. One of the most important events in the ancient Olympic Games was a footrace exactly one *stadion* long. The course on which the race was run, including artificial embankments around the sides to accommodate spectators, also became known as a *stadion*. The Romans borrowed the word as *stadium*. When *stadium* first appeared in English-language contexts, in the 14th century, it was with reference to the Greco-Roman unit of measurement or to the racecourse at Olympia or one modeled after it. Over time *stadium* has come to be used of variously sized arenas surrounded by tiered seating and used for a variety of athletic contests.

---

\ə\ abut \ᵊ\ kitten \ər\ further \a\ ash \ā\ ace
\ä\ mop, mar \aú\ out \ch\ chin \e\ bet \ē\ easy
\g\ go \i\ hit \ī\ ice \j\ job \ŋ\ sing \ō\ go
\ó\ law \ói\ boy \th\ thin \t̷h\ the \ü\ loot \ú\ foot
\y\ yet \zh\ vision    *see also* Guide to Pronunciation

**stag beetle** *noun* (1681)
: any of a family (Lucanidae) of mostly large lamellicorn beetles having males with long and often branched mandibles suggesting the antlers of a stag

¹**stage** \'stāj\ *noun* [Middle English, from Middle French *estage*, from (assumed) Vulgar Latin *staticum*, from Latin *stare* to stand — more at STAND] (14th century)
**1 a** : one of a series of positions or stations one above the other : STEP **b** : the height of the surface of a river above an arbitrary zero point ⟨flood *stage*⟩
**2 a** (1) : a raised platform (2) : the part of a theater on which the acting takes place and which often includes the wings (3) : the acting profession : the theater as an occupation or activity (4) : SOUNDSTAGE **b** : a center of attention or scene of action
**3 a** : a scaffold for workmen **b** : the small platform of a microscope on which an object is placed for examination
**4 a** : a place of rest formerly provided for those traveling by stagecoach : STATION **b** : the distance between two stopping places on a road **c** : STAGECOACH
**5 a** : a period or step in a progress, activity, or development; *especially* : one of the distinguishable periods of growth and development of a plant or animal ⟨the larval *stage* of an insect⟩ **b** : one passing through a (specified) stage
**6** : an element or part of an electronic device (as an amplifier)
**7** : one of two or more sections of a rocket that have their own fuel and engine
— **stage·ful** \-,ful\ *noun*
— **stage·like** \-,līk\ *adjective*
— **on the stage** : in or into the acting profession

²**stage** *transitive verb* **staged; stag·ing** (1879)
**1** : to produce (as a play) on a stage
**2** : to produce or cause to happen for public view or public effect ⟨*stage* a track meet⟩ ⟨*stage* a hunger strike⟩
— **stage·able** \'stā-jə-bəl\ *adjective*

³**stage** *adjective* (1824)
: intended to represent a type or stereotype ⟨a *stage* Irishman⟩ ⟨a *stage* French accent⟩

**stage business** *noun* (1825)
: BUSINESS 6

**stage·coach** \'stāj-,kōch\ *noun* (1658)
: a horse-drawn passenger and mail coach running on a regular schedule between established stops

**stage·craft** \-,kraft\ *noun* (1882)
: the effective management of theatrical devices or techniques

**stage direction** *noun* (1790)
: a description (as of a character or setting) or direction (as to indicate stage business) provided in the text of a play

**stage director** *noun* (1782)
**1** : DIRECTOR c
**2** : STAGE MANAGER

**stage fright** *noun* (1878)
: nervousness felt at appearing before an audience

**stage·hand** \'stāj-,hand\ *noun* (circa 1902)
: a stage worker who handles scenery, properties, or lights

**stage left** *noun* (1931)
: the left part of a stage from the viewpoint of one who faces the audience

**stage–man·age** \-,ma-nij\ *transitive verb* [back-formation from *stage manager*] (1879)
**1 a** : to arrange or exhibit so as to achieve a desired effect **b** : to arrange or direct from behind the scenes
**2** : to act as stage manager for
— **stage management** *noun*
**stage manager** *noun* (1805)

: one who supervises the physical aspects of a stage production, assists the director during rehearsals, and is in charge of the stage during a performance

**stag·er** \'stā-jər\ *noun* (1570)
: an experienced person : VETERAN

**stage right** *noun* (1931)
: the right part of a stage from the viewpoint of one who faces the audience

**stage set** *noun* (1861)
: scenery and properties designed and arranged for a particular scene in a play

**stage-struck** \'stāj-,strək\ *adjective* (1813)
: fascinated by the stage; *especially* : having an ardent desire to become an actor

**stage whisper** *noun* (circa 1865)
**1** : a loud whisper by an actor that is audible to the spectators but is supposed for dramatic effect not to be heard by one or more of the actors
**2** : an audible whisper
— **stage–whisper** *verb*

**stag·fla·tion** \,stag-'flā-shən\ *noun* [blend of *stagnation* and *inflation*] (1965)
: persistent inflation combined with stagnant consumer demand and relatively high unemployment
— **stag·fla·tion·ary** \-shə-,ner-ē\ *adjective*

¹**stag·ger** \'sta-gər\ *verb* **stag·gered; stag·ger·ing** \-g(ə-)riŋ\ [alteration of earlier *stacker*, from Middle English *stakeren*, from Old Norse *stakra*, frequentative of *staka* to push; perhaps akin to Old English *staca* stake — more at STAKE] (15th century)
*intransitive verb*
**1 a** : to reel from side to side : TOTTER **b** : to move on unsteadily
**2** : to waver in purpose or action : HESITATE
**3** : to rock violently ⟨the ship *staggered*⟩
*transitive verb*
**1** : to cause to doubt or hesitate : PERPLEX
**2** : to cause to reel or totter
**3** : to arrange in any of various zigzags, alternations, or overlappings of position or time ⟨*stagger* work shifts⟩ ⟨*stagger* teeth on a cutter⟩
— **stag·ger·er** \-gər-ər\ *noun*

²**stagger** *noun* (1577)
**1** *plural but singular or plural in construction* : an abnormal condition of domestic mammals and birds associated with damage to the central nervous system and marked by incoordination and a reeling unsteady gait
**2** : a reeling or unsteady gait or stance
**3** : an arrangement in which the leading edge of the upper wing of a biplane is advanced over that of the lower

³**stagger** *adjective* (1875)
: marked by an alternating or overlapping pattern

**stag·ger·bush** \'sta-gər-,bush\ *noun* (1847)
: a shrubby heath (*Lyonia mariana*) of the eastern U.S. that is poisonous to livestock

**staggering** *adjective* (1530)
: so great as to cause one to stagger : ASTONISHING, OVERWHELMING ⟨a *staggering* feat⟩ ⟨*staggering* medical bills⟩
— **stag·ger·ing·ly** \'sta-g(ə-)riŋ-lē\ *adverb*

**stag·gery** \'sta-g(ə-)rē\ *adjective* (1778)
: UNSTEADY

**stag·gy** \'sta-gē\ *adjective* (1918)
: having the appearance of a mature male — used of female or castrated male domestic animals

**stag·horn coral** \'stag-,hórn-\ *noun* (1884)
: any of several large branching corals (genus *Acropora* and especially *A. cervicornis*) that somewhat resemble antlers

**staghorn sumac** *noun* (circa 1868)
: a sumac (*Rhus typhina*) of eastern North America that is a shrub or small tree with velvety-pubescent branches and flower stalks, leaves turning brilliant red in fall, and dense panicles of greenish yellow flowers followed by hairy crimson fruits

**stag·hound** \'stag-,haund\ *noun* (1707)

: a hound formerly used in hunting the stag and other large animals; *specifically* : a large heavy hound resembling the English foxhound

**staghorn sumac**

**stag·ing** \'stā-jiŋ\ *noun* (14th century)
**1** : SCAFFOLDING
**2 a** : the business of running stagecoaches **b** : the act of journeying in stagecoaches
**3** : the putting of a play on the stage
**4 a** : the moving of troops or matériel forward in several stages **b** : the assembling of troops or matériel in transit in a particular place

**staging area** *noun* (1943)
: an area in which participants in a new operation or mission are assembled and readied

**Stag·i·rite** \'sta-jə-,rīt\ *noun* [Greek *Stagiritēs*, from *Stagira*, city in ancient Macedonia] (circa 1620)
: a native or resident of Stagira ⟨Aristotle the *Stagirite*⟩

**stag·nant** \'stag-nənt\ *adjective* (1666)
**1 a** : not flowing in a current or stream ⟨*stagnant* water⟩ **b** : STALE ⟨long disuse had made the air *stagnant* and foul —Bram Stoker⟩
**2** : not advancing or developing
— **stag·nan·cy** \-nən(t)-sē\ *noun*
— **stag·nant·ly** *adverb*

**stag·nate** \'stag-,nāt\ *intransitive verb* **stag·nat·ed; stag·nat·ing** [Latin *stagnatus*, past participle of *stagnare*, from *stagnum* body of standing water] (1669)
: to become or remain stagnant
— **stag·na·tion** \stag-'nā-shən\ *noun*

**stagy** \'stā-jē\ *or* **stag·ey** *adjective* **stag·i·er; -est** (1860)
: of or characteristic of the stage; *especially* : marked by pretense or artificiality : THEATRICAL
— **stag·i·ly** \-jə-lē\ *adverb*
— **stag·i·ness** \-jē-nəs\ *noun*

¹**staid** \'stād\ *adjective* [from past participle of ³*stay*] (1557)
: marked by settled sedateness and often prim self-restraint : SOBER, GRAVE
*synonym* see SERIOUS
— **staid·ly** *adverb*
— **staid·ness** *noun*

²**staid** *past and past participle of* STAY

¹**stain** \'stān\ *verb* [Middle English *steynen*, partly from Middle French *desteindre* to discolor & partly of Scandinavian origin; akin to Old Norse *steina* to paint — more at DISTAIN] (14th century)
*transitive verb*
**1** : to suffuse with color
**2** : DISCOLOR, SOIL
**3 a** : to taint with guilt, vice, or corruption **b** : to bring reproach on
**4** : to color (as wood, glass, or cloth) by processes affecting chemically or otherwise the material itself
*intransitive verb*
: to receive a stain
— **stain·able** \'stā-nə-bəl\ *adjective*
— **stain·er** \'stā-nər\ *noun*

²**stain** *noun* (1583)
**1 a** : a soiled or discolored spot **b** : a natural spot of color contrasting with the ground
**2** : a taint of guilt : STIGMA
**3 a** : a preparation (as of dye or pigment) used in staining; *especially* : one capable of penetrating the pores of wood **b** : a dye or mixture of dyes used in microscopy to make visible minute and transparent structures, to differentiate tissue elements, or to produce specific chemical reactions
— **stain-proof** \-,prüf\ *adjective*

**stain·abil·i·ty** \,stā-nə-'bi-lə-tē\ *noun* (1890)
: the capacity of cells and cell parts to stain specifically and consistently with particular dyes and stains

**stained glass** *noun* (1791)
: glass colored or stained (as by fusing metallic oxides into it) for decorative applications (as in windows)

¹**stain·less** \'stān-ləs\ *adjective* (1586)
**1 a :** free from stain or stigma **b :** highly resistant to stain or corrosion
**2 :** made from materials resistant to stain
— **stain·less·ly** *adverb*

²**stainless** *noun* (1945)
: tableware made of stainless steel

**stainless steel** *noun* (1920)
: an alloy of steel with chromium and sometimes another element (as nickel or molybdenum) that is practically immune to rusting and ordinary corrosion

**stair** \'star, 'ster\ *noun* [Middle English *steir,* from Old English *stæger;* akin to Old English & Old High German *stīgan* to rise, Greek *steichein* to walk] (before 12th century)
**1 :** a series of steps or flights of steps for passing from one level to another — often used in plural but singular or plural in construction ⟨a narrow private *stairs* —Lewis Mumford⟩
**2 :** a single step of a stairway

**stair·case** \-,kās\ *noun* (1624)
**1 :** the structure containing a stairway
**2 :** a flight of stairs with the supporting framework, casing, and balusters

**stair·way** \-,wā\ *noun* (1767)
: one or more flights of stairs usually with landings to pass from one level to another

**stair·well** \-,wel\ *noun* (1920)
: a vertical shaft in which stairs are located

¹**stake** \'stāk\ *noun* [Middle English, from Old English *staca;* akin to Middle Low German *stake* stake and perhaps to Latin *tignum* beam] (before 12th century)
**1 :** a pointed piece of wood or other material driven or to be driven into the ground as a marker or support
**2 a :** a post to which a person is bound for execution by burning **b :** execution by burning at a stake
**3 a :** something that is staked for gain or loss **b :** the prize in a contest **c :** an interest or share in an undertaking (as a commercial venture)
**4 :** a Mormon territorial jurisdiction comprising a group of wards
**5 :** an upright stick at the side or end of a vehicle to retain the load
**6 :** GRUBSTAKE
— **at stake :** at issue **:** in jeopardy

²**stake** *transitive verb* **staked; stak·ing** (14th century)
**1 :** to mark the limits of by or as if by stakes
**2 :** to tether to a stake
**3 :** BET, WAGER
**4 :** to fasten up or support (as plants) with stakes
**5 :** to back financially
**6 :** GRUBSTAKE
— **stake a claim :** to assert a title or right to something by or as if by placing stakes to satisfy a legal requirement

**stake body** *noun* (1907)
: an open motortruck body consisting of a platform with stakes inserted along the outside edges to retain a load

**stake·hold·er** \'stāk-,hōl-dər\ *noun* (1708)
: a person entrusted with the stakes of bettors

**stake·out** \'stā-,kaút\ *noun* (circa 1942)
: a surveillance maintained by the police of an area or a person suspected of criminal activity

**stake out** *transitive verb* (1951)
**1 :** to assign (as a police officer) to an area usually to conduct a surveillance
**2 :** to maintain a stakeout of

**stake race** *noun* (1896)

: a horse race in which the prize offered is made up at least in part of money (as entry fees) put up by the owners of the horses entered

**stake truck** *noun* (1907)
: a truck having a stake body

**Sta·kha·nov·ite** \stə-'kä-nə-,vīt\ *noun* [translation of Russian *stakhanovets,* from Alexei G. *Stakhanov* (died 1977) Russian miner] (1935)
: a Soviet industrial worker awarded recognition and special privileges for output beyond production norms
— **Sta·kha·nov·ism** \-,vi-zəm\ *noun*

**sta·lac·tite** \stə-'lak-,tīt *also* 'sta-lək-\ *noun* [New Latin *stalactites,* from Greek *stalaktos* dripping, from *stalassein* to let drip] (1677)
: a deposit of calcium carbonate (as calcite) resembling an icicle hanging from the roof or sides of a cavern
— **sta·lac·tit·ic** \,sta-(,)lak-'ti-tik, stə-,\ *adjective*

**sta·lag** \'stä-,läg\ *noun* [German, short for *Stammlager* base camp, from *Stamm* base + *Lager* camp] (1940)
: a German prison camp for noncommissioned officers or enlisted men; *broadly* : PRISON CAMP 2

**sta·lag·mite** \stə-'lag-,mīt *also* 'sta-ləg-\ *noun* [New Latin *stalagmites,* from Greek *stalagma* drop or *stalagmos* dripping, from *stalassein* to let drip] (1681)
: a deposit of calcium carbonate like an inverted stalactite formed on the floor of a cave by the drip of calcareous water
— **sta·lag·mit·ic** \,sta-(,)lag-'mi-tik, stə-,\ *adjective*

¹**stale** \'stā(ə)l\ *adjective* **stal·er; stal·est** [Middle English, aged (of ale), not fresh; akin to Middle Dutch *stel* stale] (15th century)
**1 :** tasteless or unpalatable from age
**2 :** tedious from familiarity
**3 :** impaired in legal force or effect by reason of being allowed to rest without timely use, action, or demand ⟨a *stale* affidavit⟩ ⟨a *stale* debt⟩
**4 :** impaired in vigor or effectiveness
— **stale·ly** \'stā(ə)l-lē\ *adverb*
— **stale·ness** *noun*

²**stale** *verb* **staled; stal·ing** (1599)
*transitive verb*
**1 :** to make stale
**2** *archaic* **:** to make common **:** CHEAPEN
*intransitive verb*
: to become stale

³**stale** *intransitive verb* **staled; stal·ing** [Middle English; akin to Middle Low German *stallen* to urinate, *stal* urine of horses] (15th century)
: URINATE — used chiefly of camels and horses

⁴**stale** *noun* (1548)
: urine of a domestic animal (as a horse)

¹**stale·mate** \'stā(ə)l-,māt\ *noun* [obsolete English *stale* stalemate + English ¹*mate*] (1765)
**1 :** a drawing position in chess in which only the king can move and although not in check can move only into check
**2 :** a drawn contest **:** DEADLOCK; *also* : the state of being stalemated

²**stalemate** *transitive verb* (1765)
: to bring into a stalemate

**Sta·lin·ism** \'stä-lə-,ni-zəm, 'sta-\ *noun* (1927)
: the political, economic, and social principles and policies associated with Stalin; *especially* : the theory and practice of communism developed by Stalin from Marxism-Leninism and marked especially by rigid authoritarianism,

widespread use of terror, and often emphasis on Russian nationalism
— **Sta·lin·ist** \-nist\ *noun or adjective*
— **Sta·lin·ize** \-,nīz\ *transitive verb*
— **Sta·lin·oid** \-,nóid\ *noun or adjective*

¹**stalk** \'stók\ *noun* [Middle English *stalke;* akin to Old English *stela* stalk, support] (14th century)
**1 :** a slender upright object or supporting or connecting part; *especially* : PEDUNCLE ⟨the *stalk* of a crinoid⟩
**2 a :** the main stem of an herbaceous plant often with its dependent parts **b :** a part of a plant (as a petiole, stipe, or peduncle) that supports another
— **stalked** \'stókt\ *adjective*
— **stalk·less** \'stó-kləs\ *adjective*
— **stalky** \'stó-kē\ *adjective*

²**stalk** *verb* [Middle English, from Old English be*stealcian;* akin to Old English *stelan* to steal — more at STEAL] (14th century)
*intransitive verb*
**1 :** to pursue quarry or prey stealthily
**2 :** to walk stiffly or haughtily
*transitive verb*
**1 :** to pursue by stalking
**2 :** to go through (an area) in search of prey or quarry ⟨*stalk* the woods for deer⟩
— **stalk·er** *noun*

³**stalk** *noun* (14th century)
**1 :** the act of stalking
**2 :** a stalking gait

**stalk·ing–horse** \'stó-kiŋ-,hórs\ *noun* (1519)
**1 :** a horse or a figure like a horse behind which a hunter stalks game
**2 :** something used to mask a purpose
**3 :** a candidate put forward to divide the opposition or to conceal someone's real candidacy

¹**stall** \'stól\ *noun* [Middle English, from Old English *steall;* akin to Old High German *stal* place, stall and perhaps to Latin *locus* (Old Latin *stlocus*) place] (before 12th century)
**1 a :** a compartment for a domestic animal in a stable or barn **b :** a space marked off for parking a motor vehicle
**2 a :** a seat in the chancel of a church with back and sides wholly or partly enclosed **b :** a church pew **c** *chiefly British* **:** a front orchestra seat in a theater — usually used in plural
**3 :** a booth, stand, or counter at which articles are displayed for sale
**4 :** a protective sheath for a finger or toe
**5 :** a small compartment ⟨a shower *stall*⟩

²**stall** (14th century)
*transitive verb*
**1 :** to put into or keep in a stall
**2** *obsolete* **:** to install in office
**3 a :** to bring to a standstill **:** BLOCK; *especially* **:** MIRE **b :** to cause (an engine) to stop usually inadvertently **c :** to cause (an aircraft or airfoil) to go into a stall
*intransitive verb*
**1 :** to come to a standstill (as from mired wheels or engine failure)
**2 :** to experience a stall in flying

³**stall** *noun* (1916)
: the condition of an airfoil or aircraft in which excessive angle of attack causes disruption of airflow with attendant loss of lift

⁴**stall** *noun* [alteration of *stale* lure] (1903)
: a ruse to deceive or delay

⁵**stall** (1903)
*intransitive verb*
: to play for time **:** DELAY
*transitive verb*
: to hold off, divert, or delay by evasion or deception

**stall–feed** \'stól-,fēd\ *transitive verb* **-fed** \-,fed\; **-feed·ing** (1554)

: to feed in a stall especially so as to fatten ⟨*stall-feed* an ox⟩

**stall·hold·er** \-ˌhōl-dər\ *noun* (1881)
*chiefly British* : one who manages a stall at which articles are sold

**stal·lion** \'stal-yən\ *noun* [Middle English *stalion,* from Middle French *estalon,* of Germanic origin; akin to Old High German *stal* stall] (14th century)
: an uncastrated male horse : a male horse kept for breeding; *also* : a male animal (as a dog or a sheep) kept primarily as a stud

¹**stal·wart** \'stȯl-wərt\ *adjective* [Middle English, alteration of *stalworth,* from Old English *stælwierthe* serviceable] (15th century)
: marked by outstanding strength and vigor of body, mind, or spirit ⟨*stalwart* common sense⟩
**synonym** see STRONG
— **stal·wart·ly** *adverb*
— **stal·wart·ness** *noun*

²**stalwart** *noun* (15th century)
**1** : a stalwart person
**2** : an unwavering partisan

**stal·worth** \'stȯl-(ˌ)wərth\ *archaic variant of* STALWART

**sta·men** \'stā-mən\ *noun, plural* **stamens** *also* **sta·mi·na** \'stā-mə-nə, 'sta-\ [Latin, warp, thread, from *stare* to stand — more at STAND] (1668)
: a microsporophyll of a seed plant; *specifically* : the pollen-producing male organ of a flower that consists of an anther and a filament — see FLOWER illustration

**stamin-** *combining form* [Latin *stamin-, stamen*]
: stamen ⟨*stamin*odium⟩

**stam·i·na** \'sta-mə-nə\ *noun* [Latin, plural of *stamen* warp, thread of life spun by the Fates] (1726)
: STAYING POWER, ENDURANCE ◆

**sta·mi·nate** \'stā-mə-nət, 'sta-, -ˌnāt\ *adjective* (circa 1850)
**1** : having or producing stamens
**2** *of a diclinous flower* : having stamens but no pistils

**sta·mi·no·di·um** \ˌstā-mə-'nō-dē-əm, ˌsta-\ *noun, plural* **-dia** \-dē-ə\ [New Latin, from *stamin-* + *-odium* thing resembling, from Greek *-ōdēs* like] (circa 1821)
: an abortive or sterile stamen

**stam·mel** \'sta-məl\ *noun* [probably from *stamin* a woolen fabric] (1530)
**1** *obsolete* : a coarse woolen clothing fabric usually dyed red and used sometimes for undershirts of penitents
**2** *archaic* : the bright red color of stammel

**stam·mer** \'sta-mər\ *verb* **stam·mered;** **stam·mer·ing** \'sta-mə-riŋ, 'stam-riŋ\ [Middle English *stameren,* from Old English *stamerian;* akin to Old High German *stamalōn* to stammer, Old Norse *stemma* to hinder, damn up — more at STEM] (before 12th century)
*intransitive verb*
: to make involuntary stops and repetitions in speaking : HALT — compare STUTTER
*transitive verb*
: to utter with involuntary stops or repetitions
— **stammer** *noun*
— **stam·mer·er** \-mər-ər\ *noun*

¹**stamp** \'stamp; *verb transitive & verb intransitive are also* 'stämp *or* 'stȯmb\ *verb* [Middle English; akin to Old High German *stampfōn* to stamp and perhaps to Greek *stembein* to shake up] (13th century)
*transitive verb*
**1** : to pound or crush with a pestle or a heavy instrument
**2 a** (1) : to strike or beat forcibly with the bottom of the foot (2) : to bring down (the foot) forcibly **b** : to extinguish or destroy by or as if by stamping with the foot — usually used with *out* ⟨*stamp* out cancer⟩
**3 a** : IMPRESS, IMPRINT ⟨*stamp* "paid" on the bill⟩ **b** : to attach a stamp to

**4** : to cut out, bend, or form with a stamp or die
**5 a** : to provide with a distinctive character ⟨*stamped* with a dreary, institutionalized look —Bernard Taper⟩ **b** : CHARACTERIZE
*intransitive verb*
**1** : POUND 1
**2** : to strike or thrust the foot forcibly or noisily downward

²**stamp** *noun* (15th century)
**1** : a device or instrument for stamping
**2** : the impression or mark made by stamping or imprinting
**3 a** : a distinctive character, indication, or mark **b** : a lasting imprint
**4** : the act of stamping
**5** : a stamped or printed paper affixed in evidence that a tax has been paid; *also* : POSTAGE STAMP
— **stamp·less** *adjective*

¹**stam·pede** \(ˌ)stam-'pēd\ *noun* [American Spanish *estampida,* from Spanish, crash, from *estampar* to stamp, of Germanic origin; akin to Old High German *stampfōn* to stamp] (1828)
**1** : a wild headlong rush or flight of frightened animals
**2** : a mass movement of people at a common impulse
**3** : an extended festival combining a rodeo with exhibitions, contests, and social events

²**stampede** *verb* **stam·ped·ed; stam·ped·ing** (1838)
*transitive verb*
**1** : to cause to run away in headlong panic
**2** : to cause (as a group of people) to act on sudden or rash impulse
*intransitive verb*
**1** : to flee headlong in panic
**2** : to act on mass impulse
— **stam·ped·er** *noun*

**stamp·er** \'stam-pər, 'stäm-, 'stȯm-; *compare* ¹STAMP\ *noun* (14th century)
: one that stamps: as **a** : a worker who performs an industrial stamping operation **b** : an implement for pounding or stamping **c** : any of various stamping machines

**stamping ground** \'stam-piŋ, 'stäm-, 'stȯm-\ *noun* (1786)
: a favorite or habitual resort; *also* : familiar territory

**stamp·ing mill** \'stam-piŋ-\ *noun* (1552)
: STAMP MILL

**stamp mill** \'stamp-\ *noun* (1749)
: a mill in which ore is crushed with stamps; *also* : a machine for stamping ore

**stamp tax** *noun* (1797)
: a tax collected by means of a stamp purchased and affixed (as to a deck of playing cards); *specifically* : such a tax on a document (as a deed or promissory note) — called also *stamp duty*

**stance** \'stan(t)s\ *noun* [Middle French *estance* position, posture, stay, from (assumed) Vulgar Latin *stantia,* from Latin *stant-, stans,* present participle of *stare* to stand] (14th century)
**1** *chiefly Scottish* **a** : STATION **b** : SITE
**2 a** : a way of standing or being placed : POSTURE **b** : intellectual or emotional attitude ⟨took an antiwar *stance*⟩
**3 a** : the position of the feet of a golfer or batter preparatory to making a swing **b** : the position of both body and feet from which an athlete starts or operates

¹**stanch** \'stȯnch, 'stänch, 'stanch\ *transitive verb* [Middle English *staunchen,* from Middle French *estancher,* perhaps from (assumed) Vulgar Latin *stanticare,* from Latin *stant-, stans,* present participle] (14th century)
**1** : to check or stop the flowing of ⟨*stanched* her tears⟩; *also* : to stop the flow of blood from (a wound)
**2** *archaic* : ALLAY, EXTINGUISH

**3 a** : to stop or check in its course ⟨trying to *stanch* the crime wave⟩ **b** : to make watertight : stop up
— **stanch·er** *noun*

²**stanch** *variant of* STAUNCH

**stan·chion** \'stan-chən\ *noun* [Middle English *stanchon,* from Middle French *estanchon,* from Old French, diminutive of *estance* stay, prop] (15th century)
**1** : an upright bar, post, or support (as for a roof)
**2** : a device that fits loosely around the neck of an animal (as a cow) and limits forward and backward motion (as in a stall)
— **stan·chioned** \-chənd\ *adjective*

¹**stand** \'stand\ *verb* **stood** \'stüd\; **standing** [Middle English, from Old English *standan;* akin to Old High German *stantan, stān* to stand, Latin *stare,* Greek *histanai* to cause to stand, set, *histasthai* to stand, be standing] (before 12th century)
*intransitive verb*
**1 a** : to support oneself on the feet in an erect position **b** : to be a specified height when fully erect ⟨*stands* six feet two⟩ **c** : to rise to an erect position
**2 a** : to take up or maintain a specified position or posture ⟨*stand* aside⟩ ⟨can you *stand* on your head⟩ **b** : to maintain one's position ⟨*stand* firm⟩
**3** : to be in a particular state or situation ⟨*stands* accused⟩
**4** : to hold a course at sea
**5** *obsolete* : HESITATE
**6 a** : to have or maintain a relative position in or as if in a graded scale ⟨*stands* first in the class⟩ **b** : to be in a position to gain or lose because of an action taken or a commitment made ⟨*stands* to make quite a profit⟩
**7** *chiefly British* : to be a candidate : RUN
**8 a** : to rest or remain upright on a base or lower end ⟨a clock *stood* on the mantle⟩ **b** : to occupy a place or location ⟨the house *stands* on a knoll⟩
**9 a** : to remain stationary or inactive ⟨the car *stood* in the garage for a week⟩ **b** : to gather slowly and remain ⟨tears *standing* in her eyes⟩
**10** : AGREE, ACCORD — used chiefly in the expression *it stands to reason*
**11 a** : to exist in a definite written or printed form ⟨copy a passage exactly as it *stands*⟩ **b** : to remain valid or efficacious ⟨the order given last week still *stands*⟩
**12** *of a male animal* : to be available as a sire — used especially of horses
*transitive verb*

**1 a :** to endure or undergo successfully ⟨this book will *stand* the test of time⟩ **b :** to tolerate without flinching **:** bear courageously ⟨*stands* pain well⟩ **c :** to endure the presence or personality of ⟨can't *stand* the boss⟩ **d :** to derive benefit or enjoyment from ⟨you look like you could *stand* a drink⟩
**2 :** to remain firm in the face of ⟨*stand* a siege⟩
**3 :** to submit to ⟨*stand* trial⟩
**4 a :** to perform the duty of ⟨*stand* guard⟩ **b :** to participate in (a military formation)
**5 :** to pay the cost of (a treat) **:** pay for ⟨I'll *stand* you a dinner⟩ ⟨*stand* drinks⟩
**6 :** to cause to stand **:** set upright
**7 :** to make available for breeding ⟨*stand* a stallion⟩
**synonym** see BEAR
— **stand·er** *noun*
— **stand a chance :** to have a chance
— **stand for 1 :** to be a symbol for **:** REPRESENT **2 :** to put up with **:** PERMIT
— **stand on 1 :** to depend on **2 :** to insist on ⟨never *stands on* ceremony⟩
— **stand one's ground :** to maintain one's position
— **stand on one's own feet :** to think or act independently
— **stand treat :** to pay the cost of food, drink, or entertainment for others in a group
²**stand** *noun* (1592)
**1 :** an act of stopping or staying in one place
**2 a :** a halt for defense or resistance **b :** an often defensive effort of some duration or degree of success ⟨a goal-line *stand*⟩ **c** (1) **:** a stop made to give a performance ⟨a 6-game *stand* at home⟩ (2) **:** a town where such a stop is made
**3 a :** a place or post where one stands **b :** a strongly or aggressively held position especially on a debatable issue
**4 a :** the place taken by a witness for testifying in court **b** *plural* (1) **:** a section of the tiered seats for spectators of a sport or spectacle (2) **:** the occupants of such seats **c :** a raised platform (as for a speaker) serving as a point of vantage
**5 a :** a small often open-air structure for a small retail business ⟨a vegetable *stand*⟩ ⟨a hot dog *stand*⟩ **b :** a site fit for business opportunity
**6 :** a place where a passenger vehicle stops or parks ⟨a taxi *stand*⟩
**7 :** HIVE 2
**8 :** a frame on or in which something may be placed for support
**9 :** a group of plants growing in a continuous area
**10 :** a standing posture
**stand–alone** \'stan-də-ˌlōn\ *adjective* (1966)
**:** SELF-CONTAINED; *especially* **:** operating or capable of operating independently of a computer system ⟨a *stand-alone* word processor⟩
¹**stan·dard** \'stan-dərd\ *noun* [Middle English, from Old French *estandard* rallying point, standard, of Germanic origin; akin to Old English *standan* to stand and to Old English *ord* point — more at ODD] (12th century)
**1 :** a conspicuous object (as a banner) formerly carried at the top of a pole and used to mark a rallying point especially in battle or to serve as an emblem
**2 a :** a long narrow tapering flag that is personal to an individual or corporation and bears heraldic devices **b :** the personal flag of the head of a state or of a member of a royal family **c :** an organization flag carried by a mounted or motorized military unit **d :** BANNER
**3 :** something established by authority, custom, or general consent as a model or example **:** CRITERION
**4 :** something set up and established by authority as a rule for the measure of quantity, weight, extent, value, or quality

**5 a :** the fineness and legally fixed weight of the metal used in coins **b :** the basis of value in a monetary system
**6 :** a structure built for or serving as a base or support
**7 a :** a shrub or herb grown with an erect main stem so that it forms or resembles a tree **b :** a fruit tree grafted on a stock that does not induce dwarfing
**8 a :** the large odd upper petal of a papilionaceous flower (as the pea) **b :** one of the three inner usually erect and incurved petals of an iris
**9 :** a musical composition (as a song) that has become a part of the standard repertoire ☆
— **stan·dard·less** *adjective*
²**standard** *adjective* (1622)
**1 a :** constituting or conforming to a standard especially as established by law or custom ⟨*standard* weight⟩ **b :** sound and usable but not of top quality ⟨*standard* beef⟩
**2 a :** regularly and widely used, available, or supplied ⟨*standard* automobile equipment⟩ **b :** well-established and very familiar ⟨the *standard* opera⟩
**3 :** having recognized and permanent value ⟨a *standard* reference work⟩
**4 :** substantially uniform and well established by usage in the speech and writing of the educated and widely recognized as acceptable ⟨*standard* pronunciation is subject to regional variations⟩
— **stan·dard·ly** *adverb*
**stan·dard–bear·er** \'stan-dərd-ˌbar-ər, -ˌber-\ *noun* (15th century)
**1 :** one that bears a standard or banner
**2 :** the leader of an organization, movement, or party
**stan·dard·bred** \-ˌbred\ *noun, often capitalized* (1921)
**:** any of a breed of trotting and pacing horses developed in the U.S., noted for speed and stamina, and used especially in harness racing

**standardbred**

**standard can·dle** *noun* (1879)
**:** CANDELA
**standard deviation** *noun* (1894)
**1 :** a measure of the dispersion of a frequency distribution that is the square root of the arithmetic mean of the squares of the deviation of each of the class frequencies from the arithmetic mean of the frequency distribution; *also* **:** a similar quantity found by dividing by one less than the number of squares in the sum of squares instead of taking the arithmetic mean
**2 :** a parameter that indicates the way in which a probability function or a probability density function is centered around its mean and that is equal to the square root of the moment in which the deviation from the mean is squared
**Standard English** *noun* (1836)
**:** the English that with respect to spelling, grammar, pronunciation, and vocabulary is substantially uniform though not devoid of regional differences, that is well established by usage in the formal and informal speech and writing of the educated, and that is widely recognized as acceptable wherever English is spoken and understood
**standard error** *noun* (1897)
**:** the standard deviation of the probability function or probability density function of a random variable and especially of a statistic; *specifically* **:** the standard error of the mean of a sample from a population with a normal distribution that is equal to the standard deviation of the normal distribution divided by the square root of the sample size

**standard gauge** *noun* (1871)
**:** a railroad gauge of 4 feet 8½ inches
**stan·dard·ise** *British variant of* STANDARDIZE
**stan·dard·ize** \'stan-dər-ˌdīz\ *transitive verb* **-ized; -iz·ing** (1873)
**1 :** to compare with a standard
**2 :** to bring into conformity with a standard
— **stan·dard·i·za·tion** \ˌstan-dər-də-ˈzā-shən\ *noun*
**standard of living** (1902)
**1 :** the necessities, comforts, and luxuries enjoyed or aspired to by an individual or group
**2 :** a minimum of necessities, comforts, or luxuries held essential to maintaining a person or group in customary or proper status or circumstances
**standard operating procedure** *noun* (1952)
**:** established or prescribed methods to be followed routinely for the performance of designated operations or in designated situations — called also *standing operating procedure*
**standard position** *noun* (1950)
**:** the position of an angle with its vertex at the origin of a rectangular-coordinate system and its initial side coinciding with the positive x-axis
**standard schnauzer** *noun* (circa 1934)
**:** any of a breed of medium-sized schnauzers that attain a height at the highest point of the shoulder blades of 18 to 20 inches (46 to 51 centimeters) and have a pepper-and-salt or black coat
**standard score** *noun* (1928)
**:** an individual test score expressed as the deviation from the mean score of the group in units of standard deviation
**standard time** *noun* (1879)
**:** the time of a region or country that is established by law or general usage as civil time; *specifically* **:** the mean solar time of a meridian that is a multiple of 15 arbitrarily applied to a local area or to one of the 24 time zones and designated as a number of hours earlier or later than Greenwich time
**stand·away** \'stan-də-ˌwā\ *adjective* (1948)
**:** standing out from the body ⟨a *standaway* skirt⟩
¹**stand·by** \'stan(d)-ˌbī\ *noun, plural* **stand·bys** \-ˌbīz\ (1796)
**1 a :** one to be relied on especially in emergencies **b :** a favorite or reliable choice or resource
**2 :** one that is held in reserve ready for use **:** SUBSTITUTE

---

☆ **SYNONYMS**
**Standard, criterion, gauge, yardstick, touchstone** mean a means of determining what a thing should be. STANDARD applies to any definite rule, principle, or measure established by authority ⟨*standards* of behavior⟩. CRITERION may apply to anything used as a test of quality whether formulated as a rule or principle or not ⟨questioned the critic's *criteria* for excellence⟩. GAUGE applies to a means of testing a particular dimension (as thickness, depth, diameter) or figuratively a particular quality or aspect ⟨polls as a *gauge* of voter dissatisfaction⟩. YARDSTICK is an informal substitute for CRITERION that suggests quantity more often than quality ⟨housing construction as a *yardstick* of economic growth⟩. TOUCHSTONE suggests a simple test of the authenticity or value of something intangible ⟨fine service is one *touchstone* of a first-class restaurant⟩.

---

\ə\ **abut** \ᵊ\ **kitten** \ər\ **further** \a\ **ash** \ā\ **ace**
\ä\ **mop, mar** \aů\ **out** \ch\ **chin** \e\ **bet** \ē\ **easy**
\g\ **go** \i\ **hit** \ī\ **ice** \j\ **job** \ŋ\ **sing** \ō\ **go**
\ȯ\ **law** \ȯi\ **boy** \th\ **thin** \t̲h̲\ **the** \ü\ **loot** \ů\ **foot**
\y\ **yet** \zh\ **vision**    *see also* Guide to Pronunciation

**— on standby** : ready or available for immediate action or use

**²standby** *adjective* (1882)
**1** : held near at hand and ready for use ⟨a *standby* power plant⟩ ⟨*standby* equipment⟩
**2** : relating to the act or condition of standing by ⟨*standby* duty⟩ ⟨a *standby* period⟩
**3** : of, relating to, or traveling by an airline service in which the passenger must wait for an available unreserved seat ⟨*standby* passengers⟩ ⟨a *standby* ticket⟩

**³standby** *adverb* (1971)
: on a standby basis ⟨fly *standby*⟩

**stand by** (13th century)
*intransitive verb*
**1** : to be present; *also* : to remain apart or aloof
**2** : to be or to get ready to act
*transitive verb*
: to remain loyal or faithful to : DEFEND

**stand–down** \'stan(d)-,daún\ *noun* (circa 1919)
: a relaxation of status of a military unit or force from an alert or operational posture

**stand down** *intransitive verb* (1681)
**1** : to leave the witness stand
**2** *chiefly British* **a** : to go off duty **b** : to withdraw from a contest or from a position of leadership

**stand–ee** \stan-'dē\ *noun* (1856)
: one who occupies standing room

**stand–in** \'stan-,din\ *noun* (circa 1928)
**1** : someone employed to occupy an actor's place while lights and camera are readied
**2** : SUBSTITUTE

**stand in** *intransitive verb* (1904)
: to act as a stand-in
**— stand in with** : to be in a specially favored position with

**¹stand·ing** \'stan-din\ *adjective* (14th century)
**1 a** : not yet cut or harvested ⟨*standing* timber⟩ ⟨*standing* grain⟩ **b** : upright on the feet or base : ERECT ⟨the *standing* audience⟩
**2 a** : not being used or operated ⟨a *standing* factory⟩ **b** : not flowing : STAGNANT ⟨*standing* water⟩
**3 a** : remaining at the same level, degree, or amount for an indeterminate period ⟨a *standing* offer⟩ **b** : continuing in existence or use indefinitely
**4** : established by law or custom
**5** : not movable
**6** : done from a standing position ⟨a *standing* jump⟩ ⟨a *standing* ovation⟩

**²standing** *noun* (15th century)
**1 a** : a place to stand in : LOCATION **b** : a position from which one may assert or enforce legal rights and duties
**2 a** : length of service or experience especially as determining rank, pay, or privilege **b** : position or condition in society or in a profession; *especially* : good reputation **c** : position relative to a standard of achievement or to achievements of competitors
**3** : maintenance of position or condition : DURATION ⟨a custom of long *standing*⟩

**standing army** *noun* (1603)
: a permanent army of paid soldiers

**standing committee** *noun* (circa 1636)
: a permanent committee especially of a legislative body

**standing crop** *noun* (1861)
: the total amount or number of living things or of one kind of living thing (as an uncut farm crop, the fish in a pond, or organisms in an ecosystem) in a particular situation at any given time

**standing O** \-'ō\ *noun* [ovation] (1975)
: a standing ovation

**standing order** *noun* (1737)
: an instruction or prescribed procedure in force permanently or until changed or canceled; *especially* : any of the rules for the guidance and government of parliamentary procedure which endure through successive sessions until vacated or repealed

**standing room** *noun* (1603)
: space for standing; *especially* : accommodation available for spectators or passengers after all seats are filled

**standing wave** *noun* (1896)
: a single-frequency mode of vibration of a body or physical system in which the amplitude varies from place to place, is constantly zero at fixed points, and has maxima at other points

**stan·dish** \'stan-dish\ *noun* [Middle English *standyshe*] (14th century)
: a stand for writing materials : INKSTAND

**¹stand–off** \'stan-,dòf\ *adjective* (1837)
**1** : STANDOFFISH
**2** : used for holding something at a distance from a surface ⟨a *standoff* insulator⟩

**²standoff** *noun* (1843)
**1 a** : TIE, DEADLOCK ⟨the two teams played to a *standoff*⟩ **b** : a counterbalancing effect
**2** : the act of standing off

**stand off** (1601)
*intransitive verb*
**1** : to stay at a distance from something
**2** : to sail away from the shore
*transitive verb*
**1** : to keep from advancing : REPEL
**2** : PUT OFF, STALL

**stand·off·ish** \stan-'dò-fish\ *adjective* (1860)
: somewhat cold and reserved
**— stand·off·ish·ly** *adverb*
**— stand·off·ish·ness** *noun*

**stand oil** *noun* (1908)
: a thickened drying oil; *especially* : linseed oil heated to about 600° F (315° C)

**stand·out** \'stan-,daút\ *noun, often attributive* (1928)
: one that is prominent or conspicuous especially because of excellence

**stand out** *intransitive verb* (15th century)
**1 a** : to appear as if in relief : PROJECT **b** : to be prominent or conspicuous
**2** : to steer away from shore
**3** : to be stubborn in resolution or resistance

**stand·pat** \'stan(d)-'pat\ *adjective* (1904)
: stubbornly conservative : resisting or opposing change

**stand pat** *intransitive verb* [⁴*pat*] (1882)
**1** : to play one's hand as dealt in draw poker without drawing
**2** : to oppose or resist change
**— stand·pat·ter** \'stan(d)-,pa-tər, -'pa-tər\ *noun*
**— stand·pat·ism** \-,pa-,ti-zəm\ *noun*

**stand·pipe** \'stan(d)-,pīp\ *noun* (circa 1850)
: a high vertical pipe or reservoir that is used to secure a uniform pressure in a water-supply system

**stand·point** \-,pòint\ *noun* (1829)
: a position from which objects or principles are viewed and according to which they are compared and judged

**stand·still** \-,stil\ *noun* (1702)
: a state characterized by absence of motion or of progress : STOP

**¹stand–up** \'stan-,dəp\ *adjective* (1812)
**1 a** : ERECT, UPRIGHT **b** : stiffened to stay upright without folding over ⟨a *stand-up* collar⟩
**2** : performed in, performing in, or requiring a standing position ⟨a *stand-up* bar⟩; *especially* : of, relating to, performing, or being a monologue of jokes, gags, or satirical comments delivered usually while standing alone on a stage or in front of a camera ⟨*stand-up* comedy⟩ ⟨a *stand-up* comedian⟩

**²stand–up** *noun* (1971)
: stand-up comedy

**stand up** (before 12th century)
*intransitive verb*
**1** : to rise to a standing position
**2** : to remain sound and intact under stress, attack, or close scrutiny
*transitive verb*
: to fail to keep an appointment with
**— stand up for** : to defend against attack or criticism

**— stand up to 1** : to meet fairly and fully
**2** : to face boldly
**— stand up with** : to be best man or maid of honor at a wedding ceremony

**stand–up·per** \'stan-,də-pər\ *noun* (1973)
: a television news report or interview by an on-camera reporter standing usually at the scene of an occurrence

**stane** \'stān\ *Scottish variant of* STONE

**Stan·ford–Bi·net test** \,stan-fərd-bi-'nā-\ *noun* [*Stanford* University + Alfred *Binet* (died 1911) French psychologist] (1918)
: an intelligence test prepared at Stanford University as a revision of the Binet-Simon scale and commonly used with children — called also *Stanford-Binet*

**¹stang** \'staŋ\ *transitive verb* [Middle English, from Old Norse *stanga* to prick; akin to Old Norse *stinga* to sting] (14th century)
*chiefly Scottish* : STING

**²stang** *noun* (1513)
*chiefly Scottish* : PANG

**³stang** *variant of* SATANG

**stan·hope** \'sta-nəp\ *noun* [Fitzroy *Stanhope* (died 1864) British clergyman] (1825)
: a gig, buggy, or phaeton typically having a high seat and closed back

**sta·nine** \'stā-,nīn\ *noun* [*sta*ndard (score) + *nine*] (1944)
: any of the nine classes into which a set of normalized standard scores arranged according to rank in educational testing are divided, which include the bottom 4% and the top 4% of the scores in the first and ninth classes and the middle 20% in the fifth, and which have a standard deviation of 2 and a mean of 5

**Sta·ni·slav·ski method** \,sta-nə-'slaf-ski-, -'slav-\ *noun* [Konstantin *Stanislavsky*] (1941)
: a technique in acting by which an actor strives to empathize with the character being portrayed so as to effect a realistic interpretation

**¹stank** \'staŋk\ *past of* STINK

**²stank** *noun* [Middle English, from Middle French *estanc*, from *estancher* to dam up, stanch — more at STANCH] (14th century)
**1** *dialect British* **a** : POND, POOL **b** : a ditch containing water
**2** *British* : a small dam : WEIR

**stan·na·ry** \'sta-nə-rē\ *noun, plural* **-ries** [Middle English *stannarie*, from Medieval Latin *stannaria* tin mine, from Late Latin *stannum* tin] (15th century)
: any of the regions in England containing establishments for the working of tin — usually used in plural

**stan·nic** \'sta-nik\ *adjective* [probably from French *stannique*, from Late Latin *stannum* tin, from Latin *stagnum*, an alloy of silver and lead] (1790)
: of, relating to, or containing tin especially with a valence of four

**stan·nite** \'sta-,nīt\ *noun* [Late Latin *stannum*] (1868)
: a mineral that is a steel-gray or iron-black sulfide of copper, iron, and tin with a metallic luster and occurs in granular masses

**stan·nous** \'sta-nəs\ *adjective* [International Scientific Vocabulary, from Late Latin *stannum*] (1849)
: of, relating to, or containing tin especially with a valence of two

**stan·za** \'stan-zə\ *noun* [Italian, stay, abode, room, stanza, from (assumed) Vulgar Latin *stantia* stay — more at STANCE] (1588)
: a division of a poem consisting of a series of lines arranged together in a usually recurring pattern of meter and rhyme : STROPHE
**— stan·za·ic** \stan-'zā-ik\ *adjective*

**sta·pe·dec·to·my** \,stā-pi-'dek-tə-mē\ *noun, plural* **-mies** [International Scientific Vocabulary, from New Latin *staped-, stapes*] (1894)
: surgical removal and prosthetic replacement of part or all of the stapes to relieve deafness

**sta·pe·di·al** \stā-'pē-dē-əl, stə-\ *adjective* (circa 1859)
: of, relating to, or located near the stapes

**sta·pe·lia** \stə-'pēl-yə\ *noun* [New Latin, from J. B. van *Stapel* (died 1636) Dutch botanist] (circa 1785)
: any of a genus (*Stapelia*) of African perennial herbs of the milkweed family with succulent typically leafless toothed stems like cactus joints and showy but usually putrid-smelling flowers

**sta·pes** \'stā-(,)pēz\ *noun, plural* **stapes** or **sta·pe·des** \'stā-pə-,dēz\ [New Latin *staped-, stapes,* from Medieval Latin, stirrup, alteration of Late Latin *stapia*] (1670)
: the innermost ossicle of the ear of mammals — called also *stirrup;* see EAR illustration

**staph** \'staf\ *noun* (circa 1933)
: STAPHYLOCOCCUS

**staph·y·li·nid** \,sta-fə-'lī-nəd\ *noun* [New Latin *Staphylinidae,* ultimately from Greek *staphylē* bunch of grapes] (circa 1891)
: ROVE BEETLE
— **staphylinid** *adjective*

**staph·y·lo·coc·cal** \,sta-f(ə-)lō-'kä-kəl\ *also* **staph·y·lo·coc·cic** \-'kä-kik, -'käk-sik\ *adjective* (1900)
: of, relating to, caused by, or being a staphylococcus

**staph·y·lo·coc·cus** \-'kä-kəs\ *noun, plural* **-coc·ci** \-'kä-,kī, -(,)kē; -'käk-,sī, -(,)sē\ [New Latin, from Greek *staphylē* bunch of grapes + New Latin *-coccus*] (1887)
: any of various nonmotile gram-positive spherical bacteria (especially genus *Staphylococcus*) that occur singly, in pairs or tetrads, or in irregular clusters and include pathogens which infect skin and mucous membranes

**¹sta·ple** \'stā-pəl\ *noun* [Middle English *stapel* post, staple, from Old English *stapol* post; akin to Middle Dutch *stapel* step, heap, emporium, Old English *steppan* to step] (13th century)
**1** : a U-shaped metal loop both ends of which are driven into a surface to hold the hook, hasp, or bolt of a lock, secure a rope, or fix a wire in place
**2** : a small U-shaped wire both ends of which are driven through layers of thin and easily penetrable material (as paper) and usually clinched to hold the layers together

**²staple** *transitive verb* **sta·pled; sta·pling** \-p(ə-)liŋ\ (14th century)
: to provide with or secure by staples

**³staple** *noun* [Middle English, from Middle French *estaple,* from Middle Dutch *stapel* emporium] (14th century)
**1** : a town used as a center for the sale or exportation of commodities in bulk
**2** : a place of supply : SOURCE
**3** : a chief commodity or production of a place
**4 a** : a commodity for which the demand is constant **b** : something having widespread and constant use or appeal **c** : the sustaining or principal element : SUBSTANCE
**5** : RAW MATERIAL
**6 a** : textile fiber (as wool and rayon) of relatively short length that when spun and twisted forms a yarn rather than a filament **b** : the length of a piece of such textile fiber

**⁴staple** *adjective* (1615)
**1** : used, needed, or enjoyed constantly usually by many individuals
**2** : produced regularly or in large quantities ⟨*staple* crops such as wheat and rice⟩
**3** : PRINCIPAL, CHIEF

**¹sta·pler** \'stā-p(ə-)lər\ *noun* (circa 1513)
: one that deals in staple goods or in staple fiber

**²stapler** *noun* (circa 1909)
: one that inserts staples; *especially* : a small usually hand-operated device for inserting wire staples

**¹star** \'stär\ *noun, often attributive* [Middle English *sterre,* from Old English *steorra;* akin to

Old High German *sterno* star, Latin *stella,* Greek *astēr, astron*] (before 12th century)
**1 a** : a natural luminous body visible in the sky especially at night **b** : a self-luminous gaseous celestial body of great mass which produces energy by means of nuclear fusion reactions, whose shape is usually spheroidal, and whose size may be as small as the earth or larger than the earth's orbit
**2 a** (1) : a planet or a configuration of the planets that is held in astrology to influence one's destiny or fortune — usually used in plural (2) : a waxing or waning fortune or fame ⟨her *star* was rising⟩ **b** *obsolete* : DESTINY
**3 a** : a conventional figure with five or more points that represents a star; *especially* : ASTERISK **b** : an often star-shaped ornament or medal worn as a badge of honor, authority, or rank or as the insignia of an order **c** : one of a group of conventional stars used to place something in a scale of value
**4** : something resembling a star ⟨was hit on the head and saw *stars*⟩
**5 a** : the principal member of a theatrical or operatic company who usually plays the chief roles **b** : a highly publicized theatrical or motion-picture performer **c** : an outstandingly talented performer ⟨a track *star*⟩ **d** : a person who is preeminent in a particular field
— **star·less** \-ləs\ *adjective*
— **star·like** \-,līk\ *adjective*

**²star** *verb* **starred; star·ring** (1718)
*transitive verb*
**1** : to sprinkle or adorn with stars
**2 a** : to mark with a star as being preeminent **b** : to mark with an asterisk
**3** : to advertise or display prominently : FEATURE ⟨the movie *stars* a famous stage personality⟩
*intransitive verb*
**1** : to play the most prominent or important role
**2** : to perform outstandingly

**³star** *adjective* (1832)
**1** : of, relating to, or being a star ⟨received *star* billing⟩
**2** : of outstanding excellence : PREEMINENT ⟨a *star* athlete⟩

**star apple** *noun* (1683)
: a tropical American tree (*Chrysophyllum cainito*) of the sapodilla family grown in warm regions for ornament or fruit; *also* : its usually green to purple apple-shaped edible fruit

**¹star·board** \'stär-bərd\ *noun* [Middle English *sterbord,* from Old English *stēorbord,* from *stēor-* steering oar + *bord* ship's side — more at STEER, BOARD] (before 12th century)
: the right side of a ship or aircraft looking forward — compare PORT ◆

**²starboard** *adjective* (15th century)
: of, relating to, or situated to starboard

**³starboard** *transitive verb* (1598)
: to turn or put (a helm or rudder) to the right

**¹starch** \'stärch\ *transitive verb* [Middle English *sterchen,* probably from (assumed) Old English *stercan* to stiffen; akin to Old English *stearc* stiff — more at STARK] (15th century)
: to stiffen with or as if with starch

**²starch** *noun* (15th century)
**1** : a white odorless tasteless granular or powdery complex carbohydrate ($C_6H_{10}O_5$)$_x$ that is the chief storage form of carbohydrate in plants, is an important foodstuff, and is used also in adhesives and sizes, in laundering, and in pharmacy and medicine
**2** : a stiff formal manner : FORMALITY
**3** : resolute vigor

**star–cham·ber** \'stär-'chām-bər\ *adjective* [*Star Chamber,* a court existing in England from the 15th century until 1641] (1800)
: characterized by secrecy and often being irresponsibly arbitrary and oppressive

**starchy** \'stär-chē\ *adjective* **starch·i·er; -est** (1802)
**1** : containing, consisting of, or resembling starch

**2** : consisting of or marked by formality or stiffness
— **starch·i·ly** \-chə-lē\ *adverb*
— **starch·i·ness** \-chē-nəs\ *noun*

**star–crossed** \'stär-,kròst\ *adjective* (1592)
: not favored by the stars : ILL-FATED ⟨a pair of *star-crossed* lovers take their life —Shakespeare⟩

**star·dom** \'stär-dəm\ *noun* (1865)
: the status or position of a star

**star·dust** \'stär-,dəst\ *noun* (1927)
: a feeling or impression of romance, magic, or ethereality

**¹stare** \'star, 'ster\ *verb* **stared; star·ing** [Middle English, from Old English *starian;* akin to Old High German *starēn* to stare, Greek *stereos* solid, Lithuanian *starinti* to stiffen] (before 12th century)
*intransitive verb*
**1** : to look fixedly often with wide-open eyes
**2** : to show oneself conspicuously ⟨the error *stared* from the page⟩
**3** *of hair* : to stand on end : BRISTLE; *also* : to appear rough and lusterless
*transitive verb*
**1** : to have an effect on by staring
**2** : to look at with a searching or earnest gaze
— **star·er** *noun*
— **stare one in the face** : to be undeniably and forcefully evident or apparent

**²stare** *noun* (15th century)
: the act or an instance of staring ⟨a blank *stare*⟩

**sta·re de·ci·sis** \,ster-ē-di-'sī-səs, ,star-, ,stär-\ *noun* [Latin, to stand by decided matters] (1782)
: a doctrine or policy of following rules or principles laid down in previous judicial decisions unless they contravene the ordinary principles of justice

**stare down** *transitive verb* (1925)
: to cause to waver or submit by or as if by staring

**sta·rets** \'stär-əts, -yəts\ *noun, plural* **star·tsy** \'stärt-sē\ [Russian, from *staryĭ* old — more at STOUR] (1917)
: a spiritual director or religious teacher in the Eastern Orthodox Church; *specifically* : a spiritual adviser who is not necessarily a priest,

◇ WORD HISTORY
**starboard** Appearances to the contrary notwithstanding, the *star-* in *starboard* has nothing to do with the stars. The word *starboard* descends from Old English *stēorbord,* a compound of *stēor* "steering oar, rudder" and *bord* "side of a ship." Early Germanic craft such as those used by the Angles and Saxons who invaded Britain were steered by means of a long oar attached to the right of the ship; the right side was hence the "steering side." *Stēor* is related to the Modern English verb *steer. Bord* is the ancestor of Modern English *board,* though the sense "side of a ship" is now rare outside of compounds such as *overboard. Starboard* used to be contrasted with *larboard,* in Middle English *laddebord,* the first element of which has never been identified with certainty. English-speaking navies replaced *larboard* in the 19th century with *port,* first attested in the verb phrase *to port the helm* (turn the ship to the left) in the 16th century. *Port,* too, is a nautical mystery, since there is no sure connection between the left side of a ship and *port* meaning "harbor" or "gate."

who is recognized for his piety, and who is turned to by monks or laymen for spiritual guidance

**star facet** *noun* (1751)
: one of the eight small triangular facets which abut on the table in the bezel of a brilliant

**star·fish** \'stär-ˌfish\ *noun* (1538)
: any of a class (Asteroidea) of echinoderms having a body of usually five radially disposed arms about a central disk and feeding largely on mollusks (as oysters) — called also *sea star*

**star·flow·er** \-ˌflaù(-ə)r\ *noun* (1629)
: any of several plants having star-shaped pentamerous flowers; *especially* : any of a genus (*Trientalis*, especially *T. borealis*) of perennial herbs of the primrose family

**star fruit** *noun* (1974)
: CARAMBOLA 1

**star·gaze** \-ˌgāz\ *intransitive verb* [back-formation from *stargazer*] (1626)
**1** : to gaze at stars
**2** : to gaze raptly or contemplatively

**star·gaz·er** \-ˌgā-zər\ *noun* (1560)
**1** : one who gazes at the stars: as **a** : ASTROLOGER **b** : ASTRONOMER
**2** : any of various marine bony fishes (families Uranoscopidae and Dactyloscopidae) with the eyes on top of a blocky or conical head

**star·gaz·ing** \-ˌgā-ziŋ\ *noun* (1576)
**1** : the act or practice of a stargazer
**2 a** : absorption in chimerical or impractical ideas : WOOLGATHERING **b** : the quality or state of being absentminded

**star grass** *noun* (1687)
: any of various grassy plants with stellate flowers or arrangement of leaves: as **a** : any of a genus (*Hypoxis*) of herbs of the amaryllis family **b** : either of two colicroots (*Aletris farinosa* and *A. aurea*)

**¹stark** \'stärk\ *adjective* [Middle English, stiff, strong, from Old English *stearc;* akin to Old High German *starc* strong, Lithuanian *starinti* to stiffen — more at STARE] (before 12th century)
**1 a** : rigid in or as if in death **b** : rigidly conforming (as to a pattern or doctrine) : ABSOLUTE ⟨*stark* discipline⟩
**2** *archaic* : STRONG, ROBUST
**3** : UTTER, SHEER ⟨*stark* nonsense⟩
**4 a** : BARREN, DESOLATE **b** (1) : having few or no ornaments : BARE ⟨a *stark* white room⟩ (2) : HARSH, BLUNT ⟨the *stark* realities of death⟩
**5** : sharply delineated ⟨a *stark* contrast⟩
— **stark·ly** *adverb*
— **stark·ness** *noun*

**²stark** *adverb* (13th century)
**1** : in a stark manner
**2** : to an absolute or complete degree : WHOLLY ⟨*stark* naked⟩ ⟨*stark* mad⟩

**stark·ers** \'stär-kərz\ *adjective* [alteration of ¹*stark*] (circa 1923)
*chiefly British* : completely unclothed : NAKED
**word history** SEE NUTS

**star·let** \'stär-lət\ *noun* (1920)
: a young movie actress being coached and publicized for starring roles

**star·light** \-ˌlīt\ *noun* (14th century)
: the light given by the stars

**star·ling** \'stär-liŋ\ *noun* [Middle English, from Old English *stærlinc*, from *stær* starling + *-ling, -linc* -ling; akin to Old High German *stara* starling, Latin *sturnus*] (before 12th century)
: any of a family (Sturnidae, especially genus *Sturnus*) of usually dark gregarious oscine birds; *especially* : a dark brown or in summer glossy greenish black European bird (*S. vulgaris*) naturalized nearly worldwide and often considered a pest

**star·lit** \'stär-ˌlit\ *adjective* (circa 1835)
: lighted by the stars

**star–nosed mole** \'stär-ˌnōz(d)-\ *noun* (1826)

: a common black long-tailed semi-aquatic mole (*Condylura cristata*) of the northeastern U.S. and adjacent Canada that has a series of pink fleshy projections surrounding the nostrils

star-nosed mole

**star–of–Beth·le·hem** \-'beth-li-ˌhem, -lē-(h)əm\ *noun* (1573)
: any of various Old World bulbous herbs (genus *Ornithogalum*) of the lily family with basal leaves resembling grass; *especially* : one (*O. umbellatum*) with white flowers that is naturalized in the eastern U.S.

**star of Bethlehem**
: a star which according to Christian tradition guided the Magi to the infant Jesus in Bethlehem

**Star of Da·vid** \-'dā-vəd\ (circa 1936)
: MAGEN DAVID

**star route** *noun* [so called from the asterisk used to designate such routes in postal publications] (1880)
: a mail-delivery route in a rural or thinly populated area served by a private carrier under contract who takes mail from one post office to another or from a railroad station to a post office and usually also delivers mail to private mailboxes along the route

**star·ry** \'stär-ē\ *adjective* **star·ri·er; -est** (14th century)
**1 a** : adorned with stars; *especially* : STAR-STUDDED **b** : of, relating to, or consisting of stars : STELLAR **c** : shining like stars : SPARKLING **d** : having parts arranged like the rays of a star : STELLATE
**2** : as high as or seemingly as high as the stars ⟨*starry* speculations⟩
**3** : STARRY-EYED

**star·ry–eyed** \'stär-ē-ˌīd\ *adjective* (1904)
: regarding an object or a prospect in an overly favorable light; *specifically* : characterized by dreamy, impracticable, or utopian thinking : VISIONARY

**Stars and Bars** *noun plural but singular in construction* (1861)
: the first flag of the Confederate States of America having three bars of red, white, and red respectively and a blue union with white stars in a circle representing the seceded states

**Stars and Stripes** *noun plural but singular in construction* (1777)
: the flag of the United States having 13 alternately red and white horizontal stripes and a blue union with white stars representing the states

**star sapphire** *noun* (circa 1817)
: a sapphire that when cut with a convex surface and polished exhibits asterism

**star shell** *noun* (circa 1876)
**1** : a shell that on bursting releases a shower of brilliant stars and is used for signaling
**2** : a shell with an illuminating projectile

**star·ship** \'stär-ˌship\ *noun* (1934)
: a spacecraft designed for interstellar travel

**star–span·gled** \'stär-ˌspaŋ-gəld\ *adjective* (1591)
: STAR-STUDDED

**star·struck** \-ˌstrək\ *adjective* (1968)
: particularly taken with celebrities (as movie stars)

**star–stud·ded** \'stär-ˌstə-dəd\ *adjective* (1955)
: abounding in or covered with stars ⟨a *star-studded* cast⟩ ⟨a *star-studded* uniform⟩

**star system** *noun* (1902)
: the practice of casting famous performers in principal roles (as in motion pictures or the theater) especially in order to capitalize on their popular appeal

**¹start** \'stärt\ *verb* [Middle English *sterten;* akin to Middle High German *sterzen* to stand up stiffly, move quickly] (14th century)
*intransitive verb*
**1 a** : to move suddenly and violently : SPRING ⟨*started* angrily to his feet⟩ **b** : to react with a sudden brief involuntary movement ⟨*started* when a shot rang out⟩
**2 a** : to issue with sudden force ⟨blood *starting* from the wound⟩ **b** : to come into being, activity, or operation ⟨when does the movie *start*⟩ ⟨the rain *started* up again⟩
**3** : to protrude or seem to protrude ⟨eyes *starting* from their sockets⟩
**4** : to become loosened or forced out of place ⟨one of the planks has *started*⟩
**5 a** : to begin a course or journey ⟨*started* toward the door⟩ ⟨just *starting* out⟩ **b** : to range from a specified initial point ⟨the rates *start* at $10⟩
**6** : to begin an activity or undertaking; *especially* : to begin work
**7** : to be a participant in a game or contest; *especially* : to be in the starting lineup
*transitive verb*
**1** : to cause to leave a place of concealment : FLUSH ⟨*start* a rabbit⟩
**2** *archaic* : STARTLE, ALARM
**3** : to bring up for consideration or discussion
**4** : to bring into being ⟨*start* a rumor⟩
**5** : to cause to become loosened or displaced
**6** : to begin the use of ⟨*start* a fresh loaf of bread⟩
**7 a** : to cause to move, act, or operate ⟨*start* the motor⟩ **b** : to cause to enter a game or contest; *especially* : to put in the starting lineup **c** : to care for or train during the early stages of growth and development ⟨*started* plants⟩ ⟨a well-*started* coonhound⟩
**8** : to do or experience the first stages or actions of ⟨*started* studying music at the age of five⟩
**synonym** see BEGIN
— **start something** *also* **start anything** : to make trouble ⟨always trying to *start something*⟩ ⟨don't *start anything*⟩
— **to start with 1** : at the beginning : INITIALLY **2** : in any event

**²start** *noun* (14th century)
**1 a** : a sudden involuntary bodily movement or reaction ⟨woke with a *start*⟩ **b** : a brief and sudden action or movement **c** : a sudden capricious impulse or outburst
**2** : a beginning of movement, activity, or development ⟨a false *start*⟩ ⟨housing *starts*⟩
**3** : HEAD START
**4** : a place of beginning
**5** : the act or an instance of being a competitor in a race or a member of a starting lineup in a game ⟨undefeated in six *starts* —*Current Biography*⟩

**start·er** \'stär-tər\ *noun* (1622)
**1** : a person who initiates or sets going: as **a** : an official who gives the signal to begin a race **b** : one who dispatches vehicles
**2 a** : one that engages in a competition; *especially* : a member of a starting lineup **b** : one that begins to engage in an activity or process
**3** : one that causes something to begin operating: as **a** : a device for starting an engine; *especially* : an electric motor used to start an internal combustion engine **b** : material containing microorganisms used to induce a desired fermentation
**4** : something that is the beginning of a process, activity, or series; *especially* : APPETIZER
— **for starters** : to begin with

**star thistle** *noun* (1578)
**1** : a widely naturalized spiny European knapweed (*Centaurea calcitrapa*) with purple flowers — called also *caltrops*
**2** : any of various knapweeds related to the star thistle

**starting block** *noun* (1937)
: a device that consists of two blocks mounted on either side of an adjustable frame which is usually anchored to the ground and that provides a runner with a rigid surface against which to brace the feet at the start of a race

**starting block**

**starting gate** *noun* (1898)
**1** : a mechanically operated barrier used as a starting device for a race
**2** : a barrier that when knocked aside by a competitor (as a skier) starts an electronic timing device

¹**star·tle** \'stär-t°l\ *verb* **star·tled; star·tling** \'stärt-liŋ, 'stär-t°l-iŋ\ [Middle English *stertlen*, frequentative of *sterten* to start] (1530)
*intransitive verb*
: to move or jump suddenly (as in surprise or alarm) ⟨the baby *startles* easily⟩
*transitive verb*
: to frighten or surprise suddenly and usually not seriously
— **star·tle·ment** \-mənt\ *noun*

²**startle** *noun* (1714)
: a sudden mild shock (as of surprise or alarm)

**star·tling** *adjective* (1714)
: causing momentary fright, surprise, or astonishment
— **star·tling·ly** \'stärt-liŋ-lē, 'stär-t°l-iŋ-\ *adverb*

**start–up** \'stärt-,əp\ *noun, often attributive* (1845)
**1** : the act or an instance of setting in operation or motion
**2** : a fledgling business enterprise

**star turn** *noun* (1898)
*chiefly British* : the featured skit or number in a theatrical production; *broadly* : the most widely publicized person or item in a group

**star·va·tion** \stär-'vā-shən\ *noun* (1778)
**1** : the act or an instance of starving
**2** : the state of being starved

**starvation wages** *noun* (1898)
: wages insufficient to provide the ordinary necessities of life

**starve** \'stärv\ *verb* **starved; starv·ing** [Middle English *sterven* to die, starve, from Old English *steorfan* to die; akin to Old High German *sterban* to die, Lithuanian *starinti* to stiffen — more at STARE] (15th century)
*intransitive verb*
**1 a** : to perish from lack of food **b** : to suffer extreme hunger
**2 a** *archaic* : to die of cold **b** *British* : to suffer greatly from cold
**3** : to suffer or perish from deprivation ⟨*starved* for affection⟩
*transitive verb*
**1 a** : to kill with hunger **b** : to deprive of nourishment **c** : to cause to capitulate by or as if by depriving of nourishment
**2** : to destroy by or cause to suffer from deprivation
**3** *archaic* : to kill with cold

¹**starve·ling** \'stärv-liŋ\ *noun* (1546)
: one that is thin from or as if from lack of food

²**starveling** *adjective* (1597)
: being a starveling; *also* : marked by poverty or inadequacy ⟨*starveling* wages⟩

¹**stash** \'stash\ *transitive verb* [origin unknown] (1785)
: to store in a usually secret place for future use — often used with *away*

²**stash** *noun* (circa 1914)
**1** : hiding place : CACHE

**2** : something stored or hidden away ⟨a *stash* of narcotics⟩

**sta·sis** \'stā-səs, 'sta-\ *noun, plural* **sta·ses** \'stā-,sēz, 'sta-\ [New Latin, from Greek, act or condition of standing, stopping, from *histasthai* to stand — more at STAND] (1745)
**1** : a slowing or stoppage of the normal flow of a bodily fluid or semifluid: as **a** : slowing of the current of circulating blood **b** : reduced motility of the intestines with retention of feces
**2** : a state of static balance or equilibrium : STAGNATION

**-stasis** *noun combining form, plural* **-stases** [New Latin, from Greek *stasis*]
**1** : stoppage : slowing ⟨hemo*stasis*⟩ ⟨bacterio*stasis*⟩
**2** : stable state ⟨homeo*stasis*⟩

**stat** \'stat\ *noun* (circa 1961)
: STATISTIC

**-stat** *noun combining form* [New Latin *-stata*, from Greek *-statēs* one that stops or steadies, from *histanai* to cause to stand — more at STAND]
**1** : stabilizing agent or device ⟨thermo*stat*⟩
**2** : instrument for reflecting (something specified) constantly in one direction ⟨helio*stat*⟩
**3** : agent causing inhibition of growth without destruction ⟨bacterio*stat*⟩

**sta·tant** \'stā-t°nt\ *adjective* [Latin *status*, past participle + English *-ant*] (circa 1500)
: standing in profile with all feet on the ground — used of a heraldic animal

¹**state** \'stāt\ *noun, often attributive* [Middle English *stat*, from Old French & Latin; Old French *estat*, from Latin *status*, from *stare* to stand — more at STAND] (13th century)
**1 a** : mode or condition of being ⟨a *state* of readiness⟩ **b** (1) : condition of mind or temperament ⟨in a highly nervous *state*⟩ (2) : a condition of abnormal tension or excitement
**2 a** : a condition or stage in the physical being of something ⟨insects in the larval *state*⟩ ⟨the gaseous *state* of water⟩ **b** : any of various conditions characterized by definite quantities (as of energy, angular momentum, or magnetic moment) in which an atomic system may exist
**3 a** : social position; *especially* : high rank **b** (1) : elaborate or luxurious style of living (2) : formal dignity : POMP — usually used with *in*
**4 a** : a body of persons constituting a special class in a society : ESTATE **3 b** *plural* : the members or representatives of the governing classes assembled in a legislative body **c** *obsolete* : a person of high rank (as a noble)
**5 a** : a politically organized body of people usually occupying a definite territory; *especially* : one that is sovereign **b** : the political organization of such a body of people **c** : a government or politically organized society having a particular character ⟨a police *state*⟩ ⟨the welfare *state*⟩
**6** : the operations or concerns of the government of a country
**7 a** : one of the constituent units of a nation having a federal government ⟨the fifty *states*⟩ **b** *plural, capitalized* : The United States of America
**8** : the territory of a state

²**state** *transitive verb* **stat·ed; stat·ing** (1647)
**1** : to set by regulation or authority
**2** : to express the particulars of especially in words : REPORT; *broadly* : to express in words
— **stat·able** *or* **state·able** \'stā-tə-bəl\ *adjective*

**state aid** *noun* (1856)
: public monies appropriated by a state government for the partial support or improvement of a public local institution

**state bank** *noun* (1815)
**1** : CENTRAL BANK
**2** : a bank chartered by and operating under the laws of a state of the U.S.

**state bird** *noun* (1910)

: a bird selected (as by the legislature) as an emblem of a state of the U.S.

**state capitalism** *noun* (1903)
: an economic system in which private capitalism is modified by a varying degree of government ownership and control

**state church** *noun, often S&C capitalized* (1726)
: ESTABLISHED CHURCH

**state college** *noun* (1831)
: a college that is financially supported by a state government, often specializes in a branch of technical or professional education, and often forms part of the state university

**state·craft** \'stāt-,kraft\ *noun* (1642)
: the art of conducting state affairs

**stat·ed** \'stā-təd\ *adjective* (circa 1641)
**1** : FIXED, REGULAR ⟨the president shall, at *stated* times, receive . . . a compensation —*U.S. Constitution*⟩
**2** : set down explicitly : DECLARED ⟨our *stated* intention⟩
— **stat·ed·ly** *adverb*

**stated clerk** *noun* (circa 1909)
: an executive officer of a Presbyterian general assembly, synod, or presbytery ranking below the moderator

**state flower** *noun* (1898)
: a flowering plant selected (as by the legislature) as an emblem of a state of the U.S.

**state·hood** \'stāt-,hud\ *noun* (1868)
: the condition of being a state; *especially* : the status of being one of the states of the U.S.

**state·house** \-,haus\ *noun* (1638)
: the building in which a state legislature sits

**state·less** \-ləs\ *adjective* (1609)
**1** : having no state
**2** : lacking the status of a national ⟨a *stateless* refugee⟩
— **state·less·ness** *noun*

**state·ly** \-lē\ *adjective* **state·li·er; -est** (15th century)
**1 a** : marked by lofty or imposing dignity **b** : HAUGHTY, UNAPPROACHABLE
**2** : impressive in size or proportions
*synonym* see GRAND
— **state·li·ness** *noun*
— **stately** *adverb*

**state·ment** \'stāt-mənt\ *noun* (circa 1775)
**1** : something stated: as **a** : a single declaration or remark : ASSERTION **b** : a report of facts or opinions
**2** : the act or process of stating or presenting orally or on paper
**3** : PROPOSITION 2a
**4** : the presentation of a theme in a musical composition
**5** : a summary of a financial account showing the balance due
**6** : an opinion, comment, or message conveyed indirectly usually by nonverbal means ⟨monuments are *statements* in form and space —O. B. Hardison, Jr.⟩
**7** : an instruction in a computer program

**state of the art** (1910)
: the level of development (as of a device, procedure, process, technique, or science) reached at any particular time usually as a result of modern methods
— **state–of–the–art** *adjective*

**state of war** (1880)
**1 a** : a state of actual armed hostilities regardless of a formal declaration of war **b** : a legal state created and ended by official declaration regardless of actual armed hostilities and usually characterized by operation of the rules of war
**2** : the period of time during which a state of war is in effect

---

\ə\ abut \ᵊ\ kitten \ər\ further \a\ ash \ā\ ace
\ä\ mop, mar \au\ out \ch\ chin \e\ bet \ē\ easy
\g\ go \i\ hit \ī\ ice \j\ job \ŋ\ sing \ō\ go
\o\ law \oi\ boy \th\ thin \th\ the \ü\ loot \u\ foot
\y\ yet \zh\ vision   *see also* Guide to Pronunciation

**sta·ter** \\'stā-tər, stä-'ter\\ *noun* [Middle English, from Late Latin, from Greek *statēr*, literally, a unit of weight, from *histanai* to cause to stand, weigh — more at STAND] (14th century)
: an ancient gold or silver coin of the Greek city-states

**state·room** \\'stāt-,rüm, -,rùm\\ *noun* (1660)
**1** : CABIN 1a(1)
**2** : a private room on a railroad car with one or more berths and a toilet

**state's attorney** *noun* (1809)
: a legal officer (as a district attorney) appointed or elected to represent a state in court proceedings within a district — called also *state attorney*

**state's evidence** *noun, often S capitalized* (1827)
: a participant in a crime or an accomplice who gives evidence for the prosecution especially in return for a reduced sentence; *also* : the evidence given — used chiefly in the phrase *turn state's evidence*

**States General** *noun plural* (1585)
**1** : the assembly of the three orders of clergy, nobility, and third estate in France before the Revolution
**2** : the legislature of the Netherlands from the 15th century to 1796

**¹state·side** \\'stāt-,sīd\\ *adjective, often capitalized* [(*United*) *States* + *side*] (1944)
: being in, going to, coming from, or characteristic of the 48 conterminous states of the U.S. ⟨transferred from Europe to *stateside* duty⟩

**²stateside** *adverb, often capitalized* (1945)
: in or to the continental U.S.

**states·man** \\'stāts-mən\\ *noun* (1592)
**1** : one versed in the principles or art of government; *especially* : one actively engaged in conducting the business of a government or in shaping its policies
**2** : one who exercises political leadership wisely and without narrow partisanship
— **states·man·like** \\-,līk\\ *adjective*
— **states·man·ly** \\-lē\\ *adjective*
— **states·man·ship** \\-,ship\\ *noun*

**state socialism** *noun* (1879)
: an economic system with limited socialist characteristics introduced by usually gradual political action

**states' right·er** \\'stāts-'rī-tər\\ *noun* (1945)
: one who advocates strict interpretation of the U.S. constitutional guarantee of states' rights

**states' rights** *noun plural* (1858)
: all rights not vested by the Constitution of the U.S. in the federal government nor forbidden by it to the separate states

**state tree** *noun* (1917)
: a tree selected (as by the legislature) as an emblem of a state of the U.S.

**state university** *noun* (1831)
: a university maintained and administered by one of the states of the U.S. as part of the state public educational system

**¹state·wide** \\'stāt-'wīd\\ *adjective* (1911)
: affecting or extending throughout all parts of a state

**²statewide** *adverb* (circa 1934)
: throughout the state

**¹stat·ic** \\'sta-tik\\ *adjective* [New Latin *staticus*, from Greek *statikos* causing to stand, skilled in weighing, from *histanai* to cause to stand, weigh — more at STAND] (1638)
**1** : exerting force by reason of weight alone without motion
**2** : of or relating to bodies at rest or forces in equilibrium
**3** : showing little change ⟨a *static* population⟩
**4 a** : characterized by a lack of movement, animation, or progression **b** : producing an effect of repose or quiescence ⟨a *static* design⟩
**5 a** : standing or fixed in one place : STATIONARY **b** *of water* : stored in a tank but not under pressure

**6** : of, relating to, or producing stationary charges of electricity : ELECTROSTATIC
**7** : of, relating to, or caused by radio static
— **stat·i·cal** \\-ti-kəl\\ *adjective*
— **stat·i·cal·ly** \\-ti-k(ə-)lē\\ *adverb*

**²static** *noun* [*static electricity*] (1913)
**1** : noise produced in a radio or television receiver by atmospheric or various natural or man-made electrical disturbances; *also* : the electrical disturbances producing this noise
**2** : heated opposition or criticism
— **stat·icky** \\'sta-ti-kē\\ *adjective*

**-static** *adjective combining form* [New Latin *-staticus*, from *staticus*]
**1** : of or relating to a position or state ⟨ortho-*static*⟩
**2** : inhibiting the growth of ⟨fungi*static*⟩

**stat·i·ce** \\'sta-tə-(,)sē\\ *noun* [New Latin, genus of herbs, from Latin, an astringent plant, from Greek *statikē*, from feminine of *statikos* causing to stand, astringent] (1745)
: SEA LAVENDER

**static electricity** *noun* (1876)
: electricity that consists of isolated motionless charges (as those produced by friction)

**static line** *noun* (1930)
: a cord attached to a parachute pack and to an airplane to open the parachute after a jumper clears the plane

**stat·ics** \\'sta-tiks\\ *noun plural but singular or plural in construction* (1837)
: mechanics dealing with the relations of forces that produce equilibrium among material bodies

**static tube** *noun* (1923)
: a tube used for indicating static as distinct from impact pressure in a stream of fluid

**¹sta·tion** \\'stā-shən\\ *noun* [Middle English *stacioun*, from Middle French *station*, from Latin *station-, statio*, from *stare* to stand — more at STAND] (14th century)
**1 a** : the place or position in which something or someone stands or is assigned to stand or remain **b** : any of the places in a manufacturing operation at which one part of the work is done **c** : equipment used usually by one person for performing a particular job
**2** : the act or manner of standing : POSTURE
**3** : a stopping place: as **a** (1) : a regular stopping place in a transportation route (2) : the building connected with such a stopping place : DEPOT 3 **b** : one of the stations of the cross
**4 a** : a post or sphere of duty or occupation **b** : a stock farm or ranch especially of Australia or New Zealand
**5** : STANDING, RANK ⟨a woman of high *station*⟩
**6** : a place for specialized observation and study of scientific phenomena ⟨a seismological *station*⟩ ⟨a marine biological *station*⟩
**7** : a place established to provide a public service: as **a** (1) : FIRE STATION (2) : POLICE STATION **b** : a branch post office
**8** : SERVICE STATION 1
**9 a** : a complete assemblage of radio or television equipment for transmitting or receiving **b** : the place in which such a station is located

**²station** *transitive verb* **sta·tioned; sta·tion·ing** \\'stā-sh(ə-)niŋ\\ (1748)
: to assign to or set in a station or position : POST

**sta·tion·al** \\'stā-shnəl, -shə-nªl\\ *adjective* (1902)
: of, relating to, or being a mass formerly celebrated by the pope at designated churches in Rome on appointed holy days

**sta·tion·ary** \\'stā-shə-,ner-ē\\ *adjective* (1626)
**1** : fixed in a station, course, or mode : IMMOBILE
**2** : unchanging in condition

**stationary bicycle** *noun* (1962)
: an exercise apparatus that can be pedaled like a bicycle — called also *stationary bike*

**stationary front** *noun* (circa 1940)
: the boundary between two air masses neither of which is replacing the other

**stationary wave** *noun* (1856)

: STANDING WAVE

**station break** *noun* (1937)
: a pause in a radio or television broadcast for announcement of the identity of the network or station; *also* : an announcement or advertisement during this pause

**sta·tio·ner** \\'stā-sh(ə-)nər\\ *noun* [Middle English *stacioner*, from Medieval Latin *stationarius*, from *station-, statio* shop, from Latin, station] (14th century)
**1** *archaic* **a** : BOOKSELLER **b** : PUBLISHER
**2** : one that sells stationery

**sta·tio·nery** \\'stā-shə-,ner-ē\\ *noun* [*stationer*] (circa 1688)
**1** : materials (as paper, pens, and ink) for writing or typing
**2** : letter paper usually accompanied with matching envelopes

**station house** *noun* (1833)
: a house at or a post or station; *especially* : POLICE STATION

**sta·tion·mas·ter** \\'stā-shən-,mas-tər\\ *noun* (1856)
: an official in charge of the operation of a railroad station

**stations of the cross** *often S&C capitalized* (circa 1890)
**1** : a series of usually 14 images or pictures especially in a church that represent the stages of Christ's passion and death
**2** : a devotion involving commemorative meditation before the stations of the cross

**station wagon** *noun* (1904)
: an automobile that has a passenger compartment which extends to the back of the vehicle, that has no trunk, that has one or more rear seats which can be folded down to make space for light cargo, and that has a tailgate or liftgate

**stat·ism** \\'stā-,ti-zəm\\ *noun* (1880)
: concentration of economic controls and planning in the hands of a highly centralized government

**stat·ist** \\'stā-tist\\ *noun* (1946)
: an advocate of statism
— **statist** *adjective*

**sta·tis·tic** \\stə-'tis-tik\\ *noun* [singular of *statistics*] (1880)
**1** : a single term or datum in a collection of statistics
**2 a** : a quantity (as the mean of a sample) that is computed from a sample; *specifically* : ESTIMATE 3b **b** : a random variable that takes on the possible values of a statistic

**sta·tis·ti·cal** \\-ti-kəl\\ *adjective* (1787)
: of, relating to, based on, or employing the principles of statistics
— **sta·tis·ti·cal·ly** \\-k(ə-)lē\\ *adverb*

**statistical mechanics** *noun plural but usually singular in construction* (1885)
: a branch of mechanics dealing with the application of the principles of statistics to the mechanics of a system consisting of a large number of parts having motions that differ by small steps over a large range

**stat·is·ti·cian** \\,sta-tə-'sti-shən\\ *noun* (1825)
: one versed in or engaged in compiling statistics

**sta·tis·tics** \\stə-'tis-tiks\\ *noun plural but singular or plural in construction* [German *Statistik* study of political facts and figures, from New Latin *statisticus* of politics, from Latin *status* state] (1770)
**1** : a branch of mathematics dealing with the collection, analysis, interpretation, and presentation of masses of numerical data
**2** : a collection of quantitative data

**sta·tive** \\'stā-tiv\\ *adjective* (1874)
: expressing a state, condition, or relation — compare ACTIVE 3b

**stato-** *combining form* [International Scientific Vocabulary, from Greek *statos* stationary, from *histasthai* to stand — more at STAND]
**1** : resting ⟨*stato*blast⟩
**2** : equilibrium ⟨*stato*cyst⟩

**sta·to·blast** \'sta-tə-ˌblast\ *noun* [International Scientific Vocabulary] (1855)
**1** : a bud in a freshwater bryozoan that over-winters in a chitinous envelope and develops into a new individual in spring
**2** : GEMMULE b

**sta·to·cyst** \-ˌsist\ *noun* [International Scientific Vocabulary] (1902)
: an organ of equilibrium occurring especially among invertebrate animals and consisting usually of a fluid-filled vesicle in which are suspended statoliths

**sta·to·lith** \'sta-tᵊl-ith\ *noun* [International Scientific Vocabulary] (1900)
**1** : any of the usually calcareous bodies suspended in a statocyst
**2** : any of various starch grains or other solid bodies in the plant cytoplasm that are held to be responsible by changes in their position for changes in orientation of a part or organ

**sta·tor** \'stā-tər\ *noun* [New Latin, from Latin, one that stands, from *stare* to stand — more at STAND] (1902)
: a stationary part in a machine in or about which a rotor revolves

**sta·to·scope** \'sta-tə-ˌskōp\ *noun* [International Scientific Vocabulary] (circa 1900)
: a sensitive aneroid barometer for recording small changes in atmospheric pressure; *especially* : one used for indicating small changes in the altitude of an aircraft

¹**stat·u·ary** \'sta-chə-ˌwer-ē\ *noun, plural* **-ar·ies** (1542)
**1** : SCULPTOR
**2 a** : the art of making statues **b** : a collection of statues : STATUES

²**statuary** *adjective* (1627)
: of, relating to, or suitable for statues

**stat·ue** \'sta-(ˌ)chü\ *noun* [Middle English, from Middle French, from Latin *statua*, from *statuere* to set up — more at STATUTE] (14th century)
: a three-dimensional representation usually of a person, animal, or mythical being that is produced by sculpturing, modeling, or casting

**Statue of Liberty** (circa 1900)
**1** : a large copper statue of a woman holding a torch aloft in her right hand located on Liberty Island in New York harbor
**2** : a trick played in football in which the ball-carrier takes the ball from the raised hand of a teammate who is faking a pass

**stat·u·esque** \ˌsta-chə-'wesk\ *adjective* (1834)
: resembling a statue especially in dignity, shapeliness, or stillness; *especially* : tall and shapely
— **stat·u·esque·ly** *adverb*

**stat·u·ette** \ˌsta-chə-'wet\ *noun* (1843)
: a small statue

**stat·ure** \'sta-chər\ *noun* [Middle English, from Middle French, from Latin *statura*, from *status*, past participle of *stare* to stand — more at STAND] (14th century)
**1** : natural height (as of a person) in an upright position
**2** : quality or status gained by growth, development, or achievement

**sta·tus** \'stā-təs, 'sta-\ *noun, plural* **sta·tus·es** *often attributive* [Latin — more at STATE] (1791)
**1** : the condition of a person or thing in the eyes of the law
**2 a** : position or rank in relation to others ⟨the *status* of a father⟩ **b** : relative rank in a hierarchy of prestige; *especially* : high prestige
**3** : state of affairs

**status offender** *noun* (circa 1976)
: a young offender (as a runaway or a truant) who is under the jurisdiction of a court for repeated offenses that are not crimes

**status quo** \-'kwō\ *noun* [Latin, state in which] (1833)
: the existing state of affairs ⟨seeks to preserve the *status quo*⟩

**status quo an·te** \-'an-tē\ *noun* [Latin, state in which previously] (1877)
: the state of affairs that existed previously

**sta·tusy** \'stā-tə-sē, 'sta-\ *adjective* (1962)
: having, showing, or conferring prestige

**stat·ut·able** \'sta-chə-tə-bəl, 'sta-ˌchü-\ *adjective* (1636)
: made, regulated, or imposed by or in conformity to statute : STATUTORY ⟨*statutable* tonnage⟩

**stat·ute** \'sta-(ˌ)chüt, -chət\ *noun* [Middle English, from Old French *statut*, from Late Latin *statutum* law, regulation, from Latin, neuter of *statutus*, past participle of *statuere* to set up, station, from *status* position, state] (14th century)
**1** : a law enacted by the legislative branch of a government
**2** : an act of a corporation or of its founder intended as a permanent rule
**3** : an international instrument setting up an agency and regulating its scope or authority
*synonym* see LAW

**statute book** *noun* (1593)
: the whole body of legislation of a given jurisdiction whether or not published as a whole — usually used in plural

**statute mile** *noun* (1862)
: MILE 1a

**statute of limitations** (1768)
: a statute assigning a certain time after which rights cannot be enforced by legal action or offenses cannot be punished

**stat·u·to·ry** \'sta-chə-ˌtōr-ē, -ˌtȯr-\ *adjective* (1766)
**1** : of or relating to statutes
**2** : enacted, created, or regulated by statute ⟨a *statutory* age limit⟩
— **stat·u·to·ri·ly** \ˌsta-chə-'tōr-ə-lē, -'tȯr-\ *adverb*

**statutory rape** *noun* (1898)
: sexual intercourse with a person who is below the statutory age of consent

¹**staunch** \'stȯnch, 'stänch\ *variant of* STANCH

²**staunch** *adjective* [Middle English, from Middle French *estanche*, feminine of *estanc*, from Old French, from *estancher* to stanch — more at STANCH] (15th century)
**1 a** : WATERTIGHT, SOUND **b** : strongly built : SUBSTANTIAL
**2** : steadfast in loyalty or principle
*synonym* see FAITHFUL
— **staunch·ly** *adverb*
— **staunch·ness** *noun*

**stau·ro·lite** \'stȯr-ə-ˌlīt\ *noun* [French, from Greek *stauros* cross + French *-lite* — more at STEER] (circa 1815)
: a mineral consisting of a basic silicate of iron and aluminum in prismatic orthorhombic crystals often twinned so as to resemble a cross
— **stau·ro·lit·ic** \ˌstȯr-ə-'li-tik\ *adjective*

¹**stave** \'stāv\ *noun* [Middle English, back-formation from *staves*, plural of *staf* staff] (13th century)
**1** : ¹STAFF 1, 2
**2** : any of the narrow strips of wood or narrow iron plates placed edge to edge to form the sides, covering, or lining of a vessel (as a barrel) or structure
**3** : STANZA
**4** : ¹STAFF 3

²**stave** *verb* **staved** *or* **stove** \'stōv\; **stav·ing** (circa 1595)
*transitive verb*
**1** : to break in the staves of (a cask)
**2** : to smash a hole in ⟨*stove* in the boat⟩; *also* : to crush or break inward ⟨*staved* in several ribs⟩
**3** : to drive or thrust away
*intransitive verb*
**1** *archaic* : to become stove in — used of a boat or ship
**2** : to walk or move rapidly

**stave off** *transitive verb* (1624)
**1** : to fend off ⟨*staving off* creditors⟩
**2** : to ward off (as something adverse) : FORESTALL ⟨trying to *stave off* disaster⟩

**staves** *plural of* STAFF

**staves·acre** \'stāv-ˌzā-kər\ *noun* [by folk etymology from Middle English *staphisagre*, from Medieval Latin *staphis agria*, from Greek, literally, wild raisin] (15th century)
: a Eurasian delphinium (*Delphinium staphisagria*); *also* : its violently emetic and cathartic seeds

¹**stay** \'stā\ *noun* [Middle English, from Old English *stæg*; akin to Old Norse *stag* stay, Old English *stēle* steel] (before 12th century)
**1** : a large strong rope usually of wire used to support a mast
**2** : ¹GUY

²**stay** (1627)
*transitive verb*
**1** : to secure upright with or as if with stays
**2** : to incline (a mast) forward, aft, or to one side by the stays
*intransitive verb*
: to go about : TACK

³**stay** *verb* **stayed** \'stād\ *also* **staid** \'stād\; **stay·ing** [Middle English, from Middle French *ester* to stand, stay, from Latin *stare* — more at STAND] (15th century)
*intransitive verb*
**1** : to stop going forward : PAUSE
**2** : to stop doing something : CEASE
**3** : to continue in a place or condition : REMAIN ⟨*stayed* up all night⟩ ⟨went for a short vacation but *stayed* on for weeks⟩ ⟨*stay* put till I come back⟩
**4** : to stand firm
**5** : to take up residence : LODGE
**6** : to keep even in a contest or rivalry ⟨*stay* with the leaders⟩
**7** : to call a poker bet without raising
**8** *obsolete* : to be in waiting or attendance
*transitive verb*
**1** : to wait for : AWAIT
**2** : to stick or remain with (as a race or trial of endurance) to the end — usually used in the phrase *stay the course*
**3** : to remain during ⟨*stayed* the whole time⟩
**4 a** : to stop or delay the proceeding or advance of by or as if by interposing an obstacle : HALT ⟨*stay* an execution⟩ **b** : to check the course of (as a disease) **c** : ALLAY, PACIFY ⟨*stayed* tempers⟩ **d** : to quiet the hunger of temporarily
*synonym* see DEFER

⁴**stay** *noun* (1536)
**1 a** : the action of halting : the state of being stopped **b** : a stopping or suspension of procedure or execution by judicial or executive order
**2** *obsolete* : SELF-CONTROL, MODERATION
**3** : a residence or sojourn in a place
**4** : capacity for endurance

⁵**stay** *noun* [Middle French *estaie*, of Germanic origin; akin to Old High German *stān* to stand — more at STAND] (1515)
**1** : one that serves as a prop : SUPPORT
**2** : a corset stiffened with bones — usually used in plural

⁶**stay** *transitive verb* (1548)
**1** : to provide physical or moral support for : SUSTAIN
**2** : to fix on something as a foundation

**stay–at–home** \'stā-ət-ˌhōm\ *adjective* (1806)
: remaining habitually in one's residence, locality, or country
— **stay–at–home** *noun*

**stay·er** \'stā-ər\ *noun* (circa 1580)
: one that stays; *especially* : one that upholds or supports

**staying power** *noun* (1859)
: capacity for endurance : STAMINA

---

\ə\ abut \ᵊ\ kitten \ər\ further \a\ ash \ā\ ace \ä\ mop, mar \au̇\ out \ch\ chin \e\ bet \ē\ easy \g\ go \i\ hit \ī\ ice \j\ job \ŋ\ sing \ō\ go \ȯ\ law \ȯi\ boy \th\ thin \th\ the \ü\ loot \u̇\ foot \y\ yet \zh\ vision    *see also* Guide to Pronunciation

**stay·sail** \'stā-ˌsāl, -səl\ *noun* (1669)
: a fore-and-aft sail hoisted on a stay — see SAIL illustration

**STD** \ˌes-(ˌ)tē-'dē\ *noun* [*sexually transmitted disease*] (1976)
: any of various diseases transmitted by direct sexual contact that include the classic venereal diseases (as syphilis, gonorrhea, and chancroid) and other diseases (as hepatitis A, hepatitis B, giardiasis, and AIDS) that are often or sometimes contracted by other than sexual means

**¹stead** \'sted\ *noun* [Middle English *stede*, from Old English; akin to Old High German *stat* place, Old English *standan* to stand — more at STAND] (before 12th century)
**1** *obsolete* : LOCALITY, PLACE
**2** : ADVANTAGE — used chiefly in the phrase *to stand one in good stead*
**3** : the office, place, or function ordinarily occupied or carried out by someone or something else ⟨acted in his brother's *stead*⟩

**²stead** *transitive verb* (13th century)
: to be of avail to : HELP

**stead·fast** \'sted-ˌfast *also* -fəst\ *adjective* [Middle English *stedefast*, from Old English *stedefæst*, from *stede* + *fæst* fixed, fast] (before 12th century)
**1 a** : firmly fixed in place : IMMOVABLE **b** : not subject to change ⟨the *steadfast* doctrine of original sin —Ellen Glasgow⟩
**2** : firm in belief, determination, or adherence : LOYAL
**synonym** see FAITHFUL
— **stead·fast·ly** *adverb*
— **stead·fast·ness** \-ˌfas(t)-nəs, -fəs(t)-\ *noun*

**stead·ing** \'ste-dᵊn, 'stē-, -diŋ\ *noun* [Middle English *steding*, from *stede* place, farm] (15th century)
**1** : a small farm
**2** *chiefly Scottish* : the service buildings or area of a farm

**¹steady** \'ste-dē\ *adjective* **steadi·er; -est** [Middle English *stedy*, from *stede*] (14th century)
**1 a** : direct or sure in movement : UNFALTERING **b** : firm in position : FIXED **c** : keeping nearly upright in a seaway ⟨a *steady* ship⟩
**2** : showing little variation or fluctuation : STABLE, UNIFORM ⟨a *steady* breeze⟩ ⟨*steady* prices⟩
**3 a** : not easily disturbed or upset ⟨*steady* nerves⟩ **b** (1) : constant in feeling, principle, purpose, or attachment (2) : DEPENDABLE **c** : not given to dissipation : SOBER ☆
— **steadi·ly** \'ste-dᵊl-ē\ *adverb*
— **steadi·ness** \'ste-dē-nəs\ *noun*

**²steady** *verb* **stead·ied; steady·ing** (1530)
*transitive verb*
: to make or keep steady
*intransitive verb*
: to become steady
— **steadi·er** *noun*

**³steady** *adverb* (circa 1605)
**1** : in a steady manner : STEADILY
**2** : on the course set — used as a direction to the helmsman of a ship

**⁴steady** *noun, plural* **stead·ies** (1792)
: one that is steady; *specifically* : a boyfriend or girlfriend with whom one goes steady

**steady state** *noun* (1885)
: a state or condition of a system or process (as one of the energy states of an atom) that does not change in time; *broadly* : a condition that changes only negligibly over a specified time

**steady state theory** *noun* (1948)
: a theory in astronomy: the universe has always existed and has always been expanding with hydrogen being created continuously — compare BIG BANG THEORY

**steak** \'stāk\ *noun* [Middle English *steke*, from Old Norse *steik*; akin to Old Norse *steikja* to roast on a stake, *stik* stick, stake — more at STICK] (15th century)
**1 a** : a slice of meat cut from a fleshy part of a beef carcass **b** : a similar slice of a specified meat other than beef ⟨ham *steak*⟩ **c** : a cross-section slice of a large fish ⟨swordfish *steak*⟩
**2** : ground beef prepared for cooking or for serving in the manner of a steak ⟨hamburger *steak*⟩

**steak house** *noun* (1762)
: a restaurant whose specialty is beefsteak

**steak knife** *noun* (1895)
: a table knife with a sharp often serrated blade

**steak tar·tare** \-tär-'tär\ *noun* [French *tartare* Tartar] (1911)
: highly seasoned ground beef eaten raw

**¹steal** \'stē(ə)l\ *verb* **stole** \'stōl\; **sto·len** \'stō-lən\; **steal·ing** [Middle English *stelen*, from Old English *stelan*; akin to Old High German *stelan* to steal] (before 12th century)
*intransitive verb*
**1** : to take the property of another wrongfully and especially as an habitual or regular practice
**2** : to come or go secretly, unobtrusively, gradually, or unexpectedly
**3** : to steal or attempt to steal a base
*transitive verb*
**1 a** : to take or appropriate without right or leave and with intent to keep or make use of wrongfully ⟨*stole* a car⟩ **b** : to take away by force or unjust means ⟨they've *stolen* our liberty⟩ **c** : to take surreptitiously or without permission ⟨*steal* a kiss⟩ **d** : to appropriate to oneself or beyond one's proper share : make oneself the focus of ⟨*steal* the show⟩
**2 a** : to move, convey, or introduce secretly : SMUGGLE **b** : to accomplish in a concealed or unobserved manner ⟨*steal* a visit⟩
**3 a** : to seize, gain, or win by trickery, skill, or daring ⟨a basketball player adept at *stealing* the ball⟩ ⟨*stole* the election⟩ **b** *of a base runner* : to reach (a base) safely solely by running and usually catching the opposing team off guard ☆
— **steal·able** \'stē-lə-bəl\ *adjective*
— **steal·er** *noun*
— **steal a march on** : to gain an advantage on unobserved
— **steal one's thunder** : to grab attention from another especially by anticipating an idea, plan, or presentation; *also* : to claim credit for another's idea

**²steal** *noun* (circa 1825)
**1** : the act or an instance of stealing
**2** : a fraudulent or questionable political deal
**3** : BARGAIN 2 ⟨it's a *steal* at that price⟩

**stealth** \'stelth\ *noun* [Middle English *stelthe*; akin to Old English *stelan* to steal] (13th century)
**1 a** *archaic* : THEFT **b** *obsolete* : something stolen
**2** : the act or action of proceeding furtively, secretly, or imperceptibly ⟨the state moves by *stealth* to gather information —Nat Hentoff⟩
**3** : the state of being furtive or unobtrusive
**4** : an aircraft-design characteristic consisting of oblique angular construction and avoidance of vertical surfaces that is intended to produce a very weak radar return

**stealthy** \'stel-thē\ *adjective* **stealth·i·er; -est** (1605)
**1** : slow, deliberate, and secret in action or character
**2** : intended to escape observation : FURTIVE
**synonym** see SECRET
— **stealth·i·ly** \-thə-lē\ *adverb*
— **stealth·i·ness** \-thē-nəs\ *noun*

**¹steam** \'stēm\ *noun* [Middle English *stem*, from Old English *stēam*; akin to Dutch *stoom* steam] (before 12th century)
**1** : a vapor arising from a heated substance
**2 a** : the invisible vapor into which water is converted when heated to the boiling point **b** : the mist formed by the condensation on cooling of water vapor
**3 a** : water vapor kept under pressure so as to supply energy for heating, cooking, or mechanical work; *also* : the power so generated **b** : active force : POWER, MOMENTUM ⟨got there under his own *steam*⟩ ⟨sales began to pick up *steam*⟩; *also* : normal force ⟨at full *steam*⟩ **c** : pent-up emotional tension ⟨needed to let off a little *steam*⟩
**4 a** : STEAMER 2a **b** : travel by or a trip in a steamer

**²steam** (15th century)
*transitive verb*
**1** : to give out as fumes : EXHALE
**2** : to apply steam to; *especially* : to expose to the action of steam (as for softening or cooking)
*intransitive verb*
**1** : to rise or pass off as vapor
**2** : to give off steam or vapor
**3 a** : to move or travel by the agency of steam **b** : to move or proceed with energy or force
**4** : to be angry : BOIL ⟨*steaming* over the insult⟩

**steam·boat** \'stēm-ˌbōt\ *noun* (1785)
: a boat driven by steam power; *specifically* : a shallow-draft vessel used on inland waterways

**steamboat Gothic** *noun* [from its use in homes of retired steamboat captains in imitation of the style of river steamboats] (1941)
: an elaborately ornamented architectural style used in homes built in the middle 19th century in the Ohio and Mississippi river valleys

**steam boiler** *noun* (1805)
: a boiler for producing steam

**steam chest** *noun* (1797)
: the chamber from which steam is distributed to a cylinder of a steam engine

**steamed** \'stēmd\ *adjective* (1802)
**1** : cooked by steam
**2** : ANGRY 1 — often used with *up*

**steam engine** *noun* (1751)
: an engine driven or worked by steam; *specifically* : a reciprocating engine having a piston driven in a closed cylinder by steam

**steam·er** \'stē-mər\ *noun* (1814)
**1** : a vessel in which articles are subjected to steam
**2 a** : a ship propelled by steam **b** : an engine, machine, or vehicle operated or propelled by steam
**3** : one that steams
**4** : SOFT-SHELL CLAM

**steamer rug** *noun* (1890)

---

☆ SYNONYMS

**Steady, even, equable** mean not varying throughout a course or extent. STEADY implies lack of fluctuation or interruption of movement ⟨*steady* progress⟩. EVEN suggests a lack of variation in quality or character ⟨an *even* distribution⟩. EQUABLE implies lack of extremes or of sudden sharp changes ⟨maintain an *equable* temper⟩.

**Steal, pilfer, filch, purloin** mean to take from another without right or without detection. STEAL may apply to any surreptitious taking of something and differs from the other terms by commonly applying to intangibles as well as material things ⟨*steal* jewels⟩ ⟨*stole* a look at the gifts⟩. PILFER implies stealing repeatedly in small amounts ⟨*pilfered* from his employer⟩. FILCH adds a suggestion of snatching quickly and surreptitiously ⟨*filched* an apple from the tray⟩. PURLOIN stresses removing or carrying off for one's own use or purposes ⟨printed a *purloined* document⟩.

: a warm covering for the lap and feet especially of a person sitting on a ship's deck

**steamer trunk** *noun* (1886)
: a trunk suitable for use in a stateroom of a steamer; *especially* : a shallow trunk that may be stowed beneath a berth

**steam·fit·ter** \'stēm-ˌfi-tər\ *noun* (circa 1890)
: one that installs or repairs equipment (as steam pipes) for heating, ventilating, or refrigerating systems
— **steam fitting** *noun*

**steam iron** *noun* (circa 1943)
: a pressing iron with a compartment holding water that is converted to steam by the iron's heat and emitted through the soleplate onto the fabric being pressed

¹**steam·roll·er** \'stēm-ˌrō-lər\ *noun* (1866)
**1** : a steam-driven road roller; *broadly* : ROAD ROLLER
**2** : a crushing force especially when ruthlessly applied to overcome opposition

²**steamroller** *or* **steam·roll** \-ˌrōl\ (1879)
*transitive verb*
**1** : to overwhelm usually by greatly superior force ⟨*steamroller* the opposition⟩
**2** : to bring or advance by overwhelming force or pressure ⟨*steamrollered* the bill through the legislature⟩
*intransitive verb*
: to move or proceed with irresistible force

**steam·ship** \'stēm-ˌship\ *noun* (1790)
: STEAMER 2a

**steamship round** *noun* (1964)
: a large beef roast consisting of the whole round with rump and heel

**steam shovel** *noun* (1879)
: a power shovel operated by steam; *broadly* : POWER SHOVEL

**steam table** *noun* (1861)
: a table having openings to hold containers of cooked food over steam or hot water circulating beneath them

**steam turbine** *noun* (1900)
: a turbine that is driven by the pressure of steam discharged at high velocity against the turbine vanes

**steam up** *transitive verb* (1860)
: to make angry or excited : AROUSE

**steamy** \'stē-mē\ *adjective* **steam·i·er; -est** (1644)
**1** : consisting of, characterized by, or full of steam
**2** : intensely or uncomfortably hot: as **a** : hot and humid ⟨a *steamy* afternoon⟩ **b** : sensually hot : EROTIC ⟨a *steamy* love scene⟩
— **steam·i·ly** \-mə-lē\ *adverb*
— **steam·i·ness** \-mē-nəs\ *noun*

**ste·ap·sin** \stē-'ap-sən\ *noun* [Greek *stear* hard fat + English *-psin* (as in *pepsin*)] (1896)
: the lipase in pancreatic juice

**stea·rate** \'stē-ə-ˌrāt, 'sti-(ə)r-ˌāt\ *noun* (1841)
: a salt or ester of stearic acid

**stea·ric acid** \stē-'ar-ik-, 'sti(ə)r-ik-\ *noun* (1831)
: a white crystalline fatty acid $C_{18}H_{36}O_2$ obtained by saponifying tallow or other hard fats containing stearin; *also* : a commercial mixture of stearic and palmitic acids

**stea·rin** \'stē-ə-rən, 'stir-ən\ *noun* [French *stéarine*, from Greek *stear*] (1817)
: an ester of glycerol and stearic acid

**ste·a·tite** \'stē-ə-ˌtīt\ *noun* [Latin *steatitis*, a precious stone, from Greek, from *steat-, stear*] (1758)
**1** : a massive talc having a grayish green or brown color : SOAPSTONE
**2** : an electrically insulating porcelain composed largely of steatite
— **ste·a·tit·ic** \ˌstē-ə-'ti-tik\ *adjective*

**steato-** *combining form* [Greek, from *steat-, stear*; perhaps akin to Sanskrit *styāyate* it hardens]
: fat ⟨*steato*rrhea⟩

**ste·a·to·py·gia** \ˌstē-a-tə-'pi-j(ē-)ə, -'pī-\ *noun* [New Latin, from *steat-, stear* + Greek *pygē* buttocks] (1879)

: an excessive development of fat on the buttocks that occurs especially among women of the Hottentots and some black peoples
— **ste·a·to·py·gous** \-gəs\ *or* **ste·a·to·py·gic** \ˌstē-ə-'tä-pə-jik, -tə-'pī-jik\ *adjective*

**ste·at·or·rhea** \(ˌ)stē-ˌa-tə-'rē-ə\ *noun* [New Latin] (circa 1859)
: an excess of fat in the stools

**stedfast** *variant of* STEADFAST

**steed** \'stēd\ *noun* [Middle English *stede,* from Old English *stēda* stallion; akin to Old English *stōd* stud — more at STUD] (before 12th century)
: HORSE; *especially* : a spirited horse (as for war)

**steek** \'stēk\ *verb* [Middle English *steken* to pierce, fix, enclose; akin to Old English *stician* to pierce — more at STICK] (13th century)
*chiefly Scottish* : SHUT, CLOSE

¹**steel** \'stē(ə)l\ *noun* [Middle English *stele,* from Old English *stȳle, stēle*; akin to Old High German *stahal* steel and perhaps to Sanskrit *stakati* he resists] (before 12th century)
**1** : commercial iron that contains carbon in any amount up to about 1.7 percent as an essential alloying constituent, is malleable when under suitable conditions, and is distinguished from cast iron by its malleability and lower carbon content
**2** : an instrument or implement of or characteristically of steel: as **a** : a thrusting or cutting weapon **b** : an instrument (as a fluted round rod with a handle) for sharpening knives **c** : a piece of steel for striking sparks from flint
**3** : a quality (as hardness of mind or spirit) that suggests steel ⟨nerves of *steel*⟩
**4 a** : the steel manufacturing industry **b** *plural* : shares of stock in steel companies

²**steel** *transitive verb* (13th century)
**1** : to overlay, point, or edge with steel
**2 a** : to cause to resemble steel (as in looks or hardness) **b** : to fill with resolution or determination

³**steel** *adjective* (13th century)
**1** : made of steel
**2** : of or relating to the production of steel
**3** : resembling steel

**steel band** *noun* (1949)
: a band of steel drums

**steel blue** *noun* (1817)
**1** : a grayish blue
**2** : any of the blue colors assumed by steel at various temperatures in tempering

**steel drum** *noun* (1952)
: a musical instrument originally developed in Trinidad that is played by hammering raised and tuned portions of the bottom of an oil drum

**steel engraving** *noun* (1824)
**1** : the art or process of engraving on steel
**2** : an impression taken from an engraved steel plate

**steel guitar** *noun* (1925)
**1** : HAWAIIAN GUITAR
**2** : PEDAL STEEL
— **steel guitarist** *noun*

**steel·head** \'stē(ə)l-ˌhed\ *noun, plural* **steelhead** *also* **steelheads** (circa 1882)
: an anadromous rainbow trout

**steel·ie** *also* **steely** \'stē-lē\ *noun, plural* **steel·ies** (1922)
: a steel playing marble

**steel·mak·er** \'stē(ə)l-ˌmā-kər\ *noun* (1839)
: a manufacturer of steel
— **steel·mak·ing** \-kiŋ\ *noun*

**steel–trap** \'stē(ə)l-'trap\ *adjective* (1945)
: QUICK, INCISIVE ⟨a *steel-trap* mind⟩

**steel wool** *noun* (1896)
: an abrasive material composed of long fine steel shavings and used especially for scouring and burnishing

**steel·work** \'stē(ə)l-ˌwərk\ *noun* (1681)
**1** : work in steel

**2** *plural but singular or plural in construction*
: an establishment where steel is made

**steel·work·er** \-ˌwər-kər\ *noun* (1884)
: one who works in steel and especially in the manufacturing of it

**steely** \'stē-lē\ *adjective* **steel·i·er; -est** (1509)
**1** : resembling or suggesting steel (as in hardness, color, strength, or coldness) ⟨*steely* determination⟩ ⟨*steely* blue⟩
**2** : made of steel
— **steel·i·ness** *noun*

**steel·yard** \'stē(ə)l-ˌyärd, 'stil-yərd\ *noun* [probably from ³*steel* + ⁴*yard* (rod)] (1639)
: a balance in which an object to be weighed is suspended from the shorter arm of a lever and the weight determined by moving a counterpoise along a graduated scale on the longer arm until equilibrium is attained

steelyard

**steen·bok** \'stēn-ˌbäk, 'stän-\ *or* **stein·bok** \'stīn-, 'stän-\ *noun* [Afrikaans *steenbok;* akin to Old English *stānbucca* ibex, *stān* stone, *bucca* buck] (1775)
: a small slender antelope (*Raphicerus campestris*) with long legs that inhabits chiefly grasslands of eastern and southern Africa

¹**steep** \'stēp\ *adjective* [Middle English *stepe,* from Old English *stēap* high, steep, deep; akin to Middle High German *stief* steep] (before 12th century)
**1** : LOFTY, HIGH — used chiefly of a sea
**2** : making a large angle with the plane of the horizon
**3 a** : mounting or falling precipitously ⟨the stairs were very *steep*⟩ **b** : being or characterized by a rapid and intensive decline or increase
**4** : extremely or excessively high ⟨*steep* prices⟩ ☆
— **steep·ish** \'stē-pish\ *adjective*
— **steep·ly** *adverb*
— **steep·ness** *noun*

²**steep** *noun* (1555)
: a precipitous place

³**steep** *verb* [Middle English *stepen;* akin to Swedish *stöpa* to steep] (14th century)
*transitive verb*
**1** : to soak in a liquid at a temperature under the boiling point (as for softening, bleaching, or extracting an essence)
**2** : to cover with or plunge into a liquid (as in bathing, rinsing, or soaking)
**3** : to saturate with or subject thoroughly to (some strong or pervading influence) ⟨practices *steeped* in tradition⟩

---

☆ SYNONYMS
**Steep, abrupt, precipitous, sheer**
mean having an incline approaching the perpendicular. STEEP implies such sharpness of pitch that ascent or descent is very difficult ⟨a *steep* hill⟩ ⟨a *steep* dive⟩. ABRUPT implies a sharper pitch and a sudden break in the level ⟨a beach with an *abrupt* drop-off⟩. PRECIPITOUS applies to an incline approaching the vertical ⟨the river winds through a *precipitous* gorge⟩. SHEER suggests an unbroken perpendicular expanse ⟨*sheer* cliffs that daunted the climbers⟩.

---

*intransitive verb*
**:** to undergo the process of soaking in a liquid
**synonym** see SOAK
— **steep·er** *noun*
⁴**steep** *noun* (15th century)
**1 :** the state or process of being steeped
**2 :** a bath or solution in which something is steeped
**steep·en** \'stē-pən, -p°m\ *verb* **steep·ened; steep·en·ing** \'stē-pə-niŋ, 'stēp-niŋ\ (1847)
*intransitive verb*
**:** to become steeper
*transitive verb*
**:** to make steeper
**stee·ple** \'stē-pəl\ *noun* [Middle English *stepel,* from Old English *stēpel* tower; akin to Old English *stēap* steep] (before 12th century)
**:** a tall structure usually having a small spire at the top and surmounting a church tower; *broadly* **:** a whole church tower
— **stee·pled** \-pəld\ *adjective*
**stee·ple·bush** \'stē-pəl-,bush\ *noun* (circa 1818)
**:** HARDHACK
**stee·ple·chase** \-,chās\ *noun* [from the use of church steeples as landmarks to guide the riders] (1793)
**1 a :** a horse race across country **b :** a horse race over a closed course with obstacles (as hedges and walls)
**2 :** a footrace of usually 3000 meters over hurdles and a water jump
— **stee·ple·chas·er** \-,chā-sər\ *noun*
— **stee·ple·chas·ing** \-siŋ\ *noun*
**stee·ple·jack** \-,jak\ *noun* (1881)
**:** one whose work is building smokestacks, towers, or steeples or climbing up the outside of such structures to paint and make repairs
¹**steer** \'stir\ *noun* [Middle English, from Old English *stēor* young ox; akin to Old High German *stior* young ox] (before 12th century)
**1 :** a male bovine animal castrated before sexual maturity — compare STAG 3
**2 :** an ox less than four years old
²**steer** *verb* [Middle English *steren,* from Old English *stīeran;* akin to Old English *stēor-* steering oar, Greek *stauros* stake, cross, *stylos* pillar, Sanskrit *sthavira, sthūra* stout, thick] (12th century)
*transitive verb*
**1 :** to control the course of **:** DIRECT; *especially* **:** to guide by mechanical means (as a rudder)
**2 :** to set and hold to (a course)
*intransitive verb*
**1 :** to direct the course (as of a ship or automobile)
**2 :** to pursue a course of action
**3 :** to be subject to guidance or direction ⟨an automobile that *steers* well⟩
**synonym** see GUIDE
— **steer·able** \'stir-ə-bəl\ *adjective*
— **steer·er** *noun*
— **steer clear :** to keep entirely away — often used with *of* ⟨trying to *steer clear* of controversy⟩
³**steer** *noun* (1894)
**:** a hint as to procedure **:** TIP
⁴**steer** *dialect British variant of* STIR
**steer·age** \'stir-ij\ *noun* (15th century)
**1 :** the act or practice of steering; *broadly* **:** DIRECTION
**2** [from its originally being located near the rudder] **:** a section of inferior accommodations in a passenger ship for passengers paying the lowest fares
**steer·age·way** \-,wā\ *noun* (1769)
**:** a rate of motion sufficient to make a ship or boat respond to movements of the rudder
**steering column** *noun* (1903)
**:** the column that encloses the connections to the steering gear of a vehicle (as an automobile)
**steering committee** *noun* (1887)
**:** a managing or directing committee; *specifically* **:** a committee that determines the order

in which business will be taken up in a U.S. legislative body
**steering gear** *noun* (1869)
**:** a mechanism by which something is steered
**steering wheel** *noun* (1750)
**:** a handwheel by means of which one steers
**steers·man** \'stirz-mən\ *noun* (before 12th century)
**:** one who steers **:** HELMSMAN
¹**steeve** \'stēv\ *transitive verb* **steeved; steev·ing** [Middle English *steven,* probably from Spanish *estibar* or Portuguese *estivar* to pack tightly, from Latin *stipare* to press together — more at STIFF] (15th century)
*archaic* **:** to stow especially in a ship's hold
²**steeve** *verb* **steeved; steev·ing** [origin unknown] (circa 1644)
*intransitive verb*
*of a bowsprit* **:** to incline upward at an angle with the horizon or the line of the keel
*transitive verb*
**:** to set (a bowsprit) at an upward inclination
**stego·saur** \'ste-gə-,sȯr\ *noun* [New Latin *Stegosauria,* from *Stegosaurus*] (1901)
**:** any of a suborder (Stegosauria) of quadrupedal ornithischian dinosaurs with strongly developed dorsal plates and spikes
**stego·sau·rus** \,ste-gə-'sȯr-əs\ *noun* [New Latin, from Greek *stegos* roof + *sauros* lizard — more at THATCH] (1892)
**:** any of a genus (*Stegosaurus*) of stegosaurs known from the Upper Jurassic rocks especially of Colorado and Wyoming
**stein** \'stīn\ *noun* [probably from German *Steingut* stoneware, from *Stein* stone + *Gut* goods] (1855)
**:** a large mug (as of earthenware) used especially for beer; *also* **:** the quantity of beer that a stein holds
**ste·la** \'stē-lə\ *or* **ste·le** \'stē-lē\ *noun, plural* **ste·lae** \-(,)lē\ [Latin & Greek; Latin *stela,* from Greek *stēlē;* akin to Old High German *stollo* pillar, Greek *stellein* to set up] (1776)
**:** a usually carved or inscribed stone slab or pillar used for commemorative purposes
**ste·lar** \'stē-lər, -,lär\ *adjective* (1901)
**:** of, relating to, or constituting a stele
**stele** \'stē(ə)l, 'stē-lē\ *noun* [New Latin, from Greek *stēlē* stela, pillar] (1895)
**:** the usually cylindrical central vascular portion of the axis of a vascular plant
**stel·la** \'ste-lə\ *noun* [Latin, star; from the star on the reverse] (1879)
**:** an experimental international coin based on the metric system that was issued by the U.S. in 1879 and 1880 and was worth about four dollars
**stel·lar** \'ste-lər\ *adjective* [Late Latin *stellaris,* from Latin *stella* star — more at STAR] (circa 1656)
**1 a :** of or relating to the stars **:** ASTRAL **b :** composed of stars
**2 :** of or relating to a theatrical or film star ⟨*stellar* names⟩
**3 a :** PRINCIPAL, LEADING ⟨a *stellar* role⟩ **b :** OUTSTANDING ⟨a *stellar* student⟩ ⟨a *stellar* performance⟩
**stellar wind** *noun* (1965)
**:** plasma continuously ejected from a star's surface into surrounding space
**stel·late** \'ste-,lāt\ *adjective* [Latin *stella*] (1661)
**:** resembling a star (as in shape) ⟨a *stellate* leaf⟩
**Stel·ler's jay** \'ste-lərz, 'shte-\ *noun* [Georg W. *Steller* (died 1746) German naturalist] (1828)
**:** a jay (*Cyanocitta stelleri*) of western North America with a high crest and black and dark blue plumage
**Steller's sea cow** *noun* (1814)
**:** an extinct very large aquatic sirenian (*Hydrodamalis gigas*) formerly common near the Asian coast of the Bering Sea
¹**stem** \'stem\ *noun* [Middle English, from Old English *stefn, stemn* stem of a plant or ship;

akin to Old High German *stam* plant stem and probably to Greek *stamnos* wine jar, *histanai* to set — more at STAND] (before 12th century)
**1 a :** the main trunk of a plant; *specifically* **:** a primary plant axis that develops buds and shoots instead of roots **b :** a plant part (as a branch, petiole, or stipe) that supports another (as a leaf or fruit) **c :** the complete fruiting stalk of a banana plant with its bananas
**2 a :** the main upright member at the bow of a ship **b :** the bow or prow of a ship — compare STERN
**3 :** a line of ancestry **:** STOCK; *especially* **:** a fundamental line from which others have arisen
**4 :** the part of an inflected word that remains unchanged except by phonetic changes or variations throughout an inflection
**5 :** something held to resemble a plant stem: as **a :** a main or heavy stroke of a letter **b :** the short perpendicular line extending from the head of a musical note **c :** the part of a tobacco pipe from the bowl outward **d :** the cylindrical support of a piece of stemware (as a goblet) **e :** a shaft of a watch used for winding
— **from stem to stern :** THROUGHOUT, THOROUGHLY
²**stem** *transitive verb* **stemmed; stemming** [Middle English (Scots) *stemmen* to keep a course, from ¹*stem* (of a ship)] (1593)
**1 :** to make headway against (as an adverse tide, current, or wind)
**2 :** to check or go counter to (something adverse)
— **stem·mer** *noun*
³**stem** *verb* **stemmed; stem·ming** [¹*stem* (of a plant)] (1724)
*transitive verb*
**1 :** to remove the stem from
**2 :** to make stems for (as artificial flowers)
*intransitive verb*
**:** to occur or develop as a consequence **:** have or trace an origin ⟨her success *stems* from hard work⟩
**synonym** see SPRING
— **stem·mer** *noun*
⁴**stem** *verb* **stemmed; stem·ming** [Middle English *stemmen* to dam up, from Old Norse *stemma;* akin to Middle High German *stemmen* to dam up and probably to Lithuanian *stumti* to shove] (14th century)
*transitive verb*
**1 a :** to stop or dam up (as a river) **b :** to stop or check by or as if by damming; *especially* **:** STANCH ⟨*stem* a flow of blood⟩
**2 :** to turn (a ski) in stemming
*intransitive verb*
**1 :** to restrain or check oneself; *also* **:** to become checked or stanched
**2 :** to slide the heel of one ski or of both skis outward usually in making or preparing to make a turn
⁵**stem** *noun* (circa 1700)
**1 :** CHECK, DAM
**2 :** an act or instance of stemming on skis
**stem cell** *noun* (1885)
**:** an unspecialized cell that gives rise to differentiated cells ⟨hematopoietic *stem cells* in bone marrow⟩
**stem christie** *noun, often C capitalized* (1936)
**:** a turn in skiing begun by stemming a ski and completed by bringing the skis parallel into a christie
**stem·less** \'stem-ləs\ *adjective* (1796)
**:** having no stem **:** ACAULESCENT
**stem·ma** \'ste-mə\ *noun, plural* **stem·ma·ta** \-mə-tə\ [Latin, wreath, pedigree (from the wreaths placed on ancestral images), from Greek, wreath, from *stephein* to crown, enwreathe] (1826)
**1 :** a simple eye present in some insects
**2 :** a scroll (as among the ancient Romans) containing a genealogical list

**3 :** a tree showing the relationships of the manuscripts of a literary work
— **stem·mat·ic** \ste-'ma-tik, stə-\ *adjective*
**stemmed** \'stemd\ *adjective* (1576)
**:** having a stem — usually used in combination ⟨long-*stemmed* roses⟩
**stem·my** \'ste-mē\ *adjective* **stem·mi·er; -est** (1863)
**:** abounding in stems
**stem rust** *noun* (1899)
**1 :** a rust attacking the stem of a plant; *especially* **:** a destructive disease especially of wheat caused by a rust fungus (*Puccinia graminis*) which produces reddish brown lesions in the uredospore stage and black lesions in the teliospore stage and has any of several plants of the barberry family as an intermediate host
**2 :** the fungus causing stem rust
**stem turn** *noun* (1922)
**:** a skiing turn executed by stemming an outside ski
**stem·ware** \'stem-,war, -,wer\ *noun* (1926)
**:** glass hollowware mounted on a stem
**stem–wind·er** \-,wīn-dər\ *noun* (1875)
**1 :** a stem-winding watch
**2** [from the superiority of the stem-winding watch over the older key-wound watch] **:** one that is first-rate of its kind; *especially* **:** a stirring speech
**stem–wind·ing** \-diŋ\ *adjective* (1867)
**:** wound by an inside mechanism turned by the knurled knob at the outside end of the stem ⟨a *stem-winding* watch⟩
**Sten** \'sten\ *noun* [R. V. Sheppard, 20th century English army officer + H. J. Turpin, 20th century English civil servant + *England*] (1942)
**:** a light simple 9-millimeter British submachine gun
**sten-** *or* **steno-** *combining form* [Greek, from *stenos*]
**:** close **:** narrow **:** little ⟨*steno*bathic⟩
**stench** \'stench\ *noun* [Middle English, from Old English *stenc;* akin to Old English *stincan* to emit a smell — more at STINK] (before 12th century)
**:** STINK
— **stench·ful** \-fəl\ *adjective*
— **stenchy** \'sten-chē\ *adjective*
¹**sten·cil** \'sten(t)-səl\ *noun* [Middle English *stanselen* to ornament with sparkling colors, from Middle French *estanceler,* from *estancele* spark, from (assumed) Vulgar Latin *stincilla,* alteration of Latin *scintilla*] (1707)
**1 :** an impervious material (as a sheet of paper, thin wax, or woven fabric) perforated with lettering or a design through which a substance (as ink, paint, or metallic powder) is forced onto a surface to be printed
**2 :** something (as a pattern, design, or print) that is produced by means of a stencil
**3 :** a printing process that uses a stencil
²**stencil** *transitive verb* **sten·ciled** *or* **sten·cilled; sten·cil·ing** *or* **sten·cil·ling** \-s(ə-)liŋ\ (circa 1828)
**1 :** to mark or paint with a stencil
**2 :** to produce by stencil
— **sten·cil·er** *or* **sten·cil·ler** \-s(ə-)lər\ *noun*
**steno** \'ste-(,)nō\ *noun, plural* **sten·os** (1913)
**1 :** STENOGRAPHER
**2 :** STENOGRAPHY
**steno·bath·ic** \,ste-nə-'ba-thik\ *adjective* [sten- + Greek *bathos* depth] (1902)
*of a pelagic organism* **:** living within narrow limits of depth
**ste·nog·ra·pher** \stə-'nä-grə-fər\ *noun* (1809)
**1 :** a writer of shorthand
**2 :** a person employed chiefly to take and transcribe dictation
**ste·nog·ra·phy** \-fē\ *noun* (1602)
**1 :** the art or process of writing in shorthand
**2 :** shorthand especially written from dictation or oral discourse
**3 :** the making of shorthand notes and subsequent transcription of them

— **steno·graph·ic** \,ste-nə-'gra-fik\ *adjective*
— **steno·graph·i·cal·ly** \-fi-k(ə-)lē\ *adverb*
**steno·ha·line** \,ste-nō-'hā-,līn, -'ha-,līn\ *adjective* [International Scientific Vocabulary sten- + Greek *halinos* of salt, from *hals* salt — more at SALT] (circa 1920)
*of an aquatic organism* **:** unable to withstand wide variation in salinity of the surrounding water
**ste·nosed** \stə-'nōzd, -'nōst\ *adjective* [from past participle of *stenose* to affect with stenosis] (1897)
**:** affected with stenosis
**ste·no·sis** \stə-'nō-səs\ *noun, plural* **-no·ses** \-,sēz\ [New Latin, from Greek *stenōsis* act of narrowing, from *stenoun* to narrow, from *stenos* narrow] (circa 1860)
**:** a narrowing or constriction of the diameter of a bodily passage or orifice
— **ste·not·ic** \-'nä-tik\ *adjective*
**steno·ther·mal** \,ste-nə-'thər-məl\ *adjective* (1881)
**:** capable of surviving over only a narrow range of temperatures ⟨*stenothermal* fish⟩
— **steno·therm** \'ste-nə-,thərm\ *noun*
**steno·top·ic** \,ste-nə-'tä-pik\ *adjective* [probably from German *stenotop* stenotopic, from sten- + Greek *topos* place] (1945)
**:** having a narrow range of adaptability to changes in environmental conditions
**steno·type** \'ste-nə-,tīp\ *noun* [steno- (as in stenography) + type] (1922)
**:** a small machine somewhat like a typewriter used to record speech by means of phonograms
— **stenotype** *transitive verb*
— **steno·typ·ist** \-,tī-pist\ *noun*
— **ste·no·ty·py** \-,tī-pē\ *noun*
**sten·tor** \'sten-,tór, -tər\ *noun* [Latin, from Greek *Stentōr* Stentor, a Greek herald in the Trojan War noted for his loud voice] (1609)
**1 :** a person having a loud voice
**2 :** any of a widely distributed genus (*Stentor*) of ciliate protozoans having a trumpet-shaped body with the mouth at the broad end and with the narrow end often attached to the substrate
**sten·to·ri·an** \sten-'tōr-ē-ən, -'tór-\ *adjective* (1605)
**:** extremely loud
*synonym* see LOUD
¹**step** \'step\ *noun* [Middle English, from Old English *stæpe;* akin to Old High German *stapfo* step, *stampfōn* to stamp] (before 12th century)
**1 :** a rest for the foot in ascending or descending: as **a :** one of a series of structures consisting of a riser and a tread **b :** a ladder rung
**2 a** (1) **:** an advance or movement made by raising the foot and bringing it down elsewhere (2) **:** a combination of foot or foot and body movements constituting a unit or a repeated pattern ⟨a dance *step*⟩ (3) **:** manner of walking **:** STRIDE **b :** FOOTPRINT 1 **c :** the sound of a footstep ⟨heard *steps* in the hall⟩
**3 a :** the space passed over in one step **b :** a short distance ⟨just a *step* away from the bank⟩
**c :** the height of one stair
**4** *plural* **:** COURSE, WAY ⟨directed his *steps* toward the river⟩
**5 a :** a degree, grade, or rank in a scale **b :** a stage in a process ⟨was guided through every *step* of my career⟩
**6 :** a frame on a ship designed to receive an upright shaft; *especially* **:** a block supporting the heel of a mast
**7 :** an action, proceeding, or measure often occurring as one in a series ⟨taking *steps* to improve the situation⟩
**8 :** a steplike offset or part usually occurring in a series
**9 :** an interval in a musical scale
— **step·like** \-,līk\ *adjective*
— **stepped** \'stept\ *adjective*

— **in step 1 :** with each foot moving to the same time as the corresponding foot of others or in time to music **2 :** in harmony or agreement
— **out of step :** not in step ⟨*out of step* with the times⟩
²**step** *verb* **stepped; step·ping** (before 12th century)
*intransitive verb*
**1 a :** to move by raising the foot and bringing it down elsewhere or by moving each foot in succession **b :** DANCE
**2 a :** to go on foot **:** WALK **b** *obsolete* **:** ADVANCE, PROCEED **c :** to be on one's way **:** LEAVE — often used with *along* **d :** to move briskly ⟨kept us *stepping*⟩
**3 :** to press down with the foot ⟨*step* on the brake⟩
**4 :** to come as if at a single step ⟨*stepped* into a good job⟩
*transitive verb*
**1 :** to take by moving the feet in succession ⟨*step* three paces⟩
**2 a :** to move (the foot) in any direction **:** SET (the first man to *step* foot on the moon) **b :** to traverse on foot
**3 :** to go through the steps of **:** PERFORM ⟨*step* a minuet⟩
**4 :** to make erect by fixing the lower end in a step ⟨*step* the mast⟩
**5 :** to measure by steps ⟨*step* off 50 yards⟩
**6 a :** to provide with steps **b :** to make steps in ⟨*step* a key⟩
**7 :** to construct or arrange in or as if in steps ⟨craggy peaks with terraces *stepped* up the sides —*Time*⟩
— **step on it :** to increase one's speed **:** hurry up
**step-** *combining form* [Middle English, from Old English *stēop-;* akin to Old High German *stiof-* step-, Old English a*stēpan* to deprive, bereave]
**:** related by virtue of a remarriage (as of a parent) and not by blood ⟨*step*parent⟩ ⟨*step*sister⟩
**step·broth·er** \'step-,brə-thər\ *noun* (15th century)
**:** a son of one's stepparent by a former marriage
**step–by–step** \,step-bī-'step\ *adjective or adverb* (1701)
**:** marked by successive degrees usually of limited extent **:** GRADUAL
**step·child** \'step-,chīld\ *noun* (before 12th century)
**1 :** a child of one's wife or husband by a former marriage
**2 :** one that fails to receive proper care or attention ⟨is no longer a *stepchild* in the family of nations —F. R. Smith⟩
**step dance** *noun* (1887)
**:** a dance in which steps are emphasized rather than gesture or posture
**step·daugh·ter** \'step-,dó-tər\ *noun* (before 12th century)
**:** a daughter of one's wife or husband by a former marriage
**step–down** \'step-,daún\ *noun* (1922)
**:** a decrease or reduction in size or amount ⟨a *step-down* in dosage⟩
**step down** (1890)
*intransitive verb*
**:** RETIRE, RESIGN
*transitive verb*
**1 :** to lower (a voltage) by means of a transformer
**2 :** to decrease or reduce especially by one or more steps
— **step–down** \'step-,daún\ *adjective*
**step·fam·i·ly** \'step-,fam-lē, -,fa-mə-\ *noun* (1966)

: a family in which there is a stepparent

**step·fa·ther** \'step-ˌfä-thər\ *noun* (before 12th century)
: the husband of one's mother by a subsequent marriage

**step function** *noun* (circa 1929)
: a mathematical function of a single real variable that remains constant within each of a series of adjacent intervals but changes in value from one interval to the next

**steph·a·no·tis** \ˌste-fə-'nō-təs\ *noun* [New Latin, from Greek *stephanōtis* fit for a crown, from *stephanos* crown, from *stephein* to crown] (1843)
: any of a genus (*Stephanotis* and especially *S. floribunda*) of Old World tropical woody vines of the milkweed family with fragrant white flowers the corolla of which has a cylindrical dilated tube and spreading limb

**stephanotis**

**step–in** \'step-ˌin\ *noun* (1921)
: an article of clothing put on by being stepped into: as **a** : a shoe resembling but usually having a higher vamp than a pump and concealed elastic to adjust the fit **b** : short panties for women — usually used in plural
— **step–in** *adjective*

**step in** *intransitive verb* (15th century)
**1** : to intervene in an affair or dispute
**2** : to make a brief informal visit

**step·lad·der** \'step-ˌla-dər\ *noun* (1751)
: a ladder that has broad flat steps and two pairs of legs connected by a hinge at the top and that opens at the bottom to become freestanding

**step·moth·er** \-ˌmə-thər\ *noun* (before 12th century)
: the wife of one's father by a subsequent marriage

**step out** *intransitive verb* (circa 1533)
**1** : to go away from a place usually for a short distance and for a short time
**2** : to go or march at a vigorous or increased pace
**3** : DIE
**4** : to lead an active social life
**5** : to be unfaithful — usually used with *on*

**step·par·ent** \'step-ˌpar-ənt, -ˌper-\ *noun* (circa 1890)
: the spouse of one's mother or father by a subsequent marriage

**step·par·ent·ing** *noun* (1979)
: the raising of a child by a stepparent

**steppe** \'step\ *noun* [Russian *step'*] (1671)
**1** : one of the vast usually level and treeless tracts in southeastern Europe or Asia
**2** : arid land with xerophilous vegetation found usually in regions of extreme temperature range and loess soil

**stepped–up** \'stept-'əp\ *adjective* (1902)
: increased in intensity : ACCELERATED, INTENSIFIED ⟨*stepped-up* security⟩

**step·per** \'ste-pər\ *noun* (1835)
: one (as a fast horse or a dancer) that steps

**stepper motor** *noun* (1961)
: a motor whose driveshaft rotates in small steps rather than continuously — called also *stepping motor*

**step·ping–stone** \'ste-piŋ-ˌstōn\ *noun* (14th century)
**1** : a stone on which to step (as in crossing a stream)
**2** : a means of progress or advancement

**step·sis·ter** \'step-ˌsis-tər\ *noun* (15th century)
: a daughter of one's stepparent by a former marriage

**step·son** \-ˌsən\ *noun* (before 12th century)
: a son of one's husband or wife by a former marriage

**step stool** *noun* (1946)
: a stool with one or two steps that often fold away beneath the seat

**step turn** *noun* (1941)
: a skiing turn executed in a downhill traverse by lifting the upper ski from the ground, placing it in the desired direction, weighting it, and bringing the other ski parallel

**step–up** \'step-ˌəp\ *noun* (1922)
: an increase or advance in size or amount

**step up** (1902)
*transitive verb*
**1** : to increase (a voltage) by means of a transformer
**2** : to increase, augment, or advance especially by one or more steps ⟨*step up* production⟩
*intransitive verb*
**1** : to come forward
**2** : to undergo an increase ⟨business is *stepping up*⟩
**3** : to receive a promotion
— **step–up** \'step-ˌəp\ *adjective*

**step·wise** \-ˌwīz\ *adjective* (1902)
**1** : marked by or proceeding in steps
**2** : moving by step to adjacent musical tones

**-ster** *noun combining form* [Middle English, from Old English *-estre* female agent; akin to Middle Dutch *-ster*]
**1** : one that does or handles or operates ⟨spin*ster*⟩ ⟨tap*ster*⟩ ⟨team*ster*⟩
**2** : one that makes or uses ⟨song*ster*⟩ ⟨pun*ster*⟩
**3** : one that is associated with or participates in ⟨game*ster*⟩ ⟨gang*ster*⟩
**4** : one that is ⟨young*ster*⟩

**ster·co·ra·ceous** \ˌstər-kə-'rā-shəs\ *adjective* [Latin *stercor-, stercus* excrement] (1731)
: relating to, being, or containing feces

**ster·cu·lia gum** \ˌstər-'k(y)ü-lē-ə-\ *noun* [New Latin *Sterculia*, genus of trees] (circa 1943)
: KARAYA GUM

**stere-** *or* **stereo-** *combining form* [New Latin, from Greek, from *stereos* solid — more at STARE]
**1** : solid : solid body ⟨*stereo*gram⟩
**2 a** : stereoscopic ⟨*stereo*psis⟩ **b** : having or dealing with three dimensions of space ⟨*stereo*chemistry⟩

**¹ste·reo** \'ster-ē-ˌō, 'stir-\ *noun, plural* **ste·re·os** (circa 1823)
**1** : STEREOTYPE
**2** [by shortening] **a** : stereophonic reproduction **b** : a stereophonic sound system

**²stereo** *adjective* (1876)
**1 a** : STEREOSCOPIC **b** : produced by or as if by means of a stereotype
**2** : STEREOPHONIC

**ste·reo·chem·is·try** \ˌster-ē-ō-'ke-mə-strē, ˌstir-\ *noun* [International Scientific Vocabulary] (1890)
**1** : a branch of chemistry that deals with the spatial arrangement of atoms and groups in molecules
**2** : the spatial arrangement of atoms and groups in a compound and its relation to the properties of the compound
— **ste·reo·chem·i·cal** \-'ke-mi-kəl\ *adjective*

**ste·reo·gram** \'ster-ē-ə-ˌgram, 'stir-\ *noun* [International Scientific Vocabulary] (1868)
**1** : a diagram or picture representing objects with an impression of solidity or relief
**2** : STEREOGRAPH

**ste·reo·graph** \-ˌgraf\ *noun* [International Scientific Vocabulary] (1859)
: a pair of stereoscopic pictures or a picture composed of two superposed stereoscopic images that gives a three-dimensional effect when viewed with a stereoscope or special spectacles
— **stereograph** *transitive verb*

**ste·reo·graph·ic** \ˌster-ē-ə-'gra-fik\ *adjective* (1704)
: of, relating to, or being a delineation of the form of a solid body (as the earth) on a plane ⟨*stereographic* projection⟩

**— ste·re·og·ra·phy** \ˌster-ē-'ä-grə-fē\ *noun*

**ste·reo·iso·mer** \ˌster-ē-ō-'ī-sə-mər, ˌstir-\ *noun* [International Scientific Vocabulary] (1894)
: any of a group of isomers in which atoms are linked in the same order but differ in their spatial arrangement
— **ste·reo·iso·mer·ic** \-ˌī-sə-'mer-ik\ *adjective*
— **ste·reo·isom·er·ism** \-ī-'sä-mə-ˌri-zəm\ *noun*

**ste·re·ol·o·gy** \ˌster-ē-'ä-lə-jē, ˌstir-\ *noun* [International Scientific Vocabulary] (1963)
: a branch of science concerned with inferring the three-dimensional properties of objects or matter ordinarily observed two-dimensionally
— **ste·reo·log·i·cal** \-ē-ə-'lä-ji-kəl\ *adjective*
— **ste·reo·log·i·cal·ly** \-ji-k(ə-)lē\ *adverb*

**ste·reo·mi·cro·scope** \-'mī-krə-ˌskōp\ *noun* (1948)
: a microscope having a set of optics for each eye to make an object appear in three dimensions
— **ste·reo·mi·cro·scop·ic** \-ˌmī-krə-'skä-pik\ *adjective*
— **ste·reo·mi·cro·scop·i·cal·ly** \-pi-k(ə-)lē\ *adverb*

**ste·reo·phon·ic** \ˌster-ē-ə-'fä-nik, ˌstir-\ *adjective* [International Scientific Vocabulary] (1927)
: of, relating to, or constituting sound reproduction involving the use of separated microphones and two transmission channels to achieve the sound separation of a live hearing
— **ste·reo·phon·i·cal·ly** \-ni-k(ə-)lē\ *adverb*
— **ste·reo·pho·ny** \ˌster-ē-'ä-fə-nē, ˌstir-; 'ster-ē-ə-ˌfō-nē, 'stir-\ *noun*

**ste·reo·pho·tog·ra·phy** \ˌster-ē-ō-fə-'tä-grə-fē, ˌstir-\ *noun* [International Scientific Vocabulary] (1903)
: stereoscopic photography
— **ste·reo·pho·to·graph·ic** \-ˌfō-tə-'gra-fik\ *adjective*

**ste·re·op·sis** \ˌster-ē-'äp-səs, ˌstir-\ *noun* [New Latin, from *stere-* + Greek *opsis* vision, appearance — more at OPTIC] (circa 1911)
: stereoscopic vision

**ste·re·op·ti·con** \-'äp-ti-kən\ *noun* [New Latin, from *stere-* + Greek *optikon*, neuter of *optikos* optic] (1863)
**1** : a projector for transparent slides often made double so as to produce dissolving views
**2** : STEREOSCOPE

**ste·reo·reg·u·lar** \ˌster-ē-ō-'re-gyə-lər, ˌstir-\ *adjective* (1958)
: of, relating to, or involving stereochemical regularity in the repeating units of a polymeric structure
— **ste·reo·reg·u·lar·i·ty** \-ˌre-gyə-'lar-ə-tē\ *noun*

**ste·reo·scope** \'ster-ē-ə-ˌskōp, 'stir-\ *noun* (1838)
: an optical instrument with two eyeglasses for helping the observer to combine the images of two pictures taken from points of view a little way apart and thus to get the effect of solidity or depth

**ste·reo·scop·ic** \ˌster-ē-ə-'skä-pik, ˌstir-\ *adjective* (1855)
**1** : of or relating to stereoscopy or the stereoscope
**2** : characterized by stereoscopy ⟨*stereoscopic* vision⟩
— **ste·reo·scop·i·cal·ly** \-pi-k(ə-)lē\ *adverb*

**ste·re·os·co·py** \ˌster-ē-'äs-kə-pē, ˌstir-; 'ster-ē-ə-ˌskō-pē, 'stir-\ *noun* [International Scientific Vocabulary] (circa 1859)
**1** : a science that deals with stereoscopic effects and methods
**2** : the seeing of objects in three dimensions

**ste·reo·spe·cif·ic** \ˌster-ē-ō-spi-'si-fik, ˌstir-\ *adjective* (1949)
: being, produced by, or involved in a stereochemically specific process ⟨many enzymes act as *stereospecific* catalysts⟩ ⟨*stereospecific* plastics⟩
— **ste·reo·spe·cif·i·cal·ly** \-fi-k(ə-)lē\ *adverb*
— **ste·reo·spec·i·fic·i·ty** \-ˌspe-sə-'fi-sə-tē\ *noun*

**ste·reo·tac·tic** \ˌster-ē-ə-'tak-tik, ˌstir-\ *adjective* (1950)
: STEREOTAXIC

**ste·reo·tax·ic** \ˌster-ē-ə-'tak-sik, ˌstir-\ *adjective* [New Latin *stereotaxis* stereotaxic technique, from *stere-* + *-taxis*] (1908)
: of, relating to, or being a technique or apparatus used in neurological research or surgery for directing the tip of a delicate instrument (as a needle or an electrode) in three planes in attempting to reach a specific locus in the brain
— **ste·reo·tax·i·cal·ly** \-si-k(ə-)lē\ *adverb*

**¹ste·reo·type** \'ster-ē-ə-ˌtīp, 'stir-\ *transitive verb* (1804)
**1** : to make a stereotype from
**2 a** : to repeat without variation : make hackneyed **b** : to develop a mental stereotype about
— **ste·reo·typ·er** *noun*

**²stereotype** *noun* [French *stéréotype,* from *stéré-* stere- + *type*] (1817)
**1** : a plate cast from a printing surface
**2** : something conforming to a fixed or general pattern; *especially* : a standardized mental picture that is held in common by members of a group and that represents an oversimplified opinion, prejudiced attitude, or uncritical judgment
**word history** see CLICHÉ
— **ste·reo·typ·i·cal** \ˌster-ē-ə-'ti-pi-kəl\ *also* **ste·reo·typ·ic** \-pik\ *adjective*
— **ste·reo·typ·i·cal·ly** \-pi-k(ə-)lē\ *adverb*
**ste·reo·typed** *adjective* (1849)
: lacking originality or individuality
**synonym** see TRITE

**ste·reo·ty·py** \'ster-ē-ə-ˌtī-pē, 'stir-\ *noun, plural* **-pies** (circa 1889)
: frequent almost mechanical repetition of the same posture, movement, or form of speech (as in schizophrenia)
**ste·ric** \'ster-ik, 'stir-\ *adjective* [International Scientific Vocabulary *stere-* + ¹*-ic*] (1898)
: relating to or involving the arrangement of atoms in space : SPATIAL
— **ste·ri·cal·ly** \'ster-i-k(ə-)lē, 'stir-\ *adverb*

**ste·rig·ma** \stə-'rig-mə\ *noun, plural* **-ma·ta** \-mə-tə\ *also* **-mas** [New Latin, from Greek *stērigma* support, from *stērizein* to prop; perhaps akin to Greek *stereos* solid — more at STARE] (circa 1866)
: one of the slender stalks at the top of the basidium of some fungi from the tips of which the basidiospores are formed; *broadly* : a stalk or filament that bears conidia or spermatia

**ster·il·ant** \'ster-ə-lənt\ *noun* (1941)
: a sterilizing agent

**ster·ile** \'ster-əl, *chiefly British* -ˌīl\ *adjective* [Middle English *steryle,* from Latin *sterilis;* akin to Gothic *stairo* barren animal, Sanskrit *starī* sterile cow] (15th century)
**1 a** : failing to bear or incapable of producing fruit or spores **b** : failing to produce or incapable of producing offspring ⟨a *sterile* hybrid⟩ **c** : incapable of germinating ⟨*sterile* spores⟩ **d** of *a flower* : neither perfect nor pistillate
**2 a** : unproductive of vegetation ⟨a *sterile* arid region⟩ **b** : free from living organisms and especially microorganisms **c** : lacking in stimulating emotional or intellectual quality : LIFELESS ⟨a *sterile* work of art⟩
— **ster·ile·ly** \-ə(l)-lē\ *adverb*
— **ste·ril·i·ty** \stə-'ri-lə-tē\ *noun*

**ster·il·ize** \'ster-ə-ˌlīz\ *transitive verb* **-ized; -iz·ing** (1695)

: to make sterile: as **a** : to cause (land) to become unfruitful **b** (1) : to deprive of the power of reproducing (2) : to make incapable of germination **c** : to make powerless or useless usually by restraining from a normal function, relation, or participation **d** : to free from living microorganisms
— **ster·il·i·za·tion** \ˌster-ə-lə-'zā-shən\ *noun*
— **ster·il·iz·er** \'ster-ə-ˌlī-zər\ *noun*

**¹ster·ling** \'stər-liŋ\ *noun* [Middle English, silver penny, probably from (assumed) Old English *steorling,* from Old English *steorra* star + ¹*-ling* — more at STAR] (14th century)
**1** : British money
**2** : sterling silver or articles of it

**²sterling** *adjective* (15th century)
**1 a** : of, relating to, or calculated in terms of British sterling **b** : payable in sterling
**2 a** *of silver* : having a fixed standard of purity usually defined legally as represented by an alloy of 925 parts of silver with 75 parts of copper **b** : made of sterling silver
**3** : conforming to the highest standard ⟨*sterling* character⟩
— **ster·ling·ly** \-liŋ-lē\ *adverb*
— **ster·ling·ness** *noun*

**sterling area** *noun* (1932)
: a former group of countries with currencies tied to the British pound sterling

**¹stern** \'stərn\ *adjective* [Middle English *sterne,* from Old English *styrne;* akin to Old English *starian* to stare — more at STARE] (before 12th century)
**1 a** : having a definite hardness or severity of nature or manner : AUSTERE **b** : expressive of severe displeasure : HARSH
**2** : forbidding or gloomy in appearance
**3** : INEXORABLE ⟨*stern* necessity⟩
**4** : STURDY, STOUT ⟨a *stern* resolve⟩
**synonym** see SEVERE
— **stern·ly** *adverb*
— **stern·ness** \'stərn-nəs\ *noun*

**²stern** *noun* [Middle English, rudder, probably of Scandinavian origin; akin to Old Norse *stjōrn* act of steering; akin to Old English *stīeran* to steer — more at STEER] (14th century)
**1** : the rear end of a boat
**2** : a hinder or rear part : the last or latter part

**ster·nal** \'stər-nᵊl\ *adjective* (1756)
: of or relating to the sternum

**stern chase** *noun* [²*stern*] (1627)
: a chase in which a pursuing ship follows in the path of another

**stern chaser** *noun* (1815)
: a gun so placed as to be able to fire astern at a pursuing ship

**stern·fore·most** \'stərn-'fōr-ˌmōst, -'fȯr-\ *adverb* (1840)
: with the stern in advance : BACKWARD

**ster·nite** \'stər-ˌnīt\ *noun* [International Scientific Vocabulary, from Greek *sternon* chest] (1868)
: the ventral part or shield of a somite of an arthropod; *especially* : the chitinous plate that forms the ventral surface of an abdominal or occasionally a thoracic segment of an insect

**stern·most** \'stərn-ˌmōst\ *adjective* (1622)
: farthest astern

**ster·no·cos·tal** \ˌstər-nō-'käs-tᵊl\ *adjective* [New Latin *sternum* + English *-o-* + *costal*] (1785)
: of, relating to, or situated between the sternum and ribs

**stern·post** \'stərn-ˌpōst\ *noun* (15th century)
: the principal member at the stern of a ship extending from keel to deck

**stern sheets** *noun plural* (15th century)
: the space in the stern of an open boat not occupied by the thwarts

**ster·num** \'stər-nəm\ *noun, plural* **sternums** *or* **ster·na** \-nə\ [New Latin, from Greek *sternon* chest, breastbone; akin to Old High German *stirna* forehead, Latin *sternere* to spread out — more at STREW] (1667)

: a compound ventral bone or cartilage of most vertebrates other than fishes that connects the ribs or the shoulder girdle or both and in humans consists of the manubrium, gladiolus, and xiphoid process — called also *breastbone*

**ster·nu·ta·tion** \ˌstər-nyə-'tā-shən\ *noun* [Middle English *sternutacion,* from Latin *sternutation-, sternutatio,* from *sternutare* to sneeze, frequentative of *sternuere* to sneeze; akin to Greek *ptarnysthai* to sneeze] (15th century)
: the act, fact, or noise of sneezing

**ster·nu·ta·tor** \'stər-nyə-ˌtā-tər\ *noun* (1922)
: an agent that induces sneezing and often lacrimation and vomiting

**stern·ward** \'stərn-wərd\ *or* **stern·wards** \-wərdz\ *adverb* (1832)
: AFT

**stern·way** \'stərn-ˌwā\ *noun* (1769)
: movement of a ship backward or with stern foremost

**stern–wheel·er** \-'hwē-lər, -'wē-\ *noun* (1855)
: a steamboat driven by a single paddle wheel at the stern

**ste·roid** \'stir-ˌoid *also* 'ster-\ *noun* [International Scientific Vocabulary *sterol* + *-oid*] (1926)
: any of numerous compounds containing a 17-carbon 4-ring system and including the sterols and various hormones and glycosides
— **steroid** *or* **ste·roi·dal** \stə-'ròi-dᵊl\ *adjective*

**ste·roido·gen·e·sis** \stə-ˌrȯi-də-'je-nə-səs, ˌstir-ˌȯid- *also* ˌster-\ *noun* [New Latin] (1951)
: synthesis of steroids
— **ste·roido·gen·ic** \-'je-nik\ *adjective*

**ste·rol** \'stir-ˌȯl, 'ster-, -ˌōl\ *noun* [International Scientific Vocabulary, from *-sterol* (as in *cholesterol*)] (1913)
: any of various solid steroid alcohols (as cholesterol) widely distributed in animal and plant lipids

**-sterone** *combining form* [*sterol* + *-one*]
: steroid hormone ⟨andro*sterone*⟩

**ster·tor** \'stər-tər, -ˌtȯr\ *noun* [New Latin, from Latin *stertere* to snore; akin to *sternuere* to sneeze] (1804)
: the act or fact of producing a snoring sound
: SNORING

**ster·to·rous** \'stər-tə-rəs\ *adjective* (1802)
: characterized by a harsh snoring or gasping sound
— **ster·to·rous·ly** *adverb*

**stet** \'stet\ *transitive verb* **stet·ted; stet·ting** [Latin, let it stand, from *stare* to stand — more at STAND] (1755)
: to direct retention of (a word or passage previously ordered to be deleted or omitted from a manuscript or printer's proof) by annotating usually with the word *stet*

**stetho·scope** \'ste-thə-ˌskōp *also* -thə-\ *noun* [French *stéthoscope,* from Greek *stēthos* chest + French *-scope*] (1820)
: an instrument used to detect and study sounds produced in the body
— **stetho·scop·ic** \ˌste-thə-'skä-pik *also* -thə-\ *adjective*

**Stet·son** \'stet-sən\ *trademark*
— used for a broad-brimmed high-crowned felt hat

**¹ste·ve·dore** \'stē-və-ˌdȯr, -ˌdȯr *also* 'stēv-\ *noun* [Spanish *estibador,* from *estibar* to pack, from Latin *stipare* to press together — more at STIFF] (1788)
: one who works at or is responsible for loading and unloading ships in port

**²stevedore** *verb* **-dored; -dor·ing** (1862) *transitive verb*

| | | | | |
|---|---|---|---|---|
| \ə\ abut | \ᵊ\ kitten | \ər\ further | \a\ ash | \ā\ ace |
| \ä\ mop, mar | \aú\ out | \ch\ chin | \e\ bet | \ē\ easy |
| \g\ go | \i\ hit | \ī\ ice | \j\ job | \ŋ\ sing |
| \ō\ law | \ȯi\ boy | \th\ thin | \t͟h\ the | \ü\ loot | \ú\ foot |
| \y\ yet | \zh\ vision | *see also* Guide to Pronunciation | | |

: to handle (cargo) as a stevedore; *also* : to load or unload the cargo of (a ship) in port
*intransitive verb*
: to work as a stevedore
**stevedore knot** *noun* (circa 1863)
: a stopper knot similar to a figure eight knot but with one or more extra turns — called also *stevedore's knot;* see KNOT illustration
**Ste·ven·graph** \'stē-vən-ˌgraf\ *or* **Ste·vens·graph** \-vənz-\ *noun* [Thomas *Stevens,* 19th century American weaver] (1879)
: a woven silk picture
**¹stew** \'stü, 'styü\ *noun* [Middle English *stewe* heated room for a steam bath, from Middle French *estuve,* from (assumed) Vulgar Latin *extufa* — more at STOVE] (13th century)
**1** *obsolete* : a utensil used for boiling
**2 :** a hot bath
**3 a :** WHOREHOUSE **b :** a district of bordellos — usually used in plural
**4 a :** fish or meat usually with vegetables prepared by stewing **b** (1) : a heterogeneous mixture (2) : a state of heat and congestion
**5 :** a state of excitement, worry, or confusion
**²stew** (14th century)
*transitive verb*
: to boil slowly or with simmering heat
*intransitive verb*
**1 :** to become cooked by stewing
**2 :** to swelter especially from confinement in a hot or stuffy atmosphere
**3 :** to be in a state of suppressed agitation, worry, or resentment
**³stew** *noun* [short for *stewardess*] (1970)
**:** FLIGHT ATTENDANT
**¹stew·ard** \'stü-ərd, 'styü-; 'st(y)u̇(-ə)rd\ *noun* [Middle English, from Old English *stīweard,* from *stī, stig* hall, sty + *weard* ward — more at STY, WARD] (before 12th century)
**1 :** one employed in a large household or estate to manage domestic concerns (as the supervision of servants, collection of rents, and keeping of accounts)
**2 :** SHOP STEWARD
**3 :** a fiscal agent
**4 a :** an employee on a ship, airplane, bus, or train who manages the provisioning of food and attends passengers **b :** one appointed to supervise the provision and distribution of food and drink in an institution
**5 :** one who actively directs affairs **:** MANAGER ◆
**²steward** (1621)
*transitive verb*
: to act as a steward for **:** MANAGE
*intransitive verb*
: to perform the duties of a steward
**stew·ard·ess** \'stü-ər-dəs, 'styü-; 'st(y)u̇(-ə)r-dəs\ *noun* (1631)
: a woman who performs the duties of a steward; *especially* : one who attends passengers (as on an airplane)
**usage** see -ESS
**stew·ard·ship** \'stü-ərd-ˌship, 'styü-; 'st(y)u̇(-ə)rd-\ *noun* (15th century)
**1 :** the office, duties, and obligations of a steward
**2 :** the conducting, supervising, or managing of something; *especially* : the careful and responsible management of something entrusted to one's care 〈*stewardship* of our natural resources〉
**stewed** *adjective* (circa 1737)
: DRUNK 1a
**stew·pan** \'stü-ˌpan, 'styü-\ *noun* (1651)
: a pan used for stewing
**stib·nite** \'stib-ˌnīt\ *noun* [alteration of obsolete English *stibine* stibnite, from French, from Latin *stibium* antimony, from Greek *stibi,* from Egyptian *sṭm*] (circa 1854)
: a mineral that consists of the trisulfide of antimony and occurs in orthorhombic lead-gray crystals of metallic luster or in massive form
**sticho·myth·ia** \ˌsti-kə-'mi-thē-ə\ *also* **stichom·y·thy** \sti-'kä-mə-thē\ *noun* [Greek *stichomythia,* from *stichomythein* to speak dia-

logue in alternate lines, from *stichos* row, verse + *mythos* speech, myth; akin to Greek *steichein* to walk, go — more at STAIR] (1861)
: dialogue especially of altercation or dispute delivered by two actors in alternating lines (as in classical Greek drama)
**— sticho·myth·ic** \ˌsti-kə-'mi-thik\ *adjective*
**¹stick** \'stik\ *noun* [Middle English *stik,* from Old English *sticca;* akin to Old Norse *stik* stick, Old English *stician* to stick] (before 12th century)
**1 :** a woody piece or part of a tree or shrub: as **a :** a usually dry or dead severed shoot, twig, or slender branch **b :** a cut or broken branch or piece of wood gathered for fuel or construction material

stick 2b: *a* lacrosse, *b* ice hockey, *c* field hockey

**2 a :** a long slender piece of wood or metal: as (1) : a club or staff used as a weapon (2) : WALKING STICK **b :** an implement used for striking or propelling an object in a game **c :** something used to force compliance **d :** a baton symbolizing an office or dignity; *also* : a person entitled to bear such a baton
**3 :** a piece of the materials composing something (as a building)
**4 a :** any of various implements resembling a stick in shape, origin, or use: as (1) : COMPOSING STICK (2) : an airplane lever operating the elevators and ailerons (3) : the gearshift lever of an automobile **b :** STICKFUL
**5 :** something prepared (as by cutting, molding, or rolling) in a relatively long and slender often cylindrical form 〈a *stick* of candy〉 〈a *stick* of butter〉
**6 a :** PERSON, CHAP **b :** a dull, inert, stiff, or spiritless person
**7** *plural* : remote usually rural districts regarded especially as backward, dull, or unsophisticated **:** BOONDOCKS
**8 :** an herbaceous stalk resembling a woody stick 〈celery *sticks*〉
**9 :** ¹MAST 1; *also* : ¹YARD 4
**10 :** a piece of furniture
**11 a :** a number of bombs arranged for release from a bombing plane in a series across a target **b :** a number of parachutists dropping together
**12** *slang* : a marijuana cigarette
**13 a :** punishment or the threat of punishment used to force compliance or cooperation 〈choosing between the carrot and the *stick*〉 **b** *British* : CRITICISM, ABUSE
**— stick·like** \-ˌlīk\ *adjective*
**²stick** *transitive verb* (1573)
**1 :** to arrange (lumber) in stacks
**2 :** to provide a stick as a support for
**³stick** *verb* **stuck** \'stək\; **stick·ing** [Middle English *stikken,* from Old English *stician;* akin to Old High German *stehhan* to prick, Latin *instigare* to urge on, goad, Greek *stizein* to tattoo] (before 12th century)
*transitive verb*
**1 a :** to pierce with something pointed **:** STAB **b :** to kill by piercing
**2 :** to push or thrust so as or as if to pierce
**3 a :** to fasten by thrusting in **b :** IMPALE **c :** PUSH, THRUST
**4 :** to put or set in a specified place or position
**5 :** to furnish with things fastened on by or as if by piercing
**6 :** to attach by or as if by causing to adhere to a surface
**7 a :** to compel to pay especially by trickery 〈got *stuck* with the bar bill〉 **b :** OVERCHARGE

**8 a :** to halt the movement or action of **b :** BAFFLE, STUMP
**9 a :** CHEAT, DEFRAUD **b :** to saddle with something disadvantageous or disagreeable 〈is still *stuck* with that lousy car〉
*intransitive verb*
**1 :** to hold to something firmly by or as if by adhesion: **a :** to become fixed in place by means of a pointed end **b :** to become fast by or as if by miring or by gluing or plastering 〈*stuck* in the mud〉
**2 a :** to remain in a place, situation, or environment **b :** to hold fast or adhere resolutely **:** CLING **c :** to remain effective **d :** to keep close in a chase or competition
**3 :** to become blocked, wedged, or jammed
**4 a :** BALK, SCRUPLE **b :** to find oneself baffled **c :** to be unable to proceed
**5 :** PROJECT, PROTRUDE ☆
**— stick in one's craw :** to irritate, nag at, or obsess one
**— stick it to :** to treat harshly or unfairly
**— stick one's neck out :** to make oneself vulnerable by taking a risk
**— stick to one's guns :** to maintain one's position especially in face of opposition
**— stuck on :** infatuated with
**⁴stick** *noun* (1633)
**1 :** a thrust with a pointed instrument **:** STAB
**2 a :** DELAY, STOP **b :** IMPEDIMENT
**3 :** adhesive quality or substance
**stick around** *intransitive verb* (circa 1912)
: to stay or wait about **:** LINGER
**stick·ball** \'stik-ˌbȯl\ *noun* (1934)
: baseball adapted for play in streets or small areas and using a broomstick and a lightweight ball
**stick·er** \'sti-kər\ *noun* (15th century)
**1 :** one that pierces with a point
**2 a :** one that adheres or causes adhesion **b :** a slip of paper with adhesive back that can be fastened to a surface
**sticker price** *noun* (1969)
: a manufacturer's suggested retail price that is printed on a sticker and affixed to a new automobile

**stick figure** *noun* (1949)
**1 :** a drawing showing the head of a human being or animal as a circle and all other parts as straight lines
**2 :** a fictional character lacking depth and believability

**stick·ful** \'stik-ˌful\ *noun* (1683)
**:** as much set type as fills a composing stick

**stick·han·dle** \'stik-ˌhan-dᵊl\ *intransitive verb* (1929)
**:** to maneuver a puck (as in hockey) or a ball (as in lacrosse) with a stick
— **stick·han·dler** \-ˌhan(d)-lər, -ˌhan-dᵊl-ər\ *noun*

**sticking plaster** *noun* (1655)
*chiefly British* **:** an adhesive plaster especially for closing superficial wounds

**sticking point** *noun* (1946)
**:** an item (as in negotiations) resulting or likely to result in an impasse

**stick insect** *noun* (1854)
**:** any of various usually wingless insects (especially family Phasmatidae) with a long cylindrical body resembling a stick

**stick-in-the-mud** \'stik-ən-thə-ˌməd\ *noun* (1733)
**:** one who is slow, old-fashioned, or unprogressive; *especially* **:** an old fogy

**stick·it** \'sti-kət\ *adjective* [Scots, from past participle of English ³*stick*] (1787)
**1** *Scottish* **:** UNFINISHED
**2** *chiefly Scottish* **:** having failed especially in an intended profession

**stick·le** \'sti-kəl\ *intransitive verb* **stick·led; stick·ling** \-k(ə-)liŋ\ [alteration of Middle English *stightlen*, frequentative of *stighten* to arrange, from Old English *stihtan*; akin to Old Norse *stētta* to found, support] (1642)
**1 :** to contend especially stubbornly and usually on insufficient grounds
**2 :** to feel scruples **:** SCRUPLE

**stick·le·back** \'sti-kəl-ˌbak\ *noun* [Middle English *stykylbak*, from Old English *sticel* goad + Middle English *bak* back; akin to Old English *stician* to stick] (15th century)
**:** any of a family (Gasterosteidae) of small scaleless bony fishes having two or more free spines in front of the dorsal fin and including marine, anadromous, and freshwater forms

**stick·ler** \'sti-k(ə-)lər\ *noun* (1644)
**1 :** one who insists on exactness or completeness in the observance of something ⟨a *stickler* for the rules⟩
**2 :** something that baffles or puzzles **:** POSER, STICKER

**stick·man** \'stik-ˌman, -mən\ *noun* (circa 1931)
**:** one who handles a stick: as **a :** one who supervises the play at a dice table, calls the decisions, and retrieves the dice **b :** a player in any of various games (as hockey or lacrosse) played with a stick

**stick out** (1567)
*intransitive verb*
**1 a :** to jut out **:** PROJECT **b :** to be prominent or conspicuous
**2 :** to be persistent (as in a demand or an opinion)
*transitive verb*
**:** ENDURE, LAST — often used with *it* ⟨*stuck* it *out* to the end⟩

**stick·pin** \'stik-ˌpin\ *noun* (1895)
**:** an ornamental pin; *especially* **:** one worn in a necktie

**stick·seed** \-ˌsēd\ *noun* (1843)
**:** any of various weedy herbs (genera *Lappula* and *Hackelia*) of the borage family with bristly adhesive fruit

**stick shift** *noun* (1959)
**:** a manually operated gearshift for a motor vehicle usually mounted on the floor

**stick·tight** \'stik-ˌtīt\ *noun* (circa 1884)
**:** BUR MARIGOLD

**stick-to-it·ive·ness** \ˌstik-ˈtü-ə-tiv-nəs\ *noun* [from the phrase *stick to it*] (1867)
**:** dogged perseverance **:** TENACITY

**stick·um** \'sti-kəm\ *noun* [³*stick* + *-um* (probably alteration of *'em* them)] (circa 1909)
**:** a substance that adheres or causes adhesion

**stick·up** \'stik-ˌəp\ *noun* (1904)
**:** a robbery at gunpoint **:** HOLDUP

**stick up** (15th century)
*intransitive verb*
**:** to stand upright or on end **:** PROTRUDE
*transitive verb*
**:** to rob at gunpoint
— **stick up for :** to speak or act in defense of **:** SUPPORT

**stick·weed** \'stik-ˌwēd\ *noun* (1743)
**:** any of several plants (as a beggar's-lice) with adhesive seeds

**stick·work** \-ˌwərk\ *noun* (1903)
**:** the use of one's stick in offensive and defensive techniques (as in hockey)

**sticky** \'sti-kē\ *adjective* **stick·i·er; -est** (circa 1735)
**1 a :** ADHESIVE **b** (1) **:** VISCOUS, GLUEY (2) **:** coated with a sticky substance
**2 :** HUMID, MUGGY; *also* **:** CLAMMY
**3 :** tending to stick
**4 a :** DISAGREEABLE, UNPLEASANT **b :** AWKWARD, STIFF **c :** DIFFICULT, PROBLEMATIC
**5 :** excessively sentimental **:** CLOYING
— **stick·i·ly** \'sti-kə-lē\ *adverb*
— **stick·i·ness** \'sti-kē-nəs\ *noun*

**sticky wicket** *noun* (1926)
**:** a difficult or delicate problem or situation

**stic·tion** \'stik-shən\ *noun* [*static* + f*riction*] (1946)
**:** the force required to cause one body in contact with another to begin to move

**¹stiff** \'stif\ *adjective* [Middle English *stif*, from Old English *stīf*; akin to Middle Dutch *stijf* stiff, Latin *stipare* to press together, Greek *steibein* to tread on] (before 12th century)
**1 a :** not easily bent **:** RIGID **b :** lacking in suppleness or responsiveness ⟨*stiff* muscles⟩ **c :** impeded in movement — used of a mechanism **d :** DRUNK 1a
**2 a :** FIRM, RESOLUTE **b :** STUBBORN, UNYIELDING **c :** PROUD **d** (1) **:** marked by reserve or decorum (2) **:** lacking in ease or grace **:** STILTED
**3 :** hard fought **:** PUGNACIOUS, SHARP
**4 a** (1) **:** exerting great force ⟨a *stiff* wind⟩ (2) **:** FORCEFUL, VIGOROUS **b :** POTENT ⟨a *stiff* dose⟩
**5 :** of a dense or glutinous consistency **:** THICK
**6 a :** HARSH, SEVERE ⟨a *stiff* penalty⟩ **b :** ARDUOUS, RUGGED ⟨*stiff* terrain⟩
**7 :** not easily heeled over by an external force (as the wind) ⟨a *stiff* ship⟩
**8 :** EXPENSIVE, STEEP ⟨paid a *stiff* price⟩ ☆
— **stiff·ish** \'sti-fish\ *adjective*
— **stiff·ly** *adverb*
— **stiff·ness** *noun*

**²stiff** *adverb* (13th century)
**1 :** in a stiff manner **:** STIFFLY
**2 :** to an extreme degree **:** SEVERELY ⟨scared *stiff*⟩ ⟨bored *stiff*⟩

**³stiff** *noun* (circa 1859)
**1 :** CORPSE
**2 a :** TRAMP, BUM **b :** HAND, LABORER **c :** PERSON ⟨a lucky *stiff*⟩
**3 :** FLOP, FAILURE

**⁴stiff** *transitive verb* (1950)
**1 a :** to refuse to pay or tip ⟨*stiffed* the doctor for the fee⟩ ⟨*stiffed* the waiter⟩ **b :** CHEAT ⟨*stiffed* him in a business deal⟩ **c :** STICK 7a ⟨*stiffed* us with the bar bill⟩
**2 :** SNUB 3 ⟨*stiffed* sportswriters after the game⟩

**stiff-arm** \'stif-ˌärm\ *verb or noun* (1909)
**:** STRAIGHT-ARM

**stiff·en** \'sti-fən\ *verb* **stiff·ened; stiff·en·ing** \'sti-fə-niŋ, 'stif-niŋ\ (15th century)
*transitive verb*
**:** to make stiff or stiffer
*intransitive verb*
**:** to become stiff or stiffer
— **stiff·en·er** \'sti-fə-nər, 'stif-nər\ *noun*

**stiff-necked** \'stif-ˈnekt\ *adjective* (1526)
**1 :** HAUGHTY, STUBBORN
**2 :** STILTED

**stiff upper lip** *noun* [from the phrase *keep a stiff upper lip*] (1815)
**:** a steady and determined attitude or manner in the face of trouble
— **stiff–upper–lip** *adjective*

**¹sti·fle** \'stī-fəl\ *noun* [Middle English] (14th century)
**:** the joint next above the hock in the hind leg of a quadruped (as a horse or dog) corresponding to the human knee — see HORSE illustration

**²stifle** *verb* **sti·fled; sti·fling** \-f(ə-)liŋ\ [alteration of Middle English *stuflen*] (1513)
*transitive verb*
**1 a :** to kill by depriving of oxygen **:** SUFFOCATE **b** (1) **:** SMOTHER (2) **:** MUFFLE
**2 a :** to cut off (as the voice or breath) **b :** to withhold from circulation or expression **:** REPRESS ⟨*stifled* our anger⟩ **c :** DETER, DISCOURAGE
*intransitive verb*
**:** to become suffocated by or as if by lack of oxygen **:** SMOTHER
— **sti·fler** \-f(ə-)lər\ *noun*
— **sti·fling·ly** \-f(ə-)liŋ-lē\ *adverb*

**stig·ma** \'stig-mə\ *noun, plural* **stig·ma·ta** \stig-ˈmä-tə, 'stig-mə-tə\ *or* **stig·mas** [Latin *stigmat-, stigma* mark, brand, from Greek, from *stizein* to tattoo — more at STICK] (circa 1593)
**1 a** *archaic* **:** a scar left by a hot iron **:** BRAND **b :** a mark of shame or discredit **:** STAIN **c :** an identifying mark or characteristic; *specifically* **:** a specific diagnostic sign of a disease
**2 a** *stigmata plural* **:** bodily marks or pains resembling the wounds of the crucified Christ and sometimes accompanying religious ecstasy **b :** PETECHIA
**3 a :** a small spot, scar, or opening on a plant or animal **b :** the usually apical part of the pistil of a flower which receives the pollen grains and on which they germinate — see FLOWER illustration ◆
— **stig·mal** \'stig-məl\ *adjective*

☆ **SYNONYMS**
**Stiff, rigid, inflexible** mean difficult to bend. STIFF may apply to any degree of this condition ⟨stretching will prevent your muscles from becoming *stiff*⟩. RIGID applies to something so stiff that it cannot be bent without breaking ⟨a *rigid* surfboard⟩. INFLEXIBLE stresses lack of suppleness or pliability ⟨ski boots with *inflexible* soles⟩.

◇ **WORD HISTORY**
**stigma** In ancient Greece and Rome runaway slaves and criminals were branded with a hot iron or needle as a sign of disgrace. The brand was called in Greek *stigma*, a derivative of the verb *stizein* "to tattoo." *Stigma* was taken into English in its original sense in the late 16th century. Soon, however, the word was being used figuratively to mean "a mark of shame or discredit." The English plural form for this sense is generally *stigmas*. The Greek and Latin plural form *stigmata* has been used since the Middle Ages specifically for the wounds that some people apparently bear on their hands and feet, and sometimes on their side and brow. Believers take these to be visible signs of the bearer's participation in Christ's sufferings on the cross. This religious sense gave rise in the 17th century to a medical sense, the disease-induced reddish spots known as petechiae.

\ə\ abut  \ᵊ\ kitten  \ər\ further  \a\ ash  \ā\ ace
\ä\ mop, mar  \au̇\ out  \ch\ chin  \e\ bet  \ē\ easy
\g\ go  \i\ hit  \ī\ ice  \j\ job  \ŋ\ sing  \ō\ go
\ȯ\ law  \ȯi\ boy  \th\ thin  \t͟h\ the  \ü\ loot  \u̇\ foot
\y\ yet  \zh\ vision  *see also* Guide to Pronunciation

**stig·mas·ter·ol** \stig-'mas-tə-ˌrȯl, -ˌrōl\ *noun* [New Latin Physo*stigma* (genus including the Calabar bean) + International Scientific Vocabulary *sterol*] (1907)
: a crystalline sterol $C_{29}H_{48}O$ obtained especially from the oils of Calabar beans and soybeans

¹**stig·mat·ic** \stig-'ma-tik\ *noun* (1594)
: one marked with stigmata

²**stigmatic** *adjective* (1607)
**1** : having or conveying a social stigma
**2** : of or relating to supernatural stigmata
**3** : ANASTIGMATIC — used especially of a bundle of light rays intersecting at a single point
— **stig·mat·i·cal·ly** \-ti-k(ə-)lē\ *adverb*

**stig·ma·tist** \'stig-mə-tist, stig-'mä-\ *noun* (1607)
: STIGMATIC

**stig·ma·tize** \'stig-mə-ˌtīz\ *transitive verb* **-tized; -tiz·ing** (1585)
**1 a** *archaic* : BRAND **b** : to describe or identify in opprobrious terms
**2** : to mark with stigmata
— **stig·ma·ti·za·tion** \ˌstig-mə-tə-'zā-shən\ *noun*

**stil·bene** \'stil-ˌbēn\ *noun* [International Scientific Vocabulary, from Greek *stilbein* to glitter] (circa 1868)
: an aromatic hydrocarbon $C_{14}H_{12}$ used as a phosphor and in making dyes; *also* : a compound derived from stilbene

**stil·bes·trol** \stil-'bes-ˌtrȯl, -ˌtrōl\ *noun* [*stilbene* + *estr*us + ¹*-ol*] (1938)
**1** : a crystalline synthetic derivative $C_{14}H_{12}O_2$ of stilbene that differs from the related diethylstilbestrol in lack of the ethyl groups and in possession of but slight estrogenic activity
**2** : DIETHYLSTILBESTROL

**stil·bite** \'stil-ˌbīt\ *noun* [French, from Greek *stilbein*] (1815)
: a mineral consisting of a hydrous silicate of aluminum, calcium, and sodium and often occurring in sheaflike aggregations of crystals

¹**stile** \'stī(ə)l\ *noun* [Middle English, from Old English *stigel*; akin to Old English *stæger* stair — more at STAIR] (before 12th century)
: a step or set of steps for passing over a fence or wall; *also* : TURNSTILE

²**stile** *noun* [probably from Dutch *stijl* post] (1678)
: one of the vertical members in a frame or panel into which the secondary members are fitted

**sti·let·to** \stə-'le-(ˌ)tō\ *noun, plural* **-tos** *or* **-toes** [Italian, diminutive of *stilo* stylus, dagger, from Latin *stilus* stylus — more at STYLE] (1611)
**1** : a slender dagger with a blade thick in proportion to its breadth
**2** : a pointed instrument for piercing holes for eyelets or embroidery
**3** : STILETTO HEEL

**stiletto heel** *noun* (1953)
: a high thin heel on women's shoes that is narrower than a spike heel

¹**still** \'stil\ *adjective* [Middle English *stille*, from Old English; akin to Old High German *stilli* still and perhaps to Old English *steall* stall — more at STALL] (before 12th century)
**1 a** : devoid of or abstaining from motion **b** *archaic* : SEDENTARY **c** : not effervescent ⟨*still* wine⟩ **d** (1) : of, relating to, or being a static photograph as contrasted with a motion picture (2) : designed for taking still photographs ⟨a *still* camera⟩ (3) : engaged in taking still photographs ⟨a *still* photographer⟩
**2 a** : uttering no sound : QUIET **b** : SUBDUED, MUTED
**3 a** : CALM, TRANQUIL **b** : free from noise or turbulence
— **still·ness** *noun*

²**still** (before 12th century)
*intransitive verb*
: to become motionless or silent : QUIET
*transitive verb*

**1 a** : ALLAY, CALM **b** : to put an end to : SETTLE
**2** : to arrest the motion of
**3** : SILENCE

³**still** *adverb* (before 12th century)
**1** : without motion ⟨sit *still*⟩
**2** *archaic* **a** : ALWAYS, CONTINUALLY **b** : in a progressive manner : INCREASINGLY
**3** — used as a function word to indicate the continuance of an action or condition ⟨*still* lives there⟩ ⟨drink it while it's *still* hot⟩
**4** : in spite of that : NEVERTHELESS ⟨those who take the greatest care *still* make mistakes⟩
**5 a** : EVEN 2c ⟨a *still* more difficult problem⟩ **b** : YET 1a

⁴**still** *noun* (13th century)
**1** : QUIET, SILENCE
**2** : a static photograph; *specifically* : a photograph of actors or scenes of a motion picture for publicity or documentary purposes

⁵**still** *verb* [Middle English *stillen*, short for *distillen* to distill] (13th century)
: DISTILL

⁶**still** *noun* (1533)
**1** : DISTILLERY
**2** : apparatus used in distillation comprising either the chamber in which the vaporization is carried out or the entire equipment

**still alarm** *noun* (1875)
: a fire alarm transmitted (as by telephone call) without sounding the signal apparatus

**still and all** *adverb* (1829)
: NEVERTHELESS, STILL

**still·birth** \'stil-ˌbərth, -'bərth\ *noun* (1785)
: the birth of a dead fetus

**still·born** \-'bȯrn\ *adjective* (1593)
**1** : dead at birth
**2** : failing from the start : ABORTIVE ⟨a *still-born* venture⟩
— **still·born** \-ˌbȯrn\ *noun*

**still–hunt** \-ˌhənt\ *noun* (1858)
*intransitive verb*
: to ambush or stalk a quarry; *especially* : to pursue game noiselessly usually without a dog
*transitive verb*
: to lie in wait for : approach by stealth

**still hunt** *noun* (1828)
: a quiet pursuing or ambushing of game

**still life** *noun, plural* **still lifes** (1695)
**1** : a picture consisting predominantly of inanimate objects
**2** : the category of graphic arts concerned with inanimate subject matter

**still·man** \'stil-mən\ *noun* (circa 1864)
: one who owns or operates a still

**still·room** \'stil-ˌrüm, -ˌrum\ *noun* [⁶*still*] (circa 1710)
*British* : a room connected with the kitchen where liqueurs, preserves, and cakes are kept and beverages (as tea) are prepared

**still water** *noun* (1832)
: a part of a stream where no current is visible

¹**still·ly** \'stil-lē\ *adverb* (before 12th century)
: in a calm manner : QUIETLY

²**stilly** \'sti-lē\ *adjective* [⁴*still* + ¹*-y*] (1776)
: STILL, QUIET

¹**stilt** \'stilt\ *noun* [Middle English *stilte*; akin to Old High German *stelza* stilt] (15th century)
**1 a** : one of two poles each with a rest or strap for the foot used to elevate the wearer above the ground in walking **b** : a pile or post serving as one of the supports of a structure above ground or water level
**2** *plural also* **stilt** : any of various notably long-legged 3-toed shorebirds (genera *Himantopus* and *Cladorhynchus*) that are related to the avocets, frequent inland ponds and marshes, and nest in small colonies

²**stilt** *transitive verb* (1649)
: to raise on or as if on stilts

**stilt·ed** \'stil-təd\ *adjective* (1820)
**1 a** : POMPOUS, LOFTY **b** : FORMAL, STIFF
**2** : having the curve beginning at some distance above the impost ⟨a *stilted* arch⟩
— **stilt·ed·ly** *adverb*
— **stilt·ed·ness** *noun*

**Stil·ton** \'stil-t°n\ *noun* [*Stilton*, Huntingdonshire, England] (1826)
: a blue-veined cheese with wrinkled rind made of whole cows' milk enriched with cream

**stime** \'stīm\ *noun* [Middle English (northern dialect)] (14th century)
*chiefly Scottish & Irish* : GLIMMER; *also* : GLIMPSE

**stim·u·lant** \'stim-yə-lənt\ *noun* (circa 1728)
**1** : an agent (as a drug) that produces a temporary increase of the functional activity or efficiency of an organism or any of its parts
**2** : STIMULUS
**3** : an alcoholic beverage — not used technically
— **stimulant** *adjective*

**stim·u·late** \-ˌlāt\ *verb* **-lat·ed; -lat·ing** [Latin *stimulatus*, past participle of *stimulare*, from *stimulus* goad; perhaps akin to Latin *stilus* stem, stylus — more at STYLE] (1619)
*transitive verb*
**1** : to excite to activity or growth or to greater activity : ANIMATE, AROUSE
**2 a** : to function as a physiological stimulus to **b** : to arouse or affect by a stimulant (as a drug)
*intransitive verb*
: to act as a stimulant or stimulus
*synonym* SEE PROVOKE
— **stim·u·la·tion** \ˌstim-yə-'lā-shən\ *noun*
— **stim·u·la·tive** \'stim-yə-ˌlā-tiv\ *adjective*
— **stim·u·la·tor** \-ˌlā-tər\ *noun*
— **stim·u·la·to·ry** \-lə-ˌtōr-ē, -ˌtȯr-\ *adjective*

**stim·u·lus** \'stim-yə-ləs\ *noun, plural* **-li** \-ˌlī, -ˌlē\ [Latin] (1684)
: something that rouses or incites to activity: as **a** : INCENTIVE **b** : STIMULANT 1 **c** : an agent (as an environmental change) that directly influences the activity of a living organism or one of its parts (as by exciting a sensory organ or evoking muscular contraction or glandular secretion)

¹**sting** \'stiŋ\ *verb* **stung** \'stəŋ\; **sting·ing** \'stiŋ-iŋ\ [Middle English, from Old English *stingan*; akin to Old Norse *stinga* to sting and probably to Greek *stachys* spike of grain, *stochos* target, aim] (before 12th century)
*transitive verb*
**1** : to prick painfully: as **a** : to pierce or wound with a poisonous or irritating process **b** : to affect with sharp quick pain or smart ⟨hail *stung* their faces⟩
**2** : to cause to suffer acutely ⟨*stung* with remorse⟩
**3** : OVERCHARGE, CHEAT
*intransitive verb*
**1** : to wound one with or as if with a sting
**2** : to feel a keen burning pain or smart; *also* : to cause such pain
— **sting·ing·ly** \-iŋ-lē\ *adverb*

²**sting** *noun* (before 12th century)
**1 a** : the act of stinging; *specifically* : the thrust of a stinger into the flesh **b** : a wound or pain caused by or as if by stinging
**2** : STINGER 2
**3** : a sharp or stinging element, force, or quality
**4** : an elaborate confidence game; *specifically* : such a game worked by undercover police in order to trap criminals

**sting·a·ree** \'stiŋ-ə-rē *also* 'stiŋ-rē\ *noun* [by alteration] (1836)
: STINGRAY

**sting·er** \'stiŋ-ər\ *noun* (circa 1552)
**1** : one that stings; *specifically* : a sharp blow or remark
**2** : a sharp organ (as of a bee, scorpion, or stingray) that is usually connected with a poison gland or otherwise adapted to wound by piercing and injecting a poison
**3** : a cocktail usually consisting of brandy and white crème de menthe

**stinging nettle** *noun* (1525)

: NETTLE 1; *especially* : one (*Urtica dioica*) established in North America that has broad coarsely toothed leaves

**sting·less** \'stiŋ-ləs\ *adjective* (1554)
: having no sting or stinger

**sting·ray** \-ˌrā\ *noun* (1624)
: any of numerous rays (as of the family Dasy-atidae) with one or more large sharp barbed dorsal spines near the base of the whiplike tail capable of inflicting severe wounds

**stin·gy** \'stin-jē\ *adjective* **stin·gi·er; -est** [perhaps from (assumed) English dialect *stinge*, noun, sting; akin to Old English *stingan* to sting] (1659)
**1** : not generous or liberal : sparing or scant in giving or spending
**2** : meanly scanty or small ☆
— **stin·gi·ly** \-jə-lē\ *adverb*
— **stin·gi·ness** \-jē-nəs\ *noun*

**stingray**

¹**stink** \'stiŋk\ *intransitive verb* **stank** \'staŋk\ *or* **stunk** \'stəŋk\; **stunk; stink·ing** [Middle English, from Old English *stincan;* akin to Old High German *stinkan* to emit a smell] (before 12th century)
**1** : to emit a strong offensive odor
**2** : to be offensive; *also* : to be in bad repute
**3** : to possess something to an offensive degree ⟨*stinking* with wealth⟩
**4** : to be extremely bad in quality
— **stinky** \'stiŋ-kē\ *adjective*

²**stink** *noun* (13th century)
**1** : a strong offensive odor : STENCH
**2** : a public outcry against something

**stink·ard** \'stiŋ-kərd\ *noun* (circa 1600)
: a mean or contemptible person

**stink bomb** *noun* (1915)
: a small bomb charged usually with chemicals that gives off a foul odor on bursting

**stink·bug** \'stiŋk-ˌbəg\ *noun* (1877)
: any of various hemipterous bugs (especially family Pentatomidae) that emit a disagreeable odor

**stink·er** \'stiŋ-kər\ *noun* (1607)
**1 a** : one that stinks **b** : an offensive or contemptible person **c** : something of very poor quality
**2** : any of several large petrels that have an offensive odor
**3** *slang* : something extremely difficult ⟨the examination was a real *stinker*⟩

**stink·horn** \'stiŋk-ˌhȯrn\ *noun* (1724)
: any of various fetid basidiomycetous fungi (order Phallales, especially *Phallus impudicus*) having spores dispersed by insects

¹**stink·ing** *adjective* (before 12th century)
**1** : strong and offensive to the sense of smell
**2** *slang* : offensively drunk
**synonym** *see* MALODOROUS
— **stink·ing·ly** \'stiŋ-kiŋ-lē\ *adverb*

²**stinking** *adverb* (1887)
: to an extreme degree ⟨got *stinking* drunk⟩

**stinking smut** *noun* (circa 1891)
: ⁴BUNT

**stink·pot** \'stiŋk-ˌpät\ *noun* (1669)
**1** : an earthen jar filled with fetid material and formerly sometimes thrown as a stink bomb on an enemy's deck
**2** : MUSK TURTLE
**3** : STINKER 1
**4** *slang* : MOTORBOAT

**stink up** *transitive verb* (1941)
: to cause to stink or be filled with a stench

**stink·weed** \'stiŋk-ˌwēd\ *noun* (1753)
: any of various strong-scented or fetid plants; *especially* : PENNYCRESS

**stink·wood** \-ˌwu̇d\ *noun* (1731)

**1** : any of several trees with a wood of unpleasant odor; *especially* : a southern African tree (*Ocotea bullata*) of the laurel family yielding a valued cabinet wood
**2** : the wood of a stinkwood

¹**stint** \'stint\ *verb* [Middle English, from Old English *styntan* to blunt, dull; akin to Old Norse *stuttr* scant] (13th century)
*intransitive verb*
**1** *archaic* : STOP, DESIST
**2** : to be sparing or frugal
*transitive verb*
**1** *archaic* : to put an end to : STOP
**2 a** : to restrain within certain limits : CONFINE
**b** : to restrict with respect to a share or allowance
**3** : to assign a task to (a person)
— **stint·er** *noun*

²**stint** *noun* (circa 1530)
**1 a** : a definite quantity of work assigned **b** : a period of time spent at a particular activity ⟨served a brief *stint* as a waiter⟩
**2** : RESTRAINT, LIMITATION
**synonym** *see* TASK

³**stint** *noun, plural* **stints** *also* **stint** [Middle English *stynte*] (15th century)
: any of several small sandpipers

**stipe** \'stīp\ *noun* [New Latin *stipes*, from Latin, tree trunk; akin to Latin *stipare* to press together — more at STIFF] (1785)
: a usually short plant stalk: as **a** : the stem supporting the cap of a fungus **b** : a part that is similar to a stipe and connects the holdfast and blade of a frondose alga **c** : the petiole of a fern frond **d** : a prolongation of the receptacle beneath the ovary of a seed plant
— **stiped** \'stīpt\ *adjective*

**sti·pend** \'stī-ˌpend, -pənd\ *noun* [Middle English, alteration of *stipendy*, from Latin *stipendium*, from *stip-, stips* gift + *pendere* to weigh, pay] (15th century)
: a fixed sum of money paid periodically for services or to defray expenses

¹**sti·pen·di·ary** \stī-'pen-dē-ˌer-ē\ *noun, plural* **-ar·ies** (15th century)
: one who receives a stipend

²**stipendiary** *adjective* (circa 1545)
**1** : receiving or compensated by wages or salary ⟨a *stipendiary* curate⟩
**2** : of or relating to a stipend

**sti·pes** \'stī-ˌpēz\ *noun, plural* **stip·i·tes** \'sti-pə-ˌtēz\ [New Latin *stipit-, stipes*, from Latin, tree trunk] (1760)
: PEDUNCLE; *especially* : the second basal segment of a maxilla of an insect or crustacean

¹**stip·ple** \'sti-pəl\ *transitive verb* **stip·pled; stip·pling** \-p(ə-)liŋ\ [Dutch *stippelen* to spot, dot] (circa 1762)
**1** : to engrave by means of dots and flicks
**2 a** : to make by small short touches (as of paint or ink) that together produce an even or softly graded shadow **b** : to apply (as paint) by repeated small touches
**3** : SPECKLE, FLECK
— **stip·pler** \-p(ə-)lər\ *noun*

²**stipple** *noun* (1837)
: production of gradation of light and shade in graphic art by stippling small points, larger dots, or longer strokes; *also* : an effect produced in this way

**stip·u·lar** \'sti-pyə-lər\ *adjective* (1793)
: of, resembling, or provided with stipules ⟨*stipular* glands⟩

¹**stip·u·late** \'sti-pyə-ˌlāt\ *verb* **-lat·ed; -lat·ing** [Latin *stipulatus*, past participle of *stipulari* to demand some term in an agreement] (circa 1624)
*intransitive verb*
**1** : to make an agreement or covenant to do or forbear something : CONTRACT
**2** : to demand an express term in an agreement — used with *for*
*transitive verb*
**1** : to specify as a condition or requirement of an agreement or offer
**2** : to give a guarantee of

— **stip·u·la·tor** \-ˌlā-tər\ *noun*

²**stip·u·late** \'sti-pyə-lət\ *adjective* [New Latin *stipula*] (1776)
: having stipules

**stip·u·la·tion** \ˌsti-pyə-'lā-shən\ *noun* (circa 1552)
**1** : an act of stipulating
**2** : something stipulated; *especially* : a condition, requirement, or item specified in a legal instrument
— **stip·u·la·to·ry** \'sti-pyə-lə-ˌtōr-ē, -ˌtȯr-\ *adjective*

**stip·ule** \'sti-(ˌ)pyü(ə)l\ *noun* [New Latin *stipula*, from Latin, stalk; akin to Latin *stipes* tree trunk] (1793)
: either of a pair of appendages borne at the base of the leaf in many plants

¹**stir** \'stər\ *verb* **stirred; stir·ring** [Middle English, from Old English *styrian;* akin to Old High German *stōren* to scatter] (before 12th century)
*transitive verb*
**1 a** : to cause an especially slight movement or change of position of **b** : to disturb the quiet of : AGITATE
**2 a** : to disturb the relative position of the particles or parts of especially by a continued circular movement **b** : to mix by or as if by stirring
**3** : BESTIR, EXERT
**4** : to bring into notice or debate : RAISE
**5 a** : to rouse to activity : evoke strong feelings in **b** : to call forth (as a memory) : EVOKE
**c** : PROVOKE
*intransitive verb*
**1 a** : to make a slight movement **b** : to begin to move (as in rousing)
**2** : to begin to be active
**3** : to be active or busy
**4** : to pass an implement through a substance with a circular movement
**5** : to be able to be stirred
— **stir·rer** *noun*

²**stir** *noun* (14th century)
**1 a** : a state of disturbance, agitation, or brisk activity **b** : widespread notice and discussion : IMPRESSION ⟨the book caused quite a *stir*⟩
**2** : a slight movement
**3** : a stirring movement

³**stir** *noun* [origin unknown] (1851)
*slang* : PRISON

**stir·about** \'stər-ə-ˌbau̇t\ *noun* (1682)
: a porridge of Irish origin consisting of oatmeal or cornmeal boiled in water or milk and stirred

**stir–cra·zy** \'stər-'krā-zē\ *adjective* [³*stir*] (circa 1908)

\ə\ abut \ᵊ\ kitten \ər\ further \a\ ash \ā\ ace
\ä\ mop, mar \au̇\ out \ch\ chin \e\ bet \ē\ easy
\g\ go \i\ hit \ī\ ice \j\ job \ŋ\ sing \ō\ go
\ȯ\ law \ȯi\ boy \th\ thin \t͟h\ the \ü\ loot \u̇\ foot
\y\ yet \zh\ vision *see also* Guide to Pronunciation

*slang* **:** distraught because of prolonged confinement

¹**stir-fry** \-'frī\ *transitive verb* (1958)
**:** to fry quickly over high heat in a lightly oiled pan (as a wok) while stirring continuously

²**stir-fry** \-ˌfrī\ *noun* (1959)
**:** a dish of something stir-fried

**stirk** \'stərk\ *noun* [Middle English, from Old English *stirc;* akin to Middle Low German *sterke* young cow and perhaps to Gothic *stairo* sterile animal — more at STERILE] (before 12th century)
*British* **:** a young bull or cow especially between one and two years old

**Stir-ling engine** \'stər-liŋ-\ *noun* [Robert *Stirling* (died 1878) Scottish engineer] (1896)
**:** an external combustion engine having an enclosed working fluid (as helium) that is alternately compressed and expanded to operate a piston

**Stir-ling's formula** \'stər-liŋz-\ *noun* [James *Stirling* (died 1770) Scottish mathematician] (1926)
**:** a formula

$$\sqrt{2\pi n}\; n^n e^{-n}$$

that approximates the value of the factorial of a very large number *n*

**stirp** \'stərp\ *noun* [Latin *stirp-, stirps*] (1502)
**:** a line descending from a common ancestor **:** STOCK, LINEAGE

**stirps** \'stirps, 'stərps\ *noun, plural* **stir-pes** \'stir-ˌpās, 'stər-(ˌ)pēz\ [Latin, literally, stem, stock] (1681)
**1 :** a branch of a family; *also* **:** the person from whom it is descended
**2 a :** a group of animals equivalent to a superfamily **b :** a race or fixed variety of plants

**stir-ring** \'stər-iŋ\ *adjective* (before 12th century)
**1 :** ACTIVE, BUSTLING
**2 :** ROUSING, INSPIRING ⟨a *stirring* speech⟩

**stir-rup** \'stər-əp *also* 'stir-əp *or* 'stə-rəp\ *noun* [Middle English *stirop*, from Old English *stigrāp*, from *stig-* (akin to Old High German *stīgan* to go up) + *rāp* rope — more at STAIR, ROPE] (before 12th century)
**1 :** either of a pair of small light frames or rings for receiving the foot of a rider that are attached by a strap to a saddle and used to aid in mounting and as a support while riding
**2 :** a piece resembling a stirrup (as a support or clamp in carpentry and machinery)
**3 :** a rope secured to a yard and attached to a thimble in its lower end for supporting a footrope
**4 :** STAPES

**stirrup cup** *noun* (1681)
**1 :** a small serving of drink (as wine) taken by a rider about to depart; *also* **:** the vessel in which it is served
**2 :** a farewell cup

**stirrup leather** *noun* (14th century)
**:** the looped strap suspending a stirrup

**stirrup pump** *noun* (1939)
**:** a portable hand pump held in position by a foot bracket and used for throwing a jet or spray of liquid

¹**stitch** \'stich\ *noun* [Middle English *stiche*, from Old English *stice*; akin to Old English *stician* to stick] (before 12th century)
**1 :** a local sharp and sudden pain especially in the side
**2 a :** one in-and-out movement of a threaded needle in sewing, embroidery, or suturing **b :** a portion of thread left in the material or suture left in the tissue after one stitch
**3 :** a least part especially of clothing
**4 :** a single loop of thread or yarn around an implement (as a knitting needle or crochet hook)
**5 :** a stitch or series of stitches formed in a particular way ⟨a basting *stitch*⟩

**— in stitches :** in a state of uncontrollable laughter

²**stitch** (13th century)
*transitive verb*
**1 a :** to fasten, join, or close with or as if with stitches **b :** to make, mend, or decorate with or as if with stitches
**2 :** to unite by means of staples
*intransitive verb*
**:** SEW

**— stitch-er** *noun*

**stitch-ery** \'stich-rē, 'sti-chə-\ *noun* (1607)
**:** NEEDLEWORK

**stitch-wort** \'stich-ˌwərt, -ˌwȯrt\ *noun* (13th century)
**:** any of several chickweeds (genus *Stellaria*)

**stithy** \'sti-thē, -ˌthē\ *noun, plural* **stith-ies** [Middle English, from Old Norse *stethi*; akin to Old English *stede* stead] (13th century)
**1** *archaic* **:** ANVIL
**2** *archaic* **:** SMITHY 1

**sti-ver** \'stī-vər\ *noun* [Dutch *stuiver*] (1502)
**1 :** a unit of value and coin of the Netherlands equal to ¹⁄₂₀ gulden
**2 :** something of little value

**stoa** \'stō-ə\ *noun* [Greek; akin to Greek *stylos* pillar — more at STEER] (1603)
**:** an ancient Greek portico usually walled at the back with a front colonnade designed to afford a sheltered promenade

**stoat** \'stōt\ *noun, plural* **stoats** *also* **stoat** [Middle English *stote*] (15th century)
**:** the common Holarctic ermine (*Mustela erminea*) especially in its brown summer coat

**stob** \'stäb\ *noun* [Middle English, stump; akin to Middle English *stubb* stub] (15th century)
*chiefly dialect* **:** STAKE, POST

**stoc-ca-do** \stə-'kä-(ˌ)dō\ *noun, plural* **-dos** [Italian *stoccata*] (1582)
*archaic* **:** a thrust with a rapier

**sto-chas-tic** \stə-'kas-tik, stō-\ *adjective* [Greek *stochastikos* skillful in aiming, from *stochazesthai* to aim at, guess at, from *stochos* target, aim, guess — more at STING] (1923)
**1 :** RANDOM; *specifically* **:** involving a random variable ⟨a *stochastic* process⟩
**2 :** involving chance or probability **:** PROBABILISTIC ⟨a *stochastic* model of radiation-induced mutation⟩

**— sto-chas-ti-cal-ly** \-ti-k(ə-)lē\ *adverb*

¹**stock** \'stäk\ *noun* [Middle English *stok*, from Old English *stocc*; akin to Old High German *stoc* stick] (before 12th century)
**1 a** *archaic* **:** STUMP **b** *archaic* **:** a log or block of wood **c** (1) *archaic* **:** something without life or consciousness (2) **:** a dull, stupid, or lifeless person
**2 :** a supporting framework or structure: as **a** *plural* **:** the frame or timbers holding a ship during construction **b** *plural* **:** a device for publicly punishing offenders consisting of a wooden frame with holes in which the feet or feet and hands can be locked **c** (1) **:** the wooden part by which a shoulder arm is held during firing (2) **:** the butt of an implement (as a whip or fishing rod) (3) **:** BITSTOCK, BRACE **d** **:** a long beam on a field gun forming the third support point in firing
**3 a :** the main stem of a plant **:** TRUNK **b** (1) **:** a plant or plant part united with a scion in grafting and supplying mostly underground parts to a graft (2) **:** a plant from which slips or cuttings are taken
**4 :** the crosspiece of an anchor — see ANCHOR illustration
**5 a :** the original (as a person, race, or language) from which others derive **:** SOURCE **b** (1) **:** the descendants of one individual **:** FAMILY, LINEAGE (2) **:** a compound organism — compare CLONE **c** **:** an infraspecific group usually having unity of descent **d** (1) **:** a related group of languages (2) **:** a language family
**6 a** (1) **:** the equipment, materials, or supplies of an establishment (2) **:** LIVESTOCK **b** **:** a store or supply accumulated; *especially* **:** the inventory of goods of a merchant or manufacturer

**7 a** *archaic* **:** a supply of capital **:** FUNDS; *especially* **:** money or capital invested or available for investment or trading **b** (1) **:** the part of a tally formerly given to the creditor in a transaction (2) **:** a debt or fund due (as from a government) for money loaned at interest; *also, British* **:** capital or a debt or fund bearing interest in perpetuity and not ordinarily redeemable as to principal **c** (1) **:** the proprietorship element in a corporation usually divided into shares and represented by transferable certificates (2) **:** a portion of such stock of one or more companies (3) **:** STOCK CERTIFICATE
**8 :** any of a genus (*Matthiola*) of Old World herbs or subshrubs of the mustard family with racemes of usually sweet-scented flowers
**9 :** a wide band or scarf worn about the neck especially by some clergymen
**10 a :** liquid in which meat, fish, or vegetables have been simmered that is used as a basis for soup, gravy, or sauce **b** (1) **:** raw material from which something is manufactured (2) **:** paper used for printing **c** **:** the portion of a pack of cards not distributed to the players at the beginning of a game
**11 a** (1) **:** an estimate or evaluation of something ⟨take *stock* of the situation⟩ (2) **:** the estimation in which someone or something is held ⟨his *stock* with the electorate remains high —*Newsweek*⟩ **b** **:** confidence or faith placed in someone or something ⟨put little *stock* in his testimony⟩
**12 :** the production and presentation of plays by a stock company
**13 :** STOCK CAR 1

**— in stock :** on hand **:** in the store and ready for delivery

**— out of stock :** having no more on hand **:** completely sold out

²**stock** (15th century)
*transitive verb*
**1 :** to make (a domestic animal) pregnant
**2 :** to fit to or with a stock
**3 :** to provide with stock or a stock **:** SUPPLY ⟨*stock* a stream with trout⟩
**4 :** to procure or keep a stock of
**5 :** to graze (livestock) on land
*intransitive verb*
**1 :** to send out new shoots
**2 :** to put in stock or supplies ⟨*stock* up on canned goods⟩

³**stock** *adjective* (1625)
**1 a :** kept regularly in stock ⟨comes in *stock* sizes⟩ ⟨a *stock* model⟩ **b** **:** commonly used or brought forward **:** STANDARD ⟨the *stock* answer⟩
**2 a :** kept for breeding purposes **:** BROOD ⟨a *stock* mare⟩ **b** **:** devoted to the breeding and rearing of livestock ⟨a *stock* farm⟩ **c** **:** used or intended for livestock ⟨a *stock* train⟩ **d** **:** used in herding livestock ⟨a *stock* horse⟩ ⟨a *stock* dog⟩
**3 :** of or relating to a stock company
**4 :** employed in handling, checking, or taking care of the stock of merchandise on hand ⟨a *stock* clerk⟩

¹**stock-ade** \stä-'kād\ *noun* [Spanish *estacada*, from *estaca* stake, pale, of Germanic origin; akin to Old English *staca* stake] (1614)
**1 :** a line of stout posts set firmly to form a defense
**2 a :** an enclosure or pen made with posts and stakes **b** **:** an enclosure in which prisoners are kept

²**stockade** *transitive verb* **stock-ad-ed; stock-ad-ing** (1677)
**:** to fortify or surround with a stockade

**stockade fence** (1985)
**:** a solid fence of half-round boards pointed at the top

**stock-breed-er** \'stäk-ˌbrē-dər\ *noun* (1815)
**:** a person engaged in the breeding and care of livestock for the market, for show purposes, or for racing

**stock-bro-ker** \-ˌbrō-kər\ *noun* (circa 1706)

: a broker who executes orders to buy and sell securities and often also acts as a security dealer

— **stock·bro·ker·age** \-k(ə-)rij\ *noun*
— **stock·brok·ing** \-ˌbrō-kiŋ\ *noun*

**stock car** *noun* (1858)
**1 :** a latticed railroad boxcar for carrying livestock
**2 :** a racing car having the basic chassis of a commercially produced assembly-line model

**stock certificate** *noun* (1863)
: an instrument evidencing ownership of one or more shares of the capital stock of a corporation

**stock company** *noun* (1827)
**1 :** a corporation or joint-stock company of which the capital is represented by stock
**2 :** a theatrical company attached to a repertory theater; *especially* **:** one without outstanding stars

**stock dividend** *noun* (circa 1902)
**1 :** the payment by a corporation of a dividend in the form of shares usually of its own stock without change in par value — compare STOCK SPLIT
**2 :** the stock distributed in a stock dividend

**stock·er** \'stä-kər\ *noun* (1881)
**1 :** a young animal (as a steer or heifer) suitable for being fed and fattened for market
**2 :** an animal (as a heifer) suitable for use in a breeding establishment
**3 :** STOCK CAR 2

**stock exchange** *noun* (1773)
**1 :** a place where security trading is conducted on an organized system
**2 :** an association of people organized to provide an auction market among themselves for the purchase and sale of securities

**stock·fish** \-ˌfish\ *noun* [Middle English *stokfish,* from Middle Dutch *stocvisch,* from *stoc* stick + *visch* fish] (13th century)
: fish (as cod, haddock, or hake) dried hard in the open air without salt

**stock·hold·er** \'stäk-ˌhōl-dər\ *noun* (circa 1776)
: an owner of corporate stock

**stock·i·nette** *or* **stock·i·net** \ˌstä-kə-'net\ *noun* [alteration of earlier *stocking net*] (1784)
: a soft elastic usually cotton fabric used especially for bandages and infants' wear

**stock·ing** \'stä-kiŋ\ *noun* [obsolete *stock* to cover with a stocking] (1583)
**1 a :** a usually knit close-fitting covering for the foot and leg **b :** SOCK
**2 :** something resembling a stocking; *especially* **:** a ring of distinctive color on the lower part of the leg of an animal
— **stock·inged** \-kiŋd\ *adjective*
— **in one's stocking feet :** having on stockings but no shoes

**stocking cap** *noun* (circa 1897)
: a long knitted cone-shaped cap with a tassel or pom-pom worn especially for winter sports or play

**stocking stuffer** *noun* (1948)
: a small gift suitable for placing in a Christmas stocking

**stock–in–trade** \ˌstäk-ən-'trād, 'stäk-ən-ˌ\ *noun* (circa 1771)
**1 :** the equipment, merchandise, or materials necessary to or used in a trade or business
**2 :** something that resembles the standard equipment of a tradesman or business ⟨humor was her *stock-in-trade* as a writer⟩

**stock·ish** \'stä-kish\ *adjective* (1596)
: like a stock **:** STUPID

**stock·ist** \'stä-kist\ *noun* (1910)
*British* **:** one (as a retailer) that stocks goods

**stock·job·ber** \'stäk-ˌjä-bər\ *noun* (circa 1626)
: one who deals in stocks: as **a :** a member of the London Stock Exchange who deals speculatively with brokers or other jobbers and usually specializes in one class of securities — called also *jobber* **b :** STOCKBROKER — usually used disparagingly

**stock·job·bing** \-ˌjä-biŋ\ *noun* (1692)
: speculative exchange dealings

**stock·keep·er** \'stäk-ˌkē-pər\ *noun* (circa 1786)
**1 :** one (as a herdsman or shepherd) having the charge or care of livestock
**2 :** one that keeps and records stock (as in a warehouse) **:** one that keeps an inventory of goods on hand, shipped, or received

**stock·man** \-mən, -ˌman\ *noun* (1806)
: one occupied as an owner or worker in the raising of livestock (as cattle or sheep)

**stock market** *noun* (1809)
**1 :** STOCK EXCHANGE 1
**2 a :** a market for particular stocks **b :** the market for stocks throughout a country

**stock option** *noun* (1945)
**1 :** an option contract involving stock
**2 :** a right granted by a corporation to officers or employees as a form of compensation that allows purchase of corporate stock at a fixed price at a specified time with reimbursement derived from the difference between purchase and market prices

**¹stock·pile** \'stäk-ˌpīl\ *noun* (1872)
: a storage pile: as **a :** a reserve supply of something essential accumulated within a country for use during a shortage **b :** a gradually accumulated reserve of something ⟨avert *stockpiles* of unsold cars —Bert Pierce⟩

**²stockpile** *transitive verb* (1921)
**1 :** to place or store in or on a stockpile
**2 :** to accumulate a stockpile of ⟨*stockpile* war materials in Europe —A. O. Wolfers⟩
— **stock·pil·er** *noun*

**stock·pot** \'stäk-ˌpät\ *noun* (1853)
**1 :** a pot in which soup stock is prepared
**2 :** an abundant supply **:** REPOSITORY

**stock·room** \-ˌrüm, -ˌrum\ *noun* (1825)
: a storage place for supplies or goods used in a business

**stock saddle** *noun* (1886)
**:** WESTERN SADDLE

**stock split** *noun* (1950)
: a division of corporate stock by the issuance to existing shareholders of a specified number of new shares with a corresponding lowering of par value for each outstanding share — compare STOCK DIVIDEND

**stock–still** \'stäk-'stil\ *adjective* (15th century)
: very still **:** MOTIONLESS ⟨stood *stock-still*⟩

**stock·tak·ing** \'stäk-ˌtā-kiŋ\ *noun* (circa 1858)
**1 :** INVENTORY 3
**2 :** the action of estimating a situation at a given moment

**stocky** \'stä-kē\ *adjective* **stock·i·er; -est** (1622)
: compact, sturdy, and relatively thick in build
— **stock·i·ly** \'stä-kə-lē\ *adverb*
— **stock·i·ness** \'stä-kē-nəs\ *noun*

**stock·yard** \'stäk-ˌyärd\ *noun* (1802)
: a yard for stock; *specifically* **:** one in which transient cattle, sheep, swine, or horses are kept temporarily for slaughter, market, or shipping

**¹stodge** \'stäj\ *transitive verb* **stodged; stodg·ing** [origin unknown] (1674)
*British* **:** to stuff full especially with food

**²stodge** *noun* (1825)
*British* **:** something or someone stodgy

**stodgy** \'stä-jē\ *adjective* **stodg·i·er; -est** (1858)
**1 :** having a rich filling quality **:** HEAVY ⟨*stodgy* bread⟩
**2 :** moving in a slow plodding way especially as a result of physical bulkiness
**3 :** BORING, DULL ⟨out on a peaceful rather *stodgy* Sunday boat trip —Edna Ferber⟩
**4 :** extremely old-fashioned **:** HIDEBOUND ⟨received a pompously Victorian letter from his *stodgy* father —E. S. Montagu⟩
**5 a :** DRAB **b :** DOWDY
— **stodg·i·ly** \'stä-jə-lē\ *adverb*
— **stodg·i·ness** \'stä-jē-nəs\ *noun*

**sto·gie** *or* **sto·gy** \'stō-gē\ *noun, plural* **stogies** [*Conestoga,* Pa.] (1853)
**1 :** a stout coarse shoe **:** BROGAN
**2 :** an inexpensive slender cylindrical cigar; *broadly* **:** CIGAR

**¹sto·ic** \'stō-ik\ *noun* [Middle English, from Latin *stoicus,* from Greek *stōikos,* literally, of the portico, from *Stoa* (*Poikilē*) the Painted Portico, portico at Athens where Zeno taught] (14th century)
**1** *capitalized* **:** a member of a school of philosophy founded by Zeno of Citium about 300 B.C. holding that the wise man should be free from passion, unmoved by joy or grief, and submissive to natural law
**2 :** one apparently or professedly indifferent to pleasure or pain ◆

**²stoic** *or* **sto·i·cal** \-i-kəl\ *adjective* (15th century)
**1** *capitalized* **:** of, relating to, or resembling the Stoics or their doctrines ⟨*Stoic* logic⟩
**2 :** not affected by or showing passion or feeling; *especially* **:** firmly restraining response to pain or distress ⟨a *stoic* indifference to cold⟩
*synonym* see IMPASSIVE
— **sto·i·cal·ly** \-i-k(ə-)lē\ *adverb*

**stoi·chio·met·ric** \ˌstȯi-kē-ō-'me-trik\ *adjective* (1892)
: of, relating to, used in, or marked by stoichiometry
— **stoi·chio·met·ri·cal·ly** \-tri-k(ə-)lē\ *adverb*

**stoi·chi·om·e·try** \ˌstȯi-kē-'ä-mə-trē\ *noun* [Greek *stoicheion* element (from *stoichos* row) + English *-metry;* akin to Greek *steichein* to walk, go — more at STAIR] (1807)
**1 :** a branch of chemistry that deals with the application of the laws of definite proportions and of the conservation of mass and energy to chemical activity
**2 a :** the quantitative relationship between constituents in a chemical substance **b :** the quantitative relationship between two or more substances especially in processes involving physical or chemical change

**sto·i·cism** \'stō-ə-ˌsi-zəm\ *noun* (1626)
**1** *capitalized* **:** the philosophy of the Stoics
**2 :** indifference to pleasure or pain **:** IMPASSIVENESS

---

◇ WORD HISTORY

**stoic** In Athens about the year 300 B.C. the philosopher Zeno began to teach a radically new doctrine that was to spread its influence throughout the Greco-Roman world for at least the next five hundred years. He gave lectures at a public hall adjacent to the agora (marketplace) called the *Stoa Poikilē* ("Painted Colonnade"). In later years Zeno's philosophical school itself became known as the *Stoa,* and the derivative adjective *stōikos,* literally, "of the colonnade," was used to refer to the school. Basically what he taught was that happiness and well-being do not depend on material things or on one's situation in life, but on one's reasoning faculty. Through reason, one can emulate the calm and order of the universe by learning to accept events with a stern and tranquil mind. Zeno's Greek followers elaborated and systematized his teachings, which were later adopted and popularized by the Roman Stoics Seneca, Epictetus, and Marcus Aurelius. Greek *stōikos* became *stoicus* in Latin, and by the 14th century had found a place in English. By the 16th century the word was also being used as a common noun for "one apparently or professedly indifferent to pleasure or pain."

---

\ə\ **abut** \ᵊ\ **kitten** \ər\ **further** \a\ **ash** \ā\ **ace**
\ä\ **mop, mar** \au̇\ **out** \ch\ **chin** \e\ **bet** \ē\ **easy**
\g\ **go** \i\ **hit** \ī\ **ice** \j\ **job** \ŋ\ **sing** \ō\ **go**
\ȯ\ **law** \ȯi\ **boy** \th\ **thin** \t̷h\ **the** \ü\ **loot** \u̇\ **foot**
\y\ **yet** \zh\ **vision** *see also* Guide to Pronunciation

**stoke** \'stōk\ *verb* **stoked; stok·ing** [Dutch *stoken;* akin to Middle Dutch *stuken* to push] (1683)
*transitive verb*
**1 :** to poke or stir up (as a fire) **:** supply with fuel
**2 :** to feed abundantly
*intransitive verb*
**:** to stir up or tend a fire (as in a furnace) **:** supply a furnace with fuel
**stoked** \'stōkt\ *adjective* (1965)
*slang* **:** being in an enthusiastic or exhilarated state
**stoke·hold** \'stōk-,hōld\ *noun* (1887)
**:** the boiler room of a ship
**stok·er** \'stō-kər\ *noun* (1660)
**1 :** one employed to tend a furnace and supply it with fuel; *specifically* **:** one that tends a marine steam boiler
**2 :** a machine for feeding a fire
**Stokes' aster** \'stōks-\ *noun* [Jonathan *Stokes* (died 1831) English botanist] (circa 1890)
**:** a perennial composite herb (*Stokesia laevis*) of the southern U.S. often grown for its large showy heads of usually blue flowers — called also *sto·ke·sia* \stō-'kē-zh(ē-)ə, -zē-ə\
**¹stole** \'stōl\ *past of* STEAL
**²stole** *noun* [Middle English, from Old English, from Latin *stola,* from Greek *stolē* equipment, robe, from *stellein* to set up, make ready] (before 12th century)
**1 :** a long loose garment **:** ROBE
**2 :** an ecclesiastical vestment consisting of a long usually silk band worn traditionally around the neck by bishops and priests and over the left shoulder by deacons
**3 :** a long wide scarf or similar covering worn by women usually across the shoulders
**stolen** *past participle of* STEAL
**stol·id** \'stä-ləd\ *adjective* [Latin *stolidus* dull, stupid] (circa 1600)
**:** having or expressing little or no sensibility **:** UNEMOTIONAL
*synonym* see IMPASSIVE
— **sto·lid·i·ty** \stä-'li-də-tē, stə-\ *noun*
— **stol·id·ly** \'stä-ləd-lē\ *adverb*
**stol·len** \'shtō-lən, 'shtō-, 'shtä-, *or with* s *for* sh\ *noun, plural* **stollen** *or* **stollens** [German, literally, post, support, from Old High German *stollo* — more at STELA] (1906)
**:** a sweet yeast bread of German origin containing fruit and nuts
**sto·lon** \'stō-lən, -,län\ *noun* [New Latin *stolon-, stolo,* from Latin, branch, sucker; akin to Old English *stela* stalk, Armenian *steln* branch] (1601)
**1 a :** a horizontal branch from the base of a plant that produces new plants from buds at its tip or nodes (as in the strawberry) — called also *runner* **b :** a hypha (as of rhizopus) produced on the surface and connecting a group of conidiophores

*s* **stolon 1a**

**2 :** an extension of the body wall (as of a hydrozoan or bryozoan) that develops buds giving rise to new zooids which usually remain united by the stolon
**sto·lon·if·er·ous** \,stō-lə-'ni-f(ə-)rəs\ *adjective* (circa 1777)
**:** bearing or developing stolons
**sto·ma** \'stō-mə\ *noun, plural* **sto·ma·ta** \-mə-tə\ *also* **stomas** [New Latin, from Greek *stomat-, stoma* mouth] (circa 1684)
**1 :** any of various small simple bodily openings especially in a lower animal
**2 :** one of the minute openings in the epidermis of a plant organ (as a leaf) through which gaseous interchange takes place; *also* **:** the opening with its associated cellular structures

**3 :** an artificial permanent opening especially in the abdominal wall made in surgical procedures
**¹stom·ach** \'stə-mək, -mik\ *noun* [Middle English *stomak,* from Middle French *estomac,* from Latin *stomachus* gullet, esophagus, stomach, from Greek *stomachos,* from *stoma* mouth; akin to Middle Breton *staffn* mouth, Avestan *staman-*] (14th century)
**1 a** (1) **:** a dilatation of the alimentary canal of a vertebrate communicating anteriorly with the esophagus and posteriorly with the duodenum (2) **:** one of the compartments of a ruminant stomach (the abomasum is the fourth *stomach* of a ruminant) **b :** a cavity in an invertebrate animal that is analogous to a stomach **c :** the part of the body that contains the stomach **:** BELLY, ABDOMEN
**2 a :** desire for food caused by hunger **:** APPETITE **b :** INCLINATION, DESIRE (had no *stomach* for an argument); *also* **:** COURAGE, GUTS
**3** *obsolete* **a :** SPIRIT, VALOR **b :** PRIDE **c :** SPLEEN, RESENTMENT
**²stomach** *transitive verb* (1523)
**1** *archaic* **:** to take offense at
**2 :** to bear without overt reaction or resentment **:** put up with (couldn't *stomach* office politics)
**stom·ach·ache** \-,āk\ *noun* (1763)
**:** pain in or in the region of the stomach
**stom·ach·er** \'stə-mi-kər, -chər\ *noun* (15th century)
**:** the center front section of a waist or underwaist or a usually heavily embroidered or jeweled separate piece for the center front of a bodice worn by men and women in the 15th and 16th centuries and later by women only
**¹sto·mach·ic** \stə-'ma-kik\ *adjective* (circa 1656)
**:** of or relating to the stomach (*stomachic* vessels)
**²stomachic** *noun* (1735)
**:** a stimulant or tonic for the stomach
**stom·achy** \'stə-mə-kē, -mi-\ *adjective* (circa 1825)
**1** *dialect British* **:** IRASCIBLE, IRRITABLE
**2 :** having a large stomach
**sto·mal** \'stō-məl\ *adjective* (circa 1941)
**:** of, relating to, or situated near a surgical stoma (a *stomal* ulcer)
**stomat-** *or* **stomato-** *combining form* [New Latin, from Greek, from *stomat-, stoma*]
**:** mouth **:** stoma (*stomatitis*)
**sto·ma·tal** \'stō-mə-t⁹l\ *adjective* (1861)
**:** of, relating to, or constituting plant stomata (*stomatal* openings) (*stomatal* transpiration)
**sto·mate** \'stō-,māt\ *noun* [irregular from New Latin *stomat-, stoma*] (1835)
**:** STOMA 2
**sto·ma·ti·tis** \,stō-mə-'tī-təs\ *noun, plural* **-tit·i·des** \-'ti-tə-,dēz\ *or* **-ti·tis·es** \-'tī-tə-səz\ [New Latin] (1859)
**:** any of numerous inflammatory diseases of the mouth
**sto·mato·pod** \stō-'ma-tə-,päd\ *noun* [New Latin *Stomatopoda,* from *stomat-* + Greek *pod-, pous* foot — more at FOOT] (1877)
**:** any of an order (Stomatopoda) of marine crustaceans (as a squilla) that have gills on the abdominal appendages
— **stomatopod** *adjective*
**sto·mo·de·um** *or* **sto·mo·dae·um** \,stō-mə-'dē-əm\ *noun, plural* **-dea** \-'dē-ə\ *or* **-daea** \-'dē-ə\ *also* **-deums** *or* **-daeums** [New Latin, from Greek *stoma* mouth + *hodaion,* neuter of *hodaios* being on the way, from *hodos* way] (1876)
**:** the embryonic anterior ectodermal part of the alimentary canal or tract
— **sto·mo·de·al** *or* **sto·mo·dae·al** \-'dē-əl\ *adjective*
**¹stomp** \'stämp, 'stȯmp\ *verb* [by alteration] (1803)
**:** STAMP 1, 2
**²stomp** *noun* (circa 1899)
**1 :** STAMP 4

**2 :** a jazz dance marked by heavy stamping
**stomping ground** *noun* (1854)
**:** STAMPING GROUND
**-stomy** *noun combining form* [International Scientific Vocabulary, from Greek *stoma* mouth, opening]
**:** surgical operation establishing a usually permanent opening into (such) a part (enterostomy)
**¹stone** \'stōn\ *noun* [Middle English, from Old English *stān;* akin to Old High German *stein* stone, Old Church Slavonic *stěna* wall, and perhaps to Sanskrit *styāyate* it hardens — more at STEATO-] (before 12th century)
**1 :** a concretion of earthy or mineral matter: **a** (1) **:** such a concretion of indeterminate size or shape (2) **:** ROCK **b :** a piece of rock for a specified function: as (1) **:** a building block (2) **:** a paving block (3) **:** a precious stone **:** GEM (4) **:** GRAVESTONE (5) **:** GRINDSTONE (6) **:** WHETSTONE (7) **:** a surface upon which a drawing, text, or design is to be lithographed is drawn or transferred
**2 :** something resembling a small stone: as **a :** CALCULUS 3a **b :** the hard central portion of a drupaceous fruit (as a peach) **c :** a hard stony seed (as of a date)
**3** *plural usually* **stone :** any of various units of weight; *especially* **:** an official British unit equal to 14 pounds (6.3 kilograms)
**4 a :** CURLING STONE **b :** a round playing piece used in various games (as backgammon or go)
**5 :** a stand or table with a smooth flat top on which to impose or set type
**²stone** *transitive verb* **stoned; ston·ing** (13th century)
**1 :** to hurl stones at; *especially* **:** to kill by pelting with stones
**2** *archaic* **:** to make hard or insensitive to feeling
**3 :** to face, pave, or fortify with stones
**4 :** to remove the stones or seeds of (a fruit)
**5 a :** to rub, scour, or polish with a stone **b :** to sharpen with a whetstone
— **ston·er** *noun*
**³stone** *adverb* (13th century)
**:** ENTIRELY, UTTERLY — used as an intensive; often used in combination (*stone*-broke) (*stone*-cold soup) (*stone*-dead)
**⁴stone** *adjective* (14th century)
**1 :** of, relating to, or made of stone
**2 :** ABSOLUTE, UTTER (pure *stone* craziness —Edwin Shrake)
**Stone Age** *noun* (1864)
**:** the first known period of prehistoric human culture characterized by the use of stone tools
**stone–blind** \'stōn-'blīnd\ *adjective* (14th century)
**:** totally blind
**stone·boat** \-,bōt\ *noun* (1859)
**:** a flat sledge or drag for transporting heavy articles (as stones)
**stone canal** *noun* (1887)
**:** a tube in many echinoderms that contains calcareous deposits and leads from the madreporite to the ring of the water-vascular system surrounding the mouth
**stone cell** *noun* (1875)
**:** SCLEREID
**stone–chat** \-,chat\ *noun* [²chat] (circa 1783)
**:** an Old World oscine songbird (*Saxicola torquata*) related to the thrushes; *also* **:** any of various related birds (genus *Saxicola*)
**stone china** *noun* (1823)
**:** a hard dense opaque feldspathic pottery developed in England; *broadly* **:** IRONSTONE CHINA
**stone–cold** \'stōn-'kōld\ *adverb* (1592)
**:** ABSOLUTELY (*stone-cold* sober)
**stone crab** *noun* (1709)
**:** a large brownish edible crab (*Menippe mercenaria*) found on the southern coast of the U.S. and in the Caribbean area
**stone·crop** \'stōn-,kräp\ *noun* (before 12th century)

**1** : SEDUM; *especially* : an Old World creeping evergreen sedum (*Sedum acre*) with pungent fleshy leaves and yellow flowers
**2** : any of various plants of the orpine family related to the sedums
**stone·cut·ter** \-,kə-tər\ *noun* (1540)
**1** : one that cuts, carves, or dresses stone
**2** : a machine for dressing stone
— **stone·cut·ting** \-,kə-tiŋ\ *noun*
**stoned** \'stōnd\ *adjective* (1952)
**1** : DRUNK 1a
**2** : being under the influence of a drug (as marijuana) taken especially for pleasure : HIGH
**stone–deaf** \-'def\ *adjective* (1837)
: totally deaf
**stone–faced** \-,fāst\ *adjective* (1932)
: showing no emotion : EXPRESSIONLESS
**stone·fish** \'stōn-,fish\ *noun* (1896)

stonefish

: any of several small spiny venomous scorpion fishes (especially genus *Synanceja*) common about coral reefs of the tropical Indo-Pacific
**stone fly** *noun* (15th century)
: any of an order (Plecoptera) of insects with an aquatic carnivorous nymph having gills and an adult having long antennae, two pairs of membranous wings, and usually long cerci
**stone fruit** *noun* (circa 1534)
: a fruit with a stony endocarp : DRUPE
**stone–ground** \'stōn-'graúnd\ *adjective* (1905)
: ground in a buhrstone mill ⟨*stone-ground* flour⟩
**stone·ma·son** \'stōn-,mā-s°n\ *noun* (1758)
: a mason who builds with stone
— **stone·ma·son·ry** \-,rē\ *noun*
**stone roller** *noun* (1878)
**1** : HOG SUCKER
**2** : a common cyprinid fish (*Campostoma anomalum*) found especially in clear streams of the central U.S.
**stone's throw** *noun* (1581)
: a short distance ⟨lives within a *stone's throw* of town⟩
**stone·wall** \'stōn-,wól\ (1880)
*intransitive verb*
**1** *chiefly British* : to engage in obstructive parliamentary debate or delaying tactics
**2** : to be uncooperative, obstructive, or evasive
*transitive verb*
: to refuse to comply or cooperate with
— **stone·wall·er** *noun*
**stone wall** *noun* (before 12th century)
**1** : a fence made of stones; *especially* : one built of rough stones without mortar to enclose a field
**2** : an immovable block or obstruction (as in public affairs)
**stone·ware** \-,war, -,wer\ *noun* (1683)
: a strong opaque ceramic ware that is high-fired, well vitrified, and nonporous
**stone·washed** \-,wósht, -,wäsht *also* -,wórsht *or* -,wärsht\ *adjective* (1982)
: subjected to a washing process during manufacture that includes the use of abrasive stones especially to create a softer fabric ⟨*stone-washed* denim jeans⟩
**stone·work** \-,wərk\ *noun* (before 12th century)
**1** : a structure or part built of stone : MASONRY
**2** : the shaping, preparation, or setting of stone
**stone·wort** \-,wərt, -,wórt\ *noun* (1816)
: any of various freshwater green algae (order Charales) that have a thallus differentiated into rhizoids and stems with whorls of branchlets and that are often encrusted with calcareous deposits
**stony** *also* **ston·ey** \'stō-nē\ *adjective* **ston·i·er; -est** (before 12th century)

**1** : abounding in or having the nature of stone : ROCKY
**2 a** : insensitive to pity or human feeling : OBDURATE **b** : manifesting no movement or reaction : DUMB, EXPRESSIONLESS **c** : fearfully gripping : PETRIFYING
**3** *archaic* : consisting of or made of stones
**4** *British* : stone-broke
— **ston·i·ly** \'stō-n°l-ē\ *adverb*
— **ston·i·ness** \'stō-nē-nəs\ *noun*
**stony·heart·ed** \'stō-nē-,här-təd\ *adjective* (1569)
: UNFEELING, CRUEL
**stood** *past and past participle of* STAND
**¹stooge** \'stüj\ *noun* [origin unknown] (1913)
**1 a** : one who plays a subordinate or compliant role to a principal **b** : PUPPET 3
**2** : STRAIGHT MAN
**3** : STOOL PIGEON
**²stooge** *intransitive verb* **stooged; stooging** (1939)
: to act as a stooge ⟨congressmen who *stooge* for the oil and mineral interests —*New Republic*⟩
**stook** \'stük, 'stùk\ *noun* [Middle English *stouk;* akin to Old English *stocc* stock — more at STOCK] (15th century)
*chiefly British* : ¹SHOCK
— **stook** *transitive verb, chiefly British*
**¹stool** \'stül\ *noun* [Middle English, from Old English *stōl;* akin to Old High German *stuol* chair, Old Church Slavonic *stolŭ* seat, throne] (before 12th century)
**1 a** : a seat usually without back or arms supported by three or four legs or by a central pedestal **b** : a low bench or portable support for the feet or knees : FOOTSTOOL
**2** : a seat used as a symbol of office or authority; *also* : the rank, dignity, office, or rule of a chieftain
**3 a** : a seat used while defecating or urinating **b** : a discharge of fecal matter
**4 a** : a stump or group of stumps of a tree especially when producing suckers **b** : a plant crown from which shoots grow out **c** : a shoot or growth from a stool
**5** : STOOL PIGEON
**²stool** *intransitive verb* (1770)
: to throw out shoots in the manner of a stool
**stool·ie** \'stü-lē\ *noun* (1924)
: STOOL PIGEON 2
**stool pigeon** *noun* [probably from the early practice of fastening the decoy bird to a stool] (1836)
**1** : a pigeon used as a decoy to draw others within a net
**2** : a person acting as a decoy or informer; *especially* : a spy sent into a group to report (as to the police) on its activities
**¹stoop** \'stüp\ *verb* [Middle English *stoupen,* from Old English *stūpian;* akin to Old English *stēap* steep, deep — more at STEEP] (before 12th century)
*intransitive verb*
**1 a** : to bend the body or a part of the body forward and downward sometimes simultaneously bending the knees **b** : to stand or walk with a forward inclination of the head, body, or shoulders
**2** : YIELD, SUBMIT
**3 a** : to descend from a superior rank, dignity, or status **b** : to lower oneself morally
**4 a** *archaic* : to move down from a height : ALIGHT **b** : to fly or dive down swiftly usually to attack prey
*transitive verb*
**1** : DEBASE, DEGRADE
**2** : to bend (a part of the body) forward and downward
**²stoop** *noun* (1571)
**1 a** : an act of bending the body forward **b** : a temporary or habitual forward bend of the back and shoulders
**2** : the descent of a bird especially on its prey
**3** : a lowering of oneself

**³stoop** *noun* [Dutch *stoep;* akin to Old English *stæpe* step — more at STEP] (1755)
: a porch, platform, entrance stairway, or small veranda at a house door
**stoop·ball** \'stüp-,ból\ *noun* (1941)
: a variation of baseball in which a player throws a ball against a stoop or building and runs to base while other players attempt to retrieve the rebound and put the runner out
**stoop labor** *noun* (1949)
: the hard labor done or required to plant, cultivate, and harvest a crop and especially a crop of vegetables
**¹stop** \'stäp\ *verb* **stopped; stop·ping** [Middle English *stoppen,* from Old English *-stoppian,* from (assumed) Vulgar Latin *stuppare* to stop with tow, from Latin *stuppa* tow, from Greek *styppē*] (13th century)
*transitive verb*
**1 a** : to close by filling or obstructing **b** : to hinder or prevent the passage of **c** : to get in the way of : be wounded or killed by ⟨easy to *stop* a bullet along a lonely . . . road —Harvey Fergusson⟩
**2 a** : to close up or block off (an opening) : PLUG **b** : to make impassable : CHOKE, OBSTRUCT **c** : to cover over or fill in (a hole or crevice)
**3 a** : to cause to give up or change a course of action **b** : to keep from carrying out a proposed action : RESTRAIN, PREVENT
**4 a** : to cause to cease : CHECK, SUPPRESS **b** : DISCONTINUE
**5 a** : to deduct or withhold (a sum due) **b** : to instruct one's bank to refuse (payment) or refuse payment of (as a check)
**6 a** : to arrest the progress or motion of : cause to halt ⟨*stopped* the car⟩ **b** : PARRY **c** : to check by means of a weapon : BRING DOWN, KILL **d** : to beat in a boxing match by a knockout; *broadly* : DEFEAT **e** : BAFFLE, NONPLUS
**7** : to change the pitch of (as a violin string) by pressing with the finger or (as a wind instrument) by closing one or more finger holes or by thrusting the hand or a mute into the bell
**8** : to hold an honor card and enough protecting cards to be able to block (a bridge suit) before an opponent can run many tricks
*intransitive verb*
**1 a** : to cease activity or operation **b** : to come to an end especially suddenly : CLOSE, FINISH
**2 a** : to cease to move on : HALT **b** : PAUSE, HESITATE
**3 a** : to break one's journey : STAY **b** *chiefly British* : REMAIN **c** : to make a brief call : drop in
**4** : to become choked : CLOG ☆

\ə\ **abut** \°\ **kitten** \ər\ **further** \a\ **ash** \ā\ **ace** \ä\ **mop, mar** \aú\ **out** \ch\ **chin** \e\ **bet** \ē\ **easy** \g\ **go** \i\ **hit** \ī\ **ice** \j\ **job** \ŋ\ **sing** \ō\ **go** \ò\ **law** \òi\ **boy** \th\ **thin** \th\ **the** \ü\ **loot** \ù\ **foot** \y\ **yet** \zh\ **vision** *see also* Guide to Pronunciation

— **stop·pa·ble** \'stä-pə-bəl\ *adjective*

²**stop** *noun* (15th century)
**1 a :** CESSATION, END **b :** a pause or breaking off in speech
**2 a** (1) **:** a graduated set of organ pipes of similar design and tone quality (2) **:** a corresponding set of vibrators or reeds of a reed organ (3) **:** STOP KNOB — often used figuratively in phrases like *pull out all the stops* to suggest holding nothing back **b :** a means of regulating the pitch of a musical instrument
**3 a :** something that impedes, obstructs, or brings to a halt **:** IMPEDIMENT, OBSTACLE **b :** the aperture of a camera lens; *also* **:** a marking of a series (as of f-numbers) on a camera for indicating settings of the diaphragm **c :** a drain plug **:** STOPPER
**4 :** a device for arresting or limiting motion
**5 :** the act of stopping **:** the state of being stopped **:** CHECK
**6 a :** a halt in a journey **:** STAY ⟨made a brief *stop* to refuel⟩ **b :** a stopping place ⟨a bus *stop*⟩
**7 a** *chiefly British* **:** any of several punctuation marks **b** — used in telegrams and cables to indicate a period **c :** a pause or break in a verse that marks the end of a grammatical unit
**8 a :** an order stopping payment (as of a check or note) by a bank **:** STOP ORDER
**9 :** a consonant characterized by complete closure of the breath passage in the course of articulation — compare CONTINUANT
**10 :** a depression in the face of an animal at the junction of forehead and muzzle

³**stop** *adjective* (1594)
**:** serving to stop **:** designed to stop ⟨*stop* line⟩ ⟨*stop* signal⟩

**stop–and–go** \,stäp-ən-'gō, -ᵊm-, *attributively* -,gō\ *adjective* (1925)
**:** of, relating to, or involving frequent stops; *especially* **:** controlled or regulated by traffic lights ⟨*stop-and-go* driving⟩

**stop bath** *noun* (1898)
**:** an acid bath used to check photographic development of a negative or print

**stop·cock** \'stäp-,käk\ *noun* (1584)
**:** a cock for stopping or regulating flow (as through a pipe)

**stop down** *transitive verb* (circa 1891)
**:** to reduce the effective aperture of (a lens) by means of a diaphragm

**stope** \'stōp\ *noun* [probably from Low German *stope*, literally, step; akin to Old English *stæpe* step — more at STEP] (1747)
**:** a usually steplike excavation underground for the removal of ore that is formed as the ore is mined in successive layers

**stop·gap** \'stäp-,gap\ *noun, often attributive* (1684)
**:** something that serves as a temporary expedient **:** MAKESHIFT ⟨*stopgap* measures⟩
*synonym* see RESOURCE

**stop knob** *noun* (1887)
**:** one of the handles by which an organist draws or shuts off a particular stop

**stop·light** \'stäp-,līt\ *noun* (1926)
**1 :** a light on the rear of a motor vehicle that is illuminated when the driver presses the brake pedal
**2 :** TRAFFIC SIGNAL

**stop order** *noun* (circa 1891)
**:** an order to a broker to buy or sell respectively at the market when the price of a security advances or declines to a designated level

**stop out** *intransitive verb* [after *drop out*] (1973)
**:** to withdraw temporarily from enrollment at a college or university
— **stop–out** \'stäp-,aut\ *noun*

**stop·over** \'stäp-,ō-vər\ *noun* (1885)
**1 :** a stop at an intermediate point in one's journey
**2 :** a stopping place on a journey

**stop·page** \'stä-pij\ *noun* (15th century)
**:** the act of stopping **:** the state of being stopped **:** HALT, OBSTRUCTION

**stop payment** *noun* (circa 1919)

**:** a depositor's order to a bank to refuse to honor a specified check drawn by him or her

¹**stop·per** \'stä-pər\ *noun* (15th century)
**1 :** one that brings to a halt or causes to stop operating or functioning **:** CHECK: as **a :** a playing card that will stop the running of a suit **b :** a baseball pitcher depended on to win important games or to stop a losing streak; *also* **:** an effective relief pitcher
**2 :** one that closes, shuts, or fills up; *specifically* **:** something (as a bung or cork) used to plug an opening

²**stopper** *transitive verb* **stop·pered; stop·per·ing** \-p(ə-)riŋ\ (circa 1769)
**:** to close or secure with or as if with a stopper

**stopper knot** *noun* (1860)
**:** a knot used to prevent a rope from passing through a hole or opening

¹**stop·ple** \'stä-pəl\ *noun* [Middle English *stoppell*, from *stoppen* to stop] (14th century)
**:** something that closes an aperture **:** STOPPER, PLUG

²**stopple** *transitive verb* **stop·pled; stop·pling** \-p(ə-)liŋ\ (1795)
**:** STOPPER

**stop·watch** \'stäp-,wäch\ *noun* (1737)
**:** a watch with a hand or a digital display that can be started and stopped at will for exact timing (as of a race)

**stor·age** \'stōr-ij, 'stor-\ *noun* (circa 1613)
**1 a :** space or a place for storing **b :** an amount stored **c :** MEMORY 4
**2 a :** the act of storing **:** the state of being stored; *especially* **:** the safekeeping of goods in a depository (as a warehouse) **b :** the price charged for keeping goods in a storehouse
**3 :** the production by means of electric energy of chemical reactions that when allowed to reverse themselves generate electricity again without serious loss

**storage battery** *noun* (1881)
**:** a cell or connected group of cells that converts chemical energy into electrical energy by reversible chemical reactions and that may be recharged by passing a current through it in the direction opposite to that of its discharge — called also *storage cell*

**sto·rax** \'stōr-,aks, 'stor-\ *noun* [Middle English, from Late Latin, alteration of Latin *styrax*, from Greek] (14th century)
**1 a :** a fragrant balsam obtained from the bark of an Asian tree (*Liquidambar orientalis*) of the witch-hazel family that is used as an expectorant and sometimes in perfumery — called also *Levant storax* **b :** a balsam from the sweet gum that is similar to storax
**2 :** any of a genus (*Styrax* of the family Styracaceae, the storax family) of trees or shrubs with usually hairy leaves and white flowers in drooping racemes — compare BENZOIN

¹**store** \'stōr, 'stor\ *transitive verb* **stored; stor·ing** [Middle English, from Old French *estorer* to construct, restore, store, from Latin *instaurare* to renew, restore] (13th century)
**1 :** LAY AWAY, ACCUMULATE ⟨*store* vegetables for winter use⟩ ⟨an organism that absorbs and *stores* DDT⟩
**2 :** FURNISH, SUPPLY; *especially* **:** to stock against a future time ⟨*store* a ship with provisions⟩
**3 :** to place or leave in a location (as a warehouse, library, or computer memory) for preservation or later use or disposal
**4 :** to provide storage room for **:** HOLD ⟨elevators for *storing* surplus wheat⟩
— **stor·able** \'stōr-ə-bəl, 'stor-\ *adjective*

²**store** *noun* (13th century)
**1 a :** something that is stored or kept for future use **b** *plural* **:** articles (as of food) accumulated for some specific object and drawn upon as needed **:** STOCK, SUPPLIES **c :** something that is accumulated **d :** a source from which things may be drawn as needed **:** a reserve fund

**2 :** STORAGE — usually used with *in* ⟨when placing eggs in *store* —*Dublin Sunday Independent*⟩
**3 :** VALUE, IMPORTANCE ⟨set great *store* by a partner's opinion⟩
**4 :** a large quantity, supply, or number **:** ABUNDANCE
**5 a :** STOREHOUSE, WAREHOUSE **b** *chiefly British* **:** MEMORY 4
**6 :** a business establishment where usually diversified goods are kept for retail sale ⟨grocery *store*⟩ — compare SHOP
— **in store :** in readiness **:** in preparation ⟨there's a surprise *in store* for you⟩

³**store** *adjective* (1602)
**1** *or* **stores :** of, relating to, kept in, or used for a store
**2 :** purchased from a store as opposed to being natural or homemade **:** MANUFACTURED, READY-MADE ⟨*store* clothes⟩ ⟨*store* bread⟩

**store–bought** \'stōr-,bot, 'stor-\ *adjective* (1905)
**:** STORE 2

**store cheese** *noun* [from its being a staple article stocked in grocery stores] (1863)
**:** CHEDDAR

¹**store·front** \'stōr-,frənt, 'stor-\ *noun* (1880)
**1 :** the front side of a store or store building facing a street
**2 :** a building, room, or suite of rooms having a storefront

²**storefront** *adjective* (1937)
**1 :** of, relating to, or characteristic of a storefront church ⟨a *storefront* evangelist⟩
**2 :** occupying a room or suite of rooms in a store building at street level and immediately behind a storefront ⟨a *storefront* school⟩
**3 :** of, relating to, or being outreach professional services ⟨*storefront* lawyers⟩ ⟨a *storefront* clinic⟩

**storefront church** *noun* (1937)
**:** a city church that utilizes storefront quarters as a meeting place

**store·house** \'stōr-,haus, 'stor-\ *noun* (14th century)
**1 :** a building for storing goods (as provisions) **:** MAGAZINE, WAREHOUSE
**2 :** an abundant supply or source **:** REPOSITORY

**store·keep·er** \-,kē-pər\ *noun* (1618)
**1 :** one that has charge of supplies (as military stores)
**2 :** one that operates a retail store

**store·room** \-,rüm, -,rum\ *noun* (1746)
**1 :** a room or space for the storing of goods or supplies
**2 :** STOREHOUSE 2

**store·ship** \-,ship\ *noun* (1693)
**:** a ship used to carry supplies

**store·wide** \-'wīd\ *adjective* (circa 1937)
**:** including all or most merchandise in a store ⟨a *storewide* sale⟩

¹**sto·ried** \'stōr-ēd, 'stor-\ *adjective* (14th century)
**1 :** decorated with designs representing scenes from story or history ⟨a *storied* tapestry⟩
**2 :** having an interesting history **:** celebrated in story or history ⟨a *storied* institution⟩

²**storied** *or* **sto·reyed** \'stōr-ēd, 'stor-\ *adjective* (1624)
**:** having stories — used in combination ⟨a two-*storied* house⟩

**stork** \'stork\ *noun* [Middle English, from Old English *storc*; akin to Old High German *storah* stork and probably to Old English *stearc* stiff — more at STARK] (before 12th century)
**:** any of various large mostly Old World wading birds (family Ciconiidae) that have long stout bills and are related to the ibises and herons

**storks·bill** \'storks-,bil\ *noun* (1562)
**:** any of several plants of the geranium family with elongate beaked fruits: **a :** PELARGONIUM **b :** ALFILARIA; *also* **:** any of several related plants (genus *Erodium*)

¹**storm** \'storm\ *noun, often attributive* [Middle English, from Old English; akin to Old

High German *sturm* storm, Old English *styrian* to stir] (before 12th century)
**1 a :** a disturbance of the atmosphere marked by wind and usually by rain, snow, hail, sleet, or thunder and lightning **b :** a heavy fall of rain, snow, or hail **c** (1) **:** wind having a speed of 64 to 72 miles (103 to 116 kilometers) per hour (2) **:** WHOLE GALE — see BEAUFORT SCALE table **d :** a serious disturbance of any element of nature
**2 :** a disturbed or agitated state **:** a sudden or violent commotion
**3 :** a heavy discharge of objects (as missiles)
**4 :** a tumultuous outburst
**5 a :** PAROXYSM, CRISIS **b :** a sudden heavy influx or onset
**6 :** a violent assault on a defended position
**7** *plural* **:** STORM WINDOW
**— by storm :** by or as if by employing a bold swift frontal movement especially with the intent of defeating or winning over quickly ⟨took the literary world *by storm*⟩
**— up a storm :** in a remarkable or energetic fashion — used as an intensifier ⟨dancing *up a storm*⟩ ⟨can write *up a storm*⟩

**²storm** (15th century)
*intransitive verb*
**1 a :** to blow with violence **b :** to rain, hail, snow, or sleet vigorously
**2 :** to attack by storm ⟨*stormed* ashore at zero hour⟩
**3 :** to be in or to exhibit a violent passion **:** RAGE ⟨*storming* at the unusual delay⟩
**4 :** to rush about or move impetuously, violently, or angrily ⟨the mob *stormed* through the streets⟩
*transitive verb*
**:** to attack, take, or win over by storm ⟨*storm* a fort⟩
**synonym** see ATTACK

**storm and stress** *noun, often both Ss capitalized* (1855)
**:** STURM UND DRANG

**storm-bound** \'storm-'bau̇nd\ *adjective* (1830)
**:** cut off from outside communication by a storm or its effects **:** stopped or delayed by storms

**storm cellar** *noun* (circa 1902)
**:** a cellar or covered excavation designed for protection from dangerous windstorms (as tornadoes)

**storm door** *noun* (1878)
**:** an additional door placed outside an ordinary outside door for protection against severe weather

**storm petrel** *noun* (circa 1833)
**:** any of various small petrels (family Hydrobatidae); *especially* **:** a small sooty black white-marked petrel (*Hydrobates pelagicus*) frequenting the north Atlantic and Mediterranean

**storm trooper** *noun* (1933)
**1 :** a member of a private Nazi army notorious for aggressiveness, violence, and brutality
**2 :** one that resembles a Nazi storm trooper

**storm window** *noun* (circa 1888)

**stork**

**storm petrel**

**:** a sash placed outside an ordinary window as a protection against severe weather — called also *storm sash*

**stormy** \'stȯr-mē\ *adjective* **storm·i·er; -est** (12th century)
**1 :** relating to, characterized by, or indicative of a storm ⟨a *stormy* day⟩ ⟨a *stormy* autumn⟩
**2 :** marked by turmoil or fury ⟨a *stormy* life⟩ ⟨a *stormy* conference⟩
**— storm·i·ly** \'stȯr-mə-lē\ *adverb*
**— storm·i·ness** \-mē-nəs\ *noun*

**stormy petrel** *noun* (circa 1776)
**1 :** STORM PETREL
**2 a :** one fond of strife **b :** a harbinger of trouble

**¹sto·ry** \'stȯr-ē, 'stȯr-\ *noun, plural* **stories** [Middle English *storie*, from Old French *estorie*, from Latin *historia* — more at HISTORY] (13th century)
**1** *archaic* **:** HISTORY 1, 3
**2 a :** an account of incidents or events **b :** a statement regarding the facts pertinent to a situation in question **c :** ANECDOTE; *especially* **:** an amusing one
**3 a :** a fictional narrative shorter than a novel; *specifically* **:** SHORT STORY **b :** the intrigue or plot of a narrative or dramatic work
**4 :** a widely circulated rumor
**5 :** LIE, FALSEHOOD
**6 :** LEGEND, ROMANCE
**7 :** a news article or broadcast
**8 :** MATTER, SITUATION

**²story** *transitive verb* **sto·ried; sto·ry·ing** (15th century)
**1** *archaic* **:** to narrate or describe in story
**2 :** to adorn with a story or a scene from history

**³story** *also* **sto·rey** \'stȯr-ē, 'stȯr-ē\ *noun, plural* **stories** *also* **storeys** [Middle English *storie*, from Medieval Latin *historia* picture, story of a building, from Latin, history, tale; probably from pictures adorning the windows of medieval buildings] (14th century)
**1 a :** the space in a building between two adjacent floor levels or between a floor and the roof **b :** a set of rooms in such a space **c :** a unit of measure equal to the height of the story of a building ⟨one *story* high⟩
**2 :** a horizontal division of a building's exterior not necessarily corresponding exactly with the stories within

**sto·ry·board** \-,bōrd, -,bȯrd\ *noun* (1942)
**:** a panel or series of panels on which a set of sketches is arranged depicting consecutively the important changes of scene and action in a series of shots (as for a film, television show, or commercial)
**— storyboard** *transitive verb*

**¹sto·ry·book** \-,bu̇k\ *noun* (1711)
**:** a book of stories ⟨*storybooks* for children⟩

**²storybook** *adjective* (1844)
**:** FAIRY-TALE

**story line** *noun* (1941)
**:** the plot of a story or drama

**sto·ry·tell·er** \'stȯr-ē-,te-lər, 'stȯr-\ *noun* (1709)
**:** a teller of stories: as **a :** a relater of anecdotes **b :** a reciter of tales (as in a children's library) **c :** LIAR, FIBBER **d :** a writer of stories
**— sto·ry·tell·ing** *noun*

**stoss** \'stäs, 'stȯs, 'stōs, 'shtōs\ *adjective* [German *stoss-*, from *stossen* to push, from Old High German *stōzen;* akin to Gothic *stautan* to strike — more at CONTUSION] (1878)
**:** facing toward the direction from which an overriding glacier impinges ⟨the *stoss* slope of a hill⟩

**sto·tin·ka** \stō-'tiŋ-kə, stə-\ *noun, plural* **-tin·ki** \-kē\ [Bulgarian] (circa 1892)
**—** see *lev* at MONEY table

**stound** \'stau̇nd, 'stünd\ *noun* [Middle English, from Old English *stund;* akin to Old High German *stunta* time, hour] (before 12th century)
*archaic* **:** TIME, WHILE

**stoup** \'stüp\ *noun* [Middle English *stowp,* probably of Scandinavian origin; akin to Old Norse *staup* cup] (14th century)
**1 a :** a beverage container (as a glass or tankard) **b :** FLAGON
**2 :** a basin for holy water at the entrance of a church

**¹stour** \'stu̇r\ *adjective* [Middle English *stor,* from Old English *stōr;* akin to Old High German *stuori* large, Russian *staryĭ* old, Old English *standan* to stand] (before 12th century)
**1** *chiefly Scottish* **:** STRONG, HARDY
**2** *chiefly Scottish* **:** STERN, HARSH

**²stour** *noun* [Middle English, from Middle French *estour,* of Germanic origin; akin to Old High German *sturm* storm, battle — more at STORM] (14th century)
**1 a** *archaic* **:** BATTLE, CONFLICT **b** *dialect British* **:** TUMULT, UPROAR
**2** *chiefly Scottish* **:** DUST, POWDER

**¹stout** \'stau̇t\ *adjective* [Middle English, from Middle French *estout,* of Germanic origin; akin to Old High German *stolz* proud; perhaps akin to Old High German *stelza* stilt — more at STILT] (14th century)
**1 :** strong of character: as **a :** BRAVE, BOLD **b :** FIRM, DETERMINED; *also* **:** OBSTINATE, UNCOMPROMISING
**2 :** physically or materially strong: **a :** STURDY, VIGOROUS **b :** STAUNCH, ENDURING **c :** sturdily constructed **:** SUBSTANTIAL
**3 :** FORCEFUL ⟨a *stout* attack⟩; *also* **:** VIOLENT ⟨a *stout* wind⟩
**4 :** bulky in body **:** FAT
**synonym** see STRONG
**— stout·ish** \'stau̇-tish\ *adjective*
**— stout·ly** *adverb*
**— stout·ness** *noun*

**²stout** *noun* (1677)
**1 :** a very dark full-bodied ale with a distinctive malty flavor
**2 a :** a fat person **b :** a clothing size designed for the large figure

**stout·en** \'stau̇-tⁿn\ *verb* **stout·ened; stout·en·ing** \'stau̇t-niŋ, 'stau̇-tⁿn-iŋ\ (1834)
*transitive verb*
**:** to make stout ⟨*stouten* a resolve⟩
*intransitive verb*
**:** to become stout

**stout-heart·ed** \'stau̇t-,här-təd\ *adjective* (1552)
**:** having a stout heart or spirit: **a :** COURAGEOUS **b :** STUBBORN
**— stout-heart·ed·ly** *adverb*
**— stout-heart·ed·ness** *noun*

**¹stove** \'stōv\ *noun* [Middle English, heated room, steam room, from Middle Dutch or Middle Low German, from (assumed) Vulgar Latin *extufa,* ultimately from Latin *ex-* + Greek *typhein* to smoke — more at DEAF] (1591)
**1 a :** a portable or fixed apparatus that burns fuel or uses electricity to provide heat (as for cooking or heating) **b :** a device that generates heat for special purposes (as for heating tools or heating air for a hot blast) **c :** KILN
**2** *chiefly British* **:** a hothouse especially for the cultivation of tropical exotics; *broadly* **:** GREENHOUSE

**²stove** *past and past participle of* STAVE

**stove·pipe** \'stōv-,pīp\ *noun* (1699)
**1 :** pipe of large diameter usually of sheet steel used as a stove chimney or to connect a stove with a flue
**2 :** SILK HAT

**sto·ver** \'stō-vər\ *noun* [Middle English, modification of Anglo-French *estovers* necessary supplies, from Old French *estoveir* to be necessary, ultimately from Latin *est opus* there is need] (14th century)

**1** *chiefly dialect English* **:** FODDER
**2 :** mature cured stalks of grain with the ears removed that are used as feed for livestock

**stow** \'stō\ *transitive verb* [Middle English, to place, from *stowe* place, from Old English *stōw;* akin to Old Frisian *stō* place, Greek *stylos* pillar — more at STEER] (14th century)
**1 :** HOUSE, LODGE
**2 a :** to put away for future use **:** STORE **b** *obsolete* **:** to lock up for safekeeping **:** CONFINE
**3 a :** to dispose in an orderly fashion **:** ARRANGE, PACK **b :** LOAD
**4** *slang* **:** to put aside **:** STOP
**5 a** *archaic* **:** CROWD **b :** to eat or drink up **:** CONSUME — usually used with *away* ⟨*stowed* away a huge dinner⟩

**stow·age** \-ij\ *noun* (14th century)
**1 a :** an act or process of stowing **b :** goods in storage or to be stowed
**2 a :** storage capacity **b :** a place or receptacle for storage
**3 :** the state of being stored

**stow·away** \'stō-ə-,wā\ *noun* (1850)
**:** one that stows away

**stow away** *intransitive verb* (1879)
**:** to secrete oneself aboard a vehicle as a means of obtaining transportation

**STP** \,es-,tē-'pē\ *noun* [probably from *STP,* a trademark for a motor fuel additive] (1967)
**:** a psychedelic drug chemically related to mescaline and amphetamine

**stra·bis·mus** \strə-'biz-məs\ *noun* [New Latin, from Greek *strabismos* condition of squinting, from *strabizein* to squint, from *strabos* squint-eyed; akin to Greek *strephein* to twist] (circa 1684)
**:** inability of one eye to attain binocular vision with the other because of imbalance of the muscles of the eyeball — called also *squint*
— **stra·bis·mic** \-mik\ *adjective*

**¹strad·dle** \'stra-dᵊl\ *verb* **strad·dled; strad·dling** \'strad-liŋ, 'stra-dᵊl-iŋ\ [irregular from *stride*] (1565)
*intransitive verb*
**1 :** to stand, sit, or walk with the legs wide apart; *especially* **:** to sit astride
**2 :** to spread out irregularly **:** SPRAWL
**3 :** to favor or seem to favor two apparently opposite sides
**4 :** to execute a commodities market spread
*transitive verb*
**1 :** to stand, sit, or be astride of ⟨*straddle* a horse⟩
**2 :** to be noncommittal in regard to ⟨*straddle* an issue⟩
— **strad·dler** \'strad-lər, 'stra-dᵊl-ər\ *noun*
— **straddle the fence :** to be in a position of neutrality or indecision

**²straddle** *noun* (1611)
**1 :** the act or position of one who straddles
**2 :** a noncommittal or equivocal position
**3 :** SPREAD 5

**Stra·di·va·ri** \,stra-də-'vär-ē, -'var-, -'ver-\ *noun* (circa 1903)
**:** STRADIVARIUS

**Strad·i·var·i·us** \,stra-də-'var-ē-əs, -'ver-\ *noun, plural* **-var·ii** \-ē-,ī\ [Latinized form of *Stradivari*] (1833)
**:** a stringed instrument (as a violin) made by Antonio Stradivari of Cremona

**strafe** \'strāf, *especially British* 'sträf\ *transitive verb* **strafed; straf·ing** [German *Gott strafe England* God punish England, German propaganda slogan during World War I] (1915)
**:** to rake (as ground troops) with fire at close range and especially with machine-gun fire from low-flying aircraft
— **strafe** *noun*
— **straf·er** *noun*

**¹strag·gle** \'stra-gəl\ *intransitive verb* **straggled; strag·gling** \-g(ə-)liŋ\ [Middle English *straglen*] (15th century)
**1 :** to wander from the direct course or way **:** ROVE, STRAY

**2 :** to trail off from others of its kind ⟨little cabins *straggling* off into the woods⟩
— **strag·gler** \-g(ə-)lər\ *noun*

**²straggle** *noun* (1865)
**:** a straggling group (as of persons or objects)

**strag·gly** \'stra-g(ə-)lē\ *adjective* **strag·gli·er; -est** (1862)
**:** spread out or scattered irregularly ⟨a *straggly* beard⟩

**¹straight** \'strāt\ *adjective* [Middle English *streght, straight,* from past participle of *strecchen* to stretch — more at STRETCH] (14th century)
**1 a :** free from curves, bends, angles, or irregularities ⟨*straight* hair⟩ ⟨*straight* timber⟩ **b :** generated by a point moving continuously in the same direction and expressed by a linear equation ⟨a *straight* line⟩ ⟨the *straight* segment of a curve⟩
**2 a :** lying along or holding to a direct or proper course or method ⟨a *straight* thinker⟩ **b :** CANDID, FRANK ⟨a *straight* answer⟩ **c :** coming directly from a trustworthy source ⟨a *straight* tip on the horses⟩ **d (1) :** having the elements in an order ⟨the *straight* sequence of events⟩ **(2) :** CONSECUTIVE ⟨12 *straight* days⟩ **e :** having the cylinders arranged in a single straight line ⟨a *straight* 8-cylinder engine⟩ **f :** PLUMB, VERTICAL ⟨the picture isn't quite *straight*⟩
**3 a :** exhibiting honesty and fairness ⟨*straight* dealing⟩ **b :** properly ordered or arranged ⟨set the kitchen *straight*⟩ ⟨set us *straight* on that issue⟩; *also* **:** CORRECT ⟨get the facts *straight*⟩ **c :** free from extraneous matter **:** UNMIXED ⟨*straight* whiskey⟩ **d :** marked by no exceptions or deviations in support of a principle or party ⟨votes a *straight* Democratic ticket⟩ **e :** having a fixed price for each regardless of the number sold **f :** not deviating from an indicated pattern ⟨writes *straight* humor⟩ ⟨a *straight*-A student⟩ **g (1) :** exhibiting no deviation from what is established or accepted as usual, normal, or proper **:** CONVENTIONAL; *also* **:** SQUARE 5f **(2) :** not using or under the influence of drugs or alcohol **h :** HETEROSEXUAL
**4 :** being the only form of remuneration ⟨on *straight* commission⟩
— **straight·ish** \'strā-tish\ *adjective*
— **straight·ly** *adverb*
— **straight·ness** *noun*

**²straight** *adverb* (14th century)
**:** in a straight manner

**³straight** *transitive verb* (15th century) *chiefly Scottish* **:** STRAIGHTEN

**⁴straight** *noun* (1645)
**1 :** something that is straight: as **a :** a straight line or arrangement **b :** STRAIGHTAWAY; *especially* **:** HOMESTRETCH **c :** a true or honest report or course
**2 a :** a sequence (as of shots, strokes, or moves) resulting in a perfect score in a game or contest **b :** first place at the finish of a horse race **:** WIN
**3 :** a poker hand containing five cards in sequence but not of the same suit — see POKER illustration
**4 :** a person who adheres to conventional attitudes and mores

**straight–ahead** \'strāt-ə-'hed\ *adjective* (1836)
**:** relating to or being music performed in an unembellished manner typical of a given idiom or performer; *broadly* **:** STRAIGHTFORWARD

**straight and narrow** *noun* [probably alteration of *strait and narrow;* from the admonition of Matthew 7:14 (Authorized Version), "strait is the gate and narrow is the way which leadeth unto life"] (1930)
**:** the way of propriety and rectitude — used with *the*

**straight angle** *noun* (1601)
**:** an angle whose sides lie in opposite directions from the vertex in the same straight line and which equals two right angles

**straight–arm** \'strāt-,ärm\ *noun* (1903)

**:** an act or instance of warding off a football tackler with the arm fully extended from the shoulder, elbow locked, and the palm of the hand placed firmly against any part of his body — called also *stiff-arm*
— **straight–arm** *verb*

**straight–arrow** \-'ar-(,)ō\ *adjective* [from the expression *straight as an arrow*] (circa 1969)
**:** rigidly proper and conventional

**¹straight·away** \,strāt-ə-'wā\ *adverb* (1662)
**:** without hesitation or delay

**²straight·away** \'strāt-ə-,wā\ *adjective* (1874)
**1 :** proceeding in a straight line **:** continuous in direction
**2 :** IMMEDIATE

**³straight·away** \'strā-tə-,wā\ *noun* (1878)
**:** a straight course: as **a :** the straight part of a closed racecourse **:** STRETCH **b :** a straight and unimpeded stretch of road or way

**straight·bred** \'strāt-'bred\ *adjective* (1898)
**:** produced by breeding a single breed, strain, or type ⟨*straightbred* cattle⟩
— **straight·bred** \-,bred\ *noun*

**straight chain** *noun* (1890)
**:** an open chain of atoms having no side chains — usually hyphenated when used attributively

**straight·edge** \'strāt-,ej\ *noun* (1812)
**:** a bar or piece of material (as of wood, metal, or plastic) with a straight edge for testing straight lines and surfaces or drawing straight lines

**straight·en** \'strā-tᵊn\ *verb* **straight·ened; straight·en·ing** \'strāt-niŋ, 'strā-tᵊn-iŋ\ (1542)
*transitive verb*
**:** to make straight — usually used with *up* or *out*
*intransitive verb*
**:** to become straight — usually used with *up* or *out*
**word history** see STRAITEN
— **straight·en·er** \'strāt-nər, 'strā-tᵊn-ər\ *noun*

**straight face** *noun* (circa 1890)
**:** a face giving no evidence of emotion and especially of merriment
— **straight–faced** \'strāt-'fāst\ *adjective*
— **straight–faced·ly** \-'fā-səd-lē, -'fāst-lē\ *adverb*

**straight flush** *noun* (1864)
**:** a poker hand containing five cards of the same suit in sequence — see POKER illustration

**¹straight·for·ward** \,strāt-'fȯr-wərd, 'strāt-,\ *adjective* (1806)
**1 a :** free from evasiveness or obscurity **:** EXACT, CANDID ⟨a *straightforward* account⟩ **b :** CLEAR-CUT, PRECISE
**2 :** proceeding in a straight course or manner **:** DIRECT, UNDEVIATING
— **straight·for·ward·ly** *adverb*
— **straight·for·ward·ness** *noun*

**²straightforward** *also* **straight·for·wards** \-wərdz\ *adverb* (1809)
**:** in a straightforward manner

**straight–line** \'strāt-'līn\ *adjective* (1843)
**1 :** being a mechanical linkage or equivalent device designed to produce or copy motion in a straight line
**2 :** having the principal parts arranged in a straight line
**3 :** marked by a uniform spread and especially in equal segments over a given term ⟨*straight-line* amortization⟩ ⟨*straight-line* depreciation⟩
**4 :** occurring, measured, or made in or along a straight line ⟨*straight-line* motion⟩ ⟨*straight-line* extrapolation⟩

**straight man** *noun* (1923)
**:** a member of a comedy team who feeds lines to his partner who in turn replies with usually humorous quips

**straight off** *adverb* (1873)
**:** at once **:** IMMEDIATELY

**straight–out** \'strāt-'au̇t\ *adjective* (1848)

**1 :** FORTHRIGHT, BLUNT ⟨gave him a *straight-out* answer⟩

**2 :** OUTRIGHT, THOROUGHGOING

— **straight–out** *adverb*

**straight poker** *noun* (1864)

**:** poker in which the players bet on the five cards dealt to them and then have a showdown without drawing — compare DRAW POKER, STUD POKER

**straight razor** *noun* (1938)

**:** a razor with a rigid steel cutting blade hinged to a case that forms a handle when the razor is open for use

**straight·way** \'strāt-'wā, -ˌwā\ *adverb* (15th century)

**1 :** in a direct course **:** DIRECTLY ⟨fell *straight-way* down the stairs⟩

**2 :** RIGHT AWAY, IMMEDIATELY, STRAIGHTAWAY ⟨*straightway* the clouds began to part⟩

¹**strain** \'strān\ *noun* [Middle English *streen* progeny, lineage, from Old English *strēon* gain, acquisition; akin to Old High German gi*striuni* gain, Latin *struere* to heap up — more at STREW] (13th century)

**1 a :** LINEAGE, ANCESTRY **b :** a group of presumed common ancestry with clear-cut physiological but usually not morphological distinctions ⟨a high-yielding *strain* of winter wheat⟩; *broadly* **:** a specified infraspecific group (as a stock, line, or ecotype) **c :** KIND, SORT ⟨discussions of a lofty *strain*⟩

**2 a :** inherited or inherent character, quality, or disposition ⟨a *strain* of madness in the family⟩ **b :** TRACE, STREAK ⟨a *strain* of fanaticism⟩

**3 a :** TUNE, AIR **b :** a passage of verbal or musical expression **c :** a stream or outburst of forceful or impassioned speech

**4 a :** the tenor, pervading note, burden, or tone of an utterance or of a course of action or conduct **b :** MOOD, TEMPER

²**strain** *verb* [Middle English, from Middle French *estraindre*, from Latin *stringere* to bind or draw tight, press together; akin to Greek *strang-*, *stranx* drop squeezed out, *strangalē* halter] (14th century)

*transitive verb*

**1 a :** to draw tight **:** cause to fit firmly ⟨*strain* the bandage over the wound⟩ **b :** to stretch to maximum extension and tautness ⟨*strain* a canvas over a frame⟩

**2 a :** to exert (as oneself) to the utmost **b :** to injure by overuse, misuse, or excessive pressure ⟨*strained* his back⟩ **c :** to cause a change of form or size in (a body) by application of external force

**3 :** to squeeze or clasp tightly: as **a :** HUG **b :** to compress painfully **:** CONSTRICT

**4 a :** to cause to pass through a strainer **:** FILTER **b :** to remove by straining ⟨*strain* lumps out of the gravy⟩

**5 :** to stretch beyond a proper limit ⟨that story *strains* my credulity⟩

**6** *obsolete* **:** to squeeze out **:** EXTORT

*intransitive verb*

**1 a :** to make violent efforts **:** STRIVE ⟨has to *strain* to reach the high notes⟩ **b :** to pull against resistance ⟨a dog *straining* at its leash⟩ **c :** to contract the muscles forcefully in attempting to defecate — often used in the phrase *strain at stool*

**2 :** to pass through or as if through a strainer ⟨the liquid *strains* readily⟩

**3 :** to make great difficulty or resistance **:** BALK

***word history*** see STRAITEN

— **strain a point :** to go beyond a usual, accepted, or proper limit or rule

³**strain** *noun* (1558)

**1 :** an act of straining or the condition of being strained: as **a :** bodily injury from excessive tension, effort, or use ⟨heart *strain*⟩; *especially* **:** one resulting from a wrench or twist and involving undue stretching of muscles or ligaments ⟨back *strain*⟩ **b :** excessive or difficult exertion or labor **c :** excessive physical or mental tension; *also* **:** a force, influence, or

factor causing such tension ⟨her responsibilities were a constant *strain*⟩ **d :** deformation of a material body under the action of applied forces

**2 :** an unusual reach, degree, or intensity **:** PITCH

**3** *archaic* **:** a strained interpretation of something said or written

**strained** \'strānd\ *adjective* (circa 1542)

**1 :** done or produced with excessive effort

**2 :** pushed by antagonism near to open conflict ⟨*strained* relations⟩

**strain·er** \'strā-nər\ *noun* (14th century)

**:** one that strains: as **a :** a device (as a sieve) to retain solid pieces while a liquid passes through **b :** any of various devices for stretching or tightening something

**strain gauge** *noun* (1910)

**:** EXTENSOMETER

¹**strait** \'strāt\ *adjective* [Middle English, from Old French *estreit*, from Latin *strictus* strait, strict, from past participle of *stringere*] (13th century)

**1** *archaic* **:** STRICT, RIGOROUS

**2** *archaic* **a :** NARROW **b :** limited in space or time **c :** closely fitting **:** CONSTRICTED, TIGHT

**3 a :** causing distress **:** DIFFICULT **b :** limited as to means or resources

— **strait·ly** *adverb*

— **strait·ness** *noun*

²**strait** *adverb* (13th century)

*obsolete* **:** in a close or tight manner

³**strait** *noun* (14th century)

**1 a** *archaic* **:** a narrow space or passage **b :** a comparatively narrow passageway connecting two large bodies of water — often used in plural but singular in construction **c :** ISTHMUS

**2 :** a situation of perplexity or distress — often used in plural ⟨in dire *straits*⟩

**synonym** see JUNCTURE

**strait·en** \'strā-tᵊn\ *transitive verb* **strait·ened; strait·en·ing** \'strāt-niŋ, 'strā-tᵊn-iŋ\ (circa 1552)

**1 a :** to make strait or narrow **b :** to hem in **:** CONFINE

**2** *archaic* **:** to restrict in freedom or scope **:** HAMPER

**3 :** to subject to distress, privation, or deficiency ⟨in *straitened* circumstances⟩ ◆

¹**strait·jack·et** *also* **straight·jack·et** \'strāt-ˌja-kət\ *noun* (1814)

**1 :** a cover or overgarment of strong material (as canvas) used to bind the body and especially the arms closely in restraining a violent prisoner or patient

**2 :** something that restricts or confines like a straitjacket

²**straitjacket** *also* **straightjacket** *transitive verb* (1863)

**:** to confine in or as if in a straitjacket

**strait·laced** *or* **straight·laced** \'strāt-'lāst\ *adjective* (1554)

**1 :** excessively strict in manners, morals, or opinion

**2 :** wearing or having a bodice or stays tightly laced

— **strait·laced·ly** \-'lā-səd-lē, -'lāst-lē\ *adverb*

— **strait·laced·ness** \-'lās(t)-nəs, -'lā-səd-nəs\ *noun*

**Straits dollar** \'strāts-\ *noun* [Straits Settlements, former British crown colony] (1908)

**:** a dollar formerly issued by British Malaya and used in much of southern and eastern Asia and the East Indies

**strake** \'strāk\ *noun* [Middle English; akin to Old English *streccan* to stretch — more at STRETCH] (14th century)

**1 :** a continuous band of hull planking or plates on a ship; *also* **:** the width of such a band

**2 :** STREAK, STRIPE

**stra·mash** \strə-'mash\ *noun* [origin unknown] (1803)

**1** *chiefly Scottish* **:** DISTURBANCE, RACKET

**2** *chiefly Scottish* **:** CRASH, SMASHUP

**stra·mo·ni·um** \strə-'mō-nē-əm\ *noun* [New Latin] (1663)

**1 :** the dried leaves of the jimsonweed or of a related plant (genus *Datura*) that contain toxic alkaloids (as atropine) and are used in medicine similarly to belladonna

**2 :** JIMSONWEED

¹**strand** \'strand\ *noun* [Middle English, from Old English; akin to Old Norse *strǫnd* shore] (before 12th century)

**:** the land bordering a body of water **:** SHORE, BEACH

²**strand** (1621)

*transitive verb*

**1 :** to run, drive, or cause to drift onto a strand **:** run aground

**2 :** to leave in a strange or an unfavorable place especially without funds or means to depart

**3 :** to leave (a base runner) on base at the end of an inning in baseball

*intransitive verb*

**:** to become stranded

³**strand** *noun* [Middle English *stronde, strande*] (13th century)

**1** *Scottish & dialect English* **:** STREAM

**2** *Scottish & dialect English* **:** SEA

⁴**strand** *noun* [Middle English *strond*] (15th century)

**1 a :** fibers or filaments twisted, plaited, or laid parallel to form a unit for further twisting or plaiting into yarn, thread, rope, or cordage **b :** one of the wires twisted together or laid parallel to form a wire rope or cable **c :** something (as a molecular chain) resembling a strand

**2 :** an element (as a yarn or thread) of a woven or plaited material

**3 :** an elongated or twisted and plaited body resembling a rope ⟨a *strand* of pearls⟩

**4 :** one of the elements interwoven in a complex whole

⁵**strand** *transitive verb* (1841)

**1 :** to break a strand of (a rope) accidentally

**2 a :** to form (as a rope) from strands **b :** to play out, twist, or arrange in a strand

**strand·ed** \'stran-dəd\ *adjective* (1875)

**:** having a strand or strands especially of a specified kind or number — usually used in combination ⟨the double-*stranded* molecule of DNA⟩

— **strand·ed·ness** *noun*

**strand·line** \'stran(d)-ˌlīn\ *noun* (1903)

**:** SHORELINE; *especially* **:** a shoreline above the present water level

**strange** \'strānj\ *adjective* **strang·er; strang·est** [Middle English, from Old

---

---

\ə\ **abut** \ᵊ\ **kitten** \ər\ **further** \a\ **ash** \ā\ **ace**
\ä\ **mop, mar** \aú\ **out** \ch\ **chin** \e\ **bet** \ē\ **easy**
\g\ **go** \i\ **hit** \ī\ **ice** \j\ **job** \ŋ\ **sing** \ō\ **go**
\ó\ **law** \ói\ **boy** \th\ **thin** \t̲h̲\ **the** \ü\ **loot** \ú\ **foot**
\y\ **yet** \zh\ **vision** *see also* Guide to Pronunciation

French *estrange*, from Latin *extraneus*, literally, external, from *extra* outside — more at EXTRA-] (13th century)
**1 a** *archaic* **:** of, relating to, or characteristic of another country **:** FOREIGN **b :** not native to or naturally belonging in a place **:** of external origin, kind, or character
**2 a :** not before known, heard, or seen **:** UNFAMILIAR **b :** exciting wonder or awe **:** EXTRAORDINARY
**3 a :** discouraging familiarities **:** RESERVED, DISTANT **b :** ILL AT EASE
**4 :** UNACCUSTOMED 2 ⟨she was *strange* to his ways⟩
**5 :** having the quantum characteristic of strangeness ⟨*strange* quark⟩ ⟨*strange* particle⟩
☆
— **strange·ly** *adverb*
**strange·ness** \'strānj-nəs\ *noun* (14th century)
**1 :** the quality or state of being strange
**2 :** a quantum characteristic of subatomic particles that accounts for the relatively long lifetime of certain particles, is conserved in interactions involving electromagnetism and the strong force, and has a value of zero for most known particles
**¹strang·er** \'strān-jər\ *noun* [Middle English, from Middle French *estrangier* foreign, foreigner, from *estrange*] (14th century)
**1 :** one who is strange: as **a** (1) **:** FOREIGNER (2) **:** a resident alien **b :** one in the house of another as a guest, visitor, or intruder **c :** a person or thing that is unknown or with whom one is unacquainted **d :** one who does not belong to or is kept from the activities of a group **e :** one not privy or party to an act, contract, or title **:** one that interferes without right
**2 :** one ignorant of or unacquainted with someone or something
**²stranger** *adjective* (15th century)
**:** of, relating to, or being a stranger **:** FOREIGN
**³stranger** *transitive verb* (1605)
*obsolete* **:** ESTRANGE, ALIENATE
**strange woman** *noun* [from the expression frequently used in Proverbs (Authorized Version)] (1535)
**:** PROSTITUTE
**stran·gle** \'straŋ-gəl\ *verb* **stran·gled; stran·gling** \-g(ə-)liŋ\ [Middle English, from Middle French *estrangler*, from Latin *strangulare*, from Greek *strangalan*, from *strangalē* halter — more at STRAIN] (14th century)
*transitive verb*
**1 a :** to choke to death by compressing the throat with something (as a hand or rope) **:** THROTTLE **b :** to obstruct seriously or fatally the normal breathing of **c :** STIFLE
**2 :** to suppress or hinder the rise, expression, or growth of
*intransitive verb*
**1 :** to become strangled
**2 :** to die from or as if from interference with breathing
— **stran·gler** \-g(ə-)lər\ *noun*
**stran·gle·hold** \'straŋ-gəl-,hōld\ *noun* (1893)
**1 :** an illegal wrestling hold by which one's opponent is choked
**2 :** a force or influence that chokes or suppresses freedom of movement or expression
**strangler fig** *noun* (1933)
**:** any of various vines and trees especially of the mulberry family (as *Ficus aurea* of the southeastern U.S.) and Saint-John's-wort family (as *Clusia rosea* of tropical America) that start as epiphytes but send down roots to the ground around the host tree
**stran·gles** \'straŋ-gəlz\ *noun plural but singular or plural in construction* [plural of obsolete *strangle* act of strangling] (circa 1706)
**:** an infectious febrile disease of horses caused by a bacterium (*Streptococcus equi*) and marked by inflammation and congestion of mucous membranes

**stran·gu·late** \'straŋ-gyə-,lāt\ *verb* **-lat·ed; -lat·ing** [Latin *strangulatus*, past participle of *strangulare*] (1665)
*transitive verb*
**:** STRANGLE, CONSTRICT
*intransitive verb*
**:** to become constricted so as to stop circulation ⟨the hernia will *strangulate*⟩
**stran·gu·la·tion** \,straŋ-gyə-'lā-shən\ *noun* (1542)
**1 :** the action or process of strangling or strangulating
**2 :** the state of being strangled or strangulated; *especially* **:** excessive or pathological constriction or compression of a bodily tube (as a blood vessel or a loop of intestine) that interrupts its ability to act as a passage
**stran·gu·ry** \'straŋ-gyə-rē, -,gyûr-ē\ *noun, plural* **-ries** [Middle English, from Latin *stranguria*, from Greek *strangouria*, from *strang-, stranx* drop squeezed out + *ourein* to urinate, from *ouron* urine — more at STRAIN, URINE] (14th century)
**:** a slow and painful spasmodic discharge of urine drop by drop
**¹strap** \'strap\ *noun* [alteration of *strop*, from Middle English, band or loop of leather or rope, from Old English, thong for securing an oar, from Latin *struppus* band, strap, from Greek *strophos* twisted band, from *strephein* to twist] (1601)
**1 a :** a narrow usually flat strip or thong of a flexible material and especially leather used for securing, holding together, or wrapping **b :** something made of a strap forming a loop ⟨a boot *strap*⟩ **c :** a strip of leather used for flogging **d :** STROP
**2 :** a band, plate, or loop of metal for binding objects together or for clamping an object in position
**3 :** a shoe fastened with a usually buckled strap
**4** *Irish* **:** TROLLOP 2
**²strap** *transitive verb* **strapped; strapping** (1711)
**1 a** (1) **:** to secure with or attach by means of a strap (2) **:** to support (as a sprained joint) with overlapping strips of adhesive plaster **b :** BIND, CONSTRICT
**2 :** to beat or punish with a strap
**3 :** STROP
**4 :** to cause to suffer from an extreme scarcity ⟨is often *strapped* for cash⟩
**strap·hang·er** \'strap-,haŋ-ər\ *noun* (1905)
**:** a standing passenger in a subway, streetcar, bus, or train who clings for support to one of the short straps or similar devices placed along the aisle
— **strap·hang** \-,haŋ\ *intransitive verb*
**strap·less** \-ləs\ *adjective* (1846)
**:** having no strap; *specifically* **:** made or worn without shoulder straps ⟨a *strapless* evening gown⟩
— **strapless** *noun*
**strap·pa·do** \stra-'pā-(,)dō, -'pä-\ *noun* [modification of Italian *strappata*, literally, sharp pull] (1560)
**:** a punishment or torture in which the subject is hoisted by rope and allowed to fall its full length; *also* **:** a machine used to inflict this torture
**strap·per** \'stra-pər\ *noun* (1675)
**:** one that is unusually large or robust
**¹strap·ping** \'stra-piŋ\ *adjective* (1657)
**:** having a vigorously sturdy constitution
**²strapping** *noun* (1818)
**1 :** material for a strap
**2 :** STRAPS
**strass** \'stras\ *noun* [French *stras, strass*] (1820)
**:** PASTE 3
**strat·a·gem** \'stra-tə-jəm, -,jem\ *noun* [Italian *stratagemma*, from Latin *strategema*, from Greek *stratēgēma*, from *stratēgein* to be a general, maneuver, from *stratēgos* general, from *stratos* camp, army (akin to Latin *stra-*

*tus*, past participle, spread out) + *agein* to lead — more at STRATUM, AGENT] (15th century)
**1 a :** an artifice or trick in war for deceiving and outwitting the enemy **b :** a cleverly contrived trick or scheme for gaining an end
**2 :** skill in ruses or trickery
*synonym* see TRICK
**stra·te·gic** \strə-'tē-jik\ *adjective* (1825)
**1 :** of, relating to, or marked by strategy ⟨a *strategic* retreat⟩
**2 a :** necessary to or important in the initiation, conduct, or completion of a strategic plan **b :** required for the conduct of war and not available in adequate quantities domestically ⟨*strategic* materials⟩ **c :** of great importance within an integrated whole or to a planned effect ⟨emphasized *strategic* points⟩
**3 :** designed or trained to strike an enemy at the sources of his military, economic, or political power ⟨a *strategic* bomber⟩
— **stra·te·gi·cal** \-ji-kəl\ *adjective*
— **stra·te·gi·cal·ly** \-ji-k(ə-)lē\ *adverb*
**strat·e·gist** \'stra-tə-jist\ *noun* (1838)
**:** one skilled in strategy
**strat·e·gize** \-,jīz\ *intransitive verb* **-gized; -giz·ing** (1921)
**:** to devise a strategy or course of action
**strat·e·gy** \-jē\ *noun, plural* **-gies** [Greek *stratēgia* generalship, from *stratēgos*] (1810)
**1 a** (1) **:** the science and art of employing the political, economic, psychological, and military forces of a nation or group of nations to afford the maximum support to adopted policies in peace or war (2) **:** the science and art of military command exercised to meet the enemy in combat under advantageous conditions **b :** a variety or instance of the use of strategy
**2 a :** a careful plan or method **:** a clever stratagem **b :** the art of devising or employing plans or stratagems toward a goal
**3 :** an adaptation or complex of adaptations (as of behavior, metabolism, or structure) that serves or appears to serve an important function in achieving evolutionary success ⟨foraging *strategies* of insects⟩
**strath** \'strath\ *noun* [Scottish Gaelic *srath*] (1540)
**:** a flat wide river valley or the low-lying grassland along it
**strath·spey** \,strath-'spā\ *noun, plural* **strathspeys** [*Strath Spey*, district of Scotland] (circa 1653)

---

☆ **SYNONYMS**
**Strange, singular, unique, peculiar, eccentric, erratic, odd, queer, quaint, outlandish** mean departing from what is ordinary, usual, or to be expected. STRANGE stresses unfamiliarity and may apply to the foreign, the unnatural, the unaccountable ⟨a journey filled with *strange* sights⟩. SINGULAR suggests individuality or puzzling strangeness ⟨a *singular* feeling of impending disaster⟩. UNIQUE implies singularity and the fact of being without a known parallel ⟨a career *unique* in the annals of science⟩. PECULIAR implies a marked distinctiveness ⟨the *peculiar* status of America's first lady⟩. ECCENTRIC suggests a wide divergence from the usual or normal especially in behavior ⟨the *eccentric* eating habits of preschoolers⟩. ERRATIC stresses a capricious and unpredictable wandering or deviating ⟨a friend's suddenly *erratic* behavior⟩. ODD applies to a departure from the regular or expected ⟨an *odd* sense of humor⟩. QUEER suggests a dubious sometimes sinister oddness ⟨*queer* happenings offering no ready explanation⟩. QUAINT suggests an old-fashioned but pleasant oddness ⟨a *quaint* fishing village⟩. OUTLANDISH applies to what is uncouth, bizarre, or barbaric ⟨the *outlandish* getups of heavy metal bands⟩.

: a Scottish dance that is similar to but slower than the reel; *also* : the music for this dance

**strati-** *combining form* [New Latin *stratum*]
: stratum ⟨*strati*form⟩

**strat·i·fi·ca·tion** \ˌstra-tə-fə-ˈkā-shən\ *noun* (circa 1617)
**1 a** : the act or process of stratifying **b** : the state of being stratified
**2** : a stratified formation

**strat·i·fi·ca·tion·al grammar** \ˌstra-tə-fə-ˈkā-shnəl-, -shə-nᵊl-\ *noun* (1962)
: a grammar based on the theory that language consists of a series of hierarchically related strata linked together by representational rules

**stratified charge engine** *noun* (1962)
: an internal-combustion engine in whose cylinders the combustion of fuel in a layer of rich fuel-air mixture promotes ignition in a greater volume of lean mixture

**strat·i·form** \ˈstra-tə-ˌfȯrm\ *adjective* (1805)
: having a stratified formation

**strat·i·fy** \ˈstra-tə-ˌfī\ *verb* **-fied; -fy·ing**
[New Latin *stratificare*, from *stratum* + Latin *-ificare* -ify] (1661)
*transitive verb*
**1** : to form, deposit, or arrange in strata
**2 a** : to divide or arrange into classes, castes, or social strata **b** : to divide into a series of graded statuses
*intransitive verb*
: to become arranged in strata

**strati·graph·ic** \ˌstra-tə-ˈgra-fik\ *adjective* (1877)
: of, relating to, or determined by stratigraphy

**stra·tig·ra·phy** \strə-ˈti-grə-fē\ *noun* [International Scientific Vocabulary] (1865)
**1** : geology that deals with the origin, composition, distribution, and succession of strata
**2** : the arrangement of strata

**strato-** *combining form* [New Latin *stratus*]
: stratus and ⟨*strato*cumulus⟩

**stra·toc·ra·cy** \strə-ˈtä-krə-sē\ *noun, plural* **-cies** [Greek *stratos* army — more at STRATAGEM] (1652)
: a military government

**stra·to·cu·mu·lus** \ˌstra-tō-ˈkyü-myə-ləs, ˌstra-\ *noun* [New Latin] (circa 1891)
: stratified cumulus consisting of large balls or rolls of dark cloud which often cover the whole sky especially in winter — see CLOUD illustration

**strato·sphere** \ˈstra-tə-ˌsfir\ *noun* [French *stratosphère*, from New Latin *stratum* + *-o-* + French *sphère* sphere, from Latin *sphaera*] (1909)
**1** : the part of the earth's atmosphere which extends from about 7 miles (11 kilometers) above the surface to 31 miles (50 kilometers) and in which temperature increases gradually to about 32° F (0° C) and clouds rarely form
**2** : a very high or the highest region on or as if on a graded scale ⟨construction costs in the *stratosphere*⟩ ⟨the celebrity *stratosphere*⟩
— **strato·spher·ic** \ˌstra-tə-ˈsfir-ik, -ˈsfer-\ *adjective*

**stra·to·vol·ca·no** \ˌstra-tō-väl-ˈkā-(ˌ)nō, ˌstra-, -vȯl-\ *noun* [New Latin *stratum* + English *-o-* + *volcano*] (1937)
: a volcano composed of explosively erupted cinders and ash with occasional lava flows

**stra·tum** \ˈstra-təm, ˈstra-\ *noun, plural* **strata** \ˈstra-tə, ˈstra-\ [New Latin, from Latin, spread, bed, from neuter of *stratus*, past participle of *sternere* to spread out — more at STREW] (1599)
**1** : a bed or layer artificially made
**2 a** : a sheetlike mass of sedimentary rock or earth of one kind lying between beds of other kinds **b** : a region of the sea or atmosphere that is analogous to a stratum of the earth **c** : a layer of tissue ⟨deep *stratum* of the skin⟩ **d** : a layer in which archaeological material (as artifacts, skeletons, and dwelling remains) is found on excavation
**3 a** : a part of a historical or sociological series representing a period or a stage of devel-

opment **b** : a socioeconomic level of society comprising persons of the same or similar status especially with regard to education or culture
**4** : one of a series of layers, levels, or gradations in an ordered system ⟨*strata* of thought⟩
**5** : a statistical subpopulation ▫

**stra·tus** \ˈstrā-təs, ˈstra-\ *noun, plural* **stra·ti** \ˈstrā-ˌtī, ˈstra-\ [New Latin, from Latin, past participle of *sternere*] (circa 1803)
: a cloud form extending over a large area at altitudes of usually 2000 to 7000 feet (600 to 2100 meters) — see CLOUD illustration

**stra·vage** *or* **stra·vaig** \strə-ˈvāg\ *intransitive verb* [probably by shortening & alteration from *extravagate*] (1773)
*chiefly Scottish* : ROAM

¹**straw** \ˈstrȯ\ *noun* [Middle English, from Old English *strēaw;* akin to Old High German *strō* straw, Old English *strewian* to strew] (before 12th century)
**1 a** : stalks of grain after threshing; *broadly* : dry stalky plant residue used like grain straw (as for bedding or packing) **b** : a natural or artificial heavy fiber used for weaving, plaiting, or braiding
**2** : a dry coarse stem especially of a cereal grass
**3 a** (1) : something of small worth or significance (2) : something too insubstantial to provide support or help in a desperate situation ⟨clutching at *straws*⟩ **b** : CHAFF 2
**4 a** : something (as a hat) made of straw **b** : a tube (as of paper, plastic, or glass) for sucking up a beverage
— **strawy** \ˈstrȯ-ē\ *adjective*
— **straw in the wind** : a slight fact that is an indication of a coming event

²**straw** *adjective* (15th century)
**1** : made of straw ⟨a *straw* rug⟩
**2** : of, relating to, or used for straw ⟨a *straw* barn⟩
**3** : of the color of straw ⟨*straw* hair⟩
**4** : of little or no value : WORTHLESS
**5** : of, relating to, resembling, or being a straw man
**6** : of, relating to, or concerned with the discovery of preferences by means of a straw vote

**straw·ber·ry** \ˈstrȯ-ˌber-ē, -b(ə-)rē\ *noun, often attributive* [Middle English, from Old English *strēawberige*, from *strēaw* straw + *berige* berry; perhaps from the appearance of the achenes on the surface] (before 12th century)
: the juicy edible usually red fruit of any of several low-growing temperate herbs (genus *Fragaria*) of the rose family that is technically an enlarged pulpy receptacle bearing numerous achenes; *also* : a plant whose fruits are strawberries

**strawberry bush** *noun* (circa 1856)
**1** : a shrubby North American spindle tree (*Euonymus americanus*) with crimson pods and seeds with a scarlet aril
**2** : ²WAHOO

**strawberry mark** *noun* (1847)
: a tumor of the skin filled with small blood vessels and appearing usually as a red and elevated birthmark

**strawberry roan** *noun* (1955)
: a roan horse with a light red ground color

**strawberry shrub** *noun* (circa 1890)
: any of a genus (*Calycanthus*) of the family Calycanthaceae, the strawberry-shrub family) of shrubs with fragrant brownish red flowers

**strawberry tomato** *noun* (circa 1847)

**strawberry**

: GROUND-CHERRY; *especially* : a stout hairy annual herb (*Physalis pruinosa*) of eastern North America with sweet globular yellow fruits

**strawberry tree** *noun* (15th century)
: a small European evergreen tree (*Arbutus unedo*) of the heath family with racemose white flowers and fruits like strawberries

**straw boss** *noun* (1894)
**1** : an assistant to a foreman in charge of supervising and expediting the work of a small gang of workers
**2** : a member of a group of workers who supervises the work of the others in addition to doing his or her own job

**straw·flow·er** \ˈstrȯ-ˌflau̇(-ə)r\ *noun* (circa 1922)
: any of several everlasting flowers; *especially* : an Australian perennial composite herb (*Helichrysum bracteatum*) that is widely cultivated for its heads of chaffy brightly colored long-keeping flowers

**straw·hat** \ˌstrȯ-ˈhat\ *adjective* [from the former fashion of wearing straw hats in summer] (1935)
: of, relating to, or being summer theater

**straw man** *noun* (1896)
**1** : a weak or imaginary opposition (as an argument or adversary) set up only to be easily confuted
**2** : a person set up to serve as a cover for a usually questionable transaction

**straw vote** *noun* (1866)
: an unofficial vote taken (as at a chance gathering) to indicate the relative strength of opposing candidates or issues — called also *straw poll*

**straw wine** *noun* (1824)
: a sweet wine produced by partially drying the grapes on beds of straw prior to vinification

**straw yellow** *noun* (circa 1796)
: a pale yellow

¹**stray** \ˈstrā\ *noun* [Middle English, from Old French *estraié*, past participle of *estraier*] (13th century)
**1 a** : a domestic animal that is wandering at large or is lost **b** : a person or thing that strays
**2** [Middle English, from *straien* to stray] *archaic* : the act of going astray

²**stray** *intransitive verb* [Middle English *straien*, from Middle French *estraier*, from (assumed) Vulgar Latin *extravagare*, from Latin *extra-* outside + *vagari* to wander — more at EXTRA-] (14th century)
: WANDER: as **a** : to wander from company, restraint, or proper limits **b** : to roam about without fixed direction or purpose **c** : to move in a winding course : MEANDER **d** : to move without conscious or intentional effort ⟨eyes *straying* absently around the room⟩ **e** : to become distracted from an argument or chain of

---

▫ USAGE

**stratum** The plural *strata* has occasionally been used as a singular since the 18th century and is sometimes given the plural *stratas* ⟨there was a *strata* of Paris which mere criticism of books fails to get hold of —Ezra Pound⟩ ⟨a Roman burial ground suggests *stratas* of corruption and decay —Connie Fletcher, *Booklist*⟩. Current evidence shows senses 2, 3b, and 4 so used, with 3b the most common. Singular *strata* is persistent but not frequent. It may someday establish itself as a singular like *agenda*, but its current status is something less than established.

---

\ə\ abut  \ᵊ\ kitten  \ər\ further  \a\ ash  \ā\ ace
\ä\ mop, mar  \au̇\ out  \ch\ chin  \e\ bet  \ē\ easy
\g\ go  \i\ hit  \ī\ ice  \j\ job  \ŋ\ sing  \ō\ go
\ȯ\ law  \ȯi\ boy  \th\ thin  \t̶h̶\ the  \ü\ loot  \u̇\ foot
\y\ yet  \zh\ vision  *see also* Guide to Pronunciation

thought ⟨*strayed* from the point⟩ **f :** to wander accidentally from a fixed or chosen route **g :** ERR, SIN

— **stray·er** *noun*

³**stray** *adjective* (1607)
**1 :** having strayed or escaped from a proper or intended place ⟨a *stray* cow⟩ ⟨hit by a *stray* bullet⟩ ⟨fixed a few *stray* hairs⟩
**2 :** occurring at random or sporadically ⟨a few *stray* thoughts⟩
**3 :** not serving any useful purpose : UNWANTED ⟨*stray* light⟩

¹**streak** \'strēk\ *noun* [Middle English *streke*, from Old English *strica*; akin to Old High German *strich* line, Latin *striga* row — more at STRIKE] (before 12th century)
**1 :** a line or mark of a different color or texture from the ground : STRIPE
**2 a :** the color of the fine powder of a mineral obtained by scratching or rubbing against a hard white surface and constituting an important distinguishing character **b :** inoculum implanted in a line on a solid medium **c :** any of several virus diseases of plants (as the potato, tomato, or raspberry) resembling mosaic but usually producing at least some linear markings
**3 a :** a narrow band of light **b :** a lightning bolt
**4 a :** a slight admixture : TRACE ⟨had a mean *streak* in him⟩ **b :** a brief run (as of luck) **c :** a consecutive series ⟨was on a winning *streak*⟩
**5 :** a narrow layer (as of ore)
**6 :** an act or instance of streaking

²**streak** (1595)
*transitive verb*
**:** to make streaks on or in ⟨tears *streaking* her face⟩
*intransitive verb*
**1 :** to move swiftly : RUSH ⟨a jet *streaking* across the sky⟩
**2 :** to have a streak (as of winning or outstanding performances)
**3 :** to run naked through a public place

— **streak·er** *noun*

**streak camera** *noun* (1959)
**:** a camera for recording very fast or short-lived phenomena (as fluorescence or shock waves)

**streaked** \'strēkt, 'strē-kəd\ *adjective* (1596)
**1 :** marked with stripes or linear discolorations
**2 :** physically or mentally disturbed : UPSET

**streak·ing** \'strē-kiŋ\ *noun* (circa 1964)
**:** the lightening (as by chemicals) of a few long strands of hair to produce a streaked effect

**streaky** \'strē-kē\ *adjective* **streak·i·er; -est** (1745)
**1 :** marked with streaks ⟨*streaky* bacon⟩
**2 :** APPREHENSIVE ⟨nervous and *streaky*⟩
**3 :** apt to vary (as in effectiveness) : UNRELIABLE

— **streak·i·ness** *noun*

¹**stream** \'strēm\ *noun* [Middle English *streme*, from Old English *strēam*; akin to Old High German *stroum* stream, Greek *rhein* to flow] (before 12th century)
**1 :** a body of running water (as a river or brook) flowing on the earth; *also* **:** any body of flowing fluid (as water or gas)
**2 a :** a steady succession (as of words or events) ⟨kept up an endless *stream* of chatter⟩ **b :** a constantly renewed supply **c :** a continuous moving procession ⟨a *stream* of traffic⟩
**3 :** an unbroken flow (as of gas or particles of matter)
**4 :** a ray of light
**5 a :** a prevailing attitude or group ⟨has always run against the *stream* of current fashion⟩ **b :** a dominant influence or line of development
**6** *British* **:** TRACK 3c

²**stream** (13th century)
*intransitive verb*

**1 a :** to flow in or as if in a stream **b :** to leave a bright trail ⟨a meteor *streamed* through the sky⟩
**2 a :** to exude a bodily fluid profusely ⟨her eyes were *streaming*⟩ **b :** to become wet with a discharge of bodily fluid ⟨*streaming* with perspiration⟩
**3 :** to trail out at full length ⟨her hair *streaming* back as she ran⟩
**4 :** to pour in large numbers ⟨complaints came *streaming* in⟩
*transitive verb*
**1 :** to emit freely or in a stream ⟨his eyes *streamed* tears⟩
**2 :** to display (as a flag) by waving

**stream·bed** \'strēm-ˌbed\ *noun* (1857)
**:** the channel occupied or formerly occupied by a stream

**stream·er** \'strē-mər\ *noun* (13th century)
**1 a :** a flag that streams in the wind; *especially* **:** PENNANT **b :** any long narrow wavy strip resembling or suggesting a banner floating in the wind **c :** BANNER 2
**2 a :** a long extension of the solar corona visible only during a total solar eclipse **b** *plural* **:** AURORA BOREALIS

**stream·ing** \'strē-miŋ\ *noun* (14th century)
**1 :** an act or instance of flowing; *specifically* **:** CYCLOSIS
**2** *British* **:** TRACKING

**stream·let** \'strēm-lət\ *noun* (circa 1552)
**:** a small stream

¹**stream·line** \'strēm-ˌlīn\ *noun* (1868)
**1 :** the path of a particle in a fluid relative to a solid body past which the fluid is moving in smooth flow without turbulence
**2 a :** a contour designed to minimize resistance to motion through a fluid (as air) **b :** a smooth or flowing line designed as if for decreasing air resistance

²**streamline** *transitive verb* (1913)
**1 :** to design or construct with a streamline
**2 :** to bring up to date : MODERNIZE
**3 a :** to put in order : ORGANIZE **b :** to make simpler or more efficient

**stream·lined** \-ˌlīnd\ *adjective* (1913)
**1 a :** contoured to reduce resistance to motion through a fluid (as air) **b :** stripped of nonessentials : COMPACT **c :** effectively integrated : ORGANIZED
**2 :** having flowing lines
**3 :** brought up to date : MODERNIZED
**4 :** of or relating to streamline flow

**streamline flow** *noun* (circa 1918)
**:** an uninterrupted flow (as of air) past a solid body in which the direction at every point remains unchanged with the passage of time

**stream·lin·er** \'strēm-ˌlī-nər\ *noun* (1934)
**:** one that is streamlined; *especially* **:** a streamlined train

**stream of consciousness** (1855)
**1 :** the continuous unedited chronological flow of conscious experience through the mind
**2 :** INTERIOR MONOLOGUE

**stream·side** \'strēm-ˌsīd\ *noun* (1844)
**:** the land bordering on a stream

**streek** \'strēk\ *transitive verb* [Middle English (northern dialect) *streken*; akin to Old English *streccan* to stretch] (13th century)
**1** *chiefly Scottish* **:** STRETCH, EXTEND
**2** *chiefly Scottish* **:** to lay out (a dead body)

¹**streel** \'strē(ə)l\ *intransitive verb* [Irish *straoill-, sraoill-* to tear apart, trail, trudge, from Old Irish *sroiglid* he scourges, from *sroigell* scourge, from Latin *flagellum* — more at FLAGELLATE] (1805)
**1** *chiefly Irish* **:** to saunter idly and aimlessly
**2** *chiefly Irish* **:** to trail or float in the manner of a streamer

²**streel** *noun* [Irish *straoill, sraoill*, from *straoill-*, verb] (1842)
*chiefly Irish* **:** an untidy slovenly person

¹**street** \'strēt\ *noun* [Middle English *strete*, from Old English *strǣt*, from Late Latin *strata* paved road, from Latin, feminine of *stratus*, past participle — more at STRATUM] (before 12th century)
**1 a :** a thoroughfare especially in a city, town, or village that is wider than an alley or lane and that usually includes sidewalks **b :** the part of a street reserved for vehicles **c :** a thoroughfare with abutting property ⟨lives on a fashionable *street*⟩
**2 :** the people occupying property on a street ⟨the whole *street* knew about the accident⟩
**3 :** a promising line of development or a channeling of effort
**4** *capitalized* **:** a district (as Wall Street or Fleet Street) identified with a particular profession
**5 :** an environment (as in a depressed neighborhood or section of a city) of prostitution, poverty, dereliction, or crime

— **on the street** *or* **in the street 1 :** idle, homeless, or out of a job **2 :** out of prison **:** at liberty

— **up one's street** *or* **down one's street :** suited to one's abilities or taste

²**street** *adjective* (15th century)
**:** of or relating to the streets: as **a :** adjoining or giving access to a street ⟨the *street* door⟩ **b :** carried on or taking place in the street ⟨*street* fighting⟩ **c :** living or working on the streets ⟨a *street* peddler⟩ ⟨*street* people⟩ **d :** located in, used for, or serving as a guide to the streets ⟨a *street* map⟩ **e :** performing in or heard on the street ⟨a *street* band⟩ **f** (1) **:** suitable for wear or use on the street ⟨*street* clothes⟩ (2) **:** not touching the ground — used of a woman's dress in lengths reaching the knee, calf, or ankle **g :** of or relating to the street environment ⟨*street* drugs⟩

**street arab** \-'ar-əb, -'ä-ˌrab\ *noun*, *often A capitalized* (1859)
**:** a homeless vagabond and especially an outcast boy or girl in the streets of a city : GAMIN

**street·car** \'strēt-ˌkär\ *noun* (1862)
**:** a vehicle on rails used primarily for transporting passengers and typically operating on city streets

**street·light** \-ˌlīt\ *noun* (1906)
**:** a light usually mounted on a pole and constituting one of a series spaced at intervals along a public street or highway — called also *streetlamp*

**street railway** *noun* (1861)
**:** a line operating streetcars or buses

**streets** \'strēts\ *adverb* (1898)
*chiefly British* **:** by a considerable margin ⟨a nice woman, *streets* above these other callers —Katherine Mansfield⟩

**street·scape** \'strēt-ˌskāp\ *noun* (1924)
**1 :** the appearance or view of a street
**2 :** a work of art depicting a view of a street

**word history** see LANDSCAPE

**street–smart** \-ˌsmärt\ *adjective* (1974)
**:** STREETWISE

**street smarts** *noun plural* (1972)
**:** the quality of being streetwise

**street theater** *noun* (1967)
**:** drama dealing with controversial social and political issues that is usually performed outdoors

**street virus** *noun* (circa 1911)
**:** a naturally occurring rabies virus as distinguished from virus attenuated in the laboratory

**street·walk·er** \'strēt-ˌwȯ-kər\ *noun* (1592)
**:** PROSTITUTE; *especially* **:** one who solicits in the streets — compare CALL GIRL

— **street·walk·ing** \-kiŋ\ *noun*

**street·wise** \-ˌwīz\ *adjective* (1965)
**:** possessing the skills and attitudes necessary to survive in an often violent urban environment

**strength** \'streŋ(k)th, 'stren(t)th\ *noun*, *plural* **strengths** \'streŋ(k)ths, 'stren(t)ths, 'streŋks\ [Middle English *strengthe*, from Old English *strengthu*; akin to Old High German *strengi* strong — more at STRONG] (before 12th century)

**1 :** the quality or state of being strong **:** capacity for exertion or endurance
**2 :** power to resist force **:** SOLIDITY, TOUGHNESS
**3 :** power of resisting attack **:** IMPREGNABILITY
**4 a :** legal, logical, or moral force **b :** a strong attribute or inherent asset ⟨the *strengths* and the weaknesses of the book are evident⟩
**5 a :** degree of potency of effect or of concentration **b :** intensity of light, color, sound, or odor **c :** vigor of expression
**6 :** force as measured in numbers **:** effective numbers of any body or organization ⟨an army at full *strength*⟩
**7 :** one regarded as embodying or affording force or firmness **:** SUPPORT
**8 :** maintenance of or a rising tendency in a price level **:** firmness of prices
**9 :** BASIS — used in the phrase *on the strength of*
**synonym** see POWER
**— from strength to strength :** vigorously forward **:** from one high point to the next
**strength·en** \'streŋ(k)-thən, 'stren(t)-\ *verb*
**strength·ened; strength·en·ing** \'streŋ(k)th-niŋ, 'stren(t)th-; 'streŋ(k)-thə-, 'stren(t)-\ (15th century)
*transitive verb*
**:** to make stronger
*intransitive verb*
**:** to become stronger
**— strength·en·er** \'streŋ(k)th-nər, 'stren(t)th-; 'streŋ(k)-thə-, 'stren(t)-\ *noun*
**stren·u·ous** \'stren-yə-wəs\ *adjective* [Latin *strenuus*] (1599)
**1 a :** vigorously active **:** ENERGETIC **b :** FERVENT, ZEALOUS
**2 :** marked by or calling for energy or stamina **:** ARDUOUS
**synonym** see VIGOROUS
**— stren·u·os·i·ty** \,stren-yə-'wä-sə-tē\ *noun*
**— stren·u·ous·ly** \'stren-yə-wəs-lē\ *adverb*
**— stren·u·ous·ness** *noun*
**strep** \'strep\ *noun, often attributive* (1927)
**:** STREPTOCOCCUS
**strep throat** *noun* (circa 1927)
**:** an inflammatory sore throat caused by hemolytic streptococci and marked by fever, prostration, and toxemia — called also *septic sore throat*
**strepto-** *combining form* [New Latin, from Greek, from *streptos* twisted, from *strephein* to twist]
**1 :** twisted **:** twisted chain ⟨*strepto*coccus⟩
**2 :** streptococcus ⟨*strepto*kinase⟩
**strep·to·ba·cil·lus** \,strep-tō-bə-'si-ləs\ *noun* [New Latin] (1897)
**:** any of a genus (*Streptobacillus*) of nonmotile gram-negative rod-shaped bacteria in which the individual cells are often joined in a chain; *especially* **:** one (*S. moniliformis*) that is the causative agent of one form of rat-bite fever
**strep·to·coc·cal** \,strep-tə-'kä-kəl\ *also* **strep·to·coc·cic** \-'kä-kik, -'käk-sik\ *adjective* (1877)
**:** of, relating to, caused by, or being streptococci ⟨a *streptococcal* sore throat⟩ ⟨*streptococcal* organisms⟩
**strep·to·coc·cus** \-'kä-kəs\ *noun, plural* **-coc·ci** \-'kä-,kī, -(,)kē; 'käk-,sī, -(,)sē\ [New Latin] (1877)
**:** any of a genus (*Streptococcus*) of spherical or ovoid chiefly nonmotile and parasitic gram-positive bacteria that divide only in one plane, occur in pairs or chains, and include important pathogens of humans and domestic animals; *broadly* **:** a coccus occurring in chains
**strep·to·ki·nase** \,strep-tō-'kī-,nās, -,nāz\ *noun* (1944)
**:** a proteolytic enzyme from hemolytic streptococci active in promoting dissolution of blood clots
**strep·to·ly·sin** \,strep-tə-'lī-s°n\ *noun* (1904)
**:** an antigenic hemolysin produced by streptococci

**strep·to·my·ces** \-'mī-,sēz\ *noun, plural* **streptomyces** [New Latin, from *strepto-* + Greek *mykēs* fungus — more at MYC-] (1951)
**:** any of a genus (*Streptomyces*) of mostly soil streptomycetes including some that form antibiotics as by-products of their metabolism
**strep·to·my·cete** \-'mī-,sēt, -,mī-'sēt\ *noun* [New Latin *Streptomycet-*, *Streptomyces*, genus name] (1948)
**:** any of a family (Streptomycetaceae) of actinomycetes (as a streptomyces) that form vegetative mycelia which rarely break up into bacillary forms, have conidia borne on sporophores, and are typically aerobic soil saprophytes but include a few parasites of plants and animals
**strep·to·my·cin** \-'mī-s°n\ *noun* (1944)
**:** an antibiotic organic base $C_{21}H_{39}N_7O_{12}$ produced by a soil actinomycete (*Streptomyces griseus*), active against many bacteria, and used especially in the treatment of infections (as tuberculosis) by gram-negative bacteria
**strep·to·thri·cin** \-'thrī-s°n, -'thri-\ *noun* [New Latin *Streptothric-*, *Streptothrix*, genus of bacteria, from *strepto-* + Greek *trich-*, *thrix* hair] (1926)
**:** any of a group of related basic antibiotics produced by a soil actinomycete (*Streptomyces lavendulae*) and active against bacteria and to some degree against fungi
**¹stress** \'stres\ *noun* [Middle English *stresse* stress, distress, short for *destresse* — more at DISTRESS] (14th century)
**1 :** constraining force or influence: as **a :** a force exerted when one body or body part presses on, pulls on, pushes against, or tends to compress or twist another body or body part; *especially* **:** the intensity of this mutual force commonly expressed in pounds per square inch **b :** the deformation caused in a body by such a force **c :** a physical, chemical, or emotional factor that causes bodily or mental tension and may be a factor in disease causation **d :** a state resulting from a stress; *especially* **:** one of bodily or mental tension resulting from factors that tend to alter an existent equilibrium **e :** STRAIN, PRESSURE ⟨the environment is under *stress* to the point of collapse —Joseph Shoben⟩
**2 :** EMPHASIS, WEIGHT ⟨lay *stress* on a point⟩
**3** *archaic* **:** intense effort or exertion
**4 :** intensity of utterance given to a speech sound, syllable, or word producing relative loudness
**5 a :** relative force or prominence of sound in verse **b :** a syllable having relative force or prominence
**6 :** ACCENT 6a
**²stress** *transitive verb* (1545)
**1 :** to subject to physical or psychological stress
**2 :** to subject to phonetic stress **:** ACCENT
**3 :** to lay stress on **:** EMPHASIZE
**stressed–out** \'strest-'aut\ *adjective* (1983)
**:** suffering from high levels of physical or especially psychological stress
**stress fracture** *noun* (1952)
**:** a usually hairline fracture of a bone that has been subjected to repeated stress
**stress·ful** \'stres-fəl\ *adjective* (1853)
**:** full of or tending to induce stress
**— stress·ful·ly** \-fə-lē\ *adverb*
**stress·less** \-ləs\ *adjective* (1885)
**:** having no stress; *specifically* **:** having no accent ⟨a *stressless* syllable⟩
**— stress·less·ness** *noun*
**stress mark** *noun* (1888)
**:** a mark used with (as before, after, or over) a written syllable in the respelling of a word to show that this syllable is to be stressed when spoken **:** ACCENT MARK
**stress·or** \'stre-sər, -,sòr\ *noun* (1950)
**:** a stimulus that causes stress
**stress test** *noun* (1975)

**:** an electrocardiographic test of heart function before, during, and after a controlled period of increasingly strenuous exercise (as on a treadmill)
**¹stretch** \'strech\ *verb* [Middle English *strecchen*, from Old English *streccan*; akin to Old High German *strecchan* to stretch, Old English *stræc* firm, severe] (before 12th century)
*transitive verb*
**1 :** to extend (as one's limbs or body) in a reclining position
**2 :** to reach out **:** EXTEND ⟨*stretched* out her arms⟩
**3 :** to extend in length ⟨*stretched* his neck to see what was going on⟩
**4 :** to fell with or as if with a blow
**5 :** to cause the limbs of (a person) to be pulled especially in torture
**6 :** to draw up (one's body) from a cramped, stooping, or relaxed position
**7 :** to pull taut ⟨canvas *stretched* on a frame⟩
**8 a :** to enlarge or distend especially by force **b :** to extend or expand as if by physical force ⟨*stretch* one's mind with a good book⟩ **c :** STRAIN ⟨*stretched* his already thin patience⟩
**9 :** to cause to reach or continue (as from one point to another or across a space) ⟨*stretch* a wire between two posts⟩
**10 a :** to amplify or enlarge beyond natural or proper limits ⟨the rules can be *stretched* this once⟩ **b :** to expand (as by improvisation) to fulfill a larger function ⟨*stretching* a dollar⟩
**11 :** to extend (a hit) to an extra base usually by fast or daring running ⟨*stretch* a single into a double⟩
*intransitive verb*
**1 a :** to become extended in length or breadth or both **:** SPREAD ⟨broad plains *stretching* to the sea⟩ **b :** to extend over a continuous period
**2 :** to become extended without breaking
**3 a :** to extend one's body or limbs **b :** to lie down at full length
**— stretch·abil·i·ty** \,stre-chə-'bi-lə-tē\ *noun*
**— stretch·able** \'stre-chə-bəl\ *adjective*
**— stretchy** \-chē\ *adjective*
**— stretch a point :** to go beyond what is strictly warranted in making a claim or concession
**— stretch one's legs 1 :** to extend the legs **2 :** to take a walk in order to relieve stiffness caused by prolonged sitting
**²stretch** *noun* (1541)
**1 a :** an exercise of something (as the understanding or the imagination) beyond ordinary or normal limits **b :** an extension of the scope or application of something ⟨a *stretch* of language⟩
**2 :** the extent to which something may be stretched
**3 :** the act of stretching **:** the state of being stretched
**4 a :** an extent in length or area ⟨a *stretch* of woods⟩ **b :** a continuous period of time ⟨can write for eight hours at a *stretch*⟩
**5 :** a walk to relieve fatigue
**6 :** a term of imprisonment
**7 a :** either of the straight sides of a racecourse; *especially* **:** HOMESTRETCH **b :** a final stage
**8 :** the capacity for being stretched **:** ELASTICITY
**9 :** STRETCH LIMO
**³stretch** *adjective* (1954)
**:** easily stretched **:** ELASTIC ⟨a *stretch* wig⟩
**stretch·er** \'stre-chər\ *noun* (15th century)
**1 a :** one that stretches; *especially* **:** a device or machine for stretching or expanding something **b :** an exaggerated story **:** a tall tale

\ə\ abut \ᵊ\ kitten \ər\ further \a\ ash \ā\ ace
\ä\ mop, mar \aù\ out \ch\ chin \e\ bet \ē\ easy
\g\ go \i\ hit \ī\ ice \j\ job \ŋ\ sing \ō\ go
\ò\ law \òi\ boy \th\ thin \th\ the \ü\ loot \ù\ foot
\y\ yet \zh\ vision *see also* Guide to Pronunciation

**2 a :** a brick or stone laid with its length parallel to the face of the wall **b :** a timber or rod used especially when horizontal as a tie in framed work
**3 :** a device for carrying a sick, injured, or dead person
**4 :** a rod or bar extending between two legs of a chair or table

**stretch limo** *noun* (1971)
: a long limousine that is luxuriously furnished (as with a TV or bar) — called also *stretch limousine*

**stretch marks** *noun plural* (1956)
: striae on the skin (as of the hips, abdomen, and breasts) from excessive stretching and rupture of elastic fibers especially due to pregnancy or obesity

**stretch–out** \'strech-ˌaut\ *noun* (1930)
**1 :** a system of industrial operation in which workers are required to do extra work with slight or with no additional pay
**2 :** the act of stretching out **:** the state of being stretched out
**3 :** an economizing measure that spreads a limited quantity over a larger field than originally intended: as **a :** a slackening of production schedules so that a quantity of goods will be produced over a longer period than initially planned **b :** a restructuring of a loan repayment schedule over an extended period of time

**stretch receptor** *noun* (1936)
: MUSCLE SPINDLE

**stretch runner** *noun* (1922)
: a racehorse that makes a strong bid in the homestretch

**stret·to** \'stre-(ˌ)tō\ *also* **stret·ta** \-tə\ *noun, plural* **stret·ti** \-(ˌ)tē\ *or* **strettos** [*stretto* from Italian, from *stretto* narrow, close, from Latin *strictus*, past participle; *stretta* from Italian, from feminine of *stretto* — more at STRICT] (circa 1740)
**1 a :** the overlapping of answer with subject in a musical fugue **b :** the part of a fugue characterized by this overlapping
**2 :** a concluding passage performed in a quicker tempo

**streu·sel** \'strü-səl, -zəl, 'stroi-, 'shtroi-\ *noun* [German, literally, something strewn, from Middle High German *ströusel*, from *ströuwen* to strew, from Old High German *strewen*] (1909)
: a crumbly mixture of fat, sugar, and flour and sometimes nuts and spices that is used as topping or filling for cake

**strew** \'strü\ *transitive verb* **strewed; strewed** *or* **strewn** \'strün\; **strew·ing** [Middle English *strewen, strowen*, from Old English *strewian, strēowian*; akin to Old High German *strewen* to strew, Latin *struere* to heap up, *sternere* to spread out, Greek *stornynai*] (before 12th century)
**1 :** to spread by scattering
**2 :** to cover by or as if by scattering something ⟨*strewing* the highways with litter⟩
**3 :** to become dispersed over as if scattered
**4 :** to spread abroad **:** DISSEMINATE

**strew·ment** \'strü-mənt\ *noun* (1602)
*archaic* **:** something (as flowers) strewed or designed for strewing

**stria** \'strī-ə\ *noun, plural* **stri·ae** \'strī-ˌē\ [Latin, furrow, channel — more at STRIKE] (1563)
**1 :** STRIATION 2
**2 :** a stripe or line (as in the skin) distinguished from the surrounding area by color, texture, or elevation — compare STRETCH MARKS

**¹stri·ate** \'strī-ət, -ˌāt\ *adjective* (1670)
: STRIATED

**²stri·ate** \-ˌāt\ *transitive verb* **stri·at·ed; stri·at·ing** (1709)
: to mark with striations or striae

**stri·at·ed** \'strī-ˌā-təd\ *adjective* (1646)
**1 :** marked with striations or striae
**2 :** of, relating to, or being striated muscle

**striated muscle** *noun* (1866)

: muscle tissue that is marked by transverse dark and light bands, that is made up of elongated multinuclear fibers, and that includes skeletal muscle, cardiac muscle, and most muscle of arthropods — compare SMOOTH MUSCLE, VOLUNTARY MUSCLE

**stri·a·tion** \strī-'ā-shən\ *noun* (circa 1847)
**1 a :** the fact or state of being striated **b :** arrangement of striations or striae
**2 :** a minute groove, scratch, or channel especially when one of a parallel series
**3 :** any of the alternate dark and light cross bands of a myofibril of striated muscle

**strick** \'strik\ *noun* [Middle English *stric, strik*, probably from Low German or Dutch origin; akin to Middle Low German *strik* rope, Middle Dutch *stric*] (14th century)
: a bunch of hackled flax, jute, or hemp

**strick·en** \'stri-kən\ *adjective* [Middle English *striken*, from past participle of *striken* to strike] (14th century)
**1 a :** afflicted or overwhelmed by or as if by disease, misfortune, or sorrow **b :** made incapable or unfit
**2 :** hit or wounded by or as if by a missile

**strick·le** \'stri-kəl\ *noun* [Middle English *strikell* a piece of wood for leveling a measure of grain; akin to Old English *strīcan* to stroke — more at STRIKE] (1688)
: a foundry tool for smoothing the surface of a core or mold
**— strickle** *transitive verb*

**strict** \'strikt\ *adjective* [Middle English *stricte*, from Latin *strictus*, from past participle of *stringere* to bind tight — more at STRAIN] (15th century)
**1** *archaic* **a :** TIGHT, CLOSE; *also* **:** INTIMATE **b :** NARROW
**2 a :** stringent in requirement or control ⟨under *strict* orders⟩ **b :** severe in discipline ⟨a *strict* teacher⟩
**3 a :** inflexibly maintained or adhered to ⟨*strict* secrecy⟩ **b :** rigorously conforming to principle or a norm or condition
**4 :** EXACT, PRECISE ⟨in the *strict* sense of the word⟩
**5 :** of narrow erect habit of growth ⟨a *strict* inflorescence⟩
**synonym** *see* RIGID
**— strict·ly** \'strik(t)-lē\ *adverb*
**— strict·ness** \-nəs\ *noun*

**strict liability** *noun* (1896)
: liability imposed without regard to fault

**stric·ture** \'strik-chər\ *noun* [Middle English, from Late Latin *strictura*, from Latin *strictus*, past participle] (14th century)
**1 a :** an abnormal narrowing of a bodily passage; *also* **:** the narrowed part **b :** a constriction of the breath passage in the production of a speech sound
**2 :** something that closely restrains or limits **:** RESTRICTION ⟨moral *strictures*⟩
**3 :** an adverse criticism **:** CENSURE

**¹stride** \'strīd\ *verb* **strode** \'strōd\; **strid·den** \'stri-dᵊn\; **strid·ing** \'strī-diŋ\ [Middle English, from Old English *strīdan*; akin to Middle Low German *striden* to straddle, Old High German *strītan* to quarrel] (before 12th century)
*intransitive verb*
**1 :** to stand astride
**2 :** to move with or as if with long steps
**3 :** to take a very long step
*transitive verb*
**1 :** BESTRIDE, STRADDLE
**2 :** to step over
**3 :** to move over or along with or as if with long measured steps
**— strid·er** \'strī-dər\ *noun*

**²stride** *noun* (before 12th century)
**1 a :** a cycle of locomotor movements (as of a horse) completed when the feet regain the initial relative positions; *also* **:** the distance traversed in a stride **b :** the most effective natural pace **:** maximum competence or capability — often used in the phrase *hit one's stride*

**2 :** a long step
**3 :** an act of striding
**4 :** a stage of progress **:** ADVANCE
**5 :** a manner of striding
**6 :** STRIDE PIANO
**— in stride 1 :** without interference with regular activities **2 :** without emotional reaction ⟨took the news *in stride*⟩

**stri·dence** \'strī-dᵊn(t)s\ *noun* (1890)
: STRIDENCY

**stri·den·cy** \'strī-dᵊn(t)-sē\ *noun* (1865)
: the quality or state of being strident

**stri·dent** \'strī-dᵊnt\ *adjective* [Latin *strident-, stridens*, present participle of *stridere, stridēre* to make a harsh noise] (circa 1656)
: characterized by harsh, insistent, and discordant sound ⟨a *strident* voice⟩; *also* **:** commanding attention by a loud or obtrusive quality ⟨*strident* slogans⟩
**synonym** *see* LOUD, VOCIFEROUS
**— stri·dent·ly** *adverb*

**stride piano** *noun* [from *stride bass* left hand part consisting of large skips] (1952)
: a style of jazz piano playing in which the right hand plays the melody while the left hand alternates between a single note and a chord played an octave or more higher

**stri·dor** \'strī-dər, -ˌdȯr\ *noun* [Latin, from *stridere, stridēre*] (1632)
**1 :** a harsh, shrill, or creaking noise
**2 :** a harsh vibrating sound heard during respiration in cases of obstruction of the air passages

**strid·u·late** \'stri-jə-ˌlāt\ *intransitive verb* **-lat·ed; -lat·ing** [back-formation from *stridulation*, from French, high-pitched sound, from Latin *stridulus* shrill] (1838)
: to make a shrill creaking noise by rubbing together special bodily structures — used especially of male insects (as crickets or grasshoppers)
**— strid·u·la·tion** \ˌstri-jə-'lā-shən\ *noun*
**— strid·u·la·to·ry** \'stri-jə-lə-ˌtōr-ē, -ˌtor-\ *adjective*

**strid·u·lous** \'stri-jə-ləs\ *adjective* [Latin *stridulus*, from *stridere, stridēre*] (1611)
: making a shrill creaking sound
**— strid·u·lous·ly** *adverb*

**strife** \'strīf\ *noun* [Middle English *strif*, from Old French *estrif*, probably from *estriver* to struggle — more at STRIVE] (13th century)
**1 a :** bitter sometimes violent conflict or dissension ⟨political *strife*⟩ **b :** an act of contention **:** FIGHT, STRUGGLE
**2 :** exertion or contention for superiority
**3** *archaic* **:** earnest endeavor
**synonym** *see* DISCORD
**— strife·less** \'strī-fləs\ *adjective*

**strig·il** \'stri-jəl\ *noun* [Latin *strigilis*; akin to Latin *stringere* to touch lightly] (1581)
: an instrument used by ancient Greeks and Romans for scraping moisture off the skin after bathing or exercising

**stri·gose** \'strī-ˌgōs\ *adjective* [New Latin *strigosus*, from *striga* row of bristles, from Latin, furrow] (1793)
: having appressed bristles or scales ⟨a *strigose* leaf⟩

**¹strike** \'strīk\ *verb* **struck** \'strək\; **struck** *also* **strick·en** \'stri-kən\; **strik·ing** \'strī-kiŋ\ [Middle English, from Old English *strīcan* to stroke, go; akin to Old High German *strīhhan* to stroke, Latin *stringere* to touch lightly, *striga, stria* furrow] (before 12th century)
*intransitive verb*
**1 :** to take a course **:** GO ⟨*struck* off through the brush⟩
**2 a :** to aim and usually deliver a blow, stroke, or thrust (as with the hand, a weapon, or a

strigil

tool) **b** : to arrive with detrimental effect ⟨disaster *struck*⟩ **c** : to attempt to undermine or harm something as if by a blow ⟨*struck* at . . . cherished notions —R. P. Warren⟩
**3** : to come into contact forcefully ⟨two ships *struck* in mid channel⟩
**4** : to delete something
**5** : to lower a flag usually in surrender
**6 a** : to become indicated by a clock, bell, or chime ⟨the hour had just *struck*⟩ **b** : to make known the time by sounding ⟨the clock *struck* as they entered⟩
**7** : PIERCE, PENETRATE ⟨the wind seemed to *strike* through our clothes⟩
**8 a** : to engage in battle **b** : to make a military attack
**9** : to become ignited
**10** : to discover something ⟨*struck* on a new plan of attack⟩
**11 a** : to pull on a fishing rod in order to set the hook **b** *of a fish* : to seize the bait
**12** : DART, SHOOT
**13 a** *of a plant cutting* : to take root **b** *of a seed* : GERMINATE
**14** : to make an impression
**15** : to stop work in order to force an employer to comply with demands
**16** : to make a beginning ⟨the need to *strike* vigorously for success⟩
**17** : to thrust oneself forward ⟨he *struck* into the midst of the argument⟩
**18** : to work diligently : STRIVE
*transitive verb*
**1 a** : to strike at : HIT **b** : to drive or remove by or as if by a blow **c** : to attack or seize with a sharp blow (as of fangs or claws) ⟨*struck* by a snake⟩ **d** : INFLICT ⟨*strike* a blow⟩ **e** : to produce by or as if by a blow or stroke ⟨Moses *struck* water from the rock⟩ **f** : to separate by a sharp blow ⟨*strike* off flints⟩
**2 a** : to haul down : LOWER ⟨*strike* the sails⟩ **b** : to dismantle and take away **c** : to strike the tents of (a camp)
**3** : to afflict suddenly ⟨*stricken* by a heart attack⟩
**4 a** : to engage in (a battle) : FIGHT **b** : to make a military attack on
**5** : DELETE, CANCEL ⟨*strike* the last paragraph⟩
**6 a** : to penetrate painfully : PIERCE **b** : to cause to penetrate **c** : to send down or out ⟨trees *struck* roots deep into the soil⟩
**7 a** : to level (as a measure of grain) by scraping off what is above the rim **b** : to smooth or form with a strickle
**8** : to indicate by sounding
**9 a** (1) : to bring into forceful contact (2) : to shake (hands) in confirming an agreement (3) : to thrust against **b** : to come into contact or collision with **c** *of light* : to fall on **d** *of a sound* : to become audible to
**10 a** : to affect with a mental or emotional state or a strong emotion ⟨*struck* with horror at the sight⟩ **b** : to affect a person with (a strong emotion) ⟨words that *struck* fear in the listeners⟩ **c** : to cause to become by or as if by a sudden blow ⟨*struck* him dead⟩
**11 a** : to produce by stamping **b** (1) : to produce (as fire) by or as if by striking (2) : to cause to ignite by friction
**12** : to make and ratify the terms of ⟨*strike* a bargain⟩
**13 a** : to play or produce by stroking keys or strings ⟨*struck* a series of chords on the piano⟩ **b** : to produce as if by playing an instrument ⟨his voice *struck* a note of concern⟩
**14 a** : to hook (a fish) by a sharp pull on the line **b** *of a fish* : to snatch at (a bait)
**15 a** : to occur to ⟨the answer *struck* me suddenly⟩ **b** : to appear to especially as a revelation or as remarkable : IMPRESS
**16** : BEWITCH
**17** : to arrive at by or as if by computation ⟨*strike* a balance⟩
**18 a** : to come to : ATTAIN **b** : to come upon : DISCOVER ⟨*strike* gold⟩

**19** : to engage in a strike against (an employer)
**20** : TAKE ON, ASSUME ⟨*strike* a pose⟩
**21 a** : to place (a plant cutting) in a medium for growth and rooting **b** : to so propagate (a plant)
**22** : to make one's way along
**23** : to cause (an arc) to form (as between electrodes of an arc lamp)
**24** *of an insect* : to oviposit on or in
**synonym** see AFFECT
— **strike it rich** : to become rich usually suddenly
²**strike** *noun* (15th century)
**1** : STRICKLE
**2** : an act or instance of striking
**3 a** : a work stoppage by a body of workers to enforce compliance with demands made on an employer **b** : a temporary stoppage of activities in protest against an act or condition
**4** : the direction of the line of intersection of a horizontal plane with an uptilted geological stratum
**5 a** : a pull on a fishing rod to strike a fish **b** : a pull on a line by a fish in striking
**6** : a stroke of good luck; *especially* : a discovery of a valuable mineral deposit
**7 a** : a pitched ball that is in the strike zone or is swung at and is not hit fair **b** : a perfectly thrown ball or pass
**8** : DISADVANTAGE, HANDICAP
**9** : an act or instance of knocking down all the bowling pins with the first bowl
**10** : establishment of roots and plant growth
**11** : cutaneous myiasis (as of sheep)
**12 a** : a military attack; *especially* : an air attack on a single objective **b** : a group of airplanes taking part in such an attack
**strike·bound** \'strīk-ˌbaund\ *adjective* (1943)
: subjected to a strike
**strike·break·er** \-ˌbrā-kər\ *noun* (1904)
: a person hired to replace a striking worker
**strike·break·ing** \-kiŋ\ *noun* (1905)
: action designed to break up a strike
**strike force** *noun* (1968)
: a team of federal agents assigned to investigate organized crime in a specific area
**strike off** *transitive verb* (1821)
**1** : to produce in an effortless manner
**2** : to depict clearly and exactly
**strike·out** \'strīk-ˌaut\ *noun* (1887)
: an out in baseball resulting from a batter's being charged with three strikes
**strike out** (1712)
*intransitive verb*
**1** : to enter upon a course of action
**2** : to set out vigorously
**3** : to make an out in baseball by a strikeout
**4** : to finish bowling a string with consecutive strikes; *specifically* : to bowl three strikes in the last frame
**5** : FAIL 2c
*transitive verb*
*of a baseball pitcher* : to retire (as a batter) by a strikeout
**strike·over** \'strīk-ˌō-vər\ *noun* (1938)
: an act or instance of striking a typewriter character on a spot occupied by another character
**strik·er** \'strī-kər\ *noun* (1581)
**1** : one that strikes: as **a** : a player in any of several games who is striking or attempting to strike a ball **b** : the hammer of the striking mechanism of a clock or watch **c** : a blacksmith's helper who swings the sledgehammer **d** : a worker on strike
**2** : a junior enlisted man in the U.S. Navy who has declared an occupational specialty
**strike up** (circa 1562)
*intransitive verb*
: to begin to sing or play or to be sung or played
*transitive verb*
**1** : to cause to begin singing or playing ⟨*strike up* the band⟩
**2** : to cause to begin ⟨*strike up* a conversation⟩

**strike zone** *noun* (1948)
: the area over home plate through which a pitched baseball must pass to be called a strike
**strik·ing** \'strī-kiŋ\ *adjective* (1752)
: attracting attention or notice through unusual or conspicuous qualities ⟨a place of *striking* beauty⟩
**synonym** see NOTICEABLE
— **strik·ing·ly** \-kiŋ-lē\ *adverb*
**striking distance** *noun* (1751)
: a distance from which something can be easily reached or attained ⟨almost within *striking distance* of their goal⟩
**striking price** *noun* (1961)
: an agreed-upon price at which an option contract can be exercised — called also *strike price*
¹**string** \'striŋ\ *noun* [Middle English, from Old English *streng;* akin to Old High German *strang* rope, Latin *stringere* to bind tight — more at STRAIN] (before 12th century)
**1** : a small cord used to bind, fasten, or tie
**2 a** *archaic* : a cord (as a tendon or ligament) of an animal body **b** : a plant fiber (as a leaf vein)
**3 a** : the gut, wire, or nylon cord of a musical instrument **b** *plural* (1) : the stringed instruments of an orchestra (2) : the players of such instruments
**4 a** : a group of objects threaded on a string ⟨a *string* of fish⟩ ⟨a *string* of pearls⟩ **b** (1) : a series of things arranged in or as if in a line ⟨a *string* of cars⟩ ⟨a *string* of names⟩ (2) : a sequence of like items (as bits, characters, or words) **c** : a group of business properties scattered geographically ⟨a *string* of newspapers⟩ **d** : the animals and especially horses belonging to or used by one individual
**5 a** : a means of recourse : EXPEDIENT **b** : a group of players ranked according to skill or proficiency
**6** : SUCCESSION 3a ⟨a *string* of successes⟩
**7 a** : one of the inclined sides of a stair supporting the treads and risers **b** : STRINGCOURSE
**8 a** : BALKLINE 1 **b** : the action of lagging for break in billiards
**9** : LINE 13
**10** *plural* **a** : contingent conditions or obligations **b** : CONTROL, DOMINATION
**11** : a scanty bikini — called also *string bikini*
**12** : a hypothetical one-dimensional object that is infinitely thin but has a length of $10^{-33}$ centimeters, that vibrates as it moves through space, and whose mode of vibration manifests itself as a subatomic particle
— **string·less** \'striŋ-ləs\ *adjective*
— **on the string** : subject to one's influences
²**string** *verb* **strung** \'strəŋ\; **string·ing** \'striŋ-iŋ\ (15th century)
*transitive verb*
**1 a** : to equip with strings **b** : to tune the strings of
**2** : to make tense : key up
**3 a** : to thread on or as if on a string **b** : to thread with objects **c** : to tie, hang, or fasten with string **d** : to put together (as words or ideas) like objects threaded on a string
**4** : to hang by the neck — used with *up*
**5** : to remove the strings of ⟨*string* beans⟩
**6 a** : to extend or stretch like a string ⟨*string* wires from tree to tree⟩ **b** : to set out in a line or series — often used with *out*
**7** : FOOL, HOAX ⟨cowboys *stringing* tenderfeet with tall tales —Carl Van Doren⟩ — often used with *along*
*intransitive verb*
**1** : to move, progress, or lie in a string
**2** : to form into strings

**3**: LAG 3

**³string** *adjective* (1712)
: of or relating to stringed musical instruments ⟨the *string* section⟩

**string along** (1914)
*transitive verb*
: to keep waiting
*intransitive verb*
: GO ALONG, AGREE

**string bass** *noun* (circa 1927)
: DOUBLE BASS

**string bean** *noun* (1759)
**1** : a bean of one of the older varieties of kidney bean that have stringy fibers on the lines of separation of the pods; *broadly*
: SNAP BEAN
**2** : a very tall thin person

**string-course** \-ˌkōrs, -ˌkȯrs\ *noun* (1825)
: a horizontal band (as of bricks) in a building forming a part of the design

**stringed** \'striŋd\ *adjective* (before 12th century)
**1** : having strings ⟨*stringed* instruments⟩
**2** : produced by strings

**strin-gen-cy** \'strin-jən(t)-sē\ *noun* (1844)
: the quality or state of being stringent

**strin-gen-do** \strin-'jen-(ˌ)dō\ *adverb* [Italian, verbal of *stringere* to press, from Latin, to bind tight — more at STRAIN] (1853)
: with quickening of tempo (as to a climax) — used as a direction in music

**strin-gent** \'strin-jənt\ *adjective* [Latin *stringent-, stringens,* present participle of *stringere*] (1736)
**1** : TIGHT, CONSTRICTED
**2** : marked by rigor, strictness, or severity especially with regard to rule or standard
**3** : marked by money scarcity and credit strictness
**synonym** see RIGID
— **strin-gent-ly** *adverb*

**string-er** \'striŋ-ər\ *noun* (14th century)
**1** : one that strings
**2** : a string, wire, or chain often with snaps on which fish are strung by a fisherman
**3** : a narrow vein or irregular filament of mineral traversing a rock mass of different material
**4 a** : a long horizontal timber to connect uprights in a frame or to support a floor **b** : STRING 7a **c** : a tie in a truss
**5 a** : a longitudinal member extending from bent to bent of a railroad bridge and carrying the track **b** : a longitudinal member (as in an airplane fuselage or wing) to reinforce the skin
**6 a** : a news correspondent who is paid space rates **b** : a reporter who works for a publication or news agency on a part-time basis; *broadly* : CORRESPONDENT
**7** : one estimated to be of specified excellence or efficiency — used in combination ⟨first-*stringer*⟩ ⟨second-*stringer*⟩

**string-halt** \'striŋ-ˌhȯlt\ *noun* (circa 1534)
: a condition of lameness in a horse's hind legs caused by muscular spasms
— **string-halt-ed** \-ˌhȯl-təd\ *adjective*

**string-ing** \'striŋ-iŋ\ *noun* (1812)
**1** : lines of inlay in furniture decoration
**2** : the material with which a racket is strung

**string line** *noun* (1867)
: BALKLINE 1

**string-piece** \'striŋ-ˌpēs\ *noun* (1769)
: the heavy squared timber lying along the top of the piles forming a dock front or timber pier

**string quartet** *noun* (1875)
**1** : a composition for string quartet
**2** : a quartet of performers on stringed instruments usually including a first and second violin, a viola, and a cello

**string tie** *noun* (1895)

: a narrow necktie

**stringy** \'striŋ-ē\ *adjective* **string-i-er; -est** (1669)
**1 a** : containing, consisting of, or resembling fibrous matter or string ⟨*stringy* hair⟩ **b** : lean and sinewy in build : WIRY
**2** : capable of being drawn out to form a string : ROPY ⟨a *stringy* precipitate⟩
— **string-i-ness** *noun*

**stringy-bark** \'striŋ-ē-ˌbärk\ *noun* (1799)
**1** : any of several Australian eucalypti with fibrous inner bark
**2** : the bark of a stringybark

**¹strip** \'strip\ *verb* **stripped** \'stript\ *also* **stript; strip-ping** [Middle English *strippen,* from Old English *-strīpan;* akin to Old High German *stroufen* to strip] (13th century)
*transitive verb*
**1 a** : to remove clothing, covering, or surface matter from **b** : to deprive of possessions **c** : to divest of honors, privileges, or functions
**2 a** : to remove extraneous or superficial matter from ⟨a prose style *stripped* to the bones⟩ **b** : to remove furniture, equipment, or accessories from ⟨*strip* a ship for action⟩
**3** : to make bare or clear (as by cutting or grazing)
**4** : to finish a milking of by pressing the last available milk from the teats ⟨*strip* a cow⟩
**5 a** : to remove cured leaves from the stalks of (tobacco) **b** : to remove the midrib from (tobacco leaves)
**6** : to tear or damage the thread of (a separable part or fitting)
**7** : to separate (components) from a mixture or solution
**8** : to press eggs or milt out of (a fish)
*intransitive verb*
**1 a** : to take off clothes **b** : to perform a striptease
**2** : PEEL 1
— **strip-pa-ble** \'stri-pə-bəl\ *adjective*

**²strip** *noun* [Middle English, perhaps from Middle Low German *strippe* strap] (15th century)
**1 a** : a long narrow piece of a material **b** : a long narrow area of land or water
**2** : AIRSTRIP
**3** : a commercially developed area especially along a highway
**4** : COMIC STRIP
**5** : STRIPTEASE

**strip–chart recorder** \'strip-ˌchärt-\ *noun* (1950)
: a device used for the continuous graphic recording of time-dependent data
— **strip–chart recording** *noun*

**strip–crop-ping** \'strip-ˌkrä-piŋ\ *noun* (1936)
: the growing of a cultivated crop (as corn) in strips alternating with strips of a sod-forming crop (as hay) arranged to follow an approximate contour of the land and minimize erosion
— **strip–crop** \'strip-ˌkräp\ *verb*

**¹stripe** \'strīp\ *noun* [Middle English; akin to Middle Dutch *stripe* strip, stripe] (15th century)
: a stroke or blow with a rod or lash

**²stripe** *transitive verb* **striped** \'strīpt\; **strip-ing** [probably from Middle Dutch; akin to Middle High German *strīfe* stripe] (15th century)
: to make stripes on or variegate with stripes

**³stripe** *noun* (1626)
**1 a** : a line or long narrow section differing in color or texture from parts adjoining **b** (1) : a textile design consisting of lines or bands against a plain background (2) : a fabric with a striped design
**2** : a narrow strip of braid or embroidery usually in the shape of a bar, arc, or chevron that is worn (as on the sleeve of a military uniform) to indicate rank or length of service
**3** : a distinct variety or sort : TYPE ⟨persons of the same political *stripe*⟩
— **stripe-less** \'strī-pləs\ *adjective*

**striped** \'strīpt, 'strī-pəd\ *adjective* (1616)

: having stripes or streaks

**striped bass** *noun* (1818)
: a large anadromous food and sport fish (*Morone saxatilis* of the family Percichthyidae) that occurs along the Atlantic coast of the U.S. and has been introduced along the Pacific coast — called also *rockfish*

**striped skunk** *noun* (1882)
: a common North American skunk (*Mephitis mephitis*) usually with white on the top of the head that extends posteriorly in two narrowly separated stripes

**strip-er** \'strī-pər\ *noun* (1937)
: STRIPED BASS

**strip-ing** \'strī-piŋ\ *noun* (1677)
**1 a** : the stripes marked or painted on something **b** : a design of stripes
**2** : the act or process of marking with stripes

**strip-ling** \'stri-pliŋ\ *noun* [Middle English] (14th century)
: YOUTH 2a

**strip mine** *noun* (1926)
: a mine that is worked from the earth's surface by the stripping of overburden; *especially* : a coal mine situated along the outcrop of a flat dipping bed
— **strip–mine** *verb*
— **strip miner** *noun*

**stripped–down** \'strip(t)-'daún\ *adjective* (1928)
: lacking any extra features : SIMPLE 2b

**strip-per** \'stri-pər\ *noun* (1581)
**1** : one that strips
**2** : STRIPTEASER
**3** : a machine that separates a desired part of an agricultural crop
**4** : an oil well that produces 10 barrels or less per day

**strip poker** *noun* (1919)
: a poker game in which players pay their losses by removing articles of clothing

**strip search** *noun* (1947)
: a search for something concealed on a person made after removal of the person's clothing
— **strip–search** *verb*

**strip-tease** \'strip-ˌtēz\ *noun* (1936)
: a burlesque act in which a performer removes clothing piece by piece

**strip-teas-er** \-ˌtē-zər\ *noun* (1930)
: one who performs a striptease

**stripy** \'strī-pē\ *adjective* **strip-i-er; -est** (1513)
: marked by stripes or streaks

**strive** \'strīv\ *intransitive verb* **strove** \'strōv\ *also* **strived** \'strīvd\; **striv-en** \'stri-vən\ *or* **strived; striv-ing** \'strī-viŋ\ [Middle English, from Old French *estriver,* of Germanic origin; akin to Middle High German *streben* to endeavor] (13th century)
**1** : to devote serious effort or energy : ENDEAVOR
**2** : to struggle in opposition : CONTEND
**synonym** see ATTEMPT
— **striv-er** \'strī-vər\ *noun*

**strobe** \'strōb\ *noun* [by shortening & alteration] (1942)
**1** : STROBOSCOPE
**2** : a device that utilizes a flashtube for high-speed illumination (as in photography)
**3** : STROBOTRON

**strobe light** *noun* (1947)
: STROBE

**stro-bi-la** \strō-'bī-lə, 'strō-bə-\ *noun, plural* **-lae** \-(ˌ)lē\ [New Latin, from Greek *strobilē* plug of lint shaped like a pinecone, from *strobilos* pinecone] (1864)
: a linear series of similar animal structures (as the proglottids of a tapeworm) produced by budding

**stro-bi-la-tion** \ˌstrō-bə-'lā-shən\ *noun* [New Latin *strobila*] (1878)

: asexual reproduction (as in various coelenterates and tapeworms) by transverse division of the body into segments which develop into separate individuals, zooids, or proglottids

**stro·bi·lus** \strō-'bī-ləs, 'strō-bə-\ *noun, plural* **-li** \-ˌlī\ [New Latin, from Late Latin, pinecone, from Greek *strobilos* twisted object, top, pinecone, from *strobos* action of whirling; akin to *strephein* to twist] (circa 1753)
**1 :** an aggregation of sporophylls resembling a cone (as in the club mosses and horsetails)
**2 :** the cone of a gymnosperm

**stro·bo·scope** \'strō-bə-ˌskōp\ *noun* [Greek *strobos* whirling + International Scientific Vocabulary *-scope*] (1896)
: an instrument for determining the speed of cyclic motion (as rotation or vibration) that causes the motion to appear slowed or stopped: as **a :** a revolving disk with holes around the edge through which an object is viewed **b :** a device that uses a flashtube to intermittently illuminate a moving object **c :** a cardboard disk with marks to be viewed under intermittent light

**stro·bo·scop·ic** \ˌstrō-bə-'skä-pik\ *adjective* (circa 1846)
: of, utilizing, or relating to a stroboscope or a strobe
— **stro·bo·scop·i·cal·ly** \-pi-k(ə-)lē\ *adverb*

**stro·bo·tron** \'strō-bə-ˌträn\ *noun* [*stroboscope* + *-tron*] (1937)
: a gas-filled electron tube used especially as a source of bright flashes of light for a stroboscope

**strode** *past of* STRIDE

**¹stroke** \'strōk\ *transitive verb* **stroked; strok·ing** [Middle English, from Old English *strācian;* akin to Old High German *strīhhan* to stroke — more at STRIKE] (before 12th century)
**1 :** to rub gently in one direction; *also* **:** CARESS
**2 :** to flatter or pay attention to in a manner designed to reassure or persuade
— **strok·er** *noun*

**²stroke** *noun* [Middle English; akin to Old English *strīcan* to stroke — more at STRIKE] (13th century)
**1 :** the act of striking; *especially* **:** a blow with a weapon or implement
**2 :** a single unbroken movement; *especially* **:** one of a series of repeated or to-and-fro movements
**3 a :** a controlled swing intended to hit a ball or shuttlecock; *also* **:** a striking of the ball **b :** such a stroke charged to a player as a unit of scoring in golf
**4 a :** a sudden action or process producing an impact ⟨*stroke* of lightning⟩ **b :** an unexpected result ⟨*stroke* of luck⟩
**5 :** sudden diminution or loss of consciousness, sensation, and voluntary motion caused by rupture or obstruction (as by a clot) of an artery of the brain — called also *apoplexy*
**6 a :** one of a series of propelling beats or movements against a resisting medium ⟨*stroke* of the oar⟩ **b :** a rower who sets the pace for a crew
**7 a :** a vigorous or energetic effort ⟨a *stroke* of genius⟩ **b :** a delicate or clever touch in a narrative, description, or construction
**8 :** HEARTBEAT
**9 :** the movement or the distance of the movement in either direction of a mechanical part (as a piston) having a reciprocating motion
**10 :** the sound of a bell being struck ⟨at the *stroke* of twelve⟩
**11 :** [¹*stroke*] : an act of stroking or caressing
**12 a :** a mark or dash made by a single movement of an implement **b :** one of the lines of a letter of the alphabet

**³stroke** *verb* **stroked; strok·ing** (1597)
*transitive verb*

**1 a :** to mark with a short line ⟨*stroke* the *t*'s⟩
**b :** to cancel by drawing a line through ⟨*stroked* out his name⟩
**2 :** to set the stroke for (a rowing crew); *also* **:** to set the stroke for the crew of (a rowing boat)
**3 :** HIT; *especially* **:** to propel (a ball) with a controlled swinging blow
*intransitive verb*
**1 :** to execute a stroke
**2 :** to row at a certain number of strokes a minute

**stroke play** *noun* (1905)
: golf competition scored by total number of strokes

**stroll** \'strōl\ *verb* [probably from German dialect *strollen*] (1680)
*intransitive verb*
**1 :** to walk in a leisurely or idle manner : RAMBLE
**2 :** to go from place to place in search of work or profit ⟨*strolling* players⟩ ⟨*strolling* musicians⟩
*transitive verb*
: to walk at leisure along or about
— **stroll** *noun*

**stroll·er** \'strō-lər\ *noun* (1608)
**1 a :** an itinerant actor **b :** VAGRANT, TRAMP
**2 :** one that strolls
**3 :** a collapsible carriage designed as a chair in which a small child may be pushed

**stro·ma** \'strō-mə\ *noun, plural* **stro·ma·ta** \-mə-tə\ [New Latin *stromat-, stroma*, from Latin, bed covering, from Greek *strōmat-, strōma*, from *stornynai* to spread out — more at STREW] (1832)
**1 a :** a compact mass of fungal hyphae producing perithecia or pycnidia **b :** the colorless proteinaceous matrix of a chloroplast in which the chlorophyll-containing lamellae are embedded
**2 a :** the supporting framework of an animal organ typically consisting of connective tissue **b :** the spongy protoplasmic framework of some cells (as a red blood cell)
— **stro·mal** \-məl\ *adjective*

**stro·mat·o·lite** \strō-'ma-tᵊl-ˌīt\ *noun* [Latin *stromat-, stroma* bed covering + English *-o-* + *-lite*] (1930)
: a laminated sedimentary fossil formed from layers of blue-green algae
— **stro·mat·o·lit·ic** \-ˌma-tᵊl-'i-tik\ *adjective*

**strong** \'strȯŋ\ *adjective* **stron·ger** \'strȯŋ-gər *also* -ər\; **stron·gest** \'strȯŋ-gəst *also* -əst\ [Middle English, from Old English *strang;* akin to Old High German *strengi* strong, Latin *stringere* to bind tight — more at STRAIN] (before 12th century)
**1 :** having or marked by great physical power
**2 :** having moral or intellectual power
**3 :** having great resources (as of wealth or talent)
**4 :** of a specified number ⟨an army ten thousand *strong*⟩
**5 a :** striking or superior of its kind ⟨a *strong* resemblance⟩ **b :** effective or efficient especially in a specified direction ⟨*strong* on watching other people work —A. Alvarez⟩
**6 :** FORCEFUL, COGENT ⟨*strong* evidence⟩ ⟨*strong* talk⟩
**7 :** not mild or weak : EXTREME, INTENSE: as **a :** rich in some active agent ⟨*strong* beer⟩ **b** *of a color* **:** high in chroma **c :** ionizing freely in solution ⟨*strong* acids and bases⟩ **d :** magnifying by refracting greatly ⟨*strong* lens⟩
**8** *obsolete* **:** FLAGRANT
**9 :** moving with rapidity or force ⟨*strong* wind⟩
**10 :** ARDENT, ZEALOUS ⟨a *strong* supporter⟩
**11 a :** not easily injured or disturbed : SOLID **b :** not easily subdued or taken ⟨a *strong* fort⟩
**12 :** well established : FIRM ⟨*strong* beliefs⟩
**13 :** not easily upset or nauseated ⟨a *strong* stomach⟩

**14 :** having an offensive or intense odor or flavor : RANK
**15 :** tending to steady or higher prices ⟨a *strong* market⟩
**16 :** of, relating to, or being a verb that is inflected by a change in the root vowel (as *strive, strove, striven*) rather than by regular affixation ☆
— **strong** *adverb*
— **strong·ish** \'strȯŋ-ish\ *adjective*
— **strong·ly** \'strȯŋ-lē\ *adverb*

**strong anthropic principle** *noun* (1985)
: ANTHROPIC PRINCIPLE b

**¹strong–arm** \'strȯŋ-'ärm\ *adjective* (1897)
: having or using undue force

**²strong–arm** *transitive verb* (1903)
**1 a :** to use force on : ASSAULT **b :** BULLY, INTIMIDATE
**2 :** to rob by force

**strong·box** \'strȯŋ-ˌbäks\ *noun* (1684)
: a strongly made chest or case for money or valuables

**strong breeze** *noun* (1867)
: wind having a speed of 25 to 31 miles (40 to 50 kilometers) per hour — see BEAUFORT SCALE table

**strong drink** *noun* (14th century)
: intoxicating liquor

**strong force** *noun* (1969)
: a fundamental physical force that acts on hadrons and is responsible for the binding together of protons and neutrons in the atomic nucleus and for processes of particle creation in high-energy collisions and that is the strongest known fundamental physical force but acts only over distances comparable to those between nucleons in an atomic nucleus — called also *strong interaction, strong nuclear force;* compare ELECTROMAGNETISM 2a, GRAVITY 3a(2), WEAK FORCE

**strong gale** *noun* (circa 1867)
: wind having a speed of 47 to 54 miles (76 to 87 kilometers) per hour — see BEAUFORT SCALE table

**strong·hold** \'strȯŋ-ˌhōld\ *noun* (15th century)
**1 :** a fortified place
**2 a :** a place of security or survival ⟨one of the last *strongholds* of the ancient Gaelic language —George Holmes⟩ **b :** a place dominated by a particular group or marked by a particular characteristic ⟨a Republican *stronghold*⟩ ⟨*strongholds* of snobbery —Lionel Trilling⟩

**strong·man** \'strȯŋ-ˌman\ *noun* (1859)
: one who leads or controls by force of will and character or by military methods

**strong–mind·ed** \'strȯŋ-'mīn-dəd\ *adjective* (1791)

---

☆ **SYNONYMS**
**Strong, stout, sturdy, stalwart, tough, tenacious** mean showing power to resist or to endure. STRONG may imply power derived from muscular vigor, large size, structural soundness, intellectual or spiritual resources ⟨*strong* arms⟩ ⟨the defense has a *strong* case⟩. STOUT suggests an ability to endure stress, pain, or hard use without giving way ⟨*stout* hiking boots⟩. STURDY implies strength derived from vigorous growth, determination of spirit, solidity of construction ⟨a *sturdy* table⟩ ⟨people of *sturdy* independence⟩. STALWART suggests an unshakable dependability ⟨*stalwart* environmentalists⟩. TOUGH implies great firmness and resiliency ⟨a *tough* political opponent⟩. TENACIOUS suggests strength in seizing, retaining, clinging to, or holding together ⟨*tenacious* farmers clinging to an age-old way of life⟩.

---

\ə\ abut \ᵊ\ kitten \ər\ further \a\ ash \ā\ ace
\ä\ mop, mar \au̇\ out \ch\ chin \e\ bet \ē\ easy
\g\ go \i\ hit \ī\ ice \j\ job \ŋ\ sing \ō\ go
\ȯ\ law \ȯi\ boy \th\ thin \th̷\ the \ü\ loot \u̇\ foot
\y\ yet \zh\ vision *see also* Guide to Pronunciation

: having a vigorous mind; *especially* : marked by independence of thought and judgment
— **strong–mind·ed·ly** *adverb*
— **strong–mind·ed·ness** *noun*

**strong room** *noun* (1761)
: a room for money or valuables specially constructed to be fireproof and burglarproof

**strong safety** *noun* (1970)
: a safety in football who plays opposite the strong side of an offensive formation

**strong side** *noun* (circa 1951)
: the side of a football formation having the greater number of players; *specifically* : the side on which the tight end plays

**strong suit** *noun* (1857)
**1** : a long suit containing high cards
**2** : something in which one excels : FORTE ⟨details of legislation have never been my *strong suit* —Tip O'Neill⟩

**stron·gyle** \'strän-ˌjīl, -jəl\ *noun* [New Latin *Strongylus*, genus of worms, from Greek *strongylos* round, compact; akin to Greek *stranx* drop squeezed out — more at STRAIN] (1847)
: any of various nematode worms (family Strongylidae) related to the hookworms and parasitic especially in the alimentary tract and tissues of horses

**stron·gy·loi·di·a·sis** \ˌsträn-jə-ˌlói-'dī-ə-səs\ *also* **stron·gy·loi·do·sis** \-'dō-səs\ *noun* [New Latin, from *Strongyloides*, genus name, from *Strongylus*] (1905)
: infestation with or disease caused by any of a genus (*Strongyloides*) of strongyles that sometimes parasitize the intestines of vertebrates including humans

**stron·tian·ite** \'strän(t)-shə-ˌnīt\ *noun* (1794)
: a mineral consisting of a carbonate of strontium and occurring in various forms and colors

**stron·tium** \'strän(t)-sh(ē-)əm, 'strän-tē-əm\ *noun* [New Latin, from *strontia* strontium oxide, from obsolete English *strontian*, from *Strontian*, village in Scotland] (1808)
: a soft malleable ductile metallic element of the alkaline-earth group occurring only in combination and used especially in color TV tubes, in crimson fireworks, and in the production of some ferrites — see ELEMENT table

**strontium 90** *noun* (1952)
: a heavy radioactive isotope of strontium of mass number 90 that has a half-life of 29 years and that is present in the fallout from nuclear explosions and is hazardous because like calcium it can be assimilated in biological processes and deposited in the bones of human beings and animals — called also *radiostrontium*

**¹strop** \'sträp\ *noun* [Middle English — more at STRAP] (before 12th century)
: STRAP: **a** : a short rope with its ends spliced to form a circle **b** : a usually leather band for sharpening a razor

**²strop** *transitive verb* **stropped; strop·ping** (1841)
: to sharpen (a razor) on a strop

**stro·phan·thin** \strō-'fan(t)-thən\ *noun* [International Scientific Vocabulary, from New Latin *Strophanthus*, from Greek *strophos* twisted band (from *strephein* to twist) + *anthos* flower — more at ANTHOLOGY] (1873)
: any of several glycosides (as ouabain) or mixtures of glycosides from African plants (genera *Strophanthus* and *Acokanthera*) of the dogbane family; *especially* : a bitter toxic glycoside $C_{36}H_{54}O_{14}$ from a woody vine (*Strophanthus kombé*) used similarly to digitalis

**stro·phe** \'strō-(ˌ)fē\ *noun* [Greek *strophē*, literally, act of turning, from *strephein* to turn, twist] (1603)
**1 a** : a rhythmic system composed of two or more lines repeated as a unit; *especially* : such a unit recurring in a series of strophic units **b** : STANZA
**2 a** : the movement of the classical Greek chorus while turning from one side to the oth-

er of the orchestra **b** : the part of a Greek choral ode sung during the strophe of the dance

**stro·phic** \'strō-fik, 'strä-\ *adjective* (1848)
**1** : relating to, containing, or consisting of strophes
**2** *of a song* : using the same music for successive stanzas — compare THROUGH-COMPOSED

**strop·py** \'strä-pē\ *adjective* [perhaps by shortening & alteration from *obstreperous*] (1951)
*British* : TOUCHY, BELLIGERENT

**stroud** \'straud\ *noun* [probably from *Stroud*, town in England] (1683)
**1** *also* **stroud·ing** \'strau-diŋ\ : a coarse woolen cloth formerly used in trade with North American Indians
**2** : a blanket or garment of stroud

**strove** *past & chiefly dialect past participle of* STRIVE

**strow** \'strō\ *transitive verb* **strowed; strown** \'strōn\ *or* **strowed; strow·ing** [Middle English — more at STREW] (14th century)
*archaic* : SCATTER

**stroy** *verb* [Middle English *stroyen*, short for *destroyen*] (13th century)
*obsolete* : DESTROY

**¹struck** \'strək\ *past and past participle of* STRIKE

**²struck** *adjective* (1894)
: closed by or subjected to a labor strike ⟨a *struck* factory⟩ ⟨a *struck* employer⟩

**struc·tur·al** \'strək-chə-rəl, 'strək-shrəl\ *adjective* (1835)
**1** : of or relating to the physical makeup of a plant or animal body
**2 a** : of, relating to, or affecting structure ⟨*structural* stability⟩ **b** : used in building structures ⟨*structural* clay⟩ **c** : involved in or caused by structure especially of the economy ⟨*structural* unemployment⟩
**3** : of, relating to, or resulting from the effects of folding or faulting of the earth's crust : TECTONIC
**4** : concerned with or relating to structure rather than history or comparison ⟨*structural* linguistics⟩
— **struc·tur·al·ly** *adverb*

**structural formula** *noun* (1872)
: an expanded molecular formula showing the arrangement within the molecule of atoms and of bonds

**structural gene** *noun* (1959)
: a gene that codes for the amino acid sequence of a protein (as an enzyme) or for a ribosomal RNA or transfer RNA

**struc·tur·al·ism** \'strək-chə-rə-ˌli-zəm, 'strək-shrə-\ *noun* (1907)
**1** : psychology concerned especially with resolution of the mind into structural elements
**2** : structural linguistics
**3** : an anthropological movement associated especially with Claude Lévi-Strauss that seeks to analyze social relationships in terms of highly abstract relational structures often expressed in a logical symbolism
**4** : a method of analysis (as of a literary text or a political system) that is related to cultural anthropology and that focuses on recurring patterns of thought and behavior
— **struc·tur·al·ist** \-list\ *noun or adjective*

**structural isomer** *noun* (1926)
: one of two or more compounds that contain the same number and kinds of atoms but that differ significantly in their geometric arrangement

**struc·tur·al·ize** \'strək-chə-rə-ˌlīz, 'strək-shrə-ˌlīz\ *transitive verb* **-ized; -iz·ing** (circa 1931)
: to organize or incorporate into a structure
— **struc·tur·al·i·za·tion** \ˌstrək-chə-rə-lə-'zā-shən, ˌstrək-shrə-\ *noun*

**structural steel** *noun* (1895)
**1** : rolled steel in structural shapes
**2** : steel suitable for structural shapes

**struc·tur·a·tion** \ˌstrək-chə-'rā-shən, -shə-'rā-\ *noun* (1925)

: the interrelation of parts in an organized whole

**¹struc·ture** \'strək-chər\ *noun* [Middle English, from Latin *structura*, from *structus*, past participle of *struere* to heap up, build — more at STREW] (15th century)
**1** : the action of building : CONSTRUCTION
**2 a** : something (as a building) that is constructed **b** : something arranged in a definite pattern of organization ⟨a rigid totalitarian *structure* —J. L. Hess⟩ ⟨leaves and other plant *structures*⟩
**3** : manner of construction : MAKEUP ⟨Gothic in *structure*⟩
**4 a** : the arrangement of particles or parts in a substance or body ⟨soil *structure*⟩ ⟨molecular *structure*⟩ **b** : organization of parts as dominated by the general character of the whole ⟨economic *structure*⟩ ⟨personality *structure*⟩
**5** : the aggregate of elements of an entity in their relationships to each other
— **struc·ture·less** \-ləs\ *adjective*
— **struc·ture·less·ness** \-nəs\ *noun*

**²structure** *transitive verb* **struc·tured; struc·tur·ing** \'strək-chə-riŋ, 'strək-shriŋ\ (circa 1693)
**1** : to form into or according to a structure
**2** : CONSTRUCT

**struc·tured** *adjective* (1966)
: of, relating to, or being a method of computer programming in which each step of the solution to a problem is contained in a separate subprogram

**stru·del** \'strü-dᵊl, 'shtrü-\ *noun* [German, literally, whirlpool] (circa 1893)
: a pastry made from a thin sheet of dough rolled up with filling and baked ⟨apple *strudel*⟩

**¹strug·gle** \'strə-gəl\ *intransitive verb* **strug·gled; strug·gling** \-g(ə-)liŋ\ [Middle English *struglen*] (14th century)
**1** : to make strenuous or violent efforts against opposition : CONTEND
**2** : to proceed with difficulty or with great effort ⟨*struggled* through the high grass⟩ ⟨*struggling* to make a living⟩
— **strug·gler** \-g(ə-)lər\ *noun*

**²struggle** *noun* (1692)
**1** : CONTEST, STRIFE ⟨armed *struggle*⟩ ⟨a power *struggle*⟩
**2** : a violent effort or exertion : an act of strongly motivated striving

**struggle for existence** (1832)
: the automatic competition (as for food, space, or light) of members of a natural population that tends to eliminate less efficient individuals and thereby increase the chance of the more efficient to pass on inherited adaptive traits

**¹strum** \'strəm\ *verb* **strummed; strum·ming** [imitative] (1777)
*transitive verb*
**1 a** : to brush the fingers over the strings of (a musical instrument) in playing ⟨*strum* a guitar⟩; *also* : ³THRUM 1 **b** : to play (music) on a stringed instrument ⟨*strum* a tune⟩
**2** : to cause to sound vibrantly ⟨winds *strummed* the rigging —H. A. Chippendale⟩
*intransitive verb*
**1** : to strum a stringed instrument
**2** : to sound vibrantly
— **strum·mer** *noun*

**²strum** *noun* (circa 1793)
: an act, instance, or sound of strumming

**stru·ma** \'strü-mə\ *noun, plural* **stru·mae** \-(ˌ)mē, -ˌmī\ *or* **strumas** [Latin, swelling of the lymph glands] (1565)
: GOITER

**strum·pet** \'strəm-pət\ *noun* [Middle English] (14th century)
: PROSTITUTE 1a

**strung** \'strəŋ\ *past and past participle of* STRING

**strung out** *adjective* (circa 1959)
**1** : physically debilitated (as from long-term drug addiction)

**2 :** addicted to a drug
**3 :** intoxicated or stupefied from drug use
**strunt** \'strənt\ *intransitive verb* [by alteration] (1786)
*Scottish* **:** STRUT
¹**strut** \'strət\ *verb* **strut·ted; strut·ting** [Middle English *strouten*, from Old English *strūtian* to exert oneself; akin to Middle High German *strozzen* to be swollen] (13th century)
*intransitive verb*
**1 :** to become turgid **:** SWELL
**2 a :** to walk with a proud gait **b :** to walk with a pompous and affected air
*transitive verb*
**:** to parade (as clothes) with a show of pride
— **strut·ter** *noun*
— **strut one's stuff :** to display one's best work **:** SHOW OFF
²**strut** *noun* (1587)
**1 :** a structural piece designed to resist pressure in the direction of its length
**2 :** a pompous step or walk
**3 :** arrogant behavior **:** SWAGGER
³**strut** *transitive verb* **strut·ted; strut·ting** (circa 1828)
**:** to provide, stiffen, support, or hold apart with or as if with a strut
**stru·thi·ous** \'strü-thē-əs, -thē-\ *adjective* [Late Latin *struthio* ostrich, irregular from Greek *strouthos*] (1773)
**:** of or relating to the ostriches and related birds
**strych·nine** \'strik-ˌnīn, -nən, -ˌnēn\ *noun* [French, from New Latin *Strychnos*, from Latin, nightshade, from Greek] (1819)
**:** a bitter poisonous alkaloid $C_{21}H_{22}N_2O_2$ that is obtained from nux vomica and related plants (genus *Strychnos*) and is used as a poison (as for rodents) and medicinally as a stimulant to the central nervous system
**Stu·art** \'stü-ərt, 'styü-; 'st(y)ü(-ə)rt\ *adjective* [Robert *Stewart* (Robert II of Scotland) (died 1390)] (1873)
**:** of or relating to the Scottish royal house to which belonged the rulers of Scotland from 1371 to 1603 and of Great Britain from 1603 to 1649 and from 1660 to 1714
— **Stuart** *noun*
¹**stub** \'stəb\ *noun* [Middle English *stubb*, from Old English *stybb;* akin to Old Norse *stūfr* stump, Greek *stypos* stem, *typtein* to beat — more at TYPE] (before 12th century)
**1 a :** STUMP 2 **b :** a short piece remaining on a stem or trunk where a branch has been lost
**2 :** something made or worn to a short or blunt shape; *especially* **:** a pen with a short blunt nib
**3 :** a short blunt part left after a larger part has been broken off or used up ⟨pencil *stub*⟩
**4 :** something cut short or stunted
**5 a :** a small part of a leaf (as of a checkbook) attached to the backbone for memoranda of the contents of the part torn away **b :** the part of a ticket returned to the user
²**stub** *transitive verb* **stubbed; stub·bing** (15th century)
**1 a :** to grub up by the roots **b :** to clear (land) by grubbing out rooted growth **c :** to hew or cut down (a tree) close to the ground
**2 :** to extinguish (as a cigarette) by crushing
**3 :** to strike (one's foot or toe) against an object
**stub·ble** \'stə-bəl\ *noun, often attributive* [Middle English *stuble*, from Old French *estuble*, from Latin *stupula* stalk, straw, alteration of *stipula* — more at STIPULE] (14th century)
**1 :** the basal part of herbaceous plants and especially cereal grasses remaining attached to the soil after harvest
**2 :** a rough surface or growth resembling stubble; *especially* **:** a short growth of beard
— **stub·bled** \-bəld\ *adjective*
— **stub·bly** \-b(ə-)lē\ *adjective*
**stubble mulch** *noun* (1942)

**:** a lightly tilled mulch of plant residue used to prevent erosion, conserve moisture, and add organic matter to the soil
**stub·born** \'stə-bərn\ *adjective* [Middle English *stuborn*] (14th century)
**1 a** (1) **:** unreasonably or perversely unyielding **:** MULISH (2) **:** justifiably unyielding **:** RESOLUTE **b :** suggestive or typical of a strong stubborn nature ⟨a *stubborn* jaw⟩
**2 :** performed or carried on in an unyielding, obstinate, or persistent manner ⟨*stubborn* effort⟩
**3 :** difficult to handle, manage, or treat ⟨a *stubborn* cold⟩
**4 :** LASTING ⟨*stubborn* facts⟩
*synonym* see OBSTINATE
— **stub·born·ly** *adverb*
— **stub·born·ness** \-bər(n)-nəs\ *noun*
**stub·by** \'stə-bē\ *adjective* **stub·bi·er; -est** (15th century)
**1 :** abounding with stubs
**2 a :** resembling a stub **:** being short and thick ⟨*stubby* fingers⟩ **b :** being short and thickset **:** SQUAT **c :** being short, broad, or blunt (as from use or wear)
**stuc·co** \'stə-(ˌ)kō\ *noun, plural* **stuccos** *or* **stuccoes** [Italian, of Germanic origin; akin to Old High German *stucki* piece, crust, Old English *stocc* stock — more at STOCK] (1598)
**1 a :** a fine plaster used in decoration and ornamentation (as of interior walls) **b :** a material usually made of portland cement, sand, and a small percentage of lime and applied in a plastic state to form a hard covering for exterior walls
**2 :** STUCCOWORK
— **stuc·coed** \-(ˌ)kōd\ *adjective*
**stuc·co·work** \'stə-kō-ˌwərk\ *noun* (1686)
**:** work done in stucco
**stuck** *past and past participle of* STICK
**stuck–up** \'stək-'əp\ *adjective* (1829)
**:** superciliously self-important **:** CONCEITED
¹**stud** \'stəd\ *noun, often attributive* [Middle English *stod*, from Old English *stōd;* akin to Old Church Slavonic *stado* flock and probably to Old High German *stān* to stand — more at STAND] (before 12th century)
**1 a :** a group of animals and especially horses kept primarily for breeding **b :** a place (as a farm) where a stud is kept
**2 :** STUDHORSE; *broadly* **:** a male animal kept for breeding
**3 a :** a young man **:** GUY; *especially* **:** one who is virile and promiscuous **b :** a tough person **c :** HUNK 2
— **at stud :** for breeding as a stud ⟨retired racehorses *at stud*⟩
²**stud** *noun* [Middle English *stode*, from Old English *studu;* akin to Middle High German *stud* prop, Old English *stōw* place — more at STOW] (before 12th century)
**1 a :** one of the smaller uprights in the framing of the walls of a building to which sheathing, paneling, or laths are fastened **:** SCANTLING **b :** height from floor to ceiling
**2 a :** a boss, rivet, or nail with a large head used (as on a shield or belt) for ornament or protection **b :** a solid button with a shank or eye on the back inserted (as through an eyelet in a garment) as a fastener or ornament **c :** a small often round earring made for a pierced ear
**3 a :** any of various infixed pieces (as a rod or pin) projecting from a machine and serving chiefly as a support or axis **b :** one of the metal cleats inserted in a snow tire to increase traction
³**stud** *transitive verb* **stud·ded; stud·ding** (circa 1506)
**1 :** to furnish (as a building or wall) with studs
**2 :** to adorn, cover, or protect with studs
**3 :** to set, mark, or decorate conspicuously often at intervals ⟨a sky *studded* with stars⟩ ⟨a career *studded* with honors⟩
**stud·book** \'stəd-ˌbuk\ *noun* (1803)

**:** an official record (as in a book) of the pedigree of purebred animals (as horses or dogs)
**stud·ding** \'stə-diŋ\ *noun* (1588)
**:** the studs of a building or wall
**stud·ding sail** \'stə-diŋ-ˌsāl, 'stən(t)-səl\ *noun* [origin unknown] (1549)
**:** a light sail set at the side of a principal square sail of a ship in free winds
**stu·dent** \'stü-d²nt, 'styü-, *chiefly Southern* -dənt\ *noun, often attributive* [Middle English, from Latin *student-, studens*, from present participle of *studēre* to study — more at STUDY] (14th century)
**1 :** SCHOLAR, LEARNER; *especially* **:** one who attends a school
**2 :** one who studies **:** an attentive and systematic observer
**student body** *noun* (1906)
**:** the students at an educational institution
**student government** *noun* (1948)
**:** the organization and management of student life by various student organizations
**student lamp** *noun* (1873)
**:** a desk reading lamp with a tubular shaft, one or two arms for a shaded light, and originally an oil reservoir
**stu·dent·ship** \'stü-d²nt-ˌship, 'styü-, -dənt-\ *noun* (circa 1782)
**1** *British* **:** a grant for university study
**2 :** the state of being a student
**stu·dent's t distribution** \'stü-d²n(t)s-, -dən(t)s-\ *noun, often S capitalized* [*Student*, pen name of W. S. Gossett (died 1937) British statistician] (1929)
**:** T DISTRIBUTION
**Student's t–test** *noun* (1935)
**:** T-TEST
**student teacher** *noun* (1909)
**:** a student who is engaged in practice teaching
**student teaching** *noun* (1929)
**:** PRACTICE TEACHING
**student union** *noun* (1949)
**:** a building on a college campus that is devoted to student activities and that usually contains lounges, auditoriums, offices, and game rooms
**stud·horse** \'stəd-ˌhȯrs\ *noun* (before 12th century)
**:** a stallion kept especially for breeding
**stud·ied** \'stə-dēd\ *adjective* (15th century)
**1 :** carefully considered or prepared **:** THOUGHTFUL
**2 :** KNOWLEDGEABLE, LEARNED
**3 :** produced or marked by conscious design or premeditation **:** CALCULATED ⟨*studied* indifference⟩
— **stud·ied·ly** *adverb*
— **stud·ied·ness** *noun*
**stu·dio** \'stü-dē-(ˌ)ō, 'styü-\ *noun, plural* **-dios** [Italian, literally, study, from Latin *studium*] (1819)
**1 a :** the working place of a painter, sculptor, or photographer **b :** a place for the study of an art (as dancing, singing, or acting)
**2 :** a place where motion pictures are made
**3 :** a place maintained and equipped for the transmission of radio or television programs
**4 :** a place where audio recordings are made
**5 :** STUDIO APARTMENT
**studio apartment** *noun* (1903)
**:** a small apartment consisting typically of a main room, kitchenette, and bathroom
**studio couch** *noun* (1931)
**:** an upholstered usually backless couch that can be made to serve as a double bed by sliding from underneath it the frame of a single cot

---

\ə\ abut \ᵊ\ kitten \ər\ further \a\ ash \ā\ ace
\ä\ mop, mar \aù\ out \ch\ chin \e\ bet \ē\ easy
\g\ go \i\ hit \ī\ ice \j\ job \ŋ\ sing \ō\ go
\ȯ\ law \ȯi\ boy \th\ thin \t͟h\ the \ü\ loot \ù\ foot
\y\ yet \zh\ vision *see also* Guide to Pronunciation

**stu·di·ous** \'stü-dē-əs, 'styü-\ *adjective* (14th century)
**1 :** assiduous in the pursuit of learning
**2 a :** of, relating to, or concerned with study **b** : favorable to study ⟨a *studious* environment⟩
**3 a :** diligent or earnest in intent ⟨made a *studious* effort⟩ **b** : marked by or suggesting purposefulness or diligence ⟨a *studious* expression on his face⟩ **c** : deliberately or consciously planned ⟨spoke with a *studious* accent⟩
— **stu·di·ous·ly** *adverb*
— **stu·di·ous·ness** *noun*
**stud·ly** \'stəd-lē\ *adjective* [¹stud] (1972) *slang* : HUNKY
**stud poker** *noun* [¹stud] (1864)
: poker in which each player is dealt the first card facedown and the other four cards faceup with a round of betting taking place after each of the last four rounds of dealing
**¹study** \'stə-dē\ *noun, plural* **stud·ies** [Middle English *studie*, from Old French *estudie*, from Latin *studium*, from *studēre* to devote oneself, study; probably akin to Latin *tundere* to beat — more at CONTUSION] (14th century)
**1 :** a state of contemplation : REVERIE
**2 a :** application of the mental faculties to the acquisition of knowledge ⟨years of *study*⟩ **b** : such application in a particular field or to a specific subject ⟨the *study* of Latin⟩ **c** : careful or extended consideration ⟨the proposal is under *study*⟩ **d** (1) : a careful examination or analysis of a phenomenon, development, or question (2) : the published report of such a study
**3 :** a building or room devoted to study or literary pursuits
**4 :** PURPOSE, INTENT
**5 a :** a branch or department of learning : SUBJECT **b** : the activity or work of a student ⟨returning to her *studies* after vacation⟩ **c** : an object of study or deliberation ⟨every gesture a careful *study* —Marcia Davenport⟩ **d** : something attracting close attention or examination
**6 :** a person who learns or memorizes something (as a part in a play) — usually used with a qualifying adjective ⟨he's a fast *study*⟩
**7 :** a literary or artistic production intended as a preliminary outline, an experimental interpretation, or an exploratory analysis of specific features or characteristics
**8 :** a musical composition for the practice of a point of technique
**²study** *verb* **stud·ied; study·ing** (14th century)
*intransitive verb*
**1 a :** to engage in study **b** : to undertake formal study of a subject
**2** *dialect* : MEDITATE, REFLECT
**3 :** ENDEAVOR, TRY
*transitive verb*
**1 :** to read in detail especially with the intention of learning
**2 :** to engage in the study of ⟨*study* biology⟩
**3 :** PLOT, DESIGN
**4 :** to consider attentively or in detail
*synonym* see CONSIDER
— **studi·er** \'stə-dē-ər\ *noun*
**study hall** *noun* (1846)
**1 :** a room in a school set aside for study
**2 :** a period in a student's day set aside for study and homework
**¹stuff** \'stəf\ *noun* [Middle English, from Middle French *estoffe*, from Old French, from *estoffer* to equip, stock, of Germanic origin; akin to Old High German *stopfōn* to stop up, from (assumed) Vulgar Latin *stuppare* — more at STOP] (14th century)
**1 :** materials, supplies, or equipment used in various activities: as *obsolete* : military baggage **b** : PERSONAL PROPERTY
**2 :** material to be manufactured, wrought, or used in construction ⟨clear half-inch pine *stuff* —Emily Holt⟩

**3 :** a finished textile suitable for clothing; especially : wool or worsted material
**4 a :** literary or artistic production **b** : writing, discourse, talk, or ideas of little value : TRASH
**5 a :** an unspecified material substance or aggregate of matter ⟨volcanic rock is curious *stuff*⟩ **b** : something (as a drug or food) consumed or introduced into the body by humans **c** : a matter to be considered ⟨the truth was heady *stuff*⟩ ⟨long-term policy *stuff*⟩ **d** : a group or scattering of miscellaneous objects or articles ⟨pick that *stuff* up off the floor⟩; *also* : nonphysical miscellaneous material
**6 a :** fundamental material : SUBSTANCE ⟨*stuff* of greatness⟩ **b** : subject matter ⟨a teacher who knows her *stuff*⟩
**7 :** special knowledge or capability ⟨showing their *stuff*⟩
**8 a :** spin imparted to a thrown or hit ball to make it curve or change course **b** : the movement of a baseball pitch out of its apparent line of flight : the liveliness of a pitch ⟨greatest pitcher of my time . . . had tremendous *stuff* —Ted Williams⟩
**9 :** DUNK SHOT
— **stuff·less** *adjective*
**²stuff** *transitive verb* (15th century)
**1 a :** to fill by packing things in : CRAM ⟨the boy *stuffed* his pockets with candy⟩ **b** : to fill to satiety : SURFEIT ⟨*stuffed* themselves with turkey⟩ **c** : to prepare (meat or vegetables) by filling or lining with a stuffing **d** : to fill (as a cushion) with a soft material **e** : to fill out the skin of (an animal) for mounting
**2 a :** to fill by intellectual effort ⟨*stuffing* their heads with facts⟩ **b** : to pack full of something immaterial ⟨a book *stuffed* with information⟩
**3 :** to fill or block up (as nasal passages)
**4 a :** to cause to enter or fill : THRUST ⟨*stuffed* a lot of clothing into a laundry bag⟩ **b** : to put (as a ball or puck) into a goal forcefully from close range
**5** — used in the imperative to express contempt ⟨if they didn't like it, *stuff* 'em —Eric Clapton⟩; often used in the phrases *stuff it* and *get stuffed*
**6 :** to stop abruptly in a football game ⟨*stuff* the run⟩
**stuffed shirt** *noun* (1913)
: a smug, conceited, and usually pompous person often with an inflexibly conservative or reactionary attitude
**stuff·er** \'stə-fər\ *noun* (1611)
**1 :** one that stuffs
**2 :** an enclosure (as a leaflet) inserted in an envelope in addition to a bill, statement, or notice
**3 :** a series of extra threads or yarn running lengthwise in a fabric to add weight and bulk and to form a backing especially for carpets
**stuff·ing** \'stə-fiŋ\ *noun* (15th century)
: material used to stuff; *especially* : a seasoned mixture used to stuff food (as meat, vegetables, or eggs)
**stuffing box** *noun* (1798)
: a device that prevents leakage along a moving part (as a connecting rod) passing through a hole in a vessel (as a cylinder) containing steam, water, or oil and that consists of a box or chamber made by enlarging the hole and a gland to compress the contained packing
**stuffy** \'stə-fē\ *adjective* **stuff·i·er; -est** (1813)
**1 :** lacking in vitality or interest : STODGY, DULL
**2 :** ILL-NATURED, ILL-HUMORED
**3 a :** oppressive to the breathing : CLOSE **b** : stuffed up ⟨a *stuffy* nose⟩
**4 :** narrowly inflexible in standards of conduct : SELF-RIGHTEOUS
— **stuff·i·ly** \'stə-fə-lē\ *adverb*
— **stuff·i·ness** \'stə-fē-nəs\ *noun*
**stul·ti·fy** \'stəl-tə-ˌfī\ *transitive verb* **-fied;**

**-fy·ing** [Late Latin *stultificare* to make foolish, from Latin *stultus* foolish; akin to Latin *stolidus* stolid] (1766)
**1 :** to allege or prove to be of unsound mind and hence not responsible
**2 :** to cause to appear or be stupid, foolish, or absurdly illogical
**3 a :** to impair, invalidate, or make ineffective : NEGATE **b** : to have a dulling or inhibiting effect on
— **stul·ti·fi·ca·tion** \ˌstəl-tə-fə-ˈkā-shən\ *noun*
**¹stum·ble** \'stəm-bəl\ *verb* **stum·bled; stum·bling** \-b(ə-)liŋ\ [Middle English, probably of Scandinavian origin; akin to Norwegian dialect *stumle* to stumble; akin to Old Norse *stemma* to hinder — more at STEM] (14th century)
*intransitive verb*
**1 a :** to fall into sin or waywardness **b** : to make an error : BLUNDER **c** : to come to an obstacle to belief
**2 :** to trip in walking or running
**3 a :** to walk unsteadily or clumsily **b** : to speak or act in a hesitant or faltering manner
**4 a :** to come unexpectedly or by chance ⟨*stumble* onto the truth⟩ **b** : to fall or move carelessly
*transitive verb*
**1 :** to cause to stumble : TRIP
**2 :** BEWILDER, CONFOUND
— **stum·bler** \-b(ə-)lər\ *noun*
— **stum·bling·ly** \-b(ə-)liŋ-lē\ *adverb*
**²stumble** *noun* (1547)
: an act or instance of stumbling
**stum·ble·bum** \'stəm-bəl-ˌbəm\ *noun* (1932)
: a clumsy or inept person; *especially* : an inept boxer
**stum·bling block** \'stəm-bliŋ-\ *noun* (1588)
**1 :** an obstacle to progress
**2 :** an impediment to belief or understanding : PERPLEXITY
**¹stump** \'stəmp\ *noun* [Middle English *stumpe;* akin to Old High German *stumpf* stump and perhaps to Middle English *stampen* to stamp] (14th century)
**1 a :** the basal portion of a bodily part remaining after the rest is removed **b** : a rudimentary or vestigial bodily part
**2 :** the part of a plant and especially a tree remaining attached to the root after the trunk is cut
**3 :** a remaining part : STUB
**4 :** one of the pointed rods stuck in the ground to form a cricket wicket
**5 :** a place or occasion for public speaking (as for a cause or candidate); *also* : the circuit followed by a maker of such speeches — used especially in the phrase *on the stump*
**²stump** (1596)
*transitive verb*
**1 :** to reduce to a stump : TRIM
**2 a :** DARE, CHALLENGE **b** : to frustrate the progress or efforts of : BAFFLE
**3 :** to clear (land) of stumps
**4 :** to travel over (a region) making political speeches or supporting a cause
**5 a :** to walk over heavily or clumsily **b** : STUB 3
*intransitive verb*
**1 :** to walk heavily or clumsily
**2 :** to go about making political speeches or supporting a cause
— **stump·er** *noun*
**³stump** *noun* [French or Flemish; French *estompe*, from Flemish *stomp*, literally, stub, from Middle Dutch; akin to Old High German *stumpf* stump] (1778)
: a short thick roll of leather, felt, or paper usually pointed at both ends and used for shading or blending a drawing in crayon, pencil, charcoal, pastel, or chalk
**⁴stump** *transitive verb* (1807)
: to tone or treat (a drawing) with a stump

**stump·age** \'stəm-pij\ *noun* (1835)
**1** : the value of standing timber
**2** : uncut marketable timber; *also* : the right to cut it

**stump–tailed macaque** \'stəmp-'tāl(d)-\ *noun* (1938)
: a dark reddish brown naked-faced short-tailed macaque (*Macaca arctoides* synonym *M. speciosa*) that is found in eastern Asia — called also *stump-tailed monkey*

**stump work** *noun* (1904)
: embroidery with intricate padded designs or scenes in high relief popular especially in the 17th century

**stumpy** \'stəm-pē\ *adjective* (1600)
**1** : being short and thick : STUBBY
**2** : full of stumps

**¹stun** \'stən\ *transitive verb* **stunned; stun·ning** [Middle English, modification of Middle French *estoner* — more at ASTONISH] (14th century)
**1** : to make senseless, groggy, or dizzy by or as if by a blow : DAZE
**2** : to shock with noise
**3** : to overcome especially with paralyzing astonishment or disbelief

**²stun** *noun* (1727)
: the effect of something that stuns : SHOCK

**stung** *past and past participle of* STING

**stun gun** *noun* (1967)
: a weapon designed to stun or immobilize (as by electric shock) rather than kill or injure the one affected

**stunk** *past and past participle of* STINK

**stun·ner** \'stə-nər\ *noun* (1829)
: one that stuns or is stunning

**stun·ning** \'stə-niŋ\ *adjective* (1667)
**1** : causing astonishment or disbelief
**2** : strikingly impressive especially in beauty or excellence
— **stun·ning·ly** \-niŋ-lē\ *adverb*

**¹stunt** \'stənt\ *transitive verb* [English dialect *stunt* stubborn, stunted, abrupt, probably of Scandinavian origin; akin to Old Norse *stuttr* scant — more at STINT] (1659)
: to hinder the normal growth, development, or progress of
— **stunt·ed·ness** *noun*

**²stunt** *noun* (1725)
**1** : one (as an animal) that is stunted
**2** : a check in growth
**3** : a plant disease in which dwarfing occurs

**³stunt** *noun* [origin unknown] (1878)
**1** : an unusual or difficult feat requiring great skill or daring; *especially* : one performed or undertaken chiefly to gain attention or publicity
**2** : a shifting or switching of the positions by defensive players at the line of scrimmage in football to disrupt the opponent's blocking efforts

**⁴stunt** *intransitive verb* (1917)
: to perform or engage in a stunt

**stunt·man** \'stənt-,man\ *noun* (1927)
: a man who performs stunts; *especially* : one who doubles for an actor during the filming of stunts and dangerous scenes

**stunt·wom·an** \-,wu̇-mən\ *noun* (1948)
: a woman who doubles for an actress during the filming of stunts and dangerous scenes

**stu·pa** \'stü-pə\ *noun* [Sanskrit *stūpa*] (1876)
: a usually dome-shaped structure (as a mound) serving as a Buddhist shrine

stupa

**¹stupe** \'stüp, 'styüp\ *noun* [Middle English, from Latin *stuppa* coarse part of flax, tow, from Greek *styppē*] (14th century)
: a hot wet often medicated cloth applied externally (as to stimulate circulation)

**²stupe** *noun* [short for *stupid*] (1762)
: a stupid person : DOLT

**stu·pe·fac·tion** \,stü-pə-'fak-shən, ,styü-\ *noun* [Middle English *stupefaccioun*, from Medieval Latin *stupefaction-, stupefactio*, from Latin *stupefacere*] (15th century)
: the act of stupefying : the state of being stupefied

**stu·pe·fy** \'stü-pə-,fī, 'styü-\ *transitive verb* **-fied; -fy·ing** [Middle English *stupifien*, from Middle French *stupefier*, modification of Latin *stupefacere*, from *stupēre* to be astonished + *facere* to make, do — more at DO] (15th century)
**1** : to make stupid, groggy, or insensible
**2** : ASTONISH, ASTOUND
— **stu·pe·fy·ing·ly** \-iŋ-lē\ *adverb*

**stu·pen·dous** \stu̇-'pen-dəs, styu̇-\ *adjective* [Latin *stupendus*, gerundive of *stupēre*] (1666)
**1** : causing astonishment or wonder : AWESOME, MARVELOUS
**2** : of amazing size or greatness : TREMENDOUS
*synonym* see MONSTROUS
— **stu·pen·dous·ly** *adverb*
— **stu·pen·dous·ness** *noun*

**¹stu·pid** \'stü-pəd, 'styü-\ *adjective* [Middle French *stupide*, from Latin *stupidus*, from *stupēre* to be numb, be astonished — more at TYPE] (1541)
**1 a** : slow of mind : OBTUSE **b** : given to unintelligent decisions or acts : acting in an unintelligent or careless manner **c** : lacking intelligence or reason : BRUTISH
**2** : dulled in feeling or sensation : TORPID ⟨still *stupid* from the sedative⟩
**3** : marked by or resulting from unreasoned thinking or acting : SENSELESS
**4 a** : lacking interest or point **b** : VEXATIOUS, EXASPERATING ⟨this *stupid* flashlight won't work⟩ ☆
— **stu·pid·ly** *adverb*
— **stu·pid·ness** *noun*

**²stupid** *noun* (1712)
: a stupid person

**stu·pid·i·ty** \stu̇-'pi-də-tē, styu̇-\ *noun, plural* **-ties** (1541)
**1** : the quality or state of being stupid
**2** : a stupid idea or act

**stu·por** \'stü-pər, 'styü-\ *noun* [Middle English, from Latin, from *stupēre*] (14th century)
**1** : a condition of greatly dulled or completely suspended sense or sensibility ⟨drunken *stupor*⟩
**2** : a state of extreme apathy or torpor resulting often from stress or shock : DAZE
*synonym* see LETHARGY

**stu·por·ous** \'stü-p(ə-)rəs, 'styü-\ *adjective* (1892)
: marked or affected by or as if by stupor

**stur·dy** \'stər-dē\ *adjective* **stur·di·er; -est** [Middle English, brave, stubborn, from Middle French *estourdi* stunned, from past participle of *estourdir* to stun, from (assumed) Vulgar Latin *exturdire*, from Latin *ex-* + (assumed) Vulgar Latin *turdus* simpleton, from Latin, thrush — more at THRUSH] (14th century)
**1 a** : firmly built or constituted : STOUT **b** : HARDY **c** : sound in design or execution : SUBSTANTIAL
**2 a** : marked by or reflecting physical strength or vigor **b** : FIRM, RESOLUTE **c** : RUGGED, STABLE ◆
*synonym* see STRONG
— **stur·di·ly** \'stər-d°l-ē\ *adverb*
— **stur·di·ness** \'stər-dē-nəs\ *noun*

**stur·geon** \'stər-jən\ *noun* [Middle English, from Middle French *estourjon*, of Germanic origin; akin to Old English *styria* sturgeon] (13th century)
: any of a family (Acipenseridae) of usually large elongate anadromous or freshwater bony fishes which are widely distributed in the

north temperate zone and whose roe is made into caviar

**Sturm und Drang** \,shtu̇rm-u̇nt-'dräŋ, ,stu̇r-, -ənt-\ *noun* [German, literally, storm and stress, from *Sturm und Drang* (1776), drama by Friedrich von Klinger (died 1831) German novelist and dramatist] (1845)
**1** : a late 18th century German literary movement characterized by works containing rousing action and high emotionalism that often deal with the individual's revolt against society
**2** : TURMOIL

**sturt** \'stərt\ *noun* [Middle English, contention, alteration of *strut*; akin to Old English *strūtian* to exert oneself — more at STRUT] (14th century)
*chiefly Scottish* : CONTENTION

**¹stut·ter** \'stə-tər\ *verb* [frequentative of English dialect *stut* to stutter, from Middle English *stutten*; akin to Dutch *stotteren* to stutter, Gothic *stautan* to strike — more at CONTUSION] (circa 1570)
*intransitive verb*
**1** : to speak with involuntary disruption or blocking of speech (as by spasmodic repetition or prolongation of vocal sounds)
**2** : to move or act in a halting or spasmodic

---

☆ **SYNONYMS**
**Stupid, dull, dense, crass, dumb** mean lacking in power to absorb ideas or impressions. STUPID implies a slow-witted or dazed state of mind that may be either congenital or temporary ⟨*stupid* students just keeping the seats warm⟩ ⟨*stupid* with drink⟩. DULL suggests a slow or sluggish mind such as results from disease, depression, or shock ⟨monotonous work that leaves the mind *dull*⟩. DENSE implies a thickheaded imperviousness to ideas ⟨too *dense* to take a hint⟩. CRASS suggests a grossness of mind precluding discrimination or delicacy ⟨a *crass*, materialistic people⟩. DUMB applies to an exasperating obtuseness or lack of comprehension ⟨too *dumb* to figure out what's going on⟩.

---

◇ **WORD HISTORY**
**sturdy** The usual modern meanings of *sturdy*, such as "firmly constituted" or "marked by physical strength or vigor," lie at the end of a long historical trail. Though these senses were already present in the English of Chaucer, Middle English also shows a wide range of other meanings now obsolete, such as "bold, valiant," "violent, furious," "severe, harsh," and "refractory, obstinate." (The latter sense long survived in the collocation *sturdy beggar*, referring to someone who lived by begging but who was able-bodied and hard to manage.) The source of *sturdy* was Old French *estourdi*, the past participle of *estourdir* "to stun, daze, befuddle." Though *estourdi* usually meant "dazed, stunned," it also is attested in the senses "giddy" or "foolish," and the association of giddiness with recklessness and recklessness with valor presumably led to the Middle English meaning "bold, valiant." Old French *estourdir*, in turn, most likely developed from an unattested spoken Latin verb *exturdire*, a derivative of Latin *turdus* "thrush." The thrush in folk belief was considered giddy or foolish, perhaps from the notion that it gorged itself on overripe and hence slightly alcoholic grapes until it became dizzy.

---

\ə\ abut \ᵊ\ kitten \ər\ **further** \a\ ash \ā\ ace
\ä\ mop, mar \au̇\ **out** \ch\ chin \e\ bet \ē\ **easy**
\g\ go \i\ hit \ī\ ice \j\ job \ŋ\ sing \ō\ go
\ȯ\ law \ȯi\ boy \th\ thin \t̲h̲\ the \ü\ loot \u̇\ foot
\y\ yet \zh\ vision *see also* Guide to Pronunciation

manner ⟨the old jalopy bucks and *stutters* up-hill —William Cleary⟩
*transitive verb*
: to say, speak, or sound with or as if with a stutter
— **stut·ter·er** \-tər-ər\ *noun*

**²stutter** *noun* (circa 1847)
**1** : an act or instance of stuttering
**2** : a speech disorder involving stuttering accompanied by fear and anxiety

**¹sty** \'stī\ *noun, plural* **sties** *also* **styes** [Middle English, from Old English *stig;* akin to Old Norse *-stī* sty] (before 12th century)
**1** : a pen or enclosed housing for swine
**2** : an unkempt filthy place ⟨this house is a *sty*⟩

**²sty** *verb* **stied** *or* **styed; sty·ing** (before 12th century)
*transitive verb*
: to lodge or keep in a sty
*intransitive verb*
: to live in a sty

**³sty** *or* **stye** \'stī\ *noun, plural* **sties** *or* **styes** [short for obsolete English *styan,* from (assumed) Middle English, alteration of Old English *stīgend,* from *stīgan* to go up, rise — more at STAIR] (1617)
: an inflamed swelling of a sebaceous gland at the margin of an eyelid

**sty·gian** \'sti-j(ē-)ən\ *adjective, often capitalized* [Latin *stygius,* from Greek *stygios,* from *Styg-, Styx* Styx] (1566)
**1** : of or relating to the river Styx
**2** : extremely dark, gloomy, or forbidding

**styl-** *or* **styli-** *or* **stylo-** *combining form* [Latin *stilus* spike, stem — more at STYLE]
: style ⟨styloid process⟨*stylo*podium⟩ ⟨*stylog*raphy⟩

**sty·lar** \'stī-lər, -,lär\ *adjective* [¹*style*] (circa 1928)
: of or relating to the style of a plant ovary

**¹style** \'stī(ə)l\ *noun* [Middle English *stile, style,* from Latin *stilus* spike, stem, stylus, style of writing; perhaps akin to Latin *instigare* to goad — more at STICK] (14th century)
**1** : DESIGNATION, TITLE
**2 a** : a distinctive manner of expression (as in writing or speech) ⟨writes with more attention to *style* than to content⟩ ⟨the flowery *style* of 18th century prose⟩ **b** : a distinctive manner or custom of behaving or conducting oneself ⟨the formal *style* of the court⟩ ⟨his *style* is abrasive⟩; *also* : a particular mode of living ⟨in high *style*⟩ **c** : a particular manner or technique by which something is done, created, or performed ⟨a unique *style* of horseback riding⟩ ⟨the classical *style* of dance⟩
**3 a** : STYLUS **b** : GNOMON 1b **c** : a filiform prolongation of a plant ovary bearing a stigma at its apex — see FLOWER illustration **d** : a slender elongated process (as a bristle) on an animal
**4** : a distinctive quality, form, or type of something ⟨a new dress *style*⟩ ⟨the Greek *style* of architecture⟩
**5 a** : the state of being popular : FASHION ⟨clothes that are always in *style*⟩ **b** : fashionable elegance **c** : beauty, grace, or ease of manner or technique ⟨an awkward moment she handled with *style*⟩
**6** : a convention with respect to spelling, punctuation, capitalization, and typographic arrangement and display followed in writing or printing
*synonym* see FASHION
— **style·less** \'stī(ə)l-ləs\ *adjective*
— **style·less·ness** *noun*

**²style** *transitive verb* **styled; styl·ing** (circa 1580)
**1** : to call or designate by an identifying term : NAME
**2 a** : to give a particular style to **b** : to design, make, or arrange in accord with the prevailing mode

— **styl·er** *noun*
**-style** *adjective or adverb combining form*
: being in the style of ⟨a Beaujolais-*style* wine⟩
**style·book** *noun* (1708)
: a book explaining, describing, or illustrating a prevailing, accepted, or authorized style
**sty·let** \'stī-,let, 'stī-lət\ *noun* [French, from Middle French *stilet* stiletto, from Old Italian *stiletto* — more at STILETTO] (1697)
**1 a** : a slender surgical probe **b** : a thin wire inserted into a catheter to maintain rigidity or into a hollow needle to maintain patency **c** : a pointed instrument (as for graving)
**2** : a relatively rigid elongated organ or appendage (as a piercing mouthpart) of an animal
**3** : STILETTO
**sty·li·form** \'stī-lə-,fòrm\ *adjective* [New Latin *stiliformis,* from Latin *stilus* + *-formis* -form] (1578)
: resembling a style : bristle-shaped ⟨a *styliform* copulatory organ⟩
**styl·ing** \'stī-liŋ\ *noun* (1928)
: the way in which something is styled
**styl·ise** *British variant of* STYLIZE
**styl·ish** \'stī-lish\ *adjective* (1785)
: having style; *specifically* : conforming to current fashion
— **styl·ish·ly** *adverb*
— **styl·ish·ness** *noun*
**styl·ist** \'stī-list\ *noun* (1795)
**1 a** : a master or model of style; *especially* : a writer or speaker who is eminent in matters of style **b** : one (as a writer or singer) noted for a distinctive style
**2 a** : one who develops, designs, or advises on styles **b** : HAIRSTYLIST
**sty·lis·tic** \stī-'lis-tik\ *adjective* (1860)
: of or relating especially to literary or artistic style
— **sty·lis·ti·cal·ly** \-ti-k(ə-)lē\ *adverb*
**sty·lis·tics** \stī-'lis-tiks\ *noun plural but singular or plural in construction* (circa 1883)
**1** : an aspect of literary study that emphasizes the analysis of various elements of style (as metaphor and diction)
**2** : the study of the devices in a language that produce expressive value
**sty·lite** \'stī-,līt\ *noun* [Late Greek *stylitēs,* from Greek *stylos* pillar — more at STEER] (circa 1638)
: a Christian ascetic living atop a pillar
— **sty·lit·ic** \stī-'li-tik\ *adjective*
**styl·ize** \'stī(-ə)-,līz\ *transitive verb* **styl·ized; styl·iz·ing** (1898)
: to conform to a conventional style; *specifically* : to represent or design according to a style or stylistic pattern rather than according to nature or tradition
— **styl·i·za·tion** \,stī-lə-'zā-shən\ *noun*
**sty·lo·bate** \'stī-lə-,bāt\ *noun* [Latin *stylobates,* from Greek, from *stylobatēs,* from *stylos* pillar + *bainein* to walk, go — more at COME] (1694)
: a continuous flat coping or pavement supporting a row of architectural columns
**sty·log·ra·phy** \stī-'lä-grə-fē\ *noun* (circa 1840)
: a mode of writing or tracing lines by means of a style or similar instrument
**sty·loid** \'stī(-ə)-,lòid\ *adjective* (1709)
: resembling a style : STYLIFORM — used especially of slender pointed skeletal processes (as on the ulna)
**sty·lo·po·di·um** \,stī-lə-'pō-dē-əm\ *noun, plural* **-dia** \-dē-ə\ [New Latin, from *styl-* + Greek *podion* small foot, base — more at PEW] (circa 1832)
: a disk-shaped or conical expansion at the base of the style in plants of the carrot family
**sty·lus** \'stī-ləs\ *noun, plural* **sty·li** \'stī-(ə)-,lī\ *also* **sty·lus·es** \'stī-lə-səz\ [Latin *stylus, stilus* spike, stylus — more at STYLE] (1807)

: an instrument for writing, marking, or incising: as **a** : an instrument used by the ancients in writing on clay or waxed tablets **b** : a hard-pointed pen-shaped instrument for marking on stencils used in a reproducing machine **c** (1) : NEEDLE 3c (2) : a cutting tool used to produce an original record groove during disc recording **d** : a pen-shaped pointing device used for entering positional information (as from a graphics tablet) into a computer
**sty·mie** \'stī-mē\ *transitive verb* **sty·mied; sty·mie·ing** [Scots *stimie, stymie* to obstruct a golf shot by interposition of the opponent's ball] (1902)
: to present an obstacle to : stand in the way of
**styp·tic** \'stip-tik\ *adjective* [Middle English *stiptik,* from Latin *stypticus,* from Greek *styptikos,* from *styphein* to contract] (14th century)
: tending to contract or bind : ASTRINGENT; *especially* : tending to check bleeding
— **styptic** *noun*
**styptic pencil** *noun* (1908)
: a stick of a medicated styptic substance for use especially in shaving to stop the bleeding from small cuts
**sty·rax** \'stī-,raks\ *noun* [Latin — more at STORAX] (1558)
: STORAX
**sty·rene** \'stī-,rēn\ *noun* [International Scientific Vocabulary, from Latin *styrax*] (1885)
: a fragrant liquid unsaturated hydrocarbon $C_8H_8$ used chiefly in making synthetic rubber, resins, and plastics and in improving drying oils; *also* : any of various synthetic plastics made from styrene by polymerization or copolymerization
**Sty·ro·foam** \'stī-rə-,fōm\ *trademark*
— used for an expanded rigid polystyrene plastic
**Styx** \'stiks\ *noun* [Latin *Styg-, Styx,* from Greek]
: the principal river of the underworld in Greek mythology
**su·able** \'sü-ə-bəl\ *adjective* (circa 1623)
: liable to be sued in court
— **su·abil·i·ty** \,sü-ə-'bi-lə-tē\ *noun*
— **su·ably** \-blē\ *adverb*
**sua·sion** \'swā-zhən\ *noun* [Middle English, from Latin *suasion-, suasio,* from *suadēre* to urge, persuade — more at SWEET] (14th century)
: the act of influencing or persuading
— **sua·sive** \'swā-siv, -ziv\ *adjective*
— **sua·sive·ly** *adverb*
— **sua·sive·ness** *noun*
**suave** \'swäv\ *adjective* **suav·er; -est** [Middle French, pleasant, sweet, from Latin *suavis* — more at SWEET] (1847)
**1** : smoothly though often superficially gracious and sophisticated
**2** : smooth in texture, performance, or style ☆
— **suave·ly** *adverb*
— **suave·ness** *noun*

---

☆ SYNONYMS
**Suave, urbane, diplomatic, bland, smooth, politic** mean pleasantly tactful and well-mannered. SUAVE suggests a specific ability to deal with others easily and without friction ⟨a *suave* public relations coordinator⟩. URBANE implies high cultivation and poise coming from wide social experience ⟨an *urbane* traveler⟩. DIPLOMATIC stresses an ability to deal with ticklish situations tactfully ⟨a *diplomatic* negotiator⟩. BLAND emphasizes mildness of manner and absence of irritating qualities ⟨a *bland* master of ceremonies⟩. SMOOTH suggests often a deliberately assumed suavity ⟨a *smooth* salesman⟩. POLITIC implies shrewd as well as tactful and suave handling of people ⟨a cunningly *politic* manager⟩.

— **sua·vi·ty** \\'swä-və-tē\ *noun*

¹**sub** \\'səb\ *noun* (1830)
: SUBSTITUTE

²**sub** *verb* **subbed; sub·bing** (1853)
*intransitive verb*
: to act as a substitute
*transitive verb*
**1** *British* : to read and edit as a copy editor
: SUBEDIT
**2** : SUBCONTRACT 1

³**sub** *noun* (1916)
: SUBMARINE

**sub-** *prefix* [Middle English, from Latin, under, below, secretly, from below, up, near, from *sub* under, close to — more at UP]
**1** : under : beneath : below ⟨*sub*soil⟩ ⟨*sub*aqueous⟩
**2 a** : subordinate : secondary : next lower than or inferior to ⟨*sub*station⟩ ⟨*sub*editor⟩ **b** : subordinate portion of : subdivision of ⟨*sub*committee⟩ ⟨*sub*species⟩ **c** : with repetition (as of a process) so as to form, stress, or deal with subordinate parts or relations ⟨*sub*let⟩ ⟨*sub*contract⟩
**3** : less than completely, perfectly, or normally : somewhat ⟨*sub*acute⟩ ⟨*sub*clinical⟩
**4 a** : almost : nearly ⟨*sub*erect⟩ **b** : falling nearly in the category of and often adjoining : bordering on ⟨*sub*arctic⟩

sub·ad·o·les·cent
sub·agen·cy
sub·agent
sub·al·lo·ca·tion
sub·ar·ea
sub·au·di·ble
sub·av·er·age
sub·base·ment
sub·ba·sin
sub·block
sub·branch
sub·caste
sub·cat·e·go·ri·za·tion
sub·cat·e·go·rize
sub·cat·e·go·ry
sub·ceil·ing
sub·cel·lar
sub·chap·ter
sub·chief
sub·clan
sub·clus·ter
sub·code
sub·col·lec·tion
sub·col·lege
sub·col·le·giate
sub·col·o·ny
sub·com·mis·sion
sub·com·po·nent
sub·cor·date
sub·co·ri·a·ceous
sub·coun·ty
sub·cult
sub·cu·ra·tive
sub·dean
sub·de·ci·sion
sub·de·part·ment
sub·de·vel·op·ment
sub·di·a·lect
sub·di·rec·tor
sub·dis·ci·pline
sub·dis·trict
sub·econ·o·my
sub·erect
sub·file
sub·frame
sub·gen·er·a·tion
sub·genre
sub·goal
sub·gov·ern·ment
sub·hu·mid
sub·in·dus·try
sub·in·hib·i·to·ry

sub·lan·guage
sub·lev·el
sub·li·brar·i·an
sub·li·cense
sub·lit·er·a·cy
sub·lit·er·ate
sub·lot
sub·man·ag·er
sub·mar·ket
sub·max·i·mal
sub·menu
sub·min·i·mal
sub·min·is·ter
sub·na·tion·al
sub·net·work
sub·niche
sub·op·ti·mal
sub·op·ti·mi·za·tion
sub·op·ti·mize
sub·op·ti·mum
sub·or·bic·u·lar
sub·or·ga·ni·za·tion
sub·pan·el
sub·par
sub·para·graph
sub·par·al·lel
sub·part
sub·pe·ri·od
sub·phase
sub·pri·mate
sub·pro·cess
sub·prod·uct
sub·proj·ect
sub·pro·le·tar·i·at
sub·ra·tio·nal
sub·sat·u·rat·ed
sub·sat·u·ra·tion
sub·scale
sub·science
sub·sea
sub·sec·re·tary
sub·sec·tor
sub·seg·ment
sub·sei·zure
sub·sense
sub·sen·tence
sub·se·ries
sub·site
sub·skill
sub·so·ci·ety
sub·spe·cial·ist
sub·spe·cial·ize
sub·spe·cial·ty

sub·state
sub·sys·tem
sub·task
sub·tax·on
sub·test
sub·theme
sub·ther·a·peu·tic
sub·top·ic
sub·trea·sury
sub·trend
sub·tribe

sub·type
sub·unit
sub·va·ri·ety
sub·vas·sal
sub·vis·i·ble
sub·vi·su·al
sub·world
sub·writ·er
sub·ze·ro
sub·zone

**sub·ac·id** \\,səb-'a-səd\ *adjective* [Latin *subacidus,* from *sub-* + *acidus* acid] (1765)
: somewhat acrimonious : CUTTING ⟨*subacid* comments⟩
— **sub·ac·id·ly** *adverb*
— **sub·ac·id·ness** *noun*

**sub·acute** \\-ə-'kyüt\ *adjective* (1822)
**1** : having a tapered but not sharply pointed form ⟨*subacute* leaves⟩
**2 a** : falling between acute and chronic in character especially when closer to acute ⟨*subacute* endocarditis⟩ **b** : less marked in severity or duration than a corresponding acute state ⟨*subacute* pain⟩
— **sub·acute·ly** *adverb*

**subacute sclerosing pan·en·ceph·a·li·tis** \\-,pan-in-,se-fə-'lī-təs\ *noun* [panencephalitis from New Latin, from *pan-* + *encephalitis*] (1950)
: a central nervous system disease of children and young adults caused by infection of the brain by measles virus or a closely related virus and marked by intellectual deterioration, convulsions, and paralysis

**sub·adult** \\,səb-ə-'dəlt; ,səb-'a-,dəlt\ *noun* (1923)
: an individual that has passed through the juvenile period but not yet attained typical adult characteristics
— **subadult** *adjective*

**sub·aer·i·al** \\-'ar-ē-əl, -'er-; -ā-'ir-ē-əl\ *adjective* (1833)
: situated, formed, or occurring on or immediately adjacent to the surface of the earth ⟨*subaerial* erosion⟩ ⟨*subaerial* roots⟩
— **sub·aer·i·al·ly** \\-ē-ə-lē\ *adverb*

**su·bah·dar** *or* **su·ba·dar** \\,sü-bə-'där\ *noun* [Persian *ṣūbadār*] (1698)
**1** : a governor of a province
**2** : the chief Indian officer of a company of Indian troops in the British army of India

**sub·al·pine** \\,səb-'al-,pīn\ *adjective* (circa 1656)
**1** : of or relating to the region about the foot and lower slopes of the Alps
**2** : of, relating to, or inhabiting high upland slopes and especially the zone just below the timberline

¹**sub·al·tern** \\sə-'bȯl-tərn, *especially British* 'sə-bəl-tərn\ *adjective* [Late Latin *subalternus,* from Latin *sub-* + *alternus* alternate, from *alter* other (of two) — more at ALTER] (1570)
**1** : particular with reference to a related universal proposition ⟨"some S is P" is a *subaltern* proposition to "all S is P"⟩
**2** : SUBORDINATE

²**subaltern** *noun* (1605)
**1** : a person holding a subordinate position; *specifically* : a junior officer (as in the British army)
**2** : a particular proposition that follows immediately from a universal

**sub·ant·arc·tic** \\,səb-ant-'ärk-tik, -'är-tik\ *adjective* (1875)
: of, relating to, characteristic of, or being a region just outside the antarctic circle

**sub·api·cal** \\-'ā-pi-kəl *also* -'a-\ *adjective* (1846)
: situated below or near an apex

**sub·aquat·ic** \\-ə-'kwä-tik, -'kwa-\ *adjective* [International Scientific Vocabulary] (1844)
: somewhat aquatic ⟨a marginal *subaquatic* flora⟩

**sub·aque·ous** \\-'ā-kwē-əs, -'a-\ *adjective* (1677)
: existing, formed, or taking place in or under water

**sub·arach·noid** \\-ə-'rak-,nȯid\ *also* **sub·arach·noid·al** \\-rak-'nȯi-d°l\ *adjective* (1843)
: of, relating to, occurring, or situated under the arachnoid membrane ⟨*subarachnoid* hemorrhage⟩

**sub·arc·tic** \\-'ärk-tik, -'är-tik\ *adjective* [International Scientific Vocabulary] (1854)
: of, relating to, characteristic of, or being regions immediately outside of the arctic circle or regions similar to these in climate or conditions of life
— **subarctic** *noun*

**sub·as·sem·bly** \\-ə-'sem-blē\ *noun* (1919)
: an assembled unit designed to be incorporated with other units in a finished product

**sub·at·mo·spher·ic** \\-,at-mə-'sfir-ik, -'sfer-\ *adjective* (1941)
: less or lower than that of the atmosphere ⟨*subatmospheric* pressure⟩

**sub·atom·ic** \\-ə-'tä-mik\ *adjective* (1903)
**1** : of or relating to the inside of the atom
**2** : of, relating to, or being particles smaller than atoms

**sub·au·di·tion** \\-ȯ-'di-shən\ *noun* [Late Latin *subaudition-, subauditio,* from *subaudire* to understand, from Latin *sub-* + *audire* to hear — more at AUDIBLE] (1798)
: the act of understanding or supplying something not expressed : a reading between the lines

**sub·base** \\'səb-,bās\ *noun* (1826)
: underlying support placed below what is normally construed as a base: as **a** : the lowest member horizontally of an architectural base or of a baseboard or pedestal **b** : pervious fill (as crushed stone) placed under a roadbed

**sub·bi·tu·mi·nous** \\,səb-bə-'tü-mə-nəs, -bī-, -'tyü-\ *adjective* (1908)
: of, relating to, or being coal of lower rank than bituminous coal but higher than lignite

**sub·cab·i·net** \\-'kab-nit, -'ka-bə-\ *adjective* (1954)
: of, relating to, or being a high administrative position in the U.S. government that ranks below the cabinet level

**sub·cap·su·lar** \\-'kap-sə-lər\ *adjective* (1889)
: situated or occurring beneath or within a capsule ⟨*subcapsular* cataracts⟩

**sub·cel·lu·lar** \\-'sel-yə-lər\ *adjective* (1948)
: of less than cellular scope or level of organization ⟨*subcellular* particles⟩ ⟨*subcellular* studies⟩

**sub·cen·ter** \\-'sen-tər\ *noun* (circa 1925)
: a secondary center; *especially* : a center (as for shopping) located outside the main business area of a city

**sub·cen·tral** \\-'trəl\ *adjective* (1822)
**1** : nearly but not quite central
**2** : located under a center
— **sub·cen·tral·ly** \\-trə-lē\ *adverb*

**sub·chas·er** \\-,chā-sər\ *noun* (circa 1918)
: a small maneuverable patrol or escort vessel used for antisubmarine warfare

**sub·class** \\'səb-,klas\ *noun* (1819)
: a primary division of a class: as **a** : a category in biological classification ranking below a class and above an order **b** : SUBSET

**sub·clas·si·fi·ca·tion** \\,səb-,kla-sə-fə-'kā-shən\ *noun* (1873)
**1** : a primary division of a classification

**2 :** arrangement into or assignment to subclassifications

— **sub·clas·si·fy** \-'kla-sə-,fī\ *transitive verb*

¹**sub·cla·vi·an** \-'klā-vē-ən\ *adjective* [New Latin *subclavius*, from *sub-* + *clavicula* clavicle] (1646)
**:** of, relating to, being, or performed on a part (as an artery, vein, or nerve) located under the clavicle ⟨*subclavian* angioplasty⟩

²**subclavian** *noun* (1719)
**:** a subclavian part (as an artery, vein, or nerve)

**subclavian artery** *noun* (1688)
**:** the proximal part of the main artery of the arm or forelimb

**subclavian vein** *noun* (1770)
**:** the proximal part of the main vein of the arm or forelimb

**sub·cli·max** \,səb-'klī-,maks\ *noun* (1916)
**:** a stage or community in an ecological succession immediately preceding a climax; *especially* **:** one held in relative stability throughout edaphic or biotic influences or by fire

**sub·clin·i·cal** \-'kli-ni-kəl\ *adjective* (circa 1935)
**:** not detectable or producing effects that are not detectable by the usual clinical tests ⟨a *subclinical* infection⟩ ⟨*subclinical* cancer⟩
— **sub·clin·i·cal·ly** \-k(ə-)lē\ *adverb*

**sub·com·mit·tee** \'səb-kə-,mi-tē, ,səb-kə-'\ *noun* (circa 1607)
**:** a subdivision of a committee usually organized for a specific purpose

**sub·com·mu·ni·ty** \,səb-kə-'myü-nə-tē\ *noun* (1966)
**:** a distinct grouping within a community

**sub·com·pact** \'səb-'käm-,pakt\ *noun* (1967)
**:** an automobile smaller than a compact

¹**sub·con·scious** \,səb-'kän(t)-shəs, 'səb-\ *adjective* (circa 1834)
**:** existing in the mind but not immediately available to consciousness ⟨a *subconscious* motive⟩
— **sub·con·scious·ly** *adverb*
— **sub·con·scious·ness** *noun*

²**subconscious** *noun* (1886)
**:** the mental activities just below the threshold of consciousness

**sub·con·ti·nent** \,səb-'kän-t°n-ənt, -'känt-nənt\ *noun* (1863)
**:** a large landmass smaller than a continent; *especially* **:** a major subdivision of a continent ⟨the Indian *subcontinent*⟩
— **sub·con·ti·nen·tal** \,səb-,kän-t°n-'en-t°l\ *adjective*

¹**sub·con·tract** \,səb-'kän-,trakt\ *noun* (1817)
**:** a contract between a party to an original contract and a third party; *especially* **:** one to provide all or a specified part of the work or materials required in the original contract

²**sub·con·tract** \,səb-'kän-,trakt, ,səb-kən-'\ (1842)
*intransitive verb*
**:** to let out or undertake work under a subcontract
*transitive verb*
**1 :** to engage a third party to perform under a subcontract all or part of (work included in an original contract) — sometimes used with *out*
**2 :** to undertake (work) under a subcontract

**sub·con·trac·tor** \,səb-'kän-,trak-tər, ,səb-kən-'\ *noun* (1842)
**:** an individual or business firm contracting to perform part or all of another's contract

**sub·con·tra·oc·tave** \,səb-,kän-trə-'äk-tiv, -təv, -,tāv\ *noun* (circa 1901)
**:** the musical octave that begins on the fourth C below middle C — see PITCH illustration

**sub·con·trary** \,səb-'kän-,trer-ē\ *noun* (1685)
**:** a proposition so related to another that though both may be true they cannot both be false

— **subcontrary** *adjective*

**sub·cool** \-'kül\ *transitive verb* (1916)
**:** SUPERCOOL

**sub·cor·ti·cal** \-'kȯr-ti-kəl\ *adjective* (1887)
**:** of, relating to, involving, or being nerve centers below the cerebral cortex ⟨*subcortical* lesions⟩

**sub·crit·i·cal** \-'kri-ti-kəl\ *adjective* (1930)
**1 :** less or lower than critical in respect to a specified factor
**2 a :** of insufficient size to sustain a chain reaction ⟨a *subcritical* mass of fissionable material⟩ **b :** designed for use with fissionable material of subcritical mass ⟨a *subcritical* reactor⟩

**sub·crust·al** \-'krəs-t°l\ *adjective* (1897)
**:** situated or occurring below a crust and especially the crust of the earth

**sub·cul·ture** \'səb-,kəl-chər\ *noun* (1886)
**1 a :** a culture (as of bacteria) derived from another culture **b :** an act or instance of producing a subculture
**2 :** an ethnic, regional, economic, or social group exhibiting characteristic patterns of behavior sufficient to distinguish it from others within an embracing culture or society ⟨a criminal *subculture*⟩
— **sub·cul·tur·al** \-'kəlch-rəl, -'kəl-chə-\ *adjective*
— **sub·cul·tur·al·ly** *adverb*
— **subculture** *transitive verb*

**sub·cu·ta·ne·ous** \,səb-kyù-'tā-nē-əs\ *adjective* [Late Latin *subcutaneus*, from Latin *sub-* + *cutis* skin — more at HIDE] (1651)
**:** being, living, used, or made under the skin ⟨*subcutaneous* parasites⟩
— **sub·cu·ta·ne·ous·ly** *adverb*

**sub·cu·tis** \,səb-'kyü-təs\ *noun* [New Latin, from Late Latin, beneath the skin, from Latin *sub-* + *cutis*] (1900)
**:** the deeper part of the dermis

**sub·dea·con** \-'dē-kən\ *noun* [Middle English *subdecon*, from Late Latin *subdiaconus*, from Latin *sub-* + Late Latin *diaconus* deacon — more at DEACON] (14th century)
**:** a cleric ranking below a deacon: as **a :** a cleric in the lowest of the former major orders of the Roman Catholic Church **b :** an Eastern Orthodox or Armenian cleric in minor orders **c :** a clergyman performing the liturgical duties of a subdeacon

**sub·deb** \'səb-,deb\ *noun* (1917)
**:** SUBDEBUTANTE

**sub·deb·u·tante** \,səb-'de-byù-,tänt\ *noun* (1919)
**:** a young girl who is about to become a debutante; *broadly* **:** a girl in her middle teens

**sub·der·mal** \-'dər-məl\ *adjective* (1887)
**:** SUBCUTANEOUS
— **sub·der·mal·ly** \-mə-lē\ *adverb*

**sub·di·vide** \,səb-də-'vīd, 'səb-də-,\ *verb* [Middle English, from Late Latin *subdividere*, from Latin *sub-* + *dividere* to divide] (15th century)
*transitive verb*
**1 :** to divide the parts of into more parts
**2 :** to divide into several parts; *especially* **:** to divide (a tract of land) into building lots
*intransitive verb*
**:** to separate or become separated into subdivisions
— **sub·di·vid·able** \-'vī-də-bəl, -,vī-\ *adjective*
— **sub·di·vid·er** *noun*

**sub·di·vi·sion** \'səb-də-,vi-zhən\ *noun* (15th century)
**1 :** an act or instance of subdividing
**2 :** something produced by subdividing; *especially* **:** a tract of land surveyed and divided into lots for purposes of sale
**3 :** a category in botanical classification ranking below a division and above a class

**sub·dom·i·nant** \,səb-'däm-nənt, -'dä-mə-\ *noun* (1793)

**1 :** the fourth tone of a diatonic scale
**2 :** something partly but incompletely dominant; *especially* **:** an ecologically important life form subordinate in influence to the dominants of a community
— **subdominant** *adjective*

**sub·duc·tion** \(,)səb-'dək-shən\ *noun* [Late Latin *subduction-, subductio* withdrawal, from Latin *subducere* to withdraw, from *sub-* + *ducere* to draw — more at TOW] (1970)
**:** the action or process of the edge of one crustal plate descending below the edge of another
— **sub·duct** \(,)səb-'dəkt\ *verb*

**sub·due** \səb-'dü, -'dyü\ *transitive verb* **subdued; sub·du·ing** [Middle English *sodewen, subduen* (influenced in form and meaning by Latin *subdere* to subject), from Middle French *soduire* to seduce (influenced in meaning by Latin *seducere* to seduce, from Latin *subducere*] (14th century)
**1 :** to conquer and bring into subjection **:** VANQUISH
**2 :** to bring under control especially by an exertion of the will **:** CURB ⟨*subdued* my foolish fears⟩
**3 :** to bring under cultivation
**4 :** to reduce the intensity or degree of **:** tone down
*synonym* see CONQUER
— **sub·du·er** *noun*

**sub·dued** \-'düd, -'dyüd\ *adjective* (1591)
**:** lacking in vitality, intensity, or strength ⟨*subdued* colors⟩
— **sub·dued·ly** \-'dü(-ə)d-lē, -'dyü(-ə)d-\ *adverb*

**sub·dur·al** \,səb-'dùr-əl, -'dyùr-; 'səb-,\ *adjective* [*sub-* + *dura (mater)*] (1875)
**:** situated or occurring beneath the dura mater or between the dura mater and the arachnoid membrane ⟨*subdural* space⟩ ⟨*subdural* hematomas⟩

**sub·ed·i·tor** \-'e-də-tər\ *noun* (1835)
*chiefly British* **:** COPY EDITOR
— **sub·ed·it** \-'e-dət\ *transitive verb, chiefly British*
— **sub·ed·i·to·ri·al** \,səb-,e-də-'tȯr-ē-əl, -tȯr-\ *adjective, chiefly British*

**sub·em·ployed** \,səb-im-'plȯid\ *adjective* (1967)
**:** UNDEREMPLOYED

**sub·em·ploy·ment** \-'plȯi-mənt\ *noun* (1967)
**:** a condition of inadequate employment in a labor force including unemployment and underemployment

**sub·en·try** \'səb-,en-trē\ *noun* (circa 1891)
**:** an entry (as in a catalog or an account) made under a more general entry

**sub·epi·der·mal** \,səb-,e-pə-'dər-məl\ *adjective* (1853)
**:** lying beneath or constituting the innermost part of the epidermis

**su·ber·in** \'sü-bə-rən\ *noun* [French *subérine*, from Latin *suber* cork tree, cork] (1830)
**:** a complex fatty substance found especially in the cell walls of cork

**su·ber·i·za·tion** \,sü-bə-rə-'zā-shən\ *noun* (1882)
**:** conversion of the cell walls into corky tissue by infiltration with suberin
— **su·ber·ized** \'sü-bə-,rīzd\ *adjective*

**sub·fam·i·ly** \'səb-,fam-lē, -,fa-mə-\ *noun* [International Scientific Vocabulary] (1833)
**1 :** a category in biological classification ranking below a family and above a genus
**2 :** a subgroup of languages within a language family

**sub·field** \-,fēld\ *noun* (circa 1949)
**1 :** a subset of a mathematical field that is itself a field
**2 :** a subdivision of a field (as of study)

**sub·floor** \-,flȯr, -,flȯr\ *noun* (1893)

**:** a rough floor laid as a base for a finished floor

**sub·fos·sil** \-ˌfä-səl\ *adjective* [International Scientific Vocabulary] (1832) **:** of less than typical fossil age but partially fossilized
— **subfossil** *noun*

**sub·freez·ing** \-ˈfrē-ziŋ\ *adjective* (1949) **:** being or marked by temperature below the freezing point (as of water) ⟨*subfreezing* weather⟩

**sub·fusc** \(ˌ)səb-ˈfəsk, ˈsəb-ˌ\ *adjective* [Latin *subfuscus* brownish, dusky, from *sub-* + *fuscus* dark brown — more at DUSK] (1710) *chiefly British* **:** DRAB, DUSKY

**sub·ge·nus** \ˈsəb-ˌjē-nəs\ *noun* [New Latin] (1813) **:** a category in biological classification ranking below a genus and above a species

**sub·gla·cial** \ˌsəb-ˈglā-shəl\ *adjective* (1820) **:** of or relating to the bottom of a glacier or the area immediately underlying a glacier
— **sub·gla·cial·ly** \-shə-lē\ *adverb*

**sub·grade** \ˈsəb-ˌgrād\ *noun* (1898) **:** a surface of earth or rock leveled off to receive a foundation (as of a road)

**sub·graph** \ˈsəb-ˌgraf\ *noun* (1963) **:** a graph all of whose points and lines are contained in a larger graph

**sub·group** \-ˌgrüp\ *noun* (1845) **1 :** a subordinate group whose members usually share some common differential quality **2 :** a subset of a mathematical group that is itself a group

**sub·gum** \ˈsəb-ˈgəm\ *noun* [Chinese (Guangdong) *sahp-gám*, literally, assorted, mixed] (1938) **:** a dish of Chinese origin prepared with a mixture of vegetables (as peppers, water chestnuts, and mushrooms)

**sub·head** \-ˌhed\ *noun* (1673) **1 :** a heading of a subdivision (as in an outline) **2 :** a subordinate caption, title, or headline

**sub·head·ing** \-ˌhe-diŋ\ *noun* (1889) **:** SUBHEAD

**¹sub·hu·man** \ˌsəb-ˈhyü-mən, -ˈyü-\ *adjective* (1793) **:** less than human: as **a :** failing to attain the level (as of morality or intelligence) associated with normal human beings **b :** unsuitable to or unfit for human beings ⟨*subhuman* living conditions⟩ **c :** of or relating to an infrahuman taxonomic group ⟨the *subhuman* primates⟩

**²subhuman** *noun* (1937) **:** a subhuman being

**sub·in·dex** \ˈsəb-ˈin-ˌdeks\ *noun* (1923) **:** an index to a division of a main classification

**sub·in·feu·da·tion** \ˌsəb-ˌin-fyü-ˈdā-shən\ *noun* [*sub-* + *infeudation* enfeoffment] (circa 1730) **:** the subdivision of a feudal estate by a vassal who in turn becomes feudal lord over his tenants
— **sub·in·feu·date** *transitive verb*

**sub·in·ter·val** \ˌsəb-ˈin-tər-vəl\ *noun* (1927) **:** an interval that is a subdivision or a subset of an interval

**sub·ir·ri·ga·tion** \-ˌir-ə-ˈgā-shən\ *noun* (1880) **:** irrigation below the surface (as by a periodic rise of the water table or by a system of underground porous pipes)
— **sub·ir·ri·gate** \-ˈir-ə-ˌgāt\ *transitive verb*

**su·bi·to** \ˈsü-bi-ˌtō\ *adverb* [Italian, from Latin, suddenly, from *subitus* sudden — more at SUDDEN] (circa 1724) **:** IMMEDIATELY, SUDDENLY — used as a direction in music

**sub·ja·cen·cy** \ˌsəb-ˈjā-sᵊn(t)-sē\ *noun* (circa 1891) **:** the quality or state of being subjacent

**sub·ja·cent** \-sᵊnt\ *adjective* [Latin *subjacent-, subjacens*, present participle of *sub-*

*jacēre* to lie under, from *sub-* + *jacēre* to lie — more at ADJACENT] (1597) **:** lying under or below; *also* **:** lower than though not directly below ⟨hills and *subjacent* valleys⟩
— **sub·ja·cent·ly** *adverb*

**¹sub·ject** \ˈsəb-jikt, -(ˌ)jekt\ *noun* [Middle English, from Middle French, from Latin *subjectus* one under authority & *subjectum* subject of a proposition, from masculine & neuter respectively of *subjectus*, past participle of *subicere* to subject, literally, to throw under, from *sub-* + *jacere* to throw — more at JET] (14th century) **1 :** one that is placed under authority or control: as **a :** VASSAL **b** (1) **:** one subject to a monarch and governed by the monarch's law (2) **:** one who lives in the territory of, enjoys the protection of, and owes allegiance to a sovereign power or state **2 a :** that of which a quality, attribute, or relation may be affirmed or in which it may inhere **b :** SUBSTRATUM; *especially* **:** material or essential substance **c :** the mind, ego, or agent of whatever sort that sustains or assumes the form of thought or consciousness **3 a :** a department of knowledge or learning **b :** MOTIVE, CAUSE **c** (1) **:** one that is acted on ⟨the helpless *subject* of their cruelty⟩ (2) **:** an individual whose reactions or responses are studied (3) **:** a dead body for anatomical study and dissection **d** (1) **:** something concerning which something is said or done ⟨the *subject* of the essay⟩ (2) **:** something represented or indicated in a work of art **e** (1) **:** the term of a logical proposition that denotes the entity of which something is affirmed or denied; *also* **:** the entity denoted (2) **:** a word or word group denoting that of which something is predicated **f :** the principal melodic phrase on which a musical composition or movement is based
*synonym* see CITIZEN
— **sub·ject·less** \-ləs\ *adjective*

**²subject** *adjective* (14th century) **1 :** owing obedience or allegiance to the power or dominion of another **2 a :** suffering a particular liability or exposure ⟨*subject* to temptation⟩ **b :** having a tendency or inclination **:** PRONE ⟨*subject* to colds⟩ **3 :** contingent on or under the influence of some later action ⟨the plan is *subject* to discussion⟩
*synonym* see LIABLE

**³sub·ject** \səb-ˈjekt, ˈsəb-ˌjekt\ *transitive verb* (14th century) **1 a :** to bring under control or dominion **:** SUBJUGATE **b :** to make (as oneself) amenable to the discipline and control of a superior **2 :** to make liable **:** PREDISPOSE **3 :** to cause or force to undergo or endure (something unpleasant, inconvenient, or trying) ⟨was *subjected* to constant verbal abuse⟩
— **sub·jec·tion** \səb-ˈjek-shən\ *noun*

**¹sub·jec·tive** \(ˌ)səb-ˈjek-tiv\ *adjective* (15th century) **1 :** of, relating to, or constituting a subject: as **a** *obsolete* **:** of, relating to, or characteristic of one that is a subject especially in lack of freedom of action or in submissiveness **b :** being or relating to a grammatical subject; *especially* **:** NOMINATIVE **2 :** of or relating to the essential being of that which has substance, qualities, attributes, or relations **3 a :** characteristic of or belonging to reality as perceived rather than as independent of mind **:** PHENOMENAL — compare OBJECTIVE 1b **b :** relating to or being experience or knowledge as conditioned by personal mental characteristics or states **4 a** (1) **:** peculiar to a particular individual **:** PERSONAL ⟨*subjective* judgments⟩ (2) **:** modified or affected by personal views, experience,

or background ⟨a *subjective* account of the incident⟩ **b :** arising from conditions within the brain or sense organs and not directly caused by external stimuli ⟨*subjective* sensations⟩ **c :** arising out of or identified by means of one's perception of one's own states and processes ⟨a *subjective* symptom of disease⟩ — compare OBJECTIVE 1c **5 :** lacking in reality or substance **:** ILLUSORY
— **sub·jec·tive·ly** *adverb*
— **sub·jec·tive·ness** *noun*
— **sub·jec·tiv·i·ty** \-ˌjek-ˈti-və-tē\ *noun*

**²subjective** *noun* (1817) **:** something that is subjective; *also* **:** NOMINATIVE

**subjective complement** *noun* (1923) **:** a grammatical complement relating to the subject of an intransitive verb (as *sick* in "he had fallen sick")

**sub·jec·tiv·ise** *British variant of* SUBJECTIVIZE

**sub·jec·tiv·ism** \(ˌ)səb-ˈjek-ti-ˌvi-zəm\ *noun* (circa 1857) **1 a :** a theory that limits knowledge to subjective experience **b :** a theory that stresses the subjective elements in experience **2 a :** a doctrine that the supreme good is the realization of a subjective experience or feeling (as pleasure) **b :** a doctrine that individual feeling or apprehension is the ultimate criterion of the good and the right
— **sub·jec·tiv·ist** \-vist\ *noun*
— **sub·jec·tiv·is·tic** \-ˌjek-ti-ˈvis-tik\ *adjective*

**sub·jec·tiv·ize** \-ti-ˌvīz\ *transitive verb* **-ized; -iz·ing** (1868) **:** to make subjective
— **sub·jec·tiv·i·za·tion** \-ˌjek-ti-və-ˈzā-shən\ *noun*

**subject matter** *noun* (1598) **:** matter presented for consideration in discussion, thought, or study

**sub·join** \(ˌ)səb-ˈjȯin\ *transitive verb* [Middle French *subjoindre*, from Latin *subjungere* to join beneath, add, from *sub-* + *jungere* to join — more at YOKE] (1573) **:** ANNEX, APPEND ⟨*subjoined* a statement of expenses to her report⟩

**sub ju·di·ce** \ˌsu̇b-ˈyü-di-ˌkā, ˈsəb-ˈjü-də-(ˌ)sē\ *adverb* [Latin] (1613) **:** before a judge or court **:** not yet judicially decided

**sub·ju·gate** \ˈsəb-ji-ˌgāt\ *transitive verb* **-gat·ed; -gat·ing** [Middle English, from Latin *subjugatus*, past participle of *subjugare*, from *sub-* + *jugum* yoke — more at YOKE] (15th century) **1 :** to bring under control and governance as a subject **:** CONQUER **2 :** to make submissive **:** SUBDUE
— **sub·ju·ga·tion** \ˌsəb-ji-ˈgā-shən\ *noun*
— **sub·ju·ga·tor** \ˈsəb-ji-ˌgā-tər\ *noun*

**sub·junc·tion** \(ˌ)səb-ˈjəŋ(k)-shən\ *noun* (1633) **1 :** an act of subjoining or the state of being subjoined **2 :** something subjoined

**¹sub·junc·tive** \səb-ˈjəŋ(k)-tiv\ *adjective* [Late Latin *subjunctivus*, from Latin *subjunctus*, past participle of *subjungere* to join beneath, subordinate] (1530) **:** of, relating to, or constituting a verb form or set of verb forms that represents a denoted act or state not as fact but as contingent or possible or viewed emotionally (as with doubt or desire) ⟨the *subjunctive* mood⟩

**²subjunctive** *noun* (1622) **1 :** the subjunctive mood of a language

\ə\ abut \ᵊ\ kitten \ər\ further \a\ ash \ā\ ace \ä\ mop, mar \au̇\ out \ch\ chin \e\ bet \ē\ easy \g\ go \i\ hit \ī\ ice \j\ job \ŋ\ sing \ō\ go \ȯ\ law \ȯi\ boy \th\ thin \tẖ\ the \ü\ loot \u̇\ foot \y\ yet \zh\ vision *see also* Guide to Pronunciation

**2 :** a form of verb or verbal in the subjective mood ◻

**sub·king·dom** \'səb-ˌkiŋ-dəm\ *noun* (1825)
**:** a category in biological classification ranking below a kingdom and above a phylum

**sub·late** \sə-'blāt\ *transitive verb* **sub·lat·ed; sub·lat·ing** [Latin *sublatus* (past participle of *tollere* to take away, lift up), from *sub-* up + *latus*, past participle of *ferre* to carry — more at SUB-, TOLERATE, BEAR] (1838)
**1 :** NEGATE, DENY
**2 :** to negate or eliminate (as an element in a dialectic process) but preserve as a partial element in a synthesis
**— sub·la·tion** \-'blā-shən\ *noun*

**¹sub·lease** \'səb-ˌlēs, -ˌlēs\ *noun* (1826)
**:** a lease by a tenant or lessee of part or all of leased premises to another person but with the original tenant retaining some right or interest under the original lease

**²sublease** *transitive verb* (circa 1843)
**:** to make or obtain a sublease of

**¹sub·let** \'səb-'let\ *verb* **-let; -let·ting** (1766)
*transitive verb*
**1 :** SUBLEASE
**2 :** SUBCONTRACT 1
*intransitive verb*
**:** to lease or rent all or part of a leased or rented property

**²sub·let** \-ˌlet\ *noun* (1906)
**:** property and especially housing obtained by or available through a sublease

**sub·le·thal** \ˌsəb-'lē-thəl\ *adjective* (1895)
**:** less than but usually only slightly less than lethal ⟨a *sublethal* dose⟩
**— sub·le·thal·ly** \-thə-lē\ *adverb*

**sub·lieu·ten·ant** \ˌsəb-lü-'te-nənt, *British* -le(f)-'ten-\ *noun* (1804)
**:** a commissioned officer in the British navy ranking immediately below lieutenant

**¹sub·li·mate** \'sə-blə-ˌmāt\ *transitive verb* **-mat·ed; -mat·ing** [Middle English, from Medieval Latin *sublimatus*, past participle of *sublimare*] (15th century)
**1 a :** SUBLIME 1 **b** *archaic* **:** to improve or refine as if by subliming
**2 :** to divert the expression of (an instinctual desire or impulse) from its primitive form to one that is considered more socially or culturally acceptable
**— sub·li·ma·tion** \ˌsə-blə-'mā-shən\ *noun*

**²sub·li·mate** \'sə-blə-ˌmāt, -mət\ *noun* (circa 1626)
**:** a chemical product obtained by sublimation

**¹sub·lime** \sə-'blīm\ *verb* **sub·limed; sub·lim·ing** [Middle English, from Middle French *sublimer*, from Medieval Latin *sublimare* to refine, sublime, from Latin, to elevate, from *sublimis*] (14th century)
*transitive verb*
**1 :** to cause to pass directly from the solid to the vapor state and condense back to solid form
**2** [French *sublimer*, from Latin *sublimare*] **a** (1) **:** to elevate or exalt especially in dignity or honor (2) **:** to render finer (as in purity or excellence) **b :** to convert (something inferior) into something of higher worth
*intransitive verb*
**:** to pass directly from the solid to the vapor state
**— sub·lim·able** \-'blī-mə-bəl\ *adjective*
**— sub·lim·er** *noun*

**²sublime** *adjective* **sub·lim·er; -est** [Latin *sublimis*, literally, high, elevated] (1586)
**1 a :** lofty, grand, or exalted in thought, expression, or manner **b :** of outstanding spiritual, intellectual, or moral worth **c :** tending to inspire awe usually because of elevated quality (as of beauty, nobility, or grandeur) or transcendent excellence
**2 a** *archaic* **:** high in place **b** *obsolete* **:** lofty of mien **:** HAUGHTY **c** *capitalized* **:** SUPREME — used in a style of address **d :** COMPLETE, UTTER ⟨*sublime* ignorance⟩
**synonym** see SPLENDID

**— sub·lime·ly** *adverb*
**— sub·lime·ness** *noun*

**sub·lim·i·nal** \(ˌ)sə-'bli-mə-n°l\ *adjective* [*sub-* + Latin *limin-, limen* threshold] (1886)
**1 :** inadequate to produce a sensation or a perception
**2 :** existing or functioning below the threshold of consciousness ⟨the *subliminal* mind⟩ ⟨*subliminal* advertising⟩
**— sub·lim·i·nal·ly** *adverb*

**sub·lim·i·ty** \sə-'bli-mə-tē\ *noun, plural* **-ties** (15th century)
**1 :** the quality or state of being sublime
**2 :** something sublime or exalted

**sub·line** \'səb-ˌlīn\ *noun* (1942)
**:** an inbred or selectively cultured line (as of cells) within a strain

**sub·lin·gual** \ˌsəb-'liŋ-gwəl, -gyə-wəl\ *adjective* [New Latin *sublingualis*, from Latin *sub-* + *lingua* tongue — more at TONGUE] (1661)
**:** situated or administered under the tongue ⟨*sublingual* tablets⟩ ⟨*sublingual* glands⟩

**sub·lit·er·ary** \-'li-tə-ˌrer-ē\ *adjective* (1936)
**:** relating to or being subliterature

**sub·lit·er·a·ture** \-'li-tə-rə-ˌchùr, -'li-trə-ˌchùr, -'li-tə(r)-ˌchùr, -chər, -ˌtyùr, -ˌtùr\ *noun* (1952)
**:** popular writing (as mystery or adventure stories) considered inferior to standard literature

**¹sub·lit·to·ral** \-'li-tə-rəl, ˌsəb-ˌli-tə-'ral, -'räl\ *adjective* (1846)
**1 :** situated, occurring, or formed on the aquatic side of a shoreline or littoral zone
**2 :** constituting the sublittoral

**²sublittoral** *noun* (circa 1935)
**:** the deeper part of the littoral portion of a body of water: **a :** the region in a lake between the deepest-growing rooted vegetation and the part of the lake below the thermocline **b :** the region in an ocean between the lowest point exposed by a low tide and the margin of the continental shelf

**sub·lu·na·ry** \ˌsəb-'lü-nə-rē, ˌsəb-lù-ˌner-ē\ *also* **sub·lu·nar** \ˌsəb-'lü-nər *also* -ˌnär\ *adjective* [modification of Late Latin *sublunaris*, from Latin *sub-* + *luna* moon — more at LUNAR] (1592)
**:** of, relating to, or characteristic of the terrestrial world ⟨dull *sublunary* lovers —John Donne⟩

**sub·lux·a·tion** \ˌsə-ˌblək-'sā-shən\ *noun* (circa 1688)
**:** partial dislocation (as of one of the bones in a joint)

**sub·ma·chine gun** \ˌsəb-mə-'shēn-ˌgən\ *noun* (1920)
**:** a portable automatic firearm that uses pistol-type ammunition and is fired from the shoulder or hip

**¹sub·man·dib·u·lar** \ˌsəb-man-'di-byə-lər\ *adjective* (1875)
**1 :** of, relating to, situated in, or performed in the region below the lower jaw
**2 :** of, relating to, or associated with the salivary glands inside of and near the lower edge of the mandible on each side

**²submandibular** *noun* (1974)
**:** a submandibular part (as an artery or bone)

**sub·mar·gin·al** \ˌsəb-'märj-nəl, -'märj-ə-n°l\ *adjective* (1829)
**1 :** adjacent to a margin or a marginal part or structure ⟨*submarginal* spots on an insect wing⟩
**2 :** falling below a necessary minimum ⟨*submarginal* economic conditions⟩

**¹sub·ma·rine** \'səb-mə-ˌrēn, ˌsəb-mə-'\ *adjective* (1648)
**:** UNDERWATER; *especially* **:** UNDERSEA ⟨*submarine* plants⟩ ⟨*submarine* minerals⟩

**²submarine** *noun* (1703)
**1 :** something that functions or operates underwater; *specifically* **:** a naval vessel designed to operate underwater
**2 :** a large sandwich on a long split roll with any of a variety of fillings (as meatballs or cold cuts, cheese, lettuce, and tomato) —

called also *grinder, hero, hoagie, Italian sandwich, poor boy, sub, torpedo*

**³submarine** *verb* **-rined; -rin·ing** (1914)
*transitive verb*
**:** to attack by or as if by a submarine **:** attack from beneath
*intransitive verb*
**:** to dive or slide under something

**sub·ma·ri·ner** \ˌsəb-mə-'rē-nər, -'mar-ə-nər\ *noun* (1914)
**:** a member of a submarine crew

**sub·max·il·lary** \ˌsəb-'mak-sə-ˌler-ē, 'səb-, *chiefly British* ˌsəb-mak-'si-lə-rē\ *adjective or noun* (1787)
**:** SUBMANDIBULAR

**sub·me·di·ant** \ˌsəb-'mē-dē-ənt\ *noun* (1806)
**:** the sixth tone of a diatonic scale

**sub·merge** \səb-'mərj\ *verb* **sub·merged; sub·merg·ing** [Latin *submergere*, from *sub-* + *mergere* to plunge — more at MERGE] (1611)
*transitive verb*
**1 :** to put under water

**2 :** to cover or overflow with water
**3 :** to make obscure or subordinate **:** SUPPRESS ⟨personal lives *submerged* by professional responsibilities⟩
*intransitive verb*
**:** to go under water
— **sub·mer·gence** \-'mər-jən(t)s\ *noun*
— **sub·merg·ible** \-'mər-jə-bəl\ *adjective*
**submerged** *adjective* (1799)
**1 :** covered with water
**2 :** SUBMERSED b
**3 :** sunk in poverty and misery ⟨the *submerged* masses⟩ ⟨the *submerged* tenth of the population⟩
**4 :** HIDDEN, SUPPRESSED ⟨*submerged* emotions⟩
**sub·merse** \səb-'mərs\ *transitive verb* **submersed; sub·mers·ing** [Latin *submersus,* past participle of *submergere*] (1837)
**:** SUBMERGE
— **sub·mer·sion** \-'mər-zhən, -shən\ *noun*
**submersed** *adjective* (circa 1727)
**:** SUBMERGED: as **a :** covered with water **b :** growing or adapted to grow underwater ⟨*submersed* weeds⟩
¹**sub·mers·ible** \səb-'mər-sə-bəl\ *adjective* (1866)
**:** capable of being submerged
²**submersible** *noun* (1900)
**:** something that is submersible; *especially* **:** a usually small underwater craft used especially for deep-sea research
**sub·meta·cen·tric** \ˌsəb-ˌme-tə-'sen-trik\ *adjective* (1962)
**:** having the centromere situated so that one chromosome is somewhat shorter than the other
— **submetacentric** *noun*
**sub·mi·cro·gram** \ˌsəb-'mī-krə-ˌgram\ *adjective* (1946)
**:** relating to or having a mass of less than one microgram ⟨*submicrogram* quantities of a chemical⟩
**sub·mi·cron** \-ˌkrän\ *adjective* (1948)
**1 :** being less than a micron in a (specified) measurement and especially in diameter ⟨a *submicron* particle⟩
**2 :** having or consisting of submicron particles ⟨a *submicron* metal powder⟩
**sub·mi·cro·scop·ic** \ˌsəb-ˌmī-krə-'skä-pik\ *adjective* [International Scientific Vocabulary] (1912)
**1 :** too small to be seen in an ordinary light microscope
**2 :** of, relating to, or dealing with the very minute ⟨the *submicroscopic* world⟩
— **sub·mi·cro·scop·i·cal·ly** \-pi-k(ə-)lē\ *adverb*
**sub·mil·li·me·ter** \ˌsəb-'mi-lə-ˌmē-tər\ *adjective* (1955)
**:** being less than a millimeter in diameter or wavelength ⟨a *submillimeter* particle⟩ ⟨a *submillimeter* radio wave⟩
**sub·min·i·a·ture** \ˌsəb-'mi-nē-ə-ˌchu̇r, -'mi-ni-ˌchu̇r, -'min-yə-, -chər, -ˌtyu̇r, -ˌtu̇r\ *adjective* [International Scientific Vocabulary] (1947)
**:** very small — used especially of a very compact assembly of electronic equipment
**sub·miss** \səb-'mis\ *adjective* [Latin *submissus,* from past participle of *submittere*] (1570)
*archaic* **:** SUBMISSIVE, HUMBLE
**sub·mis·sion** \səb-'mi-shən\ *noun* [Middle English, from Middle French, from Latin *submission-, submissio* act of lowering, from *submittere*] (14th century)
**1 a :** a legal agreement to submit to the decision of arbitrators **b :** an act of submitting something (as for consideration or inspection); *also* **:** something submitted (as a manuscript)
**2 :** the condition of being submissive, humble, or compliant
**3 :** an act of submitting to the authority or control of another
**sub·mis·sive** \-'mi-siv\ *adjective* (circa 1586)
**:** submitting to others
— **sub·mis·sive·ly** *adverb*

— **sub·mis·sive·ness** *noun*
**sub·mit** \səb-'mit\ *verb* **sub·mit·ted; sub·mit·ting** [Middle English *submitten,* from Latin *submittere* to lower, submit, from *sub-* + *mittere* to send] (14th century)
*transitive verb*
**1 a :** to yield to governance or authority **b :** to subject to a condition, treatment, or operation ⟨the metal was *submitted* to analysis⟩
**2 :** to present or propose to another for review, consideration, or decision ⟨*submit* a question to the court⟩ ⟨*submit* a bid on a contract⟩ ⟨*submit* a report⟩; *also* **:** to deliver formally ⟨*submitted* my resignation⟩
**3 :** to put forward as an opinion or contention ⟨we *submit* that the charge is not proved⟩
*intransitive verb*
**1 a :** to yield oneself to the authority or will of another **:** SURRENDER **b :** to permit oneself to be subjected to something ⟨had to *submit* to surgery⟩
**2 :** to defer to or consent to abide by the opinion or authority of another
*synonym* see YIELD
— **sub·mit·tal** \-'mi-t°l\ *noun*
**sub·mi·to·chon·dri·al** \ˌsəb-ˌmī-tə-'kän-drē-əl\ *adjective* (1963)
**:** relating to, composed of, or being parts and especially fragments of mitochondria ⟨*submitochondrial* membranes⟩ ⟨*submitochondrial* particles⟩
**sub·mu·co·sa** \ˌsəb-myü-'kō-zə\ *noun* [New Latin] (1885)
**:** a supporting layer of loose connective tissue directly under a mucous membrane
— **sub·mu·co·sal** \-zəl\ *adjective*
**sub·mul·ti·ple** \-'məl-tə-pəl\ *noun* (1758)
**:** an exact divisor of a number ⟨8 is a *submultiple* of 72⟩
**sub·mu·ni·tion** \(ˌ)səb-myü-'ni-shən\ *noun* (1975)
**:** any of a group of smaller weapons carried as a warhead by a missile or projectile and expelled as the carrier approaches its target
**sub·nor·mal** \-'nȯr-məl\ *adjective* [International Scientific Vocabulary] (circa 1890)
**1 :** lower or smaller than normal
**2 :** having less of something and especially of intelligence than is normal
— **sub·nor·mal·i·ty** \ˌsəb-nȯr-'ma-lə-tē\ *noun*
— **sub·nor·mal·ly** \ˌsəb-'nȯr-mə-lē\ *adverb*
**sub·nu·cle·ar** \ˌsəb-'nü-klē-ər, -'nyü-, ÷-kyə-lər\ *adjective* (1937)
**:** of, relating to, or being a particle smaller than the atomic nucleus
**sub·oce·an·ic** \ˌsəb-ˌō-shē-'a-nik\ *adjective* (1858)
**:** situated, taking place, or formed beneath the ocean or its bottom ⟨*suboceanic* oil resources⟩
**sub·or·bit·al** \ˌsəb-'ȯr-bə-t°l\ *adjective* (circa 1827)
**1 :** situated beneath the eye or the orbit of the eye
**2 :** being or involving less than one orbit (as of the earth or moon) ⟨a spacecraft's *suborbital* flight⟩; *also* **:** intended for suborbital flight ⟨a *suborbital* rocket⟩
**sub·or·der** \'səb-ˌȯr-dər\ *noun* (1826)
**:** a subdivision of an order ⟨a soil *suborder*⟩; *especially* **:** a taxonomic category ranking between an order and a family
¹**sub·or·di·nate** \sə-'bȯr-d°n-ət, -'bȯrd-nət\ *adjective* [Middle English *subordinat,* from Medieval Latin *subordinatus,* past participle of *subordinare* to subordinate, from Latin *sub-* + *ordinare* to order — more at ORDAIN] (15th century)
**1 :** placed in or occupying a lower class, rank, or position **:** INFERIOR
**2 :** submissive to or controlled by authority
**3 a :** of, relating to, or constituting a clause that functions as a noun, adjective, or adverb **b :** SUBORDINATING
— **sub·or·di·nate·ly** *adverb*
— **sub·or·di·nate·ness** *noun*

²**subordinate** *noun* (1640)
**:** one that is subordinate
³**sub·or·di·nate** \sə-'bȯr-d°n-ˌāt\ *transitive verb* **-nat·ed; -nat·ing** [Medieval Latin *subordinatus*] (1597)
**1 :** to make subject or subservient
**2 :** to treat as of less value or importance ⟨stylist . . . whose crystalline prose *subordinates* content to form —Susan Heath⟩
— **sub·or·di·na·tion** \-ˌbȯr-d°n-'ā-shən\ *noun*
— **sub·or·di·na·tive** \-'bȯr-d°n-ˌā-tiv\ *adjective*
**subordinating** *adjective* (1857)
**:** introducing and linking a subordinate clause to a main clause ⟨*subordinating* conjunction⟩
**sub·or·di·na·tor** \-ˌā-tər\ *noun* (1959)
**:** one that subordinates; *especially* **:** a subordinating conjunction
**sub·orn** \sə-'bȯrn\ *transitive verb* [Middle French *suborner,* from Latin *subornare,* from *sub-* secretly + *ornare* to furnish, equip — more at ORNATE] (1534)
**1 :** to induce secretly to do an unlawful thing
**2 :** to induce to commit perjury; *also* **:** to obtain (perjured testimony) from a witness
— **sub·or·na·tion** \ˌsə-ˌbȯr-'nā-shən\ *noun*
— **sub·orn·er** *noun*
**sub·phy·lum** \'səb-ˌfī-ləm\ *noun* [New Latin] (circa 1934)
**:** a category in biological classification ranking below a phylum and above a class
**sub·plot** \'səb-ˌplät\ *noun* (1916)
**1 :** a subordinate plot in fiction or drama
**2 :** a subdivision of an experimental plot of land
¹**sub·poe·na** \sə-'pē-nə, ÷-'nē-\ *noun* [Middle English *suppena,* from Latin *sub poena* under penalty] (15th century)
**:** a writ commanding a person designated in it to appear in court under a penalty for failure
²**subpoena** *transitive verb* **-naed; -na·ing** (1640)
**:** to serve or summon with a writ of subpoena
**subpoena ad tes·ti·fi·can·dum** \-ˌad-ˌtes-tə-fi-'kan-dəm\ *noun* [New Latin, under penalty to give testimony] (circa 1769)
**:** a writ commanding a person to appear in court to testify as a witness
**subpoena du·ces te·cum** \-ˌdü-səs-'tē-kəm\ *noun* [New Latin, under penalty you shall bring with you] (1768)
**:** a writ commanding a person to produce in court certain designated documents or evidence
**sub·po·lar** \ˌsəb-'pō-lər\ *adjective* (1826)
**:** SUBANTARCTIC, SUBARCTIC
**sub·pop·u·la·tion** \'səb-ˌpä-pyə-'lā-shən\ *noun* (1944)
**:** an identifiable fraction or subdivision of a population
**sub·po·tent** \ˌsəb-'pō-t°nt\ *adjective* (circa 1909)
**:** less potent than normal ⟨*subpotent* drugs⟩
— **sub·po·ten·cy** \-'pō-t°n(t)-sē\ *noun*
**sub·prin·ci·pal** \-'prin(t)-s(ə-)pəl\, -sə-bəl\ *noun* (1597)
**1 :** an assistant principal (as of a school)
**2 :** a secondary or bracing rafter
**sub·prob·lem** \ˌsəb-'prä-bləm\ *noun* (1906)
**:** a problem that is contingent on or forms a part of another more inclusive problem
**sub·pro·fes·sion·al** \ˌsəb-prə-'fesh-nəl, -'fe-shə-n°l\ *adjective* (1941)
**:** functioning or qualified to function below the professional level but distinctly above the clerical or labor level and usually under the supervision of a professionally trained person
— **subprofessional** *noun*

\ə\ abut \ᵊ\ kitten \ər\ further \a\ ash \ā\ ace
\ä\ mop, mar \au̇\ out \ch\ chin \e\ bet \ē\ easy
\g\ go \i\ hit \ī\ ice \j\ job \ŋ\ sing \ō\ go
\ȯ\ law \ȯi\ boy \th\ thin \t̲h̲\ the \ü\ loot \u̇\ foot
\y\ yet \zh\ vision    *see also* Guide to Pronunciation

**sub·pro·gram** \'səb-ˌprō-ˌgram, -grəm\ *noun* (1947)
: a semi-independent portion of a program (as for a computer)

**sub·re·gion** \'səb-ˌrē-jən\ *noun* [International Scientific Vocabulary] (1864)
**1** : a subdivision of a region
**2** : one of the primary divisions of a biogeographic region
— **sub·re·gion·al** \-ˌrēj-nəl, -ˌrē-jə-nᵊl\ *adjective*

**sub·rep·tion** \(ˌ)səb-'rep-shən\ *noun* [Late Latin *subreption-, subreptio*, from Latin, act of stealing, from *subripere, surripere* to take away secretly — more at SURREPTITIOUS] (1600)
: a deliberate misrepresentation; *also* : an inference drawn from it
— **sub·rep·ti·tious** \ˌsəb-ˌrep-'ti-shəs\ *adjective*
— **sub·rep·ti·tious·ly** *adverb*

**sub·ring** \'səb-ˌriŋ\ *noun* (1937)
: a subset of a mathematical ring which is itself a ring

**sub·ro·gate** \'sə-brō-ˌgāt\ *transitive verb* **-gat·ed; -gat·ing** [Middle English, from Latin *subrogatus*, past participle of *subrogare, surrogare* — more at SURROGATE] (15th century)
: to put in the place of another; *especially* : to substitute (as a second creditor) for another with regard to a legal right or claim

**sub·ro·ga·tion** \ˌsə-brō-'gā-shən\ *noun* (15th century)
: the act of subrogating; *specifically* : the assumption by a third party (as a second creditor or an insurance company) of another's legal right to collect a debt or damages

**sub–rosa** *adjective* (1923)
: SECRETIVE, PRIVATE

**sub ro·sa** \ˌsəb-'rō-zə\ *adverb* [New Latin, literally, under the rose; from the ancient association of the rose with secrecy] (1654)
: in confidence : SECRETLY

**sub·rou·tine** \'səb-(ˌ)rü-ˌtēn\ *noun* [International Scientific Vocabulary] (circa 1946)
: a subordinate routine; *specifically* : a sequence of computer instructions for performing a specified task that can be used repeatedly

**sub–Sa·ha·ran** \ˌsəb-sə-'har-ən, -'her-, -'här-\ *adjective* (1955)
: of, relating to, or being the part of Africa south of the Sahara

**¹sub·sam·ple** \'səb-ˌsam-pəl, ˌsəb-'sam-\ *transitive verb* (circa 1899)
: to draw samples from (a previously selected group or population) : sample a sample of

**²subsample** *noun* (circa 1899)
: a sample or specimen obtained by subsampling

**sub·sat·el·lite** \ˌsəb-'sa-tᵊl-ˌīt\ *noun* (1956)
: an object carried into orbit in and subsequently released from a satellite or spacecraft

**sub·scribe** \səb-'skrīb\ *verb* **sub·scribed; sub·scrib·ing** [Middle English, from Latin *subscribere*, literally, to write beneath, from *sub- + scribere* to write — more at SCRIBE] (15th century)
*transitive verb*
**1** : to write (one's name) underneath : SIGN
**2 a** : to sign (as a document) with one's own hand in token of consent or obligation **b** : to attest by signing **c** : to pledge (a gift or contribution) by writing one's name with the amount
**3** : to assent to : SUPPORT
*intransitive verb*
**1** : to sign one's name to a document
**2 a** : to give consent or approval to something written by signing ⟨unwilling to *subscribe* to the agreement⟩ **b** : to set one's name to a paper in token of promise to give something (as a sum of money); *also* : to give something in accordance with such a promise **c** : to enter one's name for a publication or service; *also*

: to receive a periodical or service regularly on order **d** : to agree to purchase and pay for securities especially of a new offering ⟨*subscribed* for 1000 shares⟩
**3** : to feel favorably disposed ⟨I *subscribe* to your sentiments⟩
*synonym* see ASSENT
— **sub·scrib·er** *noun*

**sub·script** \'səb-ˌskript\ *noun* [Latin *subscriptus*, past participle of *subscribere*] (1895)
: a distinguishing symbol (as a letter or numeral) written immediately below or below and to the right or left of another character
— **subscript** *adjective*

**sub·scrip·tion** \səb-'skrip-shən\ *noun* [Middle English *subscripcioun* signature, from Latin *subscription-, subscriptio*, from *subscribere*] (15th century)
**1 a** : the act of signing one's name (as in attesting or witnessing a document) **b** : the acceptance (as of ecclesiastical articles of faith) attested by the signing of one's name
**2** : something that is subscribed: as **a** : an autograph signature; *also* : a paper to which a signature is attached **b** : a sum subscribed or pledged
**3** : an arrangement for providing, receiving, or making use of something of a continuing or periodic nature on a prepayment plan: as **a** : a purchase by prepayment for a certain number of issues (as of a periodical) **b** : application to purchase securities of a new issue **c** : a method of offering or presenting a series of public performances **d** *British* : membership dues

**subscription TV** *noun* (1953)
: pay-TV that broadcasts programs directly over the air to customers provided with a special receiver — called also *subscription television*; compare PAY-CABLE, PAY-TV

**sub·sec·tion** \'səb-ˌsek-shən\ *noun* (1621)
**1** : a subdivision or a subordinate division of a section
**2** : a subordinate part or branch

**¹sub·se·quence** \'səb-sə-ˌkwen(t)s, -si-kwən(t)s\ *noun* (circa 1500)
: the quality or state of being subsequent; *also* : a subsequent event

**²sub·se·quence** \'səb-ˌsē-kwən(t)s, -ˌkwen(t)s\ *noun* (1908)
: a mathematical sequence that is part of another sequence

**sub·se·quent** \'səb-si-kwənt, -sə-ˌkwent\ *adjective* [Middle English, from Latin *subsequent-, subsequens*, present participle of *subsequi* to follow close, from *sub-* near + *sequi* to follow — more at SUB-, SUE] (15th century)
: following in time, order, or place
— **subsequent** *noun*
— **sub·se·quent·ly** \-ˌkwent-lē, -kwənt-\ *adverb*

**subsequent to** *preposition* (1647)
: at a time later or more recent than : SINCE

**sub·serve** \(ˌ)səb-'sərv\ *transitive verb* [Latin *subservire* to serve, be subservient, from *sub- + servire* to serve] (1661)
**1** : to promote the welfare or purposes of
**2** : to serve as an instrument or means in carrying out

**sub·ser·vi·ence** \səb-'sər-vē-ən(t)s\ *noun* (circa 1676)
**1** : a subservient or subordinate place or function
**2** : obsequious servility

**sub·ser·vi·en·cy** \-ən(t)-sē\ *noun* (1651)
: SUBSERVIENCE

**sub·ser·vi·ent** \-ənt\ *adjective* [Latin *subservient-, subserviens*, present participle of *subservire*] (1632)
**1** : serving to promote some end
**2** : useful in an inferior capacity : SUBORDINATE
**3** : obsequiously submissive : TRUCKLING ☆
— **sub·ser·vi·ent·ly** *adverb*

**sub·set** \'səb-ˌset\ *noun* (1902)

: a set each of whose elements is an element of an inclusive set

**sub·shrub** \-ˌshrəb, *especially Southern* -ˌsrəb\ *noun* (1851)
: a perennial plant having woody stems except for the terminal part of the new growth which is killed back annually; *also* : a low shrub

**sub·side** \səb-'sīd\ *intransitive verb* **sub·sid·ed; sub·sid·ing** [Latin *subsidere*, from *sub- + sidere* to sit down, sink; akin to Latin *sedēre* to sit — more at SIT] (1607)
**1** : to sink or fall to the bottom : SETTLE
**2** : to tend downward : DESCEND; *especially* : to flatten out so as to form a depression
**3** : to let oneself settle down : SINK ⟨*subsided* into a chair⟩
**4** : to become quiet or less ⟨as the fever *subsides*⟩ ⟨my anger *subsided*⟩
*synonym* see ABATE
— **sub·si·dence** \səb-'sī-dᵊn(t)s, 'səb-sə-dən(t)s\ *noun*

**sub·sid·i·ar·i·ty** \ˌsəb-si-dē-'er-ə-tē, səb-ˌsi-\ *noun* (1936)
**1** : the quality or state of being subsidiary
**2** : a principle in social organization: functions which subordinate or local organizations perform effectively belong more properly to them than to a dominant central organization

**¹sub·sid·i·ary** \səb-'si-dē-ˌer-ē, -'si-də-rē\ *adjective* [Latin *subsidiarius*, from *subsidium* reserve troops] (1543)
**1 a** : furnishing aid or support : AUXILIARY ⟨*subsidiary* details⟩ **b** : of secondary importance ⟨a *subsidiary* stream⟩
**2** : of, relating to, or constituting a subsidy ⟨a *subsidiary* payment to an ally⟩
— **sub·sid·i·ari·ly** \-ˌsi-dē-'er-ə-lē\ *adverb*

**²subsidiary** *noun, plural* **-ar·ies** (1603)
: one that is subsidiary; *especially* : a company wholly controlled by another

**sub·si·dise** *British variant of* SUBSIDIZE

**sub·si·dize** \'səb-sə-ˌdīz, -zə-\ *transitive verb* **-dized; -diz·ing** (1795)
: to furnish with a subsidy: as **a** : to purchase the assistance of by payment of a subsidy **b** : to aid or promote (as a private enterprise) with public money ⟨*subsidize* soybean farmers⟩ ⟨*subsidize* public transportation⟩
— **sub·si·di·za·tion** \ˌsəb-sə-də-'zā-shən, -zə-\ *noun*
— **sub·si·diz·er** *noun*

**sub·si·dy** \'səb-sə-dē, -zə-\ *noun, plural* **-dies** [Middle English, from Latin *subsidium* reserve troops, support, assistance, from *sub-* near + *sedēre* to sit — more at SUB-, SIT] (14th century)
: a grant or gift of money: as **a** : a sum of money formerly granted by the British Parliament to the crown and raised by special taxation **b** : money granted by one state to another **c** : a grant by a government to a private person or company to assist an enterprise deemed advantageous to the public

**sub·sist** \səb-'sist\ *verb* [Late Latin *subsistere* to exist, from Latin, to come to a halt, remain, from *sub- + sistere* to come to a stand; akin to Latin *stare* to stand — more at STAND] (1549)

---

☆ **SYNONYMS**
**Subservient, servile, slavish, obsequious** mean showing or characterized by extreme compliance or abject obedience. SUBSERVIENT implies the cringing manner of one very conscious of a subordinate position ⟨domestic help was expected to be properly *subservient*⟩. SERVILE suggests the mean or fawning behavior of a slave ⟨a political boss and his entourage of *servile* hangers-on⟩. SLAVISH suggests abject or debased servility ⟨the *slavish* status of migrant farm workers⟩. OBSEQUIOUS implies fawning or sycophantic compliance and exaggerated deference of manner ⟨waiters who are *obsequious* in the presence of celebrities⟩.

*intransitive verb*
**1 a :** to have existence **:** BE **b :** PERSIST, CONTINUE
**2 :** to have or acquire the necessities of life (as food and clothing); *especially* **:** to nourish oneself ⟨*subsisting* on roots, berries and grubs⟩
**3 a :** to hold true **b :** to be logically conceivable as the subject of true statements
*transitive verb*
**:** to support with provisions
**sub·sis·tence** \səb-'sis-tən(t)s\ *noun* [Middle English, from Late Latin *subsistentia,* from *subsistent-, subsistens,* present participle of *subsistere*] (15th century)
**1 a** (1) **:** real being **:** EXISTENCE (2) **:** the condition of remaining in existence **:** CONTINUATION, PERSISTENCE **b :** an essential characteristic quality of something that exists **c :** the character possessed by whatever is logically conceivable
**2 :** means of subsisting: as **a :** the minimum (as of food and shelter) necessary to support life **b :** a source or means of obtaining the necessities of life
— **sub·sis·tent** \-tənt\ *adjective*
**subsistence farming** *noun* (1939)
**1 :** farming or a system of farming that provides all or almost all the goods required by the farm family usually without any significant surplus for sale
**2 :** farming or a system of farming that produces a minimum and often inadequate return to the farmer — called also *subsistence agriculture*
— **subsistence farmer** *noun*
**sub·so·cial** \ˌsəb-'sō-shəl\ *adjective* (circa 1909)
**:** incompletely social; *especially* **:** tending to associate gregariously but lacking fixed or complex social organization ⟨*subsocial* insects⟩
**¹sub·soil** \'səb-ˌsȯil\ *noun* (1799)
**:** the stratum of weathered material that underlies the surface soil
**²subsoil** *transitive verb* (1840)
**:** to turn, break, or stir the subsoil
— **sub·soil·er** *noun*
**sub·so·lar point** \ˌsəb-'sō-lər-\ *noun* (circa 1908)
**:** the point on the surface of the earth or a planet at which the sun is at the zenith
**sub·son·ic** \ˌsəb-'sä-nik\ *adjective* [International Scientific Vocabulary] (1937)
**1 :** of, relating to, or being a speed less than that of sound in air
**2 :** moving, capable of moving, or utilizing air currents moving at a subsonic speed
**3 :** INFRASONIC 1
— **sub·son·i·cal·ly** \-ni-k(ə-)lē\ *adverb*
**sub·space** \'səb-ˌspās\ *noun* (1927)
**:** a subset of a space; *especially* **:** one that has the essential properties (as those of a vector space or topological space) of the including space
**sub spe·cie ae·ter·ni·ta·tis** \ˌsùb-'spe-kē-ˌā-ˌī-ter-nə-'tä-təs\ *adverb* [New Latin, literally, under the aspect of eternity] (1895)
**:** in its essential or universal form or nature
**sub·spe·cies** \'səb-ˌspē-shēz, -sēz\ *noun* [New Latin] (1699)
**:** a subdivision of a species: as **a :** a category in biological classification that ranks immediately below a species and designates a population of a particular geographical region genetically distinguishable from other such populations of the same species and capable of interbreeding successfully with them where its range overlaps theirs **b :** a named subdivision (as a race or variety) of a taxonomic species **c :** SUBGROUP 1 ⟨*subspecies* of economy fares —Michael DiPaola⟩
— **sub·spe·cif·ic** \ˌsəb-spi-'si-fik\ *adjective*
**sub·stage** \'səb-ˌstāj\ *noun* (1888)
**:** an attachment to a microscope by means of which accessories (as mirrors, diaphragms, or

condensers) are held in place beneath the stage of the instrument
**sub·stance** \'səb-stən(t)s\ *noun* [Middle English, from Middle French, from Latin *substantia,* from *substant-, substans,* present participle of *substare* to stand under, from *sub-* + *stare* to stand — more at STAND] (14th century)
**1 a :** essential nature **:** ESSENCE **b :** a fundamental or characteristic part or quality **c** *Christian Science* **:** GOD 1b
**2 a :** ultimate reality that underlies all outward manifestations and change **b :** practical importance **:** MEANING, USEFULNESS ⟨the . . . bill—which will be without *substance* in the sense that it will authorize nothing more than a set of ideas —Richard Reeves⟩
**3 a :** physical material from which something is made or which has discrete existence **b :** matter of particular or definite chemical constitution **c :** something (as drugs or alcoholic beverages) deemed harmful and usually subject to legal restriction ⟨possession of a controlled *substance*⟩ ⟨has a *substance* problem⟩
**4 :** material possessions **:** PROPERTY ⟨a family of *substance*⟩
— **sub·stance·less** \-ləs\ *adjective*
— **in substance :** in respect to essentials **:** FUNDAMENTALLY
**substance abuse** *noun* (1982)
**:** excessive use of a drug (as alcohol, narcotics, or cocaine) **:** use of a drug without medical justification
— **substance abuser** *noun*
**substance P** *noun* (1934)
**:** a neuropeptide that consists of 11 amino-acid residues, that is widely distributed in the brain, spinal cord, and peripheral nervous system, and that acts across nerve synapses to produce prolonged postsynaptic excitation
**sub·stan·dard** \ˌsəb-'stan-dərd\ *adjective* (1897)
**:** deviating from or falling short of a standard or norm: as **a :** of a quality lower than that prescribed by law **b :** conforming to a pattern of linguistic usage existing within a speech community but not that of the prestige group in that community **c :** constituting a greater than normal risk to an insurer
**sub·stan·tial** \səb-'stan(t)-shəl\ *adjective* (14th century)
**1 a :** consisting of or relating to substance **b :** not imaginary or illusory **:** REAL, TRUE **c :** IMPORTANT, ESSENTIAL
**2 :** ample to satisfy and nourish **:** FULL ⟨a *substantial* meal⟩
**3 a :** possessed of means **:** WELL-TO-DO **b :** considerable in quantity **:** significantly great ⟨earned a *substantial* wage⟩
**4 :** firmly constructed **:** STURDY
**5 :** being largely but not wholly that which is specified ⟨a *substantial* lie⟩
— **substantial** *noun*
— **sub·stan·ti·al·i·ty** \-ˌstan(t)-shē-'a-lə-tē\ *noun*
— **sub·stan·tial·ly** \-'stan(t)-sh(ə-)lē\ *adverb*
— **sub·stan·tial·ness** \-'stan(t)-shəl-nəs\ *noun*
**sub·stan·tia ni·gra** \səb-ˌstan(t)-shē-ə-'nī-grə, -'ni-\ *noun, plural* **sub·stan·ti·ae ni·grae** \-chē-ˌē-'nī-(ˌ)grē, -'ni-\ [New Latin, literally, black substance] (1882)
**:** a layer of deeply pigmented gray matter situated in the midbrain and containing the cell bodies of a tract of dopamine-producing nerve cells whose secretion tends to be deficient in Parkinson's disease
**sub·stan·ti·ate** \səb-'stan(t)-shē-ˌāt\ *transitive verb* **-at·ed; -at·ing** (1657)
**1 :** to give substance or form to **:** EMBODY
**2 :** to establish by proof or competent evidence **:** VERIFY ⟨*substantiate* a charge⟩
**synonym** see CONFIRM
— **sub·stan·ti·a·tion** \-ˌstan(t)-shē-'ā-shən\ *noun*

— **sub·stan·ti·a·tive** \-'stan(t)-shē-ˌā-tiv\ *adjective*
**sub·stan·ti·val** \ˌsəb-stən-'tī-vəl\ *adjective* (circa 1832)
**:** of, relating to, or serving as a substantive
— **sub·stan·ti·val·ly** \-və-lē\ *adverb*
**¹sub·stan·tive** \'səb-stən-tiv\ *noun* [Middle English *substantif,* from Middle French, from *substantif,* adjective, having or expressing substance, from Late Latin *substantivus*] (14th century)
**:** NOUN; *broadly* **:** a word or word group functioning syntactically as a noun
— **sub·stan·tiv·ize** \-ti-ˌvīz\ *transitive verb*
**²sub·stan·tive** \'səb-stən-tiv; *2c & 3 also* səb-'stan-tiv\ *adjective* [Middle English, from Late Latin *substantivus* having substance, from Latin *substantia*] (14th century)
**1 :** being a totally independent entity
**2 a :** real rather than apparent **:** FIRM; *also* **:** PERMANENT, ENDURING **b :** belonging to the substance of a thing **:** ESSENTIAL **c :** expressing existence ⟨the *substantive* verb is the verb *to be*⟩ **d :** requiring or involving no mordant ⟨a *substantive* dyeing process⟩
**3 a :** having the nature or function of a grammatical substantive ⟨a *substantive* phrase⟩ **b :** relating to or having the character of a noun or pronominal term in logic
**4 :** considerable in amount or numbers **:** SUBSTANTIAL
**5 :** creating and defining rights and duties ⟨*substantive* law⟩ — compare PROCEDURAL
**6 :** having substance **:** involving matters of major or practical importance to all concerned ⟨*substantive* discussions among world leaders⟩
— **sub·stan·tive·ly** *adverb*
— **sub·stan·tive·ness** *noun*
**substantive due process** *noun* (1954)
**:** DUE PROCESS 2
**substantive right** *noun* (1939)
**:** a right (as of life, liberty, property, or reputation) held to exist for its own sake and to constitute part of the normal legal order of society
**sub·sta·tion** \'səb-ˌstā-shən\ *noun* (1881)
**:** a subordinate or subsidiary station: as **a :** a branch post office **b :** a subsidiary station in which electric current is transformed **c :** a police station serving a particular area
**sub·stit·u·ent** \səb-'sti-chə-wənt, -'stich-wənt\ *noun* [Latin *substituent-, substituens,* present participle of *substituere*] (circa 1896)
**:** an atom or group that replaces another atom or group in a molecule
— **substituent** *adjective*
**sub·sti·tut·able** \'səb-stə-ˌtü-tə-bəl, -'tyü-\ *adjective* (1805)
**:** capable of being substituted
— **sub·sti·tut·abil·i·ty** \ˌsəb-stə-ˌtü-tə-'bi-lə-tē, -ˌtyü-\ *noun*
**¹sub·sti·tute** \'səb-stə-ˌtüt, -ˌtyüt\ *noun* [Middle English, from Latin *substitutus,* past participle of *substituere* to put in place of, from *sub-* + *statuere* to set up, place — more at STATUTE] (15th century)
**:** a person or thing that takes the place or function of another
— **substitute** *adjective*
**²substitute** *verb* **-tut·ed; -tut·ing** (1588)
*transitive verb*
**1 a :** to put or use in the place of another **b :** to introduce (an atom or group) as a substituent; *also* **:** to alter (as a compound) by introduction of a substituent ⟨a *substituted* benzene ring⟩
**2 :** to take the place of **:** REPLACE
*intransitive verb*
**:** to serve as a substitute
**sub·sti·tu·tion** \ˌsəb-stə-'tü-shən, -'tyü-\ *noun*

[Middle English *substitucion,* from Middle French *substitution,* from Late Latin *substitution-, substitutio,* from *substituere*] (14th century)

**1 a :** the act, process, or result of substituting one thing for another **b :** replacement of one mathematical entity by another of equal value
**2 :** one that is substituted for another
— **sub·sti·tu·tion·al** \-shnəl, -shə-nᵊl\ *adjective*
— **sub·sti·tu·tion·al·ly** *adverb*
— **sub·sti·tu·tion·ary** \-shə-ˌner-ē\ *adjective*

**substitution cipher** *noun* (1936)
**:** a cipher in which the letters of the plaintext are systematically replaced by substitute letters — compare TRANSPOSITION CIPHER

**sub·sti·tu·tive** \'səb-stə-ˌtü-tiv, -ˌtyü-\ *adjective* (1668)
**:** serving or suitable as a substitute
— **sub·sti·tu·tive·ly** *adverb*

**sub·strate** \'səb-ˌstrāt\ *noun* [Medieval Latin *substratum*] (1807)
**1 :** SUBSTRATUM
**2 :** the base on which an organism lives ⟨the soil is the *substrate* of most seed plants⟩
**3 :** a substance acted upon (as by an enzyme)

**sub·stra·tum** \'səb-ˌstrā-təm, -ˌstra-, ˌsəb-'\ *noun, plural* **-stra·ta** \-tə\ [Medieval Latin, from Latin, neuter of *substratus,* past participle of *substernere* to spread under, from *sub-* + *sternere* to spread — more at STREW] (1631)
**:** an underlying support : FOUNDATION: as **a :** substance that is a permanent subject of qualities or phenomena **b :** the material of which something is made and from which it derives its special qualities **c :** a layer beneath the surface soil; *specifically* : SUBSOIL **d :** SUBSTRATE 2

**sub·struc·ture** \'səb-ˌstrək-chər\ *noun* (1726)
**:** an underlying or supporting part of a structure
— **sub·struc·tur·al** \-chə-rəl, -shrəl\ *adjective*

**sub·sume** \səb-'süm\ *transitive verb* **subsumed; sub·sum·ing** [New Latin *subsumere,* from Latin *sub-* + *sumere* to take up — more at CONSUME] (1825)
**:** to include or place within something larger or more comprehensive : encompass as a subordinate or component element ⟨red, green, and yellow are *subsumed* under the term "color"⟩
— **sub·sum·able** \-'sü-mə-bəl\ *adjective*

**sub·sump·tion** \səb-'səm(p)-shən\ *noun* [New Latin *subsumption-, subsumptio,* from *subsumere*] (1651)
**:** the act or process of subsuming

**¹sub·sur·face** \'səb-ˌsər-fəs\ *noun* (1778)
**:** earth material (as rock) near but not exposed at the surface of the ground

**²sub·sur·face** \ˌsəb-'sər-fəs\ *adjective* (1875)
**:** of, relating to, or being something located beneath a surface and especially underground

**sub·teen** \'səb-ˌtēn\ *noun* (1951)
**:** a preadolescent child

**sub·tem·per·ate** \ˌsəb-'tem-p(ə-)rət\ *adjective* (1852)
**:** of or occurring in the colder parts of the temperate zones

**sub·ten·an·cy** \-'te-nən(t)-sē\ *noun* (circa 1861)
**:** the state of being a subtenant

**sub·ten·ant** \-'te-nənt\ *noun* (15th century)
**:** one who rents from a tenant

**sub·tend** \səb-'tend\ *transitive verb* [Latin *subtendere* to stretch beneath, from *sub-* + *tendere* to stretch — more at THIN] (1570)
**1 a :** to be opposite to and extend from one side to the other of ⟨a hypotenuse *subtends* a right angle⟩ **b :** to fix the angular extent of with respect to a fixed point or object taken as the vertex ⟨the angle *subtended* at the eye by an object of given width and a fixed distance away⟩ ⟨a central angle *subtended* by an arc⟩ **c**

**:** to determine the measure of by marking off the endpoints of ⟨a chord *subtends* an arc⟩
**2 a :** to underlie so as to include **b :** to occupy an adjacent and usually lower position to and often so as to embrace or enclose ⟨a bract that *subtends* a flower⟩

**sub·ter·fuge** \'səb-tər-ˌfyüj\ *noun* [Late Latin *subterfugium,* from Latin *subterfugere* to escape, evade, from *subter-* secretly (from *subter* underneath; akin to Latin *sub* under) + *fugere* to flee — more at UP, FUGITIVE] (1573)
**1 :** deception by artifice or stratagem in order to conceal, escape, or evade
**2 :** a deceptive device or stratagem
*synonym* see DECEPTION

**sub·ter·mi·nal** \ˌsəb-'tərm-nəl, -'tər-mə-nᵊl\ *adjective* (1828)
**:** situated or occurring near but not precisely at an end ⟨a *subterminal* band of color on the tail feathers⟩

**sub·ter·ra·nean** \ˌsəb-tə-'rā-nē-ən, -nyən\ *also* **sub·ter·ra·neous** \-nē-əs, -nyəs\ *adjective* [Latin *subterraneus,* from *sub-* + *terra* earth — more at THIRST] (1603)
**1 :** being, lying, or operating under the surface of the earth
**2 :** existing or working in secret : HIDDEN
— **sub·ter·ra·nean·ly** *also* **sub·ter·ra·neous·ly** *adverb*

**sub·text** \'səb-ˌtekst\ *noun* (1950)
**:** the implicit or metaphorical meaning (as of a literary text)
— **sub·tex·tu·al** \ˌsəb-'teks-chə-wəl, -chəl\ *adjective*

**sub·thresh·old** \ˌsəb-'thre-ˌshōld, -'thresh-ˌhōld\ *adjective* (1942)
**:** inadequate to produce a response ⟨subthreshold dosage⟩ ⟨a *subthreshold* stimulus⟩

**sub·tile** \'sə-tᵊl, 'səb-tᵊl\ *adjective* **sub·til·er** \'sət-lər, 'sə-tᵊl-ər; 'səb-tə-lər\; **sub·til·est** \'sət-ləst, 'sə-tᵊl-əst; 'səb-tə-ləst\ [Middle English, from Latin *subtilis*] (14th century)
**1 :** SUBTLE, ELUSIVE ⟨a *subtile* aroma⟩
**2 a :** CUNNING, CRAFTY **b :** SAGACIOUS, DISCERNING
— **sub·tile·ly** \'sət-lē, 'sə-tᵊl-(l)ē; 'səb-tə-lē\ *adverb*
— **sub·tile·ness** \'sə-tᵊl-nəs, 'səb-tᵊl-\ *noun*

**sub·til·i·sin** \ˌsəb-'ti-lə-sən\ *noun* [New Latin *subtilis,* specific epithet of *Bacillus subtilis,* species to which *Bacillus amyloliquefaciens* was once thought to belong] (1953)
**:** an extracellular protease produced by a soil bacillus (*Bacillus amyloliquefaciens*)

**sub·til·ize** \'sə-tᵊl-ˌīz, 'səb-tə-ˌlīz\ *verb* **-ized; -iz·ing** (1592)
*intransitive verb*
**:** to act or think subtly
*transitive verb*
**:** to make subtile
— **sub·til·i·za·tion** \ˌsə-tᵊl-ə-ˌzā-shən, ˌsəb-tə-lə-\ *noun*

**sub·til·ty** \'sə-tᵊl-tē, 'səb-tᵊl-\ *noun, plural* **-ties** (14th century)
**:** SUBTLETY

**¹sub·ti·tle** \'səb-ˌtī-tᵊl\ *noun* (1825)
**1 :** a secondary or explanatory title
**2 :** a printed statement or fragment of dialogue appearing on the screen between the scenes of a silent motion picture or appearing as a translation at the bottom of the screen during the scenes of a motion picture or television show in a foreign language

**²subtitle** *transitive verb* (1891)
**:** to give a subtitle to

**sub·tle** \'sə-tᵊl\ *adjective* **sub·tler** \'sət-lər, 'sə-tᵊl-ər\; **sub·tlest** \'sət-ləst, 'sə-tᵊl-əst\ [Middle English *sutil, sotil,* from Middle French *soutil,* from Latin *subtilis,* literally, finely textured, from *sub-* + *tela* cloth on a loom; akin to Latin *texere* to weave — more at TECHNICAL] (14th century)
**1 a :** DELICATE, ELUSIVE ⟨a *subtle* fragrance⟩ **b :** difficult to understand or perceive : OBSCURE ⟨*subtle* differences in sound⟩
**2 a :** PERCEPTIVE, REFINED ⟨a writer's sharp and

*subtle* moral sense⟩ **b :** having or marked by keen insight and ability to penetrate deeply and thoroughly ⟨a *subtle* scholar⟩
**3 a :** highly skillful : EXPERT ⟨a *subtle* craftsman⟩ **b :** cunningly made or contrived : INGENIOUS
**4 :** ARTFUL, CRAFTY ⟨a *subtle* rogue⟩
**5 :** operating insidiously ⟨*subtle* poisons⟩
— **sub·tle·ness** \'sə-tᵊl-nəs\ *noun*
— **sub·tly** \'sət-lē, 'sə-tᵊl-(l)ē\ *adverb*

**sub·tle·ty** \'sət-ᵊl-tē\ *noun, plural* **-ties** [Middle English *sutilte,* from Middle French *sutilté,* from Latin *subtilitat-, subtilitas,* from *subtilis*] (14th century)
**1 :** the quality or state of being subtle
**2 :** something subtle

**sub·ton·ic** \ˌsəb-'tä-nik\ *noun* [from its being a half tone below the upper tonic] (circa 1854)
**:** LEADING TONE

**¹sub·to·tal** \'səb-ˌtō-tᵊl\ *noun* (1906)
**:** the sum of part of a series of figures

**²sub·to·tal** \ˌsəb-'tō-tᵊl\ *adjective* (1908)
**:** somewhat less than complete : nearly total ⟨*subtotal* thyroidectomy⟩
— **sub·to·tal·ly** *adverb*

**sub·tract** \səb-'trakt\ *verb* [Latin *subtractus,* past participle of *subtrahere* to draw from beneath, withdraw, from *sub-* + *trahere* to draw] (1557)
*transitive verb*
**:** to take away by or as if by deducting ⟨*subtract* 5 from 9⟩ ⟨*subtract* funds from the project⟩
*intransitive verb*
**:** to perform a subtraction
— **sub·tract·er** *noun*

**sub·trac·tion** \səb-'trak-shən\ *noun* [Middle English *subtraccion,* from Late Latin *subtraction-, subtractio,* from *subtrahere*] (15th century)
**:** an act, operation, or instance of subtracting: as **a :** the withdrawing or withholding of a right to which an individual is entitled **b :** the operation of deducting one number from another

**sub·trac·tive** \-'trak-tiv\ *adjective* (1690)
**1 :** tending to subtract
**2 :** constituting or involving subtraction

**sub·tra·hend** \'səb-trə-ˌhend\ *noun* [Latin *subtrahendus,* gerundive of *subtrahere*] (1674)
**:** a number that is to be subtracted from a minuend

**sub·trop·i·cal** \ˌsəb-'trä-pi-kəl\ *also* **sub·trop·ic** \-pik\ *adjective* [International Scientific Vocabulary] (1842)
**:** of, relating to, or being the regions bordering on the tropical zone ⟨*subtropical* environment⟩ ⟨*subtropical* grasses⟩

**sub·trop·ics** \-piks\ *noun plural* (1886)
**:** subtropical regions

**su·bu·late** \'sü-byə-lət, 'sə-, -ˌlāt\ *adjective* [New Latin *subulatus,* from Latin *subula* awl, from *suere* to sew — more at SEW] (circa 1760)
**:** linear and tapering to a fine point ⟨a *subulate* leaf⟩

**sub·um·brel·la** \ˌsəb-(ˌ)əm-'bre-lə\ *noun* (1878)
**:** the concave undersurface of a jellyfish

**sub·urb** \'sə-ˌbərb\ *noun* [Middle English, from Latin *suburbium,* from *sub-* near + *urbs* city — more at SUB-] (14th century)
**1 a :** an outlying part of a city or town **b :** a smaller community adjacent to or within commuting distance of a city **c** *plural* **:** the residential area on the outskirts of a city or large town
**2** *plural* **:** the near vicinity : ENVIRONS
— **sub·ur·ban** \sə-'bər-bən\ *adjective or noun*
— **sub·ur·ban·ite** \-bə-ˌnīt\ *noun*

**sub·ur·ban·ise** *British variant of* SUBURBANIZE

**sub·ur·ban·ize** \sə-'bər-bə-ˌnīz\ *transitive verb* **-ized; -iz·ing** (1893)

: to make suburban : give a suburban character to

— **sub·ur·ban·i·za·tion** \-ˌbər-bə-nə-'zā-shən\ *noun*

**sub·ur·bia** \sə-'bər-bē-ə\ *noun* [New Latin, from English *suburb*] (1895)
**1** : the suburbs of a city
**2** : people who live in the suburbs
**3** : suburban life

**sub·ven·tion** \səb-'ven(t)-shən\ *noun* [Middle English *subvencion*, from Old French & Late Latin; Old French *subvención*, from Late Latin *subvention-, subventio* assistance, from Latin *subvenire* to come up, come to the rescue, from *sub-* up + *venire* to come — more at SUB-, COME] (15th century)
: the provision of assistance or financial support: as **a** : ENDOWMENT **b** : a subsidy from a government or foundation

— **sub·ven·tion·ary** \-shə-ˌner-ē\ *adjective*

**sub·ver·sion** \səb-'vər-zhən, -shən\ *noun* [Middle English, from Middle French, from Late Latin *subversion-, subversio*, from Latin *subvertere*] (14th century)
**1** : the act of subverting : the state of being subverted; *especially* : a systematic attempt to overthrow or undermine a government or political system by persons working secretly from within
**2** *obsolete* : a cause of overthrow or destruction

— **sub·ver·sion·ary** \-zhə-ˌner-ē, -shə-\ *adjective*
— **sub·ver·sive** \-'vər-siv, -ziv\ *adjective or noun*
— **sub·ver·sive·ly** *adverb*
— **sub·ver·sive·ness** *noun*

**sub·vert** \səb-'vərt\ *transitive verb* [Middle English, from Middle French *subvertir*, from Latin *subvertere*, literally, to turn from beneath, from *sub-* + *vertere* to turn — more at WORTH] (14th century)
**1** : to overturn or overthrow from the foundation : RUIN
**2** : to pervert or corrupt by an undermining of morals, allegiance, or faith

— **sub·vert·er** *noun*

**sub·vi·ral** \ˌsəb-'vī-rəl\ *adjective* (1963)
: relating to, being, or caused by a piece or a structural part (as a protein) of a virus ⟨*subviral* infection⟩

**sub·vo·cal** \-'vō-kəl\ *adjective* (1924)
: characterized by the occurrence in the mind of words in speech order with or without inaudible articulation of the speech organs

— **sub·vo·cal·ly** \-kə-lē\ *adverb*

**sub·vo·cal·i·za·tion** \ˌsəb-ˌvō-kə-lə-'zā-shən\ *noun* (1947)
: the act or process of inaudibly articulating speech with the speech organs

— **sub·vo·cal·ize** \ˌsəb-'vō-kə-ˌlīz\ *verb*

**sub·way** \'səb-ˌwā\ *noun* (1825)
: an underground way: as **a** : a passage under a street (as for pedestrians, power cables, or water or gas mains) **b** : a usually electric underground railway **c** : UNDERPASS

— **subway** *intransitive verb*

**suc·ce·da·ne·um** \ˌsək-sə-'dā-nē-əm\ *noun, plural* **-ne·ums** *or* **-nea** \-nē-ə\ [New Latin, from Latin, neuter of *succedaneus* substituted, from *succedere* to follow after] (1641)
: SUBSTITUTE

— **suc·ce·da·ne·ous** \-nē-əs\ *adjective*

**suc·ce·dent** \sək-'sē-dᵊnt\ *adjective* [Middle English, from Latin *succedent-, succedens*, present participle of *succedere*] (15th century)
: coming next : SUCCEEDING, SUBSEQUENT

**suc·ceed** \sək-'sēd\ *verb* [Middle English *succeden*, from Old French *succeder* to go up, follow after, succeed, from *sub-* near + *cedere* to go — more at SUB-] (14th century)
*intransitive verb*
**1 a** : to come next after another in office or position or in possession of an estate; *especially* : to inherit sovereignty, rank, or title **b** : to follow after another in order

**2 a** : to turn out well **b** : to attain a desired object or end
**3** *obsolete* : to pass to a person by inheritance
*transitive verb*
**1** : to follow in sequence and especially immediately
**2** : to come after as heir or successor

**synonym** see FOLLOW

— **suc·ceed·er** *noun*

**suc·cès de scan·dale** \sək-ˌsā-də-skä�207-'däl, (ˌ)sük-\ *noun* [French, literally, success of scandal] (1896)
: something (as a work of art) that wins popularity or notoriety because of its scandalous nature; *also* : the reception accorded such a piece

**suc·cès d'es·time** \-ˌdes-'tēm\ *noun* [French, literally, success of esteem] (1859)
: something (as a work of art) that wins critical respect but not popular success; *also* : the reception accorded such a piece

**suc·cès fou** \-'fü\ *noun* [French, literally, mad success] (1878)
: an extraordinary success

**suc·cess** \sək-'ses\ *noun* [Latin *successus*, from *succedere*] (1537)
**1** *obsolete* : OUTCOME, RESULT
**2 a** : degree or measure of succeeding **b** : favorable or desired outcome; *also* : the attainment of wealth, favor, or eminence
**3** : one that succeeds

**suc·cess·ful** \-fəl\ *adjective* (1588)
**1** : resulting or terminating in success
**2** : gaining or having gained success

— **suc·cess·ful·ly** \-fə-lē\ *adverb*
— **suc·cess·ful·ness** *noun*

**suc·ces·sion** \sək-'se-shən\ *noun* [Middle English, from Middle French or Latin; Middle French, from Latin *succession-, successio*, from *succedere*] (14th century)
**1 a** : the order in which or the conditions under which one person after another succeeds to a property, dignity, title, or throne **b** : the right of a person or line to succeed **c** : the line having such a right
**2 a** : the act or process of following in order : SEQUENCE **b** (1) : the act or process of one person's taking the place of another in the enjoyment of or liability for rights or duties or both (2) : the act or process of a person's becoming beneficially entitled to a property or property interest of a deceased person **c** : the continuance of corporate personality **d** : unidirectional change in the composition of an ecosystem as the available competing organisms and especially the plants respond to and modify the environment
**3 a** : a number of persons or things that follow each other in sequence **b** : a group, type, or series that succeeds or displaces another

— **suc·ces·sion·al** \-'sesh-nəl, -'se-shə-nᵊl\ *adjective*
— **suc·ces·sion·al·ly** *adverb*

**succession duty** *noun* (1853)
*chiefly British* : INHERITANCE TAX

**suc·ces·sive** \sək-'se-siv\ *adjective* (15th century)
**1** : following in order : following each other without interruption
**2** : characterized by or produced in succession

— **suc·ces·sive·ly** *adverb*
— **suc·ces·sive·ness** *noun*

**suc·ces·sor** \sək-'se-sər\ *noun* [Middle English *successour*, from Old French, from Latin *successor*, from *succedere*] (14th century)
: one that follows; *especially* : one who succeeds to a throne, title, estate, or office

**suc·ci·nate** \'sək-sə-ˌnāt\ *noun* (1790)
: a salt or ester of succinic acid

**succinate dehydrogenase** *noun* (1962)
: an iron-containing flavoprotein enzyme that catalyzes often reversibly the dehydrogenation of succinic acid to fumaric acid in the Krebs cycle and that is widely distributed especially in animal tissues, bacteria, and yeast — called also *succinic dehydrogenase*

**suc·cinct** \(ˌ)sək-'siŋ(k)t, sə-'siŋ(k)t\ *adjective* [Middle English, from Latin *succinctus*, past participle of *succingere* to gird from below, tuck up, from *sub-* + *cingere* to gird — more at CINCTURE] (15th century)
**1** *archaic* **a** : being girded **b** : close-fitting
**2** : marked by compact precise expression without wasted words

**synonym** see CONCISE

— **suc·cinct·ly** \-'siŋ(k)t-lē, -'siŋ-klē\ *adverb*
— **suc·cinct·ness** \-'siŋt-nəs, -'siŋk-nəs\ *noun*

**suc·cin·ic acid** \(ˌ)sək-'si-nik-\ *noun* [French *succinique*, from Latin *succinum* amber] (circa 1790)
: a crystalline dicarboxylic acid $C_4H_6O_4$ found widely in nature and active in energy-yielding metabolic reactions

**suc·ci·nyl** \'sək-sə-nᵊl, -ˌnil\ *noun* [International Scientific Vocabulary] (circa 1868)
: either of two groups of succinic acid: **a** : a bivalent group $OCCH_2CH_2CO$ **b** : a univalent group $HOOCCH_2CH_2CO$

**suc·ci·nyl·cho·line** \ˌsək-sə-nᵊl-'kō-ˌlēn, -ˌnil-\ *noun* (1950)
: a basic compound that is used intravenously chiefly in the form of a hydrated chloride $C_{14}H_{30}Cl_2N_2O_4 \cdot 2H_2O$ as a muscle relaxant in surgery

**¹suc·cor** \'sə-kər\ *noun* [Middle English *succur*, from earlier *sucurs*, taken as plural, from Old French *sucors*, from Medieval Latin *succursus*, from Latin *succurrere* to run up, run to help, from *sub-* up + *currere* to run — more at CAR] (13th century)
**1** : RELIEF; *also* : AID, HELP
**2** : something that furnishes relief

**²succor** *transitive verb* **suc·cored; suc·cor·ing** \'sə-k(ə-)riŋ\ (13th century)
: to go to the aid of : RELIEVE

— **suc·cor·er** \'sə-kər-ər\ *noun*

**suc·co·ry** \'sə-k(ə-)rē\ *noun* [alteration of Middle English *cicoree*] (1533)
: CHICORY

**suc·co·tash** \'sə-kə-ˌtash\ *noun* [Narraganset *msíckquatash* boiled corn kernels] (1751)
: lima or shell beans and green corn cooked together

**suc·cour** \'sə-kər\ *chiefly British variant of* SUCCOR

**suc·cu·ba** \'sə-kyə-bə\ *noun, plural* **-bae** \-ˌbē, -ˌbī\ [Latin, paramour] (1559)
: SUCCUBUS

**suc·cu·bus** \-bəs\ *noun, plural* **-bi** \-ˌbī, -ˌbē\ [Middle English, from Medieval Latin, alteration of Latin *succuba* paramour, from *succubare* to lie under, from *sub-* + *cubare* to lie, recline] (14th century)
: a demon assuming female form to have sexual intercourse with men in their sleep — compare INCUBUS

**suc·cu·lence** \'sə-kyə-lən(t)s\ *noun* (1787)
**1** : the state of being succulent
**2** : succulent feed ⟨wild game subsisting on *succulence*⟩

**¹suc·cu·lent** \-lənt\ *adjective* [Latin *suculentus*, from *sucus* juice, sap; perhaps akin to Latin *sugere* to suck — more at SUCK] (1601)
**1 a** : full of juice : JUICY **b** : moist and tasty : TOOTHSOME **c** *of a plant* : having fleshy tissues that conserve moisture
**2** : rich in interest

— **suc·cu·lent·ly** *adverb*

**²succulent** *noun* (1825)
: a succulent plant (as a cactus)

**suc·cumb** \sə-'kəm\ *intransitive verb* [French & Latin; French *succomber*, from Latin *succumbere*, from *sub-* + *-cumbere* to lie down; akin to Latin *cubare* to lie] (1604)

---

\ə\ **abut** \ᵊ\ **kitten** \ər\ **further** \a\ **ash** \ā\ **ace** \ä\ **mop, mar** \au̇\ **out** \ch\ **chin** \e\ **bet** \ē\ **easy** \g\ **go** \i\ **hit** \ī\ **ice** \j\ **job** \ŋ\ **sing** \ō\ **go** \ȯ\ **law** \ȯi\ **boy** \th\ **thin** \t͟h\ **the** \ü\ **loot** \u̇\ **foot** \y\ **yet** \zh\ **vision** *see also* Guide to Pronunciation

**1** : to yield to superior strength or force or overpowering appeal or desire
**2** : to be brought to an end (as death) by the effect of destructive or disruptive forces
*synonym* see YIELD

**¹such** \'səch, 'sich\ *adjective* [Middle English, from Old English *swilc;* akin to Old High German *sulīh* such, Old English *swā* so, *gelīk* like — more at SO, LIKE] (before 12th century)
**1 a** : of a kind or character to be indicated or suggested ⟨a bag *such* as a doctor carries⟩ **b** : having a quality to a degree to be indicated ⟨his excitement was *such* that he shouted⟩
**2** : of the character, quality, or extent previously indicated or implied ⟨in the past few years many *such* women have shifted to full-time jobs⟩
**3** : of so extreme a degree or quality ⟨never heard *such* a hubbub⟩
**4** : of the same class, type, or sort ⟨other *such* clinics throughout the state⟩
**5** : not specified

**²such** *pronoun* (before 12th century)
**1** : such a person or thing
**2** : someone or something stated, implied, or exemplified ⟨*such* was the result⟩
**3** : someone or something similar : similar persons or things ⟨tin and glass and *such*⟩
**— as such** : intrinsically considered : in itself ⟨*as such* the gift was worth little⟩

**³such** *adverb* (before 12th century)
**1 a** : to such a degree : so ⟨*such* tall buildings⟩ ⟨*such* a fine person⟩ **b** : VERY, ESPECIALLY ⟨hasn't been in *such* good spirits lately⟩
**2** : in such a way ⟨related *such* that each excludes the other⟩

**¹such and such** *adjective* (13th century)
: not named or specified

**²such and such** *pronoun* (15th century)
: something not specified

**¹such·like** \'səch-ˌlīk\ *adjective* (15th century)
: of like kind : SIMILAR

**²suchlike** *pronoun* (15th century)
: SUCH 3

**¹suck** \'sək\ *verb* [Middle English *suken,* from Old English *sūcan;* akin to Old High German *sūgan* to suck, Latin *sugere*] (before 12th century)
*transitive verb*
**1 a** : to draw (as liquid) into the mouth through a suction force produced by movements of the lips and tongue ⟨*sucked* milk from his mother's breast⟩ **b** : to draw something from or consume by such movements ⟨*suck* an orange⟩ ⟨*suck* a lollipop⟩ **c** : to apply the mouth to or to or as if to suck out a liquid ⟨*sucked* his burned finger⟩
**2 a** : to draw by or as if by suction ⟨when a receding wave *sucks* the sand from under your feet —Kenneth Brower⟩ ⟨inadvertently *sucked* into the . . . intrigue —Martin Levin⟩ **b** : to take in and consume by or as if by suction ⟨a vacuum cleaner *sucking* up dirt⟩ ⟨*suck* up a few beers⟩ ⟨opponents say that malls *suck* the life out of downtown areas —Michael Knight⟩
*intransitive verb*
**1** : to draw something in by or as if by exerting a suction force; *especially* : to draw milk from a breast or udder with the mouth
**2** : to make a sound or motion associated with or caused by suction ⟨his pipe *sucked* wetly⟩ ⟨flanks *sucked* in and out, the long nose resting on his paws —Virginia Woolf⟩
**3** : to act in an obsequious manner ⟨when they want votes . . . the candidates come *sucking* around —W. G. Hardy⟩ ⟨*sucked* up to the boss⟩
**4** *slang* : to be objectionable or inadequate ⟨our lifestyle *sucks* —*Playboy*⟩ ⟨people who went said it *sucked* —H. S. Thompson⟩

**²suck** *noun* (13th century)
**1** : a sucking movement or force
**2** : the act of sucking

**¹suck·er** \'sə-kər\ *noun* (14th century)
**1 a** : one that sucks especially a breast or udder : SUCKLING **b** : a device for creating or reg-

ulating suction (as a piston or valve in a pump) **c** : a pipe or tube through which something is drawn by suction **d** (1) : an organ in various animals for adhering or holding (2) : a mouth (as of a leech) adapted for sucking or adhering
**2** : a shoot from the roots or lower part of the stem of a plant
**3** : any of numerous chiefly North American freshwater bony fishes (family Catostomidae) closely related to the carps but distinguished from them especially by the structure of the mouth which usually has thick soft lips
**4** : LOLLIPOP 1
**5 a** : a person easily cheated or deceived **b** : a person irresistibly attracted by something specified ⟨a *sucker* for ghost stories⟩ **c** — used as generalized term of reference ⟨see if you can get that *sucker* working again⟩

**²sucker** *verb* **suck·ered; suck·er·ing** \'sə-k(ə-)riŋ\ (circa 1661)
*transitive verb*
**1** : to remove suckers from ⟨*sucker* tobacco⟩
**2** : HOODWINK
*intransitive verb*
: to send out suckers

**sucker punch** *transitive verb* (1964)
: to punch (a person) suddenly without warning and often without apparent provocation
**— sucker punch** *noun*

**suck in** *transitive verb* (1840)
**1** : DUPE, HOODWINK
**2** : to contract, flatten, and tighten (the abdomen) especially by inhaling deeply

**suck·ing** *adjective* (before 12th century)
: not yet weaned; *broadly* : very young

**sucking louse** *noun* (circa 1907)
: any of an order (Anoplura) of wingless insects comprising the true lice with mouthparts adapted to sucking body fluids

**suck·le** \'sə-kəl\ *verb* **suck·led; suck·ling** \-k(ə-)liŋ\ [Middle English *suklen,* probably back-formation from *suklyng*] (14th century)
*transitive verb*
**1 a** : to give milk to from the breast or udder ⟨a mother *suckling* her child⟩ **b** : to nurture as if by giving milk from the breast ⟨was *suckled* on pulp magazines⟩
**2** : to draw milk from the breast or udder of ⟨lambs *suckling* the ewes⟩
*intransitive verb*
: to draw milk from the breast or udder

**suck·ling** \'sə-kəl\ *noun* [Middle English *suklyng,* from *suken* to suck] (13th century)
: a young unweaned animal

**su·crase** \'sü-ˌkrās, -ˌkrāz\ *noun* [International Scientific Vocabulary, from French *sucre* sugar, from Middle French — more at SUGAR] (circa 1900)
: INVERTASE

**su·cre** \'sü-(ˌ)krā\ *noun* [Spanish, from Antonio José de *Sucre*] (1886)
— see MONEY table

**su·crose** \'sü-ˌkrōs, -ˌkrōz\ *noun* [International Scientific Vocabulary, from French *sucre* sugar] (1857)
: a sweet crystalline dextrorotatory disaccharide sugar $C_{12}H_{22}O_{11}$ that occurs naturally in most plants and is obtained commercially especially from sugarcane or sugar beets

**¹suc·tion** \'sək-shən\ *noun* [Late Latin *suction-, suctio,* from Latin *sugere* to suck — more at SUCK] (1626)
**1** : the act or process of sucking
**2 a** : the act or process of exerting a force upon a solid, liquid, or gaseous body by reason of reduced air pressure over part of its surface **b** : force so exerted
**3** : a device (as a pipe or fitting) used in a machine that operates by suction
**— suc·tion·al** \-shə-nᵊl, -shnəl\ *adjective*

**²suction** *transitive verb* (1954)
: to remove (as from a body cavity or passage) by suction

**suction cup** *noun* (1942)

: a cup-shaped device in which a partial vacuum can be produced when applied to a surface

**suction pump** *noun* (1825)
: a common pump in which the liquid to be raised is pushed by atmospheric pressure into the partial vacuum under a retreating valved piston on the upstroke and reflux is prevented by a check valve in the pipe

**suction stop** *noun* (1887)
: a voice stop in the formation of which air behind the articulation is rarefied with consequent inrush of air when articulation is broken

**suc·to·ri·al** \sək-'tōr-ē-əl, -'tȯr-\ *adjective* [New Latin *suctorius,* from Latin *sugere*] (1833)
: adapted for sucking; *especially* : serving to draw up fluid or to adhere by suction ⟨*suctorial* mouths⟩

**suc·to·ri·an** \-ē-ən\ *noun* [New Latin *Suctoria,* from neuter plural of *suctorius* suctorial] (circa 1842)
: any of a class or subclass (Suctoria) of complex protozoans which are ciliated only early in development and in which the mature form is fixed to the substrate, lacks locomotor organelles or a mouth, and obtains food through specialized suctorial tentacles

**Su·dan grass** \sü-'dan-, -'dän-\ *noun* [the *Sudan,* region in Africa] (1911)
: a vigorous tall-growing annual sorghum grass (*Sorghum bicolor sudanese*) widely grown for hay and fodder

**Su·dan·ic** \sü-'da-nik\ *noun* [the *Sudan* region] (1912)
: a group of languages neither Bantu nor Afro-Asiatic spoken in central and western Africa that were formerly considered a residual category and are now divided among the Niger-Congo and other families
**— Sudanic** *adjective*

**su·da·to·ri·um** \ˌsü-də-'tōr-ē-əm, -'tȯr-\ *noun* [Latin, from *sudare* to sweat — more at SWEAT] (circa 1757)
: a sweat room in a bath

**su·da·to·ry** \'sü-də-ˌtōr-ē, -ˌtȯr-\ *noun, plural* **-ries** (1615)
: SUDATORIUM

**sudd** \'səd\ *noun* [Arabic, literally, obstruction] (1874)
: floating vegetable matter that forms obstructive masses especially in the upper White Nile

**¹sud·den** \'sə-dᵊn\ *adjective* [Middle English *sodain,* from Middle French, from Latin *subitaneus,* from *subitus* sudden, from past participle of *subire* to come up, from *sub-* up + *ire* to go — more at SUB-, ISSUE] (14th century)
**1 a** : happening or coming unexpectedly ⟨a *sudden* shower⟩ **b** : changing angle or character all at once
**2** : marked by or manifesting abruptness or haste
**3** : made or brought about in a short time : PROMPT
*synonym* see PRECIPITATE
**— sud·den·ly** *adverb*
**— sud·den·ness** \'sə-dᵊn-(n)əs\ *noun*

**²sudden** *noun* (1559)
*obsolete* : an unexpected occurrence : EMERGENCY
**— all of a sudden** *or* **on a sudden** : sooner than was expected : at once

**sudden death** *noun* (14th century)
**1** : unexpected death that is instantaneous or occurs within minutes from any cause other than violence ⟨*sudden death* following coronary occlusion⟩

**2 :** extra play to break a tie in a sports contest in which the first to go ahead wins

**sudden infant death syndrome** *noun* (1970)
**:** death of an apparently healthy infant usually before one year of age that is of unknown cause and occurs especially during sleep — called also *crib death*; abbreviation *SIDS*

**su·do·rif·er·ous** \ˌsü-də-ˈri-f(ə-)rəs\ *adjective* [Late Latin *sudorifer*, from Latin *sudor* sweat (from *sudare* to sweat) + *-ifer* -iferous — more at SWEAT] (1597)
**:** producing or conveying sweat ⟨*sudoriferous* glands⟩ ⟨a *sudoriferous* duct⟩

**su·do·rif·ic** \-ˈri-fik\ *adjective* [New Latin *sudorificus*, from Latin *sudor*] (1626)
**:** causing or inducing sweat **:** DIAPHORETIC ⟨*sudorific* herbs⟩
**— sudorific** *noun*

**Su·dra** \ˈsü-drə, ˈshü-\ *noun* [Sanskrit *śūdra*] (1630)
**:** a Hindu of a lower caste traditionally assigned to menial occupations
**— Sudra** *adjective*

**¹suds** \ˈsədz\ *noun plural but singular or plural in construction* [probably from Middle Dutch *sudse* marsh; akin to Old English *sēothan* to seethe — more at SEETHE] (1581)
**1 :** water impregnated with soap or a synthetic detergent compound and worked up into froth; *also* **:** the lather or froth on such water
**2 a :** FOAM, FROTH **b :** BEER
**— suds·less** \-ləs\ *adjective*

**²suds** (1834)
*transitive verb*
**:** to wash in suds
*intransitive verb*
**:** to form suds

**suds·er** \ˈsəd-zər\ *noun* (1967)
**:** SOAP OPERA

**sudsy** \ˈsəd-zē\ *adjective* **suds·i·er; -est** (1866)
**1 :** full of suds **:** FROTHY, FOAMY
**2 :** SOAPY 4

**sue** \ˈsü\ *verb* **sued; su·ing** [Middle English, from Middle French *suivre*, from (assumed) Vulgar Latin *sequere*, from Latin *sequi* to follow, come or go after; akin to Greek *hepesthai* to follow, Sanskrit *sacate* he accompanies] (14th century)
*transitive verb*
**1** *obsolete* **:** to make petition to or for
**2** *archaic* **:** to pay court or suit to **:** WOO
**3 a :** to seek justice or right from (a person) by legal process; *specifically* **:** to bring an action against **b :** to proceed with and follow up (a legal action) to proper termination
*intransitive verb*
**1 :** to make a request or application **:** PLEAD — usually used with *for* or *to*
**2 :** to pay court **:** WOO
**3 :** to take legal proceedings in court
**— su·er** *noun*

**¹suede** *or* **suède** \ˈswād\ *noun* [French *gants de Suède* Swedish gloves] (1884)
**1 :** leather with a napped surface
**2 :** a fabric finished with a nap to simulate suede

**²suede** *verb* **sued·ed; sued·ing** (1921)
*transitive verb*
**:** to give a suede finish or nap to (a fabric or leather)
*intransitive verb*
**:** to give cloth or leather a suede finish

**su·et** \ˈsü-ət\ *noun* [Middle English *sewet*, from (assumed) Anglo-French, diminutive of Anglo-French *sue*, from Latin *sebum* tallow] (14th century)
**:** the hard fat about the kidneys and loins in beef and mutton that yields tallow

**suf·fer** \ˈsə-fər\ *verb* **suf·fered; suf·fer·ing** \-f(ə-)riŋ\ [Middle English *suffren*, from Old French *souffrir*, from (assumed) Vulgar Latin *sufferire*, from Latin *sufferre*, from *sub-* up + *ferre* to bear — more at SUB-, BEAR] (13th century)
*transitive verb*
**1 a :** to submit to or be forced to endure ⟨*suffer* martyrdom⟩ **b :** to feel keenly **:** labor under ⟨*suffer* thirst⟩
**2 :** UNDERGO, EXPERIENCE
**3 :** to put up with especially as inevitable or unavoidable
**4 :** to allow especially by reason of indifference ⟨the eagle *suffers* little birds to sing —Shakespeare⟩
*intransitive verb*
**1 :** to endure death, pain, or distress
**2 :** to sustain loss or damage
**3 :** to be subject to disability or handicap
*synonym* see BEAR
**— suf·fer·able** \ˈsə-f(ə-)rə-bəl\ *adjective*
**— suf·fer·able·ness** *noun*
**— suf·fer·ably** \-blē\ *adverb*
**— suf·fer·er** \ˈsə-fər-ər\ *noun*

**suf·fer·ance** \ˈsə-f(ə-)rən(t)s\ *noun* (14th century)
**1 :** patient endurance **:** LONG-SUFFERING
**2 :** PAIN, MISERY
**3 :** consent or sanction implied by a lack of interference or failure to enforce a prohibition
**4 :** power or ability to withstand **:** ENDURANCE

**suffering** *noun* (14th century)
**1 :** the state or experience of one that suffers
**2 :** PAIN
*synonym* see DISTRESS

**suf·fice** \sə-ˈfīs *also* -ˈfīz\ *verb* **suf·ficed; suf·fic·ing** [Middle English, from Middle French *suffis-*, stem of *suffire*, from Latin *sufficere* to provide, be adequate, from *sub-* + *facere* to make, do — more at DO] (14th century)
*intransitive verb*
**1 :** to meet or satisfy a need **:** be sufficient ⟨a brief note will *suffice*⟩ — often used with an impersonal *it* ⟨*suffice* it to say that they are dedicated, serious personalities —Cheryl Aldridge⟩
**2 :** to be competent or capable
*transitive verb*
**:** to be enough for
**— suf·fic·er** *noun*

**suf·fi·cien·cy** \sə-ˈfi-shən(t)-sē\ *noun* (15th century)
**1 :** sufficient means to meet one's needs **:** COMPETENCY; *also* **:** a modest but adequate scale of living
**2 :** the quality or state of being sufficient **:** ADEQUACY

**suf·fi·cient** \sə-ˈfi-shənt\ *adjective* [Middle English, from Latin *sufficient-, sufficiens*, from present participle of *sufficere*] (14th century)
**1 a :** enough to meet the needs of a situation or a proposed end ⟨*sufficient* provisions for a month⟩ **b :** being a sufficient condition
**2** *archaic* **:** QUALIFIED, COMPETENT ☆
**— suf·fi·cient·ly** *adverb*

**sufficient condition** *noun* (1914)
**1 :** a proposition whose truth assures the truth of another proposition
**2 :** a state of affairs whose existence assures the existence of another state of affairs

**¹suf·fix** \ˈsə-fiks\ *noun* [New Latin *suffixum*, from Latin, neuter of *suffixus*, past participle of *suffigere* to fasten underneath, from *sub-* + *figere* to fasten — more at FIX] (1778)
**:** an affix occurring at the end of a word, base, or phrase — compare PREFIX
**— suf·fix·al** \ˈsə-fik-səl, (ˌ)sə-ˈfik-səl\ *adjective*

**²suf·fix** \ˈsə-fiks, (ˌ)sə-ˈfiks\ *transitive verb* (1778)
**:** to attach as a suffix
**— suf·fix·a·tion** \ˌsə-fik-ˈsā-shən\ *noun*

**suf·fo·cate** \ˈsə-fə-ˌkāt\ *verb* **-cat·ed; -cat·ing** [Middle English, from Latin *suffocatus*, past participle of *suffocare* to choke, stifle, from *sub-* + *fauces* throat] (15th century)
*transitive verb*
**1 a :** to stop the respiration of (as by strangling or asphyxiation) **b :** to deprive of oxy-

gen **c :** to make uncomfortable by want of cool fresh air
**2 :** to impede or stop the development of
*intransitive verb*
**1 :** to become suffocated: **a :** to die from being unable to breathe **b :** to be uncomfortable through lack of air
**2 :** to become checked in development
**— suf·fo·cat·ing·ly** \-ˌkā-tiŋ-lē\ *adverb*
**— suf·fo·ca·tion** \ˌsə-fə-ˈkā-shən\ *noun*
**— suf·fo·ca·tive** \ˈsə-fə-ˌkā-tiv\ *adjective*

**Suf·folk** \ˈsə-fək, -ˌfók\ *noun* [*Suffolk,* England] (1831)
**1 :** any of a breed of chestnut-colored draft horses of English origin — called also *Suffolk punch*
**2 :** any of a breed of large hornless black-faced sheep of English origin raised chiefly for mutton

**¹suf·fra·gan** \ˈsə-fri-gən, -jən\ *noun* [Middle English, from Middle French, from Medieval Latin *suffraganeus*, from *suffragium* support, prayer] (14th century)
**1 :** a diocesan bishop (as in the Roman Catholic Church and the Church of England) subordinate to a metropolitan
**2 :** an Anglican or Episcopal bishop assisting a diocesan bishop and not having the right of succession

**²suffragan** *adjective* (15th century)
**1 :** of or being a suffragan
**2 :** subordinate to a metropolitan or archiepiscopal see

**suf·frage** \ˈsə-frij, *sometimes* -fə-rij\ *noun* [in sense 1, from Middle English, from Middle French, from Medieval Latin *suffragium*, from Latin, vote, political support, from *suffragari* to support with one's vote; in other senses, from Latin *suffragium*] (14th century)
**1 :** a short intercessory prayer usually in a series
**2 :** a vote given in deciding a controverted question or in the choice of a person for an office or trust
**3 :** the right of voting **:** FRANCHISE; *also* **:** the exercise of such right

**suf·frag·ette** \ˌsə-fri-ˈjet\ *noun* (1906)
**:** a woman who advocates suffrage for women

**suf·frag·ist** \ˈsəf-ri-jist\ *noun* (1822)
**:** one who advocates extension of suffrage especially to women

**suf·fuse** \sə-ˈfyüz\ *transitive verb* **suf·fused; suf·fus·ing** [Latin *suffusus*, past participle of *suffundere*, literally, to pour beneath, from *sub-* + *fundere* to pour — more at FOUND] (1590)
**:** to spread over or through in the manner of fluid or light **:** FLUSH, FILL
*synonym* see INFUSE
**— suf·fu·sion** \-ˈfyü-zhən\ *noun*
**— suf·fu·sive** \-ˈfyü-siv, -ziv\ *adjective*

**Su·fi** \ˈsü-(ˌ)fē\ *noun* [Arabic *ṣūfīy*, perhaps from *ṣūf* wool] (1653)

---

☆ **SYNONYMS**
**Sufficient, enough, adequate, competent** mean being what is necessary or desirable. SUFFICIENT suggests a close meeting of a need ⟨*sufficient* savings⟩. ENOUGH is less exact in suggestion than SUFFICIENT ⟨do you have *enough* food?⟩. ADEQUATE may imply barely meeting a requirement ⟨the service was *adequate*⟩. COMPETENT suggests measuring up to all requirements without question or being adequately adapted to an end ⟨had no *competent* notion of what was going on⟩.

---

\ə\ abut \ᵊ\ kitten \ər\ further \a\ ash \ā\ ace \ä\ mop, mar \au̇\ out \ch\ chin \e\ bet \ē\ easy \g\ go \i\ hit \ī\ ice \j\ job \ŋ\ sing \ō\ go \ȯ\ law \ȯi\ boy \th\ thin \t̲h̲\ the \ü\ loot \u̇\ foot \y\ yet \zh\ vision    *see also* Guide to Pronunciation

: a Muslim mystic
— **Su·fi** *adjective*
— **Su·fic** \-fik\ *adjective*
— **Su·fism** \-,fi-zəm\ *noun*

**¹sug·ar** \'shů-gər\ *noun* [Middle English *sugre, sucre,* from Middle French *sucre,* from Medieval Latin *zuccarum,* from Old Italian *zucchero,* from Arabic *sukkar,* from Persian *shakar,* from Sanskrit *śarkarā;* akin to Sanskrit *śarkara* pebble — more at CROCODILE] (14th century)
**1 a :** a sweet crystallizable material that consists wholly or essentially of sucrose, is colorless or white when pure tending to brown when less refined, is obtained commercially from sugarcane or sugar beet and less extensively from sorghum, maples, and palms, and is important as a source of dietary carbohydrate and as a sweetener and preservative of other foods **b :** any of various water-soluble compounds that vary widely in sweetness and include the oligosaccharides (as sucrose)
**2 :** a unit (as a spoonful, cube, or lump) of sugar
**3 :** a sugar bowl
— **sug·ar·less** \-ləs\ *adjective*

**²sugar** *verb* **sug·ared; sug·ar·ing** \'shůg(ə-)riŋ\ (15th century)
*transitive verb*
**1 :** to make palatable or attractive : SWEETEN
**2 :** to sprinkle or mix with sugar
*intransitive verb*
**1 :** to form or be converted into sugar
**2 :** to become granular : GRANULATE
**3 :** to make maple syrup or maple sugar

**sugar apple** *noun* (1738)
: a tropical American tree (*Annona squamosa*) of the custard apple family; *also* : its edible sweet pulpy fruit with thick green scaly rind and shining black seeds

**sugar beet** *noun* (1817)
: a white-rooted beet grown for the sugar in its roots

**sug·ar·ber·ry** \'shů-gər-,ber-ē\ *noun* (circa 1818)
: any of several hackberries (especially *Celtis laevigata* and *C. occidentalis*) with sweet edible fruits

**sugar bush** *noun* (1823)
: a woods in which sugar maples predominate

**sug·ar·cane** \'shů-gər-,kān\ *noun* (15th century)
: a stout tall perennial grass (*Saccharum officinarum*) that has a large terminal panicle and is widely grown in warm regions as a source of sugar

**sug·ar·coat** \'shů-gər-,kōt\ *transitive verb* [back-formation from *sugarcoated*] (1870)
**1 :** to coat with sugar
**2 :** to make superficially attractive or palatable ⟨tried to *sugarcoat* an unpleasant truth⟩

**sugar daddy** *noun* (1926)
**1 :** a well-to-do usually older man who supports or spends lavishly on a mistress or girlfriend
**2 :** a generous benefactor of a cause

**sug·ar·house** \'shů-gər-,haůs\ *noun* (1600)
: a building where sugar is made or refined; *specifically* : one where maple sap is boiled and maple syrup and maple sugar are made

**sugaring off** *noun* (1836)
**1 :** the act or process of converting maple syrup into sugar
**2 :** a party held at the time of sugaring off

**sug·ar·loaf** \'shů-gər-,lōf\ *noun* (15th century)
**1 :** refined sugar molded into a cone
**2 :** a hill or mountain shaped like a sugarloaf
— **sugar–loaf** *adjective*

sugarcane

**sugar maple** *noun* (1731)
**1 :** a maple (*Acer saccharum*) of eastern North America with 3- to 5-lobed leaves, hard close-grained wood much used for cabinetwork, and sap that is the chief source of maple syrup and maple sugar — called also *rock maple, hard maple*
**2 :** any of several maples (especially *Acer nigrum* and *A. grandidentatum*) sometimes considered subspecies of the sugar maple

**sugar off** *intransitive verb* (1836)
**1 :** to complete the process of boiling down the syrup in making maple sugar until it is thick enough to crystallize
**2 :** to approach or reach the state of granulation

**sugar orchard** *noun* (1833)
*chiefly New England* : SUGAR BUSH

**sugar pea** *noun* (1707)
: SNOW PEA

**sugar pine** *noun* (1846)
: a very tall pine (*Pinus lambertiana*) found from Oregon to Baja California and having needles in clusters of five, cones up to 18 inches (46 cm) long, and soft reddish brown wood; *also* : its wood

**sug·ar·plum** \'shů-gər-,pləm\ *noun* (circa 1668)
: a small candy in the shape of a ball or disk : SWEETMEAT

**sugar snap pea** *noun* (1979)
: SNAP PEA

**sug·ary** \'shů-g(ə-)rē\ *adjective* (1591)
**1 a :** exaggeratedly sweet : HONEYED ⟨his *sugary* deprecating voice —D. H. Lawrence⟩ **b :** cloyingly sweet : SENTIMENTAL
**2 :** containing, resembling, or tasting of sugar

**sug·gest** \səg-'jest, sə-'jest\ *transitive verb* [Latin *suggestus,* past participle of *suggerere* to pile up, furnish, suggest, from *sub-* + *gerere* to carry] (1526)
**1 a** *obsolete* **:** to seek to influence : SEDUCE **b :** to call forth : EVOKE **c :** to mention or imply as a possibility ⟨*suggested* that he might bring his family⟩ **d :** to propose as desirable or fitting ⟨*suggest* a stroll⟩ **e :** to offer for consideration or as a hypothesis ⟨*suggest* a solution to a problem⟩
**2 a :** to call to mind by thought or association ⟨the explosion . . . *suggested* sabotage —F. L. Paxson⟩ **b :** to serve as a motive or inspiration for ⟨a play *suggested* by a historic incident⟩ ☆
— **sug·gest·er** *noun*

**sug·gest·ible** \səg-'jes-tə-bəl, sə-'jes-\ *adjective* (1890)
: easily influenced by suggestion
— **sug·gest·ibil·i·ty** \-,jes-tə-'bi-lə-tē\ *noun*

**sug·ges·tion** \səg-'jes-chən, sə-'jes-, -'jesh-\ *noun* (14th century)
**1 a :** the act or process of suggesting **b :** something suggested
**2 a :** the process by which a physical or mental state is influenced by a thought or idea ⟨the power of *suggestion*⟩ **b :** the process by which one thought leads to another especially through association of ideas
**3 :** a slight indication : TRACE ⟨a *suggestion* of a smile⟩

**sug·ges·tive** \səg-'jes-tiv, sə-'jes-\ *adjective* (1631)
**1 a :** giving a suggestion : INDICATIVE ⟨*suggestive* of a past era⟩ **b :** full of suggestions : stimulating thought ⟨provided a *suggestive* . . . commentary on the era —Lloyd Morris⟩ **c :** stirring mental associations : EVOCATIVE
**2 :** suggesting or tending to suggest something improper or indecent : RISQUÉ
— **sug·ges·tive·ly** *adverb*
— **sug·ges·tive·ness** *noun*

**sui·cid·al** \,sü-ə-'sī-d°l\ *adjective* (1777)
**1 a :** dangerous especially to life **b :** destructive to one's own interests
**2 :** relating to or of the nature of suicide
**3 :** marked by an impulse to commit suicide
— **sui·cid·al·ly** *adverb*

**¹sui·cide** \'sü-ə-,sīd\ *noun* [Latin *sui* (genitive) of oneself + English *-cide;* akin to Old English & Old High German *sīn* his, Latin *suus* one's own, *sed, se* without, Sanskrit *sva* oneself, one's own] (1643)
**1 a :** the act or an instance of taking one's own life voluntarily and intentionally especially by a person of years of discretion and of sound mind **b :** ruin of one's own interests ⟨political *suicide*⟩
**2 :** one that commits or attempts suicide

**²suicide** *verb* **sui·cid·ed; sui·cid·ing** (1841)
*intransitive verb*
: to commit suicide
*transitive verb*
: to put (oneself) to death

**suicide squad** *noun* [from the fact that kickoffs are more dangerous than other plays] (circa 1966)
: a special squad used on kickoffs in football

**suicide squeeze** *noun* (1955)
: a squeeze play in which the runner runs all out at the pitch without knowing whether the batter will contact the ball

**sui ge·ner·is** \,sü-,ī-'je-nə-rəs, ,sü-ē-'je-, -'ge-\ *adjective* [Latin, of its own kind] (1787)
: constituting a class alone : UNIQUE, PECULIAR

**sui ju·ris** \,sü-,ī-'jůr-əs, ,sü-ē-'yůr-\ *adjective* [Latin, of one's own right] (1675)
: having full legal rights or capacity

**su·int** \'sü-ənt, 'swint\ *noun* [French, from Middle French, from *suer* to sweat, from Latin *sudare* — more at SWEAT] (1791)
: dried perspiration of sheep deposited in the wool and rich in potassium salts

**¹suit** \'süt\ *noun* [Middle English *siute* act of following, retinue, sequence, set, from Old French, act of following, retinue, from (assumed) Vulgar Latin *sequita,* from feminine of *sequitus,* past participle of *sequere* to follow — more at SUE] (14th century)
**1** *archaic* **:** SUITE 1
**2 a :** recourse or appeal to a feudal superior for justice or redress **b :** an action or process in a court for the recovery of a right or claim
**3 :** an act or instance of suing or seeking by entreaty : APPEAL; *specifically* : COURTSHIP
**4 :** SUITE 2 — used chiefly of armor, sails, and counters in games
**5 :** a set of garments: as **a :** an outer costume of two or more pieces **b :** a costume to be worn for a special purpose or under particular conditions ⟨gym *suit*⟩
**6 a :** all the playing cards in a pack bearing the same symbol **b :** all the dominoes bearing the same number **c :** all the cards or counters in a particular suit held by one player ⟨a 5-card *suit*⟩ **d :** the suit led ⟨follow *suit*⟩
**7** *slang* **:** a business executive — usually used in plural

☆ **SYNONYMS**
**Suggest, imply, hint, intimate, insinuate** mean to convey an idea indirectly. SUGGEST may stress putting into the mind by association of ideas, awakening of a desire, or initiating a train of thought ⟨a film title that *suggests* its subject matter⟩. IMPLY is close to SUGGEST but may indicate a more definite or logical relation of the unexpressed idea to the expressed ⟨measures *implying* that bankruptcy was imminent⟩. HINT implies the use of slight or remote suggestion with a minimum of overt statement ⟨*hinted* that she might have a job lined up⟩. INTIMATE stresses delicacy of suggestion without connoting any lack of candor ⟨*intimates* that there is more to the situation than meets the eye⟩. INSINUATE applies to the conveying of a usually unpleasant idea in a sly underhanded manner ⟨*insinuated* that there were shady dealings⟩.

**²suit** (14th century)
*transitive verb*
**1 a :** to be becoming to **b :** to be proper for **:** BEFIT
**2 :** to outfit with clothes **:** DRESS
**3 :** ACCOMMODATE, ADAPT ⟨*suit* the action to the word⟩
**4 :** to meet the needs or desires of **:** PLEASE ⟨*suits* me fine⟩
*intransitive verb*
**1 :** to be in accordance **:** AGREE ⟨the position *suits* with your abilities⟩
**2 :** to be appropriate or satisfactory ⟨these prices don't *suit*⟩
**3 :** to put on specially required clothing (as a uniform or protective garb) — usually used with *up*
**suit·able** \'sü-tə-bəl\ *adjective* (1582)
**1** *obsolete* **:** SIMILAR, MATCHING
**2 a :** adapted to a use or purpose **b :** satisfying propriety **:** PROPER **c :** ABLE, QUALIFIED
**synonym** see FIT
— **suit·abil·i·ty** \ˌsü-tə-'bi-lə-tē\ *noun*
— **suit·able·ness** *noun*
— **suit·ably** \-blē\ *adverb*
**suit·case** \'süt-ˌkās\ *noun* (1897)
**:** a bag or case carried by hand and designed to hold a traveler's clothing and personal articles
**suite** \'swēt, *2d is also* 'süt\ *noun* [French, alteration of Old French *siute* — more at SUIT] (1673)
**1 :** RETINUE; *especially* **:** the personal staff accompanying a ruler, diplomat, or dignitary on official business
**2 :** a group of things forming a unit or constituting a collection **:** SET: as **a :** a group of rooms occupied as a unit **b** (1) **:** a 17th and 18th century instrumental musical form consisting of a series of dances in the same or related keys (2) **:** a modern instrumental composition in several movements of different character (3) **:** a long orchestral concert arrangement in suite form of material drawn from a longer work (as a ballet) **c :** a collection of minerals or rocks having some characteristic in common (as type or origin) **d :** a set of matched furniture
**suit·er** \'sü-tər\ *noun* (1952)
**:** a suitcase for holding a specified number of suits — usually used in combination ⟨a two-*suiter*⟩
**suit·ing** \'sü-tiŋ\ *noun* (1883)
**1 :** fabric for suits
**2 :** a suit of clothes
**suit·or** \'sü-tər\ *noun* [Middle English, follower, pleader, from Anglo-French, from Latin *secutor* follower, from *sequi* to follow — more at SUE] (15th century)
**1 :** one that petitions or entreats
**2 :** a party to a suit at law
**3 :** one who courts a woman or seeks to marry her
**4 :** one who seeks to take over a business
**su·ki·ya·ki** \ˌskē-'yä-kē, ˌsü-kē-', ˌsü-\ *noun* [Japanese, from *suki-* slice + *yaki* broil] (1920)
**:** a dish consisting of thin slices of meat, bean curd, and vegetables cooked in soy sauce and sugar
**suk·kah** \'sù-kə\ *noun* [Hebrew *sukkāh*] (1875)
**:** a booth or shelter with a roof of branches and leaves that is used especially for meals during the Sukkoth
**Suk·koth** *or* **Suk·kot** \'sù-kəs, -ˌkōt, -ˌkōth, -ˌkōs\ *noun* [Hebrew *sukkōth*, plural of *sukkāh*] (1882)
**:** a Jewish harvest festival beginning on the 15th of Tishri and commemorating the temporary shelters used by the Jews during their wandering in the wilderness
**sul·cate** \'səl-ˌkāt\ *adjective* [Latin *sulcatus*, past participle of *sulcare* to furrow, from *sulcus*] (1760)
**:** scored with usually longitudinal furrows ⟨a *sulcate* seedpod⟩

**sul·cus** \'səl-kəs\ *noun, plural* **sul·ci** \-ˌkī, -ˌkē, -ˌsī\ [Latin; akin to Old English *sulh* plow, Greek *holkos* furrow, *helkein* to pull] (1662)
**:** FURROW, GROOVE; *especially* **:** a shallow furrow on the surface of the brain separating adjacent convolutions
**sulf-** *or* **sulfo-** *combining form* [French *sulf-*, *sulfo-*, from Latin *sulfur*]
**:** sulfur **:** containing sulfur ⟨*sulf*ide⟩
**sul·fa** \'səl-fə\ *adjective* [short for *sulfanilamide*] (1940)
**1 :** related chemically to sulfanilamide
**2 :** of, relating to, or containing sulfa drugs
**sul·fa·di·a·zine** \ˌsəl-fə-'dī-ə-ˌzēn\ *noun* [*sulfa* + *diazine* ($C_4H_4N_2$)] (1940)
**:** a sulfa drug $C_{10}H_{10}N_4O_2S$ that is used especially in the treatment of meningitis, pneumonia, and intestinal infections
**sulfa drug** *noun* (1940)
**:** any of various synthetic organic bacteria-inhibiting drugs that are sulfonamides closely related chemically to sulfanilamide
**sul·fa·nil·amide** \ˌsəl-fə-'ni-lə-ˌmīd, -ˌməd\ *noun* [*sulfanilic* + *amide*] (1937)
**:** a crystalline sulfonamide $C_6H_8N_2O_2S$ that is the amide of sulfanilic acid and the parent compound of most of the sulfa drugs
**sul·fa·nil·ic acid** \ˌsəl-fə-'ni-lik-\ *noun* [International Scientific Vocabulary *sulf-* + *aniline* + *-ic*] (1856)
**:** a crystalline acid $C_6H_7NO_3S$ obtained from aniline
**sul·fa·tase** \'səl-fə-ˌtās, -ˌtāz\ *noun* [¹*sulfate*] (1924)
**:** any of various esterases that accelerate the hydrolysis of sulfuric esters and that are found in animal tissues and in microorganisms
**¹sul·fate** \'səl-ˌfāt\ *noun* [French, from Latin *sulfur*] (1790)
**1 :** a salt or ester of sulfuric acid
**2 :** a bivalent group or anion $SO_4$ characteristic of sulfuric acid and the sulfates
**²sulfate** *transitive verb* **sul·fat·ed; sul·fat·ing** (1802)
**:** to treat or combine with sulfuric acid or a sulfate
**sulf·hy·dryl** \ˌsəlf-'(h)ī-drəl\ *noun* [International Scientific Vocabulary] (circa 1901)
**:** THIOL 2 — used chiefly in molecular biology
**sul·fide** \'səl-ˌfīd\ *noun* (1836)
**1 :** any of various organic compounds characterized by a sulfur atom attached to two carbon atoms
**2 :** a binary compound (as CuS) of sulfur usually with a more electropositive element or group **:** a salt of hydrogen sulfide
**sul·fin·py·ra·zone** \ˌsəl-fən-'pī-rə-ˌzōn\ *noun* [*sulfinic* acid (RSO₂H) + *pyr-* + *azole* + *-one*] (1958)
**:** a uricosuric drug $C_{23}H_{20}N_2O_3S$ used in long-term treatment of chronic gout
**sul·fite** \'səl-ˌfīt\ *noun* [French *sulfite*, alteration of *sulfate*] (1790)
**:** a salt or ester of sulfurous acid
— **sul·fit·ic** \ˌsəl-'fi-tik\ *adjective*
**sulfon-** *combining form* [International Scientific Vocabulary]
**:** sulfonic ⟨*sulfon*amide⟩
**sul·fon·amide** \ˌsəl-'fä-nə-ˌmīd, -məd; -'fō-nə-ˌmīd\ *noun* (1881)
**:** any of various amides (as sulfanilamide) of a sulfonic acid; *also* **:** SULFA DRUG
**¹sul·fo·nate** \'səl-fə-ˌnāt\ *noun* (1876)
**:** a salt or ester of a sulfonic acid
**²sulfonate** *transitive verb* **-nat·ed; -nat·ing** (1882)
**:** to introduce the $SO_3H$ group into; *broadly* **:** to treat (an organic substance) with sulfuric acid
— **sul·fo·na·tion** \ˌsəl-fə-'nā-shən\ *noun*
**sul·fone** \'səl-ˌfōn\ *noun* (1872)
**:** any of various compounds containing the sulfonyl group with its sulfur atom having two bonds with carbon

**sul·fon·ic** \ˌsəl-'fä-nik, -'fō-\ *adjective* (circa 1891)
**:** of, relating to, being, or derived from the univalent acid group $SO_3H$
**sulfonic acid** *noun* (1873)
**:** any of numerous acids that contain the $SO_3H$ group and may be derived from sulfuric acid by replacement of a hydroxyl group by either an inorganic anion or a univalent organic group
**sul·fo·ni·um** \ˌsəl-'fō-nē-əm\ *noun* [New Latin, from *sulf-* + *-onium*] (1885)
**:** a univalent group or cation $SH_3$ or derivative $SR_3$
**sul·fo·nyl** \'səl-fə-ˌnil\ *noun* (1920)
**:** the bivalent group $SO_2$
**sul·fo·nyl·urea** \ˌsəl-fə-ˌnil-'yùr-ē-ə\ *noun* [New Latin, from International Scientific Vocabulary *sulfonyl* + New Latin *urea*] (1956)
**:** any of several hypoglycemic compounds related to the sulfonamides and used in the oral treatment of diabetes
**sulf·ox·ide** \ˌsəl-'fäk-ˌsīd\ *noun* [International Scientific Vocabulary] (circa 1894)
**:** any of a class of organic compounds characterized by an SO group with its sulfur atom having two bonds with carbon
**sul·fur** *also* **sul·phur** \'səl-fər\ *noun* [Middle English *sulphur* brimstone, from Latin *sulpur, sulphur, sulfur*] (14th century)
**1 :** a nonmetallic element that occurs either free or combined especially in sulfides and sulfates, is a constituent of proteins, exists in several allotropic forms including yellow orthorhombic crystals, resembles oxygen chemically but is less active and more acidic, and is used especially in the chemical and paper industries, in rubber vulcanization, and in medicine for treating skin diseases — see ELEMENT table
**2 :** something (as scathing language) that suggests sulfur
— **sul·fury** *or* **sul·phury** \-ē\ *adjective*
**sulfur bacterium** *noun* (1891)
**:** any of various bacteria (especially genus *Thiobacillus*) capable of metabolizing sulfur compounds
**sulfur dioxide** *noun* (1869)
**:** a heavy pungent toxic gas $SO_2$ that is easily condensed to a colorless liquid, is used especially in making sulfuric acid, in bleaching, as a preservative, and as a refrigerant, and is a major air pollutant especially in industrial areas
**sul·fu·ric** \ˌsəl-'fyùr-ik\ *adjective* (1790)
**:** of, relating to, or containing sulfur especially with a higher valence than sulfurous compounds ⟨*sulfuric* esters⟩
**sulfuric acid** *or* **sul·phu·ric acid** \ˌsəl-'fyùr-ik-\ *noun* (1790)
**:** a heavy corrosive oily dibasic strong acid $H_2SO_4$ that is colorless when pure and is a vigorous oxidizing and dehydrating agent
**usage** see SULFUR
**sul·fu·rize** \'səl-fə-ˌrīz, -fyə-\ *transitive verb* **-rized; -riz·ing** (1794)
**:** to treat with sulfur or a sulfur compound
**sul·fu·rous** *also* **sul·phu·rous** \'səl-fə-rəs,

☐ USAGE
**sulfur** The spelling *sulfur* predominates in U.S. technical usage, while both *sulfur* and *sulphur* are common in general usage. British usage tends to favor *sulphur* for all applications. The same pattern is seen in most of the words derived from *sulfur*.

\ə\ abut \ᵊ\ kitten \ər\ further \a\ ash \ā\ ace
\ä\ mop, mar \aù\ out \ch\ chin \e\ bet \ē\ easy
\g\ go \i\ hit \ī\ ice \j\ job \ŋ\ sing \ō\ go
\ò\ law \òi\ boy \th\ thin \t͟h\ the \ü\ loot \ù\ foot
\y\ yet \zh\ vision    *see also* Guide to Pronunciation

-fyə- *also especially for 1b* ˌsəl-ˈfyu̇r-əs\ *adjective* (15th century) **1 a :** of, relating to, or containing sulfur especially with a lower valence than sulfuric compounds ⟨*sulfurous* esters⟩ **b :** resembling or emanating from sulfur and especially burning sulfur
**2 a :** of, relating to, or dealing with the fire of hell **b :** SCATHING, VIRULENT ⟨*sulfurous* denunciations⟩ **c :** PROFANE, BLASPHEMOUS ⟨*sulfurous* language⟩
*usage* see SULFUR
— **sul·fu·rous·ly** *adverb*
— **sul·fu·rous·ness** *noun*
**sulfurous acid** *noun* (1790)
**:** a weak unstable dibasic acid $H_2SO_3$ known in solution and through its salts and used as a reducing and bleaching agent
**sul·fu·ryl** \ˈsəl-fə-ˌril, -fyə-\ *noun* [International Scientific Vocabulary] (1867)
**:** SULFONYL — used especially in names of inorganic compounds
**¹sulk** \ˈsəlk\ *intransitive verb* [back-formation from *sulky*] (1781)
**:** to be moodily silent
**²sulk** *noun* (1804)
**1 :** the state of one sulking — often used in plural ⟨had a case of the *sulks*⟩
**2 :** a sulky mood or spell ⟨in a *sulk*⟩
**¹sulky** \ˈsəl-kē\ *adjective* [probably alteration of obsolete *sulke* sluggish] (1744)
**1 a :** sulking or given to spells of sulking **b :** relating to or indicating a sulk ⟨a *sulky* expression⟩
**2** [²*sulky*] **:** having wheels and usually a seat for the driver ⟨a *sulky* plow⟩
*synonym* see SULLEN
— **sulk·i·ly** \-kə-lē\ *adverb*
— **sulk·i·ness** \-kē-nəs\ *noun*
**²sulky** *noun, plural* **sulkies** [probably from ¹*sulky;* from its having room for only one person] (1756)
**:** a light 2-wheeled vehicle (as for harness racing) having a seat for the driver only and usually no body
**sul·lage** \ˈsə-lij\ *noun* [probably from Middle French *soiller, souiller* to soil — more at SOIL] (1553)
**:** REFUSE, SEWAGE
**sul·len** \ˈsə-lən\ *adjective* [Middle English *solain* solitary, probably from (assumed) Anglo-French *solein*, alteration of Old French *soltain*, from Late Latin *solitaneus* private, ultimately from Latin *solus* alone] (14th century)
**1 a :** gloomily or resentfully silent or repressed **b :** suggesting a sullen state : LOWERING
**2 :** dull or somber in sound or color
**3 :** DISMAL, GLOOMY
**4 :** moving sluggishly ☆
— **sul·len·ly** *adverb*
— **sul·len·ness** \ˈsə-lə(n)-nəs\ *noun*
**¹sul·ly** \ˈsə-lē\ *transitive verb* **sul·lied; sul·ly·ing** [Middle English *sollyen*, probably from Middle French *soiller* to soil] (15th century)
**:** to make soiled or tarnished : DEFILE
**²sully** *noun, plural* **sullies** (1602)
*archaic* **:** SOIL, STAIN
**sulph-** *or* **sulpho-** *chiefly British variant of* SULF-
**sul·phate, sul·phide** *chiefly British variant of* SULFATE, SULFIDE
**sulphur butterfly** *noun* (1879)
**:** any of numerous butterflies (especially *Colias* and related genera of the family Pieridae) having the wings usually yellow or orange with a black border — called also *sulphur*
**sul·phu·re·ous** *adjective* (circa 1552)
**:** SULFUROUS
**sul·phu·rise** *British variant of* SULFURIZE
**sulphur yellow** *noun* (1816)
**:** a brilliant greenish yellow
**Sul·pi·cian** \ˌsəl-ˈpi-shən\ *noun* [French *sulpicien*, from Compagnie de Saint-*Sulpice* Society of Saint Sulpice] (1786)

**:** a member of the Society of Priests of Saint Sulpice founded by Jean Jacques Olier in Paris, France, in 1642 and dedicated to the teaching of seminarians
**sul·tan** \ˈsəl-tᵊn\ *noun* [Middle French, from Arabic *sulṭān*] (1555)
**:** a king or sovereign especially of a Muslim state
— **sul·tan·ic** \ˌsəl-ˈta-nik\ *adjective*
**sul·ta·na** \ˌ(ˌ)səl-ˈta-nə\ *noun* [Italian, feminine of *sultano* sultan, from Arabic *sulṭān*] (1585)
**1 :** a female member of a sultan's family; *especially* **:** a sultan's wife
**2 a :** a pale yellow seedless grape grown for raisins and wine **b :** the raisin of a sultana
**sul·tan·ate** \ˈsəl-tᵊn-ˌāt\ *noun* (1822)
**1 :** a state or country governed by a sultan
**2 :** the office, dignity, or power of a sultan
**sul·tan·ess** \ˈsəl-tᵊn-əs\ *noun* (1611)
*archaic* **:** SULTANA 1
**sul·try** \ˈsəl-trē\ *adjective* **sul·tri·er; -est** [obsolete English *sulter* to swelter, alteration of English *swelter*] (1594)
**1 a :** very hot and humid : SWELTERING ⟨a *sultry* day⟩ **b :** burning hot : TORRID
**2 a :** hot with passion or anger **b :** exciting or capable of exciting strong sexual desire ⟨*sultry* glances⟩
— **sul·tri·ly** \-trə-lē\ *adverb*
— **sul·tri·ness** \-trē-nəs\ *noun*
**¹sum** \ˈsəm\ *noun* [Middle English *summe*, from Old French, from Latin *summa*, from feminine of *summus* highest; akin to Latin *super* over — more at OVER] (14th century)
**1 :** an indefinite or specified amount of money
**2 :** the whole amount : AGGREGATE
**3 :** the utmost degree : SUMMIT ⟨reached the *sum* of human happiness⟩
**4 a :** a summary of the chief points or thoughts : SUMMATION ⟨the *sum* of this criticism follows —C. W. Hendel⟩ **b :** GIST ⟨the *sum* and substance of an argument⟩
**5 a** (1) **:** the result of adding numbers ⟨*sum* of 5 and 7 is 12⟩ (2) **:** the limit of the sum of the first *n* terms of an infinite series as *n* increases indefinitely **b :** numbers to be added; *broadly* **:** a problem in arithmetic **c** (1) **:** DISJUNCTION 2 (2) **:** UNION 2d
— **sum·ma·bil·i·ty** \ˌsə-mə-ˈbi-lə-tē\ *noun*
— **sum·ma·ble** \ˈsə-mə-bəl\ *adjective*
— **in sum :** in short : BRIEFLY
**²sum** *verb* **summed; sum·ming** (14th century)
*transitive verb*
**1 :** to calculate the sum of : TOTAL
**2 :** SUMMARIZE
*intransitive verb*
**:** to reach a sum : AMOUNT
**su·mac** *also* **su·mach** \ˈshü-ˌmak, ˈsü-\ *noun* [Middle English *sumac*, from Middle French, from Arabic *summāq*] (14th century)
**1 :** a material used in tanning and dyeing that consists of dried powdered leaves and flowers of various sumacs
**2 :** any of a genus (*Rhus*) of trees, shrubs, and woody vines of the cashew family that have pinnately compound leaves turning to brilliant colors in the autumn, dioecious flowers, spikes or loose clusters of red or whitish berries, and in some cases foliage poisonous to the touch — compare POISON IVY, POISON OAK
**Su·me·ri·an** \sü-ˈmer-ē-ən, -ˈmir-\ *noun* (1878)
**1 :** a native of Sumer
**2 :** the language of the Sumerians that has no known linguistic affinities
— **Sumerian** *adjective*
**Su·me·rol·o·gy** \ˌsü-mə-ˈrä-lə-jē\ *noun* (1897)
**:** the study of Sumerian culture, language, and history
— **Su·me·rol·o·gist** \-jist\ *noun*
**sum·ma** \ˈsu̇-mə, ˈsü-, ˈsə-\ *noun, plural* **sum·mae** \ˈsu̇-ˌmī, ˈsü-, -ˌmā; ˈsə-ˌmē, -ˌmī\ [Medieval Latin, from Latin, sum] (1725)

**:** a comprehensive treatise; *especially* **:** one by a scholastic philosopher
**sum·ma cum lau·de** \ˌsu̇-mə-(ˌ)ku̇m-ˈlau̇-də, ˌsü-, -ˈlau̇-dē; ˌsə-mə-ˌkəm-ˈlȯ-dē\ *adverb or adjective* [Latin, with highest praise] (1900)
**:** with highest distinction ⟨graduated *summa cum laude*⟩ — compare CUM LAUDE, MAGNA CUM LAUDE
**sum·mand** \ˈsə-ˌmand, sə-ˈmand\ *noun* [Medieval Latin *summandus*, gerund of *summare* to sum, from *summa*] (1893)
**:** a term in a summation : ADDEND
**sum·ma·rise** *British variant of* SUMMARIZE
**sum·ma·ri·za·tion** \ˌsə-mə-rə-ˈzā-shən, ˌsəm-rə-\ *noun* (1865)
**1 :** the act of summarizing
**2 :** SUMMARY
**sum·ma·rize** \ˈsə-mə-ˌrīz\ *verb* **-rized; -riz·ing** (1871)
*transitive verb*
**:** to tell in or reduce to a summary
*intransitive verb*
**:** to make a summary
— **sum·ma·riz·able** \ˌsə-mə-ˈrī-zə-bəl\ *adjective*
— **sum·ma·riz·er** *noun*
**¹sum·ma·ry** \ˈsə-mə-rē *also* ˈsəm-rē *or* -ˌmer-ē\ *adjective* [Middle English, from Medieval Latin *summarius*, from Latin *summa* sum] (15th century)
**1 :** COMPREHENSIVE; *especially* **:** covering the main points succinctly
**2 a :** done without delay or formality : quickly executed ⟨a *summary* dismissal⟩ **b :** of, relating to, or using a summary proceeding ⟨a *summary* trial⟩
*synonym* see CONCISE
— **sum·mar·i·ly** \(ˌ)sə-ˈmer-ə-lē\ *adverb*
**²sum·ma·ry** \ˈsə-mə-rē *also* ˈsəm-rē\ *noun, plural* **-ries** (1509)
**:** an abstract, abridgment, or compendium especially of a preceding discourse
**sum·mate** \ˈsə-ˌmāt\ *verb* **sum·mat·ed; sum·mat·ing** [back-formation from *summation*] (1900)
*transitive verb*
**:** to add together : SUM UP
*intransitive verb*
**:** to form a sum or cumulative effect
**sum·ma·tion** \(ˌ)sə-ˈmā-shən\ *noun* (1760)
**1 :** the act or process of forming a sum : ADDITION
**2 :** SUM, TOTAL
**3 :** cumulative action or effect; *especially* **:** the process by which a sequence of stimuli that are individually inadequate to produce a response are cumulatively able to induce a nerve impulse

---

☆ SYNONYMS
**Sullen, glum, morose, surly, sulky, crabbed, saturnine, gloomy** mean showing a forbidding or disagreeable mood. SULLEN implies a silent ill humor and a refusal to be sociable ⟨remained *sullen* amid the festivities⟩. GLUM suggests a silent dispiritedness ⟨a *glum* candidate left to ponder a stunning defeat⟩. MOROSE adds to GLUM an element of bitterness or misanthropy ⟨*morose* job seekers who are inured to rejection⟩. SURLY implies gruffness and sullenness of speech or manner ⟨a typical *surly* teenager⟩. SULKY suggests childish resentment expressed in peevish sullenness ⟨grew *sulky* after every spat⟩. CRABBED applies to a forbidding morose harshness of manner ⟨the school's notoriously *crabbed* headmaster⟩. SATURNINE describes a heavy forbidding aspect or suggests a bitter disposition ⟨a *saturnine* cynic always finding fault⟩. GLOOMY implies a depression in mood making for seeming sullenness or glumness ⟨a *gloomy* mood ushered in by bad news⟩.

**4** : a final part of an argument reviewing points made and expressing conclusions
— **sum·ma·tion·al** \-shnəl, -shə-nᵊl\ *adjective*
**sum·ma·tive** \'sə-mə-tiv, -,mā-\ *adjective* (1881)
: ADDITIVE, CUMULATIVE
**¹sum·mer** \'sə-mər\ *noun* [Middle English *sumer,* from Old English *sumor;* akin to Old High German & Old Norse *sumer* summer, Sanskrit *samā* year, season] (before 12th century)
**1** : the season between spring and autumn comprising in the northern hemisphere usually the months of June, July, and August or as reckoned astronomically extending from the June solstice to the September equinox
**2** : the warmer half of the year
**3** : YEAR ⟨a girl of seventeen *summers*⟩
**4** : a period of maturing powers
— **sum·mer·like** \-,līk\ *adjective*
**²summer** *adjective* (14th century)
**1** : of, relating to, or suitable for summer ⟨*summer* vacation⟩ ⟨a *summer* home⟩
**2** : sown in the spring and harvested in the same year as sown ⟨*summer* wheat⟩ — compare WINTER
**³summer** *verb* **sum·mered; sum·mer·ing** \'sə-mə-riŋ, 'səm-riŋ\ (15th century)
*intransitive verb*
: to pass the summer
*transitive verb*
: to keep or carry through the summer; *especially* : to provide (as cattle or sheep) with pasture during the summer
**summer cypress** *noun* (1767)
: a densely branched Eurasian herb (*Kochia scoparia*) of the goosefoot family grown for its foliage which turns red in autumn
**sum·mer·house** \'sə-mər-,haüs\ *noun* (before 12th century)
**1** : a country house for summer residence
**2** : a covered structure in a garden or park designed to provide a shady resting place in summer
**summer kitchen** *noun* (1874)
: a small building or shed that is usually adjacent to a house and is used as a kitchen in warm weather
**sum·mer·long** \-,lȯŋ, -'lȯŋ\ *adjective* (1960)
: lasting through the summer
**sum·mers** \'sə-mərz\ *adverb* (1907)
: during the summers ⟨worked *summers* as a waiter⟩
**sum·mer·sault** *variant of* SOMERSAULT
**summer savory** *noun* (circa 1573)
: an annual European mint (*Satureja hortensis*) used in cookery — compare WINTER SAVORY
**summer school** *noun* (1860)
: a school or school session conducted in summer enabling students to accelerate progress toward a degree, to make up credits lost through absence or failure, or to round out professional education
**summer squash** *noun* (1815)
: any of various garden squashes derived from a variety (*Cucurbita pepo* variety *melopepo*) and used as a vegetable while immature and before hardening of the seeds and rind
**summer stock** *noun* (1927)
: theatrical productions of stock companies presented during the summer
**summer theater** *noun* (1801)
: a theater that presents several different plays or musicals during the summer
**sum·mer·time** \'sə-mər-,tīm\ *noun* (14th century)
: the summer season or a period like summer
**summer time** *noun* (1916)
*chiefly British* : DAYLIGHT SAVING TIME
**sum·mer·wood** \'sə-mər-,wùd\ *noun* (1902)
: the harder less porous portion of an annual ring of wood that develops late in the growing season — compare SPRINGWOOD
**sum·mery** \'sə-mə-rē, 'səm-rē\ *adjective* (1824)

: of, resembling, or fit for summer
**sum·ming-up** \,sə-miŋ-'əp\ *noun, plural* **sum·mings-up** \-miŋz-\ (1790)
: the act or statement of one who sums up
**¹sum·mit** \'sə-mət\ *noun* [Middle English *somete,* from Middle French, from Old French, diminutive of *sum* top, from Latin *summum,* neuter of *summus* highest — more at SUM] (15th century)
**1** : TOP, APEX; *especially* : the highest point : PEAK
**2** : the topmost level attainable ⟨the *summit* of human fame⟩
**3 a** : the highest level of officials; *especially* : the diplomatic level of heads of government
**b** : a conference of highest-level officials (as heads of government) ⟨an economic *summit*⟩
☆
**²summit** *intransitive verb* (1972)
: to participate in a summit conference
**sum·mit·eer** \,sə-mə-'tir\ *noun* (1957)
: one who takes part in a summit
**sum·mit·ry** \'sə-mə-trē\ *noun* (1958)
: the use of a summit conference for international negotiation
**sum·mon** \'sə-mən\ *transitive verb* **sum·moned; sum·mon·ing** \'sə-mə-niŋ, 'səm-niŋ\ [Middle English *somonen,* from Old French *somondre,* from (assumed) Vulgar Latin *summonere,* alteration of Latin *summonēre* to remind secretly, from *sub-* secretly + *monēre* to warn — more at SUB-, MIND] (13th century)
**1** : to issue a call to convene : CONVOKE
**2** : to command by service of a summons to appear in court
**3** : to call upon for specified action
**4** : to bid to come : send for ⟨*summon* a physician⟩
**5** : to call forth : EVOKE — often used with *up*
☆
— **sum·mon·able** \'sə-mə-nə-bəl\ *adjective*
— **sum·mon·er** \'sə-mə-nər, 'səm-nər\ *noun*
**¹sum·mons** \'sə-mənz\ *noun, plural* **sum·mons·es** [Middle English *somouns,* from Old French *somonse,* from past participle of *somondre*] (13th century)
**1** : the act of summoning; *especially* : a call by authority to appear at a place named or to attend to a duty
**2** : a warning or citation to appear in court: as **a** : a written notification to be served on a person as a warning to appear in court at a day specified to answer to the plaintiff **b** : a subpoena to appear as a witness
**3** : something (as a call) that summons
**²summons** *transitive verb* (1683)
: SUMMON 2
**sum·mum bo·num** \,sù-məm-'bō-nəm, ,sü-, ,sə-\ *noun* [Latin] (1563)
: the supreme good from which all others are derived
**su·mo** \'sü-(,)mō\ *noun* [Japanese *sumō*] (1880)
: a Japanese form of wrestling in which a contestant loses if he is forced out of the ring or if any part of his body except the soles of his feet touches the ground
**sump** \'səmp\ *noun* [Middle English *sompe* swamp — more at SWAMP] (1653)
**1** : a pit or reservoir serving as a drain or receptacle for liquids: as **a** : CESSPOOL **b** : a pit at the lowest point in a circulating or drainage system (as the oil-circulating system of an internal combustion engine) **c** *chiefly British* : OIL PAN
**2** *British* : CRANKCASE
**3** [German *Sumpf,* literally, marsh, from Middle High German — more at SWAMP] **a** : the lowest part of a mine shaft into which water drains **b** : an excavation ahead of regular work in driving a mine tunnel or sinking a mine shaft
**4** : something resembling a sump : SINK 2

**sump pump** *noun* (circa 1899)
: a pump (as in a basement) to remove accumulations of liquid from a sump pit
**sump·ter** \'səm(p)-tər\ *noun* [Middle English, short for *sumpter horse,* from *sumpter* driver of a packhorse, from Middle French *sometier,* from (assumed) Vulgar Latin *sagmatarius,* from Late Latin *sagmat-, sagma* packsaddle, from Greek; akin to Greek *sattein* to pack, stuff] (15th century)
: a pack animal
**sump·tu·ary** \'səm(p)-chə-,wer-ē\ *adjective* [Latin *sumptuarius,* from *sumptus* expense, from *sumere* to take, spend — more at CONSUME] (1600)
**1** : relating to personal expenditures and especially to prevent extravagance and luxury ⟨conservative *sumptuary* tastes —John Cheever⟩
**2** : designed to regulate extravagant expenditures or habits especially on moral or religious grounds ⟨*sumptuary* laws⟩ ⟨*sumptuary* tax⟩
**sump·tu·ous** \'səm(p)(t)-shə-wəs, -shəs, -shwəs\ *adjective* [Middle English, from Middle French *sumptueux,* from Latin *sumptuosus,* from *sumptus*] (15th century)
: extremely costly, rich, luxurious, or magnificent ⟨*sumptuous* banquets⟩ ⟨a *sumptuous* residence⟩; *also* : MAGNIFICENT 4
— **sump·tu·ous·ly** *adverb*
— **sump·tu·ous·ness** *noun*
**sum total** *noun* (14th century)
**1** : a total arrived at through the counting of sums
**2** : total result : TOTALITY
**sum-up** \'səm-,əp\ *noun* (1894)
: SUMMARY

---

☆ **SYNONYMS**
**Summit, peak, pinnacle, climax, apex, acme, culmination** mean the highest point attained or attainable. SUMMIT implies the topmost level attainable ⟨at the *summit* of the Victorian social scene⟩. PEAK suggests the highest among other high points ⟨an artist working at the *peak* of her powers⟩. PINNACLE suggests a dizzying and often insecure height ⟨the *pinnacle* of worldly success⟩. CLIMAX implies the highest point in an ascending series ⟨the war was the *climax* to a series of hostile actions⟩. APEX implies the point where all ascending lines converge ⟨the *apex* of Dutch culture⟩. ACME implies a level of quality representing the perfection of a thing ⟨a statue that was once deemed the *acme* of beauty⟩. CULMINATION suggests the outcome of a growth or development representing an attained objective ⟨the *culmination* of years of effort⟩.

**Summon, call, cite, convoke, convene, muster** mean to demand the presence of. SUMMON implies the exercise of authority ⟨was *summoned* to answer charges⟩. CALL may be used less formally for SUMMON ⟨*called* the legislature into special session⟩. CITE implies a summoning to court usually to answer a charge ⟨*cited* for drunken driving⟩. CONVOKE implies a summons to assemble for deliberative or legislative purposes ⟨*convoked* a Vatican council⟩. CONVENE is somewhat less formal than CONVOKE ⟨*convened* the students⟩. MUSTER suggests a calling up of a number of things that form a group in order that they may be exhibited, displayed, or utilized as a whole ⟨*mustered* the troops⟩.

---

\ə\ abut \ᵊ\ kitten \ər\ **further** \a\ ash \ā\ ace
\ä\ mop, mar \aù\ **out** \ch\ chin \e\ bet \ē\ **easy**
\g\ go \i\ hit \ī\ ice \j\ job \ŋ\ sing \ō\ go
\ȯ\ law \ȯi\ boy \th\ thin \ṯh\ **the** \ü\ loot \ù\ foot
\y\ yet \zh\ vision *see also* Guide to Pronunciation

**sum up** (15th century)
*transitive verb*
**1 :** to be the sum of **:** bring to a total ⟨10 victories *summed up* his record⟩
**2 a :** to present or show succinctly **:** SUMMARIZE ⟨*sum up* the evidence presented⟩ **b :** to assess and then describe briefly **:** size up
*intransitive verb*
**:** to present a summary or recapitulation

¹**sun** \'sən\ *noun* [Middle English *sunne,* from Old English; akin to Old High German *sunna* sun, Latin *sol* — more at SOLAR] (before 12th century)
**1 a** *often capitalized* **:** the luminous celestial body around which the earth and other planets revolve, from which they receive heat and light, and which has a mean distance from earth of 93,000,000 miles (150,000,000 kilometers), a linear diameter of 864,000 miles (1,390,000 kilometers), a mass 332,000 times greater than earth, and a mean density about one fourth that of earth **b :** a celestial body like the sun
**2 :** the heat or light radiated from the sun
**3 :** one resembling the sun (as in warmth or brilliance)
**4 :** the rising or setting of the sun ⟨from *sun* to *sun*⟩
**5 :** GLORY, SPLENDOR
**— in the sun :** in the public eye
**— under the sun :** in the world **:** on earth

²**sun** *verb* **sunned; sun·ning** (15th century)
*transitive verb*
**:** to expose to or as if to the rays of the sun
*intransitive verb*
**:** to sun oneself

**sun-baked** \'sən-,bākt\ *adjective* (1628)
**1 :** heated, parched, or compacted especially by excessive sunlight
**2 :** baked by exposure to sunshine

**sun·bath** \'sən-,bath, -,bàth\ *noun* (1866)
**:** an exposure to sunlight or a sunlamp

**sun·bathe** \-,bāth\ *intransitive verb* [back-formation from *sunbather*] (1600)
**:** to take a sunbath
**— sun·bath·er** \-,bā-thər\ *noun*

**sun·beam** \-,bēm\ *noun* (before 12th century)
**:** a ray of sunlight

**sun bear** *noun* (1842)
**:** a small forest-dwelling bear (*Ursus malayanus* synonym *Helarctos malayanus*) that is found from Myanmar to Borneo and has short glossy black fur with a lighter muzzle and often an orange or white breast mark

**sun·bird** \-,bərd\ *noun* (1826)
**:** any of numerous small brilliantly colored oscine birds (family Nectariniidae) of the tropical Old World somewhat resembling hummingbirds

**sun·block** \-,bläk\ *noun* (1972)
**:** a preparation designed to block out more of the sun's rays than a sunscreen; *also* **:** its active ingredient (as para-aminobenzoic acid)

**sun·bon·net** \-,bä-nət\ *noun* (1824)
**:** a woman's bonnet with a wide brim framing the face and usually having a ruffle at the back to protect the neck from the sun

**sun·bow** \-,bō\ *noun* (1816)
**:** an arch resembling a rainbow made by the sun shining through vapor or mist

sunbonnet

¹**sun·burn** \-,bərn\ *verb* **-burned** \-,bərnd\ *or* **-burnt** \-,bərnt\; **-burn·ing** [back-formation from *sunburned,* from *sun* + *burned*] (1530)
*transitive verb*
**:** to burn or discolor by the sun
*intransitive verb*
**:** to become sunburned

²**sunburn** *noun* (1652)
**:** inflammation of the skin caused by overexposure to sunlight

**sun·burst** \'sən-,bərst\ *noun, often attributive* (1816)
**1 :** a flash of sunlight especially through a break in clouds
**2 a :** a jeweled brooch representing a sun surrounded by rays **b :** a design in the form of rays diverging from a central point

**sun·choke** \-,chōk\ *noun* (1980)
**:** JERUSALEM ARTICHOKE

**sun·dae** \'sən-dē, -(,)dā\ *noun* [probably alteration of *Sunday*] (1897)
**:** ice cream served with topping (as crushed fruit, syrup, nuts, or whipped cream)

**sun dance** *noun, often S&D capitalized* (1849)
**:** a solo or group solstice rite of American Indians

¹**Sun·day** \'sən-dē, -(,)dā\ *noun* [Middle English, from Old English *sunnandæg* (akin to Old High German *sunnūntag*), from *sunne* sun + *dæg* day] (before 12th century)
**:** the first day of the week **:** the Christian analogue of the Jewish Sabbath
**— Sun·days** \-dēz, -(,)dāz\ *adverb*

²**Sunday** *adjective* (14th century)
**1 :** of, relating to, or associated with Sunday
**2 :** [from the practice of wearing one's best clothes on Sunday to attend church] **:** BEST ⟨*Sunday* suit⟩
**3 :** AMATEUR ⟨*Sunday* painters⟩

**Sun·day-go-to-meet·ing** \'sən-dē-,gō-tə-'mē-tiŋ\ *adjective* (1831)
**:** appropriate for Sunday churchgoing

**Sunday punch** *noun* (1929)
**1 :** a powerful or devastating blow; *especially* **:** a knockout punch
**2 :** something capable of delivering a powerful or devastating blow to the opposition ⟨saving his *Sunday punch* for the end of the campaign —*Newsweek*⟩

**Sunday school** *noun* (1783)
**:** a school held on Sunday for religious education; *also* **:** the teachers and pupils of such a school

**sun·deck** \'sən-,dek\ *noun* (1897)
**1 :** the usually upper deck of a ship that is exposed to the most sun
**2 :** a roof, deck, or terrace for sunning

**sun·der** \'sən-dər\ *verb* **sun·dered; sun·der·ing** \-d(ə-)riŋ\ [Middle English, from Old English ge*sundrian, syndrian;* akin to Old High German *suntarōn* to sunder, Old English *sundor* apart, Latin *sine* without, Sanskrit *sanutar* away] (before 12th century)
*transitive verb*
**:** to break apart or in two **:** separate by or as if by violence or by intervening time or space
*intransitive verb*
**:** to become parted, disunited, or severed
**synonym** see SEPARATE

**sun·dew** \'sən-(,)dü, -(,)dyü\ *noun* (1578)
**:** any of a genus (*Drosera* of the family Droseraceae, the sundew family) of bog-inhabiting insectivorous herbs having viscid glands on the leaves

**sun·di·al** \-,dī(-ə)l\ *noun* (1599)
**:** an instrument to show the time of day by the shadow of a gnomon on a usually horizontal plate or on a cylindrical surface

**sun disk** *noun* (1877)
**:** an ancient Near Eastern symbol consisting of a disk with conventionalized wings emblematic of the sun-god (as Ra in Egypt)

sun disk

**sun dog** *noun* (1635)
**1 :** PARHELION
**2 :** a small nearly round halo on the parhelic circle most frequently just outside the halo of 22 degrees

**sun·down** \'sən-,daún\ *noun* (1620)
**:** SUNSET 2

**sun·down·er** \-,daú-nər\ *noun* (1868)
**1** [from his habit of arriving at a place where he hopes to obtain food and lodging too late to do any work] *Australian* **:** HOBO, TRAMP
**2** *chiefly British* **:** a drink taken at sundown

**sun·dress** \-,dres\ *noun* (1942)
**:** a dress with an abbreviated bodice usually exposing the shoulders, arms, and back

**sun·dries** \'sən-drēz\ *noun plural* [¹*sundry*] (1755)
**:** miscellaneous small articles, details, or items

**sun·drops** \'sən-,dräps\ *noun plural but singular or plural in construction* (1784)
**:** any of several day-flowering herbs (genus *Oenothera*) of the evening-primrose family

¹**sun·dry** \'sən-drē\ *adjective* [Middle English, different for each, from Old English *syndrig,* from *sundor* apart — more at SUNDER] (13th century)
**:** MISCELLANEOUS, VARIOUS ⟨*sundry* articles⟩

²**sundry** *pronoun, plural in construction* (15th century)
**:** an indeterminate number ⟨recommended for reading by all and *sundry* —Edward Huberman⟩

**sun·fish** \-,fish\ *noun* (1629)
**1 :** OCEAN SUNFISH
**2 :** any of numerous American freshwater bony fishes (family Centrarchidae, especially genus *Lepomis*) usually with a deep compressed body and metallic luster

**Sunfish** *trademark*
**—** used for a light sailboat that has one sail and is designed for use by no more than two people

**sun·flow·er** \-,flaú(-ə)r\ *noun* (1597)
**:** any of a genus (*Helianthus*) of New World composite plants with large yellow-rayed flower heads bearing edible seeds that yield an edible oil

**sung** \'səŋ\ *past and past participle of* SING
**Sung** \'súŋ\ *noun* [Chinese (Beijing) *Sòng*] (1673)
**:** a Chinese dynasty dated A.D. 960–1280 and marked by cultural refinement and achievements in philosophy, literature, and art
**— Sung** *adjective*

**sun·glass** \'sən-,glas\ *noun* (1804)
**1 :** a convex lens for converging the sun's rays
**2** *plural* **:** glasses to protect the eyes from the sun

**sung mass** *noun* (1931)
**:** HIGH MASS

**sun god** *noun, often capitalized* (1592)
**:** a god that represents or personifies the sun in various religions

**sun goddess** *noun, often capitalized* (1861)
**:** a goddess that represents or personifies the sun in various religions

**sun–grebe** \'sən-,grēb\ *noun* (circa 1889)
**:** any of a small family (Heliornithidae) of African, Asian, and American tropical birds related to the rails

¹**sunk** \'səŋk\ *past and past participle of* SINK
²**sunk** *adjective* (1719)
**1 :** depressed in spirits
**2 :** DONE FOR, RUINED

**sunk·en** \'səŋ-kən\ *adjective* [Middle English *sonkyn,* past participle of *sinken* to sink] (14th century)
**1 :** SUBMERGED; *especially* **:** lying at the bottom of a body of water
**2 a :** HOLLOW, RECESSED ⟨*sunken* cheeks⟩ **b :** lying in a depression ⟨a *sunken* garden⟩ **c :** settled below the normal level ⟨a *sunken* living room⟩ **d :** constructed below the normal floor level ⟨a *sunken* living room⟩

**sunk fence** *noun* (circa 1771)
**:** a ditch with a retaining wall used to divide lands without defacing a landscape — called also *ha-ha*

**sun·lamp** \'sən-,lamp\ *noun* (1885)
**:** an electric lamp designed to emit radiation of wavelengths from ultraviolet to infrared

**sun·less** \-ləs\ *adjective* (1589)
: lacking sunshine : DARK, CHEERLESS
**sun·light** \-ˌlīt\ *noun* (13th century)
: the light of the sun : SUNSHINE
**sun·lit** \-ˌlit\ *adjective* (1822)
: lighted by or as if by the sun
**sunn** \ˈsən\ *noun* [Hindi *san,* from Sanskrit *śaṇa*] (1774)
: an East Indian leguminous plant (*Crotalaria juncea*) with slender branches, simple leaves, and yellow flowers; *also* : its valuable fiber resembling hemp that is lighter and stronger than jute
**sun·na** *also* **sun·nah** \ˈsu̇(n)-(ˌ)nə, ˈsə(n)-\ *noun, often capitalized* [Arabic *sunnah*] (1728)
: the body of Islamic custom and practice based on Muhammad's words and deeds
**sunn hemp** *noun* (1849)
: SUNN
**Sun·ni** \ˈsu̇(n)-(ˌ)nē\ *noun* [Arabic *sunnīy,* from *sunnah*] (1595)
**1** : the Muslims of the branch of Islam that adheres to the orthodox tradition and acknowledges the first four caliphs as rightful successors of Muhammad — compare SHIA
**2** : a Sunni Muslim
— **Sunni** *adjective*
**Sun·nism** \ˈsu̇(n)-ˌni-zəm\ *noun* (1892)
: the religious system or distinctive tenets of the Sunni
**Sun·nite** \-ˌnīt\ *noun* (1718)
: SUNNI 2
— **Sun·nite** \ˈsu̇(n)-ˌnīt\ *adjective*
**sun·ny** \ˈsə-nē\ *adjective* **sun·ni·er; -est** (14th century)
**1** : marked by brilliant sunlight : full of sunshine
**2** : CHEERFUL, OPTIMISTIC ⟨a *sunny* disposition⟩
**3** : exposed to, brightened, or warmed by the sun ⟨a *sunny* room⟩
— **sun·ni·ly** \ˈsə-nᵊl-ē\ *adverb*
— **sun·ni·ness** \ˈsə-nē-nəs\ *noun*
**sun·ny–side up** \ˌsə-nē-ˌsīd-ˈəp\ *adjective* (circa 1901)
*of an egg* : fried on one side only
**sun·porch** \-ˌpōrch, -ˌpȯrch\ *noun* (1918)
: a screened-in or glassed-in porch with a sunny exposure
**sun·rise** \ˈsən-ˌrīz\ *noun* (15th century)
**1** : the apparent rising of the sun above the horizon; *also* : the accompanying atmospheric effects
**2** : the time when the upper limb of the sun appears above the horizon as a result of the diurnal rotation of the earth
**sun·roof** \-ˌrüf, -ˌru̇f\ *noun* (1952)
: a panel in an automobile roof that can be opened
**sun·room** \-ˌrüm, -ˌru̇m\ *noun* (1917)
: a glass-enclosed porch or living room with a sunny exposure — called also *sun parlor*
**sun·scald** \-ˌskȯld\ *noun* (1855)
: an injury of woody plants (as fruit or forest trees) characterized by localized death of the tissues and sometimes by cankers and caused when it occurs in the summer by the combined action of both the heat and light of the sun and in the winter by the combined action of sun and low temperature to produce freezing of bark and underlying tissues
**sun·screen** \-ˌskrēn\ *noun* (1738)
: a screen to protect against sun; *especially* : a substance (as para-aminobenzoic acid) used in suntan preparations to protect the skin from excessive ultraviolet radiation
— **sun·screen·ing** *adjective*
**sun·seek·er** \-ˌsē-kər\ *noun* (1954)
: a person who travels to an area of warmth and sun especially in winter
**¹sun·set** \-ˌset\ *noun* (14th century)
**1** : the apparent descent of the sun below the horizon; *also* : the accompanying atmospheric effects

**2** : the time when the upper limb of the sun disappears below the horizon as a result of the diurnal rotation of the earth
**3** : a period of decline; *especially* : old age
**²sunset** *adjective* (1976)
: stipulating the periodic review of government agencies and programs in order to continue their existence ⟨*sunset* law⟩
**sun·shade** \ˈsən-ˌshād\ *noun* (1842)
: something used as a protection from the sun's rays: as **a** : PARASOL **b** : AWNING
**¹sun·shine** \-ˌshīn\ *noun* (13th century)
**1 a** : the sun's light or direct rays **b** : the warmth and light given by the sun's rays **c** : a spot or surface on which the sun's light shines
**2** : something (as a person, condition, or influence) that radiates warmth, cheer, or happiness
— **sun·shiny** \-ˌshī-nē\ *adjective*
**²sunshine** *adjective* (1972)
: forbidding or restricting closed meetings of legislative or executive bodies and sometimes providing for public access to records ⟨*sunshine* law⟩
**sun·spot** \-ˌspät\ *noun* (1868)
: any of the dark spots that appear from time to time on the sun's surface and are usually visible only through a telescope
**sun·stroke** \-ˌstrōk\ *noun* (1851)
: heatstroke caused by direct exposure to the sun
**sun·struck** \-ˌstrək\ *adjective* (1794)
: affected or touched by the sun
**sun·suit** \-ˌsüt\ *noun* (1929)
: an outfit worn usually for sunbathing and play
**sun·tan** \-ˌtan\ *noun* (1904)
**1** : a browning of the skin from exposure to the rays of the sun
**2** *plural* : a tan-colored summer uniform
— **sun·tanned** \-ˌtand\ *adjective*
**sun·up** \-ˌəp\ *noun* (1712)
: SUNRISE
**¹sun·ward** \ˈsən-wərd\ *or* **sun·wards** \-wərdz\ *adverb* (1611)
: toward the sun
**²sunward** *adjective* (1769)
: facing the sun
**sun·wise** \ˈsən-ˌwīz\ *adverb* (circa 1864)
: CLOCKWISE
**¹sup** \ˈsəp\ *verb* **supped; sup·ping** [Middle English *suppen,* from Old English *sūpan, suppan;* akin to Old High German *sūfan* to drink, sip, Old English *sopp* sop] (before 12th century)
*transitive verb*
: to take or drink in swallows or gulps
*intransitive verb*
*chiefly dialect* : to take food and especially liquid food into the mouth a little at a time
**²sup** *noun* (circa 1570)
: a mouthful especially of liquor or broth : SIP; *also* : a small quantity of liquid ⟨pour me just a *sup* of tea⟩
**³sup** *intransitive verb* **supped; sup·ping** [Middle English *soupen, suppen,* from Old French *souper,* from *soupe* sop, soup — more at SOUP] (14th century)
**1** : to eat the evening meal
**2** : to make one's supper — used with *on* or *off* ⟨*sup* on roast beef⟩
**¹su·per** \ˈsü-pər\ *adjective* [*super-*] (1837)
**1 a** : — used as a generalized term of approval ⟨a *super* cook⟩ **b** : of high grade or quality
**2** : very large or powerful ⟨a *super* atomic bomb⟩
**3** : exhibiting the characteristics of its type to an extreme or excessive degree ⟨*super* secrecy⟩
**²super** *noun* (1838)
**1** [by shortening] **a** : SUPERNUMERARY; *especially* : a supernumerary actor **b** : SUPERINTENDENT, SUPERVISOR; *especially* : the superintendent of an apartment building
**2** [short for obsolete *superhive*] : a removable upper story of a beehive

**3** [¹*super*] : a superfine grade or extra large size
**4** [origin unknown] : a thin loosely woven open-meshed starched cotton fabric used especially for reinforcing books
**³super** *adverb* [*super-*] (1946)
**1** : VERY, EXTREMELY ⟨a *super* fast car⟩
**2** : to an excessive degree
**super-** *prefix* [Latin *super,* over, above, in addition, from *super* over, above, on top of — more at OVER]
**1 a** (1) : over and above : higher in quantity, quality, or degree than : more than ⟨*super*human⟩ (2) : in addition : extra ⟨*super*tax⟩ **b** (1) : exceeding or so as to exceed a norm ⟨*super*heat⟩ (2) : in or to an extreme or excessive degree or intensity ⟨*super*subtle⟩ **c** : surpassing all or most others of its kind ⟨*super*highway⟩
**2 a** : situated or placed above, on, or at the top of ⟨*super*lunary⟩; *specifically* : situated on the dorsal side of **b** : next above or higher ⟨*super*tonic⟩
**3** : having the (specified) ingredient present in a large or unusually large proportion ⟨*super*phosphate⟩
**4** : constituting a more inclusive category than that specified ⟨*super*family⟩
**5** : superior in status, title, or position ⟨*super*power⟩

su·per·ab·sor·bent
su·per·achiev·er
su·per·ac·tiv·i·ty
su·per·ad·di·tion
su·per·ad·min·is·tra·tor
su·per·agent
su·per·am·bi·tious
su·per·ath·lete
su·per·bad
su·per·bank
su·per·bil·lion·aire
su·per·bitch
su·per·board
su·per·bomb
su·per·bomb·er
su·per·bright
su·per·bu·reau·crat
su·per·cab·i·net
su·per·car
su·per·car·ri·er
su·per·cau·tious
su·per·cen·ter
su·per·chic
su·per·church
su·per·civ·i·li·za·tion
su·per·civ·i·lized
su·per·clean
su·per·club
su·per·co·los·sal
su·per·com·fort·able
su·per·com·pet·i·tive
su·per·con·fi·dent
su·per·con·glom·er·ate
su·per·con·ser·va·tive
su·per·con·ve·nient
su·per·cop
su·per·cor·po·ra·tion
su·per·crim·i·nal
su·per·cute
su·per·de·luxe
su·per·dip·lo·mat
su·per·ef·fec·tive
su·per·ef·fi·cien·cy
su·per·ef·fi·cient
su·per·ego·ist
su·per·elite
su·per·em·i·nence

su·per·em·i·nent
su·per·em·i·nent·ly
su·per·ex·pen·sive
su·per·ex·press
su·per·fan
su·per·farm
su·per·fast
su·per·firm
su·per·flack
su·per·fund
su·per·good
su·per·gov·ern·ment
su·per·growth
su·per·hard·en
su·per·heavy
su·per·her·o·ine
su·per·hit
su·per·hot
su·per·hype
su·per·in·su·lat·ed
su·per·in·tel·lec·tu·al
su·per·in·tel·li·gence
su·per·in·tel·li·gent
su·per·in·ten·si·ty
su·per·jock
su·per·jum·bo
su·per·large
su·per·law·yer
su·per·light
su·per·lob·by·ist
su·per·loy·al·ist
su·per·lux·u·ri·ous
su·per·lux·u·ry
su·per·ma·cho
su·per·ma·jor·i·ty
su·per·male
su·per·mas·cu·line
su·per·mas·sive
su·per·mil·i·tant
su·per·mil·lion·aire
su·per·mind
su·per·min·is·ter
su·per·mod·el
su·per·mod·ern
su·per·mom
su·per·na·tion
su·per·na·tion·al
su·per·nu·tri·tion
su·per·or·gan·ic
su·per·or·gasm

\ə\ abut \ᵊ\ kitten \ər\ further \a\ ash \ā\ ace
\ä\ mop, mar \au̇\ out \ch\ chin \e\ bet \ē\ easy
\g\ go \i\ hit \ī\ ice \j\ job \ŋ\ sing \ō\ go
\ȯ\ law \ȯi\ boy \th\ thin \th\ the \ü\ loot \u̇\ foot
\y\ yet \zh\ vision *see also* Guide to Pronunciation

su·per·pa·tri·ot
su·per·pa·tri·ot·ic
su·per·pa·tri·o·tism
su·per·per·son
su·per·per·son·al
su·per·phe·nom·e·non
su·per·pimp
su·per·plane
su·per·play·er
su·per·po·lite
su·per·port
su·per·pow·er·ful
su·per·pre·mi·um
su·per·pro
su·per·prof·it
su·per·qual·i·ty
su·per·race
su·per·real
su·per·re·al·ism
su·per·re·gion·al
su·per·rich
su·per·road
su·per·ro·man·tic
su·per·ro·man·ti·cism
su·per·safe
su·per·sale
su·per·sales·man
su·per·scale
su·per·school
su·per·scout
su·per·se·cre·cy
su·per·se·cret
su·per·sell
su·per·sell·er
su·per·sex·u·al·i·ty
su·per·sharp
su·per·show
su·per·sing·er
su·per·size
su·per·sized

su·per·sleuth
su·per·slick
su·per·smart
su·per·smooth
su·per·soft
su·per·so·phis·ti·cat·ed
su·per·spe·cial
su·per·spe·cial·ist
su·per·spe·cial·i·za·tion
su·per·spe·cial·ized
su·per·spec·ta·cle
su·per·spec·tac·u·lar
su·per·spec·u·la·tion
su·per·spy
su·per·state
su·per·sta·tion
su·per·stim·u·late
su·per·stock
su·per·stra·tum
su·per·strength
su·per·strike
su·per·strong
su·per·stud
su·per·sub·tle
su·per·sub·tle·ty
su·per·sur·geon
su·per·sweet
su·per·tank·er
su·per·ter·rif·ic
su·per·thick
su·per·thin
su·per·thril·ler
su·per·tight
su·per·vir·ile
su·per·vir·tu·o·so
su·per·wave
su·per·weap·on
su·per·wide
su·per·wife

**su·per·a·ble** \'sü-p(ə-)rə-bəl\ *adjective* [Latin *superabilis,* from *superare* to surmount — more at INSUPERABLE] (1629)
**:** capable of being overcome or conquered
— **su·per·a·ble·ness** *noun*
— **su·per·a·bly** \-blē\ *adverb*
**su·per·abound** \,sü-pər-ə-'baùnd\ *intransitive verb* [Middle English, from Late Latin *superabundare,* from Latin *super-* + *abundare* to abound] (14th century)
**:** to abound or prevail in greater measure or to excess
**su·per·abun·dant** \-'bən-dənt\ *adjective* [Middle English, from Late Latin *superabundant-, superabundans,* from present participle of *superabundare*] (15th century)
**:** more than ample **:** EXCESSIVE
— **su·per·abun·dance** \-dən(t)s\ *noun*
— **su·per·abun·dant·ly** *adverb*
**su·per·add** \,sü-pər-'ad\ *transitive verb* [Middle English, from Latin *superaddere,* from *super-* + *addere* to add] (15th century)
**:** to add especially in a way that compounds an effect ⟨the loss of his job was *superadded* to the loss of his house⟩
**su·per·agen·cy** \'sü-pər-,ā-jən(t)-sē\ *noun* (1943)
**:** a large complex governmental agency especially when set up to supervise other agencies
**su·per·al·loy** \,sü-pər-'a-,lòi, -ə-'lòi\ *noun* (1948)
**:** any of various high-strength often complex alloys resistant to high temperature
**su·per·al·tern** \,sü-pər-'òl-tərn\ *noun* [*super-* + sub*altern*] (1921)
**:** a universal proposition in traditional logic that is a ground for the immediate inference of a corresponding subaltern
**su·per·an·nu·ate** \,sü-pər-'an-yə-,wāt\ *verb* **-at·ed; -at·ing** [back-formation from *superannuated*] (1649)
*transitive verb*

**1 :** to make, declare, or prove obsolete or out-of-date
**2 :** to retire and pension because of age or infirmity
*intransitive verb*
**1 :** to become retired
**2 :** to become antiquated
— **su·per·an·nu·a·tion** \-,an-yə-'wā-shən\ *noun*
**superannuated** *adjective* [Medieval Latin *superannuatus,* past participle of *superannuari* to be too old, from Latin *super-* + *annus* year — more at ANNUAL] (1740)
**:** incapacitated or disqualified for active duty by advanced age
**su·perb** \sù-'pərb\ *adjective* [Latin *superbus* excellent, proud, from *super* above + *-bus* (akin to Old English *bēon* to be) — more at OVER, BE] (1549)
**:** marked to the highest degree by grandeur, excellence, brilliance, or competence
*synonym* see SPLENDID
— **su·perb·ly** *adverb*
— **su·perb·ness** *noun*
**Su·per·ball** \'sü-pər-,bòl\ *trademark*
— used for a toy rubber ball with a high bounce
**su·per·block** \-,bläk\ *noun* (1928)
**:** a very large commercial or residential block barred to through traffic, crossed by pedestrian walks and sometimes access roads, and often spotted with grassed malls
**Super Bowl** *noun* [from the *Super Bowl,* annual championship game of the National Football League] (1969)
**:** a contest or event that is the most important or prestigious of its kind ⟨the 2,500-mile, 24-day *Super Bowl* of bicycle racing —John Krakauer⟩
**¹su·per·cal·en·der** \'sü-pər-,ka-lən-dər\ *transitive verb* (1888)
**:** to process (paper) in a supercalender
**²supercalender** *noun* (1894)
**:** a stack of highly polished calender rolls used to give an extra finish to paper
**su·per·car·go** \,sü-pər-'kär-(,)gō, 'sü-pər-,\ *noun* [Spanish *sobrecargo,* from *sobre-* over (from Latin *super-*) + *cargo* cargo] (1697)
**:** an officer on a merchant ship in charge of the commercial concerns of the voyage
**supercede** *variant of* SUPERSEDE
**su·per·charge** \'sü-pər-,chärj\ *transitive verb* (1876)
**1 :** to charge greatly or excessively (as with vigor or tension)
**2 :** to supply a charge to the intake of (as an engine) at a pressure higher than that of the surrounding atmosphere
**3 :** PRESSURIZE 1
— **supercharge** *noun*
**su·per·charg·er** \-,chär-jər\ *noun* (1921)
**:** a device (as a blower or compressor) for pressurizing the cabin of an airplane or for increasing the volume air charge of an internal combustion engine over that which would normally be drawn in through the pumping action of the pistons
**su·per·cil·i·ary** \,sü-pər-'si-lē-,er-ē\ *adjective* [New Latin *superciliaris,* from Latin *supercilium*] (1732)
**:** of, relating to, or adjoining the eyebrow **:** SUPRAORBITAL
**su·per·cil·ious** \-'si-lē-əs, -'sil-yəs\ *adjective* [Latin *superciliosus,* from *supercilium* eyebrow, haughtiness, from *super-* + *-cilium* eyelid (akin to *celare* to hide) — more at HELL] (1598)
**:** coolly and patronizingly haughty ◆
*synonym* see PROUD
— **su·per·cil·ious·ly** *adverb*
— **su·per·cil·ious·ness** *noun*
**su·per·city** \'sü-pər-,si-tē\ *noun* (1925)
**:** MEGALOPOLIS
**su·per·class** \-,klas\ *noun* (circa 1891)

**:** a category in biological classification ranking below a phylum or division and above a class
**su·per·clus·ter** \'sü-pər-,kləs-tər\ *noun* (1926)
**:** a group of gravitationally associated clusters of galaxies
**su·per·coil** \-,kòi(ə)l\ *noun* (1965)
**:** SUPERHELIX
— **supercoil** *verb*
**su·per·col·lid·er** \-kə-,lī-dər\ *noun* (1984)
**:** a very large collider capable of accelerating particles to very high energies
**su·per·com·put·er** \-kəm-,pyü-tər\ *noun* (1968)
**:** a large very fast mainframe used especially for scientific computations
**su·per·con·duct** \,sü-pər-kən-'dəkt\ *intransitive verb* (1952)
**:** to exhibit superconductivity
— **su·per·con·duc·tive** \-'dək-tiv\ *adjective*
**su·per·con·duc·tiv·i·ty** \-,kän-,dək-'ti-və-tē, -kən-\ *noun* (1913)
**:** a complete disappearance of electrical resistance in a substance especially at very low temperatures
— **su·per·con·duc·tor** \-kən-'dək-tər\ *noun*
**su·per·con·ti·nent** \'sü-pər-,kän-tᵊn-ənt, -,känt-nənt\ *noun* (1960)
**:** a former large continent from which other continents are held to have broken off and drifted away
**su·per·cool** \,sü-pər-'kül\ (1906)
*transitive verb*
**:** to cool below the freezing point without solidification or crystallization
*intransitive verb*
**:** to become supercooled
**su·per·crit·i·cal** \-'kri-ti-kəl\ *adjective* (1934)
**:** being or having a temperature above a critical temperature ⟨*supercritical* fluid⟩
**su·per·cur·rent** \'sü-pər-,kər-ənt, -,kə-rənt\ *noun* (1940)
**:** a current of electricity flowing in a superconductor
**su·per–du·per** \'sü-pər-,dü-pər\ *adjective* [reduplication of ¹*super*] (1940)
**:** of the greatest excellence, size, effectiveness, or impressiveness
**su·per·ego** \,sü-pər-'ē-(,)gō *also* -'e-(,)gō\ *noun* [New Latin, translation of German *Überich,* from *über* over + *ich* I] (1919)
**:** the one of the three divisions of the psyche in psychoanalytic theory that is only partly conscious, represents internalization of parental conscience and the rules of society, and functions to reward and punish through a system of moral attitudes, conscience, and a sense of guilt — compare EGO, ID
**su·per·el·e·vate** \-'e-lə-,vāt\ *transitive verb* (circa 1945)
**:** BANK 1c
**su·per·el·e·va·tion** \-,e-lə-'vā-shən\ *noun* (1889)

**1 :** the vertical distance between the heights of inner and outer edges of highway pavement or railroad rails
**2 :** additional elevation

**su·per·er·o·ga·tion** \ˌsü-pə-ˌrer-ə-'gā-shən\ *noun* [Medieval Latin *supererogation-, supererogatio,* from *supererogare* to perform beyond the call of duty, from Late Latin, to expend in addition, from Latin *super-* + *erogare* to expend public funds after asking the consent of the people, from *e-* + *rogare* to ask — more at RIGHT] (1526)
**:** the act of performing more than is required by duty, obligation, or need

**su·per·erog·a·to·ry** \ˌsü-pə-ri-'rä-gə-ˌtōr-ē, -ˌtȯr-\ *adjective* (1593)
**1 :** observed or performed to an extent not enjoined or required
**2 :** exceeding what is needed **:** SUPERFLUOUS

**su·per·fam·i·ly** \'sü-pər-ˌfam-lē, -'fa-mə-\ *noun* (circa 1890)
**:** a category of biological classification ranking below an order and above a family

**su·per·fat·ted** \-ˌfa-təd\ *adjective* (1891)
**:** containing extra oil or fat ⟨*superfatted* soap⟩

**su·per·fe·cun·da·tion** \ˌsü-pər-ˌfe-kən-'dā-shən, -ˌfē-\ *noun* (circa 1855)
**1 :** successive fertilization of two or more ova from the same ovulation especially by different sires
**2 :** fertilization at one time of a number of ova excessive for the species

**su·per·fe·ta·tion** \-fē-'tā-shən\ *noun* [Medieval Latin *superfetation-, superfetatio,* from Latin *superfetare* to conceive while already pregnant, from *super-* + *fetus* act of bearing young, offspring — more at FETUS] (1603)
**:** a progressive accumulation or accretion reaching an extreme or excessive degree

**su·per·fi·cial** \ˌsü-pər-'fi-shəl\ *adjective* [Middle English, from Late Latin *superficialis,* from Latin *superficies*] (15th century)
**1 a** (1) **:** of or relating to a surface (2) **:** lying on, not penetrating below, or affecting only the surface ⟨*superficial* wounds⟩ **b** *British, of a unit of measure* **:** SQUARE ⟨*superficial* foot⟩
**2 a :** concerned only with the obvious or apparent **:** SHALLOW **b :** lying on the surface **:** EXTERNAL **c :** presenting only an appearance without substance or significance ☆
— **su·per·fi·cial·ly** \-'fi-sh(ə-)lē\ *adverb*

**superficial fascia** *noun* (1876)
**:** the thin layer of loose fatty connective tissue underlying the skin and binding it to the parts beneath — called also *hypodermis*

**su·per·fi·ci·al·i·ty** \ˌsü-pər-ˌfi-shē-'a-lə-tē\ *noun, plural* **-ties** (1530)
**1 :** the quality or state of being superficial
**2 :** something superficial

**su·per·fi·cies** \-'fi-(ˌ)shēz, -shē-ˌēz\ *noun, plural* **superficies** [Latin, surface, from *super-* + *facies* face, aspect — more at FACE] (1530)
**1 :** a surface of a body or a region of space
**2 :** the external aspects or appearance of a thing

**su·per·fine** \ˌsü-pər-'fīn\ *adjective* (1575)
**1 :** overly refined or nice
**2 :** of extremely fine size or texture ⟨*superfine* toothbrush bristles⟩ ⟨*superfine* sugar⟩
**3 :** of high quality or grade — used especially of merchandise

**su·per·fix** \'sü-pər-ˌfiks\ *noun* [*super-* + *-fix* (as in *prefix*)] (circa 1948)
**:** a morpheme consisting of a pattern of stress, intonation, or juncture features that are associated with the syllables of a word or phrase (as the distinctive stress patterns of the noun *subject* and the verb *subject*)

**su·per·flu·id** \ˌsü-pər-'flü-əd\ *noun* (1938)
**:** an unusual state of matter noted only in liquid helium cooled to near absolute zero and characterized by apparently frictionless flow (as through fine holes)
— **superfluid** *adjective*
— **su·per·flu·id·i·ty** \-flü-'i-də-tē\ *noun*

**su·per·flu·i·ty** \ˌsü-pər-'flü-ə-tē\ *noun, plural* **-ties** [Middle English *superfluitee,* from Middle French *superfluité,* from Late Latin *superfluitat-, superfluitas,* from Latin *superfluus*] (14th century)
**1 a :** EXCESS, OVERSUPPLY **b :** something unnecessary or superfluous
**2 :** immoderate and especially luxurious living, habits, or desires

**su·per·flu·ous** \sü-'pər-flü-əs\ *adjective* [Middle English, from Latin *superfluus,* literally, running over, from *superfluere* to overflow, from *super-* + *fluere* to flow — more at FLUID] (15th century)
**1 a :** exceeding what is sufficient or necessary **:** EXTRA **b :** not needed **:** UNNECESSARY
**2** *obsolete* **:** marked by wastefulness **:** EXTRAVAGANT
— **su·per·flu·ous·ly** *adverb*
— **su·per·flu·ous·ness** *noun*

**su·per·gene** \'sü-pər-ˌjēn\ *noun* (circa 1949)
**:** a group of linked genes acting as an allelic unit especially when due to the suppression of crossing-over

**su·per·gi·ant** \-ˌjī-ənt\ *noun* (1926)
**:** something that is extremely large; *especially* **:** a star of very great intrinsic luminosity and enormous size
— **supergiant** *adjective*

**su·per·glue** *noun* (1946)
**:** a very strong glue; *specifically* **:** a glue whose chief ingredient is a cyanoacrylate that becomes adhesive through polymerization rather than evaporation of a solvent

**su·per·graph·ics** \-ˌgra-fiks\ *noun plural but singular or plural in construction* (1969)
**:** billboard-sized graphic shapes usually of bright color and simple design

**su·per·grav·i·ty** \ˌsü-pər-'gra-və-tē\ *noun* (1976)
**:** any of various theories in physics that are based on supersymmetry and attempt to unify general relativity and quantum theory and that state that the principle transmitter of gravity is the graviton

**su·per·group** \'sü-pər-ˌgrüp\ *noun* (1968)
**:** a rock group made up of prominent former members of other rock groups; *also* **:** an extremely successful rock group

¹**su·per·heat** \ˌsü-pər-'hēt\ *transitive verb* (1859)
**1 :** to heat (a vapor not in contact with its own liquid) so as to cause to remain free from suspended liquid droplets ⟨*superheated* steam⟩
**2 :** to heat (a liquid) above the boiling point without converting into vapor
— **su·per·heat·er** *noun*

²**su·per·heat** \'sü-pər-ˌhēt, ˌsü-pər-'\ *noun* (1884)
**:** the extra heat imparted to a vapor in superheating it from a dry and saturated condition; *also* **:** the corresponding rise of temperature

**su·per·heat·ed** \-ˌhē-təd, -'hē-\ *adjective* (1857)
**:** very hot; *also* **:** exceedingly emotional or intense

**su·per·hea·vy·weight** \ˌsü-pər-'he-vē-ˌwāt\ *noun* (1971)
**:** an athlete (as an Olympic weightlifter, boxer, or wrestler) who competes in the heaviest class or division

**su·per·he·lix** \'sü-pər-ˌhē-liks\ *noun* (1964)
**:** a helix (as of DNA) which has its axis arranged in a helical coil
— **su·per·he·li·cal** \ˌsü-pər-'he-li-kəl, -'hē-\ *adjective*

**su·per·hero** \-ˌhir-(ˌ)ō, -ˌhē-(ˌ)rō\ *noun* (1917)
**:** a fictional hero having extraordinary or superhuman powers; *also* **:** an exceptionally skillful or successful person

**su·per·het·ero·dyne** \ˌsü-pər-'he-tə-rə-ˌdīn, -'he-trə-\ *adjective* [*super*sonic + *heterodyne*] (1922)
**:** used in or being a radio receiver in which an incoming signal is mixed with a locally generated frequency to produce an ultrasonic signal at a fixed frequency that is then rectified, amplified, and rectified again to reproduce the sound
— **superheterodyne** *noun*

**su·per·high frequency** \'sü-pər-ˌhī-\ *noun* (circa 1945)
**:** a radio frequency in the next to the highest range of the radio spectrum — see RADIO FREQUENCY table

**su·per·high·way** \ˌsü-pər-'hī-ˌwā, 'sü-pər-ˌ\ *noun* (1925)
**:** a multilane highway (as an expressway or turnpike) designed for high-speed traffic

**su·per·hu·man** \ˌsü-pər-'hyü-mən, -'yü-\ *adjective* (1633)
**1 :** being above the human **:** DIVINE ⟨*superhuman* beings⟩
**2 :** exceeding normal human power, size, or capability **:** HERCULEAN ⟨a *superhuman* effort⟩; *also* **:** having such power, size, or capability
— **su·per·hu·man·i·ty** \-hyü-'ma-nə-tē, -yü-\ *noun*
— **su·per·hu·man·ly** \-'hyü-mən-lē, -'yü-\ *adverb*
— **su·per·hu·man·ness** \-mən-nəs\ *noun*

**su·per·im·pose** \ˌsü-pər-im-'pōz\ *transitive verb* (1794)
**:** to place or lay over or above something ⟨*superimposed* images⟩ ⟨*superimposed* a formula on the stories⟩
— **su·per·im·pos·able** \-'pō-zə-bəl\ *adjective*
— **su·per·im·po·si·tion** \-ˌim-pə-'zi-shən\ *noun*

**su·per·in·cum·bent** \-in-'kəm-bənt\ *adjective* [Latin *superincumbent-, superincumbens,* present participle of *superincumbere* to lie on top of, from *super-* + *incumbere* to lie down on — more at INCUMBENT] (1664)
**:** lying or resting and usually exerting pressure on something else
— **su·per·in·cum·bent·ly** *adverb*

**su·per·in·di·vid·u·al** \ˌsü-pər-ˌin-də-'vij-wəl, -'vi-jə-wəl, -'vi-jəl\ *adjective* (1916)
**:** of, relating to, or being an organism, entity, or complex of more than individual complexity or nature

**su·per·in·duce** \-in-'düs, -'dyüs\ *transitive verb* [Latin *superinducere,* from *super-* + *inducere* to lead in — more at INDUCE] (circa 1555)
**1 :** to introduce as an addition over or above something already existing
**2 :** BRING ON, INDUCE
— **su·per·in·duc·tion** \-'dək-shən\ *noun*

**su·per·in·fec·tion** \-in-'fek-shən\ *noun* (circa 1922)
**:** reinfection or a second infection with a microbial agent (as a bacterium, fungus, or virus)
— **su·per·in·fect** \-'fekt\ *transitive verb*

**su·per·in·tend** \ˌsü-p(ə-)rin-'tend, ˌsü-pərn-\ *transitive verb* [Late Latin *superintendere,*

☆ **SYNONYMS**
**Superficial, shallow, cursory** mean lacking in depth or solidity. SUPERFICIAL implies a concern only with surface aspects or obvious features ⟨a *superficial* analysis of the problem⟩. SHALLOW is more generally derogatory in implying lack of depth in knowledge, reasoning, emotions, or character ⟨a light, *shallow,* and frivolous review⟩. CURSORY suggests a lack of thoroughness or a neglect of details ⟨gave the letter only a *cursory* reading⟩.

\ə\ abut   \ᵊ\ kitten   \ər\ further   \a\ ash   \ā\ ace
\ä\ mop, mar   \au̇\ out   \ch\ chin   \e\ bet   \ē\ easy
\g\ go   \i\ hit   \ī\ ice   \j\ job   \ŋ\ sing   \ō\ go
\ȯ\ law   \ȯi\ boy   \th\ thin   \t͟h\ the   \ü\ loot   \u̇\ foot
\y\ yet   \zh\ vision   *see also* Guide to Pronunciation

from Latin *super-* + *intendere* to stretch out, direct — more at INTEND] (circa 1615)
**:** to have or exercise the charge and oversight of **:** DIRECT
**su·per·in·ten·dence** \-'ten-dən(t)s\ *noun* (1603)
**:** the act or function of superintending or directing **:** SUPERVISION
**su·per·in·ten·den·cy** \-dən(t)-sē\ *noun, plural* **-cies** (1598)
**:** the office, post, or jurisdiction of a superintendent; *also* **:** SUPERINTENDENCE
**su·per·in·ten·dent** \-dənt\ *noun* [Medieval Latin *superintendent-, superintendens,* from Late Latin, present participle of *superintendere*] (1554)
**:** one who has executive oversight and charge
**— superintendent** *adjective*
**¹su·pe·ri·or** \su̇-'pir-ē-ər\ *adjective* [Middle English, from Middle French *superieur,* from Latin *superior,* comparative of *superus* upper, from *super* over, above — more at OVER] (14th century)
**1 :** situated higher up **:** UPPER
**2 :** of higher rank, quality, or importance
**3 :** courageously or serenely indifferent (as to something painful or disheartening)
**4 a :** greater in quantity or numbers ⟨escaped by *superior* speed⟩ **b :** excellent of its kind **:** BETTER ⟨her *superior* memory⟩
**5 :** being a superscript
**6 a** *of an animal structure* **:** situated above or anterior or dorsal to another and especially a corresponding part ⟨a *superior* artery⟩ **b** *of a plant structure* **:** situated above or near the top of another part: as (1) *of a calyx* **:** attached to and apparently arising from the ovary (2) *of an ovary* **:** free from the calyx or other floral envelope
**7 :** more comprehensive ⟨a genus is *superior* to a species⟩
**8 :** affecting or assuming an air of superiority **:** SUPERCILIOUS
**— su·pe·ri·or·ly** *adverb*
**²superior** *noun* (15th century)
**1 :** one who is above another in rank, station, or office; *especially* **:** the head of a religious house or order
**2 :** one that surpasses another in quality or merit
**3 :** SUPERSCRIPT
**superior conjunction** *noun* (1833)
**:** a conjunction in which the primary of an orbiting celestial body is aligned between the celestial body and an observer
**superior court** *noun* (1686)
**1 :** a court of general jurisdiction intermediate between the inferior courts (as a justice of the peace court) and the higher appellate courts
**2 :** a court with juries having original jurisdiction
**superior general** *noun, plural* **superiors general** (1775)
**:** the superior of a religious order or congregation
**su·pe·ri·or·i·ty** \su̇-,pir-ē-'ȯr-ə-tē, ,su̇-, -'är-\ *noun, plural* **-ties** (15th century)
**:** the quality or state of being superior; *also* **:** a superior characteristic
**superiority complex** *noun* (circa 1924)
**:** an exaggerated opinion of oneself
**superior planet** *noun* (1583)
**:** a planet whose orbit lies outside that of the earth
**superior vena cava** *noun* (1901)
**:** the branch of the vena cava of a vertebrate that brings blood back from the head and anterior part of the body to the heart
**su·per·ja·cent** \,su̇-pər-'jā-s°nt\ *adjective* [Latin *superjacent-, superjacens,* present participle of *superjacēre* to lie over or upon, from *super-* + *jacēre* to lie; akin to Latin *jacere* to throw — more at JET] (1610)
**:** lying above or upon **:** OVERLYING ⟨*superjacent* rocks⟩

**su·per·jet** \'su̇-pər-,jet\ *noun* (1958)
**:** a very large jet airplane
**¹su·per·la·tive** \su̇-'pər-lə-tiv\ *adjective* [Middle English *superlatif,* from Middle French, from Late Latin *superlativus,* from Latin *superlatus* (past participle of *superferre* to carry over, raise high), from *super-* + *latus,* past participle of *ferre* to carry — more at TOLERATE, BEAR] (14th century)
**1 :** of, relating to, or constituting the degree of grammatical comparison that denotes an extreme or unsurpassed level or extent
**2 a :** surpassing all others **:** SUPREME **b :** of very high quality **:** EXCELLENT
**3 :** EXCESSIVE, EXAGGERATED
**— su·per·la·tive·ly** *adverb*
**— su·per·la·tive·ness** *noun*
**²superlative** *noun* (15th century)
**1 a :** the superlative degree of comparison in a language **b :** a superlative form of an adjective or adverb
**2 :** the superlative or utmost degree of something **:** ACME
**3 :** a superlative person or thing
**4 :** an admiring sometimes exaggerated expression especially of praise ▪
**su·per·lin·er** \'su̇-pər-,lī-nər\ *noun* (1919)
**:** a fast luxurious passenger liner of great size
**su·per·lu·na·ry** \,su̇-pər-'lü-nə-rē\ *or* **su·per·lu·nar** \-nər, -,när\ *adjective* [Latin *super-* + *luna* moon — more at LUNAR] (1614)
*archaic* **:** being above the moon **:** CELESTIAL
**su·per·man** \'su̇-pər-,man\ *noun* [translation of German *Übermensch,* from *über* over, super- + *Mensch* man] (1903)
**1 :** a superior man that according to Nietzsche has learned to forgo fleeting pleasures and attain happiness and dominance through the exercise of creative power
**2 :** a person of extraordinary or superhuman power or achievements
**su·per·mar·ket** \-,mär-kət\ *noun, often attributive* (1933)
**1 :** a self-service retail market selling especially foods and household merchandise
**2 :** something resembling a supermarket especially in the variety or volume of its goods or services
**su·per·mi·cro** \-,mī-(,)krō\ *noun* (1982)
**:** a very fast and powerful microcomputer
**su·per·mini·com·put·er** \-'mi-nē-kəm-,pyü-tər\ *noun* (1980)
**:** a very fast and powerful minicomputer — called also *supermini*
**su·per·nal** \su̇-'pər-n°l\ *adjective* [Middle English, from Middle French, from Latin *supernus,* from *super* over, above — more at OVER] (15th century)
**1 a :** being or coming from on high **b :** HEAVENLY, ETHEREAL ⟨*supernal* melodies⟩ **c :** superlatively good ⟨*supernal* trumpet playing⟩
**2 :** located in or belonging to the sky
**— su·per·nal·ly** \-n°l-ē\ *adverb*
**su·per·na·tant** \,su̇-pər-'nā-t°nt\ *noun* [Latin *supernatant-, supernatans,* present participle of *supernatare* to float, from *super-* + *natare* to swim — more at NATANT] (1922)
**:** the usually clear liquid overlying material deposited by settling, precipitation, or centrifugation
**— supernatant** *adjective*
**su·per·nat·u·ral** \,su̇-pər-'na-chə-rəl, -'nach-rəl\ *adjective* [Medieval Latin *supernaturalis,* from Latin *super-* + *natura* nature] (15th century)
**1 :** of or relating to an order of existence beyond the visible observable universe; *especially* **:** of or relating to God or a god, demigod, spirit, or devil
**2 a :** departing from what is usual or normal especially so as to appear to transcend the laws of nature **b :** attributed to an invisible agent (as a ghost or spirit)

**— supernatural** *noun*
**— su·per·nat·u·ral·ly** \-'na-chər-ə-lē, -'nach-rə-, -'na-chər-lē\ *adverb*
**— su·per·nat·u·ral·ness** *noun*
**su·per·nat·u·ral·ism** \,su̇-pər-'na-chə-rə-,li-zəm, -'nach-rə-\ *noun* (1799)
**1 :** the quality or state of being supernatural
**2 :** belief in a supernatural power and order of existence
**— su·per·nat·u·ral·ist** \-list\ *noun or adjective*
**— su·per·nat·u·ral·is·tic** \-,na-chə-rə-'lis-tik, -,nach-rə-\ *adjective*
**su·per·na·ture** \'su̇-pər-,nā-chər\ *noun* [back-formation from *supernatural*] (1844)
**:** the realm of the supernatural
**su·per·nor·mal** \,su̇-pər-'nȯr-məl\ *adjective* (1868)
**1 :** exceeding the normal or average
**2 :** being beyond normal human powers **:** PARANORMAL
**— su·per·nor·mal·i·ty** \-nȯr-'ma-lə-tē\ *noun*
**— su·per·nor·mal·ly** \-'nȯr-mə-lē\ *adverb*
**su·per·no·va** \,su̇-pər-'nō-və\ *noun* [New Latin] (1926)
**1 :** the explosion of a very large star in which the star may reach a maximum intrinsic luminosity one billion times that of the sun
**2 :** one that explodes into prominence or popularity; *also* **:** SUPERSTAR
**¹su·per·nu·mer·ary** \,su̇-pər-'nü-mə-,rer-ē, -'nyü-, -mə-rē; -'n(y)üm-rē\ *adjective* [Late Latin *supernumerarius,* from Latin *super-* + *numerus* number] (1605)
**1 a :** exceeding the usual, stated, or prescribed number ⟨a *supernumerary* tooth⟩ **b :** not enumerated among the regular components of a group and especially of a military organization
**2 :** exceeding what is necessary, required, or desired
**3 :** more numerous
**²supernumerary** *noun, plural* **-ar·ies** (1639)
**1 :** a supernumerary person or thing
**2 :** an actor employed to play a walk-on
**su·per·or·der** \'su̇-pər-,ȯr-dər\ *noun* (circa 1890)
**:** a category of biological classification ranking below a class and above an order
**su·per·or·di·nate** \,su̇-pər-'ȯrd-nət, -'ȯr-d°n-ət, -'ȯr-d°n-,āt\ *adjective* [*super-* + sub*ordinate*] (1620)
**:** superior in rank, class, or status

□ USAGE
**superlative** "Miss Fletcher and I were very thick, but I am the thinnest of the two," wrote Jane Austen in 1796, unmindful of having committed one of the newest improprieties of the grammarians, using the superlative of two. Just how this subject became a staple of handbooks and schoolbooks for two centuries is not entirely clear, for two of the earliest and most widely copied commentators found it a trivial matter. However, one man's preference became another man's rule soon enough, and we can still find warnings against using the superlative of two in present-day handbooks for student writers. Jane Austen's little joke is perfectly understandable even though she used the superlative, and it does not become any more understandable (or any funnier) if the comparative is substituted for the superlative. Thus the rule serves no useful purpose. Nor has it reflected real usage accurately; examples of the superlative used of two abound in literature from Shakespeare to the present. When a rule serves no purpose other than to divide those who observe it from those who don't, it has little authority.

**su·per·or·gan·ism** \-'ȯr-gə-,ni-zəm\ *noun* (circa 1899)
: an organized society (as of a social insect) that functions as an organic whole

**su·per·ovu·la·tion** \-,äv-yə-'lā-shən, -,ōv-\ *noun* (1927)
: production of exceptional numbers of ova at one time
— **su·per·ovu·late** \-'äv-yə-,lāt, -'ōv-\ *verb*

**su·per·ox·ide** \-'äk-,sīd\ *noun* (circa 1847)
: the univalent anion $O_2^-$ or a compound containing it ⟨potassium *superoxide* $KO_2$⟩

**superoxide dis·mut·ase** \-dis-'myü-,tās, -,tāz\ *noun* [*dismutation* (simultaneous oxidation and reduction) + *-ase*] (1969)
: a metal-containing enzyme that reduces potentially harmful free radicals of oxygen formed during normal metabolic cell processes to oxygen and hydrogen peroxide

**su·per·par·a·sit·ism** \,sü-pər-'par-ə-,sī-,ti-zəm, -sə-\ *noun* (circa 1899)
: parasitization of a host by more than one parasitic individual usually of one kind — used especially of parasitic insects

**su·per·phos·phate** \,sü-pər-'fäs-,fāt\ *noun* (1797)
**1** : an acid phosphate
**2** : a soluble mixture of phosphates used as fertilizer and made from insoluble mineral phosphates by treatment with sulfuric acid

**su·per·phys·i·cal** \-'fi-zi-kəl\ *adjective* (circa 1603)
: being above or beyond the physical world or explanation on physical principles

**su·per·plas·tic** \-'plas-tik\ *adjective* (1947)
**1** : capable of plastic deformation under low stress at an elevated temperature — used of metals and alloys
**2** : of or relating to superplastic materials ⟨*superplastic* forming⟩
— **su·per·plas·tic·i·ty** \-pla-'sti-sə-tē\ *noun*

**su·per·pose** \,sü-pər-'pōz\ *transitive verb* **-posed; -pos·ing** [probably from French *superposer*, back-formation from *superposition*, from Late Latin *superposition-, superpositio*, from Latin *superponere* to superpose, from *super-* + *ponere* to place — more at POSITION] (1823)
**1** : to place or lay over or above whether in or not in contact : SUPERIMPOSE
**2** : to lay (as a geometric figure) upon another so as to make all like parts coincide
— **su·per·pos·able** \-'pō-zə-bəl\ *adjective*
— **su·per·po·si·tion** \-pə-'zi-shən\ *noun*

**su·per·posed** \-'pōzd\ *adjective* (1823)
: situated vertically over another layer or part

**su·per·pow·er** \'sü-pər-,paù(-ə)r\ *noun* (1922)
**1** : excessive or superior power
**2 a** : an extremely powerful nation; *specifically* : one of a very few dominant states in an era when the world is divided politically into these states and their satellites **b** : an international governing body able to enforce its will upon the most powerful states
— **su·per·pow·ered** \-,paù(-ə)rd\ *adjective*

**su·per·sat·u·rate** \,sü-pər-'sa-chə-,rāt\ *transitive verb* (1788)
: to add to (a solution) beyond saturation

**su·per·sat·u·rat·ed** *adjective* (1854)
: containing an amount of a substance greater than that required for saturation as a result of having been cooled from a higher temperature to a temperature below that at which saturation occurs ⟨a *supersaturated* solution⟩ ⟨air *supersaturated* with water vapor⟩

**su·per·sat·u·ra·tion** \-,sa-chə-'rā-shən\ *noun* (1836)
: the state of being supersaturated

**su·per·scribe** \'sü-pər-,skrīb, ,sü-pər-'\ *transitive verb* **-scribed; -scrib·ing** [Middle English, from Latin *superscribere*, from *super-* + *scribere* to write — more at SCRIBE] (15th century)
**1** : to write (as a name or address) on the outside or cover of : ADDRESS
**2** : to write or engrave on the top or outside

**su·per·script** \'sü-pər-,skript\ *noun* [Latin *superscriptus*, past participle of *superscribere*] (1901)
: a distinguishing symbol (as a numeral or letter) written immediately above or above and to the right or left of another character
— **superscript** *adjective*

**su·per·scrip·tion** \,sü-pər-'skrip-shən\ *noun* [Middle English, from Middle French, from Late Latin *superscription-, superscriptio*, from Latin *superscribere*] (14th century)
**1** : something written or engraved on the surface of, outside, or above something else : INSCRIPTION; *also* : ADDRESS
**2** : the act of superscribing

**su·per·sede** \,sü-pər-'sēd\ *transitive verb* **-sed·ed; -sed·ing** [Middle English *superceden*, from Middle French *superseder* to refrain from, from Latin *supersedēre* to be superior to, refrain from, from *super-* + *sedēre* to sit — more at SIT] (15th century)
**1 a** : to cause to be set aside **b** : to force out of use as inferior
**2** : to take the place, room, or position of
**3** : to displace in favor of another : SUPPLANT
**synonym** see REPLACE
— **su·per·sed·er** *noun*

**su·per·se·de·as** \-'sē-dē-əs\ *noun, plural* **supersedeas** [Middle English, from Latin, you shall refrain, from *supersedēre*] (14th century)
**1** : a common-law writ commanding a stay of legal proceedings that is issued under various conditions and especially to stay an officer from proceeding under another writ
**2** : an order staying proceedings of an inferior court

**su·per·se·dure** \-'sē-jər\ *noun* (1788)
: the act or process of superseding; *especially* : the replacement of an old or inferior queen bee by a young or superior queen

**su·per·sen·si·ble** \,sü-pər-'sen(t)-sə-bəl\ *adjective* (1798)
: being above or beyond that which is apparent to the senses : SPIRITUAL

**su·per·sen·si·tive** \-'sen(t)-sə-tiv, -'sen(t)-stiv\ *adjective* (1839)
: HYPERSENSITIVE ⟨a *supersensitive* palate⟩
— **su·per·sen·si·tive·ly** *adverb*
— **su·per·sen·si·tiv·i·ty** \-,sen(t)-sə-'ti-və-tē\ *noun*

**su·per·sen·so·ry** \-'sen(t)-sə-rē, -'sen(t)s-rē\ *adjective* (1883)
: SUPERSENSIBLE

**su·per·ser·vice·able** \-'sər-və-sə-bəl\ *adjective* (1605)
: offering unwanted services : OFFICIOUS

**su·per·ses·sion** \,sü-pər-'se-shən\ *noun* [Medieval Latin *supersession-, supersessio*, from Latin *supersedēre*] (1790)
: the act of superseding : the state of being superseded

¹**su·per·son·ic** \-'sä-nik\ *adjective* [Latin *super-* + *sonus* sound — more at SOUND] (1919)
**1** : ULTRASONIC
**2** : of, being, or relating to speeds from one to five times the speed of sound in air — compare SONIC
**3** : moving, capable of moving, or utilizing air currents moving at supersonic speed
**4** : relating to supersonic airplanes or missiles ⟨the *supersonic* age⟩
— **su·per·son·i·cal·ly** \-ni-k(ə-)lē\ *adverb*

²**supersonic** *noun* (circa 1924)
**1** : a supersonic wave or frequency
**2** : a supersonic airplane

**su·per·son·ics** \,sü-pər-'sä-niks\ *noun plural but singular in construction* (1925)
: the science of supersonic phenomena

**supersonic transport** *noun* (1961)
: a supersonic transport airplane

**su·per·star** \'sü-pər-,stär\ *noun* (1924)
**1** : a star (as in sports or the movies) who is considered extremely talented, has great public appeal, and can usually command a high salary
**2** : one that is very prominent or is a prime attraction
— **su·per·star·dom** \-dəm\ *noun*

**su·per·sti·tion** \,sü-pər-'sti-shən\ *noun* [Middle English *supersticion*, from Middle French, from Latin *superstition-, superstitio*, from *superstit-, superstes* standing over (as witness or survivor), from *super-* + *stare* to stand — more at STAND] (13th century)
**1 a** : a belief or practice resulting from ignorance, fear of the unknown, trust in magic or chance, or a false conception of causation **b** : an irrational abject attitude of mind toward the supernatural, nature, or God resulting from superstition
**2** : a notion maintained despite evidence to the contrary

**su·per·sti·tious** \-'sti-shəs\ *adjective* [Middle English *supersticious*, from Middle French *supersticieux*, from Latin *superstitiosus*, from *superstitio*] (14th century)
: of, relating to, or swayed by superstition
— **su·per·sti·tious·ly** *adverb*

**su·per·store** \'sü-pər-,stōr, -,stȯr\ *noun* (1943)
: a very large store offering a wide variety of merchandise for sale

**su·per·string** \-,striŋ\ *noun* (1983)
: a hypothetical string obeying the rules of supersymmetry whose vibrations manifest themselves as particles existing in ten dimensions of which only four are evident

**su·per·struc·ture** \-,strək-chər\ *noun* (1641)
**1 a** : an entity, concept, or complex based on a more fundamental one **b** : social institutions (as the law or politics) that are in Marxist theory erected upon the economic base
**2** : a structure built as a vertical extension of something else: as **a** : all of a building above the basement **b** : the structural part of a ship above the main deck
— **su·per·struc·tur·al** \,sü-pər-'strək-chə-rəl, -'strək-shrəl\ *adjective*

**su·per·sub·stan·tial** \,sü-pər-səb-'stan(t)-shəl\ *adjective* [Late Latin *supersubstantialis*, from Latin *super-* + *substantia* substance] (1534)
: being above material substance : of a transcending substance

**su·per·sym·me·try** \-'si-mə-trē\ *noun* (1974)
: the correspondence between fermions and bosons of identical mass that is postulated to have existed during the opening moments of the big bang and that relates gravity to the other forces of nature
— **su·per·sym·met·ric** \-sə-'me-trik\ *adjective*

**su·per·sys·tem** \'sü-pər-,sis-təm\ *noun* (circa 1928)
: a system that is made up of systems

**su·per·tax** \-,taks\ *noun* (1906)
: SURTAX

**su·per·ton·ic** \,sü-pər-'tä-nik\ *noun* (1806)
: the second tone of a diatonic scale

**su·per·vene** \,sü-pər-'vēn\ *intransitive verb* **-vened; -ven·ing** [Latin *supervenire*, from *super-* + *venire* to come — more at COME] (circa 1648)

---

\ə\ abut \ᵊ\ kitten \ər\ further \a\ ash \ā\ ace
\ä\ mop, mar \aù\ out \ch\ chin \e\ bet \ē\ easy
\g\ go \i\ hit \ī\ ice \j\ job \ŋ\ sing \ō\ go
\ȯ\ law \ȯi\ boy \th\ thin \t͟h\ the \ü\ loot \ù\ foot
\y\ yet \zh\ vision *see also* Guide to Pronunciation

: to follow or result as an additional, adventitious, or unlooked-for development
**synonym** see FOLLOW
— **su·per·ven·tion** \-'ven(t)-shən\ noun
**su·per·ve·nient** \-'vē-nyənt\ adjective [Latin supervenient-, superveniens, present participle of supervenire] (1594)
: coming or occurring as something additional, extraneous, or unexpected
**su·per·vise** \'sü-pər-ˌvīz\ transitive verb **-vised; -vis·ing** [Medieval Latin supervisus, past participle of supervidēre, from Latin super- + vidēre to see — more at WIT] (1588)
: SUPERINTEND, OVERSEE
**su·per·vi·sion** \ˌsü-pər-'vi-zhən\ noun (1640)
: the action, process, or occupation of supervising; especially : a critical watching and directing (as of activities or a course of action)
**su·per·vi·sor** \'sü-pər-ˌvī-zər\ noun (15th century)
: one that supervises; especially : an administrative officer in charge of a business, government, or school unit or operation
— **su·per·vi·so·ry** \ˌsü-pər-'vī-zə-rē, -'vīz-rē\ adjective
**su·per·wom·an** \'sü-pər-ˌwu̇-mən\ noun (1906)
: an exceptional woman; especially : a woman who succeeds in having a career and raising a family
**su·pi·nate** \'sü-pə-ˌnāt\ verb **-nat·ed; -nat·ing** [Latin supinatus, past participle of supinare to lay backward or on the back, from supinus] (1831)
transitive verb
: to cause to undergo supination
intransitive verb
: to undergo supination
**su·pi·na·tion** \ˌsü-pə-'nā-shən\ noun (1666)
**1** : rotation of the forearm and hand so that the palm faces forward or upward and the radius lies parallel to the ulna; also : a corresponding movement of the foot and leg
**2** : the position resulting from supination
**su·pi·na·tor** \'sü-pə-ˌnā-tər\ noun [New Latin, from Latin supinare] (1615)
: a muscle that produces the motion of supination
¹**su·pine** \'sü-ˌpīn\ noun [Middle English supyn, from Late Latin supinum, from Latin, neuter of supinus, adjective] (15th century)
**1** : a Latin verbal noun having an accusative of purpose in -um and an ablative of specification in -u
**2** : an English infinitive with to
²**su·pine** \sù-'pīn, attributive also 'sü-ˌpīn\ adjective [Middle English supyne, from Latin supinus; akin to Latin sub under, up to — more at UP] (15th century)
**1 a** : lying on the back or with the face upward **b** : marked by supination
**2** : exhibiting indolent or apathetic inertia or passivity; especially : mentally or morally slack
**3** archaic : leaning or sloping backward
**synonym** see PRONE, INACTIVE
**usage** see PRONE
— **su·pine·ly** \sù-'pīn-lē\ adverb
— **su·pine·ness** \-'pīn-nəs\ noun
**sup·per** \'sə-pər\ noun [Middle English, from Old French souper, from souper to sup — more at SUP] (13th century)
**1 a** : the evening meal especially when dinner is taken at midday **b** : a social affair featuring a supper; especially : an evening social especially for raising funds ⟨a church supper⟩
**2** : the food served as a supper ⟨eat your supper⟩
**3** : a light meal served late in the evening
**supper club** noun (1925)
: NIGHTCLUB
**sup·plant** \sə-'plant\ transitive verb [Middle English, from Middle French supplanter, from Latin supplantare to overthrow by tripping up,

from sub- + planta sole of the foot — more at PLACE] (14th century)
**1** : to supersede (another) especially by force or treachery
**2 a** (1) obsolete : UPROOT (2) : to eradicate and supply a substitute for ⟨efforts to supplant the vernacular⟩ **b** : to take the place of and serve as a substitute for especially by reason of superior excellence or power
**synonym** see REPLACE
— **sup·plan·ta·tion** \ˌ(ˌ)sə-ˌplan-'tā-shən\ noun
— **sup·plant·er** \sə-'plan-tər\ noun
¹**sup·ple** \'sə-pəl also 'sü-\ adjective **sup·pler** \-p(ə-)lər\; **sup·plest** \-p(ə-)ləst\ [Middle English souple, from Middle French, from Latin supplic-, supplex entreating for mercy, suppliant, perhaps from sub- + -plic- (akin to plicare to fold) — more at PLY] (14th century)
**1 a** : compliant often to the point of obsequiousness **b** : readily adaptable or responsive to new situations
**2 a** : capable of being bent or folded without creases, cracks, or breaks : PLIANT ⟨supple leather⟩ **b** : able to perform bending or twisting movements with ease and grace : LIMBER ⟨supple legs of a dancer⟩ **c** : easy and fluent without stiffness or awkwardness ⟨sang with a lively, supple voice —Douglas Watt⟩
**synonym** see ELASTIC
— **sup·ple·ly** \-pə(l)-lē\ or **sup·ply** \-p(ə-)lē\ adverb
— **sup·ple·ness** \-pəl-nəs\ noun
²**supple** verb **sup·pled; sup·pling** \-p(ə-)liŋ\ (14th century)
transitive verb
**1** : to make pacific or complaisant ⟨supple the tempers of your race —Laurence Sterne⟩
**2** : to alleviate with a salve
**3** : to make flexible or pliant
intransitive verb
: to become soft and pliant
**sup·ple·jack** \'sə-pəl-ˌjak also 'sü-\ noun (circa 1725)
: any of various woody climbers having tough pliant stems; especially : a southern U.S. vine (Berchemia scandens) of the buckthorn family
¹**sup·ple·ment** \'sə-plə-mənt\ noun [Middle English, from Latin supplementum, from supplēre to fill up, complete — more at SUPPLY] (14th century)
**1** : something that completes or makes an addition ⟨dietary supplements⟩
**2** : a part added to or issued as a continuation of a book or periodical to correct errors or make additions
**3** : an angle or arc that when added to a given angle or arc equals 180°
²**sup·ple·ment** \'sə-plə-ˌment\ transitive verb (1829)
: to add or serve as a supplement to ⟨does odd jobs to supplement his income⟩
— **sup·ple·men·ta·tion** \ˌsə-plə-ˌmen-'tā-shən, -mən-\ noun
— **sup·ple·ment·er** \'sə-plə-ˌmen-tər\ noun
**sup·ple·men·tal** \ˌsə-plə-'men-tᵊl\ adjective (1605)
**1** : serving to supplement
**2** : NONSCHEDULED ⟨a supplemental airline⟩
— **supplemental** noun
**sup·ple·men·ta·ry** \ˌsə-plə-'men-tə-rē, -'men-trē\ adjective (1667)
**1** : added or serving as a supplement : ADDITIONAL ⟨supplementary reading⟩
**2** : being or relating to a supplement or a supplementary angle
**supplementary angle** noun (circa 1924)
: one of two angles or arcs whose sum is 180° — usually used in plural
**sup·ple·tion** \sə-'plē-shən\ noun [Medieval Latin suppletion-, suppletio act of supplementing, from Latin supplēre] (1914)

: the occurrence of phonemically unrelated allomorphs of the same morpheme (as went as the past tense of go or better as the comparative form of good)
— **sup·ple·tive** \sə-'plē-tiv, 'sə-plə-\ adjective
**sup·ple·to·ry** \sə-'plē-tə-rē; 'sə-plə-ˌtȯr-ē, -ˌtȯr-\ adjective [Latin supplēre] (1628)
: supplying deficiencies : SUPPLEMENTARY
**sup·pli·ance** \'sə-plē-ən(t)s\ noun (circa 1611)
: ENTREATY, SUPPLICATION
¹**sup·pli·ant** \-ənt\ noun [Middle English, from Middle French, from present participle of supplier to supplicate, from Latin supplicare] (15th century)
: one who supplicates
²**suppliant** adjective [Middle French, present participle] (circa 1586)
**1** : humbly imploring : ENTREATING ⟨a suppliant sinner seeking forgiveness —O. J. Baab⟩
**2** : expressing supplication ⟨upraised to the heavens . . . suppliant arms —William Styron⟩
— **sup·pli·ant·ly** adverb
¹**sup·pli·cant** \'sə-pli-kənt\ adjective (1597)
: SUPPLIANT
²**supplicant** noun (1597)
: SUPPLIANT
**sup·pli·cate** \'sə-plə-ˌkāt\ verb **-cat·ed; -cat·ing** [Middle English, from Latin supplicatus, past participle of supplicare, from supplic-, supplex suppliant — more at SUPPLE] (15th century)
intransitive verb
: to make a humble entreaty; especially : to pray to God
transitive verb
**1** : to ask humbly and earnestly of
**2** : to ask for earnestly and humbly
**synonym** see BEG
— **sup·pli·ca·tion** \ˌsə-plə-'kā-shən\ noun
**sup·pli·ca·to·ry** \'sə-pli-kə-ˌtȯr-ē, -ˌtȯr-\ adjective (15th century)
: expressing supplication : SUPPLIANT ⟨a supplicatory prayer⟩
¹**sup·ply** \sə-'plī\ verb **sup·plied; sup·ply·ing** [Middle English supplien, from Middle French soupleier, from Latin supplēre to fill up, supplement, supply, from sub- up + plēre to fill — more at SUB-, FULL] (14th century)
transitive verb
**1** : to add as a supplement
**2 a** : to provide for : SATISFY ⟨laws by which the material wants of men are supplied —Bulletin of Bates College⟩ **b** : to make available for use : PROVIDE ⟨supplied the necessary funds⟩ **c** : to satisfy the needs or wishes of **d** : to furnish (organs, tissues, or cells) with a vital element (as blood or nerve fibers)
**3** : to substitute for another in; specifically : to serve as a supply in (a church or pulpit)
intransitive verb
: to serve as a supply or substitute
— **sup·pli·er** \-'plī(-ə)r\ noun
²**supply** noun, plural **supplies** (15th century)
**1** obsolete : ASSISTANCE, SUCCOR
**2 a** obsolete : REINFORCEMENTS — often used in plural **b** : a clergyman filling a vacant pulpit temporarily **c** : the quantity or amount (as of a commodity) needed or available ⟨beer was in short supply in that hot weather —Nevil Shute⟩ **d** : PROVISIONS, STORES — usually used in plural
**3** : the act or process of filling a want or need ⟨engaged in the supply of raw materials to industry⟩
**4** : the quantities of goods or services offered for sale at a particular time or at one price
**5** : something that maintains or constitutes a supply
**sup·ply–side** \sə-'plī-ˌsīd\ adjective (1976)
: of, relating to, or being an economic theory that reduction of tax rates encourages more

earnings, savings, and investment and thereby expands economic activity and the total taxable national income
— **sup·ply–sid·er** \-'sī-dər\ *noun*

¹**sup·port** \sə-'pōrt, -'pȯrt\ *transitive verb* [Middle English, from Middle French *supporter*, from Late Latin *supportare*, from Latin, to carry, from *sub-* + *portare* to carry — more at FARE] (14th century)
**1 :** to endure bravely or quietly **:** BEAR
**2 a** (1) **:** to promote the interests or cause of (2) **:** to uphold or defend as valid or right **:** ADVOCATE (3) **:** to argue or vote for **b** (1) **:** ASSIST, HELP (2) **:** to act with (a star actor) (3) **:** to bid in bridge so as to show support for **c :** to provide with substantiation **:** CORROBORATE ⟨*support* an alibi⟩
**3 a :** to pay the costs of **:** MAINTAIN **b :** to provide a basis for the existence or subsistence of ⟨the island could probably *support* three —A. B. C. Whipple⟩
**4 a :** to hold up or serve as a foundation or prop for **b :** to maintain (a price) at a desired level by purchases or loans; *also* **:** to maintain the price of by purchases or loans
**5 :** to keep from fainting, yielding, or losing courage **:** COMFORT
**6 :** to keep (something) going ☆
— **sup·port·abil·i·ty** \sə-ˌpōr-tə-'bi-lə-tē, -ˌpȯr-\ *noun*
— **sup·port·able** \-'pōr-tə-bəl, -'pȯr-\ *adjective*
— **sup·port·ive** \-'pōr-tiv, -'pȯr-\ *adjective*
— **sup·port·ive·ness** \-nəs\ *noun*

²**support** *noun* (14th century)
**1 :** the act or process of supporting **:** the condition of being supported
**2 :** one that supports
**3 :** sufficient strength in a suit bid by one's partner in bridge to justify raising the suit

**sup·port·er** *noun* (15th century)
**:** one that supports or acts as a support: as **a :** ADHERENT, PARTISAN **b :** one of two figures (as of men or animals) placed one on each side of an escutcheon and exterior to it **c :** GARTER 1 **d :** ATHLETIC SUPPORTER

**support group** *noun* (1969)
**:** a group of people with common experiences and concerns who provide emotional and moral support for one another

**support hose** *noun* (1963)
**:** elastic stockings

**support level** *noun* (1953)
**:** a price level on a declining market at which a security resists further decline due to increased attractiveness to traders and investors — called also *support area*

**support system** *noun* (1980)
**:** a network of people who provide an individual with practical or emotional support

**sup·pos·able** \sə-'pō-zə-bəl\ *adjective* (1643)
**:** capable of being supposed **:** CONCEIVABLE
— **sup·pos·ably** \-blē\ *adverb*

**sup·pos·al** \-'pō-zəl\ *noun* (14th century)
**1 :** the act or process of supposing
**2 :** something supposed **:** HYPOTHESIS, SUPPOSITION

**sup·pose** \sə-'pōz, *oftenest after* "*I*" 'spōz\ *verb* **sup·posed; sup·pos·ing** [Middle English, from Middle French *supposer*, from Medieval Latin *supponere* (perfect indicative stem *supposui*), from Latin, to put under, substitute, from *sub-* + *ponere* to put — more at POSITION] (14th century)
*transitive verb*
**1 a :** to lay down tentatively as a hypothesis, assumption, or proposal ⟨*suppose* a fire broke out⟩ ⟨*suppose* you bring the salad⟩ **b** (1) **:** to hold as an opinion **:** BELIEVE ⟨they *supposed* they were early⟩ (2) **:** to think probable or in keeping with the facts ⟨seems reasonable to *suppose* that he would profit⟩
**2 a :** CONCEIVE, IMAGINE **b :** to have a suspicion of

**3 :** PRESUPPOSE
*intransitive verb*
**:** CONJECTURE, OPINE

**sup·posed** \sə-'pōzd; *1b* & *2a usually* -'pōzəd, *3* & *4 often* -'pōst\ *adjective* (1566)
**1 a :** PRETENDED ⟨twelve hours are *supposed* to elapse between Acts I and II —A. S. Sullivan⟩ **b :** ALLEGED ⟨trusted my *supposed* friends⟩
**2 a :** held as an opinion **:** BELIEVED; *also* **:** mistakenly believed **:** IMAGINED ⟨the sight which makes *supposed* terror true —Shakespeare⟩ **b :** considered probable or certain **:** EXPECTED ⟨it was not *supposed* that everybody could master the technical aspects —J. C. Murray⟩ **c :** UNDERSTOOD ⟨you will be *supposed* to refer to my grandaunt —G. B. Shaw⟩
**3 :** made or fashioned by intent or design ⟨what's that button *supposed* to do⟩
**4 a :** required by or as if by authority ⟨soldiers are *supposed* to obey their commanding officers⟩ **b :** given permission **:** PERMITTED ⟨was not *supposed* to have visitors⟩
— **sup·pos·ed·ly** \-'pō-zəd-lē *also* -'pōzd-lē\ *adverb*

**sup·pos·ing** \sə-'pō-ziŋ\ *conjunction* (circa 1843)
**:** if by way of hypothesis **:** on the assumption that

**sup·po·si·tion** \ˌsə-pə-'zi-shən\ *noun* [Middle English, from Late Latin *supposition-, suppositio*, from Latin, act of placing beneath, from *supponere*] (15th century)
**1 :** something that is supposed **:** HYPOTHESIS
**2 :** the act of supposing
— **sup·po·si·tion·al** \-'zish-nəl, -'zi-shən-ᵊl\ *adjective*

**sup·po·si·tious** \-'zi-shəs\ *adjective* [by contraction] (1624)
**:** SUPPOSITITIOUS

**sup·po·si·ti·tious** \sə-ˌpä-zə-'ti-shəs\ *adjective* [Latin *suppositicius*, from *suppositus*, past participle of *supponere* to substitute] (1611)
**1 a :** fraudulently substituted **:** SPURIOUS **b** *of a child* (1) **:** falsely presented as a genuine heir (2) **:** ILLEGITIMATE
**2** [influenced in meaning by *supposition*] **a :** IMAGINARY **b :** of the nature of or based on a supposition **:** HYPOTHETICAL
— **sup·po·si·ti·tious·ly** *adverb*

**sup·pos·i·to·ry** \sə-'pä-zə-ˌtōr-ē, -ˌtȯr-\ *noun*, *plural* **-ries** [Middle English, from Medieval Latin *suppositorium*, from Late Latin, neuter of *suppositorius* placed beneath, from Latin *supponere* to put under] (14th century)
**:** a solid but readily meltable cone or cylinder of usually medicated material for insertion into a bodily passage or cavity (as the rectum)

**sup·press** \sə-'pres\ *transitive verb* [Middle English, from Latin *suppressus*, past participle of *supprimere*, from *sub-* + *premere* to press — more at PRESS] (14th century)
**1 :** to put down by authority or force **:** SUBDUE
**2 :** to keep from public knowledge: as **a :** to keep secret **b :** to stop or prohibit the publication or revelation of
**3 a :** to exclude from consciousness **b :** to keep from giving vent to **:** CHECK
**4** *obsolete* **:** to press down
**5 a :** to restrain from a usual course or action **:** ARREST ⟨*suppress* a cough⟩ **b :** to inhibit the growth or development of **:** STUNT
**6 :** to inhibit the genetic expression of ⟨*suppress* a mutation⟩
— **sup·press·ibil·i·ty** \-ˌpre-sə-'bi-lə-tē\ *noun*
— **sup·press·ible** \-'pre-sə-bəl\ *adjective*
— **sup·pres·sive** \-'pre-siv\ *adjective*
— **sup·pres·sive·ness** \-nəs\ *noun*

**sup·pres·sant** \sə-'pre-sᵊnt\ *noun* (1942)
**:** an agent (as a drug) that tends to suppress or reduce in intensity rather than eliminate something (as appetite)

**sup·pres·sion** \sə-'pre-shən\ *noun* (15th century)

**1 :** an act or instance of suppressing **:** the state of being suppressed
**2 :** the conscious intentional exclusion from consciousness of a thought or feeling

**sup·pres·sor** \-'pre-sər\ *noun* (1560)
**:** one that suppresses; *especially* **:** a mutant gene that suppresses the expression of another nonallelic mutant gene when both are present

**suppressor T cell** *noun* (1972)
**:** a T cell that suppresses the immune response of B cells and other T cells to an antigen — called also *suppressor cell*

**sup·pu·rate** \'sə-pyə-ˌrāt\ *intransitive verb* **-rat·ed; -rat·ing** [Latin *suppuratus*, past participle of *suppurare*, from *sub-* + *pur-*, *pus* pus — more at FOUL] (1656)
**:** to form or discharge pus
— **sup·pu·ra·tion** \ˌsə-pyə-'rā-shən\ *noun*
— **sup·pu·ra·tive** \'sə-pyə-rə-tiv, -ˌrā-; 'sə-prə-tiv\ *adjective*

**su·pra** \'sü-prə, -ˌprä\ *adverb* [Latin] (1526)
**:** earlier in this writing **:** ABOVE

**supra-** *prefix* [Latin, from *supra* above, beyond, earlier; akin to Latin *super* over — more at OVER]
**1 :** SUPER- 2a ⟨*supra*orbital⟩
**2 :** transcending ⟨*supra*molecular⟩

**su·pra·lim·i·nal** \ˌsü-prə-'li-mə-nᵊl, -ˌprä-\ *adjective* [*supra-* + Latin *limin-, limen* threshold] (1892)
**1 :** existing above the threshold of consciousness
**2 :** adequate to evoke a response or induce a sensation ⟨*supraliminal* stimulus⟩

**su·pra·mo·lec·u·lar** \-mə-'le-kyə-lər\ *adjective* (circa 1909)
**:** more complex than a molecule; *also* **:** composed of many molecules

**su·pra·na·tion·al** \-'nash-nəl, -'na-shə-nᵊl\ *adjective* (1908)
**:** transcending national boundaries, authority, or interests ⟨a *supranational* authority, regulating ocean usage —N. H. Jacoby⟩
— **su·pra·na·tion·al·ism** \-'nash-nə-ˌli-zəm, -'na-shə-nᵊl-ˌi-\ *noun*
— **su·pra·na·tion·al·ist** \-list, -ist\ *noun*
— **su·pra·na·tion·al·i·ty** \-ˌna-shə-'na-lə-tē\ *noun*

**su·pra·op·tic** \-'äp-tik\ *adjective* (1921)
**:** situated above the optic chiasma; *also* **:** being a small nucleus of closely packed neurons overlying the optic chiasma and intimately connected with the neurohypophysis

**su·pra·or·bit·al** \-'ȯr-bə-tᵊl\ *adjective* [New Latin *supraorbitalis*, from Latin *supra-* + Medieval Latin *orbita* orbit] (1828)
**:** situated or occurring above the orbit of the eye

☆ **SYNONYMS**
**Support, uphold, advocate, back, champion** mean to favor actively one that meets opposition. SUPPORT is least explicit about the nature of the assistance given ⟨*supports* waterfront development⟩. UPHOLD implies extended support given to something attacked ⟨*upheld* the legitimacy of the military action⟩. ADVOCATE stresses urging or pleading ⟨*advocated* prison reform⟩. BACK suggests supporting by lending assistance to one failing or falling ⟨refusing to *back* the call for sanctions⟩. CHAMPION suggests publicly defending one unjustly attacked or too weak to advocate his or her own cause ⟨*championed* the rights of children⟩.

\ə\ abut \ᵊ\ kitten \ər\ further \a\ ash \ā\ ace
\ä\ mop, mar \au̇\ out \ch\ chin \e\ bet \ē\ easy
\g\ go \i\ hit \ī\ ice \j\ job \ŋ\ sing \ō\ go
\ȯ\ law \ȯi\ boy \th\ thin \t͟h\ the \ü\ loot \u̇\ foot
\y\ yet \zh\ vision *see also* Guide to Pronunciation

**su·pra·ra·tio·nal** \-'rash-nəl, -'ra-shə-nᵊl\ *adjective* (1894)
: transcending the rational : based on or involving factors not to be comprehended by reason alone ⟨the stars inspire *suprarational* dreams —R. J. Dubos⟩

¹**su·pra·re·nal** \-'rē-nᵊl\ *adjective* [New Latin *suprarenalis,* from Latin *supra-* + *renes* kidneys] (1828)
: situated above or anterior to the kidneys

²**suprarenal** *noun* (1841)
: a suprarenal part; *especially* : ADRENAL GLAND

**suprarenal gland** *noun* (1876)
: ADRENAL GLAND

**su·pra·seg·men·tal** \,sü-prə-seg-'men-tᵊl, -,prä-\ *adjective* (1941)
: of or relating to significant features (as stress, pitch, or juncture) that occur simultaneously with vowels and consonants in an utterance

**su·pra·ven·tric·u·lar** \-ven-'tri-kyə-lər, -vən-\ *adjective* (1951)
: relating to or being a rhythmic abnormality of the heart caused by impulses originating above the ventricles ⟨*supraventricular* tachycardia⟩

**su·pra·vi·tal** \-'vī-tᵊl\ *adjective* [International Scientific Vocabulary] (1919)
: constituting or relating to the staining of living tissues or cells surviving after removal from a living body by dyes that penetrate living substance but induce more or less rapid degenerative changes — compare INTRAVITAL 2
— **su·pra·vi·tal·ly** \-tᵊl-ē\ *adverb*

**su·prem·a·cist** \sə-'pre-mə-sist, sü-\ *noun* (1949)
1 : an advocate or adherent of group supremacy
2 : WHITE SUPREMACIST

**su·prem·a·cy** \sə-'pre-mə-sē, sü- *also* -'prē-\ *noun, plural* **-cies** [*supreme* + *-acy* (as in *primacy*)] (1537)
: the quality or state of being supreme; *also* : supreme authority or power

**su·prem·a·tism** \-mə-,ti-zəm\ *noun, often capitalized* [Russian *suprematizm,* from French *suprématie* supremacy + Russian *-izm -ism*] (1933)
: an early 20th-century art movement in Russia producing abstract works featuring flat geometric forms
— **su·prem·a·tist** \-tist\ *adjective or noun, often capitalized*

**su·preme** \sə-'prēm, sü-\ *adjective* [Latin *supremus,* superlative of *superus* upper — more at SUPERIOR] (circa 1533)
1 : highest in rank or authority ⟨the *supreme* commander⟩
2 : highest in degree or quality ⟨*supreme* endurance in war and in labour —R. W. Emerson⟩
3 : ULTIMATE, FINAL ⟨the *supreme* sacrifice⟩
— **su·preme·ly** *adverb*
— **su·preme·ness** *noun*

**Supreme Being** *noun* (1699)
: GOD 1

**supreme court** *noun, often S&C capitalized* (1709)
1 : the highest judicial tribunal in a political unit (as a nation or state)
2 : a court of original jurisdiction in New York state subordinate to a final court of appeals

**Supreme Soviet** *noun* (1936)
: the highest legislative body of a nation (as Russia or the former Soviet Union)

**su·pre·mo** \sə-'prē-(,)mō, sü-\ *noun, plural* **-mos** [Spanish & Italian, from *supremo,* adjective, supreme, from Latin *supremus*] (1937) *British* : one who is highest in rank or authority

**suq** \'sük\ *variant of* SOUK

**sur-** *prefix* [Middle English, from Old French, from Latin *super-*]
1 : over : SUPER- ⟨*sur*print⟩ ⟨*sur*tax⟩
2 : above : up ⟨*sur*base⟩

**su·ra** \'sur-ə\ *noun* [Arabic *sūrah,* literally, row] (1661)
: a chapter of the Koran

**su·rah** \'sur-ə\ *noun* [probably alteration of *surat,* a cotton produced in Surat, India] (1873)
: a soft twilled fabric of silk or rayon

**sur·base** \'sər-,bās\ *noun* (1678)
: a molding just above the base of a wall, pedestal, or podium

¹**sur·cease** \(,)sər-'sēs, 'sər-,\ *verb* **sur·ceased; sur·ceas·ing** [Middle English *sursesen, surcesen,* from Middle French *sursis,* past participle of *surseoir,* from Latin *supersedēre* — more at SUPERSEDE] (15th century)
*intransitive verb*
: to desist from action; *also* : to come to an end : CEASE
*transitive verb*
: to put an end to : DISCONTINUE

²**sur·cease** \'sər-,sēs, (,)sər-'\ *noun* (1586)
: CESSATION; *especially* : a temporary respite or end ⟨to borrow from my books *surcease* of sorrow —E. A. Poe⟩

¹**sur·charge** \'sər-,chärj\ *transitive verb* [Middle English, from Middle French *surchargier,* from *sur-* + *chargier* to charge, from Old French — more at CHARGE] (15th century)
1 a : OVERCHARGE b : to charge an extra fee c : to show an omission in (an account) for which credit ought to have been given
2 *British* : OVERSTOCK
3 : to fill or load to excess ⟨the atmosphere . . . was *surcharged* with war hysteria —H. A. Chippendale⟩
4 a : to mark a surcharge on (a stamp) b : OVERPRINT ⟨*surcharge* a banknote⟩

²**surcharge** *noun* (15th century)
1 a : an additional tax, cost, or impost b : an extra fare ⟨a sleeping car *surcharge*⟩ c : an instance of surcharging an account
2 : an excessive load or burden
3 : the action of surcharging : the state of being surcharged
4 a (1) : an overprint on a stamp; *specifically* : one that alters the denomination (2) : a stamp bearing such an overprint b : an overprint on a currency note

**sur·cin·gle** \'sər-,siŋ-gəl\ *noun* [Middle English *surcengle,* from Middle French *surcengle,* from *sur-* + *cengle* girdle, from Latin *cingulum* — more at CINGULUM] (14th century)
1 : a belt, band, or girth passing around the body of a horse to bind a saddle or pack fast to the horse's back
2 *archaic* : the cincture of a cassock

**sur·coat** \'sər-,kōt\ *noun* [Middle English *surcote,* from Middle French, from *sur-* + *cote* coat] (13th century)
: an outer coat or cloak; *specifically* : a tunic worn over armor

¹**surd** \'sərd\ *adjective* [Latin *surdus* deaf, silent, stupid] (1551)
1 : lacking sense : IRRATIONAL ⟨the *surd* mystery and the strange forces of existence —D. C. Williams⟩
2 : VOICELESS — used of speech sounds

²**surd** *noun* (1557)
1 a : an irrational root (as √3) b : IRRATIONAL NUMBER
2 : a surd speech sound

¹**sure** \'shur, *especially Southern* 'shōr\ *adjective* **sur·er; sur·est** [Middle English *sur,* from Middle French, from Latin *securus* secure] (13th century)
1 *obsolete* : safe from danger or harm
2 : firmly established : STEADFAST ⟨a *sure* hold⟩
3 : RELIABLE, TRUSTWORTHY

4 : marked by or given to feelings of confident certainty ⟨I'm *sure* I'm right⟩
5 : admitting of no doubt : INDISPUTABLE ⟨spoke from *sure* knowledge⟩
6 a : bound to happen : INEVITABLE ⟨*sure* disaster⟩ b : BOUND, DESTINED ⟨is *sure* to win⟩
7 : careful to remember, attend to, or find out something ⟨be *sure* to lock the door⟩ ☆
— **sure·ness** *noun*
— **for sure** : without doubt or question : CERTAINLY
— **to be sure** : it must be acknowledged : ADMITTEDLY

²**sure** *adverb* (14th century)
: SURELY ▫

**sure–enough** \'shur-ə-'nəf\ *adjective* (circa 1846)
: ACTUAL, GENUINE, REAL

**sure enough** *adverb* (circa 1545)
: as one might expect : CERTAINLY

**sure·fire** \'shur-'fīr\ *adjective* (circa 1909)
: certain to get successful or expected results ⟨a *surefire* recipe⟩

**sure·foot·ed** \-'fu-təd\ *adjective* (1633)
: not liable to stumble, fall, or err
— **sure·foot·ed·ly** *adverb*
— **sure·foot·ed·ness** *noun*

**sure·hand·ed** \-'han-dəd\ *adjective* (1930)
: proficient and confident in performance especially using the hands
— **sure·hand·ed·ness** *noun*

**sure·ly** \'shur-lē, *especially Southern* 'shōr-\ *adverb* (14th century)

---

☆ **SYNONYMS**
**Sure, certain, positive, cocksure** mean having no doubt or uncertainty. SURE usually stresses the subjective or intuitive feeling of assurance ⟨felt *sure* that I had forgotten something⟩. CERTAIN may apply to a basing of a conclusion or conviction on definite grounds or indubitable evidence ⟨police are *certain* about the cause of the fire⟩. POSITIVE intensifies sureness or certainty and may imply opinionated conviction or forceful expression of it ⟨I'm *positive* that's the person I saw⟩. COCKSURE implies presumptuous or careless positiveness ⟨you're always so *cocksure* about everything⟩.

---

□ **USAGE**
**sure** Most commentators consider the adverb *sure* to be something less than completely standard; *surely* is usually recommended as a substitute. Our current evidence shows, however, that *sure* and *surely* have become differentiated in use. *Sure* is used in much more informal contexts than *surely*. It is used as a simple intensive ⟨I can never know how much I bored her, but, be certain, she *sure* amused me —Norman Mailer⟩ and, because it connotes strong affirmation, it is used when the speaker or writer expects to be agreed with ⟨it's a moot point whether politicians are less venal than in Twain's day. But they're *sure* as the devil more intrusive —Alan Abelson⟩ ⟨he *sure* gets them to play —D. S. Looney⟩. *Surely,* like *sure,* is used as a simple intensive ⟨I *surely* don't want to leave the impression that I had an unhappy childhood —E. C. Welsh⟩ but it occurs in more formal contexts than *sure.* Unlike *sure* it may be used neutrally—the reader or hearer may or may not agree ⟨it would *surely* be possible, within a few years, to program a computer to construct a grammar —Noam Chomsky⟩ and it is often used when the writer is trying to persuade ⟨*surely* a book on the avant-garde cannot be so conventional —Karl Shapiro⟩.

**1 :** in a sure manner: **a** *archaic* **:** without danger or risk of injury or loss **:** SAFELY **b** (1) **:** with assurance **:** CONFIDENTLY ⟨answered quickly and *surely*⟩ (2) **:** without doubt **:** CERTAINLY ⟨they will *surely* be heard from in the future —R. J. Lifton⟩ **2 :** INDEED, REALLY — often used as an intensive ⟨you *surely* don't believe that⟩
*usage* see ²SURE
**sure thing** *noun* (1836)
**:** one that is certain to succeed **:** a sure bet
**sure·ty** \'shùr(-ə)-tē\ *noun, plural* **-ties** [Middle English *surte*, from Middle French *surté*, from Latin *securitat-, securitas* security, from *securus*] (14th century) **1 :** the state of being sure: as **a :** sure knowledge **:** CERTAINTY **b :** confidence in manner or behavior **:** ASSURANCE **2 a :** a formal engagement (as a pledge) given for the fulfillment of an undertaking **:** GUARANTEE **b :** ground of confidence or security **3 :** one who has become legally liable for the debt, default, or failure in duty of another
— **sure·ty·ship** \-,ship\ *noun*
**surety bond** *noun* (1911)
**:** a bond guaranteeing performance of a contract or obligation
¹**surf** \'sərf\ *noun* [origin unknown] (1685) **1 :** the swell of the sea that breaks upon the shore **2 :** the foam, splash, and sound of breaking waves
²**surf** *intransitive verb* (1926)
**:** to ride the surf (as on a surfboard)
— **surf·er** *noun*
¹**sur·face** \'sər-fəs\ *noun* [French, from *sur-* + *face* face, from Old French — more at FACE] (circa 1604) **1 :** the exterior or upper boundary of an object or body **2 :** a plane or curved two-dimensional locus of points (as the boundary of a three-dimensional region) ⟨plane *surface*⟩ ⟨*surface* of a sphere⟩ **3 a :** the external or superficial aspect of something **b :** an external part or layer
— **on the surface :** to all outward appearances
²**surface** *adjective* (1664) **1 a :** of, located on, or designed for use at the surface of something **b :** situated, transported, or employed on the surface of the earth ⟨*surface* mail⟩ ⟨*surface* vehicles⟩ **2 :** appearing to be such on the surface only **:** SUPERFICIAL ⟨*surface* friendships⟩
³**surface** *verb* **sur·faced; sur·fac·ing** (1778)
*transitive verb* **1 :** to give a surface to: as **a :** to plane or make smooth **b :** to apply the surface layer to ⟨*surface* a highway⟩ **2 :** to bring to the surface
*intransitive verb* **1 :** to work on or at the surface **2 :** to come to the surface **3 :** to come into public view **:** SHOW UP
— **sur·fac·er** *noun*
**surface–active** *adjective* (1920)
**:** altering the properties and especially lowering the tension at the surface of contact between phases ⟨soaps and wetting agents are typical *surface-active* substances⟩
**surface of revolution** (1840)
**:** a surface formed by the revolution of a plane curve about a line in its plane
**sur·face–rip·ened** \'sər-fəs-,rī-pənd, -,rī-p°md\ *adjective* (1945)
*of cheese* **:** ripened by the action of microorganisms (as molds) on the surface
**surface structure** *noun* (1964)
**:** a formal representation of the phonetic form of a sentence; *also* **:** the structure which such a representation describes
**surface tension** *noun* (1876)
**:** the attractive force exerted upon the surface molecules of a liquid by the molecules beneath that tends to draw the surface molecules

into the bulk of the liquid and makes the liquid assume the shape having the least surface area
**surface–to–air** *adjective* (1949)
**:** launched from the ground against a target in the air
**surfacing** *noun* (1882)
**:** material forming or used to form a surface
**sur·fac·tant** \(,)sər-'fak-tənt, 'sər-,\ *noun* [*surface-active* + *-ant*] (1950)
**:** a surface-active substance (as a detergent)
— **surfactant** *adjective*
**surf and turf** *noun* (1973)
**:** seafood and steak served as a single course
**surf·bird** \'sərf-,bərd\ *noun* (1839)
**:** a shorebird (*Aphriza virgata*) of the Pacific coasts of America that has a black-tipped white tail
**surf·board** \-,bōrd, -,bȯrd\ *noun* (circa 1826)
**:** a long narrow buoyant board (as of lightweight wood or fiberglass-covered foam) used in the sport of surfing
— **surfboard** *intransitive verb*
— **surf·board·er** *noun*
**surf·boat** \-,bōt\ *noun* (1847)
**:** a boat for use in heavy surf
**surf casting** *noun* (1928)
**:** a method of fishing in which artificial or natural bait is cast into the open ocean or in a bay where waves break on a beach
— **surf caster** *noun*
**surf clam** *noun* (1884)
**:** any of various typically rather large surf-dwelling edible clams (family Mactridae); *especially* **:** a common clam (*Spisula solidissima*) of the Atlantic coast chiefly from Nova Scotia to South Carolina
¹**sur·feit** \'sər-fət\ *noun* [Middle English *surfait*, from Middle French, from *surfaire* to overdo, from *sur-* + *faire* to do, from Latin *facere* — more at DO] (14th century) **1 :** an overabundant supply **:** EXCESS **2 :** an intemperate or immoderate indulgence in something (as food or drink) **3 :** disgust caused by excess
²**surfeit** (14th century)
*transitive verb*
**:** to feed, supply, or give to surfeit
*intransitive verb*
*archaic* **:** to indulge to satiety in a gratification (as indulgence of the appetite or senses)
**synonym** see SATIATE
— **sur·feit·er** *noun*
**surf fish** *noun* (1882)
**:** SURFPERCH
**sur·fi·cial** \,sər-'fi-shəl\ *adjective* [*surface* + *-icial* (as in *superficial*)] (1892)
**:** of or relating to a surface ⟨*surficial* geologic processes⟩
**surf·ing** \'sər-fiŋ\ *noun* (1926)
**:** the sport of riding the surf especially on a surfboard
**surf·perch** \'sərf-,pərch\ *noun* (1885)
**:** any of a family (Embiotocidae) of small or medium-sized viviparous bony fishes chiefly of shallow water along the Pacific coast of North America that resemble the perches
¹**surge** \'sərj\ *verb* **surged; surg·ing** [Middle French *sourge-*, stem of *sourdre* to rise, surge, from Latin *surgere* to go straight up, rise, from *sub-* up + *regere* to lead straight — more at SUB-, RIGHT] (1511)
*intransitive verb* **1 :** to rise and fall actively **:** TOSS ⟨a ship *surging* in heavy seas⟩ **2 :** to rise and move in waves or billows **:** SWELL **3 :** to slip around a windlass, capstan, or bitts — used especially of a rope **4 :** to rise suddenly to an excessive or abnormal value ⟨the stock market *surged* to a record high⟩ **5 :** to move with a surge or in surges ⟨felt the blood *surging* into his face —Harry Hervey⟩
*transitive verb*

**:** to let go or slacken gradually (as a rope)
²**surge** *noun* (1520)
**1 :** a swelling, rolling, or sweeping forward like that of a wave or series of waves ⟨a *surge* of interest⟩ **2 a :** a large wave or billow **:** SWELL **b** (1) **:** a series of such swells or billows (2) **:** the resulting elevation of water level **3 :** the tapered part of a windlass barrel or a capstan **4 a :** a movement (as a slipping or slackening) of a rope or cable **b :** a sudden jerk or strain caused by such a movement **5 :** a transient sudden rise of current or voltage in an electrical circuit
**sur·geon** \'sər-jən\ *noun* [Middle English *surgien*, from Anglo-French, from Old French *cirurgien*, from *cirurgie* surgery] (14th century)
**:** a medical specialist who practices surgery
**sur·geon·fish** \-,fish\ *noun* (1871)
**:** any of a family (Acanthuridae) of tropical bony fishes that have toxic flesh and typically a movable spine on each side of the body near the base of the tail capable of inflicting a painful wound
**surgeon general** *noun, plural* **surgeons general** (1706)
**:** the chief medical officer of a branch of the armed services or of a public health service
**surgeon's knot** *noun* (1733)
**:** any of several knots used in tying ligatures or surgical stitches; *especially* **:** a reef knot in which the first knot has two turns — see KNOT illustration
**sur·gery** \'sərj-rē, 'sər-jə-\ *noun, plural* **-ger·ies** [Middle English *surgerie*, from Middle French *cirurgie, surgerie*, from Latin *chirurgia*, from Greek *cheirourgia*, from *cheirourgos* surgeon, from *cheirourgos* doing by hand, from *cheir* hand + *ergon* work — more at CHIR-, WORK] (14th century) **1 :** a branch of medicine concerned with diseases and conditions requiring or amenable to operative or manual procedures **2 :** alterations made as if by surgery ⟨literary *surgery*⟩ **3 a** *British* **:** a physician's or dentist's office **b :** a room or area where surgery is performed **4 a :** the work done by a surgeon **b :** OPERATION
**sur·gi·cal** \'sər-ji-kəl\ *adjective* [*surgeon* + *-ical*] (1770) **1 a :** of or relating to surgeons or surgery ⟨*surgical* skills⟩ **b :** used in or in connection with surgery **c :** characteristic of or resembling surgery or a surgeon especially in control or incisiveness ⟨*surgical* precision⟩ **2 :** following or resulting from surgery ⟨*surgical* fevers⟩
— **sur·gi·cal·ly** \-k(ə-)lē\ *adverb*
**su·ri·mi** \sù-'rē-mē\ *noun* [Japanese, chopped meat or fish] (1976)
**:** a fish product made from inexpensive whitefish and often processed to resemble more expensive seafood (as crabmeat)
**sur·jec·tion** \(,)sər-'jek-shən\ *noun* [probably from *sur-* + *-jection* (as in *projection*)] (1964)
**:** a mathematical function that is an onto mapping — compare BIJECTION, INJECTION 3
**sur·jec·tive** \-'jek-tiv\ *adjective* (1964)
**:** ONTO ⟨a set of *surjective* functions⟩
**sur·ly** \'sər-lē\ *adjective* **sur·li·er; -est** [alteration of Middle English *sirly* lordly, imperious, from *sir*] (circa 1572) **1** *obsolete* **:** ARROGANT, IMPERIOUS **2 :** irritably sullen and churlish in mood or manner **:** CRABBED

---

\ə\ abut \ᵊ\ kitten \ər\ further \a\ ash \ā\ ace \ä\ mop, mar \aú\ out \ch\ chin \e\ bet \ē\ easy \g\ go \i\ hit \ī\ ice \j\ job \ŋ\ sing \ō\ go \ȯ\ law \ȯi\ boy \th\ thin \th\ the \ü\ loot \ù\ foot \y\ yet \zh\ vision     *see also* Guide to Pronunciation

**3 :** menacing or threatening in appearance ⟨*surly* weather⟩ ◆
**synonym** see SULLEN
— **sur·li·ly** \-lə-lē\ *adverb*
— **sur·li·ness** \-lē-nəs\ *noun*
— **surly** *adverb*
¹**sur·mise** \sər-'mīz, 'sər-\ *noun* (1569)
: a thought or idea based on scanty evidence
**:** CONJECTURE
²**sur·mise** \sər-'mīz\ *transitive verb* **sur·mised; sur·mis·ing** [Middle English, to accuse, from Middle French *surmis,* past participle of *surmetre,* from Latin *supermittere* to throw on, from *super-* + *mittere* to send] (1700)
: to imagine or infer on slight grounds
**sur·mount** \sər-'maůnt\ *transitive verb* [Middle English, from Middle French *surmonter,* from *sur-* + *monter* to mount] (14th century)
**1** *obsolete* **:** to surpass in quality or attainment **:** EXCEL
**2 :** to prevail over **:** OVERCOME ⟨*surmount* an obstacle⟩
**3 :** to get to the top of **:** CLIMB
**4 :** to stand or lie at the top of
— **sur·mount·able** \-'maůn-tə-bəl\ *adjective*
¹**sur·name** \'sər-ˌnām\ *noun* (14th century)
**1 :** an added name derived from occupation or other circumstance **:** NICKNAME 1
**2 :** the name borne in common by members of a family
²**surname** *transitive verb* (15th century)
: to give a surname to
**sur·pass** \sər-'pas\ *transitive verb* [Middle French *surpasser,* from *sur-* + *passer* to pass] (1555)
**1 :** to become better, greater, or stronger than **:** EXCEED
**2 :** to go beyond **:** OVERSTEP
**3 :** to transcend the reach, capacity, or powers of
**synonym** see EXCEED
— **sur·pass·able** \-'pa-sə-bəl\ *adjective*
**sur·pass·ing** *adjective* (circa 1580)
: greatly exceeding others **:** of a very high degree
— **sur·pass·ing·ly** \-'pa-siŋ-lē\ *adverb*
¹**sur·plice** \'sər-pləs\ *noun* [Middle English *surplis,* from Old French *surpliz,* from Medieval Latin *superpellicium,* from *super-* + *pellicium* coat of skins, from Latin, neuter of *pellicius* made of skins, from *pellis* skin — more at FELL] (13th century)
: a loose white outer ecclesiastical vestment usually of knee length with large open sleeves
²**surplice** *adjective* (1845)
: having a diagonally overlapping neckline or closing ⟨a *surplice* collar⟩ ⟨*surplice* sweaters⟩
**sur·plus** \'sər-ˌpləs\ *noun* [Middle English, from Middle French, from Medieval Latin *superplus,* from Latin *super-* + *plus* more — more at PLUS] (14th century)
**1 a :** the amount that remains when use or need is satisfied **b :** an excess of receipts over disbursements
**2 :** the excess of a corporation's net worth over the par or stated value of its capital stock
— **surplus** *adjective*
**sur·plus·age** \-(ˌ)plə-sij\ *noun* (15th century)
**1 :** SURPLUS 1a
**2 a :** excessive or nonessential matter **b :** matter introduced in legal pleading which is not necessary or relevant to the case
**surplus value** *noun* (1887)
: the difference in Marxist theory between the value of work done or of commodities produced by labor and the usually subsistence wages paid by the employer
**sur·print** \'sər-ˌprint\ *transitive verb or noun* (1917)
**:** OVERPRINT
**sur·pris·al** \sə(r)-'prī-zəl\ *noun* (1591)
: the action of surprising **:** the state of being surprised

¹**sur·prise** *also* **sur·prize** \sə(r)-'prīz\ *noun* [Middle English, from Middle French, from feminine of *surpris,* past participle of *surprendre* to take over, surprise, from *sur-* + *prendre* to take — more at PRIZE] (15th century)
**1 a :** an attack made without warning **b :** a taking unawares
**2 :** something that surprises
**3 :** the state of being surprised **:** ASTONISHMENT
²**surprise** *also* **surprize** *verb* **sur·prised; sur·pris·ing** (15th century)
*transitive verb*
**1 :** to attack unexpectedly; *also* **:** to capture by an unexpected attack
**2 a :** to take unawares **b :** to detect or elicit by a taking unawares
**3 :** to strike with wonder or amazement especially because unexpected
*intransitive verb*
: to cause astonishment or surprise ⟨her success didn't *surprise*⟩ ☆
— **sur·pris·er** *noun*
**sur·pris·ing** *adjective* (1645)
: of a nature that excites surprise
**sur·pris·ing·ly** \sə(r)-'prī-ziŋ-lē\ *adverb* (1661)
**1 :** in a surprising manner **:** to a surprising degree ⟨a *surprisingly* fast runner⟩
**2 :** it is surprising that ⟨*surprisingly,* voter turnout was high⟩
**sur·ra** \'sůr-ə\ *noun* [Marathi *sūra* wheezing sound] (1883)
: a severe Old World febrile and hemorrhagic disease of domestic animals that is caused by a flagellate protozoan (*Trypanosoma evansi*) and is transmitted by biting insects
**sur·re·al** \sə-'rē(-ə)l, -'ri-əl *also* -'rā-əl\ *adjective* [back-formation from *surrealism*] (1937)
**1 :** having the intense irrational reality of a dream
**2 :** SURREALISTIC
— **sur·re·al·ly** *adverb*
**sur·re·al·ism** \sə-'rē-ə-ˌli-zəm, -'ri- *also* -'rā-\ *noun* [French *surréalisme,* from *sur-* + *réalisme* realism] (1925)
: the principles, ideals, or practice of producing fantastic or incongruous imagery or effects in art, literature, film, or theater by means of unnatural juxtapositions and combinations
— **sur·re·al·ist** \-list\ *noun or adjective*
**sur·re·al·is·tic** \-ˌrē-ə-'lis-tik, -ˌri- *also* -ˌrā-\ *adjective* (1925)
**1 :** of or relating to surrealism
**2 :** having a strange dreamlike atmosphere or quality like that of a surrealist painting
— **sur·re·al·is·ti·cal·ly** \-ti-k(ə-)lē\ *adverb*
**sur·re·but·ter** \ˌsər-(r)i-'bə-tər\ *noun* (circa 1601)
: the reply in common law pleading of a plaintiff to a defendant's rebutter
**sur·re·join·der** \-(r)i-'join-dər\ *noun* (circa 1543)
: the reply in common law pleading of a plaintiff to a defendant's rejoinder
¹**sur·ren·der** \sə-'ren-dər\ *verb* **-dered; -der·ing** \-d(ə-)riŋ\ [Middle English, from Middle French *surrendre,* from *sur-* + *rendre* to give back, yield — more at RENDER] (15th century)
*transitive verb*
**1 a :** to yield to the power, control, or possession of another upon compulsion or demand ⟨*surrendered* the fort⟩ **b :** to give up completely or agree to forgo especially in favor of another
**2 a :** to give (oneself) up into the power of another especially as a prisoner **b :** to give (oneself) over to something (as an influence)
*intransitive verb*
: to give oneself up into the power of another **:** YIELD
**synonym** see RELINQUISH
²**surrender** *noun* (15th century)
**1 a :** the action of yielding one's person or giving up the possession of something espe-

cially into the power of another **b :** the relinquishment by a patentee of rights or claims under a patent **c :** the delivery of a principal into lawful custody by bail — called also *surrender by bail* **d :** the voluntary cancellation of the legal liability of an insurance company by the insured and beneficiary for a consideration **e :** the delivery of a fugitive from justice by one government to another
**2 :** an instance of surrendering
**sur·rep·ti·tious** \ˌsər-əp-'ti-shəs, ˌsə-rəp-, sə-ˌrep-\ *adjective* [Middle English, from Latin *surrepticius,* from *surreptus,* past participle of *surripere* to snatch secretly, from *sub-* + *rapere* to seize — more at RAPID] (15th century)
**1 :** done, made, or acquired by stealth **:** CLANDESTINE
**2 :** acting or doing something clandestinely **:** STEALTHY
**synonym** see SECRET
— **sur·rep·ti·tious·ly** *adverb*
**sur·rey** \'sər-ē, 'sə-rē\ *noun, plural* **surreys** [*Surrey,* England] (circa 1891)
: a four-wheel two-seated horse-drawn pleasure carriage
**sur·ro·ga·cy** \'sər-ə-gə-sē\ *noun* (1984)
: the practice of serving as a surrogate mother
¹**sur·ro·gate** \'sər-ə-ˌgāt, 'sə-rə-\ *transitive verb* **-gat·ed; -gat·ing** [Latin *surrogatus,* past participle of *surrogare* to choose in place of another, substitute, from *sub-* + *rogare* to ask — more at RIGHT] (1533)
: to put in the place of another: **a :** to appoint as successor, deputy, or substitute for oneself **b :** SUBSTITUTE
²**sur·ro·gate** \-ˌgāt, -gət\ *noun, often attributive* (1603)
**1 a :** one appointed to act in place of another **:** DEPUTY **b :** a local judicial officer in some states (as New York) who has jurisdiction over the probate of wills, the settlement of estates, and the appointment and supervision of guardians
**2 :** one that serves as a substitute
**3 :** SURROGATE MOTHER
**surrogate mother** *noun* (1978)
: a woman who becomes pregnant usually by artificial insemination or surgical implantation of a fertilized egg for the purpose of carrying the fetus to term for another woman

☆ SYNONYMS
**Surprise, astonish, astound, amaze, flabbergast** mean to impress forcibly through unexpectedness. SURPRISE stresses causing an effect through being unexpected at a particular time or place rather than by being essentially unusual or novel ⟨*surprised* to find them at home⟩. ASTONISH implies surprising so greatly as to seem incredible ⟨a discovery that *astonished* the world⟩. ASTOUND stresses the shock of astonishment ⟨too *astounded* to respond⟩. AMAZE suggests an effect of bewilderment ⟨*amazed* by the immense size of the place⟩. FLABBERGAST may suggest thorough astonishment and bewilderment or dismay ⟨*flabbergasted* by his angry refusal⟩.

◇ WORD HISTORY
**surly** To the highborn an association between good manners and aristocratic birth might seem obvious and inescapable, but the fact that the two do not inevitably go together is evidenced by the word *surly*. In Middle English the word was spelled *sirly,* thus making clearer its connection to *sir,* the traditional title of respect. *Sirly* had much the same meaning as *lordly* has today, that is, "proud, haughty." Although its meaning has evolved into "sullen," *surly* still refers to a disposition that is less than noble.

— **surrogate motherhood** *noun*

**¹sur·round** \sə-'raund\ *transitive verb* [Middle English, tо overflow, from Middle French *suronder,* from Late Latin *superundare,* from Latin *super-* + *unda* wave; influenced in meaning by ⁵*round* — more at WATER] (circa 1616)
**1 a** (1) : to enclose on all sides : ENVELOP ⟨the crowd *surrounded* her⟩ (2) : to enclose so as to cut off communication or retreat : INVEST **b** : to form or be a member of the entourage of ⟨flatterers who *surround* the king⟩ **c** : to constitute part of the environment of ⟨*surrounded* by poverty⟩ **d** : to extend around the margin or edge of : ENCIRCLE ⟨a wall *surrounds* the old city⟩
**2** : to cause to be surrounded by something ⟨*surrounded* himself with friends⟩

**²surround** *noun* (1825)
: something (as a border or ambient environment) that surrounds ⟨from urban centre to rural *surround* —Emrys Jones⟩

**sur·round·ings** \sə-'raun-dinz\ *noun plural* (1861)
: the circumstances, conditions, or objects by which one is surrounded : ENVIRONMENT

**sur·roy·al** \'sər-,rȯi(-ə)l\ *noun* [Middle English *surryal,* from *sur-* + *ryall* royal antler] (15th century)
: one of the terminal tines above the royal antler of a large deer (as a stag) usually grown by four years of age

**sur·sum cor·da** \,sùr-səm-'kȯr-də, -,dä\ *noun* [Late Latin, (lift) up (your) hearts; from the opening words] (1537)
**1** *often S&C capitalized* : a versicle that in traditional eucharistic liturgies exhorts the faithful to enthusiastic worship
**2** : something inspiriting

**sur·tax** \'sər-,taks\ *noun* (1881)
**1** : an extra tax or charge
**2** : a graduated income tax in addition to the normal income tax imposed on the amount by which one's net income exceeds a specified sum

**sur·tout** \(,)sər-'tü, 'sər-\ *noun* [French, from *sur* over (from Latin *super*) + *tout* all, from Latin *totus* whole — more at OVER] (1686)
: a man's long close-fitting overcoat

**sur·veil** \sər-'vā(ə)l\ *transitive verb* **surveilled; sur·veil·ling** [back-formation from *surveillance*] (1949)
: to subject to surveillance

**sur·veil·lance** \sər-'vā-lən(t)s *also* -'vāl-yən(t)s *or* -'vā-ən(t)s\ *noun* [French, from *surveiller* to watch over, from *sur-* + *veiller* to watch, from Latin *vigilare,* from *vigil* watchful — more at VIGIL] (1802)
: close watch kept over someone or something (as by a detective); *also* : SUPERVISION

**sur·veil·lant** \-'vā-lənt *also* -'vāl-yənt *or* -'vā-ənt\ *noun* (1819)
: one that exercises surveillance

**¹sur·vey** \sər-'vā, 'sər-\ *verb* **sur·veyed; sur·vey·ing** [Middle English, from Middle French *surveeir* to look over, from *sur-* + *veeir* to see — more at VIEW] (15th century)
*transitive verb*
**1 a** : to examine as to condition, situation, or value : APPRAISE **b** : to query (someone) in order to collect data for the analysis of some aspect of a group or area
**2** : to determine and delineate the form, extent, and position of (as a tract of land) by taking linear and angular measurements and by applying the principles of geometry and trigonometry
**3** : to view or consider comprehensively
**4** : INSPECT, SCRUTINIZE ⟨he *surveyed* us in a lordly way —Alan Harrington⟩
*intransitive verb*
: to make a survey

**²sur·vey** \'sər-,vā, sər-'\ *noun, plural* **surveys** (1548)
**1** : the act or an instance of surveying: as **a** : a broad treatment of a subject **b** : POLL 5a

**2** : something that is surveyed

**survey course** \'sər-,vā-\ *noun* (1916)
: a course treating briefly the chief topics of a broad field of knowledge

**sur·vey·ing** \sər-'vā-in\ *noun* (1682)
: a branch of applied mathematics that teaches the art of determining the area of any portion of the earth's surface, the lengths and directions of the bounding lines, and the contour of the surface and of accurately delineating the whole on paper

**sur·vey·or** \sər-'vā-ər\ *noun* (15th century)
: one that surveys; *especially* : one whose occupation is surveying land

**sur·viv·able** \sər-'vī-və-bəl\ *adjective* (1955)
: resulting in or permitting survival
— **sur·viv·abil·i·ty** \-,vī-və-'bi-lə-tē\ *noun*

**sur·viv·al** \sər-'vī-vəl\ *noun, often attributive* (1598)
**1 a** : a living or continuing longer than another person or thing **b** : the continuation of life or existence ⟨problems of *survival* in arctic conditions⟩
**2** : one that survives

**sur·viv·al·ist** \-və-list\ *noun* (1970)
: one who views survival as a primary objective; *especially* : one who has prepared to survive in the anarchy of an anticipated breakdown of society
— **survivalist** *adjective*

**survival of the fittest** (1864)
: NATURAL SELECTION

**sur·viv·ance** \sər-'vī-vən(t)s\ *noun* (circa 1623)
: SURVIVAL

**sur·vive** \sər-'vīv\ *verb* **sur·vived; sur·viv·ing** [Middle English, from Middle French *survivre* to outlive, from Latin *supervivere,* from *super-* + *vivere* to live — more at QUICK] (15th century)
*intransitive verb*
**1** : to remain alive or in existence : live on
**2** : to continue to function or prosper
*transitive verb*
**1** : to remain alive after the death of ⟨he is *survived* by his wife⟩
**2** : to continue to exist or live after ⟨*survived* the earthquake⟩
**3** : to continue to function or prosper despite : WITHSTAND
— **sur·vi·vor** \-'vī-vər\ *noun*

**sur·viv·er** \-'vī-vər\ *noun* (1602)
*archaic* : one that survives : SURVIVOR

**sur·vi·vor·ship** \-'vī-vər-,ship\ *noun* (circa 1625)
**1** : the legal right of the survivor of persons having joint interests in property to take the interest of the person who has died
**2** : the state of being a survivor
**3** : the probability of surviving to a particular age; *also* : the number or proportion of survivors (as of an age group)

**Su·san B. An·tho·ny Day** \'sü-z°n-,bē-'an(t)-thə-nē-\ *noun* (circa 1951)
: February 15 observed to commemorate the birth of Susan B. Anthony

**sus·cep·ti·bil·i·ty** \sə-,sep-tə-'bi-lə-tē\ *noun, plural* **-ties** (1644)
**1** : the quality or state of being susceptible; *especially* : lack of ability to resist some extraneous agent (as a pathogen or drug) : SENSITIVITY
**2 a** : a susceptible temperament or constitution **b** *plural* : FEELINGS, SENSIBILITIES
**3 a** : the ratio of the magnetization in a substance to the corresponding magnetizing force **b** : the ratio of the electric polarization to the electric intensity in a polarized dielectric

**sus·cep·ti·ble** \sə-'sep-tə-bəl\ *adjective* [Late Latin *susceptibilis,* from Latin *susceptus,* past participle of *suscipere* to take up, admit, from *sub-, sus-* up + *capere* to take — more at SUB-, HEAVE] (1605)
**1** : capable of submitting to an action, process, or operation ⟨a theory *susceptible* to proof⟩

**2** : open, subject, or unresistant to some stimulus, influence, or agency
**3** : IMPRESSIONABLE, RESPONSIVE
*synonym* see LIABLE
— **sus·cep·ti·ble·ness** *noun*
— **sus·cep·ti·bly** \-blē\ *adverb*

**sus·cep·tive** \-tiv\ *adjective* (15th century)
**1** : RECEPTIVE
**2** : SUSCEPTIBLE
— **sus·cep·tive·ness** *noun*
— **sus·cep·tiv·i·ty** \sə-,sep-'ti-və-tē\ *noun*

**su·shi** \'sü-shē *also* 'sù-\ *noun* [Japanese] (1893)
: cold rice dressed with vinegar, formed into any of various shapes, and garnished especially with bits of raw fish or shellfish

**su·slik** \'sü-slik\ *noun* [Russian] (1774)
**1** : any of several rather large short-tailed ground squirrels (genus *Citellus*) of eastern Europe or northern Asia
**2** : the mottled grayish black fur of a suslik

**¹sus·pect** \'səs-,pekt, sə-'spekt\ *adjective* [Middle English, from Middle French, from Latin *suspectus,* from past participle of *suspicere*] (14th century)
**1** : regarded or deserving to be regarded with suspicion : SUSPECTED ⟨investigates *suspect* employees⟩
**2** : DOUBTFUL, QUESTIONABLE ⟨whose skills are *suspect* —Peter Vecsey⟩

**²sus·pect** \'səs-,pekt\ *noun* (1591)
: one who is suspected; *especially* : one suspected of a crime

**³sus·pect** \sə-'spekt\ *verb* [Middle English, from Latin *suspectare,* frequentative of *suspicere* to look up at, regard with awe, suspect, from *sub-, sus-* up, secretly + *specere* to look at — more at SUB-, SPY] (15th century)
*transitive verb*
**1** : to imagine (one) to be guilty or culpable on slight evidence or without proof ⟨*suspect* him of giving false information⟩
**2** : to have doubts of : DISTRUST
**3** : to imagine to exist or be true, likely, or probable
*intransitive verb*
: to imagine something to be true or likely

**sus·pend** \sə-'spend\ *verb* [Middle English, from Old French *suspendre* to hang up, interrupt, from Latin *suspendere,* from *sub-, sus-* up + *pendere* to cause to hang, weigh] (14th century)
*transitive verb*
**1** : to debar temporarily from a privilege, office, or function ⟨*suspend* a student from school⟩
**2 a** : to cause to stop temporarily ⟨*suspend* bus service⟩ **b** : to set aside or make temporarily inoperative ⟨*suspend* the rules⟩
**3** : to defer to a later time on specified conditions ⟨*suspend* sentence⟩
**4** : to hold in an undetermined or undecided state awaiting further information ⟨*suspend* judgment⟩ ⟨*suspend* disbelief⟩
**5 a** : HANG; *especially* : to hang so as to be free on all sides except at the point of support ⟨*suspend* a ball by a thread⟩ **b** : to keep from falling or sinking by some invisible support (as buoyancy) ⟨dust *suspended* in the air⟩
**6 a** : to keep fixed or lost (as in wonder or contemplation) **b** : to keep waiting in suspense or indecision
**7** : to hold (a musical note) over into the following chord
*intransitive verb*
**1** : to cease operation temporarily
**2** : to stop payment or fail to meet obligations
**3** : HANG
*synonym* see DEFER

\ə\ abut \°\ kitten \ər\ further \a\ ash \ā\ ace \ä\ mop, mar \au̇\ out \ch\ chin \e\ bet \ē\ easy \g\ go \i\ hit \ī\ ice \j\ job \ŋ\ sing \ō\ go \ȯ\ law \ȯi\ boy \th\ thin \t̲h̲\ the \ü\ loot \u̇\ foot \y\ yet \zh\ vision   *see also* Guide to Pronunciation

**suspended animation** *noun* (1795)
: temporary suspension of the vital functions (as in persons nearly drowned)
**sus·pend·er** \sə-'spen-dər\ *noun* (1524)
**1** : one that suspends
**2** : a device by which something may be suspended: as **a** : one of two supporting bands worn across the shoulders to support trousers, skirt, or belt — usually used in plural and often with *pair* **b** *British* : a fastener attached to a garment or garter to hold up a stocking or sock; *also* : a device consisting of garter and fastener
— **sus·pend·ered** \-dərd\ *adjective*
**sus·pense** \sə-'spen(t)s\ *noun* [Middle English, from Middle French, from *suspendre*] (15th century)
**1** : the state of being suspended : SUSPENSION
**2 a** : mental uncertainty : ANXIETY **b** : pleasant excitement as to a decision or outcome ⟨a novel of *suspense*⟩
**3** : the state or character of being undecided or doubtful : INDECISIVENESS
— **sus·pense·ful** \-fəl\ *adjective*
— **sus·pense·ful·ly** \-fə-lē\ *adverb*
— **sus·pense·ful·ness** \-fəl-nəs\ *noun*
— **sus·pense·less** \-ləs\ *adjective*
**suspense account** *noun* (1869)
: an account for the temporary entry of charges or credits or especially of doubtful accounts receivable pending determination of their ultimate disposition
**sus·pens·er** \sə-'spen(t)-sər\ *noun* (circa 1960)
: a suspenseful film
**sus·pen·sion** \sə-'spen(t)-shən\ *noun* [Middle English *suspensyon*, from Middle French *suspension*, from Late Latin *suspension-, suspensio*, from Latin *suspendere*] (15th century)
**1** : the act of suspending : the state or period of being suspended: as **a** : temporary removal from office or privileges **b** : temporary withholding (as of belief or decision) **c** : temporary abrogation of a law or rule **d** (1) : the holding over of one or more musical tones of a chord into the following chord producing a momentary discord and suspending the concord which the ear expects; *specifically* : such a dissonance which resolves downward — compare ANTICIPATION, RETARDATION (2) : the tone thus held over **e** : stoppage of payment of business obligations — used especially of a business or a bank **f** : a rhetorical device whereby the principal idea is deferred to the end of a sentence or longer unit
**2 a** : the act of hanging : the state of being hung **b** (1) : the state of a substance when its particles are mixed with but undissolved in a fluid or solid (2) : a substance in this state (3) : a system consisting of a solid dispersed in a solid, liquid, or gas usually in particles of larger than colloidal size — compare EMULSION
**3** : something suspended
**4 a** : a device by which something (as a magnetic needle) is suspended **b** : the system of devices (as springs) supporting the upper part of a vehicle on the axles **c** : the act, process, or manner in which the pendulum of a timepiece is suspended
**suspension bridge** *noun* (1821)
: a bridge that has its roadway suspended from two or more cables usually passing over towers and securely anchored at the ends — see BRIDGE illustration
**suspension points** *noun plural* (1919)
: usually three spaced periods used to show the omission of a word or word group from a written context
**sus·pen·sive** \sə-'spen(t)-siv\ *adjective* (15th century)
**1** : stopping temporarily : SUSPENDING ⟨a *suspensive* veto⟩
**2** : characterized by suspense, suspended judgment, or indecisiveness
**3** : characterized by suspension
— **sus·pen·sive·ly** *adverb*

**sus·pen·sor** \sə-'spen(t)-sər\ *noun* [New Latin, from Latin *suspendere*] (1832)
: a suspending part or structure: as **a** : a group or chain of cells that is produced from the zygote of a heterosporous plant and serves to push the embryo which arises at its extremity deeper into the embryo sac and into contact with the food supply of the megaspore **b** : either of a pair of gametangia-bearing hyphal outgrowths in fungi (order Mucorales) that extend from two sexually compatible hyphae and support the resulting zygospore
¹**sus·pen·so·ry** \sə-'spen(t)-sə-rē, -'spen(t)s-rē\ *adjective* (15th century)
**1** : held in suspension; *also* : fitted or serving to suspend
**2** : temporarily leaving undetermined : SUSPENSIVE 1
²**suspensory** *noun, plural* **-ries** (15th century)
: something that suspends or holds up; *especially* : a fabric supporter for the scrotum
**suspensory ligament** *noun* (1831)
: a ligament or fibrous membrane suspending an organ or part; *especially* : a ringlike fibrous membrane connecting the ciliary body and the lens of the eye and holding the lens in place — see EYE illustration
¹**sus·pi·cion** \sə-'spi-shən\ *noun* [Middle English, from Latin *suspicion-, suspicio*, from *suspicere* to suspect — more at SUSPECT] (14th century)
**1 a** : the act or an instance of suspecting something wrong without proof or on slight evidence : MISTRUST **b** : a state of mental uneasiness and uncertainty : DOUBT
**2** : a barely detectable amount : TRACE ⟨just a *suspicion* of garlic⟩
*synonym* see UNCERTAINTY
²**suspicion** *transitive verb* **sus·pi·cioned**; **sus·pi·cion·ing** \-'spi-sh(ə-)niŋ\ (circa 1637)
*chiefly dialect* : SUSPECT
**sus·pi·cious** \sə-'spi-shəs\ *adjective* (14th century)
**1** : tending to arouse suspicion : QUESTIONABLE
**2** : disposed to suspect : DISTRUSTFUL ⟨*suspicious* of strangers⟩
**3** : expressing or indicative of suspicion ⟨a *suspicious* glance⟩
— **sus·pi·cious·ly** *adverb*
— **sus·pi·cious·ness** *noun*
**sus·pi·ra·tion** \,səs-pə-'rā-shən\ *noun* (15th century)
: a long deep breath : SIGH
**sus·pire** \sə-'spīr\ *intransitive verb* **sus·pired**; **sus·pir·ing** [Middle English, from Latin *suspirare*, from *sub-* + *spirare* to breathe] (15th century)
: to draw a long deep breath : SIGH
**suss** \'səs\ *transitive verb* [by shortening & alteration from *suspect*] (1966)
**1** *chiefly British* : to inspect or investigate so as to gain more knowledge — usually used with *out*
**2** *chiefly British* : FIGURE OUT — usually used with *out*
**Sus·sex spaniel** \'sə-siks-, -,seks-\ *noun* [*Sussex*, England] (1856)
: any of a breed of short-legged short-necked long-bodied spaniels of English origin with a flat or slightly wavy golden liver-colored coat
**sus·tain** \sə-'stān\ *transitive verb* [Middle English *sustenen*, from Old French *sustenir*, from Latin *sustinēre* to hold up, sustain, from *sub-, sus-* up + *tenēre* to hold — more at SUB-, THIN] (13th century)
**1** : to give support or relief to
**2** : to supply with sustenance : NOURISH
**3** : KEEP UP, PROLONG
**4** : to support the weight of : PROP; *also* : to carry or withstand (a weight or pressure)
**5** : to buoy up ⟨*sustained* by hope⟩
**6 a** : to bear up under **b** : SUFFER, UNDERGO ⟨*sustained* heavy losses⟩
**7 a** : to support as true, legal, or just **b** : to al-

low or admit as valid ⟨the court *sustained* the motion⟩
**8** : to support by adequate proof : CONFIRM ⟨testimony that *sustains* our contention⟩ ▪
— **sus·tained·ly** \-'stā-nəd-lē, -'stānd-lē\ *adverb*
— **sus·tain·er** *noun*
**sus·tain·able** \səs-'stā-nə-bəl\ *adjective* (circa 1727)
**1** : capable of being sustained
**2 a** : of, relating to, or being a method of harvesting or using a resource so that the resource is not depleted or permanently damaged ⟨*sustainable* techniques⟩ ⟨*sustainable* agriculture⟩ **b** : of or relating to a lifestyle involving the use of sustainable methods ⟨*sustainable* society⟩
— **sus·tain·abil·i·ty** \-,stā-nə-'bi-lə-tē\ *noun*
**sustained yield** *noun* (circa 1905)
: production of a biological resource (as timber or fish) under management procedures which insure replacement of the part harvested by regrowth or reproduction before another harvest occurs
— **sustained–yield** *adjective*
**sus·tain·ing** *adjective* (1605)
**1** : serving to sustain
**2** : aiding in the support of an organization through a special fee ⟨a *sustaining* member⟩
**sus·te·nance** \'səs-tə-nən(t)s\ *noun* [Middle English, from Old French, from *sustenir*] (14th century)
**1 a** : means of support, maintenance, or subsistence : LIVING **b** : FOOD, PROVISIONS; *also* : NOURISHMENT
**2 a** : the act of sustaining : the state of being sustained **b** : a supplying or being supplied with the necessaries of life
**3** : something that gives support, endurance, or strength
**sus·ten·tac·u·lar cell** \,səs-tən-'ta-kyə-lər-, -,ten-\ *noun* [New Latin *sustentaculum* supporting part, from Latin, prop, from *sustentare*] (1901)
: a supporting epithelial cell (as a Sertoli cell or a cell of the olfactory epithelium) that lacks a specialized function (as nerve-impulse conduction)
**sus·ten·ta·tion** \-'tā-shən\ *noun* [Middle English, from Middle French, from Latin *sustentation-, sustentatio* act of holding up, from *sustentare* to hold up, frequentative of *sustinēre* to sustain] (14th century)
**1** : the act of sustaining : the state of being sustained: as **a** : MAINTENANCE, UPKEEP **b** : PRESERVATION, CONSERVATION **c** : maintenance of life, growth, or morale **d** : provision with sustenance

☐ **USAGE**

**sustain**   Sense 6b of *sustain* has been around since the 1400s and has been given without stigma in dictionaries at least since Johnson's of 1755, yet a few commentators have found fault with it. The earliest of these was evidently offended by the frequency with which the word was used in English newspapers in the 1860s. More recent commentators content themselves with finding something vaguely pretentious about the use; a few call it formal, which is odd, since it is commonly found in journalistic surroundings ⟨the company *sustained* operating losses totalling more than $30 million —Richard A. Lester *(New Republic)*⟩ ⟨from injuries *sustained* before and during arrest —E. J. Kahn, Jr. *(New Yorker)*⟩ and especially in sportswriting ⟨in a 1983 game against the Eagles, he *sustained* a concussion —Jill Lieber *(Sports Illustrated)*⟩. It has also been considered a bit of a cliché ⟨is man ever hurt in a motor smash? No. He *sustains* an injury —Flann O'Brien⟩ but is nonetheless standard.

**2 :** something that sustains **:** SUPPORT
— **sus·ten·ta·tive** \'səs-tən-ˌtā-tiv, sə-'sten-tə-tiv\ *adjective*

**Su·su** \'sü-(ˌ)sü\ *noun, plural* **Susu** or **Susus** (1786)
**1 :** a member of a West African people of Mali, Guinea, and the area along the northern border of Sierra Leone
**2 :** the Mande language of the Susu people

**su·sur·ra·tion** \ˌsü-sə-'rā-shən\ *noun* (14th century)
**:** a whispering sound **:** MURMUR

**su·sur·rous** \sù-'sər-əs, -'sə-rəs\ *adjective* (1859)
**:** full of whispering sounds

**su·sur·rus** \sù-'sər-əs, -'sə-rəs\ *noun* [Latin, hum, whisper — more at SWARM] (1826)
**:** a whispering or rustling sound
— **su·sur·rant** \-'sər-ənt, -'sə-rənt\ *adjective*

**sut·ler** \'sət-lər\ *noun* [obsolete Dutch *soeteler,* from Low German *suteler* sloppy worker, camp cook] (1599)
**:** a civilian provisioner to an army post often with a shop on the post

**su·tra** \'sü-trə\ *noun* [Sanskrit *sūtra* precept, literally, thread; akin to Latin *suere* to sew — more at SEW] (1801)
**1 :** a precept summarizing Vedic teaching; *also* **:** a collection of these precepts
**2 :** a discourse of the Buddha

**sut·tee** \(ˌ)sə-'tē, 'sə-ˌtē\ *noun* [Sanskrit *satī* wife who performs suttee, literally, devoted woman, from feminine of *sat* true, good; akin to Old English *sōth* true — more at SOOTH] (1786)
**:** the act or custom of a Hindu widow willingly being cremated on the funeral pyre of her husband as an indication of her devotion to him; *also* **:** a woman cremated in this way

¹**su·ture** \'sü-chər\ *noun* [Middle French & Latin; Middle French, from Latin *sutura* seam, suture, from *sutus,* past participle of *suere* to sew — more at SEW] (1541)
**1 a :** a strand or fiber used to sew parts of the living body; *also* **:** a stitch made with a suture
**b :** the act or process of sewing with sutures
**2 a :** a uniting of parts **b :** the seam or seamlike line along which two things or parts are sewed or united
**3 a :** the line of union in an immovable articulation (as between the bones of the skull); *also* **:** such an articulation **b :** a furrow at the junction of adjacent bodily parts; *especially* **:** a line of dehiscence (as on a fruit)
— **su·tur·al** \'sü-chə-rəl, 'süch-rəl\ *adjective*
— **su·tur·al·ly** \-rə-lē\ *adverb*

²**suture** *transitive verb* **su·tured; su·tur·ing** \'sü-chə-riŋ, 'süch-riŋ\ (1777)
**:** to unite, close, or secure with sutures ⟨*suture* a wound⟩

**su·zer·ain** \'sü-zə-rən, -ˌrān; 'süz-rən\ *noun* [French, from (assumed) Middle French *suserain,* from Middle French *sus* up (from Latin *sursum,* from *sub-* up + *versum* -ward, from neuter of *versus,* past participle of *vertere* to turn) + *-erain* (as in *soverain* sovereign) — more at SUB-, WORTH] (1807)
**1 :** a superior feudal lord to whom fealty is due **:** OVERLORD
**2 :** a dominant state controlling the foreign relations of a vassal state but allowing it sovereign authority in its internal affairs

**su·zer·ain·ty** \-tē\ *noun* [French *suzeraineté,* from Middle French *suseraineté,* from (assumed) Middle French *suserain*] (1823)
**:** the dominion of a suzerain **:** OVERLORDSHIP

**sved·berg** \'sved-ˌbərg, 'sfed-, -ˌber-ē\ *noun* [The *Svedberg*] (1939)
**:** a unit of time amounting to $10^{-13}$ second that is used to measure the sedimentation velocity of a colloidal solution (as of a protein) in an ultracentrifuge and to determine molecular weight by substitution in an equation — called also *svedberg unit*

**svelte** \'svelt, 'sfelt\ *adjective* [French, from

Italian *svelto,* from past participle of *svellere* to pluck out, modification of Latin *evellere,* from *e-* + *vellere* to pluck — more at VULNERABLE] (circa 1817)
**1 a :** SLENDER, LITHE **b :** having clean lines **:** SLEEK
**2 :** URBANE, SUAVE
— **svelte·ly** *adverb*
— **svelte·ness** *noun*

**Sven·ga·li** \sven-'gä-lē, sfen-\ *noun* [*Svengali,* maleficent hypnotist in the novel *Trilby* (1894) by George du Maurier] (1919)
**:** one who attempts usually with evil intentions to persuade or force another to do his bidding

¹**swab** \'swäb\ *noun* [probably from obsolete Dutch *swabbe;* akin to Low German *swabber* mop] (1653)
**1 a :** MOP; *especially* **:** a yarn mop **b** (1) **:** a wad of absorbent material usually wound around one end of a small stick and used for applying medication or for removing material from an area (2) **:** a specimen taken with a swab **c :** a sponge or cloth patch attached to a long handle and used to clean the bore of a firearm
**2 a :** a useless or contemptible person **b :** SAILOR, GOB

²**swab** *transitive verb* **swabbed; swab·bing** [back-formation from *swabber*] (1719)
**1 :** to clean with or as if with a swab
**2 :** to apply medication to with a swab ⟨*swabbed* the wound with iodine⟩

**swab·ber** \'swä-bər\ *noun* [akin to Low German *swabber* mop, Middle English *swabben* to sway] (1592)
**1 :** one that swabs
**2 :** SWAB 2a

**swab·bie** *also* **swab·by** \'swä-bē\ *noun, plural* **swabbies** (1944)
*slang* **:** SWAB 2b

**swad·dle** \'swä-dᵊl\ *transitive verb* **swad·dled; swad·dling** \'swäd-liŋ, 'swä-dᵊl-iŋ\ [Middle English *swadelen, swathelen,* probably alteration of *swedelen, swethelen,* from *swethel* swaddling band, from Old English; akin to Old English *swathian* to swathe] (14th century)
**1 a :** to wrap (an infant) with swaddling clothes **b :** ENVELOP, SWATHE ⟨*swaddled* ourselves in sleeping bags⟩
**2 :** RESTRAIN, RESTRICT ⟨marriage . . . *swaddled* him in a domesticity he came to loathe —Nina Auerbach⟩

**swaddling clothes** *noun plural* (1535)
**1 :** narrow strips of cloth wrapped around an infant to restrict movement
**2 :** limitations or restrictions imposed on the immature or inexperienced

¹**swag** \'swag\ *verb* **swagged; swag·ging** [probably of Scandinavian origin; akin to Old Norse *sveggja* to cause to sway; akin to Old High German *swingan* to swing] (1530)
*intransitive verb*
**1 :** SWAY, LURCH
**2 :** SAG
*transitive verb*
**1 :** to adorn with swags
**2 :** to arrange (as drapery) in swags

²**swag** *noun* (1660)
**1 :** SWAY
**2 a :** something (as a decoration) hanging in a curve between two points **:** FESTOON **b :** a suspended cluster (as of evergreen branches)
**3 a :** goods acquired by unlawful means **:** LOOT **b :** SPOILS, PROFITS
**4 :** a depression in the earth
**5** *chiefly Australian* **:** a pack of personal belongings

¹**swage** \'swāj, 'swej\ *noun* [Middle English, ornamental border, from Middle French *souage*] (circa 1812)
**:** a tool used by metalworkers for shaping their work by holding it on the work or the work on it and striking with a hammer or sledge

²**swage** *transitive verb* **swaged; swag·ing** (1831)

**:** to shape by or as if by means of a swage

**swage block** *noun* (1843)
**:** a perforated cast-iron or steel block with grooved sides that is used in heading bolts and swaging bars by hand

¹**swag·ger** \'swa-gər\ *verb* **swag·gered; swag·ger·ing** \-g(ə-)riŋ\ [probably from ¹*swag* + *-er* (as in *chatter*)] (1590)
*intransitive verb*
**1 :** to conduct oneself in an arrogant or superciliously pompous manner; *especially* **:** to walk with an air of overbearing self-confidence
**2 :** BOAST, BRAG
*transitive verb*
**:** to force by argument or threat **:** BULLY
— **swag·ger·er** \-gər-ər\ *noun*
— **swag·ger·ing·ly** \-g(ə-)riŋ-lē\ *adverb*

²**swagger** *noun* (1725)
**1 a :** an act or instance of swaggering **b :** arrogant or conceitedly self-assured behavior **c :** ostentatious display or bravado
**2 :** a self-confident outlook **:** COCKINESS

³**swagger** *adjective* (1879)
**:** marked by elegance or showiness **:** POSH

**swagger stick** *noun* (1887)
**:** a short light stick usually covered with leather and tipped with metal at each end and intended for carrying in the hand (as by military officers)

**swag·gie** \'swa-gē\ *noun* [by shortening & alteration] (1891)
*chiefly Australian* **:** SWAGMAN

**swag·man** \'swag-mən\ *noun* (1851)
*chiefly Australian* **:** DRIFTER; *especially* **:** one who carries a swag when traveling

**Swa·hi·li** \swä-'hē-lē\ *noun, plural* **Swahili** or **Swahilis** [Arabic *sawāḥil,* plural of *sāḥil* coast] (1814)
**1 :** a member of a Bantu-speaking people of Zanzibar and the adjacent coast
**2 :** a Bantu language that is a trade and governmental language over much of East Africa and in the Congo region

**swain** \'swān\ *noun* [Middle English *swein* boy, servant, from Old Norse *sveinn;* akin to Old English *swān* swain, Latin *suus* one's own — more at SUICIDE] (14th century)
**1 :** RUSTIC, PEASANT; *specifically* **:** SHEPHERD
**2 :** a male admirer or suitor
— **swain·ish** \'swä-nish\ *adjective*
— **swain·ish·ness** *noun*

**Swain·son's hawk** \'swān(t)-sənz-\ *noun* [William *Swainson* (died 1855) English naturalist] (1895)
**:** a buteo (*Buteo swainsonii*) chiefly of western North America and South America having pointed wings and usually a dark breast

**swale** \'swā(ə)l\ *noun* [origin unknown] (1584)
**:** a low-lying or depressed and often wet stretch of land; *also* **:** a shallow depression on a golf fairway or green

¹**swal·low** \'swä-(ˌ)lō\ *noun* [Middle English *swalowe,* from Old English *swealwe;* akin to Old High German *swalawa* swallow] (before 12th century)
**1 :** any of numerous small widely distributed oscine birds (family Hirundinidae) that have a short bill, long pointed wings, and often a deeply forked tail and that feed on insects caught on the wing
**2 :** any of several swifts that superficially resemble swallows

**swallow 1**

**²swallow** *verb* [Middle English *swalowen,* from Old English *swelgan;* akin to Old High German *swelgan* to swallow] (before 12th century)
*transitive verb*
**1 :** to take through the mouth and esophagus into the stomach
**2 :** to envelop or take in as if by swallowing **:** ABSORB
**3 :** to accept without question, protest, or resentment ⟨*swallow* an insult⟩ ⟨a hard story to *swallow*⟩
**4 :** TAKE BACK, RETRACT ⟨had to *swallow* my words⟩
**5 :** to keep from expressing or showing **:** REPRESS ⟨*swallowed* my anger⟩
**6 :** to utter (as words) indistinctly
*intransitive verb*
**1 :** to receive something into the body through the mouth and esophagus
**2 :** to perform the action characteristic of swallowing something especially under emotional stress
— **swal·low·able** \'swä-lō-ə-bəl\ *adjective*
— **swal·low·er** \'swä-lə-wər\ *noun*
**³swallow** *noun* (14th century)
**1 :** the passage connecting the mouth to the stomach
**2 :** a capacity for swallowing
**3 a :** an act of swallowing **b :** an amount that can be swallowed at one time
**4 :** an aperture in a block on a ship between the sheave and frame through which the rope reeves
**swal·low·tail** \'swä-lō-ˌtāl, -lə-\ *noun* (1703)
**1 :** a deeply forked and tapering tail (as of a swallow)
**2 :** TAILCOAT
**3 :** any of various large butterflies (family Papilionidae and especially genus *Papilio*) with each hind wing usually having an elongated process

swallowtail 3

— **swal·low–tailed** \-ˌtāld\ *adjective*
**swam** *past of* SWIM
**swa·mi** \'swä-mē\ *noun* [Hindi *svāmī,* from Sanskrit *svāmin* owner, lord, from *sva* one's own — more at SUICIDE] (1895)
**1 :** a Hindu ascetic or religious teacher; *specifically* **:** a senior member of a religious order — used as a title
**2 :** one that resembles or emulates a swami **:** PUNDIT, SEER
**¹swamp** \'swämp, 'swȯmp\ *noun* [perhaps alteration of Middle English *sompe;* from Middle Dutch *somp* morass; akin to Middle High German *sumpf* marsh, Greek *somphos* spongy] (1624)
**1 :** a wetland often partially or intermittently covered with water; *especially* **:** one dominated by woody vegetation
**2 :** a tract of swamp
**3 :** a difficult or troublesome situation or subject
— **swamp** *adjective*
**²swamp** (1784)
*transitive verb*
**1 a :** to fill with or as if with water **:** INUNDATE, SUBMERGE **b :** to overwhelm numerically or by an excess of something **:** FLOOD ⟨*swamped* with work⟩
**2 :** to open by removing underbrush and debris
*intransitive verb*
**:** to become submerged
**swamp buggy** *noun* (1941)
**:** a vehicle designed to travel over swampy terrain; *especially* **:** a four-wheel motor vehicle with oversize tires
**swamp·er** \'swäm-pər, 'swȯm-\ *noun* (1775)

**1 a :** an inhabitant of swamps or lowlands **b** **:** one familiar with swampy terrain
**2 :** a general assistant **:** HANDYMAN, HELPER
**swamp·land** \'swämp-ˌland, 'swȯmp-\ *noun* (1662)
**:** SWAMP 1
**swampy** \'swäm-pē, 'swȯm-\ *adjective* **swamp·i·er; -est** (1649)
**:** consisting of, suggestive of, or resembling swamp **:** MARSHY
— **swamp·i·ness** *noun*
**¹swan** \'swän\ *noun, plural* **swans** [Middle English, from Old English; akin to Middle High German *swan* and perhaps to Latin *sonus* sound — more at SOUND] (before 12th century)
**1** *plural also* **swan :** any of various large heavy-bodied long-necked mostly pure white aquatic birds (family Anatidae and especially genus *Cygnus*) that are related to but larger than the geese
**2 :** one that resembles or is likened to a swan
**3** *capitalized* **:** the constellation Cygnus
**²swan** *intransitive verb* **swanned; swan·ning** (1942)
**:** to wander aimlessly or idly **:** DALLY
**³swan** *intransitive verb* **swanned; swan·ning** [perhaps euphemism for *swear*] (1784)
*dialect* **:** DECLARE, SWEAR
**swan boat** *noun* (1953)
**:** a small boat usually for children or sightseers pedaled by an operator who sits aft in a large model of a swan
**swan dive** *noun* (1898)
**:** a front dive executed with the head back, back arched, and arms spread sideways and then brought together above the head to form a straight line with the body as the diver enters the water
**¹swank** \'swaŋk\ *adjective* [Middle Low German or Middle Dutch *swanc* supple; akin to Old High German *swingan* to swing] (1773)
*Scottish* **:** full of life or energy **:** ACTIVE
**²swank** *intransitive verb* [perhaps akin to Middle High German *swanken* to sway; akin to Middle Dutch *swanc* supple] (circa 1809)
**:** SHOW OFF, SWAGGER; *also* **:** BOAST 1
**³swank** *or* **swanky** \'swaŋ-kē\ *adjective* **swank·er** *or* **swank·i·er; -est** (circa 1842)
**1 :** characterized by showy display **:** OSTENTATIOUS ⟨a *swank* limousine⟩
**2 :** fashionably elegant **:** SMART ⟨a *swank* restaurant⟩
— **swank·i·ly** \-kə-lē\ *adverb*
— **swank·i·ness** \-kē-nəs\ *noun*
**⁴swank** *noun* (circa 1854)
**1 :** arrogance or ostentation of dress or manner **:** PRETENTIOUSNESS, SWAGGER
**2 :** ELEGANCE, FASHIONABLENESS
**swan·nery** \'swä-nə-rē, 'swän-rē\ *noun, plural* **-ner·ies** (1754)
**:** a place where swans are bred or kept
**swans·down** \'swänz-ˌdaůn\ *noun* (1606)
**1 :** the soft downy feathers of the swan often used as trimming on articles of dress
**2 :** a heavy cotton flannel that has a thick nap on the face and is made with sateen weave
**swan·skin** \'swän-ˌskin\ *noun* (1610)
**1 :** the skin of a swan with the down or feathers on it
**2 :** fabric resembling flannel and having a soft nap or surface
**swan song** *noun* (1831)
**1 :** a song of great sweetness said to be sung by a dying swan
**2 :** a farewell appearance or final act or pronouncement
**¹swap** \'swäp\ *verb* **swapped; swap·ping** [Middle English *swappen* to strike; from the practice of striking hands in closing a business deal] (14th century)
*transitive verb*
**1 a :** to give in trade **:** BARTER **b :** EXCHANGE 2

**2 :** to take turns in telling ⟨*swap* stories⟩
*intransitive verb*
**:** to make an exchange
— **swap·per** *noun*
**²swap** *noun* (1625)
**:** an act, instance, or process of exchanging one thing for another
**swap meet** *noun* (1965)
**:** a gathering for the sale or barter of usually secondhand objects
**swa·raj** \swə-'räj\ *noun* [Hindi *svarāj,* from Sanskrit *sva* own + Hindi *rāj* rule — more at SUICIDE, RAJ] (1908)
**:** national or local self-government in India
— **swa·raj·ist** \-'rä-jist\ *noun*
**sward** \'swȯrd\ *noun* [Middle English, from Old English *sweard, swearth* skin, rind; akin to Middle High German *swart* skin, hide] (15th century)
**1 :** a portion of ground covered with grass
**2 :** the grassy surface of land
— **sward·ed** \'swȯr-dəd\ *adjective*
**swarf** \'swȯrf\ *noun* [of Scandinavian origin; akin to Old Norse *svarf* file dust; akin to Old English *sweorfan* to file away — more at SWERVE] (1587)
**:** material (as metallic particles and abrasive fragments) removed by a cutting or grinding tool
**¹swarm** \'swȯrm\ *noun* [Middle English, from Old English *swearm;* akin to Old High German *swaram* swarm and probably to Latin *susurrus* hum] (before 12th century)
**1 a (1) :** a great number of honeybees emigrating together from a hive in company with a queen to start a new colony elsewhere **(2) :** a colony of honeybees settled in a hive **b :** an aggregation of free-floating or free-swimming unicellular organisms — usually used of zoospores
**2 a :** a large number of animate or inanimate things massed together and usually in motion **:** THRONG ⟨*swarms* of sightseers⟩ ⟨a *swarm* of locusts⟩ ⟨a *swarm* of meteors⟩ **b :** a number of similar geological features or phenomena close together in space or time ⟨a *swarm* of dikes⟩ ⟨an earthquake *swarm*⟩
**²swarm** (14th century)
*intransitive verb*
**1 :** to form and depart from a hive in a swarm
**2 a :** to move or assemble in a crowd **:** THRONG **b :** to hover about in the manner of a bee in a swarm
**3 :** to contain a swarm **:** TEEM
*transitive verb*
**1 :** to fill with a swarm
**2 :** to beset or surround in a swarm ⟨players *swarming* the quarterback⟩
— **swarm·er** *noun*
**³swarm** *verb* [origin unknown] (14th century)
*intransitive verb*
**:** to climb with the hands and feet; *specifically* **:** SHIN ⟨*swarm* up a pole⟩
*transitive verb*
**:** to climb up **:** MOUNT
**swarm spore** *noun* (1859)
**:** any of various minute motile sexual or asexual spores; *especially* **:** ZOOSPORE
**swart** \'swȯrt\ *adjective* [Middle English, from Old English *sweart;* akin to Old High German *swarz* black, Latin *sordes* dirt] (before 12th century)
**1 a :** SWARTHY **b** *archaic* **:** producing a swarthy complexion
**2 :** BANEFUL, MALIGNANT
— **swart·ness** *noun*
**swar·thy** \'swȯr-thē, -thē\ *adjective* **swar·thi·er; -est** [alteration of obsolete *swarty,* from *swart*] (1587)
**:** of a dark color, complexion, or cast
— **swar·thi·ness** *noun*
**¹swash** \'swäsh, 'swȯsh\ *verb* [probably imitative] (1556)
*intransitive verb*
**1 :** BLUSTER, SWAGGER
**2 :** to make violent noisy movements

**3 :** to move with a splashing sound
*transitive verb*
**:** to cause to splash
²**swash** *noun* (1593)
**1 :** SWAGGER
**2 :** a narrow channel of water lying within a sandbank or between a sandbank and the shore
**3 :** a dashing of water against or on something; *especially* **:** the rush of water up a beach from a breaking wave
³**swash** *noun* [obsolete English *swash* slanting] (1683)
**:** an extended flourish on a printed character
⁴**swash** *adjective* (1683)
**:** having one or more swashes ⟨*swash* capitals⟩
**swash·buck·le** \'swäsh-ˌbə-kəl, 'swȯsh-\ *intransitive verb* **-led; -ling** \-ˌbə-k(ə-)liŋ\ [back-formation from *swashbuckler*] (1897)
**:** to act the part of a swashbuckler
**swash·buck·ler** \-ˌbə-klər\ *noun* [¹*swash* + *buckler*] (1560)
**1 :** a swaggering or daring soldier or adventurer
**2 :** a novel or drama dealing with a swashbuckler
**swash·buck·ling** \-ˌbə-k(ə-)liŋ\ *adjective* [*swashbuckler*] (circa 1693)
**1 :** acting in the manner of a swashbuckler
**2 :** characteristic of, marked by, or done by swashbucklers
**swash·er** \'swä-shər, 'swȯ-\ *noun* (1589)
**:** SWASHBUCKLER
**swas·ti·ka** \'swäs-ti-kə *also* swä-'stē-\ *noun* [Sanskrit *svastika*, from *svasti* well-being, from *su-* well + *as-* to be; akin to Sanskrit *asti* he is, Old English *is;* from its being regarded as a good luck symbol] (1871)
**1 :** a symbol or ornament in the form of a Greek cross with the ends of the arms extended at right angles all in the same rotary direction
**2 :** a swastika used as a symbol of anti-Semitism or of Nazism
¹**swat** \'swät\ *transitive verb* **swat·ted; swat·ting** [English dialect, to squat, alteration of English *squat*] (circa 1796)
**:** to hit with a sharp slapping blow usually with an instrument (as a bat or swatter)
²**swat** *noun* (circa 1800)
**1 :** a powerful or crushing blow
**2 :** a long hit in baseball; *especially* **:** HOME RUN
**swatch** \'swäch\ *noun* [origin unknown] (1647)
**1 a :** a sample piece (as of fabric) or a collection of samples **b :** a characteristic specimen
**2 :** PATCH
**3 :** a small collection
**4 :** SWATH 2
**swath** \'swäth, 'swȯth\ *or* **swathe** \'swäth, 'swȯth, 'swäth\ *noun* [Middle English, from Old English *swæth* footstep, trace; akin to Middle High German *swade* swath] (14th century)
**1 a :** a row of cut grain or grass left by a scythe or mowing machine **b :** the sweep of a scythe or a machine in mowing or the path cut in one course
**2 :** a long broad strip or belt
**3 :** a stroke of or as if of a scythe
**4 :** a space devastated as if by a scythe
¹**swathe** \'swäth, 'swȯth, 'swäth\ *or* **swath** \'swäth, 'swäth, 'swȯth, 'swȯth\ *noun* [Middle English, from (assumed) Old English *swæth;* akin to Old English *swathian* to swathe] (before 12th century)
**1 :** a band used in swathing
**2 :** an enveloping medium
²**swathe** \'swäth, 'swȯth, 'swäth\ *transitive verb* **swathed; swath·ing** [Middle English, from Old English *swathian*] (12th century)
**1 :** to bind, wrap, or swaddle with or as if with a bandage
**2 :** ENVELOP

**swath·er** \'swä-thər, -thər\ *noun* (circa 1875)
**:** a harvesting machine that cuts and windrows grain and seed crops; *also* **:** a mower attachment that windrows the swath
**swathing clothes** *noun plural* [Middle English] (14th century)
*obsolete* **:** SWADDLING CLOTHES
**swats** \'swäts\ *noun plural* [probably from Old English *swātan*, plural, beer] (1508)
*Scottish* **:** DRINK; *especially* **:** new ale
**swat·ter** \'swä-tər\ *noun* (1912)
**:** one that swats; *especially* **:** FLYSWATTER
**S wave** *noun* [secondary] (1937)
**:** a wave (as from an earthquake) in which the propagated disturbance is a shear in an elastic medium (as the earth) — compare PRESSURE WAVE
¹**sway** \'swā\ *noun* (14th century)
**1 :** the action or an instance of swaying or of being swayed **:** an oscillating, fluctuating, or sweeping motion
**2 :** an inclination or deflection caused by or as if by swaying
**3 a :** a controlling influence **b :** sovereign power **:** DOMINION **c :** the ability to exercise influence or authority **:** DOMINANCE
**synonym** see POWER
²**sway** *verb* [alteration of earlier *swey* to fall, swoon, from Middle English *sweyen*, probably of Scandinavian origin; akin to Old Norse *sveigja* to sway; akin to Lithuanian *svaigti* to become dizzy] (circa 1500)
*intransitive verb*
**1 a :** to swing slowly and rhythmically back and forth from a base or pivot **b :** to move gently from an upright to a leaning position
**2 :** to hold sway **:** act as ruler or governor
**3 :** to fluctuate or veer between one point, position, or opinion and another
*transitive verb*
**1 a :** to cause to sway **:** set to swinging, rocking, or oscillating **b :** to cause to bend downward to one side **c :** to cause to turn aside **:** DEFLECT, DIVERT
**2** *archaic* **a :** WIELD **b :** GOVERN, RULE
**3 a :** to cause to vacillate **b :** to exert a guiding or controlling influence on
**4 :** to hoist in place ⟨*sway* up a mast⟩
**synonym** see SWING, AFFECT
— **sway·er** *noun*
**sway·backed** \'swā-ˌbakt\ *also* **sway·back** \-ˌbak\ *adjective* (1680)
**:** having an abnormally hollow or sagging back ⟨a *swaybacked* mare⟩
— **sway·back** *noun*
**sway bar** *noun* (1949)
**:** a bar that torsionally couples the right and left front-wheel suspensions of an automobile to reduce roll and sway
**Swa·zi** \'swä-zē\ *noun, plural* **Swazi** *or* **Swazis** (1878)
**1 :** a member of a Bantu people of southeastern Africa
**2 :** a Bantu language of the Swazi people
¹**swear** \'swar, 'swer\ *verb* **swore** \'swōr, 'swȯr\; **sworn** \'swōrn, 'swȯrn\; **swear·ing** [Middle English *sweren*, from Old English *swerian;* akin to Old High German *swerien* to swear and perhaps to Old Church Slavonic *svarŭ* quarrel] (before 12th century)
*transitive verb*
**1 :** to utter or take solemnly (an oath)
**2 a :** to assert as true or promise under oath ⟨a *sworn* affidavit⟩ **b :** to assert or promise emphatically or earnestly ⟨*swore* to uphold the Constitution⟩
**3 a :** to put to an oath **:** administer an oath to **b :** to bind by an oath ⟨*swore* them to secrecy⟩
**4** *obsolete* **:** to invoke the name of (a sacred being) in an oath
**5 :** to bring into a specified state by swearing ⟨*swore* his life away⟩
*intransitive verb*
**1 :** to take an oath

**2 :** to use profane or obscene language **:** CURSE
— **swear·er** *noun*
— **swear by :** to place great confidence in
— **swear for :** to give assurance for **:** GUARANTEE
— **swear off :** to vow to abstain from **:** RENOUNCE ⟨*swear off* smoking⟩
²**swear** *noun* (14th century)
**:** OATH, SWEARWORD
**swear in** *transitive verb* (1536)
**:** to induct into office by administration of an oath
**swear out** *transitive verb* (1895)
**:** to procure (a warrant for arrest) by making a sworn accusation
**swear·word** \'swar-ˌwərd, 'swer-\ *noun* (1883)
**:** a profane or obscene oath or word
¹**sweat** \'swet\ *verb* **sweat** *or* **sweat·ed; sweat·ing** [Middle English *sweten*, from Old English *swǣtan*, from *swāt* sweat; akin to Old High German *sweiz* sweat, Latin *sudare* to sweat, Greek *hidrōs* sweat] (before 12th century)
*intransitive verb*
**1 a :** to excrete moisture in visible quantities through the openings of the sweat glands **:** PERSPIRE **b :** to labor or exert oneself so as to cause perspiration
**2 a :** to emit or exude moisture ⟨cheese *sweats* in ripening⟩ **b :** to gather surface moisture in beads as a result of condensation ⟨stones *sweat* at night⟩ **c** (1) **:** FERMENT (2) **:** PUTREFY
**3 :** to undergo anxiety or mental or emotional distress
**4 :** to become exuded through pores or a porous surface **:** OOZE
*transitive verb*
**1 :** to emit or seem to emit from pores **:** EXUDE
**2 :** to manipulate or produce by hard work or drudgery
**3 :** to get rid of or lose (weight) by or as if by sweating or being sweated
**4 :** to make wet with perspiration
**5 a :** to cause to excrete moisture from the skin **b :** to drive hard **:** OVERWORK **c :** to exact work from at low wages and under unfair or unhealthful conditions **d** *slang* **:** to give the third degree to
**6 :** to cause to exude or lose moisture; *especially* **:** to subject (as tobacco leaves) to fermentation
**7 a :** to extract something valuable from by unfair or dishonest means **:** FLEECE **b :** to remove particles of metal from (a coin) by abrasion
**8 a :** to heat (as solder) so as to melt and cause to run especially between surfaces to unite them; *also* **:** to unite by such means ⟨*sweat* a pipe joint⟩ **b :** to heat so as to extract an easily fusible constituent ⟨*sweat* bismuth ore⟩ **c :** to sauté in a covered vessel until natural juices are exuded
**9** *slang* **:** to worry about ⟨doesn't *sweat* the small stuff —Barry McDermott⟩
— **sweat blood :** to work or worry intensely ⟨in preparing speeches each *sweats* blood in his own way —Stewart Cockburn⟩
²**sweat** *noun* (13th century)
**1 :** hard work **:** DRUDGERY
**2 :** the fluid excreted from the sweat glands of the skin **:** PERSPIRATION
**3 :** moisture issuing from or gathering in drops on a surface
**4 a :** the condition of one sweating or sweated **b :** a spell of sweating
**5 :** a state of anxiety or impatience
**6** *plural* **a :** SWEAT SUIT **b :** SWEATPANTS
— **no sweat** *slang* **:** with little or no difficulty **:** EASILY; *also* **:** EASY — often used interjectionally

\ə\ **abut** \ᵊ\ **kitten** \ər\ **further** \a\ **ash** \ā\ **ace** \ä\ **mop, mar** \au̇\ **out** \ch\ **chin** \e\ **bet** \ē\ **easy** \g\ **go** \i\ **hit** \ī\ **ice** \j\ **job** \ŋ\ **sing** \ō\ **go** \ȯ\ **law** \ȯi\ **boy** \th\ **thin** \t̷h\ **the** \ü\ **loot** \u̇\ **foot** \y\ **yet** \zh\ **vision** *see also* Guide to Pronunciation

**sweat·band** \'swet-ˌband\ *noun* (1891)
**1 :** a usually leather band lining the inner edge of a hat or cap to prevent sweat damage
**2 :** a band of material worn around the head or wrist to absorb sweat
**sweat bee** *noun* (1894)
**:** any of various small black or brownish bees (family Halictidae) that are attracted to perspiration
**sweat·box** \-ˌbäks\ *noun* (1864)
**1 :** a place in which one is made to sweat; *especially* **:** a narrow box or cell in which a prisoner is placed for punishment
**2 :** a device for sweating something (as hides in tanning or dried figs)
**sweat·ed** \'swe-təd\ *adjective* (1882)
**:** of, subjected to, or produced under sweatshop conditions ⟨*sweated* labor⟩ ⟨*sweated* goods⟩
**sweat equity** *noun* (1966)
**:** equity in a property resulting from labor invested in improvements that increase its value; *also* **:** the labor so invested
**sweat·er** \'swe-tər\ *noun* (15th century)
**1 :** one that sweats or causes sweating
**2 :** a knitted or crocheted jacket or pullover
**sweat·er·dress** \-ˌdres\ *noun* (1952)
**:** a knitted or crocheted dress
**sweater girl** *noun* (1940)
**:** a woman with a shapely bust
**sweat·er·vest** \'swe-tər-ˌvest\ *noun* (1952)
**:** a sleeveless pullover or buttoned sweater
**sweat gland** *noun* (1845)
**:** a simple tubular gland of the skin that secretes perspiration, is widely distributed in nearly all parts of the human skin, and consists typically of an epithelial tube extending spirally from a minute pore on the surface of the skin into the dermis or subcutaneous tissues where it ends in a convoluted tuft
**sweat lodge** *noun* (1850)
**:** a hut, lodge, or cavern heated by steam from water poured on hot stones and used especially by American Indians for ritual or therapeutic sweating
**sweat out** *transitive verb* (1589)
**1 :** to work one's way painfully through or to
**2 :** to endure or wait through the course of
**sweat·pants** \'swet-ˌpan(t)s\ *noun plural* (1925)
**:** pants having a drawstring or elastic waist and elastic cuffs at the ankle that are worn especially by athletes in warming up
**sweat·shirt** \-ˌshərt\ *noun* (1925)
**:** a loose collarless pullover usually of heavy cotton jersey
**sweat·shop** \-ˌshäp\ *noun* (1892)
**:** a shop or factory in which workers are employed for long hours at low wages and under unhealthy conditions
**sweat suit** *noun* (1930)
**:** a suit worn usually for exercise that consists of a sweatshirt and sweatpants
**sweat test** *noun* (1978)
**:** a test for cystic fibrosis that involves measuring the subject's sweat for abnormally high sodium chloride content
**sweaty** \'swe-tē\ *adjective* **sweat·i·er; -est** (14th century)
**1 :** causing sweat ⟨a *sweaty* day⟩ ⟨*sweaty* work⟩
**2 :** wet or stained with or smelling of sweat
— **sweat·i·ly** \'swe-tᵊl-ē\ *adverb*
— **sweat·i·ness** \'swe-tē-nəs\ *noun*
**swede** \'swēd\ *noun* [Low German or obsolete Dutch] (1589)
**1** *capitalized* **a :** a native or inhabitant of Sweden **b :** a person of Swedish descent
**2** *chiefly British* **:** RUTABAGA
**Swe·den·bor·gian** \ˌswē-dᵊn-'bȯr-j(ē-)ən, -'bȯr-gē-ən\ *adjective* (1807)
**:** of or relating to the teachings of Emanuel Swedenborg or the Church of the New Jerusalem based on his teachings
— **Swedenborgian** *noun*

— **Swe·den·bor·gian·ism** \-j(ē-)ə-ˌni-zəm, -gē-ə-\ *noun*
**Swed·ish** \'swē-dish\ *noun* (1605)
**1 :** the North Germanic language spoken in Sweden and a part of Finland
**2** *plural in construction* **:** the people of Sweden
— **Swedish** *adjective*
**Swedish massage** *noun* (1911)
**:** massage involving a system of active and passive exercise of muscles and joints
**¹sweep** \'swēp\ *verb* **swept** \'swept\; **sweep·ing** [Middle English *swepen*; akin to Old English *swāpan* to sweep, Old High German *sweifen* to wander] (14th century)
*transitive verb*
**1 a :** to remove from a surface with or as if with a broom or brush ⟨*swept* the crumbs from the table⟩ **b :** to destroy completely **:** WIPE OUT — usually used with *away* ⟨everything she cherished, might be *swept* away overnight —Louis Bromfield⟩ **c :** to remove or take with a single continuous forceful action ⟨*swept* the books off the desk⟩ **d :** to remove from sight or consideration ⟨the problem can't be *swept* under the rug⟩ **e :** to drive or carry along with irresistible force ⟨a wave of protest that *swept* the opposition into office⟩
**2 a :** to clean with or as if with a broom or brush **b :** to clear by repeated and forcible action **c :** to move across or along swiftly, violently, or overwhelmingly ⟨fire *swept* the business district —*American Guide Series: Maryland*⟩ **d :** to win an overwhelming victory in or on ⟨*sweep* the elections⟩ **e :** to win all the games or contests of ⟨*sweep* a double-header⟩ ⟨*sweep* a series⟩
**3 :** to touch in passing with a swift continuous movement
**4 :** to trace or describe the locus or extent of (as a line, circle, or angle)
**5 :** to cover the entire range of ⟨his eyes *swept* the horizon⟩
*intransitive verb*
**1 a :** to clean a surface with or as if with a broom **b :** to move swiftly, forcefully, or devastatingly ⟨the wind *swept* through the treetops⟩
**2 :** to go with stately or sweeping movements ⟨proudly *swept* into the room⟩
**3 :** to move or extend in a wide curve or range
— **sweep one off one's feet :** to gain immediate and unquestioning support, approval, or acceptance by a person
— **sweep the board** *or* **sweep the table 1 :** to win all the bets on the table **2 :** to win everything **:** beat all competitors
**²sweep** *noun* (1548)
**1 :** something that sweeps or works with a sweeping motion: as **a :** a long pole or timber pivoted on a tall post and used to raise and lower a bucket in a well **b :** a triangular cultivator blade that cuts off weeds under the soil surface **c :** a windmill sail

sweep 1a

**2 a :** an instance of sweeping; *especially* **:** a clearing out or away with or as if with a broom **b :** the removal from the table in one play in casino of all the cards by pairing or combining **c :** an overwhelming victory **d :** a winning of all the contests or prizes in a competition **e :** a wide-ranging search of an area (as by police)
**3 a :** a movement of great range and force **b :** a curving or circular course or line **c :** the compass of a sweeping movement **:** SCOPE **d**

**:** a broad unbroken area or extent **e :** an end run in football in which one or more linemen pull back and run interference for the ballcarrier
**4 :** CHIMNEY SWEEP
**5 :** SWEEPSTAKES
**6 :** obliquity with respect to a reference line ⟨*sweep* of an airplane wing⟩; *especially* **:** SWEEPBACK
**7** *plural* **:** a television ratings period during which surveys are taken to determine advertising rates
**synonym** see RANGE
**sweep·back** \'swēp-ˌbak\ *noun* (1914)
**:** the backward slant of an airplane wing in which the outer portion of the wing is downstream from the inner portion
**sweep·er** \'swē-pər\ *noun* (15th century)
**1 :** one that sweeps
**2 :** a lone back in soccer who plays between the line of the defenders and the goal
**sweep hand** *noun* (1943)
**:** SWEEP-SECOND HAND
**¹sweep·ing** *noun* (14th century)
**1 :** the act or action of one that sweeps ⟨gave the room a good *sweeping*⟩
**2** *plural* **:** things collected by sweeping **:** REFUSE
**²sweeping** *adjective* (1610)
**1 a :** moving or extending in a wide curve or over a wide area **b :** having a curving line or form
**2 a :** EXTENSIVE ⟨*sweeping* reforms⟩ **b :** marked by wholesale and indiscriminate inclusion ⟨*sweeping* generalities⟩
— **sweep·ing·ly** \'swē-piŋ-lē\ *adverb*
— **sweep·ing·ness** *noun*
**sweep–sec·ond hand** \'swēp-ˌse-kənd-, -kənt-\ *noun* (circa 1940)
**:** a hand marking seconds on a timepiece mounted concentrically with the other hands and read from the same dial as the minute hand
**sweep·stakes** \-ˌstāks\ *noun plural but singular or plural in construction, also* **sweep–stake** \-ˌstāk\ [Middle English *swepestake* one who wins all the stakes in a game, from *swepen* to sweep + *stake*] (1785)
**1 a :** a race or contest in which the entire prize may be awarded to the winner; *specifically* **:** STAKE RACE **b :** CONTEST, COMPETITION
**2 :** any of various lotteries
**sweepy** \'swē-pē\ *adjective* **sweep·i·er; -est** (1697)
**:** sweeping in motion, line, or force
**¹sweet** \'swēt\ *adjective* [Middle English *swete*, from Old English *swēte*; akin to Old High German *suozi* sweet, Latin *suadēre* to urge, *suavis* sweet, Greek *hēdys*] (before 12th century)
**1 a** (1) **:** pleasing to the taste (2) **:** being or inducing the one of the four basic taste sensations that is typically induced by disaccharides and is mediated especially by receptors in taste buds at the front of the tongue — compare BITTER, SALT, SOUR **b** (1) *of a beverage* **:** containing a sweetening ingredient **:** not dry (2) *of wine* **:** retaining a portion of natural sugar
**2 a :** pleasing to the mind or feelings **:** AGREEABLE, GRATIFYING — often used as a generalized term of approval ⟨how *sweet* it is⟩ **b :** marked by gentle good humor or kindliness **c :** FRAGRANT **d** (1) **:** delicately pleasing to the ear or eye (2) **:** played in a straightforward melodic style ⟨*sweet* jazz⟩ **e :** SACCHARINE, CLOYING
**3 :** much loved **:** DEAR
**4 a :** not sour, rancid, decaying, or stale **:** WHOLESOME ⟨*sweet* milk⟩ **b :** not salt or salted **:** FRESH ⟨*sweet* butter⟩ **c** *of land* **:** free from excessive acidity **d :** free from noxious gases and odors **e :** free from excess of acid, sulfur, or corrosive salts ⟨*sweet* crude oil⟩

**5 :** SKILLFUL, PROFICIENT ⟨a *sweet* golf swing⟩
**6** — used as an intensive ⟨take your own *sweet* time⟩
— **sweet·ly** *adverb*
— **sweet·ness** *noun*
— **sweet on :** having a crush on
²**sweet** *adverb* (13th century)
**:** in a sweet manner
³**sweet** *noun* (14th century)
**1 :** something that is sweet to the taste: as **a :** a food (as a candy or preserve) having a high sugar content ⟨fill up on *sweets*⟩ **b** *British* **:** DESSERT **c** *British* **:** HARD CANDY
**2 :** a sweet taste sensation
**3 :** a pleasant or gratifying experience, possession, or state
**4 :** DARLING, SWEETHEART
**5 a** *archaic* **:** FRAGRANCE **b** *plural, archaic* **:** things having a sweet smell
**sweet alyssum** *noun* (1822)
**:** a widely cultivated perennial European herb (*Lobularia maritima*) of the mustard family having narrow leaves and clusters of small fragrant usually white or pink flowers
**sweet–and–sour** \,swē-t⁸n-'sau̇(ə)r\ *adjective* (1928)
**:** seasoned with a sauce containing sugar and vinegar or lemon juice ⟨*sweet-and-sour* shrimp⟩
**sweet basil** *noun* (circa 1647)
**:** a basil (*Ocimum basilicum*) with whitish or purple flowers that includes several cultivars (as bush basil)
**sweet bay** *noun* (1716)
**1 :** LAUREL 1
**2 :** a magnolia (*Magnolia virginiana*) of the eastern U.S. that has fragrant white flowers and leaves with glaucous undersides
**sweet birch** *noun* (1785)
**:** a common birch (*Betula lenta*) of the eastern U.S. that has spicy brown bark when young, hard dark-colored wood, and a volatile oil in its bark resembling wintergreen — called also *black birch*
**sweet·bread** \'swēt-,bred\ *noun* (1565)
**:** the thymus or pancreas of a young animal (as a calf) used for food
**sweet·bri·er** *also* **sweet·bri·ar** \-,brī(-ə)r\ *noun* (1538)
**:** an Old World rose (especially *Rosa eleganteria*) with stout recurved prickles and white to deep rosy pink single flowers — called also *eglantine*
**sweet cherry** *noun* (circa 1901)
**:** a white-flowered Eurasian cherry (*Prunus avium*) widely grown for its large sweet-flavored fruits; *also* **:** its fruit
**sweet chocolate** *noun* (1897)
**:** chocolate that contains added sugar
**sweet cic·e·ly** \-'si-s(ə-)lē\ *noun* [*cicely* from Latin *seselis*, from Greek] (1668)
**:** any of a genus (*Osmorhiza*) of American and eastern Asian herbs of the carrot family that typically have thick fleshy roots and grow in moist woodlands
**sweet clover** *noun* (1868)
**:** any of a genus (*Melilotus*) of Old World legumes that have trifoliolate leaves and are widely grown for soil improvement or hay
**sweet corn** *noun* (1646)
**:** an Indian corn (especially *Zea mays rugosa*) with kernels containing a high percentage of sugar and adapted for table use when the kernels are unripe
**sweet·en** \'swē-t⁸n\ *verb* **sweet·ened; sweet·en·ing** \'swēt-niŋ, 'swē-t⁸n-iŋ\ (circa 1552)
*transitive verb*
**1 :** to make sweet
**2 :** to soften the mood or attitude of
**3 :** to make less painful or trying
**4 :** to free from a harmful or undesirable quality or substance; *especially* **:** to remove sulfur compounds from ⟨*sweeten* natural gas⟩

**5 :** to make more valuable or attractive: as **a :** to increase (a pot not won on the previous deal) by anteing prior to another deal **b :** to place additional securities as collateral for (a loan)
*intransitive verb*
**:** to become sweet
— **sweet·en·er** \'swēt-nər, 'swē-t⁸n-ər\ *noun*
**sweetening** *noun* (1819)
**:** something that sweetens
**sweet fern** *noun* (1654)
**:** a small North American shrub (*Comptonia peregrina*) of the wax-myrtle family with aromatic leaves
**sweet flag** *noun* (1784)
**:** a perennial marsh herb (*Acorus calamus*) of the arum family with long narrow leaves and an aromatic rootstock — called also *calamus*
**sweet gum** *noun* (1700)
**1 :** a North American tree (*Liquidambar styraciflua*) of the witch-hazel family with palmately lobed leaves, corky branches, and hard wood
**2 :** heartwood of the sweet gum or reddish brown lumber sawed from it

sweet gum 1

¹**sweet·heart** \'swēt-,härt\ *noun* (14th century)
**1 :** DARLING
**2 :** one who is loved
**3 :** a generally likable person
**4 :** a remarkable one of its kind
²**sweetheart** *adjective* (1942)
**:** of or relating to an agreement between an employer and a labor union official arranged privately for their benefit usually at the expense of the workers ⟨a *sweetheart* contract⟩; *broadly* **:** arranged in private for the benefit of a few at the expense of many ⟨a *sweetheart* deal⟩
**sweetheart neckline** *noun* (1941)
**:** a neckline for women's clothing that is high in back and low in front where it is scalloped to resemble the top of a heart
**sweet·ie** \'swē-tē\ *noun* (1705)
**1** *plural, British* **:** SWEET 1a
**2 :** SWEETHEART
**sweetie pie** *noun* (1928)
**:** SWEETHEART
**sweet·ing** \'swē-tiŋ\ *noun* (13th century)
**1** *archaic* **:** SWEETHEART
**2 :** a sweet apple
**sweet·ish** \-tish\ *adjective* (1580)
**1 :** somewhat sweet
**2 :** unpleasantly sweet
— **sweet·ish·ly** *adverb*
**sweet marjoram** *noun* (1565)
**:** a perennial marjoram (*Origanum majorana* synonym *Majorana hortensis*) with dense spikelike flower clusters
**sweet·meat** \'swēt-,mēt\ *noun* (14th century)
**:** a food rich in sugar: as **a :** a candied or crystallized fruit **b :** CANDY, CONFECTION
**sweetness and light** *noun* (1704)
**1 :** a harmonious combination of beauty and enlightenment viewed as a hallmark of culture
**2 a :** amiable reasonableness of disposition ⟨they were all *sweetness and light*⟩ **b :** an untroubled or harmonious state or condition ⟨but all was not *sweetness and light*⟩
**sweet orange** *noun* (1538)
**1 a :** an orange (*Citrus sinensis*) that is probably native to southeastern Asia, has a fruit with a pithy central axis, and is the source of the widely cultivated oranges of commerce **b :** a cultivated orange derived from the sweet orange and usually having fruit with a relatively thin skin and sweet juicy edible pulp
**2 :** the fruit of a sweet orange

**sweet pea** *noun* (1732)
**1 :** a widely cultivated Italian legume (*Lathyrus odoratus*) having slender usually climbing stems, ovate leaves, and large fragrant flowers
**2 :** the flower of a sweet pea
**sweet pepper** *noun* (1814)
**:** a large mild thick-walled capsicum fruit; *also* **:** a pepper plant bearing this fruit
**sweet potato** *noun* (1750)
**1 :** a tropical vine (*Ipomoea batatas*) related to the morning glory with variously shaped leaves and purplish flowers; *also* **:** its large thick sweet and nutritious tuberous root that is cooked and eaten as a vegetable — compare YAM 2
**2 :** OCARINA
**sweet·shop** \'swēt-,shäp\ *noun* (1879)
*chiefly British* **:** a candy store
**sweet·sop** \-,säp\ *noun* (1696)
**:** SUGAR APPLE
**sweet sorghum** *noun* (1867)
**:** SORGO
**sweet spot** *noun* (circa 1949)
**:** the area around the center of mass of a bat, racket, or head of a club that is the most effective part with which to hit a ball
**sweet–talk** \'swēt-,tȯk\ (1928)
*transitive verb*
**:** CAJOLE, COAX
*intransitive verb*
**:** to use flattery
**sweet talk** *noun* (1926)
**:** FLATTERY
**sweet tooth** *noun* (14th century)
**:** a craving or fondness for sweet food
**sweet wil·liam** \,swēt-'wil-yəm\ *noun, often W capitalized* [from the name *William*] (1573)
**:** a widely cultivated Old World pink (*Dianthus barbatus*) with small white to deep red or purple flowers often showily spotted, banded, or mottled and borne in flat bracteate heads on erect stalks

sweet william

¹**swell** \'swel\ *verb* **swelled; swelled** *or* **swol·len** \'swō-lən\; **swell·ing** [Middle English, from Old English *swellan*; akin to Old High German *swellan* to swell] (before 12th century)
*intransitive verb*
**1 a :** to expand (as in size, volume, or numbers) gradually beyond a normal or original limit ⟨the population *swelled*⟩ **b :** to become distended or puffed up ⟨her ankle is badly *swollen*⟩ **c :** to form a bulge or rounded elevation
**2 a :** to become filled with pride and arrogance **b :** to behave or speak in a pompous, blustering, or self-important manner **c :** to play the swell
**3 :** to become distended with emotion
*transitive verb*
**1 :** to affect with a powerful or expansive emotion
**2 :** to increase the size, number, or intensity of
**synonym** see EXPAND
²**swell** *noun* (1606)
**1 :** a long often massive and crestless wave or succession of waves often continuing beyond or after its cause (as a gale)
**2 a :** the condition of being protuberant **b :** a rounded elevation
**3 a :** the act or process of swelling **b** (1) **:** a gradual increase and decrease of the loudness of a musical sound; *also* **:** a sign indicating a swell (2) **:** a device used in an organ for governing loudness

---

\ə\ **abut** \⁸\ **kitten** \ər\ **further** \a\ **ash** \ā\ **ace**
\ä\ **mop, mar** \au̇\ **out** \ch\ **chin** \e\ **bet** \ē\ **easy**
\g\ **go** \i\ **hit** \ī\ **ice** \j\ **job** \ŋ\ **sing** \ō\ **go**
\ȯ\ **law** \ȯi\ **boy** \th\ **thin** \ṯẖ\ **the** \ü\ **loot** \u̇\ **foot**
\y\ **yet** \zh\ **vision**    *see also* Guide to Pronunciation

**4 a** *archaic* **:** an impressive, pompous, or fashionable air or display **b :** a person dressed in the height of fashion **c :** a person of high social position or outstanding competence
³**swell** *adjective* (1785)
**1 a :** STYLISH **b :** socially prominent
**2 :** EXCELLENT — used as a generalized term of enthusiasm
**swell box** *noun* (circa 1801)
**:** a chamber in an organ containing a set of pipes and having shutters that open or shut to regulate the volume of tone
**swelled head** *noun* (1891)
**:** an exaggerated opinion of oneself **:** SELF-CONCEIT
— **swelled–head·ed** \'sweld-,he-dəd\ *adjective*
— **swelled–head·ed·ness** *noun*
**swell·fish** \'swel-,fish\ *noun* (1807)
**:** PUFFER 2a
**swell–front** \'swel-,frənt\ *adjective* (1914)
**:** BOWFRONT 1
**swell·head** \-,hed\ *noun* (1845)
**:** one who has a swelled head
— **swell·head·ed** \-,he-dəd\ *adjective*
— **swell·head·ed·ness** *noun*
**swell·ing** \'swe-liŋ\ *noun* (before 12th century)
**1 :** something that is swollen; *specifically* **:** an abnormal bodily protuberance or localized enlargement
**2 :** the condition of being swollen
¹**swel·ter** \'swel-tər\ *verb* **swel·tered; swel·ter·ing** \-t(ə-)riŋ\ [Middle English *sweltren,* frequentative of *swelten* to die, be overcome by heat, from Old English *sweltan* to die; akin to Gothic *swiltan* to die] (14th century)
*intransitive verb*
**1 :** to suffer, sweat, or be faint from heat
**2 :** to become exceedingly hot ⟨in summer, the place *swelters*⟩
*transitive verb*
**1 :** to oppress with heat
**2** *archaic* **:** EXUDE ⟨*sweltered* venom —Shakespeare⟩
²**swelter** *noun* (1851)
**1 :** a state of oppressive heat
**2 :** WELTER
**3 :** an excited or overwrought state of mind **:** SWEAT ⟨in a *swelter*⟩
**swel·ter·ing** *adjective* (1586)
**:** oppressively hot
— **swel·ter·ing·ly** \-t(ə-)riŋ-lē\ *adverb*
**swept** \'swept\ *adjective* [*swept,* past participle of *sweep*] (1903)
**:** slanted backward
**swept–back** \'swep(t)-'bak\ *adjective* (1914)
**:** possessing sweepback
**swerve** \'swərv\ *verb* **swerved; swerv·ing** [Middle English, from Old English *sweorfan* to wipe, file away; akin to Old High German *swerban* to wipe off, Welsh *chwerfu* to whirl] (14th century)
*intransitive verb*
**:** to turn aside abruptly from a straight line or course **:** DEVIATE
*transitive verb*
**:** to cause to turn aside or deviate ☆
— **swerve** *noun*
**swev·en** \'swe-vən\ *noun* [Middle English, from Old English *swefn* sleep, dream, vision — more at SOMNOLENT] (before 12th century)
*archaic* **:** DREAM, VISION
**swid·den** \'swi-dᵊn\ *noun, often attributive* [English dialect, burned clearing, probably from Old Norse *svithinn,* past participle of *svitha* to burn, singe] (circa 1868)
**:** a temporary agricultural plot produced by cutting back and burning off vegetative cover
¹**swift** \'swift\ *adjective* [Middle English, from Old English; akin to Old English *swīfan* to revolve — more at SWIVEL] (before 12th century)
**1 :** moving or capable of moving with great speed

**2 :** occurring suddenly or within a very short time
**3 :** quick to respond **:** READY
*synonym* see FAST
²**swift** *adverb* (14th century)
**:** SWIFTLY ⟨*swift*-flowing⟩
³**swift** *noun* (15th century)
**1 :** any of several lizards (especially of the genus *Sceloporus*) that run swiftly
**2 :** a reel for winding yarn or thread
**3 :** any of numerous small plainly colored birds (family Apodidae) that are related to the hummingbirds but superficially much resemble swallows
**swift fox** *noun* (1869)
**:** a small fox (*Vulpes velox*) with large ears that occurs on the plains of western North America
**swift·let** \'swif(t)-lət\ *noun* (circa 1890)
**:** any of various cave-dwelling swifts (genus *Collocalia*) of Asia including one (*C. unicolor*) that produces the nest used in bird's nest soup
**swift·ly** *adverb* (before 12th century)
**:** in a swift manner **:** with speed **:** QUICKLY
**swift·ness** \'swif(t)-nəs\ *noun* (before 12th century)
**1 :** the quality or state of being swift **:** CELERITY
**2 :** the fact of being swift
¹**swig** \'swig\ *noun* [origin unknown] (circa 1623)
**:** a quantity drunk at one time
²**swig** *verb* **swigged; swig·ging** (circa 1650)
*transitive verb*
**:** to drink in long drafts ⟨*swig* cider⟩
*intransitive verb*
**:** to take a swig **:** DRINK
— **swig·ger** *noun*
¹**swill** \'swil\ *verb* [Middle English *swilen,* from Old English *swillan*] (before 12th century)
*transitive verb*
**1 :** WASH, DRENCH
**2 :** to drink great drafts of **:** GUZZLE
**3 :** to feed (as a pig) with swill
*intransitive verb*
**1 :** to drink or eat freely, greedily, or to excess
**2 :** SWASH
— **swill·er** *noun*
²**swill** *noun* (1553)
**1 :** something suggestive of slop or garbage **:** REFUSE
**2 a :** a semiliquid food for animals (as swine) composed of edible refuse mixed with water or skimmed or sour milk **b :** GARBAGE
¹**swim** \'swim\ *verb* **swam** \'swam\; **swum** \'swəm\; **swim·ming** [Middle English *swimmen,* from Old English *swimman;* akin to Old High German *swimman* to swim] (before 12th century)
*intransitive verb*
**1 a :** to propel oneself in water by natural means (as movements of the limbs, fins, or tail) **b :** to play in the water (as at a beach or swimming pool)
**2 :** to move with a motion like that of swimming **:** GLIDE ⟨a cloud *swam* slowly across the moon⟩
**3 a :** to float on a liquid **:** not sink **b :** to surmount difficulties **:** not go under ⟨sink or *swim,* live or die, survive or perish —Daniel Webster⟩
**4 :** to become immersed in or flooded with or as if with a liquid ⟨potatoes *swimming* in gravy⟩
**5 :** to have a floating or reeling appearance or sensation
*transitive verb*
**1 a :** to cross by propelling oneself through water ⟨*swim* a stream⟩ **b :** to execute in swimming
**2 :** to cause to swim or float
— **swim·mer** *noun*
²**swim** *noun* (1599)

**1 :** a smooth gliding motion
**2 :** an act or period of swimming
**3 :** a temporary dizziness or unconsciousness
**4 a :** an area frequented by fish **b :** the main current of activity ⟨in the *swim*⟩
³**swim** *adjective* (1924)
**:** of, relating to, or used in or for swimming ⟨a *swim* meet⟩
**swim bladder** *noun* (1837)
**:** the air bladder of a fish
**swim fin** *noun* (1947)
**:** FLIPPER 1b
**swim·ma·ble** \'swi-mə-bəl\ *adjective* (1852)
**:** that can be swum
**swim·mer·et** \,swi-mə-'ret, 'swi-mə-,\ *noun* (1840)
**:** one of a series of small unspecialized appendages under the abdomen of many crustaceans that are best developed in some decapods (as a lobster) and usually function in locomotion or reproduction
**swimmer's itch** *noun* (1928)
**:** a severe urticarial reaction to the presence in the skin of larval schistosomes that are not normally human parasites
¹**swimming** *adjective* (before 12th century)
**1** [present participle of *swim*] **:** that swims ⟨a *swimming* bird⟩
**2** [gerund of *swim*] **:** adapted to or used in or for swimming
²**swimming** *noun* (14th century)
**:** the act, art, or sport of one that swims and dives
**swim·ming·ly** \'swi-miŋ-lē\ *adverb* (1622)
**:** very well **:** SPLENDIDLY
**swimming pool** *noun* (1899)
**:** a pool suitable for swimming; *especially* **:** a tank (as of concrete or plastic) made for swimming
**swim·my** \'swi-mē\ *adjective* **swim·mi·er; -est** (1836)
**1 :** verging on, causing, or affected by dizziness or giddiness
**2** *of vision* **:** UNSTEADY, BLURRED
— **swim·mi·ly** \'swi-mə-lē\ *adverb*
**swim·suit** \'swim-,süt\ *noun* (1926)
**:** a suit for swimming or bathing
**swim·wear** \-,war, -,wer\ *noun* (1935)
**:** clothing suitable for wear while swimming or bathing
¹**swin·dle** \'swin-dᵊl\ *verb* **swin·dled; swin·dling** \'swin(d)-liŋ, 'swin-dᵊl-iŋ\ [back-formation from *swindler,* from German *Schwindler* giddy person, from *schwindeln* to be dizzy, from Old High German *swintilōn,* frequentative of *swintan* to diminish, vanish; akin to Old English *swindan* to vanish] (circa 1782)
*intransitive verb*
**:** to obtain money or property by fraud or deceit
*transitive verb*

---

☆ SYNONYMS
**Swerve, veer, deviate, depart, digress, diverge** mean to turn aside from a straight course. SWERVE may suggest a physical, mental, or moral turning away from a given course, often with abruptness ⟨*swerved* to avoid hitting the dog⟩. VEER implies a major change in direction ⟨at that point the path *veers* to the right⟩. DEVIATE implies a turning from a customary or prescribed course ⟨never *deviated* from her daily routine⟩. DEPART suggests a deviation from a traditional or conventional course or type ⟨occasionally *departs* from his own guidelines⟩. DIGRESS applies to a departing from the subject of one's discourse ⟨a professor prone to *digress*⟩. DIVERGE may equal DEPART but usually suggests a branching of a main path into two or more leading in different directions ⟨after school their paths *diverged*⟩.

: to take money or property from by fraud or deceit ◆
***synonym*** see CHEAT
— **swin·dler** \'swin(d)-lər, 'swin-d°l-ər\ *noun*

**²swindle** *noun* (1833)
: an act or instance of swindling : FRAUD

**swine** \'swīn\ *noun, plural* **swine** [Middle English, from Old English *swīn;* akin to Old High German *swīn* swine, Latin *sus* — more at SOW] (before 12th century)
**1 :** any of various stout-bodied short-legged omnivorous mammals (family Suidae) with a thick bristly skin and a long mobile snout; *especially* **:** a domesticated member of the species (*Sus scrofa*) that includes the European wild boar
**2 :** a contemptible person

**swine·herd** \-,hərd\ *noun* (before 12th century)
: one who tends swine

**¹swing** \'swiŋ\ *verb* **swung** \'swəŋ\; **swing·ing** \'swiŋ-iŋ\ [Middle English, to beat, fling, hurl, rush, from Old English *swingan* to beat, fling oneself, rush; akin to Old High German *swingan* to fling, rush] (13th century)
*transitive verb*
**1 a :** to cause to move vigorously through a wide arc or circle ⟨*swing* an ax⟩ **b :** to cause to sway to and fro **c** (1) **:** to cause to turn on an axis (2) **:** to cause to face or move in another direction ⟨*swing* the car into a side road⟩
**2 :** to suspend so as to permit swaying or turning
**3 :** to convey by suspension ⟨cranes *swinging* cargo into the ship's hold⟩
**4 a** (1) **:** to influence decisively ⟨*swing* a lot of votes⟩ (2) **:** to bring around by influence **b :** to handle successfully **:** MANAGE ⟨wasn't able to *swing* a new car on his income⟩ ⟨*swing* a deal⟩
**5 :** to play or sing (as a melody) in the style of swing music
*intransitive verb*
**1 :** to move freely to and fro especially in suspension from an overhead support
**2 a :** to die by hanging **b :** to hang freely from a support
**3 :** to move in or describe a circle or arc: **a :** to turn on a hinge or pivot **b :** to turn in place **c :** to convey oneself by grasping a fixed support ⟨*swing* aboard the train⟩
**4 a :** to have a steady pulsing rhythm **b :** to play or sing with a lively compelling rhythm; *specifically* **:** to play swing music
**5 :** to shift or fluctuate from one condition, form, position, or object of attention or favor to another ⟨*swing* constantly from optimism to pessimism and back —Sinclair Lewis⟩
**6 a :** to move along rhythmically **b :** to start up in a smooth vigorous manner ⟨ready to *swing* into action⟩
**7 :** to hit or aim at something with a sweeping arm movement
**8 a :** to be lively and up-to-date **b :** to engage freely in sex ☆ ☆

**²swing** *noun* (14th century)
**1 :** an act or instance of swinging **:** swinging movement: as **a** (1) **:** a stroke or blow delivered with a sweeping arm movement ⟨a batter with a powerful *swing*⟩ (2) **:** a sweeping or rhythmic movement of the body or a bodily part (3) **:** a dance figure in which two dancers revolve with joined arms or hands (4) **:** jazz dancing in moderate tempo with a lilting syncopation **b** (1) **:** the regular movement of a freely suspended object (as a pendulum) along an arc and back (2) **:** back and forth sweep (the *swing* of the tides) **c** (1) **:** steady pulsing rhythm (as in poetry or music) (2) **:** a steady vigorous movement characterizing an activity or creative work **d** (1) **:** a trend toward a high or low point in a fluctuating cycle (as of business activity) (2) **:** an often periodic shift from one condition, form, position, or object of attention or favor to another

**2 a :** liberty of action **b** (1) **:** the driving power of something swung or hurled (2) **:** steady vigorous advance **:** driving speed ⟨a train approaching at full *swing*⟩
**3 :** the progression of an activity, process, or phase of existence ⟨the work is in full *swing*⟩
**4 :** the arc or range through which something swings
**5 :** something that swings freely from or on a support; *especially* **:** a seat suspended by a rope or chains for swinging to and fro on for pleasure
**6 a :** a curving course or outline **b :** a course from and back to a point **:** a circular tour
**7 :** jazz played usually by a large dance band and characterized by a steady lively rhythm, simple harmony, and a basic melody often submerged in improvisation
**8 :** a short pass in football thrown to a back running to the outside

**³swing** *adjective* (1934)
**1 :** of or relating to musical swing ⟨a *swing* band⟩ ⟨*swing* music⟩
**2 :** that may swing often decisively either way on an issue or in an election ⟨*swing* voters⟩ ⟨a *swing* state⟩

**¹swinge** \'swinj\ *transitive verb* **swinged; swinge·ing** [Middle English *swengen* to shake, from Old English *swengan;* akin to Old English *swingan*] (12th century)
*chiefly dialect* **:** BEAT, SCOURGE

**²swinge** *transitive verb* **swinged; swinge·ing** [alteration of *singe*] (1590)
*dialect* **:** SINGE, SCORCH

**¹swinge·ing** *also* **swing·ing** \'swin-jiŋ\ *adjective* [from present participle of ¹*swinge*] (circa 1590)
*chiefly British* **:** very large, high, or severe ⟨*swingeing* fines⟩ ⟨*swingeing* taxes⟩

**²swingeing** *or* **swinging** *adverb* (1690)
*chiefly British* **:** VERY, SUPERLATIVELY

**¹swing·er** \'swiŋ-ər\ *noun* (1543)
: one that swings: as **a :** a lively up-to-date person who indulges in what is considered fashionable **b :** one who engages freely in sex

**²swing·er** \'swin-jər\ *noun* [¹*swinge*] (1599)
**:** WHOPPER 1

**swing·ing** \'swiŋ-iŋ\ *adjective* [present participle of ¹*swing*] (1956)
**:** being lively and up-to-date; *also* **:** abounding in swingers and swinging entertainment ⟨a *swinging* coffeehouse⟩

**¹swing·ing·ly** \'swiŋ-jiŋ-lē\ *adverb* (1672)
*chiefly British* **:** VERY, EXTREMELY

**²swing·ing·ly** \'swiŋ-iŋ-lē\ *adverb* (1882)
**:** in a swinging manner **:** with a swinging movement

**swin·gle·tree** \'swiŋ-gəl-(,)trē\ *noun* [Middle English *swyngyll tre,* from *swyngyll* rod for beating flax (from Middle Dutch *swengel*) + *tre* tree] (15th century)
**:** WHIFFLETREE

**swing·man** \'swiŋ-,man, -mən\ *noun* (1965)
: a player capable of playing effectively in two different positions and especially of playing both guard and forward on a basketball team

**swing shift** *noun* (1940)
**1 :** the work shift between the day and night shifts (as from 4 P.M. to midnight)
**2 :** a group of workers in a factory operating seven days a week that work as needed to permit the regular shift workers to have one or more free days per week

**swingy** \'swiŋ-ē\ *adjective* **swing·i·er; -est** (1915)
: marked by swing

**swin·ish** \'swī-nish\ *adjective* (13th century)
: of, suggesting, or characteristic of swine
**:** BEASTLY
— **swin·ish·ly** *adverb*
— **swin·ish·ness** *noun*

**¹swink** \'swiŋk\ *intransitive verb* [Middle English, from Old English *swincan;* akin to Old High German *swingan* to rush — more at SWING] (before 12th century)
*archaic* **:** TOIL, SLAVE

**²swink** *noun* (12th century)
*archaic* **:** LABOR, DRUDGERY

**¹swipe** \'swīp\ *noun* [probably alteration of *sweep*] (1739)
**1 :** a strong sweeping blow
**2 :** a sharp often critical remark ⟨took a parting *swipe* at management⟩

**²swipe** *verb* **swiped; swip·ing** (circa 1825)
*intransitive verb*
: to strike or move with a sweeping motion
*transitive verb*
**1 :** to strike or wipe with a sweeping motion
**2 :** STEAL, PILFER

**swipes** \'swīps\ *noun plural* [origin unknown] (circa 1796)
*British* **:** poor, thin, or spoiled beer; *also* **:** BEER

**¹swirl** \'swər(-ə)l\ *verb* [Middle English] (14th century)

---

☆ **SYNONYMS**
**Swing, wave, flourish, brandish, thrash** mean to wield or cause to move to and fro or up and down. SWING implies regular or uniform movement ⟨*swing* the rope back and forth⟩. WAVE usually implies smooth or continuous motion ⟨*waving* the flag⟩. FLOURISH suggests vigorous, ostentatious, graceful movement ⟨*flourished* the winning lottery ticket⟩. BRANDISH implies threatening or menacing motion ⟨*brandishing* a knife⟩. THRASH suggests vigorous, abrupt, violent movement ⟨an infant *thrashing* his arms about⟩.

**Swing, sway, oscillate, vibrate, fluctuate, waver, undulate** mean to move from one direction to its opposite. SWING implies a movement of something attached at one end or one side ⟨the door suddenly *swung* open⟩. SWAY implies a slow swinging or teetering movement ⟨trees *swaying* in the breeze⟩. OSCILLATE stresses a usually regular alternation of direction ⟨an *oscillating* fan⟩. VIBRATE suggests the rapid oscillation of an elastic body under stress or impact ⟨the *vibrating* strings of a piano⟩. FLUCTUATE suggests constant irregular changes of level, intensity, or value ⟨*fluctuating* interest rates⟩. WAVER stresses irregular motion suggestive of reeling or tottering ⟨the exhausted runner *wavered* before collapsing⟩. UNDULATE suggests a gentle wavelike motion ⟨an *undulating* sea of grass⟩.

---

◇ **WORD HISTORY**
**swindle** One would hardly think that someone whose head is whirling could be convincing enough to perpetrate a swindle. However, the original meaning of the German noun *Schwindler* was "giddy person." In the same way that *giddy* has been extended in English to describe someone who is frivolous or foolish, *Schwindler* was extended to individuals given to habitual flights of fancy. The Germans applied the word as well to a fantastic schemer, then to a participant in shaky business deals, and finally to a cheat. The word *Schwindler* is a derivative of the verb *schwindeln,* first used to mean "to be dizzy" and then "to cheat." *Swindler* appeared first in English in the second half of the 18th century, and *swindle* was created from it by removal of the suffix. At first they were slang terms associated with the criminal underworld, but they soon became standard.

---

\ə\ **abut** \°\ **kitten** \ər\ **further** \a\ **ash** \ā\ **ace**
\ä\ **mop, mar** \aú\ **out** \ch\ **chin** \e\ **bet** \ē\ **easy**
\g\ **go** \i\ **hit** \ī\ **ice** \j\ **job** \ŋ\ **sing** \ō\ **go**
\ò\ **law** \òi\ **boy** \th\ **thin** \t̲h̲\ **the** \ü\ **loot** \ú\ **foot**
\y\ **yet** \zh\ **vision** *see also* Guide to Pronunciation

*intransitive verb*
**1 a :** to move with an eddying or whirling motion **b :** to pass in whirling confusion
**2 :** to have a twist or convolution
*transitive verb*
**:** to cause to swirl
— **swirl·ing·ly** \'swər-liŋ-lē\ *adverb*
²**swirl** *noun* (15th century)
**1 a :** a whirling mass or motion **:** EDDY **b :** whirling confusion ⟨a *swirl* of events⟩
**2 :** a twisting shape, mark, or pattern
**3 :** an act or instance of swirling
**swirly** \'swər-lē\ *adjective* **swirl·i·er; -est** (1785)
**1** *Scottish* **:** KNOTTED, TWISTED
**2 :** that swirls **:** SWIRLING ⟨the *swirly* water of the rapids⟩
¹**swish** \'swish\ *verb* [imitative] (1756)
*intransitive verb*
**:** to move, pass, swing, or whirl with the sound of a swish
*transitive verb*
**1 :** to move, cut, or strike with a swish ⟨the horse *swished* its tail⟩
**2 :** to make (a basketball shot) so that the ball falls through the rim without touching it ⟨*swished* a three-point jumper⟩
— **swish·er** *noun*
— **swish·ing·ly** \'swi-shiŋ-lē\ *adverb*
²**swish** *noun* (1820)
**1 a :** a prolonged hissing sound (as of a whip cutting the air) **b :** a light sweeping or brushing sound (as of a full silk skirt in motion)
**2 :** a swishing movement
**3 :** an effeminate homosexual — usually used disparagingly
³**swish** *adjective* [origin unknown] (1879)
**:** SMART, FASHIONABLE
**swishy** \'swi-shē\ *adjective* **swish·i·er; -est** (1828)
**1 :** producing a swishing sound
**2 :** characterized by effeminate behavior
¹**Swiss** \'swis\ *noun* [Middle French *Suisse*, from Middle High German *Swīzer*, from *Swīz* Switzerland] (1515)
**1** *plural* **Swiss a :** a native or inhabitant of Switzerland **b :** one that is of Swiss descent
**2** *often not capitalized* **:** any of various fine sheer fabrics of cotton originally made in Switzerland; *especially* **:** DOTTED SWISS
**3 :** SWISS CHEESE
²**Swiss** *adjective* (1530)
**:** of, relating to, or characteristic of Switzerland or the Swiss
**Swiss chard** *noun* (1832)
**:** a beet (*Beta vulgaris cicla*) having large leaves and succulent stalks often cooked as a vegetable — called also *chard*
**Swiss cheese** *noun* (1822)
**:** a hard cheese characterized by elastic texture, mild nutlike flavor, and large holes that form during ripening
**Swiss steak** *noun* (1924)
**:** a slice of steak pounded with flour and braised usually with vegetables and seasonings
¹**switch** \'swich\ *noun* [perhaps from Middle Dutch *swijch* twig] (1592)
**1 :** a slender flexible whip, rod, or twig ⟨a riding *switch*⟩
**2 :** an act of switching: as **a :** a blow with a switch **b :** a shift from one to another **c :** a change from the usual
**3 :** a tuft of long hairs at the end of the tail of an animal (as a cow) — see COW illustration
**4 a :** a device made usually of two movable rails and necessary connections and designed to turn a locomotive or train from one track to another **b :** a railroad siding
**5 :** a device for making, breaking, or changing the connections in an electrical circuit
**6 :** a heavy strand of hair used in addition to a person's own hair for some coiffures
²**switch** (circa 1611)
*transitive verb*
**1 :** to strike or beat with or as if with a switch

**2** WHISK, LASH ⟨a cat *switching* its tail⟩
**3 a (1) :** to turn from one railroad track to another **:** SHUNT **(2) :** to move (cars) to different positions on the same track within terminal areas **b :** to make a shift in or exchange of ⟨*switch* seats⟩
**4 a :** to shift to another electrical circuit by means of a switch **b :** to operate an electrical switch so as to turn (as a light) off or on
*intransitive verb*
**1 :** to lash from side to side
**2 :** to make a shift or exchange
— **switch·able** \'swi-chə-bəl\ *adjective*
— **switch·er** *noun*
¹**switch·back** \'swich-,bak\ *noun* (1863)
**:** a zigzag road, trail, or section of railroad tracks for climbing a steep hill
²**switchback** *adjective* (1887)
**:** resembling a switchback (as in taking a zigzag course) ⟨a *switchback* career⟩
³**switchback** *intransitive verb* (1903)
**:** to follow a zigzag course especially in ascending or descending
**switch·blade** \-,blād\ *noun* (1932)
**:** a pocketknife having the blade spring-operated so that pressure on a release catch causes it to fly open — called also *switchblade knife*
**switch·board** \-,bōrd, -,bórd\ *noun* (1873)
**:** an apparatus (as in a telephone exchange) consisting of a panel on which are mounted electric switches so arranged that a number of circuits may be connected, combined, and controlled
**switch engine** *noun* (1867)
**:** a railroad engine used in switching cars
**switch·er·oo** \,swi-chə-'rü\ *noun, plural* **-oos** [alteration of *switch*] (1933)
*slang* **:** a surprising variation **:** REVERSAL
**switch·grass** \'swich-,gras\ *noun* (1840)
**:** a panic grass (*Panicum virgatum*) of the western U.S. that is used for hay
**switch–hit** \-'hit\ *intransitive verb* **-hit; -hit·ting** [back-formation from *switch-hitter*] (1938)
**:** to bat right-handed against a left-hander and left-handed against a right-hander in baseball
**switch–hit·ter** \-'hi-tər\ *noun* (1948)
**1 :** a baseball player who switch-hits
**2** *slang* **:** BISEXUAL
**switch knife** *noun* (1950)
**:** SWITCHBLADE
**switch·man** \'swich-mən\ *noun* (1843)
**:** one who attends a switch (as in a railroad yard)
**switch·yard** \-,yärd\ *noun* (1943)
**:** a usually enclosed area for the switching facilities of a power station
**swith** \'swith\ *adverb* [Middle English, strongly, quickly, from Old English *swīthe* strongly, from *swīth* strong; akin to Gothic *swinths* strong, Old English *gesund* sound — more at SOUND] (13th century)
*chiefly dialect* **:** INSTANTLY, QUICKLY
**swith·er** \'swi-thər\ *intransitive verb* [origin unknown] (1501)
*dialect chiefly British* **:** DOUBT, WAVER
— **swither** *noun, dialect chiefly British*
**Swit·zer** \'swit-sər\ *noun* [Middle High German *Swīzer*] (1549)
**:** SWISS
¹**swiv·el** \'swi-vəl\ *noun, often attributive* [Middle English; akin to Old English *swīfan* to revolve, Old High German *swebōn* to roll, heave] (14th century)
**:** a device joining two parts so that one or both can pivot freely (as on a bolt or pin)
²**swivel** *verb* **-eled** *or* **-elled; -el·ing** *or* **-el·ling** \'swi-və-liŋ, 'swiv-liŋ\ (1794)
*transitive verb*
**:** to turn on or as if on a swivel ⟨*swiveled* his eyes in various directions⟩
*intransitive verb*
**:** to swing or turn on or as if on a swivel
**swivel chair** *noun* (1860)
**:** a chair that swivels on its base

**swiv·el–hipped** \'swi-vəl-,hipt\ *adjective* (1947)
**:** moving with or characterized by movement with a twisting motion of the hips
**swiv·et** \'swi-vət\ *noun* [origin unknown] (circa 1892)
**:** a state of extreme agitation
¹**swiz·zle** \'swi-zəl\ *noun* [origin unknown] (1813)
**:** an iced whiskey sour churned with a swizzle stick until the glass or pitcher becomes frosted
²**swizzle** *verb* **swiz·zled; swiz·zling** \'swi-zə-liŋ, 'swiz-liŋ\ (circa 1847)
*intransitive verb*
**:** to drink especially to excess **:** GUZZLE
*transitive verb*
**:** to mix or stir with or as if with a swizzle stick
— **swiz·zler** \'swi-zə-lər, 'swiz-lər\ *noun*
**swizzle stick** *noun* (1879)
**:** a stick used to stir mixed drinks
**swob** *archaic variant of* SWAB
**swollen** *past participle of* SWELL
¹**swoon** \'swün\ *intransitive verb* [Middle English *swounen*] (13th century)
**1 a :** FAINT **b :** to become enraptured ⟨*swooning* with joy⟩
**2 :** DROOP, FADE
— **swoon·er** *noun*
— **swoon·ing·ly** \'swü-niŋ-lē\ *adverb*
²**swoon** *noun* (13th century)
**1 a :** a partial or total loss of consciousness **b :** a state of bewilderment or ecstasy **:** DAZE, RAPTURE
**2 :** a state of suspended animation **:** TORPOR
¹**swoop** \'swüp\ *verb* [alteration of Middle English *swopen* to sweep, from Old English *swāpan* — more at SWEEP] (1566)
*intransitive verb*
**:** to move with a sweep ⟨the eagle *swooped* down on its prey⟩
*transitive verb*
**:** to gain or carry off in or as if in a swoop — usually used with *up*
— **swoop·er** *noun*
²**swoop** *noun* (1605)
**:** an act or instance of swooping
**swoop·stake** \'swüp-,stāk\ *adverb* [from alteration of *sweepstake*] (1602)
*obsolete* **:** in an indiscriminate manner
¹**swoosh** \'swüsh, 'swush\ *verb* [imitative] (1867)
*intransitive verb*
**1 :** to make or move with a rushing sound ⟨a car *swooshed* by⟩
**2 :** GUSH, SWIRL
*transitive verb*
**:** to discharge or transport with a rushing sound
²**swoosh** *noun* (1885)
**:** an act or instance of swooshing
**swop** *chiefly British variant of* SWAP
**sword** \'sōrd, 'sórd\ *noun, often attributive* [Middle English, from Old English *sweord*; akin to Old High German *swert* sword] (before 12th century)
**1 :** a weapon (as a cutlass or rapier) with a long blade for cutting or thrusting that is often used as a symbol of honor or authority
**2 a :** an agency or instrument of destruction or combat **b :** the use of force ⟨the pen is mightier than the *sword* —E. G. Bulwer-Lytton⟩
**3 :** coercive power
**4 :** something that resembles a sword
— **sword·like** \-,līk\ *adjective*
— **at swords' points :** mutually antagonistic **:** ready to fight
**sword cane** *noun* (1837)
**:** a cane in which a sword blade is concealed
**sword dance** *noun* (1604)
**1 :** a dance performed by men in a circle holding a sword in the right hand and grasping the tip of a neighbor's sword in the left hand
**2 :** a dance performed over or around swords
— **sword dancer** *noun*

**sword fern** *noun* (circa 1829)
: any of several ferns with long narrow more or less sword-shaped fronds: as **a** : a tropical fern (*Nephrolepis exaltata*) from which the Boston fern has been developed **b** : a fern (*Polystichum munitum*) of western North America with a large fleshy rhizome

**sword·fish** \'sōrd-,fish, 'sȯrd-\ *noun* (15th century)
: a very large oceanic bony fish (*Xiphias gladius* of the family Xiphiidae) that has a long swordlike beak formed by the bones of the upper jaw and is an important food and game fish

swordfish

**sword grass** *noun* (1598)
: any of various grasses or sedges having leaves with a sharp or toothed edge

**sword knot** *noun* (1694)
: an ornamental cord or tassel tied to the hilt of a sword

**sword of Dam·o·cles** \-'da-mə-,klēz\ *often S capitalized* (1820)
: an impending disaster

**sword·play** \'sōrd-,plā, 'sȯrd-\ *noun* (1627)
**1** : the art or skill of wielding a sword especially in fencing
**2** : an exhibition of swordplay
&mdash; **sword·play·er** *noun*

**swords·man** \'sōrdz-mən, 'sȯrdz-\ *noun* (circa 1680)
**1** : one skilled in swordplay; *especially* : a saber fencer
**2** *archaic* : a soldier armed with a sword

**swords·man·ship** \-,ship\ *noun* (circa 1852)
: SWORDPLAY

**sword·tail** \'sōrd-,tāl, 'sȯrd-\ *noun* (circa 1928)
: a small brightly marked Central American live-bearer (*Xiphophorus helleri* of the family Poeciliidae) often kept in tropical aquariums and bred in many colors

**swore** *past of* SWEAR

**sworn** *past participle of* SWEAR

**¹swot** \'swät\ *noun* [English dialect, sweat, from Middle English *swot*, from Old English *swāt* &mdash; more at SWEAT] (1850)
*British* : GRIND 2b

**²swot** *intransitive verb* **swot·ted; swot·ting** (circa 1860)
*British* : GRIND 4

**¹swound** \'swaund, 'swünd\ *noun* [Middle English, alteration of *swoun* swoon, from *swounen* to swoon] (15th century)
*archaic* : SWOON 1a

**²swound** *intransitive verb* (1530)
*archaic* : SWOON

**swum** *past participle of* SWIM

**swung** *past and past participle of* SWING

**swung dash** *noun* (1951)
: a character ~ used in printing to conserve space by representing part or all of a previously spelled-out word

**syb·a·rite** \'si-bə-,rīt\ *noun* (circa 1555)
**1** [from the notorious luxury of the Sybarites]
: VOLUPTUARY, SENSUALIST
**2** *capitalized* : a native or resident of the ancient city of Sybaris
&mdash; **syb·a·rit·ic** \,si-bə-'ri-tik\ *adjective*
&mdash; **syb·a·rit·i·cal·ly** \-ti-k(ə-)lē\ *adverb*
&mdash; **syb·a·rit·ism** \'si-bə-,rī-,tī-zəm\ *noun*

**syc·a·mine** \'si-kə-,mīn, -mən\ *noun* [Latin *sycaminus*, from Greek *sykaminos*, of Semitic

origin; akin to Hebrew *shiqmāh* mulberry tree, sycamore] (1526)
: a tree of the Bible that is usually considered a mulberry (*Morus nigra*)

**syc·a·more** \'si-kə-,mōr, -,mȯr\ *noun* [Middle English *sicamour*, from Middle French *sicamor*, from Latin *sycomorus*, from Greek *sykomoros*, probably modification of a Semitic word akin to Hebrew *shiqmāh* sycamore] (14th century)
**1** *also* **syc·o·more** \'si-kə-,\ : a fig tree (*Ficus sycomorus*) of Africa and the Middle East that is the sycamore of Scripture and has sweet and edible fruit similar but inferior to the common fig
**2** : a Eurasian maple (*Acer pseudoplatanus*) with long racemes of showy yellowish green flowers that is widely planted as a shade tree
**3** : ²PLANE; *especially* : a very large spreading tree (*Platanus occidentalis*) of eastern and central North America with 3- to 5-lobed broadly ovate leaves

**syce** \'sīs\ *noun* [Hindi *sāīs*, from Arabic *sā'is*] (1653)
: an attendant (as a groom) especially in India

**sy·cee** \'sī-,sē\ *noun* [Chinese (Guangdong) *sai-sì*, literally, fine silk] (1711)
: silver money made in the form of ingots and formerly used in China

**sy·co·ni·um** \sī-'kō-nē-əm\ *noun, plural* **-nia** \-nē-ə\ [New Latin, from Greek *sykon* fig + New Latin *-ium*] (circa 1856)
: the multiple fleshy fruit of a fig in which the ovaries are borne within an enlarged succulent concave or hollow receptacle

**sy·co·phan·cy** \'si-kə-fən(t)-sē *also* 'sī- & -,fan(t)-sē\ *noun* (1672)
: obsequious flattery; *also* : the character or behavior of a sycophant

**sy·co·phant** \-fənt *also* -,fant\ *noun* [Latin *sycophanta* slanderer, swindler, from Greek *sykophantēs* slanderer, from *sykon* fig + *phainein* to show &mdash; more at FANCY] (1575)
: a servile self-seeking flatterer
***synonym*** *see* PARASITE
&mdash; **sycophant** *adjective*

**sy·co·phan·tic** \,si-kə-'fan-tik *also* ,sī-\ *adjective* (1676)
: of, relating to, or characteristic of a sycophant : FAWNING, OBSEQUIOUS
&mdash; **sy·co·phan·ti·cal·ly** \-'fan-ti-k(ə-)lē\ *adverb*

**sy·co·phant·ish** \,si-kə-'fan-tish *also* ,sī-\ *adjective* (1794)
: SYCOPHANTIC
&mdash; **sy·co·phant·ish·ly** *adverb*

**sy·co·phant·ism** \'si-kə-fən-,ti-zəm *also* 'sī- & -,fan-\ *noun* (1821)
: SYCOPHANCY

**sy·co·phant·ly** \-lē\ *adverb* (1672)
: in a sycophantic manner

**sy·co·sis** \sī-'kō-səs\ *noun* [New Latin, from Greek *sykōsis*, from *sykon* fig] (circa 1827)
: a chronic inflammatory disorder of the hair follicles marked by papules, pustules, and tubercles with crusting

**sy·e·nite** \'sī-ə-,nīt\ *noun* [Latin *Syenites* (*lapis*) stone of Syene, from *Syene*, ancient city in Egypt] (circa 1796)
: an igneous rock composed chiefly of feldspar
&mdash; **sy·e·nit·ic** \,sī-ə-'ni-tik\ *adjective*

**sy·li** \'sē-lē\ *noun, plural* **sylis** [Susu *sílí*, literally, elephant] (1974)
: the monetary unit of Guinea from 1972 to 1986

**syl·la·bary** \'si-lə-,ber-ē\ *noun, plural* **-bar·ies** [New Latin *syllabarium*, from Latin *syllaba* syllable] (1586)
: a table or listing of syllables; *specifically* : a series or set of written characters each one of which is used to represent a syllable

**¹syl·lab·ic** \sə-'la-bik\ *adjective* [Late Latin *syllabicus*, from Greek *syllabikos*, from *syllabē* syllable] (1728)
**1** : constituting a syllable or the nucleus of a

syllable: **a** : not accompanied in the same syllable by a vowel ⟨a *syllabic* consonant⟩ **b** : having vowel quality more prominent than that of another vowel in the syllable ⟨the first vowel of a falling diphthong, as \ȯ\ in \ȯi\, is *syllabic*⟩
**2** : of, relating to, or denoting syllables ⟨*syllabic* accent⟩
**3** : characterized by distinct enunciation or separation of syllables
**4** : of, relating to, or constituting a type of verse distinguished primarily by count of syllables rather than by rhythmical arrangement of accents or quantities
&mdash; **syl·lab·i·cal·ly** \-bi-k(ə-)lē\ *adverb*

**²syllabic** *noun* (1880)
: a syllabic character or sound

**syl·lab·i·cate** \sə-'la-bə-,kāt\ *transitive verb* **-cat·ed; -cat·ing** (circa 1654)
: SYLLABIFY

**syl·lab·i·ca·tion** \sə-,la-bə-'kā-shən\ *noun* (15th century)
: the act, process, or method of forming or dividing words into syllables

**syl·la·bic·i·ty** \,si-lə-'bi-sə-tē\ *noun* (1933)
: the state of being or the power of forming a syllable

**syl·lab·i·fi·ca·tion** \sə-,la-bə-fə-'kā-shən\ *noun* (1838)
: SYLLABICATION

**syl·lab·i·fy** \sə-'la-bə-,fī\ *transitive verb* **-fied; -fy·ing** [Latin *syllaba* syllable] (circa 1859)
: to form or divide into syllables

**¹syl·la·ble** \'si-lə-bəl\ *noun* [Middle English, from Middle French *sillabe*, from Latin *syllaba*, from Greek *syllabē*, from *syllambanein* to gather together, from *syn-* + *lambanein* to take &mdash; more at LATCH] (14th century)
**1** : a unit of spoken language that is next bigger than a speech sound and consists of one or more vowel sounds alone or of a syllabic consonant alone or of either with one or more consonant sounds preceding or following
**2** : one or more letters (as *syl, la,* and *ble*) in a word (as *syl·la·ble*) usually set off from the rest of the word by a centered dot or a hyphen and roughly corresponding to the syllables of spoken language and treated as helps to pronunciation or as guides to placing hyphens at the end of a line
**3** : the smallest conceivable expression or unit of something : JOT
**4** : SOL-FA SYLLABLES

**²syllable** *transitive verb* **syl·la·bled; syl·la·bling** \-b(ə-)liŋ\ (15th century)
**1** : to give a number or arrangement of syllables to (a word or verse)
**2** : to express or utter in or as if in syllables

**syl·la·bub** \'si-lə-,bəb\ *noun* [origin unknown] (circa 1537)
**1** : a drink made by curdling milk or cream with an acid beverage (as wine or cider)
**2** : a sweetened drink or topping made of milk or cream beaten with wine or liquor and sometimes further thickened with gelatin and served as a dessert

**syl·la·bus** \'si-lə-bəs\ *noun, plural* **-bi** \-,bī, -,bē\ *or* **-bus·es** [Late Latin, alteration of Latin *sillybus* label for a book, from Greek *sillybos*] (circa 1656)
**1** : a summary outline of a discourse, treatise, or course of study or of examination requirements
**2** : HEADNOTE 2

**syl·lep·sis** \sə-'lep-səs\ *noun, plural* **-lep·ses** \-,sēz\ [Latin, from Greek *syllēpsis*, from *syllambanein*] (circa 1550)
**1** : the use of a word to modify or govern syntactically two or sometimes more words with only one of which it formally agrees in gender, number, or case

**2** : the use of a word in the same grammatical relation to two adjacent words in the context with one literal and the other metaphorical in sense
— **syl·lep·tic** \-'lep-tik\ *adjective*

**syl·lo·gism** \'si-lə-,ji-zəm\ *noun* [Middle English *silogisme*, from Middle French, from Latin *syllogismus*, from Greek *syllogismos*, from *syllogizesthai* to syllogize, from *syn-* + *logizesthai* to calculate, from *logos* reckoning, word — more at LEGEND] (14th century)
**1** : a deductive scheme of a formal argument consisting of a major and a minor premise and a conclusion (as in "every virtue is laudable; kindness is a virtue; therefore kindness is laudable")
**2** : a subtle, specious, or crafty argument
**3** : deductive reasoning
— **syl·lo·gis·tic** \,si-lə-'jis-tik\ *adjective*
— **syl·lo·gis·ti·cal·ly** \-ti-k(ə-)lē\ *adverb*

**syl·lo·gist** \'si-lə-jist\ *noun* (1799)
: one who applies or is skilled in syllogistic reasoning

**syl·lo·gize** \'si-lə-,jīz\ *verb* **-gized; -giz·ing** [Middle English *sylogysen*, from Late Latin *syllogizare*, from Greek *syllogizesthai*] (15th century)
*intransitive verb*
: to reason by means of syllogisms
*transitive verb*
: to deduce by syllogism ⟨*syllogizes* moral laws⟩

**sylph** \'silf\ *noun* [New Latin *sylphus*] (1657)
**1** : an elemental being in the theory of Paracelsus that inhabits air
**2** : a slender graceful woman or girl
— **sylph·like** \'sil-,flīk\ *adjective*

**sylph·id** \'sil-fəd\ *noun* (1680)
: a young or diminutive sylph

**sylva, sylviculture** *variant of* SILVA, SILVICULTURE

**¹syl·van** \'sil-vən\ *noun* (1565)
: one that frequents groves or woods

**²sylvan** *adjective* [Medieval Latin *silvanus*, *sylvanus*, from Latin *silva, sylva* wood] (circa 1583)
**1 a** : living or located in the woods or forest **b** : of, relating to, or characteristic of the woods or forest
**2 a** : made, shaped, or formed of woods or trees **b** : abounding in woods, groves, or trees : WOODED

**syl·va·nite** \'sil-və-,nīt\ *noun* [French *sylvanite*, from New Latin *sylvanium* tellurium, from *Transylvania*, region in Romania] (1796)
: a mineral that is a gold silver telluride and often occurs in crystals resembling written characters

**syl·vat·ic** \sil-'va-tik\ *adjective* [Latin *silvaticus* of the woods, wild — more at SAVAGE] (1661)
**1** : SYLVAN ⟨*sylvatic* rodents⟩
**2** : occurring in or affecting wild animals ⟨*sylvatic* diseases⟩

**syl·vite** \'sil-,vīt\ *also* **syl·vine** \-,vēn\ *noun* [alteration of *sylvine*, from French, from New Latin *sal digestivus Sylvii* digestive salt of Sylvius, from *Sylvius* latinized name of Jacques Dubois (died 1555) French physician] (1868)
: a mineral that is a natural potassium chloride and occurs in colorless cubes or crystalline masses

**sym-** — see SYN-

**sym·bi·ont** \'sim-bē-,änt\ *noun* [probably from German, modification of Greek *symbiount-, symbiōn*, present participle of *symbioun*] (1887)
: an organism living in symbiosis; *especially* : the smaller member of a symbiotic pair

**sym·bi·o·sis** \,sim-bē-'ō-səs, -,bī-\ *noun*, *plural* **-bi·o·ses** \-,sēz\ [New Latin, from German *Symbiose*, from Greek *symbiōsis* state of living together, from *symbioun* to live together, from *symbios* living together, from *sym-* + *bios* life — more at QUICK] (1622)

**1** : the living together in more or less intimate association or close union of two dissimilar organisms
**2** : the intimate living together of two dissimilar organisms in a mutually beneficial relationship; *especially* : MUTUALISM
**3** : a cooperative relationship (as between two persons or groups) ⟨the *symbiosis* . . . between the resident population and the immigrants —John Geipel⟩
— **sym·bi·ot·ic** \-'ä-tik\ *adjective*
— **sym·bi·ot·i·cal·ly** \-ti-k(ə-)lē\ *adverb*

**sym·bi·ote** \'sim-bē-,ōt, -,bī-\ *noun* [French, from Greek *symbiōtēs* companion, from *symbioun* to live together] (circa 1909)
: SYMBIONT

**¹sym·bol** \'sim-bəl\ *noun* [in sense 1, from Late Latin *symbolum*, from Late Greek *symbolon*, from Greek, token, sign; in other senses from Latin *symbolum* token, sign, symbol, from Greek *symbolon*, literally, token of identity verified by comparing its other half, from *symballein* to throw together, compare, from *syn-* + *ballein* to throw — more at DEVIL] (15th century)
**1** : an authoritative summary of faith or doctrine : CREED
**2** : something that stands for or suggests something else by reason of relationship, association, convention, or accidental resemblance; *especially* : a visible sign of something invisible ⟨the lion is a *symbol* of courage⟩
**3** : an arbitrary or conventional sign used in writing or printing relating to a particular field to represent operations, quantities, elements, relations, or qualities
**4** : an object or act representing something in the unconscious mind that has been repressed ⟨phallic *symbols*⟩
**5** : an act, sound, or object having cultural significance and the capacity to excite or objectify a response

**²symbol** *verb* **-boled** *or* **-bolled; -bol·ing** *or* **-bol·ling** (1832)
: SYMBOLIZE

**sym·bol·ic** \sim-'bä-lik\ *also* **sym·bol·i·cal** \-li-kəl\ *adjective* (1610)
**1 a** : using, employing, or exhibiting a symbol **b** : consisting of or proceeding by means of symbols
**2** : of, relating to, or constituting a symbol
**3** : characterized by or terminating in symbols ⟨*symbolic* thinking⟩
**4** : characterized by symbolism ⟨a *symbolic* dance⟩
— **sym·bol·i·cal·ly** \-li-k(ə-)lē\ *adverb*

**symbolic logic** *noun* (1856)
: a science of developing and representing logical principles by means of a formalized system consisting of primitive symbols, combinations of these symbols, axioms, and rules of inference

**sym·bol·ise** *British variant of* SYMBOLIZE

**sym·bol·ism** \'sim-bə-,li-zəm\ *noun* (1654)
**1** : the art or practice of using symbols especially by investing things with a symbolic meaning or by expressing the invisible or intangible by means of visible or sensuous representations: as **a** : artistic imitation or invention that is a method of revealing or suggesting immaterial, ideal, or otherwise intangible truth or states **b** : the use of conventional or traditional signs in the representation of divine beings and spirits
**2** : a system of symbols or representations

**sym·bol·ist** \'sim-bə-list\ *noun* (1812)
**1** : one who employs symbols or symbolism
**2** : one skilled in the interpretation or explication of symbols
**3** : one of a group of writers and artists in France after 1880 reacting against realism, concerning themselves with general truths instead of actualities, exalting the metaphysical and the mysterious, and aiming to unify and blend the arts and the functions of the senses
— **symbolist** *adjective*

**sym·bol·is·tic** \,sim-bə-'lis-tik\ *adjective* (circa 1864)
: SYMBOLIC

**sym·bol·i·za·tion** \,sim-bə-lə-'zā-shən\ *noun* (1603)
**1** : an act or instance of symbolizing
**2** : the human capacity to develop a system of meaningful symbols

**sym·bol·ize** \'sim-bə-,līz\ *verb* **-ized; -iz·ing** (1603)
*transitive verb*
**1** : to serve as a symbol of
**2** : to represent, express, or identify by a symbol
*intransitive verb*
: to use symbols or symbolism
— **sym·bol·iz·er** *noun*

**sym·bol·o·gy** \sim-'bä-lə-jē\ *noun*, *plural* **-gies** [*symbol* + *-logy*] (1840)
**1** : the art of expression by symbols
**2** : the study or interpretation of symbols
**3** : a system of symbols

**sym·met·al·ism** \(,)si(m)-'me-t°l-,i-zəm\ *noun* [*syn-* + *-metallism* (as in *bimetallism*)] (circa 1895)
: a system of coinage in which the unit of currency consists of a particular weight of an alloy of two or more metals

**sym·met·ri·cal** \sə-'me-tri-kəl\ *or* **sym·met·ric** \-trik\ *adjective* (1751)
**1** : having, involving, or exhibiting symmetry
**2** : having corresponding points whose connecting lines are bisected by a given point or perpendicularly bisected by a given line or plane ⟨*symmetrical* curves⟩
**3** *symmetric* : being such that the terms or variables may be interchanged without altering the value, character, or truth ⟨*symmetric* equations⟩ ⟨$R$ is a *symmetric* relation if $aRb$ implies $bRa$⟩
**4 a** : capable of division by a longitudinal plane into similar halves ⟨*symmetrical* plant parts⟩ **b** : having the same number of members in each whorl of floral leaves ⟨*symmetrical* flowers⟩
**5** : affecting corresponding parts simultaneously and similarly ⟨*symmetrical* rash⟩
**6** : exhibiting symmetry in a structural formula; *especially* : being a derivative with groups substituted symmetrically in the molecule
— **sym·met·ri·cal·ly** \-tri-k(ə-)lē\ *adverb*
— **sym·met·ri·cal·ness** \-kəl-nəs\ *noun*

**symmetric group** *noun* (1897)
: a permutation group that is composed of all of the permutations of $n$ things

**symmetric matrix** *noun* (circa 1949)
: a matrix that is its own transpose

**sym·me·trize** \'si-mə-,trīz\ *transitive verb* **-trized; -triz·ing** (1796)
: to make symmetrical
— **sym·me·tri·za·tion** \,si-mə-trə-'zā-shən\ *noun*

**sym·me·try** \'si-mə-trē\ *noun*, *plural* **-tries** [Latin *symmetria*, from Greek, from *symmetros*, from *syn-* + *metron* measure — more at MEASURE] (1541)
**1** : balanced proportions; *also* : beauty of form arising from balanced proportions
**2** : the property of being symmetrical; *especially* : correspondence in size, shape, and relative position of parts on opposite sides of a dividing line or median plane or about a center or axis — compare BILATERAL SYMMETRY, RADIAL SYMMETRY
**3** : a rigid motion of a geometric figure that determines a one-to-one mapping onto itself
**4** : the property of remaining invariant under certain changes (as of orientation in space, of the sign of the electric charge, of parity, or of the direction of time flow) — used of physical phenomena and of equations describing them

**sympath-** *or* **sympatho-** *combining form* [International Scientific Vocabulary, from *sympathetic*]
: sympathetic nerve ⟨*sympatho*lytic⟩

**sym·pa·thec·to·my** \,sim-pə-'thek-tə-mē\ *noun, plural* **-mies** [International Scientific Vocabulary] (1900)
: surgical interruption of sympathetic nerve pathways
— **sym·pa·thec·to·mized** \-,mīzd\ *adjective*

¹**sym·pa·thet·ic** \,sim-pə-'the-tik\ *adjective* [New Latin *sympatheticus,* from Latin *sympathia* sympathy] (1644)
**1** : existing or operating through an affinity, interdependence, or mutual association
**2 a** : not discordant or antagonistic **b** : appropriate to one's mood, inclinations, or disposition **c** : marked by kindly or pleased appreciation
**3** : given to, marked by, or arising from sympathy, compassion, friendliness, and sensitivity to others' emotions ⟨a *sympathetic* gesture⟩
**4** : favorably inclined : APPROVING ⟨not *sympathetic* to the idea⟩
**5 a** : showing empathy **b** : arousing sympathy or compassion ⟨a *sympathetic* role in the play⟩
**6 a** : of or relating to the sympathetic nervous system **b** : mediated by or acting on the sympathetic nerves
**7** : relating to musical tones produced by sympathetic vibration or to strings so tuned as to sound by sympathetic vibration
— **sym·pa·thet·i·cal·ly** \-ti-k(ə-)lē\ *adverb*

²**sympathetic** *noun* (1808)
: a sympathetic structure; *especially* : SYMPATHETIC NERVOUS SYSTEM

**sympathetic magic** *noun* (1905)
: magic based on the assumption that a person or thing can be supernaturally affected through its name or an object representing it

**sympathetic nervous system** *noun* (circa 1891)
: the part of the autonomic nervous system that contains chiefly adrenergic fibers and tends to depress secretion, decrease the tone and contractility of smooth muscle, and increase heart rate — compare PARASYMPATHETIC NERVOUS SYSTEM

**sympathetic strike** *noun* (1895)
: SYMPATHY STRIKE

**sympathetic vibration** *noun* (1898)
: a vibration produced in one body by the vibrations of exactly the same period in a neighboring body

**sym·pa·thin** \'sim-pə-thən\ *noun* [International Scientific Vocabulary] (1931)
: a substance (as norepinephrine) that is secreted by sympathetic nerve endings and acts as a chemical mediator

**sym·pa·thise** *chiefly British variant of* SYMPATHIZE

**sym·pa·thize** \'sim-pə-,thīz\ *intransitive verb* **-thized; -thiz·ing** (1591)
**1** : to be in keeping, accord, or harmony
**2** : to react or respond in sympathy
**3** : to share in suffering or grief : COMMISERATE ⟨*sympathize* with a friend in trouble⟩; *also* : to express such sympathy
**4** : to be in sympathy intellectually ⟨*sympathize* with a proposal⟩
— **sym·pa·thiz·er** *noun*

**sym·pa·tho·lyt·ic** \,sim-pə-thō-'li-tik\ *adjective* [International Scientific Vocabulary] (1943)
: tending to oppose the physiological results of sympathetic nervous activity or of sympathomimetic drugs
— **sympatholytic** *noun*

**sym·pa·tho·mi·met·ic** \-mə-'me-tik, -(,)mī-\ *adjective* [International Scientific Vocabulary] (1910)
: simulating sympathetic nervous action in physiological effect
— **sympathomimetic** *noun*

**sym·pa·thy** \'sim-pə-thē\ *noun, plural* **-thies** [Latin *sympathia,* from Greek *sympatheia,* from *sympathēs* having common feelings, sympathetic, from *syn-* + *pathos* feelings,

emotion, experience — more at PATHOS] (1579)
**1 a** : an affinity, association, or relationship between persons or things wherein whatever affects one similarly affects the other **b** : mutual or parallel susceptibility or a condition brought about by it **c** : unity or harmony in action or effect
**2 a** : inclination to think or feel alike : emotional or intellectual accord **b** : feeling of loyalty : tendency to favor or support ⟨republican *sympathies*⟩
**3 a** : the act or capacity of entering into or sharing the feelings or interests of another **b** : the feeling or mental state brought about by such sensitivity ⟨have *sympathy* for the poor⟩
**4** : the correlation existing between bodies capable of communicating their vibrational energy to one another through some medium
*synonym* see ATTRACTION, PITY

**sympathy strike** *noun* (1912)
: a strike in which the strikers have no direct grievance against their own employer but attempt to support or aid usually another group of workers on strike

**sym·pat·ric** \sim-'pa-trik\ *adjective* [*syn-* + Greek *patra* fatherland, from *patēr* father — more at FATHER] (circa 1904)
: occurring in the same area; *specifically* : occupying the same range without loss of identity from interbreeding ⟨*sympatric* species⟩ — compare ALLOPATRIC
— **sym·pat·ri·cal·ly** \-tri-k(ə-)lē\ *adverb*
— **sym·pat·ry** \'sim-,pa-trē\ *noun*

**sym·pet·al·ous** \(,)sim-'pe-tᵊl-əs\ *adjective* (circa 1877)
: GAMOPETALOUS
— **sym·pet·aly** \-tᵊl-ē, 'sim-,\ *noun*

**sym·phon·ic** \sim-'fä-nik\ *adjective* (1856)
**1** : HARMONIOUS, SYMPHONIOUS
**2** : relating to or having the form or character of a symphony ⟨*symphonic* music⟩
**3** : suggestive of a symphony especially in form, interweaving of themes, or harmonious arrangement ⟨a *symphonic* drama⟩
— **sym·phon·i·cal·ly** \-ni-k(ə-)lē\ *adverb*

**symphonic poem** *noun* (1873)
: an extended programmatic composition for symphony orchestra usually freer in form than a symphony

**sym·pho·ni·ous** \sim-'fō-nē-əs\ *adjective* (1652)
: agreeing especially in sound : HARMONIOUS
— **sym·pho·ni·ous·ly** *adverb*

**sym·pho·nist** \'sim(p)-fə-nist\ *noun* (1767)
**1** : a member of a symphony orchestra
**2** : a composer of symphonies

**sym·pho·ny** \-nē\ *noun, plural* **-nies** [Middle English *symphonie,* from Middle French, from Latin *symphonia,* from Greek *symphōnia,* from *symphōnos* concordant in sound, from *syn-* + *phōnē* voice, sound — more at BAN] (15th century)
**1** : consonance of sounds
**2 a** : RITORNELLO 1 **b** : SINFONIA 1 **c** (1) : a usually long and complex sonata for symphony orchestra (2) : a musical composition (as for organ) resembling such a symphony in complexity or variety
**3** : consonance or harmony of color (as in a painting)
**4 a** : SYMPHONY ORCHESTRA **b** : a symphony orchestra concert
**5** : something that in its harmonious complexity or variety suggests a symphonic composition

**symphony orchestra** *noun* (circa 1881)
: a large orchestra of winds, strings, and percussion that plays symphonic works

**sym·phy·se·al** \,sim(p)-fə-'sē-əl\ *also* **sym·phys·i·al** \sim-'fi-zē-əl\ *adjective* [Greek *symphyse-, symphysis* symphysis] (circa 1836)
: of, relating to, or constituting a symphysis

**sym·phy·sis** \'sim(p)-fə-səs\ *noun, plural* **-phy·ses** \-,sēz\ [New Latin, from Greek, state of growing together, from *symphyesthai*

to grow together, from *syn-* + *phyein* to make grow, bring forth — more at BE] (circa 1578)
**1** : an immovable or more or less movable articulation of various bones in the median plane of the body
**2** : an articulation in which the bony surfaces are connected by pads of fibrous cartilage without a synovial membrane

**sym·po·di·al** \sim-'pō-dē-əl\ *adjective* [New Latin *sympodium* apparent main axis formed from secondary axes, from Greek *syn-* + *podion* base — more at -PODIUM] (1875)
: having or involving the formation of an apparent main axis from successive secondary axes ⟨*sympodial* branching of a cyme⟩

**sym·po·si·arch** \sim-'pō-zē-,ärk\ *noun* [Greek *symposiarchos,* from *symposion* symposium + *-archos* -arch] (1603)
: one who presides over a symposium

**sym·po·si·ast** \-zē-,ast, -əst\ *noun* [Greek *symposiazein* to take part in a symposium, from *symposion*] (circa 1656)
: a contributor to a symposium

**sym·po·sium** \sim-'pō-zē-əm *also* -zh(ē-)əm\ *noun, plural* **-sia** \-zē-ə, -zh(ē-)ə\ *or* **-siums** [Latin, from Greek *symposion,* from *sympinein* to drink together, from *syn-* + *pinein* to drink — more at POTABLE] (1711)
**1 a** : a convivial party (as after a banquet in ancient Greece) with music and conversation **b** : a social gathering at which there is free interchange of ideas
**2 a** : a formal meeting at which several specialists deliver short addresses on a topic or on related topics — compare COLLOQUIUM **b** : a collection of opinions on a subject; *especially* : one published by a periodical **c** : DISCUSSION
◆

**symp·tom** \'sim(p)-təm\ *noun* [Late Latin *symptomat-, symptoma,* from Greek *symptōmat-, symptōma* happening, attribute, symptom, from *sympiptein* to happen, from *syn-* + *piptein* to fall — more at FEATHER] (1541)
**1 a** : subjective evidence of disease or physical disturbance; *broadly* : something that indicates the presence of bodily disorder **b** : an evident reaction by a plant to a pathogen

---

◇ WORD HISTORY

**symposium** In ancient Greece the evening meal was often followed by a drinking party, attended only by men, that usually featured songs, games, and performances by hired entertainers. This party was called in Greek *symposion,* a derivative of *sympotēs* "drinking companion," itself formed from the prefix *syn-* "together" and *po-,* a variant stem of the verb *pinein* "to drink." For Greeks with somewhat loftier aspirations, the drinking became subordinate to the entertainment, which at its most exalted might take the form of philosophical discussion. The Platonic dialogue known as the *Symposium* is one example of a Greek literary genre that used conversation at a drinking party as a frame for extended treatment of a serious topic—in the case of Plato's work, love and beauty. The Greek word has been borrowed into English via Latin, but the *symposion* as philosophical discussion has influenced the modern use of English *symposium* more than actual Greek practice, and the stuffy academic connotations the word now has could hardly be further from the riotous excess more typical of the ancient *symposion.*

---

\ə\ **abut** \ᵊ\ **kitten** \ər\ **further** \a\ **ash** \ā\ **ace**
\ä\ **mop, mar** \aů\ **out** \ch\ **chin** \e\ **bet** \ē\ **easy**
\g\ **go** \i\ **hit** \ī\ **ice** \j\ **job** \ŋ\ **sing** \ō\ **go**
\ò\ **law** \òi\ **boy** \th\ **thin** \t̲h̲\ **the** \ü\ **loot** \ů\ **foot**
\y\ **yet** \zh\ **vision** *see also* Guide to Pronunciation

**2 a :** something that indicates the existence of something else ⟨*symptoms* of the time⟩ **b :** a slight indication **:** TRACE
**synonym** see SIGN
— **symp·tom·less** \-ləs\ *adjective*
**symp·tom·at·ic** \ˌsim(p)-tə-ˈma-tik\ *adjective* (1698)
**1 a :** being a symptom of a disease **b :** having the characteristics of a particular disease but arising from another cause
**2 :** concerned with or affecting symptoms
**3 :** CHARACTERISTIC, INDICATIVE ⟨his behavior was *symptomatic* of his character⟩
— **symp·tom·at·i·cal·ly** \-ti-k(ə-)lē\ *adverb*
**symp·tom·atol·o·gy** \ˌsim(p)-tə-mə-ˈtä-lə-jē\ *noun* (1798)
**1 :** the symptom complex of a disease
**2 :** a branch of medical science concerned with symptoms of diseases
— **symp·tom·at·o·log·i·cal** \-ˌma-tᵊl-ˈä-ji-kəl\ *or* **symp·tom·at·o·log·ic** \-ˈä-jik\ *adjective*
— **symp·tom·at·o·log·i·cal·ly** \-ji-k(ə-)lē\ *adverb*
**syn-** *or* **sym-** *prefix* [Middle English, from Old French, from Latin, from Greek, from *syn* with, together with]
**1 :** with **:** along with **:** together ⟨*synclinal*⟩ ⟨*sympetalous*⟩
**2 :** at the same time ⟨*synesthesia*⟩
**syn·ae·re·sis** *variant of* SYNERESIS
**syn·aes·the·sia** *variant of* SYNESTHESIA
**syn·aes·the·sis** \ˌsi-nəs-ˈthē-səs\ *noun* [Greek *synaisthēsis* joint perception, from *synaisthanesthai* to perceive simultaneously, from *syn-* + *aisthanesthai* to perceive — more at AUDIBLE] (1922)
**:** harmony of different or opposing impulses produced by a work of art
**syn·a·gogue** *or* **syn·a·gog** \ˈsi-nə-ˌgäg\ *noun* [Middle English *synagoge*, from Old French, from Late Latin *synagoga*, from Greek *synagōgē* assembly, synagogue, from *synagein* to bring together, from *syn-* + *agein* to lead — more at AGENT] (13th century)
**1 :** a Jewish congregation
**2 :** the house of worship and communal center of a Jewish congregation
— **syn·a·gog·al** \ˌsi-nə-ˈgä-gəl\ *adjective*
**syn·a·loe·pha** *or* **syn·a·le·pha** \ˌsi-nə-ˈlē-fə\ *noun* [New Latin, from Greek *synaloiphē*, from *synaleiphein* to clog up, coalesce, unite two syllables into one, from *syn-* + *aleiphein* to anoint — more at ALIPHATIC] (1540)
**:** the reduction to one syllable of two vowels of adjacent syllables (as in *th' army* for *the army*)
**¹syn·apse** \ˈsi-ˌnaps, sə-ˈnaps\ *noun* [New Latin *synapsis*, from Greek, juncture, from *synaptein* to fasten together, from *syn-* + *haptein* to fasten] (1899)
**:** the point at which a nervous impulse passes from one neuron to another
**²synapse** *intransitive verb* **syn·apsed; syn·aps·ing** (1910)
**1 :** to form a synapse
**2 :** to come together in synapsis
**syn·ap·sid** \sə-ˈnap-səd\ *noun* [New Latin *Synapsida*, from Greek *syn-* + *apsid-*, *apsis* arch, vault — more at APSIS] (1956)
**:** any of a subclass (Synapsida) of extinct reptiles existing during the Pennsylvanian, Permian, and Jurassic, having a single pair of lateral temporal openings in the skull, and usually held to be ancestral to mammals
— **synapsid** *adjective*
**syn·ap·sis** \sə-ˈnap-səs\ *noun, plural* **-ap·ses** \-ˌsēz\ [New Latin] (circa 1892)
**:** the association of homologous chromosomes that is characteristic of the first meiotic prophase
**syn·ap·tic** \sə-ˈnap-tik\ *adjective* [New Latin *synapsis*] (1895)
**1 :** of or relating to a synapsis
**2 :** of or relating to a synapse

— **syn·ap·ti·cal·ly** \-ti-k(ə-)lē\ *adverb*
**syn·ap·to·ne·mal complex** \sə-ˌnap-tə-ˈnē-məl-\ *noun* [*synaptic* + *-o-* or *-i-* + Greek *nēma* thread — more at NEMAT-] (1958)
**:** a complex tripartite protein structure that spans the region between synapsed chromosomes in meiotic prophase — called also *synap·ti·ne·mal complex* \sə-ˌnap-tə-ˈnē-məl-\
**syn·ap·to·some** \sə-ˈnap-tə-ˌsōm\ *noun* [*synaptic* + *-o-* + ³*-some*] (1964)
**:** a nerve ending that is isolated from homogenized nerve tissue
— **syn·ap·to·som·al** \-ˌnap-tə-ˈsō-məl\ *adjective*
**syn·ar·thro·di·al** \ˌsin-är-ˈthrō-dē-əl\ *adjective* [New Latin *synarthrodia* synarthrosis] (1830)
**:** of, relating to, or being a synarthrosis
**syn·ar·thro·sis** \-ˈthrō-səs\ *noun, plural* **-thro·ses** \-ˌsēz\ [Greek *synarthrōsis*, from *syn-* + *arthrōsis* arthrosis] (1578)
**:** an immovable articulation in which the bones are united by intervening fibrous connective tissues
**syn·car·pous** \(ˌ)sin-ˈkär-pəs\ *adjective* (circa 1830)
**:** having the carpels of the gynoecium united in a compound ovary
— **syn·car·py** \ˈsin-ˌkär-pē\ *noun*
**syn·cat·e·gor·e·mat·ic** \ˌsin-ˌka-tə-ˌgȯr-ə-ˈma-tik, -ˌgȯr-ē-\ *adjective* [Late Latin *syncategoremat-, syncategorema* syncategorematic term, from Greek *synkatēgorēma,* from *synkatēgorein* to predicate jointly, from *syn-* + *katēgorein* to predicate — more at CATEGORY] (1827)
**:** forming a meaningful expression only in conjunction with a denotative expression (as a content word) ⟨logical operators and function words are *syncategorematic*⟩
— **syn·cat·e·gor·e·mat·i·cal·ly** \-ti-k(ə-)lē\ *adverb*
**¹syn·chro** \ˈsiŋ-(ˌ)krō, ˈsin-\ *noun, plural* **synchros** [*synchronous*] (1943)
**:** SELSYN
**²synchro** *adjective* [*synchro-*] (1947)
**:** adapted to synchronization
**synchro-** *combining form* [*synchronized & synchronous*]
**:** synchronized **:** synchronous ⟨*synchromesh*⟩
**syn·chro·cy·clo·tron** \ˌsiŋ-(ˌ)krō-ˈsī-klə-ˌträn, ˌsin-\ *noun* (1947)
**:** a modified cyclotron that achieves greater energies for the charged particles by compensating for the variation in mass that the particles experience with increasing velocity
**syn·chro·mesh** \ˈsiŋ-krō-ˌmesh, ˈsin-\ *adjective* (1928)
**:** designed for effecting synchronized shifting of gears
— **synchromesh** *noun*
**syn·chro·nal** \ˈsiŋ-krə-nᵊl, ˈsin-\ *adjective* (1660)
**:** SYNCHRONOUS
**syn·chro·ne·ity** \ˌsiŋ-krə-ˈnē-ə-tē, ˌsin-, -ˈnā-\ *noun* [*synchron*ous + *-eity* (as in *spontaneity*)] (circa 1909)
**:** the state of being synchronous
**syn·chron·ic** \sin-ˈkrä-nik, siŋ-\ *adjective* (1833)
**1 :** SYNCHRONOUS
**2 a :** DESCRIPTIVE 4 ⟨*synchronic* linguistics⟩ **b :** concerned with events existing in a limited time period and ignoring historical antecedents
— **syn·chron·i·cal** \-ni-kəl\ *adjective*
— **syn·chron·i·cal·ly** \-ni-k(ə-)lē\ *adverb*
**syn·chro·nic·i·ty** \ˌsiŋ-krə-ˈni-sə-tē, ˌsin-\ *noun* (circa 1889)

**1 :** the quality or fact of being synchronous
**2 :** the coincidental occurrence of events and especially psychic events (as similar thoughts in widely separated persons or a mental image of an unexpected event before it happens) that seem related but are not explained by conventional mechanisms of causality — used especially in the psychology of C. G. Jung
**syn·chro·ni·sa·tion, syn·chro·nise** *British variant of* SYNCHRONIZATION, SYNCHRONIZE
**syn·chro·nism** \ˈsiŋ-krə-ˌni-zəm, ˈsin-\ *noun* (1588)
**1 :** the quality or state of being synchronous **:** SIMULTANEOUSNESS
**2 :** chronological arrangement of historical events and personages so as to indicate coincidence or coexistence; *also* **:** a table showing such concurrences
— **syn·chro·nis·tic** \ˌsiŋ-krə-ˈnis-tik, ˌsin-\ *adjective*
**syn·chro·ni·za·tion** \ˌsiŋ-krə-nə-ˈzā-shən, ˌsin-\ *noun* (1828)
**1 :** the act or result of synchronizing
**2 :** the state of being synchronous
**syn·chro·nize** \ˈsiŋ-krə-ˌnīz, ˈsin-\ *verb* **-nized; -niz·ing** (circa 1624)
*intransitive verb*
**:** to happen at the same time
*transitive verb*
**1 :** to represent or arrange (events) to indicate coincidence or coexistence
**2 :** to make synchronous in operation
**3 :** to make (motion picture sound) exactly simultaneous with the action
— **syn·chro·niz·er** *noun*
**synchronized swimming** *noun* (1950)
**:** swimming in which the movements of one or more swimmers are synchronized with a musical accompaniment so as to form changing patterns
**syn·chro·nous** \ˈsiŋ-krə-nəs, ˈsin-\ *adjective* [Late Latin *synchronos*, from Greek, from *syn-* + *chronos* time] (1669)
**1 :** happening, existing, or arising at precisely the same time
**2 :** recurring or operating at exactly the same periods
**3 :** involving or indicating synchronism
**4 a :** having the same period; *also* **:** having the same period and phase **b :** GEOSTATIONARY
**5 :** of, used in, or being digital communication (as between computers) in which a common timing signal is established that dictates when individual bits can be transmitted, in which characters are not individually delimited, and which allows for very high rates of data transfer
**synonym** see CONTEMPORARY
— **syn·chro·nous·ly** *adverb*
— **syn·chro·nous·ness** *noun*
**synchronous motor** *noun* (1897)
**:** an electric motor having a speed strictly proportional to the frequency of the operating current
**syn·chro·ny** \ˈsiŋ-krə-nē, ˈsin-\ *noun, plural* **-nies** (1848)
**:** synchronistic occurrence, arrangement, or treatment
**syn·chro·scope** \-ˌskōp\ *noun* (1907)
**:** any of several devices for showing whether two associated machines or moving parts are operating in synchronism with each other
**syn·chro·tron** \ˈsiŋ-krə-ˌträn, ˈsin-\ *noun* (1945)
**1 :** an apparatus for imparting very high speeds to charged particles by means of a combination of a high-frequency electric field and a low-frequency magnetic field
**2 :** SYNCHROTRON RADIATION
**synchrotron radiation** *noun* [from its having been first observed in a synchrotron] (1956)
**:** radiation emitted by high-energy charged relativistic particles (as electrons) when they are accelerated by a magnetic field (as in a nebula)

**¹sync** *also* **synch** \ˈsiŋk\ *transitive verb* **synced** *also* **synched** \ˈsiŋ(k)t\; **sync·ing** *also* **synch·ing** \ˈsiŋ-kiŋ\ (1929)
**:** SYNCHRONIZE
**²sync** *also* **synch** *noun* (1937)
**:** SYNCHRONIZATION, SYNCHRONISM
— **sync** *adjective*

**syn·cli·nal** \(,)sin-'klī-n°l\ *adjective* [Greek *syn-* + *klinein* to lean — more at LEAN] (1833)
**1 :** inclined down from opposite directions so as to meet
**2 :** having or relating to a folded rock structure in which the sides dip toward a common line or plane
**syn·cline** \'sin-,klīn\ *noun* [back-formation from synclinal] (1873)
**:** a trough of stratified rock in which the beds dip toward each other from either side — compare ANTICLINE

cross section of strata showing syncline

**syn·co·pate** \'siŋ-kə-,pāt, 'sin-\ *transitive verb* **-pat·ed; -pat·ing** (1605)
**1 a :** to shorten or produce by syncope ⟨*syncopate suppose* to *s'pose*⟩ **b :** to cut short : CLIP, ABBREVIATE
**2 :** to modify or affect (musical rhythm) by syncopation
— **syn·co·pa·tor** \-,pā-tər\ *noun*
**syncopated** *adjective* (1665)
**1 :** cut short : ABBREVIATED
**2 :** marked by or exhibiting syncopation ⟨*syncopated* rhythm⟩
**syn·co·pa·tion** \,siŋ-kə-'pā-shən, ,sin-\ *noun* (1597)
**1 :** a temporary displacement of the regular metrical accent in music caused typically by stressing the weak beat
**2 :** a syncopated rhythm, passage, or dance step
— **syn·co·pa·tive** \'siŋ-kə-,pā-tiv, 'sin-\ *adjective*
**syn·co·pe** \'siŋ-kə-(,)pē, 'sin-\ *noun* [Late Latin, from Greek *synkopē*, literally, cutting short, from *synkoptein* to cut short, from *syn-* + *koptein* to cut — more at CAPON] (circa 1550)
**1 :** loss of consciousness resulting from insufficient blood flow to the brain : FAINT
**2 :** the loss of one or more sounds or letters in the interior of a word (as in *fo'c'sle* for *forecastle*)
— **syn·co·pal** \-kə-pəl\ *adjective*
**syn·cret·ic** \sin-'kre-tik, siŋ-\ *adjective* (1840)
**:** characterized or brought about by syncretism
**:** SYNCRETISTIC
**syn·cre·tise** *British variant of* SYNCRETIZE
**syn·cre·tism** \'siŋ-krə-,ti-zəm, 'sin-\ *noun* [New Latin *syncretismus*, from Greek *synkrētismos* federation of Cretan cities, from *syn-* + *Krēt-, Krēs* Cretan] (1618)
**1 :** the combination of different forms of belief or practice
**2 :** the fusion of two or more originally different inflectional forms
— **syn·cre·tist** \-tist\ *noun or adjective*
— **syn·cre·tis·tic** \,siŋ-krə-'tis-tik, ,sin-\ *adjective*
**syn·cre·tize** \'siŋ-krə-,tīz, 'sin-\ *transitive verb* **-tized; -tiz·ing** (circa 1891)
**:** to attempt to unite and harmonize especially without critical examination or logical unity
**syn·cy·tium** \sin-'si-sh(ē-)əm\ *noun, plural* **-tia** \-sh(ē-)ə\ [New Latin, from *syn-* + *cyt-*] (1877)
**1 :** a multinucleate mass of protoplasm (as in the plasmodium of a slime mold) resulting from fusion of cells
**2 :** COENOCYTE 1
— **syn·cy·tial** \-'si-sh(ē-)əl\ *adjective*
**syn·dac·ty·lism** \(,)sin-'dak-tə-,li-zəm\ *noun* (1889)
**:** SYNDACTYLY
**syn·dac·ty·ly** \-lē\ *noun* [New Latin *syndactylia*, from *syn-* + Greek *daktylos* finger] (1864)
**:** a union of two or more digits that is normal in some animals (as various marsupials) and

occurs as a human hereditary disorder marked by webbing of two or more fingers or toes
**syn·des·mo·sis** \,sin-,dez-'mō-səs, -,des-\ *noun, plural* **-mo·ses** \-,sēz\ [New Latin, from Greek *syndesmos* fastening, ligament, from *syndein*] (1726)
**:** an articulation in which the contiguous surfaces of the bones are rough and are bound together by a ligament
**syn·det·ic** \sin-'de-tik\ *adjective* [Greek *syndetikos*, from *syndein* to bind together — more at ASYNDETON] (1621)
**:** CONNECTIVE, CONNECTING ⟨*syndetic* pronoun⟩; *also* **:** marked by a conjunctive ⟨*syndetic* relative clause⟩
— **syn·det·i·cal·ly** \-ti-k(ə-)lē\ *adverb*
**syn·dic** \'sin-dik\ *noun* [French, from Late Latin *syndicus* representative of a corporation, from Greek *syndikos* assistant at law, advocate, representative of a state, from *syn-* + *dikē* judgment, case at law — more at DICTION] (1601)
**1 :** a municipal magistrate in some countries
**2 :** an agent of a university or corporation
**syn·di·cal** \-di-kəl\ *adjective* (1864)
**1 :** of or relating to a syndic or to a committee that assumes the powers of a syndic
**2 :** of or relating to syndicalism
**syn·di·cal·ism** \'sin-di-kə-,li-zəm\ *noun* [French *syndicalisme*, from *chambre syndicale* trade union] (1907)
**1 :** a revolutionary doctrine by which workers seize control of the economy and the government by direct means (as a general strike)
**2 :** a system of economic organization in which industries are owned and managed by the workers
**3 :** a theory of government based on functional rather than territorial representation
— **syn·di·cal·ist** \-list\ *adjective or noun*
**¹syn·di·cate** \'sin-di-kət\ *noun* [French *syndicat*, from *syndic*] (1624)
**1 a :** a council or body of syndics **b :** the office or jurisdiction of a syndic
**2 :** an association of persons officially authorized to undertake a duty or negotiate business
**3 a :** a group of persons or concerns who combine to carry out a particular transaction **b :** CARTEL 2 **c :** a loose association of racketeers in control of organized crime
**4 :** a business concern that sells materials for publication in a number of newspapers or periodicals simultaneously
**5 :** a group of newspapers under one management
**²syn·di·cate** \'sin-də-,kāt\ *verb* **-cat·ed; -cat·ing** (1882)
*transitive verb*
**1 :** to subject to or manage as a syndicate
**2 a :** to sell (as a cartoon) to a syndicate or for publication in many newspapers or periodicals at once **b :** to sell (as a series of television programs) directly to local stations
*intransitive verb*
**:** to unite to form a syndicate
— **syn·di·ca·tion** \,sin-də-'kā-shən\ *noun*
— **syn·di·ca·tor** \'sin-də-,kā-tər\ *noun*
**syn·drome** \'sin-,drōm *also* -drəm\ *noun* [New Latin, from Greek *syndromē* combination, syndrome, from *syn-* + *dramein* to run — more at DROMEDARY] (1541)
**1 :** a group of signs and symptoms that occur together and characterize a particular abnormality
**2 :** a set of concurrent things (as emotions or actions) that usually form an identifiable pattern
**¹syne** \'sīn\ *adverb* [Middle English (northern), probably from Old Norse *sīthan;* akin to Old English *siththan* since — more at SINCE] (14th century)
*chiefly Scottish* **:** since then **:** AGO
**²syne** *conjunction or preposition* (14th century)
*Scottish* **:** SINCE

**syn·ec·do·che** \sə-'nek-də-(,)kē\ *noun* [Latin, from Greek *synekdochē*, from *syn-* + *ekdochē* sense, interpretation, from *ekdechesthai* to receive, understand, from *ex* + *dechesthai* to receive; akin to Greek *dokein* to seem good — more at EX-, DECENT] (15th century)
**:** a figure of speech by which a part is put for the whole (as *fifty sail* for *fifty ships*), the whole for a part (as *society* for *high society*), the species for the genus (as *cutthroat* for *assassin*), the genus for the species (as *a creature* for *a man*), or the name of the material for the thing made (as *boards* for *stage*)
— **syn·ec·doch·ic** \,si-,nek-'dä-kik\ *adjective*
— **syn·ec·doch·i·cal** \-'dä-ki-kəl\ *adjective*
— **syn·ec·doch·i·cal·ly** \-ki-k(ə-)lē\ *adverb*
**syn·ecol·o·gy** \,si-ni-'kä-lə-jē, ,si-ne-\ *noun* [German *Synökologie*, from *syn-* syn- + *Ökologie* ecology] (1910)
**:** a branch of ecology that deals with the structure, development, and distribution of ecological communities
— **syn·eco·log·i·cal** \,si-,nē-kə-'lä-ji-kəl, ,si-ne-\ *adjective*
**syn·er·e·sis** \sə-'ner-ə-səs, -'nir-, *especially for 2* ,si-nə-'rē-\ *noun* [Late Latin *synaeresis*, from Greek *synairesis*, from *synairein* to contract, from *syn-* + *hairein* to take] (circa 1577)
**1 :** SYNIZESIS
**2 :** the separation of liquid from a gel caused by contraction
**syn·er·get·ic** \,si-nər-'je-tik\ *adjective* [Greek *synergētikos*, from *synergein* to work with, cooperate, from *synergos* working together, from *syn-* + *ergon* work — more at WORK] (circa 1836)
**:** SYNERGIC
**syn·er·gic** \sə-'nər-jik\ *adjective* (circa 1859)
**:** working together **:** COOPERATING
— **syn·er·gi·cal·ly** \-ji-k(ə-)lē\ *adverb*
**syn·er·gid** \sə-'nər-jəd, 'si-nər-\ *noun* [New Latin *synergida*, from Greek *synergos* working together] (1898)
**:** one of two small cells lying near the micropyle of the embryo sac of an angiosperm
**syn·er·gism** \'si-nər-,ji-zəm\ *noun* [New Latin *synergismus*, from Greek *synergos*] (1910)
**:** interaction of discrete agencies (as industrial firms), agents (as drugs), or conditions such that the total effect is greater than the sum of the individual effects
**syn·er·gist** \-jist\ *noun* (1876)
**:** something (as a chemical or a muscle) that enhances the effectiveness of an active agent; *broadly* **:** either member of a synergistic pair
**syn·er·gis·tic** \,si-nər-'jis-tik\ *adjective* (circa 1847)
**1 :** having the capacity to act in synergism ⟨*synergistic* drugs⟩
**2 :** of, relating to, or resembling synergism ⟨a *synergistic* reaction⟩
— **syn·er·gis·ti·cal·ly** \-ti-k(ə-)lē\ *adverb*
**syn·er·gy** \'si-nər-jē\ *noun* [New Latin *synergia*, from Greek *synergos* working together] (1660)
**:** SYNERGISM; *broadly* **:** combined action or operation
**syn·e·sis** \'si-nə-səs\ *noun* [New Latin, from Greek, understanding, sense, from *synienai* to bring together, understand, from *syn-* + *hienai* to send — more at JET] (circa 1891)
**:** a grammatical construction in which agreement or reference is according to sense rather than strict syntax (as *anyone* and *them* in "if anyone calls, tell them I am out")

**syn·es·the·sia** \,si-nəs-'thē-zh(ē-)ə\ *noun* [New Latin, from *syn-* + *-esthesia* (as in *anesthesia*)] (circa 1891)
: a concomitant sensation; *especially* : a subjective sensation or image of a sense (as of color) other than the one (as of sound) being stimulated
— **syn·es·thet·ic** \-'the-tik\ *adjective*

**syn·fu·el** \'sin-,fyü(-ə)l\ *noun* [synthetic + fuel] (1976)
: a liquid or gaseous fuel derived especially from a fossil fuel that is a solid (as coal) or part of a solid (as tar sand or oil shale)

**syn·ga·my** \'sin-gə-mē\ *noun* [International Scientific Vocabulary] (1904)
: sexual reproduction by union of gametes

**syn·gas** \'sin-,gas\ *noun* (1975)
: SYNTHESIS GAS

**syn·ge·ne·ic** \,sin-jə-'nē-ik\ *adjective* [*syn-* + *-geneic* (as in *isogeneic*)] (1961)
: genetically identical or similar especially with respect to antigens or immunological reactions ⟨*syngeneic* tumor cells⟩ ⟨grafts between *syngeneic* mice⟩ — compare ALLOGENEIC, XENOGENEIC

**syn·i·ze·sis** \,si-nə-'zē-səs\ *noun* [Late Latin, from Greek *synizēsis*, from *synizein* to sit down together, collapse, blend, from *syn-* + *hizein* to sit down; akin to Latin *sidere* to sit down — more at SUBSIDE] (1846)
: contraction of two syllables into one by uniting in pronunciation two adjacent vowels

**syn·kary·on** \sin-'kar-ē-,än, -ē-ən\ *noun* [New Latin, from Greek *syn-* + *karyon* nut — more at CAREEN] (1905)
: a cell nucleus formed by the fusion of two preexisting nuclei

**syn·od** \'si-nəd *also* -,äd\ *noun* [Middle English *sinod*, from Late Latin *synodus*, from Late Greek *synodos*, from Greek, meeting, assembly, from *syn-* + *hodos* way, journey] (14th century)
**1** : an ecclesiastical governing or advisory council: as **a** : the governing assembly of an Episcopal province **b** : a Presbyterian governing body ranking between the presbytery and the general assembly **c** : a regional or national organization of Lutheran congregations
**2** : the ecclesiastical district governed by a synod
— **syn·od·al** \'si-nə-dᵊl, -,nä-; sə-'nä-dᵊl\ *adjective*

**syn·od·ic** \sə-'nä-dik *or* **syn·od·i·cal** \-di-kəl\ *adjective* (1561)
**1** : of or relating to a synod : SYNODAL
**2** *usually* synodic [Greek *synodikos*, from *synodos* meeting, conjunction] : relating to conjunction; *especially* : relating to the period between two successive conjunctions of the same celestial bodies (as the moon and the sun)

**synodic month** *noun* (1654)
: a lunar month

**syn·o·nym** \'si-nə-,nim\ *noun* [Middle English *sinonyme*, from Latin *synonymum*, from Greek *synōnymon*, from neuter of *synōnymos* synonymous, from *syn-* + *onyma* name — more at NAME] (15th century)
**1** : one of two or more words or expressions of the same language that have the same or nearly the same meaning in some or all senses
**2** : a symbolic or figurative name : METONYM
**3** : a taxonomic name rejected as being incorrectly applied or incorrect in form — compare HOMONYM
— **syn·o·nym·ic** \,si-nə-'ni-mik\ *also* **syn·o·nym·i·cal** \-mi-kəl\ *adjective*
— **syn·o·nym·i·ty** \-'ni-mə-tē\ *noun*

**syn·on·y·mist** \sə-'nä-nə-mist\ *noun* (circa 1753)
: one who lists, studies, or discriminates synonyms

**syn·on·y·mize** \-,mīz\ *transitive verb* **-mized; -miz·ing** (circa 1595)

**1 a** : to give or analyze the synonyms of (a word) **b** : to provide (as a dictionary) with synonymies
**2** : to demonstrate (a taxonomic name) to be a synonym

**syn·on·y·mous** \-məs\ *adjective* (1610)
**1** : having the character of a synonym; *also* : alike in meaning or significance
**2** : having the same connotations, implications, or reference ⟨to runners, Boston is *synonymous* with marathon —*Runners World*⟩
— **syn·on·y·mous·ly** *adverb*

**syn·on·y·my** \-mē\ *noun, plural* **-mies** (1683)
**1 a** : a list or collection of synonyms often defined and discriminated from each other **b** : the study or discrimination of synonyms
**2** : the scientific names that have been used in different publications to designate a taxonomic group (as a species); *also* : a list of these
**3** : the quality or state of being synonymous

**syn·op·sis** \sə-'näp-səs\ *noun, plural* **-op·ses** \-,sēz\ [Late Latin, from Greek, literally, comprehensive view, from *synopsesthai* to be going to see together, from *syn-* + *opsesthai* to be going to see — more at OPTIC] (1611)
**1** : a condensed statement or outline (as of a narrative or treatise) : ABSTRACT
**2** : the abbreviated conjugation of a verb in one person only

**syn·op·size** \-,sīz\ *transitive verb* **-sized; -siz·ing** (1882)
**1** : EPITOMIZE
**2** : to make a synopsis of (as a novel)

**syn·op·tic** \sə-'näp-tik\ *also* **syn·op·ti·cal** \-ti-kəl\ *adjective* [Greek *synoptikos*, from *synopsesthai*] (1763)
**1** : affording a general view of a whole
**2** : manifesting or characterized by comprehensiveness or breadth of view
**3** : presenting or taking the same or common view; *specifically, often capitalized* : of or relating to the first three Gospels of the New Testament
**4** : relating to or displaying conditions (as of the atmosphere or weather) as they exist simultaneously over a broad area
— **syn·op·ti·cal·ly** \-ti-k(ə-)lē\ *adverb*

**syn·os·to·sis** \,si-,näs-'tō-səs\ *noun, plural* **-to·ses** \-,sēz\ [New Latin] (circa 1848)
: union of two or more separate bones to form a single bone

**sy·no·via** \sə-'nō-vē-ə, sī-\ *noun* [New Latin] (1726)
: a transparent viscid lubricating fluid secreted by a membrane of an articulation, bursa, or tendon sheath

**sy·no·vi·al** \-vē-əl\ *adjective* (1756)
: of, relating to, secreting, or being synovia ⟨*synovial* membranes⟩ ⟨*synovial* fluid⟩

**sy·no·vi·tis** \,sī-nə-'vī-təs\ *noun* (circa 1836)
: inflammation of a synovial membrane

**syn·tac·tic** \sin-'tak-tik\ *or* **syn·tac·ti·cal** \-ti-kəl\ *adjective* [New Latin *syntacticus*, from Greek *syntaktikos* arranging together, from *syntassein*] (1577)
: of, relating to, or according to the rules of syntax or syntactics
— **syn·tac·ti·cal·ly** \-ti-k(ə-)lē\ *adverb*

**syn·tac·tics** \-tiks\ *noun plural but singular or plural in construction* (1937)
: a branch of semiotic that deals with the formal relations between signs or expressions in abstraction from their signification and their interpreters

**syn·tag·ma** \sin-'tag-mə\ *noun, plural* **-mas** *or* **-ma·ta** \-mə-tə\ [Greek, from *syntassein*] (1937)
: a syntactic element
— **syn·tag·mat·ic** \,sin-,tag-'ma-tik\ *adjective*

**syn·tax** \'sin-,taks\ *noun* [French or Late Latin; French *syntaxe*, from Late Latin *syntaxis*, from Greek, from *syntassein* to arrange together, from *syn-* + *tassein* to arrange] (1574)
**1 a** : the way in which linguistic elements (as

words) are put together to form constituents (as phrases or clauses) **b** : the part of grammar dealing with this
**2** : a connected or orderly system : harmonious arrangement of parts or elements
**3** : syntactics especially as dealing with the formal properties of languages or calculi

**synth** \'sin(t)th\ *noun, often attributive* (1976)
: SYNTHESIZER 2

**syn·the·sis** \'sin(t)-thə-səs\ *noun, plural* **-the·ses** \-,sēz\ [Greek, from *syntithenai* to put together, from *syn-* + *tithenai* to put, place — more at DO] (1589)
**1 a** : the composition or combination of parts or elements so as to form a whole **b** : the production of a substance by the union of chemical elements, groups, or simpler compounds or by the degradation of a complex compound **c** : the combining of often diverse conceptions into a coherent whole; *also* : the complex so formed
**2 a** : deductive reasoning **b** : the dialectic combination of thesis and antithesis into a higher stage of truth
**3** : the frequent and systematic use of inflected forms as a characteristic device of a language
— **syn·the·sist** \-sist\ *noun*

**synthesis gas** *noun* (circa 1941)
: a mixture of carbon monoxide and hydrogen used especially in chemical synthesis

**syn·the·size** \-,sīz\ *verb* **-sized; -siz·ing** (1830)
*transitive verb*
**1** : to combine or produce by synthesis
**2** : to make a synthesis of
*intransitive verb*
: to make a synthesis

**syn·the·siz·er** \-,sī-zər\ *noun* (1869)
**1** : one that synthesizes ⟨an expert *synthesizer* of diverse views⟩
**2** : a usually computerized electronic apparatus for the production and control of sound (as for producing music)

**syn·the·tase** \'sin-thə-,tās, -,tāz\ *noun* [*synthetic* + *-ase*] (1947)
: an enzyme that catalyzes the linking together of two molecules usually using the energy derived from the concurrent splitting off of a pyrophosphate group from a triphosphate (as ATP) — called also *ligase*

**¹syn·thet·ic** \sin-'the-tik\ *adjective* [Greek *synthetikos* of composition, component, from *syntithenai* to put together] (1697)
**1** : relating to or involving synthesis : not analytic
**2** : attributing to a subject something determined by observation rather than analysis of the nature of the subject and not resulting in self-contradiction if negated — compare ANALYTIC
**3** : characterized by frequent and systematic use of inflected forms to express grammatical relationships
**4 a** (1) : of, relating to, or produced by chemical or biochemical synthesis; *especially* : produced artificially ⟨*synthetic* drugs⟩ ⟨*synthetic* silk⟩ (2) : of or relating to a synfuel **b** : devised, arranged, or fabricated for special situations to imitate or replace usual realities **c** : FACTITIOUS, BOGUS
— **syn·thet·i·cal·ly** \-ti-k(ə-)lē\ *adverb*

**²synthetic** *noun* (1946)
: something resulting from synthesis rather than occurring naturally; *especially* : a product (as a drug or plastic) of chemical synthesis

**synthetic division** *noun* (1904)
: a simplified method for dividing a polynomial by another polynomial of the first degree by writing down only the coefficients of the several powers of the variable and changing the sign of the constant term in the divisor so as to replace the usual subtractions by additions

**synthetic geometry** *noun* (1889)
: elementary euclidean geometry or projective geometry as distinguished from analytic geometry

**synthetic resin** *noun* (1907)
: RESIN 2

**syph** \'sif\ *noun* (circa 1914)
*slang* : SYPHILIS

**syph·i·lis** \'si-f(ə-)ləs\ *noun* [New Latin, from *Syphilus*, hero of the poem *Syphilis sive Morbus Gallicus* (*Syphilis or the French disease*) (1530) by Girolamo Fracastoro (died 1553) Italian poet, physician, and astronomer] (1718)
: a chronic contagious usually venereal and often congenital disease caused by a spirochete (*Treponema pallidum*) and if left untreated producing chancres, rashes, and systemic lesions in a clinical course with three stages continued over many years — compare PRIMARY SYPHILIS, SECONDARY SYPHILIS, TERTIARY SYPHILIS ◆
— **syph·i·lit·ic** \,si-fə-'li-tik\ *adjective or noun*

**sy·phon** *variant of* SIPHON

**Sy·rette** \sə-'ret\ *trademark*
— used for a small collapsible tube fitted with a hypodermic needle for injecting a single dose of a medicinal agent

**Syr·i·ac** \'sir-ē-,ak\ *noun* [Latin *syriacus* Syrian, from Greek *syriakos*, from *Syria*, ancient country in Asia] (1605)
**1** : a literary language based on an eastern Aramaic dialect and used as the literary and liturgical language by several eastern Christian churches
**2** : Aramaic spoken by Christian communities
— **Syriac** *adjective*

**Syr·i·an hamster** \'sir-ē-ən-\ *noun* [*Syria*, Asia] (circa 1949)
: GOLDEN HAMSTER

**sy·rin·ga** \sə-'riŋ-gə\ *noun* [New Latin, genus name, from Greek *syring-*, *syrinx* panpipe] (1664)
: MOCK ORANGE 1

¹**sy·ringe** \sə-'rinj *also* 'sir-inj\ *noun* [Middle English *syring*, from Medieval Latin *syringa*, from Late Latin, injection, from Greek *syring-*, *syrinx* panpipe, tube] (14th century)
: a device used to inject fluids into or withdraw them from something (as the body or its cavities): as **a** : a device that consists of a nozzle of varying length and a compressible rubber bulb and is used for injection or irrigation **b** : an instrument (as for the injection of medicine or the withdrawal of bodily fluids) that consists of a hollow barrel fitted with a plunger and a hollow needle **c** : a gravity device consisting of a reservoir fitted with a long rubber tube ending with an exchangeable nozzle that is used for irrigation of the vagina or bowel

²**syringe** *transitive verb* **sy·ringed; sy·ring·ing** (1610)
: to irrigate or spray with or as if with a syringe

**sy·rin·go·my·e·lia** \sə-,riŋ-gō-mī-'ē-lē-ə\ *noun* [New Latin, from Greek *syring-*, *syrinx* tube, fistula + New Latin *myel-* + *-ia*] (1897)
: a chronic progressive disease of the spinal cord associated with sensory disturbances, muscle atrophy, and spasticity
— **sy·rin·go·my·el·ic** \-'e-lik\ *adjective*

**syr·inx** \'sir-iŋ(k)s\ *noun, plural* **sy·rin·ges** \sə-'rin-,gēz, -'rin-,jēz\ *or* **syr·inx·es** (1606)
**1** [Late Latin, from Greek] : PANPIPE
**2** [New Latin, from Greek] : the vocal organ of birds that is a special modification of the lower part of the trachea or of the bronchi or of both

**syr·phid fly** \'sər-fəd-, 'sir-\ *noun* [New Latin *Syrphidae*, from *Syrphus*, genus of flies, from Greek *syrphos* gnat] (circa 1891)
: any of a family (Syrphidae) of dipteran flies which frequent flowers and some of whose larvae prey on plant lice — called also *syrphid*

— **syrphid** *adjective*

**syr·up** \'sər-əp, 'sir-əp, 'sə-rəp\ *noun* [Middle English *sirup*, from Middle French *sirop*, from Medieval Latin *syrupus*, from Arabic *sharāb*] (14th century)
**1 a** : a thick sticky solution of sugar and water often flavored or medicated **b** : the concentrated juice of a fruit or plant
**2** : cloying sweetness or sentimentality
— **syr·upy** *adjective*

**sys·op** \'sis-(,)äp\ *noun* [*sys*tem *op*erator] (1983)
: the administrator of a computer bulletin board

**sys·tal·tic** \sis-'tól-tik, -'tal-\ *adjective* [Late Latin *systalticus*, from Greek *systaltikos*, from *systellein* to contract — more at SYSTOLE] (1676)
: marked by regular contraction and dilatation : PULSING

**sys·tem** \'sis-təm\ *noun* [Late Latin *systemat-*, *systema*, from Greek *systēmat-*, *systēma*, from *synistanai* to combine, from *syn-* + *histanai* to cause to stand — more at STAND] (1603)
**1** : a regularly interacting or interdependent group of items forming a unified whole (a number *system*): as **a** (1) : a group of interacting bodies under the influence of related forces (a gravitational *system*) (2) : an assemblage of substances that is in or tends to equilibrium (a thermodynamic *system*) **b** (1) : a group of body organs that together perform one or more vital functions (the digestive *system*) (2) : the body considered as a functional unit **c** : a group of related natural objects or forces (a river *system*) **d** : a group of devices or artificial objects or an organization forming a network especially for distributing something or serving a common purpose (a telephone *system*) (a heating *system*) (a highway *system*) (a data processing *system*) **e** : a major division of rocks usually larger than a series and including all formed during a period or era **f** : a form of social, economic, or political organization or practice (the capitalist *system*)
**2** : an organized set of doctrines, ideas, or principles usually intended to explain the arrangement or working of a systematic whole (the Newtonian *system* of mechanics)
**3 a** : an organized or established procedure (the touch *system* of typing) **b** : a manner of classifying, symbolizing, or schematizing (a taxonomic *system*) (the decimal *system*)
**4** : harmonious arrangement or pattern : ORDER (bring *system* out of confusion —Ellen Glasgow)
**5** : an organized society or social situation regarded as stultifying : ESTABLISHMENT 2 — usually used with *the*
**synonym** see METHOD
— **sys·tem·less** \-ləs\ *adjective*

**sys·tem·at·ic** \,sis-tə-'ma-tik\ *adjective* [Late Latin *systematicus*, from Greek *systēmatikos*, from *systēmat-*, *systēma*] (circa 1680)
**1** : relating to or consisting of a system
**2** : presented or formulated as a coherent body of ideas or principles (*systematic* thought)
**3 a** : methodical in procedure or plan (a *systematic* approach) (a *systematic* scholar) **b** : marked by thoroughness and regularity (*systematic* efforts)
**4** : of, relating to, or concerned with classification; *specifically* : TAXONOMIC
— **sys·tem·at·i·cal·ly** \-ti-k(ə-)lē\ *adverb*
— **sys·tem·at·ic·ness** \-tik-nəs\ *noun*

**systematic error** *noun* (1891)
: an error that is not determined by chance but is introduced by an inaccuracy (as of observation or measurement) inherent in the system

**sys·tem·at·ics** \,sis-tə-'ma-tiks\ *noun plural but singular in construction* (1888)
**1** : the science of classification
**2 a** : a system of classification **b** : the classification and study of organisms with regard to their natural relationships : TAXONOMY

**systematic theology** *noun* (1836)
: a branch of theology concerned with summarizing the doctrinal traditions of a religion (as Christianity) especially with a view to relating the traditions convincingly to the religion's present-day setting

**sys·tem·a·tise** *British variant of* SYSTEMATIZE

**sys·tem·a·tism** \'sis-tə-mə-,ti-zəm, sis-'te-mə-\ *noun* (1846)
: the practice of forming intellectual systems

**sys·tem·a·tist** \'sis-tə-mə-tist, sis-'te-mə-\ *noun* (1700)
**1** : a maker or follower of a system
**2** : a specialist in taxonomy : TAXONOMIST

**sys·tem·a·tize** \'sis-tə-mə-,tīz\ *transitive verb* **-tized; -tiz·ing** (circa 1767)
: to arrange in accord with a definite plan or scheme : order systematically (the need to *systematize* their work)
**synonym** see ORDER
— **sys·tem·a·ti·za·tion** \,sis-tə-mə-tə-'zā-shən, sis-,te-mə-\ *noun*
— **sys·tem·a·tiz·er** *noun*

¹**sys·tem·ic** \sis-'te-mik\ *adjective* (1803)
: of, relating to, or common to a system: as **a** : affecting the body generally **b** : supplying those parts of the body that receive blood through the aorta rather than through the pulmonary artery **c** : of, relating to, or being a pesticide that as used is harmless to the plant or higher animal but when absorbed into its sap or bloodstream makes the entire organism toxic to pests (as an insect or fungus)
— **sys·tem·i·cal·ly** \-mi-k(ə-)lē\ *adverb*

²**systemic** *noun* (1951)
: a systemic pesticide

**systemic lupus er·y·the·ma·to·sus** \-,er-ə-,thē-mə-'tō-səs\ *noun* (1951)
: an inflammatory connective tissue disease of unknown cause that occurs chiefly in women, is characterized especially by fever, skin rash, and arthritis, often by acute hemolytic anemia, by small hemorrhages in the skin and mucous membranes, by inflammation of the pericardium, and in serious cases by involvement of the kidneys and central nervous system

**sys·tem·ize** \'sis-tə-,mīz\ *transitive verb* **-ized; -iz·ing** (1778)
: SYSTEMATIZE

---

◇ WORD HISTORY

**syphilis** In 1530 the Italian physician and poet Girolamo Fracastoro (circa 1478–1553) published a medical poem entitled *Syphilis, sive morbus Gallicus* ("Syphilis or the French Disease"). The "hero" of the poem is an unfortunate swineherd named Syphilus, whose name in Greek literally means "swine lover." The poem is actually a mythological tale that purports to tell how the disease first came into being. In the course of the poem Syphilus offends the sun god; for his punishment he becomes the first person to be afflicted with the fearsome contagion. In a way the poem also serves as a kind of digest of all that was then known about the disease. It discusses the venereal nature of syphilis and its symptoms and stages. Fracastoro's title gave us our name for the disease, but his work is also notable for contributing to the time-honored tradition of blaming the disease on some other country than one's own.

---

\ə\ abut \ᵊ\ kitten \ər\ further \a\ ash \ā\ ace
\ä\ mop, mar \aú\ out \ch\ chin \e\ bet \ē\ easy
\g\ go \i\ hit \ī\ ice \j\ job \ŋ\ sing \ō\ go
\ó\ law \ói\ boy \th\ thin \t̷h\ the \ü\ loot \ú\ foot
\y\ yet \zh\ vision   *see also* Guide to Pronunciation

— **sys·tem·i·za·tion** \,sis-tə-mə-'zā-shən\ *noun*

**systems analysis** *noun* (1950)
: the act, process, or profession of studying an activity (as a procedure, a business, or a physiological function) typically by mathematical means in order to define its goals or purposes and to discover operations and procedures for accomplishing them most efficiently

— **systems analyst** *noun*

**sys·to·le** \'sis-tə-(,)lē\ *noun* [Greek *systolē*, from *systellein* to contract, from *syn-* + *stellein* to send] (1578)
: a rhythmically recurrent contraction; *especially* : the contraction of the heart by which the blood is forced onward and the circulation kept up

— **sys·tol·ic** \sis-'tä-lik\ *adjective*

**syz·y·gy** \'si-zə-jē\ *noun, plural* **-gies** [Late Latin *syzygia* conjunction, from Greek, from *syzygos* yoked together, from *syn-* + *zygon* yoke — more at YOKE] (circa 1847)
: the nearly straight-line configuration of three celestial bodies (as the sun, moon, and earth during a solar or lunar eclipse) in a gravitational system

**Szech·uan** *or* **Szech·wan** \'sech-,wän, 'sesh-\ *adjective* [*Szechwan* or *Szechuan* (Sichuan), province in China] (1956)
: of, relating to, or being a style of Chinese cooking that is spicy, oily, and especially peppery

**T** *is the twentieth letter of the English alphabet. It came through Etruscan and Latin from the Greek tau, which itself was taken from Phoenician tāw. In modern English, t usually represents an alveolar stop, that is, a consonant produced by touching the tongue against the upper gum ridge (or alveolus) so as to stop the air flow through the mouth. In many other languages it is dental, or pronounced by pressing the tongue against the teeth. Unlike the otherwise identical sound of d, it is voiceless, that is, pronounced without vibration of the vocal cords. With i it often represents the sound of sh, as in nation and palatial; before u it often represents the sound of ch, as in nature and mutual. With h it forms the digraph th, which has two sounds, one voiceless, as in thin, the other voiced, as in then. T is frequently silent before syllabic n, as in chasten and soften. Small t came into being when medieval scribes began forming the miniaturized variant of the letter with two pen strokes, thus allowing the vertical stroke to emerge above the letter's crossbar.*

---

**t** \'tē\ *noun, plural* **t's** *or* **ts** \'tēz\ *often capitalized, often attributive* (before 12th century)
**1 a :** the 20th letter of the English alphabet **b :** a graphic representation of this letter **c :** a speech counterpart of orthographic *t*
**2 :** a graphic device for reproducing the letter *t*
**3 :** one designated *t* especially as the 20th in order or class
**4 :** something shaped like the letter T
**5 :** T FORMATION
**6 :** TECHNICAL FOUL
**— to a T** [short for *to a tittle*] **:** to perfection
**'t** \t\ *pronoun*
**:** IT ⟨my country, 'tis of thee —S. F. Smith⟩
**ta** \'tä\ *noun* [baby talk] (1772)
*British* **:** THANKS
**Taal** \'täl\ *noun* [Afrikaans, from Dutch, language; akin to Old English *talu* talk — more at TALE] (1896)
**:** AFRIKAANS — usually used with *the*
**¹tab** \'tab\ *noun, often attributive* [origin unknown] (1607)
**1 a :** a short projecting device: as (1) **:** a small flap or loop by which something may be grasped or pulled (2) **:** a projection from a card used as an aid in filing **b :** a small insert, addition, or remnant **c :** APPENDAGE, EXTENSION; *especially* **:** one of a series of small pendants forming a decorative border or edge of a garment **d :** a small auxiliary airfoil hinged to a control surface (as a trailing edge) to help stabilize an airplane in flight — see AIRPLANE illustration
**2** [partly short for ¹*table*; partly from sense 1] **a :** close surveillance **:** WATCH ⟨keep *tabs* on trends⟩ **b :** a creditor's statement **:** BILL, CHECK **c :** COST ⟨the *tab* for the new program⟩
**3** [by shortening] **a :** TABLOID **b :** TABLET
**4** [short for *tabulator*] **:** a device (as on a typewriter) for arranging data in columns
**²tab** *transitive verb* **tabbed; tab·bing** (1872)
**1 :** to furnish or ornament with tabs
**2 :** to single out **:** DESIGNATE
**3 :** TABULATE
**ta·ba·nid** \tə-'bā-nəd, -'ba-\ *noun* [ultimately from Latin *tabanus* horsefly] (circa 1891)
**:** HORSEFLY
**tab·ard** \'ta-bərd *also* -ˌbärd\ *noun* [Middle English, from Middle French *tabart*] (14th century)
**:** a short loose-fitting sleeveless or short-sleeved coat or cape: as **a :** a tunic worn by a knight over his armor and emblazoned with his arms **b :** a herald's official cape or coat emblazoned with his lord's arms **c :** a woman's sleeveless outer garment often with side slits

**Ta·bas·co** \tə-'bas-(ˌ)kō\ *trademark*
**—** used for a pungent condiment sauce made from hot peppers
**tab·bou·leh** \tə-'bü-lə, -lē\ *noun* [Arabic *tabbūla*] (1955)
**:** a salad of Lebanese origin consisting chiefly of cracked wheat, tomatoes, parsley, mint, onions, lemon juice, and olive oil
**¹tab·by** \'ta-bē\ *noun, plural* **tabbies** [French *tabis*, from Medieval Latin *attabi*, from Arabic *'attābī*, from Al-'*Attābīya*, quarter in Baghdad] (1638)
**1 a** *archaic* **:** a plain silk taffeta especially with moiré finish **b :** a plain-woven fabric
**2** [²*tabby*] **a :** a domestic cat with a striped and mottled coat **b :** a domestic cat; *especially* **:** a female cat ◆

tabby 2a

**²tabby** *adjective* (1661)
**1 :** of, relating to, or made of tabby
**2 :** striped and mottled with darker color **:** BRINDLED ⟨a *tabby* cat⟩
**³tabby** *noun* [Gullah *tabi*, ultimately from Spanish *tapia* adobe wall] (1775)
**:** a cement made of lime, sand or gravel, and oyster shells and used chiefly along the coast of Georgia and South Carolina in the 17th and 18th centuries
**¹tab·er·na·cle** \'ta-bər-ˌna-kəl\ *noun* [Middle English, from Old French, from Late Latin *tabernaculum*, from Latin, tent, from *taberna* hut] (13th century)
**1 a** *often capitalized* **:** a tent sanctuary used by the Israelites during the Exodus **b** *archaic* **:** a dwelling place **c** *archaic* **:** a temporary shelter **:** TENT
**2 :** a receptacle for the consecrated elements of the Eucharist; *especially* **:** an ornamental locked box used for reserving the Communion hosts
**3 :** a house of worship; *specifically* **:** a large building or tent used for evangelistic services
**— tab·er·nac·u·lar** \ˌta-bər-'na-kyə-lər\ *adjective*
**²tabernacle** *intransitive verb* **tab·er·na·cled; tab·er·na·cling** \-na-k(ə-)liŋ\ (1653)
**:** to take up temporary residence; *especially* **:** to inhabit a physical body
**ta·bes** \'tā-(ˌ)bēz\ *noun, plural* **tabes** [Latin, wasting disease, decay, from *tabēre* to decay — more at THAW] (1651)
**:** wasting accompanying a chronic disease

**— ta·bet·ic** \tə-'be-tik\ *adjective or noun*
**tabes dor·sa·lis** \-dor-'sa-ləs, -'sā-, -'sä-\ *noun* [New Latin, dorsal tabes] (circa 1681)
**:** a syphilitic disorder of the nervous system marked by wasting, pain, lack of coordination of voluntary movements and reflexes, and disorders of sensation, nutrition, and vision — called also *locomotor ataxia*
**ta·bla** \'tä-blə\ *noun* [Hindi *tablā*, from Arabic *tabla*] (1865)
**:** a pair of small different-sized hand drums used especially in music of India

tabla

**tab·la·ture** \'ta-blə-ˌchur, -chər, -ˌtyur, -ˌtur\ *noun* [Middle French, from Medieval Latin *tabulatus* tablet, from Latin *tabula*] (1574)
**:** an instrumental notation indicating the string, fret, key, or finger to be used instead of the tone to be sounded
**¹ta·ble** \'tā-bəl\ *noun, often attributive* [Middle English, from Old English *tabule* & Old French *table*; both from Latin *tabula* board, tablet, list] (before 12th century)
**1 :** TABLET 1a
**2 a** *plural* **:** BACKGAMMON **b :** one of the two leaves of a backgammon board or either half of a leaf
**3 a :** a piece of furniture consisting of a smooth flat slab fixed on legs **b** (1) **:** a supply or source of food (2) **:** an act or instance of assembling to eat **:** MEAL ⟨sit down to *table*⟩ **c** (1) **:** a group of people assembled at or as if at a table (2) **:** a legislative or negotiating session ⟨the bargaining *table*⟩
**4 :** STRINGCOURSE
**5 a :** a systematic arrangement of data usually in rows and columns for ready reference **b :** a condensed enumeration **:** LIST ⟨a *table* of contents⟩
**6 :** something that resembles a table especially in having a plane surface: as **a :** the upper flat surface of a cut precious stone **b** (1) **:** TABLELAND (2) **:** a horizontal stratum ⟨water *table*⟩
**— under the table 1 :** into a stupor ⟨can drink you *under the table*⟩ **2 :** in a covert manner ⟨took money *under the table*⟩
**²table** *transitive verb* **ta·bled; ta·bling** \-b(ə-)liŋ\ (15th century)
**1 :** to enter in a table
**2 a** *British* **:** to place on the agenda **b :** to remove (as a parliamentary motion) from consideration indefinitely **c :** to put on a table
**³table** *adjective* (1547)

◇ **WORD HISTORY**
**tabby** A silk cloth with a moiré or wavy pattern was once made in a quarter of the city of Baghdad, now the capital of the modern nation of Iraq. In Arabic the cloth was known as '*attābī*, from *Al-'Attābīya*, the name of its place of origin. The name for the cloth passed into Medieval Latin as *attabi* and then into French as *tabis*. When the word was borrowed into English as *tabby* in the 17th century, it was solely with reference to a plain-woven silk cloth with a moiré pattern. Before long, however, people noted a resemblance between the cloth's pattern and the striped or mottled markings on the coats of their domestic cats. *Tabby* has been the standard name for this type of cat ever since.

---

\ə\ **abut** \ᵊ\ **kitten** \ər\ **further** \a\ **ash** \ā\ **ace**
\ä\ **mop, mar** \au̇\ **out** \ch\ **chin** \e\ **bet** \ē\ **easy**
\g\ **go** \i\ **hit** \ī\ **ice** \j\ **job** \ŋ\ **sing** \ō\ **go**
\o̅\ **law** \o̅i\ **boy** \th\ **thin** \t͟h\ **the** \ü\ **loot** \u̇\ **foot**
\y\ **yet** \zh\ **vision** *see also* Guide to Pronunciation

**1** : suitable for a table or for use at a table ⟨a *table* lamp⟩
**2** : suitable for serving at a table ⟨*table* grapes⟩
**3** : proper for conduct at a table ⟨*table* manners⟩

**tab·leau** \'ta-ˌblō, ta-'blō\ *noun, plural* **tableaux** \-ˌblōz, -'blōz\ *also* **tableaus** [French, from Middle French *tablel*, diminutive of *table*, from Old French] (1699)
**1** : a graphic description or representation : PICTURE ⟨winsome *tableaux* of old-fashioned literary days —J. D. Hart⟩
**2** : a striking or artistic grouping
**3** [short for *tableau vivant* (from French, literally, living picture)] : a depiction of a scene usually presented on a stage by silent and motionless costumed participants

**tableau curtain** *noun* (1881)
: a stage curtain that opens in the center and has its sections drawn upward as well as to the side

**ta·ble·cloth** \'tā-bəl-ˌklȯth\ *noun* (15th century)
: a covering spread over a dining table before the tableware is set

**ta·ble d'hôte** \ˌtā-bəl-'dōt, ˌta-\ *noun* [French, literally, host's table] (1617)
**1** : a meal served to all guests at a stated hour and fixed price
**2** : a complete meal of several courses offered at a fixed price

**ta·ble·ful** \'tā-bəl-ˌfu̇l\ *noun* (1535)
: as much or as many as a table can hold or accommodate

**ta·ble·hop** \'tā-bəl-ˌhäp\ *intransitive verb* (1942)
: to move from table to table (as in a restaurant) in order to chat with friends
— **ta·ble·hop·per** *noun*

**ta·ble·land** \-bə(l)-ˌland\ *noun* (1697)
: a broad level elevated area : PLATEAU

**table linen** *noun* (1629)
: linen (as tablecloths and napkins) for the table

**ta·ble·mate** \'tā-bəl-ˌmāt\ *noun* (1624)
: a dining companion

**table of organization** (circa 1918)
: a table listing the number and duties of personnel and the major items of equipment authorized for a military unit

**table salt** *noun* (1878)
: salt suitable for use at the table and in cooking

**ta·ble·spoon** \'tā-bəl-ˌspün\ *noun* (1763)
**1** : a large spoon used for serving
**2** : a unit of measure used especially in cookery equal to ½ fluid ounce (15 milliliters)

**ta·ble·spoon·ful** \ˌtā-bəl-'spün-ˌfu̇l, 'tā-bəl-ˌ\ *noun, plural* **tablespoonfuls** \-ˌfu̇lz\ *also* **ta·ble·spoons·ful** \-'spünz-ˌfu̇l, -ˌspünz-\ (1772)
**1** : enough to fill a tablespoon
**2** : TABLESPOON 2

**table sugar** *noun* (1958)
: SUGAR 1a; *especially* : granulated white sugar

**tab·let** \'ta-blət\ *noun* [Middle English *tablett*, from Middle French *tablete*, diminutive of *table* table] (14th century)
**1 a** : a flat slab or plaque suited for or bearing an inscription **b** : a thin slab or one of a set of portable sheets used for writing **c** : PAD 4
**2 a** : a compressed or molded block of a solid material **b** : a small mass of medicated material ⟨an aspirin *tablet*⟩
**3** : GRAPHICS TABLET

**table talk** *noun* (1569)
: informal conversation at or as if at a dining table; *especially* : the social talk of a celebrity recorded for publication

**table tennis** *noun* (1901)
: a game resembling tennis that is played on a tabletop with wooden paddles and a small hollow plastic ball

**ta·ble·top** \'tā-bəl-ˌtäp\ *noun* (1807)
**1** : the top of a table

**2** : a photograph of small objects or a miniature scene arranged on a table
— **table·top** *adjective*

**ta·ble·ware** \-ˌwar, -ˌwer\ *noun* (1832)
: utensils (as of china, glass, or silver) for table use

**table wine** *noun* (circa 1827)
: an unfortified wine averaging 12 percent alcohol by volume and usually suitable for serving with food

**¹tab·loid** \'ta-ˌblȯid\ *adjective* [from *Tabloid*, a trademark] (1901)
**1** : compressed or condensed into small scope ⟨*tabloid* criticism⟩
**2** : of, relating to, or characteristic of tabloids; *especially* : featuring stories of violence, crime, or scandal presented in a sensational manner

**²tabloid** *noun* (1906)
**1** : DIGEST, SUMMARY
**2** : a newspaper that is about half the page size of an ordinary newspaper and that contains news in condensed form and much photographic matter

**¹ta·boo** *also* **ta·bu** \tə-'bü, ta-\ *adjective* [Tongan *tabu*] (1777)
**1** : forbidden to profane use or contact because of what are held to be dangerous supernatural powers
**2 a** : banned on grounds of morality or taste ⟨the subject is *taboo*⟩ **b** : banned as constituting a risk ⟨the area beyond is *taboo*, still alive with explosives —Robert Leckie⟩

**²taboo** *also* **tabu** *noun, plural* **taboos** *also* **tabus** (1777)
**1** : a prohibition against touching, saying, or doing something for fear of immediate harm from a supernatural force
**2** : a prohibition imposed by social custom or as a protective measure
**3** : belief in taboos

**³taboo** *also* **tabu** *transitive verb* (1777)
**1** : to set apart as taboo especially by marking with a ritualistic symbol
**2** : to avoid or ban as taboo

**ta·bor** *also* **ta·bour** \'tā-bər\ *noun* [Middle English, from Old French] (14th century)
: a small drum with one head of soft calfskin used to accompany a pipe or fife played by the same person

**ta·bor·er** *also* **ta·bour·er** \-bər-ər\ *noun* (15th century)
: one that plays on the tabor

**tab·o·ret** *or* **tab·ou·ret** \ˌta-bə-'ret, -'rā\ *noun* [French *tabouret*, literally, small drum, from Middle French, diminutive of *tabor*, *tabour* drum] (1630)
**1** : a cylindrical seat or stool without arms or back
**2** : a small portable stand or cabinet

**ta·bou·li** *variant of* TABBOULEH

**Ta·briz** \tə-'brēz\ *noun, plural* **Tabriz** [*Tabriz*, Iran] (1904)
: a Persian rug usually having a cotton warp, firm wool pile, and a medallion design

**tab·u·lar** \'ta-byə-lər\ *adjective* [Latin *tabularis* of boards, from *tabula* board, tablet] (circa 1656)
**1** : having a flat surface : LAMINAR ⟨a *tabular* crystal⟩
**2 a** : of, relating to, or arranged in a table; *specifically* : set up in rows and columns **b** : computed by means of a table

**ta·bu·la ra·sa** \ˌta-byə-lə-'rä-zə, -sə\ *noun, plural* **ta·bu·lae ra·sae** \-ˌlī-'rä-ˌzī, -ˌsī\ [Latin, smoothed or erased tablet] (1607)
**1** : the mind in its hypothetical primary blank or empty state before receiving outside impressions
**2** : something existing in its original pristine state

**tab·u·late** \'ta-byə-ˌlāt\ *transitive verb* **-lat·ed; -lat·ing** [Latin *tabula* tablet] (1734)

**1** : to put into tabular form
**2** : to count, record, or list systematically
— **tab·u·la·tion** \ˌta-byə-'lā-shən\ *noun*
— **tab·u·la·tor** \'ta-byə-ˌlā-tər\ *noun*

**ta·bun** \'tä-ˌbu̇n\ *noun* [German] (1948)
: a liquid organophosphate $C_5H_{11}N_2O_2P$ that acts as a nerve gas

**tac·a·ma·hac** \'ta-kə-mə-ˌhak\ *noun* [Spanish *tacamahaca*, from Nahuatl *tecamac*] (1739)
: BALSAM POPLAR

**TACAN** \'ta-ˌkan\ *noun, often attributive* [*tac*tical *a*ir *na*vigation] (1955)
: a system of navigation that uses ultrahigh frequency signals to determine the distance and bearing of an aircraft from a transmitting station

**ta·cet** \'tä-ˌket; 'tā-sət, 'ta-sət\ [Latin, literally, (it) is silent, from *tacēre* to be silent — more at TACIT] (circa 1724)
— used as a direction in music to indicate that an instrument is not to play during a movement or long section

**tach** \'tak\ *noun* (circa 1930)
: TACHOMETER

**tach·i·nid** \'ta-kə-nəd, -ˌnid\ *noun* [New Latin *Tachinidae*, from *Tachina*, genus of flies, from Greek *tachinos* fleet, from *tachys* swift] (1888)
: any of a family (Tachinidae) of bristly usually grayish or black dipteran flies whose parasitic larvae are often used in the biological control of insect pests
— **tachinid** *adjective*

**tach·ism** \'ta-ˌshi-zəm\ *noun, often capitalized* [French *tachisme*, from *tache* stain, spot, blob, from Middle French *teche, tache*, of Germanic origin; akin to Old Saxon *tēkan* sign, Old High German *zeihhan* — more at TOKEN] (1955)
: ACTION PAINTING
— **tach·ist** \'ta-shist\ *also* **ta·chiste** \ta-'shēst\ *adjective or noun, often capitalized*

**ta·chis·to·scope** \tə-'kis-tə-ˌskōp, ta-\ *noun* [Greek *tachistos* (superlative of *tachys* swift) + International Scientific Vocabulary *-scope*] (circa 1890)
: an apparatus for the brief exposure of visual stimuli that is used in the study of learning, attention, and perception
— **ta·chis·to·scop·ic** \-ˌkis-tə-'skä-pik\ *adjective*
— **ta·chis·to·scop·i·cal·ly** \-pi-k(ə-)lē\ *adverb*

**ta·chom·e·ter** \ta-'kä-mə-tər, tə-\ *noun* [Greek *tachos* speed + English *-meter*] (1810)
: a device for indicating speed of rotation

**tachy-** *combining form* [Greek, from *tachys*]
: rapid : accelerated ⟨*tachy*cardia⟩

**tachy·ar·rhyth·mia** \ˌta-kē-ā-'rith-mē-ə\ *noun* [New Latin] (1926)
: arrhythmia characterized by a rapid irregular heartbeat

**tachy·car·dia** \ˌta-ki-'kär-dē-ə\ *noun* [New Latin] (1889)
: relatively rapid heart action whether physiological (as after exercise) or pathological — compare BRADYCARDIA

**tachy·on** \'ta-kē-ˌän\ *noun* [*tachy*- + ²*-on*] (1967)
: a hypothetical particle held to travel only faster than light

**tac·it** \'ta-sət\ *adjective* [French or Latin; French *tacite*, from Latin *tacitus* silent, from past participle of *tacēre* to be silent; akin to Old High German *dagēn* to be silent] (circa 1604)
**1** : expressed or carried on without words or speech
**2 a** : implied or indicated but not actually expressed ⟨*tacit* consent⟩ **b** (1) : arising without express contract or agreement (2) : arising by operation of law ⟨*tacit* mortgage⟩
— **tac·it·ly** *adverb*
— **tac·it·ness** *noun*

tabor

**tac·i·turn** \'ta-sə-ˌtərn\ *adjective* [French or Latin; French *taciturne*, from Latin *taciturnus*, from *tacitus*] (1771)
: temperamentally disinclined to talk
**synonym** see SILENT
— **tac·i·tur·ni·ty** \ˌta-sə-'tər-nə-tē\ *noun*

**¹tack** \'tak\ *verb* [Middle English *takken*, from *tak*] (14th century)
*transitive verb*
**1** : ATTACH; *especially* : to fasten or affix with tacks
**2** : to join in a slight or hasty manner
**3 a** : to add as a supplement **b** : to add (a rider) to a parliamentary bill
**4** : to change the direction of (a sailing ship) when sailing close-hauled by turning the bow to the wind and shifting the sails so as to fall off on the other side at about the same angle as before
*intransitive verb*
**1 a** : to tack a sailing ship **b** *of a ship* : to change to an opposite tack by turning the bow to the wind **c** : to follow a course against the wind by a series of tacks
**2 a** : to follow a zigzag course **b** : to modify one's policy or attitude abruptly
— **tack·er** *noun*

**²tack** *noun* [Middle English *tak* something that attaches; akin to Middle Dutch *tac* sharp point] (1574)
**1** : a small short sharp-pointed nail usually having a broad flat head
**2 a** : the direction of a ship with respect to the trim of her sails (starboard *tack*) **b** : the run of a sailing ship on one tack **c** : a change when close-hauled from the starboard to the port tack or vice versa **d** : a zigzag movement on land **e** : a course or method of action; *especially* : one sharply divergent from that previously followed
**3** : any of various usually temporary stitches
**4** : the lower forward corner of a fore-and-aft sail
**5** : a sticky or adhesive quality or condition

**³tack** *noun* [origin unknown] (1841)
: HARDTACK 1

**⁴tack** *noun* [perhaps short for *tackle*] (1924)
: stable gear; *especially* : articles of harness (as saddle and bridle) for use on a saddle horse

**tack·board** \'tak-ˌbōrd, -ˌbȯrd\ *noun* (circa 1927)
: a board (as of cork) for tacking up notices and display materials

**tack claw** *noun* (circa 1876)
: a small hand tool for removing tacks

**tack·i·fy** \'ta-kə-ˌfī\ *transitive verb* **-fied; -fy·ing** (1942)
: to make (as a resin adhesive) tacky or more tacky
— **tack·i·fi·er** \-ˌfī(-ə)r\ *noun*

**tack·i·ly** \'ta-kə-lē\ *adverb* (1903)
: in a tacky manner : so as to be tacky

**tack·i·ness** \'ta-kē-nəs\ *noun* (1883)
: the quality or state of being tacky

**¹tack·le** \'ta-kəl, *nautical often* 'tā-\ *noun* [Middle English *takel*; akin to Middle Dutch *takel* ship's rigging] (13th century)
**1** : a set of the equipment used in a particular activity : GEAR (fishing *tackle*)
**2 a** : a ship's rigging **b** : an assemblage of ropes and pulleys arranged to gain mechanical advantage for hoisting and pulling
**3 a** : the act or an instance of tackling **b** (1) : either of two offensive football players positioned on each side of the center and between guard and end (2) : either of two football players positioned on the inside of a defensive line

**²tackle** *verb* **tack·led; tack·ling** \-k(ə-)liŋ\ (1714)
*transitive verb*
**1** : to attach or secure with or as if with tackle

**2 a** : to seize, take hold of, or grapple with especially with the intention of stopping or subduing **b** : to seize and throw down or stop (an opposing player with the ball) in football
**3** : to set about dealing with (*tackle* the problem)
*intransitive verb*
: to tackle an opposing player in football
— **tack·ler** \-k(ə-)lər\ *noun*

**tack·ling** \'ta-kliŋ, *nautical often* 'tā-\ *noun* (15th century)
: TACKLE, GEAR

**¹tacky** \'ta-kē\ *adjective* **tack·i·er; -est** [²*tack*] (1788)
: somewhat sticky to the touch (*tacky* varnish); *also* : characterized by tack : ADHESIVE

**²tacky** *adjective* **tacki·er; -est** [*tacky* a low-class person] (1862)
**1 a** : characterized by lack of good breeding : COMMON (couldn't run around downtown . . . in a bikini, which was *tacky* —Cyra McFadden) **b** : SHABBY, SEEDY (a *tacky* town whose citrus groves were blighted by smoke —Bryce Nelson)
**2** : not having or exhibiting good taste (hopelessly *tacky* bric-a-brac —T. C. Boyle): as **a** : marked by lack of style : DOWDY **b** : marked by cheap showiness : GAUDY

**ta·co** \'tä-(ˌ)kō\ *noun, plural* **tacos** \-(ˌ)kōz\ [Mexican Spanish] (1934)
: a usually fried tortilla that is folded or rolled and stuffed with a mixture (as of seasoned meat, cheese, and lettuce)

**tac·o·nite** \'ta-kə-ˌnīt\ *noun* [*Taconic* Range, mountains in U.S.] (1892)
: a flintlike rock high enough in iron content to constitute a low-grade iron ore

**tact** \'takt\ *noun* [French, sense of touch, from Latin *tactus*, from *tangere* to touch — more at TANGENT] (1797)
**1** : sensitive mental or aesthetic perception (converted the novel into a play with remarkable skill and *tact*)
**2** : a keen sense of what to do or say in order to maintain good relations with others or avoid offense ☆

**tact·ful** \'takt-fəl\ *adjective* (1864)
: having or showing tact
— **tact·ful·ly** \-fə-lē\ *adverb*
— **tact·ful·ness** *noun*

**¹tac·tic** \'tak-tik\ *noun* [New Latin *tactica*, from Greek *taktikē*, from feminine of *taktikos*] (1640)
**1** : a device for accomplishing an end
**2** : a method of employing forces in combat

**²tactic** *adjective* [New Latin *tacticus*, from Greek *taktikos*] (1871)
: of or relating to arrangement or order

**-tactic** *adjective combining form* [Greek *taktikos*]
**1** : of, relating to, or having (such) an arrangement or pattern (para*tactic*)
**2** : showing orientation or movement directed by a (specified) force or agent (geo*tactic*)

**tac·ti·cal** \'tak-ti-kəl\ *adjective* (1570)
**1** : of or relating to combat tactics: as **a** (1) : of or occurring at the battlefront (*tactical* defense) (*tactical* first strike) (2) : using or being weapons or forces employed at the battlefront (*tactical* missiles) **b** : of an air force : of, relating to, or designed for air attack in close support of friendly ground forces
**2 a** : of or relating to tactics: as (1) : of or relating to small-scale actions serving a larger purpose (2) : made or carried out with only a limited or immediate end in view **b** : adroit in planning or maneuvering to accomplish a purpose
— **tac·ti·cal·ly** \-k(ə-)lē\ *adverb*

**tac·ti·cian** \tak-'ti-shən\ *noun* (1798)
: one versed in tactics

**tac·tics** \'tak-tiks\ *noun plural but singular or*

*plural in construction* [New Latin *tactica*, plural, from Greek *taktika*, from neuter plural of *taktikos* of order, of tactics, fit for arranging, from *tassein* to arrange, place in battle formation] (1626)
**1 a** : the science and art of disposing and maneuvering forces in combat **b** : the art or skill of employing available means to accomplish an end
**2** : a system or mode of procedure
**3** : the study of the grammatical relations within a language including morphology and syntax

**tac·tile** \'tak-t³l, -ˌtīl\ *adjective* [French or Latin; French, from Latin *tactilis*, from *tangere* to touch — more at TANGENT] (1615)
**1** : perceptible by touch : TANGIBLE
**2** : of or relating to the sense of touch
— **tac·tile·ly** \-tə-lē, -ˌtīl-lē\ *adverb*

**tactile corpuscle** *noun* (1873)
: an end organ of touch

**tac·til·i·ty** \tak-'ti-lə-tē\ *noun* (1659)
**1** : the capability of being felt or touched
**2** : responsiveness to stimulation of the sense of touch

**tac·tion** \'tak-shən\ *noun* [Latin *taction-, tactio*, from *tangere*] (circa 1623)
: TOUCH

**tact·less** \'takt-ləs\ *adjective* (circa 1847)
: marked by lack of tact
— **tact·less·ly** *adverb*
— **tact·less·ness** *noun*

**tac·tu·al** \'tak-chə-wəl, -chəl\ *adjective* [Latin *tactus* sense of touch — more at TACT] (1642)
: TACTILE 2
— **tac·tu·al·ly** *adverb*

**tad** \'tad\ *noun* [probably from English dialect, toad, from Middle English *tode* — more at TOAD] (circa 1877)
**1** : a small child; *especially* : BOY
**2** : a small or insignificant amount or degree : BIT (might give him some water and a *tad* to eat —C. T. Walker)
— **a tad** : SOMEWHAT, RATHER (looked a *tad* bigger than me —Larry Hodgson)

**tad·pole** \'tad-ˌpōl\ *noun* [Middle English *taddepol*, from *tode* toad + *polle* head] (15th century)
: a larval amphibian; *specifically* : a frog or toad larva that has a rounded body with a long tail bordered by fins and external gills soon replaced by

**tadpole**

\ə\ abut \ᵊ\ kitten \ər\ further \a\ ash \ā\ ace
\ä\ mop, mar \au̇\ out \ch\ chin \e\ bet \ē\ easy
\g\ go \i\ hit \ī\ ice \j\ job \ŋ\ sing \ō\ go
\ȯ\ law \ȯi\ boy \th\ thin \t͟h\ the \ü\ loot \u̇\ foot
\y\ yet \zh\ vision   *see also* Guide to Pronunciation

**tackle 2b**

internal gills and that undergoes a metamorphosis to the adult

**Ta·dzhik** *variant of* TAJIK

**tae·di·um vi·tae** \ˌtē-dē-əm-ˈvī-ˌtē, ˌtī-dē-əm-ˈwē-ˌtī\ *noun* [Latin] (1759)
: weariness or loathing of life

**tae kwon do** \ˈtī-ˈkwän-ˈdō\ *noun, often T&K&D capitalized* [Korean *t'aekwŏndo*, from *t'ae-* to trample + *kwŏn* fist + *to* way] (1967)
: a Korean martial art resembling karate

**tael** \ˈtā(ə)l\ *noun* [Portuguese, from Malay *tahil*] (1588)
**1 :** any of various Chinese units of value based on the value of a tael weight of silver
**2 :** any of various units of weight of eastern Asia

**tae·nia** \ˈtē-nē-ə\ *noun, plural* **-ni·ae** \-nē-ˌī, -ˌē\ *or* **-nias** [Latin, ribbon, fillet, from Greek *tainia;* akin to Greek *teinein* to stretch — more at THIN] (1563)
**1 :** a band on a Doric order separating the frieze from the architrave
**2 :** TAPEWORM
**3 :** an ancient Greek fillet
**4** [New Latin, from Latin, fillet, band] **:** a band of nervous tissue or muscle

**tae·ni·a·sis** \tē-ˈnī-ə-səs\ *noun* [New Latin, from Latin *taenia* tapeworm] (circa 1890)
: infestation with or disease caused by tapeworms

**taf·fe·ta** \ˈta-fə-tə\ *noun* [Middle English, from Middle French *taffetas,* from Old Italian *taffettà,* from Turkish *tafta,* from Persian *tāftah* woven] (14th century)
: a crisp plain-woven lustrous fabric of various fibers used especially for women's clothing

**taf·fe·tized** \ˈta-fə-ˌtīzd\ *adjective* (1949)
*of cloth* **:** having a crisp finish

**taff·rail** \ˈtaf-ˌrāl, -rəl\ *noun* [modification of Dutch *tafereel,* from Middle Dutch, panel, from Old French *tablel* — more at TABLEAU] (circa 1704)
**1 :** the upper part of the stern of a wooden ship
**2 :** a rail around the stern of a ship

**taf·fy** \ˈta-fē\ *noun, plural* **taffies** [origin unknown] (circa 1817)
**1 :** a boiled candy usually of molasses or brown sugar that is pulled until porous and light-colored
**2 :** insincere flattery

**¹tag** \ˈtag\ *noun* [Middle English *tagge,* probably of Scandinavian origin; akin to Swedish *tagg* barb] (15th century)
**1 :** a loose hanging piece of cloth **:** TATTER
**2 :** a metal or plastic binding on an end of a shoelace
**3 :** a piece of hanging or attached material; *specifically* **:** a loop, knot, or tassel on a garment
**4 a :** a brief quotation used for rhetorical emphasis or sententious effect **b :** a recurrent or characteristic verbal expression **c :** TAG LINE 1
**5 a :** a cardboard, plastic, or metal marker used for identification or classification ⟨license *tags*⟩ **b :** a descriptive or identifying epithet **c :** something used for identification or location **:** FLAG **d :** LABEL 3d **e :** PRICE TAG
**6 :** a detached fragmentary piece **:** BIT

**²tag** *verb* **tagged; tag·ging** (15th century)
*transitive verb*
**1 :** to provide or mark with or as if with a tag: as **a :** to supply with an identifying marker or price ⟨*tagged* every item in the store⟩ ⟨was *tagged* at $4.95⟩ **b :** to provide with a name or epithet **:** LABEL, BRAND ⟨*tagged* him a has-been⟩ **c :** to put a ticket on (a motor vehicle) for a traffic violation
**2 :** to attach as an addition **:** APPEND
**3 :** to follow closely and persistently
**4 :** to hold to account; *especially* **:** to charge with violating the law ⟨was *tagged* for . . . assault —Burt Woolis⟩
**5 :** LABEL 2

*intransitive verb*
**:** to keep close ⟨*tagging* at their heels —Corey Ford⟩

**³tag** *noun* [origin unknown] (1738)
**1 :** a game in which the player who is it chases others and tries to touch one of them who then becomes it
**2 :** an act or instance of tagging a runner in baseball

**⁴tag** *transitive verb* **tagged; tag·ging** (1878)
**1 a :** to touch in or as if in a game of tag **b :** to put out (a runner) in baseball by a touch with the ball or the gloved hand containing the ball
**2 :** to hit solidly
**3 :** to choose usually for a special purpose **:** SELECT
**4 :** to make a hit or run off (a pitcher) in baseball

**Ta·ga·log** \tə-ˈgä-ˌlòg\ *noun, plural* **Tagalog** *or* **Tagalogs** [Tagalog] (circa 1808)
**1 :** a member of a people of central Luzon
**2 :** an Austronesian language of the Tagalog people — compare PILIPINO

**tag·along** \ˈta-gə-ˌlòn\ *noun* (1935)
**:** one that persistently and often annoyingly follows the lead of another

**tag along** *intransitive verb* (1900)
**:** to follow another's lead especially in going from one place to another

**tag·board** \ˈtag-ˌbòrd, -ˌbòrd\ *noun* (1904)
**:** strong cardboard used especially for making shipping tags

**tag end** *noun* (1807)
**1 :** the last part
**2 :** a miscellaneous or random bit

**ta·glia·tel·le** \ˌtäl-yä-ˈte-(ˌ)lā\ *noun* [Italian, from *tagliare* to cut, from Late Latin *taliare* — more at TAILOR] (1899)
**:** FETTUCCINE

**tag line** *noun* (1926)
**1 :** a final line (as in a play or joke); *especially* **:** one that serves to clarify a point or create a dramatic effect
**2 :** a reiterated phrase identified with an individual, group, or product **:** SLOGAN

**tag question** *noun* (1933)
**:** a question (as *isn't it* in "it's fine, isn't it?") added to a statement or command (as to gain the assent of or challenge the person addressed); *also* **:** a sentence ending in a tag question

**tag, rag, and bobtail** *or* **tagrag and bobtail** \ˌtag-ˌrag-ən-ˈbäb-ˌtāl, -ˌrag-ᵊŋ-\ *noun* (1645)
**:** RABBLE

**tag sale** *noun* [from the price tag on each item] (1955)
**:** GARAGE SALE

**tag team** *noun* [⁴*tag*] (1952)
**:** a team of two or more professional wrestlers who spell each other during a match

**tag up** *intransitive verb* (1942)
**:** to touch a base before running in baseball after a fly ball is caught

**ta·hi·ni** \tə-ˈhē-nē, tä-\ *noun* [Arabic dialect *ṭaḥīna,* from *ṭaḥana* to grind] (1950)
**:** a smooth paste of sesame seeds

**Ta·hi·tian** \tə-ˈhē-shən\ *noun* (1825)
**1 :** a native or inhabitant of Tahiti
**2 :** the Polynesian language of the Tahitians
**— Tahitian** *adjective*

**tahr** \ˈtär\ *noun* [Nepali *thār*] (1835)
**:** any of a genus (*Hemitragus*) of wild Asian goats; *especially* **:** one (*H. jemlahicus*) of the Himalayas having a reddish brown to dark brown coat and a long shaggy mane

**tah·sil** \tä-ˈsē(ə)l\ *noun* [Urdu *taḥsīl,* from Arabic, collection of revenue] (1846)
**:** a district administration or revenue subdivision in India

**Tai** \ˈtī\ *noun, plural* **Tai** (1693)
**:** a widespread group of peoples in southeast Asia associated ethnically with valley paddy-rice culture

**tai chi chuan** *or* **t'ai chi ch'uan** \ˈtī-ˈjē-chü-ˈän, ˈtī-ˈchē-\ *noun, often T and both Cs capitalized* [Chinese (Beijing) *tàijíquán,* from *tàijí* the Absolute in Chinese cosmology + *quán* fist, boxing] (1954)
**:** an ancient Chinese discipline of meditative movements practiced as a system of exercises — called also *tai chi, t'ai chi*

**tai·ga** \ˈtī-gə\ *noun* [Russian *taĭga*] (1888)
**:** a moist subarctic forest dominated by conifers (as spruce and fir) that begins where the tundra ends

**¹tail** \ˈtā(ə)l\ *noun, often attributive* [Middle English, from Old English *tægel;* akin to Old High German *zagal* tail, Middle Irish *dúal* lock of hair] (before 12th century)
**1 :** the rear end or a process or prolongation of the rear end of the body of an animal
**2 :** something resembling an animal's tail in shape or position: as **a :** the luminous train of a comet **b :** the rear part of an airplane consisting usually of horizontal and vertical stabilizing surfaces with attached control surfaces
**3 :** RETINUE
**4** *plural* **a :** TAILCOAT **b :** full evening dress for men
**5 a :** BUTTOCKS, BUTT **b :** a female sexual partner — usually considered vulgar
**6 :** the back, last, lower, or inferior part of something
**7 :** TAILING 1 — usually used in plural
**8 :** the reverse of a coin — usually used in plural ⟨*tails,* I win⟩
**9 :** one (as a detective) who follows or keeps watch on someone
**10 :** the blank space at the bottom of a page
**11 :** a location immediately or not far behind ⟨had a posse on his *tail*⟩
**— tailed** \ˈtā(ə)ld\ *adjective*
**— tail·less** \ˈtā(ə)l-ləs\ *adjective*
**— tail·like** \-ˌlīk\ *adjective*

**²tail** (1523)
*transitive verb*
**1 :** to connect end to end
**2 a :** to remove the tail of (an animal) **:** DOCK **b :** to remove the stem or bottom part of ⟨topping and *tailing* gooseberries⟩
**3 a :** to make or furnish with a tail **b :** to follow or be drawn behind like a tail
**4 :** to follow for purposes of surveillance
*intransitive verb*
**1 :** to form or move in a straggling line
**2 :** to grow progressively smaller, fainter, or more scattered **:** ABATE — usually used with *off* ⟨productivity is *tailing* off —Tom Nicholson⟩
**3 :** to swing or lie with the stern in a named direction — used of a ship at anchor
**4 :** ²TAG
**— tail·er** *noun*

**³tail** *noun* [Middle English, from Middle French, from Old French, from *taillier*] (14th century)
**:** ENTAIL 1a

**⁴tail** *adjective* [Middle English *taille,* from Anglo-French *taylé,* from Old French *taillié,* past participle of *taillier* to cut, limit — more at TAILOR] (15th century)
**:** limited as to tenure **:** ENTAILED

**tail·back** \ˈtā(ə)l-ˌbak\ *noun* (1930)
**:** the offensive football back farthest from the line of scrimmage

**tail·board** \-ˌbòrd, -ˌbòrd\ *noun* (1805)
*chiefly British* **:** TAILGATE 1

**tail·bone** \-ˌbōn\ *noun* (circa 1577)
**1 :** a caudal vertebra
**2 :** COCCYX

**tail·coat** \-ˌkōt\ *noun* (1847)
**:** a coat with tails; *especially* **:** a man's full-dress coat with two long tapering skirts at the back
**— tail·coat·ed** \-ˌkō-təd\ *adjective*

**tail covert** *noun* (1815)
**:** one of the coverts of the tail quills

**tail end** *noun* (14th century)

**1 :** BUTTOCKS, RUMP
**2 :** the hindmost end
**3 :** the concluding period ⟨the *tail end* of the session⟩

**tail·end·er** \'tā(ə)l-ˌen-dər\ *noun* (1885)
: one positioned at the end or in last place ⟨the *tailenders* in a race⟩

**tail fin** *noun* (1681)
**1 :** the terminal fin of a fish or cetacean
**2 :** FIN 2b

**¹tail·gate** \'tā(ə)l-ˌgāt\ *noun* (1868)
**1 :** a board or gate at the rear of a vehicle that can be removed or let down (as for loading)
**2** [from the custom of seating trombonists at the rear of trucks carrying jazz bands in parades] **:** a jazz trombone style marked by much use of slides to and from long sustained tones

**²tailgate** *verb* **tail·gat·ed; tail·gat·ing** (1949)
*intransitive verb*
**1 :** to drive dangerously close behind another vehicle
**2 :** to hold a tailgate picnic
*transitive verb*
: to drive dangerously close behind
— **tail·gat·er** *noun*

**³tailgate** *adjective* (1965)
: relating to or being a picnic set up on the tailgate especially of a station wagon

**tail·ing** \'tā-liŋ\ *noun* (1764)
**1 :** residue separated in the preparation of various products (as grain or ores) — usually used in plural
**2 :** the part of a projecting stone or brick inserted in a wall

**taille** \'tä-yə, 'tī-, 'tä(ə)l\ *noun* [Middle French, from Old French, from *taillier* to cut, tax] (circa 1533)
: a tax formerly levied by a French king or seigneur on his subjects or on lands held of him

**tail·light** \'tā(ə)l-ˌlīt\ *noun* (1844)
: a usually red warning light mounted at the rear of a vehicle — called also *taillamp*

**¹tai·lor** \'tā-lər\ *noun* [Middle English *taillour*, from Old French *tailleur*, from *taillier* to cut, from Late Latin *taliare*, from Latin *talea* twig, cutting] (14th century)
: a person whose occupation is making or altering outer garments

**²tailor** (1719)
*intransitive verb*
: to do the work of a tailor
*transitive verb*
**1 a :** to make or fashion as the work of a tailor **b :** to make or adapt to suit a special need or purpose
**2 :** to fit with clothes
**3 :** to style with trim straight lines and finished handwork

**tai·lor·bird** \'tā-lər-ˌbərd\ *noun* (1769)
: any of a genus (*Orthotomus* of the family Sylviidae) of chiefly Asian warblers that stitch leaves together to support and hide their nests

**tai·lored** \'tā-lərd\ *adjective* (1862)
**1 :** fashioned or fitted to resemble a tailor's work
**2 :** CUSTOM-MADE
**3 :** having the look of one fitted by a custom tailor

**tai·lor·ing** \'tā-lə-riŋ\ *noun* (1662)
**1 a :** the business or occupation of a tailor **b :** the work or workmanship of a tailor
**2 :** the making or adapting of something to suit a particular purpose

**¹tai·lor–made** \ˌtā-lər-'mād\ *adjective* (1832)
**1 :** made by a tailor or with a tailor's care and style
**2 :** made or fitted especially to a particular use or purpose
**3 :** factory made rather than hand-rolled ⟨*tailor-made* cigarettes⟩

**²tailor–made** *noun* (1892)

: one that is tailor-made; *specifically* **:** a woman's garment styled for a trim fit and with stiff straight lines

**tail·piece** \'tā(ə)l-ˌpēs\ *noun* (1601)
**1 :** a piece added at the end
**2 :** a device from which the strings of a stringed instrument are stretched to the pegs — see VIOLIN illustration
**3 :** an ornament placed below the text matter of a page

**tail·pipe** \-ˌpīp\ *noun* (1922)
: an outlet by which the exhaust gases are removed from an engine (as of an automobile or jet aircraft)

**tail·plane** \-ˌplān\ *noun* (1909)
: the horizontal tail surfaces of an airplane including the stabilizer and the elevator

**tail·race** \'tā(ə)l-ˌrās\ *noun* (1776)
: a race for conveying water away from a point of industrial application (as a waterwheel or turbine) after use

**tail·slide** \-ˌslīd\ *noun* (1916)
: an aerobatic maneuver in which an aircraft that has been pulled into a steep climb stalls and then loses altitude by dropping backward

**tail·spin** \-ˌspin\ *noun* (circa 1917)
**1 :** SPIN 2a
**2 :** a mental or emotional letdown or collapse
**3 :** a sustained and usually severe decline or downturn ⟨stock prices in a *tailspin*⟩

**tail·wa·ter** \-ˌwȯ-tər, -ˌwä-\ *noun* (1759)
**1 :** water below a dam or waterpower development
**2 :** excess surface water draining especially from a field under cultivation

**tail·wind** \-ˌwind\ *noun* (1897)
: a wind having the same general direction as a course of movement (as of an aircraft)

**Tai·no** \'tī-(ˌ)nō\ *noun, plural* **Taino** or **Tainos** [Spanish] (circa 1895)
**1 :** a member of an aboriginal Arawakan people of the Greater Antilles and the Bahamas
**2 :** the extinct language of the Taino people

**¹taint** \'tānt\ *verb* [Middle English *tainten* to color & *taynten* to attaint; Middle English *tainten*, from Anglo-French *teinter*, from Middle French *teint*, past participle of *teindre*, from Latin *tingere*; Middle English *taynten*, from Middle French *ataint*, past participle of *ataindre* — more at TINGE, ATTAIN] (1573)
*transitive verb*
**1 :** to contaminate morally **:** CORRUPT ⟨scholarship *tainted* by envy⟩
**2 :** to affect with putrefaction **:** SPOIL
**3 :** to touch or affect slightly with something bad ⟨persons *tainted* with prejudice⟩
*intransitive verb*
**1** *obsolete* **:** to become weak
**2 :** to become affected with putrefaction **:** SPOIL
*synonym* see CONTAMINATE

**²taint** *noun* (1601)
: a contaminating mark or influence
— **taint·less** \-ləs\ *adjective*

**'tain't** \'tānt\ (1818)
: it ain't

**¹tai·pan** \'tī-ˌpan, 'tī-'pän\ *noun* [Chinese (Guangdong) *daaih-bāan*, from *daaih* big + *bāan* class] (1834)
: a powerful businessman and especially formerly a foreigner living and operating in Hong Kong or China

**²tai·pan** \'tī-ˌpan\ *noun* [Wik Munkan (Australian aboriginal language of northern Queensland) *dhayban*] (1933)
: an exceedingly venomous elapid snake (*Oxyuranus scutellatus*) of northern Australia and New Guinea

**Ta·jik** \tä-'jik, tə-, -'jēk\ *noun* (1815)
**1 :** a member of a Persian-speaking ethnic group living in Tajikistan, Afghanistan, and adjacent areas of central Asia
**2 :** the form of Persian spoken by the Tajiks

**ta·ka** \'tä-kə, -(ˌ)kä\ *noun* [Bengali *ṭākā* rupee, taka, from Sanskrit *ṭaṅka* stamped coin] (1972)

— see MONEY table

**ta·ka·he** \tä-'kä-(ˌ)hä\ *noun* [Maori] (1851)
: a flightless bird (*Notornis mantelli* synonym *Porphyrio mantelli*) of New Zealand that is related to the gallinules

**¹take** \'tāk\ *verb* **took** \'tu̇k\; **tak·en** \'tā-kən\; **tak·ing** [Middle English, from Old English *tacan*, from Old Norse *taka*; akin to Middle Dutch *taken* to take] (before 12th century)
*transitive verb*
**1 :** to get into one's hands or into one's possession, power, or control: as **a :** to seize or capture physically ⟨*took* them as prisoners⟩ **b :** to get possession of (as fish or game) by killing or capturing **c** (1) **:** to move against (as an opponent's piece in chess) and remove from play (2) **:** to win in a card game ⟨able to *take* 12 tricks⟩ **d :** to acquire by eminent domain
**2 :** GRASP, GRIP ⟨*take* the ax by the handle⟩
**3 a :** to catch or attack through the effect of a sudden force or influence ⟨*taken* with a fit of laughing⟩ ⟨*taken* ill⟩ **b :** to catch or come upon in a particular situation or action ⟨was *taken* unawares⟩ **c :** to gain the approval or liking of **:** CAPTIVATE, DELIGHT ⟨was quite *taken* with her at their first meeting⟩
**4 a :** to receive into one's body (as by swallowing, drinking, or inhaling) ⟨*take* a pill⟩ **:** to expose oneself to (as sun or air) for pleasure or physical benefit **c :** to partake of **:** EAT ⟨*takes* dinner about seven⟩
**5 a :** to bring or receive into a relation or connection ⟨*takes* just four students a year⟩ ⟨it's time he *took* a wife⟩ **b :** to copulate with
**6 :** to transfer into one's own keeping: **a :** APPROPRIATE **b :** to obtain or secure for use (as by lease, subscription, or purchase) ⟨*take* a cottage for the summer⟩ ⟨I'll *take* the red one⟩ ⟨*took* an ad in the paper⟩
**7 a :** ASSUME ⟨gods often *took* the likeness of a human being⟩ ⟨when the college *took* its present form⟩ **b** (1) **:** to enter into or undertake the duties of ⟨*take* a job⟩ ⟨*take* office⟩ ⟨*took* command of the fleet⟩ (2) **:** to move onto or into **:** move into position on ⟨the home team *took* the field⟩ **c** (1) **:** to bind oneself by ⟨*take* the oath of office⟩ (2) **:** to make (a decision) especially with finality or authority **d :** to impose upon oneself ⟨*take* the trouble to do good work⟩ **e** (1) **:** to adopt as one's own ⟨*take* a stand on the issue⟩ ⟨*take* an interest⟩ (2) **:** to align or ally oneself with ⟨mother *took* his side⟩ **f :** to assume as if rightfully one's own or as if granted ⟨*take* the credit⟩ **g :** to have or assume as a proper part of or accompaniment to itself ⟨transitive verbs *take* an object⟩
**8 a :** to secure by winning in competition ⟨*took* first place⟩ **b :** DEFEAT
**9 :** to pick out **:** CHOOSE, SELECT
**10 :** to adopt, choose, or avail oneself of for use: as **a :** to have recourse to as an instrument for doing something ⟨*take* a scythe to the weeds⟩ **b :** to use as a means of transportation or progression ⟨*take* the bus⟩ **c :** to have recourse to for safety or refuge ⟨*take* shelter⟩ **d :** to go along, into, or through ⟨*took* a different route⟩ **e** (1) **:** to proceed to occupy ⟨*take* a seat in the rear⟩ (2) **:** to use up (as space or time) ⟨*takes* a long time to dry⟩ (3) **:** NEED, REQUIRE ⟨*takes* a size nine shoe⟩ ⟨it *takes* two to start a fight⟩
**11 a :** to obtain by deriving from a source **:** DRAW ⟨*takes* its title from the name of the hero⟩ **b** (1) **:** to obtain as the result of a special procedure **:** ASCERTAIN ⟨*take* the temperature⟩ ⟨*take* a census⟩ (2) **:** to get in or as if in writing ⟨*take* notes⟩ ⟨*take* an inventory⟩ (3) **:** to get by drawing or painting or by photography ⟨*take* a

snapshot) (4) **:** to get by transference from one surface to another ⟨*take* a proof⟩ ⟨*take* finger-prints⟩ **12 :** to receive or accept whether willingly or reluctantly ⟨*take* a bribe⟩ ⟨will you *take* this call⟩ ⟨*take* a bet⟩: as **a** (1) **:** to submit to **:** ENDURE ⟨*take* a cut in pay⟩ (2) **:** WITHSTAND ⟨it will *take* a lot of punishment⟩ (3) **:** SUFFER ⟨*took* a direct hit⟩ **b** (1) **:** to accept as true **:** BELIEVE ⟨I'll *take* your word for it⟩ (2) **:** FOLLOW ⟨*take* my advice⟩ (3) **:** to accept with the mind in a specified way ⟨*took* the news hard⟩ **c :** to indulge in and enjoy ⟨was *taking* his ease on the porch⟩ **d :** to receive or accept as a return (as in payment, compensation, or reparation) **e :** to accept in a usually professional relationship — often used with *on* ⟨agreed to *take* him on as a client⟩ **f :** to refrain from hitting at ⟨a pitched ball⟩ **13 a** (1) **:** to let in **:** ADMIT ⟨the boat was *taking* water fast⟩ (2) **:** ACCOMMODATE ⟨the suitcase wouldn't *take* another thing⟩ **b :** to be affected injuriously by (as a disease) **:** CONTRACT ⟨*take* cold⟩; *also* **:** to be seized by ⟨*take* a fit⟩ ⟨*take* fright⟩ **c :** to absorb or become impregnated with (as dye); *also* **:** to be effectively treated by ⟨a surface that *takes* a fine polish⟩ **14 a :** APPREHEND, UNDERSTAND ⟨how should I *take* your remark⟩ **b :** CONSIDER, SUPPOSE ⟨I *take* it you're not going⟩ **c :** RECKON, ACCEPT ⟨*taking* a stride at 30 inches⟩ **d :** FEEL, EXPERIENCE ⟨*take* pleasure⟩ ⟨*take* an instant dislike to someone⟩ ⟨*take* offense⟩ **15 :** to lead, carry, or cause to go along to another place ⟨this bus will *take* you into town⟩ ⟨*took* an umbrella with her⟩ **16 a :** REMOVE ⟨*take* eggs from a nest⟩ **b :** to put an end to ⟨life⟩ (2) **:** to remove by death ⟨was *taken* in his prime⟩ **c :** SUBTRACT ⟨*take* two from four⟩ **d :** EXACT ⟨the weather *took* its toll⟩ **17 a :** to undertake and make, do, or perform ⟨*take* a walk⟩ ⟨*take* aim⟩ ⟨*take* legal action⟩ ⟨*take* a test⟩ ⟨*take* a look⟩ **b :** to participate in ⟨*take* a meeting⟩ **18 a :** to deal with ⟨*take* first things first⟩ **b :** to consider or view in a particular relation ⟨*taken* together, the details were significant⟩; *especially* **:** to consider as an example ⟨*take* style, for instance⟩ **c** (1) **:** to apply oneself to the study of ⟨*take* music lessons⟩ ⟨*take* French⟩ (2) **:** to study for especially successfully ⟨*taking* a degree in engineering⟩ ⟨*took* holy orders⟩ **19 :** to obtain money from especially fraudulently ⟨*took* me for all I had⟩ **20 :** to pass or attempt to pass through, along, or over ⟨*took* the curve too fast⟩ *intransitive verb* **1 :** to obtain possession: as **a :** CAPTURE **b :** to receive property under law as one's own **2 :** to lay hold **:** CATCH, HOLD **3 :** to establish a take especially by uniting or growing ⟨90 percent of the grafts *take*⟩ **4 a :** to betake oneself **:** set out **:** GO ⟨*take* after a purse snatcher⟩ **b** *chiefly dialect* — used as an intensifier or redundantly with a following verb ⟨*took* and swung at the ball⟩ **5 a :** to take effect **:** ACT, OPERATE ⟨hoped the lesson he taught would *take*⟩ **b :** to show the natural or intended effect ⟨dry fuel *takes* readily⟩ **6 :** CHARM, CAPTIVATE ⟨a *taking* smile⟩ **7 :** DETRACT **8 :** to be seized or attacked in a specified way **:** BECOME ⟨*took* sick⟩ *usage* see BRING ☆
— **tak·er** *noun*
— **take a back seat :** to have or assume a secondary position or status
— **take a bath :** to suffer a heavy financial loss
— **take account of :** to take into account
— **take advantage of 1 :** to use to advantage **:** profit by **2 :** to impose on **:** EXPLOIT
— **take after :** to resemble in features, build, character, or disposition

— **take apart 1 :** to disconnect the pieces of **:** DISASSEMBLE **2 :** to treat roughly or harshly **:** tear into
— **take a powder :** to leave hurriedly
— **take care :** to be careful or watchful **:** exercise caution or prudence
— **take care of :** to attend to or provide for the needs, operation, or treatment of
— **take charge :** to assume care, custody, command, or control
— **take effect 1 :** to become operative **2 :** to be effective
— **take exception :** OBJECT ⟨*took* exception to the remark⟩
— **take five** *or* **take ten :** to take a break especially from work
— **take for :** to suppose to be; *especially* **:** to suppose mistakenly to be
— **take for granted 1 :** to assume as true, real, or expected **2 :** to value too lightly
— **take heart :** to gain courage or confidence
— **take hold 1 :** GRASP, GRIP, SEIZE **2 :** to become attached or established **:** take effect
— **take into account :** to make allowance for
— **take in vain :** to use (a name) profanely or without proper respect
— **take issue :** DISAGREE
— **take it on the chin :** to suffer from the results of a situation
— **take kindly to :** to show an inclination to accept or approve
— **take notice of :** to observe or treat with special attention
— **take one's time :** to be leisurely about doing something
— **take part :** JOIN, PARTICIPATE, SHARE
— **take place :** HAPPEN, OCCUR
— **take root 1 :** to become rooted **2 :** to become fixed or established
— **take shape :** to assume a definite or distinctive form
— **take stock :** to make an assessment
— **take the cake :** to carry off the prize **:** rank first
— **take the count 1** *of a boxer* **:** to be counted out **2 :** to go down in defeat
— **take the floor :** to rise (as in a meeting or a legislative assembly) to make a formal address
— **take to 1 :** to go to or into ⟨*take to* the woods⟩ **2 :** to apply or devote oneself to (as a practice, habit, or occupation) ⟨*take to* begging⟩ **3 :** to adapt oneself to **:** respond to ⟨*takes to* water like a duck⟩ **4 :** to conceive a liking for
— **take to task :** to call to account for a shortcoming **:** CRITICIZE
— **take turns :** ALTERNATE

²**take** *noun* (1654)
**1 :** something that is taken: **a :** the amount of money received **:** PROCEEDS, RECEIPTS, INCOME **b :** SHARE, CUT ⟨wanted a bigger *take*⟩ **c :** the number or quantity (as of animals, fish, or pelts) taken at one time **:** CATCH, HAUL **d :** a section or installment done as a unit or at one time **e** (1) **:** a scene filmed or televised at one time without stopping the camera (2) **:** a sound recording made during a single recording period; *especially* **:** a trial recording **2 :** an act or the action of taking: as **a :** the action of killing, capturing, or catching (as game or fish) **b** (1) **:** the uninterrupted photographing or televising of a scene (2) **:** the making of a sound recording **3 a :** a local or systemic reaction indicative of successful vaccination (as against smallpox) **b :** a successful union (as of a graft) **4 :** a visible response or reaction (as to something unexpected) ⟨a delayed *take*⟩ **5 :** a distinct or personal point of view, outlook, or assessment ⟨was asked for her *take* on recent developments⟩; *also* **:** a distinct treatment or variation ⟨a new *take* on an old style⟩
— **on the take :** illegally paid for favors

**take–away** \'tāk-ə-ˌwā\ *adjective* (1964)
*British* **:** TAKE-OUT
— **take–away** *noun*
**take back** *transitive verb* (1775)
**:** to make a retraction of **:** WITHDRAW
**take–charge** \'tāk-'chärj\ *adjective* (1954)
**:** having the qualities of a forceful leader ⟨a *take-charge* executive⟩
¹**take–down** \'tāk-ˌdaŭn\ *noun* (1893)
**1 :** the action or an act of taking down
**2 :** something (as a rifle) having takedown construction
²**take–down** \'tāk-'daŭn\ *adjective* (1907)
**:** constructed so as to be readily taken apart ⟨a *takedown* rifle⟩
**take down** (15th century)
*transitive verb*
**1 :** to lower without removing ⟨*took down* his pants⟩
**2 a :** to pull to pieces ⟨*take down* a building⟩ **b :** DISASSEMBLE ⟨*take* a rifle *down*⟩
**3 :** to lower the spirit or vanity of
**4 a :** to write down **b :** to record by mechanical means
*intransitive verb*
**:** to become seized or attacked especially by illness
**take–home pay** \'tāk-ˌhōm-\ *noun* (1943)
**:** income remaining from salary or wages after deductions (as for income-tax withholding)
**take–in** \'tā-ˌkin\ *noun* (1778)
**:** an act of taking in especially by deceiving
**take in** *transitive verb* (circa 1515)
**1 :** to draw into a smaller compass ⟨*take in* the slack of a line⟩: **a :** FURL **b :** to make (a garment) smaller by enlarging seams or tucks
**2 a :** to receive as a guest or lodger **b :** to give shelter to **c :** to take to a police station as a prisoner
**3 :** to receive as payment or proceeds
**4 :** to receive (work) into one's house to be done for pay ⟨*take in* washing⟩
**5 :** to encompass within its limits
**6 a :** to include in an itinerary **b :** ATTEND ⟨*take in* a movie⟩
**7 :** to receive into the mind **:** PERCEIVE
**8 :** DECEIVE, DUPE
**taken** *past participle of* TAKE
**take–off** \'tā-ˌkȯf\ *noun* (1846)
**1 :** an imitation especially in the way of caricature
**2 a :** a spot at which one takes off **b :** a starting point **:** point of departure
**3 a :** a rise or leap from a surface in making a jump or flight or an ascent in an aircraft or in the launching of a rocket **b :** an action of starting out **c :** a rapid rise in activity, growth, or popularity ⟨an economic *takeoff*⟩
**4 :** an action of removing something
**5 :** a mechanism for transmission of the power of an engine or vehicle to operate some other mechanism

☆ SYNONYMS
**Take, seize, grasp, clutch, snatch, grab** mean to get hold of by or as if by catching up with the hand. TAKE is a general term applicable to any manner of getting something into one's possession or control ⟨*take* some salad from the bowl⟩. SEIZE implies a sudden and forcible movement in getting hold of something tangible or an apprehending of something fleeting or elusive when intangible ⟨*seized* the suspect⟩. GRASP stresses a laying hold so as to have firmly in possession ⟨*grasp* the handle and pull⟩. CLUTCH suggests avidity or anxiety in seizing or grasping and may imply less success in holding ⟨*clutching* her purse⟩. SNATCH suggests more suddenness or quickness but less force than SEIZE ⟨*snatched* a doughnut and ran⟩. GRAB implies more roughness or rudeness than SNATCH ⟨*grabbed* roughly by the arm⟩.

**take off** (14th century)
*transitive verb*
**1 :** REMOVE ⟨*take* your shoes *off*⟩
**2 a :** RELEASE ⟨*took off* the morning train⟩ **b :** DISCONTINUE, WITHDRAW ⟨*took off* the morning train⟩ **c :** to take or allow as a discount : DEDUCT ⟨*took* 10 percent *off*⟩ **d :** to spend (a period of time) away from a usual occupation or activity ⟨*took* two weeks *off*⟩
**3** *slang* **:** ROB
*intransitive verb*
**1 :** to take away **:** DETRACT
**2 a :** to start off or away **:** SET OUT, DEPART **b** (1) **:** to branch off (as from a main stream or stem) (2) **:** to take a point of origin **c :** to begin a leap or spring **d :** to leave the surface **:** begin flight **e :** to embark on rapid activity, development, or growth **f :** to spring into wide use or popularity

**take on** (15th century)
*transitive verb*
**1 a :** to begin to perform or deal with **:** UNDERTAKE ⟨*took on* new responsibilities⟩ **b :** to contend with as an opponent ⟨*took on* the neighborhood bully⟩
**2 :** ENGAGE, HIRE
**3 a :** to assume or acquire as or as if one's own ⟨the city's plaza *takes on* a carnival air —W. T. LeViness⟩ **b :** to have as a mathematical domain or range ⟨what values does the function *take on*⟩
*intransitive verb*
**:** to show one's feelings especially of grief or anger in a demonstrative way ⟨they cried and *took on* something terrible —Bob Hope⟩

**take·out** \'tā-ˌkau̇t\ *noun* (circa 1917)
**1 :** the action or an act of taking out
**2 a :** something taken out or prepared to be taken out **b** (1) **:** an article (as in a newspaper) printed on consecutive pages so as to be conveniently removed (2) **:** an intensive study or report
**3 :** CARRYOUT 1

**take·out** \'tā-ˌkau̇t\ *adjective* (1965)
**:** of, relating to, selling, or being food not to be consumed on the premises ⟨*take-out* counter⟩ ⟨a *take-out* supper⟩

**take out** (13th century)
*transitive verb*
**1 a** (1) **:** DEDUCT, SEPARATE (2) **:** EXCLUDE, OMIT (3) **:** WITHDRAW, WITHHOLD **b :** to find release for **:** VENT ⟨*take out* their resentments on one another —J. W. Aldridge⟩ **c** (1) **:** ELIMINATE (2) **:** KILL, DESTROY (3) **:** KNOCK OUT
**2 :** to take as an equivalent in another form ⟨*took* the debt *out* in trade⟩
**3 a :** to obtain from the proper authority ⟨*take out* a charter⟩ **b :** to arrange for (insurance)
**4 :** to overcall (a bridge partner) in a different suit
*intransitive verb*
**:** to start on a course **:** SET OUT
**— take it out on :** to expend anger, vexation, or frustration in harassment of

**take·out double** \'tā-ˌkau̇t-\ *noun* (circa 1944)
**:** a double made in bridge to convey information to and request a bid from one's partner

**take·over** \'tā-ˌkō-vər\ *noun* (circa 1917)
**:** the action or an act of taking over

**take over** (1884)
*transitive verb*
**:** to assume control or possession of or responsibility for ⟨military leaders *took over* the government⟩
*intransitive verb*
**1 :** to assume control or possession
**2 :** to become dominant

**take–up** \'tā-ˌkəp\ *noun* (1838)
**:** the action or act of taking up

**take up** (14th century)
*transitive verb*
**1 :** PICK UP, LIFT
**2 a :** to begin to occupy (land) **b :** to gather from a number of sources ⟨*took up* a collection⟩

**3 a :** to accept or adopt for the purpose of assisting **b :** to accept or adopt as one's own ⟨*took up* the life of a farmer⟩ ⟨*took up* Irish citizenship⟩ **c :** to absorb or incorporate into itself ⟨plants *taking up* nutrients⟩
**4 a :** to enter upon (as a business, hobby, or subject of study) ⟨*take up* skiing⟩ ⟨*took up* the trumpet⟩ ⟨had *taken up* Marxism⟩ **b :** to proceed to consider or deal with ⟨*take up* one problem at a time⟩
**5 :** to establish oneself in ⟨*took up* residence in town⟩
**6 :** to occupy entirely or exclusively **:** fill up ⟨the meeting was *taken up* with old business⟩
**7 :** to make tighter or shorter ⟨*take up* the slack⟩
**8 :** to respond favorably to (as a person offering a bet, challenge, or proposal) ⟨*took* me *up* on it⟩
**9 :** to begin again or take over from another ⟨we must *take* the good work *up* again⟩
*intransitive verb*
**1 :** to make a beginning where another has left off
**2 :** to become shortened **:** draw together **:** SHRINK
**— take up the cudgels :** to engage vigorously in a defense or dispute
**— take up with 1 :** to become interested or absorbed in **2 :** to begin to associate or consort with

**ta·kin** \'tä-ˌkēn\ *noun* [Mishmi (Tibeto-Burman language of northeast India)] (1850)
**:** a large heavily built ruminant (*Budorcas taxicolor*) of Tibet and adjacent areas of Asia that is related to the goats but in some respects resembles the antelopes

takin

**tak·ings** \'tā-kiŋz\ *noun plural* (1632)
*chiefly British* **:** receipts especially of money

**¹ta·la** \'tä-lə\ *noun* [Sanskrit *tāla*, literally, hand-clapping] (1891)
**:** one of the ancient traditional rhythmic patterns of Indian music — compare RAGA

**²ta·la** \'tä-lə, -ˌ)lä\ *noun, plural* **tala** [Samoan, from English *dollar*] (1967)
**—** see MONEY table

**Tal·bot** \'tȯl-bət, 'tal-\ *noun* [probably from *Talbot*, name of a Norman family in England] (1562)
**:** a large heavy mostly white hound with pendulous ears and drooping flews held to be ancestral to the bloodhound

**talc** \'talk\ *noun* [Middle French *talc* mica, from Medieval Latin *talk*, from Arabic *ṭalq*] (1610)
**1 :** a very soft mineral that is a basic silicate of magnesium, has a soapy feel, and is used especially in making talcum powder
**2 :** TALCUM POWDER
**— talc·ose** \'tal-ˌkōs\ *adjective*

**tal·cum powder** \'tal-kəm-\ *noun* [Medieval Latin *talcum* mica, alteration of earlier *talk*] (circa 1890)
**1 :** powdered talc
**2 :** a toilet powder composed of perfumed talc or talc and a mild antiseptic

**tale** \'tā(ə)l\ *noun* [Middle English, from Old English *talu;* akin to Old Norse *tala* talk] (before 12th century)
**1** *obsolete* **:** DISCOURSE, TALK
**2 a :** a series of events or facts told or presented **b :** ACCOUNT **b** (1) **:** a report of a private or confidential matter ⟨dead men tell no *tales*⟩ (2) **:** a libelous report or piece of gossip
**3 a :** a usually imaginative narrative of an event **:** STORY **b :** an intentionally untrue report **:** FALSEHOOD ⟨always preferred the *tale* to the truth —Sir Winston Churchill⟩
**4 a :** COUNT, TALLY **b :** TOTAL

**tale·bear·er** \-ˌbar-ər, -ˌber-\ *noun* (15th century)
**:** one that spreads gossip or rumors; *also* **:** TATTLETALE
**— tale·bear·ing** \-iŋ\ *adjective or noun*

**tal·ent** \'ta-lənt\ *noun* [Middle English, from Old English *talente*, from Latin *talenta*, plural of *talentum* unit of weight or money, from Greek *talanton* pan of a scale, weight; akin to Greek *tlēnai* to bear; in senses 2–5, from the parable of the talents in Matthew 25:14–30 — more at TOLERATE] (before 12th century)
**1 a :** any of several ancient units of weight **b :** a unit of value equal to the value of a talent of gold or silver
**2** *archaic* **:** a characteristic feature, aptitude, or disposition of a person or animal
**3 :** the natural endowments of a person
**4 a :** a special often creative or artistic aptitude **b :** general intelligence or mental power **:** ABILITY
**5 :** a person of talent or a group of persons of talent in a field or activity ◆
*synonym* see GIFT
**— tal·ent·ed** \-lən-təd\ *adjective*
**— tal·ent·less** \-lənt-ləs\ *adjective*

**talent scout** *noun* (1936)
**:** a person engaged in discovering and recruiting people of talent for a specialized field or activity

**talent show** *noun* (1953)
**:** a show consisting of a series of individual performances (as singing) by amateurs who may be selected for special recognition as performing talent

**ta·ler** \'tä-lər\ *noun* [German — more at DOLLAR] (circa 1905)
**:** any of numerous silver coins issued by various German states from the 15th to the 19th centuries

**tales·man** \'tā(ə)lz-mən, 'tā-ˌlēz-\ *noun* [Middle English *tales* talesmen, from Medieval Latin *tales de circumstantibus* such (persons) of the bystanders; from the wording of the writ summoning them] (1679)
**1 :** a person added to a jury usually from among bystanders to make up a deficiency in the available number of jurors
**2 :** a member of a large pool of persons called for jury duty from which jurors are selected

◇ WORD HISTORY
**talent**    The ancient Greek word *talanton,* originally denoting the pan of a scale, was also applied to a unit of weight and then a monetary unit. Borrowed into English through Latin as *talent,* the word has developed several figurative meanings based on its use in the New Testament parable of the talents (Matthew 25:14–30). In the parable a master gives money to his servants: five talents to one, two talents to another, and finally a single talent to a third. The first two doubled their capital, and the master was pleased. The third servant, however, buried his talent in the earth for fear of losing it. This made the master very angry since he expected his servant at least to have invested his talent with bankers so that it would gain interest. The master then took back the one talent and gave it to the servant who had ten. Traditionally the talent has been taken as a metaphor for a God-given endowment that if not used would be lost. The English word *talent* has had this metaphorical sense since the 15th century, and several centuries later it gave rise to the extended meaning "mental ability or aptitude."

\ə\ **abut** \ᵊ\ **kitten** \ər\ **further** \a\ **ash** \ā\ **ace**
\ä\ **mop, mar** \au̇\ **out** \ch\ **chin** \e\ **bet** \ē\ **easy**
\g\ **go** \i\ **hit** \ī\ **ice** \j\ **job** \ŋ\ **sing** \ō\ **go**
\ȯ\ **law** \ȯi\ **boy** \th\ **thin** \th̲\ **the** \ü\ **loot** \u̇\ **foot**
\y\ **yet** \zh\ **vision**    *see also* Guide to Pronunciation

**tale–tell·er** \'tā(ə)l-,te-lər\ *noun* (14th century)
**1** : one who tells tales or stories
**2** : TALEBEARER
— **tale–tell·ing** \-,te-liŋ\ *adjective or noun*
**tali** *plural of* TALUS
**ta·li·pes** \'ta-lə-,pēz\ *noun* [New Latin, from Latin *talus* ankle + *pes* foot — more at FOOT] (circa 1841)
: CLUBFOOT
**tal·is·man** \'ta-ləs-mən, -ləz-\ *noun, plural* **-mans** [French *talisman* or Spanish *talismán* or Italian *talismano;* all from Arabic *tilsam,* from Middle Greek *telesma,* from Greek, consecration, from *telein* to initiate into the mysteries, complete, from *telos* end — more at TELOS] (1638)
**1** : an object held to act as a charm to avert evil and bring good fortune
**2** : something producing apparently magical or miraculous effects
— **tal·is·man·ic** \,ta-ləs-'ma-nik, -ləz-\ *adjective*
— **tal·is·man·i·cal·ly** \-ni-k(ə-)lē\ *adverb*
**¹talk** \'tȯk\ *verb* [Middle English; akin to Old English *talu* tale] (13th century)
*transitive verb*
**1** : to deliver or express in speech : UTTER
**2** : to make the subject of conversation or discourse : DISCUSS ⟨*talk* business⟩
**3** : to influence, affect, or cause by talking ⟨*talked* them into going⟩
**4** : to use (a language) for conversing or communicating : SPEAK
*intransitive verb*
**1 a** : to express or exchange ideas by means of spoken words **b** : to convey information or communicate in any way (as with signs or sounds) ⟨can make a trumpet *talk*⟩
**2** : to use speech : SPEAK
**3 a** : to speak idly : PRATE **b** : GOSSIP **c** : to reveal secret or confidential information
**4** : to give a talk : LECTURE
— **talk·er** *noun*
— **talk back** : to answer impertinently
— **talk sense** : to voice rational, logical, or sensible thoughts
— **talk through one's hat** : to voice irrational, illogical, or erroneous ideas
— **talk turkey** : to speak frankly or bluntly
**²talk** *noun* (15th century)
**1** : the act or an instance of talking : SPEECH
**2** : a way of speaking : LANGUAGE
**3** : pointless or fruitless discussion : VERBIAGE
**4** : a formal discussion, negotiation, or exchange of views — often used in plural
**5 a** : MENTION, REPORT **b** : RUMOR, GOSSIP
**6** : the topic of interested comment, conversation, or gossip ⟨it's the *talk* of the town⟩
**7 a** : ADDRESS, LECTURE **b** : written analysis or discussion presented in an informal or conversational manner
**8** : communicative sounds or signs resembling or functioning as talk ⟨bird *talk*⟩
**talk·a·thon** \'tȯ-kə-,thän\ *noun* (1934)
: a long session of discussion or speech-making
**talk·a·tive** \'tȯ-kə-tiv\ *adjective* (15th century)
: given to talking; *also* : full of talk ☆
— **talk·a·tive·ly** *adverb*
— **talk·a·tive·ness** *noun*
**talk down** (1901)
*intransitive verb*
: to speak in a condescending or oversimplified fashion
*transitive verb*
: to disparage or belittle by talking
**talk·ie** \'tȯ-kē\ *noun* (1913)
: a motion picture with a synchronized sound track
**talking book** *noun* (1932)
: a phonograph or tape recording of a reading of a book or magazine designed chiefly for the use of the blind
**talking head** *noun* (1968)

: the televised head and shoulders shot of a person talking; *also* : a television personality who appears in such shots
**talking machine** *noun* (1890)
: an early phonograph
**talking point** *noun* (circa 1914)
: something that lends support to an argument; *also* : a subject of discussion
**talk·ing–to** \'tȯ-kiŋ-,tü\ *noun* (1884)
: REPRIMAND, LECTURE
**talk out** *transitive verb* (1954)
: to clarify or settle by oral discussion
**talk over** *transitive verb* (1734)
: to review or consider in conversation : DISCUSS
**talk radio** *noun* (1972)
: radio programming consisting of call-in shows
**talk show** *noun* (1965)
: a radio or television program in which usually well-known persons engage in discussions or are interviewed
**talk up** (1722)
*transitive verb*
: to discuss favorably : ADVOCATE, PROMOTE
*intransitive verb*
: to speak up plainly or directly
**talky** \'tȯ-kē\ *adjective* **talk·i·er; -est** (1815)
**1** : TALKATIVE
**2** : containing too much talk
— **talk·i·ness** \-nəs\ *noun*
**tall** \'tȯl\ *adjective* [Middle English, probably from Old English *getæl* quick, ready; akin to Old High German *gizal* quick] (15th century)
**1** *obsolete* : BRAVE, COURAGEOUS
**2 a** : high in stature **b** : of a specified height ⟨five feet *tall*⟩
**3 a** : of considerable height ⟨*tall* trees⟩ **b** : long from bottom to top ⟨a *tall* book⟩ **c** : of a higher growing variety or species of plant
**4 a** : large or formidable in amount, extent, or degree ⟨a *tall* order to fill⟩ **b** : POMPOUS, HIGH-FLOWN ⟨*tall* talk about the vast mysteries of life —W. A. White⟩ **c** : highly exaggerated : INCREDIBLE, IMPROBABLE ⟨a *tall* story⟩
**synonym** see HIGH
— **tall** *adverb*
— **tall·ish** \'tȯ-lish\ *adjective*
— **tall·ness** \'tȯl-nəs\ *noun*
**tal·lage** \'ta-lij\ *noun* [Middle English *taillage, tallage,* from Old French *taillage,* from *taillier* to cut, limit, tax — more at TAILOR] (14th century)
: an impost or due levied by a lord upon his tenants
**tall·boy** \'tȯl-,bȯi\ *noun* (1769)
**1 a** : HIGHBOY **b** : a double chest of drawers usually with the upper section slightly smaller than the lower
**2** *British* : CLOTHESPRESS
**tall fescue** *noun* (circa 1762)
: a European fescue (*Festuca elatior*) with erect smooth stems 3 to 4 feet (about 1 meter) high that has been introduced into North America — called also *tall fescue grass;* compare FESCUE FOOT
**tall·grass prairie** \'tȯl-,gras-\ *noun* (1920)
: PRAIRIE 2a
**tal·lith** \'tä-ləs, 'ta-, -lət, -ləth\ *or* **tal·lis** \-ləs\ *noun* [Hebrew *tallīth* cover, cloak] (1613)
: a shawl with fringed corners worn over the head or shoulders by Jewish men especially during morning prayers
**tall oil** \'täl-, 'tȯl-\ *noun* [part translation of German *Tallöl,* part translation of Swedish *tallolja,* from *tall* pine + *olja* oil] (circa 1926)
: a resinous by-product from the manufacture of chemical wood pulp used especially in making soaps, coatings, and oils

tallith

**¹tal·low** \'ta-(,)lō\ *noun* [Middle English *talgh, talow;* akin to Middle Dutch *talch* tallow] (14th century)
: the white nearly tasteless solid rendered fat of cattle and sheep used chiefly in soap, candles, and lubricants
— **tal·lowy** \'ta-lə-wē\ *adjective*
**²tallow** *transitive verb* (15th century)
: to grease or smear with tallow
**tall ship** *noun* (circa 1548)
: a sailing vessel with at least two masts; *especially* : SQUARE-RIGGER
**¹tal·ly** \'ta-lē\ *noun, plural* **tallies** [Middle English *talye,* from Medieval Latin *talea, tallia,* from Latin *talea* twig, cutting] (15th century)
**1** : a device (as a notched rod or mechanical counter) for visibly recording or accounting especially business transactions
**2 a** : a recorded reckoning or account (as of items or charges) ⟨keep a daily *tally* of accidents⟩ **b** : a score or point made (as in a game)
**3 a** : a part that corresponds to an opposite or companion member : COMPLEMENT **b** : a state of correspondence or agreement
**²tally** *verb* **tal·lied; tal·ly·ing** (15th century)
*transitive verb*
**1 a** : to record on or as if on a tally : TABULATE **b** : to list or check off (as a cargo) by items **c** : to register (as a score) in a contest
**2** : to make a count of : RECKON
**3** : to cause to correspond
*intransitive verb*
**1 a** : to make a tally by or as if by tabulating **b** : to register a point in a contest : SCORE
**2** : CORRESPOND, MATCH
**tal·ly·ho** \,ta-lē-'hō\ *noun, plural* **-hos** [probably from French *taïaut,* a cry used to excite hounds in deer hunting] (1772)
**1** : a call of a huntsman at sight of the fox
**2** [*Tally-ho,* name of a coach formerly plying between London and Birmingham] : a four-in-hand coach
**tal·ly·man** \'ta-lē-mən, -,man\ *noun* (1654)
**1** *British* : one who sells goods on the installment plan
**2** : one who tallies, checks, or keeps an account or record (as of receipt of goods)
**Tal·mud** \'täl-,mùd, 'tal-məd\ *noun* [Late Hebrew *talmūdh,* literally, instruction] (1532)
: the authoritative body of Jewish tradition comprising the Mishnah and Gemara
— **Tal·mu·dic** \tal-'mü-dik, -'myü-, -'mə-; täl-'mù-\ *adjective*
— **tal·mud·ism** \'täl-,mù-,di-zəm, 'tal-, -mə-\ *noun, often capitalized*
**Tal·mud·ist** \'täl-,mü-dist, 'tal-, -mə-\ *noun* (1569)
: a specialist in Talmudic studies
**tal·on** \'ta-lən\ *noun* [Middle English, from Middle French, heel, spur, from (assumed) Vulgar Latin *talon-, talo,* from Latin *talus* ankle, anklebone] (15th century)
**1 a** : the claw of an animal and especially of a bird of prey **b** : a finger or hand of a human being
**2** : a part or object shaped like or suggestive of a heel or claw: as **a** : an ogee molding **b** : the shoulder of the bolt of a lock on which the key acts to shoot the bolt

☆ **SYNONYMS**
**Talkative, loquacious, garrulous, voluble** mean given to talk or talking. TALKATIVE may imply a readiness to engage in talk or a disposition to enjoy conversation ⟨a *talkative* neighbor⟩. LOQUACIOUS suggests the power of expressing oneself articulately, fluently, or glibly ⟨a *loquacious* spokesperson⟩. GARRULOUS implies prosy, rambling, or tedious loquacity ⟨*garrulous* traveling companions⟩. VOLUBLE suggests a free, easy, and unending loquacity ⟨a *voluble* raconteur⟩.

**3 a :** cards laid aside in a pile in solitaire **b** **:** STOCK 10c
— **tal·oned** \-lənd\ *adjective*

¹**ta·lus** \'tā-ləs, 'ta-\ *noun* [French, from Latin *talutium* slope indicating presence of gold under the soil] (1645)
**1 :** a slope formed especially by an accumulation of rock debris
**2 :** rock debris at the base of a cliff

²**ta·lus** \'tā-ləs\ *noun, plural* **ta·li** \'tā-,lī\ [New Latin, from Latin] (circa 1693)
**1 :** the human tarsal bone that bears the weight of the body and that together with the tibia and fibula forms the ankle joint
**2 :** the entire ankle

**tam** \'tam\ *noun* (1895)
**:** TAM-O'-SHANTER

**ta·ma·le** \tə-'mä-lē\ *noun* [Mexican Spanish *tamales*, plural of *tamal* tamale, from Nahuatl *tamalli* steamed cornmeal dough] (1854)
**:** ground meat seasoned usually with chili, rolled in cornmeal dough, wrapped in corn husks, and steamed

**ta·man·dua** \tə-'man-də-wə, -,man-də-'wä\ *noun* [Portuguese *tamanduá*, from Tupi] (1834)
**:** either of two arboreal anteaters (*Tamandua mexicana* and *T. tetradactyla*) of Central and South America having a nearly hairless tail

**tam·a·rack** \'ta-mə-,rak, 'tam-rak\ *noun* [origin unknown] (1805)
**1 :** any of several American larches; *especially* **:** a larch (*Larix laricina*) of northern North America that inhabits usually moist or wet areas
**2 :** the wood of a tamarack

**tam·a·rau** \,ta-mə-'raù\ *noun* [Tagalog *tamaráw*] (1898)
**:** a small dark sturdily built buffalo (*Bubalus mindorensis*) native to Mindoro

**ta·ma·ri** \tə-'mär-ē\ *noun* [Japanese] (1965)
**:** an aged soy sauce prepared with little or no added wheat

**tam·a·ril·lo** \,ta-mə-'ri-(,)lō\ *noun* [alteration of *tomatillo*] (1966)
**:** the reddish edible fruit of an arborescent shrub (*Cyphomandra betacea*) of the nightshade family that is native to South America but is grown commercially elsewhere; *also* **:** the shrub itself

**tam·a·rin** \'ta-mə-rən, -,ran\ *noun* [French, from Carib] (1780)
**:** any of numerous small chiefly South American monkeys (genera *Saguinus* and *Leontopithecus*) that are related to the marmosets and have silky fur, a long tail, and lower canine teeth that are longer than the incisors

**tam·a·rind** \'ta-mə-rənd, -,rind\ *noun* [Spanish & Portuguese *tamarindo*, from Arabic *tamr hindī*, literally, Indian date] (1533)
**:** a tropical Old World leguminous tree (*Tamarindus indica*) with hard yellowish wood, pinnate leaves, and red-striped yellow flowers; *also* **:** its fruit which has an acid pulp often used for preserves or in a cooling laxative drink

**tam·a·risk** \'ta-mə-,risk\ *noun* [Middle English *tamarisc*, from Late Latin *tamariscus*, from Latin *tamaric-, tamarix*] (14th century)
**:** any of a genus (*Tamarix* of the family Tamaricaceae, the tamarisk family) of chiefly Old World desert shrubs and trees having tiny narrow leaves and masses of minute flowers with five stamens and a one-celled ovary

**tam·ba·la** \täm-'bä-lə\ *noun, plural* **-la** *or* **-las** [Nyanja (Bantu language of Malawi), literally, cockerel] (1970)
— see *kwacha* at MONEY table

¹**tam·bour** \'tam-,bùr, tam-'\ *noun* [Middle French, drum, from Arabic *ṭanbūr*, modification of Persian *tabīr*] (15th century)
**1 :** ¹DRUM 1
**2 a :** an embroidery frame; *especially* **:** a set of two interlocking hoops between which cloth is stretched before stitching **b :** embroidery made on a tambour frame

**3 :** a shallow metallic cup or drum with a thin elastic membrane supporting a writing lever used to transmit and register slight motions (as arterial pulsations)
**4 :** a rolling top or front (as of a rolltop desk) of narrow strips of wood glued on canvas

²**tambour** (1774)
*transitive verb*
**:** to embroider (cloth) with tambour
*intransitive verb*
**:** to work at a tambour frame
— **tam·bour·er** *noun*

**tam·bou·ra** *or* **tam·bu·ra** \tam-'bùr-ə\ *noun* [Persian *ṭambūra*] (1585)
**:** an Asian musical instrument resembling a lute in construction but without frets and used to produce a drone accompaniment to singing

**tam·bou·rine** \,tam-bə-'rēn\ *noun* [Middle French *tambourin*, diminutive of *tambour*] (1579)
**:** a small drum; *especially* **:** a shallow one-headed drum with loose metallic disks at the sides played especially by shaking or striking with the hand

**tambourine**

¹**tame** \'tām\ *adjective* **tam·er; tam·est** [Middle English, from Old English *tam;* akin to Old High German *zam* tame, Latin *domare* to tame, Greek *damnanai*] (before 12th century)
**1 :** reduced from a state of native wildness especially so as to be tractable and useful to humans **:** DOMESTICATED ⟨*tame* animals⟩
**2 :** made docile and submissive **:** SUBDUED
**3 :** lacking spirit, zest, interest, or the capacity to excite **:** INSIPID ⟨a *tame* campaign⟩
— **tame·ly** *adverb*
— **tame·ness** *noun*

²**tame** *verb* **tamed; tam·ing** (14th century)
*transitive verb*
**1 a :** to reduce from a wild to a domestic state **b :** to subject to cultivation **c :** to bring under control **:** HARNESS
**2 :** to deprive of spirit **:** HUMBLE, SUBDUE ⟨the once revolutionary . . . party, long since *tamed* —*Times Literary Supplement*⟩
**3 :** to tone down **:** SOFTEN ⟨*tamed* the language in the play⟩
*intransitive verb*
**:** to become tame
— **tam·able** *or* **tame·able** \'tā-mə-bəl\ *adjective*
— **tam·er** *noun*

**tame·less** \'tām-ləs\ *adjective* (circa 1598)
**:** not tamed or not capable of being tamed

**Tam·il** \'ta-məl, 'tä-\ *noun* (1734)
**1 :** a Dravidian language of Tamil Nadu state, India, and of northern and eastern Sri Lanka
**2 :** a Tamil-speaking person or a descendant of Tamil-speaking ancestors

**Tam·ma·ny** \'ta-mə-nē\ *adjective* [*Tammany Hall*, headquarters of the Tammany Society, political organization in New York City] (1872)
**:** of, relating to, or constituting a group or organization exercising or seeking municipal political control by methods often associated with corruption and bossism
— **Tam·ma·ny·ism** \-,i-zəm\ *noun*

**Tam·muz** \'tä-,mùz\ *noun* [Hebrew *Tammūz*] (1614)
**:** the 10th month of the civil year or the 4th month of the ecclesiastical year in the Jewish calendar — see MONTH table

**Tam o' Shan·ter** *noun*
**1** \,ta-mə-'shan-tər\ **:** the hero of Burns's poem *Tam o' Shanter*
**2** *usually* **tam–o'–shanter** \'ta-mə-,\ **:** a woolen cap of Scottish origin with a tight headband, wide flat circular crown, and usually a pompon in the center

**ta·mox·i·fen** \tə-'mäk-sə-,fen\ *noun* [perhaps from *trans-* + *amine* + *oxi-* (alteration of *oxy*) + *-fen* (alteration of *phenyl*)] (1972)

**:** an estrogen antagonist $C_{26}H_{29}NO$ used especially to treat postmenopausal breast cancer

¹**tamp** \'tamp\ *transitive verb* [probably back-formation from obsolete *tampion, tampin* plug, from Middle English, from Middle French *tapon, tampon*, from (assumed) Old French *taper* to plug, of Germanic origin; akin to Old English *tæppa* tap] (1834)
**1 :** to drive in or down by a succession of light or medium blows ⟨*tamp* wet concrete⟩
**2 :** to put a check on **:** REDUCE, LESSEN
— **tamp·er** *noun*

²**tamp** *noun* (1920)
**:** a tool for tamping

**tam·per** \'tam-pər\ *intransitive verb* **tampered; tam·per·ing** \-p(ə-)riŋ\ [probably from Middle French *temprer* to temper, mix, meddle — more at TEMPER] (1567)
**1 :** to carry on underhand or improper negotiations (as by bribery)
**2 a :** to interfere so as to weaken or change for the worse — used with *with* **b :** to try foolish or dangerous experiments — used with *with*
— **tam·per·er** \-pər-ər\ *noun*
— **tam·per·proof** \'tam-pər-,prüf\ *adjective*

**tam·pi·on** \'tam-pē-ən, 'täm-\ *noun* [obsolete *tampion, tampin* plug — more at TAMP] (circa 1625)
**:** a wooden plug or a metal or canvas cover for the muzzle of a gun

¹**tam·pon** \'tam-,pän\ *noun* [French, literally, plug, from Middle French — more at TAMP] (1848)
**:** a plug (as of cotton) introduced into a body cavity usually to absorb secretions (as from menstruation) or to arrest hemorrhaging

²**tampon** *transitive verb* (1860)
**:** to plug with a tampon

**tam–tam** \'tam-,tam, 'täm-,täm\ *noun* [Hindi *ṭamṭam*] (1782)
**1 :** TOM-TOM
**2 :** GONG; *especially* **:** one of a tuned set in a gamelan orchestra

**Tam·worth** \'tam-(,)wərth\ *noun* [*Tamworth*, borough in Staffordshire, England] (1860)
**:** any of a breed of large long-bodied red swine developed in England especially for the production of bacon

¹**tan** \'tan\ *verb* **tanned; tan·ning** [Middle English *tannen*, from Middle French *tanner*, from Medieval Latin *tannare*, from *tanum, tannum* tanbark] (14th century)
*transitive verb*
**1 a :** to convert (hide) into leather by treatment with an infusion of tannin-rich bark or other agent of similar effect **b :** to convert (protein) to leather or a similar substance
**2 :** to make (skin) tan especially by exposure to the sun
**3 :** THRASH, WHIP
*intransitive verb*
**:** to get or become tanned

²**tan** *adjective* **tan·ner; tan·nest** (1586)
**1 :** of, relating to, or used for tan or tanning
**2 :** of the color tan

³**tan** *noun* [French, tanbark, from Old French, from Medieval Latin *tanum*] (1674)
**1 :** a tanning material or its active agent (as tannin)
**2 :** a brown color imparted to the skin by exposure to the sun or wind
**3 :** a light yellowish brown
**4** *plural* **:** tan-colored articles of clothing

**tan·a·ger** \'ta-ni-jər\ *noun* [New Latin *tanagra*, from Portuguese *tangará*, from Tupi] (1688)
**:** any of numerous chiefly tropical American oscine birds (family Thraupidae) that are often

brightly colored and usually unmusical and inhabit mostly woodlands

**tan·bark** \'tan-ˌbärk\ *noun* (1799)
**1** : a bark rich in tannin bruised or cut into small pieces and used in tanning
**2** : a surface (as a circus ring) covered with spent tanbark

**¹tan·dem** \'tan-dəm\ *noun* [Latin, at last, at length (taken to mean "lengthwise"), from *tam* so; akin to Old English *thæt* that] (circa 1785)
**1 a** (1) : a 2-seated carriage drawn by horses harnessed one before the other (2) : a team so harnessed **b** : TANDEM BICYCLE **c** : a vehicle (as a motortruck) having close-coupled pairs of axles
**2** : a group of two or more arranged one behind the other or used or acting in conjunction
◆
— **in tandem 1** : in a tandem arrangement
**2** : in partnership or conjunction

**²tandem** *adverb* (circa 1795)
: one after or behind another ⟨ride *tandem*⟩

**³tandem** *adjective* (1801)
**1** : consisting of things or having parts arranged one behind the other
**2** : working or occurring in conjunction with each other

**tandem bicycle** *noun* (circa 1890)
: a bicycle for usually two persons sitting tandem

**tan·door** \tän-'dur\ *noun* [Hindi *tandūr, tannūr*, from Persian *tanūr*, from Arabic *tannūr*] (1840)
: a cylindrical clay oven in which food is cooked over charcoal

**tan·doori** \tän-'dur-ē\ *adjective* [Hindi *tandurī*, from *tandūr*] (circa 1968)
: cooked in a tandoor ⟨*tandoori* chicken⟩
— **tandoori** *noun*

**¹tang** \'taŋ\ *noun* [Middle English, of Scandinavian origin; akin to Old Norse *tangi* point of land, tang] (15th century)
**1** : a projecting shank, prong, fang, or tongue (as on a knife, file, or sword) to connect with the handle
**2 a** : a sharp distinctive often lingering flavor **b** : a pungent odor **c** : something having the effect of a tang (as in stimulation of the senses)
**3 a** : a faint suggestion : TRACE **b** : a distinguishing characteristic that sets apart or gives a special individuality
— **tanged** \'taŋd\ *adjective*

**²tang** *transitive verb* (1566)
**1** : to furnish with a tang
**2** : to affect with a tang

**³tang** *verb* [imitative] (1556)
: CLANG, RING

**⁴tang** *noun* (circa 1625)
: a sharp twanging sound

**Tang** *or* **T'ang** \'täŋ\ *noun* [Chinese (Beijing) *Táng*] (1669)
: a Chinese dynasty dated A.D. 618–907 and marked by wide contacts with other cultures and by the development of printing and the flourishing of poetry and art

**tan·ge·lo** \'tan-jə-ˌlō\ *noun, plural* **-los** [*tangerine* + pom*elo*] (1904)
: the fruit of a hybrid (*Citrus tangelo*) between a tangerine or mandarin orange and a grapefruit; *also* : the tree

**tan·gen·cy** \'tan-jən(t)-sē\ *noun* (1819)
: the quality or state of being tangent

**¹tan·gent** \-jənt\ *adjective* [Latin *tangent-, tangens*, present participle of *tangere* to touch; perhaps akin to Old English *thaccian* to touch gently, stroke] (1594)
**1 a** : meeting a curve or surface in a single point if a sufficiently small interval is considered ⟨straight line *tangent* to a curve⟩ **b** (1) : having a common tangent line at a point ⟨*tangent* curves⟩ (2) : having a common tangent plane at a point ⟨*tangent* surfaces⟩
**2** : diverging from an original purpose or course : IRRELEVANT ⟨*tangent* remarks⟩

**²tangent** *noun* [New Latin *tangent-, tangens*, from *linea tangens* tangent line] (1594)
**1 a** : the trigonometric function that for an acute angle is the ratio between the leg opposite to the angle when it is considered part of a right triangle and the leg adjacent **b** : a trigonometric function that is equal to the sine divided by the cosine for all real numbers $\theta$ for which the cosine is not equal to zero and is exactly equal to the tangent of an angle of measure $\theta$ in radians
**2** : a line that is tangent; *specifically* : a straight line that is the limiting position of a secant of a curve through a fixed point and a variable point on the curve as the variable point approaches the fixed point — see CIRCLE illustration
**3** : an abrupt change of course : DIGRESSION ⟨the speaker went off on a *tangent*⟩
**4** : a small upright flat-ended metal pin at the inner end of a clavichord key that strikes the string to produce the tone

**tan·gen·tial** \tan-'jen(t)-shəl\ *adjective* (1630)
**1** : of, relating to, or of the nature of a tangent
**2** : acting along or lying in a tangent ⟨*tangential* forces⟩
**3 a** : DIVERGENT, DIGRESSIVE **b** : touching lightly : INCIDENTAL, PERIPHERAL ⟨*tangential* involvement⟩
— **tan·gen·tial·ly** \-'jen(t)-sh(ə-)lē\ *adverb*

**tangent plane** *noun* (1856)
: the plane through a point of a surface that contains the tangent lines to all the curves on the surface through the same point

**tan·ger·ine** \'tan-jə-ˌrēn, ˌtan-jə-'\ *noun* [French *Tanger* Tangier, Morocco] (1842)
**1 a** : any of various mandarins that have usually deep orange skin and pulp; *broadly* : MANDARIN 3b **b** : a tree producing tangerines
**2** : a moderate to strong reddish orange

**¹tan·gi·ble** \'tan-jə-bəl\ *adjective* [Late Latin *tangibilis*, from Latin *tangere* to touch] (1589)
**1 a** : capable of being perceived especially by the sense of touch : PALPABLE **b** : substantially real : MATERIAL
**2** : capable of being precisely identified or realized by the mind ⟨her grief was *tangible*⟩
**3** : capable of being appraised at an actual or approximate value ⟨*tangible* assets⟩
**synonym** see PERCEPTIBLE
— **tan·gi·bil·i·ty** \ˌtan-jə-'bi-lə-tē\ *noun*
— **tan·gi·ble·ness** \'tan-jə-bəl-nəs\ *noun*
— **tan·gi·bly** \-blē\ *adverb*

**²tangible** *noun* (1890)
: something tangible; *especially* : a tangible asset

**¹tan·gle** \'tan-gəl\ *verb* **tan·gled; tan·gling** \-g(ə-)liŋ\ [Middle English *tangilen*, probably of Scandinavian origin; akin to Swedish dialect *taggla* to tangle] (14th century)
*transitive verb*
**1** : to involve so as to hamper, obstruct, or embarrass
**2** : to seize and hold in or as if in a snare : ENTRAP
**3** : to unite or knit together in intricate confusion
*intransitive verb*
**1** : to interact in a contentious or conflicting way
**2** : to become entangled

**²tangle** *noun* (1615)
**1** : a tangled twisted mass : SNARL
**2 a** : a complicated or confused state or condition **b** : a state of perplexity or complete bewilderment
**3** : a serious altercation : DISPUTE

**³tangle** *noun* [of Scandinavian origin; akin to Old Norse *thongull* tangle, *thang* kelp] (1536)
: a large seaweed

**tan·gled** \'taŋ-gəld\ *adjective* (1590)
**1** : existing in or giving the appearance of a state of utter disorder
**2** : very involved : exceedingly complex

**tan·gle·ment** \-gəl-mənt\ *noun* (1831)
: ENTANGLEMENT

**tan·gly** \'taŋ-g(ə-)lē\ *adjective* (1813)
: full of tangles or knots : INTRICATE

**¹tan·go** \'taŋ-(ˌ)gō\ *noun, plural* **tangos** [American Spanish] (1913)
: a ballroom dance of Latin-American origin in ¾ time with a basic pattern of step-step-step-step-close and characterized by long pauses and stylized body positions; *also* : the music for this dance

**²tango** *intransitive verb* (1913)
: to dance the tango

**Tan·go** (1952)
— a communications code word for the letter *t*

**tan·gram** \'taŋ-grəm, 'tan-\ *noun* [perhaps from Chinese (Beijing) *táng* Chinese + English *-gram*] (circa 1864)
: a Chinese puzzle made by cutting a square of thin material into five triangles, a square, and a rhomboid which are capable of being recombined in many different figures

**tangy** \'taŋ-ē\ *adjective* **tang·i·er; -est** (1875)
: having or suggestive of a tang

tangram

**¹tank** \'taŋk\ *noun* [Portuguese *tanque*, alteration of *estanque*, from *estancar* to stanch, perhaps from (assumed) Vulgar Latin *stanticare* — more at STANCH] (circa 1616)
**1** *dialect* : POND, POOL; *especially* : one built as a water supply
**2** : a usually large receptacle for holding, transporting, or storing liquids (as water or fuel)
**3** : an enclosed heavily armed and armored combat vehicle that moves on tracks
**4** : a prison cell or enclosure used especially for receiving prisoners
**5** : TANK TOP
— **tank·ful** \-ˌful\ *noun*
— **tank·like** \-ˌlīk\ *adjective*

**²tank** (1863)
*transitive verb*
**1** : to place, store, or treat in a tank
**2** : to make no effort to win : lose intentionally ⟨*tanked* the match⟩
*intransitive verb*
: to lose intentionally : give up in competition

**tan·ka** \'tän-kə\ *noun* [Japanese] (circa 1877)
: an unrhymed Japanese verse form of five lines containing 5, 7, 5, 7, and 7 syllables respectively; *also* : a poem in this form — compare HAIKU

**tank·age** \'taŋ-kij\ *noun* (1866)
**1 a** : the aggregate of tanks required for a purpose **b** : the capacity or contents of a tank

**2 :** dried animal residues usually freed from the fat and gelatin and used as fertilizer and feedstuff
**3 :** the act or process of putting or storing in tanks
**tank·ard** \'taŋ-kərd\ noun [Middle English] (15th century)
**:** a tall one-handled drinking vessel; *especially* **:** a silver or pewter mug with a lid

**tank destroyer** noun (1941)
**:** a highly mobile lightly armored vehicle usually on a half-track or a tank chassis and mounting a cannon

tankard

**tanked** \'taŋ(k)t\ adjective (1893)
*slang* **:** DRUNK 1a — often used with *up*
**tank·er** \'taŋ-kər\ noun (1900)
**1 a :** a cargo ship fitted with tanks for carrying liquid in bulk **b :** a vehicle on which a tank is mounted to carry fluids; *also* **:** a cargo airplane for transporting fuel
**2 :** a member of a military tank crew
**tank suit** noun (1940)
**:** a one-piece bathing suit with usually wide shoulder straps
**tank top** noun (1950)
**:** a sleeveless collarless shirt with usually wide shoulder straps and no front opening
**tank town** noun [from the fact that formerly trains stopped at such towns only to take on water] (1906)
**:** a small town
**tan·nage** \'ta-nij\ noun (1662)
**:** the act, process, or result of tanning
**tan·nate** \'ta-ˌnāt\ noun [French, from *tannin*] (1802)
**:** a compound of a tannin
**¹tan·ner** \'ta-nər\ noun (before 12th century)
**1 :** one that tans hides
**2 :** one who acquires or seeks to acquire a suntan
**²tanner** noun [origin unknown] (circa 1811)
*British* **:** SIXPENCE
**tanner crab** noun [probably from New Latin *tanneri*, specific epithet of *Chionoecetes tanneri*, from Zera L. Tanner (died 1906) American naval officer] (1947)
**:** any of several spider crabs (genus *Chionoecetes*); *especially* **:** SNOW CRAB
**tan·nery** \'ta-nə-rē, 'tan-rē\ noun, plural **-ner·ies** (1736)
**:** a place where tanning is carried on
**tan·nic** \'ta-nik\ adjective [French *tannique*, from *tannin*] (circa 1859)
**1 :** of, resembling, or derived from tan or a tannin
**2** *of wine* **:** containing an abundance of tannins **:** markedly astringent
**tannic acid** noun (1836)
**:** TANNIN 1
**tan·nin** \'ta-nən\ noun [French, from *tanner* to tan] (1802)
**1 :** any of various soluble astringent complex phenolic substances of plant origin used especially in tanning, dyeing, the making of ink, and in medicine
**2 :** a substance that has a tanning effect
**tan·ning** \'ta-niŋ\ noun (15th century)
**1 :** the art or process by which a skin is tanned
**2 :** a browning of the skin especially by exposure to sun
**3 :** a sound spanking
**4 :** a natural darkening and hardening of the cuticle of an insect immediately after molting
**tan·nish** \'ta-nish\ adjective (1935)
**:** somewhat tan
**tan oak** noun (circa 1925)
**:** a U.S. Pacific coast evergreen tree (*Lithocarpus densiflora*) of the beech family that has erect staminate catkins and is rich in tannins
**Ta·no·an** \tə-'nō-ən, 'tä-nə-wən\ noun [*Tano*, a group of former pueblos in New Mexico] (1891)

**:** a family of American Indian languages spoken in New Mexico and Arizona
— **Tanoan** adjective
**tan·sy** \'tan-zē\ noun, plural **tansies** [Middle English *tanesey*, from Middle French *tanesie*, from Medieval Latin *athanasia*, from Greek, immortality, from *athanatos* immortal, from *a-* + *thanatos* death — more at THANATOS] (15th century)
**:** a common aromatic Old World composite herb (*Tanacetum vulgare*) that is naturalized in North America and has bitter-tasting finely divided leaves; *broadly* **:** a plant of the same genus
**tansy ragwort** noun (circa 1900)
**:** an Old World yellow-flowered senecio (*Senecio jacobaea*) that is naturalized in North America and is toxic to livestock
**tan·ta·late** \'tan-tᵊl-ˌāt\ noun (1849)
**:** a salt containing tantalum in combination with oxygen
**tan·ta·lise** *British variant of* TANTALIZE
**tan·ta·lite** \'tan-tᵊl-ˌīt\ noun (1805)
**:** a mineral consisting of a heavy dark lustrous oxide of tantalum and usually other metals (as iron or manganese)
**tan·ta·lize** \'tan-tᵊl-ˌīz\ verb **-lized; -liz·ing** [*Tantalus*] (1597)
*transitive verb*
**:** to tease or torment by or as if by presenting something desirable to the view but continually keeping it out of reach
*intransitive verb*
**:** to cause one to be tantalized
— **tan·ta·liz·er** noun
**tantalizing** adjective (circa 1683)
**:** possessing a quality that arouses or stimulates desire or interest; *also* **:** mockingly or teasingly out of reach
— **tan·ta·liz·ing·ly** \-ˌī-ziŋ-lē\ adverb
**tan·ta·lum** \'tan-tᵊl-əm\ noun [New Latin, from Latin *Tantalus*; from its inability to absorb acid] (1802)
**:** a hard ductile gray-white acid-resisting metallic element of the vanadium family found combined in rare minerals (as tantalite and columbite) — see ELEMENT table
**Tan·ta·lus** \'tan-tᵊl-əs\ noun [Latin, from Greek *Tantalos*]
**1 :** a legendary king of Lydia condemned to stand up to the chin in a pool of water in Hades and beneath fruit-laden boughs only to have the water or fruit recede at each attempt to drink or eat
**2** *not capitalized* **:** a locked cellarette with contents visible but not obtainable without a key
**tan·ta·mount** \'tan-tə-ˌmaůnt\ adjective [obsolete *tantamount*, noun, equivalent, from Anglo-French *tant amunter* to amount to as much] (1641)
**:** equivalent in value, significance, or effect
**tan·ta·ra** \tan-'tar-ə, -'tär-\ noun [Latin *taratantara*, of imitative origin] (1584)
**:** the blare of a trumpet or horn
**¹tan·tivy** \tan-'ti-vē\ adverb [origin unknown] (1641)
**:** at a gallop
**²tantivy** noun, plural **-tiv·ies** (circa 1658)
**1 :** a rapid gallop or ride
**2 :** TANTARA
**tan·tra** \'tən-trə, 'tän-, 'tan-\ noun, often capitalized [Sanskrit, literally, warp, from *tanoti* he stretches, weaves; akin to Greek *teinein* to stretch — more at THIN] (1799)
**:** one of the later Hindu or Buddhist scriptures dealing especially with techniques and rituals including meditative and sexual practices; *also* **:** the rituals or practices outlined in the tantra
— **tan·tric** \-trik\ adjective, often capitalized
— **Tan·trism** \-ˌtri-zəm\ noun
— **Tan·trist** \-trist\ noun
**tan·trum** \'tan-trəm\ noun [origin unknown] (1714)
**:** a fit of bad temper

**ta·nu·ki** \tä-'nü-kē\ noun [Japanese, raccoon dog] (circa 1929)
**:** the fur of a raccoon dog; *also* **:** RACCOON DOG
**tan·yard** \'tan-ˌyärd\ noun (1666)
**:** the section or part of a tannery housing tanning vats
**tan·za·nite** \'tan-zə-ˌnīt\ noun [*Tanzania*, Africa] (1968)
**:** a mineral that is a deep blue variety of zoisite and is used as a gemstone
**Tao** \'daů, 'taů\ noun [Chinese (Beijing) *dào*, literally, way] (1736)
**1 a :** the unconditional and unknowable source and guiding principle of all reality as conceived by Taoists **b :** the process of nature by which all things change and which is to be followed for a life of harmony
**2** *often not capitalized* **:** the path of virtuous conduct as conceived by Confucians
**3** *often not capitalized* **:** the art or skill of doing something in harmony with the essential nature of the thing ⟨the *tao* of archery⟩
**Tao·ism** \-ˌi-zəm\ noun [*Tao*] (1838)
**1 :** a Chinese mystical philosophy traditionally founded by Lao-tzu in the 6th century B.C. that teaches conformity to the Tao by unassertive action and simplicity
**2 :** a religion developed from Taoist philosophy and folk and Buddhist religion and concerned with obtaining long life and good fortune often by magical means
— **Tao·ist** \-ist\ adjective or noun
— **Tao·is·tic** \daů-'is-tik, taů-\ adjective
**¹tap** \'tap\ noun [Middle English *tappe*, from Old English *tæppa*; akin to Old High German *zapho* tap] (before 12th century)
**1 a :** a plug for a hole (as in a cask) **:** SPIGOT **:** a device consisting of a spout and valve attached to the end of a pipe to control the flow of a fluid **:** FAUCET
**2 a :** a liquor drawn through a tap **b :** the procedure of removing fluid (as from a body cavity)
**3 :** a tool for forming an internal screw thread
**4 :** an intermediate point in an electric circuit where a connection may be made
**5 :** WIRETAP
— **on tap 1 :** ready to be drawn from a large container (as a cask or keg) ⟨ale *on tap*⟩ **:** broached or furnished with a tap **3 :** on hand **:** AVAILABLE ⟨services instantly *on tap* —Hugh Dwan⟩ **4 :** coming up ⟨other matches *on tap* —H. W. Wind⟩
**²tap** transitive verb **tapped; tap·ping** (15th century)
**1 :** to let out or cause to flow by piercing or by drawing a plug from the containing vessel ⟨*tap* wine from a cask⟩
**2 a :** to pierce so as to let out or draw off a fluid ⟨*tap* maple trees⟩ **b :** to draw out, from, or upon ⟨*tap* new sources of revenue⟩
**3 a :** to cut in on (a telephone or telegraph wire) to get information **b :** to cut in (an electrical circuit) on another circuit
**4 :** to form an internal screw thread in by means of a tap
**5 :** to get money from as a loan or gift
**6 :** to connect (a street gas or water main) with a local supply
— **tap·per** noun
— **tap into :** to make a usually advantageous connection with ⟨clothing that . . . *taps into* the currents of popular culture —John Duka⟩
**³tap** verb **tapped; tap·ping** [Middle English *tappen*, from Middle French *taper* to strike with the flat of the hand, of Germanic origin; akin to Middle High German *tāpe* paw, blow dealt with the paw] (13th century)
*transitive verb*

---

**1 :** to strike lightly especially with a slight sound
**2 :** to give a light blow with ⟨*tap* a pencil on the table⟩
**3 :** to bring about by repeated light blows ⟨*tap* out a story on the typewriter⟩
**4 :** to repair by putting a tap on
**5 :** SELECT, DESIGNATE ⟨was *tapped* for police commissioner⟩; *specifically* **:** to elect to membership (as in a fraternity)
*intransitive verb*
**1 :** to strike a light audible blow **:** RAP
**2 :** to walk with light audible steps
**3 :** TAP-DANCE
— **tap·per** *noun*
⁴**tap** *noun* (14th century)
**1 a :** a light usually audible blow; *also* **:** its sound **b :** one of several usually rapid drumbeats on a snare drum
**2 :** HALF SOLE
**3 :** a small metal plate for the sole or heel of a shoe
**4 :** TAP DANCE 1
**5 :** FLAP 7
¹**ta·pa** \'tä-pə, 'ta-\ *noun* [Marquesan & Tahitian] (1823)
**:** a coarse cloth made in the Pacific islands from the pounded bark especially of the paper mulberry and usually decorated with geometric patterns
²**tapa** *noun* [Spanish, literally, cover, lid, probably of Germanic origin; akin to Old English *tæppa* tap] (1953)
**:** an hors d'oeuvre served with drinks in Spanish bars — usually used in plural
**tap dance** *noun* (1928)
**1 :** a step dance tapped out audibly by means of shoes with hard soles or soles and heels to which taps have been added
**2 :** something suggesting a tap dance; *especially* **:** an action or discourse intended to rationalize or distract ⟨does a clever *tap dance* to explain —Campbell Geeslin⟩
— **tap–dance** *intransitive verb*
— **tap dancer** *noun*
— **tap dancing** *noun*
¹**tape** \'tāp\ *noun* [Middle English, from Old English *tæppe*] (before 12th century)
**1 :** a narrow woven fabric
**2 :** a string or ribbon stretched breast-high above the finish line of a race
**3 :** a narrow flexible strip or band: as **a :** ADHESIVE TAPE **b :** MAGNETIC TAPE
**4 :** TAPE RECORDING
²**tape** *verb* **taped; tap·ing** (1609)
*transitive verb*
**1 :** to fasten, tie, bind, cover, or support with tape
**2 :** to record on tape and especially magnetic tape ⟨*tape* an interview⟩
*intransitive verb*
**:** to record something on tape and especially magnetic tape
³**tape** *adjective* (1947)
**1 :** recorded on tape ⟨*tape* music⟩
**2 :** intended for use with recording (as magnetic) tape ⟨a *tape* cartridge⟩
**tape deck** *noun* (1949)
**:** a device used to play back and often to record on magnetic tape that usually has to be connected to an audio system
**tape grass** *noun* (circa 1818)
**:** any of several submerged aquatic monocotyledonous plants (genus *Vallisneria* of the family Hydrocharitaceae) with long ribbonlike leaves — called also *eelgrass, wild celery*
**tape measure** *noun* (1845)
**:** a narrow strip (as of a limp cloth or steel tape) marked off in units (as inches or centimeters) for measuring
¹**ta·per** \'tā-pər\ *noun* [Middle English, from Old English *tapor* candle, wick, perhaps modification of Latin *papyrus* papyrus] (before 12th century)
**1 a :** a slender candle **b :** a long waxed wick used especially for lighting candles, lamps,

pipes, or fires **c :** a feeble light
**2 a :** a tapering form or figure **b :** gradual diminution of thickness, diameter, or width in an elongated object **c :** a gradual decrease
²**taper** *adjective* (15th century)
**1 :** progressively narrowed toward one end
**2 :** furnished with or adjusted to a scale **:** GRADUATED ⟨*taper* freight rates⟩
³**taper** *verb* **ta·pered; ta·per·ing** \'tā-p(ə-)riŋ\ (1610)
*intransitive verb*
**1 :** to become progressively smaller toward one end
**2 :** to diminish gradually
*transitive verb*
**:** to cause to taper
⁴**tap·er** \'tā-pər\ *noun* [¹*tape*] (circa 1920)
**:** one that applies or dispenses tape
**tape–re·cord** \,tā-pri-'kȯrd, 'tā-pri-,\ *transitive verb* [back-formation from *tape recording*] (1950)
**:** to make a recording of on magnetic tape
**tape recorder** *noun* (1932)
**:** a device for recording on and playing back magnetic tape
**tape recording** *noun* (1940)
**:** magnetic recording on magnetic tape; *also* **:** a recording made by this process
**ta·per·er** \'tā-pər-ər\ *noun* (15th century)
**:** one who bears a taper in a religious procession
**taper off** *verb* (1848)
**:** TAPER ⟨business growth had *tapered off* seriously while the unemployment rate had climbed —*Current Biography*⟩
**ta·per·stick** \'tā-pər-,stik\ *noun* (1546)
**:** a candlestick that holds tapers
**tap·es·tried** \'ta-pə-strēd\ *adjective* (1769)
**1 :** covered or decorated with or as if with tapestry
**2 :** woven or depicted in tapestry
**tap·es·try** \'ta-pə-strē\ *noun, plural* **-tries** [Middle English *tapistry*, modification of Middle French *tapisserie*, from *tapisser* to carpet, cover with tapestry, from Old French *tapis* carpet, from Greek *tapēt-, tapēs* rug, carpet] (15th century)
**1 a :** a heavy handwoven reversible textile used for hangings, curtains, and upholstery and characterized by complicated pictorial designs **b :** a nonreversible imitation of tapestry used chiefly for upholstery **c :** embroidery on canvas resembling woven tapestry (needlepoint *tapestry*)
**2 :** something resembling tapestry (as in complexity or richness of design)
**tapestry carpet** *noun* (1852)
**:** a carpet in which the designs are printed in colors on the threads before the fabric is woven
**ta·pe·tum** \tə-'pē-təm\ *noun, plural* **ta·pe·ta** \-'pē-tə\ [New Latin, from Latin *tapete* carpet, tapestry, from Greek *tapēt-, tapēs* rug, carpet] (1713)
**1 :** any of various membranous layers or areas especially of the choroid coat and retina of the eye
**2 :** a layer of nutritive cells that invests the sporogenous tissue in the sporangium of higher plants
**tape·worm** \'tāp-,wərm\ *noun* [from its shape] (1752)
**:** any of a class (Cestoda) of platyhelminthic worms parasitic especially in the intestines of vertebrates — called also *cestode*
**tap·hole** \'tap-,hōl\ *noun* (1594)
**:** a hole for a tap; *specifically* **:** a hole at or near the bottom of a furnace or ladle through which molten metal, matte, or slag can be tapped
**ta·phon·o·my** \tə-'fä-nə-mē, ta-\ *noun* [Greek *taphē* burial + English *-nomy*] (1940)
**:** the study of the processes (as burial, decay, and preservation) that affect animal and plant remains as they become fossilized
— **taph·o·nom·ic** \,ta-fə-'nä-mik\ *adjective*

— **ta·phon·o·mist** \tə-'fä-nə-mist, ta-\ *noun*
**tap–in** \'tap-,in\ *noun* (1948)
**1 :** TIP-IN
**2 :** a short putt in golf
**tap·i·o·ca** \,ta-pē-'ō-kə\ *noun* [Spanish & Portuguese, from Tupi *tipióka*] (1707)
**1 :** a usually granular preparation of cassava starch used especially in puddings and as a thickening in liquid food; *also* **:** a dish (as pudding) containing tapioca
**2 :** CASSAVA
**ta·pir** \'tā-pər *also* 'tā-,pir *or* tə-'pir\ *noun, plural* **tapir** *or* **tapirs** [Portuguese *tapira*, from Tupi *tapiíra*] (1774)
**:** any of a genus (*Tapirus*) of chiefly nocturnal perissodactyl ungulates of tropical America and Myanmar to Sumatra that have the snout and upper lip prolonged into a short flexible proboscis

tapir

**tap·is** \'ta-,pē, ta-'pē\ *noun* [Middle English, from Middle French — more at TAPESTRY] (15th century)
*archaic* **:** a small tapestry used for hangings and floor and table coverings
— **on the tapis :** under consideration
**tap–off** \'tap-,ȯf\ *noun* (circa 1932)
**:** ²TIP-OFF
**tap out** *intransitive verb* (1939)
**:** to run out of money by betting
**tap pants** *noun plural* (1977)
**:** a loose-fitting woman's undergarment of a style similar to shorts formerly worn for tap dancing
**tapped out** *adjective* (1950)
**:** out of money **:** BROKE
**tap·pet** \'ta-pət\ *noun* [irregular from ³*tap*] (1745)
**:** a lever or projection moved by some other piece (as a cam) or intended to tap or touch something else to cause a particular motion
**tapping** *noun* (1597)
**:** the act, process, or means by which something is tapped
**tap·pit hen** \'ta-pət-\ *noun* [Scots *tappit*, alteration of English *topped*] (1721)
*Scottish* **:** a drinking vessel with a knob on the lid
**tap·room** \'tap-,rüm, -,rùm\ *noun* (1807)
**:** BARROOM
**tap·root** \-,rüt; -,rùt\ *noun* [¹*tap*] (1601)
**1 :** a primary root that grows vertically downward and gives off small lateral roots
**2 :** the central element or position in a line of growth or development
**taps** \'taps\ *noun plural but singular or plural in construction* [probably alteration of earlier *taptoo* tattoo — more at TATTOO] (1824)
**:** the last bugle call at night blown as a signal that lights are to be put out; *also* **:** a similar call blown at military funerals and memorial services
**tap·sal·tee·rie** \,tap-səl-'tē-rē\ *adverb* [by alteration] (1784)
*Scottish* **:** TOPSY-TURVY
**tap·ster** \'tap-stər\ *noun* (before 12th century)
**:** BARTENDER
**tap water** *noun* (1881)
**:** water as it comes from a tap (as in a home)
¹**tar** \'tär\ *noun* [Middle English *terr, tarr*, from Old English *teoru*; akin to Old English *trēow* tree — more at TREE] (before 12th century)
**1 a :** a dark brown or black bituminous usually odorous viscous liquid obtained by destructive distillation of organic material (as wood, coal, or peat) **b :** a substance in some respects resembling tar; *especially* **:** a condensable residue present in smoke from burning tobacco

that contains combustion by-products (as resins, acids, phenols, and essential oils)
**2** [short for *tarpaulin*] **:** SAILOR

**²tar** *transitive verb* **tarred; tar·ring** (13th century)
**1 :** to cover with tar
**2 :** to defile as if with tar ⟨least *tarred* by the scandal —*Newsweek*⟩
— **tar and feather :** to smear (a person) with tar and cover with feathers as a punishment or indignity
— **tar with the same brush :** to mark or stain with the same fault or characteristic

**³tar** *or* **tarre** \'tär\ *transitive verb* **tarred; tar·ring; tars** *or* **tarres** [Middle English *terren, tarren*, from Old English *tyrwan*] (before 12th century)
**:** to urge to action — usually used with *on*

**tar·a·did·dle** *or* **tar·ra·did·dle** \,tar-ə-'di-dºl, 'tar-ə-,\ *noun* [origin unknown] (circa 1796)
**1 :** FIB
**2 :** pretentious nonsense

**Tar·a·hu·ma·ra** \,tar-ə-hü-'mär-ə\ *noun, plural* **Tarahumara** *or* **Tarahumaras** [Spanish] (1874)
**1 :** a member of an American Indian people living in the state of Chihuahua, Mexico
**2 :** the Uto-Aztecan language of the Tarahumara people

**tar·an·tel·la** \,tar-ən-'te-lə\ *noun* [Italian, from *Taranto*, Italy] (1782)
**:** a lively folk dance of southern Italy in ⁶⁄₈ time

**tar·an·tism** \'tar-ən-,ti-zəm\ *noun* [New Latin *tarantismus*, from *Taranto*, Italy] (circa 1656)
**:** a dancing mania or malady of late medieval Europe

**ta·ran·tu·la** \tə-'ran-chə-lə, -tə-lə; -'ranch-lə, -'rant-\ *noun, plural* **ta·ran·tu·las** *also* **ta·ran·tu·lae** \-,lē\ [Medieval Latin, from Old Italian *tarantola*, from *Taranto*] (1561)
**1 :** a European wolf spider (*Lycosa tarentula*) popularly held to be the cause of tarantism
**2 :** any of a family (Theraphosidae) of large hairy American spiders that are typically rather sluggish and capable of biting sharply though most forms are not significantly poisonous to humans

**Ta·ras·can** \tə-'ras-kən, -'räs-\ *noun* [Spanish *tarasco*] (1922)
**1 :** a member of an American Indian people of the state of Michoacán, Mexico
**2 :** the language of the Tarascan people

**tar baby** *noun* [from the tar baby that trapped Brer Rabbit in an Uncle Remus story by Joel Chandler Harris] (1924)
**:** something from which it is nearly impossible to extricate oneself

**tar·boosh** *also* **tar·bush** \tär-'büsh, 'tär-,\ *noun* [Arabic *ṭarbūsh*] (1702)
**:** a red hat similar to the fez worn especially by Muslim men

**tar·di·grade** \'tär-də-,grād\ *noun* [ultimately from Latin *tardigradus* slow-moving, from *tardus* slow + *gradi* to step, go — more at GRADE] (1860)
**:** any of a phylum (Tardigrada) of microscopic arthropods with four pairs of stout legs that live usually in water or damp moss — called also *water bear*

**tar·di·ly** \'tär-dºl-ē\ *adverb* (1597)
**1 :** at a slow pace
**2 :** LATE

**tar·dive dyskinesia** \'tär-div-\ *noun* [*tardive* tending toward late development (from French, feminine of *tardif*, from Middle French) + *dyskinesia*] (1964)
**:** a central nervous system disorder characterized by twitching of the face and tongue and involuntary motor movements of the trunk and limbs and occurring especially as a side effect of prolonged use of antipsychotic drugs (as phenothiazine)

**tar·do** \'tär-(,)dō\ *adjective* [Italian, from Latin *tardus*] (circa 1843)

**:** SLOW — used as a direction in music

**¹tar·dy** \'tär-dē\ *adjective* **tar·di·er; -est** [alteration of earlier *tardif*, from Middle French, from (assumed) Vulgar Latin *tardivus*, from Latin *tardus*] (15th century)
**1 :** moving slowly **:** SLUGGISH
**2 :** delayed beyond the expected or proper time **:** LATE
— **tar·di·ness** \'tär-dē-nəs\ *noun*

**²tardy** *noun, plural* **tardies** (1960)
**:** an instance of being tardy (as to a class)

**¹tare** \'tar, 'ter\ *noun* [Middle English; probably akin to Middle Dutch *tarwe* wheat] (14th century)
**1 a :** the seed of a vetch **b :** any of several vetches (especially *Vicia sativa* and *V. hirsuta*)
**2 :** a weed of grainfields usually held to be the darnel
**3** *plural* **:** an undesirable element

**²tare** *noun* [Middle English, from Middle French, from Old Italian *tara*, from Arabic *ṭarḥa*, literally, that which is removed] (15th century)
**1 :** a deduction from the gross weight of a substance and its container made in allowance for the weight of the container; *also* **:** the weight of the container
**2 :** COUNTERWEIGHT

**³tare** *transitive verb* **tared; tar·ing** (1812)
**:** to ascertain or mark the tare of; *especially*
**:** to weigh so as to determine the tare

**targe** \'tärj\ *noun* [Middle English, from Old French] (14th century)
**:** a light shield used especially by the Scots

**¹tar·get** \'tär-gət\ *noun, often attributive* [Middle English, from Middle French *targette*, diminutive of *targe* light shield, of Germanic origin; akin to Old Norse *targa* shield] (15th century)
**1 :** a small round shield
**2 a :** a mark to shoot at **b :** a target marked by shots fired at it **c :** something or someone fired at or marked for attack **d :** a goal to be achieved
**3 a :** an object of ridicule or criticism **b** **:** something or someone to be affected by an action or development
**4 a :** a railroad day signal that is attached to a switch stand and indicates whether the switch is open or closed **b :** a sliding sight on a surveyor's leveling rod
**5 a :** the metallic surface (as of platinum or tungsten) upon which the stream of electrons within an X-ray tube is focused and from which the X rays are emitted **b :** a body, surface, or material bombarded with nuclear particles or electrons; *especially* **:** fluorescent material on which desired visual effects are produced in electronic devices (as in radar) ◆
— **off target :** not valid **:** INACCURATE
— **on target :** precisely correct or valid especially in interpreting or addressing a problem or vital issue

**²target** *transitive verb* (1837)
**1 :** to make a target of; *especially* **:** to set as a goal
**2 :** to direct or use toward a target

**tar·get·able** \'tär-gə-tə-bəl\ *adjective* (1964)
**:** capable of being aimed at a target ⟨missiles with *targetable* warheads⟩

**target date** *noun* (1945)
**:** the date set for an event or for the completion of a project, goal, or quota

**target language** *noun* (1953)
**1 :** a language into which another language is to be translated — compare SOURCE LANGUAGE
**2 :** a language other than one's native language that is being learned

**Tar·gum** \'tär-,gùm, -,güm\ *noun* [Late Hebrew *targūm*, from Aramaic, translation] (1587)
**:** an Aramaic translation or paraphrase of a portion of the Old Testament

**Tar·heel** \'tär-,hēl\ *noun* (1864)

**:** a native or resident of North Carolina — used as a nickname

**¹tar·iff** \'tar-əf\ *noun* [Italian *tariffa*, from Arabic *ta'rīf* notification] (1592)
**1 a :** a schedule of duties imposed by a government on imported or in some countries exported goods **b :** a duty or rate of duty imposed in such a schedule
**2 :** a schedule of rates or charges of a business or a public utility
**3 :** PRICE, CHARGE

**²tariff** *transitive verb* (circa 1828)
**:** to subject to a tariff

**tar·la·tan** \'tär-lə-tºn\ *noun* [French *tarlatane*] (circa 1741)
**:** a sheer cotton fabric in open plain weave usually heavily sized for stiffness

**tar·mac** \'tär-,mak\ *noun* [from *Tarmac*, a trademark] (1919)
**:** a tarmacadam road, apron, or runway

**Tarmac** *trademark*
— used for a bituminous binder for roads

**tar·mac·ad·am** \,tär-mə-'ka-dəm\ *noun* (1882)
**1 :** a pavement constructed by spraying or pouring a tar binder over layers of crushed stone and then rolling
**2 :** a material of tar and aggregates mixed in a plant and shaped on the roadway

**tarn** \'tärn\ *noun* [Middle English *tarne*, of Scandinavian origin; akin to Old Norse *tjǫrn* small lake] (14th century)
**:** a small steep-banked mountain lake or pool

**tar·na·tion** \tär-'nā-shən\ *noun* [alteration of *darnation*, euphemism for *damnation*] (1790)
**:** DAMNATION — often used as an interjection or intensive; often used with *in* ⟨*tarnation* strike me —James Joyce⟩ ⟨where in *tarnation* you from? —Jessamyn West⟩

**¹tar·nish** \'tär-nish\ *verb* [Middle French *terniss-*, stem of *ternir*; probably of Germanic origin; akin to Old High German *ternen* to hide] (1598)
*transitive verb*
**1 :** to dull or destroy the luster of by or as if by air, dust, or dirt **:** SOIL, STAIN
**2 a :** to detract from the good quality of **:** VITIATE ⟨his fine dreams now slightly *tarnished*⟩ **b** **:** to bring disgrace on **:** SULLY
*intransitive verb*
**:** to become tarnished
— **tar·nish·able** \-ni-shə-bəl\ *adjective*

**²tarnish** *noun* (1713)
**:** something that tarnishes; *especially* **:** a film of chemically altered material on the surface of a metal (as silver)

**tarnished plant bug** *noun* (circa 1890)

---

◇ WORD HISTORY
**target** Old French *targe*, a name for a small leather-covered shield carried by a foot soldier, is probably of Frankish origin and hence akin to Old Norse *targa* "round shield." *Targe* and its diminutive form *targette* were both borrowed into Middle English. Our pronunciation of the modern word *target* with \g\ rather than \j\, as well as occasional Middle English variants such as *targatte*, shows the influence of forms with a "hard *g*" such as Middle French *targuete* or late Old Provençal *targueta*. Not until the later 18th century was *target* used with reference to something to be aimed at, originally a shieldlike object used in archery practice. During the 19th century the word acquired the general sense "a mark to shoot at," either literal or figurative.

---

: a common hemipterous bug (*Lygus lineolaris*) of eastern North America that causes injury to plants by sucking sap from buds, leaves, and fruits and that carries plant diseases

**ta·ro** \'tär-(,)ō, 'tar-, 'ter-\ *noun, plural* **taros** [Tahitian & Maori] (1769)
: a plant (*Colocasia esculenta*) of the arum family grown throughout the tropics for its edible starchy tuberous rootstocks and in temperate regions for ornament; *also* : its rootstock

**tar·ok** \'tar-,äk\ *noun* [Italian *tarocchi* tarots] (1739)
: an old card game popular in central Europe and played with a pack containing 40, 52, or 56 cards equivalent to modern playing cards plus the 22 tarots

**tar·ot** \'tar-(,)ō\ *noun* [Middle French, from Italian *tarocchi* (plural)] (circa 1623)
: any of a set of usually 78 playing cards including 22 pictorial cards used for fortune-telling; *also* : the 22 pictorial cards serving as trumps in tarok

**tarp** \'tärp\ *noun* (1906)
: TARPAULIN

**tar paper** *noun* (1891)
: a heavy paper coated or impregnated with tar for use especially in building

**tar·pau·lin** \tär-'pȯ-lən, 'tär-pə-; ÷tär-'pȯl-yən\ *noun* [probably from [1]*tar* + *-palling, -pauling* (from *pall*)] (1605)
**1** : a piece of material (as durable plastic) used for protecting exposed objects or areas
**2** : SAILOR

**tar pit** *noun* (1839)
: an area in which natural bitumens collect and are exposed at the earth's surface and which tends to trap animals and preserve their hard parts (as bones or teeth)

**tar·pon** \'tär-pən\ *noun, plural* **tarpon** *or* **tarpons** [origin unknown] (1685)
: a large silvery elongate anadromous bony fish (*Megalops atlanticus* of the family Elopidae) that occurs especially in the Gulf of Mexico, Caribbean, and warm coastal waters of the Atlantic, reaches a length of about six feet (two meters), and is often caught for sport

**tar·ra·gon** \'tar-ə-gən\ *noun* [Middle French *targon*, from Medieval Latin *tarchon*, from Arabic *ṭarkhūn*] (1538)
: a small widely cultivated perennial artemisia (*Artemisia dracunculus*) having pungent narrow usually entire leaves; *also* : its leaves used as a flavoring

**tarre** *variant of* TAR

**tar·ri·ance** \'tar-ē-ən(t)s\ *noun* (15th century)
: the act or an instance of tarrying

**[1]tar·ry** \'tar-ē\ *intransitive verb* **tar·ried; tar·ry·ing** [Middle English *tarien*] (14th century)
**1 a** : to delay or be tardy in acting or doing **b** : to linger in expectation : WAIT
**2** : to abide or stay in or at a place

**[2]tarry** *noun, plural* **tarries** (14th century)
: STAY, SOJOURN

**[3]tar·ry** \'tär-ē\ *adjective* (1552)
: of, resembling, or covered with tar

**[1]tar·sal** \'tär-səl\ *adjective* (1817)
**1** : of or relating to the tarsus
**2** : being or relating to plates of dense connective tissue that serve to stiffen the eyelids

**[2]tarsal** *noun* (1881)
: a tarsal part (as a bone or cartilage)

**tar sand** *noun* (1899)
: a natural impregnation of sand or sandstone with petroleum from which the lighter portions have escaped

**tar·si·er** \'tär-sē-ər, -sē-,ā\ *noun* [French, from *tarse* tarsus, from New Latin *tarsus*] (1774)
: any of a family (Tarsiidae) of small chiefly nocturnal and arboreal carnivorous primates of the Malay Archipelago that have large round eyes, long legs, and a long nearly hairless tail

**tar·so·meta·tar·sus** \'tär-(,)sō-'me-tə-,tär-səs\ *noun* [New Latin, from *tarsus* + *-o-* + *metatarsus*] (1854)

: the large compound bone of the tarsus of a bird; *also* : the segment of the limb it supports

**tar·sus** \'tär-səs\ *noun, plural* **tar·si** \-,sī, -,sē\ [New Latin, from Greek *tarsos* wickerwork mat, flat of the foot, ankle, edge of the eyelid; akin to Greek *tersesthai* to become dry — more at THIRST] (1676)
**1** : the part of the foot of a vertebrate between the metatarsus and the leg; *also* : the small bones that support this part of the limb
**2** : the tarsal plate of the eyelid
**3** : the distal part of the limb of an arthropod
**4** : TARSOMETATARSUS

**[1]tart** \'tärt\ *adjective* [Middle English, from Old English *teart* sharp, severe; akin to Middle High German *traz* spite] (14th century)
**1** : agreeably sharp or acid to the taste
**2** : marked by a biting, acrimonious, or cutting quality
— **tart·ish** \'tär-tish\ *adjective*
— **tart·ly** *adverb*
— **tart·ness** *noun*

**[2]tart** *noun* [Middle English *tarte*, from Middle French] (15th century)
**1** : a dish baked in a pastry shell : PIE: as **a** : a small pie or pastry shell without a top containing jelly, custard, or fruit **b** : a small pie made of pastry folded over a filling
**2** : PROSTITUTE

**tar·tan** \'tär-t°n\ *noun* [probably from Middle French *tiretaine* linsey-woolsey] (circa 1500)
**1** : a plaid textile design of Scottish origin consisting of stripes of varying width and color usually patterned to designate a distinctive clan
**2 a** : a twilled woolen fabric with tartan design **b** : a fabric with tartan design
**3** : a garment of tartan design

**[1]tar·tar** \'tär-tər\ *noun* [Middle English, from Medieval Latin *tartarum*] (14th century)
**1** : a substance consisting essentially of cream of tartar that is derived from the juice of grapes and deposited in wine casks together with yeast and other suspended matters as a pale or dark reddish crust or sediment; *especially* : a recrystallized product yielding cream of tartar on further purification
**2** : an incrustation on the teeth consisting of salivary secretion, food residue, and various salts (as calcium carbonate)

**[2]tartar** *noun* [Middle English *Tartre*, from Middle French *Tartare*, probably from Medieval Latin *Tartarus*, modification of Persian *Tātār* — more at TATAR] (14th century)
**1** *capitalized* : a native or inhabitant of Tatary
**2** *capitalized* : TATAR 2
**3** *often capitalized* : a person of irritable or violent temper
**4** : one that proves to be unexpectedly formidable
— **Tartar** *adjective*
— **Tar·tar·i·an** \tär-'tar-ē-ən, -'ter-\ *adjective*

**Tar·tar·e·an** \tär-'tar-ē-ən, -'ter-\ *adjective* [Latin *tartareus*, from Greek *tartareios*, from *Tartaros* Tartarus] (circa 1623)
: of, relating to, or resembling Tartarus : INFERNAL

**tartar emetic** *noun* (1704)
: a poisonous efflorescent crystalline salt $KSbOC_4H_4O_6 \cdot \frac{1}{2}H_2O$ of sweetish metallic taste that is used in dyeing as a mordant and in medicine especially in the treatment of amebiasis

**tar·tar·ic acid** \(,)tär-'tar-ik-\ *noun* (1810)
: a strong dicarboxylic acid $C_4H_6O_6$ of plant origin that occurs in three optically isomeric forms, is usually obtained from tartar, and is used especially in food and medicines, in photography, and in making salts and esters

**tar·tar sauce** *or* **tar·tare sauce** \'tär-tər-\ *noun* [French *sauce tartare*] (1855)
: a sauce made principally of mayonnaise and chopped pickles

**Tar·ta·rus** \'tär-tə-rəs\ *noun* [Latin, from Greek *Tartaros*]

: a section of Hades reserved for punishment of the wicked

**tart·let** \'tärt-lət\ *noun* (15th century)
: a small tart

**tar·trate** \'tär-,trāt\ *noun* [International Scientific Vocabulary, from French *tartre* tartar, from Medieval Latin *tartarum*] (1794)
: a salt or ester of tartaric acid

**Tar·tuffe** \,tär-'túf, -'tüf\ *noun* [French *Tartufe*]
: a religious hypocrite and protagonist in Molière's play *Tartuffe*

**tart up** *transitive verb* (1938)
: DRESS UP, FANCY UP ⟨*tarted up* pubs and restaurants for the spenders —Arnold Ehrlich⟩

**tarty** \'tär-(,)tē\ *adjective* [[2]*tart*] (1918)
: resembling or suggestive of a prostitute (as in clothing or manner)

**[1]task** \'task\ *noun* [Middle English *taske*, from Old North French *tasque*, from Medieval Latin *tasca* tax or service imposed by a feudal superior, from *taxare* to tax] (14th century)
**1 a** : a usually assigned piece of work often to be finished within a certain time **b** : something hard or unpleasant that has to be done **c** : DUTY, FUNCTION
**2** : subjection to adverse criticism : REPRIMAND — used in the expressions *to take, call,* or *bring to task* ☆

**[2]task** *transitive verb* (15th century)
**1** *obsolete* : to impose a tax on
**2** : to assign a task to
**3** : to oppress with great labor ⟨*tasks* his mind with petty details⟩

**task force** *noun* (1941)
: a temporary grouping under one leader for the purpose of accomplishing a definite objective

**task·mas·ter** \'task-,mas-tər\ *noun* (1530)
: one that imposes a task or burdens another with labor

**task·mis·tress** \-,mis-trəs\ *noun* (1603)
: a woman who is a taskmaster

**Tas·ma·ni·an devil** \(,)taz-'mā-nē-ən-, -nyən-\ *noun* (1867)
: a powerful heavily built carnivorous terrestrial Tasmanian marsupial (*Sarcophilus harrisii*) that is about the size of a badger and has a chiefly black coat marked with white on the chest

**Tasmanian wolf** *noun* (circa 1890)
: a somewhat doglike carnivorous marsupial (*Thylacinus cynocephalus*) that formerly inhabited Tasmania but is now considered extinct — called also *Tasmanian tiger*

**tasse** \'tas\ *noun* [perhaps from Middle French *tasse* purse, pouch] (circa 1548)
: one of a series of overlapping metal plates in a suit of armor that form a short skirt over the body below the waist — see ARMOR illustration

---

☆ **SYNONYMS**
**Task, duty, job, chore, stint, assignment** mean a piece of work to be done. TASK implies work imposed by a person in authority or an employer or by circumstance ⟨charged with a variety of *tasks*⟩. DUTY implies an obligation to perform or responsibility for performance ⟨the *duties* of a lifeguard⟩. JOB applies to a piece of work voluntarily performed; it may sometimes suggest difficulty or importance ⟨the *job* of turning the company around⟩. CHORE implies a minor routine activity necessary for maintaining a household or farm ⟨every child was assigned *chores*⟩. STINT implies a carefully allotted or measured quantity of assigned work or service ⟨a two-month *stint* as a reporter⟩. ASSIGNMENT implies a definite limited task assigned by one in authority ⟨a reporter's *assignment*⟩.

**¹tas·sel** \'ta-səl, *oftenest of corn* 'tä-, 'tȯ-\ *noun* [Middle English, clasp, tassel, from Middle French, from (assumed) Vulgar Latin *tassellus*, alteration of Latin *taxillus* small die; akin to Latin *talus* anklebone, die] (14th century)
**1 :** a dangling ornament made by laying parallel a bunch of cords or threads of even length and fastening them at one end
**2 :** something resembling a tassel; *especially* **:** the terminal male inflorescence of some plants and especially Indian corn

tassel 1

**²tassel** *verb* **-seled** *or* **-selled; -sel·ing** *or* **-sel·ling** \-s(ə-)liŋ\ (14th century)
*transitive verb*
**:** to adorn with tassels
*intransitive verb*
**:** to put forth tassel inflorescences

**¹taste** \'tāst\ *verb* **tast·ed; tast·ing** [Middle English, to touch, test, taste, from Middle French *taster*, from (assumed) Vulgar Latin *taxitare*, frequentative of Latin *taxare* to touch, feel — more at TAX] (14th century)
*transitive verb*
**1 :** to become acquainted with by experience ⟨has *tasted* the frustration of defeat⟩
**2 :** to ascertain the flavor of by taking a little into the mouth
**3 :** to eat or drink especially in small quantities
**4 :** to perceive or recognize as if by the sense of taste
**5** *archaic* **:** APPRECIATE, ENJOY
*intransitive verb*
**1 :** to eat or drink a little
**2 :** to test the flavor of something by taking a small part into the mouth
**3 :** to have perception, experience, or enjoyment **:** PARTAKE — often used with *of*
**4 :** to have a specific flavor ⟨the apple *tastes* sour⟩

**²taste** *noun* (14th century)
**1** *obsolete* **:** TEST
**2 a** *obsolete* **:** the act of tasting **b :** a small amount tasted **c :** a small amount **:** BIT; *especially* **:** a sample of experience ⟨first *taste* of success⟩
**3 :** the one of the special senses that perceives and distinguishes the sweet, sour, bitter, or salty quality of a dissolved substance and is mediated by taste buds on the tongue
**4 :** the objective sweet, sour, bitter, or salty quality of a dissolved substance as perceived by the sense of taste
**5 a :** a sensation obtained from a substance in the mouth that is typically produced by the stimulation of the sense of taste combined with those of touch and smell **:** FLAVOR **b :** the distinctive quality of an experience ⟨that gruesome scene left a bad *taste* in my mouth⟩
**6 :** individual preference **:** INCLINATION
**7 a :** critical judgment, discernment, or appreciation **b :** manner or aesthetic quality indicative of such discernment or appreciation
**taste bud** *noun* (1879)
**:** an end organ mediating the sensation of taste and lying chiefly in the epithelium of the tongue
**taste·ful** \'tāst-fəl\ *adjective* (1611)
**1 :** TASTY 1a
**2 :** having, exhibiting, or conforming to good taste
— **taste·ful·ly** \-fə-lē\ *adverb*
— **taste·ful·ness** *noun*
**taste·less** \'tāst-ləs\ *adjective* (1603)
**1 a :** having no taste **:** INSIPID ⟨*tasteless* vegetables⟩ **b :** arousing no interest **:** DULL ⟨the tale comes to a flat and *tasteless* end —R. C. Carpenter⟩
**2 :** not having or exhibiting good taste
— **taste·less·ly** *adverb*
— **taste·less·ness** *noun*
**taste·mak·er** \-ˌmā-kər\ *noun* (1954)

**:** one who sets the standards of what is currently popular or fashionable
**tast·er** \'tā-stər\ *noun* (15th century)
**1 :** one that tastes: as **a :** one that tests (as tea) for quality by tasting **b :** a person who is able to taste the chemical phenylthiocarbamide
**2 :** a device for tasting or sampling
**tasty** \'tā-stē\ *adjective* **tast·i·er; -est** (1617)
**1 a :** having a marked and appetizing flavor **b :** strikingly attractive or interesting ⟨a *tasty* bit of gossip⟩
**2 :** TASTEFUL
*synonym* see PALATABLE
— **tast·i·ly** \-stə-lē\ *adverb*
— **tast·i·ness** \-stē-nəs\ *noun*
**tat** \'tat\ *verb* **tat·ted; tat·ting** [back-formation from *tatting*] (1882)
*intransitive verb*
**:** to work at tatting
*transitive verb*
**:** to make by tatting
**ta·ta·mi** \tä-'tä-mē, ta-\ *noun, plural* **-mi** *or* **-mis** [Japanese] (1614)
**:** straw matting used as a floor covering in a Japanese home
**Ta·tar** \'tä-tər\ *noun* [Persian *Tātār*, of Turkic origin; akin to Turkish *Tatar* Tatar] (1811)
**1 :** a member of any of a group of Turkic peoples found mainly in the Tatar Republic of Russia and parts of Siberia and central Asia
**2 :** any of the Turkic languages spoken by the Tatar peoples
**ta·ter** \'tā-tər\ *noun* [by shortening & alteration] (1759)
*dialect* **:** POTATO
**¹tat·ter** \'ta-tər\ (14th century)
*transitive verb*
**:** to make ragged
*intransitive verb*
**:** to become ragged
**²tatter** *noun* [Middle English, of Scandinavian origin; akin to Old Norse *tǫturr* tatter; akin to Old English *tætteca* rag, Old High German *zotta* matted hair, tuft] (15th century)
**1 :** a part torn and left hanging **:** SHRED
**2** *plural* **:** tattered clothing **:** RAGS
**¹tat·ter·de·ma·lion** \ˌta-tər-di-'māl-yən, -'mal-, -'ma-lē-ən\ *noun* [origin unknown] (1611)
**:** a person dressed in ragged clothing **:** RAGAMUFFIN
**²tatterdemalion** *adjective* (1614)
**1 a :** ragged or disreputable in appearance **b :** being in a decayed state or condition **:** DILAPIDATED
**2 :** BEGGARLY, DISREPUTABLE
**tat·tered** \'ta-tərd\ *adjective* (14th century)
**1 :** wearing ragged clothes ⟨a *tattered* barefoot boy⟩
**2 :** torn into shreds **:** RAGGED ⟨a *tattered* flag⟩
**3 a :** broken down **:** DILAPIDATED ⟨decaying houses along *tattered* paved streets —P. B. Martin⟩ **b :** being in a shattered condition **:** DISRUPTED ⟨led their *tattered* party to victory⟩
**tat·ter·sall** \'ta-tər-ˌsȯl, -səl\ *noun* [*Tattersall's* horse market, London, England] (1891)
**1 :** a pattern of colored lines forming squares of solid background
**2 :** a fabric woven or printed in a tattersall pattern
**tat·tie** \'ta-tē\ *noun* [by shortening & alteration] (1788)
*Scottish* **:** POTATO
**tat·ting** \'ta-tiŋ\ *noun* [origin unknown] (1842)
**1 :** a delicate handmade lace formed usually by looping and knotting with a single cotton thread and a small shuttle

tatting 1

**2 :** the act or process of making tatting
**¹tat·tle** \'ta-tᵊl\ *noun* (circa 1529)
**1 :** idle talk **:** CHATTER
**2 :** GOSSIP

**²tattle** *verb* **tat·tled; tat·tling** \'tat-liŋ, 'ta-tᵊl-iŋ\ [Middle Dutch *tatelen;* akin to Middle English *tateren* to tattle] (1547)
*intransitive verb*
**1 :** CHATTER, PRATE
**2 :** to tell secrets **:** BLAB
*transitive verb*
**:** to utter or disclose in gossip or chatter
**tat·tler** \'tat-lər, 'ta-tᵊl-ər\ *noun* (1550)
**1 :** TATTLETALE
**2 :** any of various slender long-legged shorebirds (as the willet, yellowlegs, and redshank) with a loud and frequent call
**tat·tle·tale** \'ta-tᵊl-ˌtāl\ *noun* (1888)
**:** one that tattles **:** INFORMER
**¹tat·too** \ta-'tü\ *noun, plural* **tattoos** [alteration of earlier *taptoo*, from Dutch *taptoe*, from the phrase *tap toe!* taps shut!] (circa 1627)
**1 :** a rapid rhythmic rapping
**2 a :** a call sounded shortly before taps as notice to go to quarters **b :** outdoor military exercise given by troops as evening entertainment
**²tattoo** (1780)
*transitive verb*
**:** to beat or rap rhythmically on **:** drum on
*intransitive verb*
**:** to give a series of rhythmic taps
**³tattoo** *transitive verb* [Tahitian *tatau*, noun, tattoo] (1769)
**1 :** to mark or color (the skin) with tattoos
**2 :** to mark the skin with (a tattoo) ⟨*tattooed* a flag on his chest⟩
— **tat·too·er** *noun*
— **tat·too·ist** \-'tü-ist\ *noun*
**⁴tattoo** *noun, plural* **tattoos** (1777)
**1 :** the act of tattooing **:** the fact of being tattooed
**2 :** an indelible mark or figure fixed upon the body by insertion of pigment under the skin or by production of scars
**tat·ty** \'ta-tē\ *adjective* **tat·ti·er; -est** [perhaps akin to Old English *tætteca* rag — more at TATTER] (1513)
**:** rather worn, frayed, or dilapidated **:** SHABBY
— **tat·ti·ness** \-nəs\ *noun*
**tau** \'taù, 'tȯ\ *noun* [Middle English *taw*, from Latin *tau*, from Greek, of Semitic origin; akin to Hebrew *tāw* taw] (14th century)
**1 :** the 19th letter of the Greek alphabet — see ALPHABET table
**2 :** a short-lived elementary particle of the lepton family that exists in positive and negative charge states and has a mass about 3500 times heavier than an electron — called also *tau particle*
**tau cross** *noun* (15th century)
**:** a T-shaped cross sometimes having expanded ends and foot — see CROSS illustration
**taught** *past and past participle of* TEACH
**¹taunt** \'tȯnt, 'tänt\ *noun* (circa 1529)
**:** a sarcastic challenge or insult
**²taunt** *transitive verb* [perhaps from Middle French *tenter* to try, tempt — more at TEMPT] (1539)
**:** to reproach or challenge in a mocking or insulting manner **:** jeer at
*synonym* see RIDICULE
— **taunt·er** *noun*
— **taunt·ing·ly** \'tȯn-tiŋ-lē, 'tän-\ *adverb*
**taupe** \'tōp\ *noun* [French, literally, mole, from Latin *talpa*] (circa 1909)
**:** a brownish gray
**Tau·re·an** \'tȯr-ē-ən\ *noun* (1911)
**:** TAURUS 2b
**¹tau·rine** \'tȯ-ˌrīn\ *adjective* [Latin *taurinus*, from *taurus* bull; akin to Greek *tauros* bull, Middle Irish *tarb*] (1613)
**:** of or relating to a bull **:** BOVINE

**²tau·rine** \'tȯ-ˌrēn\ *noun* [International Scientific Vocabulary, from Latin *taurus;* from its having been discovered in ox bile] (1845)
: a colorless crystalline cysteine derivative $C_2H_7NO_3S$ of neutral reaction found in the juices of muscle especially in invertebrates, nerve tissue, and bile

**tau·ro·cho·lic acid** \ˌtȯr-ə-ˈkō-lik-, -ˈkä-\ *noun* [Latin *taurus* + International Scientific Vocabulary *-o-* + *cholic (acid)*] (1857)
: a deliquescent acid $C_{26}H_{45}NO_7S$ occurring as the sodium salt in the bile of the ox, humans, and various carnivores

**Tau·rus** \'tȯr-əs\ *noun* [Middle English, from Latin (genitive *Tauri*), literally, bull]
**1** : a zodiacal constellation that contains the Pleiades and Hyades and is represented pictorially by a bull's forequarters
**2 a** : the 2d sign of the zodiac in astrology **b** : one born under the sign of Taurus — see ZODIAC table

**¹taut** \'tȯt\ *adjective* [Middle English *tought*] (14th century)
**1 a** : having no give or slack : tightly drawn **b** : HIGH-STRUNG, TENSE ⟨*taut* nerves⟩
**2 a** : kept in proper order or condition ⟨a *taut* ship⟩ **b** (1) : not loose or flabby (2) : marked by economy of structure and detail ⟨a *taut* story⟩
— **taut·ly** *adverb*
— **taut·ness** *noun*

**²taut** *transitive verb* [origin unknown] (1721) *Scottish* : MAT, TANGLE

**taut-** *or* **tauto-** *combining form* [Late Latin, from Greek, from *tauto* the same, contraction of *to auto*]
: same ⟨*taut*omerism⟩ ⟨*tauto*nym⟩

**taut·en** \'tȯ-t°n\ *verb* **taut·ened; taut·en·ing** \'tȯt-niŋ, 'tȯ-t°n-iŋ\ (circa 1814)
*transitive verb*
: to make taut
*intransitive verb*
: to become taut

**tau·tog** \tȯ-'tȯg, -ˌtäg, tȯ-'\ *noun* [Narraganset *tautaŭog,* plural] (1643)
: an edible fish (*Tautoga onitis*) of the wrasse family found along the Atlantic coast of the U.S. and adjacent Canada — called also *blackfish*

**tau·to·log·i·cal** \ˌtȯ-t°l-'ä-ji-kəl\ *adjective* (1620)
: TAUTOLOGOUS
— **tau·to·log·i·cal·ly** \-k(ə-)lē\ *adverb*

**tau·tol·o·gous** \tȯ-'tä-lə-gəs\ *adjective* [Greek *tautologos,* from *taut-* + *legein* to say — more at LEGEND] (1714)
**1** : involving or containing rhetorical tautology : REDUNDANT
**2** : true by virtue of its logical form alone
— **tau·tol·o·gous·ly** *adverb*

**tau·tol·o·gy** \tȯ-'tä-lə-jē\ *noun, plural* **-gies** [Late Latin *tautologia,* from Greek, from *tautologos*] (1574)
**1 a** : needless repetition of an idea, statement, or word **b** : an instance of tautology
**2** : a tautologous statement

**tau·to·mer** \'tȯ-tə-mər\ *noun* [International Scientific Vocabulary, from *tautomeric*) (1903)
: any of the forms of a tautomeric compound

**tau·to·mer·ic** \ˌtȯ-tə-'mer-ik\ *adjective* [International Scientific Vocabulary] (circa 1890)
: of, relating to, or marked by tautomerism

**tau·tom·er·ism** \tȯ-'tä-mə-ˌri-zəm\ *noun* (circa 1890)
: isomerism in which the isomers change into one another with great ease so that they ordinarily exist together in equilibrium

**taut·o·nym** \'tȯ-tə-ˌnim\ *noun* (1899)
: a taxonomic binomial in which the generic name and specific epithet are alike and which is common in zoology especially to designate a typical form but is forbidden in botany under the International Code of Botanical Nomenclature

— **tau·ton·y·my** \tȯ-'tä-nə-mē\ *noun*

**tav·ern** \'ta-vərn\ *noun* [Middle English *taverne,* from Old French, from Latin *taberna* hut, shop] (14th century)
**1** : an establishment where alcoholic beverages are sold to be drunk on the premises
**2** : INN

**ta·ver·na** \tä-'ver-nə\ *noun* [New Greek *taberna,* probably from Late Greek, drinking establishment, from Latin *taberna*] (1914)
: a café in Greece

**tav·ern·er** \'tav-ə(r)-nər\ *noun* (14th century)
: one who keeps a tavern

**¹taw** \'tȯ\ *transitive verb* [Middle English, to prepare for use, from Old English *tawian;* akin to Old High German *zawjan* to hasten, Gothic *taujan* to do, make] (before 12th century)
: to dress (skins) usually by a dry process (as with alum or salt)

**²taw** \'täf, 'tȯf, 'täv, 'tȯv\ *noun* [Hebrew *tāw,* literally, mark, cross] (1701)
: the 23d letter of the Hebrew alphabet — see ALPHABET table

**³taw** *noun* [origin unknown] (1709)
**1 a** : a marble used as a shooter **b** : RINGTAW
**2** : the line from which players shoot at marbles
**3** : a square-dance partner

**⁴taw** *intransitive verb* (1863)
: to shoot a marble

**¹taw·dry** \'tȯ-drē, 'tä-\ *adjective* **taw·dri·er; -est** [*tawdry lace* a tie of lace for the neck, from *Saint Audrey* (Saint Etheldreda) (died 679) queen of Northumbria] (1676)
: cheap and gaudy in appearance or quality; *also* : IGNOBLE
**synonym** see GAUDY
— **taw·dri·ly** \-drə-lē\ *adverb*
— **taw·dri·ness** \-drē-nəs\ *noun*

**²tawdry** *noun* (circa 1680)
: cheap showy finery

**¹taw·ny** \'tȯ-nē, 'tä-nē\ *adjective* **taw·ni·er; -est** [Middle English, from Middle French *tanné,* past participle of *tanner* to tan] (14th century)
**1** : of the color tawny
**2** : of a warm sandy color like that of well-tanned skin ⟨the lion's *tawny* coat⟩
— **taw·ni·ness** *noun*

**²tawny** *noun, plural* **tawnies** (15th century)
: a brownish orange to light brown color

**taw·pie** \'tȯ-pē\ *noun* [of Scandinavian origin; akin to Norwegian *tåpe* simpleton] (1728) *chiefly Scottish* : a foolish or awkward young person

**tawse** *also* **taws** \'tȯz\ *noun plural but singular or plural in construction* [probably from plural of obsolete *taw* tawed leather] (circa 1585)
*British* : a leather strap slit into strips at the end and used especially for disciplining children

**¹tax** \'taks\ *transitive verb* [Middle English, to estimate, assess, tax, from Old French *taxer,* from Medieval Latin *taxare,* from Latin, to feel, estimate, censure, frequentative of *tangere* to touch — more at TANGENT] (14th century)
**1** : to assess or determine judicially the amount of (costs in a court action)
**2** : to levy a tax on
**3** *obsolete* : to enter (a name) in a list ⟨there went out a decree . . . that all the world should be *taxed* —Luke 2:1 (Authorized Version)⟩
**4** : CHARGE, ACCUSE ⟨*taxed* him with neglect of duty⟩; *also* : CENSURE
**5** : to make onerous and rigorous demands on ⟨the job *taxed* her strength⟩
— **tax·able** \'tak-sə-bəl\ *adjective*
— **tax·er** *noun*

**²tax** *noun, often attributive* (14th century)
**1 a** : a charge usually of money imposed by authority on persons or property for public purposes **b** : a sum levied on members of an organization to defray expenses
**2** : a heavy demand

**tax-** *or* **taxo-** *also* **taxi-** *combining form* [Greek *taxi-,* from *taxis*]
: arrangement ⟨*tax*eme⟩ ⟨*taxi*dermy⟩

**taxa** *plural of* TAXON

**tax·a·tion** \tak-'sā-shən\ *noun* (14th century)
**1** : the action of taxing; *especially* : the imposition of taxes
**2** : revenue obtained from taxes
**3** : the amount assessed as a tax

**tax base** *noun* (circa 1943)
: the wealth (as real estate or income) within a jurisdiction that is liable to taxation

**tax·eme** \'tak-ˌsēm\ *noun* [*tax-*] (1933)
: a minimum grammatical feature of selection, order, stress, pitch, or phonetic modification
— **tax·e·mic** \tak-'sē-mik\ *adjective*

**tax–ex·empt** \ˌtaks-ig-'zem(p)t\ *adjective* (1923)
**1** : exempted from a tax
**2** : bearing interest that is free from federal or state income tax

**¹taxi** \'tak-sē\ *noun, plural* **tax·is** \-sēz\ *also* **tax·ies** (circa 1907)
: TAXICAB; *also* : a similarly operated boat or aircraft ◆

**²taxi** *verb* **tax·ied; taxi·ing** *or* **taxy·ing; tax·is** *or* **tax·ies** (1916)
*intransitive verb*
**1 a** *of an aircraft* : to go at low speed along the surface of the ground or water **b** : to operate an aircraft on the ground under its own power
**2** : to ride in a taxicab
*transitive verb*
**1** : to transport by or as if by taxi
**2** : to cause (an aircraft) to taxi

**taxi·cab** \'tak-sē-ˌkab\ *noun* [*taxi*meter *cab*] (circa 1907)
: an automobile that carries passengers for a fare usually determined by the distance traveled

**taxi dancer** *noun* (circa 1927)
: a girl employed by a dance hall, café, or cabaret to dance with patrons who pay a certain amount for each dance

**taxi·der·my** \'tak-sə-ˌdər-mē\ *noun* [*tax-* + *derm-* + *²-y*] (1820)

---

◇ WORD HISTORY

**taxi** *Taxi* in the sense "an automobile that carries passengers for a fare usually determined by distance" is shortened from *taxicab,* itself shortened from *taximeter cab.* The taximeter is the mechanical device in a taxi that is activated when the ride starts and automatically shows the fare due at the end of the ride. Meters of this kind were first used in 19th century Germany under the name *Taxameter,* attached to horsedrawn vehicles for hire. *Taxameter* was made up irregularly in terms of the rules of Greco-Latin word formation from *Taxe* "fee, tax," Latinized to *taxa* (which happens to be the original Medieval Latin form from which *Taxe* was ultimately borrowed), and *-meter,* which as in English is used in names of measuring instruments. (The regular outcome would have been *Taxometer.*) The word soon showed up in French as *taxamètre* and in English as *taxameter,* but both languages then altered the internal *-a-* to *-i-,* yielding French *taximètre* and English *taximeter.* Though these forms violate no rules of the classical languages, they assume a nonexistent connection with Greek *taxis* "arrangement." Etymological confusion notwithstanding, *taxi* has become an international word, finding its way into languages as diverse as Arabic (*taksi*) and Japanese (*takushī*).

: the art of preparing, stuffing, and mounting the skins of animals and especially vertebrates
— **taxi·der·mic** \ˌtak-sə-'dər-mik\ *adjective*
— **taxi·der·mist** \'tak-sə-ˌdər-mist\ *noun*
**taxi·man** \'tak-sē-mən\ *noun* (1909)
*chiefly British* : the operator of a taxi
**taxi·me·ter** \'tak-sē-ˌmē-tər\ *noun* [French *taximètre*, modification of German *Taxameter*, from Medieval Latin *taxa* tax, charge (from *taxare* to tax) + German *-meter*] (1894)
: an instrument for use in a hired vehicle (as a taxicab) for automatically showing the fare due
**word history** see TAXI
**tax·ing** \'tak-siŋ\ *adjective* (1841)
: ONEROUS, WEARING ⟨a *taxing* operatic role⟩
— **tax·ing·ly** \-siŋ-lē\ *adverb*
**tax·is** \'tak-səs\ *noun, plural* **tax·es** \-ˌsēz\ [Greek, literally, arrangement, order, from *tassein* to arrange] (1758)
**1** : reflex translational or orientational movement by a freely motile and usually simple organism in relation to a source of stimulation (as a light or a temperature or chemical gradient)
**2** : a reflex reaction involving a taxis
**-taxis** *noun combining form, plural* **-taxes** [New Latin, from Greek, from *taxis*]
**1** : arrangement : ordering ⟨thermo*taxis*⟩
**2** : physiological taxis ⟨chemo*taxis*⟩
**taxi stand** *noun* (1922)
: a place where taxis may park while awaiting hire
**taxi·way** \'tak-sē-ˌwā\ *noun* (circa 1933)
: a usually paved strip for taxiing (as from the terminal to a runway) at an airport
**tax·on** \'tak-ˌsän\ *noun, plural* **taxa** \-sə\ *also* **tax·ons** [New Latin, from International Scientific Vocabulary *taxonomy*] (1929)
**1** : a taxonomic group or entity
**2** : the name applied to a taxonomic group in a formal system of nomenclature
**tax·on·o·my** \tak-'sä-nə-mē\ *noun* [French *taxonomie*, from *tax-* + *-nomie* -nomy] (circa 1828)
**1** : the study of the general principles of scientific classification : SYSTEMATICS
**2** : CLASSIFICATION; *especially* : orderly classification of plants and animals according to their presumed natural relationships
— **tax·o·nom·ic** \ˌtak-sə-'nä-mik\ *adjective*
— **tax·o·nom·i·cal·ly** \-mi-k(ə-)lē\ *adverb*
— **tax·on·o·mist** \tak-'sä-nə-mist\ *noun*
**tax·pay·er** \'taks-ˌpā-ər\ *noun* (1816)
: one that pays or is liable for a tax
**tax·pay·ing** \-ˌpā-iŋ\ *adjective* (1832)
: of, relating to, or subject to the paying of a tax
**tax selling** *noun* (1963)
: concerted selling of securities late in the year to establish gains and losses for income-tax purposes
**tax shelter** *noun* (1952)
: a strategy, investment, or tax code provision that reduces tax liability
— **tax–shel·tered** \'taks-ˌshel-tərd\ *adjective*
**tax stamp** *noun* (circa 1929)
: a stamp marked on or affixed to a taxable item as evidence that the tax has been paid
**tax·us** \'tak-səs\ *noun, plural* **tax·us** \-səs\ [New Latin, genus comprising the yews, from Latin, yew] (circa 1945)
: YEW 1a
**-taxy** *noun combining form* [Greek *-taxia*, from *taktos*, verbal of *tassein* to arrange]
: -TAXIS ⟨epi*taxy*⟩
**Tay·lor's series** \'tā-lərz-\ *noun* [Brook *Taylor* (died 1731) English mathematician] (1842)
: a power series that gives the expansion of a function *f*(*x*) in the neighborhood of a point *a* provided that in the neighborhood the function is continuous, all its derivatives exist, and the

series converges to the function in which case it has the form

$$f(x) = f(a) + \frac{f^{[1]}(a)}{1!}(x-a) + \frac{f^{[2]}(a)}{2!}(x-a)^2 + \dots$$
$$+ \frac{f^{[n]}(a)}{n!}(x-a)^n + \dots$$

where $f^{[n]}(a)$ is the derivative of nth order of $f(x)$ evaluated at $a$ — called also *Taylor series*
**Tay–Sachs disease** \'tā-'saks-\ *noun* [Warren *Tay* (died 1927) British physician & Bernard P. *Sachs* (died 1944) American neurologist] (1907)
: a hereditary disorder of lipid metabolism typically affecting individuals of eastern European Jewish ancestry that is characterized by the accumulation of lipids especially in nervous tissue due to a deficiency of hexosaminidase and causes death in early childhood — called also *Tay-Sachs*
**taz·za** \'tät-sə\ *noun* [Italian, cup, from Arabic *ṭassah*] (1824)
: a shallow cup or vase on a pedestal
**TB** \ˌtē-'bē\ *noun* [TB (abbreviation for *tubercle bacillus*)] (1912)
: TUBERCULOSIS
**T–ball** \'tē-ˌbȯl\ *noun* [²tee] (1976)
: baseball modified for youngsters in which the ball is batted from a tee rather than being pitched
**T–bar** \'tē-ˌbär\ *noun* (1948)
: a ski lift having a series of T-shaped bars each of which pulls two skiers — called also *T-bar lift*
**T–bill** \'tē-ˌbil\ *noun* [Treasury] (1973)
: a U.S. treasury note
**T–bone** \'tē-ˌbōn\ *noun* (circa 1916)
: a small steak from the thin end of the short loin containing a T-shaped bone and a small piece of tenderloin; *also* : this bone — see BEEF illustration
**TCDD** \ˌtē-(ˌ)sē-(ˌ)dē-'dē\ *noun* [tetra- + chlor- + *d*ibenzo- (containing two benzene rings) + *d*ioxin] (1971)
: a carcinogenic dioxin $C_{12}H_4O_2Cl_4$ found especially as a contaminant in 2,4,5-T
**T cell** *noun* [*t*hymus-derived *cell*] (1970)
: any of several lymphocytes (as a helper T cell) that differentiate in the thymus, possess highly specific cell-surface antigen receptors, and include some that control the initiation or suppression of cell-mediated and humoral immunity (as by the regulation of T and B cell maturation and proliferation) and others that lyse antigen-bearing cells — called also *T lymphocyte*; compare B CELL
**tchotch·ke** \'chäch-kə, 'tsäts-\ *noun* [Yiddish *tshatshke* trinket, from obsolete Polish *czaczko*] (1971)
: KNICKKNACK, TRINKET
**t distribution** *noun* (circa 1957)
: a probability density function that is used especially in testing hypotheses concerning means of normal distributions whose standard deviations are unknown and that is the distribution of a random variable

$$t = \frac{u\sqrt{n}}{v}$$

where *u* and *v* are themselves independent random variables and *u* has a normal distribution with mean 0 and a standard deviation of 1 and $v^2$ has a chi-square distribution with *n* degrees of freedom — called also *student's t distribution*
**tea** \'tē\ *noun* [Chinese (Xiamen) *t'e*] (circa 1655)
**1 a** : a shrub (*Camellia sinensis* of the family Theaceae, the tea family) cultivated especially in China, Japan, and the East Indies **b** : the leaves, leaf buds, and internodes of the tea plant prepared and cured for the market, classed according to method of manufacture

into one set of types (as green tea, black tea, or oolong), and graded according to leaf size into another (as orange pekoe, pekoe, or souchong)
**2** : an aromatic beverage prepared from tea leaves by infusion with boiling water
**3** : any of various plants somewhat resembling tea in properties; *also* : an infusion of their leaves used medicinally or as a beverage
**4 a** : refreshments usually including tea with sandwiches, crackers, or cookies served in late afternoon **b** : a reception at which tea is served
**5** *slang* : MARIJUANA
— **tea·like** \-ˌlīk\ *adjective*
**tea bag** *noun* (1935)
: a bag usually of filter paper holding enough tea for an individual serving
**tea ball** *noun* (1895)
: a perforated metal ball that holds tea leaves and is used in brewing tea in a pot or cup
**tea·ber·ry** \'tē-ˌber-ē\ *noun* [from the use of its leaves as a substitute for tea] (1818)
: CHECKERBERRY
**tea caddy** *noun* (1790)
: CADDY
**tea cake** *noun* (1824)
**1** : a small flat cake usually made with raisins
**2** : COOKIE
**tea cart** *noun* (1817)
: TEA WAGON
**teach** \'tēch\ *verb* **taught** \'tȯt\; **teach·ing** [Middle English *techen* to show, instruct, from Old English *tǣcan*; akin to Old English *tācn* sign — more at TOKEN] (before 12th century)
*transitive verb*
**1 a** : to cause to know something ⟨*taught* them a trade⟩ **b** : to cause to know how ⟨is *teaching* me to drive⟩ **c** : to accustom to some action or attitude ⟨*teach* students to think for themselves⟩ **d** : to cause to know the disagreeable consequences of some action ⟨I'll *teach* you to come home late⟩
**2** : to guide the studies of
**3** : to impart the knowledge of ⟨*teach* algebra⟩
**4 a** : to instruct by precept, example, or experience **b** : to make known and accepted ⟨experience *teaches* us our limitations⟩
**5** : to conduct instruction regularly in ⟨*teach* school⟩
*intransitive verb*
: to provide instruction : act as a teacher ☆
*usage* see LEARN
**teach·able** \'tē-chə-bəl\ *adjective* (15th century)
**1 a** : capable of being taught **b** : apt and willing to learn
**2** : favorable to teaching
— **teach·able·ness** *noun*
— **teach·ably** \-blē\ *adverb*

☆ SYNONYMS
**Teach, instruct, educate, train, discipline, school** mean to cause to acquire knowledge or skill. TEACH applies to any manner of imparting information or skill so that others may learn ⟨*taught* us a lot about our planet⟩. INSTRUCT suggests methodical or formal teaching ⟨*instructs* raw recruits in military drill⟩. EDUCATE implies development of the mind ⟨more things than formal schooling serve to *educate* a person⟩. TRAIN stresses instruction and drill with a specific end in view ⟨*trained* foreign pilots to operate the new aircraft⟩. DISCIPLINE implies training in habits of order and precision ⟨a *disciplined* mind⟩. SCHOOL implies training or disciplining especially in what is hard to master ⟨*schooled* the horse in five gaits⟩.

**teach·er** \'tē-chər\ *noun* (14th century)
**1 :** one that teaches; *especially* **:** one whose occupation is to instruct
**2 :** a Mormon ranking above a deacon in the Aaronic priesthood
**teach·er·ly** \-lē\ *adjective* (circa 1683)
**:** resembling, characteristic of, or befitting a teacher
**teachers college** *noun* (circa 1911)
**:** a college for the training of teachers usually offering a full 4-year course and granting a bachelor's degree
**teacher's pet** *noun* (1914)
**1 :** a pupil who has won his teacher's special favor
**2 :** one who has ingratiated himself with an authority
**teach–in** \'tēch-,in\ *noun* (1965)
**:** an extended meeting usually held on a college campus for lectures, debates, and discussions to raise awareness of or express a position on a social or political issue
**¹teaching** *noun* (13th century)
**1 :** the act, practice, or profession of a teacher
**2 :** something taught; *especially* **:** DOCTRINE ⟨the *teachings* of Confucius⟩
**²teaching** *adjective* (1642)
**:** of, relating to, used for, or engaged in teaching ⟨a *teaching* aid⟩ ⟨the *teaching* profession⟩ ⟨a *teaching* assistant⟩
**teaching hospital** *noun* (circa 1951)
**:** a hospital that is affiliated with a medical school and provides means for medical education
**tea·cup** \'tē-,kəp\ *noun* (1700)
**:** a small cup usually with a handle used with a saucer for hot beverages
**— tea·cup·ful** *noun*
**tea dance** *noun* (1885)
**:** a dance held in the late afternoon
**tea garden** *noun* (1802)
**1 :** a public garden where tea and light refreshments are served
**2 :** a tea plantation
**tea gown** *noun* (1878)
**:** a semiformal gown of fine materials in graceful flowing lines worn especially for afternoon entertaining at home
**tea·house** \'tē-,haus\ *noun* (1689)
**:** a public house or restaurant where tea and light refreshments are sold
**teak** \'tēk\ *noun* [Portuguese *teca*, from Malayalam *tēkka*] (1698)
**1 :** a tall East Indian timber tree (*Tectona grandis*) of the vervain family
**2 :** the hard yellowish brown wood of teak used especially for furniture and shipbuilding
**tea·ket·tle** \'tē-,ke-t³l\ *noun* (1705)
**:** a covered kettle with a handle and spout for boiling water
**teak·wood** \'tēk-,wud\ *noun* (1783)
**:** TEAK 2
**teal** \'tē(ə)l\ *noun, plural* **teal** *or* **teals** [Middle English *tele*; akin to Middle Dutch *teling* teal] (14th century)
**1 :** any of various widely distributed small short-necked dabblers (genus *Anas*) — compare GREEN-WINGED TEAL
**2 :** TEAL BLUE

teal 1

**teal blue** *noun* (1938)
**:** a dark greenish blue
**¹team** \'tēm\ *noun* [Middle English *teme*, from Old English *tēam* offspring, lineage, group of draft animals; akin to Old High German *zoum* rein, Old English *tēon* to draw, pull — more at TOW] (before 12th century)
**1 a :** two or more draft animals harnessed to the same vehicle or implement; *also* **:** these with their harness and attached vehicle **b :** a draft animal often with harness and vehicle
**2** *obsolete* **:** LINEAGE, RACE

**3 :** a group of animals: as **a :** a brood especially of young pigs or ducks **b :** a matched group of animals for exhibition
**4 :** a number of persons associated together in work or activity: as **a :** a group on one side (as in football or a debate) **b :** CREW, GANG
**²team** (1552)
*transitive verb*
**1 :** to yoke or join in a team; *also* **:** to put together in a coordinated ensemble
**2 :** to convey or haul with a team
*intransitive verb*
**1 :** to drive a team or motortruck
**2 :** to form a team or association **:** COLLABORATE ⟨*teamed* up to write a book⟩
**³team** *adjective* (1886)
**:** of or performed by a team ⟨a *team* effort⟩; *also* **:** marked by devotion to teamwork rather than individual achievement ⟨a *team* player⟩
**team foul** *noun* (1966)
**:** one of a designated number of personal fouls the players on a basketball team may commit during a given period of play before the opposing team begins receiving bonus free throws
**team handball** *noun* (1970)
**:** a game developed from soccer which is played between two teams of seven players each and in which the ball is thrown, caught, and dribbled with the hands
**team·mate** \'tēm-,māt\ *noun* (1915)
**:** a fellow member of a team
**team·ster** \'tēm(p)-stər\ *noun* (1777)
**:** one who drives a team or motortruck especially as an occupation
**team·work** \'tēm-,wərk\ *noun* (circa 1828)
**:** work done by several associates with each doing a part but all subordinating personal prominence to the efficiency of the whole
**tea party** *noun* (1778)
**1 :** an afternoon social gathering at which tea is served
**2** [from the Boston Tea Party, name applied to the occasion in 1773 when a shipment of tea was thrown into Boston harbor in protest against the tax on imports] **:** an exciting disturbance or proceeding
**tea·pot** \'tē-,pät\ *noun* (1705)
**:** a vessel with a spout and a handle in which tea is brewed and from which it is served
**tea·poy** \'tē-,poi\ *noun* [Hindi *tipāī*] (1828)
**1 :** a 3-legged ornamental stand
**2** [influenced by *tea*] **:** a stand or table containing a tea chest or caddy and used for supporting a tea set; *also* **:** TEA CADDY
**¹tear** \'tir\ *noun* [Middle English, from Old English *tæhher, tēar*; akin to Old High German *zahar* tear, Greek *dakry*] (before 12th century)
**1 a :** a drop of clear saline fluid secreted by the lacrimal gland and diffused between the eye and eyelids to moisten the parts and facilitate their motion **b** *plural* **:** a secretion of profuse tears that overflow the eyelids and dampen the face
**2 :** a transparent drop of fluid or hardened fluid matter (as resin)
**3** *plural* **:** an act of weeping or grieving ⟨broke into *tears*⟩
**— tear·less** *adjective*
**²tear** *intransitive verb* (before 12th century)
**:** to fill with tears **:** shed tears ⟨eyes *tearing* in the November wind —Saul Bellow⟩
**³tear** \'tar, 'ter\ *verb* **tore** \'tōr, 'tor\; **torn** \'tōrn, 'torn\; **tear·ing** [Middle English *teren*, from Old English *teran*; akin to Old High German *zeran* to destroy, Greek *derein* to skin, Sanskrit *dṛṇāti* he bursts, tears] (before 12th century)
*transitive verb*
**1 a :** to separate parts of or pull apart by force **:** REND **b :** to wound by or as if by tearing **:** LACERATE ⟨*tear* the skin⟩
**2 :** to divide or disrupt by the pull of contrary forces ⟨a mind *torn* with doubts⟩

**3 a :** to remove by force **:** WRENCH — often used with *off* ⟨*tear* a cover off a box⟩ **b :** to remove as if by wrenching ⟨*tear* your thoughts away from the scene⟩
**4 :** to make or effect by or as if by tearing ⟨*tear* a hole in the wall⟩
*intransitive verb*
**1 :** to separate on being pulled **:** REND ⟨this cloth *tears* easily⟩
**2 a :** to move or act with violence, haste, or force ⟨went *tearing* down the street⟩ **b :** to smash or penetrate something with violent force ⟨the bullet *tore* through his leg⟩ ☆
**— tear·able** \'tar-ə-bəl, 'ter-\ *adjective*
**— tear·er** *noun*
**— tear at :** to cause anguish to **:** DISTRESS ⟨her grief *tore at* his heart⟩
**— tear into :** to attack without restraint or caution
**— tear it :** to cause frustration, defeat, or an end to plans or hopes ⟨that *tears it*⟩
**— tear one's hair :** to pull one's hair as an expression of grief, rage, frustration, desperation, or anxiety
**⁴tear** \'tar, 'ter\ *noun* (1611)
**1 a :** damage from being torn; *especially* **:** a hole or flaw made by tearing **b :** the act of tearing
**2 a :** a tearing pace **:** HURRY **b :** SPREE ⟨go on a *tear*⟩ **c :** a run of unusual success ⟨the team was on a *tear*⟩
**tear·away** \'tar-ə-,wā, 'ter-\ *noun* (1950)
*British* **:** a rebellious and unruly or reckless young person
**tear away** *transitive verb* (circa 1699)
**:** to remove (as oneself) reluctantly
**tear·down** \'tar-,daun, 'ter-\ *noun* (1926)
**:** the act or process of disassembling
**tear down** *transitive verb* (1614)
**1 a :** to cause to decompose or disintegrate **b :** VILIFY, DENIGRATE
**2 :** to take apart **:** DISASSEMBLE
**tear·drop** \'tir-,dräp\ *noun* (1789)
**1 :** ¹TEAR 1a
**2 :** something shaped like a dropping tear; *specifically* **:** a pendent gem (as on an earring)
**tear·ful** \'tir-fəl\ *adjective* (circa 1586)
**1 :** flowing with or accompanied by tears ⟨*tearful* entreaties⟩
**2 :** causing tears **:** TEARY
**— tear·ful·ly** \-fə-lē\ *adverb*
**— tear·ful·ness** *noun*
**tear·gas** \-,gas\ *transitive verb* (1946)
**:** to use tear gas on
**tear gas** *noun* (1917)
**:** a solid, liquid, or gaseous substance that on dispersion in the atmosphere blinds the eyes with tears and is used chiefly in dispelling mobs
**tear·ing** \'tar-iŋ, 'ter-\ *adjective* (1606)
**1 :** causing continued or repeated pain or distress
**2 :** HASTY, VIOLENT
**3** *chiefly British* **:** SPLENDID
**tear·jerk·er** \'tir-,jər-kər\ *noun* (1912)

---

☆ **SYNONYMS**
**Tear, rip, rend, split, cleave, rive** mean to separate forcibly. TEAR implies pulling apart by force and leaving jagged edges ⟨*tear* up the letter⟩. RIP implies a pulling apart in one rapid uninterrupted motion often along a line or joint ⟨*ripped* the shirt on a nail⟩. REND implies very violent or ruthless severing or sundering ⟨an angry mob *rent* the prisoner's clothes⟩. SPLIT implies a cutting or breaking apart in a continuous, straight, and usually lengthwise direction or in the direction of grain or layers ⟨*split* logs for firewood⟩. CLEAVE implies very forceful splitting or cutting with a blow ⟨a bolt of lightning *cleaved* the giant oak⟩. RIVE occurs most often in figurative use ⟨a political party *riven* by conflict⟩.

: an extravagantly pathetic story, song, play, film, or broadcast
— **tear–jerk·ing** \-kiŋ\ *adjective*
**tea·room** \'tē-,rüm, -,rüm\ *noun* (1778)
: a small restaurant or café with service and decor designed primarily for a female clientele
**tea rose** *noun* (1850)
: a garden bush rose (*Rosa odorata*) of Chinese origin that includes several cultivars and is valued especially for its abundant large usually tea-scented blossoms — compare HYBRID TEA ROSE
**tear sheet** *noun* (circa 1924)
: a sheet torn from a publication
**tear·stain** \'tir-,stān\ *noun* (1922)
: a spot or streak left by tears
— **tear·stained** \-,stānd\ *adjective*
**tear up** *transitive verb* (1699)
: to damage, remove, or effect an opening in ⟨*tore up* the street to lay a new water main⟩
**teary** \'tir-ē\ *adjective* **tear·i·er; -est** (14th century)
**1 a :** wet or stained with tears : TEARFUL **b** : consisting of tears or drops resembling tears **2 :** causing tears : PATHETIC ⟨a *teary* story⟩
¹**tease** \'tēz\ *transitive verb* **teased; teas·ing** [Middle English *tesen,* from Old English *tǣsan;* akin to Old High German *zeisan* to tease] (before 12th century)
**1 a :** to disentangle and lay parallel by combing or carding ⟨*tease* wool⟩ **b :** TEASEL **2 :** to tear in pieces; *especially* : to shred (a tissue or specimen) for microscopic examination
**3 a :** to disturb or annoy by persistent irritating or provoking especially in a petty or mischievous way **b :** to annoy with petty persistent requests : PESTER; *also* : to obtain by repeated coaxing **c :** to persuade to acquiesce especially by persistent small efforts : COAX **d** : to manipulate or influence as if by teasing
**4 :** to comb (hair) by taking hold of a strand and pushing the short hairs toward the scalp with the comb
**5 :** to tantalize especially by arousing desire or curiosity without intending to satisfy it
**synonym** see WORRY
— **teas·ing·ly** \'tē-ziŋ-lē\ *adverb*
²**tease** *noun* (1693)
**1 :** the act of teasing : the state of being teased **2 :** one that teases
¹**tea·sel** \'tē-zəl\ *noun* [Middle English *tesel,* from Old English *tǣsel;* akin to Old English *tǣsan* to tease] (before 12th century)
**1 a :** an Old World prickly herb (*Dipsacus fullonum* of the family Dipsacaceae, the teasel family) with flower heads that are covered with stiff hooked bracts and are used in the woolen industry — called also *fuller's teasel* **b :** a plant of the same genus as the teasel
**2 a :** a flower head of the fuller's teasel used when dried to raise a nap on woolen cloth **b** : a wire substitute for the teasel

teasel 1a

²**teasel** *transitive verb* **tea·seled** *or* **tea·selled; tea·sel·ing** *or* **tea·sel·ling** \'tēz-liŋ, 'tē-zə-\ (1543)
: to nap (cloth) with teasels
**tease out** *transitive verb* (1828)
: to obtain by or as if by disentangling or freeing with a pointed instrument
**teas·er** \'tē-zər\ *noun* (1659)
**1 :** one that teases
**2 :** an advertising or promotional device intended to arouse interest or curiosity especially in something to follow
**tea service** *noun* (1809)
: TEA SET
**tea set** *noun* (1849)
: a matching set of metalware or china (as a teapot, sugar bowl, creamer, and often plates, cups, and saucers) for serving tea and sometimes coffee at table

**tea shop** *noun* (1856)
*chiefly British* : a small restaurant or café
: TEAROOM
**tea·spoon** \'tē-,spün, -'spün\ *noun* (1686)
**1 :** a small spoon that is used especially for eating soft foods and stirring beverages and that holds one third of a tablespoon
**2 :** a unit of measure especially in cookery equal to ⅙ fluid ounces or ⅓ tablespoon (5 milliliters)
**tea·spoon·ful** \-,fül\ *noun, plural* **tea·spoonfuls** \-,fülz\ *also* **tea·spoons·ful** \-,spünz-,fül, -'spünz-\ (1731)
**1 :** as much as a teaspoon can hold
**2 :** TEASPOON 2
*usage* see ²-FUL
**teat** \'tit, 'tēt\ *noun* [Middle English *tete,* from Old French, of Germanic origin; akin to Old English *tit* teat, Middle High German *zitze*] (13th century)
**1 :** the protuberance through which milk is drawn from an udder or breast : NIPPLE
**2 :** a small projection or a nib (as on a mechanical part)
— **teat·ed** \'ti-təd, 'tē-\ *adjective*
**tea table** *noun* (1688)
: a table used or spread for tea; *specifically* : a small table for serving afternoon tea
**tea·time** \'tē-,tīm\ *noun* (1741)
: the customary time for tea : late afternoon or early evening
**tea towel** *noun* (1871)
: a cloth for drying dishes
**tea tray** *noun* (1773)
: a tray that accommodates a tea set
**tea wagon** *noun* (1921)
: a small table on wheels used in serving tea
**Te·bet** \tā-'vāt, -'vāth, 'tā-,ves\ *noun* [Hebrew *Ṭēbhēth*] (14th century)
: the 4th month of the civil year or the 10th month of the ecclesiastical year in the Jewish calendar — see MONTH table
**teched** \'techt\ *adjective* [alteration of *touched*] (1921)
: mentally unbalanced
**tech·ie** \'te-kē\ *noun* [by shortening & alteration] (1982)
: TECHNICIAN 1
**tech·ne·tium** \tek-'nē-sh(ē-)əm\ *noun* [New Latin, from Greek *technētos* artificial, from *technasthai* to devise by art, from *technē*] (circa 1946)
: a metallic element obtained by bombarding molybdenum with deuterons or neutrons and in the fission of uranium — see ELEMENT table
**tech·ne·tron·ic** \,tek-nə-'trä-nik\ *adjective* [*techn*ological + *electronic*] (1967)
: shaped or influenced by the changes wrought by advances in technology and communications ⟨our modern *technetronic* society⟩
**tech·nic** \'tek-nik, *for 1 also* tek-'nēk\ *noun* (1855)
**1 :** TECHNIQUE 1
**2** *plural but singular or plural in construction* : TECHNOLOGY 1a
**tech·ni·cal** \'tek-ni-kəl\ *adjective* [Greek *technikos* of art, skillful, from *technē* art, craft, skill; akin to Greek *tektōn* builder, carpenter, Latin *texere* to weave, Sanskrit *takṣati* he fashions] (1617)
**1 a :** having special and usually practical knowledge especially of a mechanical or scientific subject ⟨a *technical* consultant⟩ **b** : marked by or characteristic of specialization ⟨*technical* language⟩
**2 a :** of or relating to a particular subject **b** : of or relating to a practical subject organized on scientific principles ⟨a *technical* school⟩ **c** : TECHNOLOGICAL 1
**3 a :** based on or marked by a strict or legal interpretation **b :** LEGAL 6
**4 :** of or relating to technique
**5 :** of, relating to, or produced by ordinary commercial processes without being subjected to special purification ⟨*technical* sulfuric acid⟩

**6 :** relating to or caused by the functioning of the market as a discrete mechanism not influenced by macroeconomic factors ⟨*technical* rally⟩ ⟨*technical* analysis⟩
— **tech·ni·cal·ly** \-k(ə-)lē\ *adverb*
**technical foul** *noun* (circa 1929)
: a foul (as in basketball) that involves no physical contact with an opponent and that usually is incurred by unsportsmanlike conduct — called also *technical*; compare PERSONAL FOUL
**tech·ni·cal·i·ty** \,tek-nə-'ka-lə-tē\ *noun, plural* **-ties** (1814)
**1 :** something technical; *especially* : a detail meaningful only to a specialist ⟨a legal *technicality*⟩
**2 :** the quality or state of being technical
**tech·ni·cal·ize** \'tek-ni-kə-,līz\ *transitive verb* **-ized; -iz·ing** (1852)
: to give a technical slant to
— **tech·ni·cal·i·za·tion** \,tek-ni-kə-lə-'zā-shən\ *noun*
**technical knockout** *noun* (1921)
: the termination of a boxing match when a boxer is unable or is declared by the referee to be unable (as because of injuries) to continue the fight
**technical sergeant** *noun* (circa 1956)
: a noncommissioned officer in the air force ranking above a staff sergeant and below a master sergeant
**tech·ni·cian** \tek-'ni-shən\ *noun* (1833)
**1 :** a specialist in the technical details of a subject or occupation ⟨a computer *technician*⟩
**2 :** one who has acquired the technique of an art or other area of specialization ⟨a superb *technician* and a musician of integrity —Irving Kolodin⟩
**Tech·ni·col·or** \'tek-ni-,kə-lər\ *trademark*
— used for a process of color cinematography
**tech·nique** \tek-'nēk\ *noun* [French, from *technique* technical, from Greek *technikos*] (1817)
**1 :** the manner in which technical details are treated (as by a writer) or basic physical movements are used (as by a dancer); *also* : ability to treat such details or use such movements ⟨good piano *technique*⟩
**2 a :** a body of technical methods (as in a craft or in scientific research) **b :** a method of accomplishing a desired aim
**techno-** *combining form* [*technology*]
: technical : technological ⟨*techno*cracy⟩
**tech·no·bab·ble** \'tek-nə-,ba-bəl\ *noun* (1981)
: technical jargon
**tech·noc·ra·cy** \tek-'nä-krə-sē\ *noun* (circa 1919)
: government by technicians; *specifically* : management of society by technical experts
**tech·no·crat** \'tek-nə-,krat\ *noun* (1932)
**1 :** an adherent of technocracy
**2 :** a technical expert; *especially* : one exercising managerial authority
**tech·no·crat·ic** \,tek-nə-'kra-tik\ *adjective* (1932)
: of, relating to, or suggestive of a technocrat or a technocracy
**tech·no·log·i·cal** \,tek-nə-'lä-ji-kəl\ *also* **tech·no·log·ic** \-'lä-jik\ *adjective* (1800)
**1 :** of, relating to, or characterized by technology ⟨*technological* advances⟩
**2 :** resulting from improvements in technical processes that increase productivity of machines and eliminates manual operations or operations done by older machines ⟨*technological* unemployment⟩
— **tech·no·log·i·cal·ly** \-ji-k(ə-)lē\ *adverb*
**tech·nol·o·gize** \tek-'nä-lə-,jīz\ *transitive verb* **-gized; -giz·ing** (1954)

: to affect or alter by technology

**tech·nol·o·gy** \-jē\ *noun, plural* **-gies** [Greek *technologia* systematic treatment of an art, from *technē* art, skill + *-o-* + *-logia* -logy] (1859)
**1 a :** the practical application of knowledge especially in a particular area : ENGINEERING 2 ⟨*medical technology*⟩ **b :** a capability given by the practical application of knowledge ⟨a car's fuel-saving *technology*⟩
**2 :** a manner of accomplishing a task especially using technical processes, methods, or knowledge ⟨new *technologies* for information storage⟩
**3 :** the specialized aspects of a particular field of endeavor ⟨educational *technology*⟩
— **tech·nol·o·gist** \-jist\ *noun*

**tech·no·phile** \'tek-nə-ˌfīl\ *noun* (1968)
: an enthusiast of technology

**tech·no·pho·bia** \ˌtek-nə-'fō-bē-ə\ *noun* (1965)
: fear or dislike of advanced technology or complex devices and especially computers
— **tech·no·phobe** \'tek-nə-ˌfōb\ *noun*
— **tech·no·pho·bic** \ˌtek-nə-'fō-bik\ *adjective*

**tech·no–pop** \'tek-(ˌ)nō-ˌpäp\ *noun* (1980)
: pop music featuring extensive use of synthesizers

**tech·no·struc·ture** \'tek-nō-ˌstrək-chər\ *noun* (1967)
: the network of professionally skilled managers (as scientists, engineers, and administrators) that tends to control the economy both within and beyond individual corporate groups

**tech·no–thrill·er** \'tek-nō-ˌthri-lər, -nə-\ *noun* (1989)
: a thriller whose plot relies on modern technology

**tec·ton·ic** \tek-'tä-nik\ *adjective* [Late Latin *tectonicus*, from Greek *tektonikos* of a builder, from *tektōn* builder — more at TECHNICAL] (1894)
: of or relating to tectonics
— **tec·ton·i·cal·ly** \-ni-k(ə-)lē\ *adverb*

**tec·ton·ics** \-niks\ *noun plural but singular or plural in construction* (1899)
**1 :** geological structural features as a whole
**2 a :** a branch of geology concerned with the structure of the crust of a planet (as earth) or moon and especially with the formation of folds and faults in it **b :** DIASTROPHISM

**tec·to·nism** \'tek-tə-ˌni-zəm\ *noun* [International Scientific Vocabulary] (1948)
: DIASTROPHISM

**tec·tum** \'tek-təm\ *noun, plural* **tec·ta** \-tə\ [New Latin, from Latin, roof, dwelling, from neuter of *tectus*, past participle of *tegere* to cover — more at THATCH] (circa 1905)
: a bodily structure resembling or serving as a roof; *especially* : the dorsal part of the midbrain
— **tec·tal** \'tek-tᵊl\ *adjective*

**ted** \'ted\ *transitive verb* **ted·ded; ted·ding** [(assumed) Middle English *tedden*, probably from Old Norse *tethja* to manure; akin to Old Norse *tath* spread dung, Old High German *zetten* to spread] (15th century)
: to spread or turn from the swath and scatter (as new-mown grass) for drying

**ted·der** \'te-dər\ *noun* (15th century)
: one that teds; *specifically* : a machine for stirring and spreading hay to hasten drying and curing

**ted·dy** \'te-dē\ *noun, plural* **teddies** [origin unknown] (1924)
: CHEMISE 1

**ted·dy bear** \'te-dē-ˌ\ *noun* [*Teddy*, nickname of Theodore Roosevelt; from a cartoon depicting the president sparing the life of a bear cub while hunting] (1906)
: a stuffed toy bear

**teddy boy** *noun* [*Teddy*, nickname for Edward] (1954)
: a young British hoodlum affecting Edwardian dress

**Te De·um** \ˌtā-'dā-əm, ˌtē-'dē-\ *noun, plural* **Te Deums** [Middle English, from Late Latin *te deum laudamus* thee, God, we praise; from the opening words of the hymn] (before 12th century)
: a liturgical Christian hymn of praise to God

**te·dious** \'tē-dē-əs, 'tē-jəs\ *adjective* [Middle English, from Late Latin *taediosus*, from Latin *taedium*] (15th century)
: tiresome because of length or dullness : BORING ⟨a *tedious* public ceremony⟩
— **te·dious·ly** *adverb*
— **te·dious·ness** *noun*

**te·di·um** \'tē-dē-əm\ *noun* [Latin *taedium* disgust, irksomeness, from *taedēre* to disgust, weary] (1662)
**1 :** the quality or state of being tedious : TEDIOUSNESS; *also* : BOREDOM
**2 :** a tedious period of time ⟨long *tediums* of strained anxiety —H. G. Wells⟩

**¹tee** \'tē\ *noun* [Middle English] (15th century)
**1 :** the letter *t*
**2 :** something shaped like a capital T
**3 :** a mark aimed at in various games (as curling)
— **to a tee :** EXACTLY, PRECISELY

**²tee** *noun* [origin unknown] (1673)
**1 a :** a small mound or a peg on which a golf ball is placed before being struck at the beginning of play on a hole **b :** a device for holding a football in position for kicking
**2 :** the area from which a golf ball is struck at the beginning of play on a hole

**³tee** *transitive verb* **teed; tee·ing** (1673)
: to place (a ball) on a tee — often used with *up*

**teed off** *adjective* [probably from *tee off* (on)] (1951)
: ANGRY, ANNOYED

**¹teem** \'tēm\ *verb* [Middle English *temen*, from Old English *tīman, tǣman;* akin to Old English *tēam* offspring — more at TEAM] (before 12th century)
*transitive verb*
*archaic* : BRING FORTH : give birth to : PRODUCE
*intransitive verb*
**1** *obsolete* : to become pregnant : CONCEIVE
**2 a :** to become filled to overflowing : ABOUND **b :** to be present in large quantity
— **teem·ing·ly** \'tē-miŋ-lē\ *adverb*
— **teem·ing·ness** *noun*

**²teem** *transitive verb* [Middle English *temen*, from Old Norse *tœma;* akin to Old English *tōm* empty] (14th century)
: EMPTY, POUR ⟨*teem* molten metal into a mold⟩

**¹teen** \'tēn\ *noun* [Middle English *tene*, from Old English *tēona* injury, grief; akin to Old Norse *tjōn* loss, damage] (14th century)
*archaic* : MISERY, AFFLICTION

**²teen** *noun* (1818)
: TEENAGER
— **teen** *adjective*

**teen·age** \'tē-ˌnāj\ *or* **teen·aged** \-ˌnājd\ *adjective* (1921)
: of, being, or relating to people in their teens
— **teen·ag·er** \-ˌnā-jər\ *noun*

**teen·er** \'tē-nər\ *noun* (1894)
: a teenage person

**teens** \'tēnz\ *noun plural* [*-teen* (as in *thirteen*)] (1673)
: the numbers 13 to 19 inclusive; *specifically* : the years 13 to 19 in a lifetime or century

**teen·sy** \'tēn(t)-sē\ *adjective* **teen·si·er; -est** [baby-talk alteration of *teeny*] (1899)
: TINY

**teen·sy–ween·sy** \ˌtēn(t)-sē-'wēn(t)-sē\ *adjective* [baby-talk alteration of *teeny-weeny*] (circa 1906)
: TINY

**tee·ny** \'tē-nē\ *adjective* **tee·ni·er; -est** [by alteration] (1825)
: TINY

**teeny–bop** \'tē-nē-ˌbäp\ *adjective* [back-formation from *teenybopper*] (1967)
: of, relating to, or being a teenybopper

**teeny·bop·per** \-ˌbä-pər\ *noun* [*teeny* teenager + *-bopper*, perhaps from ⁴*bop*] (1966)
**1 :** a teenage girl
**2 :** a young teenager who is enthusiastically devoted to pop music and to current fads

**tee·ny–wee·ny** \ˌtē-nē-'wē-nē\ *adjective* [*teeny* + *weeny*] (circa 1879)
: TINY

**tee off** *intransitive verb* (1895)
**1 :** to drive from a tee
**2 :** BEGIN, START
**3 :** to hit hard
**4 :** to make an angry denunciation — often used with *on*

**tee·pee** *variant of* TEPEE

**tee shirt** *variant of* T-SHIRT

**¹tee·ter** \'tē-tər\ *intransitive verb* [Middle English *titeren* to totter, reel; akin to Old High German *zittarōn* to shiver] (1844)
**1 a :** to move unsteadily : WOBBLE **b :** WAVER, VACILLATE ⟨*teetered* on the brink of bankruptcy⟩
**2 :** SEESAW

**²teeter** *noun* (1863)
: SEESAW 2b

**tee·ter·board** \-ˌbōrd, -ˌbȯrd\ *noun* (1855)
**1 :** SEESAW 2b
**2 :** a board placed on a raised support so that a person standing on one end of the board is thrown into the air if another jumps on the opposite end

**tee·ter–tot·ter** \'tē-tər-ˌtä-tər\ *noun* (circa 1905)
: SEESAW 2b

**teeth** *plural of* TOOTH

**teethe** \'tēth\ *intransitive verb* **teethed; teeth·ing** [back-formation from *teething*] (15th century)
: to cut one's teeth : grow teeth

**teeth·er** \'tē-thər\ *noun* (1946)
: an object (as a teething ring) designed for a baby to bite on during teething

**teeth·ing** \'tē-thiŋ\ *noun* [*teeth*] (1732)
**1 :** the first growth of teeth
**2 :** the phenomena accompanying growth of teeth through the gums

**teething ring** *noun* (1872)
: a usually rubber or plastic ring for a teething infant to bite on

**teeth·ridge** \'tēth-ˌrij\ *noun* (1928)
: the inner surface of the gums of the upper front teeth

**tee·to·tal** \'tē-'tō-tᵊl, -ˌtō-\ *adjective* [total + total (abstinence)] (1834)
**1 :** of, relating to, or practicing teetotalism
**2 :** TOTAL, COMPLETE
— **tee·to·tal·ly** \-tᵊl-ē\ *adverb*

**tee·to·tal·er** *or* **tee·to·tal·ler** \-'tō-tᵊl-ər\ *noun* (1834)
: one who practices or advocates teetotalism

**tee·to·tal·ism** \-tᵊl-ˌi-zəm\ *noun* (1834)
: the principle or practice of complete abstinence from alcoholic drinks
— **tee·to·tal·ist** \-tᵊl-ist\ *noun*

**tee·to·tum** \'tē-ˌtō-təm\ *noun* [¹*tee* + Latin *totum* all, from neuter of *totus* whole; from the letter *T* inscribed on one side as an abbreviation of *totum* (take) all] (1720)
: a small top usually inscribed with letters and used in put-and-take

**teff** \'tef\ *noun* [Amharic *ṭef*] (1790)
: an economically important African cereal grass (*Eragrostis tef* synonym *E. abyssinica*) that is grown for its grain which yields a white flour and as a forage and hay crop

**te·fil·lin** \tə-'fi-lən *also* -ˌlam\ *noun plural but sometimes singular in construction* [Late Hebrew *těphīlīn*, from Aramaic, attachments] (1613)
: the phylacteries worn by Jews

**Tef·lon** \'te-ˌflän\ *trademark*
— used for synthetic fluorine-containing resins used especially for molding articles and for coatings to prevent sticking (as of food in cookware)

**teg·men** \'teg-mən\ *noun, plural* **teg·mi·na** \-mə-nə\ [New Latin *tegmin-, tegmen,* from Latin, covering, from *tegere* to cover — more at THATCH] (1807)
**:** a superficial layer or cover usually of a plant or animal part

**teg·men·tal** \teg-'men-tᵊl\ *adjective* (circa 1890)
**:** of, relating to, or associated with an integument or a tegmentum

**teg·men·tum** \teg-'men-təm\ *noun, plural* **-men·ta** \-'men-tə\ [New Latin, from Latin *tegumentum, tegmentum,* covering, from *tegere*] (1832)
**:** an anatomical covering **:** TEGMEN; *especially* **:** the part of the ventral midbrain above the substantia nigra formed of longitudinal white fibers with arched transverse fibers and gray matter

**teg·u·ment** \'te-gyə-mənt\ *noun* [Middle English, from Latin *tegumentum*] (15th century)
**:** INTEGUMENT

**te·iid** \'tē-əd, 'tī-\ *noun* [New Latin *Teiidae,* from *Teius,* genus of lizards, from Portuguese *teiu,* a lizard, from Tupi *tejú*] (1956)
**:** any of a family (Teiidae) of mostly tropical American lizards (as the race runner) with a flat elongate scaly forked tongue
— **teiid** *adjective*

**tek·tite** \'tek-,tīt\ *noun* [International Scientific Vocabulary, from Greek *tēktos* molten, from *tēkein* to melt — more at THAW] (1909)
**:** a glassy body of probably meteoritic origin and of rounded but indefinite shape
— **tek·tit·ic** \tek-'ti-tik\ *adjective*

**tel-** *or* **telo-** *combining form* [International Scientific Vocabulary, from Greek *telos* — more at TELOS]
**:** end ⟨*tel*angiectasia⟩

**tel·a·mon** \'te-lə-,män\ *noun, plural* **tel·a·mo·nes** \,te-lə-'mō-(,)nēz\ [Latin, from Greek *telamōn* bearer, supporter; akin to Greek *tlēnai* to bear — more at TOLERATE] (circa 1706)
**:** ATLAS 5

**tel·an·gi·ec·ta·sia** \,te-,lan-jē-,ek-'tā-zh(ē-)ə, ,tē-, tə-\ *or* **tel·an·gi·ec·ta·sis** \-'ek-tə-səs\ *noun, plural* **-ta·sias** *or* **-ta·ses** \-tə-,sēz\ [New Latin, from *tel-* + *angi-* + *ectasia, ectasis* (as in *atelectasis*)] (1831)
**:** an abnormal dilatation of capillary vessels and arterioles that often forms an angioma
— **tel·an·gi·ec·tat·ic** \-,ek-'ta-tik\ *adjective*

**tele** \'te-lē\ *noun* (1936)
*British* **:** TELEVISION

**tele-** *or* **tel-** *combining form* [New Latin, from Greek *tēle-, tēl-,* from *tēle* far off — more at PALE-]
**1 :** distant **:** at a distance **:** over a distance ⟨*tele*gram⟩
**2 a :** telegraph ⟨*tele*typewriter⟩ **b :** television ⟨*tele*cast⟩ **c :** telecommunication ⟨*tele*marketing⟩

**tele·cast** \'te-li-,kast\ *verb* **-cast** *also* **-cast·ed; -cast·ing** [*tele-* + broad*cast*] (1937)
*transitive verb*
**:** to broadcast by television
*intransitive verb*
**:** to broadcast a television program
— **telecast** *noun*
— **tele·cast·er** *noun*

**tele·com·mu·ni·ca·tion** \,te-li-kə-,myü-nə-'kā-shən\ *noun* [International Scientific Vocabulary] (1932)
**1 :** communication at a distance (as by telephone)
**2 :** a science that deals with telecommunication — usually used in plural

**tele·com·mute** \'te-li-kə-,myüt\ *intransitive verb* (1974)
**:** to work at home by the use of an electronic linkup with a central office
— **tele·com·mut·er** *noun*

**tele·con·fer·enc·ing** \'te-li-,kän-f(ə-)rən(t)-siŋ, -fərn(t)-\ *noun* (1974)
**:** the holding of a conference among people remote from one another by means of telecommunication devices (as telephones or computer terminals)
— **tele·con·fer·ence** \-f(ə-)rən(t)s, -fərn(t)s\ *noun*

**Tele·copi·er** \'te-lə-,kä-pē-ər\ *trademark*
— used for transmitting and receiving equipment for producing facsimile copies of documents

**tele·course** \'te-li-,kōrs, -,kȯrs\ *noun* (1950)
**:** a course of study conducted over television; *especially* **:** such a course taken at home for academic credit

**tele·fac·sim·i·le** \,te-li-fak-'si-mə-(,)lē\ *noun* (1952)
**:** FACSIMILE 2

**tele·film** \'te-li-,film\ *noun* (1939)
**:** a motion picture made to be telecast

**tele·ge·nic** \,te-lə-'je-nik, -'jē-\ *adjective* (1939)
**:** well-suited to the medium of television; *especially* **:** having an appearance and manner that are markedly attractive to television viewers

**¹tele·gram** \'te-lə-,gram, *Southern also* -grəm\ *noun* (circa 1852)
**:** a telegraphic dispatch

**²tele·gram** \-,gram\ *transitive verb* **-grammed; -gram·ming** (1864)
**:** TELEGRAPH

**¹tele·graph** \-,graf\ *noun* [French *télégraphe,* from *télé-* tele- (from Greek *tēle-*) + *-graphe* -graph] (1794)
**1 :** an apparatus for communication at a distance by coded signals; *especially* **:** an apparatus, system, or process for communication at a distance by electric transmission over wire
**2 :** TELEGRAM

**²telegraph** *transitive verb* (1805)
**1 a :** to send or communicate by or as if by telegraph **b :** to send a telegram to **c :** to send by means of a telegraphic order ⟨*telegraph* flowers to a sick friend⟩
**2 :** to make known by signs especially unknowingly and in advance ⟨*telegraph* a punch⟩
— **te·leg·ra·pher** \tə-'le-grə-fər\ *noun*
— **te·leg·ra·phist** \-fist\ *noun*

**tele·graph·ese** \,te-lə-gra-'fēz, -'fēs\ *noun* (1885)
**:** language characterized by the terseness and ellipses that are common in telegrams

**tele·graph·ic** \,te-lə-'gra-fik\ *adjective* (1794)
**1 :** of or relating to the telegraph
**2 :** CONCISE, TERSE
— **tele·graph·i·cal·ly** \-fi-k(ə-)lē\ *adverb*

**te·leg·ra·phy** \tə-'le-grə-fē\ *noun* (1795)
**:** the use or operation of a telegraph apparatus or system for communication

**tele·ki·ne·sis** \,te-li-kə-'nē-səs, -kī-\ *noun* [New Latin] (1890)
**:** the production of motion in objects (as by a spiritualistic medium) without contact or other physical means
— **tele·ki·net·ic** \-'ne-tik\ *adjective*
— **tele·ki·net·i·cal·ly** \-ti-k(ə-)lē\ *adverb*

**Te·lem·a·chus** \tə-'le-mə-kəs\ *noun* [Latin, from Greek *Tēlemachos*]
**:** the son of Odysseus and Penelope who contrives with his father to slay his mother's suitors

**tel·e·mark** \'te-lə-,märk\ *noun, often capitalized* [Norwegian, from *Telemark,* region in Norway] (1904)
**:** a turn in skiing in which the outside ski is advanced considerably ahead of the other ski and then turned inward at a steadily widening angle until the turn is completed

**tele·mar·ket·ing** \,te-lə-'mär-kə-tiŋ\ *noun* (1980)
**:** the marketing of goods or services by telephone
— **tele·mar·ket·er** \-tər\ *noun*

**¹tele·me·ter** \'te-lə-,mē-tər\ *noun* [International Scientific Vocabulary] (1860)

**1 :** an instrument for measuring the distance of an object from an observer
**2 :** an electrical apparatus for measuring a quantity (as pressure, speed, or temperature), transmitting the result especially by radio to a distant station, and there indicating or recording the quantity measured

**²telemeter** (1925)
*transitive verb*
**:** to transmit (as the measurement of a quantity) by telemeter
*intransitive verb*
**:** to telemeter the measurement of a quantity

**te·lem·e·try** \tə-'le-mə-trē\ *noun* (1885)
**1 :** the science or process of telemetering data
**2 :** data transmitted by telemetry
**3 :** BIOTELEMETRY
— **tele·met·ric** \,te-lə-'me-trik\ *adjective*
— **tele·met·ri·cal·ly** \-tri-k(ə-)lē\ *adverb*

**tel·en·ceph·a·lon** \,te-len-'se-fə-,län, -lən\ *noun* [New Latin] (1897)
**:** the anterior subdivision of the embryonic forebrain or the corresponding part of the adult forebrain that includes the cerebral hemispheres and associated structures
— **tel·en·ce·phal·ic** \-,len(t)-sə-'fa-lik\ *adjective*

**tel·e·o·log·i·cal** \,te-lē-ə-'lä-ji-kəl, ,tē-\ *also* **tel·e·o·log·ic** \-'lä-jik\ *adjective* (1798)
**:** exhibiting or relating to design or purpose especially in nature
— **tel·e·o·log·i·cal·ly** \-ji-k(ə-)lē\ *adverb*

**tel·e·ol·o·gy** \,te-lē-'ä-lə-jē, ,tē-\ *noun* [New Latin *teleologia,* from Greek *tele-, telos* end, purpose + *-logia* -logy — more at WHEEL] (1740)
**1 a :** the study of evidences of design in nature **b :** a doctrine (as in vitalism) that ends are immanent in nature **c :** a doctrine explaining phenomena by final causes
**2 :** the fact or character attributed to nature or natural processes of being directed toward an end or shaped by a purpose
**3 :** the use of design or purpose as an explanation of natural phenomena
— **tel·e·ol·o·gist** \-jist\ *noun*

**tel·e·on·o·my** \,te-lē-'ä-nə-mē, ,tē-\ *noun* [*teleo-* (as in *teleology*) + *-nomy*] (1958)
**:** the quality of apparent purposefulness in living organisms that derives from their evolutionary adaptation
— **tel·e·o·nom·ic** \,te-lē-ə-'nä-mik, ,tē-\ *adjective*

**tel·e·ost** \'te-lē-,äst, 'tē-\ *noun* [ultimately from Greek *teleios* complete, perfect (from *telos* end) + *osteon* bone — more at OSSEOUS] (1862)
**:** BONY FISH
— **teleost** *adjective*
— **tel·e·os·te·an** \,te-lē-'äs-tē-ən, ,tē-\ *adjective*

**tele·path** \'te-lə-,path\ *noun* (1904)
**:** one who is able to communicate by telepathy

**te·lep·a·thy** \tə-'le-pə-thē\ *noun* (1882)
**:** communication from one mind to another by extrasensory means
— **tele·path·ic** \,te-lə-'pa-thik\ *adjective*
— **tele·path·i·cal·ly** \-thi-k(ə-)lē\ *adverb*

**¹tele·phone** \'te-lə-,fōn\ *noun, often attributive* (1849)
**:** an instrument for reproducing sounds at a distance; *specifically* **:** one in which sound is converted into electrical impulses for transmission by wire

**²telephone** *verb* **-phoned; -phon·ing** (1877)
*transitive verb*
**1 :** to speak to or attempt to reach by telephone
**2 :** to send by telephone

---

\ə\ abut \ᵊ\ kitten \ər\ further \a\ ash \ā\ ace
\ä\ mop, mar \au̇\ out \ch\ chin \e\ bet \ē\ easy
\g\ go \i\ hit \ī\ ice \j\ job \ŋ\ sing \ō\ go
\ȯ\ law \ȯi\ boy \th\ thin \t͟h\ the \ü\ loot \u̇\ foot
\y\ yet \zh\ vision *see also* Guide to Pronunciation

*intransitive verb*
**:** to communicate by telephone
— **tele·phon·er** *noun*
**telephone book** *noun* (1915)
**:** a book listing the names, addresses, and telephone numbers of telephone customers
**telephone booth** *noun* (circa 1895)
**:** an enclosure within which one may stand or sit while making a telephone call
**telephone box** *noun* (1904)
*British* **:** a public telephone booth
**telephone directory** *noun* (1907)
**:** TELEPHONE BOOK
**telephone number** *noun* (1885)
**:** a number assigned to a telephone line for a specific location that is used to call that location
**telephone tag** *noun* (1980)
**:** telephoning back and forth by parties trying to reach each other without success
**tele·phon·ic** \ˌte-lə-'fä-nik\ *adjective* (1877)
**:** of, relating to, or conveyed by a telephone
— **tele·phon·i·cal·ly** \-ni-k(ə-)lē\ *adverb*
**te·le·pho·nist** \tə-'le-fə-nist, 'te-lə-ˌfō-nist\ *noun* (1880)
*British* **:** a telephone switchboard operator
**te·le·pho·ny** \tə-'le-fə-nē *also* 'te-lə-ˌfō-\ *noun* (1835)
**:** the use or operation of an apparatus for transmission of sounds between widely removed points with or without connecting wires
¹**tele·pho·to** \ˌte-lə-'fō-(ˌ)tō\ *adjective* (circa 1895)
**:** being a camera lens system designed to give a large image of a distant object; *also* **:** relating to or being photography in which a telephoto lens is used
²**telephoto** *noun, plural* **-tos** (1904)
**1 :** a telephoto lens
**2 :** a photograph taken with a camera having a telephoto lens
**Telephoto** *trademark*
— used for an apparatus for transmitting photographs electrically or for a photograph so transmitted
**tele·pho·tog·ra·phy** \-fə-'tä-grə-fē\ *noun* [International Scientific Vocabulary] (1892)
**:** the photography of distant objects (as by a camera provided with a telephoto lens)
**tele·play** \'te-li-ˌplā\ *noun* (1952)
**:** a play written for television
**tele·port** \'te-lə-ˌpōrt, -ˌpȯrt\ *transitive verb* [back-formation from *teleportation*] (1947)
**:** to transfer by teleportation
**tele·por·ta·tion** \ˌte-lə-ˌpȯr-'tā-shən, -ˌpȯr-, -pər-\ *noun* [*tele-* + *transportation*] (1931)
**:** the act or process of moving an object or person by psychokinesis
**tele·print·er** \'te-lə-ˌprin-tər\ *noun* (1929)
**:** a device capable of producing hard copy from signals received over a communications circuit; *especially* **:** TELETYPEWRITER
**tele·pro·cess·ing** \-'prä-ˌse-siŋ, -'prō-, -sə-siŋ\ *noun* (1962)
**:** computer processing via remote terminals
**Tele·Promp·Ter** \'te-lə-ˌpräm(p)-tər\ *trademark*
— used for a device for unrolling a magnified script in front of a speaker on television
¹**tele·scope** \'te-lə-ˌskōp\ *noun, often attributive* [New Latin *telescopium*, from Greek *tēleskopos* farseeing, from *tēle-* tele- + *skopos* watcher; akin to Greek *skopein* to look — more at SPY] (1648)
**1 :** a usually tubular optical instrument for viewing distant objects by means of the refraction of light rays through a lens or the reflection of light rays by a concave mirror — compare REFLECTOR, REFRACTOR
**2 :** any of various tubular magnifying optical instruments
**3 :** RADIO TELESCOPE
²**telescope** *verb* **-scoped; -scop·ing** (1867)
*intransitive verb*

**1 :** to become forced together lengthwise with one part entering another as the result of collision
**2 :** to slide or pass one within another like the cylindrical sections of a collapsible hand telescope
**3 :** to become compressed or condensed
*transitive verb*
**1 :** to cause to telescope
**2 :** COMPRESS, CONDENSE ⟨the book arbitrarily *telescopes* time and space, and as arbitrarily extends them —Phoebe Adams⟩
**tele·scop·ic** \ˌte-lə-'skä-pik\ *adjective* (1705)
**1 a :** of, relating to, or performed with a telescope **b :** suitable for seeing or magnifying distant objects
**2 :** seen or discoverable only by a telescope ⟨*telescopic* stars⟩
**3 :** able to discern objects at a distance
**4 :** having parts that telescope
— **tele·scop·i·cal·ly** \-pi-k(ə-)lē\ *adverb*
**tele·sis** \'te-lə-səs\ *noun, plural* **-e·ses** \-ˌsēz\ [New Latin, from Greek, fulfillment, from *telein* to complete, from *telos* end — more at TELOS] (1896)
**:** progress that is intelligently planned and directed **:** the attainment of desired ends by the application of intelligent human effort to the means
**tele·text** \'te-lə-ˌtekst\ *noun* (1974)
**:** a system for broadcasting text over an unused portion of a television signal and displaying it on a decoder-equipped television set — compare VIDEOTEX
**tele·thon** \'te-lə-ˌthän\ *noun* [*tele-* + *-thon*] (1949)
**:** a long television program usually to solicit funds especially for a charity
**Tele·type** \'te-lə-ˌtīp\ *trademark*
— used for a teletypewriter
**Tele·type·set·ter** \ˌte-lə-'tīp-ˌse-tər\ *trademark*
— used for a telegraphic apparatus for the automatic operation of a keyboard typesetting machine
**tele·type·writ·er** \-ˌrī-tər\ *noun* (1903)
**:** a printing device resembling a typewriter that is used to send and receive telephonic signals
**te·leu·to·spore** \tə-'lü-tə-ˌspōr, -ˌspȯr\ *noun* [Greek *teleutē* end (akin to Greek *telos* end) + International Scientific Vocabulary *spore* — more at TELIOSPORE] (1874)
**:** TELIOSPORE
**tel·evan·ge·list** \ˌte-li-'van-jə-list\ *noun* (1973)
**:** an evangelist who conducts regularly televised religious programs
— **tel·evan·ge·lism** \-ˌli-zəm\ *noun*
**tele·view** \'te-li-ˌvyü\ *intransitive verb* (1935)
**:** to observe or watch by means of a television receiver
— **tele·view·er** *noun*
**tele·vise** \'te-lə-ˌvīz\ *verb* **-vised; -vis·ing** [back-formation from *television*] (1927)
*transitive verb*
**:** to broadcast (as a baseball game) by television
*intransitive verb*
**:** to broadcast by television
**tele·vi·sion** \'te-lə-ˌvi-zhən *especially British* ˌte-lə-'\ *noun, often attributive* [French *télévision*, from *télé-* tele- + *vision* vision] (1907)
**1 :** an electronic system of transmitting transient images of fixed or moving objects together with sound over a wire or through space by apparatus that converts light and sound into electrical waves and reconverts them into visible light rays and audible sound
**2 :** a television receiving set
**3 a :** the television broadcasting industry **b :** television as a medium of communication
**television tube** *noun* (1937)
**:** PICTURE TUBE
**tele·vi·su·al** \ˌte-lə-'vi-zhə-wəl, -zhəl; -'vizh-wəl\ *adjective* (1926)

*chiefly British* **:** of, relating to, or suitable for broadcast by television
¹**tel·ex** \'te-ˌleks\ *noun* [*teleprinter* + *exchange*] (1932)
**1 :** a communication service involving teletypewriters connected by wire through automatic exchanges; *also* **:** a teletypewriter used in telex
**2 :** a message sent by telex
²**telex** *transitive verb* (1960)
**1 :** to send (as a message) by telex
**2 :** to communicate with by telex
**te·lic** \'te-lik, 'tē-\ *adjective* [Greek *telikos*, from *telos* end — more at TELOS] (1889)
**:** tending toward an end
— **te·li·cal·ly** \-li-k(ə-)lē\ *adverb*
**te·lio·spore** \'tē-lē-ə-ˌspōr, -ˌspȯr\ *noun* [Greek *teleios* complete (from *telos* end) + English *spore*] (1905)
**:** a chlamydospore that is the final stage in the life cycle of a rust fungus and that after nuclear fusion gives rise to the basidium
**te·li·um** \'tē-lē-əm\ *noun, plural* **te·lia** \-lē-ə\ [New Latin, from Greek *teleios* complete] (circa 1905)
**:** a teliospore-producing sorus or pustule on the host plant of a rust fungus
— **te·li·al** \'tē-lē-əl\ *adjective*
¹**tell** \'tel\ *verb* **told** \'tōld\; **tell·ing** [Middle English, from Old English *tellan;* akin to Old High German *zellen* to count, tell, Old English *talu* tale] (before 12th century)
*transitive verb*
**1 :** COUNT, ENUMERATE
**2 a :** to relate in detail **:** NARRATE **b :** to give utterance to **:** SAY ⟨who dares think one thing, and another *tell* —Alexander Pope⟩
**3 a :** to make known **:** DIVULGE, REVEAL **b :** to express in words ⟨she never *told* her love —Shakespeare⟩
**4 a :** to report to **:** INFORM **b :** to assure emphatically ⟨they did not do it, I *tell* you⟩
**5 :** ORDER, DIRECT ⟨*told* me to wait⟩
**6 :** to find out by observing **:** RECOGNIZE ⟨you can *tell* it's a masterpiece⟩
*intransitive verb*
**1 :** to give an account
**2 :** to act as an informer — often used with *on* ⟨I'll get even with you if you ever *tell* on me —*Inside Detective*⟩
**3 :** to have a marked effect
**4 :** to serve as evidence or indication
**synonym** *see* REVEAL
²**tell** *noun* [Arabic *tall*] (1864)
**:** HILL, MOUND; *specifically* **:** an ancient mound in the Middle East composed of remains of successive settlements
**tell-all** \'tel-ˌȯl\ *noun* (1954)
**:** a written account (as a biography) that contains revealing and often scandalous information
— **tell-all** *adjective*
**tell·er** \'te-lər\ *noun* (14th century)
**1 :** one that relates or communicates ⟨a *teller* of stories⟩
**2 :** one that reckons or counts: as **a :** one appointed to count votes **b :** a member of a bank's staff concerned with the direct handling of money received or paid out
**tell·ing** \'te-liŋ\ *adjective* (1851)
**:** carrying great weight and producing a marked effect **:** EFFECTIVE, EXPRESSIVE ⟨the most *telling* evidence⟩
**synonym** *see* VALID
— **tell·ing·ly** \-liŋ-lē\ *adverb*
**tell off** *transitive verb* (1804)
**1 :** to number and set apart; *especially* **:** to assign to a special duty ⟨*told off* a detail and put them to opening a trench —J. F. Dobie⟩
**2 :** REPRIMAND, EXCORIATE ⟨*told* him *off* for his arrogance⟩
**tell·tale** \'tel-ˌtāl\ *noun* (circa 1548)
**1 a :** TALEBEARER, INFORMER **b :** an outward sign **:** INDICATION

**2 :** a device for indicating or recording something: as **a :** a wind-direction indicator often in the form of a ribbon **b :** a strip of metal on the front wall of a racquets or squash court above which the ball must be hit
— **telltale** adjective

**tellur-** or **telluro-** combining form [Latin tellur-, tellus — more at THILL]
**1 :** earth ⟨telluric⟩
**2** [New Latin tellurium] **:** tellurium ⟨telluride⟩
**tel·lu·ric** \tə-'lùr-ik, te-\ adjective (1836)
**1 :** of or relating to the earth **:** TERRESTRIAL
**2 :** being or relating to a usually natural electric current flowing near the earth's surface
**tel·lu·ride** \'tel-yə-,rīd\ noun [International Scientific Vocabulary] (1849)
**:** a binary compound of tellurium with a more electropositive element or group
**tel·lu·ri·um** \tə-'lùr-ē-əm, te-\ noun [New Latin, from Latin tellur-, tellus earth] (1800)
**:** a semimetallic element related to selenium and sulfur that occurs in a silvery white brittle crystalline form of metallic luster, in a dark amorphous form, or combined with metals and that is used especially in alloys — see ELEMENT table
**tel·lu·rom·e·ter** \,tel-yə-'rä-mə-tər\ noun (1957)
**:** a device that measures distance by means of microwaves
**tel·ly** \'te-lē\ noun, plural **tellys** also **tellies** [by shortening & alteration] (1939)
chiefly British **:** TELEVISION
**telo-** — see TEL-
**telo·cen·tric** \,te-lə-'sen-trik, ,tē-\ adjective [International Scientific Vocabulary tel- + centromere + -ic] (1939)
**:** having the centromere terminally situated so that there is only one chromosomal arm ⟨a telocentric chromosome⟩
— **telocentric** noun
**te·lome** \'tē-,lōm\ noun [International Scientific Vocabulary tel- + -ome] (1935)
**:** a hypothetical plant structure in a theory of the evolution of leaves and sporophylls in vascular plants that consists of one of the vegetative or reproductive terminal branchlets of a dichotomously branched axis
**telo·mere** \'te-lə-,mir, 'tē-\ noun [International Scientific Vocabulary] (1940)
**:** the natural end of a eukaryotic chromosome
**telo·phase** \'te-lə-,fāz, 'tē-\ noun [International Scientific Vocabulary] (1895)
**1 :** the final stage of mitosis and of the second division of meiosis in which the spindle disappears and the nuclear envelope reforms around each set of chromosomes
**2 :** the final stage in the first division of meiosis that may be missing in some organisms and is characterized by the gathering at opposite poles of the cell of half the original number of chromosomes including one from each homologous pair
**te·los** \'te-,läs, 'tē-\ noun [Greek; probably akin to Greek tellein to accomplish, tlēnai to bear — more at TOLERATE] (1904)
**:** an ultimate end
**telo·tax·is** \,te-lə-'tak-səs, ,tē-\ noun [New Latin] (1934)
**:** a taxis in which an organism orients itself in respect to a stimulus (as a light source) as though that were the only stimulus acting on it
**tel·son** \'tel-sən\ noun [New Latin, from Greek, end of a plowed field; perhaps akin to Greek telos end] (1855)
**:** the terminal segment of the body of an arthropod or segmented worm; especially **:** that of a crustacean forming the middle lobe of the tail
**Tel·u·gu** \'te-lə-,gü\ noun, plural **Telugu** or **Telugus** (1789)
**1 :** a member of the largest group of people in Andhra Pradesh, India
**2 :** the Dravidian language of the Telugu people

**tem·blor** \'tem-blər; 'tem-,blór, -,blōr, tem-'\ noun [Spanish, literally, trembling, from temblar to tremble, from Medieval Latin tremulare — more at TREMBLE] (1876)
**:** EARTHQUAKE
**tem·er·ar·i·ous** \,te-mə-'rer-ē-əs, -'rar-\ adjective [Latin temerarius, from temere] (1532)
**:** marked by temerity **:** rashly or presumptuously daring
— **tem·er·ar·i·ous·ly** adverb
— **tem·er·ar·i·ous·ness** noun
**te·mer·i·ty** \tə-'mer-ə-tē\ noun, plural **-ties** [Middle English temeryte, from Latin temeritas, from temere blindly, recklessly; akin to Old High German demar darkness, Latin tenebrae, Sanskrit tamas] (15th century)
**1 :** unreasonable or foolhardy contempt of danger or opposition **:** RASHNESS, RECKLESSNESS
**2 :** an act or instance of temerity ☆
**¹temp** \'temp\ noun (1886)
**1 :** TEMPERATURE 2a, c
**2 :** a temporary worker
**²temp** intransitive verb (1973)
**:** to work as a temp
**tem·peh** \'tem-,pā\ noun [Javanese témpé] (1961)
**:** an Asian food prepared by fermenting soybeans with a rhizopus
**¹tem·per** \'tem-pər\ transitive verb **tempered; tem·per·ing** \-p(ə-)riŋ\ [Middle English, from Old English & Old French; Old English temprian & Old French temprer, from Latin temperare to moderate, mix, temper; probably akin to Latin tempor-, tempus time] (before 12th century)
**1 :** to dilute, qualify, or soften by the addition or influence of something else **:** MODERATE ⟨temper justice with mercy⟩
**2** archaic **a :** to exercise control over **:** GOVERN, RESTRAIN **b :** to cause to be well disposed **:** MOLLIFY ⟨tempered and reconciled them both —Richard Steele⟩
**3 :** to bring to a suitable state by mixing in or adding a usually liquid ingredient: as **a :** to mix (clay) with water or a modifier (as grog) and knead to a uniform texture **b :** to mix oil with (colors) in making paint ready for use
**4 a** (1) **:** to soften (as hardened steel or cast iron) by reheating at a lower temperature (2) **:** to harden (as steel) by reheating and cooling in oil **b :** to anneal or toughen (glass) by a process of gradually heating and cooling
**5 :** to make stronger and more resilient through hardship **:** TOUGHEN ⟨troops tempered in battle⟩
**6 a :** to put in tune with something **:** ATTUNE **b :** to adjust the pitch of (a note, chord, or instrument) to a temperament
— **tem·per·able** \-p(ə-)rə-bəl\ adjective
— **tem·per·er** \-pər-ər\ noun
**²temper** noun (14th century)
**1 a** archaic **:** a suitable proportion or balance of qualities **:** a middle state between extremes **:** MEAN, MEDIUM ⟨virtue is . . . a just temper between propensities —T. B. Macaulay⟩ **b** archaic **:** CHARACTER, QUALITY ⟨the temper of the land you design to sow —John Mortimer⟩ **c :** characteristic tone **:** TREND, TENDENCY ⟨the temper of the times⟩ **d :** high quality of mind or spirit **:** COURAGE, METTLE
**2 a :** the state of a substance with respect to certain desired qualities (as hardness, elasticity, or workability); especially **:** the degree of hardness or resiliency given steel by tempering **b :** the feel and relative solidity of leather
**3 a :** a characteristic cast of mind or state of feeling **:** DISPOSITION **b :** calmness of mind **:** COMPOSURE, EQUANIMITY **c :** state of feeling or frame of mind at a particular time usually dominated by a single strong emotion **d :** heat of mind or emotion **:** proneness to anger **:** PASSION
**4 :** a substance (as a metal) added to or mixed with something else (as another metal) to

modify the properties of the latter
synonym see DISPOSITION
**tem·pera** \'tem-pə-rə\ noun [Italian tempera, literally, temper, from temperare to temper, from Latin] (1832)
**1 :** a process of painting in which an albuminous or colloidal medium (as egg yolk) is employed as a vehicle instead of oil; also **:** a painting done in tempera
**2 :** POSTER COLOR
**tem·per·a·ment** \'tem-p(ə-)rə-mənt, -pər-mənt\ noun [Middle English, from Latin temperamentum, from temperare to mix, temper] (15th century)
**1** obsolete **a :** constitution of a substance, body, or organism with respect to the mixture or balance of its elements, qualities, or parts **:** MAKEUP **b :** COMPLEXION 1
**2** obsolete **a :** CLIMATE **b :** TEMPERATURE 2
**3 a :** the peculiar or distinguishing mental or physical character determined by the relative proportions of the humors according to medieval physiology **b :** characteristic or habitual inclination or mode of emotional response ⟨a nervous temperament⟩ **c :** extremely high sensibility; especially **:** excessive sensitiveness or irritability
**4 a :** the act or process of tempering or modifying **:** ADJUSTMENT, COMPROMISE **b :** middle course **:** MEAN
**5 :** the process of slightly modifying the musical intervals of the pure scale to produce a set of 12 equally spaced tones to the octave which enables a keyboard instrument to play in all keys
synonym see DISPOSITION
**tem·per·a·men·tal** \,tem-p(ə-)rə-'men-t°l, ,tem-pər-'\ adjective (1646)
**1 :** of, relating to, or arising from temperament **:** CONSTITUTIONAL ⟨temperamental peculiarities⟩
**2 a :** marked by excessive sensitivity and impulsive changes of mood ⟨a temperamental child⟩ **b :** unpredictable in behavior or performance
— **tem·per·a·men·tal·ly** \-t°l-ē\ adverb
**tem·per·ance** \'tem-p(ə-)rən(t)s, -pərn(t)s\ noun [Middle English, from Latin temperantia, from temperant-, temperans, present participle of temperare to moderate, be moderate] (14th century)
**1 :** moderation in action, thought, or feeling **:** RESTRAINT
**2 a :** habitual moderation in the indulgence of the appetites or passions **b :** moderation in or abstinence from the use of intoxicating drink

---

☆ **SYNONYMS**
**Temerity, audacity, hardihood, effrontery, nerve, cheek, gall, chutzpah** mean conspicuous or flagrant boldness. TEMERITY suggests boldness arising from rashness and contempt of danger ⟨had the temerity to refuse⟩. AUDACITY implies a disregard of restraints commonly imposed by convention or prudence ⟨an entrepreneur with audacity and vision⟩. HARDIHOOD suggests firmness in daring and defiance ⟨admired for her hardihood⟩. EFFRONTERY implies shameless, insolent disregard of propriety or courtesy ⟨outraged at his effrontery⟩. NERVE, CHEEK, GALL, and CHUTZPAH are informal equivalents for EFFRONTERY ⟨the nerve of that guy⟩ ⟨has the cheek to call herself a singer⟩ ⟨had the gall to demand proof⟩ ⟨the chutzpah needed for a career in show business⟩.

---

\ə\ abut \ᵊ\ kitten \ər\ further \a\ ash \ā\ ace
\ä\ mop, mar \aù\ out \ch\ chin \e\ bet \ē\ easy
\g\ go \i\ hit \ī\ ice \j\ job \ŋ\ sing \ō\ go
\ó\ law \ói\ boy \th\ thin \th\ the \ü\ loot \ù\ foot
\y\ yet \zh\ vision *see also* Guide to Pronunciation

**tem·per·ate** \'tem-p(ə-)rət\ *adjective* [Middle English *temperat*, from Latin *temperatus*, from past participle of *temperare*] (14th century)
**1 :** marked by moderation: as **a :** keeping or held within limits **:** not extreme or excessive **:** MILD **b :** moderate in indulgence of appetite or desire **c :** moderate in the use of intoxicating liquors **d :** marked by an absence or avoidance of extravagance, violence, or extreme partisanship **:** RESTRAINED
**2 a :** having a moderate climate **b :** found in or associated with a moderate climate ⟨*temperate* insects⟩
**3 :** existing as a prophage in infected cells and rarely causing lysis ⟨*temperate* bacteriophages⟩
— **tem·per·ate·ly** *adverb*
— **tem·per·ate·ness** *noun*
**temperate rain forest** *noun* (circa 1930)
**:** woodland of a usually rather mild climatic area within the temperate zone that receives heavy rainfall, usually includes numerous kinds of trees, and is distinguished from a tropical rain forest by the presence of a dominant tree
**temperate zone** *noun, often T&Z capitalized* (1551)
**:** the area or region between the tropic of Cancer and the arctic circle or between the tropic of Capricorn and the antarctic circle
**tem·per·a·ture** \'tem-pə(r)-ˌchu̇r, -p(ə-)rə-, -chər, -ˌtyu̇r, -ˌtu̇r\ *noun* [Latin *temperatura* mixture, moderation, from *temperatus*, past participle of *temperare*] (1533)
**1** *archaic* **a :** COMPLEXION 1 **b :** TEMPERAMENT 3b
**2 a :** degree of hotness or coldness measured on a definite scale — compare THERMOMETER **b :** the degree of heat that is natural to the body of a living being **c :** abnormally high body heat **d :** relative state of emotional warmth ⟨aware of a change in the *temperature* of our friendship —Christopher Isherwood⟩
**temperature inversion** *noun* (1921)
**:** INVERSION 6
**tem·pered** \'tem-pərd\ *adjective* (14th century)
**1 a :** having the elements mixed in satisfying proportions **:** TEMPERATE **b :** qualified, lessened, or diluted by the mixture or influence of an additional ingredient **:** MODERATED ⟨a pale gleam of *tempered* sunlight fell through the leaves —W. H. Hudson (died 1922)⟩
**2 :** treated by tempering; *especially, of glass* **:** treated so as to impart increased strength and the property of shattering into pellets when broken
**3 :** having a specified temper — used in combination ⟨short-*tempered*⟩
**4 :** conforming to adjustment by temperament — used of a musical interval, intonation, semitone, or scale
**¹tem·pest** \'tem-pəst\ *noun* [Middle English, from Old French *tempeste*, from (assumed) Vulgar Latin *tempesta*, alteration of Latin *tempestas* season, weather, storm, from *tempus* time] (13th century)
**1 :** a violent storm
**2 :** TUMULT, UPROAR
**²tempest** *transitive verb* (14th century)
**:** to raise a tempest in or around
**tem·pes·tu·ous** \tem-'pes-chə-wəs, -'pesh-\ *adjective* [Late Latin *tempestuosus*, from Old Latin *tempestus* season, weather, storm, from *tempus*] (1509)
**:** of, relating to, or resembling a tempest **:** TURBULENT, STORMY ⟨*tempestuous* weather⟩ ⟨a *tempestuous* relationship⟩
— **tem·pes·tu·ous·ly** *adverb*
— **tem·pes·tu·ous·ness** *noun*
**Tem·plar** \'tem-plər\ *noun* [Middle English *templer*, from Old French *templier*, from Medieval Latin *templarius*, from Latin *templum* temple] (13th century)

**1 :** a knight of a religious military order established in the early 12th century in Jerusalem for the protection of pilgrims and the Holy Sepulcher
**2** *not capitalized* **:** a barrister or student of law in London
**3 :** KNIGHT TEMPLAR 2
**tem·plate** *also* **tem·plet** \'tem-plət\ *noun* [probably from French *templet*, diminutive of *temple*, part of a loom, probably from Latin *templum*] (1677)
**1 :** a short piece or block placed horizontally in a wall under a beam to distribute its weight or pressure (as over a door)
**2 a** (1) **:** a gauge, pattern, or mold (as a thin plate or board) used as a guide to the form of a piece being made (2) **:** a molecule (as of DNA) that serves as a pattern for the generation of another macromolecule (as messenger RNA) **b :** OVERLAY c
**3 :** something that establishes or serves as a pattern
**¹tem·ple** \'tem-pəl\ *noun* [Middle English, from Old English & Old French; Old English *tempel* & Old French *temple*, both from Latin *templum* space marked out for observation of auguries, temple, small timber; probably akin to Greek *temenos* sacred precinct, *temnein* to cut — more at TOME] (before 12th century)
**1 :** an edifice for religious exercises: as **a** *often capitalized* **:** one of three successive national sanctuaries in ancient Jerusalem **b :** a building for Mormon sacred ordinances **c :** a Reform or Conservative synagogue
**2 :** a local lodge of any of various fraternal orders; *also* **:** the building housing it
**3 :** a place devoted to a special purpose
— **tem·pled** \-pəld\ *adjective*
**²temple** *noun* [Middle English, from Middle French, from (assumed) Vulgar Latin *tempula*, alteration of Latin *tempora* (plural) temples] (14th century)
**1 :** the flattened space on each side of the forehead of some mammals including humans
**2 :** one of the side supports of a pair of glasses jointed to the bows and passing on each side of the head
**tem·po** \'tem-(ˌ)pō\ *noun, plural* **tem·pi** \-(ˌ)pē\ *or* **tempos** [Italian, literally, time, from Latin *tempus*] (circa 1724)
**1 :** the rate of speed of a musical piece or passage indicated by one of a series of directions (as largo, presto, or allegro) and often by an exact metronome marking
**2 :** rate of motion or activity **:** PACE
**¹tem·po·ral** \'tem-p(ə-)rəl\ *adjective* [Middle English, from Latin *temporalis*, from *tempor-, tempus* time] (14th century)
**1 a :** of or relating to time as opposed to eternity **b :** of or relating to earthly life **c :** lay or secular rather than clerical or sacred **:** CIVIL ⟨lords *temporal*⟩
**2 :** of or relating to grammatical tense or a distinction of time
**3 a :** of or relating to time as distinguished from space **b :** of or relating to the sequence of time or to a particular time **:** CHRONOLOGICAL
— **tem·po·ral·ly** *adverb*
**²temporal** *noun* [Middle French, from *temporal*, adjective] (1541)
**:** a temporal part (as a bone or muscle)
**³temporal** *adjective* [Middle French, from Late Latin *temporalis*, from Latin *tempora* temples] (1597)
**:** of or relating to the temples or the sides of the skull behind the orbits
**temporal bone** *noun* (1771)
**:** a compound bone of the side of the skull of some mammals including humans
**tem·po·ral·i·ty** \ˌtem-pə-'ra-lə-tē\ *noun, plural* **-ties** (14th century)
**1 a :** civil or political as distinguished from spiritual or ecclesiastical power or authority **b :** an ecclesiastical property or revenue — often used in plural

**2 :** the quality or state of being temporal
**tem·po·ral·ize** \'tem-p(ə-)rə-ˌlīz\ *transitive verb* **-ized; -iz·ing** (1828)
**1 :** SECULARIZE
**2 :** to place or define in time relations
**temporal lobe** *noun* (circa 1891)
**:** a large lobe of each cerebral hemisphere that is situated in front of the occipital lobe and contains a sensory area associated with the organ of hearing
**temporal summation** *noun* (1950)
**:** sensory summation that involves the addition of single stimuli over a short period of time
**tem·po·rar·i·ly** \ˌtem-pə-'rer-ə-lē\ *adverb* (1534)
**:** during a limited time
**¹tem·po·rary** \'tem-pə-ˌrer-ē\ *adjective* [Latin *temporarius*, from *tempor-, tempus* time] (circa 1564)
**:** lasting for a limited time
— **tem·po·rar·i·ness** *noun*
**²temporary** *noun, plural* **-rar·ies** (1848)
**:** one serving for a limited time ⟨adding several *temporaries* as typists during the summer⟩
**temporary duty** *noun* (1945)
**:** temporary military service away from one's permanent duty station
**tem·po·rise** *British variant of* TEMPORIZE
**tem·po·rize** \'tem-pə-ˌrīz\ *intransitive verb* **-rized; -riz·ing** [Middle French *temporiser*, from Medieval Latin *temporizare* to pass the time, from Latin *tempor-, tempus*] (1579)
**1 :** to act to suit the time or occasion **:** yield to current or dominant opinion **:** COMPROMISE
**2 :** to draw out discussions or negotiations so as to gain time ⟨you'd have to *temporize* until you found out how she wanted to be advised —Mary Austin⟩
— **tem·po·ri·za·tion** \ˌtem-pə-rə-'zā-shən\ *noun*
— **tem·po·riz·er** *noun*
**tem·po·ro·man·dib·u·lar** \ˌtem-pə-rō-man-'di-byə-lər\ *adjective* [³*temporal* + *-o-* + *mandibular*] (1889)
**:** of, relating to, being, or affecting the joint between the temporal bone and the mandible ⟨*temporomandibular* dysfunction⟩
**tempt** \'tem(p)t\ *transitive verb* [Middle English, from Old French *tempter, tenter*, from Latin *temptare, tentare* to feel, try] (13th century)
**1 :** to entice to do wrong by promise of pleasure or gain
**2 a** *obsolete* **:** to make trial of **:** TEST **b :** to try presumptuously **:** PROVOKE **c :** to risk the dangers of
**3 a :** to induce to do something **b :** to cause to be strongly inclined ⟨was *tempted* to call it quits⟩
*synonym* see LURE
— **tempt·able** \'tem(p)-tə-bəl\ *adjective*
**temp·ta·tion** \tem(p)-'tā-shən\ *noun* (13th century)
**1 :** the act of tempting or the state of being tempted especially to evil **:** ENTICEMENT
**2 :** something tempting **:** a cause or occasion of enticement
**tempt·er** \'tem(p)-tər\ *noun* (14th century)
**:** one that tempts or entices
**tempt·ing** *adjective* (1596)
**:** having an appeal **:** ENTICING ⟨a *tempting* offer⟩
— **tempt·ing·ly** \-tiŋ-lē\ *adverb*
**tempt·ress** \'tem(p)-trəs\ *noun* (1594)
**:** a woman who tempts or entices
**tem·pu·ra** \'tem-pə-rə, -ˌrä; tem-'pu̇r-ə\ *noun* [Japanese *tenpura*] (1920)
**:** seafood or vegetables dipped in batter and fried in deep fat
**ten** \'ten\ *noun* [Middle English, from Old English *tīene*, from *tīen*, adjective; akin to Old High German *zehan* ten, Latin *decem*, Greek *deka*] (before 12th century)
**1 —** see NUMBER table
**2 :** the 10th in a set or series ⟨wears a *ten*⟩
**3 :** something having 10 units or members

**4** : a 10-dollar bill
— **ten** *adjective*
— **ten** *pronoun, plural in construction*

**ten·a·ble** \'te-nə-bəl\ *adjective* [Middle French, from Old French, from *tenir* to hold, from Latin *tenēre* — more at THIN] (1579) : capable of being held, maintained, or defended : DEFENSIBLE, REASONABLE
— **ten·a·bil·i·ty** \,te-nə-'bi-lə-tē\ *noun*
— **ten·a·ble·ness** *noun*
— **ten·a·bly** \'te-nə-blē\ *adverb*

**ten·ace** \'te-,nās, te-'nās, 'te-nəs\ *noun* [modification of Spanish *tenaza*, literally, forceps, probably from Latin *tenacia*, neuter plural of *tenax*] (1655) : a combination of two high or relatively high cards (as ace and queen) of the same suit in one hand with one ranking two degrees below the other

**te·na·cious** \tə-'nā-shəs\ *adjective* [Latin *tenac-, tenax* tending to hold fast, from *tenēre* to hold] (1607) **1 a** : not easily pulled apart : COHESIVE, TOUGH ⟨a *tenacious* metal⟩ **b** : tending to adhere or cling especially to another substance : STICKY ⟨*tenacious* burs⟩ ⟨*tenacious* clay⟩ **2 a** : persistent in maintaining or adhering to something valued or habitual ⟨a man very *tenacious* of his rights⟩ **b** : RETENTIVE ⟨a *tenacious* memory⟩
**synonym** see STRONG
— **te·na·cious·ly** *adverb*
— **te·na·cious·ness** *noun*

**te·nac·i·ty** \tə-'na-sə-tē\ *noun* (1526) : the quality or state of being tenacious
**synonym** see COURAGE

**te·nac·u·lum** \tə-'na-kyə-ləm\ *noun, plural* **-la** \-lə\ *or* **-lums** [New Latin, from Late Latin, instrument for holding, from Latin *tenēre*] (circa 1693) **1** : a slender sharp-pointed hook attached to a handle and used mainly in surgery for seizing and holding parts (as arteries) **2** : an adhesive animal structure

**ten·an·cy** \'te-nən(t)-sē\ *noun, plural* **-cies** (1590) : a holding of an estate or a mode of holding an estate : the temporary possession or occupancy of something (as a house) that belongs to another; *also* : the period of a tenant's occupancy or possession

**¹ten·ant** \'te-nənt\ *noun* [Middle English, from Middle French, from present participle of *tenir* to hold] (14th century) **1 a** : one who holds or possesses real estate or sometimes personal property (as an annuity) by any kind of right **b** : one who has the occupation or temporary possession of lands or tenements of another; *specifically* : one who rents or leases (as a house) from a landlord **2** : OCCUPANT, DWELLER
— **ten·ant·less** \-ləs\ *adjective*

**²tenant** *transitive verb* (1634) : to hold or occupy as a tenant : INHABIT
— **ten·ant·able** \-nən-tə-bəl\ *adjective*

**tenant farmer** *noun* (1748) : a farmer who works land owned by another and pays rent either in cash or in shares of produce

**ten·ant·ry** \'te-nən-trē\ *noun, plural* **-ries** (14th century) **1** : TENANCY **2** : a body of tenants

**ten–cent store** \'ten-'sent-\ *noun* (1901) : FIVE-AND-TEN

**tench** \'tench\ *noun, plural* **tench** *or* **tench·es** [Middle English, from Middle French *tenche*, from Late Latin *tinca*] (14th century) : a cyprinid fish (*Tinca tinca*) native to Eurasia but introduced in the U.S. and noted for its ability to survive outside water

**Ten Commandments** *noun plural* (13th century) : the ethical commandments of God given according to biblical accounts to Moses by voice and by writing on stone tablets on Mount Sinai

**¹tend** \'tend\ *verb* [Middle English, short for *attenden* to attend] (14th century)
*intransitive verb*
**1** *archaic* : LISTEN
**2** : to pay attention : apply oneself ⟨*tend* to your own affairs⟩
**3** : to act as an attendant : SERVE
**4** *obsolete* : AWAIT
*transitive verb*
**1** *archaic* : to attend as a servant
**2 a** : to apply oneself to the care of : watch over **b** : to have or take charge of as a caretaker or overseer **c** : CULTIVATE, FOSTER **d** : to manage the operations of : MIND ⟨*tend* the store⟩
**3** : to stand by (as a rope) in readiness to prevent mischance (as fouling)

**²tend** *intransitive verb* [Middle English, from Middle French *tendre* to stretch, from Latin *tendere* — more at THIN] (14th century)
**1** : to move, direct, or develop one's course in a particular direction ⟨cannot tell where society is *tending*⟩
**2** : to exhibit an inclination or tendency : CONDUCE ⟨*tends* to be optimistic⟩

**ten·dance** \'ten-dən(t)s\ *noun* [short for *attendance*] (1573) **1** : watchful care **2** *archaic* : persons in attendance : RETINUE

**ten·den·cious** *chiefly British variant of* TENDENTIOUS

**ten·den·cy** \'ten-dən(t)-sē\ *noun, plural* **-cies** [Medieval Latin *tendentia*, from Latin *tendent-, tendens*, present participle of *tendere*] (1628) **1 a** : direction or approach toward a place, object, effect, or limit **b** : a proneness to a particular kind of thought or action **2 a** : the purposeful trend of something written or said : AIM **b** : deliberate but indirect advocacy ☆

**ten·den·tious** \ten-'den(t)-shəs\ *adjective* (1900) : marked by a tendency in favor of a particular point of view : BIASED
— **ten·den·tious·ly** *adverb*
— **ten·den·tious·ness** *noun*

**¹ten·der** \'ten-dər\ *adjective* [Middle English, from Old French *tendre*, from Latin *tener*; perhaps akin to Latin *tenuis* thin, slight — more at THIN] (13th century) **1 a** : having a soft or yielding texture : easily broken, cut, or damaged : DELICATE, FRAGILE ⟨*tender* feet⟩ **b** : easily chewed : SUCCULENT **2 a** : physically weak : not able to endure hardship **b** : IMMATURE, YOUNG ⟨children of *tender* years⟩ **c** : incapable of resisting cold : not hardy **3** : marked by, responding to, or expressing the softer emotions : FOND, LOVING ⟨a *tender* lover⟩ **4 a** : showing care : CONSIDERATE, SOLICITOUS ⟨*tender* regard⟩ **b** : highly susceptible to impressions or emotions : IMPRESSIONABLE ⟨a *tender* conscience⟩ **5 a** : appropriate or conducive to a delicate or sensitive constitution or character : GENTLE, MILD ⟨*tender* breeding⟩ ⟨*tender* irony⟩ **b** : delicate or soft in quality or tone ⟨never before heard the piano sound so *tender* —Elva S. Daniels⟩ **6** *obsolete* : DEAR, PRECIOUS **7 a** : sensitive to touch or palpation ⟨the bruise was still *tender*⟩ **b** : sensitive to injury or insult : TOUCHY ⟨*tender* pride⟩ **c** : demanding careful and sensitive handling : TICKLISH ⟨a *tender* situation⟩ **d** *of a ship* : ⁵CRANK
— **ten·der·ly** *adverb*
— **ten·der·ness** *noun*

**²tender** *verb* **ten·dered; ten·der·ing** \-d(ə-)riŋ\ (14th century)
*transitive verb*

**1** : to make tender : SOFTEN, WEAKEN
**2** *archaic* : to regard or treat with tenderness
*intransitive verb*
: to become tender

**³tender** *verb* **ten·dered; ten·der·ing** \-d(ə-)riŋ\ [Middle French *tendre* to stretch, stretch out, offer — more at TEND] (1535)
*transitive verb*
**1** : to make a tender of
**2** : to present for acceptance : OFFER ⟨*tendered* my resignation⟩
*intransitive verb*
: to make a bid or tender ⟨*tender* for a building contract⟩ ⟨*tendered* for 6% of the stock⟩

**⁴tender** *noun, often attributive* (circa 1543) **1** : an unconditional offer of money or service in satisfaction of a debt or obligation made to save a penalty or forfeiture for nonpayment or nonperformance **2** : an offer or proposal made for acceptance: as **a** : an offer of a bid for a contract **b** : a public expression of willingness to buy not less than a specified number of shares of a stock at a fixed price from stockholders usually in an attempt to gain control of the issuing company **3** : something that may be offered in payment; *specifically* : MONEY

**⁵tender** *noun* [¹*tender*] (1596) *obsolete* : CONSIDERATION, REGARD

**⁶tend·er** \'ten-dər\ *noun* (1675) : one that tends: as **a** (1) : a ship employed to attend other ships (as to supply provisions) (2) : a boat for communication between shore and a larger ship (3) : a warship that provides logistic support **b** : a car attached to a steam locomotive for carrying a supply of fuel and water

**ten·der·foot** \'ten-dər-,fut\ *noun, plural* **ten·der·feet** \-,fēt\ *also* **ten·der·foots** \-,futs\ (1849) **1** : a newcomer in a comparatively rough or newly settled region; *especially* : one not hardened to frontier or outdoor life **2** : an inexperienced beginner : NOVICE ⟨a political *tenderfoot*⟩

**ten·der·heart·ed** \'ten-dər-,här-təd\ *adjective* (15th century) : easily moved to love, pity, or sorrow : COMPASSIONATE, IMPRESSIONABLE
— **ten·der·heart·ed·ly** *adverb*
— **ten·der·heart·ed·ness** *noun*

**ten·der·ize** \'ten-də-,rīz\ *transitive verb* **-ized; -iz·ing** (1930) : to make (meat or meat products) tender by applying a process or substance that breaks down connective tissue
— **ten·der·i·za·tion** \,ten-d(ə-)rə-'zā-shən\ *noun*

---

☆ **SYNONYMS**
**Tendency, trend, drift, tenor, current** mean movement in a particular direction. TENDENCY implies an inclination sometimes amounting to an impelling force ⟨a general *tendency* toward inflation⟩. TREND applies to the general direction maintained by a winding or irregular course ⟨the long-term *trend* of the stock market is upward⟩. DRIFT may apply to a tendency determined by external forces ⟨the *drift* of the population away from large cities⟩ or it may apply to an underlying or obscure trend of meaning or discourse ⟨got the *drift* of her argument⟩. TENOR stresses a clearly perceptible direction and a continuous, undeviating course ⟨the *tenor* of the times⟩. CURRENT implies a clearly defined but not necessarily unalterable course ⟨an encounter that changed the *current* of my life⟩.

---

\ə\ abut \ᵊ\ kitten \ər\ further \a\ ash \ā\ ace
\ä\ mop, mar \aú\ out \ch\ chin \e\ bet \ē\ easy
\g\ go \i\ hit \ī\ ice \j\ job \ŋ\ sing \ō\ go
\ó\ law \ói\ boy \th\ thin \th\ the \ü\ loot \ú\ foot
\y\ yet \zh\ vision *see also* Guide to Pronunciation

— **ten·der·iz·er** \'ten-də-ˌrī-zər\ *noun*

**ten·der·loin** \'ten-dər-ˌlȯin\ *noun* (circa 1828)
**1** : a strip of tender meat consisting of a large internal muscle of the loin on each side of the vertebral column
**2** [from its making possible a luxurious diet for a corrupt police officer] : a district of a city largely devoted to vice

**ten·der–mind·ed** \'ten-dər-ˌmīn-dəd\ *adjective* (1605)
: marked by idealism, optimism, and dogmatism

**ten·der·om·e·ter** \ˌten-də-'rä-mə-tər\ *noun* (1938)
: a device for determining the maturity and tenderness of samples of fruits and vegetables

**ten·di·ni·tis** *or* **ten·don·itis** \ˌten-də-'nī-təs\ *noun* [*tendinitis* from New Latin, from *tendin, tendo* + *-itis; tendonitis* from *tendon* + *-itis*] (circa 1900)
: inflammation of a tendon

**ten·di·nous** \'ten-də-nəs\ *adjective* [New Latin *tendinosus*, from *tendin-, tendo* tendon, alteration of Medieval Latin *tendon-, tendo*] (1658)
**1** : consisting of tendons : SINEWY ⟨*tendinous* tissue⟩
**2** : of, relating to, or resembling a tendon

**ten·don** \'ten-dən\ *noun* [Medieval Latin *tendon-, tendo*, from Latin *tendere* to stretch — more at THIN] (1541)
: a tough cord or band of dense white fibrous connective tissue that unites a muscle with some other part (as a bone) and transmits the force which the muscle exerts

**tendon of Achil·les** \-ə-'ki-lēz\ (circa 1885)
: ACHILLES TENDON

**ten·dresse** \tän-dres\ *noun* [Middle English, from Middle French, from *tendre* tender] (14th century)
: FONDNESS

**ten·dril** \'ten-drəl\ *noun* [probably modification of Middle French *tendron, tendrum* bud, cartilage, from (assumed) Vulgar Latin *tenerumen*, from Latin *tener* tender — more at TENDER] (1538)
**1** : a leaf, stipule, or stem modified into a slender spirally coiling sensitive organ serving to attach a climbing plant to its support
**2** : something suggestive of a tendril ⟨hair hanging in *tendrils*⟩ ⟨creeping *tendrils* of fog⟩
— **ten·driled** *or* **ten·drilled** \-drəld\ *adjective*
— **ten·dril·ous** \-drə-ləs\ *adjective*

**tendril 1**

¹**-tene** *adjective combining form* [French *-tène*, from Latin *taenia* ribbon, band — more at TAENIA]
: having (such or so many) chromosomal filaments ⟨poly*tene*⟩ ⟨pachy*tene*⟩

²**-tene** *noun combining form*
: stage of meiotic prophase characterized by (such) chromosomal filaments ⟨diplo*tene*⟩ ⟨pachy*tene*⟩

**Ten·e·brae** \'te-nə-ˌbrā, -ˌbrī, -ˌbrē\ *noun plural but singular or plural in construction* [Medieval Latin, from Latin, darkness — more at TEMERITY] (1651)
: a church service observed during the final part of Holy Week commemorating the sufferings and death of Christ

**ten·e·brif·ic** \ˌte-nə-'bri-fik\ *adjective* [Latin *tenebrae* darkness] (1785)
**1** : GLOOMY
**2** : causing gloom or darkness

**te·ne·bri·o·nid** \tə-'ne-brē-ə-nəd, ˌte-nə-'brī-ə-nəd\ *noun* [New Latin *Tenebrionidae*, from *Tenebrion-, Tenebrio*, type genus, from Latin, one that shuns the light, from *tenebrae* darkness — more at TEMERITY] (1902)
: any of a family (Tenebrionidae) of firm-bodied mostly dark-colored vegetable-feeding beetles which often have vestigial and functionless wings and whose larvae are usually hard cylindrical worms (as a mealworm) — called also *darkling beetle*
— **tenebrionid** *adjective*

**te·neb·ri·ous** \tə-'ne-brē-əs\ *adjective* [by alteration] (1594)
: TENEBROUS

**ten·e·brism** \'te-nə-ˌbri-zəm\ *noun, often capitalized* [Latin *tenebrae* darkness] (1954)
: a style of painting especially associated with the Italian painter Caravaggio and his followers in which most of the figures are engulfed in shadow but some are dramatically illuminated by a concentrated beam of light usually from an identifiable source
— **ten·e·brist** \-brist\ *noun or adjective, often capitalized*

**ten·e·brous** \'te-nə-brəs\ *adjective* [Middle English, from Middle French *tenebreus*, from Latin *tenebrosus*, from *tenebrae*] (15th century)
**1** : shut off from the light : DARK, MURKY
**2** : hard to understand : OBSCURE
**3** : causing gloom

**1080** *also* **ten–eighty** \(ˌ)ten-'ā-tē\ *noun* [from its laboratory serial number] (1945)
: a poisonous preparation of sodium fluoroacetate used as a rodenticide and pesticide

**ten·e·ment** \'te-nə-mənt\ *noun* [Middle English, from Middle French, from Medieval Latin *tenementum*, from Latin *tenēre* to hold — more at THIN] (14th century)
**1** : any of various forms of corporeal property (as land) or incorporeal property that is held by one person from another
**2** : DWELLING
**3 a** : a house used as a dwelling : RESIDENCE **b** : APARTMENT, FLAT **c** : TENEMENT HOUSE

**tenement house** *noun* (1858)
: APARTMENT HOUSE; *especially* : one meeting minimum standards of sanitation, safety, and comfort and usually located in a city

**te·nes·mus** \tə-'nez-məs\ *noun* [Latin, from Greek *teinesmos*, from *teinein* to stretch, strain — more at THIN] (1527)
: a distressing but ineffectual urge to evacuate the rectum or bladder

**te·net** \'te-nət *also* 'tē-nət\ *noun* [Latin, he holds, from *tenēre* to hold] (circa 1600)
: a principle, belief, or doctrine generally held to be true; *especially* : one held in common by members of an organization, movement, or profession

**ten·fold** \'ten-ˌfōld, -'fōld\ *adjective* (before 12th century)
**1** : being 10 times as great or as many
**2** : having 10 units or members
— **ten·fold** \-'fōld\ *adverb*

**ten–gallon hat** *noun* (1927)
: COWBOY HAT

**te·nia, te·ni·a·sis** *variant of* TAENIA, TAENIASIS

**ten·ner** \'te-nər\ *noun* (1845)
**1** : a 10-pound note
**2** : a 10-dollar bill

**Ten·nes·see walking horse** \'te-nə-ˌsē-\ *noun* [*Tennessee*, state of U.S.] (1938)
: any of an American breed of large easy-gaited saddle horses largely of standardbred and Morgan ancestry — called also *Tennessee walker*

**ten·nies** \'te-nēz\ *noun plural* [by shortening & alteration] (1951)
: TENNIS SHOES, SNEAKERS

**Tennessee walking horse**

**ten·nis** \'te-nəs\ *noun, often attributive* [Middle English *tenetz, tenys*, probably from Anglo-French *tenetz*, 2d person plural imperative of *tenir* to hold — more at TENABLE] (15th century)
**1** : COURT TENNIS
**2** : an indoor or outdoor game that is played with rackets and a light elastic ball by two players or pairs of players on a level court (as of clay or grass) divided by a low net

**tennis elbow** *noun* (1883)
: inflammation and pain over the outer side of the elbow usually resulting from excessive strain on and twisting of the forearm

**tennis shoe** *noun* (1886)
: a lightweight usually low-cut sneaker

**ten·nist** \'te-nist\ *noun* [blend of *tennis* and *-ist*] (1932)
: a tennis player

¹**ten·on** \'te-nən\ *noun* [Middle English, from Middle French, from *tenir* to hold — more at TENABLE] (15th century)
: a projecting member in a piece of wood or other material for insertion into a mortise to make a joint — see DOVETAIL illustration

²**tenon** *transitive verb* (1596)
**1** : to unite by a tenon
**2** : to cut or fit for insertion in a mortise

¹**ten·or** \'te-nər\ *noun* [Middle English, from Middle French, from Latin *tenor* uninterrupted course, from *tenēre* to hold — more at THIN] (14th century)
**1 a** : the drift of something spoken or written : PURPORT **b** : an exact copy of a writing : TRANSCRIPT **c** : the concept, object, or person meant in a metaphor
**2 a** : the melodic line usually forming the cantus firmus in medieval music **b** : the voice part next to the lowest in a 4-part chorus **c** : the highest natural adult male singing voice; *also* : a person having this voice **d** : a member of a family of instruments having a range next lower than that of the alto
**3** : a continuance in a course, movement, or activity
**4** : habitual condition : CHARACTER
**synonym** see TENDENCY

²**tenor** *adjective* (1522)
: relating to or having the range or part of a tenor

**ten·or·ist** \'te-nə-rist\ *noun* (1865)
: one who sings tenor or plays a tenor instrument

**te·no·syn·o·vi·tis** \ˌte-nō-ˌsi-nə-'vī-təs, ˌtē-\ *noun* [New Latin, from Greek *tenōn* tendon (akin to Greek *teinein* to stretch) + New Latin *synovitis* — more at THIN] (circa 1860)
: inflammation of a tendon sheath

**ten·our** \'te-nər\ *chiefly British variant of* TENOR

**ten·pen·ny** \'ten-ˌpe-nē, *British* -pə-nē\ *adjective* (1592)
: amounting to, worth, or costing 10 pennies

**tenpenny nail** *noun* [from its original price per hundred] (15th century)
: a nail three inches (7.6 centimeters) long

**ten·pin** \'ten-ˌpin\ *noun* (1807)
**1** : a bottle-shaped bowling pin 15 inches high
**2** *plural but singular in construction* : a bowling game using 10 tenpins and a large ball 27 inches in circumference and allowing each player to bowl 2 balls in each of 10 frames

**ten·pound·er** \'ten-'paún-dər\ *noun* (1699)
: LADYFISH 2

**ten·rec** \'ten-ˌrek\ *noun* [French, from Malagasy *tàndraka*] (1785)
: any of numerous small often spiny mammalian insectivores (family Tenrecidae) chiefly of Madagascar

¹**tense** \'ten(t)s\ *noun* [Middle English *tens* time, tense, from Middle French, from Latin *tempus*] (14th century)
**1** : a distinction of form in a verb to express distinctions of time or duration of the action or state it denotes
**2 a** : a set of inflectional forms of a verb that express distinctions of time **b** : an inflectional form of a verb expressing a specific time distinction

**²tense** *adjective* **tens·er; tens·est** [Latin *tensus,* from past participle of *tendere* to stretch — more at THIN] (1670)
**1 :** stretched tight **:** made taut **:** RIGID
**2 a :** feeling or showing nervous tension **b :** marked by strain or suspense
**3 :** produced with the muscles involved in a relatively tense state ⟨the vowels \ē\ and \ü\ in contrast with the vowels \i\ and \u̇\ are *tense*⟩
— **tense·ly** *adverb*
— **tense·ness** *noun*
**³tense** *verb* **tensed; tens·ing** (1676)
*transitive verb*
**:** to make tense
*intransitive verb*
**:** to become tense
**ten·sile** \'ten(t)-səl *also* 'ten-ˌsīl\ *adjective* [New Latin *tensilis,* from Latin *tensus,* past participle] (1626)
**1 :** capable of tension **:** DUCTILE
**2 :** of, relating to, or involving tension ⟨*tensile* stress⟩
— **ten·sil·i·ty** \ten-'si-lə-tē\ *noun*
**tensile strength** *noun* (circa 1864)
**:** the greatest longitudinal stress a substance can bear without tearing apart
**ten·si·om·e·ter** \ˌten(t)-sē-'ä-mə-tər\ *noun* [*tension*] (1912)
**1 :** a device for measuring tension (as of structural material)
**2 :** an instrument for determining the moisture content of soil
**3 :** an instrument for measuring the surface tension of liquids
— **ten·sio·met·ric** \-sē-ō-'me-trik\ *adjective*
— **ten·si·om·e·try** \-sē-'ä-mə-trē\ *noun*
**¹ten·sion** \'ten(t)-shən\ *noun* [Middle French or Latin; Middle French, from Latin *tension-, tensio,* from *tendere*] (1533)
**1 a :** the act or action of stretching or the condition or degree of being stretched to stiffness **:** TAUTNESS **b :** STRESS 1b
**2 a :** either of two balancing forces causing or tending to cause extension **b :** the stress resulting from the elongation of an elastic body
**3 a :** inner striving, unrest, or imbalance often with physiological indication of emotion **b :** a state of latent hostility or opposition between individuals or groups **c :** a balance maintained in an artistic work between opposing forces or elements
**4 :** a device to produce a desired tension (as in a loom)
— **ten·sion·al** \'ten(t)-sh(ə-)nəl\ *adjective*
— **ten·sion·less** \'ten(t)-shən-ləs\ *adjective*
**²tension** *transitive verb* **ten·sioned; ten·sion·ing** \'ten(t)-sh(ə-)niŋ\ (1891)
**:** to subject to tension; *especially* **:** to tighten to a desired or appropriate degree
— **ten·sion·er** \-sh(ə-)nər\ *noun*
**ten·si·ty** \'ten(t)-sə-tē\ *noun, plural* **-ties** (circa 1658)
**:** the quality or state of being tense **:** TENSENESS
**ten·sive** \'ten(t)-siv\ *adjective* (1702)
**:** of, relating to, or causing tension
**ten·sor** \'ten(t)-sər, 'ten-ˌsȯr\ *noun* [New Latin, from Latin *tendere*] (circa 1704)
**1 :** a muscle that stretches a part
**2 :** a generalized vector with more than three components each of which is a function of the coordinates of an arbitrary point in space of an appropriate number of dimensions
**ten–speed** \'ten-ˌspēd\ *noun* (1971)
**:** a bicycle with 10 gear combinations
**tens place** \'tenz-\ *noun* (1937)
**:** the place two to the left of the decimal point in a number expressed in the Arabic system of writing numbers
**ten–strike** \'ten-ˌstrīk\ *noun* (1840)
**1 :** a strike in tenpins
**2 :** a highly successful stroke or achievement
**¹tent** \'tent\ *noun* [Middle English *tente,* from Old French, from Latin *tenta,* feminine of *ten-*

*tus,* past participle of *tendere* to stretch — more at THIN] (14th century)
**1 :** a collapsible shelter of fabric (as nylon or canvas) stretched and sustained by poles and used for camping outdoors or as a temporary building
**2 :** DWELLING
**3 a :** something that resembles a tent or that serves as a shelter; *especially* **:** a canopy or enclosure placed over the head and shoulders to retain vapors or oxygen during medical administration **b :** the web of a tent caterpillar
— **tent·less** \'tent-ləs\ *adjective*
— **tent·like** \-ˌlīk\ *adjective*
**²tent** (1607)
*intransitive verb*
**1 :** to reside for the time being **:** LODGE
**2 :** to live in a tent
*transitive verb*
**1 :** to cover with or as if with a tent
**2 :** to lodge in tents
**³tent** *transitive verb* [Middle English, from *tent* attention, short for *attent,* from Old French *attente,* from *atendre* to attend] (14th century)
*chiefly Scottish* **:** to attend to
**ten·ta·cle** \'ten-ti-kəl\ *noun* [New Latin *tentaculum,* from Latin *tentare* to feel, touch — more at TEMPT] (1762)
**1 :** any of various elongate flexible usually tactile or prehensile processes borne by animals and especially invertebrates chiefly on the head or about the mouth
**2 a :** something that resembles a tentacle especially in or as if in grasping or feeling out **b :** a sensitive hair or emergence on a plant (as the sundew)
— **ten·ta·cled** \-kəld\ *adjective*
**ten·tac·u·lar** \ten-'ta-kyə-lər\ *adjective* [New Latin *tentaculum*] (1828)
**1 :** of, relating to, or resembling tentacles
**2 :** equipped with tentacles
**tent·age** \'ten-tij\ *noun* (1603)
**:** a collection of tents **:** tent equipment
**ten·ta·tive** \'ten-tə-tiv\ *adjective* [Medieval Latin *tentativus,* from Latin *tentatus,* past participle of *tentare, temptare* to feel, try] (1626)
**1 :** not fully worked out or developed ⟨*tentative* plans⟩
**2 :** HESITANT, UNCERTAIN ⟨a *tentative* smile⟩
— **tentative** *noun*
— **ten·ta·tive·ly** *adverb*
— **ten·ta·tive·ness** *noun*
**tent caterpillar** *noun* (1854)
**:** any of several destructive gregarious caterpillars (genus *Malacosoma* and especially *M. americanum* of the family Lasiocampidae) that construct large silken webs on trees
**tent·ed** \'ten-təd\ *adjective* (1604)
**1 :** covered with a tent or tents
**2 :** shaped like a tent
**¹ten·ter** \'ten-tər\ *noun* [Middle English *teyntur, tentowre*] (14th century)
**1 :** a frame or endless track with hooks or clips along two sides that is used for drying and stretching cloth
**2** *archaic* **:** TENTERHOOK
**²tenter** *noun* (1846)
**:** one who lives in or occupies a tent
**ten·ter·hook** \'ten-tər-ˌhuk\ *noun* (15th century)
**:** a sharp hooked nail used especially for fastening cloth on a tenter
— **on tenterhooks :** in a state of uneasiness, strain, or suspense
**tenth** \'ten(t)th\ *noun, plural* **tenths** \'ten(t)s, 'ten(t)ths\ (15th century)
**1** — see NUMBER table
**2 a :** a musical interval embracing an octave and a third **b :** the tone at this interval
— **tenth** *adjective or adverb*
**tenth–rate** \'tenth-'rāt\ *adjective* (1834)
**:** of the lowest character or quality
**tent stitch** *noun* (1639)

**:** a short stitch slanting to the right that is used in embroidery to form even lines of solid background
**ten·ty** *also* **tent·ie** \'ten-tē\ *adjective* [³*tent*] (circa 1555)
*Scottish* **:** ATTENTIVE, WATCHFUL
**ten·u·is** \'ten-yə-wəs\ *noun, plural* **-u·es** \-yə-ˌwēz, -ˌwās\ [Medieval Latin, from Latin, thin, slight] (1650)
**:** an unaspirated voiceless stop
**te·nu·ity** \te-'nü-ə-tē, tə-, -'nyü-\ *noun* [Latin *tenuitas,* from *tenuis* thin, tenuous] (circa 1536)
**1 :** lack of substance or strength
**2 :** lack of thickness **:** SLENDERNESS, THINNESS
**3 :** lack of density **:** rarefied quality or state
**ten·u·ous** \'ten-yə-wəs\ *adjective* [Latin *tenuis* thin, slight, tenuous — more at THIN] (1597)
**1 :** not dense **:** RARE ⟨a *tenuous* fluid⟩
**2 :** not thick **:** SLENDER ⟨a *tenuous* rope⟩
**3 a :** having little substance or strength **:** FLIMSY, WEAK ⟨*tenuous* influences⟩ **b :** SHAKY 2a ⟨*tenuous* reasons⟩ ⟨on grounds that were *tenuous*⟩
**synonym** see THIN
— **ten·u·ous·ly** *adverb*
— **ten·u·ous·ness** *noun*
**ten·ure** \'ten-yər *also* -ˌyu̇r\ *noun* [Middle English, from Middle French *teneüre, tenure,* from Medieval Latin *tenitura,* from (assumed) Vulgar Latin *tenitus,* past participle of Latin *tenēre* to hold — more at THIN] (15th century)
**1 :** the act, right, manner, or term of holding something (as a landed property, a position, or an office); *especially* **:** a status granted after a trial period to a teacher that gives protection from summary dismissal
**2 :** GRASP, HOLD
— **ten·ur·able** \-ə-bəl\ *adjective*
— **te·nur·ial** \te-'nyu̇r-ē-əl\ *adjective*
— **te·nur·ial·ly** \-ə-lē\ *adverb*
**ten·ured** \'ten-yərd\ *adjective* (1965)
**:** having tenure ⟨*tenured* faculty members⟩
**ten·ure–track** \'ten-yər-ˌtrak *also* -ˌyu̇r-\ *adjective* (1976)
**:** relating to or being a teaching position that may lead to a grant of tenure
**te·nu·to** \tä-'nü-(ˌ)tō\ *adverb or adjective* [Italian, from past participle of *tenere* to hold, from Latin *tenēre*] (1762)
**:** in a manner so as to hold a tone or chord to its full value — used as a direction in music
**te·o·cal·li** \ˌtē-ə-'ka-lē, ˌtā-ə-'kä-\ *noun* [Nahuatl *teōcalli,* from *teōtl* god + *calli* house] (1613)
**:** an ancient temple of Mexico or Central America usually built upon the summit of a truncated pyramidal mound; *also* **:** the mound itself
**te·o·sin·te** \ˌtā-ō-'sin-tē\ *noun* [Mexican Spanish, from Nahuatl *teōcintli,* from *teōtl* god + *cintli* dried ears of maize] (circa 1877)
**:** a tall annual grass (*Zea mexicana* synonym *Euchlaena mexicana*) of Mexico and Central America that is closely related to and sometimes considered ancestral to maize
**te·pa** \'tē-pə\ *noun* [*tri-* + *ethylene* + *phosphor-* + *amide*] (1953)
**:** a soluble crystalline compound $C_6H_{12}N_3OP$ that is used especially as a chemical sterilizing agent of insects, a palliative in some kinds of cancer, and in finishing and flame-proofing textiles
**te·pa·ry bean** \'te-pə-rē-\ *noun* [origin unknown] (1912)
**:** an annual twining bean (*Phaseolus acutifolius* variety *latifolius*) that is native to the

\ə\ abut \ᵊ\ kitten \ər\ further \a\ ash \ā\ ace
\ä\ mop, mar \au̇\ out \ch\ chin \e\ bet \ē\ easy
\g\ go \i\ hit \ī\ ice \j\ job \ŋ\ sing \ō\ go
\ȯ\ law \ȯi\ boy \th\ thin \th\ the \ü\ loot \u̇\ foot
\y\ yet \zh\ vision *see also* Guide to Pronunciation

southwestern U.S. and Mexico and is cultivated for its roundish white, yellow, brown, or bluish black edible seeds; *also* **:** the seed

**te·pee** \'tē-(ˌ)pē\ *noun* [Dakota *thípi*, from *thi*-to dwell] (1743)
**:** a conical tent usually consisting of skins and used especially by American Indians of the Plains

**teph·ra** \'te-frə\ *noun* [New Latin, from Greek, ashes; akin to Sanskrit *dahati* it burns — more at FOMENT] (1944)
**:** solid material ejected into the air during a volcanic eruption; *especially* **:** [2]ASH 2b

**tepee**

**tep·id** \'te-pəd\ *adjective* [Middle English *teped*, from Latin *tepidus*, from *tepēre* to be moderately warm; akin to Sanskrit *tapati* it heats, Old Irish *tess* heat] (14th century)
**1 :** moderately warm **:** LUKEWARM ⟨a *tepid* bath⟩
**2 a :** lacking in passion, force, or zest ⟨a *tepid* joke⟩ **b :** marked by an absence of enthusiasm or conviction ⟨a *tepid* interest⟩
— **te·pid·i·ty** \tə-'pi-də-tē, te-\ *noun*
— **tep·id·ly** \'te-pəd-lē\ *adverb*
— **tep·id·ness** *noun*

**TEPP** \ˌtē-(ˌ)ē-(ˌ)pē-'pē\ *noun* [tetra- + ethyl + pyrophosphate] (1948)
**:** a mobile hygroscopic corrosive liquid organophosphate $C_8H_{20}O_7P_2$ that is a powerful anticholinesterase and is used especially as an insecticide

**te·qui·la** \tə-'kē-lə, tā-\ *noun* [Spanish, from *Tequila*, town in Jalisco state, Mexico] (1849)
**:** a Mexican liquor distilled from pulque

**tequila sunrise** *noun* (1965)
**:** a cocktail consisting of tequila, orange juice, and grenadine

**ter-** *combining form* [Latin, from *ter*; akin to Greek & Sanskrit *tris* three times, Latin *tres* three — more at THREE]
**:** three times **:** threefold **:** three ⟨*tercentenary*⟩

**tera-** *combining form* [International Scientific Vocabulary, from Greek *terat-, teras* monster]
**:** trillion ⟨*terawatt*⟩

**te·rai** \tə-'rī\ *noun* [*Tarai*, lowland belt of India] (1888)
**:** a wide-brimmed double felt sun hat worn especially in subtropical regions

**ter·aph** \'ter-əf\ *noun, plural* **ter·a·phim** \'ter-ə-ˌfim\ [Hebrew *tĕrāphīm* (plural in form but singular in meaning)] (14th century)
**:** an image of a Semitic household god

**terat-** *or* **terato-** *combining form* [Greek, from *terat-, teras* marvel, portent, monster]
**:** developmental malformation ⟨*teratogenic*⟩

**te·rato·car·ci·no·ma** \ˌter-ə-tō-ˌkär-sᵊn-'ō-mə\ *noun* (1946)
**:** a malignant teratoma; *especially* **:** one involving germinal cells of the testis

**te·rato·gen** \tə-'ra-tə-jən\ *noun* (1959)
**:** a teratogenic agent

**ter·a·to·gen·e·sis** \ˌter-ə-tə-'je-nə-səs\ *noun* [New Latin] (1901)
**:** production of developmental malformations

**ter·a·to·gen·ic** \-'je-nik\ *adjective* (1879)
**:** of, relating to, or causing developmental malformations ⟨*teratogenic* substances⟩ ⟨*teratogenic* effects⟩
— **ter·a·to·ge·nic·i·ty** \-jə-'ni-sə-tē\ *noun*

**ter·a·to·log·i·cal** \ˌter-ə-tᵊl-'ä-ji-kəl\ *or* **ter·a·to·log·ic** \-jik\ *adjective* (1857)
**1 :** abnormal in growth or structure
**2 :** of or relating to teratology

**ter·a·tol·o·gy** \ˌter-ə-'tä-lə-jē\ *noun* (circa 1842)
**:** the study of malformations or serious deviations from the normal type in organisms
— **ter·a·tol·o·gist** \-jist\ *noun*

**ter·a·to·ma** \ˌter-ə-'tō-mə\ *noun* [New Latin] (1879)
**:** a tumor made up of a heterogeneous mixture of tissues

**tera·watt** \'ter-ə-ˌwät\ *noun* (1970)
**:** a unit of power equal to one trillion watts

**ter·bi·um** \'tər-bē-əm\ *noun* [New Latin, from *Ytterby*, Sweden] (1843)
**:** a usually trivalent metallic element of the rare-earth group — see ELEMENT table

**terce** \'tərs\ *noun, often capitalized* [Middle English, third, terce — more at TIERCE] (14th century)
**:** the third of the canonical hours

**ter·cel** \'tər-səl\ *variant of* TIERCEL

**ter·cen·te·na·ry** \ˌtər-(ˌ)sen-'te-nə-rē, (ˌ)tər-'sen-tᵊn-ˌer-ē\ *noun, plural* **-ries** (1855)
**:** a 300th anniversary or its celebration
— **tercentenary** *adjective*

**ter·cen·ten·ni·al** \ˌtər-(ˌ)sen-'te-nē-əl\ *adjective or noun* (1872)
**:** TERCENTENARY

**ter·cet** \'tər-sət\ *noun* [Italian *terzetto*, from diminutive of *terzo* third, from Latin *tertius* — more at THIRD] (1598)
**:** a unit or group of three lines of verse: **a :** one of the 3-line stanzas in terza rima **b :** one of the two groups of three lines forming the sestet in an Italian sonnet

**ter·e·binth** \'ter-ə-ˌbin(t)th\ *noun* [Middle English *terebynt*, from Middle French *terebinthe*, from Latin *terebinthus* — more at TURPENTINE] (14th century)
**:** a small European tree (*Pistacia terebinthus*) of the cashew family yielding turpentine

**te·re·do** \tə-'rē-(ˌ)dō, -'rā-\ *noun, plural* **teredos** *or* **te·red·i·nes** \-'re-dᵊn-ˌēz\ [Middle English, from Latin *teredin-, teredo*, from Greek *terēdōn*; akin to Greek *tetrainein* to bore — more at THROW] (14th century)
**:** SHIPWORM

**tere·phthal·ate** \ˌter-ə(f)-'tha-ˌlāt\ *noun* (1868)
**:** a salt or ester of terephthalic acid; *especially* **:** a dimethyl-ester that is a major starting material for polyester fibers and coatings

**tere·phthal·ic acid** \ˌter-ə(f)-'tha-lik-\ *noun* [International Scientific Vocabulary *terebene*, mixture of terpenes from distilled turpentine + *phthalic acid*] (1857)
**:** a *p*-dicarboxylic acid $C_8H_6O_4$ that is obtained especially by oxidation of xylene and is used chiefly in the synthesis of polyesters

**te·rete** \tə-'rēt, te-\ *adjective* [Latin *teret-, teres* well turned, rounded; akin to Latin *terere* to rub — more at THROW] (circa 1619)
**:** approximately cylindrical but usually tapering at both ends ⟨a *terete* seedpod⟩

**Te·reus** \'tir-ˌyüs, 'tē-ˌrüs\ *noun* [Latin, from Greek *Tēreus*]
**:** the husband of Procne who rapes his sister-in-law Philomela

**ter·gite** \'tər-ˌgīt\ *noun* [New Latin *tergum*] (1885)
**:** the dorsal plate or dorsal portion of the covering of a metameric segment of an arthropod; *especially* **:** one on the abdomen

**ter·gi·ver·sate** \'tər-jə-vər-ˌsāt, ˌtər-'ji-vər-ˌsāt, -'gi-; ˌtər-jə-'vər-\ *intransitive verb* **-sat·ed; -sat·ing** [Latin *tergiversatus*, past participle of *tergiversari* to show reluctance, from *tergum* back + *versare* to turn, frequentative of *vertere* to turn — more at WORTH] (1654)
**:** to engage in tergiversation
— **ter·gi·ver·sa·tor** \-ˌsā-tər\ *noun*

**ter·gi·ver·sa·tion** \ˌtər-ji-vər-'sā-shən, -ˌgi-; ˌtər-ji-(ˌ)vər-\ *noun* (1570)
**1 :** evasion of straightforward action or clear-cut statement **:** EQUIVOCATION
**2 :** desertion of a cause, position, party, or faith

**ter·gum** \'tər-gəm\ *noun, plural* **ter·ga** \-gə\ [New Latin, from Latin, back] (circa 1826)
**:** the dorsal part or plate of a segment of an arthropod **:** TERGITE, NOTUM
— **ter·gal** \-gəl\ *adjective*

**ter·i·ya·ki** \ˌter-ē-'yä-kē\ *noun* [Japanese, from *teri* glaze + *yaki* broil] (1962)
**:** a Japanese dish of meat or fish that is grilled or broiled after being soaked in a seasoned soy sauce marinade

**[1]term** \'tərm\ *noun* [Middle English *terme* boundary, end, from Old French, from Latin *terminus*; akin to Greek *termōn* boundary, end, Sanskrit *tarman* top of a post] (13th century)
**1 a :** END, TERMINATION; *also* **:** a point in time assigned to something (as a payment) **b :** the time at which a pregnancy of normal length terminates ⟨had her baby at full *term*⟩
**2 a :** a limited or definite extent of time; *especially* **:** the time for which something lasts **:** DURATION, TENURE ⟨*term* of office⟩ ⟨lost money in the short *term*⟩ **b :** the whole period for which an estate is granted; *also* **:** the estate or interest held by one for a term **c :** the time during which a court is in session
**3** *plural* **:** provisions that determine the nature and scope of an agreement **:** CONDITIONS ⟨*terms* of sale⟩ ⟨liberal credit *terms*⟩
**4 a :** a word or expression that has a precise meaning in some uses or is peculiar to a science, art, profession, or subject ⟨legal *terms*⟩ **b** *plural* **:** expression of a specified kind ⟨described in glowing *terms*⟩
**5 a :** a unitary or compound expression connected with another by a plus or minus sign **b :** an element of a fraction or proportion or of a series or sequence
**6** *plural* **a :** mutual relationship **:** FOOTING ⟨on good *terms*⟩ **b :** AGREEMENT, CONCORD ⟨come to *terms*⟩
**7 :** any of the three substantive elements of a syllogism
**8 :** a quadrangular pillar often tapering downward and adorned on the top with the figure of a head or the upper part of the body
**9 :** division in a school year during which instruction is regularly given to students
— **in terms of :** with respect to or in relation to ⟨thinks of everything *in terms of* money⟩
— **on one's own terms :** in accordance with one's wishes **:** in one's own way ⟨prefers to live *on his own terms*⟩

**[2]term** *transitive verb* (circa 1557)
**:** to apply a term to **:** CALL, NAME

**[1]ter·ma·gant** \'tər-mə-gənt\ *noun* [Middle English]
**1** *capitalized* **:** a deity erroneously ascribed to Islam by medieval European Christians and represented in early English drama as a violent character
**2 :** an overbearing or nagging woman **:** SHREW

**[2]termagant** *adjective* (1596)
**:** OVERBEARING, SHREWISH

**term·er** \'tər-mər\ *noun* (1634)
**:** a person serving for a specified term (as in a political office or in prison) ⟨a first *termer*⟩

**ter·mi·na·ble** \'tər-mə-nə-bəl, 'tərm-nə-\ *adjective* [Middle English, from *terminen* to terminate, from Middle French *terminer*, from Latin *terminare*] (15th century)
**:** capable of being terminated
— **ter·mi·na·ble·ness** *noun*
— **ter·mi·na·bly** \-blē\ *adverb*

**[1]ter·mi·nal** \'tər-mə-nᵊl, 'tər-mə-nᵊl\ *adjective* [Latin *terminalis*, from *terminus*] (1744)
**1 a :** of or relating to an end, extremity, boundary, or terminus ⟨a *terminal* pillar⟩ **b :** growing at the end of a branch or stem ⟨a *terminal* bud⟩
**2 a :** of, relating to, or occurring in a term or each term ⟨*terminal* payments⟩ **b :** leading ultimately to death ⟨*terminal* cancer⟩ **c :** approaching or close to death **:** being in the final stages of a fatal disease ⟨a *terminal* patient⟩ **d :** extremely or hopelessly severe ⟨*terminal* boredom⟩
**3 a :** occurring at or constituting the end of a period or series **:** CONCLUDING ⟨the *terminal*

moments of life⟩ **b :** not intended as preparation for further academic work ⟨a *terminal* curriculum⟩
**synonym** see LAST
— **ter·mi·nal·ly** *adverb*
²**terminal** *noun* (1831)
**1 :** a part that forms the end **:** EXTREMITY, TERMINATION
**2 :** a terminating usually ornamental detail **:** FINIAL
**3 :** a device attached to the end of a wire or cable or to an electrical apparatus for convenience in making connections
**4 a :** either end of a carrier line having facilities for the handling of freight and passengers **b :** a freight or passenger station that is central to a considerable area or serves as a junction at any point with other lines **c :** a town or city at the end of a carrier line **:** TERMINUS
**5 :** a combination of a keyboard and output device (as a video display unit) by which data can be entered into or output from a computer or electronic communications system
**terminal leave** *noun* (1944)
**:** a final leave consisting of accumulated unused leave granted to a member of the armed forces just prior to separation or discharge from service
**terminal side** *noun* (1927)
**:** a straight line that has been rotated around a point on another line to form an angle measured in a clockwise or counterclockwise direction — compare INITIAL SIDE
¹**ter·mi·nate** \'tər-mə-nət\ *adjective* [Middle English, from Latin *terminatus*, past participle of *terminare*, from *terminus*] (15th century)
**:** coming to an end or capable of ending
²**ter·mi·nate** \-ˌnāt\ *verb* **-nat·ed; -nat·ing** (1610)
*intransitive verb*
**1 :** to extend only to a limit (as a point or line); *especially* **:** to reach a terminus
**2 :** to form an ending
**3 :** to come to an end in time
*transitive verb*
**1 a :** to bring to an end **:** CLOSE ⟨*terminate* a marriage by divorce⟩ ⟨*terminate* a transmission line⟩ **b :** to form the conclusion of ⟨review questions *terminate* each chapter⟩ **c :** to discontinue the employment of ⟨workers *terminated* because of slow business⟩
**2 :** to serve as an ending, limit, or boundary of **:** CLOSE
**synonym** see CLOSE
**terminating decimal** *noun* (circa 1909)
**:** a decimal which can be expressed in a finite number of figures or for which all figures to the right of some place are zero — compare REPEATING DECIMAL
**ter·mi·na·tion** \ˌtər-mə-'nā-shən\ *noun* (circa 1500)
**1 :** end in time or existence **:** CONCLUSION ⟨the *termination* of life⟩
**2 :** the last part of a word; *especially* **:** an inflectional ending
**3 :** the act of terminating
**4 :** a limit in space or extent **:** BOUND
**5 :** OUTCOME, RESULT
— **ter·mi·na·tion·al** \-shnəl, -shə-nᵊl\ *adjective*
**ter·mi·na·tive** \'tər-mə-ˌnā-tiv\ *adjective* (15th century)
**:** tending or serving to terminate **:** ENDING
— **ter·mi·na·tive·ly** *adverb*
**ter·mi·na·tor** \-ˌnā-tər\ *noun* (1770)
**1 :** the dividing line between the illuminated and the unilluminated part of the moon's or a planet's disk
**2 :** one that terminates
**ter·mi·nol·o·gy** \ˌtər-mə-'nä-lə-jē\ *noun, plural* **-gies** [Medieval Latin *terminus* term, expression (from Latin *terminus* boundary, limit) + English *-o-* + *-logy*] (1801)
**1 :** the technical or special terms used in a business, art, science, or special subject
**2 :** nomenclature as a field of study

— **ter·mi·no·log·i·cal** \-mə-nᵊl-'ä-ji-kəl\ *adjective*
— **ter·mi·no·log·i·cal·ly** \-ji-k(ə-)lē\ *adverb*
**term insurance** *noun* (1897)
**:** insurance for a specified period that provides for no payment to the insured except on losses during the period and that becomes void upon its expiration
**ter·mi·nus** \'tər-mə-nəs\ *noun, plural* **-ni** \-ˌnī, -ˌnē\ *or* **-nus·es** [Latin, boundary, end — more at TERM] (circa 1617)
**1 :** a final goal **:** a finishing point
**2 :** a post or stone marking a boundary
**3 :** either end of a transportation line or travel route; *also* **:** the station, town, or city at such a place **:** TERMINAL
**4 :** an extreme point or element **:** TIP ⟨the *terminus* of a glacier⟩
**terminus ad quem** \-ˌäd-'kwem\ *noun* [New Latin, literally, limit to which] (circa 1555)
**1 :** a goal, object, or course of action **:** DESTINATION, PURPOSE
**2 :** a final limiting point in time
**terminus a quo** \-ˌä-'kwō\ *noun* [New Latin, literally, limit from which] (circa 1555)
**1 :** a point of origin
**2 :** a first limiting point in time
**ter·mi·tar·i·um** \ˌtər-mə-'ter-ē-əm, -ˌmī-\ *noun, plural* **-ia** \-ē-ə\ [New Latin] (1863)
**:** a termites' nest
**ter·mi·tary** \'tər-mə-ˌter-ē, -ˌmī-ˌter-ē\ *noun, plural* **-tar·ies** (1826)
**:** TERMITARIUM
**ter·mite** \'tər-ˌmīt\ *noun* [New Latin *Termit-, Termes*, genus of termites, from Late Latin, a worm that eats wood, alteration of Latin *tarmit-, tarmes;* akin to Greek *tetrainein* to bore — more at THROW] (1781)
**:** any of numerous pale-colored soft-bodied social insects (order Isoptera) that live in colonies consisting usually of winged sexual forms, wingless sterile workers, and soldiers, feed on wood, and include some which are very destructive to wooden structures and trees — called also *white ant*
**term·less** \'tərm-ləs\ *adjective* (circa 1541)
**1 :** having no term or end **:** BOUNDLESS, UNENDING
**2 :** UNCONDITIONED, UNCONDITIONAL
**term paper** *noun* (1926)
**:** a major written assignment in a school or college course representative of a student's achievement during a term
**tern** \'tərn\ *noun* [of Scandinavian origin; akin to Danish *terne* tern] (1678)
**:** any of various chiefly marine birds (subfamily Sterninae of the family Laridae and especially genus *Sterna*) that differ from the related gulls in usually smaller size, a more slender build, a sharply pointed bill, narrower wings, and an often forked tail
**ter·na·ry** \'tər-nə-rē\ *adjective* [Middle English, from Latin *ternarius*, from *terni* three each; akin to Latin *tres* three — more at THREE] (15th century)
**1 a :** of, relating to, or proceeding by threes **b :** having three elements, parts, or divisions **:** THREEFOLD **c :** arranged in threes ⟨*ternary* petals⟩
**2 :** using three as the base ⟨a *ternary* logarithm⟩
**3 a :** being or consisting of an alloy of three elements **b :** of, relating to, or containing three different elements, atoms, radicals, or groups ⟨sulfuric acid is a *ternary* acid⟩
**4 :** third in order or rank
**ter·nate** \'tər-ˌnāt, -nət\ *adjective* [New Latin *ternatus*, from Medieval Latin, past participle of *ternare* to treble, from *terni*] (1760)
**:** arranged in threes or in subdivisions so arranged ⟨a *ternate* leaf⟩
— **ter·nate·ly** *adverb*
**terne** \'tərn\ *noun* [*terneplate*] (1891)

**1 :** an alloy of lead and tin typically in a ratio of four to one that is used as a coating in producing terneplate
**2 :** TERNEPLATE
**terne·plate** \-ˌplāt\ *noun* [probably from French *terne* dull (from Middle French, from *ternir* to tarnish) + English *plate*] (circa 1858)
**:** sheet iron or steel coated with an alloy of about four parts lead to one part tin
**ter·pene** \'tər-ˌpēn\ *noun* [International Scientific Vocabulary *terp-* (from German *Terpentin* turpentine, from Medieval Latin *terbentina*) + *-ene* — more at TURPENTINE] (1873)
**:** any of various isomeric hydrocarbons $C_{10}H_{16}$ found present in essential oils (as from conifers) and used especially as solvents and in organic synthesis; *broadly* **:** any of numerous hydrocarbons $(C_5H_8)n$ found especially in essential oils, resins, and balsams
— **ter·pene·less** \-ləs\ *adjective*
— **ter·pe·noid** \'tər-pə-ˌnȯid, ˌtər-'pē-\ *adjective or noun*
**ter·pin·e·ol** \ˌtər-'pi-nē-ˌȯl, -ˌōl\ *noun* [International Scientific Vocabulary, from *terpine* $(C_{10}H_{18}(OH)_2)$] (1894)
**:** any of three fragrant isomeric alcohols $C_{10}H_{17}OH$ found in essential oils or made artificially and used especially in perfume or as solvents
**ter·poly·mer** \ˌtər-'pä-lə-mər\ *noun* (1947)
**:** a polymer (as a complex resin) that results from copolymerization of three discrete monomers
**Terp·si·cho·re** \ˌtərp-'si-kə-(ˌ)rē\ *noun* [Latin, from Greek *Terpsichorē*]
**:** the Greek Muse of dancing and choral song
**terp·si·cho·re·an** \ˌtərp-(ˌ)si-kə-'rē-ən; -sə-'kȯr-ē-, -'kȯr-\ *adjective* (1825)
**:** of or relating to dancing
**ter·ra** \'ter-ə\ *noun, plural* **ter·rae** \-(ˌ)ē, -ˌī\ [New Latin, from Latin, land] (1946)
**:** any of the relatively light-colored highland areas on the surface of the moon or a planet
¹**ter·race** \'ter-əs\ *noun* [Middle French, pile of earth, platform, terrace, from Old Provençal *terrassa*, from *terra* earth, from Latin, earth, land; akin to Latin *torrēre* to parch — more at THIRST] (1515)
**1 a :** a colonnaded porch or promenade **b :** a flat roof or open platform **c :** a relatively level paved or planted area adjoining a building
**2 a :** a raised embankment with the top leveled **b :** one of usually a series of horizontal ridges made in a hillside to increase cultivable land, conserve moisture, or minimize erosion
**3 :** a level ordinarily narrow plain usually with steep front bordering a river, lake, or sea; *also* **:** a similar undersea feature
**4 a :** a row of houses or apartments on raised ground or a sloping site **b :** a group of row houses **c :** a strip of park in the middle of a street often planted with trees or shrubs **d :** STREET
**5 :** a section of a British soccer stadium set aside for standing spectators
²**terrace** *transitive verb* **ter·raced; ter·rac·ing** (1615)
**1 :** to provide (as a building or hillside) with a terrace
**2 :** to make into a terrace
**ter·ra-cot·ta** \ˌter-ə-'kä-tə\ *noun, often attributive* [Italian *terra cotta*, literally, baked earth] (1722)
**1 :** a glazed or unglazed fired clay used especially for statuettes and vases and architectural purposes (as roofing, facing, and relief ornamentation)
**2 :** a brownish orange

\ə\ **abut** \ᵊ\ **kitten** \ər\ **further** \a\ **ash** \ā\ **ace**
\ä\ **mop, mar** \au̇\ **out** \ch\ **chin** \e\ **bet** \ē\ **easy**
\g\ **go** \i\ **hit** \ī\ **ice** \j\ **job** \ŋ\ **sing** \ō\ **go**
\ȯ\ **law** \ȯi\ **boy** \th\ **thin** \t͟h\ **the** \ü\ **loot** \u̇\ **foot**
\y\ **yet** \zh\ **vision** *see also* Guide to Pronunciation

**terra fir·ma** \-'fər-mə *also* -'fir-\ *noun* [New Latin, literally, solid land] (1693)
: dry land : solid ground

**ter·rain** \tə-'rān *also* te-\ *noun* [French, land, ground, from (assumed) Vulgar Latin *terranum*, alteration of Latin *terrenum*, from neuter of *terrenus* of earth — more at TERRENE] (1766)
**1 a** (1) : a geographical area (2) : a piece of land : GROUND **b** : the physical features of a tract of land
**2** : TERRANE 1
**3 a** : a field of knowledge or interest : TERRITORY **b** : ENVIRONMENT, MILIEU

**ter·ra in·cog·ni·ta** \'ter-ə-,in-,käg-'nē-tə, -in-'käg-nə-tə\ *noun, plural* **ter·rae in·cog·ni·tae** \'ter-,ī-,in-,käg-'nē-,tī, -in-'käg-nə-,tī\ [Latin] (1616)
: unknown territory : an unexplored country or field of knowledge

**Ter·ra·my·cin** \,ter-ə-'mī-sᵊn\ *trademark*
— used for oxytetracycline

**ter·rane** \tə-'rān, te-\ *noun* [alteration of *terrain*] (1864)
**1** : the area or surface over which a particular rock or group of rocks is prevalent
**2** : TERRAIN 1a

**ter·ra·pin** \'ter-ə-pən, 'tar-\ *noun* [of Algonquian origin; akin to Delaware (dialect of New York) *tó'lpe'w*, a kind of turtle] (1613)
: any of various aquatic turtles (family Emydidae); *especially* : DIAMONDBACK TERRAPIN

terrapin

**ter·ra·que·ous** \te-'rā-kwē-əs, tə-, -'ra-\ *adjective* [Latin *terra* land + English *aqueous*] (circa 1658)
: consisting of land and water

**ter·rar·i·um** \tə-'rar-ē-əm, -'rer-\ *noun, plural* **-ia** \-ē-ə\ *or* **-i·ums** [New Latin, from Latin *terra* + *-arium* (as in *vivarium*)] (1890)
: a usually transparent enclosure for keeping or raising plants or usually small animals (as turtles) indoors

**ter·raz·zo** \tə-'ra-(,)zō, -'rät-(,)sō\ *noun* [Italian, literally, terrace, perhaps from Old Provençal *terrassa*] (1897)
: a mosaic flooring consisting of small pieces of marble or granite set in mortar and given a high polish

**¹ter·rene** \te-'rēn, tə-; 'ter-,ēn\ *adjective* [Middle English, from Latin *terrenus* of earth, from *terra* earth] (14th century)
: MUNDANE, EARTHLY

**²terrene** *noun* (1667)
: a land area : EARTH, TERRAIN

**ter·re·plein** \'ter-ə-,plān\ *noun* [Middle French, from Old Italian *terrapieno*, from Medieval Latin *terraplenum*, from *terra plenus* filled with earth] (1591)
: the level space behind a parapet of a rampart where guns are mounted

**ter·res·tri·al** \tə-'res-t(r)ē-əl; -'res-chəl, -'resh-\ *adjective* [Middle English, from Latin *terrestris*, from *terra* earth — more at TERRACE] (15th century)
**1 a** : of or relating to the earth or its inhabitants ⟨*terrestrial* magnetism⟩ **b** : mundane in scope or character : PROSAIC
**2 a** : of or relating to land as distinct from air or water ⟨*terrestrial* transportation⟩ **b** (1) : living on or in or growing from land ⟨*terrestrial* plants⟩ (2) : of or relating to terrestrial organisms ⟨*terrestrial* habits⟩
**3** : belonging to the class of planets that are like the earth (as in density and silicate composition) ⟨the *terrestrial* planets Mercury, Venus, and Mars⟩
— **terrestrial** *noun*
— **ter·res·tri·al·ly** *adverb*

**ter·ret** \'ter-ət\ *noun* [Middle English *turette*, alteration of *toret*, from Middle French, from Old French, diminutive of *tour* circuit, ring — more at TURN] (15th century)

: one of the rings on the top of a harness pad through which the reins pass

**ter·ri·ble** \'ter-ə-bəl\ *adjective* [Middle English, from Middle French, from Latin *terribilis*, from *terrēre* to frighten — more at TERROR] (15th century)
**1 a** : exciting extreme alarm or intense fear : TERRIFYING **b** : formidable in nature : AWESOME ⟨a *terrible* responsibility⟩ **c** : DIFFICULT ⟨in a *terrible* bind⟩
**2** : EXTREME, GREAT ⟨a *terrible* disappointment⟩
**3** : extremely bad: as **a** : strongly repulsive : OBNOXIOUS ⟨a *terrible* smell⟩ **b** : notably unattractive or objectionable **c** : of very poor quality ⟨a *terrible* movie⟩
— **ter·ri·ble·ness** *noun*
— **ter·ri·bly** \-blē\ *adverb*

**ter·ric·o·lous** \te-'ri-kə-ləs, tə-\ *adjective* [Latin *terricola* earth dweller, from *terra* earth + *colere* to inhabit — more at WHEEL] (circa 1836)
: living on or in the ground

**ter·ri·er** \'ter-ē-ər\ *noun* [Middle English, from Middle French (*chien*) *terrier*, literally, earth dog, from *terrier* of earth, from Medieval Latin *terrarius*, from Latin *terra*] (15th century)
: any of various usually small dogs originally used by hunters to dig for small furred game and engage the quarry underground or drive it out

**ter·rif·ic** \tə-'ri-fik\ *adjective* [Latin *terrificus*, from *terrēre* to frighten] (1667)
**1 a** : very bad : FRIGHTFUL **b** : exciting or fit to excite fear or awe
**2** : EXTRAORDINARY ⟨*terrific* speed⟩
**3** : unusually fine : MAGNIFICENT ⟨*terrific* weather⟩
— **ter·rif·i·cal·ly** \-fi-k(ə-)lē\ *adverb*

**ter·ri·fy** \'ter-ə-,fī\ *transitive verb* **-fied; -fy·ing** [Latin *terrificare*, from *terrificus*] (1575)
**1 a** : to drive or impel by menacing : SCARE **b** : DETER, INTIMIDATE
**2** : to fill with terror

**ter·ri·fy·ing** \-,fī-iŋ\ *adjective* (circa 1586)
**1** : causing terror or apprehension
**2** : of a formidable nature
— **ter·ri·fy·ing·ly** \-iŋ-lē\ *adverb*

**ter·rig·e·nous** \te-'ri-jə-nəs, tə-\ *adjective* [Latin *terrigena* earthborn, from *terra* earth + *gignere* to beget — more at KIN] (1882)
: being or relating to oceanic sediment derived directly from the destruction of rocks on the earth's surface

**ter·rine** \tə-'rēn, ter-'ēn\ *noun* [French — more at TUREEN] (circa 1706)
**1 a** : TUREEN 1 **b** : a usually earthenware dish in which foods are cooked and served
**2** : a mixture of chopped meat, fish, or vegetables cooked and served in a terrine

**¹ter·ri·to·ri·al** \,ter-ə-'tōr-ē-əl, -'tòr-\ *adjective* (1625)
**1 a** : NEARBY, LOCAL **b** : serving outlying areas : REGIONAL
**2 a** : of or relating to a territory ⟨*territorial* government⟩ **b** : of or relating to or organized chiefly for home defense ⟨a *territorial* army⟩ **c** : of or relating to private property
**3 a** : of or relating to an assigned or preempted area ⟨*territorial* commanders⟩ **b** : exhibiting territoriality ⟨*territorial* birds⟩
— **ter·ri·to·ri·al·ly** \-ē-ə-lē\ *adverb*

**²territorial** *noun* (1907)
: a member of a territorial military unit

**territorial court** *noun* (1857)
: a court in a U.S. territory that has jurisdiction over local and federal cases

**ter·ri·to·ri·al·ism** \,ter-ə-'tōr-ē-ə-,li-zəm, -'tòr-\ *noun* (1881)
**1** : LANDLORDISM
**2** : the principle established in 1555 requiring the inhabitants of a territory of the Holy Roman Empire to conform to the religion of their ruler or emigrate
— **ter·ri·to·ri·al·ist** \-list\ *noun*

**ter·ri·to·ri·al·i·ty** \,tōr-ē-'a-lə-tē, -,tòr-\ *noun* (1894)

**1** : territorial status
**2 a** : persistent attachment to a specific territory **b** : the pattern of behavior associated with the defense of a territory

**ter·ri·to·ri·al·ize** \-'tōr-ē-ə-,līz, -'tòr-\ *transitive verb* **-ized; -iz·ing** (1818)
: to organize on a territorial basis
— **ter·ri·to·ri·al·i·za·tion** \-,tōr-ē-ə-lə-'zā-shən, -,tòr-\ *noun*

**territorial waters** *noun plural* (1841)
: the waters under the sovereign jurisdiction of a nation or state including both marginal sea and inland waters

**ter·ri·to·ry** \'ter-ə-,tōr-ē, -,tòr-\ *noun, plural* **-ries** [Middle English, from Latin *territorium*, literally, land around a town, from *terra* land — more at TERRACE] (15th century)
**1 a** : a geographical area belonging to or under the jurisdiction of a governmental authority **b** : an administrative subdivision of a country **c** : a part of the U.S. not included within any state but organized with a separate legislature **d** : a geographical area (as a colonial possession) dependent on an external government but having some degree of autonomy
**2 a** : an indeterminate geographical area **b** : a field of knowledge or interest
**3 a** : an assigned area; *especially* : one in which a sales representative or distributor operates **b** : an area often including a nesting or denning site and a variable foraging range that is occupied and defended by an animal or group of animals
— **go with the territory** *or* **come with the territory** : to be a natural or unavoidable aspect or accompaniment of a particular situation, position, or field ⟨criticism *goes with the territory* in this job⟩

**ter·ror** \'ter-ər\ *noun* [Middle English, from Middle French *terreur*, from Latin *terror*, from *terrēre* to frighten; akin to Greek *trein* to be afraid, flee, *tremein* to tremble — more at TREMBLE] (14th century)
**1** : a state of intense fear
**2 a** : one that inspires fear : SCOURGE **b** : a frightening aspect ⟨the *terrors* of invasion⟩ **c** : a cause of anxiety : WORRY **d** : an appalling person or thing; *especially* : BRAT
**3** : REIGN OF TERROR
**4** : violence (as bombing) committed by groups in order to intimidate a population or government into granting their demands ⟨insurrection and revolutionary *terror*⟩
*synonym* see FEAR
— **ter·ror·less** \-ləs\ *adjective*

**ter·ror·ise** *chiefly British variant of* TERRORIZE

**ter·ror·ism** \'ter-ər-,i-zəm\ *noun* (1795)
: the systematic use of terror especially as a means of coercion
— **ter·ror·ist** \-ər-ist\ *adjective or noun*
— **ter·ror·is·tic** \,ter-ər-'is-tik\ *adjective*

**ter·ror·ize** \'ter-ər-,īz\ *transitive verb* **-ized; -iz·ing** (1823)
**1** : to fill with terror or anxiety : SCARE
**2** : to coerce by threat or violence
— **ter·ror·i·za·tion** \,ter-ər-ə-'zā-shən\ *noun*

**ter·ry** \'ter-ē\ *noun, plural* **terries** [perhaps modification of French *tiré*, past participle of *tirer* to draw] (1784)
**1** : the loop forming the pile in uncut pile fabrics
**2** : an absorbent fabric with such loops — called also *terry cloth*

**terse** \'tərs\ *adjective* **ters·er; ters·est** [Latin *tersus* clean, neat, from past participle of *tergēre* to wipe off] (1601)
**1** : smoothly elegant : POLISHED
**2** : devoid of superfluity ⟨a *terse* summary⟩; *also* : SHORT, BRUSQUE ⟨dismissed me with a *terse* "no"⟩
*synonym* see CONCISE
— **terse·ly** *adverb*
— **terse·ness** *noun*

**¹ter·tian** \'tər-shən\ *adjective* [Middle English *tercian,* from Latin *tertianus,* literally, of the third, from *tertius* third — more at THIRD] (14th century)
: recurring at approximately 48-hour intervals — used of malaria

**²tertian** *noun* (14th century)
: a tertian fever (as vivax malaria)

**¹ter·tia·ry** \'tər-shē-,er-ē, -shə-rē\ *noun, plural* **-ries** (circa 1550)
**1** [Medieval Latin *tertiarius,* from Latin, of a third] : a member of a monastic third order especially of lay people
**2** *capitalized* : the Tertiary period or system of rocks

**²tertiary** *adjective* [Latin *tertiarius* of or containing a third, from *tertius* third] (circa 1656)
**1 a** : of third rank, importance, or value **b** *chiefly British* : of, relating to, or being higher education **c** : of, relating to, or constituting the third strongest of the three or four degrees of stress recognized by most linguists (as the stress of the third syllable of *basketball team*)
**2** *capitalized* : of, relating to, or being the first period of the Cenozoic era or the corresponding system of rocks marked by the formation of high mountains (as the Alps, Caucasus, and Himalayas) and the dominance of mammals on land — see GEOLOGIC TIME table
**3 a** : involving or resulting from the substitution of three atoms or groups ⟨a *tertiary* salt⟩ ⟨*tertiary* amine⟩ **b** : being or containing a carbon atom having bonds to three other carbon atoms ⟨an acid containing a *tertiary* carbon⟩ ⟨*tertiary* alcohols⟩
**4** : occurring in or being a third stage: as **a** : being or relating to the recovery of oil and gas from old wells by means of the underground application of heat and chemicals **b** : being or relating to the purification of wastewater by removal of fine particles, nitrates, and phosphates

**tertiary color** *noun* (circa 1864)
**1** : a color produced by mixing two secondary colors
**2** : a color produced by an equal mixture of a primary color with a secondary color adjacent to it on the color wheel

**tertiary syphilis** *noun* (1875)
: the third stage of syphilis that develops after the disappearance of the secondary symptoms and is marked by ulcers in and gummas under the skin and commonly by involvement of the skeletal, cardiovascular, and nervous systems

**ter·ti·um quid** \,tər-shē-əm-'kwid, ,tər-tē-\ *noun* [Late Latin, literally, third something; from its failing to fit into a dichotomy] (circa 1724)
**1** : a middle course or an intermediate component ⟨where there are two systems of law and two orders of courts, there must . . . be some *tertium quid* to deal with conflicts of law and jurisdiction —Ernest Baker⟩
**2** : a third party of ambiguous status ⟨there was a man and his wife and a *tertium quid* —Rudyard Kipling⟩

**ter·va·lent** \,tər-'vā-lənt, 'tər-\ *adjective* (circa 1903)
: TRIVALENT

**ter·za ri·ma** \,tert-sə-'rē-mə\ *noun* [Italian, literally, third rhyme] (1819)
: a verse form consisting of tercets usually in iambic pentameter in English poetry with an interlaced rhyme scheme (as *aba, bcb, cdc*)

**tes·la** \'tes-lə\ *noun* [Nikola *Tesla*] (1958)
: a unit of magnetic flux density in the meter-kilogram-second system equivalent to one weber per square meter

**tes·sel·late** \'te-sə-,lāt\ *transitive verb* **-lat·ed; -lat·ing** [Late Latin *tessellatus,* past participle of *tessellare* to pave with tesserae, from Latin *tessella,* diminutive of *tessera*] (1789)
: to form into or adorn with mosaic

**tes·sel·lat·ed** \-,lā-təd\ *adjective* (1695)
: having a checkered appearance

**tes·sel·la·tion** \,te-sə-'lā-shən\ *noun* (1660)
**1** : MOSAIC; *especially* : a covering of an infinite geometric plane without gaps or overlaps by congruent plane figures of one type or a few types
**2** : an act of tessellating : the state of being tessellated

**tes·sera** \'te-sə-rə\ *noun, plural* **-ser·ae** \-,rē, -,rī\ [Latin, probably ultimately from Greek *tessares* four; from its having four corners — more at FOUR] (circa 1656)
**1** : a small tablet (as of wood, bone, or ivory) used by the ancient Romans as a ticket, tally, voucher, or means of identification
**2** : a small piece (as of marble, glass, or tile) used in mosaic work

**tes·ser·act** \'te-sə-,rakt\ *noun* [Greek *tessares* four + *aktis* ray — more at ACTIN-] (1888)
: the four-dimensional analogue of a cube

**tes·si·tu·ra** \,te-sə-'túr-ə\ *noun* [Italian, literally, texture, from Latin *textura*] (circa 1891)
: the general range of a melody or voice part; *specifically* : the part of the register in which most of the tones of a melody or voice part lie

**¹test** \'test\ *noun* [Middle English, vessel in which metals were assayed, cupel, from Middle French, from Latin *testum* earthen vessel; akin to Latin *testa* earthen pot, shell] (14th century)
**1 a** *chiefly British* : CUPEL **b** (1) : a critical examination, observation, or evaluation : TRIAL; *specifically* : the procedure of submitting a statement to such conditions or operations as will lead to its proof or disproof or to its acceptance or rejection ⟨a *test* of a statistical hypothesis⟩ (2) : a basis for evaluation : CRITERION **c** : an ordeal or oath required as proof of conformity with a set of beliefs
**2 a** : a means of testing: as (1) : a procedure, reaction, or reagent used to identify or characterize a substance or constituent (2) : something (as a series of questions or exercises) for measuring the skill, knowledge, intelligence, capacities, or aptitudes of an individual or group **b** : a positive result in such a test
**3** : a result or value determined by testing
**4** : TEST MATCH ◆

**²test** (1689)
*transitive verb*
**1** : to put to test or proof : TRY
**2** : to require a doctrinal oath of
*intransitive verb*
**1 a** : to undergo a test **b** : to be assigned a standing or evaluation on the basis of tests ⟨*tested* positive for cocaine⟩ ⟨the cake *tested* done⟩
**2** : to apply a test as a means of analysis or diagnosis — used with *for* ⟨*test* for mechanical aptitude⟩
— **test·abil·i·ty** \,tes-tə-'bi-lə-tē\ *noun*
— **test·able** \'tes-tə-bəl\ *adjective*
— **test the waters** *also* **test the water**
: to make a preliminary test or survey (as of reaction or interest) before embarking on a course of action

**³test** *noun* [Latin *testa* shell] (circa 1842)
: an external hard and firm covering (as a shell) of many invertebrates (as a foraminifer or a mollusk)

**tes·ta** \'tes-tə\ *noun, plural* **tes·tae** \-,tē, -,tī\ [New Latin, from Latin, shell] (1796)
: the hard external coating or integument of a seed

**tes·ta·ceous** \tes-'tā-shəs\ *adjective* [Latin *testaceus,* from *testa* shell, earthen pot, brick] (1646)
**1** : having a shell ⟨a *testaceous* protozoan⟩
**2** : of any of the several light colors of bricks

**tes·ta·cy** \'tes-tə-sē\ *noun, plural* **-cies** (circa 1864)
: the state of being testate

**tes·ta·ment** \'tes-tə-mənt\ *noun* [Middle English, from Late Latin & Latin; Late Latin *testamentum* covenant with God, holy scripture, from Latin, last will, from *testari* to be a witness, call to witness, make a will, from *testis* witness; akin to Latin *tres* three & to Latin *stare* to stand; from the witness's standing by as a third party in a litigation — more at THREE, STAND] (14th century)
**1 a** *archaic* : a covenant between God and the human race **b** *capitalized* : either of two main divisions of the Bible
**2 a** : a tangible proof or tribute **b** : an expression of conviction : CREDO
**3 a** : an act by which a person determines the disposition of his or her property after death **b** : WILL
— **tes·ta·men·ta·ry** \,tes-tə-'men-tə-rē, -'men-trē\ *adjective*

**tes·tate** \'tes-,tāt, -tət\ *adjective* [Middle English, from Latin *testatus,* past participle of *testari* to make a will] (14th century)
: having left a valid will ⟨she died *testate*⟩

**tes·ta·tor** \'tes-,tā-tər, tes-'\ *noun* [Middle English *testatour,* from Anglo-French, from Late Latin *testator,* from Latin *testari*] (15th century)
: a person who dies leaving a will or testament in force

**tes·ta·trix** \'tes-,tā-triks, tes-'\ *noun* [Late Latin, feminine of *testator*] (1591)
: a female testator

**test ban** *noun* (1958)
: a self-imposed partial or complete ban on the testing of nuclear weapons that is mutually agreed to by countries possessing such weapons

**test bed** *noun* (1914)
: a vehicle (as an airplane) used for testing new equipment (as engines or weapons systems)

**test case** *noun* (1894)
**1** : a representative case whose outcome is likely to serve as a precedent
**2** : a proceeding brought by agreement or on an understanding of the parties to obtain a decision as to the constitutionality of a statute

**test·cross** \'tes(t)-,krós\ *noun* (1934)
: a genetic cross between a homozygous recessive individual and a corresponding suspected heterozygote to determine the genotype of the latter
— **testcross** *transitive verb*

**test-drive** \'tes(t)-,drīv\ *transitive verb* **-drove** \-,drōv\; **-driv·en** \-,dri-vən\; **-driv·ing** \-,drī-viŋ\ (1950)

◇ **WORD HISTORY**
**test** Latin *testu* or *testum* was a generally used word for an earthenware pot. In the Middle Ages its descendant in Old French, *test,* denoted a specific type of vessel that was used in the assaying of precious metals, namely, a cupel. The cupel or test is a shallow, porous cup. When impure silver or gold is heated in it, the impurities are absorbed in the porous material, leaving a relatively pure button of silver or gold. As the name for a cupel, *test* was borrowed into later Middle English as *test* or *teste.* By about 1600 it was being used figuratively: *to put to the test* or *to bring to the test* was to make trial of something, to determine its quality or genuineness, as a precious metal might be tried in a cupel. The sense "trial, critical examination" soon became the most common meaning of *test.* French *têt,* the modern outcome of Old French *test,* has retained only its limited reference to an assayer's cupel; but Latin *testa* "earthenware jar, shard, shell," a feminine noun closely related to *testu,* went off in a quite different figurative direction, developing in French into *tête,* the usual word for "head."

: to drive (a motor vehicle) in order to evaluate performance
— **test–drive** *noun*

**test·ed** \'tes-təd\ *adjective* (1748)
: subjected to or qualified through testing — often used in combination ⟨time-*tested* principles⟩

**test·ee** \tes-'tē\ *noun* (1930)
: one who takes an examination

¹**tes·ter** \'tes-tər, 'tes-\ *noun* [Middle English, from Middle French *testiere* headpiece, head covering, from *teste* head, from Late Latin *testa* skull, from Latin, shell] (14th century)
: the canopy over a bed, pulpit, or altar

²**tes·ter** \'tes-tər\ *noun* [modification of Middle French *testart*, from *teston*] (1546)
: TESTON a

³**test·er** \'tes-tər\ *noun* (1661)
: one that tests or is used for testing

**test–fly** \-,flī\ *transitive verb* **-flew** \-,flü\; **-flown** \-,flōn\; **-fly·ing** (1936)
: to subject to a flight test ⟨*test-fly* an experimental plane⟩

**tes·ti·cle** \'tes-ti-kəl\ *noun* [Middle English *testicule*, from Latin *testiculus*, diminutive of *testis*] (15th century)
: TESTIS; *especially* : one of a higher mammal usually with its enclosing structures
— **tes·tic·u·lar** \tes-'ti-kyə-lər\ *adjective*

**tes·ti·fy** \'tes-tə-,fī\ *verb* **-fied; -fy·ing** [Middle English *testifien*, from Latin *testificari*, from *testis* witness] (14th century)
*intransitive verb*
**1 a** : to make a statement based on personal knowledge or belief : bear witness **b** : to serve as evidence or proof
**2** : to express a personal conviction
**3** : to make a solemn declaration under oath for the purpose of establishing a fact (as in a court)
*transitive verb*
**1 a** : to bear witness to : ATTEST **b** : to serve as evidence of : PROVE
**2** *archaic* **a** : to make known (a personal conviction) **b** : to give evidence of : SHOW
**3** : to declare under oath before a tribunal or officially constituted public body
— **tes·ti·fi·er** \-,fī-(ə)r\ *noun*

¹**tes·ti·mo·ni·al** \,tes-tə-'mō-nē-əl, -nyəl\ *adjective* (15th century)
**1** : of, relating to, or constituting testimony
**2** : expressive of appreciation or esteem ⟨a *testimonial* dinner⟩

²**testimonial** *noun* (15th century)
**1** : EVIDENCE, TESTIMONY
**2 a** : a statement testifying to benefits received **b** : a character reference : letter of recommendation
**3** : an expression of appreciation : TRIBUTE

**tes·ti·mo·ny** \'tes-tə-,mō-nē\ *noun, plural* **-nies** [Middle English, from Latin & Late Latin; Late Latin *testimonium* Decalogue, from Latin, evidence, witness, from *testis* witness — more at TESTAMENT] (14th century)
**1 a** (1) : the tablets inscribed with the Mosaic law (2) : the ark containing the tablets **b** : a divine decree attested in the Scriptures
**2 a** : firsthand authentication of a fact : EVIDENCE **b** : an outward sign **c** : a solemn declaration usually made orally by a witness under oath in response to interrogation by a lawyer or authorized public official
**3 a** : an open acknowledgment **b** : a public profession of religious experience

**test·ing** *adjective* (1878)
: requiring maximum effort or ability ⟨a most difficult and *testing* problem —Ernest Bevin⟩

**tes·tis** \'tes-təs\ *noun, plural* **tes·tes** \'tes-,tēz\ [Latin, witness, testis] (circa 1704)
: a typically paired male reproductive gland that produces sperm and that in most mammals is contained within the scrotum at sexual maturity

**test–mar·ket** \'tes(t)-,mär-kət\ *transitive verb* (1953)
: to subject (a product) to trial in a limited market

**test match** *noun* (1862)
**1** : any of a series of championship cricket matches played between teams representing Australia and England
**2** : a championship game or series (as of cricket) played between teams representing different countries

**tes·ton** \'tes-,tän\ *or* **tes·toon** \tes-'tün\ *noun* [Middle French, from Old Italian *testone*, augmentative of *testa* head, from Late Latin, skull — more at TESTER] (1536)
: any of several old European coins: as **a** : a shilling of Henry VIII of England decreasing in value to ninepence and then to sixpence in Shakespeare's time **b** : a French silver coin of the 16th century worth between 10 and 14½ sous

**tes·tos·ter·one** \te-'stäs-tə-,rōn\ *noun* [*testis* + *-o-* + *-sterone*] (1935)
: a hormone that is a hydroxy steroid ketone $C_{19}H_{28}O_2$ produced especially by the testes or made synthetically and that is responsible for inducing and maintaining male secondary sex characters

**test pattern** *noun* (circa 1946)
: a fixed picture broadcast by a television station to assist viewers in adjusting their receivers

**test pilot** *noun* (1917)
: a pilot who specializes in putting new or experimental airplanes through maneuvers designed to test them (as for strength) by producing strains in excess of normal

**test–tube** *adjective* (1935)
: produced by fertilization in laboratory apparatus and implantation in the uterus, by fertilization and growth in laboratory apparatus, or sometimes by artificial insemination ⟨*test-tube* babies⟩

**test tube** *noun* (1846)
: a plain or lipped tube usually of thin glass closed at one end and used especially in chemistry and biology

**tes·tu·do** \tes-'tü-(,)dō, -'tyü-\ *noun, plural* **-dos** [Latin *testudin-, testudo*, literally, tortoise, tortoise shell; akin to Latin *testa* shell] (1609)
: a cover of overlapping shields or a shed wheeled up to a wall used by the ancient Romans to protect an attacking force

**tes·ty** \'tes-tē\ *adjective* **tes·ti·er; -est** [Middle English *testif*, from Anglo-French, headstrong, from Old French *teste* head — more at TESTER] (1526)
**1** : easily annoyed : IRRITABLE
**2** : marked by impatience or ill humor ⟨*testy* remarks⟩
— **tes·ti·ly** \-tə-lē\ *adverb*
— **tes·ti·ness** \-tē-nəs\ *noun*

**Tet** \'tet\ *noun* [Vietnamese *tết*] (1885)
: the Vietnamese New Year observed for three days beginning at the first new moon after January 20

**tet·a·nal** \'te-tᵊn-əl\ *adjective* (1939)
: of, relating to, or derived from tetanus ⟨*tetanal* toxin⟩

**te·tan·ic** \te-'ta-nik\ *adjective* (circa 1727)
: of, relating to, being, or tending to produce tetany or tetanus
— **te·tan·i·cal·ly** \-ni-k(ə-)lē\ *adverb*

**tet·a·nize** \'te-tᵊn-,īz\ *transitive verb* **-nized; -niz·ing** (1849)
: to induce tetanus in ⟨*tetanize* a muscle⟩
— **tet·a·ni·za·tion** \,te-tᵊn-ə-'zā-shən, ,tet-nə-\ *noun*

**tet·a·nus** \'te-tᵊn-əs, 'tet-nəs\ *noun* [Middle English, from Latin, from Greek *tetanos*, from *tetanos* stretched, rigid; akin to Greek *teinein* to stretch — more at THIN] (14th century)
**1 a** : an acute infectious disease characterized by tonic spasm of voluntary muscles especially of the jaw and caused by the specific toxin of a bacterium (*Clostridium tetani*) which is usually introduced through a wound — compare LOCKJAW **b** : the bacterium that causes tetanus
**2** : prolonged contraction of a muscle resulting from rapidly repeated motor impulses

**tet·a·ny** \'te-tᵊn-ē, 'tet-nē\ *noun* [International Scientific Vocabulary, from Latin *tetanus*] (circa 1885)
: a condition of physiologic calcium imbalance marked by tonic spasm of muscles and often associated with deficient parathyroid secretion

**te·tar·to·he·dral** \te-,tär-tə-'hē-drəl\ *adjective* [Greek *tetartos* fourth; akin to Greek *tettares* four — more at FOUR] (circa 1858)
*of a crystal* : having one fourth the number of planes required by complete symmetry — compare HEMIHEDRAL, HOLOHEDRAL

**tetched** *variant of* TECHED

**tetchy** \'te-chē\ *adjective* **tetch·i·er; -est** [perhaps from obsolete *tetch* habit] (1592)
: irritably or peevishly sensitive : TOUCHY ⟨the *tetchy* manner of two women living in the same house —Elizabeth Taylor (died 1975)⟩
— **tetch·i·ly** \-chə-lē\ *adverb*
— **tetch·i·ness** \-chē-nəs\ *noun*

¹**tête–à–tête** \,tet-ə-'tet, ,tāt-ə-'tāt, *2 is also* 'tēt-ə-,tēt\ *noun* [French, literally, head to head] (1697)
**1** : a private conversation between two persons
**2** : a short piece of furniture (as a sofa) intended to seat two persons especially facing each other

²**tête–à–tête** \,tet-ə-'tet, ,tāt-ə-'tāt\ *adverb* (1700)
: in private

³**tête–à–tête** \,tet-ə-,tet, ,tāt-ə-,tāt\ *adjective* (1728)
: FACE-TO-FACE, PRIVATE

**tête–bêche** \'tet-'besh\ *adjective* [French, noun, pair of inverted stamps, from *tête* head + *-bêche*, alteration of Middle French *bechevet* head against foot] (circa 1913)
: of or relating to a pair of stamps inverted in relation to one another either through a printing error or intentionally

**teth** \'tāt, 'tāth, 'tās\ *noun* [Hebrew *ṭēth*] (circa 1823)
: the 9th letter of the Hebrew alphabet — see ALPHABET table

¹**teth·er** \'te-thər\ *noun* [Middle English *tethir*, probably of Scandinavian origin; akin to Old Norse *tjōthr* tether; akin to Old High German *zeotar* pole of a wagon] (14th century)
**1** : something (as a rope or chain) by which an animal is fastened so that it can range only within a set radius
**2** : the limit of one's strength or resources ⟨at the end of my *tether*⟩

²**tether** *transitive verb* **teth·ered; teth·er·ing** \-th(ə-)riŋ\ (15th century)
: to fasten or restrain by or as if by a tether

**teth·er·ball** \'te-thər-,bȯl\ *noun* (circa 1900)
: a game played with a ball suspended by a string from an upright pole in which the object for each contestant is to wrap the string around the pole by striking the ball in a direction opposite to that of the other contestant; *also* : the ball used in this game

**Te·thys** \'tē-thəs\ *noun* [Latin, from Greek *Tēthys*]
: a Titaness and wife of Oceanus

**tet·ra** \'te-trə\ *noun* [by shortening from New Latin *Tetragonopterus*, former genus name, from Late Latin *tetragonum* quadrangle + Greek *pteron* wing — more at TETRAGONAL, FEATHER] (1931)
: any of numerous small often brightly colored South American characin fishes often bred in tropical aquariums

**tetra-** *or* **tetr-** *combining form* [Middle English, from Latin, from Greek; akin to Greek *tettares* four — more at FOUR]
**1** : four : having four : having four parts ⟨*tetra*valent⟩

**2 :** containing four atoms or groups (of a specified kind) ⟨*tetra*chloride⟩

**tet·ra·caine** \'te-trə-ˌkān\ *noun* [*tetra-* + *-caine*] (circa 1935)
: a crystalline basic ester $C_{15}H_{24}N_2O_2$ that is closely related chemically to procaine and is used chiefly in the form of its hydrochloride as a local anesthetic

**tet·ra·chlo·ride** \ˌte-trə-'klōr-ˌīd, -'klȯr-\ *noun* (1866)
: a chloride containing four atoms of chlorine

**tet·ra·chord** \'te-trə-ˌkȯrd\ *noun* [Greek *tetrachordon*, from neuter of *tetrachordos* of four strings, from *tetra-* + *chordē* string — more at YARN] (1603)
: a diatonic series of four tones with an interval of a perfect fourth between the first and last

**tet·ra·cy·cline** \ˌte-trə-'sī-ˌklēn\ *noun* [International Scientific Vocabulary *tetracyclic* having four fused hydrocarbon rings + ²-*ine*] (1952)
: a yellow crystalline broad-spectrum antibiotic $C_{22}H_{24}N_2O_8$ produced by streptomyces or synthetically

**tet·rad** \'te-ˌtrad\ *noun* [Greek *tetrad-, tetras*, from *tetra-*] (1653)
: a group or arrangement of four: as **a :** a group of four cells produced by the successive divisions of a mother cell ⟨a *tetrad* of spores⟩ **b :** a group of four synapsed chromatids that become visibly evident in the pachytene stage of meiotic prophase
— **te·trad·ic** \te-'tra-dik\ *adjective*

**tet·ra·drachm** \'te-trə-ˌdram\ *noun* [Greek *tetradrachmon*, from *tetra-* + *drachmē* drachma] (circa 1580)
: an ancient Greek silver coin worth four drachmas

**tet·ra·dy·na·mous** \ˌte-trə-'dī-nə-məs\ *adjective* [International Scientific Vocabulary *tetra-* + Greek *dynamis* power — more at DYNAMIC] (1830)
: having six stamens four of which are longer than the others ⟨*tetradynamous* plants of the mustard family⟩

**tet·ra·eth·yl lead** \ˌte-trə-ˌe-thəl-'led\ *noun* (1923)
: a heavy oily poisonous liquid $Pb(C_2H_5)_4$ used as an antiknock agent

**tet·ra·flu·o·ride** \ˌte-trə-'flȯr-ˌīd, -'flu̇r-\ *noun* (circa 1909)
: a fluoride containing four atoms of fluorine

**tet·rag·o·nal** \te-'tra-gə-n°l\ *adjective* [Late Latin *tetragonalis* having four angles and four sides, from *tetragonum* quadrangle, from Greek *tetragōnon*, from neuter of *tetragōnos* tetragonal, from *tetra-* + *gōnia* angle — more at -GON] (1868)
: of, relating to, or characteristic of the tetragonal system
— **te·trag·o·nal·ly** \-n°l-ē\ *adverb*

**tetragonal system** *noun* (1879)
: a crystal system characterized by three axes at right angles of which only the two lateral axes are equal

**tet·ra·gram·ma·ton** \ˌte-trə-'gra-mə-ˌtän\ *noun* [Middle English, from Greek, from neuter of *tetragrammatos* having four letters, from *tetra-* + *grammat-, gramma* letter — more at GRAM] (15th century)
: the four Hebrew letters usually transliterated YHWH or JHVH that form a biblical proper name of God — compare YAHWEH

**tet·ra·he·dral** \ˌte-trə-'hē-drəl\ *adjective* (1794)
**1 :** being a polyhedral angle with four faces **2 :** relating to, forming, or having the form of a tetrahedron
— **tet·ra·he·dral·ly** \-drə-lē\ *adverb*

**tet·ra·he·drite** \-ˌdrīt\ *noun* [German *Tetraëdrit*, from Late Greek *tetraedros* having four faces] (1868)
: a fine-grained gray mineral that consists of a sulfide of copper, iron, and antimony, often

contains other elements (as silver), and occurs in tetrahedral crystals or in massive form

**tet·ra·he·dron** \ˌte-trə-'hē-drən\ *noun, plural* **-drons** *or* **-dra** \-drə\ [New Latin, from Late Greek *tetraedron*, neuter of *tetraedros* having four faces, from Greek *tetra-* + *hedra* seat, face — more at SIT] (1570)
: a polyhedron that has four faces

**tet·ra·hy·dro·can·nab·i·nol** \-ˌhī-drə-kə-'na-bə-ˌnȯl, -ˌnōl\ *noun* [*tetrahydro-* (combined with four atoms of hydrogen) + *cannabin* + ¹-*ol*] (1940)
: THC

**tetrahedron**

**tet·ra·hy·dro·fu·ran** \-'fyu̇r-ˌan, -fyu̇-'ran\ *noun* [*tetrahydro-* + *furan*] (circa 1943)
: a flammable liquid heterocyclic ether $C_4H_8O$ that is derived from furan and used as a solvent and as an intermediate in organic synthesis

**tet·ra·hy·me·na** \ˌte-trə-'hī-mə-nə\ *noun* [New Latin, from *tetra-* + Greek *hymēn* membrane] (1962)
: any of a genus (*Tetrahymena*) of ciliate protozoans

**te·tral·o·gy** \te-'trä-lə-jē, -'tra-\ *noun, plural* **-gies** [Greek *tetralogia*, from *tetra-* + *-logia* -logy] (1656)
**1 :** a group of four dramatic pieces presented consecutively on the Attic stage at the Dionysiac festival
**2 :** a series of four connected works (as operas or novels)

**tet·ra·mer** \'te-trə-mər\ *noun* (1929)
: a molecule (as an enzyme or a polymer) that consists of four structural subunits (as peptide chains or condensed monomers)
— **tet·ra·mer·ic** \ˌte-trə-'mer-ik\ *adjective*

**te·tram·er·ous** \te-'tra-mə-rəs\ *adjective* [New Latin *tetramerus*, from Greek *tetramerēs*, from *tetra-* + *meros* part — more at MERIT] (1826)
: having or characterized by the presence of four parts or of parts arranged in sets or multiples of four ⟨*tetramerous* flowers⟩

**te·tram·e·ter** \te-'tra-mə-tər\ *noun* [Greek *tetrametron*, from neuter of *tetrametros* having four measures, from *tetra-* + *metron* measure — more at MEASURE] (1612)
: a line of verse consisting either of four dipodies (as in classical iambic, trochaic, and anapestic verse) or four metrical feet (as in modern English verse)

**tet·ra·meth·yl·lead** \ˌte-trə-ˌme-thəl-'led\ *noun* (1964)
: a volatile poisonous liquid $Pb(CH_3)_4$ used as an antiknock agent

**¹tet·ra·ploid** \'te-trə-ˌplȯid\ *adjective* [International Scientific Vocabulary] (1912)
: having or being a chromosome number four times the monoploid number ⟨a *tetraploid* cell⟩
— **tet·ra·ploi·dy** \-ˌplȯi-dē\ *noun*

**²tetraploid** *noun* (1921)
: a tetraploid individual

**tet·ra·pod** \'te-trə-ˌpäd\ *noun* [New Latin *tetrapodus*, from Greek *tetrapod-, tetrapous* four-footed, from *tetra-* + *pod-, pous* foot — more at FOOT] (circa 1891)
: a vertebrate (as a frog, bird, or cat) with two pairs of limbs

**tet·ra·pyr·role** \ˌte-trə-'pir-ˌōl\ *noun* (circa 1928)
: a chemical group consisting of four pyrrole rings joined either in a straight chain or in a ring (as in chlorophyll)

**te·trarch** \'te-ˌträrk, 'tē-\ *noun* [Middle English, from Latin *tetrarcha*, from Greek *tetrarchēs*, from *tetra-* + *-archēs* -arch] (14th century)
**1 :** a governor of the fourth part of a province **2 :** a subordinate prince
— **te·trar·chic** \te-'trär-kik, tē-\ *adjective*

**te·trar·chy** \'te-ˌträr-kē, 'tē-\ *noun, plural* **-chies** (circa 1630)
: government by four persons ruling jointly

**tet·ra·spore** \'te-trə-ˌspȯr, -ˌspȯr\ *noun* [International Scientific Vocabulary] (1857)
: one of the haploid asexual spores developed meiotically in the red algae usually in groups of four
— **tet·ra·spor·ic** \ˌte-trə-'spȯr-ik, -'spȯr-\ *adjective*

**tet·ra·va·lent** \ˌte-trə-'vā-lənt\ *adjective* [International Scientific Vocabulary] (1868)
: having a valence of four

**te·traz·zi·ni** \ˌte-trə-'zē-nē\ *adjective, often capitalized* [Luisa *Tetrazzini* (died 1940) Italian opera singer] (1951)
: prepared with pasta and a white sauce seasoned with sherry and served au gratin ⟨chicken *tetrazzini*⟩

**tet·ra·zo·li·um** \ˌte-trə-'zō-lē-əm\ *noun* [New Latin, from International Scientific Vocabulary *tetrazole* $(CH_2N_4)$] (1895)
: a univalent cation or group $CH_3N_4$ that is analogous to ammonium; *also* : any of several of its derivatives used especially as electron acceptors to test for metabolic activity in living cells

**te·trode** \'te-ˌtrōd\ *noun* (1902)
: a vacuum tube with a cathode, an anode, a control grid, and an additional grid or other electrode

**te·tro·do·tox·in** \ˌte-ˌtrō-də-'täk-sən\ *noun* [International Scientific Vocabulary *tetrodo-* (from New Latin *Tetrodon*, genus of tropical marine fishes) + *toxin*] (1911)
: a neurotoxin $C_{11}H_{17}N_3O_8$ found especially in puffer fish that blocks nerve conduction by suppressing permeability of the nerve fiber to sodium ions

**te·trox·ide** \te-'träk-ˌsīd\ *noun* [International Scientific Vocabulary] (1866)
: a compound of an element or group with four atoms of oxygen

**tet·ryl** \'te-trəl\ *noun* [International Scientific Vocabulary] (1909)
: a pale yellow crystalline explosive $C_7H_5N_5O_8$ used especially as a detonator

**tet·ter** \'te-tər\ *noun* [Middle English *teter*, from Old English; akin to Old High German *zittaroh* tetter, Sanskrit *dadru* leprosy, *dṛṇāti* he tears — more at TEAR] (before 12th century)
: any of various vesicular skin diseases (as ringworm, eczema, and herpes)

**Teu·ton** \'tü-t°n, 'tyü-\ *noun* [Latin *Teutoni*, plural] (circa 1741)
**1 :** a member of an ancient probably Germanic or Celtic people
**2 :** a member of a people speaking a language of the Germanic branch of the Indo-European language family; *especially* : GERMAN

**¹Teu·ton·ic** \tü-'tä-nik, tyü-\ *noun* (1612)
: GERMANIC

**²Teutonic** *adjective* (1618)
: of, relating to, or characteristic of the Teutons
— **Teu·ton·i·cal·ly** \-ni-k(ə-)lē\ *adverb*

**Teu·ton·ism** \'tü-t°n-ˌi-zəm, 'tyü-\ *noun* (1854)
: GERMANISM

**Teu·ton·ist** \-ist\ *noun* (1882)
: GERMANIST

**teu·ton·ize** \-ˌīz\ *transitive verb* **-ized; -izing** *often capitalized* (1845)
: GERMANIZE

**tex·as** \'tek-səs, -siz\ *noun* [*Texas*, state of U.S.; from the naming of cabins on Mississippi steamboats after states, the officers' cabins being the largest] (1857)

: a structure on the awning deck of a steamer that contains the officers' cabins and has the pilothouse in front or on top

**Texas fever** *noun* (1866)

: an infectious disease of cattle transmitted by the cattle tick and caused by a protozoan (*Babesia bigemina*) that multiplies in the blood and destroys the red blood cells

**Texas Independence Day** *noun* (circa 1928)

: March 2 observed as the anniversary of the declaration of independence of Texas from Mexico in 1836 and also as the birthday of Sam Houston

**Texas leaguer** *noun* [*Texas League,* a baseball minor league] (1905)

: a fly in baseball that falls too far out to be caught by an infielder and too close in to be caught by an outfielder

**Texas longhorn** *noun* (1908)

**1 :** LONGHORN 1a
**2 :** any of a breed of relatively small cattle developed in the U.S. from descendants of the original longhorns and typically having a 40 inch (one meter) horn spread and a highly variable color pattern

**Texas Ranger** *noun* (1846)

: a member of a formerly mounted police force in Texas

**Tex–Mex** \'teks-'meks\ *adjective* [*Tex*as + *Mex*ico] (1949)

: of, relating to, or being the Mexican-American culture or cuisine existing or originating in especially southern Texas ⟨*Tex-Mex* cooking⟩ ⟨*Tex-Mex* music⟩

**text** \'tekst\ *noun* [Middle English, from Middle French *texte,* from Medieval Latin *textus,* from Latin, texture, context, from *texere* to weave — more at TECHNICAL] (14th century)

**1 a** (1) **:** the original words and form of a written or printed work (2) **:** an edited or emended copy of an original work **b :** a work containing such text
**2 a :** the main body of printed or written matter on a page **b :** the principal part of a book exclusive of front and back matter **c :** the printed score of a musical composition
**3 a** (1) **:** a verse or passage of Scripture chosen especially for the subject of a sermon or for authoritative support (as for a doctrine) (2) **:** a passage from an authoritative source providing an introduction or basis (as for a speech) **b :** a source of information or authority
**4 :** THEME, TOPIC
**5 a :** the words of something (as a poem) set to music **b :** matter chiefly in the form of words that is treated as data for processing by computerized equipment ⟨a *text*-editing typewriter⟩
**6 :** a type suitable for printing running text
**7 :** TEXTBOOK
**8 a :** something written or spoken considered as an object to be examined, explicated, or deconstructed **b :** something likened to a text ⟨the surfaces of daily life are *texts* to be explicated —Michiko Kakutani⟩ ⟨he ceased to be a teacher as he became a *text* —D. J. Boorstin⟩

**¹text·book** \'teks(t)-ˌbu̇k\ *noun* (1779)

: a book used in the study of a subject: as **a** : one containing a presentation of the principles of a subject **b :** a literary work relevant to the study of a subject

**²textbook** *adjective* (1905)

: of, suggesting, or suitable to a textbook; *especially* **:** CLASSIC ⟨a *textbook* example of bureaucratic waste⟩

**text·book·ish** \-ˌbu̇-kish\ *adjective* (1914)

: of, relating to, or having the characteristics of a textbook ⟨the style is heavy and *textbookish* —*Nation*⟩

**text edition** *noun* (1895)

: an edition of a book prepared for use especially in schools and colleges — compare TRADE EDITION

**tex·tile** \'tek-ˌstīl, 'teks-t⁹l\ *noun* [Latin, from neuter of *textilis* woven, from *texere*] (1626)

**1 :** CLOTH 1a; *especially* **:** a woven or knit cloth
**2 :** a fiber, filament, or yarn used in making cloth

**tex·tu·al** \'teks-chə-wəl, -chəl\ *adjective* [Middle English, from Medieval Latin *textus* text] (15th century)

: of, relating to, or based on a text
**— tex·tu·al·ly** *adverb*

**textual critic** *noun* (1938)

: a practitioner of textual criticism

**textual criticism** *noun* (1859)

**1 :** the study of a literary work that aims to establish the original text
**2 :** a critical study of literature emphasizing a close reading and analysis of the text

**¹tex·tu·ary** \'teks-chə-ˌwer-ē\ *noun, plural* **-ar·ies** [Medieval Latin *textus*] (1608)

: one who is well informed in the Bible or in biblical scholarship

**²textuary** *adjective* (1646)

: TEXTUAL

**¹tex·ture** \'teks-chər\ *noun* [Latin *textura,* from *textus,* past participle of *texere* to weave — more at TECHNICAL] (1578)

**1 a :** something composed of closely interwoven elements; *specifically* **:** a woven cloth **b** : the structure formed by the threads of a fabric
**2 a :** essential part **:** SUBSTANCE **b :** identifying quality **:** CHARACTER
**3 a :** the disposition or manner of union of the particles of a body or substance **b :** the visual or tactile surface characteristics and appearance of something ⟨the *texture* of an oil painting⟩
**4 a :** a composite of the elements of prose or poetry ⟨all these words . . . meet violently to form a *texture* impressive and exciting —John Berryman⟩ **b :** a pattern of musical sound created by tones or lines played or sung together
**5 a :** basic scheme or structure **b :** overall structure
**— tex·tur·al** \-chə-rəl\ *adjective*
**— tex·tur·al·ly** \-rə-lē\ *adverb*
**— tex·tured** \-chərd\ *adjective*
**— tex·ture·less** \-chər-ləs\ *adjective*

**²texture** *transitive verb* **tex·tured; tex·tur·ing** (1694)

: to give a particular texture to

**tex·tur·ize** \'teks-chə-ˌrīz\ *transitive verb* **-ized; -iz·ing** (circa 1950)

: TEXTURE ⟨*texturize* a polyester yarn⟩

**tex·tus re·cep·tus** \ˌtek-stəs-ri-'sep-təs\ *noun* [New Latin, literally, received text] (1856)

: the generally accepted text of a literary work (as the Greek New Testament)

**T formation** *noun* (1930)

: an offensive football formation in which the fullback lines up behind the center and quarterback with one halfback stationed on each side of the fullback

**T4 cell** \ˌtē-'fȯr-, -'fȯr-\ *noun* [*T cell* + *CD4*] (1983)

: any of the T cells (as a helper T cell) that bear the CD4 molecular marker and become severely depleted in AIDS — called also *T4 lymphocyte*

**T–group** \'tē-ˌgrüp\ *noun* [*t*raining *group*] (1950)

: a group of people under the leadership of a trainer who seek to develop self-awareness and sensitivity to others by verbalizing feelings uninhibitedly at group sessions — compare ENCOUNTER GROUP

**¹-th** — see -ETH

**²-th** *or* **-eth** *adjective suffix* [Middle English *-the, -te,* from Old English *-tha, -ta;* akin to Old High German *-do* -th, Latin *-tus,* Greek *-tos,* Sanskrit *-tha*]

— used in forming ordinal numbers ⟨hundred*th*⟩ ⟨forti*eth*⟩

**³-th** *noun suffix* [Middle English, from Old English; akin to Old High German *-ida,* suffix forming abstract nouns, Latin *-ta,* Greek *-tē,* Sanskrit *-tā*]

**1 :** act or process ⟨spil*th*⟩
**2 :** state or condition ⟨dear*th*⟩

**⁴-th** *symbol* [²-th]

— used with the figures 4, 5, 6, 7, 8, 9, and 0 and related Roman numerals to indicate an ordinal number ⟨25*th*⟩ ⟨50*th* wedding anniversary⟩ ⟨XXV*th* Olympiad⟩

**¹Thai** \'tī\ *noun, plural* **Thai** *or* **Thais** (1808)

**1 :** a family of languages including Thai and Shan spoken in southeast Asia and China
**2 a :** a native or inhabitant of Thailand **b :** one who is descended from a Thai
**3 :** the official language of Thailand

**²Thai** *adjective* (1808)

: of or relating to Thailand, its people, or their language or culture

**thal·a·mus** \'tha-lə-məs\ *noun, plural* **-mi** \-ˌmī, -ˌmē\ [New Latin, from Greek *thalamos* chamber] (1756)

: the largest subdivision of the diencephalon that consists chiefly of an ovoid mass of nuclei in each lateral wall of the third ventricle and functions in the integration of sensory information — see BRAIN illustration
**— tha·lam·ic** \thə-'la-mik\ *adjective*

**thal·as·sae·mia** *chiefly British variant of* THALASSEMIA

**thal·as·se·mia** \ˌtha-lə-'sē-mē-ə\ *noun* [New Latin, from Greek *thalassa* sea + New Latin *-emia*] (1932)

: any of a group of inherited disorders of hemoglobin synthesis affecting the globin chain that are characterized usually by mild to severe hemolytic anemia, are caused by a series of allelic genes, and tend to occur especially in individuals of Mediterranean, black, or southeast Asian ancestry; *especially* **:** COOLEY'S ANEMIA
**— thal·as·se·mic** \-mik\ *adjective or noun*

**thalassemia major** *noun* [New Latin, greater thalassemia] (1944)

: COOLEY'S ANEMIA

**thalassemia minor** *noun* [New Latin, lesser thalassemia] (1944)

: a mild form of thalassemia associated with the heterozygous condition for the gene involved

**tha·las·sic** \thə-'la-sik\ *adjective* [French *thalassique,* from Greek *thalassa* sea] (1883)

: of, relating to, or situated or developed about inland seas ⟨*thalassic* civilizations of the Aegean⟩

**thal·as·soc·ra·cy** \ˌtha-lə-'sä-krə-sē\ *noun* [Greek *thalassokratia,* from *thalassa* + *-kratia* -cracy] (1846)

: maritime supremacy

**tha·las·so·crat** \thə-'la-sə-ˌkrat\ *noun* (1846)

: one who has maritime supremacy

**tha·ler** \'tä-lər\ *variant of* TALER

**Tha·lia** \thə-'lī-ə\ *noun* [Latin, from Greek *Thaleia*]

**1 :** the Greek Muse of comedy
**2 :** one of the three Graces

**tha·lid·o·mide** \thə-'li-də-ˌmīd, -məd\ *noun* [ph*thal*ic acid + *-id-* (from *imide*) + *-o-* + *imide*] (1958)

: a sedative and hypnotic drug $C_{13}H_{10}N_2O_4$ that has been the cause of malformation of infants born to mothers using it during pregnancy

**thal·li·um** \'tha-lē-əm\ *noun* [New Latin, from Greek *thallos* green shoot; from the bright green line in its spectrum] (1861)

: a sparsely but widely distributed poisonous metallic element that resembles lead in physical properties and is used chiefly in the form of compounds in photoelectric cells or as a pesticide — see ELEMENT table

**thal·loid** \'tha-ˌlȯid\ *adjective* (1857)

: of, relating to, resembling, or consisting of a thallus ⟨*thalloid* liverworts⟩

**thal·lo·phyte** \'tha-lə-ˌfīt\ *noun* [ultimately from Greek *thallos* + *phyton* plant — more at PHYT-] (1854)
: any of a primary division (Thallophyta) of the plant kingdom comprising plants with single-celled sex organs or with many-celled sex organs of which all cells give rise to gametes, including the algae, fungi, and lichens, and usually held to be a heterogeneous assemblage
— **thal·lo·phyt·ic** \ˌtha-lə-'fi-tik\ *adjective*

**thal·lus** \'tha-ləs\ *noun, plural* **thal·li** \'tha-ˌlī, -ˌlē\ *or* **thal·lus·es** [New Latin, from Greek *thallos,* from *thallein* to sprout; akin to Armenian *dalar* green, fresh, Albanian *dal* I come forth] (1829)
: a plant body that is characteristic of thallophytes, lacks differentiation into distinct members (as stem, leaves, and roots), and does not grow from an apical point

**¹than** \thən, 'than\ *conjunction* [Middle English *than, then* then, than — more at THEN] (before 12th century)
**1 a** — used as a function word to indicate the second member or the member taken as the point of departure in a comparison expressive of inequality; used with comparative adjectives and comparative adverbs ⟨older *than* I am⟩ ⟨easier said *than* done⟩ **b** — used as a function word to indicate difference of kind, manner, or identity; used especially with some adjectives and adverbs that express diversity ⟨anywhere else *than* at home⟩
**2** : rather than — usually used only after *prefer, preferable,* and *preferably*
**3** : other than
**4** : WHEN — used especially after *scarcely* and *hardly*

**²than** *preposition* (1560)
: in comparison with ⟨you are older *than* me⟩
▪

**than·a·tol·o·gy** \ˌtha-nə-'tä-lə-jē\ *noun* [Greek *thanatos* + English *-logy*] (circa 1842)
: the description or study of the phenomena of death and of psychological mechanisms for coping with them
— **than·a·to·log·i·cal** \ˌtha-nə-tᵊl-'ä-ji-kəl\ *adjective*
— **than·a·tol·o·gist** \-ə-'tä-lə-jist\ *noun*

**Than·a·tos** \'tha-nə-ˌtäs\ *noun* [Greek, death; akin to Sanskrit *adhvanīt* it vanished] (1935)
: DEATH INSTINCT

**thane** \'thān\ *noun* [Middle English *theyn,* from Old English *thegn;* akin to Old High German *thegan* thane and perhaps to Greek *tiktein* to bear, beget] (before 12th century)
**1** : a free retainer of an Anglo-Saxon lord; *especially* : one resembling a feudal baron by holding lands of and performing military service for the king
**2** : a Scottish feudal lord
— **thane·ship** \-ˌship\ *noun*

**thank** \'thaŋk\ *transitive verb* [Middle English, from Old English *thancian;* akin to Old English *thanc* gratitude — more at THANKS] (before 12th century)
**1** : to express gratitude to ⟨*thanked* her for the present⟩ — used in the phrase *thank you* usually without a subject to politely express gratitude ⟨*thank* you for your consideration⟩; used in such phrases as *thank God, thank goodness* usually without a subject to express gratitude or more often only the speaker's or writer's pleasure or satisfaction in something
**2** : to hold responsible ⟨had only himself to *thank* for his loss⟩
— **thank·er** *noun*

**thank·ful** \'thaŋk-fəl\ *adjective* (before 12th century)
**1** : conscious of benefit received ⟨for what we are about to receive make us truly *thankful*⟩
**2** : expressive of thanks ⟨*thankful* service⟩
**3** : well pleased : GLAD ⟨was *thankful* that it didn't rain⟩
— **thank·ful·ness** *noun*

**thank·ful·ly** \-f(ə-)lē\ *adverb* (before 12th century)
**1** : in a thankful manner ⟨spoke *thankfully*⟩
**2** : as makes one thankful ⟨graceless stadiums . . . *thankfully* going out of fashion —R. G. Echevarriá⟩ ⟨*thankfully,* those opinions are advanced with graceful prose —Ken Auletta⟩

**thank·less** \'thaŋk-kləs\ *adjective* (1536)
**1** : not expressing or feeling gratitude : UNGRATEFUL ⟨how sharper than a serpent's tooth it is to have a *thankless* child —Shakespeare⟩
**2** : not likely to obtain thanks : UNAPPRECIATED ⟨a *thankless* task⟩
— **thank·less·ly** *adverb*
— **thank·less·ness** *noun*

**thanks** \'thaŋ(k)s\ *noun plural* [plural of Middle English *thank,* from Old English *thanc* thought, gratitude; akin to Old High German *dank* gratitude, Latin *tongēre* to know] (before 12th century)
**1** : kindly or grateful thoughts : GRATITUDE
**2** : an expression of gratitude ⟨return *thanks* before the meal⟩ — often used in an utterance containing no verb and serving as a courteous and somewhat informal expression of gratitude ⟨many *thanks*⟩
— **no thanks to** : not as a result of any benefit conferred by ⟨he feels better now, *no thanks to* you⟩
— **thanks to** : with the help of : owing to ⟨arrived early, *thanks to* good weather⟩

**thanks·giv·ing** \thaŋ(k)s-'gi-viŋ *also* 'thaŋ(k)s-ˌ\ *noun* (1533)
**1** : the act of giving thanks
**2** : a prayer expressing gratitude
**3 a** : a public acknowledgment or celebration of divine goodness **b** *capitalized* : THANKSGIVING DAY

**Thanksgiving Day** *noun* (1674)
: a day appointed for giving thanks for divine goodness: as **a** : the fourth Thursday in November observed as a legal holiday in the U.S. **b** : the second Monday in October observed as a legal holiday in Canada

**thank·wor·thy** \'thaŋk-ˌkwər-thē\ *adjective* (14th century)
: worthy of thanks or gratitude : MERITORIOUS

**thank-you** \'thaŋk-ˌkyü\ *noun* [from the phrase *thank you* used in expressing gratitude] (1792)
: a polite expression of one's gratitude

**thank-you-ma'am** \'thaŋk-yü-ˌmam, -ˌ(y)ē-\ *noun* [probably from its causing a nodding of the head] (1849)
: a bump or depression in a road; *especially* : a ridge or hollow made across a road on a hillside to cause water to run off

**¹that** \'that, thət\ *pronoun, plural* **those** \'thōz\ [Middle English, from Old English *thæt,* neuter demonstrative pronoun & definite article; akin to Old High German *daz,* neuter demonstrative pronoun & definite article, Greek *to,* Latin i*stud,* neuter demonstrative pronoun] (before 12th century)
**1 a** : the person, thing, or idea indicated, mentioned, or understood from the situation ⟨*that* is my father⟩ **b** : the time, action, or event specified ⟨after *that* I went to bed⟩ **c** : the kind or thing specified as follows ⟨the purest water is *that* produced by distillation⟩ **d** : one or a group of the indicated kind ⟨*that*'s a cat — quick and agile⟩
**2 a** : the one farther away or less immediately under observation or discussion ⟨*those* are maples and these are elms⟩ **b** : the former one
**3 a** — used as a function word after *and* to indicate emphatic repetition of the idea expressed by a previous word or phrase ⟨he was helpful, and *that* to an unusual degree⟩ **b** — used as a function word immediately before or after a word group consisting of a verbal auxiliary or a form of the verb *be* preceded by *there* or a personal pronoun subject to indicate emphatic repetition of the idea expressed by a previous verb or predicate noun or predicate adjective ⟨is she capable? She is *that*⟩

**4 a** : the one : the thing : the kind : SOMETHING, ANYTHING ⟨the truth of *that* which is true⟩ ⟨the senses are *that* whereby we experience the world⟩ ⟨what's *that* you say⟩ **b** *plural* : some persons ⟨*those* who think the time has come⟩
— **all that** : everything of the kind indicated ⟨tact, discretion, and *all that*⟩
— **at that 1** : in spite of what has been said or implied **2** : in addition : ²BESIDES

**²that** \thət, 'that\ *conjunction* (before 12th century)
**1 a** (1) — used as a function word to introduce a noun clause that is usually the subject or object of a verb or a predicate nominative ⟨said *that* he was afraid⟩ (2) — used as a function word to introduce a subordinate clause that is anticipated by the expletive *it* occurring as subject of the verb ⟨it is unlikely *that* he'll be in⟩ (3) — used as a function word to introduce a subordinate clause that is joined as complement to a noun or adjective ⟨we are certain *that* this is true⟩ ⟨the fact *that* you are here⟩ (4) — used as a function word to introduce a subordinate clause modifying an adverb or adverbial expression ⟨will go anywhere *that* he is invited⟩ **b** — used as a function word to introduce an exclamatory clause expressing a strong emotion especially of surprise, sorrow, or indignation ⟨*that* it should come to this!⟩
**2 a** (1) — used as a function word to introduce a subordinate clause expressing purpose or desired result ⟨cutting down expenses *that* her son might inherit an unencumbered estate —W. B. Yeats⟩ (2) — used as a function word to introduce a subordinate clause expressing a reason or cause ⟨rejoice *that* you are lightened of a load —Robert Browning⟩ (3) — used as a function word to introduce a subordinate clause expressing consequence, result, or effect ⟨are of sufficient importance *that* they cannot be neglected —Hannah Wormington⟩ **b** — used as a function word to introduce an exclamatory clause expressing a wish ⟨oh, *that* he would come⟩
**3** — used as a function word after a subordinating conjunction without modifying its

\ə\ **abut** \ᵊ\ **kitten** \ər\ **further** \a\ **ash** \ā\ **ace**
\ä\ **mop, mar** \au̇\ **out** \ch\ **chin** \e\ **bet** \ē\ **easy**
\g\ **go** \i\ **hit** \ī\ **ice** \j\ **job** \ŋ\ **sing** \ō\ **go**
\ȯ\ **law** \ȯi\ **boy** \th\ **thin** \t͟h\ **the** \ü\ **loot** \u̇\ **foot**
\y\ **yet** \zh\ **vision**   *see also* Guide to Pronunciation

meaning ⟨if *that* thy bent of love be honorable —Shakespeare⟩
³**that** *adjective, plural* **those** (13th century)
**1 a :** being the person, thing, or idea specified, mentioned, or understood **b :** being the one specified — usually used for emphasis ⟨*that* rarity among leaders⟩ ⟨*that* brother of yours⟩ **c :** so great a **:** SUCH
**2 :** the farther away or less immediately under observation or discussion ⟨this chair or *that* one⟩
⁴**that** \thət, 'that\ *pronoun* [Middle English, from Old English *thæt,* neuter relative pronoun, from *thæt,* neuter demonstrative pronoun] (before 12th century)
**1** — used as a function word to introduce a restrictive relative clause and to serve as a substitute within that clause for the substantive modified by the clause ⟨the house *that* Jack built⟩ ⟨I'll make a ghost of him *that* lets me —Shakespeare⟩
**2 a :** at which **:** in which **:** on which **:** by which **:** with which **:** to which ⟨each year *that* the lectures are given⟩ **b :** according to which **:** to the extent of what — used after a negative ⟨has never been here *that* I know of⟩
**3 a** *archaic* **:** that which **b** *obsolete* **:** the person who ▢ ▢
⁵**that** \'that\ *adverb* (15th century)
**1 :** to such an extent ⟨a nail about *that* long⟩
**2 :** VERY, EXTREMELY — usually used with the negative ⟨did not take the festival *that* seriously —Eric Goldman⟩
**that·a·way** \'tha-də-ˌwā\ *adverb* [alteration of *that way*] (1839)
**:** in that direction
¹**thatch** \'thach\ *transitive verb* [Middle English *thecchen,* from Old English *theccan* to cover; akin to Old High German *decchen* to cover, Latin *tegere,* Greek *stegein* to cover, *stegos* roof, Sanskrit *sthagati* he covers] (14th century)
**:** to cover with or as if with thatch
— **thatch·er** *noun*
²**thatch** *noun* (14th century)
**1 a :** a plant material (as straw) used as a sheltering cover especially of a house **b :** a sheltering cover (as a house roof) made of such material **c :** a mat of undecomposed plant material (as grass clippings) accumulated next to the soil in a grassy area (as a lawn)
**2 :** something likened to the thatch of a house; *especially* **:** the hair of one's head
**thau·ma·turge** \'thȯ-mə-ˌtərj\ *noun* [French, from New Latin *thaumaturgus,* from Greek *thaumatourgos* working miracles, from *thaumat-, thauma* miracle + *ergon* work — more at THEATER, WORK] (1715)
**:** THAUMATURGIST
**thau·ma·tur·gic** \ˌthȯ-mə-'tər-jik\ *adjective* (1680)
**1 :** performing miracles
**2 :** of, relating to, or dependent on thaumaturgy
**thau·ma·tur·gist** \'thȯ-mə-ˌtər-jist\ *noun* (1829)
**:** a performer of miracles; *especially* **:** MAGICIAN
**thau·ma·tur·gy** \-jē\ *noun* (circa 1727)
**:** the performance of miracles; *specifically* **:** MAGIC
¹**thaw** \'thȯ\ *verb* [Middle English, from Old English *thawian;* akin to Old High German *douwen* to thaw, Greek *tēkein* to melt, Latin *tabēre* to waste away] (before 12th century) *transitive verb*
**:** to cause to thaw
*intransitive verb*
**1 a :** to go from a frozen to a liquid state **:** MELT **b :** to become free of the effect (as stiffness, numbness, or hardness) of cold as a result of exposure to warmth
**2 :** to be warm enough to melt ice and snow — used with *it* in reference to the weather
**3 :** to abandon aloofness, reserve, or hostility **:** UNBEND

**4 :** to become mobile, active, or susceptible to change
²**thaw** *noun* (15th century)
**1 :** the action, fact, or process of thawing
**2 :** a period of weather warm enough to thaw ice ⟨the January *thaw*⟩
**3 :** the action or process of becoming less aloof, less hostile, or more genial ⟨a *thaw* in international relations⟩
**THC** \ˌtē-ˌ)āch-'sē\ *noun* [tetrahydrocannabinol] (1967)
**:** a physiologically active chemical $C_{21}H_{30}O_2$ from hemp plant resin that is the chief intoxicant in marijuana — called also *tetrahydrocannabinol*
¹**the** \*before consonants usually* thə, *before vowels usually* thē, *especially Southern before vowels also* thə; *for emphasis before titles and names or to suggest uniqueness often* 'thē\ *definite article* [Middle English, from Old English *thē,* masculine demonstrative pronoun & definite article, alteration (influenced by oblique cases — as *thæs,* genitive — & neuter, *thæt*) of *sē;* akin to Greek *ho,* masculine demonstrative pronoun & definite article — more at THAT] (before 12th century)
**1 a** — used as a function word to indicate that a following noun or noun equivalent is definite or has been previously specified by context or by circumstance ⟨put *the* cat out⟩ **b** — used as a function word to indicate that a following noun or noun equivalent is a unique or a particular member of its class ⟨*the* President⟩ ⟨*the* Lord⟩ **c** — used as a function word before nouns that designate natural phenomena or points of the compass ⟨*the* night is cold⟩ **d** — used as a function word before a noun denoting time to indicate reference to what is present or immediate or is under consideration ⟨in *the* future⟩ **e** — used as a function word before names of some parts of the body or of the clothing as an equivalent of a possessive adjective ⟨how's *the* arm today⟩ **f** — used as a function word before the name of a branch of human endeavor or proficiency ⟨*the* law⟩ **g** — used as a function word in prepositional phrases to indicate that the noun in the phrase serves as a basis for computation ⟨sold by *the* dozen⟩ **h** — used as a function word before a proper name (as of a ship or a well-known building) ⟨*the* Mayflower⟩ **i** — used as a function word before the plural form of a numeral that is a multiple of ten to denote a particular decade of a century or of a person's life ⟨life in *the* twenties⟩ **j** — used as a function word before the name of a commodity or any familiar appurtenance of daily life to indicate reference to the individual thing, part, or supply thought of as at hand ⟨talked on *the* telephone⟩ **k** — used as a function word to designate one of a class as the best, most typical, best known, or most worth singling out ⟨this is *the* life⟩ ⟨*the* Pill⟩; sometimes used before a personal name to denote the most prominent bearer of that name
**2 a** (1) — used as a function word with a noun modified by an adjective or by an attributive noun to limit the application of the modified noun to that specified by the adjective or by the attributive noun ⟨*the* right answer⟩ ⟨Peter *the* Great⟩ (2) — used as a function word before an absolute adjective or an ordinal number ⟨nothing but *the* best⟩ ⟨due on *the* first⟩ **b** (1) — used as a function word before a noun to limit its application to that specified by a succeeding element in the sentence ⟨*the* poet Wordsworth⟩ ⟨*the* days of our youth⟩ ⟨didn't have *the* time to write⟩ (2) — used as a function word after a person's name to indicate a characteristic trait or notorious activity specified by the succeeding noun ⟨Jack *the* Ripper⟩
**3 a** — used as a function word before a singular noun to indicate that the noun is to be understood generically ⟨*the* dog is a domestic

animal⟩ **b** — used as a function word before a singular substantivized adjective to indicate an abstract idea ⟨an essay on *the* sublime⟩
**4** — used as a function word before a noun or a substantivized adjective to indicate reference to a group as a whole ⟨*the* elite⟩
²**the** *adverb* [Middle English, from Old English *thȳ* by that, instrumental of *thæt* that] (before 12th century)
**1 :** than before **:** than otherwise — used before a comparative ⟨none *the* wiser for attending⟩
**2 a :** to what extent ⟨*the* sooner the better⟩ **b :** to that extent ⟨the sooner *the* better⟩
**3 :** beyond all others ⟨likes this *the* best⟩
³**the** *preposition* [¹*the*] (15th century)
**:** PER 2 ⟨a dollar *the* dozen⟩
**the-** *or* **theo-** *combining form* [Middle English *theo-,* from Latin, from Greek *the-, theo-,* from *theos*]
**:** god **:** God ⟨*the*ism⟩ ⟨*theo*centric⟩
¹**the·ater** *or* **the·atre** \'thē-ə-tər, 'thi-ə-, *oftenest in Southern* 'thē-ˌā- *also* thē-'ā-\ *noun* [Middle English *theatre,* from Middle French, from Latin *theatrum,* from Greek *theatron,* from *theasthai* to view, from *thea* act of seeing; akin to Greek *thauma* miracle] (14th century)
**1 a :** an outdoor structure for dramatic performances or spectacles in ancient Greece and Rome **b :** a building for dramatic performances **c :** a building or area for showing motion pictures
**2 :** a place or sphere of enactment of usually significant events or action ⟨the *theater* of public life⟩
**3 a :** a place rising by steps or gradations ⟨a woody *theater* of stateliest view —John Milton⟩ **b :** a room often with rising tiers of seats for assemblies (as for lectures or surgical demonstrations)
**4 a :** dramatic literature **:** PLAYS **b :** dramatic representation as an art or profession **:** DRAMA
**5 a :** dramatic or theatrical quality or effectiveness **b :** SPECTACLE 1a
²**theater** *adjective* (1977)
**:** of, relating to, or appropriate for use in a theater of operations ⟨*theater* nuclear weapons⟩
**the·ater·go·er** \'thē-ə-tər-ˌgō(-ə)r\ *noun* (1870)
**:** a person who frequently goes to the theater
— **the·ater·go·ing** \-ˌgō-iŋ, -gȯ(-)iŋ\ *noun or adjective*
**theater–in–the–round** *noun, plural* **theaters–in–the–round** (1948)
**:** a theater in which the stage is located in the center of the auditorium — called also *arena theater*
**theater of operations** (circa 1879)

□ USAGE
**that** *That, which, who:* In current usage *that* refers to persons or things, *which* chiefly to things and rarely to subhuman entities, *who* chiefly to persons and sometimes to animals. The notion that *that* should not be used to refer to persons is without foundation; such use is entirely standard. Because *that* has no genitive form or construction, *of which* or *whose* must be substituted for it in contexts that call for the genitive. See in addition WHOSE.

**that** *That, which:* Although some handbooks say otherwise, *that* and *which* are both regularly used to introduce restrictive clauses in edited prose. *Which* is also used to introduce nonrestrictive clauses. *That* was formerly used to introduce nonrestrictive clauses; such use is virtually nonexistent in present-day edited prose, though it may occasionally be found in poetry.

: the part of a theater of war in which active combat operations are conducted

**theater of the absurd** (1961)
: theater that seeks to represent the absurdity of human existence in a meaningless universe by bizarre or fantastic means

**theater of war** (circa 1890)
: the entire land, sea, and air area that is or may become involved directly in war operations

**The·a·tine** \'thē-ə-ˌtīn, -ˌtēn\ *noun* [New Latin *Theatinus*, from Latin *Teatinus* inhabitant of Chieti, from *Teate* Chieti, Italy] (circa 1598)
: a priest of the Order of Clerks Regular founded in 1524 in Italy by Saint Cajetan and Gian Pietro Caraffa to reform Catholic morality and combat Lutheranism
— **Theatine** *adjective*

¹**the·at·ri·cal** \thē-'a-tri-kəl\ *also* **the·at·ric** \-trik\ *adjective* (1558)
**1** : of or relating to the theater or the presentation of plays ⟨a *theatrical* costume⟩
**2** : marked by pretense or artificiality of emotion
**3 a** : HISTRIONIC ⟨a *theatrical* gesture⟩ **b** : marked by extravagant display or exhibitionism
*synonym* see DRAMATIC
— **the·at·ri·cal·ism** \-kə-ˌli-zəm\ *noun*
— **the·at·ri·cal·i·ty** \-ˌa-trə-'ka-lə-tē\ *noun*
— **the·at·ri·cal·ly** \-'a-tri-k(ə-)lē\ *adverb*

²**theatrical** *noun* (circa 1683)
**1** *plural* **a** : the performance of plays **b** : DRAMATICS
**2** *British* : a professional actor
**3** *plural* : showy or extravagant gestures

**the·at·ri·cal·ize** \thē-'a-tri-kə-ˌlīz\ *transitive verb* **-ized; -iz·ing** (1778)
**1** : to adapt to the theater : DRAMATIZE
**2** : to display in showy fashion
— **the·at·ri·cal·i·za·tion** \-ˌa-tri-kə-lə-'zā-shən\ *noun*

**the·at·rics** \thē-'a-triks\ *noun plural* (1807)
**1** : THEATRICAL 1
**2** : staged or contrived effects

**the·be** \'thā-(ˌ)bā\ *noun, plural* **thebe** [Tswana, literally, shield] (1967)
— see *pula* at MONEY table

**the·ca** \'thē-kə\ *noun, plural* **the·cae** \'thē-ˌsē, -ˌkē\ [New Latin, from Greek *thēkē* case — more at TICK] (circa 1666)
: an enveloping sheath or case of an animal or animal part
— **the·cal** \'thē-kəl\ *adjective*

**-thecium** *noun combining form, plural* **-thecia** [New Latin, from Greek *thēkion*, diminutive of *thēkē* case]
: small containing structure ⟨endo*thecium*⟩

¹**the·co·dont** \'thē-kə-ˌdänt\ *adjective* [International Scientific Vocabulary *thec-* (from New Latin *theca*) + *-odont*] (1840)
: having the teeth inserted in sockets

²**thecodont** *noun* (1840)
: any of an order (Thecodontia) of Triassic diapsid thecodont reptiles that were presumably on the common ancestral line of the dinosaurs, birds, and crocodiles

**thé dan·sant** \tā-dänⁿ-säⁿ\ *noun, plural* **thés dansants** \*same*\ [French] (circa 1845)
: TEA DANCE

**thee** \'thē\ *pronoun, archaic objective case of* THOU
**1 a** — used especially in ecclesiastical or literary language and by Friends especially among themselves in contexts where the objective case form would be expected **b** — used by Friends especially among themselves in contexts where the subjective case form would be expected
**2** : THYSELF
*word history* see YOU

**thee·lin** \'thē-(ə-)lən\ *noun* [irregular from Greek *thēlys* female; akin to Greek *thēlē* nipple — more at FEMININE] (1930)
: ESTRONE

**theft** \'theft\ *noun* [Middle English *thiefthe*, from Old English *thīefth*; akin to Old English *thēof* thief] (before 12th century)
**1 a** : the act of stealing; *specifically* : the felonious taking and removing of personal property with intent to deprive the rightful owner of it **b** : an unlawful taking (as by embezzlement or burglary) of property
**2** *obsolete* : something stolen
**3** : a stolen base in baseball

**thegn** \'thān\ *noun* [Old English — more at THANE] (1848)
: THANE 1

**thegn·ly** \-lē\ *adjective* (1876)
: of, relating to, or befitting a thegn

**their** \thər, 'ther, 'thar\ *adjective* [Middle English, from *their*, pronoun, from Old Norse *theirra*, genitive plural demonstrative & personal pronoun; akin to Old English *thæt* that] (13th century)
**1** : of or relating to them or themselves especially as possessors, agents, or objects of an action ⟨*their* furniture⟩ ⟨*their* verses⟩ ⟨*their* being seen⟩
**2** : his or her : HIS, HER, ITS — used with an indefinite third person singular antecedent ⟨anyone in *their* senses —W. H. Auden⟩
*usage* see ANYBODY, EVERYBODY, NOBODY, SOMEBODY, THEY

**theirs** \'therz, 'tharz\ *pronoun, singular or plural in construction* (14th century)
**1** : that which belongs to them — used without a following noun as a pronoun equivalent in meaning to the adjective *their*
**2** : his or hers : HIS, HERS — used with an indefinite third person singular antecedent ⟨I will do my part if everybody else will do *theirs*⟩

**their·selves** \thər-'selvz, (ˌ)ther-, (ˌ)thar-, *Southern also* -'sevz\ *pronoun plural* (14th century)
*chiefly dialect* : THEMSELVES

**the·ism** \'thē-ˌi-zəm\ *noun* (1678)
: belief in the existence of a god or gods; *specifically* : belief in the existence of one God viewed as the creative source of man and the world who transcends yet is immanent in the world
— **the·ist** \-ist\ *noun or adjective*
— **the·is·tic** \thē-'is-tik\ *also* **the·is·ti·cal** \-ti-kəl\ *adjective*
— **the·is·ti·cal·ly** \-ti-k(ə-)lē\ *adverb*

**T–help·er cell** \'tē-ˌhel-pər-\ *noun* (1980)
: HELPER T CELL

¹**them** \(th)əm, 'them, *after* p, b, v, f, *also* ᵐ\ *pronoun, objective case of* THEY
*usage* see ANYBODY, EVERYBODY, NOBODY, SOMEBODY

²**them** \'them\ *adjective* (1594)
*nonstandard* : THOSE — used chiefly in the speech of less educated people and in the familiar speech of educated people especially when they are being humorous

**the·mat·ic** \thi-'ma-tik\ *adjective* [Greek *thematikos*, from *themat-, thema* theme] (1861)
**1 a** : of or relating to the stem of a word **b** *of a vowel* : being the last part of a word stem before an inflectional ending
**2** : of, relating to, or constituting a theme
— **the·mat·i·cal·ly** \-ti-k(ə-)lē\ *adverb*

**thematic apperception test** *noun* (1941)
: a projective technique that is widely used in clinical psychology to make personality, psychodynamic, and diagnostic assessments based on the subject's verbal responses to a series of black and white pictures

**theme** \'thēm\ *noun* [Middle English *teme, theme*, from Middle French & Latin; Middle French *teme*, from Latin *thema*, from Greek, literally, something laid down, from *tithenai* to place — more at DO] (14th century)
**1 a** : a subject or topic of discourse or of artistic representation **b** : a specific and distinctive quality, characteristic, or concern ⟨the campaign has lacked a *theme*⟩

**2** : STEM 4
**3** : a written exercise : COMPOSITION ⟨a research *theme*⟩
**4** : a melodic subject of a musical composition or movement
— **themed** \'thēmd\ *adjective*

**theme park** *noun* (1960)
: an amusement park in which the structures and settings are based on a central theme

**theme song** *noun* (1929)
**1** : a melody recurring so often in a musical play that it characterizes the production or one of its characters
**2** : a song used as a signature

**them·selves** \thəm-'selvz, them-\ *pronoun plural* (14th century)
**1 a** : those identical ones that are they — compare THEY 1a; used reflexively, for emphasis, or in absolute constructions ⟨nations that govern *themselves*⟩ ⟨they *themselves* were present⟩ ⟨*themselves* busy, they disliked idleness in others⟩ **b** : himself or herself : HIMSELF, HERSELF — used with an indefinite third person singular antecedent ⟨nobody can call *themselves* oppressed —Leonard Wibberley⟩
**2** : their normal, healthy, or sane condition ⟨were *themselves* again after a night's rest⟩
*usage* see THEY

¹**then** \'then\ *adverb* [Middle English *than, then* then, than, from Old English *thonne, thænne*; akin to Old High German *denne* then, than, Old English *thæt* that] (before 12th century)
**1** : at that time
**2 a** : soon after that : next in order of time ⟨walked to the door, *then* turned⟩ **b** : following next after in order of position, narration, or enumeration : being next in a series ⟨first came the clowns, *then* came the elephants⟩ **c** : in addition : BESIDES ⟨*then* there is the interest to be paid⟩
**3 a** (1) : in that case ⟨take it, *then*, if you want it so much⟩ (2) — used after *but* to qualify or offset a preceding statement ⟨she lost the race, but *then* she never really expected to win⟩ **b** : according to that : as may be inferred ⟨your mind is made up, *then*⟩ **c** : as it appears : by way of summing up ⟨the cause of the accident, *then*, is established⟩ **d** : as a necessary consequence ⟨if the angles are equal, *then* the complements are equal⟩
— **and then some** : with much more in addition ⟨would require all his strength *and then some*⟩

²**then** *noun* (14th century)
: that time ⟨since *then*, he's been more cautious⟩

³**then** *adjective* (1584)
: existing or acting at or belonging to the time mentioned ⟨the *then* secretary of state⟩

**then and there** *adverb* (15th century)
: on the spot : IMMEDIATELY ⟨wanted the money right *then and there*⟩

**the·nar** \'thē-ˌnär, -nər\ *adjective* [New Latin, palm of the hand, from Greek; akin to Old High German *tenar* palm of the hand] (circa 1857)
: of, relating to, involving, or constituting the ball of the thumb or the intrinsic musculature of the thumb ⟨*thenar* muscles⟩

**thence** \'then(t)s *also* 'then(t)s\ *adverb* [Middle English *thannes*, from *thanne* from that place, from Old English *thanon*; akin to Old High German *thanan* from that place, Old English *thænne* then — more at THEN] (14th century)
**1** : from that place
**2** *archaic* : from that time : THENCEFORTH
**3** : from that fact or circumstance : THEREFROM
— **from thence** : from that place

---

\ə\ abut \ᵊ\ kitten \ər\ further \a\ ash \ā\ ace
\ä\ mop, mar \aủ\ out \ch\ chin \e\ bet \ē\ easy
\g\ go \i\ hit \ī\ ice \j\ job \ŋ\ sing \ō\ go
\ȯ\ law \ȯi\ boy \th\ thin \t͟h\ the \ü\ loot \ủ\ foot
\y\ yet \zh\ vision     *see also* Guide to Pronunciation

**thence·forth** \-ˌfȯrth, -ˌfōrth\ *adverb* (14th century)
**:** from that time forward
**thence·for·ward** \then(t)s-ˈfȯr-wərd *also* then(t)s-\ *also* **thence·for·wards** \-wərdz\ *adverb* (15th century)
**:** onward from that place or time
**theo-** — see THE-
**theo·bro·mine** \ˌthē-ə-ˈbrō-ˌmēn, -mən\ *noun* [New Latin *Theobroma*, genus that includes the cacao, from *the-* + Greek *brōma* food, from *bibrōskein* to devour — more at VORACIOUS] (1842)
**:** a bitter alkaloid $C_7H_8N_4O_2$ closely related to caffeine that occurs especially in cacao beans and has stimulant and diuretic properties
**theo·cen·tric** \-ˈsen-trik\ *adjective* (1886)
**:** having God as the central interest and ultimate concern ⟨a *theocentric* culture⟩
— **theo·cen·tric·i·ty** \-ˌsen-ˈtri-sə-tē\ *noun*
— **theo·cen·trism** \-ˈsen-ˌtri-zəm\ *noun*
**the·oc·ra·cy** \thē-ˈä-krə-sē\ *noun, plural* **-cies** [Greek *theokratia*, from *the-* + *-kratia* -cracy] (1622)
**1 :** government of a state by immediate divine guidance or by officials who are regarded as divinely guided
**2 :** a state governed by a theocracy
**theo·crat** \ˈthē-ə-ˌkrat\ *noun* (1827)
**1 :** one who rules in or lives under a theocratic form of government
**2 :** one who favors a theocratic form of government
**theo·crat·ic** \ˌthē-ə-ˈkra-tik\ *also* **theo·crat·i·cal** \-ti-kəl\ *adjective* (1690)
**:** of, relating to, or being a theocracy
— **theo·crat·i·cal·ly** \-ti-k(ə-)lē\ *adverb*
**the·od·i·cy** \thē-ˈä-də-sē\ *noun, plural* **-cies** [modification of French *théodicée*, from *théo-* the- (from Latin *theo-*) + Greek *dikē* judgment, right — more at DICTION] (1797)
**:** defense of God's goodness and omnipotence in view of the existence of evil
**the·od·o·lite** \thē-ˈä-dᵊl-ˌīt\ *noun* [New Latin *theodelitus*] (1571)
**:** a surveyor's instrument for measuring horizontal and usually also vertical angles
**the·og·o·ny** \thē-ˈä-gə-nē\ *noun, plural* **-nies** [Greek *theogonia*, from *the-* + *-gonia* -gony] (1612)
**:** an account of the origin and descent of the gods
— **theo·gon·ic** \ˌthē-ə-ˈgä-nik\ *adjective*
**theo·lo·gian** \ˌthē-ə-ˈlō-jən\ *noun* (15th century)
**:** a specialist in theology
**theo·log·i·cal** \-ˈlä-ji-kəl\ *also* **theo·log·ic** \-jik\ *adjective* (15th century)
**1 :** of or relating to theology
**2 :** preparing for a religious vocation ⟨a *theological* student⟩
— **theo·log·i·cal·ly** \-ji-k(ə-)lē\ *adverb*
**theological virtue** *noun* (1526)
**:** one of the three spiritual graces faith, hope, and charity drawing the soul to God according to scholastic theology
**the·ol·o·gise** *British variant of* THEOLOGIZE
**the·ol·o·gize** \thē-ˈä-lə-ˌjīz\ *verb* **-gized; -giz·ing** (1649)
*transitive verb*
**:** to make theological **:** give a religious significance to
*intransitive verb*
**:** to theorize theologically
— **the·ol·o·giz·er** *noun*
**theo·logue** *also* **theo·log** \ˈthē-ə-ˌlȯg, -ˌläg\ *noun* [Latin *theologus* theologian, from Greek *theologos*, from *the-* + *legein* to speak — more at LEGEND] (1663)
**:** a theological student or specialist
**the·ol·o·gy** \thē-ˈä-lə-jē\ *noun, plural* **-gies** [Middle English *theologie*, from Latin *theologia*, from Greek, from *the-* + *-logia* -logy] (14th century)

**1 :** the study of religious faith, practice, and experience; *especially* **:** the study of God and of God's relation to the world
**2 a :** a theological theory or system ⟨Thomist *theology*⟩ ⟨a *theology* of atonement⟩ **b :** a distinctive body of theological opinion ⟨Catholic *theology*⟩
**3 :** a usually 4-year course of specialized religious training in a Roman Catholic major seminary
**the·on·o·mous** \thē-ˈä-nə-məs\ *adjective* [*the-* + *-nomous* (as in *autonomous*)] (1947)
**:** governed by God **:** subject to God's authority
**the·on·o·my** \-mē\ *noun* [German *theonomie*, from *theo-* the- (from Latin) + *-nomie* -nomy] (1890)
**:** the state of being theonomous **:** government by God
**the·oph·a·ny** \thē-ˈä-fə-nē\ *noun, plural* **-nies** [Medieval Latin *theophania*, from Late Greek *theophaneia*, from Greek *the-* + *-phaneia* (as in *epiphaneia* appearance) — more at EPIPHANY] (circa 1633)
**:** a visible manifestation of a deity
— **theo·phan·ic** \ˌthē-ə-ˈfa-nik\ *adjective*
**the·oph·yl·line** \thē-ˈä-fə-lən\ *noun* [International Scientific Vocabulary *theo-* (from New Latin *thea* tea) + *phyll-* + ²-*ine*] (circa 1894)
**:** a feebly basic bitter crystalline compound $C_7H_8N_4O_2$ from tea leaves that is isomeric with theobromine and is used in medicine especially as a bronchodilator
**the·or·bo** \thē-ˈȯr-(ˌ)bō\ *noun, plural* **-bos** [modification of Italian *tiorba, teorba*] (1605)
**:** a stringed instrument of the 17th century resembling a large lute but having an extra set of long bass strings
**the·o·rem** \ˈthē-ə-rəm, ˈthi(-ə)r-əm\ *noun* [Late Latin *theorema*, from Greek *theōrēma*, from *theōrein* to look at, from *theōros* spectator, from *thea* act of seeing — more at THEATER] (1551)
**1 :** a formula, proposition, or statement in mathematics or logic deduced or to be deduced from other formulas or propositions
**2 :** an idea accepted or proposed as a demonstrable truth often as a part of a general theory **:** PROPOSITION ⟨the *theorem* that the best defense is offense⟩
**3 :** STENCIL
**4 :** a painting produced especially on velvet by the use of stencils for each color
— **the·o·rem·at·ic** \ˌthē-ə-rə-ˈma-tik, ˌthi(-ə)r-ə-\ *adjective*
**the·o·ret·i·cal** \ˌthē-ə-ˈre-ti-kəl, ˌthi(-ə)r-ˈe-\ *also* **the·o·ret·ic** \-tik\ *adjective* [Late Latin *theoreticus*, from Greek *theōrētikos*, from *theōrein* to look at] (1601)
**1 a :** relating to or having the character of theory **:** ABSTRACT **b :** confined to theory or speculation often in contrast to practical applications **:** SPECULATIVE ⟨*theoretical* physics⟩
**2 :** given to or skilled in theorizing ⟨a brilliant *theoretical* physicist⟩
**3 :** existing only in theory **:** HYPOTHETICAL ⟨gave as an example a *theoretical* situation⟩
**the·o·ret·i·cal·ly** \-ti-k(ə-)lē\ *adverb* (1701)
**1 :** in a theoretical way
**2 :** according to an ideal or assumed set of facts or principles **:** in theory
**the·o·re·ti·cian** \ˌthē-ə-rə-ˈti-shən, -re-; ˌthi(-ə)r-ə-\ *noun* (1886)
**:** THEORIST
**the·o·rise** *British variant of* THEORIZE
**the·o·rist** \ˈthē-ə-rist, ˈthi(-ə)r-ist\ *noun* (1646)
**:** a person who theorizes
**the·o·rize** \ˈthē-ə-ˌrīz\ *verb* **-rized; -riz·ing** (1638)
*intransitive verb*
**:** to form a theory **:** SPECULATE
*transitive verb*
**1 :** to form a theory about

**2 :** to propose as a theory
— **the·o·ri·za·tion** \ˌthē-ə-rə-ˈzā-shən, ˌthi(-ə)r-ə-\ *noun*
— **the·o·riz·er** *noun*
**the·o·ry** \ˈthē-ə-rē, ˈthi(-ə)r-ē\ *noun, plural* **-ries** [Late Latin *theoria*, from Greek *theōria*, from *theōrein*] (1592)
**1 :** the analysis of a set of facts in their relation to one another
**2 :** abstract thought **:** SPECULATION
**3 :** the general or abstract principles of a body of fact, a science, or an art ⟨music *theory*⟩
**4 a :** a belief, policy, or procedure proposed or followed as the basis of action ⟨her method is based on the *theory* that all children want to learn⟩ **b :** an ideal or hypothetical set of facts, principles, or circumstances — often used in the phrase *in theory* ⟨in *theory*, we have always advocated freedom for all⟩
**5 :** a plausible or scientifically acceptable general principle or body of principles offered to explain phenomena ⟨wave *theory* of light⟩
**6 a :** a hypothesis assumed for the sake of argument or investigation **b :** an unproved assumption **:** CONJECTURE **c :** a body of theorems presenting a concise systematic view of a subject ⟨*theory* of equations⟩
*synonym* see HYPOTHESIS
**theory of games** (1951)
**:** GAME THEORY
**theory of numbers** (1811)
**:** NUMBER THEORY
**the·os·o·phist** \thē-ˈä-sə-fist\ *noun* (1656)
**1 :** an adherent of theosophy
**2** *capitalized* **:** a member of a theosophical society
**the·os·o·phy** \-fē\ *noun* [Medieval Latin *theosophia*, from Late Greek, from Greek *the-* + *sophia* wisdom — more at -SOPHY] (1650)
**1 :** teaching about God and the world based on mystical insight
**2** *often capitalized* **:** the teachings of a modern movement originating in the U.S. in 1875 and following chiefly Buddhist and Brahmanic theories especially of pantheistic evolution and reincarnation
— **theo·soph·i·cal** \ˌthē-ə-ˈsä-fi-kəl\ *adjective*
— **theo·soph·i·cal·ly** \-k(ə-)lē\ *adverb*
**Theo·to·kos** \ˌthē-ə-ˈtō-(ˌ)kös, ˌthä-, -kəs\ *noun* [Late Greek, from Greek *the-* + *tokos* childbirth; akin to Greek *tiktein* to beget — more at THANE]
**:** VIRGIN MARY
**ther·a·peu·sis** \ˌther-ə-ˈpyü-səs\ *noun* [New Latin, from Greek, treatment, from *therapeuein*] (circa 1857)
**:** THERAPEUTICS
**ther·a·peu·tic** \-ˈpyü-tik\ *adjective* [Greek *therapeutikos*, from *therapeuein* to attend, treat, from *theraps* attendant] (1646)
**1 :** of or relating to the treatment of disease or disorders by remedial agents or methods ⟨a *therapeutic* rather than a diagnostic specialty⟩
**2 :** providing or assisting in a cure **:** CURATIVE, MEDICINAL ⟨*therapeutic* diets⟩ ⟨a *therapeutic* investigation of government waste⟩
— **ther·a·peu·ti·cal·ly** \-ti-k(ə-)lē\ *adverb*
**therapeutic index** *noun* (1926)
**:** a measure of the relative desirability of a drug for the attaining of a particular medical end that is usually expressed as the ratio of the largest dose producing no toxic symptoms to the smallest dose routinely producing cures
**ther·a·peu·tics** \ˌther-ə-ˈpyü-tiks\ *noun plural but singular or plural in construction* (1671)
**:** a branch of medical science dealing with the application of remedies to diseases
**ther·a·pist** \ˈther-ə-pist\ *noun* (1886)
**:** one specializing in therapy; *especially* **:** a person trained in methods of treatment and rehabilitation other than the use of drugs or surgery ⟨a speech *therapist*⟩
**the·rap·sid** \thə-ˈrap-səd\ *noun* [New Latin *Therapsida*, from *ther-* mammal (from Greek

theorbo

*thēr* wild animal) + *apsid-, apsis* arch, vault — more at FIERCE, APSIS] (1912)
**:** any of an order (Therapsida) of Permian and Triassic reptiles that are considered ancestors of the mammals
— **therapsid** *adjective*

**ther·a·py** \'ther-ə-pē\ *noun, plural* **-pies** [New Latin *therapia,* from Greek *therapeia,* from *therapeuein*] (circa 1846)
**:** therapeutic treatment especially of bodily, mental, or behavioral disorder

**Ther·a·va·da** \,ther-ə-'vä-də\ *noun* [Pali *theravāda,* literally, doctrine of the elders] (1882)
**:** a conservative branch of Buddhism comprising sects chiefly in Sri Lanka, Myanmar, Thailand, Laos, and Cambodia and adhering to the original Pali scriptures alone and to the nontheistic ideal of nirvana for a limited select number — compare MAHAYANA

**¹there** \'thar, 'ther\ *adverb* [Middle English, from Old English *thǣr;* akin to Old High German *dār* there, Old English *thæt* that] (before 12th century)
**1 :** in or at that place ⟨stand over *there*⟩ — often used interjectionally
**2 :** to or into that place **:** THITHER ⟨went *there* after church⟩
**3 :** at that point or stage ⟨stop right *there* before you say something you'll regret⟩
**4 :** in that matter, respect, or relation ⟨*there* is where I disagree with you⟩
**5** — used interjectionally to express satisfaction, approval, encouragement or sympathy, or defiance ⟨*there,* it's finished⟩

**²there** \'thar, 'ther, *1 is also* thər\ *pronoun* (before 12th century)
**1** — used as a function word to introduce a sentence or clause ⟨*there* shall come a time⟩
**2** — used as an indefinite substitute for a name ⟨hi *there*⟩

**³there** \*same as* ¹\ *noun* (1588)
**1 :** that place or position ⟨there is no here and no *there* . . . in pure space —James Ward⟩
**2 :** that point ⟨you take it from *there*⟩

**⁴there** \*same as* ¹\ *adjective* (1590)
**1** — used for emphasis especially after a demonstrative pronoun or a noun modified by a demonstrative adjective ⟨those men *there* can tell you⟩
**2** *nonstandard* — used for emphasis after a demonstrative adjective but before the noun modified ⟨I bet I cussed that *there* blamed mule five hundred times —Elizabeth M. Roberts⟩
**3 :** capable of being relied on for support or aid ⟨she is always *there* for him⟩
**4 :** fully conscious, rational, or aware ⟨not all *there*⟩

**there·abouts** *also* **there·about** \,thar-ə-'baut(s), ,ther-ə-,; ,ther-ə-'baut(s), 'ther-ə-,\ *adverb* (before 12th century)
**1 :** near that place or time
**2 :** near that number, degree, or quantity ⟨a boy of 18 or *thereabouts*⟩

**there·af·ter** \tha-'raf-tər, the-\ *adverb* (before 12th century)
**1 :** after that
**2** *archaic* **:** according to that **:** ACCORDINGLY

**there·at** \-'rat\ *adverb* (before 12th century)
**1 :** at that place
**2 :** at that occurrence

**there·by** \thar-'bī, ther-, 'thar-,, 'ther-,\ *adverb* (before 12th century)
**1 :** by that **:** by that means ⟨*thereby* lost her chance to win⟩
**2 :** connected with or with reference to that ⟨*thereby* hangs a tale —Shakespeare⟩

**there·for** \thar-'fòr, ther-\ *adverb* (12th century)
**:** for or in return for that ⟨ordered a change and gave his reasons *therefor*⟩

**there·fore** \'thar-,fòr, 'ther-, -,fòr\ *adverb* (14th century)
**1 a :** for that reason **:** CONSEQUENTLY **b :** because of that **c :** on that ground

**2 :** to that end

**there·from** \thar-'frəm, ther-, -'främ\ *adverb* (13th century)
**:** from that or it

**there·in** \tha-'rin, the-\ *adverb* (before 12th century)
**1 :** in or into that place, time, or thing
**2 :** in that particular or respect ⟨*therein* lies the problem⟩

**there·in·af·ter** \,thar-in-'af-tər, ,ther-\ *adverb* (1818)
**:** in the following part of that matter (as writing, document, or speech)

**there·in·to** \tha-'rin-(,)tü, the-\ *adverb* (14th century)
*archaic* **:** into that or it

**the·re·min** \'ther-ə-mən\ *noun* [Lev Theremin (born 1896) Russian engineer & inventor] (1927)
**:** a purely melodic electronic musical instrument typically played by moving a hand between two projecting electrodes

**there·of** \tha-'rəv, -'räv, the-\ *adverb* (before 12th century)
**1 :** of that or it
**2 :** from that cause or particular **:** THEREFROM

**there·on** \-'ròn, -'rän\ *adverb* (before 12th century)
**1 :** on that ⟨a text with a commentary *thereon*⟩
**2** *archaic* **:** THEREUPON

**there·to** \thar-'tü, ther-\ *adverb* (before 12th century)
**:** to that ⟨a text and the notes *thereto*⟩

**there·to·fore** \'thar-tə-,fōr, 'ther-, -,fòr; ,thar-tə-', ,ther-\ *adverb* (14th century)
**:** up to that time ⟨a *theretofore* unknown author⟩

**there·un·der** \tha-'rən-dər, the-\ *adverb* (before 12th century)
**:** under that

**there·un·to** \-'rən-(,)tü; ,thar-ən-'tü, ,ther-\ *adverb* (14th century)
*archaic* **:** THERETO

**there·up·on** \'thar-ə-,pòn, 'ther-, -,pän; ,thar-ə-', ,ther-\ *adverb* (13th century)
**1 :** on that matter
**2 :** THEREFORE
**3 :** immediately after that

**there·with** \thar-'with, ther-, -'with\ *adverb* (before 12th century)
**1 :** with that
**2** *archaic* **:** THEREUPON, FORTHWITH

**there·with·al** \'thar-wi-,thòl, 'ther-, -,thòl\ *adverb* (14th century)
**1** *archaic* **:** BESIDES
**2 :** THEREWITH

**the·ri·ac** \'thir-ē-,ak\ *noun* [New Latin *theriaca*] (1568)
**1 :** THERIACA
**2 :** CURE-ALL

**the·ri·a·ca** \thi-'rī-ə-kə\ *noun* [New Latin, from Latin, antidote against poison — more at TREACLE] (1562)
**:** a mixture of many drugs and honey formerly held to be an antidote to poison
— **the·ri·a·cal** \-kəl\ *adjective*

**the·rio·mor·phic** \thir-ē-ō-'mòr-fik\ *adjective* [Greek *thēriomorphos,* from *thērion* beast + *morphē* form — more at TREACLE] (1882)
**:** having an animal form ⟨*theriomorphic* gods⟩

**therm** \'thərm\ *noun* [Greek *thermē* heat, from *thermos* hot; akin to Latin *formus* warm, Sanskrit *gharma* heat] (1888)
**:** a unit used to measure quantity of heat that equals 100,000 British thermal units

**therm-** *or* **thermo-** *combining form* [Greek, from *thermē*]
**1 :** heat ⟨*therm*ostat⟩
**2 :** thermoelectric ⟨*thermo*pile⟩

**-therm** *noun combining form* [Greek *thermē* heat]
**:** animal having a (specified) body temperature ⟨ecto*therm*⟩

**¹ther·mal** \'thər-məl\ *adjective* [Greek *thermē*] (1756)

**1** [Latin *thermae* public baths, from Greek *thermai,* plural of *thermē*] **:** of, relating to, or marked by the presence of hot springs ⟨*thermal* waters⟩
**2 a :** of, relating to, or caused by heat ⟨*thermal* stress⟩ ⟨*thermal* insulation⟩ **b :** being or involving a state of matter dependent upon temperature ⟨*thermal* conductivity⟩ ⟨*thermal* agitation of molecular structure⟩
**3 :** designed (as with insulating air spaces) to prevent the dissipation of body heat ⟨*thermal* underwear⟩
**4 :** having energies of the order of those due to thermal agitation ⟨*thermal* neutrons⟩
— **ther·mal·ly** \-mə-lē\ *adverb*

**²thermal** *noun* (1933)
**:** a rising body of warm air

**ther·mal·ize** \'thər-mə-,līz\ *transitive verb* **-ized; -iz·ing** (1948)
**:** to change the effective speed of (a particle) to a thermal value ⟨*thermalize* a neutron⟩
— **ther·mal·i·za·tion** \,thər-mə-lə-'zā-shən\ *noun*

**thermal pollution** *noun* (1966)
**:** the discharge of heated liquid (as wastewater from a factory) into natural waters at a temperature harmful to the environment

**thermal printer** *noun* (1966)
**:** a dot matrix printer (as for a computer) in which heat is applied to the pins of the matrix to form dots on usually heat-sensitive paper

**ther·mic** \'thər-mik\ *adjective* (1842)
**:** ¹THERMAL 2 ⟨*thermic* energy⟩
— **ther·mi·cal·ly** \-mi-k(ə-)lē\ *adverb*

**therm·ion·ic** \,thər-(,)mī-'ä-nik\ *adjective* [*thermion* charged particle from an incandescent source, from *therm-* + *ion*] (1909)
**:** relating to, using, or being the emission of charged particles (as electrons) by an incandescent material

**therm·ion·ics** \,thər-(,)mī-'ä-niks\ *noun plural but singular in construction* (1909)
**:** physics dealing with thermionic phenomena

**therm·is·tor** \'thər-mis-tər\ *noun* [*therm*al re*sistor*] (1940)
**:** an electrical resistor making use of a semiconductor whose resistance varies sharply in a known manner with the temperature

**Ther·mit** \'thər-mət, -,mīt\ *trademark*
— used for thermite

**ther·mite** \'thər-,mīt\ *noun* [*therm-* + ¹*-ite*] (1900)
**:** a mixutre of aluminum powder and a metal oxide (as iron oxide) that when ignited evolves a great deal of heat and is used in welding and in incendiary bombs

**ther·mo·chem·is·try** \,thər-mō-'ke-mə-strē\ *noun* (1844)
**:** a branch of chemistry that deals with the interrelation of heat with chemical reaction or physical change of state
— **ther·mo·chem·i·cal** \-'ke-mi-kəl\ *adjective*
— **ther·mo·chem·ist** \-'ke-mist\ *noun*

**ther·mo·cline** \'thər-mə-,klīn\ *noun* (1898)
**:** the region in a thermally stratified body of water which separates warmer oxygen-rich surface water from cold oxygen-poor deep water and in which temperature decreases rapidly with depth

**ther·mo·cou·ple** \'thər-mə-,kə-pəl\ *noun* (1890)
**:** a device for measuring temperature in which a pair of wires of dissimilar metals (as copper and iron) are joined and the free ends of the wires are connected to an instrument (as a voltmeter) that measures the difference in potential created at the junction of the two metals

**ther·mo·du·ric** \,thər-mō-'dùr-ik, -'dyùr-\ *adjective* [*therm-* + Latin *durare* to last — more at DURING] (1927)
: able to survive high temperatures; *specifically* : able to survive pasteurization — used of microorganisms

**ther·mo·dy·nam·ic** \,thər-mō-dī-'na-mik, -də-\ *also* **ther·mo·dy·nam·i·cal** \-mi-kəl\ *adjective* (1849)
**1** : of or relating to thermodynamics
**2** : being or relating to a system of atoms, molecules, colloidal particles, or larger bodies considered as an isolated group in the study of thermodynamic processes
— **ther·mo·dy·nam·i·cal·ly** \-mi-k(ə-)lē\ *adverb*

**ther·mo·dy·nam·ics** \-miks\ *noun plural but singular or plural in construction* (1854)
**1** : physics that deals with the mechanical action or relations of heat
**2** : thermodynamic processes and phenomena
— **ther·mo·dy·nam·i·cist** \-'na-mə-sist\ *noun*

**ther·mo·elec·tric** \,thər-mō-i-'lek-trik\ *adjective* (1823)
: of, relating to, or dependent on phenomena that involve relations between the temperature and the electrical condition in a metal or in contacting metals

**ther·mo·elec·tric·i·ty** \,thər-mō-i-,lek-'tri-sə-tē, -'tris-tē\ *noun* (1823)
: electricity produced by the direct action of heat (as by the unequal heating of a circuit composed of two dissimilar metals)

**ther·mo·el·e·ment** \-'e-lə-mənt\ *noun* (circa 1888)
: a device for measuring small currents consisting of a wire heating element and a thermocouple in electrical contact with it

**ther·mo·form** \'thər-mə-,förm\ *transitive verb* (1956)
: to give a final shape to (as a plastic) with the aid of heat and usually pressure
— **ther·mo·form·able** \-,för-mə-bəl\ *adjective*

**ther·mo·gram** \-,gram\ *noun* (1883)
**1** : the record made by a thermograph
**2** : a photographic record made by thermography

**ther·mo·graph** \-,graf\ *noun* [International Scientific Vocabulary] (1843)
**1** : THERMOGRAM
**2** : a self-recording thermometer
**3** : the apparatus used in thermography

**ther·mog·ra·phy** \(,)thər-'mä-grə-fē\ *noun* (1840)
**1** : a process of writing or printing involving the use of heat; *especially* : a raised-printing process in which matter printed by letterpress is dusted with powder and heated to make the lettering rise
**2** : a technique for detecting and measuring variations in the heat emitted by various regions of the body and transforming them into visible signals that can be recorded photographically (as for diagnosing abnormal or diseased underlying conditions); *also* : a similar technique used elsewhere (as on buildings)
— **ther·mo·graph·ic** \,thər-mə-'gra-fik\ *adjective*
— **ther·mo·graph·i·cal·ly** \-fi-k(ə-)lē\ *adverb*

**ther·mo·ha·line** \,thər-mō-'hā-,līn, -'ha-\ *adjective* [*therm-* + Greek *hal-, hals* salt — more at SALT] (1942)
: involving or dependent upon the conjoint effect of temperature and salinity (*thermohaline* circulation in the eastern Pacific)

**ther·mo·junc·tion** \-'jən(k)-shən\ *noun* (1889)
: a junction of two dissimilar conductors used to produce a thermoelectric current

**ther·mo·la·bile** \-'lā-,bīl, -bəl\ *adjective* [International Scientific Vocabulary] (1904)
: unstable when heated; *specifically* : subject to loss of characteristic properties on being

heated to or above 55°C (many immune bodies, enzymes, and vitamins are *thermolabile*)
— **ther·mo·la·bil·i·ty** \-lā-'bi-lə-tē\ *noun*

**ther·mo·lu·mi·nes·cence** \-,lü-mə-'nes-°n(t)s\ *noun* [International Scientific Vocabulary] (1897)
**1** : phosphorescence developed in a previously excited substance upon gentle heating
**2** : the determination of the age of old material (as pottery) by the amount of thermoluminescence it produces — called also *thermoluminescence dating*
— **ther·mo·lu·mi·nes·cent** \-s°nt\ *adjective*

**ther·mo·mag·net·ic** \-mag-'ne-tik\ *adjective* (1823)
: of or relating to the effects of heat upon the magnetic properties of substances or to the effects of a magnetic field upon thermal conduction

**ther·mom·e·ter** \thə(r)-'mä-mə-tər\ *noun* [French *thermomètre*, from Greek *thermē* heat + French *-o-* + *-mètre* -meter — more at THERM] (1633)
: an instrument for determining temperature consisting typically of a glass bulb attached to a fine tube of glass with a numbered scale and containing a liquid (as mercury or colored alcohol) that is sealed in and rises and falls with changes of temperature
— **ther·mo·met·ric** \,thər-mə-'me-trik\ *adjective*
— **ther·mo·met·ri·cal·ly** \-tri-k(ə-)lē\ *adverb*

**ther·mom·e·try** \thə(r)-'mä-mə-trē\ *noun* [International Scientific Vocabulary] (1858)
: the measurement of temperature

**ther·mo·nu·cle·ar** \,thər-mō-'nü-klē-ər, -'nyü-, ÷-'n(y)ü-kyə-lər\ *adjective* [International Scientific Vocabulary] (1938)
**1** : of or relating to the transformations in the nucleus of atoms of low atomic weight (as hydrogen) that require a very high temperature for their inception (as in the hydrogen bomb or in the sun) (*thermonuclear* reaction) (*thermonuclear* weapon)
**2** : of, utilizing, or relating to a thermonuclear bomb (*thermonuclear* war) (*thermonuclear* attack)

**ther·mo·pe·ri·od·ic·i·ty** \-,pir-ē-ə-'di-sə-tē\ *noun* (1944)
: THERMOPERIODISM

**ther·mo·pe·ri·od·ism** \,thər-mō-'pir-ē-ə-,di-zəm\ *noun* (1937)
: the sum of the responses of an organism and especially a plant to appropriately fluctuating temperatures

**ther·mo·phil·ic** \,thər-mə-'fi-lik\ *also* **ther·moph·i·lous** \(,)thər-'mä-fə-ləs\ *or* **ther·mo·phile** \'thər-mə-,fīl\ *adjective* (1894)
: of, relating to, or being an organism growing at a high temperature (*thermophilic* fermentation) (*thermophilic* bacteria)
— **thermophile** *noun*

**ther·mo·pile** \'thər-mə-,pīl\ *noun* [[4]*pile*] (1849)
: an apparatus that consists of a number of thermocouples combined so as to multiply the effect and is used for generating electric currents or for determining intensities of radiation

**ther·mo·plas·tic** \,thər-mə-'plas-tik\ *adjective* (1883)
: capable of softening or fusing when heated and of hardening again when cooled (*thermoplastic* synthetic resins) — compare THERMOSETTING
— **thermoplastic** *noun*
— **ther·mo·plas·tic·i·ty** \-,pla-'sti-sə-tē\ *noun*

**ther·mo·re·cep·tor** \,thər-mō-ri-'sep-tər\ *noun* (1937)
: a sensory end organ that is stimulated by heat or cold

**ther·mo·reg·u·la·tion** \-,re-gyə-'lā-shən\ *noun* [International Scientific Vocabulary] (1927)

: the maintenance or regulation of temperature; *specifically* : the maintenance of a particular temperature of the living body
— **ther·mo·reg·u·late** \-'re-gyə-,lāt\ *verb*

**ther·mo·reg·u·la·tor** \-'re-gyə-,lā-tər\ *noun* [International Scientific Vocabulary] (1875)
: a device (as a thermostat) for the regulation of temperature

**ther·mo·reg·u·la·to·ry** \-'re-gyə-lə-,tōr-ē, -,tör-\ *adjective* (1941)
: tending to maintain a body at a particular temperature whatever its environmental temperature (*thermoregulatory* adjustments)

**ther·mo·rem·a·nent** \-'re-mə-nənt\ *adjective* (1951)
: being or relating to magnetic remanence (as in a rock cooled from a molten state or in a baked clay object containing magnetic minerals) that indicates the strength and direction of the earth's magnetic field at a former time
— **ther·mo·rem·a·nence** \-nən(t)s\ *noun*

**ther·mos** \'thər-məs\ *noun* [from *Thermos,* a trademark] (1907)
: a container (as a bottle or jar) with a vacuum between an inner and outer wall used to keep material and especially liquids either hot or cold for considerable periods

**ther·mo·scope** \'thər-mə-,skōp\ *noun* [New Latin *thermoscopium,* from *therm-* + *-scopium* -scope] (1804)
: an instrument for indicating changes of temperature by accompanying changes in volume (as of a gas)

**ther·mo·set** \'thər-mō-,set\ *noun* (1947)
: a thermosetting resin or plastic

**ther·mo·set·ting** \-,se-tiŋ\ *adjective* (circa 1931)
: capable of becoming permanently rigid when heated or cured (a *thermosetting* resin) — compare THERMOPLASTIC

**ther·mo·sphere** \'thər-mə-,sfir\ *noun* [International Scientific Vocabulary] (1950)
: the part of the earth's atmosphere that begins at about 50 miles (80 kilometers) above the earth's surface, extends to outer space, and is characterized by steadily increasing temperature with height
— **ther·mo·spher·ic** \,thər-mə-'sfir-ik, -'sfer-\ *adjective*

**ther·mo·sta·ble** \,thər-mō-'stā-bəl\ *adjective* (1904)
: stable when heated; *specifically* : retaining characteristic properties on being moderately heated (a *thermostable* bacterial protease)
— **ther·mo·sta·bil·i·ty** \-stə-'bi-lə-tē\ *noun*

**¹ther·mo·stat** \'thər-mə-,stat\ *noun* (1831)
: an automatic device for regulating temperature (as by controlling the supply of gas or electricity to a heating apparatus); *also* : a similar device for actuating fire alarms or for controlling automatic sprinklers
— **ther·mo·stat·ic** \,thər-mə-'sta-tik\ *adjective*
— **ther·mo·stat·i·cal·ly** \-ti-k(ə-)lē\ *adverb*

**²thermostat** *transitive verb* **-stat·ed** \-,sta-təd\ *also* **-stat·ted; -stat·ing** *also* **-stat·ting** (1924)
: to provide with or control the temperature of by a thermostat

**ther·mo·tac·tic** \,thər-mə-'tak-tik\ *adjective* (1839)
: of, relating to, or exhibiting thermotaxis

**ther·mo·tax·is** \-'tak-səs\ *noun* [New Latin] (circa 1891)
**1** : the regulation of body temperature
**2** : a taxis in which a temperature gradient constitutes the directive factor

**ther·mo·trop·ic** \-'trä-pik\ *adjective* [International Scientific Vocabulary] (1885)
: of, relating to, or exhibiting thermotropism

**ther·mot·ro·pism** \(,)thər-'mä-trə-,pi-zəm\ *noun* [International Scientific Vocabulary] (circa 1890)

: a tropism in which a temperature gradient determines the orientation

**-ther·my** *noun combining form* [New Latin *-thermia*, from Greek *thermē* heat — more at THERM]
**1** : state of heat ⟨endo*thermy*⟩
**2** : generation of heat ⟨dia*thermy*⟩

**the·ro·pod** \'thir-ə-ˌpäd\ *noun* [New Latin *Theropoda*, from Greek *thēr* wild animal + *pod-, pous* foot — more at FIERCE, FOOT] (circa 1891)
: any of a suborder (Theropoda) of carnivorous bipedal saurischian dinosaurs (as a tyrannosaur or allosaurus) usually having small forelimbs

**Ther·si·tes** \(ˌ)thər-'sī-(ˌ)tēz\ *noun* [Latin, from Greek *Thersitēs*]
: a Greek warrior at Troy known as a carping critic and slain by Achilles for mocking him

**the·sau·rus** \thi-'sȯr-əs\ *noun, plural* **-sau·ri** \-'sȯr-ˌī, -ˌē\ *or* **-sau·rus·es** \-'sȯr-ə-səz\ [New Latin, from Latin, treasure, collection, from Greek *thēsauros*] (circa 1823)
**1** : TREASURY, STOREHOUSE
**2 a** : a book of words or of information about a particular field or set of concepts; *especially* : a book of words and their synonyms **b** : a list of subject headings or descriptors usually with a cross-reference system for use in the organization of a collection of documents for reference and retrieval
— **the·sau·ral** \-'sȯr-əl\ *adjective*

**these** *plural of* THIS
**The·seus** \'thē-ˌsüs, -sē-əs\ *noun* [Latin, from Greek *Thēseus*]
: a king of Athens in Greek mythology who kills Procrustes and the Minotaur before defeating the Amazons and marrying their queen

**the·sis** \'thē-səs, *British especially for 1* 'the-sis\ *noun, plural* **the·ses** \'thē-ˌsēz\ [in sense 1, Middle English, from Late Latin & Greek; Late Latin, lowering of the voice, from Greek, downbeat, more important part of a foot, literally, act of laying down; in other senses, Latin, from Greek, literally, act of laying down, from *tithenai* to put, lay down — more at DO] (14th century)
**1 a** (1) : the unstressed part of a poetic foot especially in accentual verse (2) : the longer part of a poetic foot especially in quantitative verse **b** : the accented part of a musical measure : DOWNBEAT — compare ARSIS
**2 a** : a position or proposition that a person (as a candidate for scholastic honors) advances and offers to maintain by argument **b** : a proposition to be proved or one advanced without proof : HYPOTHESIS
**3** : the first and least adequate stage of dialectic — compare SYNTHESIS
**4** : a dissertation embodying results of original research and especially substantiating a specific view; *especially* : one written by a candidate for an academic degree

**¹thes·pi·an** \'thes-pē-ən\ *adjective* (1675)
**1** *capitalized* : of or relating to Thespis
**2** *often capitalized* [from the tradition that Thespis was the originator of the actor's role] : relating to the drama : DRAMATIC

**²thespian** *noun* (1827)
: ACTOR

**Thes·sa·lo·nians** \ˌthe-sə-'lō-nyənz, -nē-ənz\ *noun plural but singular in construction* [*Thessalonian* inhabitant of ancient Thessalonica, irregular from *Thessalonica*]
: either of two letters written by Saint Paul to the Christians of Thessalonica and included as books in the New Testament — see BIBLE table

**the·ta** \'thā-tə, *chiefly British* 'thē-tə\ *noun* [Greek *thēta*, of Semitic origin; akin to Hebrew *ṭēth* teth] (1603)
**1** : the 8th letter of the Greek alphabet — see ALPHABET table
**2** : THETA RHYTHM

**theta rhythm** *noun* (1944)

: a relatively high amplitude brain wave pattern between approximately 4 and 9 hertz that is characteristic especially of the hippocampus but occurs in many regions of the brain including the cortex — called also *theta wave*

**thet·ic** \'the-tik, 'thē-\ *adjective* [Greek *thetikos* of a proposition, from *tithenai* to lay down — more at DO] (1815)
: constituting or beginning with a poetic thesis ⟨a *thetic* syllable⟩
— **thet·i·cal·ly** \-ti-k(ə-)lē\ *adverb*

**The·tis** \'thē-təs\ *noun* [Latin, from Greek]
: a sea goddess who marries Peleus and becomes the mother of Achilles

**the·ur·gist** \'thē-(ˌ)ər-jist\ *noun* (1652)
: WONDER-WORKER, MAGICIAN

**the·ur·gy** \'thē-(ˌ)ər-jē\ *noun* [Late Latin *theurgia*, from Late Greek *theourgia*, from *theourgos* miracle worker, from Greek *the-* + *ergon* work — more at WORK] (1569)
: the art or technique of compelling or persuading a god or beneficent or supernatural power to do or refrain from doing something
— **the·ur·gic** \thē-'ər-jik\ *or* **the·ur·gi·cal** \-ji-kəl\ *adjective*

**thew** \'thü, 'thyü\ *noun* [Middle English, personal quality, virtue, from Old English *thēaw*; akin to Old High German *thau* custom] (15th century)
**1 a** : muscular power or development **b** : STRENGTH, VITALITY
**2** : MUSCLE, SINEW — usually used in plural

**they** \'thā\ *pronoun, plural in construction* [Middle English, from Old Norse *their*, masculine plural demonstrative & personal pronoun; akin to Old English *thæt* that] (13th century)
**1 a** : those ones — used as third person pronoun serving as the plural of *he, she,* or *it* or referring to a group of two or more individuals not all of the same sex ⟨*they* dance well⟩ **b** : ¹HE 2 — often used with an indefinite third person singular antecedent ⟨everyone knew where *they* stood —E. L. Doctorow⟩ ⟨nobody has to go to school if *they* don't want to — *N. Y. Times*⟩
**2** : PEOPLE 2 — used in a generic sense ⟨as lazy as *they* come⟩ ■ ■

**they'd** \'thād\ (1676)
: they had : they would
**they'll** \'thā(ə)l, thel\ (1607)
: they will : they shall
**they're** \thər, 'ther\ (circa 1594)
: they are
**they've** \'thāv\ (1611)
: they have

**thi-** *or* **thio-** *combining form* [International Scientific Vocabulary, from Greek *thei-, theio-* sulfur, from *theion*]
: containing sulfur ⟨*thia*mine⟩ ⟨*thio*cyanate⟩

**thia·ben·da·zole** \ˌthī-ə-'ben-də-ˌzōl\ *noun* [*thiazole* + *benz-* + *imide* + *azole*] (1961)
: a drug C₁₀H₇N₃S used in the control of parasitic nematode worms, in the treatment of fungus infections, and as an agricultural fungicide

**thi·ami·nase** \thī-'a-mə-ˌnās, 'thī-ə-mə-, -ˌnāz\ *noun* [International Scientific Vocabulary] (1938)
: an enzyme that catalyzes the breakdown of thiamine

**thi·a·mine** \'thī-ə-mən, -ˌmēn\ *also* **thi·a·min** \-mən\ *noun* [*thiamine* alteration of *thiamin*, from *thi-* + *-amin* (as in *vitamin*)] (1937)
: a vitamin (C₁₂H₁₇N₄OS)Cl of the B complex that is essential to normal metabolism and nerve function and is widespread in plants and animals — called also *vitamin B₁*

**thi·a·zide** \'thī-ə-ˌzīd, -zəd\ *noun* [*thi-* + diazine + dioxide] (1959)
: any of a group of drugs used as oral diuretics especially in the control of high blood pressure

**thi·a·zine** \'thī-ə-ˌzēn\ *noun* [International Scientific Vocabulary] (1900)
: any of various compounds that are characterized by a ring composed of four carbon atoms, one sulfur atom, and one nitrogen atom and

include some important as dyes and others as tranquilizers — compare PHENOTHIAZINE

**thi·a·zole** \'thī-ə-ˌzōl\ *noun* [International Scientific Vocabulary] (1888)
**1** : a colorless basic liquid C₃H₃NS consisting of a 5-membered ring and having an odor like pyridine
**2** : any of various thiazole derivatives including some used in medicine and others important as chemical accelerators

**¹thick** \'thik\ *adjective* [Middle English *thikke*, from Old English *thicce*; akin to Old High German *dicki* thick, Old Irish *tiug*] (before 12th century)
**1 a** : having or being of relatively great depth or extent from one surface to its opposite ⟨a *thick* plank⟩ **b** : heavily built : THICKSET
**2 a** : close-packed with units or individuals ⟨the air was *thick* with snow⟩ **b** : occurring in large numbers : NUMEROUS **c** : viscous in consistency ⟨*thick* syrup⟩ **d** : SULTRY, STUFFY **e** : marked by haze, fog, or mist ⟨*thick* weather⟩ **f** : impenetrable to the eye : PROFOUND ⟨*thick* darkness⟩ **g** : extremely intense ⟨*thick* silence⟩
**3** : measuring in thickness ⟨12 inches *thick*⟩
**4 a** : imperfectly articulated : INDISTINCT ⟨*thick* speech⟩ **b** : plainly apparent : DECIDED ⟨a *thick* French accent⟩ **c** : producing inarticulate speech ⟨a *thick* tongue⟩
**5** : OBTUSE, STUPID
**6** : associated on close terms : INTIMATE ⟨was quite *thick* with his pastor⟩
**7** : exceeding bounds of propriety or fitness : EXCESSIVE ⟨called it a bit *thick* to be fired without warning⟩
— **thick·ish** \'thi-kish\ *adjective*
— **thick·ly** *adverb*

\ə\ abut \ᵊ\ kitten \ər\ further \a\ ash \ā\ ace
\ä\ mop, mar \aù\ out \ch\ chin \e\ bet \ē\ easy
\g\ go \i\ hit \ī\ ice \j\ job \ŋ\ sing \ō\ go
\ȯ\ law \ȯi\ boy \th\ thin \t͟h\ the \ü\ loot \ù\ foot
\y\ yet \zh\ vision    *see also* Guide to Pronunciation

²**thick** *adverb* (before 12th century)
: in a thick manner : THICKLY

³**thick** *noun* (13th century)
**1** : the most crowded or active part ⟨in the *thick* of the battle⟩
**2** : the part of greatest thickness ⟨the *thick* of the thumb⟩

**thick and thin** *noun* (14th century)
: every difficulty and obstacle — used especially in the phrase *through thick and thin*

**thick·en** \'thi-kən\ *verb* **thick·ened; thick·en·ing** \'thik-niŋ, 'thi-kə-\ (15th century)
*transitive verb*
**1 a** : to make thick, dense, or viscous in consistency ⟨*thicken* gravy with flour⟩ **b** : to make close or compact
**2** : to increase the depth or diameter of
**3** : to make inarticulate : BLUR ⟨alcohol *thickened* his speech⟩
*intransitive verb*
**1 a** : to become dense ⟨the mist *thickened*⟩ **b** : to become concentrated in numbers, mass, or frequency
**2** : to grow blurred or obscure
**3** : to grow broader or bulkier
**4** : to grow complicated or keen ⟨the plot *thickens*⟩
— **thick·en·er** \'thik-nər, 'thi-kə-\ *noun*

**thickening** *noun* (circa 1580)
**1** : the act of making or becoming thick
**2** : a thickened part or place
**3** : something used to thicken

**thick·et** \'thi-kət\ *noun* [(assumed) Middle English *thikket*, from Old English *thiccet*, from *thicce* thick] (before 12th century)
**1** : a dense growth of shrubbery or small trees : COPPICE
**2** : something resembling a thicket in density or impenetrability : TANGLE
— **thick·ety** \-kə-tē\ *adjective*

**thick·et·ed** \'thi-kə-təd\ *adjective* (circa 1624)
: dotted or covered with thickets

**thick·head** \'thik-,hed\ *noun* (1824)
: a stupid person : BLOCKHEAD

**thick·head·ed** \-,he-dəd\ *adjective* (1707)
**1** : having a thick head
**2** : sluggish and obtuse of mind

**thick·ness** \-nəs\ *noun* (before 12th century)
**1** : the smallest of three dimensions ⟨length, width, and *thickness*⟩
**2** : the quality or state of being thick
**3 a** : viscous consistency ⟨boiled to the *thickness* of honey⟩ **b** : the condition of being smoky, foul, or foggy
**4** : the thick part of something
**5** : CONCENTRATION, DENSITY
**6** : STUPIDITY, DULLNESS
**7** : LAYER, PLY, SHEET ⟨a single *thickness* of canvas⟩

**thick·set** \-,set\ *adjective* (14th century)
**1** : closely placed; *also* : growing thickly ⟨a *thickset* wood⟩
**2** : having a thick body : BURLY

**thick–skinned** \-,skind\ *adjective* (1545)
**1** : having a thick skin : PACHYDERMATOUS
**2 a** : CALLOUS, INSENSITIVE **b** : impervious to criticism

**thick–wit·ted** \-,wi-təd\ *adjective* (1634)
: dull or slow of mind : STUPID

**thief** \'thēf\ *noun, plural* **thieves** \'thēvz\ [Middle English *theef*, from Old English *thēof*; akin to Old High German *diob* thief] (before 12th century)
: one that steals especially stealthily or secretly; *also* : one who commits theft or larceny

**thieve** \'thēv\ *verb* **thieved; thiev·ing** (before 12th century)
: STEAL, ROB

**thiev·ery** \'thēv-rē, 'thē-və-\ *noun, plural* **-er·ies** (1568)
: the act or practice or an instance of stealing : THEFT

**thiev·ish** \'thē-vish\ *adjective* (1538)
**1** : given to stealing
**2** : of, relating to, or characteristic of a thief

— **thiev·ish·ly** *adverb*
— **thiev·ish·ness** *noun*

**thigh** \'thī\ *noun* [Middle English, from Old English *thēoh*; akin to Old High German *dioh* thigh, Lithuanian *taukai*, plural, fat] (before 12th century)
**1 a** : the proximal segment of the vertebrate hind limb extending from the hip to the knee and supported by a single large bone **b** : the segment of the leg immediately distal to the thigh in a bird or in a quadruped in which the true thigh is obscured **c** : the femur of an insect
**2** : something resembling or covering a thigh
— **thighed** \'thīd\ *adjective*

**thigh·bone** \'thī-,bōn\ *noun* (15th century)
: FEMUR 1

**thig·mo·tax·is** \,thig-mə-'tak-səs\ *noun* [New Latin, from Greek *thigma* touch (from *thinganein* to touch) + New Latin *-taxis*; akin to Latin *fingere* to shape — more at DOUGH] (1903)
: a taxis in which contact especially with a solid body is the directive factor

**thig·mot·ro·pism** \thig-'mä-trə-,pi-zəm\ *noun* [Greek *thigma* + International Scientific Vocabulary *-o-* + *-tropism*] (circa 1900)
: a tropism in which contact especially with a solid or a rigid surface is the orienting factor

**thill** \'thil\ *noun* [Middle English *thille*, perhaps from Old English, plank; akin to Old English *thel* board, Old High German *dili*, and probably to Latin *tellus* earth] (14th century)
: a shaft of a vehicle

**thim·ble** \'thim-bəl\ *noun* [Middle English *thymbyl*, probably alteration of Old English *thȳmel* covering for the thumb, from *thūma* thumb] (15th century)
**1** : a pitted cap or cover worn on the finger to push the needle in sewing
**2 a** : a grooved ring of thin metal used to fit in a spliced loop in a rope as protection from chafing **b** : a lining (as of metal) for an opening (as in a roof or wall) through which a stovepipe or chimney passes

**thim·ble·ber·ry** \-,ber-ē\ *noun* (1788)
: any of several American raspberries or blackberries (especially *Rubus occidentalis, R. parviflorus,* and *R. odoratus*) having thimble-shaped fruit

**thim·ble·ful** \-,ful\ *noun* (1607)
**1** : as much as a thimble will hold
**2** : a very small quantity

¹**thim·ble·rig** \-,rig\ *noun* (1826)
**1** : a swindling trick in which a small ball or pea is quickly shifted from under one to another of three small cups to fool the spectator guessing its location
**2** : one who manipulates the cup in thimblerig : THIMBLERIGGER

²**thimblerig** *transitive verb* (1839)
**1** : to cheat by trickery
**2** : to swindle by thimblerig
— **thim·ble·rig·ger** *noun*

**thim·ble·weed** \'thim-bəl-,wēd\ *noun* (1833)
: any of various anemones (as *Anemone virginiana* and *A. cylindrica*)

**thi·mer·o·sal** \thī-'mer-ə-,sal\ *noun* [probably from *thi-* + *mercury* + *-o-* + *salicylate*] (1949)
: a crystalline organic mercurial antiseptic $C_9H_9HgNaO_2S$ used especially for its antifungal and bacteriostatic properties

¹**thin** \'thin\ *adjective* **thin·ner; thin·nest** [Middle English *thinne*, from Old English *thynne*; akin to Old High German *dunni* thin, Latin *tenuis*, *tenēre* to hold, *tendere* to stretch, Greek *teinein*] (before 12th century)
**1 a** : having little extent from one surface to its opposite ⟨*thin* paper⟩ **b** : measuring little in cross section or diameter ⟨*thin* rope⟩
**2** : not dense in arrangement or distribution ⟨*thin* hair⟩
**3** : not well fleshed : LEAN

**4 a** : more fluid or rarefied than normal ⟨*thin* air⟩ **b** : having less than the usual number : SCANTY ⟨*thin* attendance⟩ **c** : few in number : SCARCE **d** : scantily supplied **e** : characterized by a paucity of bids or offerings ⟨a *thin* market⟩
**5 a** : lacking substance or strength ⟨*thin* broth⟩ ⟨a *thin* plot⟩ **b** *of a soil* : INFERTILE, POOR
**6 a** : FLIMSY, UNCONVINCING ⟨a *thin* disguise⟩ **b** : disappointingly poor or hard ⟨had a *thin* time of it⟩
**7** : somewhat feeble, shrill, and lacking in resonance ⟨a *thin* voice⟩
**8** : lacking in intensity or brilliance ⟨*thin* light⟩
**9** : lacking sufficient photographic density or contrast ☆
— **thin·ly** *adverb*
— **thin·ness** \'thin-nəs\ *noun*
— **thin·nish** \'thi-nish\ *adjective*

²**thin** *verb* **thinned; thin·ning** (before 12th century)
*transitive verb*
: to make thin or thinner: **a** : to reduce in thickness or depth : ATTENUATE **b** : to make less dense or viscous **c** : DILUTE, WEAKEN **d** : to cause to lose flesh ⟨*thinned* by weeks of privation⟩ **e** : to reduce in number or bulk
*intransitive verb*
**1** : to become thin or thinner
**2** : to become weak

³**thin** *adverb* **thin·ner; thin·nest** (13th century)
: in a thin manner : THINLY — used especially in combinations ⟨*thin*-clad⟩ ⟨*thin*-flowing⟩

¹**thine** \'thīn\ *adjective* [Middle English *thin*, from Old English *thīn*] (before 12th century)
*archaic* : THY — used especially before a word beginning with a vowel or *h*

²**thine** *pronoun, singular or plural in construction* [Middle English *thin*, from Old English *thīn*, from *thīn* thy — more at THY] (before 12th century)
*archaic* : that which belongs to thee — used without a following noun as a pronoun equivalent in meaning to the adjective *thy;* used especially in ecclesiastical or literary language and still surviving in the speech of Friends especially among themselves

**thin film** *noun* (1944)
: a very thin layer of a substance on a supporting material; *especially* : a coating (as of a semiconductor) that is deposited in a layer one atom or one molecule thick

**thing** \'thiŋ\ *noun* [Middle English, from Old English, thing, assembly; akin to Old High German *ding* thing, assembly, Gothic *theihs* time] (before 12th century)
**1 a** : a matter of concern : AFFAIR ⟨many *things* to do⟩ **b** *plural* : state of affairs in general or within a specified or implied sphere ⟨*things* are improving⟩ **c** : a particular state of affairs : SITUATION ⟨look at this *thing* another way⟩ **d** : EVENT, CIRCUMSTANCE ⟨that shooting was a terrible *thing*⟩

---

☆ **SYNONYMS**
**Thin, slender, slim, slight, tenuous**
mean not thick, broad, abundant, or dense. THIN implies comparatively little extension between surfaces or in diameter, or it may imply lack of substance, richness, or abundance ⟨*thin* wire⟩ ⟨a *thin* soup⟩. SLENDER implies leanness or spareness often with grace and good proportion ⟨the *slender* legs of a Sheraton chair⟩. SLIM applies to slenderness that suggests fragility or scantiness ⟨a *slim* volume of poetry⟩ ⟨a *slim* chance⟩. SLIGHT implies smallness as well as thinness ⟨a *slight* build⟩. TENUOUS implies extreme thinness, sheerness, or lack of substance and firmness ⟨a *tenuous* thread⟩.

**2 a :** DEED, ACT, ACCOMPLISHMENT ⟨do great *things*⟩ **b :** a product of work or activity ⟨likes to build *things*⟩ **c :** the aim of effort or activity ⟨the *thing* is to get well⟩
**3 a :** a separate and distinct individual quality, fact, idea, or usually entity **b :** the concrete entity as distinguished from its appearances **c :** a spatial entity **d :** an inanimate object distinguished from a living being
**4 a** *plural* **:** POSSESSIONS, EFFECTS ⟨pack your *things*⟩ **b :** whatever may be possessed or owned or be the object of a right **c :** an article of clothing ⟨not a *thing* to wear⟩ **d** *plural* **:** equipment or utensils especially for a particular purpose ⟨bring the tea *things*⟩
**5 :** an object or entity not precisely designated or capable of being designated ⟨use this *thing*⟩
**6 a :** DETAIL, POINT ⟨checks every little *thing*⟩ **b :** a material or substance of a specified kind ⟨avoid fatty *things*⟩
**7 a :** a spoken or written observation or point **b :** IDEA, NOTION ⟨says the first *thing* he thinks of⟩ **c :** a piece of news or information ⟨couldn't get a *thing* out of him⟩
**8 :** INDIVIDUAL ⟨not a living *thing* in sight⟩
**9 :** the proper or fashionable way of behaving, talking, or dressing — used with *the*
**10 a :** a mild obsession or phobia ⟨has a *thing* about driving⟩; *also* **:** the object of such an obsession or phobia **b :** something (as an activity) that makes a strong appeal to the individual **:** FORTE, SPECIALTY ⟨letting students do their own *thing* —*Newsweek*⟩ ⟨I think travelling is very much a novelist's *thing* —Philip Larkin⟩
◆
**thing·am·a·bob**   \'thiŋ-ə-mə-ˌbäb\   *noun* (1832)
**:** THINGAMAJIG
**thing·am·a·jig** *or* **thing·um·a·jig** \'thiŋ-ə-mə-ˌjig\ *noun* [alteration of earlier *thingum*, from *thing*] (1828)
**:** something that is hard to classify or whose name is unknown or forgotten
**thing–in–itself** *noun*, *plural* **things–in–themselves** [translation of German *Ding an sich*] (1798)
**:** NOUMENON
**thing·ness** \'thiŋ-nəs\ *noun* (1896)
**:** the quality or state of objective existence or reality
**thing·um·my** \'thiŋ-ə-mē\ *noun*, *plural* **-mies** [alteration of earlier *thingum*] (1796)
**:** THINGAMAJIG
**¹think** \'thiŋk\ *verb* **thought** \'thȯt\; **thinking** [Middle English *thenken*, from Old English *thencan*; akin to Old High German *denken* to think, Latin *tongēre* to know — more at THANKS] (before 12th century)
*transitive verb*
**1 :** to form or have in the mind
**2 :** to have as an intention ⟨*thought* to return early⟩
**3 a :** to have as an opinion ⟨*think* it's so⟩ **b :** to regard as **:** CONSIDER ⟨*think* the rule unfair⟩
**4 a :** to reflect on **:** PONDER ⟨*think* the matter over⟩ **b :** to determine by reflecting ⟨*think* what to do next⟩
**5 :** to call to mind **:** REMEMBER ⟨he never *thinks* to ask how we do⟩
**6 :** to devise by thinking — usually used with *up* ⟨*thought* up a plan to escape⟩
**7 :** to have as an expectation **:** ANTICIPATE ⟨we didn't *think* we'd have any trouble⟩
**8 a :** to center one's thoughts on ⟨talks and *thinks* business⟩ **b :** to form a mental picture of
**9 :** to subject to the processes of logical thought ⟨*think* things out⟩
*intransitive verb*
**1 a :** to exercise the powers of judgment, conception, or inference **:** REASON **b :** to have in the mind or call to mind a thought
**2 a :** to have the mind engaged in reflection **:** MEDITATE **b :** to consider the suitability ⟨*thought* of her for president⟩

**3 :** to have a view or opinion ⟨*thinks* of himself as a poet⟩
**4 :** to have concern — usually used with *of* ⟨a man must *think* first of his family⟩
**5 :** to consider something likely **:** SUSPECT ⟨may happen sooner than you *think*⟩ ☆ ☆
— **think·er** *noun*
— **think better of :** to reconsider and make a wiser decision
— **think much of :** to view with satisfaction **:** APPROVE — usually used in negative constructions ⟨I didn't *think much of* the new car⟩
**²think** *noun* (1834)
**:** an act of thinking ⟨has another *think* coming⟩
**³think** *adjective* (1906)
**:** relating to, requiring, or stimulating thinking
**think·able** \'thiŋ-kə-bəl\ *adjective* (1854)
**1 :** capable of being comprehended or reasoned about ⟨the ultimate nature of Deity is scarcely *thinkable*⟩
**2 :** conceivably possible
— **think·able·ness** *noun*
— **think·ably** \-blē\ *adverb*
**¹thinking** *noun* (14th century)
**1 :** the action of using one's mind to produce thoughts
**2 a :** OPINION, JUDGMENT ⟨I'd like to know your *thinking* on this⟩ **b :** thought that is characteristic (as of a period, group, or person) ⟨the current student *thinking* on fraternities⟩
**²thinking** *adjective* (1681)
**:** marked by use of the intellect **:** RATIONAL ⟨*thinking* citizens⟩
— **think·ing·ly** \'thiŋ-kiŋ-lē\ *adverb*
— **think·ing·ness** *noun*
**thinking cap** *noun* (1874)
**:** a state or mood in which one thinks — usually used in the phrase *put one's thinking cap on*
**think piece** *noun* (1941)
**:** a piece of writing meant to be thought-provoking and speculative that consists chiefly of background material and personal opinion and analysis
**think tank** *noun* (1959)
**:** an institute, corporation, or group organized for interdisciplinary research (as in technological and social problems) — called also *think factory*
**thin–layer chromatography** *noun* (1957)
**:** chromatography in which the stationary phase is an absorbent medium (as alumina or silica gel) arranged as a thin layer on a rigid support (as a glass plate)
**thin·ner** \'thi-nər\ *noun* (1832)
**:** one that thins; *specifically* **:** a volatile liquid (as turpentine) used especially to thin paint
**thin–skinned** \'thin-ˌskind\ *adjective* (1598)
**1 :** having a thin skin or rind
**2 :** unduly susceptible to criticism or insult **:** TOUCHY
**thio-** — see THI-
**thio acid** \'thī-ō-\ *noun* [International Scientific Vocabulary, from *thi-*] (circa 1891)
**:** an acid in which oxygen is partly or wholly replaced by sulfur
**thio·cy·a·nate** \ˌthī-ō-'sī-ə-ˌnāt, -nət\ *noun* [International Scientific Vocabulary] (1877)
**:** a compound that consists of the chemical group SCN bonded by the sulfur atom to a group or an atom other than a hydrogen atom
**thi·ol** \'thī-ˌȯl, -ˌōl\ *noun* [International Scientific Vocabulary *thi-* + *¹-ol*] (circa 1890)
**1 :** any of various compounds having the general formula RSH which are analogous to alcohols but in which sulfur replaces the oxygen of the hydroxyl group and which have disagreeable odors
**2 :** the functional group — SH characteristic of thiols
— **thi·o·lic** \thī-'ō-lik\ *adjective*
**thion-** *combining form* [International Scientific Vocabulary, from Greek *theion*]
**:** sulfur ⟨me*thion*ine⟩

---

☆ SYNONYMS
**Think, conceive, imagine, fancy, realize, envisage, envision** mean to form an idea of. THINK implies the entrance of an idea into one's mind with or without deliberate consideration or reflection ⟨I just *thought* of a good joke⟩. CONCEIVE suggests the forming and bringing forth and usually developing of an idea, plan, or design ⟨*conceived* of a new marketing approach⟩. IMAGINE stresses a visualization ⟨*imagine* you're at the beach⟩. FANCY suggests an imagining often unrestrained by reality but spurred by desires ⟨*fancied* himself a super athlete⟩. REALIZE stresses a grasping of the significance of what is conceived or imagined ⟨*realized* the enormity of the task ahead⟩. ENVISAGE and ENVISION imply a conceiving or imagining that is especially clear or detailed ⟨*envisaged* a totally computerized operation⟩ ⟨*envisioned* a cure for the disease⟩.

**Think, cogitate, reflect, reason, speculate, deliberate** mean to use one's powers of conception, judgment, or inference. THINK is general and may apply to any mental activity, but used alone often suggests attainment of clear ideas or conclusions ⟨teaches students how to *think*⟩. COGITATE implies deep or intent thinking ⟨*cogitated* on the mysteries of nature⟩. REFLECT suggests unhurried consideration of something recalled to the mind ⟨*reflecting* on fifty years of married life⟩. REASON stresses consecutive logical thinking ⟨able to *reason* brilliantly in debate⟩. SPECULATE implies reasoning about things theoretical or problematic ⟨*speculated* on the fate of the lost explorers⟩. DELIBERATE suggests slow or careful reasoning before forming an opinion or reaching a conclusion or decision ⟨the jury *deliberated* for five hours before reaching a verdict⟩.

---

◇ WORD HISTORY
**thing** Old English *thing* and its cognates in other early Germanic languages meant "assembly, court." This meaning has long fallen into disuse in English, German, and Dutch, but the Scandinavian languages preserve it, notably in the names of national legislatures, such as the *Althing* ("general assembly") in Iceland and the *Storting* ("big assembly") in Norway. The passage of Old English *thing* from "assembly" to a meaning as nebulous as "thing" seems peculiar, but is actually fairly straightforward given some intermediary steps. The sequence runs from "assembly, court" to "matter before an assembly, case before a court" to the more general "matter, affair, concern" and finally to "thing" in its many and varied modern applications. Parallel shifts of meaning can be found in the histories of English *sake* and its German cognate *Sache* "thing, affair," both of whose antecedents meant "action at law," and French *chose* "thing," from Latin *causa* "legal case." Before it meant "assembly" the common Germanic word represented by Old English *thing* most likely meant simply "something fixed, fixed time" (hence, "meeting at a fixed time"). A hint of this earlier meaning is given by the cognate word *theihs* "time, occasion" in Gothic, the oldest fully attested Germanic language.

---

\ə\ abut \ᵊ\ kitten \ər\ further \a\ ash \ā\ ace
\ä\ mop, mar \aů\ out \ch\ chin \e\ bet \ē\ easy
\g\ go \i\ hit \ī\ ice \j\ job \ŋ\ sing \ō\ go
\ȯ\ law \ȯi\ boy \th\ thin \t͟h\ the \ü\ loot \ů\ foot
\y\ yet \zh\ vision   *see also* Guide to Pronunciation

**thi·o·pen·tal** \ˌthī-ō-'pen-ˌtal, -ˌtȯl\ *noun* [*thi-* + *pento*barbi*tal*] (1947)
: a barbiturate $C_{11}H_{18}N_2O_2S$ used in the form of its sodium salt especially as an intravenous anesthetic — compare PENTOTHAL

**thio·phene** \'thī-ə-ˌfēn\ *noun* [International Scientific Vocabulary *thi-* + *phene* benzene] (1883)
: a heterocyclic liquid $C_4H_4S$ from coal tar that resembles benzene

**thi·o·rid·a·zine** \ˌthī-ə-'ri-də-ˌzēn, -zən\ *noun* [*thi-* + *piperid*ine + phenothia*zine*] (1959)
: a phenothiazine tranquilizer used as the hydrochloride $C_{21}H_{26}N_2S_2·HCl$ for relief of anxiety states and in the treatment of schizophrenia

**thio·sul·fate** \-'səl-ˌfāt\ *noun* [International Scientific Vocabulary] (1873)
: a salt containing the anion $S_2O_3^{2-}$

**thio·te·pa** \ˌthī-ə-'tē-pə\ *noun* (1953)
: a sulfur analogue of tepa $C_6H_{12}N_3PS$ that is used especially as an antineoplastic agent

**thio·ura·cil** \ˌthī-ō-'yùr-ə-ˌsil\ *noun* [International Scientific Vocabulary] (1905)
: a bitter crystalline compound $C_4H_4N_2OS$ that depresses the function of the thyroid gland

**thio·urea** \-yù-'rē-ə\ *noun* [New Latin] (1894)
: a colorless crystalline bitter compound $CS(NH_2)_2$ analogous to and resembling urea that is used especially as a photographic and organic chemical reagent; *also* : a substituted derivative of this compound

**thir** \thər, 'thi(ə)r, 'thùr\ *pronoun or adjective* [Middle English (northern), perhaps irregular from Middle English *this*] (14th century)
*dialect British* : THESE

**thi·ram** \'thī-ˌram\ *noun* [probably by alteration from *thiuram* the chemical group $NH_2CS$] (1949)
: a compound $C_6H_{12}N_2S_4$ used as a fungicide and seed disinfectant

**¹third** \'thərd\ *adjective* [Middle English *thridde, thirde*, from Old English *thridda, thirdda*; akin to Latin *tertius* third, Greek *tritos, treis* three — more at THREE] (before 12th century)
**1 a :** being next after the second in place or time ⟨the *third* taxi in line⟩ **b :** ranking next after the second of a grade or degree in authority or precedence ⟨*third* mate⟩ **c :** being the forward speed or gear next higher than second especially in a motor vehicle
**2 a :** being one of three equal parts into which something is divisible **b :** being the last in each group of three in a series ⟨take out every *third* card⟩
**— third** *or* **third·ly** *adverb*

**²third** *noun* (14th century)
**1 :** one of three equal parts of something
**2 a —** see NUMBER table **b :** one that is next after second in rank, position, authority, or precedence ⟨the *third* in line⟩
**3 a :** the musical interval embracing three diatonic degrees **b :** a tone at this interval; *specifically* : MEDIANT **c :** the harmonic combination of two tones a third apart
**4** *plural* : merchandise whose quality falls below the manufacturer's standard for seconds
**5 :** THIRD BASE
**6 :** the third forward gear or speed especially of a motor vehicle

**third base** *noun* (1845)
**1 :** the base that must be touched third by a base runner in baseball
**2 :** the player position for defending the area around third base
**— third baseman** *noun*

**third–class** *adjective* (1839)
: of or relating to a class, rank, or grade next below the second
**— third–class** *adverb*

**third class** *noun* (1844)
**1 :** the third and usually next below second class in a classification
**2 :** the least expensive class of accommodations (as on a passenger ship)

**3 a :** a class of U.S. mail comprising printed matter exclusive of regularly issued periodicals and merchandise less than 16 ounces (454 grams) in weight that is not sealed against inspection **b :** a similar class of Canadian mail with different weight limits

**third degree** *noun* (1900)
: the subjection of a prisoner to mental or physical torture to extract a confession

**third–degree burn** *noun* (1930)
: a severe burn characterized by destruction of the skin through its deeper layers and possibly into underlying tissues, loss of fluid, and sometimes shock

**third dimension** *noun* (1858)
**1 :** THICKNESS, DEPTH; *also* : a dimension that adds the effect of solidity to a two-dimensional system
**2 :** a quality that confers reality or lifelikeness ⟨night sounds that stick in the mind and give a *third dimension* to the memory —Adie Suehsdorf⟩
**— third–dimensional** *adjective*

**third estate** *noun, often T&E capitalized* (1604)
: the third of the traditional political orders; *specifically* : the commons

**third force** *noun* [translation of French *troisième force*] (1936)
: a grouping (as of political parties or international powers) intermediate between two opposing political forces

**third·hand** \'thərd-'hand\ *adjective* (1599)
**1 :** received from or through two intermediaries ⟨*thirdhand* information⟩
**2 a :** acquired after being used by two previous owners **b :** dealing in thirdhand merchandise

**third house** *noun* (1849)
: a legislative lobby

**third market** *noun* (1964)
: the over-the-counter market in listed securities

**third order** *noun, often T&O capitalized* (1629)
**1 :** an organization composed of lay people living in secular society under a religious rule and directed by a religious order
**2 :** a congregation especially of teaching or nursing sisters affiliated with a religious order

**third party** *noun* (1801)
**1 a :** a major political party operating over a limited period of time in addition to two other major parties in a nation or state normally characterized by a two-party system **b :** MINOR PARTY
**2 :** a person other than the principals ⟨a *third party* to a divorce proceeding⟩

**third person** *noun* (circa 1586)
**1 a :** a set of linguistic forms (as verb forms, pronouns, and inflectional affixes) referring to one that is neither the speaker or writer of the utterance in which they occur nor the one to whom that utterance is addressed **b :** a linguistic form belonging to such a set
**2 :** reference of a linguistic form to one that is neither the speaker or writer of the utterance in which it occurs nor the one to whom that utterance is addressed

**third rail** *noun* (1890)
: a metal rail through which electric current is led to the motors of an electric vehicle (as a subway car)

**third–rate** \'thərd-'rāt\ *adjective* (1814)
: of third quality or value; *specifically* : worse than second-rate
**— third–rat·er** \-'rā-tər\ *noun*

**third reading** *noun* (circa 1571)
: the final stage of the consideration of a legislative bill before a vote on its final disposition

**third–stream** *adjective* (1962)
: of, relating to, or being music that incorporates elements of classical music and jazz

**third ventricle** *noun* (circa 1860)

: the median unpaired ventricle of the brain bounded by parts of the telencephalon and diencephalon

**third world** *noun, often T&W capitalized* [translation of French *tiers monde*] (1963)
**1 :** a group of nations especially in Africa and Asia not aligned with either the Communist or the non-Communist blocs
**2 :** an aggregate of minority groups within a larger predominant culture
**3 :** the aggregate of the underdeveloped nations of the world
**— third world·er** \-'wər(-ə)l-dər\ *noun, often T&W capitalized*

**¹thirl** \'thər(-ə)l\ *noun* [Middle English, from Old English *thyrel*, from *thurh* through — more at THROUGH] (before 12th century)
*dialect* : HOLE, PERFORATION, OPENING

**²thirl** *transitive verb* (before 12th century)
*dialect British* : PIERCE, PERFORATE

**¹thirst** \'thərst\ *noun* [Middle English, from Old English *thurst*; akin to Old High German *durst* thirst, Latin *torrēre* to dry, parch, Greek *tersesthai* to become dry] (before 12th century)
**1 a :** a sensation of dryness in the mouth and throat associated with a desire for liquids; *also* : the bodily condition (as of dehydration) that induces this sensation ⟨a desire or need to drink⟩
**2 :** an ardent desire : CRAVING, LONGING

**²thirst** *intransitive verb* (before 12th century)
**1 :** to feel thirsty : suffer thirst
**2 :** to crave vehemently and urgently
**synonym** see LONG
**— thirst·er** *noun*

**thirst·i·ly** \'thər-stə-lē\ *adverb* (1549)
: with or on account of thirst

**thirsty** \'thər-stē\ *adjective* **thirst·i·er; -est** (before 12th century)
**1 a :** feeling thirst **b :** deficient in moisture : PARCHED ⟨*thirsty* land⟩ **c :** highly absorbent ⟨*thirsty* towels⟩
**2 :** having a strong desire : AVID ⟨*thirsty* for knowledge⟩
**— thirst·i·ness** \-stē-nəs\ *noun*

**thir·teen** \ˌthər(t)-'tēn, 'thər(t)-\ *noun* [Middle English *thrittene*, from *thrittene*, adjective, from Old English *thrēotīne*; akin to Old English *tīen* ten — more at TEN] (14th century)
**—** see NUMBER table
**— thirteen** *adjective*
**— thirteen** *pronoun, plural in construction*
**— thir·teenth** \-'tēn(t)th, -ˌtēn(t)th\ *adjective or noun*

**thir·ty** \'thər-tē\ *noun, plural* **thirties** [Middle English *thritty*, from *thritty*, adjective, from Old English *thrītig*, from *thrītig* group of 30, from *thrīe* three + *-tig* group of ten; akin to Old English *tīen* ten] (before 12th century)
**1 —** see NUMBER table
**2** *plural* : the numbers 30 to 39; *specifically* : the years 30 to 39 in a lifetime or century
**3 :** a sign of completion : END — usually written 30 ⟨wrote *thirty* on the last page of the story⟩
**4 :** the second point scored by a side in a game of tennis
**— thir·ti·eth** \-tē-əth\ *adjective or noun*
**— thirty** *adjective*
**— thirty** *pronoun, plural in construction*
**— thir·ty·ish** \-ish\ *adjective*

**thir·ty–eight** \ˌthər-tē-'āt\ *noun* (circa 1934)
**1 —** see NUMBER table
**2 :** a handgun nominally of .38 caliber — usually written .38
**— thirty–eight** *adjective*
**— thirty–eight** *pronoun, plural in construction*

**thir·ty–sec·ond note** \-'se-kən(d)-ˌnōt, -kən(t)-\ *noun* (circa 1890)
: a musical note with the time value of $\frac{1}{32}$ of a whole note — see NOTE illustration

**thirty–second rest** *noun* (circa 1903)
: a musical rest corresponding in time value to a thirty-second note

**thir·ty–thir·ty** \,thər-tē-'thər-tē\ *noun* (1929)
: a rifle that fires a .30 caliber cartridge having a 30 grain powder charge — usually written .30–30

**thir·ty–three** \,thər-tē-'thrē\ *noun* (1902)
**1** — see NUMBER table
**2 :** a microgroove phonograph record designed to be played at 33⅓ revolutions per minute — usually written 33
— **thirty–three** *adjective*
— **thirty–three** *pronoun, plural in construction*

**thir·ty–two** \-'tü\ *noun* (1904)
**1** — see NUMBER table
**2 :** a .32 caliber handgun — usually written .32
— **thirty–two** *adjective*
— **thirty–two** *pronoun, plural in construction*

**thir·ty–two·mo** \-(,)mō\ *noun, plural* **-mos** (circa 1841)
: the size of a piece of paper cut 32 from a sheet; *also* **:** a book, a page, or paper of this size

**¹this** \'this, thəs\ *pronoun, plural* **these** \'thēz\ [Middle English, pronoun & adjective, from Old English *thes* (masculine), *this* (neuter); akin to Old High German *dese* this, Old English *thæt* that] (before 12th century)
**1 a** (1) **:** the person, thing, or idea that is present or near in place, time, or thought or that has just been mentioned ⟨*these* are my hands⟩ (2) **:** what is stated in the following phrase, clause, or discourse ⟨I can only say *this*: it wasn't here yesterday⟩ **b :** this time or place ⟨expected to return before *this*⟩
**2 a :** the one nearer or more immediately under observation or discussion ⟨*this* is iron and that is tin⟩ **b :** the one more recently referred to

**²this** *adjective, plural* **these** (before 12th century)
**1 a :** being the person, thing, or idea that is present or near in place, time, or thought or that has just been mentioned ⟨*this* book is mine⟩ ⟨early *this* morning⟩ **b :** constituting the immediately following part of the present discourse **c :** constituting the immediate past or future ⟨friends all *these* years⟩ **d :** being one not previously mentioned — used especially in narrative to give a sense of immediacy or vividness ⟨then *this* guy runs in⟩
**2 :** being the nearer at hand or more immediately under observation or discussion ⟨*this* car or that one⟩

**³this** \'this\ *adverb* (15th century)
**:** to the degree or extent indicated by something in the immediate context or situation ⟨didn't expect to wait *this* long⟩

**This·be** \'thiz-bē\ *noun* [Latin, from Greek *Thisbē*]
**:** a legendary young woman of Babylon who dies for love of Pyramus

**this·tle** \'thi-səl\ *noun* [Middle English *thistel*, from Old English; akin to Old High German *distill* thistle] (before 12th century)
**:** any of various prickly composite plants (especially genera *Carduus, Cirsium,* and *Onopordum*) with often showy heads of mostly tubular flowers; *also*
**:** any of various other prickly plants
— **this·tly** \'thi-s(ə-)lē\ *adjective*

**this·tle·down** \'thi-səl-,daůn\ *noun* (1561)
**:** the typically plumose pappus from the ripe flower head of a thistle

thistle

**thistle tube** *noun* (circa 1891)
**:** a funnel tube usually of glass with a bulging top and flaring mouth

**this–world·li·ness** \'this-'wərld-lē-nəs\ *noun* (1887)
**:** interest in, concern with, or devotion to things of this world especially as opposed to a future stage of existence (as after death)

**this–world·ly** \-lē\ *adjective* (1883)
**:** characterized by or manifesting this-worldliness

**¹thith·er** \'thi-thər *also* 'thi-\ *adverb* [Middle English, from Old English *thider*; akin to Old Norse *thathra* there, Old English *thæt* that] (before 12th century)
**:** to that place **:** THERE

**²thither** *adjective* (1830)
**:** being on the other and farther side **:** more remote

**thith·er·to** \-,tü; ,thi-thər-', ,thi-\ *adverb* (15th century)
**:** until that time

**thith·er·ward** \'thi-thər-wərd, 'thi-\ *also* **thith·er·wards** \-wərdz\ *adverb* (before 12th century)
**:** toward that place **:** THITHER

**thix·ot·ro·py** \thik-'sä-trə-pē\ *noun* [International Scientific Vocabulary *thixo-* (from Greek *thixis* act of touching, from *thinganein* to touch) + *-tropy* — more at THIGMOTAXIS] (1927)
**:** the property of various gels of becoming fluid when disturbed (as by shaking)
— **thixo·tro·pic** \,thik-sə-'trō-pik, -'trä-\ *adjective*

**tho** *variant of* THOUGH

**¹thole** \'thōl\ *verb* **tholed; thol·ing** [Middle English, from Old English *tholian* — more at TOLERATE] (before 12th century)
*chiefly dialect* **:** ENDURE

**²thole** *noun* [Middle English *tholle*, from Old English *thol*; akin to Old Norse *thollr* fir tree, peg, Greek *tylos* knob, callus] (before 12th century)
**1 :** either of a pair of pins set in the gunwale of a boat to hold an oar in place
**2 :** PEG, PIN

**tho·lei·ite** \'tō-lə-,īt, 'thō-\ *noun* [German *Tholeiit*, from *Tholey*, village in Saarland, Germany + German *-it* -ite] (1866)
**:** a basaltic rock that is rich in aluminum and low in potassium, is found typically in the ocean floor, and is probably derived from the earth's mantle
— **tho·lei·it·ic** \,tō-lə-'i-tik, ,thō-\ *adjective*

**thole·pin** \'thōl-,pin\ *noun* (1598)
**:** THOLE 1

**Thom·as** \'tä-məs\ *noun* [Greek *Thōmas*, from Hebrew *t'ōm* twin]
**:** an apostle who demanded proof of Christ's resurrection

**Thom·as Jef·fer·son's Birthday** \'tä-məs-'je-fər-sənz-\ *noun* (circa 1928)
**:** April 13 observed as a legal holiday in Alabama

**Tho·mism** \'tō-,mi-zəm\ *noun* [New Latin *Thomista* Thomist, from Saint *Thomas* Aquinas] (circa 1731)
**:** the scholastic philosophical and theological system of Saint Thomas Aquinas
— **Tho·mist** \-mist\ *noun or adjective*
— **Tho·mis·tic** \tō-'mis-tik\ *adjective*

**Thomp·son submachine gun** \'täm(p)-sən-\ *noun* [John T. *Thompson* (died 1940) American army officer] (1920)
**:** a .45 caliber submachine gun with a drum or stick magazine, a pistol grip, and a detachable buttstock

**Thom·son's gazelle** \'täm(p)-sənz-\ *noun* [Joseph *Thomson* (died 1895) Scottish explorer] (1897)
**:** a small gazelle (*Gazella thomsoni*) of eastern Africa that is tan above and white below with a broad black stripe on each side

**thong** \'thȯŋ\ *noun* [Middle English, from Old English *thwong*; akin Old Norse *thvengr* thong] (before 12th century)
**1 :** a strip especially of leather or hide
**2 :** a sandal held on the foot by a thong fitting between the toes and connected to a strap across the top or around the sides of the foot

— **thonged** \'thȯŋd\ *adjective*

**Thor** \'thȯr\ *noun* [Old Norse *Thōrr*]
**:** the Norse god of thunder, weather, and crops

**tho·rac·ic** \thə-'ra-sik\ *adjective* (circa 1658)
**:** of, relating to, located within, or involving the thorax
— **tho·rac·i·cal·ly** \-si-k(ə-)lē\ *adverb*

**thoracic duct** *noun* (circa 1741)
**:** the main trunk of the system of lymphatic vessels that lies along the front of the spinal column and opens into the left subclavian vein

**tho·ra·cot·o·my** \,thȯr-ə-'kä-tə-mē, ,thȯr-\ *noun, plural* **-mies** [Latin *thorac-, thorax* + International Scientific Vocabulary *-tomy*] (circa 1857)
**:** surgical incision of the chest wall

**tho·rax** \'thȯr-,aks, 'thȯr-\ *noun, plural* **tho·rax·es** *or* **tho·ra·ces** \'thȯr-ə-,sēz, 'thȯr-\ [Middle English, from Latin *thorac-, thorax* breastplate, thorax, from Greek *thōrak-, thōrax*] (15th century)
**1 :** the part of the mammalian body between the neck and the abdomen; *also* **:** its cavity in which the heart and lungs lie
**2 :** the middle of the three chief divisions of the body of an insect; *also* **:** the corresponding part of a crustacean or an arachnid

**Tho·ra·zine** \'thȯr-ə-,zēn, 'thȯr-\ *trademark*
— used for chlorpromazine

**tho·ria** \'thȯr-ē-ə, 'thȯr-\ *noun* [New Latin, from *thorium* + *-a*] (circa 1841)
**:** a powdery white oxide of thorium $ThO_2$ used especially as a catalyst and in crucibles and refractories and optical glass

**tho·ri·a·nite** \-ē-ə-,nīt\ *noun* [irregular from *thoria*] (1904)
**:** a strongly radioactive mineral that is an oxide of thorium and often contains rare-earth metals

**tho·rite** \'thȯr-,īt, 'thȯr-\ *noun* [Swedish *thorit*, from New Latin *thorium*] (1832)
**:** a rare mineral that is a brown to black or sometimes orange-yellow silicate of thorium resembling zircon

**tho·ri·um** \'thȯr-ē-əm, 'thȯr-\ *noun* [New Latin, from Old Norse *Thōrr* Thor] (1832)
**:** a radioactive metallic element that occurs combined in minerals and is usually associated with rare earths — see ELEMENT table

**thorn** \'thȯrn\ *noun, often attributive* [Middle English, from Old English; akin to Old High German *dorn* thorn, Sanskrit *tṛṇa* grass, blade of grass] (before 12th century)
**1 :** a woody plant bearing sharp impeding processes (as briers, prickles, or spines); *especially* **:** HAWTHORN
**2 a :** a sharp rigid process on a plant; *specifically* **:** a short, indurated, sharp-pointed, and leafless modified branch **b :** any of various sharp spinose structures on an animal
**3 :** the runic letter þ used in Old English, Middle English, and Icelandic to represent either of the fricatives \th\ or \th\
**4 :** something that causes distress or irritation — often used in the phrase *thorn in one's side*
— **thorned** \'thȯrnd\ *adjective*
— **thorn·less** \'thȯrn-ləs\ *adjective*
— **thorn·like** \-,līk\ *adjective*

**thorn apple** *noun* (1578)
**1 :** JIMSONWEED; *also* **:** any plant of the same genus
**2 :** the fruit of a hawthorn; *also* **:** HAWTHORN

**thorn·back** \'thȯrn-,bak\ *noun* (14th century)
**:** any of various rays having spines on the back

**thorn·bush** \-,bůsh\ *noun* (1535)
**1 :** any of various spiny or thorny shrubs or small trees
**2 :** a low growth of thorny shrubs especially of dry tropical regions

\ə\ **abut** \ᵊ\ **kitten** \ər\ **further** \a\ **ash** \ā\ **ace**
\ä\ **mop, mar** \au̇\ **out** \ch\ **chin** \e\ **bet** \ē\ **easy**
\g\ **go** \i\ **hit** \ī\ **ice** \j\ **job** \ŋ\ **sing** \ō\ **go**
\ȯ\ **law** \ȯi\ **boy** \th\ **thin** \th\ **the** \ü\ **loot** \ů\ **foot**
\y\ **yet** \zh\ **vision** *see also* Guide to Pronunciation

**thorny** \'thȯr-nē\ *adjective* **thorn·i·er; -est** (before 12th century)
**1** : full of thorns
**2** : full of difficulties or controversial points : TICKLISH ⟨a *thorny* problem⟩
— **thorn·i·ness** *noun*

**thoro** *nonstandard variant of* THOROUGH

**¹thor·ough** \'thər-(ˌ)ō, *sometimes* 'thȯr-; 'thə-(ˌ)rō\ *preposition* [Middle English *thorow*, from Old English *thurh, thuruh,* preposition & adverb] (before 12th century)
*archaic* : THROUGH

**²thorough** *adverb* (before 12th century)
*archaic* : THROUGH

**³thorough** *adjective* (15th century)
**1** : carried through to completion : EXHAUSTIVE ⟨a *thorough* search⟩
**2 a** : marked by full detail ⟨a *thorough* description⟩ **b** : careful about detail : PAINSTAKING ⟨a *thorough* scholar⟩ **c** : complete in all respects ⟨*thorough* pleasure⟩ **d** : having full mastery (as of an art) ⟨a *thorough* musician⟩
**3** : passing through
— **thor·ough·ly** *adverb*
— **thor·ough·ness** *noun*

**thor·ough·bass** \'thər-ə-ˌbās, 'thə-rə-\ *noun* (1662)
: CONTINUO

**thor·ough·brace** \-ˌbrās\ *noun* (1837)
: any of several leather straps supporting the body of a carriage and serving as springs

**¹thor·ough·bred** \-ˌbred\ *adjective* (1701)
**1** : thoroughly trained or skilled
**2** : bred from the best blood through a long line : PUREBRED ⟨*thoroughbred* dogs⟩
**3 a** *capitalized* : of, relating to, or being a member of the Thoroughbred breed of horses **b** : having characteristics resembling those of a Thoroughbred

**²thoroughbred** *noun* (1842)
**1** *capitalized* : any of an English breed of light speedy horses kept chiefly for racing that originated from crosses between English mares of uncertain ancestry and Arabian stallions
**2** : a purebred or pedigreed animal
**3** : one that has characteristics resembling those of a Thoroughbred

Thoroughbred

**thor·ough·fare** \-ˌfar, -ˌfer\ *noun* (14th century)
**1** : a way or place for passage: as **a** : a street open at both ends **b** : a main road
**2 a** : PASSAGE, TRANSIT **b** : the conditions necessary for passing through

**thor·ough·go·ing** \ˌthər-ə-'gō-iŋ, ˌthə-rə-, -'gó(-)iŋ\ *adjective* (1800)
: marked by thoroughness or zeal : THOROUGH, COMPLETE

**thor·ough·paced** \-'pāst\ *adjective* (1646)
**1** : THOROUGH, COMPLETE
**2** : thoroughly trained : ACCOMPLISHED

**thor·ough·pin** \'thər-ə-ˌpin, 'thə-rə-\ *noun* (1789)
: a synovial swelling just above the hock of a horse on both sides of the leg and slightly anterior to the hamstring tendon that is often associated with lameness

**thor·ough·wort** \-ˌwərt, -ˌwȯrt\ *noun* (1814)
: BONESET

**thorp** \'thȯrp\ *noun* [Middle English, from Old English, perhaps from Old Norse; akin to Old High German *dorf* village, Latin *trabs* beam, roof] (before 12th century)
*archaic* : VILLAGE, HAMLET

**those** [Middle English, from *those* these, from Old English *thās,* plural of *thes* this — more at THIS] *plural of* THAT

**¹thou** \'thaủ\ *pronoun* [Middle English, from Old English *thū;* akin to Old High German *dū* thou, Latin *tu,* Greek *sy*] (before 12th century)
: the one addressed ⟨*thou* shalt have no other gods before me —Exodus 20:3 (Authorized Version)⟩ — used especially in ecclesiastical or literary language and by Friends as the universal form of address to one person; compare THEE, THINE, THY, YE, YOU
***word history*** *see* YOU

**²thou** *transitive verb* (15th century)
: to address as *thou*

**³thou** \'thaủ\ *noun, plural* **thou** [short for *thousand*] (1867)
: a thousand of something (as dollars)

**¹though** \'thō\ *conjunction* [Middle English, adverb & conjunction, of Scandinavian origin; akin to Old Norse *thō* nevertheless; akin to Old English *thēah* nevertheless, Old High German *doh*] (before 12th century)
**1** : in spite of the fact that : WHILE ⟨*though* they know the war is lost, they continue to fight —Bruce Bliven (died 1977)⟩
**2** : in spite of the possibility that : even if ⟨*though* I may fail, I will try⟩

**²though** *adverb* (13th century)
: HOWEVER, NEVERTHELESS ⟨It's hard work. I enjoy it *though*⟩

**¹thought** \'thȯt\ *past and past participle of* THINK

**²thought** *noun* [Middle English, from Old English *thōht;* akin to Old English *thencan* to think — more at THINK] (before 12th century)
**1 a** : the action or process of thinking : COGITATION **b** : serious consideration : REGARD **c** *archaic* : RECOLLECTION, REMEMBRANCE
**2 a** : reasoning power **b** : the power to imagine : CONCEPTION
**3** : something that is thought: as **a** : an individual act or product of thinking **b** : a developed intention or plan ⟨had no thought of leaving home⟩ **c** : something (as an opinion or belief) in the mind ⟨he spoke his *thoughts* freely⟩ **d** : the intellectual product or the organized views and principles of a period, place, group, or individual ⟨contemporary Western *thought*⟩
***synonym*** *see* IDEA
— **a thought** : a little : SOMEWHAT ⟨a *thought* too much vinegar in the dressing⟩

**thought experiment** *noun* (1945)
: GEDANKENEXPERIMENT

**thought·ful** \'thȯt-fəl\ *adjective* (13th century)
**1 a** : absorbed in thought : MEDITATIVE **b** : characterized by careful reasoned thinking
**2 a** : having thoughts : HEEDFUL ⟨became *thoughtful* about religion⟩ **b** : given to or chosen or made with heedful anticipation of the needs and wants of others
— **thought·ful·ly** \-fə-lē\ *adverb*
— **thought·ful·ness** *noun*

**thought·less** \-ləs\ *adjective* (1592)
**1 a** : insufficiently alert : CARELESS **b** : RECKLESS, RASH
**2** : devoid of thought : INSENSATE
**3** : lacking concern for others : INCONSIDERATE
— **thought·less·ly** *adverb*
— **thought·less·ness** *noun*

**thought–out** \-'aủt\ *adjective* (1870)
: produced or arrived at through mental effort and especially through careful and thorough consideration

**thought·way** \-ˌwā\ *noun* (circa 1944)
: a way of thinking that is characteristic of a particular group, time, or culture

**thou·sand** \'thaủ-zᵊn(d)\ *noun, plural* **thousands** *or* **thousand** [Middle English, from Old English *thūsend;* akin to Old High German *dūsunt* thousand, Lithuanian *tūkstantis,* and probably to Sanskrit *tavas* strong, Latin *tumēre* to swell — more at THUMB] (before 12th century)
**1** — *see* NUMBER table
**2** : a very large number ⟨*thousands* of ants⟩
— **thousand** *adjective*

— **thou·sand·fold** \-z°n(d)-ˌfōld\ *adjective or adverb*

— **thou·sandth** \-z°n(t)th\ *adjective or noun*

**Thousand Island dressing** *noun* [*Thousand Islands,* islands in the Saint Lawrence River] (1924)
: mayonnaise with chili sauce and seasonings (as chopped pimientos, green peppers, and onion)

**thousand–leg·ger** \ˌthaủ-z°n(d)-'le-gər, -'lā-\ *noun* (1914)
: MILLIPEDE

**thousands place** *noun* (1937)
: the place four to the left of the decimal point in a number expressed in the Arabic system of writing numbers

**Thra·cian** \'thrā-shən\ *noun* (1569)
**1** : a native or inhabitant of Thrace
**2** : the Indo-European language of the ancient Thracians — *see* INDO-EUROPEAN LANGUAGES table
— **Thracian** *adjective*

**¹thrall** \'thrȯl\ *noun* [Middle English *thral,* from Old English *thræl,* from Old Norse *thræll*] (before 12th century)
**1 a** : a servant slave : BONDMAN; *also* : SERF **b** : a person in moral or mental servitude
**2 a** : a state of servitude or submission ⟨in *thrall* to his emotions⟩ **b** : a state of complete absorption ⟨mountains could hold me in *thrall* with a subtle attraction of their own —Elyne Mitchell⟩
— **thrall** *adjective*
— **thrall·dom** *or* **thral·dom** \'thrȯl-dəm\ *noun*

**²thrall** *transitive verb* (13th century)
*archaic* : ENTHRALL, ENSLAVE

**¹thrash** \'thrash\ *verb* [alteration of *thresh*] (1588)
*transitive verb*
**1** : to separate the seeds of from the husks and straw by beating : THRESH 1
**2 a** : to beat soundly with or as if with a stick or whip : FLOG **b** : to defeat decisively or severely ⟨*thrashed* the visiting team⟩
**3** : to swing, beat, or strike in the manner of a rapidly moving flail ⟨*thrashing* his arms⟩
**4 a** : to go over again and again ⟨*thrash* the matter over inconclusively⟩ **b** : to hammer out : FORGE ⟨*thrash* out a plan⟩
*intransitive verb*
**1** : THRESH 1
**2** : to deal blows or strokes like one using a flail or whip
**3** : to move or stir about violently : toss about ⟨*thrash* in bed with a fever⟩
***synonym*** *see* SWING

**²thrash** *noun* (1840)
: an act of thrashing

**¹thrash·er** \'thra-shər\ *noun* (1632)
: one that thrashes or threshes

**²thrasher** *noun* [perhaps alteration of dialect *thresher* thrush] (circa 1814)
: any of various American oscine birds (family Mimidae and especially genus *Toxostoma*) related to the mockingbird that resemble thrushes but have a curved bill and long tail

**thra·son·i·cal** \thrā-'sä-ni-kəl, thrə-\ *adjective* [Latin *Thrason-, Thraso* Thraso, braggart soldier in the comedy *Eunuchus* by Terence] (1564)
: of, relating to, resembling, or characteristic of Thraso : BRAGGING, BOASTFUL
— **thra·son·i·cal·ly** \-k(ə-)lē\ *adverb*

**¹thraw** \'thrȧ\ *verb* [Middle English — more at THROW] (before 12th century)
*transitive verb*
**1** *chiefly Scottish* : to cause to twist or turn
**2** *chiefly Scottish* : CROSS, THWART
*intransitive verb*
**1** *chiefly Scottish* : TWIST, TURN
**2** *chiefly Scottish* : to be in disagreement

**²thraw** *noun* (circa 1585)
**1** *chiefly Scottish* : TWIST, TURN

**2** *chiefly Scottish* **:** ill humor

**thra·wart** \'thrȯ-wərt\ *adjective* [Middle English (Scots), alteration of Middle English *fraward, froward* froward] (15th century)
**1** *chiefly Scottish* **:** STUBBORN
**2** *Scottish* **:** CROOKED

**thrawn** \'thrȯn\ *adjective* [Middle English (Scots), from past participle of Middle English *thrawen* to twist] (15th century)
*chiefly Scottish* **:** lacking in pleasing or attractive qualities: as **a :** PERVERSE, RECALCITRANT **b :** CROOKED, MISSHAPEN
— **thrawn·ly** *adverb, chiefly Scottish*

**¹thread** \'thred\ *noun* [Middle English *thred,* from Old English *thrǣd;* akin to Old High German *drāt* wire, Old English *thrāwan* to cause to twist or turn — more at THROW] (before 12th century)
**1 a :** a filament, a group of filaments twisted together, or a filamentous length formed by spinning and twisting short textile fibers into a continuous strand **b :** a piece of thread
**2 a :** any of various natural filaments ⟨the *threads* of a spiderweb⟩ **b :** a slender stream (as of water) **c :** a streak of light or color **d :** a projecting helical rib (as in a fitting or on a pipe) by which parts can be screwed together **:** SCREW THREAD
**3 :** something continuous or drawn out: as **a :** a train of thought **b :** a continuing element ⟨a *thread* of melancholy marked all his writing⟩
**4 :** a tenuous or feeble support
**5** *plural* **:** CLOTHING
— **thread·less** \-ləs\ *adjective*
— **thread·like** \-,līk\ *adjective*

**²thread** (14th century)
*transitive verb*
**1 a :** to pass a thread through the eye of (a needle) **b :** to arrange a thread, yarn, or lead-in piece in working position for use in (a machine)
**2 a** (1) **:** to pass something through in the manner of a thread ⟨*thread* a pipe with wire⟩ (2) **:** to pass (as a tape, line, or film) into or through something ⟨*threaded* a fresh film into the camera⟩ **b :** to make one's way through or between ⟨*threading* narrow alleys⟩; *also* **:** to make (one's way) usually cautiously through a hazardous situation
**3 :** to put together on or as if on a thread **:** STRING ⟨*thread* beads⟩
**4 :** to interweave with or as if with threads **:** INTERSPERSE ⟨dark hair *threaded* with silver⟩
**5 :** to form a screw thread on or in
*intransitive verb*
**1 :** to make one's way
**2 :** to form a thread
— **thread·er** *noun*

**thread·bare** \'thred-,bar, -,ber\ *adjective* (14th century)
**1 :** having the nap worn off so that the thread shows **:** SHABBY
**2 :** exhausted of interest or freshness
**synonym** SEE TRITE
— **thread·bare·ness** *noun*

**thread·fin** \-,fin\ *noun* (circa 1890)
**:** any of various bony fishes (family Polynemidae and especially genus *Polydactylus*) having filamentous rays on the lower part of the pectoral fin

**thread·worm** \-,wərm\ *noun* (1802)
**:** a long slender nematode worm

**thready** \'thre-dē\ *adjective* (1597)
**1 :** consisting of or bearing fibers or filaments ⟨a *thready* bark⟩
**2 a :** resembling a thread **:** FILAMENTOUS **b :** tending to form or draw out into strands **:** ROPY
**3 :** lacking in fullness, body, or vigor **:** THIN ⟨a *thready* voice⟩
— **thread·i·ness** *noun*

**threap** \'thrēp\ *transitive verb* [Middle English *threpen,* from Old English *thrēapian*] (before 12th century)
**1** *chiefly Scottish* **:** SCOLD, CHIDE
**2** *chiefly Scottish* **:** to maintain persistently

**¹threat** \'thret\ *noun* [Middle English *thret* coercion, threat, from Old English *thrēat* coercion; akin to Middle High German *drōz* annoyance, Latin *trudere* to push, thrust] (before 12th century)
**1 :** an expression of intention to inflict evil, injury, or damage
**2 :** one that threatens
**3 :** an indication of something impending ⟨the sky held a *threat* of rain⟩

**²threat** *verb* (before 12th century)
*archaic* **:** THREATEN

**threat·en** \'thre-tᵊn\ *verb* **threat·ened; threat·en·ing** \'thret-niŋ, 'thre-tᵊn-iŋ\ (13th century)
*transitive verb*
**1 :** to utter threats against
**2 a :** to give signs or warning of **:** PORTEND ⟨the clouds *threatened* rain⟩ **b :** to hang over dangerously **:** MENACE
**3 :** to announce as intended or possible ⟨the workers *threatened* a strike⟩
*intransitive verb*
**1 :** to utter threats
**2 :** to portend evil
— **threat·en·er** \'thret-nər, 'thre-tᵊn-ər\ *noun*
— **threat·en·ing·ly** \'thret-niŋ-lē, 'thre-tᵊn-iŋ-\ *adverb*

**threatened** *adjective* (1960)
**:** having an uncertain chance of continued survival ⟨a *threatened* species of owls⟩; *specifically* **:** likely to become an endangered species

**three** \'thrē\ *noun* [Middle English, from *three,* adjective, from Old English *thrīe* (masculine), *thrēo* (feminine & neuter); akin to Old High German *drī* three, Latin *tres,* Greek *treis*] (before 12th century)
**1** — see NUMBER table
**2 :** the third in a set or series ⟨the *three* of hearts⟩
**3 :** something having three units or members
— **three** *adjective*
— **three** *pronoun, plural in construction*

**three–bag·ger** \-,ba-gər\ *noun* (1881)
**:** TRIPLE

**three–ball** \-,bȯl\ *adjective* (circa 1890)
**:** relating to or being a golf match in which three players compete against one another with each playing a single ball

**three–card monte** \'thrē-'kärd-\ *noun* (1854)
**:** a gambling game in which the dealer shows three cards, shuffles them, places them face down, and invites spectators to bet they can identify the location of a particular card

**three–col·or** \'thrē-'kə-lər\ *adjective* (1893)
**:** being or relating to a printing or photographic process wherein three primary colors are used to reproduce all the colors of the subject

**3–D** \'thrē-'dē\ *noun* [D, abbreviation of *dimensional*] (1951)
**:** the three-dimensional form; *also* **:** an image or a picture produced in it
— **3–D** *adjective*

**three–deck·er** \'thrē-'de-kər\ *noun* (1795)
**1 :** a wooden warship carrying guns on three decks
**2 :** TRIPLE-DECKER

**three–dimensional** *adjective* (circa 1891)
**1 :** of or relating to three dimensions
**2 :** giving the illusion of depth or varying distances — used of an image or a pictorial representation especially when this illusion is enhanced by stereoscopic means
**3 :** describing or being described in well-rounded completeness ⟨a *three-dimensional* analysis of multiple historical processes —L. L. Snyder⟩
**4 :** true to life **:** LIFELIKE

**three–fold** \'thrē-,fōld, -'fōld\ *adjective* (before 12th century)
**1 :** having three units or members **:** TRIPLE
**2 :** being three times as great or as many
— **three·fold** \-'fōld\ *adverb*

**three–gait·ed** \-'gā-təd\ *adjective* (1948)
*of a horse* **:** trained to use the walk, trot, and canter

**three–hand·ed** \-'han-dəd\ *adjective* (1719)
**:** played by three players ⟨*three-handed* bridge⟩

**Three Hours** *noun* (circa 1891)
**:** a service of devotion between noon and three o'clock on Good Friday

**three–legged** \'thrē-'legd, -'lāgd; -'le-gəd, -'lā-\ *adjective* (1596)
**:** having three legs ⟨a *three-legged* stool⟩

**three–legged race** *noun* (1903)
**:** a race between pairs of competitors with each pair having their adjacent legs bound together

**three–line octave** *noun* (circa 1931)
**:** the musical octave that begins on the second C above middle C — see PITCH illustration

**three–mile limit** *noun* (circa 1891)
**:** the limit of the marginal sea of three miles included in the territorial waters of a state

**three of a kind** (circa 1897)
**:** three cards of the same rank in one hand — see POKER illustration

**three·pence** \'thre-pən(t)s, 'thri-, 'thrə-, *US also* 'thrē-pen(t)s\ *noun* (1589)
**1** *plural* **threepence** *or* **three·penc·es** **:** a coin worth threepence
**2 :** the sum of three British pennies

**three·pen·ny** \'thre-p(ə-)nē, 'thri-, 'thrə-, *US also* 'thrē-,pe-nē\ *adjective* (15th century)
**1 :** costing or worth threepence
**2 :** POOR

**three–phase** *adjective* (circa 1900)
**:** of, relating to, or operating by means of a combination of three circuits energized by alternating electromotive forces that differ in phase by one third of a cycle

**three–piece** *adjective* (circa 1909)
**:** consisting of or made in three pieces ⟨a *three-piece* suit⟩

**three–point landing** *noun* (1918)
**:** an airplane landing in which the two main wheels of the landing gear and the tail wheel or skid or nose wheel touch the ground simultaneously

**three–quarter** *adjective* (1677)
**:** extending to three-quarters of the normal full length ⟨a *three-quarter* sleeve⟩

**three–quarter–bound** *adjective* (circa 1951)
*of a book* **:** bound like a half-bound book but having the material on the spine extended to cover about one third of the boards
— **three–quarter binding** *noun*

**three–ring circus** *noun* (1904)
**1 :** a circus with simultaneous performances in three rings
**2 :** something wild, confusing, engrossing, or entertaining

**three R's** *noun plural* [from the facetiously used phrase *reading, 'riting, and 'rithmetic*] (1828)
**1 :** the fundamentals taught in elementary school; *especially* **:** reading, writing, and arithmetic
**2 :** the fundamental skills in a field of endeavor

**three·score** \'thrē-'skōr, -'skȯr\ *adjective* (14th century)
**:** being three times twenty **:** SIXTY

**three·some** \'thrē-səm\ *noun* (14th century)
**1 :** a group of three persons or things **:** TRIO
**2 :** a golf match in which one person plays his ball against the ball of two others playing each stroke alternately

**three–spined stickleback** \'thrē-'spin(d)-\ *noun* (1769)
: a stickle-back (*Gasterosteus aculeatus*) chiefly of fresh and brackish waters that typically has three dorsal spines

three-spined stickleback

**three–toed sloth** \'thrē-'tōd\ *noun* (1879)
: any of a genus (*Bradypus*) of sloths having three clawed digits on each foot and nine vertebrae in the neck — compare TWO-TOED SLOTH

**three–wheel·er** \-,hwē-lər, -,wē-\ *noun* (1886)
: any of various vehicles having three wheels

**thre·node** \'thrē-,nōd, 'thre-\ *noun* (1858)
: THRENODY
— **thre·nod·ic** \thri-'nä-dik\ *adjective*
— **thren·o·dist** \'thre-nə-dist\ *noun*

**thren·o·dy** \'thre-nə-dē\ *noun, plural* **-dies** [Greek *thrēnōidia,* from *thrēnos* dirge + *aeidein* to sing — more at DRONE, ODE] (1634)
: a song of lamentation for the dead : ELEGY

**three·o·nine** \'thrē-ə-,nēn\ *noun* [probably from *threonic acid* ($C_4H_8O_5$)] (1936)
: a colorless crystalline essential amino acid $C_4H_9NO_3$

**thresh** \'thrash, 'thresh\ *verb* [Middle English *thresshen,* from Old English *threscan;* akin to Old High German *dreskan* to thresh] (before 12th century)
*transitive verb*
**1** : to separate seed from (a harvested plant) mechanically; *also* : to separate (seed) in this way
**2** : THRASH 4
**3** : to strike repeatedly
*intransitive verb*
**1** : to thresh grain
**2** : THRASH 2, 3

**thresh·er** *noun* (14th century)
**1** : one that threshes; *especially* : THRESHING MACHINE
**2** : THRESHER SHARK

**thresher shark** *noun* (1888)
: a large nearly cosmopolitan shark (*Alopias vulpinus*) having a greatly elongated curved upper lobe of its tail with which it is said to thresh the water to round up the fish on which it feeds — see SHARK illustration

**threshing machine** *noun* (1775)
: a machine for separating grain crops into grain or seeds and straw

**thresh·old** \'thresh-,hōld, 'thre-,shōld\ *noun* [Middle English *thresshold,* from Old English *threscwald;* akin to Old Norse *threskjǫldr* threshold, Old English *threscan* to thresh] (before 12th century)
**1** : the plank, stone, or piece of timber that lies under a door : SILL
**2 a** : GATE, DOOR **b** (1) : END, BOUNDARY; *specifically* : the end of a runway (2) : the place or point of entering or beginning : OUTSET ⟨on the *threshold* of a new age⟩
**3 a** : the point at which a physiological or psychological effect begins to be produced **b** : a level, point, or value above which something is true or will take place and below which it is not or will not

**threw** *past of* THROW

**thrice** \'thrīs\ *adverb* [Middle English *thrie, thries,* from Old English *thriga;* akin to Old Frisian *thria* three times, Old English *thrīe* three] (13th century)
**1** : three times
**2 a** : in a threefold manner or degree **b** : to a high degree

**thrift** \'thrift\ *noun* [Middle English, from Old Norse, prosperity, from *thrīfask* to thrive] (13th century)
**1** : healthy and vigorous growth
**2** : careful management especially of money

**3** *chiefly Scottish* : gainful occupation
**4** : any of a genus (*Armeria*) of the plumbago family of perennial evergreen acaulescent herbs; *especially* : a scapose herb (*A. maritima*) with pink or white flower heads
**5** : a savings bank or savings and loan association — called also *thrift institution*

**thrift·less** \'thrift-ləs\ *adjective* (1568)
**1** : lacking usefulness or worth
**2** : careless, wasteful, or incompetent in handling money or resources : IMPROVIDENT
— **thrift·less·ly** *adverb*
— **thrift·less·ness** *noun*

**thrift shop** *noun* (1944)
: a shop that sells secondhand articles and especially clothes and is often run for charitable purposes

**thrifty** \'thrif-tē\ *adjective* **thrift·i·er; -est** (15th century)
**1** : thriving by industry and frugality : PROSPEROUS
**2** : growing vigorously
**3** : given to or marked by economy and good management
**synonym** see SPARING
— **thrift·i·ly** \-tə-lē\ *adverb*
— **thrift·i·ness** \-tē-nəs\ *noun*

**thrill** \'thril\ *verb* [Middle English *thirlen, thrillen* to pierce, from Old English *thyrlian,* from *thyrel* hole, from *thurh* through — more at THROUGH] (1592)
*transitive verb*
**1 a** : to cause to experience a sudden sharp feeling of excitement **b** : to cause to have a shivering or tingling sensation
**2** : to cause to vibrate or tremble perceptibly
*intransitive verb*
**1** : to move or pass so as to cause a sudden wave of emotion
**2** : to become thrilled: **a** : to experience a sudden sharp excitement **b** : TINGLE, THROB
**3** : TREMBLE, VIBRATE ◆
— **thrill** *noun*
— **thrill·ing·ly** \'thri-liŋ-lē\ *adverb*

**thril·ler** \'thri-lər\ *noun* (1889)
: one that thrills; *especially* : a work of fiction or drama designed to hold the interest by the use of a high degree of intrigue, adventure, or suspense

**thrips** \'thrips\ *noun, plural* **thrips** [Latin, woodworm, from Greek] (1795)
: any of an order (Thysanoptera) of small to minute sucking insects most of which feed often destructively on plant juices

**thrive** \'thrīv\ *intransitive verb* **throve** \'thrōv\ *or* **thrived; thriv·en** \'thri-vən\ *also* **thrived; thriv·ing** \'thrī-viŋ\ [Middle English, from Old Norse *thrīfask,* probably reflexive of *thrīfa* to grasp] (13th century)
**1** : to grow vigorously : FLOURISH
**2** : to gain in wealth or possessions : PROSPER
**3** : to progress toward or realize a goal
— **thriv·er** \'thrī-vər\ *noun*

**thriving** *adjective* (1607)
: characterized by success or prosperity
— **thriv·ing·ly** \'thrī-viŋ-lē\ *adverb*

**thro** \'thrü\ *preposition* (15th century)
*archaic* : THROUGH

**¹throat** \'thrōt\ *noun* [Middle English *throte,* from Old English; akin to Old High German *drozza* throat] (before 12th century)
**1 a** (1) : the part of the neck in front of the spinal column (2) : the passage through the neck to the stomach and lungs **b** (1) : VOICE (2) : the seat of the voice
**2** : something resembling the throat especially in being an entrance, a passageway, a constriction, or a narrowed part: as **a** : the orifice of a tubular organ especially of a plant **b** : the opening in the vamp of a shoe at the instep **c** : the part of a tennis racket that connects the head with the shaft
**3** : the curved part of an anchor's arm where it joins the shank — see ANCHOR illustration
— **at each other's throats** : in open and aggressive conflict

**²throat** *transitive verb* (circa 1611)
**1** : to utter in the throat : MUTTER
**2** : to sing or enunciate in a throaty voice

**throat·ed** \'thrō-təd\ *adjective* (circa 1530)
: having a throat especially of a specified kind — usually used in combination ⟨white-*throated*⟩

**throat·latch** \'thrōt-,lach\ *noun* (1794)
**1** : a strap of a bridle or halter passing under a horse's throat
**2** : the part of a horse's throat around which the throatlatch passes — see HORSE illustration

**throaty** \'thrō-tē\ *adjective* **throat·i·er; -est** (circa 1645)
**1** : uttered or produced from low in the throat ⟨a *throaty* voice⟩
**2** : heavy, thick, and deep as if from the throat ⟨*throaty* notes of a horn⟩
— **throat·i·ly** \'thrō-t°l-ē\ *adverb*
— **throat·i·ness** \'thrō-tē-nəs\ *noun*

**¹throb** \'thräb\ *intransitive verb* **throbbed; throb·bing** [Middle English *throbben*] (14th century)
**1** : to pulsate or pound with abnormal force or rapidity
**2** : to beat or vibrate rhythmically
— **throb·ber** *noun*

**²throb** *noun* (1579)
: BEAT, PULSE

**throe** \'thrō\ *noun* [Middle English *thrawe, throwe,* from Old English *thrawu, thrēa* threat, pang; akin to Old High German *drawa* threat] (13th century)
**1** : PANG, SPASM ⟨death *throes*⟩ ⟨*throes* of childbirth⟩
**2** *plural* : a hard or painful struggle ⟨the *throes* of revolutionary social change —M. D. Geismar⟩

**thromb-** *or* **thrombo-** *combining form* [Greek *thrombos* clot]
: blood clot : clotting of blood ⟨*thrombin*⟩ ⟨*thrombo*plastic⟩

**throm·bin** \'thräm-bən\ *noun* [International Scientific Vocabulary] (1898)
: a proteolytic enzyme that is formed from prothrombin and facilitates the clotting of blood by catalyzing conversion of fibrinogen to fibrin

**throm·bo·cyte** \-bə-,sīt\ *noun* [International Scientific Vocabulary] (1893)
: BLOOD PLATELET; *also* : an invertebrate cell with similar function
— **throm·bo·cyt·ic** \,thräm-bə-'si-tik\ *adjective*

**throm·bo·cy·to·pe·nia** \,thräm-bə-,sī-tə-'pē-nē-ə, -nyə\ *noun* [New Latin, from International Scientific Vocabulary *thrombocyte* + New Latin *-o-* + *-penia*] (1923)
: persistent decrease in the number of blood platelets that is often associated with hemorrhagic conditions
— **throm·bo·cy·to·pe·nic** \-nik\ *adjective*

**throm·bo·em·bo·lism** \ˌthräm-bō-'em-bə-ˌli-zəm\ *noun* (1907)
: the blocking of a blood vessel by a particle that has broken away from a blood clot at its site of formation
— **throm·bo·em·bol·ic** \-em-'bä-lik\ *adjective*

**throm·bo·ki·nase** \ˌthräm-bō-'kī-ˌnās, -ˌnāz\ *noun* [International Scientific Vocabulary] (1908)
: THROMBOPLASTIN

**throm·bo·lyt·ic** \ˌthräm-bə-'li-tik\ *adjective* (1929)
: destroying or breaking up a thrombus ⟨a *thrombolytic* agent⟩ ⟨*thrombolytic* therapy⟩

**throm·bo·phle·bi·tis** \ˌthräm-bō-fli-'bī-təs\ *noun* [New Latin] (circa 1890)
: inflammation of a vein with formation of a thrombus

**throm·bo·plas·tic** \-'plas-tik\ *adjective* [International Scientific Vocabulary] (1911)
: initiating or accelerating the clotting of blood

**throm·bo·plas·tin** \-'plas-tən\ *noun* [International Scientific Vocabulary, from *thromboplastic*] (1911)
: a complex enzyme found especially in blood platelets that functions in the conversion of prothrombin into thrombin in the clotting of blood

**throm·bo·sis** \thräm-'bō-səs, thrəm-\ *noun, plural* **-bo·ses** \-ˌsēz\ [New Latin, from Greek *thrombōsis* clotting, from *thromboustai* to become clotted, from *thrombos* clot] (1866)
: the formation or presence of a blood clot within a blood vessel
— **throm·bot·ic** \-'bä-tik\ *adjective*

**throm·box·ane** \thräm-'bäk-ˌsān\ *noun* [*thromb-* + *ox-* + *-ane*] (1975)
: any of several substances that are formed from endoperoxides, cause constriction of vascular and bronchial smooth muscle, and promote blood coagulation

**throm·bus** \'thräm-bəs\ *noun, plural* **throm·bi** \-ˌbī, -ˌbē\ [New Latin, from Greek *thrombos* clot] (circa 1693)
: a clot of blood formed within a blood vessel and remaining attached to its place of origin — compare EMBOLUS

**¹throne** \'thrōn\ *noun* [Middle English *trone*, *throne*, from Old French *trone*, from Latin *thronus*, from Greek *thronos* — more at FIRM] (13th century)
**1 a :** the chair of state of a sovereign or high dignitary (as a bishop) **b :** the seat of a deity
**2 :** royal power and dignity : SOVEREIGNTY
**3** *plural* : an order of angels — see CELESTIAL HIERARCHY

**²throne** *verb* **throned; thron·ing** (14th century)
*transitive verb*
**1 :** to seat on a throne
**2 :** to invest with kingly rank or power
*intransitive verb*
**1 :** to sit on a throne
**2 :** to hold kingly power

**throne room** *noun* (1864)
: a formal audience room containing the throne of a sovereign

**¹throng** \'thrȯŋ\ *noun* [Middle English *thrang*, *throng*, from Old English *thrang*, *gethrang*; akin to Old English *thringan* to press, crowd, Old High German *dringan*, Lithuanian *trenkti* to jolt] (before 12th century)
**1 a :** a multitude of assembled persons **b :** a large number : HOST
**2 a :** a crowding together of many persons **b :** PRESSURE ⟨this *throng* of business —S. R. Crockett⟩
**synonym** see CROWD

**²throng** *verb* **thronged; throng·ing** \'thrȯŋ-iŋ\ (1534)
*transitive verb*
**1 :** to crowd upon : PRESS
**2 :** to crowd into : PACK ⟨shoppers *thronging* the streets⟩

*intransitive verb*
: to crowd together in great numbers

**thros·tle** \'thrä-səl\ *noun* [Middle English, from Old English — more at THRUSH] (before 12th century)
: ¹THRUSH 1; *specifically* : SONG THRUSH

**¹throt·tle** \'thrä-t³l\ *verb* **throt·tled; throt·tling** \'thrät-liŋ, 'thrä-t³l-iŋ\ [Middle English *throtlen*, from *throte* throat] (15th century)
*transitive verb*
**1 a** (1) **:** to compress the throat of : CHOKE (2) **:** to kill by such action **b :** to prevent or check expression or activity of : SUPPRESS
**2 a :** to decrease the flow of (as steam or fuel to an engine) by a valve **b :** to regulate and especially to reduce the speed of (as an engine) by such means **c :** to vary the thrust of (a rocket engine) during flight
*intransitive verb*
: to throttle something (as an engine) — usually used with *back* or *down* ⟨the pilot *throttled* back⟩
— **throt·tler** \'thrät-lər, 'thrä-t³l-ər\ *noun*

**²throttle** *noun* [perhaps from (assumed) Middle English, diminutive of Middle English *throte* throat] (circa 1547)
**1 a :** THROAT 1a **b :** TRACHEA 1
**2 a :** a valve for regulating the supply of a fluid (as steam) to an engine; *especially* : the valve controlling the volume of vaporized fuel charge delivered to the cylinders of an internal combustion engine **b :** the lever controlling this valve **c :** the condition of being throttled
— **at full throttle :** at full speed

**throt·tle·able** \'thrä-t³l-ə-bəl\ *adjective* (1960)
: capable of having the thrust varied — used of a rocket engine

**throt·tle·hold** \'thrä-t³l-ˌhōld\ *noun* (1935)
: a vicious, strangling, or stultifying control

**¹through** \'thrü\ *preposition* [Middle English *thurh*, *thruh*, *through*, from Old English *thurh*; akin to Old High German *durh* through, Latin *trans* across, beyond, Sanskrit *tarati* he crosses over] (before 12th century)
**1 a** (1) — used as a function word to indicate movement into at one side or point and out at another and especially the opposite side of ⟨drove a nail *through* the board⟩ (2) **:** by way of ⟨left *through* the door⟩ (3) — used as a function word to indicate passage from one end or boundary to another ⟨a highway *through* the forest⟩ ⟨a road *through* the desert⟩ (4) **:** without stopping for : PAST ⟨drove *through* a red light⟩ **b** — used as a function word to indicate passage into and out of a treatment, handling, or process ⟨the matter has already passed *through* her hands⟩
**2** — used as a function word to indicate means, agency, or intermediacy: as **a :** by means of **:** by the agency of **b :** because of ⟨failed *through* ignorance⟩ **c :** by common descent from or relationship with ⟨related *through* their grandfather⟩
**3 a :** over the whole surface or extent of **:** THROUGHOUT ⟨homes scattered *through* the valley⟩ **b** — used as a function word to indicate movement within a large expanse ⟨flew *through* the air⟩ **c** — used as a function word to indicate exposure to a specified set of conditions ⟨put him *through* hell⟩
**4** — used as a function word to indicate a period of time: as **a :** during the entire period of ⟨all *through* her life⟩ **b :** from the beginning to the end of ⟨the tower stood *through* the earthquake⟩ **c :** to and including ⟨Monday *through* Friday⟩
**5 a** — used as a function word to indicate completion or exhaustion ⟨got *through* the book⟩ ⟨went *through* the money in a year⟩ **b** — used as a function word to indicate acceptance or approval especially by an official body ⟨got the bill *through* the legislature⟩

**²through** \'thrü\ *adverb* (before 12th century)
**1 :** from one end or side to the other

**2 a :** from beginning to end **b :** to completion, conclusion, or accomplishment ⟨see it *through*⟩
**3 :** to the core : COMPLETELY ⟨soaked *through*⟩
**4 :** into the open : OUT ⟨break *through*⟩

**³through** \'thrü\ *adjective* (1523)
**1 a :** extending from one surface to another ⟨a *through* mortise⟩ **b :** admitting free or continuous passage : DIRECT ⟨a *through* road⟩
**2 a** (1) **:** going from point of origin to destination without change or reshipment ⟨a *through* train⟩ (2) **:** of or relating to such movement ⟨a *through* ticket⟩ **b :** initiated at and destined for points outside a local zone ⟨*through* traffic⟩
**3 a :** arrived at completion or accomplishment ⟨is *through* with the job⟩ **b :** WASHED-UP, FINISHED

**through and through** *adverb* (15th century)
: in every way : THOROUGHLY

**through–com·posed** \ˌthrü-kəm-'pōzd\ *adjective* [translation of German *durchkomponiert*] (1884)
*of a song* : having new music provided for each stanza — compare STROPHIC

**through·ith·er** *or* **through·oth·er** \'thrü-(ə-)thər\ *adverb* [¹*through* + *other*] (1596)
*chiefly Scottish* : in confusion : PROMISCUOUSLY

**through·ly** \'thrü-lē\ *adverb* (15th century)
*archaic* : in a thorough manner

**¹through·out** \thrü-'aůt\ *adverb* (13th century)
**1 :** in or to every part : EVERYWHERE ⟨of one color *throughout*⟩
**2 :** during the whole time or action : from beginning to end ⟨remained loyal *throughout*⟩

**²throughout** *preposition* (13th century)
**1 :** all the way from one end to the other of **:** in or to every part of ⟨cities *throughout* the United States⟩
**2 :** during the whole course or period of ⟨troubled her *throughout* her life⟩

**through·put** \'thrü-ˌpůt\ *noun* (circa 1915)
: OUTPUT, PRODUCTION ⟨the *throughput* of a computer⟩

**through street** *noun* (1930)
: a street on which the through movement of traffic is given preference

**throve** *past of* THRIVE

**¹throw** \'thrō\ *verb* **threw** \'thrü\; **thrown** \'thrōn\; **throw·ing** [Middle English *thrawen*, *throwen* to cause to twist, throw, from Old English *thrāwan* to cause to twist or turn; akin to Old High German *drāen* to turn, Latin *terere* to rub, Greek *tribein* to rub, *tetrainein* to bore, pierce] (14th century)
*transitive verb*
**1 a :** to propel through the air by a forward motion of the hand and arm ⟨*throw* a baseball⟩ **b :** to propel through the air in any manner ⟨a rifle that can *throw* a bullet a mile⟩
**2 a :** to cause to fall ⟨*threw* his opponent⟩ **b :** to cause to fall off : UNSEAT ⟨the horse *threw* its rider⟩ **c :** to get the better of : OVERCOME ⟨the problem didn't *throw* her⟩
**3 a :** to fling (oneself) precipitately ⟨*threw* herself down on the sofa⟩ **b :** to drive or impel violently : DASH ⟨the ship was *thrown* on a reef⟩
**4 a** (1) **:** to put in a particular position or condition ⟨*threw* her arms around him⟩ (2) **:** to put on or off hastily or carelessly ⟨*threw* on a coat⟩ **b :** to bring to bear : EXERT ⟨*threw* all his efforts into the boy's defense⟩ **c :** BUILD, CONSTRUCT ⟨*threw* a pontoon bridge over the river⟩
**5 :** to form or shape on a potter's wheel
**6 :** to deliver (a blow) in or as if in boxing
**7 :** to twist two or more filaments of into a thread or yarn

\ə\ abut \ᵊ\ kitten \ər\ further \a\ ash \ā\ ace \ä\ mop, mar \aů\ out \ch\ chin \e\ bet \ē\ easy \g\ go \i\ hit \ī\ ice \j\ job \ŋ\ sing \ō\ go \ȯ\ law \ȯi\ boy \th\ thin \t͟h\ the \ü\ loot \ů\ foot \y\ yet \zh\ vision *see also* Guide to Pronunciation

**8 a :** to make a cast of (dice or a specified number on dice) **b :** ROLL 1a ⟨*throw* a bowling ball⟩
**9 :** to give up : ABANDON
**10 :** to send forth : PROJECT ⟨the setting sun *threw* long shadows⟩
**11 :** to make (oneself) dependent : commit (oneself) for help, support, or protection ⟨*threw* himself on the mercy of the court⟩
**12 :** to indulge in : give way to ⟨*threw* a temper tantrum⟩
**13 :** to bring forth : give birth to : SIRE, PRODUCE ⟨*throws* a good crop⟩ ⟨*threw* large litters⟩
**14 :** to lose intentionally ⟨*throw* a game⟩
**15 :** to move (a lever) so as to connect or disconnect parts of a clutch or switch; *also* **:** to make or break (a connection) with a lever
**16 :** to give by way of entertainment ⟨*throw* a party⟩
*intransitive verb*
**:** CAST, HURL ☆
— **throw·er** \'thrō(-ə)r\ *noun*
— **throw one's weight around** *or* **throw one's weight about :** to exercise influence or authority especially to an excessive degree or in an objectionable manner
— **throw together 1 :** to put together in a hurried and usually careless manner ⟨a bookshelf hastily *thrown together*⟩ **2 :** to bring into casual association ⟨different kinds of people are *thrown together* —Richard Sennett⟩
**²throw** *noun* (1530)
**1 a :** an act of throwing, hurling, or flinging **b** (1) **:** an act of throwing dice (2) **:** the number thrown with a cast of dice **c :** a method of throwing an opponent in wrestling or judo
**2 :** the distance a missile may be thrown or light rays may be projected
**3 :** an undertaking involving chance or danger **:** RISK, VENTURE
**4 :** the amount of vertical displacement produced by a geological fault
**5 a :** the extreme movement given to a pivoted or reciprocating piece by a cam, crank, or eccentric : STROKE **b :** the length of the radius of a crank or the virtual crank radius of an eccentric or cam
**6 a :** a light coverlet (as for a bed) **b :** a woman's scarf or light wrap
— **a throw :** for each one : APIECE ⟨copies are to be sold at $5 *a throw* —Harvey Breit⟩
**¹throw·away** \'thrō-ə-,wā\ *noun* (1903)
**1 :** one that is or is designed to be thrown away: as **a :** a free handbill or circular **b :** a line of dialogue (as in a play) de-emphasized by casual delivery; *especially* **:** a joke or witticism delivered casually
**2 :** something made or done without care or interest
**²throwaway** *adjective* (1928)
**1 :** designed to be thrown away : DISPOSABLE ⟨*throwaway* containers⟩
**2 :** written or spoken (as in a play) in a low-key or unemphatic manner ⟨*throwaway* lines⟩
**3 :** NONCHALANT, CASUAL
**throw away** *transitive verb* (1530)
**1 a :** to get rid of as worthless or unnecessary **b :** DISCARD 2b
**2 a :** to use in a foolish or wasteful manner **:** SQUANDER **b :** to fail to take advantage of **:** WASTE
**3 :** to make (as a line in a play) unemphatic by casual delivery
**throw·back** \'thrō-,bak\ *noun* (1888)
**1 a :** reversion to an earlier type or phase : ATAVISM **b :** an instance or product of atavistic reversion
**2 :** one that is suggestive of or suited to an earlier time or style ⟨his manners were a *throwback* to a more polite era⟩
**throw back** (1840)
*transitive verb*
**1 :** to delay the progress or advance of : CHECK
**2 :** to cause to rely : make dependent ⟨they are *thrown back* upon . . . native intelligence —Michael Novak⟩

**3 :** REFLECT
*intransitive verb*
**:** to revert to an earlier type or phase
**throw down** *transitive verb* (14th century)
**1 :** to cause to fall : OVERTHROW
**2 :** PRECIPITATE
**3 :** to cast off : DISCARD
**throw–in** \'thrō-,in\ *noun* (1881)
**:** an act or instance of throwing a ball in: as **a :** a throw made from the touchline in soccer to put the ball back in play after it has gone into touch **b :** a throw from an outfielder to the infield in baseball **c :** an inbounds pass in basketball
**throw in** (1678)
*transitive verb*
**1 :** to add as a gratuity or supplement
**2 :** to introduce or interject in the course of something **:** CONTRIBUTE ⟨they *throw in* some . . . sound effects on several songs —Tom Phillips⟩
**3 :** DISTRIBUTE 3b
**4 :** ENGAGE ⟨*throw in* the clutch⟩
*intransitive verb*
**:** to enter into association or partnership : JOIN ⟨agrees to *throw in* with a crooked ex-cop —Newsweek⟩
— **throw in the towel** *also* **throw in the sponge :** to abandon a struggle or contest : acknowledge defeat : GIVE UP
**throw off** (1618)
*transitive verb*
**1 a :** to free oneself from : get rid of ⟨*threw off* his inhibitions⟩ **b :** to cast off often in a hurried or vigorous manner : ABANDON ⟨*threw off* all restraint⟩ **c :** DISTRACT, DIVERT ⟨dogs *thrown off* by a false scent⟩
**2 :** EMIT, GIVE OFF ⟨stacks *throwing off* plumes of smoke⟩
**3 :** to produce in an offhand manner : execute with speed or facility ⟨some little . . . tune that the composer had *thrown off* —James Hilton⟩
**4 a :** to cause to depart from an expected or desired course ⟨mistakes *threw* his calculations *off* a bit⟩ **b :** to cause to make a mistake : MISLEAD
*intransitive verb*
**1 :** to begin hunting
**2 :** to make derogatory comments
**throw out** *transitive verb* (1526)
**1 a :** to remove from a place, office, or employment usually in a sudden or unexpected manner **b :** to get rid of as worthless or unnecessary
**2 :** to give expression to : UTTER ⟨*threw out* a remark . . . that utterly confounded him —Jean Stafford⟩
**3 :** to dismiss from acceptance or consideration : REJECT ⟨the testimony was *thrown out*⟩
**4 :** to make visible or manifest : DISPLAY ⟨the signal was *thrown out* for the . . . fleet to prepare for action —Archibald Duncan⟩
**5 :** to leave behind : OUTDISTANCE
**6 :** to give forth from within : EMIT
**7 a :** to send out **b :** to cause to project : EXTEND
**8 :** CONFUSE, DISCONCERT ⟨automobiles in line blocking the road . . . *threw* the whole schedule *out* —F. D. Roosevelt⟩
**9 :** to cause to stand out : make prominent
**10 :** to make a throw that enables a teammate to put out (a base runner)
**throw over** *transitive verb* (1835)
**1 :** to forsake despite bonds of attachment or duty
**2 :** to refuse to accept : REJECT
**throw pillow** *noun* (1956)
**:** a small pillow used especially as a decorative accessory
**throw rug** *noun* (1928)
**:** SCATTER RUG
**throw·ster** \'thrō-stər\ *noun* (15th century)
**:** one who throws textile filaments
**throw up** (15th century)
*transitive verb*

**1 :** to raise quickly
**2 :** GIVE UP, QUIT ⟨the urge . . . to *throw up* all intellectual work —Norman Mailer⟩
**3 :** to build hurriedly ⟨new houses *thrown up* almost overnight⟩
**4 :** VOMIT
**5 :** to bring forth : PRODUCE
**6 :** to make distinct especially by contrast **:** cause to stand out
**7 :** to mention repeatedly by way of reproach
*intransitive verb*
**:** VOMIT
— **throw up one's hands :** to admit defeat ⟨in the end *throws up his hands* in despair —Frank Conroy⟩
**throw weight** *noun* (1969)
**:** the maximum payload of an ICBM
**thru** *variant of* THROUGH
**¹thrum** \'thrəm\ *noun* [Middle English, from Old English -*thrum* (in *tungethrum* ligament of the tongue); akin to Old High German *drum* fragment] (14th century)
**1 a** (1) **:** a fringe of warp threads left on the loom after the cloth has been removed (2) **:** one of these warp threads **b :** a tuft or short piece of rope yarn used in thrumming canvas — usually used in plural **c :** BIT, PARTICLE
**2 :** a hair, fiber, or threadlike leaf on a plant; *also* **:** a tuft or fringe of such structures
— **thrum** *adjective*
**²thrum** *transitive verb* **thrummed; thrumming** (15th century)
**1 :** to furnish with thrums : FRINGE
**2 :** to insert short pieces of rope yarn or spun yarn in (a piece of canvas) to make a rough surface or a mat which can be wrapped about rigging to prevent chafing
**³thrum** *verb* **thrummed; thrum·ming** [imitative] (1592)
*intransitive verb*
**1 :** to play or pluck a stringed instrument idly **:** STRUM
**2 :** to sound with a monotonous hum
*transitive verb*
**1 :** to play (as a stringed instrument) in an idle or relaxed manner
**2 :** to recite tiresomely or monotonously
**⁴thrum** *noun* (1798)
**:** the monotonous sound of thrumming
**¹thrush** \'thrəsh\ *noun* [Middle English *thrusche*, from Old English *thrysce*; akin to Old English *throstle* thrush, Old High German *droscala*, Latin *turdus*] (before 12th century)
**1 :** any of numerous small or medium-sized oscine birds (families Turdidae and Muscicapidae) which are mostly of a plain color often with spotted underparts and many of which are excellent singers
**2 :** a bird held to resemble a thrush
**²thrush** *noun* [probably of Scandinavian origin; akin to Danish & Norwegian *trøske* thrush] (1665)

☆ **SYNONYMS**
**Throw, cast, toss, fling, hurl, pitch, sling** mean to cause to move swiftly through space by a propulsive movement or a propelling force. THROW is general and interchangeable with the other terms but may specifically imply a distinctive motion with bent arm ⟨can *throw* a fastball and a curve⟩. CAST usually implies lightness in the thing thrown and sometimes a scattering ⟨*cast* it to the winds⟩. TOSS suggests a light or careless or aimless throwing and may imply an upward motion ⟨*tossed* the coat on the bed⟩. FLING stresses a violent throwing ⟨*flung* the ring back in his face⟩. HURL implies power as in throwing a massive weight ⟨*hurled* himself at the intruder⟩. PITCH suggests throwing carefully at a target ⟨*pitch* horseshoes⟩. SLING stresses either the use of whirling momentum in throwing or directness of aim ⟨*slung* the bag over his shoulder⟩.

**1** : a disease that is caused by a fungus (*Candida albicans*), occurs especially in infants and children, and is marked by white patches in the oral cavity; *broadly* : CANDIDIASIS ⟨vaginal *thrush*⟩
**2** : a suppurative disorder of the feet in various animals (as a horse)
**¹thrust** \'thrəst\ *verb* **thrust; thrust·ing** [Middle English *thrusten, thristen*, from Old Norse *thrȳsta;* probably akin to Old Norse *thrjōta* to tire, Old English *thrēat* coercion — more at THREAT] (13th century)
*transitive verb*
**1** : to push or drive with force : SHOVE
**2** : to cause to enter or pierce something by or as if by pushing ⟨*thrust* a dagger into his heart⟩
**3** : EXTEND, SPREAD
**4** : STAB, PIERCE
**5 a** : to put (as an unwilling person) forcibly into a course of action or position ⟨was *thrust* into the job⟩ **b** : to introduce often improperly into a position : INTERPOLATE
**6** : to press, force, or impose the acceptance of upon someone ⟨*thrust* new responsibilities upon her⟩
*intransitive verb*
**1 a** : to force an entrance or passage **b** : to push forward : press onward **c** : to push upward : PROJECT
**2** : to make a thrust, stab, or lunge with or as if with a pointed weapon ⟨*thrust* at them with a knife⟩
**²thrust** *noun* (circa 1586)
**1 a** : a push or lunge with a pointed weapon **b** (1) : a verbal attack (2) : a military assault
**2 a** : a strong continued pressure **b** : the sideways force or pressure of one part of a structure against another part (as of an arch against an abutment) **c** : the force produced by a propeller or by a jet or rocket engine that drives a vehicle (as an aircraft) forward **d** : a nearly horizontal geological fault
**3 a** : a forward or upward push **b** : a movement (as by a group of people) in a specified direction
**4 a** : salient or essential element or meaning **b** : principal concern or objective
**thrust·er** *also* **thrust·or** \'thrəs-tər\ *noun* (1597)
: one that thrusts; *especially* : an engine (as a jet engine) that develops thrust by expelling a jet of fluid or a stream of particles
**thrust·ful** \'thrəst-fəl\ *adjective* (1909)
*British* : characterized by thrust : AGGRESSIVE ⟨*thrustful* young man on the make —*Current Literature*⟩
**thrust stage** *noun* [*thrust*, past participle of ¹*thrust*] (1965)
: a stage that projects beyond the proscenium so that the audience sits around the projection; *also* : a forestage that is extended into the auditorium to increase the stage area
**thru·way** \'thrü-ˌwā\ *noun* (1930)
: EXPRESSWAY
**¹thud** \'thəd\ *noun* [imitative] (1787)
**1** : BLOW
**2** : a dull sound : THUMP
**²thud** *intransitive verb* **thud·ded; thud·ding** (1796)
: to move or strike so as to make a thud
**thug** \'thəg\ *noun* [Hindi *thag*, literally, thief] (1810)
: a brutal ruffian or assassin : GANGSTER, KILLER ◆
— **thug·gery** \'thə-g(ə-)rē\ *noun*
— **thug·gish** \'thə-gish\ *adjective*
**thu·ja** \'thü-jə, 'thyü-\ *noun* [New Latin *Thuja*, from Medieval Latin *thuia*, a cedar, from Greek *thyia*, from *thyein* to sacrifice — more at THYME] (circa 1760)
: any of a genus (*Thuja*) of evergreen shrubs and trees (as an arborvitae) of the cypress family having scalelike closely imbricated or compressed leaves

**¹Thu·le** \'thü-lē, 'thyü-\ *noun* [Middle English *Tyle*, from Old English, from Latin *Thule, Thyle*, from Greek *Thoulē, Thylē*] (before 12th century)
: the northernmost part of the habitable ancient world
**²Thu·le** \'tü-lē\ *adjective* [*Thule*, Greenland] (1925)
: of, relating to, or being the culture existing in the arctic lands from Alaska to Greenland from about 500 A.D. to 1400 A.D.
**thu·li·um** \'thü-lē-əm, 'thyü-\ *noun* [New Latin, from Latin *Thule*] (1879)
: a trivalent metallic element of the rare-earth group — see ELEMENT table
**¹thumb** \'thəm\ *noun* [Middle English *thoume, thoumbe*, from Old English *thūma;* akin to Old High German *thūmo* thumb, Latin *tumēre* to swell] (before 12th century)
**1** : the short thick digit of the human hand that is analogous in position to the big toe and differs from the other fingers in having only two phalanges, allowing greater freedom of movement, and being opposable to each of them; *also* : a corresponding digit in lower animals
**2** : the part of a glove or mitten that covers the thumb
**3** : a convex molding : OVOLO
— **all thumbs** : extremely awkward or clumsy
— **under one's thumb** *or* **under the thumb** : under control : in a state of subservience ⟨her father did not have her that much *under his thumb* —Hamilton Basso⟩
**²thumb** (circa 1647)
*transitive verb*
**1 a** : to leaf through (pages) with the thumb : TURN **b** : to soil or wear by or as if by repeated thumbing ⟨a badly *thumbed* book⟩
**2** : to request or obtain (a ride) in a passing automobile by signaling with the thumb
*intransitive verb*
**1** : to turn over pages ⟨*thumb* through a book⟩
**2** : to travel by thumbing rides : HITCHHIKE ⟨*thumbed* across the country⟩
— **thumb one's nose 1** : to place the thumb at one's nose and extend the fingers as a gesture of scorn or defiance **2** : to express disdain or defiance ⟨*thumb their nose* at opulence —*Sales Management*⟩
**thumb·hole** \'thəm-ˌhōl\ *noun* (1859)
**1** : an opening in which to insert the thumb
**2** : a hole in a wind musical instrument opened or closed by the thumb
**thumb index** *noun* (1903)
: a series of notches cut in the fore edge of a book to facilitate reference
**¹thumb·nail** \'thəm-ˌnāl, -'nā(ə)l\ *noun* (1604)
: the nail of the thumb
**²thumbnail** *adjective* (1852)
: CONCISE, BRIEF ⟨a *thumbnail* sketch⟩
**thumb piano** *noun* (1949)
: MBIRA
**thumb·print** \'thəm-ˌprint\ *noun* (1900)
: an impression made by the thumb; *especially* : a print made by the inside of the first joint
**thumb·screw** \-ˌskrü\ *noun* (1794)
**1** : a screw having a flat-sided or knurled head so that it may be turned by the thumb and forefinger
**2** : an instrument of torture for compressing the thumb by a screw
**thumbs–down** \'thəmz-'daun\ *noun* (1889)
: an instance or gesture of rejection, disapproval, or condemnation

thumbscrew 1

**thumbs–up** \-'əp\ *noun* (circa 1917)
: an instance or gesture of approval or encouragement
**¹thumb·tack** \'thəm-ˌtak\ *noun* (1884)
: a tack with a broad flat head for pressing into a surface with the thumb
**²thumbtack** *transitive verb* (1914)

: to fasten with a thumbtack
**thumb·wheel** \'thəm-ˌhwēl, -ˌwēl\ *noun* (1903)
: a control for various devices consisting of a partially exposed wheel that can be turned by moving the exposed edge with a finger
**¹thump** \'thəmp\ *verb* [imitative] (1548)
*transitive verb*
**1** : to strike or beat with or as if with something thick or heavy so as to cause a dull sound
**2** : POUND, KNOCK
**3** : WHIP, THRASH
**4** : to produce (music) mechanically or in a mechanical manner — usually used with *out* ⟨*thumped* out a tune on the piano⟩
*intransitive verb*
**1 a** : to inflict a thump **b** : to make or move with a thumping sound
**2** : to make a vigorous endorsement ⟨got a couple of . . . senators to *thump* for him —*N.Y. Herald Tribune*⟩
— **thump·er** *noun*
**²thump** *noun* (1552)
: a blow or knock with or as if with something blunt or heavy; *also* : the sound made by such a blow
**thump·ing** *adjective* [*thumping*, present participle of ¹*thump*] (1576)
: impressively large, great, or excellent ⟨a *thumping* majority⟩
**¹thun·der** \'thən-dər\ *noun* [Middle English *thoner, thunder*, from Old English *thunor;* akin to Old High German *thonar* thunder, Latin *tonare* to thunder] (before 12th century)
**1** : the sound that follows a flash of lightning and is caused by sudden expansion of the air in the path of the electrical discharge
**2** : a loud utterance or threat
**3** : BANG, RUMBLE ⟨the *thunder* of big guns⟩
**²thunder** *verb* **thun·dered; thun·der·ing** \-d(ə-)riŋ\ (before 12th century)
*intransitive verb*

◇ WORD HISTORY
**thug** In the 1830s British officials in India launched a vigorous campaign against bands of highway robbers known as *thugs* (from Hindi *thag* "thief"). The *thugs* were supposedly members of a centuries-old hereditary criminal caste who befriended travelers and after winning their trust strangled them and plundered their goods. With the aid of *thugs* who confessed in return for reduced sentences, over a thousand men were convicted under an extraordinary legal measure that made simple membership in a *thug* gang punishable by life imprisonment. Numerous popular accounts of *thuggee*, as the phenomenon was called, that appeared in England, especially the novel *Confessions of a Thug* (1839) by an Indian civil servant named Meadows Taylor, made *thug* a well-known word that was soon generalized to refer to any brutal ruffian. It now appears that *thuggee* was largely a product of British imagination, created by combining the embellished accounts of *thug* informers with Britons' own preconceptions of mysterious evil lurking below the surface of exotic Asian societies. An actual increase in the 1830s of vagrant groups of armed men preying on travelers probably resulted from the disbanding of militias in the service of local rulers, as the British subdued one native state after another.

**1 a :** to produce thunder — usually used impersonally ⟨it *thundered*⟩ **b :** to give forth a sound that resembles thunder ⟨horses *thundered* down the road⟩
**2 :** ROAR, SHOUT
*transitive verb*
**1 :** to utter loudly **:** ROAR
**2 :** to strike with a sound likened to thunder
— **thun·der·er** \-dər-ər\ *noun*

**thun·der·bird** \'thən-dər-ˌbərd\ *noun* (1871)
**:** a bird that causes lightning and thunder in American Indian myth

**thun·der·bolt** \-ˌbōlt\ *noun* (15th century)
**1 a :** a single discharge of lightning with the accompanying thunder **b :** an imaginary elongated mass cast as a missile to earth in the lightning flash
**2 a :** a person or thing that resembles lightning in suddenness, effectiveness, or destructive power **b :** a vehement threat or censure

**thun·der·clap** \-ˌklap\ *noun* (14th century)
**1 :** a clap of thunder
**2 :** something sharp, loud, or sudden like a clap of thunder

**thun·der·cloud** \-ˌklaud\ *noun* (1697)
**:** a cloud charged with electricity and producing lightning and thunder

**thunder egg** *noun* (1941)
**:** chalcedony in rounded concretionary nodules

**thun·der·head** \-ˌhed\ *noun* (1853)
**:** a rounded mass of cumulus cloud often appearing before a thunderstorm

**thun·der·ing** *adjective* [*thundering*, present participle of ²*thunder*] (1543)
**:** awesomely great, intense, or unusual
— **thun·der·ing·ly** \-d(ə-)riŋ-lē\ *adverb*

**thunder lizard** *noun* [translation of New Latin *Brontosaurus*] (1960)
**:** BRONTOSAURUS

**thun·der·ous** \'thən-d(ə-)rəs\ *adjective* (1582)
**1 a :** producing thunder **b :** making or accompanied by a noise like thunder ⟨*thunderous* applause⟩
**2 :** THUNDERING
— **thun·der·ous·ly** *adverb*

**thun·der·show·er** \-ˌshau(-ə)r\ *noun* (1699)
**:** a shower accompanied by lightning and thunder

**thun·der·stone** \-ˌstōn\ *noun* (1598)
**1** *archaic* **:** THUNDERBOLT 1b
**2 :** any of various stones (as a meteorite or an ancient artifact) that are the probable source of the imaginary thunderbolt

**thun·der·storm** \-ˌstȯrm\ *noun* (1652)
**:** a storm accompanied by lightning and thunder

**thun·der·strike** \-ˌstrīk\ *transitive verb* -struck \-ˌstrək\; -struck *also* -strick·en \-ˌstri-kən\; -strik·ing \-ˌstrī-kiŋ\ (circa 1586)
**1 :** to strike dumb **:** ASTONISH ⟨was *thunderstruck* at the news⟩
**2** *archaic* **:** to strike by or as if by lightning

**thun·der·stroke** \-ˌstrōk\ *noun* (1587)
**:** a stroke of or as if of lightning with the attendant thunder

¹**thunk** \'thəŋk\ *dialect past and past participle of* THINK

²**thunk** *noun* [imitative] (1947)
**:** a flat hollow sound

**thu·ri·ble** \'thur-ə-bəl, 'thyur-, 'thər-\ *noun* [Middle English *turrible*, from Middle French *thurible*, from Latin *thuribulum*, from *thur-*, *thus* incense, from Greek *thyos* incense, sacrifice, from *thyein* to sacrifice — more at THYME] (15th century)
**:** CENSER

**thu·ri·fer** \-ə-fər\ *noun* [New Latin *thurifer*, adjective, incense-bearing, from *thur-*, *thus* + *-ifer* *-iferous*] (1853)
**:** one who carries a censer in a liturgical service

**Thu·rin·ger** \'thur-ən-jər, 'thyur-\ *noun* [German *Thüringerwurst*, from *Thüringer* Thuringian + *Wurst* sausage] (circa 1923)
**:** a mildly seasoned fresh or smoked sausage

**Thu·rin·gian** \thu-'rin-j(ē-)ən, thyur-\ *noun* (1618)
**1 :** a member of an ancient Germanic people whose kingdom was overthrown by the Franks in the 6th century
**2 :** a native or inhabitant of Thuringia
— **Thuringian** *adjective*

**thurl** \'thər(-ə)l\ *noun* [perhaps from English dialect, gaunt]
**:** the hip joint in cattle — see COW illustration

**Thurs·day** \'thərz-dē, -ˌdā\ *noun* [Middle English, from Old English *thursdæg*, from Old Norse *thōrsdagr*; akin to Old English *thunresdæg* Thursday, Old Norse *Thōrr* Thor, Old English *thunor* thunder — more at THUNDER] (before 12th century)
**:** the fifth day of the week
— **Thurs·days** \-dēz, -ˌdāz\ *adverb*

**thus** \'thəs\ *adverb* [Middle English, from Old English; akin to Old Saxon *thus* thus] (before 12th century)
**1 :** in this or that manner or way
**2 :** to this degree or extent **:** SO
**3 :** because of this or that **:** HENCE, CONSEQUENTLY
**4 :** as an example

**thus·ly** \-lē\ *adverb* (1865)
**:** in this manner **:** THUS ▢

¹**thwack** \'thwak\ *transitive verb* [imitative] (circa 1530)
**:** to strike with or as if with something flat or heavy **:** WHACK

²**thwack** *noun* (1587)
**:** a heavy blow **:** WHACK; *also* **:** the sound of or as if of such a blow

¹**thwart** \'thwȯrt\ *transitive verb* [Middle English *thwerten*, from *thwert*, adverb] (13th century)
**1 a :** to run counter to so as to effectively oppose or baffle **:** CONTRAVENE **b :** to oppose successfully **:** defeat the hopes or aspirations of
**2 :** to pass through or across
*synonym* see FRUSTRATE
— **thwart·er** *noun*

²**thwart** \'thwȯrt, *nautical often* 'thȯrt\ *adverb* [Middle English *thwert*, from Old Norse *thvert*, from neuter of *thverr* transverse, oblique; akin to Old High German *dwerah* transverse, oblique] (14th century)
**:** ATHWART

³**thwart** *adjective* (15th century)
**:** situated or placed across something else **:** TRANSVERSE
— **thwart·ly** *adverb*

⁴**thwart** *noun* [alteration of obsolete *thought*, *thoft*, from Middle English *thoft*, from Old English *thofte*; akin to Old High German *dofta* rower's seat] (circa 1736)
**:** a rower's seat extending athwart a boat

**thwart·wise** \-ˌwīz\ *adverb or adjective* (1589)
**:** CROSSWISE

**thy** \'thī\ *adjective* [Middle English *thin*, *thy*, from Old English *thīn*, genitive of *thū* thou — more at THOU] (12th century)
*archaic* **:** of or relating to thee or thyself especially as possessor or agent or as object of an action — used especially in ecclesiastical or literary language and sometimes by Friends especially among themselves

**Thy·es·te·an** \thī-'es-tē-ən\ *adjective* [*Thyestes*, brother of Atreus who unwittingly ate the flesh of his children] (1667)
**:** of or relating to the eating of human flesh **:** CANNIBAL

**thy·la·cine** \'thī-lə-ˌsīn\ *noun* [New Latin *Thylacinus*, genus of marsupials, from Greek *thylakos* sack, pouch] (1838)
**:** TASMANIAN WOLF

**thy·la·koid** \'thī-lə-ˌkȯid\ *noun* [International Scientific Vocabulary *thylak-* (from Greek *thylakos* sack) + *-oid*] (1966)
**:** any of the membranous disks of lamellae within plant chloroplasts that are composed of protein and lipid and are the sites of the photochemical reactions of photosynthesis

**thym-** *or* **thymo-** *combining form* [New Latin *thymus*]
**:** thymus ⟨*thymic*⟩ ⟨*thymocyte*⟩

**thyme** \'tīm *also* 'thīm\ *noun* [Middle English, from Middle French *thym*, from Latin *thymum*, from Greek *thymon*, probably from *thyein* to make a burnt offering, sacrifice; akin to Latin *fumus* smoke — more at FUME] (14th century)
**1 :** any of a genus (*Thymus*) of Eurasian mints with small pungent aromatic leaves; *especially* **:** a garden herb (*T. vulgaris*)
**2 :** thyme leaves used as a seasoning

**thy·mec·to·my** \thī-'mek-tə-mē\ *noun, plural* -mies (circa 1905)
**:** excision of the thymus
— **thy·mec·to·mize** \-ˌmīz\ *transitive verb*

**-thymia** *noun combining form* [New Latin, from Greek, from *thymos* mind]
**:** condition of mind and will ⟨cyclo*thymia*⟩

**thy·mic** \'thī-mik\ *adjective* (circa 1656)
**:** of or relating to the thymus

**thy·mi·dine** \'thī-mə-ˌdēn\ *noun* [*thymine* + *-idine*] (1912)
**:** a nucleoside $C_{10}H_{14}N_2O_5$ that is composed of thymine and deoxyribose and occurs as a structural part of DNA

**thy·mine** \'thī-ˌmēn\ *noun* [International Scientific Vocabulary, from New Latin *thymus*] (1894)
**:** a pyrimidine base $C_5H_6N_2O_2$ that is one of the four bases coding genetic information in the polynucleotide chain of DNA — compare ADENINE, CYTOSINE, GUANINE, URACIL

**thy·mo·cyte** \'thī-mə-ˌsīt\ *noun* [International Scientific Vocabulary] (circa 1923)
**:** a cell of the thymus; *especially* **:** a thymic lymphocyte

**thy·mol** \'thī-ˌmȯl, -ˌmōl\ *noun* [International Scientific Vocabulary, from Latin *thymum* thyme] (1857)
**:** a crystalline phenol $C_{10}H_{14}O$ of aromatic odor and antiseptic properties found especially in thyme oil or made synthetically and used chiefly as a fungicide and preservative

**thy·mo·sin** \'thī-mə-sən\ *noun* [Greek *thymos* thymus + English ¹*-in*] (1966)
**:** a mixture of polypeptides isolated from the thymus; *also* **:** any of these

**thy·mus** \'thī-məs\ *noun* [New Latin, from Greek *thymos* warty excrescence, thymus] (circa 1693)

---

: a glandular structure of largely lymphoid tissue that functions especially in the development of the body's immune system, is present in the young of most vertebrates typically in the upper anterior chest or at the base of the neck, and tends to atrophy in the adult

**thy·my** or **thym·ey** \'tī-mē also \'thī-\ adjective (1727)
: abounding in or fragrant with thyme

**thyr-** or **thyro-** combining form [thyroid]
: thyroid ⟨thyrotoxicosis⟩ ⟨thyroxine⟩

**thy·ra·tron** \'thī-rə-ˌträn\ noun [from Thyratron, a trademark] (1929)
: a gas-filled hot-cathode electron tube in which the grid controls only the start of a continuous current thus giving the tube a trigger effect

**thy·ris·tor** \thī-'ris-tər\ noun [thyratron + transistor] (1958)
: any of several semiconductor devices that act as switches, rectifiers, or voltage regulators

**thy·ro·cal·ci·to·nin** \ˌthī-rō-ˌkal-sə-'tō-nən\ noun (1963)
: CALCITONIN

**thy·ro·glob·u·lin** \-'glä-byə-lən\ noun [International Scientific Vocabulary] (circa 1905)
: an iodine-containing protein of the thyroid gland that is the precursor of thyroxine and triiodothyronine

**¹thy·roid** \'thī-ˌroid\ also **thy·roi·dal** \thī-'roi-dᵊl\ adjective [New Latin thyroides, from Greek thyreoeidēs shield-shaped, thyroid, from thyreos shield shaped like a door, from thyra door — more at DOOR] (circa 1741)
**1 a :** of, relating to, or being a large bilobed endocrine gland of craniate vertebrates lying at the base of the neck and producing especially the hormones thyroxine and triiodothyronine **b :** suggestive of a disordered thyroid ⟨a thyroid personality⟩
**2 :** of, relating to, or being the chief cartilage of the larynx

**²thyroid** noun (1840)
**1 :** a thyroid gland or cartilage; also : a part (as an artery or nerve) associated with either of these
**2 :** a preparation of mammalian thyroid gland used in treating thyroid disorders

**thy·roid·ec·to·my** \ˌthī-ˌroi-'dek-tə-mē, ˌthī-rə-\ noun, plural **-mies** (1889)
: surgical removal of thyroid gland tissue
— **thy·roid·ec·to·mized** \-ˌmīzd\ adjective

**thy·roid·itis** \ˌthī-ˌroi-'dī-təs, ˌthī-rə-\ noun [New Latin] (circa 1885)
: inflammation of the thyroid gland

**thyroid–stimulating hormone** noun (1941)
: THYROTROPIN

**thy·ro·tox·i·co·sis** \ˌthī-rō-ˌtäk-sə-'kō-səs\ noun [New Latin] (circa 1911)
: HYPERTHYROIDISM

**thy·ro·tro·pic** \ˌthī-rə-'trō-pik, -'trä-\ also **thy·ro·tro·phic** \-'trō-fik\ adjective (circa 1923)
: exerting or characterized by a direct influence on the secretory activity of the thyroid gland ⟨thyrotropic functions⟩

**thy·ro·tro·pin** \ˌthī-rə-'trō-pən\ also **thy·ro·tro·phin** \-fən\ noun [thyrotropic, thyrotrophic] (1939)
: a hormone secreted by the anterior pituitary that stimulates the thyroid gland — called also thyroid-stimulating hormone, thyrotropic hormone

**thyrotropin–releasing hormone** noun (1968)
: a tripeptide hormone synthesized in the hypothalamus that stimulates secretion of thyrotropin by the anterior lobe of the pituitary gland — called also thyrotropin-releasing factor

**thy·rox·ine** or **thy·rox·in** \thī-'räk-ˌsēn, -sən\ noun [International Scientific Vocabulary] (1918)

: an iodine-containing hormone $C_{15}H_{11}I_4NO_4$ that is an amino acid produced by the thyroid gland as a product of the cleavage of thyroglobulin, increases metabolic rate, and is used to treat thyroid disorders

**thyrse** \'thərs\ noun [New Latin thyrsus, from Latin, thyrsus] (1744)
: an inflorescence (as in the lilac and horse chestnut) in which the main axis is racemose and the secondary and later axes are cymose

**thyr·sus** \'thər-səs\ noun, plural **thyr·si** \-ˌsī, -ˌsē\ [Latin, from Greek thyrsos] (1591)
: a staff surmounted by a pinecone or by a bunch of vine or ivy leaves with grapes or berries that is carried by Bacchus and by satyrs and others engaging in bacchic rites

**thy·sa·nu·ran** \ˌthī-sə-'nu̇r-ən, -'nyu̇r-\ noun [ultimately from Greek thysanos tassel + oura tail — more at ASS] (1835)
: BRISTLETAIL
— **thysanuran** adjective

**thy·self** \thī-'self\ pronoun (before 12th century)
archaic : YOURSELF — used especially in ecclesiastical or literary language and sometimes by Friends especially among themselves

**¹ti** \'tē\ noun [Tahitian, Marquesan, Samoan, & Maori] (1832)
: any of several Asian and Pacific trees or shrubs (genus Cordyline) of the agave family with leaves in terminal tufts

**²ti** noun [alteration of si] (1839)
: the seventh tone of the diatonic scale in solmization

**ti·ara** \tē-'ar-ə, -'er-, -'är-\ noun [Latin, royal Persian headdress, from Greek] (1616)
**1 :** a 3-tiered crown worn by the pope
**2 :** a decorative jeweled or flowered headband or semicircle for formal wear by women

**Ti·bet·an** \tə-'be-tᵊn\ noun (1747)
**1 a :** a member of the predominant people of Tibet and adjacent areas of Asia **b :** a native or inhabitant of Tibet
**2 :** the Tibeto-Burman language of the Tibetan people
— **Tibetan** adjective

tiara 2

**Tibetan terrier** noun (1905)
: any of a breed of terriers resembling Old English sheepdogs but having a curled well-feathered tail

**Ti·be·to–Bur·man** \tə-ˌbe-tō-'bər-mən\ noun (1901)
**1 :** a language family that includes Tibetan, Burmese, and related languages of southern and eastern Asia
**2 :** a member of a people speaking a Tibeto-Burman language

Tibetan terrier

**tib·ia** \'ti-bē-ə\ noun, plural **-i·ae** \-bē-ˌē, -bē-ˌī\ also **-i·as** [Latin] (circa 1706)
**1 :** the inner and usually larger of the two bones of the vertebrate hind limb between the knee and ankle
**2 :** the fourth joint of the leg of an insect between the femur and tarsus
— **tib·i·al** \-bē-əl\ adjective

**tib·io·fib·u·la** \ˌti-bē-ō-'fi-byə-lə\ noun [New Latin] (circa 1909)
: a bone especially in frogs and toads that is formed by fusion of the tibia and fibula

**tic** \'tik\ noun [French] (circa 1834)
**1 :** local and habitual spasmodic motion of particular muscles especially of the face
: TWITCHING

**2 :** a frequent usually unconscious quirk of behavior or speech ("you know" is a verbal tic)

**ti·cal** \'ti-ˌkäl, 'ti-kəl\ noun, plural **ticals** or **ti·cal** [Thai, from Portuguese, from Malay tikal, a monetary unit] (1662)
: BAHT

**tic dou·lou·reux** \ˌtik-ˌdü-lə-'rü, -'rə(r)\ noun [French, painful twitch] (1800)
: TRIGEMINAL NEURALGIA

**¹tick** \'tik\ noun [Middle English tyke, teke; akin to Middle High German zeche tick, Armenian tiz] (14th century)
**1 :** any of a superfamily (Ixodoidea of the order Acarina) of bloodsucking arachnids that are larger than the related mites, attach themselves to warm-blooded vertebrates to feed, and include important vectors of infectious diseases
**2 :** any of various usually wingless parasitic dipteran flies — compare SHEEP KED

¹tick 1

**²tick** noun [Middle English tike, probably from Middle Dutch (akin to Old High German ziahha tick), from Latin theca cover, from Greek thēkē case; akin to Greek tithenai to place — more at DO] (15th century)
**1 :** the fabric case of a mattress, pillow, or bolster; also : a mattress consisting of a tick and its filling
**2 :** TICKING

**³tick** noun [Middle English tek pat, light stroke; akin to Middle High German zic light push] (1680)
**1 a :** a light rhythmic audible tap or beat; also : a series of such ticks **b** chiefly British : the time taken by the tick of a clock : MOMENT
**2 :** a small spot or mark; especially : one used to direct attention to something, to check an item on a list, or to represent a point on a scale

**⁴tick** (1721)
intransitive verb
**1 :** to make the sound of a tick or a series of ticks
**2 :** to operate as a functioning mechanism : RUN ⟨tried to understand what made him tick⟩ ⟨the motor was ticking over quietly⟩
transitive verb
**1 :** to mark with a written tick : CHECK — usually used with off ⟨ticked off each item in the list⟩
**2 :** to mark, count, or announce by or as if by ticking beats ⟨a meter ticking off the cab fare⟩
**3 :** to touch with a momentary glancing blow ⟨ticked the ball⟩

**⁵tick** noun [short for ¹ticket] (1642)
chiefly British : CREDIT, TRUST; also : a credit account

**tick–borne** \'tik-ˌbōrn, -ˌbȯrn\ adjective (1921)
: capable of being transmitted by the bites of ticks ⟨tick-borne encephalitis⟩

**¹ticked** \'tikt\ adjective (circa 1688)
**1 :** marked with ticks : FLECKED
**2 :** having or made of hair banded with two or more colors ⟨a ticked cat⟩ ⟨a ticked coat⟩

**²ticked** adjective [tick off] (circa 1959)
: ANGRY, UPSET

**tick·er** \'ti-kər\ noun (1828)
: something that ticks or produces a ticking sound: as **a :** WATCH **b :** a telegraphic receiving instrument that automatically prints off information (as stock quotations or news) on a paper ribbon **c** slang : HEART

**ticker tape** noun (1902)
: the paper ribbon on which a telegraphic ticker prints off its information

**¹tick·et** \'ti-kət\ noun [Middle French etiquet, estiquette notice attached to something, from estiquier to attach, from Middle Dutch steken to stick; akin to Old High German sticken to prick — more at STICK] (1529)
**1 a :** a document that serves as a certificate, license, or permit; especially **:** a mariner's or airman's certificate **b :** TAG, LABEL
**2 a :** a certificate or token showing that a fare or admission fee has been paid **b :** a means of access or passage 〈education is the ticket to a good job〉
**3 :** a list of candidates for nomination or election **:** SLATE
**4 :** the correct or desirable thing 〈cooperation, that's the ticket —K. E. Trombley〉
**5 :** a slip or card recording a transaction or undertaking or giving instructions 〈a savings deposit ticket〉
**6 :** a summons or warning issued to a traffic-law violator
— **tick·et·less** \-ləs\ adjective
**²ticket** transitive verb (1611)
**1 :** to attach a ticket to **:** LABEL; also **:** DESIGNATE
**2 :** to furnish or serve with a ticket 〈ticketed for illegal parking〉
**ticket agency** noun (1923)
**:** an agency selling transportation or theater and entertainment tickets
**ticket agent** noun (1861)
**:** one who sells transportation or theater and entertainment tickets
**ticket office** noun (circa 1667)
**:** an office of a transportation company, theatrical or entertainment enterprise, or ticket agency where tickets are sold and reservations made
**tick·et–of–leave** \,ti-kət-ə(v)-'lēv\ noun, plural **tickets–of–leave** (1732)
**:** a license or permit formerly given in the United Kingdom and the Commonwealth to a convict under imprisonment to go at large and to get work subject to certain specific conditions
**tick fever** noun (circa 1897)
**1 :** TEXAS FEVER
**2 :** a febrile disease (as Rocky Mountain spotted fever) transmitted by the bites of ticks
**¹tick·ing** \'ti-kiŋ\ noun [²tick] (1649)
**:** a strong linen or cotton fabric used in upholstering and as a covering for a mattress or pillow
**²ticking** noun [³tick] (1885)
**:** ticked marking on a bird or mammal or on individual hairs
**¹tick·le** \'ti-kəl\ verb **tick·led; tick·ling** \-k(ə-)liŋ\ [Middle English tikelen; akin to Old English tinclian to tickle] (14th century)
transitive verb
**1 a :** to excite or stir up agreeably **:** PLEASE 〈music . . . does more than tickle our sense of rhythm —Edward Sapir〉 **b :** to provoke to laughter or merriment **:** AMUSE 〈were tickled by the clown's antics〉
**2 :** to touch (as a body part) lightly so as to excite the surface nerves and cause uneasiness, laughter, or spasmodic movements
intransitive verb
**1 :** to have a tingling or prickling sensation 〈my back tickles〉
**2 :** to excite the surface nerves to prickle
**²tickle** noun (1801)
**1 :** the act of tickling
**2 :** a tickling sensation
**3 :** something that tickles
**tick·ler** \'ti-k(ə-)lər\ noun (1680)
**1 :** a person or device that tickles
**2 :** a device for jogging the memory; specifically **:** a file that serves as a reminder and is arranged to bring matters to timely attention
**tick·lish** \'ti-k(ə-)lish\ adjective (1581)
**1 a :** TOUCHY, OVERSENSITIVE 〈ticklish about his baldness〉 **b :** easily overturned 〈a canoe is a ticklish craft〉

**2 :** requiring delicate handling 〈a ticklish subject〉
**3 :** sensitive to tickling
— **tick·lish·ly** adverb
— **tick·lish·ness** noun
**tick off** transitive verb [⁴tick] (circa 1919)
**1 :** REPRIMAND, REBUKE 〈his father ticked him off for his impudence〉
**2 :** to make angry or indignant 〈the cancellation really ticked me off〉
**tick·seed** \'tik-,sēd\ noun [¹tick] (circa 1562)
**:** COREOPSIS
**tick·tack** or **tic·tac** \'tik-,tak\ noun [reduplication of tick] (1549)
**1 :** a ticking or tapping beat like that of a clock or watch
**2 :** a contrivance used by children to tap on a window from a distance
**tick·tack·toe** also **tic–tac–toe** \,tik-,tak-'tō\ noun [tic-tac-toe, former game in which players with eyes shut brought a pencil down on a slate marked with numbers and scored the number hit] (circa 1866)
**:** a game in which two players alternately put Xs and Os in compartments of a figure formed by two vertical lines crossing two horizontal lines and each tries to get a row of three Xs or three Os before the opponent does
**tick·tock** \'tik-'täk, -,täk\ noun [imitative] (1848)
**:** the ticking sound of a clock
**tick trefoil** noun [¹tick] (1857)
**:** any of various leguminous plants (genus Desmodium) with trifoliolate leaves and rough sticky loments
**¹ticky–tacky** \'ti-kē-'ta-kē\ also **ticky–tack** \-'tak\ noun, plural **ticky–tackies** also **ticky–tacks** [reduplication of tacky] (1962)
**:** sleazy or shoddy material used especially in the construction of look-alike tract houses; also **:** something built of ticky-tacky
**²ticky–tacky** also **ticky–tack** adjective (1964)
**1 :** of an uninspired or monotonous sameness
**2 :** TACKY
**3 :** built of ticky-tacky
**tid·al** \'tī-d°l\ adjective (1807)
**1 a :** of, relating to, caused by, or having tides 〈tidal cycles〉 〈tidal erosion〉 **b :** periodically rising and falling or flowing and ebbing 〈tidal waters〉
**2 :** dependent (as to the time of arrival or departure) upon the state of the tide 〈a tidal steamer〉
— **tid·al·ly** \-d°l-ē\ adverb
**tidal wave** noun (1830)
**1 a :** an unusually high sea wave that sometimes follows an earthquake **b :** an unusual rise of water alongshore due to strong winds
**2 :** something overwhelming especially in quantity or volume 〈a tidal wave of tourists〉
**tid·bit** \'tid-,bit\ noun [perhaps from tit- (as in titmouse) + bit] (circa 1640)
**1 :** a choice morsel of food
**2 :** a choice or pleasing bit (as of information)
**tid·dle·dy–winks** \'ti-d°l-dē-,win(k)s\ or **tid·dly–winks** \'ti-d°l-ē-, 'tid-lē-\ noun plural but singular in construction [probably from English dialect tiddly little, alteration of little] (1898)
**:** a game whose object is to snap small disks from a flat surface into a small container
**tid·dler** \'ti-d°l-ər, 'tid-lər\ noun [probably from English dialect tiddly little] (1885)
British **:** a small fish (as a stickleback or minnow)
**tid·dly** \'ti-d°l-ē, 'tid-lē\ adjective [tiddly an alcoholic drink, probably from English dialect tiddly] (1905)
chiefly British **:** slightly drunk
**¹tide** \'tīd\ noun [Middle English, time, from Old English tīd; akin to Old High German zīt time and perhaps to Greek daiesthai to divide] (before 12th century)

**1 a** obsolete **:** a space of time **:** PERIOD **b :** a fit or opportune time **:** OPPORTUNITY **c :** an ecclesiastical anniversary or festival; also **:** its season — usually used in combination 〈Eastertide〉
**2 a** (1) **:** the alternate rising and falling of the surface of the ocean and of water bodies (as gulfs and bays) connected with the ocean that occurs usually twice a day and is caused by the gravitational attraction of the sun and moon occurring unequally on different parts of the earth (2) **:** a less marked rising and falling of an inland body of water (3) **:** a periodic movement in the earth's crust caused by the same forces that produce ocean tides (4) **:** a tidal distortion on one celestial body caused by the gravitational attraction of another (5) **:** one of the tidal movements of the atmosphere resembling those of the ocean and produced by gravitation or diurnal temperature changes **b :** FLOOD TIDE 1
**3 a :** something that fluctuates like the tides of the sea 〈the tide of public opinion〉 **b :** a surging movement of a group 〈a tide of opportunists〉
**4 a :** a flowing stream **:** CURRENT **b :** the waters of the ocean **c :** the overflow of a flooding stream
— **tide·less** \-ləs\ adjective
**²tide** verb **tid·ed; tid·ing** (1593)
intransitive verb
**:** to flow as or in a tide **:** SURGE
transitive verb
**:** to cause to float with or as if with the tide
**³tide** intransitive verb **tid·ed; tid·ing** [Middle English, from Old English tīdan; akin to Middle Dutch tiden to go, come, Old English tīd time] (before 12th century)
archaic **:** BETIDE, BEFALL
**tide·land** \'tīd-,land, -lənd\ noun (1802)
**1 :** land overflowed during flood tide
**2 :** land underlying the ocean and lying beyond the low-water limit of the tide but being within the territorial waters of a nation — often used in plural
**tide·mark** \-,märk\ noun (1799)
**1 a :** a high-water or sometimes low-water mark left by tidal water or a flood **b :** a mark placed to indicate this point
**2 :** the point to which something has attained or below which it has receded 〈the tidemark of tolerance has risen —New Republic〉
**tide over** transitive verb [²tide] (1821)
**:** to enable to surmount or endure a difficulty 〈money to tide us over the emergency〉
**tide table** noun (1594)
**:** a table that indicates the height of the tide at one place at different times of day throughout one year
**tide·wa·ter** \-,wȯ-tər, -,wä-\ noun (1772)
**1 :** water overflowing land at flood tide; also **:** water affected by the ebb and flow of the tide
**2 :** low-lying coastal land
**tide·way** \-,wā\ noun (1798)
**:** a channel in which the tide runs
**tid·ing** \'tī-diŋ\ noun [Middle English, from Old English tīdung, from tīdan to betide] (12th century)
**:** a piece of news — usually used in plural 〈good tidings〉
**¹ti·dy** \'tī-dē\ adjective **ti·di·er; -est** [Middle English, timely, in good condition, from tide time] (13th century)
**1 :** properly filled out **:** PLUMP
**2 :** adequately satisfactory **:** ACCEPTABLE, FAIR 〈a tidy solution to their problem〉
**3 a :** neat and orderly in appearance or habits **:** well ordered and cared for **b :** METHODICAL, PRECISE 〈a tidy mind〉
**4 :** LARGE, SUBSTANTIAL 〈a tidy profit〉
— **ti·di·ly** \'tī-d°l-ē\ adverb
— **ti·di·ness** \'tī-dē-nəs\ noun
**²tidy** verb **ti·died; ti·dy·ing** (1821)
transitive verb
**:** to put in order 〈tidy up a room〉

*intransitive verb*
: to make things tidy ⟨*tidying* up after supper⟩
— **ti·di·er** *noun*

³**tidy** *noun, plural* **tidies** (circa 1828)
**1** : a usually compartmentalized receptacle for various small objects
**2** : a piece of fancywork used to protect the back, arms, or headrest of a chair or sofa from wear or soil

**ti·dy·tips** \'tī-dē-,tips\ *noun plural but singular or plural in construction* (1888)
: an annual California composite herb (*Layia platyglossa*) having yellow-rayed flower heads often tipped with white

¹**tie** \'tī\ *noun* [Middle English *teg, tye,* from Old English *tēag;* akin to Old Norse *taug* rope, Old English *tēon* to pull — more at TOW] (before 12th century)
**1 a** : a line, ribbon, or cord used for fastening, uniting, or drawing something closed; *especially* : SHOELACE **b** (1) : a structural element (as a rod or angle iron) holding two pieces together : a tension member in a construction (2) : any of the transverse supports to which railroad rails are fastened to keep them in line
**2** : something that serves as a connecting link: as **a** : a moral or legal obligation to someone or something typically constituting a restraining power, influence, or duty **b** : a bond of kinship or affection
**3** : a curved line that joins two musical notes of the same pitch to denote a single tone sustained through the time value of the two
**4 a** : an equality in number (as of votes or scores) **b** : equality in a contest; *also* : a contest that ends in a draw
**5** : a method or style of tying or knotting
**6** : something that is knotted or is to be knotted when worn: as **a** : NECKTIE **b** : a low laced shoe : OXFORD
— **tie·less** \-ləs\ *adjective*

²**tie** *verb* **tied; ty·ing** \'tī-iŋ\ *or* **tie·ing** (before 12th century)
*transitive verb*
**1 a** : to fasten, attach, or close by means of a tie **b** : to form a knot or bow in ⟨*tie* your scarf⟩ **c** : to make by tying constituent elements ⟨*tied* a wreath⟩ ⟨*tie* a fishing fly⟩
**2 a** : to place or establish in relationship : CONNECT **b** : to unite in marriage **c** : to unite (musical notes) by a tie **d** : to join (power systems) electrically
**3** : to restrain from independence or freedom of action or choice : constrain by or as if by authority, influence, agreement, or obligation
**4 a** (1) : to make or have an equal score with in a contest (2) : to equalize (the score) in a game or contest (3) : to equalize the score of (a game) **b** : to provide or offer something equal to : EQUAL
*intransitive verb*
: to make a tie: as **a** : to make a bond or connection **b** : to make an equal score **c** : to become attached **d** : to close by means of a tie
— **tie into** : to attack with vigor
— **tie one on** *slang* : to get drunk
— **tie the knot** : to perform a marriage ceremony; *also* : to get married

**tie–and–dye** \'tī-ən-,dī\ *noun* (1928)
: TIE-DYEING

**tie–back** \'tī-,bak\ *noun* (1926)
**1** : a decorative strip or device of cloth, cord, or metal for draping a curtain to the side of a window
**2** : a curtain with a tieback — usually used in plural

**tie–break·er** \'tī-,brā-kər\ *noun* (circa 1932)
: a contest used to select a winner from among contestants with tied scores at the end of a previous contest

**tied cottage** *noun* (1899)
*British* : a cottage or house owned by an employer (as a farmer) and reserved for occupancy by an employee

**tie–down** \-,daún\ *noun* (circa 1942)

: a fitting or a system of lines and fittings used to secure something (as an aircraft or cargo)

**tie–dye** \'tī-,dī\ *noun* (circa 1939)
**1** : TIE-DYEING
**2** : a tie-dyed garment or fabric

**tie–dyed** *adjective* (1904)
: having patterns produced by tie-dyeing ⟨*tie-dyed* shirts⟩

**tie–dye·ing** *noun* (1904)
: a hand method of producing patterns in textiles by tying portions of the fabric or yarn so that they will not absorb the dye

**tie–in** \'tī-,in\ *noun* (1925)
**1** : something that ties in, relates, or connects especially in a promotional campaign
**2** : a book that inspired or was inspired by a motion picture or television program

**tie in** (1793)
*transitive verb*
: to bring into connection with something relevant: as **a** : to make the final connection of ⟨*tied in* the new branch pipeline⟩ **b** : to coordinate in such a manner as to produce balance and unity ⟨the illustrations were *tied in* with the text⟩ **c** : to use as a tie-in especially in advertising
*intransitive verb*
: to become tied in

**tie–line** \'tī-,līn\ *noun* (1923)
: a telephone line that directly connects two or more private branch exchanges

**tie·mann·ite** \'tē-mə-,nīt\ *noun* [German *Tiemannit,* from W. *Tiemann* (died 1899) German scientist] (1868)
: a mineral that consists of mercuric selenide and occurs in dark gray or nearly black masses of metallic luster

**tie·pin** \'tī-,pin\ *noun* (1780)
: an ornamental straight pin that has usually a sheath for the point and is used to hold the ends of a necktie in place

¹**tier** \'tir\ *noun* [Middle French *tire* rank, from Old French — more at ATTIRE] (1569)
**1 a** : a row, rank, or layer of articles; *especially* : one of two or more rows, levels, or ranks arranged one above another **b** : a group of political or geographical divisions that form a row across the map ⟨the southern *tier* of states⟩
**2** : CLASS, CATEGORY

²**tier** (circa 1889)
*transitive verb*
: to place or arrange in tiers
*intransitive verb*
: to rise in tiers

³**ti·er** \'tī(-ə)r\ *noun* (1633)
: one that ties

¹**tierce** \'tirs\ *variant of* TERCE

²**tierce** *noun* [Middle English *terce, tierce,* from Middle French, from feminine of *terz,* adjective, third, from Latin *tertius* — more at THIRD] (15th century)
**1** *obsolete* : THIRD 2
**2** : a sequence of three playing cards of the same suit

**tier·cel** \'tir-səl\ *noun* [Middle English *tercel,* from Middle French, from (assumed) Vulgar Latin *tertiolus,* from diminutive of Latin *tertius* third] (14th century)
: a male hawk

**tiered** \'tird\ *adjective* (1807)
: having or arranged in tiers, rows, or layers — often used in combination ⟨triple-*tiered*⟩

**tie–rod** \'tī-,räd\ *noun* (1839)
: a rod (as of steel) used as a connecting member or brace

**tie silk** *noun* (circa 1915)
: a silk fabric of firm resilient pliable texture used for neckties and for blouses and accessories

**tie tack** *or* **tie tac** \-,tak\ *noun* (1954)
: an ornamented pin with a receiving button or clasp that is used to attach the two parts of a necktie together or to attach a necktie to a shirt

**tie–up** \'tī-,əp\ *noun* (1851)

**1 a** : a cow stable; *also* : a space for a single cow in a stable **b** : a mooring place for a boat
**2** : a slowdown or stoppage of traffic, business, or operation (as by a mechanical breakdown)
**3** : CONNECTION, ASSOCIATION ⟨helpful financial *tie-ups*⟩

**tie up** (1530)
*transitive verb*
**1** : to attach, fasten, or bind securely; *also* : to wrap up and fasten
**2 a** : to connect closely : JOIN ⟨*tie up* the loose ends⟩ **b** : to cause to be linked so as to depend on or relate to something
**3 a** : to place or invest in such a manner as to make unavailable for other purposes ⟨their money was *tied up* in stocks⟩ **b** : to restrain from normal movement, operation, or progress ⟨traffic was *tied up* for miles⟩
**4 a** : to keep busy ⟨was *tied up* in conference all day⟩ **b** : to preempt the use of ⟨*tied up* the phone for an hour⟩
*intransitive verb*
**1** : DOCK ⟨the ferry *ties up* at the south slip⟩
**2** : to assume a definite relationship ⟨this *ties up* with what I told you before⟩

¹**tiff** \'tif\ *intransitive verb* [origin unknown] (1700)
: to have a petty quarrel

²**tiff** *noun* (1754)
: a petty quarrel

**tif·fa·ny** \'ti-fə-nē\ *noun, plural* **-nies** [perhaps from obsolete French *tiphanie* Epiphany, from Late Latin *theophania,* from Late Greek, ultimately from Greek *theos* god + *phainein* to show] (1601)
**1** : a sheer silk gauze formerly used for clothing and trimmings
**2** : a plain-woven open-mesh cotton fabric (as cheesecloth)

**Tif·fa·ny** \'ti-fə-nē\ *adjective* (1936)
: being glass or an article of glass made by or in the manner of Louis C. Tiffany; *especially* : made of pieces of stained glass ⟨a *Tiffany-*style lamp⟩ ⟨a *Tiffany* window⟩

**tif·fin** \'ti-fən\ *noun* [probably alteration of *tiffing,* gerund of obsolete English *tiff* to eat between meals] (1800)
*chiefly British* : a light midday meal : LUNCHEON

**ti·ger** \'tī-gər\ *noun, plural* **tigers** [Middle English *tigre,* from Old English *tiger* & Old French *tigre,* both from Latin *tigris,* from Greek, probably of Iranian origin; akin to Avestan *tighra-* pointed; akin to Greek *stizein* to tattoo — more at STICK] (before 12th century)

**1** *plural also* **ti·ger a** : a large Asian carnivorous mammal (*Panthera tigris*) of the cat family having a usually tawny coat transversely striped with black **b** : any of several large wildcats (as the jaguar or cougar) **c** : a domestic cat with striped pattern **d** *Australian* : TASMANIAN WOLF
**2 a** : a fierce, daring, or aggressive person or quality ⟨aroused the *tiger* in him⟩ ⟨a *tiger* for work⟩ **b** : one (as a situation) that is formidable or impossible to control ⟨how the *tiger* of inflation can be tamed —J. A. Davenport⟩ — often used in the phrases *ride a tiger* and *have a tiger by the tail*
**3** *British* : a groom in livery
— **ti·ger·ish** \-g(ə-)rish\ *adjective*
— **ti·ger·ish·ly** *adverb*

*tiger 1a*

---

\ə\ abut  \ᵊ\ kitten  \ər\ further  \a\ ash  \ā\ ace
\ä\ mop, mar  \aú\ out  \ch\ chin  \e\ bet  \ē\ easy
\g\ go  \i\ hit  \ī\ ice  \j\ job  \ŋ\ sing  \ō\ go
\ò\ law  \òi\ boy  \th\ thin  \t̲h̲\ the  \ü\ loot  \ù\ foot
\y\ yet  \zh\ vision  *see also* Guide to Pronunciation

— **ti·ger·ish·ness** *noun*
— **ti·ger·like** \-gər-ˌlīk\ *adjective*

**tiger beetle** *noun* (1826)
: any of numerous active carnivorous beetles (family Cicindelidae) having larvae that tunnel in the soil

**tiger cat** *noun* (1699)
**1** : any of various wildcats (as the serval, ocelot, or margay) of moderate size and variegated coloration
**2** : a striped or sometimes blotched tabby cat

**ti·ger-eye** \'tī-gər-ˌī\ *or* **ti·ger's-eye** \-gərz-\ *noun* (circa 1891)
: a usually yellowish to grayish brown chatoyant stone that is much used for ornament and is a silicified crocidolite

**tiger lily** *noun* (1824)
: a common Asian garden lily (*Lilium lancifolium* synonym *L. tigrinum*) having nodding orange-colored flowers densely spotted with black; *also* : any of various lilies with similar flowers

**tiger maple** *noun* (1952)
: maple lumber having a distinct irregularly striped pattern and much used for furniture

**tiger lily**

**tiger moth** *noun* (1816)
: any of a family (Arctiidae) of stout-bodied moths usually with broad striped or spotted wings

**tiger salamander** *noun* (circa 1909)
: a large widely distributed North American salamander (*Ambystoma tigrinum*) that is variably colored with contrasting blotches, spots, or bars

**tiger shark** *noun* (circa 1785)
: a large gray or brown stocky-bodied requiem shark (*Galeocerdo cuvieri*) that is nearly cosmopolitan especially in warm seas and can be dangerous to humans — see SHARK illustration

**tiger shrimp** *noun* (1979)
: a large shrimp (*Penaeus monodon*) of the Indian and Pacific oceans that is often farmed and widely sold as food

**tiger swallowtail** *noun* (circa 1890)
: a large widely distributed swallowtail (*Papilio glaucus*) of eastern North America that in the male is largely yellow with black margins and black stripes on the wings and in the female is usually similarly marked in the north but is very often all or mostly black in the south; *also* : any of several closely related black and yellow swallowtails (as *P. rutulus* of western North America)

**¹tight** \'tīt\ *adjective* [alteration of earlier *thight* close set, dense, of Scandinavian origin; akin to Old Norse *thēttr* tight; akin to Middle High German *dīhte* thick, Sanskrit *tanakti* it causes to coagulate] (1507)
**1 a** : so close in structure as to prevent passage or escape (as of liquid, gas, or light) ⟨a *tight* ship⟩ ⟨a *tight* seal⟩ — compare LIGHTPROOF, WATERTIGHT **b** : fitting very close to the body ⟨*tight* jeans⟩; *also* : too snug ⟨*tight* shoes⟩ **c** (1) : closely packed : very full ⟨a *tight* bale of hay⟩ (2) : barely allowing time for completion ⟨a *tight* schedule⟩ ⟨*tight* deadlines⟩ **d** : having elements close together ⟨a *tight* formation⟩ ⟨a *tight* line of type⟩ **e** : allowing little or no room for free motion or movement ⟨a *tight* connection⟩ ⟨a *tight* crawl space⟩; *also* : having a small radius ⟨a *tight* turn⟩
**2 a** : strongly fixed or held : SECURE ⟨a *tight* jar lid⟩ ⟨a *tight* grip on the ladder⟩ **b** (1) : not slack or loose : TAUT ⟨kept the reins *tight*⟩ ⟨a *tight* knot⟩ ⟨a *tight* drumhead⟩; *also* : marked by firmness and muscle tone ⟨a *tight* stomach⟩

(2) : marked by unusual tension (as in the face or body) ⟨lips *tight* with anger⟩ ⟨a family *tight* with fear⟩
**3** *chiefly dialect* **a** : CAPABLE, COMPETENT **b** : having a graceful or shapely form : COMELY
**4 a** : difficult to cope with ⟨in a *tight* spot financially⟩ **b** : relatively difficult to obtain ⟨money is *tight* just now⟩; *also* : characterized by such difficulty ⟨a *tight* job market⟩ **c** : not liberal in giving : STINGY ⟨*tight* with a penny⟩
**5** : characterized by little difference in the relative positions of contestants with respect to final outcome : CLOSE ⟨a *tight* race for mayor⟩
**6** : somewhat drunk
**7 a** : characterized by firmness or strictness in control or application or in attention to details ⟨*tight* zoning codes⟩ ⟨*tight* security⟩ ⟨ran a *tight* newsroom⟩ ⟨keeps a *tight* hand on her investments⟩ **b** : marked by control or discipline in expression or style : having little or no extraneous matter ⟨*tight* writing⟩ **c** : characterized by a polished style and precise arrangements in music performance
**8** : having a close personal or working relationship : INTIMATE ⟨in *tight* with the boss⟩
**9** : being such that the subject fills the frame ⟨filming a *tight* close-up⟩
— **tight·ly** *adverb*
— **tight·ness** *noun*

**²tight** *adverb* (1680)
**1** : FAST, TIGHTLY, FIRMLY ⟨the door was shut *tight*⟩
**2** : in a sound manner : SOUNDLY ⟨sleep *tight*⟩

**tight·en** \'tī-tᵊn\ *verb* **tight·ened; tight·en·ing** \'tīt-niŋ, 'tī-tᵊn-iŋ\ (circa 1727)
*transitive verb*
: to make tight or tighter
*intransitive verb*
: to become tight or tighter
— **tight·en·er** \'tīt-nər, 'tī-tᵊn-ər\ *noun*
— **tighten one's belt** : to practice strict economy

**tight end** *noun* (1962)
: an offensive football end who lines up within two yards of the tackle

**tight·fist·ed** \'tīt-'fis-təd\ *adjective* (1844)
: reluctant to part with money
— **tight·fist·ed·ness** \-nəs\ *noun*

**tight-knit** \-'nit\ *adjective* (1946)
: closely integrated and bound in love or friendship ⟨a *tight-knit* family⟩

**tight-lipped** \-'lipt\ *adjective* (1876)
**1** : having the lips closed tight (as in determination)
**2** : reluctant to speak : TACITURN

**tight-mouthed** \-'maủthd, -'maủtht\ *adjective* (1926)
: CLOSEMOUTHED

**tight·rope** \'tīt-ˌrōp\ *noun* (1801)
**1** : a rope or wire stretched taut for acrobats to perform on
**2** : a dangerously precarious situation — usually used in the phrase *walk a tightrope*

**tights** \'tīts\ *noun plural* (circa 1837)
: a skintight garment covering the body from the neck down or from the waist down; *also*, *British* : PANTY HOSE

**tight·wad** \'tīt-ˌwäd\ *noun* (1906)
: a close or miserly person

**tight·wire** \-ˌwīr\ *noun* (1928)
: a tightrope made of wire

**ti·glon** \'tī-glən\ *noun* [*tiger* + *lion*] (1942)
: a hybrid between a male tiger and a female lion

**ti·gon** \'tī-gən\ *noun* [*tiger* + *lion*] (1926)
: TIGLON

**Ti·gre** \'ti-(ˌ)grā, 'tē-; tē-'\ *noun* (1878)
: a Semitic language of northern Ethiopia

**ti·gress** \'tī-grəs\ *noun* (1611)
: a female tiger; *also* : a tigerish woman

**Ti·gri·nya** \tə-'grē-nyə\ *noun* (1878)
: a Semitic language of northern Ethiopia

**tike** *variant of* TYKE

**ti·ki** \'tē-kē\ *noun* [Maori & Marquesan, from *Tiki*, first man or creator of first man] (1777)
: a wood or stone image of a Polynesian supernatural power

**til** \'til\ *noun* [Hindi, from Sanskrit *tila*] (1840)
: SESAME

**'til** *or* **til** \'til\ *variant of* ¹TILL 2, ²TILL

**ti·la·pia** \tə-'lä-pē-ə, -'lā-\ *noun* [New Latin, genus name] (1849)
: any of a genus (*Tilapia*) of African freshwater cichlid fishes often raised for food

**til·bury** \'til-ˌber-ē, -b(ə-)rē\ *noun, plural* **-buries** [*Tilbury*, 19th century English coach builder] (1814)
: a light 2-wheeled carriage

**til·de** \'til-də\ *noun* [Spanish, from Medieval Latin *titulus* tittle] (circa 1864)
**1** : a mark ~ placed especially over the letter *n* (as in Spanish *señor* sir) to denote the sound \nʸ\ or over vowels (as in Portuguese *irmã* sister) to indicate nasality
**2** : the mark ~ used to indicate negation in logic and the geometric relation "is similar to" in mathematics

**¹tile** \'tī(ə)l\ *noun, often attributive* [Middle English, from Old English *tigele*, from Latin *tegula* tile; akin to Latin *tegere* to cover — more at THATCH] (before 12th century)
**1** *plural* **tiles** *or* **tile a** : a flat or curved piece of fired clay, stone, or concrete used especially for roofs, floors, or walls and often for ornamental work **b** : a hollow or a semicircular and open earthenware or concrete piece used in constructing a drain **c** : a hollow building unit made of fired clay or of shale or gypsum
**2** : TILING
**3** : HAT; *especially* : a high silk hat
**4** : a thin piece of resilient material (as cork, linoleum, or rubber) used especially for covering floors or walls
**5** : a thin piece resembling a ceramic tile that usually bears a mark or letter and is used as a playing piece in a board game (as mah-jongg)
— **on the tiles** *British* : engaged in late-night carousing

**²tile** *transitive verb* **tiled; til·ing** (14th century)
**1** : to cover with tiles
**2** : to install drainage tile in
— **til·er** *noun*

**tile·fish** \'tī(ə)l-ˌfish\ *noun* [*tile-* modification of New Latin *Lopholatilus*] (1881)
: any of various marine bony fishes (family Malacanthidae) used as food; *especially* : a large fish (*Lopholatilus chamaeleonticeps*) of deep waters of the Atlantic and Gulf of Mexico with a fleshy appendage on the head and yellow spots on the upper body and some of its fins

**til·ing** \'tī-liŋ\ *noun* (15th century)
**1** : the action or work of one who tiles
**2 a** : TILES **b** : a surface of tiles

**¹till** \tᵊl, təl, 'til\ *preposition* [Middle English, from Old English *til;* akin to Old Norse *til* to, till, Old English *til* good] (before 12th century)
**1** *chiefly Scottish* : TO
**2** : UNTIL

**²till** *conjunction* (12th century)
: UNTIL

**³till** \'til\ *transitive verb* [Middle English *tilien, tillen*, from Old English *tilian;* akin to Old English *til* good, suitable, Old High German *zil* goal] (13th century)
: to work by plowing, sowing, and raising crops : CULTIVATE
— **till·able** \'ti-lə-bəl\ *adjective*

**⁴till** \'til\ *noun* [Anglo-French *tylle*] (15th century)
**1 a** : a box, drawer, or tray in a receptacle (as a cabinet or chest) used especially for valuables **b** : a money drawer in a store or bank; *also* : CASH REGISTER

**2 a :** the money contained in a till **b :** a supply of especially ready money

**⁵till** \'til\ *noun* [origin unknown] (1842)
: unstratified glacial drift consisting of clay, sand, gravel, and boulders intermingled

**till·age** \'ti-lij\ *noun* (15th century)
**1 :** the operation of tilling land
**2 :** cultivated land

**til·land·sia** \tə-'lan(d)-zē-ə\ *noun* [New Latin, from Elias *Tillands* (died 1693) Finnish botanist] (1759)
: any of a large genus (*Tillandsia*) of chiefly epiphytic plants of the pineapple family native to tropical and subtropical America

**¹til·ler** \'ti-lər\ *noun* [from (assumed) Middle English, from Old English *telgor, telgra* twig, shoot; akin to Old High German *zelga* twig, Old Irish *dlongaid* he splits] (before 12th century)
: STALK, SPROUT; *especially* : one from the base of a plant or from the axils of its lower leaves

**²til·ler** *intransitive verb* **til·lered; til·ler·ing** \'ti-lə-riŋ, 'til-riŋ\ (1677)
*of a plant* : to put forth tillers

**³till·er** \'ti-lər\ *noun* (13th century)
: one that tills : CULTIVATOR

**⁴til·ler** \'ti-lər\ *noun* [Middle English *tiler* stock of a crossbow, from Middle French *telier*, literally, beam of a loom, from Medieval Latin *telarium*, from Latin *tela* web — more at TOIL] (circa 1625)
: a lever used to turn the rudder of a boat from side to side; *broadly* : a device or system that plays a part in steering something

**til·ler·man** \'ti-lər-mən\ *noun* (circa 1934)
: one in charge of a tiller : STEERSMAN

**Til·sit** \'til-sət\ *also* **Til·sit·er** \-sə-tər\ *noun* [German *Tilsiter*, from *Tilsit* (now Sovetsk, Russia) (circa 1932)
: a semisoft porous light yellow cheese with a flavor that ranges from mild to sharp

**¹tilt** \'tilt\ *noun* [Middle English *teld, telte* tent, canopy, from Old English *teld*; akin to Old High German *zelt* tent] (15th century)
: a canopy for a wagon, boat, or stall

**²tilt** *transitive verb* (15th century)
: to cover or provide with a tilt

**³tilt** *noun* [⁴tilt] (1511)
**1 a :** a contest on horseback in which two combatants charging with lances or similar weapons try to unhorse each other : JOUST **b :** a tournament of tilts
**2 a :** DISPUTE, CONTENTION **b :** SPEED — used in the phrase *full tilt*
**3 a :** the act of tilting : the state or position of being tilted **b :** a sloping surface **c :** SLANT, BIAS ⟨a *tilt* toward military involvement⟩
**4 :** any of various contests resembling or suggesting tilting with lances
— **tilt** *adjective*

**⁴tilt** *verb* [Middle English *tulten, tilten* to cause to fall; akin to Swedish *tulta* to waddle] (1594)
*transitive verb*
**1 :** to cause to have an inclination
**2 a :** to point or thrust in or as if in a tilt ⟨*tilt* a lance⟩ **b :** to charge against ⟨*tilt* an adversary⟩
*intransitive verb*
**1 a :** to move or shift so as to lean or incline : SLANT **b :** to incline, tend, or become drawn toward an opinion, course of action, or one side of a controversy
**2 a :** to engage in a combat with lances : JOUST **b :** to make an impetuous attack ⟨*tilt* at social evils⟩
— **tilt·able** \'til-tə-bəl\ *adjective*
— **tilt·er** *noun*

**tilth** \'tilth\ *noun* [Middle English, from Old English, from *tilian* to till] (before 12th century)
**1 :** cultivated land : TILLAGE
**2 :** the state of aggregation of a soil especially in relation to its suitability for crop growth

**tilt·me·ter** \'tilt-,mē-tər\ *noun* (1932)
: an instrument to measure the tilting of the earth's surface

**tilt–ro·tor** \-,rō-tər\ *noun* (1980)
: an aircraft that has rotors at the end of each wing which can be oriented vertically for vertical takeoffs and landings, horizontally for forward flight, or to any position in between

**tilt·yard** \'tilt-,yärd\ *noun* (1528)
: a yard or place for tilting contests

**tim·bal** \'tim-bəl\ *noun* [French *timbale*, from Middle French, alteration of *tamballe*, modification of Old Spanish *atabal*, from Arabic *aṭ-ṭablative* the drum] (1680)
: KETTLEDRUM

**tim·bale** \'tim-bəl; tim-'bäl, tam-\ *noun* [French, literally, kettledrum] (1824)
**1 :** a creamy mixture (as of meat or vegetables) baked in a mold; *also* : the mold in which it is baked
**2 :** a small pastry shell filled with a cooked timbale mixture

**¹tim·ber** \'tim-bər\ *noun* [Middle English, from Old English, building, wood; akin to Old High German *zimbar* wood, room, Greek *demein* to build, *domos* course of stones or bricks] (before 12th century)
**1 a :** growing trees or their wood **b** — used interjectionally to warn of a falling tree
**2 :** wood suitable for building or for carpentry
**3 :** MATERIAL, STUFF; *especially* : personal qualification for a particular position or status
**4 a :** a large squared or dressed piece of wood ready for use or forming part of a structure **b** *British* : LUMBER 2a **c :** a curving frame branching outward from the keel of a ship and bending upward in a vertical direction that is usually composed of several pieces united : RIB
— **timber** *adjective*

**²timber** *transitive verb* **tim·bered; tim·ber·ing** \-b(ə-)riŋ\ (before 12th century)
: to frame, cover, or support with timbers

**tim·ber·doo·dle** \,tim-bər-'dü-dᵊl\ *noun* [¹*timber* + *doodle* cock] (1856)
: the American woodcock

**tim·bered** \'tim-bərd\ *adjective* (15th century)
**1 :** having walls framed by exposed timbers
**2 :** having a specified structure or constitution
**3 :** covered with growing timber : WOODED

**tim·ber·head** \'tim-bər-,hed\ *noun* (1794)
**1 :** the top end of a ship's timber used above the gunwale (as for belaying ropes)
**2 :** a bollard bolted to the deck where the end of a timber would come

**timber hitch** *noun* (circa 1815)
: a knot used to secure a line to a log or spar — see KNOT illustration

**tim·ber·ing** \'tim-b(ə-)riŋ\ *noun* (15th century)
: a set or arrangement of timbers

**tim·ber·land** \-bər-,land\ *noun* (1654)
: wooded land especially with marketable timber

**tim·ber·line** \-,līn\ *noun* (1867)
: the upper limit of arboreal growth in mountains or high latitudes — called also *tree line*

**tim·ber·man** \-mən\ *noun* (1889)
: LUMBERMAN

**timber rattlesnake** *noun* (1895)
: a widely distributed rattlesnake (*Crotalus horridus*) of the eastern U.S.

**timber wolf** *noun* (1860)
: GRAY WOLF

**tim·ber·work** \'tim-bər-,wərk\ *noun* (14th century)
: timber construction

**tim·bre** *also* **tim·ber** \'tam-bər, 'tim-; 'tam-(brᵊ)\ *noun* [French, from Middle French, bell struck by a hammer, from Old French, drum, from Middle Greek *tymbanon* kettledrum, from Greek *tympanon* — more at TYMPANUM] (1849)

: the quality given to a sound by its overtones: as **a :** the resonance by which the ear recognizes and identifies a voiced speech sound **b** : the quality of tone distinctive of a particular singing voice or musical instrument
— **tim·bral** \'tam-brəl, 'tim-\ *adjective*

**tim·brel** \'tim-brəl\ *noun* [diminutive of obsolete English *timbre* tambourine, from Middle English, from Old French, drum] (circa 1520)
: a small hand drum or tambourine
— **tim·brelled** \-brəld\ *adjective*

**¹time** \'tīm\ *noun* [Middle English, from Old English *tīma*; akin to Old Norse *tīmiles* time, Old English *tīd* — more at TIDE] (before 12th century)
**1 a :** the measured or measurable period during which an action, process, or condition exists or continues : DURATION **b :** a nonspatial continuum that is measured in terms of events which succeed one another from past through present to future **c :** LEISURE ⟨*time* for reading⟩
**2 :** the point or period when something occurs : OCCASION
**3 a :** an appointed, fixed, or customary moment or hour for something to happen, begin, or end ⟨arrived ahead of *time*⟩ **b :** an opportune or suitable moment ⟨decided it was *time* to retire⟩ — often used in the phrase *about time* ⟨about *time* for a change⟩
**4 a :** an historical period : AGE **b :** a division of geologic chronology **c :** conditions at present or at some specified period — usually used in plural ⟨*times* are hard⟩ ⟨move with the *times*⟩ **d :** the present time ⟨issues of the *time*⟩
**5 a :** LIFETIME **b :** a period of apprenticeship **c** : a term of military service **d :** a prison sentence
**6 :** SEASON ⟨very hot for this *time* of year⟩
**7 a :** rate of speed : TEMPO **b :** the grouping of the beats of music : RHYTHM
**8 a :** a moment, hour, day, or year as indicated by a clock or calendar ⟨what *time* is it⟩ **b :** any of various systems (as sidereal or solar) of reckoning time
**9 a :** one of a series of recurring instances or repeated actions ⟨you've been told many *times*⟩ **b** *plural* (1) : added or accumulated quantities or instances ⟨five *times* greater⟩ (2) : equal fractional parts of which an indicated number equal a comparatively greater quantity ⟨seven *times* smaller⟩ ⟨three *times* closer⟩ **c** : TURN ⟨three *times* at bat⟩
**10 :** finite as contrasted with infinite duration
**11 :** a person's experience during a specified period or on a particular occasion ⟨a good *time*⟩ ⟨a hard *time*⟩
**12 a :** the hours or days required to be occupied by one's work ⟨make up *time*⟩ ⟨on company *time*⟩ **b :** an hourly pay rate ⟨straight *time*⟩ **c :** wages paid at discharge or resignation ⟨pick up your *time* and get out⟩
**13 a :** the playing time of a game **b :** TIME-OUT
**14 :** a period during which something is used or available for use ⟨computer *time*⟩
— **at the same time :** NEVERTHELESS, YET ⟨slick and *at the same time* strangely unprofessional —Gerald Weaks⟩
— **at times :** at intervals : OCCASIONALLY
— **for the time being :** for the present
— **from time to time :** once in a while : OCCASIONALLY
— **in no time :** very quickly or soon
— **in time 1 :** sufficiently early **2 :** EVENTUALLY **3 :** in correct tempo ⟨learn to play *in time*⟩
— **on time 1 a :** at the appointed time **b** : on schedule **2 :** on the installment plan
— **time and again :** FREQUENTLY, REPEATEDLY

**²time** *verb* **timed; tim·ing** (14th century)
*transitive verb*
**1 a :** to arrange or set the time of **:** SCHEDULE **b
:** to regulate (a watch) to keep correct time
**2 :** to set the tempo, speed, or duration of
⟨*timed* his leap perfectly —Neil Amdur⟩
**3 :** to cause to keep time with something
**4 :** to determine or record the time, duration,
or rate of ⟨*time* a horse⟩
**5 :** to dispose (as a mechanical part) so that an
action occurs at a desired instant or in a desired way
*intransitive verb*
**:** to keep or beat time
**³time** *adjective* (circa 1711)
**1 a :** of or relating to time **b :** recording time
**2 :** timed to ignite or explode at a specific moment ⟨a *time* bomb⟩
**3 a :** payable on a specified future day or a
certain length of time after presentation for acceptance ⟨a *time* draft⟩ ⟨*time* deposits⟩ **b
:** based on installment payments ⟨a *time* sale⟩
**time and a half** *noun* (1888)
**:** payment for work (as overtime or holiday
work) at one and a half times the worker's
regular wage rate
**time bomb** *noun* (1893)
**1 :** a bomb so made as to explode at a predetermined time
**2 :** something with a potentially dangerous or
detrimental delayed reaction
**time capsule** *noun* (1938)
**1 :** a container holding historical records or
objects representative of current culture that is
deposited (as in a cornerstone) for preservation until discovery by some future age
**2 :** something resembling a time capsule
⟨sunken vessels are archaeological *time capsules* —Philip Trupp⟩
**time card** *noun* (circa 1891)
**:** a card used with a time clock to record an
employee's starting and quitting times each
day or on each job
**time chart** *noun* (circa 1830)
**1 :** a chart showing the standard times in various parts of the world with reference to a
specified time at a specified place
**2 :** TIME LINE 1
**time clock** *noun* (1887)
**:** a clock that stamps starting and quitting
times on an employee's time card
**time–con·sum·ing** \'tīm-kən-ˌsü-miŋ\ *adjective* (1890)
**1 :** using or taking up a great deal of time
⟨*time-consuming* chores⟩
**2 :** wasteful of time ⟨*time-consuming* tactics⟩
**timed** \'tīmd\ *adjective* (circa 1760)
**1 :** made to occur at or in a set time ⟨a *timed*
explosion⟩
**2 :** done or taking place at a time of a specified sort ⟨an ill-*timed* arrival⟩
**time dilation** *noun* (1934)
**:** a slowing of time in accordance with the theory of relativity that occurs in a system in motion relative to an outside observer and that
becomes apparent especially as the speed of
the system approaches that of light — called
also *time dilatation*
**timed–re·lease** \'tīmd-ri-ˈlēs\ *or* **time–release** \'tīm-\ *adjective* (1966)
**:** consisting of or containing a drug that is released in small amounts over time (as by dissolution of a coating) usually in the gastrointestinal tract ⟨*timed-release* capsules⟩
**time exposure** *noun* (1893)
**:** exposure of a photographic film for a definite time usually of more than one half second; *also* **:** a photograph taken by such exposure
**time frame** *noun* (1964)
**:** a period of time especially with respect to
some action or project
**time–hon·ored** \'tīm-ˌä-nərd\ *adjective*
(1593)

**:** honored because of age or long usage ⟨*time-
honored* traditions⟩
**time immemorial** *noun* (1602)
**1 :** time antedating a period legally fixed as
the basis for a custom or right
**2 :** time so long past as to be indefinite in history or tradition — called also *time out of
mind*
**time·keep·er** \'tīm-ˌkē-pər\ *noun* (1686)
**1 :** TIMEPIECE
**2 :** a clerk who keeps records of the time
worked by employees
**3 :** a person appointed to mark and announce
the time in an athletic game or contest
**— time·keep·ing** \-piŋ\ *noun*
**time killer** *noun* (1751)
**1 :** a person with free time
**2 :** something that passes the time **:** DIVERSION
**time lag** *noun* (1892)
**:** an interval of time between two related phenomena (as a cause and its effect)
**time-lapse** \'tīm-ˌlaps\ *adjective* (1927)
**:** of, relating to, or constituting a motion picture made so that when projected a slow action (as the opening of a flower bud) appears
to be speeded up
**time·less** \'tīm-ləs\ *adjective* (circa 1560)
**1** *archaic* **:** PREMATURE, UNTIMELY
**2 a :** having no beginning or end **:** ETERNAL **b
:** not restricted to a particular time or date ⟨the
*timeless* themes of love, solitude, joy, and nature —*Writer*⟩
**3 :** not affected by time **:** AGELESS
**— time·less·ly** *adverb*
**— time·less·ness** *noun*
**time line** *noun* (1951)
**1 :** a table listing important events for successive years within a particular historical period
**2** *usually* **time·line** \'tīm-ˌlīn\ **:** a schedule of
events and procedures **:** TIMETABLE 2
**time lock** *noun* (circa 1871)
**:** a lock controlled by clockwork to prevent its
being opened before a set time
**¹time·ly** \'tīm-lē\ *adverb* (before 12th century)
**1** *archaic* **:** EARLY, SOON
**2 :** in time **:** OPPORTUNELY ⟨the question was
not . . . *timely* raised in the state court —W.
O. Douglas⟩
**²timely** *adjective* **time·li·er; -est** (13th century)
**1 :** coming early or at the right time **:** OPPOR-
TUNE
**2 :** appropriate or adapted to the times or the
occasion ⟨a *timely* book⟩
**— time·li·ness** *noun*
**time machine** *noun* (1895)
**:** a hypothetical device that permits travel into
the past and future
**time-of–flight** \'tīm-ə(v)-ˈflīt\ *adjective*
(1945)
**:** of, relating to, being, or done with an instrument (as a mass spectrometer) that separates
particles (as ions) according to the time required for them to traverse a tube of a certain
length
**time·ous** \'tī-məs\ *adjective* (circa 1520)
*chiefly British* **:** TIMELY
**— time·ous·ly** *adverb*
**time-out** \'tīm-ˈaůt\ *noun* (1926)
**:** a brief suspension of activity **:** BREAK; *especially* **:** a suspension of play in an athletic
game
**time out of mind** (15th century)
**:** TIME IMMEMORIAL 2
**time·piece** \'tīm-ˌpēs\ *noun* (1765)
**:** a device (as a clock or watch) to measure or
show progress of time; *especially* **:** one that
does not chime
**time·pleas·er** \-ˌplē-zər\ *noun* (1601)
*obsolete* **:** TIMESERVER
**tim·er** \'tī-mər\ *noun* (1841)
**:** one that times: as **a :** TIMEPIECE; *especially*
**:** a stopwatch for timing races **b :** TIMEKEEPER
**c :** a device (as a clock) that indicates by a
sound the end of an interval of time or that
starts or stops a device at predetermined times

**time reversal** *noun* (1955)
**:** a formal operation in mathematical physics
that reverses the order in which a sequence of
events occurs
**times** \'tīmz\ *preposition* (14th century)
**:** multiplied by ⟨two *times* two is four⟩
**time·sav·ing** \'tīm-ˌsā-viŋ\ *adjective* (1865)
**:** intended or serving to expedite something
⟨*timesaving* kitchen appliances⟩
**— time–sav·er** \-ˌsā-vər\ *noun*
**time·scale** \-ˌskā(ə)l\ *noun* (1890)
**:** an arrangement of events used as a measure
of the relative or absolute duration or antiquity
of a period of history or geologic or cosmic
time
**time series** *noun* (1919)
**:** a set of data collected sequentially usually at
fixed intervals of time
**time·serv·er** \-ˌsər-vər\ *noun* (1584)
**:** a person whose behavior is adjusted to the
pattern of the times or to please superiors
**:** TEMPORIZER
**¹time·serv·ing** \-viŋ\ *noun* (1621)
**:** the behavior or practice of a timeserver
**²timeserving** *adjective* (1630)
**:** marked by or revealing a lack of independence or integrity ⟨a mean, *timeserving* little
man, grovelling odiously before the wealthy
people —Peter Forster⟩
**time–shar·ing** \'tīm-ˌsher-iŋ, -ˌshar-\ *noun*
(1953)
**1 :** simultaneous use of a central computer by
many users at remote locations
**2** *or* **time–share** \-ˌsher, -ˌshar\ **:** joint ownership or rental of a vacation lodging (as a
condominium) by several persons with each
occupying the premises in turn for short periods
**— time–share** *transitive verb*
**time sheet** *noun* (circa 1909)
**1 :** a sheet for recording the time of arrival
and departure of workers and for recording the
amount of time spent on each job
**2 :** a sheet for summarizing hours worked by
each worker during a pay period
**time signature** *noun* (1875)
**:** a sign used in music to indicate meter and
usually written as a fraction with the bottom
number indicating the kind of note used as a
unit of time and the top number indicating the
number of units in each measure
**times sign** *noun* (1948)
**:** the symbol × used to indicate multiplication
**time stamp** *noun* (1892)
**:** a device for recording the date and time of
day that letters or papers are received or sent
out
**— time–stamp** *transitive verb*
**time·ta·ble** \'tīm-ˌtā-bəl\ *noun* (1838)
**1 :** a table of departure and arrival times of
trains, buses, or airplanes
**2 a :** a schedule showing a planned order or
sequence **b :** PROGRAM 3
**— time–table** *transitive verb*
**time–test·ed** \-ˌtes-təd\ *adjective* (1930)
**:** having effectiveness that has been proved
over a long period of time ⟨*time-tested* meth-
ods⟩
**time trial** *noun* (circa 1949)
**:** a competitive event (as in auto racing) in
which individuals are successively timed over
a set course or distance
**time warp** *noun* (1954)
**:** an anomaly, discontinuity, or suspension held
to occur in the progress of time
**time·work** \'tīm-ˌwərk\ *noun* (1829)
**:** work paid for at a standard rate for the hour
or the day
**— time·work·er** \-ˌwər-kər\ *noun*
**time·worn** \-ˌwōrn, -ˌwȯrn\ *adjective* (1729)
**1 :** worn or impaired by time ⟨*timeworn* man-
sions⟩
**2 a :** AGE-OLD, ANCIENT ⟨*timeworn* procedures⟩
**b :** HACKNEYED, STALE ⟨a *timeworn* joke⟩

**time zone** *noun* (1892)
: a geographical region within which the same standard time is used

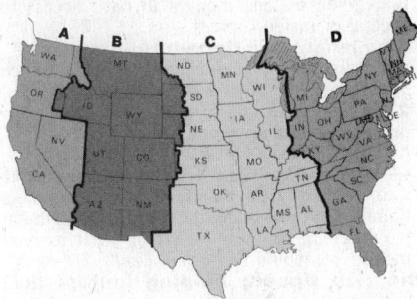

**time zones in the conterminous United States:**
*A* Pacific time, *B* mountain time, *C* central time, *D* eastern time

**tim·id** \'ti-məd\ *adjective* [Latin *timidus*, from *timēre* to fear] (1549)
**1 :** lacking in courage or self-confidence ⟨a *timid* person⟩
**2 :** lacking in boldness or determination ⟨a *timid* policy⟩
— **ti·mid·i·ty** \tə-'mi-də-tē\ *noun*
— **tim·id·ly** \'ti-məd-lē\ *adverb*
— **tim·id·ness** *noun*

**tim·ing** \'tī-miŋ\ *noun* (1597)
**1 :** selection or the ability to select for maximum effect of the precise moment for beginning or doing something ⟨haven't got my *timing* down⟩
**2 :** observation and recording (as by a stopwatch) of the elapsed time of an act, action, or process

**ti·moc·ra·cy** \tī-'mä-krə-sē\ *noun* [Middle French *tymocracie*, from Medieval Latin *timocratia*, from Greek *timokratia*, from *timē* price, value, honor + *-kratia* -cracy; akin to Greek *tiein* to honor, Sanskrit *cāyati* he respects] (1586)
**1 :** government in which a certain amount of property is necessary for office
**2 :** government in which love of honor is the ruling principle
— **ti·mo·crat·ic** \,tī-mə-'kra-tik\ *or* **ti·mo·crat·i·cal** \-ti-kəl\ *adjective*

**ti·mo·lol** \'tī-mə-,lōl, -,lȯl\ *noun* [*tim-* (of unknown origin) + *-olol* (as in *propranolol*)] (1973)
: a beta-blocker $C_{13}H_{24}N_4O_3S$ used in the form of its maleate salt to treat glaucoma and to reduce the risk of second heart attacks

**tim·o·rous** \'ti-mə-rəs, 'tim-rəs\ *adjective* [Middle English, from Middle French *timoureus*, from Medieval Latin *timorosus*, from Latin *timor* fear, from *timēre* to fear] (15th century)
**1 :** of a timid disposition **:** FEARFUL
**2 :** expressing or suggesting timidity ⟨proceed with doubtful and *timorous* steps —Edward Gibbon⟩
— **tim·o·rous·ly** *adverb*
— **tim·o·rous·ness** *noun*

**tim·o·thy** \'ti-mə-thē\ *noun* [probably after *Timothy* Hanson, 18th century American farmer said to have introduced it from New England to the southern states] (1747)
: a European grass (*Phleum pratense*) that has long cylindrical spikes and is widely grown for hay

**Tim·o·thy** \'ti-mə-thē\ *noun* [Latin *Timotheus*, from Greek *Timotheos*]
**1 :** a disciple of the apostle Paul
**2 :** either of two letters written with regard to pastoral care in the early Church and included as books in the New Testament — see BIBLE table

**tim·pa·ni** \'tim-pə-nē\ *noun plural but singular or plural in construction* [Italian, plural of *timpano* kettledrum, from Latin *tympanum* drum — more at TYMPANUM] (circa 1854)

: a set of two or more kettledrums played by one performer in an orchestra or band

**tim·pa·nist** \-nist\ *noun* (1906)
: one who plays the timpani

**¹tin** \'tin\ *noun* [Middle English, from Old English; akin to Old High German *zin* tin] (before 12th century)
**1 :** a soft faintly bluish white lustrous low-melting crystalline metallic element that is malleable and ductile at ordinary temperatures and that is used as a protective coating, in tinfoil, and in soft solders and alloys — see ELEMENT table
**2 a :** a box, can, pan, vessel, or a sheet made of tinplate; *broadly* **:** such a container of any metal (as aluminum) **b :** a metal container and its contents ⟨a *tin* of tomatoes⟩
— **tin** *adjective*
— **tin·ful** \-,fùl\ *noun*

**²tin** *transitive verb* **tinned; tin·ning** (14th century)
**1 :** to cover or plate with tin or a tin alloy
**2 :** to put up or pack in tins **:** CAN

**tin·a·mou** \'ti-nə-,mü\ *noun* [French, from Carib *tinamu*] (circa 1783)
: any of a family (Tinamidae) of South and Central American game birds that have a deeply keeled sternum and a rudimentary tail and that produce eggs with a surface resembling enamel

**tin can** *noun* (1770)
**1 :** a can made of tinplate; *broadly* **:** CAN 1c
**2** *slang* **:** DESTROYER 2

**¹tinct** \'tiŋ(k)t\ *adjective* [Latin *tinctus*, past participle] (1579)
**:** COLORED, TINGED

**²tinct** *noun* (1602)
**:** TINCTURE, TINGE

**tinc·to·ri·al** \tiŋ(k)-'tōr-ē-əl, -'tȯr-\ *adjective* [Latin *tinctorius*, from *tingere* to tinge] (1655)
**:** of or relating to colors or to dyeing or staining; *also* **:** imparting color
— **tinc·to·ri·al·ly** \-ē-ə-lē\ *adverb*

**¹tinc·ture** \'tiŋ(k)-chər\ *noun* [Middle English, from Latin *tinctura* act of dyeing, from *tinctus*, past participle of *tingere* to tinge] (14th century)
**1 a** *archaic* **:** a substance that colors, dyes, or stains **b :** COLOR, TINT
**2 a :** a characteristic quality **:** CAST **b :** a slight admixture **:** TRACE
**3** *obsolete* **:** an active principle or extract
**4 :** a heraldic metal, color, or fur
**5 :** a solution of a medicinal substance in an alcoholic menstruum

**²tincture** *transitive verb* **tinc·tured; tinc·tur·ing** \'tiŋ(k)-chə-riŋ, -shriŋ\ (1616)
**1 :** to tint or stain with a color **:** TINGE
**2 a :** to infuse or instill with a property or entity **:** IMPREGNATE **b :** to imbue with a quality **:** AFFECT ⟨writing *tinctured* with wit and wisdom⟩

**tin·der** \'tin-dər\ *noun* [Middle English, from Old English *tynder*; akin to Old High German *zuntra* tinder, Old English *tendan* to kindle] (before 12th century)
**1 :** a very flammable substance adaptable for use as kindling
**2 :** something that serves to incite or inflame

**tin·der·box** \'tin-dər-,bäks\ *noun* (1530)
**1 a :** a metal box for holding tinder and usually a flint and steel for striking a spark **b :** a highly inflammable object or place
**2 :** a potentially explosive place or situation

**¹tine** \'tīn\ *noun* [Middle English *tind*, from Old English; akin to Old High German *zint* point, tine] (before 12th century)
**1 :** a slender pointed projecting part **:** PRONG
**2 :** a pointed branch of an antler
— **tined** \'tīnd\ *adjective*

**²tine** *verb* **tined** \'tīnd\ *or* **tint** \'tint\; **tin·ing** \'tī-niŋ\ [Middle English, of Scandinavian origin; akin to Old Norse *tȳna* to lose, destroy, *tjōn* injury, loss — more at TEEN] (13th century)

*transitive verb*
*dialect British* **:** LOSE
*intransitive verb*
*dialect British* **:** to become lost

**tin·ea** \'ti-nē-ə\ *noun* [Middle English, from Medieval Latin, from Latin, worm, moth] (14th century)
**:** any of several fungal diseases of the skin; *especially* **:** RINGWORM
— **tin·e·al** \-nē-əl\ *adjective*

**tinea cru·ris** \-'krùr-əs\ *noun* [New Latin, literally, tinea of the leg] (circa 1923)
**:** a fungal infection involving especially the groin and perineum

**tin ear** *noun* (1935)
**:** a deafened or insensitive ear

**tin·foil** \'tin-,fȯil\ *noun* (15th century)
**:** a paper-thin metal sheeting usually of aluminum or tin-lead alloy

**ting** *noun* [*ting*, verb, from Middle English *tingen*, of imitative origin] (1602)
**:** a high-pitched sound like that made by a light stroke on a crystal goblet
— **ting** *intransitive verb*

**¹tinge** \'tinj\ *transitive verb* **tinged; tinge·ing** *or* **ting·ing** \'tin-jiŋ\ [Middle English, from Latin *tingere* to dip, moisten, tinge; akin to Greek *tengein* to moisten and probably to Old High German *dunkōn* to dip] (15th century)
**1 a :** to color with a slight shade or stain **:** TINT
**b :** to affect or modify with a slight odor or taste
**2 :** to affect or modify in character

**²tinge** *noun* (1752)
**1 :** a slight staining or suffusing shade or color
**2 :** an affective or modifying property or influence **:** TOUCH

**tin·gle** \'tiŋ-gəl\ *intransitive verb* **tin·gled; tin·gling** \-g(ə-)liŋ\ [Middle English, alteration of *tinklen* to tinkle, tingle] (14th century)
**1 a :** to feel a ringing, stinging, prickling, or thrilling sensation **b :** to cause such a sensation
**2 :** TINKLE
— **tingle** *noun*
— **tin·gling·ly** \-g(ə-)liŋ-lē\ *adverb*
— **tin·gly** \-g(ə-)lē\ *adjective*

**tin hat** *noun* (1903)
**:** a metal helmet

**tin·horn** \'tin-,hȯrn\ *noun* (1885)
**:** one (as a gambler) who pretends to have money, ability, or influence

**¹tin·ker** \'tiŋ-kər\ *noun* [Middle English *tinkere*] (14th century)
**1 a :** a usually itinerant mender of household utensils **b :** an unskillful mender **:** BUNGLER
**2** *chiefly Irish* **:** GYPSY

**²tinker** *verb* **tin·kered; tin·ker·ing** \-k(ə-)riŋ\ (1592)
*intransitive verb*
**:** to work in the manner of a tinker; *especially* **:** to repair, adjust, or work with something in an unskilled or experimental manner **:** FIDDLE
*transitive verb*
**:** to repair, adjust, or experiment with
— **tin·ker·er** \-kər-ər\ *noun*

**tinker's damn** *also* **tinker's dam** \-'dam\ *noun* [probably from the tinkers' reputation for blasphemy] (1839)
**:** a minimum amount or degree (as of care) ⟨didn't give a *tinker's damn* about poetry —James Blish⟩

**Tin·ker·toy** \'tiŋ-kər-,tȯi\ *trademark*
— used for a construction toy of fitting parts

**¹tin·kle** \'tiŋ-kəl\ *verb* **tin·kled; tin·kling** \-k(ə-)liŋ\ [Middle English, frequentative of *tinken* to tinkle, of imitative origin] (15th century)
*intransitive verb*

**1 :** to make or emit a tinkle or a sound suggestive of a tinkle
**2 :** URINATE
*transitive verb*
**1 :** to sound or make known (the time) by a tinkle
**2 a :** to cause to make a tinkle **b :** to produce by tinkling ⟨*tinkle* a tune⟩
²**tinkle** *noun* (1725)
**1 :** a jingling effect in verse or prose
**2 :** a series of short high ringing or clinking sounds
**tin·kly** \'tiŋ-k(ə-)lē\ *adjective* (1892)
**:** that tinkles **:** TINKLING
**tin liz·zie** \-'li-zē\ *noun* [from *Tin Lizzie*, nickname for the Model T Ford automobile] (1915)
**:** a small inexpensive early automobile
**tin·ner** \'ti-nər\ *noun* (1512)
**1 :** a tin miner
**2 :** TINSMITH
**tin·ni·tus** \'ti-nə-təs, tə-'nī-təs\ *noun* [Latin, ringing, tinnitus, from *tinnire* to ring, of imitative origin] (1843)
**:** a sensation of noise (as a ringing or roaring) that is caused by a bodily condition (as a disturbance of the auditory nerve or wax in the ear) and can usually be heard only by the one affected
**tin·ny** \'ti-nē\ *adjective* **tin·ni·er; -est** (1552)
**1 :** of, abounding in, or yielding tin
**2 a :** resembling tin **b :** LIGHT, CHEAP
**3 :** thin in tone ⟨a *tinny* voice⟩
— **tin·ni·ly** \'ti-nᵊl-ē\ *adverb*
— **tin·ni·ness** \'ti-nē-nəs\ *noun*
**Tin Pan Alley** *noun* (1908)
**:** a district that is a center for composers and publishers of popular music; *also* **:** the body of such composers and publishers
**tin·plate** \'tin-'plāt\ *noun* (1677)
**:** thin sheet iron or steel coated with tin
**tin–plate** *transitive verb* (1890)
**:** to plate or coat (as a metal sheet) with tin
**tin–pot** \'tin-'pät\ *adjective* (1838)
**:** SMALL-TIME
¹**tin·sel** \'tin(t)-səl *also* 'tin-zəl\ *noun* [Middle French *estincelle, estancele, etincelle* spark, glitter, spangle — more at STENCIL] (1538)
**1 :** a thread, strip, or sheet of metal, paper, or plastic used to produce a glittering and sparkling appearance in fabrics, yarns, or decorations
**2 :** something superficially attractive or glamorous but of little real worth ⟨disfigured by no gaudy *tinsel* of rhetoric or declamation —Thomas Jefferson⟩
²**tinsel** *adjective* (1575)
**1 :** made of or covered with tinsel
**2 a :** cheaply gaudy **:** TAWDRY **b :** SPECIOUS ⟨*tinsel* promises⟩
³**tinsel** *transitive verb* **tin·seled** *or* **tin·selled; tin·sel·ing** *or* **tin·sel·ling** \'tin(t)-s(ə-)liŋ *also* 'tin-zə-liŋ\ (1594)
**1 :** to interweave, overlay, or adorn with or as if with tinsel
**2 :** to impart a specious brightness to
**tin·sel·ly** \'tin(t)-s(ə-)lē *also* 'tin-zə-lē\ *adjective* (1811)
**:** TINSEL
**tin·smith** \'tin-,smith\ *noun* (1812)
**:** a worker who makes or repairs things of sheet metal (as tinplate)
— **tin·smith·ing** \-,smi-thiŋ\ *noun*
**tin·stone** \'tin-,stōn\ *noun* (1602)
**:** CASSITERITE
¹**tint** \'tint\ *noun* [alteration of earlier *tinct*, from Latin *tinctus* act of dyeing, from *tingere* to tinge] (1717)
**1 a :** a usually slight or pale coloration **:** HUE **b :** any of various lighter or darker shades of a color **:** TINGE
**2 :** a variation of a color produced by adding white to it and characterized by a low saturation with relatively high lightness
**3 :** a usually slight modifying quality or characteristic **:** TOUCH

**4 :** a shaded effect in engraving produced by fine parallel lines close together
**5 :** a panel of light color serving as background
**6 :** dye for the hair
— **tint·er** *noun*
²**tint** *transitive verb* (1791)
**:** to impart or apply a tint to **:** COLOR
**tint·ing** *noun* (circa 1841)
**1 :** the act or process of one that tints
**2 :** the engraved or colored tint produced by tinting
**tin·tin·nab·u·lary** \,tin-tə-'na-byə-,ler-ē\ *adjective* [Latin *tintinnabulum* bell] (1787)
**:** of, relating to, or characterized by bells or their sounds
**tin·tin·nab·u·la·tion** \,tin-tə-,na-byə-'lā-shən\ *noun* [Latin *tintinnabulum* bell, from *tintinnare* to ring, jingle, from *tinnire*] (1831)
**1 :** the ringing or sounding of bells
**2 :** a jingling or tinkling sound as if of bells
**tint·less** \'tint-ləs\ *adjective* (1789)
*archaic* **:** having no tints **:** lacking color
**tin·type** \-,tīp\ *noun* (1864)
**:** FERROTYPE 1
**tin·ware** \'tin-,war, -,wer\ *noun* (1758)
**:** articles and especially utensils made of tinplate
**tin·work** \-,wərk\ *noun* (circa 1934)
**:** work in tin
**ti·ny** \'tī-nē\ *adjective* **ti·ni·er; -est** [alteration of Middle English *tine*] (1598)
**:** very small or diminutive **:** MINUTE
*synonym* see SMALL
— **ti·ni·ly** \'tī-nᵊl-ē\ *adverb*
— **ti·ni·ness** \'tī-nē-nəs\ *noun*
¹**tip** \'tip\ *verb* **tipped; tip·ping** [Middle English] (14th century)
*transitive verb*
**1 :** OVERTURN, UPSET — usually used with *over*
**2 a :** CANT, TILT **b :** to raise and tilt forward in salute ⟨*tipped* his hat⟩
*intransitive verb*
**1 :** to become tipped **:** TOPPLE
**2 :** LEAN, SLANT
— **tip the scales 1 :** to register weight ⟨*tips the scales* at 285 pounds⟩ **2 :** to shift the balance of power or influence ⟨*tipped the scales* in favor of a declaration of war —S. F. Bemis⟩
²**tip** *noun* (1673)
**1 :** the act or an instance of tipping **:** TILT
**2** *chiefly British* **:** a place for depositing something (as rubbish) by dumping
³**tip** *transitive verb* **tipped; tip·ping** [Middle English *tipped* having a tip, from ⁴*tip*] (14th century)
**1 a :** to furnish with a tip **b** (1) **:** to cover or adorn the tip of (2) **:** to blend (furs) for improved appearance by brushing the tips of the hair with dye
**2 :** to affix (an insert) in a book — often used with *in*
**3 :** to remove the ends of ⟨*tip* raspberries⟩
⁴**tip** *noun* [Middle English; akin to Middle High German *zipf* tip, Old English *tæppa* tap — more at TAP] (15th century)
**1 :** the usually pointed end of something
**2 :** a small piece or part serving as an end, cap, or point
— **tipped** \'tipt\ *adjective*
— **on the tip of one's tongue 1 :** about to be uttered ⟨it was *on the tip of my tongue* to tell him exactly what I thought⟩ **2 :** just eluding recall
⁵**tip** *noun* [Middle English *tippe*; akin to Low German *tippen* to tap] (15th century)
**:** a light touch or blow
⁶**tip** *verb* **tipped; tip·ping** (1567)
*transitive verb*
**1 :** to strike lightly **:** TAP
**2 :** to give (a baseball) a glancing blow
*intransitive verb*
**:** TIPTOE
⁷**tip** *noun* [origin unknown] (1567)

**1 :** a piece of advice or expert or authoritative information
**2 :** a piece of advance or confidential information given by one thought to have access to special or inside sources
⁸**tip** *transitive verb* **tipped; tip·ping** (1883)
**1 :** to impart a piece of information or advice about or to — often used with *off*
**2** *chiefly British* **:** to mention as a likely candidate, prospective winner, or profitable investment **:** TOUT 4
— **tip one's hand** *also* **tip one's mitt** **:** to declare one's intentions or reveal one's opinions or resources ⟨the Justice Department wouldn't *tip its hand* by saying what its next move . . . would be —*Newsweek*⟩
⁹**tip** *verb* **tipped; tip·ping** [perhaps from ⁶*tip*] (circa 1610)
*transitive verb*
**1 :** GIVE, PRESENT
**2 :** to give a gratuity to
*intransitive verb*
**:** to bestow a gratuity
¹⁰**tip** *noun* (1755)
**:** a gift or a sum of money tendered for a service performed or anticipated **:** GRATUITY
**tip-cart** \'tip-,kärt\ *noun* (circa 1877)
**:** a cart whose body can be tipped on the frame to empty its contents
**tip·cat** \-,kat\ *noun* [⁶*tip*] (1676)
**:** a game in which one player using a bat strikes lightly a tapered wooden peg and as it flies up strikes it again to drive it as far as possible while fielders try to recover it; *also* **:** the peg used in this game
**ti·pi** \'tē-(,)pē\ *variant of* TEPEE
**tip–in** \'tip-,in\ *noun* [⁶*tip*] (1948)
**:** a goal in basketball made by deflecting a rebound into the basket with the fingertips
¹**tip–off** \'tip-,óf\ *noun* [⁸*tip*] (1901)
**1 :** WARNING, TIP
**2 :** a telltale sign
²**tip–off** *noun* [⁶*tip*] (1922)
**:** the act or an instance of putting the ball in play in basketball by a jump ball
**tip of the iceberg** [from an iceberg being mostly submerged] (1969)
**:** the earliest, most obvious, or most superficial manifestation of some phenomenon
**tip·per** \'ti-pər\ *noun* (1819)
**:** one that tips
**tip·pet** \'ti-pət\ *noun* [Middle English *tipet*] (14th century)
**1 :** a long hanging end of cloth attached to a sleeve, cap, or hood
**2 :** a shoulder cape of fur or cloth often with hanging ends
**3 :** a long black scarf worn over the robe by Anglican clergymen during morning and evening prayer
¹**tip·ple** \'ti-pəl\ *verb* **tip·pled; tip·pling** \-p(ə-)liŋ\ [back-formation from obsolete *tippler* barkeeper] (1560)
*intransitive verb*
**:** to drink liquor especially by habit or to excess
*transitive verb*
**:** to drink (liquor) especially continuously in small amounts
— **tip·pler** \-p(ə-)lər\ *noun*
²**tipple** *noun* (1581)
**:** DRINK 1, 2
³**tipple** *noun* [English dialect *tipple* to tip over, frequentative of English ¹*tip*] (1880)
**1 :** a place where or an apparatus by which cars (as for coal) are loaded or emptied
**2 :** a coal-screening plant
**tip·py** \'ti-pē\ *adjective* **tip·pi·er; -est** (1886)
**:** liable to tip ⟨a *tippy* boat⟩
**tip·staff** \'tip-,staf\ *noun, plural* **tip·staves** \-,stavz, -,stāvz\ [obsolete *tipstaff* staff tipped with metal] (1535)
**:** an officer (as a constable or bailiff) who bears a staff
**tip·ster** \'tip-stər\ *noun* (1862)

: one who gives or sells tips especially for gambling or speculation

**tip·sy** \'tip-sē\ *adjective* **tip·si·er; -est** [¹*tip* + *-sy* (as in *tricksy*)] (1577)
**1** : unsteady, staggering, or foolish from the effects of liquor : FUDDLED
**2** : UNSTEADY, ASKEW ⟨a *tipsy* angle⟩
— **tip·si·ly** \-sə-lē\ *adverb*
— **tip·si·ness** \-sē-nəs\ *noun*

¹**tip·toe** \'tip-₁tō, -₁tō\ *noun* (14th century)
: the position of being balanced on the balls of the feet and toes with the heels raised — usually used with *on*; *also* : the ends of the toes
— **on tiptoe** : ALERT, AROUSED ⟨the contest of skill that puts one *on tiptoe* to win —*Deerfield (Wisconsin) Independent*⟩

²**tiptoe** *adverb* (1592)
: on or as if on tiptoe

³**tiptoe** *adjective* (1593)
**1** : standing or walking on or as if on tiptoe
**2** : CAUTIOUS, STEALTHY

⁴**tiptoe** *intransitive verb* **tip·toed; tip·toe·ing** (circa 1661)
**1** : to stand or raise oneself on tiptoe
**2** : to walk or proceed quietly or cautiously on or as if on tiptoe

¹**tip-top** \'tip-₁täp, -₁täp\ *noun* [⁴*tip* + *top*] (1702)
: the highest point

²**tip-top** *adjective* (1722)
: EXCELLENT, FIRST-RATE ⟨*tip-top* working conditions⟩

³**tip-top** *adverb* (1882)
: very well

**ti·rade** \'tī-₁rād *also* ti-'\ *noun* [French, shot, tirade, from Middle French, from Old Italian *tirata,* from *tirare* to draw, shoot] (1802)
: a protracted speech usually marked by intemperate, vituperative, or harshly censorious language

**tir·a·mi·su** \₁tir-ə-'mē-(₁)sü, -'mi-; -mē-'sü\ *noun* [Italian *tiramisù,* from *tirami su!,* literally, pull me up!] (1982)
: a dessert made with ladyfingers, mascarpone, chocolate, and espresso

¹**tire** \'tīr\ *verb* **tired; tir·ing** [Middle English *tyren,* from Old English *tēorian, tȳrian* (before 12th century)
*intransitive verb*
: to become weary
*transitive verb*
**1** : to exhaust or greatly decrease the physical strength of : FATIGUE
**2** : to wear out the patience of : BORE ☆

²**tire** *noun* [Middle English, short for *attire*] (14th century)
**1** *obsolete* : ATTIRE
**2** *archaic* : a woman's headband or hair ornament

³**tire** *transitive verb* **tired; tir·ing** (14th century)
**1** *obsolete* : ATTIRE
**2** *archaic* : to adorn (the hair) with an ornament

⁴**tire** *noun, often attributive* [Middle English, probably from ²*tire*] (15th century)
**1** : a metal hoop forming the tread of a wheel
**2** : a rubber cushion that fits around a wheel (as of an automobile) and usually contains compressed air

**tired** \'tīrd\ *adjective* (15th century)
**1** : drained of strength and energy : fatigued often to the point of exhaustion
**2** : obviously worn by hard use : RUN-DOWN
**3** : TRITE, HACKNEYED
— **tired·ly** *adverb*
— **tired·ness** *noun*

**tire·less** \'tīr-ləs\ *adjective* (1591)
: seemingly incapable of tiring : INDEFATIGABLE
— **tire·less·ly** *adverb*
— **tire·less·ness** *noun*

**Ti·re·si·as** \tī-'rē-sē-əs, -zē-\ *noun* [Latin, from Greek *Teiresias*]

: a blind seer of Thebes who in one Greek myth is changed into a woman for several years and then changed back to a man

**tire·some** \'tīr-səm\ *adjective* (circa 1520)
: WEARISOME, TEDIOUS
— **tire·some·ly** *adverb*
— **tire·some·ness** *noun*

**tir·ing–house** \'tī-riŋ-₁haüs\ *noun* [³*tire*] (1590)
: a section of a theater reserved for the actors and used especially for dressing for stage entrances

**tir·ing–room** \-₁rüm, -₁rüm\ *noun* [³*tire*] (1623)
: a dressing room especially in a theater

**tirl** \'tərl\ *verb* [alteration of ¹*trill*] (circa 1550)
*intransitive verb*
*chiefly Scottish* : to make a rattling sound (as with a door latch)
*transitive verb*
*chiefly Scottish* : TWIRL

**tiro** *chiefly British variant of* TYRO

**'tis** \'tiz, (₁)tiz, təz\ [contraction] (15th century)
: it is

**ti·sane** \ti-'zan, -'zän\ *noun* [Middle English, from Middle French, from Latin *ptisana,* from Greek *ptisanē,* literally, crushed barley, from *ptissein* to crush — more at PESTLE] (14th century)
: an infusion (as of dried herbs) used as a beverage or for medicinal effects

**Tish·ah–b'Ab** \'ti-shə-₁bäv, -₁bȯv\ *noun* [Hebrew *tish'āh bĕ Ābh* ninth in Ab] (circa 1902)
: a Jewish holiday observed with fasting on the 9th of Ab in commemoration of the destruction of the temples at Jerusalem

**Tish·ri** \'tish-rē\ *noun* [Hebrew *tishrī*] (circa 1771)
: the 1st month of the civil year or the 7th month of the ecclesiastical year in the Jewish calendar — see MONTH table

**tis·sue** \'ti-(₁)shü, *chiefly British* 'tis-(₁)yü\ *noun* [Middle English *tissu,* a rich fabric, from Old French, from past participle of *tistre* to weave, from Latin *texere* — more at TECHNICAL] (1563)
**1 a** : a fine lightweight often sheer fabric **b** : MESH, NETWORK, WEB ⟨a *tissue* of lies⟩
**2** : a piece of soft absorbent tissue paper used especially as a handkerchief or for removing cosmetics
**3** : an aggregate of cells usually of a particular kind together with their intercellular substance that form one of the structural materials of a plant or an animal
— **tis·su·ey** \'ti-shə-wē\ *adjective*

**tissue culture** *noun* (1912)
: the process or technique of making body tissue grow in a culture medium outside the organism; *also* : a culture of tissue (as epithelium)

**tissue fluid** *noun* (1900)
: a fluid that permeates the spaces between individual cells, that is in osmotic contact with the blood and lymph, and that serves in interstitial transport of nutrients and waste

**tissue paper** *noun* (1777)
: a thin gauzy paper used especially for protecting something (as by covering or wrapping)

**tissue plasminogen activator** *noun* (1981)
: a clot-dissolving enzyme with an affinity for fibrin that is produced naturally in blood vessel linings and is used in a genetically engineered form to prevent damage to heart muscle following a heart attack — abbreviation *TPA*

**tis·su·lar** \'ti-shə-lər\ *adjective* [*tissue* + *-lar* (as in *cellular*)] (circa 1935)
: of, relating to, or affecting organismic tissue ⟨*tissular* grafts⟩ ⟨*tissular* lesions⟩

¹**tit** \'tit\ *noun* [Middle English, from Old English — more at TEAT] (before 12th century)
**1** : TEAT

**2** : BREAST — usually used in plural; usually considered vulgar

²**tit** *noun* (circa 1706)
: TITMOUSE; *broadly* : any of various small plump often long-tailed birds

**ti·tan** \'tī-tⁿn\ *noun* [Greek] (circa 1741)
**1** *capitalized* : any of a family of giants born of Uranus and Gaea and ruling the earth until overthrown by the Olympian gods
**2** : one that is gigantic in size or power : one that stands out for greatness of achievement

**titan-** *or* **titani-** *combining form* [New Latin *titanium*]
: titanium ⟨*titanate*⟩

**ti·ta·nate** \'tī-tⁿn-₁āt\ *noun* (1839)
**1** : any of various multiple oxides of titanium dioxide with other metallic oxides
**2** : a titanium ester of the general formula Ti(OR)₄

**ti·tan·ess** \'tī-tⁿn-əs\ *noun, often capitalized* (1596)
: a female titan

**ti·ta·nia** \tī-'tā-nē-ə, tə-, -'tän-yə *also* -'ta-nē-ə *or* -'tan-yə\ *noun* [New Latin] (1922)
: TITANIUM DIOXIDE

**Ti·ta·nia** \tə-'tän-yə, -'tän-; tī-'tän-\ *noun*
: the wife of Oberon and queen of the fairies in Shakespeare's *A Midsummer Night's Dream*

**ti·tan·ic** \tī-'ta-nik *also* tə-\ *adjective* [Greek *titanikos* of the Titans] (1709)
: having great magnitude, force, or power : COLOSSAL
— **ti·tan·i·cal·ly** \-ni-k(ə-)lē\ *adverb*

**ti·ta·nif·er·ous** \₁tī-tⁿn-'i-f(ə-)rəs\ *adjective* (circa 1828)
: containing or yielding titanium ⟨*titaniferous* minerals⟩

**ti·tan·ism** \'tī-tⁿn-₁i-zəm\ *noun, often capitalized* [from the Titans' rebellion against their father Uranus] (1867)
: defiance of and revolt against social or artistic conventions

**ti·ta·ni·um** \tī-'tā-nē-əm, tə- *also* -'ta-nē-əm, -'tan-yəm\ *noun* [New Latin, from Greek *Titan*] (circa 1796)
: a silvery gray light strong metallic element found combined in ilmenite and rutile and used especially in alloys (as steel) and combined in refractory materials and in coatings — see ELEMENT table

**titanium dioxide** *noun* (1877)
: an oxide TiO₂ of titanium that occurs in rutile, anatase, or ilmenite and is used especially as a pigment

**titanium white** *noun* (1920)
: TITANIUM DIOXIDE; *also* : a brilliant white lead-free pigment consisting of titanium dioxide often together with barium sulfate and zinc oxide

**tit·bit** \'tit-₁bit\ *variant of* TIDBIT

---

☆ **SYNONYMS**

**Tire, weary, fatigue, exhaust, jade, fag** mean to make or become unable or unwilling to continue. TIRE implies a draining of one's strength or patience ⟨the long ride *tired* us out⟩. WEARY stresses tiring until one is unable to endure more of the same thing ⟨*wearied* of the constant arguing⟩. FATIGUE suggests causing great lassitude through excessive strain or undue effort ⟨*fatigued* by the day's chores⟩. EXHAUST implies complete draining of strength by hard exertion ⟨shoveling snow *exhausted* him⟩. JADE suggests the loss of all freshness and eagerness ⟨*jaded* by overindulgence⟩. FAG implies a drooping with fatigue ⟨shoppers all *fagged* out by the Christmas rush⟩.

---

\ə\ **abut** \ᵊ\ **kitten** \ər\ **further** \a\ **ash** \ā\ **ace**
\ä\ **mop, mar** \aü\ **out** \ch\ **chin** \e\ **bet** \ē\ **easy**
\g\ **go** \i\ **hit** \ī\ **ice** \j\ **job** \ŋ\ **sing** \ō\ **go**
\ȯ\ **law** \ȯi\ **boy** \th\ **thin** \th̲\ **the** \ü\ **loot** \ů\ **foot**
\y\ **yet** \zh\ **vision**   *see also* Guide to Pronunciation

**ti·ter** \'tī-tər\ *noun* [French *titre* title, proportion of gold or silver in a coin, from Old French *title* inscription, title] (1888)
: the strength of a solution or the concentration of a substance (as an antibody) in solution as determined by titration

**tit·fer** \'tit-fər\ *noun* [by shortening & alteration from *tit for tat*, rhyming slang for *hat*] (circa 1930)
*British* : HAT

**tit for tat** \,tit-fər-'tat\ [alteration of earlier *tip for tap*, from *tip* (blow) + *for* + *tap*] (1556)
: an equivalent given in return (as for an injury) : retaliation in kind
— **tit-for-tat** *adjective*

**tith·able** \'tī-thə-bəl\ *adjective* (15th century)
: subject or liable to payment of tithes

**¹tithe** \'tīth\ *verb* **tithed; tith·ing** [Middle English, from Old English *teogothian*, from *teogotha* tenth] (before 12th century)
*transitive verb*
**1** : to pay or give a tenth part of especially for the support of the church
**2** : to levy a tithe on
*intransitive verb*
: to give a tenth of one's income as a tithe

**²tithe** *noun* [Middle English, from Old English *teogotha* tenth; akin to Middle Low German *tegede* tenth, Old English *tīen* ten — more at TEN] (before 12th century)
**1** : a tenth part of something paid as a voluntary contribution or as a tax especially for the support of a religious establishment
**2** : the obligation represented by individual tithes
**3** : TENTH; *broadly* : a small part
**4** : a small tax or levy

**tith·er** \'tī-thər\ *noun* (14th century)
**1** : one that pays tithes
**2** : one that collects or advocates the payment of tithes

**tith·ing** \'tī-thiŋ\ *noun* [Middle English, from Old English *tēothung*, from *teogothian*, *tēothian* to tithe, take one tenth] (before 12th century)
: a small administrative division preserved in parts of England apparently originally made up of ten men with their families

**ti·tho·nia** \tə-'thō-nyə, tī-, -nē-ə\ *noun* [New Latin, probably from Latin *Tithonia*, poetical name of Aurora] (1940)
: any of a genus (*Tithonia*) of tall composite herbs or shrubs of Mexico and Central America that have flower heads resembling sunflowers and that are sometimes grown as ornamentals

**¹ti·ti** \'tī-,tī\ *noun* [origin unknown] (1827)
**1** : a tree (*Cliftonia monophylla* of the family Cyrillaceae) of the southeastern U.S. with leathery leaves and racemes of fragrant white flowers
**2** : LEATHERWOOD 2

**²ti·ti** \tē-'tē\ *noun* [American Spanish *tití*] (1832)
: any of a genus (*Callicebus*) of small South American monkeys having long thick variably colored fur and a tail that is not prehensile

**ti·tian** \'ti-shən\ *adjective, often capitalized* [*Titian* (Tiziano Vecellio)] (1896)
: of a brownish orange color

**tit·il·late** \'ti-t°l-,āt\ *verb* **-lat·ed; -lat·ing** [Latin *titillatus*, past participle of *titillare*] (1620)
*transitive verb*
**1** : to excite pleasurably : arouse by stimulation
**2** : TICKLE

*titi*

*intransitive verb*
: to act as a stimulant to pleasurable excitement
— **tit·il·la·tion** \,ti-t°l-'ā-shən\ *noun*
— **tit·il·la·tive** \'ti-t°l-,ā-tiv\ *adjective*

**tit·il·lat·ing** \'ti-t°l-,ā-tiŋ\ *adjective* (circa 1714)
: pleasantly stimulating or exciting ⟨*titillating* reading⟩; *also* : EROTIC
— **tit·il·lat·ing·ly** \-tiŋ-lē\ *adverb*

**tit·i·vate** *or* **tit·ti·vate** \'ti-tə-,vāt\ *verb* **-vat·ed; -vat·ing** [perhaps from ¹*tidy* + renovate] (1824)
*transitive verb*
: to make smart or spruce
*intransitive verb*
: SMARTEN, SPRUCE
— **tit·i·va·tion** \,ti-tə-'vā-shən\ *noun*

**tit·lark** \'tit-,lärk\ *noun* [*tit-* (as in *titmouse*) + *lark*] (1688)
: PIPIT

**¹ti·tle** \'tī-t°l\ *noun* [Middle English, from Middle French, from Latin *titulus* inscription, title] (14th century)
**1 a** *obsolete* : INSCRIPTION **b** : written material introduced into a motion picture or television program to give credits, explain an action, or represent dialogue — usually used in plural
**2 a** : all the elements constituting legal ownership **b** : a legally just cause of exclusive possession **c** : the instrument (as a deed) that is evidence of a right
**3 a** : something that justifies or substantiates a claim **b** : an alleged or recognized right
**4 a** : a descriptive or general heading (as of a chapter in a book) **b** : the heading which names an act or statute **c** : the heading of a legal action or proceeding
**5 a** : the distinguishing name of a written, printed, or filmed production **b** : a similar distinguishing name of a musical composition or a work of art
**6** : a descriptive name : APPELLATION
**7** : a division of an instrument, book, or bill; *especially* : one larger than a section or article
**8 a** : an appellation of dignity, honor, distinction, or preeminence attached to a person or family by virtue of rank, office, precedent, privilege, attainment, or lands **b** : a person holding a title especially of nobility
**9** : a written work as distinguished from a particular copy ⟨published 25 *titles* last year⟩
**10** : CHAMPIONSHIP 1 ⟨won the batting *title*⟩

**²title** *transitive verb* **ti·tled; ti·tling** \'tīt-liŋ, 'tī-t°l-iŋ\ (14th century)
**1** : to provide a title for
**2** : to designate or call by a title : TERM, STYLE

**³title** *adjective* (1886)
: of or relating to a title: as **a** : having the same name as the title of a production ⟨did the *title* role in *Hamlet*⟩ **b** : having the same title as or providing the title for the collection or production of which it forms a part ⟨the *title* song⟩ **c** : of, relating to, or involving a championship ⟨a *title* match⟩ **d** : of, relating to, or used with the titles that introduce a motion picture or television program ⟨*title* music⟩

**ti·tled** \'tī-t°ld\ *adjective* (1593)
: having a title especially of nobility

**title deed** *noun* (circa 1768)
: the deed constituting the evidence of a person's legal ownership

**ti·tle·hold·er** \'tī-t°l-,hōl-dər\ *noun* (1904)
: one that holds a title; *specifically* : CHAMPION

**title page** *noun* (1594)
: a page of a book bearing the title and usually the names of the author and publisher and the place and sometimes date of publication

**ti·tlist** \'tī-t°l-ist, 'tīt-list\ *noun* (1924)
: TITLEHOLDER

**tit·mouse** \'tit-,maús\ *noun, plural* **tit·mice** \-,mīs\ [by folk etymology from Middle English *titmose*, from (assumed) Middle English *tit* any small object or creature + Middle English *mose* titmouse, from Old English *māse*;

akin to Old High German *meisa* titmouse] (14th century)
: any of numerous small widely distributed insectivorous oscine birds (family Paridae and especially genus *Parus*) that are related to the chickadees and have small bills and relatively long tails

**Ti·to·ism** \'tē-(,)tō-,i-zəm\ *noun* (1949)
: the political, economic, and social policies associated with Tito; *specifically* : nationalistic policies and practices followed by a communist state or group independently of and often in opposition to the U.S.S.R.
— **Ti·to·ist** \-,ō-ist\ *noun or adjective*

**ti·trant** \'tī-trənt\ *noun* (1939)
: a substance (as a reagent solution of precisely known concentration) that is added in titration

**ti·trate** \'tī-,trāt\ *verb* **ti·trat·ed; ti·trat·ing** [*titer*] (circa 1859)
*transitive verb*
: to subject to titration
*intransitive verb*
: to perform titration
— **ti·trat·able** \-,trā-tə-bəl\ *adjective*
— **ti·tra·tor** \-,trā-tər\ *noun*

**ti·tra·tion** \tī-'trā-shən\ *noun* (circa 1859)
: a method or the process of determining the concentration of a dissolved substance in terms of the smallest amount of a reagent of known concentration required to bring about a given effect in reaction with a known volume of the test solution

**ti·tre** \'tī-tər\ *variant of* TITER

**ti·tri·met·ric** \,tī-trə-'me-trik\ *adjective* [*titration* + *-i-* + *-metric*] (1902)
: employing or determined by titration

**tit–tat–toe** \,ti-,ta(t)-'tō\ *variant of* TICKTACK-TOE

**tit·ter** \'ti-tər\ *intransitive verb* [imitative] (circa 1619)
: to laugh in a nervous, affected, or partly suppressed manner : GIGGLE, SNICKER
— **titter** *noun*

**tit·tie** \'ti-tē\ *noun* [probably baby talk alteration of *sister*] (circa 1700)
*chiefly Scottish* : SISTER

**tit·tle** \'ti-t°l\ *noun* [Middle English *titel*, from Medieval Latin *titulus*, from Latin, title] (14th century)
**1** : a point or small sign used as a diacritical mark in writing or printing
**2** : a very small part

**tit·tle–tat·tle** \'ti-t°l-,ta-t°l\ *noun* [reduplication of ¹*tattle*] (circa 1529)
: GOSSIP, PRATTLE
— **tittle–tattle** *intransitive verb*

**¹tit·tup** \'ti-təp\ *noun* [imitative of the sound of a horse's hooves] (1703)
: lively, gay, or restless behavior

**²tittup** *intransitive verb* **-tupped** *or* **-tuped; -tup·ping** *or* **-tup·ing** (1785)
: to move in a lively manner often with an exaggerated or affected action

**¹tit·u·lar** \'ti-chə-lər, 'tich-lər\ *adjective* [Latin *titulus* title] (1611)
**1 a** : existing in title only; *especially* : bearing a title derived from a defunct ecclesiastical jurisdiction (as an episcopal see) ⟨a *titular* bishop⟩ **b** : having the title and usually the honors belonging to an office or dignity without the duties, functions, or responsibilities ⟨the *titular* head of a political party⟩
**2** : bearing a title : TITLED
**3** : of, relating to, or constituting a title ⟨the *titular* hero of the play⟩
— **tit·u·lar·ly** *adverb*

**²titular** *noun* (1613)
: a person holding a title

**Ti·tus** \'tī-təs\ *noun* [Late Latin, from Greek *Titos*]
**1** : an early Christian convert who assisted Paul in his missionary work

**2 :** a letter written on the subject of pastoral care in the early Church and included as a book in the New Testament — see BIBLE table

**Tiu** \'tē-(,)ü\ *noun* [Old English *Tīw* — more at DEITY]
**:** an ancient Germanic god of war identified with Tyr

**tiz·zy** \'ti-zē\ *noun, plural* **tizzies** [origin unknown] (1935)
**:** a highly excited and distracted state of mind

**TKO** \,tē-,kā-'ō\ *noun* [*technical knockout*] (1941)
**:** TECHNICAL KNOCKOUT

**Tlin·git** \'tlin-kət, -gət *also* 'kliŋ-\ *noun, plural* **Tlingit** *or* **Tlingits** (1865)
**1 :** a member of a group of American Indian peoples of the islands and coast of southern Alaska
**2 :** the language of the Tlingit peoples
— **Tlingit** *adjective*

**T lymphocyte** *noun* [*thymus*-derived] (1972)
**:** T CELL

**T–man** \'tē-,man\ *noun* [*Treasury man*] (1937)
**:** a special agent of the U.S. Treasury Department

**tme·sis** \(tə-)'mē-səs\ *noun* [Late Latin, from Greek *tmēsis* act of cutting, from *temnein* to cut — more at TOME] (1550)
**:** separation of parts of a compound word by the intervention of one or more words (as *what place soever* for *whatsoever place*)

**TNT** \,tē-(,)en-'tē\ *noun* [*trinitrotoluene*] (1915)
**:** a flammable toxic compound $C_7H_5N_3O_6$ used as a high explosive and in chemical synthesis

**¹to** \tə, tü, 'tü\ *preposition* [Middle English, from Old English *tō;* akin to Old High German *zuo* to, Latin *donec* as long as, until] (before 12th century)
**1 a** — used as a function word to indicate movement or an action or condition suggestive of movement toward a place, person, or thing reached ⟨drove *to* the city⟩ ⟨went back *to* the original idea⟩ **b** — used as a function word to indicate direction ⟨a mile *to* the south⟩ ⟨turned his back *to* the door⟩ ⟨a tendency *to* silliness⟩ **c** — used as a function word to indicate contact or proximity ⟨applied polish *to* the table⟩ ⟨put her hand *to* her heart⟩ **d** (1) — used as a function word to indicate the place or point that is the far limit ⟨100 miles *to* the nearest town⟩ (2) — used as a function word to indicate the limit of extent ⟨stripped *to* the waist⟩ **e** — used as a function word to indicate relative position ⟨perpendicular *to* the floor⟩
**2 a** — used as a function word to indicate purpose, intention, tendency, result, or end ⟨came *to* our aid⟩ ⟨drink *to* his health⟩ **b** — used as a function word to indicate the result of an action or a process ⟨broken all *to* pieces⟩ ⟨go *to* seed⟩ ⟨*to* their surprise, the train left on time⟩
**3** — used as a function word to indicate position or relation in time: as **a :** BEFORE ⟨five minutes *to* five⟩ **b :** TILL ⟨from eight *to* five⟩ ⟨up *to* now⟩
**4** — used as a function word to indicate addition, attachment, connection, belonging, possession, accompaniment, or response ⟨the key *to* the door⟩ ⟨danced *to* live music⟩ ⟨comes *to* her call⟩
**5** — used as a function word (1) to indicate the extent or degree (as of completeness or accuracy) ⟨loyal *to* a man⟩ ⟨generous *to* a fault⟩ or the extent and result (as of an action or a condition) ⟨beaten *to* death⟩ (2) to indicate the last or an intermediate point of a series ⟨moderate *to* cool temperatures⟩
**6 a** — used as a function word (1) to indicate a relation to one that serves as a standard ⟨inferior *to* her earlier works⟩ (2) to indicate similarity, correspondence, dissimilarity, or proportion ⟨compared him *to* a god⟩ **b** — used as a function word to indicate agreement or conformity ⟨add salt *to* taste⟩ ⟨*to* my knowledge⟩

**c** — used as a function word to indicate a proportion in terms of numbers or quantities ⟨400 *to* the box⟩ ⟨odds of ten *to* one⟩
**7 a** — used as a function word (1) to indicate the application of an adjective or a noun ⟨agreeable *to* everyone⟩ ⟨attitude *to* friends⟩ ⟨title *to* the property⟩ (2) to indicate the relation of a verb to its complement or to a complementary element ⟨refers *to* the traditions⟩ ⟨refers us *to* the traditions⟩ (3) to indicate the receiver of an action or the one for which something is done or exists ⟨spoke *to* his mother⟩ ⟨gives a dollar *to* the man⟩ and often used with a reflexive pronoun to indicate exclusiveness (as of possession) or separateness ⟨had the house *to* themselves⟩ ⟨thought *to* herself⟩ **b** — used as a function word to indicate agency ⟨falls *to* his opponent's blows⟩
**8** — used as a function word to indicate that the following verb is an infinitive ⟨wants *to* go⟩ and often used by itself at the end of a clause in place of an infinitive suggested by the preceding context ⟨knows more than she seems *to*⟩

**²to** \'tü\ *adverb* (before 12th century)
**1 a** — used as a function word to indicate direction toward ⟨feathers wrong end *to*⟩ ⟨run *to* and fro⟩ **b :** close to the wind ⟨the gale having gone over, we came *to* —R. H. Dana⟩
**2 a :** into contact especially with the frame — used of a door or a window ⟨the door snapped *to*⟩ **b** — used as a function word to indicate physical application or attachment ⟨he . . . hath set *to* his seal —John 3:33 (Authorized Version)⟩
**3** — used as a function word to indicate application or attention ⟨will stand *to* —Shakespeare⟩
**4 :** to a state of consciousness or awareness ⟨brings her *to* with smelling salts⟩
**5 :** at hand **:** BY ⟨get *to* see 'em close *to* —Richard Llewellyn⟩

**toad** \'tōd\ *noun* [Middle English *tode*, from Old English *tāde, tādige*] (before 12th century)
**1 :** any of numerous anuran amphibians (especially family Bufonidae) that as compared with the related frogs are generally more terrestrial in habit though returning to water to lay their eggs, squatter and shorter in build and with weaker hind limbs, and rough, dry, and warty rather than smooth and moist of skin
**2 :** a contemptible person or thing

toad 1

**toad·eat·er** \-,ē-tər\ *noun* (circa 1572)
*archaic* **:** TOADY

**toad·fish** \-,fish\ *noun* (1704)
**:** any of a family (Batrachoididae) of chiefly marine bony fishes with jugular pelvic fins, a large thick head, a wide mouth, and usually scaleless slimy skin

**toad·flax** \-,flaks\ *noun* (1578)
**:** BUTTER-AND-EGGS; *also* **:** any of several related plants (especially genus *Linaria*) of the snapdragon family

**toad·stone** \-,stōn\ *noun* (1558)
**:** a stone or similar object held to have formed in the head or body of a toad and formerly often worn as a charm or antidote to poison

**toad·stool** \-,stül\ *noun* (14th century)
**:** a fungus having an umbrella-shaped pileus **:** MUSHROOM; *especially* **:** a poisonous or inedible one as distinguished from an edible mushroom

**¹toady** \'tō-dē\ *noun, plural* **toad·ies** [by shortening & alteration from *toadeater*] (1826)
**:** one who flatters in the hope of gaining favors **:** SYCOPHANT
*synonym* see PARASITE

**²toady** *intransitive verb* **toad·ied; toady·ing** (circa 1859)
**:** to behave as a toady **:** engage in sycophancy
*synonym* see FAWN
— **toady·ism** \-ē-,i-zəm\ *noun*

**¹to–and–fro** \,tü-ən-'frō\ *adjective* (1749)
**:** forward and backward ⟨*to-and-fro* motion⟩

**²to–and–fro** *noun* (1847)
**:** activity involving alternating movement in opposite directions ⟨the busy *to-and-fro* of the holiday shoppers⟩

**to and fro** *adverb* (14th century)
**:** from one place to another

**¹toast** \'tōst\ *verb* [Middle English *tosten*, from Middle French *toster*, from Late Latin *tostare* to roast, from Latin *tostus*, past participle of *torrēre* to dry, parch — more at THIRST] (14th century)
*transitive verb*
**1 :** to warm thoroughly
**2 :** to make (as bread) crisp, hot, and brown by heat
*intransitive verb*
**:** to become toasted; *especially* **:** to warm thoroughly

**²toast** *noun* (15th century)
**1 a :** sliced bread browned on both sides by heat **b :** food prepared with toasted bread
**2** [from the use of pieces of spiced toast to flavor drinks] **a :** someone or something in honor of which persons usually drink **b :** one that is highly admired ⟨she's the *toast* of society⟩
**3** [³*toast*] **:** an act of proposing or of drinking in honor of a toast
**4 :** a rhyming narrative poem existing in oral tradition among black Americans

**³toast** *transitive verb* (1640)
**:** to propose or drink to as a toast

**toast·er** \'tō-stər\ *noun* (1582)
**:** one that toasts; *especially* **:** an electrical appliance for toasting

**toaster oven** *noun* (1961)
**:** a portable electrical appliance that can function as an oven or a toaster

**toast·mas·ter** \'tōs(t)-,mas-tər\ *noun* (1749)
**:** one who presides at a banquet and introduces the after-dinner speakers

**toast·mis·tress** \-,mis-trəs\ *noun* (1921)
**:** a woman who acts as toastmaster

**toasty** \'tō-stē\ *adjective* **toast·i·er; -est** (1953)
**:** pleasantly or comfortably warm ⟨felt snug and *toasty* by the fire⟩

**to·bac·co** \tə-'ba-(,)kō\ *noun, plural* **-cos** [Spanish *tabaco*, probably from Taino, roll of tobacco leaves] (circa 1565)
**1 :** any of a genus (*Nicotiana*) of chiefly American plants of the nightshade family with viscid foliage and tubular flowers; *especially* **:** a tall erect annual tropical American herb (*N. tabacum*) cultivated for its leaves
**2 :** the leaves of cultivated tobacco prepared for use in smoking or chewing or as snuff
**3 :** manufactured products of tobacco (as cigars or cigarettes); *also* **:** smoking as a practice ⟨has sworn off *tobacco*⟩

tobacco 1

**tobacco budworm** *noun* (1918)
**:** a noctuid moth (*Heliothis virescens* synonym *Helicoverpa virescens*) whose small rusty often green-striped caterpillar feeds on buds and young leaves especially of tobacco and cotton

**tobacco hornworm** *noun* (circa 1909)
**:** a hawkmoth (*Manduca sexta*) whose large usually green larva is a hornworm that feeds on plants of the nightshade family

---

**tobacco juice** *noun* (1833)
: saliva colored brown by tobacco or snuff

**tobacco mosaic** *noun* (1914)
: any of a complex of virus diseases of plants of the nightshade family and especially of tobacco

**to·bac·co·nist** \tə-'ba-kə-nist\ *noun* [irregular from *tobacco* + *-ist*] (1657)
: a dealer in tobacco especially at retail

**tobacco road** *noun, often T&R capitalized* [from *Tobacco Road,* novel (1932) by Erskine Caldwell and play (1933) by Jack Kirkland (died 1969) American playwright] (1937)
: a squalid poverty-stricken rural area or community

**to·be** \tə-'bē\ *adjective* (circa 1600)
: that is to be : FUTURE — usually used postpositively and often in combination ⟨a bride*to-be*⟩

**To·bi·as** \tə-'bī-əs\ *noun* [Greek *Tobias*]
**1** : a Jewish hero who with divine aid marries his kinswoman Sarah in spite of a jealous evil spirit and restores his father Tobit's sight
**2** : TOBIT 2

**To·bit** \'tō-bət\ *noun* [Greek *Tōbit*]
**1** : the elderly father of Tobias
**2** : a book of Scripture included in the Roman Catholic canon of the Old Testament and in the Protestant Apocrypha — see BIBLE table

**¹to·bog·gan** \tə-'bä-gən\ *noun* [Canadian French *tobogan,* of Algonquian origin; akin to Micmac *tobâgun* drag made of skin] (circa 1820)
**1** : a long flat-bottomed light sled made usually of thin boards curved up at one end with usually low handrails at the sides

toboggan 1

**2** : a downward course or a sharp decline

**²toboggan** *intransitive verb* (1846)
**1** : to coast on or as if on a toboggan
**2** : to decline suddenly and sharply
— **to·bog·gan·er** *noun*
— **to·bog·gan·ist** \-gə-nist\ *noun*

**to·bog·gan·ing** *noun* (1849)
: the act, art, or sport of riding a toboggan

**to·by jug** \'tō-bē-\ *noun, often capitalized* [*Toby,* nickname from the name *Tobias*] (1840)
: a small jug, pitcher, or mug shaped somewhat like a stout man with a cocked hat for the brim — called also *toby*

**toc·ca·ta** \tə-'kä-tə\ *noun* [Italian, from *toccare* to touch, from (assumed) Vulgar Latin — more at TOUCH] (circa 1724)
: a musical composition usually for organ or harpsichord in a free style and characterized by full chords, rapid runs, and high harmonies

**To·char·i·an** \tō-'kar-ē-ən, -'ker-, -'kär-\ *noun* [Greek *Tocharoi*] (circa 1926)
**1 a** : a language of central Asia known from documents from the sixth to eighth centuries A.D. **b** : a branch of the Indo-European language family containing Tocharian — see INDO-EUROPEAN LANGUAGES table
**2** : a member of a people of presumably European origin dwelling in central Asia during the first millennium of the Christian era

**Tocharian A** *noun* (1926)
: the eastern dialect of Tocharian — see INDO-EUROPEAN LANGUAGES table

**Tocharian B** *noun* (1926)
: the western dialect of Tocharian — see INDO-EUROPEAN LANGUAGES table

**toch·er** \'tä-kər\ *noun* [Middle English (Scots) *tochir,* from Scottish Gaelic *tochar*] (15th century)
*chiefly Scottish* : DOWRY 2, 3

**to·coph·er·ol** \tō-'kä-fə-ˌról, -ˌrōl\ *noun* [International Scientific Vocabulary, ultimately from Greek *tokos* childbirth, offspring (akin to Greek *tiktein* to beget) + *pherein* to carry, bear — more at THANE, BEAR] (1936)

: any of several fat-soluble oily phenolic compounds with varying degrees of antioxidant vitamin E activity; *especially* : one $C_{29}H_{50}O_2$ of high vitamin E potency obtained from germ oils or by synthesis

**toc·sin** \'täk-sən\ *noun* [Middle French *toquassen,* from Old Provençal *tocasenh,* from *tocar* to touch, ring a bell (from assumed Vulgar Latin *toccare*) + *senh* sign, bell, from Medieval Latin & Latin *signum;* Medieval Latin, bell, from Late Latin, ringing of a bell, from Latin, mark, sign — more at TOUCH, SIGN] (1586)
**1** : an alarm bell or the ringing of it
**2** : a warning signal

**¹tod** \'täd\ *noun* [Middle English] (12th century)
*chiefly Scottish* : FOX

**²tod** *noun* [Middle English *todd, todde;* probably akin to Old High German *zotta* tuft of hair] (15th century)
**1** *archaic* : any of various units of weight for wool; *especially* : one equal to 28 pounds (13 kilograms)
**2** *British* : a bushy clump (as of ivy)

**¹to·day** \tə-'dā\ *adverb* (before 12th century)
**1** : on or for this day
**2** : at the present time

**²today** *noun* (1535)
: the present day, time, or age ⟨*today's* youth⟩

**³today** *adjective* (1966)
: of or characteristic of today : NOW

**tod·dle** \'tä-dºl\ *intransitive verb* **tod·dled; tod·dling** \'täd-liŋ, 'tä-dºl-iŋ\ [origin unknown] (circa 1600)
**1** : to walk with short tottering steps in the manner of a young child
**2** : to take a stroll : SAUNTER
— **toddle** *noun*

**tod·dler** \'täd-lər, 'tä-dºl-ər\ *noun* (1793)
: one that toddles; *especially* : a young child
— **tod·dler·hood** \-ˌhùd\ *noun*

**tod·dy** \'tä-dē\ *noun, plural* **toddies** [Hindi *tāṛī* juice of the palmyra palm, from *tāṛ* palmyra palm, from Sanskrit *tāla*] (circa 1610)
**1** : the fresh or fermented sap of various chiefly East Indian palms
**2** : a usually hot drink consisting of liquor (as rum), water, sugar, and spices

**to·do** \tə-'dü\ *noun, plural* **to·dos** \-'düz\ (circa 1576)
: BUSTLE, STIR, FUSS

**¹toe** \'tō\ *noun* [Middle English *to,* from Old English *tā;* akin to Old High German *zēha* toe] (before 12th century)
**1 a** (1) : one of the terminal members of a vertebrate's foot (2) : the fore end of a foot or hoof **b** : a terminal segment of a limb of an invertebrate **c** : the forepart of something worn on the foot ⟨the *toe* of a boot⟩
**2** : a part that by its position or form is felt to resemble a toe ⟨the *toe* of Italy⟩: as **a** : a lateral projection at one end or between the ends of a piece (as a rod or bolt) **b** : the lowest part (as of an embankment, dam, or cliff)
**3** : TOE DANCE
— **toe·less** \-ləs\ *adjective*
— **on one's toes** : ALERT 1
— **toe to toe** : facing one another

**²toe** *verb* **toed; toe·ing** (1607)
*transitive verb*
**1** : to furnish with a toe ⟨*toe* a sock⟩
**2** : to touch, reach, or drive with the toe ⟨*toe* a football⟩
**3** : to drive (as a nail) obliquely; *also* : to clinch or fasten by or with nails or rods so driven
*intransitive verb*
**1** : TIPTOE
**2** : to stand, walk, or be placed so that the toes assume an indicated position or direction ⟨*toe* in⟩
— **toe the line** *or* **toe the mark** : to conform rigorously to a rule or standard

**toea** \'tói-ə\ *noun, plural* **toea** [Hiri Motu (pidgin of Papua New Guinea based on Motu, an Austronesian language), a kind of shell] (1975)
— see *kina* at MONEY table

**toe cap** *noun* (1797)
: a piece of leather covering the toe of a shoe and reinforcing or decorating it

**toed** \'tōd\ *adjective* [¹*toe*] (1611)
**1** : having a toe or toes especially of a specified kind or number — usually used in combination ⟨five-*toed*⟩ ⟨round-*toed* shoes⟩
**2** [from past participle of ²*toe*] : driven obliquely ⟨a *toed* nail⟩; *also* : secured by diagonal or oblique nailing

**toe dance** *noun* (1898)
: a dance executed on the tips of the toes by means of a ballet slipper with a reinforced toe
— **toe-dance** *intransitive verb*
— **toe dancer** *noun*
— **toe dancing** *noun*

**toe·hold** \'tō-ˌhōld\ *noun* (1880)
**1 a** : a hold or place of support for the toes (as in climbing) **b** (1) : a means of progressing (as in surmounting barriers) (2) : a slight footing ⟨used his money to get a *toehold,* then a foothold, then a near stranglehold on the political economy —R. W. Armstrong⟩
**2** : a wrestling hold in which the aggressor bends or twists his opponent's foot

**toe-in** \'tō-ˌin\ *noun* (1928)
**1** : CAMBER 3
**2** : adjustment of the front wheels of an automotive vehicle so that they are closer together at the front than at the back

**¹toe·nail** \'tō-ˌnāl, -'nā(ə)l\ *noun* (1841)
: a nail of a toe

**²toenail** *transitive verb* (1900)
: to fasten by toed nails : TOE

**toe·piece** \'tō-ˌpēs\ *noun* (1879)
: a piece designed to form a toe (as of a shoe) or cover the toes of the foot

**toe·plate** \-ˌplāt\ *noun* (1894)
: a tab attached to the toe of a shoe (as to prevent wear due to heavy use)

**toe-to-toe** *adjective or adverb* (circa 1942)
: slugging it out at or as if at close range ⟨a *toe-to-toe* confrontation over the new policy⟩

**toff** \'täf\ *noun* [probably alteration of *tuft* titled college student] (1851)
*chiefly British* : DANDY, SWELL

**tof·fee** *or* **tof·fy** \'tó-fē, 'tä-\ *noun, plural* **toffees** *or* **toffies** [alteration of *taffy*] (circa 1825)
: candy of brittle but tender texture made by boiling sugar and butter together

**tof·fee-nosed** \-ˌnōzd\ *adjective* (circa 1925)
*chiefly British* : STUCK-UP

**toft** \'tóft, 'täft\ *noun* [Middle English, from Old English, from Old Norse *topt;* probably akin to Greek *dapedon* floor, *demein* to build, *pedon* ground — more at TIMBER, PED] (before 12th century)
*British* : a site for a dwelling and its outbuildings; *also* : an entire holding comprising a homestead and additional land

**to·fu** \'tō-(ˌ)fü\ *noun* [Japanese *tōfu*] (1771)
: BEAN CURD

**tog** \'täg, 'tóg\ *transitive verb* **togged; tog·ging** [*togs*] (circa 1785)
: to dress especially in fine clothing — usually used with *up* or *out*

**to·ga** \'tō-gə\ *noun* [Latin; akin to Latin *tegere* to cover — more at THATCH] (1600)
: the loose outer garment worn in public by citizens of ancient Rome; *also* : a similar loose wrap or a professional, official, or academic gown

toga

— **to·gaed** \-gəd\ *adjective*

**to·ga vi·ri·lis** \ˌtō-gə-və-ˈrē-ləs, -ˈri-\ *noun, plural* **to·gae vi·ri·les** \ˈtō-ˌgī-və-ˈrē-ˌlās, -ˈri-\ [Latin, men's toga] (1600)
: the white toga of manhood assumed by boys of ancient Rome at age 15

**¹to·geth·er** \tə-ˈge-thər\ *adverb* [Middle English *togedere*, from Old English *togædere*, from *tō* to + *gædere* together; akin to Middle High German *gater* together, Old English *gaderian* to gather] (before 12th century)
**1 a :** in or into one place, mass, collection, or group ⟨the men get *together* every Thursday for poker⟩ **b :** in a body : as a group ⟨students and faculty *together* presented the petition⟩
**2 a :** in or into contact (as connection, collision, or union) ⟨mix these ingredients *together*⟩ **b :** in or into association or relationship ⟨colors that go well *together*⟩ ⟨went to school *together*⟩
**3 a :** at one time : SIMULTANEOUSLY ⟨events that happened *together*⟩ **b :** in succession : without intermission ⟨was depressed for days *together*⟩
**4 a :** by combined action : JOINTLY ⟨*together* we forced the door⟩ **b :** in or into agreement or harmony ⟨the soloist and the orchestra weren't quite *together*⟩ **c :** in or into a unified or coherent structure or an integrated whole ⟨can't even put a simple sentence *together*⟩ ⟨pull yourself *together*⟩
**5 a :** with each other — used as an intensive after certain verbs ⟨join *together*⟩ ⟨add *together*⟩ **b :** as a unit : in the aggregate ⟨these arguments taken *together* make a convincing case⟩ **c :** considered as a whole : counted or summed up ⟨all *together*, there were 21 entries⟩
— **to·geth·er·ness** *noun*
— **together with :** in addition to : in association with

**²together** *adjective* (1963)
**1 :** appropriately prepared, organized, or balanced
**2 :** composed in mind or manner : SELF-POSSESSED ⟨a warm, sensitive, reasonably *together* girl —*East Village Other*⟩

**Tog·gen·burg** \ˈtä-gən-ˌbərg\ *noun* [*Toggenburg*, district in northeastern Switzerland] (1886)
: any of a breed of brown hornless dairy goats of Swiss origin with white stripes on the face

**tog·gery** \ˈtä-g(ə-)rē, ˈtò-\ *noun* [*togs*] (circa 1811)
: CLOTHING

**¹tog·gle** \ˈtä-gəl\ *noun* [origin unknown] (circa 1775)
**1 :** a piece or device for holding or securing: as **a :** a pin inserted in a nautical knot to make it more secure or easier to slip **b :** a crosspiece attached to the end of or to a loop in something (as a chain, rope, line, strap, or belt) usually to prevent slipping, to serve in twisting or tightening, or to hold something attached
**2 :** a device consisting of two bars jointed together end to end but not in line so that when a force is applied to the joint tending to straighten it pressure will be exerted on the parts adjacent or fixed to the outer ends of the bars; *also* : a device with a joint using a toggle

**²toggle** *transitive verb* **tog·gled; tog·gling** \-g(ə-)liŋ\ (1836)
**1 :** to fasten with or as if with a toggle
**2 :** to furnish with a toggle

**toggle bolt** *noun* (1906)
: a bolt that has a nut with wings which close for passage through a small hole and spring open after passing through the hole to keep the bolt from slipping back through

**toggle switch** *noun* (circa 1924)
: an electric switch operated by pushing a projecting lever through a small arc

**togs** \ˈtägz, ˈtògz\ *noun plural* [plural of English slang *tog* coat, short for obsolete English cant *togeman, togman*] (1779)
: CLOTHING; *especially* : a set of clothes and accessories for a specified use ⟨riding *togs*⟩

**togue** \ˈtōg\ *noun* [Canadian French] (1839)
: LAKE TROUT

**¹toil** \ˈtòi(ə)l\ *noun* [Middle English *toile*, from Anglo-French *toyl*, from Old French *toeil* battle, confusion, from *toeillier*] (14th century)
**1** *archaic* **a :** STRUGGLE, BATTLE **b :** laborious effort
**2 :** long strenuous fatiguing labor
**synonym** see WORK
— **toil·ful** \-fəl\ *adjective*
— **toil·ful·ly** \-fə-lē\ *adverb*

**²toil** *verb* [Middle English, to argue, struggle, from Anglo-French *toiller*, from Old French *toeillier* to stir, disturb, dispute, from Latin *tudiculare* to crush, grind, from *tudicula* machine for crushing olives, diminutive of *tudes* hammer; akin to Latin *tundere* to beat — more at CONTUSION] (14th century)
*intransitive verb*
**1 :** to work hard and long : LABOR
**2 :** to proceed with laborious effort : PLOD ⟨*toiling* wearily up the hill⟩
*transitive verb*
**1** *archaic* : OVERWORK
**2** *archaic* : to get or accomplish with great effort
— **toil·er** \ˈtòi-lər\ *noun*

**³toil** *noun* [Middle French *toile* cloth, net, from Latin *tela* cloth on a loom — more at SUBTLE] (circa 1529)
**1 :** a net to trap game
**2 :** something by which one is held fast or inextricably involved : SNARE, TRAP — usually used in plural ⟨caught in the *toils* of the law⟩

**toile** \ˈtwäl\ *noun* [French, cloth, linen, from Middle French] (1794)
**1 :** any of many plain or simple twill weave fabrics; *especially* : LINEN
**2 :** a mock-up model of a garment

**toile de Jouy** \ˌtwäl-də-ˈzhwē\ *noun* [French, literally, cloth of Jouy, from *Jouy*-en-Josas, France] (circa 1920)
: an 18th century French scenic pattern usually printed on cotton, linen, or silk in one color on a light ground; *broadly* : a similar printed fabric

**¹toi·let** \ˈtòi-lət\ *noun* [Middle French *toilette* cloth put over the shoulders while dressing the hair or shaving, diminutive of *toile* cloth] (circa 1695)
**1** *archaic* : DRESSING TABLE
**2 :** the act or process of dressing and grooming oneself
**3 a** (1) : BATHROOM, LAVATORY 2 (2) : PRIVY **b** : a fixture that consists usually of a water-flushed bowl and seat and is used for defecation and urination
**4 :** cleansing in preparation for or in association with a medical or surgical procedure ⟨a pharyngeal *toilet*⟩ ◆

**²toilet** (1840)
*intransitive verb*
**1 :** to dress and groom oneself
**2 :** to use the toilet — usually used of a child
*transitive verb*
**1 :** DRESS, GARB
**2 :** to help (as a child or sick person) use the toilet

**toilet paper** *noun* (1884)
: a thin sanitary absorbent paper for bathroom use chiefly after defecation and urination

**toilet powder** *noun* (1840)
: a fine powder usually with soothing or antiseptic ingredients for sprinkling or rubbing (as after bathing) over the skin

**toi·let·ry** \ˈtòi-lə-trē\ *noun, plural* **-ries** (1892)
: an article or preparation (as toothpaste, shaving cream, or cologne) used in making one's toilet — usually used in plural

**toilet soap** *noun* (1839)
: a mild soap that is often perfumed and colored and stabilized with preservatives

**toi·lette** \twä-ˈlet\ *noun* [French, from Middle French] (1681)
**1 :** TOILET 2

**2 a :** formal or fashionable attire or style of dressing **b :** a particular costume or outfit
**word history** see TOILET

**toilet training** *noun* (1940)
: the process of training a child to control bladder and bowel movements and to use the toilet
— **toilet train** *transitive verb*

**toilet water** *noun* (1855)
: a perfumed liquid containing a high percentage of alcohol for use in or after a bath or as a skin freshener

**toil·some** \-səm\ *adjective* (1581)
: marked by or full of toil or fatigue : LABORIOUS
— **toil·some·ly** *adverb*
— **toil·some·ness** *noun*

**toil·worn** \-ˌwòrn, -ˌwórn\ *adjective* (1751)
: showing the effects of or worn out with toil ⟨*toilworn* hands⟩

**to-ing and fro-ing** \ˈtü-iŋ-ən(d)-ˈfrō-iŋ\ *noun, plural* **to-ings and fro-ings** [*to and fro*] (1847)
: a passing back and forth

**to·ka·mak** *also* **to·ko·mak** \ˈtō-kə-ˌmak, ˈtä-\ *noun* [Russian, from *toroidal'naya kamera s aksial'nym magnitnym polem* (toroidal chamber with an axial magnetic field)] (1965)
: a toroidal device for producing controlled nuclear fusion that involves the confining and heating of a gaseous plasma by means of an electric current and magnetic field

**To·kay** \tō-ˈkā\ *noun* (1710)
**1 :** a naturally sweet wine from the area around Tokaj, Hungary
**2 :** a blend of Angelica, port, and sherry made in California

**toke** \ˈtōk\ *noun* [American Spanish *toque*, from Spanish, touch, test, from *tocar* to touch, from Vulgar Latin *toccare* — more at TOUCH] (1968)
*slang* : a puff on a marijuana cigarette or pipe
— **toke** *intransitive verb, slang*

**¹to·ken** \ˈtō-kən\ *noun* [Middle English, from Old English *tācen, tācn* sign, token; akin to Old High German *zeihhan* sign, Greek *deiknynai* to show — more at DICTION] (before 12th century)
**1 :** an outward sign or expression ⟨his tears were *tokens* of his grief⟩

---

◇ WORD HISTORY

**toilet** Latin *tela* "cloth on a loom," ultimately a derivative of *texere* "to weave," developed in Old French into *toile*. From *toile* was formed the diminutive *toilette* in Middle French, which could mean simply "small piece of cloth" though it also came to be used in more specific senses, such as a wrapper for clothing or a cover for a dressing table on which items used in dressing oneself could be placed. By the 17th century, *toilette* could refer to the dressing table itself or the act of grooming that takes place at it. English borrowed the word in the late 17th century and developed the spelling *toilet* from it. Both forms have flourished with some overlap and some differentiation of meaning. *Toilet*, however, has had its other meanings overshadowed by one particular sense development, from "dressing room" through "dressing room with bath facilities" through "lavatory" and finally to "water closet." Amusingly, while English uses a French word to designate euphemistically this homely fixture, French has repaid the compliment by calling it *le water-closet* or *le w.c.*

---

\ə\ abut \ə\ kitten \ər\ further \a\ ash \ā\ ace \ä\ mop, mar \aú\ out \ch\ chin \e\ bet \ē\ easy \g\ go \i\ hit \ī\ ice \j\ job \ŋ\ sing \ō\ go \ò\ law \òi\ boy \th\ thin \t͟h\ the \ü\ loot \ù\ foot \y\ yet \zh\ vision   *see also* Guide to Pronunciation

**2 a :** SYMBOL, EMBLEM ⟨a white flag is a *token* of surrender⟩ **b :** an instance of a linguistic expression
**3 :** a distinguishing feature **:** CHARACTERISTIC
**4 a :** SOUVENIR, KEEPSAKE **b :** a small part representing the whole **:** INDICATION ⟨this is only a *token* of what we hope to accomplish⟩ **c :** something given or shown as a guarantee (as of authority, right, or identity)
**5 a :** a piece resembling a coin issued as money by some person or body other than a de jure government **b :** a piece resembling a coin issued for use (as for fare on a bus) by a particular group on specified terms
**6 :** a member of a group (as a minority) that is included within a larger group through tokenism; *especially* **:** a token employee
**synonym** see SIGN
— **by the same token :** for the same reason

**²token** *adjective* (1547)
**1 :** done or given as a token especially in partial fulfillment of an obligation or engagement ⟨a *token* payment⟩
**2 a :** representing no more than a symbolic effort **:** MINIMAL, PERFUNCTORY ⟨*token* resistance⟩ ⟨*token* integration⟩ **b :** serving or intended to show absence of discrimination ⟨a *token* female employee⟩

**to·ken·ism** \'tō-kə-ˌni-zəm\ *noun* (1961)
**:** the policy or practice of making only a symbolic effort (as to desegregate)

**token money** *noun* (1889)
**:** money of regular government issue (as paper currency or coins) having a greater face value than intrinsic value

**To·khar·i·an** *variant of* TOCHARIAN

**to·ko·no·ma** \ˌtō-kə-'nō-mə\ *noun* [Japanese] (1871)
**:** a niche or alcove in the wall of a Japanese house for the display of a decorative object

**Tok Pis·in** \'tȯk-'pi-zən, -sən\ *noun* [Tok Pisin, literally, pidgin talk] (1974)
**:** an English-based creole that is a national language of Papua New Guinea

**tol-** *or* **tolu-** *combining form* [International Scientific Vocabulary, from *toluene*]
**:** toluene ⟨*tolyl*⟩

**to·la** \'tō-lə, tō-'lä\ *noun* [Hindi *tolā*, from Sanskrit *tulā* weight; akin to Latin *tollere* to lift up] (1614)
**:** a unit of weight of India equal to 180 grains troy or 0.4114 ounce (11.7 grams)

**tol·booth** \'tō(l)-ˌbüth, 'täl-, 'tȯl-\ *noun* [Middle English *tolbothe, tollbothe* tollbooth, town hall, jail] (15th century)
**1** *Scottish* **:** a town or market hall
**2** *Scottish* **:** JAIL, PRISON

**tol·bu·ta·mide** \täl-'byü-tə-ˌmīd\ *noun* [*tol-* + *butyric* + *amide*] (1956)
**:** a sulfonylurea $C_{12}H_{18}N_2O_3S$ used in the treatment of diabetes

**told** *past and past participle of* TELL

**tole** \'tōl\ *noun, often attributive* [French *tôle*, from Middle French dialect *taule*, from Latin *tabula* board, tablet] (1927)
**:** sheet metal and especially tinplate for use in domestic and ornamental wares in which it is usually japanned or painted and often elaborately decorated; *also* **:** objects made of tole

**To·le·do** \tə-'lē-(ˌ)dō\ *noun, plural* **-dos** (1596)
**:** a finely tempered sword of a kind made in Toledo, Spain

**tol·er·a·ble** \'tä-lə-rə-bəl, 'täl-rə-; 'tä-lər-bəl\ *adjective* (15th century)
**1 :** capable of being borne or endured ⟨*tolerable* pain⟩
**2 :** moderately good or agreeable **:** PASSABLE ⟨a *tolerable* singing voice⟩
— **tol·er·a·bil·i·ty** \ˌtä-lə-rə-'bi-lə-tē, ˌtäl-rə-\ *noun*
— **tol·er·a·bly** \'tä-lə-rə-blē, 'täl-rə-; 'tä-lər-blē\ *adverb*

**tol·er·ance** \'tä-lə-rən(t)s, 'täl-rən(t)s\ *noun* (15th century)

---

**1 :** capacity to endure pain or hardship **:** ENDURANCE, FORTITUDE, STAMINA
**2 a :** sympathy or indulgence for beliefs or practices differing from or conflicting with one's own **b :** the act of allowing something **:** TOLERATION
**3 :** the allowable deviation from a standard; *especially* **:** the range of variation permitted in maintaining a specified dimension in machining a piece
**4 a** (1) **:** the capacity of the body to endure or become less responsive to a substance (as a drug) or a physiological insult with repeated use or exposure ⟨immunological *tolerance* to a virus⟩ ⟨an addict's increasing *tolerance* for a drug⟩ (2) **:** relative capacity of an organism to grow or thrive when subjected to an unfavorable environmental factor **b :** the maximum amount of a pesticide residue that may lawfully remain on or in food

**tol·er·ant** \-rənt\ *adjective* (1784)
**1 :** inclined to tolerate; *especially* **:** marked by forbearance or endurance
**2 :** exhibiting tolerance (as for a drug or an environmental factor)
— **tol·er·ant·ly** *adverb*

**tol·er·ate** \'tä-lə-ˌrāt\ *transitive verb* **-at·ed; -at·ing** [Latin *toleratus*, past participle of *tolerare* to endure, put up with; akin to Old English *tholian* to bear, Latin *tollere* to lift up, *latus* carried (suppletive past participle of *ferre*), Greek *tlēnai* to bear] (1531)
**1 :** to exhibit physiological tolerance for (as a drug)
**2 a :** to suffer to be or to be done without prohibition, hindrance, or contradiction **b :** to put up with
**synonym** see BEAR
— **tol·er·a·tive** \-ˌrā-tiv\ *adjective*
— **tol·er·a·tor** \-ˌrā-tər\ *noun*

**tol·er·a·tion** \ˌtä-lə-'rā-shən\ *noun* (1531)
**1 a :** the act or practice of tolerating something **b :** a government policy of permitting forms of religious belief and worship not officially established
**2 :** TOLERANCE 4a(1)

**tol·i·dine** \'tä-lə-ˌdēn\ *noun* [International Scientific Vocabulary *tol-* + *-idine*] (1879)
**:** any of several isomeric aromatic diamines $C_{14}H_{16}N_2$ that are homologues of benzidine and used especially as dye intermediates

**¹toll** \'tōl\ *noun* [Middle English, from Old English, from (assumed) Vulgar Latin *tolonium*, alteration of Late Latin *telonium* customhouse, from Greek *tolōnion*, from *telōnēs* collector of tolls, from *telos* tax, toll; perhaps akin to Greek *tlēnai* to bear] (before 12th century)
**1 :** a tax or fee paid for some liberty or privilege (as of passing over a highway or bridge)
**2 :** compensation for services rendered: as **a :** a charge for transportation **b :** a charge for a long-distance telephone call
**3 :** a grievous or ruinous price ⟨inflation has taken its *toll*⟩; *especially* **:** cost in life or health ⟨the death *toll* from the hurricane⟩

**²toll** (14th century)
*intransitive verb*
**:** to take or levy toll
*transitive verb*
**1 a :** to exact part of as a toll **b :** to take as toll
**2 :** to exact a toll from (someone)

**³toll** *or* **tole** \'tōl\ *transitive verb* **tolled** *or* **toled; toll·ing** *or* **tol·ing** [Middle English *tollen, tolen;* akin to Old English for*tyllan* to seduce] (13th century)
**1 :** ALLURE, ENTICE
**2 a :** to entice (game) to approach **b :** to attract (fish) with scattered bait **c :** to lead or attract (domestic animals) to a desired point

**⁴toll** *verb* [Middle English, perhaps from *tollen* to entice] (15th century)
*transitive verb*
**1 :** to sound (a bell) by pulling the rope
**2 a :** to give signal or announcement of ⟨the clock *tolled* each hour⟩ **b :** to announce by tolling ⟨church bells *tolled* the death of the

---

bishop⟩ **c :** to call to or from a place or occasion ⟨bells *tolled* the congregation to church⟩
*intransitive verb*
**:** to sound with slow measured strokes ⟨the bell *tolls* solemnly⟩

**⁵toll** *noun* (15th century)
**:** the sound of a tolling bell

**toll·booth** \'tōl-ˌbüth\ *noun* [Middle English *tolbothe, tollbothe* tollbooth, town hall, jail, from *tol, toll* toll + *bothe* booth] (14th century)
**:** a booth (as on a highway or bridge) where tolls are paid

**toll call** *noun* (1928)
**:** a long-distance telephone call at charges above a local rate

**toll·gate** \'tōl-ˌgāt\ *noun* (1773)
**:** a point where the driver of a vehicle must pay a toll

**toll·house** \-ˌhaus\ *noun* (15th century)
**:** a house or booth where tolls are taken

**Toll House** *trademark*
— used for cookies containing chocolate morsels

**toll·way** \-ˌwā\ *noun* (1949)
**:** TURNPIKE 2a(1)

**Tol·tec** \'tōl-ˌtek, 'täl-\ *noun* [Spanish *tolteca*, from Nahuatl *tōltēcah*, plural of *tōltēcatl*, literally, person from *Tōllān* (now Tula de Allende, Mexico)] (1787)
**:** a member of a people that dominated central and southern Mexico prior to the Aztecs
— **Tol·tec·an** \-ən\ *adjective*

**tol·u·ene** \'täl-yə-ˌwēn\ *noun* [French *toluène*, from *tolu* balsam from the tropical American tree *Myroxylon balsamum*, from Spanish *tolú*, from Santiago de *Tolú*, Colombia] (1871)
**:** a liquid aromatic hydrocarbon $C_7H_8$ that resembles benzene but is less volatile, flammable, and toxic and is used as a solvent, in organic synthesis, and as an antiknock agent for gasoline

**to·lu·i·dine** \tə-'lü-ə-ˌdēn\ *noun* [International Scientific Vocabulary] (1850)
**:** any of three isomeric amino derivatives of toluene $C_7H_9N$ that are analogous to aniline and are used as dye intermediates

**toluidine blue** *noun* (1898)
**:** a basic thiazine dye that is related to methylene blue and is used as a biological stain

**tol·u·ol** \'täl-yə-ˌwȯl, -ˌwōl\ *noun* (circa 1848)
**:** toluene especially of commercial grade

**tol·yl** \'tä-ləl\ *noun* [International Scientific Vocabulary] (circa 1868)
**:** any of three univalent groups $CH_3C_6H_4$ derived from toluene

**tom** \'täm\ *noun* [*Tom*, nickname for *Thomas*] (1762)
**1 :** the male of various animals: as **a :** TOMCAT **b :** a male turkey
**2** *capitalized* **:** UNCLE TOM 2

**¹tom·a·hawk** \'tä-mi-ˌhȯk\ *noun* [Virginia Algonquian *tomahack*] (circa 1612)
**:** a light ax used as a missile and as a hand weapon especially by North American Indians

**²tomahawk** *transitive verb* (circa 1650)
**:** to cut, strike, or kill with a tomahawk

**to·mal·ley** \tə-'ma-lē; 'tä-ˌma-lē, -mə-lē\ *noun, plural* **-leys** [Carib *tumali* sauce of lobster livers] (circa 1666)
**:** the liver of the lobster

**Tom and Jer·ry** \ˌtäm-ən(d)-'jer-ē\ *noun* [Corinthian *Tom & Jerry* Hawthorne, characters in *Life in London* (1821) by Pierce Egan (died 1849) English sportswriter] (1845)
**:** a hot drink that is a combination of a toddy and an eggnog

**to·ma·til·lo** \ˌtō-mə-'tē-(ˌ)yō, -'tēl-(ˌ)yō\ *noun, plural* **-los** [Spanish, diminutive of *tomate*] (circa 1913)
**:** the small round pale green or yellow or purplish edible viscid fruit of a Mexican ground-cherry (*Physalis ixocarpa*); *also* **:** the plant

**to·ma·to** \tə-'mā-(ˌ)tō; *chiefly British, eastern New England, northeastern Virginia, and sometimes elsewhere in cultivated speech*

-'mä- *or* -'mä-; *chiefly Northern* -'ma-\ *noun,*
*plural* **-toes** [alteration of earlier *tomate,*
from Spanish, from Nahuatl *tomatl*] (1604)
**1 :** the usually large rounded typically red or
yellow pulpy berry of a tomato
**2 :** any of a genus (*Lycopersicon*) of South
American herbs of the nightshade family; *es-*
*pecially* **:** one (*L. lycopersicum* synonym *L.*
*esculentum*) that is more or less perennial in
its native habitat but is widely cultivated as an
annual for its edible fruit ▫
**to·ma·to·ey** \-tə-wē\ *adjective* (1972)
**1 :** of, relating to, or characteristic of a tomato
**2 :** richly flavored with tomatoes
**tomato fruitworm** *noun* (circa 1891)
**:** CORN EARWORM
**tomato hornworm** *noun* (1921)
**:** a hawkmoth (*Manduca quinquemaculata*)
whose larva is a hornworm feeding on plants
of the nightshade family and especially tobacco and tomato
**¹tomb** \'tüm\ *noun* [Middle English *tombe,*
from Anglo-French *tumbe,* from Late Latin
*tumba* sepulchral mound, from Greek *tymbos;*
perhaps akin to Latin *tumēre* to be swollen —
more at THUMB] (13th century)
**1 a :** an excavation in which a corpse is buried
**:** GRAVE **b :** a place of interment
**2 :** a house, chamber, or vault for the dead
**3 :** a building or structure resembling a tomb
(as in appearance)
— **tomb·less** \-ləs\ *adjective*
**²tomb** *transitive verb* (14th century)
**:** BURY, ENTOMB
**tom·bac** \'täm-,bak\ *noun* [French, from
Dutch *tombak,* from Malay *těmbaga* copper]
(1602)
**:** an alloy essentially of copper and zinc and
sometimes tin or arsenic that is used especially
for cheap jewelry and gilding
**tom·bo·lo** \'töm-bə-,lō, 'täm-\ *noun, plural*
**-los** [Italian, from Latin *tumulus* mound, tu-
mulus] (1899)
**:** a sand or gravel bar connecting an island
with the mainland or another island
**tom·boy** \'täm-,bȯi\ *noun* (1592)
**:** a girl who behaves in a manner usually considered boyish **:** HOYDEN
— **tom·boy·ish** \-ish\ *adjective*
— **tom·boy·ish·ness** *noun*
**tomb·stone** \'tüm-,stōn\ *noun* (1565)
**:** GRAVESTONE
**tom·cat** \'täm-,kat\ *noun* (1789)
**:** a male domestic cat
**tom·cod** \-,käd\ *noun* (1722)
**:** either of two small fishes (*Microgadus tom-*
*cod* of the Atlantic and *M. proximus* of the Pacific) of the cod family
**Tom Col·lins** \'täm-'kä-lənz\ *noun* [from the
name *Tom Collins*] (circa 1909)
**:** a collins with a base of gin
**Tom, Dick, and Har·ry** \,täm-,dik-ən(d)-
'har-ē\ *noun, plural* **Toms, Dicks, and**
**Harrys** (1815)
**:** the common man **:** ANYONE — often used
with *every* ⟨helps every *Tom, Dick, and Harry*
in need⟩
**tome** \'tōm\ *noun* [Middle French or Latin;
Middle French, from Latin *tomus,* from Greek
*tomos* section, roll of papyrus, tome, from
*temnein* to cut; akin to Middle Irish *tamnaid*
he lops, Polish *ciąć* to cut, and perhaps to Latin *tondēre* to shear] (1519)
**1 :** a volume forming part of a larger work
**2 :** BOOK; *especially* **:** a large or scholarly book
**-tome** *noun combining form* [Greek *tomos*]
**1 :** part **:** segment ⟨myo*tome*⟩
**2 :** cutting instrument ⟨micro*tome*⟩
**to·men·tose** \tō-'men-,tōs, 'tō-mən-\ *adjec-*
*tive* [New Latin *tomentosus,* from *tomentum*]
(1698)
**:** covered with densely matted hairs ⟨a *tomen-*
*tose* leaf⟩
**to·men·tum** \tō-'men-təm\ *noun, plural* **-ta**
\-tə\ [New Latin, from Latin, cushion stuffing]
(1699)

**:** pubescence composed of densely matted
woolly hairs
**¹tom·fool** \'täm-'fül\ *noun* (circa 1709)
**:** a great fool **:** BLOCKHEAD
**²tomfool** *adjective* (1819)
**:** extremely foolish, stupid, or doltish
**tom·fool·ery** \,täm-'fül-rē, -'fü-lə-\ *noun*
(1812)
**:** playful or foolish behavior
**Tom·my** \'tä-mē\ *noun, plural* **Tommies**
[*Thomas* Atkins, name used as model in official army forms] (1892)
**:** a British soldier
**Tommy At·kins** \-'at-kənz\ *noun* (1883)
**:** TOMMY
**tom·my–gun** \'tä-mē-,gən\ *transitive verb*
(1942)
**:** to shoot with a tommy gun
**tommy gun** *noun* [by shortening & alteration]
(1929)
**:** THOMPSON SUBMACHINE GUN; *broadly* **:** SUB-
MACHINE GUN
**tom·my·rot** \'tä-mē-,rät\ *noun* [English dialect
*tommy* fool + English *rot*] (1884)
**:** utter foolishness or nonsense
**to·mo·gram** \'tō-mə-,gram\ *noun* (1936)
**:** a roentgenogram made by tomography
**to·mog·ra·phy** \tō-'mä-grə-fē\ *noun* [Greek
*tomos* section + International Scientific Vocabulary *-graphy* — more at TOME] (1935)
**:** a method of producing a three-dimensional
image of the internal structures of a solid object (as the human body or the earth) by the
observation and recording of the differences in
the effects on the passage of waves of energy
impinging on those structures — compare
COMPUTED TOMOGRAPHY
— **to·mo·graph·ic** \,tō-mə-'gra-fik\ *adjec-*
*tive*
**¹to·mor·row** \tə-'mär-(,)ō, -'mȯr-\ *adverb*
[Middle English *to morgen,* from Old English
*tō morgen,* from *tō* to + *morgen* morrow,
morning — more at MORN] (13th century)
**:** on or for the day after today ⟨will do it *to-*
*morrow*⟩
**²tomorrow** *noun* (14th century)
**1 :** the day after the present ⟨the court will recess until *tomorrow*⟩
**2 :** FUTURE 1a ⟨the world of *tomorrow*⟩
**tom·pi·on** \'täm-pē-ən\ *variant of* TAMPION
**Tom Thumb** \'täm-'thəm\ *noun*
**1 :** a legendary English dwarf
**2 :** a dwarf type, race, or individual
**tom·tit** \'täm-,tit, täm-'\ *noun* [probably short
for *tomtitmouse,* from the name *Tom* + *tit-*
*mouse*] (1700)
**:** any of various small active birds
**tom–tom** \'täm-,täm, 'təm-,təm\ *noun* [Hindi
*tamṭam*] (1693)
**1 :** a usually long and narrow small-headed
drum commonly beaten with the hands
**2 :** a monotonous beating, rhythm, or rhythmical sound
**-tomy** *noun combining form* [New Latin
*-tomia,* from Greek, from *-tomos* that cuts,
from *temnein* to cut — more at TOME]
**:** incision **:** section ⟨laparo*tomy*⟩
**¹ton** \'tən\ *noun, plural* **tons** *also* **ton** [Middle
English *tunne* unit of weight or capacity —
more at TUN] (14th century)
**1 a :** a unit of internal capacity for ships equal
to 100 cubic feet — called also *register ton* **b**
**:** a unit approximately equal to the volume of
a long ton weight of seawater used in reckoning the displacement of ships and equal to 35
cubic feet **c :** a unit of volume for cargo
freight usually reckoned at 40 cubic feet —
called also *measurement ton*
**2 :** any of various units of weight: **a** — see
WEIGHT table **b :** METRIC TON
**3 :** a great quantity **:** LOT — often used in plural ⟨ate *tons* of hamburgers⟩ ⟨has *tons* of mon-
ey⟩
**²ton** \'tōⁿ\ *noun* [French, literally, tone, from
Latin *tonus*] (1765)
**1 :** the prevailing fashion **:** VOGUE

**2 :** the quality or state of being smart or fashionable
**ton·al** \'tō-n°l\ *adjective* (1776)
**1 :** of or relating to tone, tonality, or tonicity
**2 :** having tonality
— **ton·al·ly** \-n°l-ē\ *adverb*
**to·nal·i·ty** \tō-'na-lə-tē\ *noun, plural* **-ties**
(1838)
**1 :** tonal quality
**2 a :** KEY 7 **b :** the organization of all the tones
and harmonies of a piece of music in relation
to a tonic
**3 :** the arrangement or interrelation of the
tones of a work of visual art
**ton·do** \'tän-(,)dō\ *noun, plural* **ton·di** \-(,)dē\
[Italian, from *tondo* round, short for *rotondo,*
from Latin *rotundus* — more at ROTUND]
(1890)
**1 :** a circular painting
**2 :** a sculptured medallion
**¹tone** \'tōn\ *noun* [Middle English, from Latin
*tonus* tension, tone, from Greek *tonos,* literally, act of stretching; akin to Greek *teinein* to
stretch — more at THIN] (14th century)
**1 :** vocal or musical sound of a specific quality ⟨spoke in low *tones*⟩ ⟨masculine *tones*⟩; *es-*
*pecially* **:** musical sound with respect to timbre
and manner of expression
**2 a :** a sound of definite pitch and vibration **b**
**:** WHOLE STEP
**3 :** accent or inflection expressive of a mood
or emotion
**4 :** the pitch of a word often used to express
differences of meaning
**5 :** a particular pitch or change of pitch constituting an element in the intonation of a phrase
or sentence ⟨high *tone*⟩ ⟨low *tone*⟩ ⟨mid *tone*⟩
⟨low-rising *tone*⟩ ⟨falling *tone*⟩
**6 :** style or manner of expression in speaking
or writing ⟨seemed wise to adopt a conciliatory *tone*⟩
**7 a** (1) **:** color quality or value (2) **:** a tint or
shade of color **b :** the color that appreciably
modifies a hue or white or black ⟨gray walls
of greenish *tone*⟩
**8 :** the effect in painting of light and shade together with color
**9 a :** the state of a living body or of any of its
organs or parts in which the functions are

---

\ə\ abut \ᵊ\ kitten \ər\ further \a\ ash \ā\ ace
\ä\ mop, mar \au̇\ out \ch\ chin \e\ bet \ē\ easy
\g\ go \i\ hit \ī\ ice \j\ job \ŋ\ sing \ō\ go
\ȯ\ law \ȯi\ boy \th\ thin \t̲h̲\ the \ü\ loot \u̇\ foot
\y\ yet \zh\ vision *see also* Guide to Pronunciation

healthy and performed with due vigor **b :** normal tension or responsiveness to stimuli; *specifically* **:** muscular tonus
**10 a :** healthy elasticity **:** RESILIENCY **b :** general character, quality, or trend ⟨a city's upbeat *tone*⟩ **c :** frame of mind **:** MOOD

**²tone** *verb* **toned; ton·ing** (1660)
*transitive verb*
**1 :** INTONE
**2 :** to give a particular intonation or inflection to
**3 a :** to impart tone to **:** STRENGTHEN ⟨medicine to *tone* up the system⟩ **b :** to soften or reduce in intensity, color, appearance, or sound **:** MELLOW — often used with *down* **c :** to change the normal silver image of (as a photographic print) into a colored image
*intransitive verb*
**1 :** to assume a pleasing color quality or tint
**2 :** to blend or harmonize in color

**tone·arm** \'tōn-ˌärm\ *noun* (1913)
**:** the movable part of a phonograph or record player that carries the pickup and permits the needle to follow the record groove

**tone color** *noun* (1881)
**:** TIMBRE

**toned** \'tōnd\ *adjective* (15th century)
**1 :** having tone or a specified tone **:** characterized or distinguished by a tone
**2** *of paper* **:** having a slight tint

**tone–deaf** \'tōn-ˌdef\ *adjective* (1894)
**:** relatively insensitive to differences in musical pitch
**— tone deafness** *noun*

**tone language** *noun* (circa 1909)
**:** a language (as Chinese or Zulu) in which variations in tone distinguish words or phrases of different meaning that otherwise would sound alike

**tone·less** \'tōn-ləs\ *adjective* (1773)
**:** lacking in tone, modulation, or expression
**— tone·less·ly** *adverb*
**— tone·less·ness** *noun*

**to·neme** \'tō-ˌnēm\ *noun* (1923)
**:** an intonation phoneme in a tone language
**— to·ne·mic** \tō-'nē-mik\ *adjective*

**tone poem** *noun* (1902)
**:** SYMPHONIC POEM
**— tone poet** *noun*

**ton·er** \'tō-nər\ *noun* (1888)
**:** one that tones or is a source of tones: as **a :** a solution used to impart color to a silver photographic image **b :** a substance used to develop a latent xerographic image **c :** a liquid cosmetic for cleansing the skin and contracting the pores

**tone row** *noun* (1936)
**:** the chosen sequence of tones that serves as the basis for a work of serial music; *specifically* **:** TWELVE-TONE ROW

**to·net·ic** \tō-'ne-tik\ *adjective* (1922)
**1 :** relating to linguistic tones or to tone languages
**2 :** of or relating to intonation ⟨*tonetic* notation⟩
**— to·net·i·cal·ly** \-ti-k(ə-)lē\ *adverb*

**to·net·ics** \-tiks\ *noun plural but singular in construction* (1921)
**:** the use or study of linguistic tones

**to·nette** \tō-'net\ *noun* [¹*tone* + *-ette*] (1939)
**:** a simple fipple flute with a range somewhat larger than an octave that is often used in elementary music education

**ton·ey** *variant of* TONY

**¹tong** \'täŋ, 'tȯŋ\ *noun* [Chinese (Guangdong) *tòhng,* literally, hall] (1883)
**:** a secret society or fraternal organization especially of Chinese in the U.S. formerly notorious for gang warfare

**²tong** *verb* [*tongs*] (1901)
*transitive verb*
**:** to take, gather, hold, or handle with tongs ⟨*tong* oysters⟩
*intransitive verb*
**:** to use tongs especially in taking or gathering something

**— tong·er** \'täŋ-ər, 'tȯŋ-\ *noun*

**ton·ga** \'täŋ-gə\ *noun* [Hindi *tāṅgā*] (1874)
**:** a light 2-wheeled vehicle for two or four persons drawn by one horse and common in India

**Ton·gan** \'täŋ-gən *also* -ən\ *noun* (1853)
**1 :** a member of a Polynesian people of Tonga
**2 :** the Polynesian language of the Tongans
**— Tongan** *adjective*

**tongs** \'täŋz, 'tȯŋz\ *noun plural but singular or plural in construction* [Middle English *tonges,* plural of *tonge,* from Old English *tang;* akin to Old High German *zanga* tongs and perhaps to Greek *daknein* to bite] (before 12th century)
**:** any of numerous grasping devices consisting commonly of two pieces joined at one end by a pivot or hinged like scissors

**¹tongue** \'təŋ\ *noun* [Middle English *tunge,* from Old English; akin to Old High German *zunga* tongue, Latin *lingua*] (before 12th century)
**1 a :** a fleshy movable process of the floor of the mouths of most vertebrates that bears sensory end organs and small glands and functions especially in taking and swallowing food and in humans as a speech organ **b :** a part of various invertebrate animals that is analogous to the tongue
**2 :** the flesh of a tongue (as of the ox or sheep) used as food
**3 :** the power of communication through speech
**4 a :** LANGUAGE; *especially* **:** a spoken language **b :** manner or quality of utterance with respect to tone or sound, the sense of what is expressed, or the intention of the speaker ⟨she has a clever *tongue*⟩ ⟨a sharp *tongue*⟩ **c :** ecstatic usually unintelligible utterance accompanying religious excitation — usually used in plural **d :** the cry of or as if of a hound pursuing or in sight of game — used especially in the phrase *to give tongue*
**5 :** a tapering flame ⟨*tongues* of fire⟩
**6 :** a long narrow strip of land projecting into a body of water
**7 :** something resembling an animal's tongue in being elongated and fastened at one end only: as **a :** a movable pin in a buckle **b :** a metal ball suspended inside a bell so as to strike against the sides as the bell is swung **c :** the pole of a vehicle **d :** the flap under the lacing or buckles of a shoe at the throat of the vamp
**8 a :** the rib on one edge of a board that fits into a corresponding groove in an edge of another board to make a flush joint **b :** FEATHER 4
**— tongue·like** \-ˌlīk\ *adjective*

**²tongue** *verb* **tongued; tongu·ing** \'təŋ-iŋ\ (14th century)
*transitive verb*
**1** *archaic* **:** SCOLD
**2 :** to touch or lick with or as if with the tongue
**3 a :** to cut a tongue on ⟨*tongue* a board⟩ **b :** to join (as boards) by means of a tongue and groove ⟨*tongue* flooring together⟩
**4 :** to articulate (notes) by tonguing
*intransitive verb*
**1 :** to project in a tongue
**2 :** to articulate notes on a wind instrument by successively interrupting the stream of wind with the action of the tongue

**tongue and groove** *noun* (circa 1876)
**:** a joint made by a tongue on one edge of a board fitting into a corresponding groove on the edge of another board
**— tongue–and–groove** *adjective*

**tongued** \'təŋd\ *adjective* (14th century)
**:** having a tongue especially of a specified kind — often used in combination ⟨sharp-*tongued*⟩

**tongue–in–cheek** *adjective* (1933)
**:** characterized by insincerity, irony, or whimsical exaggeration

**tongue in cheek** *adverb* (circa 1934)
**:** with insincerity, irony, or whimsical exaggeration

**tongue–lash** \'təŋ-ˌlash\ *verb* [back-formation from *tongue-lashing*] (1881)
**:** CHIDE, SCOLD
**— tongue–lash·ing** *noun*

**tongue·less** \'təŋ-ləs\ *adjective* (14th century)
**1 :** having no tongue
**2 :** lacking power of speech **:** MUTE

**¹tongue–tie** \'təŋ-ˌtī\ *transitive verb* [back-formation from *tongue-tied*] (1555)
**:** to deprive of speech or the power of distinct articulation

**²tongue–tie** *noun* (circa 1852)
**:** limited mobility of the tongue due to shortness of its frenulum

**tongue–tied** \-ˌtīd\ *adjective* (1529)
**1 :** unable or disinclined to speak freely (as from shyness)
**2 :** affected with tongue-tie

**tongue twister** *noun* (1904)
**:** a word, phrase, or sentence difficult to articulate because of a succession of similar consonantal sounds (as in "twin-screw steel cruiser")

**-tonia** *noun combining form* [New Latin, from *tonus*]
**:** condition or degree of tonus ⟨myo*tonia*⟩

**¹ton·ic** \'tä-nik\ *adjective* [Greek *tonikos,* from *tonos* tension, tone] (1649)
**1 a :** characterized by tonus ⟨*tonic* contraction of muscle⟩; *also* **:** marked by prolonged muscular contraction ⟨*tonic* convulsions⟩ **b :** producing or adapted to produce healthy muscular condition and reaction of organs (as muscles)
**2 a :** increasing or restoring physical or mental tone **:** REFRESHING **b :** yielding a tonic substance
**3 :** relating to or based on the first tone of a scale ⟨*tonic* harmony⟩
**4** *of a syllable* **:** bearing a principal stress or accent
**5 :** of or relating to speech tones or to languages using them to distinguish words otherwise identical
**— ton·i·cal·ly** \'tä-ni-k(ə-)lē\ *adverb*

**²tonic** *noun* (1799)
**1 a :** an agent (as a drug) that increases body tone **b :** one that invigorates, restores, refreshes, or stimulates ⟨a day in the country was a *tonic* for him⟩ **c :** a liquid preparation for the scalp or hair **d** *chiefly New England* **:** a carbonated flavored beverage **e :** TONIC WATER
**2 :** the first tone of a diatonic scale **:** KEYNOTE
**3 :** a voiced sound

**tonic accent** *noun* (1867)
**1 :** relative phonetic prominence (as from greater stress or higher pitch) of a spoken syllable or word
**2 :** accent depending on pitch rather than stress

**to·nic·i·ty** \tō-'ni-sə-tē\ *noun* (1824)
**1 :** the property of possessing tone; *especially* **:** healthy vigor of body or mind
**2 :** muscular tonus

**tonic sol–fa** *noun* (1852)
**:** a system of solmization based on key relationships that replaces the normal notation with sol-fa syllables or their initials

**tonic water** *noun* (1926)
**:** a carbonated beverage flavored with a small amount of quinine, lemon, and lime

**¹to·night** \tə-'nīt\ *adverb* (before 12th century)
**:** on this present night or the night following this present day ⟨will do it *tonight*⟩

**²tonight** *noun* (14th century)
**:** the present night or the night following this present day

**ton·ka bean** \'täŋ-kə-\ *noun* [probably from Tupi *tonka*] (1796)
**:** the coumarin-containing seed of any of several tropical American leguminous trees (genus *Dipteryx*) that is used in perfumes and as an artificial vanilla flavoring; *also* **:** a tree bearing tonka beans

**ton·nage** \'tə-nij\ *noun* [in sense 1, from Middle English, from Middle French, from *tonne* tun; in other senses, from ¹*ton* — more at TUNNEL] (15th century)

**1 :** a duty formerly levied on every tun of wine imported into England
**2 a :** a duty or impost on vessels based on cargo capacity **b :** a duty on goods per ton transported
**3 :** ships in terms of the total number of tons registered or carried or of their carrying capacity
**4 a :** the cubical content of a merchant ship in units of 100 cubic feet **b :** the displacement of a warship
**5 a :** total weight in tons shipped, carried, or produced **b :** impressively large amount or weight

**tonne** \'tən\ *noun* [French, from *tonne* tun, from Old French — more at TUNNEL] (1877)
**:** METRIC TON

**ton·neau** \'tä-ˌnō, tə-'nō\ *noun, plural* **tonneaus** [French, literally, tun, from Old French *tonel* — more at TUNNEL] (1901)
**1 :** the rear seating compartment of an automobile; *also* **:** the entire seating compartment
**2 :** a shape of watch case or dial resembling a barrel in profile

**ton·ner** \'tə-nər\ *noun* (1851)
**:** an object (as a ship) having a specified tonnage — used in combination ⟨a thousand-*tonner*⟩

**to·nom·e·ter** \tō-'nä-mə-tər\ *noun* [Greek *tonos* tone + English *-meter*] (1725)
**1 :** an instrument or device for determining the exact pitch or the vibration rate of tones
**2 :** an instrument for measuring tension or pressure and especially intraocular pressure
— **to·nom·e·try** \tō-'nä-mə-trē\ *noun*

**to·no·plast** \'tō-nə-ˌplast\ *noun* [International Scientific Vocabulary *tono-* (from Greek *tonos* tension) + *-plast* — more at TONE] (circa 1888)
**:** a semipermeable membrane surrounding a plant-cell vacuole

**ton·sil** \'tän(t)-səl\ *noun* [Latin *tonsillae*, plural, *tonsils*] (1601)
**1 :** either of a pair of prominent masses of lymphoid tissue that lie one on each side of the throat between the anterior and posterior pillars of the fauces
**2 :** any of various masses of lymphoid tissue that are similar to tonsils
— **ton·sil·lar** \'tän(t)-s(ə-)lər\ *adjective*

**tonsill-** *combining form* [Latin *tonsillae*]
**:** tonsil ⟨*tonsillectomy*⟩

**ton·sil·lec·to·my** \ˌtän(t)-sə-'lek-tə-mē\ *noun, plural* **-mies** (1899)
**:** the surgical removal of the tonsils

**ton·sil·li·tis** \-'lī-təs\ *noun* [New Latin] (1801)
**:** inflammation of the tonsils

**ton·so·ri·al** \tän-'sōr-ē-əl, -'sȯr-\ *adjective* [Latin *tonsorius*, from *tondēre*] (1813)
**:** of or relating to a barber or the work of a barber

**¹ton·sure** \'tän(t)-shər\ *noun* [Middle English, from Medieval Latin *tonsura*, from Latin, act of shearing, from *tonsus*, past participle of *tondēre* to shear — more at TOME] (14th century)
**1 :** the Roman Catholic or Eastern rite of admission to the clerical state by the clipping or shaving of a portion of the head
**2 :** the shaven crown or patch worn by monks and other clerics
**3 :** a bald spot resembling a tonsure

**²tonsure** *transitive verb* **ton·sured; ton·sur·ing** \'tän(t)-sh(ə-)riŋ\ (1706)
**:** to shave the head of; *especially* **:** to confer the tonsure upon

**ton·tine** \'tän-ˌtēn, tän-'\ *noun* [French, from Lorenzo *Tonti* (died 1695) Italian banker] (1765)
**:** a joint financial arrangement whereby the participants usually contribute equally to a prize that is awarded entirely to the participant who survives all the others

**to·nus** \'tō-nəs\ *noun* [New Latin, from Latin, tension, tone] (1876)
**:** TONE 9a; *especially* **:** a state of partial contraction characteristic of normal muscle

**tony** \'tō-nē\ *adjective* **ton·i·er; -est** (1877)
**:** marked by an aristocratic or high-toned manner or style ⟨*tony* private schools⟩

**To·ny** \'tō-nē\ *noun, plural* **Tonys** [*Tony*, nickname of Antoinette Perry (died 1946) American actress & producer] (1947)
**:** a medallion awarded annually by a professional organization for notable achievement in the theater

**too** \'tü\ *adverb* [Middle English, from Old English *tō* to, too — more at TO] (before 12th century)
**1 :** BESIDES, ALSO ⟨sell the house and furniture *too*⟩
**2 a :** to an excessive degree **:** EXCESSIVELY ⟨*too* large a house for us⟩ **b :** to such a degree as to be regrettable ⟨this time he has gone *too* far⟩ **c :** VERY ⟨didn't seem *too* interested⟩
**3 :** so 2d ⟨"I didn't do it." "You did *too*."⟩

**took** *past of* TAKE

**¹tool** \'tül\ *noun* [Middle English, from Old English *tōl*; akin to Old English *tawian* to prepare for use — more at TAW] (before 12th century)
**1 a :** a handheld device that aids in accomplishing a task **b** (1) **:** the cutting or shaping part in a machine or machine tool (2) **:** a machine for shaping metal **:** MACHINE TOOL
**2 a :** something (as an instrument or apparatus) used in performing an operation or necessary in the practice of a vocation or profession ⟨a scholar's books are his *tools*⟩ **b :** a means to an end ⟨a book's cover can be a marketing *tool*⟩ **c :** PENIS — often considered vulgar
**3 :** one that is used or manipulated by another
**4** *plural* **:** natural ability ⟨has all the *tools*⟩
**synonym** see IMPLEMENT

**²tool** (1812)
*transitive verb*
**1 a :** to cause (a vehicle) to go **:** DRIVE **b :** to convey in a vehicle
**2 :** to shape, form, or finish with a tool; *especially* **:** to letter or ornament (as leather or gold) by means of hand tools
**3 :** to equip (as a plant or industry) with tools, machines, and instruments for production
*intransitive verb*
**1 :** DRIVE, RIDE
**2 :** to equip a plant or industry with the means (as machines, machine tools, and instruments) of production — often used with *up*

**³tool** *noun* (1881)
**:** a design (as on the binding of a book) made by tooling

**tool·box** \'tül-ˌbäks\ *noun* (1832)
**:** a chest for tools

**tool·hold·er** \-ˌhōl-dər\ *noun* (circa 1876)
**:** a short steel bar having a shank at one end by which it is clamped to a machine and a clamp at the other end to hold small interchangeable cutting bits

**tool·house** \-ˌhau̇s\ *noun* (1818)
**:** TOOLSHED

**tool·mak·er** \'tül-ˌmā-kər\ *noun* (1844)
**:** one that makes tools; *especially* **:** a machinist who specializes in the construction, repair, maintenance, and calibration of the tools, jigs, fixtures, and instruments of a machine shop

**tool·mak·ing** \-kiŋ\ *noun* (1893)
**:** the action, process, or art of making tools; *also* **:** the trade of a toolmaker

**tool·room** \'tül-ˌrüm, -ˌru̇m\ *noun* (1878)
**:** a room where tools are kept; *especially* **:** a room in a machine shop in which tools are made, stored, and issued for use by workers

**tool·shed** \-ˌshed\ *noun* (1840)
**:** an outbuilding for storing tools

**tools of ignorance** [from the notion that a smart athlete would not play such a grueling position] (1939)
**:** a baseball catcher's equipment

**tool subject** *noun* (1925)

**:** a subject studied to gain competence in a skill used in other subjects

**toom** \'tüm\ *adjective* [Middle English, from Old English *tōm* — more at TEEM] (before 12th century)
*chiefly Scottish* **:** EMPTY

**toon** \'tün\ *noun* [Hindi *tūn*, from Sanskrit *tunna*] (1810)
**:** a southeast Asian and Australian tree (*Cedrela toona*) of the mahogany family with fragrant dark red wood and flowers that yield a dye; *also* **:** its wood

**¹toot** \'tüt\ *verb* [probably imitative] (circa 1510)
*intransitive verb*
**1 a :** to sound a short blast ⟨the horn *tooted*⟩ **b :** to sound a note or call suggesting the short blast of a wind instrument
**2 :** to blow or sound an instrument (as a horn) especially so as to produce short blasts
*transitive verb*
**:** to cause to sound ⟨*toot* a whistle⟩
— **toot·er** *noun*

**²toot** *noun* (1641)
**:** a short blast (as on a horn); *also* **:** a sound resembling such a blast

**³toot** *noun* [Scots *toot* to drink heavily] (circa 1790)
**:** a drinking bout **:** SPREE

**tooth** \'tüth\ *noun, plural* **teeth** \'tēth\ [Middle English, from Old English *tōth*; akin to Old High German *zand* tooth, Latin *dent-, dens*, Greek *odont-, odous*] (before 12th century)
**1 a :** one of the hard bony appendages that are borne on the jaws or in many of the lower vertebrates on other bones in the walls of the mouth or pharynx and serve especially for the prehension and mastication of food and as weapons of offense and defense **b :** any of various usually hard and sharp processes especially about the mouth of an invertebrate
**2 :** TASTE, LIKING
**3 :** a projection resembling or

tooth 1a: *A* outside of a molar: *1* crown, *2* neck, *3* roots; *B* cross section of a molar: *1* enamel, *2* dentin, *3* pulp, *4* cementum, *5* gum; *C* dentition of adult human, upper; *D* dentition of adult human, lower: *1* incisors, *2* canines, *3* bicuspids, *4* molars

suggesting the tooth of an animal in shape, arrangement, or action ⟨a saw *tooth*⟩: as **a :** any of the regular projections on the circumference or sometimes the face of a wheel that engage with corresponding projections on another wheel especially to transmit force **:** COG **b :** a small sharp-pointed marginal lobe or process on a plant
**4 a :** something that injures, tortures, devours, or destroys **b** *plural* **:** effective means of enforcement
**5 :** a roughness of surface produced by mechanical or artificial means
— **tooth·like** \'tüth-ˌlīk\ *adjective*
— **in the teeth of 1 :** in or into direct contact or collision with ⟨found themselves sailing *in the teeth of* a hurricane —*Current Biography*⟩ **2 :** in direct opposition to ⟨rule had . . . been imposed by conquest *in the teeth of* obstinate resistance —A. J. Toynbee⟩

**— to the teeth :** FULLY, COMPLETELY ⟨armed *to the teeth*⟩

**tooth·ache** \'tüth-,āk\ *noun* (14th century)
: pain in or about a tooth

**tooth and nail** *adverb* (1550)
: with every available means : ALL OUT ⟨fight *tooth and nail*⟩

**tooth·brush** \'tüth-,brəsh\ *noun* (1690)
: a brush for cleaning the teeth

**tooth·brush·ing** *noun* (1920)
: the action of using a toothbrush to clean teeth

**toothed** \'tütht, *uncompounded also* 'tü-thəd\ *adjective* (14th century)
: having teeth especially of a specified kind or number — often used in combination ⟨buck-*toothed*⟩

**toothed whale** \'tütht-, 'tü-thəd-\ *noun* (1843)
: any of a suborder (Odontoceti) of cetaceans (as a dolphin, porpoise, or killer whale) bearing usually numerous simple conical teeth — compare BALEEN WHALE

**tooth fairy** *noun* (1962)
: a fairy believed by children to leave money while they sleep in exchange for a tooth that has come out

**tooth·less** \'tüth-ləs\ *adjective* (14th century)
**1 :** having no teeth
**2 a :** lacking in sharpness or bite ⟨spoke in *toothless* generalities —Arthur Hepner⟩ **b** : lacking in means of enforcement or coercion : INEFFECTUAL

**tooth·paste** \-,pāst\ *noun* (1832)
: a paste for cleaning the teeth

**tooth·pick** \-,pik\ *noun* (15th century)
: a pointed instrument (as a slender tapering piece of wood) for removing food particles lodged between the teeth

**tooth powder** *noun* (1542)
: a powder for cleaning the teeth

**tooth shell** *noun* (circa 1711)
: any of a class (Scaphopoda) of burrowing marine mollusks with a tapering tubular shell; *also* : this shell

**tooth·some** \'tüth-səm\ *adjective* (1551)
**1 a :** AGREEABLE, ATTRACTIVE **b :** sexually attractive ⟨a *toothsome* blonde⟩
**2 :** of palatable flavor and pleasing texture : DELICIOUS ⟨crisp *toothsome* fried chicken⟩
**synonym** see PALATABLE
**— tooth·some·ly** *adverb*
**— tooth·some·ness** *noun*

**tooth·wort** \-,wərt, -,wȯrt\ *noun* (1597)
**1 :** a European parasitic plant (*Lathraea squamaria*) of the broomrape family having a rootstock covered with tooth-shaped scales
**2 :** any of various cresses (genus *Dentaria*) including several cultivated for their showy flowers

**toothy** \'tü-thē\ *adjective* **tooth·i·er; -est** (1530)
**1 :** having or showing prominent teeth ⟨*toothy* grin⟩
**2 :** TOOTHSOME 2
**— tooth·i·ly** \-thə-lē\ *adverb*

**too·tle** \'tü-t°l\ *verb* **too·tled; too·tling** \'tüt-liŋ, 'tü-t°l-iŋ\ [frequentative of ¹*toot*] (1820)
*intransitive verb*
**1 :** to toot gently, repeatedly, or continuously
**2 :** to drive or move along in a leisurely manner
*transitive verb*
: to toot continuously on
**— tootle** *noun*
**— too·tler** \'tüt-lər, 'tü-t°l-ər\ *noun*

**too–too** \'tü-'tü\ *adjective* (1881)
**1 :** going beyond the bounds of convention, good taste, or common sense : EXTREME
**2 :** LA-DI-DA

**toot·sie** \'tút-sē\ *noun* [origin unknown] (1905)
**1 :** DEAR, SWEETHEART
**2 :** PROSTITUTE

**toot·sy** *also* **toot·sie** \'tút-sē\ *noun, plural* **tootsies** [baby-talk alteration of *foot*] (1854)
: FOOT

**¹top** \'täp\ *noun* [Middle English, from Old English; akin to Old High German *zopf* tip, tuft of hair] (before 12th century)
**1 a** (1) : the highest point, level, or part of something : SUMMIT, CROWN (2) : the head or top of the head — used especially in the phrase *top to toe* (3) : the head of a plant and especially one with edible roots ⟨beet *tops*⟩ (4) : a garment worn on the upper body **b** (1) : the highest or uppermost region or part (2) : the upper end, edge, or surface
**2 :** a fitted, integral, or attached part or unit serving as an upper piece, lid, or covering
**3 a :** a platform surrounding the head of a lower mast that serves to spread the topmast rigging, strengthen the mast, and furnish a standing place for men aloft **b** : a comparable part of the superstructure; *especially* : such a part on a warship used as a fire-control station or antiaircraft gun platform
**4 a :** the highest degree or pitch conceivable or attained : ACME, PINNACLE **b** : the loudest or highest range of a sound
**5 a :** the part that is nearest in space or time to the source or beginning **b** : the first half of an inning in baseball
**6 a** (1) : the highest position (as in rank or achievement) (2) : a person or thing at the top **b** *plural* : aces and kings in a hand or the three highest honors in a suit
**7 :** the choicest part : CREAM, PICK
**8 :** a forward spin given to a ball (as in golf or billiards) by striking it on or near the top or above the center; *also* : the stroke so given
**— topped** \'täpt\ *adjective*
**— off the top of one's head :** in an impromptu manner ⟨sat down and wrote the . . . story *off the top of his head* —Jerome Beatty, Jr.⟩
**— on top of 1 a :** in control of ⟨acted like a man *on top of* his job —*Newsweek*⟩ **b** : informed about ⟨tried to keep *on top of* new developments⟩ **2 :** in sudden and unexpected proximity to ⟨the deadline was *on top of* them⟩ **3 :** in addition to
**— on top of the world :** in a position of eminent success, happiness, or fame
**— over the top :** beyond the bounds of what is expected, usual, normal, or appropriate

**²top** *verb* **topped; top·ping** (1509)
*transitive verb*
**1 :** to remove or cut the top of: as **a** : to shorten or remove the top of (a plant) : PINCH 1b **b** : to remove the most volatile parts from (as crude petroleum)
**2 a :** to cover with a top or on the top : provide, form, or serve as a top for **b** : to supply with a decorative or protective finish or final touch **c** : to resupply or refill to capacity — usually used with *off* ⟨*topped* off the tank⟩ **d** : to complete the basic structure of (as a highrise building) by putting on a cap or uppermost section — usually used with *out* or *off* **e** : to bring to an end or climax — usually used with *off* ⟨the event was *topped* off with a relay race —Paula Rodenas⟩
**3 a :** to be or become higher than : OVERTOP ⟨*tops* the previous record⟩ **b** : to be superior to : EXCEL, SURPASS **c** : to gain ascendancy over : DOMINATE
**4 a :** to rise to, reach, or be at the top of **b** : to go over the top of : CLEAR, SURMOUNT
**5 :** to strike (a ball) above the center thereby imparting topspin
*intransitive verb*
**1 :** to make an end, finish, or conclusion
**2 :** to reach a summit or crest — usually used with *off* or *out*

**³top** *adjective* (1593)
**1 :** of, relating to, or being at the top : UPPERMOST
**2 :** CHIEF, LEADING ⟨one of the world's *top* journalists⟩

**3 :** of the highest quality, amount, or degree ⟨*top* value⟩ ⟨*top* form⟩
**4 :** having a quantum characteristic whose existence was postulated on the basis of the discovery of the bottom quark ⟨*top* quark⟩

**⁴top** *noun* [Middle English, from Old English, plaything] (14th century)
: a commonly cylindrical or conoidal device that has a tapering usually steel-shod point on which it is made to spin and that is used especially as a toy

**top-** *or* **topo-** *combining form* [Middle English, from Late Latin, from Greek, from *topos*]
: place : locality ⟨*top*ology⟩ ⟨*top*onymy⟩

**to·paz** \'tō-,paz\ *noun* [Middle English *topace*, from Old French, from Latin *topazus*, from Greek *topazos*] (13th century)
**1 a :** a mineral that is essentially a silicate of aluminum and usually occurs in orthorhombic translucent or transparent crystals or in white translucent masses **b** : a usually yellow to brownish yellow transparent mineral topaz used as a gem **c** : a yellow sapphire **d** : a yellow quartz
**2 :** either of two large brilliantly colored South American hummingbirds (*Topaza pella* and *T. pyra*)

**top banana** *noun* [from a burlesque routine involving three comedians in which the one that gets the punch line also gets a banana] (1952)
: the leading comedian in a burlesque show; *broadly* : KINGPIN 2

**top billing** *noun* (1945)
**1 :** prominent emphasis, featuring, or advertising
**2 :** the position at the top of a theatrical bill usually featuring the star's name

**top boot** *noun* (1768)
: a high boot often with light-colored leather bands around the upper part

**top·coat** \'täp-,kōt\ *noun* (1804)
**1 :** a lightweight overcoat
**2 :** OVERCOAT 2

**top·cross** \-,krȯs\ *noun* (1890)
: a cross between a superior or purebred male and inferior female stock to improve the average quality of the progeny; *also* : the product of such a cross

**top dog** *noun* (1900)
: a person or group in a position of authority especially through victory in a hard-fought competition

**top dollar** *noun* (1970)
: the highest amount being paid for a commodity or service ⟨willing to pay *top dollar* to get them —Dean Failey⟩

**top–down** \'täp-'daún\ *adjective* [from the phrase *from the top down*] (1941)
**1 :** controlled, directed, or instituted from the top level ⟨a *top-down* corporate structure⟩
**2 :** proceeding by breaking large general aspects (as of a problem) into smaller more detailed constituents : working from the general to the specific ⟨*top-down* programming⟩ ⟨*top-down* design⟩

**top drawer** *noun* (1905)
: the highest level of society, authority, or excellence
**— top–draw·er** \-'drȯ(-ə)r\ *adjective*

**top–dress** \'täp-,dres\ *transitive verb* (1733)
: to apply material to (as land or a road) without working it in; *especially* : to scatter fertilizer over (land)

**top–dress·ing** \-,dre-siŋ\ *noun* (1744)
: a material used to top-dress soil

**¹tope** \'tōp\ *intransitive verb* **toped; top·ing** [obsolete English *tope*, interjection used to wish good health before drinking] (1667)
: to drink liquor to excess

**²tope** *noun* [origin unknown] (1686)
: a small cosmopolitan shark (*Galeorhinus galeus*) with a liver very rich in vitamin A

**³tope** *noun* [perhaps from Panjabi *ṭop* hat] (1815)

: STUPA

**to·pee** *or* **to·pi** \tō-'pē, 'tō-(‚)pē\ *noun* [Hindi *topī*] (1835)
: a lightweight helmet-shaped hat made of pith or cork

**top·er** \'tō-pər\ *noun* (1673)
: one that topes; *especially* : DRUNKARD

**top·flight** \'täp-'flīt\ *adjective* (1931)
: of, relating to, or being the highest level of achievement, excellence, or eminence
— **top flight** *noun*

**¹Top 40** *noun plural* (1966)
: the forty best-selling phonograph records for a given period

**²Top 40** *adjective* (1966)
: constituting, playing, listing, or relating to the Top 40 ⟨*Top 40* hits⟩ ⟨*Top 40* stations⟩ ⟨*Top 40* charts⟩

**top·ful** *or* **top·full** \'täp-'fùl\ *adjective* (1553)
: BRIMFUL

**¹top·gal·lant** \(‚)täp-'ga-lənt, tə-'ga-\ *adjective* [¹*top* + ²*gallant*] (1514)
: of, relating to, or being a part next above the topmast and below the royal mast ⟨*topgallant* sails⟩ ⟨the *topgallant* mast⟩

**²topgallant** *noun* (1581)
**1** *archaic* : the topmost point : SUMMIT ⟨the high *topgallant* of my joy —Shakespeare⟩
**2** : a topgallant mast or sail

**top gun** *noun* (1976)
: one who is at the top (as in ability, rank, or prestige)

**top–ham·per** \'täp-'ham-pər\ *noun* (1791)
**1** : matter or weight (as spars or rigging) in the upper part of a ship
**2** : unnecessary cumbersome matter

**top hat** *noun* (1881)
: a tall-crowned hat usually of beaver or silk

**top–heavy** \'täp-‚he-vē\ *adjective* (circa 1533)
**1** : having the top part too heavy for the lower part
**2** : having too high a proportion of administrators ⟨a *top-heavy* bureaucracy⟩
**3** : oversupplied with one element at the expense of others : lacking balance ⟨a novel *top-heavy* with description⟩

**To·phet** \'tō-fət\ *noun* [Middle English, shrine south of ancient Jerusalem where human sacrifices were performed to Moloch in Jeremiah 7:31, Gehenna, from Late Latin *Topheth,* from Hebrew *tōpheth*] (14th century)
: HELL, GEHENNA

**top–hole** \'täp-'hōl\ *adjective* (1908)
*chiefly British* : EXCELLENT, FIRST-CLASS

**to·phus** \'tō-fəs\ *noun, plural* **to·phi** \'tō-‚fī, -‚fē\ [Latin, tufa] (1607)
: a deposit of urates in tissues (as cartilage) characteristic of gout

**to·pi** \'tō-pē\ *noun, plural* **topi** *or* **topis** [perhaps from Swahili] (1894)
: a sub-Saharan antelope (*Damaliscis lunatus* synonym *D. korrigum*) having a glossy reddish brown coat with purplish black and yellowish markings

**¹to·pi·ary** \'tō-pē-‚er-ē\ *adjective* [Latin *topiarius,* from *topia* ornamental gardening, irregular from Greek *topos* place] (1592)
: of, relating to, or being the practice or art of training, cutting, and trimming trees or shrubs into odd or ornamental shapes; *also* : characterized by such work

**²topiary** *noun, plural* **-ar·ies** (1908)
**1** : topiary art or gardening; *also* : a topiary garden
**2 a** : a plant shaped by topiary art **b** : topiary plants

**top·ic** \'tä-pik\ *noun* [Latin *Topica* Topics (work by Aristotle), from Greek *Topika,* from *topika,* neuter plural of *topikos* of a place, of a topos, from *topos* place, topos] (1603)
**1 a** : one of the general forms of argument employed in probable reasoning **b** : ARGUMENT, REASON
**2 a** : a heading in an outlined argument or exposition **b** : the subject of a discourse or of a section of a discourse

**top·i·cal** \-pi-kəl\ *adjective* (1588)
**1** : designed for or involving local application and action (as on the body) ⟨a *topical* anesthetic⟩ ⟨a *topical* remedy⟩
**2 a** : of, relating to, or arranged by topics ⟨set down in *topical* form⟩ **b** : referring to the topics of the day or place : of local or temporary interest ⟨a *topical* novel⟩ ⟨*topical* references⟩
— **top·i·cal·ly** \-k(ə-)lē\ *adverb*

**top·i·cal·i·ty** \‚tä-pə-'ka-lə-tē\ *noun, plural* **-ties** (1904)
**1** : the quality or state of being topical
**2** : an item of topical interest

**topic sentence** *noun* (1885)
: a sentence that states the main thought of a paragraph or of a larger unit of discourse and is usually placed at or near the beginning

**top·kick** \'täp-‚kik\ *noun* (1918)
: FIRST SERGEANT 1

**top·knot** \-‚nät\ *noun* (circa 1688)
**1** : an ornament (as a knot of ribbons or a pompom) forming a headdress or worn as part of a coiffure
**2** : a crest of feathers or tuft of hair on the top of the head

**top·less** \-ləs\ *adjective* (1589)
**1** *archaic* : so high as to reach up beyond sight ⟨and burnt the *topless* towers of Ilium —Christopher Marlowe⟩
**2** : being without a top
**3 a** : wearing no clothing on the upper body **b** : featuring topless waitresses or entertainers ⟨*topless* bars⟩ **c** : being a place where topless women are permitted ⟨a *topless* beach⟩
— **top·less·ness** \-nəs\ *noun*

**top·line** \-‚līn\ *noun* (circa 1909)
: the outline of the top of the body of an animal (as a dog or horse)

**top·lofty** \'täp-‚lòf-tē\ *also* **top·loft·i·cal** \täp-'lòf-ti-kəl\ *adjective* [probably from the phrase *top loft*] (1823)
: very superior in air or attitude
— **top·loft·i·ly** \täp-'lòf-tə-lē\ *adverb*
— **top·loft·i·ness** \'täp-‚lòf-tē-nəs\ *noun*

**top·mast** \'täp-‚mast, -məst\ *noun* (15th century)
: the mast that is next above the lower mast and is topmost in a fore-and-aft rig

**top milk** *noun* (1891)
: the upper layer of milk in a container enriched by whatever cream has risen

**top·min·now** \'täp-‚mi-(‚)nō\ *noun* (1884)
: any of several live-bearers (family Poeciliidae) or killifish (family Cyprinodontidae)

**top·most** \'täp-‚mōst\ *adjective* (1697)
: highest of all : UPPERMOST

**top–notch** \-'näch\ *adjective* (1900)
: of the highest quality : FIRST-RATE
— **top–notch·er** \-'nä-chər\ *noun*

**to·po·cen·tric** \‚tä-pə-'sen-trik, ‚tō-\ *adjective* (circa 1942)
: relating to, measured from, or as if observed from a particular point on the earth's surface
: having or relating to such a point as origin ⟨*topocentric* coordinates⟩ — compare GEOCENTRIC

**to·pog·ra·pher** \tə-'pä-grə-fər\ *noun* (1603)
: one skilled in topography

**to·po·graph·ic** \‚tä-pə-'gra-fik, ‚tō-\ *adjective* (1632)
: of, relating to, or concerned with topography ⟨*topographic* maps⟩

**to·po·graph·i·cal** \-fi-kəl\ *adjective* (circa 1576)
**1** : TOPOGRAPHIC
**2** : of, relating to, or concerned with the artistic representation of a particular locality ⟨a *topographical* poem⟩ ⟨*topographical* painting⟩
— **to·po·graph·i·cal·ly** \-k(ə-)lē\ *adverb*

**to·pog·ra·phy** \tə-'pä-grə-fē\ *noun* [Middle English *topographie,* from Late Latin *topographia,* from Greek, from *topographein* to describe a place, from *topos* place + *graphein* to write — more at CARVE] (15th century)
**1 a** : the art or practice of graphic delineation in detail usually on maps or charts of natural

and man-made features of a place or region especially in a way to show their relative positions and elevations **b** : topographical surveying
**2 a** : the configuration of a surface including its relief and the position of its natural and man-made features **b** : the physical or natural features of an object or entity and their structural relationships

**to·po·log·i·cal** \‚tä-pə-'lä-ji-kəl\ *adjective* (1715)
**1** : of or relating to topology
**2** : being or involving properties unaltered under a homeomorphism ⟨continuity and connectedness are *topological* properties⟩
— **to·po·log·i·cal·ly** \-k(ə-)lē\ *adverb*

**topological group** *noun* (1946)
: a mathematical group which is also a topological space, whose multiplicative operation is continuous such that given any neighborhood of a product there exist neighborhoods of the elements composing the product with the property that any pair of elements representing each of these neighborhoods form a product belonging to the given neighborhood, and whose operation of taking inverses is continuous such that for any neighborhood of the inverse of an element there exists a neighborhood of the element itself in which every element has its inverse in the other neighborhood

**topologically equivalent** *adjective* (1915)
: related by a homeomorphism

**topological space** *noun* (1926)
: a set with a collection of subsets satisfying the conditions that both the empty set and the set itself belong to the collection, the union of any number of the subsets is also an element of the collection, and the intersection of any finite number of the subsets is an element of the collection

**topological transformation** *noun* (1946)
: HOMEOMORPHISM

**to·pol·o·gy** \tə-'pä-lə-jē, tä-\ *noun, plural* **-gies** [International Scientific Vocabulary] (1850)
**1** : topographic study of a particular place; *specifically* : the history of a region as indicated by its topography
**2 a** (1) : a branch of mathematics concerned with those properties of geometric configurations (as point sets) which are unaltered by elastic deformations (as a stretching or a twisting) that are homeomorphisms (2) : the set of all open subsets of a topological space **b** : CONFIGURATION ⟨*topology* of a molecule⟩ ⟨*topology* of a magnetic field⟩
— **to·pol·o·gist** \-jist\ *noun*

**top·o·nym** \'tä-pə-‚nim, 'tō-\ *noun* [International Scientific Vocabulary, back-formation from *toponymy*] (1899)
: PLACE-NAME

**top·o·nym·ic** \‚tä-pə-'ni-mik, ‚tō-\ *adjective* (1896)
: of or relating to toponyms or toponymy
— **top·o·nym·i·cal** \-mi-kəl\ *adjective*

**to·pon·y·my** \tə-'pä-nə-mē, tō-\ *noun* [International Scientific Vocabulary, from *top-* + Greek *onyma, onoma* name — more at NAME] (1876)
: the place-names of a region or language or especially the etymological study of them
— **to·pon·y·mist** \-mist\ *noun*

**to·pos** \'tō-‚päs, 'tä-\ *noun, plural* **to·poi** \-‚pòi\ [Greek, short for *koinos topos,* literally, common place] (1936)
: a traditional or conventional literary or rhetorical theme or topic

**top·per** \'tä-pər\ *noun* (1688)
**1** : one that puts on or takes off tops

\ə\ abut \ᵊ\ kitten \ər\ further \a\ ash \ā\ ace \ä\ mop, mar \aù\ out \ch\ chin \e\ bet \ē\ easy \g\ go \i\ hit \ī\ ice \j\ job \ŋ\ sing \ō\ go \ò\ law \òi\ boy \th\ thin \th\ the \ü\ loot \ù\ foot \y\ yet \zh\ vision *see also* Guide to Pronunciation

**2 :** one that is at or on the top
**3 a :** SILK HAT **b :** OPERA HAT
**4 :** something (as a joke) that caps everything preceding
**5 :** a woman's usually short and loose-fitting lightweight outer coat
**¹top·ping** \'tä-piŋ\ *noun* (14th century)
**1 :** something that forms a top; *especially* **:** a garnish (as a sauce, bread crumbs, or whipped cream) placed on top of a food for flavor or decoration
**2 :** the action of one that tops
**3 :** something removed by topping
**²topping** *adjective* (circa 1685)
**1 :** highest in rank or eminence
**2** *New England* **:** PROUD, ARROGANT
**3** *chiefly British* **:** EXCELLENT
**top·ple** \'tä-pəl\ *verb* **top·pled; top·pling** \-p(ə-)liŋ\ [frequentative of ²*top*] (1590)
*intransitive verb*
**:** to fall from or as if from being top-heavy
*transitive verb*
**1 :** to cause to topple
**2 a :** OVERTHROW 2 **b :** DEFEAT 3
**top round** *noun* (1903)
**:** meat from the inner part of a round of beef
**¹tops** \'täps\ *adjective* [plural of ¹*top*] (1935)
**:** topmost in quality, ability, popularity, or importance — used predicatively ⟨is *tops* in his field⟩
**²tops** *adverb* (1956)
**:** at the very most ⟨will cost $50, *tops*⟩
**top·sail** \'täp-,sāl, -səl\ *also* **top-s'l** \-səl\ *noun* (14th century)
**1 :** the sail next above the lowermost sail on a mast in a square-rigged ship
**2 :** the sail set above and sometimes on the gaff in a fore-and-aft rigged ship
**top secret** *adjective* (1944)
**1 :** protected by a high degree of secrecy ⟨a *top secret* weapon⟩ ⟨a *top secret* meeting⟩
**2 a :** containing or being information whose unauthorized disclosure could result in exceptionally grave danger to the nation ⟨*top secret* messages⟩ — compare CONFIDENTIAL, SECRET
**b :** of or relating to top secret documents ⟨a *top secret* clearance⟩
**top sergeant** *noun* (1898)
**:** FIRST SERGEANT 1
**top–shelf** \'täp-'shelf\ *adjective* (circa 1892)
**:** of the best quality
**¹top·side** \'täp-'sīd\ *noun* (1815)
**1** *plural* **:** the top portion of the outer surface of a ship on each side above the waterline
**2 :** the highest level of authority
**3 :** the upper portion of the ionosphere
**²topside** *adverb or adjective* (1873)
**1 :** to or on the top or surface
**2 :** in a position of authority
**3 :** on deck
**Top–Sid·er** \'täp-,sī-dər\ *trademark*
**—** used for a low casual shoe having a rubber sole
**top·soil** \'täp-,soil\ *noun* (1836)
**:** surface soil usually including the organic layer in which plants have most of their roots and which the farmer turns over in plowing
**top·spin** \-,spin\ *noun* [¹*top*] (1902)
**:** a rotary motion imparted to a ball that causes it to rotate forward in the direction it is traveling
**top·stitch** \'täp-,stich\ *transitive verb* (1934)
**:** to make a line of stitching on the outside of (a garment) close to a seam
**top·sy·tur·vi·ness** \,täp-sē-'tər-vē-nəs\ *noun* (1842)
**:** the quality or state of being topsy-turvy
**¹top·sy–tur·vy** \,täp-sē-'tər-vē\ *adverb* [probably ultimately from *tops* (plural of ¹*top*) + obsolete English *terve* to turn upside down] (1528)
**1 :** in utter confusion or disorder
**2 :** with the top or head downward **:** UPSIDE DOWN
**²topsy–turvy** *adjective* (1612)
**:** turned topsy-turvy **:** totally disordered

**— top·sy·tur·vi·ly** \-'tər-və-lē\ *adverb*
**— top·sy·tur·vy·dom** \-vē-dəm\ *noun*
**³topsy–turvy** *noun* (1655)
**:** TOPSY-TURVINESS
**top up** (1937)
*transitive verb*
*British* **:** to make up to the full quantity, capacity, or amount
*intransitive verb*
*British* **:** to replenish a supply
**— top–up** \'täp-,əp\ *noun, British*
**top·work** \'täp-,wərk\ *transitive verb* (1882)
**:** to graft scions of another variety on the main branches of (as fruit trees) usually to obtain more desirable fruit
**toque** \'tōk\ *noun* [Middle French, soft hat with a narrow brim worn especially in the 16th century, from Old Spanish *toca* headdress] (1505)
**1 :** a woman's small hat without a brim made in any of various soft close-fitting shapes
**2 :** TUQUE
**3 :** a tall brimless hat worn by a chef — called also *toque blanche*
**tor** \'tor\ *noun* [Middle English, from Old English *torr*] (before 12th century)
**:** a high craggy hill
**To·rah** \'tōr-ə, 'tor-; 'toi-rə\ *noun* [Hebrew *tōrāh*] (1577)
**1 :** the five books of Moses constituting the Pentateuch
**2 :** the body of wisdom and law contained in Jewish Scripture and other sacred literature and oral tradition
**3 :** a leather or parchment scroll of the Pentateuch used in a synagogue for liturgical purposes
**¹torch** \'torch\ *noun, often attributive* [Middle English *torche*, from Old French, bundle of twisted straw or tow, torch, from (assumed) Vulgar Latin *torca;* akin to Latin *torquēre* to twist — more at TORTURE] (14th century)
**1 :** a burning stick of resinous wood or twist of tow used to give light and usually carried in the hand **:** FLAMBEAU
**2 :** something (as tradition, wisdom, or knowledge) likened to a torch as giving light or guidance
**3 :** any of various portable devices for emitting an unusually hot flame — compare BLOWTORCH
**4** *chiefly British* **:** FLASHLIGHT 2
**5 :** INCENDIARY 1a
**²torch** *transitive verb* (1901)
**:** to set fire to with or as if with a torch
**torch·bear·er** \-,bar-ər, -,ber-\ *noun* (1538)
**1 :** one that carries a torch
**2 :** someone in the forefront of a campaign, crusade, or movement
**tor·chère** \,tor-'sher\ *noun* [French, from *torche* torch] (1904)
**1 :** a tall ornamental stand for a candlestick or candelabra
**2 :** an electric floor lamp giving indirect light
**torch·light** \-,līt\ *noun* (15th century)
**1 :** light given by torches
**2 :** TORCH
**tor·chon** \'tor-,shän\ *noun* [French, duster, from Old French, bundle of twisted straw, from *torche*] (1865)
**:** a coarse bobbin or machine-made lace made with fan-shaped designs forming a scalloped edge
**torch singer** *noun* (circa 1932)
**:** a singer of torch songs
**torch song** *noun* [from the phrase *to carry a torch for* (to be in love)] (1930)
**:** a popular sentimental song of unrequited love
**torch·wood** \'torch-,wud\ *noun* (1833)
**1 :** any of a genus (*Amyris*) of tropical American trees and shrubs of the rue family with hard heavy fragrant resinous streaky yellowish brown wood
**2 :** the wood of a torchwood

**torchy** \'tor-chē\ *adjective* **torch·i·er; -est** (1941)
**:** of, relating to, or characteristic of a torch song or torch singer
**tore** *past of* TEAR
**to·re·a·dor** \'tor-ē-ə-,dor, 'tor-, 'tär-\ *noun* [Spanish, from *torear* to fight bulls, from *toro* bull, from Latin *taurus* — more at TAURINE] (1618)
**:** TORERO, BULLFIGHTER
**to·re·ro** \tə-'rer-(,)ō\ *noun, plural* **-ros** [Spanish, from Latin *taurarius* bullfighter, from Latin *taurus* bull] (1728)
**:** a matador or a member of the attending cuadrilla
**to·reu·tics** \tə-'rü-tiks\ *noun plural but singular in construction* [*toreutic*, adjective, from Greek *toreutikos*, from *toreuein* to bore through, chase, from *toreus* boring tool; akin to Greek *tetrainein* to bore — more at THROW] (1847)
**:** the art or process of working in metal especially by embossing or chasing
**— to·reu·tic** \-'rü-tik\ *adjective*
**tori** *plural of* TORUS
**to·ric** \'tor-ik, 'tor-\ *adjective* (circa 1898)
**:** of, relating to, or shaped like a torus or segment of a torus ⟨a *toric* lens⟩
**to·rii** \'tor-ē-,ē, 'tor-\ *noun, plural* **torii** [Japanese] (1727)
**:** a Japanese gateway of light construction commonly built at the approach to a Shinto shrine
**¹tor·ment** \'tor-,ment\ *noun* [Middle English, from Old French, from Latin *tormentum* torture; akin to Latin *torquēre* to twist — more at TORTURE] (14th century)
**1 :** the infliction of torture (as by rack or wheel)
**2 :** extreme pain or anguish of body or mind **:** AGONY
**3 :** a source of vexation or pain
**²tor·ment** \tor-'ment, 'tor-\ *transitive verb* (14th century)
**1 :** to cause severe usually persistent or recurrent distress of body or mind to ⟨cattle *tormented* by flies⟩
**2 :** DISTORT, TWIST
**synonym** see AFFLICT
**tor·men·til** \'tor-mən-,til\ *noun* [Middle English *turmentill*, from Medieval Latin *tormentilla*, from Latin *tormentum;* from its use in allaying pain] (15th century)
**:** a yellow-flowered Eurasian cinquefoil (*Potentilla erecta* synonym *P. tormentilla*) with a root sometimes used in tanning and dyeing
**tor·men·tor** *also* **tor·ment·er** \tor-'men-tər, 'tor-\ *noun* (14th century)
**1 :** one that torments
**2 :** a fixed curtain or flat on each side of a theater stage that prevents the audience from seeing into the wings
**torn** *past participle of* TEAR
**tor·na·dic** \tor-'na-dik, -'na-\ *adjective* (1884)
**:** relating to, characteristic of, or constituting a tornado
**tor·na·do** \tor-'nā-(,)dō\ *noun, plural* **-does** *or* **-dos** [modification of Spanish *tronada* thunderstorm, from *tronar* to thunder, from Latin *tonare* — more at THUNDER] (1556)
**1** *archaic* **:** a tropical thunderstorm
**2 a :** a squall accompanying a thunderstorm in Africa **b :** a violent destructive whirling wind accompanied by a funnel-shaped cloud that progresses in a narrow path over the land
**3 :** a violent windstorm **:** WHIRLWIND
**tor·nil·lo** \tor-'nē-(,)yō, -'ni-(,)lō\ *noun, plural* **-los** [Spanish, literally, small lathe, screw, diminutive of *torno* lathe, from Latin *tornus* — more at TURN] (circa 1844)
**:** SCREWBEAN 1
**to·roid** \'tor-,oid, 'tor-\ *noun* [New Latin *torus*] (circa 1900)
**1 :** a surface generated by a plane closed curve rotated about a line that lies in the same plane as the curve but does not intersect it

**2 :** a body whose surface has the form of a toroid

**to·roi·dal** \tȯ-'rȯi-dᵊl\ *adjective* (circa 1889)
**:** of, relating to, or shaped like a torus or toroid **:** doughnut-shaped ⟨a *toroidal* resistance coil⟩
— **to·roi·dal·ly** \-dᵊl-ē\ *adverb*

**¹tor·pe·do** \tȯr-'pē-(,)dō\ *noun, plural* **-does** [Latin, literally, stiffness, numbness, from *torpēre* to be sluggish or numb — more at TORPID] (circa 1520)
**1 :** ELECTRIC RAY
**2 :** a weapon for destroying ships by rupturing their hulls below the waterline: as **a :** a submarine mine **b :** a thin cylindrical self-propelled underwater projectile
**3 :** a small firework that explodes when thrown against a hard object
**4 :** a professional gunman or assassin
**5 :** SUBMARINE 2 ◆

**²torpedo** *transitive verb* **tor·pe·doed; tor·pe·do·ing** \-'pē-də-wiŋ\ (circa 1879)
**1 :** to hit or sink (a ship) with a naval torpedo **:** strike or destroy by torpedo
**2 :** to destroy or nullify altogether **:** WRECK ⟨*torpedo* a plan⟩

**torpedo boat** *noun* (1810)
**:** a boat designed for launching torpedoes; *specifically* **:** a small very fast boat with one or more torpedo tubes

**torpedo bomber** *noun* (1930)
**:** a military airplane designed to carry torpedoes — called also *torpedo plane*

**torpedo tube** *noun* (circa 1891)
**:** a tube from which torpedoes are fired

**tor·pid** \'tȯr-pəd\ *adjective* [Latin *torpidus*, from *torpēre* to be sluggish or numb; akin to Lithuanian *tirpti* to become numb] (1613)
**1 a :** having lost motion or the power of exertion or feeling **:** DORMANT, NUMB **b :** sluggish in functioning or acting ⟨a *torpid* frog⟩ ⟨a *torpid* mind⟩
**2 :** lacking in energy or vigor **:** APATHETIC, DULL
— **tor·pid·i·ty** \tȯr-'pi-də-tē\ *noun*

**tor·por** \'tȯr-pər\ *noun* [Latin, from *torpēre*] (1607)
**1 :** APATHY, DULLNESS
**2 :** a state of mental and motor inactivity with partial or total insensibility **:** extreme sluggishness or stagnation of function
**synonym** see LETHARGY

**¹torque** \'tȯrk\ *noun* [French, from Latin *torques*, from *torquēre* to twist — more at TORTURE] (1695)
**:** a usually metal collar or neck chain worn by the ancient Gauls, Germans, and Britons

**²torque** *noun* [Latin *torquēre* to twist] (circa 1884)
**1 :** a force that produces or tends to produce rotation or torsion ⟨an automobile engine delivers *torque* to the drive shaft⟩; *also* **:** a measure of the effectiveness of such a force that consists of the product of the force and the perpendicular distance from the line of action of the force to the axis of rotation
**2 :** a turning or twisting force

**³torque** *transitive verb* **torqued; torqu·ing** (1959)
**:** to impart torque to **:** cause to twist (as about an axis)
— **torqu·er** *noun*

**torque converter** *noun* (1927)
**:** a device for transmitting and amplifying torque especially by hydraulic means

**torr** \'tȯr\ *noun, plural* **torr** [Evangelista *Torricelli*] (1949)
**:** a unit of pressure equal to ¹/₇₆₀ of an atmosphere (about 133.3 pascals)

**¹tor·rent** \'tȯr-ənt, 'tär-\ *noun* [Middle French, from Latin *torrent-, torrens* from *torrent-, torrens*, adjective, burning, seething, rushing, from present participle of *torrēre* to parch, burn — more at THIRST] (1582)
**1 :** a tumultuous outpouring **:** RUSH

**2 :** a violent stream of a liquid (as water or lava)
**3 :** a channel of a mountain stream

**²torrent** *adjective* (1667)
**:** TORRENTIAL

**tor·ren·tial** \tȯ-'ren(t)-shəl, tə-\ *adjective* (1849)
**1 a :** relating to or having the character of a torrent ⟨*torrential* rains⟩ **b :** caused by or resulting from action of rapid streams ⟨*torrential* gravel⟩
**2 :** resembling a torrent in violence or rapidity of flow
— **tor·ren·tial·ly** \-'ren(t)-sh(ə-)lē\ *adverb*

**tor·rid** \'tȯr-əd, 'tär-\ *adjective* [Latin *torridus*, from *torrēre*] (1545)
**1 a :** parched with heat especially of the sun **:** HOT ⟨*torrid* sands⟩ **b :** giving off intense heat **:** SCORCHING
**2 :** ARDENT, PASSIONATE ⟨*torrid* love letters⟩
— **tor·rid·i·ty** \tȯ-'ri-də-tē\ *noun*
— **tor·rid·ly** \'tȯr-əd-lē, 'tär-\ *adverb*
— **tor·rid·ness** *noun*

**torrid zone** *noun, often T&Z capitalized* (1586)
**:** the region of the earth between the tropic of Cancer and the tropic of Capricorn

**tor·sade** \tȯr-'säd, -'sād\ *noun* [French, from obsolete French *tors* twisted, from (assumed) Vulgar Latin *torsus*, alteration of Latin *tortus*, past participle of *torquēre* to twist] (1882)
**:** a twisted cord or ribbon used especially as a hat ornament

**tor·sion** \'tȯr-shən\ *noun* [Late Latin *torsion-, torsio* torment, alteration of Latin *tortio*, from *torquēre* to twist] (1543)
**1 :** the twisting or wrenching of a body by the exertion of forces tending to turn one end or part about a longitudinal axis while the other is held fast or turned in the opposite direction; *also* **:** the state of being twisted
**2 :** the twisting of a bodily organ or part on its own axis
**3 :** the reactive torque that an elastic solid exerts by reason of being under torsion
— **tor·sion·al** \'tȯr-shnəl, -shə-nᵊl\ *adjective*
— **tor·sion·al·ly** *adverb*

**torsion bar** *noun* (1948)
**:** a long metal element in an automobile suspension that has one end held rigidly to the frame end and the other twisted and connected to the axle and that acts as a spring

**tor·so** \'tȯr-(,)sō\ *noun, plural* **torsos** *or* **tor·si** \'tȯr-,sē\ [Italian, literally, stalk, from Latin *thyrsus* stalk, thyrsus] (1722)
**1 :** a sculptured representation of the trunk of a human body
**2 :** something (as a piece of writing) that is mutilated or left unfinished
**3 :** the human trunk

**tort** \'tȯrt\ *noun* [Middle English, injury, from Middle French, from Medieval Latin *tortum*, from Latin, neuter of *tortus* twisted, from past participle of *torquēre*] (1586)
**:** a wrongful act other than a breach of contract for which relief may be obtained in the form of damages or an injunction

**torte** \'tȯrt-ə, 'tȯrt\ *noun, plural* **tor·ten** \'tȯrt-ᵊn\ *or* **tortes** [German, probably from Italian *torta* cake, from Late Latin, round loaf of bread] (1555)
**:** a cake made with many eggs and often grated nuts or dry bread crumbs and usually covered with a rich frosting

**tor·tel·li·ni** \,tȯr-tᵊl-'ē-nē\ *noun* [Italian, plural of *tortellino* pasta round, diminutive of *tortello*, from *torta* cake] (circa 1911)
**:** pasta cut in rounds, folded around a filling (as of meat or cheese), formed into rings, and boiled

**tor·ti·col·lis** \,tȯr-tə-'kä-ləs\ *noun* [New Latin, from Latin *tortus* twisted + *-i-* + *collum* neck — more at COLLAR] (circa 1811)

**:** a twisting of the neck to one side that results in abnormal carriage of the head and is usually caused by muscle spasms — called also *wryneck*

**tor·ti·lla** \tȯr-'tē-yə\ *noun* [American Spanish, from Spanish, diminutive of *torta* cake, from Late Latin, round loaf of bread] (circa 1699)
**:** a round thin cake of unleavened cornmeal or wheat flour bread usually eaten hot with a topping or filling (as of ground meat or cheese)

**tor·tious** \'tȯr-shəs\ *adjective* (1544)
**:** implying or involving tort
— **tor·tious·ly** *adverb*

**tor·toise** \'tȯr-təs\ *noun* [Middle English *tortu, tortuce*, from Middle French *tortue* — more at TURTLE] (14th century)
**1 :** any of a family (Testudinidae) of terrestrial turtles; *broadly* **:** TURTLE
**2 :** someone or something regarded as slow or laggard

**tortoise beetle** *noun* (circa 1711)
**:** any of various chrysomelid beetles (subfamily Cassidinae) with leaf-eating larvae

**¹tor·toise·shell** \'tȯr-tə-,shel, -əsh-,shel\ *noun* (1632)
**1 :** the mottled horny substance of the shell of some turtles (as the hawksbill turtle) used in inlaying and in making various ornamental articles
**2 :** any of several showy nymphalid butterflies (genus *Nymphalis*)

**²tortoiseshell** *adjective* (1651)
**1 :** made of or resembling tortoiseshell especially in mottled brown and yellow coloring
**2 :** of, relating to, or being a color pattern of the domestic cat consisting of patches of black, orange, and cream

**tor·to·ni** \tȯr-'tō-nē\ *noun* [probably from *Tortoni* 19th century Italian restaurateur in Paris] (1922)
**:** ice cream made of heavy cream often with minced almonds and chopped maraschino cherries and often flavored with rum

**tor·tri·cid** \'tȯr-trə-səd\ *noun* [New Latin *Tortricidae*, from *Tortric-, Tortrix*] (circa 1891)

◇ **WORD HISTORY**
**torpedo** In 1776, David Bushnell, a Connecticut native and supporter of the American cause in the Revolutionary War, devised and built a wooden submarine with a detachable powder magazine that was to be hooked to an enemy ship and set to explode after the submarine had steered clear. According to later accounts, Bushnell dubbed his magazine, with a mixture of learning and whimsy, with the Latin word *torpedo* "electric ray," a fish that delivers an electric shock. The following year Bushnell experimented with floating mines—powder kegs set off by a spring-released flintlock—but neither his submarine nor his mines succeeded in damaging a British ship. Both of Bushnell's innovations were taken up in the early 1800s by the American inventor Robert Fulton, who also employed *torpedo* as the name for a "submarine bomb." Though Fulton's schemes came to naught as well, *torpedo* became fixed as the term for a naval mine. This situation changed in the late 1860s, when the British engineer Robert Whitehead perfected the cylindrical, self-propelled underwater projectile to which the word *torpedo* soon referred exclusively. Bushnell's crude experiments bore awful fruit in World War I, when submarine-launched torpedoes sank hundreds of ships and changed the character of warfare.

: any of a family (Tortricidae) of small stout-bodied moths many of whose larvae feed in fruits
— **tortricid** *adjective*

**tor·trix** \ˈtȯr-triks\ *noun* [New Latin *Tortric-, Tortrix*, genus of moths, from Latin *tortus*, past participle of *torquēre* to twist; from the habit of twisting or rolling leaves to make a nest] (circa 1797)
: a tortricid moth

**tor·tu·os·i·ty** \ˌtȯr-chə-ˈwä-sə-tē\ *noun, plural* **-ties** (1603)
**1** : the quality or state of being tortuous
**2** : something winding or twisted : BEND

**tor·tu·ous** \ˈtȯrch-wəs, ˈtȯr-chə-\ *adjective* [Middle English, from Middle French *tortueux*, from Latin *tortuosus*, from *tortus* twist; from *torquēre* to twist] (15th century)
**1** : marked by repeated twists, bends, or turns : WINDING ⟨a *tortuous* path⟩
**2 a** : marked by devious or indirect tactics : CROOKED, TRICKY ⟨a *tortuous* conspiracy⟩ **b** : CIRCUITOUS, INVOLVED ⟨the *tortuous* jargon of legal forms⟩
— **tor·tu·ous·ly** *adverb*
— **tor·tu·ous·ness** *noun*

**¹tor·ture** \ˈtȯr-chər\ *noun* [French, from Late Latin *tortura*, from Latin *tortus*, past participle of *torquēre* to twist; probably akin to Old High German *drāhsil* turner, Greek *atraktos* spindle] (1540)
**1 a** : anguish of body or mind : AGONY **b** : something that causes agony or pain
**2** : the infliction of intense pain (as from burning, crushing, or wounding) to punish, coerce, or afford sadistic pleasure
**3** : distortion or overrefinement of a meaning or an argument : STRAINING

**²torture** *transitive verb* **tor·tured; tor·tur·ing** \ˈtȯrch-riŋ, ˈtȯr-chə-\ (1588)
**1** : to cause intense suffering to : TORMENT
**2** : to punish or coerce by inflicting excruciating pain
**3** : to twist or wrench out of shape : DISTORT, WARP
**synonym** see AFFLICT
— **tor·tur·er** \ˈtȯr-chər-ər\ *noun*

**tor·tur·ous** \ˈtȯrch-rəs, ˈtȯr-chə-\ *adjective* (15th century)
**1 a** : causing torture ⟨*torturous* inquisitions⟩ **b** : very unpleasant or painful ⟨a *torturous* day⟩ ⟨*torturous* self-doubts⟩
**2** : painfully difficult or slow ⟨the *torturous* course of the negotiations⟩
— **tor·tur·ous·ly** *adverb*

**tor·u·la** \ˈtȯr-yə-lə, ˈtär-, -ə-lə\ *noun, plural* **-lae** \-ˌlē, -ˌlī\ *also* **-las** [New Latin, from Latin *torus* protuberance] (1861)
: any of various fungi and especially yeasts that lack sexual spores, do not produce alcoholic fermentations, and are typically acid formers — called also *torula yeast*

**to·rus** \ˈtȯr-əs, ˈtȯr-\ *noun, plural* **to·ri** \ˈtȯr-ˌī, ˈtȯr-, -ˌē\ [New Latin, from Latin, protuberance, bulge, torus molding] (1563)
**1** : a large molding of convex profile commonly occurring as the lowest molding in the base of a column — see BASE illustration
**2** : the thickening of a membrane closing a wood-cell pit (as of gymnosperm tracheids) having the secondary cell wall arched over the pit cavity
**3** : a doughnut-shaped surface generated by a circle rotated about an axis in its plane that does not intersect the circle; *broadly* : TOROID
**4** : a smooth rounded anatomical protuberance (as a bony ridge on the skull)

**To·ry** \ˈtȯr-ē, ˈtȯr-\ *noun, plural* **Tories** [Irish *tóraidhe* outlaw, robber, from Middle Irish *tóir* pursuit] (1646)
**1** : a dispossessed Irishman subsisting as an outlaw chiefly in the 17th century
**2** *obsolete* : BANDIT, OUTLAW
**3 a** : a member or supporter of a major British political group of the 18th and early 19th centuries favoring at first the Stuarts and later

royal authority and the established church and seeking to preserve the traditional political structure and defeat parliamentary reform — compare WHIG **b** : CONSERVATIVE 1b
**4** : an American upholding the cause of the British Crown against the supporters of colonial independence during the American Revolution : LOYALIST
**5** *often not capitalized* : an extreme conservative especially in political and economic principles
— **Tory** *adjective*

**Tory Democracy** *noun* (1879)
: a political philosophy advocating preservation of established institutions and traditional principles combined with political democracy and a social and economic program designed to benefit the common man

**To·ry·ism** \ˈtȯr-ē-ˌi-zəm, ˈtȯr-\ *noun* (1682)
**1** : the principles and practices of or associated with Tories
**2** : the British Tory party or its members

**tosh** \ˈtäsh\ *noun* [origin unknown] (1528)
: sheer nonsense : BOSH, TWADDLE

**¹toss** \ˈtȯs, ˈtäs\ *verb* [probably of Scandinavian origin; akin to Swedish dialect *tossa* to spread, scatter] (1506)
*transitive verb*
**1 a** : to fling or heave continuously about, to and fro, or up and down ⟨a ship *tossed* by waves⟩ **b** : BANDY 2b, c, d **c** : to mix lightly until well coated with a dressing or until the elements are thoroughly combined ⟨*toss* a salad⟩
**2** : to make uneasy : stir up : DISTURB
**3 a** : to throw with a quick, light, or careless motion or with a sudden jerk ⟨*toss* a ball around⟩ **b** : to throw up in the air ⟨*tossed* by a bull⟩ **c** : MATCH 5a **d** : to send as if by throwing ⟨*tossed* in jail⟩ **e** : to get rid of : THROW AWAY
**4 a** : to fling or lift with a sudden motion ⟨*tosses* her head angrily⟩ **b** : to tilt suddenly so as to empty by drinking ⟨*tossed* his glass⟩; *also* : to consume by drinking ⟨*toss* down a drink⟩
**5** : to accomplish, provide, or produce readily or easily ⟨*toss* off a few verses⟩
**6** : THROW 16 ⟨*toss* a party⟩
**7** : VOMIT 1 — often used in the phrase *toss one's cookies*
*intransitive verb*
**1 a** : to move restlessly or turbulently; *especially* : to twist and turn repeatedly ⟨*tossed* sleeplessly all night⟩ **b** : to move with a quick or spirited gesture
**2** : to decide an issue by flipping a coin
**synonym** see THROW
— **toss·er** *noun*

**²toss** *noun* (1634)
**1** : the state or fact of being tossed
**2** : an act or instance of tossing: as **a** : an abrupt tilting or upward fling **b** : a deciding by chance and especially by flipping a coin **c** : THROW, PITCH

**toss·pot** \-ˌpät\ *noun* (1568)
: DRUNKARD, SOT

**toss-up** \-ˌəp\ *noun* (1812)
**1** : TOSS 2b
**2** : an even chance
**3** : something that offers no clear basis for choice

**tos·ta·da** \tō-ˈstä-də\ *also* **tos·ta·do** \-(ˌ)dō\ *noun* [Mexican Spanish *tostada*, from Spanish, feminine of *tostado*, past participle of *tostar* to toast, roast, from Late Latin *tostare* — more at TOAST] (1939)
: a tortilla fried in deep fat

**¹tot** \ˈtät\ *noun* [origin unknown] (1725)
**1** : a small child : TODDLER
**2** : a small drink or allowance of liquor : SHOT

**²tot** *verb* **tot·ted; tot·ting** [*tot.*, abbreviation of *total*] (circa 1772)
*transitive verb*
: to add together : TOTAL — usually used with *up* ⟨*tots* up the score⟩

*intransitive verb*
: ADD

**¹to·tal** \ˈtō-t°l\ *adjective* [Middle English, from Middle French, from Medieval Latin *totalis*, from Latin *totus* whole, entire] (15th century)
**1** : comprising or constituting a whole : ENTIRE ⟨the *total* amount⟩
**2** : ABSOLUTE, UTTER ⟨a *total* failure⟩
**3** : involving a complete and unified effort especially to achieve a desired effect ⟨*total* war⟩ ⟨*total* theater⟩
**synonym** see WHOLE

**²total** *noun* (1557)
**1** : a product of addition : SUM
**2** : an entire quantity : AMOUNT

**³total** *adverb* (1601)
: TOTALLY

**⁴total** *transitive verb* **to·taled** *or* **to·talled; to·tal·ing** *or* **to·tal·ling** (1716)
**1** : to add up : COMPUTE
**2** : to amount to : NUMBER
**3** : to make a total wreck of : DEMOLISH ⟨*totaled* the car⟩

**total depravity** *noun* (1794)
: a state of corruption due to original sin held in Calvinism to infect every part of man's nature and to make the natural man unable to know or obey God

**total eclipse** *noun* (1671)
: an eclipse in which one celestial body is completely obscured by the shadow or body of another

**to·tal·ism** \ˈtō-t°l-ˌi-zəm\ *noun* (1941)
: TOTALITARIANISM
— **to·tal·is·tic** \ˌtō-t°l-ˈis-tik\ *adjective*

**¹to·tal·i·tar·i·an** \(ˌ)tō-ˌta-lə-ˈter-ē-ən\ *adjective* [Italian *totalitario*, from *totalità* totality] (1926)
**1 a** : of or relating to centralized control by an autocratic leader or hierarchy : AUTHORITARIAN, DICTATORIAL; *especially* : DESPOTIC **b** : of or relating to a political regime based on subordination of the individual to the state and strict control of all aspects of the life and productive capacity of the nation especially by coercive measures (as censorship and terrorism)
**2 a** : advocating or characteristic of totalitarianism **b** : completely regulated by the state especially as an aid to national mobilization in an emergency **c** : exercising autocratic powers : tending toward monopoly

**²totalitarian** *noun* (circa 1934)
: an advocate or practitioner of totalitarianism

**to·tal·i·tar·i·an·ism** \(ˌ)tō-ˌta-lə-ˈter-ē-ə-ˌni-zəm\ *noun* (1926)
**1** : centralized control by an autocratic authority
**2** : the political concept that the citizen should be totally subject to an absolute state authority

**to·tal·i·tar·i·an·ize** \-ˌnīz\ *transitive verb* **-ized; -iz·ing** (1935)
: to make totalitarian ⟨a society *totalitarianized* by the military-industrial complex —W. F. Buckley (born 1925)⟩

**to·tal·i·ty** \tō-ˈta-lə-tē\ *noun, plural* **-ties** (1598)
**1** : an aggregate amount : SUM, WHOLE
**2 a** : the quality or state of being total : WHOLENESS **b** : the phase of an eclipse during which it is total : state of total eclipse

**to·tal·iza·tor** *or* **to·tal·isa·tor** \ˈtō-t°l-ə-ˌzā-tər\ *noun* (1879)
: PARI-MUTUEL 2

**to·tal·ize** \ˈtō-t°l-ˌīz\ *transitive verb* **-ized; -iz·ing** (1818)
**1** : to add up : TOTAL
**2** : to express as a whole

**to·tal·iz·er** \-ˌī-zər\ *noun* (1887)
: one that totalizes: as **a** : PARI-MUTUEL 2 **b** : a device (as a meter) that records a remaining total (as of fuel)

**to·tal·ly** \ˈtō-t°l-ē\ *adverb* (1509)
: in a total manner : to a total or complete degree : WHOLLY, ENTIRELY

**total recall** *noun* (1926)

**:** the faculty of remembering with complete clarity and in complete detail

**¹tote** \'tōt\ *transitive verb* **tot·ed; tot·ing** [perhaps from an English-based creole; akin to Gullah & Krio *tot* to carry] (1677)
**1 :** to carry by hand **:** bear on the person **:** LUG, PACK
**2 :** HAUL, CONVEY ◆
**— tot·er** \'tō-tər\ *noun*

**²tote** *noun* (circa 1772)
**1 :** BURDEN, LOAD
**2 :** TOTE BAG

**³tote** *transitive verb* **tot·ed; tot·ing** [English dialect *tote*, noun, total] (1888)
**:** ADD, TOTAL — usually used with *up* ⟨*toted* up his accomplishments —G. P. Morrill⟩

**⁴tote** *noun* [short for *totalizator*] (1891)
**:** PARI-MUTUEL 2

**tote bag** *noun* (1900)
**:** a large 2-handled open-topped bag (as of canvas)

**tote board** *noun* [⁴*tote*] (circa 1949)
**:** an electrically operated board (as at a race-track) on which pertinent information (as betting odds and race results) is posted

**to·tem** \'tō-təm\ *noun* [Ojibwa *oto'te'man* his totem] (circa 1776)
**1 a :** an object (as an animal or plant) serving as the emblem of a family or clan and often as a reminder of its ancestry; *also* **:** a usually carved or painted representation of such an object **b :** a family or clan identified by a common totemic object
**2 :** something that serves as an emblem or revered symbol

**to·tem·ic** \tō-'te-mik\ *adjective* (1846)
**1 :** of, relating to, suggestive of, or characteristic of a totem or totemism ⟨a *totemic* animal⟩
**2 :** based on or practicing totemism ⟨*totemic* clan structure⟩

**to·tem·ism** \'tō-tə-ˌmi-zəm\ *noun* (1791)
**1 :** belief in kinship with or a mystical relationship between a group or an individual and a totem
**2 :** a system of social organization based on totemic affiliations

**to·tem·is·tic** \ˌtō-tə-'mis-tik\ *adjective* (1873)
**:** TOTEMIC

**totem pole** *noun* (1897)
**1 :** a pole or pillar carved and painted with a series of totemic symbols representing family lineage and often mythical or historical incidents and erected before the houses of Indian tribes of the northwest coast of North America
**2 :** an order of rank **:** HIERARCHY

**toth·er** *or* **t'oth·er** \'tə-thər\ *pronoun or adjective* [Middle English *tother*, alteration (resulting from misdivision of *thet other* the other, from *thet* the— from Old English *thæt* — + *other*) — more at THAT] (13th century)
*chiefly dialect* **:** the other

**to·ti·po·ten·cy** \tō-'ti-pə-tən(t)-sē, ˌtō-tə-'pō-t°n-\ *noun* (1909)
**:** ability to generate or regenerate a whole organism from a part

**to·ti·po·tent** \-tənt, -t°nt\ *adjective* [Latin *totus* whole, entire + English *-i-* + *potent*] (circa 1899)
**:** capable of developing into a complete organism or differentiating into any of its cells or tissues ⟨*totipotent* blastomeres⟩

**¹tot·ter** \'tä-tər\ *intransitive verb* [Middle English *toteren*] (15th century)
**1 a :** to tremble or rock as if about to fall **:** SWAY **b :** to become unstable **:** threaten to collapse
**2 :** to move unsteadily **:** STAGGER, WOBBLE

**²totter** *noun* (1747)
**:** an unsteady gait **:** WOBBLE

**tot·ter·ing** *adjective* (1534)
**1 a :** being in an unstable condition ⟨a *tottering* building⟩ **b :** walking unsteadily

**2 :** lacking firmness or stability **:** INSECURE ⟨a *tottering* regime⟩
**— tot·ter·ing·ly** \-tə-riŋ-lē\ *adverb*

**tot·tery** \'tä-tə-rē\ *adjective* (circa 1755)
**:** of an infirm or precarious nature

**Toua·reg** *variant of* TUAREG

**tou·can** \'tü-ˌkan, -ˌkän, tü-'\ *noun* [French, from Portuguese *tucano*, from Tupi *tukána*] (1568)
**:** any of a family (Ramphastidae) of fruit-eating birds of tropical America with brilliant coloring and a very large but light and thin-walled beak

**¹touch** \'təch\ *verb* [Middle English, from Old French *tuchier*, from (assumed) Vulgar Latin *toccare* to knock, strike a bell, touch, probably of imitative origin] (14th century)
*transitive verb*
**1 :** to bring a bodily part into contact with especially so as to perceive through the tactile sense **:** handle or feel gently usually with the intent to understand or appreciate ⟨loved to *touch* the soft silk⟩
**2 :** to strike or push lightly especially with the hand or foot or an implement
**3 :** to lay hands upon (one afflicted with scrofula) with intent to heal
**4** *archaic* **a :** to play on (a stringed instrument) **b :** to perform (a melody) by playing or singing
**5 a :** to take into the hands or mouth ⟨never *touches* alcohol⟩ **b :** to put hands upon in any way or degree ⟨don't *touch* anything before the police come⟩; *especially* **:** to commit violence upon ⟨swears he never *touched* the child⟩
**6 :** to deal with **:** become involved with ⟨a sticky situation and I wouldn't *touch* it with a 10-foot pole⟩
**7 :** to induce to give or lend ⟨*touched* him for ten dollars⟩
**8 :** to cause to be briefly in contact or conjunction with something ⟨*touched* her spurs to the horse⟩ ⟨*touched* his hand to his hat⟩
**9 a** (1) **:** to meet without overlapping or penetrating **:** ADJOIN (2) **:** to get to **:** REACH ⟨the speedometer needle *touched* 80⟩ **b :** to be tangent to **c :** to rival in quality or value ⟨nothing can *touch* that cloth for durability⟩
**10 :** to speak or tell of especially in passing ⟨barely *touched* the incident in the speech⟩
**11 a :** to relate to **:** CONCERN **b :** to have an influence on **:** AFFECT
**12 a :** to leave a mark or impression on ⟨few reagents will *touch* gold⟩; *also* **:** TINGE **b :** to harm slightly by or as if by contact **:** TAINT, BLEMISH ⟨fruit *touched* by frost⟩ **c :** to give a delicate tint, line, or expression to ⟨a smile *touched* her lips⟩
**13 :** to draw or delineate with light strokes
**14 a :** to hurt the feelings of **:** WOUND **b :** to move to sympathetic feeling
*intransitive verb*
**1 a :** to feel something with a body part (as the hand or foot) **b :** to lay hand or finger on a person to cure disease (as scrofula)
**2 :** to be in contact
**3 :** to come close **:** VERGE ⟨your actions *touch* on treason⟩
**4 :** to have a bearing **:** RELATE — used with *on* or *upon*
**5 a :** to make a brief or incidental stop on shore during a trip by water ⟨*touched* at several ports⟩ **b :** to treat a topic in a brief or casual manner — used with *on* or *upon* ⟨*touched* upon many points⟩
**synonym** see AFFECT
**— touch·able** \'tə-chə-bəl\ *adjective*
**— touch·er** *noun*
**— touch base :** to come in contact or communication ⟨coming in from the cold to *touch base* with civilization —Carla Hunt⟩

**²touch** *noun* (14th century)
**1 :** a light stroke, tap, or push
**2 :** the act or fact of touching

**3 :** the special sense by which pressure or traction exerted on the skin or mucous membrane is perceived
**4 :** mental or moral sensitiveness, responsiveness, or tact ⟨has a wonderful *touch* with children⟩
**5 :** a specified sensation that arises in response to stimulation of the tactile receptors **:** FEEL ⟨the velvety *touch* of velour⟩
**6 a :** the act of rubbing gold or silver on a touchstone to test its quality **b :** TEST, TRIAL — used chiefly in the phrase *put to the touch*
**7 a :** a visible effect **:** MARK ⟨a *touch* of the tropical sun⟩ **b :** WEAKNESS, DEFECT
**8 :** something slight of its kind: as **a :** a light attack ⟨a *touch* of fever⟩ **b :** a small quantity or indication **:** HINT ⟨a *touch* of spring in the air⟩ **c :** a transient emotion ⟨a momentary *touch* of compunction⟩ **d :** a near approach **:** CLOSE CALL ⟨beaten in the championships by a mere *touch*⟩
**9 a** *archaic* **:** the playing of an instrument (as a lute or piano) with the fingers; *also* **:** musical notes or strains so produced **b :** particular action of a keyboard with reference to the resistance of its keys to pressure ⟨piano with a stiff *touch*⟩
**10 :** control of the hands: as **a :** a manner or method of touching or striking especially the keys of a keyboard instrument **b :** ability to control the distance something (as a ball) is propelled ⟨developed his putting *touch*⟩
**11 :** a set of changes in change ringing that is less than a peal
**12 a :** an effective and subtle detail ⟨applies the finishing *touches* to the story⟩ **b :** distinctive and often effective manner or method ⟨the *touch* of a master⟩ **c :** a characteristic or distinguishing trait or quality
**13** *slang* **:** an act of soliciting or getting a gift or loan
**14 :** the state or fact of being in contact or communication or of having awareness ⟨lost *touch* with her cousin⟩ ⟨let's keep in *touch*⟩ ⟨out of *touch* with modern times⟩

◇ WORD HISTORY
**tote** *Tote*, meaning "to carry by hand," first appears in the spelling *toat* in a document of 1677 from Gloucester County, Virginia. It is next documented a century later from Boston and subsequently turns up throughout the eastern U.S. Today *tote* is fairly general in American English. The origin of this word has prompted much debate. Since early in the century it has been known that *tote* has close phonetic counterparts in western Bantu languages of Africa, such as Kikongo *tota* "pick up" and Kimbundu *tuta* "carry." *Tote* has a long record of use in African-American vernacular and occurs in Sea Islands Creole (Gullah) as well as in English-based creoles of Sierra Leone and Cameroon. Though the case for an English creole, if not Bantu, origin for *tote* looks strong, it has been objected that the early appearance of the word in New England and its general use in places such as 19th century Maine (where it usually meant "haul" rather than "carry by hand") argue against an African origin. *Tote* may have diffused into both colonial American English and Atlantic English creoles from some earlier speech form, perhaps 17th century nautical English, though unless further evidence surfaces we can only speculate on the prehistory of the word.

totem pole
1

\ə\ abut \ᵊ\ kitten \ər\ further \a\ ash \ā\ ace
\ä\ mop, mar \aú\ out \ch\ chin \e\ bet \ē\ easy
\g\ go \i\ hit \ī\ ice \j\ job \ŋ\ sing \ō\ go
\ó\ law \oi\ boy \th\ thin \t͟h\ the \ü\ loot \ú\ foot
\y\ yet \zh\ vision *see also* Guide to Pronunciation

**15 :** the area outside of the touchlines in soccer or outside of and including the touchlines in rugby

— **a touch :** SOMEWHAT, RATHER ⟨aimed *a touch* too low and missed⟩

**touch–and–go** \,təch-ən(d)-'gō\ *noun* (1953)
: an airplane landing followed immediately by application of power and a takeoff and usually executed as one of a series for practice at landings

**touch and go** *adjective* (1815)
: unpredictable as to outcome : UNCERTAIN ⟨it was *touch and go* there for a while⟩

**touch·back** \'təch-,bak\ *noun* (circa 1890)
: a situation in football in which the ball is down behind the goal line after a kick or intercepted forward pass after which it is put in play by the team defending the goal on its own 20-yard line — compare SAFETY

**touch·down** \'təch-,daùn\ *noun* (1876)
**1 :** the act of touching a football to the ground behind an opponent's goal; *specifically* : the act of scoring six points in American football by being lawfully in possession of the ball on, above, or behind an opponent's goal line when the ball is declared dead
**2 :** the act or moment of touching down (as with an airplane or spacecraft)

**touch down** (1864)
*transitive verb*
: to place (the ball in rugby) by hand on the ground on or over an opponent's goal line in scoring a try or behind one's own goal line as a defensive measure
*intransitive verb*
: to reach the ground : LAND

**tou·ché** \tü-'shā\ *interjection* [French, from past participle of *toucher* to touch, from Old French *tuchier*] (1904)
— used to acknowledge a hit in fencing or the success or appropriateness of an argument, an accusation, or a witty point

**touched** \'təcht\ *adjective* (14th century)
**1 :** emotionally stirred (as with gratitude)
**2 :** slightly unbalanced mentally

**touch football** *noun* (1933)
: football played informally and chiefly characterized by the substitution of touching for tackling

**touch·hole** \'təch-,hōl\ *noun* (1501)
: the vent in muzzle-loading guns through which the charge is ignited

**¹touch·ing** *preposition* (14th century)
: in reference to : CONCERNING

**²touching** *adjective* (1601)
: capable of arousing emotions of tenderness or compassion
**synonym** see MOVING
— **touch·ing·ly** \'tə-chiŋ-lē\ *adverb*

**touch·line** \'təch-,līn\ *noun* (1868)
: either of the lines that bound the long sides of the field of play in rugby and soccer

**touch·mark** \-,märk\ *noun* (1904)
: an identifying maker's mark impressed on pewter

**touch·me·not** \'təch-mē-,nät\ *noun* [from the bursting of the ripe pods and scattering of their seeds when touched] (1659)
: either of two North American impatiens growing in moist areas: as **a :** one (*Impatiens capensis*) typically having crimson-spotted orange flowers **b :** one (*I. pallida*) having yellow to white flowers sometimes spotted with brownish red

**touch off** *transitive verb* (circa 1765)
**1 :** to describe or characterize with precision
**2 a :** to cause to explode by or as if by touching with fire **b :** to provoke or initiate with sudden intensity ⟨the verdict *touched off* local riots⟩

**touch pad** *noun* (1979)
: a keypad for an electronic device (as a microwave oven) that consists of a flat surface divided into several differently marked areas which are touched to choose options

**touch screen** *noun* (1974)

: a display screen on which the user selects options (as from a menu) by touching the screen

**touch·stone** \'təch-,stōn\ *noun* (1530)
**1 :** a black siliceous stone related to flint and formerly used to test the purity of gold and silver by the streak left on the stone when rubbed by the metal
**2 :** a test or criterion for determining the quality or genuineness of a thing
**3 :** a fundamental or quintessential part or feature
**synonym** see STANDARD

**touch system** *noun* (1918)
: a method of typing that assigns a particular finger to each key and makes it possible to type without looking at the keyboard

**Touch-Tone** \'təch-'tōn, -,tōn\ *trademark*
— used for a telephone having push buttons that produce tones corresponding to numbers

**touch–type** \'təch-,tīp\ *intransitive verb* (1943)
: to type by the touch system
— **touch typist** *noun*

**touch–up** \'təch-,əp\ *noun* (1885)
: an act or instance of touching up

**touch up** *transitive verb* (1715)
**1 :** to improve or perfect by small additional strokes or alterations : fix the minor and usually visible defects or damages of
**2 :** to stimulate by or as if by a flick of a whip

**touch–wood** \'təch-,wùd\ *noun* (1579)
: ³PUNK

**touchy** \'tə-chē\ *adjective* **touch·i·er; -est** (1605)
**1 :** marked by readiness to take offense on slight provocation
**2 a** *of a body part* : acutely sensitive or irritable **b** *of a chemical* : highly explosive or inflammable
**3 :** calling for tact, care, or caution in treatment ⟨a *touchy* subject⟩
— **touch·i·ly** \'tə-chə-lē\ *adverb*
— **touch·i·ness** \'tə-chē-nəs\ *noun*

**touchy–feely** \,tə-chē-'fē-lē\ *adjective* (1968)
: characterized by or encouraging interpersonal touching especially in the free expression of emotions ⟨*touchy-feely* therapy⟩; *also* : openly or excessively emotional and personal ⟨*touchy-feely* management⟩

**¹tough** \'təf\ *adjective* [Middle English, from Old English *tōh*; akin to Old High German *zāhi* tough] (before 12th century)
**1 a :** strong or firm in texture but flexible and not brittle **b :** not easily chewed
**2 :** GLUTINOUS, STICKY
**3 :** characterized by severity or uncompromising determination
**4 :** capable of enduring strain, hardship, or severe labor
**5 :** very hard to influence : STUBBORN
**6 :** difficult to accomplish, resolve, endure, or deal with ⟨a *tough* question⟩ ⟨*tough* luck⟩
**7 :** stubbornly fought ⟨a *tough* contest⟩
**8 :** UNRULY, ROWDYISH
**9 :** marked by absence of softness or sentimentality
**synonym** see STRONG
— **tough·ly** *adverb*
— **tough·ness** *noun*

**²tough** *adverb* (14th century)
: in a tough manner ⟨talks *tough* and insensitively —A. E. Stevenson (died 1965)⟩

**³tough** *transitive verb* (1830)
: to bear unflinchingly : ENDURE — usually used with *out* especially in the phrase *tough it out*

**⁴tough** *noun* (1866)
: a tough person : ROWDY

**tough·en** \'tə-fən\ *verb* **tough·ened; tough·en·ing** \'tə-fə-niŋ, 'təf-niŋ\ (1582)
*transitive verb*
: to make tough
*intransitive verb*
: to become tough

**tough·ie** *also* **toughy** \'tə-fē\ *noun, plural* **tough·ies** (1921)
: one that is tough: as **a :** a loud rough rowdy person **b :** a difficult problem or question

**tough–mind·ed** \'təf-,mīn-dəd\ *adjective* (1909)
: realistic or unsentimental in temper or outlook
— **tough–mind·ed·ness** *noun*

**tou·pee** \tü-'pā\ *noun* [French *toupet* forelock, from Old French, diminutive of *top, toup,* of Germanic origin; akin to Old High German *zopf* tuft of hair — more at TOP] (1728)
**1 :** a curl or lock of hair made into a topknot on a periwig or natural coiffure; *also* : a periwig with such a topknot
**2 :** a wig or section of hair worn to cover a bald spot

**¹tour** \'tùr, *1 is also* 'taùr\ *noun* [Middle English, from Middle French, from Old French *tourn, tour* lathe, circuit, turn — more at TURN] (14th century)
**1 a :** one's turn in an orderly schedule : SHIFT **b :** a period during which an individual or unit is on a specific duty or at one place ⟨a *tour* of duty⟩
**2 a :** a journey for business, pleasure, or education often involving a series of stops and ending at the starting point; *also* : something resembling such a tour ⟨a *tour* of the history of philosophy⟩ **b :** a brief turn : ROUND **c :** a series of professional tournaments (as in golf or tennis)

**²tour** (1789)
*intransitive verb*
: to make a tour
*transitive verb*
**1 :** to make a tour of
**2 :** to present (as a theatrical production) on a tour

**tou·ra·co** \'tùr-ə-,kō\ *noun, plural* **-cos** [origin unknown] (circa 1743)
: any of a family (Musophagidae) of African birds that are related to the cuckoos and have a long tail, a short stout often colored bill, and red wing feathers

**tour·bil·lion** \tùr-'bil-yən\ *or* **tour·bil·lon** \tùr-bē-yōⁿ\ *noun* [Middle English, from Middle French *tourbillon,* from Latin *turbin-, turbo* — more at TURBINE] (15th century)
**1 :** WHIRLWIND
**2 :** a vortex especially of a whirlwind or whirlpool

**tour de force** \,tùr-də-'fōrs, -'fòrs\ *noun, plural* **tours de force** \*same*\ [French] (1802)
: a feat of strength, skill, or ingenuity

**tour·er** \'tùr-ər\ *noun* (1926)
**1 :** TOURING CAR
**2 :** one that tours

**Tou·rette's syndrome** \tü-'rets-\ *noun* [Georges Gille de la *Tourette* (died 1904) French physician] (1970)
: a rare disease characterized by involuntary tics and by uncontrollable verbalization involving especially echolalia and the use of obscene language — called also *Tou·rette syndrome* \-'ret-\

**tour·ing** \'tùr-iŋ\ *noun* (1794)
**1 :** participation in a tour
**2 :** cross-country skiing for pleasure

**touring car** *noun* (1903)
: an automobile suitable for distance driving: as **a :** a vintage automobile with two cross seats, usually four doors, and a folding top : PHAETON **2 b :** a modern usually 2-door sedan as distinguished from a sports car

touring car a

**tour·ism** \'tùr-,i-zəm\ *noun* (1811)
**1 :** the practice of traveling for recreation
**2 :** the guidance or management of tourists

**3 a :** the promotion or encouragement of touring **b :** the accommodation of tourists

**tour·ist** \'tu̇r-ist\ *noun* (1780)
**1 :** one that makes a tour for pleasure or culture
**2 :** TOURIST CLASS
— **tourist** *adjective or adverb*

**tourist card** *noun* (1948)
**:** a citizenship identity card issued to a tourist usually for a stated period of time in lieu of a passport or a visa

**tourist class** *noun* (1935)
**:** economy accommodations (as on a ship)

**tourist court** *noun* (1937)
**:** MOTEL

**tour·is·tic** \tu̇r-'is-tik\ *adjective* (1848)
**:** of or relating to a tour, tourism, or tourists
— **tour·is·ti·cal·ly** \-ti-k(ə-)lē\ *adverb*

**tourist trap** *noun* (1939)
**:** a place that attracts and exploits tourists

**tour·isty** \'tu̇r-əs-tē\ *adjective* (1906)
**:** of or relating to tourists: as **a :** patronized by tourists **b :** of a type appealing to tourists

**tour·ma·line** \'tu̇r-mə-lən, -,lēn\ *noun* [Sinhalese *toramalli* carnelian] (1759)
**:** a mineral of variable color that consists of a complex borosilicate and makes a striking gem when transparent and cut

**tour·na·ment** \'tu̇r-nə-mənt *also* 'tər- *or* 'tȯr-\ *noun* [Middle English *tornement,* from Old French *torneiement,* from *torneier*] (14th century)
**1 a :** a knightly sport of the middle ages between mounted combatants armed with blunted lances or swords and divided into two parties contesting for a prize or favor bestowed by the lady of the tournament **b :** the whole series of knightly sports, jousts, and tilts occurring at one time and place
**2 :** a series of games or contests that make up a single unit of competition (as on the professional golf tour), the championship play-offs of a league or conference, or an invitational event

**tour·ne·dos** \,tu̇r-nə-'dō\ *noun, plural* **tour·ne·dos** \-'dō(z)\ [French, from *tourner* to turn + *dos* back] (1877)
**:** a small fillet of beef usually cut from the tip of the tenderloin

**¹tour·ney** \'tu̇r-nē, 'tər- *also* 'tȯr-\ *intransitive verb* **tour·neyed; tour·ney·ing** [Middle English, from Middle French *torneier,* from Old French, from *torn, tourn* lathe, circuit] (14th century)
**:** to perform in a tournament

**²tourney** *noun, plural* **tourneys** (14th century)
**:** TOURNAMENT

**tour·ni·quet** \'tu̇r-ni-kət, 'tər-\ *noun* [French, turnstile, tourniquet, from *tourner* to turn, from Old French — more at TURN] (1695)
**:** a device (as a bandage twisted tight with a stick) to check bleeding or blood flow

**¹touse** \'tau̇z\ *transitive verb* **toused; tousing** [Middle English *-tousen;* akin to Old High German *zirzūsōn* to pull to pieces] (1598)
**:** RUMPLE, TOUSLE

**²touse** *noun* (1795)
**:** a noisy disturbance

**¹tou·sle** \'tau̇-zəl, -səl\ *transitive verb* **tousled; tou·sling** \'tau̇z-liŋ, 'tau̇s-; 'tau̇-zə-, -sə-\ [Middle English *touselen,* frequentative of *-tousen*] (15th century)
**:** DISHEVEL, RUMPLE

**²tou·sle** \'tau̇-zəl, *l is also* 'tü-\ *noun* (1788)
**1** *Scottish* **:** rough dalliance **:** TUSSLE
**2 :** a tangled mass (as of hair)

**¹tout** \'tau̇t, *in sense 4 also* 'tüt\ *verb* [Middle English *tuten* to peer; probably akin to Old English *tōtian* to stick out, Norwegian *tyte*] (circa 1700)
*transitive verb*
**1 :** to spy on **:** WATCH

**2 a** *British* **:** to spy out information about (as a racing stable or horse) **b :** to give a tip or solicit bets on (a racehorse)
**3 :** to solicit, peddle, or persuade importunately (not meant to *tout* you off the movie —Russell Baker)
**4 :** to praise or publicize loudly or extravagantly (*touted* as the . . . most elaborate suburban shopping development —*Wall Street Journal*)
*intransitive verb*
**1 :** to solicit patronage
**2 a** *chiefly British* **:** to spy on racehorses in training to gain information for betting **b :** to give a tip or solicit bets on a racehorse

**²tout** *noun* (1853)
**:** one who touts: as **a :** one who solicits patronage **b** *chiefly British* **:** one who spies out racing information for betting purposes **c :** one who gives tips or solicits bets on a racehorse

**tout·er** \'tau̇-tər\ *noun* (circa 1754)
**:** one that touts

**to·va·rich** *or* **to·va·rish** \tə-'vär-ish, -ich\ *noun* [Russian *tovarishch*] (circa 1917)
**:** COMRADE

**¹tow** \'tō\ *verb* [Middle English, from Old English *togian;* akin to Old English *tēon* to draw, pull, Old High German *ziohan* to draw, pull, Latin *ducere* to draw, lead] (before 12th century)
*transitive verb*
**:** to draw or pull along behind **:** HAUL
*intransitive verb*
**:** to move in tow (trailers that *tow* behind the family auto —Bob Munger)

**²tow** *noun* (1600)
**1 :** a rope or chain for towing
**2 a :** the act or an instance of towing **b :** the fact or state of being towed
**3 a :** something towed (as a boat or car) **b :** a group of barges lashed together and usually pushed
**4 a :** something (as a tugboat) that tows **b :** SKI TOW
— **in tow 1 :** under guidance or protection (taken *in tow* by a friendly native) **2 :** in the position of a dependent or devoted follower or admirer

**³tow** *noun* [Middle English, from Old English *tow-* spinning; akin to Old Norse *tō* tuft of wool for spinning, Old English *tawian* to prepare for use — more at TAW] (14th century)
**1 :** short or broken fiber (as of flax, hemp, or synthetic material) that is used especially for yarn, twine, or stuffing
**2 a :** yarn or cloth made of tow **b :** a loose essentially untwisted strand of synthetic fibers

**⁴tow** *noun* [Middle English, probably from Old English *toh-* (in *tohlīne* towline); akin to Old English *togian* to tow] (15th century)
*chiefly Scottish & dialect English* **:** ROPE

**tow·age** \'tō-ij\ *noun* (14th century)
**1 :** the act of towing
**2 :** a charge for towing

**¹to·ward** \'tō-(ə)rd, 'tȯ(-ə)rd\ *adjective* [Middle English *toward,* from Old English *tōweard* facing, imminent, from *tō,* preposition, to + *-weard* -ward] (before 12th century)
**1** *also* **to·wards** \'tō-(ə)rdz, 'tȯ(-ə)rdz\ [Middle English *towardes,* from Old English *tōweardes,* preposition, toward, from *tōweard,* adjective] **a :** coming soon **:** IMMINENT **b :** happening at the moment **:** AFOOT
**2 a** *obsolete* **:** quick to learn **:** APT **b :** PROPITIOUS, FAVORING (a *toward* breeze)

**²to·ward** *or* **to·wards** \'tō-(ə)rd(z), 'tȯ(-ə)rd(z), tə-'wȯrd(z), 'twȯrd(z), 'twōrd(z)\ *preposition* (before 12th century)
**1 :** in the direction of (driving *toward* town)
**2 a :** along a course leading to (a long stride *toward* disarmament) **b :** in relation to (an attitude *toward* life)

**3 a :** at a point in the direction of **:** NEAR (a cottage somewhere up *toward* the lake) **b :** in such a position so as to be in the direction of (your back was *toward* me)
**4 :** not long before (*toward* the end of the afternoon)
**5 a :** in the way of help or assistance in (did all he could *toward* raising campaign funds) **b :** for the partial payment of (proceeds go *toward* the establishment of a scholarship)

**to·ward·li·ness** \'tȯrd-lē-nəs, 'tȯrd-\ *noun* (1566)
*archaic* **:** the quality or state of being toward or towardly

**to·ward·ly** \'tō(-ə)rd-lē, 'tȯ(-ə)rd-\ *adjective* (1513)
*archaic*
**1 :** PLEASANT, AFFABLE
**2 :** FAVORABLE, PROPITIOUS
**3 :** developing favorably **:** PROMISING
— **towardly** *adverb*

**tow·boat** \'tō-,bōt\ *noun* (1815)
**1 :** TUGBOAT
**2 :** a compact shallow-draft boat with a squared bow designed and fitted for pushing tows of barges on inland waterways

**tow·el** \'tau̇(-ə)l\ *noun* [Middle English *towaille,* from Old French *toaille,* of Germanic origin; akin to Old High German *dwahila* towel; akin to Old High German *dwahan* to wash] (13th century)
**:** an absorbent cloth or paper for wiping or drying

**²towel** *verb* **-eled** *or* **-elled; -el·ing** *or* **-el·ling** (circa 1839)
*transitive verb*
**:** to rub or dry (as the body) with a towel
*intransitive verb*
**:** to use a towel to dry oneself

**tow·el·ette** \,tau̇-(ə-)'let\ *noun* (1902)
**:** a small usually premoistened piece of material used for personal cleansing (as of the hands)

**tow·el·ing** *or* **tow·el·ling** \'tau̇-(ə-)liŋ\ *noun* (1583)
**:** a cotton or linen fabric often used for making towels

**¹tow·er** \'tau̇(-ə)r\ *noun* [Middle English *tour, tor,* from Old English *torr* & Old French *tor, tur,* both from Latin *turris,* from Greek *tyrris, tyrsis*] (before 12th century)
**1 :** a building or structure typically higher than its diameter and high relative to its surroundings that may stand apart (as a campanile), or be attached (as a church belfry) to a larger structure, and that may be fully walled in or of skeleton framework (as an observation or transmission tower)
**2 :** a towering citadel **:** FORTRESS
**3 :** one that provides support or protection **:** BULWARK (a *tower* of strength)
— **tow·ered** \'tau̇(-ə)rd\ *adjective*
— **tow·er·like** \'tau̇(-ə)r-,līk\ *adjective*

**²tower** *intransitive verb* (1582)
**1 :** to reach or rise to a great height
**2 :** to exhibit superior qualities **:** SURPASS (her intellect *towered* over the others')

**tower block** *noun* (1966)
*chiefly British* **:** a tall building (as a high-rise apartment building)

**tower house** *noun* (1687)
**:** a medieval fortified castle (as in Scotland)

**tow·er·ing** *adjective* (1592)
**1 :** impressively high or great **:** IMPOSING (*towering* pines)
**2 :** reaching a high point of intensity **:** OVERWHELMING (a *towering* rage)
**3 :** going beyond proper bounds **:** EXCESSIVE (*towering* ambitions)
— **tow·er·ing·ly** \'tau̇(-ə)r-iŋ-lē\ *adverb*

---

\ə\ abut \ᵊ\ kitten \ər\ further \a\ ash \ā\ ace
\ä\ mop, mar \au̇\ out \ch\ chin \e\ bet \ē\ easy
\g\ go \i\ hit \ī\ ice \j\ job \ŋ\ sing \ō\ go
\ȯ\ law \ȯi\ boy \th\ thin \th\ the \ü\ loot \u̇\ foot
\y\ yet \zh\ vision *see also* Guide to Pronunciation

**Tower of Babel** (circa 1887)
: BABEL 2

**tow-head** \'tō-,hed\ *noun* (1829)
**1** : a low alluvial island or shoal in a river
: SANDBAR
**2** : a head of hair resembling tow especially in being flaxen or tousled; *also* : a person having such a head of hair
— **tow-head-ed** \-,he-dəd\ *adjective*

**to-whee** \'tō-,hē, 'tō-(,)ē, tō-'hē\ *noun* [imitative] (circa 1729)
**1** : a common finch (*Pipilo erythrophthalmus*) of eastern North America having the male black, white, and rufous — called also *chewink*
**2** : any of the North American finches belonging to the same genus (*Pipilo*) as the towhee

**to wit** \tə-'wit\ *adverb* [Middle English *to witen*, literally, to know — more at WIT] (14th century)
: that is to say : NAMELY

**tow-line** \'tō-,līn\ *noun* (1719)
: TOWROPE

**tow-mond** \'tō-,mänd\ *noun* [Middle English *towlmonyth*, from Old English *twelf mōnath*, from *twelf* twelve + *mōnath* month] (15th century)
*Scottish* : YEAR, TWELVEMONTH

**town** \'taún\ *noun* [Middle English, from Old English *tūn* enclosure, village, town; akin to Old High German *zūn* enclosure, Old Irish *dún* fortress] (before 12th century)
**1** *dialect English* : a cluster or aggregation of houses recognized as a distinct place with a place-name : HAMLET
**2 a** : a compactly settled area as distinguished from surrounding rural territory **b** : a compactly settled area usually larger than a village but smaller than a city **c** : a large densely populated urban area : CITY **d** : an English village having a periodic fair or market
**3** : a neighboring city, capital city, or metropolis
**4** : the city or urban life as contrasted with the country
**5** : the inhabitants of a city or town
**6** : a New England territorial and political unit usually containing both rural and unincorporated urban areas under a single town government; *also* : a New England community governed by a town meeting
**7** : a group of prairie dog burrows
— **town** *adjective*
— **on the town** : in usually carefree pursuit of entertainment or amusement (as city nightlife) especially as a relief from routine

**town car** *noun* (1907)
: a 4-door automobile with a usually open driver's compartment and a separate enclosed passenger compartment

**town clerk** *noun* (14th century)
: a public officer charged with recording the official proceedings and vital statistics of a town

**town crier** *noun* (1602)
: a town officer who makes public proclamations

**town-ee** \taú-'nē\ *noun* (1897)
*chiefly British* : TOWNIE

**town hall** *noun* (15th century)
: a public building used for town-government offices and meetings

**town house** *noun* (1803)
**1** : a house in town; *specifically* : the city residence of one having a countryseat or having a chief residence elsewhere (stayed at their *town house* during the social season)
**2** : a usually single-family house of two or sometimes three stories that is usually connected to a similar house by a common sidewall; *also* : ROW HOUSE

**town-ie** *or* **towny** \'taú-nē\ *noun, plural* **townies** (1852)
: TOWNSMAN; *especially* : a permanent inhabitant of a town as distinguished from a member of another group (as the academic community)

**town-let** \'taún-lət\ *noun* (circa 1552)
: a very small town

**town manager** *noun* (1922)
: an official appointed to direct the administration of a town government

**town meeting** *noun* (1636)
: a meeting of inhabitants or taxpayers constituting the legislative authority of a town

**town-scape** \-,skāp\ *noun* (1880)
**1** : a representation of an urban scene
**2** : a town or city viewed as a scene

**towns-folk** \'taúnz-,fōk\ *noun plural* (1737)
: TOWNSPEOPLE

**town-ship** \'taún-,ship\ *noun* (15th century)
**1** : an ancient unit of administration in England identical in area with or a division of a parish
**2 a** : TOWN 6 **b** : a unit of local government in some northeastern and north central states usually having a chief administrative officer or board **c** : an unorganized subdivision of the county in Maine, New Hampshire, and Vermont **d** : an electoral and administrative district of the county in the southern U.S.
**3** : a division of territory in surveys of U.S. public land containing 36 sections or 36 square miles
**4** : an area in the Republic of South Africa segregated for occupation by persons of non-European descent

**towns-man** \'taúnz-mən\ *noun* (before 12th century)
**1 a** : a native or resident of a town or city **b** : an urban or urbane person
**2** : a fellow citizen of a town

**towns-peo-ple** \-,pē-pəl\ *noun plural* (1648)
**1** : the inhabitants of a town or city : TOWNSMEN
**2** : town-dwelling or town-bred persons

**towns-wom-an** \-,wú-mən\ *noun* (1684)
**1** : a woman who is a native or resident of a town or city
**2** : a woman born or residing in the same town or city as another

**tow-path** \'tō-,path, -,páth\ *noun* (1788)
: a path (as along a canal) traveled especially by draft animals towing boats — called also *towing path*

**tow-rope** \-,rōp\ *noun* (1743)
: a line used in towing something (as a boat)

**tow sack** \'tō-'sak\ *noun* [³tow] (1926)
*Midland & Southern* : GUNNYSACK

**tow truck** *noun* (1944)
: a truck with winches and hoist mechanisms for freeing stuck vehicles and towing wrecked or disabled vehicles

**tox-** *or* **toxi-** *or* **toxo-** *combining form* [Late Latin, from Latin *toxicum* poison]
: poisonous : poison (*toxemia*)

**tox-a-phene** \'täk-sə-,fēn\ *noun* [from *Toxaphene*, a trademark] (1947)
: an insecticide with the approximate empirical formula $C_{10}H_{10}Cl_8$ that is a complex mixture of chlorinated compounds

**tox-e-mia** \täk-'sē-mē-ə\ *noun* [New Latin] (circa 1860)
: an abnormal condition associated with the presence of toxic substances in the blood
— **tox-e-mic** \-mik\ *adjective*

**¹tox-ic** \'täk-sik\ *adjective* [Late Latin *toxicus*, from Latin *toxicum* poison, from Greek *toxikon* arrow poison, from neuter of *toxikos* of a bow, from *toxon* bow, arrow] (1664)
**1** : of, relating to, or caused by a poison or toxin
**2** : affected by a poison or toxin (*toxic* pregnant women)
**3** : POISONOUS
— **tox-ic-i-ty** \täk-'si-sə-tē\ *noun*

**²toxic** *noun* (1890)
: a toxic substance

**toxic-** *or* **toxico-** *combining form* [New Latin, from Latin *toxicum*]
: poison (*toxico*logy)

**tox-i-cant** \'täk-si-kənt\ *noun* [Medieval Latin *toxicant-, toxicans*, present participle of *toxicare* to poison, from Latin *toxicum*] (circa 1882)
: a toxic agent; *especially* : PESTICIDE

**tox-i-co-log-i-cal** \,täk-si-kə-'lä-ji-kəl\ *or* **tox-i-co-log-ic** \-jik\ *adjective* (1839)
: of or relating to toxicology or toxins
— **tox-i-co-log-i-cal-ly** \-ji-k(ə-)lē\ *adverb*

**tox-i-col-o-gy** \-'kä-lə-jē\ *noun* (circa 1799)
: a science that deals with poisons and their effect and with the problems involved (as clinical, industrial, or legal)
— **tox-i-col-o-gist** \-jist\ *noun*

**tox-i-co-sis** \,täk-sə-'kō-səs\ *noun, plural* **-co-ses** \-,sēz\ [New Latin] (circa 1857)
: a pathological condition caused by the action of a poison or toxin

**toxic shock syndrome** *noun* (1978)
: an acute disease that is characterized by fever, diarrhea, nausea, diffuse erythema, and shock, that is associated especially with the presence of a bacterium (*Staphylococcus aureus*), and that occurs especially in menstruating females using tampons — called also *toxic shock*

**toxi-gen-ic** \,täk-sə-'je-nik\ *adjective* (circa 1923)
: producing toxin (*toxigenic* bacteria and fungi)
— **toxi-ge-nic-i-ty** \,täk-si-jə-'ni-sə-tē\ *noun*

**tox-in** \'täk-sən\ *noun* [International Scientific Vocabulary] (1886)
: a poisonous substance that is a specific product of the metabolic activities of a living organism and is usually very unstable, notably toxic when introduced into the tissues, and typically capable of inducing antibody formation

**tox-in-an-ti-tox-in** \'täk-sən-'an-ti-,täk-sən\ *noun* (1904)
: a mixture of toxin and antitoxin used especially formerly in immunizing against a disease (as diphtheria) for which they are specific

**tox-oid** \'täk-,sóid\ *noun* [International Scientific Vocabulary] (circa 1894)
: a toxin of a pathogenic organism treated so as to destroy its toxicity but leave it capable of inducing the formation of antibodies on injection

**tox-oph-i-lite** \täk-'sä-fə-,līt\ *noun* [Greek *toxon* bow, arrow + *philos* dear, loving] (1794)
: a person fond of or expert at archery
— **toxophilite** *adjective*
— **tox-oph-i-ly** \-lē\ *noun*

**toxo-plas-ma** \,täk-sə-'plaz-mə\ *noun* [New Latin] (1926)
: any of a genus (*Toxoplasma*) of sporozoans that are typically serious pathogens of vertebrates
— **toxo-plas-mic** \-mik\ *adjective*

**toxo-plas-mo-sis** \-,plaz-'mō-səs\ *noun, plural* **-mo-ses** \-,sēz\ [New Latin] (1926)
: infection of humans, other mammals, or birds with disease caused by a toxoplasma (*Toxoplasma gondii*) that invades the tissues and may seriously damage the central nervous system especially of infants

**¹toy** \'tói\ *noun* [Middle English *toye*] (15th century)
**1** *obsolete* **a** : flirtatious or seductive behavior **b** : PASTIME; *also* : a sportive or amusing act : ANTIC
**2 a** : something (as a preoccupation) that is paltry or trifling **b** : a literary or musical trifle or diversion **c** : TRINKET, BAUBLE
**3** : something for a child to play with
**4** : something diminutive; *especially* : a diminutive animal (as of a small breed or variety)
**5** : something that can be toyed with
**6** *Scottish* : a headdress of linen or woolen hanging down over the shoulders and formerly worn by old women of the lower classes

— **toy·like** \-,līk\ *adjective*

**²toy** *intransitive verb* (circa 1529)
**1 :** to act or deal with something lightly or without vigor or purpose
**2 :** to engage in flirtation
**3 :** to amuse oneself as if with a toy **:** PLAY
**synonym** see TRIFLE
— **toy·er** \'tȯi-ər\ *noun*

**³toy** *adjective* (1801)
**1 :** resembling a toy especially in diminutive size
**2 :** designed or made for use as a toy ⟨a *toy* stove⟩

**toy Man·ches·ter terrier** \-'man-,ches-tər-, -chə-stər-\ *noun* (1935)
**:** any of a breed of toy dogs developed from the Manchester terrier that have erect ears of moderate size and weigh not more than 12 pounds (5.4 kilograms) — called also *toy Manchester*

toy Manchester terrier

**toy·on** \'tȯi-,än\ *noun* [American Spanish *tollon*] (1848)
**:** a chiefly Californian ornamental evergreen shrub (*Heteromeles arbutifolia*) of the rose family having white flowers succeeded by persistent usually bright red berries

**toy poodle** *noun* (1935)
**:** any of a breed of toy dogs developed from the standard poodle that are not more than 10 inches (25 centimeters) high at the withers

**TPN** \,tē-,pē-'en\ *noun* [*triphosphopyridine nu*cleotide] (1938)
**:** NADP

**tra·be·at·ed** \'trā-bē-,ā-təd\ *also* **tra·be·ate** \-,āt\ *adjective* [Latin *trabs, trabes* beam — more at THORP] (1843)
**:** designed or constructed with horizontal beams or lintels
— **tra·be·a·tion** \,trā-bē-'ā-shən\ *noun*

**tra·bec·u·la** \trə-'be-kyə-lə\ *noun, plural* **-lae** \-,lē, -,lī\ *also* **-las** [New Latin, from Latin, little beam, diminutive of *trabs, trabes* beam] (circa 1866)
**1 :** a small bar, rod, bundle of fibers, or septal membrane in the framework of a body organ or part
**2 :** a fold, ridge, or bar projecting into or extending from a plant part; *especially* **:** a row of cells bridging an intercellular space
— **tra·bec·u·lar** \-lər\ *adjective*
— **tra·bec·u·late** \-lət\ *adjective*

**¹trace** \'trās\ *noun* [Middle English, from Middle French, from *tracier* to trace] (14th century)
**1** *archaic* **:** a course or path that one follows
**2 a :** a mark or line left by something that has passed; *also* **:** FOOTPRINT **b :** a path, trail, or road made by the passage of animals, people, or vehicles
**3 a :** a sign or evidence of some past thing **:** VESTIGE **b :** ENGRAM
**4 :** something (as a line) traced or drawn: as **a :** the marking made by a recording instrument (as a seismograph or kymograph) **b :** the ground plan of a military installation or position either on a map or on the ground
**5 a :** the intersection of a line or plane with a plane **b :** the usually bright line or spot that moves across the screen of a cathode-ray tube; *also* **:** the path taken by such a line or spot
**6 a :** a minute and often barely detectable amount or indication ⟨a *trace* of a smile⟩ **b :** an amount of a chemical constituent not always quantitatively determinable because of minuteness ☆
— **trace·less** \-ləs\ *adjective*

**²trace** *verb* **traced; trac·ing** [Middle English, from Middle French *tracier*, from (assumed) Vulgar Latin *tractiare* to drag, from Latin *tractus*, past participle of *trahere* to pull] (14th century)
*transitive verb*
**1 a :** DELINEATE, SKETCH **b :** to form (as letters or figures) carefully or painstakingly **c :** to copy (as a drawing) by following the lines or letters as seen through a transparent superimposed sheet **d :** to impress or imprint (as a design or pattern) with a tracer **e :** to record a tracing of in the form of a curved, wavy, or broken line ⟨*trace* the heart action⟩ **f :** to adorn with linear ornamentation (as tracery or chasing)
**2** *archaic* **:** to travel over **:** TRAVERSE
**3 a :** to follow the footprints, track, or trail of **b :** to follow or study out in detail or step by step ⟨*trace* the history of the labor movement⟩ **c :** to discover by going backward over the evidence step by step ⟨*trace* your ancestry⟩ **d :** to discover signs, evidence, or remains of
**4 :** to lay out the trace of (a military installation)
*intransitive verb*
**1 :** to make one's way; *especially* **:** to follow a track or trail
**2 :** to be traceable historically
— **trace·abil·i·ty** \,trā-sə-'bi-lə-tē\ *noun*
— **trace·able** \'trā-sə-bəl\ *adjective*

**³trace** *noun* [Middle English *trais*, plural, *traces*, from Middle French, plural of *trait* pull, draft, trace — more at TRAIT] (14th century)
**1 :** either of two straps, chains, or lines of a harness for attaching a draft animal to something (as a vehicle) to be drawn
**2 :** LEADER 1e(2)
**3 :** one or more vascular bundles supplying a leaf or twig
**4 :** a connecting bar or rod pivoted at each end to another piece and used for transmitting motion

**trace element** *noun* (1932)
**:** a chemical element present in minute quantities; *especially* **:** one used by organisms and held essential to their physiology

**trac·er** \'trā-sər\ *noun* (circa 1552)
**1 :** one that traces, tracks down, or searches out: as **a :** a person who traces missing persons or property and especially goods lost in transit **b :** an inquiry sent out in tracing a shipment lost in transit
**2 :** one who traces designs, patterns, or markings
**3 :** a device (as a stylus) used in tracing
**4 a :** ammunition containing a chemical composition to mark the flight of projectiles by a trail of smoke or fire **b :** a substance used to trace the course of a chemical or biological process; *especially* **:** LABEL 3d

**trac·ery** \'trā-sə-rē, 'trās-rē\ *noun, plural* **-er·ies** (1669)
**1 :** architectural ornamental work with branching lines; *especially* **:** decorative open-work in the head of a Gothic window
**2 :** a decorative interlacing of lines suggestive of Gothic tracery
— **trac·er·ied** \-rēd\ *adjective*

tracery 1

**trache-** *or* **tracheo-** *combining form* [New Latin, from Medieval Latin *trachea*]
**1 :** trachea ⟨*trache*itis⟩ ⟨*tracheo*tomy⟩
**2 :** tracheal and ⟨*tracheo*bronchial⟩

**tra·chea** \'trā-kē-ə\ *noun, plural* **-che·ae** \-kē-,ē, -kē-,ī\ *also* **-che·as** [Middle English, from Medieval Latin, from Late Latin *trachia*, from Greek *tracheia* (*artēria*) rough (artery), from feminine of *trachys* rough] (14th century)
**1 :** the main trunk of the system of tubes by which air passes to and from the lungs in vertebrates
**2** [New Latin, from Medieval Latin] **:** VESSEL 3b; *also* **:** one of its constituent cellular elements
**3** [New Latin] **:** one of the air-conveying tubules forming the respiratory system of most insects and many other arthropods
— **tra·che·al** \-kē-əl\ *adjective*

**tra·che·ary** \'trā-kē-,er-ē\ *adjective* (1885)
**:** of, relating to, or being plant tracheae ⟨*tracheary* elements⟩

**tra·che·ate** \-kē-,āt, -ət\ *or* **tra·che·at·ed** \-,ā-təd\ *adjective* (1877)
**:** having tracheae as breathing organs

**tra·cheid** \'trā-kē-əd, -,kēd\ *noun* [International Scientific Vocabulary] (1875)
**:** a long tubular pitted cell that is peculiar to xylem, functions in conduction and support, and has tapering closed ends and thickened lignified walls

**tra·che·i·tis** \,trā-kē-'ī-təs\ *noun* [New Latin] (1859)
**:** inflammation of the trachea

**tra·cheo·bron·chi·al** \,trā-kē-ō-'bräŋ-kē-əl\ *adjective* (1896)
**:** of or relating to both trachea and bronchi ⟨*tracheobronchial* lesions⟩

**tra·che·ole** \'trā-kē-,ōl\ *noun* [New Latin *tracheola*, diminutive of *trachea*] (1901)
**:** one of the minute delicate endings of a branched trachea of an insect
— **tra·che·o·lar** \trā-'kē-ə-lər\ *adjective*

**tra·cheo·phyte** \'trā-kē-ə-,fīt\ *noun* [New Latin *Tracheophyta*, from *trache-* + Greek *phyton* plant; akin to Greek *phyein* to bring forth — more at BE] (1937)
**:** any of a division (Tracheophyta) comprising green plants (as ferns and seed plants) with a vascular system that contains tracheids or tracheary elements

**tra·che·os·to·my** \,trā-kē-'äs-tə-mē\ *noun, plural* **-mies** (circa 1923)
**:** the surgical formation of an opening into the trachea through the neck especially to allow the passage of air

**tra·che·ot·o·my** \,trā-kē-'ä-tə-mē\ *noun, plural* **-mies** (circa 1726)
**:** the surgical operation of cutting into the trachea especially through the skin

**tra·cho·ma** \trə-'kō-mə\ *noun* [New Latin, from Greek *trachōma*, from *trachys* rough] (circa 1693)
**:** a chronic contagious bacterial conjunctivitis marked by inflammatory granulations on the conjunctival surfaces, caused by a chlamydia (*Chlamydia trachomatis*), and commonly resulting in blindness if left untreated

**tra·chyte** \'tra-,kīt, 'trā-\ *noun* [French, from Greek *trachys* rough] (1821)
**:** a usually light-colored volcanic rock consisting chiefly of potash feldspar

\ə\ abut \ᵊ\ kitten \ər\ further \a\ ash \ā\ ace \ä\ mop, mar \au̇\ out \ch\ chin \e\ bet \ē\ easy \g\ go \i\ hit \ī\ ice \j\ job \ŋ\ sing \ō\ go \ȯ\ law \ȯi\ boy \th\ thin \t͟h\ the \ü\ loot \u̇\ foot \y\ yet \zh\ vision *see also* Guide to Pronunciation

**tra·chyt·ic** \trə-'ki-tik\ *adjective* (1827)
: of or relating to a texture of igneous rocks in which lath-shaped feldspar crystals are in almost parallel lines

**trac·ing** \'trā-siŋ\ *noun* (15th century)
**1** : the act of one that traces
**2** : something that is traced: as **a** : a copy made on a superimposed transparent sheet **b** : a graphic record made by an instrument (as a seismograph) that registers some movement

**tracing paper** *noun* (1824)
: a semitransparent paper for tracing drawings; *also* : a thin paper containing a clothing pattern to be transferred to fabric (as through carbon paper) by tracing

**tracing wheel** *noun* (circa 1891)
: a usually toothed wheel with a handle that is used on tracing paper to trace a pattern

**¹track** \'trak\ *noun* [Middle English *trak*, from Middle French *trac*, perhaps of Germanic origin; akin to Middle Dutch *tracken*, *trecken* to pull, haul — more at TREK] (15th century)
**1 a** : detectable evidence (as the wake of a ship, a line of footprints, or a wheel rut) that something has passed **b** : a path made by repeated footfalls : TRAIL **c** : a course laid out especially for racing **d** : the parallel rails of a railroad **e** (1) : one of a series of parallel or concentric paths along which material (as music or information) is recorded (as on a phonograph record or magnetic tape) (2) : a group of grooves on a phonograph record containing recorded sound (3) : material recorded especially on a track **f** : a usually metal way (as a groove) serving as a guide (as for a movable lighting fixture)
**2** : a footprint whether recent or fossil ⟨the huge *track* of a dinosaur⟩
**3 a** : the course along which something moves **b** : a way of life, conduct, or action **c** : one of several curricula of study to which students are assigned according to their needs or levels of ability **d** : the projection on the earth's surface of the path along which something (as a missile or an airplane) has flown
**4 a** : a sequence of events : a train of ideas : SUCCESSION **b** : an awareness of a fact, progression, or condition ⟨keep *track* of the costs⟩ ⟨lose *track* of the time⟩
**5 a** : the width of a wheeled vehicle from wheel to wheel and usually from the outside of the rims **b** : the tread of an automobile tire **c** : either of two endless metal belts on which a tracklaying vehicle travels
**6** : track-and-field sports; *especially* : those performed on a running track
**synonym** see TRACE
— **track·less** \'trak-ləs\ *adjective*
— **in one's tracks** : where one stands or is at the moment : on the spot ⟨was stopped *in his tracks*⟩

**²track** (1565)
*transitive verb*
**1 a** : to follow the tracks or traces of : TRAIL **b** : to search for by following evidence until found ⟨*track* down the source⟩
**2 a** : to follow by vestiges : TRACE **b** : to observe or plot the moving path of (as a spacecraft or missile) instrumentally
**3** : to travel over : TRAVERSE ⟨*track* a desert⟩
**4 a** : to make tracks upon **b** : to carry (as mud) on the feet and deposit
**5** : to keep track of (as a trend) : FOLLOW
*intransitive verb*
**1** : TRAVEL ⟨comet *tracks* eastward⟩
**2 a** *of a phonograph needle* : to follow the groove undulations of a recording **b** *of a pair of wheels* (1) : to maintain a constant distance apart on the straightaway (2) : to fit a track or rails **c** *of a rear wheel of a vehicle* : to follow accurately the corresponding fore wheel on a straightaway
**3** : to leave tracks (as on a floor)
— **track·er** *noun*

**track·age** \'tra-kij\ *noun* (1880)
**1** : lines of railway track
**2 a** : a right to use the tracks of another railroad line **b** : the charge for such right

**track–and–field** \ˌtrak-ən-'fē(ə)ld\ *adjective* (1905)
: of, relating to, or being any of various competitive athletic events (as running, jumping, and weight throwing) performed on a running track and on the adjacent field

**track·ball** \'trak-ˌbȯl\ *noun* (1967)
: a ball that is mounted within a computer console so as to be only partially exposed and is rotated to control the movement of a cursor on a display

**tracked** \'trakt\ *adjective* (1926)
**1** : traveling on endless metal belts instead of wheels
**2** : moving along a rail ⟨a *tracked* air-cushion vehicle⟩

**track·ing** \'tra-kiŋ\ *noun* (circa 1929)
: the assigning of students to a curricular track

**tracking shot** *noun* (circa 1940)
: a scene photographed from a moving dolly

**track·lay·er** \'trak-ˌlā-ər, -ˌle(-ə)r\ *noun* (circa 1861)
**1** : a worker engaged in tracklaying
**2** : a tracklaying vehicle

**¹track·lay·ing** \-ˌlā-iŋ\ *noun* (1857)
: the laying of tracks on a railway line

**²tracklaying** *adjective* (1884)
: of, relating to, or being a vehicle that travels on two or more endless usually metal belts

**trackless trolley** *noun* (1921)
: TROLLEYBUS

**track lighting** *noun* (1972)
: adjustable lamps mounted along an electrified metal track

**track·man** \'trak-mən, -ˌman\ *noun* (1922)
: a runner on a track team

**track record** *noun* [¹*track* (track-and-field sports)] (1952)
: a record of past performance often taken as an indicator of likely future performance

**track·side** \'trak-ˌsīd\ *adjective* (1886)
: of, relating to, or situated in the area immediately adjacent to a track
— **trackside** *noun*

**track·suit** \'trak-ˌsüt\ *noun* (1922)
: a suit of clothing consisting usually of a jacket and pants that is often worn by athletes when working out

**track·walk·er** \-ˌwȯ-kər\ *noun* (1872)
: a worker employed to walk over and inspect a section of railroad tracks

**track·way** \-ˌwā\ *noun* (1818)
**1** : a beaten or trodden path
**2** : a series of fossil footprints of a dinosaur

**¹tract** \'trakt\ *noun, often capitalized* [Middle English *tracte*, from Medieval Latin *tractus*, from Latin, action of drawing, extension; perhaps from its being sung without a break by one voice] (14th century)
: verses of Scripture (as from the Psalms) used between the gradual and the Gospel at some masses (as during penitential seasons)

**²tract** *noun* [Middle English *tracte*, from Latin *tractus* action of drawing, extension, from *trahere* to pull, draw] (15th century)
**1** : extent or lapse of time
**2** : an area either large or small: as **a** : an indefinite stretch of land **b** : a defined area of land
**3 a** : a system of body parts or organs that act together to perform some function ⟨the digestive *tract*⟩ **b** : a bundle of nerve fibers having a common origin, termination, and function

**³tract** *noun* [Middle English, treatise, modification of Latin *tractatus* tractate] (1760)
: a pamphlet or leaflet of political or religious propaganda; *also* : a piece of writing that is suggestive of such a tract

**trac·ta·ble** \'trak-tə-bəl\ *adjective* [Latin *tractabilis*, from *tractare* to handle, treat] (1502)
**1** : capable of being easily led, taught, or controlled : DOCILE ⟨a *tractable* horse⟩
**2** : easily handled, managed, or wrought : MALLEABLE
**synonym** see OBEDIENT
— **trac·ta·bil·i·ty** \ˌtrak-tə-'bi-lə-tē\ *noun*
— **trac·ta·ble·ness** \'trak-tə-bəl-nəs\ *noun*
— **trac·ta·bly** \-blē\ *adverb*

**Trac·tar·i·an** \trak-'ter-ē-ən\ *noun* [from *Tracts for the Times*, series of pamphlets expounding the Oxford movement] (circa 1839)
: a promoter or supporter of the Oxford movement

**Trac·tar·i·an·ism** \-ē-ə-ˌni-zəm\ *noun* (1840)
: a system of High Church principles set forth in a series of tracts at Oxford (1833–41)

**trac·tate** \'trak-ˌtāt\ *noun* [Latin *tractatus*, from *tractare* to draw out, handle, treat — more at TREAT] (15th century)
: TREATISE, DISSERTATION

**tract house** *noun* (1956)
: any of many similarly designed houses built on a tract of land

**trac·tion** \'trak-shən\ *noun* [Medieval Latin *traction-, tractio*, from Latin *trahere*] (1615)
**1** : the act of drawing : the state of being drawn; *also* : the force exerted in drawing
**2** : the drawing of a vehicle by motive power; *also* : the motive power employed
**3 a** : the adhesive friction of a body on a surface on which it moves ⟨the *traction* of a wheel on a rail⟩ **b** : a pulling force exerted on a skeletal structure (as in a fracture) by means of a special device ⟨a *traction* splint⟩; *also* : a state of tension created by such a pulling force ⟨a leg in *traction*⟩
— **trac·tion·al** \-shnəl, -shə-nºl\ *adjective*

**trac·tive** \'trak-tiv\ *adjective* [Latin *tractus*, past participle] (1615)
**1** : serving to draw
**2** : of or relating to traction : TRACTIONAL

**trac·tor** \'trak-tər\ *noun* [New Latin, from Latin *trahere*] (1900)
**1 a** : a 4-wheeled or tracklaying automotive vehicle used especially for drawing farm equipment **b** : a smaller 2-wheeled apparatus controlled through handlebars by a walking operator **c** : ³TRUCK 3f
**2** : an airplane having the propeller forward of the main supporting surfaces

**trad** \'trad\ *adjective* (1958)
*chiefly British* : TRADITIONAL

**¹trade** \'trād\ *noun* [Middle English, from Middle Low German; akin to Old High German *trata* track, course, Old English *tredan* to tread] (14th century)
**1 a** *obsolete* : a path traversed : WAY **b** *archaic* : a track or trail left by a person or animal : TREAD 1
**2** : a customary course of action : PRACTICE ⟨thy sin's not accidental, but a *trade* —Shakespeare⟩
**3 a** : the business or work in which one engages regularly : OCCUPATION **b** : an occupation requiring manual or mechanical skill : CRAFT **c** : the persons engaged in an occupation, business, or industry
**4 a** *obsolete* : dealings between persons or groups **b** (1) : the business of buying and selling or bartering commodities : COMMERCE (2) : BUSINESS; MARKET ⟨novelties for the tourist *trade*⟩ ⟨did a good *trade* in small appliances⟩
**5 a** : an act or instance of trading : TRANSACTION; *also* : an exchange of property usually without use of money **b** : a firm's customers : CLIENTELE **c** : the group of firms engaged in a business or industry
**6** : TRADE WIND — usually used in plural
**7** : a publication intended for persons in the entertainment business — usually used in plural
**synonym** see BUSINESS

²**trade** *verb* **trad·ed; trad·ing** (1553)
*intransitive verb*
**1** *obsolete* **:** to have dealings **:** NEGOTIATE
**2 a :** to engage in the exchange, purchase, or sale of goods **b :** to make one's purchases **:** SHOP ⟨*trades* at his store⟩
**3 :** to give one thing in exchange for another
**4 :** SELL 3
*transitive verb*
**1** *archaic* **:** to do business with
**2 a :** to give in exchange for another commodity **:** BARTER; *also* **:** to make an exchange of ⟨*traded* places⟩ **b :** to engage in frequent buying and selling of (as stocks or commodities) usually in search of quick profits
**— trad·able** *also* **trade·able** \'trā-də-bəl\ *adjective*
**— trade on :** to take often unscrupulous advantage of **:** EXPLOIT ⟨*traded on* their influence . . . in securing special favors —T. C. Pease⟩

³**trade** *adjective* (1633)
**1 :** of, relating to, or used in trade
**2 a :** intended for or limited to persons in a business or industry ⟨a *trade* publication⟩ ⟨*trade* sales⟩ **b :** serving others in the same business rather than the ultimate user or consumer ⟨a *trade* printing house⟩
**3** *also* **trades :** of, composed of, or representing the trades or trade unions ⟨a *trade* committee⟩
**4 :** of a larger softcover format than mass-market paperbacks and usually sold only in bookstores ⟨*trade* paperbacks⟩; *also* **:** of or relating to the publishing of such books

**trade acceptance** *noun* (1916)
**:** a time draft or bill of exchange for the amount of a specific purchase drawn by the seller on the buyer, bearing the buyer's acceptance, and often noting the place of payment (as a bank)

**trade agreement** *noun* (circa 1921)
**1 :** an international agreement on conditions of trade in goods and services
**2 :** an agreement resulting from collective bargaining

**trade book** *noun* (circa 1945)
**1 :** a book intended for general readership
**2 :** TRADE EDITION

**trade·craft** \'trād-ˌkraft\ *noun* (1961)
**:** the techniques and procedures of espionage

**trade discount** *noun* (1901)
**:** a deduction from the list price of goods allowed by a manufacturer or wholesaler to a retailer

**trade dollar** *noun* (1873)
**:** a U.S. silver dollar weighing 420 grains .900 fine issued 1873–85 for use in oriental trade

**trade down** *intransitive verb* (1942)
**1 :** to trade something in (as an automobile) for something less expensive or valuable of its kind
**2 :** to stock or purchase lower-priced items **:** ECONOMIZE

**trade edition** *noun* (1930)
**:** an edition of a book intended for general distribution — compare TEXT EDITION

**trade–in** \'trād-ˌin\ *noun* (1917)
**:** an item of merchandise (as an automobile or refrigerator) taken as payment or part payment for a purchase

**trade in** *transitive verb* (1923)
**1 :** to turn in as payment or part payment for a purchase or bill ⟨*trade* the old car *in* on a new one⟩
**2 :** EXCHANGE 2

**trade language** *noun* (1662)
**:** a restructured language (as a lingua franca or pidgin) used especially in commercial communication

**trade–last** \'trād-ˌlast\ *noun* (1891)
**:** a complimentary remark by a third person that a hearer offers to repeat to the person complimented if he or she will first report a compliment made about the hearer

¹**trade·mark** \-ˌmärk\ *noun* (1838)
**1 :** a device (as a word) pointing distinctly to the origin or ownership of merchandise to which it is applied and legally reserved to the exclusive use of the owner as maker or seller
**2 :** a distinguishing characteristic or feature firmly associated with a person or thing ⟨derringers . . . became almost a *trademark* of gamblers —Elmer Keith⟩ ⟨wearing his *trademark* bow tie and derby hat⟩

²**trademark** *transitive verb* (1906)
**:** to secure trademark rights for **:** register the trademark of

¹**trade name** *noun* (1861)
**1 a :** the name used for an article among traders **b :** an arbitrarily adopted name that is given by a manufacturer or merchant to an article or service to distinguish it as produced or sold by him and that may be used and protected as a trademark
**2 :** the name or style under which a concern does business

²**trade name** *transitive verb* (1945)
**:** to designate with a trade name

**trade–off** \'trād-ˌȯf\ *noun* (1961)
**1 :** a balancing of factors all of which are not attainable at the same time ⟨the education versus experience *trade-off* which governs personnel practices —H. S. White⟩
**2 :** a giving up of one thing in return for another **:** EXCHANGE
**— trade off** *transitive verb*

**trad·er** \'trā-dər\ *noun* (1585)
**1 :** a person whose business is buying and selling or barter: as **a :** MERCHANT **b :** a person who buys and sells (as stocks or commodities futures) in search of short-term profits
**2 :** a ship engaged in the coastal or foreign trade

**trade route** *noun* (1876)
**1 :** a route followed by traders (as in caravans)
**2 :** one of the sea-lanes ordinarily used by merchant ships

**trad·es·can·tia** \ˌtra-də-'skan(t)-sh(ē-)ə\ *noun* [New Latin, genus name, from John Tradescant (died 1638) English traveler & gardener] (circa 1909)
**:** SPIDERWORT

**trade school** *noun* (1889)
**:** a secondary school teaching the skilled trades

**trade secret** *noun* (1895)
**:** a formula, process, or device used in a business that is not published or divulged and that thereby gives an advantage over competitors

**trades·man** \'trādz-mən\ *noun* (1597)
**1 :** a worker in a skilled trade **:** CRAFTSMAN
**2 :** one who runs a retail store **:** SHOPKEEPER

**trades·peo·ple** \-ˌpē-pəl\ *noun plural* (1728)
**:** people engaged in trade

**trade union** *also* **trades union** *noun* (1835)
**:** LABOR UNION
**— trade unionism** *noun*
**— trade unionist** *noun*

**trade up** *intransitive verb* (1926)
**1 :** to trade something in (as an automobile) for something more expensive or valuable of its kind
**2 :** to stock or purchase higher-priced items

**trade wind** *noun* (1650)
**:** a wind blowing almost constantly in one direction; *especially* **:** a wind blowing almost continually toward the equator from the northeast in the belt between the northern horse latitudes and the doldrums and from the southeast in the belt between the southern horse latitudes and the doldrums — usually used in plural

**trading post** *noun* (1796)
**1 :** a station of a trader or trading company established in a sparsely settled region where trade in products of local origin (as furs) is carried on

**2 :** ⁶POST 3b

**trading stamp** *noun* (1897)
**:** a printed stamp of value given as a premium to a retail customer to be redeemed in merchandise when accumulated in numbers

**tra·di·tion** \trə-'di-shən\ *noun* [Middle English *tradicioun*, from Middle French & Latin; Middle French *tradition*, from Latin *tradition-*, *traditio* action of handing over, tradition — more at TREASON] (14th century)
**1 :** an inherited, established, or customary pattern of thought, action, or behavior (as a religious practice or a social custom)
**2 :** the handing down of information, beliefs, and customs by word of mouth or by example from one generation to another without written instruction
**3 :** cultural continuity in social attitudes, customs, and institutions
**4 :** characteristic manner, method, or style
*word history* see TREASON
**— tra·di·tion·al** \-'dish-nəl, -'di-shə-nᵊl\ *adjective*
**— tra·di·tion·al·ly** *adverb*
**— tra·di·tion·less** \-'di-shən-ləs\ *adjective*

**tra·di·tion·al·ism** \trə-'dish-nə-ˌli-zəm, -'di-shə-nᵊl-ˌi-\ *noun* (circa 1859)
**1 :** adherence to the doctrines or practices of a tradition
**2 :** the beliefs of those opposed to modernism, liberalism, or radicalism
**— tra·di·tion·al·ist** \-list, -ist\ *noun or adjective*
**— tra·di·tion·al·is·tic** \-ˌdish-nə-'lis-tik, -ˌdi-shə-nᵊl-'is-\ *adjective*

**tra·di·tion·al·ize** \trə-'dish-nə-ˌlīz, -'di-shə-nᵊl-ˌīz\ *transitive verb* **-ized; -iz·ing** (1882)
**:** to make traditional **:** imbue with traditions or traditionalism

**tra·di·tion·ary** \trə-'di-shə-ˌner-ē\ *adjective* (1661)
**:** TRADITIONAL

**tra·duce** \trə-'düs, -'dyüs\ *transitive verb* **tra·duced; tra·duc·ing** [Latin *traducere* to lead across, transfer, degrade, from *tra-*, *trans-* trans- + *ducere* to lead — more at TOW] (1592)
**1 :** to expose to shame or blame by means of falsehood and misrepresentation
**2 :** VIOLATE, BETRAY ⟨*traduce* a principle of law⟩
*synonym* see MALIGN
**— tra·duce·ment** \-mənt\ *noun*
**— tra·duc·er** *noun*

¹**traf·fic** \'tra-fik\ *noun, often attributive* [Middle French *trafique*, from Old Italian *traffico*, from *trafficare* to traffic] (1506)
**1 a :** import and export trade **b :** the business of bartering or buying and selling **c :** illegal or disreputable usually commercial activity ⟨the drug *traffic*⟩
**2 a :** communication or dealings especially between individuals or groups **b :** EXCHANGE ⟨a lively *traffic* in ideas —F. L. Allen⟩
**3** *archaic* **:** WARES, GOODS
**4 a :** the movement (as of vehicles or pedestrians) through an area or along a route **b :** the vehicles, pedestrians, ships, or planes moving along a route **c :** the information or signals transmitted over a communications system **:** MESSAGES
**5 a :** the passengers or cargo carried by a transportation system **b :** the business of transporting passengers or freight
**6 :** the volume of customers visiting a business establishment
*synonym* see BUSINESS
**— the traffic will bear :** existing conditions will allow or permit ⟨charge what the *traffic will bear*⟩

---

\ə\ abut \ᵊ\ kitten \ər\ further \a\ ash \ā\ ace
\ä\ mop, mar \aù\ out \ch\ chin \e\ bet \ē\ easy
\g\ go \i\ hit \ī\ ice \j\ job \ŋ\ sing \ō\ go
\ȯ\ law \ȯi\ boy \th\ thin \t͟h\ the \ü\ loot \ù\ foot
\y\ yet \zh\ vision    *see also* Guide to Pronunciation

**²traffic** *verb* **traf·ficked; traf·fick·ing** (1540)
*intransitive verb*
: to carry on traffic
*transitive verb*
**1** : to travel over ⟨heavily *trafficked* highways⟩
**2** : TRADE, BARTER
— **traf·fick·er** *noun*
**traf·fic·abil·i·ty** \,tra-fi-kə-'bi-lə-tē\ *noun* (1899)
: the quality of a terrain that permits passage (as of vehicles and troops)
— **traf·fic·able** \'tra-fi-kə-bəl\ *adjective*
**traffic circle** *noun* (1942)
: ROTARY 2
**traffic cone** *noun* (1953)
: a conical marker used on a road or highway (as for indicating an area under repair)
**traffic court** *noun* (1919)
: a minor court for disposition of petty prosecutions for violations of statutes, ordinances, and local regulations governing the use of highways and motor vehicles
**traffic engineering** *noun* (1931)
: engineering dealing with the design of streets and control of traffic
— **traffic engineer** *noun*
**traffic island** *noun* (1931)
: ISLAND 2a
**traffic light** *noun* (1912)
: an electrically operated visual signal (as a system of colored lights) for controlling traffic
**traffic manager** *noun* (1862)
**1** : a supervisor of the traffic functions of a commercial or industrial organization
**2** : the director of a large telegraph office
**traffic signal** *noun* (1917)
: a signal (as a traffic light) for controlling traffic
**trag·a·canth** \'tra-jə-,kan(t)th, 'tra-gə-, -kən(t)th; *also* 'tra-gə-,san(t)th\ *noun* [Middle French *tragacanthe*, from Latin *tragacantha*, from Greek *tragakantha*, from *tragos* goat + *akantha* thorn] (1573)
: a gum obtained from various Asian or East European leguminous plants (genus *Astragalus* and especially *A. gummifer*) that swells in water and is used chiefly as an emulsifying, suspending, or thickening agent
**tra·ge·di·an** \trə-'jē-dē-ən\ *noun* [Middle English *tragedien*, from Middle French, from *tragedie*] (14th century)
**1** : a writer of tragedies
**2** : an actor specializing in tragic roles
**tra·ge·di·enne** \trə-,jē-dē-'en\ *noun* [French *tragédienne*, from Middle French, from *tragedie*] (1851)
: an actress who plays tragic roles
**trag·e·dy** \'tra-jə-dē\ *noun, plural* **-dies** [Middle English *tragedie*, from Middle French, from Latin *tragoedia*, from Greek *tragōidia*, from *tragos* goat (akin to Greek *trōgein* to gnaw) + *aeidein* to sing — more at TROGLODYTE, ODE] (14th century)
**1 a** : a medieval narrative poem or tale typically describing the downfall of a great man **b** : a serious drama typically describing a conflict between the protagonist and a superior force (as destiny) and having a sorrowful or disastrous conclusion that excites pity or terror **c** : the literary genre of tragic dramas
**2 a** : a disastrous event : CALAMITY **b** : MISFORTUNE
**3** : tragic quality or element
**trag·ic** \'tra-jik\ *also* **trag·i·cal** \-ji-kəl\ *adjective* [Middle English, from Latin *tragicus*, from Greek *tragikos*, irregular from *tragōidia* tragedy] (15th century)
**1** : of, marked by, or expressive of tragedy ⟨the *tragic* significance of the atomic bomb —H. S. Truman⟩
**2 a** : dealing with or treated in tragedy ⟨the *tragic* hero⟩ **b** : appropriate to or typical of tragedy

**3 a** : regrettably serious or unpleasant : DEPLORABLE, LAMENTABLE ⟨a *tragic* mistake⟩ **b** : marked by a sense of tragedy
— **trag·i·cal·ly** \-ji-k(ə-)lē\ *adverb*
**tragic flaw** *noun* (1913)
: a flaw in character that brings about the downfall of the hero of a tragedy
**tragic irony** *noun* (1833)
: IRONY 3b
**tragi·com·e·dy** \,tra-ji-'kä-mə-dē\ *noun* [Middle French *tragicomedie*, from Old Italian *tragicomedia*, from Old Spanish, from Latin *tragicomoedia*, from *tragicus* + *comoedia* comedy] (circa 1580)
: a drama or a situation blending tragic and comic elements
— **tragi·com·ic** \-'kä-mik\ *also* **tragi·com·i·cal** \-mi-kəl\ *adjective*
**tra·gus** \'trā-gəs\ *noun, plural* **tra·gi** \-,gī, -,jī\ [New Latin, from Greek *tragos*, a part of the ear, literally, goat] (circa 1693)
: the prominence in front of the external opening of the ear
**¹trail** \'trā(ə)l\ *verb* [Middle English, from Middle French *trailler* to tow, from (assumed) Vulgar Latin *tragulare*, from Latin *tragula* sledge, dragnet; akin to Latin *trahere* to pull] (14th century)
*intransitive verb*
**1 a** : to hang down so as to drag along or sweep the ground **b** : to extend over a surface in a loose or straggling manner ⟨a vine that *trails* over the ground⟩ **c** : to grow to such length as to droop over toward the ground ⟨*trailing* branches of a weeping birch⟩
**2 a** : to walk or proceed draggingly, heavily, or wearily : PLOD, TRUDGE **b** : to lag behind : do poorly in relation to others
**3** : to move, flow, or extend slowly in thin streams ⟨smoke *trailing* from chimneys⟩
**4 a** : to extend in an erratic or uneven course or line : STRAGGLE **b** : DWINDLE ⟨voice *trailing* off⟩
**5** : to follow a trail : track game
*transitive verb*
**1 a** : to draw or drag loosely along a surface : allow to sweep the ground **b** : HAUL, TOW
**2 a** : to drag (as a limb or the body) heavily or wearily **b** : to carry or bring along as an addition, burden, or encumbrance **c** : to draw along in one's wake
**3 a** : to follow upon the scent or trace of : TRACK **b** : to follow in the footsteps of : PURSUE **c** : to follow along behind **d** : to lag behind (as a competitor)
*synonym* see CHASE
**²trail** *noun* (14th century)
**1** : something that trails or is trailed: as **a** : a trailing plant **b** : the train of a gown **c** : a trailing arrangement (as of flowers) : SPRAY **d** : the part of a gun carriage that rests on the ground when the piece is unlimbered
**2 a** : something that follows or moves along as if being drawn along : TRAIN ⟨a *trail* of admirers⟩ **b** (1) : the streak produced by a meteor (2) : a continuous line produced photographically by permitting the image of a celestial body (as a star) to move over the plate **c** : a chain of consequences : AFTERMATH ⟨the . . . movement left a *trail* of bitterness and prejudice behind it —Paul Blanshard⟩
**3 a** : a trace or mark left by something that has passed or been drawn along : SCENT, TRACK ⟨a *trail* of blood⟩ **b** (1) : a track made by passage especially through a wilderness (2) : a marked or established path or route especially through a forest or mountainous region **c** : a course followed or to be followed ⟨hit the campaign *trail*⟩
— **trail·less** \'trā(ə)l-ləs\ *adjective*
**trail bike** *noun* (1966)
: a small motorcycle designed for off-road use
**trail·blaz·er** \'trā(ə)l-,blā-zər\ *noun* (1908)
**1** : one that blazes a trail to guide others : PATHFINDER

**2** : PIONEER 2 ⟨a *trailblazer* in astrophysics⟩
**trail·blaz·ing** \-ziŋ\ *adjective* (1951)
: making or pointing a new way ⟨*trailblazing* legislation⟩
**trail·break·er** \-,brā-kər\ *noun* (1925)
: TRAILBLAZER
**¹trail·er** \'trā-lər\ *noun* (1590)
**1** : one that trails
**2** : a trailing plant
**3** : a nonautomotive vehicle designed to be hauled by road: as **a** : a vehicle for transporting something ⟨a boat *trailer*⟩; *especially* : SEMITRAILER 1 **b** : a vehicle designed to serve wherever parked as a temporary dwelling or place of business **c** : MOBILE HOME
**4 a** : PREVIEW 2 **b** : a short blank strip of film attached to the end of a reel
**²trailer** (1938)
*intransitive verb*
**1** : to live or travel in or with a trailer
**2** : to be transportable by trailer ⟨a light boat that *trailers* easily⟩
*transitive verb*
: to transport (as a boat) by means of a trailer
— **trail·er·able** \-lə-rə-bəl\ *adjective*
— **trail·er·ing** *noun*
**trail·er·ist** \-lə-rist\ *noun* (1950)
**1** : a person traveling or vacationing with a trailer
**2** : TRAILERITE 1
**trail·er·ite** \-,rīt\ *noun* (1936)
**1** : a person living in a mobile home
**2** : TRAILERIST 1
**trailer park** *noun* (1942)
: an area equipped to accommodate mobile homes — called also *trailer camp, trailer court*
**trail·head** \'trāl-,hed\ *noun* (1948)
: the point at which a trail begins
**trailing arbutus** *noun* (1785)
: ARBUTUS 2
**trailing edge** *noun* (1909)
: the rearmost edge of an object that moves and especially of an airfoil
**trail mix** *noun* (1979)
: a mixture of seeds, nuts, and dried fruits eaten as a snack especially by hikers
**trail·side** \'trāl-,sīd\ *adjective* (1923)
: of, relating to, or situated in the area immediately adjacent to a trail
**¹train** \'trān\ *noun* [Middle English *traine*, from Middle French, from Old French, from *traïr* to betray, from Latin *tradere* — more at TRAITOR] (14th century)
*obsolete* : SCHEME; TRICK
**²train** *noun* [Middle English, from Middle French, from Old French, from *trainer* to draw, drag] (15th century)
**1** : a part of a gown that trails behind the wearer
**2 a** : RETINUE, SUITE **b** : a moving file of persons, vehicles, or animals
**3** : the vehicles, personnel, and sometimes animals that furnish supply, maintenance, and evacuation services to a combat unit
**4 a** : order of occurrence leading to some result — often used in the phrase *in train* ⟨this humiliating process had been in *train* for decades —Paul Fussell⟩ **b** : an orderly succession ⟨a *train* of thought⟩ **c** : accompanying or resultant circumstances : AFTERMATH ⟨consequences the discovery will bring in its *train*⟩
**5** : a line of combustible material laid to lead fire to a charge
**6** : a series of moving mechanical parts (as gears) that transmit and modify motion
**7 a** : a connected line of railroad cars with or without a locomotive **b** : an automotive tractor with one or more trailer units
**8** : a series of parts or elements that together constitute a system for producing a result and

especially for carrying on a process (as of manufacture) automatically ◆
— **train·ful** \'trān-ˌfül\ *noun*

³**train** *verb* [Middle English, from Middle French *trainer*, from Old French, from (assumed) Vulgar Latin *traginare;* akin to Latin *trahere* to draw] (15th century)
*transitive verb*
**1 :** TRAIL, DRAG
**2 :** to direct the growth of (a plant) usually by bending, pruning, and tying
**3 a :** to form by instruction, discipline, or drill **b :** to teach so as to make fit, qualified, or proficient
**4 :** to make prepared (as by exercise) for a test of skill
**5 :** to aim at an object or objective **:** DIRECT ⟨*trained* his camera on the deer⟩ ⟨*training* every effort toward success⟩
*intransitive verb*
**1 :** to undergo instruction, discipline, or drill
**2 :** to go by train
**synonym** see TEACH
— **train·abil·i·ty** \ˌtrā-nə-'bi-lə-tē\ *noun*
— **train·able** \'trā-nə-bəl\ *adjective*
**train·band** \'trān-ˌband\ *noun* [alteration of *trained band*] (1630)
**:** a 17th or 18th century militia company in England or America
**train·bear·er** \'trān-ˌbar-ər, -ˌber-\ *noun* (1722)
**:** an attendant who holds up (as on a ceremonial occasion) the train of a robe or gown
**train case** *noun* (1948)
**:** a small boxlike piece of luggage used especially for toilet articles
**train dispatcher** *noun* (1857)
**:** a railroad employee who directs the movement of trains within a division and coordinates their movement from one division to another
**train·ee** \trā-'nē\ *noun* (1841)
**:** one that is being trained especially for a job
— **train·ee·ship** \-'nē-ˌship\ *noun*
**train·er** \'trā-nər\ *noun* (1598)
**1 :** one that trains
**2 :** one (as a machine or vehicle) used in training
**3 :** a person who treats the ailments and minor injuries of the members of an athletic team
**train·ing** *noun* (1548)
**1 a :** the act, process, or method of one that trains **b :** the skill, knowledge, or experience acquired by one that trains
**2 :** the state of being trained
**training college** *noun* (circa 1829)
*British* **:** TEACHERS COLLEGE
**training school** *noun* (1829)
**1 :** a school preparing students for a particular occupation
**2 :** a correctional institution for the custody and reeducation of juvenile delinquents
**training table** *noun* (1893)
**:** a table where athletes under a training regimen eat meals planned to help in their conditioning
**training wheels** *noun plural* (1964)
**:** a pair of small wheels connected to the rear axle of a bicycle to help a beginning bicyclist maintain balance
**train·load** \'trān-ˌlōd\ *noun* (1876)
**:** the full freight or passenger capacity of a railroad train; *also* **:** a load that fills a train
**train·man** \'trān-mən, -ˌman\ *noun* (1877)
**:** a member of a train crew supervised by a conductor
**train oil** \'trān-\ *noun* [obsolete *train* train oil, from Middle English *trane*, from Middle Dutch *trane* or Middle Low German *trān;* akin to Old High German *trahan* tear] (circa 1553)
**:** oil from a marine animal (as a whale)
**traipse** \'trāps\ *verb* **traipsed; traips·ing** [origin unknown] (1647)
*intransitive verb*

**:** to go on foot **:** WALK ⟨*traipsed* over to the restaurant⟩ ⟨children *traipsing* at her heels⟩; *also* **:** to walk or travel about without apparent plan but with or without a purpose ⟨a week *traipsing* through the Ozarks⟩ ⟨*traipsing* from office to office⟩
*transitive verb*
**:** TRAMP, WALK
**synonym** see WANDER
— **traipse** *noun*
**trait** \'trāt, *British usually* 'trā\ *noun* [Middle French, literally, act of drawing, from Latin *tractus* — more at TRACT] (1589)
**1 a :** a stroke of or as if of a pencil **b :** TOUCH, TRACE
**2 a :** a distinguishing quality (as of personal character) **:** PECULIARITY **b :** an inherited characteristic
**trai·tor** \'trā-tər\ *noun* [Middle English *traitre*, from Old French, from Latin *traditor*, from *tradere* to hand over, deliver, betray, from *trans-, tra-* trans- + *dare* to give — more at DATE] (13th century)
**1 :** one who betrays another's trust or is false to an obligation or duty
**2 :** one who commits treason
**word history** see TREASON
**trai·tor·ous** \'trā-tə-rəs, 'trā-trəs\ *adjective* (14th century)
**1 :** guilty or capable of treason
**2 :** constituting treason ⟨*traitorous* activities⟩
**synonym** see FAITHLESS
— **trai·tor·ous·ly** *adverb*
**trai·tress** \'trā-trəs\ *or* **trai·tor·ess** \'trā-tə-rəs, 'trā-trəs\ *noun* (14th century)
**:** a female traitor
**tra·ject** \trə-'jekt\ *transitive verb* [Latin *trajectus*, past participle of *traicere*] (1657)
**:** TRANSMIT
**tra·jec·tion** \-'jek-shən\ *noun*
**tra·jec·to·ry** \trə-'jek-t(ə-)rē\ *noun, plural* **-ries** [New Latin *trajectoria*, from feminine of *trajectorius* of passing, from Latin *traicere* to cause to cross, cross, from *trans-, tra-* trans- + *jacere* to throw — more at JET] (1696)
**1 :** the curve that a body (as a planet or comet in its orbit or a rocket) describes in space
**2 :** a path, progression, or line of development resembling a physical trajectory
**Tra·keh·ner** \tra-'kā-nər\ *noun* [German, from *Trakehnen*, site of the Prussian royal stud in East Prussia] (1926)
**:** any of a breed of large powerful saddle horses that originated in East Prussia and excel in dressage and jumping
¹**tram** \'tram\ *noun* [English dialect, shaft of a wheelbarrow, probably from Low German *traam*, literally, beam] (circa 1517)
**1 :** any of various vehicles: as **a :** a boxlike wagon running on rails (as in a mine) **b** *chiefly British* **:** STREETCAR **c :** a carrier that travels on an overhead cable or rails
**2** *plural, chiefly British* **:** a streetcar line
²**tram** *transitive verb* **trammed; tram·ming** (1874)
**:** to haul in a tram or over a tramway
**tram·car** \'tram-ˌkär\ *noun* (1873)
**1** *chiefly British* **:** STREETCAR
**2 :** TRAM 1a
**tram·line** \-ˌlīn\ *noun* (1886)
*British* **:** a streetcar line
¹**tram·mel** \'tra-məl\ *noun* [Middle English *tramayle*, a kind of net, from Middle French *tremail*, from Late Latin *tremaculum*, from Latin *tres* three + *macula* mesh, spot — more at THREE] (15th century)
**1 :** a net for catching birds or fish; *especially* **:** one having three layers with the middle one finer-meshed and slack so that fish passing through carry some of the center net through the coarser opposite net and are trapped
**2 :** an adjustable pothook for a fireplace crane
**3 :** a shackle used for making a horse amble
**4 :** something impeding activity, progress, or freedom **:** RESTRAINT — usually used in plural

**5 a :** an instrument for drawing ellipses **b :** a compass for drawing large circles that consists of a beam with two sliding parts — usually used in plural **c :** any of various gauges used for aligning or adjusting machine parts
²**trammel** *transitive verb* **-meled** *or* **-melled; -mel·ing** *or* **-mel·ling** \'tra-mə-liŋ, 'tram-liŋ\ (1605)
**1 :** to catch or hold in or as if in a net **:** ENMESH
**2 :** to prevent or impede the free play of **:** CONFINE
**synonym** see HAMPER
¹**tra·mon·tane** \trə-'män-ˌtān, ˌtra-mən-'\ *noun* (1593)
**:** one dwelling in a tramontane region; *broadly* **:** FOREIGNER
²**tramontane** *adjective* [Italian *tramontano*, from Latin *transmontanus*, from *trans-* + *mont-, mons* mountain — more at MOUNT] (1596)
**1 :** TRANSALPINE
**2 :** lying on or coming from the other side of a mountain range
¹**tramp** \'tramp, *verb intransitive 1 & verb transitive 1 are also* 'trämp, 'trȯmp\ *verb* [Middle English; akin to Middle Low German *trampen* to stamp] (14th century)
*intransitive verb*
**1 :** to walk, tread, or step especially heavily
**2 a :** to travel about on foot **:** HIKE **b :** to journey as a tramp
*transitive verb*
**1 :** to tread on forcibly and repeatedly
**2 :** to travel or wander through or over on foot ⟨have *tramped* all the woods on their property⟩
— **tramp·er** *noun*
²**tramp** \'tramp, *3, 4 are also* 'trämp, 'trȯmp\ *noun* (1664)
**1 a :** a foot traveler **b :** a begging or thieving vagrant **c :** a woman of loose morals; *specifically* **:** PROSTITUTE
**2 :** a walking trip **:** HIKE
**3 :** the succession of sounds made by the beating of feet on a surface (as a road, pavement, or floor)
**4 :** an iron plate to protect the sole of a shoe

---

◇ WORD HISTORY

**train** The word *train* in the sense "a connected series of railroad cars" has given rise to words with the same meaning in a number of European languages, though sometimes in a rather roundabout way. Railways and trains with their associated vocabulary were British inventions, spreading from Britain to the continent. In English, *train* in its railway sense was shortened from phrases such as *train of carriages* or *train of wagons*, with *train* used in its long-established sense "a set of objects linked in succession." French had given English the word centuries before and now borrowed this particular meaning back. *Train* is first noted in French with the sense "series of railroad cars" in 1829, about five years after the meaning first appeared in English. Spanish and Italian borrowed the French or English word directly as, respectively, *tren* and *treno*. In central Europe, however, a different kind of borrowing took place. Because French *train* is a transparent derivative of the verb *trainer* "to pull, drag," German translated *train* with the noun *Zug*, which functions as a derivative of the verb *ziehen* "to pull, draw"—appropriate enough since a locomotive pulls a series of cars.

---

\ə\ **abut** \ᵊ\ **kitten** \ər\ **further** \a\ **ash** \ā\ **ace**
\ä\ **mop, mar** \au̇\ **out** \ch\ **chin** \e\ **bet** \ē\ **easy**
\g\ **go** \i\ **hit** \ī\ **ice** \j\ **job** \ŋ\ **sing** \ō\ **go**
\ȯ\ **law** \ȯi\ **boy** \th\ **thin** \t̲h̲\ **the** \ü\ **loot** \u̇\ **foot**
\y\ **yet** \zh\ **vision** *see also* **Guide to Pronunciation**

**5 :** a ship not making regular trips but taking cargo when and where it offers and to any port — called also **tramp steamer**

**³tramp** \'tramp\ *adjective* (1873)
: having no fixed abode, connection, or destination ⟨a *tramp* dog⟩

**tramp art** *noun* (1974)
: a style of wood carving flourishing in the U.S. from about 1875 to 1930 that is characterized by ornate layered whittling often of cigar boxes or fruit crates; *also* : an object carved in this style

**tram·ple** \'tram-pəl\ *verb* **tram·pled; tram·pling** \-p(ə-)liŋ\ [Middle English, frequentative of *trampen* to tramp] (14th century)
*intransitive verb*
**1 :** TRAMP; *especially* : to tread heavily so as to bruise, crush, or injure
**2 :** to inflict injury or destruction especially contemptuously or ruthlessly — usually used with *on, over,* or *upon* ⟨*trampling* on the rights of others⟩
*transitive verb*
: to crush, injure, or destroy by or as if by treading
— **trample** *noun*
— **tram·pler** \-p(ə-)lər\ *noun*

**tram·po·line** \,tram-pə-'lēn, 'tram-pə-,\ *noun* [Italian *trampolino* springboard, from *trampoli* stilts, of Germanic origin; akin to Middle Low German *trampen* to stamp] (1928)
: a resilient sheet or web (as of nylon) supported by springs in a metal frame and used as a springboard and landing area in tumbling
— **tram·po·lin·er** \-'lē-nər, -,lē-\ *noun*
— **tram·po·lin·ist** \-nist\ *noun*

**tram·po·lin·ing** *noun* (1949)
: the sport of jumping and tumbling on a trampoline

**tram·way** \'tram-,wā\ *noun* (1825)
**1 a :** a railway for trams **b** *British* : a streetcar line
**2 :** an overhead cable for trams

**¹trance** \'tran(t)s\ *noun* [Middle English, from Middle French *transe*, from *transir* to pass away, swoon, from Latin *transire* to pass, pass away — more at TRANSIENT] (14th century)
**1 :** a state of partly suspended animation or inability to function
**2 :** a somnolent state (as of deep hypnosis)
**3 :** a state of profound abstraction or absorption
— **trance·like** \-,līk\ *adjective*

**²trance** *transitive verb* **tranced; tranc·ing** (circa 1598)
: ENTRANCE, ENRAPTURE

**tranche** \'träⁿsh\ *noun* [French, literally, slice, from Old French, from *trenchier, trancher* to cut — more at TRENCH] (1930)
: a bond series issued for sale in a foreign country

**tran·gam** \'traŋ-gəm\ *noun* [origin unknown] (circa 1658)
*archaic* : TRINKET, GIMCRACK

**tran·quil** \'traŋ-kwəl, 'tran-\ *adjective* [Latin *tranquillus*] (1604)
**1 a :** free from agitation of mind or spirit ⟨a *tranquil* self-assurance⟩ **b** : free from disturbance or turmoil ⟨a *tranquil* scene⟩
**2 :** unvarying in aspect : STEADY, STABLE
*synonym* see CALM
— **tran·quil·ly** \-kwə-lē\ *adverb*
— **tran·quil·ness** *noun*

**tran·quil·ize** *also* **tran·quil·lize** \'traŋ-kwə-,līz, 'tran-\ *verb* **-ized** *also* **-lized; -iz·ing** *also* **-liz·ing** (1623)
*transitive verb*
: to make tranquil or calm : PACIFY; *especially* : to relieve of mental tension and anxiety by means of drugs
*intransitive verb*
**1 :** to become tranquil : RELAX 1
**2 :** to make one tranquil

**tran·quil·iz·er** *also* **tran·quil·liz·er** \-,līzər\ *noun* (1800)
**1 :** one that tranquilizes

**2 :** a drug used to reduce mental disturbance (as anxiety and tension)

**tran·quil·li·ty** *or* **tran·quil·i·ty** \tran-'kwi-lə-tē, traŋ-\ *noun* (14th century)
: the quality or state of being tranquil

**trans** \'tran(t)s, 'tranz\ *adjective* (1892)
: characterized by having certain groups of atoms on opposite sides of the longitudinal axis of a double bond or of the plane of a ring in a molecule

**trans-** *prefix* [Latin *trans-, tra-* across, beyond, through, so as to change, from *trans* across, beyond — more at THROUGH]
**1 :** on or to the other side of : across : beyond ⟨*trans*atlantic⟩
**2 a :** beyond (a specified chemical element) in the periodic table ⟨*trans*uranium⟩ **b** *usually italic* : trans ⟨*trans*-dichloro-ethylene⟩ — compare CIS- 2
**3 :** through ⟨*trans*cutaneous⟩
**4 :** so or such as to change or transfer ⟨*trans*literate⟩ ⟨*trans*location⟩ ⟨*trans*amination⟩ ⟨*trans*ship⟩

**trans·act** \tran-'zakt, tran(t)-'sakt\ *verb* [Latin *transactus*, past participle of *transigere* to drive through, complete, transact, from *trans-* + *agere* to drive, do — more at AGENT] (circa 1585)
*intransitive verb*
: to carry on business
*transitive verb*
**1 :** to carry to completion ⟨*transact* a sale⟩
**2 :** to carry on the operation or management of : DO ⟨*transact* business⟩
— **trans·ac·tor** \-'zak-tər, -'sak-tər\ *noun*

**trans·ac·ti·nide** \tran(t)-'sak-tə-,nīd, tran-'zak-\ *adjective* (1969)
: of, relating to, or being actual or hypothetical elements with atomic weights higher than those of the actinide series ⟨*transactinide* chemistry⟩

**trans·ac·tion** \tran-'zak-shən, tran(t)-'sak-\ *noun* (1647)
**1 a :** something transacted; *especially* : an exchange or transfer of goods, services, or funds ⟨electronic *transactions*⟩ **b** *plural* : the often published record of the meeting of a society or association
**2 a :** an act, process, or instance of transacting **b** : a communicative action or activity involving two parties or things that reciprocally affect or influence each other
— **trans·ac·tion·al** \-shnəl, -shə-nᵊl\ *adjective*

**transactional analysis** *noun* (1961)
: a system of psychotherapy involving analysis of individual episodes of social interaction for insight that will aid communication

**trans·al·pine** \tran(t)s-'al-,pīn, tranz-\ *adjective* [Latin *transalpinus*, from *trans-* + *Alpes* the Alps] (1590)
: situated on the north side of the Alps ⟨*Transalpine* Gaul⟩ — compare CISALPINE

**trans·am·i·nase** \tran(t)s-'a-mə-,nās, tranz-, -,nāz\ *noun* (1940)
: an enzyme promoting transamination — called also *aminotransferase*

**trans·am·i·na·tion** \,tran(t)s-,a-mə-'nā-shən, ,tranz-\ *noun* (1939)
: a reversible oxidation-reduction reaction in which an amino group is transferred typically from an alpha-amino acid to the carbonyl carbon atom of an alpha-keto acid

**trans·at·lan·tic** \,tran(t)s-ət-'lan-tik, ,tranz-\ *adjective* (1779)
**1 a :** crossing or extending across the Atlantic Ocean ⟨a *transatlantic* cable⟩ **b** : relating to or involving crossing the Atlantic Ocean ⟨*transatlantic* air fares⟩
**2 a :** situated or originating from beyond the Atlantic Ocean **b** : of, relating to, or involving countries on both sides of the Atlantic Ocean and especially the U.S. and Great Britain ⟨*transatlantic* cooperation⟩

**trans·ax·le** \tran(t)s-'ak-səl, tranz-\ *noun* [*trans*mission + *axle*] (1958)

: a unit that consists of a combination of transmission and front axle used in front-wheel-drive automobiles

**trans·ceiv·er** \tran(t)-'sē-vər\ *noun* [*trans*mitter + re*ceiver*] (1934)
: a radio transmitter-receiver that uses many of the same components for both transmission and reception

**tran·scend** \tran(t)-'send\ *verb* [Middle English, from Latin *transcendere* to climb across, transcend, from *trans-* + *scandere* to climb — more at SCAN] (14th century)
*transitive verb*
**1 a :** to rise above or go beyond the limits of **b** : to triumph over the negative or restrictive aspects of : OVERCOME **c** : to be prior to, beyond, and above (the universe or material existence)
**2 :** to outstrip or outdo in some attribute, quality, or power
*intransitive verb*
: to rise above or extend notably beyond ordinary limits
*synonym* see EXCEED

**tran·scen·dence** \-'sen-dən(t)s\ *noun* (1601)
: the quality or state of being transcendent

**tran·scen·den·cy** \-dən(t)-sē\ *noun* (1615)
: TRANSCENDENCE

**tran·scen·dent** \-dənt\ *adjective* [Latin *transcendent-, transcendens*, present participle of *transcendere*] (1598)
**1 a :** exceeding usual limits : SURPASSING **b** : extending or lying beyond the limits of ordinary experience **c** *in Kantian philosophy* : being beyond the limits of all possible experience and knowledge
**2 :** being beyond comprehension
**3 :** transcending the universe or material existence
— **tran·scen·dent·ly** *adverb*

**tran·scen·den·tal** \,tran(t)-,sen-'den-tᵊl, -sən-\ *adjective* (1624)
**1 a :** TRANSCENDENT 1b **b** : SUPERNATURAL **c** : ABSTRUSE, ABSTRACT **d** : of or relating to transcendentalism
**2 a :** incapable of being the root of an algebraic equation with rational coefficients ⟨π is a *transcendental* number⟩ **b** : being, involving, or representing a function (as sin $x$, log $x$, $e^x$) that cannot be expressed by a finite number of algebraic operations ⟨*transcendental* curves⟩
**3** *in Kantian philosophy* **a :** of or relating to experience as determined by the mind's make-up **b** : transcending experience but not human knowledge
**4 :** TRANSCENDENT 1a
— **tran·scen·den·tal·ly** \-tᵊl-ē\ *adverb*

**tran·scen·den·tal·ism** \-tᵊl-,i-zəm\ *noun* (1803)
**1 :** a philosophy that emphasizes the a priori conditions of knowledge and experience or the unknowable character of ultimate reality or that emphasizes the transcendent as the fundamental reality
**2 :** a philosophy that asserts the primacy of the spiritual and transcendental over the material and empirical
**3 :** the quality or state of being transcendental; *especially* : visionary idealism
— **tran·scen·den·tal·ist** \-tᵊl-ist\ *adjective or noun*

**transcendental meditation** *noun* (1966)
: a technique of meditation in which a mantra is chanted in order to foster calm, creativity, and spiritual well-being

**trans·con·ti·nen·tal** \,tran(t)s-,kän-tᵊn-'en-tᵊl, ,tranz-\ *adjective* (1853)
: extending or going across a continent ⟨a *transcontinental* railroad⟩

**tran·scribe** \tran(t)-'skrīb\ *transitive verb* **tran·scribed; tran·scrib·ing** [Latin *transcribere*, from *trans-* + *scribere* to write — more at SCRIBE] (1552)

**1 a :** to make a written copy of **b :** to make a copy of (dictated or recorded matter) in longhand or on a machine (as a typewriter) **c :** to paraphrase or summarize in writing **d :** WRITE DOWN, RECORD
**2 a :** to represent (speech sounds) by means of phonetic symbols **b :** TRANSLATE 2a **c :** to transfer (data) from one recording form to another **d :** to record (as on magnetic tape) for later broadcast
**3 :** to make a musical transcription of
**4 :** to cause (as DNA) to undergo genetic transcription
— **tran·scrib·er** noun

**tran·script** \'tran(t)-ˌskript\ noun [Middle English, from Medieval Latin transcriptum, from Latin, neuter of transcriptus, past participle of transcribere] (14th century)
**1 a :** a written, printed, or typed copy; especially : a usually typewritten copy of dictated or recorded material **b :** an official or legal and often published copy ⟨a court reporter's transcript⟩; especially : an official copy of a student's educational record
**2 :** a representation (as of experience) in an art form
**3 :** a sequence of RNA produced by transcription from a DNA template

**tran·scrip·tase** \tran-'skrip-ˌtās, -ˌtāz\ noun [transcription + -ase] (1963)
**:** RNA POLYMERASE; also : REVERSE TRANSCRIPTASE

**tran·scrip·tion** \tran(t)-'skrip-shən\ noun (1598)
**1 :** an act, process, or instance of transcribing
**2 :** COPY, TRANSCRIPT: as **a :** an arrangement of a musical composition for some instrument or voice other than the original **b :** a recording (as on magnetic tape) made especially for use in radiobroadcasting
**3 :** the process of constructing a messenger RNA molecule using a DNA molecule as a template with resulting transfer of genetic information to the messenger RNA — compare TRANSLATION 2, REVERSE TRANSCRIPTION
— **tran·scrip·tion·al** \-shnəl, -shə-nºl\ adjective
— **tran·scrip·tion·al·ly** adverb

**tran·scrip·tion·ist** \-shə-nist\ noun (1963)
**:** one that transcribes; especially : a typist who transcribes dictated medical reports

**trans·cul·tur·al** \tran(t)s-'kəl-chə-rəl, tranz-, -'kəlch-rəl\ adjective (1951)
**:** involving, encompassing, or extending across two or more cultures ⟨transcultural problems⟩

**trans·cu·ta·ne·ous** \ˌtran(t)s-kyu-'tā-nē-əs\ adjective (circa 1941)
**:** passing, entering, or made by penetration through the skin ⟨transcutaneous infection⟩ ⟨transcutaneous inoculation⟩

**trans·der·mal** \tran(t)s-'dər-məl, tranz-\ adjective (1944)
**:** relating to, being, or supplying a medication in a form for absorption through the skin into the bloodstream ⟨transdermal drug delivery⟩ ⟨transdermal nitroglycerin⟩ ⟨transdermal nicotine patch⟩

**trans·dis·ci·plin·ary** \-'di-sə-plə-ˌner-ē\ adjective (1948)
**:** INTERDISCIPLINARY

**trans·duce** \tran(t)s-'düs, tranz-, -'dyüs\ transitive verb **trans·duced; trans·duc·ing** [Latin transducere to lead across, transfer, from trans- + ducere to lead — more at TOW] (1947)
**1 :** to convert (as energy or a message) into another form ⟨essentially sense organs transduce physical energy into a nervous signal⟩
**2 :** to bring about the transfer of (as a gene) from one microorganism to another by means of a viral agent

**trans·duc·er** \-'dü-sər, -'dyü-\ noun (1924)
**:** a device that is actuated by power from one system and supplies power usually in another form to a second system ⟨a loudspeaker is a

transducer that transforms electrical signals into sound energy⟩

**trans·duc·tion** \-'dək-shən\ noun [Latin transducere] (1947)
**:** the action or process of transducing; especially : the transfer of genetic determinants from one microorganism to another by a viral agent (as a bacteriophage)
— **trans·duc·tant** \-tənt\ noun
— **trans·duc·tion·al** \-shnəl, -shə-nºl\ adjective

**¹tran·sect** \tran(t)-'sekt\ transitive verb [trans- + intersect] (1634)
**:** to cut transversely
— **tran·sec·tion** \-'sek-shən\ noun

**²tran·sect** \'tran(t)-ˌsekt\ noun (1905)
**:** a sample area (as of vegetation) usually in the form of a long continuous strip

**tran·sept** \'tran(t)-ˌsept\ noun [New Latin transeptum, from Latin trans- + septum, saeptum enclosure, wall] (circa 1542)
**:** the part of a cruciform church that crosses at right angles to the greatest length between the nave and the apse or choir; also : either of the projecting ends of a transept
— **tran·sep·tal** \tran(t)-'sep-tºl\ adjective

**trans·fec·tion** \tran(t)s-'fek-shən, tranz-\ noun [trans- + infection] (1964)
**:** infection of a cell with isolated viral nucleic acid followed by production of the complete virus in the cell; also : the incorporation of exogenous DNA into a cell
— **trans·fect** \-'fekt\ transitive verb

**¹trans·fer** \tran(t)s-'fər, 'tran(t)s-ˌ\ verb **trans·ferred; trans·fer·ring** [Middle English transferren, from Latin transferre, from trans- + ferre to carry — more at BEAR] (14th century)
transitive verb
**1 a :** to convey from one person, place, or situation to another : TRANSPORT **b :** to cause to pass from one to another : TRANSMIT **c :** TRANSFORM, CHANGE
**2 :** to make over the possession or control of : CONVEY
**3 :** to print or otherwise copy from one surface to another by contact
intransitive verb
**1 :** to move to a different place, region, or situation; especially : to withdraw from one educational institution to enroll at another
**2 :** to change from one vehicle or transportation line to another
— **trans·fer·abil·i·ty** \(ˌ)tran(t)s-ˌfər-ə-'bi-lə-tē\ noun
— **trans·fer·able** also **trans·fer·ra·ble** \tran(t)s-'fər-ə-bəl\ adjective
— **trans·fer·al** \-əl\ noun
— **trans·fer·rer** \-ər\ noun

**²trans·fer** \'tran(t)s-ˌfər\ noun (1674)
**1 a :** conveyance of right, title, or interest in real or personal property from one person to another **b :** removal or acquisition of property by mere delivery with intent to transfer title
**2 a :** an act, process, or instance of transferring : TRANSFERENCE 2 **b :** the carryover or generalization of learned responses from one type of situation to another
**3 :** one that transfers or is transferred; especially : a graphic image transferred by contact from one surface to another
**4 :** a place where a transfer is made (as of trains to ferries or as where one form of power is changed to another)
**5 :** a ticket entitling a passenger on a public conveyance to continue the trip on another route

**trans·fer·ase** \'tran(t)s-(ˌ)fər-ˌās, -ˌāz\ noun (1948)
**:** an enzyme that promotes transfer of a group from one molecule to another

**trans·fer·ee** \ˌtran(t)s-(ˌ)fər-'ē\ noun (circa 1736)
**1 :** a person to whom a conveyance is made
**2 :** one who is transferred

**trans·fer·ence** \tran(t)s-'fər-ən(t)s, 'tran(t)s-(ˌ)\ noun (1681)
**1 :** an act, process, or instance of transferring : CONVEYANCE, TRANSFER
**2 :** the redirection of feelings and desires and especially of those unconsciously retained from childhood toward a new object (as a psychoanalyst conducting therapy)
— **trans·fer·en·tial** \ˌtran(t)s-fə-'ren(t)-shəl\ adjective

**transfer factor** noun (1956)
**:** a substance that is produced and secreted by a lymphocyte functioning in cell-mediated immunity and that upon incorporation into a lymphocyte which has not been sensitized confers on it the same immunological specificity as the sensitized cell

**trans·fer·or** \ˌtran(t)s-(ˌ)fər-'ȯr\ noun (1875)
**:** one that conveys a title, right, or property

**transfer payment** noun (circa 1945)
**1 :** a public expenditure made for a purpose (as unemployment compensation) other than procuring goods or services — usually used in plural
**2** plural : money (as welfare payments) that is received by individuals and that is neither compensation for goods or services currently supplied nor income from investments

**trans·fer·rin** \tran(t)s-'fer-ən\ noun [trans- + Latin ferrum iron] (1947)
**:** a beta globulin in blood plasma capable of combining with ferric ions and transporting iron in the body

**transfer RNA** \'tran(t)s-ˌfər-\ noun (1961)
**:** a relatively small RNA that transfers a particular amino acid to a growing polypeptide chain at the ribosomal site of protein synthesis during translation — compare MESSENGER RNA

**trans·fig·u·ra·tion** \(ˌ)tran(t)s-ˌfi-gyə-'rā-shən, -gə-\ noun (14th century)
**1 a :** a change in form or appearance : METAMORPHOSIS **b :** an exalting, glorifying, or spiritual change
**2** capitalized : August 6 observed as a Christian feast in commemoration of the transfiguration of Christ on a mountaintop in the presence of three disciples

**trans·fig·ure** \tran(t)s-'fi-gyər, especially British -'fi-gər\ transitive verb **-ured; -ur·ing** [Middle English, from Latin transfigurare, from trans- + figurare to shape, fashion, from figura figure] (14th century)
**:** to give a new and typically exalted or spiritual appearance to : transform outwardly and usually for the better
**synonym** see TRANSFORM

**trans·fi·nite** \(ˌ)tran(t)s-'fī-ˌnīt\ adjective [German transfinit, from trans- (from Latin) + finit finite, from Latin finitus] (1902)
**1 :** going beyond or surpassing any finite number, group, or magnitude
**2 :** being or relating to cardinal and ordinal numbers of sets with an infinite number of elements

**trans·fix** \tran(t)s-'fiks\ transitive verb [Latin transfixus, past participle of transfigere, from trans- + figere to fasten, pierce — more at FIX] (1590)
**1 :** to pierce through with or as if with a pointed weapon : IMPALE
**2 :** to hold motionless by or as if by piercing
— **trans·fix·ion** \-'fik-shən\ noun

**¹trans·form** \tran(t)s-'fȯrm\ verb [Middle English, from Latin transformare, from trans- + formare to form, from forma form] (14th century)
transitive verb
**1 a :** to change in composition or structure **b :** to change the outward form or appearance of

**c :** to change in character or condition **:** CONVERT

**2 :** to subject to mathematical transformation

**3 :** to cause (a cell) to undergo genetic transformation

*intransitive verb*

**:** to become transformed **:** CHANGE ☆

— **trans·form·able** \-'fȯr-mə-bəl\ *adjective*

— **trans·for·ma·tive** \-'fȯr-mə-tiv\ *adjective*

²**trans·form** \'tran(t)s-ˌfȯrm\ *noun* (1853)

**1 :** a mathematical element obtained from another by transformation

**2 :** TRANSFORMATION 3a(1), (2)

**3 :** a linguistic structure (as a sentence) produced by means of a transformation ⟨"the duckling is killed by the farmer" is a *transform* of "the farmer kills the duckling"⟩

**trans·for·ma·tion** \ˌtran(t)s-fər-'mā-shən, -fȯr-\ *noun* (15th century)

**1 :** an act, process, or instance of transforming or being transformed

**2 :** false hair worn especially by a woman to replace or supplement natural hair

**3 a** (1) **:** the operation of changing (as by rotation or mapping) one configuration or expression into another in accordance with a mathematical rule; *especially* **:** a change of variables or coordinates in which a function of new variables or coordinates is substituted for each original variable or coordinate (2) **:** the formula that effects a transformation **b :** FUNCTION 5a

**c :** an operation that converts (as by insertion, deletion, or permutation) one grammatical string (as a sentence) into another; *also* **:** a formal statement of such an operation

**4 a :** genetic modification of a bacterium by incorporation of free DNA from another ruptured bacterial cell — compare TRANSDUCTION **b :** genetic modification of a cell by the uptake and incorporation of exogenous DNA

**trans·for·ma·tion·al** \-shnəl, -shə-nᵊl\ *adjective* (1894)

**:** of, relating to, characterized by, or concerned with transformation and especially linguistic transformation

— **trans·for·ma·tion·al·ly** *adverb*

**transformational grammar** *noun* (1961)

**:** a grammar that generates the deep structures of a language and converts these to the surface structures by means of transformations

**trans·for·ma·tion·al·ist** \ˌtran(t)s-fər-'māshnə-list, -shə-nᵊl-ist\ *noun* (1964)

**:** an exponent of transformational grammar

**trans·form·er** \tran(t)s-'fȯr-mər\ *noun* (1596)

**:** one that transforms; *specifically* **:** a device employing the principle of mutual induction to convert variations of current in a primary circuit into variations of voltage and current in a secondary circuit

**trans·fuse** \tran(t)s-'fyüz\ *transitive verb* **trans·fused; trans·fus·ing** [Middle English, from Latin *transfusus,* past participle of *transfundere,* from *trans-* + *fundere* to pour — more at FOUND] (15th century)

**1 a :** to cause to pass from one to another **:** TRANSMIT **b :** to diffuse into or through **:** PERMEATE ⟨sunlight *transfuses* the bay⟩

**2 a :** to transfer (as blood) into a vein of a person or animal **b :** to subject (a patient) to transfusion

— **trans·fus·ible** *or* **trans·fus·able** \-'fyü-zə-bəl\ *adjective*

**trans·fu·sion** \tran(t)s-'fyü-zhən\ *noun* (1578)

**1 :** an act, process, or instance of transfusing; *especially* **:** the process of transfusing fluid into a vein or artery

**2 :** something transfused

— **trans·fu·sion·al** \-'fyüzh-nəl, -'fyü-zhə-nᵊl\ *adjective*

**trans·gen·ic** \tran(t)s-'je-nik\ *adjective* (1982)

**:** having chromosomes into which one or more heterologous genes have been incorporated either artificially or naturally ⟨*transgenic* mice⟩

**trans·gress** \tran(t)s-'gres, tranz-\ *verb* [Middle French *transgresser,* from Latin *transgressus,* past participle of *transgredi* to step beyond or across, from *trans-* + *gradi* to step — more at GRADE] (1526)

*transitive verb*

**1 :** to go beyond limits set or prescribed by **:** VIOLATE ⟨*transgress* divine law⟩

**2 :** to pass beyond or go over (a limit or boundary)

*intransitive verb*

**1 :** to violate a command or law **:** SIN

**2 :** to go beyond a boundary or limit

— **trans·gres·sive** \-'gre-siv\ *adjective*

— **trans·gres·sor** \-'gre-sər\ *noun*

**trans·gres·sion** \-'gre-shən\ *noun* (15th century)

**:** an act, process, or instance of transgressing: as **a :** infringement or violation of a law, command, or duty **b :** the spread of the sea over land areas and the consequent unconformable deposit of sediments on older rocks

**tran·ship** *variant of* TRANSSHIP

**trans·his·tor·i·cal** \ˌtran(t)s-(h)is-'tȯr-i-kəl, ˌtranz-, -'tär-\ *adjective* (1909)

**:** transcending historical bounds

**trans·hu·mance** \ˌtran(t)s-'hyü-mən(t)s, tranz-, -'yü-\ *noun* [French, from *transhumer* to practice transhumance, from Spanish *trashumar,* from *tras-* trans- (from Latin *trans-*) + Latin *humus* earth — more at HUMBLE] (circa 1901)

**:** seasonal movement of livestock and especially sheep between mountain and lowland pastures either under the care of herders or in company with the owners

— **trans·hu·mant** \-mənt\ *adjective or noun*

**tran·sience** \'tran(t)-sh(ē-)ən(t)s; 'tran-zēən(t)s, 'tran(t)-sē-; 'tran-zhən(t)s, -jən(t)s\ *noun* (1745)

**:** the quality or state of being transient

**tran·sien·cy** \-sh(ē-)ən(t)-sē, -zē-ən(t)-, -sēən(t)-; -zhən(t)-sē, -jən(t)-\ *noun* (1652)

**:** TRANSIENCE

¹**tran·sient** \-sh(ē-)ənt, -zē-ənt, -sē-; -zhənt, -jənt\ *adjective* [Latin *transeunt-, transiens,* present participle of *transire* to go across, pass, from *trans-* + *ire* to go — more at ISSUE] (1599)

**1 a :** passing especially quickly into and out of existence **:** TRANSITORY **b :** passing through or by a place with only a brief stay or sojourn

**2 :** affecting something or producing results beyond itself ☆

— **tran·sient·ly** *adverb*

²**transient** *noun* (1652)

**1 :** one that is transient: as **a :** a transient guest **b :** a person traveling about usually in search of work

**2 a :** a temporary oscillation that occurs in a circuit because of a sudden change of voltage or of load **b :** a transient current or voltage

**transient ischemic attack** *noun* (1966)

**:** a brief episode of cerebral ischemia that is usually characterized by temporary blurring of vision, slurring of speech, numbness, paralysis, or syncope and that is often predictive of more serious cerebral accidents — abbreviation TIA

**trans·il·lu·mi·nate** \ˌtran(t)s-ə-'lü-mə-ˌnāt, ˌtranz-\ *transitive verb* (1900)

**:** to cause light to pass through; *especially* **:** to pass light through (a body part) for medical examination

— **trans·il·lu·mi·na·tion** \-ˌlü-mə-'nāshən\ *noun*

— **trans·il·lu·mi·na·tor** \-'lü-mə-ˌnā-tər\ *noun*

**tran·sis·tor** \tran-'zis-tər, tran(t)-'sis-tər\ *noun* [¹*transfer* + *resistor;* from its transferring an electrical signal across a resistor] (1948)

**1 :** a solid-state electronic device that is used to control the flow of electricity in electronic equipment and consists of a small block of a semiconductor (as germanium) with at least three electrodes

**2 :** a transistorized radio

**tran·sis·tor·ise** *British variant of* TRANSISTORIZE

**tran·sis·tor·ize** \-tə-ˌrīz\ *transitive verb* **-ized; -iz·ing** (circa 1952)

**:** to equip (a device) with transistors

— **tran·sis·tor·i·za·tion** \-ˌzis-tə-rə-'zāshən\ *noun*

¹**tran·sit** \'tran(t)-sət, 'tran-zət\ *noun* [Middle English *transite,* from Latin *transitus,* from *transire* to go across, pass] (15th century)

**1 a :** an act, process, or instance of passing through or over **:** PASSAGE **b :** CHANGE, TRANSITION **c** (1) **:** conveyance of persons or things from one place to another (2) **:** usually local transportation especially of people by public conveyance; *also* **:** vehicles or a system engaged in such transportation

**2 a :** passage of a celestial body over the meridian of a place or through the field of a telescope **b :** passage of a smaller body (as Venus) across the disk of a larger (as the sun)

**3 :** a theodolite with the telescope mounted so that it can be transited

²**transit** (15th century)

*intransitive verb*

**:** to make a transit

*transitive verb*

**1 a :** to pass over or through **:** TRAVERSE **b :** to cause to pass over or through

**2 :** to pass across (a meridian, a celestial body, or the field of view of a telescope)

**3 :** to turn (a telescope) over about the horizontal transverse axis in surveying

---

☆ SYNONYMS

**Transform, metamorphose, transmute, convert, transmogrify, transfigure** mean to change a thing into a different thing. TRANSFORM implies a major change in form, nature, or function ⟨*transformed* a small company into a corporate giant⟩. METAMORPHOSE suggests an abrupt or startling change induced by or as if by magic or a supernatural power ⟨awkward girls *metamorphosed* into graceful ballerinas⟩. TRANSMUTE implies transforming into a higher element or thing ⟨attempted to *transmute* lead into gold⟩. CONVERT implies a change fitting something for a new or different use or function ⟨*converted* the study into a nursery⟩. TRANSMOGRIFY suggests a strange or preposterous metamorphosis ⟨a story in which a frog is *transmogrified* into a prince⟩. TRANSFIGURE implies a change that exalts or glorifies ⟨joy *transfigured* her face⟩.

**Transient, transitory, ephemeral, momentary, fugitive, fleeting, evanescent** mean lasting or staying only a short time. TRANSIENT applies to what is actually short in its duration or stay ⟨a hotel catering primarily to *transient* guests⟩. TRANSITORY applies to what is by its nature or essence bound to change, pass, or come to an end ⟨fame in the movies is *transitory*⟩. EPHEMERAL implies striking brevity of life or duration ⟨many slang words are *ephemeral*⟩. MOMENTARY suggests coming and going quickly and therefore being merely a brief interruption of a more enduring state ⟨my feelings of guilt were only *momentary*⟩. FUGITIVE and FLEETING imply passing so quickly as to make apprehending difficult ⟨let a *fugitive* smile flit across his face⟩ ⟨*fleeting* moments of joy⟩. EVANESCENT suggests a quick vanishing and an airy or fragile quality ⟨the story has an *evanescent* touch of whimsy that is lost in translation⟩.

**tran·si·tion** \tran(t)-'si-shən, tran-'zi-, *chiefly British* tran(t)-'si-zhən\ *noun* [Latin *transition-, transitio,* from *transire*] (1551)
**1 a :** passage from one state, stage, subject, or place to another **:** CHANGE **b :** a movement, development, or evolution from one form, stage, or style to another
**2 a :** a musical modulation **b :** a musical passage leading from one section of a piece to another
**3 :** an abrupt change in energy state or level (as of an atomic nucleus or a molecule) usually accompanied by loss or gain of a single quantum of energy
— **tran·si·tion·al** \-'sish-nəl, -'sizh-, -'zish-; -'si-shə-nᵊl, -'zi-, -zhə-\ *adjective*
— **tran·si·tion·al·ly** *adverb*
**transition metal** *noun* [from their being transitional between the more highly electropositive and the less highly electropositive elements] (1940)
**:** any of various metallic elements (as chromium, iron, and nickel) that have valence electrons in two shells instead of only one — called also *transition element*
**tran·si·tive** \'tran(t)-sə-tiv, 'tran-zə-; 'tran(t)stiv\ *adjective* [Late Latin *transitivus,* from Latin *transitus,* past participle of *transire*] (1590)
**1 :** characterized by having or containing a direct object ⟨a *transitive* verb⟩ ⟨a *transitive* construction⟩
**2 :** being or relating to a relation with the property that if the relation holds between a first element and a second and between the second element and a third, it holds between the first and third elements ⟨equality is a *transitive* relation⟩
**3 :** of, relating to, or characterized by transition
— **tran·si·tive·ly** *adverb*
— **tran·si·tive·ness** *noun*
— **tran·si·tiv·i·ty** \,tran(t)-sə-'ti-və-tē, ,tran-zə-\ *noun*
**tran·si·to·ry** \'tran(t)-sə-,tōr-ē, 'tran-zə-, -,tòr-\ *adjective* [Middle English *transitorie,* from Middle French *transitoire,* from Late Latin *transitorius,* from Latin, of or allowing passage, from *transire*] (14th century)
**1 :** tending to pass away **:** not persistent
**2 :** of brief duration **:** TEMPORARY ⟨the *transitory* nature of earthly joy⟩
**synonym** see TRANSIENT
— **tran·si·to·ri·ly** \,tran(t)-sə-'tōr-ə-lē, ,tran-zə-, -'tòr-\ *adverb*
— **tran·si·to·ri·ness** \'tran(t)-sə-,tōr-ē-nəs, 'tran-zə-, -,tòr-\ *noun*
**trans·late** \tran(t)s-'lāt, tranz-; 'tran(t)s-,lāt, 'tranz-\ *verb* **trans·lat·ed; trans·lat·ing** [Middle English, from Latin *translatus* (past participle of *transferre* to transfer, translate), from *trans-* + *latus,* past participle of *ferre* to carry — more at TOLERATE, BEAR] (14th century)
*transitive verb*
**1 a :** to bear, remove, or change from one place, state, form, or appearance to another **:** TRANSFER, TRANSFORM ⟨a country boy *translated* to the city⟩ ⟨*translate* ideas into action⟩ **b :** to convey to heaven or to a nontemporal condition without death **c :** to transfer (a bishop) from one see to another
**2 a :** to turn into one's own or another language **b :** to transfer or turn from one set of symbols into another **:** TRANSCRIBE **c** (1) **:** to express in different terms and especially different words **:** PARAPHRASE (2) **:** to express in more comprehensible terms **:** EXPLAIN, INTERPRET
**3 :** ENRAPTURE
**4 :** to subject to mathematical translation
**5 :** to subject (as genetic information) to translation in protein synthesis
*intransitive verb*

**1 :** to practice translation or make a translation; *also* **:** to admit of or be adaptable to translation ⟨a word that doesn't *translate* easily⟩
**2 :** to undergo a translation
**3 :** LEAD, RESULT — usually used with *into* ⟨tax cuts *translate* into bigger savings⟩
— **trans·lat·abil·i·ty** \(,)tran(t)s-,lā-tə-'bi-lə-tē, (,)tranz-\ *noun*
— **trans·lat·able** \tran(t)s-'lā-tə-bəl, tranz-\ *adjective*
— **trans·la·tor** \-'lā-tər\ *noun*
**trans·la·tion** \tran(t)s-'lā-shən, tranz-\ *noun* (14th century)
**1 :** an act, process, or instance of translating: as **a :** a rendering from one language into another; *also* **:** the product of such a rendering **b :** a change to a different substance, form, or appearance **:** CONVERSION **c** (1) **:** a transformation of coordinates in which the new axes are parallel to the old ones (2) **:** uniform motion of a body in a straight line
**2 :** the process of forming a protein molecule at a ribosomal site of protein synthesis from information contained in messenger RNA — compare TRANSCRIPTION 3
— **trans·la·tion·al** \-shnəl, -shə-nᵊl\ *adjective*
**trans·la·tive** \-'lā-tiv\ *adjective* (circa 1682)
**1 :** of, relating to, or involving removal or transference from one person or place to another
**2 :** of, relating to, or serving to translate from one language or system into another
**trans·la·to·ry** \'tran(t)s-lə-,tōr-ē, 'tranz-, -,tòr-; tran(t)s-'lā-tə-rē, tranz-\ *adjective* (1849)
**:** of, relating to, or involving uniform motion in one direction
**trans·lit·er·ate** \tran(t)s-'li-tə-,rāt, tranz-\ *transitive verb* **-at·ed; -at·ing** [*trans-* + Latin *littera* letter] (1861)
**:** to represent or spell in the characters of another alphabet
— **trans·lit·er·a·tion** \(,)tran(t)s-,li-tə-'rā-shən, (,)tranz-\ *noun*
**trans·lo·ca·tion** \tran(t)s-lō-'kā-shən, ,tranz-\ *noun* (1624)
**:** a change of location **:** DISPLACEMENT: as **a :** the conduction of soluble material (as metabolic products) from one part of a plant to another **b :** transfer of part of a chromosome to a different position especially on a nonhomologous chromosome; *especially* **:** the exchange of parts between nonhomologous chromosomes
— **trans·lo·cate** \'trans(t)s-lō-,kāt, 'tranz-, (,)tran(t)s-', (,)tranz-\ *verb*
**trans·lu·cence** \tran(t)s-'lü-sᵊn(t)s, tranz-\ *noun* (1755)
**:** the quality or state of being translucent
**trans·lu·cen·cy** \-sᵊn(t)-sē\ *noun, plural* **-cies** (circa 1610)
**1 :** TRANSLUCENCE
**2 :** something that is translucent
**trans·lu·cent** \-sᵊnt\ *adjective* [Latin *translucent-, translucens,* present participle of *translucēre* to shine through, from *trans-* + *lucēre* to shine — more at LIGHT] (1607)
**1 :** permitting the passage of light: **a :** CLEAR, TRANSPARENT ⟨*translucent* water⟩ **b :** transmitting and diffusing light so that objects beyond cannot be seen clearly
**2 :** free from disguise or falseness ⟨his *translucent* patriotism —*Newsweek*⟩
**synonym** see CLEAR
— **trans·lu·cent·ly** *adverb*
**trans·ma·rine** \,tran(t)s-mə-'rēn, ,tranz-\ *adjective* [Latin *transmarinus,* from *trans-* + *mare* sea — more at MARINE] (1583)
**1 :** being or coming from beyond or across the sea ⟨a *transmarine* people⟩
**2 :** passing over or extending across the sea
**trans·mem·brane** \(,)tran(t)s-'mem-,brān, (,)tranz-\ *adjective* (1944)
**:** taking place or existing across a membrane ⟨a *transmembrane* potential⟩

**trans·mi·grate** \(,)tran(t)s-'mī-,grāt, (,)tranz-, 'tran(t)s-,, 'tranz-\ *verb* [Latin *transmigratus,* past participle of *transmigrare* to migrate to another place, from *trans-* + *migrare* to migrate] (circa 1559)
*transitive verb*
**:** to cause to go from one state of existence or place to another
*intransitive verb*
**1** *of the soul* **:** to pass at death from one body or being to another
**2 :** MIGRATE
— **trans·mi·gra·tion** \,tran(t)s-mī-'grā-shən, ,tranz-\ *noun*
— **trans·mi·gra·tor** \(,)tran(t)s-'mī-,grā-tər, (,)tranz-, 'tran(t)s-,, 'tranz-\ *noun*
— **trans·mi·gra·to·ry** \tran(t)s-'mī-grə-,tōr-ē, tranz-, -,tòr-\ *adjective*
**trans·mis·si·ble** \tran(t)s-'mi-sə-bəl, tranz-\ *adjective* (1644)
**:** capable of being transmitted ⟨*transmissible* diseases⟩
— **trans·mis·si·bil·i·ty** \(,)tran(t)s-,mi-sə-'bi-lə-tē, (,)tranz-\ *noun*
**trans·mis·sion** \tran(t)s-'mi-shən, tranz-\ *noun* [Latin *transmission-, transmissio,* from *transmittere* to transmit] (1611)
**1 :** an act, process, or instance of transmitting ⟨*transmission* of a nerve impulse across a synapse⟩
**2 :** the passage of radio waves in the space between transmitting and receiving stations; *also* **:** the act or process of transmitting by radio or television
**3 :** an assembly of parts including the speed-changing gears and the propeller shaft by which the power is transmitted from an automobile engine to a live axle; *also* **:** the speed-changing gears in such an assembly
**4 :** something that is transmitted **:** MESSAGE
— **trans·mis·sive** \-'mi-siv\ *adjective*
— **trans·mis·siv·i·ty** \,tran(t)s-(,)mi-'si-və-tē, ,tranz-\ *noun*
**trans·mis·som·e·ter** \,tran(t)s-(,)mi-'sä-mə-tər, ,tranz-\ *noun* (circa 1931)
**:** an instrument for measuring the transmission of light through a fluid (as the atmosphere)
**trans·mit** \tran(t)s-'mit, tranz-\ *verb* **trans·mit·ted; trans·mit·ting** [Middle English *transmitten,* from Latin *transmittere,* from *trans-* + *mittere* to send] (15th century)
*transitive verb*
**1 a :** to send or convey from one person or place to another **:** FORWARD **b :** to cause or allow to spread: as (1) **:** to convey by or as if by inheritance or heredity **:** HAND DOWN (2) **:** to convey (infection) abroad or to another
**2 a** (1) **:** to cause (as light or force) to pass or be conveyed through space or a medium (2) **:** to admit the passage of **:** CONDUCT ⟨glass *transmits* light⟩ **b :** to send out (a signal) either by radio waves or over a wire
*intransitive verb*
**:** to send out a signal either by radio waves or over a wire
— **trans·mit·ta·ble** \-'mi-tə-bəl\ *adjective*
— **trans·mit·tal** \-'mi-tᵊl\ *noun*
**trans·mit·tance** \-'mi-tᵊn(t)s\ *noun* (circa 1855)
**1 :** TRANSMISSION
**2 :** the fraction of radiant energy that having entered a layer of absorbing matter reaches its farther boundary
**trans·mit·ter** \tran(t)s-'mi-tər, tranz-; 'tran(t)s-,, 'tranz-\ *noun* (1727)
**:** one that transmits: as **a :** an apparatus for transmitting radio or television signals **b :** NEUROTRANSMITTER
**trans·mog·ri·fy** \tran(t)s-'mä-grə-,fī, tranz-\ *verb* **-fied; -fy·ing** [origin unknown] (1656)

\ə\ abut \ᵊ\ kitten \ər\ further \a\ ash \ā\ ace
\ä\ mop, mar \aù\ out \ch\ chin \e\ bet \ē\ easy
\g\ go \i\ hit \ī\ ice \j\ job \ŋ\ sing \ō\ go
\ò\ law \òi\ boy \th\ thin \t̲h̲\ the \ü\ loot \ù\ foot
\y\ yet \zh\ vision    *see also* Guide to Pronunciation

*transitive verb*
: to change or alter greatly and often with grotesque or humorous effect
*intransitive verb*
: to become transmogrified
**synonym** see TRANSFORM
— **trans·mog·ri·fi·ca·tion** \(,)tran(t)s-,mä-grə-fə-'kā-shən, (,)tranz-\ *noun*

**trans·mon·tane** \(,)tran(t)s-'män-,tān, (,)tranz-; ,tran(t)s-(,)män-', ,tranz-\ *adjective* [Latin *transmontanus*] (1727)
: TRAMONTANE

**trans·moun·tain** \tran(t)s-'maùn-t°n, ,tranz-\ *adjective* (1929)
: crossing or extending over or through a mountain ⟨a *transmountain* road⟩ ⟨a *transmountain* tunnel⟩

**trans·mu·ta·tion** \,tran(t)s-myù-'tā-shən, ,tranz-\ *noun* [Middle English *transmutacioun,* from Middle French or Latin; Middle French *transmutation,* from Latin *transmutation-, transmutatio,* from *transmutare*] (14th century)
: an act or instance of transmuting or being transmuted: as **a** : the conversion of base metals into gold or silver **b** : the conversion of one element or nuclide into another either naturally or artificially
— **trans·mut·a·tive** \tran(t)s-'myü-tə-tiv, tranz-\ *adjective*

**trans·mute** \tran(t)s-'myüt, tranz-\ *verb* **trans·mut·ed; trans·mut·ing** [Middle English, from Latin *transmutare,* from *trans-* + *mutare* to change — more at MUTABLE] (15th century)
*transitive verb*
**1** : to change or alter in form, appearance, or nature and especially to a higher form
**2** : to subject (as an element) to transmutation
*intransitive verb*
: to undergo transmutation
**synonym** see TRANSFORM
— **trans·mut·able** \-'myü-tə-bəl\ *adjective*

**trans·na·tion·al** \(,)tran(t)s-'nash-nəl, (,)tranz-, -'na-shə-n°l\ *adjective* (1921)
: extending or going beyond national boundaries ⟨*transnational* corporations⟩
— **trans·na·tion·al·ism** \-'nash-nə-,li-zəm, -'na-shə-n°l-,i-zəm\ *noun*

**trans·nat·u·ral** \-'na-chə-rəl, -'nach-rəl\ *adjective* (1569)
: being above or beyond nature

**trans·oce·an·ic** \,tran(t)s-,ō-shē-'a-nik, ,tranz-\ *adjective* (1827)
**1** : lying or dwelling beyond the ocean
**2** : crossing or extending across the ocean ⟨a *transoceanic* telephone cable⟩

**tran·som** \'tran(t)-səm\ *noun* [Middle English *traunsom, transyn,* probably alteration of *traversayn,* from Middle French *traversin,* from *traverse* traverse] (15th century)
**1** : a transverse piece in a structure : CROSSPIECE: as **a** : LINTEL **b** : a horizontal crossbar in a window, over a door, or between a door and a window or fanlight above it **c** : the horizontal bar or member of a cross or gallows **d** : any of several transverse timbers or beams secured to the sternpost of a boat; *also* : the planking forming the stern of a square-ended boat
**2** : a window above a door or other window built on and commonly hinged to a transom
— **over the transom** : without solicitation or prior arrangement ⟨the manuscript arrived *over the transom*⟩

*T:* transom 1b

**tran·son·ic** *also* **trans·son·ic** \tran(t)s-'sä-nik, tran-'sä-\ *adjective* [*trans-* + *super*sonic] (1945)
**1** : being or relating to speeds near that of sound in air or about 741 miles (1,185 kilometers) per hour at sea level and especially to speeds slightly below the speed of sound at which the speed of airflow varies from subsonic to supersonic at different points along the surface of a body in motion relative to the surrounding air
**2** : moving, capable of moving, or utilizing air currents moving at a transonic speed

**trans·pa·cif·ic** \,tran(t)s-pə-'si-fik\ *adjective* (1891)
**1 a** : crossing or extending across the Pacific Ocean ⟨*transpacific* airlines⟩ **b** : relating to or involving crossing the Pacific Ocean ⟨*transpacific* airfares⟩
**2 a** : situated or occurring beyond the Pacific Ocean **b** : of, relating to, or involving countries on both sides of the Pacific Ocean ⟨the *transpacific* economy⟩

**trans·par·ence** \tran(t)s-'par-ən(t)s, -'per-\ *noun* (1594)
: TRANSPARENCY 1

**trans·par·en·cy** \-ən(t)-sē\ *noun, plural* **-cies** (1615)
**1** : the quality or state of being transparent
**2** : something transparent; *especially* : a picture (as on film) viewed by light shining through it or by projection

**trans·par·ent** \-ənt\ *adjective* [Middle English, from Medieval Latin *transparent-, transparens,* present participle of *transparēre* to show through, from Latin *trans-* + *parēre* to show oneself] (15th century)
**1 a** (1) : having the property of transmitting light without appreciable scattering so that bodies lying beyond are seen clearly : PELLUCID (2) : allowing the passage of a specified form of radiation (as X rays or ultraviolet light) **b** : fine or sheer enough to be seen through : DIAPHANOUS
**2 a** : free from pretense or deceit : FRANK **b** : easily detected or seen through : OBVIOUS **c** : readily understood
**synonym** see CLEAR
— **trans·par·ent·ly** *adverb*
— **trans·par·ent·ness** *noun*

**trans·par·ent·ize** \-ən-,tīz\ *transitive verb* **-ized; -iz·ing** (1925)
: to make transparent or more nearly transparent ⟨*transparentize* tracing paper⟩

**trans·per·son·al** \(,)tran(t)s-'pərs-nəl, -'pər-sə-n°l\ *adjective* (circa 1906)
**1** : extending or going beyond the personal or individual
**2** : of, relating to, or being psychology concerned especially with esoteric mental experience (as mysticism and altered states of consciousness) beyond the usual limits of ego and personality

**trans·spic·u·ous** \tran(t)s-'pi-kyə-wəs\ *adjective* [New Latin *transpicuus,* from Latin *transpicere* to look through, from *trans-* + *specere* to look, see — more at SPY] (1638)
: clearly seen through or understood

**trans·pierce** \tran(t)s-'pirs\ *transitive verb* [Middle French *transpercer,* from Old French, from *trans-* (from Latin) + *percer* to pierce] (1592)
: to pierce through : PENETRATE

**tran·spi·ra·tion** \,tran(t)s-pə-'rā-shən\ *noun* (1551)
: the act or process or an instance of transpiring; *especially* : the passage of watery vapor from a living body through a membrane or pores
— **tran·spi·ra·tion·al** \-shnəl, -shə-n°l\ *adjective*

**tran·spire** \tran(t)-'spīr\ *verb* **tran·spired; tran·spir·ing** [Middle French *transpirer,* from Latin *trans-* + *spirare* to breathe] (1597)
*transitive verb*
: to pass off or give passage to (a fluid) through pores or interstices; *especially* : to excrete (as water) in the form of a vapor through a living membrane (as the skin)
*intransitive verb*
**1** : to give off vaporous material; *specifically* : to give off or exude watery vapor especially from the surfaces of leaves
**2** : to pass in the form of a vapor from a living body
**3 a** : to be revealed : come to light **b** : to become known or apparent : DEVELOP
**4** : to take place : GO ON, OCCUR ▪

**trans·pla·cen·tal** \,tran(t)s-plə-'sen-t°l\ *adjective* [International Scientific Vocabulary] (circa 1929)
: passing through or occurring by way of the placenta ⟨*transplacental* immunization⟩
— **trans·pla·cen·tal·ly** \-t°l-ē\ *adverb*

**¹trans·plant** \tran(t)s-'plant\ *verb* [Middle English *transplaunten,* from Late Latin *transplantare,* from Latin *trans-* + *plantare* to plant] (15th century)
*transitive verb*
**1** : to lift and reset (a plant) in another soil or situation
**2** : to remove from one place or context and settle or introduce elsewhere : RELOCATE
**3** : to transfer (an organ or tissue) from one part or individual to another
*intransitive verb*
: to admit of being transplanted
— **trans·plant·abil·i·ty** \,tran(t)s-,plan-tə-'bi-lə-tē\ *noun*
— **trans·plant·able** \,tran(t)s-'plan-tə-bəl\ *adjective*
— **trans·plan·ta·tion** \,tran(t)s-,plan-'tā-shən\ *noun*
— **trans·plant·er** \tran(t)s-'plan-tər\ *noun*

**²trans·plant** \'tran(t)s-,plant\ *noun* (1756)
**1** : a person or thing that is transplanted
**2** : the act or process of transplanting

**trans·po·lar** \(,)tran(t)s-'pō-lər\ *adjective* (1850)
: crossing or extending across either of the polar regions

**tran·spon·der** \tran(t)-'spän-dər\ *noun* [*transmitter* + *responder*] (circa 1944)
: a radio or radar set that upon receiving a designated signal emits a radio signal of its own and that is used especially for the detection, identification, and location of objects

**trans·pon·tine** \tran(t)s-'pän-,tīn\ *adjective* [*trans-* + Latin *pont-, pons* bridge — more at FIND] (1844)
**1** : situated on the farther side of a bridge
**2** *British* : situated on the south side of the Thames

**¹trans·port** \tran(t)s-'pōrt, -'pȯrt, 'tran(t)s-,\ *transitive verb* [Middle English, from Middle French or Latin; Middle French *transporter,* from Latin *transportare,* from *trans-* + *portare* to carry — more at FARE] (14th century)

**1 :** to transfer or convey from one place to another ⟨*transporting* ions across a living membrane⟩
**2 :** to carry away with strong and often intensely pleasant emotion
**3 :** to send to a penal colony overseas
*synonym* see BANISH
— **trans·port·abil·i·ty** \(ˌ)tran(t)s-ˌpōr-tə-'bi-lə-tē, -ˌpȯr-\ *noun*
— **trans·port·able** \tran(t)s-'pōr-tə-bəl, -'pȯr-\ *adjective*
²**trans·port** \'tran(t)s-ˌpōrt, -ˌpȯrt\ *noun* (1611)
**1 :** an act or process of transporting **:** TRANSPORTATION
**2 :** strong or intensely pleasurable emotion ⟨*transports* of joy⟩
**3 a :** a ship for carrying soldiers or military equipment **b :** a vehicle (as a truck or airplane) used to transport persons or goods **c :** TRANSPORTATION 3
**4 :** a transported convict
**5 :** a mechanism for moving magnetic tape past a recording head
*synonym* see ECSTASY
**trans·por·ta·tion** \ˌtran(t)s-pər-'tā-shən\ *noun* (1540)
**1 :** an act, process, or instance of transporting or being transported
**2 :** banishment to a penal colony
**3 a :** means of conveyance or travel from one place to another **b :** public conveyance of passengers or goods especially as a commercial enterprise
— **trans·por·ta·tion·al** \-shnəl, -shə-nᵊl\ *adjective*
**transport café** \-ka-'fā, -'kaf\ *noun* (1938)
*British* **:** a roadside restaurant frequented chiefly by truck drivers
**trans·port·er** \tran(t)s-'pōr-tər, -'pȯr-, 'tran(t)s-ˌ\ *noun* (1535)
**:** one that transports; *especially* **:** a vehicle for transporting large or heavy loads
**transposable element** *noun* (1979)
**:** a segment of genetic material that is capable of changing its location in the genome or in some bacteria of undergoing transfer between an extrachromosomal plasmid and a chromosome
¹**trans·pose** \tran(t)s-'pōz\ *transitive verb*
**trans·posed; trans·pos·ing** [Middle English, from Middle French *transposer*, from Latin *transponere* (perfect indicative *transposui*) to change the position of, from *trans-* + *ponere* to put, place — more at POSITION] (14th century)
**1 :** to change in form or nature **:** TRANSFORM
**2 :** to render into another language, style, or manner of expression **:** TRANSLATE
**3 :** to transfer from one place or period to another **:** SHIFT
**4 :** to change the relative place or normal order of **:** alter the sequence of ⟨*transpose* letters to change the spelling⟩
**5 :** to write or perform (a musical composition) in a different key
**6 :** to bring (a term) from one side of an algebraic equation to the other with change of sign
*synonym* see REVERSE
— **trans·pos·able** \-'pō-zə-bəl\ *adjective*
²**trans·pose** \'tran(t)s-ˌpōz\ *noun* (1937)
**:** a matrix formed from another matrix by interchanging the rows and columns
**trans·po·si·tion** \ˌtran(t)s-pə-'zi-shən\ *noun* [Medieval Latin *transposition-, transpositio*, from Latin *transponere* to transpose] (1538)
**1 :** an act, process, or instance of transposing or being transposed
**2 a :** the transfer of any term of an equation from one side over to the other side with a corresponding change of the sign **b :** a mathematical permutation or interchange of two letters or symbols
— **trans·po·si·tion·al** \-'zish-nəl, -'zi-shə-nᵊl\ *adjective*

**transposition cipher** *noun* (1939)
**:** a cipher in which the letters of the plaintext are systematically rearranged into another sequence — compare SUBSTITUTION CIPHER
**trans·po·son** \tran(t)s-'pō-zän\ *noun* [*transpose* + ²*-on*] (1974)
**:** a transposable element especially when it contains genetic material controlling functions other than those related to its relocation
**trans·sex·u·al** \(ˌ)tran(t)s-'sek-sh(ə-)wəl, -shəl\ *noun* (1957)
**:** a person with a psychological urge to belong to the opposite sex that may be carried to the point of undergoing surgery to modify the sex organs to mimic the opposite sex
— **trans·sex·u·al·ism** \-sh(ə-)wə-ˌli-zəm, -shə-ˌli-\ *noun*
— **trans·sex·u·al·i·ty** \-ˌsek-shə-'wa-lə-tē\ *noun*
**trans·shape** \tran(sh)-'shāp, tran(t)s-\ *transitive verb* (1575)
*archaic* **:** to change into another shape **:** TRANSFORM
**trans·ship** \tran(sh)-'ship, tran(t)s-\ (1792)
*transitive verb*
**:** to transfer for further transportation from one ship or conveyance to another
*intransitive verb*
**:** to change from one ship or conveyance to another
— **trans·ship·ment** \-mənt\ *noun*
**trans·tho·rac·ic** \ˌtran(t)s-thə-'ra-sik\ *adjective* (1905)
**:** done or made by way of the thoracic cavity
— **trans·tho·rac·i·cal·ly** \-si-k(ə-)lē\ *adverb*
**tran·sub·stan·tial** \ˌtran(t)-səb-'stan(t)-shəl\ *adjective* (1567)
**:** changed or capable of being changed from one substance to another
**tran·sub·stan·ti·ate** \ˌtran(t)-səb-'stan(t)-shē-ˌāt\ *verb* **-at·ed; -at·ing** [Medieval Latin *transubstantiatus*, past participle of *transubstantiare*, from Latin *trans-* + *substantia* substance] (1533)
*transitive verb*
**1 :** to change into another substance **:** TRANSMUTE
**2 :** to effect transubstantiation in (sacramental bread and wine)
*intransitive verb*
**:** to undergo transubstantiation
**tran·sub·stan·ti·a·tion** \-ˌstan(t)-shē-'ā-shən\ *noun* (14th century)
**1 :** an act or instance of transubstantiating or being transubstantiated
**2 :** the miraculous change by which according to Roman Catholic and Eastern Orthodox dogma the eucharistic elements at their consecration become the body and blood of Christ while keeping only the appearances of bread and wine
**tran·su·date** \'tran(t)-sü-ˌdāt, -syü-; 'tran-zü-, -zyü-\ *noun* (1876)
**:** a transuded substance
**tran·su·da·tion** \ˌtran(t)-sü-'dā-shən, -syü-; ˌtran-zü-, -zyü-\ *noun* (1617)
**1 :** the act or process of transuding or being transuded
**2 :** TRANSUDATE
**tran·sude** \tran(t)-'süd, -'syüd; tran-'züd, -'zyüd\ *verb* **tran·sud·ed; tran·sud·ing** [New Latin *transudare*, from Latin *trans-* + *sudare* to sweat — more at SWEAT] (1664)
*intransitive verb*
**:** to pass through a membrane or permeable substance **:** EXUDE
*transitive verb*
**:** to permit passage of
¹**trans·ura·nic** \ˌtran(t)-syü-'ra-nik, -shə-, -'rā-; ˌtran-zyü-, -zhə-\ *or* **trans·ura·ni·um** \-'rā-nē-əm\ *adjective* (1935)
**:** of, relating to, or being an element with an atomic number greater than that of uranium

²**transuranic** *noun* (1950)
**:** a transuranic element
**trans·val·u·ate** \(ˌ)tran(t)s-'val-yə-ˌwāt, (ˌ)tranz-\ *transitive verb* **-at·ed; -at·ing** [back-formation from *transvaluation*] (1912)
**:** TRANSVALUE
**trans·val·u·a·tion** \ˌtran(t)s-ˌval-yə-'wā-shən, ˌtranz-\ *noun* (1898)
**:** the act or process of transvaluing
**trans·val·ue** \(ˌ)tran(t)s-'val-(ˌ)yü, (ˌ)tranz-\ *transitive verb* **-val·ued; -valu·ing** (1911)
**:** to reevaluate especially on a basis that repudiates accepted standards
**trans·ver·sal** \tran(t)s-'vər-səl, tranz-\ *noun* [*transversal*, adjective, transverse, from Middle English, from Medieval Latin *transversalis*, from Latin *transversus*] (circa 1847)
**:** a line that intersects a system of lines
¹**trans·verse** \tran(t)s-'vərs, 'tran(t)s-ˌ, 'tranz-ˌ\ *adjective* [Latin *transversus*, from *trans-* + *-versus* (as in *adversus* adverse)] (1621)
**1 :** acting, lying, or being across **:** set crosswise
**2 :** made at right angles to the anterior-posterior axis of the body ⟨a *transverse* section⟩
— **trans·verse·ly** *adverb*
²**trans·verse** \'tran(t)s-ˌvərs, 'tranz-\ *noun* (circa 1633)
**:** something (as a piece, section, or part) that is transverse
**transverse colon** *noun* (circa 1860)
**:** the middle portion of the colon that extends across the abdominal cavity
**transverse process** *noun* (1696)
**:** a lateral process of a vertebra
**transverse wave** *noun* (1922)
**:** a wave in which the vibrating element moves in a direction perpendicular to the direction of advance of the wave
**trans·ves·tite** \tran(t)s-'ves-ˌtīt, tranz-\ *noun* [German *Transvestit*, from Latin *trans-* + *vestire* to clothe — more at VEST] (circa 1922)
**:** a person and especially a male who adopts the dress and often the behavior typical of the opposite sex especially for purposes of emotional or sexual gratification
— **trans·ves·tism** \-'ves-ˌti-zəm\ *noun*
— **transvestite** *adjective*
¹**trap** \'trap\ *noun* [Middle English, from Old English *treppe* & Old French *trape* (of Germanic origin); akin to Middle Dutch *trappe* trap, stair, Old English *treppan* to tread] (before 12th century)
**1 :** a device for taking game or other animals; *especially* **:** one that holds by springing shut suddenly
**2 a :** something by which one is caught or stopped unawares; *also* **:** a position or situation from which it is difficult or impossible to escape **b :** a football play in which a defensive player is allowed to cross the line of scrimmage and then is blocked from the side while the ballcarrier advances through the spot vacated by the defensive player
**3 a :** a device for hurling clay pigeons into the air **b :** SAND TRAP **c :** a piece of leather or section of interwoven leather straps between the thumb and forefinger of a baseball glove that forms an extension of the pocket
**4** *slang* **:** MOUTH
**5 :** a light usually one-horse carriage with springs
**6 :** any of various devices for preventing passage of something often while allowing other matter to proceed; *especially* **:** a device for

\ə\ abut \ᵊ\ kitten \ər\ further \a\ ash \ā\ ace
\ä\ mop, mar \aú\ out \ch\ chin \e\ bet \ē\ easy
\g\ go \i\ hit \ī\ ice \j\ job \ŋ\ sing \ō\ go
\ȯ\ law \ȯi\ boy \th\ thin \t̲h̲\ the \ü\ loot \ú\ foot
\y\ yet \zh\ vision *see also* Guide to Pronunciation

drains or sewers consisting of a bend or partitioned chamber in which the liquid forms a seal to prevent the passage of sewer gas
**7** *plural* **:** a group of percussion instruments (as a bass drum, snare drums, and cymbals) used especially in a dance or jazz band
**8 :** an arrangement of rock strata that favors the accumulation of oil and gas
**9** *plural* [*speed trap*] **:** a measured stretch of a course over which electronic timing devices measure the speed of a vehicle (as a racing car or dragster)
²**trap** *verb* **trapped; trap·ping** (14th century)
*transitive verb*
**1 a :** to catch or take in or as if in a trap **:** ENTRAP **b :** to place in a restricted position **:** CONFINE ⟨*trapped* in the burning wreck⟩
**2 :** to provide or set (a place) with traps
**3 a :** STOP, HOLD ⟨these mountains *trap* rains and fogs generated over the ocean —*American Guide Series: California*⟩ **b :** to separate out (as water from steam)
**4 a :** to catch (as a baseball) immediately after a bounce **b :** to block out (a defensive football player) by means of a trap
*intransitive verb*
**:** to engage in trapping animals (as for furs)
**synonym** see CATCH
— **trap·per** *noun*
³**trap** *transitive verb* **trapped; trap·ping** [Middle English *trappen*, from *trappe* cloth, perhaps modification of Middle French *drap* — more at DRAB] (14th century)
**:** to adorn with or as if with trappings
⁴**trap** *noun* [Swedish *trapp*, from *trappa* stair, from Middle Low German *trappe*; akin to Middle Dutch *trappe* stair] (1794)
**:** TRAPROCK
**trap·door** \'trap-'dōr, -'dȯr\ *noun* (14th century)
**:** a lifting or sliding door covering an opening (as in a roof, ceiling, or floor)
**trap–door spider** *noun* (1826)
**:** any of various often large burrowing spiders (especially family Ctenizidae) that construct a tubular subterranean silk-lined nest topped with a hinged lid
**tra·peze** \tra-'pēz *also* trȧ-\ *noun* [French *trapèze*, from New Latin *trapezium*] (1861)
**:** a gymnastic or acrobatic apparatus consisting of a short horizontal bar suspended by two parallel ropes

trap-door spider

**tra·pez·ist** \-'pē-zist\ *noun* (1875)
**:** a performer on the trapeze — called also *trapeze artist*
**tra·pe·zi·um** \tra-'pē-zē-əm, tra-\ *noun, plural* **-zi·ums** *or* **-zia** \-zē-ə\ [New Latin, from Greek *trapezion*, literally, small table, diminutive of *trapeza* table, from *tra-* four (akin to *tettares* four) + *peza* foot; akin to Greek *pod-, pous* foot — more at FOUR, FOOT] (1570)
**1 a :** a quadrilateral having no two sides parallel **b** *British* **:** TRAPEZOID 1b
**2 :** a bone in the wrist at the base of the thumb
**tra·pe·zi·us** \-zē-əs\ *noun* [New Latin, from *trapezium;* from the pair on the back forming together the figure of a trapezium] (circa 1704)
**:** a large flat triangular superficial muscle of each side of the upper back
**tra·pe·zo·he·dron** \trə-,pē-zō-'hē-drən, ,tra-pə-\ *noun, plural* **-drons** *or* **-dra** \-dra\ [New Latin, from *trapezium* + *-o-* + *-hedron*] (1822)

**:** a crystalline form whose faces are trapezi-
**trap·e·zoid** \'tra-pə-,zȯid\ *noun* [New Latin *trapezoïdes,* from Greek *trapezoeidēs* trapezium-shaped, from *trapeza* table] (circa 1706)
**1 a** *British* **:** TRAPEZIUM 1a
**b :** a quadrilateral having only two sides parallel
**2 :** a bone in the wrist at the base of the forefinger
— **trap·e·zoi·dal** \,tra-pə-'zȯi-d°l\ *adjective*

trapezoid 1b

**trap·line** \'trap-,līn\ *noun* (1920)
**:** a line or series of traps; *also* **:** the route along which such a line is set
**trap·ping** \'tra-piŋ\ *noun* [Middle English, from gerund of *trappen* to adorn] (14th century)
**1 :** CAPARISON 1 — usually used in plural
**2** *plural* **:** outward decoration or dress **:** ornamental equipment; *also* **:** outward signs ⟨conventional men with all the *trappings* . . . of banality —Robert Plank⟩
**Trap·pist** \'tra-pist\ *noun* [French *trappiste,* from La *Trappe,* France] (1814)
**:** a member of a reformed branch of the Roman Catholic Cistercian Order established by the Abbot de Rancé in 1664 at the monastery of La Trappe in Normandy
— **Trappist** *adjective*
**trap·rock** \'trap-'räk\ *noun* [⁴*trap*] (1813)
**:** any of various dark-colored fine-grained igneous rocks (as basalt) used especially in road making
**traps** \'traps\ *noun plural* [Middle English *trappe* cloth — more at TRAP] (1813)
**:** personal belongings **:** LUGGAGE
**trap·shoot·er** \'trap-,shü-tər\ *noun* (1875)
**:** a person who engages in trapshooting
**trap·shoot·ing** \-,shü-tiŋ\ *noun* (1875)
**:** shooting at clay pigeons sprung from a trap into the air away from the shooter
**tra·pun·to** \trə-'pün-(,)tō, -'pùn-\ *noun, plural* **-tos** [Italian, from past participle of *trapungere* to embroider, from *tra-* across (from Latin *trans-*) + *pungere* to prick, from Latin — more at TRANS-, PUNGENT] (circa 1924)
**:** a decorative quilted design in high relief worked through at least two layers of cloth by outlining the design in running stitch and padding it from the underside
¹**trash** \'trash\ *noun* [of Scandinavian origin; akin to Norwegian *trask* trash; akin to Old Norse *tros* fallen leaves and twigs, Old English *tros*] (circa 1518)
**1 :** something worth little or nothing: as **a** **:** JUNK, RUBBISH **b** (1) **:** empty talk **:** NONSENSE (2) **:** inferior or worthless writing or artistic matter; *also* **:** such material intended purely for entertainment
**2 :** something in a crumbled or broken condition or mass; *especially* **:** debris from pruning or processing plant material
**3 :** a worthless person; *also* **:** such persons as a group **:** RIFFRAFF
²**trash** (circa 1859)
*transitive verb*
**1 :** VANDALIZE, DESTROY
**2 :** ATTACK, ASSAULT
**3 :** SPOIL, RUIN ⟨*trashing* the environment⟩
**4 :** to subject to criticism or invective; *especially* **:** to disparage strongly ⟨a film *trashed* by the critics⟩
**5 :** THROW AWAY 1 ⟨standards of reality and truth were *trashed* —Edwin Diamond⟩
*intransitive verb*
**:** to trash something or someone
**trash fish** *noun* (1944)
**1 :** ROUGH FISH
**2 :** any of various sea fishes that have no market value as human food but are sometimes processed for use in animal feed, fertilizers, and paints

**trash·man** \'trash-,man, -mən\ *noun* (1951)
**:** a worker who collects and hauls away trash
**trashy** \'tra-shē\ *adjective* **trash·i·er; -est** (circa 1620)
**:** resembling or containing trash **:** of inferior quality
— **trash·i·ness** *noun*
**trat·to·ria** \,trä-tə-'rē-ə\ *noun, plural* **-ri·as** *or* **-rie** \-'rē-,ā\ [Italian, from *trattore* restaurateur, from French *traiteur,* from *traiter* to treat, from Old French *traitier* — more at TREAT] (1832)
**:** RESTAURANT; *specifically* **:** a usually small modest Italian restaurant
**word history** see RESTAURANT
**trau·ma** \'trau̇-mə, 'trȯ-\ *noun, plural* **trau·mas** *also* **trau·ma·ta** \-mə-tə\ [Greek *traumat-, trauma* wound, alteration of *trōma;* akin to Greek *titrōskein* to wound, *tetrainein* to pierce — more at THROW] (circa 1693)
**1 a :** an injury (as a wound) to living tissue caused by an extrinsic agent ⟨surgical *trauma*⟩ **b :** a disordered psychic or behavioral state resulting from mental or emotional stress or physical injury
**2 :** an agent, force, or mechanism that causes trauma
— **trau·mat·ic** \trə-'ma-tik, trȯ-, trau̇-\ *adjective*
— **trau·mat·i·cal·ly** \-ti-k(ə-)lē\ *adverb*
**trau·ma·tise** *British variant of* TRAUMATIZE
**trau·ma·tism** \'trau̇-mə-,ti-zəm, 'trȯ-\ *noun* (1857)
**:** the development or occurrence of trauma; *also* **:** TRAUMA
**trau·ma·tize** \-,tīz\ *transitive verb* **-tized; -tiz·ing** (1903)
**:** to inflict a trauma upon
— **trau·ma·ti·za·tion** \,trau̇-mə-tə-'zā-shən, ,trȯ-\ *noun*
¹**tra·vail** \trə-'vā(ə)l, 'tra-,vāl\ *noun* [Middle English, from Old French, from *travaillier* to torture, labor, from (assumed) Vulgar Latin *trepaliare* to torture, from Late Latin *trepalium* instrument of torture, from Latin *tripalis* having three stakes, from *tri-* + *palus* stake — more at POLE] (13th century)
**1 a :** work especially of a painful or laborious nature **:** TOIL **b :** a physical or mental exertion or piece of work **:** TASK, EFFORT **c :** AGONY, TORMENT
**2 :** LABOR, PARTURITION
**synonym** see WORK
**word history** see TRAVEL
²**travail** \*same as* ¹; in prayer-book communion service usually 'tra-,vāl\ *intransitive verb* [Middle English, from Old French *travaillier*] (13th century)
**1 :** to labor hard **:** TOIL
**2 :** LABOR 3
¹**trav·el** \'tra-vəl\ *verb* **-eled** *or* **-elled; -el·ing** *or* **-el·ling** \'tra-və-liŋ, 'trav-liŋ\ [Middle English *travailen* to labor, journey, from Old French *travaillier* to labor] (14th century)
*intransitive verb*
**1 a :** to go on or as if on a trip or tour **:** JOURNEY **b** (1) **:** to go as if by traveling **:** PASS ⟨the news *traveled* fast⟩ (2) **:** ASSOCIATE ⟨*travels* with a sophisticated crowd⟩ **c :** to go from place to place as a sales representative or business agent
**2 a :** to move or undergo transmission from one place to another ⟨goods *traveling* by plane⟩ **b :** to move in a given direction or path or through a given distance ⟨the stylus *travels* in a groove⟩ **c :** to move rapidly ⟨a car that can really *travel*⟩
**3 :** to walk or run with a basketball in violation of the rules
*transitive verb*
**1 a :** to journey through or over **b :** to follow (a course or path) as if by traveling
**2 :** to traverse (a specified distance)

**3** : to cover (a place or region) as a commercial traveler ◆

— **travel light** : to travel with a minimum of equipment or baggage

**²travel** *noun* (14th century)
**1 a** : the act of traveling : PASSAGE **b** : a journey especially to a distant or unfamiliar place : TOUR, TRIP — often used in plural
**2** *plural* : an account of one's travels
**3** : the number traveling : TRAFFIC
**4 a** : MOVEMENT, PROGRESSION ⟨the *travel* of satellites around the earth⟩ **b** : the motion of a piece of machinery; *especially* : reciprocating motion

**travel agency** *noun* (1927)
: an agency engaged in selling and arranging personal transportation and accommodations for travelers — called also *travel bureau*

**travel agent** *noun* (1925)
: a person engaged in selling and arranging transportation, tours, or trips for travelers

**trav·eled** *or* **trav·elled** \'tra-vəld\ *adjective* (15th century)
**1** : experienced in travel ⟨a widely *traveled* journalist⟩
**2** : used by travelers ⟨a well-*traveled* highway⟩

**trav·el·er** *or* **trav·el·ler** \'tra-və-lər, 'trav-lər\ *noun* (14th century)
**1** : one that travels: as **a** : one that goes on a trip or journey **b** : TRAVELING SALESMAN
**2 a** : an iron ring sliding along a rope, bar, or rod of a ship **b** : a rod on the deck on which such a ring slides
**3** : any of various devices for handling something that is being transported laterally

**traveler's check** *noun* (1891)
: a draft purchased from a bank or express company and signed by the purchaser at the time of purchase and again at the time of cashing as a precaution against forgery

**trav·el·ing** *or* **trav·el·ling** \'tra-və-liŋ, 'trav-liŋ\ *adjective* (14th century)
**1** : that travels ⟨a *traveling* opera company⟩ ⟨a *traveling* executive⟩
**2** : carried, used by, or accompanying a traveler ⟨a *traveling* alarm clock⟩ ⟨a *traveling* companion⟩

**traveling bag** *noun* (1838)
: SUITCASE

**traveling case** *noun* (1744)
: a usually rigid and box-shaped suitcase

**traveling fellowship** *noun* (1789)
: a fellowship whose terms permit or direct the holder to travel or go abroad for study or research

**traveling salesman** *noun* (1885)
: a traveling representative of a business concern who solicits orders usually in an assigned territory

**trav·el·ogue** *or* **trav·el·og** \'tra-və-ˌlóg, -ˌläg\ *noun* [travel + -logue] (1903)
**1** : a talk or lecture on travel usually accompanied by a film or slides
**2** : a narrated motion picture about travel
**3** : a piece of writing about travel

**travel trailer** *noun* (1961)
: a trailer drawn especially by a passenger automobile and equipped for use (as while traveling) as a dwelling

**tra·vers·al** \trə-'vər-səl *also* tra-' *or* 'tra-\ *noun* (1897)
: the act or an instance of traversing

**¹tra·verse** \'tra-vərs *also* -ˌvərs, *especially for* 6 & 8 *also* trə-' *or* tra-'\ *noun* [Middle English *travers,* from Middle French *traverse,* from *traverser* to cross, from Late Latin *transversare,* from Latin *transversus* transverse — more at TRANSVERSE] (14th century)
**1** : something that crosses or lies across
**2** : OBSTACLE, ADVERSITY
**3** : a formal denial of a matter of fact alleged by the opposite party in a legal pleading

**4 a** : a compartment or recess formed by a partition, curtain, or screen **b** : a gallery or loft of communication from side to side in a large building
**5** : a route or way across or over: as **a** : a zigzag course of a sailing ship with contrary winds **b** : a curving or zigzag way up a steep grade **c** : the course followed in traversing
**6** : the act or an instance of traversing : CROSSING
**7** : a protective projecting wall or bank of earth in a trench
**8 a** : a lateral movement (as of the saddle of a lathe carriage); *also* : a device for imparting such movement **b** : the lateral movement of a gun about a pivot or on a carriage to change direction of fire
**9** : a line surveyed across a plot of ground

**²tra·verse** \trə-'vərs *also* tra-' *or* 'tra-ˌ\ *verb* **tra·versed; tra·vers·ing** (14th century)
*transitive verb*
**1 a** : to go against or act in opposition to : OPPOSE, THWART **b** : to deny (as an allegation of fact or an indictment) formally at law
**2 a** : to go or travel across or over **b** : to move or pass along or through ⟨light rays *traversing* a crystal⟩
**3** : to make a study of : EXAMINE
**4** : to lie or extend across : CROSS ⟨the bridge *traverses* a brook⟩
**5 a** : to move to and fro over or along **b** : to ascend, descend, or cross (a slope or gap) at an angle **c** : to move (a gun) to right or left on a pivot
**6** : to make or carry out a survey of by using traverses
*intransitive verb*
**1** : to move back and forth or from side to side
**2** : to move or turn laterally : SWIVEL
**3 a** : to climb at an angle or in a zigzag course **b** : to ski across rather than straight down a hill
**4** : to make a survey by using traverses
— **tra·vers·able** \-'vər-sə-bəl, -(ˌ)vər-\ *adjective*
— **tra·vers·er** *noun*

**³tra·verse** \'tra-(ˌ)vərs, trə-', tra-'\ *adjective* (15th century)
: lying across : TRANSVERSE

**trav·erse jury** \'trav-ərs-\ *noun* (1823)
: PETIT JURY

**traverse rod** *noun* (1948)
: a metal rod or track with a pulley mechanism for drawing curtains

**trav·er·tine** \'trav-ər-ˌtēn, -tən\ *noun* [French *travertin,* from Italian *travertino, trevertino,* from Latin *tiburtinus,* adjective, of travertine, literally, of Tibur (Tivoli)] (1797)
: a mineral consisting of a massive usually layered calcium carbonate (as aragonite or calcite) formed by deposition from spring waters or especially from hot springs

**¹trav·es·ty** \'tra-və-stē\ *transitive verb* **-tied; -ty·ing** (1673)
: to make a travesty of : PARODY

**²travesty** *noun, plural* **-ties** [obsolete English *travesty,* disguised, parodied, from French *travesti,* past participle of *travestir* to disguise, from Italian *travestire,* from *tra-* across (from Latin *trans-*) + *vestire* to dress, from Latin — more at VEST] (1674)
**1** : a burlesque translation or literary or artistic imitation usually grotesquely incongruous in style, treatment, or subject matter
**2** : a debased, distorted, or grossly inferior imitation ⟨a *travesty* of justice⟩
**synonym** see CARICATURE

**tra·vois** \trə-'vói, 'tra-ˌvói\ *noun, plural* **tra·vois** *also* **tra·voises** \-'vóiz, -ˌvóiz\ [American French *travail,* from Canadian French, shaft of a cart, from French *travail* catafalque, prop, from Late Latin *trepalium* instrument of torture — more at TRAVAIL] (1847)

travois

: a simple vehicle used by Plains Indians consisting of two trailing poles serving as shafts and bearing a platform or net for the load

**¹trawl** \'tról\ *verb* [probably from obsolete Dutch *tragelen*] (1561)
*intransitive verb*
**1** : to fish with a trawl
**2** : TROLL 2
*transitive verb*
: to catch (fish) with a trawl

**²trawl** *noun* (1759)
**1** : a large conical net dragged along the sea bottom in gathering fish or other marine life
**2** : SETLINE

**trawl·er** \'tró-lər\ *noun* (1630)
**1** : a person who fishes by trawling
**2** : a boat used in trawling

**trawl·er·man** \-mən\ *noun* (1633)
: a fisherman who trawls or one who mans a trawler

**tray** \'trā\ *noun* [Middle English, from Old English *trĩg, trēg;* akin to Old Swedish *trō* wooden grain measure and probably to Old English *trēow* tree — more at TREE] (before 12th century)
: an open receptacle with a flat bottom and a low rim for holding, carrying, or exhibiting articles
— **tray·ful** \-ˌfúl\ *noun*

**treach·er·ous** \'tre-chə-rəs, 'trech-rəs\ *adjective* (14th century)
**1** : characterized by or manifesting treachery : PERFIDIOUS
**2 a** : likely to betray trust : UNRELIABLE ⟨a *treacherous* memory⟩ **b** : providing insecure footing or support ⟨*treacherous* quicksand⟩ **c** : marked by hidden dangers, hazards, or perils
**synonym** see FAITHLESS
— **treach·er·ous·ly** *adverb*
— **treach·er·ous·ness** *noun*

**treach·ery** \-rē\ *noun, plural* **-er·ies** [Middle English *trecherie,* from Old French, from *trechier, trichier* to deceive, from (assumed) Vulgar Latin *triccare* — more at TRICK] (13th century)

◇ WORD HISTORY
**travel** For many of us in the U.S. travel is usually for pleasure and work is not very taxing physically, so that we are unlikely to associate travel with hard labor, and labor with torture. However, travel, labor, and torture are all bound up in the history of the word *travel.* The ultimate source of both *travel* and *travail* is an unattested spoken Latin verb *trepaliare* "to torture," a derivative of Late Latin *trepalium,* a name for an instrument of torture. *Trepaliare* developed into Old French *travaillier,* which meant "to torture, torment" and intransitively "to suffer, labor." Middle English borrowed the Old French verb as well as its noun derivative *travail,* and Modern English *travail* preserves the original sense "torment." But the difficulties of getting from place to place in the Middle Ages, when any journey was a wearisome effort and a pilgrimage to a distant religious shrine a real act of devotion, led medieval Englishmen to apply *travailen* "to labor" to the act of making a trip. Shift in stress and a weakening of the vowel in the second syllable eventually led to a distinction between *travail* and *travel.*

**1** : violation of allegiance or of faith and confidence **:** TREASON
**2** : an act of perfidy or treason
**trea·cle** \'trē-kəl\ *noun* [Middle English *triacle*, from Middle French, from Latin *theriaca*, from Greek *thēriakē* antidote against a poisonous bite, from feminine of *thēriakos* of a wild animal, from *thērion* wild animal, diminutive of *thēr* wild animal — more at FIERCE] (14th century)
**1** : a medicinal compound formerly in wide use as a remedy against poison
**2** *chiefly British* **a :** MOLASSES **b :** a blend of molasses, invert sugar, and corn syrup used as syrup at the table — called also *golden syrup*
**3** : something (as a tone of voice) heavily sweet and cloying
**trea·cly** \-k(ə-)lē\ *adjective* (1733)
: resembling treacle (as in quality or appearance) ⟨*treacly* sentimentality⟩
**¹tread** \'tred\ *verb* **trod** \'träd\ *also* **tread·ed; trod·den** \'trä-d⁰n\ *or* **trod; tread·ing** [Middle English *treden*, from Old English *tredan*; akin to Old High German *tretan* to tread] (before 12th century)
*transitive verb*
**1 a :** to step or walk on or over **b :** to walk along **:** FOLLOW
**2 a :** to beat or press with the feet **:** TRAMPLE **b :** to subdue or repress as if by trampling **:** CRUSH
**3 :** to copulate with — used of a male bird
**4 a :** to form by treading **:** BEAT ⟨*tread* a path⟩ **b :** to execute by stepping or dancing ⟨*tread* a measure⟩
*intransitive verb*
**1 :** to move on foot **:** WALK
**2 a :** to set foot **b :** to put one's foot **:** STEP
**3 :** COPULATE
— **tread·er** *noun*
— **tread on one's toes** : to give offense (as by encroaching on one's rights or feelings)
— **tread water** : to keep the body nearly upright in the water and the head above water by a treading motion of the feet usually aided by the hands
**²tread** *noun* (13th century)
**1 :** a mark (as a footprint or the imprint of a tire) made by or as if by treading
**2 a** (1) : the action of treading (2) : an act or instance of treading **:** STEP **b :** manner of stepping **c :** the sound of treading
**3 a :** the part of a shoe or boot sole that touches the ground; *also* : the pattern on the bottom of a sole **b** (1) : the part of a wheel or tire that makes contact with a road or rail (2) : the pattern of ridges or grooves made or cut in the face of a tire
**4 :** the distance between the points of contact with the ground of the two front wheels or the two rear wheels of a vehicle
**5 a :** the upper horizontal part of a step **b :** the width of such a tread
— **tread·less** \-ləs\ *adjective*
**¹trea·dle** \'tre-d⁰l\ *noun* [Middle English *tredel* step of a stair, from Old English, from *tredan*] (15th century)
: a swiveling or lever device pressed by the foot to drive a machine
**²treadle** *verb* **trea·dled; trea·dling** \'tred-liŋ, 'tre-d⁰l-iŋ\ (1891)
*intransitive verb*
: to operate a treadle
*transitive verb*
: to operate (as a machine) by a treadle
**tread·mill** \'tred-ˌmil\ *noun* (1822)
**1 a :** a mill worked by persons treading on steps on the periphery of a wide wheel having a horizontal axis and used formerly in prison punishment **b :** a mill worked by an animal treading an endless belt **c :** a device having an endless belt on which an individual walks or runs in place for exercise or physiological testing
**2 :** a wearisome or monotonous routine resembling continued activity on a treadmill

**trea·son** \'trē-z⁰n\ *noun* [Middle English *tresoun*, from Old French *traison*, from Latin *tradition-, traditio* act of handing over, from *tradere* to hand over, betray — more at TRAITOR] (13th century)
**1 :** the betrayal of a trust **:** TREACHERY
**2 :** the offense of attempting by overt acts to overthrow the government of the state to which the offender owes allegiance or to kill or personally injure the sovereign or the sovereign's family ◆
**trea·son·able** \'trēz-nə-bəl, 'trē-z⁰n-ə-bəl\ *adjective* (14th century)
: relating to, consisting of, or involving treason
— **trea·son·ably** \-blē\ *adverb*
**trea·son·ous** \'trēz-nəs, 'trē-z⁰n-əs\ *adjective* (1593)
: TREASONABLE
**trea·sur·able** \'tre-zhə-rə-bəl, 'trā-; 'trezh-rə-, 'trāzh-rə-\ *adjective* (1607)
: worthy of being treasured **:** PRECIOUS
**¹trea·sure** \'tre-zhər, 'trā-\ *noun* [Middle English *tresor*, from Old French, from Latin *thesaurus* — more at THESAURUS] (12th century)
**1 a** (1) : wealth (as money, jewels, or precious metals) stored up or hoarded ⟨buried *treasure*⟩ (2) : wealth of any kind or in any form **:** RICHES **b :** a store of money in reserve
**2 :** something of great worth or value; *also* : a person esteemed as rare or precious
**3 :** a collection of precious things
**²treasure** *transitive verb* **trea·sured; trea·sur·ing** \-zh(ə-)riŋ\ (14th century)
**1 :** to collect and store up (something of value) for future use **:** HOARD
**2 :** to hold or keep as precious **:** CHERISH, PRIZE ⟨she *treasured* those memories⟩
**synonym** see APPRECIATE
**trea·sure–house** \'tre-zhər-ˌhaús, 'trā-\ *noun* (15th century)
**1 :** a building where treasure is kept **:** TREASURY
**2 :** a place or source (as a collection) where many things of value can be found
**trea·sur·er** \'tre-zhə-rər, 'trā-; 'trezh-rər, 'trāzh-\ *noun* (14th century)
**1 :** a guardian of a collection of treasures **:** CURATOR
**2 :** an officer entrusted with the receipt, care, and disbursement of funds: as **a :** a governmental officer charged with receiving, keeping, and disbursing public revenues **b :** the executive financial officer of a club, society, or business corporation
— **trea·sur·er·ship** \-ˌship\ *noun*
**treasure trove** \-ˌtrōv\ *noun* [Anglo-French *tresor trové*, literally, found treasure] (1523)
**1 :** treasure that anyone finds; *specifically* : gold or silver in the form of money, plate, or bullion which is found hidden and whose ownership is not known
**2 :** a valuable discovery, resource, or collection
**trea·sury** \'tre-zh(ə-)rē, 'trā-\ *noun, plural* **-sur·ies** [Middle English *tresorie*, from Old French, from *tresor* treasure] (14th century)
**1 a :** a place in which stores of wealth are kept **b :** the place of deposit and disbursement of collected funds; *especially* : one where public revenues are deposited, kept, and disbursed **c :** funds kept in such a depository
**2** *obsolete* **:** TREASURE
**3** *capitalized* **a :** a governmental department in charge of finances and especially the collection, management, and expenditure of public revenues **b :** the building in which the business of such a governmental department is transacted
**4** *capitalized* **:** a government security (as a note or bill) issued by the Treasury
**5 :** a repository for treasures ⟨a *treasury* of poems⟩
**treasury note** *noun* (1890)

**1 :** a currency note issued by the U.S. Treasury in payment for silver bullion purchased under the Sherman Silver Purchase Act of 1890
**2 :** a U.S. government bond usually with a maturity of not less than one year or more than seven years
**treasury of merits** (1884)
: the superabundant satisfaction of Christ for human sins and the excess of merit of the saints which according to Roman Catholic theology is effective for salvation of others and is available for dispensation through indulgences
**treasury stock** *noun* (1903)
: issued stock reacquired by a corporation and held as an asset
**¹treat** \'trēt\ *verb* [Middle English *treten*, from Old French *traitier*, from Latin *tractare* to drag about, handle, deal with, frequentative of *trahere* to drag, pull] (14th century)
*intransitive verb*
**1 :** to discuss terms of accommodation or settlement **:** NEGOTIATE
**2 :** to deal with a matter especially in writing **:** DISCOURSE — usually used with *of* ⟨a book *treating* of conservation⟩
**3 :** to pay another's expenses (as for a meal or drink) especially as a compliment or as an expression of regard or friendship
*transitive verb*
**1 a :** to deal with in speech or writing **:** EXPOUND **b :** to present or represent artistically **c :** to deal with **:** HANDLE ⟨food is plentiful and *treated* with imagination —Cecil Beaton⟩
**2 a :** to bear oneself toward **:** USE ⟨*treat* a horse cruelly⟩ **b :** to regard and deal with in a specified manner — usually used with *as*
**3 a :** to provide with free food, drink, or entertainment **b :** to provide with enjoyment or gratification
**4 :** to care for or deal with medically or surgically ⟨*treat* a disease⟩
**5 :** to act upon with some agent especially to improve or alter ⟨*treat* a metal with acid⟩
— **treat·er** *noun*
**²treat** *noun* (1651)
**1 :** an entertainment given without expense to those invited
**2 :** an especially unexpected source of joy, delight, or amusement
**treat·able** \'trē-tə-bəl\ *adjective* (14th century)
: capable of being treated **:** yielding or responsive to treatment ⟨a *treatable* disease⟩
— **treat·abil·i·ty** \ˌtrē-tə-ˈbi-lə-tē\ *noun*
**trea·tise** \'trē-təs *also* -təz\ *noun* [Middle English *tretis*, from Anglo-French *tretiz*, from Old French *traitier* to treat] (14th century)

◇ WORD HISTORY
**treason** In some circumstances *treason* may seem to be subverting the forces of *tradition,* yet both of these words come from the same Latin source. Latin *traditio* means "transmission of knowledge" or "teaching," but these senses developed from its more literal meaning "the act of handing over a person or thing." Thus *tradition* is maintained by passing information from one generation to another, whereas *treason* is committed when someone who has been entrusted with information passes it on to someone who is not supposed to have it. The difference in form between the two words is accounted for by the fact that *treason* came to us via Old French, after many generations of speakers had altered Latin *traditio* into Old French *traison*, while *tradition* was borrowed into English directly from Latin. Latin *traditio* is itself a derivative of the verb *tradere*, meaning "to hand over, deliver." Through another derivative, *traditor*, this verb is also the ultimate source of English *traitor*.

**1 :** a systematic exposition or argument in writing including a methodical discussion of the facts and principles involved and conclusions reached ⟨a *treatise* on higher education⟩
**2** *obsolete* **:** ACCOUNT, TALE

**treat·ment** \'trēt-mənt\ *noun* (circa 1560)
**1 a :** the act or manner or an instance of treating someone or something **:** HANDLING, USAGE
**b :** the techniques or actions customarily applied in a specified situation
**2 a :** a substance or technique used in treating
**b :** an experimental condition

**trea·ty** \'trē-tē\ *noun, plural* **treaties** [Middle English *tretee,* from Middle French *traité,* from Medieval Latin *tractatus,* from Latin, handling, treatment, from *tractare* to treat, handle] (14th century)
**1 :** the action of treating and especially of negotiating
**2 a :** an agreement or arrangement made by negotiation: (1) **:** PRIVATE TREATY (2) **:** a contract in writing between two or more political authorities (as states or sovereigns) formally signed by representatives duly authorized and usually ratified by the lawmaking authority of the state **b :** a document in which such a contract is set down

**treaty port** *noun* (1863)
**:** any of numerous ports and inland cities in China, Japan, and Korea formerly open by treaty to foreign commerce

¹**tre·ble** \'tre-bəl\ *noun* [Middle English, perhaps from Middle French, trio, from *treble,* adjective] (14th century)
**1 a :** the highest voice part in harmonic music **:** SOPRANO **b :** one that performs a treble part; *also* **:** a member of a family of instruments having the highest range **c :** a high-pitched or shrill voice, tone, or sound **d :** the upper half of the whole vocal or instrumental tonal range — compare BASS **e :** the higher portion of the audio frequency range in sound recording and broadcasting
**2 :** something treble in construction, uses, amount, number, or value

²**treble** *adjective* [Middle English, from Middle French, from Latin *triplus* — more at TRIPLE] (14th century)
**1 a :** having three parts or uses **:** THREEFOLD **b :** triple in number or amount
**2 a :** relating to or having the range or part of a treble **b :** HIGH-PITCHED, SHRILL **c :** of, relating to, or having the range of treble in sound recording and broadcasting ⟨*treble* frequencies⟩
— **tre·bly** \'tre-b(ə-)lē\ *adverb*

³**treble** *verb* **tre·bled; tre·bling** \'tre-b(ə-)liŋ\ (14th century)
*transitive verb*
**:** to increase threefold
*intransitive verb*
**1 :** to sing treble
**2 :** to grow to three times the size, amount, or number

**treble clef** *noun* [¹*treble;* from its use for the notation of treble parts] (circa 1854)
**1 :** a clef that places G above middle C on the second line of the staff
**2 :** TREBLE STAFF

**treble staff** *noun* (circa 1854)
**:** the musical staff carrying the treble clef

**treb·u·chet** \,tre-byə-'shet, -bə-, -'chet\ *or* **treb·uc·ket** \,tre-bə-'ket\ *noun* [Middle English *trebochet,* from Middle French *trebuchet*] (15th century)
**:** a medieval military engine for hurling heavy missiles (as rocks)

**tre·cen·to** \trā-'chen-(,)tō\ *noun* [Italian, literally, three hundred, from Latin *tres* three + *centum* hundred — more at THREE, HUNDRED] (1841)
**:** the 14th century; *specifically* **:** the 14th century in Italian literature and art

**tre·de·cil·lion** \,trē-di-'sil-yən\ *noun, often attributive* [Latin *tredecim* thirteen (from *tres*

three + *decem* ten) + English *-illion* (as in *million*) — more at THREE, TEN] (circa 1934)
— see NUMBER table

¹**tree** \'trē\ *noun* [Middle English, from Old English *trēow;* akin to Old Norse *trē* tree, Greek *drys,* Sanskrit *dāru* wood] (before 12th century)
**1 a :** a woody perennial plant having a single usually elongate main stem generally with few or no branches on its lower part **b :** a shrub or herb of arborescent form ⟨rose *trees*⟩ ⟨a banana *tree*⟩
**2 a** (1) **:** a piece of wood (as a post or pole) usually adapted to a particular use or forming part of a structure or implement (2) *archaic* **:** the cross on which Jesus was crucified **b** *archaic* **:** GALLOWS
**3 :** something in the form of or resembling a tree: as **a :** a diagram or graph that branches usually from a simple stem without forming loops or polygons ⟨genealogical *tree*⟩ **b :** a much-branched system of channels especially in an animal body ⟨the vascular *tree*⟩
**4 :** SADDLETREE
— **tree·less** \-ləs\ *adjective*
— **tree·like** \-,līk\ *adjective*

²**tree** *transitive verb* **treed; tree·ing** (1575)
**1 a :** to drive to or up a tree ⟨*treed* by a bull⟩ ⟨dogs *treeing* game⟩ **b :** to put into a position of extreme disadvantage **:** CORNER; *especially* **:** to bring to bay
**2 :** to furnish or fit (as a shoe) with a tree

**treed** \'trēd\ *adjective* (1860)
**:** planted or grown with trees **:** WOODED

**tree ear** *noun* (1967)
**:** any of several large ear-shaped basidiomycetous fungi (genus *Auricularia*); *especially* **:** one (*A. polytricha*) used especially in Chinese cooking

**tree farm** *noun* (1941)
**:** an area of forest land managed to ensure continuous commercial production

**tree fern** *noun* (1832)
**:** any of various ferns (especially families Cyatheaceae and Marattiaceae) of arborescent habit with a woody stem

**tree frog** *noun* (1738)
**:** any of numerous small anuran amphibians (especially family Hylidae) of usually arboreal habits that typically have adhesive suckers on the toes

**tree·hop·per** \'trē-,hä-pər\ *noun* (circa 1839)
**:** any of a family (Membracidae) of small leaping homopterous insects that feed on the sap especially of shrubs and trees

**tree house** *noun* (circa 1899)
**:** a structure (as a playhouse) built among the branches of a tree

**tree line** *noun* (1893)
**:** TIMBERLINE

**treen** \'trēn\ *noun, singular or plural in construction* [*treen* wooden, from Middle English, from Old English *trēowen,* from *treow* tree, wood] (1927)
**:** small woodenware — called also *treenware*

**tree·nail** *also* **tre·nail** \'trə-nᵊl\ *noun* (13th century)
**:** a wooden peg made usually of dry compressed timber so as to swell in its hole when moistened

**tree of heaven** (1845)
**:** a Chinese ailanthus (*Ailanthus altissima* synonym *A. glandulosa*) that has foliage similar to that of the sumacs, has ill-scented staminate flowers, and is grown as a shade and ornamental tree

**tree of life** (1880)
**:** a conventionalized and often ornate representation of a tree used as a decorative motif

**tree peony** *noun* (circa 1891)
**:** a shrubby Chinese peony (*Paeonia suffruticosa*) that has large showy flowers and is the source of many horticultural varieties

**tree ring** *noun* (1919)
**:** ANNUAL RING

**tree shrew** *noun* (circa 1893)
**:** any of an order (Scandentia) of arboreal insectivorous mammals of southeastern Asia often classified as true insectivores or sometimes as primitive primates

tree shrew

**tree sparrow** *noun* (circa 1770)
**1 :** a European sparrow (*Passer montanus*) that has a black spot on the ear coverts
**2 :** a North American sparrow (*Spizella arborea*) that has a single dark spot on the breast and breeds in northern North America and winters in the U.S.

**tree surgeon** *noun* (1908)
**:** a specialist in tree surgery — compare ARBORIST

**tree surgery** *noun* (1902)
**:** operative treatment of diseased trees especially for control of decay; *broadly* **:** practices forming part of the professional care of specimen or shade trees

**tree swallow** *noun* (1873)
**:** an American swallow (*Tachycineta bicolor* synonym *Iridoprocne bicolor*) with iridescent greenish blue upperparts and white underparts

**tree toad** *noun* (1778)
**:** TREE FROG

**tree tomato** *noun* (circa 1881)
**:** TAMARILLO

**tree·top** \'trē-,täp\ *noun* (1530)
**1 :** the topmost part of a tree
**2** *plural* **:** the height or line marked by the tops of a group of trees

**tre·foil** \'trē-,fȯil, 'tre-\ *noun* [Middle English, from Middle French *trefeuil,* from Latin *trifolium,* from *tri-* + *folium* leaf — more at BLADE] (15th century)
**1 a :** CLOVER; *broadly* **:** any of several trifoliolate leguminous herbs **b :** a trifoliolate leaf
**2 :** an ornament or symbol in the form of a stylized trifoliolate leaf

trefoil 2

**tre·ha·lose** \tri-'hä-,lōs, -,lōz\ *noun* [International Scientific Vocabulary *trehala* (a sweet substance constituting the pupal covering of a beetle) + ²*-ose*] (1862)
**:** a crystalline disaccharide $C_{12}H_{22}O_{11}$ stored instead of starch by many fungi and found in the blood of many insects

**treil·lage** \tre-'yäzh\ *noun* [French, from Middle French, from *treille* vine arbor, from Latin *trichila*] (1698)
**:** latticework for vines **:** TRELLIS 1

¹**trek** \'trek\ *intransitive verb* **trekked; trek·king** [Afrikaans, from Dutch *trecken* to pull, haul, migrate; akin to Old High German *trechan* to pull] (1821)
**1** *chiefly South African* **a :** to travel by ox wagon **b :** to migrate by ox wagon or in a train of such
**2 :** to make one's way arduously; *broadly* **:** to go on a journey
— **trek·ker** *noun*

²**trek** *noun* [Afrikaans, from Dutch *treck* pull, haul, from *trecken*] (1835)
**1** *chiefly South African* **:** a journey by ox wagon; *especially* **:** an organized migration by a group of settlers

\ə\ abut \ᵊ\ kitten \ər\ further \a\ ash \ā\ ace
\ä\ mop, mar \aủ\ out \ch\ chin \e\ bet \ē\ easy
\g\ go \i\ hit \ī\ ice \j\ job \ŋ\ sing \ō\ go
\ȯ\ law \ȯi\ boy \th\ thin \th\ the \ü\ loot \ủ\ foot
\y\ yet \zh\ vision    *see also* Guide to Pronunciation

**2** : a trip or movement especially when involving difficulties or complex organization

**¹trel·lis** \'tre-ləs\ noun [Middle English trelis, from Middle French treliz fabric of coarse weave, trellis, from (assumed) Vulgar Latin trilicius woven with triple thread, from Latin tri- + licium thread] (15th century)
**1** : a frame of latticework used as a screen or as a support for climbing plants
**2** : a construction (as a summerhouse) chiefly of latticework
**3** : an arrangement that forms or gives the effect of a lattice ⟨a trellis of interlacing streams⟩
— **trel·lised** \'tre-ləst\ adjective

**²trellis** transitive verb (15th century)
**1** : to provide with a trellis; especially : to train (as a vine) on a trellis
**2** : to cross or interlace on or through : INTERWEAVE

**trel·lis·work** \'tre-ləs-ˌwərk\ noun (1712)
: LATTICEWORK

**trem·a·tode** \'tre-mə-ˌtōd\ noun [ultimately from Greek trēmatōdēs pierced with holes, from trēmat-, trēma hole, from tetrainein to bore — more at THROW] (circa 1859)
: any of a class (Trematoda) of parasitic platyhelminthic flatworms including the flukes
— **trematode** adjective

**¹trem·ble** \'trem-bəl\ intransitive verb **trembled; trem·bling** \-b(ə-)liŋ\ [Middle English, from Middle French trembler, from Medieval Latin tremulare, from Latin tremulus tremulous, from tremere to tremble; akin to Greek tremein to tremble] (14th century)
**1** : to shake involuntarily (as with fear or cold) : SHIVER
**2** : to move, sound, pass, or come to pass as if shaken or tremulous ⟨the building trembled from the blast⟩
**3** : to be affected with fear or doubt ⟨tremble for the safety of another⟩
— **trem·bler** \-b(ə-)lər\ noun

**²tremble** noun (1609)
**1** : an act or instance of trembling; especially : a fit or spell of involuntary shaking or quivering
**2** plural but singular in construction : severe poisoning of livestock and especially cattle by a toxic alcohol present in a snakeroot (Eupatorium rugosum) and rayless goldenrod that is characterized by muscular tremors, weakness, and constipation

**trem·bly** \'trem-b(ə-)lē\ adjective (1848)
: marked by trembling : TREMULOUS

**tre·men·dous** \tri-'men-dəs\ adjective [Latin tremendus, from gerundive of tremere] (1632)
**1** : being such as may excite trembling or arouse dread, awe, or terror
**2 a** : notable by reason of extreme size, power, greatness, or excellence — often used as a generalized term of approval **b** : unusually large : HUGE
**synonym** see MONSTROUS
— **tre·men·dous·ly** adverb
— **tre·men·dous·ness** noun

**trem·o·lite** \'tre-mə-ˌlīt\ noun [French trémolite, from Tremola, valley in Switzerland] (1799)
: a white or gray mineral of the amphibole group that is a silicate of calcium and magnesium
— **trem·o·lit·ic** \ˌtre-mə-'li-tik\ adjective

**trem·o·lo** \'tre-mə-ˌlō\ noun, plural **-los** [Italian, from tremolo tremulous, from Latin tremulus] (circa 1801)
**1 a** : the rapid reiteration of a musical tone or of alternating tones to produce a tremulous effect **b** : vocal vibrato especially when prominent or excessive
**2** : a mechanical device in an organ for causing a tremulous effect

**trem·or** \'tre-mər\ noun [Middle English tremour terror, from Middle French, from Latin tremor trembling, from tremere] (1615)

**1** : a trembling or shaking usually from physical weakness, emotional stress, or disease
**2** : a quivering or vibratory motion; especially : a discrete small movement following or preceding a major seismic event
**3 a** : a feeling of uncertainty or insecurity **b** : a cause of such a feeling

**trem·u·lant** \'trem-yə-lənt\ adjective [Medieval Latin tremulant-, tremulans, present participle of tremulare — more at TREMBLE] (1837)
: TREMULOUS, TREMBLING

**trem·u·lous** \-ləs\ adjective [Latin tremulus — more at TREMBLE] (1611)
**1** : characterized by or affected with trembling or tremors
**2** : affected with timidity : TIMOROUS
**3** : such as is or might be caused by nervousness or shakiness ⟨a tremulous smile⟩ ⟨tremulous handwriting⟩
**4** : exceedingly sensitive : easily shaken or disordered
— **trem·u·lous·ly** adverb
— **trem·u·lous·ness** noun

**¹trench** \'trench\ noun [Middle English trenche track cut through a wood, from Middle French, act of cutting, from trenchier to cut, probably from (assumed) Vulgar Latin trinicare to cut in three, from Latin trini three each — more at TRINE] (15th century)
**1 a** : a long cut in the ground : DITCH; especially : one used for military defense often with the excavated dirt thrown up in front **b** plural : a place, position, or level at which an activity is carried on in a manner likened to trench warfare — often used in the phrase in the trenches
**2** : a long, narrow, and usually steep-sided depression in the ocean floor — compare TROUGH
**3** : TRENCH COAT

**²trench** (15th century)
transitive verb
**1** : to make a cut in : CARVE
**2 a** : to protect with or as if with a trench **b** : to cut a trench in : DITCH
intransitive verb
**1 a** : ENTRENCH, ENCROACH ⟨trenching on other domains which were more vital —Sir Winston Churchill⟩ **b** : to come close : VERGE
**2** : to dig a trench

**tren·chan·cy** \'tren-chən(t)-sē\ noun (1866)
: the quality or state of being trenchant

**tren·chant** \-chənt\ adjective [Middle English, from Middle French, present participle of trenchier] (14th century)
**1** : KEEN, SHARP
**2** : vigorously effective and articulate ⟨a trenchant analysis⟩; also : CAUSTIC ⟨trenchant remarks⟩
**3 a** : sharply perceptive : PENETRATING **b** : CLEAR-CUT, DISTINCT ⟨the trenchant divisions between right and wrong —Edith Wharton⟩
— **tren·chant·ly** adverb

**trench coat** noun (1916)
**1** : a waterproof overcoat with a removable lining designed for wear in trenches
**2** : a usually double-breasted raincoat with deep pockets, wide belt, and often straps on the shoulders

**trenched** \'trencht\ adjective (1541)
**1** : furrowed or drained by trenches
**2** : provided with protective trenches

**¹tren·cher** \'tren-chər\ noun [Middle English, from Middle French trencheoir, from trenchier to cut] (14th century)
: a wooden platter for serving food

**²trencher** adjective (15th century)
**1** : of or relating to a trencher or to meals
**2** archaic : having the nature of a parasite : SYCOPHANTIC

**³trench·er** \'tren-chər\ noun [²trench] (circa 1864)
: one that digs trenches; specifically : a usually self-propelled excavating machine typically

employing a bucket conveyor and used to dig trenches especially for pipelines and cables

**tren·cher·man** \'tren-chər-mən\ noun (1590)
**1** : a hearty eater
**2** archaic : HANGER-ON, SPONGER

**trench fever** noun (1915)
: a disease that is marked by fever and pain in muscles, bones, and joints and that is caused by a bacterium (Rochalimaea quintana) transmitted by the human body louse (Pediculus humanus)

**trench foot** noun (1915)
: a painful foot disorder resembling frostbite and resulting from exposure to cold and wet

**trench mouth** noun (1918)
**1** : VINCENT'S ANGINA
**2** : VINCENT'S INFECTION

**trench warfare** noun (1917)
: warfare in which the opposing forces attack and counterattack from a relatively permanent system of trenches protected by barbed-wire entanglements

**¹trend** \'trend\ intransitive verb [Middle English, to turn, revolve, from Old English trendan; akin to Middle High German trendel disk, spinning top] (1598)
**1 a** : to extend in a general direction : follow a general course ⟨mountain ranges trending north and south⟩ **b** : to veer in a new direction : BEND ⟨coastline that trends westward⟩
**2 a** : to show a tendency : INCLINE ⟨prices trending upward⟩ **b** : to become deflected : SHIFT ⟨opinions trending toward conservatism⟩

**²trend** noun (1777)
**1** : a line of general direction or movement ⟨the trend of the coast turned toward the west⟩
**2 a** : a prevailing tendency or inclination : DRIFT **b** : a general movement : SWING ⟨the trend toward suburban living⟩ **c** : a current style or preference : VOGUE ⟨new fashion trends⟩ **d** : a line of development : APPROACH
**3** : the general movement in the course of time of a statistically detectable change; also : a statistical curve reflecting such a change
**synonym** see TENDENCY

**trend·set·ter** \'tren(d)-ˌse-tər\ noun (1960)
: one that sets a trend

**trend·set·ting** \-ˌse-tiŋ\ adjective (1960)
: that sets a trend ⟨a trendsetting fashion look⟩

**trendy** \'tren-dē\ adjective **trend·i·er; -est** (1962)
**1** : very fashionable : UP-TO-DATE ⟨he's a trendy dresser —Sunday Mirror⟩
**2** : marked by ephemeral, superficial, or faddish appeal or taste ⟨a newspaper of trendy triviality —J.H. Plumb⟩
— **trend·i·ly** \-də-lē\ adverb
— **trend·i·ness** \-dē-nəs\ noun
— **trendy** \-dē\ noun

**¹tre·pan** \tri-'pan\ transitive verb **tre·panned; tre·pan·ning** [Middle English, from trepane trephine] (15th century)
**1** : to use a trephine on (the skull)
**2** : to remove a disk or cylindrical core (as from metal for testing)
— **trep·a·na·tion** \ˌtre-pə-'nā-shən\ noun

**²tre·pan** \'trē-ˌpan, tri-'pan\ noun [Middle English trepane trephine, from Medieval Latin trepanum, from Greek trypanon auger, from trypan to bore] (circa 1877)
: a heavy tool used in boring mine shafts

**³tre·pan** \tri-'pan\ noun [origin unknown] (1641)
**1** archaic : TRICKSTER
**2** archaic : a deceptive device : SNARE

**⁴tre·pan** \tri-'pan\ transitive verb **tre·panned; tre·pan·ning** (circa 1656)
archaic : ENTRAP, LURE

**tre·pang** \tri-'paŋ, 'trē-ˌ\ noun [Malay těripang] (1783)
: any of several large sea cucumbers (especially genera Actinopyga and Holothuria) that are taken mostly in the southwestern Pacific and

are boiled, dried, and used especially by the Chinese for making soup — called also *bêche-de-mer*

**treph·i·na·tion** \,tre-fə-'nā-shən\ *noun* (1874)
: an act or instance of perforating the skull with a surgical instrument

**tre·phine** \'trē-,fīn\ *noun* [French *tréphine,* from obsolete English *trefine, trafine,* from Latin *tres fines* three ends, from *tres* three + *fines,* plural of *finis* end — more at THREE] (1628)
: a surgical instrument for cutting out circular sections (as of bone or corneal tissue)
— **trephine** *transitive verb*

**trep·id** \'tre-pəd\ *adjective* [Latin *trepidus*] (1650)
: TIMOROUS, FEARFUL

**trep·i·dant** \'tre-pə-dənt\ *adjective* [Latin *trepidant-, trepidans,* present participle of *trepidare*] (1892)
: TIMID, TREMBLING

**trep·i·da·tion** \,tre-pə-'dā-shən\ *noun* [Latin *trepidation-, trepidatio,* from *trepidare* to tremble, from *trepidus* agitated; probably akin to Old English *thrafian* to urge, push, Greek *trapein* to press grapes] (1605)
**1** *archaic* : a tremulous motion : TREMOR
**2** : timorous uncertain agitation : APPREHENSION

*synonym* see FEAR

**trep·o·ne·ma** \,tre-pə-'nē-mə\ *noun, plural* **-ma·ta** \-mə-tə\ *or* **-mas** [New Latin *Treponemat-, Treponema,* from Greek *trepein* to turn + *nēma* thread, from *nēn* to spin — more at NEEDLE] (circa 1908)
: any of a genus (*Treponema*) of spirochetes that are pathogenic in humans and other warm-blooded animals and include organisms causing syphilis and yaws
— **trep·o·ne·mal** \-məl\ *adjective*

**trep·o·ne·ma·to·sis** \-,nē-mə-'tō-səs, -,ne-\ *noun, plural* **-to·ses** \-,sēz\ [New Latin] (1927)
: infection with or disease caused by treponemata

**trep·o·neme** \'tre-pə-,nēm\ *noun* (1919)
: TREPONEMA

**¹tres·pass** \'tres-pəs, -,pas\ *noun* [Middle English *trespas,* from Old French, crossing, trespass, from *trespasser* to go across] (14th century)
**1 a** : a violation of moral or social ethics : TRANSGRESSION; *especially* : SIN **b** : an unwarranted infringement
**2 a** : an unlawful act committed on the person, property, or rights of another; *especially* : a wrongful entry on real property **b** : the legal action for injuries resulting from trespass

**²trespass** \-,pas *also* -pəs\ *verb* [Middle English, from Middle French *trespasser,* from Old French, literally, to go across, from *tres* across (from Latin *trans*) + *passer* to pass — more at THROUGH, PASS] (14th century)
*intransitive verb*
**1 a** : ERR, SIN **b** : to make an unwarranted or uninvited incursion
**2** : to commit a trespass; *especially* : to enter unlawfully upon the land of another
*transitive verb*
: VIOLATE ⟨*trespass* the bounds of good taste⟩
☆
— **tres·pass·er** *noun*

**tress** \'tres\ *noun* [Middle English *tresse,* from Middle French *trece*] (14th century)
**1** : a long lock of hair; *especially* : the long unbound hair of a woman — usually used in plural
**2** *archaic* : a plait of hair : BRAID

**tressed** \'trest\ *adjective* (14th century)
**1** *obsolete* : being braided : PLAITED
**2** : having tresses — usually used in combination ⟨golden-*tressed*⟩

**tres·tle** *also* **tres·sel** \'tre-səl *also* 'trə-\ *noun* [Middle English *trestel,* from Middle French, from (assumed) Vulgar Latin *transtellum,* from Latin *transtillum,* diminutive of *tran-*

*strum* traverse beam, from *translation* across — more at THROUGH] (14th century)
**1** : HORSE 2b
**2** : a braced frame serving as a support
**3** : a braced framework of timbers, piles, or steelwork for carrying a road or railroad over a depression

**trestle table** *noun* (circa 1891)
: a table supported on trestles

**tres·tle·work** \-,wərk\ *noun* (1848)
: a system of connected trestles supporting a structure (as a railroad bridge)

**tre·tin·o·in** \tre-'ti-nə-win\ *noun* [perhaps from *trans-* + *retino*ic acid] (1980)
: RETINOIC ACID

**trews** \'trüz\ *noun plural* [Scottish Gaelic *triubhas*] (circa 1568)
**1** *chiefly British* : ³PANT 1; *especially* : tight-fitting trousers usually of tartan
**2** : close-cut tartan shorts worn under the kilt in Highland dress

**trey** \'trā\ *noun, plural* **treys** [Middle English *treye, treis,* from Middle French *treie, treis,* from Latin *tres* three] (14th century)
**1** : the side of a die or domino that has three spots
**2** : a card numbered three or having three main pips

**tri-** *combining form* [Middle English, from Latin (from *tri-, tres*) & Greek, from *tri-, treis* — more at THREE]
**1** : three : having three elements or parts ⟨*tri*graph⟩
**2 a** : into three ⟨*tri*sect⟩
**3 a** : thrice ⟨*tri*weekly⟩ **b** : every third ⟨*tri*monthly⟩

**tri·able** \'trī-ə-bəl\ *adjective* (15th century)
: liable or subject to judicial or quasi-judicial examination or trial

**tri·ac·e·tate** \(,)trī-'a-sə-,tāt\ *noun* [International Scientific Vocabulary] (1885)
**1** : an acetate containing three CH₃COO— groups
**2** : a textile fiber or fabric consisting of cellulose that is completely or almost completely acetylated

**tri·ad** \'trī-,ad *also* -əd\ *noun* [Latin *triad-, trias,* from Greek, from *treis* three] (1546)
**1** : a union or group of three : TRINITY
**2** : a chord of three tones consisting of a root with its third and fifth and constituting the harmonic basis of tonal music
— **tri·ad·ic** \trī-'a-dik\ *adjective*
— **tri·ad·i·cal·ly** \-di-k(ə-)lē\ *adverb*

**tri·age** \trē-'äzh, 'trē-,\ *noun* [French, sorting, sifting, from *trier* to sort, from Old French — more at TRY] (1918)
: the sorting of and allocation of treatment to patients and especially battle and disaster victims according to a system of priorities designed to maximize the number of survivors; *broadly* : the assigning of priority order to projects on the basis of where funds and resources can be best used or are most needed
— **triage** *transitive verb*

**¹tri·al** \'trī(-ə)l\ *noun* [Anglo-French, from *trier* to try] (15th century)
**1 a** : the action or process of trying or putting to the proof : TEST **b** : a preliminary contest (as in a sport)
**2** : the formal examination before a competent tribunal of the matter in issue in a civil or criminal cause in order to determine such issue
**3** : a test of faith, patience, or stamina through subjection to suffering or temptation; *broadly* : a source of vexation or annoyance
**4 a** : a tryout or experiment to test quality, value, or usefulness **b** : one of a number of repetitions of an experiment
**5** : ATTEMPT

**²trial** *adjective* (1555)
**1** : of, relating to, or used in a trial
**2** : made or done as a test or experiment
**3** : used or tried out in a test or experiment

**trial and error** *noun* (1806)

: a finding out of the best way to reach a desired result or a correct solution by trying out one or more ways or means and by noting and eliminating errors or causes of failure; *also* : the trying of one thing or another until something succeeds

**trial balance** *noun* (1838)
: a list of the debit and credit balances of accounts in a double-entry ledger at a given date prepared primarily to test their equality

**trial balloon** *noun* (1935)
: a project or scheme tentatively announced in order to test public opinion

**trial court** *noun* (1890)
: the court before which issues of fact and law are first determined as distinguished from an appellate court

**trial examiner** *noun* (1949)
: a person appointed to hold hearings and to investigate and report facts sometimes with recommendations to an administrative or quasi-judicial agency or tribunal

**trial horse** *noun* (1901)
: one set up as an opponent for a champion in trial competitions or workouts

**trial jury** *noun* (1884)
: a jury impaneled to try a cause : PETIT JURY

**trial lawyer** *noun* (circa 1914)
: a lawyer who engages chiefly in the trial of cases before courts of original jurisdiction

**tri·a·logue** \'trī-ə-,lòg, -,läg\ *noun* [*tri-* + *-alogue* (as in *dialogue*)] (1532)
: a scene, discourse, or colloquy in which three persons share

**trial run** *noun* (1903)
: a testing exercise : EXPERIMENT

**tri·am·cin·o·lone** \,trī-am-'si-nᵊl-,ōn\ *noun* [*tri-* + *-amcin-* (alteration of *American Cyanimid Company*) + ¹-*ol* + -*one*] (1957)
: a glucocorticoid drug $C_{21}H_{27}FO_6$ used especially in treating psoriasis and allergic skin and respiratory disorders

**tri·an·gle** \'trī-,aŋ-gəl\ *noun* [Middle English, from Latin *triangulum,* from neuter of *triangulus* triangular, from *tri-* + *angulus* angle] (14th century)
**1** : a polygon having three sides — compare SPHERICAL TRIANGLE
**2 a** : a percussion instrument consisting of a rod of steel bent into the form of a triangle open at one angle and sounded by striking with a small metal rod **b** : a drafting instrument consisting of a thin flat right-angled

triangle 1: *1* equilateral, *2* acute, *3* obtuse, *4* scalene, *5* isosceles, *6* right triangle

triangle of wood or plastic with acute angles of 45 degrees or of 30 degrees and 60 degrees **3 :** a situation in which one member of a couple is involved in a love affair with a third person

**triangle inequality** *noun* [from its application to the distances between three points in a coordinate system] (1941)
**:** an inequality stating that the absolute value of a sum is less than or equal to the sum of the absolute value of the terms

**tri·an·gu·lar** \trī-'aŋ-gyə-lər\ *adjective* [Late Latin *triangularis,* from Latin *triangulum*] (1541)
**1 a :** of, relating to, or having the form of a triangle ⟨a *triangular* plot of land⟩ **b :** having a triangular base or principal surface ⟨a *triangular* table⟩ ⟨a *triangular* pyramid⟩
**2 a** (1) **:** of, relating to, or involving three elements ⟨a *triangular* agreement⟩ (2) **:** *of a military group* **:** based primarily on three units **b :** of or relating to a love triangle
**— tri·an·gu·lar·i·ty** \(,)trī-,aŋ-gyə-'lar-ə-tē\ *noun*
**— tri·an·gu·lar·ly** \trī-'aŋ-gyə-lər-lē\ *adverb*

**triangular number** *noun* (1796)
**:** any of the numbers (as 1, 3, 6, 10, 15) that represent the number of dots in the figures formed starting with one dot and adding rows one after another to form triangles each row of which has one more dot than the one before and are of the general form

$$\frac{n(n+1)}{2} \text{ where } n = 1, 2, 3, \dots$$

**¹tri·an·gu·late** \trī-'aŋ-gyə-lət\ *adjective* [Medieval Latin *triangulatus,* past participle of *triangulare* to make triangles, from Latin *triangulum*] (1766)
**:** consisting of or marked with triangles
**²tri·an·gu·late** \-,lāt\ *transitive verb* **-lat·ed; -lat·ing** (1833)
**1 :** to survey, map, or determine by triangulation
**2 a :** to divide into triangles **b :** to give triangular form to

**tri·an·gu·la·tion** \(,)trī-,aŋ-gyə-'lā-shən\ *noun* (1818)
**:** the measurement of the elements necessary to determine the network of triangles into which any part of the earth's surface is divided in surveying; *broadly* **:** any similar trigonometric operation for finding a position or location by means of bearings from two fixed points a known distance apart

**tri·ar·chy** \'trī-,är-kē\ *noun, plural* **-chies** [Greek *triarchia,* from *tri-* + *-archia* -archy] (circa 1656)
**1 :** government by three persons **:** TRIUMVIRATE
**2 :** a country under three rulers

**Tri·as·sic** \trī-'a-sik\ *adjective* [International Scientific Vocabulary, from Latin *trias* triad; from the three subdivisions of the European Triassic — more at TRIAD] (1841)
**:** of, relating to, or being the earliest period of the Mesozoic era or the corresponding system of rocks marked by the first appearance of the dinosaurs — see GEOLOGIC TIME table
**— Triassic** *noun*

**tri·ath·lete** \trī-'ath-,lēt, ÷'a-thə-\ *noun* (1982)
**:** an athlete who competes in a triathlon
**tri·ath·lon** \trī-'ath-lən, -,län, ÷-'a-thə-\ *noun* [*tri-* + *-athlon* (as in decathlon)] (1978)
**:** an athletic contest that is a long-distance race consisting of three phases (as swimming, bicycling, and running)

**tri·atom·ic** \,trī-ə-'tä-mik\ *adjective* [International Scientific Vocabulary] (1862)
**:** having three atoms in the molecule ⟨ozone is *triatomic* oxygen⟩

**tri·ax·i·al** \(,)trī-'ak-sē-əl\ *adjective* [International Scientific Vocabulary] (1886)

**:** having or involving three axes
**— tri·ax·i·al·i·ty** \-,ak-sē-'a-lə-tē\ *noun*

**tri·azine** \'trī-ə-,zēn, trī-'a-,zēn\ *noun* [International Scientific Vocabulary] (1894)
**:** any of three compounds $C_3H_3N_3$ containing a ring composed of three carbon and three nitrogen atoms; *also* **:** any of various derivatives of these including several used as herbicides
**trib·al** \'trī-bəl\ *adjective* (1632)
**:** of, relating to, or characteristic of a tribe ⟨*tribal* customs⟩
**— trib·al·ly** \-bə-lē\ *adverb*
**trib·al·ism** \-bə-,li-zəm\ *noun* (1886)
**1 :** tribal consciousness and loyalty; *especially* **:** exaltation of the tribe above other groups
**2 :** strong in-group loyalty
**tri·ba·sic** \(,)trī-'bā-sik\ *adjective* (1837)
**:** having three replaceable hydrogen atoms — used of acids

**tribe** \'trīb\ *noun* [Middle English, from Latin *tribus,* a division of the Roman people, tribe] (13th century)
**1 a :** a social group comprising numerous families, clans, or generations together with slaves, dependents, or adopted strangers **b :** a political division of the Roman people originally representing one of the three original tribes of ancient Rome **c :** PHYLE
**2 :** a group of persons having a common character, occupation, or interest
**3 :** a category of taxonomic classification ranking below a subfamily; *also* **:** a natural group irrespective of taxonomic rank ⟨the cat *tribe*⟩ ⟨rose *tribe*⟩

**tribes·man** \'trībz-mən\ *noun* (1798)
**:** a member of a tribe
**tribes·peo·ple** \-,pē-pəl\ *noun plural* (1888)
**:** members of a tribe
**tribo-** *combining form* [French, from Greek *tribein* to rub; probably akin to Latin *terere* to rub — more at THROW]
**:** friction ⟨*tribo*luminescence⟩
**tri·bo·elec·tric·i·ty** \,trī-bō-i-,lek-'tri-sə-tē, ,trī-, -'tris-tē\ *noun* (circa 1917)
**:** a charge of electricity generated by friction (as by rubbing glass with silk)
**— tri·bo·elec·tric** \-'lek-trik\ *adjective*
**tri·bol·o·gy** \trī-'bä-lə-jē, tri-\ *noun* (1966)
**:** a study that deals with the design, friction, wear, and lubrication of interacting surfaces in relative motion (as in bearings or gears)
**— tri·bo·log·i·cal** \,trī-bə-'lä-ji-kəl, ,tri-\ *adjective*
**— tri·bol·o·gist** \trī-'bä-lə-jist, tri-\ *noun*
**tri·bo·lu·mi·nes·cence** \,trī-bō-,lü-mə-'ne-sᵊn(t)s, ,tri-\ *noun* [International Scientific Vocabulary] (1889)
**:** luminescence due to friction
**— tri·bo·lu·mi·nes·cent** \-sᵊnt\ *adjective*
**tri·brach** \'trī-,brak\ *noun* [Latin *tribrachys,* from Greek, having three short syllables, from *tri-* + *brachys* short — more at BRIEF] (1589)
**:** a metrical foot of three short syllables of which two belong to the thesis and one to the arsis
**— tri·brach·ic** \trī-'bra-kik\ *adjective*
**trib·u·late** \'tri-byə-,lāt\ *transitive verb* **-lat·ed; -lat·ing** [Late Latin *tribulatus,* past participle of *tribulare*] (circa 1637)
**:** to cause to endure tribulation
**trib·u·la·tion** \,tri-byə-'lā-shən\ *noun* [Middle English *tribulacion,* from Old French, from Latin *tribulation-, tribulatio,* from *tribulare* to press, oppress, from *tribulum* drag used in threshing, from *terere* to rub — more at THROW] (13th century)
**:** distress or suffering resulting from oppression or persecution; *also* **:** a trying experience
**tri·bu·nal** \trī-'byü-nᵊl, tri-\ *noun* [Latin, platform for magistrates, from *tribunus* tribune] (1526)
**1 :** ²TRIBUNE
**2 :** a court or forum of justice
**3 :** something that decides or determines ⟨the *tribunal* of public opinion⟩

**tri·bu·nate** \'tri-byə-,nāt, tri-'byü-nət\ *noun* (1546)
**:** the office, function, or term of office of a tribune
**¹tri·bune** \'tri-,byün, tri-\ *noun* [Middle English, from Latin *tribunus,* from *tribus* tribe] (14th century)
**1 :** a Roman official under the monarchy and the republic with the function of protecting the plebeian citizen from arbitrary action by the patrician magistrates
**2 :** an unofficial defender of the rights of the individual
**— tri·bune·ship** \-,ship\ *noun*
**²tribune** *noun* [French, from Italian *tribuna,* from Latin *tribunal*] (circa 1771)
**:** a dais or platform from which an assembly is addressed
**¹trib·u·tary** \'tri-byə-,ter-ē\ *adjective* (14th century)
**1 :** paying tribute to another to acknowledge submission, to obtain protection, or to purchase peace **:** SUBJECT
**2 :** paid or owed as tribute
**3 :** channeling material or supplies into something more inclusive **:** CONTRIBUTORY
**²tributary** *noun, plural* **-tar·ies** (15th century)
**1 :** a ruler or state that pays tribute to a conqueror
**2 :** a stream feeding a larger stream or a lake
**trib·ute** \'tri-(,)byüt, -byət\ *noun* [Middle English *tribut,* from Latin *tributum,* from neuter of *tributus,* past participle of *tribuere* to allot, bestow, grant, pay, from *tribus* tribe] (14th century)
**1 a :** a payment by one ruler or nation to another in acknowledgment of submission or as the price of protection; *also* **:** the tax levied for such a payment **b** (1) **:** an excessive tax, rental, or tariff imposed by a government, sovereign, lord, or landlord (2) **:** an exorbitant charge levied by a person or group having the power of coercion **c :** the liability to pay tribute
**2 a :** something given or contributed voluntarily as due or deserved; *especially* **:** a gift or service showing respect, gratitude, or affection ⟨floral *tribute*⟩ **b :** something (as material evidence or a formal attestation) that indicates the worth, virtue, or effectiveness of the one in question ⟨the product is a *tribute* to their ingenuity⟩
*synonym* see ENCOMIUM
**tri·car·box·yl·ic** \,trī-,kär-,bäk-'si-lik\ *adjective* (1894)
**:** containing three carboxyl groups in the molecule ⟨*tricarboxylic* acid⟩
**tricarboxylic acid cycle** *noun* (1945)
**:** KREBS CYCLE
**¹trice** \'trīs\ *transitive verb* **triced; tric·ing** [Middle English *trisen, tricen* to pull, trice, from Middle Dutch *trisen* to hoist, from *trise* windlass] (15th century)
**:** to haul up or in and lash or secure (as a sail) with a small rope
**²trice** *noun* [Middle English *trise,* literally, pull, from *trisen*] (15th century)
**:** a brief space of time **:** INSTANT — used chiefly in the phrase *in a trice*
**tri·ceps** \'trī-,seps\ *noun, plural* **triceps** [New Latin *tricipit-, triceps,* from Latin, three-headed, from *tri-* + *capit-, caput* head — more at HEAD] (circa 1704)
**:** a muscle that arises from three heads; *especially* **:** the great extensor muscle along the back of the upper arm
**tri·cer·a·tops** \(,)trī-'ser-ə-,täps\ *noun, plural* **-tops** *also* **-tops·es** \-,täp-səz\ [New Latin, from *tri-* + Greek *kerat-, keras* horn + *ōps* face — more at HORN, EYE] (1892)
**:** any of a genus (*Triceratops*) of large herbivorous Cretaceous dinosaurs with three horns, a bony hood or crest on the neck, and hoofed toes

**-trices** *plural of* -TRIX

**trich-** *or* **tricho-** *combining form* [New Latin, from Greek, from *trich-, thrix* hair]
**:** hair **:** filament ⟨*trichogyne*⟩

**tri·chi·a·sis** \tri-'kī-ə-səs\ *noun* [Late Latin, from Greek, from *trich-* + *-iasis*] (1661)
**:** a turning inward of the eyelashes often causing irritation of the eyeball

**tri·chi·na** \tri-'kī-nə\ *noun, plural* **-nae** \-(,)nē\ *also* **-nas** [New Latin, from Greek *trichinos* made of hair, from *trich-, thrix* hair] (1857)
**:** a small slender nematode worm (*Trichinella spiralis*) that in the larval state is parasitic in the voluntary muscles of flesh-eating mammals (as humans and swine)
— **tri·chi·nal** \-n°l\ *adjective*

**trich·i·nize** \'tri-kə-,nīz\ *transitive verb* **-nized; -niz·ing** (1864)
**:** to infest with trichinae ⟨*trichinized* pork⟩

**trich·i·no·sis** \,tri-kə-'nō-səs\ *noun* [New Latin] (1866)
**:** infestation with or disease caused by trichinae and marked especially by muscular pain, dyspnea, fever, and edema

**tri·chi·nous** \'tri-kə-nəs, tri-'kī-\ *adjective* [International Scientific Vocabulary] (1857)
**1 :** infested with trichinae ⟨*trichinous* meat⟩
**2 :** of, relating to, or involving trichinae or trichinosis ⟨*trichinous* infection⟩

**tri·chlor·fon** *also* **tri·chlor·phon** \(,)trī-'klȯr-,fän, -'klȯr-\ *noun* [*tri-* + *chlor-* + *-fon* (irregular from *phosphonate* — a salt derived from phosphine)] (1960)
**:** a crystalline compound $C_4H_8Cl_3O_4P$ used especially as an insecticide

**tri·chlo·ro·ace·tic acid** \,trī-,klȯr-ō-ə-'sē-tik-, -,klȯr-\ *noun* [International Scientific Vocabulary] (1885)
**:** a strong vesicant pungent acid $C_2Cl_3HO_2$ used in weed control and in medicine as a caustic and astringent

**tri·chlo·ro·eth·y·lene** \-'e-thə-,lēn\ *noun* (circa 1919)
**:** a nonflammable liquid $C_2HCl_3$ used especially as a solvent and in dry cleaning and for the removal of grease from metal

**tricho·cyst** \'tri-kə-,sist\ *noun* (1859)
**:** any of the minute lassoing or stinging organelles of protozoans and especially of many ciliates

**tricho·gyne** \-,jīn, -,gīn\ *noun* [International Scientific Vocabulary] (circa 1875)
**:** a slender terminal prolongation of the ascogonium of a fungus or lichen that may serve as a fertilization tube; *also* **:** a similar reproductive structure in a red alga

**tri·chol·o·gist** \tri-'kä-lə-jist\ *noun* (1887)
**:** a person who cares for and dresses hair
**:** HAIRDRESSER
— **tri·chol·o·gy** \-jē\ *noun*

**tri·chome** \'tri-,kōm, 'trī-\ *noun* [German *Trichom*, from Greek *trichōma* growth of hair, from *trichoun* to cover with hair, from *trich-, thrix* hair] (1875)
**:** a filamentous outgrowth; *especially* **:** an epidermal hair structure on a plant

**tricho·mo·na·cide** \,tri-kə-'mō-nə-,sīd\ *noun* [*trichomonad* + *-cide*] (1949)
**:** an agent used to destroy trichomonads
— **tricho·mo·na·cid·al** \-,mō-nə-'sī-d°l\ *adjective*

**tricho·mo·nad** \,tri-kə-'mō-,nad, -nəd\ *noun* [New Latin *Trichomonad-, Trichomonas*, from *trich-* + Late Latin *monad-, monas* monad] (1861)
**:** any of a genus (*Trichomonas*) of flagellated protozoans parasitic in many animals
— **trichomonad** *or* **tricho·mo·nal** \-'mō-n°l\ *adjective*

**tricho·mo·ni·a·sis** \,tri-kə-mə-'nī-ə-səs\ *noun, plural* **-a·ses** \-,sēz\ [New Latin, from *Trichomonas* + *-iasis*] (1915)
**:** infection with or disease caused by trichomonads: as **a :** a human sexually transmitted disease occurring especially as vaginitis with a persistent discharge and caused by a

trichomonad (*Trichomonas vaginalis*) that may also invade the male urethra and bladder **b :** a venereal disease of domestic cattle marked by abortion and sterility **c :** one or more diseases of various birds resembling blackhead — called also *roup*

**tri·chop·ter·an** \tri-'käp-tə-rən\ *noun* [ultimately from Greek *trich-, thrix* hair + *pteron* wing — more at FEATHER] (circa 1842)
**:** CADDIS FLY
— **trichopteran** *adjective*

**tricho·the·cene** \,tri-kə-'thē-,sēn\ *noun* [New Latin *Trichothecium* (from *trich-* + *-thecium*) + English *-ene*] (1971)
**:** any of several mycotoxins that are produced by imperfect fungi (genera *Fusarium* and *Trichothecium*) and that include some contaminants of livestock feed and some held to be found in yellow rain

**tri·chot·o·mous** \trī-'kä-tə-məs\ *adjective* [Late Greek *trichotomein* to trisect, from Greek *tricha* in three (akin to *treis* three) + *-tomein* (akin to *temnein* to cut) — more at THREE, TOME] (1800)
**:** divided or dividing into three parts or into threes ⟨*trichotomous* branching⟩
— **tri·chot·o·mous·ly** *adverb*

**tri·chot·o·my** \-mē\ *noun, plural* **-mies** (1610)
**:** division into three parts, elements, or classes

**tri·chro·mat** \'trī-krō-,mat, ·(,)trī-'\ *noun* [back-formation from *trichromatic*] (1929)
**:** a person with trichromatism

**tri·chro·mat·ic** \,trī-krō-'ma-tik\ *adjective* (circa 1890)
**1 :** of, relating to, or consisting of three colors ⟨*trichromatic* light⟩
**2 a :** relating to or being the theory that human color vision involves three types of retinal sensory receptors **b :** characterized by trichromatism ⟨*trichromatic* vision⟩

**tri·chro·ma·tism** \(,)trī-'krō-mə-,ti-zəm\ *noun* (circa 1895)
**:** color vision based on the perception of three primary colors and especially red, green, and blue

**¹trick** \'trik\ *noun* [Middle English *trik,* from Old North French *trique,* from *trikier* to deceive, cheat, from (assumed) Vulgar Latin *triccare,* alteration of Latin *tricari* to behave evasively, shuffle, from *tricae* complications, trifles] (15th century)
**1 a :** a crafty procedure or practice meant to deceive or defraud **b :** a mischievous act **:** PRANK **c :** an indiscreet or childish action **d :** a deceptive, dexterous, or ingenious feat; *especially* **:** one designed to puzzle or amuse ⟨a juggler's *tricks*⟩
**2 a :** a habitual peculiarity of behavior or manner ⟨a horse with the *trick* of shying⟩ **b :** a characteristic and identifying feature ⟨a *trick* of speech⟩ **c :** a delusive appearance especially when caused by art or legerdemain **:** an optical illusion ⟨a mere *trick* of the light⟩
**3 a :** a quick or artful way of getting a result **:** KNACK **b :** a technical device (as of an art or craft) ⟨the *tricks* of stage technique⟩
**4 :** the cards played in one round of a card game often used as a scoring unit
**5 a :** a turn of duty at the helm usually lasting for two hours **b :** SHIFT 4b(1) **c :** a trip taken as part of one's employment **d :** a sexual act performed by a prostitute; *also* **:** JOHN 2
**6 :** an attractive child or woman ⟨a cute little *trick*⟩ ☆

**²trick** *transitive verb* (circa 1500)
**1 :** to dress or adorn fancifully or ornately **:** ORNAMENT ⟨*tricked* out in a gaudy uniform⟩
**2 :** to deceive by cunning or artifice **:** CHEAT
**synonym** *see* DUPE

**³trick** *adjective* (circa 1530)
**1 :** TRIG
**2 a :** of or relating to or involving tricks or trickery ⟨*trick* photography⟩ ⟨*trick* dice⟩ **b :** skilled in or used for tricks ⟨a *trick* horse⟩

**3 a :** somewhat defective and unreliable ⟨a *trick* lock⟩ **b :** inclined to give way unexpectedly ⟨a *trick* knee⟩

**trick·er** \'tri-kər\ *noun* (circa 1553)
**:** one that tricks **:** TRICKSTER

**trick·ery** \'tri-k(ə-)rē\ *noun* (1800)
**:** the practice of crafty underhanded ingenuity to deceive or cheat
**synonym** *see* DECEPTION

**trick·ish** \'tri-kish\ *adjective* (1705)
**:** given to or characterized by tricks or trickery **:** TRICKY
— **trick·ish·ly** *adverb*
— **trick·ish·ness** *noun*

**¹trick·le** \'tri-kəl\ *intransitive verb* **trick·led; trick·ling** \-k(ə-)liŋ\ [Middle English, of imitative origin] (14th century)
**1 a :** to issue or fall in drops **b :** to flow in a thin gentle stream
**2 a :** to move or go one by one or little by little **b :** to dissipate slowly ⟨his enthusiasm *trickled* away⟩

**²trickle** *noun* (1580)
**:** a thin, slow, or intermittent stream or movement

**trickle–down** *adjective* (1944)
**1 :** relating to or working on the principle of trickle-down theory
**2 :** relating to or being an effect caused gradually by remote or indirect influences

**trickle–down theory** *noun* (1954)
**:** a theory that financial benefits given to big business will in turn pass down to smaller businesses and consumers

**trick or treat** *noun* (circa 1941)
**:** a children's Halloween practice of asking for treats from door to door under threat of playing tricks on householders who refuse
— **trick–or–treat** *intransitive verb*
— **trick–or–treater** *noun*

**trick·ster** \'trik-stər\ *noun* (1711)
**:** one who tricks: as **a :** a dishonest person who defrauds others by trickery **b :** a person (as a stage magician) skilled in the use of tricks and illusion **c :** a deceptive character appearing in various forms in the folklore of many cultures

**tricksy** \'trik-sē\ *adjective* **tricks·i·er; -est** [*tricks,* plural of *trick*] (1552)
**1** *archaic* **:** smartly attired **:** SPRUCE
**2 :** full of tricks **:** PRANKISH
**3 a** *archaic* **:** having the craftiness of a trickster **b :** difficult to cope with or handle **:** TRYING ⟨a *tricksy* job⟩
— **tricks·i·ness** *noun*

---

☆ **SYNONYMS**

**Trick, ruse, stratagem, maneuver, artifice, wile, feint** mean an indirect means to gain an end. TRICK may imply deception, roguishness, illusion, and either an evil or harmless end ⟨the *tricks* of the trade⟩. RUSE stresses an attempt to mislead by a false impression ⟨the *ruses* of smugglers⟩. STRATAGEM implies a ruse used to entrap, outwit, circumvent, or surprise an opponent or enemy ⟨the *stratagem*-filled game⟩. MANEUVER suggests adroit and skillful avoidance of difficulty ⟨last-minute *maneuvers* to avert bankruptcy⟩. ARTIFICE implies ingenious contrivance or invention ⟨the clever *artifices* of the stage⟩. WILE suggests an attempt to entrap or deceive with false allurements ⟨used all of his *wiles* to ingratiate himself⟩. FEINT implies a diversion or distraction of attention away from one's real intent ⟨a *feint* toward the enemy's left flank⟩.

---

\ə\ abut \ᵊ\ kitten \ər\ further \a\ ash \ā\ ace
\ä\ mop, mar \au̇\ out \ch\ chin \e\ bet \ē\ easy
\g\ go \i\ hit \ī\ ice \j\ job \ŋ\ sing \ō\ go
\ȯ\ law \ȯi\ boy \th\ thin \th̲\ the \ü\ loot \u̇\ foot
\y\ yet \zh\ vision *see also* Guide to Pronunciation

**tricky** \'tri-kē\ *adjective* **trick·i·er; -est** (1786)
**1 :** inclined to or marked by trickery
**2 a :** giving a deceptive impression of easiness, simplicity, or order **:** TICKLISH 〈a *tricky* path through the swamp〉 **b :** TRICK 3
**3 :** requiring skill, knack, or caution (as in doing or handling) **:** DIFFICULT; *also* **:** INGENIOUS 〈a *tricky* rhythm〉
**synonym** see SLY
— **trick·i·ly** \'tri-kə-lē\ *adverb*
— **trick·i·ness** \'tri-kē-nəs\ *noun*

**tri·clad** \'tri-ˌklad\ *noun* [New Latin *Tricladida*, from *tri-* + Greek *klados* branch — more at CLAD-] (1888)
**:** any of an order (Tricladida) of turbellarian flatworms (as a planarian) that have the intestine composed of a median anterior division and two lateral posterior divisions with side branches
— **triclad** *adjective*

**tri·clin·ic** \(ˌ)trī-'kli-nik\ *adjective* [International Scientific Vocabulary] (1854)
**:** having three unequal axes intersecting at oblique angles — used especially of a crystal

**tri·clin·i·um** \trī-'kli-nē-əm\ *noun, plural* **-ia** \-nē-ə\ [Latin, from Greek *triklinion*, from *tri-* + *klinein* to lean, recline — more at LEAN] (1646)
**1 :** a couch extending round three sides of a table used by the ancient Romans for reclining at meals
**2 :** a dining room furnished with a triclinium

**tric·o·lette** \ˌtri-kə-'let\ *noun* [tricot + -lette (as in *flannelette*)] (1919)
**:** a usually silk or rayon knitted fabric used especially for women's clothing

**¹tri·col·or** \'trī-ˌkə-lər *also* 'trē-, *especially British* 'tri-kə-lər\ *adjective* [French *tricolore* three-colored, from Late Latin *tricolor*, from Latin *tri-* + *color* color] (1795)
**1 a** *or* **tri·col·ored** \'trī-'kəl-ərd\ **:** having, using, or marked with three colors **b** *of a dog* **:** having a coat of black, tan, and white
**2 :** of, relating to, or characteristic of a tricolor or a nation whose flag is a tricolor; *especially* **:** FRENCH

**²tricolor** *noun* (1797)
**1 :** a flag of three colors arranged in equal horizontal or vertical bands 〈the French *tricolor*〉
**2 :** a tricolor animal; *especially* **:** a tricolor dog

**tri·corn** \'trī-ˌkȯrn\ *adjective* [Latin *tricornis*] (circa 1844)
**:** having three horns or corners

**tri·corne** *or* **tri·corn** \'trī-ˌkȯrn\ *noun* [French *tricorne*, from *tricorne* three-cornered, from Latin *tricornis*, from *tri-* + *cornu* horn — more at HORN] (1876)
**:** COCKED HAT 1

**tri·cor·nered** \'trī-'kȯ(r)-nərd\ *adjective* (1819)
**:** having three corners

**tri·cot** \'trē-(ˌ)kō, 'trī-kət\ *noun* [French, from *tricoter* to knit, from Middle French, to agitate, hop, ultimately from Old French *estriquier* to stroke, of Germanic origin; akin to Old English *strīcan* to stroke — more at STRIKE] (1872)
**1 :** a plain warp-knitted fabric (as of nylon, wool, rayon, silk, or cotton) with a close inelastic knit and used especially in clothing (as underwear)
**2 :** a twilled clothing fabric of wool with fine warp ribs or of wool and cotton with fine weft ribs

**tri·co·tine** \ˌtri-kə-'tēn, ˌtrē-\ *noun* [French, from *tricot*] (circa 1899)
**:** a sturdy suiting woven of tightly twisted yarns in a double twill

**tric·trac** \'trik-ˌtrak\ *noun* [French, of imitative origin] (1687)
**:** an old form of backgammon played with pegs

**¹tri·cus·pid** \(ˌ)trī-'kəs-pəd\ *adjective* [Latin *tricuspid-, tricuspis*, from *tri-* + *cuspid-, cuspis* point] (1834)
**:** having three cusps 〈a *tricuspid* molar〉

**²tricuspid** *noun* (circa 1860)
**:** a tricuspid anatomical structure; *especially* **:** a tooth having three cusps

**tricuspid valve** *noun* (1670)
**:** a valve of three flaps that prevents reflux of blood from the right ventricle to the right atrium

**tri·cy·cle** \'trī-sə-kəl, -ˌsi-kəl\ *noun* [French, from *tri-* + Greek *kyklos* wheel — more at WHEEL] (1868)
**:** a 3-wheeled vehicle propelled by pedals or a motor

**tri·cy·clic** \(ˌ)trī-'sī-klik, -'si-klik\ *adjective* [tri- + cyclic] (1891)
**:** being a chemical with three usually fused rings in the molecular structure and especially a tricyclic antidepressant

**tricyclic antidepressant** *noun* (1966)
**:** any of a group of antidepressant drugs (as imipramine, amitriptyline, desipramine, and nortriptyline) that potentiate the action of catecholamines and do not inhibit the action of monoamine oxidase — called also *tricyclic*

**¹tri·dent** \'trī-dᵊnt\ *adjective* [Latin *trident-, tridens*] (1589)
**:** having three teeth, processes, or points

**²trident** *noun* [Latin *trident-, tridens, from trident-, tridens* having three teeth, from *tri-* + *dent-, dens* tooth — more at TOOTH] (1599)
**1 :** a 3-pronged spear serving in classical mythology as the attribute of a sea god (as Neptune)
**2 :** a 3-pronged spear (as for fishing)

**Tri·den·tine** \trī-'den-ˌtīn, -ˌtēn; 'trī-dᵊn-, 'tri-\ *adjective* [New Latin *Tridentinus*, from Latin *Tridentum* Trent, Italy] (1561)
**:** of or relating to the Roman Catholic Church council held at Trent from 1545 to 1563

**tri·di·men·sion·al** \ˌtrī-də-'mench-nəl, -ˌdī-, -'men(t)-shə-nᵊl\ *adjective* [International Scientific Vocabulary] (1858)
**:** of, relating to, or concerned with three dimensions 〈*tridimensional* space〉
— **tri·di·men·sion·al·i·ty** \-ˌmen(t)-shə-'na-lə-tē\ *noun*

**trid·u·um** \'tri-jə-wəm, 'tri-dyə-\ *noun* [Latin, space of three days, from *tri-* + *-duum* (akin to *dies* day) — more at DEITY] (1873)
**:** a period of three days of prayer usually preceding a Roman Catholic feast

**tried** \'trīd\ *adjective* [Middle English, from past participle of *trien* to try, test] (15th century)
**1 :** found good, faithful, or trustworthy through experience or testing 〈a *tried* recipe〉
**2 :** subjected to trials or distress 〈a kind but much-*tried* father〉

**tried–and–true** *adjective* (1935)
**:** proved good, desirable, or feasible **:** shown or known to be worthy 〈a *tried-and-true* sales technique〉

**tri·ene** \'trī-ˌēn\ *noun* (1917)
**:** a chemical compound containing three double bonds

**tri·en·ni·al** \(ˌ)trī-'e-nē-əl\ *adjective* (1562)
**1 :** occurring or being done every three years 〈the *triennial* convention〉
**2 :** consisting of or lasting for three years 〈a *triennial* contract〉
— **triennial** *noun*
— **tri·en·ni·al·ly** \-nē-ə-lē\ *adverb*

**tri·en·ni·um** \trī-'e-nē-əm\ *noun, plural* **-ni·ums** *or* **-nia** \-nē-ə\ [Latin, from *tri-* + *annus* year — more at ANNUAL] (1847)
**:** a period of three years

**tri·er** \'trī(-ə)r\ *noun* (14th century)
**1 :** someone or something that tries
**2 :** an implement (as a tapered hollow tube) used in obtaining samples of bulk material for examination and testing

**tri·er·arch** \'trī-(ə)-ˌrärk\ *noun* [Latin *trierarchus*, from Greek *triērarchos*, from *triērēs* tri-

reme (from *tri-* + *-ērēs* — akin to Latin *remus* oar) + *-archos* -arch — more at ROW] (circa 1656)
**1 :** the commander of a trireme
**2 :** an Athenian citizen who had to fit out a trireme for the public service

**tri·er·ar·chy** \-ˌrär-kē\ *noun* (1837)
**:** the ancient Athenian plan whereby individual citizens furnished and maintained triremes as a civic duty

**tri·eth·yl** \(ˌ)trī-'e-thəl\ *adjective* [International Scientific Vocabulary] (1858)
**:** containing three ethyl groups in the molecule

**tri·fec·ta** \trī-'fek-tə, 'trī-ˌ\ *noun* [tri- + per-fecta] (1974)
**:** a variation of the perfecta in which a bettor wins by selecting the first three finishers of a race in the correct order of finish

**tri·fid** \'trī-ˌfid, -fəd\ *adjective* [Latin *trifidus* split into three, from *tri-* + *findere* to split — more at BITE] (1753)
**:** being deeply and narrowly cleft into three teeth, processes, or points 〈a spoon with a *trifid* top〉

**¹tri·fle** \'trī-fəl\ *noun* [Middle English *trufle, trifle*, from Old French *trufe, trufle* mockery] (13th century)
**1 :** something of little value, substance, or importance
**2 :** a dessert of many varieties typically including plain or sponge cake, sherry, rum, or brandy, jam or jelly, fruit, custard, and whipped cream
— **a trifle :** to some small degree **:** SLIGHTLY 〈a *trifle* annoyed〉

**²trifle** *verb* **tri·fled; tri·fling** \-f(ə-)liŋ\ [Middle English *truflen, triflen*, from Old French *trufer, trufler* to mock, trick] (14th century)
*intransitive verb*
**1 a :** to talk in a jesting or mocking manner or with intent to delude or mislead **b :** to treat someone or something as unimportant
**2 :** to handle something idly
*transitive verb*
**:** to spend or waste in trifling or on trifles ☆
— **tri·fler** \-f(ə-)lər\ *noun*

**tri·fling** \'trī-fliŋ\ *adjective* (1535)
**:** lacking in significance or solid worth: as **a** **:** FRIVOLOUS 〈*trifling* talk〉 **b** **:** TRIVIAL 〈a *trifling* gift〉 **c** *chiefly dialect* **:** LAZY, SHIFTLESS 〈a *trifling* fellow〉

**tri·fluo·per·a·zine** \ˌtrī-ˌflü-ō-'per-ə-ˌzēn, -zən\ *noun* [tri- + fluor- + piperazine] (circa 1957)
**:** a phenothiazine tranquilizer $C_{21}H_{24}F_3N_3S$ used to treat psychotic conditions and especially schizophrenia

**tri·flu·ra·lin** \trī-'flur-ə-lən\ *noun* [tri- + fluor- + aniline] (circa 1961)
**:** an herbicide $C_{13}H_{16}F_3N_3O_4$ used in the control of weeds

**¹tri·fo·cal** \(ˌ)trī-'fō-kəl\ *adjective* (1826)
**:** having three focal lengths

**²trifocal** *noun* (1899)
**1** *plural* **:** eyeglasses with trifocal lenses
**2 :** a trifocal glass or lens

---

☆ SYNONYMS
**Trifle, toy, dally, flirt, coquet** mean to deal with or act toward without serious purpose. TRIFLE may imply playfulness, unconcern, indulgent contempt 〈to *trifle* with a lover's feelings〉. TOY implies acting without full attention or serious exertion of one's powers 〈a political novice *toying* with great issues〉. DALLY suggests indulging in thoughts or plans merely as an amusement 〈*dallying* with the idea of building a boat someday〉. FLIRT implies an interest or attention that soon passes to another object 〈*flirted* with one fashionable ism after another〉. COQUET implies attracting interest or admiration without serious intention 〈companies that *coquet* with environmentalism solely for public relations〉.

**tri·fo·li·ate** \(ˌ)trī-'fō-lē-ət\ *adjective* [*tri-* + Latin *folium* leaf — more at BLADE] (1753)
**1** : having three leaves ⟨a *trifoliate* plant⟩
**2** : TRIFOLIOLATE

**trifoliate orange** *noun* (circa 1900)
: a Chinese citrus (*Poncirus trifoliata*) with trifoliolate leaves that is widely grown for ornament and especially as a stock for budding oranges

**tri·fo·li·o·late** \(ˌ)trī-'fō-lē-ə-ˌlāt\ *adjective* [International Scientific Vocabulary *tri-* + Late Latin *foliolum* leaflet, diminutive of Latin *folium* leaf] (circa 1828)
: having three leaflets ⟨a *trifoliolate* leaf⟩ — see LEAF illustration

**tri·fo·li·um** \trī-'fō-lē-əm\ *noun* [New Latin, from Latin, trefoil — more at TREFOIL] (1541)
: CLOVER 1

**tri·fo·ri·um** \trī-'fōr-ē-əm, -'fòr-\ *noun, plural* **-ria** \-ē-ə\ [Medieval Latin] (1703)
: a gallery forming an upper story to the aisle of a church and typically an arcaded story between the nave arches and clerestory

**tri·form** \'trī-ˌfòrm\ *adjective* [Middle English *triforme*, from Latin *triformis*, from *tri-* + *forma* form] (15th century)
: having a triple form or nature

**tri·fur·cate** \(ˌ)trī-'fər-kət, -ˌkāt; 'trī-(ˌ)fər-ˌkāt\ *adjective* [Latin *trifurcus*, from *tri-* + *furca* fork] (circa 1831)
: having three branches or forks : TRICHOTOMOUS
— **tri·fur·cate** \'trī-(ˌ)fər-ˌkāt, trī-'fər-\ *intransitive verb*
— **tri·fur·ca·tion** \ˌtrī-(ˌ)fər-'kā-shən\ *noun*

**¹trig** \'trig\ *adjective* [Middle English, trusty, nimble, of Scandinavian origin; akin to Old Norse *tryggr* faithful; akin to Old English *trēowe* faithful — more at TRUE] (1513)
**1** : stylishly or jauntily trim
**2** : extremely precise : PRIM
**3** *dialect chiefly British* : FIRM, VIGOROUS

**²trig** *noun* [by shortening] (circa 1895)
: TRIGONOMETRY

**tri·gem·i·nal** \trī-'je-mə-nᵊl\ *adjective* [New Latin *trigeminus* trigeminal nerve, from Latin, threefold, from *tri-* + *geminus* twin] (1872)
: of or relating to the trigeminal nerve

**trigeminal nerve** *noun* (1830)
: either of a pair of large mixed nerves that are the 5th cranial nerves and supply motor and sensory fibers mostly to the face — called also *trigeminal*

**trigeminal neuralgia** *noun* (1874)
: an intense paroxysmal neuralgia involving one or more branches of the trigeminal nerve

**¹trig·ger** \'tri-gər\ *noun* [alteration of earlier *tricker*, from Dutch *trekker*, from Middle Dutch *trecker* one that pulls, from *trecken* to pull — more at TREK] (1621)
**1 a** : a piece (as a lever) connected with a catch or detent as a means of releasing it; *especially* : the part of the action moved by the finger to fire a gun **b** : a similar movable part by which a mechanism is actuated ⟨*trigger* of a spray gun⟩
**2** : something that acts like a mechanical trigger in initiating a process or reaction
— **trigger** *adjective*
— **trig·gered** \-gərd\ *adjective*

**²trigger** *verb* **trig·gered; trig·ger·ing** \'tri-g(ə-)riŋ\ (1916)
*transitive verb*
**1 a** : to release or activate by means of a trigger; *especially* : to fire by pulling a mechanical trigger ⟨*trigger* a rifle⟩ **b** : to cause the explosion of ⟨*trigger* a missile with a proximity fuze⟩
**2** : to initiate, actuate, or set off by a trigger ⟨an indiscreet remark that *triggered* a fight⟩ ⟨a stimulus that *triggered* a reflex⟩
*intransitive verb*
: to release a mechanical trigger

**trig·ger·fish** \'tri-gər-ˌfish\ *noun* (1849)
: any of various deep-bodied bony fishes (family Balistidae, especially genus *Balistes*) of warm seas having an anterior dorsal fin with two or three stout erectile spines

triggerfish

**trig·ger–hap·py** \-ˌha-pē\ *adjective* (1943)
**1** : irresponsible in the use of firearms; *especially* : inclined to shoot before clearly identifying the target
**2 a** : inclined to be irresponsible in matters that might precipitate war **b** : aggressively belligerent in attitude

**trig·ger·man** \-ˌmən, -ˌman\ *noun* (circa 1930)
: a gunman who shoots the victim (as in a gangland murder)

**tri·glyc·er·ide** \(ˌ)trī-'gli-sə-ˌrīd\ *noun* [International Scientific Vocabulary] (circa 1860)
: an ester formed from glycerol by reacting all three of its alcohol hydroxy groups with fatty acids

**tri·glyph** \'trī-ˌglif\ *noun* [Latin *triglyphus*, from Greek *triglyphos*, from *tri-* + *glyphein* to carve — more at CLEAVE] (1563)
: a slightly projecting rectangular tablet in a Doric frieze with two vertical channels of V section and two corresponding chamfers or half channels on the vertical sides
— **tri·glyph·ic** \trī-'gli-fik\ *or* **tri·glyph·i·cal** \-fi-kəl\ *adjective*

**tri·gon** \'trī-ˌgän\ *noun* [Latin *trigonum*, from Greek *trigōnon*, from neuter of *trigōnos* triangular, from *tri-* + *gōnia* angle — more at -GON] (1563)
: TRIPLICITY 1

**tri·go·nal** \trī-'gō-nᵊl\ *adjective* (1878)
: of, relating to, or being the division of the hexagonal crystal system or the forms belonging to it characterized by a vertical axis of threefold symmetry
— **tri·go·nal·ly** \-nᵊl-ē\ *adverb*

**trig·o·no·met·ric** \ˌtri-gə-nə-'me-trik\ *also* **trig·o·no·met·ri·cal** \-tri-kəl\ *adjective* (1690)
: of, relating to, or being in accordance with trigonometry
— **trig·o·no·met·ri·cal·ly** \-tri-k(ə-)lē\ *adverb*

**trigonometric function** *noun* (1909)
**1** : a function (as the sine, cosine, tangent, cotangent, secant, or cosecant) of an arc or angle most simply expressed in terms of the ratios of pairs of sides of a right-angled triangle — called also *circular function*
**2** : the inverse (as the arcsine, arccosine, or arctangent) of a trigonometric function

**trig·o·nom·e·try** \ˌtri-gə-'nä-mə-trē\ *noun* [New Latin *trigonometria*, from Greek *trigōnon* + *-metria* -metry] (1614)
: the study of the properties of triangles and trigonometric functions and of their applications

**tri·gram** \'trī-ˌgram\ *noun* (1606)
**1** : TRIGRAPH 2
**2** : any of the eight possible combinations of three whole or broken lines used especially in Chinese divination

**tri·graph** \'trī-ˌgraf\ *noun* (circa 1836)
**1** : three letters spelling a single consonant, vowel, or diphthong ⟨*eau* of *beau* is a *trigraph*⟩
**2** : a cluster of three successive letters ⟨*the, ion,* and *ing* are high frequency *trigraphs*⟩
— **tri·graph·ic** \(ˌ)trī-'gra-fik\ *adjective*

**tri·halo·meth·ane** \(ˌ)trī-ˌha-lə-'me-ˌthān, *British usually* -'mē-\ *noun* (1969)
: any of various derivatives CHX₃ of methane (as chloroform) that have three halogen atoms per molecule and are formed especially during the chlorination of drinking water

**tri·he·dral** \trī-'hē-drəl\ *adjective* (1789)
**1** : having three faces ⟨*trihedral* angle⟩
**2** : of or relating to a trihedral angle
— **trihedral** *noun*

**tri·hy·brid** \-'hī-brəd\ *noun* (1903)
: an individual or strain that is heterozygous for three pairs of genes
— **trihybrid** *adjective*

**tri·hy·droxy** \ˌtrī-hī-'dräk-sē, -hə-\ *adjective* [International Scientific Vocabulary] (1903)
: containing three hydroxyl groups in the molecule

**tri·io·do·thy·ro·nine** \ˌtrī-ˌī-ə-dō-'thī-rə-ˌnēn\ *noun* [*tri-* + *iod-* + *thyronine* (an amino acid of which thyroxine is a derivative)] (1952)
: an iodine-containing hormone $C_{15}H_{12}I_3NO_4$ that is an amino acid derived from thyroxine

**tri·jet** \'trī-ˌjet\ *noun* (1967)
: an aircraft powered with three jet engines

**trike** \'trīk\ *noun* [by shortening & alteration] (1884)
: TRICYCLE

**tri·lat·er·al** \(ˌ)trī-'la-tə-rəl, -'la-trəl\ *adjective* [Latin *trilaterus*, from *tri-* + *later-, latus* side] (1660)
: having three sides or parties ⟨*trilateral* business ventures⟩ ⟨*trilateral* discussions⟩

**tril·by** \'tril-bē\ *noun, plural* **tril·bies** [from the fact that such a hat was worn in the London stage version of the novel *Trilby* (1894) by George du Maurier] (1897)
*chiefly British* : a soft felt hat with indented crown

**tri·lin·e·ar** \(ˌ)trī-'li-nē-ər\ *adjective* (1715)
: of, relating to, or involving three lines ⟨*trilinear* coordinates⟩

**tri·lin·gual** \-'liŋ-gwəl *also* -'liŋ-gyə-wəl\ *adjective* (1834)
: consisting of, having, or expressed in three languages; *also* : familiar with or able to use three languages
— **tri·lin·gual·ly** *adverb*

**¹tri·lit·er·al** \-'li-t(ə-)rəl\ *adjective* [*tri-* + Latin *littera* letter] (1751)
: consisting of three letters and especially of three consonants ⟨*triliteral* roots in Semitic languages⟩
— **tri·lit·er·al·ism** \-t(ə-)rə-ˌli-zəm\ *noun*

**²triliteral** *noun* (circa 1828)
: a root or word that is triliteral

**¹trill** \'tril\ *verb* [Middle English, probably of Scandinavian origin; akin to Swedish *trilla* to roll; akin to Middle Dutch *trillen* to vibrate] (14th century)
*intransitive verb*
**1** : to flow in a small stream or in drops : TRICKLE
**2** : TWIRL, REVOLVE
*transitive verb*
: to cause to flow in a small stream

**²trill** *noun* [Italian *trillo* probably of imitative origin] (1649)
**1 a** : the alternation of two musical tones a diatonic second apart — called also *shake* **b** : VIBRATO **c** : a rapid reiteration of the same tone especially on a percussion instrument
**2** : a sound resembling a musical trill : WARBLE
**3 a** : the rapid vibration of one speech organ against another (as of the tip of the tongue against the teethridge) **b** : a speech sound made by a trill

**³trill** (circa 1667)
*intransitive verb*
: to play or sing with a trill : QUAVER
*transitive verb*
: to utter as or with or as if with a trill ⟨*trill* the *r*⟩
— **trill·er** *noun*

**tril·lion** \'tri(l)-yən\ *noun* [French, from *tri-* + *-illion* (as in *million*)] (circa 1690)

---

\ə\ abut \ᵊ\ kitten \ər\ further \a\ ash \ā\ ace
\ä\ mop, mar \aù\ out \ch\ chin \e\ bet \ē\ easy
\g\ go \i\ hit \ī\ ice \j\ job \ŋ\ sing \ō\ go
\ò\ law \òi\ boy \th\ thin \t̲h̲\ the \ü\ loot \ù\ foot
\y\ yet \zh\ vision *see also* Guide to Pronunciation

**1** — see NUMBER table
**2 :** a very large number
— **trillion** *adjective*
— **tril·lionth** \-yən(t)th\ *adjective or noun*
**tril·li·um** \'tri-lē-əm\ *noun* [New Latin, from Swedish *trilling* triplet; from its three leaves] (circa 1760)
**:** any of a genus (*Trillium*) of herbs of the lily family with an erect stem bearing a whorl of three leaves and a large solitary typically spring-blooming flower
**tri·lo·bate** \(ˌ)trī-'lō-ˌbāt\ *adjective* (1785)
**:** TRILOBED
**tri·lobed** \'trī-'lōbd\ *adjective* (1826)
**:** having three lobes ⟨a *trilobed* leaf⟩
**tri·lo·bite** \'trī-lə-ˌbīt\ *noun* [ultimately from Greek *trilobos* three-lobed, from *tri-* + *lobos* lobe] (1832)
**:** any of numerous extinct Paleozoic marine arthropods (group Trilobita) having the segments of the body divided by furrows on the dorsal surface into three lobes
**tril·o·gy** \'tri-lə-jē\ *noun*, *plural* **-gies** [Greek *trilogia*, from *tri-* + *-logia* -logy] (circa 1661)
**:** a series of three dramas or literary works or sometimes three musical compositions that are closely related and develop a single theme
**¹trim** \'trim\ *verb* **trimmed; trim·ming** [probably from (assumed) Middle English *trimmen* to prepare, put in order, from Old English *trymian, tryman* to strengthen, arrange, from *trum* strong, firm; probably akin to Old English *trēo* tree, wood — more at TREE] (circa 1521)
*transitive verb*
**1 :** to embellish with or as if with ribbons, lace, or ornaments ⟨*trim* the Christmas tree⟩ ⟨the coat was *trimmed* with fur⟩
**2 a :** to administer a beating to **:** THRASH **b :** DEFEAT ⟨*trimmed* me at chess⟩
**3 a :** to make trim and neat especially by cutting or clipping ⟨*trim* the hedges⟩ **b :** to free of excess or extraneous matter by or as if by cutting ⟨*trim* a budget⟩ ⟨*trim* down the inventory⟩ **c :** to remove by or as if by cutting ⟨*trimmed* thousands from federal payrolls —*Grit*⟩
**4 a** (1) **:** to cause (as a ship) to assume a desirable position in the water by arrangement of ballast, cargo, or passengers (2) **:** to adjust (as an airplane or submarine) for horizontal movement or for motion upward or downward **b :** to adjust (as cargo or a sail) to a desired position
**5 :** to adjust (as one's opinions) for reasons of expediency — often used in the phrase *trim one's sails*
*intransitive verb*
**1 a :** to maintain neutrality between opposing parties or to favor each equally **b :** to change one's views for reasons of expediency
**2 :** to assume or cause a boat to assume a desired position in the water ⟨a boat that *trims* badly⟩
— **trim one's sails :** to adjust oneself or one's actions to prevailing conditions
**²trim** *adjective* **trim·mer; trim·mest** (circa 1521)
**1** *obsolete* **:** EXCELLENT, FINE
**2 :** ready for service or use; *also* **:** in good physical condition ⟨keeps *trim* by jogging⟩
**3 :** exhibiting neatness, good order, or compactness of line or structure ⟨*trim* houses⟩
— **trim·ly** *adverb*
— **trim·ness** *noun*

**³trim** *adverb* (1529)
**:** in a trim manner **:** TRIMLY — used chiefly in combination ⟨the *trim*-cut forest vistas —W. M. Thackeray⟩
**⁴trim** *noun* (1590)
**1 :** suitable or excellent condition ⟨tries to keep in *trim*⟩
**2 a :** one's clothing or appearance **b :** material used for ornament or trimming **c :** the lighter woodwork in the finish of a building especially around openings **d :** the interior furnishings of an automobile
**3 a :** the position of a ship or boat especially with reference to the horizontal; *also* **:** the difference between the draft of a ship forward and that aft **b :** the relation between the plane of a sail and the direction of the ship **c :** the buoyancy status of a submarine **d :** the attitude of a lighter-than-air craft relative to a fore-and-aft horizontal plane **e :** the attitude with respect to wind axes at which an airplane will continue in level flight with free controls
**4 :** something that is trimmed off or cut out
**5 :** a haircut that neatens a previous haircut
**tri·ma·ran** \'trī-mə-ˌran, ˌtrī-mə-'\ *noun* [*tri-* + cata*maran*] (1949)
**:** a fast pleasure sailboat with three hulls side by side
**tri·mer** \'trī-mər\ *noun* [International Scientific Vocabulary] (circa 1930)
**:** a polymer formed from three molecules of a monomer
— **tri·mer·ic** \trī-'mer-ik\ *adjective*
**trim·er·ous** \'tri-mə-rəs\ *adjective* [New Latin *trimerus*, from Greek *tri-* + *meros* part — more at MERIT] (1826)
**:** having the parts in threes — used of a flower and often written *3-merous*
**tri·mes·ter** \(ˌ)trī-'mes-tər, 'trī-ˌ\ *noun* [French *trimestre*, from Latin *trimestris* of three months, from *tri-* + *mensis* month — more at MOON] (1821)
**1 :** a period of three or about three months; *especially* **:** any of three periods of approximately three months each into which a human pregnancy is divided
**2 :** one of three terms into which the academic year is sometimes divided
**trim·e·ter** \'tri-mə-tər\ *noun* [Latin *trimetrus*, from Greek *trimetros* having three measures, from *tri-* + *metron* measure — more at MEASURE] (1567)
**:** a line of verse consisting of three dipodies or three metrical feet
**tri·meth·o·prim** \trī-'me-thə-ˌprim\ *noun* [*tri-* + *meth-* + *-prim* (by shortening & alteration from *pyrimidine*)] (1964)
**:** a synthetic antibacterial and antimalarial drug $C_{14}H_{18}N_4O_3$ often used with a sulfa drug
**tri·met·ro·gon** \trī-'me-trə-ˌgän\ *noun* [*tri-* + Greek *metron* measure + English *-gon*] (1943)
**:** a system of aerial mapping involving the use of sets of one vertical and two oblique aerial photographs taken simultaneously over the area being mapped
**trim·mer** \'tri-mər\ *noun* (1555)
**1 a** (1) **:** one that trims articles (2) **:** one that stows coal or freight on a ship so as to distribute the weight properly **b :** an instrument or machine with which trimming is done **c :** a circuit element (as a capacitor) used to tune a circuit to a desired frequency
**2 :** a beam that receives the end of a header in floor framing
**3 :** a person who modifies a policy, position, or opinion especially out of expediency
**trim·ming** *noun* (circa 1518)
**1 :** DEFEAT, BEATING
**2 :** the act of one who trims
**3 a :** a decorative accessory or additional item ⟨*trimmings* for a hat⟩ **b :** an additional garnishing ⟨turkey and all the *trimmings*⟩
**tri·month·ly** \(ˌ)trī-'mən(t)th-lē\ *adjective* (1856)
**:** occurring every three months

**tri·mor·phic** \(ˌ)trī-'mȯr-fik\ *adjective* [Greek *trimorphos* having three forms, from *tri-* + *-morphos* -morphous] (1866)
**:** occurring in or having three distinct forms
**tri·mo·tor** \'trī-ˌmō-tər, -'mō-\ *noun* (1923)
**:** an airplane powered by three engines
**trim size** *noun* (circa 1929)
**:** the actual size (as of a book page) after excess material required in production has been cut off
**Tri·mur·ti** \tri-'mȯr-tē\ *noun* [Sanskrit *-trimūrti*, from *trimūrti* having three forms, from *tri-* tri- + *mūrti* body, form] (1810)
**:** the great triad of Hindu gods comprising Brahma, Vishnu, and Siva
**tri·nal** \'trī-nᵊl\ *adjective* [Late Latin *trinalis*, from Latin *trini* three each] (1590)
**:** THREEFOLD
**¹trine** \'trīn\ *adjective* [Middle English, from Middle French *trin*, from Latin *trinus*, from *trini* three each; akin to Latin *tres* three — more at THREE] (14th century)
**1 :** THREEFOLD, TRIPLE
**2 :** of, relating to, or being the favorable astrological aspect of two celestial bodies 120 degrees apart
**²trine** *noun* (1552)
**1 :** a group of three **:** TRIAD
**2 :** the trine astrological aspect of two celestial bodies
**trine immersion** *noun* (1637)
**:** the practice of immersing a candidate for baptism three times in the names of the members of the Trinity
**trin·i·tar·i·an** \ˌtri-nə-'ter-ē-ən\ *adjective* (1628)
**1** *capitalized* **:** of or relating to the Trinity, the doctrine of the Trinity, or adherents to that doctrine
**2 :** having three parts or aspects **:** THREEFOLD
**Trinitarian** *noun* (1628)
**1 :** a member of a religious teaching and nursing order for men founded in France in 1198 by John of Matha and Philip of Valois
**2 :** one who subscribes to the doctrine of the Trinity
— **Trin·i·tar·i·an·ism** \-ē-ə-ˌni-zəm\ *noun*
**tri·ni·tro·tol·u·ene** \(ˌ)trī-ˌnī-trō-'täl-yə-ˌwēn\ *noun* [International Scientific Vocabulary] (circa 1900)
**:** TNT
**Trin·i·ty** \'tri-nə-tē\ *noun* [Middle English *trinite*, from Old French *trinité*, from Late Latin *trinitat-, trinitas* state of being threefold, from Latin *trinus* threefold] (13th century)
**1 :** the unity of Father, Son, and Holy Spirit as three persons in one Godhead according to Christian dogma
**2** *not capitalized* **:** a group of three closely related persons or things
**3 :** the Sunday after Whitsunday observed as a feast in honor of the Trinity
**Trin·i·ty·tide** \-ˌtīd\ *noun* (1511)
**:** the season of the church year between Trinity Sunday and Advent
**¹trin·ket** \'triŋ-kət\ *noun* [origin unknown] (circa 1533)
**1 :** a small ornament (as a jewel or ring)
**2 :** a small article of equipment
**3 :** a thing of little value **:** TRIFLE
**²trinket** *intransitive verb* [perhaps from ¹*trinket*] (1646)
**:** to deal clandestinely **:** INTRIGUE
— **trin·ket·er** *noun*
**trin·ket·ry** \-kə-trē\ *noun* (1810)
**:** small items of personal ornament
**trin·oc·u·lar** \(ˌ)trī-'nä-kyə-lər\ *adjective* [*tri-* + *binocular*] (1960)
**:** relating to or being a binocular microscope equipped with a lens for photographic recording during direct visual observation
**¹tri·no·mi·al** \trī-'nō-mē-əl\ *noun* [*tri-* + *-nomial* (as in *binomial*)] (1674)
**1 :** a polynomial of three terms
**2 :** a biological taxonomic name of three terms of which the first designates the genus, the

second the species, and the third the subspecies or variety

**²trinomial** *adjective* (circa 1704)
**1 :** consisting of three mathematical terms
**2 :** of, relating to, or being a biological trinomial

**tri·nu·cle·o·tide** \(ˌ)trī-ˈnü-klē-ə-ˌtīd, -ˈnyü-\ *noun* (1918)
**:** a nucleotide consisting of three mononucleotides in combination **:** CODON

**trio** \ˈtrē-(ˌ)ō\ *noun, plural* **tri·os** [French, from Italian, from *tri-* (from Latin)] (circa 1724)
**1 a :** a musical composition for three voice parts or three instruments **b :** the secondary or episodic division of a minuet or scherzo, a march, or of various dance forms
**2 :** the performers of a musical or dance trio
**3 :** a group or set of three

**tri·ode** \ˈtrī-ˌōd\ *noun* (1922)
**:** an electron tube with an anode, a cathode, and a controlling grid

**tri·ol** \ˈtrī-ˌól, -ˌōl\ *noun* (1936)
**:** a chemical compound containing three hydroxyl groups

**tri·o·let** \ˈtrē-ə-lət, ˈtrī-\ *noun* [French, from Middle French, literally, clover leaf, clover, ultimately from Greek *triphyllon,* from *tri-* tri- + *phyllon* leaf — more at BLADE] (1651)
**:** a poem or stanza of eight lines in which the first line is repeated as the fourth and seventh and the second line as the eighth with a rhyme scheme of *ABaAabAB*

**tri·ose** \ˈtrī-ˌōs, -ˌōz\ *noun* [International Scientific Vocabulary] (1894)
**:** either of two simple sugars $C_3H_6O_3$ containing three carbon atoms

**tri·ox·ide** \(ˌ)trī-ˈäk-ˌsīd\ *noun* [International Scientific Vocabulary] (circa 1868)
**:** an oxide containing three atoms of oxygen

**¹trip** \ˈtrip\ *verb* **tripped; trip·ping** [Middle English *trippen,* from Middle French *triper,* of Germanic origin; akin to Old English *treppan* to tread — more at TRAP] (14th century)
*intransitive verb*
**1 a :** to dance, skip, or caper with light quick steps **b :** to walk with light quick steps
**2 :** to catch the foot against something so as to stumble
**3 :** to make a mistake or false step (as in morality or accuracy)
**4 :** to stumble in articulation when speaking
**5 :** to make a journey
**6 :** to run past the pallet of an escapement without previously locking — used of a tooth of the escapement wheel of a watch
**7 a :** to actuate a mechanism **b :** to become operative
**8 :** to get high on a psychedelic drug (as LSD) **:** TURN ON — often used with *out*
*transitive verb*
**1 a :** to cause to stumble — often used with *up* **b :** to cause to fail **:** OBSTRUCT — often used with *up*
**2 :** to detect in a misstep, fault, or blunder; *also* **:** EXPOSE — usually used with *up*
**3** *archaic* **:** to perform (as a dance) lightly or nimbly
**4 :** to raise (an anchor) from the bottom so as to hang free
**5 a :** to pull (a yard) into a perpendicular position for lowering **b :** to hoist (a topmast) far enough to enable the fid to be withdrawn preparatory to housing or lowering
**6 :** to release or operate (a mechanism) especially by releasing a catch or detent
**— trip the light fantastic :** DANCE

**²trip** *noun* (15th century)
**1 :** a stroke or catch by which a wrestler is made to lose footing
**2 a :** VOYAGE, JOURNEY **b :** a single round or tour on a business errand
**3 :** ERROR, MISSTEP
**4 :** a quick light step
**5 :** a faltering step caused by stumbling

**6 a :** the action of tripping mechanically **b** (1) **:** a device for tripping a mechanism (as a catch or detent) (2) **:** TUP 2
**7 :** an intense visionary experience undergone by a person who has taken a psychedelic drug (as LSD)
**8 :** absorption in or obsession with an interest, attitude, or state of mind ⟨a guilt *trip*⟩ ⟨on a nostalgia *trip*⟩
**9 :** SCENE, LIFESTYLE

**tri·pack** \ˈtrī-ˌpak\ *noun* (1911)
**:** a combination of three superposed films or emulsions each sensitive to a different primary color for simultaneous exposure in one camera

**tri·par·tite** \(ˌ)trī-ˈpär-ˌtīt\ *adjective* [Middle English, from Latin *tripartitus,* from *tri-* + *partitus* divided — more at PARTITE] (15th century)
**1 :** divided into or composed of three parts
**2 :** having three corresponding parts or copies
**3 :** made between or involving three parties ⟨a *tripartite* treaty⟩

**tripe** \ˈtrīp\ *noun* [Middle English, from Middle French] (14th century)
**1 :** stomach tissue of a ruminant and especially of the ox used as food
**2 :** something poor, worthless, or offensive

**¹trip-ham·mer** \ˈtrip-ˌha-mər\ *noun* (1781)
**:** a massive power hammer having a head that is tripped and allowed to fall by cam or lever action

**²trip–hammer** *adjective* (circa 1864)
**:** suggesting a trip-hammer in loud pounding or persistent action

**tri·phe·nyl·meth·ane** \ˌtrī-ˌfe-nᵊl-ˈme-ˌthān, -ˌfē-\ *noun* [International Scientific Vocabulary] (circa 1885)
**:** a crystalline hydrocarbon $CH(C_6H_5)_3$ that is the parent compound of many dyes

**tri·phos·phate** \(ˌ)trī-ˈfäs-ˌfāt\ *noun* (circa 1826)
**:** a salt or acid that contains three phosphate groups — compare ATP, GTP

**tri·phos·pho·pyr·i·dine nucleotide** \ˌtrī-ˌfäs-fō-ˈpir-ə-ˌdēn-\ *noun* (1937)
**:** NADP

**triph·thong** \ˈtrif-ˌthóŋ, ˈtrip-\ *noun* [*tri-* + *-phthong* (as in *diphthong*)] (circa 1599)
**1 :** a phonological unit consisting of three successive vocalic sounds in one syllable
**2 :** TRIGRAPH
**— triph·thon·gal** \trif-ˈthóŋ-gəl, trip-, -əl\ *adjective*

**tri·pin·nate** \(ˌ)trī-ˈpi-ˌnāt\ *adjective* (circa 1760)
**:** bipinnate with each division pinnate
**— tri·pin·nate·ly** *adverb*

**tri·plane** \ˈtrī-ˌplān\ *noun* (1909)
**:** an airplane with three main supporting surfaces superposed

**¹tri·ple** \ˈtri-pəl\ *verb* **tri·pled; tri·pling** \-p(ə-)liŋ\ [Middle English, from Late Latin *triplare,* from Latin *triplus,* adjective] (14th century)
*transitive verb*
**1 :** to make three times as great or as many
**2 a :** to score (a base runner) by a triple **b :** to bring about the scoring of (a run) by a triple
*intransitive verb*
**1 :** to become three times as great or as numerous
**2 :** to make a triple in baseball

**²triple** *noun* [Middle English, from Latin *triplus,* adjective] (15th century)
**1 a :** a triple sum, quantity, or number **b :** a combination, group, or series of three
**2 :** a base hit that allows the batter to reach third base safely
**3 :** TRIFECTA

**³triple** *adjective* [Middle French or Latin; Middle French, from Latin *triplus,* from *tri-* + *-plus* multiplied by — more at -FOLD] (1550)
**1 :** being three times as great or as many
**2 :** having three units or members

**3 :** having a threefold relation or character ⟨worked as a double or even *triple* agent —*Time*⟩
**4 :** three times repeated **:** TREBLE
**5 :** marked by three beats per musical measure ⟨*triple* meter⟩
**6 a :** having units of three components ⟨*triple* feet⟩ **b** *of rhyme* **:** involving correspondence of three syllables (as in *unfortunate-importunate*)

**triple bond** *noun* (1889)
**:** a chemical bond in which three pairs of electrons are shared by two atoms in a molecule — compare DOUBLE BOND, SINGLE BOND

**triple counterpoint** *noun* (circa 1869)
**:** three-part musical counterpoint so written that any part may be transposed above or below any other

**Triple Crown** *noun* (circa 1897)
**1 :** an unofficial title in horse racing representing the championship achieved by a horse that wins the three classic races for a designated category
**2 :** the unofficial title signifying the achievement of a baseball player who at the end of a season leads the league in batting average, home runs, and runs batted in

**tri·ple-deck·er** \ˌtri-pəl-ˈde-kər\ *noun, often attributive* (1938)
**:** something having three basic components or levels: as **a :** TRILOGY **b :** a sandwich consisting of three pieces of bread and two layers of filling **c :** a 3-story dwelling with an apartment on each floor

**tri·ple-head·er** \-ˈhe-dər\ *noun* (circa 1949)
**:** a program consisting of three consecutive games, contests, or events

**triple jump** *noun* (1964)
**:** a jump for distance in track-and-field athletics usually from a running start and combining a hop, a stride, and a jump in succession
**— triple jumper** *noun*

**triple play** *noun* (1869)
**:** a play in baseball by which three players are put out

**triple point** *noun* (1872)
**:** the condition of temperature and pressure under which the gaseous, liquid, and solid phases of a substance can exist in equilibrium

**triple sec** \-ˈsek\ *noun* [from *Triple Sec,* a trademark] (1943)
**:** a colorless orange-flavored liqueur

**tri·ple-space** \ˌtri-pəl-ˈspās\ (circa 1939)
*transitive verb*
**:** to type (text) leaving two blank lines between lines of copy
*intransitive verb*
**:** to type on every third line

**trip·let** \ˈtri-plət\ *noun* [²*triple*] (1656)
**1 :** a unit of three lines of verse
**2 a :** a combination, set, or group of three **b :** a group of three elementary particles (as positive, negative, and neutral pions) with different charge states but otherwise similar properties **c :** an atom or molecule with an even number of electrons that have a net magnetic moment **d :** CODON
**3 :** one of three children or offspring born at one birth
**4 :** a group of three musical notes or tones performed in the time of two of the same value

**tri·ple-tail** \ˈtri-pəl-ˌtāl\ *noun* (circa 1803)
**:** a large marine bony fish (*Lobotes surinamensis* of the family Lobotidae) of warm and tropical waters that has long dorsal and anal fins which extend backward and together with the caudal fin appear like a 3-lobed tail

**triple threat** *noun* (1924)
**1 :** a football player adept at running, kicking, and passing

\ə\ **abut** \ᵊ\ **kitten** \ər\ **further** \a\ **ash** \ā\ **ace**
\ä\ **mop, mar** \au̇\ **out** \ch\ **chin** \e\ **bet** \ē\ **easy**
\g\ **go** \i\ **hit** \ī\ **ice** \j\ **job** \ŋ\ **sing** \ō\ **go**
\ò\ **law** \ói\ **boy** \th\ **thin** \t̲h̲\ **the** \ü\ **loot** \u̇\ **foot**
\y\ **yet** \zh\ **vision**   *see also* Guide to Pronunciation

**2 :** a person adept in three different fields of activity
— **triple–threat** *adjective*

**tri·ple–tongue** \ˌtri-pəl-'təŋ\ *intransitive verb* (1879)
: to articulate the notes of triplets in fast tempo on a wind instrument by using the tongue positions especially for *t, k, t* for the notes of each successive triplet

**¹tri·plex** \'tri-ˌpleks, 'trī-\ *noun* (1601)
: something (as an apartment) that is triplex

**²triplex** *adjective* [Latin, from *tri-* + *-plex* -fold — more at -FOLD] (1655)
**1 :** THREEFOLD, TRIPLE ⟨*triplex* windows⟩
**2 :** having three apartments, floors, or sections ⟨*triplex* buildings⟩ ⟨*triplex* apartments⟩ ⟨a *triplex* theater⟩

**¹trip·li·cate** \'tri-pli-kət\ *adjective* [Middle English, from Latin *triplicatus*, past participle of *triplicare* to triple, from *triplic-, triplex* threefold] (15th century)
: consisting of or existing in three corresponding or identical parts or examples ⟨*triplicate* invoices⟩

**²trip·li·cate** \-plə-ˌkāt\ *transitive verb* **-cat·ed; -cat·ing** (circa 1623)
**1 :** to make triple or threefold
**2 :** to prepare in triplicate
— **trip·li·ca·tion** \ˌtri-plə-'kā-shən\ *noun*

**³trip·li·cate** \-pli-kət\ *noun* (1810)
: three copies all alike — used with *in* ⟨typed in *triplicate*⟩

**tri·plic·i·ty** \tri-'pli-sə-tē, trī-\ *noun, plural* **-ties** [Middle English *triplicite*, from Late Latin *triplicitas* condition of being threefold, from Latin *triplic-, triplex*] (14th century)
**1 :** one of the groups of three signs each distant 120 degrees from the other two into which the signs of the zodiac are divided — called also *trigon*
**2 :** the quality or state of being triple or three-fold

**trip·lo·blas·tic** \ˌtri-plō-'blas-tik\ *adjective* [Latin *triplus* + English *-o-* + *-blastic*] (circa 1888)
: having three primary germ layers

**trip·loid** \'tri-ˌplȯid\ *adjective* [International Scientific Vocabulary, from Latin *triplus* triple] (1911)
: having or being a chromosome number three times the monoploid number
— **trip·loid** *noun*
— **trip·loi·dy** \-ˌplȯi-dē\ *noun*

**trip·ly** \'tri-p(ə-)lē\ *adverb* (1660)
: in a triple degree, amount, or manner

**tri·pod** \'trī-ˌpäd\ *noun* [Latin *tripod-, tripus*, from Greek *tripod-, tripous*, from *tri-* + *pod-, pous* foot — more at FOOT] (1603)
**1 :** a vessel (as a cauldron) resting on three legs
**2 :** a stool, table, or altar with three legs
**3 :** a three-legged stand (as for a camera)
— **tripod** *or* **tri·po·dal** \'trī-pə-dᵊl, 'trī-ˌpä-\ *adjective*

**trip·o·li** \'tri-pə-lē\ *noun* [French, from *Tripoli*, region of Africa] (circa 1601)
**1 :** an earth consisting of very friable soft schistose deposits of silica and including diatomite and kieselguhr
**2 :** an earth consisting of friable dustlike silica not of diatomaceous origin

**tri·pos** \'trī-ˌpäs\ *noun* [modification of Latin *tripus*] (1589)
**1** *archaic* **:** TRIPOD
**2** [from the three-legged stool occupied by a participant in a disputation at the degree ceremonies] **:** a final honors examination at Cambridge university originally in mathematics

**trip·per** \'tri-pər\ *noun* (1813)
**1** *chiefly British* **:** one that takes a trip **:** TOURIST
**2 :** a tripping device (as for operating a railroad signal)

**trip·ping·ly** \'tri-piŋ-lē\ *adverb* (1590)

: in a nimble or lively manner ⟨the new name . . . may not roll *trippingly* off the tongue —Paul B. Carroll⟩

**trip·py** \'tri-pē\ *adjective* (1968)
: of, relating to, or suggesting a trip on psychedelic drugs or the culture associated with such drugs

**trip·tych** \'trip-(ˌ)tik\ *noun* [Greek *triptychos* having three folds, from *tri-* + *ptychē* fold] (1731)
**1 :** an ancient Roman writing tablet with three waxed leaves hinged together
**2 a :** a picture (as an altarpiece) or carving in three panels side by side **b :** something composed or presented in three parts or sections; *especially* **:** TRILOGY

**trip wire** *noun* (1916)
**1 :** a low-placed concealed wire used especially in warfare to trip an enemy or trespasser and usually to trigger an alarm or explosive device when moved
**2 :** something (as a small military force) intended to function like a trip wire (as to set a larger military force in motion)

**tri·que·trous** \trī-'kwē-trəs, -'kwe-\ *adjective* [Latin *triquetrus* three-cornered, from *tri-* + *-quetrus*; probably akin to Old High German *waz* sharp — more at WHET] (circa 1879)
: having three acute angles ⟨*triquetrous* stems⟩

**tri·ra·di·ate** \(ˌ)trī-'rā-dē-ət, -dē-ˌāt\ *adjective* (1846)
: having three rays or radiating branches ⟨a *triradiate* sponge spicule⟩

**tri·reme** \'trī-ˌrēm\ *noun* [Latin *triremis*, from *tri-* + *remus* oar — more at ROW] (1601)
: an ancient galley having three banks of oars

**tri·sac·cha·ride** \(ˌ)trī-'sa-kə-ˌrīd\ *noun* [International Scientific Vocabulary] (circa 1899)
: a sugar that yields on complete hydrolysis three monosaccharide molecules

**tri·sect** \'trī-ˌsekt, trī-'\ *transitive verb* [*tri-* + inter*sect*] (1695)
: to divide into three usually equal parts
— **tri·sec·tion** \'trī-ˌsek-shən, trī-'\ *noun*
— **tri·sec·tor** \'trī-ˌsek-tər, trī-'\ *noun*

**tri·shaw** \'trī-ˌshȯ\ *noun* [*tri-* + rick*shaw*] (1946)
: PEDICAB

**tris·kai·deka·pho·bia** \ˌtris-ˌkī-ˌde-kə-'fō-bē-ə, ˌtris-kə-\ *noun* [New Latin, from Greek *treiskaideka* thirteen (from *treis* three + *kai* and + *deka* ten) + New Latin *phobia* — more at THREE, TEN] (circa 1911)
: fear of the number 13

**tri·skel·i·on** \trī-'ske-lē-ən, tri-\ *or* **tri·skele** \'trī-ˌskēl, 'tri-\ *noun* [*triskelion* from New Latin, from Greek *triskelēs* three-legged, from *tri-* + *skelos* leg; *triskele* from Greek *triskelēs* — more at ISOSCELES] (1857)
: a figure composed of three usually curved or bent branches radiating from a center

**tris·mus** \'triz-məs\ *noun* [New Latin, from Greek *trismos* gnashing (of teeth), from *trizein* to squeak, gnash; akin to Latin *stridēre* to creak — more at STRIDENT] (circa 1693)
: spasm of the muscles of mastication **:** LOCKJAW

**triskelion**

**tris·oc·ta·he·dron** \ˌtri-ˌsäk-tə-'hē-drən\ *noun* [Greek *tris* thrice + English *octahedron* — more at TER-] (circa 1847)
: a solid (as a crystal) having 24 congruent faces meeting on the edges of a regular octahedron

**tri·so·di·um phosphate** \ˌtrī-'sō-dē-əm-\ *noun* (1900)
: a crystalline compound $Na_3PO_4$ that is used especially in cleaning compositions

**tri·so·my** \'trī-ˌsō-mē\ *noun, plural* **-mies** [*tri-* + ³-*some* + ²-*y*] (1930)

: the condition (as in Down's syndrome) of having one or a few chromosomes triploid in an otherwise diploid set
— **tri·so·mic** \(ˌ)trī-'sō-mik\ *adjective or noun*

**Tris·tan** \'tris-tən, -ˌtän, -ˌtan\ *noun*
: TRISTRAM

**tri·state** \'trī-ˌstāt, -ˌstāt\ *adjective* (1900)
: of, relating to, or consisting of three adjoining states ⟨the *tristate* area⟩

**triste** \'trēst\ *adjective* [French, from Latin *tristis*] (1756)
: SAD, MOURNFUL; *also* **:** WISTFUL

**tri·stea·rin** \(ˌ)trī-'stē-ə-rən, -'sti-(ə)r-ən\ *noun* [International Scientific Vocabulary] (circa 1856)
: the crystallizable triglyceride $C_{57}H_{110}O_6$ of stearic acid that is found especially in hard fats

**tris·te·za** \ˌtri-'stā-zə\ *noun* [Portuguese, literally, sadness, from Latin *tristitia*, from *tristis* sad] (circa 1902)
: a highly infectious virus disease of citrus trees grafted on sour orange rootstocks that is characterized by rotting of the rootlets and eventually causes the death of the trees

**trist·ful** \'trist-fəl\ *adjective* [Middle English *trist* sad, from Middle French *triste*] (15th century)
: SAD, MELANCHOLY
— **trist·ful·ly** \-fə-lē\ *adverb*
— **trist·ful·ness** *noun*

**tri·stim·u·lus** \(ˌ)trī-'stim-yə-ləs\ *adjective* (1933)
: of or relating to values giving the amounts of the three colored lights red, green, and blue that when combined additively produce a match for the color being considered

**Tris·tram** \'tris-trəm\ *noun* [Middle English *Tristrem*, from Anglo-French *Tristan*, from Old Welsh *Trystan*]
: the lover of Isolde of Ireland and husband of Isolde of Brittany in medieval legend

**tri·sub·sti·tut·ed** \'trī-ˌsəb-stə-ˌtü-təd, -ˌtyü-\ *adjective* (circa 1899)
: having three substituent atoms or groups in the molecule

**tri·sul·fide** \-'səl-ˌfīd\ *noun* (1866)
: a compound of an element or radical with three atoms of sulfur

**tri·syl·lab·ic** \ˌtrī-sə-'la-bik\ *adjective* [Latin *trisyllabus*, from Greek *trisyllabos*, from *tri-* + *syllabē* syllable] (1637)
: having three syllables ⟨a *trisyllabic* word⟩

**tri·syl·la·ble** \'trī-ˌsi-lə-bəl, (ˌ)trī-'\ *noun* (1589)
: a word of three syllables

**trite** \'trīt\ *adjective* **trit·er; trit·est** [Latin *tritus*, from past participle of *terere* to rub, wear away — more at THROW] (1548)
: hackneyed or boring from much use **:** not fresh or original ☆
— **trite·ly** *adverb*
— **trite·ness** *noun*

**tri·the·ism** \'trī-thē-ˌi-zəm\ *noun* (1678)

: the doctrine that the Father, Son, and Holy Spirit are three distinct Gods
— **tri·the·ist** \-(ˌ)thē-ist\ *noun or adjective*
— **tri·the·is·tic** \ˌtrī-thē-'is-tik\ *or* **tri·the·is·ti·cal** \-'is-ti-kəl\ *adjective*

**tri·thing** \'trī-thiŋ\ *noun* [Middle English, alteration of (assumed) Old English *thrithing, thriding*] (13th century)
*archaic* : ³RIDING 1

**tri·ti·at·ed** \'tri-tē-ˌā-təd, 'tri-shē-\ *adjective* (1953)
: containing and especially labeled with tritium

**trit·i·ca·le** \ˌtri-tə-'kā-lē\ *noun* [New Latin, blend of *Triticum*, genus of wheat, and *Secale*, genus of rye] (1952)
: an amphidiploid hybrid between wheat and rye that has a high yield and rich protein content

**tri·ti·um** \'tri-tē-əm, 'tri-shē-\ *noun* [New Latin, from Greek *tritos* third — more at THIRD] (1933)
: a radioactive isotope of hydrogen with atoms of three times the mass of ordinary light hydrogen atoms

**trit·o·ma** \'tri-tə-mə\ *noun* [New Latin, genus name, from Greek *tritomos* thrice cut, from *tri-* + *temnein* to cut; from their trimerous flowers — more at TOME] (1804)
: any of a genus (*Khiphofia*) of African herbs of the lily family that are often grown for their spikes of showy red or yellow flowers

¹**tri·ton** \'trī-tⁿ\ *noun* [Latin, from Greek *Trītōn*]
**1** *capitalized* : a son of Poseidon described as a demigod of the sea with the lower part of his body like that of a fish
**2** [New Latin, genus name, from Latin *Triton*] : any of various large marine gastropod mollusks (especially family Ranellidae) with a heavy elongated conical shell; *also* : the shell

²**tri·ton** \'trī-ˌtän\ *noun* [tritium + ²-*on*] (1934)
: the nucleus of tritium

**tri·tone** \'trī-ˌtōn\ *noun* [Greek *tritonon*, from *tri-* + *tonos* tone] (1609)
: a musical interval of three whole steps

¹**trit·u·rate** \'tri-chə-ˌrāt\ *transitive verb* -**rat·ed**; -**rat·ing** [Late Latin *trituratus*, past participle of *triturare* to thresh, from Latin *tritura* act of rubbing, threshing, from *tritus*, past participle — more at TRITE] (circa 1755)
**1** : CRUSH, GRIND
**2** : to pulverize and comminute thoroughly by rubbing or grinding
— **trit·u·ra·ble** \'tri-chə-rə-bəl\ *adjective*
— **trit·u·ra·tor** \-ˌrā-tər\ *noun*

²**trit·u·rate** \-rət\ *noun* (circa 1891)
: a triturated substance : TRITURATION 2

**trit·u·ra·tion** \ˌtri-chə-'rā-shən\ *noun* (1646)
**1** : the act or process of triturating : the state of being triturated : COMMINUTION
**2** : a triturated medicinal powder made by triturating a substance with a diluent

¹**tri·umph** \'trī-əm(p)f\ *noun, plural* **tri·umphs** \-əm(p)fs, -əm(p)s\ [Middle English *triumphe*, from Middle French, from Latin *triumphus*] (14th century)
**1** : a ceremony attending the entering of Rome by a general who had won a decisive victory over a foreign enemy — compare OVATION 1
**2** : the joy or exultation of victory or success
**3 a** : a victory or conquest by or as if by military force **b** : a notable success
— **tri·um·phal** \trī-'əm(p)-fəl\ *adjective*

²**triumph** *intransitive verb* (1508)
**1** : to obtain victory : PREVAIL
**2 a** : to receive the honor of a triumph **b** : to celebrate victory or success boastfully or exultingly

**tri·um·phal·ism** \trī-'əm(p)-fə-ˌli-zəm\ *noun* (1964)
: the doctrine, attitude, or belief that one religious creed is superior to all others
— **tri·um·phal·ist** \-fə-list\ *noun or adjective*

**tri·um·phant** \trī-'əm(p)-fənt\ *adjective* (15th century)
**1** : VICTORIOUS, CONQUERING
**2** *archaic* : of or relating to a triumph
**3** : rejoicing for or celebrating victory
**4** : notably successful
— **tri·um·phant·ly** *adverb*

**tri·um·vir** \trī-'əm-vər\ *noun, plural* -**virs** *also* -**vi·ri** \-və-ˌrī, -ˌrē\ [Latin, back-formation from *triumviri*, plural, commission of three men, from *trium virum* of three men] (circa 1580)
: one of a commission or ruling body of three

**tri·um·vi·rate** \-və-rət\ *noun* (1584)
**1** : a body of triumvirs
**2** : the office or government of triumvirs
**3** : a group or association of three

¹**tri·une** \'trī-ˌyün\ *noun, often capitalized* [Latin *tri-* + *unus* one — more at ONE] (1605)
: TRINITY 1

²**triune** *adjective* (1635)
: three in one: **a** *often capitalized* : of or relating to the Trinity ⟨the *triune* God⟩ **b** : consisting of three parts, members, or aspects

**tri·va·lent** \(ˌ)trī-'vā-lənt\ *adjective* [International Scientific Vocabulary] (1868)
**1** : having a chemical valence of three
**2** : reacting immunologically with three different combining sites (as of antigens or antibodies) ⟨*trivalent* oral polio vaccine⟩

**triv·et** \'tri-vət\ *noun* [Middle English *trevet*, from Old English *trefet*, probably modification of Late Latin *triped-, tripes*, from Latin, three-footed, from *tri-* + *ped-, pes* foot — more at FOOT] (before 12th century)
**1** : a three-legged stand : TRIPOD
**2** : a usually metal stand with short feet for use under a hot dish at table

**triv·ia** \'tri-vē-ə\ *noun plural but singular or plural in construction* [(assumed) New Latin, back-formation from Latin *trivialis*] (1920)
: unimportant matters : trivial facts or details; *also, singular in construction* : a quizzing game involving obscure facts

**triv·i·al** \'tri-vē-əl\ *adjective* [Latin *trivialis* found everywhere, commonplace, from *trivium* crossroads, from *tri-* + *via* way — more at WAY] (1589)
**1** : COMMONPLACE, ORDINARY
**2 a** : of little worth or importance **b** : relating to or being the mathematically simplest case; *specifically* : characterized by having all variables equal to zero ⟨a *trivial* solution to a linear equation⟩
**3** : SPECIFIC 4 ◆
— **triv·i·al·ist** \-ə-list\ *noun*
— **triv·i·al·ly** \-ə-lē\ *adverb*

**triv·i·al·ise** *British variant of* TRIVIALIZE

**triv·i·al·i·ty** \ˌtri-vē-'a-lə-tē\ *noun, plural* -**ties** (1598)
**1** : the quality or state of being trivial
**2** : something trivial : TRIFLE

**triv·i·al·ize** \'tri-vē-ə-ˌlīz\ *transitive verb* -**ized**; -**iz·ing** (1846)
: to make trivial : reduce to triviality
— **triv·i·al·i·za·tion** \ˌtri-vē-ə-lə-'zā-shən\ *noun*

**trivial name** *noun* (1759)
**1** : SPECIFIC EPITHET
**2** : a common or vernacular name of an organism or chemical

**triv·i·um** \'tri-vē-əm\ *noun, plural* **triv·ia** \-vē-ə\ [Medieval Latin, from Latin, meeting of three ways, crossroads] (1804)
: a group of studies consisting of grammar, rhetoric, and logic and forming the lower division of the seven liberal arts in medieval universities — compare QUADRIVIUM

¹**tri·week·ly** \(ˌ)trī-'wē-klē\ *adjective* (1832)
**1** : occurring or appearing three times a week
**2** : occurring or appearing every three weeks
— **triweekly** *adverb*

²**triweekly** *noun, plural* -**lies** (1851)
: a triweekly publication

-**trix** *noun suffix, plural* -**trices** *or* -**trixes** [Middle English, from Latin, feminine of -*tor*, suffix denoting an agent]
**1** : female that does or is associated with a (specified) thing ⟨avia*trix*⟩
**2** : geometric line, point, or surface ⟨genera*trix*⟩

**tRNA** \ˌtē-ˌär-ˌen-'ā, 'tē-ˌär-ˌen-ˌā\ *noun* (1962)
: TRANSFER RNA

**tro·car** *also* **tro·char** \'trō-ˌkär\ *noun* [French *trocart*, from *trois* three (from Latin *tres*) + *carre* side of a sword blade, from *carrer* to make square, from Latin *quadrare* — more at THREE, QUADRATE] (circa 1706)
: a sharp-pointed surgical instrument fitted with a cannula and used especially to insert the cannula into a body cavity as a drainage outlet

**tro·cha·ic** \trō-'kā-ik\ *adjective* [Middle French *trochaïque*, from Latin *trochaicus*, from Greek *trochaikos*, from *trochaios* trochee] (1589)
: of, relating to, or consisting of trochees
— **trochaic** *noun*

**tro·chan·ter** \trō-'kan-tər\ *noun* [Greek *trochantēr*; akin to Greek *trechein* to run] (1615)
**1** : a rough prominence at the upper part of the femur of many vertebrates
**2** : the second segment counting from the base of the leg of an insect
— **tro·chan·ter·al** \-tə-rəl\ *adjective*
— **tro·chan·ter·ic** \ˌtrō-kən-'ter-ik, -ˌkan-\ *adjective*

**tro·che** \'trō-kē, *British usually* 'trōsh\ *noun* [alteration of earlier *trochisk*, from Late Latin *trochiscus*, from Greek *trochiskos*, from diminutive of *trochos* wheel] (1597)
: a usually circular medicinal tablet or lozenge for slow dissolution in the mouth; *especially* : one used as a demulcent

**tro·chee** \'trō-(ˌ)kē\ *noun* [probably from Middle French *trochée*, from Latin *trochaeus*, from Greek *trochaios*, from *trochaios* running, from *trochē* run, course, from *trechein* to run; akin to Greek *trochos* wheel, Old Irish *droch*] (1589)
: a metrical foot consisting of one long syllable followed by one short syllable or of one stressed syllable followed by one unstressed syllable (as in *apple*)

◇ **WORD HISTORY**
**trivial** The ancient Romans used the adjective *trivialis* to refer to what is commonplace or ordinary. Literally meaning "pertaining to a crossroads," *trivialis* is a derivative of *trivium*, which was compounded from *tri-* "three" and *via* "way, road." Thus *trivium* might be rendered literally as "a place where three roads meet." The extended sense of *trivialis* rested on the belief that things found at such a public place as a crossroads, where all the world may pass by, are generally common things. The notion that people often stop where roads meet to pass the time of day with inconsequential talk may also have influenced the development of this sense. This is the source for the modern senses of *trivial* such as "commonplace" or "of little importance." It was not until the 1920s that the word *trivia* began being used for "unimportant matters." Its form is just like that of the plural of Latin *trivium*, but its meaning is dependent on Modern English senses of *trivial*.

\ə\ **abut** \ᵊ\ **kitten** \ər\ **further** \a\ **ash** \ā\ **ace**
\ä\ **mop, mar** \au̇\ **out** \ch\ **chin** \e\ **bet** \ē\ **easy**
\g\ **go** \i\ **hit** \ī\ **ice** \j\ **job** \ŋ\ **sing** \ō\ **go**
\ȯ\ **law** \ȯi\ **boy** \th\ **thin** \t͟h\ **the** \ü\ **loot** \u̇\ **foot**
\y\ **yet** \zh\ **vision**    *see also* Guide to Pronunciation

**troch·lea** \'trä-klē-ə\ *noun* [New Latin, from Latin, block of pulleys, from Greek *trochileia*, from *trochilos* sheave, from *trochos* wheel] (circa 1693)
: an anatomical structure that is held to resemble a pulley; *especially* : the articular surface on the medial condyle of the humerus that articulates with the ulna

**troch·le·ar** \-ər\ *adjective* (circa 1681)
**1** : of, relating to, or being a trochlea
**2** : of, relating to, or being a trochlear nerve

**trochlear nerve** *noun* (circa 1890)
: either of the 4th pair of cranial nerves that supply some of the eye muscles with motor fibers — called also *trochlear*

**tro·choid** \'trō-ˌkȯid, 'trä-ˌkȯid\ *noun* [Greek *trochoeidēs* like a wheel, from *trochos* wheel] (circa 1704)
: the curve generated by a point on the radius of a circle or the radius extended as the circle rolls on a fixed straight line
— **tro·choi·dal** \trō-'kȯi-dᵊl, trä-\ *adjective*

**trocho·phore** \'trä-kə-ˌfōr, -ˌfȯr\ *noun* [ultimately from Greek *trochos* wheel + *pherein* to carry — more at BEAR] (1892)
: a free-swimming ciliate larva occurring in several invertebrate groups (as the polychaete worms and mollusks)

**trod** *past and past participle of* TREAD
**trodden** *past participle of* TREAD

**trof·fer** \'trä-fər, 'trō-\ *noun* [blend of *trough* and *coffer*] (1942)
: an inverted trough serving as a support and reflector usually for a fluorescent lighting unit

**trog·lo·dyte** \'trä-glə-ˌdīt\ *noun* [Latin *troglodytae*, plural, from Greek *trōglodytai*, from *trōglē* hole, cave (akin to Greek *trōgein* to gnaw, Armenian *aracem* I lead to pasture, graze) + *dyein* to enter] (1558)
**1** : a member of a primitive people dwelling in caves
**2** : a person resembling a troglodyte (as in reclusive habits or outmoded or reactionary attitudes)
— **trog·lo·dyt·ic** \ˌträ-glə-'di-tik\ *adjective*

**tro·gon** \'trō-ˌgän\ *noun* [New Latin, genus name, from Greek *trōgōn*, present participle of *trōgein* to gnaw] (1792)
: any of numerous nonpasserine tropical birds (family Trogonidae) with brilliant often iridescent plumage

**troi·ka** \'trȯi-kə\ *noun* [Russian *troĭka*, from *troe* three; akin to Old English *thrīe* three] (1842)
**1** : a Russian vehicle drawn by three horses abreast; *also* : a team for such a vehicle
**2** : a group of three; *especially* : an administrative or ruling body of three

**troi·lite** \'trō-ə-ˌlīt, 'trȯi-ˌlīt\ *noun* [German *Troilit*, from Domenico *Troili*, 18th century Italian scientist + German *-it* -ite] (circa 1868)
: a mineral that is a variety of pyrrhotite and that is widely but sparsely distributed (as on earth, in meteorites, and in lunar soil samples)

**Troi·lus** \'trȯi-ləs, 'trō-ə-ləs\ *noun* [Middle English, from Latin, from Greek *Trōïlos*]
: a son of Priam who in medieval legend loved Cressida and lost her to Diomedes

**¹Tro·jan** \'trō-jən\ *noun* [Middle English, from Latin *trojanus* of Troy, from *Troia, Troja* Troy, from Greek *Trōïa*] (14th century)
**1** : a native or inhabitant of Troy
**2** : one who shows qualities (as pluck, endurance, or determined energy) attributed to the defenders of ancient Troy
**3** : a gay, irresponsible, or disreputable companion

**²Trojan** *adjective* (14th century)
**1** : of, relating to, or resembling ancient Troy or its inhabitants
**2** : of, relating to, or constituting a Trojan horse

**Trojan horse** *noun* [from the large hollow wooden horse filled with Greek soldiers and introduced within the walls of Troy by a stratagem] (1837)
**1** : someone or something intended to defeat or subvert from within
**2** : a seemingly useful computer program that contains concealed instructions which when activated perform an illicit or malicious action (as destroying data files); *also* : the concealed instructions of such a program — compare VIRUS

**Trojan War** *noun*
: a 10-year war between the Greeks and Trojans brought on by the abduction of Helen by Paris and ended with the destruction of Troy

**¹troll** \'trōl\ *verb* [Middle English] (15th century)
*transitive verb*
**1** : to cause to move round and round : ROLL
**2 a** : to sing the parts of (as a round or catch) in succession **b** : to sing loudly **c** : to celebrate in song
**3 a** : to fish for by trolling **b** : to fish by trolling in ⟨*troll* lakes⟩ **c** : to pull through the water in trolling ⟨*troll* a lure⟩
*intransitive verb*
**1** : to move around : RAMBLE
**2** : to fish by trailing a lure or baited hook from a moving boat
**3** : to sing or play in a jovial manner
**4** : to speak rapidly
— **troll·er** *noun*

**²troll** *noun* (1869)
: a lure or a line with its lure and hook used in trolling

**³troll** *noun* [Norwegian *troll* & Danish *trold*, from Old Norse *troll* giant, demon; probably akin to Middle High German *trolle* lout] (1616)
: a dwarf or giant in Scandinavian folklore inhabiting caves or hills

**¹trol·ley** *also* **trol·ly** \'trä-lē\ *noun, plural* **trolleys** *also* **trollies** [probably from ¹*troll*] (1823)
**1** *dialect English* : a cart of any of various kinds
**2 a** : a device that carries electric current from an overhead wire to an electrically driven vehicle **b** : a streetcar powered electrically through a trolley — called also *trolley car*
**3** : a wheeled carriage running on an overhead rail or track
**4** *chiefly British* : a cart or wheeled stand used for conveying something (as food or books)

**²trolley** *also* **trolly** *verb* **trol·leyed** *also* **trol·lied; trol·ley·ing** *also* **trol·ly·ing** (1882)
*transitive verb*
: to convey by a trolley
*intransitive verb*
: to ride on a trolley

**trol·ley·bus** \'trä-lē-ˌbəs\ *noun* (1921)
: a bus powered electrically from two overhead wires

**trol·lop** \'trä-ləp\ *noun* [perhaps irregular from *trull*] (1621)
: a vulgar or disreputable woman; *especially* : one who engages in sex promiscuously or for money

**Trombe wall** \'trȯmb-, 'trämb-, 'trōⁿb-\ *noun* [Félix *Trombe* 20th century French designer] (1978)
: a masonry wall that is usually separated from the outdoors by a glass wall and is designed to absorb solar heat and release it into the interior of a building

**trom·bone** \träm-'bōn, (ˌ)tröm-', 'träm-ˌ\ *noun* [Italian, augmentative of *tromba* trumpet, of Germanic origin; akin to Old High German *trumba, trumpa* trumpet] (circa 1724)
: a brass instrument consisting of a long cylindrical metal tube with two turns and having a movable slide or valves for varying the tone and a usual range one octave lower than that of the trumpet
— **trom·bon·ist** \-'bō-nist, -ˌbō-\ *noun*

trombone

**trom·mel** \'trä-məl\ *noun* [German, drum, from Middle High German *trummel*, diminutive of *trumme* drum — more at DRUM] (circa 1877)
: a usually cylindrical or conical revolving screen used especially for screening or sizing rock, ore, or coal

**tromp** \'trämp, 'trȯmp\ *verb* [by alteration] (1883)
*intransitive verb*
**1** : TRAMP 1 ⟨a lot of knocking on doors, *tromping* from room to room —Sara Davidson⟩
**2** : to step hard : STAMP ⟨*tromped* on the brake⟩
*transitive verb*
**1** : TRAMP
**2** : STAMP ⟨*tromps* the accelerator to the floor —Jim Becker⟩
**3 a** : to give a physical beating to **b** : to defeat decisively

**trompe l'oeil** \(ˌ)trȯmp-'lȯi, trȯⁿp-lœ̄i\ *noun, often attributive* [French *trompe-l'œil*, literally, deceive the eye] (1889)
**1** : a style of painting in which objects are depicted with photographically realistic detail; *also* : the use of similar technique in interior decorating
**2** : a trompe l'oeil painting or effect

**-tron** *noun suffix* [Greek, suffix denoting an instrument; akin to Old English *-thor*, suffix denoting an instrument, Latin *-trum*]
**1** : vacuum tube ⟨magne*tron*⟩
**2** : device for the manipulation of subatomic particles ⟨cyclo*tron*⟩

**tro·na** \'trō-nə\ *noun* [Swedish, probably from Arabic *natrūn* natron — more at NATRON] (1799)
: a gray-white or yellowish white monoclinic mineral consisting of a hydrous acid sodium carbonate

**¹troop** \'trüp\ *noun* [Middle French *trope, troupe* company, herd, of Germanic origin; akin to Old English *thorp, throp* village — more at THORP] (1545)
**1 a** : a group of soldiers **b** : a cavalry unit corresponding to an infantry company **c** *plural* : ARMED FORCES, SOLDIERS
**2** : a collection of people or things : CREW 2
**3** : a flock of mammals or birds
**4** : the basic organizational unit of Boy Scouts or Girl Scouts under an adult leader

**²troop** *intransitive verb* (1565)
**1** : to move or gather in crowds
**2** : to go one's way : WALK
**3** : to spend time together : ASSOCIATE
**4** : to move in large numbers

**troop·er** \'trü-pər\ *noun* (1640)
**1 a** (1) : an enlisted cavalryman (2) : the horse of a cavalryman **b** : PARATROOPER **c** : SOLDIER
**2 a** : a mounted police officer **b** : a state police officer
**3** : TROUPER 2

**troop·ship** \'trüp-ˌship\ *noun* (1862)
: a ship for carrying troops : TRANSPORT

**trop-** *or* **tropo-** *combining form* [International Scientific Vocabulary, from Greek *tropos*]
**1** : turn : turning : change ⟨*tropo*sphere⟩
**2** : tropism ⟨*tropic*⟩

**trope** \'trōp\ *noun* [Latin *tropus*, from Greek *tropos* turn, way, manner, style, trope, from *trepein* to turn] (1533)
**1** : the use of a word or expression in a figurative sense : FIGURE OF SPEECH
**2** : a phrase or verse added as an embellishment or interpolation to the sung parts of the Mass in the medieval period

**troph-** *or* **tropho-** *combining form* [French, from Greek, from *trophē* nourishment]
: nutritive ⟨*tropho*blast⟩

**troph·al·lax·is** \ˌtrō-fə-ˈlak-səs\ *noun* [New Latin, from *troph-* + Greek *allaxis* exchange, from *allassein* to change, exchange, from *allos* other — more at ELSE] (1918)
**:** exchange of food (as from special glands) between social insects (as ants or termites)

**tro·phic** \ˈtrō-fik\ *adjective* [French *trophique*, from Greek *trophikos*, from *trophē* nourishment, from *trephein* to nourish] (1873)
**1 :** of or relating to nutrition **:** NUTRITIONAL ⟨*trophic* disorders⟩
**2 :** ³TROPIC
— **tro·phi·cal·ly** \-fi-k(ə-)lē\ *adverb*

**-trophic** *adjective combining form* [New Latin *-trophia* -trophy]
**1 a :** of, relating to, or characterized by (such) nutrition ⟨ecto*trophic*⟩ **b :** requiring or utilizing (such) a kind of nutrition ⟨hetero*trophic*⟩
**2 :** -TROPIC 2 ⟨gonado*trophic*⟩

**trophic level** *noun* (1942)
**:** one of the hierarchical strata of a food web characterized by organisms which are the same number of steps removed from the primary producers

**tro·pho·blast** \ˈtrō-fə-ˌblast\ *noun* [International Scientific Vocabulary] (1889)
**:** a thin layer of ectoderm that forms the wall of many mammalian blastulas and functions in the nutrition and implantation of the embryo
— **tro·pho·blas·tic** \ˌtrō-fə-ˈblas-tik\ *adjective*

**tro·pho·zo·ite** \ˌtrō-fə-ˈzō-ˌīt\ *noun* [*troph-* + *zo-* + ¹*-ite*] (circa 1909)
**:** a protozoan of a vegetative form as distinguished from one of a reproductive or resting form

**tro·phy** \ˈtrō-fē\ *noun, plural* **trophies** [Middle French *trophee*, from Latin *tropaeum, trophaeum*, from Greek *tropaion*, from neuter of *tropaios* of a turning, of a rout, from *tropē* turn, rout, from *trepein* to turn] (15th century)
**1 :** something gained or given in victory or conquest especially when preserved or mounted as a memorial
**2 a :** a memorial of an ancient Greek or Roman victory raised on the field of battle or in case of a naval victory on the nearest land **b :** a representation of such a memorial (as on a medal); *also* **:** an architectural ornament representing a group of military weapons
**3 :** a game animal or fish suitable for mounting as a trophy — usually used attributively
◆
— **trophy** *transitive verb*

**-trophy** *noun combining form* [New Latin *-trophia*, from Greek, from *-trophos* nourishing, from *trephein*]
**:** nutrition **:** nurture **:** growth ⟨dys*trophy*⟩

**¹trop·ic** \ˈträ-pik\ *noun* [Middle English *tropik*, from Latin *tropicus* of the solstice, from Greek *tropikos*, from *tropē* turn] (1527)
**1 :** either of the two parallels of terrestrial latitude at a distance of about 23½ degrees north or south of the equator where the sun is directly overhead when it reaches its most northerly or southerly point in the sky — compare TROPIC OF CANCER, TROPIC OF CAPRICORN
**2** *plural, often capitalized* **:** the region lying between the tropics

**²tropic** *adjective* (1551)
**:** of, relating to, or occurring in the tropics **:** TROPICAL

**³tro·pic** \ˈtrō-pik\ *adjective* [*trop-*] (1903)
**1 :** of, relating to, or characteristic of tropism or of a tropism
**2** *of a hormone* **:** influencing the activity of a specified gland

**-tropic** *adjective combining form* [French *-tropique*, from Greek *-tropos* -tropous]
**1 :** turning, changing, or tending to turn or change in a (specified) manner or in response to a (specified) stimulus ⟨geo*tropic*⟩
**2 :** attracted to or acting upon (something specified) ⟨neuro*tropic*⟩

**trop·i·cal** \for 1 ˈträ-pi-kəl, for 2 ˈtrō- *also* ˈträ-\ *adjective* (1527)

**1 a :** of, relating to, occurring in, or suitable for use in the tropics **b :** of, being, or characteristic of a region or climate that is frost-free with temperatures high enough to support year-round plant growth given sufficient moisture ⟨*tropical* Florida⟩
**2** [Latin *tropicus*, from Greek *tropikos*, from *tropos* trope] **:** FIGURATIVE 2
— **trop·i·cal·ly** \-pi-k(ə-)lē\ *adverb*

**tropical aquarium** *noun* (circa 1948)
**:** an aquarium kept at a uniform warmth and used especially for tropical fish

**tropical cyclone** *noun* (1920)
**:** a cyclone in the tropics characterized by winds rotating at a rate of 74 miles (119 kilometers) an hour or more

**tropical fish** *noun* (1931)
**:** any of various small usually showy fishes of tropical origin often kept in the tropical aquarium

**trop·i·cal·ize** \ˈträ-pi-kə-ˌlīz\ *transitive verb* **-ized; -iz·ing** (1885)
**1 :** to make tropical (as in character, conditions, or appearance)
**2 :** to fit or adapt for use in a tropical climate especially by measures designed to combat the effects of fungi and moisture

**tropical oil** *noun* (1988)
**:** any of several oils (as coconut oil and palm oil) that are high in saturated fatty acids

**tropical rain forest** *noun* (1926)
**:** RAIN FOREST 1

**tropical sprue** *noun* (circa 1955)
**:** SPRUE 2

**tropical storm** *noun* (circa 1945)
**:** a tropical cyclone with strong winds of less than hurricane intensity

**tropic bird** *noun* (circa 1681)
**:** any of a genus (*Phaethon* of the family Phaethontidae) of web-footed birds that are related to the pelicans, are found chiefly in tropical seas often far from land, and have mostly white satiny plumage marked with a little black, a greatly elongated central pair of tail feathers, and a bright-colored bill

**tropic bird**

**tropic of Cancer** [from the sign of the zodiac which its celestial projection intersects] (1555)
**:** the parallel of latitude that is approximately 23½ degrees north of the equator and that is the northernmost latitude reached by the overhead sun

**tropic of Capricorn** [from the sign of the zodiac which its celestial projection intersects] (1545)
**:** the parallel of latitude that is approximately 23½ degrees south of the equator and that is the southernmost latitude reached by the overhead sun

**-tropin** *or* **-trophin** *noun combining form* [*-tropin*, alteration of *-trophin*, from *-trophic* + ¹*-in*]
**:** hormone ⟨gonado*tropin*⟩ ⟨somato*tropin*⟩

**tro·pism** \ˈtrō-ˌpi-zəm\ *noun* [International Scientific Vocabulary *-tropism*] (1899)
**1 a :** involuntary orientation by an organism or one of its parts that involves turning or curving by movement or by differential growth and is a positive or negative response to a source of stimulation **b :** a reflex reaction involving a tropism
**2 :** an innate tendency to react in a definite manner to stimuli; *broadly* **:** a natural inclination **:** PROPENSITY
— **tro·pis·tic** \trō-ˈpis-tik\ *adjective*

**-tropism** *noun combining form* [International Scientific Vocabulary, from *trop-*]
**:** tropism ⟨helio*tropism*⟩

**tropo-** — see TROP-

**tro·po·col·la·gen** \ˌträ-pə-ˈkä-lə-jən, ˌtrō-\ *noun* (1954)
**:** a subunit of collagen fibrils consisting of three polypeptide strands arranged in a helix

**tro·po·log·i·cal** \ˌtrō-pə-ˈlä-ji-kəl, ˌträ-\ *also* **tro·po·log·ic** \-jik\ *adjective* (14th century)
**1 :** of, relating to, or involving biblical interpretation stressing moral metaphor; *also* **:** MORAL
**2 :** characterized or varied by tropes **:** FIGURATIVE
— **tro·po·log·i·cal·ly** \-ji-k(ə-)lē\ *adverb*

**tropo·my·o·sin** \ˌträ-pə-ˈmī-ə-sən, ˌtrō-\ *noun* (1946)
**:** a protein of muscle that forms a complex with troponin regulating the interaction of actin and myosin in muscular contraction

**tro·po·nin** \ˈtrō-pə-nən, ˈträ-, -ˌnin\ *noun* [by shortening & alteration from *tropomyosin*] (1966)
**:** a protein of muscle that together with tropomyosin forms a regulatory protein complex controlling the interaction of actin and myosin and that when combined with calcium ions permits muscular contraction

**tro·po·pause** \ˈtrō-pə-ˌpóz, ˈträ-\ *noun* [International Scientific Vocabulary *tropo*sphere + *pause*] (1918)
**:** the region at the top of the troposphere; *also* **:** a comparable layer of a celestial body

**tro·po·sphere** \ˈtrō-pə-ˌsfir, ˈträ-\ *noun* [International Scientific Vocabulary] (1909)
**:** the lowest densest part of the earth's atmosphere in which most weather changes occur and temperature generally decreases rapidly with altitude and which extends from the surface to the bottom of the stratosphere
— **tro·po·spher·ic** \ˌtrō-pə-ˈsfir-ik, ˌträ-, -ˈsfer-\ *adjective*

**tro·po·tax·is** \ˌtrō-pə-ˈtak-səs, ˌträ-\ *noun* [New Latin] (1934)
**:** a taxis in which an organism orients itself by the simultaneous comparison of stimuli of different intensity acting on separate end organs

**-tropous** *adjective combining form* [Greek *-tropos*, from *trepein* to turn]
**:** turning or curving in (such) a way **:** exhibiting (such) a tropism ⟨ana*tropous*⟩

**-tropy** *noun combining form* [French *-tropie*, from Greek *-tropia*, from *-tropos*]
**1 :** condition of exhibiting (such) a behavior ⟨allo*tropy*⟩

◇ **WORD HISTORY**
**trophy** After a military victory, the ancient Greeks had a custom of hanging captured enemy arms and armor from a stake or tree somewhere on the battlefield, ideally at the spot where the enemy had first turned in retreat. The Greek name for such a memorial was *tropaion*, from the neuter form of the adjective *tropaios* "of or relating to a turn or rout," a derivative of *tropē* "turn, rout." Eventually *tropaion* was applied to much more elaborate and permanent victory memorials of stone or bronze, ones not necessarily erected on the actual battlefield. From Hellenistic Greece the ancient Romans took the custom as well as the word, which was Latinized as *tropaeum*, later *trophaeum*. English borrowed the word via French as *trophe* in the 16th century. From its original classical reference, the meaning of *trophy* has been generalized to apply to anything that could be displayed as a reminder of success, whether in war, sports, or life.

\ə\ abut \ᵊ\ kitten \ər\ further \a\ ash \ā\ ace
\ä\ mop, mar \aù\ out \ch\ chin \e\ bet \ē\ easy
\g\ go \i\ hit \ī\ ice \j\ job \ŋ\ sing \ō\ go
\ò\ law \òi\ boy \th\ thin \t̷h\ the \ü\ loot \ù\ foot
\y\ yet \zh\ vision *see also* Guide to Pronunciation

**2 :** change in a (specified) way or in response to a (specified) stimulus ⟨thixo*tropy*⟩

**¹trot** \'trät\ *noun* [Middle English, from Middle French, from *troter* to trot, of Germanic origin; akin to Old High German *trottōn* to tread, Old English *tredan*] (14th century) **1 a** (1) **:** a moderately fast gait of a quadruped (as a horse) in which the legs move in diagonal pairs (2) **:** a jogging gait of a human that falls between a walk and a run **b :** a ride on horseback **2 :** an old woman **3 :** a literal translation of a foreign text **4** *plural* **:** DIARRHEA

**²trot** *verb* **trot·ted; trot·ting** (14th century) *intransitive verb* **1 :** to ride, drive, or proceed at a trot ⟨the fox *trotted* over the knoll⟩ **2 :** to proceed briskly **:** HURRY ~ *transitive verb* **1 :** to cause to go at a trot **2 :** to traverse at a trot

**³trot** *noun* (1883) **:** TROTLINE; *also* **:** one of the short lines with hooks that are attached to it at intervals

**¹troth** \'träth, 'tròth, 'trōth, *or with* th\ *noun* [Middle English *trouth*, from Old English *trēowth* — more at TRUTH] (13th century) **1 :** loyal or pledged faithfulness **:** FIDELITY **2 :** one's pledged word; *also* **:** BETROTHAL

**²troth** *transitive verb* (15th century) **:** PLEDGE, BETROTH

**¹troth·plight** \'träth-,plīt, 'tròth-, 'trōth-\ *transitive verb* (15th century) **:** BETROTH

**²trothplight** *noun* (1513) **:** BETROTHAL

**trot·line** \'trät-,līn\ *noun* [probably from ²*trot*] (1826) **:** SETLINE; *especially* **:** a comparatively short setline used near shore or along streams

**trot out** *transitive verb* (1838) **1 :** to lead out and show the paces of (as a horse) **2 :** to bring forward for display ⟨always *trots out* some new excuse⟩

**Trots·ky·ism** \'trät-skē-,i-zəm, 'tròt-\ *noun* (1925) **:** the political, economic, and social principles advocated by Trotsky; *especially* **:** the theory and practice of communism developed by or associated with Trotsky and usually including adherence to the concept of worldwide revolution as opposed to socialism in one country — **Trots·ky·ist** \-skē-ist\ *noun or adjective* — **Trots·ky·ite** \-skē-,īt\ *noun or adjective*

**trot·ter** \'trä-tər\ *noun* (14th century) **1 :** one that trots; *specifically* **:** a standardbred horse trained for harness racing **2 :** a pig's foot used as food

**trou·ba·dour** \'trü-bə-,dōr, -,dòr, -,dùr\ *noun* [French, from Old Provençal *trobador*, from *trobar* to compose, probably from (assumed) Vulgar Latin *tropare*, from Latin *tropus* trope] (circa 1741) **:** one of a class of lyric poets and poet-musicians often of knightly rank who flourished from the 11th to the end of the 13th century chiefly in the south of France and the north of Italy and whose major theme was courtly love — compare TROUVÈRE

**¹trou·ble** \'trə-bəl\ *verb* **trou·bled; troubling** \'trə-b(ə-)liŋ\ [Middle English, from Old French *tourbler*, *troubler*, from (assumed) Vulgar Latin *turbulare*, from *turbulus* agitated, alteration of Latin *turbulentus* — more at TURBULENT] (13th century) *transitive verb* **1 a :** to agitate mentally or spiritually **:** WORRY, DISTURB **b** (1) *archaic* **:** MISTREAT, OPPRESS (2) **:** to produce physical disorder in **:** AFFLICT ⟨*troubled* by a cold⟩ **c :** to put to exertion or inconvenience **2 :** to put into confused motion ⟨the wind *troubled* the sea⟩ *intransitive verb*

**1 :** to become mentally agitated **:** WORRY ⟨refused to *trouble* over trifles⟩ **2 :** to make an effort **:** be at pains ⟨did not *trouble* to come⟩ — **trou·bler** \-b(ə-)lər\ *noun*

**²trouble** *noun* (13th century) **1 :** the quality or state of being troubled especially mentally **2 :** public unrest or disturbance ⟨there's *trouble* brewing downtown⟩ **3 :** an instance of trouble ⟨used to disguise her frustrations and despair by making light of her *troubles* —*Current Biography*⟩ **4 :** a state or condition of distress, annoyance, or difficulty ⟨in *trouble* with the law⟩ ⟨heading for *trouble*⟩ ⟨got into financial *trouble*⟩: as **a :** a condition of physical distress or ill health **:** AILMENT ⟨back *trouble*⟩ ⟨heart *trouble*⟩ **b :** a condition of mechanical malfunction ⟨engine *trouble*⟩ **c :** a condition of doing something badly or only with great difficulty ⟨has *trouble* reading⟩ ⟨has *trouble* breathing⟩ **d :** pregnancy out of wedlock ⟨got a girl in *trouble*⟩ **5 :** an effort made **:** PAINS ⟨took the *trouble* to do it right⟩ **6 a :** a cause of distress, annoyance, or inconvenience ⟨don't mean to be any *trouble*⟩ ⟨what's the *trouble?*⟩ **b :** a negative feature **:** DRAWBACK ⟨the *trouble* with you is you're too honest⟩ ⟨the main *trouble* with electronic systems is the overreliance on them —John Perham⟩ **c :** the unhappy or sad fact ⟨the *trouble* is, I need the money⟩

**trou·bled** \'trə-bəld\ *adjective* (14th century) **1 a :** CONCERNED, WORRIED ⟨*troubled* feelings about the decision⟩ **b :** emotionally or mentally disturbed ⟨a home for *troubled* children⟩ **2 :** characterized by or indicative of trouble ⟨our *troubled* cities⟩ ⟨a gray and *troubled* sky⟩

**trou·ble·mak·er** \'trə-bəl-,mā-kər\ *noun* (circa 1914) **:** a person who consciously or unconsciously causes trouble — **trou·ble·mak·ing** \-kiŋ\ *adjective or noun*

**trou·ble·shoot** \-,shüt\ *verb* **-shot** \-,shät\; **-shoot·ing** [back-formation from *troubleshooter*] (1918) *intransitive verb* **:** to operate or serve as a troubleshooter ⟨is *troubleshooting* for an electronics firm⟩ *transitive verb* **:** to investigate or deal with in the role of troubleshooter ⟨*troubleshoots* TV receivers⟩

**trou·ble·shoot·er** \-,shü-tər\ *noun* (1905) **1 :** a skilled worker employed to locate trouble and make repairs in machinery and technical equipment **2 :** an expert in resolving diplomatic or political disputes **:** a mediator of disputes that are at an impasse **3 :** a person skilled at solving or anticipating problems or difficulties

**trou·ble·some** \-səm\ *adjective* (1542) **1 :** DIFFICULT, BURDENSOME **2 :** giving trouble or anxiety **:** VEXATIOUS — **trou·ble·some·ly** *adverb* — **trou·ble·some·ness** *noun*

**trou·blous** \'trə-b(ə-)ləs\ *adjective* (15th century) **1 :** full of trouble **:** STORMY ⟨these *troublous* times⟩ **2 :** causing trouble **:** TROUBLESOME ⟨inflation is a *troublous* matter⟩ — **trou·blous·ly** *adverb* — **trou·blous·ness** *noun*

**trough** \'tròf, 'tròth, *by bakers often* 'trō\ *noun, plural* **troughs** \'tròfs, 'tròvz; 'tròths, 'trò(th)z; 'tròz\ [Middle English, from Old English *trog;* akin to Old High German *trog* trough, Old English *trēow* tree, wood — more at TREE] (before 12th century) **1 a :** a long shallow often V-shaped receptacle for the drinking water or feed of domestic animals **b :** any of various domestic or industrial containers

**2 a :** a conduit, drain, or channel for water; *especially* **:** a gutter along the eaves of a building **b :** a long and narrow or shallow channel or depression (as between waves or hills); *especially* **:** a long but shallow depression in the bed of the sea — compare TRENCH **3 :** the minimum point of a complete cycle of a periodic function: as **a :** an elongated area of low barometric pressure **b :** the low point in a business cycle

**trounce** \'traůn(t)s\ *transitive verb* **trounced; trounc·ing** [origin unknown] (1868) **:** to thrash or punish severely; *especially* **:** to defeat decisively

**¹troupe** \'trüp\ *noun* [French, from Middle French — more at TROOP] (1825) **:** COMPANY, TROOP; *especially* **:** a group of theatrical performers

**²troupe** *intransitive verb* **trouped; troup·ing** (1900) **:** to travel in a troupe; *also* **:** to perform as a member of a theatrical troupe

**troup·er** \'trü-pər\ *noun* (1890) **1 :** a member of a troupe; *especially* **:** ACTOR **2 :** a person who deals with and persists through difficulty or hardship without complaint ⟨you're a real *trouper* to wait so long⟩

**trou·pi·al** \'trü-pē-əl\ *noun* [French *troupiale*, from *troupe;* from its living in flocks] (1825) **:** a large showy oriole (*Icterus icterus*) of Central and South America; *also* **:** any of various related birds (family Icteridae)

**¹trou·ser** \'traů-zər\ *noun* [alteration of earlier *trouse*, from Scottish Gaelic *triubhas*] (1613) **:** ³PANT 1 — usually used in plural

**²trouser** *adjective* (circa 1771) **1 :** of, relating to, or designed for trousers ⟨*trouser* pockets⟩ **2 :** of or relating to a male dramatic role played by a woman

**trouser suit** *noun* (1939) *chiefly British* **:** PANTSUIT

**trous·seau** \'trü-(,)sō, trü-'\ *noun, plural* **trous·seaux** \-(,)sōz, -'sōz\ *or* **trousseaus** [French, from Old French, diminutive of *trousse* bundle, from *trousser* to truss] (1833) **:** the personal possessions of a bride usually including clothes, accessories, and household linens and wares

**trout** \'traůt\ *noun, plural* **trout** *also* **trouts** [Middle English, from Old English *trūht*, from Late Latin *trocta, tructa*, a fish with sharp teeth, from Greek *trōktēs*, literally, gnawer, from *trōgein* to gnaw — more at TROGLODYTE] (before 12th century) **1 :** any of various salmonid food and sport fishes that are mostly smaller than the typical salmons and are anadromous or restricted to cool clear fresh waters: **a :** any of various Old or New World fishes (genera *Salmo* and *Oncorhynchus*) — compare BROWN TROUT, RAINBOW TROUT **b :** ¹CHAR **2 :** any of various fishes (as the largemouth bass) held to resemble the true trouts

**trout lily** *noun* [probably from its speckled leaves] (circa 1898) **:** DOGTOOTH VIOLET

**trout–perch** \'traůt-,pərch\ *noun* (1883) **:** a small freshwater fish (*Percopsis omiscomaycus* of the family Percopsidae) chiefly of northern North America having a scaleless head and large eyes

**trouty** \'traů-tē\ *adjective* **trout·i·er; -est** (1676) **:** containing or likely to contain abundant trout

**trou·vère** \trü-'ver\ *noun* [French, from Old French *troveor, troverre*, from *trover* to compose, find, from (assumed) Vulgar Latin *tropare* — more at TROUBADOUR] (1795) **:** one of a school of poets who flourished from the 11th to the 14th centuries and who composed mostly narrative works (as chansons de geste and fabliaux) — compare TROUBADOUR

**trove** \'trōv\ *noun* [short for *treasure trove*] (1888)
**1** : DISCOVERY, FIND
**2** : a valuable collection : TREASURE; *also* : HAUL, COLLECTION

**tro·ver** \'trō-vər\ *noun* [Middle French *trover* to find, from Old French] (1594)
: a common law action to recover the value of goods wrongfully converted to another's own use

**trow** \'trō\ *verb* [Middle English, from Old English *trēowan;* akin to Old English *trēowe* faithful, true — more at TRUE] (before 12th century)
**1** *obsolete* : BELIEVE
**2** *archaic* : THINK

**¹trow·el** \'trau̇(-ə)l\ *noun* [Middle English *truel,* from Middle French *truelle,* from Late Latin *truella,* from Latin *trulla* ladle] (14th century)
: any of various hand tools used to apply, spread, shape, or smooth loose or plastic material; *also* : a scoop-shaped or flat-bladed garden tool for taking up and setting small plants

**²trowel** *transitive verb* **-eled** *or* **-elled; -el·ing** *or* **-el·ling** (circa 1670)
: to smooth, mix, or apply with or as if with a trowel
— **trow·el·er** *noun*

trowel: *1* gardener's, *2* plasterer's, *3* bricklayer's

**troy** \'troi\ *adjective* [Middle English *troye,* from *Troyes,* France] (15th century)
: expressed in troy weight

**troy weight** *noun* (15th century)
: a series of units of weight based on a pound of 12 ounces and an ounce of 480 grains — see WEIGHT table

**tru·an·cy** \'trü-ən(t)-sē\ *noun, plural* **-cies** (1784)
: an act or instance of playing truant : the state of being truant

**¹tru·ant** \'trü-ənt\ *noun* [Middle English, vagabond, idler, from Old French, vagrant, of Celtic origin; akin to Old Irish *trógán* wretch, *trúag* wretched] (15th century)
: one who shirks duty; *especially* : one who stays out of school without permission

**²truant** *adjective* (1561)
**1** : shirking responsibility
**2** : being, resembling, or characteristic of a truant

**³truant** *intransitive verb* (1580)
: to idle away time especially while playing truant

**truant officer** *noun* (1872)
: ATTENDANCE OFFICER

**tru·ant·ry** \'trü-ən-trē\ *noun, plural* **-ries** (15th century)
: TRUANCY

**¹truce** \'trüs\ *noun* [Middle English *trewes,* plural of *trewe* agreement, from Old English *trēow* fidelity; akin to Old English *trēowe* faithful — more at TRUE] (13th century)
**1** : a suspension of fighting especially of considerable duration by agreement of opposing forces : ARMISTICE, CEASE-FIRE
**2** : a respite especially from a disagreeable or painful state or action

**²truce** *verb* **truced; truc·ing** (1569)
*intransitive verb*
: to make a truce
*transitive verb*
: to end with a truce

**¹truck** \'trək\ *verb* [Middle English *trukken,* from Old French *troquer*] (13th century)
*transitive verb*
**1** : to give in exchange : SWAP
**2** : to barter or dispose of by barter
*intransitive verb*
**1** : to exchange commodities : BARTER
**2** : to negotiate or traffic especially in an underhanded way : have dealings

**²truck** *noun* (1553)

**1** : BARTER
**2** : commodities appropriate for barter or for small trade
**3** : close association or connection ⟨will have no *truck* with crooks⟩
**4** : payment of wages in goods instead of cash
**5** : vegetables grown for market
**6** : heterogeneous small articles often of little value; *also* : RUBBISH

**³truck** *noun* [probably back-formation from *truckle* small wheel — more at TRUCKLE BED] (1611)
**1** : a small wheel; *specifically* : a small strong wheel for a gun carriage
**2** : a small wooden cap at the top of a flagstaff or masthead usually having holes for reeving flag or signal halyards
**3** : a wheeled vehicle for moving heavy articles: as **a** : a strong horse-drawn or automotive vehicle for hauling **b** : a small barrow consisting of a rectangular frame having at one end a pair of handles and at the other end a pair of small heavy wheels and a projecting edge to slide under a load — called also *hand truck* **c** : a small heavy rectangular frame supported on four wheels for moving heavy objects **d** : a small flat-topped car pushed or pulled by hand **e** : a shelved stand mounted on casters **f** : an automotive vehicle with a short chassis equipped with a swivel for attaching a trailer and used especially for the highway hauling of freight; *also* : a truck with attached trailer
**4 a** *British* : an open railroad freight car **b** : a swiveling carriage consisting of a frame with one or more pairs of wheels and springs to carry and guide one end (as of a railroad car) in turning sharp curves
— **truck·ful** \-ˌfu̇l\ *noun*

**⁴truck** (1748)
*transitive verb*
: to load or transport on a truck
*intransitive verb*
**1** : to transport goods by truck
**2** : to be employed in driving a truck
**3** : to roll along especially in an easy untroubled way

**truck·age** \'trə-kij\ *noun* (1830)
**1** : conveyance by truck
**2** : money paid for conveyance on a truck

**¹truck·er** \'trə-kər\ *noun* [¹*truck*] (1598)
**1** : one that barters
**2** *Scottish* : PEDDLER

**²trucker** *noun* [⁴*truck*] (1878)
**1** : one whose business is transporting goods by truck
**2** : a truck driver

**truck farm** *noun* [²*truck*] (1866)
: a farm devoted to the production of vegetables for the market
— **truck farmer** *noun*

**truck·ing** *noun* (1809)
: the process or business of transporting goods on trucks

**truck·le** \'trə-kəl\ *intransitive verb* **truck·led; truck·ling** \-k(ə-)liŋ\ [from the lower position of the truckle bed] (1667)
: to act in a subservient manner : SUBMIT
*synonym* see FAWN
— **truck·ler** \-k(ə-)lər\ *noun*

**truckle bed** *noun* [*truckle* small wheel, pulley, from Middle English *trocle,* from Latin *trochlea* block of pulleys — more at TROCHLEA] (15th century)
: TRUNDLE BED

**truck·line** \'trək-ˌlīn\ *noun* (1924)
: a transportation line using trucks

**truck·load** \-'lōd, -ˌlōd\ *noun* (1862)
**1** : a load or amount that fills or could fill a truck
**2** : the minimum weight required for shipping at truckload rates

**truck·man** \-mən\ *noun* (1787)
**1** : ²TRUCKER
**2** : a member of a fire department unit that operates a hook and ladder truck

**truck·mas·ter** \-ˌmas-tər\ *noun* (1637)
*archaic* : an officer in charge of trade with Indians especially among the early settlers

**truck stop** *noun* (circa 1951)
: a facility especially for truckers that is usually by a highway and that includes a diner, fuel pumps, and a garage

**truck system** *noun* (1830)
: the system of paying wages in goods instead of cash

**tru·cu·lence** \'trə-kyə-lən(t)s *also* 'trü-\ *noun* (circa 1727)
: the quality or state of being truculent

**tru·cu·len·cy** \-lən(t)-sē\ *noun* (1569)
: TRUCULENCE

**tru·cu·lent** \-lənt\ *adjective* [Latin *truculentus,* from *truc-, trux* savage; perhaps akin to Middle Irish *trú* doomed person] (circa 1540)
**1** : feeling or displaying ferocity : CRUEL, SAVAGE
**2** : DEADLY, DESTRUCTIVE
**3** : scathingly harsh : VITRIOLIC
**4** : aggressively self-assertive : BELLIGERENT
— **tru·cu·lent·ly** *adverb*

**¹trudge** \'trəj\ *verb* **trudged; trudg·ing** [origin unknown] (1547)
*intransitive verb*
: to walk or march steadily and usually laboriously ⟨*trudged* through deep snow⟩
*transitive verb*
: to trudge along or over
— **trudg·er** *noun*

**²trudge** *noun* (1835)
: a long tiring walk : TRAMP

**trud·gen stroke** \'trə-jən-\ *noun* [John *Trudgen* (died 1902) English swimmer] (1893)
: a swimming stroke consisting of alternating overarm strokes and a scissors kick

**¹true** \'trü\ *adjective* **tru·er; tru·est** [Middle English *trewe,* from Old English *trēowe* faithful; akin to Old High German *gitriuwi* faithful, Old Irish *derb* sure, and probably to Sanskrit *dāruṇa* hard, *dāru* wood — more at TREE] (before 12th century)
**1 a** : STEADFAST, LOYAL **b** : HONEST, JUST **c** *archaic* : TRUTHFUL
**2 a** (1) : being in accordance with the actual state of affairs ⟨*true* description⟩ (2) : conformable to an essential reality (3) : fully realized or fulfilled ⟨dreams come *true*⟩ **b** : IDEAL, ESSENTIAL **c** : being that which is the case rather than what is manifest or assumed ⟨the *true* dimension of the problem⟩ **d** : CONSISTENT ⟨*true* to character⟩
**3 a** : properly so called ⟨*true* love⟩ ⟨the *true* faith⟩ ⟨the *true* stomach of ruminant mammals⟩ **b** (1) : possessing the basic characters of and belonging to the same natural group as ⟨a whale is a *true* but not a typical mammal⟩ (2) : TYPICAL ⟨the *true* cats⟩
**4** : LEGITIMATE, RIGHTFUL ⟨our *true* and lawful king⟩
**5 a** : that is fitted or formed or that functions accurately **b** : conformable to a standard or pattern : ACCURATE
**6** : determined with reference to the earth's axis rather than the magnetic poles ⟨*true* north⟩
**7** : logically necessary
**8** : NARROW, STRICT ⟨in the *truest* sense⟩
**9** : corrected for error
— **true·ness** *noun*

**²true** *adverb* (14th century)
**1** : in accordance with fact or reality
**2 a** : without deviation ⟨the bullet flew straight and *true*⟩ **b** : without variation from type ⟨breed *true*⟩

**³true** *noun* (1812)
**1** : TRUTH, REALITY — usually used with *the*

---

\ə\ abut \ᵊ\ kitten \ər\ further \a\ ash \ā\ ace
\ä\ mop, mar \au̇\ out \ch\ chin \e\ bet \ē\ easy
\g\ go \i\ hit \ī\ ice \j\ job \ŋ\ sing \ō\ go
\ȯ\ law \ȯi\ boy \th\ thin \t̷h\ the \ü\ loot \u̇\ foot
\y\ yet \zh\ vision   *see also* Guide to Pronunciation

**2 :** the quality or state of being accurate (as in alignment or adjustment) — used in the phrases *in true* and *out of true*

**⁴true** *transitive verb* **trued; true·ing** *also* **tru·ing** (1841)
**:** to make level, square, balanced, or concentric : bring or restore to a desired mechanical accuracy or form ⟨*true* up a board⟩ ⟨*true* up an engine cylinder⟩

**true believer** *noun* (circa 1820)
**1 :** one who professes absolute belief in something
**2 :** a zealous supporter of a particular cause

**true bill** *noun* (1769)
**:** a bill of indictment endorsed by a grand jury as warranting prosecution of the accused

**true–blue** *adjective* (1674)
**1 :** marked by unswerving loyalty (as to a party)
**2 :** GENUINE ⟨a *true-blue* romantic⟩

**true blue** *noun* [from the association of blue with constancy] (1762)
**:** one who is true-blue

**true–born** \'trü-'bȯrn\ *adjective* (1591)
**:** genuinely such by birth ⟨a *trueborn* Englishman —Shakespeare⟩

**true bug** *noun* (1895)
**:** BUG 1c

**true–false test** \'trü-'fȯls-\ *noun* (1924)
**:** a test consisting of a series of statements to be marked as true or false

**true·heart·ed** \-'här-təd\ *adjective* (15th century)
**:** FAITHFUL, LOYAL
— **true·heart·ed·ness** *noun*

**true–life** \'trü-'līf\ *adjective* (1926)
**:** true to life ⟨a *true-life* story⟩

**true·love** \'trü-,ləv\ *noun* (14th century)
**:** one truly beloved or loving : SWEETHEART

**true lover's knot** *noun* (1615)
**:** a complicated ornamental knot not readily untied and symbolic of mutual love — called also *truelove knot;* see KNOT illustration

**true·pen·ny** \'trü-,pe-nē\ *noun* (1595)
**:** an honest or trusty person

**true rib** *noun* (1741)
**:** any of the ribs having costal cartilages connected directly with the sternum and in humans constituting the first seven pairs

**true seal** *noun* (1923)
**:** HAIR SEAL

**truf·fle** \'trə-fəl, 'trü-\ *noun* [modification of Middle French *truffe,* from Old Provençal *trufa,* from (assumed) Vulgar Latin *tufera;* akin to Latin *tuber* swelling, truffle — more at TUBER] (1591)
**1 :** the usually dark and rugose edible subterranean fruiting body of several European ascomycetous fungi (especially genus *Tuber*); *also* **:** one of these fungi
**2 :** a candy made of chocolate, butter, sugar, and sometimes liqueur shaped into balls and often coated with cocoa

**truf·fled** \-fəld\ *adjective* (1837)
**:** cooked, stuffed, or garnished with truffles

**trug** \'trəg\ *noun* [origin unknown] (circa 1864)
*chiefly British* **:** a shallow rectangular gardening basket

**tru·ism** \'trü-,i-zəm\ *noun* (1708)
**:** an undoubted or self-evident truth; *especially* **:** one too obvious for mention
— **tru·is·tic** \trü-'is-tik\ *adjective*

**trull** \'trəl\ *noun* [German *Trulle,* from Middle High German; akin to Middle High German *trolle* lout — more at TROLL] (1519)
**:** PROSTITUTE, STRUMPET

**tru·ly** \'trü-lē\ *adverb* (13th century)
**1 a :** INDEED — often used as an intensive ⟨*truly,* she is fair⟩ or interjectionally to express astonishment or doubt **b :** without feigning, falsity, or inaccuracy in truth or fact
**2 :** in all sincerity : SINCERELY — often used with *yours* as a complimentary close
**3 :** in agreement with fact : TRUTHFULLY
**4 :** with exactness of construction or operation
**5 :** in a proper or suitable manner

**¹trump** \'trəmp\ *noun* [Middle English *trompe,* from Old French, of Germanic origin; akin to Old High German *trumba, trumpa* trumpet] (14th century)
**1 a :** TRUMPET **b** *chiefly Scottish* **:** JEW'S HARP
**2 :** a sound of or as if of trumpeting ⟨the *trump* of doom⟩

**²trump** *noun* [alteration of ¹*triumph*] (1529)
**1 a :** a card of a suit any of whose cards will win over a card that is not of this suit **b :** the suit whose cards are trumps for a particular hand — often used in plural
**2 :** a decisive overriding factor or final resource
**3 :** a dependable and exemplary person

**³trump** (1586)
*transitive verb*
**1 :** to get the better of : OUTDO
**2 :** to play a trump on (a card or trick) when another suit was led
*intransitive verb*
**:** to play a trump when another suit was led

**trump card** *noun* (1822)
**1 :** ²TRUMP 1a, 2

**trumped–up** \'trəm(p)t-'əp\ *adjective* (1728)
**:** fraudulently concocted : SPURIOUS ⟨*trumped-up* charges⟩

**trum·pery** \'trəm-p(ə-)rē\ *noun* [Middle English *tromperie* deceit, from Middle French, from *tromper* to deceive] (15th century)
**1 a :** worthless nonsense **b :** trivial or useless articles : JUNK ⟨a wagon loaded with household *trumpery* —Washington Irving⟩
**2** *archaic* **:** tawdry finery
— **trumpery** *adjective*

**¹trum·pet** \'trəm-pət\ *noun* [Middle English *trompette,* from Middle French, from Old French *trompe* trump] (14th century)
**1 a :** a wind instrument consisting of a conical or cylindrical usually metal tube, a cup-shaped mouthpiece, and a flared bell; *specifically* **:** a valved brass instrument having a cylindrical tube with two turns and a usual range from F sharp below middle C upward for 2½ octaves **b :** a musical instrument (as a cornet) resembling a trumpet
**2 :** a trumpet player
**3 :** something that resembles a trumpet or its tonal quality: as **a :** a funnel-shaped instrument (as a megaphone) for collecting, directing, or intensifying sound **b** (1) **:** a stentorian voice (2) **:** a penetrating cry (as of an elephant)
— **trum·pet·like** *adjective*

trumpet 1a

**²trumpet** (1530)
*intransitive verb*
**1 :** to blow a trumpet
**2 :** to make a sound suggestive of that of a trumpet
*transitive verb*
**:** to sound or proclaim on or as if on a trumpet

**trumpet creeper** *noun* (1818)
**:** a North American woody vine (*Campsis radicans* of the family Bignoniaceae, the trumpet-creeper family) having pinnate leaves and large typically red trumpet-shaped flowers

**trum·pet·er** \'trəm-pə-tər\ *noun* (15th century)
**1 a :** a trumpet player; *specifically* **:** one that gives signals with a trumpet **b :** one that praises or advocates : EULOGIST, SPOKESMAN
**2 a :** any of a genus (*Psophia* of the family Psophiidae) of several large gregarious long-legged long-necked South American birds related to the cranes **b :** any of an Asian breed of pigeons with a rounded crest and heavily feathered feet

trumpet creeper

**trumpeter swan** *noun* (1834)
**:** a rare pure white North American wild swan (*Cygnus buccinator*) that is noted for its sonorous voice and is sometimes considered a subspecies (*C. cygnus buccinator*) of the whooper swan

**trumpet flower** *noun* (circa 1731)
**1 :** any of various plants (as a trumpet creeper or a datura) with trumpet-shaped flowers
**2 :** the flower of a trumpet flower

**trumpet honeysuckle** *noun* (1731)
**:** a North American honeysuckle (*Lonicera sempervirens*) with coral-red or orange flowers having a trumpet-shaped corolla

**trumpet vine** *noun* (1709)
**:** TRUMPET CREEPER

**trump up** *transitive verb* (1695)
**1 :** to concoct especially with intent to deceive : FABRICATE, INVENT
**2** *archaic* **:** to cite as support for an action or claim

**¹trun·cate** \'trəŋ-,kāt, 'trən-\ *adjective* [Latin *truncatus,* past participle of *truncare* to shorten, from *truncus* trunk] (1716)
**:** having the end square or even ⟨the *truncate* leaves of the tulip tree⟩

**²truncate** *transitive verb* **trun·cat·ed; trun·cat·ing** (circa 1727)
**1 :** to shorten by or as if by cutting off
**2 :** to replace (an edge or corner of a crystal) by a plane
— **trun·ca·tion** \trəŋ-'kā-shən, trən-\ *noun*

**trun·cat·ed** \-,kā-təd\ *adjective* (circa 1704)
**1 :** having the apex replaced by a plane section and especially by one parallel to the base ⟨*truncated* cone⟩
**2 a :** cut short : CURTAILED **b :** lacking an expected or normal element (as a syllable) at the beginning or end : CATALECTIC

**¹trun·cheon** \'trən-chən\ *noun* [Middle English *tronchoun,* from Middle French *tronchon,* from (assumed) Vulgar Latin *truncion-, truncio,* from Latin *truncus* trunk] (14th century)
**1 :** a shattered spear or lance
**2 a** *obsolete* **:** CLUB, BLUDGEON **b :** BATON 2 **c :** a police officer's billy club

**²truncheon** *transitive verb* (1597)
*archaic* **:** to beat with a truncheon

**¹trun·dle** \'trən-dᵊl\ *verb* **trun·dled; trun·dling** \'trən(d)-liŋ, 'trən-dᵊl-iŋ\ [²*trundle*] (1598)
*transitive verb*
**1 a :** to propel by causing to rotate : ROLL **b** *archaic* **:** to cause to revolve : SPIN
**2 :** to transport in or as if in a wheeled vehicle : HAUL, WHEEL
*intransitive verb*
**1 :** to progress by revolving
**2 :** to move on or as if on wheels : ROLL
— **trun·dler** \'trən(d)-lər, 'trən-dᵊl-ər\ *noun*

**²trundle** *noun* [from *trundle* small wheel, alteration of earlier *trendle,* from Middle English, circle, ring, wheel, from Old English *trendel;* akin to Old English *trendan* to revolve — more at TREND] (1851)
**1 :** TRUNDLE BED
**2 :** the motion or sound of something rolling
**3 :** a round or oval wooden tub

**trundle bed** *noun* (1542)
**:** a low bed usually on casters that can be rolled or slid under a higher bed when not in use — called also *truckle bed*

**trun·dle–tail** \'trən-dᵊl-,tāl\ *noun* (15th century)
*archaic* **:** a curly-tailed dog

**trunk** \'trəŋk\ *noun* [Middle English *tronke* box, trunk, from Middle French *tronc,* from Latin *truncus* trunk, torso] (15th century)
**1 a :** the main stem of a tree apart from limbs and roots — called also *bole* **b** (1) **:** the human or animal body apart from the head and appendages : TORSO (2) **:** the thorax of an insect **c :** the central part of anything; *specifically* **:** the shaft of a column or pilaster

**2 a** (1) : a large rigid piece of luggage used usually for transporting clothing and personal effects (2) : the luggage compartment of an automobile **b** (1) : a superstructure over a ship's hatches usually level with the poop deck (2) : the part of the cabin of a boat projecting above the deck (3) : the housing for a centerboard or rudder
**3** : PROBOSCIS; *especially* : the long muscular proboscis of the elephant
**4** *plural* : men's shorts worn chiefly for sports
**5 a** : a usually major channel or passage (as a chute or shaft) **b** : a circuit between two telephone exchanges for making connections between subscribers; *broadly* : a usually electronic path over which information is transmitted (as between computer memories)
**6 a** : the principal channel of a tributary system ⟨an arterial *trunk*⟩ ⟨*trunk* of a river⟩ **b** : TRUNK LINE
— **trunk·ful** \'trəŋk-,fůl\ *noun*

**trunked** \'trəŋ(k)t\ *adjective* (1640)
: having a trunk especially of a specified kind — usually used in combination ⟨a gray-*trunked* tree⟩

**trunk·fish** \'trəŋk-,fish\ *noun* (circa 1804)
: any of numerous small often bright-colored bony fishes (family Ostraciidae) of tropical seas with the body and head enclosed in a bony carapace

**trunk hose** \'trəŋk-\ *noun plural* [probably from obsolete English *trunk* to truncate] (1637)
: short full breeches reaching about halfway down the thigh that were worn chiefly in the late 16th and early 17th centuries

**trunk line** *noun* (1843)
**1** : a transportation system (as an airline, railroad, or highway) handling long-distance through traffic
**2 a** : a main supply channel (as for gas or oil) **b** : TRUNK 5b

**trun·nel** \'trə-n°l\ *variant of* TREENAIL

**trun·nion** \'trən-yən\ *noun* [French *trognon* core, stump] (circa 1625)
: a pin or pivot on which something can be rotated or tilted; *especially* : either of two opposite gudgeons on which a cannon is swiveled

**¹truss** \'trəs\ *transitive verb* [Middle English, from Old French *trousser, tourser* to bundle, pack, from (assumed) Vulgar Latin *torsare*, from *torsus* twisted — more at TORSADE] (13th century)
**1 a** : to secure tightly : BIND **b** : to arrange for cooking by binding close the wings or legs of (a fowl)
**2** : to support, strengthen, or stiffen by or as if by a truss
— **truss·er** *noun*

**²truss** *noun* (13th century)
**1** : an iron band around a lower mast with an attachment by which a yard is secured to the mast
**2 a** : BRACKET 1 **b** : an assemblage of members (as beams) forming a rigid framework
**3** : a device worn to reduce a hernia by pressure
**4** : a compact flower or fruit cluster

**truss bridge** *noun* (1840)
: a bridge supported mainly by trusses — see BRIDGE illustration

**truss·ing** \'trə-siŋ\ *noun* (1840)
**1** : the members forming a truss
**2** : the trusses and framework of a structure

**¹trust** \'trəst\ *noun* [Middle English, probably of Scandinavian origin; akin to Old Norse *traust* trust; akin to Old English *trēowe* faithful — more at TRUE] (13th century)
**1 a** : assured reliance on the character, ability, strength, or truth of someone or something **b** : one in which confidence is placed
**2 a** : dependence on something future or contingent : HOPE **b** : reliance on future payment for property (as merchandise) delivered : CREDIT

**3 a** : a property interest held by one person for the benefit of another **b** : a combination of firms or corporations formed by a legal agreement; *especially* : one that reduces or threatens to reduce competition
**4** *archaic* : TRUSTWORTHINESS
**5 a** (1) : a charge or duty imposed in faith or confidence or as a condition of some relationship (2) : something committed or entrusted to one to be used or cared for in the interest of another **b** : responsible charge or office **c** : CARE, CUSTODY ⟨the child committed to her *trust*⟩
— **in trust** : in the care or possession of a trustee

**²trust** (13th century)
*intransitive verb*
**1 a** : to place confidence : DEPEND ⟨*trust* in God⟩ ⟨*trust* to luck⟩ **b** : to be confident : HOPE
**2** : to sell or deliver on credit
*transitive verb*
**1 a** : to commit or place in one's care or keeping : ENTRUST **b** : to permit to stay or go or to do something without fear or misgiving
**2 a** : to rely on the truthfulness or accuracy of : BELIEVE **b** : to place confidence in : rely on **c** : to hope or expect confidently
**3** : to extend credit to
— **trust·abil·i·ty** \,trəs-tə-'bi-lə-tē\ *noun*
— **trust·able** \'trəs-tə-bəl\ *adjective*
— **trust·er** *noun*
— **trust·ing·ly** \'trəs-tiŋ-lē\ *adverb*
— **trust·ing·ness** *noun*

**trust-bust·er** \'trəs(t)-,bəs-tər\ *noun* (1903)
: one who seeks to break up business trusts; *specifically* : a federal official who prosecutes trusts under the antitrust laws
— **trust–bust·ing** \-tiŋ\ *noun*

**trust company** *noun* (1834)
: an incorporated trustee; *broadly* : a corporation that functions as a corporate and personal trustee and usually also engages in the normal activities of a commercial bank

**¹trust·ee** \,trəs-'tē\ *noun* (1647)
**1 a** : one to whom something is entrusted **b** : a country charged with the supervision of a trust territory
**2 a** : a natural or legal person to whom property is legally committed to be administered for the benefit of a beneficiary (as a person or a charitable organization) **b** : one (as a corporate director) occupying a position of trust and performing functions comparable to those of a trustee

**²trustee** *verb* **trust·eed; trust·ee·ing** (1818)
*transitive verb*
: to commit to the care of a trustee
*intransitive verb*
: to serve as trustee

**trust·ee·ship** \,trəs-'tē-,ship\ *noun* (circa 1736)
**1** : the office or function of a trustee
**2** : supervisory control by one or more countries over a trust territory

**trust·ful** \'trəst-fəl\ *adjective* (1834)
: full of trust : CONFIDING
— **trust·ful·ly** \-fə-lē\ *adverb*
— **trust·ful·ness** *noun*

**trust fund** *noun* (1780)
: property (as money or securities) settled or held in trust

**trust·less** \'trəst-ləs\ *adjective* (circa 1530)
**1** : not deserving of trust : FAITHLESS
**2** : DISTRUSTFUL

**trust territory** *noun* (1945)
: a non-self-governing territory placed under an administrative authority by the Trusteeship Council of the United Nations

**trust·wor·thy** \'trəst-,wər-thē\ *adjective* (1829)
: worthy of confidence : DEPENDABLE
— **trust·wor·thi·ly** \-thə-lē\ *adverb*
— **trust·wor·thi·ness** *noun*

**¹trusty** \'trəs-tē\ *adjective* **trust·i·er; -est** (14th century)

: TRUSTWORTHY, DEPENDABLE
— **trust·i·ness** *noun*

**²trusty** \'trəs-tē *also* ,trəs-'tē\ *noun, plural* **trust·ies** (1573)
: a trusty or trusted person; *specifically* : a convict considered trustworthy and allowed special privileges

**truth** \'trüth\ *noun, plural* **truths** \'trüthz, 'trüths\ [Middle English *trewthe*, from Old English *trēowth* fidelity; akin to Old English *trēowe* faithful — more at TRUE] (before 12th century)
**1 a** *archaic* : FIDELITY, CONSTANCY **b** : sincerity in action, character, and utterance
**2 a** (1) : the state of being the case : FACT (2) : the body of real things, events, and facts : ACTUALITY (3) *often capitalized* : a transcendent fundamental or spiritual reality **b** : a judgment, proposition, or idea that is true or accepted as true ⟨*truths* of thermodynamics⟩ **c** : the body of true statements and propositions
**3 a** : the property (as of a statement) of being in accord with fact or reality **b** *chiefly British* : TRUE 2 **c** : fidelity to an original or to a standard
**4** *capitalized, Christian Science* : GOD
— **in truth** : in accordance with fact : ACTUALLY

**truth·ful** \'trüth-fəl\ *adjective* (1596)
: telling or disposed to tell the truth
— **truth·ful·ly** \-fə-lē\ *adverb*
— **truth·ful·ness** *noun*

**truth serum** *noun* (1925)
: a hypnotic or anesthetic held to induce a subject under questioning to talk freely

**truth set** *noun* (1940)
: a mathematical or logical set containing all the elements that make a given statement of relationships true when substituted in it ⟨the equation $x + 7 = 10$ has as its *truth set* the single number 3⟩

**truth table** *noun* (1921)
: a table that shows the truth-value of a compound statement for every truth-value of its component statements; *also* : a similar table (as for a computer logic circuit) showing the value of the output for each value of each input

## TRUTH TABLE

| a statement | a statement | not *p* denial | *p* and *q* conjunction | *p* or *q* (inclusive) inclusive disjunction | *p* or *q* (exclusive) exclusive disjunction | if *p* then *q* conditional | *p* if and only if *q* biconditional |
|---|---|---|---|---|---|---|---|
| *p* | *q* | ~*p* | *p* · *q* | *p* ∨ *q* | | *p* ⊃ *q* | *p* ≡ *q* |
| T | T | F | T | T | F | T | T |
| T | F | F | F | T | T | F | F |
| F | T | T | F | T | T | T | F |
| F | F | T | F | F | F | T | T |

T = true  F = false

**truth–value** *noun* (1903)
: the truth or falsity of a proposition or statement

**¹try** \'trī\ *verb* **tried; try·ing** [Middle English *trien*, from Anglo-French *trier*, from Old French, to pick out, sift, probably from Late

Latin *tritare* to grind, frequentative of Latin *terere* to rub — more at THROW] (14th century)
*transitive verb*
**1 a :** to examine or investigate judicially **b** (1) : to conduct the trial of (2) : to participate as counsel in the judicial examination of
**2 a :** to put to test or trial ⟨*try* one's luck⟩ — often used with *out* **b :** to subject to something (as undue strain or excessive hardship or provocation) that tests the powers of endurance **c :** DEMONSTRATE, PROVE
**3 a** *obsolete* **:** PURIFY, REFINE **b :** to melt down and procure in a pure state **:** RENDER ⟨*try* out whale oil from blubber⟩
**4 :** to fit or finish with accuracy
**5 :** to make an attempt at — often used with an infinitive
*intransitive verb*
**:** to make an attempt ☐
**synonym** see AFFLICT, ATTEMPT
**— try one's hand :** to attempt something for the first time
²**try** *noun, plural* **tries** (1607)
**1 :** an experimental trial **:** ATTEMPT
**2 :** a play in rugby that is similar to a touchdown in football, scores usually four points, and entitles the scoring side to attempt a placekick at the goal for additional points; *also* **:** the score made on a try
**try for point** (1929)
**:** an attempt made after scoring a touchdown in football to score one or two additional points by kicking the ball over the crossbar or again carrying it into the opponents' end zone
**try·ing** \'trī-iŋ\ *adjective* (1718)
**:** severely straining the powers of endurance
**— try·ing·ly** \-iŋ-lē\ *adverb*
**try on** *transitive verb* (1693)
**1 :** to put on (a garment) in order to test the fit
**2 :** to use or test experimentally
**— try–on** \'trī-ˌȯn, -ˌän\ *noun*
**try·out** \'trī-ˌau̇t\ *noun* (1903)
**:** an experimental performance or demonstration: as **a :** a test of the ability (as of an athlete or actor) to fill a part or meet standards **b :** a performance of a play prior to its official opening to determine response and discover weaknesses
**try out** *intransitive verb* (1909)
**:** to compete for a position especially on an athletic team or for a part in a play
**try·pano·some** \tri-'pa-nə-ˌsōm\ *noun* [New Latin *Trypanosoma*, from Greek *trypanon* auger + New Latin *-soma* -some — more at TREPAN] (1903)
**:** any of a genus (*Trypanosoma*) of parasitic flagellate protozoans that infest the blood of various vertebrates including humans, are usually transmitted by the bite of an insect, and include some that cause serious disease (as sleeping sickness)
**try·pano·so·mi·a·sis** \tri-ˌpa-nə-sə-'mī-ə-səs\ *noun, plural* **-a·ses** \-ˌsēz\ [New Latin] (1902)
**:** infection with or disease caused by trypanosomes
**try·pot** \'trī-ˌpät\ *noun* (1795)
**:** a metallic pot used on a whaler or on shore to render whale oil from blubber
**tryp·sin** \'trip-sən\ *noun* [perhaps from Greek *tryein* to wear down + English pe*psin*; akin to Latin *terere* to rub — more at THROW] (1876)
**:** a proteolytic enzyme from pancreatic juice active in an alkaline medium — compare CHYMOTRYPSIN
**tryp·sin·o·gen** \trip-'si-nə-jən\ *noun* [International Scientific Vocabulary] (circa 1890)
**:** the inactive substance released by the pancreas into the duodenum to form trypsin
**trypt·amine** \'trip-tə-ˌmēn\ *noun* [*trypt*ophan + *amine*] (1929)
**:** a crystalline amine $C_{10}H_{12}N_2$ derived from tryptophan
**tryp·tic** \'trip-tik\ *adjective* [International Scientific Vocabulary, from *trypsin*] (1888)

**:** of, relating to, or produced by trypsin or its action
**tryp·to·phan** \'trip-tə-ˌfan\ *also* **tryp·to·phane** \-ˌfän\ *noun* [International Scientific Vocabulary *tryp*tic + *-o-* + *-phane*] (1890)
**:** a crystalline essential amino acid $C_{11}H_{12}N_2O_2$ that is widely distributed in proteins
**try·sail** \'trī-ˌsāl, -səl\ *noun* [obsolete *at* try lying to] (1769)
**:** a fore-and-aft sail bent to a gaff and hoisted on a lower mast or a small mast close abaft
**try square** *noun* (circa 1877)
**:** an instrument consisting of two straightedges fixed at right angles to each other and used for laying off right angles and testing whether work is square
¹**tryst** \'trist, *especially British* 'trīst\ *noun* [Middle English, from Middle French *triste* watch post, probably of Scandinavian origin; akin to Old Norse *traust* trust] (14th century)
**1 :** an agreement (as between lovers) to meet
**2 :** an appointed meeting or meeting place
²**tryst** *intransitive verb* (14th century)
**:** to make or keep a tryst
**— tryst·er** \'tris-tər, 'trīs-\ *noun*
**try·works** \'trī-ˌwərks\ *noun plural* (1792)
**:** a brick furnace in which try-pots are placed; *also* **:** the furnace with the pots
**tsa·de** \'(t)sä-də, -dē\ *variant of* SADHE
**tsar** \'zär, '(t)sär\ *variant of* CZAR
**tset·se fly** \'(t)set-sē-, 'tet-, '(t)sēt-, 'tēt-\ *noun* [Afrikaans, from Tswana *tsètsè* fly] (1865)
**:** any of several dipteran flies (genus *Glossina*) that occur in Africa south of the Sahara and include vectors of human and animal trypanosomes — called also *tsetse*; compare SLEEPING SICKNESS
**Tshi** \'chwē, chə-'wē, 'twē, 'chē\ *variant of* TWI
**Tshi·lu·ba** \chi-'lü-bə\ *noun* (circa 1961)
**:** a Bantu language used as a lingua franca in southeastern Zaire
**T-shirt** \'tē-ˌshərt\ *noun* (1920)
**:** a collarless short-sleeved or sleeveless usually cotton undershirt; *also* **:** an outer shirt of similar design
**— T-shirt·ed** *adjective*
**T square** *noun* (1785)
**:** a ruler with a crosspiece or head at one end used in making parallel lines
**tsu·na·mi** \(t)su̇-'nä-mē\ *noun, plural* **tsuna·mis** *also* **tsunami** [Japanese, from *tsu* harbor + *nami* wave] (1897)
**:** a great sea wave produced by submarine earth movement or volcanic eruption **:** TIDAL WAVE
**— tsu·na·mic** \-mik\ *adjective*
**tsu·tsu·ga·mu·shi disease** \ˌ(t)süt-sə-gə-'mü-shē-, ˌtüt-\ *noun* [Japanese *tsutsugamushi* scrub typhus mite, from *tsutsuga* sickness + *mushi* insect] (1906)
**:** an acute febrile bacterial disease that is caused by a rickettsia (*Rickettsia tsutsugamushi*) transmitted by mite larvae, resembles louse-borne typhus, and is widespread in the western Pacific area — called also *scrub typhus, tsutsugamushi*
**Tswa·na** \'(t)swä-nə\ *noun, plural* **Tswana** *or* **Tswanas** (1937)
**1 :** the language of the Tswana people
**2 :** a member of a Bantu-speaking people of Botswana and the Republic of South Africa
**t-test** \'tē-ˌtest\ *noun* (1932)
**:** a statistical test involving confidence limits for the random variable $t$ of a t distribution and used especially in testing hypotheses about means of normal distributions when the standard deviations are unknown
**T₃** *also* **T-3** \'tē-'thrē\ *noun* [*T,* abbreviation for *thyronine* + *3*, number of iodine atoms attached to the thyronine nucleus] (1956)
**:** TRIIODOTHYRONINE
**Tua·reg** \'twä-ˌreg\ *noun, plural* **Tuareg** *or* **Tuaregs** [Arabic *Tawāriq*] (1821)
**:** a member of a nomadic people of the central and western Sahara and along the middle Niger from Tombouctou to Nigeria

**tu·a·ta·ra** \ˌtü-ə-'tär-ə\ *noun* [Maori *tuatàra*] (1890)
**:** a large spiny quadrupedal reptile (*Sphenodon punctatum*) of islands off the coast of New Zealand that has a vestigial third eye in the middle of the forehead representing the pineal gland and that is the only surviving rhynchocephalian

tuatara

¹**tub** \'təb\ *noun* [Middle English *tubbe*, from Middle Dutch; akin to Middle Low German *tubbe* tub] (14th century)
**1 a :** a wide low vessel originally formed with wooden staves, round bottom, and hoops **b :** a small round container in which a product is sold ⟨a *tub* of oleo⟩
**2 :** an old or slow boat
**3 :** BATHTUB; *also* **:** BATH
**4 :** the amount that a tub will hold
**— tub·ful** \-ˌfu̇l\ *noun*
**— tub·like** \-ˌlīk\ *adjective*
²**tub** *verb* **tubbed; tub·bing** (1610)
*transitive verb*
**1 :** to wash or bathe in a tub
**2 :** to put or store in a tub
*intransitive verb*
**1 :** BATHE
**2 :** to undergo washing
**— tub·ba·ble** \'tə-bə-bəl\ *adjective*
**— tub·ber** *noun*
**tu·ba** \'tü-bə, 'tyü-\ *noun* [Italian, from Latin, trumpet] (1852)
**:** a large low-pitched brass instrument usually oval in shape and having a conical tube, a cup-shaped mouthpiece, and a usual range an octave lower than that of the euphonium
**— tu·ba·ist** \-bə-(i)st\ *or* **tub·ist** \-bist\ *noun*
**tub·al** \'tü-bəl, 'tyü-\ *adjective* (circa 1736)

tuba

: of, relating to, or involving a tube and especially a fallopian tube ⟨*tubal* infection⟩

**tubal ligation** *noun* (1948)
: ligation of the fallopian tubes to prevent passage of ova from the ovaries to the uterus used as a method of female sterilization

**tub·by** \'tə-bē\ *adjective* **tub·bi·er; -est** (circa 1807)
**1** : sounding dull and without proper resonance or freedom of sound ⟨a *tubby* violin⟩
**2** : PUDGY, FAT

**tube** \'tüb, 'tyüb\ *noun* [French, from Latin *tubus*; akin to Latin *tuba* trumpet] (1651)
**1** : any of various usually cylindrical structures or devices: as **a** : a hollow elongated cylinder; *especially* : one to convey fluids **b** : a soft tubular container whose contents (as toothpaste) can be removed by squeezing **c** (1) : TUNNEL (2) *British* : SUBWAY b **d** : the basically cylindrical section between the mouthpiece and bell that is the fundamental part of a wind instrument
**2 a** : a slender channel within a plant or animal body : DUCT — compare FALLOPIAN TUBE **b** : the narrow basal portion of a gamopetalous corolla or a calyx with united sepals
**3** : INNER TUBE
**4 a** : ELECTRON TUBE; *especially* : VACUUM TUBE **b** : CATHODE-RAY TUBE; *especially* : a television picture tube **c** : TELEVISION
**5** : an article of clothing shaped like a tube ⟨*tube* top⟩ ⟨*tube* socks⟩
— **tubed** \'tübd, 'tyübd\ *adjective*
— **tube·like** \'tüb-,līk, 'tyüb-\ *adjective*
— **down the tube** *or* **down the tubes** : into a state of collapse, deterioration, or ruin

**tube foot** *noun* (1888)
: one of the small flexible tubular processes of most echinoderms that are extensions of the water-vascular system and are used especially in locomotion and grasping

**tube·less** \'tü-bləs, 'tyüb-\ *adjective* (1855)
: lacking a tube; *specifically* : being a pneumatic tire that does not depend on an inner tube for airtightness

**tube nucleus** *noun* (1939)
: the one of the two nuclei formed by mitotic division of a microspore during the formation of a pollen grain that is held to control subsequent growth of the pollen tube and that does not divide again — compare GENERATIVE NUCLEUS

**tube pan** *noun* (1926)
: a round cake pan having a hollow tube in the center

**tu·ber** \'tü-bər, 'tyü-\ *noun* [Latin, swelling, truffle; perhaps akin to Latin *tumēre* to swell — more at THUMB] (1668)
**1 a** : a short fleshy usually underground stem bearing minute scale leaves each of which bears a bud in its axil and is potentially able to produce a new plant — compare BULB, CORM **b** : a fleshy root or rhizome resembling a tuber
**2** : an anatomical prominence : TUBEROSITY

**tu·ber·cle** \'tü-bər-kəl, 'tyü-\ *noun* [Latin *tuberculum*, diminutive of *tuber*] (1578)
**1** : a small knobby prominence or excrescence especially on a plant or animal : NODULE: as **a** : a protuberance near the head of a rib that articulates with the transverse process of a vertebra **b** : any of several prominences in the central nervous system **c** : NODULE b
**2** : a small abnormal discrete lump in the substance of an organ or in the skin; *especially* : the specific lesion of tuberculosis

**tubercle bacillus** *noun* (circa 1890)
: a bacterium (*Mycobacterium tuberculosis*) that is a major cause of tuberculosis

**tubercul-** *combining form* [New Latin, from Latin *tuberculum*]
**1** : tubercle ⟨*tubercular*⟩
**2** : tubercle bacillus ⟨*tuberculin*⟩
**3** : tuberculosis ⟨*tuberculoid*⟩

**¹tu·ber·cu·lar** \tü-'bər-kyə-lər, tyü-\ *adjective* (1799)

**1 a** : of, relating to, or affected with tuberculosis : TUBERCULOUS **b** : caused by the tubercle bacillus ⟨*tubercular* meningitis⟩
**2** : characterized by lesions that are or resemble tubercles ⟨*tubercular* leprosy⟩
**3** : relating to, resembling, or constituting a tubercle : TUBERCULATED

**²tubercular** *noun* (1925)
: a person with tuberculosis

**tu·ber·cu·lat·ed** \tü-'bər-kyə-,lā-təd, tyü-\ *also* **tu·ber·cu·late** \-lət\ *adjective* (1771)
: having tubercles : characterized by or beset with tubercles

**tu·ber·cu·lin** \tü-'bər-kyə-lən, tyü-\ *noun* [International Scientific Vocabulary] (circa 1890)
: a sterile liquid containing the growth products of or specific substances extracted from the tubercle bacillus and used in the diagnosis of tuberculosis especially in children and cattle

**tuberculin test** *noun* (circa 1900)
: a test for hypersensitivity to tuberculin as an indication of past or present tubercular infection

**tu·ber·cu·loid** \tü-'bər-kyə-,lȯid, tyü-\ *adjective* [International Scientific Vocabulary] (circa 1923)
: resembling tuberculosis especially in the presence of tubercles ⟨*tuberculoid* leprosy⟩

**tu·ber·cu·lo·sis** \tü-,bər-kyə-'lō-səs, tyü-\ *noun, plural* **-lo·ses** \-,sēz\ [New Latin] (1860)
: a highly variable communicable disease of humans and some other vertebrates caused by the tubercle bacillus and rarely in the U.S. by a related mycobacterium (*Mycobacterium bovis*) and characterized by toxic symptoms or allergic manifestations which in humans primarily affect the lungs

**tu·ber·cu·lous** \tü-'bər-kyə-ləs, tyü-\ *adjective* (1891)
**1** : constituting or affected with tuberculosis ⟨a *tuberculous* process⟩
**2** : caused by or resulting from the presence or products of the tubercle bacillus ⟨*tuberculous* peritonitis⟩

**tube·rose** \'tü-,brōz, 'tyü-, *also* -bə-,rōz, -bə-,rōs\ *noun* [New Latin *tuberosa*, specific epithet, from Latin, feminine of *tuberosus* tuberous, from *tuber* tuber] (1664)
: a Mexican bulbous herb (*Polianthes tuberosa*) of the agave family cultivated for its spike of fragrant white single or double flowers

**tu·ber·os·i·ty** \,tü-bə-'rä-sə-tē, ,tyü-\ *noun, plural* **-ties** (1611)
: a rounded prominence; *especially* : a large prominence on a bone usually serving for the attachment of muscles or ligaments

**tu·ber·ous** \'tü-b(ə-)rəs, 'tyü-\ *adjective* (1650)
**1** : consisting of, bearing, or resembling a tuber
**2** : of, relating to, or being a plant tuber or tuberous root of a plant

**tuberous root** *noun* (circa 1668)
: a thick fleshy storage root like a tuber but lacking buds or scale leaves
— **tuberous–rooted** *adjective*

**tube worm** *noun* (circa 1819)
: a worm that lives in a tube: as **a** : any of various polychaetes or oligochaetes **b** : a pogonophoran and especially an extremely large one that is found near deep-ocean hydrothermal vents

**tu·bi·fex** \'tü-bə-,feks, 'tyü-\ *noun* [New Latin *Tubific-, Tubifex*, from Latin *tubus* tube + *facere* to make — more at DO] (1948)
: any of a genus (*Tubifex*) of slender reddish oligochaete worms that live in tubes in fresh or brackish water and are widely used as food for aquarium fish

**tu·bi·fi·cid** \tü-'bi-fə-səd, tyü-; ,t(y)ü-bə-'fi-səd\ *noun* [New Latin *Tubificidae*, from *Tubific-, Tubifex*] (1950)

: any of a family (Tubificidae) of aquatic oligochaetes including the tubifex worms
— **tubificid** *adjective*

**tub·ing** \'tü-biŋ, 'tyü-\ *noun* (1845)
**1** : material in the form of a tube; *also* : a length or piece of tube
**2** : a series or system of tubes

**tu·bo·cu·ra·rine** \,tü-bō-kyü-'rär-ən, ,tyü-, -,ēn\ *noun* [International Scientific Vocabulary *tubo-* (from Latin *tubus* tube) + *curare* + *-ine*; from its being shipped in sections of hollow bamboo] (1898)
: a toxic alkaloid or its crystalline hydrated hydrochloride salt $C_{37}H_{42}Cl_2N_2O_6 \cdot 5H_2O$ that is obtained chiefly from the bark and stems of a South American vine (*Chondrodendron tomentosum* of the family Menispermaceae) and in its dextrorotatory form constitutes the chief active constituent of curare and is used especially as a skeletal muscle relaxant

**tub–thump·er** \'təb-,thəm-pər\ *noun* (1662)
: a vociferous supporter (as of a cause)
— **tub–thump** \-,thəmp\ *verb*

**tu·bu·lar** \'tü-byə-lər, 'tyü-\ *adjective* (1673)
**1 a** : having the form of or consisting of a tube ⟨a *tubular* calyx⟩ **b** : made or provided with tubes
**2** : of, relating to, or sounding as if produced through tubes

**tu·bule** \'tü-(,)byü(ə)l, 'tyü-\ *noun* [Latin *tubulus*, diminutive of *tubus*] (1677)
: a small tube; *especially* : a slender elongated anatomical channel

**tu·bu·lin** \'tü-byə-lən, 'tyü-\ *noun* [*tubule* + *¹-in*] (1968)
: a globular protein that polymerizes to form microtubules

**tu·chun** \'dü-'jün, -'jŭen\ *noun* [Chinese (Beijing) *dūjūn*] (1917)
**1** : a Chinese military governor (as of a province)
**2** : a Chinese warlord

**¹tuck** \'tək\ *verb* [Middle English *tuken* to pull up sharply, scold, from Old English *tūcian* to ill-treat; akin to Old High German *zuhhen* to jerk, Old English *togian* to pull — more at TOW] (15th century)
*transitive verb*
**1 a** : to pull up into a fold **b** : to make a tuck
**2** : to put into a snug often concealing or isolating place ⟨cottage *tucked* away in the hill⟩
**3 a** : to push in the loose end of so as to hold tightly ⟨*tuck* in your shirt⟩ **b** : to cover by tucking in bedclothes — usually used with *in*
**4** : EAT — usually used with *away* or *in* ⟨*tucked* away a big lunch⟩
**5** : to put into a tuck position
*intransitive verb*
**1** : to draw together into tucks or folds
**2** : to eat or drink heartily — usually used with *into* ⟨*tucked* into their beer and pretzels⟩
**3** : to fit snugly

**²tuck** *noun* (1532)
**1** : a fold stitched into cloth to shorten, decorate, or control fullness
**2** : the part of a vessel where the ends of the lower planks meet under the stern
**3 a** : an act or instance of tucking **b** : something tucked or to be tucked in
**4 a** : a body position (as in diving) in which the knees are bent, the thighs drawn tightly to the chest, and the hands clasped around the shins **b** : a skiing position in which the skier squats forward and holds the ski poles under the arms and parallel to the ground
**5** : a cosmetic surgical operation for the removal of excess skin or fat from a body part ⟨a tummy *tuck*⟩

\ə\ abut \ᵊ\ kitten \ər\ further \a\ ash \ā\ ace
\ä\ mop, mar \aů\ out \ch\ chin \e\ bet \ē\ easy
\g\ go \i\ hit \ī\ ice \j\ job \ŋ\ sing \ō\ go
\ȯ\ law \ȯi\ boy \th\ thin \t̲h̲\ the \ü\ loot \ů\ foot
\y\ yet \zh\ vision *see also* Guide to Pronunciation

³**tuck** *noun* [Middle English (Scots) *tuicke* beat, stroke] (15th century)
: a sound of or as if of a drumbeat

⁴**tuck** *noun* [Middle French *estoc*, from Old French, tree trunk, sword point, of Germanic origin; akin to Old English *stocc* stump of a tree — more at STOCK] (1508)
*archaic* : RAPIER

⁵**tuck** *noun* [probably from ²*tuck*] (1878)
: VIGOR, ENERGY ⟨seemed to kind of take the *tuck* all out of me —Mark Twain⟩

**tuck·a·hoe** \'tə-kə-ˌhō\ *noun* [Virginia Algonquian *tockawhoughe*] (1612)
**1** : either of two arums (*Peltandra virginica* and *Orontium aquaticum*) of the U.S. with rootstocks used as food by American Indians
**2** : the large edible sclerotium of a subterranean fungus (*Poria cocos*)

¹**tuck·er** \'tə-kər\ *noun* (1688)
**1** : a piece of lace or cloth in the neckline of a dress
**2** : one that tucks
**3** *chiefly Australian* : FOOD

²**tucker** *transitive verb* **tuck·ered; tuck·er·ing** \'tə-k(ə-)riŋ\ [obsolete English *tuck* to reproach + -*er* (as in ¹*batter*)] (1833)
: EXHAUST — often used with *out*

**tuck·er–bag** \'tə-kər-ˌbag\ *noun* (1885)
*chiefly Australian* : a bag used especially by travelers in the bush to hold food

**tuck·et** \'tə-kət\ *noun* [probably from obsolete English *tuk* to beat the drum, sound the trumpet] (1593)
: a fanfare on a trumpet

**tuck–point** \'tək-ˌpȯint\ *transitive verb* (1881)
: to finish (the mortar joints between bricks or stones) with a narrow ridge of putty or fine lime mortar

**tuckshop** \-ˌshäp\ *noun* [British *tuck* food, confectionery] (1857)
*British* : a confectioner's shop : CONFECTIONERY

**Tu·dor** \'tü-dər, 'tyü-\ *adjective* [Henry *Tudor* (Henry VII of England)] (1779)
**1** : of or relating to the English royal house that ruled from 1485 to 1603
**2** : of, relating to, or characteristic of the Tudor period
— **Tudor** *noun*

**Tudor arch** *noun* (1815)
: a low elliptical 3-, 4-, or 5-centered arch; *especially* : a 4-centered pointed arch — see ARCH illustration

**Tues·day** \'tüz-dē, 'tyüz-, -(ˌ)dā\ *noun* [Middle English *tiwesday*, from Old English *tiwesdæg* (akin to Old High German *zīostag* Tuesday), from Old English *Tīw* Tiu + *dæg* day — more at DEITY] (before 12th century)
: the third day of the week
— **Tues·days** \-dēz, -(ˌ)dāz\ *adverb*

**tu·fa** \'tü-fə, 'tyü-\ *noun* [Italian *tufo*, from Latin *tofus*] (1770)
**1** : TUFF
**2** : a porous rock formed as a deposit from springs or streams
— **tu·fa·ceous** \tü-'fā-shəs, tyü-\ *adjective*

**tuff** \'təf\ *noun* [Middle French *tuf*, from Old Italian *tufo*] (1815)
: a rock composed of the finer kinds of volcanic detritus usually fused together by heat
— **tuff·a·ceous** \ˌtə-'fā-shəs\ *adjective*

**tuf·fet** \'tə-fət\ *noun* [alteration of ¹*tuft*] (1553)
**1** : TUFT 1a
**2** : a low seat

¹**tuft** \'təft\ *noun* [Middle English, modification of Middle French *tufe*] (14th century)
**1 a** : a small cluster of elongated flexible outgrowths attached or close together at the base and free at the opposite ends; *especially* : a growing bunch of grasses or close-set plants **b** : a bunch of soft fluffy threads cut off short and used as ornament
**2** : CLUMP, CLUSTER
**3** : MOUND

**4** : any of the projections of yarns drawn through a fabric or making up a fabric so as to produce a surface of raised loops or cut pile
— **tuft·ed** \'təf-təd\ *adjective*
— **tufty** \'təf-tē\ *adjective*

²**tuft** (1535)
*transitive verb*
**1 a** : to provide or adorn with a tuft **b** : to make (a fabric) of or with tufts
**2** : to make (as a mattress) firm by stitching at intervals and sewing on tufts
*intransitive verb*
: to form into or grow in tufts
— **tuft·er** *noun*

¹**tug** \'təg\ *verb* **tugged; tug·ging** [Middle English *tuggen*; akin to Old English *togian* to pull — more at TOW] (14th century)
*intransitive verb*
**1** : to pull hard
**2** : to struggle in opposition : CONTEND
**3** : to exert oneself laboriously : LABOR
*transitive verb*
**1** : to pull or strain hard at
**2 a** : to move by pulling hard : HAUL **b** : to carry with difficulty : LUG
**3** : to tow with a tugboat
— **tug·ger** *noun*

²**tug** *noun* (15th century)
**1 a** : ³TRACE 1 **b** : a short leather strap or loop **c** : a rope or chain used for pulling
**2 a** : an act or instance of tugging : PULL **b** : a strong pulling force
**3 a** : a straining effort **b** : a struggle between two people or opposite forces
**4** : TUGBOAT

**tug·boat** \'təg-ˌbōt\ *noun* (1830)
: a strongly built powerful boat used for towing and pushing — called also *towboat*

**tug-of-war** \ˌtəg-ə(v)-'wȯr\ *noun, plural* **tugs-of-war** (1677)
**1** : a struggle for supremacy or control usually involving two antagonists
**2** : a contest in which two teams pull against each other at opposite ends of a rope with the object of pulling the middle of the rope over a mark on the ground

**tu·grik** *or* **tu·ghrik** \'tü-grik\ *noun* [Mongolian *tögrig*, literally, circle, wheel] (1927)
— see MONEY table

**tuille** \'twē(ə)l\ *noun* [Middle English *toile*, from Middle French *tuille* tile, from Latin *tegula* — more at TILE] (15th century)
: one of the hinged plates before the thigh in plate armor — see ARMOR illustration

**tu·ition** \tə-'wi-shən, tyü-\ *noun* [Middle English *tuicioun* protection, from Old French *tuicion*, from Latin *tuition-, tuitio*, from *tueri* to look at, look after] (15th century)
**1** *archaic* : CUSTODY, GUARDIANSHIP
**2** : the act or profession of teaching : INSTRUCTION ⟨pursued his studies under private *tuition*⟩
**3** : the price of or payment for instruction
— **tu·ition·al** \-'wish-nəl, -'wi-shə-nᵊl\ *adjective*

**tu·la·re·mia** \ˌtü-lə-'rē-mē-ə, ˌtyü-\ *noun* [New Latin, from *Tulare* County, Calif.] (1921)
: an infectious disease especially of wild rabbits, rodents, humans, and some domestic animals that is caused by a bacterium (*Francisella tularensis*), is transmitted especially by the bites of insects, and in humans is marked by symptoms (as fever) of toxemia
— **tu·la·re·mic** \-mik\ *adjective*

**tu·le** \'tü-lē\ *noun* [Spanish, from Nahuatl *tōllin*] (1837)
: either of two large New World bulrushes (*Scirpus californicus* and *S. acutus*)

**tu·lip** \'tü-ləp, 'tyü-\ *noun* [New Latin *tulipa*, from Turkish *tülbent* turban — more at TURBAN] (1578)
: any of a genus (*Tulipa*) of Eurasian bulbous herbs of the lily family that have linear or broadly lanceolate leaves and are widely grown for their showy flowers; *also* : the flower or bulb of a tulip ◆

**tulip tree** *noun* (1705)
**1** : a tall North American timber tree (*Liriodendron tulipifera*) of the magnolia family having large greenish yellow tulip-shaped flowers and soft white wood used especially for cabinetwork and woodenware — called also *tulip poplar, yellow poplar*
**2** : any of various trees other than the tulip tree with tulip-shaped flowers

**tu·lip·wood** \'tü-ləp-ˌwùd, 'tyü-\ *noun* (1843)
**1** : wood of the North American tulip tree
**2 a** : any of several showily striped or variegated woods; *especially* : the rose-colored wood of a Brazilian tree (*Physocalymma scabberimum* of the family Lythraceae) that is much used by cabinetmakers for inlaying **b** : a tree that yields tulipwood

**tulle** \'tül\ *noun* [French, from *Tulle,* France] (circa 1818)
: a sheer often stiffened silk, rayon, or nylon net used chiefly for veils or ballet costumes

¹**tum·ble** \'təm-bəl\ *verb* **tum·bled; tum·bling** \-b(ə-)liŋ\ [Middle English, frequentative of *tumben* to dance, from Old English *tumbian*; akin to Old High German *tūmōn* to reel] (14th century)
*intransitive verb*
**1 a** : to fall suddenly and helplessly **b** : to suffer a sudden downfall, overthrow, or defeat **c** : to decline suddenly and sharply (as in price) : DROP ⟨the stock market *tumbled*⟩ **d** : to fall into ruin : COLLAPSE
**2 a** : to perform gymnastic feats in tumbling **b** : to turn end over end in falling or flight
**3** : to roll over and over, to and fro, or end over end : TOSS
**4** : to issue forth hurriedly and confusedly
**5** : to come by chance : STUMBLE
**6** : to come to understand : CATCH ON ⟨didn't *tumble* to the seriousness of the problem⟩
*transitive verb*
**1** : to cause to tumble (as by pushing or toppling)
**2 a** : to throw together in a confused mass : RUMPLE, DISORDER
**3** : to whirl in a tumbling barrel

²**tumble** *noun* (1634)
**1 a** : a disordered mass of objects or material **b** : a disorderly state
**2** : an act or instance of tumbling

**tum·ble·bug** \'təm-bəl-ˌbəg\ *noun* (1805)

: any of various scarabaeid beetles (especially genera *Scarabaeus, Canthon, Copris,* or *Phanaeus*) that roll dung into small balls, bury them in the ground, and lay eggs in them

**tum·ble·down** \'təm-bəl-'daún\ *adjective* (1818)
: DILAPIDATED, RAMSHACKLE ⟨a *tumbledown* house at the edge of town —Sherwood Anderson⟩

**tumble dry** *transitive verb* (1962)
: to dry (as clothes) by tumbling in a dryer
— **tumble dryer** *noun*
— **tumble drying** *noun*

**tum·bler** \'təm-blər\ *noun* (14th century)
**1** : one that tumbles: as **a** : one that performs tumbling feats : ACROBAT **b** : any of various domestic pigeons that tumble or somersault backward in flight or on the ground
**2** : a drinking glass without foot or stem and originally with pointed or convex base
**3 a** : a movable obstruction in a lock (as a lever, latch, wheel, slide, or pin) that must be adjusted to a particular position (as by a key) before the bolt can be thrown **b** : a piece on which the mainspring acts in a gun's lock
**4** : a device or mechanism for tumbling (as a revolving cage in which clothes are dried)
**5** : a worker that operates a tumbler
— **tum·bler·ful** \-,fúl\ *noun*

**tum·ble·weed** \'təm-bəl-,wēd\ *noun* (1887)
: a plant (as Russian thistle or any of several amaranths) that breaks away from its roots in the autumn and is driven about by the wind as a light rolling mass

**¹tum·bling** \'təm-b(ə-)liŋ\ *noun* (1604)
: the skill, practice, or sport of executing gymnastic feats (as somersaults and handsprings) without the use of apparatus

**²tumbling** *adjective* (circa 1916)
: tipped or slanted out of the vertical — used especially of a cattle brand

**tumbling barrel** *noun* (circa 1890)
: a revolving cask in which objects or materials undergo a process (as drying or polishing) by being whirled about

**tumbling verse** *noun* (1585)
: an early modern English type of verse having four stresses but no prevailing type of foot and no regular number of syllables

**tum·brel** *or* **tum·bril** \'təm-brəl\ *noun* [Middle English *tombrel,* from Old French *tumberel* tipcart, from *tomber* to tumble, of Germanic origin; akin to Old High German *tūmōn* to reel — more at TUMBLE] (15th century)
**1** : a farm tipcart
**2** : a vehicle carrying condemned persons (as political prisoners during the French Revolution) to a place of execution

**tu·me·fac·tion** \,tü-mə-'fak-shən, ,tyü-\ *noun* [Middle French, from Latin *tumefacere* to cause to swell, from *tumēre* to swell + *facere* to make, do — more at THUMB, DO] (1597)
**1** : an action or process of swelling or becoming tumorous
**2** : SWELLING

**tu·mes·cence** \tü-'me-s²n(t)s, tyü-\ *noun* (1859)
: the quality or state of being tumescent; *especially* : readiness for sexual activity marked especially by vascular congestion of the sex organs

**tu·mes·cent** \-s²nt\ *adjective* [Latin *tumescent-, tumescens,* present participle of *tumescere* to swell up, inchoative of *tumēre* to swell] (1882)
: somewhat swollen ⟨*tumescent* tissue⟩

**tu·mid** \'tü-məd, 'tyü-\ *adjective* [Latin *tumidus,* from *tumēre*] (1541)
**1** : marked by swelling : SWOLLEN, ENLARGED ⟨a badly infected *tumid* leg⟩
**2** : PROTUBERANT, BULGING ⟨sails *tumid* in the breeze⟩
**3** : BOMBASTIC, TURGID

**tum·my** \'tə-mē\ *noun, plural* **tummies** [baby-talk alteration of *stomach*] (1867)

: STOMACH 1c

**tu·mor** \'tü-mər, 'tyü-\ *noun* [Latin *tumor,* from *tumēre*] (1597)
**1** : a swollen or distended part
**2** : an abnormal benign or malignant mass of tissue that is not inflammatory, arises without obvious cause from cells of preexistent tissue, and possesses no physiologic function
— **tu·mor·al** \-mə-rəl\ *adjective*
— **tu·mor·like** \-mər-,līk\ *adjective*

**tu·mor·i·gen·ic** \,tü-mə-rə-'je-nik, ,tyü-\ *adjective* (1941)
: producing or tending to produce tumors; *also* : CARCINOGENIC
— **tu·mor·i·gen·e·sis** \-'je-nə-səs\ *noun*
— **tu·mor·i·ge·nic·i·ty** \-jə-'ni-sə-tē\ *noun*

**tumor necrosis factor** *noun* (1975)
: a protein that is produced by monocytes and macrophages in response especially to endotoxins and that activates leukocytes and has antitumor activity

**tu·mor·ous** \'tü-mə-rəs, 'tyü-; 'tüm-rəs, 'tyüm-\ *adjective* (1547)
: of, relating to, or resembling a tumor

**tu·mour** \'tyü-mər\ *chiefly British variant of* TUMOR

**¹tump** \'təmp\ *noun* [origin unknown] (1589)
**1** *chiefly dialect English* : MOUND, HUMMOCK
**2** : a clump of vegetation

**²tump** *verb* [perhaps akin to British dialect *tumpoke* to fall head over heels] (1967)
*intransitive verb*
*chiefly Southern* : to tip or turn over especially accidentally — usually used with *over* ⟨sooner or later everybody *tumps* over. Nothing to worry about if you don't get caught under the canoe —Don Kennard⟩
*transitive verb*
*chiefly Southern* : to cause to tip over : OVERTURN, UPSET — usually used with *over*

**tump·line** \'təm-,plīn\ *noun* [*tump,* of Algonquian origin; akin to Eastern Abenaki *mádûmbí* pack strap] (1796)
: a sling formed by a strap slung over the forehead or chest and used for carrying or helping to support a pack on the back or in hauling loads

**tu·mult** \'tü-,məlt, 'tyü- *also* 'tə-\ *noun* [Middle English *tumulte,* from Middle French, from Latin *tumultus;* perhaps akin to Sanskrit *tumula* noisy] (15th century)
**1 a** : disorderly agitation or milling about of a crowd usually with uproar and confusion of voices : COMMOTION **b** : a turbulent uprising : RIOT
**2** : HUBBUB, DIN
**3 a** : violent agitation of mind or feelings **b** : a violent outburst

**tu·mul·tu·ary** \tü-'məl-chə-,wer-ē, tyü-, tə-\ *adjective* (1590)
: attended or marked by tumult, riot, lawlessness, confusion, or impetuosity

**tu·mul·tu·ous** \tü-'məl-chə-wəs, tyü-, tə-, -chəs; -'məlch-wəs\ *adjective* (circa 1548)
**1** : marked by tumult
**2** : tending or disposed to cause or incite a tumult
**3** : marked by violent or overwhelming turbulence or upheaval
— **tu·mul·tu·ous·ly** *adverb*
— **tu·mul·tu·ous·ness** *noun*

**tu·mu·lus** \'tü-myə-ləs, 'tyü-, 'tə-\ *noun, plural* **-li** \-,lī, -,lē\ [Latin; akin to Latin *tumēre* to swell — more at THUMB] (1686)
: an artificial hillock or mound (as over a grave); *especially* : an ancient grave : BARROW

**tun** \'tən\ *noun* [Middle English *tunne,* from Old English, from Medieval Latin *tunna*] (before 12th century)
**1** : a large cask especially for wine
**2** : any of various units of liquid capacity; *especially* : one equal to 252 gallons

**¹tu·na** \'tü-nə\ *noun* [Spanish, from Taino] (circa 1555)
**1** : any of various flat-jointed prickly pears

(genus *Opuntia*); *especially* : one (*O. tuna*) of tropical America
**2** : the edible fruit of a tuna

**²tu·na** \'tü-nə, 'tyü-\ *noun, plural* **tuna** *or* **tunas** [American Spanish, alteration of Spanish *atún,* modification of Arabic *tūn,* from Latin *thunnus,* from Greek *thynnos*] (1881)
**1** : any of numerous large vigorous scombroid food and sport fishes (as an albacore or a bluefin tuna)
**2** : the flesh of a tuna especially when canned for use as food — called also *tuna fish*

**tun·able** \'tü-nə-bəl, 'tyü-\ *adjective* (circa 1500)
**1** *archaic* **a** : TUNEFUL **b** : sounding in tune : CONCORDANT
**2** : capable of being tuned
— **tun·abil·i·ty** \,tü-nə-'bi-lə-tē, ,tyü-\ *noun*
— **tun·able·ness** \'tü-nə-bəl-nəs, 'tyü-\ *noun*
— **tun·ably** \-blē\ *adverb*

**tun·dish** \'tən-,dish\ *noun* [Middle English, funnel for filling a tun] (14th century)
**1** : FUNNEL 1a
**2** : a reservoir in the top part of a mold into which molten metal is poured

**tun·dra** \'tən-drə *also* 'tün-\ *noun* [Russian, of Lappish origin; akin to Kola Lappish *tundar* hill] (circa 1841)
: a level or rolling treeless plain that is characteristic of arctic and subarctic regions, consists of black mucky soil with a permanently frozen subsoil, and has a dominant vegetation of mosses, lichens, herbs, and dwarf shrubs; *also* : a similar region confined to mountainous areas above timberline

**¹tune** \'tün, 'tyün\ *noun* [Middle English, alteration of *tone*] (14th century)
**1 a** *archaic* : quality of sound : TONE **b** : manner of utterance : INTONATION; *specifically* : phonetic modulation
**2 a** : a succession of pleasing musical tones : MELODY **b** : a dominant theme
**3** : correct musical pitch or consonance — used chiefly in the phrases *in tune* and *out of tune*
**4 a** *archaic* : a frame of mind : MOOD **b** : AGREEMENT, HARMONY ⟨in *tune* with the times⟩ **c** : general attitude : APPROACH ⟨changed his *tune* when the going got rough⟩
**5** : AMOUNT, EXTENT ⟨custom-made to the *tune* of $40 to $50 apiece —*American Fabrics*⟩

**²tune** *verb* **tuned; tun·ing** (15th century)
*transitive verb*
**1** : to adjust in musical pitch or cause to be in tune ⟨*tuned* her guitar⟩
**2 a** : to bring into harmony : ATTUNE **b** : to adjust for precise functioning — often used with *up* ⟨*tune* up an engine⟩ **c** : to make more precise, intense, or effective
**3** : to adjust with respect to resonance at a particular frequency: as **a** : to adjust (a radio or television receiver) to respond to waves of a particular frequency — often used with *in* **b** : to establish radio contact with ⟨*tune* in a directional beacon⟩
**4** : to adjust the frequency of the output of (a device) to a chosen frequency or range of frequencies; *also* : to alter the frequency of (radiation)
*intransitive verb*
**1** : to become attuned
**2** : to adjust a radio or television receiver to respond to waves of a particular frequency

**tuned–in** \'tünd-'in; 'tyünd-\ *adjective* (1963)
: TURNED-ON

**tune·ful** \'tün-fəl, 'tyün-\ *adjective* (1591)
: MELODIOUS, MUSICAL
— **tune·ful·ly** \-fə-lē\ *adverb*
— **tune·ful·ness** *noun*

\ə\ abut \ᵊ\ kitten \ər\ further \a\ ash \ā\ ace \ä\ mop, mar \aú\ out \ch\ chin \e\ bet \ē\ easy \g\ go \i\ hit \ī\ ice \j\ job \ŋ\ sing \ō\ go \ó\ law \ói\ boy \th\ thin \th̲\ the \ü\ loot \ú\ foot \y\ yet \zh\ vision *see also* Guide to Pronunciation

**tune in** (1913)
*transitive verb*
**:** to listen to or view a broadcast of ⟨*tuned in* the weather report⟩
*intransitive verb*
**:** to listen to or view a broadcast ⟨*tune in* next week for the conclusion⟩
**tune·less** \'tün-ləs, 'tyün-\ *adjective* (1591)
**1 :** not tuneful
**2 :** not producing music
— **tune·less·ly** *adverb*
**tune out** (1910)
*transitive verb*
**:** to become unresponsive to **:** IGNORE
*intransitive verb*
**:** to dissociate oneself from what is happening or one's surroundings
**tun·er** \'tü-nər, 'tyü-\ *noun* (circa 1801)
**1 :** one that tunes ⟨a piano *tuner*⟩
**2 :** something used for tuning; *specifically* **:** the part of a receiving set that converts radio signals into audio or video signals
**tune·smith** \'tün-ˌsmith, 'tyün-\ *noun* (1926)
**:** a composer especially of popular songs
**tune–up** \-ˌəp\ *noun* (1933)
**1 :** a general adjustment to insure operation at peak efficiency
**2 :** a preliminary trial **:** WARM-UP
**tung** \'təŋ\ *noun* (1914)
**:** TUNG TREE
**tung oil** *noun* [part translation of Chinese (Beijing) *tóngyóu*] (1881)
**:** a pale yellow pungent drying oil obtained from the seeds of tung trees and used chiefly in quick-drying varnishes and paints and as a waterproofing agent
**tung·state** \'təŋ-ˌstāt\ *noun* (1800)
**:** a salt or ester of a tungstic acid and especially of $H_2WO_4$
**tung·sten** \'təŋ-stən\ *noun* [Swedish, from *tung* heavy + *sten* stone] (1796)
**:** a gray-white heavy high-melting ductile hard polyvalent metallic element that resembles chromium and molybdenum in many of its properties and is used especially for electrical purposes and in hardening alloys (as steel) — called also *wolfram;* see ELEMENT table
**tung·stic acid** \'təŋ-stik-\ *noun* [*tungsten*] (1796)
**:** a yellow crystalline powder $WO_3$ that is the trioxide of tungsten; *also* **:** an acid (as $H_2WO_4$) derived from this
**tung tree** *noun* [Chinese (Beijing) *tóng*] (1895)
**:** any of several trees (genus *Aleurites*) of the spurge family whose seeds yield tung oil; *especially* **:** an Asian tree (*A. fordii*) widely grown in warm regions
**Tun·gus** \tûŋ-'gûz, tən-\ *noun, plural* **Tungus** or **Tun·gus·es** [Russian] (1674)
**1 :** a member of an indigenous people of central and southeastern Siberia
**2 :** the Tungusic language of the Tungus people
**Tun·gu·sic** \-'gü-zik\ *noun* (circa 1867)
**:** a family of Altaic languages spoken in Manchuria and northward
— **Tungusic** *adjective*
**tu·nic** \'tü-nik, 'tyü-\ *noun* [Latin *tunica,* of Semitic origin; akin to Hebrew *kuttōneth* coat] (circa 1609)
**1 a :** a simple slip-on garment made with or without sleeves and usually knee-length or longer, belted at the waist, and worn as an under or outer garment by men and women of ancient Greece and Rome **b :** SURCOAT
**2 :** an enclosing or covering membrane or tissue ⟨the *tunic* of a seed⟩
**3 :** a long usually plain close-fitting jacket with high collar worn especially as part of a uniform
**4 :** TUNICLE
**5 a :** a short overskirt **b :** a hip-length or longer blouse or jacket

**tu·ni·ca** \'tü-ni-kə, 'tyü-\ *noun, plural* **tu·ni·cae** \-nə-ˌkē, -ˌkī, -ˌsē\ [Latin, tunic, membrane] (circa 1828)
**:** an enveloping membrane or layer of body tissue
**¹tu·ni·cate** \'tü-ni-kət, 'tyü-, -nə-ˌkāt\ *also* **tu·ni·cat·ed** \-nə-ˌkā-təd\ *adjective* [Latin *tunicatus,* from *tunica*] (circa 1623)
**1 a :** having or covered with a tunic or tunica **b :** having, arranged in, or made up of concentric layers ⟨a *tunicate* bulb⟩
**2 :** of or relating to the tunicates
**²tu·ni·cate** \-nə-ˌkāt, -nə-kət\ *noun* [New Latin *Tunicata,* from neuter plural of Latin *tunicatus*] (1889)
**:** any of a subphylum (Urochordata synonym Tunicata) of marine chordate animals that have a thick secreted covering layer, a greatly reduced nervous system, a heart able to reverse the direction of blood flow, and only in the larval stage a notochord
**tu·ni·cle** \'tü-ni-kəl, 'tyü-\ *noun* [Middle English, from Latin *tunicula,* diminutive of *tunica*] (15th century)
**:** a short vestment worn by a subdeacon over the alb during mass and by a bishop under the dalmatic at pontifical ceremonies
**tuning fork** *noun* (1799)
**:** a 2-pronged metal implement that gives a fixed tone when struck and is useful for tuning musical instruments and ascertaining standard pitch
**tuning pipe** *noun* (1897)
**:** PITCH PIPE; *specifically* **:** one of a set of pitch pipes used especially for tuning stringed musical instruments
**¹tun·nel** \'tə-n°l\ *noun* [Middle English *tonel* tube-shaped net, from Middle French, from *tun,* from Old French, from *tonne* tun, from Medieval Latin *tunna*] (1548)
**1 :** a hollow conduit or recess **:** TUBE, WELL
**2 a :** a covered passageway; *specifically* **:** a horizontal passageway through or under an obstruction **b :** a subterranean gallery (as in a mine) **c :** BURROW
— **tun·nel·like** \-n°l-ˌ(l)īk\ *adjective*
**²tunnel** *verb* **-neled** *or* **-nelled; -nel·ing** *or* **-nel·ling** \'tən-liŋ, 'tə-n°l-iŋ\ (1795)
*intransitive verb*
**1 :** to make or use a tunnel
**2** *physics* **:** to pass through a potential barrier ⟨electrons *tunneling* through an insulator between semiconductors⟩
*transitive verb*
**:** to make a tunnel or similar opening through or under; *also* **:** to make (one's way) by or as if by making a tunnel
— **tun·nel·er** \'tən-lər, 'tə-n°l-ər\ *noun*
**tunnel vision** *noun* (circa 1942)
**1 :** constriction of the visual field resulting in loss of peripheral vision
**2 :** extreme narrowness of viewpoint **:** NARROWMINDEDNESS; *also* **:** single-minded concentration on one objective
— **tun·nel–vi·sioned** \-'vi-zhənd\ *adjective*
**tun·ny** \'tə-nē\ *noun, plural* **tunnies** *also* **tunny** [modification of Middle French *thon* or Old Italian *tonno;* both from Old Provençal *ton,* from Latin *thunnus* — more at TUNA] (circa 1530)
**:** TUNA
**¹tup** \'təp\ *noun* [Middle English *tupe*] (14th century)
**1** *chiefly British* **:** RAM 1a
**2 :** a heavy metal body (as the weight of a pendulum)
**²tup** *transitive verb* **tupped; tup·ping** (1604)
*chiefly British* **:** to copulate with (a ewe)
**tu·pe·lo** \'tü-pə-ˌlō, 'tyü-\ *noun, plural* **-los** [perhaps from Creek *ito opilwa* swamp tree] (circa 1730)
**1 :** any of a genus (*Nyssa* of the family Nyssaceae) of North American and Asian deciduous trees that have simple alternate leaves,

small greenish dioecious stalked flowers, and a rounded drupe; *especially* **:** BLACK GUM
**2 :** the pale soft wood of a tupelo
**Tu·pi** \tü-'pē, 'tü-(ˌ)\ *noun, plural* **Tupi** *or* **Tu·pis** (1842)
**1 :** the language of the Tupi people
**2 :** a member of a group of Tupi-Guaranian peoples of Brazil living especially in the Amazon valley
**Tu·pi·an** \tü-'pē-ən, 'tü-(ˌ)\ *adjective* (1902)
**:** of, relating to, or constituting the Tupi or other Tupi-Guaranian peoples or their languages
**Tu·pi–Gua·ra·ni** \tü-ˌpē-gwär-ə-'nē, 'tü-(ˌ)pē-\ *noun* (1850)
**1 :** a member of a group of South American Indian peoples spread over an area from eastern Brazil to the Peruvian Andes and from the Guianas to Uruguay
**2 :** TUPI-GUARANIAN
**Tupi–Gua·ra·ni·an** \-'nē-ən\ *noun* (circa 1902)
**:** a language family widely distributed in tropical South America
**-tu·ple** \ˌtə-pəl, ˌtü-\ *noun combining form* [quin*tuple,* sex*tuple*]
**:** set of (so many) elements — usually used of sets with ordered elements ⟨the ordered 2-*tuple* (*a, b*)⟩
**tup·pence** *variant of* TWOPENCE
**tuque** \'tük, 'tyük\ *noun* [Canadian French, from French *toque* — more at TOQUE] (1871)
**:** a warm knitted usually pointed stocking cap
**tu quo·que** \tü-'kwō-kwē, 'tyü-, -'kō-\ *noun* [Latin, you too] (1614)
**:** a retort charging an adversary with being or doing what he criticizes in others
**tu·ra·co** \'tür-ə-(ˌ)kō\ *noun, plural* **-cos** [origin unknown] (1743)
**:** any of a family (Musophagidae) of African birds that are related to the cuckoos and have a long tail, a short stout often colored bill, and red wing feathers
**Tu·ra·ni·an** \tü-'rä-nē-ən, tyü-, -'rä-\ *noun* [Persian *Tūrān* Turkestan, the region north of the Amu Darya] (circa 1777)
**1 :** a member of any of various peoples speaking Ural-Altaic languages
**2 :** URAL-ALTAIC
— **Turanian** *adjective*
**tur·ban** \'tər-bən\ *noun* [Middle French *turbant,* from Italian *turbante,* from Turkish *tülbent,* from Persian *dulband*] (1588)
**1 :** a headdress worn chiefly in countries of the eastern Mediterranean and southern Asia especially by Muslims and made of a cap around which is wound a long cloth
**2 :** a headdress resembling a turban; *specifically* **:** a woman's close-fitting hat without a brim
**3 :** a rolled stuffed fillet of fish ⟨*turban* of sole⟩
***word history*** SEE TULIP
— **tur·baned** *or* **tur·banned** \-bənd\ *adjective*

turban 1

**tur·bel·lar·i·an** \ˌtər-bə-'ler-ē-ən, -'lar-\ *noun* [ultimately from Latin *turbellae* (plural) bustle, stir, diminutive of *turba* confusion, crowd; from the tiny eddies created in water by the cilia] (1883)
**:** any of a class (Turbellaria) of mostly aquatic and free-living flatworms (as a planarian)
— **turbellarian** *adjective*
**tur·bid** \'tər-bəd\ *adjective* [Latin *turbidus* confused, turbid, from *turba* confusion, crowd, probably from Greek *tyrbē* confusion] (1626)
**1 a :** thick or opaque with or as if with roiled sediment ⟨a *turbid* stream⟩ **b :** heavy with smoke or mist
**2 a :** deficient in clarity or purity **:** FOUL, MUDDY ⟨*turbid* depths of degradation and misery —C. I. Glicksberg⟩ **b :** characterized by or producing obscurity (as of mind or emotions) ⟨an emotionally *turbid* response⟩

— **tur·bid·i·ty** \ˌtər-'bi-də-tē\ *noun*

— **tur·bid·ly** \'tər-bəd-lē\ *adverb*

— **tur·bid·ness** *noun*

**tur·bi·dim·e·ter** \ˌtər-bə-'di-mə-tər\ *noun* [International Scientific Vocabulary *turbid*ity + -*meter*] (1905)
**1 :** an instrument for measuring and comparing the turbidity of liquids by viewing light through them and determining how much light is cut off
**2 :** NEPHELOMETER

— **tur·bi·di·met·ric** \ˌtər-bə-də-'me-trik, ˌtər-ˌbi-də-\ *adjective*

— **tur·bi·di·met·ri·cal·ly** \-tri-k(ə-)lē\ *adverb*

— **tur·bi·dim·e·try** \ˌtər-bə-'di-mə-trē\ *noun*

**tur·bi·dite** \'tər-bə-ˌdīt\ *noun* [*turbid*ity current (a current flowing down a slope and spreading out on the ocean floor) + [1]-*ite*] (1957)
**:** a sedimentary deposit consisting of material that has moved down the steep slope at the edge of a continental shelf; *also* **:** a rock formed from this deposit

[1]**tur·bi·nate** \'tər-bə-nət, -ˌnāt\ *also* **tur·bi·nat·ed** \-ˌnā-təd\ *adjective* [Latin *turbinatus*, from *turbin-, turbo*] (1661)
**1 :** shaped like a top or an inverted cone ⟨*turbinate* seed capsule⟩
**2 :** relating to or being a turbinate

[2]**turbinate** *noun* (circa 1803)
**:** one of usually several thin plicated membrane-covered bony or cartilaginous plates on the walls of the nasal chambers

**tur·bine** \'tər-bən, -ˌbīn\ *noun* [French, from Latin *turbin-, turbo* top, whirlwind, whirl, from *turba* confusion — more at TURBID] (1842)
**:** a rotary engine actuated by the reaction or impulse or both of a current of fluid (as water, steam, or air) subject to pressure and usually made with a series of curved vanes on a central rotating spindle

**tur·bo** \'tər-(ˌ)bō\ *noun, plural* **turbos** [*turbo-*] (1904)
**1 :** TURBINE
**2** [by shortening] **:** TURBOCHARGER

**turbo-** *combining form* [*turbine*]
**1 :** coupled directly to a driving turbine ⟨*turbo*fan⟩
**2 :** consisting of or incorporating a turbine ⟨*turbo*jet engine⟩

**tur·bo·car** \'tər-bō-ˌkär\ *noun* (1950)
**:** an automotive vehicle propelled by a gas turbine

**tur·bo·charged** \-ˌchärjd\ *adjective* (1945)
**:** equipped with a turbocharger

**tur·bo·charg·er** \-ˌchär-jər\ *noun* (1934)
**:** a centrifugal blower driven by exhaust gas turbines and used to supercharge an engine

**tur·bo·elec·tric** \ˌtər-bō-i-'lek-trik\ *adjective* (1904)
**:** using or being a turbine generator that produces electricity usually for motive power

**tur·bo·fan** \'tər-bō-ˌfan\ *noun* (1911)
**1 :** a fan that is directly connected to and driven by a turbine and is used to supply air for cooling, ventilation, or combustion
**2 :** a jet engine having a turbofan

**tur·bo·gen·er·a·tor** \ˌtər-bō-'je-nə-ˌrā-tər\ *noun* (1898)
**:** an electric generator driven by a turbine

**tur·bo·jet** \-ˌjet\ *noun* (1945)
**1 :** an airplane powered by turbojet engines
**2 :** TURBOJET ENGINE

**turbojet engine** *noun* (1944)
**:** a jet engine in which a turbine drives a compressor that supplies air to a burner and hot gases from the burner drive the turbine before being discharged rearward

**tur·bo·ma·chin·ery** \ˌtər-bō-mə-'shēn-rē, -'shē-nə-\ *noun* (1948)
**:** machinery consisting of, incorporating, or constituting a turbine

**tur·bo·prop** \'tər-bō-ˌpräp\ *noun* (1945)
**1 :** TURBOPROP ENGINE

**2 :** an airplane powered by turboprop engines

**turboprop engine** *noun* (1947)
**:** a jet engine designed to produce thrust principally by means of a propeller driven by a turbine with additional thrust usually obtained by the rearward discharge of hot exhaust gases

**tur·bo·shaft** \'tər-bō-ˌshaft\ *noun* (1958)
**:** a gas turbine engine that is similar in operation to a turboprop engine but instead of being used to power a propeller is used through a transmission system for powering other devices (as helicopter rotors and pumps)

**tur·bot** \'tər-bət\ *noun, plural* **turbot** *also* **turbots** [Middle English, from Old French *tourbot*] (14th century)
**1 :** a large European flatfish (*Psetta maxima*) that is a popular food fish and has a brownish upper surface marked with scattered tubercles and a white undersurface
**2 :** any of various flatfishes resembling the turbot

**tur·bu·lence** \'tər-byə-lən(t)s\ *noun* (1598)
**:** the quality or state of being turbulent: as **a :** wild commotion **b :** irregular atmospheric motion especially when characterized by up-and-down currents **c :** departure in a fluid from a smooth flow

**tur·bu·len·cy** \-lən(t)-sē\ *noun, plural* **-cies** (1607)
*archaic* **:** TURBULENCE

**tur·bu·lent** \-lənt\ *adjective* [Latin *turbulentus*, from *turba* confusion, crowd — more at TURBID] (1538)
**1 :** causing unrest, violence, or disturbance
**2 a :** characterized by agitation or tumult **:** TEMPESTUOUS **b :** exhibiting physical turbulence

— **tur·bu·lent·ly** *adverb*

**turbulent flow** *noun* (1895)
**:** a fluid flow in which the velocity at a given point varies erratically in magnitude and direction — compare LAMINAR FLOW

**Tur·co-** *or* **Tur·ko-** \'tər-(ˌ)kō\ *combining form* [*Turco-* from Medieval Latin *Turcus* Turk; *Turko-* from *Turk*]
**1 :** Turkic **:** Turkish **:** Turk ⟨*Turco*phil⟩
**2 :** Turkish and ⟨*Turco*-Greek⟩

**turd** \'tərd\ *noun* [Middle English *tord, turd*, from Old English *tord*; akin to Middle Dutch *tort* dung and probably to Old English *teran* to tear — more at TEAR] (before 12th century)
**1 :** a piece of excrement — sometimes considered vulgar
**2 :** a contemptible person — usually considered vulgar

**tu·reen** \tə-'rēn, tyů-\ *noun* [French *terrine*, from Middle French, from feminine of *terrin* of earth, from (assumed) Vulgar Latin *terrinus*, from Latin *terra* earth — more at TERRACE] (circa 1706)
**1 :** a deep and usually covered bowl from which foods (as soup) are served
**2 :** CASSEROLE 1

[1]**turf** \'tərf\ *noun, plural* **turfs** \'tərfs\ *also* **turves** \'tərvz\ [Middle English, from Old English; akin to Old High German *zurba* turf, Sanskrit *darbha* tuft of grass] (before 12th century)
**1 a :** the upper stratum of soil bound by grass and plant roots into a thick mat; *also* **:** a piece of this **b :** an artificial substitute for this (as on a playing field)
**2 a :** PEAT 2 **b :** a piece of peat dried for fuel
**3 a :** a track or course for horse racing **b :** the sport or business of horse racing
**4 a :** territory considered by a teenage gang to be under its control **b :** TERRITORY 2 ⟨have to play two of the last three games on hostile *turf* —Joe Klein⟩ ⟨points toward the biographer's *turf*, not the critic's —Hugh Kenner⟩; *also* **:** a sphere of activity or influence ⟨people who could hurt him on his own foreign-policy *turf* —*Wall Street Journal*⟩

— **turfy** \'tər-fē\ *adjective*

[2]**turf** *transitive verb* (15th century)
**1 :** to cover with turf

**2** *chiefly British* **:** to eject forcibly **:** KICK — usually used with *out*

**turf accountant** *noun* (1915)
*British* **:** BOOKMAKER 2

**turf·man** \'tərf-mən\ *noun* (1818)
**:** a devotee of horse racing; *especially* **:** a person who owns and races horses

**turf·ski** \-ˌskē\ *noun* (1967)
**:** a short ski with rollers on the bottom that can be used to ski down a grassy slope

— **turf·ski·ing** *noun*

**tur·ges·cent** \ˌtər-'je-s°nt\ *adjective* [Latin *turgescent-, turgescens*, present participle of *turgescere* to swell, inchoative of *turgēre* to be swollen] (circa 1727)
**:** becoming turgid, distended, or inflated **:** SWELLING

— **tur·ges·cence** \-s°n(t)s\ *noun*

**tur·gid** \'tər-jəd\ *adjective* [Latin *turgidus*, from *turgēre* to be swollen] (1620)
**1 :** being in a state of distension **:** SWOLLEN, TUMID ⟨*turgid* limbs⟩; *especially* **:** exhibiting turgor
**2 :** excessively embellished in style or language **:** BOMBASTIC, POMPOUS

— **tur·gid·i·ty** \ˌtər-'ji-də-tē\ *noun*

— **tur·gid·ly** \'tər-jəd-lē\ *adverb*

— **tur·gid·ness** *noun*

**tur·gor** \'tər-gər, -ˌgȯr\ *noun* [Late Latin, turgidity, swelling, from Latin *turgēre*] (1876)
**:** the normal state of turgidity and tension in living cells; *especially* **:** the distension of the protoplasmic layer and wall of a plant cell by the fluid contents

**Tu·ring machine** \'tůr-iŋ-, 'tyůr-\ *noun* [A. M. *Turing* (died 1954) English mathematician] (1937)
**:** a hypothetical computing machine that has an unlimited amount of information storage

**tu·ris·ta** \tů-'rē-stə\ *noun* [Spanish, tourist] (1962)
**:** intestinal sickness and diarrhea commonly affecting a tourist in a foreign country; *especially* **:** MONTEZUMA'S REVENGE

**Turk** \'tərk\ *noun* [Middle English, from Middle French or Turkish; Middle French *Turc*, from Medieval Latin or Turkish; Medieval Latin *Turcus*, from Turkish *Türk*] (14th century)
**1 :** a member of any of numerous Asian peoples speaking Turkic languages who live in a region extending from the Balkans to eastern Siberia and western China
**2 :** a native or inhabitant of Turkey
**3** *archaic* **:** one who is cruel or tyrannical
**4 :** MUSLIM; *specifically* **:** a Muslim subject of the Turkish sultan
**5 :** a Turkish horse; *specifically* **:** a Turkish strain of Arab and crossbred horses
**6** *often not capitalized* **:** a usually young dynamic person eager for change; *especially* **:** YOUNG TURK

**tur·key** \'tər-kē\ *noun, plural* **turkeys** [*Turkey*, country in western Asia and southeastern Europe; from confusion with the guinea fowl, supposed to be imported from Turkish territory] (1555)

**1** *plural also* **turkey**
**:** a large North American gallinaceous bird (*Meleagris gallopavo*) that is domesticated in most parts of the world
**2 :** FAILURE, FLOP; *especially* **:** a theatrical production that has failed

turkey 1

**3 :** three successive strikes in bowling
**4 :** a stupid, foolish, or inept person
**tur·key-cock** \'tər-kē-,käk\ *noun* (1578)
**1 :** GOBBLER
**2 :** a strutting pompous person
**turkey oak** *noun* (1709)
**:** a small oak (*Quercus laevis* synonym *Q. catesbaei*) of the southeastern U.S.; *also* **:** a Eurasian oak (*Q. cerris*)
**Tur·key red** \'tər-kē-\ *noun* [*Turkey*] (1789)
**:** a brilliant durable red produced on cotton by means of alizarin in connection with an aluminum mordant and fatty matter
**tur·key shoot** \'tər-kē-\ *noun* (1845)
**:** a marksmanship contest using a moving target with a turkey offered as a prize
**turkey trot** *noun* (1908)
**:** a ragtime dance danced with the feet well apart and with a characteristic rise on the ball of the foot followed by a drop upon the heel
**turkey vulture** *noun* (1823)
**:** an American vulture (*Cathartes aura*) with a red head and whitish bill — called also *turkey buzzard*
**Turk·ic** \'tər-kik\ *adjective* (1859)
**1 a :** of, relating to, or constituting a family of Altaic languages including Turkish **b :** of or relating to the peoples speaking Turkic
**2 :** TURKISH 1
**— Turkic** *noun*
**¹Turk·ish** \'tər-kish\ *adjective* (1545)
**1 :** of, relating to, or characteristic of Turkey, the Turks, or Turkish
**2 :** TURKIC 1a
**²Turkish** *noun* (1677)
**:** the Turkic language of the Republic of Turkey
**Turkish bath** *noun* (1644)
**:** a bath in which the bather passes through a series of steam rooms of increasing temperature and then receives a rubdown, massage, and cold shower
**Turkish coffee** *noun* (1854)
**:** a sweetened decoction of pulverized coffee
**Turkish delight** *noun* (1877)
**:** a jellylike or gummy confection usually cut in cubes and dusted with sugar — called also *Turkish paste*
**Turkish towel** *noun* (1862)
**:** a towel made of cotton terry cloth
**Turk·ism** \'tər-,ki-zəm\ *noun* (1595)
**:** the customs, beliefs, institutions, and principles of the Turks
**Tur·ko·man** *or* **Tur·co·man** \'tər-kə-mən\ *noun, plural* **Turkomans** *or* **Turcomans** [Medieval Latin *Turcomannus,* from Persian *Turkmān,* from *turkmān* resembling a Turk, from *Turk*] (circa 1520)
**:** a member of a Turkic-speaking traditionally nomadic people living chiefly in Turkmenistan, Afghanistan, and Iran
**— Turkoman** *or* **Turcoman** *adjective*
**Turk's head** *noun* (1833)
**:** a turban-shaped knot worked on a rope with a piece of small line — see KNOT illustration
**tur·mer·ic** \'tər-mə-rik *also* 'tü-mə- *or* 'tyü-\ *noun* [modification of Middle French *terre merite* saffron, from Medieval Latin *terra merita,* literally, deserving or deserved earth] (1545)
**1 :** an East Indian perennial herb (*Curcuma domestica* synonym *C. longa*) of the ginger family with a large aromatic yellow rhizome
**2 :** the cleaned, boiled, dried, and usually pulverized rhizome of the turmeric plant used as a coloring agent, a flavoring, or a stimulant
**3 :** a yellow to reddish brown dyestuff obtained from turmeric
**tur·moil** \'tər-,mȯil\ *noun* [origin unknown] (1526)
**:** a state or condition of extreme confusion, agitation, or commotion
**¹turn** \'tərn\ *verb* [Middle English; partly from Old English *tyrnan & turnian* to turn, from Medieval Latin *tornare,* from Latin, to turn on a lathe, from *tornus* lathe, from Greek *tornos*;

partly from Old French *torner, tourner* to turn, from Medieval Latin *tornare;* akin to Latin *terere* to rub — more at THROW] (before 12th century)
*transitive verb*
**1 a :** to cause to move around an axis or a center **:** make rotate or revolve ⟨*turn* a wheel⟩ ⟨*turn* a crank⟩ **b (1) :** to cause to move around so as to effect a desired end (as of locking, opening, or shutting) ⟨*turned* the knob till the door opened⟩ **(2) :** to affect or alter the functioning of (as a mechanical device) by such movement ⟨*turn* the oven to a higher temperature⟩ **c :** to execute or perform by rotating or revolving ⟨*turn* handsprings⟩ **d :** to twist out of line or shape **:** WRENCH ⟨had *turned* his ankle⟩
**2 (1) :** to cause to change position by moving through an arc of a circle ⟨*turned* her chair to the fire⟩ **(2) :** to cause to move around a center so as to show another side of ⟨*turn* the page⟩ **(3) :** to cause (as a scale) to move so as to register weight **b :** to revolve mentally **:** think over **:** PONDER
**3 a :** to reverse the sides or surfaces of **:** INVERT ⟨*turn* pancakes⟩ ⟨*turn* the shirt inside out⟩: as **(1) :** to dig or plow so as to bring the lower soil to the surface **(2) :** to make (as a garment) over by reversing the material and resewing ⟨*turn* a collar⟩ **(3) :** to invert feet up and face down (as a character, rule, or slug) in setting type **b :** to reverse or upset the order or disposition of ⟨everything was *turned* topsy-turvy⟩ **c :** to disturb or upset the mental balance of **:** DERANGE, UNSETTLE ⟨a mind *turned* by grief⟩ **d :** to set in another especially contrary direction
**4 a :** to bend or change the course of **:** DIVERT **b :** to cause to retreat ⟨used fire hoses to *turn* the mob⟩ **c :** to alter the drift, tendency, or expected result of **d :** to bend a course around or about **:** ROUND ⟨*turned* the corner at full speed⟩
**5 a (1) :** to direct or point (as the face) in a specified way or direction **(2) :** to present by a change in direction or position ⟨*turning* his back to his guests⟩ **b :** to bring to bear (as by aiming, pointing, or focusing) **:** TRAIN ⟨*turned* the light into the dark doorway⟩ ⟨*turned* a questioning eye toward her⟩ **c :** to direct (as the attention or mind) toward or away from something **d :** to direct the employment of **:** APPLY, DEVOTE ⟨*turned* his skills to the service of mankind⟩ **e (1) :** to cause to rebound or recoil ⟨*turns* their argument against them⟩ **(2) :** to make antagonistic **:** PREJUDICE ⟨*turn* a child against its mother⟩ **f (1) :** to cause to go in a particular direction ⟨*turned* our steps homeward⟩ **(2) :** DRIVE, SEND ⟨*turn* cows to pasture⟩ ⟨*turning* hunters off his land⟩ **(3) :** to convey or direct into or out of a receptacle by inverting
**6 a (1) :** to make acid or sour **(2) :** to change the color of (as foliage) **b (1) :** CONVERT, TRANSFORM ⟨*turn* defeat into victory⟩ **(2) :** TRANSLATE, PARAPHRASE **c :** to cause to become of a specified nature or appearance ⟨*turned* him into a frog⟩ ⟨illness *turned* her hair white⟩ **d :** to exchange for something else ⟨*turn* coins into paper money⟩ **e :** to cause to defect to another side
**7 a :** to shape especially in a rounded form by applying a cutting tool while revolving in a lathe **b :** to give a rounded form to by any means ⟨*turn* the heel of a sock⟩ **c :** to shape or mold artistically, gracefully, or neatly ⟨a well *turned* phrase⟩
**8 :** to make a fold, bend, or curve in: **a :** to form by bending ⟨*turn* a lead pipe⟩ **b :** to cause (the edge of a blade) to bend back or over **:** BLUNT, DULL
**9 a :** to keep (as money or goods) moving; *specifically* **:** to dispose of (a stock) to make room for another **b :** to gain in the course of business ⟨*turning* a quick profit⟩ **c :** to make use of ⟨*turned* her education to advantage⟩ **d :** to carry to completion ⟨*turned* a double play⟩

**10 :** to engage in (an act of prostitution) ⟨*turn* tricks⟩
*intransitive verb*
**1 a :** to move around on an axis or through an arc of a circle **:** ROTATE **b :** to become giddy or dizzy **:** SPIN ⟨heights always made his head *turn*⟩ **c (1) :** to have as a decisive factor **:** HINGE ⟨the argument *turns* on a point of logic⟩ ⟨the outcome of the game *turned* on an interception⟩ **(2) :** to have a center (as of interest) in something specified
**2 a :** to direct one's course **b (1) :** to reverse a course or direction **(2) :** to have a reactive usually adverse effect **:** RECOIL **c :** to take a different course or direction ⟨*turned* toward home⟩ ⟨the main road *turns* sharply to the right⟩
**3 a :** to change position so as to face another way **b :** to face toward or away from someone or something **c :** to change one's attitude or reverse one's course of action to one of opposition or hostility ⟨felt the world had *turned* against him⟩ **d :** to make a sudden violent assault especially without evident cause ⟨dogs *turning* on their owners⟩
**4 a :** to direct one's attention or thoughts to or away from someone or something **b (1) :** to change one's religion **(2) :** to go over to another side or party **:** DEFECT **c :** to have recourse **:** REFER, RESORT ⟨*turned* to a friend for help⟩ ⟨*turned* to his notes for the exact figures⟩ **d :** to direct one's efforts or interests **:** devote or apply oneself ⟨*turned* to the study of the law⟩
**5 a :** to become changed, altered, or transformed: as **(1)** *archaic* **:** to become different **(2) :** to change color ⟨the leaves have *turned*⟩ **(3) :** to become sour, rancid, or tainted ⟨the milk had *turned*⟩ **(4) :** to be variable or inconstant **(5) :** to become mentally unbalanced **:** become deranged **b (1) :** to pass from one state to another **:** CHANGE ⟨water had *turned* to ice⟩ **(2) :** BECOME, GROW ⟨his hair had *turned* gray⟩ ⟨the weather *turned* bad⟩ ⟨just *turned* twenty⟩ **(3) :** to become someone or something specified by change from another state **:** change into ⟨*turn* pro⟩ ⟨doctors *turned* authors⟩
**6 :** to become curved or bent (as from pressure); *especially* **:** to become blunted by bending ⟨edge of the knife had *turned*⟩
**7 :** to operate a lathe
**8** *of merchandise* **:** to be stocked and disposed of **:** change hands
**— turn·able** \'tər-nə-bəl\ *adjective*
**— turn a blind eye :** to refuse to see **:** be oblivious ⟨might *turn a blind eye* to the use of violence —Arthur Krock⟩
**— turn a deaf ear :** to refuse to listen
**— turn a hair :** to give a sign of distress or disturbance ⟨did not *turn a hair* when told of the savage murder —*Times Literary Supplement*⟩
**— turn color 1 :** to become of a different color **2 a :** BLUSH, FLUSH **b :** to grow pale
**— turn loose 1 a :** to set free ⟨*turned loose* the captured animal⟩ **b :** to free from all restraints ⟨*turned* them *loose* with a pile of theme paper to write whatever they liked —Elizabeth P. Schafer⟩ **2 :** to fire off **:** DISCHARGE **3 :** to open fire
**— turn one's back on 1 :** REJECT, DENY ⟨would be *turning one's back on* history —Pius Walsh⟩ **2 :** FORSAKE ⟨*turned his back on* his obligations⟩
**— turn one's hand** *or* **turn a hand :** to set to work **:** apply oneself
**— turn one's head :** to cause to become infatuated or conceited ⟨success had not *turned his head*⟩
**— turn one's stomach :** to disgust completely **:** SICKEN, NAUSEATE ⟨the foul smell *turned his stomach*⟩
**— turn tail :** to turn away so as to flee ⟨*turned tail* and ran⟩
**— turn the other cheek :** to respond to injury or unkindness with patience **:** forgo retaliation

— **turn the tables :** to bring about a reversal of the relative conditions or fortunes of two contending parties

— **turn the trick :** to bring about the desired result or effect

— **turn turtle :** CAPSIZE, OVERTURN

**²turn** *noun* [Middle English; partly from Old French *tourn, tour* lathe, circuit, turn (partly from Latin *tornus* lathe; partly from Old French *torner, tourner* to turn); partly from Middle English *turnen* to turn] (13th century) **1 a :** the action or an act of turning about a center or axis **:** REVOLUTION, ROTATION **b :** any of various rotating or pivoting movements in dancing or gymnastics **2 a :** the action or an act of giving or taking a different direction **:** change of course or posture ⟨illegal left *turn*⟩: as (1) **:** a drill maneuver in which troops in mass formation change direction without preserving alignment (2) **:** any of various shifts of direction in skiing (3) **:** an interruption of a curve in figure skating **b :** DEFLECTION, DEVIATION **c :** the action or an act of turning so as to face in the opposite direction **:** reversal of posture or course ⟨an about *turn*⟩ ⟨*turn* of the tide⟩ **d :** a change effected by turning over to another side ⟨*turn* of the cards⟩ **e :** a place at which something turns, turns off, or turns back **:** BEND, CURVE **3 :** a short trip out and back or round about ⟨took a *turn* through the park⟩ **4 :** an act or deed affecting another especially when incidental or unexpected ⟨one good *turn* deserves another⟩ **5 a :** a period of action or activity **:** GO, SPELL **b :** a place, time, or opportunity accorded an individual or unit of a series in simple succession or in a scheduled order ⟨waiting her *turn* in line⟩ **c :** a period or tour of duty **:** SHIFT **d :** a short act or piece (as for a variety show); *also* **:** PERFORMANCE 3 **e** (1) **:** an event in any gambling game after which bets are settled (2) **:** the order of the last three cards in faro — used in the phrase *call the turn* **6 :** something that revolves around a center: as **a** (1) **:** LATHE (2) **:** a catch or latch for a cupboard or cabinet door operated by turning a handle **b :** a musical ornament consisting of a group of four or more notes that wind about the principal note by including the notes next above and next below **7 :** a special purpose or requirement — used chiefly in the phrase *serve one's turn* **8 a :** an act of changing **:** ALTERATION, MODIFICATION ⟨a nasty *turn* in the weather⟩ **b :** a change in tendency, trend, or drift ⟨hoped for a *turn* in his luck⟩ ⟨a *turn* for the better⟩ **c :** the beginning of a new period of time ⟨the *turn* of the century⟩ **9 a :** distinctive quality or character **b** (1) **:** a skillful fashioning of language or arrangement of words (2) **:** a particular form of expression or peculiarity of phrasing **c :** the shape or mold in which something is fashioned **:** CAST **10 a :** the state or manner of being coiled or twisted **b :** a single round (as of rope passed about an object or of wire wound on a core) **11 :** natural or special ability or aptitude **:** BENT, INCLINATION ⟨a *turn* for logic⟩ ⟨an optimistic *turn* of mind⟩ **12 :** a special twist, construction, or interpretation ⟨gave the old yarn a new *turn*⟩ **13 a :** a disordering spell or attack (as of illness, faintness, or dizziness) **b :** a nervous start or shock **14 a :** a complete transaction involving a purchase and sale of securities; *also* **:** a profit from such a transaction **b :** TURNOVER 7b **15 :** something turned or to be turned: as **a :** a character or slug inverted in setting type **b :** a piece of type placed bottom up

— **at every turn :** on every occasion **:** CONTINUALLY ⟨they opposed her at *every turn*⟩

— **by turns 1 :** one after another in regular succession **2 :** VARIOUSLY, ALTERNATELY ⟨a book that is *by turns* pedantic, delightful, and infuriating⟩

— **in turn :** in due order of succession

— **on the turn :** at the point of turning ⟨tide is *on the turn*⟩

— **out of turn 1 :** not in due order of succession ⟨play *out of turn*⟩ **2 :** at a wrong time or place and usually imprudently ⟨talking *out of turn*⟩

— **to a turn :** to perfection

**turn·about** \'tər-nə-ˌbau̇t\ *noun* (1789) **1 :** MERRY-GO-ROUND **2 a :** a change or reversal of direction, trend, policy, role, or character **b :** a changing from one allegiance to another **c :** TURNCOAT, RENEGADE **d :** an act or instance of retaliating ⟨*turnabout* is fair play⟩

**turn·around** \-ˌrau̇nd\ *noun* (1926) **1 a :** the process of readying a vehicle for departure after its arrival especially without any intervening delays; *also* **:** the time spent in this process **b :** the action of receiving, processing, and returning something **2 :** a space permitting the turning around of a vehicle **3 :** TURNABOUT 2a, b

**turn around** (1949) *intransitive verb* **1 :** to act in an abrupt, different, or surprising manner — used with *and* ⟨after three years he just *turned around* and left school⟩ **2 :** to become changed for the better *transitive verb* **:** to change for the better ⟨*turned* her life *around*⟩

**turn away** (13th century) *transitive verb* **1 :** DEFLECT, AVERT **2 a :** to send away **:** REJECT, DISMISS **b :** REPEL **c :** to refuse admittance or acceptance to *intransitive verb* **:** to start to go away **:** DEPART

**turn back** (1535) *intransitive verb* **1 a :** to go in the reverse direction **b :** to stop going forward **2 :** to refer to an earlier time or place *transitive verb* **1 :** to drive back or away **2 :** to stop the advance of **3 :** to fold back **4 :** GIVE BACK, RETURN

— **turn back the clock :** to revert to or remind of a condition existing in the past

**turn·buck·le** \'tərn-ˌbə-kəl\ *noun* (circa 1877) **:** a device that usually consists of a link with screw threads at both ends, that is turned to bring the ends closer together, and that is used for tightening a rod or stay

**turnbuckles**

**turn·coat** \-ˌkōt\ *noun* (1557) **:** one who switches to an opposing side or party; *specifically* **:** TRAITOR

**¹turn·down** \'tərn-'dau̇n\ *adjective* (1840) **:** capable of being turned down; *especially* **:** worn turned down ⟨*turndown* collar⟩

**²turn·down** \'tərn-ˌdau̇n\ *noun* (1849) **1 :** something turned down; *also* **:** an instance of turning something (as a bed sheet) down ⟨hotel *turndown* service⟩ **2 :** REJECTION **3 :** DOWNTURN

**turn down** (1601) *transitive verb* **1 :** to fold or double down **2 :** to turn (a card) face downward

**3 :** to reduce the height or intensity of by turning a control ⟨*turn down* the radio⟩ **4 :** to decline to accept **:** REJECT ⟨*turned down* the offer⟩ *intransitive verb* **:** to be capable of being folded or doubled down ⟨the collar *turns down*⟩

**turned-on** \'tərnd-'ȯn, -'än\ *adjective* (1966) **:** keenly aware of and responsive to what is new and fashionable **:** HIP

**¹turn·er** \'tər-nər\ *noun* (15th century) **:** one that turns or is used for turning ⟨a pancake *turner*⟩; *especially* **:** a person who forms articles with a lathe

**²tur·ner** \'tər-nər, 'tu̇r-\ *noun* [German, from *turnen* to perform gymnastic exercises, from Old High German *turnēn* to turn, from Medieval Latin *tornare* — more at TURN] (1854) **:** a member of a turnverein **:** GYMNAST

**Tur·ner's syndrome** \'tər-nərz-\ *noun* [Henry Hubert *Turner* (died 1970) American physician] (1942) **:** a genetically determined condition that is associated with the presence of only one complete X chromosome and no Y chromosome and that is characterized by a female phenotype with underdeveloped and infertile ovaries

**turn·ery** \'tər-nə-rē\ *noun, plural* **-er·ies** (1644) **:** the work, products, or shop of a turner

**turn–in** \'tər-ˌnin\ *noun* (1902) **:** something that turns in or is turned in

**turn in** (1535) *intransitive verb* **1 :** to make an entrance by turning from a road or path **2 :** to go to bed ⟨*turned in* early⟩ *transitive verb* **1 :** to deliver up **:** HAND OVER ⟨*turned in* his badge and quit⟩ **2 a :** to inform on **:** BETRAY **b :** to deliver to an authority ⟨urged the wanted man to *turn* himself *in*⟩ **3 :** to acquit oneself of **:** PUT ON, PRODUCE ⟨*turned in* a good performance⟩

**turn·ing** *noun* (14th century) **1 :** the act or course of one that turns **2 :** a place of a change in direction **3 a :** a forming by use of a lathe; *broadly* **:** TURNERY **b** *plural* **:** waste produced in turning

**turning chisel** *noun* (circa 1877) **:** a chisel used for shaping or finishing work in a lathe

**turning point** *noun* (1851) **:** a point at which a significant change occurs

**tur·nip** \'tər-nəp\ *noun* [probably from ¹*turn* + *neep;* from the well-rounded root] (1533) **1 a :** either of two biennial herbs of the mustard family with thick edible roots: (1) **:** one (*Brassica rapa rapifera*) with usually flattened roots and leaves that are cooked as a vegetable (2) **:** RUTABAGA **b :** the root of a turnip **2 :** a large pocket watch

**¹turn·key** \'tərn-ˌkē\ *noun, plural* **turnkeys** (1654) **:** one who has charge of a prison's keys

**²turnkey** *adjective* (1927) **:** built, supplied, or installed complete and ready to operate ⟨a *turnkey* nuclear plant⟩ ⟨a *turnkey* computer system⟩; *also* **:** of or relating to a turnkey building or installation ⟨a *turnkey* contract⟩ ⟨*turnkey* vendors⟩

**turn-off** \'tər-ˌnȯf\ *noun* (circa 1852) **1 :** a turning off **2 :** a place where one turns off; *especially* **:** EXIT 4 **3 :** one that causes loss of interest or enthusiasm ⟨the music was a *turnoff*⟩

**turn off** (1564) *transitive verb*

**1 a :** DISMISS, DISCHARGE **b :** to dispose of **:** SELL
**2 :** DEFLECT, EVADE
**3 :** PRODUCE, ACCOMPLISH
**4 :** to stop the flow of or shut off by or as if by turning a control ⟨*turn* the water *off*⟩
**5 :** HANG 1b
**6 a :** to remove (material) by the process of turning **b :** to shape or produce by turning
**7 :** to cause to lose interest **:** BORE ⟨economics *turns* me *off*⟩; *also* **:** to evoke a negative feeling in
*intransitive verb*
**1 :** to deviate from a straight course or from a main road ⟨*turn off* into a side road⟩
**2 a** *British* **:** to turn bad **:** SPOIL **b :** to change to a specified state **:** BECOME
**3 :** to lose interest **:** WITHDRAW

**turn on** (1833)
*transitive verb*
**1 :** to activate or cause to flow, operate, or function by or as if by turning a control ⟨*turn* the water *on* full⟩ ⟨*turn on* the power⟩
**2 a :** to cause to undergo an intense often visionary experience by taking a drug; *broadly* **:** to cause to get high **b :** to move pleasurably ⟨rock music *turns* her *on*⟩; *also* **:** to excite sexually **c :** to cause to gain knowledge or appreciation of something specified ⟨*turned* her *on* to ballet⟩
*intransitive verb*
**:** to become turned on
— **turn–on** \'tər-,nȯn, -,nän\ *noun*

**turn-out** \'tər-,naut\ *noun* (1688)
**1 :** an act of turning out
**2** *chiefly British* **a :** STRIKE 3a **b :** STRIKER 1d
**3 :** the number of people who participate in or attend an event ⟨a heavy voter *turnout*⟩
**4 a :** a place where something (as a road) turns out or branches off **b :** a space adjacent to a highway in which vehicles may park or pull into to enable others to pass **c :** a railroad siding
**5 :** a clearing out and cleaning
**6 a :** a coach or carriage together with the horses, harness, and attendants **b :** EQUIPMENT, RIG **c :** manner of dress **:** GETUP
**7 :** net quantity of produce yielded

**turn out** (1546)
*transitive verb*
**1 a :** EXPEL, EVICT **b :** to put (as a horse) to pasture
**2 a :** to turn inside out ⟨*turning out* his pockets⟩ **b :** to empty the contents of especially for cleaning or rearranging; *also* **:** CLEAN
**3 :** to produce often rapidly or regularly by or as if by machine ⟨a writer *turning out* stories⟩
**4 :** to equip, dress, or finish in a careful or elaborate way
**5 :** to put out by turning a switch ⟨*turn out* the lights⟩
**6 :** to call (as the guard or a company) out from rest or shelter and into formation
*intransitive verb*
**1 a :** to come or go out from home in or as if in answer to a summons ⟨voters *turned out* in droves⟩ **b :** to get out of bed
**2 a :** to prove to be in the result or end ⟨the play *turned out* to be a flop⟩ ⟨it *turned out* that we were both wrong⟩ **b :** to become in maturity ⟨nobody thought he'd *turn out* like this⟩ **c :** END ⟨stories that *turn out* happily⟩

**¹turn-over** \'tər-,nō-vər\ *noun* (14th century)
**1 :** an act or result of turning over **:** UPSET
**2 :** a turning from one side, place, or direction to its opposite **:** SHIFT, REVERSAL
**3 :** a reorganization with a view to a shift in personnel **:** SHAKE-UP
**4 :** something that is turned over
**5 :** a filled pastry made by folding half of the crust over the other half
**6 :** the amount of business done; *especially* **:** the volume of shares traded on a stock exchange

**7 a :** movement (as of goods or people) into, through, and out of a place **b :** a cycle of purchase, sale, and replacement of a stock of goods; *also* **:** the ratio of sales for a stated period to average inventory **c :** the number of persons hired within a period to replace those leaving or dropped from a workforce; *also* **:** the ratio of this number to the number in the average force maintained
**8 :** the act or an instance of a team's losing possession of a ball through error or a minor violation of the rules (as in basketball or football)

**²turnover** *adjective* (circa 1849)
**:** capable of being turned over

**turn over** (14th century)
*transitive verb*
**1 a :** to turn from an upright position **:** OVERTURN **b :** ROTATE ⟨*turn over* a stiff valve with a wrench⟩; *also* **:** to cause (an internal combustion engine) to begin firing
**2 :** to search (as clothes or papers) by lifting or moving one by one
**3 :** to read or examine (as a book) slowly or idly
**4 :** DELIVER, SURRENDER ⟨I'm *turning* the job *over* to you⟩; *also* **:** to lose possession of ⟨*turned* the ball *over* three times⟩
**5 a :** to receive and dispose of (a stock of merchandise) **b :** to do business to the amount of ⟨*turning over* $1000 a week⟩
*intransitive verb*
**1 :** UPSET, CAPSIZE
**2 a :** ROTATE **b** *of an engine* **:** to have crankshaft rotation especially by external means (as by a starter) ⟨the engine *turned over* but didn't start⟩
**3 a** *of one's stomach* **:** to heave with nausea **b** *of one's heart* **:** to seem to leap or lurch convulsively with sudden fright
— **turn over a new leaf :** to make a change for the better especially in one's way of living

**turn-pike** \'tərn-,pīk\ *noun* [Middle English *turnepike* revolving frame bearing spikes and serving as a barrier, from *turnen* to turn + *pike*] (1533)
**1 :** TOLLGATE
**2 a** (1) **:** a road (as an expressway) for the use of which tolls are collected (2) **:** a road formerly maintained as a turnpike **b :** a main road; *especially* **:** a paved highway with crowned surface

**turn-sole** \'tərn-,sōl\ *noun* [Middle English *turnesole*, from Middle French *tournesol*, from Old Italian *tornasole*, from *tornare* to turn (from Medieval Latin) + *sole* sun, from Latin *sol* — more at TURN, SOLAR] (14th century)
**1 :** a European herb (*Chrozophora tinctoria*) of the spurge family with juice that is turned blue by ammonia; *also* **:** a purple dye obtained from it
**2 :** HELIOTROPE 1

**turn-spit** \-,spit\ *noun* (1570)
**1 a :** one that turns a spit; *specifically* **:** a small dog formerly used in a treadmill to turn a spit **b :** a roasting jack
**2 :** a rotatable spit

**turn-stile** \-,stīl\ *noun* (1643)
**:** a post with arms pivoted on the top set in a passageway so that persons can pass through only on foot one by one

**turn-stone** \-,stōn\ *noun* [from a habit of turning over stones to find food] (circa 1674)
**:** either of two shorebirds (genus *Arenaria*) that resemble the related plovers and sandpipers: **a :** a bird (*A. interpres*) of worldwide distribution that has black and chestnut upperparts and a black breast **b :** a North American bird (*A. melanocephala*) with black upperparts and breast

**turn-ta-ble** \-,tā-bəl\ *noun* (1835)

**:** a revolvable platform: as **a :** a platform with a track for turning wheeled vehicles **b :** LAZY SUSAN **c :** a rotating platform that carries a phonograph record

**turn to** *intransitive verb* (1813)
**:** to apply oneself to work **:** act vigorously

**¹turn-up** \'tər-'nəp\ *adjective* (1685)
**1 :** turned up ⟨a *turnup* nose⟩
**2 :** made or fitted to be turned up ⟨a *turnup* collar⟩

**²turn-up** \'tər-,nəp\ *noun* (1688)
**:** something that is turned up

**turn up** (1563)
*transitive verb*
**1 :** FIND, DISCOVER
**2 :** to raise or increase by or as if by turning a control ⟨*turn up* the volume on the radio⟩
**3** *British* **a :** to look up (as a word or fact) in a book **b :** to refer to or consult (a book)
**4 :** to turn (a card) face upward
*intransitive verb*
**1 :** to appear or come to light unexpectedly or after being lost ⟨new evidence has *turned up*⟩
**2 a** (1) **:** to turn out to be ⟨he *turned up* missing at roll call⟩ (2) **:** APPEAR 4 ⟨her name is always *turning up* in the newspapers⟩ **b :** to arrive or show up at an appointed or expected time or place ⟨*turned up* half an hour late⟩
**3 :** to happen or occur unexpectedly ⟨something always *turned up* to prevent their meeting⟩
**4** *of a ship* **:** TACK 1b
— **turn up one's nose :** to show scorn or disdain

**turn-ver-ein** \'tərn-və-,rīn, 'tùrn-\ *noun* [German, from *turnen* to perform gymnastic exercises + *Verein* club] (1852)
**:** an athletic club

**tu-ro-phile** \'tùr-ə-,fīl, 'tyùr-\ *noun* [irregular from Greek *tyros* cheese + English *-phile* — more at BUTTER] (1938)
**:** a connoisseur of cheese **:** a cheese fancier

**¹tur-pen-tine** \'tər-pən-,tīn, 'tər-pᵊm-\ *noun* [Middle English *terbentyne, turpentyne*, from Middle French & Medieval Latin; Middle French *terbentine, tourbentine*, from Medieval Latin *terbentina*, from Latin *terebinthina*, feminine of *terebinthinus* of terebinth, from *terebinthus* terebinth, from Greek *terebinthos*] (14th century)
**1 a :** a yellow to brown semifluid oleoresin obtained as an exudate from the terebinth **b :** an oleoresin obtained from various conifers (as some pines and firs)
**2 a :** an essential oil obtained from turpentines by distillation and used especially as a solvent and thinner — called also *gum turpentine* **b :** a similar oil obtained by distillation or carbonization of pinewood — called also *wood turpentine*

**²turpentine** *transitive verb* -tined; -tin-ing (1759)
**1 :** to apply turpentine to
**2 :** to extract turpentine from; *especially* **:** to tap (pine trees) in order to obtain turpentine

**tur-pi-tude** \'tər-pə-,tüd, -,tyüd\ *noun* [Middle French, from Latin *turpitudo*, from *turpis* vile, base] (15th century)
**:** inherent baseness **:** DEPRAVITY ⟨moral *turpitude*⟩; *also* **:** a base act

**turps** \'tərps\ *noun plural but singular in construction* [by shortening & alteration] (circa 1823)
**:** TURPENTINE

**tur-quoise** *also* **tur-quois** \'tər-,kȯiz, -,kwȯiz\ *noun* [Middle English *turkeis, turcas*, from Middle French *turquoyse*, from feminine of *turquoys* Turkish, from Old French, from *Turc* Turk] (14th century)

turnstone

**1 :** a mineral that is a blue, bluish green, or greenish gray hydrous basic phosphate of copper and aluminum, takes a high polish, and is valued as a gem when skyblue
**2 :** a light greenish blue

**turquoise blue** noun (1799)
**:** a light greenish blue that is paler and slightly bluer than average turquoise

**turquoise green** noun (1886)
**:** a light bluish green

**tur·ret** \'tər-ət, 'tə-rət, 'tùr-ət\ noun [Middle English touret, from Middle French torete, tourete, from Old French, diminutive of tor, tur tower — more at TOWER] (14th century)
**1 :** a little tower; specifically **:** an ornamental structure at an angle of a larger structure
**2 a :** a pivoted and revolvable holder in a machine tool **b :** a device (as on a microscope or a television camera) holding several lenses
**3 a :** a tall building usually moved on wheels and formerly used for carrying soldiers and equipment for breaching or scaling a wall **b** (1) **:** a gunner's fixed or movable enclosure in an airplane (2) **:** a revolving armored structure on a warship that protects one or more guns mounted within it (3) **:** a similar upper structure usually for one gun on a tank

**tur·ret·ed** \'tər-ə-təd, 'tə-rə-, 'tùr-ə-\ adjective (1550)
**:** furnished with or as if with turrets

**¹tur·tle** \'tər-t°l\ noun [Middle English, from Old English turtla, from Latin turtur] (before 12th century)
archaic **:** TURTLEDOVE

**²turtle** noun, plural **turtles** also **turtle** often attributive [modification of French tortue, from Late Latin tartarucha, feminine of tartaruchus of Tartarus, from Greek tartarouchos, from Tartaros Tartarus] (1657)
**:** any of an order (Testudines) of terrestrial, freshwater, and marine reptiles that have a toothless horny beak and a shell of bony dermal plates usually covered with horny shields enclosing the trunk and into which the head, limbs, and tail usually may be withdrawn ◆

**³turtle** noun (1952)
**:** TURTLENECK

**tur·tle·back** \'tər-t°l-,bak\ noun (1881)
**:** a raised convex surface
— **turtleback** or **tur·tle–backed** \-,bakt\ adjective

**tur·tle·dove** \-,dəv\ noun (14th century)
**:** any of several small wild pigeons (genus Streptopelia and especially S. turtur) noted for plaintive cooing

**tur·tle·head** \-,hed\ noun (1857)
**:** any of a genus (Chelone) of perennial herbs of the snapdragon family with spikes of showy white or purple flowers

**tur·tle·neck** \-,nek\ noun (1897)
**1 :** a high close-fitting turnover collar used especially for sweaters
**2 :** a sweater with a turtleneck
— **tur·tle·necked** \-,nekt\ adjective

**tur·tling** \'tərt-liŋ, 'tər-t°l-iŋ\ noun (1726)
**:** the action or process of catching turtles

**turves** plural of TURF

**¹Tus·can** \'təs-kən\ adjective [Latin tuscanus Etruscan, from Tusci Etruscans] (1563)
**1 :** of or relating to one of the five classical orders of architecture that is of Roman origin and plain in style
**2 :** of, relating to, or characteristic of Tuscany, the Tuscans, or Tuscan

**²Tuscan** noun (1568)
**1 a :** the Italian language as spoken in Tuscany **b :** the standard literary dialect of Italian
**2 :** a native or inhabitant of Tuscany

**Tus·ca·ro·ra** \,təs-kə-'rōr-ə, -'ror-\ noun, plural **Tuscarora** or **Tuscaroras** [Tuscarora skarò'r₂°] (1650)
**1 :** a member of an American Indian people originally of North Carolina and later of New York and Ontario
**2 :** the Iroquoian language of the Tuscarora people

**tu·sche** \'tüsh, 'tü-shə\ noun [German, from tuschen to lay on color, from French toucher, literally, to touch, from Old French tuchier — more at TOUCH] (1885)
**:** a black liquid used in lithography for drawing and painting and in etching and the silk-screen process as a resist

**¹tush** \'təsh\ noun [Middle English tusch, from Old English tūsc; akin to Old Frisian tusk tooth, Old English tōth tooth] (before 12th century)
**:** a long pointed tooth; especially **:** a horse's canine

**²tush** interjection [Middle English tussch] (15th century)
— used to express disdain or reproach

**³tush** \'tùsh\ noun [perhaps modification of Yiddish tokhes, from Hebrew taḥath under, beneath] (1962)
slang **:** BUTTOCKS

**¹tusk** \'təsk\ noun [Middle English, alteration of tux, from Old English tūx; akin to Old English tūsc tush] (before 12th century)
**1 :** an elongated greatly enlarged tooth (as of an elephant or walrus) that projects when the mouth is closed and serves for digging food or as a weapon; broadly **:** a long protruding tooth
**2 :** one of the small projections on a tusk tenon
— **tusked** \'təskt\ adjective
— **tusk·like** \'təsk-,līk\ adjective

**²tusk** transitive verb (1629)
**:** to dig up with a tusk; also **:** to gash with a tusk

**tusk·er** \'təs-kər\ noun (1859)
**:** an animal with tusks; especially **:** a male elephant with two normally developed tusks

**tusk tenon** noun (circa 1825)
**:** a tenon strengthened by one or more smaller tenons underneath forming a steplike outline

**tus·sah** \'tə-sə, -,sò\ or **tus·sore** \-,sōr, -,sor\ noun [Hindi tasar] (1590)
**:** silk or silk fabric from the brownish fiber produced by larvae of some saturniid moths (as Antheraea paphia)

**tus·sive** \'tə-siv\ adjective [Latin tussis cough] (circa 1857)
**:** of, relating to, or involved in coughing

**¹tus·sle** \'tə-səl\ noun (1629)
**1 :** a physical contest or struggle **:** SCUFFLE
**2 :** an intense argument, controversy, or struggle

**²tussle** intransitive verb **tus·sled; tus·sling** \-s(ə-)liŋ\ [Middle English tussillen, frequentative of Middle English -tusen, -tousen to tousle — more at TOUSE] (1638)
**:** to struggle roughly **:** SCUFFLE

**tus·sock** \'tə-sək\ noun [origin unknown] (1580)
**:** a compact tuft especially of grass or sedge; also **:** an area of raised solid ground in a marsh or bog that is bound together by roots of low vegetation
— **tus·socky** \-sə-kē\ adjective

**tussock grass** noun (1842)
**:** a grass or sedge that typically grows in tussocks

**tussock moth** noun (1826)
**:** any of numerous dull-colored moths (family Lymantriidae) that usually have wingless females and larvae with long tufts of hair

**tut** \a t-sound made by suction rather than explosion; often read as 'tət\ interjection (circa 1529)
— used to express disapproval or disbelief

**tu·tee** \tü-'tē, tyü-\ noun [tutor + -ee] (circa 1927)
**:** one who is being tutored

**tu·te·lage** \'tü-t°l-ij, 'tyü-\ noun [Latin tutela protection, guardian (from tutari to protect, frequentative of tueri to look at, guard) + English -age] (1605)
**1 a :** an act or process of serving as guardian or protector **:** GUARDIANSHIP **b :** hegemony over a foreign territory **:** TRUSTEESHIP 2
**2 :** the state of being under a guardian or tutor

**3 a :** instruction especially of an individual **b :** a guiding influence

**tu·te·lar** \'tü-t°l-ər, 'tyü-, -,är\ adjective or noun (1600)
**:** TUTELARY

**¹tu·te·lary** \'tü-t°l-,er-ē, 'tyü-\ adjective (1611)
**1 :** having the guardianship of a person or a thing ⟨a tutelary goddess⟩
**2 :** of or relating to a guardian

**²tutelary** noun, plural **-lar·ies** (1652)
**:** a tutelary power (as a deity)

**¹tu·tor** \'tü-tər, 'tyü-\ noun [Middle English, from Middle French & Latin; Middle French tuteur, from Latin tutor, from tueri] (14th century)
**:** a person charged with the instruction and guidance of another: as **a :** a private teacher **b :** a teacher in a British university who gives individual instruction to undergraduates

**²tutor** (1592)
transitive verb
**1 :** to have the guardianship, tutelage, or care of
**2 :** to teach or guide usually individually in a special subject or for a particular purpose **:** COACH
intransitive verb
**1 :** to do the work of a tutor
**2 :** to receive instruction especially privately

**tu·tor·age** \'tü-tə-rij, 'tyü-\ noun (1617)
**:** the function or work of a tutor

**tu·tor·ess** \'tü-tə-rəs, 'tyü-\ noun (1614)
**:** a woman or girl who is a tutor

**¹tu·to·ri·al** \tü-'tōr-ē-əl, tyü-, -'tor-\ adjective (1822)
**:** of, relating to, or involving a tutor

**²tutorial** noun (1923)
**1 :** a class conducted by a tutor for one student or a small number of students
**2 :** a paper, book, film, or computer program that provides practical information about a specific subject

**tu·tor·ship** \'tü-tər-,ship, 'tyü-\ noun (1581)
**1 :** the office, function, or work of a tutor
**2 :** TUTELAGE 3

**tu·toy·er** \tŒ-twä-yā\ transitive verb [French, to address with the familiar pronoun tu thou,

---

◇ **WORD HISTORY**
**turtle** The word turtle appears to have developed in 17th century nautical English out of an earlier word tortu, or its French source tortue, from which English tortoise is also derived. French tortue as a name for this animal, like Spanish tortuga and Italian tartaruga, ultimately descends from Late Latin tartarucha. This word is short for bestia tartarucha (or a similar collocation), literally, "infernal beast" or "beast of the nether regions." Such a humble and generally inoffensive animal hardly seems to deserve this epithet, but in early Christian literature and art the turtle, thought because of its lowness to the ground to wallow in mud and filth, was taken as a symbol of heresy and evil. A mosaic of the late 3rd century A.D. in Aquileia, northern Italy, depicts a turtle partly withdrawn into its shell aggressively confronted by a rooster, symbolic of goodness. Both rooster and turtle as emblems of light and darkness were taken from the pre-Christian cult of Mithras popular in the Roman empire. This demonic characterization of the animal was pervasive enough to affect everyday speech, and the Romance descendants of tartarucha largely ousted the descendants of the classical Latin word for "turtle," testudo.

---

from Middle French, from *tu* thou (from Latin) + *toi* thee, from Latin *te* (accusative of *tu*) — more at THOU] (1697)
: to address familiarly

**Tut·si** \'tü-sē, 'tüt-\ *noun, plural* **Tutsi** *or* **Tut·sis** (1950)
: a member of a Nilotic people of Rwanda and Burundi

¹**tut·ti** \'tü-tē, 'tü-; 'tü-,tē, 'tü-\ *adjective or adverb* [Italian, masculine plural of *tutto* all, from (assumed) Vulgar Latin *tottus*, alteration of Latin *totus*] (circa 1724)
: with all voices or instruments performing together — used as a direction in music

²**tutti** *noun* (1816)
: a passage or section performed by all the performers

**tut·ti–frut·ti** \,tü-ti-'frü-tē, ,tü-\ *noun* [Italian *tutti frutti* all fruits] (1834)
: a confection or ice cream containing chopped usually candied fruits

¹**tut–tut** \*two t-sounds made by suction rather than explosion; often read as* 'tət-'tət\ *interjection* (1591)
: TUT

²**tut–tut** \'tət-'tət\ *intransitive verb* **tut–tut·ted; tut–tut·ting** (1873)
: to express disapproval or disbelief by or as if by uttering tut ⟨the civilian press corps *tut-tutted* over the officers' equivocation, ignorance and bigotry —M. B. Duberman⟩

**tu·tu** \'tü-(,)tü\ *noun* [French, from (baby talk) *tutu* backside] (1913)
: a short projecting skirt worn by a ballerina

**tu–whit tu–whoo** \tə-,(h)wit-tə-'(h)wü\ *noun* [imitative] (1588)
: the cry of an owl

**tux** \'təks\ *noun* (1922)
: TUXEDO

**tux·e·do** \,tək-'sē-(,)dō\ *noun, plural* **-dos** *or* **-does** [Tuxedo Park, N.Y.] (1889)
**1** : a single-breasted or double-breasted usually black or blackish blue jacket
**2** : semiformal evening clothes for men
— **tux·e·doed** \-(,)dōd\ *adjective*

tutu

**tu·yere** \twē-'er\ *noun* [French *tuyère*, from Middle French, from *tuyau* pipe] (1781)
: a nozzle through which an air blast is delivered to a forge or blast furnace

**TV** \'tē-'vē\ *noun* [television] (1947)
: TELEVISION

**TV dinner** *noun* [from its saving the television viewer from having to interrupt viewing to prepare and serve a meal] (1954)
: a quick-frozen packaged dinner (as of meat, potatoes, and a vegetable) that requires only heating before it is served

**twa** \'twä\ *or* **twae** \'twä, 'twē\ *Scottish variant of* TWO

¹**twad·dle** \'twä-d°l\ *noun* [probably alteration of English dialect *twattle* idle talk] (1782)
**1** : silly idle talk : DRIVEL
**2** : one that twaddles : TWADDLER

²**twaddle** *verb* **twad·dled; twad·dling** \'twäd-liŋ, 'twä-d°l-iŋ\ (1826)
: PRATE, BABBLE
— **twad·dler** \'twäd-lər, 'twä-d°l-ər\ *noun*

¹**twain** \'twān\ *adjective* [Middle English, from Old English *twēgen* — more at TWO] (before 12th century)
*archaic* : TWO

²**twain** *pronoun* (before 12th century)
: TWO; *especially* : two fathoms ⟨mark *twain*⟩

³**twain** *noun* (14th century)
**1** : TWO
**2** : COUPLE, PAIR

¹**twang** \'twaŋ\ *noun* [imitative] (circa 1553)
**1** : a harsh quick ringing sound like that of a plucked banjo string
**2 a** : nasal speech or resonance **b** : the charac-

teristic speech of a region, locality, or group of people
**3 a** : an act of plucking **b** : PANG, TWINGE
— **twangy** \'twaŋ-ē\ *adjective*

²**twang** *verb* **twanged; twang·ing** \'twaŋ-iŋ\ (1567)
*intransitive verb*
**1** : to sound with a twang ⟨the couch *twanged* when he sat down⟩
**2** : to speak or sound with a nasal intonation
**3** : to throb or twitch with pain or tension
*transitive verb*
**1** : to cause to sound with a twang
**2** : to utter or pronounce with a nasal twang
**3** : to pluck the string of
— **twang·er** *noun*

³**twang** *noun* [alteration of *tang*] (1611)
**1** : a persisting flavor, taste, or odor : TANG
**2** : SUGGESTION, TRACE

**'twas** \'twəz, 'twäz\ [by contraction] (1588)
: it was

**twat** \'twät\ *noun* [origin unknown] (1656)
: VULVA — usually considered vulgar

**tway–blade** \'twā-,blād\ *noun* [English dialect *tway* two] (1578)
: any of various orchids (genera *Listera* and *Liparis*) often having two leaves

¹**tweak** \'twēk\ *verb* [probably alteration of Middle English *twikken* to pull sharply, from Old English *twiccian* to pluck — more at TWITCH] (1601)
*transitive verb*
**1** : to pinch and pull with a sudden jerk and twist : TWITCH ⟨*tweaked* a bud from the stem⟩
**2** : to pinch (a person or a body part) lightly or playfully ⟨*tweaked* the baby's ear affectionately⟩
**3** : to make small adjustments in or to ⟨*tweak* the controls⟩; *especially* : FINE-TUNE
*intransitive verb*
: PULL 1a, PLUCK

²**tweak** *noun* (1609)
: an act of tweaking : PINCH

**twee** \'twē\ *adjective* [baby-talk alteration of *sweet*] (1905)
*chiefly British* : affectedly or excessively dainty, delicate, cute, or quaint ⟨such a theme might sound *twee* or corny —*Times Literary Supplement*⟩

**tweed** \'twēd\ *noun* [probably short for Scots *tweedling, twidling* twilled cloth] (1841)
**1** : a rough woolen fabric made usually in twill weaves and used especially for suits and coats
**2** *plural* : tweed clothing; *specifically* : a tweed suit

**Twee·dle·dum and Twee·dle·dee** \,twē-d°l-'dəm-ən(d)-,twē-d°l-'dē\ *noun* [English *tweedle* to chirp + *dum* (imitative of a low musical note) & *dee* (imitative of a high musical note)] (1725)
: two individuals or groups that are practically indistinguishable

**tweedy** \'twē-dē\ *adjective* **tweed·i·er; -est** (1912)
**1** : of or resembling tweed
**2 a** : given to wearing tweeds **b** : informal or suggestive of the outdoors in taste or habits
— **tweed·i·ness** *noun*

**tween** \'twēn\ *preposition* [Middle English *twene*, short for *betwene*] (14th century)
: BETWEEN

**tweet** \'twēt\ *noun* [imitative] (1845)
: a chirping note
— **tweet** *intransitive verb*

**tweet·er** \'twē-tər\ *noun* (1934)
: a small loudspeaker responsive only to the higher acoustic frequencies and reproducing sounds of high pitch — compare WOOFER

**tweeze** \'twēz\ *transitive verb* **tweezed; tweez·ing** [back-formation from *tweezers*] (1932)
: to pluck, remove, or handle with tweezers

**twee·zer** \'twē-zər\ *noun* (1904)
: TWEEZERS

**twee·zers** \-zərz\ *noun plural but singular or*

plural *in* construction [obsolete English *tweeze*, noun, *etui*, short for obsolete English *etweese*, from plural of obsolete English *etwee*, from French *étui*] (1654)
: any of various small metal instruments that are usually held between the thumb and forefinger, are used for plucking, holding, or manipulating, and consist of two legs joined at one end

**Twelfth Day** *noun* [from its being the 12th day after Christmas] (before 12th century)
: EPIPHANY 1

**Twelfth Night** *noun* (before 12th century)
: the evening or sometimes the eve of Epiphany

**twelve** \'twelv\ *noun* [Middle English, from Old English *twelf*; akin to Old High German *zwelif* twelve, Old English *twā* two, *-leofan* (as in *endleofan* eleven) — more at TWO, ELEVEN] (before 12th century)
**1** — see NUMBER table
**2** *capitalized* **a** : the twelve original disciples of Jesus **b** : the books of the Minor Prophets in the Jewish Scriptures
**3** : the 12th in a set or series
**4** : something having 12 units or members
**5** *plural* : TWELVEMO
— **twelfth** \'twelf(t)th\ *adjective or noun*
— **twelve** *adjective*
— **twelve** *pronoun, plural in construction*

**twelve·mo** \'twelv-(,)mō\ *noun, plural* **-mos** (1819)
: the size of a piece of paper cut 12 from a sheet; *also* : a book, a page, or paper of this size

**twelve·month** \-,mən(t)th\ *noun* (13th century)
: YEAR

**twelve–tone** \-'tōn\ *adjective* (1926)
: of, relating to, or being serial music utilizing the 12 chromatic tones

**twelve–tone row** *noun* (1941)
: the 12 chromatic tones of the octave placed in a chosen fixed order and constituting with some permitted permutations and derivations the melodic and harmonic material of a serial musical piece

**twen·ty** \'twen-tē, 'twən-\ *noun, plural* **twen·ties** [Middle English, from *twenty*, adjective, from Old English *twēntig*, noun, group of 20, from *twēn-* (akin to Old English *twā* two) + *-tig* group of 10; akin to Old English *tīen* ten — more at TWO, TEN] (15th century)
**1** — see NUMBER table
**2** : the numbers 20 to 29; *specifically* : the years 20 to 29 in a lifetime or century
**3** : a 20-dollar bill
— **twen·ti·eth** \-tē-əth\ *adjective or noun*
— **twenty** *adjective*
— **twenty** *pronoun, plural in construction*

**twen·ty–four·mo** \,twen-tē-'fōr-(,)mō, ,twən-, -'for-\ *noun, plural* **-mos** (circa 1841)
: the size of a piece of paper cut 24 from a sheet; *also* : a book, a page, or paper of this size

**twen·ty–one** \,twen-tē-'wən, ,twən-\ *noun* (1611)
**1** — see NUMBER table
**2** [translation of French *vingt-et-un*] : BLACKJACK
— **twenty–one** *adjective*
— **twenty–one** *pronoun, plural in construction*

**twen·ty–twen·ty** *or* **20/20** \-'twen-tē, -'twən-\ *adjective* [from the testing of vision by reading letters at a distance of 20 feet] (1875)
*of the human eye* : meeting a standard of normal visual acuity ⟨*twenty-twenty* vision⟩

**twen·ty–two** \-'tü\ *noun* (1526)
**1** — see NUMBER table
**2** : a .22-caliber firearm; *especially* : one firing rimfire cartridges — usually written .22
— **twenty–two** *adjective*
— **twenty–two** *pronoun, plural in construction*

**¹twere** \'twər\ [by contraction] (1588)
: it were

**twerp** \'twərp\ *noun* [origin unknown] (circa 1923)
: a silly, insignificant, or contemptible person

**Twi** \'chwē, chə-'wē, 'twē, 'chē\ *noun* (1874)
**1** : a dialect of Akan
**2** : a literary language based on the Twi dialect and used by the Akan-speaking peoples (as the Ashanti)

**twi-** \'twī\ *prefix* [Middle English, from Old English; akin to Old High German *zwi-* twi-, Latin *bi-*, Greek *di-*, Old English *twā* two]
: two : double : doubly : twice ⟨*twi*-headed⟩

**twice** \'twīs\ *adverb* [Middle English *twiges, twies,* from Old English *twiga;* akin to Old English *twi-*] (12th century)
**1** : on two occasions ⟨*twice* absent⟩
**2** : two times : in doubled quantity or degree ⟨*twice* two is four⟩ ⟨*twice* as much⟩

**twice–born** \-'bȯrn\ *adjective* (15th century)
**1** : born a second time
**2** : having undergone a definite experience of fundamental moral and spiritual renewal : REGENERATE
**3** : of or forming one of the three upper Hindu caste groups in which boys undergo an initiation symbolizing spiritual birth

**twice–laid** \-'lād\ *adjective* (circa 1593)
: made from the ends of rope and strands of used rope ⟨*twice-laid* rope⟩

**twice–told** \-'tōld\ *adjective* (1595)
: well known from repeated telling — used chiefly in the phrase *a twice-told tale*

**¹twid·dle** \'twi-dᵊl\ *verb* **twid·dled; twid·dling** \'twid-liŋ, 'twi-dᵊl-iŋ\ [origin unknown] (circa 1540)
*intransitive verb*
**1** : to play negligently with something : FIDDLE
**2** : to turn or jounce lightly ⟨*twiddles* round and round in the water —J. B. S. Haldane⟩
*transitive verb*
: to rotate lightly or idly ⟨*twiddled* his cigar —James Lord⟩
— **twiddle one's thumbs** : to spend time idly : do nothing

**²twiddle** *noun* (1774)
: TURN, TWIST

**¹twig** \'twig\ *noun* [Middle English *twigge,* from Old English; akin to Old High German *zwīg* twig, Old English *twā* two] (before 12th century)
**1** : a small shoot or branch usually without its leaves
**2** : a minute branch of a nerve or artery
— **twigged** \'twigd\ *adjective*
— **twig·gy** \'twi-gē\ *adjective*

**²twig** *verb* **twigged; twig·ging** [perhaps from Irish & Scottish Gaelic *tuig-* understand] (1764)
*transitive verb*
**1** : NOTICE, OBSERVE
**2** : to understand the meaning of : COMPREHEND
*intransitive verb*
: to gain a grasp : UNDERSTAND ⟨*twigged* instinctively about things —H. E. Bates⟩

**³twig** *noun* [origin unknown] (circa 1811)
*British* : FASHION, STYLE

**twi·light** \'twī-,līt\ *noun, often attributive* (15th century)
**1** : the light from the sky between full night and sunrise or between sunset and full night produced by diffusion of sunlight through the atmosphere and its dust
**2 a** : an intermediate state that is not clearly defined ⟨lived in the *twilight* of neutrality —*Newsweek*⟩ **b** : a period of decline ⟨the *twilight* of a great career⟩

**twilight glow** *noun* (1819)
: airglow seen at twilight

**Twilight of the Gods**
: RAGNAROK

**twilight zone** *noun* (1909)
**1 a** : TWILIGHT 2a **b** : an area just beyond ordinary legal and ethical limits

**2** : a world of fantasy, illusion, or unreality

**twi-lit** \'twī-,lit\ *adjective* [*twilight* + *lit*] (1869)
: lighted by or as if by twilight

**twill** \'twil\ *noun* [Middle English *twyll, twylle,* from Old English *twilic* having a double thread, part translation of Latin *bilic-, bilix,* from *bi-* + *licium* thread] (14th century)
**1** : a fabric with a twill weave
**2** : a textile weave in which the filling threads pass over one and under two or more warp threads to give an appearance of diagonal lines

**twilled** \'twild\ *adjective* (15th century)
: made with a twill weave

**twill·ing** \'twi-liŋ\ *noun* (circa 1859)
: twilled fabric; *also* : the process of making it

**¹twin** \'twin\ *noun* [Middle English, from *twin* twofold] (14th century)
**1 a** : either of two offspring produced at a birth **b** *plural, capitalized* : GEMINI
**2** : one of two persons or things closely related to or resembling each other
**3** : a compound crystal composed of two adjoining crystals or parts of crystals of the same kind that share a common plane of atoms
— **twin·ship** \-,ship\ *noun*

**²twin** *verb* **twinned; twin·ning** (14th century)
*transitive verb*
**1** : to bring together in close association : COUPLE
**2** : DUPLICATE, MATCH
*intransitive verb*
**1** : to bring forth twins
**2** : to grow as a twin crystal

**³twin** *adjective* [Middle English, twofold, double, from Old English *twinn;* akin to Old Norse *tvinnr* two by two, Old English *twā* two] (1590)
**1** : born with one other or as a pair at one birth ⟨*twin* brother⟩ ⟨*twin* girls⟩
**2 a** : made up of two similar, related, or connected members or parts : DOUBLE **b** : paired in a close or necessary relationship : MATCHING **c** : having or consisting of two identical units **d** : being one of a pair

**twin bed** *noun* (1919)
: one of a pair of matching single beds

**twin·ber·ry** \'twin-,ber-ē\ *noun* [from the occurrence of the berries in pairs] (1821)
**1** : a shrubby North American honeysuckle (*Lonicera involucrata*) with yellowish involucrate flowers
**2** : PARTRIDGEBERRY

**twin bill** *noun* (circa 1939)
: DOUBLEHEADER

**twin-born** \'twin-'bȯrn\ *adjective* (1598)
: born at the same birth

**twin double** *noun* (1960)
: a system of betting (as on horse races) in which the bettor must pick the winners of four stipulated races in order to win — compare DAILY DOUBLE

**¹twine** \'twīn\ *noun* [Middle English *twin,* from Old English *twīn;* akin to Middle Dutch *twijn* twine, Old English *twā* two] (before 12th century)
**1** : a strong string of two or more strands twisted together
**2** : a twined or interlaced part or object
**3** : an act of twining, interlacing, or embracing
— **twiny** \'twī-nē\ *adjective*

**²twine** *verb* **twined; twin·ing** (13th century)
*transitive verb*
**1 a** : to twist together **b** : to form by twisting : WEAVE
**2 a** : INTERLACE ⟨the girl *twined* her hands —John Buchan⟩ **b** : to cause to encircle or enfold something **c** : to cause to be encircled
*intransitive verb*
**1** : to coil about a support
**2** : to stretch or move in a sinuous manner : MEANDER ⟨the river *twines* through the valley⟩
— **twin·er** *noun*

**³twine** *verb* **twined; twin·ing** [alteration of

Scots *twin,* from Middle English *twinnen,* from *twin* double] (1722)
*transitive verb*
*chiefly Scottish* : to cause (one) to lose possession : DEPRIVE ⟨*twined* him of his nose —J. C. Ransom⟩
*intransitive verb*
*chiefly Scottish* : PART ⟨you and me must *twine* —R. L. Stevenson⟩

**twin-flow·er** \'twin-,flaȯ(-ə)r\ *noun* (circa 1818)
: a low prostrate subshrub (*Linnaea borealis*) of the honeysuckle family that is found in cool regions of the northern hemisphere and has fragrant usually pink flowers

**¹twinge** \'twinj\ *verb* **twinged; twing·ing** \'twin-jiŋ\ *or* **twinge·ing** [Middle English *twengen,* from Old English *twengan;* akin to Old High German *zwengen* to pinch] (before 12th century)
*transitive verb*
**1** *dialect* : PLUCK, TWEAK
**2** : to affect with a sharp pain or pang
*intransitive verb*
: to feel a sudden sharp local pain

**²twinge** *noun* (1608)
**1** : a sudden sharp stab of pain
**2** : a moral or emotional pang ⟨a *twinge* of conscience⟩

**twi-night** \'twī-,nīt\ *adjective* [*twilight* + *night*] (1946)
: of, relating to, or being a baseball doubleheader in which the first game is played in the late afternoon and the second continues into the evening

**¹twin·kle** \'twiŋ-kəl\ *verb* **twin·kled; twin·kling** \-k(ə-)liŋ\ [Middle English, from Old English *twinclian;* akin to Middle High German *zwinken* to blink] (before 12th century)
*intransitive verb*
**1** : to shine with a flickering or sparkling light : SCINTILLATE
**2 a** : to flutter the eyelids **b** : to appear bright especially with merriment ⟨his eyes *twinkled*⟩
**3** : to flutter or flit rapidly
*transitive verb*
**1** : to cause to shine with fluctuating light
**2** : to flicker or flirt rapidly ⟨*twinkled* the straight, red-lacquered toes —Glenway Wescott⟩
— **twin·kler** \-k(ə-)lər\ *noun*

**²twinkle** *noun* (1548)
**1** : a wink of the eyelids
**2** : the instant's duration of a wink : TWINKLING
**3** : an intermittent radiance : FLICKER, SPARKLE
**4** : a rapid flashing motion : FLIT
— **twin·kly** \-k(ə-)lē\ *adjective*

**twin·kling** \'twiŋ-kliŋ\ *noun* (14th century)
: the time required for a wink : INSTANT ⟨the kettle will boil in a *twinkling* —*Punch*⟩

**twin·set** \'twin-'set\ *noun* (1937)
: a combination of a matching pullover and cardigan worn together

**twin–size** \'twin-'sīz\ *adjective* [*twin bed*] (1926)
: having the dimensions 39 inches by 75 inches (about 99 centimeters by 191 centimeters) — used of a bed; compare FULL-SIZE, KING-SIZE, QUEEN-SIZE

**¹twirl** \'twər(-ə)l\ *verb* [perhaps of Scandinavian origin; akin to Norwegian dialect *tvirla* to twirl; akin to Old High German *dweran* to stir] (1598)
*intransitive verb*
**1** : to revolve rapidly
**2** : to pitch in a baseball game
*transitive verb*
**1** : to cause to rotate rapidly
**2** : PITCH 2a

\ə\ abut \ᵊ\ kitten \ər\ further \a\ ash \ā\ ace
\ä\ mop, mar \aȯ\ out \ch\ chin \e\ bet \ē\ easy
\g\ go \i\ hit \ī\ ice \j\ job \ŋ\ sing \ō\ go
\ȯ\ law \ȯi\ boy \th\ thin \ṯẖ\ the \ü\ loot \u̇\ foot
\y\ yet \zh\ vision *see also* Guide to Pronunciation

— **twirl·er** \'twər-lər\ *noun*

²**twirl** *noun* (1598)
**1** : an act of twirling
**2** : COIL, WHORL
— **twirly** \'twər-lē\ *adjective*

**twirp** *variant of* TWERP

¹**twist** \'twist\ *verb* [Middle English, from Old English *-twist* rope; akin to Middle Dutch *twist* quarrel, twine, Old English *twā* two] (15th century)
*transitive verb*
**1 a** : to unite by winding ⟨*twisting* strands together⟩ **b** : to make by twisting strands together ⟨*twist* thread from yarn⟩ **c** : to mingle by interlacing
**2** : TWINE, COIL
**3 a** : to wring or wrench so as to dislocate or distort; *especially* : SPRAIN ⟨*twisted* my ankle⟩ **b** : to alter the meaning of : DISTORT, PERVERT ⟨*twisted* the facts⟩ **c** : CONTORT ⟨*twisted* his face into a grin⟩ **d** : to pull off, turn, or break by torsion **e** : to cause to move with a turning motion **f** : to form into a spiral shape **g** : to cause to take on moral, mental, or emotional deformity **h** : to make (one's way) in a winding or devious manner to a destination or objective
*intransitive verb*
**1** : to follow a winding course : SNAKE
**2 a** : to turn or change shape under torsion **b** : to assume a spiral shape **c** : SQUIRM, WRITHE **d** : to dance the twist
**3** *of a ball* : to rotate while taking a curving path or direction
**4** : TURN 3a ⟨*twisted* around to see behind him⟩
— **twist one's arm** : to bring strong pressure to bear on one

²**twist** *noun* (1555)
**1** : something formed by twisting or winding: as **a** : a thread, yarn, or cord formed by twisting two or more strands together **b** : a strong tightly twisted sewing silk **c** : a baked piece of twisted dough **d** : tobacco leaves twisted into a thick roll **e** : a strip of citrus peel used to flavor a drink
**2 a** : an act of twisting : the state of being twisted **b** : a dance performed with strenuous gyrations especially of the hips **c** : the spin given the ball in any of various games **d** : a spiral turn or curve **e** (1) : torque or torsional stress applied to a body (as a rod or shaft) (2) : torsional strain (3) : the angle through which a thing is twisted
**3 a** : a turning off a straight course **b** : ECCENTRICITY, IDIOSYNCRASY **c** : a distortion of meaning or sense
**4 a** : an unexpected turn or development ⟨weird *twists* of fate —W. L. Shirer⟩ **b** : a clever device : TRICK ⟨questions demanding special *twists* of thinking —*New Yorker*⟩ **c** : a variant approach or method : GIMMICK ⟨a kind of *twist* on the old triangle theme —Dave Fedo⟩
**5** : a front or back dive in which the diver twists sideways a half or full turn before entering the water
— **twisty** \'twis-tē\ *adjective*

**twist drill** *noun* (circa 1875)
: a drill having deep helical grooves extending from the point to the smooth portion of the shank

**twist·ed** \'twis-təd\ *adjective* (circa 1890)
: mentally or emotionally unsound or disturbed : SICK

**twist·er** \'twis-tər\ *noun* (1579)
**1** : one that twists; *especially* : a ball with a forward and spinning motion
**2** : a tornado, waterspout, or dust devil in which the rotatory ascending movement of a column of air is especially apparent

**twist·ing** \'twis-tiŋ\ *noun* (circa 1905)
: the use of misrepresentation or trickery to get someone to lapse a life insurance policy and buy another usually in another company

¹**twit** \'twit\ *noun* (1528)
**1** : an act of twitting : TAUNT

**2** : a silly annoying person : FOOL

²**twit** *transitive verb* **twit·ted; twit·ting** [Middle English *atwiten* to reproach, from Old English *ætwītan*, from *æt* at + *wītan* to reproach; akin to Old High German *wīzan* to punish, Old English *witan* to know] (1530)
**1** : to subject to light ridicule or reproach : RALLY
**2** : to make fun of as a fault

¹**twitch** \'twich\ *verb* [Middle English *twicchen;* akin to Old English *twiccian* to pluck, Old High German *gizwickan* to pinch] (14th century)
*transitive verb*
: to move or pull with a sudden motion : JERK
*intransitive verb*
**1** : PULL 1a, PLUCK ⟨*twitched* at my sleeve⟩
**2** : to move jerkily : QUIVER
— **twitch·er** *noun*

²**twitch** *noun* (1523)
**1** : an act of twitching; *especially* : a short sudden pull or jerk
**2** : a physical or mental pang
**3** : a loop of rope or strap that is tightened over a horse's lip as a restraining device
**4 a** : a short spastic contraction of the muscle fibers **b** : a slight jerk of a body part
— **twitch·i·ly** \'twi-chə-lē\ *adverb*
— **twitchy** \'twi-chē\ *adjective*

³**twitch** *noun* [alteration of *quitch*] (1598)
: QUACK GRASS

¹**twit·ter** \'twi-tər\ *verb* [Middle English *twiteren;* akin to Old High German *zwizzirōn* to twitter] (14th century)
*intransitive verb*
**1** : to utter successive chirping noises
**2 a** : to talk in a chattering fashion **b** : GIGGLE, TITTER
**3** : to tremble with agitation : FLUTTER
*transitive verb*
**1** : to utter in chirps or twitters ⟨the robin *twittered* its morning song⟩
**2** : to shake rapidly back and forth : FLUTTER

²**twitter** *noun* (1678)
**1** : a trembling agitation : QUIVER
**2** : a small tremulous intermittent sound (as of birds)
**3 a** : a light chattering **b** : a light silly laugh : GIGGLE
— **twit·tery** \'twi-tə-rē\ *adjective*

**twixt** \'twikst\ *or* ¹**'twixt** *preposition* [Middle English *twix,* short for *betwix, betwixt*] (14th century)
: BETWEEN

¹**two** \'tü\ *adjective* [Middle English *twa, two,* from Old English *twā* (feminine & neuter); akin to Old English *twēgen* two (masculine), *tū* (neuter), Old High German *zwēne,* Latin *duo,* Greek *dyo*] (before 12th century)
**1** : being one more than one in number
**2** : being the second — used postpositively ⟨section *two* of the instructions⟩

²**two** *pronoun, plural in construction* (before 12th century)
**1** : two countable individuals not specified ⟨only *two* were found⟩
**2** : a small approximate number of indicated things ⟨only a shot or *two* were fired⟩

³**two** *noun, plural* **twos** (circa 1585)
**1** — see NUMBER table
**2** : the second in a set or series ⟨the *two* of spades⟩
**3** : a 2-dollar bill
**4** : something having two units or members

**two-bag·ger** \-'ba-gər\ *noun* (1880)
: DOUBLE 1b

**two-bit** \'tü-'bit\ *adjective* (1802)
**1** : of the value of two bits
**2** : cheap or trivial of its kind : PETTY, SMALL-TIME

**two bits** *noun plural but singular or plural in construction* (1730)
**1** : the value of a quarter of a dollar
**2** : something of small worth or importance

¹**two-by-four** \,tü-bī-'fōr, -'fȯr\ *noun* (1884)
: a piece of lumber approximately 2 by 4 inch-

es as sawed and usually 1⅝ by 3⅝ inches if dressed

²**two-by-four** *adjective* (1897)
**1** : measuring two units (as inches) by four
**2** : small or petty of its kind ⟨this house and its *two-by-four* garden —Philip Barry⟩

**two cents** *noun* (1947)
**1** : a sum or object of very small value : practically nothing ⟨said angrily that for *two cents* he'd punch your nose⟩
**2** *or* **two cents worth** : an opinion offered on a topic under discussion ⟨each speaker . . . is getting in his *two cents worth* —Dwight Macdonald⟩

**two-cycle** *adjective* (1902)
*of an internal combustion engine* : having a 2-stroke cycle

**two-dimensional** *adjective* (1883)
**1** : having two dimensions
**2** : lacking depth of characterization ⟨*two-dimensional* characters⟩
— **two-dimensionality** *noun*

**two-edged sword** \'tü-'ejd-, -'e-jəd-\ *noun* (1526)
: DOUBLE-EDGED SWORD

**two-faced** \'tü-'fāst\ *adjective* (1609)
**1** : DOUBLE-DEALING, FALSE
**2** : having two faces
— **two-faced·ness** \-'fāst-nəs, -'fā-səd-nəs\ *noun*

**two·fer** \'tü-fər\ *noun* [alteration of *two for (one)*] (1890)
**1** : a cheap item of merchandise; *especially* : a cigar selling at two for a nickel
**2** : a free coupon entitling the bearer to purchase two tickets to a specified theatrical production for the price of one
**3** : two articles available for the price of one or about the price of one

**two-fist·ed** \-'fis-təd\ *adjective* (1774)
: marked by vigorous often virile energy : HARD-HITTING

**two·fold** \'tü-,fōld, -'fōld\ *adjective* (1559)
**1** : having two parts or aspects
**2** : being twice as great or as many
— **twofold** \-'fōld\ *adverb*

**2,4-D** \,tü-,fȯr-'dē, -,fȯr-\ *noun* [*di-*] (circa 1945)
: a white crystalline irritant compound $C_8H_6Cl_2O_3$ used especially as a weed killer

**2,4,5-T** \-,fīv-'tē\ *noun* [*tri-*] (1946)
: an irritant compound $C_8H_5Cl_3O_3$ used especially as an herbicide and defoliant

**two-hand·ed** \'tü-'han-dəd\ *adjective* (15th century)
**1** : used with both hands ⟨a *two-handed* sword⟩
**2** : requiring two persons ⟨a *two-handed* saw⟩
**3** *archaic* : STOUT, STRONG
**4 a** : having two hands **b** : efficient with either hand

**two-line octave** *noun* (circa 1931)
: the musical octave that begins on the first C above middle C — see PITCH illustration

**two-party** *adjective* (1925)
: characterized by two major political parties of comparable strength

**two·pence** \'tə-pən(t)s, *US also* 'tü-,pen(t)s\ *noun* (15th century)
**1** : the sum of two British pennies
**2** *plural* **twopence** *or* **two·pen·ces** : a coin worth twopence

**two·pen·ny** \'tə-pən-nē, 'tə-pə-, *US also* 'tü-,pe-nē\ *adjective* (1532)
: costing or worth twopence

**two-phase** *adjective* (circa 1896)
: DIPHASIC

¹**two-piece** \'tü-'pēs\ *adjective* (1910)
: forming a clothing ensemble with matching top and bottom parts

²**two-piece** \'tü-,pēs\ *noun* (1930)
: a garment (as a bathing suit) that is two-piece

**two-piec·er** \'tü-'pē-sər\ *noun* (1943)
: TWO-PIECE

**two-ply** \-'plī\ *adjective* (circa 1847)

**1** : consisting of two thicknesses
**2 a** : woven with two sets of warp thread and two of filling ⟨a *two-ply* carpet⟩ **b** : consisting of two strands ⟨*two-ply* yarn⟩

**two–sid·ed** \-'sī-dəd\ *adjective* (1884)
: having two sides : BILATERAL

**two·some** \'tü-səm\ *noun* (14th century)
**1** : a group of two persons or things : COUPLE
**2** : a golf singles match

**two–spot·ted spider mite** \'tü-'spä-təd-\ *noun* (1947)
: a widely distributed mite (*Tetranychus urticae*) that feeds on soft plant parts and is a serious pest in greenhouses and gardens

**two–step** \'tü-,step\ *noun* (1895)
**1** : a ballroom dance in ⅔ or 4/4 time having a basic pattern of step-close-step
**2** : a piece of music for the two-step
— **two–step** *intransitive verb*

**two–suit·er** \-'sü-tər\ *noun* (1948)
: a man's suitcase designed to hold two suits and accessories

**two–tailed** \'tü-'tāl(d)\ *also* **two–tail** \-'tā(ə)l\ *adjective* (1945)
: being a statistical test for which the critical region consists of all values of the test statistic greater than a given value plus the values less than another given value — compare ONE-TAILED

**two–time** \'tü-,tīm\ *transitive verb* (1924)
**1** : DOUBLE-CROSS
**2** : to betray (a spouse or lover) by secret lovemaking with another
— **two–tim·er** *noun*

**two–toed sloth** \'tü-'tōd-\ *noun* (1781)
: any of a genus (*Choloepus*) of sloths having two clawed digits on each forefoot, three clawed digits on each hind foot, and usually six or seven vertebrae in the neck — compare THREE-TOED SLOTH

**two–tone** \'tü-'tōn\ *adjective* (1906)
: colored in two colors or in two shades of one color ⟨*two-tone* shoes⟩

**two–toned** \'tü-'tōnd\ *adjective* (1897)
: TWO-TONE

**two–way** *adjective* (1571)
**1** : being a cock or valve that will connect a pipe or channel with either of two others
**2** : moving or allowing movement in either direction ⟨a *two-way* bridge⟩
**3 a** : involving or allowing an exchange between two individuals or groups ⟨there must be good *two-way* communication —Jerrold Orne⟩; *especially* : designed for both sending and receiving messages ⟨*two-way* radio⟩ **b** : involving mutual responsibility or reciprocal relationships ⟨political alliance is a *two-way* thing —T. H. White (died 1986)⟩
**4** : involving two participants ⟨a *two-way* race⟩
**5** : usable in either of two manners ⟨a *two-way* lamp⟩

**two–way street** *noun* (1948)
: a situation or relationship requiring give-and-take ⟨marriage is a *two-way street*⟩

**two–wheel·er** \-'hwē-lər, -'wē-\ *noun* (1861)
: a 2-wheeled vehicle (as a bicycle)

**two–winged fly** \'tü-'win(d)-\ *noun* (1753)
: ⁴FLY 2a

**-ty** *noun suffix* [Middle English *-te,* from Old French *-té,* from Latin *-tat-, -tas* — more at -ITY]
: quality : condition : degree ⟨apriori*ty*⟩

**ty·coon** \tī-'kün\ *noun* [Japanese *taikun*] (1857)
**1** : SHOGUN
**2 a** : a top leader (as in politics) **b** : a businessman of exceptional wealth and power
: MAGNATE ◆

**ty·er** \'tī(-ə)r\ *variant of* ³TIER

**tying** *present participle of* TIE

**tyke** \'tīk\ *noun* [Middle English *tyke,* from Old Norse *tík* bitch; akin to Middle Low German *tīke* bitch] (15th century)
**1** : DOG; *especially* : an inferior or mongrel dog

**2 a** *chiefly British* : a clumsy, churlish, or eccentric person **b** : a small child

**tym·bal** \'tim-bəl\ *noun* [alteration of *timbal*] (1929)
: the vibrating membrane in the shrilling organ of a cicada

**tym·pan** \'tim-pən\ *noun* [in sense 1, from Middle English, from Old English *timpana,* from Latin *tympanum;* in other senses, from Medieval Latin & Latin *tympanum*] (before 12th century)
**1** : DRUM
**2** : a sheet (as of paper or cloth) placed between the impression surface of a press and the paper to be printed
**3** : TYMPANUM 2

**tym·pa·ni, tym·pa·nist** *variant of* TIMPANI, TIMPANIST

**tym·pan·ic** \tim-'pa-nik\ *adjective* [Latin & New Latin *tympanum*] (1808)
: of, relating to, or being a tympanum

**tympanic membrane** *noun* (1860)
: a thin membrane that closes externally the cavity of the middle ear and functions in the mechanical reception of sound waves and in their transmission to the site of sensory reception — called also *eardrum;* see EAR illustration

**tym·pa·ni·tes** \,tim-pə-'nī-tēz\ *noun* [Middle English, from Late Latin, from Greek *tympanitēs,* from *tympanon*] (14th century)
: a distension of the abdomen caused by accumulation of gas in the intestinal tract or peritoneal cavity
— **tym·pa·nit·ic** \-'ni-tik\ *adjective*

**tym·pa·num** \'tim-pə-nəm\ *noun, plural* **-na** \-nə\ *also* **-nums** [Medieval Latin & Latin; Medieval Latin, eardrum, from Latin, drum, architectural panel, from Greek *tympanon* drum, kettledrum, from Latin, drum; perhaps akin to Greek *typtein* to beat] (1619)
**1 a** (1) : TYMPANIC MEMBRANE (2) : MIDDLE EAR **b** : a thin tense membrane covering an organ of hearing of an insect — see INSECT illustration **c** : a membranous resonator in a sound-producing organ
**2 a** : the recessed usually triangular face of a pediment within the frame made by the upper and lower cornices **b** : the space within an arch and above a lintel or a subordinate arch

*1 tympanum 2a*

**tym·pa·ny** \-nē\ *noun, plural* **-nies** [Medieval Latin *tympanias,* from Greek, from *tympanon*] (1528)
**1** : TYMPANITES
**2** : BOMBAST, TURGIDITY

**Tyn·dar·e·us** \tin-'dar-ē-əs\ *noun* [Latin, from Greek]
: a king of Sparta and husband of Leda in Greek mythology

**tyne** *variant of* TINE

**typ·al** \'tī-pəl\ *adjective* (1853)
**1** : serving as a type : TYPICAL
**2** : of or relating to a type

**¹type** \'tīp\ *noun, often attributive* [Middle English, from Late Latin *typus,* from Latin & Greek; Latin *typus* image, from Greek *typos* blow, impression, model, from *typtein* to strike, beat; akin to Sanskrit *tupati* he injures and probably to Latin *stupēre* to be benumbed] (15th century)
**1 a** : a person or thing (as in the Old Testament) believed to foreshadow another (as in the New Testament) **b** : one having qualities of a higher category : MODEL **c** : a lower taxonomic category selected as a standard of reference for a higher category; *also* : a specimen or series of specimens on which a taxonomic species or subspecies is actually based

**2** : a distinctive mark or sign
**3 a** (1) : a rectangular block usually of metal bearing a relief character from which an inked print can be made (2) : a collection of such blocks ⟨a font of *type*⟩ (3) : alphanumeric characters for printing ⟨the *type* for this book has been photoset⟩ **b** : TYPEFACE ⟨italic *type*⟩ **c** : printed letters **d** : matter set in type
**4 a** : qualities common to a number of individuals that distinguish them as an identifiable class: as (1) : the morphological, physiological, or ecological characters by which relationship between organisms may be recognized (2) : the form common to all instances of a linguistic element **b** : a typical and often superior specimen **c** : a member of an indicated class or variety of people ⟨the guests were mostly urban *types* —Lucy Cook⟩ **d** : a particular kind, class, or group ⟨oranges of the seedless *type*⟩ ⟨leaders of the new *type* . . . did England yeoman's service —G. M. Trevelyan⟩ **e** : something distinguishable as a variety : SORT ⟨what *type* of food do you like?⟩ ☆

²**type** *verb* **typed; typ·ing** (1596)
*transitive verb*
**1 :** to represent beforehand as a type **:** PREFIGURE
**2 a :** to produce a copy of **b :** to represent in terms of typical characteristics **:** TYPIFY
**3 :** to produce (as a character or document) on a typewriter; *also* **:** KEYBOARD
**4 :** to identify as belonging to a type: as **a :** to determine the natural type of (as a blood sample) **b :** TYPECAST
*intransitive verb*
**:** to write something on a typewriter or enter data into a computer by way of a keyboard
— **type·able** \'tī-pə-bəl\ *adjective*
**type A** *adjective* (1970)
**:** relating to, characteristic of, having, or being a personality that is marked by impatience, aggressiveness, and competitiveness and that is held to be associated with increased risk of cardiovascular disease ⟨*type A* behavior⟩
**type·cast** \'tīp-ˌkast\ *transitive verb* **-cast; -cast·ing** (1927)
**1 :** to cast (an actor or actress) in a part calling for the same characteristics as those possessed by the performer
**2 :** to cast (an actor or actress) repeatedly in the same type of role
**3 :** STEREOTYPE ⟨*typecast* as the grubby, unbeautiful place which is full of life —Miles Kington⟩
**type·face** \-ˌfās\ *noun* (1887)
**1 :** the face of printing type
**2 :** all type of a single design
**type·found·er** \-ˌfauṅ-dər\ *noun* (1797)
**:** one engaged in the design and production of metal printing type for hand composition
— **type·found·ing** \-diŋ\ *noun*
**type genus** *noun* (1840)
**:** the genus of a taxonomic family or subfamily from which the name of the family or subfamily is formed
**type I error** \'tīp-'wən-\ *noun* (1947)
**:** rejection of the null hypothesis in statistical testing when it is true
**type·script** \'tīp-ˌskript\ *noun* [*type* + *manuscript*] (1893)
**:** a typewritten manuscript; *especially* **:** one intended for use as printer's copy
**type·set** \-ˌset\ *transitive verb* **-set; -set·ting** (1945)
**:** to set in type **:** COMPOSE
**type·set·ter** \-ˌse-tər\ *noun* (1883)
**:** one that sets type
**type·set·ting** \-ˌse-tiŋ\ *noun* (1846)
**:** the process of setting material in type or into a form to be used in printing; *also* **:** the process of producing graphic matter (as through a computer system)
**type species** *noun* (1840)
**:** the species of a genus with which the generic name is permanently associated
**type specimen** *noun* (circa 1891)
**:** a specimen or individual designated as type of a species or lesser group and serving as the final criterion of the characteristics of that group
**type·style** \'tīp-ˌstī(ə)l\ *noun* (1954)
**:** TYPEFACE
**type II error** \-'tü-\ *noun* (1947)
**:** acceptance of the null hypothesis in statistical testing when it is false
**type·write** \'tīp-ˌrīt\ *verb* **-wrote** \-ˌrōt\; **-writ·ten** \-ˌri-t³n\ [back-formation from *typewriter*] (1887)
*transitive verb*
**:** TYPE 3
*intransitive verb*
**:** TYPE
**type·writ·er** \-ˌrī-tər\ *noun* (1868)
**1 :** a machine for writing in characters similar to those produced by printer's type by means of keyboard-operated types striking a ribbon to transfer ink or carbon impressions onto the paper
**2 :** TYPIST

**type·writ·ing** \-ˌrī-tin\ *noun* (1867)
**1 :** the act or study of or skill in using a typewriter
**2 :** writing produced with a typewriter
**typ·ey** *also* **typy** \'tī-pē\ *adjective* **typ·i·er; -est** [¹*type*] (1923)
**:** characterized by strict conformance to type; *also* **:** exhibiting superior bodily conformation ⟨a sound *typey* heifer⟩
**typh·lo·sole** \'ti-flə-ˌsōl\ *noun* [Greek *typhlos* blind + *sōlēn* pipe, channel — more at DEAF] (1859)
**:** a longitudinal fold of the intestinal wall that projects into the cavity especially in bivalve mollusks, annelids, and starfishes
**Ty·pho·eus** \tī-'fō-ˌyüs, -yəs\ *noun* [Latin, from Greek *Typhōeus*]
**:** TYPHON
— **Ty·phoe·an** \-'fē-ən\ *adjective*
¹**ty·phoid** \'tī-ˌfȯid, (ˌ)tī-'\ *adjective* [New Latin *typhus*] (1800)
**1 :** of, relating to, or suggestive of typhus
**2** [²*typhoid*] **:** of, relating to, or constituting typhoid
²**typhoid** *noun* (1861)
**1 :** TYPHOID FEVER
**2 :** a disease of domestic animals resembling human typhus or typhoid
**typhoid fever** *noun* (1845)
**:** a communicable disease marked especially by fever, diarrhea, prostration, headache, and intestinal inflammation and caused by a bacterium (*Salmonella typhi*)
**Typhoid Mary** *noun, plural* **Typhoid Marys** [*Typhoid Mary,* nickname of Mary Mallon (died 1938) Irish cook in U.S. who was found to be a typhoid carrier] (1931)
**:** one that is by force of circumstances a center from which something undesirable spreads
**Ty·phon** \'tī-ˌfän\ *noun* [Latin, from Greek *Typhōn*]
**:** a monster with a tremendous voice who according to classical mythology was father of Cerberus, the Chimera, and the Sphinx
**ty·phoon** \tī-'fün\ *noun* [alteration (influenced by Chinese — Guangdong — *daaih-fùng,* from *daaih* big + *fùng* wind) of earlier *touffon,* from Arabic *ṭūfān* hurricane, from Greek *typhōn* violent storm] (1771)
**1 :** a tropical cyclone occurring in the region of the Philippines or the China sea
**2 :** WHIRLWIND 2a ⟨a veritable *typhoon* of interest and corporate investment —Norman Sklarewitz⟩
**ty·phus** \'tī-fəs\ *noun* [New Latin, from Greek *typhos* fever; akin to Greek *typhein* to smoke — more at DEAF] (1785)
**:** any of various bacterial diseases caused by rickettsias: as **a :** a severe human febrile disease that is caused by one (*Rickettsia prowazekii*) transmitted especially by body lice and is marked by high fever, stupor alternating with delirium, intense headache, and a dark red rash **b :** MURINE TYPHUS **c :** TSUTSUGAMUSHI DISEASE
**typ·ic** \'ti-pik\ *adjective* (1610)
**:** TYPICAL 1
**typ·i·cal** \'ti-pi-kəl\ *adjective* [Late Latin *typicalis,* from *typicus,* from Greek *typikos,* from *typos* model — more at TYPE] (1612)
**1 :** constituting or having the nature of a type **:** SYMBOLIC
**2 a :** combining or exhibiting the essential characteristics of a group ⟨*typical* suburban houses⟩ **b :** conforming to a type ⟨a specimen *typical* of the species⟩
*synonym* see REGULAR
— **typ·i·cal·i·ty** \ˌti-pə-'ka-lə-tē\ *noun*
— **typ·i·cal·ness** \'ti-pi-kəl-nəs\ *noun*
**typ·i·cal·ly** \'ti-pi-k(ə-)lē\ *adverb* (1605)
**1 :** in a typical manner ⟨*typically* American⟩
**2 :** on a typical occasion **:** in typical circumstances ⟨*typically,* members of our staff receive little . . . recognition —Brendan Gill⟩
**typ·i·fy** \'ti-pə-ˌfī\ *transitive verb* **-fied; -fy·ing** (1634)

**1 :** to represent in typical fashion **:** to constitute a typical mark or instance of ⟨realism . . . that *typified* his earlier work —*Current Biography*⟩
**2 :** to embody the essential or salient characteristics of **:** be the type of
— **typ·i·fi·ca·tion** \ˌti-pə-fə-'kā-shən\ *noun*
**typ·ist** \'tī-pist\ *noun* (1885)
**:** one who types or enters data into a computer especially as a job
**ty·po** \'tī-(ˌ)pō\ *noun, plural* **typos** [short for *typographical (error)*] (1892)
**:** an error (as of spelling) in typed or typeset material
**ty·po·graph** \'tī-pə-ˌgraf\ *transitive verb* (circa 1933)
**:** to produce (stamps) by letterpress
**ty·pog·ra·pher** \tī-'pä-grə-fər\ *noun* (1643)
**:** a person (as a compositor, printer, or designer) who specializes in the design, choice, and arrangement of type matter
**ty·po·graph·ic** \ˌtī-pə-'gra-fik\ *or* **ty·po·graph·i·cal** \-fi-kəl\ *adjective* (1593)
**:** of, relating to, or occurring or used in typography or typeset matter ⟨a *typographic* character⟩ ⟨a *typographical* error⟩
— **ty·po·graph·i·cal·ly** \-fi-k(ə-)lē\ *adverb*
**ty·pog·ra·phy** \tī-'pä-grə-fē\ *noun* [Medieval Latin *typographia,* from Greek *typos* impression, cast + *-graphia* -graphy — more at TYPE] (1610)
**1 :** letterpress printing
**2 :** the style, arrangement, ˌor appearance of typeset matter
**ty·po·log·i·cal** \ˌtī-pə-'lä-ji-kəl\ *adjective* (1845)
**:** of or relating to typology or types
— **ty·po·log·i·cal·ly** \-ji-k(ə-)lē\ *adverb*
**ty·pol·o·gy** \tī-'pä-lə-jē\ *noun, plural* **-gies** (1845)
**1 :** a doctrine of theological types; *especially* **:** one holding that things in Christian belief are prefigured or symbolized by things in the Old Testament
**2 :** study of or analysis or classification based on types or categories
— **ty·pol·o·gist** \-jist\ *noun*
**Tyr** \'tir\ *noun* [Old Norse *Tȳr;* akin to Old English *Tīw* Tiu — more at DEITY]
**:** a god of war in Norse mythology
**ty·ra·mine** \'tī-rə-ˌmēn\ *noun* [International Scientific Vocabulary *tyrosine* + *amine*] (1910)
**:** a phenolic amine $C_8H_{11}NO$ found in various foods and beverages (as cheese and red wine) that has a sympathomimetic action and is derived from tyrosine
**ty·ran·ni·cal** \tə-'ra-ni-kəl, tī-\ *also* **ty·ran·nic** \-nik\ *adjective* [Latin *tyrannicus,* from Greek *tyrannikos,* from *tyrannos* tyrant] (15th century)
**:** being or characteristic of a tyrant or tyranny **:** DESPOTIC ⟨*tyrannical* rule⟩ ⟨a *tyrannical* ruler⟩
— **ty·ran·ni·cal·ly** \-ni-k(ə-)lē\ *adverb*
— **ty·ran·ni·cal·ness** \-kəl-nəs\ *noun*
**ty·ran·ni·cide** \tə-'ra-nə-ˌsīd, tī-\ *noun* [in sense 1, from French, from Latin *tyrannicidium,* from *tyrannus* + *-i- + -cidium* -cide (killing); in sense 2, from French, from Latin *tyrannicida,* from *tyrannus* + *-i- + -cida* -cide (killer)] (1650)
**1 :** the act of killing a tyrant
**2 :** the killer of a tyrant
**tyr·an·nise** *British variant of* TYRANNIZE
**tyr·an·nize** \'tir-ə-ˌnīz\ *verb* **-nized; -niz·ing** (15th century)
*intransitive verb*
**:** to exercise arbitrary oppressive power or severity ⟨some ways the living *tyrannize* over the dying —Thomas Powers⟩

*transitive verb*
**:** to treat tyrannically **:** OPPRESS
— **tyr·an·niz·er** *noun*

**ty·ran·no·saur** \tə-'ra-nə-ˌsȯr, tī-\ *noun* [New Latin *Tyrannosaurus,* genus name, from Greek *tyrannos* tyrant + *sauros* lizard] (1924)
**:** a very large bipedal carnivorous dinosaur (*Tyrannosaurus rex*) with small forelegs that occurs in the Upper Cretaceous of North America

**ty·ran·no·sau·rus** \tə-ˌra-nə-'sȯr-əs, (ˌ)tī-\ *noun* [New Latin] (1905)
**:** TYRANNOSAUR

**tyr·an·nous** \'tir-ə-nəs\ *adjective* (15th century)
**:** marked by tyranny; *especially* **:** unjustly severe
— **tyr·an·nous·ly** *adverb*

**tyr·an·ny** \'tir-ə-nē\ *noun, plural* **-nies** [Middle English *tyrannie,* from Middle French, from Medieval Latin *tyrannia,* from Latin *tyrannus* tyrant] (14th century)
**1 :** oppressive power ⟨every form of *tyranny* over the mind of man —Thomas Jefferson⟩; *especially* **:** oppressive power exerted by government ⟨the *tyranny* of a police state⟩
**2 a :** a government in which absolute power is vested in a single ruler; *especially* **:** one characteristic of an ancient Greek city-state **b :** the office, authority, and administration of a tyrant
**3 :** a rigorous condition imposed by some outside agency or force ⟨living under the *tyranny* of the clock —Dixon Wecter⟩
**4 :** a tyrannical act

**ty·rant** \'tī-rənt\ *noun* [Middle English *tirant,* from Old French *tyran, tyrant,* from Latin *tyr-*

*annus,* from Greek *tyrannos*] (14th century)
**1 a :** an absolute ruler unrestrained by law or constitution **b :** a usurper of sovereignty
**2 a :** a ruler who exercises absolute power oppressively or brutally **b :** one resembling an oppressive ruler in the harsh use of authority or power

**tyrant flycatcher** *noun* (circa 1783)
**:** any of various large American flycatchers (family Tyrannidae) that are usually strictly insectivorous and have a flattened bill often hooked at the tip and usually bristly at the gape

**tyre** *chiefly British variant of* TIRE

**Tyr·i·an purple** \'tir-ē-ən-\ *noun* [*Tyre,* maritime city of ancient Phoenicia] (circa 1586)
**:** a crimson or purple dye that is related to indigo, obtained by the ancient Greeks and Romans from gastropod mollusks, and now made synthetically

**ty·ro** \'tī-(ˌ)rō\ *noun, plural* **tyros** *often attributive* [Medieval Latin, from Latin *tiro* young soldier, tyro] (1611)
**:** a beginner in learning **:** NOVICE
*synonym* SEE AMATEUR

**ty·ro·ci·dine** *also* **ty·ro·ci·din** \ˌtī-rə-'sī-dᵊn\ *noun* [*tyrothricin* + *gramicidin*] (1940)
**:** a basic polypeptide antibiotic produced by a soil bacillus (*Bacillus brevis*)

**Ty·ro·le·an** *also* **Ty·ro·li·an** \tə-'rō-lē-ən, tī-\ *adjective* (1805)
**1 :** of or relating to the Tirol
**2** *of a hat* **:** of a style originating in the Tirol and marked by soft often green felt, a narrow brim and pointed crown, and an ornamental feather

**ty·ros·i·nase** \tə-'rä-sə-ˌnās, tī-, -ˌnāz\ *noun* (1896)
**:** a copper-containing enzyme that promotes the oxidation of phenols (as tyrosine) and is widespread in plants and animals

**ty·ro·sine** \'tī-rə-ˌsēn\ *noun* [International Scientific Vocabulary, irregular from Greek *tyros* cheese — more at BUTTER] (1857)
**:** a phenolic amino acid $C_9H_{11}NO_3$ that is a precursor of several important substances (as epinephrine and melanin)

**ty·ro·thri·cin** \ˌtī-rə-'thrī-sᵊn\ *noun* [New Latin *Tyrothoric-, Tyrothrix,* genus name formerly applied to various bacteria including *Bacillus brevis*] (1940)
**:** an antibiotic mixture that consists chiefly of tyrocidine and gramicidin, is usually extracted from a soil bacillus (*Bacillus brevis*) as a gray to brown powder, and is used for local applications especially for infection caused by gram-positive bacteria

**tzaddik** *noun, plural* **tzaddikim** *variant of* ZADDIK

**tzar** \'zär, '(t)sär\ *variant of* CZAR

**tzi·gane** \(t)sē-'gän\ *noun* [French, from Hungarian *cigány*] (1763)
**1 :** GYPSY 1
**2 :** ROMANY 2

**tzim·mes** \'tsi-məs\ *noun* [Yiddish *tsimes,* from Middle High German *z, zuo* at, too + *imbīz* light meal] (1892)
**:** a sweetened combination of vegetables (as carrots and potatoes) or of meat and carrots often with dried fruits (as prunes) that is stewed or baked in a casserole

**tzi·tzis, tzi·tzit** *variant of* ZIZITH

# U

U *is the twenty-first letter of the English alphabet. It is a cursive form of the letter V, with which it was once used interchangeably, both letters having the value of either the modern vowel U or the modern consonant V. By the 10th century, V came to be preferred as the capital form used at the beginning of a word, and U as the cursive form used in the middle of a word. Since the consonant sound usually occurred at the beginning and the vowel sound in the middle of words, V gradually became specialized to represent the former and U the latter, but small u and small v were used interchangeably as late as the 13th century. In dictionaries of English, U and V were not given separate alphabetical positions until about 1800. The vowel sounds of* u *in Old English were the ones which it still retains in most of the languages of Europe, that of the vowel in* tool, *and the vowel in* wood, *but Modern English* u *represents various other sounds as well.*

**u** \'yü\ *noun, plural* **u's** *or* **us** \'yüz\ *often capitalized, often attributive* (before 12th century)
**1 a :** the 21st letter of the English alphabet **b :** a graphic representation of this letter **c :** a speech counterpart of orthographic *u*
**2 :** a graphic device for reproducing the letter *u*
**3 :** one designated *u* especially as the 21st in order or class
**4** [abbreviation for *unsatisfactory*] **a :** a grade rating a student's work as unsatisfactory **b :** one graded or rated with a U
**5 :** something shaped like the letter U
**U** \'yü\ *adjective* [upper class] (1954)
**:** characteristic of the upper classes
**Uban·gi** \yü-'baŋ-gē, ü-, -'baŋ-ē\ *noun* [*Ubangi-Shari,* Africa] (1942)
**:** a woman of the district of Kyabé village in Chad with lips pierced and distended to unusual dimensions with wooden disks — not used technically
**ubi·qui·none** \yü-'bi-kwə-₁nōn, ₁yü-bə-kwi-'nōn\ *noun* [blend of Latin *ubique* everywhere and English *quinone;* from its widespread occurrence in nature] (1958)
**:** any of a group of lipid-soluble quinones that contain a long isoprenoid side chain and that function in the part of cellular respiration comprising oxidative phosphorylation as electron-carrying coenzymes in the transport of electrons from organic substrates to oxygen especially along the chain of reactions leading from the Krebs cycle
**ubiq·ui·tous** \yü-'bi-kwə-təs\ *adjective* (1837)
**:** existing or being everywhere at the same time : constantly encountered : WIDESPREAD
— **ubiq·ui·tous·ly** *adverb*
— **ubiq·ui·tous·ness** *noun*
**ubiq·ui·ty** \-kwə-tē\ *noun* [Latin *ubique* everywhere, from *ubi* where + *-que,* enclitic generalizing particle; akin to Latin *quis* who and to Latin *-que* and — more at WHO, SESQUI-] (1597)
**:** presence everywhere or in many places especially simultaneously : OMNIPRESENCE
**U-boat** \'yü-₁bōt\ *noun* [translation of German *U-boot,* short for *Unterseeboot,* literally, undersea boat] (1916)
**:** a German submarine
**ud·der** \'ə-dər\ *noun* [Middle English, from Old English *ūder;* akin to Old High German *ūtar* udder, Latin *uber,* Greek *outhar,* Sanskrit *ūdhar*] (before 12th century)
**1 :** a large pendulous organ consisting of two or more mammary glands enclosed in a common envelope and each provided with a single nipple — see COW illustration

**2 :** MAMMARY GLAND
**UFO** \₁yü-(₁)ef-'ō\ *noun, plural* **UFO's** *or* **UFOs** \-'ōz\ [*unidentified flying object*] (1953)
**:** an unidentified flying object; *especially* **:** FLYING SAUCER
**ufol·o·gy** \yü-'fä-lə-jē\ *noun, often UFO capitalized* [*UFO* + *-logy*] (1959)
**:** the study of unidentified flying objects
— **ufo·log·i·cal** \₁yü-fə-'lä-ji-kəl\ *adjective, often UFO capitalized*
— **ufol·o·gist** \yü-'fä-lə-jist\ *noun, often UFO capitalized*
**¹Uga·rit·ic** \₁yü-gə-'ri-tik, ₁ü-gə-\ *noun* (1936)
**:** the Semitic language of ancient Ugarit closely related to Phoenician and Hebrew
**²Ugaritic** *adjective* (1938)
**:** of, relating to, or characteristic of the ancient city of Ugarit, its inhabitants, or Ugaritic
**ugh** \*often read as* 'əg *or* 'ək *or* 'ə\ *interjection* (1837)
— used to indicate the sound of a cough or grunt or to express disgust or horror
**Ug·li** \'ə-glē\ *trademark*
— used for a tangelo
**ug·li·fy** \'ə-gli-₁fī\ *transitive verb* **-fied; -fy·ing** (1576)
**:** to make ugly
— **ug·li·fi·ca·tion** \₁ə-gli-fə-'kā-shən\ *noun*
**ug·li·ness** \'ə-glē-nəs\ *noun* (14th century)
**1 :** the quality or state of being ugly
**2 :** something that is ugly
**¹ug·ly** \'ə-glē\ *adjective* **ug·li·er; -est** [Middle English, from Old Norse *uggligr,* from *uggr* fear; akin to Old Norse *ugga* to fear] (13th century)
**1 :** FRIGHTFUL, DIRE
**2 a :** offensive to the sight : HIDEOUS **b :** offensive or unpleasant to any sense
**3 :** morally offensive or objectionable ⟨corruption—the *ugliest* stain of all⟩
**4 a :** likely to cause inconvenience or discomfort ⟨the *ugly* truth⟩ **b :** SURLY, QUARRELSOME ⟨an *ugly* disposition⟩ ⟨the crowd got *ugly*⟩
— **ug·li·ly** \-glə-lē\ *adverb*
**²ugly** *adverb* (14th century)
**:** in an ugly manner ⟨was acting *ugly*⟩
**Ugly American** *noun* [*The Ugly American* (1958), collection of stories by Eugene Burdick (died 1965) and William J. Lederer (born 1912) American authors] (1965)
**:** an American in a foreign country whose behavior is offensive to the people of that country
**ugly duckling** *noun* [*The Ugly Duckling,* story by Hans Christian Andersen] (1883)
**:** one that appears very unpromising but often has great potential

**Ugri·an** \'yü-grē-ən, 'ü-\ *noun* [Old Russian *Ugre* Hungarians] (1841)
**:** a member of a division of the Finno-Ugric peoples that includes the Hungarians and two peoples of western Siberia
— **Ugrian** *adjective*
**Ugric** \-grik\ *adjective* (1854)
**:** of, relating to, or characteristic of the languages of the Ugrians
**ug·some** \'əg-səm\ *adjective* [Middle English, from *uggen* to fear, inspire fear, from Old Norse *ugga* to fear] (15th century)
*archaic* **:** FRIGHTFUL, LOATHSOME
**uh-huh** \*two m's or two n's separated by the voiceless sound* h; 'ə̃-(₁)hə̃, (₁)ə̃-'\ *interjection* (1899)
— used to indicate affirmation, agreement, or gratification
**uh·lan** \'ü-₁län, ü-'; 'yü-lən, 'ü-\ *noun* [German, from Polish *ulan,* from Turkish *oğlan* boy, servant] (1753)
**:** any of a body of Prussian light cavalry originally modeled on Tatar lancers
**uh-oh** \'ə-₁ō, *usually with strong glottal stops before the vowels*\ *interjection* (1971)
— used to indicate dismay or concern
**uh-uh** \*two m's or two n's preceded by glottal stops;* 'ə̃-₁ə̃ⁿ\ *interjection* (circa 1924)
— used to indicate negation
**Ui·ghur** *also* **Ui·gur** \'wē-₁gu̇r\ *noun* [*Uighur Uighur*] (1747)
**1 :** a member of a Turkic people powerful in Mongolia and eastern Turkestan between the 8th and 12th centuries A.D. who constitute a majority of the population of Chinese Turkestan
**2 :** the Turkic language of the Uighurs
— **Uighur** *also* **Uigur** *adjective*
**uil·leann pipes** \'i-lən-\ *noun plural, often capitalized* [*uilleann* from Irish, genitive singular of *uillinn* elbow, from Old Irish *uilen;* akin to Old English *eln* ell — more at ELL] (1906)
**:** an Irish bagpipe with air supplied by a bellows held under and worked by the elbow
**uin·ta·ite** *also* **uin·tah·ite** \yu̇-'in-tə-₁īt\ *noun* [*Uinta, Uintah,* mountains in Utah] (1888)
**:** a black lustrous asphalt occurring especially in Utah
**Uit·land·er** \'āt-₁lan-dər, 'au̇t-, -₁län-\ *noun* [Afrikaans, from Middle Dutch *utelander* foreigner, from *utelant* foreign territory, from *ute* out + *lant* land] (1892)
**:** FOREIGNER; *especially* **:** a British resident in the former republics of the Transvaal and Orange Free State
**ukase** \yü-'kās, -'kāz, 'yü-₁; ü-'käz\ *noun* [French & Russian; French, from Russian *ukaz,* from *ukazat'* to show, order; akin to Old Church Slavonic *u-* away, Latin *au-,* Sanskrit *ava-* and to Old Church Slavonic *kazati* to show] (1729)
**1 :** a proclamation by a Russian emperor or government having the force of law
**2 :** EDICT
**uke** \'yük\ *noun* (1921)
**:** UKULELE
**uki·yo-e** *also* **uki·yo-ye** \ü-₁kē-ō-'yā, -'ā\ *noun* [Japanese *ukiyo-e* genre picture, from *ukiyo* world, life + *e* picture] (1879)
**:** a Japanese art movement that flourished from the 17th to the 19th century and produced paintings and prints depicting the everyday life and interests of the common people; *also* **:** the paintings and prints themselves
**Ukrai·ni·an** \yü-'krā-nē-ən *also* -'krī-\ *noun* (1823)
**1 :** a native or inhabitant of Ukraine
**2 :** the Slavic language of the Ukrainian people
— **Ukrainian** *adjective*
**uku·le·le** *also* **uke·le·le** \₁yü-kə-'lā-lē, ₁ü-\ *noun* [Hawaiian *'ukulele,* from *'uku* flea + *lele* jumping] (1896)

: a small guitar of Portuguese origin popularized in Hawaii in the 1880s and strung typically with four strings ◆

ukulele

**-ular** *adjective suffix* [Latin *-ularis,* from *-ulus, -ula, -ulum -ule* + *-aris -ar*]
: of, relating to, or resembling ⟨valv*ular*⟩

**ul·cer** \'əl-sər\ *noun*
[Middle English, from Latin *ulcer-, ulcus;* akin to Greek *helkos* wound] (14th century)
**1** : a break in skin or mucous membrane with loss of surface tissue, disintegration and necrosis of epithelial tissue, and often pus
**2** : something that festers and corrupts like an open sore
— **ulcer** *verb*

**ul·cer·ate** \'əl-sə-ˌrāt\ *verb* **-at·ed; -at·ing** (15th century)
*intransitive verb*
: to become affected with or as if with an ulcer
*transitive verb*
: to affect with or as if with an ulcer

**ul·cer·a·tion** \ˌəl-sə-'rā-shən\ *noun* (14th century)
**1** : the process of becoming ulcerated : the state of being ulcerated
**2** : ULCER
— **ul·cer·a·tive** \'əl-sə-ˌrā-tiv, 'əls-rə-, 'əl-sə-rə-\ *adjective*

**ulcerative colitis** *noun* (circa 1928)
: a nonspecific inflammatory disease of the colon of unknown cause characterized by diarrhea with discharge of mucus and blood, cramping abdominal pain, and inflammation and edema of the mucous membrane with patches of ulceration

**ul·cero·gen·ic** \ˌəl-sə-rō-'je-nik\ *adjective* (1950)
: tending to produce or develop into ulcers or ulceration

**ul·cer·ous** \'əls-rəs, 'əl-sə-\ *adjective* (1577)
**1** : being or marked by an ulceration ⟨*ulcerous* lesions⟩
**2** : affected with or as if with an ulcer : ULCERATED

**-ule** *noun suffix* [French & Latin; French, from Latin *-ulus,* masculine diminutive suffix, *-ula,* feminine diminutive suffix, *-ulum,* neuter diminutive suffix]
: little one ⟨duct*ule*⟩

**ule·ma** *or* **ula·ma** \ˌü-lə-'mä\ *noun* [Arabic, Turkish, & Persian; Turkish & Persian *'ulemā,* from Arabic *'ulamā*] (1688)
**1** *plural in construction* : the body of mullahs
**2** : MULLAH

**-ulent** *adjective suffix* [Latin *-ulentus*]
: that abounds in (a specified thing) ⟨flocc*ulent*⟩

**ulex·ite** \'yü-lək-ˌsīt\ *noun* [George L. *Ulex* (died 1883) German chemist] (1867)
: a mineral consisting of a hydrous borate of sodium and calcium and usually occurring in loosely packed white fibers that transmit light lengthwise with nearly undiminished intensity

**ul·lage** \'ə-lij\ *noun* [Middle English *ulage,* from Middle French *eullage* act of filling a cask, from *eullier* to fill a cask, from Old French *ouil* eye, bunghole, from Latin *oculus* eye — more at EYE] (15th century)
: the amount that a container (as a tank or cask) lacks of being full

**ul·na** \'əl-nə\ *noun* [New Latin, from Latin, elbow — more at ELL] (1541)
: the bone on the little-finger side of the human forearm; *also* : a corresponding part of the forelimb of vertebrates above fishes
— **ul·nar** \-nər, -ˌnär\ *adjective*

**ul·ster** \'əl-stər\ *noun* [*Ulster,* Ireland] (1876)
: a long loose overcoat of Irish origin made of heavy material (as frieze)

---

**ul·te·ri·or** \ˌəl-'tir-ē-ər\ *adjective* [Latin, farther, further, comparative of (assumed) Latin *ulter* situated beyond, from *uls* beyond; akin to Latin *ollus, ille,* that one, Old Irish ind*oll* beyond] (1646)
**1 a** : FURTHER, FUTURE **b** : more distant : REMOTER **c** : situated on the farther side : THITHER
**2** : going beyond what is openly said or shown and especially what is proper ⟨*ulterior* motives⟩
— **ul·te·ri·or·ly** *adverb*

**ul·ti·ma** \'əl-tə-mə\ *noun* [Latin, feminine of *ultimus* last] (circa 1864)
: the last syllable of a word

**ul·ti·ma·cy** \'əl-tə-mə-sē\ *noun, plural* **-cies** (1842)
**1** : the quality or state of being ultimate
**2** : ULTIMATE 1

**ul·ti·ma ra·tio** \ˌül-tə-mə-'rä-tē-ˌō\ *noun* [New Latin] (1780)
: the final argument; *also* : the last resort (as force)

**¹ul·ti·mate** \'əl-tə-mət\ *adjective* [Medieval Latin *ultimatus* last, final, from Late Latin, past participle of *ultimare* to come to an end, be last, from Latin *ultimus* farthest, last, final, superlative of (assumed) Latin *ulter* situated beyond] (1654)
**1 a** : most remote in space or time : FARTHEST **b** : last in a progression or series ⟨their *ultimate* destination was Paris⟩ **c** : EVENTUAL ⟨they hoped for *ultimate* success⟩ **d** : the best or most extreme of its kind : UTMOST ⟨the *ultimate* sacrifice⟩
**2** : arrived at as the last result ⟨the *ultimate* question⟩
**3 a** : BASIC, FUNDAMENTAL ⟨the *ultimate* nature of things —A. N. Whitehead⟩ **b** : ORIGINAL ⟨the *ultimate* source⟩ **c** : incapable of further analysis, division, or separation
**4** : MAXIMUM
**synonym** see LAST
— **ul·ti·mate·ness** *noun*

**²ultimate** *noun* (1681)
**1** : something ultimate; *especially* : FUNDAMENTAL
**2** : ACME

**³ul·ti·mate** \-mət, -ˌmāt\ *verb* **-mat·ed; -mat·ing** (circa 1834)
: END

**ul·ti·mate·ly** \-mət-lē\ *adverb* (1652)
**1** : in the end : FINALLY, FUNDAMENTALLY
**2** : EVENTUALLY

**ul·ti·ma Thu·le** \ˌəl-tə-mə-'thü-lē, -'thyü-\ *noun* [Latin, farthest Thule] (1665)
: THULE

**ul·ti·ma·tum** \ˌəl-tə-'mā-təm, -'mä-\ *noun, plural* **-tums** *or* **-ta** \-tə\ [New Latin, from Medieval Latin, neuter of *ultimatus* final] (1731)
: a final proposition, condition, or demand; *especially* : one whose rejection will end negotiations and cause a resort to force or other direct action

**ul·ti·mo** \'əl-tə-ˌmō\ *adjective* [Latin *ultimo mense* in the last month] (1616)
: of or occurring in the month preceding the present

**ul·ti·mo·gen·i·ture** \ˌəl-tə-mō-'je-nə-ˌchùr, -ni-chər, -nə-ˌtùr, -nə-ˌtür\ *noun* [Latin *ultimus* last + English primo*geniture*] (1882)
: a system of inheritance by which the youngest child succeeds to the estate

**¹ul·tra** \'əl-trə\ *adjective* [*ultra-*] (1818)
: going beyond others or beyond due limit : EXTREME

**²ultra** *noun* [*ultra-*] (1819)
: one that is ultra : EXTREMIST

**ultra-** *prefix* [Latin, from *ultra* beyond, adverb & preposition, from (assumed) Latin *ulter* situated beyond — more at ULTERIOR]
**1** : beyond in space : on the other side : TRANS- ⟨*ultra*violet⟩
**2** : beyond the range or limits of : transcending : SUPER- ⟨*ultra*microscopic⟩

---

**3** : beyond what is ordinary, proper, or moderate : excessively : extremely ⟨*ultra*modern⟩

| | |
|---|---|
| ul·tra·care·ful | ul·tra·na·tion·al·is·tic |
| ul·tra·ca·su·al | ul·tra·or·tho·dox |
| ul·tra·cau·tious | ul·tra·par·a·dox·i·cal |
| ul·tra·chic | ul·tra·pa·tri·ot·ic |
| ul·tra·civ·i·lized | ul·tra·phys·i·cal |
| ul·tra·clean | ul·tra·pow·er·ful |
| ul·tra·cold | ul·tra·prac·ti·cal |
| ul·tra·com·mer·cial | ul·tra·pre·cise |
| ul·tra·com·pact | ul·tra·pre·ci·sion |
| ul·tra·com·pe·tent | ul·tra·pro·fes·sion·al |
| ul·tra·con·ser·va·tism | ul·tra·pro·gres·sive |
| ul·tra·con·ser·va·tive | ul·tra·pure |
| ul·tra·con·tem·po·rary | ul·tra·qui·et |
| ul·tra·con·ve·nient | ul·tra·rad·i·cal |
| ul·tra·cool | ul·tra·rap·id |
| ul·tra·crit·i·cal | ul·tra·rare |
| ul·tra·dem·o·crat·ic | ul·tra·rar·e·fied |
| ul·tra·dense | ul·tra·ra·tio·nal |
| ul·tra·dis·tance | ul·tra·re·al·ism |
| ul·tra·dis·tant | ul·tra·re·al·ist |
| ul·tra·dry | ul·tra·re·al·is·tic |
| ul·tra·ef·fi·cient | ul·tra·re·fined |
| ul·tra·en·er·get·ic | ul·tra·re·li·able |
| ul·tra·ex·clu·sive | ul·tra·re·spect·able |
| ul·tra·fa·mil·iar | ul·tra·rev·o·lu·tion·ary |
| ul·tra·fast | ul·tra·rich |
| ul·tra·fas·tid·i·ous | ul·tra·right |
| ul·tra·fem·i·nine | ul·tra·right·ist |
| ul·tra·fine | ul·tra·ro·man·tic |
| ul·tra·glam·or·ous | ul·tra·roy·al·ist |
| ul·tra·haz·ard·ous | ul·tra·safe |
| ul·tra·heat | ul·tra·se·cret |
| ul·tra·heavy | ul·tra·seg·re·ga·tion·ist |
| ul·tra·high | ul·tra·sen·si·tive |
| ul·tra·hip | ul·tra·se·ri·ous |
| ul·tra·hot | ul·tra·sharp |
| ul·tra·hu·man | ul·tra·sim·ple |
| ul·tra·left | ul·tra·slick |
| ul·tra·left·ism | ul·tra·slow |
| ul·tra·left·ist | ul·tra·small |
| ul·tra·lib·er·al | ul·tra·smart |
| ul·tra·lib·er·al·ism | ul·tra·smooth |
| ul·tra·light·weight | ul·tra·soft |
| ul·tra·low | ul·tra·so·phis·ti·cat·ed |
| ul·tra·mas·cu·line | ul·tra·thin |
| ul·tra·mil·i·tant | ul·tra·vac·u·um |
| ul·tra·min·i·a·tur·ized | ul·tra·vi·o·lence |
| ul·tra·mod·ern | ul·tra·vi·o·lent |
| ul·tra·mod·ern·ist | ul·tra·vir·ile |
| ul·tra·na·tion·al·ism | ul·tra·vi·ril·i·ty |
| ul·tra·na·tion·al·ist | ul·tra·wide |

◇ **WORD HISTORY**
**ukulele** In Hawaiian *'ukulele* means literally "jumping flea," a creature with little resemblance to a small guitar. It is likely that this improbable name became attached to the instrument in a rather roundabout way. Edward Purvis, a former British army officer living in Hawaii as an official at the court of King Kalakaua, is said to have been given the nickname *'ukulele* because he was a small and lively man. In 1879 Portuguese immigrants to the Hawaiian Islands from Madeira brought with them several musical instruments. Among these was the *machete,* a small four-stringed guitar. Purvis, being fond of music, was taken with the new instrument and soon learned to play it. When the *machete* became a Hawaiian favorite, it took the name of its popularizer, and its Portuguese name and origin were soon forgotten.

| | | | |
|---|---|---|---|
| \ə\ abut | \ᵊ\ kitten | \ər\ further | \a\ ash \ā\ ace |
| \ä\ mop, mar | \aù\ out | \ch\ chin | \e\ bet \ē\ easy |
| \g\ go | \i\ hit | \ī\ ice | \j\ job \ŋ\ sing \ō\ go |
| \ò\ law | \òi\ boy | \th\ thin | \t̶h\ the \ü\ loot \ù\ foot |
| \y\ yet | \zh\ vision | *see also* Guide to Prŏnunciation | |

**ul·tra·ba·sic** \ˌəl-trə-ˈbā-sik\ *adjective* [International Scientific Vocabulary] (1881)
: extremely basic; *specifically* : very low in silica and rich in iron and magnesium minerals
— **ultrabasic** *noun*

**ul·tra·cen·trif·u·gal** \-ˌsen-ˈtri-fyə-gəl, -fi-gəl\ *adjective* (1930)
: of, relating to, or obtained by means of an ultracentrifuge
— **ul·tra·cen·trif·u·gal·ly** \-gə-lē\ *adverb*

**¹ul·tra·cen·tri·fuge** \-ˈsen-trə-ˌfyüj\ *noun* (1924)
: a high-speed centrifuge able to sediment colloidal and other small particles and used especially in determining sizes of such particles and molecular weights of large molecules

**²ultracentrifuge** *transitive verb* (1930)
: to subject to an ultracentrifuge
— **ul·tra·cen·tri·fu·ga·tion** \-ˌsen-trə-ˌfyü-ˈgā-shən\ *noun*

**ul·tra·fiche** \ˈəl-trə-ˌfēsh\ *noun* (1969)
: a microfiche whose microimages are of printed matter reduced 90 or more times

**ul·tra·fil·tra·tion** \ˌəl-trə-fil-ˈtrā-shən\ *noun* (1908)
: filtration through a medium (as a semipermeable capillary wall) which allows small molecules (as of water) to pass but holds back larger ones (as of protein)
— **ul·tra·fil·trate** \-ˈfil-ˌtrāt\ *noun*

**ultrahigh frequency** *noun* (1932)
: a radio frequency between superhigh frequency and very high frequency — see RADIO FREQUENCY table

**ul·tra·ism** \ˈəl-trə-ˌi-zəm\ *noun* (1821)
**1** : the principles of those who advocate extreme measures (as radicalism)
**2** : an instance or example of radicalism
— **ul·tra·ist** \-trə-ist\ *adjective or noun*
— **ul·tra·is·tic** \ˌəl-trə-ˈis-tik\ *adjective*

**¹ul·tra·light** \ˈəl-trə-ˌlīt\ *adjective* (1974)
: extremely light in mass or weight ⟨an *ultralight* alloy⟩ ⟨an *ultralight* pullover⟩

**²ultralight** *noun* (1980)
: a very light recreational aircraft typically for one person that is powered by a small gasoline engine

**ul·tra·maf·ic** \ˌəl-trə-ˈma-fik\ *adjective* (1933)
: ULTRABASIC

**ul·tra·mar·a·thon** \-ˈmar-ə-ˌthän\ *noun* (1977)
: a footrace longer than a marathon
— **ul·tra·mar·a·thon·er** \-ˌthä-nər\ *noun*

**¹ul·tra·ma·rine** \-mə-ˈrēn\ *noun* [Medieval Latin *ultramarinus* coming from beyond the sea, from Latin *ultra-* + *mare* sea — more at MARINE] (1598)
**1 a** (1) : a blue pigment prepared by powdering lapis lazuli (2) : a similar pigment prepared from kaolin, soda ash, sulfur, and charcoal **b** : any of several related pigments
**2** : a vivid blue

**²ultramarine** *adjective* (1652)
: situated beyond the sea

**ul·tra·mi·cro** \ˌəl-trə-ˈmī-(ˌ)krō\ *adjective* (1937)
: being or dealing with something smaller than micro

**ul·tra·mi·cro·scope** \ˌəl-trə-ˈmī-krə-ˌskōp\ *noun* [back-formation from *ultramicroscopic*] (1906)
: an apparatus for making visible by scattered light particles too small to be perceived by an ordinary microscope

**ul·tra·mi·cro·scop·ic** \-ˌmī-krə-ˈskä-pik\ *also* **ul·tra·mi·cro·scop·i·cal** \-pi-kəl\ *adjective* [International Scientific Vocabulary] (1870)
**1** : too small to be seen with an ordinary microscope
**2** : of or relating to an ultramicroscope
— **ul·tra·mi·cro·scop·i·cal·ly** \-pi-k(ə-)lē\ *adverb*

**ul·tra·mi·cro·tome** \-ˈmī-krə-ˌtōm\ *noun* (1946)
: a microtome for cutting extremely thin sections for electron microscopy
— **ul·tra·mi·crot·o·my** \-mī-ˈkrä-tə-mē\ *noun*

**ul·tra·min·i·a·ture** \-ˈmi-nē-ə-ˌchür, -ˈmi-ni-ˌchür, -ˈmin-yə-, -chər, -ˌtyür, -ˌtür\ *adjective* (1942)
: SUBMINIATURE

**ul·tra·mon·tane** \-ˈmän-ˌtān, -ˌmän-ˈ\ *adjective* [Medieval Latin *ultramontanus*, from Latin *ultra-* + *mont-, mons* mountain — more at MOUNT] (circa 1618)
**1** : of or relating to countries or peoples beyond the mountains (as the Alps)
**2** : favoring greater or absolute supremacy of papal over national or diocesan authority in the Roman Catholic Church
— **ultramontane** *noun, often capitalized*
— **ul·tra·mon·tan·ism** \-ˈmän-tᵊn-ˌi-zəm\ *noun*

**ul·tra·short** \-ˈshȯrt\ *adjective* (1926)
**1** : having a wavelength below 10 meters ⟨*ultrashort* radiation⟩
**2** : very short in duration ⟨an *ultrashort* pulse of light⟩

**ul·tra·son·ic** \-ˈsä-nik\ *adjective* (1923)
**1** : having a frequency above the human ear's audibility limit of about 20,000 hertz — used of waves and vibrations
**2** : utilizing, produced by, or relating to ultrasonic waves or vibrations ⟨*ultrasonic* testing of metal⟩
— **ul·tra·son·i·cal·ly** \-ni-k(ə-)lē\ *adverb*

**ul·tra·son·ics** \ˌəl-trə-ˈsä-niks\ *noun plural* (1924)
**1** : ultrasonic vibrations or compressional waves
**2** *singular in construction* : the study of ultrasonic vibrations and their associated phenomena
**3** : ultrasonic devices

**ul·tra·so·nog·ra·phy** \-sə-ˈnä-grə-fē, -sō-\ *noun* [*ultrasonic* + *-o-* + *-graphy*] (1951)
: ULTRASOUND 2
— **ul·tra·so·nog·ra·pher** \-fər\ *noun*
— **ul·tra·so·no·graph·ic** \-ˌsō-nə-ˈgra-fik, -ˌsä-\ *adjective*

**ul·tra·sound** \ˈəl-trə-ˌsaund\ *noun* (1923)
**1** : vibrations of the same physical nature as sound but with frequencies above the range of human hearing
**2** : the diagnostic or therapeutic use of ultrasound and especially a technique involving the formation of a two-dimensional image used for the examination and measurement of internal body structures and the detection of bodily abnormalities — called also *sonography*
**3** : a diagnostic examination using ultrasound

**ul·tra·struc·ture** \ˈəl-trə-ˌstrək-chər\ *noun* (1939)
: biological structure and especially fine structure (as of a cell) not visible through an ordinary microscope
— **ul·tra·struc·tur·al** \ˌəl-trə-ˈstrək-chə-rəl, -ˈstrək-shrəl\ *adjective*
— **ul·tra·struc·tur·al·ly** *adverb*

**ul·tra·vi·o·let** \ˌəl-trə-ˈvī-(ə-)lət\ *adjective* (1840)
**1** : situated beyond the visible spectrum at its violet end — used of radiation having a wavelength shorter than wavelengths of visible light and longer than those of X rays
**2** : relating to, producing, or employing ultraviolet radiation
— **ultraviolet** *noun*

**ul·tra vi·res** \ˌəl-trə-ˈvī-(ˌ)rēz\ *adverb or adjective* [New Latin, literally, beyond power] (1793)
: beyond the scope or in excess of legal power or authority

**ul·u·lant** \ˈəl-yə-lənt\ *adjective* (1868)
: having a howling sound : WAILING ⟨dark wasteland . . . *ululant* with bitter wind —Rudi Blesh⟩

**ul·u·late** \-ˌlāt\ *intransitive verb* **-lat·ed; -lat·ing** [Latin *ululatus*, past participle of *ululare*, of imitative origin] (1623)
: HOWL, WAIL
— **ul·u·la·tion** \-yə-ˈlā-shən\ *noun*

**ul·va** \ˈəl-və\ *noun* [New Latin, genus name, from Latin, sedge] (1706)
: SEA LETTUCE

**Ulys·ses** \yu̇-ˈli-(ˌ)sēz\ *noun* [Latin *Ulysses, Ulixes,* from Greek *Oulixes, Olysseus, Odysseus*]
: ODYSSEUS

**um·bel** \ˈəm-bəl\ *noun* [New Latin *umbella,* from Latin, umbrella — more at UMBRELLA] (1597)
: a racemose inflorescence typical of the carrot family in which the axis is very much contracted so that the pedicels appear to spring from the same point to form a flat or rounded flower cluster — see INFLORESCENCE illustration

**um·bel·late** \ˈəm-bə-ˌlāt, ˌəm-ˈbe-lət\ *adjective* (1760)
**1** : bearing, consisting of, or arranged in umbels
**2** : resembling an umbel in form

**um·bel·li·fer** \ˌəm-ˈbe-lə-fər\ *noun* [New Latin *Umbelliferae,* group name, feminine plural of *umbellifer* bearing umbels] (1718)
: a plant of the carrot family

**um·bel·lif·er·ous** \ˌəm-bə-ˈli-f(ə-)rəs\ *adjective* (1662)
: of or relating to the carrot family ⟨*umbelliferous* flower heads⟩

**¹um·ber** \ˈəm-bər\ *noun* [probably from obsolete English, shade, color, from Middle English *umbre* shade, shadow, from Middle French, from Latin *umbra* — more at UMBRAGE] (1568)
**1** : a brown earth that is darker in color than ocher and sienna because of its content of manganese and iron oxides and is highly valued as a permanent pigment either in the raw or burnt state
**2 a** : a moderate to dark yellowish brown **b** : a moderate brown

**²umber** *transitive verb* **um·bered; um·ber·ing** \-b(ə-)riŋ\ (1610)
: to darken with or as if with umber

**³umber** *adjective* (1802)
: of, relating to, or having the characteristics of umber; *specifically* : of the color of umber

**¹um·bil·i·cal** \ˌəm-ˈbi-li-kəl, *British also* ˌəm-bə-ˈlī-kəl\ *adjective* (1541)
**1** : of, relating to, or used at the navel
**2** : of or relating to the central region of the abdomen

**²umbilical** *noun* (1774)
: UMBILICAL CORD 2

**umbilical cord** *noun* (1753)
**1** : a cord arising from the navel that connects the fetus with the placenta; *also* : YOLK STALK
**2** : a tethering or supply line (as for an astronaut outside a spacecraft or a diver underwater)

**um·bil·i·cate** \ˌəm-ˈbi-li-kət\ *or* **um·bil·i·cat·ed** \-lə-ˌkā-təd\ *adjective* (1698)
**1** : depressed like a navel
**2** : having an umbilicus
— **um·bil·i·ca·tion** \ˌəm-ˌbi-lə-ˈkā-shən\ *noun*

**um·bi·li·cus** \ˌəm-ˈbi-li-kəs, ˌəm-bə-ˈlī-\ *noun, plural* **um·bi·li·ci** \ˌəm-ˈbi-li-ˌkī, -ˌkē; ˌəm-bə-ˈlī-ˌkī, -ˌsī\ *or* **um·bi·li·cus·es** [Latin — more at NAVEL] (circa 1615)
**1 a** : NAVEL 1 **b** : any of several morphological depressions; *especially* : HILUM 1
**2** : a central point : CORE, HEART

**um·bles** \ˈəm-bəlz\ *noun plural* [Middle English, alteration of *nombles,* from Middle French, plural of *nomble* fillet of beef, pork loin, modification of Latin *lumbulus,* diminutive of *lumbus* loin — more at LOIN] (15th century)
: the edible viscera of an animal and especially of a deer or hog

**um·bo** \'əm-(,)bō\ *noun, plural* **um·bo·nes** \,əm-'bō-(,)nēz\ *or* **umbos** [Latin; akin to Latin *umbilicus* — more at NAVEL] (1721)
**1** : the boss of a shield
**2 a** : a rounded elevation: as **a** : an inward projection of the tympanic membrane of the ear **b** : one of the lateral prominences just above the hinge of a bivalve shell
— **um·bo·nal** \'əm-bə-nᵊl, ,əm-'bō-\ *adjective*
— **um·bo·nate** \'əm-bə-,nāt, ,əm-'bō-nət\ *adjective*

**um·bra** \'əm-brə\ *noun, plural* **umbras** *or* **um·brae** \-(,)brē, -,brī\ [Latin] (1638)
**1** : a shaded area
**2 a** : a conical shadow excluding all light from a given source; *specifically* : the conical part of the shadow of a celestial body excluding all light from the primary source **b** : the central dark part of a sunspot
— **um·bral** \-brəl\ *adjective*

**um·brage** \'əm-brij\ *noun* [Middle English, from Middle French, from Latin *umbraticum,* neuter of *umbraticus* of shade, from *umbratus,* past participle of *umbrare* to shade, from *umbra* shade, shadow; akin to Lithuanian *unksmė* shadow] (15th century)
**1** : SHADE, SHADOW
**2** : shady branches : FOLIAGE
**3 a** : an indistinct indication : vague suggestion : HINT **b** : a reason for doubt : SUSPICION
**4** : a feeling of pique or resentment at some often fancied slight or insult ⟨took *umbrage* at the speaker's remarks⟩
*synonym* see OFFENSE

**um·bra·geous** \,əm-'brā-jəs\ *adjective* (1587)
**1 a** : affording shade **b** : spotted with shadows
**2** : inclined to take offense easily
— **um·bra·geous·ly** *adverb*
— **um·bra·geous·ness** *noun*

**¹um·brel·la** \,əm-'bre-lə, *especially Southern* 'əm-\ *noun* [Italian *ombrella,* modification of Latin *umbella,* diminutive of *umbra*] (1611)
**1** : a collapsible shade for protection against weather consisting of fabric stretched over hinged ribs radiating from a central pole; *especially* : a small one for carrying in the hand
**2** : the bell-shaped or saucer-shaped largely gelatinous structure that forms the chief part of the body of most jellyfishes
**3** : something which provides protection: as **a** : defensive air cover (as over a battlefront) **b** : a heavy barrage
**4** : something which covers or embraces a broad range of elements or factors ⟨decided to expand . . . by building new colleges under a federation *umbrella* —Diane Ravitch⟩

**²umbrella** *transitive verb* **-laed; -la·ing** (circa 1800)
: to protect, cover, or provide with an umbrella

**umbrella plant** *noun* (1874)
: an African sedge (*Cyperus alternifolius*) that has large terminal whorls of slender leaves and is often grown as an ornamental

**umbrella tree** *noun* (1738)
**1** : a magnolia (*Magnolia tripetala*) of the eastern U.S. having large leaves clustered at the ends of the branches
**2** : any of various trees or shrubs resembling an umbrella especially in the arrangement of leaves or the shape of the crown

**Um·bri·an** \'əm-brē-ən\ *noun* (1601)
**1** : a native or inhabitant of Umbria
**2** : the Italic language of ancient Umbria — see INDO-EUROPEAN LANGUAGES table
— **Umbrian** *adjective*

**Um·bun·du** \,əm-'bùn-(,)dü\ *noun* (circa 1895)
: a Bantu language of central Angola

**umi·ak** \'ü-mē-,ak\ *noun* [Inuit *umiaq*] (1769)
: an open Eskimo boat made of a wooden frame covered with hide

**¹um·laut** \'üm-,laùt, 'ùm-\ *noun* [German, from *um-* around, transformation + *Laut* sound] (1852)
**1 a** : the change of a vowel that is caused by partial assimilation to a succeeding sound or that occurs as a reflex of the former presence of a succeeding sound which has been lost or altered (as to mark pluralization in *goose, geese* or *mouse, mice*) **b** : a vowel resulting from such partial assimilation
**2** : a diacritical mark ¨ placed over a vowel to indicate a more central or front articulation — compare DIAERESIS

**²umlaut** *transitive verb* (1879)
**1** : to produce by umlaut
**2** : to write or print an umlaut over

**¹ump** \'əmp\ *noun* (1912)
: UMPIRE 2

**²ump** *intransitive verb* (1928)
: to act as umpire

**¹um·pire** \'əm-,pīr\ *noun* [Middle English *oumpere,* alteration (from misdivision of *a noumpere*) of *noumpere,* from Middle French *nomper* not equal, not paired, from *non-* + *per* equal, from Latin *par*] (15th century)
**1** : one having authority to decide finally a controversy or question between parties: as **a** : one appointed to decide between arbitrators who have disagreed **b** : an impartial third party chosen to arbitrate disputes arising under the terms of a labor agreement
**2** : an official in a sport who rules on plays
**3** : a military officer who evaluates maneuvers

**²umpire** *verb* **um·pired; um·pir·ing** (1609)
*transitive verb*
: to supervise or decide as umpire
*intransitive verb*
: to act as umpire

**ump·teen** \'əm(p)-,tēn, ,əm(p)-'\ *adjective* [blend of *umpty* (such and such) and *-teen* (as in *thirteen*)] (1918)
: very many : indefinitely numerous
— **ump·teenth** \-,tēn(t)th, -'tēn(t)th\ *adjective*

**¹un-** \,ən, *often* 'ən *before* '-*stressed syllable*\ *prefix* [Middle English, from Old English; akin to Old High German *un-* un-, Latin *in-*, Greek *a-, an-*, Old English *ne* not — more at NO]
**1** : not : IN-, NON- — in adjectives formed from adjectives ⟨*unambitious*⟩ ⟨*unskilled*⟩ or participles ⟨*undressed*⟩, in nouns formed from nouns ⟨*unavailability*⟩, and rarely in verbs formed from verbs ⟨*unbe*⟩; sometimes in words that have a meaning that merely negates that of the base word and are thereby distinguished from words that prefix in- or a variant of it (as im-) to the same base word and have a meaning positively opposite to that of the base word ⟨*unartistic*⟩ ⟨*unmoral*⟩
**2** : opposite of : contrary to — in adjectives formed from adjectives ⟨*unconstitutional*⟩ ⟨*ungraceful*⟩ ⟨*unmannered*⟩ or participles ⟨*unbelieving*⟩ and in nouns formed from nouns ⟨*unrest*⟩

**²un-** *prefix* [Middle English, from Old English *un-, on-*, alteration of *and-* against — more at ANTE-]
**1** : do the opposite of : reverse (a specified action) : DE- 1a, DIS- 1a — in verbs formed from verbs ⟨*unbend*⟩ ⟨*undress*⟩ ⟨*unfold*⟩
**2 a** : deprive of : remove (a specified thing) from : remove — in verbs formed from nouns ⟨*unfrock*⟩ ⟨*unsex*⟩ **b** : release from : free from — in verbs formed from nouns ⟨*unhand*⟩ **c** : remove from : extract from : bring out of — in verbs formed from nouns ⟨*unbosom*⟩ **d** : cause to cease to be — in verbs formed from nouns ⟨*unman*⟩
**3** : completely ⟨*unloose*⟩

un·abrad·ed
un·ab·sorbed
un·ab·sor·bent
un·ac·a·dem·ic
un·ac·a·dem·i·cal·ly
un·ac·cent·ed
un·ac·cept·ed
un·ac·cli·mat·ed
un·ac·cli·ma·tized
un·ac·com·mo·dat·ed
un·ac·com·mo·dat·ing
un·ac·cred·it·ed
un·ac·cul·tur·at·ed
un·achieved
un·ac·knowl·edged
un·ac·quaint·ed

un·act·able
un·act·ed
un·ac·tor·ish
un·adapt·able
un·adapt·ed
un·ad·dressed
un·ad·ju·di·cat·ed
un·ad·just·ed
un·ad·mired
un·ad·mit·ted
un·adopt·able
un·adult
un·ad·ven·tur·ous
un·ad·ver·tised
un·aes·thet·ic
un·af·fect·ing
un·af·fec·tion·ate
un·af·fec·tion·ate·ly
un·af·fil·i·at·ed
un·af·flu·ent
un·af·ford·able
un·afraid
un·ag·gres·sive
un·aid·ed
un·air–con·di·tioned
un·akin
un·alien·at·ed
un·alike
un·al·le·vi·at·ed
un·al·lo·cat·ed
un·al·lur·ing
un·al·tered
un·am·bi·tious
un·ame·na·ble
un·amend·ed
un·ami·a·ble
un·am·or·tized
un·am·pli·fied
un·amus·ing
un·an·a·lyz·able
un·an·a·lyzed
un·an·no·tat·ed
un·an·nounced
un·apol·o·giz·ing
un·ap·par·ent
un·ap·peased
un·ap·pre·ci·at·ed
un·ap·pre·cia·tive
un·ap·pro·pri·at·ed

un·ap·proved
un·ar·gu·able
un·ar·gu·ably
un·ar·mored
un·ar·ro·gant
un·ar·tis·tic
un·as·pi·rat·ed
un·as·sailed
un·as·sem·bled
un·as·signed
un·as·sim·i·la·ble
un·as·sim·i·lat·ed
un·as·so·ci·at·ed
un·as·suaged
un·ath·let·ic
un·at·tain·able
un·at·tend·ed
un·at·ten·u·at·ed
un·at·test·ed
un·at·trib·ut·able
un·at·trib·ut·ed
un·at·tuned
un·au·dit·ed
un·au·then·tic
un·au·tho·rized
un·au·to·mat·ed
un·avail·abil·i·ty
un·avail·able
un·avowed
un·awak·ened
un·award·ed
un·awe·some
un·ban
un·bap·tized
un·barbed
un·bar·ri·cad·ed
un·be·hold·en
un·bel·lig·er·ent
un·be·loved
un·be·mused
un·billed
un·bit·ten
un·bit·ter
un·bleached
un·blem·ished
un·blend·ed
un·blood·ed
un·book·ish
un·bought

◇ WORD HISTORY

**umpire** The medieval French adjective *nonper* was a compound formed from *non* "not" and *per* "equal" and it meant "not paired, odd (of a number)" or "not equaled, incomparable." It was adopted into Middle English as *noumpere,* a noun meaning "arbitrator," in other words, someone not equal to the parties in a dispute and thus able to mediate between them. Early on, English speakers must have lost any sense of the word's French etymological components, because not long after *noumpere* appears in the late 14th century, a variant *oumpere* is also found in manuscripts. This new form resulted from misplacing the boundary between the noun and a preceding indefinite article: *a noumpere* was understood as *an oumpere.* By the 16th century no further trace of the word with an initial *n* is found, and spellings such as *umpier* and *umpire* reflect a change in the quality of the second vowel that must have begun shortly after the word was first borrowed. (The same change is evident in Modern English *briar, choir,* and *contrive* from Middle English *brere, quer,* and *contreven.*) In reference to an arbiter in a sporting event, *umpire* is first recorded in 1714.

\ə\ abut \ᵊ\ kitten \ər\ further \a\ ash \ā\ ace
\ä\ mop, mar \aù\ out \ch\ chin \e\ bet \ē\ easy
\g\ go \i\ hit \ī\ ice \j\ job \ŋ\ sing \ō\ go
\ò\ law \òi\ boy \th\ thin \th̲\ the \ü\ loot \ù\ foot
\y\ yet \zh\ vision *see also* Guide to Pronunciation

un·bowd·ler·ized
un·brack·et·ed
un·brake
un·breach·able
un·break·able
un·bridge·able
un·bridged
un·briefed
un·bright
un·bril·liant
un·bruised
un·brushed
un·bud·get·ed
un·buf·fered
un·build·able
un·bulky
un·bu·reau·crat·ic
un·bur·ied
un·burn·able
un·burned
un·burnt
un·busi·ness·like
un·busy
un·but·tered
un·cal·ci·fied
un·cal·cined
un·cal·i·brat·ed
un·called
un·cal·loused
un·can·celed
un·can·did
un·can·did·ly
un·ca·non·i·cal
un·cap
un·cap·i·tal·ized
un·cap·tioned
un·cap·tur·able
un·cared—for
un·car·ing
un·car·pet·ed
un·case
un·cas·trat·ed
un·cat·a·loged
un·catch·able
un·catchy
un·cat·e·go·riz·able
un·caught
un·cen·sored
un·cen·so·ri·ous
un·cen·sured
un·cer·ti·fied
un·chal·lenge·able
un·chal·lenged
un·chal·leng·ing
un·changed
un·chan·neled
un·chap·er·oned
un·char·is·mat·ic
un·charm·ing
un·chart·ered
un·chau·vin·is·tic
un·check·able
un·checked
un·chew·able
un·chewed
un·chic
un·child·like
un·chlo·ri·nat·ed
un·cho·reo·graphed
un·chris·tened
un·chron·i·cled
un·chro·no·log·i·cal
un·church·ly
un·cil·i·at·ed
un·cin·e·mat·ic
un·clad
un·claimed
un·clar·i·fied
un·clas·si·fi·able
un·cleaned
un·clear
un·cli·chéd
un·clip
un·cloy·ing
un·co·alesce
un·coat·ed

un·coat·ing
un·cod·ed
un·cod·i·fied
un·co·erced
un·co·er·cive
un·co·er·cive·ly
un·col·lect·ed
un·col·lect·ible
un·co·lored
un·com·bat·ive
un·combed
un·com·bined
un·come·ly
un·com·ic
un·com·mer·cial·ized
un·com·pas·sion·ate
un·com·pel·ling
un·com·pen·sat·ed
un·com·pla·cent
un·com·plet·ed
un·com·pound·ed
un·com·pre·hend·ed
un·com·pu·ter·ized
un·con·cealed
un·con·fessed
un·con·fined
un·con·firmed
un·con·found·ed
un·con·fuse
un·con·ju·gat·ed
un·con·nect·ed
un·con·quered
un·con·se·crat·ed
un·con·strained
un·con·strict·ed
un·con·struc·tive
un·con·sumed
un·con·sum·mat·ed
un·con·tain·able
un·con·tam·i·nat·ed
un·con·tem·plat·ed
un·con·tem·po·rary
un·con·ten·tious
un·con·test·ed
un·con·tract·ed
un·con·tra·dict·ed
un·con·trived
un·con·trolled
un·con·tro·ver·sial
un·con·tro·ver·sial·ly
un·con·vert·ed
un·con·vinced
un·con·voyed
un·cooked
un·cooled
un·co·op·er·a·tive
un·co·or·di·nat·ed
un·copy·right·able
un·cor·rect·able
un·cor·rect·ed
un·cor·re·lat·ed
un·cor·rob·o·rat·ed
un·cor·rupt
un·count·able
un·cou·ra·geous
un·cov·e·nant·ed
un·coy
un·cracked
un·crate
un·cra·zy
un·cre·a·tive
un·cre·den·tialed
un·cred·it·ed
un·crip·pled
un·cropped
un·cross·able
un·crowd·ed
un·crush·able
un·cuff
un·cul·ti·va·ble
un·cul·ti·vat·ed
un·cul·tured
un·cured
un·cu·ri·ous
un·cur·rent

un·cur·tained
un·cus·tom·ar·i·ly
un·cus·tom·ary
un·cute
un·cyn·i·cal
un·cyn·i·cal·ly
un·dam·aged
un·damped
un·dance·able
un·dat·ed
un·dec·a·dent
un·de·cid·abil·i·ty
un·de·cid·able
un·de·cid·ed
un·de·ci·pher·able
un·de·ci·phered
un·de·clared
un·de·com·posed
un·dec·o·rat·ed
un·ded·i·cat·ed
un·de·feat·ed
un·de·fend·ed
un·de·filed
un·de·fin·able
un·de·fined
un·de·fo·li·at·ed
un·de·formed
un·del·e·gat·ed
un·de·liv·er·able
un·de·liv·ered
un·de·lud·ed
un·de·mand·ing
un·de·nom·i·na·tion·al
un·de·pend·able
un·de·scrib·able
un·de·served
un·de·serv·ing
un·des·ig·nat·ed
un·de·sired
un·de·tect·able
un·de·tect·ed
un·de·ter·min·able
un·de·ter·mined
un·de·terred
un·de·vel·oped
un·di·ag·nos·able
un·di·ag·nosed
un·di·a·lec·ti·cal
un·di·dac·tic
un·dif·fer·en·ti·at·ed
un·di·gest·ed
un·di·gest·ible
un·dig·ni·fied
un·di·lut·ed
un·di·min·ished
un·dimmed
un·dis·charged
un·dis·ci·plined
un·dis·closed
un·dis·cour·aged
un·dis·cov·er·able
un·dis·cov·ered
un·dis·crim·i·nat·ing
un·dis·cussed
un·dis·mayed
un·dis·pu·ta·ble
un·dis·put·ed
un·dis·solved
un·dis·tort·ed
un·dis·tract·ed
un·dis·trib·ut·ed
un·dis·turbed
un·di·vid·ed
un·do·able
un·doc·ile
un·doc·tored
un·doc·tri·naire
un·doc·u·ment·ed
un·do·mes·tic
un·do·mes·ti·cat·ed
un·dot·ted
un·doubt·able
un·doubt·ing
un·drained

un·dra·ma·tized
un·drilled
un·dubbed
un·dulled
un·du·pli·cat·ed
un·dyed
un·dy·nam·ic
un·ea·ger
un·ear·marked
un·eat·able
un·eat·en
un·ec·cen·tric
un·eco·log·i·cal
un·ed·i·fy·ing
un·ed·u·ca·ble
un·ed·u·cat·ed
un·elab·o·rate
un·elect·able
un·elect·ed
un·elec·tri·fied
un·em·bar·rassed
un·em·bel·lished
un·em·bit·tered
un·em·phat·ic
un·em·phat·i·cal·ly
un·em·pir·i·cal
un·en·chant·ed
un·en·closed
un·en·cour·ag·ing
un·en·dear·ing
un·en·dur·able
un·en·dur·able·ness
un·en·dur·ably
un·en·force·able
un·en·forced
un·en·larged
un·en·light·ened
un·en·light·en·ing
un·en·riched
un·en·ter·pris·ing
un·en·thu·si·as·tic
un·en·thu·si·as·ti·cal·ly
un·en·vi·able
un·en·vi·ous
un·erot·ic
un·es·cap·able
un·es·tab·lished
un·eth·i·cal
un·eval·u·at·ed
un·ex·am·ined
un·ex·celled
un·ex·cit·able
un·ex·cit·ed
un·ex·cit·ing
un·ex·cused
un·ex·ot·ic
un·ex·pend·ed
un·ex·pired
un·ex·plain·able
un·ex·plained
un·ex·plod·ed
un·ex·plored
un·ex·posed
un·ex·pressed
un·ex·pur·gat·ed
un·ex·traor·di·nary
un·faked
un·fa·mous
un·fan·cy
un·fas·tid·i·ous
un·fea·si·ble
un·felt
un·fem·i·nine
un·fenced
un·fer·ment·ed
un·fer·tile
un·fer·til·ized
un·filled
un·fired
un·flam·boy·ant
un·flashy
un·fly·able
un·fond
un·forced
un·fore·see·able

un·fore·seen
un·for·est·ed
un·for·giv·able
un·forked
un·for·mu·lat·ed
un·forth·com·ing
un·for·ti·fied
un·fos·sil·if·er·ous
un·framed
un·free
un·free·dom
un·friv·o·lous
un·ful·fill·able
un·ful·filled
un·fun·ny
un·fur·nished
un·fused
un·gal·lant
un·gal·lant·ly
un·gar·nished
un·ge·nial
un·gen·teel
un·gen·tle
un·gen·tle·man·ly
un·gen·tri·fied
un·ger·mi·nat·ed
un·gift·ed
un·gim·micky
un·glam·or·ized
un·glam·or·ous
un·glazed
un·grace·ful
un·grace·ful·ly
un·grad·ed
un·grasp·able
un·ground
un·grouped
un·guess·able
un·guid·ed
un·hack·neyed
un·ham·pered
un·harmed
un·har·ness
un·har·vest·ed
un·hatched
un·healed
un·health·ful
un·heat·ed
un·hedged
un·heed·ed
un·heed·ing
un·help·ful
un·help·ful·ly
un·her·ald·ed
un·he·ro·ic
un·hin·dered
un·hip
un·his·tor·i·cal
un·ho·mog·e·nized
un·hon·ored
un·hope·ful
un·housed
un·hu·mor·ous
un·hurt
un·hy·dro·lyzed
un·hy·gien·ic
un·hy·phen·at·ed
un·hys·ter·i·cal
un·hys·ter·i·cal·ly
un·iden·ti·fi·able
un·iden·ti·fied
un·ideo·log·i·cal
un·id·i·om·at·ic
un·ig·nor·able
un·il·lu·mi·nat·ing
un·imag·i·na·tive
un·imag·i·na·tive·ly
un·im·mu·nized
un·im·paired
un·im·pas·sioned
un·im·ped·ed
un·im·por·tant
un·im·pos·ing
un·im·pressed
un·im·pres·sive
un·in·cor·po·rat·ed

un·in·dexed
un·in·dict·ed
un·in·dus·tri·al·ized
un·in·fect·ed
un·in·flat·ed
un·in·flect·ed
un·in·flu·enced
un·in·for·ma·tive
un·in·for·ma·tive·ly
un·in·formed
un·in·gra·ti·at·ing
un·in·hab·it·able
un·in·hab·it·ed
un·ini·ti·at·ed
un·in·jured
un·in·oc·u·lat·ed
un·in·spect·ed
un·in·spired
un·in·spir·ing
un·in·struct·ed
un·in·struc·tive
un·in·su·lat·ed
un·in·sur·able
un·in·sured
un·in·te·grat·ed
un·in·tel·lec·tu·al
un·in·tel·li·gent
un·in·tel·li·gent·ly
un·in·tel·li·gi·bil·i·ty
un·in·tel·li·gi·ble
un·in·tel·li·gi·ble-ness
un·in·tel·li·gi·bly
un·in·tend·ed
un·in·ten·tion·al
un·in·ten·tion·al·ly
un·in·ter·est·ing
un·in·ter·rupt·ed
un·in·ter·rupt·ed·ly
un·in·tim·i·dat·ed
un·in·ven·tive
un·in·vit·ed
un·in·vit·ing
un·in·volved
un·iron·i·cal·ly
un·ir·ra·di·at·ed
un·ir·ri·gat·ed
un·is·sued
un·jad·ed
un·joint·ed
un·jus·ti·fi·able
un·jus·ti·fi·ably
un·jus·ti·fied
un·kept
un·knot
un·knowl·edge·able
un·ko·sher
un·la·beled
un·la·dy·like
un·la·ment·ed
un·laun·dered
un·learn·able
un·leav·ened
un·lib·er·at·ed
un·li·censed
un·lik·able
un·lined
un·lis·ten·able
un·lit
un·lit·er·ary
un·liv·able
un·lo·cal·ized
un·lov·able
un·loved
un·lov·ing
un·lyr·i·cal
un·ma·cho
un·mag·ni·fied
un·ma·li·cious
un·ma·li·cious·ly
un·man·age·able
un·man·age·ably
un·man·aged
un·ma·nip·u·lat·ed
un·mapped
un·marked

un·mar·ket·able
un·marred
un·mas·cu·line
un·match·able
un·matched
un·meant
un·mea·sur·able
un·mea·sured
un·mech·a·nized
un·med·i·cat·ed
un·me·lo·di·ous
un·me·lo·di·ous·ness
un·mem·o·ra·ble
un·mem·o·ra·bly
un·mer·it·ed
un·mer·ry
un·met
un·me·tab·o·lized
un·mil·i·tary
un·milled
un·mined
un·mix
un·mix·able
un·mixed
un·mod·ern·ized
un·mod·i·fied
un·mod·ish
un·mo·lest·ed
un·mon·i·tored
un·mo·ti·vat·ed
un·mount·ed
un·mov·able
un·moved
un·mu·si·cal
un·name·able
un·named
un·need·ed
un·ne·go·tia·ble
un·neu·rot·ic
un·news·wor·thy
un·no·tice·able
un·no·ticed
un·nour·ish·ing
un·ob·jec·tion·able
un·ob·serv·able
un·ob·served
un·ob·struct·ed
un·ob·tain·able
un·of·fi·cial
un·of·fi·cial·ly
un·open·able
un·opened
un·op·posed
un·or·dered
un·orig·i·nal
un·or·na·ment·ed
un·os·ten·ta·tious
un·os·ten·ta·tious·ly
un·owned
un·ox·y·gen·at·ed
un·paint·ed
un·par·a·sit·ized
un·par·don·able
un·pass·able
un·pas·teur·ized
un·pas·to·ral
un·pat·ent·able
un·pa·tri·ot·ic
un·paved
un·pe·dan·tic
un·peeled
un·per·ceived
un·per·cep·tive
un·per·form·able
un·per·formed
un·per·suad·ed
un·per·sua·sive
un·per·turbed
un·pic·tur·esque
un·planned
un·plau·si·ble
un·play·able
un·pleased
un·pleas·ing
un·plowed

un·po·et·ic
un·po·liced
un·pol·ished
un·pol·lut·ed
un·posed
un·prac·ti·cal
un·pre·dict·abil·i·ty
un·pre·dict·able
un·pre·dict·ably
un·prej·u·diced
un·pre·med·i·tat·ed
un·pre·pared
un·pre·pared·ness
un·pre·pos·sess·ing
un·pressed
un·pres·sured
un·pres·sur·ized
un·pret·ty
un·priv·i·leged
un·prob·lem·at·ic
un·pro·cessed
un·pro·duced
un·pro·duc·tive
un·pro·fes·sion·al
un·pro·gram·ma·ble
un·pro·grammed
un·pro·gres·sive
un·prompt·ed
un·pro·nounce·able
un·pro·pi·tious
un·pros·per·ous
un·pro·tect·ed
un·prov·able
un·proved
un·prov·en
un·pro·voked
un·pruned
un·pub·li·cized
un·pub·lished
un·punc·tu·al
un·punc·tu·al·i·ty
un·punc·tu·at·ed
un·pun·ished
un·quan·ti·fi·able
un·quench·able
un·ques·tioned
un·raised
un·ranked
un·rat·ed
un·rav·ished
un·reach·able
un·reached
un·read·able
un·read·i·ness
un·ready
un·re·al·iz·able
un·re·al·ized
un·re·cep·tive
un·re·claim·able
un·re·claimed
un·rec·og·niz·able
un·rec·og·niz·ably
un·rec·og·nized
un·rec·on·cil·able
un·rec·on·ciled
un·re·cord·ed
un·re·cov·er·able
un·re·cov·ered
un·re·cy·cla·ble
un·re·deem·able
un·re·deemed
un·re·dressed
un·re·fined
un·re·flec·tive
un·re·formed
un·re·frig·er·at·ed
un·reg·is·tered
un·reg·u·lat·ed
un·re·hearsed
un·re·in·forced
un·re·lat·ed
un·re·laxed
un·re·li·abil·i·ty
un·re·li·able
un·re·lieved
un·re·liev·ed·ly

un·re·luc·tant
un·re·mark·able
un·re·mark·ably
un·re·mem·bered
un·rem·i·nis·cent
un·re·mov·able
un·re·peat·able
un·re·pen·tant
un·re·pen·tant·ly
un·re·port·ed
un·rep·re·sen·ta·tive
un·rep·re·sen·ta·tive·ness
un·rep·re·sent·ed
un·re·pressed
un·re·sis·tant
un·re·solv·able
un·re·solved
un·re·spect·able
un·re·spon·sive
un·re·spon·sive·ly
un·re·spon·sive·ness
un·rest·ful
un·re·stored
un·re·strict·ed
un·re·touched
un·re·turn·able
un·re·vealed
un·re·view·able
un·re·viewed
un·re·vised
un·rev·o·lu·tion·ary
un·re·ward·ed
un·re·ward·ing
un·rhe·tor·i·cal
un·rhymed
un·rhyth·mic
un·rid·able
un·ri·fled
un·rip·ened
un·ro·man·tic
un·ro·man·ti·cal·ly
un·ro·man·ti·cized
un·roofed
un·rushed
un·safe
un·sal·able
un·sal·a·ried
un·salt·ed
un·sal·vage·able
un·sanc·tioned
un·san·i·tary
un·sat·is·fied
un·scal·able
un·scarred
un·scent·ed
un·sched·uled
un·schol·ar·ly
un·screened
un·scrip·tur·al
un·sea·soned
un·sea·wor·thy
un·se·cured
un·seed·ed
un·seg·ment·ed
un·self–con·scious
un·self–con·scious·ly
un·self–con·scious·ness
un·sell·able
un·sen·sa·tion·al
un·sen·si·tized
un·sent
un·sen·ti·men·tal
un·sep·a·rat·ed
un·se·ri·ous
un·se·ri·ous·ness
un·served
un·ser·vice·able
un·sex·u·al
un·sexy
un·shad·ed
un·shak·able
un·shak·ably

un·shak·en
un·shape·ly
un·shared
un·sharp
un·shav·en
un·shelled
un·shock·able
un·shorn
un·showy
un·signed
un·sink·able
un·size
un·slaked
un·smart
un·smil·ing
un·smoothed
un·soiled
un·sol·dier·ly
un·so·lic·it·ed
un·solv·able
un·solved
un·sort·ed
un·sound·ed
un·sown
un·spe·cial·ized
un·spec·i·fi·able
un·spe·cif·ic
un·spec·i·fied
un·spec·tac·u·lar
un·spent
un·spir·i·tu·al
un·split
un·spoiled
un·spoilt
un·spo·ken
un·sprayed
un·stained
un·stan·dard·ized
un·star·tling
un·stat·ed
un·stayed
un·ster·ile
un·ster·il·ized
un·stint·ed
un·stitch
un·stop·per
un·strained
un·strat·i·fied
un·stuffy
un·styl·ish
un·sub·dued
un·sub·si·dized
un·sub·stan·ti·at·ed
un·sub·tle
un·sub·tly
un·suit·abil·i·ty
un·suit·able
un·suit·ably
un·suit·ed
un·sul·lied
un·su·per·vised
un·sup·port·able
un·sup·port·ed
un·sure
un·sur·pass·able
un·sur·passed
un·sur·prised
un·sus·cep·ti·ble
un·sus·pect·ed
un·sus·pect·ing
un·sus·pi·cious
un·sus·tain·able
un·sweet·ened
un·sym·pa·thet·ic
un·sym·pa·thet·i·cal·ly
un·syn·chro·nized
un·sys·tem·at·ic
un·sys·tem·at·i·cal·ly
un·sys·tem·a·tized
un·tact·ful
un·tagged
un·taint·ed
un·tal·ent·ed
un·tam·able

un·tamed
un·tanned
un·tar·nished
un·taxed
un·teach·able
un·tech·ni·cal
un·tem·pered
un·ten·ant·ed
un·tend·ed
un·ten·ured
un·test·able
un·test·ed
un·the·o·ret·i·cal
un·threat·en·ing
un·thrifty
un·till·able
un·tilled
un·to·geth·er
un·trace·able
un·tra·di·tion·al
un·tra·di·tion·al·ly
un·trained
un·tram·meled
un·trans·formed
un·trans·lat·abil·i·ty
un·trans·lat·able
un·trans·lat·ed
un·trav·eled
un·tra·versed
un·treat·ed
un·trendy
un·trimmed
un·trust·ing
un·trust·wor·thy
un·tuck
un·tuft·ed
un·typ·i·cal

un·typ·i·cal·ly
un·un·der·stand·able
un·us·able
un·uti·lized
un·vac·ci·nat·ed
un·var·ied
un·vary·ing
un·ven·ti·lat·ed
un·ver·bal·ized
un·ver·i·fi·able
un·versed
un·vi·a·ble
un·vis·it·ed
un·want·ed
un·war·like
un·war·rant·ed
un·wa·ver·ing
un·wa·ver·ing·ly
un·waxed
un·weaned
un·wear·able
un·weath·ered
un·wed
un·weight·ed
un·wel·come
un·white
un·willed
un·win·na·ble
un·wom·an·ly
un·won
un·work·abil·i·ty
un·work·able
un·worked
un·wor·ried
un·wound·ed
un·wo·ven
un·young

**un·abashed** \ˌən-ə-ˈbasht\ *adjective* (1571)
: not abashed : UNDISGUISED, UNAPOLOGETIC
— **un·abash·ed·ly** \-ˈbash-əd-lē\ *adverb*

**un·abat·ed** \ˌən-ə-ˈbā-təd\ *adjective* (circa 1611)
: not abated : being at full strength or force
— **un·abat·ed·ly** *adverb*

**un·able** \ˌən-ˈā-bəl\ *adjective* (14th century)
: not able : INCAPABLE: as **a** : UNQUALIFIED, INCOMPETENT **b** : IMPOTENT, HELPLESS

**un·abridged** \ˌən-ə-ˈbrijd\ *adjective* (1599)
**1** : not abridged : COMPLETE ⟨an *unabridged* reprint of a novel⟩
**2** : being the most complete of its class : not based on one larger ⟨an *unabridged* dictionary⟩

**un·ac·cept·able** \ˌən-ik-ˈsep-tə-bəl, -ak-\ *adjective* (15th century)
: not acceptable : not pleasing or welcome
— **un·ac·cept·abil·i·ty** \-ˌsep-tə-ˈbi-lə-tē\ *noun*
— **un·ac·cept·ably** \-ˈsep-tə-blē\ *adverb*

**un·ac·com·pa·nied** \ˌən-ə-ˈkəmp-nēd, -ˈkämp-; -ˈkəm-pə-, -ˈkäm-\ *adjective* (1545)
: not accompanied; *especially* : being without instrumental accompaniment

**un·ac·count·able** \ˌən-ə-ˈkaůn-tə-bəl\ *adjective* (1643)
**1** : not to be accounted for : INEXPLICABLE, STRANGE
**2** : not to be called to account : not responsible
— **un·ac·count·abil·i·ty** \-ˌkaůn-tə-ˈbi-lə-tē\ *noun*

**un·ac·count·ably** \-ˈkaůn-tə-blē\ *adverb* (1694)
**1** : in an unaccountable manner ⟨looking *unaccountably* upset⟩ ⟨heat was *unaccountably* disappearing⟩
**2** : for reasons that are hard to understand ⟨*unaccountably*, he stayed right there⟩

**un·ac·count·ed** \-ˈkaůn-təd\ *adjective* (1689)

: not accounted : UNEXPLAINED — often used with *for*

**un·ac·cus·tomed** \,ən-ə-'kəs-təmd\ *adjective* (1526)
**1** : not customary : not usual or common
**2** : not habituated — usually used with *to*
— **un·ac·cus·tomed·ly** \-təmd-lē\ *adverb*

**una cor·da** \,ü-nə-'kȯr-də, -(,)dä\ *adverb or adjective* [Italian, literally, one string] (circa 1849)
: with soft pedal depressed — used as a direction in piano music

**un·adorned** \,ən-ə-'dȯrnd\ *adjective* (1634)
: not adorned : lacking embellishment or decoration : PLAIN, SIMPLE

**un·adul·ter·at·ed** \,ən-ə-'dəl-tə-,rā-təd\ *adjective* (circa 1719)
**1** : not adulterated : PURE ⟨*unadulterated* food⟩
**2** : COMPLETE, UNQUALIFIED ⟨an *unadulterated* fool⟩
— **un·adul·ter·at·ed·ly** *adverb*

**un·ad·vised** \,ən-əd-'vīzd\ *adjective* (14th century)
**1** : done without due consideration : RASH ⟨*unadvised* and dangerous dealings with the terrorists⟩
**2** : not prudent : ILL-ADVISED ⟨done with *unadvised* haste⟩
— **un·ad·vis·ed·ly** \-'vī-zəd-lē\ *adverb*

**un·af·fect·ed** \,ən-ə-'fek-təd\ *adjective* (circa 1586)
**1** : not influenced or changed mentally, physically, or chemically
**2** : free from affectation : GENUINE
— **un·af·fect·ed·ly** *adverb*
— **un·af·fect·ed·ness** *noun*

**un·ag·ing** *or* **un·age·ing** \,ən-'ā-jiŋ\ *adjective* (1860)
: AGELESS

**una·kite** \'yü-nə-,kīt\ *noun* [*Unaka* Mountains, Tenn. & N.C. + [1]-*ite*] (1874)
: an altered igneous rock that is usually opaque with green, black, pink, and white flecks and is usually used as a gemstone

**un·alien·able** \,ən-'āl-yə-nə-bəl, -'ā-lē-ə-\ *adjective* (1611)
: INALIENABLE

**un·aligned** \,ən-ə-'līnd\ *adjective* (circa 1934)
: NONALIGNED

**un·al·loyed** \,ən-ə-'lȯid\ *adjective* (1667)
: not alloyed : UNMIXED, UNQUALIFIED, PURE ⟨*unalloyed* metals⟩ ⟨*unalloyed* happiness⟩

**un·al·ter·able** \,ən-'ȯl-t(ə)rə-bəl\ *adjective* (1611)
: not capable of being altered or changed ⟨an *unalterable* resolve⟩ ⟨*unalterable* hatred⟩
— **un·al·ter·abil·i·ty** \,ən-,ȯl-t(ə-)rə-'bi-lə-tē\ *noun*
— **un·al·ter·able·ness** \,ən-'ȯl-t(ə)rə-bəl-nəs\ *noun*
— **un·al·ter·ably** \-blē\ *adverb*

**un·am·big·u·ous** \,ən-am-'bi-gyə-wəs\ *adjective* (1751)
: not ambiguous : CLEAR, PRECISE
— **un·am·big·u·ous·ly** *adverb*

**un·am·biv·a·lent** \-'bi-və-lənt\ *adjective* (1945)
: not ambivalent : CLEAR-CUT, DEFINITE
— **un·am·biv·a·lent·ly** *adverb*

**un–Amer·i·can** \,ən-ə-'mer-ə-kən\ *adjective* (1818)
: not American : not characteristic of or consistent with American customs, principles, or traditions

**un·an·chored** \,ən-'aŋ-kərd\ *adjective* (1651)
**1** : not anchored : not at anchor
**2** : not having a firm basis or foundation

**un·aneled** \,ən-ə-'nē(ə)ld\ *adjective* [*un-* + *aneled,* past participle of *anele* to anoint, from Middle English, from *an* on + *elen* to anoint, from *ele* oil, from Old English, from Latin *oleum* — more at OIL] (1602)
*archaic* : not having received extreme unction

**un·anes·the·tized** \,ən-ə-'nes-thə-,tīzd\ *adjective* (1950)
: not having been subjected to an anesthetic

**una·nim·i·ty** \,yü-nə-'ni-mə-tē\ *noun* (15th century)
: the quality or state of being unanimous

**unan·i·mous** \yü-'na-nə-məs\ *adjective* [Latin *unanimus,* from *unus* one + *animus* mind — more at ONE, ANIMATE] (1624)
**1** : being of one mind : AGREEING
**2** : formed with or indicating unanimity : having the agreement and consent of all
— **unan·i·mous·ly** *adverb*

**un·an·swer·able** \,ən-'an(t)s-rə-bəl, -'an(t)sə-\ *adjective* (1613)
: not capable of being answered; *also* : IRREFUTABLE
— **un·an·swer·abil·i·ty** \,ən-,an(t)s-rə-'bi-lə-tē, -,an(t)-sə-\ *noun*
— **un·an·swer·ably** \,ən-'an(t)s-rə-blē, -'an(t)-sə-\ *adverb*

**un·an·swered** \,ən-'an(t)-sərd\ *adjective* (14th century)
**1** : not answered ⟨*unanswered* letters⟩
**2** : scored in succession during a period in which an opponent fails to score ⟨scored 20 *unanswered* points in the last quarter⟩

**un·an·tic·i·pat·ed** \,ən-an-'ti-sə-,pā-təd\ *adjective* (circa 1779)
: not anticipated : UNEXPECTED, UNFORESEEN
— **un·an·tic·i·pat·ed·ly** *adverb*

**un·apol·o·get·ic** \,ən-ə-,pä-lə-'je-tik\ *adjective* (1834)
: not apologetic : offered, put forward, or being such without apology or qualification ⟨an *unapologetic* liberal⟩
— **un·apol·o·get·i·cal·ly** \-ti-k(ə-)lē\ *adverb*

**un·ap·peal·able** \,ən-ə-'pē-lə-bəl\ *adjective* (1635)
: not appealable : not subject to appeal

**un·ap·peal·ing** \-'pē-liŋ\ *adjective* (circa 1846)
: not appealing : UNATTRACTIVE
— **un·ap·peal·ing·ly** \-liŋ-lē\ *adverb*

**un·ap·peas·able** \-'pē-zə-bəl\ *adjective* (1561)
: not to be appeased : IMPLACABLE
— **un·ap·peas·ably** \-blē\ *adverb*

**un·ap·pe·tiz·ing** \,ən-'a-pə-,tī-ziŋ\ *adjective* (1884)
: not appetizing : INSIPID, UNATTRACTIVE
— **un·ap·pe·tiz·ing·ly** \-ziŋ-lē\ *adverb*

**un·ap·pre·ci·a·tion** \,ən-ə-,prē-shē-'ā-shən\ *noun* (1886)
: failure to appreciate something

**un·ap·proach·able** \,ən-ə-'prō-chə-bəl\ *adjective* (1581)
**1** : not approachable : physically inaccessible
**2** : discouraging intimacies : RESERVED
— **un·ap·proach·abil·i·ty** \-,prō-chə-'bi-lə-tē\ *noun*
— **un·ap·proach·ably** \-'prō-chə-blē\ *adverb*

**un·apt** \,ən-'apt\ *adjective* (circa 1513)
**1** : INAPPROPRIATE, UNSUITABLE ⟨an *unapt* quote⟩
**2** : not accustomed and not likely ⟨a teacher *unapt* to tolerate carelessness⟩
**3** : DULL, BACKWARD ⟨*unapt* scholars⟩
— **un·apt·ly** \-'ap(t)-lē\ *adverb*
— **un·apt·ness** \-nəs\ *noun*

**un·arm** \,ən-'ärm\ *transitive verb* (1560)
: DISARM

**un·armed** \-'ärmd\ *adjective* (14th century)
**1** : not armed or armored
**2** : having no hard and sharp projections (as spines, spurs, or claws)

**un·ar·tic·u·lat·ed** \,ən-är-'ti-kyə-,lā-təd\ *adjective* (circa 1700)
: not articulated; *especially* : not carefully reasoned or analyzed

**una·ry** \'yü-nə-rē\ *adjective* [Latin *unus* one + English *-ary*] (1576)
: having, consisting of, or acting on a single element, item, or component : MONADIC

**un·ashamed** \,ən-ə-'shāmd\ *adjective* (1600)
: not ashamed : being without guilt, self-consciousness, or doubt

— **un·asham·ed·ly** \-'shā-məd-lē\ *adverb*

**un·asked** \,ən-'as(k)t\ *adjective* (13th century)
**1** : not being asked : UNINVITED
**2** : not asked ⟨*unasked* questions⟩
**3** : not asked for ⟨*unasked* advice⟩

**un·as·sail·able** \,ən-ə-'sā-lə-bəl\ *adjective* (1596)
: not assailable : not liable to doubt, attack, or question
— **un·as·sail·abil·i·ty** \-,sā-lə-'bi-lə-tē\ *noun*
— **un·as·sail·able·ness** \-'sā-lə-bəl-nəs\ *noun*
— **un·as·sail·ably** \-blē\ *adverb*

**un·as·ser·tive** \,ən-ə-'sər-tiv\ *adjective* (1861)
: not assertive : MODEST, SHY
— **un·as·ser·tive·ly** *adverb*

**un·as·sist·ed** \,ən-ə-'sis-təd\ *adjective* (1614)
**1** : not assisted : lacking help
**2** : made or performed without an assist ⟨an *unassisted* double play⟩

**un·as·suage·able** \,ən-ə-'swā-jə-bəl\ *adjective* (circa 1611)
: not capable of being assuaged

**un·as·sum·ing** \,ən-ə-'sü-miŋ\ *adjective* (1726)
: not assuming : not arrogant or presuming : MODEST, RETIRING
— **un·as·sum·ing·ness** *noun*

**un·at·tached** \,ən-ə-'tacht\ *adjective* (1796)
**1 a** : not assigned or committed (as to a particular task, organization, or person); *especially* : not married or engaged **b** : not seized as security for a legal judgment
**2** : not joined or united ⟨*unattached* buildings⟩

**un·at·trac·tive** \-'trak-tiv\ *adjective* (circa 1775)
: not attractive : PLAIN, DULL
— **un·at·trac·tive·ly** *adverb*
— **un·at·trac·tive·ness** *noun*

**un·avail·ing** \-'vā-liŋ\ *adjective* (1670)
: not availing : FUTILE, USELESS
— **un·avail·ing·ly** \-liŋ-lē\ *adverb*
— **un·avail·ing·ness** *noun*

**un·av·er·age** \,ən-'a-v(ə-)rij\ *adjective* (1962)
: not average : UNUSUAL, OUTSTANDING

**un·avoid·able** \,ən-ə-'vȯi-də-bəl\ *adjective* (1577)
: not avoidable : INEVITABLE
— **un·avoid·ably** \-blē\ *adverb*

[1]**un·aware** \-ə-'war, -'wer\ *adverb* (1592)
: UNAWARES

[2]**unaware** *adjective* (1704)
: not aware : IGNORANT
— **un·aware·ly** *adverb*
— **un·aware·ness** *noun*

**un·awares** \-'warz, -'werz\ *adverb* [*un-* + *aware* + *-s,* adverb suffix, from Middle English, from *-s,* genitive singular ending of nouns — more at -S] (1535)
**1** : without design, attention, preparation, or premeditation
**2** : without warning : SUDDENLY, UNEXPECTEDLY

**un·backed** \,ən-'bakt\ *adjective* (1609)
: lacking support or aid

[1]**un·bal·ance** \-'ba-lən(t)s\ *transitive verb* (1856)
: to put out of balance; *especially* : to derange mentally

[2]**unbalance** *noun* (1887)
: lack of balance : IMBALANCE

**un·bal·anced** \-'ba-lən(t)st\ *adjective* (1650)
: not balanced: as **a** : not in equilibrium **b** : mentally disordered or deranged **c** : not adjusted so as to make credits equal to debits ⟨an *unbalanced* account⟩

**un·bal·last·ed** \-'ba-lə-stəd\ *adjective* (1657)
: not furnished with or steadied by ballast : UNSTEADY

**un·ban·dage** \-'ban-dij\ *transitive verb* (1840)
: to remove a bandage from

**un·bar** \,ən-'bär\ *transitive verb* (14th century)
: to remove a bar from : UNBOLT, OPEN

**un·bar·bered** \-'bär-bərd\ *adjective* (1845)
: having long and especially unkempt hair

**un·barred** \-'bärd\ *adjective* (1603)
**1** : not secured by a bar : UNLOCKED
**2** : not marked with bars

**un·bat·ed** \-'bā-təd\ *adjective* (1596)
**1** : UNABATED
**2** *archaic* : not blunted

**un·be** \-'bē\ *intransitive verb* (15th century)
*archaic* : to lack or cease to have being

**un·bear·able** \ˌən-'bar-ə-bəl, -'ber-\ *adjective* (15th century)
: not bearable : UNENDURABLE
— **un·bear·ably** \-blē\ *adverb*

**un·beat·able** \-'bē-tə-bəl\ *adjective* (1897)
**1** : not capable of being defeated
**2** : possessing unsurpassable qualities
— **un·beat·ably** \-blē\ *adverb*

**un·beat·en** \-'bē-tᵊn\ *adjective* (13th century)
**1** : not pounded or beaten : not whipped
**2** : not traversed : UNTROD
**3** : not defeated

**un·beau·ti·ful** \-'byü-ti-fəl\ *adjective* (15th century)
: not beautiful : UNATTRACTIVE
— **un·beau·ti·ful·ly** \-f(ə-)lē\ *adverb*

**un·be·com·ing** \ˌən-bi-'kə-miŋ\ *adjective* (1598)
: not becoming ⟨an *unbecoming* dress⟩; *especially* : not according with the standards appropriate to one's position or condition of life ⟨*unbecoming* conduct⟩
**synonym** see INDECOROUS
— **un·be·com·ing·ly** \-miŋ-lē\ *adverb*
— **un·be·com·ing·ness** *noun*

**un·be·knownst** \ˌən-bi-'nōn(t)st\ *also* **un·be·known** \-'nōn\ *adjective* [¹un- + obsolete English *beknown* known; *unbeknownst*, irregular from *unbeknown*] (1636)
: happening without one's knowledge : UNKNOWN — usually used with *to*

**un·be·lief** \ˌən-bə-'lēf\ *noun* (12th century)
: incredulity or skepticism especially in matters of religious faith

**un·be·liev·able** \-'lē-və-bəl\ *adjective* (1548)
: too improbable for belief ⟨the plot is unreal and *unbelievable*⟩; *also* : of such a superlative degree as to be hard to believe ⟨the destruction was *unbelievable*⟩ ⟨made an *unbelievable* catch in center field⟩
— **un·be·liev·ably** \-blē\ *adverb*

**un·be·liev·er** \-'lē-vər\ *noun* (1526)
**1** : one that does not believe : an incredulous person : DOUBTER, SKEPTIC
**2** : one that does not believe in a particular religious faith

**un·be·liev·ing** \-'lē-viŋ\ *adjective* (14th century)
: marked by unbelief : INCREDULOUS, SKEPTICAL
— **un·be·liev·ing·ly** \-viŋ-lē\ *adverb*

**un·belt·ed** \ˌən-'bel-təd\ *adjective* (1814)
: not furnished with a belt

**un·bend** \-'bend\ *verb* **-bent** \-'bent\; **-bend·ing** (13th century)
*transitive verb*
**1** : to free from flexure : make or allow to become straight ⟨*unbend* a bow⟩
**2** : to cause (as the mind) to relax
**3 a** : to unfasten (as a sail) from a spar or stay **b** : to cast loose (as a rope) : UNTIE
*intransitive verb*
**1** : to relax one's severity, stiffness, or austerity
**2** : to cease to be bent : become straight

**un·bend·able** \-'ben-də-bəl\ *adjective* (circa 1775)
: SINGLE-MINDED, FIRM

**un·bend·ing** \-'ben-diŋ\ *adjective* [¹un-] (circa 1688)
**1** : not bending : UNYIELDING, INFLEXIBLE ⟨an *unbending* will⟩
**2** : aloof or unsocial in manner : RESERVED

**un·be·seem·ing** \ˌən-bi-'sē-miŋ\ *adjective* (1583)
: not befitting : UNBECOMING

**un·bi·ased** \ˌən-'bī-əst\ *adjective* (1647)
**1** : free from bias; *especially* : free from all prejudice and favoritism : eminently fair
**2** : having an expected value equal to a population parameter being estimated ⟨an *unbiased* estimate of the population mean⟩
**synonym** see FAIR
— **un·bi·ased·ness** \-əs(t)-nəs\ *noun*

**un·bib·li·cal** \ˌən-'bi-bli-kəl\ *adjective* (1828)
: contrary to or unsanctioned by the Bible

**un·bid·den** \-'bi-dᵊn\ *also* **un·bid** \-'bid\ *adjective* [Middle English *unbiden, unbeden*, from Old English *unbeden*, from *un-* + *beden*, past participle of *biddan* to entreat — more at BID] (before 12th century)
: not bidden : UNASKED, UNINVITED

**un·bind** \-'bīnd\ *transitive verb* **-bound** \-'baund\; **-bind·ing** (before 12th century)
**1** : to remove a band from : free from fastenings : UNTIE, UNFASTEN
**2** : to set free : RELEASE

**un·bit·ted** \-'bi-təd\ *adjective* [²*bit*] (circa 1586)
: UNBRIDLED, UNCONTROLLED

**un·blenched** \-'blencht\ *adjective* (1634)
: not disconcerted : UNDAUNTED

**un·blessed** *also* **un·blest** \ˌən-'blest\ *adjective* (14th century)
**1** : not blessed
**2** : EVIL, ACCURSED

**un·blind·ed** \-'blīn-dəd\ *adjective* (circa 1611)
: not blinded; *especially* : free from illusion

**un·blink·ing** \-'bliŋ-kiŋ\ *adjective* (circa 1909)
**1** : not blinking
**2** : not showing signs of emotion, doubt, or confusion
— **un·blink·ing·ly** \-kiŋ-lē\ *adverb*

**un·block** \-'bläk\ *transitive verb* (1611)
: to free from being blocked

**un·blush·ing** \-'blə-shiŋ\ *adjective* (1595)
**1** : not blushing
**2** : SHAMELESS, UNABASHED
— **un·blush·ing·ly** \-shiŋ-lē\ *adverb*

**un·bod·ied** \-'bä-dēd\ *adjective* (1532)
**1** : having no body : INCORPOREAL; *also* : freed from the body ⟨*unbodied* souls⟩
**2** : FORMLESS

**un·bolt** \ˌən-'bōlt\ *transitive verb* (circa 1598)
: to open or unfasten by withdrawing a bolt

**¹un·bolt·ed** \-'bōl-təd\ *adjective* [²*bolt*] (circa 1580)
: not fastened by bolts

**²unbolted** *adjective* [⁴*bolt*] (1598)
: not sifted ⟨*unbolted* flour⟩

**un·bon·net·ed** \ˌən-'bä-nə-təd\ *adjective* (1604)
: BAREHEADED

**un·born** \-'bȯrn\ *adjective* (before 12th century)
**1** : not born : not brought into life
**2** : still to appear : FUTURE
**3** : existing without birth

**un·bos·om** \-'bu̇-zəm *also* -'bü-\ (1588)
*transitive verb*
**1** : to give expression to : DISCLOSE, REVEAL
**2** : to disclose the thoughts or feelings of (oneself)
*intransitive verb*
: to unbosom oneself

**un·bound** \-'baund\ *adjective* (before 12th century)
: not bound: as **a** (1) : not fastened (2) : not confined **b** : not having the leaves fastened together ⟨an *unbound* book⟩ **c** : not bound together with other issues ⟨*unbound* periodicals⟩ **d** : not held in chemical or physical combination

**un·bound·ed** \-'baun-dəd\ *adjective* (1593)
**1** : having no limit
**2** : UNRESTRAINED, UNCONTROLLED
— **un·bound·ed·ness** *noun*

**un·bowed** \ˌən-'baud\ *adjective* (14th century)
**1** : not bowed down
**2** : not subdued ⟨bloodied but *unbowed*⟩

**un·box** \-'bäks\ *transitive verb* (1611)

: to remove from a box

**un·brace** \-'brās\ *transitive verb* (1593)
**1** : to free or detach by or as if by untying or removing a brace or bond
**2** : ENFEEBLE, WEAKEN

**un·braid** \-'brād\ *transitive verb* (circa 1828)
: to separate the strands of : UNRAVEL

**un·branched** \-'brancht\ *adjective* (1665)
**1** : having no branches ⟨a straight *unbranched* trunk⟩
**2** : not divided into branches ⟨a leaf with *unbranched* veins⟩

**un·brand·ed** \-'bran-dəd\ *adjective* (1886)
**1** : not marked with the owner's name or mark ⟨*unbranded* cattle⟩
**2** : not sold under a brand name

**un·breath·able** \-'brē-thə-bəl\ *adjective* (1846)
: not fit for being breathed

**un·bred** \-'bred\ *adjective* (1662)
**1** *obsolete* : ILL-BRED
**2** : not taught : UNTRAINED
**3** : not bred : never having been bred ⟨an *unbred* heifer⟩

**un·bri·dle** \ˌən-'brī-dᵊl\ *transitive verb* (15th century)
: to free or loose from a bridle; *broadly* : to set loose : free from restraint

**un·bri·dled** \-'brī-dᵊld\ *adjective* (14th century)
**1** : UNRESTRAINED ⟨*unbridled* enthusiasm⟩
**2** : not confined by a bridle

**un·broke** \-'brōk\ *adjective* (14th century)
: UNBROKEN

**un·bro·ken** \-'brō-kən\ *adjective* (14th century)
: not broken: as **a** : not violated **b** : WHOLE, INTACT **c** : not subdued : UNTAMED; *especially* : not trained for service or use ⟨*unbroken* colts⟩ **d** : CONTINUOUS ⟨miles of *unbroken* forest⟩ **e** : not plowed **f** : not disorganized ⟨advanced in *unbroken* ranks⟩

**un·buck·le** \-'bə-kəl\ (14th century)
*transitive verb*
: to loose the buckle of : UNFASTEN
*intransitive verb*
**1** : to loosen buckles
**2** : RELAX

**un·budge·able** \-'bə-jə-bəl\ *adjective* (1929)
: not able to be budged or changed : INFLEXIBLE
— **un·budge·ably** \-blē\ *adverb*

**un·budg·ing** \-'bə-jiŋ\ *adjective* (circa 1934)
: not budging : resisting movement or change
— **un·budg·ing·ly** \-jiŋ-lē\ *adverb*

**un·build** \ˌən-'bild\ *verb* **-built** \-'bilt\; **-build·ing** (1607)
*transitive verb*
: to pull down : DEMOLISH, RAZE
*intransitive verb*
: to destroy something

**un·built** \-'bilt\ *adjective* (15th century)
**1** : not built : not yet constructed
**2** : not built on ⟨an *unbuilt* plot⟩

**un·bun·dle** \-'bən-dᵊl\ (1969)
*intransitive verb*
: to give separate prices for equipment and supporting services
*transitive verb*
: to price separately

**un·bur·den** \-'bər-dᵊn\ *transitive verb* (1538)
**1** : to free or relieve from a burden
**2** : to relieve oneself of (as cares, fears, or worries) : cast off

**un·bur·dened** \-'bər-dᵊnd\ *adjective* (1548)
: not burdened : having no weight or load

**un·but·ton** \-'bə-tᵊn\ (14th century)
*transitive verb*
**1** : to loose the buttons of
**2** : to open by or as if by loosing buttons

*intransitive verb*
: to undo buttons
**un·but·toned** \-'t°nd\ *adjective* (1583)
**1 a** : not buttoned **b** : not provided with buttons
**2** : not under constraint : free and unrestricted in action and expression
**un·cage** \,ən-'kāj\ *transitive verb* (1620)
: to release from or as if from a cage : free from restraint
**un·cal·cu·lat·ed** \-'kal-kyə-,lā-təd\ *adjective* (circa 1828)
: not planned or thought out beforehand : SPONTANEOUS
**un·cal·cu·lat·ing** \-,lā-tiŋ\ *adjective* (circa 1828)
: not based on or marked by calculation
**un·called–for** \,ən-'kȯl(d)-,fȯr\ *adjective* (circa 1656)
**1** : not called for or needed : UNNECESSARY
**2** : being or offered without provocation or justification ⟨an *uncalled-for* display of temper⟩ ⟨*uncalled-for* insults⟩
**un·can·ny** \-'ka-nē\ *adjective* (1843)
**1 a** : seeming to have a supernatural character or origin : EERIE, MYSTERIOUS **b** : being beyond what is normal or expected : suggesting superhuman or supernatural powers ⟨an *uncanny* sense of direction⟩
**2** *chiefly Scottish* : SEVERE, PUNISHING
**synonym** SEE WEIRD
— **un·can·ni·ly** \-'ka-n°l-ē\ *adverb*
— **un·can·ni·ness** \-'ka-nē-nəs\ *noun*
**un·caused** \-'kȯzd\ *adjective* (circa 1628)
: having no antecedent cause
**un·ceas·ing** \-'sē-iŋ\ *adjective* (14th century)
: never ceasing : CONTINUOUS, INCESSANT
— **un·ceas·ing·ly** \-siŋ-lē\ *adverb*
**un·cel·e·brat·ed** \-'se-lə-,brā-təd\ *adjective* (1660)
**1** : not formally honored or commemorated
**2** : not famous : OBSCURE
**un·cer·e·mo·ni·ous** \,ən-,ser-ə-'mō-nē-əs\ *adjective* (1598)
**1** : not ceremonious : INFORMAL
**2** : ABRUPT, RUDE ⟨an *unceremonious* dismissal⟩
— **un·cer·e·mo·ni·ous·ly** *adverb*
— **un·cer·e·mo·ni·ous·ness** *noun*
**un·cer·tain** \,ən-'sər-t°n\ *adjective* (14th century)
**1** : INDEFINITE, INDETERMINATE ⟨the time of departure is *uncertain*⟩
**2** : not certain to occur : PROBLEMATICAL
**3** : not reliable : UNTRUSTWORTHY
**4 a** : not known beyond doubt : DUBIOUS **b** : not having certain knowledge : DOUBTFUL **c** : not clearly identified or defined
**5** : not constant : VARIABLE, FITFUL
— **un·cer·tain·ly** *adverb*
— **un·cer·tain·ness** \-t°n-(n)əs\ *noun*
**un·cer·tain·ty** \-t°n-tē\ *noun* (14th century)
**1** : the quality or state of being uncertain : DOUBT
**2** : something that is uncertain ☆
**uncertainty principle** *noun* (1929)
: a principle in quantum mechanics: it is impossible to discern simultaneously and with high accuracy both the position and the momentum of a particle (as an electron) — called also *Heisenberg uncertainty principle*
**un·chain** \,ən-'chān\ *transitive verb* (1582)
: to free by or as if by removing a chain : set loose
**un·chancy** \-'chan(t)-sē\ *adjective* (1533)
**1** *chiefly Scottish* : ILL-FATED
**2** *chiefly Scottish* : DANGEROUS
**un·change·able** \-'chān-jə-bəl\ *adjective* (14th century)
: not changing or to be changed : IMMUTABLE
— **un·change·abil·i·ty** \,ən-,chān-jə-'bi-lə-tē\ *noun*
— **un·change·able·ness** \,ən-'chān-jə-bəl-nəs\ *noun*
— **un·change·ably** \-blē\ *adverb*
**un·chang·ing** \-'chān-jiŋ\ *adjective* (1593)
: CONSTANT, INVARIABLE

— **un·chang·ing·ly** \-jiŋ-lē\ *adverb*
— **un·chang·ing·ness** *noun*
**un·char·ac·ter·is·tic** \,ən-,kar-ik-tə-'ris-tik\ *adjective* (1753)
: not characteristic : not typical or distinctive
— **un·char·ac·ter·is·ti·cal·ly** \-ti-k(ə-)lē\ *adverb*
**un·charge** \,ən-'chärj\ *transitive verb* (1602)
*obsolete* : ACQUIT
**un·charged** \-'chärjd\ *adjective* (1815)
: not charged; *specifically* : having no electric charge
**un·char·i·ta·ble** \-'char-ə-tə-bəl\ *adjective* (15th century)
: lacking in charity : severe in judging : HARSH
— **un·char·i·ta·ble·ness** *noun*
— **un·char·i·ta·bly** \-blē\ *adverb*
**un·chart·ed** \-'chär-təd\ *adjective* (circa 1847)
: not recorded or plotted on a map, chart, or plan; *broadly* : UNKNOWN ⟨*uncharted* territory⟩
**un·chaste** \-'chāst\ *adjective* (14th century)
: not chaste : lacking in chastity
— **un·chaste·ly** *adverb*
— **un·chaste·ness** \-'chās(t)-nəs\ *noun*
**un·chas·ti·ty** \-'chas-tə-tē\ *noun* (14th century)
: the quality or state of being unchaste
**un·chiv·al·rous** \-'shi-vəl-rəs\ *adjective* (circa 1846)
: not chivalrous : lacking in chivalry
— **un·chiv·al·rous·ly** *adverb*
**un·choke** \-'chōk\ *transitive verb* (1588)
: to clear of obstruction
**un·chris·tian** \-'kris-chən, -'krish-\ *adjective* (1555)
**1** : not of the Christian faith
**2 a** : contrary to the Christian spirit or character **b** : UNCIVILIZED, BARBAROUS
**un·church** \-'chərch\ *transitive verb* (circa 1620)
**1** : to expel from a church : EXCOMMUNICATE
**2** : to deprive of a church or of status as a church
**un·churched** \-'chərcht\ *adjective* (1681)
: not belonging to or connected with a church
**unci** *plural of* UNCUS
¹**un·cial** \'ən(t)-shəl, -sē-əl\ *adjective* [Late Latin *unciales* (*litterae*) uncial (letters), from Latin, plural of *uncialis* weighing an ounce, from *uncia* twelfth part, ounce — more at OUNCE] (1712)
: written in the style or size of uncials
— **un·cial·ly** *adverb*
²**uncial** *noun* (circa 1775)
**1** : a handwriting used especially in Greek and Latin manuscripts of the 4th to the 8th centuries A.D. and made with somewhat rounded separated majuscules but having cursive forms for some letters

ROMAN UNCIAL

uncials

**2** : an uncial letter
**3** : a manuscript written in uncial
**un·ci·form** \'ən(t)-sə-,fȯrm\ *adjective* [New Latin *unciformis*, from Latin *uncus* hook + *-formis* -form — more at ANGLE] (circa 1734)
: hook-shaped : UNCINATE
**un·ci·na·ri·a·sis** \,ən-,si-nə-'rī-ə-səs\ *noun* [New Latin, from *Uncinaria*, genus that includes hookworms, from Latin *uncinus* hook] (1903)
: ANCYLOSTOMIASIS
**un·ci·nate** \'ən(t)-sə-,nāt\ *adjective* [Latin *uncinatus*, from *uncinus* hook, from *uncus*] (circa 1760)
: bent at the tip like a hook : HOOKED ⟨an *uncinate* achene⟩
**un·cir·cu·lat·ed** \,ən-'sər-kyə-,lā-təd\ *adjective* (1917)
: issued for use as money but kept out of circulation ⟨saved for preservation in a collection⟩
**un·cir·cum·cised** \,ən-'sər-kəm-,sīzd\ *adjective* (14th century)

**1** : not circumcised
**2** : spiritually impure : HEATHEN
— **un·cir·cum·ci·sion** \,ən-,sər-kəm-'si-zhən\ *noun*
**un·civ·il** \,ən-'si-vəl\ *adjective* (1553)
**1** : not civilized : BARBAROUS
**2** : lacking in courtesy : ILL-MANNERED, IMPOLITE
**3** : not conducive to civic harmony and welfare
— **un·civ·il·ly** \-və-lē\ *adverb*
**un·civ·i·lized** \-'si-və-,līzd\ *adjective* (1607)
**1** : not civilized : BARBAROUS
**2** : remote from settled areas : WILD
**un·clamp** \-'klamp\ *transitive verb* (1809)
: to loosen the clamp of : to free from a clamp
**un·clar·i·ty** \-'klar-ə-tē\ *noun, plural* **-ties** (1923)
: lack of clarity : AMBIGUITY, OBSCURITY
**un·clasp** \-'klasp\ (1530)
*transitive verb*
**1** : to open the clasp of
**2** : to open or cause to be opened (as a clenched hand)
*intransitive verb*
: to loosen a hold
**un·clas·si·cal** \-'kla-si-kəl\ *adjective* (1725)
: not classical; *especially* : unconcerned with the classics
**un·clas·si·fied** \-'kla-sə-,fīd\ *adjective* (1865)
**1** : not placed or belonging in a class
**2** : not subject to a security classification
**un·cle** \'ən-kəl\ *noun* [Middle English, from Old French, from Latin *avunculus* mother's brother; akin to Old English *ēam* uncle, Welsh *ewythr* uncle, Latin *avus* grandfather] (14th century)
**1 a** : the brother of one's father or mother **b** : the husband of one's aunt
**2** : one who helps, advises, or encourages
**3** — used as a cry of surrender ⟨was forced to cry *uncle*⟩
**4** *capitalized* : UNCLE SAM
**un·clean** \,ən-'klēn\ *adjective* (before 12th century)
**1** : morally or spiritually impure
**2** : infected with a harmful supernatural contagion; *also* : prohibited by ritual law for use or contact
**3** : DIRTY, FILTHY
**4** : lacking in clarity and precision of conception or execution
— **un·clean·ness** \-'klēn-nəs\ *noun*
¹**un·clean·ly** \-'klen-lē\ *adjective* (before 12th century)
: morally or physically unclean
— **un·clean·li·ness** *noun*
²**un·clean·ly** \-'klēn-lē\ *adverb* (before 12th century)
: in an unclean manner
**un·clench** \-'klench\ (1699)

---

☆ **SYNONYMS**
**Uncertainty, doubt, dubiety, skepticism, suspicion, mistrust** mean lack of sureness about someone or something. UNCERTAINTY may range from a falling short of certainty to an almost complete lack of conviction or knowledge especially about an outcome or result ⟨assumed the role of manager without hesitation or *uncertainty*⟩. DOUBT suggests both uncertainty and inability to make a decision ⟨plagued by *doubts* as to what to do⟩. DUBIETY stresses a wavering between conclusions ⟨felt some *dubiety* about its practicality⟩. SKEPTICISM implies unwillingness to believe without conclusive evidence ⟨an economic forecast greeted with *skepticism*⟩. SUSPICION stresses lack of faith in the truth, reality, fairness, or reliability of something or someone ⟨regarded the stranger with *suspicion*⟩. MISTRUST implies a genuine doubt based upon suspicion ⟨had a great *mistrust* of doctors⟩.

*transitive verb*
**1 :** to open from a clenched position
**2 :** to release from a grip
*intransitive verb*
**:** to become unclasped or relaxed
**Un·cle Sam** \ˌəŋ-kəl-'sam\ *noun* [expansion of *U.S.*, abbreviation of *United States*] (1813)
**1 :** the U.S. government
**2 :** the American nation or people
**¹Uncle Tom** \-'täm\ *noun* [*Uncle Tom,* pious and faithful black slave in *Uncle Tom's Cabin* (1851–52) by Harriet Beecher Stowe] (1922)
**1 :** a black who is overeager to win the approval of whites (as by obsequious behavior or uncritical acceptance of white values and goals)
**2 :** a member of a low-status group who is overly subservient to or cooperative with authority ⟨the worst floor managers and supervisors by far are women . . . Some of them are regular *Uncle Toms* —Jane Fonda⟩
**— Uncle Tom·ism** \-'tä-ˌmi-zəm\ *noun*
**²Uncle Tom** *intransitive verb* **Uncle Tommed; Uncle Tom·ming** (1947)
**:** to behave like an Uncle Tom
**un·climb·able** \ˌən-'klī-mə-bəl\ *adjective* (1553)
**:** not able to be climbed
**— un·climb·able·ness** *noun*
**un·clinch** \ˌən-'klinch\ *transitive verb* (1598)
**:** UNCLENCH
**un·cloak** \-'klōk\ (1598)
*transitive verb*
**1 :** to remove a cloak or cover from
**2 :** REVEAL, UNMASK
*intransitive verb*
**:** to take off a cloak
**un·clog** \-'kläg\ *transitive verb* (1607)
**:** to free from a difficulty or obstruction
**un·close** \-'klōz\ (14th century)
*transitive verb*
**1 :** OPEN
**2 :** DISCLOSE, REVEAL
*intransitive verb*
**:** to become opened
**un·closed** \-'klōzd\ *adjective* (15th century)
**:** not closed or settled **:** not concluded
**un·clothe** \-'klōth\ *transitive verb* (14th century)
**1 :** to strip of clothes
**2 :** DIVEST, UNCOVER
**un·clothed** \-'klōthd\ *adjective* (15th century)
**:** not clothed
**un·cloud·ed** \-'klaủ-dəd\ *adjective* (1594)
**:** not covered by clouds **:** not darkened or obscured **:** CLEAR
**— un·cloud·ed·ly** *adverb*
**un·club·ba·ble** \ˌən-'klə-bə-bəl\ *adjective* (circa 1764)
**:** UNSOCIABLE 1
**un·clut·ter** \-'klə-tər\ *transitive verb* (1930)
**:** to remove clutter from **:** make neat and orderly
**un·clut·tered** \-'tərd\ *adjective* (1925)
**:** not cluttered
**¹un·co** \'əŋ-(ˌ)kō, -kə\ *adjective* [Middle English (Scots) *unkow,* alteration of Middle English *uncouth*] (15th century)
**1** *chiefly Scottish* **a :** STRANGE, UNKNOWN **b :** UNCANNY, WEIRD
**2** *chiefly Scottish* **:** EXTRAORDINARY
**²unco** *adverb* (1724)
**:** EXTREMELY, REMARKABLY, UNCOMMONLY
**³unco** *noun, plural* **uncos** (1785)
**1** *plural, chiefly Scottish* **:** NEWS, TIDINGS
**2** *chiefly Scottish* **:** STRANGER
**un·cock** \ˌən-'käk\ *transitive verb* (circa 1775)
**:** to remove the hammer of (a firearm) from a cocked position
**un·cof·fin** \-'kȯ-fən\ *transitive verb* (1836)
**:** to remove from or as if from a coffin
**un·cof·fined** \-fənd\ *adjective* (1648)
**:** not placed in a coffin
**un·coil** \ˌən-'kȯi(ə)l\ (1713)
*transitive verb*
**:** to release from a coiled state **:** UNWIND

*intransitive verb*
**:** to become uncoiled
**un·coiled** \-'kȯi(ə)ld\ *adjective* (1713)
**:** not coiled
**un·coined** \-'kȯind\ *adjective* (15th century)
**1 :** not minted ⟨*uncoined* metal⟩
**2 :** not fabricated **:** NATURAL
**un·com·fort·able** \ˌən-'kəm(p)(f)-tə(r)-bəl, -'kəm(p)-fə(r)-tə-bəl, -'kəm-fə(r)-bəl\ *adjective* (1592)
**1 :** causing discomfort or annoyance ⟨an *uncomfortable* chair⟩ ⟨an *uncomfortable* performance⟩
**2 :** feeling discomfort **:** UNEASY ⟨was *uncomfortable* with them⟩
**— un·com·fort·ably** \-blē\ *adverb*
**un·com·mer·cial** \ˌən-kə-'mər-shəl\ *adjective* (1768)
**1 :** not engaged in or related to commerce
**2 :** not based on commercial principles
**3 :** not likely to result in financial success ⟨an *uncommercial* book⟩
**un·com·mit·ted** \ˌən-kə-'mi-təd\ *adjective* (1598)
**:** not committed; *specifically* **:** not pledged to a particular belief, allegiance, or program
**un·com·mon** \ˌən-'kä-mən\ *adjective* (1611)
**1 :** not ordinarily encountered **:** UNUSUAL
**2 :** REMARKABLE, EXCEPTIONAL
**synonym** see INFREQUENT
**— un·com·mon·ly** *adverb*
**— un·com·mon·ness** \-mən-nəs\ *noun*
**un·com·mu·ni·ca·ble** \ˌən-kə-'myü-ni-kə-bəl\ *adjective* (14th century)
**:** INCOMMUNICABLE
**un·com·mu·ni·ca·tive** \-'myü-nə-ˌkā-tiv, -ni-kə-tiv\ *adjective* (1691)
**:** not disposed to talk or impart information **:** RESERVED
**un·com·pet·i·tive** \-'pe-tə-tiv\ *adjective* (1885)
**:** not competitive **:** unable to compete
**— un·com·pet·i·tive·ness** *noun*
**un·com·plain·ing** \-'plā-niŋ\ *adjective* (1744)
**:** not complaining **:** PATIENT
**— un·com·plain·ing·ly** \-niŋ-lē\ *adverb*
**un·com·pli·cat·ed** \ˌən-'käm-plə-ˌkā-təd\ *adjective* (circa 1775)
**1 a :** not complicated by something outside itself **b :** not involving medical complications ⟨an *uncomplicated* peptic ulcer⟩
**2 :** not complex **:** SIMPLE ⟨*uncomplicated* machinery⟩
**un·com·pli·men·ta·ry** \ˌən-ˌkäm-plə-'men-tə-rē, -'men-trē\ *adjective* (1842)
**:** not complimentary **:** DEROGATORY
**un·com·pre·hend·ing** \-pri-'hen-diŋ\ *adjective* (1838)
**:** not comprehending **:** lacking understanding
**— un·com·pre·hend·ing·ly** \-diŋ-lē\ *adverb*
**un·com·pro·mis·able** \ˌən-'käm-prə-ˌmī-zə-bəl\ *adjective* (1958)
**:** not able to be compromised
**un·com·pro·mis·ing** \-ˌmī-ziŋ\ *adjective* (circa 1828)
**:** not making or accepting a compromise **:** making no concessions **:** INFLEXIBLE, UNYIELDING
**— un·com·pro·mis·ing·ly** \-ziŋ-lē\ *adverb*
**— un·com·pro·mis·ing·ness** \-nəs\ *noun*
**un·con·ceiv·able** \ˌən-kən-'sē-və-bəl\ *adjective* (circa 1607)
**:** INCONCEIVABLE
**un·con·cern** \ˌən-kən-'sərn\ *noun* (1711)
**1 :** lack of care or interest **:** INDIFFERENCE
**2 :** freedom from excessive concern or anxiety
**un·con·cerned** \-'sərnd\ *adjective* (circa 1635)
**1 :** not involved **:** not having any part or interest
**2 :** not anxious or upset **:** free of worry
**synonym** see INDIFFERENT
**— un·con·cerned·ly** \-'sər-nəd-lē, -'sərnd-lē\ *adverb*

**— un·con·cerned·ness** \-'sər-nəd-nəs, -'sərn(d)-nəs\ *noun*
**un·con·di·tion·al** \ˌən-kən-'dish-nəl, -'di-shə-nºl\ *adjective* (1666)
**1 :** not conditional or limited **:** ABSOLUTE, UNQUALIFIED ⟨*unconditional* surrender⟩
**2 :** UNCONDITIONED 2
**— un·con·di·tion·al·ly** *adverb*
**un·con·di·tioned** \-'di-shənd\ *adjective* (circa 1631)
**1 :** not subject to conditions or limitations
**2 a :** not dependent on or subjected to conditioning or learning **:** NATURAL ⟨*unconditioned* responses⟩ **b :** producing an unconditioned response ⟨*unconditioned* stimuli⟩
**un·con·form·able** \-'fȯr-mə-bəl\ *adjective* (1594)
**1 :** not conforming
**2 :** exhibiting geological unconformity
**— un·con·form·ably** \-blē\ *adverb*
**un·con·for·mi·ty** \-'fȯr-mə-tē\ *noun* (circa 1600)
**1** *archaic* **:** lack of conformity
**2 a :** lack of continuity in deposition between rock strata in contact corresponding to a period of nondeposition, weathering, or erosion **b :** the surface of contact between unconformable strata
**un·con·ge·nial** \-'jē-nyəl, -nē-əl\ *adjective* (circa 1775)
**1 :** not sympathetic or compatible ⟨*uncongenial* roommates⟩
**2 a :** not fitted **:** UNSUITABLE ⟨a soil *uncongenial* to most crops⟩ **b :** not to one's taste **:** DISAGREEABLE ⟨an *uncongenial* task⟩
**— un·con·ge·nial·i·ty** \-ˌjē-nē-'a-lə-tē, -ˌjēn-'ya-\ *noun*
**un·con·quer·able** \ˌən-'käŋ-k(ə-)rə-bəl\ *adjective* (1598)
**1 :** incapable of being conquered **:** INDOMITABLE ⟨an *unconquerable* will⟩
**2 :** incapable of being surmounted ⟨*unconquerable* difficulties⟩
**— un·con·quer·ably** \-blē\ *adverb*
**un·con·scio·na·ble** \-'kän(t)-sh(ə-)nə-bəl\ *adjective* (1570)
**1 :** not guided or controlled by conscience **:** UNSCRUPULOUS ⟨an *unconscionable* villain⟩
**2 a :** EXCESSIVE, UNREASONABLE ⟨found an *unconscionable* number of defects in the car⟩ **b :** shockingly unfair or unjust ⟨*unconscionable* sales practices⟩
**— un·con·scio·na·bil·i·ty** \ˌən-ˌkän(t)-sh(ə-)nə-'bi-lə-tē\ *noun*
**— un·con·scio·na·ble·ness** \ˌən-'kän(t)-sh(ə-)nə-bəl-nəs\ *noun*
**— un·con·scio·na·bly** \-blē\ *adverb*
**¹un·con·scious** \ˌən-'kän(t)-shəs\ *adjective* (1712)
**1 a :** not knowing or perceiving **:** not aware **b :** free from self-awareness
**2 a :** not possessing mind or consciousness ⟨*unconscious* matter⟩ **b (1) :** not marked by conscious thought, sensation, or feeling ⟨*unconscious* motivation⟩ **(2) :** of or relating to the unconscious **c :** having lost consciousness ⟨was *unconscious* for three days⟩
**3 :** not consciously held or deliberately planned or carried out ⟨*unconscious* bias⟩
**— un·con·scious·ly** *adverb*
**— un·con·scious·ness** *noun*
**²unconscious** *noun* (1912)
**:** the part of the psychic apparatus that does not ordinarily enter the individual's awareness and that is manifested especially by slips of the tongue or dissociated acts or in dreams
**un·con·sid·ered** \ˌən-kən-'si-dərd\ *adjective* (1587)
**1 :** not considered or worth consideration
**2 :** not resulting from consideration

**un·con·sol·i·dat·ed** \-'sä-lə-ˌdā-təd\ *adjective* (circa 1775)
: loosely arranged ⟨*unconsolidated* subsidiaries⟩; *especially* : not stratified ⟨*unconsolidated* soil⟩

**un·con·sti·tu·tion·al** \ˌən-ˌkän(t)-stə-'tü-shnəl, -'tyü-, -shə-n°l\ *adjective* (1734)
: not according or consistent with the constitution of a body politic (as a nation)
— **un·con·sti·tu·tion·al·i·ty** \-ˌtü-shə-'na-lə-tē, -ˌtyü-\ *noun*
— **un·con·sti·tu·tion·al·ly** *adverb*

**un·con·straint** \ˌən-kən-'stränt\ *noun* (1711)
: freedom from constraint : EASE

**un·con·struct·ed** \-'strək-təd\ *adjective* (1970)
*of clothing* : manufactured without added material for padding, stiffening, or shape retention

**un·con·trol·la·ble** \-'trō-lə-bəl\ *adjective* (1593)
**1** *archaic* : free from control by a superior power : ABSOLUTE
**2** : incapable of being controlled : UNGOVERNABLE
— **un·con·trol·la·bil·i·ty** \-ˌtrō-lə-'bi-lə-tē\ *noun*
— **un·con·trol·la·bly** \-'trō-lə-blē\ *adverb*

**un·con·ven·tion·al** \-'vench-nəl, -'ven(t)-shə-n°l\ *adjective* (1839)
: not conventional : not bound by or in accordance with convention : being out of the ordinary
— **un·con·ven·tion·al·i·ty** \-ˌven(t)-shə-'na-lə-tē\ *noun*
— **un·con·ven·tion·al·ly** *adverb*

**un·con·vinc·ing** \-'vin(t)-siŋ\ *adjective* (1653)
: not convincing : IMPLAUSIBLE
— **un·con·vinc·ing·ly** \-siŋ-lē\ *adverb*
— **un·con·vinc·ing·ness** *noun*

**un·cool** \ˌən-'kül\ *adjective* (1953)
**1** : lacking in assurance
**2** : failing to accord with the current styles (as of dress or behavior) of a particular group

**un·cork** \ˌən-'kȯrk\ *transitive verb* (1727)
**1** : to draw a cork from
**2 a** : to release from a sealed or pent-up state ⟨*uncork* a surprise⟩ **b** : to let go : RELEASE ⟨*uncork* a wild pitch⟩

**un·corked** \-'kȯrkt\ *adjective* (1791)
: not provided with a cork

**un·cor·set·ed** \-'kȯr-sə-təd\ *adjective* (1856)
**1** : not wearing a corset
**2** : not controlled or inhibited ⟨*uncorseted* freedom⟩

**un·count·ed** \-'kaȯn-təd\ *adjective* (15th century)
**1** : not counted
**2** : INNUMERABLE

**un·cou·ple** \-'kə-pəl\ *transitive verb* (14th century)
**1** : to release (dogs) from a couple
**2** : DETACH, DISCONNECT ⟨*uncouple* railroad cars⟩
— **un·cou·pler** \-p(ə-)lər\ *noun*

**un·couth** \-'küth\ *adjective* [Middle English, from Old English *uncūth*, from *un-* + *cūth* familiar, known; akin to Old High German *kund* known, Old English *can* know — more at CAN] (before 12th century)
**1 a** *archaic* : not known or not familiar to one : seldom experienced : UNCOMMON, RARE **b** *obsolete* : MYSTERIOUS, UNCANNY
**2 a** : strange or clumsy in shape or appearance : OUTLANDISH **b** : lacking in polish and grace : RUGGED ⟨*uncouth* verse⟩ **c** : awkward and uncultivated in appearance, manner, or behavior
— **un·couth·ly** *adverb*
— **un·couth·ness** *noun*

**un·cov·er** \-'kə-vər\ (14th century)
*transitive verb*
**1** : to make known : bring to light : DISCLOSE, REVEAL
**2** : to expose to view by removing some covering

**3 a** : to take the cover from **b** : to remove the hat from
**4** : to deprive of protection
*intransitive verb*
**1** : to remove a cover or covering
**2** : to take off the hat as a token of respect

**un·cov·ered** \-'vərd\ *adjective* (15th century)
: not covered: as **a** : not supplied with a covering **b** : not covered by insurance or included in a social insurance or welfare program **c** : not covered by collateral ⟨an *uncovered* note⟩

**un·cre·at·ed** \ˌən-krē-'ā-təd\ *adjective* (circa 1549)
**1** : not existing by creation : ETERNAL, SELF-EXISTENT
**2** : not yet created

**un·crit·i·cal** \ˌən-'kri-ti-kəl\ *adjective* (1659)
**1** : not critical : lacking in discrimination
**2** : showing lack or improper use of critical standards or procedures
— **un·crit·i·cal·ly** \-k(ə-)lē\ *adverb*

**un·cross** \-'krȯs\ *transitive verb* (1599)
: to change from a crossed position

**un·crown** \-'kraȯn\ *transitive verb* (14th century)
: to take the crown from : DEPOSE, DETHRONE

**un·crum·ple** \-'krəm-pəl\ *transitive verb* (1611)
: to restore to an original smooth condition

**un·crys·tal·ized** \-'kris-tə-ˌlīzd\ *adjective* (1759)
: not crystallized; *also* : not finally or definitely formed

**unc·tion** \'əŋ(k)-shən\ *noun* [Middle English *unctioun*, from Latin *unction-, unctio*, from *unguere* to anoint — more at OINTMENT] (14th century)
**1** : the act of anointing as a rite of consecration or healing
**2** : something used for anointing : OINTMENT, UNGUENT
**3 a** : religious or spiritual fervor or the expression of such fervor **b** : exaggerated, assumed, or superficial earnestness of language or manner : UNCTUOUSNESS

**unc·tu·ous** \'əŋ(k)-chə-wəs, -chəs, -shwəs\ *adjective* [Middle English, from Middle French or Medieval Latin; Middle French *unctueux*, from Medieval Latin *unctuosus*, from Latin *unctus* act of anointing, from *unguere* to anoint] (14th century)
**1 a** : FATTY, OILY **b** : smooth and greasy in texture or appearance
**2** : PLASTIC ⟨fine *unctuous* clay⟩
**3** : full of unction; *especially* : revealing or marked by a smug, ingratiating, and false earnestness or spirituality
— **unc·tu·ous·ly** *adverb*
— **unc·tu·ous·ness** *noun*

**un·curl** \ˌən-'kər(-ə)l\ (1588)
*intransitive verb*
: to become straightened out from a curled or coiled position
*transitive verb*
: to straighten the curls of : UNROLL

**un·cus** \'əŋ-kəs\ *noun, plural* **un·ci** \'əŋ-ˌkī, -ˌkē; 'ən-ˌsī\ [New Latin, from Latin, hook — more at ANGLE] (1826)
: a hooked anatomical part or process

**un·cut** \ˌən-'kət\ *adjective* (1548)
**1** : not cut down or cut into
**2** : not shaped by cutting ⟨an *uncut* diamond⟩
**3** *of a book* : not having the folds of the leaves slit
**4** : not abridged, curtailed, or expurgated ⟨the *uncut* version of the film⟩
**5** : not diluted or adulterated ⟨*uncut* vinegar⟩ ⟨*uncut* heroin⟩

**un·daunt·able** \ˌən-'dȯn-tə-bəl, -'dän-\ *adjective* (1587)
: incapable of being daunted : FEARLESS

**un·daunt·ed** \-təd\ *adjective* (1587)
: courageously resolute especially in the face of danger or difficulty : not discouraged
— **un·daunt·ed·ly** *adverb*

**un·dead** \ˌən-'ded\ *noun, plural* **undead** (1897)
**1** : VAMPIRE 1
**2** : ZOMBIE 1b

**un·de·bat·able** \ˌən-di-'bā-tə-bəl\ *adjective* (1869)
: not subject to debate : INDISPUTABLE
— **un·de·bat·ably** \-blē\ *adverb*

**un·de·ceive** \ˌən-di-'sēv\ *transitive verb* (1598)
: to free from deception, illusion, or error

**un·de·cil·lion** \ˌən-di-'sil-yən\ *noun, often attributive* [Latin *undecim* eleven (from *unus* one + *decem* ten) + English *-illion* (as in *million*) — more at ONE, TEN] (1931)
— see NUMBER table

**un·dec·y·le·nic acid** \ˌən-ˌde-sə-'le-nik-, -'lē-\ *noun* [*undecylene* (C₁₁H₂₂)] (1879)
: an acid $C_{11}H_{20}O_2$ found in perspiration, obtained commercially from castor oil, and used in the treatment of fungal infections (as ringworm) of the skin

**un·dem·o·crat·ic** \ˌən-ˌde-mə-'kra-tik\ *adjective* (1839)
: not democratic : not agreeing with democratic practice or ideals
— **un·dem·o·crat·i·cal·ly** \-ti-k(ə-)lē\ *adverb*

**un·de·mon·stra·tive** \ˌən-di-'män(t)-strə-tiv\ *adjective* (1846)
: restrained in expression of feeling : RESERVED
— **un·de·mon·stra·tive·ly** *adverb*
— **un·de·mon·stra·tive·ness** *noun*

**un·de·ni·able** \ˌən-di-'nī-ə-bəl\ *adjective* (1547)
**1** : plainly true : INCONTESTABLE
**2** : unquestionably excellent or genuine ⟨an applicant with *undeniable* references⟩
— **un·de·ni·able·ness** *noun*
— **un·de·ni·ably** \-blē\ *adverb*

**¹un·der** \'ən-dər\ *adverb* [Middle English, adverb & preposition, from Old English; akin to Old High German *untar* under, Latin *inferus* situated beneath, lower, *infra* below, Sanskrit *adha*] (before 12th century)
**1** : in or into a position below or beneath something
**2** : below or short of some quantity, level, or limit ⟨$10 or *under*⟩ — often used in combination ⟨*under*staffed⟩
**3** : in or into a condition of subjection, subordination, or unconsciousness
**4** : down to defeat, ruin, or death
**5** : so as to be covered

**²under** *preposition* (before 12th century)
**1** : below or beneath so as to be overhung, surmounted, covered, protected, or concealed by ⟨*under* sunny skies⟩ ⟨a soft heart *under* a stern exterior⟩ ⟨*under* cover of darkness⟩
**2 a** : subject to the authority, control, guidance, or instruction of ⟨served *under* the general⟩ ⟨*under* the terms of the contract⟩ **b** : receiving or undergoing the action or effect of ⟨*under* pressure⟩ ⟨courage *under* fire⟩ ⟨*under* the influence of alcohol⟩ ⟨the image of a point *under* a mapping⟩
**3** : within the group or designation of ⟨*under* this heading⟩
**4** : less or lower than (as in size, amount, or rank); *especially* : falling short of a standard or required degree ⟨*under* the legal age⟩ ⟨*under* par⟩

**³under** *adjective* (14th century)
**1 a** : lying or placed below, beneath, or on the ventral side — often used in combination ⟨*under*lip⟩ **b** : facing or protruding downward
**2** : lower in rank or authority : SUBORDINATE
**3** : lower than usual, proper, or desired in amount, quality, or degree ⟨an *under* dose of medicine⟩

**un·der·achiev·er** \ˌən-dər-ə-'chē-vər\ *noun* (1952)
: a person and especially a student who fails to attain a predicted level of achievement or does not do as well as expected

— **un·der·achieve** \-ə-'chēv\ *intransitive verb*

— **un·der·achieve·ment** \-mənt\ *noun*

**un·der·act** \ˌən-dər-'akt\ (circa 1623)
*transitive verb*
: to perform (a dramatic part) with restraint for effect : UNDERPLAY
*intransitive verb*
: to perform feebly or with restraint

**un·der·ac·tive** \-'ak-tiv\ *adjective* (1959)
: characterized by an abnormally low level of activity ⟨an *underactive* thyroid gland⟩
— **un·der·ac·tiv·i·ty** \-'ti-və-tē\ *noun*

**un·der·age** \ˌən-dər-'āj\ *adjective* (1594)
**1** : of less than mature or legal age
**2** : done by or involving underage persons ⟨*underage* drinking⟩

**un·der·ap·pre·ci·at·ed** \ˌən-dər-ə-'prē-shē-ˌā-təd\ *adjective* (1968)
: not duly appreciated

¹**un·der·arm** \'ən-dər-ˌärm\ *adjective* (1816)
**1** : UNDERHAND 4
**2** : placed under or on the underside of the arm ⟨*underarm* seams⟩

²**un·der·arm** \ˌən-dər-'ärm\ *adverb* (circa 1909)
: UNDERHAND

³**un·der·arm** \'ən-dər-ˌärm\ *noun* (1923)
**1** : ARMPIT 1
**2** : the part of a garment that covers the underside of the arm

**un·der·bel·ly** \'ən-dər-ˌbe-lē\ *noun* (1607)
**1** : the underside of a body or mass
**2** : a vulnerable area

**un·der·bid** \ˌən-dər-'bid\ *verb* **-bid; -bid·ding** (circa 1677)
*transitive verb*
**1** : to bid less than (a competing bidder)
**2** : to bid (a hand of cards) at less than the strength of the hand warrants
*intransitive verb*
: to bid too low
— **un·der·bid·der** *noun*

**un·der·body** \'ən-dər-ˌbä-dē\ *noun* (1879)
: the lower part of something: as **a** : the lower part of an animal's body : UNDERPARTS **b** : the lower parts of the body of a vehicle

**un·der·boss** \'ən-dər-ˌbȯs\ *noun* (1942)
: a boss ranking next below the head of a branch of a crime syndicate

**un·der·bred** \ˌən-dər-'bred\ *adjective* (1650)
: marked by lack of good breeding : ILL-BRED

**un·der·brim** \'ən-dər-ˌbrim\ *noun* (1886)
: a facing on the underside of a hat brim

**un·der·brush** \'ən-dər-ˌbrəsh\ *noun* (1775)
**1** : shrubs, bushes, or small trees growing beneath large trees in a wood or forest : BRUSH
**2** : a tangled, obstructing, or impeding mass

**un·der·bud·get·ed** \ˌən-dər-'bə-jə-təd\ *adjective* (1965)
: provided with an inadequate budget

**un·der·cap·i·tal·ized** \-'ka-pə-t²l-ˌīzd, -'kap-t²l-\ *adjective* (1967)
: having too little capital for efficient operation

**un·der·card** \'ən-dər-ˌkärd\ *noun* (1948)
: a program (as of boxing matches) supporting the featured match

**un·der·car·riage** \'ən-dər-ˌkar-ij\ *noun* (circa 1796)
**1** : a supporting framework (as of an automobile)
**2** *chiefly British* : the landing gear of an airplane

**un·der·charge** \ˌən-dər-'chärj\ *transitive verb* (1633)
: to charge (as a person) too little
— **undercharge** \'ən-dər-ˌ\ *noun*

**un·der·class** \'ən-dər-ˌklas\ *noun* (1918)
: the lowest social stratum usually made up of disadvantaged minority groups

**un·der·class·man** \ˌən-dər-'klas-mən\ *noun* (1871)
: a member of the freshman or sophomore class in a school or college

**un·der·clothes** \'ən-dər-ˌklō(th)z\ *noun plural* (circa 1859)
: UNDERWEAR

**un·der·cloth·ing** \-ˌklō-thiŋ\ *noun* (1835)
: UNDERWEAR

**un·der·coat** \-ˌkōt\ *noun* (1648)
**1** : a coat or jacket worn under another
**2** : a growth of short hair or fur partly concealed by the longer and usually coarser guard hairs of a mammal
**3 a** : a coat (as of paint) applied as a base for another coat **b** : UNDERCOATING
**4** *dialect* : PETTICOAT

**un·der·coat·ing** \-ˌkō-tiŋ\ *noun* (1922)
: a usually asphalt-based waterproof coating applied to the underside of a vehicle

**un·der·cool** \ˌən-dər-'kül\ *transitive verb* (1902)
: SUPERCOOL

**un·der·count** \-'kaunt\ *transitive verb* (1951)
: to count fewer than the actual number of
— **undercount** *noun*

**un·der·cov·er** \-'kə-vər\ *adjective* (1920)
: acting or executed in secret; *specifically* : employed or engaged in spying or secret investigation ⟨an *undercover* agent⟩

**un·der·croft** \'ən-dər-ˌkrȯft\ *noun* [Middle English, from *under* + *crofte* crypt, from Middle Dutch, from Medieval Latin *crupta,* from Latin *crypta* — more at CRYPT] (14th century)
: a subterranean room; *especially* : a vaulted chamber under a church

**un·der·cur·rent** \-ˌkər-ənt, -ˌkə-rənt\ *noun* (1683)
**1** : a current below the upper currents or surface
**2** : a hidden opinion, feeling, or tendency often contrary to the one publicly shown
— **undercurrent** *adjective*

¹**un·der·cut** \ˌən-dər-'kət\ *verb* **-cut; -cut·ting** (1598)
*transitive verb.*
**1** : to cut away the underpart of ⟨*undercut* a vein of ore⟩
**2** : to cut away material from the underside of (an object) so as to leave an overhanging portion in relief
**3** : to offer to sell at lower prices than or to work for lower wages than (a competitor)
**4** : to cut obliquely into (a tree) below the main cut and on the side toward which the tree will fall
**5** : to strike (a ball) with a downward glancing blow so as to give a backspin or elevation to the shot
**6** : to undermine or destroy the force, value, or effectiveness of ⟨inflation *undercuts* consumer buying power⟩
*intransitive verb*
: to perform the action of cutting away beneath

²**un·der·cut** \'ən-dər-ˌkət\ *noun* (1859)
**1** *British* : TENDERLOIN 1
**2** : the action or result of cutting away from the underside or lower part of something
**3** : a notch cut in the base of a tree before felling to determine the direction of falling and to prevent splitting

**un·der·de·vel·oped** \ˌən-dər-di-'ve-ləpt\ *adjective* (1892)
**1** : not normally or adequately developed ⟨*underdeveloped* muscles⟩ ⟨an *underdeveloped* film⟩
**2** : having a relatively low economic level of industrial production and standard of living (as from lack of capital) ⟨*underdeveloped* nations⟩
— **un·der·de·vel·op·ment** \-ləp-mənt\ *noun*

**un·der·dog** \'ən-dər-ˌdȯg\ *noun* (1887)
**1** : a loser or predicted loser in a struggle or contest
**2** : a victim of injustice or persecution

**un·der·done** \ˌən-dər-'dən\ *adjective* (1683)
: not thoroughly cooked : RARE

**un·der·draw·ers** \'ən-dər-ˌdrȯ(-ə)rz\ *noun plural* (1894)
: an article of underwear for the lower body

**un·der·ed·u·cat·ed** \ˌən-dər-'e-jə-ˌkā-təd\ *adjective* (1856)
: poorly educated

**un·der·em·pha·sis** \ˌən-dər-'em(p)-fə-səs\ *noun* (1964)
: less emphasis than is possible or desirable

**un·der·em·pha·size** \-ˌsīz\ *transitive verb* (1967)
: to fail to emphasize adequately

**un·der·em·ployed** \ˌən-dər-im-'plȯid\ *adjective* (1908)
: having less than full-time, regular, or adequate employment

**un·der·em·ploy·ment** \-'plȯi-mənt\ *noun* (1910)
**1** : the condition in which people in a labor force are employed at less than full-time or regular jobs or at jobs inadequate with respect to their training or economic needs
**2** : the condition of being underemployed

**un·der·es·ti·mate** \ˌən-dər-'es-tə-ˌmāt\ *transitive verb* (1812)
**1** : to estimate as being less than the actual size, quantity, or number
**2** : to place too low a value on : UNDERRATE
— **un·der·es·ti·mate** \-mət\ *noun*
— **un·der·es·ti·ma·tion** \-ˌes-tə-'mā-shən\ *noun*

**un·der·ex·pose** \ˌən-dər-ik-'spōz\ *transitive verb* (1861)
: to expose insufficiently; *especially* : to expose (as film) to insufficient radiation (as light)
— **un·der·ex·po·sure** \-'spō-zhər\ *noun*

**un·der·feed** \ˌən-dər-'fēd\ *transitive verb* **-fed** \-'fed\; **-feed·ing** (1659)
: to feed with too little food

**un·der·fi·nanced** \-fə-'nan(t)st, -'fī-ˌ, -fī-'\ *adjective* (1922)
: inadequately financed

**un·der·foot** \-'fut\ *adverb* (13th century)
**1** : under the foot especially against the ground ⟨trampled the flowers *underfoot*⟩
**2** : below, at, or before one's feet ⟨warm sand *underfoot*⟩
**3** : in the way ⟨children always getting *underfoot*⟩

**un·der·fund** \-'fənd\ *transitive verb* (1968)
: to provide insufficient funds for

**un·der·fur** \'ən-dər-ˌfər\ *noun* (1877)
: an undercoat of fur especially when thick and soft

**un·der·gar·ment** \-ˌgär-mənt\ *noun* (1530)
: a garment to be worn under another

**un·der·gird** \ˌən-dər-'gərd\ *transitive verb* (1526)
**1** *archaic* : to make secure underneath ⟨took measures to *undergird* the ship —Acts 27:17 (Revised Standard Version)⟩
**2** : to form the basis or foundation of : STRENGTHEN, SUPPORT ⟨facts and statistics subtly *undergird* his commentary —Susan Q. Stranahan⟩

**un·der·glaze** \'ən-dər-ˌglāz\ *adjective* (1879)
: applied or suitable for applying before the glaze is put on ⟨*underglaze* decorations⟩ ⟨*underglaze* colors⟩
— **underglaze** *noun*

**un·der·go** \ˌən-dər-'gō\ *transitive verb* **-went** \-'went\; **-gone** \-'gȯn *also* -'gän\; **-go·ing** \-'gō-iŋ, -'gȯ(-)iŋ\ (14th century)
**1** : to submit to : ENDURE
**2** : to go through : EXPERIENCE
**3** *obsolete* : UNDERTAKE
**4** *obsolete* : to partake of

**un·der·grad** \'ən-dər-ˌgrad\ *noun* (1827)
: UNDERGRADUATE

**un·der·grad·u·ate** \ˌən-dər-'gra-jə-wət, -ˌwāt; -'graj-wət\ *noun* (1630)
: a student at a college or university who has not taken a first and especially a bachelor's degree
— **undergraduate** *adjective*

**¹un·der·ground** \ˌən-dər-'graùnd\ *adverb* (1571)
**1** : beneath the surface of the earth
**2** : in or into hiding or secret operation

**²underground** \'ən-dər-ˌ\ *noun* (1594)
**1** : a subterranean space or channel
**2** : an underground city railway system
**3 a** : a movement or group organized in strict secrecy among citizens especially in an occupied country for maintaining communications, popular solidarity, and concerted resistive action pending liberation **b** : a clandestine conspiratorial organization set up for revolutionary or other disruptive purposes especially against a civil order **c** : an unofficial, unsanctioned, or illegal but informal movement or group; *especially* : a usually avant-garde group or movement that functions outside the establishment

**³un·der·ground** \'ən-dər-ˌgraùnd\ *adjective* (1610)
**1** : being, growing, operating, or situated below the surface of the ground
**2** : conducted by secret means
**3 a** : existing outside the establishment ⟨an *underground* literary reputation⟩ **b** : existing outside the purview of tax collectors or statisticians ⟨the *underground* economy⟩
**4 a** : produced or published outside the establishment especially by the avant-garde ⟨*underground* movies⟩ ⟨*underground* newspapers⟩ **b** : of or relating to the avant-garde underground ⟨an *underground* moviemaker⟩ ⟨an *underground* theater⟩

**un·der·ground·er** \'ən-dər-ˌgraùn-dər\ *noun* (1882)
: a member of the underground

**Underground Railroad** *noun* (1842)
: a system of cooperation among active antislavery people in the U.S. before 1863 by which fugitive slaves were secretly helped to reach the North or Canada — called also *Underground Railway*

**un·der·growth** \'ən-dər-ˌgrōth\ *noun* (1600)
: low growth on the floor of a forest including seedlings and saplings, shrubs, and herbs

**¹un·der·hand** \'ən-dər-ˌhand\ *adverb* (1538)
**1 a** : in a clandestine manner **b** *archaic* : in a quiet or unobtrusive manner
**2** : with the target seen below the hand holding the bow
**3** : with an underhand motion ⟨bowl *underhand*⟩ ⟨pitch *underhand*⟩

**²underhand** *adjective* (1545)
**1** : aimed so that the target is seen below the hand holding the bow ⟨*underhand* shooting at long range⟩
**2** : UNDERHANDED
**3** : done so as to evade notice
**4** : made with the hand brought forward and up from below the shoulder level

**¹un·der·hand·ed** \ˌən-dər-'han-dəd\ *adverb* (circa 1822)
: UNDERHAND

**²underhanded** *adjective* (1853)
: marked by secrecy, chicanery, and deception
: not honest and aboveboard : SLY
*synonym* see SECRET
— **un·der·hand·ed·ly** *adverb*
— **un·der·hand·ed·ness** *noun*

**un·der·in·flat·ed** \ˌən-dər-in-'flā-təd\ *adjective* (1928)
: not sufficiently inflated ⟨*underinflated* tires⟩
— **un·der·in·fla·tion** \-'flā-shən\ *noun*

**un·der·in·sured** \-'shùrd\ *adjective* (1893)
: not sufficiently insured

**un·der·in·vest·ment** \ˌən-dər-in-'ves(t)-mənt\ *noun* (1940)
: an insufficient amount of investment

**un·der·laid** \ˌən-dər-'lād\ *adjective* (before 12th century)
**1** : laid or placed underneath
**2** : having something laid or lying underneath

**¹un·der·lay** \-'lā\ *transitive verb* **-laid** \-'lād\; **-lay·ing** (before 12th century)
**1** : to cover, line, or traverse the bottom of : give support to on the underside or below
**2** : to raise or support by something laid under

**²un·der·lay** \'ən-dər-ˌlā\ *noun* (1612)
: something that is or is designed to be laid under

**un·der·lay·ment** \ˌən-dər-'lā-mənt\ *noun* (1949)
: UNDERLAY

**un·der·let** \ˌən-dər-'let\ *transitive verb* **-let; -let·ting** (1677)
**1** : to let below the real value
**2** : SUBLET

**un·der·lie** \-'lī\ *transitive verb* **-lay** \-'lā\; **-lain** \-'lān\; **-ly·ing** \-'lī-iŋ\ (before 12th century)
**1** *archaic* : to be subject or amenable to
**2** : to lie or be situated under
**3** : to be at the basis of : form the foundation of : SUPPORT ⟨ideas *underlying* the revolution⟩
**4** : to exist as a claim or security superior and prior to (another)

**¹un·der·line** \'ən-dər-ˌlīn, ˌən-dər-'\ *transitive verb* (1721)
**1** : to mark (as a word) with a line underneath
**2** : to put emphasis on : STRESS
**3** : to show clearly or emphatically

**²un·der·line** \'ən-dər-ˌlīn\ *noun* (1886)
**1** : the outline of a quadruped's underbody; *also* : the ventral surface of a quadruped's body
**2** : a horizontal line placed underneath something

**un·der·ling** \'ən-dər-liŋ\ *noun* (12th century)
: one who is under the orders of another : SUBORDINATE, INFERIOR

**un·der·lip** \ˌən-dər-'lip\ *noun* (1669)
: the lower lip

**un·der·ly·ing** \ˌən-dər-'lī-iŋ\ *adjective* (1611)
**1 a** : lying beneath or below ⟨the *underlying* rock is shale⟩ **b** : BASIC, FUNDAMENTAL ⟨an investigation of the *underlying* issues⟩
**2** : evident only on close inspection : IMPLICIT
**3** : anterior and prior in claim ⟨*underlying* mortgage⟩
**4** : of or being present in deep structure ⟨*underlying* word order⟩

**un·der·ly·ing·ly** \-'lī-iŋ-lē\ *adverb* (1973)
: in deep structure

**un·der·manned** \ˌən-dər-'mand\ *adjective* (circa 1867)
: inadequately staffed

**un·der·mine** \-'mīn\ *transitive verb* (14th century)
**1** : to excavate the earth beneath : form a mine under : SAP
**2** : to wash away supporting material from under
**3** : to subvert or weaken insidiously or secretly
**4** : to weaken or ruin by degrees
*synonym* see WEAKEN

**un·der·most** \'ən-dər-ˌmōst\ *adjective* (1555)
: lowest in relative position
— **undermost** *adverb*

**¹un·der·neath** \ˌən-dər-'nēth\ *preposition* [Middle English *undernethe*, preposition & adverb, from Old English *underneothan*, from *under* + *neothan* below — more at BENEATH] (before 12th century)
**1 a** : directly beneath ⟨write the date *underneath* the address⟩ **b** : close under especially so as to be hidden ⟨treachery lying *underneath* a mask of friendliness⟩ ⟨wore a swimsuit *underneath* his slacks⟩
**2** : under subjection to

**²underneath** *adverb* (before 12th century)
**1** : under or below an object or a surface : BENEATH
**2** : on the lower side

**— underneath** *adjective*

**un·der·nour·ished** \ˌən-dər-'nər-isht, -'nə-risht\ *adjective* (1910)
**1** : supplied with less than the minimum amount of the foods essential for sound health and growth
**2** : poorly supplied with vital elements or qualities ⟨*undernourished* independent libraries⟩
— **un·der·nour·ish·ment** \-'nər-ish-mənt, -'nə-rish-\ *noun*

**un·der·nu·tri·tion** \-nù-'tri-shən, -nyü-\ *noun* (circa 1889)
: deficient bodily nutrition due to inadequate food intake or faulty assimilation

**un·der·paint·ing** \'ən-dər-ˌpān-tiŋ\ *noun* (1866)
: preliminary painting; *especially* : such painting done on a canvas or panel and covered completely or partially by the final layers of paint

**un·der·pants** \'ən-dər-ˌpan(t)s\ *noun plural* (1925)
: a usually short undergarment for the lower trunk : DRAWERS
*word history* see PANTALOON

**un·der·part** \-ˌpärt\ *noun* (1662)
**1** : a part lying on the lower side especially of a bird or mammal
**2** : a subordinate or auxiliary part or role

**un·der·pass** \-ˌpas\ *noun* (1903)
: a crossing of a highway and another way (as a road or railroad) at different levels; *also* : the lower level of such a crossing

**un·der·pay** \ˌən-dər-'pā\ *transitive verb* **-paid** \-'pād\; **-pay·ing** (1817)
: to pay less than what is normal or required ⟨*underpay* taxes⟩
— **un·der·pay·ment** *noun*

**un·der·pin** \-'pin\ *transitive verb* (1522)
**1** : SUPPORT, SUBSTANTIATE ⟨*underpin* a thesis with evidence⟩
**2** : to form part of, strengthen, or replace the foundation of ⟨*underpin* a structure⟩ ⟨*underpin* a sagging building⟩

**un·der·pin·ning** \'ən-dər-ˌpi-niŋ\ *noun* (1538)
**1** : the material and construction (as a foundation) used for support of a structure
**2** : something that serves as a foundation : BASIS, SUPPORT — often used in plural ⟨the philosophical *underpinnings* of educational methods⟩
**3** : UNDERWEAR — usually used in plural
**4** : a person's legs — usually used in plural

**un·der·play** \ˌən-dər-'plā\ (1896)
*intransitive verb*
: to play a role with subdued force
*transitive verb*
**1** : to act or present (as a role or a scene) with restraint : PLAY DOWN
**2** : to play a card lower than (a held high card)

**un·der·plot** \'ən-dər-ˌplät\ *noun* (1668)
: SUBPLOT 1

**un·der·pop·u·lat·ed** \ˌən-dər-'pä-pyə-ˌlā-təd\ *adjective* (1884)
: having a lower density of population than is normal or desirable

**un·der·pow·ered** \-'paù(-ə)rd\ *adjective* (1905)
**1** : driven by an engine of insufficient power
**2** : having or supplied with insufficient power

**un·der·pre·pared** \-prə-'pard, -'perd\ *adjective* (1964)
: inadequately prepared

**un·der·price** \-'prīs\ *transitive verb* (1756)
**1** : to price below what is normal or below the real value
**2** : to undercut (a competitor) in prices

**un·der·priv·i·leged** \-'priv-lijd, -'pri-və-\ *adjective* (1896)
**1** : deprived through social or economic condition of some of the fundamental rights of all members of a civilized society
**2** : of or relating to underprivileged people ⟨*underprivileged* areas of the city⟩

**un·der·pro·duc·tion** \-prə-'dək-shən\ *noun* (1887)
: the production of less than enough to satisfy the demand or of less than the usual amount

**un·der·proof** \ˌən-dər-'prüf\ *adjective* (1857)
: containing less alcohol than proof spirit

**un·der·pub·li·cized** \-'pə-blə-ˌsīzd\ *adjective* (1966)
: insufficiently publicized

**un·der·rate** \ˌən-də(r)-'rāt\ *transitive verb* (1650)
: to rate too low : UNDERVALUE

**un·der·re·act** \-rē-'akt\ *intransitive verb* (1965)
: to react with less than appropriate force or intensity

**un·der·re·port** \-ri-'pōrt, -'pȯrt\ *transitive verb* (1949)
: to report to be less than is actually the case : UNDERSTATE ⟨*underreports* his income⟩ ⟨the number of cases has been *underreported*⟩

**un·der·rep·re·sent·ed** \-ˌre-pri-'zen-təd\ *adjective* (1884)
: inadequately represented
— **un·der·rep·re·sen·ta·tion** \-ˌzen-'tā-shən, -zən-\ *noun*

¹**un·der·run** \-'rən\ *transitive verb* **-ran** \-'ran\; **-run; -run·ning** (1547)
**1** : to pass along under in order to examine (a cable)
**2** : to pass or extend under

²**un·der·run** \'ən-də(r)-ˌrən\ *noun* (1926)
: the amount by which something produced (as a cut of lumber) falls below an estimate

**un·der·sat·u·rat·ed** \ˌən-dər-'sa-chə-ˌrā-təd\ *adjective* (circa 1828)
: less than normally or adequately saturated

¹**un·der·score** \'ən-dər-ˌskōr, -ˌskȯr\ *transitive verb* (1771)
**1** : to draw a line under : UNDERLINE
**2** : to make evident : EMPHASIZE, STRESS
**3** : to provide (action on film) with accompanying music

²**underscore** *noun* (1901)
**1** : a line drawn under a word or line especially for emphasis or to indicate intent to italicize
**2** : music accompanying the action and dialogue of a film

¹**un·der·sea** \ˌən-dər-'sē\ *adjective* (1613)
**1** : being or carried on under the sea or under the surface of the sea ⟨*undersea* oil deposits⟩ ⟨*undersea* fighting⟩
**2** : designed for use under the surface of the sea ⟨an *undersea* fleet⟩

²**undersea** *or* **un·der·seas** \-'sēz\ *adverb* (1684)
: under the sea : beneath the surface of the sea ⟨photographs taken *undersea*⟩

**un·der·sec·re·tary** \ˌən-dər-'se-krə-ˌter-ē, -'se-kə-\ *noun* (1687)
: a secretary immediately subordinate to a principal secretary ⟨*undersecretary* of health⟩

**un·der·sell** \ˌən-dər-'sel\ *transitive verb* **-sold** \-'sōld\; **-sell·ing** (1622)
**1** : to sell articles cheaper than ⟨*undersell* a competitor⟩ ⟨we will not be *undersold*⟩
**2** : to sell cheaper than ⟨imported cars that *undersell* domestic ones⟩

**un·der·served** \ˌən-dər-'sərvd\ *adjective* (1710)
: provided with inadequate service

**un·der·sexed** \-'sekst\ *adjective* (1931)
: deficient in sexual desire

**un·der·shirt** \'ən-dər-ˌshərt\ *noun* (1648)
: a collarless undergarment with or without sleeves
— **un·der·shirt·ed** *adjective*

**un·der·shoot** \ˌən-dər-'shüt\ *transitive verb* **-shot** \-'shät\; **-shoot·ing** (circa 1661)
**1** : to shoot short of or below (a target)
**2** : to fall short of (a runway) in landing an airplane

**un·der·shorts** \'ən-dər-ˌshȯrts\ *noun plural* (1949)
: SHORT 4b

**un·der·shot** \'ən-dər-ˌshät\ *adjective* (1610)

**1** : moved by water passing beneath ⟨an *undershot* wheel⟩
**2** : having the lower incisor teeth or lower jaw projecting beyond the upper when the mouth is closed

**un·der·shrub** \'ən-dər-ˌshrəb, *especially Southern* -ˌsrəb\ *noun* (1598)
: SUBSHRUB

**un·der·side** \'ən-dər-ˌsīd, ˌən-dər-'\ *noun* (1680)
**1** : the side or surface lying underneath
**2** : a side usually hidden from sight; *specifically* : the more unpleasant or reprehensible side ⟨the *underside* of politics⟩

**un·der·signed** \'ən-dər-ˌsīnd\ *noun, plural* **undersigned** (1643)
: one whose name is signed at the end of a document ⟨the *undersigned* all agree⟩

**un·der·sized** \ˌən-dər-'sīzd\ *also* **un·der·size** \-'sīz\ *adjective* (1706)
: of a size less than is common, proper, normal, or average ⟨*undersized* trout⟩

**un·der·skirt** \'ən-dər-ˌskərt\ *noun* (1861)
: a skirt worn under an outer skirt; *especially* : PETTICOAT

**un·der·slung** \ˌən-dər-'sləŋ\ *adjective* (1903)
**1** *of a vehicle frame* : suspended below the axles
**2** : having a low center of gravity

**un·der·spin** \'ən-dər-ˌspin\ *noun* (1901)
: BACKSPIN

**un·der·staffed** \ˌən-dər-'staft\ *adjective* (1891)
: inadequately staffed
— **un·der·staff·ing** \-'sta-fiŋ\ *noun*

**un·der·stand** \ˌən-dər-'stand\ *verb* **-stood** \-'stüd\; **-stand·ing** [Middle English, from Old English *understandan*, from *under* + *standan* to stand] (before 12th century)
*transitive verb*
**1 a** : to grasp the meaning of ⟨*understand* Russian⟩ **b** : to grasp the reasonableness of ⟨his behavior is hard to *understand*⟩ **c** : to have thorough or technical acquaintance with or expertness in the practice of ⟨*understand* finance⟩ **d** : to be thoroughly familiar with the character and propensities of ⟨*understands* children⟩
**2** : to accept as a fact or truth or regard as plausible without utter certainty ⟨we *understand* that he is returning from abroad⟩
**3** : to interpret in one of a number of possible ways
**4** : to supply in thought as though expressed ⟨"to be married" is commonly *understood* after the word *engaged*⟩
*intransitive verb*
**1** : to have understanding : have the power of comprehension
**2** : to achieve a grasp of the nature, significance, or explanation of something
**3** : to believe or infer something to be the case
**4** : to show a sympathetic or tolerant attitude toward something ☆
— **un·der·stand·abil·i·ty** \-ˌstan-də-'bi-lə-tē\ *noun*
— **un·der·stand·able** \-'stan-də-bəl\ *adjective*

**un·der·stand·ably** \ˌən-dər-'stan-də-blē\ *adverb* (circa 1921)
: as can be easily understood : for understandable reasons ⟨is *understandably* nervous⟩

¹**un·der·stand·ing** \ˌən-dər-'stan-diŋ\ *noun* (before 12th century)
**1** : a mental grasp : COMPREHENSION
**2 a** : the power of comprehending; *especially* : the capacity to apprehend general relations of particulars **b** : the power to make experience intelligible by applying concepts and categories
**3 a** : friendly or harmonious relationship **b** : an agreement of opinion or feeling : adjustment of differences **c** : a mutual agreement not formally entered into but in some degree binding on each side
**4** : EXPLANATION, INTERPRETATION

**5** : SYMPATHY 3a

²**understanding** *adjective* (13th century)
**1** *archaic* : KNOWING, INTELLIGENT
**2** : endowed with understanding : TOLERANT, SYMPATHETIC
— **un·der·stand·ing·ly** \-'stan-diŋ-lē\ *adverb*

**un·der·state** \ˌən-dər-'stāt\ *transitive verb* (1824)
**1** : to represent as less than is the case
**2** : to state or present with restraint especially for effect
— **un·der·state·ment** \-mənt\ *noun*

**un·der·stat·ed** \-'stā-təd\ *adjective* (circa 1909)
: avoiding obvious emphasis or embellishment
— **un·der·stat·ed·ly** *adverb*

**un·der·steer** \'ən-dər-ˌstir\ *noun* (1936)
: the tendency of an automobile to turn less sharply than the driver intends
— **un·der·steer** \ˌən-dər-'\ *intransitive verb*

**un·der·stood** \ˌən-dər-'stüd\ *adjective* (1605)
**1** : fully apprehended
**2** : agreed upon
**3** : IMPLICIT

**un·der·sto·ry** \'ən-dər-ˌstōr-ē, -ˌstȯr-\ *noun* (1902)
**1** : an underlying layer of vegetation; *specifically* : the vegetative layer and especially the trees and shrubs between the forest canopy and the ground cover
**2** : the plants that form the understory

**un·der·strap·per** \-ˌstra-pər\ *noun* [³*under* + *strapper* one who harnesses horses] (circa 1704)
: a petty agent or subordinate : UNDERLING

**un·der·strength** \ˌən-dər-'streŋ(k)th\ *adjective* (1925)
: deficient in strength; *especially* : lacking sufficient or prescribed personnel

¹**un·der·study** \'ən-dər-ˌstə-dē, ˌən-dər-'\ (1874)
*intransitive verb*
: to study another actor's part in order to substitute in an emergency
*transitive verb*
: to prepare (as a part) as understudy; *also* : to prepare as understudy to (as an actor)

²**un·der·study** \'ən-dər-ˌstə-dē\ *noun* (1882)
: one who is prepared to act another's part or take over another's duties

**un·der·sup·ply** \ˌən-dər-sə-'plī\ *noun* (1848)
: an inadequate supply or amount

¹**un·der·sur·face** \'ən-dər-ˌsər-fəs\ *noun* (1733)
: UNDERSIDE

²**un·der·sur·face** \ˌən-dər-'sər-fəs\ *adjective* (circa 1934)
: existing or moving below the surface

**un·der·take** \ˌən-dər-'tāk\ *verb* **-took** \-'tùk\; **-tak·en** \-'tā-kən\; **-tak·ing** (14th century)

---

☆ **SYNONYMS**
**Understand, comprehend, appreciate** mean to have a clear or complete idea of. UNDERSTAND and COMPREHEND are very often interchangeable. UNDERSTAND may, however, stress the fact of having attained a firm mental grasp of something ⟨orders that were fully *understood* and promptly obeyed⟩. COMPREHEND may stress the process of coming to grips with something intellectually ⟨I have trouble *comprehending* your reasons for doing this⟩. APPRECIATE implies a just evaluation or judgment of a thing's value or nature ⟨failed to *appreciate* the risks involved⟩.

---

\ə\ abut \ᵊ\ kitten \ər\ further \a\ ash \ā\ ace
\ä\ mop, mar \aù\ out \ch\ chin \e\ bet \ē\ easy
\g\ go \i\ hit \ī\ ice \j\ job \ŋ\ sing \ō\ go
\ȯ\ law \ȯi\ boy \th\ thin \th̲\ the \ü\ loot \ù\ foot
\y\ yet \zh\ vision    *see also* Guide to Pronunciation

*transitive verb*
**1 :** to take upon oneself : set about : ATTEMPT ⟨*undertake* a task⟩ ⟨*undertake* to learn to swim⟩
**2 :** to put oneself under obligation to perform; *also* **:** to accept as a charge or responsibility ⟨the lawyer who *undertook* the case⟩
**3 :** GUARANTEE, PROMISE
*intransitive verb*
*archaic* **:** to give surety or assume responsibility

**un·der·tak·er** \ˌən-dər-ˈtā-kər, *2 is* ˈən-dər-\ *noun* (1615)
**1 :** one that undertakes : one that takes the risk and management of business : ENTREPRENEUR
**2 :** one whose business is to prepare the dead for burial and to arrange and manage funerals
**3 :** an Englishman taking over forfeited lands in Ireland in the 16th and 17th centuries

**un·der·tak·ing** \ˈən-dər-ˌtā-kiŋ, ˌən-dər-ˈ; *1b is* ˈən-dər-, *only*\ *noun* (15th century)
**1 a :** the act of one who undertakes or engages in a project or business **b :** the business of an undertaker
**2 :** something undertaken : ENTERPRISE
**3 :** PLEDGE, GUARANTEE

**un·der·ten·ant** \ˈən-dər-ˌte-nənt\ *noun* (1546)
**:** one who holds lands or tenements by a sub-lease

**under–the–counter** *adjective* [from the hiding of illicit wares under the counter of stores where they are sold] (1926)
**:** surreptitious and usually irregular or illicit ⟨*under-the-counter* liquor sales⟩

**under–the–table** *adjective* (1948)
**:** covert and usually unlawful ⟨*under-the-table* payoffs⟩

**un·der·thrust** \ˌən-dər-ˈthrəst\ *transitive verb* **-thrust; -thrust·ing** (1893)
**:** to insert (a faulted rock mass) into position under a passive rock mass

**un·der·tone** \ˈən-dər-ˌtōn\ *noun* (1806)
**1 :** a low or subdued utterance or accompanying sound
**2 :** a quality (as of emotion) underlying the surface of an utterance or action
**3 :** a subdued color; *specifically* **:** a color seen through and modifying another color

**un·der·tow** \-ˌtō\ *noun* (1817)
**1 :** the current beneath the surface that sets seaward or along the beach when waves are breaking upon the shore
**2 :** an underlying current, force, or tendency that is in opposition to what is apparent

**un·der·trick** \-ˌtrik\ *noun* (1903)
**:** any of the tricks by which a declarer in bridge falls short of making the contract

**un·der·used** \ˌən-dər-ˈyüzd\ *adjective* (1960)
**:** not fully used

**un·der·uti·lize** \ˌən-dər-ˈyü-t°l-ˌīz\ *transitive verb* (1951)
**:** to utilize less than fully or below the potential use
— **un·der·uti·li·za·tion** \ˈən-dər-ˌyü-t°l-ə-ˈzā-shən\ *noun*

**un·der·val·u·a·tion** \ˌən-dər-ˌval-yə-ˈwā-shən\ *noun* (1653)
**1 :** the act of undervaluing
**2 :** a value below the real worth

**un·der·val·ue** \-ˈval-(ˌ)yü\ *transitive verb* (1599)
**1 :** to value, rate, or estimate below the real worth ⟨*undervalue* stock⟩
**2 :** to treat as having little value ⟨was *undervalued* as a poet⟩

**un·der·wa·ter** \ˌən-dər-ˈwȯ-tər, -ˈwä-\ *adjective* (1627)
**1 :** lying, growing, worn, or operating below the surface of the water
**2 :** being below the waterline of a ship
— **underwater** *adverb*

**un·der·way** \ˌən-dər-ˈwā\ *adjective* (1743)
**:** occurring, performed, or used while traveling or in motion ⟨*underway* replenishment of fuel⟩

**under way** *adverb* [probably from Dutch *onderweg*, from Middle Dutch *onderwegen*, literally, under or among the ways] (1751)
**1 :** in motion : not at anchor or aground
**2 :** into motion from a standstill
**3 :** in progress : AFOOT ⟨preparations were *under way*⟩ ⟨the season got *under way* with a bang⟩

**un·der·wear** \ˈən-dər-ˌwar, -ˌwer\ *noun* (circa 1879)
**:** clothing or an article of clothing worn next to the skin and under other clothing

**under weigh** *adverb* [by folk etymology] (1777)
**:** UNDER WAY

**¹un·der·weight** \ˌən-dər-ˈwāt\ *noun* (1596)
**:** weight below normal, average, or requisite weight

**²underweight** *adjective* (1890)
**:** weighing less than the normal or requisite amount

**un·der·whelm** \-ˈhwelm, -ˈwelm\ *transitive verb* [*under* + over*whelm*] (1949)
**:** to fail to impress or stimulate

**¹un·der·wing** \ˈən-dər-ˌwiŋ\ *noun* (1535)
**1 :** one of the posterior wings of an insect
**2 :** any of various noctuid moths (especially genus *Catocala*) that have the hind wings banded with contrasting colors (as red and black) — called also *underwing moth*
**3 :** the underside of a bird's wing

**²underwing** *adjective* (1896)
**:** placed or growing underneath the wing ⟨*underwing* rockets⟩

**un·der·wood** \ˈən-dər-ˌwùd\ *noun* (14th century)
**:** UNDERGROWTH, UNDERBRUSH

**un·der·wool** \-ˌwùl\ *noun* (1939)
**:** short woolly underfur

**un·der·world** \-ˌwərld\ *noun* (1608)
**1 :** the place of departed souls : HADES
**2** *archaic* **:** EARTH
**3 :** the side of the earth opposite to one : ANTIPODES
**4 :** a social sphere below the level of ordinary life; *especially* **:** the world of organized crime

**un·der·write** \ˈən-də(r)-ˌrīt, ˌən-də(r)-ˈ\ *verb* **-wrote** \-ˌrōt, -ˈrōt\; **-writ·ten** \-ˌri-t°n, -ˈri-t°n\; **-writ·ing** \-ˌrī-tiŋ, -ˈrī-\ (15th century)
*transitive verb*
**1 :** to write under or at the end of something else
**2 :** to set one's name to (an insurance policy) for the purpose of thereby becoming answerable for a designated loss or damage on consideration of receiving a premium percent : insure on life or property; *also* **:** to assume liability for (a sum or risk) as an insurer
**3 :** to subscribe to : agree to
**4 a :** to agree to purchase (as security issue) usually on a fixed date at a fixed price with a view to public distribution **b :** to guarantee financial support of
*intransitive verb*
**:** to work as an underwriter

**un·der·writ·er** \ˈən-də(r)-ˌrī-tər\ *noun* (1622)
**1 :** one that underwrites : GUARANTOR
**2 a :** one that underwrites a policy of insurance : INSURER **b :** one who selects risks to be solicited or rates the acceptability of risks solicited
**3 :** one that underwrites a security issue

**un·de·scend·ed** \ˌən-di-ˈsen-dəd\ *adjective* (1701)
**:** retained within the inguinal region rather than descending into the scrotum ⟨an *undescended* testis⟩

**un·de·sign·ing** \ˌən-di-ˈzī-niŋ\ *adjective* (1697)
**:** having no ulterior or fraudulent purpose : SINCERE

**¹un·de·sir·able** \-ˈzī-rə-bəl\ *adjective* (1667)
**:** not desirable : UNWANTED
— **un·de·sir·abil·i·ty** \-ˌzī-rə-bi-lə-tē\ *noun*

— **un·de·sir·able·ness** \-ˈzī-rə-bəl-nəs\ *noun*
— **un·de·sir·ably** \-blē\ *adverb*

**²undesirable** *noun* (1883)
**:** one that is undesirable

**un·de·vi·at·ing** \ˌən-ˈdē-vē-ˌā-tiŋ\ *adjective* (1732)
**:** keeping a true course : UNSWERVING ⟨served their country with *undeviating* loyalty and devotion⟩
— **un·de·vi·at·ing·ly** \-tiŋ-lē\ *adverb*

**un·dies** \ˈən-dēz\ *noun plural* [by shortening & alteration] (1900)
**:** UNDERWEAR; *especially* **:** women's underwear

**un·dine** \ˌən-ˈdēn, ˈən-\ *noun* [New Latin *undina*, from Latin *unda* wave — more at WATER] (1657)
**:** an elemental being in the theory of Paracelsus inhabiting water : WATER NYMPH

**un·dip·lo·mat·ic** \ˌən-ˌdi-plə-ˈma-tik\ *adjective* (circa 1828)
**:** not diplomatic; *especially* **:** TACTLESS
— **un·dip·lo·mat·i·cal·ly** \-ti-k(ə-)lē\ *adverb*

**un·di·rect·ed** \ˌən-də-ˈrek-təd, -dī-\ *adjective* (1596)
**:** not directed : not planned or guided ⟨*undirected* efforts⟩

**un·dis·guised** \ˌən-dis-ˈgīzd\ *adjective* (circa 1500)
**:** not disguised or concealed : FRANK, OPEN
— **un·dis·guis·ed·ly** \-ˈgī-zəd-lē\ *adverb*

**un·dis·so·ci·at·ed** \ˌən-di-ˈsō-shē-ˌā-təd, -sē-\ *adjective* (1899)
**:** not electrolytically dissociated

**un·do** \ˌən-ˈdü, ˈən-\ *verb* **-did** \-ˈdid\; **-done** \-ˈdən\; **-do·ing** \-ˈdü-iŋ\ (before 12th century)
*transitive verb*
**1 :** to open or loose by releasing a fastening
**2 :** to make of no effect or as if not done : make null : REVERSE
**3 a :** to ruin the worldly means, reputation, or hopes of **b :** to disturb the composure of : UPSET ⟨she's come *undone*⟩ **c :** SEDUCE 3
*intransitive verb*
**:** to come open or apart
— **un·do·er** \-ˈdü-ər\ *noun*

**un·dock** \-ˈdäk\ (1750)
*intransitive verb*
**:** to move away from a dock (as at sailing time)
*transitive verb*
**:** UNCOUPLE ⟨*undock* the shuttle from the space station⟩

**un·dog·mat·ic** \ˌən-dȯg-ˈma-tik, -däg-\ *adjective* (1857)
**:** not dogmatic : not committed to dogma
— **un·dog·mat·i·cal·ly** \-ti-k(ə-)lē\ *adverb*

**un·do·ing** \-ˈdü-iŋ\ *noun* (14th century)
**1 :** an act of loosening : UNFASTENING
**2 :** RUIN; *also* **:** a cause of ruin ⟨greed was to prove his *undoing*⟩
**3 :** ANNULMENT, REVERSAL

**un·done** \-ˈdən\ *adjective* (14th century)
**:** not done : not performed or finished

**un·dou·ble** \ˌən-ˈdə-bəl\ *verb* (circa 1611)
**:** UNFOLD, UNCLENCH

**un·dou·bled** \-ˈdə-bəld\ *adjective* (1598)
**:** not doubled

**un·doubt·ed** \-ˈdaù-təd\ *adjective* (15th century)
**:** not doubted : GENUINE, UNDISPUTED
— **un·doubt·ed·ly** *adverb*

**un·dra·mat·ic** \ˌən-drə-ˈma-tik\ *adjective* (1754)
**:** lacking dramatic force or quality : UNSPECTACULAR
— **un·dra·mat·i·cal·ly** \-ti-k(ə-)lē\ *adverb*

**un·drape** \ˌən-ˈdrāp\ *transitive verb* (1869)
**:** to strip of drapery : UNVEIL

**un·draw** \-ˈdrȯ\ *transitive verb* **-drew** \-ˈdrü\; **-drawn** \-ˈdrȯn\; **-draw·ing** (1677)
**:** to draw aside (as a curtain) : OPEN

**un·dreamed** \-'drem(p)t, -'drēmd\ *also* **un·dreamt** \-'drem(p)t\ *adjective* (1611)
: not dreamed : not thought of : UNIMAGINED ⟨technical advances *undreamed* of a few years ago⟩

¹**un·dress** \-'dres\ (1596)
*transitive verb*
**1** : to remove the clothes or covering of : DIVEST, STRIP
**2** : EXPOSE, REVEAL
*intransitive verb*
: to take off one's clothes : DISROBE

²**undress** *noun* (1683)
**1** : informal dress: as **a** : a loose robe or dressing gown **b** : ordinary dress — compare FULL DRESS
**2** : the state of being undressed

**un·dressed** \,ən-'drest\ *adjective* (1535)
: not dressed: as **a** : partially, improperly, or informally clothed **b** : not fully processed or finished ⟨*undressed* hides⟩ **c** : not cared for or tended ⟨an *undressed* wound⟩ ⟨*undressed* fields⟩

**un·drink·able** \,ən-'driŋ-kə-bəl\ *adjective* (1611)
: unsuitable or unpleasant to drink

**un·drunk** \-'drəŋk\ *adjective* (1637)
: not swallowed

**un·due** \-'dü, -'dyü\ *adjective* (14th century)
**1** : not due : not yet payable
**2** : exceeding or violating propriety or fitness : EXCESSIVE

**un·du·lant** \'ən-jə-lənt, 'ən-dyə-, 'ən-də-\ *adjective* (circa 1830)
**1** : rising and falling in waves
**2** : having a wavy form, outline, or surface ⟨played her approach shot onto the *undulant* green⟩

**undulant fever** *noun* (1896)
: a persistent human brucellosis marked by remittent fever, pain and swelling in the joints, and great weakness and contracted by contact with infected domestic animals or consumption of their products

¹**un·du·late** \'ən-jə-lət, 'ən-dyə-, 'ən-də-, -,lāt\ *or* **un·du·lat·ed** \-,lā-təd\ *adjective* [Latin *undulatus*, from (assumed) Latin *undula*, diminutive of Latin *unda* wave — more at WATER] (1658)
: having a wavy surface, edge, or markings ⟨the *undulate* margin of a leaf⟩

²**un·du·late** \-,lāt\ *verb* **-lat·ed; -lat·ing** [Late Latin *undula* small wave, from (assumed) Latin] (1664)
*intransitive verb*
**1** : to form or move in waves : FLUCTUATE
**2** : to rise and fall in volume, pitch, or cadence
**3** : to present a wavy appearance
*transitive verb*
: to cause to move in a wavy, sinuous, or flowing manner
*synonym* see SWING

**un·du·la·tion** \,ən-jə-'lā-shən, ,ən-dyə-, ,ən-də-\ *noun* (1646)
**1 a** : a rising and falling in waves **b** : a wavelike motion to and fro in a fluid or elastic medium propagated continuously among its particles but with little or no permanent translation of the particles in the direction of the propagation : VIBRATION
**2** : the pulsation caused by the vibrating together of two tones not quite in unison
**3** : a wavy appearance, outline, or form : WAVINESS

**un·du·la·to·ry** \'ən-jə-lə-,tōr-ē, 'ən-dyə-, 'ən-də-, -,tȯr-\ *adjective* (1728)
: of or relating to undulation : moving in or resembling waves : UNDULATING

**undulatory theory** *noun* (circa 1828)
: WAVE THEORY

**un·du·ly** \,ən-'dü-lē, -'dyü-\ *adverb* (14th century)
: in an undue manner : EXCESSIVELY

**un·du·ti·ful** \-'dü-ti-fəl, -'dyü-\ *adjective* (1582)
: not dutiful

— **un·du·ti·ful·ly** \-fə-lē\ *adverb*
— **un·du·ti·ful·ness** *noun*

**un·dy·ing** \-'dī-iŋ\ *adjective* (14th century)
: not dying : IMMORTAL, PERPETUAL

**un·earned** \-'ərnd\ *adjective* (13th century)
**1** : not gained by labor, service, or skill ⟨*unearned* income⟩
**2** : scored as a result of an error by the opposing team ⟨an *unearned* run⟩

**unearned increment** *noun* (1871)
: an increase in the value of property (as land) that is due to no labor or expenditure of the owner but to natural causes (as the increase of population) that create an increased demand for it

**un·earth** \,ən-'ərth\ *transitive verb* (15th century)
**1** : to dig up out of or as if out of the earth : EXHUME ⟨*unearth* a hidden treasure⟩ ⟨*unearth* a forgotten photo album⟩
**2** : to make known or public : bring to light ⟨*unearth* a plot⟩
*synonym* see DISCOVER

**un·earth·ly** \-lē\ *adjective* (1611)
: not earthly: as **a** : not terrestrial ⟨*unearthly* radio sources⟩ **b** : PRETERNATURAL, SUPERNATURAL ⟨an *unearthly* light⟩ **c** : WEIRD, EERIE ⟨*unearthly* howls⟩ **d** : not mundane : IDEAL ⟨*unearthly* love⟩ **e** : ABSURD 1, UNGODLY ⟨getting up at an *unearthly* hour⟩
— **un·earth·li·ness** *noun*

**un·ease** \,ən-'ēz\ *noun* (14th century)
: mental or spiritual discomfort: as **a** : vague dissatisfaction : MISGIVING **b** : ANXIETY, DISQUIET **c** : lack of ease (as in social relations) : EMBARRASSMENT

**un·eas·i·ly** \-'ē-zə-lē\ *adverb* (14th century)
: in an uneasy manner

¹**un·easy** \-'ē-zē\ *adjective* (13th century)
**1** : causing physical or mental discomfort ⟨*uneasy* news of captures and killings —Marjory S. Douglas⟩
**2** : not easy : DIFFICULT
**3** : marked by lack of ease : AWKWARD, EMBARRASSED ⟨gave an *uneasy* laugh⟩
**4** : APPREHENSIVE, WORRIED
**5** : RESTLESS, UNQUIET
**6** : PRECARIOUS, UNSTABLE ⟨an *uneasy* truce⟩
— **un·eas·i·ness** *noun*

²**uneasy** *adverb* (1596)
: UNEASILY

**un·eco·nom·ic** \,ən-,e-kə-'nä-mik, -,ē-kə-\ *or* **un·eco·nom·i·cal** \-mi-kəl\ *adjective* (1840)
: not economically practicable ⟨*uneconomic* transportation routes⟩; *also* : COSTLY, WASTEFUL ⟨an *uneconomic* nuclear technology⟩

**un·ed·it·ed** \,ən-'e-də-təd\ *adjective* (1829)
: not edited: as **a** : left unrevised **b** : not yet edited ⟨*unedited* books⟩ ⟨*unedited* films⟩

**un·emo·tion·al** \,ən-i-'mō-shnəl, -shə-n°l\ *adjective* (1876)
: not emotional: as **a** : not easily aroused or excited : COLD **b** : involving a minimum of emotion : INTELLECTUAL
— **un·emo·tion·al·ly** *adverb*

**un·em·ploy·able** \,ən-im-'plȯi-ə-bəl\ *adjective* (1887)
: not acceptable for employment
— **un·em·ploy·abil·i·ty** \-,plȯi-ə-'bi-lə-tē\ *noun*
— **unemployable** *noun*

**un·em·ployed** \-'plȯid\ *adjective* (1600)
: not employed: **a** : not being used **b** : not engaged in a gainful occupation **c** : not invested
— **unemployed** *noun*

**un·em·ploy·ment** \-'plȯi-mənt\ *noun* (1888)
**1** : the state of being unemployed : involuntary idleness of workers; *also* : the rate of such unemployment
**2** : UNEMPLOYMENT COMPENSATION

**unemployment compensation** *noun* (1944)
: compensation paid at regular intervals (as by a government agency) to an unemployed worker and especially one who has been laid off — called also *unemployment benefit*

**unemployment insurance** *noun* (1923)
: social insurance against involuntary unemployment that provides unemployment compensation for a limited period to unemployed workers; *also* : UNEMPLOYMENT COMPENSATION

**un·en·cum·bered** \,ən-in-'kəm-bərd\ *adjective* (1722)
: free of encumbrance

**un·end·ing** \,ən-'en-diŋ\ *adjective* (1661)
: never ending : ENDLESS
— **un·end·ing·ly** \-diŋ-lē\ *adverb*

**un–En·glish** \,ən-'iŋ-glish *also* -'iŋ-lish\ *adjective* (1633)
**1** : not characteristically English
**2** : not agreeing with standard or generally accepted usage of the English language

¹**un·equal** \,ən-'ē-kwəl\ *adjective* (1565)
**1 a** : not of the same measurement, quantity, or number as another **b** : not like or not the same as another in degree, worth, or status
**2** : not uniform : VARIABLE, UNEVEN
**3 a** : badly balanced or matched ⟨an *unequal* contest⟩ **b** : contracted between unequals ⟨*unequal* marriages⟩ **c** *archaic* : not equable
**4** *archaic* : not equitable : UNJUST
**5** : INADEQUATE, INSUFFICIENT ⟨*unequal* to the task⟩
— **un·equal·ly** \-kwə-lē\ *adverb*

²**unequal** *noun* (1600)
: one that is not equal to another

³**unequal** *adverb* (1602)
*archaic* : in an unequal manner ⟨*unequal* match'd —Shakespeare⟩

**un·equaled** *or* **un·equalled** \-kwəld\ *adjective* (1600)
: not equaled : UNPARALLELED

**un·equiv·o·ca·bly** \,ən-i-'kwi-və-kə-blē\ *adverb* [by alteration] (1917)
*nonstandard* : UNEQUIVOCALLY

**un·equiv·o·cal** \,ən-i-'kwi-və-kəl\ *adjective* (1784)
**1** : leaving no doubt : CLEAR, UNAMBIGUOUS
**2** : UNQUESTIONABLE ⟨production of *unequivocal* masterpieces —Carole Cook⟩

**un·equiv·o·cal·ly** \-kə-lē, -klē\ *adverb* (1794)
: in an unequivocal manner

**un·err·ing** \,ən-'er-iŋ, ,ən-'ər-\ *adjective* (1621)
: committing no error : FAULTLESS, UNFAILING
— **un·err·ing·ly** \-iŋ-lē\ *adverb*

**un·es·sen·tial** \,ən-ə-'sen(t)-shəl\ *adjective* (circa 1656)
**1** : not essential : DISPENSABLE, UNIMPORTANT
**2** *archaic* : void of essence : INSUBSTANTIAL

**un–Eu·ro·pe·an** \,ən-,yur-ə-'pē-ən\ *adjective* (1846)
: not characteristically European

**un·even** \,ən-'ē-vən\ *adjective* (before 12th century)
**1 a** *archaic* : UNEQUAL 1a **b** : ODD 3a
**2 a** : not even : not level or smooth : RUGGED, RAGGED ⟨large *uneven* teeth⟩ ⟨*uneven* handwriting⟩ **b** : varying from the straight or parallel **c** : not uniform : IRREGULAR ⟨*uneven* combustion⟩ **d** : varying in quality ⟨an *uneven* performance⟩
**3** : UNEQUAL 3a ⟨an *uneven* confrontation⟩
*synonym* see ROUGH
— **un·even·ly** *adverb*
— **un·even·ness** \-və(n)-nəs\ *noun*

**un·event·ful** \,ən-i-'vent-fəl\ *adjective* (1800)
: marked by no noteworthy or untoward incidents : PLACID
— **un·event·ful·ly** \-fə-lē\ *adverb*
— **un·event·ful·ness** \-fəl-nəs\ *noun*

**un·ex·am·pled** \,ən-ig-'zam-pəld\ *adjective* (1610)

| | | | |
|---|---|---|---|
| \ə\ abut | \ᵊ\ kitten | \ər\ further | \a\ ash \ā\ ace |
| \ä\ mop, mar | \au̇\ out | \ch\ chin | \e\ bet \ē\ easy |
| \g\ go | \i\ hit \ī\ ice | \j\ job | \ŋ\ sing \ō\ go |
| \ȯ\ law \ȯi\ boy | \th\ thin | \th\ the | \ü\ loot \u̇\ foot |
| \y\ yet | \zh\ vision | *see also* Guide to Pronunciation | |

: having no example or parallel : UNPRECE-DENTED

**un·ex·cep·tion·able** \ˌən-ik-ˈsep-sh(ə-)nə-bəl\ *adjective* [*un-* + obsolete *exception* to take exception, object] (1664)
: not open to objection or criticism : beyond reproach : UNIMPEACHABLE
— **un·ex·cep·tion·able·ness** *noun*
— **un·ex·cep·tion·ably** \-blē\ *adverb*
**un·ex·cep·tion·al** \-shnəl, -shə-nᵊl\ *adjective* (1806)
: not out of the ordinary : COMMONPLACE
**un·ex·er·cised** \ˌən-ˈek-sər-ˌsīzd\ *adjective* (14th century)
**1** : having terms that are not implemented ⟨*unexercised* options⟩
**2** : not subjected to exercise ⟨*unexercised* muscles⟩
**un·ex·pect·ed** \ˌən-ik-ˈspek-təd\ *adjective* (circa 1586)
: not expected : UNFORESEEN
— **un·ex·pect·ed·ly** *adverb*
— **un·ex·pect·ed·ness** *noun*
**un·ex·ploit·ed** \ˌən-ik-ˈsplȯi-təd\ *adjective* (1888)
: not exploited or developed : not taken advantage of
**un·ex·pres·sive** \ˌən-ik-ˈspre-siv\ *adjective* (1600)
**1** *obsolete* : INEFFABLE
**2** : not expressive : failing to convey the feeling or meaning intended
**un·fad·ing** \ˌən-ˈfā-diŋ\ *adjective* (1652)
**1** : not losing color or freshness
**2** : not losing value or effectiveness
— **un·fad·ing·ly** \-diŋ-lē\ *adverb*
**un·fail·ing** \ˌən-ˈfā-liŋ\ *adjective* (14th century)
: not failing or liable to fail: **a** : CONSTANT, UN-FLAGGING ⟨*unfailing* courtesy⟩ **b** : EVERLAST-ING, INEXHAUSTIBLE ⟨a subject of *unfailing* interest⟩ **c** : INFALLIBLE, SURE ⟨an *unfailing* test⟩
— **un·fail·ing·ly** \-liŋ-lē\ *adverb*
**un·fair** \ˌən-ˈfar, -ˈfer\ *adjective* (1700)
**1** : marked by injustice, partiality, or deception : UNJUST
**2** : not equitable in business dealings
— **un·fair·ness** *noun*
**un·fair·ly** *adverb* (1713)
: in an unfair manner
**un·faith** \ˌən-ˈfāth, ˈən-ˌ\ *noun* (15th century)
: absence of faith : DISBELIEF
**un·faith·ful** \ˌən-ˈfāth-fəl\ *adjective* (15th century)
: not faithful: **a** : not adhering to vows, allegiance, or duty : DISLOYAL **b** : not faithful to marriage vows **c** : INACCURATE, UNTRUSTWOR-THY
— **un·faith·ful·ly** \-fə-lē\ *adverb*
— **un·faith·ful·ness** *noun*
**un·fall·en** \ˌən-ˈfȯ-lən\ *adjective* (1653)
: not morally fallen : INNOCENT 1a
**un·fal·si·fi·able** \ˌən-ˌfȯl-sə-ˈfī-ə-bəl\ *adjective* (circa 1934)
: not capable of being proved false ⟨*unfalsifiable* hypotheses⟩
**un·fal·ter·ing** \ˌən-ˈfȯl-t(ə-)riŋ\ *adjective* (1727)
: not wavering or weakening : FIRM
— **un·fal·ter·ing·ly** \-t(ə-)riŋ-lē\ *adverb*
**un·fa·mil·iar** \ˌən-fə-ˈmil-yər\ *adjective* (1594)
: not familiar: **a** : not well-known : STRANGE ⟨an *unfamiliar* place⟩ **b** : not well acquainted ⟨*unfamiliar* with the subject⟩
— **un·fa·mil·iar·i·ty** \-ˌmil-ˈyar-ə-tē, -ˌmi-lē-ˈyar-\ *noun*
— **un·fa·mil·iar·ly** \-ˈmil-yər-lē\ *adverb*
**un·fash·ion·able** \ˌən-ˈfa-sh(ə-)nə-bəl\ *adjective* (1648)
**1** : not in keeping with the current fashion ⟨*unfashionable* clothes⟩
**2** : not favored socially ⟨*unfashionable* neighborhoods⟩
— **un·fash·ion·able·ness** \-bəl-nəs\ *noun*
— **un·fash·ion·ably** \-blē\ *adverb*

**un·fas·ten** \-ˈfa-sᵊn\ *transitive verb* (15th century)
: to make loose: as **a** : UNPIN, UNBUCKLE **b** : UN-DO ⟨*unfasten* a button⟩ **c** : DETACH ⟨*unfasten* a boat from its moorings⟩
**un·fa·thered** \-ˈfä-thərd\ *adjective* (1597)
**1** : having no father : ILLEGITIMATE, BASTARD
**2** : having no known origin ⟨*unfathered* slanders⟩
**un·fath·om·able** \-ˈfa-thə-mə-bəl\ *adjective* (1640)
: not capable of being fathomed: **a** : impossible to comprehend **b** : IMMEASURABLE
**un·fa·vor·able** \ˌən-ˈfā-v(ə-)rə-bəl, -ˈfā-vər-bəl\ *adjective* (1548)
**1 a** : OPPOSED, CONTRARY **b** : expressing disapproval : NEGATIVE ⟨*unfavorable* reviews⟩
**2** : not propitious : DISADVANTAGEOUS
**3** : not pleasing
— **un·fa·vor·able·ness** *noun*
— **un·fa·vor·ably** \-blē\ *adverb*
**un·fa·vor·ite** \-ˈfā-v(ə-)rət, -ˈfā-vərt\ *adjective* (circa 1934)
: not being a favorite; *especially* : being regarded with special disfavor or dislike
**un·fazed** \ˌən-ˈfāzd\ *adjective* (1945)
: not fazed : UNDAUNTED
**un·feel·ing** \-ˈfē-liŋ\ *adjective* (before 12th century)
**1** : devoid of feeling : INSENSATE ⟨an *unfeeling* corpse⟩
**2** : devoid of kindness or sympathy : HARD-HEARTED, CRUEL ⟨an *unfeeling* wretch⟩
— **un·feel·ing·ly** \-liŋ-lē\ *adverb*
— **un·feel·ing·ness** *noun*
**un·feigned** \-ˈfānd\ *adjective* (14th century)
: not feigned or hypocritical : GENUINE
**synonym** see SINCERE
— **un·feign·ed·ly** \-ˈfā-nəd-lē, -ˈfānd-lē\ *adverb*
**un·fet·ter** \-ˈfe-tər\ *transitive verb* (14th century)
**1** : to free from fetters ⟨*unfetter* a prisoner⟩
**2** : EMANCIPATE, LIBERATE ⟨*unfetter* the mind from prejudice⟩
**un·fet·tered** \-tərd\ *adjective* (1601)
: FREE, UNRESTRAINED
**un·fil·ial** \ˌən-ˈfi-lē-əl, -ˈfil-yəl\ *adjective* (1611)
: not observing the obligations of a child to a parent : UNDUTIFUL
— **un·fil·ial·ly** *adverb*
**un·fil·tered** \ˌən-ˈfil-tərd\ *adjective* (circa 1775)
**1** : not filtered ⟨*unfiltered* wine⟩; *also* : not modified, processed, or refined ⟨*unfiltered* commercial publicity material —Paul Grimes⟩
**2** : lacking a filter ⟨an *unfiltered* cigarette⟩
**un·find·able** \ˌən-ˈfin-də-bəl\ *adjective* (1791)
: not capable of being found
**un·fin·ished** \-ˈfi-nisht\ *adjective* (1539)
: not finished: **a** : not brought to an end or to the desired final state **b** : being in a rough state : UNPOLISHED **c** : subjected to no other processes (as bleaching or dyeing) after coming from the loom
**¹un·fit** \-ˈfit\ *adjective* (1545)
: not fit: **a** : not adapted to a purpose : UNSUIT-ABLE **b** : not qualified : INCAPABLE, INCOMPE-TENT **c** : physically or mentally unsound
— **un·fit·ly** *adverb*
— **un·fit·ness** *noun*
**²unfit** *transitive verb* (1611)
: to make unfit : DISABLE, DISQUALIFY
**un·fit·ted** \ˌən-ˈfi-təd\ *adjective* (1592)
: not adapted : UNQUALIFIED
**un·fit·ting** \-ˈfi-tiŋ\ *adjective* (1534)
: not fitting : UNSUITABLE
**un·fix** \-ˈfiks\ *transitive verb* (1597)
**1** : to loosen from a fastening : DETACH, DISEN-GAGE
**2** : to make unstable : UNSETTLE
**un·flag·ging** \-ˈfla-giŋ\ *adjective* (1715)
**1** : not flagging : TIRELESS
**2** : UNRELENTING 2

— **un·flag·ging·ly** \-giŋ-lē\ *adverb*
**un·flap·pa·ble** \-ˈfla-pə-bəl\ *adjective* [¹*un-* + ¹*flap* (state of excitement) + *-able*] (1954)
: marked by assurance and self-control
— **un·flap·pa·bil·i·ty** \-ˌfla-pə-ˈbi-lə-tē\ *noun*
— **un·flap·pa·bly** \-ˈfla-pə-blē\ *adverb*
**un·flat·ter·ing** \-ˈfla-tə-riŋ\ *adjective* (1581)
: not flattering; *especially* : UNFAVORABLE
— **un·flat·ter·ing·ly** \-riŋ-lē\ *adverb*
**un·fledged** \ˌən-ˈflejd\ *adjective* (1611)
**1** : not feathered : not ready for flight
**2** : not fully developed : IMMATURE ⟨an *unfledged* writer⟩
**un·flinch·ing** \-ˈflin-chiŋ\ *adjective* (1728)
: not flinching or shrinking : STEADFAST, UN-COMPROMISING
— **un·flinch·ing·ly** \-chiŋ-lē\ *adverb*
**un·fo·cused** *also* **un·fo·cussed** \-ˈfō-kəst\ *adjective* (1886)
**1** : not adjusted to a focus
**2** : not concentrated on one point or objective ⟨*unfocused* rage⟩
**un·fold** \-ˈfōld\ (before 12th century)
*transitive verb*
**1 a** : to open the folds of : spread or straighten out : EXPAND ⟨*unfolded* the map⟩ **b** : to remove (as a package) from the folds : UNWRAP
**2** : to open to the view : REVEAL; *especially* : to make clear by gradual disclosure and often by recital
*intransitive verb*
**1 a** : to open from a folded state : open out : EXPAND **b** : BLOSSOM
**2** : DEVELOP, EVOLVE ⟨as the story *unfolds*⟩
**3** : to open out gradually to the view or understanding : become known ⟨a panorama *unfolds* before their eyes⟩
— **un·fold·ment** \-ˈfōl(d)-mənt\ *noun*
**un·fold·ed** *adjective* (1683)
: not folded
**un·for·get·ta·ble** \ˌən-fər-ˈge-tə-bəl\ *adjective* (1806)
: incapable of being forgotten : MEMORABLE
— **un·for·get·ta·bly** \-ˈge-tə-blē\ *adverb*
**un·for·giv·ing** \ˌən-fər-ˈgi-viŋ\ *adjective* (1713)
**1** : unwilling or unable to forgive
**2** : having or making no allowance for error or weakness ⟨an *unforgiving* environment where false moves can prove fatal —Jaclyn Fierman⟩
— **un·for·giv·ing·ness** *noun*
**un·formed** \-ˈfȯrmd\ *adjective* (14th century)
: not arranged in regular shape, order, or relations; *especially* : IMMATURE, UNDEVELOPED
**¹un·for·tu·nate** \-ˈfȯrch-nət, -ˈfȯr-chə-\ *adjective* (15th century)
**1 a** : not favored by fortune : UNSUCCESSFUL, UNLUCKY ⟨an *unfortunate* young man⟩ **b** : marked or accompanied by or resulting in misfortune ⟨an *unfortunate* decision⟩
**2 a** : INFELICITOUS, UNSUITABLE ⟨an *unfortunate* choice of words⟩ **b** : DEPLORABLE, REGRETTA-BLE ⟨an *unfortunate* lack of taste⟩
**²unfortunate** *noun* (1683)
: an unfortunate person
**un·for·tu·nate·ly** \-lē\ *adverb* (circa 1548)
**1** : in an unfortunate manner ⟨the marriage turned out *unfortunately*⟩
**2** : it is unfortunate ⟨*unfortunately* for him your letter has let the cat out of the bag —G. B. Shaw⟩
**un·found·ed** \ˌən-ˈfaun-dəd\ *adjective* (1648)
: lacking a sound basis : GROUNDLESS, UNWAR-RANTED
**un·freeze** \-ˈfrēz\ *transitive verb* **-froze** \-ˈfrōz\; **-fro·zen** \-ˈfrō-zᵊn\; **-freez·ing** (1584)
**1** : to cause to thaw
**2** : to remove from a freeze
**un·fre·quent·ed** \ˌən-frē-ˈkwen-təd; ˌən-ˈfrē-kwən-\ *adjective* (1588)
: not often visited or traveled over
**un·friend·ed** \ˌən-ˈfren-dəd\ *adjective* (1513)
: having no friends : not befriended

**un·friend·li·ness** \-'fren(d)-lē-nəs\ *noun* (circa 1684)
: the quality or state of being unfriendly : HOSTILITY

**un·friend·ly** \-'fren(d)-lē\ *adjective* (15th century)
: not friendly: as **a** : HOSTILE, UNSYMPATHETIC **b** : INHOSPITABLE, UNFAVORABLE

**un·frock** \-'fräk\ *transitive verb* (1644)
: DEFROCK

**un·froz·en** \-'frō-z°n\ *adjective* (1596)
: not frozen ⟨*unfrozen* ground⟩

**un·fruit·ful** \-'früt-fəl\ *adjective* (14th century)
: not fruitful: as **a** : not producing offspring : BARREN **b** : yielding no valuable result : UNPROFITABLE ⟨an *unfruitful* conference⟩
— **un·fruit·ful·ly** \-fə-lē\ *adverb*
— **un·fruit·ful·ness** *noun*

**un·fund·ed** \-'fən-dəd\ *adjective* (circa 1775)
**1** : not funded : FLOATING ⟨an *unfunded* debt⟩
**2** : not provided with funds ⟨*unfunded* schools⟩

**un·furl** \-'fər(-ə)l\ (1641)
*transitive verb*
: to release from a furled state
*intransitive verb*
: to open out from or as if from a furled state : UNFOLD

**un·fussy** \-'fə-sē\ *adjective* (1825)
: not fussy: as **a** : not particular : UNCONCERNED **b** : not cluttered with pretentious or nonessential matters : UNCOMPLICATED
— **un·fuss·i·ly** \-'fə-sə-lē\ *adverb*

**un·gain·ly** \-'gān-lē\ *adjective* (1611)
**1 a** : lacking in smoothness or dexterity : CLUMSY **b** : hard to handle : UNWIELDY
**2** : having an awkward appearance : UGLY
— **un·gain·li·ness** *noun*

**un·gen·er·os·i·ty** \,ən-,je-nə-'rä-sə-tē, -'räs-tē\ *noun* (1757)
: lack of generosity

**un·gen·er·ous** \-ən-'jen-rəs, -'je-nə-\ *adjective* (1641)
: not generous: **a** : PETTY, MEAN **b** : deficient in liberality : STINGY
— **un·gen·er·ous·ly** *adverb*

**un·gird** \-'gərd\ *transitive verb* (before 12th century)
: to divest of a restraining band or girdle : UNBIND

**un·girt** \-'gərt\ *adjective* (14th century)
**1** : having the belt or girdle off or loose
**2** : lacking in discipline or compactness : LOOSE, SLACK

**un·glue** \-'glü\ *transitive verb* (circa 1548)
: to separate by or as if by dissolving an adhesive

**un·glued** \-'glüd\ *adjective* (1922)
: UPSET, DISORDERED

**un·god·li·ness** \,ən-'gäd-lē-nəs *also* -'gȯd-\ *noun* (1526)
: the quality or state of being ungodly

**un·god·ly** \-lē\ *adjective* (1526)
**1 a** : denying or disobeying God : IMPIOUS, IRRELIGIOUS **b** : contrary to moral law : SINFUL, WICKED
**2** : OUTRAGEOUS ⟨gets up at an *ungodly* hour⟩

**un·got·ten** \-'gä-t°n\ *or* **un·got** \-'gät\ *adjective* (15th century)
**1** *obsolete* : not begotten
**2** : not obtained

**un·gov·ern·able** \-'gə-vər-nə-bəl\ *adjective* (1673)
: not capable of being governed, guided, or restrained
**synonym** see UNRULY

**un·gra·cious** \-'grā-shəs\ *adjective* (13th century)
**1** *archaic* : WICKED
**2** : not courteous : RUDE
**3** : not pleasing : DISAGREEABLE
— **un·gra·cious·ly** *adverb*
— **un·gra·cious·ness** *noun*

**un·gram·mat·i·cal** \,ən-grə-'ma-ti-kəl\ *adjective* (1654)
: not following rules of grammar
— **un·gram·mat·i·cal·i·ty** \-,ma-tə-'ka-lə-tē\ *noun*

**un·grate·ful** \,ən-'grāt-fəl\ *adjective* (1533)
**1** : showing no gratitude : making a poor return
**2** : DISAGREEABLE; *also* : THANKLESS
— **un·grate·ful·ly** \-fə-lē\ *adverb*
— **un·grate·ful·ness** *noun*

**un·grudg·ing** \-'grə-jiŋ\ *adjective* (circa 1774)
: being without envy or reluctance

**un·gual** \'əŋ-gwəl, 'ən-\ *adjective* [Latin *unguis* nail, claw, hoof — more at NAIL] (1834)
: of, relating to, or resembling a nail, claw, or hoof

**un·guard** \,ən-'gärd\ *transitive verb* [back-formation from *unguarded*] (1745)
: to leave unprotected

**un·guard·ed** \-'gär-dəd\ *adjective* (circa 1593)
**1** : vulnerable to attack : UNPROTECTED
**2** : free from guile or wariness : DIRECT, INCAUTIOUS
— **un·guard·ed·ly** *adverb*
— **un·guard·ed·ness** *noun*

**un·guent** \'əŋ-gwənt, 'ən-; 'ən-jənt\ *noun* [Middle English, from Latin *unguentum* — more at OINTMENT] (15th century)
: a soothing or healing salve : OINTMENT

**un·guis** \'əŋ-gwəs, 'ən-\ *noun, plural* **un·gues** \-,gwēz\ [Latin — more at NAIL] (circa 1790)
: a nail, claw, or hoof especially on a digit of a vertebrate

**¹un·gu·late** \'əŋ-gyə-lət, 'ən-, -,lāt\ *adjective* [Late Latin *ungulatus,* from Latin *ungula* hoof, from *unguis* nail, hoof] (1839)
**1** : having hoofs
**2** : of or relating to the ungulates

**²ungulate** *noun* [New Latin *Ungulata,* from Late Latin, neuter plural of *ungulatus*] (circa 1842)
: a hoofed typically herbivorous quadruped mammal (as a ruminant, swine, camel, hippopotamus, horse, tapir, rhinoceros, elephant, or hyrax) of a polyphyletic group formerly considered a major mammalian taxon (Ungulata)

**un·hair** \,ən-'har, -'her\ *transitive verb* (14th century)
*archaic* : to deprive of hair

**un·hal·low** \-'ha-(,)lō\ *transitive verb* (1535)
*archaic* : to make profane

**un·hal·lowed** \-(,)lōd\ *adjective* (before 12th century)
**1** : not blessed : UNCONSECRATED, UNHOLY
**2 a** : unsanctioned by or showing lack of reverence for religion : IMPIOUS, PROFANE **b** : contrary to accepted standards : IMMORAL

**un·hand** \,ən-'hand\ *transitive verb* (1602)
: to remove the hand from : let go

**un·hand·some** \-'han(t)-səm\ *adjective* (1530)
: not handsome: as **a** : not beautiful : HOMELY **b** : UNBECOMING, UNSEEMLY **c** : lacking in courtesy or taste : RUDE
— **un·hand·some·ly** *adverb*

**un·handy** \-'han-dē\ *adjective* (1664)
**1** : hard to handle : INCONVENIENT
**2** : lacking in skill or dexterity : AWKWARD
— **un·hand·i·ly** \-də-lē\ *adverb*
— **un·hand·i·ness** \-dē-nəs\ *noun*

**un·hap·pi·ly** \,ən-'ha-pə-lē\ *adverb* (14th century)
**1** : UNFORTUNATELY **2** ⟨*unhappily,* medicine has not yet found a cure —Diana Trilling⟩
**2** : in an unhappy manner : without pleasure ⟨practiced law *unhappily* for a few years⟩

**un·hap·py** \-'ha-pē\ *adjective* (14th century)
**1** : not fortunate : UNLUCKY
**2** : not cheerful or glad : SAD, WRETCHED
**3 a** : causing or subject to misfortune : INAUSPICIOUS **b** : INFELICITOUS, INAPPROPRIATE
— **un·hap·pi·ness** *noun*

**un·healthy** \-'hel-thē\ *adjective* (1595)

**1** : not conducive to health ⟨an *unhealthy* climate⟩
**2** : not in good health : SICKLY, DISEASED
**3 a** : DANGEROUS, RISKY **b** : BAD, INJURIOUS **c** : morally contaminated : CORRUPT, UNWHOLESOME ⟨an *unhealthy* imagination⟩
— **un·health·i·ly** \-thə-lē\ *adverb*
— **un·health·i·ness** \-thē-nəs\ *noun*

**un·heard** \-'hərd\ *adjective* (14th century)
**1 a** : not perceived by the ear **b** : not given a hearing
**2** *archaic* : UNHEARD-OF

**un·heard-of** \-,əv, -,äv\ *adjective* (1592)
: previously unknown; *especially* : UNPRECEDENTED

**un·hes·i·tat·ing** \-'he-zə-,tā-tiŋ\ *adjective* (1753)
: not hesitating : not checked or qualified
— **un·hes·i·tat·ing·ly** \-tiŋ-lē\ *adverb*

**un·hinge** \-'hinj\ *transitive verb* (1616)
**1** : to remove (as a door) from the hinges
**2** : to make unstable : UNSETTLE, DISRUPT ⟨*unhinge* the balance of world peace⟩ ⟨pressure that would *unhinge* a less experienced person⟩

**un·hitch** \-'hich\ *transitive verb* (1706)
: to free from or as if from being hitched

**un·ho·ly** \,ən-'hō-lē\ *adjective* (before 12th century)
**1** : showing disregard for what is holy : WICKED
**2** : SHOCKING, OUTRAGEOUS
— **un·ho·li·ness** *noun*

**un·hood** \-'hu̇d\ *transitive verb* (1575)
: to remove a hood or covering from

**un·hook** \-'hu̇k\ *transitive verb* (1611)
**1** : to remove from a hook
**2** : to unfasten by disengaging a hook
**3** : to free from a habit or dependency

**un·hoped** \-'hōpt\ *adjective* (14th century)
*archaic* : not hoped for or expected

**un·horse** \-'hȯrs\ *transitive verb* (14th century)
: to dislodge from or as if from a horse

**un·hou·seled** \-'hau̇-zəld\ *adjective* (1532)
*archaic* : not having received the Eucharist especially shortly before death

**un·hur·ried** \-'hər-ēd, -'hə-rēd\ *adjective* (circa 1774)
: not hurried : LEISURELY
— **un·hur·ried·ly** *adverb*

**uni-** *prefix* [Middle English, from Middle French, from Latin, from *unus* — more at ONE]
: one : single ⟨*unicellular*⟩

**uni·al·gal** \,yü-nē-'al-gəl\ *adjective* (1914)
: of, relating to, or derived from a single algal individual or cell ⟨a *unialgal* culture⟩

**Uni·ate** *or* **Uni·at** \'yü-nē-,at, 'ü-\ *noun* [Ukrainian *uniat, uniyat* one in favor of the union of the Greek and Roman Catholic churches, from *uniya* union, from Polish *unija,* from Late Latin *unio* — more at UNION] (1833)
: a Christian of a church adhering to an Eastern rite and discipline but submitting to papal authority
— **Uniate** *adjective*

**uni·ax·i·al** \,yü-nē-'ak-sē-əl\ *adjective* (circa 1828)
**1** : having only one axis
**2** : of or relating to only one axis

**uni·cam·er·al** \,yü-ni-'kam-rəl, -'ka-mə-\ *adjective* [*uni-* + Late Latin *camera* room, chamber — more at CHAMBER] (1853)
: having or consisting of a single legislative chamber
— **uni·cam·er·al·ly** *adverb*

**uni·cel·lu·lar** \,yü-ni-'sel-yə-lər\ *adjective* (1858)
: having or consisting of a single cell

\ə\ abut \°\ kitten \ər\ further \a\ ash \ā\ ace
\ä\ mop, mar \au̇\ out \ch\ chin \e\ bet \ē\ easy
\g\ go \i\ hit \ī\ ice \j\ job \ŋ\ sing \ō\ go
\ȯ\ law \ȯi\ boy \th\ thin \t͟h\ the \ü\ loot \u̇\ foot
\y\ yet \zh\ vision   *see also* Guide to Pronunciation

**uni·corn** \'yü-nə-ˌkȯrn\ *noun* [Middle English *unicorne,* from Old French, from Late Latin *unicornis,* from Latin, having one horn, from *uni-* + *cornu* horn — more at HORN] (13th century) : a mythical animal generally depicted with the body and head of a horse, the hind legs of a stag, the tail of a lion, and a single horn in the middle of the forehead ◆

unicorn

**unicorn plant** *noun* (1796) : DEVIL'S CLAW

**uni·cy·cle** \'yü-ni-ˌsī-kəl\ *noun* [*uni* + *-cycle* (as in *tricycle*)] (1869) : a vehicle that has a single wheel and is usually propelled by pedals
— **uni·cy·clist** \-ˌsī-k(ə-)list\ *noun*

**uni·di·men·sion·al** \ˌyü-ni-də-'mench-nəl, -'men(t)-sh(ə-)nᵊl *also* -ˌdī-\ *adjective* (1883) : ONE-DIMENSIONAL
— **uni·di·men·sion·al·i·ty** \-ˌmen(t)-shə-'na-lə-tē\ *noun*

**uni·di·rec·tion·al** \ˌyü-ni-də-'rek-shnəl, -dī-, -shə-nᵊl\ *adjective* (1883)
**1** : involving, functioning, moving, or responsive in a single direction
**2** : not subject to change or reversal of direction
— **uni·di·rec·tion·al·ly** *adverb*

**unidirectional current** *noun* (1883) : DIRECT CURRENT

**uni·fi·ca·tion** \ˌyü-nə-fə-'kā-shən\ *noun* (1851) : the act, process, or result of unifying : the state of being unified

**uni·fo·li·ate** \-'fō-lē-ət\ *adjective* [*uni-* + Latin *folium* leaf — more at BLADE] (1849)
**1** : having only one leaf
**2** : UNIFOLIOLATE

**uni·fo·li·o·late** \-'fō-lē-ə-ˌlāt\ *adjective* [*uni-* + Late Latin *foliolum* leaflet, diminutive of Latin *folium* leaf] (circa 1859) *of a leaf* : compound but having only a single leaflet and distinguishable from a simple leaf by the basal joint

**¹uni·form** \'yü-nə-ˌfȯrm\ *adjective* [Middle French *uniforme,* from Latin *uniformis,* from *uni-* + *-formis* -form] (1538)
**1** : consistent in conduct or opinion ⟨*uniform* interpretation of laws⟩
**2** : having always the same form, manner, or degree : not varying or variable
**3** : of the same form with others : conforming to one rule or mode : CONSONANT
**4** : presenting an unvaried appearance of surface, pattern, or color ⟨*uniform* red brick houses⟩
**5** : relating to or being convergence of a series whose terms are functions in such manner that the absolute value of the difference between the sum of the first *n* terms of the series and the sum of all terms can be made arbitrarily small for all values of the domain of the functions by choosing the *n*th term sufficiently far along in the series
— **uni·form·ly** \'yü-nə-ˌfȯrm-lē, ˌyü-nə-'\ *adverb*
— **uni·form·ness** \'yü-nə-ˌfȯrm-nəs\ *noun*

**²uniform** *transitive verb* (circa 1681)
**1** : to bring into uniformity
**2** : to clothe with a uniform

**³uniform** *noun* (1748) : dress of a distinctive design or fashion worn by members of a particular group and serving as a means of identification; *broadly* : distinctive or characteristic clothing

**Uniform** (circa 1956) — a communication code word for the letter *u*

**uni·for·mi·tar·i·an** \ˌyü-nə-ˌfȯr-mə-'ter-ē-ən\ *noun* (1840)
**1** : an adherent of the doctrine of uniformitarianism
**2** : an advocate of uniformity
— **uniformitarian** *adjective*

**uni·for·mi·tar·i·an·ism** \-ē-ə-ˌni-zəm\ *noun* (1865) : a geological doctrine that existing processes acting in the same manner as at present are sufficient to account for all geological changes — compare CATASTROPHISM

**uni·for·mi·ty** \ˌyü-nə-'fȯr-mə-tē\ *noun, plural* **-ties** (15th century)
**1** : the quality or state of being uniform
**2** : an instance of uniformity

**uni·fy** \'yü-nə-ˌfī\ *transitive verb* **-fied; -fy·ing** [Late Latin *unificare,* from Latin *uni-* + *-ficare* -fy] (1502) : to make into a unit or a coherent whole : UNITE
— **uni·fi·able** \-ˌfī-ə-bəl\ *adjective*
— **uni·fi·er** \-ˌfī(-ə)r\ *noun*

**uni·lat·er·al** \ˌyü-ni-'la-tə-rəl, -'la-trəl\ *adjective* (1802)
**1 a** : done or undertaken by one person or party **b** : of, relating to, or affecting one side of a subject : ONE-SIDED **c** : constituting or relating to a contract or engagement by which an express obligation to do or forbear is imposed on only one party
**2 a** : having parts arranged on one side ⟨a *unilateral* raceme⟩ **b** : occurring on, performed on, or affecting one side of the body or one of its parts ⟨*unilateral* exophthalmos⟩
**3** : UNILINEAL
**4** : having only one side
— **uni·lat·er·al·ly** *adverb*

**uni·lin·e·al** \-'li-nē-əl\ *adjective* (1952) : tracing descent through either the maternal or paternal line only

**uni·lin·e·ar** \ˌyü-ni-'li-nē-ər\ *adjective* (1851) : developing in or involving a series of stages usually from the primitive to the more advanced ⟨a *unilinear* cultural sequence⟩

**uni·lin·gual** \ˌyü-ni-'liŋ-gwəl, -gyə-wəl\ *adjective* [*uni-* + Latin *lingua* tongue, language — more at TONGUE] (1866) : composed in or using one language only

**un·il·lu·sioned** \ˌən-i-'lü-zhənd\ *adjective* (1926) : free from illusion

**uni·loc·u·lar** \ˌyü-ni-'lä-kyə-lər\ *adjective* (1753) : containing a single cavity

**un·imag·in·able** \ˌən-ə-'maj-nə-bəl, -'ma-jə-\ *adjective* (1611) : not imaginable or comprehensible
— **un·imag·in·ably** \-blē\ *adverb*

**un·im·peach·able** \ˌən-im-'pē-chə-bəl\ *adjective* (1784) : not impeachable : not to be called in question : not liable to accusation : IRREPROACHABLE, BLAMELESS
— **un·im·peach·ably** \-blē\ *adverb*

**¹un·im·proved** \-'prüvd\ *adjective* (1602) *obsolete* : not reproved or admonished

**²unimproved** *adjective* (1665) : not improved: as **a** : not tilled, built on, or otherwise improved for use ⟨*unimproved* land⟩ **b** : not used or employed advantageously ⟨wasted time and *unimproved* opportunities⟩ **c** : not selectively bred for better quality or productiveness

**un·in·hib·it·ed** \ˌən-in-'hi-bə-təd\ *adjective* (1880) : free from inhibition; *also* : boisterously informal
— **un·in·hib·it·ed·ly** *adverb*
— **un·in·hib·it·ed·ness** *noun*

**un·ini·ti·ate** \ˌən-ə-'ni-sh(ē-)ət\ *adjective* (1801) : not initiated : INEXPERIENCED
— **uninitiate** *noun*

**un·in·ter·est** \ˌən-'in-trəst; -'in-tə-rəst, -tə-ˌrest, -tərst; -'in-ˌtrest\ *noun* (1890) : lack of interest

**uninterested** *adjective* (1661) : not interested : not having the mind or feelings engaged
*usage* see DISINTERESTED

**uni·nu·cle·ate** \ˌyü-ni-'nü-klē-ət, -'nyü-\ *adjective* (1885) : having a single nucleus ⟨a *uninucleate* yeast cell⟩

**¹union** \'yün-yən\ *noun* [Middle English, from Middle French, from Late Latin *union-, unio* oneness, union, from Latin *unus* one — more at ONE] (15th century)
**1 a** : an act or instance of uniting or joining two or more things into one: as (1) : the formation of a single political unit from two or more separate and independent units (2) : a uniting in marriage; *also* : SEXUAL INTERCOURSE (3) : the growing together of severed parts **b** : a unified condition : COMBINATION, JUNCTION ⟨a gracious *union* of excellence and strength⟩
**2** : something that is made one : something formed by a combining or coalition of parts or members: as **a** : a confederation of independent individuals (as nations or persons) for some common purpose **b** (1) : a political unit constituting an organic whole formed usually from previously independent units (as England and Scotland in 1707) which have surrendered their principal powers to the government of the whole or to a newly created government (as the U.S. in 1789) (2) *capitalized* : the federal union of states during the period of the U.S. Civil War **c** *capitalized* : an organization on a college or university campus providing recreational, social, cultural, and sometimes dining facilities; *also* : the building housing such an organization **d** : the set of all elements belonging to one or more of a given collection of two or more sets — called also *join,* sum **e** : LABOR UNION
**3 a** : a device emblematic of the union of two or more sovereignties borne on a national flag typically in the upper inner corner or constituting the whole design of the flag **b** : the upper inner corner of a flag
**4** : any of various devices for connecting parts (as of a machine); *especially* : a coupling for pipes or pipes and fittings

◇ WORD HISTORY
**unicorn** The two-horned African rhinoceros was quite familiar in the ancient Mediterranean world, even to the urban populaces of Alexandria and Rome, where specimens are reported to have been exhibited. The Greeks dubbed the animal *rhinokerōs,* literally, "nose-horned one"—an appropriate name, since the rhinoceros's primary horn protrudes from above its snout, unlike the horns of other ungulates, which grow above the brow. The single-horned Indian rhinoceros, on the other hand, was never observed firsthand by ancient authors, and descriptions of it are rather garbled. By late antiquity legend had shaped out of the Indian rhinoceros a mythical animal, the *monokerōs* ("single-horned one"). This animal is described in the *Physiologus,* an anonymous 4th century Greek prototype of the medieval bestiary, as having most of the physical features we now associate with the unicorn. The *Physiologus* introduces as well the belief that the fierce unicorn can only be subdued by a virgin, and attaches to this trait a Christian interpretation, that the taming of the unicorn symbolizes Christ's incarnation in a virgin. Authors writing in Latin translated Greek *monokerōs* as *unicornis* or *unicornuus,* the ultimate source of English *unicorn.*

**²union** *adjective* (1707)
: of, relating to, dealing with, or constituting a union; *especially, capitalized* : of, relating to, or being the side favoring the Union in the U.S. Civil War ⟨*Union* troops⟩

**union card** *noun* (1874)
**1** : a card certifying personal membership in good standing in a labor union
**2** : something that resembles a union card especially in being necessary for employment or in providing evidence of in-group status

**union church** *noun* (1847)
: a local church uniting members of diverse denominational backgrounds in an interdenominational congregation

**un·ion·i·sa·tion, union·ise** *British variant of* UNIONIZATION, UNIONIZE

**union·ism** \'yün-yə-,ni-zəm\ *noun* (1845)
: the principle or policy of forming or adhering to a union: as **a** *capitalized* : adherence to the policy of a firm federal union between the states of the United States especially during the Civil War period **b** : the principles, theory, advocacy, or system of trade unions

**union·ist** \-nist\ *noun* (1799)
: an advocate or supporter of union or unionism

**union·i·za·tion** \,yün-yə-nə-'zā-shən\ *noun* (1896)
**1** : the quality or state of being unionized
**2** : the action of unionizing

**union·ize** \'yün-yə-,nīz\ *verb* **-ized; -iz·ing** (1890)
*transitive verb*
: to organize into a labor union
*intransitive verb*
: to form or join a labor union

**unionized** *adjective* (1900)
: characterized by the presence of labor unions ⟨*unionized* states⟩

**union jack** *noun* (1674)
**1** : a jack consisting of the union of a national ensign
**2** *U&J capitalized* : the state flag of the United Kingdom consisting of the union of the British national ensign

**union shop** *noun* (1904)
: an establishment in which the employer by agreement is free to hire nonmembers as well as members of the union but retains nonmembers on the payroll only on condition of their becoming members of the union within a specified time

**union suit** *noun* (1892)
: an undergarment with shirt and drawers in one piece

**uni·pa·ren·tal** \,yü-ni-pə-'ren-t°l\ *adjective* (1900)
: having or involving a single parent; *especially* : PARTHENOGENETIC
— **uni·pa·ren·tal·ly** \-t°l-ē\ *adverb*

**unique** \yù-'nēk\ *adjective* [French, from Latin *unicus,* from *unus* one — more at ONE] (1602)
**1** : being the only one : SOLE ⟨his *unique* concern was his own comfort⟩ ⟨I can't walk away with a *unique* copy. Suppose I lost it? —Kingsley Amis⟩ ⟨the *unique* factorization of a number into prime factors⟩
**2 a** : being without a like or equal : UNEQUALED ⟨could stare at the flames, each one new, violent, *unique* —Robert Coover⟩ **b** : distinctively characteristic : PECULIAR 1 ⟨this is not a condition *unique* to California —Ronald Reagan⟩
**3** : UNUSUAL ⟨a very *unique* ball-point pen⟩ ⟨we were fairly *unique,* the sixty of us, in that there wasn't one good mixer in the bunch —J. D. Salinger⟩ ▪
**synonym** see STRANGE
— **unique·ly** *adverb*

union suit

— **unique·ness** *noun*

**¹uni·sex** \'yü-nə-,seks\ *noun* (1966)
: the state or condition of not being distinguishable (as by hair or clothing) as to sex

**²unisex** *adjective* (1968)
**1** : not distinguishable as male or female ⟨a *unisex* face⟩
**2** : suitable or designed for both males and females ⟨*unisex* clothes⟩

**uni·sex·u·al** \,yü-nə-'sek-sh(ə-)wəl, -shəl\ *adjective* (circa 1802)
**1** : of, relating to, or restricted to one sex: **a** : male or female but not hermaphroditic **b** : DICLINOUS ⟨a *unisexual* flower⟩
**2** : UNISEX
— **uni·sex·u·al·i·ty** \-,sek-shə-'wa-lə-tē\ *noun*

**uni·son** \'yü-nə-sən, -nə-zən\ *noun* [Middle French, from Medieval Latin *unisonus* having the same sound, from Latin *uni-* + *sonus* sound — more at SOUND] (1575)
**1 a** : identity in musical pitch; *specifically* : the interval of a perfect prime **b** : the state of being so tuned or sounded **c** : the writing, playing, or singing of parts in a musical passage at the same pitch or in octaves
**2** : a harmonious agreement or union : CONCORD
— **unison** *adjective*
— **in unison 1** : in perfect agreement : so as to harmonize exactly **2** : at the same time : SIMULTANEOUSLY

**¹unit** \'yü-nət\ *noun* [back-formation from *unity*] (1570)
**1 a** : the first and least natural number : ONE **b** : a single quantity regarded as a whole in calculation
**2** : a determinate quantity (as of length, time, heat, or value) adopted as a standard of measurement: as **a** : an amount of work used in education in calculating student credits **b** : an amount of a biologically active agent (as a drug or antigen) required to produce a specific result under strictly controlled conditions
**3 a** : a single thing, person, or group that is a constituent of a whole **b** : a part of a military establishment that has a prescribed organization (as of personnel and materiel) **c** : a piece or complex of apparatus serving to perform one particular function **d** : a part of a school course focusing on a central theme **e** : a local congregation of Jehovah's Witnesses

**²unit** *adjective* (1844)
: being, relating to, or measuring one unit

**unit·age** \'yü-nə-tij\ *noun* (1935)
**1** : specifications of the amount constituting a unit
**2** : amount in units

**uni·tard** \'yü-nə-,tärd\ *noun* [*uni-* + leo*tard*] (1961)
: a close-fitting one-piece garment for the torso, legs, feet, and often the arms

**uni·tar·i·an** \,yü-nə-'ter-ē-ən\ *noun* [New Latin *unitarius,* from Latin *unitas* unity] (1687)
**1 a** *often capitalized* : one who believes that the deity exists only in one person **b** *capitalized* : a member of a denomination that stresses individual freedom of belief, the free use of reason in religion, a united world community, and liberal social action
**2** : an advocate of unity or a unitary system
— **unitarian** *adjective, often capitalized*
— **uni·tar·i·an·ism** \-ē-ə-,ni-zəm\ *noun, often capitalized*

**uni·tary** \'yü-nə-,ter-ē\ *adjective* (1861)
**1 a** : of or relating to a unit **b** : based on or characterized by unity or units
**2** : having the character of a unit : UNDIVIDED, WHOLE
— **uni·tar·i·ly** \,yü-nə-'ter-ə-lē\ *adverb*

**unit cell** *noun* (1915)
: the simplest polyhedron that embodies all the structural characteristics of and by indefinite repetition makes up the lattice of a crystal

**unit character** *noun* (1902)
: a natural character inherited on an all-or-none basis; *especially* : one dependent on the presence or absence of a single gene

**unit circle** *noun* (1955)
: a circle having a radius of 1

**¹unite** \yù-'nīt\ *verb* **unit·ed; unit·ing** [Middle English, from Latin *unire,* from *unus* one — more at ONE] (15th century)
*transitive verb*
**1 a** : to put together to form a single unit **b** : to cause to adhere **c** : to link by a legal or moral bond
**2** : to possess (as qualities) in combination
*intransitive verb*
**1 a** : to become one or as if one **b** : to become combined by or as if by adhesion or mixture
**2** : to act in concert
**synonym** see JOIN
— **unit·er** *noun*

**²unite** \'yü-,nīt\ *noun* [obsolete *unite* united, from Middle English *unit,* from Late Latin *unitus,* past participle] (1604)
: an old British gold 20-shilling piece issued first by James I in 1604 for the newly united England and Scotland — called also *Jacobus*

**unit·ed** \yù-'nī-təd\ *adjective* (1552)
**1** : made one : COMBINED
**2** : relating to or produced by joint action
**3** : being in agreement : HARMONIOUS
— **unit·ed·ly** *adverb*

**United Nations Day** *noun* (1947)
: October 24 observed in commemoration of the founding of the United Nations

**Unit·ed States** \yù-'nī-təd-, *especially Southern* 'yü-,\ *noun plural but singular or plural in construction* (1617)
: a federation of states especially when forming a nation in a usually specified territory ⟨advocating a *United States* of Europe⟩

**uni·tive** \'yü-nə-tiv, yù-'nī-\ *adjective* (1526)
: characterized by or tending to produce union

**unit·ize** \'yü-nə-,tīz\ *transitive verb* **-ized; -iz·ing** (1860)
**1** : to form or convert into a unit
**2** : to divide into units ⟨the added cost of *unitizing* bulk products⟩
— **unit·i·za·tion** \,yü-nə-tə-'zā-shən\ *noun*

**unit membrane** *noun* [from its being the basic structural unit of the cell] (1959)

---

☐ USAGE
**unique** Many commentators have objected to the comparison or modification (as by *somewhat* or *very*) of *unique;* the statement that a thing is either unique or it is not has often been repeated by them. Objections are based chiefly on the assumption that *unique* has but a single absolute sense, an assumption contradicted by information readily available in a dictionary. *Unique* dates back to the 17th century but was little used until the end of the 18th when, according to the Oxford English Dictionary, it was reacquired from French. H. J. Todd entered it as a foreign word in his edition (1818) of Johnson's Dictionary, characterizing it as "affected and useless." Around the middle of the 19th century it ceased to be considered foreign and came into considerable popular use. With popular use came a broadening of application beyond the original two meanings (here numbered 1 and 2a). In modern use both comparison and modification are widespread and standard but are confined to the extended senses 2b and 3. When sense 1 or sense 2a is intended, *unique* is used without qualifying modifiers.

---

\ə\ abut \ᵊ\ kitten \ər\ further \a\ ash \ā\ ace
\ä\ mop, mar \au̇\ out \ch\ chin \e\ bet \ē\ easy
\g\ go \i\ hit \ī\ ice \j\ job \ŋ\ sing \ō\ go
\ȯ\ law \ȯi\ boy \th\ thin \th\ the \ü\ loot \u̇\ foot
\y\ yet \zh\ vision *see also* Guide to Pronunciation

: a 3-layered membrane that consists of an inner lipid layer surrounded by a protein layer on each side

**unit rule** *noun* (1884)
: a rule under which a delegation to a national political convention casts its entire vote as a unit as determined by a majority vote

**uni·trust** \'yü-ni-ˌtrəst\ *noun* (1970)
: a trust from which the beneficiary receives annually a fixed percentage of the fair market value of its assets

**units place** *noun* (1937)
: the place just to the left of the decimal point in a number expressed in the Arabic system of writing numbers

**unit train** *noun* (1964)
: a railway train that transports a single commodity directly from producer to consumer

**unit trust** *noun* (1936)
**1** *British* : MUTUAL FUND
**2** : an investment company whose portfolio consists of long-term bonds that are held to maturity

**uni·ty** \'yü-nə-tē\ *noun, plural* **-ties** [Middle English *unite*, from Middle French *unité*, from Latin *unitat-, unitas*, from *unus* one — more at ONE] (14th century)
**1 a** : the quality or state of not being multiple : ONENESS **b** (1) : a definite amount taken as one or for which 1 is made to stand in calculation ⟨in a table of natural sines the radius of the circle is regarded as *unity*⟩ (2) : IDENTITY ELEMENT
**2 a** : a condition of harmony : ACCORD **b** : continuity without deviation or change (as in purpose or action)
**3 a** : the quality or state of being made one : UNIFICATION **b** : a combination or ordering of parts in a literary or artistic production that constitutes a whole or promotes an undivided total effect; *also* : the resulting singleness of effect or symmetry and consistency of style and character
**4** : a totality of related parts : an entity that is a complex or systematic whole
**5** : any of three principles of dramatic structure derived by French classicists from Aristotle's *Poetics* and requiring a play to have a single action represented as occurring in one place and within one day
**6** *capitalized* : a 20th century American religious movement that emphasizes spiritual sources of health and prosperity

**¹uni·va·lent** \ˌyü-ni-'vā-lənt\ *adjective* (1898)
**1** : MONOVALENT 1
**2** : being a chromosomal univalent

**²univalent** *noun* (1912)
: a chromosome that lacks a synaptic mate

**uni·valve** \'yü-ni-ˌvalv\ *noun* (1668)
**1** : a mollusk with a shell consisting of one valve; *especially* : GASTROPOD
**2** : the shell of a univalve
— **univalve** *adjective*

**uni·var·i·ate** \ˌyü-ni-'ver-ē-ət, -'var-\ *adjective* (1928)
: characterized by or depending on only one random variable ⟨a *univariate* linear model⟩

**¹uni·ver·sal** \ˌyü-nə-'vər-səl\ *adjective* [Middle English, from Middle French, from Latin *universalis*, from *universum* universe] (14th century)
**1** : including or covering all or a whole collectively or distributively without limit or exception
**2 a** : present or occurring everywhere **b** : existent or operative everywhere or under all conditions ⟨*universal* cultural patterns⟩
**3 a** : embracing a major part or the greatest portion (as of mankind) ⟨a *universal* state⟩ ⟨*universal* practices⟩ **b** : comprehensively broad and versatile ⟨a *universal* genius⟩
**4 a** : affirming or denying something of all members of a class or of all values of a variable **b** : denoting every member of a class ⟨a *universal* term⟩

**5** : adapted or adjustable to meet varied requirements (as of use, shape, or size) ⟨a *universal* gear cutter⟩
— **uni·ver·sal·ly** \-s(ə-)lē\ *adverb*
— **uni·ver·sal·ness** \-səl-nəs\ *noun*

**²universal** *noun* (1553)
**1** : one that is universal: as **a** : a universal proposition in logic **b** : a predicable of traditional logic **c** : a general concept or term or something in reality to which it corresponds : ESSENCE
**2 a** : a behavior pattern or institution (as the family) existing in all cultures **b** : a culture trait characteristic of all normal adult members of a particular society

**universal donor** *noun* (1922)
: a person who belongs to ABO blood group O and can donate blood to any recipient

**universal grammar** *noun* (1751)
: the study of general principles believed to underlie the grammatical phenomena of all languages; *also* : such principles viewed as part of an innate human capacity for learning a language

**uni·ver·sal·ism** \ˌyü-nə-'vər-sə-ˌli-zəm\ *noun* (1805)
**1** *often capitalized* **a** : a theological doctrine that all human beings will eventually be saved **b** : the principles and practices of a liberal Christian denomination founded in the 18th century originally to uphold belief in universal salvation and now united with Unitarianism
**2** : something that is universal in scope
**3** : the state of being universal : UNIVERSALITY
— **uni·ver·sal·ist** \-s(ə-)list\ *noun or adjective, often capitalized*

**uni·ver·sal·is·tic** \-ˌvər-sə-'lis-tik\ *adjective* (1872)
: of or relating to the whole : universal in scope or nature

**uni·ver·sal·i·ty** \-(ˌ)vər-'sa-lə-tē\ *noun* (14th century)
**1** : the quality or state of being universal
**2** : universal comprehensiveness in range

**uni·ver·sal·ize** \-'vər-sə-ˌlīz\ *transitive verb* **-ized; -iz·ing** (1642)
: to make universal : GENERALIZE
— **uni·ver·sal·i·za·tion** \-ˌvər-sə-lə-'zā-shən\ *noun*

**universal joint** *noun* (1676)
: a shaft coupling capable of transmitting rotation from one shaft to another not collinear with it — called also *universal coupling*

universal joint

**universal motor** *noun* (1925)
: an electric motor that can be used on either an alternating or a direct current supply

**Universal Product Code** *noun* (1974)
: a combination of a bar code and numbers by which a scanner can identify a product and usually assign a price

**universal recipient** *noun* (1922)
: a person who belongs to ABO blood group AB and can receive blood from any donor

**Universal time** *noun* (1882)
: GREENWICH MEAN TIME

**uni·verse** \'yü-nə-ˌvərs\ *noun* [Latin *universum*, from neuter of *universus* entire, whole, from *uni-* + *versus* turned toward, from past participle of *vertere* to turn — more at WORTH] (1589)
**1** : the whole body of things and phenomena observed or postulated : COSMOS: as **a** : a systematic whole held to arise by and persist through the direct intervention of divine power **b** : the world of human experience **c** (1) : the entire celestial cosmos (2) : MILKY WAY GALAXY (3) : an aggregate of stars comparable to the Milky Way galaxy

**2** : a distinct field or province of thought or reality that forms a closed system or self-inclusive and independent organization
**3** : POPULATION 4
**4** : a set that contains all elements relevant to a particular discussion or problem
**5** : a great number or quantity ⟨a large enough *universe* of stocks . . . to choose from —G. B. Clairmont⟩

**universe of discourse** (1881)
: an inclusive class of entities that is tacitly implied or explicitly delineated as the subject of a statement, discourse, or theory

**uni·ver·si·ty** \ˌyü-nə-'vər-sə-tē, -'vər-stē\ *noun, plural* **-ties** [Middle English *universite*, from Middle French *université*, from Medieval Latin *universitat-, universitas*, from Latin *universus*] (14th century)
**1** : an institution of higher learning providing facilities for teaching and research and authorized to grant academic degrees; *specifically* : one made up of an undergraduate division which confers bachelor's degrees and a graduate division which comprises a graduate school and professional schools each of which may confer master's degrees and doctorates
**2** : the physical plant of a university

**univ·o·cal** \yü-'ni-və-kəl\ *adjective* [Late Latin *univocus*, from Latin *uni-* + *voc-, vox* voice — more at VOICE] (1599)
: having one meaning only
— **univ·o·cal·ly** \-k(ə-)lē\ *adverb*

**un·joined** \ˌən-'jȯind\ *adjective* (1538)
: not joined

**un·just** \ˌən-'jəst\ *adjective* (14th century)
**1** : characterized by injustice : UNFAIR
**2** *archaic* : DISHONEST, FAITHLESS
— **un·just·ly** *adverb*
— **un·just·ness** \-'jəs(t)-nəs\ *noun*

**un·kempt** \ˌən-'kem(p)t\ *adjective* [*un-* + *kempt* combed, neat] (1579)
**1** : deficient in order or neatness ⟨*unkempt* individuals⟩ ⟨*unkempt* hotel rooms⟩; *also* : ROUGH, UNPOLISHED ⟨*unkempt* prose⟩
**2** : not combed ⟨*unkempt* hair⟩

**un·kenned** \ˌən-'kend\ *adjective* (14th century) *chiefly dialect* : UNKNOWN, STRANGE

**un·ken·nel** \ˌən-'ke-nᵊl\ *transitive verb* (1575)
**1 a** : to drive (as a fox) from a hiding place or den **b** : to free (dogs) from a kennel
**2** : to bring out into the open : UNCOVER

**un·kind** \ˌən-'kīnd\ *adjective* (13th century)
**1** : not pleasing or mild : INCLEMENT ⟨an *unkind* climate⟩
**2** : lacking in kindness or sympathy : HARSH, CRUEL
— **un·kind·ness** \-'kīn(d)-nəs\ *noun*

**¹un·kind·ly** \ˌən-'kīn(d)-lē\ *adjective* (13th century)
: not kindly
— **un·kind·li·ness** *noun*

**²unkindly** *adverb* (14th century)
: in an unkind manner ⟨dwells *unkindly* long on his final decline —A. H. Johnston⟩

**un·kink** \ˌən-'kiŋk\ (1891)
*transitive verb*
: to free from kinks : STRAIGHTEN
*intransitive verb*
: to become lax or loose : RELAX

**un·knit** \ˌən-'nit\ *verb* **-knit** *or* **-knit·ted; -knit·ting** (before 12th century)
: UNDO, UNRAVEL

**un·know·able** \ˌən-'nō-ə-bəl\ *adjective* (14th century)
: not knowable; *especially* : lying beyond the limits of human experience or understanding
— **un·know·abil·i·ty** \-ˌnō-ə-'bi-lə-tē\ *noun*

**¹un·know·ing** \ˌən-'nō-iŋ\ *adjective* (14th century)
: not knowing
— **un·know·ing·ly** \-iŋ-lē\ *adverb*

**²unknowing** *noun* (14th century)
: IGNORANCE

**¹un·known** \ˌən-'nōn\ *adjective* (14th century)

: not known or not well-known; *also* : having an unknown value ⟨an *unknown* quantity⟩
²**unknown** *noun* (1597)
**1** : one that is not known or not well-known; *especially* : a person who is little known (as to the public)
**2** : something that requires discovery, indentification, or clarification: as **a** : a symbol (as *x, y,* or *z*) in a mathematical equation representing an unknown quantity **b** : a specimen (as of bacteria or mixed chemicals) required to be identified as an exercise in appropriate laboratory techniques
**Unknown Soldier** *noun* (1923)
: an unidentified soldier whose body is selected to receive national honors as a representative of all of the same nation who died in a war and especially in one of the world wars
**un·lace** \ˌən-ˈlās\ *transitive verb* (14th century)
**1** : to loose by undoing a lacing
**2** *obsolete* : UNDO, DISGRACE
**un·lade** \-ˈlād\ *verb* **-lad·ed; -laded** *or* **-laden** \-ˈlā-dᵊn\; **-lad·ing** (14th century)
*transitive verb*
**1** : to take the load or cargo from
**2** : DISCHARGE, UNLOAD
*intransitive verb*
: to discharge cargo
**un·lash** \-ˈlash\ *transitive verb* (1748)
: to untie the lashing of
**un·latch** \-ˈlach\ (1642)
*transitive verb*
: to open or loose by lifting the latch
*intransitive verb*
: to become loosed or opened
**un·law·ful** \ˌən-ˈlò-fəl\ *adjective* (14th century)
**1** : not lawful : ILLEGAL
**2** : not morally right or conventional
— **un·law·ful·ly** \-f(ə-)lē\ *adverb*
— **un·law·ful·ness** \-fəl-nəs\ *noun*
**un·lay** \-ˈlā\ *verb* **-laid** \-ˈlād\; **-lay·ing** (1726)
*transitive verb*
: to untwist the strands of (as a rope)
*intransitive verb*
: UNTWIST
**un·lead·ed** \-ˈle-dəd\ *adjective* (circa 1891)
**1** : not having leads between the lines in printing
**2** : not treated or mixed with lead or lead compounds ⟨*unleaded* fuels⟩
**un·learn** \-ˈlərn\ *transitive verb* (15th century)
**1** : to put out of one's knowledge or memory
**2** : to undo the effect of : discard the habit of
**un·learned** \-ˈlər-nəd *for 1, 2,* -ˈlərnd *for 3*\ *adjective* (15th century)
**1** : possessing inadequate learning or education; *especially* : deficient in scholarly attainments
**2** : characterized by or revealing ignorance
**3** : not gained by study or training
**synonym** see IGNORANT
**un·leash** \-ˈlēsh\ *transitive verb* (circa 1671)
: to free from or as if from a leash : let loose
¹**un·less** \ən-ˈles, ˈən-ˌ\ *conjunction* [Middle English *unlesse,* alteration of *onlesse,* from *on + lesse* less] (1509)
**1** : except on the condition that : under any other circumstance than
**2** : without the accompanying circumstance or condition that : but that : BUT
²**unless** *preposition* (circa 1532)
: except possibly : EXCEPT
**un·let·tered** \ˌən-ˈle-tərd\ *adjective* (14th century)
**1 a** : lacking facility in reading and writing and ignorant of the knowledge to be gained from books **b** : ILLITERATE
**2** : not marked with letters
**synonym** see IGNORANT
**un·licked** \-ˈlikt\ *adjective* (1593)
**1** : lacking proper form or shape
**2** *archaic* : not licked dry
¹**un·like** \-ˈlīk\ *adjective* (13th century)

: not like: as **a** : marked by lack of resemblance : DIFFERENT ⟨the two books are quite *unlike*⟩ **b** : marked by inequality : UNEQUAL ⟨contributed *unlike* amounts⟩
— **un·like·ness** *noun*
²**unlike** *preposition* (1593)
: not like: as **a** : different from **b** : not characteristic of **c** : in a different manner from
**un·like·li·hood** \ˌən-ˈlī-klē-ˌhùd\ *noun* (1548)
**1** : IMPROBABILITY
**2** : something unlikely
**un·like·li·ness** \-nəs\ *noun* (1614)
: IMPROBABILITY
**un·like·ly** \-ˈlī-klē\ *adjective* (14th century)
**1** : not likely : IMPROBABLE
**2** : likely to fail : UNPROMISING
**un·lim·ber** \ˌən-ˈlim-bər\ (1802)
*transitive verb*
**1** : to detach the limber from and so make ready ⟨*unlimber* a gun for action⟩
**2** : to prepare for operation or performance ⟨*unlimbered* his banjo and began to play⟩
*intransitive verb*
: to perform the task of preparing something for action
**un·lim·it·ed** \-ˈli-mə-təd\ *adjective* (15th century)
**1** : lacking any controls : UNRESTRICTED
**2** : BOUNDLESS, INFINITE
**3** : not bounded by exceptions : UNDEFINED
— **un·lim·it·ed·ly** *adverb*
**un·link** \-ˈliŋk\ (1600)
*transitive verb*
: to unfasten the links of : SEPARATE, DISCONNECT
*intransitive verb*
: to become detached
**un·linked** \-ˈliŋ(k)t\ *adjective* (1966)
: not belonging to the same genetic linkage group ⟨*unlinked* genes⟩
**un·list·ed** \-ˈlis-təd\ *adjective* (1644)
**1** : not appearing on a list; *especially* : not appearing in a telephone book ⟨*unlisted* numbers⟩
**2** : being or involving a security not listed formally on an organized exchange : OVER-THE-COUNTER
**un·live** \-ˈliv\ *transitive verb* (1614)
: ANNUL, REVERSE
**un·load** \ˌən-ˈlōd\ (1523)
*transitive verb*
**1 a** (1) : to take off : DELIVER (2) : to take the cargo from **b** : to give outlet to : pour forth ⟨*unloaded* her bitter feelings⟩
**2** : to relieve of something burdensome, unwanted, or oppressive ⟨*unloaded* the pack animals⟩ ⟨*unloaded* himself to his friend⟩
**3** : to draw the charge from ⟨*unloaded* the gun⟩
**4** : to sell or dispose of especially in large quantities : DUMP
**5** : to hit or propel with a great release of power ⟨*unloaded* his ninth homer⟩
*intransitive verb*
**1** : to perform the act of unloading
**2** : to release or deliver something especially with power ⟨*unloaded* on the ball⟩
— **un·load·er** *noun*
**un·lock** \-ˈläk\ (15th century)
*transitive verb*
**1** : to unfasten the lock of
**2** : OPEN, UNDO
**3** : to free from restraints or restrictions ⟨the shock *unlocked* a flood of tears⟩
**4** : to furnish a key to : DISCLOSE
*intransitive verb*
: to become unfastened or freed from restraints
**un·looked–for** \-ˈlùkt-ˌfòr\ *adjective* (1535)
: not foreseen : UNEXPECTED
**un·loose** \ˌən-ˈlüs\ *transitive verb* (14th century)
**1** : to relax the strain of ⟨*unloose* a grip⟩
**2** : to release from or as if from restraints : set free

**3** : to loosen the ties of ⟨*unloose* traditional social bonds⟩
**un·loos·en** \-ˈlü-sᵊn\ *transitive verb* (15th century)
: UNLOOSE
**un·love·ly** \-ˈləv-lē\ *adjective* (14th century)
: not likable : DISAGREEABLE, UNPLEASANT
— **un·love·li·ness** \-lē-nəs\ *noun*
**un·luck·i·ly** \ˌən-ˈlə-kə-lē\ *adverb* (1530)
: UNFORTUNATELY ⟨*unluckily,* it has a nasty way of turning to rain —Ambrose Bierce⟩ ⟨his ascent being *unluckily* a little out of the perpendicular —T. L. Peacock⟩
**un·lucky** \-ˈlə-kē\ *adjective* (1530)
**1** : marked by adversity or failure ⟨an *unlucky* year⟩
**2** : likely to bring misfortune : INAUSPICIOUS
**3** : having or meeting with bad luck ⟨*unlucky* people⟩
**4** : producing dissatisfaction : REGRETTABLE
— **un·luck·i·ness** \-ˈlə-kē-nəs\ *noun*
**un·made** \ˌən-ˈmād\ *adjective* (13th century)
: not made ⟨an *unmade* bed⟩
**un·make** \-ˈmāk\ *transitive verb* **-made** \-ˈmād\; **-mak·ing** (15th century)
**1** : to cause to disappear : DESTROY
**2** : to deprive of rank or office : DEPOSE
**3** : to deprive of essential characteristics : change the nature of
**un·man** \ˌən-ˈman\ *transitive verb* (circa 1600)
**1** : to deprive of manly vigor, fortitude, or spirit
**2** : CASTRATE, EMASCULATE
**synonym** see UNNERVE
**un·man·ly** \-ˈman-lē\ *adjective* (circa 1547)
: not manly: as **a** : being of weak character : COWARDLY **b** : EFFEMINATE
— **un·man·li·ness** \-lē-nəs\ *noun*
**un·manned** \-ˈmand\ *adjective* (1544)
**1** : not manned ⟨an *unmanned* spaceflight⟩
**2** *of a hawk* : not trained
**un·man·nered** \-ˈma-nərd\ *adjective* (1594)
**1** : marked by a lack of good manners : RUDE
**2** : characterized by an absence of artificiality : UNAFFECTED
— **un·man·nered·ly** *adverb*
¹**un·man·ner·ly** \-ˈma-nər-lē\ *adverb* (14th century)
: in an unmannerly fashion
²**unmannerly** *adjective* (14th century)
: not mannerly : DISCOURTEOUS
— **un·man·ner·li·ness** \-lē-nəs\ *noun*
**un·mar·ried** \-ˈmar-ēd\ *adjective* (14th century)
: not married : **a** : not now or previously married **b** : being divorced or widowed
— **unmarried** *noun*
**un·mask** \ˌən-ˈmask\ (1602)
*transitive verb*
**1** : to remove a mask from
**2** : to reveal the true nature of : EXPOSE
*intransitive verb*
: to remove one's mask
**un·mean·ing** \-ˈmē-niŋ\ *adjective* (1704)
**1** : lacking intelligence : VAPID
**2** : having no meaning : SENSELESS
**un·me·di·at·ed** \ˌən-ˈmē-dē-ˌā-təd\ *adjective* (1648)
: not mediated : not communicated or transformed by an intervening agency ⟨experience *unmediated* by artifice⟩
**un·meet** \-ˈmēt\ *adjective* (circa 1529)
: not meet : UNSUITABLE, IMPROPER
¹**un·men·tion·able** \-ˈmen(t)-sh(ə-)nə-bəl\ *adjective* (1837)
: not fit or allowed to be mentioned or discussed : UNSPEAKABLE
²**unmentionable** *noun* (1928)
: one that is not to be mentioned or discussed: as **a** *plural* : ³PANT 1 **b** *plural* : UNDERWEAR

\ə\ abut \ᵊ\ kitten \ər\ further \a\ ash \ā\ ace
\ä\ mop, mar \aù\ out \ch\ chin \e\ bet \ē\ easy
\g\ go \i\ hit \ī\ ice \j\ job \ŋ\ sing \ō\ go
\ò\ law \òi\ boy \th\ thin \th̲\ the \ü\ loot \ù\ foot
\y\ yet \zh\ vision      *see also* Guide to Pronunciation

**un·mer·ci·ful** \ˌən-'mər-si-fəl\ *adjective* (15th century)
**1 :** not merciful **:** MERCILESS
**2 :** EXCESSIVE, EXTREME ⟨chatted for an *unmerciful* length of time⟩
— **un·mer·ci·ful·ly** \-f(ə-)lē\ *adverb*

**un·mind·ful** \-'mīn(d)-fəl\ *adjective* (14th century)
**:** not consciously aware, attentive, or heedful **:** INATTENTIVE, CARELESS

**un·mis·tak·able** \ˌən-mə-'stā-kə-bəl\ *adjective* (1666)
**:** not capable of being mistaken or misunderstood **:** CLEAR
— **un·mis·tak·ably** \-blē\ *adverb*

**un·mit·i·gat·ed** \ˌən-'mi-tə-ˌgā-təd\ *adjective* (1599)
**1 :** not lessened **:** UNRELIEVED ⟨sufferings *unmitigated* by any hope of early relief⟩
**2 :** being so definitely what is stated as to offer little chance of change or relief ⟨an *unmitigated* evil⟩
— **un·mit·i·gat·ed·ly** *adverb*
— **un·mit·i·gat·ed·ness** *noun*

**un·mold** \ˌən-'mōld\ *transitive verb* (circa 1900)
**:** to remove from a mold

**un·moor** \-'mu̇r\ (15th century)
*transitive verb*
**:** to loosen from or as if from moorings
*intransitive verb*
**:** to cast off moorings

**un·mor·al** \-'mȯr-əl, -'mär-\ *adjective* (1841)
**1 :** having no moral perception or quality; *also* **:** not influenced or guided by moral considerations
**2 :** lying outside the bounds of morals or ethics **:** AMORAL
— **un·mo·ral·i·ty** \ˌən-mə-'ra-lə-tē, -mȯ-\ *noun*

**un·muf·fle** \ˌən-'mə-fəl\ *transitive verb* (1611)
**:** to free from something that muffles

**un·muz·zle** \-'mə-zəl\ *transitive verb* (1601)
**:** to free from or as if from a muzzle

**un·my·elin·at·ed** \-'mī-ə-lə-ˌnā-təd\ *adjective* (1919)
**:** lacking a myelin sheath

**un·nail** \ˌən-'nā(ə)l\ *transitive verb* (15th century)
**:** to unfasten by removing nails

**un·nat·u·ral** \ˌən-'na-chə-rəl, -'nach-rəl\ *adjective* (15th century)
**1 :** not being in accordance with nature or consistent with a normal course of events
**2 a :** not being in accordance with normal human feelings or behavior **:** PERVERSE **b :** lacking ease and naturalness **:** CONTRIVED ⟨her manner was forced and *unnatural*⟩ **c :** inconsistent with what is reasonable or expected ⟨an *unnatural* alliance⟩
*synonym* see IRREGULAR
— **un·nat·u·ral·ly** \-'na-chə-rə-lē, -'nach-rə-, -'na-chər-\ *adverb*
— **un·nat·u·ral·ness** \-'na-chə-rəl-nəs, -'nach-rəl-\ *noun*

**un·nec·es·sar·i·ly** \ˌən-ˌne-sə-'ser-ə-lē\ *adverb* (1594)
**:** not by necessity **:** to an unnecessary degree

**un·nec·es·sary** \ˌən-'ne-sə-ˌser-ē\ *adjective* (1548)
**:** not necessary

**un·nerve** \-'nərv\ *transitive verb* (1601)
**1 :** to deprive of courage, strength, or steadiness
**2 :** to cause to become nervous **:** UPSET ☆
— **un·nerv·ing·ly** \-'nər-viṅ-lē\ *adverb*

**un·nil·hex·i·um** \ˌyü-nᵊl-'hek-sē-əm\ *noun* [New Latin, from *unnil-* (from Latin *unus* one + *nil* nothing, zero) + Greek *hex* six + New Latin *-ium* — more at ONE, NIL, SIX] (1981)
**:** the chemical element of atomic number 106
— see ELEMENT table

**un·nil·pen·ti·um** \-'pen-tē-əm\ *noun* [New Latin, from *unnil-* + Greek *pente* five + New Latin *-ium* — more at FIVE] (1981)

**:** the chemical element of atomic number 105
— see ELEMENT table

**un·nil·qua·di·um** \-'kwä-dē-əm\ *noun* [New Latin, from *unnil-* + *quadri-* + *-ium*] (1979)
**:** the chemical element of atomic number 104
— see ELEMENT table

**un·num·bered** \ˌən-'nəm-bərd\ *adjective* (14th century)
**1 :** INNUMERABLE
**2 :** not having an identifying number ⟨*unnumbered* pages⟩

**un·ob·tru·sive** \ˌən-əb-'trü-siv, -ziv\ *adjective* (1743)
**:** not obtrusive **:** not blatant, arresting, or aggressive **:** INCONSPICUOUS
— **un·ob·tru·sive·ly** *adverb*
— **un·ob·tru·sive·ness** *noun*

**un·oc·cu·pied** \ˌən-'ä-kyə-ˌpīd\ *adjective* (14th century)
**:** not occupied: as **a :** not busy **:** UNEMPLOYED **b :** not lived in **:** EMPTY

**un·or·ga·nized** \-'ȯr-gə-ˌnīzd\ *adjective* (circa 1828)
**1 :** not organized: as **a :** not brought into a coherent or well-ordered whole **b :** not belonging to a labor union
**2 :** not having the characteristics of a living organism

**un·or·tho·dox** \-'ȯr-thə-ˌdäks\ *adjective* (1657)
**:** not orthodox
— **un·or·tho·dox·ly** *adverb*

**un·or·tho·doxy** \-ˌdäk-sē\ *noun* (circa 1704)
**1 :** the quality or state of being unorthodox
**2 :** something (as an opinion or doctrine) that is unorthodox

**un·pack** \ˌən-'pak\ (15th century)
*transitive verb*
**1 a :** to remove the contents of ⟨*unpack* a trunk⟩ **b :** UNBURDEN, REVEAL ⟨must . . . *unpack* my heart with words —Shakespeare⟩
**2 :** to remove or undo from packing or a container ⟨*unpacked* his gear⟩
**3 :** to analyze the nature of by examining in detail **:** EXPLICATE ⟨*unpack* a concept⟩
*intransitive verb*
**:** to engage in unpacking a container
— **un·pack·er** *noun*

**un·paged** \-'pājd\ *adjective* (1874)
**:** having no page numbers

**un·paid** \-'pād\ *adjective* (14th century)
**1 :** not paid ⟨an *unpaid* volunteer⟩
**2 :** not paying a salary ⟨an *unpaid* position⟩

**un·paired** \-'pard, -'perd\ *adjective* (1648)
**1 :** not paired; *especially* **:** not matched or mated
**2 :** characterized by the absence of pairing ⟨electrons in the *unpaired* state⟩

**un·pal·at·able** \-'pa-lə-tə-bəl\ *adjective* (1682)
**1 :** not palatable **:** DISTASTEFUL
**2 :** UNPLEASANT, DISAGREEABLE
— **un·pal·at·abil·i·ty** \ˌən-ˌpa-lə-tə-'bi-lə-tē\ *noun*

**un·par·al·leled** \ˌən-'par-ə-ˌleld, -ləld\ *adjective* (1594)
**:** having no parallel; *especially* **:** having no equal or match **:** unique in kind or quality

**un·par·lia·men·ta·ry** \ˌən-ˌpär-lə-'men-tə-rē, -ˌpärl-yə-, -'men-trē\ *adjective* (1626)
**:** contrary to the practice of parliamentary bodies

**un·peg** \ˌən-'peg\ *transitive verb* (1602)
**1 :** to remove a peg from
**2 :** to unfasten by or as if by removing a peg

**un·peo·ple** \-'pē-pəl\ *transitive verb* (circa 1533)
**:** DEPOPULATE

**un·peo·pled** \ˌən-'pē-pəld\ *adjective* (circa 1586)
**:** not filled with or occupied by people

**un·per·fect** \-'pər-fikt\ *adjective* (14th century)
**:** IMPERFECT

**un·per·son** \'ən-'pər-sᵊn, -ˌpər-\ *noun* (1949)

**:** an individual who usually for political or ideological reasons is removed completely from recognition or consideration

**un·pick** \ˌən-'pik\ *transitive verb* (circa 1775)
**:** to undo (as sewing) by taking out stitches

**un·pile** \-'pī(ə)l\ *transitive verb* (1611)
**:** to take or disentangle from a pile

**un·pin** \-'pin\ *transitive verb* (14th century)
**1 :** to remove a pin from
**2 :** to loosen, free, or unfasten by or as if by removing a pin

**un·placed** \ˌən-'plāst\ *adjective* (1512)
**1 :** not placed **:** not having a definite or assigned place ⟨taxonomically *unplaced* organisms⟩
**2 :** not finishing in one of the first three places in a horse race

**un·pleas·ant** \-'ple-zᵊnt\ *adjective* (1538)
**:** not pleasant **:** not amiable or agreeable **:** DISPLEASING ⟨*unpleasant* odors⟩
— **un·pleas·ant·ly** *adverb*

**un·pleas·ant·ness** *noun* (1548)
**1 :** the quality or state of being unpleasant
**2 :** an unpleasant situation, experience, or event

**un·plug** \ˌən-'pləg\ *transitive verb* (circa 1775)
**1 a :** to take a plug out of **b :** to remove an obstruction from
**2 a :** to remove (as an electric plug) from a socket or receptacle **b :** to disconnect from an electric circuit by removing a plug ⟨*unplug* the refrigerator⟩

**un·plumbed** \-'pləmd\ *adjective* (1623)
**1 :** not tested with a plumb line
**2 a :** not measured with a plumb **b :** not thoroughly explored

**un·po·lar·ized** \-'pō-lə-ˌrīzd\ *adjective* (circa 1828)
**:** not polarized; *specifically* **:** having a random pattern of vibrations

**un·po·lit·i·cal** \ˌən-pə-'li-ti-kəl\ *adjective* (1643)
**:** APOLITICAL 1

**un·pop·u·lar** \ˌən-'pä-pyə-lər\ *adjective* (1647)
**:** not popular **:** viewed or received unfavorably by the public
— **un·pop·u·lar·i·ty** \ˌən-ˌpä-pyə-'lar-ə-tē\ *noun*

**un·prec·e·dent·ed** \ˌən-'pre-sə-ˌden-təd\ *adjective* (1623)
**:** having no precedent **:** NOVEL, UNEXAMPLED
— **un·prec·e·dent·ed·ly** *adverb*

**un·preg·nant** \ˌən-'preg-nənt\ *adjective* (1602)
*obsolete* **:** INEPT 1

**un·pre·tend·ing** \ˌən-pri-'ten-diṅ\ *adjective* (1697)
**:** UNPRETENTIOUS

**un·pre·ten·tious** \-'ten(t)-shəs\ *adjective* (1859)
**:** free from ostentation, elegance, or affectation **:** MODEST ⟨*unpretentious* homes⟩
— **un·pre·ten·tious·ly** *adverb*
— **un·pre·ten·tious·ness** *noun*

---

☆ **SYNONYMS**
**Unnerve, enervate, unman, emasculate** mean to deprive of strength or vigor and the capacity for effective action. UNNERVE implies marked often temporary loss of courage, self-control, or power to act ⟨*unnerved* by the near collision⟩. ENERVATE suggests a gradual physical or moral weakening (as through luxury or indolence) until one is too feeble to make an effort ⟨a nation's youth *enervated* by affluence and leisure⟩. UNMAN implies a loss of manly vigor, fortitude, or spirit ⟨a soldier *unmanned* by the terrors of battle⟩. EMASCULATE stresses a depriving of characteristic force by removing something essential ⟨an amendment that *emasculates* existing safeguards⟩.

**un·prin·ci·pled** \ˌən-ˈprin(t)-s(ə-)pəld, -sə-bəld\ *adjective* (1644)
: lacking moral principles : UNSCRUPULOUS
— **un·prin·ci·pled·ness** *noun*

**un·print·able** \-ˈprin-tə-bəl\ *adjective* (1871)
: unfit to be printed

**un·pro·fessed** \ˌən-prə-ˈfest\ *adjective* (15th century)
: not professed ⟨an *unprofessed* aim⟩

**un·prof·it·able** \ˌən-ˈprä-fə-tə-bəl, -ˈpräf-tə-bəl\ *adjective* (14th century)
: not profitable : producing no gain, good, or result
— **un·prof·it·able·ness** *noun*
— **un·prof·it·ably** \-blē\ *adverb*

**un·prom·is·ing** \-ˈprä-mə-siŋ\ *adjective* (1663)
: appearing unlikely to prove worthwhile or result favorably
— **un·prom·is·ing·ly** \-siŋ-lē\ *adverb*

**un·pro·nounced** \ˌən-prə-ˈnaun(t)st\ *adjective* (1611)
: not pronounced; *especially* : MUTE

**un·pub·lish·able** \-ˈpə-bli-shə-bəl\ *adjective* (1815)
: UNPRINTABLE

**un·qual·i·fied** \ˌən-ˈkwä-lə-ˌfīd\ *adjective* (1556)
**1** : not fit : not having requisite qualifications
**2** : not modified or restricted by reservations : COMPLETE ⟨an *unqualified* denial⟩
— **un·qual·i·fied·ly** \-ˌfī(-ə)d-lē\ *adverb*

**un·ques·tion·able** \-ˈkwes-chə-nə-bəl, -ˈkwesh-\ *adjective* (1631)
: not questionable : INDISPUTABLE ⟨*unquestionable* evidence⟩
— **un·ques·tion·ably** \-blē\ *adverb*

**un·ques·tion·ing** \-ˈkwes-chə-niŋ, -ˈkwesh-\ *adjective* (circa 1828)
: not questioning : not expressing or marked by doubt or hesitation ⟨*unquestioning* obedience⟩
— **un·ques·tion·ing·ly** \-niŋ-lē\ *adverb*

**un·qui·et** \-ˈkwī-ət\ *adjective* (1523)
**1** : not quiet : AGITATED, TURBULENT
**2** : physically, emotionally, or mentally restless : UNEASY
— **un·qui·et·ly** *adverb*
— **un·qui·et·ness** *noun*

**un·quote** \ˈən-ˌkwōt *also* -ˌkōt\ *noun* (1915)
— used orally to indicate the end of a direct quotation

**un·rav·el** \ˌən-ˈra-vəl\ (1603)
*transitive verb*
**1 a** : to disengage or separate the threads of : DISENTANGLE **b** : to cause to come apart by or as if by separating the threads of
**2** : to resolve the intricacy, complexity, or obscurity of : clear up ⟨*unravel* a mystery⟩
*intransitive verb*
: to become unraveled

**un·read** \-ˈred\ *adjective* (15th century)
**1** : not read : left unexamined
**2** : lacking the experience or the benefits of reading ⟨*unread* in political science⟩

**un·re·al** \-ˈrē(-ə)l, -ˈri(-ə)l\ *adjective* (1605)
: lacking in reality, substance, or genuineness : ARTIFICIAL, ILLUSORY; *also* : INCREDIBLE, FANTASTIC

**un·re·al·is·tic** \ˌən-ˌrē-ə-ˈlis-tik, -ˌri-ə-\ *adjective* (1865)
: not realistic : inappropriate to reality or fact
— **un·re·al·is·ti·cal·ly** \-ti-k(ə-)lē\ *adverb*

**un·re·al·i·ty** \ˌən-rē-ˈa-lə-tē\ *noun* (1751)
**1 a** : the quality or state of being unreal : lack of substance or validity **b** : something unreal, insubstantial, or visionary : FIGMENT
**2** : ineptitude in dealing with reality

**un·rea·son** \ˌən-ˈrē-zᵊn, ˈən-ˌ\ *noun* (1827)
: the absence of reason or sanity : IRRATIONALITY, MADNESS

**un·rea·son·able** \-ˈrēz-nə-bəl, -ˈrē-zᵊn-ə-bəl\ *adjective* (14th century)
**1 a** : not governed by or acting according to reason ⟨*unreasonable* people⟩ **b** : not conformable to reason : ABSURD ⟨*unreasonable* beliefs⟩

**2** : exceeding the bounds of reason or moderation ⟨working under *unreasonable* pressure⟩
— **un·rea·son·able·ness** \-nəs\ *noun*
— **un·rea·son·ably** \-blē\ *adverb*

**un·rea·soned** \-ˈrē-zᵊnd\ *adjective* (1790)
: not founded on reason or reasoning

**un·rea·son·ing** \-ˈrēz-niŋ, -ˈrē-zᵊn-iŋ\ *adjective* (1751)
: not reasoning; *especially* : not moderated or controlled by reason ⟨*unreasoning* fear⟩
— **un·rea·son·ing·ly** \-ˈrēz-niŋ-lē, -ˈrē-zᵊn-iŋ-\ *adverb*

**un·re·con·struct·ed** \ˌən-ˌrē-kən-ˈstrək-təd\ *adjective* (1867)
: not reconciled to some political, economic, or social change ⟨an *unreconstructed* rebel⟩; *also* : holding stubbornly to a particular belief, view, place, or style ⟨an *unreconstructed* New Yorker⟩

**un·reel** \ˌən-ˈrē(ə)l\ (1567)
*transitive verb*
**1** : to unwind from a reel
**2** : to perform successfully ⟨*unreeled* a 66-yard pass play⟩
**3** : REEL OFF 2
*intransitive verb*
**1** : to become unwound
**2** : to be presented ⟨the dress rehearsal *unreeled* flawlessly⟩

**un·reeve** \-ˈrēv\ *transitive verb* **-rove** \-ˈrōv\ *or* **-reeved; -reev·ing** (1600)
: to withdraw (a rope) from an opening (as a ship's block or thimble)

**un·re·gen·er·ate** \ˌən-ri-ˈje-nə-rət, -ˈjen-rət\ *adjective* (1589)
**1** : not regenerate ⟨the *unregenerate* condition of humanity⟩ ⟨*unregenerate* pagans⟩
**2 a** : not reformed : UNRECONSTRUCTED ⟨*unregenerate* liberals⟩ ⟨*unregenerate* Confederates⟩ **b** : OBSTINATE, STUBBORN ⟨struggling against *unregenerate* impulses⟩ ⟨his *unregenerate* competitiveness⟩
— **un·re·gen·er·ate·ly** *adverb*

**un·re·lent·ing** \-ˈlen-tiŋ\ *adjective* (1588)
**1** : not softening or yielding in determination : HARD, STERN ⟨an *unrelenting* leader⟩
**2** : not letting up or weakening in vigor or pace : CONSTANT ⟨the *unrelenting* struggle⟩
— **un·re·lent·ing·ly** \-tiŋ-lē\ *adverb*

**un·re·marked** \-ˈmärkt\ *adjective* (circa 1775)
: not remarked : UNNOTICED

**un·re·mit·ting** \-ˈmi-tiŋ\ *adjective* (1728)
: not remitting : CONSTANT, INCESSANT
— **un·re·mit·ting·ly** \-tiŋ-lē\ *adverb*

**un·re·quit·ed** \ˌən-ri-ˈkwī-təd\ *adjective* (circa 1542)
: not requited : not reciprocated or returned in kind ⟨*unrequited* love⟩

**un·re·serve** \-ˈzərv\ *noun* (1751)
: absence of reserve : FRANKNESS

**un·re·served** \-ˈzərvd\ *adjective* (1539)
**1** : not limited or partial : ENTIRE, UNQUALIFIED ⟨*unreserved* enthusiasm⟩
**2** : not cautious or reticent : FRANK, OPEN
**3** : not set aside for special use
— **un·re·serv·ed·ly** \-ˈzər-vəd-lē\ *adverb*
— **un·re·served·ness** \-ˈzər-vəd-nəs, -ˈzərv(d)-nəs\ *noun*

**un·rest** \ˌən-ˈrest\ *noun* (14th century)
: a disturbed or uneasy state : TURMOIL

**un·re·strained** \ˌən-ri-ˈstrānd\ *adjective* (circa 1600)
**1** : not restrained : IMMODERATE, UNCONTROLLED ⟨*unrestrained* proliferation of technology⟩
**2** : free of constraint : SPONTANEOUS ⟨felt happy and *unrestrained*⟩
— **un·re·strain·ed·ly** \-ˈstrā-nəd-lē\ *adverb*
— **un·re·strained·ness** \-ˈstrā-nəd-nəs, -ˈstrān(d)-nəs\ *noun*

**un·re·straint** \-ˈstrānt\ *noun* (1804)
: freedom from or lack of restraint

**un·rid·dle** \ˌən-ˈri-dᵊl\ *transitive verb* (circa 1586)

: to find the explanation of : FIGURE OUT, SOLVE ⟨*unriddle* a puzzle⟩ ⟨no trouble *unriddling* three-part syllogisms —*New Yorker*⟩; *also* : to make understandable : EXPLAIN ⟨just trying to *unriddle* the man —Helen Dudar⟩

**un·rig** \-ˈrig\ *transitive verb* (circa 1580)
: to strip of rigging ⟨*unrig* a ship⟩

**un·right·eous** \-ˈrī-chəs\ *adjective* (before 12th century)
**1** : not righteous : SINFUL, WICKED
**2** : UNJUST, UNMERITED ⟨intolerable and *unrighteous* interference in their lives —W. W. Wagar⟩
— **un·right·eous·ly** *adverb*
— **un·right·eous·ness** *noun*

**un·ripe** \-ˈrīp\ *adjective* (13th century)
**1** : not ripe : IMMATURE
**2** : not ready : UNPREPARED
— **un·ripe·ness** *noun*

**un·ri·valed** *or* **un·ri·valled** \ˌən-ˈrī-vəld\ *adjective* (1591)
: having no rival : INCOMPARABLE, SUPREME

**un·roll** \-ˈrōl\ (15th century)
*transitive verb*
**1** : to unwind a roll of : open out : UNCOIL
**2** : to spread out like a scroll for reading or inspection : UNFOLD, REVEAL
*intransitive verb*
: to be unrolled : UNWIND

**un·roof** \-ˈrüf, -ˈruf\ *transitive verb* (1598)
: to strip off the roof or covering of

¹**un·round** \ˌən-ˈraund\ *transitive verb* (1874)
**1** : to pronounce (a sound) without lip rounding or with decreased lip rounding
**2** : to spread (the lips) laterally ⟨necessary to *unround* the lips in pronouncing \ē\⟩

²**unround** *adjective* (1958)
: pronounced with the lips not rounded

**un·ruf·fled** \ˌən-ˈrə-fəld\ *adjective* (1659)
**1** : poised and serene especially in the face of setbacks or confusion
**2** : not ruffled : SMOOTH ⟨*unruffled* water⟩
*synonym* SEE COOL

**un·ru·ly** \-ˈrü-lē\ *adjective* [Middle English *unreuly*, from *un-* + *reuly* disciplined, from *reule* rule] (15th century)
: not readily ruled, disciplined, or managed ⟨an *unruly* crowd⟩ ⟨a mane of *unruly* hair⟩ ☆
— **un·rul·i·ness** *noun*

**un·sad·dle** \ˌən-ˈsa-dᵊl\ (14th century)
*transitive verb*
**1** : to take the saddle from

---

☆ **SYNONYMS**
**Unruly, ungovernable, intractable, refractory, recalcitrant, willful, headstrong** mean not submissive to government or control. UNRULY implies lack of discipline or incapacity for discipline and often connotes waywardness or turbulence of behavior ⟨*unruly* children⟩. UNGOVERNABLE implies either an escape from control or guidance or a state of being unsubdued and incapable of controlling oneself or being controlled by others ⟨*ungovernable* rage⟩. INTRACTABLE suggests stubborn resistance to guidance or control ⟨*intractable* opponents of the hazardous-waste dump⟩. REFRACTORY stresses resistance to attempts to manage or to mold ⟨special schools for *refractory* children⟩. RECALCITRANT suggests determined resistance to or defiance of authority ⟨acts of sabotage by a *recalcitrant* populace⟩. WILLFUL implies an obstinate determination to have one's own way ⟨a *willful* disregard for the rights of others⟩. HEADSTRONG suggests self-will impatient of restraint, advice, or suggestion ⟨a *headstrong* young calvary officer⟩.

---

\ə\ abut   \ᵊ\ kitten   \ər\ further   \a\ ash   \ā\ ace
\ä\ mop, mar   \au̇\ out   \ch\ chin   \e\ bet   \ē\ easy
\g\ go   \i\ hit   \ī\ ice   \j\ job   \ŋ\ sing   \ō\ go
\ȯ\ law   \ȯi\ boy   \th\ thin   \th\ the   \ü\ loot   \u̇\ foot
\y\ yet   \zh\ vision   *see also* Guide to Pronunciation

**2 :** to throw from the saddle
*intransitive verb*
**:** to remove the saddle from a horse
**un·said** \-'sed\ *adjective* (before 12th century)
**:** not said; *especially* **:** not spoken aloud
**un·sat·is·fac·to·ry** \-ˌsa-təs-'fak-t(ə-)rē\ *adjective* (circa 1650)
**:** not satisfactory
— **un·sat·is·fac·to·ri·ly** \-t(ə-)rə-lē\ *adverb*
— **un·sat·is·fac·to·ri·ness** \-t(ə-)rē-nəs\ *noun*
**un·sat·u·rate** \-'sa-chə-rət, -'sach-rət\ *noun* (1934)
**:** an unsaturated chemical compound
**un·sat·u·rat·ed** \-'sa-chə-ˌrā-təd\ *adjective* (1758)
**:** not saturated: as **a :** capable of absorbing or dissolving more of something ⟨an *unsaturated* solution⟩ **b :** able to form products by chemical addition; *especially* **:** containing double or triple bonds between carbon atoms
**un·saved** \-ən-'sāvd\ *adjective* (1648)
**:** not saved; *especially* **:** not absolved from eternal punishment **:** not regenerate
**un·sa·vory** \-'sā-və-rē, -'sāv-rē\ *adjective* (13th century)
**1 :** INSIPID, TASTELESS
**2 a :** unpleasant to taste or smell **b :** DISAGREEABLE, DISTASTEFUL ⟨an *unsavory* assignment⟩; *especially* **:** morally offensive
**un·say** \-'sā, *Southern also* -'se\ *transitive verb* **-said** \-'sed\; **-say·ing** \-'sā-iŋ\ (15th century)
**:** to make as if not said **:** RECANT, RETRACT
**un·say·able** \-'sā-ə-bəl\ *adjective* (1870)
**:** not sayable **:** not easily expressed or related
**un·scathed** \-'skāthd\ *adjective* (14th century)
**:** wholly unharmed **:** not injured
**un·schooled** \-'sküld\ *adjective* (1589)
**1 :** not schooled **:** UNTAUGHT, UNTRAINED ⟨an *unschooled* woodsman⟩
**2 :** not artificial **:** NATURAL ⟨*unschooled* talent⟩
**un·sci·en·tif·ic** \ˌən-ˌsī-ən-'ti-fik\ *adjective* (circa 1775)
**:** not scientific: as **a :** not used in scientific work **b :** not being in accord with the principles and methods of science ⟨*unscientific* management of woodlands⟩ ⟨an *unscientific* survey⟩ **c :** not showing scientific knowledge or familiarity with scientific methods
— **un·sci·en·tif·i·cal·ly** \-fi-k(ə-)lē\ *adverb*
**un·scram·ble** \ˌən-'skram-bəl\ *transitive verb* (circa 1920)
**1 :** to separate (as a conglomeration or tangle) into original components **:** RESOLVE, CLARIFY
**2 :** to restore (scrambled communication) to intelligible form
— **un·scram·bler** \-b(ə-)lər\ *noun*
**un·screw** \-'skrü\ (1605)
*transitive verb*
**1 :** to draw the screws from
**2 :** to loosen or withdraw by turning
*intransitive verb*
**:** to become or admit of being unscrewed
**un·script·ed** \-'skrip-təd\ *adjective* (circa 1950)
**:** not following a prepared script
**un·scru·pu·lous** \-'skrü-pyə-ləs\ *adjective* (1803)
**:** not scrupulous **:** UNPRINCIPLED
— **un·scru·pu·lous·ly** *adverb*
— **un·scru·pu·lous·ness** *noun*
**un·seal** \-'sē(ə)l\ *transitive verb* (15th century)
**:** to break or remove the seal of **:** OPEN
**un·sealed** \-'sē(ə)ld\ *adjective* (14th century)
**:** not sealed
**un·seam** \ən-'sēm\ *transitive verb* (1592)
**:** to open the seams of
**un·search·able** \-'sər-chə-bəl\ *adjective* (14th century)
**:** not capable of being searched or explored **:** INSCRUTABLE
— **un·search·ably** \-blē\ *adverb*

**un·sea·son·able** \-'sēz-nə-bəl, -'sē-z°n-ə-\ *adjective* (15th century)
**1 :** occurring at other than the proper time **:** UNTIMELY
**2 :** not being in season
**3 a :** not normal for the season of the year ⟨*unseasonable* weather⟩ **b :** marked by unseasonable weather ⟨an *unseasonable* summer⟩
— **un·sea·son·able·ness** *noun*
— **un·sea·son·ably** \-blē\ *adverb*
**un·seat** \-'sēt\ *transitive verb* (1596)
**1 :** to dislodge from one's seat especially on horseback
**2 :** to remove from a place or position; *especially* **:** to remove from political office
**¹un·seem·ly** \-'sēm-lē\ *adjective* (14th century)
**:** not seemly: as **a :** not according with established standards of good form or taste ⟨*unseemly* bickering⟩ **b :** not suitable for time or place **:** INAPPROPRIATE, UNSEASONABLE
*synonym* see INDECOROUS
— **un·seem·li·ness** \-lē-nəs\ *noun*
**²unseemly** *adverb* (14th century)
**:** in an unseemly manner
**un·seen** \ˌən-'sēn\ *adjective* (13th century)
**1 :** not seen or perceived
**2 :** SIGHT 1 ⟨an *unseen* translation⟩
**un·seg·re·gat·ed** \-'se-gri-ˌgā-təd\ *adjective* (1905)
**:** not segregated; *especially* **:** free from racial segregation
**un·se·lect·ed** \ˌən-sə-'lek-təd\ *adjective* (circa 1891)
**:** not selected **:** chosen at random
**un·se·lec·tive** \-'lek-tiv\ *adjective* (circa 1925)
**:** not marked by selection **:** RANDOM, INDISCRIMINATE
— **un·se·lec·tive·ly** \-lē\ *adverb*
**un·self·ish** \ˌən-'sel-fish\ *adjective* (1698)
**:** not selfish **:** GENEROUS
— **un·self·ish·ly** *adverb*
— **un·self·ish·ness** *noun*
**un·sell** \-'sel\ *transitive verb* **-sold** \-'sōld\; **-sel·ling** (circa 1929)
**1 :** to dissuade from a belief in the truth, value, or desirability of something ⟨ads that *unsell* the public on energy consumption⟩
**2 :** to discourage a belief in the truth, value, or desirability of ⟨I *unsold* the coat he wanted and sold him another⟩
**un·set** \-'set\ *adjective* (14th century)
**:** not set: as **a :** not fixed in a setting **:** UNMOUNTED ⟨*unset* diamonds⟩ **b :** not firmed or solidified ⟨*unset* concrete⟩
**un·set·tle** \ˌən-'se-t°l\ (1598)
*transitive verb*
**1 :** to loosen or move from a settled state or condition **:** make unstable **:** DISORDER
**2 :** to perturb or agitate mentally or emotionally **:** DISCOMPOSE
*intransitive verb*
**:** to become unsettled
**un·set·tled** \-'se-t°ld\ *adjective* (1591)
**:** not settled: as **a** (1) **:** not calm or tranquil **:** DISTURBED ⟨*unsettled* political conditions⟩ (2) **:** likely to vary widely especially in the near future **:** VARIABLE ⟨*unsettled* weather⟩ (3) **:** not settled down ⟨*unsettled* dust⟩ **b** (1) **:** not decided or determined **:** DOUBTFUL ⟨an *unsettled* state of mind⟩ (2) **:** not resolved or worked out **:** UNDECIDED ⟨an *unsettled* question⟩ **c :** characterized by irregularity ⟨an *unsettled* life⟩ **d :** not inhabited or populated ⟨*unsettled* land⟩ **e :** mentally unbalanced **f** (1) **:** not disposed of according to law ⟨an *unsettled* estate⟩ (2) **:** not paid or discharged ⟨*unsettled* debts⟩
— **un·set·tled·ness** \-t°l(d)-nəs\ *noun*
**un·set·tling** \ˌən-'set-liŋ, -'se-t°l-iŋ\ *adjective* (1665)
**:** having the effect of upsetting, disturbing, or discomposing ⟨*unsettling* images of the war⟩
— **un·set·tling·ly** \-lē\ *adverb*
**un·set·tle·ment** \-t°l-mənt\ *noun* (1648)
**1 :** an act, process, or instance of unsettling

**2 :** the quality or state of being unsettled
**un·sew** \ˌən-'sō\ *transitive verb* **-sewed**; **-sewn** \-'sōn\ *or* **-sewed**; **-sew·ing** (14th century)
**:** to undo the sewing of
**un·sex** \-'seks\ *transitive verb* (1605)
**1 :** to deprive of sex or sexual power
**2 :** to deprive of the qualities typical of one's sex
**un·shack·le** \-'sha-kəl\ *transitive verb* (1611)
**:** to free from shackles
**un·shaped** \-'shāpt\ *adjective* (1572)
**:** not shaped: as **a :** not dressed or finished to final form ⟨an *unshaped* timber⟩ **b :** imperfect in form or formulation ⟨*unshaped* ideas⟩
**un·shap·en** \-'shā-pən\ *adjective* [Middle English, from ¹*un-* + *shapen,* past participle of *shapen* to shape] (14th century)
**:** UNSHAPED
**un·sheathe** \ˌən-'shēth\ *transitive verb* (circa 1542)
**:** to draw from or as if from a sheath or scabbard
**un·ship** \-'ship\ (15th century)
*transitive verb*
**1 :** to take out of a ship **:** DISCHARGE, UNLOAD
**2 :** to remove (as an oar or tiller) from position **:** DETACH
*intransitive verb*
**:** to become or admit of being detached or removed
**un·shod** \ˌən-'shäd\ *adjective* (before 12th century)
**:** not wearing or provided with shoes
**¹un·sight** \-'sīt\ *transitive verb* (1615)
**:** to prevent from seeing
**²unsight** *adjective* (circa 1622)
**:** not sighted or examined
**un·sight·ly** \ˌən-'sīt-lē\ *adjective* (15th century)
**:** not pleasing to the sight **:** not comely
— **un·sight·li·ness** \-lē-nəs\ *noun*
**un·skilled** \-'skild\ *adjective* (1581)
**1 :** not skilled in a branch of work **:** lacking technical training ⟨an *unskilled* worker⟩
**2 :** not requiring skill ⟨*unskilled* jobs⟩
**3 :** marked by lack of skill ⟨produced *unskilled* poems⟩
**un·skill·ful** \-'skil-fəl\ *adjective* (1565)
**:** not skillful **:** lacking in skill or proficiency
— **un·skill·ful·ly** \-fə-lē\ *adverb*
— **un·skill·ful·ness** *noun*
**un·slak·able** \ˌən-'slā-kə-bəl\ *adjective* (1820)
**:** unable to be slaked **:** UNQUENCHABLE ⟨an *unslakable* thirst⟩ ⟨an *unslakable* desire for excellence⟩
**un·sling** \-'sliŋ\ *transitive verb* **-slung** \-'sləŋ\; **-sling·ing** \-'sliŋ-iŋ\ (1630)
**1 :** to take off the slings of especially aboard ship **:** release from slings
**2 :** to remove from being slung ⟨*unslung* the carbine⟩
**un·snap** \-'snap\ *transitive verb* (1862)
**:** to loosen or free by or as if by undoing a snap
**un·snarl** \-'snär(-ə)l\ *transitive verb* (1555)
**:** to disentangle a snarl in
**un·so·cia·ble** \ˌən-'sō-shə-bəl\ *adjective* (1600)
**1 :** having or showing a disinclination for social activity **:** SOLITARY, RESERVED
**2 :** not conducive to sociability
— **un·so·cia·bil·i·ty** \ˌən-ˌsō-shə-'bi-lə-tē\ *noun*
— **un·so·cia·ble·ness** \ˌən-'sō-shə-bəl-nəs\ *noun*
— **un·so·cia·bly** \-blē\ *adverb*
**un·so·cial** \-'sō-shəl\ *adjective* (1731)
**:** lacking a taste or desire for society or close association; *also* **:** marked by or arising from such a lack ⟨an *unsocial* disposition⟩
— **un·so·cial·ly** \-'sō-sh(ə-)lē\ *adverb*
**un·sold** \-'sōld\ *adjective* (14th century)
**:** not sold

**un·so·phis·ti·cat·ed** \ˌən-sə-'fis-tə-ˌkā-təd\ *adjective* (1630)
: not sophisticated: as **a** : not changed or corrupted : GENUINE **b** (1) : not worldly-wise : lacking social or economic sophistication (2) : lacking complexity of structure : SIMPLE, STRAIGHTFORWARD ⟨an *unsophisticated* analysis⟩ ⟨*unsophisticated* rhythms⟩
*synonym* see NATURAL

**un·so·phis·ti·ca·tion** \-ˌfis-tə-'kā-shən\ *noun* (1825)
: lack of or freedom from sophistication

**un·sought** \ˌən-'sȯt\ *adjective* (13th century)
: not searched for or sought out ⟨*unsought* compliments⟩

**un·sound** \-'saund\ *adjective* (14th century)
: not sound: as **a** : not healthy or whole **b** : not mentally normal : not wholly sane **c** : not firmly made, placed, or fixed **d** : not valid or true : INVALID, SPECIOUS
— **un·sound·ly** \-'saun(d)-lē\ *adverb*

**un·sound·ness** \-'saun(d)-nəs\ *noun* (1586)
**1** : the quality or state of being unsound
**2** : something (as a disease, injury, or defect) that causes one to be unsound

**un·spar·ing** \-'spar-iŋ, -'sper-\ *adjective* (circa 1586)
**1** : not merciful or forbearing : HARD, RUTHLESS
**2** : not frugal : LIBERAL, PROFUSE
— **un·spar·ing·ly** \-iŋ-lē\ *adverb*

**un·speak** \-'spēk\ *transitive verb* (1605)
*obsolete* : UNSAY

**un·speak·able** \-'spē-kə-bəl\ *adjective* (14th century)
**1 a** : incapable of being expressed in words : UNUTTERABLE **b** : inexpressibly bad : HORRENDOUS
**2** : that may not or cannot be spoken ⟨the bawdy thoughts that come into one's head — the *unspeakable* words —L. P. Smith⟩ ⟨*unspeakable* collections of consonants —Rosemary Jellis⟩
— **un·speak·ably** \-blē\ *adverb*

**un·sports·man·like** \-'spȯrts-mən-ˌlīk, -'spȯrts-\ *adjective* (1754)
: not characteristic of or exhibiting good sportsmanship : not sportsmanlike

**un·spot·ted** \-'spä-təd\ *adjective* (14th century)
: not spotted : free from spot or stain; *especially* : free from moral stain

**un·sprung** \-'sprəŋ\ *adjective* (1600)
: not sprung; *especially* : not equipped with springs

**un·sta·ble** \-'stā-bəl\ *adjective* (13th century)
: not stable : not firm or fixed : not constant: as **a** : not steady in action or movement : IRREGULAR ⟨an *unstable* pulse⟩ **b** : wavering in purpose or intent : VACILLATING **c** : lacking steadiness : apt to move, sway, or fall ⟨an *unstable* tower⟩ **d** (1) : liable to change or alteration ⟨an *unstable* economy⟩ ⟨*unstable* weather⟩ (2) : readily changing (as by decomposing) in chemical composition or biological activity **e** : characterized by lack of emotional control
*synonym* see INCONSTANT
— **un·sta·ble·ness** *noun*
— **un·sta·bly** \-b(ə-)lē\ *adverb*

**¹un·steady** \ˌən-'ste-dē\ *transitive verb* (1532)
: to make unsteady

**²unsteady** *adjective* (1598)
: not steady: as **a** : not firm or solid : not fixed in position : UNSTABLE **b** : marked by change or fluctuation : CHANGEABLE **c** : not uniform or even : IRREGULAR
— **un·stead·i·ly** \-'ste-d°l-ē\ *adverb*
— **un·stead·i·ness** \-'ste-dē-nəs\ *noun*

**un·step** \ˌən-'step\ *transitive verb* (1853)
: to remove (a mast) from a step

**un·stick** \-'stik\ *transitive verb* **-stuck** \-'stək\; **-stick·ing** (1706)
: to release from a state of adhesion

**un·stint·ing** \-'stin-tiŋ\ *adjective* (1845)
: not restricting or holding back : giving or being given freely or generously ⟨an *unstinting* volunteer⟩ ⟨*unstinting* praise⟩
— **un·stint·ing·ly** *adverb*

**un·stop** \-'stäp\ *transitive verb* (14th century)
**1** : to free from an obstruction : OPEN
**2** : to remove a stopper from

**un·stop·pa·ble** \-'stä-pə-bəl\ *adjective* (1836)
: incapable of being stopped
— **un·stop·pa·bly** \-blē\ *adverb*

**un·strap** \-'strap\ *transitive verb* (1828)
: to remove or loose a strap from

**un·stressed** \ˌən-'strest\ *adjective* (1883)
**1** : not bearing a stress or accent ⟨*unstressed* syllables⟩
**2** : not subjected to stress ⟨*unstressed* wires⟩

**un·string** \-'striŋ\ *transitive verb* **-strung** \-'strəŋ\; **-string·ing** \-'striŋ-iŋ\ (1611)
**1** : to loosen or remove the strings of
**2** : to remove from a string
**3** : to make weak, disordered, or unstable ⟨was *unstrung* by the news⟩

**un·struc·tured** \-'strək-chərd\ *adjective* (1936)
: lacking structure or organization: as **a** : not formally organized in a set or conventional pattern ⟨an *unstructured* question⟩ ⟨feel insecure in an *unstructured* situation⟩ **b** : not having a system or hierarchy typical of an organized society

**un·stuck** \ˌən-'stək\ *adjective* (1934)
: brought into a state of disarray, discomposure, or incoherence ⟨the deal came *unstuck*⟩

**un·stud·ied** \-'stə-dēd\ *adjective* (14th century)
: not studied: as **a** : not acquired by study **b** : not forced : not done or planned for effect

**un·sub·stan·tial** \ˌən-səb-'stan(t)-shəl\ *adjective* (15th century)
: not substantial : lacking substance, firmness, or strength
— **un·sub·stan·ti·al·i·ty** \-ˌstan(t)-shē-'a-lə-tē\ *noun*
— **un·sub·stan·tial·ly** \ˌən-səb-'stan(t)-sh(ə-)lē\ *adverb*

**un·suc·cess** \ˌən-sək-'ses\ *noun* (circa 1586)
: lack of success : FAILURE

**un·suc·cess·ful** \-fəl\ *adjective* (1617)
: not successful : not meeting with or producing success
— **un·suc·cess·ful·ly** \-fə-lē\ *adverb*

**un·sung** \ˌən-'səŋ\ *adjective* (15th century)
**1** : not sung
**2** : not celebrated or praised (as in song or verse) ⟨an *unsung* hero⟩

**un·sur·pris·ing** \ˌən-sə(r)-'prī-ziŋ\ *adjective* (1671)
: not surprising or unexpected

**un·sur·pris·ing·ly** \-ziŋ-lē\ *adverb* (1950)
**1** : as is not surprising ⟨matters complicate, *unsurprisingly* —Stanley Kauffmann⟩
**2** : in an unsurprising manner ⟨the story ended *unsurprisingly*⟩

**un·swathe** \-'swäth, -'swȯth, -'swāth\ *transitive verb* (14th century)
: to free from something that swathes

**un·swear** \-swar, -'swer\ *verb* **-swore** \-'swȯr, -'swȯr\; **-sworn** \-'swȯrn, -'swȯrn\; **swear·ing** (1596)
*intransitive verb*
*archaic* : to unsay or retract something sworn
*transitive verb*
*archaic* : to recant or recall (as an oath) especially by a second oath

**un·swerv·ing** \-'swər-viŋ\ *adjective* (1694)
**1** : not swerving or turning aside
**2** : STEADY, UNFALTERING ⟨*unswerving* loyalty⟩

**un·sym·met·ri·cal** \ˌən-sə-'me-tri-kəl\ *adjective* (circa 1755)
: ASYMMETRIC
— **un·sym·met·ri·cal·ly** \-k(ə-)lē\ *adverb*

**un·tan·gle** \ˌən-'taŋ-gəl\ *transitive verb* (1550)
**1** : to loose from tangles or entanglement
**2** : straighten out
*synonym* see EXTRICATE

**un·tapped** \-'tapt\ *adjective* (circa 1775)

**1** : not subjected to tapping ⟨an *untapped* keg⟩
**2** : not drawn upon or utilized ⟨as yet *untapped* markets⟩

**un·taught** \-'tȯt\ *adjective* (14th century)
**1** : not instructed or trained : IGNORANT
**2** : NATURAL, SPONTANEOUS ⟨*untaught* kindness⟩

**un·teach** \-'tēch\ *transitive verb* **-taught** \-'tȯt\; **-teach·ing** (1532)
**1** : to cause to unlearn something
**2** : to teach the contrary of

**un·ten·a·ble** \-'te-nə-bəl\ *adjective* (1647)
**1** : not able to be defended
**2** : not able to be occupied
— **un·ten·a·bil·i·ty** \ˌən-ˌte-nə-'bi-lə-tē\ *noun*

**un·tent·ed** \-'ten-təd\ *adjective* [¹un- + obsolete English *tented,* past participle of *tent* to probe] (1605)
*archaic* : not probed or dressed ⟨the *untented* woundings of a father's curse —Shakespeare⟩

**un·teth·er** \-'te-thər\ *transitive verb* (circa 1775)
: to free from a tether

**un·think** \-'thiŋk\ *transitive verb* **-thought** \-'thȯt\; **-think·ing** (circa 1600)
: to put out of mind

**un·think·able** \-'thiŋ-kə-bəl\ *adjective* (15th century)
**1** : not capable of being grasped by the mind
**2** : being contrary to what is reasonable, desirable, or probable : being out of the question
— **un·think·abil·i·ty** \ˌən-ˌthiŋ-kə-'bi-lə-tē\ *noun*
— **un·think·ably** \ˌən-'thiŋ-kə-blē\ *adverb*

**un·think·ing** \ˌən-'thiŋ-kiŋ\ *adjective* (1676)
**1** : not taking thought : HEEDLESS, UNMINDFUL
**2** : not indicating thought or reflection
**3** : not having the power of thought
— **un·think·ing·ly** \-kiŋ-lē\ *adverb*

**un·thought** \-'thȯt\ *adjective* (circa 1548)
: not anticipated : UNEXPECTED — often used with of ⟨an *unthought*-of development⟩

**un·thread** \ˌən-'thred\ *transitive verb* (1595)
**1** : to draw or take out a thread from
**2** : to loosen the threads or connections of
**3** : to make one's way through ⟨*unthread* a maze⟩

**un·throne** \-'thrōn\ *transitive verb* (1611)
: to remove from or as if from a throne

**un·ti·dy** \-'tī-dē\ *adjective* (14th century)
**1 a** : not neat : SLOVENLY **b** : not neat or orderly in habits or procedure ⟨an *untidy* mind⟩
**2 a** : not neatly organized or carried out ⟨an *untidy* manuscript⟩ **b** : conducive to a lack of neatness ⟨*untidy* tasks like bathing the baby —New Yorker⟩
— **un·ti·di·ly** \-'tī-d°l-ē\ *adverb*
— **un·ti·di·ness** \-'tī-dē-nəs\ *noun*

**un·tie** \-'tī\ *verb* **-tied; -ty·ing** *or* **-tie·ing** (before 12th century)
*transitive verb*
**1** : to free from something that ties, fastens, or restrains : UNBIND
**2 a** : to disengage the knotted parts of **b** : DISENTANGLE, RESOLVE ⟨*untie* a traffic jam⟩
*intransitive verb*
: to become loosened or unbound

**¹un·til** \ən-'til, -'tel; 'ən-ˌ, -t°l\ *preposition* [Middle English, from *un-* up to, until (akin to Old English *oth* to, until, Old High German *unt* up to, until, Old English *ende* end) + *til, till* till] (13th century)
**1** *chiefly Scottish* : TO
**2** — used as a function word to indicate continuance (as of an action or condition) to a specified time ⟨stayed *until* morning⟩
**3** : BEFORE 2 ⟨not available *until* tomorrow⟩ ⟨we don't open *until* ten⟩

**²until** *conjunction* (14th century)

---

\ə\ abut \ᵊ\ kitten \ər\ further \a\ ash \ā\ ace \ä\ mop, mar \aů\ out \ch\ chin \e\ bet \ē\ easy \g\ go \i\ hit \ī\ ice \j\ job \ŋ\ sing \ō\ go \ȯ\ law \ȯi\ boy \th\ thin \t͟h\ the \ü\ loot \ů\ foot \y\ yet \zh\ vision *see also* Guide to Pronunciation

: up to the time that : up to such time as ⟨play continued *until* it got dark⟩ ⟨never able to relax *until* he took up fishing⟩ ⟨ran *until* he was breathless⟩

**¹un·time·ly** \ˌən-ˈtīm-lē\ *adverb* (13th century)
**1** : at an inopportune time : UNSEASONABLY
**2** : before the due, natural, or proper time : PREMATURELY ⟨went *untimely* to the grave⟩

**²untimely** *adjective* (1535)
**1** : occurring or done before the due, natural, or proper time : too early : PREMATURE ⟨*untimely* death⟩
**2** : INOPPORTUNE, UNSEASONABLE ⟨an *untimely* joke⟩ ⟨*untimely* frost⟩
— **un·time·li·ness** *noun*

**un·time·ous** \-ˈtī-məs\ *adjective* (15th century)
*chiefly Scottish* : UNTIMELY

**un·tir·ing** \-ˈtī-riŋ\ *adjective* (1822)
: not becoming tired : INDEFATIGABLE ⟨an *untiring* worker⟩
— **un·tir·ing·ly** *adverb*

**un·ti·tled** \-ˈtī-t³ld\ *adjective* (1590)
**1** *obsolete* : having no title or right to rule
**2** : not named ⟨an *untitled* novel⟩
**3** : not called by a title ⟨*untitled* nobility⟩

**un·to** \ˈən-(ˌ)tü\ *preposition* [Middle English, from un- up to, until + to] (14th century)
**1** : TO
**2** — used as a function word to indicate reference or concern ⟨they became a world *unto* themselves —Anne T. Fleming⟩

**un·told** \ˌən-ˈtōld\ *adjective* (15th century)
**1** : too great or numerous to count : INCALCULABLE, VAST
**2 a** : not told or related **b** : kept secret

**un·touch·abil·i·ty** \ˌən-ˌtə-chə-ˈbi-lə-tē\ *noun* (1919)
: the quality or state of being untouchable; *especially* : the state of being an untouchable

**¹un·touch·able** \ˌən-ˈtə-chə-bəl\ *adjective* (1567)
**1 a** : forbidden to the touch : not to be handled **b** : exempt from criticism or control
**2** : lying beyond reach
**3** : disagreeable or defiling to the touch

**²untouchable** *noun* (1909)
: one that is untouchable; *specifically* : a member of a large formerly segregated hereditary group in India having in traditional Hindu belief the quality of defiling by contact a member of a higher caste

**un·touched** \ˌən-ˈtəcht\ *adjective* (14th century)
**1** : not subjected to touching : not handled
**2** : not described or dealt with
**3 a** : not tasted **b** : being in the first or a primeval state or condition
**4** : not influenced : UNAFFECTED

**un·to·ward** \ˌən-ˈtō(-ə)rd, -ˈtȯ(-ə)rd; ˌən-tə-ˈwȯrd\ *adjective* (1526)
**1** : difficult to guide, manage, or work with : UNRULY, INTRACTABLE
**2 a** : marked by trouble or unhappiness : UNLUCKY **b** : not favorable : ADVERSE, UNPROPITIOUS ⟨*untoward* side effects⟩
**3** : IMPROPER, INDECOROUS
— **un·to·ward·ly** *adverb*
— **un·to·ward·ness** *noun*

**un·tread** \ˌən-ˈtred\ *transitive verb* (1592)
*archaic* : to tread back : RETRACE

**un·tried** \-ˈtrīd\ *adjective* (1526)
**1** : not tested or proved by experience or trial
**2** : not tried in court

**un·trod** \-ˈträd\ *or* **un·trod·den** \-ˈträ-d³n\ *adjective* (1593)
: not trod : UNTRAVERSED

**un·trou·bled** \-ˈtrə-bəld\ *adjective* (15th century)
**1** : not given trouble : not made uneasy
**2** : CALM, TRANQUIL

**un·true** \-ˈtrü\ *adjective* (before 12th century)
**1** : not faithful : DISLOYAL
**2** : not according with a standard of correctness : not level or exact

**3** : not according with the facts : FALSE
— **un·tru·ly** \-ˈtrü-lē\ *adverb*

**un·truss** \-ˈtrəs\ (1577)
*transitive verb*
**1** *archaic* : UNTIE, UNFASTEN — used in the phrase *untruss one's points*
**2** *archaic* : UNDRESS
*intransitive verb*
*archaic* : to unfasten or take off one's clothes and especially one's breeches

**un·truth** \ˌən-ˈtrüth, ˈən-ˌ\ *noun* (before 12th century)
**1** *archaic* : DISLOYALTY
**2** : lack of truthfulness : FALSITY
**3** : something that is untrue : FALSEHOOD

**un·truth·ful** \-ˈtrüth-fəl\ *adjective* (circa 1843)
: not containing or telling the truth : FALSE, INACCURATE ⟨*untruthful* report⟩
**synonym** see DISHONEST
— **un·truth·ful·ly** \-fə-lē\ *adverb*
— **un·truth·ful·ness** *noun*

**un·tune** \-ˈtün, -ˈtyün\ *transitive verb* (1598)
**1** : to put out of tune
**2** : DISARRANGE, DISCOMPOSE

**un·tu·tored** \-ˈtü-tərd, -ˈtyü-\ *adjective* (1593)
**1 a** : having no formal learning or training **b** : NAIVE, UNSOPHISTICATED
**2** : not produced or developed by instruction : NATIVE ⟨*untutored* shrewdness⟩
**synonym** see IGNORANT

**un·twine** \-ˈtwīn\ (15th century)
*transitive verb*
**1** : to unwind the twisted or tangled parts of : DISENTANGLE
**2** : to remove by unwinding
*intransitive verb*
: to become disentangled or unwound

**un·twist** \ˌən-ˈtwist\ (1538)
*transitive verb*
: to separate the twisted parts of : UNTWINE
*intransitive verb*
: to become untwined

**un·twist·ed** \-ˈtwis-təd\ *adjective* (1575)
: not twisted

**un·used** \-ˈyüzd, *in the phrase "unused to"* usually -ˈyüs(t)\ *adjective* (14th century)
**1** : not habituated : UNACCUSTOMED ⟨*unused* to crowds⟩
**2** : not used: as **a** : FRESH, NEW ⟨set an *unused* canvas on the easel⟩ **b** : not put to use : IDLE ⟨*unused* land⟩ **c** : not consumed : ACCRUED ⟨*unused* sick leave⟩

**un·usu·al** \-ˈyü-zhə-wəl, -zhəl; -ˈyüzh-wəl\ *adjective* (1582)
: not usual : UNCOMMON, RARE
— **un·usu·al·ly** *adverb*
— **un·usu·al·ness** *noun*

**un·ut·ter·able** \ˌən-ˈə-tə-rə-bəl\ *adjective* (circa 1586)
: being beyond the powers of description : INEXPRESSIBLE
— **un·ut·ter·ably** \-blē\ *adverb*

**un·val·ued** \-ˈval-(ˌ)yüd, -yəd\ *adjective* (1586)
**1** *obsolete* : INVALUABLE
**2 a** : not important or prized : DISREGARDED **b** : not appraised

**un·var·nished** \-ˈvär-nisht\ *adjective* (1604)
**1 a** : not adorned or glossed : PLAIN, STRAIGHTFORWARD ⟨told the *unvarnished* truth⟩ **b** : ARTLESS, FRANK ⟨the *unvarnished* candor of old people and children —Janet Flanner⟩
**2** : not coated with or as if with varnish : CRUDE, UNFINISHED

**un·veil** \ˌən-ˈvā(ə)l\ (1599)
*transitive verb*
**1** : to remove a veil or covering from
**2** : to make public : DIVULGE, REVEAL
*intransitive verb*
: to throw off a veil or protective cloak

**un·veiled** \-ˈvā(ə)ld\ *adjective* (1606)
: not veiled : OPEN, REVEALED

**un·vo·cal** \ˌən-ˈvō-kəl\ *adjective* (1773)
**1** : not eloquent or outspoken : INARTICULATE
**2** : not musical : DISCORDANT

**un·voice** \-ˈvȯis\ *transitive verb* (1637)

: DEVOICE

**un·voiced** \-ˈvȯist\ *adjective* (1859)
**1** : not verbally expressed
**2** : VOICELESS 2

**un·war·rant·able** \-ˈwȯr-ən-tə-bəl, -ˈwär-\ *adjective* (1612)
: not justifiable : INEXCUSABLE
— **un·war·rant·ably** \-blē\ *adverb*

**un·wary** \ˌən-ˈwar-ē, -ˈwer-\ *adjective* (1579)
: not alert : easily fooled or surprised : HEEDLESS, GULLIBLE
— **un·wari·ly** \-ˈwar-ə-lē, -ˈwer-\ *adverb*
— **un·wari·ness** \-ˈwar-ē-nəs, -ˈwer-\ *noun*

**¹un·washed** \-ˈwȯsht, -ˈwäsht\ *adjective* (14th century)
**1** : not cleaned with or as if with soap and water
**2** : IGNORANT, PLEBEIAN
— **un·washed·ness** *noun*

**²unwashed** *noun* (1830)
: an ignorant or underprivileged group : RABBLE — usually used with *great* ⟨the great *unwashed*⟩

**un·watch·able** \ˌən-ˈwä-chə-bəl, -ˈwȯ-\ *adjective* (1886)
: not suitable or fit for watching : tending to discourage watching

**un·wea·ried** \-ˈwir-ēd\ *adjective* (13th century)
: not tired or jaded : FRESH
— **un·wea·ried·ly** *adverb*

**un·weave** \-ˈwēv\ *transitive verb* -wove \-ˈwōv\; -wo·ven \-ˈwō-vən\; -weav·ing (1542)
: DISENTANGLE, UNRAVEL

**un·weet·ing** \-ˈwē-tiŋ\ *adjective* (14th century)
*archaic* : UNWITTING
— **un·weet·ing·ly** \-tiŋ-lē\ *adverb, archaic*

**un·weight** \-ˈwāt\ (circa 1939)
*transitive verb*
: to reduce momentarily the force exerted by (as a ski) upon a surface by shifting the weight or position of one's body
*intransitive verb*
: to unweight something by shifting the weight or position of one's body

**un·well** \ˌən-ˈwel\ *adjective* (15th century)
**1** : being in poor health : AILING, SICK
**2** : undergoing menstruation

**un·whole·some** \-ˈhōl-səm\ *adjective* (13th century)
**1** : detrimental to physical, mental, or moral well-being : UNHEALTHY ⟨*unwholesome* food⟩ ⟨*unwholesome* pastimes⟩
**2 a** : CORRUPT, UNSOUND **b** : offensive to the senses : LOATHSOME
— **un·whole·some·ly** *adverb*

**un·wieldy** \-ˈwē(ə)l-dē\ *adjective* (1530)
: not easily managed, handled, or used (as because of bulk, weight, complexity, or awkwardness) : CUMBERSOME
— **un·wield·i·ly** \-ˈwēl-də-lē\ *adverb*
— **un·wield·i·ness** \-dē-nəs\ *noun*

**un·will·ing** \-ˈwi-liŋ\ *adjective* (before 12th century)
: not willing: **a** : LOATH, RELUCTANT ⟨was *unwilling* to learn⟩ **b** : done or given reluctantly ⟨*unwilling* approval⟩ **c** : offering opposition : OBSTINATE ⟨an *unwilling* student⟩
— **un·will·ing·ly** \-liŋ-lē\ *adverb*
— **un·will·ing·ness** *noun*

**un·wind** \-ˈwīnd\ *verb* -wound \-ˈwau̇nd\; -wind·ing (14th century)
*transitive verb*
**1 a** : to cause to uncoil : wind off : UNROLL **b** : to free from or as if from a binding or wrapping **c** : to release from tension : RELAX
**2** *archaic* : to trace to the end ⟨*unwinding* the labyrinth and bringing the hero out —Laurence Sterne⟩
*intransitive verb*
**1** : to become uncoiled or disentangled : UNFOLD
**2** : to become released from tension

**un·wis·dom** \,ən-'wiz-dəm\ *noun* (before 12th century)
: lack of wisdom : FOOLISHNESS, FOLLY

**un·wise** \-'wīz\ *adjective* (before 12th century)
: lacking wisdom or good sense : FOOLISH, IMPRUDENT
— **un·wise·ly** *adverb*

**un·wish** \-'wish\ *transitive verb* (1594)
*obsolete* : to wish away

**un·wit·ting** \-'wi-tiŋ\ *adjective* (before 12th century)
**1** : not knowing : UNAWARE ⟨kept the truth from their *unwitting* friends⟩
**2** : not intended : INADVERTENT ⟨an *unwitting* mistake⟩
— **un·wit·ting·ly** \-tiŋ-lē\ *adverb*

**un·wont·ed** \-'wȯn-təd, -'wōn- *also* -'wən- *or* -'wän-\ *adjective* (1553)
**1** : being out of the ordinary : RARE, UNUSUAL
**2** : not accustomed by experience
— **un·wont·ed·ly** *adverb*
— **un·wont·ed·ness** *noun*

**un·world·ly** \-'wər(-ə)l-dlē, -'wərl-lē\ *adjective* (1707)
**1** : not of this world : UNEARTHLY; *specifically* : SPIRITUAL
**2 a** : not wise in the ways of the world : NAIVE
**b** : not swayed by mundane considerations
— **un·world·li·ness** \-'wərl(d)-lē-nəs\ *noun*

**un·worn** \-'wȯrn, -'wȯrn\ *adjective* (circa 1586)
**1 a** : not impaired by use : not worn away **b** : not worn : NEW
**2** : not jaded : FRESH, ORIGINAL

**un·wor·thy** \,ən-'wər-thē\ *adjective* (13th century)
**1 a** : lacking in excellence or value : POOR, WORTHLESS **b** : BASE, DISHONORABLE
**2** : not meritorious : UNDESERVING ⟨*unworthy* of attention⟩
**3** : not deserved : UNMERITED ⟨*unworthy* treatment⟩
**4** : inappropriate to one's condition or station ⟨actions *unworthy* of a gentleman⟩
— **un·wor·thi·ly** \-thə-lē\ *adverb*
— **un·wor·thi·ness** \-thē-nəs\ *noun*

**un·wrap** \-'rap\ *transitive verb* (14th century)
: to remove the wrapping from : DISCLOSE ⟨*unwrap* a package⟩ ⟨*unwrap* evidence in a criminal case⟩

**un·wreathe** \-'rēth\ *transitive verb* (1591)
: UNCOIL, UNTWIST

**un·writ·ten** \-'ri-tᵊn\ *adjective* (14th century)
**1** : not expressed in writing : ORAL, TRADITIONAL
**2** : containing no writing : BLANK

**unwritten constitution** *noun* (1890)
: a constitution not embodied in a single document but based chiefly on custom and precedent as expressed in statutes and judicial decisions

**unwritten law** *noun* (1641)
: law based chiefly on custom rather than legislative enactments

**un·yield·ing** \,ən-'yē(ə)l-diŋ\ *adjective* (1658)
**1** : characterized by lack of softness or flexibility
**2** : characterized by firmness or obduracy
— **un·yield·ing·ly** \-diŋ-lē\ *adverb*

**un·yoke** \-'yōk\ (before 12th century)
*transitive verb*
**1** : to free from a yoke or harness
**2** : to take apart : DISJOIN
*intransitive verb*
**1** *archaic* : to unharness a draft animal
**2** *archaic* : to cease from work

**un·zip** \-'zip\ (1939)
*transitive verb*
: to zip open
*intransitive verb*
: to open by or as if by means of a zipper

**¹up** \'əp\ *adverb* [partly from Middle English *up* upward, from Old English *ūp;* partly from Middle English *uppe* on high, from Old English; both akin to Old High German *ūf* up and

probably to Latin *sub* under, Greek *hypo* under, *hyper* over — more at OVER] (before 12th century)
**1 a** (1) : in or into a higher position or level; *especially* : away from the center of the earth (2) : from beneath the ground or water to the surface (3) : from below the horizon (4) : UPSTREAM (5) : in or into an upright position ⟨sit *up*⟩; *especially* : out of bed **b** : upward from the ground or surface ⟨pull *up* a daisy⟩ **c** : so as to expose a particular surface
**2** : with greater intensity ⟨speak *up*⟩
**3 a** : in or into a better or more advanced state **b** : at an end ⟨your time is *up*⟩ **c** : in or into a state of greater intensity or excitement **d** : in a continual sequence : in continuance from a point or to a point ⟨from third grade *up*⟩ ⟨at prices of $10 and *up*⟩ ⟨*up* until now⟩
**4 a** (1) : into existence, evidence, prominence, or prevalence ⟨put *up* several new buildings⟩ (2) : into operation or practical form **b** : into consideration or attention ⟨bring *up* for discussion⟩
**5** : into possession or custody
**6 a** : ENTIRELY, COMPLETELY ⟨button *up* your coat⟩ **b** — used as an intensifier ⟨clean *up* the house⟩
**7** : in or into storage : BY ⟨lay *up* supplies⟩
**8 a** : so as to arrive or approach **b** : in a direction conventionally the opposite of down: (1) : to windward (2) : NORTHWARD (3) : to or at the top (4) : to or at the rear of a theatrical stage
**9** : in or into parts
**10** : to a stop — usually used with *draw, bring, fetch,* or *pull*
**11** : for each side ⟨the score is 15 *up*⟩

**²up** *adjective* (before 12th century)
**1 a** : risen above the horizon ⟨the sun is *up*⟩ **b** : STANDING **c** : being out of bed **d** : relatively high ⟨the river is *up*⟩ ⟨was well *up* in her class⟩ **e** : being in a raised position : LIFTED ⟨windows are *up*⟩ **f** : being in a state of completion : CONSTRUCTED, BUILT **g** : having the face upward **h** : mounted on a horse ⟨a new jockey *up*⟩ **i** : grown above a surface ⟨the corn is *up*⟩ **j** (1) : moving, inclining, or directed upward ⟨the *up* escalator⟩ (2) : bound in a direction regarded as up
**2 a** (1) : marked by agitation, excitement, or activity (2) : positive or upbeat in mood or demeanor **b** : being above a former or normal level (as of quantity or intensity) ⟨attendance is *up*⟩ ⟨the wind is *up*⟩ **c** : exerting enough power (as for operation) ⟨sail when steam is *up*⟩ **d** : READY; *specifically* : highly prepared **e** : going on : taking place ⟨find out what is *up*⟩
**3 a** : risen from a lower position ⟨men *up* from the ranks⟩ **b** : being at the same level or point ⟨did not feel *up* to par⟩ **c** (1) : well informed : ABREAST ⟨*up* on the news⟩ (2) : being on schedule ⟨*up* on his homework⟩ **d** : being ahead of one's opponent
**4 a** : presented for or undergoing consideration ⟨contract *up* for negotiation⟩; *also* : charged before a court ⟨*up* for robbery⟩ **b** : being the one whose turn it is ⟨you're *up* next⟩
**5** *of a quark* : having an electric charge of +²⁄₃, zero charm, and zero strangeness — compare ⁴DOWN 6
— **up against** : confronted with : face-to-face with ⟨the problem we are *up against*⟩
— **up to 1** : capable of performing or dealing with ⟨feels *up to* her role⟩ **2** : engaged in ⟨what is he *up to*⟩ **3** : being the responsibility of ⟨it's *up to* me⟩

**³up** *preposition* (1509)
**1 a** — used as a function word to indicate motion to or toward or situation at a higher point of ⟨went *up* the stairs⟩ **b** : up into or in the ⟨went *up* an attic⟩
**2 a** : in a direction regarded as being toward or near the upper end or part of ⟨lives a few

miles *up* the coast⟩ ⟨walked *up* the street⟩ **b** : toward or near a point closer to the source or beginning of ⟨sail *up* the river⟩
**3** : in the direction opposite to ⟨sailed *up* the wind⟩

**⁴up** *noun* (1536)
**1** : one in a high or advantageous position
**2** : an upward slope
**3** : a period or state of prosperity or success
**4** : ³UPPER

**⁵up** *verb* **upped** \'əpt\ *or in intransitive verb 2* **up; upped; up·ping; ups** *or in intransitive verb 2* **up** (1643)
*intransitive verb*
**1 a** : to rise from a lying or sitting position **b** : to move upward : ASCEND
**2** — used with *and* and another verb to indicate that the action of the following verb was either surprisingly or abruptly initiated ⟨he *up* and married a showgirl⟩
*transitive verb*
**1** : RAISE, LIFT
**2 a** : to advance to a higher level: (1) : INCREASE (2) : PROMOTE 1a **b** : RAISE 8d, e

**up–and–com·ing** \,əp-ən(d)-'kə-miŋ, ,əp-ᵊm-\ *adjective* (1926)
: gaining prominence and likely to advance or succeed
— **up–and–com·er** \-'kə-mər\ *noun*

**up–and–down** \-'daůn\ *adjective* (circa 1755)
**1** : marked by alternate upward and downward movement, action, or surface
**2** : PERPENDICULAR

**up and down** *adverb* (12th century)
**1** : TO AND FRO ⟨paced *up and down*⟩
**2** : alternately upward and downward ⟨jump *up and down*⟩
**3** *archaic* : here and there especially throughout an area
**4** : with regard to every particular : THOROUGHLY ⟨knew the territory *up and down*⟩
— **up and down** *preposition*

**up–and–up** \'əp-ən-'əp\ *noun* (1863)
: an honest or respectable course — used in the phrase *on the up-and-up*

**Upa·ni·shad** \ü-'pä-ni-,shäd, yü-'pa-nə-,shad\ *noun* [Sanskrit *upaniṣad*] (1805)
: one of a class of Vedic treatises dealing with broad philosophic problems
— **Upa·ni·shad·ic** \(,)ü-,pä-ni-'shä-dik, (,)yü-,pa-nə-'sha-dik\ *adjective*

**upas** \'yü-pəs\ *noun* [Indonesian Malay *pohon upas* poison tree] (1783)
**1** : a tall tropical Asian tree (*Antiaris toxicaria*) of the mulberry family with a latex that contains poisonous glucosides used as an arrow poison; *also* : a poisonous concentrate of the juice or latex of a upas
**2** : a poisonous or harmful influence or institution

**¹up·beat** \'əp-,bēt\ *noun* (1869)
**1** : an unaccented beat in a musical measure; *specifically* : the last beat of the measure
**2** : an increase in activity or prosperity ⟨business that is on the *upbeat*⟩

**²upbeat** *adjective* (1947)
: CHEERFUL, OPTIMISTIC

**up–bow** \'əp-,bō\ *noun* (circa 1890)
: a stroke in playing a bowed instrument in which the bow is moved across the strings from the tip to the heel

**up·braid** \,əp-'brād\ *transitive verb* [Middle English *upbreyden,* from Old English *ūpbregdan,* probably from *ūp* up + *bregdan* to snatch, move suddenly — more at BRAID] (14th century)
**1** : to criticize severely : find fault with
**2** : to reproach severely : scold vehemently
**synonym** see SCOLD
— **up·braid·er** *noun*

---

\ə\ abut \ᵊ\ kitten \ər\ further \a\ ash \ā\ ace
\ä\ mop, mar \aů\ out \ch\ chin \e\ bet \ē\ easy
\g\ go \i\ hit \ī\ ice \j\ job \ŋ\ sing \ō\ go
\ȯ\ law \ȯi\ boy \th\ thin \th\ the \ü\ loot \ů\ foot
\y\ yet \zh\ vision *see also* Guide to Pronunciation

**up·bring·ing** \'əp-ˌbriŋ-iŋ\ *noun* (1520)
: early training; *especially* : a particular way of bringing up a child ⟨had a strict *upbringing*⟩
**up·build** \ˌəp-'bild\ *transitive verb* **-built** \-'bilt\; **-build·ing** (1513)
: BUILD UP
**up·cast** \'əp-ˌkast\ *noun* (1890)
: something cast up
**up·chuck** \'əp-ˌchək\ *verb* (1936)
: VOMIT
**up close** *adverb or adjective* (1851)
: at close range
**up·coast** \'əp-ˌkōst\ *adverb* (1909)
: up the coast
**up·com·ing** \'əp-ˌkə-miŋ\ *adjective* (1944)
: FORTHCOMING, APPROACHING
**up–coun·try** \'əp-ˌkən-trē\ *adjective* (1835)
: of, relating to, or characteristic of an inland, upland, or outlying region
— **up–country** \'əp-ˈ\ *noun*
— **up–country** \'əp-ˈ\ *adverb*
¹**up·date** \ˌəp-'dāt\ *transitive verb* (1910)
: to bring up to date
²**up·date** \'əp-ˌdāt\ *noun* (1965)
**1** : an act or instance of updating
**2** : current information for updating something
**3** : an up-to-date version, account, or report
**up·do** \'əp-(ˌ)dü\ *noun, plural* **updos** [*up*-swept hair*do*] (1938)
: an upswept hairdo
**up·draft** \'əp-ˌdraft, -ˌdråft\ *noun* (circa 1887)
: an upward movement of gas (as air)
**up·end** \ˌəp-'end\ (1823)
*transitive verb*
**1** : to set or stand on end; *also* : OVERTURN 1
**2 a** : to affect to the point of being upset or flurried ⟨a . . . literary shocker, designed to *upend* the credulous matrons —Wolcott Gibbs⟩ **b** : DEFEAT, BEAT
*intransitive verb*
: to rise on an end
**up·field** \'əp-'fē(ə)ld\ *adverb or adjective* (circa 1934)
: in or into the part of the field toward which the offensive team is headed
**up–front** \ˌəp-'frənt, 'əp-ˌ\ *adjective* (1945)
: being or coming in or at the front: as **a** (1) : being in a conspicuous or leading position (2) : FRANK, FORTHRIGHT **b** : playing in a front line (as in football) **c** : paid or payable in advance
**up front** *adverb* (1937)
**1** : in or at the front
**2** : in advance
**3** : in an up-front manner : FRANKLY
¹**up·grade** \'əp-ˌgrād\ *noun* (1873)
**1** : an upward grade or slope
**2** : INCREASE, RISE
**3** : IMPROVEMENT 2b
²**up·grade** \'əp-ˌgrād, ˌəp-'\ *transitive verb* (1901)
: to raise or improve the grade of: as **a** : to improve (livestock) by use of purebred sires **b** : to advance to a job requiring a higher level of skill especially as part of a training program **c** : to raise the quality of **d** : to raise the classification and usually the price of without improving the quality **e** : to extend the usefulness of (as a device)
— **up·grad·abil·i·ty** *or* **up·grade·abil·i·ty** \ˌəp-ˌgrā-də-'bi-lə-tē\ *noun*
— **up·grad·able** *or* **up·grade·able** \ˌəp-'grā-də-bəl\ *adjective*
**up·growth** \'əp-ˌgrōth\ *noun* (1844)
: the process of growing upward : DEVELOPMENT; *also* : a product or result of this
**up·heav·al** \ˌəp-'hē-vəl, (ˌ)ə-'pē-\ *noun* (1838)
**1** : the action or an instance of upheaving especially of part of the earth's crust
**2** : extreme agitation or disorder : radical change; *also* : an instance of this
**up·heave** \ˌəp-'hēv, (ˌ)ə-'pēv\ (14th century)
*transitive verb*
: to heave up : LIFT
*intransitive verb*
: to move upward especially with power

— **up·heav·er** *noun*
¹**up·hill** \'əp-ˌhil\ *noun* (1548)
: rising ground : ASCENT
²**up·hill** \-'hil\ *adverb* (1607)
**1** : upward on a hill or incline
**2** : against difficulties ⟨seemed to be talking *uphill* —Willa Cather⟩
³**up·hill** \-ˌhil\ *adjective* (1613)
**1** : situated on elevated ground
**2 a** : going up : ASCENDING **b** : being the higher one or part especially of a set; *specifically* : being nearer the top of an incline
**3** : DIFFICULT, LABORIOUS
**up·hold** \(ˌ)əp-'hōld\ *transitive verb* **-held** \-'held\; **-hold·ing** (13th century)
**1 a** : to give support to **b** : to support against an opponent
**2 a** : to keep elevated **b** : to lift up
*synonym* see SUPPORT
— **up·hold·er** *noun*
**up·hol·ster** \(ˌ)əp-'hōl-stər, (ˌ)ə-'pōl-\ *transitive verb* **-stered**; **-ster·ing** \-st(ə-)riŋ\ [back-formation from *upholstery*] (1864)
: to furnish with or as if with upholstery
— **up·hol·ster·er** \-stər-ər\ *noun*
**up·hol·stery** \-st(ə-)rē\ *noun, plural* **-ster·ies** [Middle English *upholdester* upholsterer, from *upholden* to uphold, from *up* + *holden* to hold] (1649)
: materials (as fabric, padding, and springs) used to make a soft covering especially for a seat
**up·keep** \'əp-ˌkēp\ *noun* (1884)
**1** : the act of maintaining in good condition : the state of being maintained in good condition
**2** : the cost of maintaining in good condition
**up·land** \'əp-lənd, -ˌland\ *noun* (1566)
**1** : high land especially at some distance from the sea : PLATEAU
**2** : ground elevated above the lowlands along rivers or between hills
— **upland** *adjective*
— **up·land·er** \-lən-dər, -ˌlan-\ *noun*
**upland cotton** *noun* (1819)
: a widely cultivated American cotton plant (*Gossypium hirsutum*) having short- to medium-staple fibers
**upland sandpiper** *noun* (circa 1890)
: a large North American sandpiper (*Bartramia longicauda*) that frequents fields and prairies — called also *upland plover*
¹**up·lift** \(ˌ)əp-'lift\ (14th century)
*transitive verb*
**1** : to lift up : ELEVATE; *especially* : to cause (a portion of the earth's surface) to rise above adjacent areas
**2** : to improve the spiritual, social, or intellectual condition of
*intransitive verb*
: RISE
— **up·lift·er** *noun*
²**up·lift** \'əp-ˌlift\ *noun* (circa 1845)
**1** : an act, process, result, or cause of uplifting: as **a** (1) : the uplifting of a part of the earth's surface (2) : an uplifted mass of land **b** : a bettering of a condition especially spiritually, socially, or intellectually **c** (1) : influences intended to uplift (2) : a social movement to improve especially morally or culturally
**2** : a brassiere designed to hold the breasts up
**up·link** \'əp-ˌliŋk\ *noun* (1968)
**1** : a communications channel for transmissions to a spacecraft; *also* : the transmissions themselves
**2** : a facility on earth for transmitting to a spacecraft
**up·load** \(ˌ)əp-'lōd, 'əp-ˌ\ *transitive verb* (1983)

upland sandpiper

: to transfer (information) from a microcomputer to a remote computer usually with a modem
**up·man·ship** \'əp-mən-ˌship\ *noun* (1959)
: ONE-UPMANSHIP
**up·mar·ket** \'əp-'mär-kət\ *adjective* (1972)
: UPSCALE
— **upmarket** *adverb*
**up·most** \'əp-ˌmōst\ *adjective* (1560)
: UPPERMOST
¹**up·on** \ə-'pȯn, -'pän\ *preposition* (13th century)
: ON
²**up·on** \ə-'pȯn, -'pän\ *adverb* (14th century)
**1** *obsolete* : on the surface : on it
**2** *obsolete* : THEREAFTER, THEREON
¹**up·per** \'ə-pər\ *adjective* [Middle English, comparative of ²*up*] (14th century)
**1 a** : higher in physical position, rank, or order **b** : farther inland ⟨the *upper* Mississippi⟩
**2** : constituting the branch of a bicameral legislature that is usually smaller and more restricted in membership and possesses greater traditional prestige than the lower house
**3 a** : constituting a stratum relatively near the earth's surface **b** *capitalized* : being a later epoch or series of the period or system named ⟨*Upper* Cretaceous⟩ ⟨*Upper* Paleolithic⟩
**4** : NORTHERN ⟨*upper* Manhattan⟩
²**upper** *noun* (1789)
: one that is upper: as **a** : the parts of a shoe or boot above the sole **b** : an upper tooth or denture **c** : an upper berth
— **on one's uppers** : in straitened circumstances : DESTITUTE
³**upper** *noun* [*up* + ²-*er*] (circa 1968)
**1** : a stimulant drug; *especially* : AMPHETAMINE
**2** : something that induces a state of good feeling or exhilaration
¹**up·per·case** \ˌə-pər-'kās\ *adjective* [from the compositor's practice of keeping capital letters in the upper of a pair of type cases] (1738)
: CAPITAL 1
²**uppercase** *noun* (circa 1916)
: capital letters
³**uppercase** *transitive verb* **-cased; -casing** (1949)
: to print or set in capital letters
**upper case** *noun* (1683)
: a type case containing capitals and usually small capitals, fractions, symbols, and accents
**upper–class** *adjective* (1837)
: of, relating to, or characteristic of the upper class
**upper class** *noun* (1839)
: a social class occupying a position above the middle class and having the highest status in a society
**up·per·class·man** \ˌə-pər-'klas-mən\ *noun* (1871)
: a member of the junior or senior class in a school or college
**upper crust** *noun* (1836)
: the highest social class or group; *especially* : the highest circle of the upper class
— **upper–crust** *adjective*
**up·per·cut** \'ə-pər-ˌkət\ *noun* (1842)
: a swinging blow (as in boxing) directed upward with a bent arm
— **uppercut** *verb*
**upper hand** *noun* (15th century)
: MASTERY, ADVANTAGE, CONTROL ⟨was determined not to let the opposition get the *upper hand*⟩
**up·per·most** \'ə-pər-ˌmōst\ *adverb* (15th century)
: in or into the highest or most prominent position
— **uppermost** *adjective*
**up·per·part** \-ˌpärt\ *noun* (1526)
: a part lying on the upper side (as of a bird)
**upper respiratory** *adjective* (1950)
: of, affecting, or being the part of the respiratory system that includes the nose, nasal passages, and nasopharynx ⟨*upper respiratory* tract⟩ ⟨*upper respiratory* infection⟩

**up·pish** \'ə-pish\ *adjective* (circa 1734)
: UPPITY
— **up·pish·ly** *adverb*
— **up·pish·ness** *noun*
**up·pi·ty** \'ə-pə-tē\ *adjective* [probably from *up* + *-ity* (as in *persnickity,* variant of *persnickety*)] (1880)
: putting on or marked by airs of superiority : ARROGANT, PRESUMPTUOUS ⟨*uppity* technicians⟩ ⟨a small *uppity* country⟩
— **up·pi·ti·ness** *also* **up·pi·ty·ness** *noun*
**up·raise** \(ˌ)əp-'rāz\ *transitive verb* (14th century)
: to raise or lift up : ELEVATE
**up·rate** \'əp-ˌrāt\ *transitive verb* (1965)
: UPGRADE; *specifically* : to improve the power output of (as an engine)
**up·rear** \-'rir\ (14th century)
*transitive verb*
1 : to lift up
2 : ERECT
*intransitive verb*
: RISE
¹**up·right** \'əp-ˌrīt\ *adjective* (before 12th century)
1 a : PERPENDICULAR, VERTICAL b : erect in carriage or posture c : having the main axis or a main part perpendicular ⟨*upright* freezer⟩
2 : marked by strong moral rectitude ☆
— **up·right·ly** *adverb*
— **up·right·ness** *noun*
²**upright** *adverb* (1590)
: vertically upward : in an upright position
³**upright** *noun* (1683)
1 : the state of being upright : PERPENDICULAR ⟨a pillar out of *upright*⟩
2 : something that stands upright; *especially* : a football goalpost — usually used in plural
3 : UPRIGHT PIANO
**upright piano** *noun* (circa 1890)
: a piano with vertical frame and strings — compare GRAND PIANO
¹**up·rise** \ˌəp-'rīz\ *intransitive verb* **up·rose** \-'rōz\; **up·ris·en** \-'ri-zᵊn\; **up·ris·ing** \-'rī-ziŋ\ (14th century)
1 a : to rise to a higher position b (1) : STAND UP (2) : to get out of bed c : to come into view especially from below the horizon
2 : to rise up in sound
— **up·ris·er** \ˌəp-'rī-zər, 'əp-ˌ\ *noun*
²**up·rise** \'əp-ˌrīz\ *noun* (15th century)
1 : an act or instance of uprising
2 : an upward slope
**up·ris·ing** \'əp-ˌrī-ziŋ\ *noun* (13th century)
: an act or instance of rising up; *especially* : a usually localized act of popular violence in defiance usually of an established government
*synonym* see REBELLION
**up·riv·er** \'əp-'ri-vər\ *adverb or adjective* (1774)
: toward or at a point nearer the source of a river
**up·roar** \'əp-ˌrōr, -ˌrȯr\ *noun* [by folk etymology from Dutch *oproer,* from Middle Dutch, from *op* up (akin to Old English *ūp*) + *roer* motion; akin to Old English *hrēran* to stir] (1526)
: a state of commotion, excitement, or violent disturbance ◆
**up·roar·i·ous** \ˌəp-'rōr-ē-əs, -'rȯr-\ *adjective* (1819)
1 : marked by uproar
2 : very noisy and full
3 : extremely funny ⟨an *uproarious* comedy⟩
— **up·roar·i·ous·ly** *adverb*
— **up·roar·i·ous·ness** *noun*
**up·root** \(ˌ)əp-'rüt, -'rùt\ *transitive verb* (circa 1620)
1 : to remove as if by pulling up
2 : to pull up by the roots
3 : to displace from a country or traditional habitat
*synonym* see EXTERMINATE
— **up·root·ed·ness** *noun*
— **up·root·er** *noun*
**up·rush** \'əp-ˌrəsh\ *noun* (1871)

1 : an upward rush (as of gas or liquid)
2 : a sudden increase
**ups and downs** *noun plural* (1659)
: alternating rise and fall especially in fortune
**up·scale** \'əp-ˌskāl\ *adjective* (1966)
: relating to, being, or appealing to affluent consumers; *also* : of a superior quality
— **upscale** *adverb or transitive verb*
¹**up·set** \(ˌ)əp-'set\ *verb* **-set; -set·ting** (1677)
*transitive verb*
1 : to thicken and shorten (as a heated bar of iron) by hammering on the end : SWAGE
2 : to force out of the usual upright, level, or proper position : OVERTURN
3 a : to trouble mentally or emotionally : disturb the poise of b : to throw into disorder c : INVALIDATE d : to defeat unexpectedly
4 : to cause a physical disorder in; *specifically* : to make somewhat ill
*intransitive verb*
: to become overturned
*synonym* see DISCOMPOSE
— **up·set·ter** *noun*
²**up·set** \'əp-ˌset\ *noun* (1804)
1 : an act of overturning : OVERTURN
2 a (1) : an act of throwing into disorder : DERANGEMENT (2) : a state of disorder : CONFUSION b : an unexpected defeat
3 a : a minor physical disorder ⟨a stomach *upset*⟩ b : an emotional disturbance ⟨went through a big *upset* after his father's death⟩
4 a : a part of a rod (as the head on a bolt) that is upset b : the expansion of a bullet on striking
³**up·set** \(ˌ)əp-'set\ *adjective* (1805)
: emotionally disturbed or agitated ⟨was too *upset* to speak to him⟩
**up·set price** \'əp-ˌset-\ *noun* (1814)
: the minimum price set for property offered at auction or public sale
**up·shift** \'əp-ˌshift\ *intransitive verb* (1952)
: to shift an automotive vehicle into a higher gear
— **upshift** *noun*
**up·shot** \'əp-ˌshät\ *noun* (1604)
: the final result : OUTCOME
¹**up·side** \'əp-ˌsīd\ *noun* [²*up* + ¹*side*] (1927)
1 : an upward trend (as of prices)
2 : a positive aspect
²**up·side** \'əp-ˌsīd\ *preposition* [perhaps from ¹*up* + *-side* (as in *alongside*)] (1929)
: up on or against the side of ⟨layin' in this death cell, writin' my time *upside* the wall —Lonnie Johnson⟩ ⟨if they wish to knock a thug *upside* the head, they do so —Robert MacKenzie⟩
**up·side down** \'əp-ˌsīd-'daùn\ *adverb* [alteration of Middle English *up so doun,* from *up + so + doun* down] (15th century)
1 : in such a way that the upper and the lower parts are reversed in position
2 : in or into great disorder
— **upside–down** *adjective*
**upside–down cake** *noun* (1930)
: a cake baked with its batter covering an arrangement of fruit (as pineapple) and served fruit side up
**up·si·lon** \'üp-sə-ˌlän, 'yüp-, 'əp-, -lən, *British* usually yüp-'sī-lən\ *noun* [Middle Greek y psi-lon, literally, simple y; from the desire to distinguish it from *oi,* which was pronounced the same in later Greek] (1621)
1 : the 20th letter of the Greek alphabet — see ALPHABET table
2 : any of a group of unstable electrically neutral elementary particles of the meson family that have a mass about 10 times that of a proton
**up·spring** \ˌəp-'spriŋ\ *intransitive verb* **-sprang** \-'spraŋ\ *or* **-sprung** \-'sprəŋ\; **-sprung; -spring·ing** \-'spriŋ-iŋ\ (before 12th century)
1 : to spring up
2 : to come into being
¹**up·stage** \'əp-ˌstāj\ *adverb* (1870)

1 : toward or at the rear of a theatrical stage
2 : away from a motion-picture or television camera
²**upstage** *adjective* (1918)
1 [³*upstage*] : HAUGHTY
2 : of or relating to the rear of a stage
³**up·stage** \ˌəp-'stāj\ *transitive verb* (1921)
1 : to draw attention away from
2 : to force (an actor) to face away from the audience by staying upstage
3 : to treat snobbishly
⁴**up·stage** \'əp-ˌstāj\ *noun* (circa 1931)
: the part of a stage that is farthest from the audience or camera
¹**up·stairs** \'əp-'starz, -'sterz\ *adverb* (1596)
1 : up the stairs : on or to a higher floor
2 : to or at a high altitude or higher position ⟨kicked *upstairs* to company management⟩
3 : in the head : INTELLECTUALLY ⟨a little slow *upstairs* —Tom Clancy⟩
²**up·stairs** \'əp-'\ *adjective* (1782)
: situated above the stairs especially on an upper floor ⟨an *upstairs* bedroom⟩
³**up·stairs** \'əp-', -əp-\ *noun plural but singular or plural in construction* (1842)
: the part of a building above the ground floor
**up·stand·ing** \ˌəp-'stan-diŋ, 'əp-ˌ\ *adjective* (before 12th century)
1 : ERECT, UPRIGHT
2 : marked by integrity
— **up·stand·ing·ness** *noun*
¹**up·start** \ˌəp-'stärt\ *intransitive verb* (14th century)
: to jump up (as to one's feet) suddenly
²**up·start** \'əp-ˌstärt\ *noun* (1555)

---

☆ SYNONYMS
**Upright, honest, just, conscientious, scrupulous, honorable** mean having or showing a strict regard for what is morally right. UPRIGHT implies a strict adherence to moral principles ⟨a stern and *upright* minister⟩. HONEST stresses adherence to such virtues as truthfulness, candor, fairness ⟨known for being *honest* in business dealings⟩. JUST stresses conscious choice and regular practice of what is right or equitable ⟨workers given *just* compensation⟩. CONSCIENTIOUS and SCRUPULOUS imply an active moral sense governing all one's actions and painstaking efforts to follow one's conscience ⟨*conscientious* in the completion of her assignments⟩ ⟨*scrupulous* in carrying out the terms of the will⟩. HONORABLE suggests a firm holding to codes of right behavior and the guidance of a high sense of honor and duty ⟨a difficult but *honorable* decision⟩.

---

◇ WORD HISTORY
**uproar**   Despite appearances to the contrary, the *-roar* part of the word *uproar* has no etymological connection with the sound made by some animals. In Dutch *oproer* means "revolt, uprising," having been compounded from *op* "up," and *roer* "motion." When the word was borrowed into English, its Dutch meaning was initially retained, but through the process known as folk etymology its spelling and meaning were altered to fit already familiar English words. English speakers assumed that the *-roar* in *uproar* did indeed refer to loud cries or sounds, and so the word went from meaning "uprising" to meaning "a state of commotion."

---

\ə\ **abut** \ᵊ\ **kitten** \ər\ **further** \a\ **ash** \ā\ **ace**
\ä\ **mop, mar** \aù\ **out** \ch\ **chin** \e\ **bet** \ē\ **easy**
\g\ **go** \i\ **hit** \ī\ **ice** \j\ **job** \ŋ\ **sing** \ō\ **go**
\ȯ\ **law** \ȯi\ **boy** \th\ **thin** \th\ **the** \ü\ **loot** \ù\ **foot**
\y\ **yet** \zh\ **vision**    *see also* Guide to Pronunciation

**1** : one that has risen suddenly (as from a low position to wealth or power) : PARVENU; *especially* : one that claims more personal importance than is warranted
**2** : a start-up enterprise
— **up·start** \'əp-,\ *adjective*

**up·state** \'əp-,stāt\ *noun* (1901)
: the chiefly northerly sections of a state; *also* : the chiefly rural part of a state when the major metropolitan area is in the south
— **up·state** \-'stāt\ *adverb or adjective*
— **up·stat·er** \-'stā-tər\ *noun*

**up·stream** \'əp-'strēm\ *adverb or adjective* (1681)
**1** : in the direction opposite to the flow of a stream
**2** : toward a portion of the production stream closer to basic extractive or manufacturing processes ⟨make most of its money *upstream*, selling cheap crude . . . to refineries —John Quirt⟩

**up·stroke** \'əp-,strōk\ *noun* (1828)
: a stroke (as of a pen) made in an upward direction

**up·surge** \'əp-,sərj\ *noun* (1917)
: a rapid or sudden rise

**¹up·sweep** \'əp-,swēp\ *intransitive verb* **-swept** \-,swept\; **-sweep·ing** (1791)
: to sweep upward

**²upsweep** *noun* (circa 1891)
**1** : an upward sweep
**2** : an upswept hairdo

**up·swept** \'əp-,swept\ *adjective* (1938)
: swept-upward; *especially* : brushed up to the top of the head ⟨*upswept* hair⟩

**up·swing** \'əp-,swiŋ\ *noun* (1924)
**1** : an upward swing
**2** : a marked increase or improvement — often used in the phrase *on the upswing*

**up·take** \'əp-,tāk\ *noun* [Scots *uptake* to understand] (1816)
**1** : UNDERSTANDING, COMPREHENSION ⟨quick on the *uptake*⟩
**2** : a flue leading upward
**3** : an act or instance of absorbing and incorporating especially into a living organism

**up–tem·po** \'əp-,tem-(,)pō\ *adjective* (1948)
: having a fast-moving tempo (as in jazz)

**¹up·throw** \'əp-,thrō\ *transitive verb* **-threw** \-,thrü\; **-thrown** \-,thrōn\; **-throw·ing** (1600)
: to throw or thrust upward

**²upthrow** *noun* (1807)
: an upward displacement (as of a rock stratum) : UPHEAVAL, UPTHRUST

**¹up·thrust** \'əp-,thrəst\ (1845)
*transitive verb*
: to thrust up; *especially* : to elevate (a part of the earth's surface) in an upthrust
*intransitive verb*
: to rise with an upward thrust

**²upthrust** *noun* (1846)
: an upward thrust; *specifically* : an uplift of part of the earth's crust

**up·tick** \'əp-,tik\ *noun* [²up + ³tick] (1955)
: INCREASE, RISE

**up·tight** \'əp-'tīt\ (,)əp-'\ *adjective* (1934)
**1 a** : being tense, nervous, or uneasy **b** : ANGRY, INDIGNANT **c** : rigidly conventional
**2** : being in financial difficulties
— **up·tight·ness** \(,)əp-'tīt-nəs\ *noun*

**up·tilt** \'əp-'tilt\ *transitive verb* (1849)
: to tilt upward

**up·time** \'əp-,tīm\ *noun* (1958)
: time during which a piece of equipment (as a computer) is functioning or able to function

**up to** *preposition* (13th century)
**1** — used as a function word to indicate extension as far as a specified place ⟨sank *up to* his knees in the mud⟩
**2** — used as a function word to indicate a limit or boundary ⟨*up to* 50,000 copies a month⟩ ⟨worked *up to* the last minute⟩

**up–to–date** *adjective* (1888)
**1** : extending up to the present time : including the latest information ⟨*up-to-date* maps⟩

**2** : abreast of the times : MODERN ⟨*up-to-date* methods⟩
— **up–to–date·ly** *adverb*
— **up–to–date·ness** *noun*

**up–to–the–minute** *adjective* (1912)
**1** : extending up to the immediate present : including the very latest information
**2** : marked by complete up-to-dateness

**¹up·town** \'əp-'taùn\ *adjective* (1838)
**1** : of or relating to uptown
**2** : UPSCALE, FASHIONABLE
— **uptown** *adverb*

**²up·town** \'əp-'taùn\ *noun* (1844)
: the upper part of a town or city; *especially* : the residential district

**up·trend** \'əp-,trend\ *noun* (1926)
: an upturn especially in business or economic activity

**¹up·turn** \'əp-'tərn, ,əp-'\ (1567)
*transitive verb*
**1** : to turn up or over
**2** : to direct upward
*intransitive verb*
: to turn upward

**²up·turn** \'əp-,tərn\ *noun* (1864)
: an upward turn especially toward better conditions or higher prices

**¹up·ward** \'əp-wərd\ *or* **up·wards** \-wərdz\ *adverb* (before 12th century)
**1 a** : in a direction from lower to higher ⟨the kite rose *upward*⟩ **b** (1) : toward the source (as of a river) (2) : toward the interior (as of a region) **c** : in a higher position ⟨held out his hand, palm *upward*⟩ **d** : in the upper parts : toward the head : ABOVE ⟨from the waist *upward*⟩
**2** : toward a higher or better condition or level ⟨young lawyers moving *upward*⟩
**3 a** : to an indefinitely greater amount, figure, or rank ⟨from $5 *upward*⟩ **b** : toward a greater amount or higher number, degree, or rate ⟨attendance figures have risen *upward*⟩
**4** : toward or into later years ⟨from youth *upward*⟩

**²upward** *adjective* (1607)
**1** : directed toward or situated in a higher place or level : ASCENDING
**2** : rising to a higher pitch
— **up·ward·ly** *adverb*
— **up·ward·ness** *noun*

**upward mobility** *noun* (1949)
: the capacity or facility for rising to a higher social or economic position
— **upwardly mobile** *adjective*

**upwards of** *also* **upward of** *adverb* (1721)
: more than : in excess of ⟨they cost *upwards of* $25⟩

**up·well** \,əp-'wel\ *intransitive verb* (1885)
: to well up; *specifically* : to move or flow upward

**up·well·ing** \-'we-liŋ\ *noun* (1868)
: the process or an instance of rising or appearing to rise to the surface and flowing outward; *especially* : the process of upward movement to the surface of marine often nutrient-rich lower waters especially along some shores due to the offshore drift of surface water (as from the action of winds and the Coriolis force)

**up·wind** \'əp-'wind\ *adverb or adjective* (1838)
: in the direction from which the wind is blowing

**¹ur- or uro-** *combining form* [New Latin, from Greek *our-, ouro-,* from *ouron* urine, from *ourein* to urinate — more at URINE]
**1** : urine ⟨*uric*⟩
**2** : urinary tract ⟨*urology*⟩
**3** : urinary and ⟨*urogenital*⟩
**4** : urea ⟨*uracil*⟩

**²ur- or uro-** *combining form* [New Latin, from Greek *our-, ouro-,* from *oura* tail — more at ASS]
: tail ⟨*uropod*⟩

**³ur-** \'ùr\ *prefix, often capitalized* [German, from Old High German *ir-, ur-* thoroughly (perfective prefix) — more at ABIDE]
**1** : original : primitive ⟨*ur*-form⟩
**2** : original version of ⟨*urtext*⟩
**3** : prototypical : ARCH- ⟨*ur*-anticommunist⟩

**ura·cil** \'yùr-ə-,sil, -səl\ *noun* [International Scientific Vocabulary ¹*ur-* + *acetic* + *-il* (substance relating to)] (1890)
: a pyrimidine base $C_4H_4N_2O_2$ that is one of the four bases coding genetic information in the polynucleotide chain of RNA — compare ADENINE, CYTOSINE, GUANINE, THYMINE

**urae·us** \yù-'rē-əs\ *noun, plural* **uraei** \-'rē-,ī\ [New Latin, from Late Greek *ouraios,* a kind of snake] (1832)
: a representation of the sacred asp (*Naja haje*) appearing in ancient Egyptian art and especially on the headdress of rulers and serving as a symbol of sovereignty

**uraeus**

**Ural–Al·ta·ic** \,yùr-əl-al-'tā-ik\ *noun* (1853)
: a postulated language family comprising the Uralic and Altaic languages
— **Ural–Altaic** *adjective*

**Ura·li·an** \yù-'rā-lē-ən, -'ra-\ *adjective* (1801)
**1** : of or relating to the Ural mountains
**2** : URALIC

**¹Ural·ic** \yù-'ra-lik\ *noun* (1861)
: a language family comprising the Finno-Ugric and Samoyed languages

**²Uralic** *adjective* (1880)
: of, relating to, or constituting the Finno-Ugric and Samoyed languages

**Ura·nia** \yù-'rā-nē-ə, -nyə\ *noun* [Latin, from Greek *Ourania*]
: the Greek Muse of astronomy

**Ura·ni·an** \yù-'rā-nē-ən, -nyən\ *adjective* (1844)
: of or relating to the planet Uranus

**ura·ni·nite** \yù-'rā-nə-,nīt\ *noun* [German *Uranin* uraninite (from New Latin *uranium*) + English *-ite*] (1879)
: a mineral that is basically a black octahedral or cubic oxide of uranium which contains thorium, lead, and rare earth elements and is the chief ore of uranium

**ura·ni·um** \yù-'rā-nē-əm\ *noun, often attributive* [New Latin, from *Uranus*] (circa 1797)
: a silvery heavy radioactive polyvalent metallic element that is found especially in pitchblende and uraninite and exists naturally as a mixture of three isotopes of mass number 234, 235, and 238 in the proportions of 0.006 percent, 0.71 percent, and 99.28 percent respectively — see ELEMENT table ◆

**uranium hexa·flu·o·ride** \-,hek-sə-'flòr-,īd, -'flùr-\ *noun* (1899)

---

◇ WORD HISTORY

**uranium** In Greek mythology the god of the heavens was known as *Ouranos,* literally "sky, heaven," and the muse of astronomy as *Ourania.* The Romans latinized these figures as *Uranus* and *Urania.* Uranus was the father of the god Saturn and the grandfather of Jupiter. In 1781 the English astronomer Sir William Herschel discovered by telescope the seventh planet of our solar system. Because the planets long familiar to astronomy were named after Roman gods, the German astronomer Johann Bode suggested the name *Uranus,* an especially apt choice since the fifth and sixth planets are Jupiter and Saturn respectively. In 1789 the German chemist Martin Klaproth discovered a new element and later gave it the name *uranium,* after the planet that had been recently discovered.

: a volatile compound $UF_6$ of uranium and fluorine that is used in one major process of enriching uranium in uranium 235

**uranium 238** *noun* (1942)
: an isotope of uranium of mass number 238 that is the most abundant and stable uranium isotope, that is not fissionable but can be used to produce a fissionable isotope of plutonium, and that has a half-life of $4.51 \times 10^9$ years

**uranium 235** *noun* (1940)
: a light isotope of uranium of mass number 235 that when bombarded with slow neutrons undergoes rapid fission into smaller atoms with the release of neutrons and energy and that is used in nuclear power plants and atomic bombs

**ura·nog·ra·phy** \,yuṙ-ə-'nä-grə-fē\ *noun* [Greek *ouranographia* description of the heavens, from *ouranos* sky + *-graphia* -graphy] (1675)
: the construction of celestial representations (as maps)

**Ura·nus** \'yuṙ-ə-nəs, yu̇-'rā-\ *noun* [Late Latin, from Greek *Ouranos*]
**1** : the sky personified as a god and father of the Titans in Greek mythology
**2** : the planet seventh in order from the sun — see PLANET table ■

**ura·nyl** \'yuṙ-ə-,nil, yu̇-'rā-n°l\ *noun* [International Scientific Vocabulary, from New Latin *uranium* + International Scientific Vocabulary *-yl*] (1850)
: a bivalent radical $UO_2$

**urate** \'yuṙ-,āt\ *noun* [French, from *urique* uric, from English *uric*] (1800)
: a salt of uric acid
— **urat·ic** \yu̇-'ra-tik\ *adjective*

**ur·ban** \'ər-bən\ *adjective* [Latin *urbanus*, from *urbs* city] (1619)
: of, relating to, characteristic of, or constituting a city

**ur·bane** \,ər-'bān\ *adjective* [Latin *urbanus* urban, urbane] (circa 1623)
: notably polite or finished in manner
: POLISHED
**synonym** see SUAVE
— **ur·bane·ly** *adverb*

**ur·ban·i·sa·tion, ur·ban·ise** *British variant of* URBANIZATION, URBANIZE

**ur·ban·ism** \'ər-bə-,ni-zəm\ *noun* (1889)
**1** : the characteristic way of life of city dwellers
**2 a** : the study of the physical needs of urban societies **b** : CITY PLANNING
**3** : URBANIZATION

**ur·ban·ist** \'ər-bə-nist\ *noun* (1930)
: a specialist in city planning
— **ur·ban·is·tic** \,ər-bə-'nis-tik\ *adjective*
— **ur·ban·is·ti·cal·ly** \-ti-k(ə-)lē\ *adverb*

**ur·ban·ite** \'ər-bə-,nīt\ *noun* (1897)
: a person who lives in a city

**ur·ban·i·ty** \,ər-'ba-nə-tē\ *noun, plural* **-ties** (1535)
**1** : the quality or state of being urbane
**2** *plural* : urbane acts or conduct

**ur·ban·i·za·tion** \,ər-bə-nə-'zā-shən\ *noun* (1888)
: the quality or state of being urbanized or the process of becoming urbanized

**ur·ban·ize** \'ər-bə-,nīz\ *transitive verb* **-ized; -iz·ing** (1884)
**1** : to cause to take on urban characteristics ⟨*urbanized* areas⟩
**2** : to impart an urban way of life to ⟨*urbanize* migrants from rural areas⟩

**ur·ban·ol·o·gy** \,ər-bə-'nä-lə-jē\ *noun* (1961)
: a study dealing with specialized problems of cities (as planning, education, sociology, and politics)
— **ur·ban·ol·o·gist** \-jist\ *noun*

**urban renewal** *noun* (1954)
: a construction program to replace or restore substandard buildings in an urban area

**urban sprawl** *noun* (1958)

: the spreading of urban developments (as houses and shopping centers) on undeveloped land near a city

**ur·ce·o·late** \,ər-'sē-ə-lət, 'ər-sē-ə-,lāt\ *adjective* [New Latin *urceolatus*, from Latin *urceolus*, diminutive of *urceus* pitcher] (1760)
: shaped like an urn ⟨the *urceolate* corolla of a blueberry⟩

**ur·chin** \'ər-chən\ *noun* [Middle English, from Middle French *herichon, heriçon,* from (assumed) Old French *eriz,* from Latin *ericius,* from *eris;* akin to Greek *chēr* hedgehog] (14th century)
**1** *archaic* : HEDGEHOG 1a
**2** : a mischievous youngster : SCAMP
**3** : SEA URCHIN

**urd** \'uṙd, 'ərd\ *noun* [Hindi] (circa 1934)
: an annual Asian legume (*Vigna mungo* synonym *Phaseolus mungo*) widely grown in warm regions for its edible blackish seed, for green manure, or for forage; *also* : the seed

**Ur·du** \'uṙ-(,)dü, 'ər-\ *noun* [Hindi *urdū,* from Persian *zabān-e-urdū-e-muallā* language of the Exalted Camp (the imperial bazaar in Delhi)] (1796)
: an Indo-Aryan language that has the same colloquial basis as standard Hindi, is an official language of Pakistan, and is widely used by Muslims in urban areas of India

**-ure** *noun suffix* [Middle English, from Old French, from Latin *-ura*]
**1** : act : process ⟨expos*ure*⟩
**2** : office : function; *also* : body performing (such) a function ⟨legisla*ture*⟩

**urea** \yu̇-'rē-ə\ *noun* [New Latin, from French *urée,* from *urine*] (1806)
: a soluble weakly basic nitrogenous compound $CO(NH_2)_2$ that is the chief solid component of mammalian urine and an end product of protein decomposition, is synthesized from carbon dioxide and ammonia, and is used especially in synthesis (as of resins and plastics) and in fertilizers and animal rations

**urea–formaldehyde** *noun* (1928)
: a thermosetting synthetic resin made by condensing urea with formaldehyde

**ure·ase** \'yuṙ-ē-,ās, -,āz\ *noun* (1892)
: an enzyme that catalyzes the hydrolysis of urea

**ure·din·i·um** \,yuṙ-ə-'di-nē-əm\ *noun, plural* **-ia** \-nē-ə\ [New Latin, from Latin *uredin-, uredo* burning, blight, from *urere* to burn — more at EMBER] (1905)
: a usually reddish or black mass of hyphae and spores of a rust fungus forming pustules that rupture the host's cuticle
— **ure·din·i·al** \-nē-əl\ *adjective*

**ure·do·spore** \yu̇-'rē-də-,spōr, -,spór\ *also* **ure·dio·spore** \-'rē-dē-ə-\ *or* **ure·din·io·spore** \yu̇r-'di-nē-ə-\ *noun* [New Latin *ure*dium *uredinium* (from Latin *uredo*) + English *-o-* + *spore*] (1875)
: one of the thin-walled spores that are produced by the uredinial hyphae of rust fungi and spread the fungus vegetatively

**ure·ide** \'yuṙ-ē-,īd\ *noun* (1857)
: a cyclic or acyclic acyl derivative of urea

**ure·mia** \yu̇-'rē-mē-ə\ *noun* [New Latin] (circa 1857)
**1** : accumulation in the blood of constituents normally eliminated in the urine that produces a severe toxic condition and usually occurs in severe kidney disease
**2** : the toxic bodily condition associated with uremia ⟨the patient was in *uremia*⟩
— **ure·mic** \-mik\ *adjective*

**ureo·tel·ic** \yu̇-,rē-ə-'te-lik, ,yuṙ-ē-ō-\ *adjective* [urea + *-o-* + *tel-* + *-ic*; from the fact that urea is the end product] (1924)
: excreting nitrogen mostly in the form of urea ⟨*ureotelic* mammals⟩
— **ureo·te·lism** \-'te-,li-zəm, ,yuṙ-ē-'ä-t°l-,i-zəm\ *noun*

**ure·ter** \'yuṙ-ə-tər\ *noun* [New Latin, from Greek *ourētēr,* from *ourein* to urinate — more at URINE] (1543)

: a duct that carries away the urine from a kidney to the bladder or cloaca
— **ure·ter·al** \yu̇-'rē-tə-rəl\ *or* **ure·ter·ic** \,yuṙ-ə-'ter-ik\ *adjective*

**ure·thane** \'yuṙ-ə-,thān\ *or* **ure·than** \-,than\ *noun* [French *uréthane,* from *ur-* [1]*ur-* + *éth-* eth- + *-ane*] (1838)
**1 a** : a crystalline compound $C_3H_7NO_2$ that is the ethyl ester of carbamic acid and is used especially as a solvent and medicinally as an antineoplastic agent **b** : an ester of carbamic acid other than the ethyl ester
**2** : POLYURETHANE

**ure·thra** \yu̇-'rē-thrə\ *noun, plural* **-thras** *or* **-thrae** \-(,)thrē\ [Late Latin, from Greek *ourēthra,* from *ourein* to urinate] (1634)
: the canal that in most mammals carries off the urine from the bladder and in the male serves also as a genital duct
— **ure·thral** \-thrəl\ *adjective*

**ure·thri·tis** \,yuṙ-i-'thrī-təs\ *noun* [New Latin] (circa 1823)
: inflammation of the urethra

**ure·thro·scope** \yu̇-'rē-thrə-,skōp\ *noun* [International Scientific Vocabulary] (1868)
: an instrument for viewing the interior of the urethra

**¹urge** \'ərj\ *verb* **urged; urg·ing** [Latin *urgēre* to press, push, entreat — more at WREAK] (1560)
*transitive verb*
**1** : to present, advocate, or demand earnestly or pressingly ⟨his conviction was upheld on a theory never *urged* at his . . . trial —Leon Friedman⟩
**2** : to undertake the accomplishment of with energy, swiftness, or enthusiasm ⟨*urge* the attack⟩
**3 a** : SOLICIT, ENTREAT **b** : to serve as a motive or reason for
**4** : to force or impel in an indicated direction or into motion or greater speed ⟨the dog *urged* the sheep toward the gate⟩
**5** : STIMULATE, PROVOKE
*intransitive verb*
: to declare, advance, or press earnestly a statement, argument, charge, or claim
— **urg·er** *noun*

**²urge** *noun* (circa 1618)
**1** : the act or process of urging
**2** : a force or impulse that urges; *especially* : a continuing impulse toward an activity or goal

**ur·gen·cy** \'ər-jən(t)-sē\ *noun, plural* **-cies** (1540)
**1** : the quality or state of being urgent : INSISTENCE
**2** : a force or impulse that impels or constrains : URGE

---

□ USAGE

**Uranus** The name of a god and a celestial body can be both heavenly and earthy in the case of *Uranus.* Some critics perceive the variant \yu̇-'rā-nəs\ to be a vulgar pun, and yet evidence in the Merriam-Webster citation files suggests that this newer variant has been gaining popularity since the beginning of the 20th century. The Greek word for "heaven" from which Uranus descended has stress on the final syllable, a fact which supports neither side in the modern English dispute. For those who would avoid distractions from or misperceptions of their speech, the older variant with first-syllable stress is advised, although this pronunciation is itself just like the pronunciation of the rare word *urinous.*

---

\ə\ **abut** \°\ **kitten** \ər\ **further** \a\ **ash** \ā\ **ace**
\ä\ **mop, mar** \au̇\ **out** \ch\ **chin** \e\ **bet** \ē\ **easy**
\g\ **go** \i\ **hit** \ī\ **ice** \j\ **job** \ŋ\ **sing** \ō\ **go**
\ȯ\ **law** \ȯi\ **boy** \th\ **thin** \t͟h\ **the** \ü\ **loot** \u̇\ **foot**
\y\ **yet** \zh\ **vision** *see also* Guide to Pronunciation

**ur·gent** \'ər-jənt\ *adjective* [Middle English, from Middle French, from Latin *urgent-, urgens,* present participle of *urgēre*] (15th century)
**1 a** : calling for immediate attention : PRESSING ⟨*urgent* appeals⟩ **b** : conveying a sense of urgency
**2** : urging insistently : IMPORTUNATE
— **ur·gent·ly** *adverb*

**-urgy** *noun combining form* [New Latin *-urgia,* from Greek *-ourgia,* from *-ourgos* working, from *-o-* + *ergon* work — more at WORK]
: technique or art of dealing or working with (such) a product, matter, or tool ⟨metall*urgy*⟩

**-uria** *noun combining form* [New Latin, from Greek *-ouria,* from *ouron* urine, from *ourein* to urinate — more at URINE]
**1** : presence of (a specified substance) in urine ⟨albumin*uria*⟩
**2** : condition of having (such) urine ⟨poly*uria*⟩; *especially* : abnormal or diseased condition marked by the presence of (a specified substance) ⟨py*uria*⟩

**uri·al** \'ùr-ē-əl, -äl\ *noun* [Panjabi *huṛeāl*] (1860)
: an upland wild sheep (*Ovis vignei*) of southern and central Asia which is reddish brown and the males of which have a beard from the neck to the chest

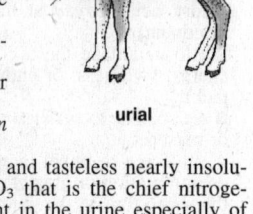
**urial**

**uric** \'yùr-ik\ *adjective* (1797)
: of, relating to, or found in urine

**uric acid** *noun* (1800)
: a white odorless and tasteless nearly insoluble acid $C_5H_4N_4O_3$ that is the chief nitrogenous waste present in the urine especially of lower vertebrates (as birds and reptiles), is present in small quantity in human urine, and occurs pathologically in renal calculi and the tophi of gout

**uri·co·su·ric** \,yùr-i-kə-'shùr-ik, -'sùr-\ *adjective* [irregular from *uric*] (circa 1947)
: relating to or promoting the excretion of uric acid in the urine

**uri·co·tel·ic** \,yùr-i-kō-'te-lik\ *adjective* [*uric* + *-o-* + *tel-* + *-ic;* from the fact that uric acid is the end product] (1924)
: excreting nitrogen mostly in the form of uric acid ⟨birds are typical *uricotelic* animals⟩
— **uri·co·tel·ism** \-'te-,li-zəm, -'kä-t°l-,i-zəm\ *noun*

**uri·dine** \'yùr-ə-,dēn\ *noun* [International Scientific Vocabulary [1]*ur-* + *-idine*] (1911)
: a pyrimidine nucleoside $C_9H_{12}N_2O_6$ that is composed of uracil attached to ribose, is derived by hydrolysis from nucleic acids, and in the form of phosphate derivatives plays an important role in carbohydrate metabolism

**Uri·el** \'yùr-ē-əl\ *noun* [Hebrew *Ūrī'ēl*]
: one of the four archangels named in Hebrew tradition

**Urim and Thum·mim** \,yùr-ə-mən(d)-'thə-məm, ,ùr-; ,ùr-ēm-ən(d)-'tù-mēm\ *noun plural* [part translation of Hebrew *ūrīm wěthummīm*] (1537)
: sacred lots used in early times by the Hebrews

**urin-** *or* **urino-** *combining form* [Middle English, from Old French, from Latin, from *urina* urine]
: [1]UR- ⟨*urino*genital⟩ ⟨*urinary*⟩

**uri·nal** \'yùr-ə-n°l, *British also* yù-'rī-n°l\ *noun* [Middle English, from Middle French, from Late Latin *urina*] (13th century)
**1** : a vessel for receiving urine
**2 a** : a building or enclosure with facilities for urinating **b** : a fixture used for urinating

**uri·nal·y·sis** \,yùr-ə-'na-lə-səs\ *noun, plural* **-y·ses** [New Latin, irregular from *urin-* + *analysis*] (1889)
: chemical analysis of urine

**uri·nary** \'yùr-ə-,ner-ē\ *adjective* (1578)
**1** : relating to, occurring in, affecting, or constituting the organs concerned with the formation and discharge of urine ⟨*urinary* system⟩ ⟨*urinary* calculi⟩
**2** : of, relating to, or for urine
**3** : excreted as or in urine

**urinary bladder** *noun* (1728)
: a membranous sac in many vertebrates that serves for the temporary retention of urine and discharges by the urethra

**uri·nate** \'yùr-ə-,nāt\ *intransitive verb* **-nat·ed; -nat·ing** (1599)
: to discharge urine : MICTURATE
— **uri·na·tion** \,yùr-ə-'nā-shən\ *noun*

**urine** \'yùr-ən\ *noun* [Middle English, from Middle French, from Latin *urina,* from *urinari* to dive; akin to Sanskrit *vār* water and perhaps to Sanskrit *varṣati* it rains, Greek *ourein* to urinate] (14th century)
: waste material that is secreted by the kidney in vertebrates, is rich in end products of protein metabolism together with salts and pigments, and forms a clear amber and usually slightly acid fluid in mammals but is semisolid in birds and reptiles
— **urin·ous** \'yùr-ə-nəs\ *adjective*

**uri·no·gen·i·tal** \,yùr-ə-nō-'je-nə-t°l\ *adjective* (1836)
: UROGENITAL

**uri·nom·e·ter** \,yùr-ə-'nä-mə-tər\ *noun* [International Scientific Vocabulary] (1843)
: a small hydrometer for determining the specific gravity of urine

**urn** \'ərn\ *noun* [Middle English *urne,* from Latin *urna*] (14th century)
**1** : a vessel that is typically an ornamental vase on a pedestal and that is used for various purposes (as preserving the ashes of the dead after cremation)
**2** : a closed vessel usually with a spigot for serving a hot beverage ⟨a coffee *urn*⟩

**uro-** — see UR-

**uro·ca·nic acid** \,yùr-ə-'kā-nik-, -'ka-\ *noun* [[1]*ur-* + *canine* + *-ic;* from its being first obtained from the urine of a dog] (circa 1903)
: a crystalline acid $C_6H_6N_2O_2$ that is normally present in human skin

**uro·chor·date** \,yùr-ə-'kòr-dət, -,dāt\ *noun* [New Latin *Urochordata,* former group name, from [2]*ur-* + *chordatus* having a notochord, from *chorda* notochord, from Latin, string, cord — more at CORD] (1948)
: TUNICATE
— **urochordate** *adjective*

**uro·chrome** \'yùr-ə-,krōm\ *noun* (1864)
: a yellow pigment to which the color of normal urine is principally due

**uro·dele** \'yùr-ə-,dēl\ *noun* [French *urodèle,* ultimately from Greek *oura* tail + *dēlos* evident, showing — more at ASS] (1842)
: any of an order (Caudata synonym Urodela) of amphibians (as newts) that have a tail throughout life
— **urodele** *adjective*

**uro·gen·i·tal** \,yùr-ō-'je-nə-t°l\ *adjective* [International Scientific Vocabulary] (1848)
: of, relating to, or being the organs or functions of excretion and reproduction

**uro·ki·nase** \,yùr-ō-'kī-,nās, -,nāz\ *noun* (1952)
: an enzyme that is produced by the kidney and found in urine, that activates plasminogen, and that is used therapeutically to dissolve blood clots (as in the heart)

**uro·lith** \'yùr-ə-,lith\ *noun* [International Scientific Vocabulary] (circa 1900)
: a calculus in the urinary tract

**uro·lith·ia·sis** \,yùr-ə-li-'thī-ə-səs\ *noun* [New Latin] (circa 1860)
: a condition that is characterized by the formation or presence of calculi in the urinary tract

**uro·log·ic** \,yùr-ə-'lä-jik\ *also* **uro·log·i·cal** \-ji-kəl\ *adjective* (1855)
: of or relating to the urinary tract or to urology

**urol·o·gist** \yù-'rä-lə-jist\ *noun* (1889)
: a physician who specializes in the urinary or urogenital tract
— **urol·o·gy** \-jē\ *noun*

**-uronic** *adjective suffix* [Greek *ouron* urine]
: connected with urine — in names of certain aldehyde-acids derived from sugars or compounds of such acids ⟨hyal*uronic*⟩

**uron·ic acid** \yù-'rä-nik-\ *noun* (1925)
: any of a class of acidic compounds of the general formula $HOOC(CHOH)_nCHO$ that contain both carboxylic and aldehydic groups, are oxidation products of sugars, and occur combined in many polysaccharides and in urine

**uro·pod** \'yùr-ə-,päd\ *noun* [International Scientific Vocabulary [2]*ur-* + Greek *pod-, pous* foot — more at FOOT] (circa 1890)
: either of the flattened lateral appendages of the last abdominal segment of a crustacean; *broadly* : an abdominal appendage of a crustacean

**uro·py·gi·al gland** \,yùr-ə-'pī-jē-əl-\ *noun* (1870)
: a large gland that occurs in most birds, opens dorsally at the base of the tail feathers, and usually secretes an oily fluid which the bird uses in preening its feathers — called also *oil gland*

**uro·py·gi·um** \,yùr-ə-'pī-jē-əm\ *noun* [New Latin, from Greek *ouropygion,* from *ouro-* [2]*ur-* + *pygē* rump] (1771)
: the fleshy and bony prominence at the posterior extremity of a bird's body that supports the tail feathers

**uro·style** \'yùr-ə-,stīl\ *noun* [International Scientific Vocabulary [2]*ur-* + Greek *stylos* pillar — more at STEER] (1875)
: a long unsegmented bone that represents a number of fused vertebrae and forms the posterior part of the vertebral column of frogs and toads

**Ur·sa Ma·jor** \,ər-sə-'mā-jər\ *noun* [Latin (genitive *Ursae Majoris*), literally, greater bear]
: a constellation that is the most conspicuous of the northern constellations, is situated near the north pole of the heavens, and contains the stars forming the Big Dipper two of which are in a line indicating the direction of the North Star — called also *Great Bear*

**Ursa Mi·nor** \-'mī-nər\ *noun* [Latin (genitive *Ursae Minoris*), literally, lesser bear]
: a constellation that includes the north pole of the heavens and the stars which form the Little Dipper with the North Star at the tip of the handle — called also *Little Bear*

**ur·sine** \'ər-,sīn\ *adjective* [Latin *ursinus,* from *ursus* bear — more at ARCTIC] (circa 1550)
**1** : of or relating to a bear or the bear family (Ursidae)
**2** : suggesting or characteristic of a bear ⟨a lumbering *ursine* gait⟩

**Ur·su·line** \'ər-sə-lən, -,līn, -,lēn\ *noun* [New Latin *Ursulina,* from *Ursula* Saint Ursula, legendary Christian martyr] (1693)
: a member of any of several Roman Catholic teaching orders of nuns; *especially* : a member of a teaching order founded by Saint Angela Merici in Brescia, Italy, in 1535

**ur·text** \'ùr-,tekst\ *noun* [German, from [3]*ur-* + *Text* text] (circa 1932)
: the original text (as of a musical score)

**ur·ti·car·ia** \,ər-tə-'kar-ē-ə, -'ker-\ *noun* [New Latin, from Latin *urtica* nettle] (circa 1771)
: an allergic disorder marked by raised edematous patches of skin or mucous membrane and usually intense itching and caused by contact

with a specific precipitating factor (as a food, drug, or inhalant) either externally or internally
— **ur·ti·car·i·al** \-ē-əl\ *adjective*
**ur·ti·cate** \'ər-tə-ˌkāt\ *intransitive verb* **-cated; -cat·ing** [Medieval Latin *urticatus,* past participle of *urticare* to sting, from Latin *urtica*] (1843)
: to produce wheals or itching; *especially* : to induce urticaria
— **ur·ti·ca·tion** \ˌər-tə-'kā-shən\ *noun*
**urus** \'yur-əs\ *noun* [Latin, of Germanic origin; akin to Old High German *ūro* aurochs — more at AUROCHS] (1601)
: AUROCHS 1
**uru·shi·ol** \yu̇-'rü-shē-ˌȯl, u̇-', -ˌōl\ *noun* [International Scientific Vocabulary, from Japanese *urushi* lacquer + International Scientific Vocabulary [1]*-ol*] (1908)
: a mixture of pyrocatechol derivatives with saturated or unsaturated side chains of 15 or 17 carbon atoms that is an oily toxic irritant principle present in poison ivy and some related plants (genus *Rhus*) and in oriental lacquers derived from such plants
**us** \'əs\ *pronoun* [Middle English, from Old English *ūs;* akin to Old High German *uns* us, Latin *nos*] *objective case of* WE
**us·able** *also* **use·able** \'yü-zə-bəl\ *adjective* (14th century)
**1** : capable of being used
**2** : convenient and practicable for use
— **us·abil·i·ty** \ˌyü-zə-'bi-lə-tē\ *noun*
— **us·able·ness** \'yü-zə-bəl-nəs\ *noun*
— **us·ably** \-blē\ *adverb*
**us·age** \'yü-sij, -zij\ *noun* [Middle English, from Middle French, from *us* use] (14th century)
**1 a** : firmly established and generally accepted practice or procedure **b** : a uniform certain reasonable lawful practice existing in a particular locality or occupation and binding persons entering into transactions chiefly on the basis of presumed familiarity **c** : the way in which words and phrases are actually used (as in a particular form or sense) in a language community
**2 a** : the action, amount, or mode of using ⟨a decrease in the *usage* of electricity⟩ **b** : manner of treating ⟨suffered ill *usage* at the hands of his captors⟩
**synonym** see HABIT
**us·ance** \'yü-z°n(t)s\ *noun* (14th century)
**1** : USAGE 1a
**2** : USE, EMPLOYMENT
**3 a** *obsolete* : USURY **b** : INTEREST
**4** : the time allowed by custom for payment of a bill of exchange in foreign commerce
[1]**use** \'yüs\ *noun* [Middle English *us,* from Old French, from Latin *usus,* from *uti* to use] (13th century)
**1 a** : the act or practice of employing something : EMPLOYMENT, APPLICATION ⟨he made good *use* of his spare time⟩ **b** : the fact or state of being used ⟨a dish in daily *use*⟩ **c** : a method or manner of employing or applying something ⟨gained practice in the *use* of the camera⟩
**2 a** (1) : habitual or customary usage (2) : an individual habit or group custom **b** : a liturgical form or observance; *especially* : a liturgy having modifications peculiar to a local church or religious order
**3 a** : the privilege or benefit of using something ⟨gave him the *use* of her car⟩ **b** : the ability or power to use something (as a limb or faculty) **c** : the legal enjoyment of property that consists in its employment, occupation, exercise, or practice ⟨she had the *use* of the estate for life⟩
**4 a** : a particular service or end ⟨put learning to practical *use*⟩ **b** : the quality of being suitable for employment ⟨saving things that might be of *use*⟩ **c** : the occasion or need to employ ⟨took only what they had *use* for⟩

**5 a** : the benefit in law of one or more persons; *specifically* : the benefit or profit of property established in one other than the legal possessor **b** : a legal arrangement by which such benefits and profits are so established
**6** : a favorable attitude : LIKING ⟨had no *use* for modern art⟩
[2]**use** \'yüz\ *verb* **used** \'yüzd, *in the phrase* "*used to*" *usually* 'yüs(t)\; **us·ing** \'yü-ziŋ\ (14th century)
*transitive verb*
**1** *archaic* : ACCUSTOM, HABITUATE
**2** : to put into action or service : avail oneself of : EMPLOY
**3** : to consume or take (as liquor or drugs) regularly
**4** : to carry out a purpose or action by means of : UTILIZE; *also* : MANIPULATE 2b ⟨*used* him only as a means up the corporate ladder⟩
**5** : to expend or consume by putting to use — often used with *up*
**6** : to behave toward : act with regard to : TREAT ⟨*used* the prisoners cruelly⟩
**7** : STAND 1d ⟨the house could *use* a coat of paint⟩
*intransitive verb*
— used in the past with *to* to indicate a former fact or state ⟨claims winters *used* to be harder⟩ ⟨didn't *use* to smoke so much⟩ ☆
**used** \'yüzd, *in the phrase* "*used to*" *usually* 'yüs(t)\ *adjective* (14th century)
**1** : employed in accomplishing something
**2** : that has endured use; *specifically* : SECONDHAND ⟨a *used* car⟩
**3** : ACCUSTOMED, HABITUATED
**use·ful** \'yüs-fəl\ *adjective* (1595)
**1** : capable of being put to use; *especially* : serviceable for an end or purpose
**2** : of a valuable or productive kind ⟨do something *useful* with your life⟩
— **use·ful·ly** \-fə-lē\ *adverb*
**use·ful·ness** *noun* (1617)
: the quality of having utility and especially practical worth or applicability
**use·less** \'yü-sləs\ *adjective* (1593)
: having or being of no use: **a** : INEFFECTUAL **b** : not able to give service or aid : INEPT
— **use·less·ly** *adverb*
— **use·less·ness** *noun*
**us·er** \'yü-zər\ *noun* (15th century)
: one that uses
**user fee** *noun* (1967)
: an excise tax often in the form of a license or supplemental charge levied to fund a public service — called also *user's fee*
**us·er-friend·ly** \ˌyü-zər-'fren(d)-lē\ *adjective* (1977)
: easy to learn, use, understand, or deal with
— **user-friendliness** *noun*
**use up** *transitive verb* (1833)
: to exhaust of strength or useful properties ⟨land that has been *used up*⟩
**Ushak** \ü-'shäk\ *variant of* OUSHAK
[1]**ush·er** \'ə-shər\ *noun* [Middle English *ussher,* from Middle French *ussier,* from (assumed) Vulgar Latin *ustiarius* doorkeeper, from Latin *ostium, ustium* door, mouth of a river — more at OSTIUM] (14th century)
**1 a** : an officer or servant who has the care of the door of a court, hall, or chamber **b** : an officer who walks before a person of rank **c** : one who escorts persons to their seats (as in a theater)
**2** *archaic* : an assistant teacher
[2]**usher** *verb* **ush·ered; ush·er·ing** \'ə-sh(ə-)riŋ\ (1596)
*transitive verb*
**1** : to conduct to a place
**2** : to precede as an usher, forerunner, or harbinger
**3** : to cause to enter : INTRODUCE ⟨a new theory *ushered* into the world⟩
*intransitive verb*
: to serve as an usher ⟨*usher* at a wedding⟩

**ush·er·ette** \ˌə-shə-'ret\ *noun* (1925)
: a girl or woman who is an usher (as in a theater)
**usher in** *transitive verb* (circa 1600)
**1** : to serve to bring into being ⟨a discovery that *ushered in* a period of prosperity⟩
**2** : to mark or observe the beginning of ⟨*ushered in* the new year with much merrymaking⟩
**synonym** see BEGIN
**us·nea** \'əs-nē-ə, 'əz-\ *noun* [New Latin, from Arabic *ushnah* moss] (circa 1597)
: any of a genus (*Usnea*) of widely distributed lichens (as old-man's beard) that have a grayish or yellow pendulous freely branched thallus
**us·que·baugh** \'əs-kwi-ˌbȯ, -ˌbä\ *noun* [Irish *uisce beathadh*] (1581)
*Irish & Scottish* : WHISKEY
[1]**usu·al** \'yü-zhə-wəl, -zhəl; 'yüzh-wəl\ *adjective* [Middle English, from Late Latin *usualis,* from Latin *usus* use] (14th century)
**1** : accordant with usage, custom, or habit : NORMAL
**2** : commonly or ordinarily used ⟨followed his *usual* route⟩
**3** : found in ordinary practice or in the ordinary course of events : ORDINARY ☆
— **usu·al·ly** \'yü-zhə-wə-lē, -zhə-lē; 'yüzh-wə-lē, 'yüzh-lē\ *adverb*
— **usu·al·ness** \'yü-zhə-wəl-nəs, -zhəl-; 'yüzh-wəl-\ *noun*
— **as usual** : in the accustomed or habitual way ⟨*as usual* they were late⟩
[2]**usual** *noun* (1589)
: something usual
**usu·fruct** \'yü-zə-ˌfrəkt, -sə-\ *noun* [Latin *ususfructus,* from *usus et fructus* use and enjoyment] (circa 1630)
**1** : the legal right of using and enjoying the fruits or profits of something belonging to another
**2** : the right to use or enjoy something
[1]**usu·fruc·tu·ary** \ˌyü-zə-'frək-chə-ˌwer-ē, -sə-\ *noun* (circa 1618)

---

☆ **SYNONYMS**
**Use, employ, utilize** mean to put into service especially to attain an end. USE implies availing oneself of something as a means or instrument to an end ⟨willing to *use* any means to achieve her ends⟩. EMPLOY suggests the use of a person or thing that is available but idle, inactive, or disengaged ⟨looking for better ways to *employ* their skills⟩. UTILIZE may suggest the discovery of a new, profitable, or practical use for something ⟨an old wooden bucket *utilized* as a planter⟩.

**Usual, customary, habitual, wonted, accustomed** mean familiar through frequent or regular repetition. USUAL stresses the absence of strangeness or unexpectedness ⟨my *usual* order for lunch⟩. CUSTOMARY applies to what accords with the practices, conventions, or usages of an individual or community ⟨the *customary* waiting period before the application is approved⟩. HABITUAL suggests a practice settled or established by much repetition ⟨an *habitual* morning routine⟩. WONTED stresses habituation but usually applies to what is favored, sought, or purposefully cultivated ⟨his *wonted* determination⟩. ACCUSTOMED is less emphatic than WONTED or HABITUAL in suggesting fixed habit or invariable custom ⟨accepted the compliment with her *accustomed* modesty⟩.

---

\ə\ abut \ᵊ\ kitten \ər\ further \a\ ash \ā\ ace
\ä\ mop, mar \au̇\ out \ch\ chin \e\ bet \ē\ easy
\g\ go \i\ hit \ī\ ice \j\ job \ŋ\ sing \ō\ go
\ȯ\ law \ȯi\ boy \th\ thin \th\ the \ü\ loot \u̇\ foot
\y\ yet \zh\ vision *see also* Guide to Pronunciation

**1 :** one having the usufruct of property
**2 :** one having the use or enjoyment of something

**²usufructuary** *adjective* (1710)
**:** of, relating to, or having the character of a usufruct

**usu·rer** \'yü-zhər-ər, 'yüzh-rər\ *noun* (14th century)
**:** one that lends money especially at an exorbitant rate

**usu·ri·ous** \yu-'zhur-ē-əs, -'zur-\ *adjective* (1610)
**1 :** practicing usury
**2 :** involving usury **:** of the character of usury
**— usu·ri·ous·ly** *adverb*
**— usu·ri·ous·ness** *noun*

**usurp** \yu-'sərp *also* -'zərp\ *verb* [Middle English, from Middle French *usurper,* from Latin *usurpare* to take possession of without legal claim, from *usu* (ablative of *usus* use) + *rapere* to seize — more at RAPID] (14th century) *transitive verb*
**1 a :** to seize and hold (as office, place, or powers) in possession by force or without right ⟨*usurp* a throne⟩ **b :** to take or make use of without right ⟨*usurped* the rights to her life story⟩
**2 :** to take the place of by or as if by force **:** SUPPLANT ⟨must not let stock responses based on inherited prejudice *usurp* careful judgment⟩ *intransitive verb*
**:** to seize or exercise authority or possession wrongfully
**— usur·pa·tion** \,yü-sər-'pā-shən *also* ,yü-zər-\ *noun*
**— usurp·er** \yu-'sər-pər *also* -'zər-\ *noun*

**usu·ry** \'yü-zhə-rē, 'yüzh-rē\ *noun, plural* **-ries** [Middle English, from Medieval Latin *usuria,* alteration of Latin *usura,* from *usus,* past participle of *uti* to use] (14th century)
**1** *archaic* **:** INTEREST
**2 :** the lending of money with an interest charge for its use; *especially* **:** the lending of money at exorbitant interest rates
**3 :** an unconscionable or exorbitant rate or amount of interest; *specifically* **:** interest in excess of a legal rate charged to a borrower for the use of money

**ut** \'ət, 'üt, 'üt\ *noun* [Middle English, first note in the diatonic scale, from Medieval Latin, from the syllable sung to this note in a medieval hymn to Saint John the Baptist] (14th century)
**:** a syllable used for the first note in the diatonic scale in an early solmization system and later replaced by *do*

**Ute** \'yüt\ *noun, plural* **Ute** *or* **Utes** [short for earlier *Utah, Utaw,* from American Spanish *Yuta*] (1776)
**1 :** a member of an American Indian people originally ranging through Utah, Colorado, Arizona, and New Mexico
**2 :** the Uto-Aztecan language of the Ute people

**uten·sil** \yu-'ten(t)-səl, 'yü-,\ *noun* [Middle English, vessels for domestic use, from Middle French *utensile,* from Latin *utensilia,* from neuter plural of *utensilis* useful, from *uti* to use] (14th century)
**1 :** an implement, instrument, or vessel used in a household and especially a kitchen
**2 :** a useful tool or implement
**synonym** see IMPLEMENT

**uter·ine** \'yü-tə-,rīn, -rən\ *adjective* [Middle English, from Late Latin *uterinus,* from Latin *uterus*] (15th century)
**1 :** born of the same mother but by a different father
**2 :** of, relating to, or affecting the uterus ⟨*uterine* cancer⟩

**uter·us** \'yü-tə-rəs, 'yü-trəs\ *noun, plural* **uteri** \'yü-tə-,rī\ *also* **uter·us·es** [Latin, belly, womb; probably akin to Greek *hoderos* belly, Sanskrit *udara*] (1615)

**1 :** an organ of the female mammal for containing and usually for nourishing the young during development previous to birth — called also *womb*
**2 :** a structure in some lower animals analogous to the uterus in which eggs or young develop

**Uther** \'ü-thər, 'yü-\ *noun*
**:** a legendary British king and father of Arthur

**utile** \'yü-t°l, 'yü-,tīl\ *adjective* [Middle French, from Latin *utilis*] (15th century)
**:** USEFUL

**uti·lise** *British variant of* UTILIZE

**¹util·i·tar·i·an** \(,)yü-,ti-lə-'ter-ē-ən\ *noun* (circa 1780)
**:** an advocate or adherent of utilitarianism

**²utilitarian** *adjective* (1802)
**1 :** of or relating to or advocating utilitarianism
**2 :** marked by utilitarian views or practices
**3 a :** of, relating to, or aiming at utility **b :** exhibiting or preferring mere utility ⟨spare *utilitarian* furnishings⟩

**util·i·tar·i·an·ism** \-ē-ə-,ni-zəm\ *noun* (1827)
**1 :** a doctrine that the useful is the good and that the determining consideration of right conduct should be the usefulness of its consequences; *specifically* **:** a theory that the aim of action should be the largest possible balance of pleasure over pain or the greatest happiness of the greatest number
**2 :** utilitarian character, spirit, or quality

**¹util·i·ty** \yü-'ti-lə-tē\ *noun, plural* **-ties** [Middle English *utilite,* from Middle French *utilité,* from Latin *utilitat, utilitas,* from *utilis* useful, from *uti* to use] (14th century)
**1 :** fitness for some purpose or worth to some end
**2 :** something useful or designed for use
**3 a :** PUBLIC UTILITY **b** (1) **:** a service (as light, power, or water) provided by a public utility (2) **:** equipment or a piece of equipment to provide such service or a comparable service
**4 :** a program or routine designed to perform or facilitate especially routine operations (as copying files or editing text) on a computer

**²utility** *adjective* (1851)
**1 :** capable of serving as a substitute in various roles or positions ⟨a *utility* infielder⟩
**2 a :** kept to provide a useful product or service rather than for show or as a pet ⟨*utility* livestock⟩ ⟨a *utility* dog⟩ **b :** being of a usable but inferior grade ⟨*utility* beef⟩
**3 :** serving primarily for utility rather than beauty **:** UTILITARIAN
**4 :** designed or adapted for general use ⟨a *utility* knife⟩
**5 :** of or relating to a utility ⟨a *utility* company⟩

**uti·lize** \'yü-t°l-,īz\ *transitive verb* **-lized; -lizing** [French *utiliser,* from *utile*] (1807)
**:** to make use of **:** turn to practical use or account ⟨I'm a great person for *utilizing* waste power —Robert Frost⟩
**synonym** see USE
**— uti·liz·able** \-,ī-zə-bəl\ *adjective*
**— uti·li·za·tion** \,yü-t°l-ə-'zā-shən\ *noun*
**— uti·liz·er** \'yü-t°l-,ī-zər\ *noun*

**¹ut·most** \'ət-,mōst, *especially Southern* -məst\ *adjective* [Middle English, alteration of *utmest,* from Old English *ūtmest,* superlative adjective, from *ūt* out, adverb — more at OUT] (before 12th century)
**1 :** situated at the farthest or most distant point **:** EXTREME ⟨the *utmost* point of the earth —John Hunt⟩
**2 :** of the greatest or highest degree, quantity, number, or amount ⟨a matter of *utmost* concern⟩

**²utmost** *noun* (before 12th century)
**1 :** the most possible **:** the extreme limit **:** the highest attainable point or degree ⟨the *utmost* in reliability⟩
**2 :** the highest, greatest, or best of one's abilities, powers, and resources ⟨will do our *utmost* to help⟩

**Uto–Az·tec·an** \,yü-tō-'az-,te-kən\ *noun* [*Ute* + *-o-* + *Aztec*] (1891)
**:** a family of American Indian languages spoken by peoples from the U.S. Great Basin south to Central America
**— Uto–Aztecan** *adjective*

**uto·pia** \yu-'tō-pē-ə\ *noun* [*Utopia,* imaginary and ideal country in *Utopia* (1516) by Sir Thomas More, from Greek *ou* not, no + *topos* place] (1610)
**1 :** an imaginary and indefinitely remote place
**2** *often capitalized* **:** a place of ideal perfection especially in laws, government, and social conditions
**3 :** an impractical scheme for social improvement ◇

**¹uto·pi·an** \-pē-ən\ *adjective, often capitalized* (1551)
**1 :** of, relating to, or having the characteristics of a utopia; *especially* **:** having impossibly ideal conditions especially of social organization
**2 :** proposing or advocating impractically ideal social and political schemes ⟨*utopian* idealists⟩
**3 :** impossibly ideal **:** VISIONARY ⟨recognised the *utopian* nature of his hopes —C. S. Kilby⟩
**4 :** believing in, advocating, or having the characteristics of utopian socialism ⟨*utopian* doctrines⟩ ⟨*utopian* novels⟩

**²utopian** *noun* (circa 1873)
**1 :** one that believes in the perfectibility of human society
**2 :** one that proposes or advocates utopian schemes

**uto·pi·an·ism** \-pē-ə-,ni-zəm\ *noun* (circa 1661)
**1 :** a utopian idea or theory
**2** *often capitalized* **:** the body of ideas, views, or aims of a utopian

**utopian socialism** *noun* (circa 1923)
**:** socialism based on a belief that social ownership of the means of production can be achieved by voluntary and peaceful surrender of their holdings by propertied groups
**— utopian socialist** *noun*

**uto·pism** \'yü-tə-,pi-zəm, yu-'tō-\ *noun* (1888)
**:** UTOPIANISM 2
**— utopist** \yu-'tō-pist\ *noun*
**— uto·pis·tic** \,yü-tə-'pis-tik, yu-,tō-\ *adjective*

**utri·cle** \'yü-tri-kəl\ *noun* [Latin *utriculus,* diminutive of *uter* leather bag] (1731)
**:** any of various small pouches or saccate parts of an animal or plant body: as **a :** the part of the membranous labyrinth of the inner ear into which the semicircular canals open **b :** a small usually indehiscent one-seeded fruit with thin membranous pericarp
**— utric·u·lar** \yü-'tri-kyə-lər\ *adjective*

---

◇ **WORD HISTORY**
**utopia** In 1516 Sir Thomas More, the English humanist and statesman, published his book *Utopia,* in which the social and economic conditions of Europe, outlined in Book I, are compared in Book II with those of an ideal society established on an imaginary island off the shore of the New World. That such an ideal state is unattainable in reality is implied by the name More gave to this island, *Utopia,* coined from Greek *ou* "no, not" and *topos* "place." In a poem prefaced to the book, More also puns on the name, suggesting *eutopos* "good place." In Modern English *utopia* has become, through the influence of More's classic, a generic term for any place of ideal perfection, especially in laws, government, and social conditions. Less optimistically *utopia* and its adjective derivative *utopian* have also come to refer to impractical schemes for social improvement.

**utric·u·lus** \yu̇-'tri-kyə-ləs\ *noun* [Latin, small bag] (1847)
**:** UTRICLE a

**¹ut·ter** \'ə-tər\ *adjective* [Middle English, remote, from Old English *ūtera* outer, comparative adjective from *ūt* out, adverb — more at OUT] (15th century)
**:** carried to the utmost point or highest degree **:** ABSOLUTE, TOTAL ⟨*utter* darkness⟩ ⟨*utter* strangers⟩
— **ut·ter·ly** *adverb*

**²utter** *verb* [Middle English *uttren*, from *utter* outside, adverb, from Old English *ūtor*, comparative of *ūt* out] (15th century)
*transitive verb*
**1** *obsolete* **:** to offer for sale
**2 a :** to send forth as a sound **b :** to give utterance to **:** PRONOUNCE, SPEAK **c :** to give public expression to **:** express in words
**3 :** to put (as currency) into circulation; *specifically* **:** to circulate (as a counterfeit note) as if legal or genuine ⟨*utter* false tokens⟩
**4 :** to put forth or out **:** DISCHARGE
*intransitive verb*
**:** to make a statement or sound
**synonym** see EXPRESS
— **ut·ter·able** \'ə-tə-rə-bəl\ *adjective*
— **ut·ter·er** \'ə-tər-ər\ *noun*

**¹ut·ter·ance** \'ə-tə-rən(t)s, 'ə-trən(t)s\ *noun* [Middle English *uttraunce*, modification of Middle French *outrance* — more at OUTRANCE] (15th century)
*archaic* **:** the last extremity **:** BITTER END

**²ut·ter·ance** \'ə-tə-rən(t)s *also* 'ə-trən(t)s\ *noun* (15th century)

**1 :** something uttered; *especially* **:** an oral or written statement **:** a stated or published expression
**2 :** vocal expression **:** SPEECH
**3 :** power, style, or manner of speaking

**¹ut·ter·most** \'ə-tər-ˌmōst\ *adjective* [Middle English, alteration of *uttermest*, from ¹*utter* + -*mest* (as in *utmest* utmost)] (14th century)
**1 :** OUTERMOST
**2 :** EXTREME, UTMOST

**²uttermost** *noun* (14th century)
**:** UTMOST ⟨to the *uttermost* of our capacity —H. S. Truman⟩

**U-turn** \'yü-ˌtərn\ *noun* (1930)
**1 :** a turn resembling the letter U; *especially* **:** a 180-degree turn made by a vehicle in a road
**2 :** something (as a reversal of policy) resembling a U-turn

**U-val·ue** \'yü-ˌval-(ˌ)yü\ *noun* [unit] (1949)
**:** a measure of the heat transmission through a building part (as a wall or window) or a given thickness of a material (as insulation) with lower numbers indicating better insulating properties — compare R-VALUE

**uva·rov·ite** \yü-'vär-ə-ˌvīt, ü-\ *noun* [German *Uwarowit*, from Count Sergei S. *Uvarov* (died 1855) Russian statesman] (1837)
**:** an emerald green calcium-chromium garnet

**uvea** \'yü-vē-ə\ *noun* [Medieval Latin, from Latin *uva* grape] (1525)
**:** the posterior pigmented layer of the iris; *also* **:** the iris and ciliary body together with the choroid coat
— **uve·al** \-vē-əl\ *adjective*

**uve·itis** \ˌyü-vē-'ī-təs\ *noun* [New Latin] (circa 1848)
**:** inflammation of the uvea of the eye

**uvu·la** \'yü-vyə-lə\ *noun, plural* **-las** *or* **-lae** \-ˌlē, -ˌlī\ [Middle English, from Medieval Latin, diminutive of Latin *uva* cluster of grapes, uvula; probably akin to Greek *oa* service tree, Old English *īw* yew — more at YEW] (14th century)
**:** the pendent fleshy lobe in the middle of the posterior border of the soft palate

**uvu·lar** \-lər\ *adjective* (1843)
**1 :** of or relating to the uvula ⟨*uvular* glands⟩
**2 :** produced with the aid of the uvula ⟨a *uvular* sound⟩

**ux·o·ri·al** \ˌək-'sōr-ē-əl, -'sȯr-; ˌəg-'zōr-, -'zȯr-\ *adjective* [Latin *uxorius*] (1800)
**:** of, relating to, or characteristic of a wife

**ux·or·i·cide** \ˌək-'sȯr-ə-ˌsīd, -'sär-; ˌəg-'zȯr-, -'zär-\ *noun* (1860)
**1** [Medieval Latin *uxoricidium*, from Latin *uxor* wife + -*i*- + -*cidium* -cide] **:** murder of a wife by her husband
**2** [Latin *uxor* + English -*i*- + -*cide*] **:** a wife murderer

**ux·o·ri·ous** \ˌək-'sōr-ē-əs, -'sȯr-; ˌəg-'zōr-, -'zȯr-\ *adjective* [Latin *uxorius* uxorious, uxorial, from *uxor* wife] (1598)
**:** excessively fond of or submissive to a wife
— **ux·o·ri·ous·ly** *adverb*
— **ux·o·ri·ous·ness** *noun*

**Uz·bek** \'ůz-ˌbek, 'əz-, ůz-\ *or* **Uz·beg** \-ˌbeg, -'beg\ *noun* (1616)
**1 :** a member of a Turkic people of Uzbekistan and adjacent regions of central Asia
**2 :** the Turkic language of the Uzbek people

# V

V *is the twenty-second letter of the English alphabet.* V *and* U *are varieties of the same character,* U *being the cursive form, and the two letters were once used indiscriminately (see* U). *The letter* W, *a doubled* V *called "double* u," *is a survival of this interchangeable use.* V *does not occur in the oldest English texts; its sound was represented in the middle of words by* F. *The letter was probably introduced into English during the later Middle Ages by French scribes.* V *is from the Latin alphabet, where it was used both as a vowel and as a consonant (first with the value of English* w, *and later with that of* v). *Latin derived the letter from a western alphabetic form of the Greek upsilon (see* Y). *In Greek it was used as a vowel, but it originated in a Phoenician character,* wāw, *which had the value of a consonant (see* F). *In English* V *represents the sound of the second consonant in* love. *Small* v *originated as a miniaturized form of the capital letter.*

---

**v** \'vē\ *noun, plural* **v's** *or* **vs** \'vēz\ *often capitalized, often attributive* (15th century)
**1 a :** the 22d letter of the English alphabet **b :** a graphic representation of this letter **c :** a speech counterpart of orthographic *v*
**2 :** FIVE — see NUMBER table
**3 :** a graphic device for reproducing the letter *v*
**4 :** one designated *v* especially as the 22d in order or class
**5 :** something shaped like the letter V

**va·can·cy** \'vā-kən(t)-sē\ *noun, plural* **-cies** (1599)
**1** *archaic* **:** an interval of leisure
**2 :** physical or mental inactivity or relaxation **:** IDLENESS
**3 a :** a vacating of an office, post, or piece of property **b :** the time such office or property is vacant
**4 :** a vacant office, post, or tenancy
**5 :** empty space **:** VOID; *specifically* **:** an unoccupied site for an atom or ion in a crystal
**6 :** the state of being vacant **:** VACUITY

**va·cant** \'vā-kənt\ *adjective* [Middle English, from Old French, from Latin *vacant-, vacans,* present participle of *vacare* to be empty, be free] (14th century)
**1 :** not occupied by an incumbent, possessor, or officer ⟨a *vacant* office⟩ ⟨*vacant* thrones⟩
**2 :** being without content or occupant ⟨a *vacant* seat in a bus⟩ ⟨a *vacant* room⟩
**3 :** free from activity or work **:** DISENGAGED ⟨*vacant* hours⟩
**4 :** devoid of thought, reflection, or expression ⟨a *vacant* smile⟩
**5 :** not lived in ⟨*vacant* houses⟩
**6 a :** not put to use ⟨*vacant* land⟩ **b :** having no heir or claimant **:** ABANDONED ⟨a *vacant* estate⟩
***synonym*** see EMPTY
— **va·cant·ly** *adverb*
— **va·cant·ness** *noun*

**va·cate** \'vā-ˌkāt, vā-'\ *verb* **va·cat·ed; va·cat·ing** [Latin *vacatus,* past participle of *vacare*] (1643)
*transitive verb*
**1 :** to make legally void **:** ANNUL
**2 a :** to deprive of an incumbent or occupant **b :** to give up the incumbency or occupancy of
*intransitive verb*
**:** to vacate an office, post, or tenancy

**¹va·ca·tion** \vā-'kā-shən, və-\ *noun, often attributive* [Middle English *vacacioun,* from Middle French *vacation,* from Latin *vacation-, vacatio* freedom, exemption, from *vacare*] (14th century)
**1 :** a respite or a time of respite from something **:** INTERMISSION

**2 a :** a scheduled period during which activity (as of a court or school) is suspended **b :** a period of exemption from work granted to an employee for rest and relaxation
**3 :** a period spent away from home or business in travel or recreation ⟨had a restful *vacation* at the beach⟩
**4 :** an act or an instance of vacating

**²vacation** *intransitive verb* **-tioned; -tion·ing** \-sh(ə-)niŋ\ (1896)
**:** to take or spend a vacation
— **va·ca·tion·er** \-sh(ə-)nər\ *noun*

**va·ca·tion·ist** \-sh(ə-)nist\ *noun* (1885)
**:** a person taking a vacation

**va·ca·tion·land** \-shən-ˌland\ *noun* (1927)
**:** an area with recreational attractions and facilities for vacationists

**vac·ci·nal** \'vak-sə-nᵊl, vak-'sē-\ *adjective* (circa 1860)
**:** of or relating to vaccine or vaccination

**vac·ci·nate** \'vak-sə-ˌnāt\ *verb* **-nat·ed; -nat·ing** (1803)
*transitive verb*
**1 :** to inoculate (a person) with cowpox virus in order to produce immunity to smallpox
**2 :** to administer a vaccine to usually by injection
*intransitive verb*
**:** to perform or practice vaccination
— **vac·ci·na·tor** \-ˌnā-tər\ *noun*

**vac·ci·na·tion** \ˌvak-sə-'nā-shən\ *noun* (1800)
**1 :** the act of vaccinating
**2 :** the scar left by vaccinating

**vac·cine** \vak-'sēn, 'vak-ˌ\ *noun* [Latin *vaccinus,* adjective, of or from cows, from *vacca* cow; akin to Sanskrit *vaśa* cow] (1803)
**1 :** matter or a preparation containing the virus of cowpox in a form used for vaccination
**2 :** a preparation of killed microorganisms, living attenuated organisms, or living fully virulent organisms that is administered to produce or artificially increase immunity to a particular disease ◆
— **vaccine** *adjective*

**vac·ci·nee** \ˌvak-sə-'nē\ *noun* (1889)
**:** a vaccinated individual

**vac·cin·ia** \vak-'si-nē-ə\ *noun* [New Latin, from *vaccinus*] (1803)
**1 :** COWPOX
**2 :** the virus that is the causative agent of cowpox
— **vac·cin·i·al** \-nē-əl\ *adjective*

**vac·il·late** \'va-sə-ˌlāt\ *intransitive verb* **-lat·ed; -lat·ing** [Latin *vacillatus,* past participle of *vacillare* to sway, waver — more at WINK] (1597)
**1 a :** to sway through lack of equilibrium **b :** FLUCTUATE, OSCILLATE

**2 :** to waver in mind, will, or feeling **:** hesitate in choice of opinions or courses
***synonym*** see HESITATE
— **vac·il·lat·ing·ly** \-ˌlā-tiŋ-lē\ *adverb*
— **vac·il·la·tor** \-ˌlā-tər\ *noun*

**vac·il·la·tion** \ˌva-sə-'lā-shən\ *noun* (15th century)
**1 :** an act or instance of vacillating
**2 :** inability to take a stand **:** IRRESOLUTION, INDECISION

**va·cu·i·ty** \va-'kyü-ə-tē, və-\ *noun, plural* **-ties** [Latin *vacuitas,* from *vacuus* empty] (1541)
**1 :** an empty space
**2 :** the state, fact, or quality of being vacuous
**3 :** something (as an idea) that is vacuous or inane

**vac·u·o·late** \'va-kyə-(ˌ)wō-ˌlāt\ *or* **vac·u·o·lat·ed** \-ˌlā-təd\ *adjective* (1859)
**:** containing one or more vacuoles ⟨highly *vacuolated* cells⟩

**vac·u·o·la·tion** \ˌva-kyə-(ˌ)wō-'lā-shən\ *noun* (1858)
**:** the development or formation of vacuoles

**vac·u·ole** \'va-kyə-ˌwōl\ *noun* [French, literally, small vacuum, from Latin *vacuum*] (1853)
**1 :** a small cavity or space in the tissues of an organism containing air or fluid
**2 :** a cavity or vesicle in the cytoplasm of a cell usually containing fluid — see CELL illustration
— **vac·u·o·lar** \ˌva-kyə-'wō-lər, -ˌlär\ *adjective*

**vac·u·ous** \'va-kyə-wəs\ *adjective* [Latin *vacuus*] (1655)
**1 :** emptied of or lacking content
**2 :** marked by lack of ideas or intelligence **:** STUPID, INANE ⟨a *vacuous* mind⟩ ⟨a *vacuous* expression⟩
**3 :** devoid of serious occupation **:** IDLE
***synonym*** see EMPTY
— **vac·u·ous·ly** *adverb*
— **vac·u·ous·ness** *noun*

**¹vac·u·um** \'va-(ˌ)kyüm, -kyəm *also* -kyü-əm\ *noun, plural* **vac·u·ums** *or* **vac·ua** \-kyə-wə\ [Latin, from neuter of *vacuus* empty, from *vacare* to be empty] (1550)
**1 :** emptiness of space
**2 a :** a space absolutely devoid of matter **b :** a space partially exhausted (as to the highest degree possible) by artificial means (as an air pump) **c :** a degree of rarefaction below atmospheric pressure

---

◇ WORD HISTORY

**vaccine**   Toward the end of the 18th century the English physician Edward Jenner set about investigating the truth of the folk wisdom that people such as dairymaids who contracted cowpox thereby gained immunity from smallpox, a much more serious disease. Working from this premise, he inoculated an eight-year-old boy with material taken from a milkmaid's cowpox sores. After the boy contracted and recovered from cowpox, Jenner proceeded to inoculate him with smallpox. Immunity had been provided, however, and the boy did not contract the disease. When Jenner published his documentation of 23 such cases in June 1798, he employed the medical Latin name for cowpox, *variolae vaccinae,* literally, "cow pustules." This led to the use of *vaccine matter* or *vaccine virus* for the cowpox inoculum (the virus-containing material used in inoculations), and *vaccination* as a name for the inoculation procedure. French authors writing about Jenner's work used the word *vaccine* alone in 1799 as a term for cowpox, and *vaccin* (a masculine derivative of *vaccine*) in 1801 as a term for the cowpox inoculum. English began to employ *vaccine* in the same sense not long after.

**3 a :** a state or condition resembling a vacuum **:** VOID ⟨the power *vacuum* in Indochina after the departure of the French —Norman Cousins⟩ **b :** a state of isolation from outside influences ⟨people who live in a *vacuum* . . . so that the world outside them is of no moment —W. S. Maugham⟩
**4 :** a device creating or utilizing a partial vacuum; *especially* **:** VACUUM CLEANER
²**vacuum** *adjective* (1825)
**1 :** of, containing, producing, or utilizing a partial vacuum ⟨separated by means of *vacuum* distillation⟩
**2 :** of or relating to a vacuum device or system
³**vacuum** (1922)
*transitive verb*
**:** to use a vacuum device (as a vacuum cleaner) on
*intransitive verb*
**:** to operate a vacuum device
**vacuum bottle** *noun* (1910)
**:** THERMOS
**vacuum cleaner** *noun* (1903)
**:** a household appliance for cleaning (as floors, carpets, or upholstery) by suction — called also *vacuum sweeper*
**vacuum flask** *noun* (1917)
**:** THERMOS
**vacuum gauge** *noun* (circa 1864)
**:** a gauge indicating degree of rarefaction below atmospheric pressure
**vacuum–packed** *adjective* (circa 1926)
**:** having much of the air removed before being hermetically sealed
**vacuum pan** *noun* (1833)
**:** a tank with a vacuum pump for rapid evaporation and condensation (as of sugar syrup) by boiling at a low temperature
**vacuum pump** *noun* (circa 1858)
**:** a pump for exhausting gas from an enclosed space
**vacuum tube** *noun* (1859)
**:** an electron tube evacuated to a high degree of vacuum
**va·de me·cum** \ˌvā-dē-ˈmē-kəm, ˌvä-dē-ˈmā-\ *noun, plural* **vade mecums** [Latin, go with me] (1629)
**1 :** a book for ready reference **:** MANUAL
**2 :** something regularly carried about by a person
**va·dose** \ˈvā-ˌdōs\ *adjective* [Latin *vadosus* shallow, from *vadum,* noun, shallow, ford; akin to Latin *vadere* to go — more at WADE] (1894)
**:** of, relating to, or being water or solutions in the earth's crust above the permanent groundwater level
**vag-** *or* **vago-** *combining form* [International Scientific Vocabulary, from New Latin *vagus*]
**:** vagus nerve ⟨*vagal*⟩ ⟨*vago*tomy⟩
¹**vag·a·bond** \ˈva-gə-ˌbänd\ *adjective* [Middle English, from Middle French, from Late Latin *vagabundus,* from Latin *vagari* to wander] (15th century)
**1 :** moving from place to place without a fixed home **:** WANDERING
**2 a :** of, relating to, or characteristic of a wanderer **b :** leading an unsettled, irresponsible, or disreputable life
— **vag·a·bond·ish** \-ˌbän-dish\ *adjective*
²**vagabond** *noun* (15th century)
**:** one leading a vagabond life; *especially* **:** TRAMP
— **vag·a·bond·age** \-ˌbän-dij\ *noun*
— **vag·a·bond·ism** \-ˌbän-ˌdi-zəm\ *noun*
³**vagabond** *intransitive verb* (1586)
**:** to wander in the manner of a vagabond **:** roam about
**va·gal** \ˈvā-gəl\ *adjective* [International Scientific Vocabulary] (1854)
**:** of, relating to, mediated by, or being the vagus nerve
— **va·gal·ly** \-gə-lē\ *adverb*
**va·gar·i·ous** \vā-ˈger-ē-əs, və-, -ˈgar-\ *adjective* (1798)
**:** marked by vagaries **:** CAPRICIOUS, WHIMSICAL

— **va·gar·i·ous·ly** *adverb*
**va·ga·ry** \ˈvā-gə-rē; və-ˈger-ē, -ˈgar-, vā-; *also* ˈva-gə-rē\ *noun, plural* **-ries** [probably from Latin *vagari* to wander, from *vagus* wandering] (1573)
**:** an erratic, unpredictable, or extravagant manifestation, action, or notion
**synonym** see CAPRICE
**vag·ile** \ˈva-jəl, -ˌjīl\ *adjective* [International Scientific Vocabulary, from Latin *vagus* wandering] (circa 1890)
**:** free to move about ⟨*vagile* organisms⟩
— **va·gil·i·ty** \və-ˈji-lə-tē, va-\ *noun*
**va·gi·na** \və-ˈjī-nə\ *noun, plural* **-nae** \-(ˌ)nē\ *or* **-nas** [Latin, literally, sheath] (1682)
**1 :** a canal in a female mammal that leads from the uterus to the external orifice of the genital canal
**2 :** a canal that is similar in function or location to the vagina and occurs in various animals other than mammals
**vag·i·nal** \ˈva-jə-nᵊl\ *adjective* (1726)
**1 :** of or relating to a theca
**2 :** of, relating to, or affecting the genital vagina
— **vag·i·nal·ly** \-nᵊl-ē\ *adverb*
**vag·i·nis·mus** \ˌva-jə-ˈniz-məs\ *noun* [New Latin, from Latin *vagina*] (1866)
**:** a painful spasmodic contraction of the vagina
**vag·i·ni·tis** \ˌva-jə-ˈnī-təs\ *noun* [New Latin] (1846)
**:** inflammation of the vagina or of a sheath (as a tendon sheath)
**va·got·o·my** \vā-ˈgä-tə-mē\ *noun, plural* **-mies** [International Scientific Vocabulary] (circa 1903)
**:** surgical division of the vagus nerve
**va·go·to·nia** \ˌvā-gə-ˈtō-nē-ə\ *noun* [New Latin] (circa 1915)
**:** excessive excitability of the vagus nerve resulting typically in vasomotor instability, constipation, and sweating
— **va·go·ton·ic** \-ˈtä-nik\ *adjective*
**va·gran·cy** \ˈvā-grən(t)-sē\ *noun, plural* **-cies** (1641)
**1 :** VAGARY
**2 :** the state or action of being vagrant
**3 :** the offense of being a vagrant
¹**va·grant** \ˈvā-grənt\ *noun* [Middle English *vagraunt,* probably modification of Middle French *waucrant, wacrant* wandering, from Old French, from present participle of *waucrer, wacrer* to roll, wander, of Germanic origin; akin to Old English *wealcan* to roll — more at WALK] (15th century)
**1 a :** one who has no established residence and wanders idly from place to place without lawful or visible means of support **b :** one (as a prostitute or drunkard) whose conduct constitutes statutory vagrancy
**2 :** WANDERER, ROVER
²**vagrant** *adjective* (15th century)
**1 :** wandering about from place to place usually with no means of support
**2 a :** having a fleeting, wayward, or inconstant quality **b :** having no fixed course **:** RANDOM
— **va·grant·ly** *adverb*
**va·grom** \ˈvā-grəm\ *adjective* [by alteration] (1599)
**:** VAGRANT
**vague** \ˈvāg\ *adjective* **vagu·er; vagu·est** [Middle French, from Latin *vagus,* literally, wandering] (1548)
**1 a :** not clearly expressed **:** stated in indefinite terms ⟨*vague* accusation⟩ **b :** not having a precise meaning ⟨*vague* term of abuse⟩
**2 a :** not clearly defined, grasped, or understood **:** INDISTINCT ⟨only a *vague* notion of what's needed⟩; *also* **:** SLIGHT ⟨a *vague* hint of a thickening waistline⟩ ⟨hasn't the *vaguest* idea⟩ **b :** not clearly felt or sensed **:** somewhat subconscious ⟨a *vague* longing⟩
**3 :** not thinking or expressing one's thoughts clearly or precisely ⟨*vague* about dates and places⟩

**4 :** lacking expression **:** VACANT
**5 :** not sharply outlined **:** HAZY
**synonym** see OBSCURE
— **vague·ly** *adverb*
— **vague·ness** *noun*
**va·gus nerve** \ˈvā-gəs-\ *noun* [New Latin *vagus nervus,* literally, wandering nerve] (1840)
**:** either of the 10th pair of cranial nerves that arise from the medulla and supply chiefly the viscera especially with autonomic sensory and motor fibers — called also *vagus*
**vail** \ˈvā(ə)l\ *transitive verb* [Middle English *valen,* partly from Middle French *valer* (short for *avaler* to let fall) & partly short for Middle English *avalen* to let fall, from Middle French *avaler,* from Old French, from *aval* downward, from *a* to (from Latin *ad*) + *val* valley — more at AT, VALE] (14th century)
**:** to lower often as a sign of respect or submission
**vain** \ˈvān\ *adjective* [Middle English, from Middle French, from Latin *vanus* empty, vain — more at WANE] (14th century)
**1 :** having no real value **:** IDLE, WORTHLESS
**2 :** marked by futility or ineffectualness **:** UNSUCCESSFUL, USELESS ⟨*vain* efforts to escape⟩
**3** *archaic* **:** FOOLISH, SILLY
**4 :** having or showing undue or excessive pride in one's appearance or achievements **:** CONCEITED ☆
**synonym** see FUTILE
— **vain·ly** *adverb*
— **vain·ness** \ˈvān-nəs\ *noun*
— **in vain 1 :** to no end **:** without success or result **2 :** in an irreverent or blasphemous manner ⟨you shall not take the name of the Lord your God *in vain* —Deuteronomy 5:11 (Revised Standard Version)⟩
**vain·glo·ri·ous** \vān-ˈglōr-ē-əs, -ˈglȯr-\ *adjective* (15th century)
**:** marked by vainglory **:** BOASTFUL
— **vain·glo·ri·ous·ly** *adverb*
— **vain·glo·ri·ous·ness** *noun*
**vain·glo·ry** \ˈvān-ˌglōr-ē, -ˌglȯr-, ˌvān-ˈ\ *noun* (14th century)
**1 :** excessive or ostentatious pride especially in one's achievements
**2 :** vain display or show **:** VANITY
**vair** \ˈvar, ˈver\ *noun* [Middle English *veir,* from Old French *vair,* from *vair,* adjective, variegated, from Latin *varius* variegated, various] (14th century)
**:** the bluish gray and white fur of a squirrel prized for ornamental use in medieval times
**Vaish·na·va** \ˈvīsh-nə-və\ *noun* [Sanskrit *vaiṣṇava* of Vishnu, from *Viṣṇu* Vishnu] (1815)
**:** a member of a major Hindu sect devoted to the cult of Vishnu
— **Vaishnava** *adjective*
— **Vaish·na·vism** \-ˌvi-zəm\ *noun*

---

☆ **SYNONYMS**
**Vain, nugatory, otiose, idle, empty, hollow** mean being without worth or significance. VAIN implies either absolute or relative absence of value ⟨*vain* promises⟩. NUGATORY suggests triviality or insignificance ⟨a monarch with *nugatory* powers⟩. OTIOSE suggests that something serves no purpose and is either an encumbrance or a superfluity ⟨a film without a single *otiose* scene⟩. IDLE suggests being incapable of worthwhile use or effect ⟨*idle* speculations⟩. EMPTY and HOLLOW suggest a deceiving lack of real substance or soundness or genuineness ⟨an *empty* attempt at reconciliation⟩ ⟨a *hollow* victory⟩.

---

\ə\ **abut** \ᵊ\ **kitten** \ər\ **further** \a\ **ash** \ā\ **ace**
\ä\ **mop, mar** \aů\ **out** \ch\ **chin** \e\ **bet** \ē\ **easy**
\g\ **go** \i\ **hit** \ī\ **ice** \j\ **job** \ŋ\ **sing** \ō\ **go**
\ȯ\ **law** \ȯi\ **boy** \th\ **thin** \t̶h̶\ **the** \ü\ **loot** \ů\ **foot**
\y\ **yet** \zh\ **vision** *see also* Guide to Pronunciation

**Vais·ya** \'vīsh-yə, 'vī-shə\ *noun* [Sanskrit *vaiśya,* from *viś* settlement; akin to Greek *oikos* house — more at VICINITY] (1665)
: a Hindu of an upper caste traditionally assigned to commercial and agricultural occupations

**va·lance** \'va-lən(t)s, 'vā-\ *noun* [Middle English *vallance,* perhaps from *Valence,* France] (15th century)
**1** : a drapery hung along the edge of a bed, table, altar, canopy, or shelf
**2** : a short drapery or wood or metal frame used as a decorative heading to conceal the top of curtains and fixtures
— **va·lanced** \-lən(t)st\ *adjective*

**vale** \'vā(ə)l\ *noun* [Middle English, from Middle French *val,* from Old French *val,* from Latin *valles, vallis;* perhaps akin to Latin *volvere* to roll — more at VOLUBLE] (14th century)
**1** : VALLEY, DALE
**2** : WORLD ⟨this *vale* of tears⟩

**val·e·dic·tion** \,va-lə-'dik-shən\ *noun* [Latin *valedicere* to say farewell, from *vale* farewell + *dicere* to say — more at DICTION] (1614)
**1** : an act of bidding farewell
**2** : VALEDICTORY

**val·e·dic·to·ri·an** \-,dik-'tōr-ē-ən, -'tȯr-\ *noun* (1759)
: the student usually having the highest rank in a graduating class who delivers the valedictory address at the commencement exercises

**¹val·e·dic·to·ry** \-'dik-t(ə-)rē\ *adjective* [Latin *valedicere*] (1651)
: of or relating to a valediction : expressing or containing a farewell

**²valedictory** *noun, plural* **-ries** (1779)
: an address or statement of farewell or leave-taking

**va·lence** \'vā-lən(t)s\ *noun* [Late Latin *valentia* power, capacity, from Latin *valent-, valens,* present participle of *valēre* to be strong — more at WIELD] (1884)
**1** : the degree of combining power of an element as shown by the number of atomic weights of a univalent element (as hydrogen) with which the atomic weight of the element will combine or for which it can be substituted or with which it can be compared
**2 a** : relative capacity to unite, react, or interact (as with antigens or a biological substrate) **b** : the degree of attractiveness an individual, activity, or object possesses as a behavioral goal

**valence band** *noun* (1953)
: the range of permissible energy values that are the highest energies an electron of an atom can have and still be associated with the atom and be used to form bonds — compare CONDUCTION BAND

**valence electron** *noun* (1923)
: a single electron or one of two or more electrons in the outer shell of an atom that is responsible for the chemical properties of the atom

**Va·len·cia orange** \və-'len-ch(ē-)ə, -len(t)-sē-ə\ *noun* [*Valencia,* Spain] (1858)
: a sweet orange of a juicy thin-skinned cultivar grown in the U.S. — called also *Valencia*

**Va·len·ci·ennes** \və-,len(t)-sē-'en(z), ,va-lən-sē-\ *noun* [*Valenciennes,* France] (1717)
: a fine bobbin lace

**-valent** *adjective combining form* [International Scientific Vocabulary, from Latin *valent-, valens*]
**1** : having a (specified) valence or valences ⟨bi*valent*⟩ ⟨multi*valent*⟩
**2** : having (so many) chromosomal strands or homologous chromosomes ⟨uni*valent*⟩

**val·en·tine** \'va-lən-,tīn\ *noun* (15th century)
**1** : a sweetheart chosen or complimented on Saint Valentine's Day
**2 a** : a gift or greeting sent or given especially to a sweetheart on Saint Valentine's Day; es-

pecially : a greeting card sent on this day **b** : something (as a movie or piece of writing) expressing uncritical praise or affection : TRIBUTE

**Valentine's Day** *also* **Valentine Day** *noun* (1668)
: SAINT VALENTINE'S DAY

**val·er·ate** \'va-lə-,rāt\ *noun* (1852)
: a salt or ester of valeric acid

**va·le·ri·an** \və-'lir-ē-ən\ *noun* [Middle English, from Middle French or Medieval Latin; Middle French *valeriane,* from Medieval Latin *valeriana,* probably from feminine of *valerianus* of Valeria, from *Valeria,* Roman province formerly part of Pannonia] (14th century)
**1** : any of a genus (*Valeriana* of the family Valerianaceae, the valerian family) of perennial herbs many of which possess medicinal properties
**2** : a drug consisting of the dried rootstock and roots of the garden heliotrope (*Valeriana officinalis*) formerly used as a carminative and sedative

**va·le·ric acid** \və-'lir-ik-, -'ler-\ *noun* [*valerian;* from its occurrence in the root of valerian] (1857)
: any of four isomeric fatty acids $C_5H_{10}O_2$ or a mixture of these; *especially* : a liquid acid of disagreeable odor obtained from valerian or made synthetically and used especially in organic synthesis

**¹va·let** \'va-lət, 'va-(,)lā, va-'lā\ *noun* [Middle French *vaslet, varlet, valet* young nobleman, page, domestic servant, from (assumed) Medieval Latin *vassellittus,* diminutive of Medieval Latin *vassus* servant — more at VASSAL] (1567)
**1 a** : a man's male servant who performs personal services (as taking care of clothing) **b** : an employee (as of a hotel or a public facility) who performs personal services for customers
**2** : a device (as a rack or tray) for holding clothing or personal effects

**²valet** *transitive verb* (1840)
: to serve as a valet

**va·let de cham·bre** \(,)va-lā-də-'shä<sup>n</sup>br<sup>e</sup>\ *noun, plural* **va·lets de chambre** \*same*\ [French, literally, chamber valet] (1646)
: VALET 1a

**valet parking** *noun* (1960)
: a service that provides parking of motor vehicles by an attendant

**¹val·e·tu·di·nar·i·an** \,va-lə-,tü-d<sup>ə</sup>n-'er-ē-ən, -,tyü-\ *noun* [Latin *valetudinarius* sickly, infirm, from *valetudin-, valetudo* state of health, sickness, from *valēre* to be strong, be well — more at WIELD] (1703)
: a person of a weak or sickly constitution; *especially* : one whose chief concern is being or becoming a chronic invalid

**²valetudinarian** *adjective* (1713)
: of, relating to, or characteristic of a valetudinarian : SICKLY, WEAK

**val·e·tu·di·nar·i·an·ism** \-ē-ə-,ni-zəm\ *noun* (1839)
: the condition or state of mind of a valetudinarian

**¹val·e·tu·di·nary** \-'tü-d<sup>ə</sup>n-,er-ē, -'tyü-\ *adjective* [Latin *valetudinarius*] (1581)
: VALETUDINARIAN

**²valetudinary** *noun, plural* **-nar·ies** (1665)
: VALETUDINARIAN

**val·gus** \'val-gəs\ *adjective* [New Latin, from Latin, bowlegged] (1884)
: of, relating to, or being a deformity in which an anatomical part is turned outward away from the midline of the body to an abnormal degree ⟨*valgus* deformity of the ankle⟩
— **valgus** *noun*

**Val·hal·la** \val-'ha-lə *also* väl-'hä-\ *noun* [German & Old Norse; German *Walhalla,* from Old Norse *Valhǫll,* literally, hall of the slain, from *valr* the slain (akin to Old English *wæl* slaughter, the slain) + *hǫll* hall; akin to Old English *heall* hall]

: the great hall in Norse mythology where the souls of heroes slain in battle are received

**val·iance** \'val-yən(t)s\ *noun* (15th century)
: VALOR

**val·ian·cy** \-yən(t)-sē\ *noun* (15th century)
: VALOR

**¹val·iant** \'val-yənt\ *adjective* [Middle English *valiaunt,* from Middle French *vaillant,* from Old French, from present participle of *valoir* to be of worth, from Latin *valēre* to be strong — more at WIELD] (14th century)
**1** : possessing or acting with bravery or boldness : COURAGEOUS ⟨*valiant* soldiers⟩
**2** : marked by, exhibiting, or carried out with courage or determination : HEROIC ⟨*valiant* feats⟩
— **val·iant·ly** *adverb*
— **val·iant·ness** *noun*

**²valiant** *noun* (1609)
: a valiant person

**val·id** \'va-ləd\ *adjective* [Middle French or Medieval Latin; Middle French *valide,* from Medieval Latin *validus,* from Latin, strong, from *valēre*] (1571)
**1** : having legal efficacy or force; *especially* : executed with the proper legal authority and formalities ⟨a *valid* contract⟩
**2 a** : well-grounded or justifiable : being at once relevant and meaningful ⟨a *valid* theory⟩ **b** : logically correct ⟨a *valid* argument⟩ ⟨*valid* inference⟩
**3** : appropriate to the end in view : EFFECTIVE ⟨every craft has its own *valid* methods⟩
**4** *of a taxon* : conforming to accepted principles of sound biological classification ☆
— **va·lid·i·ty** \və-'li-də-tē, va-\ *noun*
— **val·id·ly** \'va-ləd-lē\ *adverb*

**val·i·date** \'va-lə-,dāt\ *transitive verb* **-dat·ed; -dat·ing** (1648)
**1 a** : to make legally valid **b** : to grant official sanction to by marking **c** : to confirm the validity of (an election); *also* : to declare (a person) elected
**2** : to support or corroborate on a sound or authoritative basis ⟨experiments designed to *validate* the hypothesis⟩
*synonym* see CONFIRM

**val·i·da·tion** \,va-lə-'dā-shən\ *noun* (circa 1656)
: an act, process, or instance of validating; *especially* : the determination of the degree of validity of a measuring device

**va·line** \'va-,lēn, 'vā-\ *noun* [International Scientific Vocabulary, from *valeric (acid)*] (1907)
: a crystalline essential amino acid $C_5H_{11}NO_2$ that is one of the building blocks of plant and animal proteins

**va·lise** \və-'lēs\ *noun* [French, from Italian *valigia*] (1615)
: SUITCASE

**Val·i·um** \'va-lē-əm, 'val-yəm\ *trademark*
— used for a preparation of diazepam

**Val·ky·rie** \val-'kir-ē *also* val-'kī-rē, 'val-kə-rē\ *noun* [German & Old Norse; German

---

☆ **SYNONYMS**
**Valid, sound, cogent, convincing, telling** mean having such force as to compel serious attention and usually acceptance. VALID implies being supported by objective truth or generally accepted authority ⟨a *valid* reason for being absent⟩ ⟨a *valid* marriage⟩. SOUND implies a basis of flawless reasoning or of solid grounds ⟨a *sound* proposal for reviving the economy⟩. COGENT may stress either weight of sound argument and evidence or lucidity of presentation ⟨the prosecutor's *cogent* summation won over the jury⟩. CONVINCING suggests a power to overcome doubt, opposition, or reluctance to accept ⟨a *convincing* argument for welfare reform⟩. TELLING stresses an immediate and crucial effect striking at the heart of a matter ⟨a *telling* example of bureaucratic waste⟩.

*Walküre,* from Old Norse *valkyrja,* literally, chooser of the slain; akin to Old English *wæl-cyrige* witch, with Old Norse *valr* the slain, Old High German *kiosan* to choose — more at CHOOSE]
: any of the maidens of Odin who choose the heroes to be slain in battle and conduct them to Valhalla

**val·late** \'va-ˌlāt\ *adjective* [Latin *vallatus,* past participle of *vallare* to surround with a wall, from *vallum* wall, rampart — more at WALL] (1878)
: having a raised edge surrounding a depression ⟨*vallate* papillae of the tongue⟩

**val·lec·u·la** \va-'le-kyə-lə, və-\ *noun, plural* **-u·lae** \-kyə-ˌlē, -ˌlī\ [New Latin, from Late Latin, little valley, diminutive of Latin *valles* valley — more at VALE] (1859)
: an anatomical groove, channel, or depression; *especially* : one between the base of the tongue and the epiglottis
— **val·lec·u·lar** \-lər\ *adjective*

**val·ley** \'va-lē\ *noun, plural* **valleys** [Middle English *valey,* from Old French *valee,* from *val* valley — more at VALE] (14th century)
**1 a** : an elongate depression of the earth's surface usually between ranges of hills or mountains **b** : an area drained by a river and its tributaries
**2** : a low point or condition
**3 a** : HOLLOW, DEPRESSION **b** : the place of meeting of two slopes of a roof that form on the plan a reentrant angle

**valley fever** *noun* [from its prevalence in the San Joaquin valley of California] (1938)
: COCCIDIOIDOMYCOSIS

**Va·lois** \'val-ˌwä, val-'\ *adjective* [Philippe de *Valois* (Philip VI of France)] (circa 1888)
: of or relating to the French royal house that ruled from 1328 to 1589

**va·lo·nia** \və-'lō-nē-ə, -nyə\ *noun* [Italian *vallonia,* from Middle Greek *balanidia,* plural of *balanidion,* diminutive of Greek *balanos* acorn — more at GLAND] (1722)
: dried acorn cups especially from a Eurasian evergreen oak (*Quercus macrolepis* synonym *Q. aegilops*) used in tanning or dressing leather

**val·or** \'va-lər\ *noun* [Middle English, from Middle French *valour,* from Medieval Latin *valor* value, valor, from Latin *valēre* to be strong — more at WIELD] (15th century)
: strength of mind or spirit that enables a person to encounter danger with firmness : personal bravery

**val·o·rize** \'va-lə-ˌrīz\ *transitive verb* **-rized; -riz·ing** [Portuguese *valorizar,* from *valor* value, price, from Medieval Latin] (circa 1906)
: to enhance or try to enhance the price, value, or status of by organized and usually governmental action ⟨using subsidies to *valorize* coffee⟩
— **val·o·ri·za·tion** \ˌva-lə-rə-'zā-shən\ *noun*

**val·or·ous** \'va-lə-rəs\ *adjective* (15th century)
: VALIANT
— **val·or·ous·ly** *adverb*

**val·our** \'va-lər\ *chiefly British variant of* VALOR

**val·po·li·cel·la** \ˌväl-ˌpō-lə-'che-lə, ˌval-\ *noun, often capitalized* [*Valpolicella,* district in northern Italy] (1903)
: a dry red Italian table wine

**Val·sal·va maneuver** \val-'sal-və-\ *noun* [Antonio Maria *Valsalva* (died 1723) Italian anatomist] (1886)
: the process of making a forceful attempt at expiration while holding the nostrils closed and keeping the mouth shut for the purpose of testing the patency of the eustachian tubes or of adjusting middle ear pressure — called also *Valsalva*

**valse** \väls\ *noun* [French, from German *Walzer* — more at WALTZ] (1796)
: WALTZ; *specifically* : a concert waltz

**¹valu·able** \'val-yə-bəl, -yə-wə-bəl\ *adjective* (1589)
**1 a** : having monetary value **b** : worth a good price
**2 a** : having desirable or esteemed characteristics or qualities ⟨*valuable* friendships⟩ **b** : of great use or service ⟨*valuable* advice⟩
— **valu·able·ness** *noun*
— **valu·ably** \-blē\ *adverb*

**²valuable** *noun* (circa 1775)
: a usually personal possession (as jewelry) of relatively great monetary value — usually used in plural

**valuable consideration** *noun* (1638)
: an equivalent or compensation having value that is given for something acquired or promised (as money or marriage) and that may consist either in a benefit accruing to one party or a loss falling upon the other

**valu·ate** \'val-yə-ˌwāt\ *transitive verb* **-at·ed; -at·ing** (1873)
: to place a value on : APPRAISE

**valu·a·tion** \ˌval-yə-'wā-shən\ *noun* [Middle French, from *valuer* to value, from *value*] (1529)
**1** : the act or process of valuing; *specifically* : appraisal of property
**2** : the estimated or determined market value of a thing
**3** : judgment or appreciation of worth or character
— **valu·a·tion·al** \-shnəl, -shə-nᵊl\ *adjective*
— **valu·a·tion·al·ly** *adverb*

**valu·a·tor** \'val-yə-ˌwā-tər\ *noun* (1731)
: one that valuates; *specifically* : one that appraises

**¹val·ue** \'val-(ˌ)yü\ *noun* [Middle English, from Middle French, from (assumed) Vulgar Latin *valuta,* from feminine of *valutus,* past participle of Latin *valēre* to be worth, be strong — more at WIELD] (14th century)
**1** : a fair return or equivalent in goods, services, or money for something exchanged
**2** : the monetary worth of something : marketable price
**3** : relative worth, utility, or importance ⟨a good *value* at the price⟩ ⟨the *value* of base stealing in baseball⟩ ⟨had nothing of *value* to say⟩
**4 a** : a numerical quantity that is assigned or is determined by calculation or measurement ⟨let *x* take on positive *values*⟩ ⟨a *value* for the age of the earth⟩ **b** : precise signification ⟨*value* of a word⟩
**5** : the relative duration of a musical note
**6 a** : relative lightness or darkness of a color : LUMINOSITY **b** : the relation of one part in a picture to another with respect to lightness and darkness
**7** : something (as a principle or quality) intrinsically valuable or desirable ⟨sought material *values* instead of human *values* —W. H. Jones⟩
**8** : DENOMINATION 2
— **val·ue·less** \-(ˌ)yü-ləs, -yə-\ *adjective*
— **val·ue·less·ness** *noun*

**²value** *transitive verb* **val·ued; val·u·ing** (15th century)
**1 a** : to estimate or assign the monetary worth of : APPRAISE ⟨*value* a necklace⟩ **b** : to rate or scale in usefulness, importance, or general worth : EVALUATE
**2** : to consider or rate highly : PRIZE, ESTEEM ⟨*values* your opinion⟩
*synonym* see ESTIMATE, APPRECIATE
— **val·u·er** \-yə-wər\ *noun*

**value–added tax** *noun* (1935)
: an incremental excise that is levied on the value added at each stage of the processing of a raw material or the production and distribution of a commodity and that typically has the impact of a sales tax on the ultimate consumer

**val·ued** \'val-(ˌ)yüd, -yəd\ *adjective* (1595)
: having a value or values especially of a specified kind or number — often used in combination ⟨real-*valued*⟩

**val·ue–free** \'val-(ˌ)yü-'frē\ *adjective* (1948)
: making or having no value judgments ⟨*value-free* distinctions⟩ ⟨*value-free* economics⟩

**value judgment** *noun* (1899)
: a judgment assigning a value (as good or bad) to something

**va·lu·ta** \və-'lü-tə, -(ˌ)tä\ *noun* [Italian, value, from (assumed) Vulgar Latin *valuta*] (1920)
**1** : the agreed upon or exchange value of a currency
**2** : FOREIGN EXCHANGE 2

**val·vate** \'val-ˌvāt\ *adjective* (1829)
: having valves or parts resembling a valve; *especially* : meeting at the edges without overlapping in the bud (as in the calyx of a mallow)

**valve** \'valv\ *noun* [Latin *valva;* akin to Latin *volvere* to roll — more at VOLUBLE] (14th century)
**1** *archaic* : a leaf of a folding or double door
**2** [New Latin *valva,* from Latin] : a structure especially in a vein or lymphatic that closes temporarily a passage or orifice or permits movement of fluid in one direction only
**3 a** : any of numerous mechanical devices by which the flow of liquid, gas, or loose material in bulk may be started, stopped, or regulated by a movable part that opens, shuts, or partially obstructs one or more ports or passageways; *also* : the movable part of such a device **b** : a device in a brass instrument for quickly channeling air flow through an added length of tube in order to change the fundamental tone by some definite interval **c** *chiefly British* : ELECTRON TUBE
**4** [New Latin *valva,* from Latin] : one of the distinct and usually movably articulated pieces of which the shell of some shell-bearing animals (as lamellibranch mollusks, brachiopods, and barnacles) consists
**5** [New Latin *valva,* from Latin] **a** : one of the segments or pieces into which a dehiscing capsule or legume separates **b** : the portion of various anthers (as of the barberry) resembling a lid **c** : one of the two encasing membranes of a diatom
— **valved** \'valvd\ *adjective*
— **valve·less** \'valv-ləs\ *adjective*

**val·vu·la** \'val-vyə-lə\ *noun, plural* **-lae** \-ˌlē, -ˌlī\ [New Latin, diminutive of Latin *valva*] (1615)
: a small valve or fold

**val·vu·lar** \'val-vyə-lər\ *adjective* (1797)
**1** : resembling or functioning as a valve; *also* : opening by valves
**2** : of, relating to, or affecting a valve especially of the heart ⟨*valvular* heart disease⟩

**val·vu·li·tis** \ˌval-vyə-'lī-təs\ *noun* [New Latin] (circa 1891)
: inflammation of a valve especially of the heart

**va·moose** \və-'müs, va-\ *intransitive verb* **va·moosed; va·moos·ing** [Spanish *vamos* let us go, suppletive 1st plural imperative (from Latin *vadere* to go) of *ir* to go, from Latin *ire* — more at WADE, ISSUE] (1840)
: to depart quickly

**¹vamp** \'vamp\ *verb* [²*vamp*] (1599)
*transitive verb*
**1 a** : to provide (a shoe) with a new vamp **b** : to piece (something old) with a new part : PATCH ⟨*vamp* up old sermons⟩
**2** : INVENT, FABRICATE ⟨*vamp* up an excuse⟩
*intransitive verb*
: to play a musical vamp
— **vamp·er** *noun*

²**vamp** *noun* [Middle English *vampe* sock, from Old French *avantpié,* from *avant-* fore- + *pié* foot, from Latin *ped-, pes* — more at VANGUARD, FOOT] (1654)
**1 :** the part of a shoe upper or boot upper covering especially the forepart of the foot and sometimes also extending forward over the toe or backward to the back seam of the upper
**2** [¹*vamp*] **:** a short introductory musical passage often repeated several times (as in vaudeville) before a solo or between verses

³**vamp** *noun* [short for *vampire*] (circa 1911)
**:** a woman who uses her charm or wiles to seduce and exploit men
— **vamp·ish** \'vam-pish\ *adjective*

⁴**vamp** *transitive verb* (circa 1915)
**:** to practice seductive wiles on

**vam·pire** \'vam-ˌpīr\ *noun* [French, from German *Vampir,* from Serbo-Croatian *vampir*] (1734)
**1 :** the reanimated body of a dead person believed to come from the grave at night and suck the blood of persons asleep
**2 a :** one who lives by preying on others **b :** a woman who exploits and ruins her lover
**3 :** VAMPIRE BAT
— **vam·pir·ish** \-ish\ *adjective*

**vampire bat** *noun* (1790)
**:** any of several Central and South American bats (*Desmodus rotundus, Diaemus youngi,* and *Diphylla ecaudata* of the subfamily Desmodontinae of the family Phyllostomidae) that feed on the blood of birds and mammals and especially domestic animals and that are sometimes vectors of equine trypanosomiasis and of rabies; *also* **:** any of several other bats (as of the families Megadermatidae and Phyllostomidae) that do not feed on blood but are sometimes reputed to do so

**vampire bat**

**vam·pir·ism** \-ˌpīr-ˌi-zəm\ *noun* (1794)
**1 :** belief in vampires
**2 :** the actions of a vampire

¹**van** \'van\ *noun* [Middle English, from Middle French, from Latin *vannus* — more at WINNOW] (14th century)
**1** *dialect English* **:** a winnowing device (as a fan)
**2 :** WING 1a

²**van** *noun* [by shortening] (1610)
**:** VANGUARD

³**van** *noun* [short for *caravan*] (1829)
**1 a :** a usually enclosed wagon or motortruck used for transportation of goods or animals; *also* **:** CARAVAN 2a **b :** a multipurpose enclosed motor vehicle having a boxlike shape, rear or side doors, and side panels often with windows **c :** a detachable passenger cabin transportable by aircraft or truck
**2** *chiefly British* **:** an enclosed railroad freight or baggage car

⁴**van** *transitive verb* **vanned; van·ning** (1840)
**:** to transport by van

**van·a·date** \'va-nə-ˌdāt\ *noun* [New Latin *vanadium* + English ¹*-ate*] (1835)
**:** a salt derived from vanadium pentoxide and containing pentavalent vanadium

**va·na·di·um** \və-'nā-dē-əm\ *noun* [New Latin, from Old Norse *Vanadīs* Freya] (1833)
**:** a grayish malleable ductile metallic element found combined in minerals and used especially to form alloys (as vanadium steel) — see ELEMENT table

**vanadium pentoxide** *noun* (1885)
**:** a yellowish red crystalline compound $V_2O_5$ used especially in glass manufacture and as a catalyst

**Van Al·len belt** \van-'a-lən-\ *noun* [James A. *Van Allen*] (1958)
**:** a belt of intense radiation in the magnetosphere composed of energetic charged particles trapped by the earth's magnetic field; *also* **:** a similar belt surrounding another planet

**va·nas·pa·ti** \və-'nəs-pə-tē, -'näs-\ *noun* [Sanskrit, forest tree, soma plant, literally, lord of the forest, from *vana* forest + *pati* lord, master — more at POTENT] (1941)
**:** a hydrogenated vegetable fat used as a butter substitute in India

**van·dal** \'van-dᵊl\ *noun* [Latin *Vandalii* (plural), of Germanic origin] (1555)
**1** *capitalized* **:** a member of a Germanic people who lived in the area south of the Baltic between the Vistula and the Oder, overran Gaul, Spain, and northern Africa in the 4th and 5th centuries A.D., and in 455 sacked Rome
**2 :** one who willfully or ignorantly destroys, damages, or defaces property belonging to another or to the public ◆
— **vandal** *adjective, often capitalized*
— **Van·dal·ic** \van-'da-lik\ *adjective*

**van·dal·ise** *British variant of* VANDALIZE

**van·dal·ism** \'van-dᵊl-ˌi-zəm\ *noun* (1798)
**:** willful or malicious destruction or defacement of public or private property

**van·dal·is·tic** \ˌvan-dᵊl-'is-tik\ *adjective* (1897)
**:** of or relating to vandalism

**van·dal·ize** \'van-dᵊl-ˌīz\ *transitive verb* **-ized; -iz·ing** (1845)
**:** to subject to vandalism **:** DAMAGE
— **van·dal·i·za·tion** \ˌvan-dᵊl-ə-'zā-shən\ *noun*

**van·da orchid** \'van-də-\ *noun* [New Latin, from Hindi *vandā* mistletoe, from Sanskrit, a parasitic plant] (1943)
**:** any of a large genus (*Vanda*) of Indo-Malayan epiphytic orchids often grown for their loose racemes of showy flowers — called also *vanda*

**Van de Graaff generator** \'van-də-ˌgraf-\ *noun* [Robert J. *Van de Graaff* (died 1967) American physicist] (1937)
**:** an apparatus for the production of electrical discharges at high voltage commonly consisting of an insulated hollow conducting sphere that accumulates in its interior the charge continuously conveyed from a source of direct current by an endless belt of flexible nonconducting material

**van der Waals forces** \'van-dər-ˌwȯlz-, 'vän-dər-ˌvälz-\ *noun plural* [Johannes D. *van der Waals* (died 1923) Dutch physicist] (1926)
**:** the relatively weak attractive forces that act on neutral atoms and molecules and that arise because of the electric polarization induced in each of the particles by the presence of other particles

**Van·dyke** \van-'dīk, vən-\ *noun* [Sir Anthony *Vandyke*] (1755)
**1 a :** a wide collar with a deeply indented edge **b :** one of several V-shaped points forming a decorative edging **c :** a border of such points
**2 :** a trim pointed beard
— **van·dyked** \-'dīkt\ *adjective*

**Vandyke brown** *noun* [from its use by the painter Vandyke] (circa 1850)
**:** a natural brown-black pigment of organic matter obtained from bog earth or peat or lignite deposits; *also* **:** any of various synthetic brown pigments

**Vandyke 2**

**vane** \'vān\ *noun* [Middle English (southern dialect), from Old English *fana* banner; akin to Old High German *fano* cloth, Latin *pannus* cloth, rag] (15th century)
**1 a :** a movable device attached to an elevated object (as a spire) for showing the direction of the wind **b :** one that is changeable or inconstant
**2 :** a thin flat or curved object that is rotated about an axis by a flow of fluid or that rotates to cause a fluid to flow or that redirects a flow of fluid (the *vanes* of a windmill)
**3 :** the web or flat expanded part of a feather — see FEATHER illustration
**4 :** a feather fastened to the shaft near the nock of an arrow
*word history* see VIXEN
— **vaned** \'vānd\ *adjective*

**van·guard** \'van-ˌgärd *also* 'vaŋ-\ *noun* [Middle English *vantgard,* from Middle French *avant-garde,* from Old French, from *avant-* fore- (from *avant* before, from Late Latin *abante*) + *garde* guard — more at ADVANCE] (15th century)
**1 :** the troops moving at the head of an army
**2 :** the forefront of an action or movement
— **van·guard·ism** \-ˌgär-ˌdi-zəm\ *noun*
— **van·guard·ist** \-dist\ *noun*

¹**va·nil·la** \və-'ni-lə, -'ne-\ *noun* [New Latin, from Spanish *vainilla* vanilla (plant and fruit), diminutive of *vaina* sheath, from Latin *vagina* sheath, vagina] (1662)
**1 a :** VANILLA BEAN **b :** a commercially important extract of the vanilla bean that is used especially as a flavoring
**2 :** any of a genus (*Vanilla*) of tropical American climbing epiphytic orchids

²**vanilla** *adjective* (1846)
**1 :** flavored with vanilla
**2 :** lacking distinction **:** PLAIN, ORDINARY

**vanilla bean** *noun* (1874)
**:** the long capsular fruit of a vanilla (especially *Vanilla planifolia*) that is an important article of commerce

**van·il·lin** \'va-nᵊl-ən\ *noun* (circa 1868)
**:** a crystalline phenolic aldehyde $C_8H_8O_3$ that is extracted from vanilla beans or prepared synthetically and is used especially in flavoring and in perfumery

**Va·nir** \'vän-ˌir\ *noun plural* [Old Norse]
**:** a race of Norse gods who become united with the Aesir

**van·ish** \'va-nish\ *verb* [Middle English *vanisshen,* from Middle French *evaniss-,* stem of *evanir,* from (assumed) Vulgar Latin *exvanire,* alteration of Latin *evanescere* to dissipate like vapor, vanish, from *e-* + *vanescere* to vanish, from *vanus* empty] (14th century)
*intransitive verb*
**1 a :** to pass quickly from sight **:** DISAPPEAR **b :** to pass completely from existence

2 : to assume the value zero
*transitive verb*
: to cause to disappear
— **van·ish·er** *noun*
**vanishing cream** *noun* (1916)
: a cosmetic preparation that is less oily than cold cream and is used chiefly as a foundation for face powder
**van·ish·ing·ly** \'va-ni-shiŋ-lē\ *adverb* (1870)
: so as to be almost nonexistent or invisible ⟨the difference is *vanishingly* small⟩
**vanishing point** *noun* (1797)
1 : a point at which receding parallel lines seem to meet when represented in linear perspective
2 : a point at which something disappears or ceases to exist
**van·i·ty** \'va-nə-tē\ *noun, plural* **-ties** [Middle English *vanite*, from Old French *vanité*, from Latin *vanitat-, vanitas* quality of being empty or vain, from *vanus* empty, vain — more at WANE] (13th century)
1 : something that is vain, empty, or valueless
2 : the quality or fact of being vain
3 : inflated pride in oneself or one's appearance : CONCEIT
4 : a fashionable trifle or knicknack
5 a : ³COMPACT a b : a small case or handbag for toilet articles used by women
6 : DRESSING TABLE
**vanity fair** *noun, often V&F capitalized* [*Vanity-Fair*, a fair held in the frivolous town of Vanity in *Pilgrim's Progress* (1678) by John Bunyan] (1816)
: a scene or place characterized by frivolity and ostentation
**vanity plate** *noun* (1966)
: a license plate bearing letters or numbers designated by the owner of the vehicle
**vanity press** *noun* (1950)
: a publishing house that publishes books at the author's expense — called also *vanity publisher*
**van·ner** \'va-nər\ *noun* (1927)
: a person who owns a usually customized van
**van·pool** \'van-,pül\ *noun* (1973)
: an arrangement by which a group of people commute to work in a van
— **van·pool·ing** *noun*
**van·quish** \'vaŋ-kwish, 'van-\ *transitive verb* [Middle English *venquissen*, from Middle French *venquis*, preterit of *veintre* to conquer, from Latin *vincere* — more at VICTOR] (14th century)
1 : to overcome in battle : subdue completely
2 : to defeat in a conflict or contest
3 : to gain mastery over (an emotion, passion, or temptation)
*synonym* see CONQUER
— **van·quish·able** \-kwi-shə-bəl\ *adjective*
— **van·quish·er** *noun*
**van·tage** \'van-tij\ *noun* [Middle English, from Anglo-French, from Middle French *avantage* — more at ADVANTAGE] (14th century)
1 *archaic* : BENEFIT, GAIN
2 : superiority in a contest
3 : a position giving a strategic advantage, commanding perspective, or comprehensive view
4 : ADVANTAGE 4
— **to the vantage** *obsolete* : in addition
**vantage point** *noun* (1865)
: a position or standpoint from which something is viewed or considered; *especially* : POINT OF VIEW
**van·ward** \'van-wərd\ *adjective* (1820)
: located in the vanguard : ADVANCED
— **vanward** *adverb*
**va·pid** \'va-pəd, 'vā-\ *adjective* [Latin *vapidus* flat-tasting; akin to Latin *vappa* vapid wine and perhaps to Latin *vapor* steam] (circa 1656)
: lacking liveliness, tang, briskness, or force : FLAT, DULL ⟨a gossipy, *vapid* woman, obsessed by her own elegance —R. F. Delder-

field⟩ ⟨London was not all *vapid* dissipation —V. S. Pritchett⟩
*synonym* see INSIPID
— **va·pid·ly** *adverb*
— **va·pid·ness** *noun*
**va·pid·i·ty** \va-'pi-də-tē, vā-, və-\ *noun, plural* **-ties** (circa 1721)
1 : the quality or state of being vapid
2 : something vapid
¹**va·por** \'vā-pər\ *noun* [Middle English *vapour*, from Middle French *vapeur*, from Latin *vapor* steam, vapor] (14th century)
1 : diffused matter (as smoke or fog) suspended floating in the air and impairing its transparency
2 a : a substance in the gaseous state as distinguished from the liquid or solid state b : a substance (as gasoline, alcohol, mercury, or benzoin) vaporized for industrial, therapeutic, or military uses; *also* : a mixture (as the explosive mixture in an internal combustion engine) of such a vapor with air
3 a : something unsubstantial or transitory : PHANTASM b : a foolish or fanciful idea
4 *plural a archaic* : exhalations of bodily organs (as the stomach) held to affect the physical or mental condition b : a depressed or hysterical nervous condition
²**vapor** *intransitive verb* **va·pored; va·por·ing** \-p(ə-)riŋ\ (15th century)
1 a : to rise or pass off in vapor b : to emit vapor
2 : to indulge in bragging, blustering, or idle talk
— **va·por·er** \-p(ə)r-ər\ *noun*
**vapor barrier** *noun* (circa 1941)
: a layer of material (as roofing paper or polyethylene film) used to retard or prevent the absorption of moisture into a construction (as a wall or floor)
**va·po·ret·to** \,vä-pə-'re-(,)tō\ *noun, plural* **-ret·ti** \-'re-tē\ *also* **-ret·tos** [Italian, diminutive of *vapore* steamboat, from French *vapeur*, from *bateau à vapeur* steamboat] (1926)
: a motorboat serving as a canal bus in Venice, Italy
**va·por·ing** \'vā-p(ə-)riŋ\ *noun* (circa 1630)
: the act or speech of one that vapors; *specifically* : an idle, extravagant, or high-flown expression or speech — usually used in plural
**va·por·ise** *British variant of* VAPORIZE
**va·por·ish** \'vā-p(ə-)rish\ *adjective* (circa 1644)
1 : resembling or suggestive of vapor
2 : given to fits of the vapors
— **va·por·ish·ness** *noun*
**va·por·ize** \'vā-pə-,rīz\ *verb* **-ized; -iz·ing** (1803)
*transitive verb*
1 : to convert (as by the application of heat or by spraying) into vapor
2 : to cause to become dissipated
*intransitive verb*
1 : to become vaporized
2 : VAPOR 2
— **va·por·iz·able** \-,rī-zə-bəl\ *adjective*
— **va·por·i·za·tion** \,vä-pər-ə-'zā-shən\ *noun*
**va·por·iz·er** \'vā-pə-,rī-zər\ *noun* (circa 1846)
: one that vaporizes: as a : ATOMIZER b : a device for converting water or a medicated liquid into a vapor for inhalation
**vapor lock** *noun* (1926)
: partial or complete interruption of flow of a fluid (as fuel in an internal combustion engine) caused by the formation of bubbles of vapor in the feeding system
**va·por·ous** \'vā-p(ə-)rəs\ *adjective* (1527)
1 : consisting or characteristic of vapor
2 : producing vapors : VOLATILE
3 : containing or obscured by vapors : MISTY
4 a : ETHEREAL, UNSUBSTANTIAL b : consisting of or indulging in vaporings
— **va·por·ous·ly** *adverb*
— **va·por·ous·ness** *noun*
**vapor pressure** *noun* (1875)

: the pressure exerted by a vapor that is in equilibrium with its solid or liquid form — called also *vapor tension*
**vapor trail** *noun* (1941)
: CONTRAIL
**va·por·ware** \'vā-pər-,war, -,wer\ *noun* (1984)
: a new computer-related product that has been widely advertised but is not yet available
**va·pory** \'vā-p(ə-)rē\ *adjective* (1598)
: VAPOROUS, MISTY
**va·pour** *chiefly British variant of* VAPOR
**va·que·ro** \vä-'ker-(,)ō\ *noun, plural* **-ros** [Spanish — more at BUCKAROO] (1826)
: HERDSMAN, COWBOY
**va·ra** \'vär-ə\ *noun* [American Spanish, from Spanish, pole, from Latin, forked pole, from feminine of *varus* bent, bow-legged] (1831)
: a Texas unit of length equal to 33.33 inches (84.66 centimeters)
**vari-** *or* **vario-** *combining form* [Latin *varius*]
1 : varied : diverse ⟨*vari*colored⟩
2 : variation : variability ⟨*vario*meter⟩
**var·ia** \'ver-ē-ə, 'var-\ *noun plural* [New Latin, from Latin, neuter plural of *varius* various] (1926)
: MISCELLANY; *especially* : a literary miscellany
¹**var·i·able** \'ver-ē-ə-bəl, 'var-\ *adjective* [Middle English, from Middle French, from Latin *variabilis*, from *variare* to vary] (14th century)
1 a : able or apt to vary : subject to variation or changes ⟨*variable* winds⟩ ⟨*variable* costs⟩ b : FICKLE, INCONSTANT
2 : characterized by variations
3 : having the characteristics of a variable
4 : not true to type : ABERRANT — used of a biological group or character
— **var·i·abil·i·ty** \,ver-ē-ə-'bi-lə-tē, ,var-\ *noun*
— **var·i·able·ness** \'ver-ē-ə-bəl-nəs, 'var-\ *noun*
— **var·i·ably** \-blē\ *adverb*
²**variable** *noun* (1816)
1 a : a quantity that may assume any one of a set of values b : a symbol representing a variable
2 : something that is variable
3 : VARIABLE STAR
**variable rate mortgage** *noun* (1975)
: ADJUSTABLE RATE MORTGAGE
**variable star** *noun* (1788)
: a star whose brightness changes usually in more or less regular periods
**var·i·ance** \'ver-ē-ən(t)s, 'var-\ *noun* (14th century)
1 : the fact, quality, or state of being variable or variant : DIFFERENCE, VARIATION ⟨yearly *variance* in crops⟩
2 : the fact or state of being in disagreement : DISSENSION, DISPUTE
3 : a disagreement between two parts of the same legal proceeding that must be consonant
4 : a license to do some act contrary to the usual rule ⟨a zoning *variance*⟩
5 : the square of the standard deviation
*synonym* see DISCORD
— **at variance** : not in harmony or agreement
¹**var·i·ant** \'ver-ē-ənt, 'var-\ *adjective* (14th century)
1 *obsolete* : VARIABLE
2 : manifesting variety, deviation, or disagreement
3 : varying usually slightly from the standard form ⟨*variant* readings⟩
²**variant** *noun* (1848)
: one of two or more persons or things exhibiting usually slight differences: as a : one that exhibits variation from a type or norm b : one of two or more different spellings (as *labor*

\ə\ abut \ᵊ\ kitten \ər\ further \a\ ash \ā\ ace \ä\ mop, mar \aů\ out \ch\ chin \e\ bet \ē\ easy \g\ go \i\ hit \ī\ ice \j\ job \ŋ\ sing \ō\ go \ò\ law \òi\ boy \th\ thin \t͟h\ the \ü\ loot \ů\ foot \y\ yet \zh\ vision *see also* Guide to Pronunciation and *labour*) or pronunciations (as of *economics* \ek-, ēk-\) of the same word **c** : one of two or more words (as *geographic* and *geographical*) or word elements (as *mon-* and *mono-*) of essentially the same meaning differing only in the presence or absence of an affix

**var·i·ate** \'ver-ē-,āt, 'var-, -ət\ *noun* (1899)
: RANDOM VARIABLE

**var·i·a·tion** \,ver-ē-'ā-shən, ,var-\ *noun* (14th century)
**1 a** : the act or process of varying : the state or fact of being varied **b** : an instance of varying **c** : the extent to which or the range in which a thing varies
**2** : DECLINATION 6
**3 a** : a change of algebraic sign between successive terms of a sequence **b** : a measure of the change in data, a variable, or a function
**4** : the repetition of a musical theme with modifications in rhythm, tune, harmony, or key
**5 a** : divergence in the characteristics of an organism from the species or population norm or average **b** : something (as an individual or group) that exhibits variation
**6 a** : a solo dance in classic ballet **b** : a repetition in modern ballet of a movement sequence with changes
— **var·i·a·tion·al** \-shnəl, -shə-n°l\ *adjective*
— **var·i·a·tion·al·ly** *adverb*

**var·i·cel·la** \,var-ə-'se-lə\ *noun* [New Latin, irregular diminutive of *variola*] (circa 1771)
: CHICKEN POX

**var·i·co·cele** \'var-ə-kō-,sēl\ *noun* [New Latin, from Latin *varic-, varix* + New Latin -*o-* + *-cele*] (1736)
: a varicose enlargement of the veins of the spermatic cord

**var·i·col·ored** \'ver-i-,kə-lərd, 'var-\ *adjective* (1665)
: having various colors : VARIEGATED ⟨the *varicolored* breeding plumage of a bird⟩; *also* : of various colors

**var·i·cose** \'var-ə-,kōs\ *also* **var·i·cosed** \-,kōst\ *adjective* [Latin *varicosus* full of dilated veins, from *varic-, varix* dilated vein] (circa 1730)
**1** : abnormally swollen or dilated ⟨*varicose* veins⟩
**2** : affected with varicose veins ⟨*varicose* legs⟩

**var·i·cos·i·ty** \,var-ə-'kä-sə-tē\ *noun, plural* **-ties** (circa 1842)
**1** : the quality or state of being abnormally or markedly swollen or dilated
**2** : VARIX

**var·ied** \'ver-ēd, 'var-\ *adjective* (1588)
**1** : VARIOUS, DIVERSE
**2** : VARIEGATED 1
— **var·ied·ly** *adverb*

**var·ie·gate** \'ver-ē-ə-,gāt, 'ver-i-,gāt, 'var-\ *transitive verb* **-gat·ed; -gat·ing** [Latin *variegatus*, past participle of *variegare*, from *varius* various + *-egare* (akin to Latin *agere* to drive) — more at AGENT] (1653)
**1** : to diversify in external appearance especially with different colors : DAPPLE
**2** : to enliven or give interest to by means of variety
— **var·ie·ga·tor** \-,gā-tər\ *noun*

**var·ie·gat·ed** \-,gā-təd\ *adjective* (1661)
**1** : having discrete markings of different colors ⟨*variegated* leaves⟩
**2** : VARIED 1

**variegated cutworm** *noun* (1922)
: a widespread noctuid moth (*Peridroma saucia*) whose larva is destructive to crops

**var·ie·ga·tion** \,ver-ē-ə-'gā-shən, ,ver-i-'gā-, ,var-\ *noun* (1646)
: the act of variegating : the state of being variegated; *especially* : diversity of colors

**var·i·er** \'ver-ē-ər, 'var-\ *noun* (1860)
: one that varies

**¹va·ri·etal** \və-'rī-ə-t°l\ *adjective* (1866)

**1** : of, relating to, or characterizing a variety ⟨*varietal* name⟩; *also* : being a variety in distinction from an individual or species
**2** : of, relating to, or producing a varietal

**²varietal** *noun* (1950)
: a wine bearing the name of the principal grape from which it is made

**va·ri·e·ty** \və-'rī-ə-tē\ *noun, plural* **-ties** [Middle French or Latin; Middle French *variété*, from Latin *varietat-, varietas*, from *varius* various] (15th century)
**1** : the quality or state of having different forms or types : MULTIFARIOUSNESS
**2** : a number or collection of different things especially of a particular class : ASSORTMENT
**3 a** : something differing from others of the same general kind : SORT **b** : any of various groups of plants or animals ranking below a species : SUBSPECIES
**4** : VARIETY SHOW

**variety meat** *noun* (circa 1946)
: an edible part (as the liver or tongue) of a slaughter animal other than skeletal muscle

**variety show** *noun* (1882)
: a theatrical entertainment of successive separate performances (as of songs, dances, skits, acrobatic feats, and trained animal acts)

**variety store** *noun* (circa 1768)
: a retail store that carries a wide variety of merchandise especially of low unit value

**vario-** — *see* VARI-

**va·ri·o·la** \və-'rī-ə-lə; ,ver-ē-'ō-lə, ,var-\ *noun* [New Latin, from Medieval Latin, pustule, pox, from Late Latin, pustule, probably from *varius* various] (1543)
: SMALLPOX

**var·i·om·e·ter** \,ver-ē-'ä-mə-tər, ,var-\ *noun* (circa 1900)
**1** : an instrument for measuring magnetic declination
**2** : an aeronautical instrument for indicating rate of climb

**¹var·i·o·rum** \,ver-ē-'ōr-əm, ,var-, -'ȯr\ *noun* [Latin *variorum* of various persons (genitive plural masculine of *varius*), in the phrase *cum notis variorum* with the notes of various persons] (1728)
**1** : an edition or text with notes by different persons
**2** : an edition containing variant readings of the text

**²variorum** *adjective* (1763)
: relating to or being a variorum; *also* : VARIANT ⟨*variorum* readings⟩

**¹var·i·ous** \'ver-ē-əs, 'var-\ *adjective* [Latin *varius*] (1552)
**1** *archaic* : VARIABLE, INCONSTANT
**2** : VARICOLORED ⟨birds of *various* plumage⟩
**3 a** : of differing kinds : MULTIFARIOUS **b** : dissimilar in nature or form : UNLIKE ⟨animals as *various* as the jaguar and the sloth⟩
**4** : having a number of different aspects or characteristics ⟨a *various* place⟩ ⟨a *various* talent⟩
**5** : of an indefinite number greater than one ⟨stop at *various* towns⟩
**6** : INDIVIDUAL, SEPARATE ⟨rate increases granted in the *various* states⟩
**synonym** *see* DIFFERENT
— **var·i·ous·ness** *noun*

**²various** *pronoun, plural in construction* (1877)
: an indefinite number of separate individuals greater than one ⟨conversations with people from *various* of the schools —Patricia Linden⟩

**var·i·ous·ly** \'ver-i-,sīzd, 'var-\ *adverb* (1627)
**1** : in various ways : at various times ⟨was *variously* occupied teaching, farming, and clerking⟩
**2** : by various designations ⟨known *variously* as principal, headmaster, and rector⟩

**vari-sized** \'ver-i-,sīzd, 'var-\ *adjective* (1936)
: of various sizes

**va·ris·tor** \va-'ris-tər, ve-\ *noun* [*vari-* + *resistor*] (1937)

: an electrical resistor whose resistance depends on the applied voltage

**var·ix** \'var-iks\ *noun, plural* **var·i·ces** \'var-ə-,sēz\ [Middle English, from Latin *varic-, varix*] (14th century)
: an abnormally dilated and lengthened vein, artery, or lymph vessel; *especially* : a varicose vein

**var·let** \'vär-lət\ *noun* [Middle English, from Middle French *vaslet, varlet* young nobleman, page — more at VALET] (15th century)
**1 a** : ATTENDANT, MENIAL **b** : a knight's page
**2** : a base unprincipled person : KNAVE

**var·let·ry** \-lə-trē\ *noun* (1606)
*archaic* : RABBLE

**var·mint** \'vär-mənt\ *noun* [alteration of *vermin*] (1539)
**1** : an animal considered a pest; *specifically* : one classed as vermin and unprotected by game law
**2** : a contemptible person : RASCAL; *broadly* : PERSON, FELLOW

**¹var·nish** \'vär-nish\ *noun* [Middle English *vernisch*, from Middle French *vernis*, from Old Italian or Medieval Latin; Old Italian *vernice*, from Medieval Latin *veronic-, veronix sandarac*] (14th century)
**1 a** : a liquid preparation that when spread and allowed to dry on a surface forms a hard lustrous typically transparent coating **b** : the covering or glaze given by the application of varnish **c** (1) : something that suggests varnish by its gloss (2) : a coating (as of deposits in an internal combustion engine) comparable to varnish
**2** : outside show : ¹GLOSS
**3** *chiefly British* : a liquid nail polish
— **var·nishy** \-ni-shē\ *adjective*

**²varnish** *transitive verb* (14th century)
**1** : to apply varnish to
**2** : to cover or conceal (as something unpleasant) with something that gives a fair appearance : ²GLOSS
**3** : ADORN, EMBELLISH
— **var·nish·er** \'vär-ni-shər\ *noun*

**varnish tree** *noun* (1758)
: any of various trees yielding a milky juice from which in some cases varnish or lacquer is prepared; *especially* : a Japanese sumac (*Rhus verniciflua*)

**var·si·ty** \'vär-sə-tē, -stē\ *noun, plural* **-ties** [by shortening & alteration from *university*] (1646)
**1** *British* : UNIVERSITY
**2 a** : the principal squad representing a university, college, school, or club especially in a sport **b** : REGULAR 1d

**Var·so·vi·an** \,vär-'sō-vē-ən\ *noun* [French *varsovien*, from *Varsovie* Warsaw] (1764)
: a native or resident of Warsaw, Poland

**Va·ru·na** \'var-ə-nə\ *noun* [Sanskrit *Varuṇa*]
: a chief Vedic god responsible for natural and moral order in the cosmos

**var·us** \'var-əs, 'ver-\ *noun* [New Latin, from Latin, bent, knock-kneed] (1800)
: a deformed position of a bodily part characterized by bending or turning inward toward the midline of the body to an abnormal degree ⟨a moderate right metatarsus *varus* —*Journal American Medical Association*⟩
— **varus** *adjective*

**varve** \'värv\ *noun* [Swedish *varv* turn, layer; akin to Old Norse *hvarf* ring, Old English *hweorfan* to turn — more at WHARF] (1912)
: a pair of layers of alternately finer and coarser silt or clay believed to comprise an annual cycle of deposition in a body of still water
— **varved** \'värvd\ *adjective*

**vary** \'ver-ē, 'var-\ *verb* **var·ied; vary·ing** [Middle English *varien*, from Middle French or Latin; Middle French *varier*, from Latin *variare*, from *varius* various] (14th century)
*transitive verb*

**1 a :** to make a partial change in **:** make different in some attribute or characteristic **b :** to make differences between items in **:** DIVERSIFY **2 :** to present under new aspects ⟨*vary* the rhythm and harmonic treatment⟩ *intransitive verb* **1 :** to exhibit or undergo change ⟨the sky was constantly *varying*⟩ **2 :** DEVIATE, DEPART **3 :** to take on successive values ⟨*y varies* inversely with *x*⟩ **4 :** to exhibit divergence in structural or physiological characters from the typical form **synonym** see CHANGE

— **vary·ing·ly** \-iŋ-lē\ *adverb*

**varying hare** *noun* (1781)
**:** SNOWSHOE HARE

**vas** \'vas\ *noun, plural* **va·sa** \'vā-zə\ [New Latin, from Latin, vessel] (1651)
**:** an anatomical vessel **:** DUCT

— **va·sal** \-zəl\ *adjective*

**vas-** *or* **vaso-** *combining form* [New Latin, from Latin *vas*]
**1 :** vessel: as **a :** blood vessel ⟨*vaso*motor⟩ **b :** vas deferens ⟨*vas*ectomy⟩ **2 :** vascular and ⟨*vaso*vagal⟩ **3 :** vasomotor ⟨*vaso*active⟩

**va·sa ef·fer·en·tia** \'vā-zə-ˌe-fə-'ren(t)-sh(ē-)ə\ *noun plural* [New Latin, literally, efferent vessels] (circa 1860)
**:** the 12 to 20 ductules that lead from the rete of the testis to the vas deferens and except near their commencement are greatly convoluted and form the compact head of the epididymis

**vas·cu·lar** \'vas-kyə-lər\ *adjective* [New Latin *vascularis*, from Latin *vasculum* small vessel, diminutive of *vas*] (1672)
**1 :** of or relating to a channel for the conveyance of a body fluid (as blood of an animal or sap of a plant) or to a system of such channels; *also* **:** supplied with or made up of such channels and especially blood vessels ⟨a *vascular* tumor⟩ ⟨a *vascular* system⟩ **2 :** marked by vigor and ardor **:** SPIRITED, PASSIONATE

— **vas·cu·lar·i·ty** \ˌvas-kyə-'lar-ə-tē\ *noun*

**vascular bundle** *noun* (circa 1884)
**:** a strand of specialized vascular tissue of higher plants consisting mostly of xylem and phloem

**vascular cylinder** *noun* (circa 1889)
**:** STELE

**vas·cu·lar·i·za·tion** \ˌvas-kyə-lə-rə-'zā-shən\ *noun* (1818)
**:** the process of becoming vascular; *also* **:** abnormal or excessive formation of blood vessels (as in the retina or on the cornea)

**vascular plant** *noun* (1861)
**:** a plant having a specialized conducting system that includes xylem and phloem **:** TRACHEOPHYTE

**vascular ray** *noun* (1672)
**:** a band of usually parenchymatous cells partly in the xylem and partly in the phloem of a plant root or stem that conducts fluids radially and appears in a cross section like a spoke of a wheel

**vascular tissue** *noun* (1815)
**:** plant tissue concerned mainly with conduction; *especially* **:** the specialized tissue of higher plants consisting essentially of phloem and xylem

**vas·cu·la·ture** \'vas-kyə-lə-ˌchúr, -ˌtyùr, -ˌtùr\ *noun* [Latin *vasculum* vessel + English *-ature* (as in *musculature*)] (circa 1927)
**:** the arrangement of blood vessels in an organ or part

**vas·cu·li·tis** \ˌvas-kyə-'lī-təs\ *noun, plural* **-lit·i·des** \-'li-tə-ˌdēz\ [New Latin, from Latin *vasculum* vessel] (circa 1900)
**:** inflammation of a blood or lymph vessel

**vas·cu·lum** \'vas-kyə-ləm\ *noun, plural* **-la** \-lə\ [New Latin, from Latin, small vessel] (1782)

**:** a usually metal and commonly cylindrical or flattened covered box used in collecting plants

**vas def·er·ens** \'vas-'de-fə-rənz, -ˌrenz\ *noun, plural* **va·sa def·er·en·tia** \'vā-zə-ˌde-fə-'ren(t)-sh(ē-)ə\ [New Latin, literally, deferent vessel] (1578)
**:** a spermatic duct especially of a higher vertebrate that in the human male is a thick-walled tube about two feet (0.61 meters) long that begins at and is continuous with the tail of the epididymis and eventually joins the duct of the seminal vesicle to form the ejaculatory duct

**vase** \US oftenest 'vās; Canadian usually & US also 'vāz; British usually, Canadian also, & US sometimes 'väz\ *noun* [French, from Latin *vas* vessel] (1563)
**:** a usually round vessel of greater depth than width used chiefly as an ornament or for holding flowers ■

— **vase·like** \-ˌlīk\ *adjective*

**va·sec·to·mize** \və-'sek-tə-ˌmīz, vā-'zek-\ *transitive verb* **-mized; -miz·ing** (1900)
**:** to perform a vasectomy on

**va·sec·to·my** \-tə-mē\ *noun, plural* **-mies** [International Scientific Vocabulary] (1899)
**:** surgical division or resection of all or part of the vas deferens usually to induce sterility

**Vas·e·line** \'va-sə-ˌlēn, ˌva-sə-'\ *trademark* — used for petroleum jelly

**va·so·ac·tive** \ˌvā-zō-'ak-tiv\ *adjective* (circa 1921)
**:** affecting the blood vessels especially in respect to the degree of their relaxation or contraction

— **va·so·ac·tiv·i·ty** \-ak-'ti-və-tē\ *noun*

**va·so·con·stric·tion** \-kən-'strik-shən\ *noun* [International Scientific Vocabulary] (1899)
**:** narrowing of the lumen of blood vessels especially as a result of vasomotor action

**va·so·con·stric·tive** \-'strik-tiv\ *adjective* (1890)
**:** inducing vasoconstriction

**va·so·con·stric·tor** \-tər\ *noun* (1877)
**:** an agent (as a sympathetic nerve fiber or a drug) that induces or initiates vasoconstriction

**va·so·di·la·tion** \-dī-'lā-shən, -də-\ *or* **va·so·di·la·ta·tion** \-ˌdi-lə-'tā-shən, -ˌdī-lə-\ *noun* [International Scientific Vocabulary] (1896)
**:** widening of the lumen of blood vessels

**va·so·di·la·tor** \-dī-'lā-tər, -'dī-ˌlā-\ *noun* (1881)
**:** an agent (as a parasympathetic nerve fiber or a drug) that induces or initiates vasodilation

**va·so·mo·tor** \ˌvā-zə-'mō-tər\ *adjective* [International Scientific Vocabulary] (1865)
**:** of, relating to, or being nerves or centers controlling the size of blood vessels

**va·so·pres·sin** \ˌvā-zō-'pre-sᵊn\ *noun* [from *Vasopressin*, a trademark] (1927)
**:** a polypeptide hormone secreted by the posterior lobe of the pituitary gland that increases blood pressure and decreases urine flow — called also *antidiuretic hormone*

**va·so·pres·sor** \-'pre-sər\ *adjective* (1928)
**:** causing a rise in blood pressure by exerting a vasoconstrictor effect

— **vasopressor** *noun*

**va·so·spasm** \'vā-zō-ˌspa-zəm\ *noun* [International Scientific Vocabulary] (circa 1909)
**:** sharp and often persistent contraction of a blood vessel reducing its caliber and blood flow

— **va·so·spas·tic** \ˌvā-zō-'spas-tik\ *adjective*

**va·so·to·cin** \ˌvā-zə-'tō-sᵊn\ *noun* [*vaso-* + *oxytocin*] (circa 1963)
**:** a polypeptide pituitary hormone of most vertebrates below mammals that is probably the phylogenetic precursor of oxytocin and vasopressin

**va·so·va·gal** \ˌvā-zō-'vā-gəl\ *adjective* (circa 1923)
**:** of, relating to, or involving both vascular and vagal factors

**vas·sal** \'va-səl\ *noun* [Middle English, from Middle French, from Medieval Latin *vassal-*

*lus,* from *vassus* servant, vassal, of Celtic origin; akin to Welsh *gwas* young man, servant] (14th century)
**1 :** a person under the protection of a feudal lord to whom he has vowed homage and fealty **:** a feudal tenant **2 :** one in a subservient or subordinate position

— **vassal** *adjective*

**vas·sal·age** \-sə-lij\ *noun* (1594)
**1 :** the state of being a vassal **2 :** the homage, fealty, or services due from a vassal **3 :** a position of subordination or submission (as to a political power)

¹**vast** \'vast\ *adjective* [Latin *vastus;* akin to Old High German *wuosti* empty, desolate, Old Irish *fás*] (1575)
**:** very great in size, amount, degree, intensity, or especially in extent or range **synonym** see ENORMOUS

— **vast·ly** *adverb*

— **vast·ness** \'vas(t)-nəs\ *noun*

²**vast** *noun* (1604)
**:** a boundless space ⟨the *vast* of heaven —John Milton⟩

**vas·ti·tude** \'vas-tə-ˌtüd, -ˌtyüd\ *noun* [Latin *vastitudo,* from *vastus*] (1623)
**:** IMMENSITY, VASTNESS

**vasty** \'vas-tē\ *adjective* (1596)
**:** VAST ⟨call spirits from the *vasty* deep —Shakespeare⟩

¹**vat** \'vat\ *noun* [Middle English *fat, vat,* from Old English *fæt;* akin to Old High German *vaz* vessel, Lithuanian *puodas* pot] (13th century)
**1 :** a large vessel (as a cistern, tub, or barrel) especially for holding liquors in an immature state or preparations for dyeing or tanning **2 :** a liquor containing a dye converted into a soluble reduced colorless or weakly colored form that on textile material steeped in the liquor and exposed to the air is converted by oxidation to the original insoluble dye and precipitated in the fiber

**word history** see VIXEN

²**vat** *transitive verb* **vat·ted; vat·ting** (1784)
**:** to put into or treat in a vat

**vat dye** *noun* (circa 1903)
**:** a water-insoluble generally fast dye used in the form of a vat liquor — called also *vat color*

**vat–dyed** \'vat-ˌdīd\ *adjective* (circa 1947)
**:** dyed with one or more vat dyes

**vat·ic** \'va-tik\ *adjective* [Latin *vates* seer, prophet; akin to Old English *wōth* poetry, Old High German *wuot* madness, Old Irish *fáith* seer, poet] (1603)
**:** PROPHETIC, ORACULAR

**Vat·i·can** \'va-ti-kən\ *noun* [Latin *Vaticanus* Vatican Hill (in Rome)] (1555)

---

◻ USAGE

**vase**   This little word of four letters, one of which is silent, provokes two long-standing pronunciation questions. Should the *a* have the sound of *a* in *are* or *ate,* and should the *s* have the sound of *s* in *case* or *rase*? Swift and Byron rhymed *vase* with *face* and *place,* but all four possibilities have been advocated in the past, along with a fifth variant which rhymed with *gauze.* One also finds a variety of spellings over the centuries to match each pronunciation. To some ears the \'väz\ variant sounds more elegant, but the others are also established by long usage and are equally acceptable. Which is the dominant form depends on where you are in the English-speaking world, as noted above.

---

\ə\ **abut**   \ᵊ\ **kitten**   \ər\ **further**   \a\ **ash**   \ā\ **ace** \ä\ **mop, mar**   \aú\ **out**   \ch\ **chin**   \e\ **bet**   \ē\ **easy** \g\ **go**   \i\ **hit**   \ī\ **ice**   \j\ **job**   \ŋ\ **sing**   \ō\ **go** \ó\ **law**   \ói\ **boy**   \th\ **thin**   \t͟h\ **the**   \ü\ **loot**   \ú\ **foot** \y\ **yet**   \zh\ **vision**   *see also* Guide to Pronunciation

**1 :** the papal headquarters in Rome
**2 :** the papal government
— **Vatican** *adjective*

**va·tic·i·nal** \və-'ti-s³n-əl, va-\ *adjective* [Latin *vaticinus,* from *vaticinari* to foretell, prophesy] (1586)
**:** PROPHETIC

**va·tic·i·nate** \-s³n-,āt\ *verb* **-nat·ed; -nat·ing** [Latin *vaticinatus,* past participle of *vaticinari,* from *vates* + *-cinari* (akin to Latin *canere* to sing) — more at CHANT] (circa 1623)
**:** PROPHESY, PREDICT
— **va·tic·i·na·tor** \-,ā-tər\ *noun*

**va·tic·i·na·tion** \-,ti-s³n-'ā-shən\ *noun* (1603)
**1 :** PREDICTION
**2 :** the act of prophesying

**va·tu** \'vä-,tü\ *noun, plural* **vatu** [probably alteration of *Vanuatu*] (1981)
— see MONEY table

**vaude·ville** \'vȯd-vəl, 'väd-, 'vȯd-, -,vil; 'vȯdə-, 'vä-, 'vō-\ *noun* [French, from Middle French, popular satirical song, alteration of *vaudevire,* from *vau-de-Vire* valley of Vire, town in northwest France where such songs were composed] (1739)
**1 :** a light often comic theatrical piece frequently combining pantomime, dialogue, dancing, and song
**2 :** stage entertainment consisting of various acts (as performing animals, acrobats, comedians, dancers, or singers)
— **vaude·vil·lian** \,vȯd-'vil-yən, ,väd-, ,vȯd-; ,vȯ-də-, ,vä-, ,vō-\ *noun or adjective*

**Vau·dois** \vō-'dwä, 'vō-,\ *noun plural* [Middle French, from Medieval Latin *Valdenses*] (1560)
**:** WALDENSES

**¹vault** \'vȯlt\ *noun* [Middle English *voute,* from Middle French, from (assumed) Vulgar Latin *volvita* turn, vault, from feminine of *volvitus,* alteration of Latin *volutus,* past participle of *volvere* to roll — more at VOLUBLE] (14th century)
**1 a :** an arched structure of masonry usually forming a ceiling or roof **b :** something (as the sky) resembling a vault **c :** an arched or dome-shaped anatomical structure
**2 a :** a space covered by an arched structure; *especially* **:** an underground passage or room **b :** an underground storage compartment **c :** a room or compartment for the safekeeping of valuables
**3 a :** a burial chamber **b :** a prefabricated container usually of metal or concrete into which a casket is placed at burial
— **vaulty** \'vȯl-tē\ *adjective*

**²vault** *transitive verb* (14th century)
**:** to form or cover with or as if with a vault **:** ARCH

**³vault** *verb* [Middle French *volter,* from Old Italian *voltare,* from (assumed) Vulgar Latin *volvitare* to turn, leap, frequentative of Latin *volvere*] (1538)
*intransitive verb*
**1 :** to bound vigorously; *especially* **:** to execute a leap using the hands or a pole
**2 :** to do or achieve something as if by a leap
*transitive verb*
**:** to leap over; *especially* **:** to leap over by or as if by aid of the hands or a pole

**⁴vault** *noun* (1576)
**:** an act of vaulting **:** LEAP

**vault·ed** \'vȯl-təd\ *adjective* (1533)
**1 :** built in the form of a vault **:** ARCHED
**2 :** covered with a vault

**vault·er** \-tər\ *noun* (circa 1552)
**:** one that vaults; *especially* **:** an athlete who competes in the pole vault

**¹vault·ing** \-tiŋ\ *noun* (1512)
**:** vaulted construction

**²vaulting** *adjective* (1593)
**1 :** reaching or stretching for the heights ⟨*vaulting* ambition⟩ ⟨a *vaulting* imagination⟩
**2 :** designed for use in vaulting or in gymnastic exercises ⟨a *vaulting* block⟩

— **vault·ing·ly** \-tiŋ-lē\ *adverb*

**vaulting horse** *noun* (circa 1875)
**1 :** a gymnastics apparatus used in vaulting that consists of a padded rectangular or cylindrical form supported in a horizontal position above the floor
**2 :** an event in which vaults are made over a vaulting horse

**¹vaunt** \'vȯnt, 'vänt\ *verb* [Middle English, from Middle French *vanter,* from Late Latin *vanitare,* frequentative of (assumed) Latin *vanare,* from Latin *vanus* vain] (15th century)
*intransitive verb*
**:** to make a vain display of one's own worth or attainments **:** BRAG
*transitive verb*
**:** to call attention to pridefully and often boastfully ⟨people who *vaunt* their ingenuity⟩
**synonym** see BOAST
— **vaunt·er** *noun*
— **vaunt·ing·ly** \'vȯn-tiŋ-lē, 'vän-\ *adverb*

**²vaunt** *noun* (15th century)
**1 :** a vainglorious display of what one is or has or has done
**2 :** a bragging assertive statement

**vaunt–cou·ri·er** \vȯnt-'kùr-ē-ər, vänt-, -'kər-ē-, -'kə-rē-\ *noun* [Middle French *avant-courier,* literally, advance courier] (1560)
*archaic* **:** FORERUNNER

**vaunt·ed** \'vȯn-təd, 'vän-\ *adjective* (1579)
**:** highly or widely praised or boasted about ⟨his own much *vaunted* ferocity —Calvin Tomkins⟩

**vaunt·ful** \'vȯnt-fəl, 'vänt-\ *adjective* (1590)
**:** VAINGLORIOUS, BOASTFUL

**vaunty** \'vȯn-tē, 'vän-\ *adjective* (1724)
*Scottish* **:** PROUD, BOASTFUL, VAIN

**vav** *variant of* WAW

**vav·a·sor** *or* **vav·a·sour** \'va-və-,sȯr, -,sùr\ *noun* [Middle English *vavasour,* from Middle French *vavassour,* probably from Medieval Latin *vassus vassorum* vassal of vassals] (14th century)
**:** a feudal tenant ranking directly below a baron

**va·ward** \'vaù-,ȯrd, -,wȯrd\ *noun* [Middle English *vauntwarde, vaward,* from Old North French *avantwarde,* from *avant* before (from Late Latin *abante*) + *warde* guard, from *warder* to guard — more at ADVANCE, REWARD] (1597)
*archaic* **:** the foremost part **:** FOREFRONT ⟨the *vaward* of our youth —Shakespeare⟩

**VCR** \,vē-(,)sē-'är\ *noun* [*videocassette recorder*] (1971)
**:** a videotape recorder that uses videocassettes

**V–day** \'vē-,dā\ *noun* [*victory day*] (1941)
**:** a day of victory

**'ve** \v, əv\ *verb* [by contraction]
**:** HAVE ⟨we*'ve* been there⟩

**Ve·adar** \'vā-,ä-,där, 'vā-ə-\ *noun* [Hebrew *wĕAdhār,* literally, and Adar (i.e., the second Adar)] (circa 1864)
**:** the intercalary month of the Jewish calendar following Adar in leap years — see MONTH table

**¹veal** \'vē(ə)l\ *noun* [Middle English *veel,* from Middle French, from Latin *vitellus* small calf, diminutive of *vitulus* calf — more at WETHER] (14th century)
**1 :** the flesh of a young calf
**2 :** CALF; *especially* **:** VEALER

**²veal** *transitive verb* (1847)
**:** to kill and dress (a calf) for veal

**veal·er** \'vē-lər\ *noun* (circa 1895)
**:** a calf grown for or suitable for veal

**vealy** \'vē-lē\ *adjective* (1769)
**1 :** resembling or suggesting veal or a calf
**2 :** IMMATURE

**¹vec·tor** \'vek-tər\ *noun* [New Latin, from Latin, carrier, from *vehere* to carry — more at WAY] (1846)
**1 a :** a quantity that has magnitude and direction and that is commonly represented by a directed line segment whose length represents the magnitude and whose orientation in space

represents the direction; *broadly* **:** an element of a vector space **b :** a course or compass direction especially of an airplane
**2 a :** an organism (as an insect) that transmits a pathogen **b :** POLLINATOR a
**3 :** a sequence of genetic material (as a transposon or the genome of a bacteriophage) used to introduce specific genes into the genome of an organism
— **vector** *adjective*
— **vec·to·ri·al** \vek-'tȯr-ē-əl, -'tȯr-\ *adjective*
— **vec·to·ri·al·ly** \-ə-lē\ *adverb*

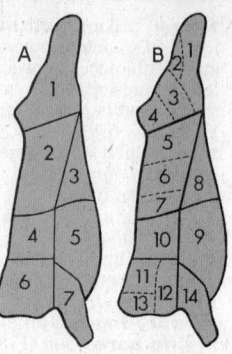

veal 1: *A* wholesale cuts: *1* leg, *2* loin, *3* flank, *4* rib, *5* breast, *6* shoulder, *7* shank; *B* retail cuts: *1* hind shank, *2* heel of round, *3* round, *4* rump roast, *5* sirloin steak, *6* loin chops, *7* kidney chops, *8* flank, *9* breast, *10* rib roast, *11* blade steak, *12* arm steak, *13* shoulder roast, *14* foreshank

**²vector** *transitive verb* **vec·tored; vec·tor·ing** \-t(ə-)riŋ\ (1941)
**1 :** to guide (as an airplane, its pilot, or a missile) in flight by means of a radioed vector
**2 :** to change the direction of (the thrust of a jet engine) for steering

**vector product** *noun* (1878)
**:** a vector *c* whose length is the product of the lengths of two vectors *a* and *b* and the sine of their included angle, whose direction is perpendicular to their plane, and whose direction is that in which a right-handed screw with axis *c* will move along *c* when *a* is rotated into *b* — called also *cross product*

**vector space** *noun* (1937)
**:** a set representing a generalization of a system of vectors and consisting of elements which comprise a commutative group under addition, each of which is left unchanged under multiplication by the multiplicative identity of a field, and for which multiplication by the multiplicative operation of the field is commutative, closed, distributive such that both $c(A + B) = cA + cB$ and $(c + d)A = cA + dA$, and associative such that $(cd)A = c(dA)$ where $A, B$ are vectors and $c, d$ are elements of the field

**vector sum** *noun* (circa 1890)
**:** the sum of a number of vectors that for the sum of two vectors is geometrically represented by the diagonal of a parallelogram whose sides represent the two vectors being added

**Ve·da** \'vā-də\ *noun* [Sanskrit, literally, knowledge; akin to Greek *eidenai* to know — more at WIT] (1734)
**:** any of four canonical collections of hymns, prayers, and liturgical formulas that comprise the earliest Hindu sacred writings

**ve·da·lia** \vi-'dāl-yə\ *noun* [New Latin, genus name] (1889)
**:** an Australian ladybug (*Rodolia cardinalis*) introduced to many countries to control scale insects

**Ve·dan·ta** \vā-'dän-tə, və-, -'dän-\ *noun* [Sanskrit *Vedānta,* literally, end of the Veda, from *Veda* + *anta* end; akin to Old English *ende* end] (1788)
**:** an orthodox system of Hindu philosophy developing especially in a qualified monism the speculations of the Upanishads on ultimate reality and the liberation of the soul
— **Ve·dan·tism** \-'dän-,ti-zəm, -'dän-\ *noun*
— **Ve·dan·tist** \-'dän-tist, -'dän-\ *noun*

**Ve·dan·tic** \-'dän-tik, -'dän-\ *adjective* (1882)
**1 :** of or relating to the Vedanta philosophy
**2 :** VEDIC

**Ved·da** *or* **Ved·dah** \'ve-də\ *noun* [Sinhalese *vedda* hunter] (1681)
: a member of an aboriginal people of Sri Lanka

**Ved·doid** \'ve-ˌdȯid\ *noun* (1928)
: a member of an ancient race of southern Asia characterized by wavy to curly hair, chocolate-brown skin color, and slender body build
— **Veddoid** *adjective*

**ve·dette** \vi-'det\ *noun* [French, from Italian *vedetta*, alteration of *veletta*, probably from Spanish *vela* watch, from *velar* to keep watch, from Latin *vigilare* to wake, watch, from *vigil* awake — more at VIGIL] (circa 1702)
: a mounted sentinel stationed in advance of pickets

**Ve·dic** \'vā-dik\ *adjective* (1848)
: of or relating to the Vedas, the language in which they are written, or Hindu history and culture between 1500 B.C. and 500 B.C.

**vee** \'vē\ *noun* (circa 1883)
**1** : something shaped like the letter V
**2** : the letter *v*

**vee·jay** \'vē-ˌjā\ *noun* [video jockey] (1981)
: an announcer of a program (as on television) that features music videos

**vee·na** *variant of* VINA

**veep** \'vēp\ *noun* [from *v. p.* (abbreviation for *vice president*)] (1949)
: VICE PRESIDENT

**¹veer** \'vir\ *transitive verb* [Middle English *veren*, of Low German or Dutch origin; akin to Middle Dutch *vieren* to slacken, Middle Low German *vīren*] (15th century)
: to let out (as a rope)

**²veer** *verb* [Middle French *virer*, from Old French, to throw with a twisting motion, perhaps modification of Latin *vibrare* to wave, propel suddenly — more at VIBRATE] (1582)
*intransitive verb*
**1** *of the wind* : to shift in a clockwise direction — compare BACK
**2** : to change direction or course
**3** : to wear ship
*transitive verb*
: to direct to a different course; *specifically* : WEAR 7
**synonym** see SWERVE
— **veer·ing·ly** \-iŋ-lē\ *adverb*

**³veer** *noun* (1611)
: a change in course or direction ⟨a *veer* to the right⟩

**vee·ry** \'vir-ē\ *noun, plural* **veeries** [probably imitative] (1838)
: a thrush (*Catharus fuscescens*) common in the eastern U.S.

**veg** \'vej\ *noun, plural* **veg** (1918)
*chiefly British* : VEGETABLE

**Ve·ga** \'vē-gə, 'vā-\ *noun* [New Latin, from Arabic (*al-Nasr*) *al-Wāqiʿ*, literally, the falling (vulture)]
: a star of the first magnitude that is the brightest in the constellation Lyra

**veg·an** \'vē-gən *also* 'vā- *also* 've-jən *or* -ˌjan\ *noun* [by contraction from *vegetarian*] (1944)
: a strict vegetarian who consumes no animal food or dairy products; *also* : one who abstains from using animal products (as leather)
— **veg·an·ism** \'vē-gə-ˌni-zəm, 'vā-gə-, 've-jə-\ *noun*

**¹veg·e·ta·ble** \'vej-tə-bəl, 've-jə-\ *adjective* [Middle English, from Medieval Latin *vegetabilis* vegetative, from *vegetare* to grow, from Latin, to animate, from *vegetus* lively, from *vegēre* to enliven — more at WAKE] (15th century)
**1 a** : of, relating to, constituting, or growing like plants **b** : consisting of plants : VEGETATIONAL
**2** : made or obtained from plants or plant products
**3** : resembling or suggesting a plant (as in inertness or passivity)

**²vegetable** *noun* (1582)
**1** : PLANT 1b

**2** : a usually herbaceous plant (as the cabbage, bean, or potato) grown for an edible part that is usually eaten as part of a meal; *also* : such edible part
**3** : a human being whose mental and physical functioning is severely impaired (as from accident or disease)

**vegetable ivory** *noun* (1842)
**1** : the hard white opaque endosperm of the ivory nut that takes a high polish and is used as a substitute for ivory
**2** : IVORY NUT

**vegetable marrow** *noun* (1816)
: any of various smooth-skinned elongated summer squashes with creamy white to deep green skins

**vegetable oil** *noun* (1797)
: an oil of plant origin; *especially* : a fatty oil from seeds or fruits

**vegetable oyster** *noun* (circa 1818)
: SALSIFY

**vegetable pear** *noun* (1887)
: CHAYOTE

**vegetable wax** *noun* (1815)
: a wax of plant origin secreted commonly in thin flakes by the walls of epidermal cells

**veg·e·ta·bly** \'vej-tə-blē, 've-jə-\ *adverb* (1651)
: in the manner of or like a vegetable

**veg·e·tal** \'ve-jə-tᵊl\ *adjective* [Medieval Latin *vegetare* to grow] (15th century)
**1** : VEGETABLE
**2** : VEGETATIVE
**3** : of or relating to the vegetal pole of an egg or to that part of an egg from which the endoderm normally develops ⟨*vegetal* blastomeres⟩

**vegetal pole** *noun* (1896)
: the point on the surface of an egg that is diametrically opposite to the animal pole and usually marks the center of the protoplasm containing more yolk, dividing more slowly and into larger blastomeres than that about the animal pole, and giving rise to the hypoblast of the embryo

**¹veg·e·tar·i·an** \ˌve-jə-'ter-ē-ən\ *noun* [²vegetable + -arian] (1839)
**1** : one who believes in or practices vegetarianism
**2** : HERBIVORE

**²vegetarian** *adjective* (1849)
**1** : of or relating to vegetarians
**2** : consisting wholly of vegetables, fruits, and sometimes eggs or dairy products ⟨a *vegetarian* diet⟩

**veg·e·tar·i·an·ism** \-ē-ə-ˌni-zəm\ *noun* (circa 1851)
: the theory or practice of living on a diet made up of vegetables, fruits, grains, nuts, and sometimes eggs or dairy products

**veg·e·tate** \'ve-jə-ˌtāt\ *verb* **-tat·ed; -tat·ing** [Medieval Latin *vegetatus*, past participle of *vegetare* to grow] (1605)
*intransitive verb*
**1 a** : to grow in the manner of a plant; *also* : to grow exuberantly or with proliferation of fleshy or warty outgrowths **b** : to produce vegetation
**2** : to lead a passive existence without exertion of body or mind
*transitive verb*
: to establish vegetation in or on

**veg·e·ta·tion** \ˌve-jə-'tā-shən\ *noun* (1564)
**1** : the act or process of vegetating
**2** : inert existence
**3** : plant life or total plant cover (as of an area)
**4** : an abnormal growth upon a body part
— **veg·e·ta·tion·al** \-shnəl, -shə-nᵊl\ *adjective*

**veg·e·ta·tive** \'ve-jə-ˌtā-tiv\ *adjective* (14th century)
**1 a** (1) : growing or having the power of growing (2) : of, relating to, or engaged in nutritive and growth functions as contrasted with reproductive functions ⟨a *vegetative* nucleus⟩

**b** : promoting plant growth ⟨the *vegetative* properties of soil⟩ **c** : of, relating to, or involving propagation by nonsexual processes or methods
**2** : relating to, composed of, or suggesting vegetation ⟨*vegetative* cover⟩
**3** : of or relating to the division of nature comprising the plant kingdom
**4** : affecting, arising from, or relating to involuntary bodily functions
**5** : VEGETABLE 3
— **veg·e·ta·tive·ly** *adverb*
— **veg·e·ta·tive·ness** *noun*

**ve·gete** \və-'jēt\ *adjective* [Latin *vegetus* — more at VEGETABLE] (1639)
*archaic* : LIVELY, HEALTHY

**veg·gie** *also* **veg·ie** \'ve-jē\ *noun* [by shortening & alteration] (1955)
**1** : VEGETABLE
**2** *slang* : VEGETARIAN

**veg out** \'vej-\ *intransitive verb* **vegged out; veg·ging out** [short for *vegetate*] (1980)
: to spend time idly or passively

**ve·he·mence** \'vē-ə-mən(t)s\ *noun* (15th century)
: the quality or state of being vehement : INTENSITY

**ve·he·ment** \-mənt\ *adjective* [Middle English, from Middle French, from Latin *vehement-, vehemens, vement-, vemens*] (15th century)
: marked by forceful energy : POWERFUL ⟨a *vehement* wind⟩: as **a** : intensely emotional : IMPASSIONED, FERVID ⟨*vehement* patriotism⟩ **b** (1) : deeply felt ⟨a *vehement* suspicion⟩ (2) : forcibly expressed ⟨*vehement* denunciations⟩ **c** : bitterly antagonistic ⟨a *vehement* debate⟩
— **ve·he·ment·ly** *adverb*

**ve·hi·cle** \'vē-ə-kəl *also* 'vē-ˌhi-kəl\ *noun* [French *véhicule*, from Latin *vehiculum* carriage, conveyance, from *vehere* to carry — more at WAY] (1612)
**1 a** : an inert medium (as a syrup) in which a medicinally active agent is administered **b** : any of various media acting usually as solvents, carriers, or binders for active ingredients or pigments
**2** : an agent of transmission : CARRIER
**3** : a medium through which something is expressed, achieved, or displayed
**4** : a means of carrying or transporting something : CONVEYANCE: as **a** : MOTOR VEHICLE **b** : a piece of mechanized equipment

**ve·hic·u·lar** \vē-'hi-kyə-lər\ *adjective* (1616)
**1 a** : of, relating to, or designed for vehicles and especially motor vehicles **b** : transported by vehicle **c** : caused by or resulting from the operation of a vehicle ⟨*vehicular* homicide⟩
**2** : serving as a vehicle

**V–8** \'vē-'āt\ *noun* (1942)
: an internal combustion engine having two banks of four cylinders each with the banks at an angle to each other; *also* : an automobile having such an engine

**¹veil** \'vā(ə)l\ *noun* [Middle English *veile*, from Old North French *vele*, from Latin *vela*, plural of *velum* sail, awning, curtain] (13th century)
**1 a** : a length of cloth worn by women as a covering for the head and shoulders and often especially in Eastern countries for the face; *specifically* : the outer covering of a nun's headdress **b** : a length of veiling or netting worn over the head or face or attached for protection or ornament to a hat or headdress **c** : any of various liturgical cloths; *especially* : a cloth used to cover the chalice
**2** : the cloistered life of a nun

\ə\ **abut** \ᵊ\ **kitten** \ər\ **further** \a\ **ash** \ā\ **ace** \ä\ **mop, mar** \au̇\ **out** \ch\ **chin** \e\ **bet** \ē\ **easy** \g\ **go** \i\ **hit** \ī\ **ice** \j\ **job** \ŋ\ **sing** \ō\ **go** \ȯ\ **law** \ȯi\ **boy** \th\ **thin** \t͟h\ **the** \ü\ **loot** \u̇\ **foot** \y\ **yet** \zh\ **vision** *see also* Guide to Pronunciation

**3 :** a concealing curtain or cover of cloth
**4 :** something that hides or obscures like a veil
**5 :** a covering body part or membrane: as **a :** VELUM **b :** CAUL
²**veil** (14th century)
*transitive verb*
**:** to cover, provide, obscure, or conceal with or as if with a veil
*intransitive verb*
**:** to put on or wear a veil
**veiled** \'vā(ə)ld\ *adjective* (1593)
**1 a :** having or wearing a veil or a concealing cover ⟨a *veiled* hat⟩ **b :** characterized by a softening tonal distortion
**2 :** obscured as if by a veil : DISGUISED ⟨*veiled* threats⟩
**veil·ing** \'vā-liŋ\ *noun* (14th century)
**1 :** VEIL
**2 :** any of various light sheer fabrics
¹**vein** \'vān\ *noun* [Middle English *veine*, from Old French, from Latin *vena*] (14th century)
**1 a :** a narrow water channel in rock or earth or in ice **b** (1) : LODE 2, 3 (2) : a bed of useful mineral matter
**2 :** BLOOD VESSEL; *especially* **:** any of the tubular branching vessels that carry blood from the capillaries toward the heart
**3 a :** any of the vascular bundles forming the framework of a leaf **b :** any of the thickened cuticular ribs that serve to stiffen the wings of an insect
**4 :** something suggesting veins (as in reticulation); *specifically* **:** a wavy variegation (as in marble)
**5 a :** a distinctive mode of expression : STYLE **b :** a pervasive element or quality : STRAIN **c :** a line of thought or action
**6 a :** a special aptitude : TALENT **b :** a usually transitory and casually attained mood **c :** top form : FETTLE
— **vein·al** \'vā-nᵊl\ *adjective*
²**vein** *transitive verb* (1502)
**:** to pattern with or as if with veins
**veined** \'vānd\ *adjective* (circa 1529)
**:** patterned with or as if with veins : having venation : STREAKED ⟨a *veined* leaf⟩ ⟨*veined* marble⟩ ⟨*veined* cheese⟩
**vein·er** \'vā-nər\ *noun* (1895)
**:** a small V gouge used in wood carving
**vein·ing** \'vā-niŋ\ *noun* (1826)
**:** a pattern of veins : VENATION
**vein·let** \'vān-lət\ *noun* (1831)
**:** a small vein
**veiny** \'vā-nē\ *adjective* (1611)
**:** full of veins : noticeably veined
**ve·la·men** \və-'lā-mən\ *noun, plural* **ve·lam·i·na** \-'la-mə-nə\ [New Latin, from Latin, covering, from *velare* to cover, from *velum* curtain] (1882)
**:** the thick corky epidermis of aerial roots of an epiphytic orchid that absorbs water from the atmosphere
**ve·lar** \'vē-lər\ *adjective* [New Latin *velaris*, from *velum*] (1876)
**1 :** formed with the back of the tongue touching or near the soft palate ⟨the *velar* \k\ of \'kül\ *cool*⟩
**2 :** of, forming, or relating to a velum and especially the soft palate
— **velar** *noun*
**ve·lar·i·um** \vi-'lar-ē-əm, -'ler-\ *noun, plural* **-ia** \-ē-ə\ [Latin, from *velum* curtain] (1834)
**:** an awning over an ancient Roman theater or amphitheater
**ve·lar·i·za·tion** \ˌvē-lə-rə-'zā-shən\ *noun* (1915)
**1 :** the quality or state of being velarized
**2 :** an act or instance of velarizing
**ve·lar·ize** \'vē-lə-ˌrīz\ *transitive verb* **-ized; -iz·ing** (1915)
**:** to modify (as the \l\ of \'pül\ *pool*) by a simultaneous velar articulation
**Vel·cro** \'vel-(ˌ)krō\ *trademark*
— used for a closure consisting of a piece of fabric of small hooks that sticks to a corresponding fabric of small loops

**veld** *or* **veldt** \'velt, 'felt\ *noun* [Afrikaans *veld*, from Dutch, field; akin to Old English *feld* field] (1835)
**:** a grassland especially of southern Africa usually with scattered shrubs or trees
**ve·li·ger** \'vē-lə-jər, 've-\ *noun* [New Latin, from *velum* + *-ger* bearing, from *gerere* to bear] (1877)
**:** a larval mollusk in the stage when it has developed the velum
**vel·le·i·ty** \ve-'lē-ə-tē, və-\ *noun, plural* **-ties** [New Latin *velleitas*, from Latin *velle* to wish, will — more at WILL] (1618)
**1 :** the lowest degree of volition
**2 :** a slight wish or tendency : INCLINATION
¹**vel·lum** \'ve-ləm\ *noun* [Middle English *vel-lim*, from Middle French *veelin*, from *veelin*, adjective, of a calf, from *veel* calf — more at VEAL] (15th century)
**1 :** a fine-grained unsplit lambskin, kidskin, or calfskin prepared especially for writing on or for binding books
**2 :** a strong cream-colored paper
²**vellum** *adjective* (1565)
**1 :** of, resembling, or bound in vellum
**2 :** slightly rough ⟨paper with a *vellum* finish⟩
**ve·lo·ce** \vā-'lō-(ˌ)chā\ *adverb or adjective* [Italian, from Latin *veloc-, velox*] (circa 1823)
**:** in a rapid manner — used as a direction in music
**ve·lo·cim·e·ter** \ˌvē-lō-'si-mə-tər, ˌve-\ *noun* [*velocity* + *-meter*] (1842)
**:** a device for measuring speed (as of fluid flow or sound)
**ve·loc·i·pede** \və-'lä-sə-ˌpēd\ *noun* [French *vélocipède*, from Latin *veloc-, velox* + *ped-, pes* foot — more at FOOT] (1818)
**:** a lightweight wheeled vehicle propelled by the rider: as **a** *archaic* **:** BICYCLE **b :** TRICYCLE **c :** a 3-wheeled railroad handcar
**ve·loc·i·ty** \və-'lä-sə-tē, -'läs-tē\ *noun, plural* **-ties** [Middle French *velocité*, from Latin *velocitat-, velocitas*, from *veloc-, velox* quick; probably akin to Latin *vegēre* to enliven — more at WAKE] (circa 1550)
**1 a :** quickness of motion : SPEED ⟨the *velocity* of sound⟩ **b :** rapidity of movement ⟨[my horse's] strong suit is grace & personal comeliness, rather than *velocity* —Mark Twain⟩ **c :** speed imparted to something ⟨the power pitcher relies on *velocity* —Tony Scherman⟩
**2 :** the rate of change of position along a straight line with respect to time : the derivative of position with respect to time
**3 a :** rate of occurrence or action : RAPIDITY ⟨the *velocity* of historical change —R. J. Lifton⟩ ⟨the narrative leaps from one frantic episode to another with impressive *velocity* —James Atlas⟩ **b :** rate of turnover ⟨the *velocity* of money⟩
**ve·lo·drome** \'vē-lə-ˌdrōm, 've-, 'vä-\ *noun* [French *vélodrome*, from *vélo* cycle (short for *vélocipède*) + *-drome*] (1895)
**:** a track designed for cycling
**ve·lour** *or* **ve·lours** \və-'lùr\ *noun, plural* **ve·lours** \-'lùrz\ [French *velours* velvet, velour, from Middle French *velours, velour*, from Old French *velous*, from Old Provençal *velos*, from Latin *villosus* shaggy, from *villus* shaggy hair — more at VELVET] (circa 1706)
**1 :** any of various fabrics with a pile or napped surface resembling velvet used in heavy weights for upholstery and curtains and in lighter weights for clothing; *also* **:** the article of clothing itself
**2 :** a fur felt (as of rabbit or nutria) finished with a long velvety nap and used especially for hats
**ve·lou·té** \və-ˌlü-'tā\ *noun* [French, literally, velvetness, from Middle French *velluté*, from Old Provençal *velut* velvety, from (assumed) Vulgar Latin *villutus*] (1830)
**:** a white sauce made of chicken, veal, or fish stock and cream and thickened with butter and flour

**ve·lum** \'vē-ləm\ *noun, plural* **ve·la** \-lə\ [New Latin, from Latin, curtain] (1753)
**1 :** a membrane or membranous part resembling a veil or curtain: as **a :** SOFT PALATE **b :** an annular membrane projecting inward from the margin of the umbrella in some jellyfishes (as the hydromedusans)
**2 :** a swimming organ that is especially well developed in the later larval stages of many marine gastropods
**ve·lure** \ve-'lùr, vel-'yùr, 'vel-yər\ *noun* [modification of Middle French *velour*] (1587)
*obsolete* **:** VELVET; *also* **:** a fabric resembling velvet
¹**vel·vet** \'vel-vət\ *noun* [Middle English *veluet, velvet*, from Middle French *velu* shaggy, from (assumed) Vulgar Latin *villutus*, from Latin *villus* shaggy hair; akin to Latin *vellus* fleece — more at WOOL] (14th century)
**1 :** a clothing and upholstery fabric (as of silk, rayon, or wool) characterized by a short soft dense warp pile
**2 a :** something suggesting velvet **b :** a characteristic (as softness or smoothness) of velvet
**3 :** the soft vascular skin that envelops and nourishes the developing antlers of deer
**4 a :** the winnings of a player in a gambling game **b :** a profit or gain beyond ordinary expectation
— **vel·vet·like** \-ˌlīk\ *adjective*
²**velvet** *adjective* (14th century)
**1 :** made of or covered with velvet; *also* **:** clad in velvet
**2 :** resembling or suggesting velvet : VELVETY ⟨a *velvet* voice⟩
**velvet ant** *noun* (1748)
**:** any of various solitary usually brightly colored and hairy fossorial wasps (family Mutillidae) with the female wingless
**velvet bean** *noun* (1898)
**:** an annual legume (*Mucuna deeringiana* synonym *Stizolobium deeringianum*) grown especially in the southern U.S. for green manure and grazing; *also* **:** its seed often used as stock feed
**vel·ve·teen** \ˌvel-və-'tēn\ *noun* (1776)
**1 :** a clothing fabric usually of cotton in twill or plain weaves made with a short close weft pile in imitation of velvet
**2** *plural* **:** clothes made of velveteen
**vel·vety** \'vel-və-tē\ *adjective* (1752)
**1 :** soft and smooth like velvet ⟨*velvety* hair⟩
**2 :** smooth to the taste : MILD ⟨a *velvety* wine⟩
**ven-** *or* **veni-** *or* **veno-** *combining form* [Latin *vena*]
**:** vein ⟨*veni*puncture⟩ ⟨*veno*graphy⟩
**ve·na** \'vē-nə\ *noun, plural* **ve·nae** \-(ˌ)nē\ [Middle English, from Latin] (14th century)
**:** VEIN
**ve·na ca·va** \ˌvē-nə-'kā-və\ *noun, plural* **ve·nae ca·vae** \-(ˌ)nē-'kā-(ˌ)vē\ [New Latin, literally, hollow vein] (1598)
**:** any of the large veins by which in air-breathing vertebrates the blood is returned to the right atrium of the heart
— **ve·na ca·val** \-vəl\ *adjective*
**ve·nal** \'vē-nᵊl\ *adjective* [Latin *venalis*, from *venum* (accusative) sale; akin to Greek *ōneisthai* to buy, Sanskrit *vasna* price] (1652)
**1 :** capable of being bought or obtained for money or other valuable consideration : PURCHASABLE; *especially* **:** open to corrupt influence and especially bribery : MERCENARY ⟨a *venal* legislator⟩
**2 :** originating in, characterized by, or associated with corrupt bribery ⟨a *venal* arrangement with the police⟩
— **ve·nal·i·ty** \vi-'na-lə-tē\ *noun*
— **ve·nal·ly** \'vē-nᵊl-ē\ *adverb*

**ve·na·tion** \ve-'nā-shən, vē-\ *noun* [Latin *vena* vein] (1646)
: an arrangement or system of veins (as in the tissue of a leaf or the wing of an insect)

**vend** \'vend\ *verb* [Latin *vendere* to sell, transitive verb, contraction for *venum dare* to give for sale] (1622) *intransitive verb*
: to dispose of something by sale : SELL; *also* : to engage in selling *transitive verb*
**1 a** : to sell especially as a hawker or peddler **b** : to sell by means of vending machines
**2** : to utter publicly

**Ven·da** \'ven-də\ *noun* (1908)
: a Bantu language spoken by a people of Northern Transvaal; *also* : a member of this people

**vend·ee** \ven-'dē\ *noun* (1547)
: one to whom a thing is sold : BUYER

**ven·det·ta** \ven-'de-tə\ *noun* [Italian, literally, revenge, from Latin *vindicta* — more at VINDICTIVE] (1855)
**1** : BLOOD FEUD
**2** : an often prolonged series of retaliatory, vengeful, or hostile acts or exchange of such acts ⟨waged a personal *vendetta* against those who opposed his nomination⟩

**ven·deuse** \vänⁿ-'də(r)z, vän-'düz\ *noun* [French, feminine of *vendeur* salesman, from Middle French] (1913)
: a saleswoman especially in the fashion industry

**vend·ible** *or* **vend·able** \'ven-də-bəl\ *adjective* (14th century)
: capable of being vended : SALABLE
— **vend·ibil·i·ty** \ˌven-də-'bi-lə-tē\ *noun*

**vending machine** *noun* (circa 1895)
: a coin-operated machine for selling merchandise

**ven·dor** \'ven-dər, *for 1 also* ven-'dȯr\ *also* **vend·er** \-dər\ *noun* [Middle French *vendeur*, from *vendre* to sell, from Latin *vendere*] (1594)
**1** : one that vends : SELLER
**2** : VENDING MACHINE

**ven·due** \'ven-ˌdü, 'vän-, 'fen-, -ˌdyü; ven-', vän-'\ *noun* [obsolete French, from Middle French, from *vendre*] (1668)
: a public sale at auction

**¹ve·neer** \və-'nir\ *noun* [German *Furnier*, from *furnieren* to veneer, from French *fournir* to furnish, equip — more at FURNISH] (1702)
**1** : a thin sheet of a material: as **a** : a layer of wood of superior value or excellent grain to be glued to an inferior wood **b** : any of the thin layers bonded together to form plywood
**2** : a protective or ornamental facing (as of brick or stone)
**3** : a superficial or deceptively attractive appearance, display, or effect : FACADE, GLOSS

**²veneer** *transitive verb* (1728)
**1** : to overlay or plate (as a common wood) with a thin layer of finer wood for outer finish or decoration; *broadly* : to face with a material giving a superior surface
**2** : to cover over with a veneer; *especially* : to conceal (as a defect of character) under a superficial and deceptive attractiveness
— **ve·neer·er** *noun*

**ve·neer·ing** *noun* (circa 1706)
**1** : a veneered surface
**2** : material used as veneer

**ven·er·a·ble** \'ve-nər-(ə-)bəl, 'ven-rə-bəl\ *adjective* (15th century)
**1** : deserving to be venerated — used as a ti-

tle for an Anglican archdeacon or for a Roman Catholic who has been accorded the lowest of three degrees of recognition for sanctity
**2** : made sacred especially by religious or historical association
**3 a** : calling forth respect through age, character, and attainments; *broadly* : conveying an impression of aged goodness and benevolence **b** : impressive by reason of age ⟨under *venerable* pines⟩
**synonym** see OLD
— **ven·er·a·bil·i·ty** \ˌve-nə-rə-'bi-lə-tē, ˌven-rə-\ *noun*
— **ven·er·a·ble·ness** \'ve-nər-(ə)-bəl-nəs, 'ven-rə-\ *noun*
— **ven·er·a·bly** \-blē\ *adverb*

**ven·er·ate** \'ve-nə-ˌrāt\ *transitive verb* **-at·ed; -at·ing** [Latin *veneratus*, past participle of *venerari*, from *vener-, venus* love, charm — more at WIN] (circa 1623)
**1** : to regard with reverential respect or with admiring deference
**2** : to honor (as an icon or a relic) with a ritual act of devotion
**synonym** see REVERE
**word history** see VENOM
— **ven·er·a·tor** \-ˌrā-tər\ *noun*

**ven·er·a·tion** \ˌve-nə-'rā-shən\ *noun* (15th century)
**1** : respect or awe inspired by the dignity, wisdom, dedication, or talent of a person
**2** : the act of venerating
**3** : the condition of one that is venerated

**ve·ne·re·al** \və-'nir-ē-əl\ *adjective* [Middle English *venerealle*, from Latin *venereus*, from *vener-, venus* love, sexual desire] (14th century)
**1** : of or relating to sexual pleasure or indulgence
**2 a** : resulting from or contracted during sexual intercourse ⟨*venereal* infections⟩ **b** : of, relating to, or affected with venereal disease ⟨a high *venereal* rate⟩ **c** : involving the genital organs ⟨*venereal* sarcoma⟩

**venereal disease** *noun* (1658)
: a contagious disease (as gonorrhea or syphilis) that is typically acquired in sexual intercourse — compare STD

**¹ven·ery** \'ve-nə-rē\ *noun* [Middle English *venerie*, from Middle French, from *vener* to hunt, from Latin *venari* — more at VENISON] (14th century)
**1** : the art, act, or practice of hunting
**2** : animals that are hunted : GAME

**²venery** *noun* [Middle English *venerie*, from Medieval Latin *veneria*, from Latin *vener-, venus* sexual desire] (15th century)
**1** : the pursuit of or indulgence in sexual pleasure
**2** : SEXUAL INTERCOURSE

**ve·ne·sec·tion** \'ve-nə-ˌsek-shən, 'vē-\ *noun* [New Latin *venae section-, venae sectio*, literally, cutting of a vein] (1661)
: the operation of opening a vein for letting blood : PHLEBOTOMY

**Ven·e·ti** \'ve-nə-ˌtī\ *noun plural* [Latin *Veneti*] (1881)
**1** : an ancient people in Gaul conquered by Caesar in 56 B.C.
**2** : an ancient people in northeastern Italy allied politically to the Romans

**ve·ne·tian blind** \və-'nē-shən-\ *noun* [*Venetian* of Venice, Italy] (1770)
: a blind (as for a window) having numerous horizontal slats that may be set simultaneously at any of several angles so as to vary the amount of light admitted

**venetian glass** *noun, often V capitalized* (circa 1845)
: often colored glassware made at Murano near Venice of a soda-lime metal and typically elaborately decorated (as with gilt, enamel, or engraving)

**Venetian red** *noun* (circa 1753)
: an earthy hematite used as a pigment; *also* : a synthetic iron oxide pigment

**Ve·net·ic** \və-'ne-tik\ *noun* [Latin *veneticus* of the Veneti, from *Veneti*] (1902)
: the language of the ancient Veneti of Italy
— see INDO-EUROPEAN LANGUAGES table
— **Venetic** *adjective*

**venge** \'venj\ *transitive verb* **venged; veng·ing** [Middle English, from Middle French *vengier*, from Old French] (14th century)
*archaic* : AVENGE

**ven·geance** \'ven-jən(t)s\ *noun* [Middle English, from Old French, from *vengier* to avenge, from Latin *vindicare* to lay claim to, avenge — more at VINDICATE] (14th century)
: punishment inflicted in retaliation for an injury or offense : RETRIBUTION
— **with a vengeance 1** : with great force or vehemence **2** : to an extreme or excessive degree

**venge·ful** \'venj-fəl\ *adjective* [obsolete English *venge* revenge] (1586)
: REVENGEFUL: as **a** : seeking to avenge **b** : serving to gain vengeance
— **venge·ful·ly** \-fə-lē\ *adverb*
— **venge·ful·ness** *noun*

**V–en·gine** \'vē-\ *noun* (circa 1922)
: an internal combustion engine whose cylinders are arranged in two banks forming an acute or right angle

**veni-** *or* **veno-** — see VEN-

**ve·ni·al** \'vē-nē-əl, -nyəl\ *adjective* [Middle English, from Middle French, from Late Latin *venialis*, from Latin *venia* favor, indulgence, pardon; akin to Latin *venus* love, charm — more at WIN] (14th century)
: of a kind that can be remitted : FORGIVABLE, PARDONABLE; *also* : meriting no particular censure or notice : EXCUSABLE ⟨*venial* faults⟩
— **ve·nial·ly** *adverb*
— **ve·nial·ness** *noun*

**venial sin** *noun* (14th century)
: a sin that is relatively slight or that is committed without full reflection or consent and so according to Thomist theology does not deprive the soul of sanctifying grace — compare MORTAL SIN

**ve·ni·punc·ture** \'vē-nə-ˌpəŋ(k)-chər, 've-\ *noun* (circa 1903)
: surgical puncture of a vein especially for the withdrawal of blood or for intravenous medication

**ve·ni·re** \və-'nī-rē\ *noun* [*venire facias*] (1665)
: an entire panel from which a jury is drawn

**ve·ni·re fa·ci·as** \-ˌnī-rē-'fā-shē-əs\ *noun* [Middle English, from Medieval Latin, you should cause to come] (15th century)
: a judicial writ directing the sheriff to summon a specified number of qualified persons to serve as jurors

**ve·ni·re·man** \və-'nī-rē-mən, -'nir-ē-\ *noun* (1776)
: a member of a venire

**ven·i·son** \'ve-nə-sən *also* -zən, *British usually* 'ven-zən\ *noun, plural* **venisons** *also* **venison** [Middle English, from Old French *veneison* hunting, game, from Latin *venation-, venatio*, from *venari* to hunt, pursue; akin to Sanskrit *vanoti* he strives for — more at WIN] (14th century)
: the edible flesh of a game animal and especially a deer

**Ve·ni·te** \və-'nī-tē, -'nē-ˌtā\ *noun* [Middle English, from Latin, O come, from *venire* to come; from the opening word of Psalms 95:1 — more at COME] (13th century)
: a liturgical chant composed of parts of Psalms 95 and 96

*venation a:
1 parallel-veined,
2 net-veined,
3 dichotomously veined*

**Venn diagram** \'ven-\ *noun* [John *Venn* (died 1923) English logician] (1918)
: a graph that employs closed curves and especially circles to represent logical relations between and operations on sets and the terms of propositions by the inclusion, exclusion, or intersection of the circles

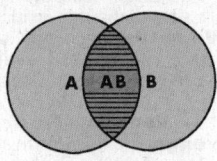

Venn diagram: *AB* represents the intersection of sets *A* and *B*

**ve·nog·ra·phy** \vi-'nä-grə-fē, vā-\ *noun* [International Scientific Vocabulary] (1935)
: roentgenography of a vein after injection of an opaque substance

**¹ven·om** \'ve-nəm\ *noun* [Middle English *venim, venom,* from Old French *venim,* from (assumed) Vulgar Latin *venimen,* alteration of Latin *venenum* magic charm, drug, poison; akin to Latin *venus* love, charm — more at WIN] (13th century)
**1** : poisonous matter normally secreted by some animals (as snakes, scorpions, or bees) and transmitted to prey or an enemy chiefly by biting or stinging; *broadly* : material that is poisonous
**2** : ILL WILL, MALEVOLENCE ◆

**²venom** *transitive verb* (14th century)
: ENVENOM

**ven·om·ous** \'ve-nə-məs\ *adjective* (14th century)
**1** : full of venom: as **a** : POISONOUS, ENVENOMED **b** : NOXIOUS, PERNICIOUS ⟨expose a *venomous* dope ring —Don Porter⟩ **c** : SPITEFUL, MALEVOLENT ⟨*venomous* criticism⟩
**2** : having a venom-producing gland and able to inflict a poisoned wound ⟨*venomous* snakes⟩
— **ven·om·ous·ly** *adverb*
— **ven·om·ous·ness** *noun*

**ve·nous** \'vē-nəs\ *adjective* [Latin *venosus,* from *vena* vein] (1626)
**1** : of, relating to, or full of veins ⟨a *venous* rock⟩ ⟨a *venous* system⟩
**2** *of blood* : having passed through the capillaries and given up oxygen for the tissues and become charged with carbon dioxide
— **ve·nous·ly** *adverb*

**¹vent** \'vent\ *transitive verb* [Middle English, probably from Middle French *esventer* to expose to the air, from *es-* (from Latin *ex-*) + *vent* wind, from Latin *ventus* — more at WIND] (14th century)
**1** : to provide with a vent
**2 a** : to serve as a vent for ⟨chimneys *vent* smoke⟩ **b** : DISCHARGE, EXPEL **c** : to give often vigorous or emotional expression to
**3** : to relieve by means of a vent
**synonym** see EXPRESS

**²vent** *noun* (1508)
**1** : an opportunity or means of escape, passage, or release : OUTLET ⟨finally gave *vent* to his pent-up hostility⟩
**2** : an opening for the escape of a gas or liquid or for the relief of pressure: as **a** : the external opening of the rectum or cloaca : ANUS **b** : PIPE 3c, FUMAROLE **c** : an opening at the breech of a muzzle-loading gun through which fire is touched to the powder **d** *chiefly Scottish* : CHIMNEY, FLUE
— **vent·less** \-ləs\ *adjective*

**³vent** *noun* [Middle English *vente,* alteration of *fente,* from Middle French, slit, fissure, from *fendre* to split, from Latin *findere* — more at BITE] (15th century)
: a slit in a garment; *specifically* : an opening in the lower part of a seam (as of a jacket or skirt)
— **vent·less** *adjective*

**vent·age** \'ven-tij\ *noun* (1602)
: a small hole (as a flute stop)

**ven·tail** \'ven-ˌtāl\ *noun* [Middle English, from Middle French *ventaille,* from *vent* wind] (15th century)
: the lower movable front of a medieval helmet

**ven·ter** \'ven-tər\ *noun* [Anglo-French, from Latin, belly, womb; perhaps akin to Old High German *wanast* paunch, Latin *vesica* bladder, Sanskrit *vasti*] (1544)
**1** : a wife or mother that is a source of offspring
**2** : a protuberant and often hollow anatomical structure: as **a** : the undersurface of the abdomen of an arthropod **b** : the swollen basal portion of an archegonium in which an egg develops

**ven·ti·fact** \'ven-tə-ˌfakt\ *noun* [Latin *ventus* + English art*ifact*] (1911)
: a stone worn, polished, or faceted by wind-blown sand

**ven·ti·late** \'ven-tᵊl-ˌāt\ *transitive verb* **-lat·ed; -lat·ing** [Late Latin *ventilatus,* past participle of *ventilare,* from Latin, to fan, winnow, from *ventus* wind — more at WIND] (1527)
**1 a** : to examine, discuss, or investigate freely and openly : EXPOSE ⟨*ventilating* family quarrels in public⟩ **b** : to make public : UTTER ⟨*ventilated* their objections at length⟩
**2** *archaic* : to free from chaff by winnowing
**3 a** : to expose to air and especially to a current of fresh air for purifying, curing, or refreshing ⟨*ventilate* stored grain⟩; *also* : OXYGENATE, AERATE ⟨*ventilate* blood in the lungs⟩ **b** : to subject the lungs to ventilation ⟨artificially *ventilate* a patient in respiratory distress⟩
**4 a** *of a current of air* : to pass or circulate through so as to freshen **b** : to cause fresh air to circulate through (as a room or mine)
**5** : to provide an opening in (a burning structure) to permit escape of smoke and heat

**ven·ti·la·tion** \ˌven-tᵊl-'ā-shən\ *noun* (1519)
**1** : the act or process of ventilating
**2 a** : circulation of air ⟨a room with good *ventilation*⟩ **b** : the circulation and exchange of gases in the lungs or gills that is basic to respiration
**3** : a system or means of providing fresh air

**ven·ti·la·tor** \'ven-tᵊl-ˌā-tər\ *noun* (1743)
: one that ventilates: as **a** : a contrivance for introducing fresh air or expelling foul or stagnant air **b** : RESPIRATOR 2

**ven·ti·la·to·ry** \'ven-tᵊl-ə-ˌtōr-ē, -ˌtor-\ *adjective* (1850)
: of, relating to, or provided with ventilation ⟨*ventilatory* capacity of the lung⟩

**ventr-** *or* **ventro-** *combining form* [Latin *ventr-, venter* belly]
: ventral and ⟨*ventro*lateral⟩

**¹ven·tral** \'ven-trəl\ *adjective* [French, from Latin *ventralis,* from *ventr-, venter*] (1739)
**1 a** : of or relating to the belly : ABDOMINAL **b** : being or located near or on the anterior or lower surface of an animal opposite the back
**2** : being or located on the lower surface of a dorsiventral plant structure
— **ven·tral·ly** \-trə-lē\ *adverb*

**²ventral** *noun* (1834)
: a ventral part (as a scale or fin)

**ventral root** *noun* (circa 1923)
: the one of the two roots of a spinal nerve that passes ventrally from the spinal cord and consists of motor fibers — compare DORSAL ROOT

**ven·tri·cle** \'ven-tri-kəl\ *noun* [Middle English, from Latin *ventriculus,* from diminutive of *ventr-, venter* belly] (14th century)
: a cavity of a bodily part or organ: as **a** : a chamber of the heart which receives blood from a corresponding atrium and from which blood is forced into the arteries — see HEART illustration **b** : any of the system of communicating cavities in the brain that are continuous with the central canal of the spinal cord — see BRAIN illustration

**ven·tri·cose** \-ˌkōs\ *adjective* [New Latin *ventricosus,* from Latin *ventr-, venter* + *-icosus* (as in *varicosus* varicose)] (1756)
: markedly swollen, distended, or inflated especially on one side ⟨*ventricose* corollas⟩

**ven·tric·u·lar** \ven-'tri-kyə-lər, vən-\ *adjective* (1822)
: of, relating to, or being a ventricle ⟨*ventricular* fibrillation⟩ ⟨*ventricular* pressure⟩ ⟨*ventricular* myocardium⟩

**ven·tric·u·lus** \ven-'tri-kyə-ləs, vən-\ *noun,* *plural* **-li** \-ˌlī, -ˌlē\ [New Latin, from Latin, diminutive of *venter*] (1693)
: a digestive cavity: as **a** : STOMACH **b** : GIZZARD 1a **c** : the digestive part of an insect's stomach

**ven·tril·o·quism** \ven-'tri-lə-ˌkwi-zəm\ *noun* [Late Latin *ventriloquus* ventriloquist, from Latin *ventr-, venter* + *loqui* to speak; from the belief that the voice is produced from the ventriloquist's stomach] (circa 1797)
: the production of the voice in such a way that the sound seems to come from a source other than the vocal organs of the speaker
— **ven·tri·lo·qui·al** \ˌven-trə-'lō-kwē-əl\ *adjective*
— **ven·tri·lo·qui·al·ly** \-ə-lē\ *adverb*

**ven·tril·o·quist** \ven-'tri-lə-kwist\ *noun* (circa 1656)
: one who uses or is skilled in ventriloquism; *especially* : one who provides entertainment by using ventriloquism to carry on an apparent conversation with a hand-manipulated dummy
— **ven·tril·o·quis·tic** \(ˌ)ven-ˌtri-lə-'kwis-tik\ *adjective*

**ven·tril·o·quize** \ven-'tri-lə-ˌkwīz\ *verb* **-quized; -quiz·ing** (1844)
*intransitive verb*
: to use ventriloquism
*transitive verb*
: to utter in the manner of a ventriloquist

**ven·tril·o·quy** \-kwē\ *noun* (1584)
: VENTRILOQUISM

**ven·tro·lat·er·al** \ˌven-trō-'la-tə-rəl, -'la-trəl\ *adjective* (1835)
: ventral and lateral

**ven·tro·me·di·al** \-'mē-dē-əl\ *adjective* (1908)
: ventral and medial

**¹ven·ture** \'ven(t)-shər\ *verb* **ven·tured; ven·tur·ing** \'ven(t)-sh(ə-)riŋ\ [Middle English *venteren,* by shortening & alteration

from *aventuren,* from *aventure* adventure]
(15th century)
*transitive verb*
**1 :** to expose to hazard **:** RISK, GAMBLE ⟨*ventured* a buck or two on the race⟩
**2 :** to undertake the risks and dangers of **:** BRAVE ⟨*ventured* the stormy sea⟩
**3 :** to offer at the risk of rebuff, rejection, or censure ⟨*venture* an opinion⟩
*intransitive verb*
**:** to proceed especially in the face of danger
— **ven·tur·er** \'ven(t)-sh(ə-)rər\ *noun*
**²venture** *noun* (15th century)
**1** *obsolete* **:** DESTINY, FORTUNE, CHANCE
**2 a :** an undertaking involving chance, risk, or danger; *especially* **:** a speculative business enterprise **b :** a venturesome act
**3 :** something (as money or property) at hazard in a speculative venture
— **at a venture** **:** at random ⟨a certain man drew a bow *at a venture,* and smote the king —1 Kings 22:34 (Authorized Version)⟩
**venture capital** *noun* (1943)
**:** capital (as retained corporate earnings or individual savings) invested or available for investment in the ownership element of new or fresh enterprise — called also *risk capital*
— **venture capitalist** *noun*
**ven·ture·some** \'ven(t)-shər-səm\ *adjective* (1661)
**1 :** involving risk **:** HAZARDOUS ⟨a *venturesome* journey⟩
**2 :** inclined to court or incur risk or danger **:** DARING ⟨a *venturesome* hunter⟩
*synonym* see ADVENTUROUS
— **ven·ture·some·ly** *adverb*
— **ven·ture·some·ness** *noun*
**ven·tu·ri** \ven-'tür-ē\ *noun* [G. B. *Venturi* (died 1822) Italian physicist] (1887)
**:** a short tube with a tapering constriction in the middle that causes an increase in the velocity of flow of a fluid and a corresponding decrease in fluid pressure and that is used especially in measuring fluid flow or for creating a suction (as for driving aircraft instruments or drawing fuel into the flow stream of a carburetor)
**ven·tur·ous** \'ven(t)-sh(ə-)rəs\ *adjective* (1565)
**:** VENTURESOME
— **ven·tur·ous·ly** *adverb*
— **ven·tur·ous·ness** *noun*
**ven·ue** \'ven-,yü\ *noun* [Middle English *venyw* action of coming, from Middle French *venue,* from *venir* to come, from Latin *venire* — more at COME] (1531)
**1 a :** the place or county in which take place the alleged events from which a legal action arises **b :** the place from which a jury is drawn and in which trial is held ⟨requested a change of *venue*⟩ **c :** a statement showing that a case is brought to the proper court or authority
**2 :** LOCALE 1
**ve·nule** \'vēn-(,)yü(ə)l, 'ven-\ *noun* [Latin *venula,* diminutive of *vena* vein] (circa 1850)
**:** a small vein; *especially* **:** any of the minute veins connecting the capillaries with the larger systemic veins
**Ve·nus** \'vē-nəs\ *noun* [Middle English, from Latin *Vener-, Venus*]
**1 :** the Roman goddess of love and beauty — compare APHRODITE
**2 :** the planet second in order from the sun — see PLANET table
**Ve·nus·berg** \-,bərg\ *noun*
**:** a mountain in central Germany containing a cavern where in medieval legend Venus held court
**Ve·nus·hair** \-,har, -,her\ *noun* (1548)
**:** a delicate maidenhair fern (*Adiantum capillus-veneris*) that grows chiefly on wet calcareous rocks
**Ve·nu·sian** \vi-'nü-zhən, -'nyü-\ *adjective* (1874)
**:** of or relating to the planet Venus

**Ve·nus's–flow·er–bas·ket** \'vē-nə-,səz-, 'vē-nəs-\ *noun* (1872)
**:** any of several glass sponges (genus *Euplectella*) of the western Pacific and Indian oceans — called also *Venus flower basket*
**Ve·nus's–fly·trap** \-'flī-,trap\ *noun* (1770)
**:** an insectivorous plant (*Dionaea muscipula*) of the sundew family of the Carolina coast with the leaf apex modified into an insect trap — called also *Venus flytrap*
**ve·ra·cious** \və-'rā-shəs\ *adjective* [Latin *verac-, verax* — more at VERY] (1677)
**1 :** TRUTHFUL, HONEST
**2 :** marked by truth **:** ACCURATE
— **ve·ra·cious·ly** *adverb*
— **ve·ra·cious·ness** *noun*
**ve·rac·i·ty** \və-'ra-sə-tē\ *noun, plural* **-ties** (circa 1623)
**1 :** devotion to the truth **:** TRUTHFULNESS
**2 :** power of conveying or perceiving truth
**3 :** conformity with truth or fact **:** ACCURACY
**4 :** something true ⟨makes lies sound like *veracities*⟩
**ve·ran·da** *or* **ve·ran·dah** \və-'ran-də\ *noun* [Hindi *varaṇḍā*] (1711)
**:** a usually roofed open gallery or portico attached to the exterior of a building
**ve·ran·daed** *also* **ve·ran·dahed** \-dəd\ *adjective* (1818)
**:** having a veranda
**ve·rap·a·mil** \və-'ra-pə-,mil\ *noun* [International Scientific Vocabulary *valeric* (acid) + *-apam-* (probably alteration of *amino + propyl*) + *nitrile*] (1967)
**:** a calcium channel blocker $C_{27}H_{38}N_2O_4$ used especially in the form of its hydrochloride
**ve·rat·ri·dine** \və-'ra-trə-,dēn\ *noun* [*veratrine + -idine*] (1907)
**:** a poisonous alkaloid $C_{36}H_{51}NO_{11}$ occurring especially in sabadilla seed
**ve·ra·trine** \'ver-ə-,trēn, və-'ra-trən\ *noun* [New Latin *veratrina,* from *Veratrum,* genus of herbs] (1822)
**:** a poisonous irritant mixture of alkaloids from sabadilla seed that has been used as a counterirritant and insecticide
**ve·ra·trum** \və-'ra-trəm\ *noun* [New Latin, genus name, from Latin, hellebore] (1577)
**:** HELLEBORE 2
**verb** \'vərb\ *noun* [Middle English *verbe,* from Middle French, from Latin *verbum* word, verb — more at WORD] (14th century)
**:** a word that characteristically is the grammatical center of a predicate and expresses an act, occurrence, or mode of being, that in various languages is inflected for agreement with the subject, for tense, for voice, for mood, or for aspect, and that typically has rather full descriptive meaning and characterizing quality but is sometimes nearly devoid of these especially when used as an auxiliary or linking verb
— **verb·less** \'vərb-ləs\ *adjective*
**¹ver·bal** \'vər-bəl\ *adjective* [Middle French or Late Latin; Middle French, from Late Latin *verbalis,* from Latin *verbum* word] (15th century)
**1 a :** of, relating to, or consisting of words ⟨*verbal* instructions⟩ **b :** of, relating to, or involving words rather than meaning or substance ⟨a consistency that is merely *verbal* and scholastic —B. N. Cardozo⟩ **c :** consisting of or using words only and not involving action ⟨a *verbal* protest⟩
**2 :** of, relating to, or formed from a verb ⟨a *verbal* adjective⟩
**3 :** spoken rather than written ⟨a *verbal* contract⟩
**4 :** VERBATIM, WORD-FOR-WORD ⟨a *verbal* translation⟩
**5 :** of or relating to facility in the use and comprehension of words ⟨*verbal* aptitude⟩ ∎

— **ver·bal·ly** \-bə-lē\ *adverb*
**²verbal** *noun* (1530)
**:** a word that combines characteristics of a verb with those of a noun or adjective — compare GERUND, INFINITIVE, PARTICIPLE
**verbal auxiliary** *noun* (circa 1958)
**:** an auxiliary verb
**ver·bal·ism** \'vər-bə-,li-zəm\ *noun* (1787)
**1 a :** a verbal expression **:** TERM **b :** PHRASING, WORDING
**2 :** words used as if they were more important than the realities they represent ⟨the emancipation of science from *verbalism* —G. A. L. Sarton⟩
**3 a :** a wordy expression of little meaning **b :** VERBOSITY
**ver·bal·ist** \-list\ *noun* (circa 1609)
**1 :** one who stresses words above substance or reality
**2 :** a person who uses words skillfully
— **ver·bal·is·tic** \,vər-bə-'lis-tik\ *adjective*
**ver·bal·ize** \'vər-bə-,līz\ *verb* **-ized; -iz·ing** (1609)
*intransitive verb*
**1 :** to speak or write verbosely
**2 :** to express something in words
*transitive verb*
**1 :** to convert into a verb
**2 :** to name or describe in words
— **ver·bal·i·za·tion** \,vər-bə-lə-'zā-shən\ *noun*
— **ver·bal·iz·er** \'vər-bə-,lī-zər\ *noun*
**verbal noun** *noun* (circa 1706)
**:** a noun derived directly from a verb or verb stem and in some uses having the sense and constructions of a verb
**¹ver·ba·tim** \(,)vər-'bā-təm\ *adverb* [Middle English, from Medieval Latin, from Latin *verbum* word] (15th century)
**:** in the exact words **:** word for word
**²verbatim** *adjective* (1737)
**:** being in or following the exact words **:** WORD-FOR-WORD
**ver·be·na** \(,)vər-'bē-nə\ *noun* [New Latin, genus of herbs or subshrubs, from Latin, leafy

— **Venus's–flytrap** (caption near illustration)

branch used ceremonially or medicinally — more at VERVAIN⟩ (1562)

: VERVAIN; *especially* : any of numerous garden plants of hybrid origin widely grown for their showy spikes of white, pink, red, or blue flowers which are borne in profusion over a long season

**ver·bi·age** \'vər-bē-ij *also* -bij\ *noun* [French, from Middle French *verbier* to chatter, from *verbe* speech, from Latin *verbum* word] (circa 1721)

**1** : a profusion of words usually of little or obscure content ⟨such a tangled maze of evasive *verbiage* as a typical party platform —Marcia Davenport⟩

**2** : manner of expressing oneself in words : DICTION ⟨sportswriters guarded their *verbiage* so jealously —Raymond Sokolov⟩

**ver·bi·cide** \'vər-bə-ˌsīd\ *noun* [Latin *verbum* word + English -*cide*] (1858)

**1** : deliberate distortion of the sense of a word (as in punning)

**2** : one who distorts the sense of a word

**ver·bid** \'vər-bəd\ *noun* (1914)

: VERBAL

**ver·big·er·a·tion** \(ˌ)vər-ˌbi-jə-'rā-shən\ *noun* [International Scientific Vocabulary, from Latin *verbigerare* to talk, chat, from *verbum* word + *gerere* to carry, wield — more at WORD] (1886)

: continual repetition of stereotyped phrases (as in some forms of mental illness)

**ver·bose** \(ˌ)vər-'bōs\ *adjective* [Latin *verbosus*, from *verbum*] (1672)

**1** : containing more words than necessary : WORDY ⟨a *verbose* reply⟩; *also* : impaired by wordiness ⟨a *verbose* style⟩

**2** : given to wordiness ⟨a *verbose* orator⟩

**synonym** see WORDY

— **ver·bose·ly** *adverb*
— **ver·bose·ness** *noun*
— **ver·bos·i·ty** \-'bä-sə-tē\ *noun*

**ver·bo·ten** \vər-'bō-tᵊn, fər-, ver-\ *adjective* [German, from Old High German *farboten*, past participle of *farbioten* to forbid (akin to Old English *forbēodan* to forbid), from *far*-, *fur*- for- + *biotan* to offer — more at BID] (1912)

: not allowed : FORBIDDEN; *especially* : prohibited by dictate

**verb sap** \'vərb-'sap\ (1841)

: VERBUM SAP

**ver·bum sap** \ˌvər-bəm-'sap\ [short for New Latin *verbum sapienti* (*sat est*) a word to the wise (is sufficient)] (1818)

: enough said — used to indicate that something left unsaid may or should be inferred

**ver·dant** \'vər-dᵊnt\ *adjective* [modification of Middle French *verdoyant*, from present participle of *verdoyer* to be green, from Old French *verdoier*, from *verd*, *vert* green, from Latin *viridis*, from *virēre* to be green] (1581)

**1 a** : green in tint or color ⟨*verdant* grass⟩ **b** : green with growing plants ⟨*verdant* fields⟩

**2** : unripe in experience or judgment : GREEN 9a, b

— **ver·dan·cy** \-dᵊn(t)-sē\ *noun*
— **ver·dant·ly** \-dᵊnt-lē\ *adverb*

**verd an·tique** *or* **verde an·tique** \ˌvərd-ˌan-'tēk\ *noun* [Italian *verde antico*, literally, ancient green] (1745)

: a green mottled or veined serpentine marble or calcareous serpentine much used for indoor decoration especially by the ancient Romans

**ver·der·er** *also* **ver·der·or** \'vər-dər-ər\ *noun* [Anglo-French, from Old French *verdier*, from *verd* green] (circa 1538)

: a onetime English judicial officer in charge of the king's forest

**ver·dict** \'vər-(ˌ)dikt\ *noun* [alteration of Middle English *verdit*, from Anglo-French, from Old French *vrai* true (from Latin *verus*) + *dit* saying, dictum, from Latin *dictum* — more at VERY] (1533)

**1** : the finding or decision of a jury on the matter submitted to it in trial

**2** : OPINION, JUDGMENT

**ver·di·gris** \'vər-də-ˌgrēs, -ˌgris, -grəs *also* -ˌgrē\ *noun* [Middle English *vertegrez*, from Old French *vert de Grice*, literally, green of Greece] (14th century)

**1 a** : a green or greenish blue poisonous pigment resulting from the action of acetic acid on copper and consisting of one or more basic copper acetates **b** : normal copper acetate $Cu(C_2H_3O_2)_2 \cdot H_2O$

**2** : a green or bluish deposit especially of copper carbonates formed on copper, brass, or bronze surfaces

**ver·din** \'vər-dᵊn\ *noun* [French, a green songbird of Indochina, alteration of *verdon*, *verdun* bunting, yellowhammer, from *vert* green, from Old French *verd*, *vert*] (1881)

: a very small yellow-headed titmouse (*Auriparus flaviceps*) found from Texas to California and southward

**ver·dure** \'vər-jər *also* -dyər\ *noun* [Middle English, from Middle French, from *verd* green] (14th century)

**1** : the greenness of growing vegetation; *also* : such vegetation itself

**2** : a condition of health and vigor

— **ver·dur·ous** \'vərj-rəs; 'ver-jə-rəs, -dyə-\ *adjective*

**ver·dured** \'vər-jərd *also* -dyərd\ *adjective* (circa 1718)

: covered with verdure

**¹verge** \'vərj\ *noun* [Middle English, from Middle French, from Latin *virga* rod, stripe] (15th century)

**1 a** (1) : a rod or staff carried as an emblem of authority or symbol of office (2) *obsolete* : a stick or wand held by a person being admitted to tenancy while he swears fealty **b** : the spindle of a watch balance; *especially* : a spindle with pallets in an old vertical escapement **c** : the male intromittent organ of any of various invertebrates

**2 a** : something that borders, limits, or bounds: as (1) : an outer margin of an object or structural part (2) : the edge of roof covering (as tiling) projecting over the gable of a roof (3) *British* : a paved or planted strip of land at the edge of a road : SHOULDER **b** : BRINK, THRESHOLD ⟨a country on the *verge* of destruction —Archibald MacLeish⟩

**²verge** *intransitive verb* **verged; verg·ing** (1787)

**1** : to be contiguous

**2** : to be on the verge or border

**³verge** *intransitive verb* **verged; verg·ing** [Latin *vergere* to bend, incline — more at WRENCH] (1610)

**1 a** *of the sun* : to incline toward the horizon : SINK **b** : to move or extend in some direction or toward some condition

**2** : to be in transition or change

**verg·er** \'vər-jər\ *noun* (15th century)

**1** *chiefly British* : an attendant that carries a verge (as before a bishop or justice)

**2** : a church official who keeps order during services or serves as an usher or a sacristan

**ve·rid·i·cal** \və-'ri-di-kəl\ *adjective* [Latin *veridicus*, from *verus* true + *dicere* to say — more at VERY, DICTION] (1653)

**1** : TRUTHFUL, VERACIOUS ⟨tried . . . to supply . . . a *veridical* background to the events and people portrayed —Laura Krey⟩

**2** : not illusory : GENUINE ⟨it is assumed that . . . perception is *veridical* —George Lakoff⟩

— **ve·rid·i·cal·i·ty** \-ˌri-də-'ka-lə-tē\ *noun*
— **ve·rid·i·cal·ly** \-'ri-di-k(ə-)lē\ *adverb*

**ver·i·fi·able** \ˌver-ə-'fī-ə-bəl\ *adjective* (1593)

: capable of being verified

— **ver·i·fi·abil·i·ty** \ˌver-ə-ˌfī-ə-'bi-lə-tē\ *noun*
— **ver·i·fi·able·ness** *noun*

**ver·i·fi·ca·tion** \ˌver-ə-fə-'kā-shən\ *noun* (1523)

: the act or process of verifying : the state of being verified

**ver·i·fy** \'ver-ə-ˌfī\ *transitive verb* **-fied; -fy·ing** [Middle English *verifien*, from Middle French *verifier*, from Medieval Latin *verificare*, from Latin *verus* true] (14th century)

**1** : to confirm or substantiate in law by oath

**2** : to establish the truth, accuracy, or reality of

**synonym** see CONFIRM

— **ver·i·fi·er** \-ˌfī-(ə)r\ *noun*

**ver·i·ly** \'ver-ə-lē\ *adverb* [Middle English *verraily*, from *verray* very] (14th century)

**1** : in truth : CERTAINLY

**2** : TRULY, CONFIDENTLY

**veri·sim·i·lar** \ˌver-ə-'si-mə-lər, -'sim-lər\ *adjective* [Latin *verisimilis*] (1681)

**1** : having the appearance of truth : PROBABLE

**2** : depicting realism (as in art or literature)

— **veri·sim·i·lar·ly** *adverb*

**veri·si·mil·i·tude** \-sə-'mi-lə-ˌtüd, -ˌtyüd\ *noun* [Latin *verisimilitudo*, from *verisimilis* verisimilar, from *veri similis* like the truth] (1603)

**1** : the quality or state of being verisimilar

**2** : something verisimilar

— **veri·si·mil·i·tu·di·nous** \-ˌmi-lə-'tüd-nəs, -'tü-dᵊn-əs, -'tyü-\ *adjective*

**ve·rism** \'ver-ˌi-zəm, 'ver-\ *noun* [Italian *verismo*, from *vero* true, from Latin *verus*] (1892)

: artistic use of contemporary everyday material in preference to the heroic or legendary especially in grand opera

— **ve·rist** \-ist\ *noun or adjective*
— **ve·ris·tic** \vir-'is-tik, ver-\ *adjective*

**ve·ris·mo** \vā-'rēz-(ˌ)mō\ *noun* [Italian] (circa 1908)

: VERISM; *also* : REALISM 3

**ver·i·ta·ble** \'ver-ə-tə-bəl\ *adjective* [Middle English, from Middle French, from *verité*] (15th century)

: being in fact the thing named and not false, unreal, or imaginary — often used to stress the aptness of a metaphor ⟨a *veritable* mountain of references⟩

— **ver·i·ta·ble·ness** *noun*
— **ver·i·ta·bly** \-blē\ *adverb*

**vé·ri·té** \ˌver-ə-'tā\ *noun* [*cinema verité*] (1966)

: the art or technique of filming (as a motion picture) so as to convey candid realism

**ver·i·ty** \'ver-ə-tē\ *noun, plural* **-ties** [Middle English *verite*, from Middle French *verité*, from Latin *veritat-, veritas*, from *verus* true] (14th century)

**1** : the quality or state of being true or real

**2** : something (as a statement) that is true; *especially* : a fundamental and inevitably true value ⟨such eternal *verities* as honor, love, and patriotism⟩

**3** : the quality or state of being truthful or honest ⟨the king-becoming graces, as justice, *verity* —Shakespeare⟩

**ver·juice** \'vər-ˌjüs\ *noun* [Middle English *verjus*, from Middle French, from *vert jus*, literally, green juice] (14th century)

**1** : the sour juice of crab apples or of unripe fruit (as grapes or apples); *also* : an acid liquor made from verjuice

**2** : acidity of disposition or manner

**ver·meil** *noun* [Middle French, from *vermeil*, adjective — more at VERMILION] (1590)

**1** \'vər-məl, -ˌmāl\ : VERMILION

**2** \ver-'mā\ : gilded silver

— **vermeil** *adjective*

**vermi-** *combining form* [New Latin, from Late Latin, from Latin *vermis* — more at WORM]

: worm ⟨*vermiform*⟩

**ver·mi·cel·li** \ˌvər-mə-'che-lē, -'se-\ *noun* [Italian, from plural of *vermicello*, diminutive of *verme* worm, from Latin *vermis*] (1669)

: pasta made in long solid strings smaller in diameter than spaghetti

**ver·mi·cide** \'vər-mə-ˌsīd\ *noun* (1849)

: an agent that destroys worms

**ver·mic·u·lar** \(ˌ)vər-'mi-kyə-lər\ *adjective* [New Latin *vermicularis*, from Latin *vermiculus*, diminutive of *vermis*] (1672)

**1 a :** resembling a worm in form or motion **b** : VERMICULATE

**2 :** of, relating to, or caused by worms

**ver·mic·u·late** \-lət\ *or* **ver·mic·u·lat·ed** \-,lā-təd\ *adjective* [Latin *vermiculatus,* from *vermiculus*] (1605)

**1 :** TORTUOUS, INVOLUTE

**2 :** full of worms : WORM-EATEN

**3 a :** VERMIFORM **b :** marked with irregular fine lines or with wavy impressed lines ⟨a *vermiculate* nut⟩

— **ver·mic·u·la·tion** \-,mi-kyə-'lā-shən\ *noun*

**ver·mic·u·lite** \(,)vər-'mi-kyə-,līt\ *noun* [Latin *vermiculus* little worm] (1824)

**:** any of various micaceous minerals that are hydrous silicates resulting usually from expansion of the granules of mica at high temperatures to give a lightweight highly water-absorbent material

**ver·mi·form** \'vər-mə-,form\ *adjective* [New Latin *vermiformis,* from *vermi-* + *-formis* -form] (circa 1730)

**:** resembling a worm in shape

**vermiform appendix** *noun* (1778)

**:** a narrow blind tube usually about three to four inches (7.6 to 10.2 centimeters) long that extends from the cecum in the lower right-hand part of the abdomen

**ver·mi·fuge** \'vər-mə-,fyüj\ *adjective* (1697)

**:** serving to destroy or expel parasitic worms : ANTHELMINTIC

— **vermifuge** *noun*

**ver·mil·ion** *also* **ver·mil·lion** \vər-'mil-yən\ *noun* [Middle English *vermilioun,* from Old French *vermeillon,* from *vermeil,* adjective, bright red, vermilion, from Late Latin *vermiculus* kermes, from Latin, little worm] (13th century)

**1 :** a bright red pigment consisting of mercuric sulfide; *broadly* **:** any of various red pigments

**2 :** a vivid reddish orange

**ver·min** \'vər-mən\ *noun, plural* **vermin** [Middle English, from Middle French, from (assumed) Vulgar Latin *verminum,* from Latin *verminare* to be infested with maggots, have racking pains, from *vermina* racking pains] (14th century)

**1 a :** small common harmful or objectionable animals (as lice or fleas) that are difficult to control **b :** birds and mammals that prey on game **c :** animals that at a particular time and place compete (as for food) with humans or domestic animals

**2 :** an offensive person

**ver·min·ous** \'vər-mə-nəs\ *adjective* (circa 1616)

**1 :** consisting of or being vermin : NOXIOUS

**2 :** forming a breeding place for or infested by vermin : FILTHY ⟨*verminous* garbage⟩

**3 :** caused by vermin ⟨*verminous* disease⟩

**ver·mouth** \vər-'müth\ *noun* [French *vermout,* from German *Wermut* wormwood, from Old High German *wermuota* — more at WORMWOOD] (1806)

**:** a dry or sweet aperitif wine flavored with aromatic herbs and often used in mixed drinks

**¹ver·nac·u·lar** \və(r)-'na-kyə-lər\ *adjective* [Latin *vernaculus* native, from *verna* slave born in the master's house, native] (1601)

**1 a :** using a language or dialect native to a region or country rather than a literary, cultured, or foreign language **b :** of, relating to, or being a nonstandard language or dialect of a place, region, or country **c :** of, relating to, or being the normal spoken form of a language

**2 :** applied to a plant or animal in the common native speech as distinguished from the Latin nomenclature of scientific classification

**3 :** of, relating to, or characteristic of a period, place, or group; *especially* **:** of, relating to, or being the common building style of a period or place ◆

— **ver·nac·u·lar·ly** *adverb*

**²vernacular** *noun* (circa 1706)

**1 :** a vernacular language, expression, or mode of expression

**2 :** the mode of expression of a group or class

**3 :** a vernacular name of a plant or animal

**ver·nac·u·lar·ism** \və(r)-'na-kyə-lə-,ri-zəm\ *noun* (circa 1841)

**:** a vernacular word or idiom

**ver·nal** \'vər-nᵊl\ *adjective* [Latin *vernalis,* alteration of *vernus,* from *ver* spring; akin to Greek *ear* spring, Sanskrit *vasanta*] (1534)

**1 :** of, relating to, or occurring in the spring ⟨*vernal* equinox⟩ ⟨*vernal* sunshine⟩

**2 :** fresh or new like the spring; *also* **:** YOUTHFUL

— **ver·nal·ly** \-nᵊl-ē\ *adverb*

**ver·nal·i·za·tion** \,vər-nᵊl-ə-'zā-shən\ *noun* (1933)

**:** the act or process of hastening the flowering and fruiting of plants by treating seeds, bulbs, or seedlings so as to induce a shortening of the vegetative period

— **ver·nal·ize** \'vər-nᵊl-,īz\ *transitive verb*

**ver·na·tion** \(,)vər-'nā-shən\ *noun* [New Latin *vernation-, vernatio,* from Latin *vernare* to behave as in spring, from *vernus* vernal] (1793)

**:** the arrangement of foliage leaves within the bud

**Ver·ner's law** \'ver-nərz-\ *noun* [Karl A. *Verner*] (1878)

**:** a statement in historical linguistics: in medial or final position in voiced environments and when the immediately preceding vowel did not bear the principal accent in Proto-Indo-European, the Proto-Germanic voiceless fricatives *f,* þ, and χ derived from the Proto-Indo-European voiceless stops *p, t,* and *k* and the Proto-Germanic voiceless fricative *s* derived from Proto-Indo-European *s* became the voiced fricatives *b,* ð, *g,* and *z* represented in various recorded Germanic languages by *b, d, g,* and *r*

**ver·ni·cle** *or* **ver·na·cle** \'vər-ni-kəl\ *noun* [Middle English *vernicle,* from Middle French *veronique, vernicle,* from Medieval Latin *veronica*] (14th century)

**:** ²VERONICA

**¹ver·ni·er** \'vər-nē-ər\ *noun* [Pierre *Vernier*] (1766)

**1 :** a short scale made to slide along the divisions of a graduated instrument for indicating parts of divisions

**2 a :** a small auxiliary device used with a main device to obtain fine adjustment **b :** any of two or more small supplementary rocket engines or gas nozzles on a missile or a rocket vehicle for making fine adjustments in the speed or course or controlling the attitude — called also *vernier engine*

**²vernier** *adjective* (1788)

**:** having or comprising a vernier

**vernier caliper** *noun* (circa 1876)

**:** a measuring device that consists of a main scale with a fixed jaw and a sliding jaw with an attached vernier

**ver·nis·sage** \,ver-ni-'säzh\ *noun* [French, day before an exhibition opens reserved for artists to varnish and put finishing touches to their paintings, literally, varnishing, from *vernis* varnish — more at VARNISH] (1912)

**:** a private showing or preview of an art exhibition

**¹ve·ron·i·ca** \və-'rä-ni-kə\ *noun* [New Latin, genus of herbs] (1527)

**:** SPEEDWELL

**²veronica** *noun* [Medieval Latin, from *Veronica,* legendary saint of the 1st century A.D.] (circa 1700)

**:** an image of Christ's face said to have been impressed on the cloth that Saint Veronica gave him to wipe his face with on the way to his crucifixion; *also* **:** a cloth resembling the legendary one of Saint Veronica

**³veronica** *noun* [Spanish *verónica,* from Saint *Veronica*] (1926)

**:** a pase in bullfighting in which the cape is swung slowly away from the charging bull while the matador keeps his feet in the same position

**Vé·ro·nique** *also* **Ve·ro·nique** \,vā-rō-'nēk\ *adjective* [French *Véronique* Veronica] (1907)

**:** prepared or garnished with usually white seedless grapes ⟨sole *Véronique*⟩

**ver·ru·ca** \və-'rü-kə\ *noun, plural* **-cae** \-(,)kē, -,kī, -,sī\ [Latin, wart, hillock; akin to Lithuanian *viršus* summit and probably to Old English *wearte* wart — more at WART] (1565)

**1 :** a wart or warty skin lesion

**2 :** a warty elevation on a plant or animal surface

**verruca vul·ga·ris** \-,vəl-'gar-əs, -'ger-\ *noun* [New Latin, literally, common verruca] (1903)

**:** WART 1a

**ver·ru·cose** \və-'rü-,kōs\ *adjective* (1686)

**:** covered with warty elevations

**ver·sal** \'vər-səl, 'vär-\ *adjective* [short for *universal*] (1592)

*archaic* **:** ENTIRE, WHOLE ⟨as pale as any clout in the *versal* world —Shakespeare⟩

**ver·sant** \'vər-sᵊnt\ *adjective* [Latin *versant-, versans,* present participle of *versare, versari* to turn, occupy oneself, meditate] (1645)

**1** *archaic* **:** EXPERIENCED, PRACTICED

**2 :** CONVERSANT

**ver·sa·tile** \'vər-sə-tᵊl, *especially British* -,tīl\ *adjective* [French or Latin; French, from Latin *versatilis* turning easily, from *versare* to turn, frequentative of *vertere*] (1605)

**1 :** changing or fluctuating readily **:** VARIABLE ⟨a *versatile* disposition⟩

**2 :** embracing a variety of subjects, fields, or skills; *also* **:** turning with ease from one thing to another

**3 a** (1) **:** capable of turning forward or backward **:** REVERSIBLE ⟨a *versatile* toe of a bird⟩ (2) **:** capable of moving laterally and up and down ⟨*versatile* antennae⟩ **b** *of an anther* **:** having the filaments attached at or near the middle so as to swing freely

**4 :** having many uses or applications ⟨*versatile* building material⟩

— **ver·sa·tile·ly** \-tᵊl-(l)ē, -,tīl-lē\ *adverb*

— **ver·sa·tile·ness** \-tᵊl-nəs, -,tīl-nəs\ *noun*

**ver·sa·til·i·ty** \,vər-sə-'ti-lə-tē\ *noun* (circa 1755)

\ə\ **abut** \ᵊ\ **kitten** \ər\ **further** \a\ **ash** \ā\ **ace** \ä\ **mop, mar** \au̇\ **out** \ch\ **chin** \e\ **bet** \ē\ **easy** \g\ **go** \i\ **hit** \ī\ **ice** \j\ **job** \ŋ\ **sing** \ō\ **go** \ȯ\ **law** \ȯi\ **boy** \th\ **thin** \t̲h̲\ **the** \ü\ **loot** \u̇\ **foot** \y\ **yet** \zh\ **vision** *see also* Guide to Pronunciation

: the quality or state of being versatile ⟨a writer of great *versatility*⟩

**vers de so·ci·é·té** \,ver-də-,sō-sē-ə-'tā\ *noun* [French, society verse] (1796)
: witty and typically ironic light verse

**¹verse** \'vərs\ *noun* [Middle English *vers*, from Old French & Old English; both from Latin *versus*, literally, turning, from *vertere* to turn — more at WORTH] (before 12th century)
**1** : a line of metrical writing
**2 a** (1) : metrical language (2) : metrical writing distinguished from poetry especially by its lower level of intensity (3) : POETRY 2 **b** : POEM **c** : a body of metrical writing (as of a period or country)
**3** : STANZA
**4** : one of the short divisions into which a chapter of the Bible is traditionally divided

**²verse** *verb* **versed; vers·ing** (before 12th century)
*intransitive verb*
: to make verse : VERSIFY
*transitive verb*
**1** : to tell or celebrate in verse
**2** : to turn into verse

**³verse** *transitive verb* **versed; vers·ing** [back-formation from *versed*, from Latin *versatus*, past participle of *versari* to be active, be occupied (in), passive of *versare* to turn] (1673)
: to familiarize by close association, study, or experience ⟨well *versed* in the theater⟩

**vers·et** \'vər-sət, -,set; ,vər-'set\ *noun* [Middle English, from Old French, diminutive of *vers* verse] (13th century)
: a short verse especially from a sacred book (as the Koran)

**ver·si·cle** \'vər-si-kəl\ *noun* [Middle English, from Latin *versiculus*, diminutive of *versus* verse] (14th century)
**1** : a short verse or sentence (as from a psalm) said or sung by a leader in public worship and followed by a response from the people
**2** : a little verse

**ver·sic·u·lar** \,vər-'si-kyə-lər\ *adjective* [Latin *versiculus* little verse] (1812)
: of or relating to verses or versicles

**ver·si·fi·ca·tion** \,vər-sə-fə-'kā-shən\ *noun* (1603)
**1** : the making of verses
**2 a** : metrical structure : PROSODY **b** : a particular metrical structure or style
**3** : a version in verse of something originally in prose

**ver·si·fi·er** \'vər-sə-,fī(-ə)r\ *noun* (14th century)
: one that versifies; *especially* : a writer of light or inferior verse

**ver·si·fy** \-,fī\ *verb* **-fied; -fy·ing** [Middle English *versifien*, from Middle French *versifier*, from Latin *versificare*, from *versus* verse, line] (14th century)
*intransitive verb*
: to compose verses
*transitive verb*
**1** : to relate or describe in verse
**2** : to turn into verse

**ver·sion** \'vər-zhən, -shən\ *noun* [Middle French, from Medieval Latin *version-, versio* act of turning, from Latin *vertere* to turn — more at WORTH] (1582)
**1** : a translation from another language; *especially* : a translation of the Bible or a part of it
**2 a** : an account or description from a particular point of view especially as contrasted with another account **b** : an adaptation of a literary work ⟨the movie *version* of the novel⟩ **c** : an arrangement of a musical composition
**3** : a form or variant of a type or original ⟨an experimental *version* of the plane⟩
**4 a** : a condition in which an organ and especially the uterus is turned from its normal position **b** : manual turning of a fetus in the uterus to aid delivery
— **ver·sion·al** \'vərzh-nəl, 'vərsh-; 'vər-zhən°l, -shə-\ *adjective*

**vers li·bre** \ver-'lēbrᵊ\ *noun, plural* **vers li·bres** \*same*\ [French] (1902)
: FREE VERSE

**vers–li·brist** \-'lē-brist\ *noun* [French *vers-libriste*] (1916)
: a writer of free verse

**ver·so** \'vər-(,)sō\ *noun, plural* **versos** [New Latin *verso* (*folio*) the page being turned] (1839)
**1** : the side of a leaf (as of a manuscript) that is to be read second
**2** : a left-hand page — compare RECTO

**verst** \'vərst\ *noun* [French *verste* & German *Werst*; both from Russian *versta*; akin to Latin *vertere* to turn] (1555)
: a Russian unit of distance equal to 0.6629 mile (1.067 kilometers)

**ver·sus** \'vər-səs, -səz\ *preposition* [Medieval Latin, towards, against, from Latin, adverb, so as to face, from past participle of *vertere* to turn] (15th century)
**1** : AGAINST
**2** : in contrast to or as the alternative of ⟨free trade *versus* protection⟩

**vert** \'vərt\ *noun* [Middle English *verte*, from Middle French *vert*, from *vert* green — more at VERDANT] (15th century)
**1 a** : green forest vegetation especially when forming cover or providing food for deer **b** : the right or privilege (as in England) of cutting living wood or sometimes of pasturing animals in a forest
**2** : the heraldic color green

**ver·te·bra** \'vər-tə-brə, -,brā\ *noun, plural* **-brae** \-,brā, -(,)brē, -brə\ *or* **-bras** [Latin, joint, vertebra, from *vertere* to turn] (1578)
: one of the bony or cartilaginous segments composing the spinal column, consisting in some lower vertebrates of several distinct elements which never become united, and in higher vertebrates having a short more or less cylindrical body whose ends articulate by pads of elastic or cartilaginous tissue with those of adjacent vertebrae and a bony arch that encloses the spinal cord

**ver·te·bral** \,(,)vər-'tē-brəl, 'vər-tə-\ *adjective* (circa 1681)
**1** : of, relating to, or being vertebrae or the vertebral column : SPINAL
**2** : composed of or having vertebrae

**vertebral canal** *noun* (1831)
: a canal that contains the spinal cord and is delimited by the arches on the dorsal side of the vertebrae — called also *spinal canal*

**vertebral column** *noun* (1822)
: SPINAL COLUMN

**¹ver·te·brate** \'vər-tə-brət, -,brāt\ *adjective* [New Latin *vertebratus*, from Latin, jointed, from *vertebra*] (1826)
**1 a** : having a spinal column **b** : of or relating to the vertebrates
**2** : organized or constructed in orderly or developed form

**²vertebrate** *noun* [New Latin *Vertebrata*, from neuter plural of *vertebratus*] (1826)
: any of a subphylum (Vertebrata) of chordates that possess a spinal column including the mammals, birds, reptiles, amphibians, and fishes

**ver·tex** \'vər-,teks\ *noun, plural* **ver·ti·ces** \'vər-tə-,sēz\ *also* **ver·tex·es** [Latin *vertic-, vertex, vortic-, vortex* whirl, whirlpool, top of the head, summit, from *vertere* to turn] (1570)
**1 a** : the point opposite to and farthest from the base in a figure **b** : a point (as of an angle, polygon, polyhedron, graph, or network) that terminates a line or curve or comprises the intersection of two or more lines or curves **c** : a point where an axis of an ellipse, parabola, or hyperbola intersects the curve itself
**2** : the top of the head
**3** : a principal or highest point : SUMMIT ⟨the *vertex* of the hill⟩

**ver·ti·cal** \'vər-ti-kəl\ *adjective* [Middle French or Late Latin; Middle French, from Late Latin *verticalis*, from Latin *vertic-, vertex*] (1559)
**1 a** : situated at the highest point : directly overhead or in the zenith **b** *of an aerial photograph* : taken with the camera pointing straight down or nearly so
**2 a** : perpendicular to the plane of the horizon or to a primary axis : UPRIGHT **b** (1) : located at right angles to the plane of a supporting surface (2) : lying in the direction of an axis : LENGTHWISE
**3 a** : relating to, involving, or integrating economic activity from basic production to point of sale ⟨*vertical* monopoly⟩ **b** : of, relating to, or comprising persons of different status ⟨the *vertical* arrangement of society⟩ ☆
— **vertical** *noun*
— **ver·ti·cal·i·ty** \,vər-tə-'ka-lə-tē\ *noun*
— **ver·ti·cal·ly** \'vər-ti-k(ə-)lē\ *adverb*
— **ver·ti·cal·ness** \-kəl-nəs\ *noun*

**vertical angle** *noun* (1571)
: either of two angles lying on opposite sides of two intersecting lines

**vertical circle** *noun* (1559)
: a great circle of the celestial sphere whose plane is perpendicular to that of the horizon

**vertical file** *noun* (1906)
: a collection of articles (as pamphlets and clippings) that is maintained (as in a library) to answer brief questions or to provide points of information not easily located

**vertical union** *noun* (1933)
: INDUSTRIAL UNION

**ver·ti·cil** \'vər-tə-,sil\ *noun* [New Latin *verticillus*, diminutive of Latin *vertex* whirl] (1793)
: a circle of similar parts (as flowers around a stem or sensory hairs around an antennal joint) about the same point on the axis : WHORL

**ver·ti·cil·late** \,vər-tə-'si-lət\ *adjective* (circa 1793)
: arranged in verticils

**ver·ti·cil·li·um wilt** \,vər-tə-'si-lē-əm-\ *noun* [New Latin *Verticillium*, from *verticillus*] (1916)
: a wilt disease of various plants that is caused by a soil-borne imperfect fungus (genus *Verticillium*)

**ver·tig·i·nous** \(,)vər-'ti-jə-nəs\ *adjective* [Latin *vertiginosus*, from *vertigin-, vertigo*] (1608)
**1 a** : characterized by or suffering from vertigo or dizziness **b** : inclined to frequent and often pointless change : INCONSTANT
**2** : causing or tending to cause dizziness ⟨the *vertiginous* heights⟩
**3** : marked by turning : ROTARY ⟨the *vertiginous* motion of the earth⟩
— **ver·tig·i·nous·ly** *adverb*

**ver·ti·go** \'vər-ti-,gō\ *noun, plural* **-goes** *or* **-gos** [Latin *vertigin-, vertigo*, from *vertere* to turn] (1528)
**1 a** : a disordered state in which the individual or the individual's surroundings seem to whirl dizzily **b** : a dizzy confused state of mind
**2** : disordered vertiginous movement as a symptom of disease in lower animals; *also* : a disease (as gid) causing this

**ver·tu** \,vər-'tü, ver-\ *variant of* VIRTU

---

☆ **SYNONYMS**
**Vertical, perpendicular, plumb** mean being at right angles to a base line. VERTICAL suggests a line or direction rising straight upward toward a zenith ⟨the side of the cliff is almost *vertical*⟩. PERPENDICULAR may stress the straightness of a line making a right angle with any other line, not necessarily a horizontal one ⟨the parallel bars are *perpendicular* to the support posts⟩. PLUMB stresses an exact verticality determined (as with a plumb line) by earth's gravity ⟨make sure that the wall is *plumb*⟩.

**ver·vain** \'vər-ˌvān\ *noun* [Middle English *verveine,* from Middle French, from Latin *verbena* leafy branch; akin to Latin *verber* rod, Lithuanian *virbas,* and perhaps to Greek *rhabdos* rod] (14th century)
: any of a genus (*Verbena* of the family Verbenaceae, the vervain family) of chiefly American plants that have bracted spicate flowers, a regular corolla with a 5-lobed limb, and a fruit that separates into four nutlets

**verve** \'vərv\ *noun* [French, fantasy, caprice, animation, from Latin *verba,* plural of *verbum* word — more at WORD] (1697)
**1** *archaic* : special ability or talent
**2 a** : the spirit and enthusiasm animating artistic composition or performance : VIVACITY **b** : ENERGY, VITALITY

**ver·vet monkey** \'vər-vət-\ *noun* [French *vervet*] (1893)
: a monkey of any of several African races of a guenon (*Cercopithecus aethiops*) having the face, chin, hands, and feet black — called also *vervet*

**vervet monkey**

**¹very** \'ver-ē\ *adjective* **veri·er; -est** [Middle English *verray, verry,* from Old French *verai,* from (assumed) Vulgar Latin *veracus,* alteration of Latin *verac-, verax* truthful, from *verus* true; akin to Old English *wǣr* true, Old High German *wāra* trust, care, Greek *ēra* (accusative) favor] (13th century)
**1 a** : properly entitled to the name or designation : TRUE ⟨the fierce hatred of a *very* woman —J. M. Barrie⟩ **b** : ACTUAL, REAL ⟨the *very* blood and bone of our grammar —H. L. Smith (died 1972)⟩ **c** : SIMPLE, PLAIN ⟨in *very* truth⟩
**2 a** : being exactly as stated ⟨the *very* heart of the city⟩ **b** : exactly suitable or necessary ⟨the *very* thing for the purpose⟩
**3 a** : ABSOLUTE, UTTER ⟨the *veriest* fool alive⟩ **b** : UNQUALIFIED, SHEER ⟨the *very* shame of it⟩
**4** — used as an intensive especially to emphasize identity ⟨before my *very* eyes⟩
**5** : MERE, BARE ⟨the *very* thought terrified him⟩
**6** : being the same one : SELFSAME ⟨the *very* man I saw⟩
**7** : SPECIAL, PARTICULAR ⟨the *very* essence of truth is plainness and brightness —John Milton⟩
**synonym** see SAME

**²very** *adverb* (14th century)
**1** : in actual fact : TRULY ⟨the *very* best store in town⟩ ⟨told the *very* same story⟩
**2** : to a high degree : EXCEEDINGLY ⟨*very* hot⟩ ⟨didn't hurt *very* much⟩ ■

**very hard** *adjective* (circa 1943)
*of cheese* : suitable chiefly for grating

**very high frequency** *noun* (1920)
: a radio frequency between ultrahigh frequency and high frequency — see RADIO FREQUENCY table

**Ve·ry light** \'ver-ē-, 'vir-ē-\ *noun* [Edward W. *Very* (died 1910) American naval officer] (1917)
: a pyrotechnic signal in a system of signaling using white or colored balls of fire projected from a special pistol

**very low-density lipoprotein** *noun* (1977)
: VLDL

**very low frequency** *noun* (1938)
: a radio frequency between low frequency and voice frequency — see RADIO FREQUENCY table

**Ve·ry pistol** \'ver-ē-, 'vir-ē-\ *noun* (1915)
: a pistol for firing Very lights

**Very Reverend** \'ver-ē-\ (circa 1828)
— used as a title for various ecclesiastical officials (as cathedral deans and canons, rectors

of Roman Catholic colleges and seminaries, and superiors of some religious houses)

**ves·i·cal** \'ve-si-kəl\ *adjective* [Latin *vesica* bladder — more at VENTER] (1797)
: of or relating to the urinary bladder ⟨*vesical* burning⟩

**ves·i·cant** \-kənt\ *noun* [Latin *vesica* bladder, blister] (1661)
: an agent (as a drug or a chemical weapon) that induces blistering
— **vesicant** *adjective*

**ves·i·cle** \'ve-si-kəl\ *noun* [Middle French *vesicule,* from Latin *vesicula* small bladder, blister, from diminutive of *vesica*] (1578)
**1 a** : a membranous and usually fluid-filled pouch (as a cyst, vacuole, or cell) in a plant or animal **b** : a small abnormal elevation of the outer layer of skin enclosing a watery liquid : BLISTER **c** : a pocket of embryonic tissue that is the beginning of an organ
**2** : a small cavity in a mineral or rock

**ve·sic·u·lar** \və-'si-kyə-lər, ve-\ *adjective* [New Latin *vesicula* vesicle, from Latin, small bladder] (1715)
**1** : containing, composed of, or characterized by vesicles ⟨*vesicular* lava⟩
**2** : having the form or structure of a vesicle
**3** : of or relating to vesicles
— **ve·sic·u·lar·i·ty** \-ˌsi-kyə-'lar-ə-tē\ *noun*

**vesicular stomatitis** *noun* (circa 1903)
: an acute virus disease especially of various domesticated animals (as horses and cows) that is marked by erosive blisters in and about the mouth and that much resembles foot-and-mouth disease

**ve·sic·u·late** \və-'si-kyə-ˌlāt, ve-\ *verb* **-lated; -lat·ing** (1865)
*transitive verb*
: to make vesicular
*intransitive verb*
: to become vesicular
— **ve·sic·u·la·tion** \-ˌsi-kyə-'lā-shən\ *noun*

**¹ves·per** \'ves-pər\ *noun* [Middle English, from Latin, evening, evening star — more at WEST] (14th century)
**1** *capitalized, archaic* : EVENING STAR
**2** : a vesper bell
**3** *archaic* : EVENING, EVENTIDE

**²vesper** *adjective* (1791)
: of or relating to vespers or the evening

**ves·per·al** \'ves-p(ə-)rəl\ *adjective* (circa 1623)
: VESPER ⟨a *vesperal* breeze⟩

**ves·pers** \'ves-pərz\ *noun plural but singular or plural in construction, often capitalized* [French *vespres,* from Medieval Latin *vesperae,* from Latin, plural of *vespera* evening; akin to Latin *vesper* evening star] (1611)
**1** : the sixth of the canonical hours that is said or sung in the late afternoon
**2** : a service of evening worship

**ves·per·til·ian** \ˌves-pər-'ti-lē-ən, -'til-yən\ *adjective* [Latin *vespertilio* bat, from *vesper*] (1874)
: of, relating to, or resembling a bat ⟨flaunts *vespertilian* wing and cloven hoof —Robert Graves⟩

**ves·per·tine** \'ves-pər-ˌtīn\ *adjective* [Latin *vespertinus,* from *vesper*] (1502)
**1** : of, relating to, or occurring in the evening ⟨*vespertine* shadows⟩
**2** : active, flowering, or flourishing in the evening : CREPUSCULAR

**ves·pid** \'ves-pəd\ *noun* [ultimately from Latin *vespa* wasp — more at WASP] (circa 1900)
: any of a cosmopolitan family (Vespidae) of chiefly social wasps that usually live in colonies like bees
— **vespid** *adjective*

**ves·pine** \'ves-ˌpīn\ *adjective* [Latin *vespa* wasp] (1843)
: of, relating to, or resembling wasps and especially vespid wasps

**ves·sel** \'ve-səl\ *noun* [Middle English, from Middle French *vaissel,* from Late Latin *vascellum,* diminutive of Latin *vas* vase, vessel] (14th century)
**1 a** : a container (as a hogshead, bottle, kettle, cup, or bowl) for holding something **b** : a person into whom some quality (as grace) is infused ⟨a child of light, a true *vessel* of the Lord —H. J. Laski⟩
**2** : a watercraft bigger than a rowboat; *especially* : SHIP 1
**3 a** : a tube or canal (as an artery) in which a body fluid is contained and conveyed or circulated **b** : a conducting tube in the xylem of a vascular plant formed by the fusion and loss of end walls of a series of cells

**¹vest** \'vest\ *verb* [Middle English, from Middle French *vestir* to clothe, invest, from Latin *vestire* to clothe, from *vestis* clothing, garment — more at WEAR] (15th century)
*transitive verb*
**1 a** : to place or give into the possession or discretion of some person or authority; *especially* : to give to a person a legally fixed immediate right of present or future enjoyment of (as an estate) **b** : to grant or endow with a particular authority, right, or property ⟨the retirement plan *vests* the workers absolutely with the company's contribution after 10 years of continuous employment⟩
**2** : to clothe with or as if with a garment; *especially* : to robe in ecclesiastical vestments
*intransitive verb*
**1** : to become legally vested
**2** : to put on garments; *especially* : to put on ecclesiastical vestments

**²vest** *noun* [French *veste,* from Italian, from Latin *vestis* garment] (1613)
**1** *archaic* **a** : a loose outer garment : ROBE **b** : CLOTHING, GARB
**2 a** : a man's sleeveless garment for the upper body usually worn under a suit coat; *also* : a similar garment for women **b** : a protective usually sleeveless garment (as a life preserver) that extends to the waist **c** : an insulated sleeveless waist-length garment often worn under or in place of a coat
**3 a** *chiefly British* : a man's sleeveless undershirt **b** : a knitted undershirt for women

---

□ USAGE
**very** The propriety of using *very* to modify a participial adjective, as in "very pleased" or "very flattering," has been the subject of considerable speculation since the 1870s. *Very,* an intensifier, does not modify verbs—you can "try hard" but you can't "try very"—and it was thus a matter of dispute whether *very* could modify participles. Many commentators believe that *very much* rather than *very* alone should be used. However, the question is not one of propriety, but of grammar. Participles have been moving into the class of adjectives since at least the 17th century. And one of the surest signs that a participle is established as an adjective is its being modified by *very.* The transition from verb form to adjective is a gradual one, and at any given time there will be participles that will sound right with *very* to some people and wrong to others. So writers have to trust their ear and use *very* where it sounds right and *very much* (or something else) where *very* alone sounds wrong. Dictionaries will not always be helpful. Participial adjectives are often omitted when their meaning is simply the meaning of the verb so that the space they would take up can be devoted to more words.

---

\ə\ **abut** \ᵊ\ **kitten** \ər\ **further** \a\ **ash** \ā\ **ace**
\ä\ **mop, mar** \au̇\ **out** \ch\ **chin** \e\ **bet** \ē\ **easy**
\g\ **go** \i\ **hit** \ī\ **ice** \j\ **job** \ŋ\ **sing** \ō\ **go**
\ȯ\ **law** \ȯi\ **boy** \th\ **thin** \t̵h\ **the** \ü\ **loot** \u̇\ **foot**
\y\ **yet** \zh\ **vision** *see also* Guide to Pronunciation

**4 :** a plain or decorative piece used to fill in the front neckline of a woman's outer garment (as a waist, coat, or gown)
— **vest·like** \-,līk\ *adjective*
**ves·ta** \'ves-tə\ *noun* [Latin *Vesta*]
**1** *capitalized* **:** the Roman goddess of the hearth — compare HESTIA
**2 :** a short match with a shank of wax-coated threads; *also* **:** a short wooden match
¹**ves·tal** \'ves-tᵊl\ *adjective* (15th century)
**1 :** of or relating to the Roman goddess Vesta
**2 a :** of or relating to a vestal virgin **b :** CHASTE
²**vestal** *noun* (1549)
**:** VESTAL VIRGIN
**vestal virgin** *noun* (1600)
**1 :** a virgin consecrated to the Roman goddess Vesta and to the service of watching the sacred fire perpetually kept burning on her altar
**2 :** a chaste woman
**vest·ed** \'ves-təd\ *adjective* (1766)
**1 :** fully and unconditionally guaranteed as a legal right, benefit, or privilege ⟨the *vested* benefits of the pension plan⟩
**2 :** having a vest ⟨a *vested* suit⟩
**vested interest** *noun* (1818)
**1 a :** an interest (as a title to an estate) carrying a legal right of present or future enjoyment **b :** a right vested in an employee under a pension plan
**2 :** a special concern or stake in maintaining or influencing a condition, arrangement, or action especially for selfish ends
**3 :** one having a vested interest in something; *specifically* **:** a group enjoying benefits from an existing economic or political privilege
**vest·ee** \ve-'stē\ *noun* (1915)
**1 :** DICKEY; *especially* **:** one made to resemble a vest and worn under a coat
**2 :** VEST 4
**ves·ti·ary** \'ves-tē-,er-ē, 'vesh-chē-\ *noun* [Middle English *vestiarie*, from Middle French, vestry — more at VESTRY] (15th century)
**1 :** a room where clothing is kept
**2 :** CLOTHING, RAIMENT
**ves·tib·u·lar** \ve-'sti-byə-lər\ *adjective* (circa 1839)
**:** of, relating to, or functioning as a vestibule
**ves·ti·bule** \'ves-tə-,byü(ə)l\ *noun* [Latin *vestibulum*] (1728)
**1 :** any of various bodily cavities especially when serving as or resembling an entrance to some other cavity or space: as **a :** the central cavity of the bony labyrinth of the ear or the parts of the membranous labyrinth that it contains **b :** the part of the left ventricle below the aortic orifice **c :** the space between the labia minora containing the orifice of the urethra **d :** the part of the mouth cavity outside the teeth and gums
**2 a :** a passage, hall, or room between the outer door and the interior of a building **:** LOBBY **b :** an enclosed entrance at the end of a railway passenger car
**3 :** a course that offers access (as to something new)
— **ves·ti·buled** \-,byü(ə)ld\ *adjective*
**vestibule school** *noun* (1918)
**:** a school organized in an industrial plant to train new workers in specific skills
**ves·tib·u·lo·co·chle·ar nerve** \ve-,sti-byə-lō-'kō-klē-ər-, -'kä-\ *noun* (1962)
**:** AUDITORY NERVE
**ves·tige** \'ves-tij\ *noun* [French, from Latin *vestigium* footstep, footprint, track, vestige] (1602)
**1 a** (1) **:** a trace, mark, or visible sign left by something (as an ancient city or a condition or practice) vanished or lost (2) **:** the smallest quantity or trace **:** FOOTPRINT 1
**2 :** a bodily part or organ that is small and degenerate or imperfectly developed in comparison to one more fully developed in an earlier stage of the individual, in a past generation, or

in closely related forms
*synonym* see TRACE
— **ves·ti·gial** \ve-'sti-jē-əl, -jəl\ *adjective*
— **ves·ti·gial·ly** *adverb*
**vest·ing** \'ves-tiŋ\ *noun* (1944)
**:** the conveying to an employee of the inalienable right to share in a pension fund especially in the event of termination of employment prior to the normal retirement age; *also* **:** the right so conveyed
**vest·ment** \'ves(t)-mənt\ *noun* [Middle English *vestement*, from Middle French, from Latin *vestimentum*, from *vestire* to clothe] (14th century)
**1 a :** an outer garment; *especially* **:** a robe of ceremony or office **b** *plural* **:** CLOTHING, GARB
**2 :** a covering resembling a garment
**3 :** one of the articles of the ceremonial attire and insignia worn by ecclesiastical officiants and assistants as indicative of their rank and appropriate to the rite being celebrated
— **vest·men·tal** \ves(t)-'men-tᵊl\ *adjective*
**vest–pocket** *adjective* (1848)
**1 :** adapted to fit into the vest pocket ⟨a *vest-pocket* edition of a book⟩
**2 :** of very small size or scope
**vest–pocket park** *noun* (1966)
**:** a very small urban park
**ves·try** \'ves-trē\ *noun, plural* **vestries** [Middle English *vestrie*, probably modification of Middle French *vestiarie*, from Medieval Latin *vestiarium*, from Latin *vestire*; from its use as a robing room for the clergy] (14th century)
**1 a :** SACRISTY **b :** a room used for church meetings and classes
**2 a :** the business meeting of an English parish **b :** an elective body in an Episcopal parish composed of the rector and a group of elected parishioners administering the temporal affairs of the parish
**ves·try·man** \-trē-mən\ *noun* (1614)
**:** a member of a vestry
¹**ves·ture** \'ves-chər, 'vesh-\ *noun* [Middle English, from Middle French, from *vestir* to clothe — more at VEST] (14th century)
**1 a :** a covering garment (as a robe or vestment) **b :** CLOTHING, APPAREL
**2 :** something that covers like a garment
²**vesture** *transitive verb* **ves·tured; ves·tur·ing** (1555)
**:** to cover with vesture **:** CLOTHE
**ve·su·vi·an** \və-'sü-vē-ən\ *noun* [*Vesuvian*] (1853)
**:** a match used especially formerly for lighting cigars
**Ve·su·vi·an** \və-'sü-vē-ən\ *adjective* (1673)
**1 :** of, relating to, or resembling the volcano Vesuvius
**2 :** marked by sudden outbursts ⟨has a *Vesuvian* temper, but quickly controls himself —Sidney Shalett⟩
**ve·su·vi·an·ite** \-vē-ə-,nīt\ *noun* (circa 1888)
**:** IDOCRASE
¹**vet** \'vet\ *noun* (1862)
**:** VETERINARIAN, VETERINARY
²**vet** *transitive verb* **vet·ted; vet·ting** (1891)
**1 a :** to provide veterinary care for (an animal) or medical care for (a person) **b :** to subject (a person or animal) to a physical examination or checkup
**2 :** to subject to expert appraisal or correction **:** EVALUATE
³**vet** *adjective or noun* (1848)
**:** VETERAN
**vetch** \'vech\ *noun* [Middle English *vecche*, from Old North French *veche*, from Latin *vicia;* perhaps akin to Latin *vincire* to bind] (14th century)
**:** any of a genus (*Vicia*) of herbaceous twining leguminous plants including some grown for fodder and green manure
**vetch·ling** \-liŋ\ *noun* (1578)
**:** any of various leguminous herbs (genus *Lathyrus* and especially *L. pratensis*)
**vet·er·an** \'ve-tə-rən, 've-trən\ *noun* [Latin *veteranus*, from *veteranus*, adjective, old, of

long experience, from *veter-, vetus* old — more at WETHER] (1509)
**1 a :** an old soldier of long service **b :** a former member of the armed forces
**2 :** a person of long experience in some occupation or skill (as politics or the arts)
— **veteran** *adjective*
**Veterans Day** *noun* (1952)
**:** November 11 set aside in commemoration of the end of hostilities in 1918 and 1945 and observed as a legal holiday in the U.S. to honor the veterans of the armed forces
**veterans' preference** *noun* (circa 1941)
**:** preferential treatment given qualified veterans of the U.S. armed forces under federal or state law; *specifically* **:** special consideration (as by allowance of points) on a civil service examination
**vet·er·i·nar·i·an** \,ve-tə-rə-'ner-ē-ən, ,ve-trə-, ,ve-tᵊn-\ *noun* (1646)
**:** a person qualified and authorized to practice veterinary medicine
¹**vet·er·i·nary** \'ve-tə-rə-,ner-ē, 've-trə-, 've-tᵊn-\ *adjective* [Latin *veterinarius* of beasts of burden, from *veterinae* beasts of burden, from feminine plural of *veterinus* of beasts of burden; akin to Latin *veter-, vetus* old] (1790)
**:** of, relating to, or being the science and art of prevention, cure, or alleviation of disease and injury in animals and especially domestic animals
²**veterinary** *noun, plural* **-nar·ies** (1861)
**:** VETERINARIAN
**veterinary surgeon** *noun* (circa 1802)
*British* **:** VETERINARIAN
**vet·i·ver** \'ve-tə-vər\ *noun* [French *vétiver*, from Tamil *veṭṭivēr*] (circa 1858)
**:** an East Indian grass (*Vetiveria zizanioides*) cultivated in warm regions especially for its fragrant roots which are used especially in woven goods (as mats) and in perfumes; *also* **:** its root
¹**ve·to** \'vē-(,)tō\ *noun, plural* **vetoes** [Latin, I forbid, from *vetare* to forbid] (1629)
**1 :** an authoritative prohibition **:** INTERDICTION
**2 a :** a power of one department or branch of a government to forbid or prohibit finally or provisionally the carrying out of projects attempted by another department; *especially* **:** a power vested in a chief executive to prevent permanently or temporarily the enactment of measures passed by a legislature **b** (1) **:** the exercise of such authority (2) **:** a message communicating the reasons of an executive and especially the president of the U.S. for vetoing a proposed law
²**veto** *transitive verb* (1706)
**:** to refuse to admit or approve **:** PROHIBIT; *also*
**:** to refuse assent to (a legislative bill) so as to prevent enactment or cause reconsideration
— **ve·to·er** \-,tō-(ə)r\ *noun*
**ve·to–proof** \-,prüf\ *adjective* (1972)
**:** having enough potential votes to be enacted over a veto or to override vetoes consistently ⟨a *veto-proof* bill⟩
**vex** \'veks\ *transitive verb* **vexed** *also* **vext; vex·ing** [Middle English, from Middle French *vexer*, from Latin *vexare* to agitate, harry; probably akin to Latin *vehere* to convey — more at WAY] (15th century)
**1 a :** to bring trouble, distress, or agitation to ⟨the restaurant is *vexed* by slow service⟩ **b :** to bring physical distress to ⟨a headache *vexed* him all morning⟩ **c :** to irritate or annoy by petty provocations **:** HARASS ⟨*vexed* by the children⟩ **d :** PUZZLE, BAFFLE ⟨a problem to *vex* the keenest wit⟩
**2 :** to shake or toss about
*synonym* see ANNOY
**vex·a·tion** \vek-'sā-shən\ *noun* (15th century)
**1 :** the act of harassing or vexing **:** TROUBLING
**2 :** the quality or state of being vexed **:** IRRITATION
**3 :** a cause of trouble **:** AFFLICTION
**vex·a·tious** \-shəs\ *adjective* (1534)

**1 a** : causing vexation : DISTRESSING **b** : intended to harass
**2** : full of disorder or stress : TROUBLED
— **vex·a·tious·ly** adverb
— **vex·a·tious·ness** noun
**vexed** \'vekst\ adjective (1657)
: debated or discussed at length ⟨a vexed question⟩
**vexed·ly** \'vek-səd-lē, 'vekst-lē\ adverb (1748)
: with vexation
**vex·il·lol·o·gy** \,vek-sə-'lä-lə-jē\ noun [Latin vexillum] (1959)
: the study of flags
— **vex·il·lo·log·ic** \(,)vek-,si-lə-'lä-jik\ or **vex·il·lo·log·i·cal** \-'lä-ji-kəl\ adjective
— **vex·il·lol·o·gist** \,vek-sə-'lä-lə-jist\ noun
**vex·il·lum** \vek-'si-ləm\ noun, plural **-la** \-lə\ [Latin; akin to Latin velum curtain, awning] (1726)
**1** : a square flag of the ancient Roman cavalry
**2** : the web or vane of a feather
**via** \'vī-ə, 'vē-ə\ preposition [Latin, ablative of via way — more at WAY] (1779)
**1** : by way of
**2** : through the medium or agency of; also : by means of
**vi·a·ble** \'vī-ə-bəl\ adjective [French, from Middle French, from vie life, from Latin vita — more at VITAL] (circa 1832)
**1** : capable of living; especially : capable of surviving outside the mother's womb without artificial support ⟨the normal human fetus is usually viable by the end of the seventh month⟩
**2** : capable of growing or developing ⟨viable seeds⟩ ⟨viable eggs⟩
**3 a** : capable of working, functioning, or developing adequately ⟨viable alternatives⟩ **b** : capable of existence and development as an independent unit ⟨the colony is now a viable state⟩ **c** (1) : having a reasonable chance of succeeding ⟨a viable candidate⟩ (2) : financially sustainable ⟨a viable enterprise⟩
— **vi·a·bil·i·ty** \,vī-ə-'bi-lə-tē\ noun
— **vi·a·bly** \'vī-ə-blē\ adverb
**via·duct** \'vī-ə-,dəkt\ noun [Latin via way, road + English aqueduct] (1816)
: a long elevated roadway usually consisting of a series of short spans supported on arches, piers, or columns

**viaduct**

**vi·al** \'vī(-ə)l\ noun [Middle English fiole, viole, from Middle French fiole, from Old Provençal fiola, from Latin phiala — more at PHIAL] (14th century)
: a small closed or closable vessel especially for liquids
**via me·dia** \,vī-ə-'mē-dē-ə; ,vē-ə-'mä-dē-ə, -'me-\ noun [Latin] (1834)
: a middle way
**vi·and** \'vī-ənd\ noun [Middle English, from Middle French viande, from Medieval Latin vivanda food, alteration of Latin vivenda, neuter plural of vivendus, gerundive of vivere to live — more at QUICK] (15th century)
**1** : an item of food; especially : a choice or tasty dish
**2** plural : PROVISIONS, FOOD
**vi·at·i·cum** \vī-'a-ti-kəm, vē-\ noun, plural **-cums** or **-ca** \-kə\ [Latin — more at VOYAGE] (1562)
**1** : the Christian Eucharist given to a person in danger of death
**2 a** : an allowance (as of transportation or supplies and money) for traveling expenses **b** : provisions for a journey
**vibe** \'vīb\ noun (1967)

: VIBRATION 4 ⟨seems to be in on every conversation, every deal, every vibe that is winging through the room —Albert Goldman⟩ — usually used in plural ⟨got bad vibes from him⟩
**vibes** \'vībz\ noun plural (1940)
: VIBRAPHONE
— **vib·ist** \'vī-bist\ noun
**vi·bra·harp** \'vī-brə-,härp\ noun [from Vibra-Harp, a trademark] (1930)
: VIBRAPHONE
— **vi·bra·harp·ist** \-,här-pist\ noun
**vi·brance** \'vī-brən(t)s\ noun (1921)
: VIBRANCY
**vi·bran·cy** \'vī-brən(t)-sē\ noun (circa 1890)
: the quality or state of being vibrant
**vi·brant** \-brənt\ adjective (1616)
**1 a** (1) : oscillating or pulsating rapidly (2) : pulsating with life, vigor, or activity ⟨a vibrant personality⟩ **b** (1) : readily set in vibration (2) : RESPONSIVE, SENSITIVE
**2** : sounding as a result of vibration : RESONANT ⟨a vibrant voice⟩
**3** : BRIGHT 4 ⟨a vibrant orange⟩
— **vi·brant·ly** adverb
**vi·bra·phone** \'vī-brə-,fōn\ noun [Latin vibrare + International Scientific Vocabulary -phone] (1926)
: a percussion instrument resembling the xylophone but having metal bars and motor-driven resonators for sustaining the tone and producing a vibrato
— **vi·bra·phon·ist** \-,fō-nist\ noun

**vibraphone**

**vi·brate** \'vī-,brāt, especially British vī-'\ verb **vi·brat·ed; vi·brat·ing** [Latin vibratus, past participle of vibrare to brandish, wave, rock — more at WIPE] (1616)
transitive verb
**1** : to swing or move to and fro
**2** : to emit with or as if with a vibratory motion
**3** : to mark or measure by oscillation ⟨a pendulum vibrating seconds⟩
**4** : to set in vibration
intransitive verb
**1 a** : to move to and fro or from side to side : OSCILLATE **b** : FLUCTUATE, VACILLATE ⟨vibrate between two choices⟩
**2** : to have an effect as or as if of vibration ⟨music, when soft voices die, vibrates in the memory —P. B. Shelley⟩
**3** : to be in a state of vibration : QUIVER
**4** : to respond sympathetically : THRILL ⟨vibrate to the opportunity⟩
**synonym** see SWING
**vi·bra·tile** \'vī-brə-t°l, -,tīl\ adjective (circa 1826)
**1** : characterized by vibration
**2** : adapted to or used in vibratory motion ⟨the vibratile organs of insects⟩
**vi·bra·tion** \vī-'brā-shən\ noun (1655)
**1 a** : a periodic motion of the particles of an elastic body or medium in alternately opposite directions from the position of equilibrium when that equilibrium has been disturbed (as when a stretched cord produces musical tones or particles of air transmit sounds to the ear) **b** : the action of vibrating : the state of being vibrated or in vibratory motion: as (1) : OSCILLATION (2) : a quivering or trembling motion : QUIVER
**2** : an instance of vibration
**3** : vacillation in opinion or action : WAVERING
**4 a** : a characteristic emanation, aura, or spirit that infuses or vitalizes someone or something and that can be instinctively sensed or experienced — often used in plural **b** : a distinctive usually emotional atmosphere capable of being sensed — usually used in plural
— **vi·bra·tion·al** \-shnəl, -shə-n°l\ adjective
— **vi·bra·tion·less** \-shən-ləs\ adjective

**vi·bra·to** \vi-'brä-(,)tō, vī-\ noun, plural **-tos** [Italian, from past participle of vibrare to vibrate, from Latin] (circa 1876)
: a slightly tremulous effect imparted to vocal or instrumental tone for added warmth and expressiveness by slight and rapid variations in pitch
— **vi·bra·to·less** \-ləs\ adjective
**vi·bra·tor** \'vī-,brā-tər\ noun (1862)
: one that vibrates or causes vibration: as **a** : a vibrating electrical apparatus used in massage or for sexual stimulation **b** : a vibrating device (as in an electric bell or buzzer)
**vi·bra·to·ry** \'vī-brə-,tōr-ē, -,tȯr-\ adjective (1728)
**1** : consisting in, capable of, or causing vibration or oscillation
**2** : characterized by vibration
**vib·rio** \'vi-brē-,ō\ noun, plural **-rios** [New Latin, Vibrion-, Vibrio, from Latin vibrare to wave] (circa 1864)
: any of a genus (Vibrio) of short rigid motile bacteria typically shaped like a comma or an S
— **vib·ri·on·ic** \,vi-brē-'ä-nik\ adjective
**vib·ri·on** \'vi-brē-,än\ noun [New Latin Vibrion-, Vibrio] (1882)
: VIBRIO; also : a motile bacterium
**vib·ri·o·sis** \,vi-brē-'ō-səs\ noun, plural **-o·ses** \-,sēz\ [New Latin, from Vibrio] (1950)
: abortion in sheep and cattle caused by a bacterium (Campylobacter fetus synonym Vibrio fetus) that invades the uterine and placental capillaries, interferes with fetal nutrition, and causes the death of the developing fetus
**vi·bris·sa** \vī-'bri-sə, və-\ noun, plural **vi·bris·sae** \vī-'bri-(,)sē; və-'bri-(,)sē, -,sī\ [Medieval Latin, from Latin vibrare] (circa 1693)
**1** : one of the stiff hairs that are located especially about the nostrils or on other parts of the face in many mammals and that often serve as tactile organs
**2** : one of the bristly feathers near the mouth of many and especially insectivorous birds that may help to prevent the escape of insects
**vi·bur·num** \vī-'bər-nəm\ noun [New Latin, from Latin, a viburnum] (circa 1731)
: any of a genus (Viburnum) of widely distributed shrubs or trees of the honeysuckle family with simple leaves and white or rarely pink cymose flowers
**vic·ar** \'vi-kər\ noun [Middle English, from Latin vicarius, from vicarius vicarious] (14th century)
**1** : one serving as a substitute or agent; specifically : an administrative deputy
**2** : an ecclesiastical agent: as **a** : a Church of England incumbent receiving a stipend but not the tithes of a parish **b** : a member of the Episcopal clergy or laity who has charge of a mission or chapel **c** : a member of the clergy who exercises a broad pastoral responsibility as the representative of a prelate
— **vic·ar·ship** \-,ship\ noun
**vic·ar·age** \'vi-k(ə-)rij\ noun (15th century)
**1** : the benefice of a vicar
**2** : the house of a vicar
**3** : VICARIATE 1
**vicar apostolic** noun, plural **vicars apostolic** (1766)
: a Roman Catholic titular bishop who administers a territory not organized as a diocese
**vic·ar·ate** \'vi-kə-rət, -,rāt\ noun (1883)
: VICARIATE
**vicar–general** noun, plural **vicars–general** (15th century)
: an administrative deputy of a Roman Catholic or Anglican bishop or of the head of a religious order
**vi·car·i·al** \vī-'ker-ē-əl, və-, -'kar-\ adjective [Latin vicarius] (1617)

\ə\ abut \°\ kitten \ər\ further \a\ ash \ā\ ace
\ä\ mop, mar \au̇\ out \ch\ chin \e\ bet \ē\ easy
\g\ go \i\ hit \ī\ ice \j\ job \ŋ\ sing \ō\ go
\ȯ\ law \ȯi\ boy \th\ thin \t͟h\ the \ü\ loot \u̇\ foot
\y\ yet \zh\ vision    see also Guide to Pronunciation

**1 :** VICARIOUS 1

**2 :** of or relating to a vicar

**vi·car·i·ance** \-ē-ən(t)s\ *noun* (1957)

**:** fragmentation of the environment (as by splitting of a tectonic plate) in contrast to dispersal as a factor in promoting biological evolution by division of large populations into isolated subpopulations — called also *vicariance biogeography*

**vi·car·i·ant** \-ē-ənt\ *adjective* [translation of German *vikarirend*, present participle of *vikarieren* to act as a substitute, from *Vikar* representative, proxy, from Middle High German *vicar*, from Latin *vicarius* substitute] (1952)

**:** of, relating to, or being the process of vicariance or organisms that evolved through this process ⟨the possible *vicariant* origin of the Antillean arthropod fauna⟩

**— vicariant** *noun*

**vi·car·i·ate** \-ē-ət\ *noun* [Medieval Latin *vicariatus*, from Latin *vicarius* vicar] (1610)

**1 :** the office, jurisdiction, or tenure of a vicar

**2 :** the office or district of a governmental administrative deputy

**vi·car·i·ous** \vī-'ker-ē-əs, və-, -'kar-\ *adjective* [Latin *vicarius*, from *vicis* change, alternation, stead — more at WEEK] (1637)

**1 a :** serving instead of someone or something else **b :** that has been delegated ⟨*vicarious* authority⟩

**2 :** performed or suffered by one person as a substitute for another or to the benefit or advantage of another **:** SUBSTITUTIONARY ⟨a *vicarious* sacrifice⟩

**3 :** experienced or realized through imaginative or sympathetic participation in the experience of another

**4 :** occurring in an unexpected or abnormal part of the body instead of the usual one ⟨bleeding from the gums sometimes occurs in the absence of the normal discharge from the uterus in *vicarious* menstruation⟩

**— vi·car·i·ous·ly** *adverb*

**— vi·car·i·ous·ness** *noun*

**Vicar of Christ** (1570)

**:** POPE 1

¹**vice** \'vīs\ *noun* [Middle English, from Old French, from Latin *vitium* fault, vice] (14th century)

**1 a :** moral depravity or corruption **:** WICKEDNESS **b :** a moral fault or failing **c :** a habitual and usually trivial defect or shortcoming **:** FOIBLE ⟨suffered from the *vice* of curiosity⟩

**2 :** BLEMISH, DEFECT

**3 :** a physical imperfection, deformity, or taint

**4 a** *often capitalized* **:** a character representing one of the vices in an English morality play **b :** BUFFOON, JESTER

**5 :** an abnormal behavior pattern in a domestic animal detrimental to its health or usefulness

**6 :** sexual immorality; *especially* **:** PROSTITUTION

**synonym** see FAULT, OFFENSE

²**vice** *chiefly British variant of* VISE

³**vice** \'vīs *also* 'vī-sē\ *preposition* [Latin, ablative of *vicis* change, alternation, stead — more at WEEK] (1770)

**:** in the place of ⟨I will preside, *vice* the absent chairman⟩; *also* **:** rather than

**vice-** \'vīs, ,vīs\ *prefix* [Middle English *vis-*, *vice-*, from Middle French, from Late Latin *vice-*, from Latin *vice*, ablative of *vicis*]

**:** one that takes the place of ⟨*vice*-chancellor⟩

**vice admiral** *noun* [Middle French *visamiral*, from *vis-* vice- + *amiral* admiral] (1520)

**:** a commissioned officer in the navy or coast guard who ranks above a rear admiral and whose insignia is three stars

**vice–chan·cel·lor** \'vīs-'chan(t)-s(ə-)lər, ,vīs-\ *noun* [Middle English *vichauncellor*, from Middle French *vischancelier*, from *vis-* + *chancelier* chancellor] (15th century)

**1 :** an officer ranking next below a chancellor and serving as deputy to the chancellor

**2 :** chief administrative officer in a British university

**3 :** a judge appointed to act for or to assist a chancellor

**vice–con·sul** \-'kän(t)-səl\ *noun* (1559)

**:** a consular officer subordinate to a consul general or to a consul

**vice·ge·ren·cy** \-'jir-ən(t)-sē\ *noun, plural* **-cies** (1596)

**:** the office or jurisdiction of a vicegerent

**vice·ge·rent** \-'jir-ənt\ *noun* [Medieval Latin *vicegerent-*, *vicegerens*, from Late Latin *vice-* + Latin *gerent-*, *gerens*, present participle of *gerere* to carry, carry on] (1536)

**:** an administrative deputy of a king or magistrate

**vi·cen·ni·al** \vī-'se-nē-əl\ *adjective* [Late Latin *vicennium* period of 20 years, from Latin *vicies* 20 times + *annus* year; akin to Latin *viginti* twenty — more at VIGESIMAL, ANNUAL] (circa 1859)

**:** occurring once every 20 years

**vice presidency** *noun* (1804)

**:** the office of vice president

**vice president** *noun* (1574)

**1 :** an officer next in rank to a president and usually empowered to serve as president in that officer's absence or disability

**2 :** any of several officers serving as a president's deputies in charge of particular locations or functions

**— vice presidential** *adjective*

**vice·re·gal** \'vīs-'rē-gəl, ,vīs-\ *adjective* (1836)

**:** of or relating to a viceroy or viceroyalty

**— vice·re·gal·ly** \-gə-lē\ *adverb*

**vice–re·gent** \-'rē-jənt\ *noun* (1556)

**:** a regent's deputy

**vice–reine** \'vīs-,rān\ *noun* [French, from *vice-* + *reine* queen, from Latin *regina*, feminine of *reg-*, *rex* king — more at ROYAL] (1823)

**1 :** the wife of a viceroy

**2 :** a woman who is a viceroy

**vice·roy** \'vīs-,rȯi\ *noun* [Middle French *viceroi*, from *vice-* + *roi* king, from Latin *reg-*, *rex*] (1524)

**1 :** the governor of a country or province who rules as the representative of a king or sovereign

**2 :** a showy American nymphalid butterfly (*Limenitis archippus*) closely mimicking the monarch in coloration but smaller

**vice·roy·al·ty** \'vīs-,rȯi(-ə)l-tē, ,vīs-'\ *noun* (1703)

**:** the office, jurisdiction, or term of service of a viceroy

**vice·roy·ship** \'vīs-,rȯi-,ship\ *noun* (1609)

**:** VICEROYALTY

**vice squad** *noun* (1905)

**:** a police squad charged with enforcement of laws concerning gambling, pornography, prostitution, and the illegal use of liquor and narcotics

**vice ver·sa** \,vī-si-'vər-sə, 'vīs-'vər-\ *adverb* [Latin] (1601)

**:** with the order changed **:** with the relations reversed **:** CONVERSELY

**vi·chys·soise** \,vi-shē-'swäz, ,vē-\ *noun* [French, from feminine of *vichyssois* of Vichy, from *Vichy*, France] (1939)

**:** a soup made of pureed leeks or onions and potatoes, cream, and chicken stock and usually served cold

**Vi·chy water** \'vi-shē-\ *noun* (circa 1858)

**:** a natural sparkling mineral water from Vichy, France; *also* **:** an imitation of or substitute for this

**vic·i·nage** \'vi-s°n-ij, 'vis-nij\ *noun* [Middle English *vesinage*, from Middle French, from *vesin* neighboring, from Latin *vicinus*] (14th century)

**:** a neighboring or surrounding district **:** VICINITY

**vic·i·nal** \'vi-s°n-əl, 'vis-nəl\ *adjective* [Latin *vicinalis*, from *vicinus* neighbor, from *vicinus*, adjective, neighboring] (circa 1623)

**1 :** of or relating to a limited district **:** LOCAL

**2 :** of, relating to, or substituted in adjacent sites in a molecule ⟨a *vicinal* disulfide group⟩

**vi·cin·i·ty** \və-'si-nə-tē\ *noun, plural* **-ties** [Middle French *vicinité*, from Latin *vicinitat-*, *vicinitas*, from *vicinus* neighboring, from *vicus* row of houses, village; akin to Gothic *weihs* village, Old Church Slavonic *vĭsĭ*, Greek *oikos, oikia* house] (1560)

**1 :** the quality or state of being near **:** PROXIMITY

**2 :** a surrounding area or district **:** NEIGHBORHOOD

**3 :** NEIGHBORHOOD 3b

**vi·cious** \'vi-shəs\ *adjective* [Middle English, from Middle French *vicieus*, from Latin *vitiosus* full of faults, corrupt, from *vitium* vice] (14th century)

**1 :** having the nature or quality of vice or immorality **:** DEPRAVED

**2 :** DEFECTIVE, FAULTY; *also* **:** INVALID

**3 :** IMPURE, NOXIOUS

**4 a :** dangerously aggressive **:** SAVAGE ⟨a *vicious* dog⟩ **b :** marked by violence or ferocity **:** FIERCE ⟨a *vicious* fight⟩

**5 :** MALICIOUS, SPITEFUL ⟨*vicious* gossip⟩

**6 :** worsened by internal causes that reciprocally augment each other ⟨a *vicious* wage-price spiral⟩ ☆

**— vi·cious·ly** *adverb*

**— vi·cious·ness** *noun*

**vicious circle** *noun* (circa 1792)

**1 :** a chain of events in which the response to one difficulty creates a new problem that aggravates the original difficulty

**2 :** an argument or definition that begs the question

**vi·cis·si·tude** \və-'si-sə-,tüd, vī-, -,tyüd\ *noun* [Middle French, from Latin *vicissitudo*, from *vicissim* in turn, from *vicis* change, alternation — more at WEEK] (circa 1576)

**1 a :** the quality or state of being changeable **:** MUTABILITY **b :** natural change or mutation visible in nature or in human affairs

**2 a :** a favorable or unfavorable event or situation that occurs by chance **:** a fluctuation of state or condition ⟨the *vicissitudes* of daily life⟩ **b :** a difficulty or hardship attendant on a way of life, a career, or a course of action and usually beyond one's control **c :** alternating change **:** SUCCESSION

**vi·cis·si·tu·di·nous** \və-,si-sə-'tüd-nəs, (,)vī-, -'tyüd-; -'tü-d°n-əs, -'tyü-\ *adjective* [Latin *vicissitudin-*, *vicissitudo*] (circa 1846)

**:** marked by or filled with vicissitudes

**vic·tim** \'vik-təm\ *noun* [Middle English *vyctym*, from Latin *victima*; perhaps akin to Old High German *wīh* holy] (15th century)

**1 :** a living being sacrificed to a deity or in the performance of a religious rite

☆ **SYNONYMS**

**Vicious, villainous, iniquitous, nefarious, corrupt, degenerate** mean highly reprehensible or offensive in character, nature, or conduct. VICIOUS may directly oppose *virtuous* in implying moral depravity, or may connote malignancy, cruelty, or destructive violence ⟨a *vicious* gangster⟩. VILLAINOUS applies to any evil, depraved, or vile conduct or characteristic ⟨a *villainous* assault⟩. INIQUITOUS implies absence of all signs of justice or fairness ⟨an *iniquitous* system of taxation⟩. NEFARIOUS suggests flagrant breaching of time-honored laws and traditions of conduct ⟨the *nefarious* rackets of organized crime⟩. CORRUPT stresses a loss of moral integrity or probity causing betrayal of principle or sworn obligations ⟨city hall was rife with *corrupt* politicians⟩. DEGENERATE suggests having sunk to an especially vicious or enervated condition ⟨a *degenerate* regime propped up by foreign powers⟩.

**2 :** one that is acted on and usually adversely affected by a force or agent ⟨the schools are *victims* of the social system⟩: as **a** (1) **:** one that is injured, destroyed, or sacrificed under any of various conditions ⟨a *victim* of cancer⟩ ⟨a *victim* of the auto crash⟩ ⟨a murder *victim*⟩ (2) **:** one that is subjected to oppression, hardship, or mistreatment ⟨a frequent *victim* of political attacks⟩ **b :** one that is tricked or duped ⟨a con man's *victim*⟩
— **vic·tim·hood** \-,hùd\ *noun*
**vic·tim·ise** *British variant of* VICTIMIZE
**vic·tim·ize** \'vik-tə-,mīz\ *transitive verb* **-ized; -iz·ing** (1830)
**1 :** to make a victim of
**2 :** to subject to deception or fraud **:** CHEAT
— **vic·tim·i·za·tion** \,vik-tə-mə-'zā-shən\ *noun*
— **vic·tim·iz·er** \'vik-tə-,mī-zər\ *noun*
**vic·tim·less** \'vik-təm-ləs\ *adjective* (1965)
**:** having no victim **:** not of a nature that may produce a complainant ⟨a *victimless* crime⟩
**vic·tim·ol·o·gy** \,vik-tə-'mä-lə-jē\ *noun* (1958)
**1 :** the study of victims and victimization
**2 :** the claim that the problems of a person or group are the result of victimization
— **vic·tim·ol·o·gist** \-jist\ *noun*
**vic·tor** \'vik-tər\ *noun* [Middle English, from Latin, from *vincere* to conquer, win; akin to Old English *wīgan* to fight, Lithuanian *veikti* to be active] (14th century)
**:** one that defeats an enemy or opponent **:** WINNER
— **victor** *adjective*
**Victor** (1942)
— a communications code word for the letter *v*
**vic·to·ria** \vik-'tōr-ē-ə, -'tòr-\ *noun* [Queen *Victoria*] (circa 1864)
**:** a low four-wheeled pleasure carriage for two with a folding top and a raised seat in front for the driver
**Victoria Cross** *noun* (1856)
**:** a bronze Maltese cross awarded to members of the British armed services for acts of remarkable valor
**Victoria Day** *noun* [Queen *Victoria*] (1901)
**1 :** formerly May 24 and now the Monday preceding May 25 observed in Canada as a legal holiday
**2 :** COMMONWEALTH DAY
¹**Vic·to·ri·an** \vik-'tōr-ē-ən, -'tòr-\ *adjective* (1839)
**1 :** of, relating to, or characteristic of the reign of Queen Victoria of England or the art, letters, or tastes of her time
**2 :** typical of the moral standards, attitudes, or conduct of the age of Victoria especially when considered stuffy or hypocritical
²**Victorian** *noun* (1876)
**1 :** a person living during Queen Victoria's reign; *especially* **:** a representative figure of that time
**2 :** a typically large and ornate house built during Queen Victoria's reign
**Vic·to·ri·ana** \(,)vik-,tōr-ē-'a-nə, -,tòr-, -'ä-, -'ā-\ *noun* [Queen *Victoria* + English *-ana*] (1940)
**:** materials concerning or characteristic of the Victorian age; *also* **:** a collection of such materials
**Vic·to·ri·an·ism** \vik-'tōr-ē-ə-,ni-zəm, -'tòr-\ *noun* (1905)
**1 :** a typical instance or product of Victorian expression, taste, or conduct
**2 :** the quality or state of being Victorian especially in taste or conduct
**vic·to·ri·ous** \vik-'tōr-ē-əs, -'tòr-\ *adjective* (14th century)
**1 a :** having won a victory **b :** of, relating to, or characteristic of victory
**2 :** evincing moral harmony or a sense of fulfillment **:** FULFILLED
— **vic·to·ri·ous·ly** *adverb*
— **vic·to·ri·ous·ness** *noun*

**vic·to·ry** \'vik-t(ə-)rē\ *noun, plural* **-ries** [Middle English, from Middle French *victorie*, from Latin *victoria*, from *victor*] (14th century)
**1 :** the overcoming of an enemy or antagonist
**2 :** achievement of mastery or success in a struggle or endeavor against odds or difficulties
**Vic·tro·la** \vik-'trō-lə\ *trademark*
— used for a phonograph
¹**vict·ual** \'vi-t°l\ *noun* [alteration of Middle English *vitaille*, from Middle French, from Late Latin *victualia*, plural, provisions, victuals, from neuter plural of *victualis* of nourishment, from Latin *victus* nourishment, way of living, from *vivere* to live — more at QUICK] (1523)
**1 :** food usable by people
**2** *plural* **:** supplies of food **:** PROVISIONS
²**victual** *verb* **-ualed** *or* **-ualled; -ual·ing** *or* **-ual·ling** (1558)
*transitive verb*
**:** to supply with food
*intransitive verb*
**1 :** EAT
**2 :** to lay in provisions
**vict·ual·ler** *or* **vict·ual·er** \'vi-t°l-ər\ *noun* (1568)
**1 :** the keeper of a restaurant or tavern
**2 :** one that provisions an army, a navy, or a ship with food
**3 :** an army or navy provision ship
**vi·cu·ña** *or* **vi·cu·na** \vi-'kün-yə, vī-; vī-'kü-nə, və-, -'kyü-\ *noun* [Spanish *vicuña*, from Quechua *wik'uña*] (1604)
**1 :** a wild ruminant (*Vicugna vicugna* synonym *Lama vicugna*) of the Andes from Peru to Argentina that is related to the llama and alpaca
**2 a :** the wool from the vicuña's fine lustrous undercoat **b :** a fabric made of vicuña wool; *also* **:** a sheep's wool imitation of this

vicuña 1

**vi·de** \'vī-dē, 'vē-,dā\ *imperative verb* [Latin, from *vidēre* to see — more at WIT] (1565)
**:** SEE — used to direct a reader to another item
**vi·de·li·cet** \və-'de-lə-,set, vī-; vi-'dā-li-,ket\ *adverb* [Middle English, from Latin, from *vidēre* to see + *licet* it is permitted, from *licēre* to be permitted] (15th century)
**:** that is to say **:** NAMELY
¹**vid·eo** \'vi-dē-,ō\ *noun* [Latin *vidēre* to see + *-o* (as in *audio*)] (1937)
**1 :** TELEVISION; *also* **:** the visual portion of television
**2 :** VIDEOTAPE: as **a :** a recording of a motion picture or television program for playing through a television set **b :** a videotaped performance of a song often featuring an interpretation of the lyrics through visual images
²**video** *adjective* (1938)
**1 :** being, relating to, or used in the transmission or reception of the television image ⟨*video* channel⟩ — compare AUDIO
**2 :** being, relating to, or involving images on a television screen or computer display ⟨*video* terminal⟩
**vid·eo·cas·sette** \,vi-dē-ō-kə-'set, -ka-\ *noun* (1970)
**1 :** a case containing videotape for use with a VCR
**2 :** a recording (as of a movie) on a videocassette
**videocassette recorder** *noun* (1976)
**:** VCR
**vid·eo·con·fer·enc·ing** \-'kän-f(ə-)rən(t)-siŋ, -fərn(t)-\ *noun* (1977)

**:** the holding of a conference among people at remote locations by means of transmitted audio and video signals
— **vid·eo·con·fer·ence** \-'kän-f(ə-)rən(t)s, -fərn(t)s\ *noun*
**vid·eo·disc** *or* **vid·eo·disk** \'vi-dē-ō-,disk\ *noun* (1967)
**1 :** a disc similar in appearance and use to a phonograph record on which programs have been recorded for playback on a television set; *also* **:** OPTICAL DISK
**2 :** a recording (as of a movie) on a videodisc
**video game** *noun* (1973)
**:** an electronic game played by means of images on a video screen and often emphasizing fast action
**vid·e·og·ra·phy** \,vi-dē-'ä-grə-fē\ *noun* (1972)
**:** the practice or art of recording images with a video camera
— **vid·e·og·ra·pher** \-fər\ *noun*
**vid·eo·land** \-,land\ *noun* (1967)
**:** television as a medium or industry
**vid·eo·phile** \'vi-dē-ə-,fīl\ *noun* (1966)
**:** a person fond of video; *especially* **:** one interested in video equipment or in producing videos
**vid·eo·phone** \'vi-dē-ə-,fōn\ *noun* (circa 1950)
**:** a telephone equipped for transmission of video as well as audio signals so that users can see each other
¹**vid·eo·tape** \'vi-dē-ō-,tāp\ *noun* (1953)
**:** a recording of visual images and sound (as of a television production) made on magnetic tape; *also* **:** the magnetic tape used for such a recording
²**videotape** *transitive verb* (1958)
**:** to make a videotape of ⟨*videotape* a show⟩ ⟨*videotape* the president's speech⟩
**videotape recorder** *noun* (1953)
**:** a device for recording and playing back videotapes — called also *video recorder*
**vid·eo·tex** \-,teks\ *also* **vid·eo·text** \-,tekst\ *noun* [²*video* + *-tex* (alteration of *text*)] (1978)
**:** an electronic data retrieval system in which usually textual information is transmitted via telephone or cable-television lines and displayed on a television set or video display terminal; *especially* **:** such a system that is interactive — compare TELETEXT
**video vé·ri·té** \-,ver-ə-'tā\ *noun* [*cinema verité*] (1969)
**:** the filming or videotaping of a television program (as a documentary) so as to convey candid realism
**vi·dette** *variant of* VEDETTE
**vid·icon** \'vi-di-,kän\ *noun, often capitalized* [²*video* + *icono*scope] (1950)
**:** a camera tube using the principle of photoconductivity
**vi·du·ity** \vi-'dü-ə-tē, -'dyü-\ *noun* [Middle English (Scots) *viduite*, from Middle French *viduite*, from Latin *viduitat-, viduitas*, from *vidua* widow — more at WIDOW] (15th century)
**:** WIDOWHOOD
**vie** \'vī\ *verb* **vied; vy·ing** \'vī-iŋ\ [modification of Middle French *envier* to invite, challenge, wager, from Latin *invitare* to invite] (1577)
*intransitive verb*
**:** to strive for superiority **:** CONTEND, COMPETE
*transitive verb*
*archaic* **:** WAGER, HAZARD; *also* **:** to exchange in rivalry **:** MATCH
— **vi·er** \'vī(-ə)r\ *noun*
**Vi·en·na sausage** \vē-'e-nə-\ *noun* [*Vienna*, Austria] (circa 1902)
**:** a short slender frankfurter

---

\ə\ abut   \°\ kitten   \ər\ further   \a\ ash   \ā\ ace
\ä\ mop, mar   \aù\ out   \ch\ chin   \e\ bet   \ē\ easy
\g\ go   \i\ hit   \ī\ ice   \j\ job   \ŋ\ sing   \ō\ go
\ò\ law   \òi\ boy   \th\ thin   \t̷h\ the   \ü\ loot   \ù\ foot
\y\ yet   \zh\ vision   *see also* Guide to Pronunciation

**Viet·cong** \vē-'et-'käŋ, vyet-, ,vē-ət-, vēt-, -'kóŋ\ *noun, plural* **Vietcong** [Vietnamese *Việt-cộng*] (1957)
: a guerrilla member of the Vietnamese communist movement

**Viet·minh** \-'min\ *noun, plural* **Vietminh** [Vietnamese *Việt-Minh*, short for *Việt-Nam Độc-Lập Đồng-Minh* League for the Independence of Vietnam] (1945)
: an adherent of the Vietnamese communist movement from 1941 to 1951

**Viet·nam·ese** \vē-,et-nə-'mēz, ,vyet-, ,vē-ət-, ,vēt-, -na-, -nä-, -'mēs\ *noun, plural* **Vietnamese** (1947)
**1** : a native or inhabitant of Vietnam
**2** : the language of the largest group in Vietnam and the official language of the country
— **Vietnamese** *adjective*

**¹view** \'vyü\ *noun* [Middle English *vewe*, from Middle French *veue, vue*, from Old French, from feminine of *veu, vu*, past participle of *veeir, voir* to see, from Latin *vidēre* — more at WIT] (15th century)
**1** : the act of seeing or examining : INSPECTION; *also* : SURVEY ⟨a *view* of English literature⟩
**2 a** : a mode or manner of looking at or regarding something **b** : an opinion or judgment colored by the feeling or bias of its holder ⟨in my *view* the conference has no chance of success⟩
**3** : SCENE, PROSPECT ⟨the lovely *view* from the balcony⟩
**4** : extent or range of vision : SIGHT ⟨tried to keep the ship in *view*⟩ ⟨sat high in the bleachers to get a good *view*⟩
**5** : something that is looked toward or kept in sight : OBJECT ⟨studied hard with a *view* to getting an A⟩
**6** : the foreseeable future ⟨no hope in *view*⟩
**7** : a pictorial representation
**synonym** see OPINION
— **in view of** : in regard to : in consideration of
— **on view** : open to public inspection : on exhibition

**²view** *transitive verb* (1523)
**1** : to look at attentively : SCRUTINIZE, OBSERVE ⟨*view* an exhibit⟩ ⟨*view* the landscape⟩
**2 a** : SEE, WATCH ⟨*view* a film⟩ **b** : to look on in a particular light : REGARD ⟨doesn't *view* himself as a rebel⟩
**3** : to survey or examine mentally : CONSIDER ⟨*view* all sides of a question⟩
— **view·able** \-ə-bəl\ *adjective*

**view·data** \'vyü-,dā-tə *also* -,da-\ *noun* (1975)
: a videotex system usually employing telephone lines

**view·er** \'vyü-ər\ *noun* (15th century)
: one that views: as **a** : a person legally appointed to inspect and report on property **b** : an optical device used in viewing **c** : a person who watches television

**view·er·ship** \-,ship\ *noun* (1954)
: a television audience especially with respect to size or makeup

**view·find·er** \'vyü-,fīn-dər\ *noun* (1889)
: a device on a camera for showing the area of the subject to be included in the picture

**view hal·loo** \,vyü-hə-'lü\ *interjection* (1761)
— used in fox hunting on seeing a fox break cover

**view·ing** *noun* (1535)
: an act of seeing, watching, or taking a look; *especially* : an instance or the practice of watching television

**view·less** \'vyü-ləs\ *adjective* (1603)
**1** : not perceivable : INVISIBLE
**2** : affording no view
**3** : expressing no views or opinions
— **view·less·ly** *adverb*

**view·point** \-,póint\ *noun* (1855)
: POINT OF VIEW, STANDPOINT

**viewy** \'vyü-ē\ *adjective* (1848)
**1** : possessing visionary, impractical, or fantastic views

**2** : spectacular or arresting in appearance : SHOWY

**vig** \'vig\ *noun* (1968)
: VIGORISH

**vi·ga** \'vē-gə\ *noun* [Spanish, beam, rafter] (1844)
: one of the heavy rafters and especially a log supporting the roof in American Indian and Spanish architecture of the Southwest

**vi·ges·i·mal** \vī-'je-sə-məl\ *adjective* [Latin *vicesimus, vigesimus* twentieth; akin to Latin *viginti* twenty, Greek *eikosi*] (circa 1656)
: based on the number 20

**vig·il** \'vi-jəl\ *noun* [Middle English *vigile*, from Old French, from Late Latin & Latin; Late Latin *vigilia* watch on the eve of a feast, from Latin, wakefulness, watch, from *vigil* awake, watchful; akin to Latin *vigēre* to be vigorous, *vegēre* to enliven — more at WAKE] (13th century)
**1 a** : a watch formerly kept on the night before a religious feast with prayer or other devotions **b** : the day before a religious feast observed as a day of spiritual preparation **c** : evening or nocturnal devotions or prayers — usually used in plural
**2** : the act of keeping awake at times when sleep is customary; *also* : a period of wakefulness
**3** : an act or period of watching or surveillance : WATCH

**vig·i·lance** \'vi-jə-lən(t)s\ *noun* (1533)
: the quality or state of being vigilant

**vigilance committee** *noun* (1835)
: a committee of vigilantes

**vig·i·lant** \'vi-jə-lənt\ *adjective* [Middle English, from Middle French, from Latin *vigilant-, vigilans*, from present participle of *vigilare* to keep watch, stay awake, from *vigil* awake] (15th century)
: alertly watchful especially to avoid danger
**synonym** see WATCHFUL
— **vig·i·lant·ly** *adverb*

**vig·i·lan·te** \,vi-jə-'lan-tē\ *noun* [Spanish, watchman, guard, from *vigilante* vigilant, from Latin *vigilant-, vigilans*] (1865)
: a member of a volunteer committee organized to suppress and punish crime summarily (as when the processes of law appear inadequate); *broadly* : a self-appointed doer of justice
— **vig·i·lan·tism** \-'lan-,ti-zəm\ *noun*

**vigil light** *noun* (circa 1931)
: a candle lighted devotionally (as in a Roman Catholic church) before a shrine or image — called also *vigil candle*

**vi·gin·til·lion** \,vī-,jin-'til-yən\ *noun, often attributive* [Latin *viginti* twenty + English *-illion* (as in *million*) — more at VIGESIMAL] (circa 1903)
— see NUMBER table

**vi·gne·ron** \,vēn-yə-'rōn\ *noun* [Middle English, from Middle French, from Old French *vineron*, from *vine, vigne* vine, vineyard] (15th century)
: WINEGROWER

**¹vi·gnette** \vin-'yet, vēn-\ *noun* [French, from Middle French *vignete*, from diminutive of *vigne* vine — more at VINE] (1751)
**1** : a running ornament (as of vine leaves, tendrils, and grapes) put on or just before a title page or at the beginning or end of a chapter; *also* : a small decorative design or picture so placed
**2 a** : a picture (as an engraving or photograph) that shades off gradually into the surrounding paper **b** : the pictorial part of a postage stamp design as distinguished from the frame and lettering
**3 a** : a short descriptive literary sketch **b** : a brief incident or scene (as in a play or movie)
— **vi·gnett·ist** \-'ye-tist\ *noun*

**²vignette** *transitive verb* **vi·gnett·ed; vi·gnett·ing** (1853)
**1** : to finish (as a photograph) in the manner of a vignette

**2** : to describe briefly
— **vi·gnett·er** *noun*

**vig·or** \'vi-gər\ *noun* [Middle English, from Middle French *vigor*, from Latin, from *vigēre* to be vigorous] (14th century)
**1** : active bodily or mental strength or force
**2** : active healthy well-balanced growth especially of plants
**3** : intensity of action or effect : FORCE
**4** : effective legal status

**vig·o·rish** \'vi-gə-rish\ *noun* [perhaps from Ukrainian *vygrash* or Russian *vyigrysh* winnings, profit] (1912)
**1** : a charge taken (as by a bookie or a gambling house) on bets; *also* : the degree of such a charge ⟨a *vigorish* of five percent⟩
**2** : interest paid to a moneylender

**vi·go·ro·so** \,vi-gə-'rō-(,)sō, ,vē-, -(,)zō\ *adjective or adverb* [Italian, literally, vigorous, from Middle French *vigorous*] (circa 1724)
: energetic in style — used as a direction in music

**vig·or·ous** \'vi-g(ə-)rəs\ *adjective* [Middle English, from Middle French, from Old French, from *vigor*] (14th century)
**1** : possessing vigor : full of physical or mental strength or active force : STRONG ⟨a *vigorous* youth⟩ ⟨a *vigorous* plant⟩
**2** : done with vigor : carried out forcefully and energetically ⟨*vigorous* exercises⟩ ☆
— **vig·or·ous·ly** *adverb*
— **vig·or·ous·ness** *noun*

**vig·our** \'vi-gər\ *chiefly British variant of* VIGOR

**Vi·king** \'vī-kiŋ\ *noun* [Old Norse *vīkingr*] (1807)
**1 a** : one of the pirate Norsemen plundering the coasts of Europe in the 8th to 10th centuries **b** *not capitalized* : SEA ROVER
**2** : SCANDINAVIAN

**vile** \'vī(ə)l\ *adjective* **vil·er** \'vī-lər\; **vil·est** \-ləst\ [Middle English, from Old French *vil*, from Latin *vilis*] (14th century)
**1 a** : morally despicable or abhorrent ⟨nothing is so *vile* as intellectual dishonesty⟩ **b** : physically repulsive : FOUL ⟨a *vile* slum⟩
**2** : of little worth or account : COMMON; *also* : MEAN
**3** : tending to degrade ⟨*vile* employments⟩
**4** : disgustingly or utterly bad : OBNOXIOUS, CONTEMPTIBLE ⟨*vile* weather⟩ ⟨had a *vile* temper⟩
**synonym** see BASE
— **vile·ly** \'vī(ə)l-lē\ *adverb*
— **vile·ness** *noun*

**vil·i·fi·ca·tion** \,vi-lə-fə-'kā-shən\ *noun* (1630)
**1** : the act of vilifying : ABUSE
**2** : an instance of vilifying : a defamatory utterance

**vil·i·fy** \'vi-lə-,fī\ *transitive verb* **-fied; -fy·ing** [Middle English *vilifien*, from Late Latin *vilificare*, from Latin *vilis* cheap, vile] (15th century)
**1** : to lower in estimation or importance

☆ SYNONYMS
**Vigorous, energetic, strenuous, lusty, nervous** mean having or showing great vitality and force. VIGOROUS further implies showing no signs of depletion or diminishing of freshness or robustness (as *vigorous* as a youth half his age). ENERGETIC suggests a capacity for intense activity ⟨an *energetic* campaigner⟩. STRENUOUS suggests a preference for coping with the arduous or the challenging ⟨the *strenuous* life on an oil rig⟩. LUSTY implies exuberant energy and capacity for enjoyment ⟨a *lusty* appetite for life⟩. NERVOUS suggests especially the forcibleness and sustained effectiveness resulting from mental vigor ⟨full of *nervous* energy⟩.

**2 :** to utter slanderous and abusive statements against : DEFAME

**synonym** see MALIGN

— **vil·i·fi·er** \-ˌfī(-ə)r\ *noun*

**vil·i·pend** \'vi-lə-ˌpend\ *transitive verb* [Middle English, from Middle French *vilipender,* from Medieval Latin *vilipendere,* from Latin *vilis* + *pendere* to weigh, estimate] (15th century)

**1 :** to hold or treat as of little worth or account : CONTEMN

**2 :** to express a low opinion of : DISPARAGE

**vill** \'vil\ *noun* [Anglo-French, from Old French *ville* village] (1596)

**1 :** a division of a hundred : TOWNSHIP

**2 :** VILLAGE

**vil·la** \'vi-lə\ *noun* [Italian, from Latin; akin to Latin *vicus* village — more at VICINITY] (1611)

**1 :** a country estate

**2 :** the rural or suburban residence of a wealthy person

**3** *British* **:** a detached or semidetached urban residence with yard and garden space

**vil·la·dom** \'vi-lə-dəm\ *noun* (1880) *British* **:** the world constituted by villas and their occupants

**vil·lage** \'vi-lij\ *noun, often attributive* [Middle English, from Middle French, from Old French, from *ville* farm, village, from Latin *villa*] (14th century)

**1 a :** a settlement usually larger than a hamlet and smaller than a town **b :** an incorporated minor municipality

**2 :** the residents of a village

**3 :** something (as an aggregation of burrows or nests) suggesting a village

**4 :** a territorial area having the status of a village especially as a unit of local government

**vil·lag·er** \'vi-li-jər\ *noun* (1570) **:** an inhabitant of a village

**vil·lag·ery** \'vi-lij-rē, -li-jə-\ *noun* (1590) **:** VILLAGES

**vil·lain** \'vi-lən\ *noun* [Middle English *vilain, vilein,* from Middle French, from Medieval Latin *villanus,* from Latin *villa*] (14th century)

**1 :** an uncouth person : BOOR

**2 :** VILLEIN

**3 :** a deliberate scoundrel or criminal

**4 :** a scoundrel in a story or play

**5 :** a person or thing blamed for a particular evil or difficulty ⟨automation as the *villain* in job . . . displacement —M. H. Goldberg⟩ ◆

**vil·lain·ess** \-lə-nəs\ *noun* (1586) **:** a woman who is a villain

**vil·lain·ous** \-lə-nəs\ *adjective* (15th century)

**1 a :** befitting a villain (as in evil, depraved, or vile character) ⟨a *villainous* attack⟩ **b :** being or having the character of a villain : DEPRAVED ⟨the *villainous* foe⟩

**2 :** highly objectionable : WRETCHED

**synonym** see VICIOUS

— **vil·lain·ous·ly** *adverb*

— **vil·lain·ous·ness** *noun*

**vil·lainy** \-lə-nē\ *noun, plural* **-lain·ies** (13th century)

**1 :** villainous conduct; *also* **:** a villainous act

**2 :** the quality or state of being villainous : DEPRAVITY

**vil·la·nel·la** \ˌvi-lə-'ne-lə\ *noun, plural* **-nel·le** \-'ne-lē\ [Italian, from *villano* villein, peasant, from Medieval Latin *villanus*] (1596)

**1 :** a 16th century Italian rustic part-song unaccompanied and in free form

**2 :** an instrumental piece in the style of a rustic dance

**vil·la·nelle** \ˌvi-lə-'nel\ *noun* [French, from Italian *villanella*] (1877) **:** a chiefly French verse form running on two rhymes and consisting typically of five tercets and a quatrain in which the first and third lines of the opening tercet recur alternately at the end of the other tercets and together as the last two lines of the quatrain

**vil·lat·ic** \vi-'la-tik\ *adjective* [Latin *villaticus,* from *villa*] (1671)

**:** RURAL

**-ville** \ˌvil, *especially Southern* vəl\ *noun suffix* [-*ville,* suffix occurring in names of towns, from French, from Old French, from *ville* village]

**:** place, category, or quality of a specified nature ⟨dulls*ville*⟩

**vil·lein** \'vi-lən, 'vi-ˌlān, vi-'lān\ *noun* [Middle English *vilain, vilein* — more at VILLAIN] (14th century)

**1 :** a free common villager or village peasant of any of the feudal classes lower in rank than the thane

**2 :** a free peasant of a feudal class lower than a sokeman and higher than a cotter

**3 :** an unfree peasant standing as the slave of a feudal lord but free in legal relations with respect to all others

**vil·len·age** \'vi-lə-nij\ *noun* [Middle English *vilenage,* from Middle French, from Old French, from *vilein, vilain*] (14th century)

**1 :** tenure at the will of a feudal lord by villein services

**2 :** the status of a villein

**vil·li·form** \'vi-lə-ˌfȯrm\ *adjective* [International Scientific Vocabulary] (1849) **:** having the form or appearance of villi

**vil·los·i·ty** \vi-'lä-sə-tē\ *noun, plural* **-ties** (1777)

**1 :** the state of being villous

**2 :** a villous patch or area

**vil·lous** \'vi-ləs\ *adjective* [Middle English, from Latin *villosus* hairy, shaggy, from *villus*] (14th century)

**1 :** covered or furnished with villi

**2 :** having soft long hairs ⟨leaves *villous* underneath⟩ — compare PUBESCENT

**vil·lus** \'vi-ləs\ *noun, plural* **vil·li** \'vi-ˌlī, -(ˌ)lē\ [New Latin, from Latin, tuft of shaggy hair — more at VELVET] (circa 1704)

**:** a small slender often vascular process: as **a** **:** one of the minute finger-shaped processes of the mucous membrane of the small intestine that serve in the absorption of nutriment **b** **:** one of the branching processes of the surface of the chorion of the developing embryo of most mammals that help to form the placenta

**vim** \'vim\ *noun* [Latin, accusative of *vis* strength; akin to Greek *is* strength, Sanskrit *vaya* meal, strength] (1843) **:** robust energy and enthusiasm

**vi·na** \'vē-nə\ *noun* [Sanskrit *vīṇā*] (1788) **:** a stringed instrument of India having usually four strings on a long bamboo fingerboard with movable frets and a gourd resonator at each end

**vina**

**vi·na·ceous** \vī-'nā-shəs, vi-\ *adjective* [Latin *vinaceus* of wine, from *vinum* wine — more at WINE] (1688) **:** of the color wine

**vin·ai·grette** \ˌvi-ni-'gret\ *noun* [French, from *vinaigre* vinegar] (1699)

**1 :** a sauce made typically of oil and vinegar, onions, parsley, and herbs and used especially on cold meats or fish — called also *vinaigrette dressing, vinaigrette sauce*

**2 :** a small ornamental box or bottle with perforated top used for holding an aromatic preparation (as smelling salts)

**vi·nal** \'vī-ˌnal\ *noun* [poly*vinyl* *al*cohol] (circa 1939) **:** a synthetic textile fiber that is a long-chain polymer consisting largely of vinyl alcohol units

**vin·blas·tine** \(ˌ)vin-'blas-ˌtēn\ *noun* [contraction of *vincaleukoblastine,* from *vinca* + *leukoblast* developing leukocyte, from *leuk-* + *-blast*] (1962) **:** an alkaloid $C_{46}H_{58}N_4O_9$ from Madagascar periwinkle used especially in the form of its sulfate to treat human neoplastic diseases

**vin·ca** \'viŋ-kə\ *noun* [New Latin, short for Latin *vincapervinca* periwinkle] (1868) **:** [1]PERIWINKLE

**Vin·cen·tian** \vin-'sen(t)-shən\ *noun* (1854)

**1 :** a member of the Roman Catholic Congregation of the Mission founded by Saint Vincent de Paul in Paris, France, in 1625 and devoted to missions and seminaries

**2 :** a native or inhabitant of the island of Saint Vincent

— **Vincentian** *adjective*

**Vin·cent's angina** \'vin(t)-sən(t)s-, (ˌ)van-'sänz-\ *noun* [Jean Hyacinthe *Vincent* (died 1950) French bacteriologist] (circa 1903) **:** Vincent's infection in which the ulceration has spread to surrounding tissues (as of the pharynx and tonsils) — called also *trench mouth*

**Vincent's infection** *noun* (circa 1922) **:** a progressive painful disease of the mouth that is marked especially by dirty gray ulceration of the mucous membranes, spontaneous hemorrhaging of the gums, and a foul odor to the breath and that is associated with the presence of large numbers of a bacillus (*Fusobacterium nucleatum* synonym *F. fusiforme*) and a spirochete (*Treponema vincentii* synonym *Borrelia vincentii*) in the lesions — called also *trench mouth*

**vin·ci·ble** \'vin(t)-sə-bəl\ *adjective* [Latin *vincibilis,* from *vincere* to conquer — more at VICTOR] (1548) **:** capable of being overcome or subdued

**vin·cris·tine** \(ˌ)vin-'kris-ˌtēn\ *noun* [*vin*circa + Latin *crista* crest + English [2]-*ine* — more at CREST] (circa 1962) **:** an alkaloid $C_{46}H_{56}N_4O_{10}$ from Madagascar periwinkle used especially in the form of its sulfate to treat some human neoplastic diseases (as leukemias)

**vin·cu·lum** \'viŋ-kyə-ləm\ *noun, plural* **-lums** *or* **-la** \-lə\ [Latin, from *vincire* to bind] (1661)

**1 :** a unifying bond : LINK, TIE

---

◇ **WORD HISTORY**

**villain** In medieval France and England a *vilain* or *vilein* was an agricultural laborer, at some times and places free and at others bound through feudal obligation to the property of his lord. *Vilain* is the Old French outcome of a spoken Latin word that appears in early Medieval Latin as *villanus,* literally, "inhabitant of a *villa.*" *Villa* in classical Latin was a large country dwelling, though by the time of Late Latin (3d to 6th centuries) the word could also refer more generally to any aggregation of rural dwellings and was nearly equivalent in sense to "village," so that a *villanus* was in effect a "villager." Because the landed aristocracy that dominated medieval society had a preponderant influence on linguistic usage, Middle English *vilain* or *vilein* developed the depreciatory sense "a person of uncouth mind and manners." This pejorative tendency gained in strength and currency through the common equation of manners with morals, so that the modern *villain* is a deliberate scoundrel or criminal, or a person or thing blamed for a particular evil or difficulty.

---

\ə\ abut \ᵊ\ kitten \ər\ further \a\ ash \ā\ ace
\ä\ mop, mar \au̇\ out \ch\ chin \e\ bet \ē\ easy
\g\ go \i\ hit \ī\ ice \j\ job \ŋ\ sing \ō\ go
\ȯ\ law \ȯi\ boy \th\ thin \th\ the \ü\ loot \u̇\ foot
\y\ yet \zh\ vision *see also* Guide to Pronunciation

**2 :** a straight horizontal mark that is placed over two or more members of a compound mathematical expression and is equivalent to parentheses or brackets placed around them (as in $a-b-c=a-[b-c]$)

**vin·da·loo** \'vin-də-ˌlü\ *noun* [probably from Konkani *vindalu,* from Indo-Portuguese (Portuguese creole of India) *vinh d'alho,* literally, wine of garlic, from Portuguese *vinho de alho*] (1888)
**:** a curried dish of Indian origin made with meat or shellfish, garlic, and wine or vinegar

**vin·di·ca·ble** \'vin-di-kə-bəl\ *adjective* (1647)
**:** capable of being vindicated

**vin·di·cate** \'vin-də-ˌkāt\ *transitive verb* **-cat·ed; -cat·ing** [Latin *vindicatus,* past participle of *vindicare* to lay claim to, avenge, from *vindic-, vindex* claimant, avenger] (1570)
**1** *obsolete* **:** to set free **:** DELIVER
**2 :** AVENGE
**3 a :** to free from allegation or blame **b** (1) **:** CONFIRM, SUBSTANTIATE (2) **:** to provide justification or defense for **:** JUSTIFY **c :** to protect from attack or encroachment **:** DEFEND
**4 :** to maintain a right to
**synonym** see EXCULPATE, MAINTAIN
— **vin·di·ca·tor** \-ˌkā-tər\ *noun*

**vin·di·ca·tion** \ˌvin-də-'kā-shən\ *noun* (1613)
**:** an act of vindicating **:** the state of being vindicated; *specifically* **:** justification against denial or censure **:** DEFENSE

**vin·dic·a·tive** \vin-'di-kə-tiv\ *adjective* (1521)
**1** *obsolete* **:** VINDICTIVE, VENGEFUL
**2** *archaic* **:** PUNITIVE

**vin·di·ca·to·ry** *adjective* (1647)
**1** \'vin-di-kə-ˌtōr-ē, -ˌtȯr-\ **:** providing vindication **:** JUSTIFICATORY
**2** \vin-'di-kə-\ **:** PUNITIVE, RETRIBUTIVE

**vin·dic·tive** \vin-'dik-tiv\ *adjective* [Latin *vindicta* revenge, vindication, from *vindicare*] (1616)
**1 a :** disposed to seek revenge **:** VENGEFUL **b :** intended for or involving revenge
**2 :** intended to cause anguish or hurt **:** SPITEFUL
— **vin·dic·tive·ly** *adverb*
— **vin·dic·tive·ness** *noun*

**¹vine** \'vīn\ *noun* [Middle English, from Middle French, from Old French *vigne,* from Latin *vinea* vine, vineyard, from feminine of *vineus* of wine, from *vinum* wine — more at WINE] (14th century)
**1 :** GRAPE 2
**2 a :** a plant whose stem requires support and which climbs by tendrils or twining or creeps along the ground; *also* **:** the stem of such a plant **b :** any of various sprawling herbaceous plants (as a tomato or potato) that lack specialized adaptations for climbing

**²vine** *intransitive verb* **vined; vin·ing** (1796)
**:** to form or grow in the manner of a vine

**vine·dress·er** \'vīn-ˌdre-sər\ *noun* (1560)
**:** a person who cultivates and prunes grapevines

**vin·e·gar** \'vi-ni-gər\ *noun* [Middle English *vinegre,* from Middle French *vinaigre,* from *vin* wine (from Latin *vinum*) + *aigre* keen, sour — more at EAGER] (14th century)
**1 :** a sour liquid obtained by fermentation of dilute alcoholic liquids and used as a condiment or preservative
**2 :** ill humor **:** SOURNESS
**3 :** VIM

**vin·e·gared** \-gərd\ *adjective* (1861)
**:** flavored or marinated with vinegar

**vinegar eel** *noun* (circa 1839)
**:** a minute nematode worm (*Turbatrix aceti*) often found in great numbers in vinegar or acid fermenting vegetable matter

**vinegar fly** *noun* [from its breeding in pickles] (1901)
**:** DROSOPHILA

**vin·e·gar·ish** \'vi-ni-g(ə-)rish\ *adjective* (1648)
**:** VINEGARY 2

**vin·e·gary** \'vi-ni-g(ə-)rē\ *adjective* (circa 1730)
**1 a :** resembling vinegar **:** SOUR **b :** flavored with vinegar
**2 :** disagreeable, bitter, or irascible in character or manner

**vin·ery** \'vīn-rē, 'vī-nə-\ *noun, plural* **-er·ies** (15th century)
**:** an area or building in which vines are grown

**vine·yard** \'vin-yərd\ *noun* (14th century)
**1 :** a planting of grapevines
**2 :** a sphere of activity **:** field of endeavor (toilers in the *vineyard* of diplomacy —Daniel Schorr)

**vine·yard·ist** \-yər-dist\ *noun* (1848)
**:** a person who owns or cultivates a vineyard

**vingt–et–un** \ˌvan-ˌtā-'ən\ *noun* [French, literally, twenty-one] (1772)
**:** BLACKJACK 5

**vi·ni·cul·ture** \'vi-nə-ˌkəl-chər, 'vī-\ *noun* [Latin *vinum* + International Scientific Vocabulary *-i-* + *culture*] (1871)
**:** VITICULTURE

**vi·nif·era** \vī-'ni-f(ə-)rə\ *adjective* [New Latin, from Latin *vinifer* wine-producing, from *vinum* wine] (1900)
**:** of, relating to, being, or derived from a common European grape (*Vitis vinifera*) that is the chief source of Old World wine grapes and table grapes
— **vinifera** *noun*

**vi·ni·fi·ca·tion** \ˌvi-nə-fə-'kā-shən, ˌvī-\ *noun* [French, from *vin* wine + *-i-* + *-fication*] (1880)
**:** the conversion of fruit juices (as grape juice) into wine by fermentation

**vin·i·fy** \'vi-nə-ˌfī, 'vī-\ *transitive verb* **-fied; -fy·ing** [probably back-formation from *vinification*] (1969)
**1 :** to make wine from (grapes often of a specified kind)
**2 :** to make (wine) from grapes

**vi·no** \'vē-(ˌ)nō\ *noun* [Italian & Spanish, from Latin *vinum*] (circa 1919)
**:** WINE

**vi·nos·i·ty** \vī-'nä-sə-tē\ *noun, plural* **-ties** (1658)
**:** the characteristic body, flavor, and color of a wine

**vi·nous** \'vī-nəs\ *adjective* [Latin *vinosus,* from *vinum* wine] (1664)
**1 :** of, relating to, or made with wine (*vinous* medications)
**2 :** showing the effects of the use of wine
**3 :** VINACEOUS
— **vi·nous·ly** *adverb*

**¹vin·tage** \'vin-tij\ *noun* [Middle English, alteration of *vendage,* from Middle French *vendenge,* from Latin *vindemia* grape-gathering, vintage, from *vinum* wine, grapes + *demere* to take off, from *de-* + *emere* to take — more at WINE, REDEEM] (15th century)
**1 a** (1) **:** a season's yield of grapes or wine from a vineyard (2) **:** WINE; *especially* **:** a usually superior wine all or most of which comes from a single year **b :** a collection of contemporaneous and similar persons or things **:** CROP
**2 :** the act or time of harvesting grapes or making wine
**3 a :** a period of origin or manufacture (a piano of 1845 *vintage*) **b :** length of existence **:** AGE

**²vintage** *adjective* (1601)
**1** *of wine* **:** of, relating to, or produced in a particular vintage
**2 :** of old, recognized, and enduring interest, importance, or quality **:** CLASSIC
**3 a :** dating from the past **:** OLD **b :** OUTMODED, OLD-FASHIONED
**4 :** of the best and most characteristic — used with a proper noun (*vintage* Shaw: a wise and winning comedy —*Time*)

**vin·tag·er** \'vin-ti-jər\ *noun* (1589)
**:** a person concerned with the production of grapes and wine

**vintage year** *noun* (1933)
**1 :** a year of outstanding distinction or success
**2 :** a year in which a vintage wine is produced

**vint·ner** \'vint-nər\ *noun* [Middle English *vineter,* from Middle French *vinetier,* from Medieval Latin *vinetarius,* from Latin *vinetum* vineyard, from *vinum* wine] (15th century)
**1 :** a wine merchant
**2 :** a person who makes wine

**viny** \'vī-nē\ *adjective* **vin·i·er; -est** (1570)
**1 :** of, relating to, or resembling vines (*viny* plants)
**2 :** covered with or abounding in vines

**vi·nyl** \'vī-nᵊl\ *noun* [International Scientific Vocabulary, from Latin *vinum* wine] (1863)
**1 :** a univalent group $CH_2$=CH derived from ethylene by removal of one hydrogen atom
**2 :** a polymer of a vinyl compound or a product (as a resin or a textile fiber) made from such a polymer
— **vi·nyl·ic** \vī-'ni-lik\ *adjective*

**vinyl alcohol** *noun* (1873)
**:** an unstable compound $CH_2$=CHOH isolated only in the form of its polymers or derivatives

**vinyl chloride** *noun* (1872)
**:** a flammable gaseous carcinogenic compound $C_2H_3Cl$ that is used especially to make vinyl resins

**vi·nyl·i·dene** \vī-'ni-lə-ˌdēn\ *noun* [International Scientific Vocabulary *vinyl* + *-ide* + *-ene*] (1898)
**:** a bivalent group $CH_2$=C derived from ethylene by removal of two hydrogen atoms from one carbon atom

**vinyl resin** *noun* (1934)
**:** any of various thermoplastic resinous materials that are essentially polymers of vinyl compounds

**vi·ol** \'vī(-ə)l, 'vī-(ˌ)ōl\ *noun* [Middle English, from Middle French *viole* viol, viola, from Old Provençal *viola* viol] (15th century)
**:** a bowed stringed instrument chiefly of the 16th and 17th centuries made in treble, alto, tenor, and bass sizes and distinguished from members of the violin family especially in having a deep body, a flat back, sloping shoulders, usually six strings, a fretted fingerboard, and a low-arched bridge

**¹vi·o·la** \vī-'ō-lə, vē-; 'vī-ə-\ *noun* [Middle English, from Latin] (15th century)
**:** VIOLET 1a; *especially* **:** any of various garden hybrids with solitary white, yellow, or purple often variegated flowers resembling but smaller than typical pansies

**²vi·o·la** \vē-'ō-lə\ *noun* [Italian & Spanish, viol, viola, from Old Provençal, viol] (circa 1724)
**:** a musical instrument of the violin family that is intermediate in size and compass between the violin and cello and is tuned a fifth below the violin
— **vi·o·list** \-list\ *noun*

**vi·o·la·ble** \'vī-ə-lə-bəl\ *adjective* (1552)
**:** capable of being or likely to be violated
— **vi·o·la·bil·i·ty** \ˌvī-ə-lə-'bi-lə-tē\ *noun*
— **vi·o·la·ble·ness** \'vī-ə-lə-bəl-nəs\ *noun*
— **vi·o·la·bly** \-blē\ *adverb*

**vi·o·la·ceous** \ˌvī-ə-'lā-shəs\ *adjective* [Latin *violaceus,* from *viola* violet] (1657)
**:** of the color violet

**vi·o·la da gam·ba** \vē-ˌō-lə-də-'gäm-bə, -'gam-\ *noun, plural* **vi·o·las da gamba** \-ləz-də-\ *or* **vi·o·le da gamba** \-(ˌ)lā-\ [Italian, leg viol] (1597)
**:** a bass member of the viol family having a range approximating the cello
— **vi·o·list da gamba** \-lis(t)-də-\ *noun*

**viola d'a·mo·re** \-də-'mȯr-ē, -'mȯr-, -(ˌ)ā\ *noun, plural* **violas d'amore** *or* **viole d'amore** [Italian, viol of love] (circa 1700)
**:** a tenor viol having usually seven gut and seven wire strings

**¹vi·o·late** \'vī-ə-ˌlāt\ *transitive verb* **-lat·ed; -lat·ing** [Middle English, from Latin *violatus,* past participle of *violare,* probably from *violentus* violent] (15th century)
**1 :** BREAK, DISREGARD (*violate* the law)

**2 :** to do harm to the person or especially the chastity of; *specifically* **:** RAPE
**3 :** to fail to show proper respect for **:** PROFANE ⟨*violate* a shrine⟩
**4 :** INTERRUPT, DISTURB ⟨*violate* the peace of a spring evening —Nancy Larter⟩
— **vi·o·la·tive** \-ˌlā-tiv\ *adjective*
— **vi·o·la·tor** \-ˌlā-tər\ *noun*
²**vi·o·late** \'vī-ə-lət\ *adjective* (1503)
*archaic* **:** subjected to violation
**vi·o·la·tion** \ˌvī-ə-'lā-shən\ *noun* (15th century)
**:** the act of violating **:** the state of being violated: as **a :** INFRINGEMENT, TRANSGRESSION; *specifically* **:** an infringement of the rules in sports that is less serious than a foul and usually involves technicalities of play **b :** an act of irreverence or desecration **:** PROFANATION **c :** DISTURBANCE, INTERRUPTION **d :** RAPE, RAVISHMENT
**vi·o·lence** \'vī-ə-lən(t)s\ *noun* (14th century)
**1 a :** exertion of physical force so as to injure or abuse (as in effecting illegal entry into a house) **b :** an instance of violent treatment or procedure
**2 :** injury by or as if by distortion, infringement, or profanation **:** OUTRAGE
**3 a :** intense, turbulent, or furious and often destructive action or force ⟨the *violence* of the storm⟩ **b :** vehement feeling or expression **:** FERVOR; *also* **:** an instance of such action or feeling **c :** a clashing or jarring quality **:** DISCORDANCE
**4 :** undue alteration (as of wording or sense in editing a text)
**vi·o·lent** \-lənt\ *adjective* [Middle English, from Middle French, from Latin *violentus;* akin to Latin *vis* strength — more at VIM] (14th century)
**1 :** marked by extreme force or sudden intense activity ⟨a *violent* attack⟩
**2 a :** notably furious or vehement ⟨a *violent* denunciation⟩ **b :** EXTREME, INTENSE ⟨*violent* pain⟩ ⟨*violent* colors⟩
**3 :** caused by force **:** not natural ⟨a *violent* death⟩
**4 a :** emotionally agitated to the point of loss of self-control ⟨a mental patient becoming *violent*⟩ **b :** prone to commit acts of violence ⟨*violent* prison inmates⟩
— **vi·o·lent·ly** *adverb*
**violent storm** *noun* (circa 1881)
**:** STORM 1c(1) — see BEAUFORT SCALE table
**vi·o·let** \'vī-(ə-)lət\ *noun* [Middle English, from Middle French *violete*, diminutive of *viole* violet, from Latin *viola*] (14th century)
**1 a :** any of a genus (*Viola* of the family Violaceae, the violet family) with alternate stipulate leaves and showy flowers in spring and cleistogamous flowers in summer; *especially* **:** one with smaller usually solid-colored flowers as distinguished from the usually larger-flowered violas and pansies **b :** any of several plants of genera other than that of the violet — compare DOGTOOTH VIOLET

violet 1a

**2 :** any of a group of colors of reddish blue hue, low lightness, and medium saturation
**vi·o·lin** \ˌvī-ə-'lin\ *noun* [Italian *violino*, diminutive of *viola*] (1579)
**:** a bowed stringed instrument having four strings tuned at intervals of a fifth and a usual range from G below middle C upward for more than 4½ octaves and having a shallow body, shoulders at right angles to the neck, a fingerboard without frets, and a curved bridge
— **vi·o·lin·ist** \-ist\ *noun*
— **vi·o·lin·is·tic** \-ə-lə-'nis-tik\ *adjective*

**vi·o·lon·cel·lo** \ˌvī-ə-lən-'che-(ˌ)lō, ˌvē-\ *noun* [Italian, diminutive of *violone*, augmentative of *viola*] (circa 1724)
**:** CELLO
— **vi·o·lon·cel·list** \-'che-list\ *noun*
**vio·my·cin** \ˌvī-ə-'mī-sᵊn\ *noun* [*violet* + *-mycin;* from the color of the soil organism] (1950)
**:** a polypeptide antibiotic $C_{25}H_{43}N_{13}O_{10}$ that is produced by several soil actinomycetes (genus *Streptomyces*) and is administered in the form of its sulfate in the treatment of tuberculosis
**VIP** \ˌvē-ˌī-'pē\ *noun, plural* **VIPs** \-'pēz\ [*very important person*] (1933)
**:** a person of great influence or prestige; *especially* **:** a high official with special privileges
**vi·per** \'vī-pər\ *noun* [Middle French *vipere*, from Latin *vipera*] (1526)
**1 a :** a common Eurasian venomous snake (*Vipera berus*) that attains a length of two feet (0.6 meter), varies in color from red, brown, or gray with dark markings to black, and is usually not fatal to humans; *broadly* **:** any of a family (Viperidae) of venomous snakes that includes Old World snakes (subfamily Viperinae) and the pit vipers **b :** a venomous or reputedly venomous snake
**2 :** a vicious or treacherous person
**vi·per·ine** \-pə-ˌrīn\ *adjective* (circa 1550)
**:** of, relating to, or resembling a viper **:** VENOMOUS
**vi·per·ish** \-p(ə-)rish\ *adjective* (1755)
**:** spitefully vituperative **:** VENOMOUS
**vi·per·ous** \-p(ə-)rəs\ *adjective* (1535)
**1 :** VIPERINE
**2 :** having the qualities attributed to a viper **:** MALIGNANT, VENOMOUS
— **vi·per·ous·ly** *adverb*
**viper's bugloss** *noun* (1597)
**:** a coarse Old World herb (*Echium vulgare*) of the borage family that is naturalized in North America and has showy blue tubular flowers with exserted stamens — called also *blueweed*
**vi·ra·go** \və-'rä-(ˌ)gō, -'rā-; 'vir-ə-ˌgō\ *noun, plural* **-goes** *or* **-gos** [Middle English, from Latin *viragin-, virago*, from *vir* man — more at VIRILE] (14th century)
**1 :** a loud overbearing woman **:** TERMAGANT
**2 :** a woman of great stature, strength, and courage
— **vi·rag·i·nous** \və-'ra-jə-nəs\ *adjective*
**vi·ral** \'vī-rəl\ *adjective* (1937)
**:** of, relating to, or caused by a virus
— **vi·ral·ly** \-rə-lē\ *adverb*
**vir·e·lay** \'vir-ə-ˌlā\ *noun* [Middle English, from Middle French *virelai*] (14th century)
**:** a chiefly French verse form consisting of stanzas of indeterminate length and number with alternating long and short lines and interlaced rhyme (as *abab bcbc cdcd dada*)
**vi·re·mia** \vī-'rē-mē-ə\ *noun* [New Latin, from *virus* + *-emia*] (1946)
**:** the presence of virus in the blood of a host
— **vi·re·mic** \-mik\ *adjective*
**vir·eo** \'vir-ē-ˌō\ *noun, plural* **-e·os** [Latin, a small bird, from *virēre* to be green] (1834)
**:** any of various small insectivorous American oscine birds (family Vireonidae and especially genus *Vireo*) that are chiefly olivaceous and grayish in color
**vires** *plural of* VIS
**vi·res·cence** \və-'re-sᵊn(t)s, vī-\ *noun* (circa 1888)
**:** the state or condition of becoming green; *especially* **:** such a condition due to the development of chloroplasts in plant organs (as petals) normally white or colored
**vi·res·cent** \-sᵊnt\ *adjective* [Latin *virescent-, virescens*, present participle of *virescere* to become green, inchoative of *virēre* to be green] (1826)
**1 :** beginning to be green **:** GREENISH
**2 :** developing or displaying virescence
**vir·ga** \'vər-gə\ *noun* [New Latin, from Latin, branch, rod, streak in the sky suggesting rain] (1938)
**:** wisps of precipitation evaporating before reaching the ground
¹**vir·gate** \'vər-ˌgāt\ *noun* [Medieval Latin *virgata*, from *virga*, a land measure, from Latin, rod] (1655)
**:** an old English unit of land area equal to one quarter of a hide or one quarter of an acre
²**virgate** *adjective* [New Latin *virgatus*, from Latin, made of twigs, from *virga*] (1821)
**:** shaped like a rod or wand ⟨a *virgate* one-flowered branch⟩
¹**vir·gin** \'vər-jən\ *noun* [Middle English, from Old French *virgine*, from Latin *virgin-, virgo* young woman, virgin] (13th century)
**1 a :** an unmarried woman devoted to religion **b** *capitalized* **:** VIRGO
**2 a :** an absolutely chaste young woman **b :** an unmarried girl or woman
**3** *capitalized* **:** VIRGIN MARY
**4 a :** a person who has not had sexual intercourse **b :** a person who is inexperienced in a usually specified sphere of activity ⟨a *virgin* in politics⟩
**5 :** a female animal that has never copulated
²**virgin** *adjective* (14th century)
**1 :** free of impurity or stain **:** UNSULLIED
**2 :** CHASTE
**3 :** characteristic of or befitting a virgin **:** MODEST
**4 :** FRESH, UNSPOILED; *specifically* **:** not altered by human activity ⟨a *virgin* forest⟩
**5 a** (1) **:** being used or worked for the first time (2) *of a metal* **:** produced directly from ore by primary smelting **b :** INITIAL, FIRST
**6** *of a vegetable oil* **:** obtained from the first light pressing and without heating
¹**vir·gin·al** \'vər-jə-nᵊl, 'vərj-nəl\ *adjective* (15th century)
**1 :** of, relating to, or characteristic of a virgin or virginity; *especially* **:** PURE, CHASTE
**2 :** PRISTINE, UNSULLIED
— **vir·gin·al·ly** *adverb*
²**virginal** *noun* [probably from Latin *virginalis* of a virgin, from *virgin-, virgo*] (1530)
**:** a small rectangular spinet having no legs and only one wire to a note and popular in the 16th and 17th centuries — often used in plural; called also *pair of virginals*
— **vir·gin·al·ist** \'vər-jə-nᵊl-ist, 'vərj-nə-list\ *noun*
**virgin birth** *noun* (1652)
**1 :** birth from a virgin
**2** *often V&B capitalized* **:** the theological doctrine that Jesus was miraculously begotten of God and born of a virgin mother
**Vir·gin·ia bluebells** \vər-'jin-yə-, -'ji-nē-ə-\ *noun plural* [*Virginia*, state of the U.S.] (circa 1922)
**:** BLUEBELL 2b
**Virginia creeper** *noun* (1704)
**:** a common North American tendril-climbing vine (*Parthenocissus quinquefolia*) of the grape family with palmately compound leaves and bluish black berries — called also *woodbine*
**Virginia fence** *noun* (1671)
**:** WORM FENCE — called also *Virginia rail fence*
**Virginia ham** *noun* (1824)

---

\ə\ abut \ᵊ\ kitten \ər\ further \a\ ash \ā\ ace
\ä\ mop, mar \au̇\ out \ch\ chin \e\ bet \ē\ easy
\g\ go \i\ hit \ī\ ice \j\ job \ŋ\ sing \ō\ go
\ȯ\ law \ȯi\ boy \th\ thin \t̲h̲\ the \ü\ loot \u̇\ foot
\y\ yet \zh\ vision *see also* Guide to Pronunciation

: a dry-cured, smoked, and aged ham especially from a peanut-fed hog

**Virginia pine** *noun* (1897)
: a pine (*Pinus virginiana*) of the eastern U.S. that has short needles occurring in pairs — called also *Jersey pine*

**Virginia rail** *noun* (1813)
: an American long-billed rail (*Rallus limicola*) that has gray cheeks

**Virginia reel** *noun* (1817)
: an American dance in which two lines of couples face each other and all couples in turn participate in a series of figures

**Virginia snakeroot** *noun* (1694)
: a birthwort (*Aristolochia serpentaria*) of the eastern U.S. with oblong leaves cordate at the base and a solitary basal very irregular flower

**vir·gin·i·ty** \(,)vər-'ji-nə-tē\ *noun, plural* **-ties** (14th century)
**1** : the quality or state of being virgin; *especially* : MAIDENHOOD
**2** : the unmarried life : CELIBACY, SPINSTERHOOD

**Virgin Mary** *noun*
: the mother of Jesus

**virgin's bower** *noun* (1597)
: any of several usually small-flowered and climbing clematises (especially *Clematis virginiana*)

**virgin wool** *noun* (1915)
: wool not used before in manufacture

**Vir·go** \'vər-(,)gō, 'vir-\ *noun* [Latin (genitive *Virginis*), literally, virgin]
**1** : a zodiacal constellation on the celestial equator that lies due south of the handle of the Big Dipper and is pictured as a woman holding a spike of grain
**2 a** : the 6th sign of the zodiac in astrology — see ZODIAC table **b** : one born under the sign of Virgo
— **Vir·go·an** *noun*

**vir·gule** \'vər-(,)gyü(ə)l\ *noun* [French, from Latin *virgula* small stripe, obelus, from diminutive of *virga* rod] (1837)
: DIAGONAL 3

**vi·ri·ci·dal** \,vī-rə-'sī-dᵊl\ *adjective* [New Latin *virus* + English -i- + -cide] (1924)
: VIRUCIDAL
— **vi·ri·cide** \'vī-rə-,sīd\ *noun*

**vir·id** \'vir-əd\ *adjective* [Latin *viridis* green] (1600)
: vividly green : VERDANT

**vir·i·des·cent** \,vir-ə-'de-sᵊnt\ *adjective* [Latin *viridis* green] (circa 1847)
: slightly green : GREENISH

**vi·rid·i·an** \və-'ri-dē-ən\ *noun* [Latin *viridis*] (1882)
: a chrome green that is a hydrated oxide of chromium

**vi·rid·i·ty** \və-'ri-də-tē\ *noun* [Middle English *viridite*, from Middle French *viridité*, from Latin *viriditat-*, *viriditas*, from *viridis*] (15th century)
**1 a** : the quality or state of being green **b** : the color of grass or foliage
**2** : naive innocence

**vir·ile** \'vir-əl, 'vir-,īl, *British also* 'vir-,īl\ *adjective* [Middle French or Latin; Middle French *viril*, from Latin *virilis*, from *vir* man, male; akin to Old English & Old High German *wer* man, Sanskrit *vīra*] (15th century)
**1** : having the nature, properties, or qualities of an adult male; *specifically* : capable of functioning as a male in copulation
**2** : ENERGETIC, VIGOROUS
**3 a** : characteristic of or associated with men : MASCULINE **b** : having traditionally masculine traits especially to a marked degree
**4** : MASTERFUL, FORCEFUL
— **vir·ile·ly** *adverb*

**vir·il·ism** \'vir-ə-,li-zəm\ *noun* (1922)
: the appearance of secondary male characteristics in the female

**vi·ril·i·ty** \və-'ri-lə-tē, *British also* vī-\ *noun* (1586)

: the quality or state of being virile: **a** : MANHOOD **b** : manly vigor : MASCULINITY

**vir·i·on** \'vī-rē-,än, 'vir-ē-\ *noun* [French, from *virien* viral (from *virus* virus) + -on ²-on] (1959)
: a complete virus particle that consists of an RNA or DNA core with a protein coat sometimes with external envelopes and that is the extracellular infective form of a virus

**virl** \'vər(-ə)l\ *noun* [Middle English *virole* — more at FERRULE] (15th century)
*Scottish* : FERRULE 1

**vi·roid** \'vī-,roid\ *noun* [New Latin *virus* + English -oid] (1971)
: any of several causative agents of plant disease that consist solely of a single-stranded RNA of low molecular weight arranged in a closed loop or a linear chain

**vi·rol·o·gy** \vī-'rä-lə-jē\ *noun* [New Latin *virus* + International Scientific Vocabulary -logy] (circa 1935)
: a branch of science that deals with viruses
— **vi·ro·log·i·cal** \,vī-rə-'lä-ji-kəl\ *or* **vi·ro·log·ic** \-jik\ *adjective*
— **vi·ro·log·i·cal·ly** \-ji-k(ə-)lē\ *adverb*
— **vi·rol·o·gist** \vī-'rä-lə-jist\ *noun*

**vir·tu** \,vər-'tü, vir-\ *noun* [Italian *virtù*, literally, virtue, from Latin *virtut-*, *virtus*] (1722)
**1** : a love of or taste for curios or objets d'art
**2** : productions of art especially of a curious or antique nature : OBJETS D'ART

**vir·tu·al** \'vər-chə-wəl, -chəl; 'vərch-wəl\ *adjective* [Middle English, possessed of certain physical virtues, from Medieval Latin *virtualis*, from Latin *virtus* strength, virtue] (1654)
**1** : being such in essence or effect though not formally recognized or admitted ⟨a *virtual* dictator⟩
**2** : of, relating to, or using virtual memory
**3** : of, relating to, or being a hypothetical particle whose existence is inferred from indirect evidence ⟨*virtual* photons⟩ — compare REAL 3

**virtual image** *noun* (1859)
: an image (as seen in a plane mirror) formed of points from which divergent rays (as of light) seem to emanate without actually doing so

**vir·tu·al·i·ty** \,vər-chə-'wa-lə-tē\ *noun, plural* **-ties** (1646)
**1** : ESSENCE
**2** : potential existence : POTENTIALITY

**vir·tu·al·ly** \'vər-chə-wə-lē, -chə-lē; 'vərch-wə-lē\ *adverb* (15th century)
**1** : almost entirely : NEARLY
**2** : for all practical purposes ⟨*virtually* unknown⟩

**virtual memory** *noun* (1959)
: external memory (as magnetic disks) for a computer that can be used as if it were an extension of the computer's internal memory — called also *virtual storage*

**virtual reality** *noun* (1989)
: an artificial environment which is experienced through sensory stimuli (as sights and sounds) provided by a computer and in which one's actions partially determine what happens in the environment

**vir·tue** \'vər-(,)chü\ *noun* [Middle English *vertu*, from Old French, from Latin *virtut-*, *virtus* strength, manliness, virtue, from *vir* man — more at VIRILE] (13th century)
**1 a** : conformity to a standard of right : MORALITY **b** : a particular moral excellence
**2** *plural* : an order of angels — see CELESTIAL HIERARCHY
**3** : a beneficial quality or power of a thing
**4** : manly strength or courage : VALOR
**5** : a commendable quality or trait : MERIT
**6** : a capacity to act : POTENCY
**7** : chastity especially in a woman
— **vir·tue·less** \-(,)chü-ləs\ *adjective*
— **by virtue of** *or* **in virtue of** : through the force of : by authority of

**vir·tu·o·sa** \,vər-chü-'ō-sə, -zə\ *noun* [Italian, feminine of *virtuoso*] (1668)

: a girl or woman who is a virtuoso

**vir·tu·os·i·ty** \-'ä-sə-tē\ *noun, plural* **-ties** (1673)
**1** : a taste for or interest in virtu
**2** : great technical skill (as in the practice of a fine art)

**vir·tu·o·so** \-'ō-(,)sō, -(,)zō\ *noun, plural* **-sos** *or* **-si** \-(,)sē, -(,)zē\ [Italian, from *virtuoso*, adjective, virtuous, skilled, from Late Latin *virtuosus* virtuous, from Latin *virtus*] (1651)
**1** : an experimenter or investigator especially in the arts and sciences : SAVANT
**2** : one skilled in or having a taste for the fine arts
**3** : one who excels in the technique of an art; *especially* : a highly skilled musical performer (as on the violin)
**4** : a person who has great skill at some endeavor ⟨a computer *virtuoso*⟩ ⟨a *virtuoso* at public relations⟩
— **vir·tu·o·sic** \-'ō-sik, -zik\ *adjective*
— **virtuoso** *adjective*

**vir·tu·ous** \'vər-chə-wəs, 'vərch-wəs\ *adjective* (14th century)
**1** : POTENT, EFFICACIOUS
**2 a** : having or exhibiting virtue **b** : morally excellent : RIGHTEOUS
**3** : CHASTE
*synonym* see MORAL
— **vir·tu·ous·ly** *adverb*
— **vir·tu·ous·ness** *noun*

**vi·ru·cid·al** \,vī-rə-'sī-dᵊl\ *adjective* [New Latin, *virus* + English -cide] (1925)
: having the capacity to or tending to destroy or inactivate viruses ⟨*virucidal* agents⟩ ⟨*virucidal* activity⟩
— **vi·ru·cide** \'vī-rə-,sīd\ *noun*

**vir·u·lence** \'vir-ə-lən(t)s, 'vir-yə-\ *noun* (1663)
: the quality or state of being virulent: as **a** : extreme bitterness or malignity of temper : RANCOR **b** : MALIGNANCY, VENOMOUSNESS ⟨ameliorate the *virulence* of a disease⟩ **c** : the relative capacity of a pathogen to overcome body defenses

**vir·u·len·cy** \-lən(t)-sē\ *noun* (circa 1617)
: VIRULENCE

**vir·u·lent** \-lənt\ *adjective* [Middle English, from Latin *virulentus*, from *virus* poison] (14th century)
**1 a** : marked by a rapid, severe, and malignant course ⟨a *virulent* infection⟩ **b** : able to overcome bodily defensive mechanisms ⟨a *virulent* pathogen⟩
**2** : extremely poisonous or venomous
**3** : full of malice : MALIGNANT ⟨*virulent* racists⟩
**4** : objectionably harsh or strong
— **vir·u·lent·ly** *adverb*

**vir·u·lif·er·ous** \,vir-ə-'li-f(ə-)rəs, ,vir-yə-\ *adjective* [*virulence* + -iferous] (circa 1899)
: containing, producing, or conveying an agent of infection and especially a virus ⟨*viruliferous* insects⟩

**vi·rus** \'vī-rəs\ *noun* [Latin, venom, poisonous emanation; akin to Greek *ios* poison, Sanskrit *viṣa;* in senses 2 & 4, from New Latin, from Latin] (1599)
**1** *archaic* : VENOM 1
**2 a** : the causative agent of an infectious disease **b** : any of a large group of submicroscopic infective agents that are regarded either as extremely simple microorganisms or as extremely complex molecules, that typically contain a protein coat surrounding an RNA or DNA core of genetic material but no semipermeable membrane, that are capable of growth and multiplication only in living cells, and that cause various important diseases in humans, lower animals, or plants; *also* : FILTERABLE VIRUS **c** : a disease caused by a virus
**3** : something that poisons the mind or soul ⟨the force of this *virus* of prejudice —V. S. Waters⟩
**4** : a computer program usually hidden within another seemingly innocuous program that

produces copies of itself and inserts them into other programs and that usually performs a malicious action (as destroying data)

**vis** \'vis\ *noun, plural* **vi·res** \'vī-ˌrēz\ [Latin — more at VIM] (1601)
: FORCE, POWER

¹**vi·sa** \'vē-zə *also* -sə\ *noun* [French, from Latin, neuter plural of *visus,* past participle] (1831)
**1** : an endorsement made on a passport by the proper authorities denoting that it has been examined and that the bearer may proceed
**2** : a signature of formal approval by a superior upon a document

²**visa** *transitive verb* **vi·saed** \-zəd, -səd\; **vi·sa·ing** \-zə-iŋ, -sə-\ (circa 1847)
: to give a visa to (a passport)

**vis·age** \'vi-zij\ *noun* [Middle English, from Old French, from *vis* face, from Latin *visus* sight, from *vidēre* to see — more at WIT] (14th century)
**1** : the face, countenance, or appearance of a person or sometimes an animal
**2** : ASPECT, APPEARANCE ⟨grimy *visage* of a mining town⟩
— **vis·aged** \-zijd\ *adjective*

¹**vis-à-vis** \ˌvēz-ə-'vē, ˌvēs- *also* -ä-'vē\ *preposition* [French, literally, face-to-face] (1755)
**1** : face-to-face with
**2** : in relation to
**3** : as compared with

²**vis-à-vis** *noun, plural* **vis-à-vis** \-ə-'vē(z), -ä-\ (circa 1757)
**1** : one that is face-to-face with another
**2 a** : ESCORT, DATE **b** : COUNTERPART
**3** : TÊTE-À-TÊTE 1

³**vis-à-vis** *adverb* (1870)
: in company : TOGETHER

**Vi·sa·yan** \və-'sī-ən\ *variant of* BISAYAN

**vis·ca·cha** \vis-'kä-chə\ *noun* [Spanish *vizcacha,* from Quechua *wisk'acha*] (1604)
: any of several South American burrowing rodents (genera *Lagostomus* and *Lagidium*) closely related to the chinchilla

viscacha

**vis·cera** *plural of* VISCUS

**vis·cer·al** \'vi-sə-rəl, 'vis-rəl\ *adjective* (1575)
**1** : felt in or as if in the viscera : DEEP ⟨*visceral* conviction⟩
**2** : not intellectual : INSTINCTIVE, UNREASONING ⟨*visceral* drives⟩
**3** : dealing with crude or elemental emotions : EARTHY ⟨a *visceral* novel⟩
**4** : of, relating to, or located on or among the viscera : SPLANCHNIC
— **vis·cer·al·ly** \-rə-lē\ *adverb*

**vis·cid** \'vi-səd\ *adjective* [Late Latin *viscidus,* from Latin *viscum* birdlime — more at VISCOUS] (1635)
**1 a** : having an adhesive quality : STICKY **b** : having a glutinous consistency : VISCOUS
**2** : covered with a sticky layer
— **vis·cid·i·ty** \vi-'si-də-tē\ *noun*
— **vis·cid·ly** \'vi-səd-lē\ *adverb*

**vis·co·elas·tic** \ˌvis-kō-ə-'las-tik\ *adjective* [*viscous* + *-o-* + *elastic*] (1935)
: having appreciable and conjoint viscous and elastic properties ⟨such *viscoelastic* materials as asphalt⟩; *also* : constituting or relating to the state of viscoelastic materials ⟨*viscoelastic* data⟩ ⟨*viscoelastic* properties⟩
— **vis·co·elas·tic·i·ty** \-ˌlas-'ti-sə-tē, -'tis-tē\ *noun*

**vis·com·e·ter** \vis-'kä-mə-tər\ *noun* [*viscosity* + *-meter*] (circa 1883)
: an instrument with which to measure viscosity
— **vis·co·met·ric** \ˌvis-kə-'me-trik\ *adjective*
— **vis·com·e·try** \-mə-trē\ *noun*

¹**vis·cose** \'vis-ˌkōs, -ˌkōz\ *noun* [obsolete *viscose,* adjective, viscous] (1896)
**1** : a viscous golden-brown solution made by treating cellulose with caustic alkali solution and carbon disulfide and used in making rayon and films of regenerated cellulose
**2** : viscose rayon

²**viscose** *adjective* (1900)
: of, relating to, or made from viscose

**vis·co·sim·e·ter** \ˌvis-kə-'si-mə-tər\ *noun* [International Scientific Vocabulary *viscosity* + *-meter*] (circa 1868)
: VISCOMETER
— **vis·cosi·met·ric** \(ˌ)vis-ˌkä-sə-'me-trik\ *adjective*

**vis·cos·i·ty** \vis-'kä-sə-tē\ *noun, plural* **-ties** [Middle English *viscosite,* from Middle French *viscosité,* from Medieval Latin *viscositat-, viscositas,* from Late Latin *viscosus* viscous] (15th century)
**1** : the quality or state of being viscous
**2** : the property of resistance to flow in a fluid or semifluid
**3** : the ratio of the tangential frictional force per unit area to the velocity gradient perpendicular to the direction of flow of a liquid — called also *coefficient of viscosity*

**viscosity index** *noun* (1929)
: an arbitrary number assigned as a measure of the constancy of the viscosity of a lubricating oil with change of temperature with higher numbers indicating viscosities that change little with temperature

**vis·count** \'vī-ˌkau̇nt\ *noun* [Middle English *viscounte,* from Middle French *viscomte,* from Medieval Latin *vicecomit-, vicecomes,* from Late Latin *vice-* vice- + *comit-, comes* count — more at COUNT] (15th century)
: a member of the peerage in Great Britain ranking below an earl and above a baron
— **vis·count·cy** \-ˌkau̇nt(t)-sē\ *noun*
— **vis·count·y** \-ˌkau̇n-tē\ *noun*

**vis·count·ess** \-ˌkau̇n-təs\ *noun* (15th century)
**1** : the wife or widow of a viscount
**2** : a woman who holds the rank of viscount in her own right

**vis·cous** \'vis-kəs\ *adjective* [Middle English *viscouse,* from Late Latin *viscosus* full of birdlime, viscous, from Latin *viscum* mistletoe, birdlime; akin to Old High German *wīhsila* cherry, Greek *ixos* mistletoe] (14th century)
**1** : VISCID
**2** : having or characterized by viscosity ⟨*viscous* flow⟩
— **vis·cous·ly** *adverb*
— **vis·cous·ness** *noun*

**vis·cus** \'vis-kəs\ *noun, plural* **vis·cera** \'vi-sə-rə\ [Latin (plural *viscera*)] (1651)
**1** : an internal organ of the body; *especially* : one (as the heart, liver, or intestine) located in the great cavity of the trunk proper
**2** *plural* : HEART 4

¹**vise** \'vīs\ *noun* [Middle French *vis* screw, something winding, from Latin *vitis* vine — more at WITHY] (1500)
**1** : any of various tools with two jaws for holding work that close usually by a screw, lever, or cam
**2** : something likened to a vise ⟨economic *vise* of slow growth and rampant price increases —David Milne⟩
— **vise·like** \-ˌlīk\ *adjective*

vise 1

²**vise** *transitive verb* **vised; vis·ing** (1602)
: to hold, force, or squeeze with or as if with a vise

¹**vi·sé** \'vē-ˌzā, vē-'\ *transitive verb* **vi·séd** *or* **vi·séed; vi·sé·ing** [French, past participle of *viser* to visa, from *visa*] (1810)
: VISA

²**visé** *noun* (1842)
: VISA

**Vish·nu** \'vish-(ˌ)nü\ *noun* [Sanskrit *Viṣṇu*] (1638)
: the preserver god of the Hindu sacred triad — compare BRAHMA, SIVA

**vis·i·bil·i·ty** \ˌvi-zə-'bi-lə-tē\ *noun, plural* **-ties** (1581)
**1** : the quality or state of being visible
**2 a** : the degree of clearness of the atmosphere; *specifically* : the greatest distance toward the horizon at which prominent objects can be identified with the naked eye **b** : capability of being readily noticed **c** : capability of affording an unobstructed view **d** : PUBLICITY 2d
**3** : a measure of the ability of radiant energy to evoke visual sensation

**vis·i·ble** \'vi-zə-bəl\ *adjective* [Middle English, from Middle French or Latin; Middle French, from Latin *visibilis,* from *visus,* past participle of *vidēre* to see] (14th century)
**1 a** : capable of being seen ⟨stars *visible* to the naked eye⟩ **b** : situated in the region of the electromagnetic spectrum perceptible to human vision ⟨*visible* light⟩ — used of radiation having a wavelength between about 400 nanometers and 700 nanometers
**2 a** : exposed to view ⟨the *visible* horizon⟩ **b** : CONSPICUOUS
**3** : capable of being discovered or perceived : RECOGNIZABLE ⟨no *visible* means of support⟩
**4** : ACCESSIBLE 4
**5** : devised to keep a particular part or item always in full view or readily seen or referred to ⟨a *visible* index⟩
— **vis·i·ble·ness** *noun*
— **vis·i·bly** \-blē\ *adverb*

**visible speech** *noun* (1865)
**1** : a set of phonetic symbols based on symbols for articulatory position
**2** : speech reproduced spectrographically

**Vis·i·goth** \'vi-zə-ˌgäth\ *noun* [Late Latin *Visigothi,* plural] (1611)
: a member of the western division of the Goths
— **Vis·i·goth·ic** \ˌvi-zə-'gä-thik\ *adjective*

¹**vi·sion** \'vi-zhən\ *noun* [Middle English, from Old French, from Latin *vision-, visio,* from *vidēre* to see — more at WIT] (14th century)
**1 a** : something seen in a dream, trance, or ecstasy; *especially* : a supernatural appearance that conveys a revelation **b** : an object of imagination **c** : a manifestation to the senses of something immaterial ⟨look, not at *visions,* but at realities —Edith Wharton⟩
**2 a** : the act or power of imagination **b** (1) : mode of seeing or conceiving (2) : unusual discernment or foresight ⟨a man of *vision*⟩ **c** : direct mystical awareness of the supernatural usually in visible form
**3 a** : the act or power of seeing : SIGHT **b** : the special sense by which the qualities of an object (as color, luminosity, shape and size) constituting its appearance are perceived and which is mediated by the eye
**4 a** : something seen **b** : a lovely or charming sight
— **vi·sion·al** \'vizh-nəl, 'vi-zhə-nᵊl\ *adjective*
— **vi·sion·al·ly** *adverb*

²**vision** *transitive verb* **vi·sioned; vi·sion·ing** \'vi-zhə-niŋ, 'vizh-niŋ\ (1795)
: ENVISION

¹**vi·sion·ary** \'vi-zhə-ˌner-ē\ *adjective* (1648)
**1 a** : of the nature of a vision : ILLUSORY **b** : incapable of being realized or achieved : UTOPIAN ⟨a *visionary* scheme⟩ **c** : existing only in imagination : UNREAL
**2 a** : able or likely to see visions **b** : disposed to reverie or imagining : DREAMY

\ə\ abut \ᵊ\ kitten \ər\ further \a\ ash \ā\ ace \ä\ mop, mar \au̇\ out \ch\ chin \e\ bet \ē\ easy \g\ go \i\ hit \ī\ ice \j\ job \ŋ\ sing \ō\ go \ȯ\ law \ȯi\ boy \th\ thin \th̲\ the \ü\ loot \u̇\ foot \y\ yet \zh\ vision *see also* Guide to Pronunciation

**3** : of, relating to, or characterized by visions or the power of vision
**4** : having or marked by foresight and imagination ⟨a *visionary* leader⟩ ⟨a *visionary* invention⟩
*synonym* see IMAGINARY
— **vi·sion·ar·i·ness** \-ē-nəs\ *noun*
²**visionary** *noun, plural* **-ar·ies** (1702)
**1** : one whose ideas or projects are impractical : DREAMER
**2** : one who sees visions : SEER
**vi·sioned** \'vi-zhənd\ *adjective* (1510)
**1** : seen in a vision ⟨a *visioned* face⟩
**2** : produced by or experienced in a vision ⟨*visioned* agony⟩
**3** : endowed with vision : INSPIRED
**vi·sion·less** \'vi-zhən-ləs\ *adjective* (1820)
**1** : SIGHTLESS, BLIND ⟨*visionless* eyes⟩
**2** : lacking vision or inspiration ⟨a *visionless* leader⟩
¹**vis·it** \'vi-zət\ *verb* **vis·it·ed** \'vi-zə-təd, 'viz-təd\; **vis·it·ing** \'vi-zə-tiŋ, 'viz-tiŋ\ [Middle English, from Old French *visiter*, from Latin *visitare*, frequentative of *visere* to go to see, frequentative of *vidēre* to see] (13th century)
*transitive verb*
**1 a** *archaic* : COMFORT — used of the Deity ⟨*visit* us with Thy salvation —Charles Wesley⟩
**b** (1) : AFFLICT ⟨*visited* his people with distempers —Tobias Smollett⟩ (2) : INFLICT, IMPOSE ⟨*visited* his wrath upon them⟩ **c** : AVENGE ⟨*visited* the sins of the fathers upon the children⟩ **d** : to present itself to or come over momentarily ⟨was *visited* by a strange notion⟩
**2** : to go to see in order to comfort or help
**3 a** : to pay a call on as an act of friendship or courtesy **b** : to reside with temporarily as a guest **c** : to go to see or stay at (a place) for a particular purpose (as business or sightseeing) **d** : to go or come officially to inspect or oversee ⟨a bishop *visiting* his parishes⟩
*intransitive verb*
**1** : to make a visit; *also* : to make frequent or regular visits
**2** : CHAT, CONVERSE
²**visit** *noun* (1621)
**1 a** : a short stay : CALL **b** : a brief residence as a guest **c** : an extended stay : SOJOURN
**2** : a journey to and stay or short sojourn at a place
**3** : an official or professional call or tour : VISITATION
**4** : the act of a naval officer in boarding a merchant ship on the high seas in exercise of the right of search
**vis·it·able** \'vi-zə-tə-bəl, 'viz-tə-\ *adjective* (1605)
**1** : subject to or allowing visitation or inspection
**2** : socially eligible to receive visits
**vis·i·tant** \'vi-zə-tənt, 'viz-tənt\ *noun* (1599)
**1** : VISITOR; *especially* : one thought to come from a spirit world
**2** : a migratory bird that appears at intervals for a limited period
— **visitant** *adjective*
**vis·i·ta·tion** \,vi-zə-'tā-shən\ *noun* (14th century)
**1** : an instance of visiting: as **a** : an official visit (as for inspection) **b** : ²WAKE **3 c** : temporary custody of a child granted to a noncustodial parent ⟨*visitation* rights⟩
**2 a** : a special dispensation of divine favor or wrath **b** : a severe trial : AFFLICTION
**3** *capitalized* : the visit of the Virgin Mary to Elizabeth recounted in Luke and celebrated July 2 by a Christian feast
**vis·i·ta·to·ri·al** \,vi-zə-tə-'tōr-ē-əl, ,viz-tə-, -'tór-\ *adjective* (1688)
: of or relating to visitation or to a judicial visitor or superintendent
**visiting** *adjective* (1949)
: invited to join or attend an institution (as a university) for a limited time ⟨a *visiting* professor⟩ ⟨a *visiting* fellow⟩
**visiting card** *noun* (1782)

: a small card presented when visiting that bears the name and sometimes the address of the visitor
**visiting fireman** *noun* (1926)
: a usually important or influential visitor whom it is desirable or expedient to entertain impressively
**visiting nurse** *noun* (circa 1924)
: a nurse employed by a hospital or social-service agency to perform public health services and especially to visit sick persons in a community
**vis·i·tor** \'vi-zə-tər, 'viz-tər\ *noun* (15th century)
: one that visits; *especially* : one that makes formal visits of inspection
**vi·sive** \'vi-ziv, 'vī-siv\ *adjective* [Medieval Latin *visivus*, from Latin *visus*, past participle of *vidēre* to see — more at WIT] (1543)
*archaic* : of, relating to, or serving for vision
**vi·sor** \'vī-zər\ *noun* [Middle English *viser*, from Anglo-French, from Old French *visiere*, from *vis* face — more at VISAGE] (14th century)
**1** : the front piece of a helmet; *especially* : a movable upper piece
**2 a** : a face mask **b** : DISGUISE
**3 a** : a projecting front on a cap for shading the eyes **b** : a usually movable flat sunshade attached at the top of an automobile windshield
— **vi·sored** \-zərd\ *adjective*
— **vi·sor·less** \-zər-ləs\ *adjective*
**vis·ta** \'vis-tə\ *noun* [Italian, sight, from *visto*, past participle of *vedere* to see, from Latin *vidēre* — more at WIT] (1644)
**1** : a distant view through or along an avenue or opening : PROSPECT
**2** : an extensive mental view (as over a stretch of time or a series of events)
**vis·taed** \'vis-təd\ *adjective* (1835)
**1** : affording or made to form a vista
**2** : seen in or as if in a vista
¹**vi·su·al** \'vi-zhə-wəl, -zhəl; 'vizh-wəl\ *adjective* [Middle English, from Late Latin *visualis*, from Latin *visus* sight, from *vidēre* to see] (1603)
**1** : of, relating to, or used in vision ⟨*visual* organs⟩
**2** : attained or maintained by sight ⟨*visual* impressions⟩
**3** : VISIBLE
**4** : producing mental images : VIVID
**5** : done or executed by sight only ⟨*visual* navigation⟩
**6** : of, relating to, or employing visual aids
— **vi·su·al·ly** \'vi-zhə-wə-lē, -zhə-lē; 'vizh-wə-lē\ *adverb*
²**visual** *noun* (1938)
: something (as a picture, chart, or film) that appeals to the sight and is variously used (as for illustration, demonstration, or promotion) — usually used in plural
**visual acuity** *noun* (1889)
: the relative ability of the visual organ to resolve detail that is usually expressed as the reciprocal of the minimum angular separation in minutes of two lines just resolvable as separate and that forms in the average human eye an angle of one minute
**visual aid** *noun* (1911)
: an instructional device (as a chart, map, or model) that appeals chiefly to vision; *especially* : an educational motion picture or filmstrip
**visual field** *noun* (1880)
: the entire expanse of space visible at a given instant without moving the eyes — called also *field of vision*
**vi·su·al·ise** *British variant of* VISUALIZE
**vi·su·al·i·za·tion** \,vi-zhə-wə-lə-'zā-shən, ,vi-zhə-lə-, ,vizh-wə-lə-\ *noun* (1883)
**1** : formation of mental visual images
**2** : the act or process of interpreting in visual terms or of putting into visible form
**3** : the process of making an internal organ visible by the introduction (as by swallowing,

by an injection, or by an enema) of a radiopaque substance followed by roentgenography
**vi·su·al·ize** \'vi-zhə-wə-,līz, 'vi-zhə-,līz, 'vizh-wə-,līz\ *verb* **-ized; -iz·ing** (1863)
*transitive verb*
: to make visible: as **a** : to see or form a mental image of **b** : to make (an organ) visible by roentgenographic visualization
*intransitive verb*
: to form a mental visual image
**vi·su·al·iz·er** \-,lī-zər\ *noun* (1886)
: one that visualizes; *especially* : a person whose mental imagery is prevailingly visual
**visual literacy** *noun* (1971)
: the ability to recognize and understand ideas conveyed through visible actions or images (as pictures)
**visual purple** *noun* (1878)
: a photosensitive red or purple pigment in the retinal rods of various vertebrates; *especially* : RHODOPSIN
**vi·ta** \'vē-tə, 'vī-tə\ *noun, plural* **vi·tae** \'vē-,tī, -tē\ [Latin, literally, life] (1939)
**1** : a brief biographical sketch
**2** : CURRICULUM VITAE
**vi·tal** \'vī-t°l\ *adjective* [Middle English, from Middle French, from Latin *vitalis* of life, from *vita* life; akin to Latin *vivere* to live — more at QUICK] (14th century)
**1 a** : existing as a manifestation of life **b** : concerned with or necessary to the maintenance of life ⟨*vital* organs⟩ ⟨blood and other *vital* fluids⟩
**2** : full of life and vigor : ANIMATED
**3** : characteristic of life or living beings
**4 a** : fundamentally concerned with or affecting life or living beings: as (1) : tending to renew or refresh the living : INVIGORATING (2) : destructive to life : MORTAL **b** : of the utmost importance
**5** : recording data relating to lives
**6** : of, relating to, or constituting the staining of living tissues
*synonym* see ESSENTIAL
— **vi·tal·ly** \-t°l-ē\ *adverb*
**vital capacity** *noun* (1852)
: the breathing capacity of the lungs expressed as the number of cubic inches or cubic centimeters of air that can be forcibly exhaled after a full inspiration
**vi·tal·ism** \'vī-t°l-,i-zəm\ *noun* (1822)
**1** : a doctrine that the functions of a living organism are due to a vital principle distinct from physicochemical forces
**2** : a doctrine that the processes of life are not explicable by the laws of physics and chemistry alone and that life is in some part self-determining
— **vi·tal·ist** \-t°l-ist\ *noun or adjective*
— **vi·tal·is·tic** \,vī-t°l-'is-tik\ *adjective*
**vi·tal·i·ty** \vī-'ta-lə-tē\ *noun, plural* **-ties** (1592)
**1 a** : the peculiarity distinguishing the living from the nonliving **b** : capacity to live and develop; *also* : physical or mental vigor especially when highly developed
**2 a** : power of enduring **b** : lively and animated character
**vi·tal·ize** \'vī-t°l-,īz\ *transitive verb* **-ized; -iz·ing** (1678)
: to endow with vitality : ANIMATE
— **vi·tal·i·za·tion** \,vī-t°l-ə-'zā-shən\ *noun*
**vi·tals** \'vī-t°lz\ *noun plural* (circa 1610)
**1** : vital organs (as the heart, liver, lungs, and brain)
**2** : essential parts
**vital signs** *noun plural* (circa 1919)
: signs of life; *specifically* : the pulse rate, respiratory rate, body temperature, and often blood pressure of a person
**vital statistics** *noun plural* (1837)
**1** : statistics relating to births, deaths, marriages, health, and disease

**2 :** facts (as physical dimensions or quantities) considered to be interesting or important; *especially* **:** a woman's bust, waist, and hip measurements

**vi·ta·min** \'vī-tə-mən, *British usually* 'vi-\ *noun* [Latin *vita* life + International Scientific Vocabulary *amine*] (1912)
**:** any of various organic substances that are essential in minute quantities to the nutrition of most animals and some plants, act especially as coenzymes and precursors of coenzymes in the regulation of metabolic processes but do not provide energy or serve as building units, and are present in natural foodstuffs or sometimes produced within the body

**vitamin A** *noun* (1920)
**:** any of several fat-soluble vitamins (as retinol) found especially in animal products (as egg yolk, milk, or fish-liver oils) or a mixture of them whose lack in the animal body causes epithelial tissues to become keratinous (as in the eye with resulting visual defects)

**vitamin B** *noun* (1920)
**1 :** VITAMIN B COMPLEX
**2** *or* **vitamin B₁** \-'bē-'wən\ **:** THIAMINE

**vitamin B complex** *noun* (1928)
**:** a group of water-soluble vitamins found especially in yeast, seed germs, eggs, liver and flesh, and vegetables that have varied metabolic functions and include coenzymes and growth factors — called also *B complex*; compare BIOTIN, CHOLINE, NICOTINIC ACID, PANTOTHENIC ACID

**vitamin B₆** \-'bē-'siks\ *noun* (1934)
**:** pyridoxine or a closely related compound found widely in combined form and considered essential to vertebrate nutrition

**vitamin B₁₂** \-'bē-'twelv\ *noun* (1948)
**1 :** a complex cobalt-containing compound $C_{63}H_{88}CoN_{14}O_{14}P$ that occurs especially in liver, is essential to normal blood formation, neural function, and growth, and is used especially in treating pernicious and related anemias and in animal feed as a growth factor — called also *cyanocobalamin*
**2 :** any of several compounds similar to vitamin B₁₂ in action but having different chemistry

**vitamin B₂** \-'bē-'tü\ *noun* (1928)
**:** RIBOFLAVIN

**vitamin C** *noun* (1920)
**:** a water-soluble vitamin $C_6H_8O_6$ found in plants and especially in fruits and leafy vegetables or made synthetically and used in the prevention and treatment of scurvy and as an antioxidant for foods — called also *ascorbic acid*

**vitamin D** *noun* (1921)
**:** any or all of several fat-soluble vitamins chemically related to steroids, essential for normal bone and tooth structure, and found especially in fish-liver oils, egg yolk, and milk or produced by activation (as by ultraviolet irradiation) of sterols: as **a** *or* **vitamin D₂** \-'dē-'tü\ **:** CALCIFEROL **b** *or* **vitamin D₃** \-'dē-'thrē\ **:** CHOLECALCIFEROL

**vitamin E** *noun* (1925)
**:** any of several fat-soluble vitamins that are chemically tocopherols, are essential in the nutrition of various vertebrates in which their absence is associated with infertility, degenerative changes in muscle, or vascular abnormalities, are found especially in leaves and in seed germ oils, and are used chiefly in animal feeds and as antioxidants

**vitamin G** *noun* (1929)
**:** RIBOFLAVIN

**vitamin H** *noun* (circa 1935)
**:** BIOTIN

**vitamin K** *noun* [Danish *koagulation* coagulation] (1935)
**1 :** either of two naturally occurring fat-soluble vitamins $C_{31}H_{46}O_2$ and $C_{41}H_{56}O_2$ essential for the clotting of blood because of their role in the production of prothrombin — called also respectively *vitamin K₁*, *vitamin K₂*

**2 :** any of several synthetic compounds closely related chemically to natural vitamins K₁ and K₂ and of similar biological activity

**vi·tel·line** \vī-'te-lən, -,lēn, -,līn\ *adjective* [Middle English, from Middle French *vitellin,* from Medieval Latin *vitellinus,* from Latin *vitellus*] (15th century)
**1 :** resembling the yolk of an egg especially in yellow color
**2 :** of, relating to, or producing yolk

**vitelline membrane** *noun* (1845)
**:** a membrane that encloses the egg proper, corresponds to the plasmalemma of an ordinary cell, and in many animals forms the fertilization membrane by separating from the plasma membrane immediately after fertilization

**vi·tel·lo·gen·e·sis** \vī-,te-lō-'je-nə-səs, və-\ *noun* [New Latin, from Latin *vitellus* + New Latin *-o-* + *genesis*] (1947)
**:** yolk formation

**vi·tel·lus** \vī-'te-ləs\ *noun* [Latin] (1728)
**:** the egg cell proper including the yolk but excluding any albuminous or membranous envelopes; *also* **:** YOLK 1c

**vi·ti·ate** \'vi-shē-,āt\ *transitive verb* **-at·ed; -at·ing** [Latin *vitiatus,* past participle of *vitiare,* from *vitium* fault, vice] (1534)
**1 :** to make faulty or defective **:** IMPAIR ⟨the comic impact is *vitiated* by obvious haste —William Styron⟩
**2 :** to debase in moral or aesthetic status ⟨a mind *vitiated* by prejudice⟩
**3 :** to make ineffective ⟨fraud *vitiates* a contract⟩
**synonym** see DEBASE
— **vi·ti·a·tion** \,vi-shē-'ā-shən\ *noun*
— **vi·ti·a·tor** \'vi-shē-,ā-tər\ *noun*

**vi·ti·cul·ture** \'vi-tə-,kəl-chər, 'vī-\ *noun* [Latin *vitis* vine + English *culture* — more at WITHY] (1872)
**:** the cultivation or culture of grapes especially for wine making
— **vi·ti·cul·tur·al** \,vi-tə-'kəl-chə-rəl, ,vī-, -'kəlch-rəl\ *adjective*
— **vi·ti·cul·tur·al·ly** *adverb*
— **vi·ti·cul·tur·ist** \-rist\ *noun*

**vit·i·li·go** \,vi-t°l-'ī-(,)gō, -'ē-\ *noun* [New Latin, from Latin, tetter] (1842)
**:** a skin disorder manifested by smooth white spots on various parts of the body

**vit·rec·to·my** \və-'trek-tə-mē\ *noun, plural* **-mies** [*vitreous* humor + *-ectomy*] (1968)
**:** surgical removal of all or part of the vitreous humor

**¹vit·re·ous** \'vi-trē-əs\ *adjective* [Latin *vitreus,* from *vitrum* glass] (1646)
**1 :** of, relating to, derived from, or consisting of glass
**2 a :** resembling glass (as in color, composition, brittleness, or luster) **:** GLASSY ⟨*vitreous* rocks⟩ **b :** characterized by low porosity and usually translucence due to the presence of a glassy phase ⟨*vitreous* china⟩
**3 :** of, relating to, or constituting the vitreous humor

**²vitreous** *noun* (1869)
**:** VITREOUS HUMOR

**vitreous humor** *noun* (1663)
**:** the clear colorless transparent jelly that fills the eyeball posterior to the lens — see EYE illustration

**vitreous silica** *noun* (1925)
**:** a chemically stable and refractory glass made from silica alone — compare QUARTZ GLASS

**vit·ri·fy** \'vi-trə-,fī\ *verb* **-fied; -fy·ing** [Middle French *vitrifier,* from Latin *vitrum* glass] (1594)
*transitive verb*
**:** to convert into glass or a glassy substance by heat and fusion
*intransitive verb*
**:** to become vitrified
— **vit·ri·fi·able** \,vi-trə-'fī-ə-bəl\ *adjective*

— **vit·ri·fi·ca·tion** \,vi-trə-fə-'kā-shən\ *noun*

**vi·trine** \və-'trēn\ *noun* [French, from *vitre* pane of glass, from Old French, from Latin *vitrum*] (1880)
**:** a glass showcase or cabinet especially for displaying fine wares or specimens

**vit·ri·ol** \'vi-trē-əl\ *noun* [Middle English, from Middle French, from Medieval Latin *vitriolum,* alteration of Late Latin *vitreolum,* neuter of *vitreolus* glassy, from Latin *vitreus* vitreous] (14th century)
**1 a :** a sulfate of any of various metals (as copper, iron, or zinc); *especially* **:** a glassy hydrate of such a sulfate **b :** OIL OF VITRIOL
**2 :** something felt to resemble vitriol especially in caustic quality; *especially* **:** virulence of feeling or of speech
— **vit·ri·ol·ic** \,vi-trē-'ä-lik\ *adjective*

**vit·ta** \'vi-tə\ *noun, plural* **vit·tae** \'vi-tē, 'vi-,tē, 'vi-,tī\ [New Latin, from Latin, fillet; akin to Latin *viēre* to plait — more at WIRE] (1819)
**1 :** STRIPE, STREAK
**2 :** one of the oil tubes in the fruits of plants of the carrot family

**vit·tles** \'vi-t°lz\ *noun plural* (14th century)
**:** VICTUALS

**vi·tu·per·ate** \vī-'tü-pə-,rāt, və-, -'tyü-\ *verb* **-at·ed; -at·ing** [Latin *vituperatus,* past participle of *vituperare,* from *vitium* fault + *parare* to make, prepare — more at PARE] (1542)
*transitive verb*
**:** to abuse or censure severely or abusively **:** BERATE
*intransitive verb*
**:** to use harsh condemnatory language
**synonym** see SCOLD
— **vi·tu·per·a·tor** \-,rā-tər\ *noun*

**vi·tu·per·a·tion** \(,)vī-,tü-pə-'rā-shən, və-, -,tyü-\ *noun* (15th century)
**1 :** sustained and bitter railing and condemnation **:** vituperative utterance
**2 :** an act or instance of vituperating
**synonym** see ABUSE

**vi·tu·per·a·tive** \vī-'tü-p(ə-)rə-tiv, -pə-,rā-\ *adjective* (1727)
**:** uttering or given to censure **:** containing or characterized by verbal abuse
— **vi·tu·per·a·tive·ly** *adverb*

**vi·tu·per·a·to·ry** \-p(ə-)rə-,tōr-ē, -,tòr-\ *adjective* (1586)
**:** VITUPERATIVE

**vi·va** \'vē-və, -,vä\ *interjection* [Italian & Spanish, long live, from 3d person singular present subjunctive of *vivere* to live, from Latin — more at QUICK] (circa 1700)
— used to express goodwill or approval

**¹vi·va·ce** \vē-'vä-(,)chä, -chē\ *adverb or adjective* [Italian, vivacious, from Latin *vivac-, vivax*] (1683)
**:** in a brisk spirited manner — used as a direction in music

**²vivace** *noun* (circa 1683)
**:** a musical composition or movement in vivace tempo

**vi·va·cious** \və-'vā-shəs *also* vī-\ *adjective* [Latin *vivac-, vivax,* literally, long-lived, from *vivere* to live] (circa 1645)
**:** lively in temper, conduct, or spirit **:** SPRIGHTLY
**synonym** see LIVELY
— **vi·va·cious·ly** *adverb*
— **vi·va·cious·ness** *noun*

**vi·vac·i·ty** \-'va-sə-tē\ *noun* (15th century)
**:** the quality or state of being vivacious

**vi·van·dière** \,vē-,vän-'dyer\ *noun* [French, feminine of Middle French *vivandier,* from Medieval Latin *vivanda* food — more at VIAND] (1848)

---

\ə\ abut \ᵊ\ kitten \ər\ further \a\ ash \ā\ ace
\ä\ mop, mar \aú\ out \ch\ chin \e\ bet \ē\ easy
\g\ go \i\ hit \ī\ ice \j\ job \ŋ\ sing \ō\ go
\ò\ law \ói\ boy \th\ thin \th\ the \ü\ loot \ú\ foot
\y\ yet \zh\ vision *see also* Guide to Pronunciation

: a female sutler

**vi·var·i·um** \vī-'var-ē-əm, -'ver-\ *noun, plural* **-ia** \-ē-ə\ *or* **-i·ums** [Latin, park, preserve, from *vivus* alive — more at QUICK] (1853)
: a terrarium used especially for small animals

¹**vi·va vo·ce** \,vī-və-'vō-(,)sē *or (as if from Italian)* ,vē-və-'vō-(,)chā\ *adverb* [Medieval Latin, with the living voice] (1563)
: by word of mouth : ORALLY

²**viva voce** *adjective* (1654)
: expressed or conducted by word of mouth : ORAL

³**viva voce** *noun* (1842)
: an examination conducted viva voce — called also *viva*

**vi·vax malaria** \'vī-,vaks-\ *noun* [New Latin *vivax*, specific epithet of *Plasmodium vivax*, parasite causing tertian] (circa 1941)
: malaria caused by a plasmodium (*Plasmodium vivax*) that induces paroxysms at 48-hour intervals

**vi·ver·rid** \vī-'ver-əd\ *noun* [New Latin *Viverridae*, from *Viverra*, type genus, from Latin *viverra* ferret; akin to Old English *ācweorna* squirrel, Lithuanian *voverė̃*] (1902)
: any of a family (*Viverridae*) of carnivorous mammals (as a civet, a genet, or a mongoose) that are rarely larger than a domestic cat but are long, slender, and like a weasel in build with short more or less retractile claws and rounded feet
— **viverrid** *adjective*

**vi·vers** \'vē-vərz, 'vī-\ *noun plural* [Middle French *vivres*, plural of *vivre* food, from *vivre* to live, from Latin *vivere*] (1536)
*chiefly Scottish* : VICTUALS, FOOD

**Viv·i·an** *or* **Viv·i·en** \'vi-vē-ən\ *noun*
: the mistress of Merlin in Arthurian legend — called also *Lady of the Lake*

**viv·id** \'vi-vəd\ *adjective* [Latin *vividus*, from *vivere* to live — more at QUICK] (1638)
**1** : having the appearance of vigorous life or freshness : LIVELY ⟨a *vivid* sketch⟩
**2** *of a color* : very strong : very high in chroma
**3** : producing a strong or clear impression on the senses : SHARP, INTENSE; *specifically* : producing distinct mental images ⟨a *vivid* description⟩
**4** : acting clearly and vigorously ⟨a *vivid* imagination⟩
*synonym* see GRAPHIC
— **viv·id·ly** *adverb*
— **viv·id·ness** *noun*

**vi·vif·ic** \vī-'vi-fik\ *adjective* [Latin *vivificus*] (1551)
: imparting spirit or vivacity

**viv·i·fy** \'vi-və-,fī\ *transitive verb* **-fied; -fy·ing** [Middle French *vivifier*, from Late Latin *vivificare*, from Latin *vivificus* enlivening, from *vivus* alive — more at QUICK] (1545)
**1** : to endue with life or renewed life : ANIMATE ⟨rains that *vivify* the barren hills⟩
**2** : to impart vitality or vividness to ⟨concentrating this union of quality and meaning in a way which *vivifies* both —John Dewey⟩
*synonym* see QUICKEN
— **viv·i·fi·ca·tion** \,vi-və-fə-'kā-shən\ *noun*
— **viv·i·fi·er** \'vi-və-,fī-(ə)r\ *noun*

**vi·vi·par·i·ty** \,vī-və-'par-ət-ē, ,vi-\ *noun* (1864)
: the quality or state of being viviparous

**vi·vip·a·rous** \vī-'vi-p(ə-)rəs, və-\ *adjective* [Latin *viviparus*, from *vivus* alive + *-parus* -parous] (1646)
**1** : producing living young instead of eggs from within the body in the manner of nearly all mammals, many reptiles, and a few fishes
**2** : germinating while still attached to the parent plant ⟨the *viviparous* seed of the mangrove⟩
— **vi·vip·a·rous·ly** *adverb*

**viv·i·sect** \'vi-və-,sekt\ *verb* [back-formation from *vivisection*] (1864)
*transitive verb*
: to perform vivisection on : subject to vivisection
*intransitive verb*
: to practice vivisection
— **viv·i·sec·tor** \-,sek-tər\ *noun*

**viv·i·sec·tion** \,vi-və-'sek-shən, 'vi-və-,\ *noun* [Latin *vivus* + English *section*] (1707)
**1** : the cutting of or operation on a living animal usually for physiological or pathological investigation; *broadly* : animal experimentation especially if considered to cause distress to the subject
**2** : minute or pitiless examination or criticism
— **viv·i·sec·tion·al** \,vi-və-'sek-shnəl, -shə-nᵊl\ *adjective*
— **viv·i·sec·tion·ist** \-'sek-sh(ə-)nist\ *noun*

**vix·en** \'vik-sən\ *noun* [[assumed] Middle English (southern dialect) *vixen*, alteration of Middle English *fixen*, from Old English *fyxe*, feminine of *fox*] (1590)
**1** : a shrewish ill-tempered woman
**2** : a female fox ◆
— **vix·en·ish** \-s(ə-)nish\ *adjective*

**viz·ard** \'vi-zərd, -,zärd\ *noun* [alteration of Middle English *viser* mask, visor] (circa 1555)
**1** : a mask for disguise or protection
**2** : DISGUISE, GUISE

**viz·ca·cha** *variant of* VISCACHA

**vi·zier** \və-'zir\ *noun* [Turkish *vezir*, from Arabic *wazīr*] (1599)
: a high executive officer of various Muslim countries and especially of the Ottoman Empire
— **vi·zier·ate** \-'zir-ət, -'zir-,āt\ *noun*
— **vi·zier·ial** \-'zir-ē-əl\ *adjective*
— **vi·zier·ship** \-'zir-,ship\ *noun*

**vi·zor** *variant of* VISOR

**vizs·la** \'vēz-lə, 'vēs-, 'vizh-\ *noun* [Hungarian] (1945)
: any of a breed of hunting dogs of Hungarian origin that resemble the weimaraner but have a rich deep red coat and brown eyes

**vizsla**

**VLDL** \,vē-(,)el-(,)dē-'el\ *noun* [*very low-density lipoprotein*] (1977)
: a plasma lipoprotein that is produced primarily by the liver with lesser amounts contributed by the intestine, that contains relatively large amounts of triglycerides compared to protein, and that leaves a residue of cholesterol in the tissues during the process of conversion to LDL — compare HDL

**V neck** *noun* (1905)
: a V-shaped neck of a garment; *also* : a garment (as a sweater) with a V-shaped neck
— **V-necked** *adjective*

**vo·ca·ble** \'vō-kə-bəl\ *noun* [Middle French, from Latin *vocabulum*, from *vocare* to call, from *vox* voice — more at VOICE] (1530)
: TERM; *specifically* : a word composed of various sounds or letters without regard to its meaning

**vo·cab·u·lar** \vō-'ka-byə-lər, və-\ *adjective* [back-formation from *vocabulary*] (1608)
: of or relating to words or phraseology : VERBAL

**vo·cab·u·lary** \vō-'ka-byə-,ler-ē, və-\ *noun, plural* **-lar·ies** [Middle French *vocabulaire*, probably from Medieval Latin *vocabularium*, from neuter of *vocabularius* verbal, from Latin *vocabulum*] (1532)
**1** : a list or collection of words or of words and phrases usually alphabetically arranged and explained or defined : LEXICON
**2 a** : a sum or stock of words employed by a language, group, individual, or work or in a field of knowledge **b** : a list or collection of terms or codes available for use (as in an indexing system)

**3** : a supply of expressive techniques or devices (as of an art form)

**vocabulary entry** *noun* (circa 1934)
: a word (as the noun *book*), hyphenated or open compound (as the verb *book-match* or the noun *book review*), word element (as the affix *pro-*), abbreviation (as *agt*), verbalized symbol (as *Na*), or term (as *man in the street*) entered alphabetically in a dictionary for the purpose of definition or identification or expressly included as an inflected form (as the noun *mice* or the verb *saw*) or as a derived form (as the noun *godlessness* or the adverb *globally*) or related phrase (as *one for the book*) run on at its base word and usually set in a type (as boldface) readily distinguishable from that of the lightface running text which defines, explains, or identifies the entry

¹**vo·cal** \'vō-kəl\ *adjective* [Middle English, from Latin *vocalis*, from *voc-, vox* voice — more at VOICE] (14th century)
**1 a** : uttered by the voice : ORAL **b** : produced in the larynx : uttered with voice
**2** : relating to, composed or arranged for, or sung by the human voice ⟨*vocal* music⟩
**3** : VOCALIC
**4 a** : having or exercising the power of producing voice, speech, or sound **b** : EXPRESSIVE **c** : full of voices : RESOUNDING **d** : given to expressing oneself freely or insistently : OUTSPOKEN **e** : expressed in words
**5** : of, relating to, or resembling the voice ⟨*vocal* impairment⟩
— **vo·cal·i·ty** \vō-'ka-lə-tē\ *noun*
— **vo·cal·ly** \'vō-kə-lē\ *adverb*

²**vocal** *noun* (1582)
**1** : a vocal sound
**2** : a usually accompanied musical composition for the human voice : SONG; *also* : a performance of such a composition

**vocal cords** *noun plural* (1852)
: either of two pairs of folds of mucous membranes that project into the cavity of the larynx and have free edges extending dorsoventrally toward the middle line

**vocal folds** *noun plural* (1924)
: the lower pair of vocal cords each of which when drawn taut, approximated to the contralateral member of the pair, and subjected to a flow of breath produces the voice

¹**vo·cal·ic** \vō-'ka-lik, və-\ *adjective* [Latin *vocalis* vowel, from *vocalis* vocal] (1814)
**1** : marked by or consisting of vowels

◇ **WORD HISTORY**

**vixen** Even though *very, voice,* and *visit* are now in everyday use, English originally had no words beginning with a \v\ sound. Almost all words beginning with *v* have been borrowed from other languages, such as French or Latin. The sound \v\ did exist in Old English, but it could only appear in the middle of words, not at the beginning or end. Because the \v\ sound was in a complementary relation with the sound \f\, which could appear at the beginning and end of words but not the middle, the single letter *f* sufficed in Old English to spell both \f\ and \v\. In parts of southern England, however, medieval speakers of English began to pronounce all instances of initial \f\ as \v\ and initial \s\ as \z\; this tendency continues today among rural dialect speakers in southwestern England, so that *finger* is pronounced as if it were spelled *vinger* and *seven* as if it were spelled *zeven*. A handful of such dialectal pronunciations with initial \v\ for \f\ became standard in early Modern English, and the words affected have consequently been respelled with *v.* These include *vat* (from Old English *fæt*), *vane* (from Old English *fana* "banner"), and *vixen* (from Old English *fyxe*). The change of consonant in *vixen* obscures the original relation of the word to *fox.*

**2 a :** being or functioning as a vowel **b :** of, relating to, or associated with a vowel
— **vo·cal·i·cal·ly** \-li-k(ə-)lē\ *adverb*
**²vocalic** *noun* (1924)
**:** a vowel sound or sequence in its function as the most sonorous part of a syllable
**vo·cal·ise** *British variant of* VOCALIZE
**vo·cal·ism** \'vō-kə-,li-zəm\ *noun* (circa 1859)
**1 :** VOCALIZATION
**2 :** vocal art or technique **:** SINGING
**3 a :** the vowel system of a language or dialect **b :** the pattern of vowels in a word or paradigm
**vo·cal·ist** \-kə-list\ *noun* (1834)
**:** ¹SINGER
**vo·cal·ize** \'vō-kə-,līz\ *verb* **-ized; -iz·ing** (1669)
*transitive verb*
**1 :** to give voice to **:** UTTER; *specifically* **:** SING
**2 a :** to make voiced rather than voiceless **:** VOICE **b :** to convert to a vowel
**3 :** to furnish (as a consonantal Hebrew or Arabic text) with vowels or vowel points
*intransitive verb*
**1 :** to utter vocal sounds
**2 :** SING; *specifically* **:** to sing without words
— **vo·cal·i·za·tion** \,vō-kə-lə-'zā-shən\ *noun*
— **vo·cal·iz·er** \'vō-kə-,lī-zər\ *noun*
**vo·ca·tion** \vō-'kā-shən\ *noun* [Middle English *vocacioun*, from Latin *vocation-*, *vocatio* summons, from *vocare* to call, from *vox* voice — more at VOICE] (15th century)
**1 a :** a summons or strong inclination to a particular state or course of action; *especially* **:** a divine call to the religious life **b :** an entry into the priesthood or a religious order
**2 a :** the work in which a person is regularly employed **:** OCCUPATION **b :** the persons engaged in a particular occupation
**3 :** the special function of an individual or group
**vo·ca·tion·al** \-shnəl, -shə-n°l\ *adjective* (1652)
**1 :** of, relating to, or concerned with a vocation
**2 :** of, relating to, or being in training in a skill or trade to be pursued as a career
— **vo·ca·tion·al·ly** *adverb*
**vo·ca·tion·al·ism** \-shnə-,li-zəm, -shə-n°l-,i-zəm\ *noun* (1924)
**:** emphasis on vocational training in education
— **vo·ca·tion·al·ist** \-list, -ist\ *noun*
**¹voc·a·tive** \'vä-kə-tiv\ *adjective* [Middle English *vocatif*, from Middle French, from Latin *vocativus*, from *vocatus*, past participle of *vocare*] (15th century)
**1 :** of, relating to, or being a grammatical case marking the one addressed (as Latin *Domine* in *miserere, Domine* "have mercy, O Lord")
**2** *of a word or word group* **:** marking the one addressed (as *mother* in "mother, come here")
— **voc·a·tive·ly** *adverb*
**²vocative** *noun* (circa 1522)
**1 :** the vocative case of a language
**2 :** a form in the vocative case
**vo·cif·er·ant** \vō-'si-fə-rənt\ *adjective* (1609)
**·** : CLAMOROUS, VOCIFEROUS
**vo·cif·er·ate** \-,rāt\ *verb* **-at·ed; -at·ing** [Latin *vociferatus*, past participle of *vociferari*, from *voc-, vox* voice + *ferre* to bear — more at VOICE, BEAR] (1599)
*transitive verb*
**:** to utter loudly **:** SHOUT
*intransitive verb*
**:** to cry out loudly **:** CLAMOR
— **vo·cif·er·a·tion** \-,si-fə-'rā-shən\ *noun*
— **vo·cif·er·a·tor** \-'si-fə-,rā-tər\ *noun*
**vo·cif·er·ous** \vō-'si-f(ə-)rəs\ *adjective* (circa 1611)
**:** marked by or given to vehement insistent outcry ☆
— **vo·cif·er·ous·ly** *adverb*
— **vo·cif·er·ous·ness** *noun*
**vo·cod·er** \'vō-'kō-dər\ *noun* [*voice coder*] (1939)

**:** an electronic mechanism that reduces speech signals to slowly varying signals transmittable over communication systems of limited frequency bandwidth
**vod·ka** \'väd-kə\ *noun* [Russian, from *voda* water; akin to Old English *wæter* water] (circa 1803)
**:** a colorless liquor of neutral spirits distilled from a mash (as of rye or wheat)
**vodka martini** *noun* (1948)
**:** a martini made with vodka instead of gin
**vo·dun** *also* **vo·doun** \vō-'dü<sup>n</sup>\ *noun* [Haitian Creole] (1920)
**:** VOODOO 1
**vo·gie** \'vō-gē\ *adjective* [origin unknown] (1712)
*Scottish* **:** PROUD, VAIN
**¹vogue** \'vōg\ *noun* [Middle French, action of rowing, course, fashion, from Old Italian *voga*, from *vogare* to row] (1571)
**1** *archaic* **:** the leading place in popularity or acceptance
**2 a :** popular acceptation or favor **:** POPULARITY **b :** a period of popularity
**3 :** one that is in fashion at a particular time
*synonym* see FASHION
— **vogue** *adjective*
**²vogue** *intransitive verb* [from *Vogue*, a fashion magazine] **vogued; vogu·ing** *or* **vogue·ing** (1989)
**:** to strike poses in campy imitation of fashion models especially as a kind of dance
— **vogu·er** \'vō-gər\ *noun*
**vogu·ish** \'vō-gish\ *adjective* (1926)
**1 :** FASHIONABLE, SMART
**2 :** suddenly or temporarily popular
— **vogu·ish·ness** *noun*
**¹voice** \'vois\ *noun* [Middle English, from Old French *vois*, from Latin *voc-, vox;* akin to Old High German gi*wahanen* to mention, Greek *epos* word, speech, Sanskrit *vāk* voice] (14th century)
**1 a :** sound produced by vertebrates by means of lungs, larynx, or syrinx; *especially* **:** sound so produced by human beings **b** (1) **:** musical sound produced by the vocal folds and resonated by the cavities of head and throat (2) **:** the power or ability to produce musical tones (3) **:** SINGER (4) **:** one of the melodic parts in a vocal or instrumental composition (5) **:** condition of the vocal organs with respect to production of musical tones (6) **:** the use of the voice (as in singing or acting) (studying *voice*) **c :** expiration of air with the vocal cords drawn close so as to vibrate audibly (as in uttering vowels and consonant sounds as \v\ or \z\) **d :** the faculty of utterance (lost my *voice*)
**2 :** a sound resembling or suggesting vocal utterance
**3 :** an instrument or medium of expression (the party became the *voice* of the workers)
**4 a :** wish, choice, or opinion openly or formally expressed (the *voice* of the people) **b :** right of expression; *also* **:** influential power
**5 :** distinction of form or a system of inflections of a verb to indicate the relation of the subject of the verb to the action which the verb expresses (active and passive *voices*)
— **with one voice :** without dissent **:** UNANIMOUSLY
**²voice** *transitive verb* **voiced; voic·ing** (15th century)
**1 :** to express in words **:** UTTER (*voice* a complaint)
**2 :** to adjust for producing the proper musical sounds
**3 :** to pronounce (as a consonant) with voice
*synonym* see EXPRESS
**voice box** *noun* (1912)
**:** LARYNX
**voiced** \'voist\ *adjective* (1593)
**1 :** having or furnished with a voice especially of a specified kind — often used in combination (soft-*voiced*)
**2 :** uttered with vocal cord vibration (a *voiced* consonant)

**voice·ful** \'vois-fəl\ *adjective* (circa 1611)
**:** having a voice or vocal quality; *also* **:** having a loud voice or many voices
— **voice·ful·ness** *noun*
**voice·less** \-ləs\ *adjective* (1535)
**1 :** having no voice **:** MUTE
**2 :** not voiced **:** SURD (a *voiceless* consonant)
— **voice·less·ly** *adverb*
— **voice·less·ness** *noun*
**voice mail** *noun* (1981)
**:** an electronic communication system in which spoken messages are recorded or digitized for later playback to the intended recipient
**voice–over** \'vois-,ō-vər\ *noun* (circa 1947)
**1 a :** the voice of an unseen narrator speaking (as in a motion picture or television commercial) **b :** the voice of a visible character (as in a motion picture) expressing unspoken thoughts
**2 :** a recording of a voice-over
**voice part** *noun* (1776)
**:** VOICE 1b(4)
**voice·print** \'vois-print\ *noun* [*voice* + *fingerprint*] (1962)
**:** an individually distinctive pattern of certain voice characteristics that is spectrographically produced
**voic·er** \'voi-sər\ *noun* (1879)
**:** one that voices; *specifically* **:** one that voices organ pipes
**voice vote** *noun* (1924)
**:** a parliamentary vote taken by calling for ayes and noes and estimating which response is stronger
**¹void** \'void\ *adjective* [Middle English *voide*, from Old French, from (assumed) Vulgar Latin *vocitus*, alteration of Latin *vocivus, vacivus* empty, from *vacare* to be empty] (14th century)
**1 a :** not occupied **:** VACANT (a *void* bishopric) **b :** not inhabited **:** DESERTED
**2 :** containing nothing (*void* space)
**3 :** IDLE, LEISURE
**4 a :** being without **:** DEVOID (a nature *void* of all malice) **b :** having no members or examples; *specifically, of a suit* **:** having no cards represented in a particular hand
**5 :** VAIN, USELESS
**6 a :** of no legal force or effect **:** NULL (a *void* contract) **b :** VOIDABLE
*synonym* see EMPTY
— **void·ness** *noun*
**²void** *noun* (1616)
**1 a :** OPENING, GAP **b :** empty space **:** EMPTINESS, VACUUM

---

☆ SYNONYMS
**Vociferous, clamorous, blatant, strident, boisterous, obstreperous** mean so loud or insistent as to compel attention. VOCIFEROUS implies a vehement shouting or calling out (*vociferous* cries of protest and outrage). CLAMOROUS may imply insistency as well as vociferousness in demanding or protesting (*clamorous* demands for prison reforms). BLATANT implies an offensive bellowing or insensitive loudness (*blatant* rock music) (a *blatant* clamor for impeachment). STRIDENT suggests harsh and discordant noise (heard the *strident* cry of the crow). BOISTEROUS suggests a noisiness and turbulence due to high spirits (a *boisterous* crowd of party goers). OBSTREPEROUS suggests unruly and aggressive noisiness and resistance to restraint (the *obstreperous* demonstrators were removed from the hall).

---

\ə\ abut \ə\ kitten \ər\ further \a\ ash \ā\ ace
\ä\ mop, mar \aú\ out \ch\ chin \e\ bet \ē\ easy
\g\ go \i\ hit \ī\ ice \j\ job \ŋ\ sing \ō\ go
\ò\ law \òi\ boy \th\ thin \th\ the \ü\ loot \ú\ foot
\y\ yet \zh\ vision *see also* Guide to Pronunciation

**2 :** the quality or state of being without something **:** LACK, ABSENCE
**3 :** a feeling of want or hollowness
**4 :** absence of cards of a particular suit in a hand originally dealt to a player
³**void** *verb* [Middle English, from Middle French *vuidier*, from (assumed) Vulgar Latin *vocitare*, from *vocitus*] (14th century)
*transitive verb*
**1 a :** to make empty or vacant **:** CLEAR **b** *archaic* **:** VACATE, LEAVE
**2 :** DISCHARGE, EMIT ⟨void excrement⟩
**3 :** NULLIFY, ANNUL ⟨void a contract⟩
*intransitive verb*
**:** to eliminate solid or liquid waste from the body
— **void·er** *noun*
**void·able** \'vȯi-də-bəl\ *adjective* (15th century)
**:** capable of being voided; *specifically* **:** capable of being adjudged void
— **void·able·ness** *noun*
**void·ance** \'vȯi-dᵊn(t)s\ *noun* (14th century)
**1 :** the act of voiding
**2** *of a benefice* **:** the state of being without an incumbent
**void·ed** \'vȯi-dəd\ *adjective* (circa 1539)
**:** having the inner part cut away or left vacant with a narrow border left at the sides — used of a heraldic charge
**voi·là** *or* **voi·la** \vwä-'lä\ *interjection* [French, literally, see there] (1739)
— used to call attention, to express satisfaction or approval, or to suggest an appearance as if by magic
**voile** \'vȯi(ə)l\ *noun* [French, veil, from Latin *vela*, neuter plural of *velum*] (1889)
**:** a fine soft sheer fabric used especially for women's summer clothing or curtains
**voir dire** \'vwär-ˌdir, 'wär-\ *noun* [Anglo-French, from Old French, to speak the truth] (1676)
**:** a preliminary examination to determine the competency of a witness or juror
**vo·lant** \'vō-lənt\ *adjective* [Middle French, from Latin *volant-, volans*, present participle of *volare* to fly] (1572)
**1 :** having the wings extended as if in flight — used of a heraldic bird
**2 :** flying or capable of flying
**3 :** QUICK, NIMBLE
**vo·lan·te** \vō-'län-(ˌ)tā\ *adjective* [Italian, literally, flying, from Latin *volant-, volans*, present participle] (circa 1854)
**:** moving with light rapidity — used as a direction in music
**Vo·la·pük** \'vō-lə-ˌpu̇k, 'vä-\ *noun* [Volapük, literally, world's speech, from *vola* of the world (genitive of *vol* world, modification of English *world*) + *pük* speech, modification of English *speak*] (1885)
**:** an artificial international language based largely on English but with some root words from German, French, and Latin
**vo·lar** \'vō-lər, -ˌlär\ *adjective* [Latin *vola* hollow in the palm of the hand or sole of the foot] (1814)
**:** relating to the palm of the hand or the sole of the foot; *specifically* **:** located on the same side as the palm of the hand ⟨the *volar* part of the forearm⟩
¹**vol·a·tile** \'vä-lə-tᵊl, *especially British* -ˌtīl\ *adjective* [French, from Latin *volatilis*, from *volare* to fly] (1605)
**1 :** readily vaporizable at a relatively low temperature
**2 :** flying or having the power to fly
**3 a :** LIGHTHEARTED, LIVELY **b :** easily aroused ⟨*volatile* suspicions⟩ **c :** tending to erupt into violence **:** EXPLOSIVE
**4 a :** unable to hold the attention fixed because of an inherent lightness or fickleness of disposition **b :** characterized by or subject to rapid or unexpected change
**5 :** difficult to capture or hold permanently **:** EVANESCENT, TRANSITORY

— **vol·a·tile·ness** *noun*
— **vol·a·til·i·ty** \ˌvä-lə-'ti-lə-tē\ *noun*
²**volatile** *noun* (1686)
**:** a volatile substance
**volatile oil** *noun* (1800)
**:** an oil that vaporizes readily; *especially* **:** ESSENTIAL OIL
**vol·a·til·ise** *British variant of* VOLATILIZE
**vol·a·til·ize** \'vä-lə-tᵊl-ˌīz, *British also* və-'la-\ *verb* **-ized; -iz·ing** (1657)
*transitive verb*
**:** to make volatile; *especially* **:** to cause to pass off in vapor
*intransitive verb*
**:** to pass off in vapor
— **vol·a·til·iz·able** \-ˌī-zə-bəl\ *adjective*
— **vol·a·til·i·za·tion** \ˌvä-lə-tᵊl-ə-'zā-shən, *British also* və-ˌla-\ *noun*
**vol-au-vent** \ˌvȯ-lō-'väⁿ\ *noun* [French, literally, flight in the wind] (1828)
**:** a baked patty shell filled with meat, fowl, game, or seafood in sauce
¹**vol·ca·nic** \väl-'ka-nik, vȯl- *also* -'kā-\ *adjective* (1774)
**1 a :** of, relating to, or produced by a volcano **b :** characterized by volcanoes ⟨a *volcanic* range⟩ **c :** made of materials from volcanoes
**2 :** explosively violent **:** VOLATILE ⟨*volcanic* emotions⟩
— **vol·ca·ni·cal·ly** \-ni-k(ə-)lē\ *adverb*
²**volcanic** *noun* (1894)
**:** a volcanic rock
**volcanic glass** *noun* (circa 1840)
**:** natural glass produced by the cooling of molten lava too rapidly to permit crystallization
**vol·ca·nic·i·ty** \ˌväl-kə-'ni-sə-tē, ˌvȯl-\ *noun* (1836)
**:** VOLCANISM
**vol·ca·nism** \'väl-kə-ˌni-zəm, 'vȯl-\ *noun* (circa 1864)
**:** volcanic action or activity
**vol·ca·no** \väl-'kā-(ˌ)nō, vȯl-\ *noun, plural* **-noes** *or* **-nos** [Italian or Spanish; Italian *vulcano*, from Spanish *volcán*, ultimately from Latin *Volcanus* Vulcan] (1613)
**1 :** a vent in the crust of the earth or another planet from which usually molten or hot rock and steam issue; *also* **:** a hill or mountain composed wholly or in part of the ejected material
**2 :** something of explosively violent potential
◆
**vol·ca·no·log·i·cal** \ˌväl-kə-nᵊl-'ä-ji-kəl, ˌvȯl-\ *also* **vol·ca·no·log·ic** \-jik\ *adjective* (circa 1891)
**:** of, relating to, or involving volcanology or volcanic phenomena ⟨*volcanological* processes that shape the planets⟩
**vol·ca·nol·o·gy** \ˌväl-kə-'nä-lə-jē, ˌvȯl-\ *noun* (1886)
**:** a branch of science that deals with volcanic phenomena
— **vol·ca·nol·o·gist** \-jist\ *noun*
¹**vole** \'vōl\ *noun* [French, probably from *voler* to fly — more at VOLLEY] (1679)
**:** GRAND SLAM 1
²**vole** *noun* [earlier *vole-mouse*, from *vole-* (of Scandinavian origin; akin to Old Norse *vǫllr* field) + *mouse;* akin to Old English *weald* forest — more at WOLD] (1805)
**:** any of various small rodents (*Microtus* and related genera) that typically have a stout body, rather blunt nose, and short ears, inhabit both moist meadows and dry uplands and do much damage to crops, and are closely related to muskrats and lemmings
**vo·li·tion** \vō-'li-shən, və-\ *noun* [French, from Medieval Latin *volition-, volitio*, from Latin *vol-* (stem of *velle* to will, wish) + *-ition-, -itio* (as in Latin *position-, positio* position) — more at WILL] (1615)
**1 :** an act of making a choice or decision; *also* **:** a choice or decision made
**2 :** the power of choosing or determining **:** WILL

— **vo·li·tion·al** \-'lish-nəl, -'li-shə-nᵊl\ *adjective*
**vol·i·tive** \'vä-lə-tiv\ *adjective* (1660)
**1 :** of or relating to the will
**2 :** expressing a wish or permission
**volks·lied** \'fōks-ˌlēt, 'fȯlks-\ *noun, plural* **volks·lie·der** \-ˌlē-dər\ [German, from *Volk* people + *Lied* song] (circa 1854)
**:** a folk song
¹**vol·ley** \'vä-lē\ *noun, plural* **volleys** [Middle French *volee* flight, from *voler* to fly, from Latin *volare*] (1573)
**1 a :** a flight of missiles (as arrows) **b :** simultaneous discharge of a number of missile weapons **c :** one round per gun in a battery fired as soon as a gun is ready without regard to order **d** (1) **:** the flight of the ball (as in volleyball or tennis) or its course before striking the ground; *also* **:** a return of the ball before it touches the ground (2) **:** a kick of the ball in soccer before it rebounds (3) **:** the exchange of the shuttlecock in badminton following the serve
**2 a :** a burst or emission of many things or a large amount at once ⟨received a *volley* of angry letters⟩ ⟨a *volley* of praise⟩ **b :** a burst of simultaneous or immediately sequential nerve impulses passing to an end organ, synapse, or center
²**volley** *verb* **vol·leyed; vol·ley·ing** (1591)
*transitive verb*
**1 :** to discharge in or as if in a volley
**2 :** to propel (an object) while in the air and before touching the ground; *especially* **:** to hit (a tennis ball) on the volley
*intransitive verb*
**1 :** to become discharged in or as if in a volley
**2 :** to make a volley; *specifically* **:** to volley an object of play (as in tennis)
— **vol·ley·er** *noun*
**vol·ley·ball** \'vä-lē-ˌbȯl\ *noun* (1896)
**:** a game played by volleying an inflated ball over a net; *also* **:** the ball used in this game
**vol·plane** \'väl-ˌplān, 'vȯl-\ *intransitive verb* **vol·planed; vol·plan·ing** [French *vol plané* gliding flight] (1909)
**1 :** to glide in or as if in an airplane
**2 :** GLIDE 3
**Vol·sci** \'vȯl-ˌskē, 'väl-ˌsī\ *noun plural* [Latin] (circa 1909)
**:** a people of ancient Italy dwelling between the Latins and Samnites

◇ **WORD HISTORY**
**volcano** Before the Age of Discoveries medieval Europe knew only the handful of active volcanoes long familiar to mariners in the Mediterranean—Vesuvius in Italy, Etna on Sicily, and the peaks of Stromboli and Vulcano among the Lipari Islands off the Sicilian coast. Apparently no need was felt for a generic word to describe a mountain that emitted fire. This situation changed in the 16th century, when the Spanish conquistadores came upon the great volcanic peaks of Mexico, Central America, and the Andes. The chroniclers of the conquistadores applied to these mountains the word *volcán*, whose roots lie in classical antiquity. *Vulcanus*, the ancient Roman god of fire, was particularly associated with the Lipari Islands—the *insulae Vulcaniae* "islands of Vulcan" to Cicero—and this association is perpetuated today in *Vulcano*, the modern Italian name of the southernmost island. Medieval Islamic authors applied *burkān*, an arabicized form of *Vulcanus*, to either Etna or the Lipari Island volcanoes, and this word appears retransformed into the latinized *vulcan* in a 13th century Spanish translation from Arabic. It resurfaces as *volcán* in a 1524 description of Guatemalan volcanoes, and from the Spanish chroniclers the word soon found its way into Italian, French, and English.

**Vol·scian** \'väl-shən, 'vȯl-skē-ən\ *noun, plural*
**Volscians** (1513)
**1 :** a member of the Volsci
**2 :** the Italic language of the Volsci
— **Volscian** *adjective*

**¹volt** \'vōlt, 'vȯlt\ *noun* [French *volte,* from
Italian *volta* turn, from *voltare* to turn, from
(assumed) Vulgar Latin *volvitare,* frequentative of Latin *volvere* to roll — more at VOLU-
BLE] (1688)
**1 :** a leaping movement in fencing to avoid a
thrust
**2 a :** a tread or gait in which a horse going
sideways makes a turn around a center **b :** a
circle traced by a horse in this movement

**²volt** \'vōlt\ *noun* [Alessandro *Volta*] (1873)
**:** the practical meter-kilogram-second unit of
electrical potential difference and electromotive force equal to the difference of potential
between two points in a conducting wire carrying a constant current of one ampere when
the power dissipated between these two points
is equal to one watt and equivalent to the potential difference across a resistance of one
ohm when one ampere is flowing through it

**volt·age** \'vōl-tij\ *noun* (1890)
**1 :** electric potential or potential difference expressed in volts
**2 :** intensity of feeling

**voltage divider** *noun* (1922)
**:** a resistor or series of resistors provided with
taps at certain points and used to provide various potential differences from a single power
source

**vol·ta·ic** \väl-'tā-ik, vōl-, vȯl-\ *adjective*
[Alessandro *Volta*] (1812)
**:** of, relating to, or producing direct electric
current by chemical action (as in a battery)
**:** GALVANIC ⟨*voltaic* cell⟩

**volt-am·pere** \'vōlt-'am-,pir *also* -,per\ *noun*
(1896)
**:** a unit of electric measurement equal to the
product of a volt and an ampere that for direct
current constitutes a measure of power equivalent to a watt

**volte–face** \,vȯlt-'fäs, ,vȯl-tə-\ *noun* [French,
from Italian *voltafaccia,* from *voltare* to turn +
*faccia* face, from (assumed) Vulgar Latin *facia*
— more at VOLT, FACE] (1819)
**:** a reversal in policy **:** ABOUT-FACE

**volt·me·ter** \'vōlt-,mē-tər\ *noun* [International
Scientific Vocabulary] (1882)
**:** an instrument (as a galvanometer) for measuring in volts the differences in potential between different points of an electrical circuit

**vol·u·ble** \'väl-yə-bəl\ *adjective* [Middle
French or Latin; Middle French, from Latin
*volubilis,* from *volvere* to roll; akin to Old English *wealwian* to roll, Greek *eilyein* to roll,
wrap] (15th century)
**1 :** easily rolling or turning **:** ROTATING
**2 :** characterized by ready or rapid speech
**:** GLIB, FLUENT
*synonym* see TALKATIVE
— **vol·u·bil·i·ty** \,väl-yə-'bi-lə-tē\ *noun*
— **vol·u·ble·ness** \'väl-yə-bəl-nəs\ *noun*
— **vol·u·bly** \-blē\ *adverb*

**¹vol·ume** \'väl-yəm, -(,)yüm\ *noun* [Middle
English, from Middle French, from Latin *volu-
men* roll, scroll, from *volvere* to roll] (14th
century)
**1 a :** a series of printed sheets bound typically
in book form **:** BOOK **b :** a series of issues of a
periodical **c :** ALBUM 1c
**2 :** SCROLL 1a
**3 :** the amount of space occupied by a three-
dimensional object as measured in cubic units
(as quarts or liters) **:** cubic capacity — see
METRIC SYSTEM table, WEIGHT table
**4 a (1) :** AMOUNT; *also* **:** BULK, MASS **(2) :** a considerable quantity **b :** the amount of a substance occupying a particular volume **c :** mass
or the representation of mass in art or architecture

**5 :** the degree of loudness or the intensity of a
sound; *also* **:** LOUDNESS
*synonym* see BULK
— **vol·umed** \-yəmd, -(,)yümd\ *adjective*

## VOLUME FORMULAS

| FIGURE | FORMULA | MEANING OF LETTERS |
|---|---|---|
| cube | $V = a^3$ | a=length of one edge |
| rectangular solid | $V = lwh$ | l=length of base; w=width of base; h=height |
| pyramid | $V = \dfrac{Ah}{3}$ | A=area of base; h=height |
| cylinder | $V = \pi r^2 h$ | $\pi = 3.1416$; r=radius of the base; h=height |
| cone | $V = \dfrac{\pi r^2 h}{3}$ | $\pi = 3.1416$; r=radius of the base; h=height |
| sphere | $V = \dfrac{4\pi r^3}{3}$ | $\pi = 3.1416$; r=radius |

**²volume** *verb* **vol·umed; vol·um·ing**
(1815)
*transitive verb*
**:** to send or give out in volume
*intransitive verb*
**:** to roll or rise in volume

**³volume** *adjective* (circa 1945)
**:** involving large quantities ⟨offered *volume*
discounts⟩

**vol·u·me·ter** \'väl-yu̇-,mē-tər\ *noun* [Interna-
tional Scientific Vocabulary, blend of *volume*
and *-meter*] (1829)
**:** an instrument for measuring volumes (as of
gases or liquids) directly or (as of solids) by
displacement of a liquid

**vol·u·met·ric** \,väl-yu̇-'me-trik\ *adjective*
(1857)
**:** of, relating to, or involving the measurement
of volume
— **vol·u·met·ri·cal·ly** \-tri-k(ə-)lē\ *adverb*

**vo·lu·mi·nos·i·ty** \və-,lü-mə-'nä-sə-tē\ *noun*
(1782)
**:** the quality or state of being voluminous

**vo·lu·mi·nous** \və-'lü-mə-nəs\ *adjective* [Late
Latin *voluminosus,* from Latin *volumin-, volu-
men*] (1611)
**1 :** consisting of many folds, coils, or convolutions **:** WINDING
**2 a :** having or marked by great volume or
bulk **:** LARGE ⟨long *voluminous* tresses⟩; *also*
**:** FULL ⟨a *voluminous* skirt⟩ **b :** NUMEROUS ⟨try-
ing to keep track of *voluminous* slips of paper⟩
**3 a :** filling or capable of filling a large volume or several volumes ⟨a *voluminous* literature on the subject⟩ **b :** writing or speaking
much or at great length
— **vo·lu·mi·nous·ly** *adverb*
— **vo·lu·mi·nous·ness** *noun*

**vol·un·ta·rism** \'vä-lən-tə-,ri-zəm\ *noun*
(1838)
**1 :** the principle or system of doing something
by or relying on voluntary action or volunteers
**2 :** a theory that conceives will to be the dominant factor in experience or in the world
— **vol·un·ta·rist** \-rist\ *noun*
— **vol·un·ta·ris·tic** \,vä-lən-tə-'ris-tik\ *adjective*

**¹vol·un·tary** \'vä-lən-,ter-ē\ *adjective* [Middle
English, from Latin *voluntarius,* from *voluntas*
will, from *velle* to will, wish — more at
WILL] (14th century)
**1 :** proceeding from the will or from one's
own choice or consent
**2 :** unconstrained by interference **:** SELF-DETER-
MINING

**3 :** done by design or intention **:** INTENTIONAL
⟨*voluntary* manslaughter⟩
**4 :** of, relating to, subject to, or regulated by
the will ⟨*voluntary* behavior⟩
**5 :** having power of free choice
**6 :** provided or supported by voluntary action
⟨a *voluntary* organization⟩
**7 :** acting or done of one's own free will without valuable consideration or legal obligation
☆
— **vol·un·tar·i·ly** *adverb*
— **vol·un·tar·i·ness** *noun*

**²voluntary** *noun, plural* **-tar·ies** (1598)
**1 a :** a prefatory often extemporized musical
piece **b :** an improvisatory organ piece played
before, during, or after a religious service
**2 :** one who participates voluntarily **:** VOLUN-
TEER

**vol·un·tary·ism** \'vä-lən-,ter-ē-,i-zəm\ *noun*
(1835)
**:** VOLUNTARISM
— **vol·un·tary·ist** \-ē-ist\ *noun*

**voluntary muscle** *noun* (1788)
**:** muscle (as most striated muscle) under voluntary control

**¹vol·un·teer** \,vä-lən-'tir\ *noun* [obsolete
French *voluntaire* (now *volontaire*), from *voluntaire,* adjective, voluntary, from Latin *voluntarius*] (circa 1618)
**1 :** a person who voluntarily undertakes or expresses a willingness to undertake a service: as
**a :** one who enters into military service voluntarily **b (1) :** one who renders a service or
takes part in a transaction while having no legal concern or interest **(2) :** one who receives a
conveyance or transfer of property without
giving valuable consideration
**2 :** a volunteer plant
**3** *capitalized* [*Volunteers of America*] **:** a
member of a quasi-military religious and philanthropic organization founded in 1896 by
Commander and Mrs. Ballington Booth

**²volunteer** *adjective* (1649)
**1 :** being, consisting of, or engaged in by volunteers ⟨a *volunteer* army⟩ ⟨*volunteer* activities to help the mentally handicapped⟩
**2 :** growing spontaneously without direct human control or supervision especially from
seeds lost from a previous crop ⟨*volunteer*
corn plants⟩

**³volunteer** (circa 1755)
*intransitive verb*
**:** to offer oneself as a volunteer
*transitive verb*
**:** to offer or bestow voluntarily ⟨*volunteer*
one's services⟩

**vol·un·teer·ism** \,vä-lən-'tir-,i-zəm\ *noun*
(1844)
**1 :** VOLUNTARISM 1
**2 :** the act or practice of doing volunteer work
in community service

---

☆ SYNONYMS
**Voluntary, intentional, deliberate,
willing** mean done or brought about of
one's own will. VOLUNTARY implies freedom
and spontaneity of choice or action without
external compulsion ⟨a *voluntary* confession⟩.
INTENTIONAL stresses an awareness of an
end to be achieved ⟨the *intentional* concealment of vital information⟩. DELIBERATE implies full consciousness of the nature of
one's act and its consequences ⟨*deliberate*
acts of sabotage⟩. WILLING implies a readiness and eagerness to accede to or anticipate the wishes of another ⟨*willing* obedi-
ence⟩.

---

\ə\ **abut** \ə̇\ **kitten** \ər\ **further** \a\ **ash** \ā\ **ace**
\ä\ **mop, mar** \au̇\ **out** \ch\ **chin** \e\ **bet** \ē\ **easy**
\g\ **go** \i\ **hit** \ī\ **ice** \j\ **job** \ŋ\ **sing** \ō\ **go**
\ȯ\ **law** \ȯi\ **boy** \th\ **thin** \t̶h̶\ **the** \ü\ **loot** \u̇\ **foot**
\y\ **yet** \zh\ **vision** *see also* Guide to Pronunciation

**vo·lup·tu·ary** \və-'ləp(t)-shə-,wer-ē\ *noun, plural* **-ar·ies** (circa 1610)
: a person whose chief interests are luxury and the gratification of sensual appetites
— **voluptuary** *adjective*

**vo·lup·tuous** \-shə-wəs, -shəs\ *adjective* [Middle English, from Latin *voluptuosus,* irregular from *voluptas* pleasure, from *volup* pleasurable; akin to Greek *elpesthai* to hope, Latin *velle* to wish — more at WILL] (14th century)
**1 a** : full of delight or pleasure to the senses : conducive to or arising from sensuous or sensual gratification : LUXURIOUS ⟨a *voluptuous* dance⟩ ⟨*voluptuous* ornamentation⟩ **b** : suggesting sensual pleasure by fullness and beauty of form ⟨*voluptuous* nudes⟩
**2** : given to or spent in enjoyments of luxury, pleasure, or sensual gratifications ⟨a long and *voluptuous* holiday —Edmund Wilson⟩
*synonym* see SENSUOUS
— **vo·lup·tuous·ly** *adverb*
— **vo·lup·tuous·ness** *noun*

**vo·lute** \və-'lüt\ *noun* [Latin *voluta,* from feminine of *volutus,* past participle of *volvere* to roll — more at VOLUBLE] (circa 1696)
**1** : a spiral or scroll-shaped form
**2** : a spiral scroll-shaped ornament forming the chief feature of the Ionic capital
**3 a** : any of various marine gastropod mollusks (family Volutidae) with a thick short-spired shell **b** : the shell of a volute
— **volute** *or* **vo·lut·ed** \-'lü-təd\ *adjective*

**vo·lu·tin** \'väl-yə-,tin, və-'lü-t°n\ *noun* [German, from New Latin *volutans,* specific epithet of the bacterium *Spirillum volutans* in which it was first found] (1908)
: a granular basophilic substance that is thought to be a nucleic acid compound and that is common in microorganisms

**vol·va** \'väl-və, 'vȯl-\ *noun* [New Latin, from Latin *volva, vulva* integument — more at VULVA] (circa 1753)
: a membranous sac or cup about the base of the stipe in many gill fungi

**vol·vox** \-,väks\ *noun* [New Latin, from Latin *volvere* to roll] (1798)
: any of a genus (*Volvox*) of flagellated unicellular green algae that form spherical colonies

volva

**vol·vu·lus** \'väl-vyə-ləs, 'vȯl-\ *noun* [New Latin, from Latin *volvere*] (1679)
: a twisting of the intestine upon itself that causes obstruction

**vo·mer** \'vō-mər\ *noun* [New Latin, from Latin, plowshare] (circa 1704)
: a bone of the skull of most vertebrates that is situated below the ethmoid region and in the human skull forms part of the nasal septum
— **vo·mer·ine** \'vō-mə-,rīn\ *adjective*

**¹vom·it** \'vä-mət\ *noun* [Middle English, from Middle French, from Latin *vomitus,* from *vomere* to vomit; akin to Old Norse *vāma* seasickness, Greek *emein* to vomit] (14th century)
**1** : an act or instance of disgorging the contents of the stomach through the mouth; *also* : the disgorged matter
**2** : EMETIC

**²vomit** (15th century)
*intransitive verb*
**1** : to disgorge the stomach contents
**2** : to spew forth : BELCH, GUSH
*transitive verb*
**1** : to disgorge (the contents of the stomach) through the mouth
**2** : to eject violently or abundantly : SPEW
**3** : to cause to vomit
— **vom·it·er** *noun*

**vom·i·to·ry** \'vä-mə-,tōr-ē, -,tȯr-\ *noun, plural* **-ries** [Late Latin *vomitorium,* from Latin *vomere;* from its disgorging the spectators] (1730)
: an entrance piercing the banks of seats of a theater, amphitheater, or stadium

**vom·i·tus** \'vä-mə-təs\ *noun* [Latin] (circa 1899)
: material discharged by vomiting

**V-1** \'vē-'wən\ *noun* [German, abbreviation for *Vergeltungswaffe 1,* literally, reprisal weapon 1] (1944)
: BUZZ BOMB

**¹voo·doo** \'vü-(,)dü\ *noun, plural* **voodoos** [Louisiana Creole *voudou,* probably from Ewe *vódū* tutelary deity, demon] (1850)
**1** : a religion that is derived from African polytheism and ancestor worship and is practiced chiefly in Haiti
**2 a** : a person who deals in spells and necromancy **b** (1) : a sorcerer's spell : HEX (2) : a hexed object : CHARM
— **voodoo** *adjective*

**²voodoo** *transitive verb* (1880)
: to bewitch by or as if by means of voodoo
: HEX

**voo·doo·ism** \'vü-(,)dü-,i-zəm\ *noun* (1865)
**1** : VOODOO 1
**2** : the practice of witchcraft
— **voo·doo·ist** \-ist\ *noun*
— **voo·doo·is·tic** \,vü-(,)dü-'is-tik\ *adjective*

**vo·ra·cious** \vȯ-'rā-shəs, və-\ *adjective* [Latin *vorac-, vorax,* from *vorare* to devour; akin to Old English *ācweorran* to guzzle, Latin *gurges* whirlpool, Greek *bibrōskein* to devour] (1635)
**1** : having a huge appetite : RAVENOUS
**2** : excessively eager : INSATIABLE ⟨a *voracious* reader⟩ ☆
— **vo·ra·cious·ly** *adverb*
— **vo·ra·cious·ness** *noun*

**vo·rac·i·ty** \vȯ-'ra-sə-tē, və-\ *noun* (1526)
: the quality or state of being voracious

**vor·la·ge** \'fȯr-,lä-gə, 'fȯr-\ *noun* [German, literally, forward position, from *vor* fore + *Lage* position] (1936)
: the position of a skier leaning forward from the ankles usually without lifting the heels from the skis

**-vorous** *adjective combining form* [Latin *-vorus,* from *vorare* to devour]
: eating : feeding on ⟨frugi*vorous*⟩

**vor·tex** \'vȯr-,teks\ *noun, plural* **vor·ti·ces** \'vȯr-tə-,sēz\ *also* **vor·tex·es** \'vȯr-,tek-səz\ [New Latin *vortic-, vortex,* from Latin *vertex, vortex* whirlpool — more at VERTEX] (1652)
**1 a** : a mass of fluid (as a liquid) with a whirling or circular motion that tends to form a cavity or vacuum in the center of the circle and to draw toward this cavity or vacuum bodies subject to its action; *especially* : WHIRLPOOL, EDDY **b** : a region within a body of fluid in which the fluid elements have an angular velocity
**2** : something that resembles a whirlpool ⟨the hellish *vortex* of battle —*Time*⟩

**vor·ti·cal** \'vȯr-ti-kəl\ *adjective* (1653)
: of, relating to, or resembling a vortex : SWIRLING
— **vor·ti·cal·ly** \-k(ə-)lē\ *adverb*

**vor·ti·cel·la** \,vȯr-tə-'se-lə\ *noun, plural* **-cel·lae** \-'se-(,)lē\ *or* **-cellas** [New Latin, from Latin *vortic-, vortex*] (1787)
: any of a genus (*Vorticella*) of stalked bell-shaped ciliates

**vor·ti·cism** \'vȯr-tə-,si-zəm\ *noun* [Latin *vortic-, vortex*] (1914)
: an English abstract art movement from about 1912–15 embracing cubist and futurist concepts
— **vor·ti·cist** \-sist\ *noun*

**vor·tic·i·ty** \vȯr-'ti-sə-tē\ *noun* (1888)
**1** : the state of a fluid in vortical motion; *broadly* : vortical motion
**2** : a measure of vortical motion; *especially* : a vector measure of local rotation in a fluid flow

**vor·ti·cose** \'vȯr-ti-,kōs\ *adjective* (1783)
*archaic* : VORTICAL

**vo·ta·ress** \'vō-tə-rəs\ *noun* (1589)
: a female votary

**vo·ta·rist** \-rist\ *noun* (1603)
: VOTARY

**vo·ta·ry** \'vō-tə-rē\ *noun, plural* **-ries** [Latin *votum* vow] (1546)
**1** *archaic* : a sworn adherent
**2 a** : ENTHUSIAST, DEVOTEE **b** : a devoted admirer
**3 a** : a devout or zealous worshiper **b** : a staunch believer or advocate

**¹vote** \'vōt\ *noun* [Middle English (Scots), from Latin *votum* vow, wish — more at VOW] (15th century)
**1 a** : a usually formal expression of opinion or will in response to a proposed decision; *especially* : one given as an indication of approval or disapproval of a proposal, motion, or candidate for office **b** : the total number of such expressions of opinion made known at a single time (as at an election) **c** : an expression of opinion or preference that resembles a vote **d** : BALLOT 1
**2** : the collective opinion or verdict of a body of persons expressed by voting
**3** : the right to cast a vote; *specifically* : the right of suffrage : FRANCHISE
**4 a** : the act or process of voting ⟨brought the question to a *vote*⟩ **b** : a method of voting
**5** : a formal expression of a wish, will, or choice voted by a meeting
**6 a** : VOTER **b** : a group of voters with some common and identifying characteristics ⟨the labor *vote*⟩
**7** *chiefly British* **a** : a proposition to be voted on; *especially* : a legislative money item **b** : APPROPRIATION

**²vote** *verb* **vot·ed; vot·ing** (1552)
*intransitive verb*
**1** : to express one's views in response to a poll; *especially* : to exercise a political franchise
**2** : to express an opinion ⟨consumers . . . *vote* with their dollars —Lucia Mouat⟩
*transitive verb*
**1** : to choose, endorse, decide the disposition of, defeat, or authorize by vote
**2 a** : to adjudge by general agreement : DECLARE **b** : to offer as a suggestion : PROPOSE ⟨I *vote* we all go home⟩
**3 a** : to cause to vote in a given way **b** : to cause to be cast for or against a proposal
**4** : to vote in accordance with or in the interest of ⟨*vote* your conscience⟩ ⟨*voted* their pocketbooks⟩

**vote·less** \'vōt-ləs\ *adjective* (1672)
: having no vote; *especially* : denied the political franchise

**vot·er** \'vō-tər\ *noun* (circa 1578)
: one that votes or has the legal right to vote

**voting machine** *noun* (1900)
: a mechanical device for recording and counting votes cast in an election

---

☆ **SYNONYMS**
**Voracious, gluttonous, ravenous, rapacious** mean excessively greedy. VORACIOUS applies especially to habitual gorging with food or drink ⟨teenagers are often *voracious* eaters⟩. GLUTTONOUS applies to one who delights in eating or acquiring things especially beyond the point of necessity or satiety ⟨an admiral who was *gluttonous* for glory⟩. RAVENOUS implies excessive hunger and suggests violent or grasping methods of dealing with food or with whatever satisfies an appetite ⟨a nation with a *ravenous* lust for territorial expansion⟩. RAPACIOUS often suggests excessive and utterly selfish acquisitiveness or avarice ⟨*rapacious* developers indifferent to environmental concerns⟩.

**vo·tive** \'vō-tiv\ adjective [Latin votivus, from votum vow] (1597)
**1** : consisting of or expressing a vow, wish, or desire ⟨a votive prayer⟩
**2** : offered or performed in fulfillment of a vow or in gratitude or devotion
— **vo·tive·ly** adverb
— **vo·tive·ness** noun
**votive candle** noun (1824)
**1** : a candle lit in devotion or gratitude
**2** : a small squat candle
**votive mass** noun (1738)
: a mass celebrated for a special intention (as for a wedding or funeral) in place of the mass of the day
**vo·tress** \'vō-trəs\ noun [by alteration] (1590) archaic : VOTARESS
**¹vouch** \'vauch\ verb [Middle English vochen, vouchen, from Middle French vocher, from Latin vocare to call, summon, from vox voice — more at VOICE] (14th century)
transitive verb
**1** : to summon into court to warrant or defend a title
**2** archaic **a** : ASSERT, AFFIRM **b** : ATTEST
**3** archaic : to cite or refer to as authority or supporting evidence
**4 a** : PROVE, SUBSTANTIATE **b** : to verify (a business transaction) by examining documentary evidence
intransitive verb
**1** : to give a guarantee : become surety
**2 a** : to supply supporting evidence or testimony **b** : to give personal assurance
**synonym** see CERTIFY
**²vouch** noun (1603)
obsolete : ALLEGATION, DECLARATION
**vouch·ee** \vau-'chē\ noun (15th century)
: a person for whom another vouches
**¹vouch·er** \'vau-chər\ noun [Middle French vocher, voucher to vouch] (circa 1523)
**1** : an act of vouching
**2 a** : a piece of supporting evidence : PROOF **b** : a documentary record of a business transaction **c** : a written affidavit or authorization : CERTIFICATE **d** : a form or check indicating a credit against future purchases or expenditures
**²voucher** transitive verb (1609)
**1** : to establish the authenticity of
**2** : to prepare a voucher for
**³voucher** noun [¹vouch + ²-er] (1612)
archaic : one that guarantees : SURETY
**vouch·safe** \vauch-'sāf, 'vauch-,\ transitive verb **vouch·safed; vouch·saf·ing** (1587)
**1 a** : to grant or furnish often in a gracious or condescending manner **b** : to give by way of reply ⟨refused to vouchsafe an explanation⟩
**2** : to grant as a privilege or special favor
**synonym** see GRANT
— **vouch·safe·ment** \vauch-'sāf-mənt\ noun
**vous·soir** \vü-'swär, 'vü-,\ noun [French, from (assumed) Vulgar Latin volsorium, from Latin volvere to roll — more at VOLUBLE] (1728)
: one of the wedge-shaped pieces forming an arch or vault — see ARCH illustration
**Vou·vray** \vü-'vrā\ noun [French, from Vouvray, village in France] (1885)
: a semidry to semisweet white wine from the Loire Valley of France that is often produced as a sparkling wine
**¹vow** \'vau\ noun [Middle English vowe, from Old French vou, from Latin votum, from neuter of votus, past participle of vovēre to vow; akin to Greek euchesthai to pray, vow, Sanskrit vāghat sacrificer] (14th century)
: a solemn promise or assertion; specifically : one by which a person is bound to an act, service, or condition
**²vow** (14th century)
transitive verb
**1** : to promise solemnly : SWEAR
**2** : to bind or consecrate by a vow
intransitive verb
: to make a vow
— **vow·er** \'vau(-ə)r\ noun

**³vow** transitive verb [Middle English, short for avowen] (14th century)
: AVOW, DECLARE
**vow·el** \'vau(-ə)l\ noun [Middle English, from Middle French vouel, from Latin vocalis — more at VOCALIC] (14th century)
**1** : one of a class of speech sounds in the articulation of which the oral part of the breath channel is not blocked and is not constricted enough to cause audible friction; broadly : the one most prominent sound in a syllable
**2** : a letter or other symbol representing a vowel — usually used in English of a, e, i, o, u, and sometimes y
**vow·el·ize** \'vau(-ə-),līz\ transitive verb **-ized; -iz·ing** (1883)
: to furnish with vowel points
**vowel point** noun (1764)
: a mark placed below or otherwise near a consonant in some languages (as Hebrew) and representing the vowel sound that precedes or follows the consonant sound
**vowel rhyme** noun (1838)
: ASSONANCE 2b
**vox po·pu·li** \'väks-'pä-pyü-,lī, -pyə-(,)lē, -pə-(,)lē\ noun [Latin, voice of the people] (circa 1550)
: popular sentiment
**¹voy·age** \'vȯi-ij, 'vȯ(-)ij\ noun [Middle English, from Old French voiage, from Late Latin viaticum, from Latin, traveling money, from neuter of viaticus of a journey, from via way — more at WAY] (14th century)
**1** : an act or instance of traveling : JOURNEY
**2** : a course or period of traveling by other than land routes
**3** : an account of a journey especially by sea
**²voyage** verb **voy·aged; voy·ag·ing** (15th century)
intransitive verb
: to take a trip : TRAVEL
transitive verb
: SAIL, TRAVERSE
— **voy·ag·er** noun
**voya·geur** \,vȯi-ə-'zhər, ,vwä-yä-\ noun [Canadian French, from French, traveler, from voyager to travel, from voyage voyage, from Old French voiage] (1793)
: a man employed by a fur company to transport goods to and from remote stations especially in the Canadian Northwest
**voy·eur** \vwä-'yər, vȯi-'ər\ noun [French, literally, one who sees, from Middle French, from voir to see, from Latin vidēre — more at WIT] (1900)
**1** : one obtaining sexual gratification from seeing sex organs and sexual acts; broadly : one who habitually seeks sexual stimulation by visual means
**2** : a prying observer who is usually seeking the sordid or the scandalous
— **voy·eur·ism** \-,i-zəm\ noun
— **voy·eur·is·tic** \,vwä-(,)yər-'is-tik, ,vȯi-ər-\ adjective
— **voy·eur·is·ti·cal·ly** \-ti-k(ə-)lē\ adverb
**vroom** \'vrüm, və-'rüm\ intransitive verb [imitative of the noise of an engine] (1965)
: to operate a motor vehicle at high speed or so as to create a great deal of engine noise
**V sign** noun (1942)
: a sign made by raising the index and middle fingers in a V and used as a victory salute or a gesture of approval
**V-2** \'vē-'tü\ noun [German, abbreviation for Vergeltungswaffe 2, literally, reprisal weapon 2] (1944)
: a rocket-propelled bomb of German invention
**vug** \'vəg\ noun [Cornish dialect vooga underground chamber, from Latin fovea small pit] (1818)
: a small unfilled cavity in a lode or in rock
— **vug·gy** \'və-gē\ adjective
**Vul·can** \'vəl-kən\ noun [Latin Volcanus, Vulcanus]

: the Roman god of fire and metalworking — compare HEPHAESTUS
**vul·ca·ni·an** \,vəl-'kā-nē-ən\ adjective (1602)
**1** capitalized : of or relating to Vulcan or to working in metals (as iron)
**2** : of or relating to a volcanic eruption in which highly viscous or solid lava is blown into fragments and dust
**vul·ca·nic·i·ty** \,vəl-kə-'ni-sə-tē\ noun (1873)
: VOLCANISM
**vul·ca·ni·sate, vul·ca·ni·sa·tion, vul·ca·nise** British variant of VULCANIZATE, VULCANIZATION, VULCANIZE
**vul·ca·nism** \'vəl-kə-,ni-zəm\ noun (1877)
: VOLCANISM
**vul·ca·ni·zate** \'vəl-kə-nə-,zāt, ,vəl-kə-'nī-\ noun [back-formation from vulcanization] (1926)
: a vulcanized product
**vul·ca·ni·za·tion** \,vəl-kə-nə-'zā-shən\ noun (1846)
: the process of treating crude or synthetic rubber or similar plastic material chemically to give it useful properties (as elasticity, strength, and stability)
**vul·ca·nize** \'vəl-kə-,nīz\ verb **-nized; -niz·ing** [International Scientific Vocabulary, from Latin Vulcanus Vulcan, fire] (1846)
transitive verb
: to subject to vulcanization
intransitive verb
: to undergo vulcanization
— **vul·ca·niz·er** noun
**vulcanized fiber** noun [from Vulcanized Fibre, a trademark] (circa 1884)
: a tough substance made by treatment of cellulose and used for luggage and electrical insulation and in packaging
**vul·ca·nol·o·gy** \,vəl-kə-'nä-lə-jē\ noun [International Scientific Vocabulary] (1858)
: VOLCANOLOGY
— **vul·ca·nol·o·gist** \-jist\ noun
**vul·gar** \'vəl-gər\ adjective [Middle English, from Latin vulgaris of the mob, vulgar, from volgus, vulgus mob, common people] (14th century)
**1 a** : generally used, applied, or accepted **b** : understood in or having the ordinary sense ⟨they reject the vulgar conception of miracle —W. R. Inge⟩
**2** : VERNACULAR ⟨the vulgar name of a plant⟩
**3 a** : of or relating to the common people : PLEBEIAN **b** : generally current : PUBLIC ⟨the vulgar opinion of that time⟩ **c** : of the usual, typical, or ordinary kind
**4 a** : lacking in cultivation, perception, or taste : COARSE **b** : morally crude, undeveloped, or unregenerate : GROSS **c** : ostentatious or excessive in expenditure or display : PRETENTIOUS
**5 a** : offensive in language : EARTHY **b** : lewdly or profanely indecent
**synonym** see COMMON, COARSE
— **vul·gar·ly** adverb
**vulgar era** noun (1716)
: CHRISTIAN ERA
**vul·gar·i·an** \,vəl-'gar-ē-ən, -'ger-\ noun (1804)
: a vulgar person
**vul·gar·ise** British variant of VULGARIZE
**vul·gar·ism** \'vəl-gə-,ri-zəm\ noun (circa 1676)
**1** : VULGARITY
**2 a** : a word or expression originated or used chiefly by illiterate persons **b** : a coarse word or phrase : OBSCENITY
**vul·gar·i·ty** \,vəl-'gar-ə-tē\ noun, plural **-ties** (1579)
**1** : something vulgar

**2 :** the quality or state of being vulgar

**vul·gar·ize** \\'vəl-gə-ˌrīz\ *transitive verb* **-ized; -iz·ing** (1709)
**1 :** to diffuse generally **:** POPULARIZE
**2 :** to make vulgar **:** COARSEN
— **vul·gar·i·za·tion** \ˌvəl-gə-rə-'zā-shən\ *noun*
— **vul·gar·iz·er** \\'vəl-gə-ˌrī-zər\ *noun*
**Vulgar Latin** *noun* (1818)
**:** the nonclassical Latin of ancient Rome including the speech of plebeians and the informal speech of the educated established by comparative evidence as the chief source of the Romance languages
**vul·gate** \\'vəl-ˌgāt, -gət\ *noun* [Medieval Latin *vulgata,* from Late Latin *vulgata editio* edition in general circulation] (1728)
**1** *capitalized* **:** a Latin version of the Bible authorized and used by the Roman Catholic Church
**2 :** a commonly accepted text or reading
**3 :** the speech of the common people and especially of uneducated people
**vul·gus** \\'vəl-gəs\ *noun* [probably alteration of obsolete *vulgars* English sentences to be translated into Latin] (1856)
**:** a short composition in Latin verse formerly common as an exercise in some English public schools

**vul·ner·a·ble** \\'vəl-n(ə-)rə-bəl, 'vəl-nər-bəl\ *adjective* [Late Latin *vulnerabilis,* from Latin *vulnerare* to wound, from *vulner-, vulnus* wound; probably akin to Latin *vellere* to pluck, Greek *oulē* wound] (1605)
**1 :** capable of being physically wounded
**2 :** open to attack or damage **:** ASSAILABLE
**3 :** liable to increased penalties but entitled to increased bonuses after winning a game in contract bridge
— **vul·ner·a·bil·i·ty** \ˌvəl-n(ə-)rə-'bi-lə-tē\ *noun*
— **vul·ner·a·ble·ness** \\'vəl-n(ə-)rə-bəl-nəs, 'vəl-nər-bəl-\ *noun*
— **vul·ner·a·bly** \-blē\ *adverb*
¹**vul·ner·ary** \\'vəl-nə-ˌrer-ē\ *adjective* [Latin *vulnerarius,* from *vulner-, vulnus*] (1599)
**:** used for or useful in healing wounds ⟨*vulnerary* plants⟩
²**vulnerary** *noun, plural* **-ar·ies** (1601)
**:** a vulnerary remedy
**vul·pine** \\'vəl-ˌpīn\ *adjective* [Latin *vulpinus,* from *vulpes* fox; perhaps akin to Greek *alōpēx* fox — more at ALOPECIA] (1628)
**1 :** of, relating to, or resembling a fox
**2 :** FOXY, CRAFTY
**vul·ture** \\'vəl-chər\ *noun* [Middle English, from Latin *vultur*] (14th century)

**1 :** any of various large raptorial birds (families Accipitridae and Cathartidae) that are related to the hawks, eagles, and falcons but have weaker claws and the head usually naked and that subsist chiefly or entirely on carrion
**2 :** a rapacious or predatory person
— **vul·tur·ish** \-chə-rish\ *adjective*
**vul·tur·ine** \-chə-ˌrīn\ *adjective* (1647)
**1 :** of, relating to, or characteristic of vultures
**2 :** RAPACIOUS, PREDATORY ⟨*vulturine* legislators⟩
**vul·tur·ous** \\'vəl-chə-rəs, 'vəlch-rəs\ *adjective* (1623)
**:** resembling a vulture especially in rapacity or scavenging habits
**vul·va** \\'vəl-və\ *noun, plural* **vul·vae** \-ˌvē, -ˌvī\ [New Latin, from Latin *volva, vulva* womb, female genitals; akin to Sanskrit *ulva* womb and perhaps to Latin *volvere* to roll — more at VOLUBLE] (circa 1577)
**:** the external parts of the female genital organs
— **vul·val** \\'vəl-vəl\ *or* **vul·var** \-vər, -ˌvär\ *adjective*
**vul·vo·vag·i·ni·tis** \ˌvəl-(ˌ)vō-ˌva-jə-'nī-təs\ *noun* [New Latin] (1897)
**:** coincident inflammation of the vulva and vagina

**vying** *present participle of* VIE

W *is the twenty-third letter of the English alphabet. In form and origin,* W *is a ligature,* VV *or* UU, *called "double* u,*" which was introduced into English by French scribes in the 11th century to replace an Old English runic character called* wynn. *The sound of* w *is usually a consonant, as in* we. *In English, with minor exceptions,* w *represents a vowel only in diphthongs, as in* few *and* how. W *appears also in the frequent consonantal group* wh, *as in* what *and* white. *Written* W *is silent in some words, as* wrist *and* answer. *Words with* W *are almost wholly of Germanic origin, either by inheritance through Old English or by borrowing from Old Norse or from Old North French. In the latter, Germanic loanwords appear with* w *instead of with the* gu *or* g *that prevails in central Old French and in Modern French (as seen in Old North French* wage *"pledge" contrasting with Old French* guage *"pledge"). Small* w *was formed by a simple reduction in the size of the capital.*

**w** \'də-bəl-(ˌ)yü, 'də-bə-; 'dəb-(ˌ)yü, -yə; 'dəb-yē\ *noun, plural* **w's** *or* **ws** \-(ˌ)yüz, -yəz, -yēz\ *often capitalized, often attributive* (15th century)
**1 a :** the 23d letter of the English alphabet **b :** a graphic representation of this letter **c :** a speech counterpart of orthographic *w*
**2 :** a graphic device for reproducing the letter *w*
**3 :** one designated *w* especially as the 23d in order or class
**4 :** something shaped like the letter W
**W** *noun* (1960)
**:** W PARTICLE
**wab·ble** \'wä-bəl\ *variant of* WOBBLE
**Wac** \'wak\ *noun* [Women's Army Corps] (1943)
**:** a member of the Women's Army Corps
**wacked–out** *variant of* WHACKED-OUT
**wacko** \'wa-(ˌ)kō\ *adjective* [by alteration] (1975)
**:** WACKY
**— wacko** *noun*
**wacky** \'wa-kē\ *adjective* **wack·i·er; -est** [perhaps from English dialect *whacky* fool] (circa 1935)
**:** absurdly or amusingly eccentric or irrational **:** CRAZY
**— wack·i·ly** \'wa-kə-lē\ *adverb*
**— wack·i·ness** \'wa-kē-nəs\ *noun*
**¹wad** \'wäd\ *noun* [Medieval Latin *wadda*] (1573)
**1 :** a small mass, bundle, or tuft: as **a :** a soft mass especially of a loose fibrous material variously used (as to stop an aperture, pad a garment, or hold grease around an axle) **b** (1) **:** a soft plug used to retain a powder charge or to avoid windage especially in a muzzle-loading gun (2) **:** a felt or paper disk used to separate the components of a shotgun cartridge **c :** a small mass of a chewing substance ⟨a *wad* of gum⟩
**2 :** a considerable amount (as of money)
**3 a :** a roll of paper money **b :** MONEY
**²wad** *transitive verb* **wad·ded; wad·ding** (1579)
**1 a :** to insert a wad into ⟨*wad* a gun⟩ **b :** to hold in by a wad ⟨*wad* a bullet in a gun⟩
**2 :** to form into a wad or wadding; *especially* **:** to roll or crush into a tight wad
**3 :** to stuff or line with some soft substance
**— wad·der** *noun*
**wad·ding** \'wä-diŋ\ *noun* (1627)
**1 :** wads or material for making wads
**2 :** a soft mass or sheet of short loose fibers used for stuffing or padding

**¹wad·dle** \'wä-d°l\ *intransitive verb* **wad·dled; wad·dling** \'wäd-liŋ, 'wä-d°l-iŋ\ [frequentative of *wade*] (1592)
**1 :** to walk with short steps swinging the forepart of the body from side to side
**2 :** to move clumsily in a manner suggesting a waddle
**— wad·dler** \'wäd-lər, 'wä-d°l-ər\ *noun*
**²waddle** *noun* (1691)
**:** an awkward clumsy swaying gait
**¹wad·dy** \'wä-dē\ *noun, plural* **waddies** [Dharuk (Australian aboriginal language of the Port Jackson area) *wadi* stick, wooden weapon] (circa 1790)
*Australian* **:** CLUB 1a
**²waddy** *transitive verb* **wad·died; wad·dy·ing** (1833)
*Australian* **:** to attack or beat with a waddy
**³wad·dy** *or* **wad·die** \'wä-dē\ *noun, plural* **waddies** [origin unknown] (1897)
*West* **:** COWBOY
**¹wade** \'wād\ *verb* **wad·ed; wad·ing** [Middle English, from Old English *wadan;* akin to Old High German *watan* to go, wade, Latin *vadere* to go] (13th century)
*intransitive verb*
**1 :** to step in or through a medium (as water) offering more resistance than air
**2 :** to move or proceed with difficulty or labor
**3 :** to set to work or attack with determination or vigor — used with *in* or *into* ⟨*wade* into a task⟩
*transitive verb*
**:** to pass or cross by wading
**— wad·able** *or* **wade·able** \'wā-də-bəl\ *adjective*
**²wade** *noun* (1665)
**:** an act of wading ⟨a *wade* in the brook⟩
**Wade–Giles** \'wād-'gīlz\ *noun* [Thomas F. *Wade* (died 1895) British diplomat & Herbert A. *Giles* (died 1935) British sinologist] (1943)
**:** a system for romanizing Chinese ideograms in which tones are indicated by superscript numbers and consonantal aspiration is indicated by an apostrophe — compare PINYIN
**wad·er** \'wā-dər\ *noun* (1673)
**1 :** one that wades
**2 :** SHOREBIRD; *also* **:** WADING BIRD
**3** *plural* **:** high waterproof boots or a one-piece waterproof garment usually consisting of pants with attached boots that are used for wading (as when fishing)
**wa·di** \'wä-dē\ *noun* [Arabic *wādiy*] (1839)
**1 :** the bed or valley of a stream in regions of southwestern Asia and northern Africa that is usually dry except during the rainy season and that often forms an oasis **:** GULLY, WASH

**2 :** a shallow usually sharply defined depression in a desert region
**wading bird** *noun* (circa 1843)
**:** any of an order (Ciconiiformes) of long-legged birds (as herons, bitterns, storks, and flamingos) that wade in water in search of food
**wading pool** *noun* (1921)
**:** a shallow pool of portable or permanent construction used by children for wading

**waders**

**wad·mal** *or* **wad·mol** *or* **wad·mel** \'wäd-məl\ *noun* [Middle English *wadmale*, from Old Norse *vathmāl*, literally, standard cloth, from *vāth* cloth, clothing + *māl* measure; akin to Latin *metiri* to measure — more at WEED, MEASURE] (14th century)
**:** a coarse rough woolen fabric formerly used in the British Isles and Scandinavia for protective coverings and warm clothing
**wae·sucks** \'wā-ˌsəks\ *interjection* [Scots *wae* woe (from Middle English *wa*) + *sucks,* alteration of English *sakes* — more at WOE] (circa 1774)
*Scottish* — used to express pity
**Waf** \'waf\ *noun* [Women in the Air Force] (1948)
**:** a member of the women's component of the air force formed after World War II
**¹wa·fer** \'wā-fər\ *noun* [Middle English, from Old North French *waufre*, of Germanic origin; akin to Middle Dutch *wafel,* wafer waffle] (14th century)
**1 a :** a thin crisp cake, candy, or cracker **b :** a round thin piece of unleavened bread used in the celebration of the Eucharist
**2 :** an adhesive disk of dried paste with added coloring matter used as a seal
**3 a :** a thin disk or ring resembling a wafer and variously used (as for a valve or diaphragm) **b :** a thin slice of semiconductor (as silicon) used as a base for an electronic component or circuit
**²wafer** *transitive verb* **wa·fered; wa·fer·ing** \-f(ə-)riŋ\ (1748)
**1 :** to seal, close, or fasten with a wafer
**2 :** to divide (as a silicon rod) into wafers
**waff** \'waf\ *noun* [English dialect *waff* to wave] (1600)
**1** *chiefly Scottish* **:** a waving motion
**2** *chiefly Scottish* **:** PUFF, GUST
**¹waf·fle** \'wä-fəl, 'wȯ-\ *noun* [Dutch *wafel,* from Middle Dutch *wafel, wafer;* akin to Old English *wefan* to weave] (1744)
**:** a crisp cake of batter baked in a waffle iron
**²waffle** *intransitive verb* **waf·fled; waf·fling** \-f(ə-)liŋ\ [frequentative of obsolete *yoff* to yelp, of imitative origin] (1868)
**1 :** EQUIVOCATE, VACILLATE; *also* **:** YO-YO, FLIP-FLOP
**2 :** to talk or write foolishly **:** BLATHER ⟨can *waffle* . . . tiresomely off the point —*Times Literary Supplement*⟩
**— waf·fler** \-f(ə-)lər\ *noun*
**³waffle** *noun* (circa 1888)
**:** empty or pretentious words **:** TRIPE
**waffle iron** *noun* (1794)
**:** a cooking utensil having two hinged metal parts that shut upon each other and impress surface projections on waffles that are being cooked
**waf·fle-stomp·er** \'wä-fəl-ˌstäm-pər, 'wȯ-, -ˌstȯm-\ *noun* [from the pattern left by the soles] (1972)

\ə\ **abut** \ᵊ\ **kitten** \ər\ **further** \a\ **ash** \ā\ **ace**
\ä\ **mop, mar** \aů\ **out** \ch\ **chin** \e\ **bet** \ē\ **easy**
\g\ **go** \i\ **hit** \ī\ **ice** \j\ **job** \ŋ\ **sing** \ō\ **go**
\ȯ\ **law** \ȯi\ **boy** \th\ **thin** \t̲h̲\ **the** \ü\ **loot** \ů\ **foot**
\y\ **yet** \zh\ **vision** *see also* Guide to Pronunciation

: a hiking boot with a lug sole

**¹waft** \'wäft, 'waft\ *verb* [[assumed] Middle English *waughten* to guard, convoy, from Middle Dutch or Middle Low German *wachten* to watch, guard; akin to Old English *wæccan* to watch — more at WAKE] (circa 1562)
*intransitive verb*
: to move or go lightly on or as if on a buoyant medium
*transitive verb*
: to cause to move or go lightly by or as if by the impulse of wind or waves
— **waft·er** *noun*

**²waft** *noun* (1607)
**1 :** something (as an odor) that is wafted : WHIFF
**2 :** a slight breeze : PUFF
**3 :** the act of waving
**4 :** a pennant or flag used to signal or to show wind direction

**waft·age** \'wäf-tij, 'waf-\ *noun* (1558)
: the act of wafting or state of being wafted; *broadly* : CONVEYANCE

**waf·ture** \'wäf(t)-shər, 'waf(t)-\ *noun* (1601)
: the act of waving or a wavelike motion

**¹wag** \'wag\ *verb* **wagged; wag·ging** [Middle English *waggen;* akin to Middle High German *wacken* to totter, Old English *wegan* to move — more at WAY] (13th century)
*intransitive verb*
**1 :** to be in motion : STIR
**2 :** to move to and fro or up and down especially with quick jerky motions
**3 :** to move in chatter or gossip ⟨scandal caused tongues to *wag*⟩
**4** *archaic* : DEPART
**5 :** WADDLE
*transitive verb*
**1 :** to swing to and fro or up and down especially with quick jerky motions : SWITCH; *specifically* : to nod (the head) or shake (a finger) at (as in assent or mild reproof)
**2 :** to move (as the tongue) animatedly in conversation
— **wag·ger** *noun*

**²wag** *noun* (1589)
: an act of wagging : SHAKE

**³wag** *noun* [probably short for obsolete English *waghalter* gallows bird, from English ¹*wag + halter*] (circa 1553)
**1 :** WIT, JOKER
**2** *obsolete* : a young man : CHAP

**¹wage** \'wāj\ *noun* [Middle English, pledge, wage, from Old North French, of Germanic origin; akin to Gothic *wadi* pledge — more at WED] (14th century)
**1 a :** a payment usually of money for labor or services usually according to contract and on an hourly, daily, or piecework basis — often used in plural **b** *plural* : the share of the national product attributable to labor as a factor in production
**2 :** RECOMPENSE, REWARD — usually used in plural but singular or plural in construction ⟨the *wages* of sin is death —Romans 6:23 (Revised Standard Version)⟩
— **wage·less** \-ləs\ *adjective*

**²wage** *verb* **waged; wag·ing** [Middle English, to pledge, give as security, from Old North French *wagier,* from *wage*] (15th century)
*transitive verb*
: to engage in or carry on ⟨*wage* war⟩ ⟨*wage* a campaign⟩
*intransitive verb*
: to be in process of occurring ⟨the riot *waged* for several hours —*American Guide Series: Maryland*⟩

**wage earner** *noun* (1885)
: a person who works for wages or salary

**¹wa·ger** \'wā-jər\ *noun* [Middle English, pledge, bet, from Anglo-French *wageure,* from Old North French *wagier* to pledge] (14th century)

**1 a :** something (as a sum of money) risked on an uncertain event : STAKE **b :** something on which bets are laid : GAMBLE ⟨do a stunt as a *wager*⟩
**2** *archaic* : an act of giving a pledge to take and abide by the result of some action

**²wager** *verb* **wa·gered; wa·ger·ing** \'wāj-riŋ, 'wā-jə-\ (1602)
*intransitive verb*
: to make a bet
*transitive verb*
: to risk or venture on a final outcome; *specifically* : to lay as a gamble : BET ⟨*wager* $5 on a horse⟩
— **wa·ger·er** \'wā-jər-ər\ *noun*

**wage scale** *noun* (1902)
: a schedule of wage rates for related tasks; *broadly* : the general level of wages in an industry or region

**wage slave** *noun* (1886)
: a person dependent on wages or a salary for a livelihood

**wage·work·er** \'wāj-,wər-kər\ *noun* (1876)
: WAGE EARNER

**wag·gery** \'wa-gə-rē\ *noun, plural* **-ger·ies** (1594)
**1 :** mischievous merriment : PLEASANTRY
**2 :** JEST; *especially* : PRACTICAL JOKE

**wag·gish** \'wa-gish\ *adjective* (1589)
**1 :** resembling or characteristic of a wag ⟨a *waggish* friend⟩ ⟨a *waggish* prose style⟩
**2 :** done or made in waggery or for sport : HUMOROUS ⟨*waggish* spoofs of popular songs⟩
— **wag·gish·ly** *adverb*
— **wag·gish·ness** *noun*

**¹wag·gle** \'wa-gəl\ *verb* **wag·gled; wag·gling** \-g(ə-)liŋ\ [frequentative of ¹*wag*] (1594)
*transitive verb*
: to move frequently one way and the other : WAG
*intransitive verb*
: to reel, sway, or move from side to side : WAG
— **wag·gly** \-g(ə-)lē\ *adjective*

**²waggle** *noun* (circa 1866)
**1 :** an instance of waggling : a jerky motion back and forth or up and down
**2 :** a preliminary swinging of a golf club head back and forth over the ball before the swing

**wag·gon** *chiefly British variant of* WAGON

**¹Wag·ne·ri·an** \väg-'nir-ē-ən, -'ner-\ *adjective* [Richard *Wagner*] (1873)
: of, relating to, characteristic, or suggestive of Wagner or his music or theories

**²Wagnerian** *noun* (1882)
: an admirer of the musical theories and style of Wagner

**Wag·ner·ite** \'väg-nə-,rīt\ *noun* (1855)
: WAGNERIAN

**¹wag·on** \'wa-gən\ *noun* [Dutch *wagen,* from Middle Dutch — more at WAIN] (15th century)
**1 a :** a usually four-wheel vehicle for transporting bulky commodities and drawn originally by animals **b :** a lighter typically horse-drawn vehicle for transporting goods or passengers **c :** PADDY WAGON
**2** *British* : a railway freight car
**3 :** a low four-wheel vehicle with an open rectangular body and a retroflex tongue made for the play or use (as for carrying newspapers) of a child
**4 :** a small wheeled table used for the service of a dining room
**5 :** a delivery truck ⟨milk *wagon*⟩
**6 :** STATION WAGON
— **off the wagon :** no longer abstaining from alcoholic beverages
— **on the wagon :** abstaining from alcoholic beverages

**²wagon** (1606)
*intransitive verb*
: to travel or transport goods by wagon

*transitive verb* : to transport (goods) by wagon

**wag·on·er** \'wa-gə-nər\ *noun* (1544)
**1 :** a person who drives a wagon or transports goods by wagon
**2** *capitalized, obsolete* : BOÖTES

**wag·on·ette** \,wa-gə-'net\ *noun* (circa 1858)
: a light wagon with two facing seats along the sides behind a transverse front seat

**wa·gon-lit** \vá-gō<sup>n</sup>-lē\ *noun, plural* **wagons–lits** *or* **wagon–lits** \-gō<sup>n</sup>-lē(z)\ [French, from *wagon* railroad car + *lit* bed] (1884)
: a railroad sleeping car

**wagon master** *noun* (1645)
: a person in charge of one or more wagons

**wagon train** *noun* (1810)
: a column of wagons (as of supplies for a group of settlers) traveling overland

**wag·tail** \'wag-,tāl\ *noun* (1510)
: any of various chiefly Old World oscine birds (family Motacillidae) related to the pipits and having a trim slender body and a very long tail that they habitually jerk up and down

**Wah·habi** *also* **Wa·habi** \wə-'hä-bē, wä-\ *noun* [Arabic *wahhābīy,* from Muḥammad born 'Abd al-*Wahhāb* (Abdul-Wahhab) (died 1787) Arabian religious reformer] (1807)
: a member of a puritanical Muslim sect founded in Arabia in the 18th century by Muhammad ibn-Abdul Wahhab and revived by ibn-Saud in the 20th century
— **Wah·hab·ism** \-'hä-,bi-zəm\ *noun*
— **Wah·hab·ite** \-,bīt\ *adjective or noun*

**wa·hi·ne** \wä-'hē-nē, -(,)nā\ *noun* [Maori & Hawaiian, woman] (1773)
**1 :** a Polynesian woman
**2 :** a female surfer

**¹wa·hoo** \'wä-,hü, 'wó-\ *noun, plural* **wa·hoos** [origin unknown] (1770)
: WINGED ELM

**²wahoo** *noun, plural* **wahoos** [Dakota *wāhu,* from *wā-* arrow + *hu* wood] (1857)
: a shrubby North American spindle tree (*Euonymus atropurpureus*) having purple capsules which in dehiscence expose the scarlet-ariled seeds — called also *burning bush*

**³wahoo** *noun, plural* **wahoos** [origin unknown] (circa 1900)
: a large vigorous mackerel (*Acanthocybium solandri*) that is common in warm seas and esteemed as a food and sport fish

**⁴wa·hoo** \'wä-hü\ *interjection* (circa 1924)
*chiefly West* — used to express exuberance or enthusiasm or to attract attention

**wah·wah pedal** *variant of* WA-WA PEDAL

**¹waif** \'wāf\ *noun* [Middle English, from Old North French, adjective, lost, unclaimed, probably of Scandinavian origin; akin to Old Norse *veif* something flapping, *veifa* to be in movement — more at WIPE] (14th century)
**1 a :** a piece of property found (as washed up by the sea) but unclaimed **b** *plural* : stolen goods thrown away by a thief in flight
**2 a :** something found without an owner and especially by chance **b :** a stray person or animal; *especially* : a homeless child
— **waif-like** \-,līk\ *adjective*

**²waif** *noun* (1530)
: WAFT 4

**¹wail** \'wā(ə)l\ *verb* [Middle English, of Scandinavian origin; akin to Old Norse *væla, vāla* to wail; akin to Old Norse *vei* woe — more at WOE] (14th century)
*intransitive verb*
**1 :** to express sorrow audibly : LAMENT
**2 :** to make a sound suggestive of a mournful cry
**3 :** to express dissatisfaction plaintively : COMPLAIN
*transitive verb*
*archaic* : BEWAIL
— **wail·er** \'wā-lər\ *noun*

²**wail** *noun* (15th century)
**1 :** the act or practice of wailing **:** loud lamentation
**2 a :** a usually prolonged cry or sound expressing grief or pain **b :** a sound suggestive of wailing ⟨the *wail* of an air-raid siren⟩ **c :** a querulous expression of grievance **:** COMPLAINT

**wail·ful** \'wā(ə)l-fəl\ *adjective* (1544)
**1 :** uttering a sound suggestive of wailing
**2 :** expressing grief or pain **:** SORROWFUL, MOURNFUL
— **wail·ful·ly** \-fə-lē\ *adverb*

**wailing wall** *noun* (1919)
**1** *capitalized* **:** a surviving section of the wall which in ancient times formed a part of the enclosure of Herod's temple near the Holy of Holies and at which Jews traditionally gather for prayer and religious lament
**2 :** a source of comfort and consolation in misfortune

**wain** \'wān\ *noun* [Middle English, wagon, chariot, from Old English *wægn;* akin to Middle Dutch *wagen* wagon, Old English *wegan* to move — more at WAY] (before 12th century)
**1 :** a usually large and heavy vehicle for farm use
**2** *capitalized* [short for *Charles's Wain*] **:** BIG DIPPER

¹**wain·scot** \'wān-skət, -ˌskōt, -ˌskät\ *noun* [Middle English, from Middle Dutch *wagenschot,* probably from *wagen* wagon + *schot* shot, crossbar] (14th century)
**1** *British* **:** a fine grade of oak imported for woodwork
**2 a** (1) **:** a usually paneled wooden lining of an interior wall (2) **:** a lining of an interior wall irrespective of material **b :** the lower three or four feet (about one meter) of an interior wall when finished differently from the remainder of the wall

²**wainscot** *transitive verb* **-scot·ed** *or* **-scot·ted; -scot·ing** *or* **-scot·ting** (circa 1570)
**:** to line with or as if with boards or paneling

**wain·scot·ing** *or* **wain·scot·ting** \-ˌskō-tiŋ, -ˌskä-, -skə-\ *noun* (1580)
**1 :** WAINSCOT 2
**2 :** material used to wainscot a surface

**wain·wright** \'wān-ˌrīt\ *noun* (before 12th century)
**:** a maker and repairer of wagons

**waist** \'wāst\ *noun* [Middle English *wast;* akin to Old English *wæstm* growth, *weaxan* to grow — more at WAX] (14th century)
**1 a :** the narrowed part of the body between the thorax and hips **b :** the greatly constricted basal part of the abdomen of some insects (as wasps and flies)
**2 :** the part of something corresponding to or resembling the human waist: as **a** (1) **:** the part of a ship's deck between the poop and forecastle (2) **:** the middle part of a sailing ship between foremast and mainmast **b :** the middle section of the fuselage of an airplane
**3 :** a garment or the part of a garment covering the body from the neck to the waistline or just below: **a :** BODICE 1 **b :** BLOUSE
**4 :** WAISTLINE 1b
— **waist·ed** \'wā-stəd\ *adjective*

**waist·band** \'wās(t)-ˌband\ *noun* (1584)
**:** a band (as of trousers or a skirt) fitting around the waist

**waist·coat** \'wes-kət, 'wās(t)-ˌkōt\ *noun* (1519)
**1 :** an ornamental garment worn under a doublet
**2** *chiefly British* **:** VEST 2a
— **waist·coat·ed** \-ˌkō-təd\ *adjective*

**waist·line** \'wāst-ˌlīn\ *noun* (1896)
**1 a :** an arbitrary line encircling the narrowest part of the waist **b :** the part of a garment that covers the waistline or may be above or below it as fashion dictates
**2 :** body circumference at the waist

¹**wait** \'wāt\ *verb* [Middle English, from Old North French *waitier* to watch, of Germanic origin; akin to Old High German *wahta* watch, Old English *wæccan* to watch — more at WAKE] (14th century)
*transitive verb*
**1 :** to stay in place in expectation of **:** AWAIT
**2 :** to delay serving (a meal)
**3 :** to serve as waiter for ⟨*wait* tables⟩
*intransitive verb*
**1 a :** to remain stationary in readiness or expectation ⟨*wait* for a train⟩ **b :** to pause for another to catch up — usually used with *up*
**2 a :** to look forward expectantly ⟨just *waiting* to see his rival lose⟩ **b :** to hold back expectantly ⟨*waiting* for a chance to strike⟩
**3 :** to serve at meals — usually used in such phrases as *wait on tables* or *wait on table*
**4 a :** to be ready and available ⟨slippers *waiting* by the bed⟩ **b :** to remain temporarily neglected or unrealized ▪
— **wait on** *also* **wait upon 1 a :** to attend as a servant **b :** to supply the wants of **:** SERVE
**2 :** to make a formal call on **3 :** to wait for
— **wait up :** to delay going to bed **:** stay up

²**wait** *noun* [Middle English *waite* watchman, public musician, wait, from Old North French, watchman, watch, of Germanic origin; akin to Old High German *wahta* watch] (14th century)
**1 a :** a hidden or concealed position — used chiefly in the expression *lie in wait* **b :** a state or attitude of watchfulness and expectancy ⟨anchored in *wait* for early morning fishing —Fred Zimmer⟩
**2 a :** one of a band of public musicians in England employed to play for processions or public entertainments **b** (1) **:** one of a group who serenade for gratuities especially at the Christmas season (2) **:** a piece of music by such a group
**3 :** an act or period of waiting ⟨a long *wait* in line⟩

**wait·er** \'wā-tər\ *noun* (15th century)
**1 :** one that waits on another; *especially* **:** a person who waits tables (as in a restaurant)
**2 :** a tray on which something (as a tea service) is carried **:** SALVER

**waiting game** *noun* (1890)
**:** a strategy in which one or more participants withhold action temporarily in the hope of having a favorable opportunity for more effective action later

**waiting list** *noun* (1897)
**:** a list or roster of those waiting (as for election to a club or admission to an educational institution)

**waiting room** *noun* (1683)
**:** a room (as in a doctor's office) for the use of persons (as patients) who are waiting

**wait out** *transitive verb* (1941)
**:** to await an end to ⟨*wait* the storm *out*⟩

**wait·per·son** \'wāt-ˌpər-s°n\ *noun* (1976)
**:** a waiter or waitress

**wait·ress** \'wā-trəs\ *noun* (1834)
**:** a woman who waits tables (as in a restaurant)
*usage* see -ESS
— **waitress** *intransitive verb*

**waive** \'wāv\ *transitive verb* **waived; waiv·ing** [Middle English *weiven,* from Old North French *weyver,* from *waif* lost, unclaimed — more at WAIF] (14th century)
**1** *archaic* **:** GIVE UP, FORSAKE
**2 :** to throw away (stolen goods)
**3** *archaic* **:** to shunt aside (as a danger or duty) **:** EVADE
**4 a :** to relinquish voluntarily (as a legal right) ⟨*waive* a jury trial⟩ **b :** to refrain from pressing or enforcing (as a claim or rule) **:** FORGO

**5 :** to put off from immediate consideration **:** POSTPONE
**6 :** to dismiss with or as if with a wave of the hand ⟨*waived* the problem aside⟩
**7 :** to place (a ball player) on waivers; *also* **:** to release after placing on waivers
*synonym* see RELINQUISH

**waiv·er** \'wā-vər\ *noun* [Anglo-French *weyver,* from Old North French *weyver* to abandon, waive] (1628)
**1 :** the act of intentionally relinquishing or abandoning a known right, claim, or privilege; *also* **:** the legal instrument evidencing such an act
**2 :** the act of a club's waiving the right to claim a professional ball player who is being removed from another club's roster — often used in the phrase *on waivers* denoting the process by which a player to be removed from a roster is made available to other clubs ⟨was placed on *waivers* before being released⟩

**Wa·kash·an** \wȯ-'ka-shən, 'wȯ-ˌ\ *noun* (circa 1895)
**:** a family of American Indian languages spoken in coastal areas of British Columbia and northwest Washington

¹**wake** \'wāk\ *verb* **woke** \'wōk\ *also* **waked** \wākt\; **wo·ken** \'wō-kən\ *or* **waked** *also* **woke; wak·ing** [partly from Middle English *waken* (past *wook,* past participle *waken*), from Old English *wacan* to awake (past *wōc,* past participle *wacen*); partly from Middle English *wakien, waken* (past & past participle *waked*), from Old English *wacian* to be awake (past *wacode,* past participle *wacod*); akin to Old English *wæccan* to watch, Latin *vegēre* to enliven] (before 12th century)
*intransitive verb*
**1 a :** to be or remain awake **b** *archaic* **:** to remain awake on watch especially over a corpse **c** *obsolete* **:** to stay up late in revelry
**2 :** AWAKE — often used with *up*
*transitive verb*
**1 :** to stand watch over (as a dead body); *especially* **:** to hold a wake over
**2 a :** to rouse from or as if from sleep **:** AWAKE — often used with *up* **b :** STIR, EXCITE ⟨*woke* up latent possibilities —Norman Douglas⟩ **c :** to arouse conscious interest in **:** ALERT — usually used with *to* ⟨*woke* the publishers to

\ə\ abut \°\ kitten \ər\ further \a\ ash \ā\ ace
\ä\ mop, mar \au̇\ out \ch\ chin \e\ bet \ē\ easy
\g\ go \i\ hit \ī\ ice \j\ job \ŋ\ sing \ō\ go
\ȯ\ law \ȯi\ boy \th\ thin \th\ the \ü\ loot \u̇\ foot
\y\ yet \zh\ vision    *see also* Guide to Pronunciation

the fact that there was an enormous . . . audience —Harrison Smith⟩ ▫
— **wak·er** *noun*

**²wake** *noun* (13th century)
**1** : the state of being awake
**2 a** (1) : an annual English parish festival formerly held in commemoration of the church's patron saint (2) : VIGIL 1a **b** : the festivities originally connected with the wake of an English parish church — usually used in plural but singular or plural in construction **c** *British* : an annual holiday or vacation — usually used in plural but singular or plural in construction
**3** : a watch held over the body of a dead person prior to burial and sometimes accompanied by festivity

**³wake** *noun* [of Scandinavian origin; akin to Old Norse *vǫk* hole in ice] (circa 1547)
**1** : the track left by a moving body (as a ship) in a fluid (as water); *broadly* : a track or path left
**2** : AFTERMATH 3
— **in the wake of 1** : close behind and in the same path of travel ⟨*in the wake of* trappers and . . . riflemen came . . . settlers —*American Guide Series: Indiana*⟩ **2** : as a result of : as a consequence of ⟨power vacuums left *in the wake of* the second world war —A. M. Schlesinger (born 1917)⟩

**wake·ful** \'wāk-fəl\ *adjective* (1549)
: not sleeping or able to sleep : SLEEPLESS
— **wake·ful·ly** \-fə-lē\ *adverb*
— **wake·ful·ness** *noun*

**wake·less** \'wā-kləs\ *adjective* (1824)
: SOUND, UNBROKEN ⟨*wakeless* sleep⟩

**wak·en** \'wā-kən\ *verb* **wak·ened; wak·en·ing** \'wāk-niŋ, 'wā-kə-\ [Middle English *waknen*, from Old English *wæcnian*; akin to Old Norse *vakna* to awaken, Old English *wæccan* to watch] (before 12th century)
*intransitive verb*
: AWAKE — often used with *up*
*transitive verb*
: to rouse especially out of sleep : WAKE

**wak·en·er** \'wāk-nər, 'wā-kə-\ *noun* (1573)
*archaic* : one that causes to waken

**wake·rife** \'wāk-ˌrīf\ *adjective* [Middle English (Scots) *walkryfe*, from *walk* awake (from *waken, walken* to wake) + *ryfe* rife] (15th century)
*Scottish* : WAKEFUL, ALERT

**wake–rob·in** \'wāk-ˌrä-bən\ *noun* (circa 1530)
**1** : TRILLIUM
**2** : JACK-IN-THE-PULPIT

**wake–up** \'wāk-ˌəp\ *adjective* (1946)
: serving to wake up ⟨a *wake-up* call⟩ ⟨a *wake-up* cup of coffee⟩

**wak·ing** \'wā-kin\ *adjective* (1567)
: passed in a conscious or alert state ⟨every *waking* hour⟩

**Wal·den·ses** \wȯl-'den(t)-(ˌ)sēz, wäl-\ *noun plural* [Medieval Latin *Waldensis*, from Medieval Latin *Waldenses, Valdenses*, from Peter *Waldo* (or *Valdo*)] (1537)
: a Christian sect arising in southern France in the 12th century, adopting Calvinist doctrines in the 16th century, and later living chiefly in Piedmont
— **Wal·den·sian** \-'den(t)-shən, -'den(t)-sē-ən\ *adjective or noun*

**Wal·dorf salad** \'wȯl-ˌdȯrf-\ *noun* [*Waldorf-Astoria* Hotel, New York City] (1902)
: a salad made typically of diced apples, celery, nuts, and mayonnaise

**¹wale** \'wā(ə)l\ *noun* [Middle English, from Old English *walu*; akin to Old Norse *vǫlr* staff and perhaps to Old Norse *valr* round, Latin *volvere* to roll — more at VOLUBLE] (before 12th century)
**1 a** : a streak or ridge made on the skin especially by the stroke of a whip : WEAL **b** : a narrow raised surface : RIDGE
**2** : any of a number of strakes usually of extra thick and strong planks in the sides of a wooden ship — usually used in plural

**3 a** : one of a series of even ribs in a fabric **b** : the texture especially of a fabric
**4** : a horizontal constructional member (as of timber or steel) used for bracing vertical members

**²wale** *transitive verb* **waled; wal·ing** (15th century)
: to mark (as the skin) with welts

**³wale** *noun* [Middle English (Scots & northern dialect) *wal*, from Old Norse *val*; akin to Old High German *wala* choice, Old English *wyllan* to wish — more at WILL] (14th century)
**1** *dialect British* : CHOICE
**2** *dialect British* : the best part : PICK

**⁴wale** *verb* (14th century)
*dialect British* : CHOOSE

**wal·er** \'wā-lər\ *noun, often capitalized* [New South *Wales*, Australia] (1849)
: a horse from New South Wales; *especially* : a rather large rugged saddle horse of mixed ancestry formerly exported in quantity from Australia to British India for military use

**Wal·hal·la** \väl-'hä-lə\ *noun* [German]
: VALHALLA

**¹walk** \'wȯk\ *verb* [partly from Middle English *walken* (past *welk*, past participle *walken*), from Old English *wealcan* to roll, toss, journey about (past *weolc*, past participle *wealcen*) and partly from Middle English *walkien* (past *walked*, past participle *walked*), from Old English *wealcian* to roll up, muffle up; akin to Middle Dutch *walken* to knead, press, full] (before 12th century)
*intransitive verb*
**1 a** *obsolete* : ROAM, WANDER **b** *of a spirit* : to move about in visible form : APPEAR **c** *of a ship* : to make headway
**2 a** : to move along on foot : advance by steps **b** : to come or go easily or readily **c** : to go on foot for exercise or pleasure **d** : to go at a walk
**3 a** : to pursue a course of action or way of life : conduct oneself : BEHAVE ⟨*walk* warily⟩ **b** : to be or act in association : continue in union ⟨the British and American peoples will . . . *walk* together side by side . . . in peace —Sir Winston Churchill⟩ **c** : WALK OUT ⟨the workers didn't like the new contract so they *walked*⟩
**4** : to go to first base as a result of a base on balls
**5** *of an inanimate object* **a** : to move in a manner that is suggestive of walking **b** : to stand with an appearance suggestive of strides ⟨pylons *walking* across the valley⟩
**6** *of an astronaut* : to move about in space outside a spacecraft
*transitive verb*
**1 a** : to pass on foot or as if on foot through, along, over, or upon : TRAVERSE, PERAMBULATE ⟨*walk* the streets⟩ ⟨*walk* a tightrope⟩ **b** : to perform or accomplish by going on foot ⟨*walk* guard⟩
**2 a** : to cause (an animal) to go at a walk : take for a walk ⟨*walking* a dog⟩ **b** (1) : to cause to move by walking ⟨*walked* her bicycle up the hill⟩ (2) : to haul (as an anchor) by walking round the capstan
**3** : to follow on foot for the purpose of measuring, surveying, or inspecting ⟨*walk* a boundary⟩
**4 a** : to accompany on foot : walk with ⟨*walked* her home⟩ **b** : to compel to walk (as by a command) **c** : to bring to a specified condition by walking ⟨*walked* us off our feet⟩
**5** : to move (an object) in a manner suggestive of walking
**6** : to perform (a dance) at a walking pace ⟨*walk* a quadrille⟩
**7** : to give a base on balls to
— **walk away from 1** : to outrun or get the better of without difficulty **2** : to survive (an accident) with little or no injury
— **walk off with 1 a** : to steal and take away **b** : to take over unexpectedly from someone else : STEAL 1d ⟨*walked off with* the

show⟩ **2** : to win or gain especially by outdoing one's competitors without difficulty
— **walk on** : to take advantage of : ABUSE
— **walk over** : to treat contemptuously
— **walk the plank 1** : to walk under compulsion over the side of a ship into the sea **2** : to resign an office or position under compulsion
— **walk through 1** : to go through (as a theatrical role or familiar activity) perfunctorily (as in an early stage of rehearsal) **2** : to guide (as a novice) through an unfamiliar or complex procedure step-by-step **3** : to deal with or carry out perfunctorily

**²walk** *noun* (14th century)
**1 a** : an act or instance of going on foot especially for exercise or pleasure ⟨go for a *walk*⟩ **b** : SPACE WALK
**2** : an accustomed place of walking : HAUNT
**3 a** : a place designed for walking : as **a** : a railed platform above the roof of a dwelling house **b** (1) : a path specially arranged or paved for walking (2) : SIDEWALK **c** : a public avenue for promenading : PROMENADE **d** : ROPEWALK
**4** : a place or area of land in which animals feed and exercise with minimal restraint
**5** : distance to be walked ⟨a quarter mile *walk* from here⟩
**6** *British* : a ceremonial procession
**7** : manner of living : CONDUCT, BEHAVIOR
**8 a** : the gait of a biped in which the feet are lifted alternately with one foot not clear of the ground before the other touches **b** : the gait of a quadruped in which there are always at least two feet on the ground; *specifically* : a four-beat gait of a horse in which the feet strike the ground in the sequence near hind, near fore, off hind, off fore **c** : a low rate of speed ⟨the shortage of raw materials slowed production to a *walk*⟩
**9** : a route regularly traversed by a person in the performance of a particular activity (as patrolling, begging, or vending)
**10** : characteristic manner of walking ⟨his *walk* is just like his father's⟩
**11 a** : social or economic status ⟨all *walks* of life⟩ **b** (1) : range or sphere of action : FIELD, PROVINCE (2) : VOCATION
**12** : BASE ON BALLS

**walk·about** \'wȯ-kə-ˌbau̇t\ *noun* (1908)
**1** : a short period of wandering bush life engaged in by an Australian aborigine as an occasional interruption of regular work

▫ USAGE
**wake**   *Wake* has such a large selection of forms for the past and past participle because it is the modern result of the coalescence of two old verbs, one with regular parts, one with irregular. What makes *wake* interesting is that preference for these forms has changed over time and is still changing. The regular *waked* was the prevalent form in the 16th, 17th, and 18th centuries. During the 19th century *woke* came into wide use for the past tense while *waked* continued as the past participle. In the 20th century *woken* has emerged as a strong contender to be the dominant past participle. These changes have not taken place uniformly, and they seem to have become prevalent in British English earlier than they did in American English. For instance *woken* seems to be the usual past participle for British writers ⟨in the mornings he was *woken* by his butler —Julian Huxley⟩ ⟨one night he was *woken* by someone coming into the bedroom —Graham Greene⟩ while in American English *waked* and *woken* are both used ⟨during the night he has *waked* up sweating —Mary McCarthy⟩ ⟨he had *woken* them, clearing his throat —John Updike⟩. *Woke* is much less frequent as a past participle than *waked* and *woken*.

**2 :** a walking tour **:** walking trip

**walk·a·thon** \'wȯ-kə-ˌthän\ *noun* [*walk* + *-athon*] (1932)
**:** a walk covering a considerable distance organized especially to raise money for a cause

**walk·away** \'wȯ-kə-ˌwā\ *noun* (1888)
**:** an easily won contest

**walk·er** \'wȯ-kər\ *noun* (14th century)
**1 :** one that walks: as **a :** a competitor in a walking race **b :** a peddler going on foot **c :** a temporary male escort of socially prominent women attending usually public events
**2 :** something used in walking: as **a :** a framework designed to support a baby learning to walk or an infirm or handicapped person **b :** a walking shoe

**walk·ie–talk·ie** \ˌwȯ-kē-'tȯ-kē, 'wȯ-kē-\ *noun* (1939)
**:** a compact easily transportable battery-operated radio transmitting and receiving set

**¹walk–in** \'wȯk-ˌin\ *adjective* (1926)
**1 :** large enough to be walked into ⟨a *walk-in* closet⟩
**2 :** arranged so as to be entered directly rather than through a lobby ⟨a *walk-in* apartment⟩
**3 a :** being a person who walks in without an appointment ⟨a *walk-in* blood donor⟩ **b :** of or relating to such persons ⟨*walk-in* clinic⟩

**²walk–in** \'wȯk-ˌin\ *noun* (1944)
**1 :** a walk-in refrigerator or cold storage room
**2 :** an easy election victory
**3 :** one who walks in without an appointment

**¹walk·ing** \'wȯ-kiŋ\ *noun* (15th century)
**1 :** the action of one that walks ⟨*walking* is good exercise⟩
**2 :** the condition of a surface for one going on foot ⟨the *walking* is slippery⟩

**²walking** *adjective* (15th century)
**1 a :** able to walk : AMBULATORY ⟨the *walking* wounded⟩ **b :** being the personification of a nonhuman quality or thing ⟨a *walking* encyclopedia⟩
**2 a :** used for or in walking ⟨*walking* shoes⟩ **b :** characterized by or consisting of the action of walking ⟨a *walking* tour⟩
**3 :** that moves or appears to move in a manner suggestive of walking; *especially* **:** that swings or rocks back and forth ⟨*walking* beam⟩
**4 :** guided or operated by a person on foot ⟨a *walking* plow⟩

**walking catfish** *noun* (1968)
**:** an Asian freshwater catfish (*Clarias batrachus* of the family Clariidae) that is able to move about on land and has become established in Florida waters

**walking delegate** *noun* (1889)
**:** a labor union representative appointed to visit members and their places of employment, to secure enforcement of union rules and agreements, and at times to represent the union in dealing with employers

**walking leaf** *noun* (1826)
**:** any of a family (Phylliidae) of phasmid insects with wings and legs resembling leaves

**walking papers** *noun plural* (1825)
**:** DISMISSAL, DISCHARGE — called also *walking ticket*

**walking pneumonia** *noun* (1964)
**:** a usually mild pneumonia caused by a mycoplasma (*Mycoplasma pneumoniae*) and characterized by malaise, cough, and often fever

**walking stick** *noun* (1580)
**1 :** a stick used in walking
**2** *usually* **walking-stick :** STICK INSECT; *especially* **:** a phasmid insect (*Diapheromera femorata*) common in parts of the U.S.

**walkingstick**

**Walk·man** \'wȯk-mən, -ˌman\ *trademark*
— used for a small portable radio or cassette player listened to by means of headphones or earphones

**walk–on** \'wȯk-ˌȯn, -ˌän\ *noun* (1902)

**1 :** a minor part (as in a dramatic production); *also* **:** an actor having such a part
**2 :** a college athlete who tries out for an athletic team without having been recruited or offered a scholarship

**walk–out** \'wȯk-ˌau̇t\ *noun* (1888)
**1 :** STRIKE 3a
**2 :** the action of leaving a meeting or organization as an expression of disapproval

**walk out** *intransitive verb* (1840)
**1 :** to leave suddenly often as an expression of disapproval
**2 :** to go on strike
— **walk out on :** to leave in the lurch **:** ABANDON, DESERT

**walk·over** \'wȯk-ˌō-vər\ *noun* (1838)
**1 :** a one-sided contest **:** an easy or uncontested victory
**2 :** a horse race with only one starter

**walk–through** \'wȯk-ˌthrü\ *noun* (1940)
**1 :** a perfunctory performance of a play or acting part (as in an early stage of rehearsal)
**2 :** a television rehearsal without cameras

**¹walk–up** \'wȯk-ˌəp\ *adjective* (1919)
**1 :** located above the ground floor in a building with no elevator ⟨a *walk-up* apartment⟩
**2 :** consisting of several stories and having no elevator ⟨a *walk-up* tenement⟩
**3 :** designed to allow pedestrians to be served without entering a building ⟨the *walk-up* window of a bank⟩

**²walk–up** *noun* (1924)
**:** a building or apartment house of several stories that has no elevator; *also* **:** an apartment or office in such a building

**walk·way** \'wȯk-ˌwā\ *noun* (1792)
**:** a passage for walking **:** WALK

**Wal·ky·rie** \val-'kir-ē *also* val-'kī-rē *or* 'väl-kə-rē\ *noun* [German *Walküre* & Old Norse *valkyrja*]
**:** VALKYRIE

**¹wall** \'wȯl\ *noun* [Middle English, from Old English *weall;* akin to Middle High German *wall;* both from Latin *vallum* rampart, from *vallus* stake, palisade; perhaps akin to Old Norse *vǫlr* staff — more at WALE] (before 12th century)
**1 a :** a high thick masonry structure forming a long rampart or an enclosure chiefly for defense — often used in plural **b :** a masonry fence around a garden, park, or estate **c :** a structure that serves to hold back pressure (as of water or sliding earth)
**2 :** one of the sides of a room or building connecting floor and ceiling or foundation and roof
**3 :** the side of a footpath next to buildings
**4 :** an extreme or desperate position or a state of defeat, failure, or ruin — usually used in the phrase *to the wall*
**5 :** a material layer enclosing space ⟨the *wall* of a container⟩ ⟨heart *walls*⟩
**6 :** something resembling a wall (as in appearance, function, or effect); *especially* **:** something that acts as a barrier or defense ⟨a *wall* of reserve⟩ ⟨tariff *wall*⟩
— **walled** \'wȯld\ *adjective*
— **wall–like** \'wȯl-ˌlīk\ *adjective*
— **up the wall** *slang* **:** into a state of intense agitation, annoyance, or frustration ⟨the noise drove me *up the wall*⟩

**²wall** *transitive verb* (13th century)
**1 a :** to provide, cover with, or surround with or as if with a wall ⟨*wall* in the garden⟩ **b :** to separate by or as if by a wall ⟨*walled* off half the house⟩
**2 a :** IMMURE **b :** to close (an opening) with or as if with a wall

**³wall** *verb* [Middle English (Scots) *wawlen,* probably from Middle English *wawil-* (in *wawil-eghed* walleyed)] (15th century)
*intransitive verb*
*of the eyes* **:** to roll in a dramatic manner
*transitive verb*
**:** to roll (one's eyes) in a dramatic manner

**wal·la·by** \'wä-lə-bē\ *noun, plural* **wal·la·bies** *also* **wallaby** [Dharuk (Australian aboriginal language of the Port Jackson area) *walaba*] (circa 1798)
**:** any of various small or medium-sized kangaroos (especially genus *Macropus*) — compare ROCK WALLABY

**Wal·lace's line** \'wä-lə-səz-\ *noun* [Alfred Russel *Wallace*] (1868)
**:** a hypothetical boundary that separates the highly distinctive floras and faunas of the Oriental and Australian biogeographic regions and passes between the islands of Bali and Lombok in Indonesia, between Borneo and Sulawesi, and between the Philippines and the Moluccas

**wallaby**

**wal·lah** \'wä-lə, *in combination usually* ˌwä-lə\ *noun* [Hindi *-vālā* one in charge, from Sanskrit *pāla* protector, from *pālayati, pārayati* he guards; akin to Sanskrit *piparti* he brings over, saves, Old English *faran* to go — more at FARE] (1782)
**:** a person who is associated with a particular work or who performs a specific duty or service — usually used in combination ⟨the book *wallah* was an itinerant peddler —George Orwell⟩

**wal·la·roo** \ˌwä-lə-'rü\ *noun, plural* **-roos** [Dharuk (Australian aboriginal language of the Port Jackson area) *walaru*] (1827)
**1 :** a large reddish gray kangaroo (*Macropus robustus*) — called also *euro*
**2 :** either of two kangaroos (*Macropus antelopinus* and *M. bernardus*) related to the wallaroo

**wall·board** \'wȯl-ˌbōrd, -ˌbȯrd\ *noun* (1906)
**:** a structural boarding of any of various materials (as wood pulp, gypsum, or plastic) made in large rigid sheets and used especially for sheathing interior walls and ceilings

**wal·let** \'wä-lət\ *noun* [Middle English *walet*] (14th century)
**1 :** a bag for carrying miscellaneous articles while traveling
**2 a :** a folding pocketbook with compartments for personal papers and usually unfolded paper money; *also* **:** BILLFOLD **b :** a container that resembles a money wallet: as (1) **:** a usually flexible folding case fitted for carrying specific items (as tools or fishing flies) (2) **:** FOLDER 3

**wall·eye** \'wȯ-ˌlī\ *noun* [back-formation from *walleyed*] (1523)
**1 a :** an eye with a whitish or bluish white iris **b :** an eye with an opaque white cornea
**2 a :** strabismus in which the eye turns outward away from the nose **b :** an eye affected with divergent strabismus
**3 :** a large vigorous North American freshwater food and sport fish (*Stizostedion vitreum*) that has prominent eyes and is related to the perches but resembles the true pike — called also *walleyed pike*

**wall–eyed** \-ˈlīd\ *adjective* [by folk etymology from Middle English *wawil-eghed,* part translation of Old Norse *vagl-eygr* walleyed, from *vagl* beam (akin to Greek *ochleus* bar, Old English *wegan* to move, carry) + *eygr* eyed — more at WAY] (15th century)
**1 :** having walleyes or affected with walleye
**2 :** marked by a wild irrational staring of the eyes

**walleye pollack** *noun* (1907)

: POLLACK 2

**wall·flow·er** \'wȯl-ˌflaü(-ə)r\ *noun* (1578)
**1 a :** any of several Old World herbaceous or somewhat woody perennial plants (genus *Cheiranthus*) of the mustard family; *especially* **:** a hardy erect herb (*C. cheiri*) widely cultivated for its showy fragrant flowers **b :** any of a related genus (*Erysimum*) of plants with showy flowers
**2 :** a person who from shyness or unpopularity remains on the sidelines of a social activity (as a dance)

**Wal·loon** \wä-'lün\ *noun* [Middle French *Wallon*, adjective & noun, of Germanic origin; probably akin to Old High German *Walah* Celtic, Roman, Old English *Wealh* Celt, Welshman — more at WELSH] (1567)
**1 :** a member of a people of southern and southeastern Belgium and adjacent parts of France
**2 :** a French dialect of the Walloons
— **Walloon** *adjective*

**¹wal·lop** \'wä-ləp\ *verb* [Middle English *walopen* to gallop, from Old North French *waloper*] (1579)
*intransitive verb*
**1 :** to boil noisily
**2 a :** to move with reckless or disorganized haste **:** advance in a headlong rush **b :** WALLOW, FLOUNDER
*transitive verb*
**1 a :** to thrash soundly **:** LAMBASTE **b :** to beat by a wide margin **:** TROUNCE
**2 :** to hit with force **:** SOCK
— **wal·lop·er** *noun*

**²wallop** *noun* [Middle English, gallop, from Old North French *walop*, from *waloper* to gallop] (circa 1823)
**1 a :** a powerful blow **:** PUNCH **b :** something resembling a wallop especially in suddenness of force **c :** the ability (as of a boxer) to hit hard
**2 a :** emotional, sensory, or psychological force or influence **:** IMPACT ⟨a novel that packs a *wallop*⟩ **b :** an exciting emotional response **:** THRILL
**3** *British* **:** BEER

**wal·lop·ing** *adjective* (circa 1847)
**1 :** LARGE, WHOPPING
**2 :** exceptionally fine or impressive **:** SMASHING

**¹wal·low** \'wä-(ˌ)lō\ *intransitive verb* [Middle English *walwen*, from Old English *wealwian* to roll — more at VOLUBLE] (before 12th century)
**1 :** to roll oneself about in an indolent or ungainly manner
**2 :** to billow forth **:** SURGE
**3 :** to devote oneself entirely; *especially* **:** to take unrestrained pleasure **:** DELIGHT
**4 a :** to become abundantly supplied **:** LUXURIATE ⟨a family that *wallows* in money⟩ **b :** to indulge oneself immoderately ⟨*wallowing* in self-pity⟩
**5 :** to become or remain helpless ⟨allowed them to *wallow* in their ignorance⟩
— **wal·low·er** \'wä-lə-wər\ *noun*

**²wallow** *noun* (15th century)
**1 :** an act or instance of wallowing
**2 a :** a muddy area or one filled with dust used by animals for wallowing **b :** a depression formed by or as if by the wallowing of animals
**3 :** a state of degradation or degeneracy

**wall painting** *noun* (1688)
**:** FRESCO

**¹wall·pa·per** \'wȯl-ˌpā-pər\ *noun* (1827)
**:** decorative paper for the walls of a room

**²wallpaper** (1924)
*transitive verb*
**:** to provide the walls of (a room) with wallpaper
*intransitive verb*
**:** to put wallpaper on a wall

**wall plate** *noun* (14th century)
**:** PLATE 5

**wall plug** *noun* (1888)
**:** an electric receptacle in a wall

**wall rock** *noun* (1876)
**:** a rock through which a fault or vein runs

**wall rocket** *noun* (1611)
**:** any of several Old World herbs (genus *Diplotaxis*) of the mustard family; *especially* **:** a yellow-flowered European herb (*D. tenuifolia*) adventive in North America

**Wall Street** \'wȯl-\ *noun* [*Wall Street*, New York City, site of the New York Stock Exchange] (1836)
**:** the influential financial interests of the U.S. economy

**Wall Street·er** \-ˌstrē-tər\ *noun* (1885)
**:** a person who is involved in Wall Street

**wall system** *noun* (1968)
**:** a set of shelves often with cabinets or bureaus that can be variously arranged along a wall

**wall–to–wall** *adjective* (1946)
**1 :** covering the entire floor ⟨*wall-to-wall* carpeting⟩
**2 a :** covering or filling one entire space or time ⟨a party crammed with *wall-to-wall* bodies⟩ **b :** occurring or found everywhere **:** UBIQUITOUS

**wal·ly** \'wä-lē\ *adjective* [probably from ³*wale*] (circa 1520)
*Scottish* **:** FINE, STURDY

**wal·ly·drai·gle** \'wä-lē-ˌdrā-gəl, 'wä-lē-\ *noun* [origin unknown] (1508)
*chiefly Scottish* **:** a feeble, imperfectly developed, or slovenly creature

**wal·nut** \'wȯl-(ˌ)nət\ *noun* [Middle English *walnot*, from Old English *wealhhnutu*, literally, foreign nut, from *Wealh* Welshman, foreigner + *hnutu* nut — more at WELSH, NUT] (before 12th century)
**1 a :** a nut of any of a genus (*Juglans* of the family Juglandaceae, the walnut family) of trees; *especially* **:** the large edible nut of a Eurasian tree (*J. regia*) with a hard richly figured wood **b :** a tree that bears walnuts **c :** the wood of a walnut that is often used for cabinetmaking and veneers
**2 :** a moderate reddish brown ◆

**Wal·pur·gis·nacht** \väl-'pür-gəs-ˌnäkt\ *noun* [German] (1822)
**:** WALPURGIS NIGHT

**Wal·pur·gis Night** \väl-'pür-gəs-\ *noun* [part translation of German *Walpurgisnacht*, from *Walpurgis* Saint Walburga (died A.D. 779) English saint whose feast day falls on May Day + German *Nacht* night] (1823)
**1 :** the eve of May Day on which witches are held to ride to an appointed rendezvous
**2 :** something (as an event or situation) having a nightmarish quality

**wal·rus** \'wȯl-rəs, 'wäl-\ *noun, plural* **walrus** *or* **wal·rus·es** [Dutch, of Scandinavian origin; akin to Danish & Norwegian *hvalros* walrus, Old Norse *rosmhvalr*] (1728)
**:** a large gregarious marine mammal (*Odobenus rosmarus* of the family Odobenidae) related to the seal that is found in Arctic seas, has long ivory tusks, a tough wrinkled hide, and stiff whiskers, and feeds mostly on bivalve mollusks

**Wal·ter Mit·ty** \ˌwȯl-tər-'mi-tē\ *noun* [*Walter Mitty*, daydreaming hero of a story by James Thurber] (1949)
**:** a commonplace unadventurous person who seeks escape from reality through daydreaming
— **Walter Mit·ty·ish** \-ish\ *adjective*

**¹waltz** \'wȯl(t)s\ *noun* [German *Walzer*, from *walzen* to roll, dance, from Old High German *walzan* to turn, roll — more at WELTER] (1781)
**1 :** a ballroom dance in ¾ time with strong accent on the first beat and a basic pattern of step-step-close
**2 :** music for a waltz or a concert composition in ¾ time

**²waltz** (circa 1794)

*intransitive verb*
**1 :** to dance a waltz
**2 :** to move or advance in a lively or conspicuous manner **:** FLOUNCE
**3 a :** to advance easily and successfully **:** BREEZE — often used with *through* **b :** to approach boldly — used with *up* ⟨can't just *waltz* up and introduce ourselves⟩
*transitive verb*
**1 :** to dance a waltz with
**2 :** to grab and lead (as a person) unceremoniously **:** MARCH
— **waltz·er** *noun*

**¹wam·ble** \'wäm-bəl\ *intransitive verb* **wam·bled; wam·bling** \-b(ə-)liŋ\ [Middle English *wamlen;* akin to Danish *vamle* to become nauseated, Latin *vomere* to vomit — more at VOMIT] (14th century)
**1 a :** to feel nausea **b** *of a stomach* **:** RUMBLE 1
**2 :** to move unsteadily or with a weaving or rolling motion

**²wamble** *noun* (1552)
**1 :** a wambling especially of the stomach
**2 :** a reeling or staggering gait or movement

**wame** \'wām\ *noun* [Middle English, alteration of *wamb* — more at WOMB] (15th century)
*chiefly Scottish* **:** BELLY

**Wam·pa·no·ag** \ˌwäm-pə-'nō-(ˌ)ag, ˌwȯm-\ *noun, plural* **Wampanoag** *or* **Wampano·ags** [Narraganset, literally, easterners] (1676)
**:** a member of an American Indian people of Rhode Island east of Narragansett Bay and neighboring parts of Massachusetts

**wam·pum** \'wäm-pəm\ *noun* [short for *wampumpeag*] (1636)
**1 :** beads of polished shells strung in strands, belts, or sashes and used by North American Indians as money, ceremonial pledges, and ornaments
**2 :** MONEY

**wam·pum·peag** \-ˌpēg\ *noun* [Massachuset *wampompeag*, from *wampan* white + *api* string + *-ag*, plural suffix] (1627)
**:** WAMPUM

**¹wan** \'wän\ *adjective* **wan·ner; wan·nest** [Middle English, from Old English *wann* dark, livid] (14th century)
**1 a :** suggestive of poor health **:** SICKLY, PALLID
**b :** lacking vitality **:** FEEBLE
**2 :** DIM, FAINT
**3 :** LANGUID ⟨a *wan* smile⟩
— **wan·ly** *adverb*
— **wan·ness** \'wän-nəs\ *noun*

◇ **WORD HISTORY**
**walnut** The English walnut (*Juglans regia*) is not native to England in spite of its name. This tree, important for both its wood and fruit, was known in southern Europe long before it was introduced to northern Europeans, to whom the only readily available nut was the hazelnut. *Wealhhnutu*, the Old English ancestor of *walnut*, reflects the foreign origin of the walnut: it is a compound of *wealh* "stranger, foreigner" and *hnutu* "nut." Other Germanic words of later date, such as Middle Low German *walnut* (from which ultimately Modern German *Walnuss* comes), Middle High German *walhisch nuz*, and Old Norse *valhnot*, contain the same elements. They have a parallel in a Medieval Latin name for the walnut, *nux gallica*, literally, "Gallic or French nut." Old English *wealh* "foreigner" is buried in other Modern English words in addition to *walnut*. *Wealh* was applied to the Celtic speakers who opposed the Anglo-Saxons' invasion of Britain—despite being the indigenous inhabitants they were "foreigners" to the Germanic tribes—and *Wealas*, the plural of *wealh*, developed into Modern English *Wales*, now designating the land where Celtic Britons took refuge and maintained their ancient speech.

²**wan** *intransitive verb* **wanned; wan·ning** (1582)
: to grow or become pale or sickly

**wand** \'wänd\ *noun* [Middle English, slender stick, from Old Norse *vǫndr;* probably akin to Old English *windan* to wind, twist — more at WIND] (15th century)
**1 :** a slender staff carried in a procession : VERGE
**2 :** a slender rod used by conjurers and magicians
**3 :** a slat 6 feet by 2 inches used as a target in archery; *also* : a narrow strip of paper pasted vertically on a target face
**4 :** any of various pipelike devices; *especially* : the rigid tube between the hose and the nozzle of a vacuum cleaner
**5 :** a handheld device used to enter information (as from a bar code) into a computer

**wan·der** \'wän-dər\ *verb* **wan·dered; wan·der·ing** \-d(ə-)riŋ\ [Middle English *wandren,* from Old English *wandrian;* akin to Middle High German *wandern* to wander, Old English *windan* to wind, twist] (before 12th century)
*intransitive verb*
**1 a :** to move about without a fixed course, aim, or goal **b :** to go idly about : RAMBLE
**2 :** to follow a winding course : MEANDER
**3 a :** to deviate (as from a course) : STRAY **b** : to go astray morally : ERR **c :** to lose normal mental contact : stray in thought
*transitive verb*
: to roam over ☆
— **wander** *noun*
— **wan·der·er** \-dər-ər\ *noun*

¹**wandering** *adjective* (before 12th century)
: characterized by aimless, slow, or pointless movement: as **a :** that winds or meanders ⟨a *wandering* course⟩ **b :** not keeping a rational or sensible course : VAGRANT **c :** NOMADIC ⟨*wandering* tribes⟩ **d** *of a plant* : having long runners or tendrils

²**wandering** *noun* (14th century)
**1 :** a going about from place to place — often used in plural
**2 :** movement away from the proper, normal, or usual course or place — often used in plural

**Wandering Jew** *noun*
**1 :** a Jew of medieval legend condemned by Christ to wander the earth till Christ's second coming
**2** *W not capitalized* : any of several plants (genera *Zebrina* and *Tradescantia*) of the spiderwort family; *especially* : either of two trailing or creeping plants (*Z. pendula* and *T. fluminensis*) cultivated for their showy and often white-striped foliage

**wan·der·lust** \'wän-dər-ˌləst\ *noun* [German, from *wandern* to wander + *Lust* desire, pleasure] (1902)
: strong longing for or impulse toward wandering

¹**wane** \'wän\ *intransitive verb* **waned; wan·ing** [Middle English, from Old English *wanian;* akin to Old High German *wanōn* to wane, Old English *wan* wanting, deficient, Latin *vanus* empty, vain] (before 12th century)
**1 :** to decrease in size, extent, or degree : DWINDLE: as **a :** to diminish in phase or intensity — used chiefly of the moon **b :** to become less brilliant or powerful : DIM **c :** to flow out : EBB
**2 :** to fall gradually from power, prosperity, or influence
**synonym** *see* ABATE

²**wane** *noun* (14th century)
**1 a :** the act or process of waning ⟨strength on the *wane*⟩ **b :** a period or time of waning; *specifically* : the period from full phase of the moon to the new moon
**2** [Middle English, defect, from Old English *wana;* akin to Old English *wan* deficient] : a defect in lumber characterized by bark or a lack of wood at a corner or edge

**wan·gle** \'waŋ-gəl\ *verb* **wan·gled; wan·gling** \-g(ə-)liŋ\ [perhaps alteration of *waggle*] (circa 1820)
*intransitive verb*
**1 :** to extricate oneself (as from difficulty) : WIGGLE
**2 :** to resort to trickery or devious methods
*transitive verb*
**1 :** SHAKE, WIGGLE
**2 :** to adjust or manipulate for personal or fraudulent ends
**3 :** to make or get by devious means : FINAGLE ⟨*wangle* an invitation⟩
— **wan·gler** \-g(ə-)lər\ *noun*

**wan·i·gan** *or* **wan·ni·gan** \'wä-ni-gən\ *noun* [Ojibwa *wa'nikka'n* pit] (circa 1848)
: a shelter (as for sleeping, eating, or storage) often mounted on wheels or tracks and towed by tractor or mounted on a raft or boat

**wan·ion** \'wän-yən\ *noun* [from the obsolete phrase *in the waniand* unluckily, literally, in the waning (moon), from Middle English, from *waniand,* northern present participle of *wanien, wanen* to wane] (1549)
*archaic* : PLAGUE, VENGEANCE — used in the phrase *with a wanion*

**Wan·kel engine** \'väŋ-kəl-, 'waŋ-\ *noun* [Felix Wankel (died 1988) German engineer] (1961)
: an internal combustion rotary engine that has a rounded triangular rotor functioning as a piston and rotating in a space in the engine and that has only two major moving parts

**wan·na–be** \'wä-nə-ˌbē\ *noun* [from the phrase *want to be*] (1981)
: a person who wants or aspires to be someone or something else or who tries to look or act like someone else

¹**want** \'wȯnt *also* 'wänt & 'wənt\ *verb* [Middle English, from Old Norse *vanta;* akin to Old English *wan* deficient] (13th century)
*intransitive verb*
**1 :** to be needy or destitute
**2 :** to have or feel need ⟨never *wants* for friends⟩
**3 :** to be necessary or needed
**4 :** to desire to come, go, or be ⟨the cat *wants* in⟩ ⟨*wants* out of the deal⟩
*transitive verb*
**1 :** to fail to possess especially in customary or required amount : LACK ⟨the answer *wanted* courtesy⟩
**2 a :** to have a strong desire for ⟨*wanted* a chance to rest⟩ **b :** to have an inclination to : LIKE ⟨say what you *want,* he is efficient⟩
**3 a :** to have need of : REQUIRE ⟨the motor *wants* a tune-up⟩ **b :** to suffer from the lack of ⟨thousands still *want* food and shelter⟩
**4 :** OUGHT — used with the infinitive ⟨you *want* to be very careful what you say —Claudia Cassidy⟩
**5 :** to wish or demand the presence of
**6 :** to hunt or seek in order to apprehend ⟨*wanted* for murder⟩
**synonym** *see* DESIRE

²**want** *noun* (14th century)
**1 a :** DEFICIENCY, LACK ⟨suffers from a *want* of good sense⟩ **b :** grave and extreme poverty that deprives one of the necessities of life
**2 :** something wanted : NEED, DESIRE
**3 :** personal defect : FAULT
**synonym** *see* POVERTY

**want ad** *noun* (1897)
: a newspaper advertisement stating that something (as an employee, employment, or a specified item) is wanted

¹**want·ing** *adjective* (15th century)
**1 :** not present or in evidence : ABSENT
**2 a :** not being up to standards or expectations **b :** lacking in ability or capacity : DEFICIENT

²**wanting** *preposition* (1693)
**1 :** LESS, MINUS ⟨a month *wanting* two days⟩
**2 :** WITHOUT ⟨a book *wanting* a cover⟩

¹**wan·ton** \'wȯn-tᵊn, 'wän-\ *adjective* [Middle English, from *wan-* deficient, wrong, mis- (from Old English *wan* deficient) + *to-*

*wen,* past participle of *teen* to draw, train, discipline, from Old English *tēon* — more at TOW] (14th century)
**1 a** *archaic* : hard to control : UNDISCIPLINED, UNRULY **b :** playfully mean or cruel : MISCHIEVOUS
**2 a :** LEWD, BAWDY **b :** causing sexual excitement : LUSTFUL, SENSUAL
**3 a :** MERCILESS, INHUMANE ⟨*wanton* cruelty⟩ **b** : having no just foundation or provocation : MALICIOUS ⟨a *wanton* attack⟩
**4 :** being without check or limitation: as **a** : luxuriantly rank ⟨*wanton* vegetation⟩ **b :** unduly lavish : EXTRAVAGANT
— **wan·ton·ly** *adverb*
— **wan·ton·ness** \-tᵊn-nəs\ *noun*

²**wanton** *noun* (1526)
**1 :** a pampered person or animal : PET; *especially* : a spoiled child
**2 :** a frolicsome child or animal
**3 a :** one given to self-indulgent flirtation or trifling — used especially in the phrase *play the wanton* **b :** a lewd or lascivious person

³**wanton** (1582)
*intransitive verb*
: to be wanton or act wantonly
*transitive verb*
: to pass or waste wantonly or in wantonness
— **wan·ton·er** *noun*

**wa·pen·take** \'wa-pən-ˌtāk, 'wä-\ *noun* [Middle English, from Old English *wǣpentæc,* from Old Norse *vāpnatak* act of grasping weapons, from *vāpn* weapon + *tak* act of grasping, from *taka* to take; probably from the brandishing of weapons as an expression of approval when the chief of the wapentake entered upon his office — more at WEAPON, TAKE] (before 12th century)
: a subdivision of some English shires corresponding to a hundred

**wa·pi·ti** \'wä-pə-tē\ *noun, plural* **wapiti** *or* **wapitis** [Shawnee *wa'piti,* literally, white rump] (1806)
: ELK 1b

**wap·pen·schaw·ing** \'wa-pən-ˌshȯ(-)iŋ, 'wä-\ *noun* [Middle English (northern dialect) *wapynschawing,* from *wapen* weapon (from Old Norse *vāpn*) + *schawing,* gerund of *schawen* to show, from Old English *scēawian* to look, look at — more at WEAPON, SHOW] (15th century)
: an inspection or muster of soldiers formerly held at various times in each district of Scotland

---

☆ **SYNONYMS**
**Wander, roam, ramble, rove, traipse, meander** mean to go about from place to place usually without a plan or definite purpose. WANDER implies an absence of or an indifference to a fixed course ⟨fond of *wandering* about the square just watching the people⟩. ROAM suggests wandering about freely and often far afield ⟨liked to *roam* through the woods⟩. RAMBLE stresses carelessness and indifference to one's course or objective ⟨the speaker *rambled* on without ever coming to the point⟩. ROVE suggests vigorous and sometimes purposeful roaming ⟨armed brigands *roved* over the countryside⟩. TRAIPSE implies a course that is erratic but may sometimes be purposeful ⟨*traipsed* all over town looking for the right dress⟩. MEANDER implies a winding or intricate course suggestive of aimless or listless wandering ⟨the river *meanders* for miles through rich farmland⟩.

---

\ə\ abut   \ᵊ\ kitten   \ər\ further   \a\ ash   \ā\ ace
\ä\ mop, mar   \au̇\ out   \ch\ chin   \e\ bet   \ē\ easy
\g\ go   \i\ hit   \ī\ ice   \j\ job   \ŋ\ sing   \ō\ go
\ȯ\ law   \ȯi\ boy   \th\ thin   \th̲\ the   \ü\ loot   \u̇\ foot
\y\ yet   \zh\ vision    *see also* Guide to Pronunciation

**¹war** \'wȯr\ *noun, often attributive* [Middle English *werre,* from Old North French, of Germanic origin; akin to Old High German *werra* strife; akin to Old High German *werran* to confuse] (12th century) **1 a** (1) **:** a state of usually open and declared armed hostile conflict between states or nations (2) **:** a period of such armed conflict (3) **:** STATE OF WAR **b :** the art or science of warfare **c** (1) *obsolete* **:** weapons and equipment for war (2) *archaic* **:** soldiers armed and equipped for war **2 a :** a state of hostility, conflict, or antagonism **b :** a struggle or competition between opposing forces or for a particular end ⟨a class *war*⟩ ⟨a *war* against disease⟩ **c :** VARIANCE, ODDS 3
— **war·less** \-ləs\ *adjective*

**²war** *intransitive verb* **warred; war·ring** (13th century) **1 :** to be in active or vigorous conflict **2 :** to engage in warfare

**³war** \'wȧr\ *adverb or adjective* [Middle English *werre,* from Old Norse *verri,* adjective, *verr,* adverb; akin to Old English *wiersa* worse — more at WORSE] (13th century) *chiefly Scottish* **:** WORSE

**⁴war** \'wȧr\ *transitive verb* **warred; war·ring** (15th century) *Scottish* **:** WORST, OVERCOME

**war baby** *noun* (1901) **:** a person born or conceived during a war

**¹war·ble** \'wȯr-bəl\ *noun* [Middle English *werble* tune, from Old North French, of Germanic origin; akin to Middle High German *wirbel* whirl, tuning peg, Old High German *wirbil* whirlwind — more at WHIRL] (14th century) **1 :** a melodious succession of low pleasing sounds **2 :** a musical trill **3 :** the action of warbling

**²warble** *verb* **war·bled; war·bling** \-b(ə-)liŋ\ (15th century) *intransitive verb* **1 :** to sing in a trilling manner or with many turns and variations **2 :** to become sounded with trills, quavers, and rapid modulations in pitch **3 :** SING *transitive verb* **:** to render with turns, runs, or rapid modulations **:** TRILL

**³warble** *noun* [perhaps of Scandinavian origin; akin to obsolete Swedish *varbulde* boil, from *var* pus + *bulde* swelling] (circa 1585) **1 :** a swelling under the hide especially of the back of cattle, horses, and wild mammals caused by the maggot of a botfly or warble fly **2 :** the maggot of a warble fly
— **war·bled** \-bəld\ *adjective*

**warble fly** *noun* (1877) **:** any of various dipteran flies (family Oestridae) whose larvae live under the skin of various mammals and cause warbles

**war·bler** \'wȯr-blər\ *noun* (1611) **1 :** one that warbles **:** SINGER, SONGSTER **2 a :** any of numerous small Old World oscine birds (family Sylviidae) many of which are noted songsters and are closely related to the thrushes **b :** any of numerous small brightly colored American oscine birds (family Parulidae) with a usually weak and unmusical song — called also *wood warbler*

**war·bon·net** \'wȯr-ˌbä-nət\ *noun* (1845) **:** an American Indian ceremonial headdress with a feathered extension down the back

**war bride** *noun* (1916) **1 :** a woman who marries a serviceman ordered into active service in time of war **2 :** a woman who marries a serviceman especially of a foreign nation met during a time of war

**war chest** *noun* (1901) **:** a fund accumulated to finance a war; *broadly* **:** a fund earmarked for a specific purpose, action, or campaign

**war club** *noun* (1776) **:** a club-shaped implement used as a weapon especially by American Indians

**war crime** *noun* (1906) **:** a crime (as genocide or maltreatment of prisoners) committed during or in connection with war — usually used in plural
— **war criminal** *noun*

**war cry** *noun* (1748) **1 :** a cry used by a body of fighters in war **2 :** a slogan used especially to rally people to a cause

**¹ward** \'wȯrd\ *noun* [Middle English, from Old English *weard;* akin to Old High German *warta* act of watching, Old English *warian* to beware of, guard, *wær* careful — more at WARY] (before 12th century) **1 a :** the action or process of guarding **b :** a body of guards **2 :** the state of being under guard; *especially* **:** CUSTODY **3 a :** the inner court of a castle or fortress **b :** a division (as a cell or block) of a prison **c :** a division in a hospital; *especially* **:** a large room in a hospital where a number of patients often requiring similar treatment are accommodated **4 a :** a division of a city for representative, electoral, or administrative purposes **b :** a division of some English and Scottish counties corresponding to a hundred **c :** the Mormon local congregation having auxiliary organizations (as Sunday schools and relief societies) and one or more quorums of each office of the Aaronic priesthood **5 :** a projecting ridge of metal in a lock casing or keyhole permitting only the insertion of a key with a corresponding notch; *also* **:** a corresponding notch in a bit of a key **6 :** a person or thing under guard, protection, or surveillance: as **a :** a minor subject to wardship **b :** a person who by reason of incapacity (as minority or lunacy) is under the protection of a court either directly or through a guardian appointed by the court — called also *ward of court* **c :** a person or body of persons under the protection or tutelage of a government **7 :** a means of defense **:** PROTECTION
— **ward·ed** \'wȯr-dəd\ *adjective*

**²ward** *transitive verb* [Middle English, from Old English *weardian;* akin to Old High German *wartēn* to watch, Old Norse *vartha* to guard, Old English *weard* ward] (before 12th century) **1 :** to keep watch over **:** GUARD **2 :** to turn aside (something threatening) **:** DEFLECT — usually used with *off*

**¹-ward** *also* **-wards** *adjective suffix* [*-ward* from Middle English, from Old English *-weard;* akin to Old High German *-wart, -wert* -ward, Latin *vertere* to turn; *-wards* from *-wards,* adverb suffix — more at WORTH] **1 :** that moves, tends, faces, or is directed toward ⟨river*ward*⟩ **2 :** that occurs or is situated in the direction of ⟨left*ward*⟩

**²-ward** *or* **-wards** *adverb suffix* [*-ward* from Middle English, from Old English *-weard,* from *-weard,* adjective suffix; *-wards* from Middle English *-wardes,* from Old English *-weardes,* genitive singular neuter of *-weard,* adjective suffix] **1 :** in a (specified) spatial or temporal direction ⟨up*ward*⟩ ⟨after*ward*⟩

**warbonnet**

**2 :** toward a (specified) point, position, or area ⟨earth*ward*⟩

**war dance** *noun* (1711) **:** a dance performed (as by American Indians) in preparation for battle or in celebration of victory

**ward·ed** \'wȯr-dəd\ *adjective* (1572) **:** provided with a ward ⟨a *warded* lock⟩

**war·den** \'wȯr-dᵊn\ *noun* [Middle English *wardein,* from Old North French, from *warder* to guard, of Germanic origin; akin to Old High German *wartēn* to watch] (13th century) **1 :** one having care or charge of something **:** GUARDIAN, KEEPER **2 a :** REGENT 2 **b :** the governor of a town, district, or fortress **c :** a member of the governing body of a guild **3 a :** an official charged with special supervisory duties or with the enforcement of specified laws or regulations ⟨game *warden*⟩ ⟨air raid *warden*⟩ **b :** an official in charge of the operation of a prison **c :** any of various British officials having designated administrative functions ⟨*warden* of the mint⟩ **4 a :** one of two ranking lay officers of an Episcopal parish **b :** any of various British college officials whose duties range from the administration of academic matters to the supervision of student discipline

**war·den·ship** \-ˌship\ *noun* (15th century) **:** the office, jurisdiction, or powers of a warden

**¹ward·er** \'wȯr-dər\ *noun* [Middle English, from Anglo-French *wardere,* from *warde* act of guarding, of Germanic origin; akin to Old High German *warta* act of watching] (15th century) **1 :** WATCHMAN, PORTER **2** *British* **a :** WARDEN **b :** a prison guard

**²war·der** *noun* [Middle English, staff, perhaps from *warden* to ward] (circa 1548) **:** a truncheon used by a king or commander in chief to signal orders

**ward heeler** *noun* (1888) **:** a worker for a political boss in a ward or other local area

**ward·ress** \'wȯr-drəs\ *noun* (1878) **:** a woman supervising female prisoners (as in a prison)

**ward·robe** \'wȯr-ˌdrōb\ *noun* [Middle English *warderobe,* from Old North French, from *warder* to guard + *robe* robe] (14th century) **1 a :** a room or closet where clothes are kept **b :** CLOTHESPRESS **c :** a large trunk in which clothes may be hung upright **2 a :** a collection of wearing apparel (as of one person or for one activity) ⟨a summer *wardrobe*⟩ **b :** a collection of stage costumes and accessories **3 :** the department of a royal or noble household entrusted with the care of wearing apparel, jewels, and personal articles

**ward·room** \'wȯr-ˌdrüm, -ˌdrum\ *noun* (1758) **:** the space in a warship allotted for living quarters to the commissioned officers excepting the captain; *specifically* **:** the mess assigned to these officers

**ward·ship** \'wȯrd-ˌship\ *noun* (15th century) **1 a :** care and protection of a ward **b :** the right to the custody of an infant heir of a feudal tenant and of the heir's property **2 :** the state of being under a guardian

**¹ware** \'war, 'wer\ *adjective* [Middle English *war, ware* careful, aware, from Old English *wær* — more at WARY] (before 12th century) **1 :** AWARE, CONSCIOUS ⟨was *ware* of black looks cast at me —Mary Webb⟩ **2** *archaic* **:** WARY, VIGILANT

**²ware** *transitive verb* **wared; war·ing** [Middle English, from Old English *warian;* akin to Old High German *biwarōn* to protect, Old English *wær* aware] (before 12th century) **:** to beware of **:** AVOID — used chiefly as a command to hunting animals

**³ware** *noun* [Middle English, from Old English *waru;* akin to Middle High German *ware* ware and probably to Sanskrit *vasna* price — more at VENAL] (before 12th century)
**1 a :** manufactured articles, products of art or craft, or farm produce **:** GOODS — often used in combination ⟨tin*ware*⟩ **b :** an article of merchandise
**2 :** articles (as pottery or dishes) of fired clay ⟨earthen*ware*⟩
**3 :** an intangible item (as a service or ability) that is a marketable commodity

**⁴ware** *transitive verb* **wared; war·ing** [Middle English, from Old Norse *verja* to clothe, invest, spend — more at WEAR] (14th century)
*Scottish* **:** SPEND, EXPEND

**¹ware·house** \'war-ˌhaus, 'wer-\ *noun* (14th century)
**:** a structure or room for the storage of merchandise or commodities

**²ware·house** \-ˌhauz, -ˌhaus\ *transitive verb* (1799)
**1 :** to deposit, store, or stock in or as if in a warehouse
**2 :** to confine or house (a person) in conditions suggestive of a warehouse

**ware·house·man** \-ˌhaus-mən\ *noun* (1635)
**:** a person who manages or works in a warehouse

**ware·hous·er** \-ˌhau-zər, -sər\ *noun* (circa 1927)
**:** WAREHOUSEMAN

**ware·room** \'war-ˌrüm, 'wer-, -ˌrum\ *noun* (1811)
**:** a room in which goods are exhibited for sale

**war·fare** \'wor-ˌfar, -ˌfer\ *noun* [Middle English, from *werre, warre* war + *fare* journey, passage — more at FARE] (15th century)
**1 :** military operations between enemies **:** HOSTILITIES, WAR; *also* **:** an activity undertaken by a political unit (as a nation) to weaken or destroy another ⟨economic *warfare*⟩
**2 :** struggle between competing entities **:** CONFLICT

**war·fa·rin** \'wor-fə-rən\ *noun* [*W*isconsin *A*lumni *R*esearch *F*oundation (its patentee) + coum*arin*] (1950)
**:** a crystalline anticoagulant compound $C_{19}H_{16}O_4$ used as a rodent poison and in medicine

**war footing** *noun* (1847)
**:** the condition of being prepared to undertake or maintain war

**war–game** (1942)
*transitive verb*
**:** to plan or conduct in the manner of a war game ⟨*war-gamed* an invasion —*Newsweek*⟩
*intransitive verb*
**:** to conduct a war game

**war game** *noun* (1828)
**1 :** a simulated battle or campaign to test military concepts and usually conducted in conferences by officers acting as the opposing staffs
**2 :** a two-sided umpired training maneuver with actual elements of the armed forces participating

**war hawk** *noun* (1798)
**:** one who clamors for war; *especially* **:** an American jingo favoring war with Britain around 1812

**war·head** \'wor-ˌhed\ *noun* (1898)
**:** the section of a missile containing the explosive, chemical, or incendiary charge

**war·horse** \-ˌhors\ *noun* (1653)
**1 :** a horse used in war **:** CHARGER
**2 :** a person with long experience in a field; *especially* **:** a veteran soldier or public person (as a politician)
**3 :** something (as a work of art or musical composition) that has become overly familiar or hackneyed due to much repetition in the standard repertoire

**war·i·son** \'war-ə-sən\ *noun* [probably a misunderstanding by Sir Walter Scott in the *Lay*

*of the Last Minstrel* (1805) of Middle English *waryson* reward, from Old North French *warison* defense, possessions, from *warir* to protect, provide, of Germanic origin; akin to Old High German *werien* to defend — more at WEIR] (1805)
**:** a bugle call to attack

**war·like** \'wor-ˌlīk\ *adjective* (15th century)
**1** *obsolete* **:** ready for war **:** equipped to fight
**2 :** fit for, disposed to, or fond of war **:** BELLICOSE
**3 :** of, relating to, or useful in war
**4 :** befitting or characteristic of war or a soldier

**war·lock** \-ˌläk\ *noun* [Middle English *warloghe,* from Old English *wǣrloga* one that breaks faith, the Devil, from *wǣr* faith, troth + *-loga* (from *lēogan* to lie); akin to Old English *wǣr* true — more at VERY, LIE] (14th century)
**1 :** a man practicing the black arts **:** SORCERER — compare WITCH
**2 :** CONJURER

**war·lord** \-ˌlord\ *noun* (1856)
**1 :** a supreme military leader
**2 :** a military commander exercising civil power by force usually in a limited area
— **war·lord·ism** \-ˌlord-ˌi-zəm\ *noun*

**¹warm** \'worm\ *adjective* [Middle English, from Old English *wearm;* akin to Old High German *warm* warm and probably to Lithuanian *virti* to cook, boil] (before 12th century)
**1 a :** having or giving out heat to a moderate or adequate degree **b :** serving to maintain or preserve heat especially to a satisfactory degree ⟨a *warm* sweater⟩ **c :** feeling or causing sensations of heat brought about by strenuous exertion
**2 :** comfortably established **:** SECURE
**3 a :** marked by strong feeling **:** ARDENT **b :** marked by excitement, disagreement, or anger ⟨the argument grew *warm*⟩
**4 :** marked by or readily showing affection, gratitude, cordiality, or sympathy ⟨a *warm* welcome⟩ ⟨*warm* regards⟩
**5 :** emphasizing or exploiting sexual imagery or incidents
**6 :** accompanied or marked by extreme danger or duress
**7 :** newly made **:** FRESH ⟨a *warm* scent⟩
**8 :** having the color or tone of something that imparts heat; *specifically* **:** of a hue in the range yellow through orange to red
**9 :** near to a goal, object, or solution sought
— **warm·ish** \'wor-mish\ *adjective*
— **warm·ness** \'worm-nəs\ *noun*

**²warm** (before 12th century)
*transitive verb*
**1 :** to make warm
**2 a :** to infuse with a feeling of love, friendship, well-being, or pleasure **b :** to fill with anger, zeal, or passion
**3 :** to reheat (cooked food) for eating — often used with *over*
**4 :** to make ready for operation or performance by preliminary exercise or operation — often used with *up*
*intransitive verb*
**1 :** to become warm
**2 a :** to become ardent, interested, or receptive — usually used with *to* or *toward* ⟨*warmed* to the idea⟩ **b :** to become filled with affection or love — used with *to* or *toward*
**3 :** to experience feelings of pleasure **:** BASK
**4 :** to become ready for operation or performance by preliminary activity — often used with *up*

**³warm** *adverb* (before 12th century)
**:** WARMLY — usually used in combination ⟨*warm*-clad⟩

**warm–blood·ed** \'worm-'blə-dəd\ *adjective* (1793)
**1 :** having warm blood; *specifically* **:** having a relatively high and constant body temperature relatively independent of the surroundings
**2 :** fervent or ardent in spirit
— **warm–blood·ed·ness** *noun*

**warmed–over** \'wormd-'ō-vər\ *adjective* (1887)
**1 :** not fresh or new **:** STALE ⟨*warmed-over* ideas⟩
**2 :** heated again ⟨*warmed-over* beans⟩

**warm·er** \'wor-mər\ *noun* (circa 1595)
**:** one that warms; *especially* **:** a device for keeping something warm ⟨a hand *warmer*⟩

**warm front** *noun* (circa 1921)
**:** an advancing edge of a warm air mass

**warm·heart·ed** \'worm-'här-təd\ *adjective* (circa 1520)
**:** marked by ready affection, cordiality, generosity, or sympathy
— **warm·heart·ed·ness** *noun*

**warming pan** *noun* (15th century)
**:** a long-handled covered pan filled with live coals that is used to warm a bed

**warm·ly** \'worm-lē\ *adverb* (1529)
**1 :** in a manner characterized or accompanied by warmth of emotion
**2 :** in a manner that causes or maintains warmth

**war·mon·ger** \'wor-ˌməŋ-gər, -ˌmäŋ-\ *noun* (1590)
**:** one who urges or attempts to stir up war **:** JINGO
— **war·mon·ger·ing** \-g(ə-)riŋ\ *noun*

**war·mouth** \'wor-ˌmauth\ *noun* [origin unknown] (circa 1883)
**:** a freshwater sunfish (*Lepomis gulosus*) chiefly of the eastern U.S. — called also *warmouth bass*

**warm spot** *noun* (1951)
**:** a lasting affection for a particular person or object

**warmth** \'worm(p)th\ *noun* (13th century)
**1 :** the quality or state of being warm in temperature
**2 :** the quality or state of being warm in feeling ⟨a child needing human *warmth* and family life⟩
**3 :** a glowing effect produced by the use of warm colors

**warm–up** \'worm-ˌəp\ *noun* (1915)
**1 :** the act or an instance of warming up; *also* **:** a preparatory activity or procedure
**2 :** a suit for exercise or casual wear consisting of a jacket or sweatshirt and pants — often used in plural; called also *warm-up suit*

**warm up** *intransitive verb* (1846)
**:** to engage in exercise or practice especially before entering a game or contest; *broadly* **:** to get ready

**warn** \'worn\ *verb* [Middle English, from Old English *warnian;* akin to Old High German *warnōn* to take heed, Old English *wǣr* careful, aware — more at WARY] (before 12th century)
*transitive verb*
**1 a :** to give notice to beforehand especially of danger or evil **b :** to give admonishing advice to **:** COUNSEL **c :** to call to one's attention **:** INFORM
**2 :** to order to go or stay away — often used with *off*
*intransitive verb*
**:** to give a warning
— **warn·er** *noun*

**¹warn·ing** \'wor-niŋ\ *noun* (before 12th century)
**1 :** the act of warning **:** the state of being warned ⟨he had *warning* of his illness⟩
**2 :** something that warns or serves to warn; *especially* **:** a notice or bulletin that alerts the public that a tornado has been reported in the immediate vicinity or that the approach of a severe storm is imminent

**²warning** *adjective* (circa 1552)
: serving as an alarm, signal, summons, or admonition ⟨*warning* bell⟩ ⟨*warning* shot⟩
— **warn·ing·ly** \ˈwȯr-niŋ-lē\ *adverb*

**warning coloration** *noun* (circa 1928)
: conspicuous coloration possessed by an animal (as an insect) otherwise effectively but not obviously defended that serves to warn off potential enemies

**warning track** *noun* (1966)
: a usually dirt or cinder strip around the outside edge of a baseball outfield to warn a fielder when running to make a catch that the fence is near — called also *warning path*

**war of nerves** (1939)
: a conflict characterized by psychological tactics (as bluff, threats, and intimidation) designed primarily to create confusion, indecision, or breakdown of morale

**¹warp** \ˈwȯrp\ *noun* [Middle English, from Old English *wearp;* akin to Old High German *warf* warp, Old English *weorpan* to throw, Old Norse *verpa*] (before 12th century)
**1 a :** a series of yarns extended lengthwise in a loom and crossed by the weft **b :** FOUNDATION, BASE ⟨the *warp* of the economic structure is agriculture —*American Guide Series: North Carolina*⟩
**2 :** a rope for warping or mooring a ship or boat
**3** [²*warp*] **a :** a twist or curve that has developed in something originally flat or straight ⟨a *warp* in a door panel⟩ **b :** a mental twist or aberration
— **warp·age** \ˈwȯr-pij\ *noun*

**²warp** (14th century)
*transitive verb*
**1 :** to arrange (yarns) so as to form a warp
**2 a :** to turn or twist out of or as if out of shape; *especially* **:** to twist or bend out of a plane **b :** to cause to judge, choose, or act wrongly or abnormally **:** PERVERT **c :** DISTORT 1 ⟨intellect and learning . . . *warped* by prejudices —Irving Wallace⟩ **d :** to deflect from a course
**3 :** to move (as a ship) by hauling on a line attached to a fixed object
*intransitive verb*
**1 :** to become warped
**2 :** to move a ship by warping
**synonym** see DEFORM
— **warp·er** *noun*

**war paint** *noun* (1826)
**1 :** paint put on parts of the body (as the face) by American Indians as a sign of going to war
**2 :** MAKEUP 3a

**warp and woof** *noun* (1842)
: FOUNDATION, BASE ⟨the vigorous Anglo-Saxon base had become the *warp and woof* of English speech —H. R. Warfel⟩

**war party** *noun* (1755)
**1 :** a group of American Indians on the warpath
**2 :** a usually jingoistic political party advocating or upholding a war

**war·path** \ˈwȯr-ˌpath, -ˌpäth\ *noun* (1755)
**1 :** the route taken by a party of American Indians going on a warlike expedition or to a war
**2 :** a hostile course of action or frame of mind

**warp beam** *noun* (circa 1833)
: a roll on which warp is wound for a loom

**warp knit** *noun* (1946)
: a knit fabric produced by machine with the yarns running in a lengthwise direction — compare WEFT KNIT
— **warp–knit·ted** \-ˈni-təd\ *adjective*
— **warp knitting** *noun*

**war·plane** \ˈwȯr-ˌplān\ *noun* (circa 1911)
: a military airplane; *specifically* **:** one armed for combat

**war power** *noun* (1766)
: the power to make war; *specifically* **:** an extraordinary power exercised usually by the executive branch of a government in the prosecution of a war

**¹war·rant** \ˈwȯr-ənt, ˈwär-\ *noun* [Middle English, protector, warrant, from Old North French *warant,* modification of a Germanic noun represented by Old High German *werēnto* guarantor, from present participle of *werēn* to warrant; akin to Old High German *wāra* trust, care — more at VERY] (14th century)
**1 a** (1) **:** SANCTION, AUTHORIZATION; *also* **:** evidence for or token of authorization (2) **:** GUARANTEE, SECURITY **b** (1) **:** GROUND, JUSTIFICATION (2) **:** CONFIRMATION, PROOF
**2 a :** a commission or document giving authority to do something; *especially* **:** a writing that authorizes a person to pay or deliver to another and the other to receive money or other consideration **b :** a precept or writ issued by a competent magistrate authorizing an officer to make an arrest, a seizure, or a search or to do other acts incident to the administration of justice **c :** an official certificate of appointment issued to an officer of lower rank than a commissioned officer **d** (1) **:** a short-term obligation of a governmental body (as a municipality) issued in anticipation of revenue (2) **:** an instrument issued by a corporation giving to the holder the right to purchase the capital stock of the corporation at a stated price either prior to a stipulated date or at any future time
— **war·rant·less** \-ləs\ *adjective*

**²warrant** *transitive verb* [Middle English, from Old North French *warantir,* from *warant*] (14th century)
**1 a :** to declare or maintain with certainty **:** be sure that ⟨I'll *warrant* he'll be here by noon⟩ **b :** to assure (a person) of the truth of what is said
**2 a :** to guarantee to a person good title to and undisturbed possession of (as an estate) **b :** to provide a guarantee of the security of (as title to property sold) usually by an express covenant in the deed of conveyance **c :** to guarantee to be as represented **d :** to guarantee (as goods sold) especially in respect of the quality or quantity specified
**3 :** to guarantee security or immunity to **:** SECURE ⟨I'll *warrant* him from drowning —Shakespeare⟩
**4 :** to give warrant or sanction to **:** AUTHORIZE ⟨the law *warrants* this procedure⟩
**5 a :** to give proof of the authenticity or truth of **b :** to give assurance of the nature of or for the undertaking of **:** GUARANTEE
**6 :** to serve as or give adequate ground or reason for ⟨promising enough to *warrant* further consideration⟩

**war·rant·able** \ˈwȯr-ən-tə-bəl, ˈwär-\ *adjective* (1581)
: capable of being warranted **:** JUSTIFIABLE
— **war·rant·able·ness** *noun*
— **war·rant·ably** \-blē\ *adverb*

**war·ran·tee** \ˌwȯr-ən-ˈtē, ˌwär-\ *noun* (1706)
: the person to whom a warranty is made

**warrant officer** *noun* (1693)
**1 :** an officer in the armed forces holding rank by virtue of a warrant and ranking above a noncommissioned officer and below a commissioned officer
**2 :** a commissioned officer ranking below an ensign in the navy or coast guard and below a second lieutenant in the marine corps

**war·ran·tor** \ˈwȯr-ən-ˌtȯr, ˌwȯr-; ˈwȯr-ən-tər, ˈwär-\ *also* **war·rant·er** \ˈwȯr-ən-tər, ˈwär-\ *noun* (1583)
: one that warrants or gives a warranty

**war·ran·ty** \ˈwȯr-ən-tē, ˈwär-\ *noun, plural* **-ties** [Middle English *warantie,* from Old North French, from *warantir* to warrant] (14th century)
**1 a :** a real covenant binding the grantor of an estate and his heirs to warrant and defend the title **b :** a collateral undertaking that a fact regarding the subject of a contract is or will be as it is expressly or by implication declared or promised to be
**2 :** something that authorizes, sanctions, supports, or justifies **:** WARRANT
**3 :** a usually written guarantee of the integrity of a product and of the maker's responsibility for the repair or replacement of defective parts

**warranty deed** *noun* (1779)
: a deed warranting that the grantor has a good title free and clear of all liens and encumbrances and will defend the grantee against all claims

**war·ren** \ˈwȯr-ən, ˈwär-\ *noun* [Middle English *warenne,* from Old North French, probably of Germanic origin; akin to Old High German *werien* to defend, protect — more at WEIR] (15th century)
**1** *chiefly British* **a :** a place legally authorized for keeping small game (as hare or pheasant) **b :** the privilege of hunting game in such a warren
**2 a** (1) **:** an area (as of uncultivated ground) where rabbits breed (2) **:** a structure where rabbits are kept or bred **b :** the rabbits of a warren
**3 a :** a crowded tenement or district **b :** a maze of passageways or cubbies

**war·ren·er** \-ə-nər\ *noun* (13th century)
**1 :** GAMEKEEPER
**2 :** a person who maintains a rabbit warren

**war·rior** \ˈwȯr-yər, ˈwȯr-ē-ər, ˈwär-ē- *also* ˈwär-yər\ *noun, often attributive* [Middle English *werriour,* from Old North French *werreieur,* from *werreier* to make war, from *werre* war — more at WAR] (14th century)
: a man engaged or experienced in warfare; *broadly* **:** a person engaged in some struggle or conflict ⟨poverty *warriors*⟩

**war room** *noun* (1914)
**1 :** a room at a military headquarters where maps showing the current status of troops in battle are maintained
**2 :** a room (as at a business headquarters) used for conferences and planning that is often specially equipped (as with computers, maps, or charts)

**war·saw grouper** \ˈwȯr-(ˌ)sȯ-\ *noun* [*warsaw* modification of American Spanish *guasa*] (1949)
: any of several large groupers (especially *Epinephelus nigritus*) — called also *warsaw*

**war·ship** \ˈwȯr-ˌship\ *noun* (1533)
: a naval vessel

**war·sle** *or* **wars·tle** \ˈwä(r)-səl\ *verb* [Middle English *werstelen, warstelen,* alteration of *wrestlen, wrastlen*] (14th century)
*Scottish* **:** WRESTLE, STRUGGLE
— **warsle** *noun, Scottish*

**war story** *noun* (1981)
: a story of a memorable personal experience typically involving an element of danger, hardship, or adventure ⟨politicians swapping *war stories* from past campaigns⟩

**wart** \ˈwȯrt\ *noun* [Middle English, from Old English *wearte;* akin to Old High German *warza* wart, Old Church Slavonic *vrědŭ* injury] (before 12th century)
**1 a :** a horny projection on the skin usually of the extremities that is caused by a virus — called also *verruca vulgaris* **b :** any of numerous similar skin lesions
**2 :** an excrescence or protuberance resembling a true wart; *especially* **:** a glandular excrescence or hardened protuberance on a plant
**3 a :** one that suggests a wart especially in smallness, unpleasantness, or unattractiveness **b :** DEFECT, IMPERFECTION — often used in the phrase *warts and all*
— **wart·ed** \ˈwȯr-təd\ *adjective*
— **wart·less** \ˈwȯrt-ləs\ *adjective*
— **warty** \ˈwȯr-tē\ *adjective*

**wart·hog** \'wȯrt-ˌhȯg, -ˌhäg\ *noun* (1840)
: a wild African hog (*Phacochoerus aethiopicus*) which has large protruding tusks and the males of which have two pairs of rough warty excrescences on the face

warthog

**war·time** \'wȯr-ˌtīm\ *noun, often attributive* (14th century)
: a period during which a war is in progress

**warts–and–all** *adjective* (1930)
: showing defects or imperfections frankly : not idealized ⟨a *warts-and-all* biography⟩

**war whoop** *noun* (1739)
: a war cry especially of American Indians

**wary** \'war-ē, 'wer-\ *adjective* **war·i·er; -est** [¹*ware*, from Middle English *war, ware,* from Old English *wær* careful, aware, wary; akin to Old High German *giwar* aware, attentive, Latin *vereri* to fear, Greek *horan* to see] (15th century)
: marked by keen caution, cunning, and watchful prudence especially in detecting and escaping danger
*synonym* see CAUTIOUS
— **war·i·ly** \'war-ə-lē, 'wer-\ *adverb*
— **war·i·ness** \'war-ē-nəs, 'wer-\ *noun*

**war zone** *noun* (1914)
**1** : a zone in which belligerents are waging war
**2** : a designated area especially on the high seas within which rights of neutrals are not respected by a belligerent nation in time of war

**was** [Middle English, from Old English, 1st & 3d singular past indicative of *wesan* to be; akin to Old Norse *vera* to be, *var* was, Sanskrit *vasati* he lives, dwells] *past 1st & 3d singular of* BE

**wa·sa·bi** \'wä-sə-bē\ *noun* [Japanese] (1903)
**1** : a condiment that is prepared from the thick pungent greenish root of an Asian herb (*Eutrema wasabi*) of the mustard family and is similar in flavor and use to horseradish; *also* : the root
**2** : the herb that yields wasabi

**¹wash** \'wȯsh, 'wäsh, *chiefly Midland also* 'wȯrsh *or* 'wärsh\ *verb* [Middle English, from Old English *wascan*; akin to Old High German *waskan* to wash and perhaps to Old English *wæter* water] (before 12th century)
*transitive verb*
**1 a** : to cleanse by or as if by the action of liquid (as water) **b** : to remove (as dirt) by rubbing or drenching with liquid
**2** : to cleanse (fur) by licking or by rubbing with a paw moistened with saliva
**3 a** : to flush or moisten (a bodily part or injury) with a liquid **b** (1) : to wet thoroughly : DRENCH (2) : to overspread with light : SUFFUSE **c** : to pass a liquid (as water) over or through especially so as to carry off material from the surface or interior
**4** : to flow along or dash or overflow against ⟨waves *washing* the shore⟩
**5** : to move, carry, or deposit by or as if by the force of water in motion ⟨houses *washed* away by the flood⟩
**6 a** : to subject (as crushed ore) to the action of water to separate valuable material **b** : to separate (particles) from a substance (as ore) by agitation with or in water **c** (1) : to pass through a bath to carry off impurities or soluble components (2) : to pass (a gas or gaseous mixture) through or over a liquid to purify it especially by removing soluble components
**7 a** : to cover or daub lightly with or as if with an application of a thin liquid (as whitewash or varnish) **b** : to depict or paint by a broad sweep of thin color with a brush
**8** : to cause to swirl ⟨*washing* coffee around in his cup⟩

**9** : LAUNDER 3 ⟨how the mob *washes* its money through corrupt bankers —Vincent Teresa⟩
*intransitive verb*
**1** : to wash oneself or a part of one's body
**2** : to become worn away by the action of water
**3** : to clean something by rubbing or dipping in water
**4 a** : to become carried along on water : DRIFT ⟨cakes of ice *washing* along⟩ **b** : to pour, sweep, or flow in a stream or current ⟨waves of pioneers *washing* westward —Green Peyton⟩
**5** : to serve as a cleansing agent ⟨this soap *washes* thoroughly⟩
**6 a** : to undergo laundering ⟨this dress doesn't *wash* well⟩ **b** (1) : to undergo testing successfully : WORK 4 ⟨an interesting theory, but it just won't *wash*⟩ (2) : to gain acceptance : inspire belief ⟨the story didn't *wash* with me⟩
— **wash one's hands of** : to disclaim interest in, responsibility for, or further connection with

**²wash** *noun* (15th century)
**1 a** : a piece of ground washed by the sea or river **b** : BOG, MARSH **c** (1) : a shallow body of water (2) : a shallow creek **d** *West* : the dry bed of a stream — called also *dry wash*
**2 a** : the act or process or an instance of washing or being washed **b** : articles to be washed, being washed, or having been washed
**3** : the surging action of waves
**4 a** : worthless especially liquid waste : REFUSE **b** : an insipid beverage **c** : vapid writing or speech
**5 a** : a sweep or splash especially of color made by or as if by a long stroke of a brush **b** : a thin coat of paint (as watercolor) **c** : a thin liquid used for coating a surface (as a wall)
**6** : LOTION
**7** : loose or eroded surface material of the earth (as rock debris) transported and deposited by running water
**8 a** : BACKWASH 1 **b** : a disturbance in the air produced by the passage of an airfoil or propeller
**9** : a situation in which losses and gains or advantages and disadvantages balance each other

**³wash** *adjective* (1634)
**1** : WASHABLE ⟨*wash* fabric⟩
**2** : involving essentially simultaneous purchase and sale of the same security ⟨spurious market activity resulting from *wash* trading⟩

**wash·able** \'wȯ-shə-bəl, 'wä-\ *adjective* (1821)
: capable of being washed without damage
— **wash·abil·i·ty** \ˌwȯ-shə-'bi-lət-ē, ˌwä-\ *noun*

**wash–and–wear** *adjective* (1956)
: of, relating to, or constituting a fabric or garment that needs little or no ironing after washing

**wash·a·te·ria** *also* **wash·e·te·ria** \ˌwä-shə-'tir-ē-ə, ˌwȯ-\ *noun* [²*wash* + *-ateria* or *-eteria* (as in *cafeteria*)] (1937)
*chiefly Southern* : a self-service laundry

**wash·ba·sin** \'wȯsh-ˌbā-sᵊn, 'wäsh-\ *noun* (1812)
: WASHBOWL

**wash·board** \'wȯsh-ˌbȯrd, 'wäsh-, -ˌbȯrd\ *noun* (1742)
**1** : a broad thin plank along a gunwale or on the sill of a lower deck port to keep out the sea
**2** : BASEBOARD
**3 a** : a corrugated rectangular surface that is used for scrubbing clothes or as a percussion instrument **b** : a road or pavement so worn by traffic as to be corrugated transversely

**wash·bowl** \-ˌbōl\ *noun* (1816)
: a large bowl for water that is used to wash one's hands and face

**wash·cloth** \-ˌklȯth\ *noun* (circa 1900)
: a cloth that is used for washing one's face and body — called also *facecloth, washrag*

**wash down** *transitive verb* (1600)

**1** : to move or carry downward by action of a liquid; *especially* : to facilitate the passage of (food) down the gullet with accompanying swallows of liquid ⟨pizza *washed down* with beer⟩
**2** : to wash the whole length or extent of ⟨*washed down* and scrubbed the front porch⟩

**wash drawing** *noun* (1889)
: watercolor painting in or chiefly in washes especially in black, white, and gray tones only

**washed–out** \'wȯsht-'aut, 'wäsht-\ *adjective* (1796)
**1** : faded in color
**2** : depleted in vigor or animation : EXHAUSTED

**washed–up** \'wȯsht-'əp, 'wäsht-\ *adjective* (1928)
: no longer successful, skillful, popular, or needed

**wash·er** \'wȯ-shər, 'wä-\ *noun* (13th century)
**1** : a flat thin ring or a perforated plate used in joints or assemblies to ensure tightness, prevent leakage, or relieve friction
**2** : one that washes; *especially* : WASHING MACHINE

**wash·er·man** \-mən\ *noun* (1715)
: LAUNDRYMAN; *also* : a man operating any of various industrial washing machines

**wash·er·wom·an** \-ˌwu̇-mən\ *noun* (1632)
: a woman whose occupation is washing clothes : LAUNDRESS

**wash·house** \'wȯsh-ˌhau̇s, 'wäsh-\ *noun* (1577)
: a building used or equipped for washing; *especially* : one for washing clothes

**wash·ing** \'wȯ-shiŋ, 'wä-\ *noun* (13th century)
**1** : the act or action of one that cleanses with water
**2** : material obtained by washing
**3** : articles washed or to be washed : WASH

**washing machine** *noun* (circa 1754)
: a machine for washing; *especially* : one for washing clothes and household linen

**washing soda** *noun* (1865)
: a transparent crystalline hydrated sodium carbonate — called also *sal soda*

**Wash·ing·ton pie** \'wȯ-shiŋ-tən-, 'wä-, *chiefly Midland also* 'wȯr-shiŋ- *or* 'wär-shiŋ-\ *noun* [George *Washington*] (1905)
: cake layers put together with a jam or jelly filling

**Washington's Birthday** *noun* [George *Washington*] (1829)
**1** : February 22 formerly observed as a legal holiday in most of the states of the U.S.
**2** : the third Monday in February observed as a legal holiday in most of the states of the U.S. — called also *Presidents' Day*

**wash·out** \'wȯsh-ˌau̇t, 'wäsh-\ *noun* (1873)
**1 a** : the washing out or away of something and especially of earth in a roadbed by a freshet **b** : a place where earth is washed away
**2** : one that fails to measure up : FAILURE: as **a** : one who fails in a course of training or study **b** : an unsuccessful enterprise or undertaking

**wash out** (1555)
*transitive verb*
**1** : to wash free of an extraneous substance (as dirt)
**2 a** : to cause to fade by or as if by laundering **b** : to deplete the strength or vitality of **c** : to eliminate as useless or unsatisfactory : REJECT
**3 a** : to destroy or make useless by the force or action of water ⟨the storm *washed out* the bridge⟩ **b** : RAIN OUT ⟨the game was *washed out*⟩
*intransitive verb*
**1** : to become depleted of color or vitality : FADE
**2** : to fail to meet requirements or measure up to a standard

**wash·rag** \'wȯsh-ˌrag, 'wäsh-\ *noun* (1890)
: WASHCLOTH

**wash·room** \-ˌrüm, -ˌru̇m\ *noun* (1806)
: a room that is equipped with washing and toilet facilities : LAVATORY

**wash·stand** \-ˌstand\ *noun* (1789)
**1** : a stand holding articles needed for washing one's face and hands
**2** : a washbowl permanently set in place and attached to water and drainpipes

**wash·tub** \-ˌtəb\ *noun* (1602)
: a tub in which clothes are washed or soaked

**wash·up** \-ˌəp\ *noun* (1884)
: the act or process of washing clean

**wash up** (1751)
*transitive verb*
**1** : to get rid of by washing ⟨*wash up* the spilled milk⟩
**2** : EXHAUST, FINISH
*intransitive verb*
**1** : to wash one's face and hands
**2** *British* : to wash the dishes after a meal
**3** : to be deposited by or as if by a swell of waves ⟨seaweed *washed up* on the shore⟩

**wash·wom·an** \'wȯsh-ˌwu̇-mən, 'wäsh-\ *noun* (1590)
: WASHERWOMAN

**washy** \'wȯ-shē, 'wä-\ *adjective* **wash·i·er; -est** (1615)
**1 a** : WEAK, WATERY ⟨*washy* tea⟩ **b** : deficient in color : PALLID **c** : lacking in vigor, individuality, or definiteness
**2** : lacking in condition and in firmness of flesh

**wasn't** \'wə-zᵊnt, 'wä-, *dialect also* 'wə-tᵊn(t)\ (circa 1849)
: was not

**wasp** \'wäsp, 'wȯsp\ *noun* [Middle English *waspe*, from Old English *wæps, wæsp;* akin to Old High German *wafsa* wasp, Latin *vespa* wasp] (before 12th century)
**1** : any of numerous social or solitary winged hymenopterous insects (especially families Sphecidae and Vespidae) that usually have a slender smooth body with the abdomen attached by a narrow stalk, well-developed wings, biting mouthparts, and in the females and workers an

**wasp 1**

often formidable sting, and that are largely carnivorous and often provision their nests with caterpillars, insects, or spiders killed or paralyzed by stinging for their larvae to feed on — compare BEE
**2** : any of various hymenopterous insects (as a chalcid or ichneumon fly) other than wasps with larvae that are parasitic on other arthropods
— **wasp·like** \-ˌlīk\ *adjective*

**WASP** *or* **Wasp** \'wäsp, 'wȯsp\ *noun, often attributive* [*w*hite *A*nglo-*S*axon *P*rotestant] (1957)
: an American of Northern European and especially British ancestry and of Protestant background; *especially* : a member of the dominant and the most privileged class of people in the U.S. — sometimes used disparagingly
— **Wasp·dom** \-dəm\ *noun*
— **Wasp·ish** \'wäs-pish, 'wȯs-\ *adjective*
— **Wasp·ish·ness** *noun*
— **Waspy** \-pē\ *adjective*

**wasp·ish** \'wäs-pish, 'wȯs-\ *adjective* (1566)
**1** : resembling a wasp in behavior; *especially* : SNAPPISH, PETULANT
**2** : resembling a wasp in form; *especially* : slightly built
— **wasp·ish·ly** *adverb*
— **wasp·ish·ness** *noun*

**wasp waist** *noun* (1870)
: a very slender waist
— **wasp–waist·ed**    \'wäsp-'wā-stəd, 'wȯsp-\ *adjective*

---

**¹was·sail** \'wä-səl *also* wä-'sā(ə)l\ *noun* [Middle English *wæs hæil*, from Old Norse *ves heill* be well, from *ves* (imperative singular of *vera* to be) + *heill* healthy — more at WAS, WHOLE] (13th century)
**1** : an early English toast to someone's health
**2** : a hot drink that is made with wine, beer, or cider, spices, sugar, and usually baked apples and is traditionally served in a large bowl especially at Christmastime
**3** : riotous drinking : REVELRY

**²wassail** (14th century)
*intransitive verb*
**1** : to indulge in wassail : CAROUSE
**2** *dialect English* : to sing carols from house to house at Christmas
*transitive verb*
: to drink to the health or thriving of

**was·sail bowl** \'wä-səl-\ *noun* (1606)
**1** : a bowl that is used for the serving of wassail
**2** : WASSAIL 2

**was·sail·er** \'wä-sə-lər *also* wä-'sā-lər\ *noun* (1634)
**1** : one that carouses : REVELER
**2** *archaic* : one who goes about singing carols

**Was·ser·mann reaction** \'wä-sər-mən-, 'vä-\ *noun* [August von *Wassermann*] (1911)
: the complement-fixing reaction that occurs in a positive complement-fixation test for syphilis using the serum of an infected individual

**Wassermann test** *noun* (1909)
: a test for the detection of syphilitic infection using the Wassermann reaction — called also *Wasserman*

**wast** \'wəst, 'wäst\ *archaic past 2d singular of* BE

**wast·age** \'wā-stij\ *noun* (1756)
: loss, decrease, or destruction of something (as by use, decay, erosion, or leakage); *especially* : wasteful or avoidable loss of something valuable

**¹waste** \'wāst\ *noun* [Middle English *waste, wast;* in sense 1, from Old North French *wast,* from *wast,* adjective, desolate, waste, from Latin *vastus;* in other senses, from Middle English *wasten* to waste — more at VAST] (13th century)
**1 a** : a sparsely settled or barren region : DESERT **b** : uncultivated land **c** : a broad and empty expanse (as of water)
**2** : the act or an instance of wasting : the state of being wasted
**3 a** : loss through breaking down of bodily tissue **b** : gradual loss or decrease by use, wear, or decay
**4 a** : damaged, defective, or superfluous material produced by a manufacturing process: as (1) : material rejected during a textile manufacturing process and used usually for wiping away dirt and oil ⟨cotton *waste*⟩ (2) : SCRAP (3) : an unwanted by-product of a manufacturing process, chemical laboratory, or nuclear reactor ⟨toxic *waste*⟩ ⟨hazardous *waste*⟩ ⟨nuclear *waste*⟩ **b** : refuse from places of human or animal habitation: as (1) : GARBAGE, RUBBISH (2) : EXCREMENT — often used in plural : SEWAGE **c** : material derived by mechanical and chemical weathering of the land and moved down sloping surfaces or carried by streams to the sea

**²waste** *verb* **wast·ed; wast·ing** [Middle English, from Old North French *waster,* from Latin *vastare,* from *vastus* desolate, waste] (13th century)
*transitive verb*
**1** : to lay waste; *especially* : to damage or destroy gradually and progressively ⟨reclaiming land *wasted* by strip-mining⟩
**2** : to cause to shrink in physical bulk or strength : EMACIATE, ENFEEBLE
**3** : to wear away or diminish gradually : CONSUME

---

**4 a** : to spend or use carelessly : SQUANDER **b** : to allow to be used inefficiently or become dissipated
**5** : KILL; *also* : to injure severely
*intransitive verb*
**1** : to lose weight, strength, or vitality — often used with *away*
**2 a** : to become diminished in bulk or substance **b** : to become consumed
**3** : to spend money or consume property extravagantly or improvidently
**synonym** *see* RAVAGE
— **waste one's breath** : to accomplish nothing by speaking

**³waste** *adjective* [Middle English *waste, wast,* from Old North French *wast*] (14th century)
**1 a** (1) : being wild and uninhabited : DESOLATE (2) : ARID, EMPTY **b** : not cultivated : not productive
**2** : being in a ruined or devastated condition
**3** [¹*waste*] **a** : discarded as worthless, defective, or of no use : REFUSE ⟨*waste* material⟩ **b** : excreted from or stored in inert form in a living body as a byproduct of vital activity ⟨*waste* disposal in birds⟩
**4** [¹*waste*] : serving to conduct or hold refuse material; *specifically* : carrying off superfluous water
**5** : WASTED 4

**waste·bas·ket** \'wās(t)-ˌbas-kət\ *noun* (1850)
: a receptacle for refuse and especially for wastepaper — called also *wastepaper basket*

**wasted** *adjective* (15th century)
**1** : laid waste : RAVAGED
**2** : impaired in strength or health : EMACIATED
**3** *archaic* : gone by : ELAPSED ⟨the chronicle of *wasted* time —Shakespeare⟩
**4** : unprofitably used, made, or expended ⟨*wasted* effort⟩
**5** *slang* : intoxicated from drugs or alcohol

**waste·ful** \'wāst-fəl\ *adjective* (14th century)
: given to or marked by waste : LAVISH, PRODIGAL
— **waste·ful·ly** \-fə-lē\ *adverb*
— **waste·ful·ness** *noun*

**waste·land** \'wāst-ˌland *also* -lənd\ *noun* (14th century)
**1** : barren or uncultivated land ⟨a desert *wasteland*⟩
**2** : an ugly often devastated or barely inhabitable place or area
**3** : something (as a way of life) that is spiritually and emotionally arid and unsatisfying

**waste·pa·per** \'wās(t)-'pā-pər\ *noun* (1585)
: paper discarded as used, superfluous, or not fit for use

**waste pipe** *noun* (circa 1512)
: a pipe for carrying off waste fluid

**wast·er** \'wā-stər\ *noun* (14th century)
**1 a** (1) : one that spends or consumes extravagantly and without thought for the future (2) : a dissolute person **b** : one that uses wastefully or causes or permits waste ⟨a procedure that is a *waster* of time⟩ **c** : one that lays waste : DESTROYER
**2** : an imperfect or inferior manufactured article or object

**waste·wa·ter** \'wāst-ˌwȯ-tər, -ˌwä-\ *noun* (15th century)
: water that has been used (as in a manufacturing process) : SEWAGE

**wast·ing** \'wā-stiŋ\ *adjective* (13th century)
**1** : laying waste : DEVASTATING
**2** : undergoing or causing decay or loss of strength ⟨*wasting* diseases such as tuberculosis⟩

**wast·rel** \'wās-trəl *also* 'wäs-\ *noun* [irregular from ²*waste*] (circa 1841)
**1** : VAGABOND, WAIF
**2** : one who dissipates resources foolishly and self-indulgently : PROFLIGATE

**¹watch** \'wäch, 'wȯch\ *verb* [Middle English *wacchen,* from Old English *wæccan* — more at WAKE] (before 12th century)
*intransitive verb*

**1 a :** to keep vigil as a devotional exercise **b :** to be awake during the night **2 a :** to be attentive or vigilant **b :** to keep guard **3 a :** to keep someone or something under close observation **b :** to observe as a spectator ⟨the country *watched* as stocks fell sharply⟩ **4 :** to be expectant : WAIT ⟨*watch* for the signal⟩
*transitive verb*
**1 :** to keep under guard **2 a :** to observe closely in order to check on action or change ⟨being *watched* by the police⟩ **b :** to look at : OBSERVE ⟨sat and *watched* the crowd⟩ **c :** to look on at ⟨*watch* television⟩ ⟨*watch* a ball game⟩ **3 a :** to take care of : TEND **b :** to be careful of ⟨*watches* his diet⟩ **4 :** to be on the alert for : BIDE ⟨*watched* her opportunity⟩
— **watch it :** look out : be careful ⟨*watch it* when you handle the glassware⟩
— **watch one's step :** to proceed with extreme care : act or talk warily
— **watch over :** to have charge of : SUPERINTEND

**²watch** *noun* (before 12th century)
**1 a :** the act of keeping awake to guard, protect, or attend **b** *obsolete* **:** the state of being wakeful **c :** a wake over a dead body **d :** a state of alert and continuous attention **e :** close observation : SURVEILLANCE **f :** a notice or bulletin that alerts the public to the possibility of severe weather conditions occurring in the near future ⟨winter storm *watch*⟩ **2 a :** any of the definite divisions of the night made by ancient peoples **b :** one of the indeterminate intervals marking the passage of night — usually used in plural ⟨the silent *watches* of the night⟩ **3 a :** LOOKOUT, WATCHMAN **b** *archaic* **:** the office or function of a sentinel or guard **4 a :** a body of soldiers or sentinels making up a guard **b :** a watchman or body of watchmen formerly assigned to patrol the streets of a town at night, announce the hours, and act as police **5 a** (1) **:** a portion of time during which a part of a ship's company is on duty (2) **:** the part of a ship's company required to be on duty during a particular watch (3) **:** a sailor's assigned duty period **b :** a period of duty : SHIFT **c :** a term as holder especially of an overseeing or managerial office ⟨the business grew on her *watch*⟩ **6 :** a portable timepiece designed to be worn (as on the wrist) or carried in the pocket — compare CLOCK

**watch·able** \'wä-chə-bəl, 'wò-\ *adjective* (1954)
**:** worth watching
— **watchable** *noun*

**watch and ward** *noun* (14th century)
**1 :** continuous unbroken vigilance and guard **2 :** service as a watchman or sentinel required from a feudal tenant

**watch·band** \'wäch-ˌband, 'wòch-\ *noun* (1924)
**:** the bracelet or strap of a wristwatch

**watch cap** *noun* (1886)
**:** a knitted close-fitting usually navy-blue cap worn especially by enlisted men in the U.S. navy in cold or stormy weather

**watch·case** \'wäch-ˌkās, 'wòch-\ *noun* (1671)
**:** the outside metal covering of a watch

**¹watch·dog** \-ˌdòg\ *noun* (1610)
**1 :** a dog kept to guard property **2 :** one that guards against loss, waste, theft, or undesirable practices

**²watchdog** *transitive verb* (1902)
**:** to act as a watchdog for

**watch·er** \'wä-chər, 'wò-\ *noun* (1509)
**:** one that watches: as **a :** one that sits up or continues awake at night **b :** WATCHMAN **c** (1) **:** one that keeps watch beside a dead person

(2) **:** one that attends a sick person at night **d :** a person who closely follows or observes someone or something ⟨a Supreme Court *watcher*⟩ — often used in combination ⟨celebrity-*watchers*⟩ **e :** a representative of a party or candidate who is stationed at the polls on an election day to watch the conduct of officials and voters

**watch fire** *noun* (1801)
**:** a fire lighted as a signal or for the use of a guard

**watch·ful** \'wäch-fəl, 'wòch-\ *adjective* (1548)
**1** *archaic* **a :** not able or accustomed to sleep or rest : WAKEFUL **b :** causing sleeplessness **c :** spent in wakefulness : SLEEPLESS **2 :** carefully observant or attentive : being on the watch ☆
— **watch·ful·ly** \-fə-lē\ *adverb*
— **watch·ful·ness** *noun*

**watch·mak·er** \-ˌmā-kər\ *noun* (1630)
**:** one that makes or repairs watches or clocks
— **watch·mak·ing** \-ˌmā-kiŋ\ *noun*

**watch·man** \-mən\ *noun* (15th century)
**:** a person who keeps watch : GUARD

**watch night** *noun* (1742)
**:** a devotional service lasting until after midnight especially on New Year's Eve

**watch out** *intransitive verb* (1845)
**:** to be vigilant or alert : be on the lookout ⟨you'd better *watch out*⟩ ⟨*watch out* for the tree!⟩

**watch pocket** *noun* (1831)
**:** a small pocket just below the front waistband of men's trousers

**watch·tow·er** \'wäch-ˌtaùr, 'wòch-\ *noun* (1544)
**:** a tower for a lookout

**watch·word** \-ˌwərd\ *noun* (15th century)
**1 :** a word or phrase used as a sign of recognition among members of the same society, class, or group **2 a :** a word or motto that embodies a principle or guide to action of an individual or group : SLOGAN ⟨"safety" is our *watchword*⟩ **b :** a guiding principle ⟨change is the *watchword* for both parties⟩

**¹wa·ter** \'wò-tər, 'wä-\ *noun, often attributive* [Middle English, from Old English *wæter*; akin to Old High German *wazzar* water, Greek *hydōr*, Latin *unda* wave] (before 12th century) **1 a :** the liquid that descends from the clouds as rain, forms streams, lakes, and seas, and is a major constituent of all living matter and that when pure is an odorless, tasteless, very slightly compressible liquid oxide of hydrogen $H_2O$ which appears bluish in thick layers, freezes at 0° C and boils at 100° C, has a maximum density at 4° C and a high specific heat, is feebly ionized to hydrogen and hydroxyl ions, and is a poor conductor of electricity and a good solvent **b :** a natural mineral water — usually used in plural **2 :** a particular quantity or body of water: as **a** (1) *plural* **:** the water occupying or flowing in a particular bed (2) *chiefly British* **:** LAKE, POND **b :** a quantity or depth of water adequate for some purpose (as navigation) **c** *plural* (1) **:** a band of seawater abutting on the land of a particular sovereignty and under the control of that sovereignty (2) **:** the sea of a particular part of the earth **d :** WATER SUPPLY ⟨threatened to turn off the *water*⟩ **3 :** travel or transportation on water ⟨we went by *water*⟩ **4 :** the level of water at a particular state of the tide : TIDE **5 :** liquid containing or resembling water: as **a** (1) **:** a pharmaceutical or cosmetic preparation made with water (2) **:** a watery solution of a gaseous or readily volatile substance — compare AMMONIA WATER **b** *archaic* **:** a distilled fluid (as an essence); *especially* **:** a distilled alcoholic liquor **c :** a watery fluid (as tears, urine, or sap) formed or circulating in a living body **d :** AMNIOTIC FLUID; *also* **:** BAG OF WATERS

**6 a :** the degree of clarity and luster of a precious stone **b :** degree of excellence ⟨a scholar of the first *water*⟩ **7 :** WATERCOLOR **8 a :** capital stock not representing assets of the issuing company and not backed by earning power **b :** fictitious or exaggerated asset entries that give a stock an unrealistic book value
— **above water :** out of difficulty

**²water** (before 12th century)
*transitive verb*
**1 :** to moisten, sprinkle, or soak with water **2 :** to supply with water for drink **3 :** to supply water to **4 :** to treat with or as if with water; *specifically* **:** to impart a lustrous appearance and wavy pattern to (cloth) by calendering **5 a :** to dilute by the addition of water — often used with *down* ⟨*water* down the punch⟩ **b :** to add to the aggregate par value of (securities) without a corresponding addition to the assets represented by the securities
*intransitive verb*
**1 :** to form or secrete water or watery matter (as tears or saliva) **2 :** to get or take water: as **a :** to take on a supply of water **b :** to drink water

**water bag** *noun* (1638)
**1 :** a bag for holding water; *especially* **:** one designed to keep water cool for drinking by evaporation through a slightly porous surface **2 :** the fetal membranes enclosing the amniotic fluid — used especially of domestic animals

**water balance** *noun* (1911)
**:** the ratio between the water assimilated into the body and that lost from the body; *also* **:** the condition of the body when this ratio approximates unity

**water ballet** *noun* (1926)
**:** a synchronized sequence of movements performed by a group of swimmers

**water bear** *noun* (1852)
**:** TARDIGRADE

**Water Bearer** *noun*
**:** AQUARIUS 1, 2a

**water bed** *noun* (1844)
**:** a bed whose mattress is a watertight bag filled with water

**water beetle** *noun* (circa 1668)
**:** any of numerous oval flattened aquatic beetles (especially family Dytiscidae) that swim by means of their fringed hind legs which act together as oars

**wa·ter·bird** \'wò-tər-ˌbərd, 'wä-\ *noun* (15th century)
**:** a swimming or wading bird — compare WATERFOWL

**water biscuit** *noun* (circa 1790)
**:** a cracker of flour and water and sometimes fat

---

☆ SYNONYMS
**Watchful, vigilant, wide-awake, alert** mean being on the lookout especially for danger or opportunity. WATCHFUL is the least explicit term ⟨the *watchful* eye of the department supervisor⟩. VIGILANT suggests intense, unremitting, wary watchfulness ⟨eternally *vigilant* in the safeguarding of democracy⟩. WIDE-AWAKE applies to watchfulness for opportunities and developments more often than dangers ⟨*wide-awake* companies latched onto the new technology⟩. ALERT stresses readiness or promptness in meeting danger or in seizing opportunity ⟨*alert* traders anticipated the stock market's slide⟩.

---

\ə\ abut \ᵊ\ kitten \ər\ further \a\ ash \ā\ ace
\ä\ mop, mar \aù\ out \ch\ chin \e\ bet \ē\ easy
\g\ go \i\ hit \ī\ ice \j\ job \ŋ\ sing \ō\ go
\ò\ law \òi\ boy \th\ thin \th\ the \ü\ loot \ù\ foot
\y\ yet \zh\ vision *see also* Guide to Pronunciation

**water blister** *noun* (1895)
: a blister with a clear watery content that is not purulent or sanguineous

**water bloom** *noun* (1903)
: an accumulation of algae and especially of blue-green algae at or near the surface of a body of water

**water boatman** *noun* (1815)
**1 :** BACK SWIMMER
**2 :** any of various aquatic bugs (family Corixidae) with one pair of legs modified into paddles

**wa·ter·borne** \'wȯ-tər-ˌbōrn, 'wä-, -ˌbȯrn\ *adjective* (circa 1559)
: supported or carried by water ⟨*waterborne* commerce⟩ ⟨*waterborne* infection⟩

**water boy** *noun* (1859)
: one who keeps a group (as of football players) supplied with drinking water

**wa·ter·buck** \'wȯ-tər-ˌbək, 'wä-\ *noun, plural* **waterbuck** *or* **waterbucks** (1850)
: an antelope (*Kobus ellipsiprymnus*) of sub-Saharan Africa that commonly frequent streams or wet areas

**water buffalo** *noun* (circa 1890)
: an often domesticated Asian buffalo (*Bubalus bubalis* synonym *B. arnee*)

water buffalo

**water bug** *noun* (1750)
: any of various small arthropods and especially insects that frequent damp or wet places: as **a** : GERMAN COCKROACH **b** : WATER BOATMAN **c** : any of various large aquatic bugs (family Belostomatidae) with the hind legs flattened and used for swimming

**water cannon** *noun* (1964)
: a large truck-mounted nozzle for directing a high-pressure stream of water (as at a crowd of rioters or demonstrators)

**water chestnut** *noun* (1854)
**1 :** any of a genus (*Trapa* and especially *T. natans* of the family Trapaceae, the water-chestnut family) of Old World aquatic herbs sometimes grown as ornamentals; *also* : its edible nutlike spiny fruit
**2 :** a whitish crunchy vegetable used especially in Chinese cooking that is the peeled and often sliced tuber of a sedge (*Eleocharis dulcis* synonym *E. tuberosa*) native to Asia but widely cultivated elsewhere; *also* : the tuber or the sedge itself

**water clock** *noun* (1601)
: an instrument designed to measure time by the fall or flow of a quantity of water — called also *clepsydra*

**water closet** *noun* (1755)
**1 :** a compartment or room for defecation and excretion into a toilet bowl
**2 :** a toilet bowl and its accessories

**wa·ter·col·or** \'wȯ-tər-ˌkə-lər, 'wä-\ *noun* (1596)
**1 :** a paint of which the liquid is a water dispersion of the binding material (as glue, casein, or gum)
**2 :** the art or method of painting with watercolors
**3 :** a picture or design executed in watercolors
— **watercolor** *adjective*
— **wa·ter·col·or·ist** \-ˌkə-lə-rist\ *noun*

**wa·ter·cool·er** \'wȯ-tər-ˌkü-lər, 'wä-\ *noun* (1846)
: a device for dispensing refrigerated drinking water

**wa·ter·course** \'wȯ-tər-ˌkōrs, -ˌkȯrs\ *noun* (1510)
**1 :** a natural or artificial channel through which water flows
**2 :** a stream of water (as a river, brook, or underground stream)

**wa·ter·craft** \-ˌkraft\ *noun* (1566)
**1 :** skill in aquatic activities (as managing boats)
**2 a :** SHIP, BOAT **b** : craft for water transport

**wa·ter·cress** \-ˌkres\ *noun* (14th century)
: any of several water-loving cresses; *especially* : a perennial European cress (*Nasturtium officinale*) naturalized in the U.S. and used especially in salads or as a potherb

**water cycle** *noun* (1928)
: HYDROLOGIC CYCLE

**water dog** *noun* (14th century)
**1 :** any of several large American salamanders; *especially* : any of a genus (*Necturus* of the family Proteidae) with external gills
**2 :** a person (as a skilled sailor) who is quite at ease in or on water

**water down** *transitive verb* (1850)
: to reduce or temper the force or effectiveness of
— **wa·tered–down** *adjective*

**wa·ter·er** \'wȯ-tər-ər, 'wä-\ *noun* (1549)
: one that waters: as **a** : a person who obtains or supplies drinking water **b** : a device used for supplying water to livestock and poultry — called also *drinker*

**wa·ter·fall** \-ˌfȯl\ *noun* (before 12th century)
**1 a :** a perpendicular or very steep descent of the water of a stream **b** : an artificial waterfall (as in a hotel lobby or a nightclub)
**2 :** something resembling a waterfall

**water flea** *noun* (circa 1585)
: any of various small active dark or brightly colored aquatic crustaceans (as a daphnia or cyclops)

**¹wa·ter·flood** \-ˌfləd\ *noun* (1928)
: the process of waterflooding an oil well

**²waterflood** *intransitive verb* (1928)
: to pump water into the ground around an oil well nearing depletion in order to loosen and force out additional oil

**wa·ter·fowl** \'wȯ-tər-ˌfau̇l, 'wä-\ *noun* (14th century)
**1 :** a bird that frequents water; *especially* : a swimming bird
**2 waterfowl** *plural* : swimming game birds as distinguished from upland game birds and shorebirds

**wa·ter·fowl·er** \-ˌfau̇-lər\ *noun* (1968)
: a hunter of waterfowl
— **wa·ter·fowl·ing** \-liŋ\ *noun*

**wa·ter·front** \-ˌfrənt\ *noun* (1766)
: land, land with buildings, or a section of a town fronting or abutting on a body of water

**water gap** *noun* (1756)
: a pass in a mountain ridge through which a stream runs — compare WIND GAP

**water garden** *noun* (1891)
**1 :** a garden in which aquatic plants predominate
**2 :** a garden built about a stream or pool as a central feature

**water gas** *noun* (1851)
: a poisonous flammable gaseous mixture that consists chiefly of carbon monoxide and hydrogen with small amounts of methane, carbon dioxide, and nitrogen, is usually made by blowing air and then steam over red-hot coke or coal, and is used as a fuel or after carbureting as an illuminant

**Wa·ter·gate** \-ˌgāt\ *noun* [*Watergate*, apartment and office complex in Washington, D.C.; from the scandal following the break-in at the Democratic National Committee headquarters there in 1972] (1973)
: a scandal usually involving abuses of office, skulduggery, and a cover-up

**water gate** *noun* (14th century)
**1 :** a gate (as of a building) giving access to a body of water
**2 :** FLOODGATE

**water gauge** *noun* (circa 1706)
: an instrument to measure or find the depth or quantity of water or to indicate the height of its surface especially in a steam boiler

**water glass** *noun* (1612)

**1 :** a glass vessel (as a drinking glass) for holding water
**2 :** an instrument consisting of an open box or tube with a glass bottom used for examining objects in or under water
**3 :** a substance that consists usually of the silicate of sodium, is found in commerce as a glassy mass, a stony powder, or dissolved in water as a viscous syrupy liquid, and is used especially as a cement, a protective coating, and as a fireproofing agent

**water gun** *noun* (1951)
: WATER PISTOL

**water hammer** *noun* (circa 1890)
: a concussion or sound of concussion of moving water against the sides of a containing pipe or vessel (as a steam pipe)

**water haul** *noun* [from the figure of a fishing net that catches nothing but water] (1823)
: a fruitless effort

**water heater** *noun* (circa 1876)
: an apparatus for heating and usually storing hot water (as for domestic use)

**water hemlock** *noun* (1764)
: a tall poisonous Eurasian perennial herb (*Cicuta virosa*) of the carrot family; *also* : any of several poisonous North American plants (especially *Cicuta maculata* and *C. douglasii*) of the same genus

**water hen** *noun* (circa 1529)
: any of various birds (as a coot or gallinule) of the rail family

**water hole** *noun* (circa 1653)
**1 :** a natural hole or hollow containing water
**2 :** a hole in a surface of ice

**water hyacinth** *noun* (circa 1890)
: a showy floating aquatic plant (*Eichhornia crassipes* of the family Pontederiaceae) of tropical America that often clogs waterways (as in the southern U.S.)

**water ice** *noun* (1818)
: a frozen dessert of water, sugar, and flavoring

**watering can** *noun* (1692)
: a vessel usually with a spout used to sprinkle or pour water especially on plants — called also *watering pot*

**watering hole** *noun* (1955)
: a place where people gather socially; *especially* : WATERING PLACE 3

**watering place** *noun* (15th century)
**1 :** a place where water may be obtained; *especially* : one where animals and especially livestock come to drink
**2 :** a health or recreational resort featuring mineral springs or bathing
**3 :** a place (as a nightclub, bar, or lounge) where drink is available

**wa·ter·ish** \'wȯ-tər-ish, 'wä-\ *adjective* (1542)
: somewhat watery
— **wa·ter·ish·ness** *noun*

**water jacket** *noun* (1869)
: an outer casing which holds water or through which water circulates to cool the interior; *specifically* : the enclosed space surrounding the cylinder block of an internal combustion engine and containing the cooling liquid

**water jump** *noun* (1875)
: an obstacle (as in a steeplechase) consisting of a pool, stream, or ditch of water

**wa·ter·leaf** \'wȯ-tər-ˌlēf, 'wä-\ *noun, plural* **-leafs** \-ˌlēfs\ (1760)
: any of a genus (*Hydrophyllum* of the family Hydrophyllaceae, the waterleaf family) of perennial North American woodland herbs with lobed or pinnate toothed leaves and cymes of bell-shaped flowers

**wa·ter·less** \-ləs\ *adjective* (before 12th century)
**1 :** lacking or destitute of water : DRY
**2 :** not requiring water (as for cooling or cooking)
— **wa·ter·less·ness** *noun*

**water level** *noun* (1563)

**1 :** an instrument to show the level by means of the surface of water in a trough or in a U-shaped tube
**2 :** the surface of still water: as **a :** the level assumed by the surface of a particular body or column of water **b :** the waterline of a vessel

**water lily** *noun* (15th century)
**:** any of various aquatic plants (especially genera *Nymphaea* and *Nuphar* of the family Nymphaeaceae, the water-lily family) with floating leaves and usually showy flowers; *broadly*
**:** an aquatic plant (as a water hyacinth) with showy flowers

**wa·ter·line** \'wȯ-tər-ˌlīn, 'wä-\ *noun* (circa 1625)
**:** a line that marks the level of the surface of water on something: as **a** (1) **:** the point on the hull of a ship or boat to which the water rises (2) **:** a line marked on the outside of a ship that corresponds with the water's surface when the ship is afloat on an even keel under specified conditions of loading **b :** SHORELINE 1

**wa·ter·log** \-ˌlȯg, -ˌläg\ *transitive verb* [back-formation from *waterlogged*] (1779)
**:** to make waterlogged

**wa·ter·logged** \-ˌlȯgd, -ˌlägd\ *adjective* [[1]water + log to accumulate in the hold] (circa 1776)
**1 :** so filled or soaked with water as to be heavy or hard to manage ⟨*waterlogged* boats⟩
**2 :** saturated with water ⟨*waterlogged* soil⟩

**wa·ter·loo** \ˌwȯ-tər-'lü, ˌwä-\ *noun, plural* **-loos** [*Waterloo*, Belgium, scene of Napoleon's defeat in 1815] (1816)
**:** a decisive or final defeat or setback

**water main** *noun* (1803)
**:** a pipe or conduit for conveying water

**wa·ter·man** \'wȯ-tər-mən, 'wä-\ *noun* (15th century)
**:** one who works or lives on the water: as **a :** a man who makes his living from the water (as by fishing) **b :** a boatman who plies for hire usually on inland waters or harbors

**wa·ter·man·ship** \-ˌship\ *noun* (1882)
**:** the business, skill, or art of a waterman: as **a :** technique or expertness in rowing **b :** technique or expertness in swimming

**[1]wa·ter·mark** \'wȯ-tər-ˌmärk, 'wä-\ *noun* (1678)
**1 :** a mark indicating the height to which water has risen
**2 :** a marking in paper resulting from differences in thickness usually produced by pressure of a projecting design in the mold or on a processing roll and visible when the paper is held up to the light; *also* **:** the design of or the metal pattern producing the marking

**[2]watermark** *transitive verb* (1866)
**1 :** to mark (paper) with a watermark
**2 :** to impress (a given design) as a watermark

**wa·ter·mel·on** \-ˌme-lən\ *noun* (1615)
**1 :** a large oblong or roundish fruit with a hard green or white rind often striped or variegated, a sweet watery pink, yellowish, or red pulp, and usually many seeds
**2 :** a widely grown African vine (*Citrullus lanatus* synonym *C. vulgaris*) of the gourd family that bears watermelons

**water meter** *noun* (circa 1858)
**:** an instrument for recording the quantity of water passing through a particular outlet

**water milfoil** *noun* (1578)
**:** any of a genus (*Myriophyllum* of the family Haloragaceae) of aquatic plants with finely pinnate submersed leaves

**water mill** *noun* (15th century)
**:** a mill whose machinery is moved by water

**water moccasin** *noun* (1821)
**1 :** a venomous semiaquatic pit viper (*Agkistrodon piscivorus*) chiefly of the southeastern U.S. that is closely related to the copperhead — called also *cottonmouth, cottonmouth moccasin*
**2 :** an American water snake (genus *Nerodia*)

**water mold** *noun* (1899)

**:** an aquatic fungus (as of the genus *Saprolegnia*)

water moccasin 1

**water nymph** *noun* (14th century)
**:** a nymph (as a naiad, Nereid, or Oceanid) associated with a body of water

**water oak** *noun* (1687)
**:** any of several American oaks (especially *Quercus nigra*) that thrive in wet soils

**water of crystallization** (1791)
**:** water of hydration present in many crystallized substances that is usually essential for maintenance of a particular crystal structure

**water of hydration** (1889)
**:** water that is chemically combined with a substance to form a hydrate and can be expelled (as by heating) without essentially altering the composition of the substance

**water on the knee** (circa 1934)
**:** an accumulation of inflammatory exudate in the knee joint often following an injury

**water ouzel** *noun* (1622)
**:** DIPPER 2

**water parting** *noun* (1859)
**:** DIVIDE 2a

**water pepper** *noun* (circa 1538)
**:** an annual smartweed (*Polygonum hydropiper*) of moist soils with extremely acrid peppery juice

**water pimpernel** *noun* (circa 1760)
**:** either of two small white-flowered herbs (*Samolus valerandi* of Eurasia and *S. floribundus* synonym *S. parviflorus* of America) of the primrose family that grow in wet places

**water pipe** *noun* (15th century)
**1 :** a pipe for conveying water
**2 :** a smoking device that consists of a bowl mounted on a vessel of water which is provided with a long tube and arranged so that smoke is drawn through the water where it is cooled and up the tube to the mouth

**water pistol** *noun* (1905)
**:** a toy pistol designed to squirt a jet of liquid — called also *water gun, squirt gun*

**water plantain** *noun* (circa 1538)
**:** any of a genus (*Alisma* of the family Alismataceae, the water-plantain family) of marsh or aquatic herbs with acrid sap and scapose 3-petaled flowers

**water polo** *noun* (1884)
**:** a goal game similar to soccer that is played in water by teams of swimmers using a ball resembling a soccer ball

**wa·ter·pow·er** \'wȯ-tər-ˌpau̇(-ə)r, 'wä-\ *noun* (1817)
**1 :** the power of water employed to move machinery
**2 :** a fall of water suitable for being used to move machinery

**water privilege** *noun* (1804)
**:** the right to use water especially as a source of mechanical power

**[1]wa·ter·proof** \'wȯ-tər-ˌprüf, 'wä-\ *adjective* (1736)
**:** impervious to water; *especially* **:** covered or treated with a material (as a solution of rubber) to prevent permeation by water
— **wa·ter·proof·ness** *noun*

**[2]waterproof** *noun* (1799)
**1 :** a waterproof fabric
**2** *chiefly British* **:** RAINCOAT

**[3]waterproof** *transitive verb* (1841)
**:** to make waterproof
— **wa·ter·proof·er** *noun*

**wa·ter·proof·ing** \-ˌprü-fiŋ\ *noun* (1845)
**1 a :** the act or process of making something waterproof **b :** the condition of being made waterproof
**2 :** something (as a coating) capable of imparting waterproofness

**water rat** *noun* (1552)
**1 :** a rodent that frequents water

**2 :** a waterfront loafer or petty thief

**wa·ter–re·pel·lent** \ˌwȯ-tə(r)-ri-'pe-lənt, ˌwä-\ *adjective* (1896)
**:** treated with a finish that is resistant but not impervious to penetration by water

**wa·ter–re·sis·tant** \-ri-'zis-tənt\ *adjective* (1921)
**:** WATER-REPELLENT

**water right** *noun* (1793)
**:** a right to the use of water (as for irrigation); *especially* **:** RIPARIAN RIGHT

**water sapphire** *noun* (circa 1741)
**:** a deep blue cordierite sometimes used as a gem

**wa·ter·scape** \'wȯ-tər-ˌskāp, 'wä-\ *noun* (circa 1854)
**:** a water or sea view **:** SEASCAPE 1

**water scorpion** *noun* (1681)
**:** any of numerous aquatic bugs (family Nepidae) with the end of the abdomen prolonged by a long breathing tube

**wa·ter·shed** \'wȯ-tər-ˌshed, 'wä-\ *noun* (1803)
**1 a :** DIVIDE 2a **b :** a region or area bounded peripherally by a divide and draining ultimately to a particular watercourse or body of water
**2 :** a crucial dividing point, line, or factor **:** TURNING POINT
— **watershed** *adjective*

**water shield** *noun* (circa 1818)
**:** an aquatic plant (*Brasenia schreberi*) of the water-lily family having floating oval leaves with a gelatinous coating and small dull purple flowers; *also* **:** any of a related genus (*Cabomba*)

**[1]wa·ter·side** \'wȯ-tər-ˌsīd, 'wä-\ *noun* (14th century)
**:** the margin of a body of water **:** WATERFRONT

**[2]waterside** *adjective* (1663)
**1 :** employed along the waterside ⟨*waterside* workers⟩; *also* **:** of or relating to the workers along the waterside ⟨a *waterside* strike⟩
**2 :** of, relating to, or located on the waterside ⟨a *waterside* café⟩

**water ski** *noun* (1931)
**:** a ski used in planing over water while being towed by a speedboat
— **wa·ter–ski** *intransitive verb*

**wa·ter–ski·er** \'wȯ-tər-ˌskē-ər, 'wä-\ *noun* (1931)
**:** one that water-skis

**wa·ter–ski·ing** \-ˌskē-iŋ\ *noun* (1931)
**:** the sport of planing and jumping on water skis

**water snake** *noun* (1601)
**:** any of various snakes (especially genus *Nerodia* formerly included in the genus *Natrix*) that frequent or inhabit fresh waters and feed largely on aquatic animals

**wa·ter–soak** \'wȯ-tər-ˌsōk, 'wä-\ *transitive verb* (1791)
**:** to soak in water

**water spaniel** *noun* (1566)
**:** a spaniel of either of two breeds: **a :** AMERICAN WATER SPANIEL **b :** IRISH WATER SPANIEL

**water spot** *noun* (1939)
**:** a physiological disorder of citrus fruits in the rainy season in which the epidermal air spaces of the rind become filled with liquid

**wa·ter·spout** \'wȯ-tər-ˌspau̇t, 'wä-\ *noun* (14th century)
**1 :** a pipe, duct, or orifice from which water is spouted or through which it is carried
**2 :** a funnel-shaped or tubular column of rotating cloud-filled wind usually extending from the underside of a cumulus or cumulonimbus cloud down to a cloud of spray torn up by the whirling winds from the surface of an ocean or lake

**water sprite** *noun* (1798)

\ə\ **abut** \ᵊ\ **kitten** \ər\ **further** \a\ **ash** \ā\ **ace**
\ä\ **mop, mar** \au̇\ **out** \ch\ **chin** \e\ **bet** \ē\ **easy**
\g\ **go** \i\ **hit** \ī\ **ice** \j\ **job** \ŋ\ **sing** \ō\ **go**
\ȯ\ **law** \ȯi\ **boy** \th\ **thin** \t͟h\ **the** \ü\ **loot** \u̇\ **foot**
\y\ **yet** \zh\ **vision** *see also* Guide to Pronunciation

: a sprite believed to inhabit or haunt water : WATER NYMPH

**water sprout** *noun* (circa 1892)
: an extremely vigorous shoot from an adventitious or latent bud on a tree — compare SUCKER 2

**water strider** *noun* (1849)
: any of various long-legged bugs (family Gerridae) that move about on the surface of the water

**water supply** *noun* (circa 1882)
: a source, means, or process of supplying water (as for a community) usually including reservoirs, tunnels, and pipelines

**water table** *noun* (15th century)
**1** : a stringcourse or similar member when projecting so as to throw off water
**2** : the upper limit of the portion of the ground wholly saturated with water

**water taxi** *noun* (1928)
: a boat functioning (as within a harbor) as a taxi

**wa·ter·thrush** \ˈwȯ-tər-ˌthrəsh, ˈwä-\ *noun* (circa 1813)
: either of two North American warblers (*Seiurus noveboracensis* and *S. motacilla*) found near freshwater (as a stream)

**wa·ter·tight** \ˌwȯ-tər-ˈtīt, ˌwä-\ *adjective* (14th century)
**1** : of such tight construction or fit as to be impermeable to water except when under sufficient pressure to produce structural discontinuity
**2** : leaving no possibility of misconstruction or evasion ⟨a *watertight* lease⟩
— **wa·ter·tight·ness** *noun*

**water tower** *noun* (circa 1883)
: a tower or standpipe serving as a reservoir to deliver water at a required head

**water turkey** *noun* (1836)
: a New World anhinga (*Anhinga anhinga*)

**water vapor** *noun* (1880)
: water in a vaporous form especially when below boiling temperature and diffused (as in the atmosphere)

**water–vascular system** *noun* (1870)
: a system of canals in echinoderms containing a circulating watery fluid that is used for the movement of the tentacles and tube feet

**water wagon** *noun* (1904)
: a wagon or motortruck equipped with a tank or barrels for hauling water or for sprinkling
— **on the water wagon** : abstaining from alcoholic beverages : on the wagon

**water wave** *noun* (1882)
: a method or style of setting hair by dampening with water and forming into waves
— **wa·ter·waved** \ˈwȯ-tər-ˌwāvd, ˈwä-\ *adjective*

**wa·ter·way** \ˈwȯ-tər-ˌwā, ˈwä-\ *noun* (15th century)
**1** : a way or channel for water
**2** : a navigable body of water

**wa·ter·weed** \-ˌwēd\ *noun* (1842)
: any of various aquatic plants (as a pondweed) with inconspicuous flowers — compare WATER LILY

**wa·ter·wheel** \-ˌhwēl, -ˌwēl\ *noun* (15th century)
**1** : a wheel made to rotate by direct action of water
**2** : a wheel for raising water

**water wings** *noun plural* (1907)
: a pneumatic device that buoys the body of a swimmer and is used especially in learning to swim

waterwheel 1

**water witch** *noun* (1817)
: one that dowses for water
— **water witch·ing** \-ˌwi-chiŋ\ *noun*

**water witch·er** \-ˌwi-chər\ *noun* (1917)
: WATER WITCH

**wa·ter·works** \ˈwȯ-tər-ˌwərks, ˈwä-\ *noun plural* (circa 1586)
**1** : an ornamental fountain or cascade
**2** : the system of reservoirs, channels, mains, and pumping and purifying equipment by which a water supply is obtained and distributed (as to a city)
**3** : the shedding of tears : TEARS

**wa·ter·worn** \-ˌwȯrn, -ˌwȯrn\ *adjective* (1815)
: worn, smoothed, or polished by the action of water

**wa·tery** \ˈwȯ-tə-rē, ˈwä-\ *adjective* (before 12th century)
**1 a** : consisting of, filled with, or surrounded by water **b** : containing, sodden with, or yielding water or a thin liquid ⟨a *watery* solution⟩ ⟨*watery* vesicles⟩
**2 a** : resembling water or watery matter especially in thin fluidity, soggy texture, paleness, or lack of savor ⟨*watery* blood⟩ ⟨*watery* sunlight⟩ ⟨a *watery* soup⟩ **b** : exhibiting weakness and vapidity : WISHY-WASHY ⟨a *watery* writing style⟩
— **wa·ter·i·ly** \-tə-rə-lē\ *adverb*
— **wa·ter·i·ness** \-tə-rē-nəs\ *noun*

**wa·ter·zooi** \ˈvä-tər-ˌzoi\ *noun* [Flemish, from *water* water + *zooi* quantity of cooked food] (1949)
: a stew of fish or chicken and vegetables in a seasoned stock thickened with cream and egg yolks

**Wat·son–Crick** \ˌwät-sən-ˈkrik\ *adjective* (1964)
: of or relating to the Watson-Crick model ⟨*Watson-Crick* helix⟩ ⟨*Watson-Crick* structure⟩ ⟨*Watson-Crick* base pairs⟩

**Watson–Crick model** *noun* [J. D. *Watson* & F. H. C. *Crick*] (1958)
: a model of DNA structure in which the molecule is a cross-linked double-stranded helix, each strand is composed of alternating links of phosphate and deoxyribose, and the strands are cross-linked by pairs of purine and pyrimidine bases projecting inward from the deoxyribose sugars and joined by hydrogen bonds with adenine paired with thymine and with cytosine paired with guanine — compare DOUBLE HELIX

**watt** \ˈwät\ *noun* [James *Watt* (died 1819)] (1882)
: the absolute meter-kilogram-second unit of power equal to the work done at the rate of one joule per second or to the power produced by a current of one ampere across a potential difference of one volt : $\frac{1}{746}$ horsepower

**watt·age** \ˈwä-tij\ *noun* (1903)
: amount of power expressed in watts

**Wat·teau** \(ˌ)wä-ˈtō\ *adjective* [Antoine *Watteau*] (1873)
**1** *of women's dress* : having back pleats falling loosely from neckline to hem
**2** *of a hat* : shallow-crowned and having a wide brim turned up at the back to hold flower trimmings

**watt–hour** \ˈwät-ˈau̇(-ə)r\ *noun* (1888)
: a unit of work or energy equivalent to the power of one watt operating for one hour

**¹wat·tle** \ˈwä-tᵊl\ *noun* [Middle English *watel*, from Old English *watel*; akin to Old High German *wadal* bandage] (before 12th century)
**1 a** : a fabrication of poles interwoven with slender branches, withes, or reeds and used especially formerly in building **b** : material for such construction **c** *plural* : poles laid on a roof to support thatch
**2** : a fleshy dependent process usually about the head or neck (as of a bird)
**3** *Australian* : ACACIA 2
— **wat·tled** \-tᵊld\ *adjective*

**²wattle** *transitive verb* **wat·tled; wat·tling** \ˈwät-liŋ, ˈwä-tᵊl-iŋ\ (14th century)
**1** : to form or build of or with wattle

**2 a** : to form into wattle : interlace to form wattle **b** : to unite or make solid by interweaving light flexible material

**wattle and daub** *noun* (1808)
: a framework of woven rods and twigs covered and plastered with clay and used in building construction

**wat·tle·bird** \ˈwä-tᵊl-ˌbərd\ *noun* (1819)
: any of several Australasian honeyeaters (genus *Anthochaera*) having fleshy pendulous ear wattles

**watt·me·ter** \ˈwät-ˌmē-tər\ *noun* [International Scientific Vocabulary] (1887)
: an instrument for measuring electric power in watts

**Wa·tu·si** \wä-ˈtü-sē\ *noun, plural* **Watusi** *also* **Watusis** (1899)
: TUTSI

**¹wave** \ˈwāv\ *verb* **waved; wav·ing** [Middle English, from Old English *wafian* to wave with the hands; akin to *wæfan* to clothe and perhaps to Old English *wefan* to weave] (before 12th century)
*intransitive verb*
**1** : to motion with the hands or with something held in them in signal or salute
**2** : to float, play, or shake in an air current : move loosely to and fro : FLUTTER
**3** *of water* : to move in waves : HEAVE
**4** : to become moved or brandished to and fro
**5** : to move before the wind with a wavelike motion ⟨field of *waving* grain⟩
**6** : to follow a curving line or take a wavy form : UNDULATE
*transitive verb*
**1** : to swing (something) back and forth or up and down
**2** : to impart a curving or undulating shape to ⟨*waved* her hair⟩
**3 a** : to motion to (someone) to go in an indicated direction or to stop : FLAG, SIGNAL ⟨checked his name and *waved* him on⟩ ⟨*waved* down a passing car⟩ **b** : to gesture with (the hand or an object) in greeting or farewell or in homage **c** : to dismiss or put out of mind : DISREGARD — usually used with *aside* or *off* **d** : to convey by waving ⟨*waved* farewell⟩
**4** : BRANDISH, FLOURISH ⟨*waved* a pistol menacingly⟩
**synonym** see SWING

**²wave** *noun* (1526)
**1 a** : a moving ridge or swell on the surface of a liquid (as of the sea) **b** : open water
**2 a** : a shape or outline having successive curves **b** : a waviness of the hair **c** : an undulating line or streak or a pattern formed by such lines
**3** : something that swells and dies away: as **a** : a surge of sensation or emotion ⟨a *wave* of anger swept over her⟩ **b** : a movement sweeping large numbers in a common direction ⟨*waves* of protest⟩ **c** : a peak or climax of activity ⟨a *wave* of buying⟩
**4** : a sweep of hand or arm or of some object held in the hand used as a signal or greeting
**5** : a rolling or undulatory movement or one of a series of such movements passing along a surface or through the air
**6** : a movement like that of an ocean wave: as **a** : a surging movement of a group ⟨a big new *wave* of women politicians⟩ **b** : one of a succession of influxes of people migrating into a region **c** (1) : a moving group of animals of one kind (2) : a sudden rapid increase in a population **d** : a line of attacking or advancing troops or airplanes **e** : a display of people in a large crowd (as at a sports event) successively rising, lifting their arms overhead, and quickly sitting so as to form a swell moving through the crowd
**7 a** : a disturbance or variation that transfers energy progressively from point to point in a medium and that may take the form of an elastic deformation or of a variation of pressure,

electric or magnetic intensity, electric potential, or temperature **b :** one complete cycle of such a disturbance
**8 :** a marked change in temperature **:** a period of hot or cold weather
**9 :** an undulating or jagged line constituting a graphic representation of an action
— **wave·less** \'wāv-ləs\ *adjective*
— **wave·less·ly** *adverb*
— **wave·like** \-,līk\ *adjective*
**Wave** \'wāv\ *noun* [*W*omen *A*ccepted for *Vol*unteer *E*mergency *S*ervice] (1942)
**:** a woman serving in the navy
**wave band** *noun* (1923)
**:** a band of radio-wave frequencies
**waved** \'wāvd\ *adjective* (1599)
**:** having a wavelike form or outline: as **a :** having wavy lines of color **:** WATERED ⟨*waved* cloth⟩ **b :** marked by undulations **:** CURVING ⟨the *waved* cutting edge of a bread knife⟩
**wave equation** *noun* (1926)
**:** a partial differential equation of the second order whose solutions describe wave phenomena
**wave·form** \'wāv-,form\ *noun* (1845)
**:** a usually graphic representation of the shape of a wave that indicates its characteristics (as frequency and amplitude) — called also *waveshape*
**wave front** *noun* (circa 1864)
**:** a surface composed at any instant of all the points just reached by a vibrational disturbance in its propagation through a medium
**wave·guide** \'wāv-,gīd\ *noun* (1932)
**:** a device (as a duct, coaxial cable, or glass fiber) designed to confine and direct the propagation of electromagnetic waves (as light); *especially* **:** a metal tube for channeling ultrahigh-frequency waves
**wave·length** \-,leŋ(k)th\ *noun* (1850)
**1 :** the distance in the line of advance of a wave from any one point to the next point of corresponding phase
**2 :** a particular course or line of thought especially as related to mutual understanding ⟨two people on different *wavelengths*⟩
**wave·let** \-lət\ *noun* (circa 1810)
**:** a little wave **:** RIPPLE
**wave mechanics** *noun plural but singular or plural in construction* (1926)
**1 :** the mathematical description of atomic and subatomic particles in terms of their wave characteristics
**2 :** QUANTUM MECHANICS
**wave number** *noun* (1873)
**:** the number of waves per unit distance of radiant energy of a given wavelength **:** the reciprocal of the wavelength
**wave of the future** (1940)
**:** an idea, product, or movement that is viewed as representing forces or a trend that will inevitably prevail
**wave packet** *noun* (1928)
**:** a pulse of radiant energy that is the resultant of a number of wave trains of differing wavelengths
**¹wa·ver** \'wā-vər\ *intransitive verb* **wavered; wa·ver·ing** \'wāv-riŋ, 'wā-və-riŋ\ [Middle English; akin to Old English *wǣfre* restless, *wafian* to wave with the hands — more at WAVE] (14th century)
**1 :** to vacillate irresolutely between choices **:** fluctuate in opinion, allegiance, or direction
**2 a :** to weave or sway unsteadily to and fro **:** REEL, TOTTER **b :** QUIVER, FLICKER ⟨*wavering* flames⟩ **c :** to hesitate as if about to give way **:** FALTER
**3 :** to give an unsteady sound **:** QUAVER
***synonym*** see SWING, HESITATE
— **wa·ver·er** \'wā-və-rər\ *noun*
— **wa·ver·ing·ly** \'wāv-riŋ-lē, 'wā-və-\ *adverb*
**²waver** *noun* (1519)
**:** an act of wavering, quivering, or fluttering
**³wav·er** \'wā-vər\ *noun* (1835)
**:** one that waves

**wa·very** \'wāv-rē, 'wā-və-rē\ *adjective* (1820)
**:** that waves **:** WAVERING
**wave·shape** \'wāv-,shāp\ *noun* (1907)
**:** WAVEFORM
**wave theory** *noun* (1833)
**:** a theory in physics: light is transmitted from luminous bodies to the eye and other objects by an undulatory movement — called also *undulatory theory*
**wave train** *noun* (1897)
**:** a succession of similar waves at equal intervals
**wavy** \'wā-vē\ *adjective* **wav·i·er; -est** (circa 1586)
**1 :** rising or swelling in waves; *also* **:** abounding in waves ⟨*wavy* hair⟩
**2 :** moving with an undulating motion **:** FLUCTUATING; *also* **:** marked by wavering
**3 :** marked by undulation **:** ROLLING
— **wav·i·ly** \'wā-və-lē\ *adverb*
— **wav·i·ness** \-vē-nəs\ *noun*
**waw** \'väv, 'vov\ *noun* [Hebrew *wāw*] (14th century)
**:** the 6th letter of the Hebrew alphabet — see ALPHABET table
**wa-wa pedal** \'wä-,wä-\ *noun* [imitative] (1968)
**:** an electronic device that is connected to an amplifier and operated by a foot pedal and that is used (as with an electric guitar) to produce a fluctuating muted effect
**¹wax** \'waks\ *noun* [Middle English, from Old English *weax*; akin to Old High German *wahs* wax, Lithuanian *vaškas*] (before 12th century)
**1 :** a substance that is secreted by bees and is used by them for constructing the honeycomb, that is a dull yellow solid plastic when warm, and that is composed of a mixture of esters, cerotic acid, and hydrocarbons — called also *beeswax*
**2 :** any of various substances resembling beeswax: as **a :** any of numerous substances of plant or animal origin that differ from fats in being less greasy, harder, and more brittle and in containing principally compounds of high molecular weight (as fatty acids, alcohols, and saturated hydrocarbons) **b :** a solid substance (as ozokerite or paraffin wax) of mineral origin consisting usually of hydrocarbons of high molecular weight **c :** a pliable or liquid composition used especially in uniting surfaces, excluding air, making patterns or impressions, or producing a polished surface
**3 :** something likened to wax as soft, impressionable, or readily molded
**4 :** a waxy secretion; *especially* **:** CERUMEN
**5 :** a phonograph recording
— **wax·like** \'waks-,līk\ *adjective*
**²wax** *transitive verb* (14th century)
**1 :** to treat or rub with wax usually for polishing or stiffening
**2 :** to record on phonograph records
**³wax** *intransitive verb* [Middle English, from Old English *weaxan*; akin to Old High German *wahsan* to increase, Greek *auxanein*, Latin *augēre* — more at EKE] (before 12th century)
**1 a :** to increase in size, numbers, strength, prosperity, or intensity **b :** to grow in volume or duration **c :** to grow toward full development
**2 :** to increase in phase or intensity — used chiefly of the moon, other satellites, and inferior planets
**3 :** to assume a (specified) characteristic, quality, or state **:** BECOME ⟨*wax* indignant⟩
**⁴wax** *noun* (14th century)
**:** INCREASE, GROWTH — usually used in the phrase *on the wax*
**⁵wax** *noun* [perhaps from ³*wax*] (1854)
**:** a fit of temper **:** RAGE
**wax bean** *noun* (1897)
**:** a kidney bean with pods that turn creamy yellow to bright yellow when mature enough for use as snap beans
**wax·bill** \'waks-,bil\ *noun* (1757)

**:** any of numerous Old World oscine birds (family Estrildidae and especially genus *Estrilda*) having white, pink, or reddish bills of a waxy appearance
**waxed paper** *noun* (1853)
**:** paper coated or treated with wax to make it resistant to water and grease and used especially as a wrapping
**wax·en** \'wak-sən\ *adjective* (before 12th century)
**1 :** made of or covered with wax
**2 :** resembling wax: as **a :** easily molded **:** PLIABLE **b :** seeming to lack vitality or animation **:** PALLID **c :** lustrously smooth
**wax·er** \-sər\ *noun* (circa 1875)
**1 :** a device for applying wax
**2 :** one whose work is applying or polishing with wax
**wax·ing** *noun* (15th century)
**1 :** the act of applying wax (as in polishing)
**2 :** the process of removing body hair with a depilatory wax
**wax light** *noun* (1599)
**:** a wax candle **:** TAPER
**wax moth** *noun* (1766)
**:** a dull brownish or ashen pyralid moth (*Galleria mellonella*) with a larva that feeds on the comb wax of the honeybee
**wax museum** *noun* (1953)
**:** a place where wax effigies (as of famous historical persons) are exhibited
**wax myrtle** *noun* (1806)
**:** any of a genus (*Myrica* of the family Myricaceae, the wax-myrtle family) of trees or shrubs with aromatic foliage; *especially* **:** a shrub (*M. cerifera*) of the eastern U.S. having small hard berries with a thick coating of white wax used for candles
**wax palm** *noun* (circa 1828)
**:** any of several palms that yield wax: as **a :** an Andean pinnate-leaved palm (*Ceroxylon alpinum* synonym *C. andicola*) whose stem yields a resinous wax used in candles **b :** CARNAUBA
**wax paper** *noun* (circa 1844)
**:** WAXED PAPER
**wax·wing** \'waks-,wiŋ\ *noun* (1817)
**:** any of a genus (*Bombycilla*) of American and Eurasian chiefly brown to gray oscine birds (as a cedar waxwing) having a showy crest, red waxy material on the tips of the secondaries, and a yellow band on the tip of the tail
**wax·work** \-,wərk\ *noun* (1697)
**1 :** an effigy in wax usually of a person
**2** *plural but singular or plural in construction* **:** WAX MUSEUM

waxwing

**waxy** \'wak-sē\ *adjective* **wax·i·er; -est** (1552)
**1 :** made of, abounding in, or covered with wax **:** WAXEN ⟨a *waxy* surface⟩ ⟨*waxy* berries⟩
**2 :** resembling wax: as **a :** readily shaped or molded **b :** marked by smooth or lustrous whiteness ⟨a *waxy* complexion⟩
— **wax·i·ness** *noun*
**¹way** \'wā\ *noun* [Middle English, from Old English *weg*; akin to Old High German *weg* way, Old English *wegan* to move, Latin *vehere* to carry, *via* way] (before 12th century)
**1 a :** a thoroughfare for travel or transportation from place to place **b :** an opening for passage ⟨this door is the only *way* out of the room⟩
**2 :** the course traveled from one place to another **:** ROUTE
**3 a :** a course (as a series of actions or se-

quence of events) leading in a direction or toward an objective ⟨led the *way* to eventual open heart operations —*Current Biography*⟩ **b** (1) : a course of action ⟨took the easy *way* out⟩ (2) : opportunity, capability, or fact of doing as one pleases ⟨always manages to get her own *way*⟩ **c** : a possible decision, action, or outcome : POSSIBILITY ⟨they were rude—no two *ways* about it⟩
**4 a** : manner or method of doing or happening; *also* : method of accomplishing : MEANS **b** : FEATURE, RESPECT ⟨in no *way* resembles her mother⟩ **c** : a usually specified degree of participation in an activity or enterprise ⟨active in real estate in a small *way*⟩
**5 a** : characteristic, regular, or habitual manner or mode of being, behaving, or happening ⟨knows nothing of the *ways* of women⟩ **b** : ability to get along well or perform well ⟨she has a *way* with kids⟩ ⟨a *way* with words⟩
**6** : the length of a course : DISTANCE ⟨has come a long *way* in her studies⟩ ⟨still have a *way* to go⟩
**7** : movement or progress along a course ⟨worked her *way* up the corporate ladder⟩
**8 a** : DIRECTION ⟨is coming this *way*⟩ **b** : PARTICIPANT — usually used in combination ⟨three-*way* discussion⟩
**9** : state of affairs : CONDITION, STATE ⟨that's the *way* things are⟩
**10 a** *plural but sometimes singular in construction* : an inclined structure upon which a ship is built or supported in launching **b** *plural* : the guiding surfaces on the bed of a machine along which a table or carriage moves
**11** : CATEGORY, KIND — usually used in the phrase *in the way of* ⟨doesn't require much in the *way* of expensive equipment —*Forbes*⟩
**12** : motion or speed of a ship or boat through the water
***synonym*** see METHOD
— **all the way** : to the full or entire extent : as far as possible ⟨ran *all the way* home⟩ ⟨seated *all the way* in the back⟩
— **by the way** : by way of interjection or digression : INCIDENTALLY
— **by way of 1** : for the purpose of **2** : by the route through : VIA
— **in a way 1** : within limits : with reservations **2** : from one point of view
— **in one's way** *also* **in the way 1** : in a position to be encountered by one : in or along one's course ⟨an opportunity had been put *in my way* —Ellen Glasgow⟩ **2** : in a position to hinder or obstruct
— **on the way** *or* **on one's way** : moving along in one's course : in progress
— **out of the way 1** : WRONG, IMPROPER ⟨didn't know I'd said anything *out of the way*⟩ **2 a** : in or to a secluded place **b** : UNUSUAL, REMARKABLE ⟨there's nothing *out of the way* about the plan⟩ **3** : DONE, COMPLETED ⟨got his homework *out of the way*⟩
— **the way 1** : in view of the manner in which ⟨you'd think she was rich, *the way* she spends money⟩ **2** : LIKE, AS ⟨we have cats *the way* other people have mice —James Thurber⟩
**²way** *adjective* (1799)
: of, connected with, or constituting an intermediate point on a route ⟨visited five major countries plus *way* points⟩
**³way** *adverb* (1849)
**1 a** : AWAY 7 ⟨is *way* ahead of the class⟩ **b** : by far : MUCH ⟨ate *way* too much⟩
**2** : all the way ⟨pull the switch *way* back⟩
— **from way back** : of long standing ⟨friends *from way back*⟩
**way·bill** \'wā-ˌbil\ *noun* (1821)
: a document prepared by the carrier of a shipment of goods that contains details of the shipment, route, and charges
**way·far·er** \'wā-ˌfar-ər, -ˌfer-\ *noun* [Middle English *weyfarere*, from *wey*, *way* way + *-farere* traveler, from *faren* to go — more at FARE] (15th century)
: a traveler especially on foot

— **way·far·ing** \-ˌfar-iŋ, -ˌfer-\ *adjective*
**wayfaring tree** *noun* (1597)
: a Eurasian shrub (*Viburnum lantana*) that has large ovate leaves and dense cymes of small white flowers and is common along waysides
**way·go·ing** \'wā-ˌgō-ən, -iŋ\ *noun* (1633)
*chiefly Scottish* : the act of leaving : DEPARTURE
**Way·land** \'wā-lən(d)\ *noun* [Old English *Wēland*]
: an heroic smith of Germanic legend
**way·lay** \'wā-ˌlā\ *transitive verb* **-laid** \-ˌlād\; **-lay·ing** (1513)
: to lie in wait for or attack from ambush
**way·less** \-ləs\ *adjective* (12th century)
: having no road or path
**Way of the Cross** (1868)
: STATIONS OF THE CROSS
**way–out** \'wā-'aút\ *adjective* (1954)
: FAR-OUT
**ways** \'wāz\ *noun plural but singular in construction* [Middle English *wayes*, from genitive of ¹*way*] (1588)
: WAY 6 ⟨a long *ways* from home⟩
**-ways** *adverb suffix* [Middle English, from *ways*, genitive of *way*]
: in (such) a way, course, direction, or manner ⟨side*ways*⟩
**ways and means** *noun plural* (15th century)
**1** : methods and resources for accomplishing something and especially for defraying expenses
**2** *W&M often capitalized* **a** : methods and resources for raising the necessary revenues for the expenses of a nation or state **b** : a legislative committee concerned with this function
**way·side** \'wā-ˌsīd\ *noun* (15th century)
: the side of or land adjacent to a road or path
— **wayside** *adjective*
— **by the wayside** : out of consideration : into a condition of neglect or disuse — usually used with *fall*
**way station** *noun* (1850)
**1** : an intermediate station between principal stations on a line of travel (as a railroad)
**2** : an intermediate stopping place
**way·ward** \'wā-wərd\ *adjective* [Middle English, short for *awayward* turned away, from *away*, adverb + *-ward*] (14th century)
**1** : following one's own capricious, wanton, or depraved inclinations : UNGOVERNABLE
**2** : following no clear principle or law : UNPREDICTABLE
**3** : opposite to what is desired or expected : UNTOWARD ⟨*wayward* fate⟩
***synonym*** see CONTRARY
— **way·ward·ly** *adverb*
— **way·ward·ness** *noun*
**way·worn** \-ˌwōrn, -ˌwòrn\ *adjective* (1788)
: wearied by traveling
**we** \'wē\ *pronoun, plural in construction* [Middle English, from Old English *wē*; akin to Old High German *wir* we, Sanskrit *vayam*] (before 12th century)
**1** : I and the rest of a group that includes me : you and I : you and I and another or others : I and another or others not including you — used as pronoun of the first person plural; compare I, OUR, OURS, US
**2** : ¹I — used by sovereigns; used by writers to keep an impersonal character
**weak** \'wēk\ *adjective* [Middle English *weike*, from Old Norse *veikr;* akin to Old English *wīcan* to yield, Greek *eikein* to give way, Sanskrit *vijate* he speeds, flees] (14th century)
**1** : lacking strength: as **a** : deficient in physical vigor : FEEBLE, DEBILITATED **b** : not able to sustain or exert much weight, pressure, or strain **c** : not able to resist external force or withstand attack
**2 a** : mentally or intellectually deficient **b** : not firmly decided : VACILLATING **c** : resulting from or indicating lack of judgment or discernment **d** : not able to withstand temptation or persuasion ⟨the spirit is willing but the flesh is *weak*⟩

**3** : not factually grounded or logically presented ⟨a *weak* argument⟩
**4 a** : not able to function properly **b** (1) : lacking skill or proficiency ⟨tutoring for *weaker* students⟩ (2) : indicative of a lack of skill or aptitude ⟨history was my *weakest* subject⟩ **c** : wanting in vigor of expression or effect
**5 a** : deficient in the usual or required ingredients : DILUTE ⟨*weak* coffee⟩ **b** : lacking normal intensity or potency ⟨*weak* strain of virus⟩
**6 a** : not having or exerting authority or political power ⟨*weak* government⟩ **b** : INEFFECTIVE, IMPOTENT
**7** : of, relating to, or constituting a verb or verb conjugation that in English forms the past tense and past participle by adding the suffix *-ed* or *-d* or *-t*
**8 a** : bearing the minimal degree of stress occurring in the language ⟨*weak* syllable⟩ **b** : having little or no stress and obscured vowel sound ⟨*'d* is the *weak* form of *would*⟩
**9** : tending toward a lower price ⟨a *weak* market⟩
**10** : ionizing only slightly in solution ⟨*weak* acids and bases⟩ ☆
— **weak·ly** *adverb*
**weak anthropic principle** *noun* (1985)
: ANTHROPIC PRINCIPLE a
**weak·en** \'wē-kən\ *verb* **weak·ened; weak·en·ing** \'wēk-niŋ, 'wē-kə-\ (1530)
*transitive verb*
**1** : to make weak : lessen the strength of
**2** : to reduce in intensity or effectiveness
*intransitive verb*
: to become weak ☆
— **weak·en·er** \'wēk-nər, 'wē-kə-\ *noun*

☆ SYNONYMS
**Weak, feeble, frail, fragile, infirm, decrepit** mean not strong enough to endure strain, pressure, or strenuous effort. WEAK applies to deficiency or inferiority in strength or power of any sort ⟨students too *weak* to resist peer pressure⟩. FEEBLE suggests extreme weakness inviting pity or contempt ⟨a *feeble* attempt to get out of bed⟩. FRAIL implies delicacy and slightness of constitution or structure ⟨a *frail* teenager who was unable to enjoy contact sports⟩. FRAGILE suggests frailty and brittleness unable to resist rough usage ⟨a reclusive poet too *fragile* for the rigors of this world⟩. INFIRM suggests instability, unsoundness, and insecurity due to old age or crippling illness ⟨*infirm* residents requiring constant care⟩. DECREPIT implies being worn-out or broken-down from long use or old age ⟨the dowager's faithful, *decrepit* retainers⟩.

**Weaken, enfeeble, debilitate, undermine, sap, cripple, disable** mean to lose or cause to lose strength or vigor. WEAKEN may imply loss of physical strength, health, soundness, or stability or of quality, intensity, or effective power ⟨a disease that *weakens* the body's defenses against infection⟩. ENFEEBLE implies an obvious and pitiable condition of weakness and helplessness ⟨*enfeebled* by starvation⟩. DEBILITATE suggests a less marked or more temporary impairment of strength or vitality ⟨the *debilitating* effects of surgery⟩. UNDERMINE and SAP suggest a weakening by something working surreptitiously and insidiously ⟨a poor diet *undermines* your health⟩ ⟨drugs had *sapped* his ability to think⟩. CRIPPLE implies causing a serious loss of functioning power through damaging or removing an essential part or element ⟨*crippled* by arthritis⟩. DISABLE suggests a usually sudden crippling or enfeebling ⟨*disabled* soldiers received an immediate discharge⟩.

**weak·fish** \'wēk-ˌfish\ *noun* [obsolete Dutch *weekvis*, from Dutch *week* soft + *vis* fish; from its tender flesh] (1791)
**1** : a common marine bony fish (*Cynoscion regalis* of the family Sciaenidae) that is a sport and food fish of the eastern coast of the U.S. — called also *sea trout*
**2** : any of several fishes congeneric with the weakfish

**weak force** *noun* (1971)
: a fundamental physical force that governs interactions between hadrons and leptons (as in the emission and absorption of neutrinos) and is responsible for particle decay processes (as beta decay) in radioactivity, that is $10^5$ times weaker than the strong force, and that acts over distances smaller than those between nucleons in an atomic nucleus — called also *weak interaction, weak nuclear force;* compare ELECTROMAGNETISM 2a, GRAVITY 3a(2), STRONG FORCE

**weak·heart·ed** \-'här-təd\ *adjective* (1549)
: lacking courage : FAINTHEARTED

**weak·ish** \'wē-kish\ *adjective* (1594)
: somewhat weak ⟨*weakish* tea⟩

**weak–kneed** \'wēk-'nēd\ *adjective* (1863)
: lacking willpower or resolution

**weak·ling** \'wē-kliŋ\ *noun* (1548)
: one that is weak in body, character, or mind
— **weakling** *adjective*

**weak·ly** \'wē-klē\ *adjective* (1577)
: FEEBLE, WEAK
— **weak·li·ness** *noun*

**weak–mind·ed** \'wēk-'mīn-dəd\ *adjective* (1716)
: having or indicating a weak mind: **a** : lacking in judgment or good sense : FOOLISH **b** : FEEBLEMINDED
— **weak–mind·ed·ness** *noun*

**weak·ness** \-nəs\ *noun* (14th century)
**1** : the quality or state of being weak; *also* : an instance or period of being weak ⟨agreed in a moment of *weakness* to go along⟩
**2** : FAULT, DEFECT
**3 a** : a special desire or fondness ⟨has a *weakness* for chocolates⟩ **b** : an object of special desire or fondness ⟨pizza is my *weakness*⟩

**weak side** *noun* (1940)
**1** : the side of a football formation having the smaller number of players; *specifically* : the side of a formation away from the tight end
**2** : the side of a court or field (as in basketball or soccer) away from the ball
— **weak·side** \'wēk-ˌsīd\ *adjective*

**weak sister** *noun* (1857)
: a member of a group who needs aid; *also* : something that is weak and ineffective as compared with others in the group

**¹weal** \'wē(ə)l\ *noun* [Middle English *wele,* from Old English *wela;* akin to Old English *wel* well] (before 12th century)
**1** : a sound, healthy, or prosperous state : WELL-BEING
**2** *obsolete* : BODY POLITIC, COMMONWEAL

**²weal** *noun* [alteration of *wale*] (circa 1798)
: WELT

**weald** \'wē(ə)ld\ *noun* [the *Weald,* England, from Middle English *weeld,* from Old English *weald* forest — more at WOLD] (before 12th century)
**1** : a heavily wooded area : FOREST ⟨the *Weald* of Kent⟩
**2** : a wild or uncultivated usually upland region

**wealth** \'welth *also* 'weltth\ *noun* [Middle English *welthe,* from *wele* weal] (13th century)
**1** *obsolete* : WEAL, WELFARE
**2** : abundance of valuable material possessions or resources
**3** : abundant supply : PROFUSION
**4 a** : all property that has a money value or an exchangeable value **b** : all material objects that have economic utility; *especially* : the stock of useful goods having economic value in existence at any one time ⟨national *wealth*⟩

**wealthy** \'wel-thē *also* 'welt-thē\ *adjective* **wealth·i·er; -est** (15th century)
**1** : having wealth : extremely affluent
**2** : characterized by abundance : AMPLE
**synonym** SEE RICH
— **wealth·i·ly** \-thə-lē\ *adverb*
— **wealth·i·ness** \-thē-nəs\ *noun*

**wean** \'wēn\ *transitive verb* [Middle English *wenen,* from Old English *wenian* to accustom, wean; akin to Old English *wunian* to be used to — more at WONT] (before 12th century)
**1** : to accustom (as a child) to take food otherwise than by nursing
**2** : to detach from a source of dependence ⟨being *weaned* off the medication⟩ ⟨*wean* the bears from human food —*Sports Illustrated*⟩; *also* : to free from a usually unwholesome habit or interest ⟨*wean* him off his excessive drinking⟩ ⟨settling his soldiers on the land . . ., *weaning* them from habits of violence —Geoffrey Carnall⟩
**3** : to accustom to something from an early age — used in the passive especially with *on* ⟨students *weaned* on the microcomputer⟩ ⟨I was *weaned* on greasepaint —Helen Hayes⟩ ⟨the principles upon which he had been *weaned* —J. A. Michener⟩

**wean·er** \'wē-nər\ *noun* (1579)
**1** : one that weans
**2** : a young animal recently weaned from its mother

**wean·ling** \'wēn-liŋ\ *noun* (1532)
: a child or animal newly weaned
— **wean·ling** *adjective*

**¹weap·on** \'we-pən\ *noun* [Middle English *wepen,* from Old English *wǣpen;* akin to Old High German *wāffan* weapon, Old Norse *vāpn*] (before 12th century)
**1** : something (as a club, knife, or gun) used to injure, defeat, or destroy
**2** : a means of contending against another

**²weapon** *transitive verb* (before 12th century)
: ARM

**weap·on·less** \-ləs\ *adjective* (before 12th century)
: lacking weapons : UNARMED

**weap·on·ry** \-rē\ *noun* (1844)
**1** : WEAPONS
**2** : the science of designing and making weapons

**¹wear** \'war, 'wer\ *verb* **wore** \'wōr, 'wȯr\; **worn** \'wōrn, 'wȯrn\; **wear·ing** [Middle English *weren,* from Old English *werian;* akin to Old Norse *verja* to clothe, invest, spend, Latin *vestis* clothing, garment, Greek *hennynai* to clothe] (before 12th century)
*transitive verb*
**1** : to bear or have on the person ⟨*wore* a coat⟩
**2 a** : to use habitually for clothing, adornment, or assistance ⟨*wears* a toupee⟩ ⟨*wear* glasses⟩ **b** : to carry on the person ⟨*wear* a sword⟩
**3 a** : to hold the rank or dignity or position signified by (an ornament) ⟨*wear* the royal crown⟩ **b** : EXHIBIT, PRESENT ⟨*wore* a happy smile⟩ ⟨commend the book for *wearing* its research so lightly —Brad Leithauser⟩ **c** : to show or fly (a flag or colors) on a ship
**4 a** : to cause to deteriorate by use **b** : to impair or diminish by use or attrition : consume or waste gradually ⟨letters on the stone *worn* away by weathering⟩
**5** : to produce gradually by friction or attrition ⟨*wear* a hole in the rug⟩
**6** : to exhaust or lessen the strength of : WEARY, FATIGUE
**7** : to cause (a ship) to go about with the stern presented to the wind
**8** *British* : to accept or tolerate without complaint : put up with — usually used in negative constructions ⟨your mates wouldn't *wear* it —Colin MacInnes⟩
*intransitive verb*
**1 a** : to endure use : last under use or the passage of time ⟨material that will *wear* for years⟩
**b** : to retain quality or vitality

**2 a** : to diminish or decay through use ⟨the heels of his shoes began to *wear*⟩ **b** : to diminish or fail with the passage of time ⟨the effect of the drug *wore* off⟩ ⟨the day *wore* on⟩ **c** : to grow or become by attrition or wear
**3** *of a ship* : to change to an opposite tack by turning the stern to the wind — compare TACK
— **wear·er** *noun*
— **wear on** : IRRITATE, FRAY
— **wear the trousers** *or* **wear the pants** : to have the controlling authority in a household
— **wear thin 1** : to become weak or ready to give way ⟨my patience was *wearing thin*⟩ **2** : to become trite, unconvincing, or out-of-date ⟨an argument that quickly *wore thin*⟩

**²wear** *noun* (15th century)
**1** : the act of wearing : the state of being worn : USE ⟨clothes for everyday *wear*⟩
**2 a** : clothing or an article of clothing usually of a particular kind; *especially* : clothing worn for a special occasion or popular during a specific period **b** : FASHION, VOGUE
**3** : wearing quality : durability under use
**4** : the result of wearing or use : diminution or impairment due to use ⟨*wear*-resistant surface⟩

**¹wear·able** \'war-ə-bəl, 'wer-\ *adjective* (1590)
: capable of being worn : suitable to be worn
— **wear·abil·i·ty** \ˌwar-ə-'bi-lə-tē, ˌwer-\ *noun*

**²wearable** *noun* (1711)
: GARMENT — usually used in plural

**wear and tear** *noun* (1666)
: the loss, injury, or stress to which something is subjected by or in the course of use; *especially* : normal depreciation

**wear down** *transitive verb* (1803)
: to weary and overcome by persistent resistance or pressure

**wea·ri·ful** \'wir-ē-fəl\ *adjective* (15th century)
**1** : causing weariness; *especially* : TEDIOUS
**2** : full of weariness : WEARIED
— **wea·ri·ful·ly** \-fə-lē\ *adverb*
— **wea·ri·ful·ness** *noun*

**wea·ri·less** \'wir-ē-ləs\ *adjective* (15th century)
: TIRELESS
— **wea·ri·less·ly** *adverb*

**¹wear·ing** \'war-iŋ, 'wer-\ *adjective* (15th century)
: intended for wear ⟨*wearing* apparel⟩

**²wearing** *adjective* (1811)
: subjecting to or inflicting wear; *especially* : causing fatigue ⟨a *wearing* journey⟩
— **wear·ing·ly** \-iŋ-lē\ *adverb*

**wea·ri·some** \'wir-ē-səm\ *adjective* (15th century)
: causing weariness : TIRESOME
— **wea·ri·some·ly** *adverb*
— **wea·ri·some·ness** *noun*

**wear out** (14th century)
*transitive verb*
**1** : TIRE, EXHAUST
**2** : to make useless especially by long or hard usage
**3** : ERASE, EFFACE
**4** : to endure through : OUTLAST ⟨*wear out* a storm⟩
**5** : to consume (as time) tediously ⟨*wear out* idle days⟩
*intransitive verb*
: to become useless from long or excessive wear or use

**¹wea·ry** \'wir-ē\ *adjective* **wea·ri·er; -est** [Middle English *wery,* from Old English *wērig;* akin to Old High German *wuorag* intoxicated and perhaps to Greek *aōros* sleep] (before 12th century)

**1 :** exhausted in strength, endurance, vigor, or freshness
**2 :** expressing or characteristic of weariness
**3 :** having one's patience, tolerance, or pleasure exhausted — used with *of*
**4 :** WEARISOME
— **wea·ri·ly** \'wir-ə-lē\ *adverb*
— **wea·ri·ness** \'wir-ē-nəs\ *noun*
²**weary** *verb* **wea·ried; wea·ry·ing** (before 12th century)
*intransitive verb*
**:** to become weary
*transitive verb*
**:** to make weary
**synonym** see TIRE
**wea·sand** \'wē-zᵊnd, 'wi-zᵊn(d)\ *noun* [Middle English *wesand,* from (assumed) Old English *wāsend* gullet; akin to Old English *wāsend* gullet, Old High German *weisunt* windpipe] (before 12th century)
**:** THROAT, GULLET; *also* **:** TRACHEA
¹**wea·sel** \'wē-zəl\ *noun, plural* **weasels** [Middle English *wesele,* from Old English *weosule;* akin to Old High German *wisula* weasel] (before 12th century)

**1** *or plural* **weasel :** any of various small slender active carnivorous mammals (genus *Mustela* of the family Mustelidae, the weasel family) that are able to prey

**weasel 1**

on animals (as rabbits) larger than themselves, are mostly reddish brown with white or yellowish underparts, and in northern forms turn white in winter
**2 :** a light self-propelled tracked vehicle built either for traveling over snow, ice, or sand or as an amphibious vehicle
²**weasel** *intransitive verb* **wea·seled; wea·sel·ing** \'wēz-liŋ, 'wē-zə-\ [*weasel word*] (1900)
**1 :** to use weasel words **:** EQUIVOCATE
**2 :** to escape from or evade a situation or obligation — often used with *out*
**wea·sel·ly** *also* **wea·sely** \'wēz-lē, 'wē-zə-\ *adjective* (1838)
**:** resembling or suggestive of a weasel
**weasel word** *noun* [from the weasel's reputed habit of sucking the contents out of an egg while leaving the shell superficially intact] (1900)
**:** a word used in order to evade or retreat from a direct or forthright statement or position
¹**weath·er** \'we-t͟hər\ *noun* [Middle English *weder,* from Old English; akin to Old High German *wetar* weather, Old Church Slavonic *vetrŭ* wind] (before 12th century)
**1 :** the state of the atmosphere with respect to heat or cold, wetness or dryness, calm or storm, clearness or cloudiness
**2 :** state or vicissitude of life or fortune
**3 :** disagreeable atmospheric conditions: as **a :** RAIN, STORM **b :** cold air with dampness
**4 :** WEATHERING
— **under the weather 1 :** ILL **2 :** DRUNK 1a
²**weather** *verb* **weath·ered; weath·er·ing** \'we-t͟h-riŋ, 'we-t͟hə-\ (15th century)
*transitive verb*
**1 :** to expose to the open air **:** subject to the action of the elements
**2 :** to bear up against and come safely through ⟨*weather* a storm⟩ ⟨*weather* a crisis⟩
*intransitive verb*
**:** to undergo or endure the action of the elements
³**weather** *adjective* (circa 1625)
**:** of or relating to the side facing the wind — compare LEE
**weath·er·abil·i·ty** \,we-t͟h-rə-'bi-lə-tē, ,we-t͟hə-\ *noun* (1947)

**:** capability of withstanding the weathering process ⟨*weatherability* of a plastic⟩
**weath·er-beat·en** \'we-t͟hər-,bē-tᵊn\ *adjective* (1530)
**1 :** toughened, tanned, or bronzed by the weather ⟨a *weather-beaten* face⟩
**2 :** worn or damaged by exposure to weather
**weath·er·board** \-,bōrd, -,bȯrd\ *noun* (circa 1540)
**1 :** CLAPBOARD, SIDING
**2 :** the weather side of a ship
— **weath·er·board·ed** *adjective*
**weath·er·board·ing** \-,bōr-diŋ, -,bȯr-\ *noun* (1632)
**:** CLAPBOARDS, SIDING
**weath·er-bound** \-,baund\ *adjective* (1590)
**:** kept in port or at anchor or from travel or sport by bad weather
**weather bureau** *noun* (1871)
**:** a bureau engaged in the collection of weather reports as a basis for weather predictions, storm warnings, and the compiling of statistical records
**weath·er-burned** \'we-t͟hər-,bərnd\ *adjective* (1906)
**:** browned by sun and wind
**weath·er·cast** \-,kast\ *noun* [¹*weather* + ²*forecast*] (1866)
**:** a weather forecast especially on radio or television
**weath·er·cast·er** \-,kas-tər\ *noun* (1607)
**:** a weather forecaster especially on radio or television
**weath·er·cock** \-,käk\ *noun* (13th century)
**1 :** a vane often in the figure of a cock mounted so as to turn freely with the wind and show its direction
**2 :** a person or thing that changes readily or often
**weather deck** *noun* (1850)
**:** a deck having no overhead protection from the weather
**weath·ered** \'we-t͟hərd\ *adjective* (1789)
**1 :** seasoned by exposure to the weather
**2 :** altered in color, texture, composition, or form by such exposure or by artificial means producing a similar effect ⟨*weathered* oak⟩
**weather eye** *noun* (1839)
**1 :** an eye quick to observe coming changes in the weather
**2 :** constant and shrewd watchfulness and alertness
**weath·er·glass** \'we-t͟hər-,glas\ *noun* (1626)
**:** a simple instrument for showing changes in atmospheric pressure by the changing level of liquid in a spout connected with a closed reservoir; *broadly* **:** BAROMETER
**weathering** *noun* (1548)
**:** the action of the elements in altering the color, texture, composition, or form of exposed objects; *specifically* **:** the physical disintegration and chemical decomposition of earth materials at or near the earth's surface
**weath·er·ize** \'we-t͟hə-,rīz\ *transitive verb* **-ized; -iz·ing** (1943)
**:** to make (as a house) better protected against winter weather (as by adding insulation)
— **weath·er·i·za·tion** \,wet͟h-rə-'za-shən, ,we-t͟hə-\ *noun*
**weath·er·ly** \'we-t͟hər-lē\ *adjective* (1729)
**:** able to sail close to the wind with little leeway
**weath·er·man** \-,man\ *noun* (1859)
**:** one who reports and forecasts the weather **:** METEOROLOGIST
**weather map** *noun* (1871)
**:** a map or chart showing the principal meteorological elements at a given hour and over an extended region
**weath·er·per·son** \'we-t͟hər-,pər-sᵊn\ *noun* (1974)
**:** a person who reports and forecasts the weather **:** METEOROLOGIST
**weath·er·proof** \'we-t͟hər-,prüf\ *adjective* (1620)

**:** able to withstand exposure to weather without damage or loss of function
— **weatherproof** *transitive verb*
— **weath·er·proof·ness** *noun*
**weather ship** *noun* (1946)
**:** a ship that makes observations for use by meteorologists
**weather station** *noun* (circa 1895)
**:** a station for taking, recording, and reporting meteorological observations
**weather strip** *noun* (1846)
**:** a strip of material to cover the joint of a door or window and the sill, casing, or threshold so as to exclude rain, snow, and cold air — called also *weather stripping*
— **weath·er-strip** *transitive verb*
**weather vane** *noun* (circa 1721)
**:** VANE 1a
**weath·er-wise** \'we-t͟hər-,wīz\ *adjective* (14th century)
**1 :** skillful in forecasting changes in the weather
**2 :** skillful in forecasting changes in opinion or feeling ⟨a *weather-wise* politician⟩
**weath·er-worn** \-,wōrn, -,wȯrn\ *adjective* (1609)
**:** worn by exposure to the weather
¹**weave** \'wēv\ *verb* **wove** \'wōv\ *or* **weaved; wo·ven** \'wō-vən\ *or* **weaved; weav·ing** [Middle English *weven,* from Old English *wefan;* akin to Old High German *weban* to weave, Greek *hyphainein* to weave, *hyphos* web] (before 12th century)
*transitive verb*
**1 a :** to form (cloth) by interlacing strands (as of yarn); *specifically* **:** to make (cloth) on a loom by interlacing warp and filling threads **b :** to interlace (as threads) into cloth **c :** to make (as a basket) by intertwining
**2 :** SPIN 2 — used of spiders and insects
**3 :** to interlace especially to form a texture, fabric, or design
**4 a :** to produce by elaborately combining elements **:** CONTRIVE **b :** to unite in a coherent whole **c :** to introduce as an appropriate element **:** work in — usually used with *in* or *into*
**5 :** to direct (as the body) in a winding or zigzag course especially to avoid obstacles
*intransitive verb*
**1 :** to work at weaving **:** make cloth
**2 :** to move in a devious, winding, or zigzag course especially to avoid obstacles
²**weave** *noun* (1581)
**1 :** something woven; *especially* **:** woven cloth
**2 :** any of the patterns or methods for interlacing the threads of woven fabrics
³**weave** *intransitive verb* **weaved; weav·ing** [Middle English *weven* to move to and fro, wave; akin to Old Norse *veifa* to be in movement — more at WIPE] (1596)
**:** to move waveringly from side to side **:** SWAY
**weav·er** \'wē-vər\ *noun* (14th century)
**1 :** one that weaves especially as an occupation
**2 :** WEAVERBIRD
**weav·er·bird** \-,bərd\ *noun* (1826)
**:** any of numerous Old World passerine birds (family Ploceidae) that resemble finches and mostly construct elaborate nests of interlaced vegetation
**weaver's knot** *noun* (1532)
**:** SHEET BEND — called also *weaver's hitch*
¹**web** \'web\ *noun* [Middle English, from Old English; akin to Old Norse *vefr* web, Old English *wefan* to weave] (before 12th century)
**1 :** a fabric on a loom or in process of being removed from a loom
**2 a :** COBWEB, SPIDERWEB **b :** a network of silken thread spun especially by the larvae of various insects (as a tent caterpillar) and usually serving as a nest or shelter
**3 :** a tissue or membrane of an animal or plant; *especially* **:** that uniting fingers or toes

either at their bases (as in humans) or for a greater part of their length (as in many water-birds)
**4 a :** a thin metal sheet, plate, or strip **b :** the plate connecting the upper and lower flanges of a girder or rail **c :** the arm of a crank
**5 :** something resembling a web: **a :** SNARE, ENTANGLEMENT ⟨a *web* of intrigue⟩ ⟨ensnarled in a *web* of folly —David A. Stockman⟩ **b :** an intricate pattern or structure suggestive of something woven **:** NETWORK ⟨a *web* of little roads⟩ ⟨a complex *web* of relationships⟩
**6 :** the series of barbs implanted on each side of the shaft of a feather **:** VANE
**7 a :** a continuous sheet of paper manufactured or undergoing manufacture on a paper machine **b :** a roll of paper for use in a rotary printing press
**8 :** the part of a ribbed vault between the ribs
— **webbed** \'webd\ *adjective*
— **web·like** \'web-,līk\ *adjective*
**²web** *verb* **webbed; web·bing** (1604)
*intransitive verb*
**:** to construct or form a web
*transitive verb*
**1 :** to cover with a web or network
**2 :** ENSNARE, ENTANGLE
**3 :** to provide with a web
**web·bing** \'we-biŋ\ *noun* (1796)
**1 :** a strong narrow closely woven tape designed for bearing weight and used especially for straps, harness, or upholstery
**2 :** TRAP 3c
**web·by** \'we-bē\ *adjective* (1661)
**:** of, relating to, or consisting of a web
**we·ber** \'we-bər, 'vā-bər\ *noun* [Wilhelm E. Weber (died 1891) German physicist] (1891)
**:** the practical meter-kilogram-second unit of magnetic flux equal to that flux which in linking a circuit of one turn produces in it an electromotive force of one volt as the flux is reduced to zero at a uniform rate in one second **:** $10^8$ maxwells
**web·fed** \'web-,fed\ *adjective* (1947)
**:** of, relating to, or printed by a web press
**web·foot** *noun* (1765)
**1** \'web-'fut\ **:** a foot having webbed toes
**2** \-,fut\ **:** an animal having web feet
— **web–foot·ed** \-'fu-təd\ *adjective*
**web member** *noun* (circa 1890)
**:** one of the several members joining the top and bottom chords of a truss or lattice girder
**web–off·set** \'web-'òf-,set\ *noun, often attributive* (1959)
**:** offset printing by web press
**web press** *noun* (1875)
**:** a press that prints a continuous roll of paper
**web spinner** *noun* (circa 1907)
**:** an insect that spins a web; *especially* **:** any of an order (Embioptera synonym Embiidina) of small slender insects with biting mouthparts that live in silken tunnels which they spin
**web·ster** \'web-stər\ *noun* [Middle English, from Old English *webbestre* female weaver, from *webbian* to weave; akin to Old English *wefan* to weave] (12th century)
*archaic* **:** WEAVER 1
**web·work** \'web-,wərk\ *noun* (1790)
**:** WEB 5b ⟨a vast *webwork* of real estate holdings⟩
**web·worm** \-,wərm\ *noun* (1797)
**:** any of various caterpillars that are more or less gregarious and spin large webs
**wed** \'wed\ *verb* **wed·ded** *also* **wed; wed·ding** [Middle English *wedden*, from Old English *weddian*; akin to Middle High German *wetten* to pledge, Old English *wedd* pledge, Old High German *wetti*, Gothic *wadi*, Latin *vad-, vas* bail, security] (before 12th century)
*transitive verb*
**1 :** to take for wife or husband by a formal ceremony **:** MARRY
**2 :** to join in marriage
**3 :** to unite as if by the bond of marriage
*intransitive verb*
**:** to enter into matrimony

— **wed·der** *noun*
**we'd** \'wēd\ (1603)
**:** we had **:** we would **:** we should
**Wed·dell seal** \wi-'del-, 'we-dᵊl-\ *noun* [James *Weddell* (died 1834) English navigator] (1914)
**:** a vocal Antarctic hair seal (*Leptonychotes weddelli*) noted for its deep dives in search of food
**wed·ding** \'we-diŋ\ *noun, often attributive* (before 12th century)
**1 :** a marriage ceremony usually with its accompanying festivities **:** NUPTIALS
**2 :** an act, process, or instance of joining in close association
**3 :** a wedding anniversary or its celebration — usually used in combination ⟨a golden *wedding*⟩
**wedding cake** *noun* (1648)
**1 :** a usually elaborately decorated and tiered cake made for the celebration of a wedding
**2 :** something (as a large building) likened to a wedding cake especially in elaborate ornamentation
**wedding march** *noun* (1850)
**:** a march of slow tempo and stately character composed or played to accompany the bridal procession
**wedding ring** *noun* (14th century)
**:** a ring often of plain gold or platinum given by the groom to the bride during the wedding service; *also* **:** a similar ring given by the bride to the groom in a double-ring service
**we·del** \'vā-dᵊl\ *intransitive verb* [German *Wedeln*] (circa 1963)
**:** to ski downhill by means of wedeln
**we·deln** \'vā-dᵊln\ *noun* [German, from *wedeln*, literally, to fan, wag the tail, from *Wedel* fan, tail, from Old High German *wadal*; akin to Old Norse *vēli* bird's tail] (circa 1957)
**:** a style of skiing in which a skier rhythmically swings the rear of the skis from side to side while following the fall line
**¹wedge** \'wej\ *noun* [Middle English *wegge*, from Old English *wecg*; akin to Old High German *wecki* wedge, Lithuanian *vagis*] (before 12th century)
**1 :** a piece of a substance (as wood or iron) that tapers to a thin edge and is used for splitting wood and rocks, raising heavy bodies, or for tightening by being driven into something
**2 a :** something (as a policy) causing a breach or separation **b :** something used to initiate an action or development
**3 :** something wedge-shaped: as **a :** an array of troops or tanks in the form of a wedge **b :** the wedge-shaped stroke in cuneiform characters **c :** a shoe having a heel extending from the back of the shoe to the front of the shank and a tread formed by an extension of the sole **d :** an iron golf club with a broad low-angled face for maximum loft
**²wedge** *verb* **wedged; wedg·ing** (15th century)
*transitive verb*
**1 :** to fasten or tighten by driving in a wedge
**2 a :** to force or press (something) into a narrow space **:** CRAM **b :** to force (one's way) into or through ⟨*wedged* his way into the crowd⟩
**3 :** to separate or force apart with or as if with a wedge
*intransitive verb*
**:** to become wedged
**wedged** \'wejd, 'we-jəd\ *adjective* (1552)
**:** shaped like a wedge
**wedg·ie** \'we-jē\ *noun* (1939)
**1 :** a shoe having a wedge-shaped piece serving as the heel and joining the half sole to form a continuous flat undersurface
**2 :** the condition of having one's clothing wedged between the buttocks especially from having one's pants or underpants yanked up from behind as a prank — often used with *get* or *give*
**Wedg·wood** \'wej-,wud\ *trademark*

— used for ceramic wares (as bone china or jasper)
**wedgy** \'we-jē\ *adjective* (1799)
**:** resembling a wedge in shape
**wed·lock** \'wed-,läk\ *noun* [Middle English *wedlok*, from Old English *wedlāc* marriage bond, from *wedd* pledge + *-lāc*, suffix denoting activity] (13th century)
**:** the state of being married **:** MARRIAGE, MATRIMONY
— **out of wedlock :** with the natural parents not legally married to each other
**Wednes·day** \'wenz-dē, -(,)dā; *British also* 'wed-nz-\ *noun* [Middle English, from Old English *wōdnesdæg* (akin to Old Norse *ōthinsdagr* Wednesday); akin to Old English *Wōden* Odin and *dæg* day] (before 12th century)
**:** the fourth day of the week
— **Wednes·days** \-dēz, -(,)dāz\ *adverb*
**wee** \'wē\ *adjective* [Middle English *we*, from *we*, noun, little bit, from Old English *wæge* weight; akin to Old English *wegan* to move, weigh — more at WAY] (15th century)
**1 :** very small **:** DIMINUTIVE
**2 :** very early ⟨*wee* hours of the morning⟩
**¹weed** \'wēd\ *noun* [Middle English, from Old English *wēod* weed, herb; akin to Old Saxon *wiod* weed] (before 12th century)
**1 a** (1) **:** a plant that is not valued where it is growing and is usually of vigorous growth; *especially* **:** one that tends to overgrow or choke out more desirable plants (2) **:** a weedy growth of plants **b :** an aquatic plant; *especially* **:** SEAWEED **c** (1) **:** TOBACCO (2) **:** MARIJUANA
**2 a :** an obnoxious growth, thing, or person **b :** something like a weed in detrimental quality; *especially* **:** an animal unfit to breed from
**²weed** (before 12th century)
*intransitive verb*
**:** to remove weeds or something harmful
*transitive verb*
**1 a :** to clear of weeds ⟨*weed* a garden⟩ **b** (1) **:** to free from something hurtful or offensive (2) **:** to remove the less desirable portions of
**2 :** to get rid of (something harmful or superfluous) — often used with *out*
**³weed** *noun* [Middle English *wede*, from Old English *wǣd, gewǣde*; akin to Old Norse *vāth* cloth, clothing and perhaps to Lithuanian *austi* to weave] (before 12th century)
**1 :** GARMENT — often used in plural
**2 a :** dress worn as a sign of mourning (as by a widow) — usually used in plural **b :** a band of crape worn on a man's hat as a sign of mourning — usually used in plural
**weed·er** \'wē-dər\ *noun* (15th century)
**:** one that weeds; *specifically* **:** any of various devices for removing weeds from an area
**weedy** \'wē-dē\ *adjective* **weed·i·er; -est** (15th century)
**1 :** abounding with or consisting of weeds
**2 :** resembling a weed especially in rank growth or ready propagation
**3 :** noticeably lean and scrawny **:** LANKY
— **weed·i·ness** *noun*
**week** \'wēk\ *noun* [Middle English *weke*, from Old English *wicu, wucu*; akin to Old High German *wehha* week and perhaps to Latin *vicis* change, alternation, Old High German *wehsal* exchange] (before 12th century)
**1 a :** any of a series of 7-day cycles used in various calendars; *especially* **:** a 7-day cycle beginning on Sunday and ending on Saturday **b** (1) **:** a week beginning with a specified day or containing a specified holiday ⟨the *week* of the 18th⟩ ⟨Easter *week*⟩ (2) **:** a week appointed for public recognition of some cause ⟨Fire Prevention *Week*⟩

\ə\ abut \ᵊ\ kitten \ər\ further \a\ ash \ā\ ace
\ä\ mop, mar \au̇\ out \ch\ chin \e\ bet \ē\ easy
\g\ go \i\ hit \ī\ ice \j\ job \ŋ\ sing \ō\ go
\ò\ law \òi\ boy \th\ thin \tẖ\ the \ü\ loot \u̇\ foot
\y\ yet \zh\ vision *see also* Guide to Pronunciation

**2 a :** any seven consecutive days **b :** a series of regular working, business, or school days during each 7-day period
**3 :** a time seven days before or after a specified day ⟨last Sunday *week*⟩
**week·day** \'wēk-ˌdā\ *noun* (15th century)
**:** a day of the week except Sunday or sometimes except Saturday and Sunday
**week·days** \-ˌdāz\ *adverb* (1777)
**:** on weekdays repeatedly **:** on any weekday ⟨takes a bus *weekdays*⟩
**¹week·end** \'wēk-ˌend\ *noun* (1638)
**:** the end of the week; *specifically* **:** the period between the close of one working or business or school week and the beginning of the next
**²weekend** *intransitive verb* (1901)
**:** to spend the weekend
**³weekend** *adjective* (1935)
**:** active in a specified role only on weekends or part-time ⟨a *weekend* father⟩ ⟨*weekend* athletes⟩
**weekend bag** *noun* (1921)
**:** a suitcase of a size to carry clothing and personal articles for a weekend trip — called also *weekend case*
**week·end·er** \'wēk-ˈen-dər\ *noun* (1880)
**1 :** one that vacations or visits for a weekend
**2 :** WEEKEND BAG
**week·ends** \'wēk-ˌen(d)z\ *adverb* (1892)
**:** on weekends repeatedly **:** on any weekend ⟨travels *weekends*⟩
**week·long** \'wēk-ˈlȯŋ\ *adjective* (1898)
**:** lasting a week
**¹week·ly** \'wē-klē\ *adverb* (15th century)
**:** every week **:** once a week **:** by the week
**²weekly** *adjective* (15th century)
**1 :** occurring, appearing, or done weekly
**2 :** reckoned by the week
**³weekly** *noun, plural* **weeklies** (1833)
**:** a weekly newspaper or periodical
**week·night** \'wēk-ˌnīt\ *noun* (1859)
**:** a weekday night
**week·nights** \-ˌnīts\ *adverb* (1965)
**:** on weeknights repeatedly **:** on any weeknight
**ween** \'wēn\ *transitive verb* [Middle English *wenen,* from Old English *wēnan;* akin to Old Norse *væna* to hope and probably to Latin *venus* love, charm — more at WIN] (before 12th century)
*archaic* **:** IMAGINE
**wee·nie** \'wē-nē\ *noun* [alteration of *wienie*] (circa 1906)
**1 :** FRANKFURTER
**2** *slang* **:** PENIS
**3 :** NERD ⟨computer *weenies*⟩
**wee·ny** \'wē-nē\ *also* **ween·sy** \'wēn(t)-sē\ *adjective* [alteration of *wee*] (circa 1781)
**:** exceptionally small **:** TINY
**weep** \'wēp\ *verb* **wept** \'wept\; **weep·ing** [Middle English *wepen,* from Old English *wēpan;* akin to Old High German *wuoffan* to weep, Old Church Slavonic *vabiti* to call to] (before 12th century)
*transitive verb*
**1 :** to express deep sorrow for usually by shedding tears **:** BEWAIL
**2 :** to pour forth (tears) from the eyes
**3 :** to exude (a fluid) slowly **:** OOZE
*intransitive verb*
**1 :** to express passion (as grief) by shedding tears
**2 a :** to give off or leak fluid slowly **:** OOZE **b :** of a fluid **:** to flow sluggishly or in drops
**3 :** to droop over **:** BEND
**weep·er** \'wē-pər\ *noun* (14th century)
**1 a :** one that weeps **b :** a professional mourner
**2 :** a small statue of a figure in mourning on a funeral monument
**3 :** a badge of mourning worn especially in the 18th and 19th centuries
**4** *plural* **:** long and flowing side-whiskers
**5 :** TEARJERKER
**weep hole** *noun* (1851)
**:** a hole (as in a wall or foundation) that is designed to drain off accumulated water

**weep·ie** \'wē-pē\ *noun* (1928)
**:** TEARJERKER
**weep·ing** \'wē-piŋ\ *adjective* (before 12th century)
**1 :** TEARFUL
**2** *archaic* **:** RAINY
**3 :** having slender pendent branches
**weeping willow** *noun* (circa 1731)
**:** an Asian willow (*Salix babylonica*) introduced into North America that has slender pendent branches
**weepy** \'wē-pē\ *adjective* (1863)
**:** inclined to weep **:** TEARFUL
**weet** \'wēt\ *verb* [Middle English *weten,* alteration of *witen* — more at WIT] (14th century)
*archaic* **:** KNOW
**wee·vil** \'wē-vəl\ *noun* [Middle English *wevel,* from Old English *wifel;* akin to Old High German *wibil* beetle, Old English *wefan* to weave] (before 12th century)
**:** any of a superfamily (Curculionoidea) of beetles which have the head prolonged into a more or less distinct snout and which include many that are injurious especially as larvae to nuts, fruit, and grain or to living plants; *especially* **:** any of a family (Curculionidae) having a well-developed snout curved downward with the jaws at the tip and clubbed usually elbowed antennae

**weevil**
— **wee·vily** *or* **wee·vil·ly** \'wēv-lē, 'wē-və-lē\ *adjective*
**weft** \'weft\ *noun* [Middle English, from Old English; akin to Old Norse *veptr* weft, Old English *wefan* to weave — more at WEAVE] (before 12th century)
**1 a :** a filling thread or yarn in weaving **b :** yarn used for the weft
**2 :** WEB, FABRIC; *also* **:** an article of woven fabric
**weft knit** *noun* (1943)
**:** a knit fabric produced in machine or hand knitting with the yarns running crosswise or in a circle — compare WARP KNIT
— **weft-knit·ted** \-ˌni-təd\ *adjective*
— **weft knit·ting** *noun*
**wei·ge·la** \wī-ˈjē-lə\ *noun* [New Latin, from Christian E. *Weigel* (died 1831) German physician] (1846)
**:** any of a genus (*Weigela*) of showy shrubs of the honeysuckle family; *especially* **:** one (*W. florida*) of China widely grown for its usually pink or red flowers
**¹weigh** \'wā\ *verb* [Middle English *weyen,* from Old English *wegan* to move, carry, weigh — more at WAY] (before 12th century)
*transitive verb*
**1 :** to ascertain the heaviness of by or as if by a balance
**2 a :** OUTWEIGH **b :** COUNTERBALANCE **c :** to make heavy **:** WEIGHT — often used with *down*
**3 :** to consider carefully especially by balancing opposing factors or aspects in order to reach a choice or conclusion **:** EVALUATE
**4 :** to heave up (an anchor) preparatory to sailing
**5 :** to measure or apportion (a definite quantity) on or as if on a scales
*intransitive verb*
**1 a :** to have a certain heaviness **:** experience a specific force due to gravity **b :** to register a weight (as on a scales) — used with *in* or *out;* compare WEIGH IN
**2 :** to merit consideration as important **:** COUNT ⟨evidence will *weigh* heavily against him⟩
**3 a :** to press down with or as if with a heavy weight **b :** to have a saddening or disheartening effect
**4 :** to weigh anchor
*synonym* see CONSIDER
— **weigh·able** \'wā-ə-bəl\ *adjective*
— **weigh·er** *noun*
**²weigh** *noun* [alteration of *way*] (1777)

**:** WAY — used in the phrase *under weigh*
**weigh down** *transitive verb* (14th century)
**1 :** to cause to bend down **:** OVERBURDEN
**2 :** OPPRESS, DEPRESS
**weigh–in** \'wā-ˌin\ *noun* (1939)
**:** an act or instance of weighing in as a contestant especially in sport
**weigh in** *intransitive verb* (1868)
**1 :** to have oneself or one's possessions (as baggage) weighed; *especially* **:** to have oneself weighed in connection with an athletic contest
**2 :** to enter as a participant
**¹weight** \'wāt\ *noun* [Middle English *wight, weght,* from Old English *wiht;* akin to Old Norse *vætt* weight, Old English *wegan* to weigh] (before 12th century)
**1 a :** the amount that a thing weighs **b** (1) **:** the standard or established amount that a thing should weigh (2) **:** one of the classes into which contestants in a sports event are divided according to body weight (3) **:** poundage required to be carried by a horse in a handicap race
**2 a :** a quantity or thing weighing a fixed and usually specified amount **b :** a heavy object (as a metal ball) thrown, put, or lifted as an athletic exercise or contest
**3 a :** a unit of weight or mass — see METRIC SYSTEM table **b :** a piece of material (as metal) of known specified weight for use in weighing articles **c :** a system of related units of weight
**4 a :** something heavy **:** LOAD **b :** a heavy object to hold or press something down or to counterbalance
**5 a :** BURDEN, PRESSURE **b :** the quality or state of being ponderous **c :** CORPULENCE
**6 a :** relative heaviness **:** MASS **b :** the force with which a body is attracted toward the earth or a celestial body by gravitation and which is equal to the product of the mass and the local gravitational acceleration
**7 a :** the relative importance or authority accorded something **b :** measurable influence especially on others
**8 :** overpowering force
**9 :** the quality (as lightness) that makes a fabric or garment suitable for a particular use or season — often used in combination ⟨summer-*weight*⟩
**10 :** a numerical coefficient assigned to an item to express its relative importance in a frequency distribution
**11 :** the degree of thickness of the strokes of a type character
*synonym* see IMPORTANCE, INFLUENCE
**²weight** *transitive verb* (1647)
**1 :** to oppress with a burden ⟨*weighted* down with cares⟩
**2 a :** to load or make heavy with or as if with a weight **b :** to increase in heaviness by adding an ingredient
**3 a :** WEIGH 1 **b :** to feel the weight of **:** HEFT
**4 :** to assign a statistical weight to
**5 :** to cause to incline in a particular direction by manipulation ⟨the tax structure . . . which was *weighted* so heavily in favor of the upper classes —A. S. Link⟩
**6 :** to shift the burden of weight upon ⟨*weight* the inside ski⟩
**weight·ed** *adjective* (circa 1732)
**1 :** made heavy **:** LOADED ⟨*weighted* silk⟩
**2 a :** having a statistical weight attached ⟨a *weighted* test score⟩ **b :** compiled or calculated from weighted data ⟨a *weighted* mean⟩
**3 :** INCLINED 1
**weight·less** \'wāt-ləs\ *adjective* (circa 1547)
**:** having little weight **:** lacking apparent gravitational pull
— **weight·less·ly** *adverb*
— **weight·less·ness** *noun*
**weight lifter** *noun* (1897)
**:** one that lifts barbells in competition or as an exercise
— **weight lifting** *noun*
**weight man** *noun* (circa 1949)

# WEIGHTS AND MEASURES[1]

| UNIT | ABBREVIATION OR SYMBOL | EQUIVALENTS IN OTHER UNITS OF SAME SYSTEM | METRIC EQUIVALENT |
|---|---|---|---|
| **WEIGHT** | | | |
| *Avoirdupois[2]* | | | |
| ton | | | |
|  short ton | | 20 short hundredweight, 2000 pounds | 0.907 metric ton |
|  long ton | | 20 long hundredweight, 2240 pounds | 1.016 metric tons |
| hundredweight | cwt | | |
|  short hundredweight | | 100 pounds, 0.05 short ton | 45.359 kilograms |
|  long hundredweight | | 112 pounds, 0.05 long ton | 50.802 kilograms |
| pound | lb or lb avdp *also* # | 16 ounces, 7000 grains | 0.454 kilogram |
| ounce | oz or oz avdp | 16 drams, 437.5 grains, 0.0625 pound | 28.350 grams |
| dram | dr or dr avdp | 27.344 grains, 0.0625 ounce | 1.772 grams |
| grain | gr | 0.037 dram, 0.002286 ounce | 0.0648 gram |
| *Troy* | | | |
| pound | lb t | 12 ounces, 240 pennyweight, 5760 grains | 0.373 kilogram |
| ounce | oz t | 20 pennyweight, 480 grains, 0.083 pound | 31.103 grams |
| pennyweight | dwt *also* pwt | 24 grains, 0.05 ounce | 1.555 grams |
| grain | gr | 0.042 pennyweight, 0.002083 ounce | 0.0648 gram |
| *Apothecaries'* | | | |
| pound | lb ap | 12 ounces, 5760 grains | 0.373 kilogram |
| ounce | oz ap or ℥ | 8 drams, 480 grains, 0.083 pound | 31.103 grams |
| dram | dr ap or ʒ | 3 scruples, 60 grains | 3.888 grams |
| scruple | s ap or ℈ | 20 grains, 0.333 dram | 1.296 grams |
| grain | gr | 0.05 scruple, 0.002083 ounce, 0.0166 dram | 0.0648 gram |
| **CAPACITY** | | | |
| *U.S. liquid measure* | | | |
| gallon | gal | 4 quarts (231 cubic inches) | 3.785 liters |
| quart | qt | 2 pints (57.75 cubic inches) | 0.946 liter |
| pint | pt | 4 gills (28.875 cubic inches) | 473.176 milliliters |
| gill | gi | 4 fluid ounces (7.219 cubic inches) | 118.294 milliliters |
| fluid ounce | fl oz or f℥ | 8 fluid drams (1.805 cubic inches) | 29.573 milliliters |
| fluid dram | fl dr or fʒ | 60 minims (0.226 cubic inch) | 3.697 milliliters |
| minim | min or ℳ | 1/60 fluid dram (0.003760 cubic inch) | 0.061610 milliliter |
| *U.S. dry measure* | | | |
| bushel | bu | 4 pecks (2150.42 cubic inches) | 35.239 liters |
| peck | pk | 8 quarts (537.605 cubic inches) | 8.810 liters |
| quart | qt | 2 pints (67.201 cubic inches) | 1.101 liters |
| pint | pt | 1/2 quart (33.600 cubic inches) | 0.551 liter |
| *British imperial liquid and dry measure* | | | |
| bushel | bu | 4 pecks (2219.36 cubic inches) | 36.369 liters |
| peck | pk | 2 gallons (554.84 cubic inches) | 9.092 liters |
| gallon | gal | 4 quarts (277.420 cubic inches) | 4.546 liters |
| quart | qt | 2 pints (69.355 cubic inches) | 1.136 liters |
| pint | pt | 4 gills (34.678 cubic inches) | 568.26 milliliters |
| gill | gi | 5 fluid ounces (8.669 cubic inches) | 142.066 milliliters |
| fluid ounce | fl oz or f℥ | 8 fluid drams (1.7339 cubic inches) | 28.412 milliliters |
| fluid dram | fl dr or fʒ | 60 minims (0.216734 cubic inch) | 3.5516 milliliters |
| minim | min or ℳ | 1/60 fluid dram (0.003612 cubic inch) | 0.059194 milliliter |
| **LENGTH** | | | |
| mile | mi | 5280 feet, 1760 yards, 320 rods | 1.609 kilometers |
| rod | rd | 5.50 yards, 16.5 feet | 5.029 meters |
| yard | yd | 3 feet, 36 inches | 0.9144 meter |
| foot | ft or ' | 12 inches, 0.333 yard | 30.48 centimeters |
| inch | in or " | 0.083 foot, 0.028 yard | 2.54 centimeters |
| **AREA** | | | |
| square mile | sq mi or mi² | 640 acres, 102,400 square rods | 2.590 square kilometers |
| acre | | 4840 square yards, 43,560 square feet | 0.405 hectare, 4047 square meters |
| square rod | sq rd or rd² | 30.25 square yards, 0.00625 acre | 25.293 square meters |
| square yard | sq yd or yd² | 1296 square inches, 9 square feet | 0.836 square meter |
| square foot | sq ft or ft² | 144 square inches, 0.111 square yard | 0.093 square meter |
| square inch | sq in or in² | 0.0069 square foot, 0.00077 square yard | 6.452 square centimeters |
| **VOLUME** | | | |
| cubic yard | cu yd or yd³ | 27 cubic feet, 46,656 cubic inches | 0.765 cubic meter |
| cubic foot | cu ft or ft³ | 1728 cubic inches, 0.0370 cubic yard | 0.028 cubic meter |
| cubic inch | cu in or in³ | 0.00058 cubic foot, 0.000021 cubic yard | 16.387 cubic centimeters |

[1]For U.S. equivalents of the metric units see Metric System table.

[2]The U.S. uses the avoirdupois units as the common system of measuring weight.

: an athlete who competes in any of the field events in which a weight is thrown or put

**weight room** *noun* (1973)
: a room containing equipment for weight training

**weight training** *noun* (1955)
: a system of conditioning involving lifting weights especially for strength and endurance

**weighty** \'wā-tē\ *adjective* **weight·i·er; -est** (15th century)
**1 a :** of much importance or consequence : MOMENTOUS **b :** SOLEMN
**2 a :** weighing a considerable amount **b :** heavy in proportion to its bulk ⟨*weighty* metal⟩
**3 :** POWERFUL, TELLING ⟨*weighty* arguments⟩
**synonym** see HEAVY
— **weight·i·ly** \'wā-t³l-ē\ *adverb*
— **weight·i·ness** \'wā-tē-nəs\ *noun*

**wei·ma·ra·ner** \,vī-mə-'rä-nər, ,wī-; 'vī-mə-, 'wī-\ *noun* [German, from *Weimar*, Germany] (1943)
: any of a breed of large light gray usually short-haired pointers of German origin

**wei·ner** *variant of* WIENER

**weir** \'war, 'wer, 'wir\ *noun* [Middle English *were*, from Old English *wer*; akin to Old Norse *ver* fishing place, Old High German *we-rien, werren* to defend] (before 12th century)
**1 :** a fence or enclosure set in a waterway for taking fish
**2 :** a dam in a stream or river to raise the water level or divert its flow

**¹weird** \'wird\ *noun* [Middle English *wird, werd*, from Old English *wyrd*; akin to Old Norse *urthr* fate, Old English *weorthan* to become — more at WORTH] (before 12th century)
**1 :** FATE, DESTINY; *especially* : ill fortune
**2 :** SOOTHSAYER ◆

**²weird** *adjective* (15th century)
**1 :** of, relating to, or caused by witchcraft or the supernatural : MAGICAL
**2 :** of strange or extraordinary character : ODD, FANTASTIC ☆
— **weird·ly** *adverb*
— **weird·ness** *noun*

**weird·ie** \'wir-dē\ *or* **weirdy** *noun, plural* **weird·ies** (1894)
: WEIRDO

**weirdo** \'wir-(,)dō\ *noun, plural* **weird·os** (circa 1955)
: a person who is extraordinarily strange or eccentric

**Weird Sisters** *noun plural*
: FATES

**wei·sen·hei·mer** *variant of* WISENHEIMER

**weka** \'we-kə\ *noun* [Maori] (1845)
: a flightless New Zealand rail (*Gallirallus australis*)

**welch** \'welch\ *variant of* WELSH
**Welch** \'welch\ *variant of* WELSH

**¹wel·come** \'wel-kəm\ *transitive verb* **wel·comed; wel·com·ing** [Middle English, from Old English *welcumian, wylcumian*, from *wilcuma*, noun] (before 12th century)
**1 :** to greet hospitably and with courtesy or cordiality
**2 :** to accept with pleasure the occurrence or presence of ⟨*welcomes* danger⟩
— **wel·com·er** *noun*

**²welcome** *interjection* [Middle English, alteration of *wilcume*, from Old English, from *wilcuma* desirable guest (akin to Old High German *willicomo* desirable guest); akin to Old English *willa*, *will* desire, *cuman* to come — more at WILL, COME] (12th century)
— used to express a greeting to a guest or newcomer upon arrival

**³welcome** *adjective* (12th century)
**1 :** received gladly into one's presence or companionship ⟨was always *welcome* in their home⟩
**2 :** giving pleasure : received with gladness or delight especially in response to a need ⟨a *welcome* relief⟩

**3 :** willingly permitted or admitted ⟨he was *welcome* to come and go —W. M. Thackeray⟩
**4 :** — used in the phrase "You're welcome" as a reply to an expression of thanks
— **wel·come·ly** *adverb*
— **wel·come·ness** *noun*

**⁴welcome** *noun* (1525)
**1 :** a greeting or reception usually upon arrival
**2 :** the state of being welcome ⟨overstayed their *welcome*⟩

**welcome mat** *noun* (1946)
: something likened to a mat placed before an entrance as a sign of welcome

**¹weld** \'weld\ *verb* [alteration of obsolete English *well* to weld, from Middle English *wellen* to boil, well, weld — more at WELL] (1599)
*intransitive verb*
: to become or be capable of being welded
*transitive verb*
**1 a :** to unite (metallic parts) by heating and allowing the metals to flow together or by hammering or compressing with or without previous heating **b :** to unite (plastics) in a similar manner by heating **c :** to repair (as an article) by this method **d :** to produce or create as if by such a process
**2 :** to unite or reunite closely or intimately
— **weld·able** \'wel-də-bəl\ *adjective*

**²weld** *noun* (1831)
**1 :** a welded joint
**2 :** union by welding : the state or condition of being welded

**weld·er** \'wel-dər\ *noun* (circa 1828)
: one that welds: as **a** *or* **wel·dor :** one whose work is welding **b :** a machine used in welding

**weld·ment** \'wel(d)-mənt\ *noun* (1941)
: a unit formed by welding together an assembly of pieces

**¹wel·fare** \'wel-,far, -,fer\ *noun* [Middle English, from the phrase *wel faren* to fare well] (14th century)
**1 :** the state of doing well especially in respect to good fortune, happiness, well-being, or prosperity
**2 a :** aid in the form of money or necessities for those in need **b :** an agency or program through which such aid is distributed

**²welfare** *adjective* (1904)
**1 :** of, relating to, or concerned with welfare and especially with improvement of the welfare of disadvantaged social groups ⟨*welfare* legislation⟩
**2 :** receiving public welfare benefits ⟨*welfare* families⟩

**welfare state** *noun* (1941)
**1 :** a social system based on the assumption by a political state of primary responsibility for the individual and social welfare of its citizens
**2 :** a nation or state characterized by the operation of the welfare state system

**wel·far·ism** \'wel-,far-,i-zəm, -,fer-\ *noun* (1949)
: the complex of policies, attitudes, and beliefs associated with the welfare state
— **wel·far·ist** \-ist\ *noun or adjective*

**wel·kin** \'wel-kən\ *noun* [Middle English, literally, cloud, from Old English *wolcen*; akin to Old High German *wolkan* cloud] (12th century)
**1 a :** the vault of the sky : FIRMAMENT **b :** the celestial abode of God or the gods : HEAVEN
**2 :** the upper atmosphere

**¹well** \'wel\ *noun* [Middle English *welle*, from Old English *welle*; akin to Old English *weallan* to bubble, boil, Old High German *wella* wave, Lithuanian *vilnis*] (before 12th century)
**1 a :** an issue of water from the earth : a pool fed by a spring **b :** SOURCE, ORIGIN
**2 a :** a pit or hole sunk into the earth to reach a supply of water **b :** a shaft or hole sunk to obtain oil, brine, or gas
**3 a :** an enclosure in the middle of a ship's hold to protect from damage and facilitate the

inspection of the pumps **b :** a compartment in the hold of a fishing boat in which fish are kept alive
**4 :** an open space extending vertically through floors of a structure
**5 :** a space having a construction or shape suggesting a well for water
**6 a :** something resembling a well in being damp, cool, deep, or dark **b :** a deep vertical hole **c :** a source from which something may be drawn as needed
**7 :** a pronounced minimum of a variable in physics ⟨a potential *well*⟩

**²well** [Middle English, from Old English *wellan* to cause to well; akin to Old English *weallan* to bubble, boil] (before 12th century)
*intransitive verb*
**1 :** to rise to the surface and usually flow forth ⟨tears *welled* from her eyes⟩
**2 :** to rise like a flood of liquid ⟨longing *welled* up in his breast⟩
*transitive verb*
: to emit in a copious free flow

**³well** *adverb* **bet·ter** \'be-tər\; **best** \'best\ [Middle English *wel*, from Old English; akin to Old High German *wela* well, Old English *wyllan* to wish — more at WILL] (before 12th century)
**1 a :** in a good or proper manner : JUSTLY, RIGHTLY **b :** satisfactorily with respect to conduct or action ⟨did *well* in math⟩
**2 :** in a kindly or friendly manner ⟨spoke *well* of your idea⟩
**3 a :** with skill or aptitude : EXPERTLY ⟨paints *well*⟩ **b :** SATISFACTORILY **c :** with good appearance or effect : ELEGANTLY ⟨carried himself *well*⟩
**4 :** with careful or close attention : ATTENTIVELY
**5 :** to a high degree ⟨*well* deserved the honor⟩ ⟨a *well*-equipped kitchen⟩ — often used as an intensifier or qualifier ⟨there are . . . vacancies pretty *well* all the time —*Listener*⟩
**6 :** FULLY, QUITE ⟨*well* worth the price⟩

---

☆ **SYNONYMS**
**Weird, eerie, uncanny** mean mysteriously strange or fantastic. WEIRD may imply an unearthly or supernatural strangeness or it may stress queerness or oddness ⟨*weird* creatures from another world⟩. EERIE suggests an uneasy or fearful consciousness that mysterious and malign powers are at work ⟨an *eerie* calm preceded the bombing raid⟩. UNCANNY implies disquieting strangeness or mysteriousness ⟨an *uncanny* resemblance between total strangers⟩.

---

◇ **WORD HISTORY**
**weird** *Weird* is a northern English and Scots outcome of Old English *wyrd*, the Anglo-Saxons' name for the unpredictable and uncontrollable force determining the outcome of human events that in Modern English we call *fate*. As early as the late 8th century, *wyrde*, the plural of *wyrd*, served as an Old English gloss for *Parcae*, the Latin name for the Fates, three goddesses who spun, measured, and cut the thread of life. In the 15th and 16th centuries Scots authors employed *werd* or *weird* attributively in the phrase *weird sisters* to refer to the Fates of classical myth. Shakespeare adopted this usage in his tragedy *Macbeth*, in which the *weird sisters* are depicted not in their ancient guise but rather as three witches. Subsequent adjectival use of *weird* to mean "unearthly," "mysterious," or "odd" has grown out of a reinterpretation of *weird* in the Shakespearean phrase, most notably by the Romantic poets Shelley and Keats in the early 19th century.

**7 a :** in a way appropriate to the facts or circumstances **:** FITTINGLY, RIGHTLY **b :** in a prudent manner **:** SENSIBLY — used with *do*
**8 :** in accordance with the occasion or circumstances **:** with propriety or good reason ⟨cannot *well* refuse⟩
**9 a :** as one could wish **:** FAVORABLY **b :** with material success **:** ADVANTAGEOUSLY ⟨married *well*⟩
**10 a :** EASILY, READILY ⟨could *well* afford a new car⟩ **b :** in all likelihood **:** INDEED ⟨it may *well* be true⟩
**11 :** in a prosperous or affluent manner ⟨he lives *well*⟩
**12 :** to an extent approaching completeness **:** THOROUGHLY ⟨after being *well* dried with a sponge⟩
**13 :** without doubt or question **:** CLEARLY ⟨*well* knew the penalty⟩
**14 :** in a familiar manner ⟨knew her *well*⟩
**15 :** to a large extent or degree **:** CONSIDERABLY, FAR ⟨*well* over a million⟩
*usage* see GOOD
— **as well 1 :** in addition **:** ALSO ⟨there were other features *as well*⟩ **2 :** to the same extent or degree **:** as much ⟨open *as well* to the poor as to the rich⟩ **3 :** with equivalent, comparable, or more favorable effect ⟨might just *as well* have stayed home⟩
**⁴well** *interjection* (before 12th century)
**1** — used to indicate resumption of discourse or to introduce a remark
**2** — used to express surprise or expostulation
**⁵well** *adjective* (before 12th century)
**1 a :** PROSPEROUS, WELL-OFF **b :** being in satisfactory condition or circumstances
**2 :** being in good standing or favor
**3 :** SATISFACTORY, PLEASING ⟨all's *well* that ends well⟩
**4 :** ADVISABLE, DESIRABLE ⟨it might be *well* for you to leave⟩
**5 a :** free or recovered from infirmity or disease **:** HEALTHY ⟨a *well* man⟩ **b :** completely cured or healed ⟨the wound is nearly *well*⟩
**6 :** pleasing or satisfactory in appearance
**7 :** being a cause for thankfulness **:** FORTUNATE ⟨it is *well* that this has happened⟩
*synonym* see HEALTHY
*usage* see GOOD
**we'll** \'wē(ə)l, wil\ (1578)
**:** we will **:** we shall
**well-ad·just·ed** \,wel-ə-'jəs-təd\ *adjective* (1692)
**:** WELL-BALANCED 2
**well-ad·vised** \'wel-əd-'vīzd\ *adjective* (14th century)
**1 :** acting with wisdom, wise counsel, or proper deliberation **:** PRUDENT
**2 :** resulting from, based on, or showing careful deliberation or wise counsel ⟨*well-advised* plans⟩
**well-ap·point·ed** \'wel-ə-'pȯin-təd\ *adjective* (1530)
**:** having good and complete equipment **:** properly fitted out ⟨a *well-appointed* house⟩
**wel·la·way** \,we-lə-'wā, 'we-lə-,\ *interjection* [Middle English *welaway,* from Old English *weilāwei,* literally, woe! lo! woe!, alteration of *wālāwā,* from *wā* woe + *lā* lo + *wā* woe — more at WOE] (before 12th century)
*archaic* — used to express sorrow or lamentation
**well-bal·anced** \'wel-'ba-lən(t)st\ *adjective* (1629)
**1 :** nicely or evenly balanced, arranged, or regulated ⟨a *well-balanced* diet⟩ ⟨a *well-balanced* attack in football⟩
**2 :** emotionally or psychologically untroubled
**well-be·ing** \'wel-'bē-iŋ\ *noun* (circa 1613)
**:** the state of being happy, healthy, or prosperous **:** WELFARE
**well-be·loved** \,wel-bi-'ləvd\ *adjective* (14th century)
**1 :** sincerely and deeply loved ⟨my *well-beloved* wife⟩

**2 :** sincerely respected — used in various ceremonial forms of address
**well-born** \'wel-'bȯrn\ *adjective* (before 12th century)
**:** born of noble or wealthy lineage
**well-bred** \-'bred\ *adjective* (1597)
**1 :** having or displaying good breeding **:** REFINED
**2 :** having a good pedigree ⟨*well-bred* swine⟩
**well-con·di·tioned** \,wel-kən-'di-shənd\ *adjective* (15th century)
**1 :** characterized by proper disposition, morals, or behavior
**2 :** having a good physical condition **:** SOUND
**well deck** *noun* (1888)
**:** a space on the weather deck of a ship lying at a lower level between a raised forecastle or poop and the bridge superstructure
**well-de·fined** \,wel-di-'fīnd\ *adjective* (1704)
**1 :** having clearly distinguishable limits, boundaries, or features ⟨a *well-defined* scar⟩
**2 :** clearly stated or described ⟨*well-defined* policies⟩
**well-dis·posed** \-dis-'pōzd\ *adjective* (14th century)
**:** having a good disposition; *especially* **:** disposed to be friendly, favorable, or sympathetic
**well-done** \'wel-'dən\ *adjective* (15th century)
**1 :** rightly or properly performed
**2 :** cooked thoroughly
**Wel·ler·ism** \'we-lə-,ri-zəm\ *noun* [Sam *Weller,* witty servant of Mr. Pickwick in the story *Pickwick Papers* (1836–37) by Charles Dickens] (1839)
**:** an expression of comparison comprising a usually well-known quotation followed by a facetious sequel (as "'every one to his own taste,' said the old woman as she kissed the cow")
**well-fa·vored** \'wel-'fā-vərd\ *adjective* (15th century)
**:** GOOD-LOOKING, HANDSOME
— **well-fa·vored·ness** *noun*
**well-fixed** \-'fikst\ *adjective* (1822)
**:** having plenty of money or property
**well-found** \-'faund\ *adjective* (1793)
**:** fully furnished **:** properly equipped ⟨a *well-found* ship⟩
**well-found·ed** \-'faun-dəd\ *adjective* (14th century)
**:** based on excellent reasoning, information, judgment, or grounds
**well-groomed** \-'grümd, -'grumd\ *adjective* (1886)
**1 :** well-dressed and scrupulously neat ⟨*well-groomed* men⟩
**2 :** made neat, tidy, and attractive down to the smallest details ⟨a *well-groomed* lawn⟩
**well-ground·ed** \-'graun-dəd\ *adjective* (14th century)
**1 :** having a firm foundation ⟨*well-grounded* in Latin and Greek⟩
**2 :** WELL-FOUNDED
**well-han·dled** \-'han-dᵊld\ *adjective* (15th century)
**1 :** managed or administered efficiently
**2 :** having been handled a great deal ⟨*well-handled* goods for sale⟩
**well·head** \'wel-,hed\ *noun* (14th century)
**1 :** the source of a spring or a stream
**2 :** principal source **:** FOUNTAINHEAD
**3 :** the top of or a structure built over a well
**wellhead price** *noun* (1953)
**:** the price less transportation costs charged by the producer for petroleum or natural gas
**well-heeled** \-'hē(ə)ld\ *adjective* (1897)
**:** having plenty of money **:** WELL-FIXED
**wel·lie** *or* **wel·ly** \'we-lē\ *noun, plural* **wel·lies** [by shortening & alteration] (1961)
*chiefly British* **:** WELLINGTON — usually used in plural
**well-in·formed** \-in-'fȯrmd\ *adjective* (15th century)
**1 :** having extensive knowledge especially of current topics and events

**2 :** thoroughly knowledgeable in a particular subject
**Wel·ling·ton** \'we-liŋ-tən\ *noun* [Arthur Wellesley, 1st Duke of *Wellington*] (1817)
**:** a boot having a loose top with the front usually coming to or above the knee — usually used in plural
**well-in·ten·tioned** \,wel-in-'ten(t)-shənd\ *adjective* (1598)
**:** WELL-MEANING
**well-knit** \'wel-'nit\ *adjective* (15th century)
**:** firmly knit ⟨a *well-knit* group⟩; *especially* **:** firmly and strongly constructed, compacted, or framed ⟨a *well-knit* drama⟩
**well-known** \-'nōn\ *adjective* (15th century)
**:** fully or widely known
**well-mean·ing** \-'mē-niŋ\ *adjective* (1532)
**1 :** having good intentions ⟨*well-meaning* but misguided idealists⟩
**2 :** based on good intentions ⟨*well-meaning* advice⟩
**well-meant** \-'ment\ *adjective* (15th century)
**:** WELL-MEANING 2
**well·ness** \'wel-nəs\ *noun* (1654)
**:** the quality or state of being in good health especially as an actively sought goal ⟨*wellness* clinics⟩ ⟨lifestyles that promote *wellness*⟩
**well-nigh** \-'nī\ *adverb* (12th century)
**:** ALMOST, NEARLY ⟨*well-nigh* impossible⟩
**well-off** \-'ȯf\ *adjective* (1733)
**1 :** being in good condition or favorable circumstances ⟨doesn't know when he's *well-off*⟩
**2 :** having no lack — usually used with *for*
**3 a :** being in easy or affluent circumstances **:** WELL-TO-DO **b :** suggesting prosperity ⟨the house had a sleek *well-off* look⟩
**well-oiled** \-'ȯild\ *adjective* (1847)
**:** smoothly functioning ⟨a *well-oiled* political machine⟩
**well-or·dered** \-'ȯr-dərd\ *adjective* (1589)
**1 :** having an orderly procedure or arrangement ⟨a *well-ordered* household⟩
**2 :** partially ordered with every subset containing a first element and exactly one of the relationships "greater than", "less than", or "equal to" holding for any given pair of elements
— **well-or·der·ing** \-'ȯrd-riŋ, -'ȯr-də-\ *noun*
**well-read** \-'red\ *adjective* (1596)
**:** well informed or deeply versed through reading ⟨*well-read* in history⟩
**well-round·ed** \-'raun-dəd\ *adjective* (1875)
**:** fully or broadly developed: as **a :** having a broad educational background ⟨schools that turn out *well-rounded* graduates⟩ **b :** COMPREHENSIVE ⟨a *well-rounded* program of activities⟩
**well-set** \-'set\ *adjective* (14th century)
**1 :** well or firmly established ⟨*well-set* in his own values —William Johnson⟩
**2 :** strongly built ⟨a *well-set* athlete⟩
**well-spo·ken** \'wel-'spō-kən\ *adjective* (15th century)
**1 :** speaking well, fitly, or courteously
**2 :** spoken with propriety ⟨*well-spoken* words⟩
**well·spring** \-,spriŋ\ *noun* (before 12th century)
**:** a source of continual supply ⟨a *wellspring* of information⟩
**well-tak·en** \-'tā-kən\ *adjective* (1761)
**:** WELL-GROUNDED, JUSTIFIABLE ⟨your point is *well-taken*⟩
**well-thought-of** \wel-'thȯt-,əv, -,äv\ *adjective* (1579)
**:** being of good repute
**well-timed** \'wel-'tīmd\ *adjective* (circa 1656)
**:** happening at an opportune moment **:** TIMELY ⟨a *well-timed* announcement⟩
**well-to-do** \,wel-tə-'dü\ *adjective* (1825)

\ə\ abut  \ᵊ\ kitten  \ər\ further  \a\ ash  \ā\ ace
\ä\ mop, mar  \au̇\ out  \ch\ chin  \e\ bet  \ē\ easy
\g\ go  \i\ hit  \ī\ ice  \j\ job  \ŋ\ sing  \ō\ go
\ȯ\ law  \ȯi\ boy  \th\ thin  \t͟h\ the  \ü\ loot  \u̇\ foot
\y\ yet  \zh\ vision  *see also* Guide to Pronunciation

: having more than adequate financial resources : PROSPEROUS ⟨a *well-to-do* family⟩

**well–turned** \'wel-'tərnd\ *adjective* (1616)
**1** : symmetrically shaped or rounded : SHAPELY
**2** : concisely and appropriately expressed ⟨a *well-turned* phrase⟩
**3** : expertly rounded or turned ⟨a *well-turned* column⟩

**well–wish·er** \'wel-,wi-shər, -'wi-\ *noun* (1590)
: one that wishes well to another
— **well–wish·ing** \-shiŋ\ *adjective or noun*

**well–worn** \-'wōrn, -'wòrn\ *adjective* (1621)
**1 a** : made trite by overuse : HACKNEYED ⟨a *well-worn* quotation⟩ **b** : having been much used or worn ⟨*well-worn* shoes⟩
**2** *archaic* : worn well or properly

**welsh** \'welsh, 'welch\ *intransitive verb* [probably from *Welsh*, adjective] (1905)
**1** : to avoid payment — used with *on* ⟨*welshed* on his debts⟩
**2** : to break one's word : RENEGE ⟨*welshed* on their promises⟩
— **welsh·er** *noun*

**Welsh** \'welsh *also* 'welch\ *noun* [Middle English *Walsche, Welsse,* from *walisch, welisch,* adjective, Welsh, from Old English *wælisc, welisc* Celtic, Welsh, foreign, from Old English *Wealh* Celtic, Welshman, foreigner, of Celtic origin; akin to the source of Latin *Volcae,* a Celtic people of southeastern Gaul] (before 12th century)
**1** : the Celtic language of the Welsh people
**2** *plural in construction* : the natives or inhabitants of Wales
**3** : WELSH PONY
— **Welsh** *adjective*

**Welsh black** *noun* (1919)
: any of a breed of hardy medium-sized thick-haired horned black cattle of Welsh origin that are raised for meat and milk

**Welsh cob** *noun* (1947)
: any of a breed of medium-sized cobby horses that were developed by interbreeding Welsh mountain ponies with larger horses

**Welsh corgi** *noun* (1926)
: a short-legged long-backed dog with foxy head of either of two breeds of Welsh origin: **a** : CARDIGAN WELSH CORGI **b** : PEMBROKE WELSH CORGI

**Welsh·man** \-mən\ *noun* (13th century)
: a native or inhabitant of Wales

**Welsh mountain pony** *noun* (1947)
: any of a breed of small sturdy ponies native to the mountains of Wales that do not exceed 12.2 hands (124 centimeters) in height

Welsh corgi: 1 Pembroke, 2 Cardigan

**Welsh pony** *noun* (1771)
: a pony of any of several breeds of Welsh origin; *especially* : any of a breed of riding and light draft ponies measuring 12.2 to 13.2 hands (124 to 134 centimeters) in height

**Welsh rabbit** *noun* (1725)
: melted often seasoned cheese poured over toast or crackers

**Welsh rare·bit** \-'rar-bət, -'rer-\ *noun* [by alteration] (1785)
: WELSH RABBIT

**Welsh springer spaniel** *noun* (circa 1929)
: any of a breed of red and white or orange and white small-eared springer spaniels of Welsh origin

**Welsh terrier** *noun* (1885)
: any of a breed of wiry-coated terriers resembling Airedales but smaller and developed in Wales for hunting

**Welsh·wom·an** \'welsh-,wu̇-mən *also* 'welch-\ *noun* (15th century)
: a woman who is a native or inhabitant of Wales

**¹welt** \'welt\ *noun* [Middle English *welte*] (15th century)
**1** : a strip between a shoe sole and upper through which they are stitched or stapled together
**2** : a doubled edge, strip, insert, or seam (as on a garment) for ornament or reinforcement
**3 a** : a ridge or lump raised on the body usually by a blow **b** : a heavy blow

**²welt** *transitive verb* (15th century)
**1** : to furnish with a welt
**2 a** : to raise a welt on the body of **b** : to hit hard

**welt·an·schau·ung** \'velt-,än-,shau̇-əŋ\ *noun, plural* **weltanschauungs** \-əŋz\ *or* **welt·an·schau·ung·en** \-əŋ-ən\ *often capitalized* [German, from *Welt* world + *Anschauung* view] (1868)
: a comprehensive conception or apprehension of the world especially from a specific standpoint

**¹wel·ter** \'wel-tər\ *intransitive verb* **wel·tered; wel·ter·ing** \-t(ə-)riŋ\ [Middle English; akin to Middle Dutch *welteren* to roll, Old High German *walzan,* Lithuanian *volioti,* Latin *volvere* — more at VOLUBLE] (14th century)
**1 a** : WRITHE, TOSS; *also* : WALLOW **b** : to rise and fall or toss about in or with waves
**2** : to become deeply sunk, soaked, or involved
**3** : to be in turmoil

**²welter** *noun* (1596)
**1** : a state of wild disorder : TURMOIL
**2** : a chaotic mass or jumble ⟨a bewildering *welter* of data⟩

**³welter** *noun* (1900)
: WELTERWEIGHT

**wel·ter·weight** \'wel-tər-,wāt\ *noun* [*welter* (probably from ¹*welt*) + *weight*] (circa 1892)
: a boxer in a weight division having a maximum limit of 147 pounds — compare LIGHTWEIGHT, MIDDLEWEIGHT

**welt·schmerz** \'velt-,shmerts\ *noun, often capitalized* [German, from *Welt* world + *Schmerz* pain] (1875)
**1** : mental depression or apathy caused by comparison of the actual state of the world with an ideal state
**2** : a mood of sentimental sadness

**¹wen** \'wen\ *noun* [Middle English *wenn,* from Old English; akin to Middle Low German *wene* wen] (before 12th century)
: an abnormal growth or a cyst protruding from a surface especially of the skin

**²wen** *variant of* WYNN

**¹wench** \'wench\ *noun* [Middle English *wenche,* short for *wenchel* child, from Old English *wencel;* akin to Old High German *wankōn* to totter, waver and probably to Old High German *winchan* to stagger — more at WINK] (14th century)
**1 a** : a young woman : GIRL **b** : a female servant
**2** : a lewd woman : PROSTITUTE

**²wench** *intransitive verb* (1599)
: to consort with lewd women; *especially* : to practice fornication
— **wench·er** *noun*

**wend** \'wend\ *verb* [Middle English, from Old English *wendan;* akin to Old High German *wenten* to turn, Old English *windan* to twist — more at WIND] (before 12th century)
*intransitive verb*
: to direct one's course : TRAVEL
*transitive verb*
: to proceed on (one's way) : DIRECT

**Wend** \'wend\ *noun* [German *Wende,* from Old High German *Winida;* akin to Old English *Winedas,* plural, Wends] (1786)
: a member of a Slavic people of eastern Germany

**¹Wend·ish** \'wen-dish\ *adjective* (1614)
: of or relating to the Wends or their language

**²Wendish** *noun* (1617)
: the West Slavic language of the Wends

**went** [Middle English, past & past participle of *wenden* to wend] *past of* GO

**wen·tle·trap** \'wen-t°l-,trap\ *noun* [Dutch *wenteltrap* winding stair, from Middle Dutch *wendeltrappe,* from *wendel* turning + *trappe* stairs] (1758)
: any of a family (Epitoniidae) of marine snails with usually white shells; *also* : one of the shells

**wept** *past and past participle of* WEEP

**were** [Middle English *were* (suppletive singular past subjunctive & 2d singular past indicative of *been* to be), *weren* (suppletive past plural of *been*), from Old English *wǣre* (singular past subjunctive & 2d singular past indicative of *wesan* to be), *wǣron* (past plural indicative of *wesan*), *wǣren* (past plural subjunctive of *wesan*) — more at WAS] *past 2d singular, past plural, or past subjunctive of* BE

**we're** \'wir, 'wər, 'wē-ər\ (1608)
: we are

**weren't** \(')wərnt, 'wər-ənt\ (1865)
: were not

**were·wolf** \'wir-,wu̇lf, 'wer-, 'wər-\ *noun, plural* **were·wolves** \-,wu̇lvz\ [Middle English, from Old English *werwulf* (akin to Old High German *werwolf* werewolf), from *wer* man + *wulf* wolf — more at VIRILE, WOLF] (before 12th century)
: a person transformed into a wolf or capable of assuming a wolf's form

**wer·gild** \'wər-,gild\ *or* **wer·geld** \-,geld\ *noun* [Middle English *wergeld,* from Old English, from *wer* man + *-geld,* alteration of *gield, geld* payment, tribute — more at GELD] (13th century)
: the value set in Anglo-Saxon and Germanic law upon human life in accordance with rank and paid as compensation to the kindred or lord of a slain person

**wert** \'wərt\ *archaic past 2d singular of* BE

**wes·kit** \'wes-kət\ *noun* [alteration of *waistcoat*] (1856)
: VEST 2a

**Wes·ley·an·ism** \'wes-lē-ə-,ni-zəm *also* 'wez-\ *noun* (1774)
: METHODISM 1; *specifically* : the system of Arminian Methodism taught by John Wesley
— **Wes·ley·an** \-lē-ən\ *adjective or noun*

**¹west** \'west\ *adverb* [Middle English, from Old English; akin to Old High German *westar* to the west and probably to Latin *vesper* evening, Greek *hesperos*] (before 12th century)
: to, toward, or in the west

**²west** *adjective* (before 12th century)
**1** : situated toward or at the west ⟨the *west* exit⟩
**2** : coming from the west ⟨a *west* wind⟩

**³west** *noun* (12th century)
**1 a** : the general direction of sunset : the direction to the left of one facing north **b** : the compass point directly opposite to east
**2** *capitalized* **a** : regions or countries lying to the west of a specified or implied point of orientation **b** : the noncommunist countries of Europe and America
**3** : the end of a church opposite the chancel
**4** *often capitalized* **a** : the one of four positions at 90-degree intervals that lies to the west or at the left of a diagram **b** : a person (as a bridge player) occupying this position during a specified activity

**west·bound** \'wes(t)-,bau̇nd\ *adjective* (1881)
: traveling or heading west

**west by north** (1760)
: a compass point that is one point north of due west : N78°45′W

**west by south** (1577)
: a compass point that is one point south of due west : S78°45′W

**west·er** \'wes-tər\ *intransitive verb* **west-ered; west·er·ing** \-t(ə-)riŋ\ [Middle English *westren*, from [1]*west*] (14th century)
: to turn or move westward ⟨the half moon *westers* low —A. E. Housman⟩

[1]**west·er·ly** \'wes-tər-lē\ *adjective or adverb* [obsolete *wester* western] (15th century)
**1** : situated toward or belonging to the west ⟨the *westerly* end of the farm⟩
**2** : coming from the west ⟨a *westerly* breeze⟩

[2]**westerly** *noun, plural* **-lies** (1876)
: a wind from the west

[1]**west·ern** \'wes-tərn\ *adjective* [Middle English *westerne*, from Old English; akin to Old High German *westrōni* western, Old English *west*] (before 12th century)
**1 a** : coming from the west ⟨a *western* storm⟩ **b** : lying toward the west
**2** *capitalized* : of, relating to, or characteristic of a region conventionally designated West: as **a** : steeped in or stemming from the Greco-Roman traditions **b** : of or relating to the non-communist countries of Europe and America **c** : of or relating to the American West
**3** *capitalized* : of or relating to the Roman Catholic or Protestant segment of Christianity ⟨*Western* liturgies⟩
— **west·ern·most** \-,mōst\ *adjective*

[2]**western** *noun* (1612)
**1** : one that is produced in or characteristic of a western region and especially the western U.S.
**2** *often capitalized* : a novel, story, motion picture, or broadcast dealing with life in the western U.S. especially during the latter half of the 19th century

**Western blot** *noun* [after *Southern blot*] (1983)
: a blot that consists of a nitrocellulose sheet containing spots of protein for identification by a suitable molecular probe and is used especially for the detection of antibodies
— **Western blotting** *noun*

**West·ern·er** \'wes-tə(r)-nər\ *noun* (1599)
**1** : a native or inhabitant of the West; *especially* : a native or resident of the western part of the U.S.
**2** : one advocating the adoption of western European culture especially in 19th century Russia

**western hemisphere** *noun, often W&H capitalized* (1624)
: the half of the earth comprising North and South America and surrounding waters

**west·ern·i·sa·tion, west·ern·ise** *British variant of* WESTERNIZATION, WESTERNIZE

**west·ern·i·za·tion** \,wes-tər-nə-'zā-shən\ *noun, often capitalized* (1904)
: conversion to, or adoption of western traditions or techniques

**west·ern·ize** \'wes-tər-,nīz\ *verb* **-ized; -iz·ing** *often capitalized* (1837)
*transitive verb*
: to imbue with qualities native to or associated with a western region and especially the noncommunist countries of Europe and America
*intransitive verb*
: to become westernized

**western omelet** *noun* (1951)
: an omelet made usually with diced ham, green pepper, and onion — called also *Denver omelet*

**western red cedar** *noun* (1886)
: RED CEDAR 2; *also* : its wood

**western saddle** *noun, often W capitalized* (1897)
: a deep-seated saddle with a high pommel and broad skirts and fenders used originally by cattlemen — called also *stock saddle;* see SADDLE illustration

**western sandwich** *noun* (1926)
: a sandwich filled with a western omelet — called also *Denver sandwich*

**western swing** *noun* (1973)
: swing music played typically on country-music instruments (as guitar, fiddle, or steel guitar)

**West Germanic** *noun* (1894)
: a subdivision of the Germanic languages including English, Frisian, Dutch, and German — see INDO-EUROPEAN LANGUAGES table

**West Highland white terrier** *noun* (circa 1904)
: any of a breed of small white long-coated terriers developed in Scotland — called also *West·ie* \'wes-tē\

**west·ing** \'wes-tiŋ\ *noun* (1628)
: westerly progress
: a going westward

**west–northwest** *noun* (15th century)
: a compass point that is two points north of due west : N67°30′W

**West·pha·lian ham** \wes(t)-'fāl-yən-, -'fā-lē-ən-\ *noun* [*Westphalia*, Germany] (1664)
: a ham of distinctive flavor produced by smoking with juniper brush

**West Saxon** *noun* (14th century)
**1** : a member or a descendant of the Saxons who occupied England largely south of the Thames, west of the Downs, and east of Dartmoor
**2** : a dialect of Old English used as the chief literary dialect in England before the Norman Conquest

**west–southwest** *noun* (1555)
: a compass point that is two points south of due west : S67°30′W

[1]**west·ward** \'wes-twərd\ *adverb or adjective* (before 12th century)
: toward the west
— **west·wards** \-twərdz\ *adverb*

[2]**westward** *noun* (1652)
: westward direction or part ⟨sail to the *westward*⟩

[1]**wet** \'wet\ *adjective* **wet·ter; wet·test** [Middle English, partly from past participle of *weten* to wet & partly from Old English *wǣt* wet; akin to Old Norse *vātr* wet, Old English *wǣter* water] (before 12th century)
**1 a** : consisting of, containing, covered with, or soaked with liquid (as water) **b** *of natural gas* : containing appreciable quantities of readily condensable hydrocarbons
**2** : RAINY
**3** : still moist enough to smudge or smear ⟨*wet* paint⟩
**4 a** : DRUNK 1a ⟨a *wet* driver⟩ **b** : having or advocating a policy permitting the manufacture and sale of alcoholic beverages ⟨a *wet* county⟩ ⟨a *wet* candidate⟩
**5** : preserved in liquid
**6** : employing or done by means of or in the presence of water or other liquid ⟨*wet* extraction of copper⟩
**7** : overly sentimental
**8** *British* **a** : lacking strength of character : WEAK, SPINELESS ⟨thought him *wet* and violence petrified him —William Golding⟩ **b** : belonging to the moderate or liberal wing of the Conservative party ☆
— **wet·ly** *adverb*
— **wet·ness** *noun*
— **all wet** : completely wrong : in error
— **wet behind the ears** : IMMATURE, INEXPERIENCED

[2]**wet** *noun* (before 12th century)
**1** : WATER; *also* : MOISTURE, WETNESS
**2** : rainy weather : RAIN
**3** : an advocate of a policy of permitting the sale of intoxicating liquors
**4** *British* : one who is wet

[3]**wet** *verb* **wet** *or* **wet·ted; wet·ting** [Middle English, from Old English *wǣtan*, from *wǣt*, adjective] (before 12th century)
*transitive verb*
**1** : to make wet
**2** : to urinate in or on
*intransitive verb*
**1** : to become wet
**2** : URINATE
— **wet one's whistle** : to take a drink especially of liquor

**wet·back** \'wet-,bak\ *noun* [from the practice of wading or swimming the Rio Grande where it forms the U.S.-Mexico border] (1929)
: a Mexican who enters the U.S. illegally — sometimes taken to be offensive

**wet bar** *noun* (1967)
: a bar for mixing drinks (as in a home) that contains a sink with running water

**wet blanket** *noun* (1857)
: one that quenches or dampens enthusiasm or pleasure

**wet down** *transitive verb* (1840)
: to dampen by sprinkling with water

**wet dream** *noun* (1851)
: an erotic dream culminating in orgasm and in the male accompanied by seminal emission

**weth·er** \'we-thər\ *noun* [Middle English, ram, from Old English; akin to Old High German *widar* ram, Latin *vitulus* calf, *vetus* old, Greek *etos* year] (before 12th century)
: a male sheep castrated before sexual maturity; *also* : a castrated male goat

**wet·land** \'wet-,land, -lənd\ *noun* (1778)
: land or areas (as tidal flats or swamps) containing much soil moisture — usually used in plural

**wet–nurse** *transitive verb* (1784)
**1** : to act as wet nurse to
**2** : to give constant and often excessive care to

**wet nurse** *noun* (1620)
: a woman who cares for and suckles children not her own

**wet suit** *noun* (1955)
: a close-fitting suit made of material (as sponge rubber) that traps a thin layer of water against the body to retain body heat and that is worn (as by a skin diver) especially in cold water

**wet·ta·bil·i·ty** \,we-tə-'bi-lə-tē\ *noun* (1913)
: the quality or state of being wettable : the degree to which something can be wet

**wet·ta·ble** \'we-tə-bəl\ *adjective* (1885)
: capable of being wetted

**wet·ter** \'we-tər\ *noun* (1737)
: one that wets; *also* : WETTING AGENT

**wetting agent** *noun* (1927)

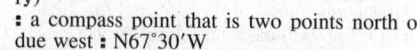
**West Highland white terrier**

---

☆ SYNONYMS
**Wet, damp, dank, moist, humid** mean covered or more or less soaked with liquid. WET usually implies saturation but may suggest a covering of a surface with water or something (as paint) not yet dry ⟨slipped on the *wet* pavement⟩. DAMP implies a slight or moderate absorption and often connotes an unpleasant degree of moisture ⟨clothes will mildew if stored in a *damp* place⟩. DANK implies a more distinctly disagreeable or unwholesome dampness ⟨a prisoner in a cold, *dank* cell⟩. MOIST applies to what is slightly damp or not felt as dry ⟨treat the injury with *moist* heat⟩. HUMID applies to the presence of much water vapor in the air ⟨a hot, *humid* climate⟩.

---

\ə\ abut \ᵊ\ kitten \ər\ further \a\ ash \ā\ ace
\ä\ mop, mar \au̇\ out \ch\ chin \e\ bet \ē\ easy
\g\ go \i\ hit \ī\ ice \j\ job \ŋ\ sing \ō\ go
\ȯ\ law \ȯi\ boy \th\ thin \th\ the \ü\ loot \u̇\ foot
\y\ yet \zh\ vision *see also* Guide to Pronunciation

: a substance that by becoming adsorbed prevents a surface from being repellent to a wetting liquid and is used especially in mixing solids with liquids or spreading liquids on surfaces

**wet·tish** \'we-tish\ *adjective* (1648)
: somewhat wet : MOIST

**wet wash** *noun* (1916)
: laundry returned damp and not ironed

**we've** \'wēv\ (1742)
: we have

¹**whack** \'hwak, 'wak\ *verb* [probably imitative of the sound of a blow] (1719)
*transitive verb*
**1 a :** to strike with a smart or resounding blow **b :** to cut with or as if with a whack : CHOP **2** *chiefly British* : to get the better of : DEFEAT
*intransitive verb*
: to strike a smart or resounding blow
— **whack·er** *noun*

²**whack** *noun* (1736)
**1 a :** a smart or resounding blow; *also* : the sound of or as if of such a blow **b :** a critical attack
**2 :** PORTION, SHARE
**3 :** CONDITION, STATE
**4 a :** an opportunity or attempt to do something ⟨take a *whack* at it⟩ **b :** a single action or occasion ⟨borrowed $50 all at one *whack*⟩
— **out of whack 1 :** out of proper order or shape ⟨threw his knee *out of whack*⟩ **2 :** not in accord ⟨feeling *out of whack* with her contemporaries —S. E. Rubin⟩

**whacked–out** \'(h)wakt-,aut, ,(h)wakt-'\ *adjective* (1967)
**1 :** WORN-OUT, EXHAUSTED
**2 :** WACKY ⟨a *whacked-out* parody⟩
**3 :** STONED ⟨*whacked-out* on drugs⟩

¹**whack·ing** \'hwa-kiŋ, 'wa-\ *adjective* (1806)
: very large : WHOPPING

²**whacking** *adverb* (1853)
: VERY ⟨a *whacking* good story⟩

**whacko** \'hwa-(,)kō, 'wa-\ *variant of* WACKO

**whack off** *verb* (1969)
: MASTURBATE — usually considered vulgar

**whack up** *transitive verb* (circa 1893)
: to divide into shares

**whacky** \'hwa-kē, 'wa-\ *variant of* WACKY

¹**whale** \'hwā(ə)l, 'wā(ə)l\ *noun, plural* **whales** *often attributive* [Middle English, from Old English *hwæl;* akin to Old High German *hwal* whale and perhaps to Latin *squalus* sea fish] (before 12th century)
**1** *or plural* **whale :** CETACEAN; *especially* : one (as a sperm whale or killer whale) of larger size
**2 :** one that is impressive especially in size ⟨a *whale* of a difference⟩ ⟨a *whale* of a good time⟩
— **whale·like** \-,līk\ *adjective*

²**whale** *intransitive verb* **whaled; whal·ing** (1700)
: to engage in whale fishing

³**whale** *transitive verb* **whaled; whal·ing** [origin unknown] (circa 1790)
**1 :** LASH, THRASH
**2 :** to strike or hit vigorously
**3 :** to defeat soundly

**whale·back** \'hwā(ə)l-,bak, 'wā(ə)l-\ *noun* (1886)
: something shaped like the back of a whale

**whale·boat** \-,bōt\ *noun* (1682)
**1 :** a long narrow rowboat made with both ends sharp and raking, often steered with an oar, and formerly used by whalers for hunting whales
**2 :** a long narrow rowboat or motorboat resembling the original whaleboats and often carried by warships and merchant ships

**whale·bone** \-,bōn\ *noun* (1601)
**1 :** BALEEN
**2 :** an article made of whalebone

**whalebone whale** *noun* (1725)
: BALEEN WHALE

**whal·er** \'hwā-lər, 'wā-\ *noun* (1684)
**1 :** a person or ship engaged in whale fishing

**2 :** WHALEBOAT 2

**whale shark** *noun* (circa 1885)
: a shark (*Rhincodon typus*) of warm waters that has small teeth, feeds chiefly on plankton strained by its gill rakers, may attain a length of up to 60 feet (18.3 meters), and is the largest known fish

**whal·ing** \'hwā-liŋ, 'wā-\ *noun* (1688)
: the occupation of catching and extracting commercial products from whales

¹**wham** \'hwam, 'wam\ *noun* [imitative] (1739)
**1 :** a solid blow
**2 :** the loud sound of a hard impact

²**wham** *or* **wham·mo** \'hwa-(,)mō, 'wa-\ *adverb* (1924)
: with violent abruptness ⟨everything seemed to be going well, when *wham* the deal fell through⟩

³**wham** *verb* **whammed; wham·ming** (1925)
*transitive verb*
: to propel, strike, or beat so as to produce a loud impact
*intransitive verb*
: to hit or explode with a loud impact

**wham·my** \'hwa-mē, 'wa-\ *noun, plural* **whammies** [probably from ¹*wham*] (1940)
**1 a :** a supernatural power bringing bad luck **b :** a magic curse or spell
**2 :** a potent force or attack; *specifically* : a paralyzing or lethal blow

¹**whang** \'hwaŋ, 'waŋ\ *noun* [alteration of Middle English *thong, thwang*] (1536)
**1** *dialect* **a :** THONG **b :** RAWHIDE
**2** *British* : a large piece : CHUNK
**3 :** PENIS — often considered vulgar

²**whang** (1684)
*transitive verb*
**1** *dialect* : BEAT, THRASH
**2 :** to propel or strike with force
*intransitive verb*
: to beat or work with force or violence

³**whang** *noun* [imitative] (circa 1824)
: a loud sharp vibrant or resonant sound

⁴**whang** (1875)
*intransitive verb*
: to make a whang
*transitive verb*
: to strike with a whang

**whan·gee** \'hwaŋ-'ē, waŋ-, -'gē\ *noun* [probably modification of Chinese (Beijing) *huáng* bamboo] (1790)
**1 :** any of several Chinese bamboos (genus *Phyllostachys*)
**2 :** a walking stick or riding crop of whangee

**whap** \'hwäp, 'wäp\ *variant of* WHOP

**wharf** \'hworf, 'worf\ *noun, plural* **wharves** \'hworvz, 'worvz\ *also* **wharfs** [Middle English, from Old English *hwearf* embankment, wharf; akin to Old English *hweorfan* to turn, Old High German *hwerban*, Greek *karpos* wrist] (before 12th century)
**1 :** a structure built along or at an angle from the shore of navigable waters so that ships may lie alongside to receive and discharge cargo and passengers
**2** *obsolete* : the bank of a river or the shore of the sea

**wharf·age** \'hwor-fij, 'wor-\ *noun* (15th century)
**1 a :** the provision or the use of a wharf **b :** the handling or stowing of goods on a wharf
**2 :** the charge for the use of a wharf
**3 :** the wharf accommodations of a place : WHARVES

**wharf·in·ger** \-fən-jər\ *noun* [irregular from *wharfage*] (1552)
: the operator or manager of a commercial wharf

**wharf·mas·ter** \'hworf-,mas-tər, 'worf-\ *noun* (1618)
: the manager of a wharf : WHARFINGER

¹**what** \'hwät, 'hwət, 'wät, 'wət\ *pronoun* [Middle English, from Old English *hwæt,* neuter of *hwā* who — more at WHO] (before 12th century)

**1 a** (1) — used as an interrogative expressing inquiry about the identity, nature, or value of an object or matter ⟨*what* is this⟩ ⟨*what* is wealth without friends⟩ ⟨*what* does he earn⟩ ⟨*what* hath God wrought⟩ (2) — often used to ask for repetition of an utterance or part of an utterance not properly heard or understood ⟨you said *what*⟩ **b** (1) *archaic* : WHO 1 — used as an interrogative expressing inquiry about the identity of a person (2) — used as an interrogative expressing inquiry about the character, nature, occupation, position, or role of a person ⟨*what* do you think I am, a fool⟩ ⟨*what* is she, that all our swains commend her —Shakespeare⟩ **c** — used as an exclamation expressing surprise or excitement and frequently introducing a question ⟨*what*, no breakfast⟩ **d** — used in expressions directing attention to a statement that the speaker is about to make ⟨you know *what*⟩ **e** — used at the end of a question to express inquiry about additional possibilities ⟨is it raining, or snowing, or *what*⟩ **f** *chiefly British* — used at the end of an utterance as a form of tag question ⟨a clever play, *what*⟩
**2** *chiefly dialect* : ⁴THAT 1, WHICH 3, WHO 3
**3 :** that which : the one or ones that ⟨no income but *what* he gets from his writings⟩ — sometimes used in reference to a clause or phrase that is yet to come or is not yet complete ⟨gave also, *what* is more valuable, understanding⟩
**4 a :** WHATEVER 1a ⟨say *what* you will⟩ **b** *obsolete* : WHOEVER
— **what for 1 :** for what purpose or reason : WHY — usually used with the other words of a question between *what* and *for* ⟨*what* did you do that *for*⟩ except when used alone **2 :** harsh treatment especially by blows or by a sharp reprimand ⟨gave him *what for* in violent Spanish —*New Yorker*⟩
— **what have you :** WHATNOT ⟨novels, plays, short stories, travelogues, and *what have you* —Haldeen Braddy⟩
— **what if 1 :** what will or would be the result if **2 :** what does it matter if
— **what of 1 :** what is the situation with respect to **2 :** what importance can be assigned to
— **what's what :** the true state of things ⟨knows *what's what* when it comes to fashion⟩
— **what though :** what does it matter if ⟨*what though* the rose have prickles, yet 'tis plucked —Shakespeare⟩

²**what** *adverb* (before 12th century)
**1** *obsolete* : WHY
**2 :** in what respect : HOW ⟨*what* does he care⟩
**3** — used to introduce prepositional phrases in parallel construction or a prepositional phrase that expresses cause and usually has more than one object; used principally before phrases beginning with *with* ⟨*what* with unemployment increasing⟩ ⟨*what* with the war, *what* with the sweat, *what* with the gallows, and *what* with poverty, I am custom-shrunk —Shakespeare⟩

³**what** *adjective* (13th century)
**1 a** — used as an interrogative expressing inquiry about the identity, nature, or value of a person, object, or matter ⟨*what* minerals do we export⟩ **b :** how remarkable or striking for good or bad qualities — used especially in exclamatory utterances and dependent clauses ⟨*what* mountains⟩ ⟨remember *what* fun we had⟩ ⟨*what* a suggestion⟩ ⟨*what* a charming girl⟩
**2 a** (1) : WHATEVER 1a (2) : ANY ⟨ornament of *what* description soever⟩ **b :** the . . . that : as much or as many . . . as ⟨rescued *what* survivors they found⟩

**what all** \'hwä-,dol, 'wä-, '(h)wə-\ *pronoun* (1702)
: WHATNOT

**what·cha·ma·call·it** \'hwä-chə-mə-,kȯ-lət, 'wä-, '(h)wə-\ *noun* [alteration of *what you may call it*] (1928)

: THINGAMAJIG

¹**what·ev·er** \hwät-'e-vər, wät-, (,)(h)wət-\ *pronoun* (14th century)
**1 a :** anything or everything that 〈take *whatever* you want〉 **b :** no matter what 〈*whatever* he says, they won't believe him〉 **c :** WHATNOT 〈buffalo or rhinoceros or *whatever* —Alan Moorehead〉
**2 :** WHAT 1a(1) — used to express astonishment or perplexity 〈*whatever* do you mean by that〉

²**whatever** *adjective* (14th century)
**1 a :** any . . . that : all . . . that 〈buy peace . . . on *whatever* terms could be obtained —C. S. Forester〉 **b :** no matter what 〈money, in *whatever* hands, will confer power —Samuel Johnson〉
**2 :** of any kind at all — used after the substantive it modifies with *any* or with an expressed or implied negative 〈in any order *whatever* —W. G. Moulton〉 〈no food *whatever*〉

³**whatever** *adverb* (1870)
**:** in any case : whatever the case may be — sometimes used interjectionally to suggest the unimportance of a decision between alternatives

**what-if** \,hwät-'if, ,wät-, ,(h)wət-\ *noun* (1970)
**:** a suppositional question

**what·ness** \'hwät-nəs, 'wät-, '(h)wət-\ *noun* (1611)
**:** QUIDDITY 1

¹**what·not** \'hwät-,nät, 'wät-, '(h)wət-\ *pronoun* [*what not?*] (1540)
**:** any of various other things that might also be mentioned 〈paper clips, pins, and *whatnot*〉

²**whatnot** *noun* (1602)
**1 :** a nondescript person or thing
**2 :** a light open set of shelves for bric-a-brac

**what-sit** \'hwät-sət, 'wät-, 'wət-\ *or* **what-sis** \-səs\ *also* **what-is-it** \-iz-ət\ *noun* [*whatsit* & *whatsis* contraction of *what-is-it*] (circa 1882)
**:** THINGAMAJIG

**what·so·ev·er** \,hwät-sə-'we-vər, ,wät-, ,(h)wət-\ *pronoun or adjective* (13th century)
**:** WHATEVER

**whaup** \'hwóp, 'wóp\ *noun, plural* **whaup** *also* **whaups** [imitative] (circa 1512)
*chiefly Scottish* **:** a European curlew (*Numenius arquata*)

**wheal** \'hwē(ə)l, 'wē(ə)l\ *noun* [alteration of ¹*wale*] (1808)
**:** a suddenly formed elevation of the skin surface: as **a :** WELT **b :** a flat burning or itching eminence on the skin

**wheat** \'hwēt, 'wēt\ *noun, often attributive* [Middle English *whete*, from Old English *hwǣte*; akin to Old High German *weizzi* wheat, *hwīz, wīz* white — more at WHITE] (before 12th century)
**1 :** a cereal grain that yields a fine white flour, is the chief breadstuff of temperate climates, is used also in pastas (as macaroni or spaghetti), and is important in animal feeds
**2 :** any of various annual grasses (genus *Triticum* and especially *T. aestivum* and *T. turgidum*) of wide climatic adaptability that are cultivated in most temperate areas for the wheat they yield
**3 :** a light yellow

**wheat bread** *noun* (14th century)
**:** a bread made of a combination of white and whole wheat flours as distinguished from bread made entirely of white or whole wheat flour

**wheat cake** *noun* (1772)
**:** a pancake made of wheat flour

**wheat·ear** \'hwēt-,ir, 'wēt-\ *noun* [back-formation from earlier *wheatears* wheatear, probably by folk etymology or euphemism from *white* + *arse*] (1591)
**:** any of various small thrushes (genus *Oenanthe*); *especially* **:** a white-rumped one (*O. oenanthe*) of Eurasia and northern North America

¹**wheat·en** \'hwē-t°n, 'wē-\ *adjective* (before 12th century)
**:** of, relating to, or made of wheat

²**wheaten** *noun* (circa 1931)
**:** a pale yellowish to ruddy fawn color characteristic of the coat of some dogs

**wheat germ** *noun* (1897)
**:** the embryo of the wheat kernel separated in milling and used especially as a source of vitamins and protein

**wheat rust** *noun* (1884)
**:** a destructive disease of wheat caused by rust fungi; *also* **:** a fungus (as *Puccinia graminis*) causing a wheat rust

**Wheat·stone bridge** \'hwēt-,stōn-, 'wēt-, *chiefly British* -stən-\ *noun* [Sir Charles Wheatstone] (1872)
**:** a bridge for measuring electrical resistances that consists of a conductor joining two branches of a circuit

**whee** \'hwē, 'wē\ *interjection* (1898)
**—** used to express delight or exuberance

**whee·dle** \'hwē-d°l, 'wē-\ *verb* **whee·dled; whee·dling** \'(h)wēd-liŋ, '(h)wē-d°l-iŋ\ [origin unknown] (circa 1661)
*transitive verb*
**1 :** to influence or entice by soft words or flattery
**2 :** to gain or get by wheedling 〈*wheedle* one's way into favor〉
*intransitive verb*
**:** to use soft words or flattery

¹**wheel** \'hwē(ə)l, 'wē(ə)l\ *noun, often attributive* [Middle English, from Old English *hweogol, hwēol*; akin to Old Norse *hvēl* wheel, Greek *kyklos* circle, wheel, Sanskrit *cakra*, Latin *colere* to cultivate, inhabit, Sanskrit *carati* he moves, wanders] (before 12th century)
**1 :** a circular frame of hard material that may be solid, partly solid, or spoked and that is capable of turning on an axle
**2 :** a contrivance or apparatus having as its principal part a wheel: as **a :** a chiefly medieval instrument of torture designed for mutilating a victim (as by stretching or disjointing) **b :** BICYCLE **c :** any of many revolving disks or drums used as gambling paraphernalia **d :** POTTER'S WHEEL **e :** STEERING WHEEL
**3 a :** an imaginary turning wheel symbolizing the inconstancy of fortune **b :** a recurring course, development, or action : CYCLE
**4 :** something resembling a wheel in shape or motion: as **a :** a round flat cheese **b :** a firework that rotates while burning **c :** a propeller on a boat
**5 a :** a curving or circular movement **b :** a rotation or turn usually about an axis or center; *specifically* **:** a turning movement of troops or ships in line in which the units preserve alignment and relative positions as they change direction
**6 a :** a moving or essential part of something compared to a machine 〈the *wheels* of government〉 **b :** a directing or controlling force **c :** a person of importance especially in an organization 〈a big *wheel*〉
**7 :** the refrain or burden of a song
**8 a :** a circuit of theaters or places of entertainment **b :** a sports league
**9** *plural, slang* **:** a wheeled vehicle; *especially* **:** AUTOMOBILE
**— wheel·less** \'hwē(ə)l-ləs, 'wē(ə)l-\ *adjective*

²**wheel** (13th century)
*intransitive verb*
**1 :** to turn on or as if on an axis : REVOLVE
**2 :** to change direction as if revolving on a pivot 〈the battalion would have *wheeled* to the

wheel 1: *1* hub,
*2* spoke, *3* felly,
*4* tire

flank —Walter Bernstein〉 〈her mind will *wheel* around to the other extreme —Liam O'Flaherty〉
**3 :** to move or extend in a circle or curve 〈birds in *wheeling* flight〉 〈valleys where young cotton *wheeled* slowly in fanlike rows —William Faulkner〉
**4 :** to drive or go on or as if on wheels or in a wheeled vehicle
*transitive verb*
**1 :** to cause to turn on or as if on an axis : ROTATE
**2 :** to convey or move on or as if on wheels or in a wheeled vehicle; *especially* **:** to drive (a vehicle) at high speed
**3 :** to cause to change direction as if revolving on a pivot
**4 :** to make or perform in a circle or curve
**— wheel and deal :** to make deals or do business especially shrewdly or briskly

**wheel and axle** *noun* (circa 1773)
**:** a mechanical device consisting of a grooved wheel turned by a cord or chain with a rigidly attached axle (as for winding up a weight) together with the supporting standards

**wheel animal** *noun* (1788)
**:** ROTIFER

**wheel animalcule** *noun* (1834)
**:** ROTIFER

¹**wheel·bar·row** \'hwē(ə)l-,bar-(,)ō, 'wē(ə)l-\ *noun* (14th century)
**:** a small usually single-wheeled vehicle that is used for carrying small loads and is fitted with handles at the rear by which it can be pushed and guided

²**wheelbarrow** *transitive verb* (1721)
**:** to convey in a wheelbarrow

**wheel·base** \'hwē(ə)l-,bās, 'wē(ə)l-\ *noun* (1886)
**:** the distance in inches between the front and rear axles of an automotive vehicle

**wheel bug** *noun* (1815)
**:** a large North American bug (*Arilus cristatus*) that has a high serrated crest on its prothorax and preys on other insects

**wheel·chair** \'hwē(ə)l-,cher, 'wē(ə)l-, -,char\ *noun* (circa 1700)
**:** a chair mounted on wheels especially for the use of disabled persons

**wheeled** \'hwē(ə)ld, 'wē(ə)ld\ *adjective* (1606)
**1 :** equipped with wheels 〈*wheeled* vehicles〉
**2 :** moving or functioning by means of wheels 〈*wheeled* traffic〉

**wheel·er** \'hwē-lər, 'wē-\ *noun* (1683)
**1 :** one that wheels
**2 :** a draft animal (as a horse) pulling in the position nearest the front wheels of a wagon
**3 :** something (as a vehicle or ship) that has wheels — used especially in combination 〈side-*wheeler*〉

**wheeler and dealer** *noun, plural* **wheelers and dealers** (1966)
**:** WHEELER-DEALER

**wheel·er–deal·er** \,hwē-lər-'dē-lər, ,wē-\ *noun* (1954)
**:** a shrewd operator especially in business or politics

**wheel·horse** \'hwē(ə)l-,hòrs, 'wē(ə)l-\ *noun* (1708)
**1 :** a horse (as in a tandem) in a position nearest the wheels
**2 :** a steady and effective worker especially in a political body

**wheel·house** \-,haùs\ *noun* (1835)
**:** PILOTHOUSE

**wheel·ie** \'hwē-lē, 'wē-\ *noun* (circa 1965)
**:** a maneuver in which a wheeled vehicle (as a bicycle) is momentarily balanced on its rear wheel or wheels

**wheel·ing** \'hwē-liŋ, 'wē-\ *noun* (15th century)
**1 :** the act or process of one that wheels
**2 :** the condition of a road relative to passage on wheels

**wheel lock** *noun* (1670)
**:** a gun's lock for a muzzle-loading firearm in which sparks are struck from a flint or a piece of iron pyrites by a revolving wheel

**wheel·man** \'hwē(ə)l-mən, 'wē(ə)l-\ *noun* (1865)
**1 a :** HELMSMAN **b :** the driver of an automobile
**2 :** CYCLIST

**wheels·man** \'hwē(ə)lz-mən, 'wē(ə)lz-\ *noun* (1866)
**:** one who steers with a wheel; *especially* **:** HELMSMAN

**wheel–thrown** \'hwēl-,thrōn, 'wēl-\ *adjective* (1975)
**:** made on a potter's wheel ⟨*wheel-thrown* pottery⟩

**wheel·work** \'hwē(ə)l-,wərk, 'wē(ə)l-\ *noun* (1670)
**:** wheels in gear and their connections in a machine or mechanism

**wheel·wright** \-,rīt\ *noun* (13th century)
**:** a maker and repairer of wheels and wheeled vehicles

**¹wheen** \'hwēn, 'wēn\ *adjective* [Middle English (Scots) *quheyne*, from Old English *hwǣne, hwēne*, adverb, somewhat, from instrumental of *hwōn* little, few] (14th century)
*dialect British* **:** FEW 2

**²wheen** *noun* (1680)
*dialect British* **:** a considerable number or amount

**¹wheeze** \'hwēz, 'wēz\ *intransitive verb*
**wheezed; wheez·ing** [Middle English *whesen*, probably of Scandinavian origin; akin to Old Norse *hvǣsa* to hiss; akin to Old English *hwǣst* action of blowing, Sanskrit *śvasiti* he blows, snorts] (15th century)
**1 :** to breathe with difficulty usually with a whistling sound
**2 :** to make a sound resembling that of wheezing

**²wheeze** *noun* (1834)
**1 :** a sound of wheezing
**2 a :** an often repeated and widely known joke used especially by entertainers **b :** a trite saying or proverb

**wheezy** \'hwē-zē, 'wē-\ *adjective* **wheez·i·er; -est** (1818)
**1 :** inclined to wheeze
**2 :** having a wheezing sound
— **wheez·i·ly** \-zə-lē\ *adverb*
— **wheez·i·ness** \-zē-nəs\ *noun*

**¹whelk** \'hwelk, 'welk, 'wilk\ *noun* [Middle English *welke*, from Old English *weoloc;* akin to Middle Dutch *willoc* whelk and perhaps to Latin *volvere* to turn — more at VOLUBLE] (before 12th century)
**:** any of numerous large marine snails (as of the genus *Buccinum*); *especially* **:** one (*B. undatum*) much used as food in Europe

**²whelk** \'hwelk, 'welk\ *noun* [Middle English *whelke*, from Old English *hwylca*, from *hwelian* to suppurate] (before 12th century)
**:** PAPULE, PUSTULE

**whelm** \'hwelm, 'welm\ *verb* [Middle English] (14th century)
*transitive verb*
**1 :** to turn (as a dish or vessel) upside down usually to cover something **:** cover or engulf completely with usually disastrous effect
**2 :** to overcome in thought or feeling **:** OVERWHELM
*intransitive verb*
**:** to pass or go over something so as to bury or submerge it

**whelk**

**¹whelp** \'hwelp, 'welp\ *noun* [Middle English, from Old English *hwelp;* akin to Old High German *hwelf* whelp] (before 12th century)
**1 :** any of the young of various carnivorous mammals and especially of the dog
**2 :** a young boy or girl

**²whelp** (13th century)
*transitive verb*
**:** to give birth to — used of various carnivores and especially the dog
*intransitive verb*
**:** to bring forth young

**¹when** \'hwen, 'wen, (h)wən\ *adverb* [Middle English, from Old English *hwanne, hwenne;* akin to Old High German *hwanne* when, Old English *hwā* who — more at WHO] (before 12th century)
**1 :** at what time ⟨*when* will you return⟩
**2 a :** at or during which time **b :** and then
**3 :** at a former and usually less prosperous time ⟨brag fondly of having known him *when* —Vance Packard⟩

**²when** *conjunction* [Middle English, from Old English *hwanne, hwenne*, from *hwanne, hwenne*, adverb] (before 12th century)
**1 a :** at or during the time that **:** WHILE ⟨went fishing *when* he was a boy⟩ **b :** just at the moment that ⟨stop writing *when* the bell rings⟩ **c :** at any or every time that ⟨*when* he listens to music, he falls asleep⟩
**2 :** in the event that **:** IF ⟨a contestant is disqualified *when* he disobeys the rules⟩
**3 a :** considering that ⟨why use water at all *when* you can drown in it —Stuart Chase⟩ **b :** in spite of the fact that **:** ALTHOUGH ⟨quit politics *when* I might have had a great career in it⟩
**4 :** the time or occasion at or in which ⟨tomorrow is *when* we must decide⟩ ⟨humor is *when* you laugh —Earl Rovit⟩

**³when** \'hwen, 'wen\ *pronoun* (14th century)
**:** what or which time ⟨life-long homes for those . . . who have lived here since *when* —Kim Waller⟩

**⁴when** *noun* (1616)
**:** the time in which something is done or comes about ⟨troubled his head very little about the hows and *whens* of life —Laurence Sterne⟩

**when·as** \hwe-'naz, we-, (h)wə-\ *conjunction* [Middle English (Scots) *when as*, from Middle English *when + as*] (15th century)
*archaic* **:** WHEN

**¹whence** \'hwen(t)s, 'wen(t)s\ *adverb* [Middle English *whennes*, from *whenne* whence (from Old English *hwanon*) + -*s*, adverb suffix, from -*s*, genitive singular ending; akin to Old High German *hwanān* whence, Old English *hwā* who] (13th century)
**:** from what place, source, or cause ⟨then *whence* comes this paradox —*Changing Times*⟩
— **from whence :** from what place, source, or cause ⟨no one could tell me *from whence* the gold had come —Graham Greene⟩

**²whence** *conjunction* (14th century)
**1 :** from what place, source, or cause ⟨inquired *whence* the water came —Maria Edgeworth⟩
**2 a :** from or out of which place, source, or cause ⟨the lawless society *whence* the ballads sprang —DeLancey Ferguson⟩ **b :** by reason of which fact **:** WHEREFORE ⟨nothing broke — *whence* I infer that my bones are not yet chalky —O. W. Holmes (died 1935)⟩

**whence·so·ev·er** \'hwen(t)s-sə-,we-vər, 'wen(t)s-\ *conjunction* (1511)
**:** from whatever place or source

**¹when·ev·er** \hwe-'ne-vər, we-, (h)wə-\ *conjunction* (14th century)
**:** at any or every time that

**²whenever** *adverb* (1667)
**:** at whatever time

**¹when·so·ev·er** \'hwen(t)s-sə-,we-vər, 'wen(t)-\ *conjunction* (14th century)
**:** WHENEVER

**²whensoever** *adverb* (1526)

*obsolete* **:** at any time whatever

**¹where** \'hwer, 'hwar, 'wer, 'war, (,)(h)wər\ *adverb* [Middle English, from Old English *hwǣr;* akin to Old High German *hwār* where, Old English *hwā* who — more at WHO] (before 12th century)
**1 a :** at, in, or to what place ⟨*where* is the house⟩ ⟨*where* are we going⟩ **b :** at, in, or to what situation, position, direction, circumstances, or respect ⟨*where* does this plan lead⟩ ⟨*where* am I wrong⟩
**2** *archaic* **:** HERE, THERE ⟨lo, *where* it comes again —Shakespeare⟩

**²where** *conjunction* (13th century)
**1 a :** at, in, or to what place ⟨knows *where* the house is⟩ **b :** at, in, or to what situation, position, direction, circumstances, or respect ⟨shows *where* the plan leads⟩ **c :** the place or point at, in, or to which ⟨couldn't see from *where* he was sitting⟩ ⟨kept that horse and gentled him to *where* I finally rode him —William Faulkner⟩
**2 :** WHEREVER ⟨goes *where* she likes⟩
**3 a :** at, in, or to which place ⟨the town *where* she lives⟩ **b :** at or in which ⟨has reached the size *where* traffic is a problem⟩ ⟨two fireplaces *where* you can bake bread in the ovens —Randall Jarrell⟩
**4 a :** at, in, or to the place at, in, or to which ⟨stay *where* you are⟩ ⟨send him away *where* he'll forget⟩ **b :** in a case, situation, or respect in which ⟨outstanding *where* endurance is called for⟩
**5 :** THAT ⟨I've read *where* they do it that way in some Middle Eastern countries —Andy Rooney⟩

**³where** \'hwer, 'hwar, 'wer, 'war\ *noun* (15th century)
**1 :** PLACE, LOCATION ⟨the *where* and the how of the accident⟩
**2 :** what place, source, or cause ⟨I know *where* that comes from⟩
— **where it's at 1 a :** a place of central interest or activity **b :** something (as a topic or field of interest) of primary concern or importance ⟨education is *where it's at*⟩ **2 :** the true nature of things
— **where one is at :** one's true position, state, or nature

**¹where·abouts** \-ə-,baůts\ *also* **whereabout** \-,baůt\ *adverb* [Middle English *wherabouts* (from *wher aboute* + -*s*, genitive suffix) & *wher aboute*, from *where, wher* where + *about, aboute* about — more at WHENCE] (14th century)
**:** about where **:** near what place ⟨*whereabouts* is the house⟩

**²whereabouts** *also* **whereabout** *conjunction* (14th century)
**1** *obsolete* **:** on what business or errand
**2 :** near what place **:** WHERE ⟨know *whereabouts* he lives⟩

**³whereabouts** *noun plural but singular or plural in construction, also* **whereabout** (1605)
**:** the place or general locality where a person or thing is ⟨their present *whereabouts* are a secret⟩

**¹where·as** \hwer-'az, hwar-, wer-, war-, (,)(h)wər-\ *conjunction* [Middle English *where as*, from *where + as*] (14th century)
**1 a :** while on the contrary **b :** ALTHOUGH
**2 :** in view of the fact that **:** SINCE — used especially to introduce a preamble

**²whereas** *noun* (1795)
**1 :** an introductory statement of a formal document **:** PREAMBLE
**2 :** a conditional or qualifying statement

**where·at** \-'at\ *conjunction* (15th century)
**1 :** at or toward which
**2 :** in consequence of which **:** WHEREUPON

**¹where·by** \-'bī\ *conjunction* (13th century)
**:** by, through, or in accordance with which

**²whereby** *adverb* (14th century)
*obsolete* **:** by what **:** HOW

**¹where·fore** \'hwer-ˌfōr, 'hwar-, 'wer-, -ˌför\ *adverb* [Middle English *wherfor, wherfore,* from *where, wher* + *for, fore* for] (13th century)
**1 :** for what reason or purpose **:** WHY
**2 :** THEREFORE
**²wherefore** *noun* (1590)
**:** an answer or statement giving an explanation **:** REASON ⟨wants to know the whys and *wherefores*⟩

**where·from** \-ˌfrəm, -ˌfräm\ *conjunction* (15th century)
**:** from which

**¹where·in** \hwer-'in, hwar-, wer-, war-, (ˌ)(h)wər-\ *adverb* (13th century)
**:** in what **:** in what particular or respect ⟨*wherein* was I wrong⟩
**²wherein** *conjunction* (15th century)
**1 a :** in which **:** WHERE ⟨the city *wherein* he lives⟩ **b :** during which
**2 :** in what way **:** HOW ⟨showed me *wherein* I was wrong⟩

**where·in·to** \-'in-(ˌ)tü\ *conjunction* (1539)
**:** into which

**¹where·of** \-'əv, -'äv\ *conjunction* (13th century)
**1** *archaic* **:** with or by which
**2 :** of what ⟨knows *whereof* she speaks⟩
**3 a :** of which ⟨books *whereof* the best are lost⟩ **b :** of whom
**²whereof** *adverb* (15th century)
*archaic* **:** of what ⟨*whereof* are you made —Shakespeare⟩

**¹where·on** \-'ón, -'än\ *conjunction* (13th century)
**1** *archaic* **:** on what ⟨tell me *whereon* the likelihood depends —Shakespeare⟩
**2 :** on which ⟨the base *whereon* it rests⟩
**²whereon** *adverb* (15th century)
*archaic* **:** on what ⟨*whereon* do you look —Shakespeare⟩

**where·so·ev·er** \'hwer-sə-ˌwe-vər, 'hwar-, 'wer-, 'war-\ *conjunction* (13th century)
**:** WHEREVER

**where·through** \'hwer-ˌthrü, 'hwar-, 'wer-, 'war-\ *conjunction* (13th century)
**:** through which

**¹where·to** \-ˌtü\ *adverb* (13th century)
**:** to what place, purpose, or end ⟨*whereto* tends all this —Shakespeare⟩
**²whereto** *conjunction* (14th century)
**:** to which

**where·un·to** \hwer-'ən-(ˌ)tü, hwar-, war-, (ˌ)(h)wər-\ *adverb or conjunction* (15th century)
**:** WHERETO

**where·up·on** \'hwer-ə-ˌpón, 'hwar-, 'wer-, 'war-, -ˌpän\ *conjunction* (14th century)
**1 :** on which
**2 :** closely following and in consequence of which

**¹wher·ev·er** \hwer-'e-vər, hwar-, wer-, war-, (ˌ)(h)wər-\ *adverb* (13th century)
**1 :** where in the world ⟨*wherever* did you get that tie⟩
**2 :** anywhere at all ⟨explore northward or *wherever* —Bernard De Voto⟩
**²wherever** *conjunction* (14th century)
**1 :** at, in, or to any or all places that ⟨thrives *wherever* he goes⟩
**2 :** in any circumstance in which ⟨*wherever* it is possible, we try to help⟩

**¹where·with** \'hwer-ˌwith, 'hwar-, 'wer-, 'war-, -ˌwith\ *pronoun* (13th century)
*archaic* **:** that with or by which — used with an infinitive ⟨so shall I have *wherewith* to answer him —Psalms 119:42 (Authorized Version)⟩
**²wherewith** *adverb* (13th century)
*obsolete* **:** with what ⟨*wherewith* shall it be salted —Matthew 5:13 (Authorized Version)⟩
**³wherewith** *conjunction* (14th century)
**:** with or by means of which ⟨metal tools *wherewith* to break ground —Russell Lord⟩

**¹where·with·al** \'hwer-wi-ˌthól, 'hwar-, 'wer-, 'war-, -ˌthól\ *conjunction* [*where* + ²*withal*] (1534)
**:** WHEREWITH
**²wherewithal** *pronoun* (1583)
**:** WHEREWITH
**³wherewithal** *noun* (1659)
**:** MEANS, RESOURCES; *specifically* **:** MONEY ⟨didn't have the *wherewithal* for an expensive dinner⟩

**wher·ry** \'hwer-ē, 'wer-\ *noun, plural* **wher·ries** [Middle English *whery*] (15th century)
**1 :** any of various light boats: as **a :** a long light rowboat made sharp at both ends and used to transport passengers on rivers and about harbors **b :** a racing scull for one person
**2 :** a large light barge, lighter, or fishing boat varying in type in different parts of Great Britain

**¹whet** \'hwet, 'wet\ *transitive verb* **whet·ted; whet·ting** [Middle English *whetten,* from Old English *hwettan;* akin to Old High German *wezzen* to whet, *waz* sharp] (before 12th century)
**1 :** to sharpen by rubbing on or with something (as a stone) ⟨*whet* a knife⟩
**2 :** to make keen or more acute **:** EXCITE, STIMULATE ⟨*whet* the appetite⟩
**— whet·ter** *noun*
**²whet** *noun* (circa 1628)
**1** *dialect* **a :** a spell of work done with a scythe between the time it is sharpened and the time it needs to be sharpened again **b :** TIME, WHILE
**2 :** something that sharpens or makes keen: **a :** GOAD, INCITEMENT **b :** APPETIZER; *also* **:** a drink of liquor

**¹wheth·er** \'hwe-thər, 'we-, (ˌ)(h)wə-\ *pronoun* [Middle English, from Old English *hwæther, hwether;* akin to Old High German *hwedar* which of two, Latin *uter,* Greek *poteros,* Old English *hwā* who — more at WHO] (before 12th century)
**1** *archaic* **:** which one of the two
**2** *archaic* **:** whichever one of the two
**²whether** *conjunction* (before 12th century)
— used as a function word usually with correlative *or* or with *or whether* to indicate (1) until the early 19th century a direct question involving alternatives; (2) an indirect question involving stated or implied alternatives ⟨decide *whether* he should agree or raise objections⟩ ⟨wondered *whether* to stay⟩; (3) alternative conditions or possibilities ⟨see me no more, *whether* he be dead or no —Shakespeare⟩ ⟨seated him next to her *whether* by accident or design⟩
**— whether or no** *or* **whether or not**
**:** in any case

**whet·stone** \'hwet-ˌstōn, 'wet-\ *noun* (before 12th century)
**:** a stone for whetting edge tools

**whew** \*often read as* 'hwü, 'wü, 'hyü; *the interjection is a whistle concluded with a voiceless* ü\ *noun* [imitative] (1513)
**:** a whistling sound or a sound like a half-formed whistle uttered as an exclamation ⟨gave a long *whew* when he realized the size of the job⟩ — used interjectionally chiefly to express amazement, discomfort, or relief

**whey** \'hwā, 'wā\ *noun* [Middle English, from Old English *hwæg;* akin to Middle Dutch *wey* whey] (before 12th century)
**:** the watery part of milk that is separated from the coagulable part or curd especially in the process of making cheese and that is rich in lactose, minerals, and vitamins and contains lactalbumin and traces of fat
**— whey·like** \-ˌlīk\ *adjective*

**whey–face** \'hwā-ˌfās, 'wā-\ *noun* (1605)
**:** a person having a pale face (as from fear)
**— whey–faced** \-ˌfāst\ *adjective*

**¹which** \'hwich, 'wich\ *adjective* [Middle English, of what kind, which, from Old English *hwilc;* akin to Old High German *wilīh* of what kind, which, Old English *hwā* who, *gelīk* like — more at WHO, LIKE] (before 12th century)
**1 :** being what one or ones out of a group — used as an interrogative ⟨*which* tie should I wear⟩ ⟨kept a record of *which* employees took their vacations in July⟩
**2 :** WHICHEVER ⟨it will not fit, turn it *which* way you like⟩
**3** — used as a function word to introduce a nonrestrictive relative clause and to modify a noun in that clause and to refer together with that noun to a word or word group in a preceding clause or to an entire preceding clause or sentence or longer unit of discourse ⟨in German, *which* language might . . . have been the medium of transmission —Thomas Pyles⟩ ⟨that this city is a rebellious city . . . : for *which* cause was this city destroyed —Ezra 4:15 (Authorized Version)⟩
**²which** *pronoun* (before 12th century)
**1 :** what one or ones out of a group — used as an interrogative ⟨*which* of those houses do you live in⟩ ⟨*which* of you want tea and *which* want lemonade⟩ ⟨he is swimming or canoeing, I don't know *which*⟩
**2 :** WHICHEVER ⟨take *which* you like⟩
**3** — used as a function word to introduce a relative clause; used in any grammatical relation except that of a possessive; used especially in reference to animals, inanimate objects, groups, or ideas ⟨the bonds *which* represent the debt —G. B. Robinson⟩ ⟨the Samnite tribes, *which* settled south and southeast of Rome —Ernst Pulgram⟩; used freely in reference to persons as recently as the 17th century ⟨our Father *which* art in heaven —Matthew 6:9 (Authorized Version)⟩, and still occasionally so used but usually with some implication of emphasis on the function or role of the person rather than on the person as such ⟨chiefly they wanted husbands, *which* they got easily —Lynn White⟩; used by speakers on all educational levels and by many reputable writers, though disapproved by some grammarians, in reference to an idea expressed by a word or group of words that is not necessarily a noun or noun phrase ⟨he resigned that post, after *which* he engaged in ranching —*Current Biography*⟩
***usage*** see ⁴THAT, WHOSE

**¹which·ev·er** \hwich-'e-vər, wich-\ *adjective* (14th century)
**:** being whatever one or ones out of a group **:** no matter which ⟨its soothing . . . effect will be the same *whichever* way you take it —*Punch*⟩
**²whichever** *pronoun* (15th century)
**:** whatever one or ones out of a group ⟨take two of the four elective subjects, *whichever* you prefer⟩

**which·so·ev·er** \ˌhwich-sə-'we-vər, ˌwich-\ *pronoun or adjective* (15th century)
*archaic* **:** WHICHEVER

**whick·er** \'hwi-kər, 'wi-\ *intransitive verb* **whick·ered; whick·er·ing** \-k(ə-)riŋ\ [imitative] (1753)
**:** NEIGH, WHINNY
**— whicker** *noun*

**whid** \'hwid, 'wid\ *intransitive verb* **whid·ded; whid·ding** [Scots *whid* silent rapid motion] (1728)
*Scottish* **:** to move nimbly and silently

**¹whiff** \'hwif, 'wif\ *noun* [origin unknown] (1591)
**1 a :** a quick puff or slight gust especially of air, odor, gas, smoke, or spray **b :** an inhalation of odor, gas, or smoke **c :** a slight puffing or whistling sound
**2 :** a slight trace or indication
**3 :** STRIKEOUT

**²whiff** (1591)
*intransitive verb*
**1 :** to move with or as if with a puff of air
**2 :** to emit whiffs **:** PUFF
**3 :** to inhale an odor
**4 :** STRIKE OUT 3
*transitive verb*
**1 a :** to carry or convey by or as if by a whiff **:** BLOW **b :** to expel or puff out in a whiff **:** EXHALE **c :** SMOKE 3
**2 :** FAN 8

**whif·fet** \'hwi-fət, 'wi-\ *noun* [probably alteration of *whippet*] (1839)
**:** a small, young, or unimportant person

**whif·fle** \'hwi-fəl, 'wi-\ *verb* **whif·fled; whif·fling** \-f(ə-)liŋ\ [probably frequentative of *whiff*] (1568)
*intransitive verb*
**1 a** *of the wind* **:** to blow unsteadily or in gusts **b :** VACILLATE
**2 :** to emit or produce a light whistling or puffing sound
*transitive verb*
**:** to blow, disperse, emit, or expel with or as if with a whiff

**¹whif·fler** \'hwi-flər, 'wi-\ *noun* [alteration of earlier *wifler*, from obsolete *wifle* battle-ax] (1539)
*British* **:** one that clears the way for a procession

**²whif·fler** \'hwi-f(ə-)lər, 'wi-\ *noun* [*whiffle*] (1607)
**1 :** a person who frequently changes opinions or course
**2 :** a person who uses shifts and evasions in argument

**whif·fle·tree** \'hwi-fəl-(,)trē, 'wi-\ *noun* [alteration of *whippletree*] (circa 1806)
**:** the pivoted swinging bar to which the traces of a harness are fastened and by which a vehicle or implement is drawn

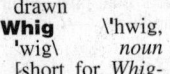

*1* whiffletree

**Whig** \'hwig, 'wig\ *noun* [short for *Whiggamore*, member of a Scottish group that marched to Edinburgh in 1648 to oppose the court party] (circa 1680)
**1 :** a member or supporter of a major British political group of the late 17th through early 19th centuries seeking to limit the royal authority and increase parliamentary power — compare TORY
**2 :** an American favoring independence from Great Britain during the American Revolution
**3 :** a member or supporter of an American political party formed about 1834 in opposition to the Jacksonian Democrats, associated chiefly with manufacturing, commercial, and financial interests, and succeeded about 1854 by the Republican party
— **Whig** *adjective*
— **Whig·gism** \'hwi-,gi-zəm\ *noun*
**Whig·gery** \'hwi-gə-rē, 'wi-\ *noun* (1714)
**:** the principles or practices of Whigs
**Whig·gish** \'hwi-gish, 'wi-\ *adjective* (1684)
**1 :** characteristic of Whigs or Whiggery
**2 :** of, relating to, or characterized by a view which holds that history follows a path of inevitable progression and improvement and which judges the past in light of the present
**whig·ma·lee·rie** \,hwig-mə-'lir-ē, ,wig-\ *noun* [origin unknown] (1730)
**1** *chiefly Scottish* **:** WHIM
**2** *chiefly Scottish* **:** an odd or fanciful contrivance **:** GIMCRACK

**¹while** \'hwī(ə)l, 'wī(ə)l\ *noun* [Middle English, from Old English *hwīl;* akin to Old High German *hwīla* time, Latin *quies* rest, quiet] (before 12th century)

**1 :** a period of time especially when short and marked by the occurrence of an action or a condition **:** TIME ⟨stay here for a *while*⟩
**2 :** the time and effort used (as in the performance of an action) **:** TROUBLE ⟨worth your *while*⟩

**²while** *conjunction* (12th century)
**1 a :** during the time that ⟨take a nap *while* I'm out⟩ **b :** as long as ⟨*while* there's life there's hope⟩
**2 a :** when on the other hand **:** WHEREAS ⟨easy for an expert, *while* it is dangerous for a novice⟩ **b :** in spite of the fact that **:** ALTHOUGH ⟨*while* respected, he is not liked⟩
**3 :** similarly and at the same time that ⟨*while* the book will be welcomed by scholars, it will make an immediate appeal to the general reader —*British Book News*⟩

**³while** *preposition* (15th century)
*dialect British* **:** UNTIL

**⁴while** *transitive verb* **whiled; whil·ing** (1635)
**:** to cause to pass especially without boredom or in a pleasant manner — usually used with *away* ⟨*while* away the time⟩

**¹whiles** \'hwī(ə)lz, 'wī(ə)lz\ *conjunction* [Middle English, from *while* + *-s*, adverb suffix — more at WHENCE] (13th century)
*archaic* **:** WHILE

**²whiles** *adverb* (15th century)
*chiefly Scottish* **:** SOMETIMES

**¹whi·lom** \'hwī-lom, 'wī-\ *adverb* [Middle English, literally, at times, from Old English *hwīlum*, dative plural of *hwīl* time, while] (13th century)
*archaic* **:** FORMERLY

**²whilom** *adjective* (1837)
**:** FORMER

**whilst** \'hwī(ə)lst, 'wī(ə)lst\ *conjunction* [Middle English *whilest*, alteration of *whiles*] (14th century)
*chiefly British* **:** WHILE

**whim** \'hwim, 'wim\ *noun* [short for *whim-wham*] (1697)
**1 :** a capricious or eccentric and often sudden idea or turn of the mind **:** FANCY
**2 :** a large capstan that is made with one or more radiating arms to which a horse may be yoked and that is used in mines for raising ore or water
*synonym* see CAPRICE

**whim·brel** \'hwim-brəl, 'wim-\ *noun* [origin unknown] (circa 1531)
**:** a small curlew (*Numenius phaeopus*) chiefly of the northern regions of North America and Eurasia; *broadly* **:** any small curlew

**¹whim·per** \'hwim-pər, 'wim-\ *intransitive verb* **whim·pered; whim·per·ing** \-p(ə-)riŋ\ [imitative] (1513)
**1 :** to make a low whining plaintive or broken sound
**2 :** to complain or protest with or as if with a whimper

**²whimper** *noun* (circa 1700)
**1 :** a whimpering cry or sound
**2 :** a petulant complaint or protest

**whim·si·cal** \'hwim-zi-kəl, 'wim-\ *adjective* [*whimsy*] (1653)
**1 :** full of, actuated by, or exhibiting whims
**2 a :** resulting from or characterized by whim or caprice; *especially* **:** lightly fanciful **b :** subject to erratic behavior or unpredictable change
— **whim·si·cal·i·ty** \,hwim-zə-'ka-lə-tē, ,wim-\ *noun*
— **whim·si·cal·ly** \'hwim-zi-k(ə-)lē, 'wim-\ *adverb*
— **whim·si·cal·ness** \-kəl-nəs\ *noun*
**whim·sy** *also* **whim·sey** \'hwim-zē, 'wim-\ *noun, plural* **whimsies** *also* **whimseys** [irregular from *whim-wham*] (1605)
**1 :** WHIM, CAPRICE
**2 :** the quality or state of being whimsical or fanciful ⟨the designer's new line showed a touch of *whimsy*⟩

**3 :** a fanciful or fantastic device, object, or creation especially in writing or art
**whim–wham** \'hwim-,hwam, 'wim-,wam\ *noun* [origin unknown] (1500)
**1 :** a whimsical object or device especially of ornament or dress
**2 :** FANCY, WHIM
**3** *plural* **:** JITTERS

**whin** \'hwin, 'win\ *noun* [Middle English *whynne*, of Scandinavian origin; akin to Norwegian *kvein* bent grass] (15th century)
**:** GORSE

**whin·chat** \'hwin-,chat, 'win-\ *noun* [*whin*] (1678)
**:** a small brown and buff European singing bird (*Saxicola rubetra*) of grassy meadows

**¹whine** \'hwīn, 'wīn\ *verb* **whined; whin·ing** [Middle English, from Old English *hwīnan* to whiz; akin to Old Norse *hvīna* to whiz] (13th century)
*intransitive verb*
**1 a :** to utter a high-pitched plaintive or distressed cry **b :** to make a sound similar to such a cry ⟨the wind *whined* in the chimney⟩
**2 :** to complain with or as if with a whine
**3 :** to move or proceed with the sound of a whine ⟨the bullet *whined* . . . across the ice —Berton Roueché⟩
*transitive verb*
**:** to utter or express with or as if with a whine
— **whin·er** *noun*
— **whin·ing·ly** \'hwī-niŋ-lē, 'wī-\ *adverb*

**²whine** *noun* (1633)
**1 a :** a prolonged high-pitched cry usually expressive of distress or pain **b :** a sound resembling such a cry
**2 :** a complaint uttered with or as if with a whine
— **whiny** *or* **whin·ey** \'hwī-nē, 'wī-\ *adjective*

**whing–ding** \'wiŋ-,diŋ, 'hwiŋ-\ *noun* [by alteration] (circa 1945)
**:** WINGDING

**whinge** \'hwinj, 'winj\ *intransitive verb* **whinged; whing·ing** *or* **whinge·ing** [from (assumed) Middle English, from Old English *hwinsian;* akin to Old High German *winsōn* to moan] (12th century)
*British* **:** to complain fretfully **:** WHINE

**¹whin·ny** \'hwi-nē, 'wi-\ *verb* **whin·nied; whin·ny·ing** [probably imitative] (1530)
*intransitive verb*
**:** to neigh especially in a low or gentle way
*transitive verb*
**:** to utter with or as if with a whinny

**²whinny** *noun, plural* **whinnies** (circa 1823)
**1 :** the neigh of a horse especially when low or gentle
**2 :** a sound resembling a neigh

**whin·stone** \'hwin-,stōn, 'win-\ *noun* [*whin*, a hard rock] (1513)
**:** basaltic rock **:** TRAP; *also* **:** any of various other dark resistant rocks (as chert)

**¹whip** \'hwip, 'wip\ *verb* **whipped; whip·ping** [Middle English *wippen, whippen;* akin to Middle Dutch *wippen* to move up and down, sway, Old English *wīpian* to wipe] (14th century)
*transitive verb*
**1 :** to take, pull, snatch, jerk, or otherwise move very quickly and forcefully ⟨*whipped* out his gun —Green Peyton⟩
**2 a** (1) **:** to strike with a slender lithe implement (as a lash or rod) especially as a punishment (2) **:** SPANK **b :** to drive or urge on by or as if by using a whip **c :** to strike as a lash does ⟨rain *whipped* the pavement⟩
**3 a :** to bind or wrap (as a rope or fishing rod) with cord for protection and strength **b :** to wind or wrap around something
**4 :** to belabor with stinging words **:** ABUSE
**5 :** to seam or hem with shallow overcasting stitches
**6 :** to overcome decisively **:** DEFEAT

**7 :** to stir up : INCITE — usually used with *up* ⟨trying to *whip* up a new emotion —Ellen Glasgow⟩
**8 :** to produce in a hurry — usually used with *up* ⟨a sketch . . . an artist might *whip* up —*N.Y. Times*⟩
**9 :** to fish (water) with rod, line, and artificial lure
**10 :** to beat (as eggs or cream) into a froth with a utensil (as a whisk or fork)
**11 :** to gather together or hold together for united action in the manner of a party whip
*intransitive verb*
**1 :** to proceed nimbly or quickly ⟨*whipping* through the supper dishes —C. B. Davis⟩
**2 :** to thrash about flexibly in the manner of a whiplash ⟨a flag . . . *whipping* out from its staff —H. A. Calahan⟩
— **whip·per** *noun*
— **whip into shape :** to bring forcefully to a desired state or condition
**²whip** *noun* (14th century)
**1 :** an instrument consisting usually of a handle and lash forming a flexible rod that is used for whipping
**2 :** a stroke or cut with or as if with a whip
**3 a :** a dessert made by whipping a portion of the ingredients ⟨prune *whip*⟩ **b :** a kitchen utensil made of braided or coiled wire or perforated metal with a handle and used in whipping
**4 :** one that handles a whip: as **a :** a driver of horses : COACHMAN **b :** WHIPPER-IN 1
**5 a :** a member of a legislative body appointed by a political party to enforce party discipline and to secure the attendance of party members at important sessions **b** *often capitalized* **:** a notice of forthcoming business sent weekly to each member of a political party in the British House of Commons
**6 :** a whipping or thrashing motion
**7 :** the quality of resembling a whip especially in being flexible
**8 :** a flexible vertical rod radio antenna — called also *whip antenna*
— **whip·like** \'hwip-ˌlīk, 'wip-\ *adjective*
**whip·cord** \'hwip-ˌkȯrd, 'wip-\ *noun* [from its use in making whips] (14th century)
**1 :** a thin tough cord made of braided or twisted hemp or catgut
**2 :** a cloth that is made of hard-twisted yarns and has fine diagonal cords or ribs
**whip hand** *noun* (1680)
**1 :** positive control : ADVANTAGE
**2 :** the hand holding the whip in driving
**whip in** *transitive verb* (1742)
**1 :** to collect or keep together (members of a political party) for legislative action
**2 :** to keep (hounds in a pack) from scattering by use of a whip
**whip·lash** \'hwip-ˌlash, 'wip-\ *noun* (circa 1580)
**1 :** the lash of a whip
**2 :** something resembling a blow from a whip ⟨the *whiplash* of fear —R. S. Banay⟩
**3 :** WHIPLASH INJURY
**whiplash injury** *noun* (circa 1953)
**:** injury resulting from a sudden sharp whipping movement of the neck and head (as of a person in a vehicle that is struck head-on or from the rear by another vehicle)
**whip·per-in** \ˌhwip-pər-'in, ˌwi-\ *noun, plural* **whip·pers-in** \-pərz-\ (1739)
**1 :** a huntsman's assistant who whips in the hounds
**2 :** WHIP 5a
**whip·per·snap·per** \'hwi-pər-ˌsna-pər, 'wi-\ *noun* [alteration of *snippersnapper*] (1700)
**:** a diminutive, insignificant, or presumptuous person
**whip·pet** \'hwi-pət, 'wi-\ *noun* [probably from ¹*whip*] (1610)
**:** any of a breed of small swift slender dogs that are widely used for racing
**whipping** *noun* (1540)

**1 :** the act of one that whips: as **a :** a severe beating or chastisement **b :** a stitching with small overcasting stitches
**2 :** material used to whip or bind
**whipping boy** *noun* (1647)
**1 :** a boy formerly educated with a prince and punished in his stead
**2 :** SCAPEGOAT 2
**whipping cream** *noun* (1921)
**:** a cream suitable for whipping that by law contains not less than 30 percent butterfat
**whipping post** *noun* (1600)
**:** a post to which offenders are tied to be legally whipped
**whip·ple·tree** \'hwi-pəl-ˌ(ˌ)trē, 'wi-\ *noun* [perhaps irregular from *whip* + *tree*] (1733)
**:** WHIFFLETREE
**whip·poor·will** \'hwi-pər-ˌwil, ˌhwi-pər-', 'wi-, ˌwi-\ *noun* [imitative] (1709)
**:** a nocturnal nightjar (*Caprimulgus vociferus*) of eastern North America with a loud repeated call suggestive of its name
**whip·py** \'hwi-pē, 'wi-\ *adjective* **whip·pi·er; -est** (1867)

whippoorwill

**1 :** unusually resilient : SPRINGY ⟨a *whippy* fishing rod⟩
**2 :** of, relating to, or resembling a whip
**whip–round** \'hwip-ˌraund, 'wip-\ *noun* (1887)
*chiefly British* **:** a collection of money made usually for a benevolent purpose ⟨had a *whip-round* to help the couple pay for a Paris honeymoon —*The People*⟩
**¹whip·saw** \'hwip-ˌsȯ, 'wip-\ *noun* [²*whip*] (1538)
**:** a narrow pit saw averaging from 5 to 7½ feet (1.5 to 2.3 meters) in length
**²whipsaw** *transitive verb* (1842)
**1 :** to saw with a whipsaw
**2 :** to beset or victimize in two opposite ways at once, by a two-phase operation, or by the collusive action of two opponents ⟨wage earners were *whipsawed* by inflation and high taxes⟩
**whip·sawed** \-ˌsȯd\ *adjective* (1892)
**:** subjected to a double market loss through trying inopportunely to recoup a loss by a subsequent short sale of the same security
**whip scorpion** *noun* (circa 1890)
**:** any of an order (Uropygi) of arachnids somewhat resembling true scorpions but having a long slender caudal process and no sting
**whip stall** *noun* (1924)
**:** a stall during a vertical climb in which the nose of the airplane whips violently forward and then downward
**¹whip·stitch** \'hwip-ˌstich, 'wip-\ *transitive verb* (1592)
**:** WHIP 5
**²whipstitch** *noun* (1640)
**:** a shallow overcasting stitch
**whip·stock** \-ˌstäk\ *noun* (circa 1530)
**:** the handle of a whip
**whip·worm** \-ˌwərm\ *noun* (1875)
**:** a parasitic nematode worm (genus *Trichuris*) with a body that is thickened posteriorly and that is very long and slender anteriorly; *especially* **:** one (*T. trichiura*) of the human intestine
**¹whir** *also* **whirr** \'hwər, 'wər\ *verb* **whirred; whir·ring** [Middle English (Scots) *quirren*, probably of Scandinavian origin; akin to Danish *hvirre* to whirl, whir] (15th century)
*intransitive verb*
**:** to fly, revolve, or move rapidly with a whir
*transitive verb*
**:** to move or carry rapidly with a whir
**²whir** *also* **whirr** *noun* (1677)
**:** a continuous fluttering or vibratory sound made by something in rapid motion

**¹whirl** \'hwər(-ə)l, 'wər(-ə)l\ *verb* [Middle English, probably of Scandinavian origin; akin to Old Norse *hvirfla* to whirl; akin to Old High German *wirbil* whirlwind, Old English *hweorfan* to turn — more at WHARF] (14th century)
*intransitive verb*
**1 :** to move in a circle or similar curve especially with force or speed
**2 a :** to turn on or around an axis like a wheel : ROTATE **b :** to turn abruptly around or aside : WHEEL
**3 :** to pass, move, or go quickly ⟨*whirled* down the hallway⟩
**4 :** to become giddy or dizzy : REEL ⟨my head is *whirling*⟩
*transitive verb*
**1 :** to drive, impel, or convey with or as if with a rotary motion
**2 a :** to cause to turn usually rapidly on or around an axis : ROTATE **b :** to cause to turn abruptly around or aside
**3** *obsolete* **:** to throw or hurl violently with a revolving motion
— **whirl·er** \'hwər-lər, 'wər-\ *noun*
**²whirl** *noun* (15th century)
**1 a :** a rapid rotating or circling movement **b :** something undergoing such a movement
**2 a :** a busy or fast-paced succession of events : BUSTLE ⟨a *whirl* of activity⟩ ⟨the social *whirl*⟩ **b :** a confused or disturbed mental state : TURMOIL ⟨a *whirl* of febrile excitement —Emily Skeel⟩
**3 :** an experimental or brief attempt : TRY ⟨gave it a whirl⟩
**whirl·i·gig** \'hwər-li-ˌgig, 'wər-\ *noun* [Middle English *whirlegigg*, from *whirlen* to whirl + *gigg* top — more at GIG] (15th century)
**1 :** a child's toy having a whirling motion
**2 :** MERRY-GO-ROUND
**3 a :** one that continuously whirls, moves, or changes **b :** a whirling or circling course (as of events)
**whirligig beetle** *noun* (1855)
**:** any of a family (Gyrinidae) of beetles with two pairs of eyes and clubbed antennae that live mostly on the surface of water where they swim swiftly about in circles
**whirl·pool** \'hwər(-ə)l-ˌpül, 'wər(-ə)l-\ *noun* (1529)
**1 a :** a confused tumult and bustle : WHIRL **b :** a magnetic or impelling force by which something may be engulfed ⟨refusing to be drawn into this *whirlpool* of intrigue —A. D. White⟩
**2 a :** water moving rapidly in a circle so as to produce a depression in the center into which floating objects may be drawn : EDDY, VORTEX **b :** WHIRLPOOL BATH
**whirlpool bath** *noun* (circa 1916)
**:** a therapeutic bath in which all or part of the body is exposed to forceful whirling currents of hot water
**¹whirl·wind** \-ˌwind\ *noun* (14th century)
**1 :** a small rotating windstorm of limited extent
**2 a :** a confused rush : WHIRL **b :** a violent or destructive force or agency
**²whirlwind** *adjective* (1614)
**:** resembling a whirlwind especially in speed or force ⟨a *whirlwind* campaign⟩ ⟨a *whirlwind* romance⟩
**¹whirly** \'hwər-lē, 'wər-\ *adjective* (15th century)
**:** marked by or exhibiting a whirling motion
**²whirly** *noun, plural* **whirl·ies** (1914)
**:** a small whirlwind
**whirly·bird** \-ˌbərd\ *noun* (1951)
**:** HELICOPTER

\ə\ abut \ᵊ\ kitten \ər\ further \a\ ash \ā\ ace
\ä\ mop, mar \au̇\ out \ch\ chin \e\ bet \ē\ easy
\g\ go \i\ hit \ī\ ice \j\ job \ŋ\ sing \ō\ go
\ȯ\ law \ȯi\ boy \th\ thin \t͟h\ the \ü\ loot \u̇\ foot
\y\ yet \zh\ vision *see also* Guide to Pronunciation

**whir·ry** \'hwər-ē, 'wər-, '(h)wə-rē\ *verb* **whir·ried; whir·ry·ing** [perhaps blend of *whir* and *hurry*] (1582)
*transitive verb*
*Scottish* : to convey quickly
*intransitive verb*
*Scottish* : HURRY

¹**whish** \'hwish, 'wish\ *verb* [imitative] (1518)
*transitive verb*
: to urge on or cause to move with a whish
*intransitive verb*
**1** : to make a sibilant sound
**2** : to move with a whish especially at high speed ⟨an elevator . . . *whishes* down to the lower level —Natalie Cooper⟩

²**whish** *noun* (circa 1802)
: a rushing sound : SWISH

**whisht** \'hwisht, 'wisht\ *intransitive verb* [Middle English; imitative] (15th century)
*chiefly Irish* : HUSH — often used interjectionally to enjoin silence

¹**whisk** \'hwisk, 'wisk\ *noun* [Middle English *wisk*, probably of Scandinavian origin; akin to Old Norse *visk* wisp; akin to Old English *wiscian* to plait] (14th century)
**1** : a quick light brushing or whipping motion
**2 a** : a usually wire kitchen utensil used for beating food by hand **b** : a flexible bunch (as of twigs, feathers, or straw) attached to a handle for use as a brush

²**whisk** (15th century)
*intransitive verb*
: to move nimbly and quickly
*transitive verb*
**1** : to move or convey briskly ⟨*whisked* the children off to bed⟩
**2** : to mix or fluff up by or as if by beating with a whisk ⟨*whisk* egg whites⟩
**3** : to brush or wipe off lightly

**whisk broom** *noun* (1857)
: a small broom with a short handle used especially as a clothes brush

**whis·ker** \'hwis-kər, 'wis-\ *noun* [singular of *whiskers* mustache, from ²*whisk*] (circa 1600)
**1 a** : a hair of the beard **b** *plural* (1) *archaic* : MUSTACHE (2) : the part of the beard growing on the sides of the face or on the chin **c** : HAIRBREADTH ⟨lost the race by a *whisker*⟩
**2** : one of the long projecting hairs or bristles growing near the mouth of an animal (as a cat or bird)
**3** : an outrigger extending on each side of the bowsprit to spread the jib and flying jib guys — usually used in plural
**4 a** : a shred or filament resembling a whisker **b** : a thin hairlike crystal (as of sapphire or copper) of exceptional mechanical strength used especially to reinforce composite structural material
— **whis·kered** \-kərd\ *adjective*
— **whis·kery** \-k(ə-)rē\ *adjective*

**whis·key** *or* **whis·ky** \'hwis-kē, 'wis-\ *noun*, *plural* **whiskeys** *or* **whiskies** [Irish *uisce beathadh* & Scottish Gaelic *uisge beatha*, literally, water of life] (1715)
**1** : a liquor distilled from the fermented mash of grain (as rye, corn, or barley)
**2** : a drink of whiskey ◆
**Whiskey** (circa 1952)
— a communication code word for the letter *w*

**whiskey sour** *noun* (circa 1889)
: a cocktail usually consisting of whiskey, sugar, and lemon juice shaken with ice

¹**whis·per** \'hwis-pər, 'wis-\ *verb* **whis·pered; whis·per·ing** \-p(ə-)riŋ\ [Middle English, from Old English *hwisperian;* akin to Old High German *hwispalōn* to whisper, Old Norse *hvīsla* — more at WHISTLE] (before 12th century)
*intransitive verb*
**1** : to speak softly with little or no vibration of the vocal cords especially to avoid being overheard
**2** : to make a sibilant sound that resembles whispering

*transitive verb*
**1** : to address in a whisper
**2** : to utter or communicate in or as if in a whisper

²**whisper** *noun* (1595)
**1** : something communicated by or as if by whispering; *especially* : RUMOR ⟨*whispers* of scandal⟩
**2 a** : an act or instance of whispering; *especially* : speech without vibration of the vocal cords **b** : a sibilant sound that resembles whispered speech
**3** : HINT, TRACE

**whis·per·er** \-pər-ər\ *noun* (1547)
: one that whispers; *specifically* : RUMORMONGER

¹**whispering** *noun* (before 12th century)
**1 a** : whispered speech **b** : GOSSIP, RUMOR
**2** : a sibilant sound : WHISPER

²**whispering** *adjective* (1547)
**1** : making a sibilant sound
**2** : spreading confidential and especially derogatory reports ⟨*whispering* tongues can poison truth —S. T. Coleridge⟩
— **whis·per·ing·ly** \-p(ə-)riŋ-lē\ *adverb*

**whispering campaign** *noun* (1920)
: the systematic dissemination by word of mouth of derogatory rumors or charges especially against a candidate for public office

**whis·pery** \'hwis-p(ə-)rē, 'wis-\ *adjective* (1834)
**1** : resembling a whisper
**2** : full of whispers

¹**whist** \'hwist, 'wist\ *intransitive verb* [Middle English; imitative] (14th century)
*dialect British* : to be silent : HUSH — often used interjectionally to enjoin silence

²**whist** *adjective* (15th century)
: QUIET, SILENT

³**whist** *noun* [alteration of earlier *whisk,* probably from ²*whisk;* from whisking up the tricks] (1663)
: a card game for four players in two partnerships that is played with a pack of 52 cards and that scores one point for each trick in excess of six

¹**whis·tle** \'hwi-səl, 'wi-\ *noun, often attributive* [Middle English, from Old English *hwistle;* akin to Old Norse *hvīsla* to whisper] (before 12th century)
**1 a** : a small wind instrument in which sound is produced by the forcible passage of breath through a slit in a short tube ⟨police *whistle*⟩ **b** : a device through which air or steam is forced into a cavity or against a thin edge to produce a loud sound ⟨a factory *whistle*⟩
**2 a** : a shrill clear sound produced by forcing breath out or air in through the puckered lips **b** : the sound produced by a whistle **c** : a signal given by, or as if by whistling
**3** : a sound that resembles a whistle; *especially* : a shrill clear note of or as if of a bird

²**whistle** *verb* **whis·tled; whis·tling** \-s(ə-)liŋ\ (before 12th century)
*intransitive verb*
**1 a** : to utter a shrill clear sound by blowing or drawing air through the puckered lips **b** : to utter a shrill note or call resembling a whistle **c** : to make a shrill clear sound especially by rapid movement ⟨the wind *whistled*⟩ **d** : to blow or sound a whistle
**2 a** : to give a signal or issue an order or summons by or as if by whistling **b** : to make a demand without result ⟨did a sloppy job so he can *whistle* for his money⟩
*transitive verb*
**1 a** : to send, bring, signal, or call by or as if by whistling **b** : to charge (as a basketball or hockey player) with an infraction
**2** : to produce, utter, or express by whistling ⟨*whistle* a tune⟩
— **whis·tle·able** \-sə-lə-bəl\ *adjective*
— **whistle in the dark** : to keep up one's courage by or as if by whistling

**whis·tle–blow·er** \-,blō(-ə)r\ *noun* (1970)
: one who reveals something covert or who informs against another ⟨pledges to protect *whistle-blowers* who fear reprisals —*Wall Street Journal*⟩
— **whis·tle–blow·ing** \-,blō-iŋ\ *noun*

**whis·tler** \'hwi-s(ə-)lər, 'wi-\ *noun* (before 12th century)
: one that whistles: as **a** : any of various birds; *especially* : any of numerous Australian and Polynesian oscine birds (especially genus *Pachycephala*) that are related to the shrikes and have a whistling call **b** : a large mountain marmot (*Marmota caligata*) of northwestern North America **c** : a broken-winded horse **d** : a very-low-frequency radio signal that is generated by lightning discharge, travels along the earth's magnetic-field lines, and produces a sound resembling a whistle of descending pitch in radio receivers

¹**whis·tle–stop** \'hwi-səl-,stäp, 'wi-\ *noun, often attributive* (circa 1925)
**1 a** : a small station at which trains stop only on signal : FLAG STOP **b** : a small community
**2** : a brief personal appearance especially by a political candidate usually on the rear platform of a train during the course of a tour

²**whistle–stop** *intransitive verb* (1952)
: to make a tour especially in a political campaign with many brief personal appearances in small communities

**whistling** *noun* (14th century)
: the act or sound of one that whistles : WHISTLE

**whistling swan** *noun* (1785)
: a native North American swan (*Cygnus columbianus* synonym *Olor columbianus*) that calls with a soft musical note, breeds in the Arctic tundra, and winters in shallow fresh or salt water especially along the eastern and western coasts of the U.S.

**whit** \'hwit, 'wit\ *noun* [Middle English, probably alteration of *wiht, wight* creature, thing — more at WIGHT] (15th century)
: the smallest part or particle imaginable : BIT ⟨what some people will do for a *whit* of publicity —Patrick Quinn⟩

¹**white** \'hwīt, 'wīt\ *adjective* **whit·er; whit·est** [Middle English, from Old English *hwīt;* akin to Old High German *hwīz* white and probably to Old Church Slavonic *světǔ* light, Sanskrit *śveta* white, bright] (before 12th century)
**1 a** : free from color **b** : of the color of new snow or milk; *specifically* : of the color white **c** : light or pallid in color ⟨*white* hair⟩ ⟨lips *white* with fear⟩ **d** : lustrous pale gray : SILVERY; *also* : made of silver
**2 a** : being a member of a group or race characterized by reduced pigmentation and usually

specifically distinguished from persons belonging to groups marked by black, brown, yellow, or red skin coloration **b** : of, relating to, characteristic of, or consisting of white people **c** : marked by upright fairness
**3** : free from spot or blemish: as **a** (1) : free from moral impurity : INNOCENT (2) : marked by the wearing of white by the woman as a symbol of purity ⟨a *white* wedding⟩ **b** : unmarked by writing or printing **c** : not intended to cause harm ⟨a *white* lie⟩ ⟨*white* magic⟩ **d** : FAVORABLE, FORTUNATE ⟨one of the *white* days of his life —Sir Walter Scott⟩
**4 a** : wearing or habited in white **b** : marked by the presence of snow : SNOWY ⟨a *white* Christmas⟩
**5 a** : heated to the point of whiteness **b** : notably ardent : PASSIONATE ⟨*white* fury⟩
**6 a** : conservative or reactionary in political outlook and action **b** : instigated or carried out by reactionary forces as a counterrevolutionary measure ⟨a *white* terror⟩
**7** : of, relating to, or constituting a musical tone quality characterized by a controlled pure sound, a lack of warmth and color, and a lack of resonance
**8** : consisting of a wide range of frequencies — used of light, sound, and electromagnetic radiation
— **whit·ish** \'hwī-tish, 'wī-\ *adjective*

**²white** *noun* (before 12th century)
**1** : the achromatic object color of greatest lightness characteristically perceived to belong to objects that reflect diffusely nearly all incident energy throughout the visible spectrum
**2 a** : a white or light-colored part of something: as (1) : a mass of albuminous material surrounding the yolk of an egg (2) : the white part of the ball of the eye (3) : the light-colored pieces in a two-handed board game; *also* : the player by whom these are played (4) : the area of a page unmarked by writing, printing, or illustration **b** (1) *archaic* : a white target (2) : the fifth or outermost circle of an archery target; *also* : a shot that hits it
**3** : one that is or approaches white in color: as **a** : white clothing — often used in plural **b** : WHITE WINE **c** : a white mammal (as a horse or a hog) **d** (1) : a white-colored product (as flour, pins, or sugar) — usually used in plural (2) : any of numerous butterflies (subfamily Pierinae of the family Pieridae) that usually have the ground color of the wings white and are related to the sulphur butterflies
**4** *plural* : LEUKORRHEA
**5** : a person belonging to a light-skinned race
**6** *often capitalized* : a member of a conservative or reactionary political group

**³white** *transitive verb* **whit·ed; whit·ing** [Middle English, from *white*, adjective] (before 12th century)
*archaic* : WHITEN

**white amur** \-ä-'mùr\ *noun* [*amur* from *Amur* River] (1968)
: GRASS CARP

**white ant** *noun* (1684)
: TERMITE

**white ash** *noun* (1683)
: an American ash (*Fraxinus americana*) having compound leaves with a pale green or silvery white underside; *also* : its hard brownish wood

**white·bait** \'hwīt-,bāt, 'wīt-\ *noun* (1758)
**1** : the young of any of several European herrings and especially of the common herring (*Clupea harengus*) or of the sprat (*C. sprattus*)
**2** : any of various small fishes likened to the European whitebait and used as food

**white bass** *noun* (1813)
: a North American freshwater bony fish (*Morone chrysops* of the family Percichthyidae) that is used for food

**white bean** *noun* (1969)
: a dried white kidney bean seed; *also* : a plant that is a source of white beans

**white·beard** \'hwīt-,bird, 'wīt-\ *noun* (15th century)
: an old man : GRAYBEARD

**white birch** *noun* (1789)
**1** : PAPER BIRCH; *also* : GRAY BIRCH
**2** : either of two European birches (*Betula pubescens* and *B. pendula*) with white or ash-colored bark that are often planted as ornamentals in the U.S.

**white blood cell** *noun* (1885)
: any of the blood cells that are colorless, lack hemoglobin, contain a nucleus, and include the lymphocytes, monocytes, neutrophils, eosinophils, and basophils — called also *white blood corpuscle*

**white book** *noun* (15th century)
: an official report of government affairs bound in white

**white–bread** \'hwīt-'bred, 'wīt-\ *adjective* (1979)
: being, typical of, or having qualities (as blandness) associated with the white middle class

**white·cap** \'hwīt-,kap, 'wīt-\ *noun* (1773)
: a wave crest breaking into white foam — usually used in plural

**white cedar** *noun* (1674)
**1** : a strong-scented evergreen swamp tree (*Chamaecyparis thyoides*) of the cypress family that occurs along the eastern coast of the U.S. and that has smaller leaves than an arborvitae and globose cones with peltate scales; *also* : its wood
**2** : NORTHERN WHITE CEDAR

**white cell** *noun* (1861)
: WHITE BLOOD CELL

**white chip** *noun* (1897)
**1** : a white-colored poker chip usually of minimum value
**2** : a thing or quantity of little worth — compare BLUE CHIP

**white chocolate** *noun* (1923)
: a confection of cocoa butter, sugar, milk solids, lecithin, and flavorings

**white clover** *noun* (before 12th century)
: a Eurasian clover (*Trifolium repens*) with round heads of white flowers that is widely used in lawn and pasture grass-seed mixtures and is an important source of nectar for bees — called also *white Dutch clover*

**white–col·lar** \'hwīt-'kä-lər, 'wīt-\ *adjective* (1920)
: of, relating to, or constituting the class of salaried employees whose duties do not call for the wearing of work clothes or protective clothing — compare BLUE-COLLAR

**white crappie** *noun* (circa 1926)
: a silvery North American sunfish (*Pomoxis annularis*) with 5 or 6 protruding spines on the dorsal fins that is used as a panfish and often for stocking small ponds

**white–crowned sparrow** \'hwīt-'kraùnd-, 'wīt-\ *noun* (1839)
: a migratory sparrow (*Zonotrichia leucophrys*) that breeds in northern and western North America and has a grayish breast, pink bill, and head striped with black and white

**whit·ed** \'hwī-təd, 'wī-\ *adjective* (14th century)
**1** : covered with white or whiting and especially with whitewash
**2** : made white : WHITENED

**whited sepulcher** *noun* [from the simile in Matthew 23:27 (Authorized Version)] (1582)
: a person inwardly corrupt or wicked but outwardly or professedly virtuous or holy : HYPOCRITE

**white dwarf** *noun, plural* **white dwarfs** (1924)
: a small whitish star of low intrinsic brightness usually with a mass approximately equal to that of the sun but with a density many times larger

**white elephant** *noun* (15th century)
**1** : an Indian elephant of a pale color that is sometimes venerated in India, Sri Lanka, Thailand, and Myanmar
**2 a** : a property requiring much care and expense and yielding little profit **b** : an object no longer of value to its owner but of value to others **c** : something of little or no value

**white·face** \'hwīt-,fās, 'wīt-\ *noun* (1709)
**1** : a white-faced animal; *specifically* : HEREFORD
**2** : dead-white facial makeup ⟨a clown in *whiteface*⟩

**white–faced** \-'fāst\ *adjective* (1595)
**1** : having a wan pale face
**2** : having the face white in whole or in part — used especially of an animal otherwise dark in color

**white feather** *noun* [from the superstition that a white feather in the plumage of a gamecock is a mark of a poor fighter] (circa 1785)
: a mark or symbol of cowardice — used chiefly in the phrase *show the white feather*

**white·fish** \'hwīt-,fish, 'wīt-\ *noun* (15th century)
**1 a** : any of various freshwater salmonid food fishes (especially of genera *Coregonus* and *Prosopium*) **b** : any of various fishes resembling the true whitefishes **c** *British* : any of various market fishes with white flesh that is not oily
**2** : the flesh of a whitefish especially as an article of food

**white flag** *noun* (1600)
**1** : a flag of plain white used as a flag of truce or as a token of surrender
**2** : a token of weakness or yielding

**white flight** *noun* (1967)
: the departure of white families usually from urban neighborhoods undergoing racial integration or from cities implementing school desegregation

**white·fly** \'hwīt-,flī, 'wīt-\ *noun* (circa 1889)
: any of numerous small homopterous insects (family Aleyrodidae) that are injurious plant pests

**white–foot·ed mouse** \'hwīt-,fù-təd-, 'wīt-\ *noun* (1869)
: any of various largely nocturnal mice (genus *Peromyscus*) of North and Central America typically having whitish feet and underparts;

**white-footed mouse**

*especially* : a common woodland mouse (*P. leucopus*) of North America

**white friar** *noun, often W&F capitalized* [from his white habit] (15th century)
: CARMELITE

**white–fringed beetle** \'hwīt-,frinj(d)-, 'wīt-\ *noun* (1939)
: any of a genus (*Graphognathus*) of South American flightless beetles of which one (*G. leucoloma*) has been accidentally introduced into the southeastern U.S. where it is a pest on cultivated plants

**white gas** *noun* (1926)
: unleaded gasoline — called also *white gasoline*

**white gold** *noun* (1666)
: a pale alloy of gold especially with nickel or palladium that resembles platinum in appearance

**white goods** *noun plural* (circa 1871)
**1 a** : white fabrics especially of cotton or linen **b** : articles (as sheets, towels, or curtains) originally or typically made of white cloth

**2 :** major household appliances (as stoves and refrigerators) that are typically finished in white enamel

**white grub** *noun* (circa 1817)
**:** a grub that is a destructive pest of grass roots and is the larva of various beetles and especially june bugs

**White·hall** \'hwīt-,hȯl, 'wīt-\ *noun* [*Whitehall,* thoroughfare of London in which are located the chief offices of British government] (1827)
**:** the British government

**white·head** \-,hed\ *noun* (circa 1931)
**:** MILIUM

**white–head·ed** \-'he-dəd\ *adjective* (1525)
**1 :** having the hair, fur, or plumage of the head white or very light
**2 :** specially favored **:** FORTUNATE — used especially in the phrase *white-headed boy*

**white heat** *noun* (circa 1710)
**1 :** a temperature (as for copper and iron from 1500° to 1600° C) which is higher than red heat and at which a body becomes brightly incandescent
**2 :** a state of intense mental or physical strain, emotion, or activity

**white hole** *noun* (1971)
**:** a hypothetical extremely dense celestial object that radiates enormous amounts of energy and matter — compare BLACK HOLE 1

**white hope** *noun* (1911)
**1 :** a white contender for a boxing championship held by a black; *also* **:** one who is felt to represent whites
**2 :** one from whom much is expected; *especially* **:** a person undertaking a difficult task

**white–hot** \'hwīt-'hät, 'wīt-\ *adjective* (1820)
**1 :** being at or radiating white heat
**2 :** ardently zealous **:** FERVID

**White House** \-,haus\ *noun* [the *White House,* mansion in Washington, D.C., assigned to the use of the president of the U.S.] (1811)
**1 :** the executive department of the U.S. government
**2 :** a residence of the president of the U.S.

**white hunter** *noun* (1945)
**:** a white man serving as guide and professional hunter to an African safari

**white knight** *noun* (1951)
**1 :** one that comes to the rescue of another; *especially* **:** a corporation invited to buy out a second corporation in order to prevent an undesired takeover by a third
**2 :** one that champions a cause

**white–knuck·le** \'hwīt-'nə-kəl, 'wīt-\ *also* **white–knuck·led** \-kəld\ *adjective* (1974)
**:** showing or causing tense nervousness ⟨a *white-knuckle* ride on a roller coaster⟩

**white lead** *noun* (15th century)
**:** any of several white lead-containing pigments; *especially* **:** a heavy poisonous basic carbonate of lead of variable composition that is marketed as a powder or as a paste in linseed oil, has good hiding power, and is used chiefly in exterior paints

**white lightning** *noun* (1915)
**:** MOONSHINE 3

**white line** *noun* (15th century)
**:** a band or edge of something white; *especially* **:** a stripe painted on a road and used to guide traffic

**white list** \-,list\ *noun* (1900)
**:** a list of approved or favored items — compare BLACKLIST
— **white–list·ed** \-,lis-təd\ *adjective*

**white–liv·ered** \-'li-vərd\ *adjective* [from the former belief that the choleric temperament depends on the body's producing large quantities of yellow bile] (1549)
**:** PUSILLANIMOUS, LILY-LIVERED

**white·ly** \'hwīt-lē, 'wīt-\ *adverb* (14th century)
**:** with an effect of whiteness **:** so as to show or appear white

**white man's burden** *noun* ["The White Man's Burden" (1899), poem by Rudyard Kipling] (1911)

**:** the alleged duty of the white peoples to manage the affairs of the less developed nonwhite peoples

**white matter** *noun* (circa 1847)
**:** neural tissue that consists largely of myelinated nerve fibers, has a whitish color, and underlies the gray matter of the brain and spinal cord or is gathered into nerves

**white metal** *noun* (1613)
**1 :** any of several light-colored alloys used especially as a base for plated silverware and ornaments and novelties
**2 :** any of several lead-base or tin-base alloys (as babbitt) used especially for bearings, fusible plugs, and type metal

**white mustard** *noun* (1731)
**:** a Eurasian mustard (*Brassica hirta*) grown for its seeds which yield mustard and mustard oil

**whit·en** \'hwī-t°n, 'wī-\ *verb* **whit·ened; whit·en·ing** \'hwīt-niŋ, 'wīt-, -°n-iŋ\ (14th century)
*transitive verb*
**:** to make white or whiter ⟨snow *whitened* the hills⟩
*intransitive verb*
**:** to become white or whiter

**whit·en·er** \'hwīt-nər, 'wīt-; 'hwī-t°n-ər, 'wī-\ *noun* (1611)
**:** one that whitens; *specifically* **:** an agent (as a bleach) used to impart whiteness to something

**white·ness** \'hwīt-nəs, 'wīt-\ *noun* (before 12th century)
**1 :** the quality or state of being white: as **a :** white color **b :** PALLOR, PALENESS **c :** freedom from stain **:** CLEANNESS
**2 :** white substance

**whitening** *noun* (1601)
**1 :** the act or process of making or becoming white
**2 :** something that is used to make white **:** WHITING

**white noise** *noun* (1943)
**:** a heterogeneous mixture of sound waves extending over a wide frequency range

**white oak** *noun* (1634)
**:** any of various oaks (especially *Quercus alba* of eastern North America) with acorns that mature in one year and leaf veins that never extend beyond the margin of the leaf; *also* **:** its hard strong durable wood

**white oil** *noun* (circa 1900)
**:** any of various colorless odorless tasteless mineral oils used especially in medicine and in pharmaceutical and cosmetic preparations

white oak: leaves and acorns

**white·out** \'hwīt-,aut, 'wīt-\ *noun* [*white* + black*out*] (1942)
**:** a surface weather condition in a snow-covered area (as a polar region) in which no object casts a shadow, the horizon cannot be seen, and only dark objects are discernible; *also* **:** a blizzard that severely reduces visibility

**white pages** *noun plural* (1952)
**:** the section of a telephone directory that lists individuals and businesses alphabetically

**white paper** *noun* (1899)
**1 :** a government report on any subject; *especially* **:** a British publication that is usually less extensive than a blue book
**2 :** a detailed or authoritative report

**white pepper** *noun* (14th century)
**:** a pungent condiment that consists of the fruit of an East Indian plant (*Piper nigrum*) ground after the black husk has been removed

**white perch** *noun* (1775)

**1 :** a silvery anadromous bass (*Morone americana*) chiefly of the coast and coastal streams of the eastern U.S.
**2 :** FRESHWATER DRUM
**3 :** WHITE CRAPPIE

**white pine** *noun* (1682)
**1 a :** a tall-growing pine (*Pinus strobus*) of eastern North America with long needles in clusters of five — called also *eastern white pine* **b :** any of several trees that resemble the white pine especially in having leaves in bundles of five
**2 :** the wood of a white pine and especially of the eastern white pine

**white–pine blister rust** *noun* (1911)
**:** a destructive disease of white pine caused by a rust fungus (*Cronartium ribicola*) that passes part of its complex life cycle on currant or gooseberry bushes; *also* **:** this fungus

**white potato** *noun* (circa 1890)
**:** POTATO 2b

**white rice** *noun* (1923)
**:** rice from which the hull and bran have been removed by milling

**white room** *noun* (1961)
**:** CLEAN ROOM

**White Russian** *noun* (1850)
**1 :** BELORUSSIAN
**2 :** a cocktail made of vodka, coffee liqueur, and cream or milk

**white rust** *noun* (circa 1848)
**:** any of various plant diseases caused by a fungus (genus *Albugo* of the order Peronosporales) and characterized by the presence of masses of white spores that escape through ruptures of the host tissue; *also* **:** a fungus causing a white rust

**white sale** *noun* (1914)
**:** a sale of white goods

**white sauce** *noun* (1723)
**:** a sauce consisting essentially of a roux with milk, cream, or stock and seasoning

**white sea bass** *noun* (1884)
**:** a large croaker (*Atractoscion nobilis*) of the Pacific coast that is an important sport and food fish

**white shark** *noun* (1674)
**:** GREAT WHITE SHARK

**white slave** *noun* (1882)
**:** a woman or girl held unwillingly for purposes of commercial prostitution

**white slav·er** \-'slā-vər\ *noun* (1912)
**:** one engaged in white-slave traffic

**white slavery** *noun* (1857)
**:** enforced prostitution

**white·smith** \'hwīt-,smith, 'wīt-\ *noun* (14th century)
**1 :** TINSMITH
**2 :** a worker in iron who finishes or polishes the work

**white space** *noun* (1849)
**:** the areas of a page without print or pictures

**white spruce** *noun* (1770)
**1 :** any of several spruces; *especially* **:** a widely distributed spruce (*Picea glauca*) of coniferous forests of Canada and the northern U.S. that has short stiff blue-green needles and slender cones
**2 :** the wood of a white spruce; *especially* **:** the light pale tough straight-grained wood of the common white spruce (*Picea glauca*) used especially for construction and as a source of paper pulp

**white sucker** *noun* (circa 1902)
**:** a common and widespread edible sucker (*Catostomus commersoni*) of the U.S. and Canada

**white supremacist** *noun* (1945)
**:** an advocate of or believer in white supremacy

**white supremacy** *noun* (1867)
**:** a doctrine based on a belief in the inherent superiority of the white race over the black race and the correlative necessity for the subordination of blacks to whites in all relationships

**white·tail** \'hwīt-ˌtāl, 'wīt-\ *noun* (1872)
: WHITE-TAILED DEER

**white–tailed deer** \-ˌtāld-\ *noun* (1849)
: a North American deer (*Odocoileus virginianus*) with a rather long tail white on the undersurface and the males of which have forward-arching antlers

white-tailed deer

**white·throat** \'hwīt-ˌthrōt, 'wīt-\ *noun* (1676)
: any of several birds with white on the throat: as **a** : an Old World warbler (*Sylvia communis*) with rusty upper parts and largely pale buff underparts **b** : WHITE-THROATED SPARROW

**white–throat·ed sparrow** \-ˌthrō-təd-\ *noun* (1811)
: a common brown sparrow (*Zonotrichia albicollis*) chiefly of eastern North America with a black-and-white striped crown and a white patch on the throat

**white–tie** *adjective* (1936)
: characterized by or requiring the wearing of formal evening clothes consisting of white tie and tailcoat for men and a formal gown for women ⟨a *white-tie* dinner⟩ — compare BLACK-TIE

**white trash** *noun singular but plural in construction* (1831)
: POOR WHITE — usually used disparagingly

**white·wall** \'hwīt-ˌwȯl, 'wīt-\ *noun* (1953)
: an automobile tire having a white band on the sidewall

**white walnut** *noun* (1743)
**1** : BUTTERNUT 1
**2** : the light-colored wood of a butternut

**1white·wash** \'hwīt-ˌwȯsh, 'wīt-, -ˌwäsh\ *transitive verb* (1591)
**1** : to whiten with whitewash
**2 a** : to gloss over or cover up (as vices or crimes) **b** : to exonerate by means of a perfunctory investigation or through biased presentation of data
**3** : to hold (an opponent) scoreless in a game or contest
— **white·wash·er** *noun*

**2whitewash** *noun* (1689)
**1** : a liquid composition for whitening a surface: as **a** : a preparation for whitening the skin **b** : a composition (as of lime and water or whiting, size, and water) for whitening structural surfaces
**2** : an act or instance of glossing over or of exonerating
**3** : a defeat in a contest in which the loser fails to score

**white·wash·ing** *noun* (1663)
: an act or instance of applying whitewash; *also* : WHITEWASH 3

**white water** *noun* (1586)
: frothy water (as in breakers, rapids, or falls)
— **white–water** *adjective*

**white way** *noun* [the *Great White Way*, nickname for the theatrical section of Broadway, New York City] (1909)
: a brilliantly lighted street or avenue especially in a city's business or theater district

**white whale** *noun* (circa 1834)
: a cetacean (*Delphinapterus leucas*) that is about 10 feet (3.0 meters) long and white when adult — called also *beluga*

white whale

**white wine** *noun* (14th century)
: a wine ranging in color from faintly yellow to amber that is produced from the juice alone of dark- or light-colored grapes

**white·wing** \'hwīt-ˌwiŋ, 'wīt-\ *noun* (1898)
: a person and especially a street sweeper wearing a white uniform

**white·wood** \-ˌwu̇d\ *noun* (1663)
**1** : any of various trees with pale or white wood: as **a** : TULIP TREE 1 **b** : an Australian tree (*Atalaya hemiglauca*) of the soapberry family
**2** : the wood of a whitewood; *especially* : TULIPWOOD 1

**whit·ey** \'hwī-tē, 'wī-\ *noun, often capitalized* (1828)
: the white man : white society — usually used disparagingly

**white zinfandel** *noun* (1976)
: a blush wine made from zinfandel grapes

**1whith·er** \'hwi-thər, 'wi-\ *adverb* [Middle English, from Old English *hwider*; akin to Latin *quis* who and to Old English *hider* hither — more at WHO, HITHER] (before 12th century)
**1** : to what place ⟨*whither* will they go⟩
**2** : to what situation, position, degree, or end ⟨*whither* will this abuse drive him⟩

**2whither** *conjunction* (before 12th century)
**1 a** : to what place ⟨knew *whither* to go —Daniel Defoe⟩ **b** : to what situation, position, degree, or end
**2 a** : to the place at, in, or to which **b** : to which place
**3** : to whatever place

**whith·er·so·ev·er** \ˌhwi-thər-sə-'we-vər, ˌwi-\ *conjunction* (14th century)
: to whatever place ⟨will go *whithersoever* you lead⟩

**whith·er·ward** \'hwi-thər-wərd, 'wi-\ *adverb* (13th century)
*archaic* : toward what or which place

**1whit·ing** \'hwī-tiŋ, 'wī-\ *noun* [Middle English, from Middle Dutch *witinc*, from *wit* white; akin to Old English *hwīt* white] (15th century)
: any of various marine food fishes: as **a** : a common European fish (*Merlangus merlangus*) of the cod family **b** : SILVER HAKE

**2whiting** *noun* [Middle English, from gerund of *whiten* to white] (15th century)
: calcium carbonate ground into fine powder, washed, and used especially as a pigment and extender, in putty, and in rubber compounding and paper coating

**whit·low** \'hwit-(ˌ)lō, 'wit-\ *noun* [Middle English *whitflawe, whitflowe, whitlowe*] (14th century)
: a deep usually suppurative inflammation of the finger or toe especially near the end or around the nail — called also *felon*

**Whit·mon·day** \'hwit-ˌmən-dē, 'wit-, -ˌmən-\ *noun* [*Whit*sunday + *Monday*] (1557)
: the day after Whitsunday observed as a legal holiday in England, Wales, and Ireland

**Whit·sun** \'hwit-sən, 'wit-\ *adjective* [Middle English *Whitson*, from *Whitsonday*] (14th century)
: of, relating to, or observed on Whitsunday or at Whitsuntide

**Whit·sun·day** \-'sən-dē, -sən-ˌdā\ *noun* [Middle English *Whitsonday*, from Old English *hwīta sunnandæg*, literally, white Sunday; probably from the custom of wearing white robes by those newly baptized at this season] (12th century)
: PENTECOST 2

**Whit·sun·tide** \-sən-ˌtīd\ *noun* (13th century)
: the week beginning with Whitsunday and especially the first three days of this week

**1whit·tle** \'hwit-ᵊl, 'wit-\ *noun* [Middle English *whittel*, alteration of *thwitel*, from *thwiten* to whittle, from Old English *thwītan*; akin to Old Norse *thveita* to hew] (15th century)
*archaic* : a large knife

**2whittle** *verb* **whit·tled; whit·tling** \'hwit-liŋ, 'wit-; 'hwi-t ᵊl-iŋ, 'wi-\ (1552)
*transitive verb*
**1 a** : to pare or cut off chips from the surface of (wood) with a knife **b** : to shape or form by so paring or cutting

**2** : to reduce, remove, or destroy gradually as if by cutting off bits with a knife : PARE ⟨*whittle* down expenses⟩
*intransitive verb*
**1** : to cut or shape something (as wood) by or as if by paring it with a knife
**2** : to wear oneself or another out with fretting
— **whit·tler** \'hwit-lər, 'wit-; 'hwi-t ᵊl-ər, 'wi-\ *noun*

**whit·tling** *noun* (1854)
**1** : the act or art of whittling
**2** : a piece cut away in whittling

**whit·tret** \'hwi-trət, 'wi-\ *noun* [Middle English *whitrat*, from *white, whit* white + *rat* rat] (15th century)
*chiefly Scottish* : WEASEL

**whity** *or* **whit·ey** \'hwī-tē, 'wī-\ *adjective* (1593)
: somewhat white : WHITISH — usually used in combination

**1whiz** *or* **whizz** \'hwiz, 'wiz\ *verb* **whizzed; whiz·zing** [imitative] (1547)
*intransitive verb*
**1** : to hum, whir, or hiss like a speeding object (as an arrow or ball) passing through air
**2** : to fly or move swiftly especially with a whiz
*transitive verb*
: to cause to whiz; *especially* : to rotate very rapidly

**2whiz** *or* **whizz** *noun, plural* **whiz·zes** (1620)
**1** : a hissing, buzzing, or whirring sound
**2** : a movement or passage of something accompanied by a whizzing sound

**3whiz** *noun, plural* **whiz·zes** [probably by shortening & alteration] (1914)
: WIZARD 3 ⟨a *whiz* at math⟩

**whiz·bang** *also* **whizz·bang** \'hwiz-ˌbaŋ, 'wiz-, -'baŋ\ *noun* (1915)
: one that is conspicuous for noise, speed, excellence, or startling effect
— **whiz–bang** *adjective*

**whiz kid** *also* **whizz kid** \'hwiz-ˌkid\ *noun* [3*whiz*] (circa 1942)
: a person who is unusually intelligent, clever, or successful especially at an early age

**whiz·zer** \'hwi-zər, 'wi-\ *noun* (1881)
: one that whizzes; *especially* : a centrifugal machine for drying something (as grain, sugar, or nitrated cotton)

**who** \'hü, ü\ *pronoun* [Middle English, from Old English *hwā*; akin to Old High German *hwer*, interrogative pronoun, who, Latin *quis*, Greek *tis*, Latin *qui*, relative pronoun, who] (before 12th century)
**1** : what or which person or persons — used as an interrogative ⟨*who* was elected?⟩ ⟨find out *who* they are⟩; used by speakers on all educational levels and by many reputable writers, though disapproved by some grammarians, as the object of a verb or a following preposition ⟨*who* did I see but a Spanish lady —Padraic Colum⟩ ⟨do not know *who* the message is from —G. K. Chesterton⟩
**2** : the person or persons that : WHOEVER
**3** — used as a function word to introduce a relative clause; used especially in reference to persons ⟨my father, *who* was a lawyer⟩ but also in reference to groups ⟨a generation *who* had known nothing but war —R. B. West⟩ or to animals ⟨dogs *who* . . . fawn all over tramps —Nigel Balchin⟩ or to inanimate objects especially with the implication that the reference is really to a person ⟨earlier sources *who* maintain a Davidic ancestry —F. M. Cross⟩; used by speakers on all educational levels and by many reputable writers, though disapproved by some grammarians, as the object of a verb or a following preposition ⟨a

\ə\ abut \ᵊ\ kitten \ər\ further \a\ ash \ā\ ace
\ä\ mop, mar \au̇\ out \ch\ chin \e\ bet \ē\ easy
\g\ go \i\ hit \ī\ ice \j\ job \ŋ\ sing \ō\ go
\ȯ\ law \ȯi\ boy \th\ thin \th\ the \ü\ loot \u̇\ foot
\y\ yet \zh\ vision    *see also* Guide to Pronunciation

character *who* we are meant to pity —*Times Literary Supplement*
*usage* see WHOM, THAT
— **as who** *archaic* : as one that : as if someone
— **as who should say** *archaic* : so to speak
— **who is who** *or* **who's who** *or* **who was who** : the identity of or the noteworthy facts about each of a number of persons
¹**whoa** \'wō, 'hō, 'hwō\ *imperative verb* [Middle English *whoo, who*] (15th century)
— a command (as to a draft animal) to stand still
**who'd** \'hüd\ (1640)
: who had : who would
**who·dun·it** *also* **who·dun·nit** \hü-'də-nət\ *noun* [alteration of *who done it?*] (1930)
: a detective story or mystery story
**who·ev·er** \hü-'e-vər\ *pronoun* (13th century)
: whatever person : no matter who — used in any grammatical relation except that of a possessive ⟨sells to *whoever* has the money to buy⟩
¹**whole** \'hōl\ *adjective* [Middle English *hool* healthy, unhurt, entire, from Old English *hāl;* akin to Old High German *heil* healthy, unhurt, Old Norse *heill,* Old Church Slavonic *cělŭ*] (before 12th century)
**1 a** (1) : free of wound or injury : UNHURT (2) : recovered from a wound or injury : RESTORED (3) : being healed ⟨*whole* of an ancient evil, I sleep sound —A. E. Housman⟩ **b** : free of defect or impairment : INTACT **c** : physically sound and healthy : free of disease or deformity **d** : mentally or emotionally sound
**2** : having all its proper parts or components : COMPLETE, UNMODIFIED ⟨*whole* milk⟩ ⟨a *whole* egg⟩
**3 a** : constituting the total sum or undiminished entirety : ENTIRE ⟨owns the *whole* island⟩ **b** : each or all of the ⟨took part in the *whole* series of athletic events⟩
**4 a** : constituting an undivided unit : UNBROKEN, UNCUT ⟨a *whole* roast suckling pig⟩ **b** : directed to one end : CONCENTRATED ⟨promised to give it his *whole* attention⟩
**5 a** : seemingly complete or total ⟨the *whole* idea is to help, not hinder⟩ **b** : very great in quantity, extent, or scope ⟨feels a *whole* lot better now⟩
**6** : constituting the entirety of a person's nature or development ⟨educate the *whole* student⟩
**7** : having the same father and mother ⟨*whole* brother⟩ ☆
*synonym* see PERFECT
— **whole·ness** *noun*
²**whole** *noun* (14th century)
**1** : a complete amount or sum : a number, aggregate, or totality lacking no part, member, or element
**2** : something constituting a complex unity : a coherent system or organization of parts fitting or working together as one
— **in whole** : to the full or entire extent : WHOLLY — usually used in the phrase *in whole or in part*
— **on the whole 1** : in view of all the circumstances or conditions : all things considered **2** : in general : in most instances : TYPICALLY
³**whole** *adverb* (14th century)
**1** : WHOLLY, ENTIRELY ⟨a *whole* new age group —Henry Chauncey⟩
**2** : as a complete entity
**whole cloth** *noun* (1840)
: pure fabrication — usually used in the phrase *out of whole cloth*
**whole gale** *noun* (circa 1805)
: wind having a speed of 55 to 63 miles (88 to 101 kilometers) per hour — see BEAUFORT SCALE table
**whole·heart·ed** \'hōl-'här-təd\ *adjective* (1840)

**1** : completely and sincerely devoted, determined, or enthusiastic ⟨a *wholehearted* student of social problems⟩
**2** : marked by complete earnest commitment : free from all reserve or hesitation ⟨gave the proposal *wholehearted* approval⟩
*synonym* see SINCERE
— **whole·heart·ed·ly** *adverb*
**whole–hog** *adjective* (1829)
: committed without reservation : THOROUGHGOING ⟨a *whole-hog* patriot⟩
¹**whole hog** *noun* (1829)
: the whole way or farthest limit — usually used adverbially in the phrase *go the whole hog*
²**whole hog** *adverb* (1844)
: to the fullest extent : without reservation : COMPLETELY ⟨accepting *whole hog* the standards . . . of the majority —R. B. Kaplan⟩
**whole–life** \'hōl-'līf\ *adjective* (1845)
: of, relating to, or being life insurance with a fixed premium for the life of the policyholder and a cash value that can be redeemed on sale of the policy or can be the basis of low-interest loans
**whole note** *noun* (1597)
: a musical note equal in time value to four quarter notes or two half notes — see NOTE illustration
**whole number** *noun* (1557)
: any of the set of nonnegative integers; *also* : INTEGER
**whole rest** *noun* (circa 1890)
: a musical rest corresponding in time value to a whole note — see REST illustration
¹**whole·sale** \'hōl-,sāl\ *noun* (15th century)
: the sale of commodities in quantity usually for resale (as by a retail merchant)
²**wholesale** *adjective* (1642)
**1** : performed or existing on a large scale especially without discrimination ⟨*wholesale* slaughter⟩
**2** : of, relating to, or engaged in the sale of commodities in quantity for resale ⟨a *wholesale* grocer⟩
³**wholesale** *adverb* (1759)
: in a wholesale manner
⁴**wholesale** *verb* **whole·saled; whole·sal·ing** (1800)
*transitive verb*
: to sell (something) in quantity usually for resale
*intransitive verb*
: to sell in quantity usually for resale
**whole·sal·er** \'hōl-,sā-lər\ *noun* (1857)
: a merchant middleman who sells chiefly to retailers, other merchants, or industrial, institutional, and commercial users mainly for resale or business use
**whole·some** \'hōl-səm\ *adjective* (13th century)
**1** : promoting health or well-being of mind or spirit
**2** : promoting health of body
**3 a** : sound in body, mind, or morals **b** : having the simple health or vigor of normal domesticity
**4 a** : based on well-grounded fear : PRUDENT ⟨a *wholesome* respect for the law⟩ **b** : SAFE ⟨it wouldn't be *wholesome* for you to go down there —Mark Twain⟩
*synonym* see HEALTHFUL, HEALTHY
— **whole·some·ly** *adverb*
— **whole·some·ness** *noun*
**whole–souled** \'hōl-'sōld\ *adjective* (1834)
: moved by ardent enthusiasm or single-minded devotion : WHOLEHEARTED
**whole step** *noun* (circa 1899)
: a musical interval (as C–D or G–A) comprising two half steps — called also *whole tone*
**whole wheat** *adjective* (1880)
: made of ground entire wheat kernels
**who·lis·tic** \hō-'lis-tik\ *variant of* HOLISTIC
**whol·ly** \'hō(l)-lē\ *adverb* [Middle English *hoolly,* from *hool* whole] (14th century)

**1** : to the full or entire extent : COMPLETELY ⟨a *wholly* owned subsidiary⟩
**2** : to the exclusion of other things : SOLELY ⟨a book dealing *wholly* with herbs⟩
**whom** \'hüm, üm\ *pronoun, objective case of* WHO [Middle English, from Old English *hwām,* dative of *hwā* who] (before 12th century)
— used as an interrogative or relative; used as object of a verb or a preceding preposition ⟨to know for *whom* the bell tolls —John Donne⟩ or less frequently as the object of a following preposition ⟨the man *whom* you wrote to⟩ though now often considered stilted especially as an interrogative and especially in oral use; occasionally used as predicate nominative with a copulative verb or as subject of a verb especially in the vicinity of a preposition or a verb of which it might mistakenly be considered the object ⟨*whom* say ye that I am —Matthew 16:15 (Authorized Version)⟩ ⟨people . . . *whom* you never thought would sympathize —Shea Murphy⟩ ◻
**whom·ev·er** \hü-'me-vər\ *pronoun, objective case of* WHOEVER
¹**whomp** \'hwämp, 'hwȯmp, 'wämp, 'wȯmp\ *noun* [imitative] (1926)
: a loud slap, crash, or crunch
²**whomp** (1942)
*intransitive verb*
: to strike with a sharp noise or thump
*transitive verb*
**1** : to hit or slap sharply
**2** : to defeat decisively : TROUNCE
**3** : to create or put together especially hastily — usually used with *up*
**whomp up** *transitive verb* (1949)

---

☆ **SYNONYMS**
**Whole, entire, total, all** mean including everything or everyone without exception. WHOLE implies that nothing has been omitted, ignored, abated, or taken away ⟨read the *whole* book⟩. ENTIRE may suggest a state of completeness or perfection to which nothing can be added ⟨the *entire* population was wiped out⟩. TOTAL implies that everything has been counted, weighed, measured, or considered ⟨the *total* number of people present⟩. ALL may equal WHOLE, ENTIRE, or TOTAL ⟨*all* proceeds go to charity⟩.

---

◻ **USAGE**
**whom** Observers of the language have been predicting the demise of *whom* from about 1870 down to the present day ⟨one of the pronoun cases is visibly disappearing—the objective case *whom* —R. G. White (1870)⟩ ⟨*whom* is dying out in England, where "Whom did you see?" sounds affected —Anthony Burgess (1980)⟩. Our evidence shows that no one—English or not—should expect *whom* to disappear momentarily; it shows every indication of persisting quite a while yet. Actual usage of *who* and *whom*—accurately described at the entries in this dictionary—does not appear to be markedly different from the usage of Shakespeare's time. But the 18th century grammarians, propounding rules and analogies, rejecting other rules and analogies, and usually justifying both with appeals to Latin or Greek, have intervened between us and Shakespeare. It seems clear that the grammarians' rules have had little effect on the traditional uses. One thing they have accomplished is to encourage hypercorrect uses of *whom* ⟨*whom* shall I say is calling⟩. Another is that they have made some people unsure of themselves ⟨said he was asked to step down, although it is not known exactly *who* or *whom* asked him —*Redding (Connecticut) Pilot*⟩.

: to stir up : AROUSE

**whom·so** \'hüm-(,)sō\ *pronoun, objective case of* WHOSO

**whom·so·ev·er** \,hüm-sə-'we-vər\ *pronoun, objective case of* WHOSOEVER

¹**whoop** \'hüp, 'hùp, 'hwüp, 'hwùp, 'wüp, 'wùp\ *verb* [Middle English *whopen,* from Middle French *houpper,* of imitative origin] (14th century)
*intransitive verb*
**1 :** to utter a whoop in expression of eagerness, enthusiasm, or enjoyment : SHOUT
**2 :** to utter the cry of an owl : HOOT
**3 :** to make the characteristic whoop of whooping cough
**4 a :** to go or pass with a loud noise **b :** to be rushed through by acclamation or with noisy support ⟨the bill *whooped* through both houses⟩
*transitive verb*
**1 a :** to utter or express with a whoop **b :** to urge, drive, or cheer on with a whoop
**2 :** to agitate in behalf of
**3 :** RAISE, BOOST ⟨*whoop* up the price⟩
**— whoop it up 1 :** to celebrate riotously : CAROUSE **2 :** to stir up enthusiasm

²**whoop** *noun* (1593)
**1 a :** a loud yell expressive of eagerness, exuberance, or jubilation — often used interjectionally **b :** a shout of hunters or of men in battle or pursuit
**2 :** the cry of an owl : HOOT
**3 :** the crowing intake of breath following a paroxysm in whooping cough
**4 :** a minimum amount or degree : the least bit ⟨not worth a *whoop*⟩

**whoop-de-do** *or* **whoop-de-doo** \,h(w)üp-dē-'dü, ,h(w)ùp-, -tē-\ *noun* [probably irregular from ²*whoop*] (1929)
**1 :** noisy and exuberant or attention-getting activity (as at a social affair or in a political campaign)
**2 :** a lively social affair
**3 :** agitated public discussion or debate

¹**whoop·ee** \'(h)wù-(,)pē, '(h)wü-; (h)wù-'pē, (h)wü-\ *interjection* [irregular from ²*whoop*] (1845)
— used to express exuberance

²**whoop·ee** \'(h)wù-(,)pē, '(h)wü-\ *noun* (1924)
**1 :** boisterous convivial fun : MERRYMAKING — usually used with *make*
**2 :** sexual play — usually used with *make*

**whoopee cushion** *noun* (1953)
: a cushion that makes a sound like the breaking of wind when sat upon

**whoop·er** \'h(w)ü-pər, 'h(w)ù-\ *noun* (1660)
: one that whoops; *specifically* : WHOOPING CRANE

**whooper swan** *noun* (1880)
: a chiefly Eurasian swan (*Cygnus cygnus*) with a yellow and black bill — compare TRUMPETER SWAN

**whooping cough** *noun* (circa 1670)
: an infectious disease especially of children caused by a bacterium (*Bordetella pertussis*) and marked by a convulsive spasmodic cough sometimes followed by a crowing intake of breath — called also *pertussis*

**whooping crane** *noun* (circa 1730)
: a large white nearly extinct North American crane (*Grus americana*) noted for its loud trumpeting call

**whoop·la** \'h(w)üp-,lä, 'h(w)ùp-\ *noun* [alteration of *hoopla*] (1931)
**1 :** HOOPLA
**2 :** boisterous merrymaking

**whoops** \'(w)ú(ə)ps\ *variant of* OOPS

whooping crane

¹**whoosh** \'hwüsh, 'wüsh, '(h)wùsh\ *noun* [imitative] (1880)
: a swift or explosive rush; *also* : the sound created by such a rush — often used interjectionally

²**whoosh** (1909)
*intransitive verb*
: to rush past or move explosively ⟨cars *whooshing* along the expressway⟩
*transitive verb*
: to move (a person or thing) with or as if with a whoosh

¹**whop** \'hwäp, 'wäp\ *transitive verb* **whopped; whop·ping** [Middle English *whappen,* alteration of *wappen* to throw violently] (15th century)
**1 :** to pull or whip out
**2 a :** BEAT, STRIKE **b :** to defeat totally

²**whop** *noun* (15th century)
: a heavy blow : THUMP

**whop·per** \'hwä-pər, 'wä-\ *noun* [¹*whop*] (circa 1785)
**1 :** something unusually large or otherwise extreme of its kind
**2 :** an extravagant or monstrous lie

**whop·ping** \'hwä-piŋ, 'wä-\ *adjective* (circa 1625)
: extremely large; *also* : EXTRAORDINARY, INCREDIBLE

¹**whore** \'hōr, 'hòr, 'hùr\ *noun* [Middle English *hore,* from Old English *hōre;* akin to Old Norse *hōra* whore, *hōrr* adulterer, Latin *carus* dear — more at CHARITY] (before 12th century)
**1 :** a woman who engages in sexual acts for money : PROSTITUTE; *also* : a promiscuous or immoral woman
**2 :** a male who engages in sexual acts for money
**3 :** a venal or unscrupulous person

²**whore** *verb* **whored; whor·ing** (1583)
*intransitive verb*
**1 :** to have unlawful sexual intercourse as or with a whore
**2 :** to pursue a faithless, unworthy, or idolatrous desire
*transitive verb*
*obsolete* : to corrupt by lewd intercourse : DEBAUCH

**whore·dom** \'hōr-dəm, 'hòr-, 'hùr-\ *noun* [Middle English *hordom* sexual immorality, idolatrous practices, from Old Norse *hōrdōmr* adultery, from *hōrr*] (12th century)
**1 :** the practice of whoring : PROSTITUTION
**2 :** faithless, unworthy, or idolatrous practices or pursuits

**whore·house** \'hōr-,haùs, 'hòr-, 'hùr-\ *noun* (14th century)
: a building in which prostitutes are available : BORDELLO

**whore·mas·ter** \-,mas-tər\ *noun* (14th century)
: a man consorting with whores or given to lechery

**whore·mon·ger** \-,məŋ-gər, -,mäŋ-\ *noun* (1526)
: WHOREMASTER

**whore·son** \'hōr-sᵊn, 'hòr-, 'hùr-\ *noun, often attributive* (14th century)
**1 :** BASTARD
**2 :** a coarse fellow — used as a generalized term of abuse

**Whorf·ian hypothesis** \'wòr-fē-ən-, 'hwòr-\ *noun* [Benjamin Lee *Whorf* (died 1941) American anthropologist] (1954)
: a theory in linguistics: one's language determines one's conception of the world

**whor·ish** \'hōr-ish, 'hòr-, 'hùr-\ *adjective* (1535)
: of or befitting a whore

**whorl** \'hwòr(-ə)l, 'wòr(-ə)l, '(h)wər(-ə)l\ *noun* [Middle English *wharle, whorle,* probably alteration of *whirle,* from *whirlen* to whirl] (15th century)
**1 :** a drum-shaped section on the lower part of a spindle in spinning or weaving machinery

serving as a pulley for the tape drive that rotates the spindle
**2 :** an arrangement of similar anatomical parts (as leaves) in a circle around a point on an axis
**3 :** something that whirls, coils, or spirals or whose form suggests such movement : SWIRL ⟨*whorls* of snow⟩
**4 :** one of the turns of a univalve shell
**5 :** a fingerprint in which the central papillary ridges turn through at least one complete circle

**whorled** \'hwòr(-ə)ld, 'wòr(-ə)ld, '(h)wər(-ə)ld\ *adjective* (circa 1776)
: having or arranged in whorls ⟨leaves *whorled* at the nodes of the stem⟩

**whor·tle·ber·ry** \'hwər-t'l-,ber-ē, 'wər-\ *noun* [alteration of earlier *hurtleberry,* from Middle English *hurtilberye,* irregular from Old English *horte* whortleberry + Middle English *berye* berry] (1578)
**1 :** a European blueberry (*Vaccinium myrtillus*); *also* : its glaucous blackish edible berry
**2 :** BLUEBERRY

¹**whose** \'hüz, üz\ *adjective* [Middle English *whos,* genitive of *who, what*] (before 12th century)
: of or relating to whom or which especially as possessor or possessors ⟨*whose* gorgeous vesture heaps the ground —Robert Browning⟩, agent or agents ⟨the law courts, *whose* decisions were important —F. L. Mott⟩, or object or objects of an action ⟨the first poem *whose* publication he ever sanctioned —J. W. Krutch⟩

²**whose** *pronoun, singular or plural in construction* (13th century)
: that which belongs to whom — used without a following noun as a pronoun equivalent in meaning to the adjective *whose* ⟨tell me *whose* it was —Shakespeare⟩ ◻

**whose·so·ev·er** \,hüz-sə-'we-vər\ *adjective* (1611)
: of or relating to whomsoever ⟨*whosesoever* sins ye remit —John 20:23 (Authorized Version)⟩

**who·so** \'hü-(,)sō\ *pronoun* (12th century)
: WHOEVER

**who·so·ev·er** \,hü-sə-'we-vər\ *pronoun* (13th century)

\ə\ **abut** \ᵊ\ **kitten** \ər\ **further** \a\ **ash** \ā\ **ace**
\ä\ **mop, mar** \aù\ **out** \ch\ **chin** \e\ **bet** \ē\ **easy**
\g\ **go** \i\ **hit** \ī\ **ice** \j\ **job** \ŋ\ **sing** \ō\ **go**
\ò\ **law** \òi\ **boy** \th\ **thin** \th\ **the** \ü\ **loot** \ù\ **foot**
\y\ **yet** \zh\ **vision** *see also* Guide to Pronunciation

: WHOEVER

**who's who** \ˌhüz-ˈhü\ *noun, often both Ws capitalized* (1917)
**1** : a compilation of brief biographical sketches of prominent persons in a particular field ⟨a *who's who* of sports figures⟩
**2** : the leaders of a group : ELITE; *also* : a listing of such figures

**whump** \ˈhwəmp, ˈwəmp\ *intransitive verb* [imitative] (1897)
: BANG, THUMP
— **whump** *noun*

¹**why** \ˈhwī, ˈwī\ *adverb* [Middle English, from Old English *hwȳ*, instrumental case of *hwæt* what — more at WHAT] (before 12th century)
: for what cause, reason, or purpose ⟨*why* did you do it?⟩

²**why** *conjunction* (before 12th century)
**1** : the cause, reason, or purpose for which ⟨know *why* you did it⟩ ⟨that is *why* you did it⟩
**2** : for which : on account of which ⟨know the reason *why* you did it⟩

³**why** *noun, plural* **whys** (14th century)
**1** : REASON, CAUSE ⟨wants to know the *whys* and wherefores⟩
**2** : a baffling problem : ENIGMA

⁴**why** *interjection* (1519)
— used to express mild surprise, hesitation, approval, disapproval, or impatience ⟨*why*, here's what I was looking for⟩

**whyd·ah** \ˈhwi-də, ˈwi-\ *noun* [alteration of *widow* (bird)] (1783)
: any of various mostly black and white African weaverbirds (genera *Euplectes* and *Vidua*) often kept as cage birds and distinguished in the male by long drooping tail feathers during the breeding season

¹**wick** \ˈwik\ *noun* [Middle English *weke, wicke,* from Old English *wēoce;* akin to Old High German *wiohha* wick, Middle Irish *figid* he weaves] (before 12th century)
: a bundle of fibers or a loosely twisted, braided, or woven cord, tape, or tube usually of soft spun cotton threads that by capillary attraction draws up to be burned a steady supply of the oil in lamps or the melted tallow or wax in candles

²**wick** *transitive verb* (1949)
: to carry (as moisture) by capillary action — often used with *away* ⟨a fabric that *wicks* away perspiration⟩

¹**wick·ed** \ˈwi-kəd\ *adjective* [Middle English, alteration of *wicke* wicked] (13th century)
**1** : morally very bad : EVIL
**2 a** : FIERCE, VICIOUS ⟨a *wicked* dog⟩ **b** : disposed to or marked by mischief : ROGUISH ⟨does *wicked* impersonations⟩
**3 a** : disgustingly unpleasant : VILE ⟨a *wicked* odor⟩ **b** : causing or likely to cause harm, distress, or trouble ⟨a *wicked* storm⟩
**4** : going beyond reasonable or predictable limits : of exceptional quality or degree ⟨throws a *wicked* fastball⟩
— **wick·ed·ly** *adverb*

²**wicked** *adverb* (1980)
: VERY, EXTREMELY ⟨*wicked* fast⟩

**wick·ed·ness** *noun* (14th century)
**1** : the quality or state of being wicked
**2** : something wicked

**wick·er** \ˈwi-kər\ *noun* [Middle English *wiker,* of Scandinavian origin; akin to Swedish dialect *vikker* willow, Old Norse *veikr* weak — more at WEAK] (14th century)
**1** : a small pliant twig or branch : OSIER, WITHE
**2 a** : WICKERWORK **b** : something made of wicker
— **wicker** *adjective*

**wick·er·work** \-ˌwərk\ *noun* (1719)
: work consisting of interlaced osiers, twigs, or rods ⟨a cage of *wickerwork*⟩

**wick·et** \ˈwi-kət\ *noun* [Middle English *wiket,* from Old North French, of Germanic origin; akin to Old Norse *vik* corner, *vīkja* to move, turn] (13th century)
**1** : a small gate or door; *especially* : one forming part of or placed near a larger gate or door

**2** : an opening like a window; *especially* : a grilled or grated window through which business is transacted
**3 a** : either of the two sets of three stumps topped by two crosspieces and set 66 feet apart at which the ball is bowled in cricket **b** : an area 10 feet wide bounded by these wickets **c** : one innings of a batsman; *specifically* : one that is not completed or never begun ⟨win by three *wickets*⟩
**4** : an arch or hoop in croquet

**wick·ing** \ˈwi-kiŋ\ *noun* (1847)
: material for wicks

**wick·i·up** \ˈwi-kē-ˌəp\ *noun* [Fox (Algonquian language of the Fox, Sauk, and Kickapoo Indians) *wi·kiya'pi* house] (1852)
: a hut used by the nomadic Indians of the arid regions of the western and southwestern U.S. with a usually oval base and a rough frame covered with reed mats, grass, or brushwood; *also* : a rude temporary shelter or hut

**wickiup**

**wid·er·shins** \ˈwi-dər-shənz\ *adverb* [Middle Low German *weddersinnes,* from Middle High German *widersinnes,* from *widersinnen* to go against, from *wider* back against (from Old High German *widar*) + *sinnen* to travel, go; akin to Old High German *sendan* to send — more at WITH, SEND] (1513)
: in a left-handed, wrong, or contrary direction : COUNTERCLOCKWISE — compare DEASIL

**wid·dy** \ˈwi-dē\ *noun, plural* **widdies** [Middle English (Scots), from Middle English *withy*] (15th century)
**1** *Scottish & dialect English* : a rope of osiers
**2** *Scottish & dialect English* : a hangman's noose

¹**wide** \ˈwīd\ *adjective* **wider; wid·est** [Middle English, from Old English *wīd;* akin to Old High German *wīt* wide] (before 12th century)
**1 a** : having great extent : VAST ⟨a *wide* area⟩ **b** : extending over a vast area : EXTENSIVE ⟨a *wide* reputation⟩ **c** : extending throughout a specified area or scope — usually used in combination ⟨nation*wide*⟩ ⟨industry-*wide*⟩ **d** : COMPREHENSIVE, INCLUSIVE ⟨a *wide* assortment⟩
**2 a** : having a specified extension from side to side ⟨3 feet *wide*⟩ **b** : having much extent between the sides : BROAD ⟨a *wide* doorway⟩ **c** : fully opened ⟨*wide*-eyed⟩ **d** : LAX 4
**3 a** : extending or fluctuating considerably between limits ⟨a *wide* variation⟩ **b** : straying or deviating from something specified — used with *of* ⟨the accusation was *wide* of the truth⟩
**4** *of an animal ration* : relatively rich in carbohydrate as compared with protein
*synonym* see BROAD
— **wide·ness** *noun*

²**wide** *adverb* **wid·er; wid·est** (before 12th century)
**1 a** : over a great distance or extent : WIDELY ⟨searched far and wide⟩ **b** : over a specified distance, area, or extent — usually in combination ⟨expanded the business country-*wide*⟩
**2 a** : so as to leave much space or distance between **b** : so as to pass at or clear by a considerable distance ⟨ran *wide* around left end⟩
**3** : to the fullest extent : COMPLETELY, FULLY ⟨*wide* open⟩

**wide–an·gle** \ˈwīd-ˈaŋ-gəl\ *adjective* (1878)
**1** : having or covering an angle of view wider than the ordinary — used especially of lenses of shorter than normal focal length
**2** : having, involving the use of, or relating to a wide-angle lens ⟨a *wide-angle* shot⟩

**wide–awake** \ˌwīd-ə-ˈwāk\ *noun* (1837)
**1** : a soft felt hat with a low crown and a wide brim

**2** : SOOTY TERN

**wide–awake** *adjective* (1818)
**1** : fully awake
**2** : alertly watchful especially for advantages or opportunities
*synonym* see WATCHFUL

**wide–band** \ˈwīd-ˌband\ *adjective* (1935)
: BROADBAND

**wide–body** \ˈwīd-ˌbä-dē\ *noun* (1968)
: a large jet aircraft

**wide–eyed** \ˈwīd-ˈīd\ *adjective* (1853)
**1** : having the eyes wide open especially with wonder or astonishment
**2** : having or marked by unsophisticated or uncritical acceptance or admiration : NAIVE ⟨*wide-eyed* innocence⟩

**wide·ly** *adverb* (1579)
**1** : over or through a wide area ⟨has traveled *widely*⟩
**2** : to a great extent ⟨departed *widely* from the previous edition⟩
**3** : by or among a large well-dispersed group of people ⟨a *widely* known political figure⟩
**4** : over a broad range ⟨persons with *widely* fluctuating incomes —*Current Biography*⟩

**wide–mouthed** \ˈwīd-ˈmaüthd, -ˈmaütht\ *adjective* (1593)
**1** : having one's mouth opened wide (as in awe)
**2** : having a wide mouth ⟨*widemouthed* jars⟩

**wid·en** \ˈwī-dᵊn\ *verb* **wid·ened; wid·en·ing** \ˈwīd-niŋ, ˈwī-dᵊn-iŋ\ (1650)
*transitive verb*
: to increase the width, scope, or extent of
*intransitive verb*
: to become wide or wider
— **wid·en·er** \ˈwīd-nər, ˈwī-dᵊn-ər\ *noun*

**wide–open** \ˈwīd-ˈō-pən, -ˌō-\ *adjective* (1852)
: having virtually no limits or restrictions ⟨a *wide-open* town⟩

**wide–out** \ˈwīd-ˌaüt\ *noun* (1979)
: WIDE RECEIVER

**wide–rang·ing** \ˈwīd-ˌrān-jiŋ\ *adjective* (1816)
: extensive in scope : COMPREHENSIVE ⟨*wide-ranging* interests⟩

**wide receiver** *noun* (1968)
: a football receiver who normally lines up several yards to the side of the offensive formation

**wide–screen** *adjective* (1931)
: of or relating to a projected picture whose aspect ratio is substantially greater than 1.33:1

**wide·spread** \ˈwīd-ˈspred\ *adjective* (1705)
**1** : widely diffused or prevalent ⟨*widespread* public interest⟩
**2** : widely extended or spread out ⟨low, *widespread* hood and fenders —*Time*⟩ ⟨a *widespread* erosion surface —C. B. Hitchcock⟩

**wide–spread·ing** \-ˌspre-diŋ\ *adjective* (1591)
: stretching or extending over a wide space or area ⟨*wide-spreading* thatch roofs —*Nat'l Geographic*⟩

**wid·get** \ˈwi-jət\ *noun* [alteration of *gadget*] (1926)
**1** : GADGET
**2** : an unnamed article considered for purposes of hypothetical example

**wid·ish** \ˈwī-dish\ *adjective* (1845)
: somewhat wide

¹**wid·ow** \ˈwi-(ˌ)dō\ *noun* [Middle English *widewe,* from Old English *wuduwe;* akin to Old High German *wituwa* widow, Latin *vidua,* Sanskrit *vidhavā,* Latin *-videre* to separate] (before 12th century)
**1 a** : a woman who has lost her husband by death and usually has not remarried **b** : GRASS WIDOW 2 **c** : a woman whose husband leaves her alone frequently or for long periods to engage in a usually specified activity ⟨a golf *widow*⟩
**2** : an extra hand or part of a hand of cards dealt face down and usually placed at the disposal of the highest bidder

**3 :** a single usually short last line (as of a paragraph) separated from its related text and appearing at the top of a printed page or column

**²widow** *transitive verb* (14th century)
**1 :** to cause to become a widow or widower
**2** *obsolete* **:** to survive as the widow of
**3 :** to deprive of something greatly valued or needed

**wid·ow·er** \'wi-də-wər\ *noun* [Middle English *widewer*, alteration of *wedow* widow, widower, from Old English *wuduwa* widower; akin to Old English *wuduwe* widow] (14th century)
**:** a man who has lost his wife by death and usually has not remarried

**wid·ow·er·hood** \-ˌhud\ *noun* (1796)
**1 :** the fact or state of being a widower
**2 :** the period during which a man remains a widower

**wid·ow·hood** \'wi-dō-ˌhud, -də-\ *noun* (before 12th century)
**1 :** the fact or state of being a widow
**2 :** the period during which a woman remains a widow
**3 :** WIDOWERHOOD

**widow's cruse** *noun* [from the widow's cruse of oil that miraculously supplies Elijah during a famine (I Kings 17:8–16)] (1816)
**:** an inexhaustible supply

**widow's peak** *noun* (1849)
**:** a point formed by the hairline in front

**widow's walk** *noun* (1937)
**:** a railed observation platform atop a usually coastal house

**width** \'width, 'witth\ *noun* [¹*wide*] (1627)
**1 :** the horizontal measurement taken at right angles to the length
**2 :** largeness of extent or scope
**3 :** a measured and cut piece of material ⟨a *width* of calico⟩

**wield** \'wē(ə)ld\ *transitive verb* [Middle English *welden* to control, from Old English *wieldan;* akin to Old High German *waltan* to rule, Latin *valēre* to be strong, be worth] (before 12th century)
**1** *chiefly dialect* **:** to deal successfully with **:** MANAGE
**2 :** to handle (as a tool) especially effectively ⟨*wield* a broom⟩
**3 a :** to exert one's authority by means of ⟨*wield* influence⟩ **b :** have at one's command or disposal ⟨did not *wield* appropriate credentials —G. W. Bonham⟩
— **wield·er** *noun*

**wieldy** \'wē(ə)l-dē\ *adjective* (14th century)
**:** capable of being wielded easily

**wie·ner** \'wē-nər, 'wē-nē *also* 'wi-nē\ *noun* [short for *wienerwurst*] (1900)
**:** FRANKFURTER

**Wie·ner schnit·zel** \'vē-nər-ˌshnit-səl, 'wē-nər-ˌsnit-\ *noun* [German, literally, Vienna cutlet] (1862)
**:** a thin breaded veal cutlet

**wie·ner·wurst** \'wē-nə(r)-ˌwərst *also* -ˌwurst *sometimes* -ˌwust *or* -ˌwust; *also with* v *for* w\ *noun* [German, from *Wiener* of Vienna + *Wurst* sausage] (1889)
**1 :** VIENNA SAUSAGE
**2 :** FRANKFURTER

**wie·nie** \'wē-nē *also* 'wi-nē\ *noun* [by shortening & alteration from *wienerwurst*] (1897)
**:** FRANKFURTER

**wife** \'wīf\ *noun, plural* **wives** \'wīvz\ [Middle English *wif*, from Old English *wīf;* akin to Old High German *wīb* wife] (before 12th century)
**1 a** *dialect* **:** WOMAN **b :** a woman acting in a specified capacity — used in combination ⟨fish*wife*⟩
**2 :** a female partner in a marriage
— **wife·hood** \'wīf-ˌhud, 'wī-ˌfud\ *noun*
— **wife·less** \'wī-fləs\ *adjective*

**¹wife·like** \'wī-ˌflīk\ *adverb* (1598)
**:** in a wifely manner
**²wifelike** *adjective* (1613)
**:** WIFELY

**wife·ly** \'wī-flē\ *adjective* (before 12th century)
**:** of, relating to, or befitting a wife
— **wife·li·ness** \-flē-nəs\ *noun*

**Wif·fle** \'wi-fᵊl\ *trademark*
— used for a hollow plastic ball with cutouts in one hemisphere

**wif·ty** \'wif-tē\ *adjective* [origin unknown] (1979)
**:** DITSY

**¹wig** \'wig\ *noun* [short for *periwig*] (1675)
**1 a :** a manufactured covering of natural or synthetic hair for the head **b :** TOUPEE 2
**2 :** an act of wigging **:** REBUKE
**²wig** *verb* **wigged; wig·ging** (1829)
*transitive verb*
**:** to scold severely **:** REBUKE
*intransitive verb*
*slang* **:** to lose one's composure or reason **:** FLIP — usually used with *out*

**wig·an** \'wi-gən\ *noun* [*Wigan*, England] (circa 1875)
**:** a stiff plain-weave cotton fabric used for interlining

**wi·geon** *or* **wid·geon** \'wi-jən\ *noun, plural* **wigeon** *or* **wigeons** *or* **widgeon** *or* **widgeons** [origin unknown] (1513)
**:** any of several freshwater ducks (genus *Anas*): as **a :** an Old World duck (*Anas penelope*) with a large white patch on each wing and in the male with a red brown head and a buff crown **b :** BALDPATE 2

**wigged** \'wigd\ *adjective* (1777)
**:** wearing a wig especially of a specified kind ⟨the mute, blond-*wigged* . . . member of the team —*Current Biography*⟩

**wigged–out** \'wigd-'aut\ *adjective* (1970)
*slang* **:** having lost touch with reality **:** CRAZY

**¹wig·gle** \'wi-gəl\ *verb* **wig·gled; wig·gling** \-g(ə-)liŋ\ [Middle English *wiglen*, from or akin to Middle Dutch or Middle Low German *wiggelen* to totter; akin to Old English *wegan* to move — more at WAY] (13th century)
*intransitive verb*
**1 :** to move to and fro with quick jerky or shaking motions **:** JIGGLE
**2 :** to proceed with or as if with twisting and turning movements **:** WRIGGLE
*transitive verb*
**:** to cause to wiggle

**²wiggle** *noun* (1816)
**1 :** the act of wiggling
**2 :** shellfish or fish in cream sauce with peas
— **wig·gly** \'wi-g(ə-)lē\ *adjective*

**wig·gler** \'wi-g(ə-)lər\ *noun* (1859)
**1 :** a larva or pupa of the mosquito — called also *wriggler*
**2 :** one that wiggles

**¹wight** \'wīt\ *noun* [Middle English, creature, thing, from Old English *wiht;* akin to Old High German *wiht* creature, thing, Old Church Slavonic *veštĭ* thing] (before 12th century)
**:** a living being **:** CREATURE; *especially* **:** a human being

**²wight** *adjective* [Middle English, of Scandinavian origin; akin to Old Norse *vīgr* skilled in fighting (neuter *vīgt*), akin to Old English *wīgan* to fight — more at VICTOR] (13th century)
*archaic* **:** VALIANT, STALWART

**wig·let** \'wi-glət\ *noun* (1831)
**:** a small wig used especially to enhance a hairstyle

**¹wig·wag** \'wig-ˌwag\ *verb* [English dialect *wig* to move + English *wag*] (1892)
*transitive verb*
**1 :** to signal by wigwagging
**2 :** to cause to wigwag
*intransitive verb*
**1 :** to send a signal by or as if by a flag or light waved according to a code
**2 :** to make a signal (as by waving the hand or arm)

**²wigwag** *noun* (1886)
**:** the art or practice of wigwagging

**wig·wam** \'wig-ˌwäm\ *noun* [Eastern Abenaki *wìkəwam* house] (1628)

wigwam

**:** a hut of the American Indians of the Great Lakes region and eastward having typically an arched framework of poles overlaid with bark, rush mats, or hides; *also* **:** a rough hut

**wil·co** \'wil-(ˌ)kō\ *interjection* [*wil*l *co*mply] (circa 1938)
— used especially in radio and signaling to indicate that a message received will be complied with

**¹wild** \'wī(ə)ld\ *adjective* [Middle English *wilde*, from Old English; akin to Old High German *wildi* wild, Welsh *gwyllt*] (before 12th century)
**1 a :** living in a state of nature and not ordinarily tame or domesticated ⟨*wild* duck⟩ **b** (1) **:** growing or produced without human aid or care ⟨*wild* honey⟩ (2) **:** related to or resembling a corresponding cultivated or domesticated organism **c :** of or relating to wild organisms ⟨the *wild* state⟩
**2 a :** not inhabited or cultivated ⟨*wild* land⟩ **b :** not amenable to human habitation or cultivation; *also* **:** DESOLATE
**3 a** (1) **:** not subject to restraint or regulation **:** UNCONTROLLED; *also* **:** UNRULY (2) **:** emotionally overcome ⟨*wild* with grief⟩; *also* **:** passionately eager or enthusiastic ⟨was *wild* to own a toy train —J. C. Furnas⟩ **b :** marked by turbulent agitation **:** STORMY ⟨a *wild* night⟩ **c :** going beyond normal or conventional bounds **:** FANTASTIC ⟨*wild* ideas⟩; *also* **:** SENSATIONAL **d :** indicative of strong passion, desire, or emotion ⟨a *wild* gleam of delight in his eyes —*Irish Digest*⟩
**4 :** UNCIVILIZED, BARBARIC
**5 :** characteristic of, appropriate to, or expressive of wilderness, wildlife, or a simple or uncivilized society
**6 a :** deviating from the intended or expected course ⟨*wild* spelling —C. W. Cunnington⟩ ⟨the throw was *wild*⟩; *also* **:** tending to throw inaccurately **b :** having no basis in known or surmised fact ⟨a *wild* guess⟩
**7** *of a playing card* **:** able to represent any card designated by the holder
— **wild·ish** \'wīl-dish\ *adjective*
— **wild·ness** \-nəs\ *noun*

**²wild** *adverb* (1549)
**:** in a wild manner: as **a :** without regulation or control **b :** off an intended or expected course

**³wild** *noun* (1596)
**1 :** a sparsely inhabited or uncultivated region or tract **:** WILDERNESS
**2 :** a wild, free, or natural state or existence

**wild bergamot** *noun* (1843)
**:** a fragrant North American herbaceous mint (*Monarda fistulosa*) having a terminal capitate cluster of rather large pink or purple flowers

**wild boar** *noun* (13th century)
**:** an Old World wild hog (*Sus scrofa*) from which most domestic swine have been derived

**wild card** *noun* [*wild card*, playing card with arbitrarily determined value] (1972)
**1 :** one picked to fill a leftover playoff or tournament berth after regularly qualifying competitors have all been determined
**2 :** an unknown or unpredictable factor

**wild carrot** *noun* (circa 1538)
**:** QUEEN ANNE'S LACE

\ə\ abut \ᵊ\ kitten \ər\ further \a\ ash \ā\ ace
\ä\ mop, mar \au\ out \ch\ chin \e\ bet \ē\ easy
\g\ go \i\ hit \ī\ ice \j\ job \ŋ\ sing \ō\ go
\o\ law \oi\ boy \th\ thin \th\ the \ü\ loot \u\ foot
\y\ yet \zh\ vision *see also* Guide to Pronunciation

**¹wild·cat** \'wī(ə)l(d)-ˌkat\ *noun, plural* **wild-cats** (14th century)
**1 a :** a cat (*Felis silvestris*) of Eurasia and Africa that resembles but is heavier in build than the domestic tabby cat and is usually held to be among the ancestors of the domestic cat **b** *or plural* **wildcat :** any of various small or medium-sized cats (as the lynx or ocelot) **c :** a feral domestic cat
**2 :** a savage quick-tempered person
**3 a :** wildcat money **b :** a wildcat oil or gas well **c :** a wildcat strike
**²wildcat** *adjective* (1838)
**1 a** (1) **:** financially irresponsible or unreliable ⟨*wildcat* banks⟩ (2) **:** issued by a financially irresponsible banking establishment ⟨*wildcat* currency⟩ **b :** operating, produced, or carried on outside the bounds of standard or legitimate business practices ⟨*wildcat* insurance schemes —H. H. Reichard⟩ **c :** of, relating to, or being an oil or gas well drilled in territory not known to be productive **d :** initiated by a group of workers without formal union approval or in violation of a contract ⟨a *wildcat* strike⟩ ⟨*wildcat* work stoppages⟩
**2 a** *of a cartridge* **:** having a bullet of standard caliber but using an expanded case or a case designed for a bullet of greater caliber necked down for the smaller bullet **b** *of a firearm* **:** using wildcat cartridges
**³wildcat** *intransitive verb* **wild·cat·ted; wild·cat·ting** (1883)
**:** to prospect and drill an experimental oil or gas well or sink a mine shaft in territory not known to be productive
**wild·cat·ter** \-ˌka-tər\ *noun* (1883)
**1 :** one that drills wells in the hope of finding oil in territory not known to be an oil field
**2 :** one that promotes unsafe and unreliable enterprises; *especially* **:** one that sells stocks in such enterprises
**3 :** one that designs, builds, or fires wildcat cartridges and firearms
**4 :** a worker who goes out on a wildcat strike
**wild celery** *noun* (1874)
**:** TAPE GRASS
**wil·de·beest** \'wil-də-ˌbēst\ *noun, plural* **wildebeests** *also* **wildebeest** [Afrikaans *wildebees*, from *wilde* wild + *bees* ox] (1824)
**:** GNU
**wil·der** \'wil-dər\ *verb* [probably irregular from *wilderness*] (1613)
*transitive verb*
**1** *archaic* **:** to lead astray
**2** *archaic* **:** BEWILDER, PERPLEX
*intransitive verb*
*archaic* **:** to move at random **:** WANDER
— **wil·der·ment** \-dər-mənt\ *noun, archaic*
**wil·der·ness** \'wil-dər-nəs\ *noun* [Middle English, from *wildern* wild, from Old English *wilddēoren* of wild beasts] (13th century)
**1 a** (1) **:** a tract or region uncultivated and uninhabited by human beings (2) **:** an area essentially undisturbed by human activity together with its naturally developed life community **b :** an empty or pathless area or region ⟨in remote *wildernesses* of vast groups of nebulae are found —G. W. Gray (died 1960)⟩ **c :** a part of a garden devoted to wild growth
**2** *obsolete* **:** wild or uncultivated state
**3 a :** a confusing multitude or mass ⟨an indefinitely great number or quantity ⟨I would not have given it for a *wilderness* of monkeys —Shakespeare⟩ **b :** a bewildering situation ⟨those moral *wildernesses* of civilized life —Norman Mailer⟩
**wilderness area** *noun, often W&A capitalized* (1928)
**:** an often large tract of public land maintained essentially in its natural state and protected against introduction of intrusive artifacts (as roads and buildings)
**wild-eyed** \'wī(ə)ld-ˈīd\ *adjective* (1817)
**1 :** having a wild expression in the eyes
**2 :** consisting of or favoring extreme or visionary ideas ⟨*wild-eyed* schemes⟩

**wild·fire** \-ˌfīr\ *noun* (12th century)
**1 :** a sweeping and destructive conflagration especially in a wilderness or a rural area
**2 :** GREEK FIRE
**3 :** a phosphorescent glow (as ignis fatuus or fox fire)
**4 :** a destructive leaf-spot disease of tobacco caused by several strains of a bacterium (*Pseudomonas syringae*)
— **like wildfire :** very rapidly
**wild-flow·er** \-ˌflaù(-ə)r\ *noun* (1797)
**:** the flower of a wild or uncultivated plant or the plant bearing it
**wild-fowl** \-ˌfaùl\ *noun* (before 12th century)
**:** a game bird; *especially* **:** a game waterfowl (as a wild duck or goose)
— **wild-fowl·er** \-ˌfaù-lər\ *noun*
— **wild-fowl·ing** \-liŋ\ *noun*
**wild geranium** *noun* (1840)
**:** a common geranium (*Geranium maculatum*) of eastern North America with deeply parted leaves and flowers of rosy purple; *also* **:** any of several related geraniums
**wild ginger** *noun* (1804)
**:** a North American perennial herb (*Asarum canadense*) of the birthwort family with a pungent creeping rhizome
**wild–goose chase** *noun* (1592)
**:** a complicated or lengthy and usually fruitless pursuit or search
**wild hyacinth** *noun* (1847)
**:** any of several plants with flowers suggestive of hyacinths: as **a :** a camas (*Camassia scilloides*) of the central U.S. and southern Ontario with white racemose flowers **b :** BLUEBELL 2a **c :** any of several western North American plants (genus *Brodiaea*) of the lily family with grasslike basal leaves and variously colored flowers
**wild indigo** *noun* (1744)
**:** BAPTISIA; *especially* **:** a tumbleweed (*Baptisia tinctoria*) with bright yellow flowers and trifoliolate leaves
**¹wild·ing** \'wīl-diŋ\ *noun* [¹wild + ²-ing] (circa 1525)
**1 a :** a plant growing uncultivated in the wild either as a native or an escape; *especially* **:** a wild apple or crab apple **b :** the fruit of a wilding
**2 :** a wild animal
**²wilding** *adjective* (1697)
**:** not domesticated or cultivated **:** WILD
**wild·land** \'wī(ə)l(d)-ˌland\ *noun* (1813)
**:** land that is uncultivated or unfit for cultivation
**wild·life** \-ˌlīf\ *noun, often attributive* (1879)
**:** living things and especially mammals, birds, and fishes that are neither human nor domesticated
**wild·ling** \-liŋ\ *noun* (1840)
**:** WILDING
**wild·ly** \'wī(ə)l(d)-lē\ *adverb* (14th century)
**1 :** in a wild manner ⟨was talking *wildly*⟩
**2 :** EXTREMELY 2 ⟨*wildly* popular⟩
**wild marjoram** *noun* (1550)
**:** OREGANO 1
**wild mustard** *noun* (1597)
**:** CHARLOCK
**wild oat** *noun* (15th century)
**1 :** any of several wild grasses (genus *Avena*); *especially* **:** a European annual weed (*A. fatua*) common in meadows and pastures
**2** *plural* **:** offenses and indiscretions ascribed to youthful exuberance — usually used in the phrase *sow one's wild oats*
**wild pansy** *noun* (circa 1900)
**:** JOHNNY-JUMP-UP
**wild pink** *noun* (1814)
**:** an American catchfly (*Silene caroliniana*) of the eastern U.S. with pink or whitish flowers
**wild pitch** *noun* (1867)
**:** a baseball pitch not hit by the batter that cannot be caught or controlled by the catcher with ordinary effort and that enables a base runner to advance — compare PASSED BALL
**wild rice** *noun* (1748)

**:** a tall aquatic North American perennial grass (*Zizania aquatica*) that yields an edible grain; *also* **:** the grain
**wild rye** *noun* (circa 1500)
**:** any of several grasses (genus *Elymus*)
**wild sarsaparilla** *noun* (1814)
**:** a common North American perennial herb (*Aralia nudicaulis*) of the ginseng family with long-stalked basal compound leaves, umbels of greenish flowers, and an aromatic root used as a substitute of true sarsaparilla
**wild type** *noun* (1914)
**:** a phenotype, genotype, or gene that predominates in a natural population of organisms or strain of organisms in contrast to that of natural or laboratory mutant forms; *also* **:** an organism or strain displaying the wild type
— **wild–type** *adjective*
**Wild West** *noun* (1849)
**:** the western U.S. in its frontier period characterized by roughness and lawlessness
— **Wild West** *adjective*
**wild-wood** \'wī(ə)l(d)-ˌwùd\ *noun* (12th century)
**:** a wood unaltered or unfrequented by humans
**¹wile** \'wī(ə)l\ *noun* [Middle English *wil*, probably of Scandinavian origin; akin to Old Norse *vēl* deceit, artifice] (12th century)
**1 :** a trick or stratagem intended to ensnare or deceive; *also* **:** a beguiling or playful trick
**2 :** skill in outwitting **:** TRICKERY, GUILE
**synonym** SEE TRICK
**²wile** *transitive verb* **wiled; wil·ing** (14th century)
**1 :** to lure by or as if by a magic spell **:** ENTICE
**2** [by alteration] **:** WHILE
**¹will** \wəl, (ə)l, ²l, 'wil\ *verb, past* **would** \wəd, (ə)d, 'wùd\; *present singular & plural* **will** [Middle English (1st & 3d singular present indicative), from Old English *wille* (infinitive *wyllan*); akin to Old High German *wili* (3d singular present indicative) wills, Latin *velle* to wish, will] (before 12th century)
*transitive verb*
**:** DESIRE, WISH ⟨call it what you *will*⟩
*verbal auxiliary*
**1** — used to express desire, choice, willingness, consent, or in negative constructions refusal ⟨no one *would* take the job⟩ ⟨if we *will* all do our best⟩ ⟨*will* you please stop that racket⟩
**2** — used to express frequent, customary, or habitual action or natural tendency or disposition ⟨*will* get angry over nothing⟩ ⟨*will* work one day and loaf the next⟩
**3** — used to express futurity ⟨tomorrow morning I *will* wake up in this first-class hotel suite —Tennessee Williams⟩
**4** — used to express capability or sufficiency ⟨the back seat *will* hold three passengers⟩
**5** — used to express probability and often equivalent to the simple verb ⟨that *will* be the milkman⟩
**6 a** — used to express determination, insistence, persistence, or willfulness ⟨I have made up my mind to go and go I *will*⟩ **b** — used to express inevitability ⟨accidents *will* happen⟩
**7** — used to express a command, exhortation, or injunction ⟨you *will* do as I say, at once⟩
*intransitive verb*
**:** to have a wish or desire ⟨whether we *will* or no⟩
**usage** SEE SHALL
— **if you will :** if you wish to call it that ⟨a kind of preoccupation, or obsession *if you will* —Louis Auchincloss⟩
**²will** \'wil\ *noun* [Middle English, from Old English *willa* will, desire; akin to Old English *wille*] (before 12th century)
**1 :** DESIRE, WISH: as **a :** DISPOSITION, INCLINATION ⟨where there's a *will* there's a way⟩ **b :** APPETITE, PASSION **c :** CHOICE, DETERMINATION
**2 a :** something desired; *especially* **:** a choice or determination of one having authority or

power **b** (1) *archaic* : REQUEST, COMMAND (2) [from the phrase *our will is* which introduces it] : the part of a summons expressing a royal command
**3** : the act, process, or experience of willing : VOLITION
**4 a** : mental powers manifested as wishing, choosing, desiring, or intending **b** : a disposition to act according to principles or ends **c** : the collective desire of a group ⟨the *will* of the people⟩
**5** : the power of control over one's own actions or emotions ⟨a man of iron *will*⟩
**6** : a legal declaration of a person's wishes regarding the disposal of his or her property or estate after death; *especially* : a written instrument legally executed by which a person makes disposition of his or her estate to take effect after death
— **at will** : as one wishes : as or when it pleases or suits oneself

**³will** \'wil\ (before 12th century)
*transitive verb*
**1 a** : to order or direct by a will **b** : to dispose of by or as if by a will : BEQUEATH
**2 a** : to determine by an act of choice **b** : DECREE, ORDAIN ⟨Providence *wills* it⟩ **c** : INTEND, PURPOSE **d** : to cause or change by an act of will; *also* : to try to do so
*intransitive verb*
**1** : to exercise the will
**2** : CHOOSE

**willed** \'wild\ *adjective* (14th century)
**1** : having a will especially of a specified kind — usually used in combination ⟨strong-*willed*⟩
**2** : DELIBERATE

**wil·lem·ite** \'wi-lə-,mīt\ *noun* [German *Willemit*, from *Willem* (William) I (died 1843) king of the Netherlands] (circa 1841)
: a mineral consisting of a silicate of zinc, occurring in hexagonal prisms and in massive or granular forms, and varying in color

**wil·let** \'wi-lət\ *noun, plural* **willet** [imitative] (1791)
: a large American shorebird (*Catoptrophorus semipalmatus*) that resembles the greater yellowlegs but has a thicker bill and gray legs and that displays a black and white wing pattern when in flight

**will·ful** *or* **wil·ful** \'wil-fəl\ *adjective* (13th century)
**1** : obstinately and often perversely self-willed
**2** : done deliberately : INTENTIONAL
*synonym* see UNRULY
— **will·ful·ly** \-fə-lē\ *adverb*
— **will·ful·ness** *noun*

**Wil·liam Tell** \,wil-yəm-'tel\ *noun*
: an heroic archer in Swiss legend who complies with an order to shoot an apple off his son's head

**wil·lies** \'wi-lēz\ *noun plural* [origin unknown] (circa 1896)
: a fit of nervousness : JITTERS — used with *the*

**will·ing** \'wi-liŋ\ *adjective* (14th century)
**1** : inclined or favorably disposed in mind : READY
**2** : prompt to act or respond
**3** : done, borne, or accepted by choice or without reluctance
**4** : of or relating to the will or power of choosing : VOLITIONAL
*synonym* see VOLUNTARY
— **will·ing·ly** \-liŋ-lē\ *adverb*
— **will·ing·ness** *noun*

**wil·li·waw** \'wi-li-,wo\ *noun* [origin unknown] (1842)
**1 a** : a sudden violent gust of cold land air common along mountainous coasts of high latitudes **b** : a sudden violent wind
**2** : a violent commotion

**will·less** \'wil-ləs\ *adjective* (1747)
**1** : involving no exercise of the will : INVOLUNTARY ⟨*will*-less obedience⟩
**2** : not exercising the will ⟨*will*-less slaves⟩

**will–o'–the–wisp** \,wil-ə-thə-'wisp\ *noun* [*Will* (nickname for *William*) + *of* + *the* + *wisp*] (1661)
**1** : IGNIS FATUUS 1
**2** : a delusive or elusive goal
— **will–o'–the–wisp** *adjective*

**wil·low** \'wi-(,)lō\ *noun* [Middle English *wilghe, wilowe*, from Old English *welig*; akin to Middle High German *wilge* willow] (before 12th century)
**1** : any of a genus (*Salix* of the family Salicaceae, the willow family) of trees and shrubs bearing catkins of apetalous flowers and including forms of value for wood, osiers, or tanbark and a few ornamentals
**2** : an object made of willow wood; *especially* : a cricket bat
— **wil·low·like** \-lō-,līk\ *adjective*

**willow herb** *noun* (1578)
: any of a genus (*Epilobium*) of herbs of the evening-primrose family; *especially* : FIREWEED b

**wil·low·ware** \'wi-lə-,war, 'wi-lō-, -,wer\ *noun* (circa 1885)
: dinnerware that is usually blue-and-white and that is decorated with a story-telling design featuring a large willow tree by a little bridge

**wil·lowy** \'wi-lə-wē\ *adjective* (1766)
**1** : abounding with willows
**2** : resembling a willow: **a** : PLIANT **b** : gracefully tall and slender

**will·pow·er** \'wil-,paů-(-ə)r\ *noun* (1874)
: energetic determination

**will to power** *noun* (1907)
**1** : the drive of the superman in the philosophy of Nietzsche to perfect and transcend the self through the possession and exercise of creative power
**2** : a conscious or unconscious desire to exercise authority over others

**wil·ly–nil·ly** \,wi-lē-'ni-lē\ *adverb or adjective* [alteration of *will I nill I* or *will ye nill ye* or *will he nill he*] (1608)
**1** : by compulsion : without choice
**2** : in a haphazard or spontaneous manner

**Wilms' tumor** \'vilm-zəz-, 'vilmz-\ *noun* [Max *Wilms* (died 1918) German surgeon] (circa 1910)
: a malignant tumor of the kidney that primarily affects children and is made up of embryonic elements

**Wil·son's disease** \'wil-sənz-\ *noun* [Samuel A. K. *Wilson* (died 1937) English neurologist] (circa 1915)
: a hereditary disease that is determined by an autosomal recessive gene and is marked especially by cirrhotic changes in the liver and severe mental disorder due to a ceruloplasmin deficiency and resulting inability to metabolize copper

**¹wilt** \'wəlt, 'wilt\ *archaic present 2d singular of* WILL

**²wilt** \'wilt\ *verb* [alteration of earlier *welk*, from Middle English *welken*, probably from Middle Dutch; akin to Old High German er-*welkēn* to wilt] (circa 1691)
*intransitive verb*
**1 a** : to lose turgor from lack of water ⟨the plants *wilted* in the heat⟩ **b** : to become limp
**2** : to grow weak or faint : LANGUISH
*transitive verb*
: to cause to wilt

**³wilt** \'wilt\ *noun* (1855)
**1** : an act or instance of wilting : the state of being wilted
**2 a** : a disorder (as a fungus disease) of plants marked by loss of turgidity in soft tissues with subsequent drooping and often shriveling — called also *wilt disease* **b** : a destructive virus disease of various caterpillars marked by visceral liquefaction and shriveling of the body

**Wil·ton** \'wil-tᵊn\ *noun* [*Wilton*, borough in England] (1774)

: a carpet woven with loops like the Brussels carpet but having a velvet cut pile and being generally of better materials

**wily** \'wī-lē\ *adjective* **wil·i·er; -est** (14th century)
: full of wiles : CRAFTY
*synonym* see SLY
— **wil·i·ly** \-lə-lē\ *adverb*
— **wil·i·ness** \-lē-nəs\ *noun*

**¹wim·ble** \'wim-bəl\ *noun* [Middle English, from Anglo-French, from Middle Dutch *wimmel* auger; akin to Middle Low German *wimmel* auger] (13th century)
: any of various instruments for boring holes

**²wimble** *transitive verb* **wim·bled; wim·bling** \-b(ə-)liŋ\ (15th century)
*archaic* : to bore with or as if with a wimble

**wimp** \'wimp\ *noun* [origin unknown] (1920)
: a weak, cowardly, or ineffectual person
— **wimp·i·ness** \'wim-pē-nəs\ *noun*
— **wimp·ish** \'wim-pish\ *adjective*
— **wimp·ish·ness** \-nəs\ *noun*
— **wimpy** \'wim-pē\ *adjective*

**¹wim·ple** \'wim-pəl\ *noun* [Middle English *wimpel*, from Old English; perhaps akin to Old English *wīpian* to wipe] (before 12th century)
**1** : a cloth covering worn over the head and around the neck and chin especially by women in the late medieval period and by some nuns
**2** *Scottish* **a** : a crafty turn : TWIST **b** : CURVE, BEND

**²wimple** *verb* **wim·pled; wim·pling** \-p(ə-)liŋ\ (13th century)
*transitive verb*
**1** : to cover with or as if with a wimple : VEIL
**2** : to cause to ripple
*intransitive verb*
**1** *archaic* : to fall or lie in folds
**2** *chiefly Scottish* : to follow a winding course : MEANDER
**3** : RIPPLE

wimple 1

**wimp out** *intransitive verb* (1982)
: to behave like a wimp : chicken out; *especially* : to choose the easiest course of action

**¹win** \'win\ *verb* **won** \'wən\; **win·ning** [Middle English *winnen*, from Old English *winnan* to struggle; akin to Old High German *winnan* to struggle and probably to Latin *venus* sexual desire, charm, Sanskrit *vanas* desire, *vanoti* he strives for] (before 12th century)
*transitive verb*
**1 a** : to get possession of by effort or fortune **b** : to obtain by work : EARN ⟨striving to *win* a living from the sterile soil⟩
**2 a** : to gain in or as if in battle or contest **b** : to be the victor in ⟨*won* the war⟩
**3 a** : to make friendly or favorable to oneself or to one's cause — often used with *over* ⟨*won* him over with persuasive arguments⟩ **b** : to induce to accept oneself in marriage
**4 a** : to obtain (as ore, coal, or clay) by mining **b** : to prepare (as a vein or bed) for regular mining **c** : to recover (metal) from ore
**5** : to reach by expenditure of effort
*intransitive verb*
**1** : to gain the victory in a contest : SUCCEED
**2** : to succeed in arriving at a place or a state
— **win·less** \'win-ləs\ *adjective*
— **win·na·ble** \'wi-nə-bəl\ *adjective*

**²win** *noun* (1862)

\ə\ abut \ᵊ\ kitten \ər\ further \a\ ash \ā\ ace
\ä\ mop, mar \aů\ out \ch\ chin \e\ bet \ē\ easy
\g\ go \i\ hit \ī\ ice \j\ job \ŋ\ sing \ō\ go
\ȯ\ law \ȯi\ boy \th\ thin \th\ the \ü\ loot \ů\ foot
\y\ yet \zh\ vision *see also* Guide to Pronunciation

: VICTORY; *especially* : first place at the finish (as of a horse race)

**wince** \'win(t)s\ *intransitive verb* **winced; winc·ing** [Middle English *wynsen* to kick impatiently, from (assumed) Old North French *wincier* to turn aside, of Germanic origin; akin to Old High German *wankōn* to totter — more at WENCH] (circa 1748)
: to shrink back involuntarily (as from pain) : FLINCH
**synonym** see RECOIL
— **wince** *noun*

**¹winch** \'winch\ *noun* [Middle English *winche* roller, reel, from Old English *wince;* akin to Old English *wincian* to wink] (before 12th century)
**1 :** any of various machines or instruments for hauling or pulling; *especially* : a powerful machine with one or more drums on which to coil a rope, cable, or chain for hauling or hoisting : WINDLASS
**2 :** a crank with a handle for giving motion to a machine (as a grindstone)

winch 1

**²winch** *transitive verb* (1529)
: to hoist or haul with or as if with a winch
— **winch·er** *noun*

**Win·ches·ter** \'win-ˌches-tər\ *adjective* [from the code name used by the original developer] (1973)
: relating to or being computer disk technology that permits high-density storage by sealing the rigid metal disks within the disk drive mechanism as protection against dust

**¹wind** \'wind, *archaic or poetic* 'wīnd\ *noun, often attributive* [Middle English, from Old English; akin to Old High German *wint* wind, Latin *ventus,* Greek *aēnai* to blow, Sanskrit *vāti* it blows] (before 12th century)
**1 a :** a natural movement of air of any velocity; *especially* : the earth's air or the gas surrounding a planet in natural motion horizontally **b :** an artificially produced movement of air **c :** SOLAR WIND, STELLAR WIND
**2 a :** a destructive force or influence **b :** a force or agency that carries along or influences : TENDENCY, TREND ⟨withstood the *winds* of popular opinion —Felix Frankfurter⟩
**3 a :** BREATH 4a **b :** BREATH 2a **c :** the pit of the stomach : SOLAR PLEXUS
**4 :** gas generated in the stomach or the intestines
**5 a :** compressed air or gas **b** *archaic* : AIR
**6 :** something that is insubstantial: as **a :** mere talk : idle words **b :** NOTHING, NOTHINGNESS **c :** vain self-satisfaction
**7 a :** air carrying a scent (as of a hunter or game) **b :** slight information especially about something secret : INTIMATION ⟨got *wind* of the plan⟩
**8 a :** musical wind instruments especially as distinguished from strings and percussion **b** *plural* : players of wind instruments
**9 a :** a direction from which the wind may blow : a point of the compass; *especially* : one of the cardinal points **b :** the direction from which the wind is blowing
— **wind·less** \-ləs\ *adjective*
— **wind·less·ly** *adverb*
— **before the wind :** in the same direction as the main force of the wind
— **close to the wind :** as nearly as possible against the main force of the wind
— **have the wind of 1 :** to be to windward of **2 :** to be on the scent of **3 :** to have a superior position to
— **in the wind :** about to happen : ASTIR, AFOOT ⟨change is *in the wind*⟩
— **near the wind 1 :** close to the wind **2 :** close to a point of danger : near the permissible limit
— **off the wind :** away from the direction from which the wind is blowing

— **on the wind :** toward the direction from which the wind is blowing
— **to the wind** *or* **to the winds :** ASIDE, AWAY ⟨threw caution *to the wind*⟩
— **under the wind 1 :** to leeward **2 :** in a place protected from the wind : under the lee

**²wind** \'wind\ (15th century)
*transitive verb*
**1 :** to detect or follow by scent
**2 :** to expose to the air or wind : dry by exposing to air
**3 :** to make short of breath
**4 :** to regulate the wind supply of (an organ pipe)
**5 :** to rest (as a horse) in order to allow the breath to be recovered
*intransitive verb*
**1 :** to scent game
**2** *dialect* : to pause for breath

**³wind** \'wīnd, 'wind\ *verb* **wind·ed** \'wīn-dəd, 'win-\ *or* **wound** \'waúnd\; **wind·ing** [¹*wind*] (1586)
*transitive verb*
**1 :** to cause (as a horn) to sound by blowing : BLOW
**2 :** to sound (as a call or note) on a horn ⟨*wound* a rousing call —R. L. Stevenson⟩
*intransitive verb*
: to produce a sound on a horn

**⁴wind** \'wīnd\ *verb* **wound** \'waúnd\ *also* **wind·ed; wind·ing** [Middle English, from Old English *windan* to twist, move with speed or force, brandish; akin to Old High German *wintan* to wind, Umbrian *oha*vendu let him turn aside] (before 12th century)
*transitive verb*
**1 a** *obsolete* : WEAVE **b :** ENTANGLE, INVOLVE **c** : to introduce sinuously or stealthily : INSINUATE
**2 a :** to encircle or cover with something pliable : bind with loops or layers **b :** to turn completely or repeatedly about an object : COIL, TWINE **c** (1) : to hoist or haul by means of a rope or chain and a windlass (2) : to move (a ship) by hauling on a capstan **d** (1) : to tighten the spring of ⟨*wind* a clock⟩ (2) *obsolete* : to make tighter : TIGHTEN, TUNE (3) : CRANK **e :** to raise to a high level (as of excitement or tension) — usually used with *up*
**3 a :** to cause to move in a curving line or path **b** *archaic* : to turn the course of; *especially* : to lead (a person) as one wishes **c** (1) : to cause (as a ship) to change direction : TURN (2) : to turn (a ship) end for end **d :** to traverse on a curving course ⟨the river *winds* the valley⟩ **e :** to effect by or as if by curving
*intransitive verb*
**1 :** BEND, WARP
**2 a :** to have a curving course or shape : extend in curves **b :** to proceed as if by winding
**3 :** to move so as to encircle something
**4 :** to turn when lying at anchor

**⁵wind** \'wīnd\ *noun* (14th century)
**1 :** a mechanism (as a winch) for winding
**2 :** an act of winding : the state of being wound
**3 :** COIL, TURN
**4 :** a particular method of winding

**wind·age** \'win-dij\ *noun* [¹*wind*] (circa 1710)
**1 a :** the space between the projectile of a smoothbore gun and the surface of the bore **b :** the difference between the diameter of the bore of a muzzle-loading rifled cannon and that of the projectile cylinder
**2 a :** the amount of sight deflection necessary to compensate for wind displacement in aiming a gun **b** (1) : the influence of the wind in deflecting the course of a projectile (2) : the amount of deflection due to the wind
**3 :** the surface exposed (as by a ship) to the wind

**wind·bag** \'win(d)-ˌbag\ *noun* (1827)
: an exhaustingly talkative person

**wind–bell** \-ˌbel\ *noun* (1901)
**1 :** WIND CHIME — usually used in plural

**2 :** a bell that is light enough to be moved and sounded by the wind

**wind·blast** \-ˌblast\ *noun* (1942)
: the destructive effect of air friction on a pilot ejected from a high-speed airplane

**wind–blown** \-ˌblōn\ *adjective* (1600)
: blown by the wind; *especially* : having a permanent set or character of growth determined by the prevailing winds ⟨*windblown* trees⟩

**wind–borne** \-ˌbōrn, -ˌbórn\ *adjective* (1842)
: carried by the wind ⟨*wind-borne* pollen⟩ ⟨*wind-borne* soil deposits⟩

**wind·break** \-ˌbrāk\ *noun* (1861)
: a growth of trees or shrubs serving to break the force of wind; *broadly* : a shelter (as a fence) from the wind

**wind·break·er** \-ˌbrā-kər\ *noun* [from a trademark] (1918)
: an outer jacket made of wind-resistant material

**wind–bro·ken** \-ˌbrō-kən\ *adjective* (1603)
*of a horse* : affected with pulmonary emphysema or heaves

**wind·burn** \-ˌbərn\ *noun* (1925)
: irritation of the skin caused by wind
— **wind·burned** \-ˌbərnd\ *adjective*

**Wind·cheat·er** \'win(d)-ˌchē-tər\ *trademark*
— used for a windbreaker

**wind·chill** \'win(d)-ˌchil\ *noun* (1939)
: a still-air temperature that would have the same cooling effect on exposed human skin as a given combination of temperature and wind speed — called also *chill factor, windchill factor, windchill index*

**wind chime** *noun* (1927)
: a cluster of small often sculptured pieces (as of metal or glass) suspended so as to chime when blown by the wind — usually used in plural

**wind down** (1952)
*intransitive verb*
**1 :** to draw gradually toward an end
**2 :** RELAX, UNWIND
*transitive verb*
: to cause a gradual lessening of usually with the intention of bringing to an end

**wind·er** \'wīn-dər\ *noun* [⁴*wind*] (1552)
: one that winds: as **a :** a worker or machine that winds thread and yarn **b :** a key for winding a mechanism (as a clock) **c :** a step that is wider at one end than at the other (as in a spiral staircase)

**wind·fall** \'win(d)-ˌfól\ *noun* (15th century)
**1 :** something (as a tree or fruit) blown down by the wind
**2 :** an unexpected, unearned, or sudden gain or advantage

**wind farm** *noun* (1980)
: an area of land with a cluster of wind turbines for driving electrical generators

**wind·flow·er** \-ˌflaú(-ə)r\ *noun* (1551)
: ANEMONE 1

**wind·gall** \-ˌgól\ *noun* (circa 1534)
: a soft tumor or synovial swelling on a horse's leg in the region of the fetlock joint

**wind gap** *noun* (1769)
: a notch in the crest of a mountain ridge : a pass not occupied by a stream — compare WATER GAP

**wind harp** *noun* (1813)
: AEOLIAN HARP

**wind·hov·er** \'wind-ˌhə-vər, -ˌhä-\ *noun* (1674)
*British* : KESTREL

**¹wind·ing** \'wīn-diŋ\ *noun* (before 12th century)
**1 :** material (as wire) wound or coiled about an object (as an armature); *also* : a single turn of the wound material
**2 a :** the act of one that winds **b :** the manner of winding something
**3 :** a curved or sinuous course, line, or progress

**²winding** *adjective* (1530)

: marked by winding: as **a** : having a curved or spiral course or form ⟨a *winding* stairway⟩ **b** : having a course that winds ⟨a *winding* road⟩

**wind·ing–sheet** \'wīn-diŋ-,shēt\ *noun* (15th century)
: a sheet in which a corpse is wrapped

**wind·ing–up** \,wīn-diŋ-'əp\ *noun* (circa 1858)
*British* : the process of liquidating the assets of a partnership or corporation in order to pay creditors and make distributions to partners or shareholders upon dissolution

**wind instrument** *noun* (1582)
: a musical instrument (as a trumpet, clarinet, or organ) sounded by wind; *especially* : one sounded by the player's breath

**wind·jam·mer** \'win(d)-,ja-mər\ *noun* (1880)
: a sailing ship; *also* : one of its crew
— **wind·jam·ming** \-miŋ\ *noun*

¹**wind·lass** \'win(d)-ləs\ *noun* [Middle English *wyndlas*, alteration of *wyndas*, from Old Norse *vindāss*, from *vinda* to wind (akin to Old High German *wintan* to wind) + *āss* pole; akin to Gothic *ans* beam] (15th century)
: any of various machines for hoisting or hauling: as **a** : a horizontal barrel supported on vertical posts and turned by a crank so that the hoisting rope is wound around the barrel **b** : a steam or electric winch with horizontal or vertical shaft and two drums used to raise a ship's anchor

²**windlass** *transitive verb* (1834)
: to hoist or haul with a windlass

**win·dle·straw** \'win-d°l-,strȯ, 'wi-n°l-\ *noun* [(assumed) Middle English, from Old English *windelstrēaw*, from *windel* basket (from *windan* to wind) + *strēaw* straw] (before 12th century)
*British* : a dry thin stalk of grass

¹**wind·mill** \'win(d)-,mil\ *noun* (14th century)
**1 a** : a mill or machine operated by the wind usually acting on oblique vanes or sails that radiate from a horizontal shaft; *especially* : a wind-driven water pump or electric generator **b** : the wind-driven wheel of a windmill
**2** : something that resembles or suggests a windmill; *especially* : a calisthenic exercise that involves alternately lowering each outstretched hand to touch the toes of the opposite foot
**3** [from the episode in *Don Quixote* by Cervantes in which the hero attacks windmills under the illusion that they are giants] : an imaginary wrong, evil, or opponent — usually used in the phrase *to tilt at windmills*

²**windmill** (1914)
*transitive verb*
: to cause to move like a windmill
*intransitive verb*
: to move like a windmill; *especially* : to spin from the force of wind

**win·dow** \'win-(,)dō\ *noun, often attributive* [Middle English *windowe*, from Old Norse *vindauga*, from *vindr* wind (akin to Old English *wind*) + *auga* eye; akin to Old English *ēage* eye — more at EYE] (13th century)
**1 a** : an opening especially in the wall of a building for admission of light and air that is usually closed by casements or sashes containing transparent material (as glass) and capable of being opened and shut **b** : WINDOWPANE **c** : a space behind a window of a retail store containing displayed merchandise **d** : an opening in a partition or wall through which business is conducted ⟨a bank teller's *window*⟩
**2** : a means of entrance or access; *especially* : a means of obtaining information ⟨a *window* on history⟩
**3** : an opening (as a shutter, slot, or valve) that resembles or suggests a window
**4** : the transparent panel or opening of a window envelope
**5** : the framework (as a shutter or sash with its fittings) that closes a window opening
**6** : CHAFF 4

**7** : a range of wavelengths in the electromagnetic spectrum to which a planet's atmosphere is transparent
**8 a** : an interval of time within which a rocket or spacecraft must be launched to accomplish a particular mission **b** : an interval of time during which certain conditions or an opportunity exists ⟨a *window* of vulnerability⟩
**9** : an area at the limits of the earth's sensible atmosphere through which a spacecraft must pass for successful reentry
**10** : any of the areas into which a computer display may be divided and on which distinctly different types of information are displayed ◆
— **win·dow·less** \-dō-ləs, -də-\ *adjective*
— **out the window** : out of existence, use, or consideration

**window box** *noun* (circa 1885)
: a box designed to hold soil for growing plants at a windowsill

**window dressing** *noun* (1895)
**1** : the display of merchandise in a retail store window
**2 a** : the act or an instance of making something appear deceptively attractive or favorable **b** : something used to create a deceptively favorable or attractive impression
— **win·dow–dress** \'win-dō-,dres\ *transitive verb*
— **window dresser** *noun*

**win·dowed** \'win-(,)dōd, -dəd\ *adjective* (15th century)
: having windows especially of a specified kind — often used in combination

**window envelope** *noun* (1914)
: an envelope having an opening through which the address on the enclosure is visible

**win·dow·pane** \'win-dō-,pān, -də-\ *noun* (1819)
**1** : a pane in a window
**2** : TATTERSALL

**window seat** *noun* (circa 1745)
**1** : a seat built into a window recess
**2** : a seat next to a window (as in a bus or airplane)

**window shade** *noun* (1810)
: a shade or curtain for a window

**win·dow–shop** \'win-dō-,shäp, -də-\ *intransitive verb* (1922)
: to look at the displays in retail store windows without going inside the stores to make purchases
— **win·dow–shop·per** *noun*

**win·dow·sill** \-,sil\ *noun* (1703)
: the horizontal member at the bottom of a window opening

**wind·pipe** \'win(d)-,pīp\ *noun* (1530)
: TRACHEA 1

**wind–pol·li·nat·ed** \-'pä-lə-,nā-təd\ *adjective* (1884)
: pollinated by wind-borne pollen

**wind·proof** \-'prüf\ *adjective* (1616)
: impervious to wind ⟨a *windproof* jacket⟩

**wind rose** \'wind-,rōz\ *noun* [German *Windrose* compass card] (1846)
: a diagram showing for a given place the relative frequency or frequency and strength of winds from different directions

¹**wind·row** \'win(d)-,rō\ *noun* (circa 1534)
**1 a** : a row of hay raked up to dry before being baled or stored **b** : a similar row of cut vegetation (as grain) for drying
**2** : a row heaped up by or as if by the wind
**3 a** : a long low ridge of road-making material scraped to the side of a road **b** : BANK, RIDGE, HEAP

²**windrow** *transitive verb* (1729)
: to form (as hay) into a windrow

**wind·screen** \'win(d)-,skrēn\ *noun* (1858)
**1** : a screen that protects against the wind
**2** *chiefly British* : WINDSHIELD

**wind shake** *noun* (1545)
: shake in timber attributed to high winds

**wind shear** *noun* (1941)

: a radical shift in wind speed and direction that occurs over a very short distance

**wind·shield** \'win(d)-,shēld\ *noun* (1902)
: a transparent screen (as of glass) in front of the occupants of a vehicle

**wind sock** *noun* (1928)
: a truncated cloth cone open at both ends and mounted in an elevated position to indicate the direction of the wind

**Wind·sor chair** \'win-zər-\ *noun* [*Windsor*, England] (1740)
: a wooden chair with spindle back, raking legs, and usually a saddle seat — called also *Windsor*

**Windsor knot** *noun* [probably after Edward, Duke of *Windsor*] (1947)
: a symmetrical necktie knot that is wider than the usual four-in-hand knot

**Windsor tie** *noun* (1895)
: a broad necktie usually tied in a loose bow

**Windsor chair**

**wind sprint** *noun* (1948)
: a sprint performed as a training exercise to develop breathing capacity especially during exertion

**wind·storm** \'win(d)-,stȯrm\ *noun* (14th century)
: a storm marked by high wind with little or no precipitation

**Wind·surf·er** \-,sər-fər\ *trademark*
— used for a sailboard

**wind·surf·ing** \-,sər-fiŋ\ *noun* (1969)
: the sport or activity of riding a sailboard
— **wind·surf** \-,sərf\ *intransitive verb*

**wind·swept** \'win(d)-,swept\ *adjective* (1812)
: swept by or as if by wind

**wind tee** *noun* (1932)
: a large weather vane shaped like a horizontal letter T on or near a landing field

**wind·throw** \'win(d)-,thrō\ *noun* (1916)
: the uprooting and overthrowing of trees by the wind

**wind tunnel** *noun* (1911)
: a tunnellike passage through which air is blown at a known velocity to investigate air flow around an object (as an airplane part or model) placed in the passage

---

◇ WORD HISTORY
**window** To the ancient inhabitants of cold regions around the world, a window in a dwelling was a practical feature only when glass had become available to provide light and a view while sealing the opening from the weather. Consequently, in English and other tongues of northern Europe words for "window" developed relatively late, being either borrowings from languages of the Mediterranean region, where glass was known much earlier, or entirely new coinages. A metaphor common to several northern European languages equated the window in a dwelling with the human or animal eye, both being means of seeing out. In Old English "window" was *ēagduru*, literally, "eye-door," or *ēagthyrel* "eye-hole." The latter survived into early Middle English as *eie thurl*, but was soon supplanted by *windowe*, a loan from Old Norse *vindauga*, literally, "wind eye." *Windowe* in its turn competed for a while with *fenestre*, a borrowing from the Old French descendant of Latin *fenestra*, but the French loan died out in early Modern English, leaving us with *window* as our usual word.

---

\ə\ abut \ᵊ\ kitten \ər\ further \a\ ash \ā\ ace
\ä\ mop, mar \au̇\ out \ch\ chin \e\ bet \ē\ easy
\g\ go \i\ hit \ī\ ice \j\ job \ŋ\ sing \ō\ go
\ȯ\ law \ȯi\ boy \th\ thin \t̲h̲\ the \ü\ loot \u̇\ foot
\y\ yet \zh\ vision *see also* Guide to Pronunciation

**wind turbine** *noun* (1909)
: a wind-driven turbine for generating electricity

¹**wind·up** \'wīn-,dəp\ *noun* (1665)
**1 a :** the act of bringing to an end **b :** a concluding act or part : FINISH
**2 a :** a series of regular and distinctive motions (as swinging the arms) made by a pitcher preparatory to releasing a pitch **b :** an exaggerated backswing (as in tennis)

²**windup** *adjective* (1784)
: operated by a spring mechanism wound by hand

**wind up** (1583)
*transitive verb*
**1 :** to bring to a conclusion : END
**2 a :** to put in order for the purpose of bringing to an end ⟨*winds up* the meeting⟩ **b** *British* : to effectuate a winding up
*intransitive verb*
**1 a :** to come to a conclusion **b :** to arrive in a place, situation, or condition at the end or as a result of a course of action ⟨*wound up* as millionaires⟩
**2 :** to make a pitching windup

¹**wind·ward** \'win-(d)wərd\ *noun* (1549)
: the side or direction from which the wind is blowing
— **to windward :** into or in an advantageous position

²**windward** *adjective* (1627)
: being in or facing the direction from which the wind is blowing — compare LEEWARD

**wind·way** \'win(d)-,wā\ *noun* (circa 1875)
: a passage for air (as in an organ pipe)

**windy** \'win-dē\ *adjective* **wind·i·er; -est** (before 12th century)
**1 a** (1) : WINDSWEPT (2) : marked by strong wind or by more wind than usual **b :** VIOLENT, STORMY
**2 :** FLATULENT 1 ⟨a *windy* bellyache⟩
**3 a :** VERBOSE, BOMBASTIC **b :** lacking substance : EMPTY
— **wind·i·ly** \-də-lē\ *adverb*
— **wind·i·ness** \-dē-nəs\ *noun*

¹**wine** \'wīn\ *noun, often attributive* [Middle English *win*, from Old English *wīn*; akin to Old High German *wīn* wine; both from Latin *vinum* wine, probably of non-Indo-European origin; akin to the source of Greek *oinos* wine] (before 12th century)
**1 a :** the fermented juice of fresh grapes used as a beverage **b :** wine or a substitute used in Christian communion services
**2 :** the usually fermented juice of a plant product (as a fruit) used as a beverage
**3 :** something that invigorates or intoxicates
**4 :** a dark red

²**wine** *verb* **wined; win·ing** (1829)
*intransitive verb*
: to drink wine
*transitive verb*
: to give wine to ⟨*wined* and dined his friends⟩

**wine cellar** *noun* (14th century)
: a room for storing wines; *also* : a stock of wines

**wine cooler** *noun* (1815)
**1 :** a vessel or container in which wine is cooled
**2 :** a usually carbonated beverage that contains a mixture of wine and fruit juice

**wine·glass** \'wīn-,glas\ *noun* (1709)
: a stemware drinking glass for wine

**wine·grow·er** \-,grō(-ə)r\ *noun* (1844)
: a person who cultivates a vineyard and makes wine

**wine·press** \'wīn-,pres\ *noun* (1526)
: a vat in which juice is expressed from grapes by treading or by means of a plunger

**win·ery** \'wī-nə-rē, 'wīn-rē\ *noun, plural* **-er·ies** (1882)
: a wine-making establishment

**wine·shop** \'wīn-,shäp\ *noun* (1848)
: a tavern that specializes in serving wine

**wine·skin** \-,skin\ *noun* (1821)

: a bag that is made from the skin of an animal (as a goat) and that is used for holding wine

**wine taster** *noun* (1632)
**1 :** one who tastes and evaluates wine especially professionally
**2 :** a small shallow vessel used to sample wine

**win·ey** *variant of* WINY

¹**wing** \'win\ *noun, often attributive* [Middle English *winge*, of Scandinavian origin; akin to Danish & Swedish *vinge* wing; akin to Sanskrit *vāti* it blows — more at WIND] (13th century)
**1 a :** one of the movable feathered or membranous paired appendages by means of which a bird, bat, or insect is able to fly; *also* : such appendage

wing 1a: *1* coverts, *2* primaries, *3* secondaries

even though rudimentary if possessed by an animal belonging to a group characterized by the power of flight **b :** any of various anatomical structures especially of a flying fish or flying lemur providing means of limited flight
**2 :** an appendage or part resembling a wing in appearance, position, or function: as **a :** a device worn under the arms to aid a person in swimming or staying afloat **b :** ALA **c :** a turned-back or extended edge on an article of clothing **d :** a sidepiece at the top of an armchair **e** (1) : a foliaceous, membranous, or woody expansion of a plant especially along a stem or on a samara or capsule (2) : either of the two lateral petals of a papilionaceous flower **f :** a vane of a windmill or arrow **g :** SAIL **h :** an airfoil that develops a major part of the lift which supports a heavier-than-air aircraft **i** *chiefly British* : FENDER d
**3 :** a means of flight or rapid progress
**4 :** the act or manner of flying : FLIGHT
**5 :** a side or outlying region or district
**6 :** a part or feature usually projecting from and subordinate to the main or central part ⟨the servants' *wing* of the mansion⟩
**7 a :** one of the pieces of scenery at the side of a stage **b** *plural* : the area at the side of the stage out of sight
**8 a :** a left or right section of an army or fleet : FLANK **b :** one of the offensive positions or players on either side of a center position in certain team sports; *also* : FLANKER
**9 a :** either of two opposing groups within an organization or society : FACTION **b :** a section of an organized body (as a legislative chamber) representing a group or faction holding distinct opinions or policies — compare LEFT WING, RIGHT WING
**10 a :** a unit of the U.S. Air Force higher than a group and lower than a division **b :** two or more squadrons of naval airplanes
**11 :** a dance step marked by a quick outward and inward rolling glide of one foot
**12** *plural* : insignia consisting of an outspread pair of stylized bird's wings which are awarded on completion of prescribed training to a qualified pilot, aircrew member, or military balloon pilot
— **wingy** \'win-ē\ *adjective*
— **in the wings 1 :** out of sight in the stage wings **2 :** close at hand in the background : readily available ⟨had a plan waiting *in the wings*⟩
— **on the wing 1 :** in flight : FLYING **2 :** in motion
— **under one's wing :** under one's protection : in one's care

²**wing** (1591)
*transitive verb*
**1 a :** to fit with wings **b :** to enable to fly or move swiftly
**2 a :** to traverse with or as if with wings **b :** to effect or achieve by flying

**3 :** to let fly : DISPATCH ⟨would start to *wing* punches —A. J. Liebling⟩
**4 a :** to wound in the wing : disable the wing of ⟨*winged* the duck⟩ **b :** to wound (as with a bullet) without killing ⟨*winged* by a sniper⟩
**5 :** to do or perform without preparation or guidelines : IMPROVISE ⟨*winging* it⟩
*intransitive verb*
: to go with or as if with wings : FLY

**wing and wing** *adverb* (1781)
: with sails extended on both sides

**wing·back** \'win-,bak\ *noun* (1933)
: an offensive back in football who lines up outside the tight end; *also* : the position of such a player

**wing bar** *noun* (1855)
: a line of contrasting color across the middle of a bird's wing made by markings on the wing coverts

**wing case** *noun* (1661)
: ELYTRON

**wing chair** *noun* (1904)
: an upholstered armchair with high solid back and sides that provide a rest for the head and protection from drafts

**wing commander** *noun* (1914)
: a commissioned officer in the British air force who ranks with a lieutenant colonel in the army

**wing covert** *noun* (1815)
: one of the feathers covering the bases of the wing quills

**wing·ding** \'win-,din\ *noun* [origin unknown] (1944)
: a wild, lively, or lavish party

**winged** \'wind *also except for* 1a(2) 'win-əd\ *adjective* (14th century)
**1 a** (1) : having wings ⟨*winged* seeds⟩ (2) : having wings of a specified kind — used in combination ⟨strong-*winged*⟩ **b :** using wings in flight
**2 a :** soaring with or as if with wings : ELEVATED **b :** SWIFT, RAPID

**winged bean** \'wind-\ *noun* (1910)
: an Asian twining legume (*Psophocarpus tetragonolobus*) cultivated in warm regions for its edible high-protein 4-winged pods; *also* : its pod

**winged elm** *noun* (1820)
: an elm (*Ulmus alata*) of the U.S. having twigs and young branches with prominent corky projections

**wing·er** \'win-ər\ *noun* (1896)
: a player (as in soccer or ice hockey) in a wing position

**wing-foot·ed** \'win-'fu-təd\ *adjective* (1591)
**1 :** having winged feet
**2 :** SWIFT

**wing·less** \'win-ləs\ *adjective* (1591)
: having no wings or very rudimentary wings
— **wing·less·ness** *noun*

**wing·let** \'win-lət\ *noun* (1816)
: a small wing; *also* : a small nearly vertical airfoil at an airplane's wingtip that reduces drag by inhibiting turbulence

**wing·like** \-,līk\ *adjective* (circa 1804)
: resembling a wing in form or lateral position

**wing·man** \-mən\ *noun* (1942)
: a pilot who flies behind and outside the leader of a flying formation

**wing nut** *noun* (circa 1900)
: a nut with wings that provide a grip for the thumb and finger

**wing·over** \'win-,ō-vər\ *noun* (1927)
: a flight maneuver in which a plane is put into a climbing turn until nearly stalled after which the nose is allowed to fall while the turn is continued until normal flight is attained in a direction opposite to that in which the maneuver was entered

**wing shooting** *noun* (1881)
: the act or practice of shooting at game birds in flight or at flying targets

**wing·span** \'win-,span\ *noun* (circa 1917)
: the distance from the tip of one of a pair of wings to that of the other; *also* : SPAN 2c

**wing·spread** \-ˌspred\ *noun* (1897)
: the spread of the wings : WINGSPAN; *specifically* : the extreme measurement between the tips or outer margins of the wings (as of a bird or insect)

**wing tip** *noun* (circa 1908)
**1** : a toe cap having a point that extends back toward the throat of the shoe and curving sides that extend toward the shank
**2** : a shoe having a wing tip
**3 a** : the edge or outer margin of a bird's wing **b** *usually* **wingtip** : the outer end of an airplane wing

¹**wink** \ˈwiŋk\ *verb* [Middle English, from Old English *wincian*; akin to Old High German *winchan* to stagger, wink and perhaps to Latin *vacillare* to sway, Sanskrit *vañcati* he goes crookedly] (before 12th century)
*intransitive verb*
**1** : to shut one eye briefly as a signal or in teasing
**2** : to close and open the eyelids quickly
**3** : to avoid seeing or noting something — usually used with *at*
**4** : to gleam or flash intermittently : TWINKLE
**5 a** : to come to an end — usually used with *out* **b** : to stop shining — usually used with *out*
**6** : to signal a message with a light
*transitive verb*
**1** : to cause to open and shut
**2** : to affect or influence by or as if by blinking the eyes

²**wink** *noun* (14th century)
**1** : a brief period of sleep : NAP
**2 a** : a hint or sign given by winking **b** : an act of winking
**3** : the time of a wink : INSTANT ⟨quick as a *wink*⟩
**4** : a flicker of the eyelids : BLINK

**wink·er** \ˈwiŋ-kər\ *noun* (1549)
**1** : one that winks
**2** : a horse's blinder

¹**win·kle** \ˈwiŋ-kəl\ *noun* [by shortening] (1585)
: ²PERIWINKLE

²**winkle** *intransitive verb* **win·kled; win·kling** \-k(ə-)liŋ\ [frequentative of *wink*] (1791)
: TWINKLE

³**winkle** *transitive verb* **win·kled; win·kling** \-k(ə-)liŋ\ [¹*winkle;* from the process of extracting a winkle from its shell] (1918)
*chiefly British* : to displace, extract, or evict from a position — usually used with *out*

**win·ner** \ˈwi-nər\ *noun* (14th century)
: one that wins: as **a** : one that is successful especially through praiseworthy ability and hard work **b** : a victor especially in games and sports **c** : one that wins admiration **d** : a shot in a court game that is not returned and that scores for the player making it

**winner's circle** *noun* (1951)
: an enclosure near a racetrack where the winning horse and jockey are brought for photographs and awards

**Win·nie** \ˈwi-nē\ *noun* [*winn*er + -*ie*] (circa 1944)
: an award presented annually by a professional organization for notable achievement in fashion design

¹**win·ning** \ˈwi-niŋ\ *noun* (14th century)
**1** : the act of one that wins : VICTORY
**2** : something won: as **a** : a captured territory : CONQUEST **b** : money won by success in a game or competition — usually used in plural

²**winning** *adjective* (15th century)
**1 a** : of or relating to winning : that wins ⟨the *winning* ticket⟩ **b** : successful especially in competition ⟨a *winning* team⟩
**2** : tending to please or delight ⟨a *winning* smile⟩
— **win·ning·ly** \-niŋ-lē\ *adverb*

**win·nock** \ˈwi-nək\ *noun* [Middle English (Scots) *windok, windowe*] (15th century)

*Scottish* : WINDOW

¹**win·now** \ˈwi-(ˌ)nō\ *verb* [Middle English *winewen*, from Old English *windwian* to fan, winnow; akin to Old High German *wintōn* to fan, Latin *vannus* winnowing fan, *ventus* wind — more at WIND] (before 12th century)
*transitive verb*
**1 a** (1) : to remove (as chaff) by a current of air (2) : to get rid of (something undesirable or unwanted) : REMOVE — often used with *out* ⟨*winnow* out certain inaccuracies —Stanley Walker⟩ **b** (1) : SEPARATE, SIFT ⟨an old hand at *winnowing* what is true and significant —Oscar Lewis⟩ (2) : SELECT
**2 a** : to treat (as grain) by exposure to a current of air so that waste matter is eliminated **b** : to free of unwanted or inferior elements : PARE
**3** : to blow on : FAN ⟨the wind *winnowing* his thin white hair —*Time*⟩
*intransitive verb*
**1** : to separate chaff from grain by fanning
**2** : to separate desirable and undesirable elements
— **win·now·er** \ˈwi-nə-wər\ *noun*

²**winnow** *noun* (1580)
**1** : a device for winnowing
**2 a** : the action of winnowing **b** : a motion resembling that of winnowing

**wino** \ˈwī-(ˌ)nō\ *noun, plural* **win·os** (circa 1915)
: one who is chronically addicted to drinking wine

**win·some** \ˈwin(t)-səm\ *adjective* [Middle English *winsum*, from Old English *wynsum*, from *wynn* joy; akin to Old High German *wunna* joy, Latin *venus* desire — more at WIN] (before 12th century)
**1** : generally pleasing and engaging often because of a childlike charm and innocence
**2** : CHEERFUL, GAY
— **win·some·ly** *adverb*
— **win·some·ness** *noun*

¹**win·ter** \ˈwin-tər\ *noun* [Middle English, from Old English; akin to Old High German *wintar* winter and perhaps to Lithuanian *vanduo* water, Old English *wæter* — more at WATER] (before 12th century)
**1** : the season between autumn and spring comprising in the northern hemisphere usually the months of December, January, and February or as reckoned astronomically extending from the December solstice to the March equinox
**2** : the colder half of the year
**3** : YEAR ⟨happened many *winters* ago⟩
**4** : a period of inactivity or decay

²**winter** *verb* **win·tered; win·ter·ing** \ˈwin-t(ə-)riŋ\ (14th century)
*intransitive verb*
**1** : to pass the winter
**2** : to feed or find food during the winter — used with *on*
*transitive verb*
: to keep, feed, or manage during the winter

³**winter** *adjective* (15th century)
**1** : of, relating to, or suitable for winter ⟨a *winter* vacation⟩ ⟨*winter* clothes⟩
**2** : sown in the autumn and harvested in the following spring or summer ⟨*winter* wheat⟩ ⟨*winter* rye⟩ — compare SUMMER

**winter aconite** *noun* (1794)
: a small European perennial herb (*Eranthis hyemalis*) of the buttercup family grown for its bright yellow flowers which often bloom through the snow

**win·ter·ber·ry** \ˈwin-tər-ˌber-ē\ *noun* (1759)
**1** : an eastern North American shrub (*Ilex verticillata*) of the holly family with clusters of axillary flowers, usually bright red berries, and deciduous leaves that turn black in the fall — called also *black alder*
**2** : a shrub (*Ilex laevigata*) of the holly family similar to the winterberry but of more restricted range

**winter crookneck** *noun* (circa 1909)

: any of several crooknecks that are winter squashes of the pumpkin group noted for their keeping qualities

**win·ter·er** \ˈwin-tər-ər\ *noun* (1783)
: one that winters; *specifically* : a winter resident or visitor

**winter flounder** *noun* (1814)
: a rusty brown flounder (*Pseudopleuronectes americanus* of the family Pleuronectidae) of the northwestern Atlantic important as a market fish especially in winter

**win·ter·green** \ˈwin-tər-ˌgrēn\ *noun* (1548)
**1** : any of a genus (*Pyrola* of the family Pyrolaceae, the wintergreen family) of evergreen perennial herbs (as the shinleafs) that have basal leaves and racemose flowers
**2 a** : any of a genus (*Gaultheria*) of evergreen plants of the heath family; *especially* : a low creeping evergreen shrub (*G. procumbens*) of North America with white flowers and spicy red berries — compare CHECKERBERRY **b** (1) : an essential oil from this plant (2) : the flavor of this oil ⟨*wintergreen* lozenges⟩

**win·ter·ize** \ˈwin-tə-ˌrīz\ *transitive verb* **-ized; -iz·ing** (1934)
: to make ready for winter or winter use and especially resistant or proof against winter weather ⟨*winterize* a car⟩
— **win·ter·i·za·tion** \ˌwin-tə-rə-ˈzā-shən\ *noun*

**win·ter–kill** \ˈwin-tər-ˌkil\ (circa 1806)
*transitive verb*
: to kill (as a plant) by exposure to winter conditions
*intransitive verb*
: to die as a result of exposure to winter conditions
— **winterkill** *noun*

**win·ter·ly** \ˈwin-tər-lē\ *adjective* (1559)
: of, relating to, or occurring in winter : WINTRY

**winter melon** *noun* (circa 1900)
**1** : any of several muskmelons (as a casaba or honeydew melon) that are fruits of a cultivated vine (*Cucumis melo indorus*)
**2** : a large white-fleshed melon that is the fruit of an Asian vine (*Benincasa hispida*) and is used especially in Chinese cooking

**winter quarters** *noun plural but singular or plural in construction* (1641)
: a winter residence or station (as of a military unit or a circus)

**winter savory** *noun* (1597)
: a perennial European mint (*Satureja montana*) with leaves used for seasoning — compare SUMMER SAVORY

**winter squash** *noun* (1775)
: any of various hard-shelled squashes that belong to cultivars derived from several species (especially *Cucurbita maxima, C. moschata,* and *C. pepo*) and that can be stored for several months

**win·ter·tide** \ˈwin-tər-ˌtīd\ *noun* (before 12th century)
: WINTERTIME

**win·ter·time** \-ˌtīm\ *noun* (14th century)
: the season of winter

**win through** *intransitive verb* (1644)
: to survive difficulties and reach a desired or satisfactory end

**win·tle** \ˈwin-nᵊl\ *intransitive verb* **win·tled; win·tling** \ˈwin(t)-liŋ; ˈwi-nᵊl-iŋ, ˈwin-nᵊl-\ [perhaps from Flemish *windtelen* to reel] (1786)
**1** *Scottish* : STAGGER, REEL
**2** *Scottish* : WRIGGLE

**win·try** \ˈwin-trē\ *also* **win·tery** \ˈwin-t(ə-)rē\ *adjective* **win·tri·er; -est** [Old English *wintrig*, from *winter*] (before 12th century)
**1** : of, relating to, or characteristic of winter

\ə\ abut \ᵊ\ kitten \ər\ further \a\ ash \ā\ ace
\ä\ mop, mar \aú\ out \ch\ chin \e\ bet \ē\ easy
\g\ go \i\ hit \ī\ ice \j\ job \ŋ\ sing \ō\ go
\ò\ law \òi\ boy \th\ thin \th\ the \ü\ loot \ú\ foot
\y\ yet \zh\ vision *see also* Guide to Pronunciation

**2 a :** weathered by or as if by winter **:** AGED, HOARY **b :** CHEERLESS, CHILLING 〈a *wintry* greeting〉
— **win·tri·ness** \'win-trē-nəs\ *noun*
**winy** \'wī-nē\ *adjective* **win·i·er; -est** (14th century)
**1 :** having the taste or qualities of wine **:** VINOUS
**2** *of the air* **:** crisply fresh **:** EXHILARATING
**¹winze** \'winz\ *noun* [alteration of earlier *winds,* probably from plural of ⁵*wind*] (1757) **:** a steeply inclined passageway in a mine
**²winze** *noun* [Flemish or Dutch *wensch* wish] (1785)
*Scottish* **:** CURSE
**¹wipe** \'wīp\ *verb* **wiped; wip·ing** [Middle English *wipen,* from Old English *wīpian;* akin to Old High German *wīfan* to wind around, Latin *vibrare* to brandish, and probably to Old Norse *veipa* to be in movement, Sanskrit *vepate* it trembles] (before 12th century)
*transitive verb*
**1 a :** to rub with or as if with something soft for cleaning **b :** to clean or dry by rubbing **c :** to draw, pass, or move for or as if for rubbing or cleaning
**2 a :** to remove by or as if by rubbing **b :** to expunge completely 〈*wipe* from memory the gruesome scenes —*American Guide Series: Delaware*〉
**3 :** to spread by or as if by wiping
*intransitive verb*
**:** to make a motion of or as if of wiping something
— **wipe one's boots on :** to treat with indignity
— **wipe the floor with** *or* **wipe the ground with :** to defeat decisively
**²wipe** *noun* (1550)
**1 a :** BLOW, STRIKE **b :** JEER, GIBE
**2 a :** an act or instance of wiping **b :** a transition from one scene or picture to another (as in movies or television) made by a line moving across the screen
**3 :** something (as a towel) used for wiping
**wiped out** *adjective* (1965)
*slang* **:** INTOXICATED, HIGH
**wipe·out** \'wīp-ˌaut\ *noun* (1921)
**1 :** the act or an instance of wiping out **:** complete or utter destruction
**2 :** a fall or crash caused usually by losing control
**wipe out** (1535)
*transitive verb*
**:** to destroy completely **:** ANNIHILATE
*intransitive verb*
**:** to fall or crash usually as a result of losing control
**wip·er** \'wī-pər\ *noun* (1552)
**1 :** one that wipes
**2 a :** something (as a towel or sponge) used for wiping **b :** a moving contact for making connections with the terminals of an electrical device (as a rheostat) **c :** a usually motor-driven arm with a flexible blade for wiping a window (as the windshield of an automobile or airplane)
**¹wire** \'wīr\ *noun, often attributive* [Middle English, from Old English *wīr;* akin to Old High German *wiara* fine gold work, Latin *viēre* to plait, and probably to Greek *iris* rainbow] (before 12th century)
**1 a :** metal in the form of a usually very flexible thread or slender rod **b :** a thread or rod of such material
**2 a :** WIREWORK **b :** the meshwork of parallel or woven wire on which the wet web of paper forms
**3 :** something (as a thin plant stem) that is wirelike
**4** *plural* **a :** a system of wires used to operate the puppets in a puppet show **b :** hidden influences controlling the action of a person or organization

**5 a :** a line of wire for conducting electrical current — compare CORD 3b **b :** a telephone or telegraph wire or system; *especially* **:** WIRE SERVICE **c :** TELEGRAM, CABLEGRAM
**6 :** fencing or a fence of usually barbed wire
**7 :** the finish line of a race
**8 :** WIREHAIR
— **wire·like** \-ˌlīk\ *adjective*
— **under the wire 1 :** at the finish line **2 :** at the last moment
**²wire** *verb* **wired; wir·ing** (15th century)
*transitive verb*
**1 :** to provide with wire **:** use wire on for a specific purpose
**2 :** to send or send word to by telegraph
**3 :** to connect by or as if by a wire
*intransitive verb*
**:** to send a telegraphic message
— **wir·er** \'wīr-ər\ *noun*
**wire cloth** *noun* (1798)
**:** a fabric of woven metallic wire (as for strainers)
**wired** \'wīrd\ *adjective* (15th century)
**1 :** reinforced by wire (as for strength)
**2 :** furnished with wires (as for electric connections)
**3 :** bound with wire 〈a *wired* container〉
**4 :** having a wirework netting or fence
**5 :** feverishly excited
**wire·draw** \'wīr-ˌdro\ *transitive verb* (1598)
**1 :** to draw or stretch forcibly **:** ELONGATE
**2 :** to draw or spin out to great length, tenuity, or overrefinement **:** ATTENUATE
— **wire·draw·er** \-dro-(-ə)r\ *noun*
**wire·drawn** \-ˌdron\ *adjective* (1603)
**:** excessively minute and subtle 〈curious speculations, *wiredrawn* comparisons, obsolete erudition —Virginia Woolf〉
**wire fox terrier** *noun* (1929)
**:** a wirehaired fox terrier
**wire fraud** *noun* (1976)
**:** fraud committed using a means of electronic communication (as a telephone)
**wire gauge** *noun* (1833)
**1 :** a gauge especially for measuring the diameter of wire or the thickness of sheet metal
**2 :** any of various systems consisting of a series of standard sizes used in describing the diameter of wire or the thickness of sheet metal
**wire gauze** *noun* (1816)
**:** a gauzelike wire cloth
**wire grass** *noun* (1751)
**:** any of various grasses or rushes having wiry culms or leaves: as **a :** a European slender-stemmed meadow grass (*Poa compressa*) widely naturalized in the U.S. and Canada **b :** any of several coarse grasses (genus *Aristida*) with a 3-awned lemma that grow extensively in open dry, sandy, or sterile areas especially of the southeastern and south-central U.S.
**wire·hair** \'wīr-ˌhar, -ˌher\ *noun* (1884)
**:** a wirehaired dog or cat
**wire·haired** \-'hard, -'herd\ *adjective* (1801)
**:** having a stiff wiry outer coat of hair — used especially of a dog or cat; compare ROUGH, SMOOTH
**wirehaired pointing griffon** *noun* (1929)
**:** any of a breed of dogs of Dutch origin that both hunt and retrieve and have a long head and a harsh wiry often chestnut or white and chestnut colored coat
**wirehaired terrier** *noun* (circa 1885)
**:** WIRE FOX TERRIER
**¹wire·less** \'wīr-ləs\ *adjective* (1894)
**1 :** having no wire or wires
**2** *chiefly British* **:** of or relating to radiotelegraphy, radiotelephony, or radio
**²wireless** *noun* (1903)
**1 :** WIRELESS TELEGRAPHY
**2 :** two-way wireless transmission of sound using radio waves
**3** *chiefly British* **:** RADIO

**wireless telegraphy** *noun* (1898)
**:** telegraphy carried on by radio waves and without connecting wires — called also *wireless telegraph*
**wireless telephone** *noun* (1894)
**:** RADIOTELEPHONE
**wire·man** \'wīr-mən\ *noun* (circa 1548)
**1 :** a maker of or worker with wire; *especially* **:** LINEMAN 1
**2 :** WIRETAPPER
**wire netting** *noun* (1801)
**:** a wire cloth coarser than wire gauze
**wire·pho·to** \'wīr-'fō-(ˌ)tō\ *noun* [from *Wirephoto,* a trademark] (1935)
**:** a photograph transmitted by electrical signals over telephone wires
**wire–pull·er** \-ˌpu-lər\ *noun* (1832)
**:** one who uses secret or underhanded means to influence the acts of a person or organization
— **wire–pull·ing** \-ˌpu-liŋ\ *noun*
**wire recorder** *noun* (1943)
**:** a magnetic recorder using a thin wire as the recording medium
— **wire–re·cord·ing** *noun*
**wire rope** *noun* (1841)
**:** a rope formed wholly or chiefly of wires
**wire service** *noun* (1944)
**:** a news agency that sends out syndicated news copy to subscribers by wire or by satellite transmission
**¹wire·tap** \'wīr-ˌtap\ (1904)
*intransitive verb*
**:** to tap a telephone or telegraph wire in order to get information
*transitive verb*
**:** to tap the telephone of
**²wiretap** *noun* (1948)
**1 :** the act or an instance of wiretapping
**2 :** an electrical connection for wiretapping
**wire·tap·per** \-ˌtap-ər\ *noun* (1893)
**:** one that taps telephone or telegraph wires
**wire·work** \-ˌwərk\ *noun* (1587)
**1 :** a work of wires; *especially* **:** meshwork, netting, or grillwork of wire 〈plan the *wirework* for new circuitry〉
**2 :** walking on wires especially by acrobats
**wire·worm** \-ˌwərm\ *noun* (1790)
**:** any of the slender hard-coated larvae of various click beetles that include some destructive especially to plant roots
**wir·ing** \'wīr-iŋ\ *noun* (1809)
**1 :** the act of providing or using wire
**2 :** a system of wires; *especially* **:** an arrangement of wires used for electric distribution
**wir·ra** \'wir-ə\ *interjection* [*oh wirra,* from Irish *a Mhuire,* literally, Mary!] (1829)
*Irish* — usually used to express lament, grief, or concern
**wiry** \'wīr-ē\ *adjective* **wir·i·er** \'wī-rē-ər\; **-est** (1588)
**1 a** *archaic* **:** made of wire **b :** resembling wire especially in form and flexibility **c** *of sound* **:** produced by or suggestive of the vibration of wire 〈the violinist . . . often let his tone go nasal and *wiry* —D. J. Henahan〉
**2 :** being lean, supple, and vigorous **:** SINEWY
— **wir·i·ly** \'wī-rə-lē\ *adverb*
— **wir·i·ness** \-rē-nəs\ *noun*
**wis** \'wis\ *verb* [by misdivision from *iwis* (understood as *I wis,* with *wis* taken to be an archaic present indicative of ¹*wit*)] (1508)
*archaic* **:** KNOW
**wis·dom** \'wiz-dəm\ *noun* [Middle English, from Old English *wīsdōm,* from *wīs* wise] (before 12th century)
**1 a :** accumulated philosophic or scientific learning **:** KNOWLEDGE **b :** ability to discern inner qualities and relationships **:** INSIGHT **c :** good sense **:** JUDGMENT **d :** generally accepted belief 〈challenges what has become accepted *wisdom* among many historians —Robert Darnton〉
**2 :** a wise attitude or course of action

**3 :** the teachings of the ancient wise men
**synonym** see SENSE
**Wisdom** *noun*
**:** a didactic book included in the Roman Catholic canon of the Old Testament and corresponding to the Wisdom of Solomon in the Protestant Apocrypha — see BIBLE table
**Wisdom of Sol·o·mon** \-'sä-lə-mən\
**:** a didactic book included in the Protestant Apocrypha — see BIBLE table
**wisdom tooth** *noun* [from being cut usually in the late teens] (1848)
**:** the third molar that is the last tooth to erupt on each side of the upper and lower jaws in humans
**¹wise** \'wīz\ *noun* [Middle English, from Old English *wīse;* akin to Old High German *wīsa* manner, Greek *eidos* form, *idein* to see — more at WIT] (before 12th century)
**:** MANNER, WAY ⟨in any *wise*⟩
**²wise** *adjective* **wis·er; wis·est** [Middle English *wis,* from Old English *wīs;* akin to Old High German *wīs* wise, Old English *witan* to know — more at WIT] (before 12th century)
**1 a :** characterized by wisdom **:** marked by deep understanding, keen discernment, and a capacity for sound judgment **b :** exercising sound judgment **:** PRUDENT
**2 a :** evidencing or hinting at the possession of inside information **:** KNOWING **b :** possessing inside information **c :** CRAFTY, SHREWD
**3** *archaic* **:** skilled in magic or divination
**4 :** INSOLENT, SMART-ALECKY, FRESH ☆
— **wise·ly** *adverb*
— **wise·ness** *noun*
**³wise** *verb* **wised; wis·ing** (1905)
*transitive verb*
**:** to give instruction or information to **:** TEACH — usually used with *up*
*intransitive verb*
**:** to become informed or knowledgeable **:** LEARN — used with *up*
**⁴wise** *transitive verb* **wised; wis·ing** [Middle English, from Old English *wīsian;* akin to Old Norse *vīsa* to show the way, Old English *wīs* wise] (before 12th century)
**1** *chiefly Scottish* **a :** DIRECT, GUIDE **b :** ADVISE, PERSUADE
**2** *chiefly Scottish* **:** to divert or impel in a given direction **:** SEND
**-wise** *adverb combining form* [Middle English, from Old English -*wīsan,* from *wīse* manner]
**1 a :** in the manner of ⟨crab*wise*⟩ ⟨fan*wise*⟩ **b :** in the position or direction of ⟨slant*wise*⟩ ⟨clock*wise*⟩
**2 :** with regard to **:** in respect of ⟨dollar*wise*⟩
**wise·acre** \'wī-,zā-kər\ *noun* [Middle Dutch *wijssegger* soothsayer, modification of Old High German *wīzzago;* akin to Old English *wītega* soothsayer, *witan* to know] (1595)
**:** one who pretends to knowledge or cleverness; *especially* **:** SMART ALECK
**wise·ass** \'wīz-,as\ *noun* (1971)
**:** SMART ALECK
**¹wise·crack** \'wīz-,krak\ *noun* (1924)
**:** a clever or sarcastic remark
**²wisecrack** *intransitive verb* (1924)
**:** to make a wisecrack
— **wise·crack·er** *noun*
**wised-up** \'wīzd-'əp\ *adjective* (1926)
**:** KNOWING 1
**wise guy** \'wīz-,gī\ *noun* (1896)
**:** SMART ALECK
**wise man** *noun* (before 12th century)
**1 :** a man of unusual learning, judgment, or insight **:** SAGE
**2 :** a man versed in esoteric lore (as of magic or astrology); *especially* **:** MAGUS 1b
**wi·sen·hei·mer** \'wī-z°n-,hī-mər\ *noun* [²*wise* + -*enheimer* (as in family names such as *Guggenheimer, Oppenheimer*)] (1904)
**:** SMART ALECK

**wi·sent** \'vē-,zent\ *noun* [German, from Old High German *wisant* — more at BISON] (1866)
**:** a European bison (*Bison bonasus*) sometimes considered conspecific with the North American buffalo (*B. bison*) — called also *aurochs*

wisent

**wise·wom·an** \'wīz-,wu̇-mən\ *noun* (14th century)
**:** a woman versed in charms, conjuring, or fortune-telling
**¹wish** \'wish\ *verb* [Middle English *wisshen,* from Old English *wȳscan;* akin to Old High German *wunsken* to wish, Sanskrit *vāñchati* he wishes, *vanoti* he strives for — more at WIN] (before 12th century)
*transitive verb*
**1 :** to have a desire for (as something unattainable) ⟨*wished* he could live his life over⟩
**2 :** to give expression to as a wish **:** BID ⟨*wish* them good night⟩
**3 a :** to give form to (a wish) **b :** to express a wish for **c :** to request in the form of a wish **:** ORDER **d :** to desire (a person or thing) to be as specified ⟨cannot *wish* our problems away⟩
**4 :** to confer (something unwanted) on someone **:** FOIST
*intransitive verb*
**1 :** to have a desire **:** WANT
**2 :** to make a wish
**synonym** see DESIRE
— **wish·er** *noun*
**²wish** *noun* (14th century)
**1 a :** an act or instance of wishing or desire **:** WANT **b :** an object of desire **:** GOAL
**2 a :** an expressed will or desire **:** MANDATE **b :** a request or command couched as a wish
**3 :** an invocation of good or evil fortune on someone
**wisha** \'wi-shə\ *interjection* [Irish *mhuise*] (1826)
*chiefly Irish* — used as an intensive or to express surprise
**wish·bone** \'wish-,bōn\ *noun* [from the superstition that when two persons pull it apart the one getting the longer fragment will have a wish granted] (1853)
**1 :** a forked bone in front of the breastbone in a bird consisting chiefly of the two clavicles fused at their median or lower end
**2 :** a variation of the T formation in which the halfbacks line up farther from the line of scrimmage than the fullback does
**wish·ful** \'wish-fəl\ *adjective* (1593)
**1 a :** expressive of a wish **:** HOPEFUL **b :** having a wish **:** DESIROUS
**2 :** according with wishes rather than reality
— **wish·ful·ly** \-fə-lē\ *adverb*
— **wish·ful·ness** *noun*
**wish fulfillment** *noun* (1908)
**:** the gratification of a desire especially symbolically (as in dreams, daydreams, or neurotic symptoms)
**wishful thinking** *noun* (1932)
**:** the attribution of reality to what one wishes to be true or the tenuous justification of what one wants to believe
**wish·ing** *adjective* (circa 1530)
**1** *archaic* **:** WISHFUL
**2 :** regarded as having the power to grant wishes ⟨threw a coin in the *wishing* well⟩
**wish list** *noun* (1972)
**:** a list of desired but often realistically unobtainable items
**wish–wash** \'wish-,wȯsh, -,wäsh\ *noun* [reduplication of ²*wash*] (1786)
**1 :** a weak drink
**2 :** insipid talk or writing

**wishy–washy** \'wi-shē-,wȯ-shē, -,wä-\ *adjective* [reduplication of *washy*] (circa 1693)
**1 :** lacking in character or determination **:** INEFFECTUAL
**2 :** lacking in strength or flavor **:** WEAK
— **wishy–wash·i·ness** *noun*
**¹wisp** \'wisp\ *noun* [Middle English] (14th century)
**1 :** a small handful (as of hay or straw)
**2 a :** a thin strip or fragment **b :** a thready streak ⟨a *wisp* of smoke⟩ **c :** something frail, slight, or fleeting ⟨a *wisp* of a girl⟩ ⟨a *wisp* of a smile⟩
**3** *archaic* **:** WILL-O'-THE-WISP
— **wisp·i·ly** \'wis-pə-lē\ *adverb*
— **wisp·i·ness** \'wis-pē-nəs\ *noun*
— **wispy** \'wis-pē\ *adjective*
**²wisp** (1753)
*transitive verb*
**1 :** to roll into a wisp
**2 :** to make wisps of ⟨a cigarette *wisping* smoke at the corner of his mouth —Raymond Chandler⟩
*intransitive verb*
**:** to emerge or drift in wisps ⟨her hair began to *wisp* into her eyes —Mary Manning⟩
**wisp·ish** \'wis-pish\ *adjective* (1896)
**:** resembling a wisp **:** INSUBSTANTIAL
**wist** \'wist\ *transitive verb* [alteration of *wis*] (1508)
*archaic* **:** KNOW
**wis·te·ria** \wis-'tir-ē-ə\ *or* **wis·tar·ia** \-'tir-ē-ə *also* -'ter-\ *noun* [New Latin *Wisteria,* from Caspar *Wistar* (died 1818) American physician] (1842)
**:** any of a genus (*Wisteria*) of chiefly Asian mostly woody leguminous vines that have pinnately compound leaves and long racemes of showy blue, white, purple, or rose papilionaceous flowers and that include several grown as ornamentals
**wist·ful** \'wist-fəl\ *adjective* [blend of *wishful* and obsolete English *wistly* intently] (1714)
**1 :** full of yearning or desire tinged with melancholy; *also* **:** inspiring such yearning ⟨a *wistful* memoir⟩

wisteria

\ə\ abut \ᵊ\ kitten \ər\ further \a\ ash \ā\ ace \ä\ mop, mar \au̇\ out \ch\ chin \e\ bet \ē\ easy \g\ go \i\ hit \ī\ ice \j\ job \ŋ\ sing \ō\ go \ȯ\ law \ȯi\ boy \th\ thin \t͟h\ the \ü\ loot \u̇\ foot \y\ yet \zh\ vision *see also* Guide to Pronunciation

**2** : musingly sad : PENSIVE
— **wist·ful·ly** \-fə-lē\ adverb
— **wist·ful·ness** noun

**¹wit** \'wit\ verb **wist** \'wist\; **wit·ting** present 1st & 3d singular **wot** \'wät\ [Middle English witen (1st & 3d singular present wot, past wiste), from Old English witan (1st & 3d singular present wāt, past wisse, wiste); akin to Old High German wizzan to know, Latin vidēre to see, Greek eidenai to know, idein to see] (before 12th century)
**1** archaic : KNOW
**2** archaic : to come to know : LEARN

**²wit** noun [Middle English, from Old English; akin to Old High German wizzi knowledge, Old English witan to know] (before 12th century)
**1 a** : MIND, MEMORY **b** : reasoning power : INTELLIGENCE
**2 a** : SENSE 2a — usually used in plural ⟨alone and warming his five wits, the white owl in the belfry sits —Alfred Tennyson⟩ **b** (1) : mental soundness : SANITY — usually used in plural (2) : mental capability and resourcefulness : INGENUITY
**3 a** : astuteness of perception or judgment : ACUMEN **b** : the ability to relate seemingly disparate things so as to illuminate or amuse **c** (1) : a talent for banter or persiflage (2) : a witty utterance or exchange **d** : clever or apt humor
**4 a** : a person of superior intellect : THINKER **b** : an imaginatively perceptive and articulate individual especially skilled in banter or persiflage ☆
— **at one's wit's end** or **at one's wits' end** : at a loss for a means of solving a problem

**wi·tan** \'wi-ˌtän\ noun plural [Old English, plural of wita sage, adviser; akin to Old High German wizzo sage, Old English witan to know] (1807)
: members of the witenagemot

**¹witch** \'wich\ noun [Middle English wicche, from Old English wicca, masculine, wizard & wicce, feminine, witch; akin to Middle High German wicken to bewitch, Old English wigle divination, and perhaps to Old High German wīh holy — more at VICTIM] (before 12th century)
**1** : one that is credited with usually malignant supernatural powers; especially : a woman practicing usually black witchcraft often with the aid of a devil or familiar : SORCERESS — compare WARLOCK
**2** : an ugly old woman : HAG
**3** : a charming or alluring girl or woman
— **witch·like** \'wich-ˌlīk\ adjective
— **witchy** \'wi-chē\ adjective

**²witch** (14th century)
transitive verb
**1** : to affect injuriously with witchcraft
**2** archaic : to influence or beguile with allure or charm
intransitive verb
: DOWSE

**witch·craft** \'wich-ˌkraft\ noun (before 12th century)
**1 a** : the use of sorcery or magic **b** : communication with the devil or with a familiar
**2** : an irresistible influence or fascination

**witch doctor** noun (1718)
: a professional worker of magic usually in a primitive society who often works to cure sickness

**witch·ery** \'wi-chə-rē, 'wich-rē\ noun, plural **-er·ies** (1546)
**1 a** : the practice of witchcraft : SORCERY **b** : an act of witchcraft
**2** : an irresistible fascination

**witches' brew** noun (1929)
: a potent or fearsome mixture ⟨a witches' brew of untamed sex and brutality —Harrison Smith⟩

**witch·es'–broom** \'wi-chəz-ˌbrüm, -ˌbrum\ noun (1881)

: an abnormal tufted growth of small branches on a tree or shrub caused especially by fungi or viruses

**witches' Sabbath** noun (circa 1676)
: a midnight assembly of witches, devils, and sorcerers for the celebration of rites and orgies

**witch·grass** \'wich-ˌgras\ noun [probably alteration of quitch (grass)] (1790)
**1** : QUACK GRASS
**2** [¹witch] : a North American grass (Panicum capillare) with slender brushy panicles that is often a weed on cultivated land

**witch ha·zel** \'wich-ˌhā-zəl\ noun [witch, a tree with pliant branches, from Middle English wyche, from Old English wice; probably akin to Old English wīcan to yield — more at WEAK] (circa 1542)
**1** : any of a genus (Hamamelis of the family Hamamelidaceae, the witch-hazel family) of shrubs or small trees with slender-petaled yellow flowers borne in late fall or early spring; especially : one (H. virginiana) of eastern North America that blooms in the fall
**2** : an alcoholic solution of a distillate of the bark of a witch hazel (H. virginiana) used as a soothing and mildly astringent lotion

**witch–hunt** \'wich-ˌhənt\ noun (1885)
**1** : a searching out for persecution of persons accused of witchcraft
**2** : the searching out and deliberate harassment of those (as political opponents) with unpopular views
— **witch–hunt·er** noun
— **witch–hunt·ing** noun or adjective

**¹witch·ing** \'wi-chiŋ\ noun (before 12th century)
: the practice of witchcraft : SORCERY

**²witching** adjective (14th century)
: of, relating to, or suitable for sorcery or supernatural occurrences ⟨the very witching time of night —Shakespeare⟩

**witch of Agne·si** \-än-ˈyā-zē\ noun [Maria Gaetana Agnesi (died 1799) Italian mathematician; witch, translation of Italian versiera cubic curve (influenced by Italian versiera female demon)] (1875)
: a plane cubic curve that is symmetric about the y-axis and approaches the x-axis as an asymptote that is constructed by drawing lines from the origin intersecting an upright circle tangent to the x-axis at the origin and taking the locus of points of intersection of pairs of lines parallel to the x-axis and y-axis each pair of which consists of a line parallel to the x-axis through the point where a line through the origin intersects the circle and a line parallel to the y-axis through the point where the same line through the origin intersects the line parallel to the x-axis through the point of intersection of the circle and the y-axis and that has the equation $x^2y = 4a^2(2a - y)$ — called also witch

**witch·weed** \'wich-ˌwēd\ noun (1904)
: any of a genus (Striga) of yellow-flowered Old World plants of the snapdragon family that are damaging root parasites of grasses (as sorghum and maize) and that include one (S. lutea) which is an introduced pest in parts of the southeastern U.S.

**¹wite** \'wīt\ transitive verb **wit·ed; wit·ing** [Middle English, from Old English wītan; akin to Old High German wīzan to blame, Old English witan to know] (before 12th century)
chiefly Scottish : BLAME

**²wite** noun (13th century)
chiefly Scottish : BLAME, RESPONSIBILITY

**wi·te·na·ge·mot** or **wi·te·na·ge·mote** \'wi-tᵊn-ə-gə-ˌmōt, -yə-ˌmōt\ noun [Old English witena gemōt, from witena (genitive plural of wita sage, adviser) + gemōt gemot] (before 12th century)
: an Anglo-Saxon council made up of a varying number of nobles, prelates, and influential officials and convened from time to time to advise the king on administrative and judicial matters

**with** \'with, 'with, wᵊth, wəth\ preposition [Middle English, against, from, with, from Old English; akin to Old English wither against, Old High German widar against, back, Sanskrit vi apart] (before 12th century)
**1 a** : in opposition to : AGAINST ⟨had a fight with his brother⟩ **b** : so as to be separated or detached from ⟨broke with her family⟩
**2 a** — used as a function word to indicate a participant in an action, transaction, or arrangement ⟨works with his father⟩ ⟨a talk with a friend⟩ ⟨got into an accident with the car⟩ **b** — used as a function word to indicate the object of attention, behavior, or feeling ⟨get tough with him⟩ ⟨angry with her⟩ **c** : in respect to : so far as concerns ⟨on friendly terms with all nations⟩ **d** — used to indicate the object of an adverbial expression of imperative force ⟨off with his head⟩ **e** : OVER, ON ⟨no longer has any influence with them⟩ **f** : in the performance, operation, or use of ⟨the trouble with this machine⟩
**3 a** — used as a function word to indicate the object of a statement of comparison or equality ⟨a dress identical with her hostess's⟩ **b** — used as a function word to express agreement or sympathy ⟨must conclude, with you, that the painting is a forgery⟩ **c** : on the side of : FOR ⟨if he's for lower taxes, I'm with him⟩ **d** : as well as ⟨can pitch with the best of them⟩
**4 a** — used as a function word to indicate combination, accompaniment, presence, or addition ⟨heat milk with honey⟩ ⟨went there with her⟩ ⟨his money, with his wife's, comes to a million⟩ **b** : inclusive of ⟨costs $5 with the tax⟩
**5 a** : in the judgment or estimation of ⟨stood well with her classmates⟩ **b** : in or according to the experience or practice of ⟨with many of us, our ideas seem to fall by the wayside —W. J. Reilly⟩
**6 a** — used as a function word to indicate the means, cause, agent, or instrumentality ⟨hit him with a rock⟩ ⟨pale with anger⟩ ⟨threatened with tuberculosis⟩ ⟨he amused the crowd with his antics⟩ **b** archaic : by the direct act of
**7 a** — used as a function word to indicate manner of action ⟨ran with effort⟩ ⟨acknowledge your contribution with thanks⟩ **b** — used as a function word to indicate an attendant fact or circumstance ⟨stood there with his hat on⟩ **c** — used as a function word to indicate a result attendant on a specified action ⟨got off with a light sentence⟩
**8 a** (1) : in possession of : HAVING ⟨came with good news⟩ (2) : in the possession or care of ⟨left the money with her mother⟩ **b** : characterized or distinguished by ⟨a person with a sharp nose⟩

---

☆ **SYNONYMS**
**Wit, humor, irony, sarcasm, satire, repartee** mean a mode of expression intended to arouse amusement. WIT suggests the power to evoke laughter by remarks showing verbal felicity or ingenuity and swift perception especially of the incongruous ⟨a playful wit⟩. HUMOR implies an ability to perceive the ludicrous, the comical, and the absurd in human life and to express these usually without bitterness ⟨a sense of humor⟩. IRONY applies to a manner of expression in which the intended meaning is the opposite of what is seemingly expressed ⟨the irony of the title⟩. SARCASM applies to expression frequently in the form of irony that is intended to cut or wound ⟨given to heartless sarcasm⟩. SATIRE applies to writing that exposes or ridicules conduct, doctrines, or institutions either by direct criticism or more often through irony, parody, or caricature ⟨a satire on the Congress⟩. REPARTEE implies the power of answering quickly, pointedly, or wittily ⟨a dinner guest noted for repartee⟩.

**9 a** — used as a function word to indicate a close association in time ⟨*with* the outbreak of war they went home⟩ ⟨mellows *with* time⟩ **b** : in proportion to ⟨the pressure varies *with* the depth⟩
**10 a** : in spite of : NOTWITHSTANDING ⟨a really tip-top man, *with* all his wrongheadedness —H. J. Laski⟩ **b** : except for ⟨finds that, *with* one group of omissions and one important addition, they reflect that curriculum —Gilbert Highet⟩
**11** : in the direction of ⟨*with* the wind⟩ ⟨*with* the grain⟩
**¹with·al** \wi-ˈthȯl, -ˈthȯl\ *adverb* [Middle English, from *with* + *all, al* all] (13th century)
**1** : together with this : BESIDES ⟨a supporter of all constructive work and *withal* an excellent businessman —A. W. Long⟩
**2** *archaic* : THEREWITH 1
**3** : on the other hand : NEVERTHELESS
**²withal** *preposition* (14th century)
*archaic* : WITH — used postpositively with a relative or interrogative pronoun as object
**with·draw** \with-ˈdrȯ, with-\ *verb* **-drew** \-ˈdrü\; **-drawn** \-ˈdrȯn\; **-draw·ing** \-ˈdrȯ(-)iŋ\ [Middle English, from *with* from + *drawen* to draw] (13th century)
*transitive verb*
**1 a** : to take back or away : REMOVE ⟨pressure upon educational administrators to *withdraw* academic credit —J. W. Scott⟩ **b** : to remove from use or cultivation **c** : to remove (money) from a place of deposit **d** : to turn away (as the eyes) from an object of attention ⟨*withdrew* her gaze⟩ **e** : to draw (as a curtain) back or aside
**2 a** : to remove from consideration or set outside a group ⟨*withdrew* his name from the list of nominees⟩ ⟨*withdrew* their child from the school⟩ **b** (1) : TAKE BACK, RETRACT (2) : to recall or remove (a motion) under parliamentary procedure
*intransitive verb*
**1 a** : to move back or away : RETIRE **b** : to draw back from a battlefield : RETREAT
**2 a** : to remove oneself from participation **b** : to become socially or emotionally detached ⟨had *withdrawn* farther and farther into herself —Ethel Wilson⟩
**3** : to recall a motion under parliamentary procedure
— **with·draw·able** \-ˈdrȯ-ə-bəl\ *adjective*
**with·draw·al** \-ˈdrȯ(-ə)l\ *noun* (1749)
**1 a** : the act of taking back or away something that has been granted or possessed **b** : removal from a place of deposit or investment **c** (1) : the discontinuance of administration or use of a drug (2) : a period following the discontinuance of an addicting drug that is marked by often painful physical and psychological symptoms ⟨a heroin addict going through *withdrawal*⟩
**2 a** : retreat or retirement especially into a more secluded or less exposed place or position **b** : an operation by which a military force disengages from the enemy **c** (1) : social or emotional detachment (2) : a pathological retreat from objective reality (as in some schizophrenic states)
**3** : RETRACTION, REVOCATION ⟨threatened us with *withdrawal* of consent⟩
**4 a** : the act of drawing someone or something back from or out of a place or position **b** : COITUS INTERRUPTUS
**withdrawing room** *noun* (1591)
: a room to retire to (as from a dining room); *especially* : DRAWING ROOM
**with·drawn** \with-ˈdrȯn, with-\ *adjective* (1615)
**1** : removed from immediate contact or easy approach : ISOLATED
**2** : socially detached and unresponsive : exhibiting withdrawal : INTROVERTED
— **with·drawn·ness** \-ˈdrȯn-nəs\ *noun*

**withe** \ˈwith, ˈwith, ˈwīth\ *noun* [Middle English, from Old English *withthe*; akin to Old English *wīthig* withy] (before 12th century)
: a slender flexible branch or twig; *especially* : one used as a band or line
**¹with·er** \ˈwi-thər\ *verb* **with·ered; with·er·ing** \ˈwith-riŋ, ˈwi-thə-\ [Middle English *widren*; probably akin to Middle English *weder* weather] (14th century)
*intransitive verb*
**1** : to become dry and sapless; *especially* : to shrivel from or as if from loss of bodily moisture
**2** : to lose vitality, force, or freshness
*transitive verb*
**1** : to cause to wither
**2** : to make speechless or incapable of action : STUN ⟨*withered* him with a look —Dorothy Sayers⟩
**²wither** *noun* (1607)
*chiefly British* : WITHERS
**withering** *adjective* (1579)
: acting or serving to cut down or destroy : DEVASTATING ⟨a *withering* fire from the enemy⟩
— **with·er·ing·ly** \ˈwith-riŋ-lē, ˈwi-thə-\ *adverb*
**with·er·ite** \ˈwi-thə-ˌrīt\ *noun* [German *Witherit*, irregular from William *Withering* (died 1799) English physician] (1794)
: a mineral consisting of a carbonate of barium in the form of white or gray twin crystals or columnar or granular masses
**withe rod** *noun* (1846)
: a North American viburnum (*Viburnum cassinoides*) with tough slender shoots
**with·ers** \ˈwi-thərz\ *noun plural* [probably from obsolete English *wither-* against, from Middle English, from Old English, from *wither* against; from the withers being the parts which resist the pull in drawing a load — more at WITH] (1580)
**1** : the ridge between the shoulder bones of a horse — see HORSE illustration
**2** : a part corresponding to the withers in a quadruped other than a horse
**with·er·shins** \ˈwi-thər-shənz\ *variant of* WIDDERSHINS
**with·hold** \with-ˈhōld, with-\ *verb* **-held** \-ˈheld\; **-hold·ing** [Middle English, from *with* from + *holden* to hold — more at WITH] (13th century)
*transitive verb*
**1** : to hold back from action : CHECK
**2** *archaic* : to keep in custody
**3** : to refrain from granting, giving, or allowing ⟨*withhold* permission⟩
**4** : to deduct (withholding tax) from income
*intransitive verb*
: FORBEAR, REFRAIN
*synonym* see KEEP
— **with·hold·er** *noun*
**withholding tax** *noun* (1940)
: a deduction (as from wages, fees, or dividends) levied at a source of income as advance payment on income tax
**¹with·in** \wi-ˈthin, -ˈthin\ *adverb* [Middle English *withinne*, from Old English *withinnan*, from *with* + *innan* inwardly, within, from *in*] (before 12th century)
**1** : in or into the interior : INSIDE
**2** : in one's inner thought, disposition, or character : INWARDLY ⟨search *within* for a creative impulse —Kingman Brewster, Jr.⟩
**²within** *preposition* (12th century)
**1** — used as a function word to indicate enclosure or containment
**2** — used as a function word to indicate situation or circumstance in the limits or compass of: as **a** : before the end of ⟨gone *within* a week⟩ **b** (1) : not beyond the quantity, degree, or limitations of ⟨live *within* your income⟩ (2) : in or into the scope or sphere of ⟨*within* the jurisdiction of the state⟩ (3) : in or into the range of ⟨*within* reach⟩ ⟨*within* sight⟩ (4) — used as a function word to indicate a specified

difference or margin ⟨came *within* two points of a perfect mark⟩ ⟨*within* a mile of the town⟩
**3** : to the inside of : INTO
**³within** *noun* (15th century)
: an inner place or area ⟨revolt from *within*⟩
**⁴within** *adjective* (1748)
: being inside : ENCLOSED ⟨the *within* indictment⟩
**with·in·doors** \wi-ˌthin-ˈdōrz, -ˌthin-, -ˈdȯrz\ *adverb* (1581)
: INDOORS
**with-it** \ˈwi-thət, -thət\ *adjective* (1959)
: socially or culturally up-to-date ⟨the intelligent, disaffected, *with-it* young —Eliot Fremont-Smith⟩
**¹with·out** \wi-ˈthaut, -ˈthaut\ *preposition* [Middle English *withoute*, from Old English *withūtan*, from *with* + *ūtan* outside, from *ūt* out — more at OUT] (before 12th century)
**1** : OUTSIDE
**2** — used as a function word to indicate the absence or lack of something or someone ⟨fight *without* fear⟩ ⟨left *without* him⟩ ⟨looks *without* seeing⟩
**²without** *adverb* (before 12th century)
**1** : on the outside : EXTERNALLY
**2** : with something lacking or absent ⟨has learned to do *without*⟩
**³without** *conjunction* (14th century)
*chiefly dialect* : UNLESS ⟨you don't know about me *without* you have read a book —Mark Twain⟩
**⁴without** *noun* (15th century)
: an outer place or area ⟨came from *without*⟩
**with·out·doors** \wi-ˌthaut-ˈdōrz, -ˌthaut-\ *adverb* (1617)
: OUTDOORS
**with·stand** \with-ˈstand, with-\ *transitive verb* **-stood** \-ˈstud\; **-stand·ing** [Middle English, from Old English *withstandan*, from *with* against + *standan* to stand] (before 12th century)
**1 a** : to stand up against : oppose with firm determination; *especially* : to resist successfully **b** : to be proof against : resist the effect of ⟨*withstand* the impact of a landing —*Current Biography*⟩
**2** *archaic* : to stop or obstruct the course of
*synonym* see OPPOSE
**¹withy** \ˈwi-thē\ *noun, plural* **with·ies** [Middle English, from Old English *wīthig*; akin to Old High German *wīda* willow, Latin *vitis* vine, *viēre* to plait — more at WIRE] (before 12th century)
**1** : WILLOW; *especially* : OSIER 1
**2** : a flexible slender twig or branch (as of osier) : WITHE
**²withy** \ˈwi-thē, ˈwi-thē, ˈwī-thē\ *adjective* [*withe*] (1598)
: flexibly tough
**wit·less** \ˈwit-ləs\ *adjective* (before 12th century)
**1** : destitute of wit or understanding : FOOLISH
**2** : mentally deranged : CRAZY ⟨drive one *witless* with anxiety —William Styron⟩
— **wit·less·ly** *adverb*
— **wit·less·ness** *noun*
**wit·ling** \-liŋ\ *noun* (1693)
**1** : a would-be wit
**2** : a person of little wit
**wit·loof** \ˈwit-ˌlōf, -ˌlüf\ *noun* [Dutch dialect *witloof* chicory, from Dutch *wit* white + *loof* foliage] (1885)
: CHICORY 1; *also* : ENDIVE 2
**¹wit·ness** \ˈwit-nəs\ *noun* [Middle English *witnesse,* from Old English *witnes* knowledge, testimony, witness, from *²wit*] (before 12th century)
**1** : attestation of a fact or event : TESTIMONY

| | | | |
|---|---|---|---|
| \ə\ abut | \ᵊ\ kitten | \ər\ further | \a\ ash | \ā\ ace |
| \ä\ mop, mar | \au̇\ out | \ch\ chin | \e\ bet | \ē\ easy |
| \g\ go | \i\ hit | \ī\ ice | \j\ job | \ŋ\ sing | \ō\ go |
| \ȯ\ law | \ȯi\ boy | \th\ thin | \th\ the | \ü\ loot | \u̇\ foot |
| \y\ yet | \zh\ vision | *see also* Guide to Pronunciation |

**2** : one that gives evidence; *specifically* : one who testifies in a cause or before a judicial tribunal
**3** : one asked to be present at a transaction so as to be able to testify to its having taken place
**4** : one who has personal knowledge of something
**5 a** : something serving as evidence or proof : SIGN **b** : public affirmation by word or example of usually religious faith or conviction ⟨the heroic *witness* to divine life —*Pilot*⟩
**6** *capitalized* : a member of the Jehovah's Witnesses
**²witness** (14th century)
*transitive verb*
**1** : to testify to : ATTEST
**2** : to act as legal witness of
**3** : to furnish proof of : BETOKEN
**4 a** : to have personal or direct cognizance of: see for oneself ⟨*witnessed* the historic event⟩ **b** : to take note of ⟨our grammar — *witness* our verb system—is a marvel of flexibility, variety, and exactitude —Charlton Laird⟩
**5** : to constitute the scene or time of ⟨structures . . . which this striking Dorset hilltop once *witnessed* —*Times Literary Supplement*⟩
*intransitive verb*
**1** : to bear witness : TESTIFY
**2** : to bear witness to one's religious convictions ⟨opportunity to *witness* for Christ —Billy Graham⟩
**synonym** see CERTIFY
**wit·ness–box** \-,bäks\ *noun* (1806)
*chiefly British* : an enclosure in which a witness sits or stands while testifying in court
**witness stand** *noun* (1853)
: a stand or an enclosure from which a witness gives evidence in a court
**wit·ted** \'wi-təd\ *adjective* (14th century)
: having wit or understanding — usually used in combination ⟨dull-*witted*⟩ ⟨quick-*witted*⟩
**wit·ti·cism** \'wi-tə-,si-zəm\ *noun* [*witty* + *-cism* (as in *criticism*)] (1651)
: a cleverly witty and often biting or ironic remark
**¹wit·ting** \'wi-t°n, -tiŋ\ *noun* (14th century)
**1** *chiefly dialect* : knowledge or awareness of something : COGNIZANCE
**2** *chiefly dialect* : information obtained or communicated : NEWS
**²wit·ting** \-tiŋ\ *adjective* (circa 1520)
**1** : cognizant or aware of something : CONSCIOUS
**2** : done deliberately : INTENTIONAL
— **wit·ting·ly** \-tiŋ-lē\ *adverb*
**wit·tol** \'wi-t°l\ *noun* [Middle English *wetewold*, from *weten*, *witen* to know + *cokewold* cuckold — more at WIT] (15th century)
**1** *archaic* : a man who knows of his wife's infidelity and puts up with it
**2** *archaic* : a witless person
**wit·ty** \'wi-tē\ *adjective* **wit·ti·er; -est** (before 12th century)
**1** *archaic* : having good intellectual capacity : INTELLIGENT
**2** : amusingly or ingeniously clever in conception or execution ⟨the costumes are sumptuous and *witty* —Virgil Thomson⟩ ⟨the musical background is . . . often *witty* —Wolcott Gibbs⟩
**3** : marked by or full of wit : smartly facetious or jocular
**4** : quick or ready to see or express illuminating or amusing relationships or insights ☆
— **wit·ti·ly** \'wi-t°l-ē\ *adverb*
— **wit·ti·ness** \'wi-tē-nəs\ *noun*
**wive** \'wīv\ *verb* **wived; wiv·ing** [Middle English, from Old English *wīfian*, from *wīf* woman, wife] (before 12th century)
*intransitive verb*
: to marry a woman
*transitive verb*
**1** : to marry to a woman
**2** : to take for a wife
**wives** *plural of* WIFE

**wiz** \'wiz\ *noun* (1902)
: WIZARD 3
**¹wiz·ard** \'wi-zərd\ *noun* [Middle English *wysard*, from *wis, wys* wise] (15th century)
**1** *archaic* : a wise man : SAGE
**2** : one skilled in magic : SORCERER
**3** : a very clever or skillful person
**²wizard** *adjective* (1579)
**1** *archaic* : having magical influence or power
**2** *archaic* : of or relating to wizardry : ENCHANTED
**3** *chiefly British* : worthy of the highest praise : EXCELLENT
**wiz·ard·ly** \'wi-zərd-lē\ *adjective* (1588)
**1** : having characteristics of a wizard
**2** : marvelous in construction or operation ⟨uses *wizardly* circuitry to distort images —*Time*⟩
**wiz·ard·ry** \'wi-zə(r)-drē\ *noun, plural* **-ries** (1583)
**1** : the art or practices of a wizard : SORCERY
**2 a** : a seemingly magical transforming power or influence ⟨electronic *wizardry*⟩ **b** : great skill or cleverness in an activity
**¹wiz·en** \'wi-z°n *also* 'wē-\ *verb* **wiz·ened; wiz·en·ing** \'wiz-niŋ *also* 'wēz-; 'wi-z°n-iŋ *also* 'wē-\ [Middle English *wisenen*, from Old English *wisnian*; akin to Old High German *wesanēn* to wither, Lithuanian *vysti*] (before 12th century)
*intransitive verb*
: to become dry, shrunken, and wrinkled often as a result of aging or of failing vitality
*transitive verb*
: to cause to wizen
**²wizen** *adjective* [alteration of *wizened*] (1786)
: that is wizened
**woad** \'wōd\ *noun* [Middle English *wod*, from Old English *wād*; akin to Old High German *weit* woad, Latin *vitrum*] (before 12th century)
: a European herb (*Isatis tinctoria*) of the mustard family formerly grown for the blue dyestuff yielded by its leaves; *also* : this dyestuff
**¹wob·ble** \'wä-bəl\ *verb* **wob·bled; wob·bling** \-b(ə-)liŋ\ [probably from Low German *wabbeln*; akin to Old English *wæfre* restless — more at WAVER] (1657)
*intransitive verb*
**1 a** : to move or proceed with an irregular rocking or staggering motion or unsteadily and clumsily from side to side **b** : TREMBLE, QUAVER
**2** : WAVER, VACILLATE
*transitive verb*
: to cause to wobble
— **wob·bler** \-b(ə-)lər\ *noun*
— **wob·bli·ness** \'wä-blē-nəs\ *noun*
— **wob·bly** \'wä-b(ə-)lē\ *adjective*
**²wobble** *noun* (1699)
**1 a** : a hobbling or rocking unequal motion (as of a wheel unevenly mounted) **b** : an uncertainly directed movement
**2** : an intermittent variation (as in volume of sound)
**Wob·bly** \'wä-blē\ *noun, plural* **Wobblies** [origin unknown] (1914)
: a member of the Industrial Workers of the World
**Wo·den** \'wō-d°n\ *noun* [Old English *Wōden*] : ODIN
**wodge** \'wäj\ *noun* [probably alteration of *wedge*] (1860)
*chiefly British* : a bulky mass or chunk : LUMP, WAD
**¹woe** \'wō\ *interjection* [Middle English *wa, wo*, from Old English *wā*; akin to Old Norse *vei*, interjection, woe, Latin *vae*] (before 12th century)
— used to express grief, regret, or distress
**²woe** *noun* (13th century)
**1** : a condition of deep suffering from misfortune, affliction, or grief
**2** : ruinous trouble : CALAMITY, AFFLICTION ⟨economic *woes*⟩
**synonym** see SORROW

**woe·be·gone** \'wō-bi-,gón *also* -,gän\ *adjective* [Middle English *wo begon*, from *wo*, + *begon*, past participle of *begon* to go about, beset, from Old English *begān*, from *be-* + *gān* to go — more at GO] (14th century)
**1** : strongly affected with woe : WOEFUL
**2 a** : exhibiting great woe, sorrow, or misery ⟨a *woebegone* expression⟩ **b** : being in a sorry state ⟨*woebegone* tattered clothes⟩
— **woe·be·gone·ness** *noun*
**woe·ful** *also* **wo·ful** \'wō-fəl\ *adjective* (14th century)
**1** : full of woe : GRIEVOUS ⟨*woeful* prophecies⟩
**2** : involving or bringing woe
**3** : lamentably bad or serious : DEPLORABLE ⟨*woeful* ignorance⟩
— **woe·ful·ly** \-f(ə-)lē\ *adverb*
— **woe·ful·ness** \-fəl-nəs\ *noun*
**wog** \'wäg, 'wóg\ *noun* [perhaps short for *golliwog*] (circa 1929)
*chiefly British* : a dark-skinned foreigner; *especially* : one from the Middle East or Far East — usually used disparagingly
**wok** \'wäk\ *noun* [Chinese (Guangdong) *wohk*] (1952)
: a bowl-shaped cooking utensil used especially in stir-frying
**woke** *past and past participle of* WAKE
**woken** *past participle of* WAKE
**wold** \'wōld\ *noun* [Middle English *wald, wold*, from Old English *weald, wald* forest; akin to Old High German *wald* forest, Old Norse *vollr* field] (before 12th century)
**1** : a usually upland area of open country
**2** *capitalized* : a hilly or rolling region — used in names of various English geographical areas ⟨Yorkshire *Wolds*⟩
**¹wolf** \'wúlf\ *noun, plural* **wolves** \'wúlvz\ *often attributive* [Middle English, from Old English *wulf*; akin to Old High German *wolf* wolf, Latin *lupus*, Greek *lykos*] (before 12th century)
**1** *plural also* **wolf a** : any of various large predatory canids (genus *Canis*) that live and hunt in packs and resemble the related dogs; *especially* : GRAY WOLF — compare COYOTE, JACKAL **b** : the fur of a wolf
**2 a** (1) : a fierce, rapacious, or destructive person (2) : a man forward, direct, and zealous in amatory attentions to women **b** : dire poverty : STARVATION ⟨keep the *wolf* from the door⟩ **c** : the maggot of a warble fly
**3** [German; from the howling sound] **a** (1) : dissonance in some chords on organs, pianos, or other instruments with fixed tones tuned by unequal temperament (2) : an instance of such dissonance **b** : a harshness due to faulty vibration in various tones in a bowed instrument
— **wolf·like** \'wúlf-,līk\ *adjective*
— **wolf in sheep's clothing** : one who cloaks a hostile intention with a friendly manner
**²wolf** *transitive verb* (1862)
: to eat greedily : DEVOUR
**wolf·ber·ry** \'wúlf-,ber-ē\ *noun* (circa 1834)

☆ **SYNONYMS**
**Witty, humorous, facetious, jocular, jocose** mean provoking or intended to provoke laughter. WITTY suggests cleverness and quickness of mind ⟨a *witty* remark⟩. HUMOROUS applies broadly to anything that evokes usually genial laughter and may contrast with *witty* in suggesting whimsicality or eccentricity ⟨*humorous* anecdotes⟩. FACETIOUS stresses a desire to produce laughter and may be derogatory in implying dubious or ill-timed attempts at wit or humor ⟨*facetious* comments⟩. JOCULAR implies a usually habitual fondness for jesting and joking ⟨a *jocular* fellow⟩. JOCOSE is somewhat less derogatory than FACETIOUS in suggesting habitual waggishness or playfulness ⟨*jocose* proposals⟩.

: a white-berried North American shrub (*Symphoricarpos occidentalis*) of the honeysuckle family

**wolf dog** *noun* (1652)
**1** : any of various large dogs formerly kept for hunting wolves
**2** : the offspring of a wolf and a domestic dog

**wolf·er** \'wul-fər\ *noun* (1872)
: a hunter of wolves

**wolff·ian body** \'wul-fē-ən-\ *noun, often W capitalized* [Kaspar Friedrich *Wolff*] (circa 1844)
: MESONEPHROS

**Wolffian duct** *noun* (1879)
: the duct of the mesonephros that persists in the female chiefly as part of a vestigial organ and in the male as the duct system leaving the testis and including the epididymis, vas deferens, and ejaculatory duct

**wolf·fish** \'wulf-,fish\ *noun* (1569)
: any of several large marine blennies (genus *Anarhichas* of the family Anarhicadidae) having strong canine teeth in the front of the jaws and molar teeth on the sides and that feed chiefly on shellfish, starfish, and sea urchins

**wolf·hound** \'wulf-,haund\ *noun* (1786)
: any of several large dogs used especially formerly in hunting large animals (as wolves)

**wolf·ish** \'wul-fish\ *adjective* (1570)
**1** : of or relating to wolves
**2 a** : suggestive of a wolf ⟨*wolfish* mongrel dogs —Hoffman Birney⟩ ⟨a *wolfish* and withdrawn youth —Marshall Frady⟩ **b** : befitting or characteristic of a wolf ⟨a *wolfish* appetite⟩
— **wolf·ish·ly** *adverb*
— **wolf·ish·ness** *noun*

**wolf pack** *noun* (1941)
: a group of submarines that make a coordinated attack on shipping

**wol·fram** \'wul-frəm\ *noun* [German] (1757)
**1** : WOLFRAMITE
**2** : TUNGSTEN

**wol·fram·ite** \'wul-frə-,mīt\ *noun* [German *Wolframit,* from *Wolfram*] (circa 1868)
: a mineral that consists of a tungstate of iron and manganese usually of a brownish or grayish black color and slightly metallic luster, occurs in monoclinic crystals and in granular or columnar masses, and is used as a source of tungsten

**wolfs·bane** \'wulfs-,bān\ *noun* (1548)
: MONKSHOOD; *especially* : a highly variable yellow-flowered poisonous European herb (*Aconitum vulparia*)

**wolf spider** *noun* (1608)
: any of various active wandering ground spiders (family Lycosidae)

**wolf whistle** *noun* (1946)
: a distinctive whistle sounded by a boy or man to express sexual admiration for a girl or woman in his vicinity

**wol·las·ton·ite** \'wul-lə-stə-,nīt, 'wä-\ *noun* [William H. *Wollaston*] (1823)
: a triclinic mineral consisting of a native calcium silicate occurring usually in cleavable masses

**Wo·lof** \'wō-,lof\ *noun* (1823)
: a Niger-Congo language of Senegambia

**wol·ver·ine** \,wul-və-'rēn\ *noun, plural* **wolverines** [probably irregular from *wolv-* (as in *wolves*)] (1574)
**1** *plural also* **wol·verine a** : a carnivorous usually solitary mammal (*Gulo gulo*) of the weasel family of northern forests and associated tundra that is blackish with a light brown band on each side of the body and is noted especially for its strength **b** : the fur of the wolverine

**wolverine 1a**

**2** *capitalized* : a native or resident of Michigan — used as a nickname

**wom·an** \'wu-mən, *especially Southern* 'wo-or 'wə-\ *noun, plural* **wom·en** \'wi-mən\ [Middle English, from Old English *wīfman,* from *wīf* woman, wife + *man* human being, man] (before 12th century)
**1 a** : an adult female person **b** : a woman belonging to a particular category (as by birth, residence, membership, or occupation) — usually used in combination ⟨council*woman*⟩
**2** : WOMENKIND
**3** : distinctively feminine nature : WOMANLINESS
**4** : a female servant or personal attendant
**5 a** *chiefly dialect* : WIFE **b** : MISTRESS **c** : GIRLFRIEND 2 ◆
— **woman** *adjective*
— **wom·an·less** \-ləs\ *adjective*

**wom·an·hood** \-,hud\ *noun* (14th century)
**1 a** : the state of being a woman **b** : the distinguishing character or qualities of a woman or of womankind
**2** : WOMEN, WOMENKIND

**wom·an·ise** *British variant of* WOMANIZE

**wom·an·ish** \'wu-mə-nish\ *adjective* (14th century)
**1** : characteristic of or suitable for a woman
**2** : unsuitable to a man or to a strong character of either sex : EFFEMINATE ⟨*womanish* fears⟩
— **wom·an·ish·ly** *adverb*
— **wom·an·ish·ness** *noun*

**wom·an·ize** \'wu-mə-,nīz\ *verb* **-ized; -izing** (1593)
*transitive verb*
: to make effeminate
*intransitive verb*
: to pursue multiple casual relationships with women
— **wom·an·iz·er** *noun*

**wom·an·kind** \'wu-mən-,kīnd\ *noun singular but singular or plural in construction* (14th century)
: WOMENKIND

**¹wom·an·like** \-,līk\ *adjective* (15th century)
: WOMANLY

**²womanlike** *adverb* (15th century)
: in the manner of a woman

**wom·an·ly** \-lē\ *adjective* (13th century)
**1** : having qualities generally associated with a woman
**2** : appropriate in character to a woman
— **wom·an·li·ness** *noun*

**woman of letters** (1818)
**1** : a woman who is a scholar
**2** : a woman who is an author

**woman of the street** (1928)
: PROSTITUTE

**wom·an·pow·er** \'wu-mən-,pau(-ə)r\ *noun* (1938)
: women available and prepared for work (as in industry or a particular line of endeavor)

**woman's rights** *noun plural* (1840)
**1** : legal, political, and social rights for women equal to those of men
**2** : FEMINISM 2

**woman suffrage** *noun* (1867)
: possession and exercise of suffrage by women

**womb** \'wüm\ *noun* [Middle English *wamb, womb,* from Old English; akin to Old High German *wamba* belly] (before 12th century)
**1** : UTERUS
**2 a** : a cavity or space that resembles a womb in containing and enveloping **b** : a place where something is generated
— **wombed** \'wümd\ *adjective*

**wom·bat** \'wäm-,bat\ *noun* [Dharuk (Australian aboriginal language of the Port Jackson area) *wambat*] (1798)
: any of several stocky Australian marsupials (genera

**wombat**

*Vombatus* and *Lasiorhinus* of the family Vombatidae) resembling small bears

**wom·en·folk** \'wi-mən-,fōk\ *also* **wom·en·folks** \-,fōks\ *noun plural* (1833)
: WOMEN

**wom·en·kind** \-,kīnd\ *noun* (14th century)
: female human beings : women especially as distinguished from men

**women's rights** *noun plural* (1632)
: WOMAN'S RIGHTS

**women's room** *noun* (circa 1937)
: LADIES' ROOM

**wom·mera** \'wä-mə-rə\ *variant of* WOOMERA

**¹won** \'wən, 'wōn\ *intransitive verb* **wonned; won·ning** [Middle English, from Old English *wunian* — more at WONT] (before 12th century)
*archaic* : DWELL 2a, ABIDE 2

**²won** \'wən\ *past and past participle of* WIN

**³won** \'won\ *noun, plural* **won** [Korean *wŏn*] (circa 1917)
— see MONEY table

**¹won·der** \'wən-dər\ *noun* [Middle English, from Old English *wundor;* akin to Old High German *wuntar* wonder] (before 12th century)
**1 a** : a cause of astonishment or admiration : MARVEL ⟨it's a *wonder* you weren't killed⟩ **b** : MIRACLE
**2** : the quality of exciting amazed admiration
**3 a** : rapt attention or astonishment at something awesomely mysterious or new to one's experience **b** : a feeling of doubt or uncertainty

**²wonder** *verb* **won·dered; won·der·ing** \-d(ə-)riŋ\ (before 12th century)
*intransitive verb*
**1 a** : to be in a state of wonder **b** : to feel surprise
**2** : to feel curiosity or doubt
*transitive verb*
: to be curious or in doubt about
— **won·der·er** \-dər-ər\ *noun*

**³wonder** *adjective* (12th century)
: WONDROUS, WONDERFUL: as **a** : exciting

\ə\ **abut** \ᵊ\ **kitten** \ər\ **further** \a\ **ash** \ā\ **ace**
\ä\ **mop, mar** \au̇\ **out** \ch\ **chin** \e\ **bet** \ē\ **easy**
\g\ **go** \i\ **hit** \ī\ **ice** \j\ **job** \ŋ\ **sing** \ō\ **go**
\ȯ\ **law** \ȯi\ **boy** \th\ **thin** \t̶h̶\ **the** \ü\ **loot** \u̇\ **foot**
\y\ **yet** \zh\ **vision** *see also* Guide to Pronunciation

amazement or admiration **b :** effective or efficient far beyond anything previously known or anticipated

**wonder drug** *noun* (1939)
**:** MIRACLE DRUG

**won·der·ful** \'wən-dər-fəl\ *adjective* (before 12th century)
**1 :** exciting wonder **:** MARVELOUS, ASTONISHING ⟨a sight *wonderful* to behold⟩
**2 :** unusually good **:** ADMIRABLE
— **won·der·ful·ly** \-f(ə-)lē\ *adverb*
— **won·der·ful·ness** \-fəl-nəs\ *noun*

**won·der·land** \'wən-dər-,land, -lənd\ *noun* (1790)
**1 :** an imaginary place of delicate beauty or magical charm
**2 :** a place that excites admiration or wonder

**won·der·ment** \-mənt\ *noun* (1535)
**1 :** ASTONISHMENT, SURPRISE
**2 :** a cause of or occasion for wonder
**3 :** curiosity about something

**won·der·work** \-də(r)-,wərk\ *noun* (before 12th century)
**:** a marvelous act, work, or accomplishment

**won·der–work·er** \-,wər-kər\ *noun* (1599)
**:** one that performs wonders

**won·der–work·ing** \-kiŋ\ *adjective* (1594)
**:** producing wonders

**won·drous** \'wən-drəs\ *adjective* [Middle English, alteration of *wonders,* from genitive of [1]*wonder*] (15th century)
**:** that is to be marveled at **:** EXTRAORDINARY
— **wondrous** *adverb, archaic*
— **won·drous·ly** *adverb*
— **won·drous·ness** *noun*

**wonk** \'wäŋk, 'wȯŋk\ *noun* [origin unknown] (1954)
**:** NERD

**won·ky** \'wäŋ-kē\ *adjective* [probably alteration of English dialect *wankle,* from Middle English *wankel,* from Old English *wancol;* akin to Old High German *wankōn* to totter — more at WENCH] (1919)
**1** *British* **:** UNSTEADY, SHAKY
**2** *British* **:** AWRY, WRONG

[1]**wont** \'wȯnt, 'wōnt *also* 'wənt, 'wänt\ *adjective* [Middle English *woned, wont,* from past participle of *wonen* to dwell, be used to, from Old English *wunian;* akin to Old High German *wonēn* to dwell, be used to, Sanskrit *vanoti* he strives for — more at WIN] (before 12th century)
**1 :** ACCUSTOMED, USED ⟨got up early as he is *wont* to do⟩
**2 :** INCLINED, APT ⟨revealing as letters are *wont* to be —Gladys M. Wrigley⟩

[2]**wont** *verb* **wont; wont** *or* **wont·ed; wont·ing** (15th century)
*transitive verb*
**:** ACCUSTOM, HABITUATE
*intransitive verb*
**:** to have the habit of doing something

[3]**wont** *noun* (1530)
**:** habitual way of doing **:** USE
**synonym** see HABIT

**won't** \'wōnt; *New England, upstate New York, northern Pennsylvania* ,wənt, 'wənt; *greater New York City* 'wŭnt; *eastern South Carolina* 'wünt, 'wŭnt\ (1652)
**:** will not

**wont·ed** \'wȯn-təd, 'wōn- *also* 'wən- *or* 'wän-\ *adjective* (15th century)
**:** usual or ordinary especially by reason of established habit ⟨flashed his *wonted* grin⟩
**synonym** see USUAL
— **wont·ed·ly** *adverb*
— **wont·ed·ness** *noun*

**won·ton** \'wän-,tän\ *noun* [Chinese (Guangdong) *wàhn-tān*] (1934)
**:** filled pockets of noodle dough served boiled in soup or fried

**woo** \'wü\ *verb* [Middle English *wowen,* from Old English *wōgian*] (before 12th century)
*transitive verb*
**1 :** to sue for the affection of and usually marriage with **:** COURT

**2 :** to solicit or entreat especially with importunity
**3 :** to seek to gain or bring about
*intransitive verb*
**:** to court a woman
— **woo·er** *noun*

[1]**wood** \'wŭd, 'wȯd, 'wŭd\ *adjective* [Middle English, from Old English *wōd* insane; akin to Old High German *wuot* madness — more at VATIC] (before 12th century)
*archaic* **:** violently mad

[2]**wood** \'wŭd\ *noun* [Middle English *wode,* from Old English *widu, wudu;* akin to Old High German *witu* wood, Old Irish *fid* tree] (before 12th century)
**1 a :** a dense growth of trees usually greater in extent than a grove and smaller than a forest — often used in plural but singular or plural in construction **b :** WOODLAND
**2 a :** the hard fibrous substance consisting basically of xylem that makes up the greater part of the stems, branches, and roots of trees or shrubs beneath the bark and is found to a limited extent in herbaceous plants **b :** wood suitable or prepared for some use (as burning or building)
**3 a :** something made of wood **b :** a golf club having a thick wooden head; *also* **:** a golf club having a similar head made of metal
— **out of the woods :** clear of danger or difficulty

[3]**wood** \'wŭd\ *adjective* (1538)
**1 :** WOODEN
**2 :** suitable for cutting or working with wood ⟨a *wood* saw⟩
**3** *or* **woods** \'wŭdz\ **:** living, growing, or existing in woods ⟨*woods* trails⟩

[4]**wood** \'wŭd\ (1630)
*intransitive verb*
**:** to gather or take on wood
*transitive verb*
**:** to cover with a growth of trees or plant with trees

**wood alcohol** *noun* (1861)
**:** METHANOL

**wood anemone** *noun* (1657)
**:** any of several anemones; *especially* **:** one (*Anemone quinquefolia*) of North America with solitary often pink-tinged flowers

**wood bet·o·ny** \-'be-t°n-ē\ *noun* [Middle English *betone,* from Old French *betoine,* from Latin *vettonica, betonica,* from *Vettones,* an ancient people inhabiting the Iberian peninsula] (1657)
**:** a lousewort (*Pedicularis canadensis*) of eastern North America with yellow or reddish flowers in bracted spikes

**wood·bine** \'wŭd-,bīn\ *noun* [Middle English *wodebinde,* from Old English *wudubinde,* from *wudu* wood + *bindan* to tie, bind; from its winding around trees] (before 12th century)
**1 :** any of several honeysuckles; *especially* **:** a Eurasian twining shrub (*Lonicera periclymenum*)
**2 :** VIRGINIA CREEPER

**wood·block** \-,bläk\ *noun* (1837)
**:** WOODCUT
— **wood–block** *adjective*

**wood–bor·ing** \-,bȯr-iŋ, -,bȯr-\ *adjective* (1815)
**:** excavating galleries in wood in feeding or in constructing a nest — used chiefly of an insect

**wood carving** *noun* (1847)
**:** the art of fashioning or ornamenting objects of wood by cutting with a sharp handheld implement; *also* **:** an object of wood so fashioned or ornamented
— **wood·carv·er** \-,kär-vər\ *noun*

**wood·chat shrike** \'wŭd-,chat-\ *noun* (1781)
**:** a European shrike (*Lanius senator*) — called also *woodchat*

**wood·chop·per** \-,chä-pər\ *noun* (1779)
**:** one engaged especially in chopping down trees

**wood·chuck** \-,chək\ *noun* [by folk etymology from a word of Algonquian origin; akin to Narraganset *ockqutchaun* woodchuck] (1674)
**:** a grizzled thickset marmot (*Marmota monax*) chiefly of Alaska, Canada, and the northeastern U.S. — called also *groundhog*

**wood·cock** \'wŭd-,käk\ *noun, plural* **wood·cocks** (before 12th century)
**1** *or plural* **woodcock :** a widespread Old World woodland bird (*Scolopax rusticola*) that is related to the sandpipers and snipes; *also* **:** a smaller related game bird (*Scolopax minor* synonym *Philohela minor*) of eastern North America
**2** [from the ease with which the woodcock is snared] *archaic* **:** SIMPLETON

**wood·craft** \-,kraft\ *noun* (14th century)
**1 :** skill and practice in anything relating to the woods and especially in maintaining oneself and making one's way in the woods
**2 :** skill in shaping or constructing articles from wood

**wood·cut** \-,kət\ *noun* (1662)
**1 :** a relief printing surface consisting of a wooden block with a usually pictorial design cut with the grain
**2 :** a print from a woodcut

**wood·cut·ter** \-,kə-tər\ *noun* (1761)
**:** one that cuts wood

**wood·cut·ting** \-,kə-tiŋ\ *noun* (1683)
**1 :** the action or occupation of cutting wood or timber
**2 :** the producing of woodcuts

**wood duck** *noun* (1777)
**:** a showy American duck (*Aix sponsa*) which nests in tree cavities and the males of which have a large crest and iridescent plumage varied with green, purple, black, white, and chestnut

wood duck

**wood ear** *noun* (1917)
**:** TREE EAR

**wood·ed** \'wŭ-dəd\ *adjective* (1605)
**:** covered with growing trees

**wood·en** \'wŭ-d°n\ *adjective* (1538)
**1 :** made or consisting of wood
**2 :** lacking ease or flexibility **:** awkwardly stiff
— **wood·en·ly** *adverb*
— **wood·en·ness** \-d°n-(n)əs\ *noun*

**wood engraving** *noun* (1816)
**1 :** a relief printing surface consisting of a wooden block with a usually pictorial design cut in the end grain
**2 :** a print from a wood engraving

**wood·en·head** \'wŭ-d°n-,hed\ *noun* (1831)
**:** BLOCKHEAD

**wood·en·head·ed** \,wŭ-d°n-'he-dəd\ *adjective* (circa 1854)
**:** DENSE, STUPID

**wooden Indian** *noun* (1879)
**:** a wooden image of a standing American Indian brave used especially formerly as a sign for a cigar store

**wood·en·ware** \'wŭ-d°n-,war, -,wer\ *noun* (1647)
**:** articles made of wood for domestic use

**wood fiber** *noun* (1875)
**:** any of various fibers in or associated with xylem

[1]**wood·land** \'wŭd-lənd, -,land\ *noun* (before 12th century)
**:** land covered with woody vegetation **:** TIMBERLAND, FOREST
— **wood·land·er** \-lən-dər, -,lan-\ *noun*

[2]**woodland** *adjective* (14th century)
**1 :** growing, living, or existing in woodland
**2 :** of, relating to, or being woodland

**wood·lore** \'wŭd-,lȯr, -,lȯr\ *noun* (1918)
**:** knowledge of the woods

**wood·lot** \-,lät\ *noun* (1643)

: a restricted area of woodland usually privately maintained as a source of fuel, posts, and lumber

**wood louse** *noun* (1611)
: a terrestrial isopod crustacean (suborder Oniscoidea) with a flattened elliptical body often capable of being rolled into a ball — called also *pill bug*, *sow bug*

**wood·man** \'wùd-mən\ *noun* (15th century)
**1** : WOODSMAN
**2** *capitalized* [Modern *Woodmen* of America & *Woodmen* of the World] : a member of either of two independent benevolent and fraternal societies

**wood·note** \-,nōt\ *noun* [from its likeness to the call of a bird in the woods] (1632)
: verbal expression that is natural and artless

**wood nymph** *noun* (1577)
: a nymph living in woods — called also *dryad*

**wood·peck·er** \'wùd-,pe-kər\ *noun* (circa 1530)
: any of numerous birds (family Picidae) with zygodactyl feet, stiff spiny tail feathers used in climbing or resting on tree trunks, a usually extensile tongue, a very hard bill used to drill the bark or wood of trees for insect food or to excavate nesting cavities, and generally showy parti-colored plumage

**wood·pile** \-,pīl\ *noun* (circa 1552)
: a pile of wood (as firewood)
**— in the woodpile** : doing or responsible for covert mischief

**wood pulp** *noun* (1866)
: pulp from wood used in making cellulose derivatives (as paper or rayon)

**wood pussy** *noun* (circa 1899)
: SKUNK

**wood rat** *noun* (1763)
: any of numerous cricetid rodents (especially genus *Neotoma*) of North and Central America with soft fur, well-furred tails, and large ears

**wood ray** *noun* (1925)
: XYLEM RAY

**wood·ruff** \'wùd-(,)rəf\ *noun* [Middle English *woderove*, from Old English *wudurofe*, from *wudu* wood + *-rofe* (of unknown origin)] (before 12th century)
**1** : any of a genus (*Asperula*) of Old World herbs of the madder family
**2** : a small Eurasian and North African sweet-scented herb (*Galium odoratum* synonym *Asperula odorata*) used in perfumery and for flavoring wine

**¹wood·shed** \-,shed\ *noun* (1844)
**1** : a shed for storing wood and especially firewood
**2** : a place, means, or session for administering discipline

**²woodshed** *intransitive verb* **-shed·ded; -shed·ding** [probably from the former use of woodsheds for private practicing] (1936)
: PRACTICE; *especially* : to practice on a musical instrument

**wood shot** *noun* (1927)
**1** : a golf shot played with a wood
**2** : a stroke in a racket game in which the ball or shuttlecock is hit with the frame of the racket rather than the strings

**woods·man** \'wùdz-mən\ *noun* (1688)
: a person who frequents or works in the woods; *especially* : one skilled in woodcraft

**wood sorrel** *noun* (1525)
: any of a genus (*Oxalis* of the family Oxalidaceae, the wood-sorrel family) of herbs with acid sap, compound leaves, and regular flowers; *especially* : either of two stemless herbs (*O. montana* of North America and *O. acetosella* of Eurasia) with trifoliolate leaves

**wood spirit** *noun* (1842)
: METHANOL

**wood stork** *noun* (1884)
: a white stork (*Mycteria americana*) with black wing flight feathers and tail that frequents wooded swamps from the southeastern U.S. to Argentina — called also *wood ibis*

**wood·stove** \'wùd-,stōv\ *noun* (1847)
: a stove that uses wood for fuel

**wood sugar** *noun* (circa 1900)
: XYLOSE

**woodsy** \'wùd-zē\ *adjective* (1860)
: characteristic or suggestive of woods

**wood tar** *noun* (1857)
: tar obtained by the destructive distillation of wood either as a deposit from pyroligneous acid or as a residue from the distillation of the acid or of wood turpentine

**wood tick** *noun* (1668)
: any of several ixodid ticks: as **a** : a widely distributed tick (*Dermacentor andersonii*) of western North America that is a vector of Rocky Mountain spotted fever **b** : AMERICAN DOG TICK

**wood turning** *noun* (circa 1876)
: the art or process of fashioning wooden pieces or blocks into various forms and shapes by means of a lathe

**wood turpentine** *noun* (circa 1909)
: TURPENTINE 2b

**wood warbler** *noun* (1817)
: WARBLER 2b

**wood·wind** \'wùd-,wind\ *noun* (1876)
**1** : any of a group of wind instruments (as a clarinet, flute, oboe, or saxophone) that are characterized by a cylindrical or conical tube of wood or metal usually ending in a slightly flared bell, that produce tones by the vibration of one or two reeds in the mouthpiece or by the passing of air over a mouth hole, and that usually have finger holes or keys by which the player may produce all the tones within an instrument's range
**2** *plural* : the woodwind section of a band or orchestra

**wood·work** \-,wərk\ *noun* (1650)
**1** : work made of wood; *especially* : interior fittings (as moldings or stairways) of wood
**2** : a place or state of concealment, seclusion, or anonymity ⟨witnesses came out of the *woodwork* when a reward was offered⟩

**¹wood·work·ing** \-,wər-kin\ *adjective* (1872)
: used for woodworking

**²woodworking** *noun* (1875)
: the act, process, or occupation of working wood into a useful or desired form
**— wood·work·er** \-kər\ *noun*

**wood·worm** \'wùd-,wərm\ *noun* (1725)
: an insect larva (as of a furniture beetle) that bores especially in dead wood; *also* : an infestation of woodworms

**¹woody** \'wù-dē\ *adjective* **wood·i·er; -est** (14th century)
**1** : abounding or overgrown with woods
**2 a** : of or containing wood or wood fibers : LIGNEOUS ⟨*woody* tissues⟩ **b** : having woody parts : rich in xylem and associated structures ⟨*woody* plants⟩
**3** : characteristic of or suggestive of wood ⟨wine with a *woody* flavor⟩
**— wood·i·ness** *noun*

**²woody** *or* **wood·ie** \'wù-dē\ *noun, plural* **woodies** [alteration of ³*wood*] (1961)
: a wood-paneled station wagon

**¹woof** \'wùf, 'wüf\ *noun* [alteration of Middle English *oof*, from Old English *ōwef*, from *ō-* (from *on*) + *wefan* to weave — more at WEAVE] (before 12th century)
**1 a** : WEFT 1a **b** : woven material; *also* : the texture of such a fabric
**2** : a basic or essential element or material

**²woof** \'wùf\ *intransitive verb* [imitative] (1804)
**1** : to make the low gruff sound typically produced by a dog
**2** : to express oneself in a usually stylized boastful, aggressive, or exaggeratedly deceitful manner

**³woof** *noun* (1839)
**1** : a low gruff sound typically produced by a dog
**2** : a low note emitted by sound reproducing equipment

**woof·er** \'wù-fər\ *noun* (1935)
: a loudspeaker usually larger than a tweeter, responsive only to the lower acoustic frequencies, and used for reproducing sounds of low pitch — compare TWEETER

**wool** \'wùl\ *noun, often attributive* [Middle English *wolle*, from Old English *wull;* akin to Old High German *wolla* wool, Latin *vellus* fleece, *lana* wool] (before 12th century)
**1** : the soft wavy or curly hypertrophied undercoat of various hairy mammals and especially the sheep made up of a matrix of keratin fibers and covered with minute scales
**2** : a product of wool; *especially* : a woven fabric or garment of such fabric
**3 a** : a dense felted pubescence especially on a plant : TOMENTUM **b** : a filamentous mass — usually used in combination; compare MINERAL WOOL, STEEL WOOL

**wooled** *also* **woolled** \'wùld\ *adjective* (circa 1859)
: having wool especially of a specified kind — used in combination ⟨long-*wooled*⟩

**¹wool·en** *or* **wool·len** \'wù-lən\ *adjective* (before 12th century)
**1** : made of wool
**2** : of or relating to the manufacture or sale of woolen products ⟨*woolen* mills⟩ ⟨the *woolen* industry⟩

**²woolen** *or* **woollen** *noun* (14th century)
**1** : a fabric made of wool and especially of woolen yarns having a fuzzy or napped face (as for use in clothing or blankets) — compare WORSTED
**2** : garments of woolen fabric — usually used in plural

**wool fat** *noun* (1875)
: wool grease especially after refining : LANOLIN

**wool–gath·er** \'wùl-,ga-thər, -,ge-thər\ *intransitive verb* (1850)
: to indulge in woolgathering
**— wool·gath·er·er** \-thər-ər\ *noun*

**wool·gath·er·ing** \-,ga-th(ə-)rin, -,geth(ə-)rin\ *noun* (1553)
: indulgence in idle daydreaming

**wool grease** *noun* (1875)
: a fatty slightly sticky wax coating the surface of the fibers of sheep's wool — compare WOOL FAT

**¹wool·ly** *also* **wooly** \'wù-lē\ *adjective* **wool·li·er; -est** (1578)
**1 a** : of, relating to, or bearing wool **b** : resembling wool
**2 a** : lacking in clearness or sharpness of outline ⟨a *woolly* TV picture⟩ **b** : marked by mental confusion ⟨*woolly* thinking⟩
**3** : marked by boisterous roughness or lack of order or restraint ⟨where the West is still *woolly* —Paul Schubert⟩ — used especially in the phrase *wild and woolly*
**— wool·li·ly** \-lə-lē\ *adverb*
**— wool·li·ness** *noun*

**²wool·ly** *also* **wool·ie** *or* **wooly** \'wù-lē\ *noun, plural* **wool·lies** *also* **wool·ies** (circa 1865)
**1** : a garment made from wool; *especially* : underclothing of knitted wool — usually used in plural
**2** *West & Australian* : SHEEP

**woolly aphid** *noun* (1842)
: any of several plant lice (especially genus *Eriosoma*) covered with a dense coat of white filaments — called also *woolly aphis*

**woolly bear** *noun* (circa 1841)
: any of various rather large very hairy moth caterpillars; *especially* : one of a tiger moth

**wool·ly–head·ed** \,wù-lē-'he-dəd\ *adjective* (1650)
**1** : having hair suggesting wool

---

\ə\ abut \ᵊ\ kitten \ər\ further \a\ ash \ā\ ace
\ä\ mop, mar \aù\ out \ch\ chin \e\ bet \ē\ easy
\g\ go \i\ hit \ī\ ice \j\ job \ŋ\ sing \ō\ go
\ò\ law \òi\ boy \th\ thin \th\ the \ü\ loot \ù\ foot
\y\ yet \zh\ vision *see also* Guide to Pronunciation

**2 :** marked by vague or confused perception or thinking

**woolly mammoth** *noun* (1933)
**:** a heavy-coated mammoth (*Mammuthus primigenius*) of the colder parts of the northern hemisphere

**wool·pack** \'wùl-,pak\ *noun* (14th century)
**1 :** a wrapper of strong fabric into which fleeces are packed for shipment
**2 :** the complete package of wool and wrapper

**wool·sack** \-,sak\ *noun* (14th century)
**1** *archaic* **:** WOOLPACK 2
**2 :** a cushion that is the official seat of the Lord Chancellor or his deputy in presiding over the House of Lords

**wool·shed** \-,shed\ *noun* (1850)
**:** a building or range of buildings (as on an Australian sheep station) in which sheep are sheared and wool is prepared for market

**wool·skin** \-,skin\ *noun* (15th century)
**:** a sheepskin having the wool still on it

**wool·sort·er's disease** \'wùl-,sòr-tərz-\ *noun* (1880)
**:** pulmonary anthrax resulting especially from inhalation of bacterial spores (*Bacillus anthracis*) from contaminated wool or hair

**wool stapler** *noun* (1709)
**:** a dealer in wool

**woom·era** \'wù-mə-rə\ *noun* [Dharvk (Australian aboriginal language of the Port Jackson area) *wumera*] (1817)
**:** a wooden rod with a hooked end used by Australian aborigines for throwing a spear

**woops** \'(w)ù(ə)ps\ *variant of* OOPS

**woo·zy** \'wü-zē, 'wù-\ *adjective* **woo·zi·er; -est** [origin unknown] (1897)
**1 :** mentally unclear or hazy ⟨seems a little *woozy*, not quite knowing what to say —J. A. Lukacs⟩
**2 :** affected with dizziness, mild nausea, or weakness
— **woo·zi·ly** *adverb*
— **woo·zi·ness** *noun*

**wop** \'wäp\ *noun, often capitalized* [Italian dialect *guappo* swaggerer, tough, from Spanish *guapo*, probably from Middle French dialect *vape, wape* weak, insipid, from Latin *vappa* wine gone flat] (1908)
**:** ITALIAN — usually used disparagingly

**Worces·ter** \'wùs-tər\ *noun* (1802)
**:** low-fired porcelain containing a frit and steatite produced at Worcester, England, from about 1751 — called also *Worcester china, Worcester porcelain*

**Worces·ter·shire sauce** \'wùs-tə(r)-,shir-, -shər- *also* -,shīr-\ *noun* [*Worcestershire*, England, where it was originally made] (1843)
**:** a pungent sauce whose ingredients include soy, vinegar, and garlic

**¹word** \'wərd\ *noun* [Middle English, from Old English; akin to Old High German *wort* word, Latin *verbum*, Greek *eirein* to say, speak, Hittite *weriya-* to call, name] (before 12th century)
**1 a :** something that is said **b** *plural* (1) **:** TALK, DISCOURSE ⟨putting one's feelings into *words*⟩ (2) **:** the text of a vocal musical composition **c :** a brief remark or conversation ⟨would like to have a *word* with you⟩
**2 a** (1) **:** a speech sound or series of speech sounds that symbolizes and communicates a meaning without being divisible into smaller units capable of independent use (2) **:** the entire set of linguistic forms produced by combining a single base with various inflectional elements without change in the part of speech elements **b** (1) **:** a written or printed character or combination of characters representing a spoken word ⟨the number of *words* to a line⟩ — sometimes used with the first letter of a real or pretended taboo word prefixed often as a humorous euphemism ⟨we were not afraid to use the d *word* and talk about death —Erma Bombeck⟩ ⟨the first man to utter the f *word* on British TV —*Time*⟩ (2) **:** any segment of written or printed discourse ordinarily appearing between spaces or between a space and a punctuation mark **c :** a number of bytes processed as a unit and conveying a quantum of information in communication and computer work
**3 :** ORDER, COMMAND ⟨don't move till I give the *word*⟩
**4** *often capitalized* **a :** LOGOS **b :** GOSPEL 1a **c :** the expressed or manifested mind and will of God
**5 a :** NEWS, INFORMATION ⟨sent *word* that he would be late⟩ **b :** RUMOR
**6 :** the act of speaking or of making verbal communication
**7 :** SAYING, PROVERB
**8 :** PROMISE, DECLARATION ⟨kept her *word*⟩
**9 :** a quarrelsome utterance or conversation — usually used in plural ⟨they had *words* and parted⟩
**10 :** a verbal signal **:** PASSWORD
— **good word 1 :** a favorable statement ⟨put in a *good word* for me⟩ **2 :** good news ⟨what's the *good word*⟩
— **in a word :** in short
— **in so many words 1 :** in exactly those terms ⟨implied that such actions were criminal but did not say so *in so many words*⟩ **2 :** in plain forthright language ⟨*in so many words*, she wasn't fit to be seen —Jean Stafford⟩
— **of few words :** not inclined to say more than is necessary **:** LACONIC
— **of one's word :** that can be relied on to keep a promise — used only after *man* or *woman*
— **upon my word :** with my assurance **:** INDEED, ASSUREDLY ⟨*upon my word*, I've never heard of such a thing⟩

**²word** (13th century)
*intransitive verb*
*archaic* **:** SPEAK
*transitive verb*
**:** to express in words **:** PHRASE

**word·age** \'wər-dij\ *noun* (1829)
**1 a :** WORDS **b :** VERBIAGE 1
**2 :** the number or quantity of words
**3 :** WORDING

**word–association test** *noun* (1946)
**:** a test of personality and mental function in which the subject is required to respond to each of a series of words with the first one that comes to mind or with one of a specified class of words

**word·book** \'wərd-,bùk\ *noun* (1598)
**:** VOCABULARY, DICTIONARY

**word class** *noun* (1914)
**:** a linguistic form class whose members are words; *especially* **:** PART OF SPEECH

**word–for–word** *adjective* (1611)
**:** being in the exact words **:** VERBATIM

**word for word** *adverb* (14th century)
**:** in the exact words **:** VERBATIM

**word–hoard** \'wərd-,hōrd, -,hòrd\ *noun* [translation of Old English *wordhord*] (circa 1869)
**:** a supply of words **:** VOCABULARY

**word·ing** \'wər-diŋ\ *noun* (1649)
**:** the act or manner of expressing in words **:** PHRASEOLOGY

**word·less** \'wərd-ləs\ *adjective* (15th century)
**1 :** not expressed in or accompanied by words
**2 :** SILENT, SPEECHLESS
— **word·less·ly** *adverb*
— **word·less·ness** *noun*

**word·mon·ger** \-,məŋ-gər, -,mäŋ-\ *noun* (1590)
**:** a writer who uses words for show or without particular regard for meaning

**word–mon·ger·ing** \-g(ə-)riŋ\ *noun* (1879)
**:** the use of empty or bombastic words

**word–of–mouth** \,wərd-ə(v)-'mauth\ *adjective* (1802)
**:** orally communicated; *also* **:** generated from or reliant on oral publicity ⟨*word-of-mouth* customers⟩ ⟨a *word-of-mouth* business⟩

**word of mouth** *noun* (1553)
**:** oral communication; *especially* **:** oral often inadvertent publicity

**word order** *noun* (1892)
**:** the order or arrangement of words in a phrase, clause, or sentence

**word–play** \'wərd-,plā\ *noun* (1855)
**:** verbal wit

**word processing** *noun* (1970)
**:** the production of typewritten documents (as business letters) with automated and usually computerized typing and text-editing equipment
— **word process** *verb*

**word processor** *noun* (1970)
**:** a keyboard-operated terminal usually with a video display and a magnetic storage device for use in word processing; *also* **:** software (as for a computer system) to perform word processing

**word·smith** \'wərd-,smith\ *noun* (1896)
**:** a person who works with words; *especially* **:** a skillful writer
— **word·smith·ery** \-,smi-thə-rē\ *noun*

**word square** *noun* (circa 1879)
**:** a series of words of equal length arranged in a square pattern to read the same horizontally and vertically

**word stress** *noun* (circa 1914)
**:** the manner in which stresses are distributed on the syllables of a word — called also *word accent*

**wordy** \'wər-dē\ *adjective* **word·i·er; -est** (12th century)
**1 :** using or containing many and usually too many words
**2 :** of or relating to words **:** VERBAL ☆
— **word·i·ly** \'wər-d°l-ē\ *adverb*
— **word·i·ness** \'wər-dē-nəs\ *noun*

**wore** *past of* WEAR

**¹work** \'wərk\ *noun* [Middle English *werk, work*, from Old English *werc, weorc;* akin to Old High German *werc, Greek ergon,* Avestan *varəzem* activity] (before 12th century)
**1 :** activity in which one exerts strength or faculties to do or perform something: **a :** sustained physical or mental effort to overcome obstacles and achieve an objective or result **b :** the labor, task, or duty that is one's accustomed means of livelihood **c :** a specific task, duty, function, or assignment often being a part or phase of some larger activity
**2 a :** energy expended by natural phenomena **b :** the result of such energy ⟨sand dunes are the *work* of sea and wind⟩ **c :** the transference of energy that is produced by the motion of the point of application of a force and is measured by multiplying the force and the displacement of its point of application in the line of action
**3 a :** something that results from a particular manner or method of working, operating, or devising ⟨careful police *work*⟩ ⟨clever camera *work*⟩ **b :** something that results from the use or fashioning of a particular material ⟨porcelain *work*⟩
**4 a :** a fortified structure (as a fort, earthen barricade, or trench) **b** *plural* **:** structures in engineering (as docks, bridges, or embankments) or mining (as shafts or tunnels)
**5** *plural but singular or plural in construction* **:** a place where industrial labor is carried on **:** PLANT, FACTORY

---

☆ **SYNONYMS**
**Wordy, verbose, prolix, diffuse** mean using more words than necessary to express thought. WORDY may also imply loquaciousness or garrulity ⟨a *wordy* speech⟩. VERBOSE suggests a resulting dullness, obscurity, or lack of incisiveness or precision ⟨the *verbose* position papers⟩. PROLIX suggests unreasonable and tedious dwelling on details ⟨habitually transformed brief anecdotes into *prolix* sagas⟩. DIFFUSE stresses lack of compactness and pointedness of style ⟨*diffuse* memoirs that are so many shaggy-dog stories⟩.

**6** *plural* **:** the working or moving parts of a mechanism ⟨*works* of a clock⟩
**7 a :** something produced or accomplished by effort, exertion, or exercise of skill ⟨this book is the *work* of many hands⟩ **b :** something produced by the exercise of creative talent or expenditure of creative effort **:** artistic production
**8** *plural* **:** performance of moral or religious acts ⟨salvation by *works*⟩
**9 a :** effective operation **:** EFFECT, RESULT ⟨wait for time to do its healing *work*⟩ **b :** manner of working **:** WORKMANSHIP, EXECUTION
**10 :** the material or piece of material that is operated upon at any stage in the process of manufacture
**11** *plural* **a :** everything possessed, available, or belonging ⟨the whole *works*, rod, reel, tackle box, went overboard⟩ ⟨ordered pizza with the *works*⟩ **b :** subjection to drastic treatment **:** all possible abuse — usually used with *get* ⟨get the *works*⟩ or *give* ⟨gave them the *works*⟩ ☆ ☆
— **at work 1 :** engaged in working **:** BUSY; *especially* **:** engaged in one's regular occupation **2 :** having effect **:** OPERATING, FUNCTIONING
— **in the works :** in process of preparation, development, or completion
— **in work 1 :** in process of being done **2** *of a horse* **:** in training
— **out of work :** without regular employment **:** JOBLESS

²**work** *adjective* (14th century)
**1 :** used for work ⟨*work* elephant⟩
**2 :** suitable or styled for wear while working ⟨*work* clothes⟩
**3 :** involving or engaged in work ⟨*work* gang⟩ ⟨*work* hours⟩

³**work** *verb* **worked** \'wərkt\ *or* **wrought** \'rȯt\; **work·ing** [Middle English *werken, worken*, from Old English *wyrcan;* akin to Old English *weorc*] (before 12th century)
*transitive verb*
**1 :** to bring to pass **:** EFFECT ⟨*work* miracles⟩
**2 a :** to fashion or create a useful or desired product by expending labor or exertion on **:** FORGE, SHAPE ⟨*work* flint into tools⟩ **b :** to make or decorate with needlework; *especially* **:** EMBROIDER
**3 a :** to prepare for use by stirring or kneading **b :** to bring into a desired form by a gradual process of cutting, hammering, scraping, pressing, or stretching ⟨*work* cold steel⟩
**4 :** to set or keep in motion, operation, or activity **:** cause to operate or produce ⟨a pump *worked* by hand⟩ ⟨*work* farmland⟩
**5 :** to solve (a problem) by reasoning or calculation — often used with *out*
**6 a :** to cause to toil or labor ⟨*worked* their horses nearly to death⟩ **b :** to make use of **:** EXPLOIT **c :** to control or guide the operation of ⟨switches are *worked* from a central tower⟩
**7 a :** to carry on an operation or perform a job through, at, in, or along ⟨the salespeople *worked* both sides of the street⟩ ⟨a sportscaster hired to *work* the game⟩ **b :** to greet and talk with in a friendly way in order to ingratiate oneself or achieve a purpose ⟨politicians *working* the crowd⟩ ⟨*worked* the room⟩
**8 :** to pay for or achieve with labor or service ⟨*worked* my way through college⟩ ⟨*worked* my way up in the company⟩
**9 a :** to get (oneself or an object) into or out of a condition or position by gradual stages **b :** CONTRIVE, ARRANGE ⟨we can *work* it so that you can take your vacation⟩
**10 a :** to practice trickery or cajolery on for some end ⟨*worked* the management for a free ticket⟩ **b :** EXCITE, PROVOKE ⟨*worked* myself into a rage⟩
*intransitive verb*
**1 a :** to exert oneself physically or mentally especially in sustained effort for a purpose or under compulsion or necessity **b :** to perform or carry through a task requiring sustained ef-

fort or continuous repeated operations ⟨*worked* all day over a hot stove⟩ **c :** to perform work or fulfill duties regularly for wages or salary
**2 :** to function or operate according to plan or design ⟨hinges *work* better with oil⟩
**3 :** to exert an influence or tendency
**4 :** to produce a desired effect or result **:** SUCCEED
**5 a :** to make way slowly and with difficulty **:** move or progress laboriously ⟨*worked* up to the presidency⟩ **b :** to sail to windward
**6 :** to permit of being worked **:** react in a specified way to being worked ⟨this wood *works* easily⟩
**7 a :** to be in agitation or restless motion **b :** FERMENT 1 **c :** to move slightly in relation to another part **d :** to get into a specified condition by slow or imperceptible movements ⟨the knot *worked* loose⟩
*usage* see WRECK
— **work on 1 :** AFFECT ⟨*worked on* my sympathies⟩ **2 :** to strive to influence or persuade
— **work upon :** to have effect upon **:** operate on **:** INFLUENCE

**work·able** \'wər-kə-bəl\ *adjective* (1545)
**1 :** capable of being worked
**2 :** PRACTICABLE, FEASIBLE ⟨a *workable* system⟩
— **work·abil·i·ty** \ˌwər-kə-'bi-lə-tē\ *noun*
— **work·able·ness** \'wər-kə-bəl-nəs\ *noun*

**work·a·day** \'wər-kə-ˌdā\ *adjective* [alteration of earlier *workday*, from obsolete *workday*, noun *workday*] (1554)
**1 :** of, relating to, or suited for working days
**2 :** ORDINARY, PROSAIC

**work·a·hol·ic** \ˌwər-kə-'hȯ-lik, -'hä-\ *noun* [*work* + *-aholic*, alteration of *-oholic* (as in *alcoholic*)] (1968)
**:** a compulsive worker
— **workaholic** *adjective*
— **work·a·hol·ism** \'wər-kə-ˌhȯ-ˌli-zəm, -ˌhä-\ *noun*

**work·bag** \'wərk-ˌbag\ *noun* (1775)
**:** a bag for implements or materials for work; *especially* **:** a bag for needlework

**work·bas·ket** \-ˌbas-kət\ *noun* (1743)
**:** a basket for needlework

**work·bench** \-ˌbench\ *noun* (1781)
**:** a bench on which work especially of mechanics, machinists, and carpenters is performed

**work·boat** \-ˌbōt\ *noun* (1937)
**:** a boat used for work purposes (as commercial fishing and ferrying supplies) rather than for sport or for passenger or naval service

**work·book** \-ˌbùk\ *noun* (1910)
**1 :** a worker's manual
**2 :** a booklet outlining a course of study
**3 :** a record of work done
**4 :** a student's book of problems to be solved directly on the pages

**work·box** \-ˌbäks\ *noun* (1605)
**:** a box for work instruments and materials

**work camp** *noun* (1933)
**:** a camp for workers: as **a :** PRISON CAMP 1 **b :** a short-term group project in which individuals from one or more religious organizations volunteer their labor

**work·day** \'wər-ˌdā\ *noun* (15th century)
**1 :** a day on which work is performed as distinguished from a day off
**2 :** the period of time in a day during which work is performed
— **workday** *adjective*

**worked** \'wərkt\ *adjective* (1740)
**:** that has been subjected to some process of development, treatment, or manufacture ⟨a newly *worked* field⟩

**worked up** *adjective* (1903)
**:** emotionally aroused **:** EXCITED

**work·er** \'wər-kər\ *noun* (14th century)
**1 a :** one that works especially at manual or industrial labor or with a particular material — often used in combination **b :** a member of the working class
**2 :** any of the sexually underdeveloped and usually sterile members of a colony of social

ants, bees, wasps, or termites that perform most of the labor and protective duties of the colony

**worker–priest** *noun* (1949)
**:** a French Roman Catholic priest who for missionary purposes spends part of each weekday as a worker in a secular job

**workers' compensation** *noun* (1948)
**:** a system of insurance that reimburses an employer for damages that must be paid to an employee for injury occurring in the course of employment

**work ethic** *noun* (1951)
**:** a belief in work as a moral good

**work·fare** \'wərk-ˌfar, -ˌfer\ *noun* [*work* + *welfare*] (1968)
**:** a welfare program in which recipients are required to perform usually public-service work

**work farm** *noun* (1953)
**:** a farm on which persons guilty of minor law violations are confined

**work·folk** \'wərk-ˌfōk\ *or* **work·folks** \-ˌfōks\ *noun plural* (15th century)
**:** working people; *especially* **:** farm workers

**work·force** \'wərk-ˌfōrs, -ˌfȯrs\ *noun* (1943)
**1 :** the workers engaged in a specific activity or enterprise ⟨the factory's *workforce*⟩
**2 :** the number of workers potentially assignable for any purpose ⟨the nation's *workforce*⟩

**work·horse** \'wərk-ˌhȯrs\ *noun* (1543)
**1 :** a horse used chiefly for labor as distinguished from driving, riding, or racing

---

☆ **SYNONYMS**
**Work, labor, travail, toil, drudgery, grind** mean activity involving effort or exertion. WORK may imply activity of body, of mind, of a machine, or of a natural force ⟨too tired to do any *work*⟩. LABOR applies to physical or intellectual work involving great and often strenuous exertion ⟨farmers demanding fair compensation for their *labor*⟩. TRAVAIL is bookish for labor involving pain or suffering ⟨years of *travail* were lost when the house burned⟩. TOIL implies prolonged and fatiguing labor ⟨his lot would be years of backbreaking *toil*⟩. DRUDGERY suggests dull and irksome labor ⟨an editorial job with a good deal of *drudgery*⟩. GRIND implies labor exhausting to mind or body ⟨the *grind* of the assembly line⟩.

**Work, employment, occupation, calling, pursuit, métier, business** mean a specific sustained activity engaged in especially in earning one's living. WORK may apply to any purposeful activity whether remunerative or not ⟨her *work* as a hospital volunteer⟩. EMPLOYMENT implies work for which one has been engaged and is being paid by an employer ⟨your *employment* with this firm is hereby terminated⟩. OCCUPATION implies work in which one engages regularly especially as a result of training ⟨his *occupation* as a trained auto mechanic⟩. CALLING applies to an occupation viewed as a vocation or profession ⟨the ministry seemed my true *calling*⟩. PURSUIT suggests a trade, profession, or avocation followed with zeal or steady interest ⟨her family considered medicine the only proper *pursuit*⟩. MÉTIER implies a calling or pursuit for which one believes oneself to be especially fitted ⟨acting was my one and only *métier*⟩. BUSINESS suggests activity in commerce or the management of money and affairs ⟨the *business* of managing a hotel⟩.

---

\ə\ abut  \ˌə, ˌᵊ\ kitten  \ər\ further  \a\ ash  \ā\ ace
\ä\ mop, mar  \aù\ out  \ch\ chin  \e\ bet  \ē\ easy
\g\ go  \i\ hit  \ī\ ice  \j\ job  \ŋ\ sing  \ō\ go
\ȯ\ law  \ȯi\ boy  \th\ thin  \t͟h\ the  \ü\ loot  \ù\ foot
\y\ yet  \zh\ vision  *see also* Guide to Pronunciation

**2 a** (1) **:** a person who performs most of the work of a group task (2) **:** a hardworking person **b :** a markedly useful or durable vehicle, craft, or machine **c :** HORSE 7

**work·house** \-,haůs\ *noun* (1652)
**1** *British* **:** POORHOUSE
**2 :** a house of correction for persons guilty of minor law violations

**work in** *transitive verb* (1675)
**1 :** to insert or cause to penetrate by repeated or continued effort
**2 :** to interpose or insinuate gradually or unobtrusively ⟨*worked in* a few topical jokes⟩

**¹work·ing** *noun* (14th century)
**1 :** the manner of functioning or operating **:** OPERATION — usually used in plural
**2 :** an excavation or group of excavations made in mining, quarrying, or tunneling — usually used in plural

**²working** *adjective* (1613)
**1 :** engaged in work ⟨a *working* journalist⟩
**2 :** adequate to permit work to be done ⟨a *working* majority⟩
**3 :** assumed or adopted to permit or facilitate further work or activity ⟨*working* draft⟩
**4 :** spent at work ⟨*working* life⟩
**5 :** being in use or operation ⟨a *working* farm⟩

**working asset** *noun* (circa 1914)
**:** an asset other than a capital asset

**working capital** *noun* (circa 1901)
**:** capital actively turned over in or available for use in the course of business activity: **a :** the excess of current assets over current liabilities **b :** all capital of a business except that invested in capital assets

**working–class** *adjective* (1839)
**:** of, relating to, deriving from, or suitable to the class of wage earners ⟨*working-class* virtues⟩ ⟨*working-class* family⟩

**working class** *noun* (1789)
**:** the class of people who work for wages usually at manual labor

**working day** *noun* (15th century)
**:** WORKDAY

**working dog** *noun* (1891)
**:** a dog fitted by size, breeding, or training for useful work (as draft or herding) especially as distinguished from one fitted primarily for pet, show, or sporting use

**working fluid** *noun* (1903)
**:** a fluid working substance

**work·ing·man** \'wər-kiŋ-,man\ *noun* (1638)
**:** one who works for wages usually at manual labor

**working papers** *noun plural* (1928)
**:** official documents legalizing the employment of a minor

**working substance** *noun* (1897)
**:** a usually fluid substance that through changes of temperature, volume, and pressure is the means of carrying out thermodynamic processes or cycles (as in a heat engine)

**work·ing·wom·an** \'wər-kiŋ-,wů-mən\ *noun* (1853)
**:** WORKWOMAN

**work·less** \'wər-kləs\ *adjective* (15th century)
**:** being without work **:** UNEMPLOYED
— **work·less·ness** *noun*

**work·load** \'wərk-,lōd\ *noun* (1943)
**1 :** the amount of work or of working time expected or assigned
**2 :** the amount of work performed or capable of being performed (as by a mechanical device) usually within a specific period

**work·man** \'wərk-mən\ *noun* (before 12th century)
**1 :** WORKINGMAN
**2 :** ARTISAN

**work·man·like** \-,līk\ *adjective* (1739)
**:** characterized by the skill and efficiency typical of a good workman

**work·man·ly** \-lē\ *adjective* (1545)
**:** WORKMANLIKE

**work·man·ship** \-,ship\ *noun* (1523)
**1 :** something effected, made, or produced **:** WORK

**2 :** the art or skill of a workman **:** CRAFTSMANSHIP; *also* **:** the quality imparted to a thing in the process of making ⟨a vase of exquisite *workmanship*⟩

**work·mate** \'wərk-,māt\ *noun* (1851)
*chiefly British* **:** a fellow worker

**workmen's compensation insurance** *noun* (circa 1917)
**:** WORKERS' COMPENSATION

**work of art** (1834)
**1 :** a product of one of the fine arts; *especially* **:** a painting or sculpture of high artistic quality
**2 :** something giving high aesthetic satisfaction to the viewer or listener

**work off** *transitive verb* (1678)
**:** to dispose of or get rid of by work or activity

**work·out** \'wərk-,aůt\ *noun* (circa 1894)
**1 :** a practice or exercise to test or improve one's fitness for athletic competition, ability, or performance
**2 :** a test of one's ability, capacity, stamina, or suitability

**work out** (1534)
*transitive verb*
**1 a :** to bring about by labor and exertion ⟨*work out* your own salvation —Philippians 2:12 (Authorized Version)⟩ **b :** to solve (as a problem) by a process of reasoning or calculation **c :** to devise, arrange, or achieve by resolving difficulties ⟨after many years of wrangling, *worked out* a definite agreement —A. A. Butkus⟩ **d :** DEVELOP ⟨the final situation is not *worked out* with psychological profundity —Leslie Rees⟩
**2 :** to discharge (as a debt) by labor
**3 :** to exhaust (as a mine) by working
*intransitive verb*
**1 a :** to prove effective, practicable, or suitable ⟨how this will actually *work out* I don't know —Milton Kotler⟩ **b :** to amount to a total or calculated figure — used with *at* or *to*
**2 :** to engage in a workout ⟨*works out* in gymnasiums . . . to keep in shape —*Current Biography*⟩

**work over** *transitive verb* (1874)
**1 :** to do over **:** REWORK ⟨saved the play by *working* the first act *over*⟩
**2 :** to subject to thorough examination, study, or treatment ⟨shelf stock *worked over* by shoppers⟩
**3 :** to beat up or manhandle with thoroughness ⟨the gang *worked* me *over*⟩

**work·peo·ple** \'wərk-,pē-pəl\ *noun plural* (1708)
*chiefly British* **:** WORKERS, EMPLOYEES

**work·piece** \-,pēs\ *noun* (1926)
**:** a piece of work in process of manufacture

**work·place** \-,plās\ *noun* (circa 1828)
**:** a place (as a shop or factory) where work is done

**work print** *noun* (1937)
**:** a completely edited motion-picture print used as a guide in cutting the original negative from which the final production prints will be made

**work·room** \'wərk-,rüm, -,rům\ *noun* (1828)
**:** a room used for work

**work·shop** \-,shäp\ *noun* (1562)
**1 :** a small establishment where manufacturing or handicrafts are carried on
**2 :** WORKROOM
**3 :** a usually brief intensive educational program for a relatively small group of people that focuses especially on techniques and skills in a particular field

**work song** *noun* (1911)
**:** a song sung in rhythm with work

**work·sta·tion** \-,stā-shən\ *noun* (1931)
**1 :** an area with equipment for the performance of a specialized task usually by a single individual
**2 a :** an intelligent terminal or personal computer usually connected to a computer network **b :** a powerful microcomputer used especially for scientific or engineering work

**work stoppage** *noun* (1945)

**:** concerted cessation of work by a group of employees usually more spontaneous and less serious than a strike

**work–study program** *noun* (1946)
**:** a program planned to give high school or college students work experience

**work·ta·ble** \'wərk-,tā-bəl\ *noun* (1790)
**:** a table for holding working materials and implements; *especially* **:** a small table with drawers and other conveniences for needlework

**work–to–rule** *noun* (1950)
**:** the practice of working to the strictest interpretation of the rules as a job action

**work–up** \'wərk-,əp\ *noun* (1939)
**:** an intensive diagnostic study

**work–up** \'wərk-,əp\ *noun* (1903)
**:** an unintended mark on a printed sheet caused by the rising of spacing material

**work up** (15th century)
*transitive verb*
**1 :** to stir up **:** ROUSE
**2 :** to produce by mental or physical work ⟨*worked up* a comedy act⟩ ⟨*worked up* a sweat in the gymnasium⟩
*intransitive verb*
**:** to rise gradually in intensity or emotional tone

**work·week** \'wərk-,wēk\ *noun* (1921)
**:** the hours or days of work in a calendar week ⟨40-hour *workweek*⟩ ⟨a 5-day *workweek*⟩ ⟨a shortened *workweek*⟩

**work·wom·an** \-,wů-mən\ *noun* (circa 1530)
**:** a woman who works

**¹world** \'wər(-ə)ld\ *noun* [Middle English, from Old English *woruld* human existence, this world, age (akin to Old High German *weralt* age, world); akin to Old English *wer* man, *eald* old — more at VIRILE, OLD] (before 12th century)
**1 a :** the earthly state of human existence **b :** life after death — used with a qualifier ⟨the next *world*⟩
**2 :** the earth with its inhabitants and all things upon it
**3 :** individual course of life **:** CAREER
**4 :** the inhabitants of the earth **:** the human race
**5 a :** the concerns of the earth and its affairs as distinguished from heaven and the life to come **b :** secular affairs
**6 :** the system of created things **:** UNIVERSE
**7 a :** a division or generation of the inhabitants of the earth distinguished by living together at the same place or at the same time ⟨the medieval *world*⟩ **b :** a distinctive class of persons or their sphere of interest ⟨the academic *world*⟩ ⟨the sports *world*⟩
**8 :** human society ⟨withdraw from the *world*⟩
**9 :** a part or section of the earth that is a separate independent unit
**10 :** the sphere or scene of one's life and action ⟨living in your own little *world*⟩
**11 :** an indefinite multitude or a great quantity or distance ⟨makes a *world* of difference⟩ ⟨a *world* away⟩
**12 :** the whole body of living persons **:** PUBLIC ⟨announced their discovery to the *world*⟩
**13 :** KINGDOM 5 ⟨the animal *world*⟩
**14 :** a celestial body (as a planet)
— **for all the world :** in every way **:** EXACTLY ⟨copies which look *for all the world* like the original⟩
— **in the world :** among innumerable possibilities **:** EVER — used as an intensive ⟨what *in the world* is it⟩
— **out of this world :** of extraordinary excellence **:** SUPERB

**²world** *adjective* (13th century)
**1 :** of or relating to the world ⟨a *world* championship⟩
**2 a :** extending or found throughout the world **:** WORLDWIDE ⟨brought about *world* peace⟩ **b :** involving or applying to part of or the whole world ⟨a *world* tour⟩ ⟨a *world* state⟩

**world–beat·er** \'wərl(d)-ˌbē-tər\ *noun* (circa 1888)
**:** one that excels all others of its kind **:** CHAMPION

**world–class** *adjective* (1950)
**:** being of the highest caliber in the world ⟨a *world-class* polo player⟩

**world federalism** *noun* (1950)
**1 :** federalism on a worldwide basis
**2** *W&F capitalized* **a :** the principles and policies of the World Federalists **b :** the body or movement composed of World Federalists

**world federalist** *noun* (1951)
**1 :** an adherent or advocate of world federalism
**2** *W&F capitalized* **:** a member of a movement arising after World War II advocating the formation of a federal union of the nations of the world with limited but positive governmental powers

**world·ling** \'wər(-ə)ld-liŋ, 'wərl-liŋ\ *noun* (1549)
**:** a person engrossed in the concerns of this present world

**world·ly** \'wər(-ə)ld-lē, 'wərl-lē\ *adjective* (before 12th century)
**1 :** of, relating to, or devoted to this world and its pursuits rather than to religion or spiritual affairs
**2 :** WORLDLY-WISE
*synonym* see EARTHLY
— **world·li·ness** *noun*

**world·ly–mind·ed** \ˌwərl(d)-lē-'mīn-dəd\ *adjective* (1601)
**:** devoted to or engrossed in worldly interests
— **world·ly–mind·ed·ness** *noun*

**world·ly–wise** \'wərl(d)-lē-ˌwīz\ *adjective* (15th century)
**:** possessing a practical and often shrewd understanding of human affairs
*synonym* see SOPHISTICATED

**world power** *noun* (1860)
**:** a political unit (as a nation or state) powerful enough to affect the entire world by its influence or actions

**world premiere** *noun* (1925)
**:** the first regular performance (as of a theatrical production) anywhere in the world

**World Series** *noun* [from *World Series,* annual championship of U.S. major-league baseball] (1951)
**:** a contest or event that is the most important or prestigious of its kind ⟨the *World Series* of the equestrian world⟩

**world's fair** *noun* (1850)
**:** an international exposition featuring exhibits and participants from all over the world

**world–shak·ing** \'wərl(d)-ˌshā-kiŋ\ *adjective* (1598)
**:** EARTHSHAKING

**world soul** *noun* (1848)
**:** an animating spirit or creative principle related to the world as the soul is to the individual being

**world–view** \-ˌvyü\ *noun* (1858)
**:** WELTANSCHAUUNG

**world war** *noun* (1909)
**:** a war engaged in by all or most of the principal nations of the world; *especially, both Ws capitalized* **:** either of two such wars of the first half of the 20th century

**world–wea·ry** \'wərld-ˌwir-ē\ *adjective* (1768)
**:** feeling or showing fatigue from or boredom with the life of the world and especially material pleasures
— **world–wea·ri·ness** *noun*

**¹world·wide** \-'wīd\ *adjective* (1632)
**:** extended throughout or involving the entire world

**²worldwide** *adverb* (1892)
**:** throughout the world

**¹worm** \'wərm\ *noun, often attributive* [Middle English, from Old English *wyrm* serpent,

worm; akin to Old High German *wurm* serpent, worm, Latin *vermis* worm] (before 12th century)
**1 a :** EARTHWORM; *broadly* **:** an annelid worm **b :** any of numerous relatively small elongated usually naked and soft-bodied animals: as (1) **:** an insect larva; *especially* **:** one that is a destructive grub, caterpillar, or maggot (2) **:** SHIPWORM (3) **:** BLINDWORM
**2 a :** a human being who is an object of contempt, loathing, or pity **:** WRETCH **b :** something that torments or devours from within
**3** *archaic* **:** SNAKE, SERPENT
**4 :** HELMINTHIASIS — usually used in plural
**5 :** something (as a mechanical device) spiral or vermiculate in form or appearance: as **a :** the thread of a screw **b :** a short revolving screw whose threads gear with the teeth of a worm wheel or a rack **c :** a spiral condensing tube used in distilling **d :** ARCHIMEDES' SCREW; *also* **:** a conveyor working on the principle of such a screw
**6 :** a usually small self-contained computer program that invades computers on a network and usually performs a malicious action
— **worm·like** \-ˌlīk\ *adjective*

**²worm** (1610)
*intransitive verb*
**:** to move or proceed sinuously or insidiously
*transitive verb*
**1 a :** to proceed or make (one's way) insidiously or deviously ⟨*worm* their way into positions of power —Bill Franzen⟩ **b :** to insinuate or introduce (oneself) by devious or subtle means **c :** to cause to move or proceed in or as if in the manner of a worm
**2 :** to wind rope or yarn spirally round and between the strands of (a cable or rope) before serving
**3 :** to obtain or extract by artful or insidious questioning or by pleading, asking, or persuading — usually used with *out of*
**4 :** to treat (an animal) with a drug to destroy or expel parasitic worms

**worm–eat·en** \'wərm-ˌē-tᵊn\ *adjective* (14th century)
**1 a :** eaten or burrowed by worms ⟨*worm-eaten* timber⟩ **b :** PITTED
**2 :** WORN-OUT, ANTIQUATED

**worm·er** \'wər-mər\ *noun* (circa 1934)
**:** a drug used in veterinary medicine to worm an animal

**worm fence** *noun* (1652)
**:** a zigzag fence consisting of interlocking rails supported by crossed poles — called also *snake fence, Virginia fence*

**worm gear** *noun* (circa 1876)
**1 :** WORM WHEEL
**2 :** a gear of a worm and a worm wheel working together

worm fence

**worm·hole** \'wərm-ˌhōl\ *noun* (1593)
**1 :** a hole or passage burrowed by a worm
**2 :** a hypothetical structure of space-time envisioned as a long thin tunnel connecting points that are separated in space and time

**worm·seed** \-ˌsēd\ *noun* (15th century)
**:** any of various plants whose seeds possess anthelmintic properties: as **a :** any of several artemisias **b :** a goosefoot (*Chenopodium ambrosioides*)

**worm's–eye** \'wərm-ˌzī\ *adjective* (1908)
**:** seen from ground level or from the lowest levels of a hierarchy ⟨the bird's-eye view of the executive and the *worm's-eye* view of the employee —Current Biography⟩

**worm snake** *noun* (1885)
**:** a reddish terrestrial colubrid snake (*Carphophis amoenus*) of the eastern U.S.

**worm wheel** *noun* (1677)
**:** a toothed wheel gearing with the thread of a worm

**worm·wood** \'wərm-ˌwu̇d\ *noun* [Middle English *wormwode,* alteration of *wermode,* from Old English *wermōd;* akin to Old High German *wermuota* wormwood] (15th century)
**1 :** ARTEMISIA; *especially* **:** a European plant (*Artemisia absinthium*) that has silvery silky-haired leaves and drooping yellow nearly globular flower heads and yields a bitter dark green oil used in absinthe
**2 :** something bitter or grievous **:** BITTERNESS

**wormy** \'wər-mē\ *adjective* **worm·i·er; -est** (15th century)
**1 :** containing, abounding in, or infested with or as if with worms ⟨*wormy* flour⟩ ⟨a *wormy* dog⟩; *also* **:** damaged by worms **:** WORM-EATEN ⟨*wormy* timbers⟩
**2 :** resembling or suggestive of a worm

**worn** *past participle of* WEAR

**worn–out** \'wōrn-'au̇t, 'wȯrn-\ *adjective* (1589)
**:** exhausted or used up by or as if by wear

**wor·ri·ment** \'wər-ē-mənt, 'wə-rē-\ *noun* (1833)
**:** an act or instance of worrying; *also* **:** TROUBLE, WORRY

**wor·ri·some** \-səm\ *adjective* (1845)
**1 :** causing distress or worry
**2 :** inclined to worry or fret
— **wor·ri·some·ly** *adverb*
— **wor·ri·some·ness** *noun*

**¹wor·ry** \'wər-ē, 'wə-rē\ *verb* **wor·ried; wor·ry·ing** [Middle English *worien,* from Old English *wyrgan;* akin to Old High German *wurgen* to strangle, Lithuanian *veržti* to constrict] (before 12th century)
*transitive verb*
**1** *dialect British* **:** CHOKE, STRANGLE
**2 a :** to harass by tearing, biting, or snapping especially at the throat **b :** to shake or pull at with the teeth ⟨a terrier *worrying* a rat⟩ **c :** to touch or disturb something repeatedly **d :** to change the position of or adjust by repeated pushing or hauling
**3 a :** to assail with rough or aggressive attack or treatment **:** TORMENT **b :** to subject to persistent or nagging attention or effort
**4 :** to afflict with mental distress or agitation **:** make anxious
*intransitive verb*
**1** *dialect British* **:** STRANGLE, CHOKE
**2 :** to move, proceed, or progress by unceasing or difficult effort **:** STRUGGLE
**3 :** to feel or experience concern or anxiety **:** FRET ☆
— **wor·ried·ly** \-(r)ēd-lē, -(r)əd-\ *adverb*

---

☆ SYNONYMS
**Worry, annoy, harass, harry, plague, pester, tease** mean to disturb or irritate by persistent acts. WORRY implies an incessant goading or attacking that drives one to desperation ⟨pursued a policy of *worrying* the enemy⟩. ANNOY implies disturbing one's composure or peace of mind by intrusion, interference, or petty attacks ⟨you're doing that just to *annoy* me⟩. HARASS implies petty persecutions or burdensome demands that exhaust one's nervous or mental power ⟨*harassed* on all sides by creditors⟩. HARRY may imply heavy oppression or maltreatment ⟨the strikers had been *harried* by thugs⟩. PLAGUE implies a painful and persistent affliction ⟨*plagued* all her life by poverty⟩. PESTER stresses the repetition of petty attacks ⟨constantly *pestered* with trivial complaints⟩. TEASE suggests an attempt to break down one's resistance or rouse to wrath ⟨children *teased* the dog⟩.

---

\ə\ abut \ᵊ\ kitten \ər\ further \a\ ash \ā\ ace
\ä\ mop, mar \au̇\ out \ch\ chin \e\ bet \ē\ easy
\g\ go \i\ hit \ī\ ice \j\ job \ŋ\ sing \ō\ go
\ȯ\ law \ȯi\ boy \th\ thin \t͟h\ the \ü\ loot \u̇\ foot
\y\ yet \zh\ vision *see also* Guide to Pronunciation

— **wor·ri·er** \-(r)ē-ər\ *noun*

²**worry** *noun, plural* **worries** (1804)
**1 a :** mental distress or agitation resulting from concern usually for something impending or anticipated : ANXIETY **b :** an instance or occurrence of such distress or agitation
**2 :** a cause of worry : TROUBLE, DIFFICULTY
*synonym* see CARE

**worry beads** *noun plural* (1956)
: a string of beads that can be fingered to keep one's hands occupied

**wor·ry·wart** \'wər-ē-ˌwȯrt, 'wə-rē-\ *noun* (1936)
: one who is inclined to worry unduly

¹**worse** \'wərs\ *adjective, comparative of* BAD *or of* ILL [Middle English *werse, worse,* from Old English *wiersa, wyrsa;* akin to Old High German *wirsiro* worse] (before 12th century)
**1 :** of more inferior quality, value, or condition
**2 a :** more unfavorable, difficult, unpleasant, or painful **b :** more faulty, unsuitable, or incorrect **c :** less skillful or efficient
**3 :** bad, evil, or corrupt in a greater degree : more reprehensible
**4 :** being in poorer health : SICKER

²**worse** *noun* (before 12th century)
: one that is worse 〈thought he was an atheist and *worse* —Van Wyck Brooks〉

³**worse** *adverb, comparative of* BAD *or of* ILL (before 12th century)
**1 :** in a worse manner : to a worse extent or degree
**2 :** what is worse

**wors·en** \'wər-sᵊn\ *verb* **wors·ened; wors·en·ing** \'wərs-niŋ, 'wər-sᵊn-iŋ\ (13th century)
*transitive verb*
: to make worse
*intransitive verb*
: to become worse

**wors·er** \'wər-sər\ *adjective or adverb* (15th century)
*archaic* : WORSE 〈I cannot hate thee *worser* than I do —Shakespeare〉

¹**wor·ship** \'wər-shəp\ *noun* [Middle English *worshipe* worthiness, respect, reverence paid to a divine being, from Old English *weorthscipe* worthiness, respect, from *weorth* worthy, worth + *-scipe* -ship] (before 12th century)
**1** *chiefly British* : a person of importance — used as a title for various officials (as magistrates and some mayors)
**2 :** reverence offered a divine being or supernatural power; *also* : an act of expressing such reverence
**3 :** a form of religious practice with its creed and ritual
**4 :** extravagant respect or admiration for or devotion to an object of esteem 〈*worship* of the dollar〉

²**worship** *verb* **-shiped** *or* **-shipped; -ship·ing** *or* **-ship·ping** (13th century)
*transitive verb*
**1 :** to honor or reverence as a divine being or supernatural power
**2 :** to regard with great or extravagant respect, honor, or devotion
*intransitive verb*
: to perform or take part in worship or an act of worship
*synonym* see REVERE
— **wor·ship·er** *or* **wor·ship·per** *noun*

**wor·ship·ful** \'wər-shəp-fəl\ *adjective* (14th century)
**1 a** *archaic* : NOTABLE, DISTINGUISHED **b** *chiefly British* — used as a title for various persons or groups of rank or distinction
**2 :** giving or expressing worship or veneration
— **wor·ship·ful·ly** \-fə-lē\ *adverb*
— **wor·ship·ful·ness** *noun*

**wor·ship·less** \-shə-pləs\ *adjective* (1765)
: lacking worship or worshipers

¹**worst** \'wərst\ *adjective, superlative of* BAD *or of* ILL [Middle English *werste, worste,* from Old English *wierresta, wyrsta,* superlative of the root of Old English *wiersa* worse] (before 12th century)
**1 :** most corrupt, bad, evil, or ill
**2 a :** most unfavorable, difficult, unpleasant, or painful **b :** most unsuitable, faulty, unattractive, or ill-conceived **c :** least skillful or efficient
**3 :** most wanting in quality, value, or condition
— **the worst way :** very much 〈such men . . . need indoctrination *the worst way* —J. G. Cozzens〉 — often used with *in* 〈wanted a new bicycle in *the worst way*〉

²**worst** *adverb, superlative of* ILL *or* ILLY *or of* BAD *or* BADLY (before 12th century)
**1 :** to the extreme degree of badness or inferiority
**2 :** to the greatest or highest degree 〈groups who need the subsidies *worst* lose out —T. W. Arnold〉

³**worst** *noun, plural* **worst** (14th century)
: one that is worst
— **at worst :** under the worst circumstances

⁴**worst** *transitive verb* (1636)
: to get the better of : DEFEAT

**worst–case** *adjective* (1964)
: involving, projecting, or providing for the worst possible circumstances or outcome of a given situation

**wor·sted** \'wu̇s-təd, 'wər-stəd\ *noun* [Middle English, from *Worsted* (now *Worstead*), England] (13th century)
: a smooth compact yarn from long wool fibers used especially for firm napless fabrics, carpeting, or knitting; *also* : a fabric made from worsted yarns
— **worsted** *adjective*

¹**wort** \'wərt, 'wȯrt\ *noun* [Middle English, from Old English *wyrt* root, herb, plant — more at ROOT] (before 12th century)
: PLANT; *especially* : an herbaceous plant — usually used in combination 〈louse*wort*〉

²**wort** *noun* [Middle English, from Old English *wyrt;* akin to Middle High German *würze* brewer's wort, Old English *wyrt* root, herb] (before 12th century)
: a liquid formed by soaking mash in hot water and then fermented to make beer

¹**worth** \'wərth\ *intransitive verb* [Middle English, from Old English *weorthan;* akin to Old High German *werdan* to become, Latin *vertere* to turn, Lithuanian *versti* to overturn, Sanskrit *vartate* he turns] (before 12th century)
*archaic* : BECOME — usually used in the phrase *woe worth*

²**worth** *adjective* [Middle English, from Old English *weorth* worthy, of (a specified) value; akin to Old High German *werd* worthy, worth] (before 12th century)
**1** *archaic* : having monetary or material value
**2** *archaic* : ESTIMABLE
— **for all one is worth :** to the fullest extent of one's value or ability

³**worth** *noun* (before 12th century)
**1 a :** monetary value 〈farmhouse and lands of little *worth*〉 **b :** the equivalent of a specified amount or figure 〈a dollar's *worth* of gas〉
**2 :** the value of something measured by its qualities or by the esteem in which it is held 〈a literary heritage of great *worth*〉
**3 a :** moral or personal value 〈trying to teach human *worth*〉 **b :** MERIT, EXCELLENCE 〈a field in which we have proved our *worth*〉
**4 :** WEALTH, RICHES

⁴**worth** *preposition* (13th century)
**1 a :** equal in value to **b :** having assets or income equal to
**2 :** deserving of 〈well *worth* the effort〉
— **worth one's salt :** of substantial or significant value or merit

**worth·ful** \'wərth-fəl\ *adjective* (before 12th century)
**1 :** full of merit 〈a good and *worthful* person〉
**2 :** having value 〈the *worthful* aspects of their culture〉

**worth·less** \'wərth-ləs\ *adjective* (1588)
**1 a :** lacking worth : VALUELESS 〈*worthless* currency〉 **b :** USELESS 〈*worthless* to continue searching〉
**2 :** CONTEMPTIBLE, DESPICABLE
— **worth·less·ly** *adverb*
— **worth·less·ness** *noun*

**worth·while** \-'hwī(ə)l, -'wī(ə)l\ *adjective* (1900)
**1 :** being worth the time or effort spent
**2 :** WORTHY 1
— **worth·while·ness** *noun*

¹**wor·thy** \'wər-thē\ *adjective* **wor·thi·er; -est** (13th century)
**1 a :** having worth or value : ESTIMABLE 〈a *worthy* cause〉 **b :** HONORABLE, MERITORIOUS 〈*worthy* candidates〉
**2 :** having sufficient worth or importance 〈*worthy* to be remembered〉
— **wor·thi·ly** \'wər-thə-lē\ *adverb*
— **wor·thi·ness** \-thē-nəs\ *noun*

²**worthy** *noun, plural* **worthies** (14th century)
: a worthy or prominent person

-**wor·thy** \ˌwər-thē\ *adjective combining form*
**1 :** fit or safe for 〈a sea*worthy* vessel〉
**2 :** of sufficient worth for 〈a news*worthy* event〉

¹**wot** *present 1st & 3d singular of* WIT

²**wot** \'wät\ *verb* **wot·ted; wot·ting** [Middle English, alteration of *witen* — more at WIT] (14th century)
*chiefly British* : KNOW — often used with *of*

**would** \wəd, əd, d, 'wu̇d\ *past of* WILL [Middle English *wolde,* from Old English; akin to Old High German *wolta* wished, desired] (before 12th century)
**1 a** *archaic* : WISHED, DESIRED **b** *archaic* : wish for : WANT **c** (1) : strongly desire : WISH 〈I *would* I were young again〉 — often used without a subject and with *that* in a past or conditional construction 〈*would* that I had heeded your advice〉 (2) — used in auxiliary function with *rather* or *sooner* to express preference 〈he *would* sooner die than face them〉
**2 a** — used in auxiliary function to express wish, desire, or intent 〈those who *would* forbid gambling〉 **b** — used in auxiliary function to express willingness or preference 〈as ye *would* that men should do to you —Luke 6:31 (Authorized Version)〉 **c** — used in auxiliary function to express plan or intention 〈said they *would* come〉
**3** — used in auxiliary function to express custom or habitual action 〈we *would* meet often for lunch〉
**4** — used in auxiliary function to express consent or choice 〈*would* put it off if he could〉
**5 a** — used in auxiliary function in the conclusion of a conditional sentence to express a contingency or possibility 〈if he were coming, he *would* be here now〉 **b** — used in auxiliary function in a noun clause 〈as one completing a statement of desire, request, or advice〉 〈wish that he *would* go〉
**6** — used in auxiliary function to express probability or presumption in past or present time 〈*would* have won if I had not tripped〉
**7 :** COULD 〈the barrel *would* hold 20 gallons〉
**8** — used in auxiliary function to express a request with which voluntary compliance is expected 〈*would* you please help us〉
**9** — used in auxiliary function to express doubt or uncertainty 〈the explanation . . . *would* seem satisfactory〉
**10 :** SHOULD 〈knew I *would* enjoy the trip〉 〈*would* be glad to know the answer〉 ◾

**would–be** \'wu̇d-ˌbē\ *adjective* (1647)
: desiring, professing, or having the potential to be

**would·est** \'wu̇-dəst\ *archaic past 2d singular of* WILL

**wouldn't** \'wu̇-dᵊnt, -dᵊn, *dialect also* 'wu̇-tᵊn(t) *or* ˌwu̇nt\ (circa 1828)
: would not

**wouldst** \wədst, 'wu̇dst, wətst\ *archaic past 2d singular of* WILL

**¹wound** \'wünd, *archaic or dialect* 'waùnd\ *noun* [Middle English, from Old English *wund;* akin to Old High German *wunta* wound] (before 12th century)
**1 a :** an injury to the body (as from violence, accident, or surgery) that involves laceration or breaking of a membrane (as the skin) and usually damage to underlying tissues **b :** a cut or breach in a plant due to external violence **2 :** a mental or emotional hurt or blow **3 :** something resembling a wound in appearance or effect; *especially* **:** a rift in or blow to a political body or social group

**²wound** (before 12th century)
*transitive verb*
**:** to cause a wound to or in
*intransitive verb*
**:** to inflict a wound

**³wound** \'waùnd\ *past and past participle of* WIND

**¹wound·ed** \'wün-dəd\ *noun plural* (before 12th century)
**:** wounded persons

**²wounded** *adjective* (14th century)
**:** injured, hurt by, or suffering from a wound

**wound·less** \'wün(d)-ləs\ *adjective* (1579)
**1 :** free from wounds **:** UNWOUNDED
**2** *obsolete* **:** INVULNERABLE (the *woundless* air —Shakespeare)

**wove** *past of* WEAVE

**¹woven** *past participle of* WEAVE

**²wo·ven** \'wō-vən\ *noun* (1930)
**:** a woven fabric

**wove paper** \'wōv-\ *noun* [*wove* (archaic past participle of *weave*)] (1815)
**:** paper made with a revolving roller covered with wires so woven as to produce no fine lines running across the grain — compare LAID PAPER

**¹wow** \'waù\ *interjection* (1513)
— used to express strong feeling (as pleasure or surprise)

**²wow** *noun* (1920)
**:** a striking success **:** HIT

**³wow** *transitive verb* (1924)
**:** to excite to enthusiastic admiration or approval

**⁴wow** *noun* [imitative] (1932)
**:** a distortion in reproduced sound consisting of a slow rise and fall of pitch caused by speed variation in the reproducing system

**wow·ser** \'waù-zər\ *noun* [origin unknown] (1899)
*chiefly Australian* **:** an obtrusively puritanical person

**W particle** *noun* [weak] (1963)
**:** either of two particles about 80 times heavier than a proton that along with the Z particle are transmitters of the weak force and that can have a positive or negative charge

**¹wrack** \'rak\ *noun* [Middle English *wrak,* from Middle Dutch or Middle Low German; akin to Old English *wræc* something driven by the sea] (14th century)
**1 a :** a wrecked ship **b :** WRECKAGE **c :** WRECK **d** *dialect* **:** the violent destruction of a structure, machine, or vehicle
**2 a :** marine vegetation; *especially* **:** KELP **b :** dried seaweeds

**²wrack** *noun* [Middle English, from Old English *wræc* misery, punishment, something driven by the sea; akin to Old English *wrecan* to drive, punish — more at WREAK] (15th century)
**1 :** RUIN, DESTRUCTION
**2 :** a remnant of something destroyed

**³wrack** *transitive verb* (1562)
**:** to utterly ruin **:** WRECK

**⁴wrack** *verb* [by alteration] (circa 1555)
**:** ⁴RACK

**⁵wrack** *noun* (1591)
**:** ³RACK 2

**⁶wrack** *noun* (1796)
**:** ¹RACK

**wrack·ful** \'rak-fəl\ *adjective* (1558)
**:** DESTRUCTIVE

**wraith** \'rāth\ *noun, plural* **wraiths** \'rāths *also* 'rāthz\ [origin unknown] (1513)
**1 a :** the exact likeness of a living person seen usually just before death as an apparition **b :** GHOST, SPECTER
**2 :** an insubstantial form or semblance **:** SHADOW
**3 :** a barely visible gaseous or vaporous column
— **wraith·like** \-ˌlīk\ *adjective*

**¹wran·gle** \'raŋ-gəl\ *verb* **wran·gled; wran·gling** \-g(ə-)liŋ\ [Middle English; akin to Old High German *ringan* to struggle — more at WRING] (14th century)
*intransitive verb*
**1 :** to dispute angrily or peevishly **:** BICKER
**2 :** to engage in argument or controversy
*transitive verb*
**1 :** to obtain by persistent arguing or maneuvering **:** WANGLE
**2** [back-formation from *wrangler*] **:** to herd and care for (livestock and especially horses) on the range

**²wrangle** *noun* (1547)
**1 :** an angry, noisy, or prolonged dispute or quarrel
**2 :** the action or process of wrangling

**wran·gler** \-g(ə-)lər\ *noun* (circa 1515)
**1 :** a bickering disputant
**2** [short for *horse-wrangler,* probably part translation of Mexican Spanish *caballerango* groom] **:** a ranch hand who takes care of the saddle horses; *broadly* **:** COWBOY

**¹wrap** \'rap\ *verb* **wrapped; wrap·ping** [Middle English *wrappen*] (14th century)
*transitive verb*
**1 a :** to cover especially by winding or folding **b :** to envelop and secure for transportation or storage **:** BUNDLE **c :** ENFOLD, EMBRACE **d :** to coil, fold, draw, or twine (as string or cloth) around something
**2 a :** SURROUND, ENVELOP **b :** to suffuse or surround with an aura or state (the affair was *wrapped* in scandal) **c :** to involve completely **:** ENGROSS — usually used with *up*
**3 :** to conceal or obscure as if by enveloping
**4 :** to enclose as if with a protective covering
**5 :** to finish filming or videotaping (*wrap* a movie)
*intransitive verb*
**1 :** to wind, coil, or twine so as to encircle or cover something
**2 :** to put on clothing **:** DRESS — usually used with *up*
**3 :** to be subject to covering, enclosing, or packaging — usually used with *up*
**4 :** to come to completion in filming or videotaping

**²wrap** *noun* (15th century)
**1 a** (1) **:** WRAPPER, WRAPPING (2) **:** material used for wrapping (plastic *wrap*) **b :** an article of clothing that may be wrapped round a person; *especially* **:** an outer garment (as a coat or shawl) **c :** BLANKET
**2 :** a single turn or convolution of something wound round an object
**3** *plural* **a :** RESTRAINT **b :** a shroud of secrecy (a plan kept under *wraps*)
**4 :** the completion of a schedule or session for filming or videotaping

**³wrap** *adjective* (1948)
**:** WRAPAROUND 1

**¹wrap·around** \'rap-ə-ˌraùnd\ *noun* (1924)
**1 :** a garment (as a dress) made with a full-length opening and adjusted to the figure by wrapping around
**2 :** an object that encircles or especially curves and laps over another

**²wraparound** *adjective* (1926)
**1 :** made to be wrapped around something and especially the body (a *wraparound* skirt)
**2 a :** shaped to follow a contour; *especially* **:** made to curve from the front around to the side (*wraparound* sunglasses) (*wraparound*

terraces) **b :** extending laterally to the outermost limits of the field of vision (a *wraparound* movie screen)

**wrap·per** \'ra-pər\ *noun* (15th century)
**1 :** that in which something is wrapped: as **a :** a tobacco leaf used for the outside covering especially of cigars **b** (1) **:** JACKET 3c(1) (2) **:** the paper cover of a book not bound in boards **c :** a paper wrapped around a newspaper or magazine in the mail
**2 :** one that wraps
**3 :** an article of clothing worn wrapped around the body

**wrap·ping** \'ra-piŋ\ *noun* (14th century)
**:** something used to wrap an object **:** WRAPPER

**wrap–up** \'rap-ˌəp\ *noun* (1951)
**1 :** a summarizing report
**2 :** a concluding part **:** FINALE

**wrap up** *transitive verb* (circa 1568)
**1 :** SUMMARIZE, SUM UP
**2 a :** to bring to a usually successful conclusion **b :** CINCH, SEW UP (has the nomination *wrapped up*)

**wrasse** \'ras\ *noun, plural* **wrasses** *also* **wrasse** [Cornish *gwragh, wragh* hag, wrasse] (circa 1672)
**:** any of a large family (Labridae) of elongate compressed usually brilliantly colored marine bony fishes that usually bury themselves in sand at night and include important food fishes as well as a number of popular aquarium fishes

**¹wrath** \'rath, *chiefly British* 'róth\ *noun* [Middle English, from Old English *wræththo,* from *wrāth* wroth — more at WROTH] (before 12th century)
**1 :** strong vengeful anger or indignation
**2 :** retributory punishment for an offense or a crime **:** divine chastisement
**synonym** see ANGER

**²wrath** *adjective* [alteration of *wroth*] (1535)
*archaic* **:** WRATHFUL

**wrath·ful** \-fəl\ *adjective* (14th century)
**1 :** filled with wrath **:** IRATE

□ USAGE
**would** *Would have* is sometimes substituted for the past subjunctive *had* in the subordinate clause of a conditional sentence ⟨if we *would have* known Max was going to die [we] should have made sound movies of him —Ernest Hemingway (letter)⟩. Most of the evidence for this construction comes from speech, and it must be common in student writing for it is mentioned as something to avoid in student handbooks dating from 1920 to the present. It is occasionally found in edited writing ⟨if the spurious signal *would have* turned up during the brief period it took to punch the keys, it would have triggered an actual abort —*N. Y. Times*⟩ ⟨if this *would have* been a real . . . test of his critical powers, in another sense it could have proved a greater surety for his critical survival —Louis Kronenberger⟩. The origin and development of this construction are imperfectly known, but it has been found as far back as the second half of the 19th century ⟨these characteristics, fixed and unchangeable as bone in Mr. Casaubon, might have remained longer unfelt by Dorothea . . . if he *would have* held her hands between his and listened —George Eliot⟩. It is apparently well established in speech, where it tends not to be noticed. It is better avoided in writing, however, where it tends to attract unfavorable notice.

\ə\ **abut** \ᵊ\ **kitten** \ər\ **further** \a\ **ash** \ā\ **ace** \ä\ **mop, mar** \aù\ **out** \ch\ **chin** \e\ **bet** \ē\ **easy** \g\ **go** \i\ **hit** \ī\ **ice** \j\ **job** \ŋ\ **sing** \ō\ **go** \ò\ **law** \òi\ **boy** \th\ **thin** \t͟h\ **the** \ü\ **loot** \ù\ **foot** \y\ **yet** \zh\ **vision** *see also* Guide to Pronunciation

**2 :** arising from, marked by, or indicative of wrath
— **wrath·ful·ly** \-fə-lē\ *adverb*
— **wrath·ful·ness** *noun*
**wrathy** \'ra-thē, *chiefly British* 'rȯ-\ *adjective* (1828)
**:** WRATHFUL
**wreak** \'rēk *also* 'rek\ *transitive verb* [Middle English *wreken*, from Old English *wrecan* to drive, punish, avenge; akin to Old High German *rehhan* to avenge and perhaps to Latin *urgēre* to drive on, urge] (before 12th century)
**1 a** *archaic* **:** AVENGE **b :** to cause the infliction of (vengeance or punishment)
**2 :** to give free play or course to (malevolent feeling)
**3 :** BRING ABOUT, CAUSE ⟨*wreak* havoc⟩
*usage* see WRECK
**wreath** \'rēth\ *noun, plural* **wreaths** \'rēthz, 'rēths\ [Middle English *wrethe*, from Old English *writha*; akin to Old English *wrīthan* to twist — more at WRITHE] (before 12th century)
**:** something intertwined into a circular shape; *especially* **:** GARLAND, CHAPLET
**wreathe** \'rēth\ *verb* **wreathed; wreath-ing** [*wreath*] (1530)
*transitive verb*
**1 a :** to shape into a wreath **b :** INTERWEAVE **c :** to cause to coil about something
**2 :** to twist or contort so as to show folds or creases
**3 :** to encircle or adorn with or as if with a wreath
*intransitive verb*
**1 :** to twist in coils **:** WRITHE
**2 a :** to take on the shape of a wreath **b :** to move or extend in circles or spirals
**wreathy** \'rē-thē, -thē\ *adjective* (1644)
**1 :** having the form of a wreath
**2 :** constituting a wreath
**¹wreck** \'rek\ *noun* [Middle English *wrek*, from Anglo-French, of Scandinavian origin; akin to Old Norse *rek* wreck; akin to Old English *wrecan* to drive] (13th century)
**1 :** something cast up on the land by the sea especially after a shipwreck
**2 a :** SHIPWRECK **b :** the action of wrecking or fact or state of being wrecked **:** DESTRUCTION
**3 a :** a hulk or the ruins of a wrecked ship **b :** the broken remains of something wrecked or otherwise ruined **c :** something disabled or in a state of ruin or dilapidation; *also* **:** a person or animal of broken constitution, health, or spirits
**²wreck** (15th century)
*transitive verb*
**1 :** to cast ashore
**2 a :** to reduce to a ruinous state by or as if by violence **b :** SHIPWRECK **c :** to ruin, damage, or imperil by a wreck **d :** to involve in disaster or ruin
**3 :** BRING ABOUT, WREAK ⟨*wreck* havoc⟩
*intransitive verb*
**1 :** to become wrecked
**2 :** to rob, salvage, or repair wreckage or a wreck ■
**wreck·age** \'re-kij\ *noun* (1837)
**1 :** the act of wrecking **:** the state of being wrecked
**2 a :** something that has been wrecked **b :** broken and disordered parts or material from something wrecked
**wreck·er** \'re-kər\ *noun* (1802)
**1 a :** one that searches for or works on the wrecks of ships (as for rescue or for plunder) **b :** TOW TRUCK
**2 :** one that wrecks; *especially* **:** one whose work is the demolition of buildings
**wrecker's ball** *noun* (1967)
**:** a heavy iron or steel ball swung or dropped by a derrick to demolish old buildings — called also *wrecking ball*
**wrecking bar** *noun* (1924)

**:** a small crowbar with a claw for pulling nails at one end and a slight bend for prying at the other end
**wren** \'ren\ *noun* [Middle English *wrenne*, from Old English *wrenna; akin to Old High German *rentilo* wren] (before 12th century)
**1 :** any of a family (Troglodytidae) of numerous small more or less brown oscine singing birds; *especially* **:** a very small widely distributed bird (*Troglodytes troglodytes*) that has a short erect tail and is noted for its song
**2 :** any of various small singing birds resembling the true wrens in size and habits

wren 1

**¹wrench** \'rench\ *verb* [Middle English, from Old English *wrencan*; akin to Old High German *renken* to twist and perhaps to Latin *vergere* to bend, incline] (before 12th century)
*intransitive verb*
**1 :** to move with a violent twist; *also* **:** to undergo twisting
**2 :** to pull or strain at something with violent twisting
*transitive verb*
**1 :** to twist violently
**2 :** to injure or disable by a violent twisting or straining
**3 :** CHANGE; *especially* **:** DISTORT, PERVERT
**4 a :** to pull or tighten by violent twisting or with violence **b :** to snatch forcibly **:** WREST
**5 :** to cause to suffer mental anguish **:** RACK
— **wrench·ing·ly** \'ren-chiŋ-lē\ *adverb*
**²wrench** *noun* (1530)
**1 a :** a violent twisting or a pull with or as if with twisting **b :** a sharp twist or sudden jerk straining muscles or ligaments; *also* **:** the resultant injury (as of a joint) **c :** a distorting or perverting alteration **d :** acute emotional distress **:** sudden violent mental change
**2 :** a hand or power tool for holding, twisting, or turning an object (as a bolt or nut)
**3 :** MONKEY WRENCH 2
**¹wrest** \'rest\ *transitive verb* [Middle English *wrasten, wresten*, from Old English *wrǣstan; akin to Old Norse *reista* to bend and probably to Old English *wrigian* to turn — more at WRY] (before 12th century)
**1 :** to pull, force, or move by violent wringing or twisting movements
**2 :** to gain with difficulty by or as if by force, violence, or determined labor
**²wrest** *noun* (14th century)
**1 :** the action of wresting **:** WRENCH
**2** *archaic* **:** a key or wrench used for turning pins in a stringed instrument (as a harp or piano)
**¹wres·tle** \'re-səl, 'ra-\ *verb* **wres·tled; wres·tling** \'res-liŋ, 'ras-; 're-s°l-iŋ, 'ra-\ [Middle English *wrastlen, wrestlen*, from Old English *wrǣstlian*, frequentative of *wrǣstan*] (before 12th century)
*intransitive verb*
**1 :** to contend by grappling with and striving to trip or throw an opponent down or off balance
**2 :** to combat an opposing tendency or force ⟨*wrestling* with his conscience⟩
**3 :** to engage in deep thought, consideration, or debate
**4 :** to engage in or as if in a violent or determined struggle ⟨*wrestling* with cumbersome luggage⟩
*transitive verb*
**1 a :** to engage in (a match, bout, or fall) in wrestling **b :** to wrestle with ⟨*wrestle* an alligator⟩
**2 :** to move, maneuver, or force with difficulty
— **wres·tler** \'res-lər, 'ras-; 're-s°l-ər, 'ra-\ *noun*

**²wrestle** *noun* (1593)
**:** the action or an instance of wrestling **:** STRUGGLE; *especially* **:** a wrestling bout
**wres·tling** \'res-liŋ, 'ras-; 're-s°l-iŋ, 'ra-\ *noun* (before 12th century)
**:** a sport or contest in which two unarmed individuals struggle hand to hand with each attempting to subdue or unbalance the other
**wretch** \'rech\ *noun* [Middle English *wrecche*, from Old English *wrecca* outcast, exile; akin to Old High German *hrechjo* fugitive, Old English *wrecan* to drive, drive out — more at WREAK] (before 12th century)
**1 :** a miserable person **:** one who is profoundly unhappy or in great misfortune
**2 :** a base, despicable, or vile person
**wretch·ed** \'re-chəd\ *adjective* [Middle English, irregular from *wretch*] (12th century)
**1 :** deeply afflicted, dejected, or distressed in body or mind
**2 :** extremely or deplorably bad or distressing ⟨was in *wretched* health⟩ ⟨a *wretched* accident⟩
**3 a :** being or appearing mean, miserable, or contemptible ⟨dressed in *wretched* old clothes⟩ **b :** very poor in quality or ability **:** INFERIOR ⟨*wretched* workmanship⟩
— **wretch·ed·ly** *adverb*
— **wretch·ed·ness** *noun*
**¹wrig·gle** \'ri-gəl\ *verb* **wrig·gled; wrig·gling** \-g(ə-)liŋ\ [Middle English, from or akin to Middle Low German *wriggeln* to wriggle; akin to Old English *wrigian* to turn — more at WRY] (15th century)
*intransitive verb*
**1 :** to move the body or a bodily part to and fro with short writhing motions like a worm **:** SQUIRM
**2 :** to move or advance by twisting and turning
**3 :** to extricate or insinuate oneself or reach a goal as if by wriggling
*transitive verb*
**1 :** to cause to move in short quick contortions
**2 :** to introduce, insinuate, or bring into a state or place by or as if by wriggling
— **wrig·gly** \-g(ə-)lē\ *adjective*
**²wriggle** *noun* (1709)
**1 :** a short or quick writhing motion or contortion
**2 :** a formation or marking of sinuous design
**wrig·gler** \'ri-g(ə-)lər\ *noun* (1631)
**:** one that wriggles; *especially* **:** WIGGLER 1
**wright** \'rīt\ *noun* [Middle English, from Old English *wyrhta, wryhta* worker, maker; akin to Old English *weorc* work — more at WORK] (before 12th century)

: a worker skilled in the manufacture especially of wooden objects — usually used in combination ⟨ship*wright*⟩ ⟨wheel*wright*⟩

**wring** \'riŋ\ *verb* **wrung** \'rəŋ\; **wring·ing** \'riŋ-iŋ\ [Middle English, from Old English *wringan*; akin to Old High German *ringan* to struggle, Lithuanian *rengtis* to bend down, Old English *wyrgan* to strangle — more at WORRY] (before 12th century)
*transitive verb*
**1 :** to squeeze or twist especially so as to make dry or to extract moisture or liquid ⟨*wring* a towel dry⟩
**2 :** to extract or obtain by or as if by twisting and compressing ⟨*wring* water from a towel⟩ ⟨*wring* a confession from the suspect⟩
**3 a :** to twist so as to strain or sprain into a distorted shape ⟨I could *wring* your neck⟩ **b :** to twist together (clasped hands) as a sign of anguish
**4 :** to affect painfully as if by wringing **:** TORMENT ⟨a tragedy that *wrings* the heart⟩
*intransitive verb*
**:** SQUIRM, WRITHE
**— wring** *noun*
**wring·er** \'riŋ-ər\ *noun* (14th century)
**:** one that wrings: as **a :** a machine or device for pressing out liquid or moisture ⟨a clothes *wringer*⟩ **b :** something that causes pain, hardship, or exertion
**¹wrin·kle** \'riŋ-kəl\ *noun* [Middle English, back-formation from *wrinkled* twisted, winding, probably from Old English *gewrinclod*, past participle of *gewrinclian* to wind, from *ge-*, perfective prefix + *-wrinclian* (akin to *wrencan* to wrench) — more at CO-] (15th century)
**1 :** a small ridge or furrow especially when formed on a surface by the shrinking or contraction of a smooth substance **:** CREASE; *specifically* **:** one in the skin especially when due to age, worry, or fatigue
**2 a :** METHOD, TECHNIQUE **b :** a change in a customary procedure or method **c :** something new or different **:** INNOVATION
**3 :** IMPERFECTION, IRREGULARITY
**— wrin·kly** \-k(ə-)lē\ *adjective*
**²wrinkle** *verb* **wrin·kled; wrin·kling** \-k(ə-)liŋ\ (1523)
*intransitive verb*
**:** to become marked with or contracted into wrinkles
*transitive verb*
**:** to contract into wrinkles **:** PUCKER
**wrist** \'rist\ *noun* [Middle English, from Old English; akin to Middle High German *rist* wrist, ankle, Old English *wrǣstan* to twist — more at WREST] (before 12th century)
**1 :** the joint or the region of the joint between the human hand and the arm or a corresponding part on a lower animal
**2 :** the part of a garment or glove covering the wrist
**wrist·band** \'ris(t)-,band\ *noun* (1571)
**1 :** the part of a sleeve covering the wrist
**2 :** a band encircling the wrist
**wrist·let** \'ris(t)-lət\ *noun* (circa 1847)
**:** a band encircling the wrist; *especially* **:** a close-fitting knitted band attached to the top of a glove or the end of a sleeve
**wrist·lock** \'rist-,läk\ *noun* (1921)
**:** a wrestling hold in which one contestant is thrown or made helpless by a twisting grip on the wrist
**wrist pin** *noun* (circa 1875)
**:** a stud or pin that forms a journal (as in a crosshead) for a connecting rod
**wrist shot** *noun* (circa 1899)
**:** a quick usually short-range shot in ice hockey made while the puck is against the blade of the stick by snapping the blade quickly forward
**wrist·watch** \'rist-,wäch\ *noun* (1896)
**:** a small watch that is attached to a bracelet or strap and is worn around the wrist
**wrist wrestling** *noun* (1968)

: a form of arm wrestling in which opponents interlock thumbs instead of gripping hands
**wristy** \'ris-tē\ *adjective* **wrist·i·er; -est** (1867)
**:** involving or using a lot of wrist movement (as in stroking a ball)
**writ** \'rit\ *noun* [Middle English, from Old English; akin to Old English *wrītan* to write] (before 12th century)
**1 :** something written **:** WRITING ⟨Sacred *Writ*⟩
**2 a :** a formal written document; *specifically* **:** a legal instrument in epistolary form issued under seal in the name of the English monarch **b :** an order or mandatory process in writing issued in the name of the sovereign or of a court or judicial officer commanding the person to whom it is directed to perform or refrain from performing an act specified therein ⟨*writ* of detinue⟩ ⟨*writ* of entry⟩ ⟨*writ* of execution⟩ **c :** the power and authority of the issuer of such a written order — usually used with *run* ⟨outside the United States where . . . our *writ* does not run —Dean Acheson⟩
**writ·able** \'rī-tə-bəl\ *adjective* (1782)
**:** capable of being put in writing
**write** \'rīt\ *verb* **wrote** \'rōt\; **writ·ten** \'ri-tᵊn\ *also* **writ** \'rit\ *or dialect* **wrote; writ·ing** \'rī-tiŋ\ [Middle English, from Old English *wrītan* to scratch, draw, inscribe; akin to Old High German *rīzan* to tear and perhaps to Greek *rhīnē* file, rasp] (before 12th century)
*transitive verb*
**1 a :** to form (as characters or symbols) on a surface with an instrument (as a pen) **b :** to form (as words) by inscribing the characters or symbols of on a surface **c :** to spell in writing ⟨words *written* alike but pronounced differently⟩ **d :** to cover, fill, or fill in by writing ⟨*wrote* ten pages⟩ ⟨*write* a check⟩
**2 :** to set down in writing: as **a :** DRAW UP, DRAFT ⟨*write* a will⟩ **b** (1) **:** to be the author of **:** COMPOSE ⟨*writes* poems and essays⟩ (2) **:** to compose in musical form ⟨*write* a string quartet⟩ **c :** to express in literary form ⟨if I could *write* the beauty of your eyes —Shakespeare⟩ **d :** to communicate by letter ⟨*writes* that they are coming⟩ **e :** to use or exhibit (a specific script, language, or literary form or style) in writing ⟨*writes* Braille⟩ ⟨*writes* French with ease⟩ **f :** to write contracts or orders for; *especially* **:** UNDERWRITE ⟨*write* life insurance⟩
**3 :** to make a permanent impression of
**4 :** to communicate with in writing ⟨we'll *write* you when we get there⟩
**5 :** ORDAIN, FATE ⟨so be it, it is *written* —D. C. Peattie⟩
**6 :** to make evident or obvious ⟨guilt *written* on his face⟩
**7 :** to force, effect, introduce, or remove by writing ⟨*write* oneself into fame and fortune —Charles Lee⟩
**8 :** to take part in or bring about (something worth recording)
**9 a :** to introduce (information) into the storage device or medium of a computer **b :** to transfer (information) from the main memory of a computer to a storage or output device
**10 :** SELL ⟨*write* a stock option⟩
*intransitive verb*
**1 a :** to make significant characters or inscriptions; *also* **:** to permit or be adapted to writing **b :** to form or produce written letters, words, or sentences
**2 :** to compose, communicate by, or send a letter
**3 a :** to produce a written work **b :** to compose music ▪
**— write one's own ticket :** to select a course of action or position entirely according to one's wishes
**— writ large :** on a larger scale or in a more prominent manner ⟨the problems of modern totalitarianism are only our own problems *writ large* —*Times Literary Supplement*⟩
**— writ small :** on a smaller scale
**write–down** \'rīt-,daûn\ *noun* (1932)

: a deliberate reduction in the book value of an asset (as to reflect the effect of obsolescence)
**write down** (1588)
*transitive verb*
**1 :** to record in written form
**2 a :** to depreciate, disparage, or injure by writing **b :** to reduce in status, rank, or value; *especially* **:** to reduce the book value of
*intransitive verb*
**:** to write so as to appeal to a lower level of taste, comprehension, or intelligence
**write–in** \'rīt-,in\ *noun* (1932)
**1 :** a vote cast by writing in the name of a candidate
**2 :** a candidate whose name is written in
**write in** *transitive verb* (14th century)
**1 :** to insert in a document or text
**2 a :** to insert (a name not listed on a ballot or voting machine) in an appropriate space **b :** to cast (a vote) in this manner
**write–off** \'rīt-,òf\ *noun* (1905)
**1 :** an elimination of an item from the books of account
**2 :** a reduction in book value of an item (as by way of depreciation)
**write off** *transitive verb* (1682)
**1 a :** to reduce the estimated or book value of **:** DEPRECIATE **b :** to take off the books **:** CANCEL ⟨*write off* a bad debt⟩
**2 :** to regard or concede to be lost ⟨most were content to *write off* 1979 and look optimistically ahead —*Money*⟩; *also* **:** DISMISS ⟨was *written off* as an expatriate highbrow —Brendan Gill⟩
**write out** *transitive verb* (1548)
**:** to write especially in a full and complete form
**writ·er** \'rī-tər\ *noun* (before 12th century)
**:** one that writes: as **a :** AUTHOR **b :** one who writes stock options
**writ·er·ly** \'rī-tər-lē\ *adjective* (1957)
**:** of, relating to, or typical of a writer
**writer's block** *noun* (1950)
**:** a psychological inhibition preventing a writer from proceeding with a piece
**writer's cramp** *noun* (1853)
**:** a painful spasmodic cramp of muscles of the hand or fingers brought on by excessive writing
**write–up** \'rīt-,əp\ *noun* (1885)
**1 :** a written account; *especially* **:** a flattering article
**2 :** a deliberate increase in the book value of an asset (as to reflect the effect of inflation)
**write up** *transitive verb* (15th century)
**1 :** to make a write-up of
**2 :** to report (a person) especially for some violation of law or rules

---

□ USAGE

**write** Back in the 18th century, the past participles *wrote* and *writ* were both in common use ⟨I have *wrote* him word —George Washington⟩ ⟨I ought to have *wrote* to you long since —Benjamin Franklin⟩ ⟨you will have thought me very inexcusable for not having *writ* to you —Richard Brinsley Sheridan⟩. We can still find *writ* in the Civil War era ⟨I have *writ* to George again —Walt Whitman⟩ and it has continued in the 20th century in much diminished use—chiefly in facetious text ⟨yes, Little Eva, the foregoing sentence was *writ* deliberate —James J. Kilpatrick⟩ and in the fixed phrase *writ large* ⟨museums are collections *writ large* —*Smithsonian*⟩. *Written* is the usual past participle now; *wrote* has dropped out of standard use.

\ə\ abut \ᵊ\ kitten \ər\ further \a\ ash \ā\ ace
\ä\ mop, mar \aù\ out \ch\ chin \e\ bet \ē\ easy
\g\ go \i\ hit \ī\ ice \j\ job \ŋ\ sing \ō\ go
\ò\ law \òi\ boy \th\ thin \t̷h\ the \ü\ loot \ù\ foot
\y\ yet \zh\ vision    *see also* Guide to Pronunciation

**writhe** \'rīth\ *verb* **writhed; writh·ing** [Middle English, from Old English *wrīthan;* akin to Old Norse *rītha* to twist] (before 12th century)
*transitive verb*
**1 a :** to twist into coils or folds **b :** to twist so as to distort **:** WRENCH **c :** to twist (the body or a bodily part) in pain
**2 :** INTERTWINE
*intransitive verb*
**1 :** to move or proceed with twists and turns
**2 :** to twist from or as if from pain or struggling
**3 :** to suffer keenly
— **writhe** *noun*

**writh·en** \'ri-thən\ *adjective* [Middle English, from Old English, from past participle of *wrīthan*] (before 12th century)
**:** being twisted or contorted ⟨*writhen* trees⟩ ⟨a *writhen* smile⟩

**writ·ing** \'rī-tiŋ\ *noun* (13th century)
**1 :** the act or process of one who writes: as **a :** the act or art of forming visible letters or characters; *specifically* **:** HANDWRITING 1 **b :** the act or practice of literary or musical composition
**2 :** something written: as **a :** letters or characters that serve as visible signs of ideas, words, or symbols **b :** a letter, note, or notice used to communicate or record **c :** a written composition **d :** INSCRIPTION
**3 :** a style or form of composition
**4 :** the occupation of a writer; *especially* **:** the profession of authorship
— **writing on the wall :** HANDWRITING ON THE WALL

**writing desk** *noun* (1611)
**:** a desk that often has a sloping top for writing on; *also* **:** a portable case that contains writing materials and has a surface for writing

**writing paper** *noun* (1548)
**:** paper that is usually finished with a smooth surface and sized and that can be written on with ink

**Writ·ings** \'rī-tiŋz\ *noun plural* [translation of Late Hebrew *kĕthūbhīm*] (14th century)
**:** HAGIOGRAPHA

**writ of assistance** (1706)
**1 :** a writ issued to a law officer (as a sheriff or marshal) for the enforcement of a court order or decree; *especially* **:** one used to enforce an order for the possession of lands
**2 :** a writ used especially in colonial America authorizing a law officer to search in unspecified locations for unspecified illegal goods

**writ of certiorari** (circa 1532)
**:** CERTIORARI

**writ of error** (15th century)
**:** a common law writ directing an inferior court to remit the record of a legal action to the reviewing court in order that an error of law may be corrected if it exists

**writ of extent** (circa 1861)
**:** a writ formerly used to recover debts of record to the British crown and under which the lands, goods, and person of the debtor might all be seized to secure payment

**writ of habeas corpus** (1771)
**:** HABEAS CORPUS

**writ of mandamus** (circa 1861)
**:** MANDAMUS

**writ of prohibition** (circa 1876)
**:** a writ issued by a superior court to prevent an inferior court from acting beyond its jurisdiction

**writ of right** *noun* (15th century)
**1 :** a common law writ for restoring to its owner property held by another
**2 :** a writ granted as a matter of right

**writ of summons** (1660)
**:** a writ issued on behalf of the British monarch summoning a lord spiritual or a lord temporal to attend parliament

**¹wrong** \'ròŋ\ *noun* [Middle English, from Old English *wrang,* from (assumed) *wrang,* adjective, wrong] (before 12th century)

**1 a :** an injurious, unfair, or unjust act **:** action or conduct inflicting harm without due provocation or just cause **b :** a violation or invasion of the legal rights of another; *especially* **:** TORT
**2 :** something wrong, immoral, or unethical; *especially* **:** principles, practices, or conduct contrary to justice, goodness, equity, or law
**3 :** the state, position, or fact of being or doing wrong: as **a :** the state of being mistaken or incorrect **b :** the state of being guilty
**synonym** see INJUSTICE

**²wrong** *adjective* **wrong·er** \'ròŋ-ər\; **wrong·est** \'ròŋ-əst\ [Middle English, from (assumed) Old English *wrang,* of Scandinavian origin; akin to Old Norse *rangr* awry, wrong; akin to Old English *wringan* to wring] (13th century)
**1 :** not according to the moral standard **:** SINFUL, IMMORAL ⟨thought that war was *wrong*⟩
**2 :** not right or proper according to a code, standard, or convention **:** IMPROPER ⟨it was *wrong* not to thank your host⟩
**3 :** not according to truth or facts **:** INCORRECT ⟨gave a *wrong* date⟩
**4 :** not satisfactory (as in condition, results, health, or temper)
**5 :** not in accordance with one's needs, intent, or expectations ⟨took the *wrong* bus⟩
**6 :** of, relating to, or constituting the side of something that is usually held to be opposite to the principal one, that is the one naturally or by design turned down, inward, or away, or that is the least finished or polished
— **wrong·ly** \'ròŋ-lē\ *adverb*
— **wrong·ness** *noun*
— **wrong side of the tracks :** a run-down or unfashionable neighborhood

**³wrong** *adverb* (13th century)
**1 :** without accuracy **:** INCORRECTLY ⟨guessed *wrong*⟩
**2 :** without regard for what is proper or just
**3 :** in a wrong direction
**4 a :** in an unsuccessful or unfortunate way **b :** out of working order or condition
**5 :** in a false light ⟨don't get me *wrong*⟩

**⁴wrong** *transitive verb* **wronged; wrong·ing** \'ròŋ-iŋ\ (14th century)
**1 a :** to do wrong to **:** INJURE, HARM **b :** to treat disrespectfully or dishonorably **:** VIOLATE
**2 :** DEFRAUD — usually used with *of*
**3 :** DISCREDIT, MALIGN ☆
— **wrong·er** \'ròŋ-ər\ *noun*

**wrong·do·er** \'ròŋ-,dü-ər\ *noun* (15th century)
**:** one that does wrong; *especially* **:** one who transgresses moral laws

**wrong·do·ing** \-,dü-iŋ\ *noun* (14th century)
**1 :** evil or improper behavior or action
**2 :** an instance of doing wrong

**wronged** *adjective* (circa 1547)
**:** being injured unjustly **:** suffering a wrong

**wrong·ful** \'ròŋ-fəl\ *adjective* (14th century)
**1 :** WRONG, UNJUST
**2 a :** having no legal sanction **:** UNLAWFUL **b :** ILLEGITIMATE
— **wrong·ful·ly** \-fə-lē\ *adverb*
— **wrong·ful·ness** *noun*

**wrong·head·ed** \'ròŋ-'he-dəd\ *adjective* (1732)
**:** stubborn in adherence to wrong opinion or principles ⟨a *wrongheaded* policy⟩
— **wrong·head·ed·ly** *adverb*
— **wrong·head·ed·ness** *noun*

**wrote** *past and dialect past participle of* WRITE

**wroth** \'ròth *also* 'rōth\ *adjective* [Middle English, from Old English *wrāth;* akin to Old High German *reid* twisted, Old English *wrīthan* to writhe] (before 12th century)
**:** intensely angry **:** highly incensed **:** WRATHFUL

**¹wrought** \'ròt\ *past and past participle of* WORK

**usage** see WRECK

**²wrought** *adjective* [Middle English, from past participle of *worken* to work] (14th centu-

**1 :** worked into shape by artistry or effort ⟨carefully *wrought* essays⟩
**2 :** elaborately embellished **:** ORNAMENTED
**3 :** processed for use **:** MANUFACTURED ⟨*wrought* silk⟩
**4 :** beaten into shape by tools **:** HAMMERED — used of metals
**5 :** deeply stirred **:** EXCITED — often used with *up* ⟨gets easily *wrought* up over nothing⟩

**wrought iron** *noun* (1678)
**:** a commercial form of iron that is tough, malleable, and relatively soft, contains less than 0.3 percent and usually less than 0.1 percent carbon, and carries 1 or 2 percent of slag mechanically mixed with it

**wrung** *past and past participle of* WRING

**¹wry** \'rī\ *verb* **wried; wry·ing** [Middle English *wrien,* from Old English *wrigian* to turn; akin to Middle High German *rigel* kerchief wound around the head, Greek *rhiknos* shriveled, Avestan *urvisyeiti* he turns] (14th century)
*intransitive verb*
**:** TWIST, WRITHE
*transitive verb*
**:** to pull out of or as if out of proper shape **:** make awry

**²wry** *adjective* **wry·er** \'rī-(ə)r\; **wry·est** \'rī-əst\ (1523)
**1 :** having a bent or twisted shape or condition ⟨a *wry* smile⟩; *especially* **:** turned abnormally to one side ⟨a *wry* neck⟩
**2 :** WRONGHEADED
**3 :** cleverly and often ironically or grimly humorous
— **wry·ly** \'rī-lē\ *adverb*
— **wry·ness** *noun*

**wry·neck** \'rī-,nek\ *noun* (1585)
**1 :** either of two Old World woodpeckers (*Jynx torquilla* or *J. ruficollis*) that differ from the typical woodpeckers in having soft tail feathers and a peculiar manner of writhing the neck
**2 :** TORTICOLLIS

**Wu** \'wü\ *noun* [Chinese (Beijing) *Wú,* historical kingdom coextensive with the dialect area] (1908)
**:** a group of Chinese dialects spoken principally in Jiangsu and Zhejiang provinces

**wud** \'wüd\ *adjective* [alteration of ¹*wood*] (1772)
*chiefly Scottish* **:** INSANE, MAD

**wul·fen·ite** \'wùl-fə-,nīt\ *noun* [German *Wulfenit,* from F. X. von *Wulfen* (died 1805) Austrian mineralogist] (1849)
**:** a tetragonal mineral that is a complex oxide of lead and molybdenum and occurs especially in bright orange-yellow tabular crystals

**wun·der·kind** \'vùn-dər-,kint\ *noun, plural* **wun·der·kin·der** \-,kin-dər\ [German, from *Wunder* wonder + *Kind* child] (1891)
**:** a child prodigy; *also* **:** one who succeeds in a competitive or highly difficult field or profession at an early age

**wurst** \'wərst *also* 'wùrst *sometimes* 'wùsht *or*

☆ **SYNONYMS**
**Wrong, oppress, persecute, aggrieve** mean to injure unjustly or outrageously. WRONG implies inflicting injury either unmerited or out of proportion to what one deserves ⟨a penal system that had *wronged* him⟩. OPPRESS suggests inhumane imposing of burdens one cannot endure or exacting more than one can perform ⟨a people *oppressed* by a warmongering tyrant⟩. PERSECUTE implies a relentless and unremitting subjection to annoyance or suffering ⟨a child *persecuted* by constant criticism⟩. AGGRIEVE implies suffering caused by an infringement or denial of rights ⟨a legal aid society representing *aggrieved* minority groups⟩.

'wu̇st; *also with* v *for* w\ *noun* [German, from Old High German] (1855)

**:** SAUSAGE

**wurzel** *noun* [short for *mangel-wurzel*] (circa 1888)

**:** MANGEL

**wuss** \'wu̇s\ *also* **wus·sy** \'wu̇-sē\ *noun, plural* **wuss·es** *also* **wus·sies** [origin unknown] (1983)

**:** WIMP

— **wussy** *adjective*

**wuth·er** \'wə-t͟hər\ *intransitive verb* [alteration of *whither* to rush, bluster, hurl] (circa 1825) *dialect English* **:** to blow with a dull roaring sound

**Wy·an·dot** \'wī-ən-ˌdät *also* 'wīn-\ *noun* (1749)

**:** a member of an American Indian group

formed in the 17th century by Hurons and other Indians fleeing the Iroquois

**wy·an·dotte** \-ˌdät\ *noun* [probably from *Wyandotte* Wyandot] (1884)

**:** any of a U.S. breed of medium-sized domestic fowls raised for meat and eggs

**Wyc·liff·ite** \'wi-klə-ˌfīt\ *noun* [John *Wycliffe*] (1580)

**:** LOLLARD

— **Wycliffite** *adjective*

**wye** \'wī\ *noun* (1857)

**1 :** a Y-shaped part or object

**2 :** the letter *y*

**wy·lie·coat** \'wī-lē-ˌkōt, 'wi-\ *noun* [Middle English (Scots) *wyle cot*] (15th century)

**1** *chiefly Scottish* **:** a warm undergarment

**2** *chiefly Scottish* **:** PETTICOAT

**wynd** \'wīnd\ *noun* [Middle English (Scots)

*wynde,* probably from *wynden* to wind, proceed, go, from Old English *windan* to twist — more at WIND] (15th century)

*chiefly Scottish* **:** a very narrow street

**wynn** *or* **wyn** \'win\ *noun* [Old English *wynn,* literally, joy — more at WINSOME] (before 12th century)

**:** a runic letter used in Old English and Middle English to represent the consonant \w\

**WYS·I·WYG** \'wi-zē-ˌwig, -zə-\ *adjective* [*what you see is what you get*] (1982)

**:** of, relating to, or being a display generated by word-processing or desktop-publishing software that exactly reflects the appearance of the printed document

**wy·vern** \'wī-vərn\ *noun* [alteration of Middle English *wyvere* viper, from Old North French *wivre,* modification of Latin *vipera*] (1610)

**:** a mythical animal usually represented as a 2-legged winged creature resembling a dragon

# X

X *is the twenty-fourth letter of the English alphabet. Its form and pronunciation are from Latin, as is its name. The letter came into Latin from a western Greek alphabet in which it had the value of* ks. *In an eastern Greek alphabet and in classical Greek, the same sign stood for the letter* chi, *which represented the breathy, guttural sound heard in English at the end of Scottish* loch, *while that of* ks *was indicated by the letter* xi. *In English,* x *represents an unusually wide variety of sounds for a consonant letter. Most prominent are these five: the sound of* ks *as in* tax, *of* z *as in* xylophone, *of* gz *as in* exact, *of* ksh *as in one pronunciation of* anxious, *and of* gzh *as in one pronunciation of* luxurious. *Initial X occurs most often in words of Greek origin, where it is pronounced like* z *and stands for classical Greek* xi. *In the middle and at the end of words, however, X appears frequently in words of Latin origin, directly or through French, such as* axis *and* mix. *Small* x *developed through the miniaturizing of the capital form.*

**¹x** \'eks\ *noun, plural* **x's** *or* **xs** \'ek-səz\ *often capitalized, often attributive* (before 12th century) **1 a :** the 24th letter of the English alphabet **b :** a graphic representation of this letter **c :** a speech counterpart of orthographic *x* **2 :** TEN — see NUMBER table **3 :** a graphic device for reproducing the letter *x* **4 :** one designated *x* especially as the 24th in order or class, or the first in an order or class that includes x, y, and sometimes z **5 :** an unknown quantity **6 :** something shaped like or marked with the letter X

**²x** *transitive verb* **x–ed** *also* **x'd** *or* **xed** \'ekst\; **x–ing** *or* **x'ing** \'ek-siŋ\ (circa 1849) **1 :** to mark with an *x* **2 :** to cancel or obliterate with a series of *x*'s — usually used with *out*

**X** \'eks\ *adjective* (1950) *of a motion picture* **:** of such a nature that admission is denied to persons under a specified age (as 17) — used before the adoption of *NC-17*

**Xan·a·du** \'za-nə-,dü, -,dyü\ *noun* [*Xanadu,* locality in *Kubla Khan* (1798), poem by Samuel T. Coleridge] (1919) **:** an idyllic, exotic, or luxurious place

**xanth-** *or* **xantho-** *combining form* [New Latin, from Greek, from *xanthos*] **:** yellow ⟨*xanth*ene⟩

**xan·than gum** \'zan-thən-\ *noun* [*xanth-* (from New Latin *Xanthomonas,* genus name) + ³*-an*] (1964) **:** a polysaccharide that is produced by fermentation of carbohydrates by a gram-negative bacterium (*Xanthomonas campestris* of the family Pseudomonadaceae) and is a thickening and suspending agent used especially in pharmaceuticals and prepared foods — called also *xanthan*

**xan·thate** \'zan-,thāt\ *noun* (1831) **:** a salt or ester of any of various thio acids and especially $C_3H_6OS_2$

**xan·thene** \-,thēn\ *noun* (1898) **1 :** a white crystalline heterocyclic compound $C_{13}H_{10}O$; *also* **:** an isomer of this that is the parent of the colored forms of the xanthene dyes **2 :** any of various derivatives of xanthene

**xanthene dye** *noun* (1930) **:** any of various brilliant fluorescent yellow to pink to bluish red dyes that are characterized by the presence of the xanthene nucleus

**xan·thine** \'zan-,thēn\ *noun* [International Scientific Vocabulary] (1857) **:** a feebly basic compound $C_5H_4N_4O_2$ that occurs especially in animal or plant tissue, is derived from guanine and hypoxanthine, and yields uric acid on oxidation; *also* **:** any of various derivatives of this

**Xan·thip·pe** \zan-'thi-pē, -'ti-\ *or* **Xan·tip·pe** \-'ti-pē\ *noun* [Greek *Xanthippē,* shrewish wife of Socrates] (1691) **:** an ill-tempered woman

**xan·thone** \'zan-,thōn\ *noun* [International Scientific Vocabulary] (circa 1894) **:** a ketone $C_{13}H_8O_2$ that is the parent of several natural yellow pigments

**xan·tho·phyll** \'zan(t)-thə-,fil\ *noun* [French *xanthophylle,* from *xanth-* + *-phylle* -phyll] (1838) **:** any of several neutral yellow to orange carotenoid pigments that are oxygen derivatives of carotenes; *especially* **:** LUTEIN

**Xa·ve·ri·an Brother** \zā-'vir-ē-ən-, za-\ *noun* [*Xaverian* of Saint Francis Xavier] (1882) **:** a member of a Roman Catholic congregation of lay brothers founded by Theodore J. Ryken in Bruges, Belgium, in 1839 and dedicated to education

**x–ax·is** \'eks-,ak-səs\ *noun* (1886) **1 :** the axis in a plane Cartesian coordinate system parallel to which abscissas are measured **2 :** one of the three axes in a three-dimensional rectangular coordinate system

**X band** *noun* (circa 1946) **:** a segment of the superhigh-frequency radio spectrum that lies between 5.2 GHz and 10.9 GHz and is used especially for radars and for spacecraft communication

**X chromosome** *noun* (1911) **:** a sex chromosome that usually occurs paired in each female cell and single in each male cell in species in which the male typically has two unlike sex chromosomes — compare Y CHROMOSOME

**x–co·or·di·nate** \,eks-kō-'ord-nət; -'ȯr-d°n-ət, -də-,nāt\ *noun* (1927) **:** a coordinate whose value is determined by measuring parallel to an x-axis; *specifically* **:** ABSCISSA

**xe·bec** \'zē-,bek, zi-'\ *noun* [modification of French *chebec,* from Arabic *shabbāk*] (1756) **:** a usually 3-masted Mediterranean sailing ship with long overhanging bow and stern

**xen-** *or* **xeno-** *combining form* [Late Latin, from Greek, from *xenos* stranger, guest, host] **1 :** guest **:** foreigner ⟨*xeno*phobia⟩ **2 :** strange **:** foreign ⟨*xeno*lith⟩

**xe·nia** \'zē-nē-ə, -nyə\ *noun* [New Latin, from Greek, hospitality, from *xenos* host] (1899) **:** the effect of genes introduced by pollen especially on endosperm and embryo development

**xe·no·bi·ot·ic** \,ze-nō-bī-'ä-tik, ,zē-, -bē-\ *noun* (1965) **:** a chemical compound (as a drug, pesticide, or carcinogen) that is foreign to a living organism — **xenobiotic** *adjective*

**xe·no·di·ag·no·sis** \-,dī-ig-'nō-səs\ *noun* [New Latin] (circa 1929) **:** the detection of a parasite (as of humans) by feeding a suitable intermediate host (as an insect) on supposedly infected material (as blood) and later examining the host for the parasite — **xe·no·di·ag·nos·tic** \-'näs-tik\ *adjective*

**xe·no·ge·ne·ic** \-jə-'nē-ik\ *adjective* [*xen-* + *-geneic* (as in *isogeneic*)] (1961) **:** derived from, originating in, or being a member of another species

**xe·no·graft** \'ze-nə-,graft, 'zē-\ *noun* (1961) **:** HETEROGRAFT

**xe·no·lith** \'ze-n°l-,ith, 'zē-\ *noun* (1894) **:** a fragment of a rock included in another rock — **xe·no·lith·ic** \,ze-n°l-'i-thik, ,zē-\ *adjective*

**xe·non** \'zē-,nän, 'ze-\ *noun* [Greek, neuter of *xenos* strange] (1898) **:** a heavy, colorless, and relatively inert gaseous element that occurs in air as about one part in 20 million by volume and is used especially in thyratrons and specialized flashtubes — see ELEMENT table

**xe·no·phile** \'ze-nə-,fīl, 'zē-\ *noun* [International Scientific Vocabulary] (1948) **:** one attracted to foreign things (as styles or people)

**xe·no·phobe** \'ze-nə-,fōb, 'zē-\ *noun* [International Scientific Vocabulary] (1922) **:** one unduly fearful of what is foreign and especially of people of foreign origin — **xe·no·pho·bic** \,ze-nə-'fō-bik, ,zē-\ *adjective* — **xe·no·pho·bi·cal·ly** \-bi-k(ə-)lē\ *adverb*

**xe·no·pho·bia** \,ze-nə-'fō-bē-ə, ,zē-\ *noun* [New Latin] (1903) **:** fear and hatred of strangers or foreigners or of anything that is strange or foreign

**xe·no·tro·pic** \-'trä-pik, -trō-\ *adjective* (1973) **:** replicating or reproducing only in cells other than those of the host species ⟨*xenotropic* viruses⟩

**xer-** *or* **xero-** *combining form* [Late Latin, from Greek *xēr-, xēro-,* from *xēros*] **:** dry ⟨*xeric*⟩ ⟨*xerophyte*⟩

**xe·ric** \'zir-ik, 'zer-\ *adjective* (1926) **:** characterized by, relating to, or requiring only a small amount of moisture ⟨a *xeric* habitat⟩ ⟨a *xeric* plant⟩ — compare HYDRIC, MESIC

**Xeri·scape** \'zir-ə-,skāp, 'zer-\ *trademark* — used for a water-conserving method of landscaping in arid or semiarid climates

**xe·ro·der·ma pig·men·to·sum** \,zir-ə-'dər-mə-,pig-mən-'tō-səm, -,men-\ *noun* [New Latin, literally, pigmented dryness of the skin] (1884) **:** a genetic condition inherited as a recessive autosomal trait that is caused by a defect in mechanisms that repair DNA mutations (as those caused by ultraviolet light) and is characterized by the development of pigment abnormalities and multiple skin cancers in body areas exposed to the sun

**xe·rog·ra·phy** \zə-'rä-grə-fē\ *noun* [International Scientific Vocabulary] (1948) **1 :** a process for copying graphic matter by the action of light on an electrically charged photoconductive insulating surface in which the latent image is developed with a resinous powder **2 :** XERORADIOGRAPHY — **xe·ro·graph·ic** \,zir-ə-'gra-fik\ *adjective* — **xe·ro·graph·i·cal·ly** \-fi-k(ə-)lē\ *adverb*

**xe·roph·i·lous** \zə-'rä-fə-ləs\ *or* **xe·ro·phile** \'zir-ə-,fīl\ *adjective* (1863)

**:** thriving in or tolerant or characteristic of a xeric environment
— **xe·roph·i·ly** \zə-'rä-fə-lē\ *noun*

**xe·roph·thal·mia** \,zir-,äf-'thal-mē-ə, -,äp-'thal-\ *noun* [Late Latin, from Greek *xē- rophthalmia,* from *xēr-* xer- + *ophthalmia* ophthalmia] (circa 1656)
**:** a dry thickened lusterless condition of the eyeball resulting especially from a severe systemic deficiency of vitamin A
— **xe·roph·thal·mic** \-mik\ *adjective*

**xe·ro·phyte** \'zir-ə-,fīt\ *noun* (1897)
**:** a plant structurally adapted for life and growth with a limited water supply especially by means of mechanisms that limit transpiration or that provide for the storage of water
— **xe·ro·phyt·ic** \,zir-ə-'fi-tik\ *adjective*
— **xe·ro·phyt·ism** \'zir-ə-,fī-,ti-zəm\ *noun*

**xe·ro·ra·di·og·ra·phy** \,zir-ō-,rā-dē-'ä-grə-fē\ *noun* (1949)
**:** radiography used especially in mammographic screening for breast cancer that produces an image using X rays in a manner similar to the way an image is produced by light in xerography

**xe·ro·ther·mic** \,zir-ə-'thər-mik\ *adjective* (1904)
**1 :** characterized by heat and dryness
**2 :** adapted to or thriving in a hot dry environment

**xe·rox** \'zir-,äks, 'zē-,räks\ *transitive verb* [from *Xerox*] (1965)
**1 :** to copy on a Xerox copier
**2 :** to make (a copy) on a Xerox copier
**Xe·rox** \'zir-,äks, 'zē-,räks\ *trademark*
— used for a xerographic copier

**x-height** \'eks-,hīt, -,hītth\ *noun* (circa 1945)
**:** the height of a lowercase x used to represent the height of the main body of a lowercase letter

**Xho·sa** \'kō-sə, 'hō-, 'kō- *or with* ȯ *for* ō\ *noun* (1801)
**1 :** a member of a Bantu-speaking people of Eastern Cape province
**2 :** a Bantu language of the Xhosas

**xi** \'zī, 'ksī\ *noun, plural* **xis** [Greek *xei*] (1823)
**:** the 14th letter of the Greek alphabet — see ALPHABET table

**x-in·ter·cept** \'eks-'in-tər-,sept\ *noun* (circa 1939)
**:** the x-coordinate of a point where a line, curve, or surface intersects the x-axis

**xi·phi·ster·num** \,zī-fə-'stər-nəm, ,zi-\ *noun, plural* **-na** \-nə\ [New Latin, from Greek *xiphos* sword + New Latin *sternum*] (circa 1860)
**:** XIPHOID PROCESS

**xi·phoid** \'zī-,fȯid, 'zi-\ *noun* [New Latin *xiphoides,* from Greek *xiphoeidēs,* from *xiphos*] (circa 1860)
**:** XIPHOID PROCESS
— **xiphoid** *adjective*

**xiphoid process** *noun* (1873)
**:** the segment of the human sternum that is the third and closest to the feet

**x-ir·ra·di·a·tion** \,eks-i-,rā-dē-'ā-shən\ *noun, often capitalized* (1927)
**:** X-RADIATION 1

**Xmas** \'kris-məs *also* 'eks-məs\ *noun* [*X* (symbol for *Christ,* from the Greek letter chi (X), initial of *Christos* Christ) + *-mas* (in *Christmas*)] (1551)
**:** CHRISTMAS

**x-ra·di·a·tion** \,eks-,rā-dē-'ā-shən\ *noun, often capitalized* (1896)
**1 :** exposure to X rays
**2 :** radiation composed of X rays

**X-rated** \'eks-'rā-təd\ *adjective* (1970)
**1 :** having a rating of X; *broadly* **:** relating to

or characterized by explicit sexual material or activity 〈an *X-rated* book〉
**2 :** OBSCENE, VULGAR 〈an *X-rated* gesture〉

**Xray** \'eks-,rā\ (1943)
— a communications code word for the letter x ◆

**x-ray** \'eks-,rā\ *transitive verb, often capitalized* (1899)
**:** to examine, treat, or photograph with X rays

**X ray** \'eks-,rā\ *noun* (1896)
**1 :** any of the electromagnetic radiations of the same nature as visible radiation but having an extremely short wavelength of less than 100 angstroms that is produced by bombarding a metallic target with fast electrons in vacuum or by transition of atoms to lower energy states and that has the properties of ionizing a gas upon passage through it, of penetrating various thicknesses of all solids, of producing secondary radiations by impinging on material bodies, of acting on photographic films and plates as light does, and of causing fluorescent screens to emit light
**2 :** a photograph obtained by use of X rays
— **X-ray** *adjective*

**X-ray astronomy** *noun* (1963)
**:** astronomy dealing with investigations of celestial bodies by means of the X rays they emit

**X-ray diffraction** *noun* (1924)
**:** a scattering of X rays by the atoms of a crystal that produces an interference effect so that the diffraction pattern gives information on the structure of the crystal or the identity of a crystalline substance

**X-ray star** *noun* (1964)
**:** a luminous celestial object emitting a major portion of its radiation in the form of X rays
— called also *X-ray source*

**X-ray therapy** *noun* (1926)
**:** medical treatment (as of cancer) by controlled application of X rays

**X-ray tube** *noun* (1896)
**:** a vacuum tube in which a concentrated stream of electrons strikes a metal target and produces X rays

**x-sec·tion** \'krȯs-'sek-shən, -,sek-\ *noun* [*x,* rebus for *cross*] (1962)
**:** CROSS SECTION
— **x-sec·tion·al** \-shnəl, -shə-n°l\ *adjective*

**xu** \'sü\ *noun, plural* **xu** [Vietnamese, from French *sou* sou] (1948)
**1 :** a coin formerly minted by South Vietnam equivalent to the cent
**2** — see *dong* at MONEY table

**xyl-** *or* **xylo-** *combining form* [Latin, from Greek, from *xylon*]
**1 :** wood 〈*xylo*phone〉
**2 :** xylene 〈*xyl*idine〉

**xy·lan** \'zī-,lan\ *noun* [International Scientific Vocabulary] (circa 1894)
**:** a yellow gummy pentosan that yields xylose on hydrolysis and is abundantly present in plant cell walls and woody tissue

**xy·lem** \'zī-ləm, -,lem\ *noun* [German, from Greek *xylon*] (1873)
**:** a complex tissue in the vascular system of higher plants that consists of vessels, tracheids, or both usually together with wood fibers and parenchyma cells, functions chiefly in conduction of water and dissolved minerals but also in support and food storage, and typically constitutes the woody element (as of a plant stem) — compare PHLOEM

**xylem ray** *noun* (1875)
**:** a vascular ray or portion of a vascular ray located in xylem — called also *wood ray;* compare PHLOEM RAY

**xy·lene** \'zī-,lēn\ *noun* [International Scientific

Vocabulary] (1851)
**:** any of three toxic flammable oily isomeric aromatic hydrocarbons $C_8H_{10}$ that are dimethyl homologues of benzene and are usually obtained from petroleum or natural gas distillates; *also* **:** a mixture of xylenes and ethyl benzene used chiefly as a solvent

**xy·li·dine** \'zī-lə-,dēn\ *noun* [International Scientific Vocabulary] (1850)
**:** any or a mixture of six toxic liquid or low-melting crystalline isomeric amino derivatives $C_8H_{11}N$ of the xylenes used chiefly as intermediates for azo dyes and in organic synthesis

**xy·li·tol** \'zī-lə-,tȯl, -,tōl\ *noun* (1891)
**:** a crystalline alcohol $C_5H_{12}O_5$ that is a derivative of xylose, is obtained especially from birch bark, and is used as a sweetener

**xy·log·ra·phy** \zī-'lä-grə-fē\ *noun* [French *xylographie,* from *xyl-* + *-graphie* -graphy] (1816)
**:** the art of making engravings on wood especially for printing
— **xy·lo·graph** \'zī-lə-,graf\ *noun*
— **xy·log·ra·pher** \zī-'lä-grə-fər\ *noun*
— **xy·lo·graph·ic** \,zī-lə-'gra-fik\ *also* **xy·lo·graph·i·cal** \-fi-kəl\ *adjective*

**xy·lol** \'zī-,lȯl, -,lōl\ *noun* [International Scientific Vocabulary] (1851)
**:** XYLENE

**xy·loph·a·gous** \zī-'lä-fə-gəs\ *adjective* [Greek *xylophagos,* from *xyl-* + *-phagos* -phagous] (1739)
**:** feeding on or in wood

**xy·lo·phone** \'zī-lə-,fōn *also* 'zi-\ *noun* (1866)
**:** a percussion instrument consisting of a series of wooden bars graduated in length to produce the musical scale, supported on belts of straw or felt, and sounded by striking with two small wooden hammers
— **xy·lo·phon·ist** \-,fō-nist\ *noun*

xylophone

**xy·lose** \'zī-,lōs, -,lōz\ *noun* [International Scientific Vocabulary] (circa 1894)
**:** a crystalline aldose sugar $C_5H_{10}O_5$ that is not fermentable with ordinary yeasts and occurs especially as a constituent of xylans from which it is obtained by hydrolysis

◇ **WORD HISTORY**
**Xray** On November 8, 1895, Wilhelm Conrad Röntgen was conducting an experimental investigation in Würzburg, Germany, of the properties of cathode rays. He noticed that a fluorescent surface in the neighborhood of a cathode-ray tube would become luminous even if shielded from the direct light of the tube. A thick metal object placed between the tube and the affected surface impaired the fluorescence and cast a dark shadow. An object made of a less dense substance such as wood cast only a weak shadow. Röntgen's explanation for this phenomenon was that the tube produced some type of invisible radiation which could pass through substances that blocked ordinary visible light. Because he did not know the nature of this radiation he had discovered, he named it *X-Strahl,* based on the mathematical use of *x* to designate an unknown quantity. His German name was translated into English as *X ray.*

# Y

**Y** *is the twenty-fifth letter of the English alphabet. It comes from the Latin, which borrowed it from the Greek* upsilon *and used it as a vowel in the writing of Greek words. In Greek,* Y *was an eastern and classical form of the* V *which had been borrowed earlier from the western Greek alphabet by Latin. In English,* Y *is used as both a consonant and a vowel. At the beginning of a word or syllable, it is usually pronounced as a consonant with slight or no audible friction (as in* yes*); in the middle or at the end of a syllable, it is usually a vowel, with various values (as in* myth, happy, my, myrrh, *and* martyr*). In certain archaic forms such as the* ye *of "ye olde tavern,"* Y *represents an Old and Middle English character called* thorn *and is pronounced like* th. *This use caused confusion in later English speakers, who interpreted words like* ye *as though pronounced with the sound of consonant* y. *Actually, such words were originally pronounced with the* th *sound.*

**y** \'wī\ *noun, plural* **y's** *or* **ys** \'wīz\ *often capitalized, often attributive* (before 12th century) **1 a** : the 25th letter of the English alphabet **b** : a graphic representation of this letter **c** : a speech counterpart of orthographic *y* **2** : a graphic device for reproducing the letter *y* **3** : one designated *y* especially as the 25th in order or class or the second in order or class when *x* is made the first **4** : something shaped like the letter Y

**Y** \'wī\ *noun* (circa 1915)
: YMCA, YWCA

**¹-y** *also* **-ey** \ē; *in some dialects, especially British, Southern, & New England, often* i *but not shown at individual entries*\ *adjective suffix* [Middle English, from Old English *-ig*; akin to Old High German *-īg* -y, Latin *-icus*, Greek *-ikos*, Sanskrit *-ika*] **1 a** : characterized by : full of ⟨blossomy⟩ ⟨dirty⟩ ⟨muddy⟩ ⟨clayey⟩ **b** : having the character of : composed of ⟨icy⟩ ⟨waxy⟩ **c** : like : like that of ⟨homey⟩ ⟨wintry⟩ — often with a disparaging connotation ⟨stagy⟩ **2 a** : tending or inclined to ⟨sleepy⟩ ⟨chatty⟩ **b** : giving occasion for (specified) action ⟨teary⟩ **c** : performing (specified) action ⟨curly⟩

**²-y** \same\ *noun suffix, plural* **-ies** [Middle English *-ie*, from Old French, from Latin *-ia*, from Greek *-ia, -eia*] **1** : state : condition : quality ⟨beggary⟩ **2** : activity, place of business, or goods dealt with ⟨chandlery⟩ ⟨laundry⟩ **3** : whole body or group ⟨soldiery⟩

**³-y** *noun suffix, plural* **-ies** [Middle English *-ie*, from Anglo-French, from Latin *-ium*] : instance of a (specified) action ⟨entreaty⟩ ⟨inquiry⟩

**⁴-y** — see -IE

**yab·ber** \'ya-bər\ *noun* [probably modification of Wuywurung (Australian aboriginal language of the Melbourne area) *yaba* speak] (1855)
*Australian* : TALK, JABBER ⟨all *yabber* and chatter ceased around the campfires —Francis Birtles⟩
— **yabber** *intransitive verb*

**¹yacht** \'yät\ *noun* [obsolete Dutch *jaght*, from Middle Low German *jacht*, short for *jacht-schip*, literally, hunting ship] (1557)
: any of various recreational watercraft: as **a** : a sailboat used for racing **b** : a large usually motor-driven craft used for pleasure cruising

**²yacht** *intransitive verb* (1836)
: to race or cruise in a yacht

**yacht club** *noun* (1834)
: a club organized to promote and regulate yachting and boating

**yacht·ing** *noun* (1836)

: the action, fact, or pastime of racing or cruising in a yacht

**yachts·man** \'yäts-mən\ *noun* (1862)
: a person who owns or sails a yacht

**YAG** \'yag\ *noun* [yttrium aluminum garnet] (1964)
: a synthetic yttrium aluminum garnet of marked hardness and high refractive index that is used especially as a gemstone and in laser technology

**ya·gi** \'yä-gē, 'ya-\ *noun* [Hidetsugu Yagi (born 1886) Japanese engineer] (1943)
: a highly directional and selective shortwave antenna consisting of a horizontal conductor of one or two dipoles connected with the receiver or transmitter and of a set of nearly equal insulated dipoles parallel to and on a level with the horizontal conductor

**ya·hoo** \'yä-(ˌ)hü, 'yä-\ *noun, plural* **yahoos** (1726)
**1** *capitalized* : a member of a race of brutes in Swift's *Gulliver's Travels* who have the form and all the vices of humans
**2** : a boorish, crass, or stupid person
— **ya·hoo·ism** \-ˌi-zəm\ *noun*

**Yah·weh** \'yä-(ˌ)wā, -(ˌ)vā\ *also* **Yah·veh** \-(ˌ)vā\ *noun* [Hebrew *Yahweh*] (1869)
: GOD 1a — used especially by the Hebrews; compare TETRAGRAMMATON

**Yah·wism** \-ˌwi-zəm, -ˌvi-\ *noun* (1867)
: the worship of Yahweh among the ancient Hebrews

**Yah·wis·tic** \yä-'wis-tik, -'vis-\ *adjective* (1874)
**1** : characterized by the use of *Yahweh* as the name of God
**2** : of or relating to Yahwism

**¹yak** \'yak\ *noun, plural* **yaks** *also* **yak** [Tibetan *gyagk*] (1795)
: a large long-haired wild or domesticated ox (*Bos grunniens* synonym *B. mutus*) of Tibet and adjacent elevated parts of central Asia

**²yak** \'yäk, 'yak\ *noun* [imitative] (1948)
**1** *slang* : LAUGH
**2** *slang* : JOKE, GAG

**³yak** *also* **yack** *intransitive verb* **yakked** *also* **yacked**; **yak·king** *also* **yack·ing** [probably imitative] (1949)
: to talk persistently : CHATTER

**⁴yak** *also* **yack** \'yak\ *noun* (1950)
: persistent or voluble talk

**Yak·i·ma** \'ya-kə-ˌmȯ\ *noun, plural* **Yakima** *or* **Yakimas** (1838)
**1** : a member of a group of Shahaptian peoples of the lower Yakima River valley, south central Washington
**2** : the language of the Yakima people

**ya·ki·to·ri** \ˌyä-ki-'tȯr-ē\ *noun* [Japanese, grilled chicken, from *yaki* broil, roast + *tori* bird] (1962)
: bite-sized marinated pieces of beef, seafood, or chicken on skewers

**y'all** \'yȯl\ *variant of* YOU-ALL

**yam** \'yam\ *noun* [earlier *iname*, from Portuguese *inhame* & Spanish *ñame*, of African origin; akin to Fulani *nyami* to eat] (1657)
**1** : the edible starchy tuberous root of various plants (genus *Dioscorea* of the family Dioscoreaceae) used as a staple food in tropical areas; *also* : a plant producing yams
**2** : a moist-fleshed and usually orange-fleshed sweet potato

**ya·men** \'yä-mən\ *noun* [Chinese (Beijing) *yámen*] (1747)
: the headquarters or residence of a Chinese government official or department

**yam·mer** \'ya-mər\ *intransitive verb* **yammered**; **yam·mer·ing** \'ya-mə-riŋ, 'yam-riŋ\ [Middle English *yameren*, alteration of *yomeren* to murmur, be sad, from Old English *gēomrian*; akin to Old High German *jāmaron* to be sad] (15th century)
**1 a** : to utter repeated cries of distress or sorrow **b** : WHIMPER
**2** : to utter persistent complaints : WHINE
**3** : to talk persistently or volubly and often loudly ⟨purists who *yammer* for censorship —D. W. Maurer⟩
— **yammer** *noun*

**yang** \'yäŋ, 'yaŋ\ *noun* [Chinese (Beijing) *yáng*] (1671)
: the masculine active principle in nature that in Chinese cosmology is exhibited in light, heat, or dryness and that combines with yin to produce all that comes to be

**¹yank** \'yaŋk\ *noun* [origin unknown] (circa 1864)
: a strong sudden pull : JERK

**²yank** (1822)
*intransitive verb*
: to pull on something with a quick vigorous movement
*transitive verb*
**1** : to pull or extract with a quick vigorous movement
**2** : to remove in or as if in an abrupt manner ⟨*yanked* the story from the evening edition⟩

**Yank** \'yaŋk\ *noun* (1778)
: YANKEE

◇ **WORD HISTORY**
**yacht** In the 16th century the Dutch developed a kind of shallow-draft, fast-moving ship for use in coastal waters and river estuaries. These vessels were called by the name *jaght*, short for Middle Low German *jachtschip* or Middle Dutch *jageschip*, literally "hunting ship" or "pursuit ship," though *jacht* may simply imply that the boat was a speedy one. The name appears in 16th and 17th century English documents in a variety of forms, such as *yoath* and *yaught*. The form *jacht* or *yacht* became widespread after 1660, when King Charles II, on his return from exile on the Continent, was given such a craft, dubbed the *Mary*, by the Dutch East India Company. The king chose to use the boat for excursions and racing, and the word *yacht* became attached to other vessels used for the same purposes, the earliest being copied after the design of the *Mary*. Today the word *yacht* is applied to a wide variety of luxuriously outfitted craft—powerboats as well as sailboats—that are designed for pleasure cruising.

yak

**¹Yan·kee** \'yaŋ-kē\ *noun* [origin unknown] (1758)
**1 a :** a native or inhabitant of New England **b** **:** a native or inhabitant of the northern U.S.
**2 :** a native or inhabitant of the U.S.
— **Yan·kee·dom** \-kē-dəm\ *noun*
— **Yan·kee·ism** \-kē-,i-zəm\ *noun*
**²Yankee** (1952)
— a communications code word for the letter *y*

**Yan·kee–Doo·dle** \,yaŋ-kē-'dü-d°l\ *noun* [*Yankee Doodle*, popular song during the American Revolution] (1770)
**:** YANKEE

**yan·qui** \'yän-kē\ *noun, often capitalized* [Spanish, from English ¹*Yankee*] (1928)
**:** a citizen of the U.S. as distinguished from a Latin American

**yan·tra** \'yən-trə, 'yan-, 'yän-\ *noun* [Sanskrit] (1877)
**:** a geometrical diagram used like an icon usually in meditation

**¹yap** \'yap\ *intransitive verb* **yapped; yap·ping** [imitative] (1668)
**1 :** to bark snappishly **:** YELP
**2 :** to talk in a shrill insistent way **:** CHATTER
— **yap·per** *noun*
**²yap** *noun* (1826)
**1 a :** a quick sharp bark **:** YELP **b :** shrill insistent talk **:** CHATTER
**2 :** an unsophisticated, ignorant, or uncouth person **:** BUMPKIN
**3** *slang* **:** MOUTH
**Ya·qui** \'yä-kē\ *noun* (1861)
**1 :** a member of an American Indian people of Sonora, Mexico
**2 :** the Uto-Aztecan language of the Yaqui people

**Yar·bor·ough** \'yär-,bər-ə, -,bə-rə, -b(ə-)rə\ *noun* [Charles Anderson Worsley, 2d Earl of *Yarborough* (died 1897) English nobleman said to have bet a thousand to one against the dealing of such a hand] (1900)
**:** a hand in bridge or whist containing no ace and no card higher than a nine

**¹yard** \'yärd\ *noun* [Middle English, from Old English *geard* enclosure, yard; akin to Old High German *gart* enclosure, Latin *hortus* garden] (before 12th century)
**1 a :** a small usually walled and often paved area open to the sky and adjacent to a building **:** COURT **b :** the grounds of a building or group of buildings
**2 :** the grounds immediately surrounding a house that are usually covered with grass
**3 a :** an enclosure for livestock (as poultry) **b** (1) **:** an area with its buildings and facilities set aside for a particular business or activity (2) **:** an assembly or storage area **c :** a system of tracks for storage and maintenance of cars and making up trains
**4 :** a locality in a forest where deer herd in winter
**²yard** *adjective* (15th century)
**1 :** of, relating to, or employed in the yard surrounding a building ⟨*yard* light⟩
**2 :** of, relating to, or employed in a railroad yard ⟨a *yard* engine⟩
**³yard** (1758)
*transitive verb*
**1 :** to drive into or confine in a restricted area **:** HERD, PEN
**2 :** to deliver to or store in a yard
*intransitive verb*
**:** to congregate in or as if in a yard
**⁴yard** *noun* [Middle English *yarde*, from Old English *gierd* twig, measure, yard; akin to Old High German *gart* stick, Latin *hasta* spear] (before 12th century)
**1 :** any of various units of measure: as **a :** a unit of length equal in the U.S. to 0.9144 meter — see WEIGHT table **b :** a unit of volume equal to a cubic yard
**2 a :** a great length or quantity ⟨remembered *yards* of facts and figures⟩ **b** *slang* **:** one hundred dollars

**3 :** a long spar tapered toward the ends to support and spread the head of a square sail, lateen, or lugsail
**4 :** a slender horn-shaped glass about three feet tall; *also* **:** the amount it contains ⟨a *yard* of ale⟩
— **the whole nine yards :** all of a related set of circumstances, conditions, or details ⟨who could learn the most about making records, about electronics and engineering, *the whole nine yards* —Stephen Stills⟩ — sometimes used adverbially with *go* to indicate an all-out effort

**¹yard·age** \'yär-dij\ *noun* [¹*yard*] (1867)
**1 :** the use of a livestock enclosure for animals in transit provided by a railroad at a station
**2 :** a charge made by a railroad for the use of a livestock enclosure
**²yardage** *noun* [⁴*yard*] (1900)
**1 a :** an aggregate number of yards **b :** the length, extent, or volume of something as measured in yards
**2 :** YARD GOODS

**yard·arm** \'yärd-,ärm\ *noun* (1553)
**:** either end of the yard of a square-rigged ship

**yard·bird** \-,bərd\ *noun* [¹*yard*] (circa 1941)
**1 :** a soldier assigned to a menial task or restricted to a limited area as a disciplinary measure
**2 :** an untrained or inept enlisted man

**yard goods** *noun plural* (1905)
**:** fabrics sold by the yard **:** PIECE GOODS

**yard grass** *noun* [¹*yard*] (1822)
**:** a coarse annual grass (*Eleusine indica*) with digitate spikes that is widely distributed as a weed — called also *goosegrass*

**yard line** *noun* (1949)
**:** any of a series of marked or imaginary lines one yard apart on a football field that are parallel to the goal lines and that indicate the distance to the nearest goal line

**yard–long bean** \'yärd-,lȯŋ-\ *noun* (1926)
**:** the edible 1- to 3-foot (0.3- to 0.9- meter) long thin stringless fruit of a plant of a subspecies (*Vigna unguiculata sesquipedalis*) of the cowpea; *also* **:** the plant

**yard·man** \'yärd-mən, -,man\ *noun* (circa 1825)
**1 :** a person employed to do outdoor work (as mowing lawns)
**2 :** a person who works in the yard of a commercial establishment; *especially* **:** one who supervises the handling of building materials in a lumberyard
**3 :** a railroad hand employed in yard service

**yard·mas·ter** \-,mas-tər\ *noun* (1864)
**:** the person in charge of operations in a railroad yard

**yard sale** *noun* (1972)
**:** GARAGE SALE

**yard·stick** \'yärd-,stik\ *noun* (1816)
**1 a :** a graduated measuring stick three feet (0.9144 meter) long **b :** a standard basis of calculation
**2 :** a standard for making a critical judgment **:** CRITERION
**synonym** see STANDARD

**yare** \'yar, 'yer, 'yär\ *adjective* [Middle English, from Old English *gearu*; akin to Old High German *garo* ready] (before 12th century)
**1** *archaic* **:** set for action **:** READY
**2** *or* **yar** \'yär\ **a :** characterized by speed and agility **:** NIMBLE, LIVELY **b :** HANDY 1c, MANEUVERABLE
— **yare** *adverb, archaic*
— **yare·ly** *adverb, archaic*

**yar·mul·ke** *also* **yar·mel·ke** \'yä-mə-kə, 'yär-mə(l)-kə\ *noun* [Yiddish *yarmlke*, from Polish *jarmułka* & Ukrainian *yarmulka* skullcap, of Turkic origin; akin to Turkish *yağmurluk* rainwear] (1903)
**:** a skullcap worn especially by Orthodox and Conservative Jewish males in the synagogue and the home

**¹yarn** \'yärn\ *noun* [Middle English, from Old English *gearn;* akin to Old High German *garn* yarn, Greek *chordē* string, Latin *hernia* rupture, Sanskrit *hira* band] (before 12th century)
**1 a :** a continuous often plied strand composed of either natural or man-made fibers or filaments and used in weaving and knitting to form cloth **b :** a similar strand of another material (as metal, glass, or plastic)
**2 :** a narrative of adventures; *especially* **:** a tall tale
**²yarn** *intransitive verb* (1812)
**:** to tell a yarn
— **yarn·er** *noun*

**yarn–dye** \'yärn-,dī\ *transitive verb* (1885)
**:** to dye before weaving or knitting

**yar·row** \'yar-(,)ō\ *noun* [Middle English *yarowe*, from Old English *gearwe;* akin to Old High German *garwa* yarrow] (before 12th century)
**:** a widely naturalized strong-scented Eurasian composite herb (*Achillea millefolium*) with finely dissected leaves and small usually white corymbose flowers; *also* **:** any of several congeneric plants

**yash·mak** *also* **yas·mak** \'yash-,mak, 'yas-\ *noun* [Turkish *yaşmak*] (1844)
**:** a veil worn by Muslim women that is wrapped around the upper and lower parts of the face so that only the eyes remain exposed to public view

**yat·a·ghan** \'ya-tə-,gan, 'ya-ti-gən\ *noun* [Turkish *yatağan*] (1819)
**:** a long knife or short saber that lacks a guard for the hand at the juncture of blade and hilt and that usually has a double curve to the edge and a nearly straight back

**yauld** \'yȯl(d)\ *adjective* [origin unknown] (1786)
*chiefly Scottish* **:** VIGOROUS, ENERGETIC

**yau·pon** \'yȯ-,pän *also* 'yō-, 'yȯ-\ *noun* [Catawba *yápą*, from *yą-* tree + *pą* leaf] (1709)
**:** a holly (*Ilex vomitoria*) of the southeastern U.S. that has smooth elliptical leaves with emetic and purgative properties

**yau·tia** \'yaủ-tē-ə\ *noun* [American Spanish *yautía*, from Taino] (1899)
**:** any of several aroid plants (genus *Xanthosoma* and especially *X. sagittifolium*) chiefly of tropical America with starchy edible shaggy brown tubers that are cooked and eaten like yams or potatoes; *especially* **:** one of these tubers

**¹yaw** \'yȯ\ *noun* [origin unknown] (1546)
**1 :** the action of yawing; *especially* **:** a side to side movement
**2 :** the extent of the movement in yawing
**²yaw** *intransitive verb* (1586)
**1 a** *of a ship* **:** to deviate erratically from a course (as when struck by a heavy sea); *especially* **:** to move from side to side **b** *of an airplane, spacecraft, or projectile* **:** to turn by angular motion about the vertical axis
**2 :** ALTERNATE ⟨restlessly *yawing* between apparent extremes —Martin Kasindorf⟩

**yawl** \'yȯl\ *noun* [Low German *jolle*] (1670)
**1 :** a ship's small boat **:** JOLLY BOAT
**2 :** a fore-and-aft rigged sailboat carrying a mainsail and one or more jibs with a mizzenmast far aft

yawl 2

**¹yawn** \\'yȯn, 'yän\ *verb* [Middle English *yenen, yanen,* from Old English *ginian;* akin to Old High German *ginēn* to yawn, Latin *hiare,* Greek *chainein*] (before 12th century)
*intransitive verb*
**1 :** to open wide **:** GAPE
**2 :** to open the mouth wide usually as an involuntary reaction to fatigue or boredom
*transitive verb*
**1 :** to utter with a yawn
**2 :** to accomplish with or impel by yawns ⟨his grandchildren *yawned* him to bed —L. L. King⟩
**²yawn** *noun* (1602)
**1 :** GAP, CAVITY
**2 :** a deep usually involuntary intake of breath through the wide open mouth often as an involuntary reaction to fatigue or boredom; *also* **:** a reaction resembling a yawn ⟨a . . . success at the box office but drew only *yawns* from critics —*Current Biography*⟩
**3 :** ⁵BORE
**yawn·er** *noun* (1687)
**1 :** one that yawns
**2 :** something that causes boredom ⟨the show was a real *yawner*⟩
**yawn·ing** *adjective* (before 12th century)
**1 :** wide open **:** CAVERNOUS ⟨a *yawning* hole⟩ ⟨a dreadful, *yawning* gap of . . . weeks —*Times Educational Supplement*⟩
**2 :** showing fatigue or boredom by yawns ⟨a *yawning* audience⟩
**— yawn·ing·ly** \\'yȯ-niŋ-lē\ *adverb*
**¹yawp** *or* **yaup** \\'yȯp\ *intransitive verb* [Middle English *yolpen*] (14th century)
**1 :** to make a raucous noise **:** SQUAWK
**2 :** CLAMOR, COMPLAIN
**— yawp·er** *noun*
**²yawp** *also* **yaup** *noun* (1824)
**1 :** a raucous noise **:** SQUAWK
**2 :** something suggestive of a raucous noise; *specifically* **:** rough vigorous language
**yawp·ing** *noun* (1876)
**:** a strident utterance
**yaws** \\'yȯz\ *noun plural but singular or plural in construction* [probably from an English-based creole of the Caribbean] (1679)
**:** an infectious contagious tropical disease caused by a spirochete (*Treponema pertenue*) closely resembling the causative agent of syphilis and marked by ulcerating lesions with later bone involvement — called also *frambesia*
**y-ax·is** \\'wī-ˌak-səs\ *noun* (1875)
**1 :** the axis of a plane Cartesian coordinate system parallel to which ordinates are measured
**2 :** one of the three axes in a three-dimensional rectangular coordinate system
**Y chromosome** *noun* (1911)
**:** a sex chromosome that is characteristic of male cells in species in which the male typically has two unlike sex chromosomes — compare X CHROMOSOME
**yclept** *or* **ycleped** [Middle English, from Old English *geclipod,* past participle of *clipian* to cry out, name] *past participle of* CLEPE
**y-co·or·di·nate** \\'wī-kō-ˌȯrd-nət, -ˈȯr-d³n-ət, -də-ˌnāt\ *noun* (1927)
**:** a coordinate whose value is determined by measuring parallel to a y-axis; *specifically* **:** ORDINATE
**¹ye** \\'yē\ *pronoun* [Middle English, from Old English *gē;* akin to Old High German *ir* you — more at YOU] (before 12th century)
**:** YOU 1 — used originally only as a plural pronoun of the second person in the subjective case and now used especially in ecclesiastical or literary language and in various English dialects
***word history*** see YOU
**²ye** \ˌyē, yə; *originally same as* ¹THE\ *definite article* [alteration of Middle English *þe* the, from Old English *þē;* from the use of the letter

y by printers and scribes of late Middle English to represent þ (*th*) of earlier manuscripts] (1551)
*archaic* **:** THE ⟨*Ye* Olde Gifte Shoppe⟩
**¹yea** \\'yā\ *adverb* [Middle English *ye, ya,* from Old English *gēa;* akin to Old High German *jā* yes] (before 12th century)
**1 :** YES — used in oral voting
**2 :** more than this **:** not only so but — used as a function word to introduce a more explicit or emphatic phrase ⟨yet the impression, *yea* the evidence, is inescapable —J. G. Harrison⟩
**²yea** *noun* (13th century)
**1 :** AFFIRMATION, ASSENT
**2 a :** an affirmative vote **b :** a person casting a yea vote
**yeah** \\'ye-ə, 'yeᵈ, 'ya-ə\ *adverb* [by alteration] (1902)
**:** YES
**yean** \\'yēn, ēn\ *intransitive verb* [Middle English *yenen,* from (assumed) Old English *geēanian,* from Old English *ge-,* perfective prefix + *ēanian* to yean; akin to Latin *agnus* lamb, Greek *amnos*] (1548)
**:** to bring forth young — used of a sheep or goat
**yean·ling** \-liŋ, -lən\ *noun* (1637)
**:** LAMB, KID 1a
**year** \\'yir\ *noun* [Middle English *yere,* from Old English *gēar;* akin to Old High German *jār* year, Greek *hōros* year, *hōra* season, hour] (before 12th century)
**1 a :** the period of about 365¼ solar days required for one revolution of the earth around the sun **b :** the time required for the apparent sun to return to an arbitrary fixed or moving reference point in the sky **c :** the time in which a planet completes a revolution about the sun ⟨a year of Jupiter⟩
**2 a :** a cycle in the Gregorian calendar of 365 or 366 days divided into 12 months beginning with January and ending with December **b :** a period of time equal to one year of the Gregorian calendar but beginning at a different time
**3 :** a calendar year specified usually by a number ⟨died in the *year* 1900⟩
**4** *plural* **:** a time or era having a special significance ⟨their glory *years*⟩
**5 a :** 12 months that constitute a measure of age or duration ⟨her 21st *year*⟩ — often used in combination ⟨a *year*-old child⟩ **b** *plural* **:** AGE ⟨an adult in *years* but a child in understanding⟩; *also* **:** the final stage of the normal life span
**6 :** a period of time (as the usually nine-month period in which a school is in session) other than a calendar year
**year·book** \-ˌbůk\ *noun* (1710)
**1 :** a book published yearly as a report or summary of statistics or facts **:** ANNUAL
**2 :** a school publication that is compiled usually by a graduating class and that serves as a record of the year's activities
**¹year–end** \\'yir-ˈend\ *noun* (1872)
**:** the end of usually the fiscal year
**²year–end** *adjective* (1899)
**:** made, occurring, or existing at the year-end ⟨a *year-end* report⟩
**year·ling** \\'yir-liŋ, 'yər-lən\ *noun* (15th century)
**:** one that is a year old: as **a :** an animal one year old or in the second year of its age **b :** a racehorse between January 1st of the year after the year in which it was foaled and the next January 1st
**— yearling** *adjective*
**year·long** \\'yir-ˈlȯŋ\ *adjective* (1813)
**:** lasting through a year
**¹year·ly** \\'yir-lē\ *adjective* (before 12th century)
**1 :** reckoned by the year
**2 :** occurring, appearing, made, done, or acted upon every year or once a year **:** ANNUAL
**²yearly** *adverb* (before 12th century)
**:** every year **:** ANNUALLY
**Yearly Meeting** *noun* (1688)

**:** an organization uniting several Quarterly Meetings of the Society of Friends
**yearn** \\'yərn\ *intransitive verb* [Middle English *yernen,* from Old English *giernan;* akin to Old High German *gerōn* to desire, Latin *hortari* to urge, encourage, Greek *chairein* to rejoice] (before 12th century)
**1 :** to long persistently, wistfully, or sadly
**2 :** to feel tenderness or compassion
***synonym*** see LONG
**— yearn·er** *noun*
**— yearn·ing·ly** \\'yər-niŋ-lē\ *adverb*
**yearn·ing** *noun* (before 12th century)
**:** a tender or urgent longing
**year of grace** (14th century)
**:** a calendar year of the Christian era ⟨the *year of grace* 1993⟩
**year–round** \\'yir-ˈraůnd\ *adjective* (1924)
**:** occurring, effective, employed, staying, or operating for the full year **:** not seasonal ⟨a *year-round* resort⟩
**— year–round** *adverb*
**— year–round·er** \-ˈraůn-dər\ *noun*
**yea–say·er** \\'yā-ˌsā-ər, -ˌse(-ə)r\ *noun* (1920)
**1 :** one whose attitude is that of confident affirmation
**2 :** YES-MAN
**¹yeast** \\'yēst, *especially Southern & Midland* 'ēst\ *noun* [Middle English *yest,* from Old English *gist;* akin to Old High German *jesen, gesen* to ferment, Greek *zein* to boil] (before 12th century)
**1 a :** a yellowish surface froth or sediment that occurs especially in saccharine liquids (as fruit juices) in which it promotes alcoholic fermentation, consists largely of cells of a fungus (family Saccharomycetaceae), and is used especially in the making of alcoholic liquors and as a leaven in baking **b :** a commercial product containing yeast plants in a moist or dry medium **c (1) :** a minute fungus (especially *Saccharomyces cerevisiae*) that is present and functionally active in yeast, usually has little or no mycelium, and reproduces by budding **(2) :** any of various similar fungi (especially orders Endomycetales and Moniliales)
**2** *archaic* **:** the foam or spume of waves
**3 :** something that causes ferment or activity ⟨were all seething with the *yeast* of revolt —J. F. Dobie⟩
**²yeast** *intransitive verb* (1819)
**:** FERMENT, FROTH
**yeasty** \\'yē-stē, 'ē-stē\ *adjective* **yeast·i·er; -est** (1598)
**1 :** of, relating to, or resembling yeast
**2 a :** IMMATURE, UNSETTLED **b :** marked by change **c :** full of vitality **d :** FRIVOLOUS 1a, 2
**— yeast·i·ness** \-stē-nəs\ *noun*
**yech** *or* **yecch** \\'yək, 'yə̱k, 'yek, 'ye̱k\ *interjection* (1969)
**—** used to express rejection or disgust
**yegg** \\'yeg, 'yäg\ *noun* [origin unknown] (1903)
**:** SAFECRACKER; *also* **:** ROBBER
**¹yell** \\'yel\ *verb* [Middle English, from Old English *giellan;* akin to Old High German *gellan* to yell, Old English *galan* to sing] (before 12th century)
*intransitive verb*
**1 :** to utter a loud cry, scream, or shout
**2 :** to give a cheer usually in unison
*transitive verb*
**:** to utter or declare with or as if with a yell **:** SHOUT
**— yell·er** *noun*
**²yell** *noun* (14th century)
**1 :** SCREAM, SHOUT
**2 :** a usually rhythmic cheer used especially in schools or colleges to encourage athletic teams
**¹yel·low** \\'ye-(ˌ)lō, *dialect* 'ye-lər *or* 'ya-\ *adjective* [Middle English *yelwe, yelow,* from Old English *geolu;* akin to Old High German *gelo* yellow, Latin *helvus* light bay, Greek *chlōros* greenish yellow, Sanskrit *hari* yellowish] (before 12th century)

**1 a :** of the color yellow **b :** become yellowish through age, disease, or discoloration **:** SALLOW **c :** having a yellow or light brown complexion or skin
**2 a :** featuring sensational or scandalous items or ordinary news sensationally distorted ⟨*yellow* journalism⟩ **b :** MEAN, COWARDLY
— **yel·low·ish** \'ye-lə-wish\ *adjective*
**²yellow** *noun* (before 12th century)
**1 :** something yellow or marked by a yellow color: as **a :** a person having yellow or light brown skin **b :** the yolk of an egg
**2 a :** a color whose hue resembles that of ripe lemons or sunflowers or is that of the portion of the spectrum lying between green and orange **b :** a pigment or dye that colors yellow
**3** *plural* **:** JAUNDICE
**4** *plural but singular in construction* **:** any of several plant diseases caused especially by mycoplasma-like organisms and marked by yellowing of the foliage and stunting
**³yellow** (1598)
*transitive verb*
**:** to make yellow **:** give a yellow tinge or color to ⟨*yellowed* by time⟩
*intransitive verb*
**:** to become or turn yellow
**yellow bile** *noun* (1881)
**:** a humor believed in medieval physiology to be secreted by the liver and to cause irascibility
**yellow birch** *noun* (1787)
**:** a North American birch (*Betula alleghaniensis* synonym *B. lutea*) with thin lustrous gray or yellow bark forming plates with ragged edges in older trees; *also* **:** its strong hard dark brown to reddish brown wood
**yel·low–dog** \,ye-lō-'dȯg, -lə-'dȯg\ *adjective* (1880)
**1 :** MEAN, CONTEMPTIBLE
**2 :** of or relating to opposition to trade unionism or a labor union
**yellow–dog contract** *noun* (1920)
**:** an employment contract in which a worker disavows membership in and agrees not to join a labor union in order to get a job
**yellow dwarf** *noun* (1928)
**:** any of several virus diseases especially of cereal grasses (as oats and barley) characterized by yellowing and stunting
**yellow fever** *noun* (1739)
**:** an acute destructive infectious disease of warm regions marked by sudden onset, prostration, fever, albuminuria, jaundice, and often hemorrhage and caused by a virus transmitted by the yellow-fever mosquito
**yellow–fever mosquito** *noun* (1905)
**:** a small dark-colored mosquito (*Aedes aegypti*) that is the usual vector of yellow fever
**yel·low·fin tuna** \'ye-lō-,fin-, 'ye-lə-\ *noun* (1922)
**:** a rather small and nearly cosmopolitan tuna (*Thunnus albacares*) with yellowish fins — called also *yellowfin*
**yellow–green alga** *noun* (1930)
**:** any of a class (Xanthophyceae of the division Chrysophyta) of algae with the chlorophyll masked by brown or yellow pigment
**yel·low·ham·mer** \'ye-lō-,ha-mər, 'ye-lə-\ *noun* [alteration of earlier *yelambre,* from (assumed) Middle English *yelwambre,* from Middle English *yelwe* yellow + (assumed) Middle English *ambre* yellowhammer, from Old English *amore*; akin to Old High German *amaro* yellowhammer, *amari* emmer] (1556)
**1 :** a common Palearctic finch (*Emberiza citrinella*) having the male largely bright yellow — called also *yellow bunting*
**2 :** YELLOW-SHAFTED FLICKER
**yellow jack** *noun* (1836)
**1 :** YELLOW FEVER
**2 :** a yellowish carangid marine food fish (*Caranx bartholomaei*) found from Massachusetts to Brazil
**yellow jacket** *noun* (1796)

**1 :** any of various small yellow-marked vespid wasps (especially genus *Vespula*) that commonly nest in the ground and can sting repeatedly and painfully
**2** *slang* **:** pentobarbital especially in a yellow capsule
**yellow jessamine** *noun* (1709)
**:** a twining evergreen shrub (*Gelsemium sempervirens* of the family Loganiaceae) with fragrant yellow flowers — called also *yellow jasmine*
**yel·low·legs** \'ye-lō-,legz, 'ye-lə-, -,lāgz\ *noun plural but singular or plural in construction* (1772)
**:** either of two American shorebirds with yellow legs: **a :** GREATER YELLOWLEGS **b :** LESSER YELLOWLEGS
**yellow ocher** *noun* (15th century)
**1 :** a mixture of limonite usually with clay and silica used as a pigment
**2 :** a moderate orange yellow
**yellow pages** *noun plural, often Y&P capitalized* (1952)
**:** the section of a telephone book that lists business and professional firms alphabetically by category and that includes classified advertising; *also* **:** a listing of products or services that is independently published
**yellow perch** *noun* (1805)
**:** a common North American freshwater bony fish (*Perca flavescens*) of the perch family that is yellowish with dark green bands and is an excellent food and sport fish
**yellow peril** *noun, often Y&P capitalized* (1898)
**1 :** a danger to Western civilization held to arise from expansion of the power and influence of eastern Asian peoples
**2 :** a threat to Western living standards from the influx of eastern Asian laborers willing to work for very low wages
**yellow pine** *noun* (1709)
**1 :** any of several North American pines (as a Ponderosa pine or longleaf pine) with yellowish wood
**2 :** the wood of a yellow pine
**yellow poplar** *noun* (1774)
**1 :** TULIP TREE 1
**2 :** TULIPWOOD 1
**yellow rain** *noun* (1979)
**:** a yellow substance reported to occur as a mist or as spots on rocks and vegetation in Southeast Asia and variously held to be a chemical warfare agent used in the Vietnam War or a natural substance similar if not identical to pollen or the feces of bees
**yel·low–shaft·ed flicker** \'ye-lō-,shaf-təd-, 'ye-lə-\ *noun* (1888)
**:** a flicker of eastern North America that is golden yellow on the underside of the tail and wings, has a red mark on the nape, and in the male has a black streak on each cheek
**yellow spot** *noun* (1869)
**:** MACULA LUTEA
**yel·low·tail** \'ye-lō-,tāl, 'ye-lə-\ *noun, plural* **yellowtail** *or* **yellowtails** (1709)
**:** any of various fishes having a yellow or yellowish tail: as **a :** any of several carangid fishes (genus *Seriola*); *especially* **:** a sport fish (*S. lalandei*) of the California coast and southward that reaches a length of about three feet (one meter) **b :** SILVER PERCH a **c :** a common snapper (*Ocyurus chrysurus*) that is a sport and food fish of the tropical western Atlantic and West Indies and is olive above and broadly striped with yellow along the sides and on the tail — called also *yellowtail snapper*
**yel·low·throat** \-,thrȯt\ *noun* (1702)
**:** any of several largely olive American warblers (genus *Geothlypis*); *especially* **:** one (*G. trichas*) with yellow breast and throat and a whitish belly
**yel·low·ware** \-,war, -,wer\ *noun* (1785)
**:** pottery made from buff clay and covered with a yellowish transparent clay
**yel·low·wood** \-,wu̇d\ *noun* (1666)

**1 :** any of various trees having yellowish wood or yielding a yellow extract; *especially* **:** a leguminous tree (*Cladrastis lutea*) of the southern U.S. having showy white fragrant flowers and yielding a yellow dye
**2 :** the wood of a yellowwood tree
**¹yelp** \'yelp\ *noun* [²*yelp*] (1501)
**:** a sharp shrill bark or cry (as of a dog); *also* **:** SQUEAL
**²yelp** *verb* [Middle English, to boast, cry out, from Old English *gielpan* to boast, exult; akin to Old High German *gelph* outcry] (1553)
*intransitive verb*
**:** to utter a sharp quick shrill cry ⟨dogs *yelp*⟩
*transitive verb*
**:** to utter with a yelp
**yelp·er** \'yel-pər\ *noun* (1673)
**1 :** one that yelps; *especially* **:** a yelping dog
**2 :** an instrument used by hunters to produce a call or whistle imitating the yelp of the wild turkey hen
**¹yen** \'yen\ *noun, plural* **yen** [Japanese *en*] (1875)
— see MONEY table
**²yen** *noun* [obsolete English argot *yen-yen* craving for opium, from Chinese (Guangdong) *yīn-yáhn,* from *yīn* opium + *yáhn* craving] (1906)
**:** a strong desire or propensity **:** LONGING; *also* **:** URGE
**³yen** *intransitive verb* **yenned; yen·ning** (1919)
**:** to have an intense desire **:** LONG, YEARN
**yen–shee** \'yen-'shē\ *noun* [Chinese (Guangdong) *yīn-sí,* from *yīn* opium + *sí* excrement, filth] (1882)
**:** the residue formed in the bowl of an opium pipe by smoking
**yen·ta** \'yen-tə\ *noun* [Yiddish *yente,* from the name *Yente*] (1923)
**:** one that meddles; *also* **:** BLABBERMOUTH, GOSSIP
**yeo·man** \'yō-mən\ *noun* [Middle English *yoman*] (14th century)
**1 a :** an attendant or officer in a royal or noble household **b :** a person attending or assisting another **:** RETAINER **c :** YEOMAN OF THE GUARD **d :** a naval petty officer who performs clerical duties
**2 a :** a person who owns and cultivates a small farm; *specifically* **:** one belonging to a class of English freeholders below the gentry **b :** a person of the social rank of yeoman
**3 :** one that performs great and loyal service ⟨did a *yeoman's* job in seeing the program through⟩
**¹yeo·man·ly** \-lē\ *adverb* (14th century)
*archaic* **:** in a manner befitting a yeoman **:** BRAVELY
**²yeomanly** *adjective* (1576)
**1 :** of, relating to, or having the rank of a yeoman
**2 :** becoming or suitable to a yeoman **:** STURDY, LOYAL
**yeoman of the guard** (circa 1520)
**:** a member of a military corps attached to the British royal household that serves as ceremonial attendants of the sovereign and as warders of the Tower of London
**yeo·man·ry** \'yō-mən-rē\ *noun* (14th century)
**1 :** the body of yeomen; *specifically* **:** the body of small landed proprietors of the middle class
**2 :** a British volunteer cavalry force created from yeomen in 1761 as a home defense force and reorganized in 1907 as part of the territorial force
**yep** \'yep, *or with glottal stop instead of* p\ *adverb* [by alteration] (1891)
**:** YES
**-yer** — see -ER

\ə\ abut \ᵊ\ kitten \ər\ further \a\ ash \ā\ ace
\ä\ mop, mar \au̇\ out \ch\ chin \e\ bet \ē\ easy
\g\ go \i\ hit \ī\ ice \j\ job \ŋ\ sing \ō\ go
\ȯ\ law \ȯi\ boy \th\ thin \t̲h̲\ the \ü\ loot \u̇\ foot
\y\ yet \zh\ vision    *see also* Guide to Pronunciation

**yer·ba ma·té** \,yer-bə-'mä-,tā, ,yər-\ *noun* [American Spanish *yerba mate,* from *yerba* herb + *mate* maté] (1839)
: MATÉ

**¹yerk** \'yərk\ *transitive verb* [Middle English, to bind tightly] (circa 1520)
**1** *dialect* : to beat vigorously : THRASH
**2** *dialect* : to attack or excite vigorously : GOAD

**²yerk** *noun* (1581)
**1** *Scottish* : a lashing out : KICK
**2** *dialect* : JERK 1

**¹yes** \'yes\ *adverb* [Middle English, from Old English *gēse*] (before 12th century)
**1** — used as a function word to express assent or agreement ⟨are you ready? *Yes,* I am⟩
**2** — used as a function word usually to introduce correction or contradiction of a negative assertion or direction ⟨don't say that! *Yes,* I will⟩
**3** — used as a function word to introduce a more emphatic or explicit phrase
**4** — used as a function word to indicate uncertainty or polite interest or attentiveness

**²yes** *noun* (1712)
: an affirmative reply : YEA

**ye·shi·va** *also* **ye·shi·vah** \yə-'shē-və\ *noun, plural* **yeshivas** *or* **ye·shi·vot** \-,shē-'vōt, -'vōth\ [Late Hebrew *yĕshībhāh*] (1851)
**1** : a school for talmudic study
**2** : an Orthodox Jewish rabbinical seminary
**3** : a Jewish day school providing secular and religious instruction

**yes–man** \'yes-,man\ *noun* (1913)
: a person who agrees with everything that is said; *especially* : one who endorses or supports without criticism every opinion or proposal of an associate or superior

**yes·ter** \'yes-tər\ *adjective* (1577)
*archaic* : of or relating to yesterday

**¹yes·ter·day** \'yes-tər-dē, -(,)dā\ *adverb* [Middle English *yisterday,* from Old English *giestran dæg,* from *giestran* yesterday + *dæg* day; akin to Old High German *gestaron* yesterday, Latin *heri,* Greek *chthes*] (before 12th century)
**1** : on the day last past : on the day preceding today
**2** : at a time not long past : only a short time ago ⟨I wasn't born *yesterday*⟩
— **yesterday** *adjective*

**²yesterday** *noun* (before 12th century)
**1** : the day last past : the day next before the present
**2** : recent time : time not long past
**3** : past time — usually used in plural

**¹yes·ter·night** \'yes-tər-,nīt\ *adverb* [Middle English, from Old English *gystran niht,* from *giestran* yesterday + *niht* night] (before 12th century)
*archaic* : on the night last past

**²yesternight** *noun* (1513)
: the night last past

**yes·ter·year** \'yes-tər-,yir\ *noun* [*yester*day + *year*] (1870)
**1** : last year
**2** : time gone by; *especially* : the recent past
— **yesteryear** *adverb*

**yes·treen** \ye-'strēn\ *noun* [Middle English (Scots) *yistrevin,* from *yisterday* + *evin* evening, alteration of Middle English *even*] (1785)
*chiefly Scottish* : last evening or night
— **yestreen** *adverb*

**¹yet** \'yet\ *adverb* [Middle English, from Old English *gīet;* akin to Old Frisian *ieta* yet] (before 12th century)
**1 a** : in addition : BESIDES ⟨gives *yet* another reason⟩ **b** : EVEN 2c ⟨a *yet* higher speed⟩ **c** : on top of everything else : no less ⟨had wells going dry. Between two large lakes, *yet* —J. H. Buzard⟩
**2 a** (1) : up to now : so far ⟨hasn't done much *yet*⟩ — often used to imply the negative of a following infinitive ⟨have *yet* to win a game⟩

(2) : at this or that time : so soon as now ⟨not time to go *yet*⟩ **b** : continuously up to the present or a specified time : STILL ⟨is *yet* a new country⟩ **c** : at a future time : EVENTUALLY ⟨may *yet* see the light⟩
**3** : NEVERTHELESS, HOWEVER
— **as yet** : up to the present or a specified time
— **yet again** : one more time ⟨arrived late *yet again*⟩

**²yet** *conjunction* (13th century)
: but nevertheless : BUT

**ye·ti** \'ye-tē, 'yā-\ *noun* [Tibetan] (1937)
: ABOMINABLE SNOWMAN

**yeuk** \'yük\ *intransitive verb* [Middle English (northern) *yukyn,* from Old English *giccan* — more at ITCH] (15th century)
*chiefly Scottish* : ITCH

**yew** \'yü\ *noun* [Middle English *ew,* from Old English *īw;* akin to Old High German *īwa* yew, Middle Irish *eó*] (before 12th century)
**1 a** : any of a genus (*Taxus* of the family Taxaceae, the yew family) of evergreen trees and shrubs with stiff linear leaves and fruits with a fleshy aril: as (1) : a long-lived Eurasian tree or shrub (*T. baccata*) — called also *English yew* (2) : a low straggling bush (*T. canadensis*) of the eastern U.S. and Canada **b** : the wood of a yew; *especially* : the heavy fine-grained wood of English yew
**2** *archaic* : an archery bow made of yew

**yew 1a**

**Ygerne** \ē-'gern\ *noun*
: IGRAINE

**Ygg·dra·sil** \'ig-drə-,sil\ *noun* [Old Norse]
: a huge ash tree in Norse mythology that overspreads the world and binds earth, hell, and heaven together

**YHWH** \'yä-(,)wä, -(,)vä\ *noun*
: YAHWEH — compare TETRAGRAMMATON

**Yid** \'yid\ *noun* [Yiddish, from Middle High German *Jüde,* from Old High German *Judeo,* from Latin *Judaeus* — more at JEW] (circa 1874)
: JEW — usually taken to be offensive

**Yid·dish** \'yi-dish\ *noun* [Yiddish *yidish,* short for *yidish daytsh,* literally, Jewish German, from Middle High German *jüdisch diutsch,* from *jüdisch* Jewish (from *Jude* Jew) + *diutsch* German] (1886)
: a High German language written in Hebrew characters that is spoken by Jews and descendants of Jews of central and eastern European origin
— **Yiddish** *adjective*

**Yid·dish·ism** \'yi-di-,shi-zəm\ *noun* (1904)
**1** : a usage, word, phrase, or idiom peculiar to Yiddish
**2** : a movement characterized by advocacy of the Yiddish language and culture
— **Yid·dish·ist** \-shist\ *noun or adjective*

**¹yield** \'yē(ə)ld\ *verb* [Middle English, from Old English *gieldan;* akin to Old High German *geltan* to pay] (before 12th century)
*transitive verb*
**1** *archaic* : RECOMPENSE, REWARD
**2** : to give or render as fitting, rightfully owed, or required
**3** : to give up possession of on claim or demand: as **a** : to give up (as one's breath) and so die **b** : to surrender or relinquish to the physical control of another : hand over possession of **c** : to surrender or submit (oneself) to another **d** : to give (oneself) up to an inclination, temptation, or habit **e** : to relinquish one's possession of (as a position of advantage or point of superiority) ⟨*yield* precedence⟩
**4 a** : to bear or bring forth as a natural product especially as a result of cultivation ⟨the tree always *yields* good fruit⟩ **b** : to produce or furnish as return ⟨this soil should *yield* good

crops⟩ **c** (1) : to produce as return from an expenditure or investment : furnish as profit or interest ⟨a bond that *yields* 12 percent⟩ (2) : to produce as revenue : BRING IN ⟨the tax is expected to *yield* millions⟩
**5** : to give up (as a hit or run) in baseball ⟨*yielded* two runs in the third inning⟩
*intransitive verb*
**1** : to be fruitful or productive : BEAR, PRODUCE
**2** : to give up and cease resistance or contention : SUBMIT, SUCCUMB
**3** : to give way to pressure or influence : submit to urging, persuasion, or entreaty
**4** : to give way under physical force (as bending, stretching, or breaking)
**5 a** : to give place or precedence : acknowledge the superiority of someone else **b** : to be inferior ⟨our dictionary *yields* to none⟩ **c** : to give way to or become succeeded by someone or something else
**6** : to relinquish the floor of a legislative assembly ☆

**²yield** *noun* (15th century)
**1** : something yielded : PRODUCT; *especially* : the amount or quantity produced or returned ⟨*yield* of wheat per acre⟩
**2** : the capacity of yielding produce

**yield·er** \'yēl-dər\ *noun* (1590)
: one that yields: as **a** : a person who surrenders, concedes, or gives in **b** : something that yields produce or products

**yield·ing** \-diŋ\ *adjective* (1533)
**1** : PRODUCTIVE ⟨a high-*yielding* wheat⟩
**2** : lacking rigidity or stiffness : FLEXIBLE
**3** : disposed to submit or comply

**yikes** \'yīks\ *interjection* [probably alteration of *yoicks*] (1957)
— used to express fear or astonishment

**yin** \'yin\ *noun* [Chinese (Beijing) *yīn*] (1671)
: the feminine passive principle in nature that in Chinese cosmology is exhibited in darkness, cold, or wetness and that combines with yang to produce all that comes to be

**Yin·glish** \'yiŋ-glish, -lish\ *noun* [blend of *Yiddish* and *English*] (1951)
: English marked by numerous borrowings from Yiddish

**y–in·ter·cept** \'wī-'in-tər-,sept\ *noun* (circa 1939)
: the y-coordinate of a point where a line, curve, or surface intersects the y-axis

**yip** \'yip\ *intransitive verb* **yipped**; **yip·ping** [imitative] (1907)
**1** : to bark sharply, quickly, and often continuously

☆ SYNONYMS
**Yield, submit, capitulate, succumb, relent, defer** mean to give way to someone or something that one can no longer resist. YIELD may apply to any sort or degree of giving way before force, argument, persuasion, or entreaty ⟨*yields* too easily in any argument⟩. SUBMIT suggests full surrendering after resistance or conflict to the will or control of another ⟨a repentant sinner vowing to *submit* to the will of God⟩. CAPITULATE stresses the fact of ending all resistance and may imply either a coming to terms (as with an adversary) or hopelessness in the face of an irresistible opposing force ⟨officials *capitulated* to the protesters' demands⟩. SUCCUMB implies weakness and helplessness to the one that gives way or an overwhelming power to the opposing force ⟨a stage actor *succumbing* to the lure of Hollywood⟩. RELENT implies a yielding through pity or mercy by one who holds the upper hand ⟨finally *relented* and let the children stay up late⟩. DEFER implies a voluntary yielding or submitting out of respect or reverence for or deference and affection toward another ⟨I *defer* to your superior expertise in these matters⟩. See in addition RELINQUISH.

**2 :** to utter a short sharp cry
— **yip** *noun*

**yip·pee** \'yi-pē\ *interjection* (1914)
— used to express exuberant delight or triumph

**yip·pie** \'yi-pē\ *noun* [*Youth International Party* + *-ie* (as in *hippie*)] (1968)
**:** a person belonging to or identified with a politically active group of hippies

**yips** \'yips\ *noun plural* [origin unknown] (1962)
**:** a state of nervous tension affecting an athlete (as a golfer) in the performance of a crucial action ⟨had a bad case of the *yips* on short putts⟩

**-yl** \əl, ᵊl, (,)il, ,ēl, *chiefly British* ,īl\ *noun combining form* [Greek *hylē* matter, material, literally, wood]
**:** chemical and usually univalent group ⟨ethyl⟩

**ylang-ylang** \ē-,läŋ-'ē-,läŋ\ *noun* [Tagalog] (1876)
**1 :** a tree (*Cananga odorata* synonym *Canangium odoratum*) of the custard-apple family of the Malay Archipelago, the Philippines, and adjacent areas that has very fragrant greenish yellow flowers
**2 :** a perfume distilled from the flowers of the ylang-ylang tree

**YMCA** \,wī-,em-(,)sē-'ā\ *noun* [*Young Men's Christian Association*] (1881)
**:** an international organization that promotes the spiritual, intellectual, social, and physical welfare originally of young men

**YMHA** \,wī-,em-,ā-'chā\ *noun* [*Young Men's Hebrew Association*] (1918)
**:** an organization that promotes the religious, intellectual, social, and physical welfare of Jewish young men

**Ymir** \'ē-,mir\ *noun* [Old Norse]
**:** a giant from whose body the gods create the world in Norse mythology

**yo** \'yō\ *interjection* [Middle English *yo, io,* interjection] (15th century)
— used especially to call attention, to indicate attentiveness, or to express affirmation

**yob** \'yäb\ *noun* [backward spelling for *boy*] (1908)
*British* **:** YOBBO

**yob·bo** \'yä-bō\ *noun, plural* **yobbos** *or* **yob·boes** [*yob* + *¹-o*] (1922)
**1** *British* **:** LOUT, YOKEL
**2** *British* **:** HOODLUM

**yock** \'yäk\ *variant of* ²YAK

**yod** \'yōd, 'yủd\ *noun* [Hebrew *yōdh*] (1735)
**:** the 10th letter of the Hebrew alphabet — see ALPHABET table

**¹yo·del** \'yō-d³l\ *verb* **-deled** *or* **-delled; -del·ing** *or* **-del·ling** \'yōd-liŋ, 'yō-d³l-iŋ\ [German *jodeln*] (1838)
*intransitive verb*
**:** to sing by suddenly changing from a natural voice to a falsetto and back; *also* **:** to shout or call in a similar manner
*transitive verb*
**:** to sing (a tune) by yodeling
— **yo·del·er** \'yōd-lər, 'yō-d³l-ər\ *noun*

**²yodel** *noun* (1849)
**:** a song or refrain sung by yodeling; *also* **:** a yodeled shout or cry

**yo·ga** \'yō-gə\ *noun* [Sanskrit, literally, yoking, from *yunakti* he yokes; akin to Latin *jungere* to join — more at YOKE] (1820)
**1** *capitalized* **:** a Hindu theistic philosophy teaching the suppression of all activity of body, mind, and will in order that the self may realize its distinction from them and attain liberation
**2 :** a system of exercises for attaining bodily or mental control and well-being
— **yo·gic** \-gik\ *adjective, often capitalized*

**yogh** \'yōk, 'yōg, 'yōk̲\ *noun* [Middle English] (14th century)
**:** the letter ȝ used especially in Middle English chiefly to represent voiced and voiceless velar and palatal fricatives

**yo·gi** \'yō-gē\ *also* **yo·gin** \-gən, -,gin\ *noun* [Sanskrit *yogin,* from *yoga*] (1619)
**1 :** a person who practices yoga
**2** *capitalized* **:** an adherent of Yoga philosophy
**3 :** a markedly reflective or mystical person

**yo·gurt** *also* **yo·ghurt** \'yō-gərt\ *noun* [Turkish *yoğurt*] (1625)
**:** a fermented slightly acid often flavored semisolid food made of whole or skimmed cow's milk and milk solids to which cultures of two bacteria (*Lactobacillus bulgaricus* and *Streptococcus thermophilus*) have been added

**yo·him·bine** \yō-'him-,bēn, -bən\ *noun* [International Scientific Vocabulary, from *yohimbé,* a tropical African tree (*Corynanthe yohimbe*) from which it is obtained] (1898)
**:** an alkaloid $C_{21}H_{26}N_2O_3$ that is a weak blocker of alpha-adrenergic receptors and has been used as an aphrodisiac

**yoicks** \'yȯiks\ *interjection* (1774)
— used as a cry of encouragement to foxhounds

**¹yoke** \'yōk\ *noun, plural* **yokes** [Middle English *yok,* from Old English *geoc;* akin to Old High German *joh* yoke, Latin *jugum,* Greek *zygon,* Sanskrit *yuga,* Latin *jungere* to join] (before 12th century)
**1 a :** a wooden bar or frame by which two draft animals (as oxen) are joined at the heads or necks for working together **b :** an arched device formerly laid on the neck of a defeated person **c :** a frame fitted to a person's shoulders to carry a load in two equal portions **d :** a bar by which the end of the tongue of a wagon or carriage is suspended from the collars of the harness **e** (1) **:** a crosspiece on the head of a boat's rudder (2) **:** the control device for an airplane's ailerons that is mounted on a column which also serves to operate the elevator **f :** a frame from which a bell is hung **g :** a clamp or similar piece that embraces two parts to hold or unite them in position
**2** *plural usually* **yoke :** two animals yoked or worked together
**3 a** (1) **:** an oppressive agency (2) **:** SERVITUDE, BONDAGE **b :** TIE, LINK; *especially* **:** MARRIAGE
**4 :** a fitted or shaped piece at the top of a skirt or at the shoulder of various garments

**²yoke** *verb* **yoked; yok·ing** (before 12th century)
*transitive verb*
**1 a** (1) **:** to put a yoke on (2) **:** to join in or with a yoke **b :** to attach a draft animal to; *also* **:** to attach (a draft animal) to something
**2 :** to join as if by a yoke
**3 :** to put to work
*intransitive verb*
**:** to become joined or linked

**yoke·fel·low** \'yōk-,fe-(,)lō\ *noun* (1526)
**:** a close companion **:** MATE

**yo·kel** \'yō-kəl\ *noun* [perhaps from English dialect *yokel* green woodpecker, of imitative origin] (circa 1812)
**:** a naive or gullible inhabitant of a rural area or small town

**yolk** \'yōk, 'yelk (*in cultivated speech, especially Southern*), *also* 'yōlk, 'yȯlk, 'yälk, 'yəlk\ *also* **yoke** \'yōk\ *noun* [Middle English *yolke,* from Old English *geoloca,* from *geolu* yellow — more at YELLOW] (before 12th century)
**1 a :** the yellow spheroidal mass of stored food that forms the inner portion of the egg of a bird or reptile and is surrounded by the white — see EGG illustration **b** *archaic* **:** the whole contents of an ovum consisting of a protoplasmic formative portion and an inert nutritive portion **c :** material stored in an ovum that supplies food to the developing embryo and consists chiefly of proteins, lecithin, and cholesterol
**2** [akin to Middle Dutch *ieke* yolk (of wool), Old English *ēowu* ewe] **:** oily material in unprocessed sheep wool consisting of wool fat, suint, and debris
— **yolked** *adjective*
— **yolky** *adjective*

**yolk sac** *noun* (1861)
**:** a membranous sac that is attached to an embryo and encloses food yolk, that is continuous in most forms through the yolk stalk with the intestinal cavity of the embryo, that being abundantly supplied with blood vessels is throughout embryonic life and in some forms later the chief organ of nutrition, and that in placental mammals is nearly vestigial and functions chiefly prior to the elaboration of the placenta

**yolk stalk** *noun* (1900)
**:** the narrow tubular stalk connecting the yolk sac with the embryo

**Yom Kip·pur** \,yȯm-ki-'pủr, ,yȯm-, ,yäm-; -'ki-pər, -(,)pủr\ *noun* [Hebrew *yōm kippūr,* literally, day of atonement] (1854)
**:** a Jewish holiday observed with fasting and prayer on the 10th day of Tishri in accordance with the rites described in Leviticus 16 — called also *Day of Atonement*

**¹yon** \'yän\ *adjective* [Middle English, from Old English *geon;* akin to Old High German *ienēr,* adjective, that, Greek *enē* day after tomorrow] (before 12th century)
**:** YONDER

**²yon** *pronoun* (14th century)
*dialect* **:** that or those yonder

**³yon** *adverb* (15th century)
**1 :** YONDER
**2 :** THITHER ⟨ran hither and *yon*⟩

**¹yond** \'yänd\ *adverb* [Middle English, from Old English *geond;* akin to Old English *geon*] (before 12th century)
*archaic* **:** YONDER

**²yond** *adjective* (13th century)
*dialect* **:** YONDER

**¹yon·der** \'yän-dər\ *adverb* [Middle English, from *yond* + *-er* (as in *hither*)] (14th century)
**:** at or in that indicated more or less distant place usually within sight

**²yonder** *adjective* (14th century)
**1 :** farther removed **:** more distant
**2 :** being at a distance within view or at a place or in a direction known or indicated

**³yonder** *pronoun* (14th century)
**:** something that is or is in an indicated more or less distant place

**yo·ni** \'yō-nē\ *noun* [Sanskrit, vulva] (1799)
**:** a stylized representation of the female genitalia symbolizing the feminine principle in Hindu cosmology — compare LINGAM
— **yo·nic** \'yō-nik\ *adjective*

**yoo-hoo** \'yü-(,)hü\ *interjection* (circa 1924)
— used to attract attention or as a call to persons

**yore** \'yōr, 'yȯr\ *noun* [Middle English, from *yore,* adverb, long ago, from Old English *gēara,* from *gēar* year — more at YEAR] (14th century)
**:** time past and especially long past — usually used in the phrase *of yore*

**York·ie** \'yȯr-kē\ *noun* [by shortening & alteration] (1946)
**:** YORKSHIRE TERRIER

**York·ist** \'yȯr-kist\ *adjective* [Edward, Duke of York (Edward IV of England)] (1823)
**:** of or relating to the English royal house that ruled from 1461 to 1485
— **Yorkist** *noun*

**York rite** \'yȯrk-\ *noun* [*York,* England] (circa 1878)
**1 :** a ceremonial observed by one of the Masonic systems
**2 :** a system or organization that observes the York rite and confers in the U.S. 13 degrees of which the last three are in commanderies of Knights Templar — compare SCOTTISH RITE

**York·shire** \'yȯrk-,shir, -shər\ *noun* (1902)

: a white swine of any of several breeds or strains originated in Yorkshire, England

**Yorkshire pudding** *noun* (1747)
: batter consisting of eggs, flour, and milk that is baked in meat drippings

**Yorkshire terrier** *noun* (1872)
: any of a breed of compact toy terriers with long straight silky hair mostly bluish gray but tan on the head and chest

**Yor·u·ba** \'yȯr-ə-bə\ *noun, plural* **Yoruba** *or* **Yorubas** (1841)
: a Niger-Congo language of southwestern Nigeria and parts of Benin and Togo; *also* : a member of any of the Yoruba-speaking peoples of this region
— **Yo·ru·ban** \'yȯr-ə-bən\ *noun or adjective*

**you** \'yü, yə *also* yē\ *pronoun* [Middle English, from Old English *ēow*, dative & accusative of *gē* you; akin to Old High German *iu*, dative of *ir* you, Sanskrit *yūyam* you] (before 12th century)
**1** : the one or ones being addressed — used as the pronoun of the second person singular or plural in any grammatical relation except that of a possessive 〈*you* may sit in that chair〉 〈*you* are my friends〉 〈can I pour *you* a cup of tea〉; used formerly only as a plural pronoun of the second person in the dative or accusative case as direct or indirect object of a verb or as object of a preposition; compare THEE, THOU, YE, YOUR, YOURS
**2** : ONE 2a ◼ ◆

**you-all** \yü-'ȯl, 'yü-,; 'yȯl\ *pronoun* (1824)
*chiefly Southern* : YOU — usually used in addressing two or more persons or sometimes one person as representing also another or others

**you'd** \'yüd, 'yu̇d, yəd\ (1602)
: you had : you would

**you'll** \'yü(ə)l, 'yu̇l, yəl\ (1592)
: you will : you shall

**¹young** \'yəŋ\ *adjective* **youn·ger** \'yəŋ-gər\ **youn·gest** \'yəŋ-gəst\ [Middle English *yong*, from Old English *geong*; akin to Old High German *jung* young, Latin *juvenis*] (before 12th century)
**1 a** : being in the first or an early stage of life, growth, or development **b** : JUNIOR 1a **c** : of an early, tender, or desirable age for use as food or drink 〈fresh *young* lamb〉 〈a *young* wine〉
**2** : having little experience
**3 a** : recently come into being : NEW **b** : YOUTHFUL 5
**4** : of, relating to, or having the characteristics of youth or a young person
**5** *capitalized* : representing a new or rejuvenated especially political group or movement
— **young·ish** \'yəŋ-ish\ *adjective*
— **young·ness** \'yəŋ-nəs\ *noun*

**²young** *noun, plural* **young** (before 12th century)
**1** *plural* **a** : young persons : YOUTH **b** : immature offspring especially of lower animals
**2** : a single recently born or hatched animal
— **with young** : PREGNANT — used of a female animal

**young·ber·ry** \'yəŋ-,ber-ē\ *noun* [B. M. *Young* (flourished 1900) American fruit grower] (1927)
: the large sweet reddish black fruit of a cultivar of a hybrid bramble closely related to the boysenberry and loganberry and grown in the western and southern U.S.; *also* : a bramble bearing youngberries

**youn·ger** \'yəŋ-gər\ *noun* (before 12th century)
: an inferior in age : JUNIOR — usually used with a possessive pronoun 〈is several years his *younger*〉

**youn·gest** \'yəŋ-gəst\ *noun, plural* **youn·gest** (13th century)
: one that is the least old; *especially* : the youngest child or member of a family

**young·ling** \'yəŋ-liŋ\ *noun* (before 12th century)

: one that is young; *especially* : a young person or animal
— **youngling** *adjective*

**young·ster** \'yəŋ(k)-stər\ *noun* (1589)
**1 a** : a young person : YOUTH **b** : CHILD
**2** : a young mammal, bird, or plant especially of a domesticated or cultivated breed or type

**Young Turk** *noun* [*Young Turks*, a 20th century revolutionary party in Turkey] (1908)
: an insurgent or a member of an insurgent group especially in a political party : RADICAL; *broadly* : one advocating changes within a usually established group

**youn·ker** \'yəŋ-kər\ *noun* [Dutch *jonker* young nobleman] (1513)
**1** : a young man
**2** : CHILD, YOUNGSTER

**your** \yər, 'yu̇r, 'yȯr, 'yȯr\ *adjective* [Middle English, from Old English *ēower*; akin to Old English *ēow* you — more at YOU] (before 12th century)
**1** : of or relating to you or yourself or yourselves especially as possessor or possessors 〈*your* bodies〉, agent or agents 〈*your* contributions〉, or object or objects of an action 〈*your* discharge〉
**2** : of or relating to one or oneself 〈when you face the north, east is at *your* right〉
**3** — used with little or no meaning almost as an equivalent to the definite article *the* 〈a trait . . . that sets him apart from *your* average professor —James Breckenridge〉

**you're** \yər, 'yu̇r, 'yȯr, 'yȯr, ,yü-ər\ *pronoun* (1593)
: you are

**yours** \'yu̇rz, 'yȯrz, 'yȯrz\ *pronoun, singular or plural in construction* [Middle English from *your* + *-s* '-s] (1526)
: that which belongs to you — used without a following noun as a pronoun equivalent in meaning to the adjective *your; often* used especially with an adverbial modifier in the complimentary close of a letter 〈*yours* truly〉
— **yours truly** : I, ME, MYSELF 〈I can take care of *yours truly*〉

**your·self** \yər-'self, *Southern also* -'sef\ *pronoun* (14th century)
**1 a** : that identical one that is you — used reflexively 〈you might hurt *yourself*〉, for emphasis 〈carry them *yourself*〉, or in absolute constructions **b** : your normal, healthy, or sane condition
**2** : ONESELF ◻

**your·selves** \-'selvz, *Southern also* -'sevz\ *pronoun plural* (1523)
**1** : those identical ones that are you — used reflexively 〈get *yourselves* a treat〉, for emphasis, or in absolute constructions
**2** : your normal, healthy, or sane condition

**youth** \'yüth\ *noun, plural* **youths** \'yüthz, 'yüths\ *often attributive* [Middle English *youthe*, from Old English *geoguth;* akin to Old English *geong* young — more at YOUNG] (before 12th century)
**1 a** : the time of life when one is young; *especially* : the period between childhood and maturity **b** : the early period of existence, growth, or development
**2 a** : a young person; *especially* : a young male between adolescence and maturity **b** : young persons or creatures — usually plural in construction
**3** : the quality or state of being youthful : YOUTHFULNESS

**youth·ful** \'yüth-fəl\ *adjective* (1590)
**1** : of, relating to, or characteristic of youth
**2** : being young and not yet mature
**3** : marked by or possessing youth
**4** : having the vitality or freshness of youth : VIGOROUS
**5** : having accomplished or undergone little erosion
— **youth·ful·ly** \-fə-lē\ *adverb*
— **youth·ful·ness** *noun*

**youth hostel** *noun* (1929)
: HOSTEL 2b

---

◻ **USAGE**

**you**    Just about everybody agrees that the use of *you* to address the reader contributes to informality and directness, and helps avoid labored circumlocutions to boot. But when *you* is used indefinitely 〈in seventh grade they were always assigning *you* to write about things like farm produce — Russell Baker〉 some commentators are reluctant to consider it acceptable, preferring *one* instead. *One* sometimes presents problems of pronoun agreement in American English; in British English "one does what one can" is normal, but the second *one* sounds a bit odd to American ears. Should it be replaced with *he, she, he or she, they*? The question is neatly sidestepped by using *you. You* is appropriately used for *one* in all contexts except the most formal.

**yourself**    *Yourself* and, less often, *yourselves* turn up in contexts in which *you* might be used 〈get me some good left-handers like *yourself* and Robinson —Robert Frost (letter)〉. Such use has been censured in handbooks by many of the same authors who have censured the similar use of *myself*. But the commentators have failed to note that such use is not random, but rather is confined to contexts in which the person addressed is the subject of the discourse rather than a participant in it. A letter written to Alfred Lord Tennyson makes this point: "How are you standing this tropical heat, and Mrs. Tennyson? Let us have a good account of yourselves." The *you* is in direct address—Tennyson is a participant here. But the *yourselves*—the plural showing more certainly than *you* alone would that Mrs. Tennyson is to be included—makes the Tennysons the subjects about whom the writer wants to hear. Substituting *you*, or even *you both*, for *yourselves* sounds awkward. This use of the reflexive is standard in English and is found especially in conversation, dialogue, and letters.

---

◇ **WORD HISTORY**

**you**    Any English speaker who has studied another European language has discovered that most foreign tongues have more than one word corresponding to *you*. Typically there are separate forms to express distinctions of number and grammatical function. Many languages also use different forms depending on degree of familiarity with the person addressed; a common pattern, exemplified by French and Russian, is to address an elder, social superior, or stranger with the plural pronoun. The leveling of all these possibilities into one word, *you*, is in fact relatively recent in our language. Early Modern English inherited four second person pronouns: *thou* and *thee* as subject and object forms for singular usage, and *ye* and *you* for plural. However, in weakly stressed positions both *ye* and *you* were pronounced \yə\, which led to the blurring of the grammatical distinction between them. *You* emerged predominant around 1600. In the 14th century English had copied French and begun to use *ye* and *you* as a polite mode of addressing a single person. *You* gradually became the common neutral form, while *thou* and *thee* conveyed either intimacy or disrespect. By the late 17th century, use of *thou* and *thee* was confined to the church, Quaker speech, and rural dialects.

**youth·quake** \-ˌkwāk\ *noun* [*youth* + *earthquake*] (1966)
: the impact of the values, tastes, and mores of youth on the established norms of society

**you've** \'yüv, yəv\ (1691)
: you have

**¹yowl** \'yaů(ə)l\ *verb* [Middle English] (13th century)
*intransitive verb*
**1 :** to utter a loud long cry of grief, pain, or distress **:** WAIL
**2 :** to complain or protest with or as if with yowls
*transitive verb*
**:** to express with yowling

**²yowl** *noun* (15th century)
: a loud long mournful wail or howl (as of a cat)

**¹yo–yo** \'yō-(ˌ)yō\ *noun, plural* **yo–yos** [perhaps from a language of the Philippines] (1915)
**1 :** a thick grooved double disk with a string attached to its center which is made to fall and rise to the hand by unwinding and rewinding on the string
**2 :** one that resembles a yo-yo especially in moving up and down unexpectedly or repeatedly
**3 :** a stupid or foolish person

**²yo–yo** *adjective* (1932)
: shifting back and forth or up and down uncertainly or unexpectedly

**³yo–yo** *intransitive verb* **yo–yoed; yo–yo·ing** (1967)
: to move from one position to another repeatedly **:** FLUCTUATE

**yt·ter·bi·um** \i-'tər-bē-əm\ *noun* [New Latin, from *Ytterby*, town in southern Sweden] (1879)
: a metallic element of the rare-earth group that resembles yttrium and occurs with it and related elements in several minerals — see ELEMENT table

**yt·tri·um** \'i-trē-əm\ *noun* [New Latin, from *yttria* yttrium oxide (Y₂O₃), irregular from *Ytterby*, town in southern Sweden] (1822)
: a metallic element usually included among the rare-earth metals which it resembles chemically and with which it usually occurs in minerals — see ELEMENT table

**yu·an** \'yü-ən, yù-'än\ *noun, plural* **yuan** [Chinese (Beijing) *yuán*] (1914)

**1** — see MONEY table
**2 :** the dollar of the Republic of China (Taiwan)

**yu·ca** \'yü-kə\ *noun* [New Latin *jucca*, from Taino *yuca*] (1555)
: CASSAVA

**Yu·ca·tec** \'yü-kə-ˌtek\ *noun* [Spanish *yucateco*] (1843)
**1 :** a member of an American Indian people of the Yucatán peninsula, Mexico
**2 :** the Mayan language of the Yucatecs
— **Yu·ca·tec·an** \ˌyü-kə-'te-kən\ *adjective or noun*

**yuc·ca** \'yə-kə\ *noun* [New Latin, from Spanish *yuca*, of unknown origin] (1664)
**1 :** any of a genus (*Yucca*) of sometimes arborescent plants of the agave family that occur in warm regions chiefly of western North America and have long often rigid fibrous-margined leaves on a woody base and bear a large panicle of white blossoms
**2 :** CASSAVA

**¹yuck** \'yək\ *variant of* ²YAK

**²yuck** *also* **yuk** *interjection* (1966)
— used to express rejection or disgust ⟨spending hours over some dish and getting, "yuck, I hate that" —Anne Dowie⟩

**yucky** \'yə-kē\ *adjective* [²*yuck*] (1970)
: OFFENSIVE, DISTASTEFUL

**yu·ga** \'yù-gə, 'yü-\ *noun* [Sanskrit, yoke, age — more at YOKE] (1784)
: one of the four ages of a Hindu world cycle

**yuk** \'yək\ *variant of* ²YAK

**yule** \'yü(ə)l\ *noun, often capitalized* [Middle English *yol*, from Old English *geōl*; akin to Old Norse *jōl*, a pagan midwinter festival] (before 12th century)
: the feast of the nativity of Jesus Christ **:** CHRISTMAS

**Yule log** *noun* (1725)
: a large log formerly put on the hearth on Christmas Eve as the foundation of the fire

**yule·tide** \'yü(ə)l-ˌtīd\ *noun, often capitalized* (15th century)

**yucca**

: CHRISTMASTIDE

**Yu·man** \'yü-mən\ *noun* (1891)
: an American Indian language family of southwestern U.S. and northern Mexico
— **Yuman** *adjective*

**yum·my** \'yə-mē\ *adjective* **yum·mi·er; -est** [*yum-yum*] (1899)
: highly attractive or pleasing; *especially* **:** DELICIOUS, DELECTABLE

**yum–yum** \'yəm-'yəm\ *interjection* (1878)
— used to express pleasurable satisfaction especially in the taste of food

**¹yup** \'yəp\ *variant of* YEP

**²yup** *noun* (1983)
: YUPPIE

**Yu·pik** \'yü-pək\ *noun, plural* **Yupiks** *or* **Yupik** [Central Alaskan Yupik *yúppik*, literally, authentic person] (1951)
**1 :** the language of the Eskimo people of southwestern Alaska
**2 :** a member of the Yupik-speaking people

**yup·pie** \'yə-pē\ *noun, often capitalized* [probably from young *urban professional* + *-ie*] (1983)
: a young college-educated adult who is employed in a well-paying profession and who lives and works in or near a large city

**yurt** \'yùrt\ *noun* [Russian dialect *yurta*, of Turkic origin; akin to Turkish *yurt* home] (1784)
: a circular domed tent of skins or felt stretched over a collapsible lattice framework and used by pastoral peoples of inner Asia; *also* **:** a structure that resembles a yurt usually in size and design

**YWCA** \ˌwī-ˌdə-bəl-yù-(ˌ)sē-'ā, -ˌdə-bə-yù-\ *noun* [*Young Women's Christian Association*] (1887)
: an international organization that promotes the spiritual, intellectual, social, and physical welfare originally of young women

**YWHA** \-ˌäch-'ā\ *noun* [*Young Women's Hebrew Association*] (1918)
: an organization that promotes the religious, intellectual, social, and physical welfare of Jewish young women

**yurt**

**Z**

Z is the twenty-sixth and last letter of the English alphabet. It comes from Latin, which borrowed it, after the Roman conquest of the eastern Mediterranean, from the Greek zeta and used it to render that letter in words from Greek. The Greek letter is from Phoenician zayin. In English, the letter is usually pronounced as in maze, but that sound is more often represented by s than by z. It sometimes has the palatalized sound of z in azure. The letter Z occurs for a Middle English character called yogh, which looked like cursive z but had the sound of y, in a few Scottish words such as capercailzie "a European grouse" and names such as Mackenzie. English Z occurs in some native words, such as graze and ooze, to represent the voiced sound of an earlier written s (that is, an s pronounced with vibration of the vocal cords), but for the most part it is restricted to loanwords, especially from Greek. Small z developed through a simple reduction in size of the capital form. The name of this letter is usually zee in American English but usually zed in other varieties. Zed comes by way of French and Latin from Greek zeta.

---

**z** \'zē, *Canadian, British, & Australian* 'zed, *chiefly dialect* 'i-zərd\ *noun, plural* **z's** *or* **zs** *often capitalized, often attributive* (before 12th century)
**1 a :** the 26th and last letter of the English alphabet **b :** a graphic representation of this letter **c :** a speech counterpart of orthographic z
**2 :** a graphic device for reproducing the letter z
**3 :** one designated z especially as the 26th in order or class or the third in order or class when x is made the first
**4 :** something shaped like the letter Z
**5 :** WINK 1 — usually used in plural ⟨catch some z's before dinner⟩

**Z** *noun* (1967)
**:** Z PARTICLE

**za·ba·glio·ne** \ˌzä-bəl-'yō-nē\ *noun* [Italian] (1899)
**:** a whipped dessert consisting of a mixture of egg yolks, sugar, and usually Marsala wine that is often served on fruit

**Zach·a·ri·as** \ˌza-kə-'rī-əs\ *noun* [Late Latin, from Greek, from Hebrew *Zĕkharyāh*]
**:** ZECHARIAH

**zad·dik** \'tsä-dik\ *noun, plural* **zad·dik·im** \tsä-'di-kəm\ [Yiddish *tsadek*, from Hebrew *ṣaddîq* just, righteous] (1873)
**1 :** a righteous and saintly person by Jewish religious standards
**2 :** the spiritual leader of a modern Hasidic community

**zaf·tig** \'zäf-tig, 'zóf-\ *adjective* [Yiddish *zaftik* juicy, succulent, from *zaft* juice, sap, from Middle High German *saf, saft*, from Old High German *saf* — more at SAP] (circa 1936)
*of a woman* **:** having a full rounded figure **:** pleasingly plump

**¹zag** \'zag\ *noun* [zig*zag*] (1793)
**1 a :** one of the sharp turns, angles, or alterations in a zigzag course **b :** one of the short straight lines or sections of a zigzag course at an angle to a zig
**2 :** ZIG 2

**²zag** *intransitive verb* **zagged; zag·ging** (1900)
**:** to execute a zag — usually contrasted with *zig*

**zaire** \'zīr, zä-'ir\ *noun, plural* **zaires** *or* **zaire** [French *zaïre*, from *Zaïre*, former country in central Africa] (1967)
— see MONEY table

**za·mia** \'zā-mē-ə\ *noun* [New Latin, from Latin *zamiae nuces*, false manuscript reading for *azaniae nuces* pine nuts] (1819)
**:** any of a genus (*Zamia* of the family Zamiaceae) of American cycads with a short thick woody base, a crown of palmlike leaves, and oblong cones

**za·min·dar** *or* **ze·min·dar** \'za-mən-ˌdär, 'ze-; zə-ˌmēn-'där\ *noun* [Hindi *zamīndār*, from Persian, from *zamīn* land + *-dār* holder] (1683)
**1 :** a collector of the land revenue of a district for the government during the period of Mogul rule in India
**2 :** a feudal landlord in British India paying the government a fixed revenue

**za·min·dari** *or* **ze·min·dary** \ˌza-mən-'där-ē, ˌze-; zə-ˌmēn-\ *noun, plural* **-dar·is** *or* **-dar·ies** [Hindi *zamīndārī*, from Persian, from *zamīndār*] (1757)
**1 :** the system of landholding and revenue collection by zamindars
**2 :** the land held or administered by a zamindar

**zan·der** \'zan-dər, 'tsän-\ *noun, plural* **zander** *or* **zanders** [German] (1854)
**:** a pike perch (*Stizostedion lucioperca*) of central Europe related to the walleye

**¹za·ny** \'zā-nē\ *noun, plural* **zanies** [Italian *zanni*, a traditional masked clown, from Italian dialect *Zanni*, nickname for Italian *Giovanni* John] (1588)
**1 :** a subordinate clown or acrobat in old comedies who mimics ludicrously the tricks of the principal **:** MERRY-ANDREW
**2 :** a slavish follower **:** TOADY
**3 a :** one who acts the buffoon to amuse others **b :** NUT, KOOK

**²zany** *adjective* **za·ni·er; -est** (1616)
**1 :** being or having the characteristics of a zany
**2 :** fantastically or absurdly ludicrous
— **za·ni·ly** \'zā-nə-lē, 'zā-nᵊl-ē\ *adverb*
— **za·ni·ness** \'zā-nē-nəs\ *noun*

**¹zap** \'zap\ *interjection* [imitative] (1929)
**1** — used to express a sound made by or as if by a gun
**2** — used to indicate a sudden or instantaneous occurrence

**²zap** *verb* **zapped; zap·ping** (1942)
*transitive verb*
**1 a :** to get rid of, destroy, or kill especially with or as if with sudden force **b :** to hit with or as if with a sudden concentrated application of force or energy **c :** to irradiate especially with microwaves
**2 a :** to propel suddenly or speedily **b :** to transport instantaneously

**3 :** to avoid watching (as a television commercial) by changing channels especially with a remote control or by fast-forwarding a videotape
*intransitive verb*
**1 :** to move with speed or force
**2 :** to change television channels using a remote control

**³zap** *noun* (1963)
**:** a pungent or zestful quality **:** ZIP; *also* **:** a sudden forceful blow

**za·pa·te·ado** \ˌzä-pə-tä-'ä-(ˌ)dō, ˌsä-pə-tä-'aù\ *noun* [Spanish, from *zapatear* to strike or tap with the shoe, from *zapato* shoe] (1845)
**:** a Latin-American dance marked by rhythmic stamping or tapping of the feet

**za·pa·teo** \ˌzä-pə-'tä-(ˌ)ō, ˌsä-\ *noun* [Spanish, from *zapatear*] (1922)
**:** ZAPATEADO

**Za·po·tec** \ˌzä-pə-'tek, ˌsä-\ *noun* (1797)
**:** a member of an American Indian people of Oaxaca state, Mexico

**zap·per** \'za-pər\ *noun* (1969)
**:** one that zaps: as **a :** an electronic device designed to attract and kill insects **b :** a person who habitually changes channels (as to avoid commercials) **c :** a remote control device used for zapping

**zap·py** \'za-pē\ *adjective* (1969)
**:** ZIPPY

**za·re·ba** *or* **za·ri·ba** \zə-'rē-bə\ *noun* [Arabic *zarībah* enclosure] (1849)
**:** an improvised stockade constructed in parts of Africa especially of thorny bushes

**zar·zue·la** \ˌzär-zə-'wä-lə, ˌzär-'zwä-\ *noun* [Spanish, probably from *La Zarzuela*, royal residence near Madrid where it was first performed] (1888)
**:** a usually comic Spanish operetta

**z–ax·is** \'zē-ˌak-səs; *Canadian, British, & Australian* 'zed-\ *noun* (circa 1949)
**:** one of the axes in a three-dimensional rectangular coordinate system

**za·yin** \'zä-yən, 'zī(-ə)n\ *noun* [Hebrew] (1823)
**:** the 7th letter of the Hebrew alphabet — see ALPHABET table

**z–co·or·di·nate** \ˌzē-kō-'órd-nət; -'ór-d°n-ət, -də-ˌnät; *Canadian, British, & Australian* ˌzed-\ *noun* (circa 1956)
**:** a coordinate whose value is determined by measuring parallel to a z-axis

**zeal** \'zē(ə)l\ *noun* [Middle English *zele*, from Late Latin *zelus*, from Greek *zēlos*] (15th century)
**:** eagerness and ardent interest in pursuit of something **:** FERVOR
*synonym* see PASSION

**zeal·ot** \'ze-lət\ *noun* [Late Latin *zelotes*, from Greek *zēlōtēs*, from *zēlos*] (1537)
**1** *capitalized* **:** a member of a fanatical sect arising in Judea during the first century A.D. and militantly opposing the Roman domination of Palestine
**2 :** a zealous person; *especially* **:** a fanatical partisan

**zeal·ot·ry** \'ze-lə-trē\ *noun, plural* **-ries** (1656)
**:** excess of zeal **:** fanatical devotion

**zeal·ous** \'ze-ləs\ *adjective* (1535)
**:** filled with or characterized by zeal ⟨*zealous* missionaries⟩
— **zeal·ous·ly** *adverb*
— **zeal·ous·ness** *noun*

**ze·a·tin** \'zē-ə-tən\ *noun* [New Latin *Zea*, genus of grasses including Indian corn + kine*tin* — more at ZEIN] (1963)
**:** a cytokinin first isolated from the endosperm of Indian corn

**ze·bra** \'zē-brə, *Canadian & British also* 'ze-\ *noun, plural* **zebras** [Portuguese *zebra, zebro* wild ass, perhaps from Latin *equiferus*, kind of wild horse, from *equus* horse + *ferus* wild — more at EQUINE, FIERCE] (1600)
**1** *plural also* **zebra :** any of several fleet African mammals (*Equus burchelli, E. grevyi*,

and *E. zebra*) related to the horse but distinctively and conspicuously patterned in stripes of black or dark brown and white or buff
**2** [from the shirts patterned in black and white stripes worn by football referees] **:** REFEREE 2
**3 :** ZEBRA CROSSING
— **ze·brine** \-ˌbrīn\ *adjective or noun*
**ze·bra crossing** \'ze-brə-, 'zē-\ *noun* (1950)
*British* **:** a crosswalk marked by a series of broad white stripes to indicate a crossing point at which pedestrians have the right of way
**zebra finch** *noun* (1889)
**:** a small largely gray-and-white Australian waxbill (*Poephila guttata*) that has black bars on the tail coverts and is often kept as a cage bird
**zebra fish** *noun* (1771)
**:** any of various barred fishes; *especially* **:** a very small blue-and-silver-striped Indian danio (*Brachydanio rerio* synonym *Danio rerio*) often kept in the tropical aquarium
**zebra mussel** *noun* (1883)
**:** a freshwater Eurasian lamellibranch mollusk (*Dreissena polymorpha*) that was accidentally introduced into the Great Lakes and is spreading to surrounding waterways where it colonizes and clogs water intake pipes and competes with native fish for food
**ze·bra·wood** \'zē-brə-ˌwud\ *noun* (1783)
**1 :** any of several trees or shrubs having mottled or striped wood: as **a :** any of various leguminous African timber trees (genus *Brachystegia*) **b :** a tall South American timber tree (*Astronium fraxinifolium*) of the cashew family
**2 :** the wood of a zebrawood
**ze·bu** \'zē-(ˌ)bü, -(ˌ)byü\ *noun* [French *zébu*] (1774)
**:** any of various breeds of domestic oxen developed in India that are often considered conspecific with the common ox (*Bos taurus*) or sometimes as a separate species (*B. indicus*) and are characterized by a large fleshy hump over the shoulders, a dewlap, pendulous ears, and marked resistance to the injurious effects of heat and insect attack

zebu

**Zeb·u·lun** \'ze-byə-lən\ *noun* [Hebrew *Zĕbhūlūn*]
**:** a son of Jacob and the traditional eponymous ancestor of one of the tribes of Israel
**zec·chi·no** \ze-'kē-(ˌ)nō, tse-\ *noun, plural* **-ni** \-(ˌ)nē\ *or* **-nos** [Italian — more at SEQUIN] (1617)
**:** SEQUIN 1
**Zech·a·ri·ah** \ˌze-kə-'rī-ə\ *noun* [Hebrew *Zĕkharyāh*]
**1 :** a Hebrew prophet of the 6th century B.C.
**2 :** a prophetic book of canonical Jewish and Christian Scripture — see BIBLE table
**zec·chin** \'ze-kən, ze-'kēn\ *noun* [Italian *zecchino*] (1575)
**:** SEQUIN 1
**zed** \'zed\ *noun* [Middle English, from Middle French *zede,* from Late Latin *zeta* zeta, from Greek *zēta*] (15th century)
*chiefly British* **:** the letter *z*
**zee** \'zē\ *noun* (1677)
**:** the letter *z*
**ze·in** \'zē-ən\ *noun* [New Latin *Zea,* genus of grasses including Indian corn, from Greek *zeai,* plural, wheat; akin to Sanskrit *yava* barley] (1822)
**:** a protein from Indian corn that lacks lysine and tryptophan and is used especially in making textile fibers, plastics, printing inks, coatings, and adhesives and sizes

**zeit·ge·ber** \'tsīt-ˌgā-bər, 'zīt-\ *noun* [German, from *Zeit* time + *Geber* giver] (1964)
**:** an environmental agent or event (as the occurrence of light or dark) that provides the stimulus setting or resetting a biological clock of an organism
**zeit·geist** \'tsīt-ˌgīst, 'zīt-\ *noun, often capitalized* [German, from *Zeit* + *Geist* spirit] (1884)
**:** the general intellectual, moral, and cultural climate of an era
**zel·ko·va** \'zel-kə-və, zel-'kō-və\ *noun* [New Latin, from Russian *zel'kova, zel'kva,* from Georgian *dzelkva*] (circa 1890)
**:** a tall widely spreading Japanese tree (*Zelkova serrata*) of the elm family that is often used as an ornamental and shade tree in place of the American elm because of its resistance to Dutch elm disease
**zemst·vo** \'zem(p)st-(ˌ)vō, -və\ *noun, plural* **zemstvos** [Russian; akin to Russian *zemlya* earth, land, Latin *humus* — more at HUMBLE] (1865)
**:** one of the district and provincial assemblies established in Russia in 1864
**Zen** \'zen\ *noun* [Japanese, religious meditation] (1727)
**:** a Japanese sect of Mahayana Buddhism that aims at enlightenment by direct intuition through meditation
**ze·na·na** \zə-'nä-nə\ *noun* [Hindi *zanāna,* from Persian, from *zan* woman] (1760)
**:** HAREM 1a
**Zend–Aves·ta** \ˌzend-ə-'ves-tə\ *noun* [French, from Middle Persian *Avastāk va Zand* Avesta and commentary] (1630)
**:** AVESTA
**ze·ner diode** \'zē-nər-, 'ze-\ *noun, often Z capitalized* [Clarence M. *Zener* (born 1905) American physicist] (1957)
**:** a silicon semiconductor device used especially as a voltage regulator
**ze·nith** \'zē-nəth, *Canadian also & British usually* 'ze-nəth, -nith\ *noun* [Middle English *senith,* from Middle French *cenith,* from Medieval Latin, from Old Spanish *zenit,* modification of Arabic *samt* (*ar-ra's*) way (over one's head)] (14th century)
**1 :** the point of the celestial sphere that is directly opposite the nadir and vertically above the observer
**2 :** the highest point reached in the heavens by a celestial body
**3 :** culminating point **:** ACME ⟨at the *zenith* of his powers —John Buchan⟩ ◆
**ze·nith·al** \-nə-thəl\ *adjective* (1860)
**1 :** of, relating to, or located at or near the zenith
**2 :** showing correct directions from the center ⟨a *zenithal* map⟩
**ze·o·lite** \'zē-ə-ˌlīt\ *noun* [Swedish *zeolit,* from Greek *zein* to boil + *-o-* + Swedish *-lit* -lite, from French *-lite* — more at YEAST] (circa 1777)
**:** any of various hydrous silicates that are analogous in composition to the feldspars, occur as secondary minerals in cavities of lavas, and can act as ion-exchangers; *also* **:** any of various natural or synthesized silicates of similar structure used especially in water softening and as adsorbents and catalysts
— **ze·o·lit·ic** \ˌzē-ə-'li-tik\ *adjective*
**Zeph·a·ni·ah** \ˌze-fə-'nī-ə\ *noun* [Hebrew *Şĕphanyāh*]
**1 :** a Hebrew prophet of the 7th century B.C.
**2 :** an apocalyptic book of canonical Jewish and Christian Scripture — see BIBLE table
**zeph·yr** \'ze-fər\ *noun* [Middle English *Zephirus,* west wind (personified), from Latin *Zephyrus,* god of the west wind & *zephyrus* west wind, zephyr, from Greek *Zephyros* & *zephyros*] (1611)
**1 a :** a breeze from the west **b :** a gentle breeze
**2 :** any of various lightweight fabrics and articles of clothing
**Zeph·y·rus** \'ze-fə-rəs\ *noun* [Latin]

**:** the Greek god of the west wind
**zep·pe·lin** \'ze-p(ə-)lən\ *noun* [Count Ferdinand von *Zeppelin*] (1900)
**:** a rigid airship consisting of a cylindrical trussed and covered frame supported by internal gas cells; *broadly* **:** AIRSHIP

zeppelin

**zerk** \'zərk\ *noun* [Oscar U. *Zerk* (died 1968) American (Austrian-born) inventor] (1926)
**:** a grease fitting
**¹ze·ro** \'zē-(ˌ)rō, 'zir-(ˌ)ō\ *noun, plural* **zeros** *also* **zeroes** [French or Italian; French *zéro,* from Italian *zero,* from Medieval Latin *zephirum,* from Arabic *şifr*] (1604)
**1 a :** the arithmetical symbol 0 or ∅ denoting the absence of all magnitude or quantity **b :** ADDITIVE IDENTITY; *specifically* **:** the number between the set of all negative numbers and the set of all positive numbers **c :** a value of an independent variable that makes a function equal to zero ⟨+2 and −2 are *zeros* of $f(x)=x^2-4$⟩
**2** — see NUMBER table
**3 a** (1) **:** the point of departure in reckoning; *specifically* **:** the point from which the graduation of a scale (as of a thermometer) begins (2) **:** the temperature represented by the zero mark on a thermometer **b :** the setting or adjustment of the sights of a firearm that causes it to shoot to point of aim at a desired range
**4 :** an insignificant person or thing **:** NONENTITY
**5 a :** a state of total absence or neutrality **b :** the lowest point **:** NADIR
**6 :** something arbitrarily or conveniently designated zero
**²zero** *adjective* (1810)
**1 a :** of, relating to, or being a zero **b :** having no magnitude or quantity **:** not any ⟨*zero* growth⟩ **c** (1) **:** having no phonetic manifestation ⟨the *zero* modification in the past tense of *cut*⟩ (2) **:** having no modified inflectional form ⟨a *zero* plural⟩
**2 a** *of a cloud ceiling* **:** limiting vision to 50 feet (15 meters) or less **b** *of horizontal visibility* **:** limited to 165 feet (50.3 meters) or less
**³zero** (1913)
*transitive verb*
**1 :** to determine or adjust the zero of (as a rifle)

---

◇ **WORD HISTORY**
**zenith** The zenith is the point of the celestial sphere vertically above the observer. The Arabs called this point *samt ar-ra's* "the way over one's head" (literally, "the way of the head"). When *samt* was borrowed into Medieval Latin, it was presumably first rendered *zemt,* in keeping with transcription conventions of the time. But most likely by a scribe's error in copying a text—*m* could easily have been misread as *ni*—it appears in manuscripts, initially in the 12th century, as *zenit,* later as *cenith* or *zenith.* The first vernacular appearance of the word was in Spanish astronomical texts of the 13th century; from Spanish or Medieval Latin the word eventually spread to most languages of Europe, appearing in English in the 14th century. By the 1600s *zenith* had acquired the additional senses "the upper region of the heavens" and then "the highest point reached in the heavens by a celestial body." The generalized meaning "culminating point, acme" soon followed.

---

\ə\ **abut** \ᵊ\ **kitten** \ər\ **further** \a\ **ash** \ā\ **ace**
\ä\ **mop, mar** \au̇\ **out** \ch\ **chin** \e\ **bet** \ē\ **easy**
\g\ **go** \i\ **hit** \ī\ **ice** \j\ **job** \ŋ\ **sing** \ō\ **go**
\ȯ\ **law** \ȯi\ **boy** \th\ **thin** \t̲h̲\ **the** \ü\ **loot** \u̇\ **foot**
\y\ **yet** \zh\ **vision** *see also* Guide to Pronunciation

**2 a :** to concentrate firepower on the exact range of — usually used with *in* **b :** to bring to bear on the exact range of a target — usually used with *in*
*intransitive verb*
**1 :** to adjust fire on a specific target — usually used with *in*
**2 :** to close in on or focus attention on an objective — usually used with *in*
**zero–based** *or* **zero–base** *adjective* (1970)
**:** having each item justified on the basis of cost or need 〈*zero-based* budgeting〉
**zero coupon** *adjective* (1979)
**:** of, relating to, or being an investment security that is sold at a deep discount, is redeemable at face value on maturity, and that pays no periodic interest 〈*zero coupon* municipal bonds〉
**zero gravity** *noun* (1951)
**:** the state or condition of lacking apparent gravitational pull : WEIGHTLESSNESS
**zero hour** *noun* [from its being marked by the count of zero in a countdown] (1917)
**1 a :** the hour at which a planned military operation is scheduled to start **b :** the time at which a usually significant or notable event is scheduled to take place
**2 :** a time when a vital decision or decisive change must be made
**zero–sum** *adjective* (1944)
**:** of, relating to, or being a situation (as a game or relationship) in which a gain for one side entails a corresponding loss for the other side
**ze·roth** \'zē-(ˌ)rōth, 'zir-(ˌ)ōth\ *adjective* (1896)
**:** being numbered zero in a series; *also* : ZERO 1 〈the *zeroth* power of a number〉
**zero tillage** *noun* (1963)
**:** NO-TILLAGE
**zero vector** *noun* (circa 1901)
**:** a vector which is of zero length and all of whose components are zero
**zero–zero** *adjective* (circa 1939)
**1 :** characterized by or being atmospheric conditions that reduce ceiling and visibility to zero
**2 :** limited to zero by atmospheric conditions
**zest** \'zest\ *noun* [obsolete French (now *zeste*), orange or lemon peel (used as flavoring)] (circa 1674)
**1 :** a piece of the peel or of the thin outer skin of an orange or lemon used as flavoring
**2 :** an enjoyably exciting quality : PIQUANCY
**3 :** keen enjoyment : RELISH, GUSTO ◆
— **zest·ful** \-fəl\ *adjective*
— **zest·ful·ly** \-fə-lē\ *adverb*
— **zest·ful·ness** *noun*
— **zest·less** \-ləs\ *adjective*
**zest·er** \'zes-tər\ *noun* (1973)
**:** a small utensil for peeling zest
**zesty** \'zes-tē\ *adjective* **zest·i·er; -est** (1930)
**:** having or characterized by zest
**ze·ta** \'zā-tə, 'zē-\ *noun* [Greek *zēta*] (1823)
**:** the 6th letter of the Greek alphabet — see ALPHABET table
**zeug·ma** \'züg-mə\ *noun* [Latin, from Greek, literally, joining, from *zeugnynai* to join; akin to Latin *jungere* to join — more at YOKE] (1523)
**:** the use of a word to modify or govern two or more words usually in such a manner that it applies to each in a different sense or makes sense with only one (as in "opened the door and her heart to the homeless boy")
**Zeus** \'züs\ *noun* [Greek]
**:** the king of the gods and husband of Hera in Greek mythology — compare JUPITER
**zib·e·line** *or* **zib·el·line** \'zi-bə-ˌlēn, -ˌlīn\ *noun* [Middle French, sable, from Old Italian *zibellino*, of Slavic origin; akin to Russian *sobol'* sable] (1892)
**:** a soft lustrous wool fabric with mohair, alpaca, or camel's hair
**zi·do·vu·dine** \zi-'dō-vyü-ˌdēn\ *noun* [by shortening & alteration from *azidothymidine*] (1987)

**:** AZIDOTHYMIDINE
**¹zig** \'zig\ *noun* [*zigzag*] (1840)
**1 a :** one of the sharp turns, angles, or alterations in a zigzag course **b :** one of the short straight lines or sections of a zigzag course at an angle to a zag
**2 :** a sharp alteration or change of direction (as in a process or policy) 〈the quick *zigs* and zags of his international maneuverings —*N.Y. Times*〉
**²zig** *intransitive verb* **zigged; zig·ging** (1940)
**:** to execute a zig — usually contrasted with *zag*
**zig·gu·rat** \'zi-gə-ˌrat\ *noun* [Akkadian *ziqqurratu*] (1877)
**:** an ancient Mesopotamian temple tower consisting of a lofty pyramidal structure built in successive stages with outside staircases and a shrine at the top

**ziggurat**

**¹zig·zag** \'zig-ˌzag\ *noun* [French] (1712)
**:** one of a series of short sharp turns, angles, or alterations in a course; *also* : something having the form or character of such a series 〈a blouse with green *zigzags*〉 〈endured the *zigzags* of policy —Richard Bernstein〉
**²zigzag** *adverb* (circa 1730)
**:** in or by a zigzag path or course
**³zigzag** *adjective* (1750)
**:** having short sharp turns or angles 〈a *zigzag* trail〉
**⁴zigzag** *verb* **zig·zagged; zig·zag·ging** (1777)
*transitive verb*
**:** to form into a zigzag or move along a zigzag course
*intransitive verb*
**:** to lie in, proceed along, or consist of a zigzag course
**zilch** \'zilch\ *adjective or noun* [origin unknown] (circa 1966)
**:** ZERO, NOTHING
**zil·lion** \'zil-yən\ *noun* [*z* + *-illion* (as in *million*)] (1934)
**:** an indeterminately large number 〈*zillions* of mosquitoes〉
— **zil·lionth** \-yən(t)th\ *adjective*
**zil·lion·aire** \ˌzil-yə-'nar, -'ner\ *noun* [*zillion* + *-aire* (as in *millionaire*)] (1946)
**:** an immeasurably wealthy person
**zin** \'zin\ *noun, often capitalized* (1980)
**:** ZINFANDEL
**¹zinc** \'ziŋk\ *noun, often attributive* [German *Zink*] (1651)
**:** a bluish white crystalline metallic element of low to intermediate hardness that is ductile when pure but in the commercial form is brittle at ordinary temperatures and becomes ductile on slight heating, occurs abundantly in minerals, is an essential micronutrient for both plants and animals, and is used especially as a protective coating for iron and steel — see ELEMENT table
**²zinc** *transitive verb* **zinced** *or* **zincked** \'ziŋ(k)t\; **zinc·ing** *or* **zinck·ing** \'ziŋ-kiŋ\ (1841)
**:** to treat or coat with zinc : GALVANIZE
**zinc blende** *noun* (1842)
**:** SPHALERITE
**zinc chloride** *noun* (1851)
**:** a poisonous caustic deliquescent salt $ZnCl_2$ used especially as a wood preservative, drying agent, and catalyst
**zinc·ite** \'ziŋ-ˌkīt\ *noun* [German *Zinkit*, from *Zink*] (1854)

**:** a brittle deep-red to orange-yellow hexagonal mineral that consists essentially of zinc oxide and occurs in massive or granular form
**zinc oxide** *noun* (1849)
**:** an infusible white solid ZnO used especially as a pigment, in compounding rubber, and in pharmaceutical and cosmetic preparations
**zinc oxide ointment** *noun* (1936)
**:** an ointment that contains about 20 percent of zinc oxide and is used in treating skin disorders
**zinc sulfate** *noun* (1851)
**:** a crystalline salt $ZnSO_4$ used especially in making a white paint pigment, in printing and dyeing, in sprays and fertilizers, and in medicine as an astringent, emetic, and weak antiseptic
**zinc sulfide** *noun* (1851)
**:** a fluorescent white to yellowish compound ZnS used especially as a white pigment and a phosphor
**zinc white** *noun* (1847)
**:** a white pigment that consists of zinc oxide
**zin·eb** \'zi-ˌneb\ *noun* [*zinc* + *ethylene* + *bis*-] (1950)
**:** a zinc-containing agricultural fungicide $C_4H_6N_2S_4Zn$ used on fruits and vegetables
**zin·fan·del** \'zin-fən-ˌdel\ *noun* [origin unknown] (1896)
**:** a dry red table wine made from a small black grape that is grown chiefly in California; *also* **:** the grape
**¹zing** \'ziŋ\ *noun* [imitative] (1911)
**1 :** a shrill humming noise
**2 a :** an enjoyably exciting or stimulating quality : ZEST 〈really put some *zing* into this industry —Erwin Fine〉 **b :** a sharply piquant flavor 〈barbecue sauce with *zing*〉
**²zing** (1920)
*intransitive verb*
**1 :** to make or move with a humming sound
**2 :** ZIP, SPEED
*transitive verb*
**1 :** to hit suddenly : ZAP
**2 :** to criticize in a pointed or witty manner
**zing·er** \'ziŋ-ər\ *noun* (1955)
**1 :** something causing or meant to cause interest, surprise, or shock
**2 :** a pointed witty remark or retort
**zingy** \'ziŋ-ē\ *adjective* **zing·i·er; -est** [¹*zing*] (1945)
**1 :** enjoyably exciting 〈a *zingy* musical〉
**2 :** strikingly attractive or appealing 〈wore a *zingy* new outfit〉
**3 :** sharply piquant 〈a *zingy* salad〉
**zin·nia** \'zi-nē-ə, 'zē-; 'zin-yə, 'zēn-\ *noun* [New Latin, from Johann G. *Zinn* (died 1759) German botanist] (1767)
**:** any of a small genus (*Zinnia*) of tropical

American composite herbs and low shrubs with showy flower heads and long-lasting ray flowers

**Zi·on** \'zī-ən\ *noun* [Middle English *Sion*, from Old English, citadel in Palestine which was the nucleus of Jerusalem, from Late Latin, from Greek *Seiōn*, from Hebrew *Ṣīyōn*] (14th century)
**1 a :** the Jewish people **:** ISRAEL **b :** the Jewish homeland that is symbolic of Judaism or of Jewish national aspiration **c :** the ideal nation or society envisaged by Judaism
**2 :** HEAVEN
**3 :** UTOPIA
**Zi·on·ism** \'zī-ə-,ni-zəm\ *noun* (1896)
**:** an international movement originally for the establishment of a Jewish national or religious community in Palestine and later for the support of modern Israel
— **Zi·on·ist** \-nist\ *adjective or noun*
— **Zi·on·is·tic** \,zī-ə-'nis-tik\ *adjective*

**¹zip** \'zip\ *verb* **zipped; zip·ping** [imitative of the sound of a speeding object] (1852)
*intransitive verb*
**1 :** to move, act, or function with speed and vigor
**2 :** to travel with a sharp hissing or humming sound
*transitive verb*
**1 :** to impart speed or force to
**2 :** to add zest, interest, or life to — often used with *up*
**3 :** to transport or propel with speed
**²zip** *noun* (1875)
**1 :** a sudden sharp hissing or sibilant sound
**2 :** ENERGY, VIM
— **zip·less** \-ləs\ *adjective*
**³zip** *noun* [origin unknown] (circa 1900)
**:** NOTHING, ZERO ⟨the final score was 27 to *zip*⟩
**⁴zip** *noun* (1920)
*chiefly British* **:** ZIPPER
**⁵zip** *verb* **zipped; zip·ping** [back-formation from *zipper*] (1932)
*transitive verb*
**1 a :** to close or open with or as if with a zipper **b :** to enclose or wrap by fastening a zipper
**2 :** to cause (a zipper) to open or shut
*intransitive verb*
**:** to become open, closed, or attached by means of a zipper
**⁶zip** *noun, often Z&I&P capitalized* (1965)
**:** ZIP CODE
**zip–code** *transitive verb* (1964)
**:** to furnish with a zip code
**zip code** *noun, often Z&I&P capitalized* [zone improvement plan] (1963)
**:** a number that identifies each postal delivery area in the U.S.
**zip fastener** *noun* (1927)
*chiefly British* **:** ZIPPER
**zip gun** *noun* (1950)
**:** a crudely homemade single-shot pistol
**¹zip·per** \'zi-pər\ *noun* [from *Zipper*, a trademark] (1926)
**:** a fastener consisting of two rows of metal or plastic teeth on strips of tape and a sliding piece that closes an opening by drawing the teeth together
**²zipper** *transitive verb* (1930)
**:** ⁵ZIP
**zip·pered** \-pərd\ *adjective* (1939)
**:** equipped with a zipper
**zip·py** \'zi-pē\ *adjective* **zip·pi·er; -est** (1904)
**:** full of zip **:** BRISK, SNAPPY
**zi·ram** \'zī-,ram\ *noun* [*zin*c + di*thioca*r*bamate*] (1949)
**:** an organic zinc salt $C_6H_{12}N_2S_4Zn$ used especially as an agricultural fungicide
**zir·con** \'zər-,kän, -kən\ *noun* [German, modification of French *jargon* jargoon, zircon, from Italian *giargone*] (1794)
**:** a tetragonal mineral consisting of a silicate of zirconium and occurring usually in brown or grayish square prisms of adamantine luster

or sometimes in transparent forms which are used as gems
**zir·co·nia** \,zər-'kō-nē-ə\ *noun* [New Latin, from International Scientific Vocabulary *zircon*] (1797)
**:** a white crystalline compound $ZrO_2$ used especially in refractories, in thermal and electric insulation, in abrasives, and in enamels and glazes — called also *zirconium oxide*
**zir·co·ni·um** \,zər-'kō-nē-əm\ *noun* [New Latin, from International Scientific Vocabulary *zircon*] (1808)
**:** a steel-gray strong ductile metallic element with a high melting point that occurs widely in combined form (as in zircon), is highly resistant to corrosion, and is used especially in alloys and in refractories and ceramics — see ELEMENT table
**zit** \'zit\ *noun* [origin unknown] (circa 1966)
*slang* **:** PIMPLE 1
**zith·er** \'zi-thər, -thər\ *noun* [German, from Latin *cithara* cithara — more at CITHER] (1850)
**:** a stringed instrument having usually 30 to 40 strings over a shallow horizontal soundboard and played with pick and fingers
— **zith·er·ist** \-thə-rist, -thə-\ *noun*

**zither**

**zi·ti** \'zē-tē\ *noun, plural* **ziti** [Italian, plural of *zito*, alteration of *zita* piece of tubular pasta, probably short for *maccheroni di zita*, literally, bride's macaroni] (circa 1845)
**:** medium-sized tubular pasta
**zi·zith** \'tsit-səs, tsēt-'sēt\ *noun plural* [Hebrew *ṣīṣīth*] (1675)
**:** the fringes or tassels worn on traditional or ceremonial garments by Jewish males as reminders of the commandments of Deuteronomy 22:12 and Numbers 15:37–41
**Z line** *noun* (1916)
**:** any of the dark thin lines across a striated muscle fiber that mark the boundaries between adjacent sarcomeres
**zlo·ty** \'zló-tē\ *noun, plural* **zlo·tys** \-tēz\ *or* **zloty** [Polish *złoty*] (1915)
— see MONEY table
**zo-** *or* **zoo-** *combining form* [Greek *zōi-, zōio-*, from *zōion*; akin to Greek *zōē* life — more at QUICK]
**1 :** animal **:** animal kingdom or kind ⟨*zoo*id⟩ ⟨*zoo*logy⟩
**2** [Greek *zō-* alive, from *zōos*; akin to Greek *zōē*] **:** motile ⟨*zoo*spore⟩
**-zoa** \'zō-ə\ *noun plural combining form* [New Latin, from Greek *zōia*, plural of *zōion*]
**:** animals — in taxa ⟨Meta*zoa*⟩ ⟨Proto*zoa*⟩
**zo·an·thar·i·an** \,zō-ən-'ther-ē-ən, -'thar-\ *noun* [ultimately from *zo-* + Greek *anthos* flower — more at ANTHOLOGY] (1887)
**:** any of a subclass (Zoantharia) of anthozoans having a hexamerous arrangement of tentacles or septa or both and including most of the recent corals and sea anemones
— **zoantharian** *adjective*
**zo·di·ac** \'zō-dē-,ak\ *noun* [Middle English, from Middle French *zodiaque*, from Latin *zodiacus*, from Greek *zōidiakos*, from *zōidiakos*, adjective, of carved figures, of the zodiac, from *zōidion* carved figure, sign of the zodiac, from diminutive of *zōion* living being, figure; akin to Greek *zōē* life] (14th century)
**1 a :** an imaginary band in the heavens centered on the ecliptic that encompasses the apparent paths of all the planets except Pluto and is divided into 12 constellations or signs each taken for astrological purposes to extend 30 degrees of longitude **b :** a figure representing the signs of the zodiac and their symbols
**2 :** a cyclic course ⟨a *zodiac* of feasts and fasts —R. W. Emerson⟩
— **zo·di·a·cal** \zō-'dī-ə-kəl; zə-\ *adjective*

## SIGNS OF THE ZODIAC

| NUMBER and NAME | SYMBOL | SUN ENTERS |
|---|---|---|
| 1 Aries the Ram | ♈ | March 21 |
| 2 Taurus the Bull | ♉ | April 20 |
| 3 Gemini the Twins | ♊ | May 21 |
| 4 Cancer the Crab | ♋ | June 22 |
| 5 Leo the Lion | ♌ | July 23 |
| 6 Virgo the Virgin | ♍ | August 23 |
| 7 Libra the Balance | ♎ | September 23 |
| 8 Scorpio the Scorpion | ♏ | October 24 |
| 9 Sagittarius the Archer | ♐ | November 22 |
| 10 Capricorn the Goat | ♑ | December 22 |
| 11 Aquarius the Water Bearer | ♒ | January 20 |
| 12 Pisces the Fishes | ♓ | February 19 |

**zodiacal light** *noun* (1734)
**:** a diffuse glow seen in the west after twilight and in the east before dawn
**zo·ea** \zō-'ē-ə\ *noun, plural* **zo·eae** \-'ē-,ē\ *or* **zo·eas** \-'ē-əz\ [New Latin, from Greek *zōē* life] (circa 1890)
**:** a free-swimming planktonic larval form of many decapod crustaceans and especially crabs that has a relatively large cephalothorax, conspicuous eyes, and fringed antennae and mouthparts
**zof·tig** \'zóf-tig\ *variant of* ZAFTIG
**¹-zoic** *adjective combining form* [Greek *zōikos* of animals, from *zōion* animal — more at ZO-]
**:** having a (specified) animal mode of existence ⟨holo*zoic*⟩
**²-zoic** *adjective combining form* [Greek *zōē* life]
**:** of, relating to, or being a (specified) geological era ⟨Archeo*zoic*⟩ ⟨Meso*zoic*⟩
**zois·ite** \'zói-,sīt\ *noun* [German *Zoisit*, from Baron Sigismund Zois von Edelstein (died 1819) Slovenian nobleman] (1805)
**:** an orthorhombic mineral that consists of a basic silicate of calcium and aluminum and is related to epidote
**zom·bie** *also* **zom·bi** \'zäm-bē\ *noun* [Louisiana Creole or Haitian Creole *zōbi*, of Bantu origin; akin to Kimbundu *nzúmbe* ghost] (circa 1871)
**1** *usually zombi* **a :** the supernatural power that according to voodoo belief may enter into and reanimate a dead body **b :** a will-less and speechless human in the West Indies capable only of automatic movement who is held to have died and been supernaturally reanimated
**2 a :** a person held to resemble the so-called walking dead; *especially* **:** AUTOMATON **b :** a

\ə\ abut \ᵊ\ kitten \ər\ further \a\ ash \ā\ ace \ä\ mop, mar \aú\ out \ch\ chin \e\ bet \ē\ easy \g\ go \i\ hit \ī\ ice \j\ job \ŋ\ sing \ō\ go \ó\ law \ói\ boy \th\ thin \t͟h\ the \ü\ loot \ü\ foot \y\ yet \zh\ vision *see also* Guide to Pronunciation

person markedly strange in appearance or behavior
**3 :** a mixed drink made of several kinds of rum, liqueur, and fruit juice ◆
— **zom·bie·like** \-bē-ˌlīk\ *adjective*
**zom·bi·fy** \ˈzäm-bə-ˌfī\ *transitive verb* **-fied; -fy·ing** (1946)
: to turn (a human being) into a zombie
— **zom·bi·fi·ca·tion** \ˌzäm-bə-fə-ˈkā-shən\ *noun*
**zom·bi·ism** \-bē-ˌi-zəm\ *noun* (1932)
: the beliefs and practices of the cult of the zombi
**zon·al** \ˈzō-nᵊl\ *adjective* (1873)
**1 :** of, relating to, affecting, or having the form of a zone ⟨a *zonal* boundary⟩
**2 :** of, relating to, or being a soil or a major soil group marked by well-developed characteristics that are determined primarily by the action of climate and organisms especially vegetation — compare AZONAL, INTRAZONAL
— **zon·al·ly** \-nᵊl-ē\ *adverb*
**zo·na pel·lu·ci·da** \ˌzō-nə-pə-ˈlü-sə-də, -pel-ˈyü-\ *noun, plural* **zo·nae pel·lu·ci·dae** \-(ˌ)nē . . . -(ˌ)dē, -ˌnī . . . -ˌdī\ [New Latin, transparent zone] (1841)
: the transparent more or less elastic outer layer or envelope of a mammalian ovum often traversed by numerous radiating striae
**zo·na·tion** \zō-ˈnā-shən\ *noun* (1902)
**1 :** structure or arrangement in zones
**2 :** distribution of kinds of organisms in biogeographic zones
**¹zone** \ˈzōn\ *noun* [Middle English, from Latin *zona* belt, zone, from Greek *zōnē;* akin to Lithuanian *juosti* to gird] (15th century)
**1 a :** any of five great divisions of the earth's surface with respect to latitude and temperature — compare FRIGID ZONE, TEMPERATE ZONE, TORRID ZONE **b :** a portion of the surface of a sphere included between two parallel planes
**2** *archaic* **:** GIRDLE, BELT
**3 a :** an encircling anatomical structure **b** (1) : a subdivision of a biogeographic region that supports a similar fauna and flora throughout its extent (2) : such a zone dominated by a particular life form **c :** a distinctive belt, layer, or series of layers of earth materials (as rock)
**4 :** a region or area set off as distinct from surrounding or adjoining parts
**5 :** one of the sections of an area or territory created for a particular purpose: as **a :** a zoned section of a city **b :** any of the eight concentric bands of territory centered on a given postal shipment point designated as a distance bracket for U.S. parcel post to which mail is charged at a single rate **c :** a distance within which the same fare is charged by a common carrier **d :** an area on a field of play **e :** a stretch of roadway or a space in which certain traffic regulations are in force
**²zone** *transitive verb* **zoned; zon·ing** (1795)
**1 :** to surround with a zone : ENCIRCLE
**2 :** to arrange in or mark off into zones; *specifically* **:** to partition (a city, borough, or township) by ordinance into sections reserved for different purposes (as residence or business)
— **zon·er** *noun*
**³zone** *adjective* (1795)
**1 :** ZONAL 1
**2 :** of, relating to, or being a system of defense (as in basketball or football) in which each player guards an assigned area rather than a specified opponent
**zone out** *intransitive verb* (1984)
: to become oblivious to one's surroundings especially in order to relax
**zone refining** *noun* (1952)
: a technique for the purification of a crystalline material and especially a metal in which a molten region travels through the material to be refined, picks up impurities at its advancing

edge, and then allows the purified part to recrystallize at its opposite edge — called also *zone melting*
— **zone–refined** *adjective*
**Zon·ian** \ˈzō-nē-ən, -nyən\ *noun* (1910)
: a U.S. citizen who lives in the Panama Canal Zone
**zonk** \ˈzäŋk, ˈzȯŋk\ *verb* [probably imitative] (1950)
*transitive verb*
: STUN, STUPEFY; *also* : STRIKE, ZAP — often used with *out*
*intransitive verb*
: to pass out from or as if from alcohol or a drug — often used with *out*
**zonked** \ˈzäŋkt, ˈzȯŋ(k)t\ *adjective* (circa 1959)
: stupefied by or as if by alcohol or a drug
**zonked–out** \-ˈaȯt\ *adjective* (1967)
: ZONKED
**Zon·ti·an** \ˈzän-tē-ən\ *noun* [*Zonta International,* a service club] (1934)
: a member of a service club made up of executive women each of whom is a sole representative of one business or profession in a community
**zoo** \ˈzü\ *noun, plural* **zoos** [short for *zoological garden*] (circa 1847)
**1 a :** ZOOLOGICAL GARDEN **b :** a collection of living animals usually for public display
**2 :** a place, situation, or group marked by crowding, confusion, or unrestrained behavior ⟨the convention was a *zoo*⟩
**zoo-** — see ZO-
**zo·oe·ci·um** *or* **zo·e·ci·um** \zō-ˈē-shē-əm\ *noun, plural* **-cia** [New Latin, from *zo-* + Greek *oikia* house — more at VICINITY] (1880)
: a sac or chamber secreted and lived in by a bryozoan zooid
**zoo·gen·ic** \ˌzō-ə-ˈje-nik\ *adjective* [International Scientific Vocabulary] (circa 1864)
: caused by or associated with animals or their activities ⟨*zoogenic* humus⟩
**zoo·ge·og·ra·phy** \ˌzō-ə-jē-ˈä-grə-fē\ *noun* [International Scientific Vocabulary] (1868)
: a branch of biogeography concerned with the geographical distribution of animals and especially with the determination of the areas characterized by special groups of animals and the study of the causes and significance of such groups
— **zoo·ge·og·ra·pher** \-fər\ *noun*
— **zoo·geo·graph·ic** \-ˌjē-ə-ˈgra-fik\ *or* **zoo·geo·graph·i·cal** \-fi-kəl\ *adjective*
— **zoo·geo·graph·i·cal·ly** \-fi-k(ə-)lē\ *adverb*
**zo·oid** \ˈzō-ˌȯid\ *noun* (1851)
: one of the asexually produced individuals of a compound organism (as a bryozoan, hydroid, or coral colony)
**zoo·keep·er** \ˈzü-ˌkē-pər\ *noun* (1924)
: one who maintains or cares for animals in a zoo
**zooks** \ˈzȯks\ *interjection* [short for *gadzooks*] (1634)
*archaic* — used as a mild oath
**zo·ol·a·try** \zō-ˈä-lə-trē, zə-ˈwä-\ *noun* [New Latin *zoolatria,* from *zo-* + Late Latin *-latria* -latry] (1817)
: animal worship
**zoo·log·i·cal** \ˌzō-ə-ˈlä-ji-kəl\ *also* **zoo·log·ic** \-jik\ *adjective* (1807)
**1 :** of, relating to, or occupied with zoology
**2 :** of, relating to, or affecting lower animals often as distinguished from humans
— **zoo·log·i·cal·ly** \-ji-k(ə-)lē\ *adverb*
**zoological garden** *noun* (1829)
: a garden or park where wild animals are kept for exhibition
**zo·ol·o·gy** \zō-ˈä-lə-jē, zə-ˈwä-\ *noun* [New Latin *zoologia,* from *zo-* + *-logia* -logy] (1669)
**1 :** a branch of biology concerned with the classification and the properties and vital phenomena of animals

**2 a :** animal life (as of a region) : FAUNA **b** : the properties and vital phenomena exhibited by an animal, animal type, or group
— **zo·ol·o·gist** \-jist\ *noun*
**¹zoom** \ˈzüm\ *verb* [imitative] (1886)
*intransitive verb*
**1 a :** to move with a loud low hum or buzz **b** : to go speedily : ZIP
**2** *of an airplane* **:** to climb for a short time at an angle greater than that which can be maintained in steady flight so that the machine is carried upward at the expense of stored kinetic energy
**3 :** to focus a camera or microscope on an object using a zoom lens so that the object's apparent distance from the observer changes — often used with *in* or *out*
**4 :** to increase sharply ⟨retail sales *zoomed*⟩
*transitive verb*
: to cause to zoom ▪
**²zoom** *noun* (1918)
**1 a :** an act or process of zooming; *especially* : a sharp upward movement **b** : an image created by zooming
**2 :** a zooming sound
**3 :** ZOOM LENS
**zoom lens** *noun* (1936)
: a lens (as of a camera or projector) in which the image size can be varied continuously while the image remains in focus
**zoo·mor·phic** \ˌzō-ə-ˈmȯr-fik\ *adjective* [International Scientific Vocabulary] (1872)
**1 :** having the form of an animal
**2 :** of, relating to, or being a deity conceived of in animal form or with animal attributes
— **zoo·morph** \ˈzō-ə-ˌmȯrf\ *noun*

□ **USAGE**
**zoom** A recent commentator tells us that it is technically correct to zoom up (although the *up* is redundant), that informally *zoom* may apply to level movement, and that *zoom* is nonstandard in reference to downward movement. The distinction is tidy but bears no relation to the real use of *zoom*. A cursory examination of the entry above will show that there is a technical meaning for airplanes but that it is neither the earliest nor the only sense. One may zoom in any direction without transgressing the bounds of standard English: skiers are unlikely to zoom up the slopes.

◇ **WORD HISTORY**
**zombie** The word *zombie* or *zombi* is now inextricably associated with the walking dead of Haitian folk belief, though its first attestation in English has no connection with Haiti. In a collection of Americanisms published in 1871, the philologist Maximilian Schele de Vere claims that *zombi,* "a phantom or ghost," is "not infrequently heard in the Southern States in nurseries and among the servants." The source of the word in the American South is the French creole spoken by African slaves and their descendants in Louisiana—a language akin to Haitian Creole. *Zombi* as an English loan from Haitian Creole was first noted in an 1884 book by Spencer St. John, British consul in Port-au-Prince. St. John's book initiated a series of naive and sensational popular depictions of Haitian life. One of the more successful such works was W. H. Seabrook's *The Magic Island* (1929), which did much to increase the currency of *zombie* in American English. The ultimate source of French creole *zōbi* is most likely Kimbundu *nzúmbe* "departed spirit," or cognate words in other Bantu languages of west central Africa. The Bantu word also surfaces as *jumby* "ghost" in English creoles of the Caribbean.

**-zoon** *noun combining form, plural* **-zoa** [New Latin, from Greek *zōion*]
**:** animal **:** zooid ⟨spermato*zoon*⟩

**zoo·no·sis** \ˌzō-'ä-nə-səs, ˌzō-ə-'nō-səs\ *noun, plural* **-no·ses** \-ˌsēz\ [New Latin, from *zo-* + Greek *nosos* disease] (1876)
**:** a disease communicable from animals to humans under natural conditions
— **zoo·not·ic** \ˌzō-ə-'nä-tik\ *adjective*

**zoo·phil·ic** \ˌzō-ə-'fi-lik\ *or* **zo·oph·i·lous** \zō-'ä-fə-ləs, zə-'wä-\ *adjective* (1886)
**:** having an attraction to or preference for animals; *especially, of an insect* **:** preferring animals to humans as a source of food

**zoo·phyte** \'zō-ə-ˌfīt\ *noun* [Greek *zōophyton,* from *zōi-, zō-* zo- + *phyton* plant — more at PHYT-] (1621)
**:** an invertebrate animal (as a coral or sponge) more or less resembling a plant in appearance or mode of growth

**zoo·plank·ter** \'zō-ə-ˌplaŋ(k)-tər\ *noun* [*zo-* + *plankter*] (1943)
**:** a planktonic animal

**zoo·plank·ton** \ˌzō-ə-'plaŋ(k)-tən, -ˌtän\ *noun* (1901)
**:** plankton composed of animals
— **zoo·plank·ton·ic** \-ˌplaŋ(k)-'tä-nik\ *adjective*

**zoo·spo·ran·gi·um** \ˌzō-ə-spə-'ran-jē-əm\ *noun* [New Latin] (1874)
**:** a spore case or sporangium bearing zoospores

**zoo·spore** \'zō-ə-ˌspōr, -ˌspȯr\ *noun* [International Scientific Vocabulary] (1846)
**:** an independently motile spore; *especially* **:** a motile usually naked and flagellated asexual spore especially of an alga or lower fungus
— **zoo·spor·ic** \ˌzō-ə-'spōr-ik, -'spȯr-\ *adjective*

**zo·os·ter·ol** \zō-'äs-tə-ˌrȯl, -ˌrōl\ *noun* (1926)
**:** a sterol (as cholesterol) of animal origin — compare PHYTOSTEROL

**zoo·tech·ni·cal** \ˌzō-ə-'tek-ni-kəl\ *adjective* (1926)
**:** of or relating to the technology of animal husbandry
— **zoo·tech·nics** \-'tek-niks\ *noun plural but singular or plural in construction*

**zoot suit** \'züt-\ *noun* [coined by Harold C. Fox (born 1910) American clothier and bandleader] (1942)
**:** a suit of extreme cut typically consisting of a thigh-length jacket with wide padded shoulders and peg pants with narrow cuffs
— **zoot–suit·er** \-ˌsü-tər\ *noun*

**zooty** \'zü-tē\ *adjective* (1946)
**:** typical of a zoot-suiter **:** flashy in manner or style ⟨a *zooty* haircut⟩

**zo·o·xan·thel·la** \ˌzō-ə-zan-'the-lə\ *noun, plural* **-lae** \-(ˌ)lē\ [New Latin, from *zo-* + *xanth-* + *-ella* (diminutive suffix)] (circa 1891)
**:** any of various symbiotic dinoflagellates that live within the cells of other organisms (as reef-building coral polyps)

**zo·ri** \'zȯr-ē, 'zȯr-\ *noun, plural* **zori** *also* **zoris** [Japanese *zōri*] (1823)
**:** a flat thonged sandal usually made of straw, cloth, leather, or rubber

**Zorn's lemma** \'zȯrnz-, 'tsȯrnz-\ *noun* [Max August *Zorn* (died 1993) German mathematician] (circa 1950)
**:** a lemma in set theory: if a set S is partially ordered and if each subset for which every pair of elements is related by exactly one of the relationships "less than," "equal to," or "greater than" has an upper bound in S, then S contains at least one element for which there is no greater element in S — compare AXIOM OF CHOICE

**Zo·ro·as·tri·an·ism** \ˌzȯr-ə-'was-trē-ə-ˌni-zəm\ *noun* (1854)
**:** a Persian religion founded in the 6th century B.C. by the prophet Zoroaster, promulgated in the Avesta, and characterized by worship of a supreme god Ahura Mazda who requires good deeds for help in his cosmic struggle against the evil spirit Ahriman
— **Zo·ro·as·tri·an** \-trē-ən\ *adjective or noun*

**zoster** *noun* [Latin, from Greek *zōstēr* girdle; akin to Greek *zōnē* zone] (circa 1706)
**:** HERPES ZOSTER

**Zou·ave** \zu̇-'äv\ *noun* [French, from Berber *Zwāwa,* Berber tribe] (1830)
**1 :** a member of a French infantry unit originally composed of Algerians wearing a brilliant uniform and conducting a quick spirited drill
**2 :** a member of a military unit adopting the dress and drill of the Zouaves

**zounds** \'zau̇n(d)z, 'zün(d)z, 'zwau̇n(d)z, 'zwün(d)z\ *interjection* [euphemism for *God's wounds*] (circa 1600)
— used as a mild oath

**zow·ie** \'zau̇-ē\ *interjection* [imitative of the sound of a speeding vehicle] (1902)
— used to express astonishment or admiration especially in response to something sudden or speedy

**zoy·sia** \'zȯi-shə, -zhə, -sē-ə, -zē-ə\ *noun* [New Latin, alteration of *Zoisia,* from Karl von *Zois* (died 1800) German botanist] (1924)
**:** any of a genus (*Zoysia*) of creeping perennial grasses of southeastern Asia and New Zealand having fine wiry leaves and including some suitable for lawn grasses especially in warm regions

**Z particle** *noun* (1979)
**:** a neutral elementary particle about 90 times heavier than a proton that along with the W particle is a transmitter of the weak force — called also $Z^0$ or $Z^0$ particle

**zuc·chet·to** \zu̇-'ke-(ˌ)tō, tsü-\ *noun, plural* **-tos** [Italian, diminutive of *zucca* gourd, head] (1853)
**:** a small round skullcap worn by Roman Catholic ecclesiastics in colors that vary according to the rank of the wearer

**zuc·chi·ni** \zu̇-'kē-nē\ *noun, plural* **-ni** *or* **-nis** [Italian, plural of *zucchino,* diminutive of *zucca* squash] (1929)
**:** a summer squash of bushy growth with smooth cylindrical usually dark green fruits; *also* **:** its fruit

**¹Zu·lu** \'zü-(ˌ)lü\ *noun, plural* **Zulu** *or* **Zulus** (1824)
**1 :** a member of a Bantu-speaking people of Natal
**2 :** the Bantu language of the Zulus
— **Zulu** *adjective*

**²Zulu** (1952)
— a communications code word for the letter *z*

**Zu·ni** \'zü-nē\ *also* **Zu·ñi** \'zün-yē\ *noun, plural* **Zuni** *or* **Zunis** *also* **Zuñi** *or* **Zuñis** [American Spanish *Zuñi*] (1834)
**1 :** a member of an American Indian people of western New Mexico
**2 :** the language of the Zuni people

**zup·pa in·gle·se** \ˌtsü-pə-iŋ-'glā-(ˌ)zā, ˌzü-, -in-, -(ˌ)sä\ *noun, often I capitalized* [Italian, literally, English soup] (1941)
**:** a dessert consisting of sponge cake and custard or pudding that is flavored with rum, covered with cream, and garnished with fruit

**zwie·back** \'swē-ˌbak, 'swī-, 'zwē-, 'zwī-, -ˌbäk\ *noun* [German, literally, twice baked, from *zwie-* twice (from Old High German *zwi-*) + *backen* to bake, from Old High German *bahhan* — more at TWI-, BAKE] (1894)
**:** a usually sweetened bread enriched with eggs that is baked and then sliced and toasted until dry and crisp

**Zwing·li·an** \'zwiŋ-glē-ən, 'swiŋ-, -lē-; 'tsfiŋ-lē-\ *adjective* (1532)
**:** of or relating to Ulrich Zwingli or his teachings and especially his doctrine that Christ's presence in the Eucharist is not corporeal but symbolic
— **Zwinglian** *noun*
— **Zwing·li·an·ism** \-ə-ˌni-zəm\ *noun*

**zwit·ter·ion** \'tsvi-tər-ˌī-ˌän *also* 'zwi-\ *noun* [German, from *Zwitter* hybrid (from Old High German *zwitaran,* from *zwi-*) + *Ion* ion — more at TWI-] (1906)
**:** a dipolar ion
— **zwit·ter·ion·ic** \ˌzwi-tər-ī-'ä-nik, ˌswi-\ *adjective*

**zy·de·co** \'zī-də-ˌkō\ *noun, often attributive* [perhaps modification of French *les haricots* beans, from the Cajun dance tune *Les Haricots Sont Pas Salés*] (1960)
**:** popular music of southern Louisiana that combines tunes of French origin with elements of Caribbean music and the blues and that features guitar, washboard, and accordion

**zyg-** *or* **zygo-** *combining form* [New Latin, from Greek, from *zygon* — more at YOKE]
**1 :** yoke ⟨*zygo*morphic⟩
**2 :** pair ⟨*zygo*dactyl⟩
**3 :** union ⟨*zygo*spore⟩

**zyg·apoph·y·sis** \ˌzī-gə-'pä-fə-səs\ *noun, plural* **-y·ses** \-ˌsēz\ [New Latin] (1854)
**:** any of the articular processes of the neural arch of a vertebra of which there are usually two anterior and two posterior

**zy·go·dac·tyl** \ˌzī-gə-'dak-t°l\ *adjective* [International Scientific Vocabulary *zyg-* + Greek *daktylos* toe] (1831)
**:** having the toes arranged two in front and two behind — used of a bird

**zy·go·dac·ty·lous** \-tə-ləs\ *adjective* (circa 1828)
**:** ZYGODACTYL

**zy·go·ma** \zī-'gō-mə\ *noun, plural* **-ma·ta** \-mə-tə\ *also* **-mas** [New Latin *zygomat-, zygoma,* from Greek *zygōma,* from *zygoun* to join, from *zygon* yoke] (circa 1684)
**1 a :** ZYGOMATIC ARCH **b :** a slender bony process of the zygomatic arch
**2 :** ZYGOMATIC BONE

**zy·go·mat·ic** \ˌzī-gə-'ma-tik\ *adjective* (1709)
**:** of, relating to, constituting, or situated in the region of the zygoma and especially the zygomatic arch

**zygomatic arch** *noun* (1825)
**:** the arch of bone that extends along the front or side of the skull beneath the orbit

**zygomatic bone** *noun* (1709)
**:** a bone of the side of the face below the eye that in mammals forms part of the zygomatic arch and part of the orbit — called also *cheekbone*

**zygomatic process** *noun* (1741)
**:** any of several bony processes that enter into or strengthen the zygomatic arch

**zy·go·mor·phic** \ˌzī-gə-'mȯr-fik\ *adjective* (1875)
**:** having one or more similar parts unequal in size or form so that the whole structure is capable of division into essentially symmetrical halves by only one longitudinal plane passing through the axis ⟨the flower of the pea is *zygomorphic*⟩
— **zy·go·mor·phy** \'zī-gə-ˌmȯr-fē\ *noun*

**zy·gos·i·ty** \zī-'gä-sə-tē\ *noun* [probably from *-zygous*] (1946)
**:** the makeup or characteristics of a particular zygote

**zy·go·spore** \'zī-gə-ˌspōr, -ˌspȯr\ *noun* [International Scientific Vocabulary] (1849)
**:** a thick-walled spore of some algae and fungi that is formed by union of two similar sexual cells, usually serves as a resting spore, and produces the sporophytic phase of the plant — compare OOSPORE

**zy·gote** \'zī-ˌgōt\ *noun* [Greek *zygōtos* yoked,

from *zygoun* to join — more at ZYGOMA] (circa 1887)
**:** a cell formed by the union of two gametes; *broadly* **:** the developing individual produced from such a cell
— **zy·got·ic** \zī-'gä-tik\ *adjective*
**zy·go·tene** \'zī-gə-ˌtēn\ *noun* [International Scientific Vocabulary] (1911)
**:** the stage of meiotic prophase which immediately follows the leptotene and during which synapsis of homologous chromosomes occurs
— **zygotene** *adjective*
**-zygous** *adjective combining form* [Greek *-zygos* yoked, from *zygon* yoke — more at YOKE]

**:** having (such) a zygotic constitution ⟨heterozygous⟩
**zym-** *or* **zymo-** *combining form* [International Scientific Vocabulary, from Greek, leaven, from *zymē* — more at JUICE]
**1 :** yeast ⟨zymosan⟩
**2 :** enzyme ⟨zymogen⟩
**zy·mase** \'zī-ˌmās, -ˌmāz\ *noun* [International Scientific Vocabulary] (1875)
**:** an enzyme or enzyme complex of yeast that promotes fermentation of sugar
**-zyme** *noun combining form* [Greek *zymē* leaven]
**:** enzyme ⟨lysozyme⟩

**zy·mo·gen** \'zī-mə-jən\ *noun* [International Scientific Vocabulary] (1877)
**:** an inactive protein precursor of an enzyme secreted by living cells and activated by catalysis (as by a kinase or an acid) — called also *proenzyme*
**zy·mo·gram** \'zī-mə-ˌgram\ *noun* (1957)
**:** an electrophoretic strip (as of starch gel) or a representation of it exhibiting the pattern of separated enzymes and especially isoenzymes after electrophoresis
**zy·mo·san** \'zī-mə-ˌsan\ *noun* [zym- + -osan (as in *hexosan*)] (1943)
**:** an insoluble largely polysaccharide fraction of yeast cell walls

# Abbreviations

## AND SYMBOLS FOR CHEMICAL ELEMENTS

The following list of abbreviations is not intended to be all-inclusive; it does, however, contain many of those most commonly used as well as all the abbreviations that are used in the text of this work. Symbols for chemical elements are also included. Most of these abbreviations have been normalized to one form. In practice, however, there is considerable variation in the use of periods and in capitalization (as *mph, m.p.h., Mph,* and *MPH*), and stylings other than those given in this dictionary are often acceptable. For a small number of abbreviations about which the question of punctuation is raised very frequently, a note is added at the entry.

**a** absent, acceleration, acre, adult, alto, anode, answer, ante, anterior, are, area, atto-, author
**A** ace, adenine, ampere, argon
**Å** angstrom unit
**aa** ana
**AA** administrative assistant, Alcoholics Anonymous, antiaircraft, associate in arts, author's alterations
**AAA** Agricultural Adjustment Administration, American Automobile Association
**AAAL** American Academy of Arts and Letters
**AAAS** American Association for the Advancement of Science
**AAFP** American Academy of Family Physicians
**AAMC** American Association of Medical Colleges
**A and M** agricultural and mechanical, ancient and modern
**A and R** artists and repertory
**AAR** against all risks
**AARP** American Association of Retired Persons
**AAS** associate in applied science
**AASCU** American Association of State Colleges and Universities
**AAU** Amateur Athletic Union
**AAUP** American Association of University Professors
**AAUW** American Association of University Women
**ab** about
**AB** able-bodied seaman, airborne, airman basic, Alberta, [New Latin *artium baccalaureus*] bachelor of arts
**ABA** Amateur Boxing Association, American Bankers Association, American Bar Association, American Booksellers Association
**abbr** abbreviation
**ABC** American Bowling Congress, American Broadcasting Companies, Australian Broadcasting Corporation
**ABCD** accelerated business collection and delivery
**abd** *or* **abdom** abdomen, abdominal
**abl** ablative
**abn** airborne
**abp** archbishop
**abr** abridged, abridgment
**abs** absolute, abstract
**ABS** American Bible Society, antilock braking system
**abstr** abstract
**ac** account, acre
**Ac** actinium, altocumulus
**AC** air-conditioning, alternating current, [Medieval Latin *ante Christum*] before Christ; [Latin *ante cibum*] before meals; area code, athletic club
**acad** academic, academy

**acc** accusative
**accel** accelerando
**acct** account, accountant
**accus** accusative
**ACE** American Council on Education
**ack** acknowledge, acknowledgment
**ACLU** American Civil Liberties Union
**ACP** African, Caribbean and Pacific (states), American College of Physicians
**acpt** acceptance
**ACS** American Chemical Society, American College of Surgeons
**act** active, actor, actual
**ACT** Action for Children's Television, American College Test, Association of Classroom Teachers, Australian Capital Territory
**actg** acting
**ACV** actual cash value, air-cushion vehicle
**AD** active duty, after date, anno Domini — often printed in small capitals and often punctuated; assembly district, assistant director, athletic director
**A/D** analog/digital
**ADA** American Dental Association, Americans for Democratic Action, average daily attendance
**ADC** aide-de-camp, Aid to Dependent Children, Air Defense Command, assistant division commander
**ADD** American Dialect Dictionary, attention deficit disorder
**addn** addition
**addnl** additional
**ADF** automatic direction finder
**ad int** ad interim
**ADIZ** air defense identification zone
**adj** adjective, adjunct, adjustment, adjutant
**ad loc** [Latin *ad locum*] to or at the place
**adm** administration, administrative
**ADM** admiral
**admin** administration, administrative
**adv** adverb, [Latin *adversus*] against; advertisement, advertising, advisory
**ad val** ad valorem
**advt** advertisement
**AEC** Atomic Energy Commission
**AEF** American Expeditionary Force
**aeq** [Latin *aequalis*] equal
**aero** aeronautical, aeronautics
**aet** *or* **aetat** [Latin *aetatis*] of age, aged
**af** affix
**AF** air force, audio frequency
**AFB** air force base
**AFC** American Football Conference, automatic frequency control
**A/1C** airman first class

**AFDC** Aid to Families with Dependent Children
**aff** affirmative
**afft** affidavit
**AFL** American Football League
**AFL–CIO** American Federation of Labor and Congress of Industrial Organizations
**AFP** alpha-fetoprotein
**Afr** Africa, African
**aft** afternoon
**AFT** American Federation of Teachers, automatic fine tuning
**AFTRA** American Federation of Television and Radio Artists
**Ag** [Latin *argentum*] silver
**AG** adjutant general, attorney general
**AGC** advanced graduate certificate
**agcy** agency
**agl** above ground level
**agr** *or* **agric** agricultural, agriculture
**agt** agent
**AH** ampere-hour, anno hegirae, arts and humanities
**AHL** American Hockey League
**AI** ad interim, airborne intercept, air interception, artificial insemination, artificial intelligence
**AIA** American Institute of Architects
**AID** Agency for International Development, artificial insemination by donor
**AIM** American Indian Movement
**AK** Alaska
**aka** also known as
**AKC** American Kennel Club
**Al** aluminum
**AL** Alabama, American League, American Legion
**Ala** Alabama
**ALA** American Library Association
**Alb** Albania, Albanian
**alc** alcohol
**ALCS** American League Championship Series
**ald** alderman
**alg** algebra
**alk** alkaline
**alky** alkalinity
**ALS** amyotrophic lateral sclerosis, autographed letter signed
**alt** alternate, altitude, alto
**Alta** Alberta
**alum** aluminum
**alw** allowance
**Am** America, American, americium
**AM** airmail, Air Medal, [Latin *anno mundi*] in the year of the world — often printed in small capitals; ante meridiem — often not capitalized and often punctuated; [New Latin *artium magister*] master of arts
**AMA** American Medical Association
**amb** ambassador

**amdt** amendment
**AmE** American English
**Amer** America, American
**AmerInd** American Indian
**AMG** allied military government
**Amn** airman
**amp hr** ampere-hour
**AMSLAN** American Sign Language
**amt** amount
**AMU** atomic mass unit
**AMVETS** American Veterans (of World War II)
**an** annum
**AN** airman (Navy)
**ANA** American Nurses Association
**anal** analogy, analysis, analytic
**anat** anatomical, anatomy
**anc** ancient
**ANC** African National Congress
**Angl** Anglican
**anhyd** anhydrous
**ann** annals, annual
**anon** anonymous, anonymously
**ANOVA** analysis of variance
**ans** answer
**ANSI** American National Standards Institute
**ant** antenna, antonym
**Ant** Antarctica, Antrim
**anthrop** anthropological, anthropology
**antiq** antiquarian, antiquary
**AO** account of, and others
**aor** aorist
**ap** apostle, apothecaries'
**AP** additional premium, adjective phrase, airplane, American plan, antipersonnel, arithmetic progression, armor-piercing, Associated Press, author's proof
**APB** all points bulletin
**APC** armored personnel carrier
**API** air position indicator
**APO** army post office
**Apoc** Apocalypse, Apocrypha, apocryphal
**app** apparatus, appendix, appliance
**appl** applied
**appro** approval
**approx** approximate, approximately
**appt** appoint, appointed, appointment
**apptd** appointed
**Apr** April
**APR** annual percentage rate
**apt** apartment, aptitude
**aq** aqua, aqueous
**ar** arrival, arrive
**Ar** Arabic, argon
**AR** accounts receivable, acknowledgment of receipt, all rail, all risks, annual return, Arkansas, army regulation, autonomous republic
**Arab** Arabian, Arabic

**ARC** AIDS-related complex, American Red Cross
**arch** archaic, archery, architect, architectural, architecture
**Arch** Archbishop
**archeol** archeology
**arg** argent, argument
**Arg** Argentina
**arith** arithmetic, arithmetical
**Ariz** Arizona
**Ark** Arkansas
**Arm** Armagh, Armenian
**ARM** adjustable rate mortgage
**ARP** air-raid precautions
**arr** arranged, arrival, arrive
**ARRT** American Registry of Radiologic Technologists
**art** article, artificial, artillery
**arty** artillery
**ARV** American Revised Version
**ARVN** Army of the Republic of Vietnam (South Vietnam)
**As** altostratus, arsenic
**AS** after sight, airspeed, American Samoa, Anglo-Saxon, antisubmarine, associate in science
**ASAP** as soon as possible
**asb** asbestos
**ASCAP** American Society of Composers, Authors and Publishers
**ASE** American Stock Exchange
**ASEAN** Association of Southeast Asian Nations
**asgd** assigned
**asgmt** assignment
**ASI** airspeed indicator
**ASL** American Sign Language
**ASPCA** American Society for the Prevention of Cruelty to Animals
**ASR** airport surveillance radar, air-sea rescue
**assn** association
**assoc** associate, associated, association
**ASSR** Autonomous Soviet Socialist Republic
**asst** assistant, assorted
**asstd** assented, assorted
**assy** assembly
**Assyr** Assyrian
**AST** Alaska standard time
**ASTM** American Society for Testing and Materials
**ASTP** army specialized training program
**astrol** astrologer, astrology
**astron** astronomer, astronomy
**ASV** American Standard Version
**ASW** antisubmarine warfare
**at** airtight, atmosphere, atomic
**At** astatine
**AT** air temperature, ampere-turn, automatic transmission
**ATC** air traffic control
**Atl** Atlantic
**atm** atmosphere, atmospheric
**ATM** automated teller machine, automatic teller machine
**at no** atomic number
**att** attached, attention, attorney
**attn** attention
**attrib** attributive, attributively
**atty** attorney
**atty gen** attorney general
**ATV** all-terrain vehicle
**at wt** atomic weight
**Au** [Latin *aurum*] gold; author
**AU** angstrom unit, astronomical unit
**AUC** [Latin *ab urbe condita*] from the year of the founding of the city (of Rome)
**aud** audit, auditor
**aug** augmentative
**Aug** August
**Aus** Austria, Austrian
**AUS** Army of the United States
**Austral** Australia, Australian
**auth** authentic, author, authorized
**auto** automatic
**aux** auxiliary verb
**av** avenue, average, avoirdupois

**AV** ad valorem, audiovisual, Authorized Version
**AVC** automatic volume control
**avdp** avoirdupois
**ave** avenue
**avg** average
**avn** aviation
**AW** actual weight, aircraft warning, articles of war, automatic weapon
**AWACS** airborne warning and control system
**ax** axiom, axis
**AYC** American Youth Congress
**AYD** American Youth for Democracy
**AYH** American Youth Hostels
**az** azimuth, azure
**AZ** Arizona
**b** bachelor, bacillus, back, bag, bale, bass, basso, bat, Baumé, before, Bible, billion, bishop, black, blue, bolivar, book, born, bottom, brick, brightness, British, bulb, butut
**B** boron
**Ba** barium
**BA** bachelor of arts, batting average, Buenos Aires
**BAA** bachelor of applied arts
**BAAE** bachelor of aeronautical and astronautical engineering
**bac** [Medieval Latin *baccalaureus*] bachelor
**bact** bacterial, bacteriology, bacterium
**BAE** bachelor of aeronautical engineering, bachelor of agricultural engineering, bachelor of architectural engineering, bachelor of art education, bachelor of arts in education
**BAEd** bachelor of arts in education
**BAeE** bachelor of aeronautical engineering
**BAEE** bachelor of arts in elementary education
**BAg** bachelor of agriculture
**bal** balance
**BAM** bachelor of applied mathematics, bachelor of arts in music
**B and B** bed-and-breakfast
**B and E** breaking and entering
**b and w** black and white
**Bap** *or* **Bapt** Baptist
**bar** barometer, barometric, barrel
**Bar** Baruch
**BAr** bachelor of architecture
**BAR** Browning automatic rifle
**Bart** baronet
**BAS** bachelor of applied science, bachelor of arts and sciences
**BAT** bachelor of arts in teaching
**Bav** Bavaria, Bavarian
**BB** bachelor of business, ball bearing, base on balls, blue book, B'nai B'rith
**BBA** bachelor of business administration
**BBB** Better Business Bureau
**BBC** British Broadcasting Corporation
**BBE** bachelor of business education
**bbl** barrel, barrels
**BBQ** barbecue
**BBS** bulletin board system
**BC** before Christ — often printed in small capitals and often punctuated; British Columbia
**BCD** bad conduct discharge
**BCE** bachelor of chemical engineering, bachelor of civil engineering, before the Christian Era — often punctuated; before the Common Era — often punctuated
**bcf** billion cubic feet
**BCh** bachelor of chemistry
**BChE** bachelor of chemical engineering
**BCL** bachelor of canon law, bachelor of civil law
**bcn** beacon
**BCS** bachelor of chemical science, bachelor of commercial science
**bd** barrels per day, board, bound, boundary, bundle

**BD** bachelor of divinity, bank draft, bills discounted, bomb disposal, brought down
**BDA** bachelor of dramatic art
**bd ft** board foot
**bdl** *or* **bdle** bundle
**bdrm** bedroom
**Be** beryllium
**BE** bachelor of education, bachelor of engineering, bill of exchange, Black English
**Bé** Baumé
**BEC** Bureau of Employees' Compensation
**BEd** bachelor of education
**Beds** Bedfordshire
**BEE** bachelor of electrical engineering
**bef** before
**BEF** British Expeditionary Force
**beg** begin, beginning
**Belg** Belgian, Belgium
**BEM** bachelor of engineering of mines, British Empire Medal
**BEngr** bachelor of engineering
**BEngS** bachelor of engineering science
**Berks** Berkshire
**bet** between
**BeV** billion electron volts
**BEV** Black English vernacular
**bf** boldface
**BF** bachelor of forestry, board foot, brought forward
**BFA** bachelor of fine arts
**bg** background, bag, beige, being
**BG** *or* **B Gen** brigadier general
**BH** bill of health, Brinell hardness
**bhd** bulkhead
**BHL** bachelor of Hebrew letters, bachelor of Hebrew literature
**BHN** Brinell hardness number
**bhp** bishop
**Bi** bismuth
**BIA** bachelor of industrial administration, Bureau of Indian Affairs
**bib** Bible, biblical
**bibliog** bibliography
**bid** [Latin *bis in die*] twice a day
**BID** bachelor of industrial design
**BIE** bachelor of industrial engineering
**bil** billion
**biog** biographer, biographical, biography
**biol** biologic, biological, biologist, biology
**BJ** bachelor of journalism
**bk** bank, book, break, brook
**Bk** berkelium
**bkg** banking, bookkeeping, breakage
**bkgd** background
**bks** barracks
**bkt** basket, bracket
**bl** bale, barrel, black, block, blue
**BL** bachelor of law, bachelor of letters, baseline, bats left, bill of lading, breadth-length
**bld** blond, blood
**bldg** building
**bldr** builder
**BLEVE** boiling liquid expanding vapor explosion
**BLitt** *or* **BLit** [Medieval Latin *baccalaureus litterarum*] bachelor of letters, bachelor of literature
**blk** black, block, bulk
**BLM** Bureau of Land Management
**BLS** bachelor of liberal studies, bachelor of library science, Bureau of Labor Statistics
**blvd** boulevard
**bm** beam
**BM** bachelor of medicine, bachelor of music, basal metabolism, bill of material, board measure, bowel movement, bronze medal
**BME** bachelor of mechanical engineering, bachelor of mining engineering, bachelor of music education
**BMOC** big man on campus
**BMR** basal metabolic rate
**BMS** bachelor of marine science
**BMT** bachelor of medical technology

**BMX** bicycle motocross
**bn** baron, battalion, beacon, been
**BN** bachelor of nursing, bank note, Bureau of Narcotics
**BNDD** Bureau of Narcotics and Dangerous Drugs
**BNS** bachelor of naval sciences
**BO** back order, best offer, body odor, box office, branch office, buyer's option
**BOD** biochemical oxygen demand, biological oxygen demand
**BOQ** bachelor officers' quarters
**bor** borough
**bot** botanical, botanist, botany, bottle, bottom, bought
**botan** botanical
**bp** baptized, base pair, birthplace, bishop
**BP** batting practice, beautiful people, before the present, bills payable, blood pressure, blueprint, boiling point
**bpd** barrels per day
**BPE** bachelor of petroleum engineering, bachelor of physical education
**BPh** bachelor of philosophy
**BPH** benign prostatic hyperplasia; benign prostatic hypertrophy
**BPharm** bachelor of pharmacy
**bpi** bits per inch, bytes per inch
**bpl** birthplace
**BPOE** Benevolent and Protective Order of Elks
**bps** bits per second
**BPW** Board of Public Works, Business and Professional Women's Clubs
**br** branch, brass, brown
**Br** Britain, British, bromine
**BR** bats right, bedroom, bills receivable
**Braz** Brazil, Brazilian
**BRE** bachelor of religious education, business reply envelope
**Breck** Brecknockshire
**brig** brigade, brigadier
**Brig Gen** brigadier general
**Brit** Britain, British
**brl** barrel
**bros** brothers
**BS** bachelor of science, balance sheet, bill of sale, British standard, bullshit — sometimes considered vulgar
**BSA** bachelor of science in agriculture, Boy Scouts of America
**BSAA** bachelor of science in applied arts
**BSAE** bachelor of science in aeronautical engineering, bachelor of science in agricultural engineering, bachelor of science in architectural engineering
**BSAg** bachelor of science in agriculture
**BSArch** bachelor of science in architecture
**BSB** bachelor of science in business
**BSc** bachelor of science
**BSCE** bachelor of science in chemical engineering
**BSCh** bachelor of science in chemistry
**BSEc** *or* **BSEcon** bachelor of science in economics
**BSEd** *or* **BSE** bachelor of science in education
**BSEE** bachelor of science in electrical engineering, bachelor of science in elementary education
**BSFor** bachelor of science in forestry
**BSFS** bachelor of science in foreign service
**BSI** British Standards Institution
**bskt** basket
**BSL** bachelor of sacred literature, bachelor of science in languages, bachelor of science in law, bachelor of science in linguistics
**BSME** bachelor of science in mechanical engineering
**bsmt** basement
**BSN** bachelor of science in nursing
**BSW** bachelor of social work

**Bt** baronet
**btry** battery
**Btu** British thermal unit
**bu** bureau, bushel
**Bucks** Buckinghamshire
**buff** buffalo
**Bulg** Bulgaria, Bulgarian
**bull** bulletin
**bur** bureau
**bus** business
**BV** Blessed Virgin
**bvt** brevet
**BW** bacteriological warfare, biological warfare, black and white
**BWI** British West Indies
**bx** box
**BX** base exchange
**by** billion years
**BYO** bring your own
**BYOB** bring your own beer, bring your own booze, bring your own bottle
**byp** bypass
**c** calm, calorie, Canadian, canceled, candle, carat, case, castle, catcher, Catholic, cedi, cent, centavo, center, centi-, centime, centimeter, centum, century, chairman, chapter, circa, circuit, circumference, clockwise, cloudy, cocaine, codex, coefficient, college, colon, color, colt, [Latin *congius*] gallon; congress, conservative, contralto, copyright, cost, cubic, cup, curie
**C** capacitance, carbon, Celsius, centigrade, Coulomb, cytosine
**ca** circa
**Ca** calcium
**CA** California, Central America, certified acupuncturist, chartered accountant, chief accountant, chronological age, commercial agent, controller of accounts, current account
**CAB** Civil Aeronautics Board
**CAD** computer-aided design
**CAF** cost and freight
**CAFE** corporate average fuel economy
**CAGS** Certificate of Advanced Graduate Study
**CAI** computer-aided instruction, computer-assisted instruction
**cal** calendar, caliber, calorie, small calorie
**Cal** California, large calorie
**calc** calculate, calculated
**Calif** California
**cam** camera
**CAM** computer-aided manufacturing
**Cambs** Cambridgeshire
**can** canceled, cancellation, cannon, canto
**Can** *or* **Canad** Canada, Canadian
**canc** canceled
**C and F** cost and freight
**C and W** country and western
**Cant** Canticle of Canticles, Cantonese
**cap** capacity, capital, capitalize, capitalized
**CAP** Civil Air Patrol
**caps** capitals, capsule
**Capt** captain
**Car** Carlow
**CAR** civil air regulations
**card** cardinal
**CARE** Cooperative for American Relief to Everywhere
**CAS** certificate of advanced study
**cat** catalog, catalyst
**CAT** clear-air turbulence, college ability test, computerized axial tomography
**cath** cathedral, cathode
**CATV** community antenna television
**caus** causative
**cav** cavalry, cavity
**CAVU** ceiling and visibility unlimited
**Cb** columbium, cumulonimbus
**CBC** Canadian Broadcasting Corporation
**CBD** cash before delivery, central business district

**CBE** commander of the Order of the British Empire, companion of the Order of the British Empire
**CBI** computer-based instruction, Cumulative Book Index
**CBO** Congressional Budget Office
**CBS** Columbia Broadcasting System
**CBW** chemical and biological warfare
**cc** cubic centimeter
**Cc** cirrocumulus
**CC** carbon copy, chief clerk, common carrier, community college, country club
**CCC** Civilian Conservation Corps
**CCD** Confraternity of Christian Doctrine
**CCF** Chinese communist forces
**cckw** counterclockwise
**CCTV** closed-circuit television
**CCU** cardiac care unit, coronary care unit, critical care unit
**ccw** counterclockwise
**cd** candela, candle, cord
**Cd** cadmium
**CD** carried down, certificate of deposit, civil defense, [French *corps diplomatique*] diplomatic corps
**CDC** Centers for Disease Control
**CDD** certificate of disability for discharge
**cdg** commanding
**Cdn** Canadian
**CDP** certificate in data processing
**CDR** commander
**CDT** central daylight time
**Ce** cerium
**CE** chemical engineer, civil engineer, Christian Era — often punctuated; Common Era — often punctuated; Corps of Engineers
**CEA** College English Association, Council of Economic Advisors
**CED** Committee for Economic Development
**cem** cement
**CEMF** counter electromotive force
**cent** centigrade, central, centum, century
**Cent** Central
**CENTO** Central Treaty Organization
**CERN** [*Conseil Européen pour la Recherche Nucléaire*] European Organization for Nuclear Research
**cert** certificate, certification, certified, certify
**CETA** Comprehensive Employment and Training Act
**CEU** continuing education credit
**cf** calf, [Latin *confer,* imperative of *conferre* to compare] compare
**Cf** californium
**CF** carried forward, centrifugal force, cost and freight, cystic fibrosis
**CFC** chlorofluorocarbon
**CFI** certified flight instructor, chief flying instructor; cost, freight, and insurance
**CFL** Canadian Football League
**cfm** cubic feet per minute
**CFO** chief financial officer
**CFP** Certified Financial Planner
**cfs** cubic feet per second
**cg** centigram
**CG** center of gravity, coast guard, commanding general
**cgs** centimeter-gram-second
**CGT** [French *Confédération Germénénérale du Travail*] General Confederation of Labor
**ch** chain, champion, chaplain, chapter, chief, child, children, church
**CH** clearinghouse, courthouse, customhouse
**chan** channel
**chap** chapter
**CHD** coronary heart disease
**chem** chemical, chemist, chemistry
**Ches** Cheshire
**chg** change, charge
**Chin** Chinese
**chm** chairman, checkmate
**Chmn** chairman

**chron** chronicle, chronological, chronology
**Chron** Chronicles
**Ci** cirrus, curie
**CI** cast iron, certificate of insurance, Channel Islands
**CIA** Central Intelligence Agency, certified internal auditor
**cía** [Spanish *compañía*] company
**CIAA** Central Intercollegiate Athletic Association
**CIC** counterintelligence corps
**CID** Criminal Investigation Department, cubic inch displacement
**cie** [French *compagnie*] company
**CIF** central information file; cost, insurance, and freight
**C in C** commander in chief
**CIP** Cataloging in Publication
**cir** circle, circuit, circular, circumference
**circ** circular
**cit** citation, cited, citizen
**civ** civil, civilian, civilization
**CIWS** close-in weapons system
**CJ** chief justice
**ck** cask, check
**cl** centiliter, claiming, class, clause, close, closet, cloth
**Cl** chlorine
**CL** carload, center line, civil law, common law
**cld** called, cleared
**CLEP** College Level Examination Program
**clin** clinical
**clk** clerk
**clo** clothing
**clr** clear, clearance
**CLU** chartered life underwriter
**cm** centimeter, cumulative
**Cm** curium
**CM** center matched, circular mil, common meter, [Commonwealth of the Northern Mariana Islands] Northern Mariana Islands, Congregation of the Mission
**CMA** certified medical assistant
**cmd** command
**cmdg** commanding
**cmdr** commander
**CMG** Companion of the Order of St. Michael and St. George
**cml** commercial
**CMSgt** chief master sergeant
**CMV** cytomegalovirus
**CN** credit note
**CNC** computer numerical control
**CNO** chief of naval operations
**CNS** central nervous system
**co** company, county
**Co** cobalt
**CO** cash order, Colorado, commanding officer, conscientious objector
**c/o** care of
**cod** codex
**COD** carrier onboard delivery, cash on delivery, collect on delivery
**coeff** *or* **coef** coefficient
**C of C** Chamber of Commerce
**C of S** chief of staff
**cog** cognate
**col** colonial, colony, color, colored, column, counsel
**col** *or* **coll** collateral, collect, collected, collection, college, collegiate
**Col** colonel, Colorado, Colossians
**COL** colonel, cost of living
**COLA** cost-of-living allowance
**collat** collateral
**colloq** colloquial
**Colo** Colorado
**colog** cologarithm
**com** comedy, comic, comma
**COM** computer output microfilm, computer output microfilmer
**comb** combination, combined, combining, combustion
**comd** command
**comdg** commanding
**comdr** commander
**comdt** commandant

**COMECON** Council for Mutual Economic Assistance
**coml** commercial
**comm** command, commandant, commander, commanding, commentary, commerce, commercial, commission, commissioned, commissioner, committee, common, commoner, commonwealth, commune, communication, communist, community
**commo** commodore
**comp** comparative, compare, compensation, compiled, compiler, composition, compositor, compound, comprehensive, comptroller
**compd** compound
**comr** commissioner
**con** [Latin *conjunx*] consort; consolidated, consul, continued
**conc** concentrate, concentrated, concentration, concrete
**concn** concentration
**cond** condition, conductivity
**conf** conference, confidential
**Confed** Confederate
**cong** congress, congressional
**conj** conjunction, conjunctive
**Conn** Connecticut
**cons** consecrated, conservative, consigned, consignment, consol, consolidated, consonant, constable, constitution, construction, consul, consulting
**consol** consolidated
**const** constant, constitution, constitutional, construction
**constr** construction
**cont** containing, contents, continent, continental, continued, control
**contd** continued
**contg** containing
**contr** contract, contraction, contralto, contrary, control, controller
**contrib** contribution, contributor
**conv** convention, conventional, convertible, convocation
**COO** chief operating officer
**cop** copper, copulative, copy, copyright
**cor** corner, coroner, corpus, corresponding
**Cor** Corinthians
**CORE** Congress of Racial Equality
**Corn** Cornish, Cornwall
**corp** corporal, corporation
**corr** correct, corrected, correction, correspondence, correspondent, corresponding, corrupt, corruption
**cos** companies, consul, consulship, cosine, counties
**COS** cash on shipment, chief of staff
**cosec** cosecant
**cot** cotangent
**cp** compare, coupon
**CP** candlepower, Cape Province, center of pressure, cerebral palsy, charter party, chemically pure, command post, Communist party, Congregation of the Passion, custom of port
**CPA** certified public accountant
**CPB** Corporation for Public Broadcasting
**CPCU** chartered property casualty underwriter
**cpd** compound
**CPFF** cost plus fixed fee
**cpi** characters per inch
**CPI** consumer price index
**cpl** complete, compline
**Cpl** corporal
**CPM** cost per thousand
**CPO** chief petty officer
**CPOM** master chief petty officer
**CPOS** senior chief petty officer
**CPR** cardiopulmonary resuscitation
**CPS** cards per second, certified professional secretary, characters per second, Civilian Public Service, cycles per second
**CPSC** Consumer Product Safety Commission
**CPT** captain
**cpu** central processing unit

**CQ** call to quarters, charge of quarters, commercial quality

**cr** center, circular, commander, cream, creased, credit, creditor, creek, crescendo

**Cr** chromium

**CR** carrier's risk, cathode ray, class rate, conditioned reflex, conditioned response, consciousness-raising, Costa Rica, current rate

**CRC** Civil Rights Commission

**cresc** crescendo

**crim** criminal

**crim con** criminal conversation

**criminol** criminologist, criminology

**crit** critical, criticism, criticized

**CRNA** certified registered nurse anesthetist

**CRT** carrier route

**cryst** crystalline, crystallized

**cs** case, cases, census, consciousness, consul

**Cs** cesium, cirrostratus

**CS** capital stock, cesarean section, chief of staff, Christian Science practitioner, civil service, conditioned stimulus, county seat

**CSA** Confederate States of America

**csc** cosecant

**CSC** Civil Service Commission

**CSF** cerebrospinal fluid

**CSM** command sergeant major

**CST** central standard time

**ct** carat, cent, count, county, court

**CT** central time, certificated teacher, certified teacher, code telegram, computed tomography, computerized tomography, Connecticut

**CTC** centralized traffic control

**ctf** certificate

**ctn** carton, cotangent

**c to c** center to center

**ctr** center, counter

**cu** cubic, cumulative

**Cu** cumulus, [Latin *cuprum*] copper

**CU** close-up

**cum** cumulative

**Cumb** Cumbria

**cur** currency, current

**cv** *or* **cvt** convertible

**CV** cardiovascular, chief value, curriculum vitae

**CVA** Columbia Valley Authority

**cw** clockwise

**CW** chemical warfare, chief warrant officer, continuous wave

**CWO** cash with order, chief warrant officer

**cwt** hundredweight

**CY** calendar year

**cyl** cylinder

**CYO** Catholic Youth Organization

**cytol** cytological, cytology

**CZ** Canal Zone

**d** date, daughter, day, dead, deceased, deci-, degree, [Latin *denarius, denarii*] penny, pence; depart, departure, diameter, differential, dimensional, distance, dorsal, drive, driving

**D** Democrat, derivative, deuterium, Dutch

**da** deka-

**DA** days after acceptance, delayed action, deposit account, Dictionary of Americanisms, district attorney, doctor of arts, documents against acceptance, documents for acceptance, don't answer

**DAB** Dictionary of American Biography

**DAE** Dictionary of American English

**dag** dekagram

**DAH** Dictionary of American History

**dal** dekaliter

**dam** dekameter

**Dan** Daniel, Danish

**D & C** dilation and curettage

**DAR** Daughters of the American Revolution

**DARE** Dictionary of American Regional English

**DARPA** Defense Advanced Research Projects Agency

**dat** dative

**DAT** differential aptitude test, digital audiotape

**dau** daughter

**DAV** Disabled American Veterans

**db** debenture

**dB** decibel

**DB** daybook

**d/b/a** doing business as

**DBA** doctor of business administration

**DBE** Dame Commander of the Order of the British Empire

**DBH** diameter at breast height

**dbl** *or* **dble** double

**DBMS** data base management system

**DBS** direct broadcast satellite

**DC** [Italian *da capo*] from the beginning; decimal classification, direct current, District of Columbia, doctor of chiropractic, double crochet

**DChE** doctor of chemical engineering

**DCL** doctor of canon law, doctor of civil law

**dd** dated, delivered

**DD** days after date, demand draft, dishonorable discharge, doctor of divinity, due date

**DDC** Dewey Decimal Classification

**DDD** direct distance dialing

**DDS** doctor of dental science, doctor of dental surgery

**DE** defensive end, Delaware, doctor of engineering

**DEA** Drug Enforcement Administration

**deb** debenture

**dec** deceased, declaration, declared, declination, decorated, decorative, decrease, decrescendo

**Dec** December

**decd** deceased

**def** defendant, defense, deferred, defined, definite, definition

**deg** degree

**del** delegate, delegation, delete

**Del** Delaware

**dely** delivery

**dem** demonstrative, demurrage

**Dem** Democrat, Democratic

**Den** Denmark

**dent** dental, dentist, dentistry

**dep** depart, department, departure, deponent, deposed, deposit, depot, deputy

**depr** depreciation, depression

**dept** department

**der** *or* **deriv** derivation, derivative

**Derbys** Derbyshire

**derm** dermatologist, dermatology

**det** detached, detachment, detail, determine

**detd** determined

**detn** detention, determination

**Deut** Deuteronomy

**dev** deviation

**Devon** Devonshire

**DEW** distant early warning

**DF** damage free, direction finder, direction finding

**DFA** doctor of fine arts

**DFC** Distinguished Flying Cross

**dft** defendant, draft

**dg** decigram

**DG** [Late Latin *Dei gratia*] by the grace of God; director general

**DH** doctor of humanities

**DHL** doctor of Hebrew letters, doctor of Hebrew literature

**DI** drill instructor

**dia** diameter

**diag** diagonal, diagram

**dial** dialect, dialectical

**diam** diameter

**dict** dictionary

**dif** *or* **diff** difference

**dig** digest

**dil** dilute

**dim** dimension, diminished, diminuendo, diminutive

**dimin** diminuendo

**din** dinar

**DIN** [German *Deutsche Industrie-Normen*] German Industrial Standards

**dip** diploma

**dir** direction, director

**dis** discharge, discount, distance

**disc** discount

**disp** dispensary

**diss** dissertation

**dist** distance, district

**distn** distillation

**distr** distribute, distribution

**div** divided, dividend, division, divorced

**DIY** do it yourself

**DJ** district judge, doctor of jurisprudence, dust jacket

**DJIA** Dow-Jones Industrial Average

**dk** dark, deck, dock

**dl** deciliter

**DL** disabled list

**DLitt** *or* **DLit** [New Latin *doctor litterarum*] doctor of letters, doctor of literature

**DLO** dead letter office, dispatch loading only

**DLS** doctor of library science

**dm** decimeter

**DM** deutsche mark

**DMA** doctor of musical arts

**DMD** [New Latin *dentariae medicinae doctor*] doctor of dental medicine

**DMin** doctor of ministry

**DML** doctor of modern languages

**DMZ** demilitarized zone

**dn** down

**DNB** Dictionary of National Biography

**DNF** did not finish

**DNR** do not resuscitate

**do** ditto

**DO** defense order, doctor of osteopathy

**DOA** dead on arrival

**DOB** date of birth

**doc** document

**DOD** Department of Defense

**DOE** Department of Energy

**dol** dollar

**dom** domestic, dominant, dominion

**Don** Donegal

**Dors** Dorset

**DOS** disk operating system

**DOT** Department of Transportation

**doz** dozen

**DP** data processing, degree of polymerization, dew point, doctor of podiatry, double play

**DPE** doctor of physical education

**DPh** doctor of philosophy

**DPH** department of public health, doctor of public health

**DPM** doctor of podiatric medicine

**dpt** department, deponent

**DPT** diphtheria, pertussis, tetanus

**DQ** disqualification, disqualify

**dr** debtor, drachma, dram, drive, drum

**Dr** doctor

**DR** dead reckoning, dining room

**dram** dramatic, dramatist

**DS** [Italian *dal segno*] from the sign; days after sight, detached service, document signed

**DSc** doctor of science

**DSC** Distinguished Service Cross, doctor of surgical chiropody

**DSM** Distinguished Service Medal

**DSO** Distinguished Service Order

**DSP** [Latin *decessit sine prole*] died without issue

**DST** daylight saving time, doctor of sacred theology

**DSW** doctor of social welfare, doctor of social work

**DT** daylight time, doctor of theology, double time

**DTh** doctor of theology

**DTP** desktop publishing; diphtheria, tetanus, pertussis

**Du** Dutch

**Dub** Dublin

**DUI** driving under the influence

**Dumf Gal** Dumfries and Galloway

**dup** duplex, duplicate

**Dur** Durham

**DV** [Latin *Deo volente*] God willing; Douay Version

**DVM** doctor of veterinary medicine

**DW** deadweight, delayed weather, distilled water, dust wrapper

**DWI** driving while intoxicated, Dutch West Indies

**dwt** deadweight ton, pennyweight

**DX** distance

**dy** delivery, deputy, duty

**Dy** dysprosium

**dynam** dynamics

**dz** dozen

**e** earth, east, easterly, eastern, edge, eldest, ell, empty, end, energy, erg, error, excellent

**E** electromotive force, energy, English, exponent

**ea** each

**E and OE** errors and omissions excepted

**EB** eastbound

**EBC** Educational Broadcasting Corporation

**EBV** Epstein-Barr virus

**EC** European Community

**eccl** ecclesiastic, ecclesiastical

**Eccles** Ecclesiastes

**Ecclus** Ecclesiasticus

**ECG** electrocardiogram

**ECM** electronic countermeasure, European Common Market

**ecol** ecological, ecology

**econ** economics, economist, economy

**ECT** electroconvulsive therapy

**Ecua** Ecuador

**ed** edited, edition, editor, education

**EDB** ethylene dibromide

**EdD** doctor of education

**EDD** English Dialect Dictionary

**EDP** electronic data processing

**EdS** specialist in education

**EDT** eastern daylight time

**educ** education, educational

**EE** electrical engineer

**EEC** European Economic Community

**EEG** electroencephalogram, electroencephalograph

**EENT** eye, ear, nose, and throat

**EEO** equal employment opportunity

**eff** efficiency

**EFT** *or* **EFTS** electronic funds transfer (system)

**e.g.** [Latin *exempli gratia*] for example

**Eg** Egypt, Egyptian

**EGF** epidermal growth factor

**Egypt** Egyptian

**EHF** extremely high frequency

**EHP** effective horsepower, electric horsepower

**EHV** extra high voltage

**EKG** [German *Elektrokardiogramm*] electrocardiogram, electrocardiograph

**el** elevation

**elec** electric, electrical, electricity

**elem** elementary

**elev** elevation

**ELF** extremely low frequency

**Eliz** Elizabethan

**EM** electromagnetic, electron microscope, electron microscopy, end matched, engineer of mines, enlisted man

**emer** emeritus

**EMG** electromyogram, electromyograph, electromyography

**emp** emperor, empress

**EMP** electromagnetic pulse

**emu** electromagnetic unit

**enc** *or* **encl** enclosure

**ency** *or* **encyc** encyclopedia

**ENE** east-northeast

**eng** engine, engineer, engineering

**Eng** England, English

**engr** engineer, engraved, engraver, engraving
**enl** enlarged, enlisted
**ENS** ensign
**ENT** ear, nose, and throat
**entom** or **entomol** entomological, entomology
**env** envelope
**EO** executive order
**EOE** equal opportunity employer
**EOM** end of month
**EP** estimated position, European plan, extended play
**EPA** Environmental Protection Agency
**Eph** or **Ephes** Ephesians
**Episc** Episcopal
**eq** equal, equation
**equip** equipment
**equiv** equivalency, equivalent
**Er** erbium
**ER** earned run, emergency room
**ERA** earned run average, Equal Rights Amendment
**ERISA** Employee Retirement Income Security Act
**Es** einsteinium
**ESB** electrical stimulation of the brain
**Esd** Esdras
**ESE** east-southeast
**Esk** Eskimo
**ESL** English as a second language
**ESOP** employee stock ownership plan
**esp** especially
**Esq** or **Esqr** esquire
**est** established, estimate, estimated
**EST** eastern standard time
**Esth** Esther
**Et** ethyl
**ET** eastern time
**ETA** estimated time of arrival
**et al** [Latin *et alii* (masculine), *et aliae* (feminine), or *et alia* (neuter)] and others
**etc** et cetera
**ETD** estimated time of departure
**ETO** European theater of operations
**et seq** [Latin *et sequens*] and the following one; [Latin *et sequentes* (masculine & feminine plural), or *et sequentia* (neuter plural)] and the following ones
**et ux** [Latin *et uxor*] and wife
**ETV** educational television
**Eu** europium
**Eur** Europe, European
**eV** electron volt
**EVA** extravehicular activity
**eval** evaluation
**evap** evaporate
**evg** evening
**EW** enlisted woman
**ex** example, exchange, executive, express, extra
**Ex** Exodus
**exc** excellent, except
**exch** exchange, exchanged
**excl** exclude, excluded, excluding
**exhbn** exhibition
**Exod** Exodus
**exor** executor
**exp** expense, experience, experiment, experimental, exponent, export, express
**expt** experiment
**exptl** experimental
**expwy** expressway
**exrx** executrix
**ext** extension, exterior, external, externally, extra, extract
**Ez** or **Ezr** Ezra
**Ezech** Ezechiel
**Ezek** Ezekiel
**f** failure, false, family, faraday, feast, female, feminine, femto-, fermi, fine, finish, fluid, fluidness, focal length, [*following*] and the following one; force, forte, fragile, frequency, from, full
**F** Fahrenheit, farad, fluorine, French, Friday

**FA** field artillery, fielding average, football association
**FAA** Federal Aviation Administration, free of all average
**fac** facsimile, faculty
**FADM** fleet admiral
**Fah** or **Fahr** Fahrenheit
**fam** familiar, family
**F and A** fore and aft
**FAO** Food and Agriculture Organization of the United Nations
**FAQ** fair average quality, frequently asked question
**far** farthing
**FAS** firsts and seconds, free alongside (ship)
**fasc** fascicle
**fath** fathom
**FB** foreign body, freight bill
**FBI** Federal Bureau of Investigation
**FC** fire control, fire controlman, follow copy, food control, footcandle
**FCA** Farm Credit Administration
**FCC** Federal Communications Commission
**fcp** foolscap
**fcy** fancy
**FD** fire department, free dock
**FDA** Food and Drug Administration
**FDIC** Federal Deposit Insurance Corporation
**Fe** [Latin *ferrum*] iron
**Feb** February
**fec** [Latin *fecit*] he made it
**fed** federal, federation
**fedn** federation
**fem** female, feminine
**FEMA** Federal Emergency Management Agency
**FEPA** Fair Employment Practices Act
**FEPC** Fair Employment Practices Commission
**Ferm** Fermanagh
**FET** Federal excise tax, field-effect transistor
**ff** folios, [*following*] and the following ones; fortissimo
**FHA** Federal Housing Administration
**FICA** Federal Insurance Contributions Act
**fict** fiction, fictitious
**fi fa** fieri facias
**FIFO** first in, first out
**fig** figurative, figuratively, figure
**fin** finance, financial, finish
**Finn** Finnish
**FIO** free in and out
**fl** flanker, floor, florin, [Latin *floruit*] flourished; fluid
**FL** Florida, focal length, foreign language
**Fla** Florida
**fl dr** fluid dram
**Flem** Flemish
**Flint** or **Flints** Flintshire
**FLIR** forward-looking infrared
**fl oz** fluid ounce
**FLSA** Fair Labor Standards Act
**fm** fathom
**Fm** fermium
**FM** field manual
**FMCS** Federal Mediation and Conciliation Service
**fn** footnote
**fo** or **fol** folio
**FO** field officer, field order, finance officer, flight officer, foreign office, forward observer
**FOB** free on board
**FOC** free of charge
**FOE** Fraternal Order of Eagles
**FOIA** Freedom of Information Act
**for** foreign, forestry
**FOR** free on rail
**forz** forzando
**FOS** free on steamer
**FOT** free on truck
**4WD** four-wheel drive
**fow** first open water
**fp** freezing point
**FPA** Foreign Press Association, free of particular average

**FPC** fish protein concentrate
**fpm** feet per minute
**FPO** fleet post office
**fps** feet per second, foot-pound-second, frames per second
**fr** father, franc, friar, from
**Fr** France, francium, French, Friday
**FRB** Federal Reserve Board
**freq** frequency, frequent, frequentative, frequently
**FRG** Federal Republic of Germany
**Fri** Friday
**FRM** fixed rate mortgage
**front** frontispiece
**FRS** Federal Reserve System
**frt** freight
**frwy** freeway
**fs** femtosecond
**FS** filmstrip, Foreign Service
**FSH** follicle-stimulating hormone
**FSLIC** Federal Savings and Loan Insurance Corporation
**FSO** Foreign Service Officer
**ft** feet, foot, fort
**FT** Fourier transform, free throw, full time
**FTC** Federal Trade Commission
**FTE** full-time equivalent
**fth** fathom
**ft lb** foot-pound
**FTP** file transfer protocol
**fund** fundamental
**fur** furlong
**fut** future
**FV** [Latin *folio verso* the page being turned] on the back of the page
**fwd** foreword, forward
**FWD** front-wheel drive
**FX** foreign exchange
**FY** fiscal year
**FYI** for your information
**g** acceleration of gravity, game, gauge, gelding, gender, good, gram, grand, gravity
**G** German, giga-, guanine, Gulf
**ga** gauge
**Ga** gallium, Georgia
**GA** Gamblers Anonymous, general agent, general assembly, general average, general of the army, Georgia
**GAAP** generally accepted accounting principles
**gal** gallery, gallon
**Gal** Galatians
**galv** galvanized
**GAO** General Accounting Office
**gar** garage
**GAR** Grand Army of the Republic
**GATT** General Agreement on Tariffs and Trade
**gaz** gazette
**GB** Great Britain
**GBF** Great Books Foundation
**GC** gas chromatograph, gas chromatography
**GCA** ground-controlled approach
**GCB** Knight Grand Cross of the Bath
**GCD** greatest common divisor
**GCF** greatest common factor
**gd** good
**Gd** gadolinium
**GDR** German Democratic Republic
**Ge** germanium
**GE** gilt edges
**GED** General Educational Development (tests), general equivalency diploma
**GEM** ground-effect machine
**gen** general, genitive, genus
**Gen** Genesis
**Gen AF** general of the air force
**genl** general
**geog** geographic, geographical, geography
**geol** geologic, geological, geology
**geom** geometric, geometrical, geometry
**ger** gerund
**Ger** German, Germany
**GeV** giga-electron-volt
**GHQ** general headquarters
**GHz** gigahertz

**gi** gill
**GI** galvanized iron, gastrointestinal, general issue, government issue
**Gib** or **Gibr** Gibraltar
**GIGO** garbage in, garbage out
**GIT** Group Inclusive Tour
**Gk** Greek
**Glos** Gloucestershire
**gm** gram
**GM** general manager, grand master, guided missile
**GMT** Greenwich mean time
**GMW** gram-molecular weight
**gn** guinea
**GNI** gross national income
**GNP** gross national product
**GO** general order
**GOP** Grand Old Party (Republican)
**Goth** Gothic
**gov** government, governor
**govt** government
**gp** group
**GP** general practice, general practitioner, geometric progression
**GPA** grade point average
**GPD** gallons per day
**GPH** gallons per hour
**GPM** gallons per minute
**GPO** general post office, Government Printing Office
**GPS** gallons per second
**GQ** general quarters
**gr** grade, grain, gram, gravity, gross
**Gr** Greece, Greek
**grad** graduate, graduated
**gram** grammar, grammatical
**Gramp** Grampian
**GRAS** generally recognized as safe
**GRE** Graduate Record Examination
**gro** gross
**GRP** glass-reinforced plastic
**GRU** [Russian *Glavnoe razvedyvatel'-noe upravlenie*] Chief Intelligence Directorate
**gr wt** gross weight
**GS** general staff, giant slalom, government service, ground speed
**GSA** General Services Administration, Girl Scouts of America
**GSC** general staff corps
**GSL** Guaranteed Student Loan
**GSO** general staff officer
**GSR** galvanic skin response
**GST** Greenwich sidereal time
**GSUSA** Girl Scouts of the United States of America
**gt** gilt top, great
**GT** gross ton
**Gt Brit** Great Britain
**gtd** guaranteed
**Gtr Man** Greater Manchester
**gtt** [Latin *gutta*, plural *guttae*] drop
**GU** genitourinary, Guam
**GUI** graphical user interface
**GUT** grand unified theory, grand unification theory
**GWRBI** game winning run batted in
**Gwyn** Gwynedd
**gyn** or **gynecol** gynecology
**Gy Sgt** gunnery sergeant
**h** half, harbor, hard, hardness, hecto-, height, high, hit, horse, hour, humidity, hundred, Hungary, husband
**H** Hamiltonian, henry, heroin, hydrogen
**ha** hectare
**HA** hour angle
**Hab** Habacuc, Habakkuk
**hab corp** habeas corpus
**Hag** Haggai
**Hants** Hampshire
**Hb** hemoglobin
**HBM** Her Britannic Majesty, His Britannic Majesty
**HC** Holy Communion, House of Commons, hydrocarbon
**HCF** highest common factor
**HCG** human chorionic gonadotropin
**HCL** high cost of living
**hd** head
**HD** heavy-duty
**hdbk** handbook

**hdkf** handkerchief
**HDTV** high-definition television
**hdwe** hardware
**He** helium
**HE** Her Excellency, high explosive, His Eminence, His Excellency
**Heb** Hebrew, Hebrews
**her** heraldry
**Heref/Worcs** Hereford and Worcester
**Herts** Hertfordshire
**HEW** Department of Health, Education, and Welfare
**hex** hexagon
**hf** half
**Hf** hafnium
**HF** height finding, high frequency, home forces
**hg** hectogram, heliogram, hemoglobin
**Hg** [New Latin *hydrargyrum,* literally, water silver] mercury
**HGH** human growth hormone
**hgt** height
**hgwy** highway
**HH** Her Highness, His Highness, His Holiness
**HHD** [New Latin *humanitatum doctor*] doctor of humanities
**HHS** Department of Health and Human Services
**HI** Hawaii, high intensity, humidity index
**hist** historian, historical, history
**Hitt** Hittite
**HJ** [Latin *hic jacet*] here lies
**HJR** House joint resolution
**hl** hectoliter
**HL** House of Lords
**hld** hold
**hlqn** harlequin
**HLS** [Latin *hoc loco situs*] laid in this place; holograph letter signed
**hlt** halt
**hm** hectometer
**HM** Her Majesty, Her Majesty's, His Majesty, His Majesty's
**HMAS** Her Majesty's Australian ship, His Majesty's Australian ship
**HMBS** Her Majesty's British ship, His Majesty's British ship
**HMC** Her Majesty's Customs, His Majesty's Customs
**HMCS** Her Majesty's Canadian ship, His Majesty's Canadian ship
**HMS** Her Majesty's ship, His Majesty's ship
**HN** head nurse
**Ho** holmium
**hom** homiletics, homily
**hon** honor, honorable, honorary
**Hon** *or* **Hond** Honduras
**HOPE** Health Opportunity for People Everywhere
**hor** horizontal
**hort** horticultural, horticulture
**Hos** Hosea
**hosp** hospital
**HOV** high-occupancy vehicle
**hp** horsepower
**HP** half pay, high pressure
**HPA** high-power amplifier
**HPF** highest possible frequency, high power field
**HPV** human-powered vehicle
**HQ** headquarters
**hr** here, hour
**HR** home run, House of Representatives
**H Res** House resolution
**HRH** Her Royal Highness, His Royal Highness
**hrzn** horizon
**HS** high school
**HSL** high-speed launch
**HST** Hawaiian standard time, hypersonic transport
**ht** height
**HT** half time, halftone, hardtop, Hawaii time, high-tension, high tide, [Latin *hoc tempore*] at this time; [Latin *hoc titulo*] under this title
**http** hypertext transfer protocol

**HUAC** House Un-American Activities Committee
**HUD** Department of Housing and Urban Development
**Humber** Humberside
**Hung** Hungarian, Hungary
**hv** have
**HV** high velocity, high voltage
**HVAC** heating, ventilating, and air-conditioning
**hvy** heavy
**hw** how
**HW** high water, highway, hot water
**HWM** high-water mark
**hwy** highway
**hyd** hydraulics, hydrostatics
**hyp** hypothesis, hypothetical
**Hz** hertz
**i** industrial, initial, intelligence, intensity, intransitive, island, isle
**I** electric current, Indian, interstate, iodine, Israeli
**Ia** *or* **IA** Iowa
**IAA** indoleacetic acid
**IAAF** International Amateur Athletic Federation
**IABA** International Amateur Boxing Association
**IAEA** International Atomic Energy Agency
**IALC** instrument approach and landing chart
**IAM** International Association of Machinists and Aerospace Workers
**IAP** international airport
**IAS** indicated airspeed
**IATA** International Air Transport Association
**IAU** International Association of Universities, International Astronomical Union
**ib** *or* **ibid** ibidem
**IB** in bond, incendiary bomb
**IBRD** International Bank for Reconstruction and Development
**ICA** International Cooperative Alliance
**ICAO** International Civil Aviation Organization
**ICC** International Chamber of Commerce, Interstate Commerce Commission
**Ice** Iceland
**ICE** internal combustion engine, International Cultural Exchange
**Icel** Icelandic
**ICF** intermediate care facility
**ICFTU** International Confederation of Free Trade Unions
**ICJ** International Court of Justice
**ICRC** International Committee of the Red Cross
**ICU** intensive care unit
**id** idem
**ID** Idaho, identification, independent distributor, industrial design, inner diameter, inside dimensions, intelligence department, internal diameter
**IDA** International Development Association
**IDP** international driving permit
**i.e.** [Latin *id est*] that is
**IE** industrial engineer
**IEEE** The Institute of Electrical and Electronics Engineers
**IF** intermediate frequency
**IFC** International Finance Corporation
**IFF** identification, friend or foe
**IFO** identified flying object
**IFR** instrument flight rules
**Ig** immunoglobulin
**IG** inspector general
**IGY** International Geophysical Year
**ihp** indicated horsepower
**IIE** Institute of Industrial Engineers
**IL** Illinois
**ILA** International Longshoremen's Association
**ILGWU** International Ladies' Garment Workers' Union
**ill** illustrated, illustration, illustrator
**Ill** Illinois

**illust** *or* **illus** illustrated, illustration
**ILO** International Labor Organization
**ILS** instrument landing system
**IL-2** interleukin-2
**IM** individual medley, intramural
**IMCO** Inter-Governmental Maritime Consultative Organization
**IMF** International Monetary Fund
**imit** imitative
**immed** immediate, immediately
**immun** immunity, immunization
**immunol** immunology
**imp** imperative, imperfect, imperial, import, imported
**IMP** international match point
**imperf** imperfect, imperforate
**in** inch, inlet
**In** indium
**IN** Indiana
**inc** incomplete, incorporated, increase
**incl** include, included, including, inclusive
**incog** incognito
**incr** increase, increased
**ind** independent, index, industrial, industry
**Ind** Indian, Indiana
**IND** investigational new drug
**IndE** industrial engineer
**indef** indefinite
**indic** indicative
**indiv** individual
**indn** indication
**Indon** Indonesia, Indonesian
**indus** industrial, industry
**inf** infantry, infinitive
**INF** intermediate range nuclear forces
**infl** influenced
**INH** [*iso-nicotinic acid hydrazide*] isoniazid
**inorg** inorganic
**INP** International News Photo
**inq** inquire
**INRI** [Latin *Iesus Nazarenus Rex Iudaeorum*] Jesus of Nazareth, King of the Jews
**ins** inches, insurance
**INS** Immigration and Naturalization Service, inertial navigation system
**insol** insoluble
**insp** inspector
**inst** instant, institute, institution, institutional
**instr** instructor, instrument, instrumental
**insur** insurance
**int** intelligence, intercept, interest, interim, interior, interjection, interleaved, intermediate, internal, international, interpreter, intersection, interval, interview, intransitive
**intel** intelligence
**interj** interjection
**Interpol** International Criminal Police Organization
**interrog** interrogative
**intl** *or* **intnl** international
**intrans** intransitive
**in trans** [Latin *in transitu*] in transit
**introd** introduction
**inv** inventor, invoice
**I/O** input/output
**IOC** International Olympic Committee
**IOM** Isle of Man
**Ion** Ionic
**IOOF** Independent Order of Odd Fellows
**IORM** Improved Order of Red Men
**IOW** Isle of Wight
**IP** initial point, innings pitched, intermediate pressure
**IPA** individual practice association
**ipm** inches per minute
**IPO** initial public offering
**ips** inches per second
**IPTS** International Practical Temperature Scale
**iq** [Latin *idem quod*] the same as
**Ir** iridium, Irish

**IR** information retrieval, infrared, inland revenue, intelligence ratio, internal revenue
**IRA** Irish Republican Army
**IRBM** intermediate range ballistic missile
**Ire** Ireland
**irid** iridescent
**irred** irredeemable
**irreg** irregular
**IRS** Internal Revenue Service
**is** island, isle
**Isa** *or* **Is** Isaiah
**ISBN** International Standard Book Number
**ISC** interstate commerce
**isl** island
**ISO** International Organization for Standardization
**isoln** isolation
**Isr** Israel, Israeli
**ISSN** International Standard Serial Number
**isth** isthmus
**ISV** International Scientific Vocabulary
**It** Italian, Italy
**ital** italic, italicized
**Ital** Italian
**ITO** International Trade Organization
**ITU** International Telecommunication Union, International Typographical Union
**ITV** instructional television
**IU** international unit
**IV** intravenous, intravenously
**IVF** in vitro fertilization
**IW** inside width, isotopic weight
**IWW** Industrial Workers of the World
**j** jack, journal, judge, justice
**J** joule, jump shot
**JA** joint account, judge advocate
**JAG** judge advocate general
**Jam** Jamaica
**Jan** January
**Jas** James
**Jav** Javanese
**JBS** John Birch Society
**JC** junior college
**JCAHO** Joint Commission on Accreditation of Healthcare Organizations
**JCB** [New Latin *juris canonici baccalaureus*] bachelor of canon law
**JCD** [New Latin *juris canonici doctor*] doctor of canon law
**JCL** [New Latin *juris canonici licentiatus*] licentiate in canon law
**JCS** joint chiefs of staff
**jct** junction
**JD** [New Latin *juris doctor*] doctor of jurisprudence, doctor of law; [New Latin *jurum doctor*] doctor of laws; justice department, juvenile delinquent
**Jer** Jeremiah, Jeremias
**jg** junior grade
**JIT** job instruction training, just in time
**Jn** *or* **Jno** John
**JND** just noticeable difference
**jnr** *British* junior
**Jo** Joel
**Jon** Jonah, Jonas
**Josh** Joshua
**jour** journal, journeyman
**Jp** Japanese
**JP** jet propulsion, justice of the peace
**Jpn** Japan, Japanese
**Jr** junior
**JSD** [New Latin *juris scientiae doctor*] doctor of science of law
**jt** *or* **jnt** joint
**Jud** Judith
**Judg** Judges
**Jul** July
**jun** junior
**Jun** June
**junc** junction
**juv** juvenile
**JV** junior varsity

**k** karat, kindergarten, king, kitchen, knit, knot, koruna, kosher — often enclosed in a circle; kyat

**K** [New Latin *kalium*] potassium; Kelvin, kilometer

**ka** [German *Kathode*] cathode

**Kan** *or* **Kans** Kansas

**kb** kilobar, kilobase

**KB** kilobyte

**kbar** kilobar

**kc** kilocycle

**KC** Kansas City, King's Counsel, Knights of Columbus

**kcal** kilocalorie, kilogram calorie

**KCB** knight commander of the Order of the Bath

**kc/s** kilocycles per second

**KD** kiln-dried, knockdown, knocked down

**Ker** Kerry

**keV** kilo-electron volt

**kg** keg, kilogram, king

**kG** kilogauss

**KG** knight of the Order of the Garter

**KGB** [Russian *Komitet gosudarstvennoĭ bezopasnosti*] (Soviet) State Security Committee

**kgps** kilograms per second

**kHz** kilohertz

**KIA** killed in action

**Kild** Kildare

**Kilk** Kilkenny

**kit** kitchen

**kJ** kilojoule

**KJV** King James Version

**KKK** Ku Klux Klan

**kl** kiloliter

**km** kilometer

**kmh** *or* **kmph** kilometers per hour

**kmps** kilometers per second

**kn** knot

**K of C** Knights of Columbus

**Kor** Korea, Korean

**kPa** kilopascal

**kpc** kiloparsec

**kph** kilometers per hour

**Kr** krypton

**KS** Kansas, Kaposi's sarcoma

**kt** karat, knight, knot

**KT** kiloton

**kV** kilovolt

**kW** kilowatt

**kWh** kilowatt-hour

**Ky** *or* **KY** Kentucky

**l** lady, lake, lambert, land, large, late, left, [Latin *libra*] pound; line, liquid, lira, lire, liter, little, low

**L** Lagrangian, Latin, long

**La** lanthanum, Louisiana

**LA** law agent, legislative assistant, Los Angeles, Louisiana

**Lab** Labrador

**lam** laminated

**Lam** Lamentations

**Lancs** Lancashire

**lang** language

**lat** latitude

**Lat** Latin, Latvia

**LAT** local apparent time

**lav** lavatory

**lb** [Latin *libra*] pound

**LB** Labrador

**LBO** leveraged buyout

**lc** lowercase

**LC** landing craft, left center, letter of credit, Library of Congress

**LCD** least common denominator, lowest common denominator

**LCDR** lieutenant commander

**LCL** less-than-carload lot

**LCM** least common multiple, lowest common multiple, [New Latin *legis comparativae magister*] master of comparative law

**LCpl** lance corporal

**LCS** League Championship Series

**LCT** local civil time

**ld** load, lord

**LD** learning disabled, learning disability; lethal dose — often used with a numerical subscript to indicate the percent of a test group of organisms

the dose is expected to kill $\langle LD_{50}\rangle$; line of departure

**LDC** less developed country

**ldg** landing, loading

**LDH** lactate dehydrogenase, lactic dehydrogenase

**ldr** leader

**LDS** Latter-day Saints

**LE** leading edge

**lea** leather

**Leb** Lebanese, Lebanon

**lect** lecture, lecturer

**leg** legal, legato, legislative, legislature

**legis** legislation, legislative, legislature

**Leics** Leicestershire

**Leit** Leitrim

**LEM** lunar excursion module

**LEP** limited English proficiency, limited English proficient

**Lev** *or* **Levit** Leviticus

**lf** lightface

**LF** ledger folio, low frequency

**lg** large, long

**LH** left hand, lower half, luteinizing hormone

**LHD** [New Latin *litterarum humaniorum doctor*] doctor of humane letters, doctor of humanities

**li** link

**Li** lithium

**LI** Long Island

**lib** liberal, librarian, library

**lic** license

**lieut** lieutenant

**LIFO** last in, first out

**Lim** Limerick

**lin** lineal, linear

**Lincs** Lincolnshire

**ling** linguistics

**liq** liquid, liquor

**lit** liter, literal, literally, literary, literature

**lith** lithographic, lithography

**Lith** Lithuanian

**Litt B** *or* **Lit B** [Medieval Latin *litterarum baccalaureus*] bachelor of letters, bachelor of literature

**Litt D** *or* **Lit D** [Medieval Latin *litterarum doctor*] doctor of letters, doctor of literature

**Lk** Luke

**ll** lines

**LL** lending library, limited liability, lower left

**LLB** [New Latin *legum baccalaureus*] bachelor of laws

**LLD** [New Latin *legum doctor*] doctor of laws

**LLM** [New Latin *legum magister*] master of laws

**lm** lumen

**LM** Legion of Merit, long meter, lunar module

**LMG** light machine gun

**LMT** local mean time

**ln** lane, natural logarithm

**lndg** landing

**LNG** liquefied natural gas

**LOA** length overall

**loc cit** [Latin *loco citato*] in the place cited

**log** logic

**Lond** London, Londonderry

**long** longitude

**Long** Longford

**loq** [Latin *loquitur*] he speaks, she speaks

**LOS** line of scrimmage, line of sight

**Loth** Lothian

**Lou** Louth

**LP** low pressure

**LPG** liquefied petroleum gas

**LPGA** Ladies Professional Golf Association

**Lr** lawrencium

**LR** living room, log run, lower right

**LRT** light-rail transit

**LRV** light-rail vehicle

**LS** left side, letter signed, library science, [Latin *locus sigilli*] place of the seal; long shot

**LSAT** Law School Admission Test

**LSI** large-scale integrated circuit, large-scale integration

**LSM** letter-sorting machine

**LSS** lifesaving service, lifesaving station, life-support system

**LST** landing ship, tank; local sidereal time

**lt** light

**Lt** lieutenant

**LT** long ton, low-tension

**LTC** lieutenant colonel, long term care

**Lt Col** lieutenant colonel

**Lt Comdr** lieutenant commander

**ltd** limited

**LTG** *or* **Lt Gen** lieutenant general

**lt gov** lieutenant governor

**LTh** licentiate in theology

**LTJG** lieutenant, junior grade

**LTL** less than truckload

**ltr** letter, lighter

**LTS** launch telemetry station, launch tracking system

**Lu** lutetium

**lub** lubricant, lubricating

**Luth** Lutheran

**lv** leave

**LVT** landing vehicle, tracked

**LW** low water

**LWM** low-water mark

**LWV** League of Women Voters

**lx** lux

**LZ** landing zone

**m** male, manual, married, martyr, masculine, mass, measure, meridian, [Latin *meridies*] noon; meter, middle, mile, [Latin *mille*] thousand; milli-, minute, molal, molality, molar, molarity, mole, month, moon, morning, muscle

**m-** meta-

**M** Mach, March, May, medium, mega-, million, monsieur

**mA** milliampere

**MA** [Medieval Latin *magister artium*] master of arts; Massachusetts, mental age, Middle Ages

**MAA** master of applied arts

**Mac** Machabees

**Mac** *or* **Macc** Maccabees

**MAC** military airlift command

**mach** machine, machinery, machinist

**MAD** mutual assured destruction

**MAE** *or* **MA Ed** master of arts in education

**mag** magnesium, magnetism, magneto, magnitude

**Maj** major

**Maj Gen** major general

**Mal** Malachi

**MALS** master of arts in liberal studies, master of arts in library science

**man** manual

**Man** Manitoba

**M&A** mergers and acquisitions

**manuf** manufacture, manufacturing

**MAO** monoamine oxidase

**MAP** modified American plan

**mar** maritime

**Mar** March

**MARC** machine readable cataloging

**MARV** maneuverable reentry vehicle

**masc** masculine

**MASH** mobile army surgical hospital

**Mass** Massachusetts

**MAT** master of arts in teaching, Miller analogy test

**math** mathematical, mathematician

**matric** matriculated, matriculation

**Matt** Matthew

**MATV** master antenna television

**max** maximum

**mb** millibar

**MB** bachelor of medicine, Manitoba, megabyte, municipal borough

**MBA** master of business administration

**mbd** million barrels per day

**MBD** minimal brain dysfunction

**MBE** member of the Order of the British Empire

**MBO** management by objective

**MBS** Mutual Broadcasting System

**mc** megacycle, millicurie

**MC** member of Congress

**MCAT** Medical College Admission Test

**MCC** mission control center

**mcf** thousand cubic feet

**mcg** microgram

**MCL** Marine Corps League, master of civil law, master of comparative law

**MCP** male chauvinist pig

**MCPO** master chief petty officer

**Md** Maryland, mendelevium

**MD** [New Latin *medicinae doctor*] doctor of medicine; [Italian *mano destra*] right hand; Maryland, medical department, months after date, muscular dystrophy

**MDC** more developed country

**MDiv** master of divinity

**mdnt** midnight

**mdse** merchandise

**MDT** mountain daylight time

**Me** Maine, methyl

**ME** Maine, managing editor, mechanical engineer, medical examiner

**Mea** Meath

**meas** measure

**mech** mechanical, mechanics

**med** medicine, medieval, medium

**Med** Mediterranean

**MEd** master of education

**meg** megohm

**MEGO** my eyes glaze over

**MEK** methyl ethyl ketone

**mem** member, memoir, memorial

**MEng** master of English

**MEP** member of the European Parliament

**mer** meridian

**Mersey** Merseyside

**met** meteorological, meteorology, metropolitan

**metal** *or* **metall** metallurgical, metallurgy

**metaph** metaphysics

**METO** Middle East Treaty Organization

**MeV** million electron volts

**Mex** Mexican, Mexico

**mf** mezzo forte

**mF** millifarad

**MF** medium frequency, microfiche

**MFA** master of fine arts

**mfd** manufactured

**mfg** manufacturing

**MFH** master of foxhounds

**MFN** most favored nation

**mfr** manufacture, manufacturer

**mg** milligram

**Mg** magnesium

**MG** machine gun, major general, military government

**mgal** milligal

**MGB** [Russian *Ministerstvo gosudarstvennoĭ bezopasnosti*] Ministry of State Security

**mgd** million gallons per day

**mgr** manager, monseigneur, monsignor

**mgt** *or* **mgmt** management

**MGy Sgt** master gunnery sergeant

**MH** medal of honor, mental health, mobile home

**MHA** master of hospital administration

**MHC** major histocompatibility complex

**MHD** magnetohydrodynamic, magnetohydrodynamics

**mhg** mahogany

**MHW** mean high water

**MHz** megahertz

**mi** mile, mileage, mill

**MI** Michigan, military intelligence

**Mic** Micah

**MIC** methyl isocyanate

**Mich** Michigan

**MICR** magnetic ink character recognition

**mid** middle

**Middx** Middlesex

**Mid Glam** Mid Glamorgan

**midn** midshipman

**mil** military, million

**min** minim, minimum, mining, minister, minor, minute

**Minn** Minnesota

**MIO** minimum identifiable odor

**MIPS** *or* **mips** million instructions per second

**misc** miscellaneous

**Miss** Mississippi

**mixt** mixture

**mk** mark, markka

**Mk** Mark

**mks** meter-kilogram-second

**mkt** market

**mktg** marketing

**ml** milliliter

**mL** millilambert

**MLA** Member of the Legislative Assembly

**MLD** median lethal dose, minimum lethal dose

**MLF** multilateral force

**Mlle** [French] mademoiselle

**Mlles** [French] mesdemoiselles

**MLS** master of library science

**MLW** mean low water

**mm** millimeter

**MM** [French] messieurs; mutatis mutandis

**Mme** [French] madame

**Mmes** [French] mesdames

**mmf** magnetomotive force

**MMPI** Minnesota Multiphasic Personality Inventory

**Mn** manganese

**MN** magnetic north, Minnesota

**MNC** multinational company, multinational corporation

**mo** month

**Mo** Missouri, molybdenum, Monday

**MO** mail order, medical officer, Missouri, modus operandi, money order

**mod** moderate, modification, modified, modulo, modulus

**modif** modification

**mol** mole, molecular, molecule

**MOL** manned orbiting laboratory

**mol wt** molecular weight

**MOM** middle of month

**mon** monastery, monetary

**Mon** Monaghan, Monday

**Mont** Montana

**mor** morocco

**MOR** middle of the road

**morph** morphology

**mos** months

**MOS** metal-oxide semiconductor, military occupational specialty

**MOSFET** metal-oxide-semiconductor field-effect transistor

**MP** melting point, member of parliament, metropolitan police, milepost, military police, military policeman

**MPA** master of public administration

**MPAA** Motion Picture Association of America

**mpg** miles per gallon

**mph** miles per hour

**MPH** master of public health

**MPhil** master of philosophy

**MPM** meters per minute

**MPS** meters per second

**MPV** multi-purpose vehicle

**MPX** multiplex

**mR** milliroentgen

**MR** map reference, mentally retarded

**MRE** meals ready to eat

**MRI** magnetic resonance imaging

**mRNA** messenger RNA

**ms** millisecond

**MS** [Italian *mano sinistra*] left hand; manuscript, master of science, military science, Mississippi, motor ship, multiple sclerosis

**MSc** master of science

**msec** millisecond

**msg** message

**MSG** master sergeant, monosodium glutamate

**msgr** monseigneur, monsignor

**MSgt** master sergeant

**MSH** melanocyte-stimulating hormone

**MSL** mean sea level

**MSN** master of science in nursing

**MSS** manuscripts

**MST** mountain standard time

**MSW** master of social welfare, master of social work

**mt** mount, mountain

**Mt** Matthew

**MT** machine translation, metric ton, Montana, mountain time

**mtg** meeting, mortgage

**mtge** mortgage

**mth** month

**mtn** mountain

**MTO** Mediterranean theater of operations

**mun** *or* **munic** municipal

**mus** museum, music, musical, musician

**mV** millivolt

**MV** main verb, mean variation, motor vessel

**MVD** [Russian *Ministerstvo vnutrennikh del*] Ministry of Internal Affairs

**MVP** most valuable player

**mW** milliwatt

**MW** megawatt

**MWe** megawatts electric

**mxd** mixed

**my** million years

**myc** *or* **mycol** mycology

**Myr** million years

**n** name, nano-, navy, net, neuter, *usually italic* neutron, noon, normal, north, northern, note, noun, number

**N** newton, nitrogen

**Na** [New Latin *natrium*] sodium

**NA** national association, no account, North America, not applicable, not available

**NAACP** National Association for the Advancement of Colored People

**NAB** New American Bible

**NAD** no appreciable disease

**Nah** Nahum

**NAIA** National Association of Intercollegiate Athletes

**NAS** National Academy of Sciences, naval air station

**NASA** National Aeronautics and Space Administration

**NASCAR** National Association for Stock Car Auto Racing

**NASD** National Association of Securities Dealers

**NASL** North American Soccer League

**NASW** National Association of Social Workers

**nat** national, native, natural

**natl** national

**NATO** North Atlantic Treaty Organization

**naut** nautical

**nav** naval, navigable, navigation

**Nb** niobium

**NB** New Brunswick, northbound, nota bene

**NBA** National Basketball Association, National Boxing Association

**NBC** National Broadcasting Company

**NBS** National Bureau of Standards

**NC** no charge, no credit, North Carolina, nurse corps

**NCAA** National Collegiate Athletic Association

**NCE** New Catholic Edition

**NCV** no commercial value

**nd** no date

**Nd** neodymium

**ND** doctor of naturopathy, North Dakota

**N Dak** North Dakota

**NDE** near-death experience

**NDP** New Democratic Party (Canadian)

**Ne** neon

**NE** Nebraska, New England, no effects, northeast

**NEA** National Education Association, National Endowment for the Arts

**Neb** *or* **Nebr** Nebraska

**NEB** New English Bible

**NED** New English Dictionary

**neg** negative, negotiable

**Neh** Nehemiah

**NEH** National Endowment for the Humanities

**NEI** not elsewhere included

**nem con** [New Latin *nemine contradicente*] no one contradicting

**nem diss** [New Latin *nemine dissentiente*] no one dissenting

**NEP** New Economic Policy

**NES** not elsewhere specified

**Neth** Netherlands

**neurol** neurological, neurology

**neut** neuter

**Nev** Nevada

**New Eng** New England

**NF** Newfoundland, no funds

**NFC** National Football Conference

**NFL** National Football League

**Nfld** Newfoundland

**NFP** natural family planning

**NFS** not for sale

**ng** nanogram

**NG** national guard, no good

**NGF** nerve growth factor

**NGO** nongovernmental organization

**NGU** nongonococcal urethritis

**NH** never hinged, New Hampshire

**NHL** National Hockey League

**Ni** nickel

**NIC** newly industrialized country, newly industrializing country

**NIH** National Institutes of Health, not invented here

**NIMBY** not in my backyard

**NIT** National Invitational Tournament

**NIU** network interface unit

**NJ** New Jersey

**NKVD** [Russian *Narodnyĭ komissariat vnutrennikh del*] People's Commissariat of Internal Affairs

**NL** National League, new line, night letter, [Latin *non licet*] it is not permitted; north latitude

**NLCS** National League Championship Series

**NLF** National Liberation Front

**NLRB** National Labor Relations Board

**NLT** night letter

**nm** nanometer

**NM** nautical mile, New Mexico, no mark, not marked

**N Mex** New Mexico

**NMHA** National Mental Health Association

**NMI** no middle initial

**NMR** nuclear magnetic resonance

**NNE** north-northeast

**NNW** north-northwest

**no** north, northern, [Latin *numero,* ablative of *numerus*] number

**No** nobelium

**NOAA** National Oceanic and Atmospheric Administration

**NOIBN** not otherwise indexed by name

**nom** nominative

**non obst** *or* **non obs** non obstante

**non seq** non sequitur

**NOP** not otherwise provided for

**Nor** Norway, Norwegian

**NORAD** North American Air Defense Command

**Norf** Norfolk

**norm** normal

**Northants** Northamptonshire

**Norw** Norway, Norwegian

**nos** numbers

**NOS** not otherwise specified

**Notts** Nottinghamshire

**nov** novelist

**Nov** November

**NOW** National Organization for Women

**NO$_x$** nitrogen oxide

**np** no pagination, no place (of publication)

**Np** neptunium

**NP** neuropsychiatric, neuropsychiatry, no protest, notary public, noun phrase

**NPF** not provided for

**NPN** nonprotein nitrogen

**NPR** National Public Radio

**NPS** National Park Service

**nr** near

**NR** not rated

**NRA** National Recovery Administration, National Rifle Association

**NRC** National Research Council, Nuclear Regulatory Commission

**ns** *also* **nsec** nanosecond

**Ns** nimbostratus

**NS** new series, new style, not specified, not sufficient, Nova Scotia

**NSA** National Security Agency

**NSC** National Security Council

**NSF** National Science Foundation, not sufficient funds

**NSW** New South Wales

**NT** New Territories, New Testament, Northern Territory, Northwest Territories

**Nthmb** Northumberland

**NTP** normal temperature and pressure

**NTSB** National Transportation Safety Board

**nt wt** *or* **n wt** net weight

**NU** name unknown

**num** numeral

**Num** *or* **Numb** Numbers

**numis** numismatic, numismatical, numismatics

**NV** Nevada, nonvoting

**NW** northwest

**NWT** Northwest Territories

**NY** New York

**NYC** New York City

**NYSE** New York Stock Exchange

**NZ** New Zealand

**o** ocean, ohm, old, order, oriental, over

**O** Ohio, oxygen, [New Latin *octarius*] pint

**o-** ortho-

**o/a** on or about

**OAS** Organization of American States

**OASDHI** Old Age, Survivors, Disability, and Health Insurance

**OAU** Organization of African Unity

**ob** [Latin *obiit*] he died, she died; observation

**Ob** *or* **Obad** Obadiah

**OB** obstetric, obstetrician, obstetrics

**OBE** officer of the Order of the British Empire, out-of-body experience

**OB–GYN** obstetrician gynecologist, obstetrics gynecology

**obj** object, objective

**obl** oblique, oblong

**obstet** obstetrical, obstetrics

**obv** obverse

**oc** ocean

**OC** off center, officer candidate, on center, on course, over-the-counter

**occas** occasionally

**oceanog** oceanography

**OCR** optical character reader, optical character recognition

**OCS** officer candidate school

**oct** octavo

**Oct** October

**OD** doctor of optometry, [Latin *oculus dexter*] right eye; officer of the day, olive drab, on demand, outside diameter, outside dimension, overdraft, overdrawn

**Oe** oersted

**OECD** Organization for Economic Cooperation and Development

**OED** Oxford English Dictionary

**OEO** Office of Economic Opportunity

**OER** officer efficiency report

**OES** Order of the Eastern Star

**OF** outfield

**off** office, officer, official

**offic** official
**OG** officer of the guard, original gum
**OH** Ohio
**OHMS** on Her Majesty's service, on His Majesty's service
**OIT** Office of International Trade
**OJ** orange juice
**OJT** on-the-job training
**OK** Oklahoma, outer keel
**Okla** Oklahoma
**OM** order of merit
**OMB** Office of Management and Budget
**ON** *or* **Ont** Ontario
**OOD** officer of the deck
**op** operation, operative, operator, opportunity, opus
**OP** observation post, out of print
**op cit** [Latin *opere citato*] in the work cited
**OPEC** Organization of Petroleum Exporting Countries
**opp** opposite
**opt** optical, optician, optics, option, optional
**OR** operating room, operational research, operations research, Oregon, owner's risk, own recognizance
**orch** orchestra
**ord** order, ordnance
**Ore** *or* **Oreg** Oregon
**org** organic, organization, organized
**orig** original, originally, originator
**Ork** Orkney
**ornith** ornithology
**ORV** off-road vehicle
**Os** osmium
**OS** [Latin *oculus sinister*] left eye; old series, old style, ordinary seaman, out of stock
**OSHA** Occupational Safety and Health Administration
**OSS** Office of Strategic Services
**OT** occupational therapy, Old Testament, overtime
**OTA** Office of Technology Assessment
**OTB** offtrack betting
**OTC** over-the-counter
**OTR** occupational therapist, registered
**OTS** officers' training school
**OW** one-way
**Oxfam** Oxford Committee for Famine Relief
**Oxon** [Medieval Latin *Oxonia*] Oxford; Oxfordshire, [Medieval Latin *Oxoniensis*] of Oxford
**oz** [obsolete Italian *onza* (now *oncia*)] ounce, ounces

**p** page, pages, parental generation, part, participle, past, pater, pawn, pence, penny, per, peseta, peso, petite, piano, pico-, pint, pipe, pitch, pole, port, power, pro, proton, purl
**P** phosphorus, pressure, [French *poids*] weight
**p-** para-
**Pa** pascal, Pennsylvania, protactinium
**PA** particular average, passenger agent, Pennsylvania, per annum, personal appearance, personal assistant, power amplifier, power of attorney, press agent, private account, professional association, public address, purchasing agent
**Pac** Pacific
**PAC** political action committee
**paleon** paleontology
**pam** pamphlet
**Pan** Panama
**p and h** postage and handling
**P&I** principal and interest
**P&L** profit and loss
**par** paragraph, parallel, parish
**para** paragraph
**part** participial, participle, particular
**PAS** para-aminosalicylic acid
**pass** passenger, passive
**pat** patent
**PAT** point after touchdown
**path** *or* **pathol** pathological, pathology

**PAYE** *British* pay as you earn
**payt** payment
**pb** paperback
**Pb** [Latin *plumbum*] lead
**PB** personal best, power brakes
**PB&J** peanut butter and jelly
**PBS** Public Broadcasting Service
**pc** parsec
**PC** Peace Corps, percent, percentage, politically correct, postcard, [Latin *post cibum*] after meals; printed circuit, professional corporation
**PCP** pneumocystis carinii pneumonia, primary care physician
**PCR** polymerase chain reaction
**pct** percent, percentage
**pd** paid
**Pd** palladium
**PD** per diem, police department, postal district, potential difference, program director, public domain
**PDA** predicted drift angle, public display of affection
**PDD** past due date
**PDT** Pacific daylight time
**PE** physical education, printer's error, probable error, professional engineer
**P/E** price/earnings
**PEI** Prince Edward Island
**pen** peninsula
**PEN** International Association of Poets, Playwrights, Editors, Essayists and Novelists
**Penn** *or* **Penna** Pennsylvania
**per** period, person
**perf** perfect, perforated, performance
**perh** perhaps
**perm** permanent
**perp** perpendicular
**pers** person, personal, personnel
**Pers** Persia, Persian
**pert** pertaining
**pet** petroleum
**Pet** Peter
**PET** positron-emission tomography
**pf** personal foul, pfennig, picofarad, preferred
**PF** power factor, pianoforte, [Italian *più forte*] louder
**PFC** *or* **Pfc** private first class
**pfd** preferred
**PFD** personal flotation device
**pg** page, picogram
**Pg** Portugal, Portuguese
**PG** paying guest, postgraduate, prostaglandin
**PGA** Professional Golfers' Association
**ph** phase
**PH** pinch hit, public health, Purple Heart
**phar** pharmacopoeia, pharmacy
**pharm** pharmaceutical, pharmacist, pharmacy
**PhB** [New Latin *philosophiae baccalaureus*] bachelor of philosophy
**PhD** [New Latin *philosophiae doctor*] doctor of philosophy
**phil** *or* **philol** philological, philology
**Phil** Philippians
**philos** philosopher, philosophy
**phon** phonetics
**photog** photographic, photography
**phr** phrase
**phys** physical, physics
**physiol** physiologist, physiology
**PI** Philippine Islands, private investigator, programmed instruction
**PID** pelvic inflammatory disease
**PIK** payment in kind
**PIN** personal identification number
**PINS** persons in need of supervision
**pinx** [Latin *pinxit*] he painted it, she painted it
**PIRG** Public Interest Research Group
**pizz** pizzicato
**pk** park, peak, peck, pike
**PK** preacher's kid
**pkg** package
**pkt** packet, pocket
**PKU** phenylketonuria
**pkwy** parkway

**pl** place, plate, plural
**PL** partial loss, private line, Public Law
**plat** plateau, platoon
**PLC** *British* public limited company
**plf** plaintiff
**PLO** Palestine Liberation Organization
**pls** please
**PLSS** portable life-support system
**pm** phase modulation, premium
**Pm** promethium
**PM** paymaster, permanent magnet, police magistrate, postmaster, post meridiem — often not capitalized and often punctuated; postmortem, prime minister, provost marshal
**pmk** postmark
**PMS** premenstrual syndrome
**pmt** payment
**PN** promissory note
**pnxt** [Latin *pinxit*] he painted it, she painted it
**Po** polonium
**PO** [Latin *per os*] by mouth, orally; petty officer, postal order, post office, purchase order
**POB** post office box
**POC** port of call
**POD** pay on delivery, post office department
**POE** port of embarkation, port of entry
**Pol** Poland, Polish
**polit** political, politician
**poly** polytechnic
**pon** pontoon
**pop** population
**POP** point of purchase
**por** portrait
**POR** pay on return, price on request
**port** portable, portrait
**Port** Portugal, Portuguese
**pos** position, positive
**POS** point of sale
**poss** possessive
**pot** potential, potentiometer
**POV** point of view
**pp** pages, [Latin *per procurationem*] by proxy; pianissimo
**PP** parcel post, past participle, postpaid, prepaid
**ppa** per power of attorney
**ppb** parts per billion
**ppd** postpaid, prepaid
**PPI** plan position indicator
**ppm** parts per million
**PPS** [New Latin *post postscriptum*] an additional postscript
**ppt** parts per thousand, parts per trillion, precipitate
**pptn** precipitation
**PQ** Province of Quebec
**pr** pair, price, printed
**Pr** praseodymium, propyl
**PR** payroll, proportional representation, public relations, Puerto Rico
**PRC** People's Republic of China
**prec** preceding
**pred** predicate
**pref** preface, preference, preferred, prefix
**prem** premium
**prep** preparatory, preposition
**prepd** prepared
**prepg** preparing
**prepn** preparation
**pres** present, president
**Presb** Presbyterian
**prev** previous, previously
**prf** proof
**prim** primary, primitive
**prin** principal, principle
**priv** private, privately, privative
**PRN** [Latin *pro re nata*] for the emergency, as needed
**PRO** public relations officer
**prob** probable, probably, probate, problem
**proc** proceedings
**prod** product, production
**prof** professional
**prog** program

**proj** project, projector
**prom** promontory
**pron** pronoun, pronounced, pronunciation
**prop** property, proposition, proprietor
**pros** prosody
**Prot** Protestant
**prov** province, provincial, provisional
**Prov** Proverbs
**prox** proximo
**Pruss** Prussian
**ps** picosecond
**Ps** *or* **Psa** Psalms
**PS** [New Latin *postscriptum*] postscript; power steering, power supply, public school
**PSA** public service announcement
**psec** picosecond
**pseud** pseudonym, pseudonymous
**psf** pounds per square foot
**PSG** platoon sergeant
**psi** pounds per square inch
**psig** pounds per square inch gauge
**PST** Pacific standard time
**psych** psychology
**psychol** psychologist, psychology
**pt** part, payment, pint, point, port
**Pt** platinum
**PT** Pacific time, part-time, physical therapy, physical training
**pta** peseta
**PTA** Parent-Teacher Association
**pte** *British* private
**ptg** printing
**PTO** Parent-Teacher Organization, please turn over, power takeoff
**PTSD** post-traumatic stress disorder
**PTV** public television
**Pty** *British* proprietary
**Pu** plutonium
**PU** pickup
**pub** public, publication, publicity, published, publisher, publishing
**publ** publication, published, publisher
**PUD** pickup and delivery
**pulv** [Latin *pulvis*] powder
**PUSH** People United to Serve Humanity
**PV** photovoltaic, polyvinyl
**PVA** polyvinyl acetate
**PVC** polyvinyl chloride
**PVO** private voluntary organization
**pvt** private
**PVT** pressure, volume, temperature
**PW** prisoner of war
**PWA** person with AIDS
**pwr** power
**PWR** pressurized water reactor
**pwt** pennyweight
**PX** please exchange, post exchange
**PYO** pick your own
**q** quart, quartile, quarto, queen, query, question, quetzal, quire
**QA** quality assurance
**QB** quarterback, queen's bench
**QC** quality control, queen's counsel
**qd** [Latin *quaque die*] daily
**QED** quantum electrodynamics, [Latin *quod erat demonstrandum*] which was to be demonstrated
**QEF** [Latin *quod erat faciendum*] which was to be done
**QEI** [Latin *quod erat inveniendum*] which was to be found out
**QF** quick-firing
**qid** [Latin *quater in die*] four times a day
**Qld** Queensland
**qm** [Latin *quoque matutino*] every morning
**QM** quartermaster
**QMC** quartermaster corps
**QMG** quartermaster general
**qp** *or* **q pl** [Latin *quantum placet*] as much as you please
**qq** questions
**qq v** [Latin *quae vide*] which (*plural*) see
**qr** quarter, quire
**qs** [Latin *quantum sufficit*] as much as suffices
**qt** quantity, quart

**qtd** quartered
**qto** quarto
**qty** quantity
**qu** or **ques** question
**quad** quadrant
**qual** qualitative, quality
**quant** quantitative
**quar** quarterly
**Que** Quebec
**quot** quotation
**qv** [Latin *quod vide*] which see
**qy** query
**r** rabbi, radius, rain, range, Rankine, rare, real, Reaumur, recto, red, repeat, rerun, resistance, right, river, roentgen, rook, rough, run
**R** radial, radical — used especially of a univalent hydrocarbon radical; recipe; registered trademark — often enclosed in a circle; regular, Republican
**ra** range
**Ra** radium
**RA** regular army, right ascension, Royal Academician, Royal Academy
**RAAF** Royal Australian Air Force
**rad** radical, radian, radiator, radio, radius, radix
**RADM** rear admiral
**RAF** Royal Air Force
**R & B** rhythm and blues
**R and R** rest and recreation, rest and recuperation
**rap** rapid
**Rb** rubidium
**RBC** red blood cells, red blood count
**RBE** relative biological effectiveness
**RC** Red Cross, resistance-capacitance, Roman Catholic
**RCAF** Royal Canadian Air Force
**RCMP** Royal Canadian Mounted Police
**RCN** Royal Canadian Navy
**rct** recruit
**rd** road, rod, round
**RD** registered dietitian, rural delivery
**RDA** recommended daily allowance, recommended dietary allowance
**RDF** radio direction finder, radio direction finding, Rapid Deployment Force, refuse-derived fuel
**Re** rhenium
**REA** Rural Electrification Administration
**reas** reasonable
**rec** receipt, record, recording, recreation
**recd** received
**recip** reciprocal, reciprocity
**rec sec** recording secretary
**rect** receipt, rectangle, rectangular, rectified
**red** reduce, reduction
**ref** reference, referred, refining, reformed, refunding
**refl** reflex, reflexive
**refr** refraction
**refrig** refrigerating, refrigeration
**reg** region, register, registered, registration, regular
**regd** registered
**regt** regiment
**REIT** real estate investment trust
**rel** relating, relative, released, religion, religious
**relig** religion
**rep** repair, repeat, report, reporter, representative, republic
**Rep** Republican
**repl** replace, replacement
**rept** report
**req** request, require, required, requisition
**reqd** required
**res** research, reservation, reserve, reservoir, residence, resident, resolution
**RES** reticuloendothelial system
**resp** respective, respectively
**ret** retain, retired, return
**retd** retained, retired, returned
**rev** revenue, reverse, review, reviewed, revised, revision, revolution
**Rev** Revelation, reverend

**Revd** *British* reverend
**rf** refunding
**RF** radio frequency
**RFD** rural free delivery
**RFP** request for proposal
**Rh** rhodium
**RH** relative humidity, right hand
**rhet** rhetoric
**RHIP** rank has its privileges
**RI** refractive index, Rhode Island
**RIA** radioimmunoassay
**RICO** Racketeer Influenced and Corrupt Organizations (Act)
**RIF** reduction in force
**RIO** radar intercept officer
**RIP** [Latin *requiescat in pace*] may he rest in peace, may she rest in peace; [Latin *requiescant in pace*] may they rest in peace
**RISC** reduced instruction-set computer; reduced instruction-set computing
**rit** ritardando
**riv** river
**RJ** road junction
**rm** ream, room
**rms** root-mean-square
**Rn** radon
**RN** Royal Navy
**rnd** round
**RNZAF** Royal New Zealand Air Force
**ROC** Republic of China (Taiwan)
**ROG** receipt of goods
**ROI** return on investment
**ROK** Republic of Korea (South Korea)
**Rom** Roman, Romance, Romania, Romanian, Romans
**ROP** record of production, run-of-paper
**ROR** release on own recognizance
**Ros** or **Rosc** Roscommon
**rot** rotating, rotation
**ROTC** Reserve Officers' Training Corps
**RP** Received Pronunciation, relief pitcher, reply paid, reprint, reprinting, Republic of the Philippines
**RPh** registered pharmacist
**rpm** revolutions per minute
**rps** revolutions per second
**rpt** repeat, report
**RQ** respiratory quotient
**RR** railroad, rural route
**RRT** registered record technician
**RS** Received Standard, recording secretary, revised statutes, right side, Royal Society
**RSA** Republic of South Africa
**RSFSR** [Russian *Rossiĭskaya Sovetskaya Federativnaya Sotsialisticheskaya Respublika*] Russian Soviet Federated Socialist Republic
**RSV** Revised Standard Version
**RSVP** [French *répondez s'il vous plaît*] please reply
**RSWC** right side up with care
**rt** right, route
**RT** radiologic technologist, radiotelephone, respiratory therapy, room temperature, round-trip
**rte** route
**rtw** ready-to-wear
**Ru** ruthenium
**Rum** Rumania, Rumanian
**Russ** Russia, Russian
**RV** Revised Version
**RW** radiological warfare, right worshipful, right worthy
**rwy** or **ry** railway
**s** sabbath, saint, schilling, scruple, second, secondary, section, senate, series, shilling, [Latin *signa*] label; siemens, signor, sine, singular, small, smooth, snow, society, son, sou, south, southern, subject, symmetrical
**S** satisfactory, short, standard deviation of a sample, sulfur, svedberg
**Sa** Saturday
**SA** Salvation Army, seaman apprentice, sex appeal, [Latin *sine anno* without year] without date; South Af-

rica, South America, South Australia, subject to approval
**sac** sacrifice
**SAC** special agent in charge, Strategic Air Command
**SAD** seasonal affective disorder
**SAE** self-addressed envelope, Society of Automotive Engineers, stamped addressed envelope
**SAG** Screen Actors Guild
**sal** salary
**SALT** Strategic Arms Limitation Talks
**Sam** or **Saml** Samuel
**san** sanatorium
**S&H** shipping and handling
**S and M** sadism and masochism, sadist and masochist
**sanit** sanitary, sanitation
**SAR** search and rescue
**SASE** self-addressed stamped envelope
**Sask** Saskatchewan
**sat** saturate, saturated, saturation
**Sat** Saturday
**satd** saturated
**S Aust** South Australia
**sb** substantive
**Sb** [Latin *stibium*] antimony
**SB** [New Latin *scientiae baccalaureus*] bachelor of science; simultaneous broadcast, southbound
**SBA** Small Business Administration
**SBN** Standard Book Number
**sc** scale, scene, science, scilicet, screw, [Latin *sculpsit*] he carved it, she carved it, he engraved it, she engraved it
**Sc** scandium, Scots, stratocumulus
**SC** small capitals, South Carolina, supercalendered, supreme court
**Scand** Scandinavia, Scandinavian
**SCAT** School and College Ability Test, supersonic commercial air transport
**ScD** doctor of science
**sch** school
**sci** science, scientific
**SCID** severe combined immune deficiency, severe combined immunodeficiency
**scil** scilicet
**SCLC** Southern Christian Leadership Conference
**Scot** Scotland, Scottish
**SCPO** senior chief petty officer
**script** scripture
**sct** scout
**sctd** scattered
**sd** said, sewed
**SD** sea-damaged, sine die, South Dakota, special delivery, stage direction, standard deviation
**S Dak** South Dakota
**SDI** Strategic Defense Initiative
**SDRs** special drawing rights
**SDS** Students for a Democratic Society
**Se** selenium
**SE** self-explanatory, southeast, Standard English, stock exchange, straight edge
**SEAL** sea, air, land (team)
**SEATO** Southeast Asia Treaty Organization
**sec** secant, second, secondary, secretary, section, [Latin *secundum*] according to; security
**SEC** Securities and Exchange Commission
**sect** section, sectional
**secy** secretary
**sed** sediment, sedimentation
**sel** select, selected, selection
**sem** semicolon, seminar, seminary
**Sem** Semitic
**sen** senate, senator, senior
**sep** separate, separated
**Sep** September
**SEP** simplified employee pension
**sepd** separated
**sepg** separating
**sepn** separation

**Sept** September
**seq** [Latin *sequens, sequentes, sequentia*] the following
**seqq** [Latin *sequentia*] the following ones
**ser** serial, series, service
**Serb** Serbian
**serg** or **sergt** sergeant
**serv** service
**SES** socioeconomic status
**sess** session
**sf** or **sfz** sforzando
**SF** sacrifice fly, science fiction, sinking fund, square feet, square foot
**SFC** sergeant first class
**SG** senior grade, sergeant, solicitor general, *often not capitalized* specific gravity; surgeon general
**sgd** signed
**Sgt** sergeant
**Sgt Maj** sergeant major
**sh** share
**Shak** Shakespeare
**shd** should
**Shet** Shetland
**SHF** superhigh frequency
**shipt** shipment
**shp** shaft horsepower
**shpt** shipment
**sht** sheet
**shtg** shortage
**Si** silicon
**SI** [French *Système International d'Unités*] International System of Units
**SIDS** sudden infant death syndrome
**sig** signal, signature, signor
**Sig** [Latin *signa*] label
**SIG** special interest group
**sigill** [Latin *sigillum*] seal
**sin** sine
**sing** singular
**SIS** Secret Intelligence Service (British)
**SJ** Society of Jesus
**SK** Saskatchewan
**sl** slightly, slip, slow
**SL** salvage loss, sea level, south latitude
**SLAN** [Latin *sine loco, anno, (vel) nomine*] without place, year, or name
**SLBM** submarine-launched ballistic missile
**sld** sailed, sealed, sold
**SLE** systemic lupus erythematosus
**Slo** Sligo
**SLR** single-lens reflex
**sm** small
**Sm** samarium
**SM** [New Latin *scientiae magister*] master of science; sergeant major, service mark, soldier's medal, stage manager, station master
**S–M** or **S/M** sadomasochism, sadomasochist
**SMA** sergeant major of the army
**SMaj** sergeant major
**SMSA** Standard Metropolitan Statistical Area
**SMSgt** senior master sergeant
**SMV** slow-moving vehicle
**Sn** [Late Latin *stannum*] tin
**SN** seaman
**SNCC** Student Nonviolent Coordinating Committee
**SNF** skilled nursing facility
**SNG** substitute natural gas, synthetic natural gas
**Snr** *British* senior
**so** south, southern
**SO** seller's option, strikeout
**soc** social, society, sociology
**sociol** sociologist, sociology
**sol** solicitor, soluble, solution
**soln** solution
**Som** Somersetshire
**SOP** standard operating procedure, standing operating procedure
**soph** sophomore
**SO**$_x$ sulfur oxide
**sp** special, species, specific, specimen, spelling, spirit

**Sp** Spain, Spanish
**SP** self-propelled, shore patrol, shore patrolman, shore police, [Latin *sine prole*] without issue; single pole, specialist
**Span** Spanish
**SPCA** Society for the Prevention of Cruelty to Animals
**SPCC** Society for the Prevention of Cruelty to Children
**spd** speed
**spec** special, specialist, specifically, specification
**specif** specific, specifically
**SPF** sun protection factor
**sp gr** specific gravity
**sp ht** specific heat
**SPOT** satellite positioning and tracking
**spp** species (*plural*)
**SPQR** [Latin *senatus populusque Romanus*] the senate and the people of Rome; small profits, quick returns
**sps** [Latin *sine prole superstite*] without surviving issue
**sq** squadron, square
**Sr** senior, senor, señor, sister, strontium
**SR** seaman recruit, sedimentation rate, shipping receipt
**Sra** senora, señora
**SRO** standing room only
**Srta** senorita, señorita
**ss** scilicet — used in legal documents, [Latin *semis*] one half
**SS** saints, same size, Social Security, steamship, sworn statement
**SSA** Social Security Administration
**SSE** south-southeast
**SSG** *or* **SSgt** staff sergeant
**SSI** supplemental security income
**SSM** staff sergeant major
**SSN** Social Security number
**ssp** subspecies
**SSPE** subacute sclerosing panencephalitis
**SSR** Soviet Socialist Republic
**SSS** Selective Service System
**SSW** south-southwest
**st** stanza, state, stitch, stone, street
**St** saint, stratus
**ST** short ton, single throw, standard time
**sta** station, stationary
**Staffs** Staffordshire
**START** strategic arms limitation talks
**stat** [Latin *statim*] immediately; statute
**STB** [New Latin *sacrae theologiae baccalaureus*] bachelor of sacred theology; [New Latin *scientiae theologicae baccalaureus*] bachelor of theology
**stbd** starboard
**std** standard
**STD** [New Latin *sacrae theologiae doctor*] doctor of sacred theology
**Ste** [French *sainte*] saint (female)
**ster** *or* **stg** sterling
**stge** storage
**stk** stock
**STL** [New Latin *sacrae theologiae licentiatus*] licentiate of sacred theology
**STM** [New Latin *sacrae theologiae magister*] master of sacred theology, scanning tunneling microscope; scanning tunneling microscopy
**STOL** short takeoff and landing
**stor** storage
**STP** standard temperature and pressure
**str** steamer, strophe
**stud** student
**STV** subscription television
**Su** Sunday
**sub** subaltern, subscription, subtract, suburb
**subj** subject, subjunctive
**suff** sufficient, suffix
**Suff** Suffolk
**Sun** Sunday

**sup** superior, supplement, supplementary, supply, supra
**supp** *or* **suppl** supplement, supplementary
**supr** supreme
**supt** superintendent
**supvr** supervisor
**sur** surface
**surg** surgeon, surgery, surgical
**surv** survey, surveying, surveyor
**Suss** Sussex
**sv** sailing vessel, saves, [Latin *sub verbo* or *sub voce*] under the word
**svc** *or* **svce** service
**svgs** savings
**sw** switch
**Sw** Sweden
**SW** seawater, shipper's weight, shortwave, southwest
**SWAK** sealed with a kiss
**SWAT** Special Weapons and Tactics
**Swed** Sweden, Swedish
**SWG** standard wire gauge
**Switz** Switzerland
**syl** *or* **syll** syllable
**sym** symbol, symmetrical
**syn** synonym, synonymous, synonymy
**syst** system
**t** metric ton, tablespoon, target, teaspoon, technical, temperature, [Latin *tempore*] in the time of; tense, tension, tertiary, time, ton, township, transitive, troy, true
**T** tera-, tesla, thymine, toddler, tritium, T-shirt
**Ta** tantalum
**TA** teaching assistant, transactional analysis
**TAC** Tactical Air Command
**TAG** the adjutant general
**tan** tangent
**TAT** thematic apperception test
**taxon** taxonomic, taxonomy
**Tay** Tayside
**tb** tablespoon, tablespoonful
**Tb** terbium
**TB** thoroughbred, trial balance, tubercle bacillus
**TBA** *often not capitalized* to be announced
**TBD** to be determined
**tbs** *or* **tbsp** tablespoon, tablespoonful
**TBS** talk between ships
**tc** tierce
**Tc** technetium
**TC** terra-cotta, till countermanded
**TCE** trichloroethylene
**tchr** teacher
**TD** tank destroyer, touchdown, Treasury Department
**TDD** telecommunications device for the deaf
**TDN** total digestible nutrients
**TDY** temporary duty
**Te** tellurium
**tec** technical, technician
**tech** technical, technically, technician, technological, technology
**technol** technological, technology
**TEFL** teaching English as a foreign language
**tel** telegram, telegraph, telephone
**teleg** telegraphy
**temp** temperance, template, temporal, temporary, [Latin *tempore*] in the time of
**Tenn** Tennessee
**ter** terrace, territory
**terr** territory
**TESL** teaching English as a second language
**TESOL** Teachers of English to Speakers of Other Languages
**Test** Testament
**Tex** Texas
**TF** task force, territorial force
**tfr** transfer
**TFR** total fertility rate
**TG** transformational grammar, type genus
**TGIF** thank God it's Friday

**tgt** target
**TGV** [French *train à grande vitesse*] high-speed train
**Th** thorium, Thursday
**TH** true heading
**Thai** Thailand
**ThD** [New Latin *theologiae doctor*] doctor of theology
**theat** theater, theatrical
**theol** theological, theology
**therm** thermometer
**Thess** Thessalonians
**ThM** [New Latin *theologiae magister*] master of theology
**Thurs** *or* **Thur** *or* **Thu** Thursday
**Ti** titanium
**TIA** transient ischemic attack
**tid** [Latin *ter in die*] three times a day
**Tim** Timothy
**TIN** taxpayer identification number
**tinc** tincture
**Tip** Tipperary
**tit** title
**Tit** Titus
**tk** tank, truck
**tkt** ticket
**Tl** thallium
**TL** total loss, truckload
**TLC** tender loving care, thin-layer chromatography
**TLO** total loss only
**tlr** tailor, trailer
**Tm** thulium
**TM** trademark, transcendental meditation
**TMJ** temporomandibular joint
**TMO** telegraph money order
**tn** ton, town, train
**TN** Tennessee, true north
**TNF** tumor necrosis factor
**tng** training
**tnpk** turnpike
**TO** table of organization, telegraph office, traditional orthography, turn over
**Tob** Tobit
**TOEFL** Test of English as a Foreign Language
**tol** tolerance
**tonn** tonnage
**topo** topographic, topographical
**topog** topography
**tot** total
**TOT** time on target
**tp** title page, township
**TP** triple play
**TPA** tissue plasminogen activator
**tpk** *or* **tpke** turnpike
**tps** townships, troops
**tr** translated, translation, translator, transpose, troop, trustee
**trag** tragedy, tragic
**trans** transaction, transitive, translated, translation, translator, transmission, transportation, transverse
**transf** transfer, transferred
**transl** translated, translation
**transp** transportation
**trav** travel, traveler, travels
**treas** treasurer, treasury
**trib** tributary
**trit** triturate
**trop** tropic, tropical
**ts** tensile strength
**TSgt** technical sergeant
**TSH** thyroid-stimulating hormone
**tsp** teaspoon, teaspoonful
**TSS** toxic shock syndrome
**TT** telegraphic transfer, teletypewriter, Trust Territories
**TTY** teletypewriter
**Tu** Tuesday
**TU** trade union, transmission unit
**TUC** Trades Union Congress
**Tues** *or* **Tue** Tuesday
**Turk** Turkey, Turkish
**TV** terminal velocity, transvestite
**TVA** Tennessee Valley Authority
**2WD** two-wheel drive
**twp** township
**TWX** teletypewriter exchange
**TX** Texas
**Tyr** Tyrone

**u** uncle, unit, unsymmetrical, upper
**U** [*Union of Orthodox Hebrew Congregations*] kosher certification — often enclosed in a circle; university, unsatisfactory, uracil, uranium
**UAE** United Arab Emirates
**UAR** United Arab Republic
**UAW** United Automobile Workers
**UC** undercharge, uppercase
**ugt** urgent
**UHF** ultrahigh frequency
**UI** unemployment insurance
**UK** United Kingdom
**ult** ultimate, ultimo
**UMWA** United Mine Workers of America
**UN** United Nations
**unan** unanimous
**Unc** uncirculated
**UNCF** United Negro College Fund
**UNESCO** United Nations Educational, Scientific, and Cultural Organization
**Unh** unnilhexium
**uni** uniform
**UNICEF** [*United Nations International Children's Emergency Fund*, its former name] United Nations Children's Fund
**univ** universal, university
**unp** unpaged
**Unp** unnilpentium
**Unq** unnilquadium
**UNRWA** United Nations Relief and Works Agency
**uns** unsymmetrical
**UP** underproof, Upper Peninsula (of Michigan)
**UPC** Universal Product Code
**UPI** United Press International
**urol** urological, urology
**US** [Latin *ubi supra*] where above mentioned; United States, [Latin *ut supra*] as above
**USA** United States Army, United States of America
**USAF** United States Air Force
**USCG** United States Coast Guard
**USDA** United States Department of Agriculture
**USES** United States Employment Service
**USG** United States government
**USGA** United States Golf Association
**USGS** United States Geological Survey
**USIA** United States Information Agency
**USMC** United States Marine Corps
**USN** United States Navy
**USNR** United States Naval Reserve
**USNS** United States Naval Ship
**USO** United Service Organizations
**USP** United States Pharmacopeia
**USPS** United States Postal Service
**USS** United States ship
**USSR** Union of Soviet Socialist Republics
**USTA** United States Tennis Association
**usu** usual, usually
**UT** Universal time, Utah
**UTC** Coordinated Universal Time
**ut dict** [Latin *ut dictum*] as directed
**util** utility
**UV** ultraviolet
**UW** underwriter
**ux** [Latin *uxor*] wife
**UXB** unexploded bomb
**v** vector, velocity, verb, verse, verso, versus, very, vice, victory, vide, voice, voltage, volume, vowel
**V** vanadium, volt
**Va** Virginia
**VA** Veterans Administration, vicar apostolic, vice admiral, Virginia, visual aid, volt-ampere
**vac** vacuum
**VADM** vice admiral
**vag** vagrancy
**val** value, valued

**var** variable, variant, variation, variety, various
**VAR** visual-aural range, volt-ampere reactive
**VAT** value-added tax
**vb** verb, verbal
**VC** veterinary corps, vice-chancellor, vice-consul, Victoria Cross, Vietcong
**VD** vapor density, various dates, venereal disease
**VDRL** venereal disease research laboratory
**VDT** video display terminal
**VDU** visual display unit
**veg** vegetable
**vel** vellum, velocity
**Ven** venerable
**ver** verse
**vert** vertebrate, vertical
**VF** very fair, very fine, video frequency, visual field, voice frequency
**VFD** volunteer fire department
**VFR** visual flight rules
**VFW** Veterans of Foreign Wars
**VG** very good, vicar-general
**VHF** very high frequency
**vi** verb intransitive, [Latin *vide infra*] see below
**VI** Virgin Islands, viscosity index, volume indicator
**vic** vicinity
**Vic** Victoria
**vil** village
**VIN** vehicle identification number
**vis** visibility, visible, visual
**VISTA** Volunteers in Service to America
**viz** videlicet
**VJ** veejay
**VLF** very low frequency
**VMD** [New Latin *veterinariae medicinae doctor*] doctor of veterinary medicine
**VNA** Visiting Nurse Association
**VOA** Voice of America
**voc** vocational, vocative
**vocab** vocabulary

**vol** volcano, volume, volunteer
**VOM** volt-ohmmeter
**VOR** very-high-frequency omnidirectional radio range
**vou** voucher
**VP** variable pitch, various places, verb phrase, vice president
**VRM** variable rate mortgage
**vs** verse, versus
**VS** veterinary surgeon, [Latin *vide supra*] see above
**vss** verses, versions
**V/STOL** vertical or short takeoff and landing
**vt** verb transitive
**Vt** Vermont
**VT** vacuum tube, variable time, Vermont, voice tube
**VTOL** vertical takeoff and landing
**VTR** videotape recorder
**VU** volume unit
**Vulg** Vulgate
**vv** verses, vice versa
**w** warden, water, week, weight, Welsh, west, western, white, wicket, wide, width, wife, with, withdrawal, work
**W** energy, [German *Wolfram*] tungsten; watt
**WA** Washington, Western Australia
**war** warrant
**Warks** Warwickshire
**Wash** Washington
**Wat** Waterford
**WATS** Wide-Area Telecommunications Service
**W Aust** Western Australia
**Wb** weber
**WB** water ballast, waybill, weather bureau, westbound, wheelbase
**WBC** white blood cells
**WBF** wood-burning fireplace
**WC** water closet, without charge
**WCTU** Women's Christian Temperance Union
**wd** wood, word, would
**WD** War Department
**We** *or* **Wed** Wednesday

**Westm** Westmeath, Westmorland
**Wex** Wexford
**wf** wrong font
**WFTU** World Federation of Trade Unions
**wh** which, white
**WH** watt-hour, withholding
**whf** wharf
**WHO** World Health Organization
**whr** watt-hour
**whs** *or* **whse** warehouse
**whsle** wholesale
**WI** West Indies, Wisconsin, wrought iron
**WIA** wounded in action
**Wick** Wicklow
**wid** widow, widower
**Wilts** Wiltshire
**Wis** *or* **Wisc** Wisconsin
**Wisd** Wisdom
**wk** week, work
**wkly** weekly
**WL** waterline, wavelength
**wm** wattmeter
**wmk** watermark
**WNW** west-northwest
**WO** warrant officer
**w/o** without
**WOC** without compensation
**WP** weather permitting, wettable powder, white phosphorus, without prejudice, word processing, word processor
**WPA** Works Progress Administration
**wpc** watts per candle, watts per channel
**WPI** Wholesale Price Index
**WPM** words per minute
**wpn** weapon
**WR** warehouse receipt, world record
**WRAC** Women's Royal Army Corps
**WRAF** Women's Royal Air Force
**WRNS** Women's Royal Naval Service
**wrnt** warrant
**WRVS** Women's Royal Voluntary Service

**WSW** west-southwest
**wt** weight
**WT** watertight, wireless telegraphy
**wtd** wanted
**WV** *or* **W Va** West Virginia
**WVS** Women's Voluntary Services
**WW** warehouse warrant, with warrants, world war
**w/w** wall-to-wall
**WWW** World Wide Web
**WY** *or* **Wyo** Wyoming
**x** cross, ex, experimental, extra
**X–C** cross-country
**XD** *or* **x div** ex dividend
**Xe** xenon
**XL** extra large, extra long
**Xn** Christian
**Xnty** Christianity
**XO** executive officer
**XS** extra small
**XW** ex warrants
**y** yard, year, yeoman
**Y** yttrium
**YA** young adult
**Yb** ytterbium
**YB** yearbook
**YBP** years before present
**yd** yard
**yeo** *or* **yeom** yeomanry
**YO** year old
**YOB** year of birth
**Yorks** Yorkshire
**yr** year, younger, your
**yrbk** yearbook
**YT** Yukon Territory
**Yug** Yugoslavia
**z** zero, zone
**Z** *or* **ZD** zenith distance
**Zach** Zacharias
**Zech** Zechariah
**Zeph** Zephaniah
**ZI** zone of interior
**Zn** [azimuth + *north*] azimuth; zinc
**zool** zoological, zoology
**ZPG** zero population growth
**Zr** zirconium

# Biographical, Biblical, and Mythological Names

This section constitutes a pronouncing dictionary of the names of important figures from contemporary life, history, biblical tradition, legend, and myth likely to be of interest to the reader. Names containing connectives like *d', de, di, van,* or *von* are alphabetized generally under the part of the name following the connective. If a person has a commonly encountered second name, a nickname, or an epithet, it is given in italics usually immediately after the life dates. When a second set of dates is given, it pertains only to the particular office, honor, or achievement which immediately precedes it.

**Aar·on** \'ar-ən, 'er-\ brother of Moses and first high priest of the Hebrews in the Bible

**Aaron** Henry Louis 1934–  *Hank* American baseball player

**Abel** \'ā-bəl\ son of Adam and Eve and brother of Cain in the Bible

**Ab·er·nathy** \'ab-ər-,nath-ē\ Ralph David 1926–1990 American clergyman and civil rights leader

**Abra·ham** \'ā-brə-,ham\ patriarch and founder of the Hebrew people in the Bible

**Achil·les** \ə-'kil-ēz\ hero of the Trojan War in Greek mythology

**Ad·am** \'ad-əm\ the first man in biblical tradition

**Ad·ams** \'ad-əmz\ Ansel Easton 1902–1984 American photographer

**Adams** John 1735–1826 2d president of the United States (1797–1801)

**Adams** John Quin·cy \'kwin-zē, -sē\ 1767–1848 6th president of the United States (1825–29); son of John Adams

**Adams** Samuel 1722–1803 American Revolutionary patriot

**Ad·dams** \'ad-əmz\ Jane 1860–1935 American social worker; Nobel prize winner (1931)

**Ad·di·son** \'ad-ə-sən\ Joseph 1672–1719 English essayist

**Ado·nis** \ə-'dän-əs, -'dō-nəs\ beautiful youth in Greek mythology who is loved by Aphrodite

**Ae·ne·as** \i-'nē-əs\ Trojan hero in classical mythology

**Ae·o·lus** \'ē-ə-ləs\ god of the winds in Greek mythology

**Aes·chy·lus** \'es-kə-ləs, 'ēs-\ 525–456 B.C. Greek dramatist

**Aes·cu·la·pi·us** \'es-kyə-'lā-pē-əs\ god of medicine in Roman mythology — compare ASCLEPIUS

**Ae·sop** \'ē-,säp, -səp\ Greek writer of fables; probably legendary

**Ag·a·mem·non** \,ag-ə-'mem-,nän, -nən\ leader of the Greeks during the Trojan War in Greek mythology

**Aggeus** — see HAGGAI

**Ag·nes** \'ag-nəs\ Saint *died* 304 A.D. Christian martyr

**Ag·rip·pi·na** \,ag-rə-'pī-nə, -'pē-\ *about* 14 B.C.–33 A.D. mother of Caligula

**Ahab** \'ā-,hab\ king of Israel in the 9th century B.C. and husband of Jezebel

**Ajax** \'ā-,jaks\ hero in Greek mythology who kills himself during the Trojan War because the armor of Achilles is awarded to Odysseus

**Alad·din** \ə-'lad-n\ youth in the *Arabian Nights' Entertainments* who comes into possession of a magic lamp and ring

**Al·a·ric** \'al-ə-rik\ *about* 370–410 A.D. king of the Visigoths

**Al·ber·tus Mag·nus** \al-'bərt-ə-'smag-nəs\ Saint *about* 1200–1280 *Albert* Count *von Boll·städt* \-'bȯl-,shtet\ German philosopher and theologian

**Al·bright** \'ȯl-,brīt\ Madeleine Korbel 1937– American scholar and government official; United States secretary of state (1997–2001)

**Al·ci·bi·a·des** \,al-sə-'bī-ə-,dēz\ *about* 450–404 B.C. Athenian general and politician

**Al·cott** \'ȯl-kət\ Louisa May 1832–1888 American author

**Al·ex·an·der** \,al-ig-'zan-der, ,el-\ name of 8 popes: especially **VI** (*Rodrigo Borgia*) 1431–1503 (pope 1492–1503)

**Alexander** name of 3 emperors of Russia: **I** 1777–1825 (reigned 1801–25); **II** 1818–1881 (reigned 1855–81); **III** 1845–1894 (reigned 1881–94)

**Alexander III of Macedon** 356–323 B.C. *the Great* king (336–323)

**Al·fred** \'al-frəd, -fərd\ 849–899 *the Great* king of Wessex (871–899)

**Ali** \ä-'lē\ Muhammad 1942– originally *Cassius Marcellus Clay* American boxer

**Al·len** \'al-ən\ Ethan 1738–1789 American Revolutionary soldier

**Am·brose** \'am-,brōz\ Saint 339–397 A.D. bishop of Milan

**Amerigo Vespucci** — see VESPUCCI

**Am·herst** \'am-ərst, -,ərst\ Baron Jeffrey 1717–1797 British general in America

**Amos** \'ā-məs\ Hebrew prophet of the 8th century B.C.

**Amund·sen** \'äm-ən-sən\ Roald 1872–1928 Norwegian explorer

**An·a·ni·as** \,an-ə-'nī-əs\ early Christian who in the Bible is struck dead for lying

**An·chi·ses** \an-'kī-sēz, ang-\ father of Aeneas in classical mythology

**An·der·sen** \'an-dər-sən\ Hans Christian 1805–1875 Danish writer of fairy tales

**An·der·son** \'an-dər-sən\ Marian 1897–1993 American contralto

**An·drea del Sar·to** \än-,drā-ə-,del-'särt-ō\ 1486–1530 Florentine painter

**An·dro·cles** \'an-drə-,klēz\ legendary Roman slave spared in the arena by a lion from whose foot he had once taken a thorn

**An·drom·a·che** \an-'dräm-ə-kē\ wife of Hector in Greek mythology

**An·drom·e·da** \an-'dräm-ə-də\ Ethiopian princess rescued from a monster by Perseus in Greek mythology

**An·gel·i·co** \än-'jā-lē-kō\ Fra *about* 1400–1455 Florentine painter

**An·ge·lou** \'an-jə-,lō\ Maya 1928– originally *Marguerite Johnson* American author

**An·nan** \ä-'nän\ Kofi 1938–  Ghanaian United Nations official; secretary-general (1997–  )

**Anne** \'an\ 1665–1714 queen of Great Britain (1702–14); daughter of James II

**An·tho·ny** \'an-thə-nē, *chiefly British* 'an-tə-nē\ Saint *about* 250–355 A.D. Egyptian monk

**Anthony** Mark — see ANTONIUS

**Anthony** Susan Brownell 1820–1906 American suffragist

**Anthony of Padua** Saint 1195–1231 Franciscan friar

**An·tig·o·ne** \an-'tig-ə-nē\ daughter of Oedipus and Jocasta in Greek mythology

**An·to·ni·nus** \,an-tə-'nī-nəs\ Marcus Au·re·li·us \ȯ-'rēl-yəs, -'rē-lē-əs\ 121–180 A.D. Roman emperor (161–180); philosopher

**An·to·ni·us** \an-'tō-nē-əs\ Marcus *about* 82–30 B.C. *Mark* or *Marc An·to·ny* or *An·tho·ny* \'an-thə-ne, *chiefly British* 'an-tə-nē\ Roman general

**Aph·ro·di·te** \,af-rə-'dīt-ē\ goddess of love and beauty in Greek mythology — compare VENUS

**Apol·lo** \ə-'päl-ō\ *or* **Phoe·bus** \'fē-bəs\ god of sunlight, prophecy, music, and poetry in classical mythology

**Apol·lyon** \ə-'päl-yən, -'päl-ē-ən\ the angel of the bottomless pit in the Book of Revelation

**Aqui·nas** \ə-'kwī-nəs\ Saint Thomas 1224 (or 1225)–1274 Italian theologian

**Arach·ne** \ə-'rak-nē\ girl in Greek mythology who is changed into a spider for challenging Athena to a contest in weaving

**Ar·chi·me·des** \,är-kə-'mēd-ēz\ *about* 287–212 B.C. Greek mathematician and inventor

**Ares** \'aər-ēz, 'eər-; 'ā-,rēz\ god of war in Greek mythology — compare MARS

**Ar·gus** \'är-gəs\ hundred-eyed monster in Greek mythology

**Ar·i·ad·ne** \,ar-ē-'ad-nē\ daughter of Minos who helps Theseus escape from a labyrinth in Greek mythology

**Ar·is·ti·des** *or* **Ar·is·tei·des** \,ar-ə-'stīd-ēz\ *about* 530–*about* 468 B.C. *the Just* Athenian statesman and general

**Ar·is·toph·a·nes** \,ar-ə-'stäf-ə-,nēz\ *about* 450–*about* 388 B.C. Greek dramatist

**Ar·is·tot·le** \'ar-ə-,stät-l\ 384–322 B.C. Greek philosopher

**Ari·us** \ə-'rī-əs; 'ar-ē-əs, 'er-\ *about* 250–336 A.D. Greek theologian

---

\ə\ abut  \ᵊ\ kitten  \ər\ further  \a\ ash  \ā\ ace
\ä\ mop, mar  \au̇\ out  \ch\ chin  \e\ bet  \ē\ easy
\g\ go  \i\ hit  \ī\ ice  \j\ job  \ŋ\ sing  \ō\ go
\ȯ\ law  \ȯi\ boy  \th\ thin  \th\ the  \ü\ loot  \u̇\ foot
\y\ yet  \zh\ vision  *see also* Guide to Pronunciation

**Arm·strong** \'ärm-ˌströng\ Louis 1901–1971 *Satchmo* \'sach-ˌmō\ American jazz musician

**Armstrong** Neil Alden 1930– American astronaut; first man on the moon (1969)

**Ar·nold** \'ärn-ld\ Benedict 1741–1801 American Revolutionary general and traitor

**Arnold** Matthew 1822–1888 English poet, essayist, and critic

**Ar·te·mis** \'ärt-ə-məs\ *or* **Phoe·be** \'fē-bē\ goddess of the moon, wild animals, and hunting in Greek mythology — compare DIANA

**Ar·thur** \'är-thər\ legendary king of the Britons whose story is based on traditions of a 6th century military leader — **Ar·thu·ri·an** \är-'thür-ē-ən, -'thyür-\ *adj*

**Arthur** Chester Alan 1829–1886 21st president of the United States (1881–85)

**As·cle·pi·us** \ə-'sklē-pē-əs\ god of medicine in Greek mythology — compare AESCULAPIUS

**As·tar·te** \ə-'stärt-ē\ Phoenician goddess of love and fertility

**As·tor** \'as-tər\ John Jacob 1763–1848 American (German-born) fur trader and capitalist

**At·a·lan·ta** \ˌat-l-'ant-ə\ beautiful fleet-footed heroine in Greek mythology who challenges her suitors to a race and is defeated when she stops to pick up three golden apples

**Ath·el·stan** \'ath-əl-ˌstan\ died 939 Anglo-Saxon ruler

**Athe·ne** \ə-'thē-nē\ *or* **Athe·na** \-nə\ *or* **Pal·las** \'pal-əs\ goddess of wisdom in Greek mythology — compare MINERVA

**At·las** \'at-ləs\ Titan in Greek mythology forced to bear the heavens on his shoulders

**Atreus** \'ā-ˌtrüs, -trē-əs\ king of Mycenae and father of Agamemnon and Menelaus in Greek mythology

**At·ti·la** \'at-l-ə, ə-'til-ə\ 406?–453 A.D. *the Scourge of God* king of the Huns

**At·tucks** \'at-əks\ Crispus 1723?–1770 American Revolutionary patriot

**Au·du·bon** \'öd-ə-bən, -ˌbän\ John James 1785–1851 American (Haitian-born) artist and ornithologist

**Au·gus·tine** \'ö-gə-ˌstēn; ö-'gəs-tən, ə-\ Saint 354–430 A.D. church father; bishop of Hippo (396–430)

**Augustine** Saint *died* 604 A.D. *Apostle of the English* 1st archbishop of Canterbury (601–604)

**Au·gus·tus** \ö-'gəs-təs, ə-\ *or* **Augustus Cae·sar** *or* **Oc·ta·vi·an** \äk-'tā-vē-ən\ 63 B.C.–14 A.D. originally *Gaius Octavius* 1st Roman emperor 27 B.C.–14 A.D.

**Au·ro·ra** \ə-'rōr-ə, ö-, -'rör-\ goddess of the dawn in Roman mythology — compare EOS

**Aus·ten** \'ös-tən, 'äs-\ Jane 1775–1817 English author

**Bac·chus** \'bak-əs\ — see DIONYSUS

**Bach** \'bäk, 'bäk\ Johann Sebastian 1685–1750 German composer and organist

**Ba·con** \'bā-kən\ Francis 1561–1626 1st Baron *Ver·u·lam* \'ver-ə-ləm, -yə-\ Viscount *Saint Al·bans* \sänt-'öl-bənz, sənt-\ English philosopher and author

**Bacon** Roger *about* 1220–1292 *Friar Bacon* English philosopher

**Ba·den–Pow·ell** \ˌbäd-n-'pō-əl\ Robert Stephenson Smyth 1857–1941 English founder of Boy Scout movement

**Bal·boa** \bal-'bō-ə\ Vasco Núñez, de 1475–1519 Spanish explorer and discoverer of the Pacific Ocean for Spain (1513)

**Bald·win** \'böld-wən\ James 1924–1987 American author

**Baltimore** Lord — see CALVERT

**Bal·zac** \'böl-ˌzak, 'bal-, *French* bál-zák\ Honoré de 1799–1850 French author

**Ba·rab·bas** \bə-'rab-əs\ prisoner in the Bible released in preference to Christ at the demand of the multitude

**Barbarossa** — see FREDERICK I

**Bar·num** \'bär-nəm\ Phineas Taylor 1810–1891 American showman

**Bar·rie** \'bar-ē\ Sir James Matthew 1860–1937 Scottish author

**Bar·ry·more** \'bar-i-ˌmōr, -ˌmör\ family of American actors: Maurice 1847–1905; his wife Georgiana Emma 1854–1893; their children Lionel 1878–1954, Ethel 1879–1959, and John Blythe 1882–1942

**Bar·thol·di** \bär-'täl-dē, -'töl-, -'thäl-, -'thöl-\ Frédéric Auguste 1834–1904 French sculptor of the Statue of Liberty

**Bar·tók** \'bar-ˌtäk, -ˌtök\ Bé·la \'bā-lə\ 1881–1945 Hungarian composer

**Bar·ton** \'bärt-n\ Clara 1821–1912 founder of American Red Cross Society

**Ba·sie** \'bā-sē\ William 1904–1984 *Count* American bandleader and composer

**Ba·sil** \'baz-əl, 'bās-, 'bas-, 'bāz-\ Saint *about* 329–379 A.D. *the Great* church father; bishop of Caesarea

**Bau·de·laire** \ˌbōd-'laər, -'leər\ Charles-Pierre 1821–1867 French poet

**Beau·re·gard** \'bōr-ə-ˌgärd, 'bör-\ Pierre Gustave Toutant 1818–1893 American Confederate general

**Beck·et, à** \ə-'bek-ət, ä-\ Saint Thomas *about* 1118–1170 archbishop of Canterbury (1162–70)

**Bede** \'bēd\ Saint *about* 672–735 A.D. *the Venerable Bede* Anglo-Saxon historian and theologian

**Beel·ze·bub** \bē-'el-zi-ˌbəb, 'bēl-zi-, 'bel-\ prince of the demons identified with Satan in the New Testament

**Bee·tho·ven** \'bā-ˌtō-vən\ Ludwig van 1770–1827 German composer

**Bell** \'bel\ Alexander Graham 1847–1922 American (Scottish-born) inventor of the telephone

**Bel·ler·o·phon** \bə-'ler-ə-fən, -ˌfän\ hero in Greek mythology who slays the monster Chimera with the help of his horse Pegasus

**Bel·li·ni** \bə-'lē-nē\ Vincenzo 1801–1835 Italian composer

**Bel·low** \'bel-ō\ Saul 1915– American (Canadian-born) author; Nobel prize winner (1976)

**Ben·e·dict** \'ben-ə-dikt\ name of 15 popes: especially **XIV** (*Prospero Lambertini*) 1675–1758 (pope 1740–58); **XV** (*Giacomo della Chiesa*) 1854–1922 (pope 1914–22)

**Benedict of Nur·sia** \'nər-shə, -shē-ə\ Saint *about* 480–*about* 547 A.D. Italian founder of Benedictine order

**Be·nét** \bə-'nā\ Stephen Vincent 1898–1943 American author

**Ben·ja·min** \'benj-mən, -ə-mən\ Jacob's youngest son and ancestor of one of the 12 tribes of Israel in the Bible

**Ben·tham** \'ben-thəm\ Jeremy 1748–1832 English jurist and philosopher

**Ben·ton** \'bent-n\ Thomas Hart 1889–1975 American painter

**Be·o·wulf** \'bā-ə-ˌwùlf\ legendary Geat warrior and hero of the Old English poem *Beowulf*

**Be·ring** \'biər-ing, 'beər-\ Vitus 1681–1741 Danish navigator and explorer of the Bering Strait and Bering Sea for Russia

**Ber·lin** \bər-'lin, ˌbər-\ Irving 1888–1989 American (Russian-born) composer and songwriter

**Ber·li·oz** \'ber-lē-ˌōz\ (Louis-) Hector 1803–1869 French composer

**Ber·ni·ni** \bər-'nē-nē\ Gian *or* Giovanni Lorenzo 1598–1680 Italian sculptor, architect, and painter

**Bern·stein** \'bərn-ˌstīn *also* -ˌstēn\ Leonard 1918–1990 American conductor and composer

**Bes·se·mer** \'bes-ə-mər\ Sir Henry 1813–1898 English engineer

**Be·thune** \bə-'thün, -'thyün\ Mary 1875–1955 née *McLeod* American educator

**Beyle** Marie-Henri — see STENDHAL

**Bierce** \'biərs\ Ambrose Gwinnett 1842–?1914 American author

**Bi·ko** \'bē-ˌkō\ (Bantu) Stephen 1946–1977 South African black nationalist

**Bis·marck** \'biz-ˌmärk\ Prince Otto Eduard Leopold von 1815–1898 1st chancellor of German Empire (1871–90)

**Bi·zet** \bē-'zā\ Alexandre-César-Léopold 1838–1875 *Georges* French composer

**Black Hawk** \'blak-ˌhök\ 1767–1838 American Indian chief

**Black·stone** \'blak-ˌstōn, *chiefly British* -stən\ Sir William 1723–1780 English jurist

**Black·well** \'blak-ˌwel, -wəl\ Elizabeth 1821–1910 American (English-born) physician

**Blair** \'blaər, 'bleər\ Anthony Charles Lynton 1953– *Tony* British prime minister (1997– )

**Blake** \'blāk\ William 1757–1827 English poet and artist

**Bloom·er** \'blü-mər\ Amelia Jenks 1818–1894 American social reformer

**Boc·cac·cio** \bō-'käch-ē-ˌō, -'käch-ō\ Giovanni 1313–1375 Italian author

**Bohr** \'bör, 'bōr\ Niels 1885–1962 Danish physicist; Nobel prize winner (1922)

**Bo·leyn** \bù-'lin, 'bùl-ən\ Anne 1507?–1536 2d wife of Henry VIII of England; mother of Elizabeth I

**Bo·lí·var** Si·món \sē-ˌmōn-bə-'lē-ˌvär, ˌsī-mən-'bäl-ə-vər\ 1783–1830 South American liberator

**Bo·na·parte** \'bō-nə-ˌpärt\ *or Italian* **Buo·na·par·te** \ˌbwön-ə-'pärt-ē\ Corsican family: Jérôme

1784–1860 king of Westphalia; Joseph 1768–1844 king of Naples and Spain; Louis 1778–1846 king of Holland; Lucien 1775–1840 prince of Canino; all brothers of Napoléon I

**Bon·i·face** \'bän-ə-fəs, -ˌfās\ Saint *about* 675–754 A.D. *Wynfrid or Wynfrith* English missionary in Germany

**Boniface** name of 9 popes: especially **VIII** (*Benedetto Caetani*) *about* 1235 (or 1240)–1303 (pope 1294–1303)

**Boone** \'bün\ Daniel 1734–1820 American pioneer

**Booth** \'büth\ John Wilkes 1838–1865 American actor and assassin of Abraham Lincoln

**Booth** \'büth, *chiefly British* 'büth\ William 1829–1912 English founder of Salvation Army

**Bo·re·as** \'bōr-ē-əs, 'bòr-\ god of the north wind in Greek mythology

**Bor·gia** \'bòr-jä, -jə, -zhə\ Cesare 1475 (or 1476)–1507 Italian cardinal and military leader; son of Rodrigo Borgia

**Borgia** Lucrezia 1480–1519 duchess of Ferrara; daughter of Rodrigo Borgia

**Borgia** Rodrigo — see Pope ALEXANDER VI

**Bo·ro·din** \ˌbòr-ə-'dēn, ˌbär-\ Aleksandr Porfirevich 1833–1887 Russian composer and chemist

**Bosch** \'bäsh, 'bösh, *Dutch* 'bäs, 'bòs\ Hieronymus *about* 1450–*about* 1516 Dutch painter

**Bos·co** \'bäs-kō, 'bòs-\ Saint Giovanni Melchior 1815–1888 Italian priest and founder of the Salesians

**Bos·well** \'bäz-ˌwel, -wəl\ James 1740–1795 Scottish biographer of Samuel Johnson

**Bot·ti·cel·li** \ˌbät-ə-'chel-ē\ Sandro 1445–1510 Italian painter

**Boyle** \'bòil\ Robert 1627–1691 British physicist and chemist

**Brad·bury** \'brad-ˌber-ē, -bə-rē, -brē\ Ray Douglas 1920– American author

**Brad·dock** \'brad-ək\ Edward 1695–1755 British general in America

**Brad·ford** \'brad-fərd\ William 1590–1657 Pilgrim father; 2d governor of Plymouth colony

**Brad·street** \'brad-ˌstrēt\ Anne *about* 1612–1672 American poet

**Brah·ma** \'bräm-ə\ creator god of the Hindu sacred triad — compare SIVA, VISHNU

**Brahms** \'brämz\ Johannes 1833–1897 German composer

**Braille** \'brāl, 'brī\ Louis 1809–1852 French blind teacher of the blind

**Bran·deis** \'bran-ˌdīs, -ˌdīz\ Louis Dembitz 1856–1941 American jurist

**Brant** \'brant\ Joseph 1742–1807 *Thayendanegea* Mohawk Indian chief

**Braun** \'braùn\ Wernher von 1912–1977 American (German-born) engineer

**Brezh·nev** \'brezh-ˌnef\ Leonid Ilyich 1906–1982 Russian politician; 1st secretary of Communist party (1964–82); president of the U.S.S.R. (1960–64; 1977–82)

**Bri·an Bo·ru** \ˌbrī-ən-bə-'rü\ 941–1014 king of Ireland (1002–14)

**Brig·id** \'brij-əd, 'brē-əd\ Saint *died about* 524–528 A.D. a patron saint of Ireland

**Brit·ten** \'brit-n\ (Edward) Benjamin 1913–1976 English composer

**Bron·të** \'bränt-ē, 'brän-ˌtā\ family of English authors: Charlotte 1816–1855 and her sisters Emily 1818–1848 and Anne 1820–1849

**Brooks** \'brùks\ Gwendolyn Elizabeth 1917–2000 American poet

**Brown** \'braùn\ John 1800–1859 *Old Brown of Osawat-o-mie* \ˌö-sə-'wät-ə-mē\ American abolitionist

**Brow·ning** \'braù-ning\ Elizabeth Barrett 1806–1861 English poet

**Browning** Robert 1812–1889 English poet; husband of Elizabeth

**Broz** Josip — see TITO

**Bruce, the** — see ROBERT I

**Bruck·ner** \'brùk-nər\ Anton 1824–1896 Austrian composer

**Brue·ghel** *or* **Breu·ghel** \'brü-gəl, 'bröi-\ Pieter *the Elder about* 1525 (or 1530)–1569 Flemish painter

**Brun·hild** \'brün-ˌhilt\ legendary Germanic queen won by Siegfried for Gunther

**Bru·tus** \'brüt-əs\ Marcus Junius 85–42 B.C. Roman politician and one of Julius Caesar's assassins

**Bry·an** \'brī-ən\ William Jennings 1860–1925 American lawyer and politician

**Bry·ant** \'brī-ənt\ William Cullen 1794–1878 American poet

**Bu·chan·an** \byü-'kan-ən, bə-\ James 1791–1868 15th president of the United States (1857–61)

**Buck** \'bək\ Pearl 1892–1973 American author; Nobel prize winner (1938)

**Buddha** — see GAUTAMA BUDDHA

**Buffalo Bill** — see William Frederick CODY

**Bunche** \'bənch\ Ralph Johnson 1904–1971 American diplomat

**Bun·yan** \'bən-yən\ John 1628–1688 English preacher and author

**Bur·bank** \'bər-,bangk\ Luther 1849–1926 American horticulturist

**Bur·ger** \'bər-gər\ Warren Earl 1907–1995 American jurist; chief justice United States Supreme Court (1969–86)

**Bur·goyne** \'bər-,góin, ,bər-\ John 1722–1792 British general in America

**Burke** \'bərk\ Edmund 1729–1797 British statesman and author

**Burns** \'bərnz\ Robert 1759–1796 Scottish poet

**Burn·side** \'bərn-,sīd\ Ambrose Everett 1824–1881 American general

**Burr** \'bər\ Aaron 1756–1836 vice president of the United States (1801–05)

**Bur·roughs** \'bər-,ōz, 'bə-,rōz\ Edgar Rice 1875–1950 American author

**Bush** \'bush\ George Herbert Walker 1924–  41st president of the United States (1989–93)

**Bush** George Walker 1946–  43rd president of the United States (2001–  ); son of George H. W. Bush

**But·ler** \'bət-lər\ Samuel 1835–1902 English author

**By·ron** \'bī-rən\ 6th Baron 1788–1824 *George Gordon Byron* English poet

**Cab·ot** \'kab-ət\ John *about* 1450–*about* 1499 Italian navigator and explorer of coast of North America for England

**Ca·bri·ni** \kə-'brē-nē\ Saint Frances Xavier 1850–1917 *Mother Cabrini* 1st American (Italian-born) to be canonized (1946)

**Cad·mus** \'kad-məs\ founder of Thebes in Greek mythology

**Caed·mon** \'kad-mən\ *flourished* 658–680 A.D. English poet

**Cae·sar** \'sē-zər\ Gaius Julius 100–44 B.C. Roman general, statesman, and writer

**Cain** \'kān\ son of Adam and Eve and brother of Abel in the Bible

**Cal·houn** \kal-'hün\ John Caldwell 1782–1850 vice president of the United States (1825–32)

**Ca·lig·u·la** \kə-'lig-yə-lə\ 12–41 A.D. *Gaius Caesar* Roman emperor (37–41)

**Cal·li·o·pe** \kə-'lī-ə-pē\ Muse of heroic poetry in Greek mythology

**Cal·vert** \'kal-vərt\ George 1580?–1632 1st Baron *Baltimore* English proprietary in America

**Cal·vin** \'kal-vən\ John 1509–1564 French theologian and reformer

**Ca·lyp·so** \kə-'lip-sō\ sea nymph in Homer's *Odyssey* who keeps Odysseus for seven years on an island

**Ca·mus** \kȧ-'mǖ\ Albert 1913–1960 French author

**Ca·nute** \kə-'nüt, -'nyüt\ *died* 1035 king of England (1016–35); of Denmark (1018–35); of Norway (1028–35)

**Ča·pek** \'chäp-,ek\ Karel 1890–1938 Czech author

**Capet** Hugh — see HUGH CAPET

**Car·lyle** \kär-'līl, 'kär-\ Thomas 1795–1881 Scottish essayist and historian

**Car·ne·gie** \'kär-nə-gē, kär-'neg-ē\ Andrew 1835–1919 American (Scottish-born) industrialist and philanthropist

**Carroll** Lewis — see DODGSON

**Car·son** \'kärs-n\ Christopher 1809–1868 *Kit* American scout

**Carson** Rachel Louise 1907–1964 American biologist and environmentalist

**Car·ter** \'kärt-ər\ James Earl, Jr. 1924–  *Jimmy* 39th president of the United States (1977–81)

**Car·tier** \kär-'tyā, 'kärt-ē-,ā\ Jacques 1491–1557 French navigator and explorer of Saint Lawrence River

**Ca·ru·so** \kə-'rü-sō, -zō\ En·ri·co \en-'rē-kō\ 1873–1921 Italian tenor

**Car·ver** \'kär-vər\ George Washington 1864–1943 American botanist

**Ca·sals** \kə-'sälz, -'zälz\ Pablo 1876–1973 Spanish-born cellist, conductor, and composer

**Ca·sa·no·va** \,kaz-ə-'nō-və, ,kas-\ Giovanni Giacomo 1725–1798 Italian adventurer

**Cas·san·dra** \kə-'san-drə\ daughter of Priam in Greek mythology who is endowed with the gift of prophecy but fated never to be believed

**Cas·satt** \kə-'sat\ Mary 1845–1926 American painter

**Cas·tor** \'kas-tər\ the mortal twin of Pollux in mythology

**Cas·tro** \'kas-trō, 'käs-\ **(Ruz)** \'rüs\ Fi·del \fē-'del\ 1926–  Cuban leader (1959–  )

**Cath·er** \'kath-ər\ Willa Sibert 1873–1947 American author

**Cath·er·ine** \'kath-rən, -ə-rən\ name of 1st, 5th, and 6th wives of Henry VIII of England: Catherine of Aragon 1485–1536; Catherine Howard 1520?–1542; Catherine Parr 1512–1548

**Catherine I** 1684–1727 wife of Peter the Great; empress of Russia (1725–27)

**Catherine II** 1729–1796 *the Great* empress of Russia (1762–96)

**Cath·er·ine de Mé·di·cis** \'kath-ə-rən-də-'mā-də-,sēs, -'med-ə-,chē\ 1519–1589 Italian *Ca·te·ri·na de' Me·di·ci* \,kä-te-'rē-nä-dā-'med-ē-,chē\ queen of Henry II of France

**Cat·i·line** \'kat-l-,īn\ *about* 108–62 B.C. Roman politician and conspirator

**Ca·to** \'kāt-ō\ Marcus Porcius 234–149 B.C. *the Elder; the Censor* Roman statesman

**Cato** Marcus Porcius 95–46 B.C. *the Younger* Roman statesman; great-grandson of the preceding

**Ca·tul·lus** \kə-'təl-əs\ Gaius Valerius *about* 84–*about* 54 B.C. Roman poet

**Cax·ton** \'kak-stən\ William *about* 1422–1491 first English printer

**Ce·ci·lia** \sə-'sēl-yə, -'sil-\ Saint 2d or 3d century A.D. Christian martyr; patron saint of music

**Cel·li·ni** \chə-'lē-nē\ Benvenuto 1500–1571 Italian goldsmith and sculptor

**Cer·ber·us** \'sər-bə-rəs, -brəs\ 3-headed dog in classical mythology who guards the entrance to Hades

**Ce·res** \'siər-,ēz\ the goddess of agriculture in Roman mythology — compare DEMETER

**Cer·van·tes (Saa·ve·dra)** \sər-'van-,tēz-,sä-ə-'vä-drə\ Miguel de 1547–1616 Spanish author

**Cé·zanne** \sā-'zan\ Paul 1839–1906 French painter

**Cha·gall** \shə-'gäl, -'gal\ Marc 1887–1985 Russian painter in France

**Cham·ber·lain** \'chäm-bər-lən\ (Arthur) Neville 1869–1940 British prime minister (1937–40)

**Cham·plain** \sham-'plān, shä"-'pla"\ Samuel de *about* 1567–1635 French navigator, explorer, and founder of Quebec

**Chap·lin** \'chap-lən\ Sir Charles Spencer 1889–1977 British film actor and producer

**Char·le·magne** \'shär-lə-,mān\ 742–814 A.D. *Charles the Great* or *Charles I* Frankish king (768–814); emperor of the West (800–814)

**Charles** \'chärlz\ name of 10 kings of France: especially **I** 823–877 A.D. (reigned 840–877) *the Bald;* Holy Roman emperor as *Charles II* (875–877); **IV** 1294–1328 (reigned 1322–28) *the Fair;* **V** 1337–1380 (reigned 1364–80) *the Wise;* **VI** 1368–1422 (reigned 1380–1422) *the Mad* or *the Beloved;* **VII** 1403–1461 (reigned 1422–61) *the Victorious;* **IX** 1550–1574 (reigned 1560–74); **X** 1757–1836 (reigned 1824–30)

**Charles** name of 2 kings of Great Britain: **I** 1600–1649 (reigned 1625–49) *Charles Stuart;* **II** 1630–1685 (reigned 1660–85) son of Charles I

**Charles** 1948–  son of Elizabeth II; prince of Wales

**Charles I** 1887–1922 *Charles Francis Joseph* emperor of Austria and (as *Charles IV*) king of Hungary (1916–18)

**Charles V** 1500–1558 Holy Roman emperor (1519–56); king of Spain as *Charles I* (1516–56)

**Charles XII** 1682–1718 king of Sweden (1697–1718)

**Charles Edward** 1720–1788 *the Young Pretender; (Bonnie) Prince Charlie* British prince

**Charles Mar·tel** \mär-'tel\ *about* 688–741 A.D. grandfather of Charlemagne; Frankish ruler (719–741)

**Char·on** \'kar-ən, 'ker-\ boatman in Greek mythology who ferries the souls of the dead across the river Styx to Hades

**Cha·teau·bri·and** \sha-,tō-brē-'ä"\ Vi·comte \vē-kō"t\ François-Auguste-René de 1768–1848 French author

**Chau·cer** \'chò-sər\ Geoffrey *about* 1342–1400 English poet

**Che·khov** \'chek-,óf, -,óv\ Anton Pavlovich 1860–1904 Russian author

**Che·ney** \'chē-nē, *commonly* 'chā-\ Richard Bruce 1941–  vice president of the United States (2001–  )

**Cheops** — see KHUFU

**Ches·ter·field** \'ches-tər-,fēld\ 4th Earl of 1694–1773 English statesman and author

**Ches·ter·ton** \'ches-tərt-n\ Gilbert Keith 1874–1936 English author

**Chiang Kai–shek** \jē-'äng-'kī-'shek, 'chang-\ 1887–1975 Chinese general and statesman; president of China (1948–49; Taiwan, 1950–75)

**Chi·ron** \'kīr-ən, 'kī-,rän\ wise centaur and tutor to many heroes in Greek mythology

**Cho·pin** \'shō-,pan, -,pa"\ Frédéric François 1810–1849 Polish pianist and composer

**Chou En–lai** \'jō-'en-'lī\ 1898–1976 Chinese Communist politician; premier (1949–76)

**Chré·tien** \krā-'tye"\ (Joseph Jacques) Jean 1934–  prime minister of Canada (1993–  )

**Christ** Jesus — see JESUS

**Chris·tie** \kris-tē\ Dame Agatha 1890–1976 English author

**Chry·sos·tom** \'kris-əs-təm, kris-'äs-təm\ Saint John *about* 347–407 A.D. church father; patriarch of Constantinople

**Chur·chill** \'chər-,chil, 'chərch-,hil\ Randolph Henry Spencer 1849–1895 *Lord Randolph Churchill* British statesman

**Churchill** Sir Winston Leonard Spencer 1874–1965 British prime minister (1940–45; 1951–55); son of Lord Randolph Churchill

**Cic·ero** \'sis-ə-,rō\ Marcus Tullius 106–43 B.C. Roman statesman, orator, and author

**Cid, El** \el-'sid\ *about* 1043–1099 *Rodrigo Díaz de Vi·var* \bē-'vär\ Spanish soldier and hero

**Cir·ce** \'sər-sē\ enchantress in Greek mythology who turns her victims into swine

**Clark** \'klärk\ George Rogers 1752–1818 American soldier and frontiersman

**Clark** William 1770–1838 American explorer (with Meriwether Lewis)

**Clay** \'klā\ Henry 1777–1852 American statesman and orator

**Cle·men·ceau** \,klem-ən-'sō, klā-mä"-'sō\ Georges 1841–1929 French statesman

**Clem·ens** \'klem-ənz\ Samuel Langhorne 1835–1910 pseudonym *Mark Twain* \'twän\ American author

**Clem·ent** \'klem-ənt\ name of 14 popes

**Cle·o·pa·tra** \,klē-ə-'pa-trə, -'pä-, -'pä-\ 69–30 B.C. queen of Egypt (51–30)

**Cleve·land** \'klēv-lənd\ (Stephen) Grover 1837–1908 22d and 24th president of the United States (1885–89; 1893–97)

**Clin·ton** \'klint-n\ William Jefferson 1946–  42d president of the United States (1993–2001)

**Clio** \'klī-ō, 'klē-\ Muse of history in Greek mythology

**Clo·vis I** \'klō-vəs\ *about* 466–511 A.D. Frankish king (481–511)

**Cly·tem·nes·tra** \,klīt-əm-'nes-trə\ wife of Agamemnon in Greek mythology

**Co·chise** \kō-'chēs\ 1812?–1874 Apache Indian chief

**Co·dy** \'kōd-ē\ William Frederick 1846–1917 *Buffalo Bill* American scout and showman

**Co·han** \'kō-,han\ George Michael 1878–1942 American actor, playwright, and songwriter

**Cole·ridge** \'kōl-rij, 'kō-lə-rij\ Samuel Taylor 1772–1834 English poet and critic

**Co·lette** \kȯ-'let\ Sidonie-Gabrielle 1873–1954 French author

**Co·lum·bus** \kə-'ləm-bəs\ Christopher 1451–1506 Italian navigator and discoverer of America for Spain (1492)

**Con·fu·cius** \kən-'fyü-shəs\ *about* 551–479 B.C. Chinese philosopher

**Con·rad** \'kän-,rad\ Joseph 1857–1924 British (Ukrainian-born of Polish parents) author

**Con·stan·tine I** \'kän-stən-,tēn, -,tīn\ *died* 337 A.D. *the Great* Roman emperor (306–337)

**Cook** \'kůk\ Captain James 1728–1779 English navigator

**Coo·lidge** \'kü-lij\ (John) Calvin 1872–1933 30th president of the United States (1923–29)

---

\ə\ abut  \ᵊ\ kitten  \ər\ further  \a\ ash  \ā\ ace
\ä\ mop, mar  \au̇\ out  \ch\ chin  \e\ bet  \ē\ easy
\g\ go  \i\ hit  \ī\ ice  \j\ job  \ŋ\ sing  \ō\ go
\ò\ law  \òi\ boy  \th\ thin  \t͟h\ the  \ü\ loot  \ů\ foot
\y\ yet  \zh\ vision  *see also* Guide to Pronunciation

**Coo·per** \'kü-pər, 'kup-ər\ James Fen·i·more \'fen-ə-‚mȯr, -‚mȯr\ 1789–1851 American author

**Co·per·ni·cus** \kō-'pər-ni-kəs\ Nicolaus 1473–1543 Polish astronomer

**Cop·land** \'kō-plənd\ Aaron 1900–1990 American composer

**Corn·plan·ter** \'kȯrn-‚plant-ər\ *about* 1732–1836 *John O'Bail* or *O'Beel* Seneca Indian leader of partly European ancestry

**Corn·wal·lis** \kȯrn-'wäl-əs\ 1st Marquis 1738–1805 *Charles Cornwallis* British general and statesman

**Co·ro·na·do** \‚kȯr-ə-'näd-ō, ‚kär-\ Francisco Vásquez de *about* 1510–1554 Spanish explorer and conquistador

**Cor·tés** or **Cor·tez** \kȯr-'tez, 'kȯr-‚\ Hernán or Hernando 1485–1547 Spanish conqueror of Mexico

**Cow·per** \'kü-pər, 'kup-ər, 'kau-pər\ William 1731–1800 English poet

**Crane** \'krān\ Stephen 1871–1900 American author

**Crazy Horse** \'krā-zē-‚hȯrs\ 1842–1877 Sioux Indian chief

**Cres·si·da** \'kres-əd-ə\ Trojan woman who in medieval legend is unfaithful to her lover Troilus

**Crock·ett** \'kräk-ət\ David 1786–1836 *Davy* American frontiersman and politician

**Croe·sus** \'krē-səs\ *died* 546 B.C. king of Lydia (560–546)

**Crom·well** \'kräm-‚wel, 'krȯm-, -wəl\ Oliver 1599–1658 English general and statesman; lord protector of England (1653–58)

**Cro·nus** \'krō-nəs\ Titan dethroned by his son Zeus in Greek mythology

**Cu·pid** \'kyü-pəd\ god of love in Roman mythology — compare EROS

**Cu·rie** \kyu-'rē, 'kyur-ē\ Marie 1867–1934 French (Polish-born) chemist; Nobel prize winner (1903, 1911)

**Curie** Pierre 1859–1906 French chemist; husband of Marie; Nobel prize winner (1903)

**Cus·ter** \'kəs-tər\ George Armstrong 1839–1876 American general

**Cyb·e·le** \'sib-ə-lē\ a nature goddess of ancient Asia Minor

**Cy·ra·no de Ber·ge·rac** \‚sir-ə-‚nō-də-'ber-zhə-‚rak\ Savinien de 1619–1655 French poet and soldier

**Cyr·il** \'sir-əl\ Saint *about* 827–869 A.D. Apostle to the Slavs; brother of Methodius

**Cy·rus II** \'sī-rəs\ *about* 585–*about* 529 B.C. *the Great* or *the Elder* king of Persia (550–529)

**Cyrus** 424?–401 B.C. *the Younger* Persian prince and satrap

**Dae·da·lus** \'ded-l-əs, 'dēd-\ builder in Greek mythology of the Cretan labyrinth and inventor of wings by which he and his son Icarus escape from it

**Dahl** \'däl\ Roald 1916–1990 British author

**Da·lí** \'dä-lē, dä-'lē\ Salvador 1904–1989 Spanish painter

**Dal·ton** \'dȯlt-n\ John 1766–1844 English chemist and physicist

**Dam·o·cles** \'dam-ə-‚klēz\ courtier of ancient Syracuse who according to legend was seated at a banquet beneath a sword hung by a single hair

**Da·mon** \'dā-mən\ a legendary Sicilian who pledges his life for that of his condemned friend Pythias

**Da·na** \'dā-nə\ Richard Henry 1815–1882 American author

**Dan·aë** \'dan-ə-‚ē\ imprisoned princess in Greek mythology who is visited by Zeus as a shower of gold

**Dan·iel** \'dan-yəl\ a prophet in the Bible who is held captive in Babylon and divinely delivered from a den of lions

**Dan·te** \'dän-tā, 'dan-, -tē\ 1265–1321 Italian poet

**Daph·ne** \'daf-nē\ nymph in Greek mythology who is transformed into a laurel tree to escape the pursuing Apollo

**Dare** \'daər, 'deər\ Virginia 1587–? first child born in America of English parents

**Da·ri·us I** \də-'rī-əs\ 550–486 B.C. *the Great* king of Persia (522–486)

**Dar·row** \'dar-ō\ Clarence Seward 1857–1938 American lawyer

**Dar·win** \'där-wən\ Charles Robert 1809–1882 English naturalist

**Da·vid** \'dā-vəd\ a youth in the Bible who slays Goliath and succeeds Saul as king of Israel

**David** Saint *about* 520–600 patron saint of Wales

**Da·vid** \dä-'vēd\ Jacques-Louis 1748–1825 French painter

**Da·vis** \'dā-vəs\ Jefferson 1808–1889 president of the Confederate States of America (1861–65)

**Davis** Miles 1926–1991 American jazz composer and musician

**Da·vy** \'dā-vē\ Sir Humphry 1778–1829 English chemist

**Debs** \'debz\ Eugene Victor 1855–1926 American socialist

**De·bus·sy** \‚deb-yü-'sē, ‚däb-; də-'byü-sē\ (Achille-) Claude 1862–1918 French composer

**De·ca·tur** \di-'kāt-ər\ Stephen 1779–1820 American naval officer

**De·foe** \di-'fō\ Daniel 1660–1731 English author

**De·gas** \də-'gä\ (Hilaire-Germain-) Edgar 1834–1917 French artist

**de Gaulle** \di-'gōl, -'gȯl\ Charles-André-Marie-Joseph 1890–1970 French general; president of Fifth Republic (1958–69)

**de Klerk** \də-'klərk\ Frederik Willem 1936– president of Republic of South Africa (1989–94); vice president (1994– )

**De·la·croix** \‚del-ə-'krwä, -'kwä\ (Ferdinand-Victor-) Eugène 1798–1863 French painter

**de la Mare** \‚del-ə-'maər, -'meər\ Walter John 1873–1956 English author

**De·li·lah** \di-'lī-lə\ mistress and betrayer of Samson in the Bible

**De·me·ter** \di-'mēt-ər\ goddess of agriculture in Greek mythology — compare CERES

**de Mille** \də-'mil\ Agnes George 1905–1993 American choreographer

**de·Mille** Cec·il \'ses-əl\ Blount \'blənt\ 1881–1959 American film director and producer

**De·mos·the·nes** \di-'mäs-thə-‚nēz\ 384–322 B.C. Athenian orator and statesman

**De·nis** or **De·nys** \'den-əs, də-'nē\ Saint *died* 258? A.D. 1st bishop of Paris; patron saint of France

**De Quin·cey** \di-'kwin-sē, -'kwin-zē\ Thomas 1785–1859 English author

**Des·cartes** \dā-'kärt\ René 1596–1650 French mathematician and philosopher

**de So·to** \di-'sōt-ō\ Hernando 1496 (or 1499 or 1500)–1542 Spanish explorer of Mississippi River (1540)

**Dew·ey** \'dü-ē, 'dyü-\ George 1837–1917 American admiral

**Dewey** John 1859–1952 American philosopher and educator

**Di·ana** \dī-'an-ə\ ancient Italian goddess of childbirth and the forest who was identified with Artemis in Roman mythology

**Di·as** or **Di·az** \'dē-‚äsh\ Bartholomeu *about* 1450–1500 Portuguese navigator

**Dick·ens** \'dik-ənz\ Charles John Huffam 1812–1870 *Boz* \'bäz, 'bōz\ English author

**Dick·in·son** \'dik-ən-sən\ Emily Elizabeth 1830–1886 American poet

**Di·de·rot** \'dē-‚drō, ‚dēd-ə-‚rō\ Denis 1713–1784 French philosopher and author

**Di·do** \'dīd-ō\ legendary queen of Carthage who entertains and falls in love with Aeneas and kills herself upon his departure

**Di·o·cle·tian** \‚dī-ə-'klē-shən\ 245 (or 248)–313 (or 316) A.D. Roman emperor (284–305)

**Di·og·e·nes** \dī-'äj-ə-‚nēz\ *died about* 320 B.C. Greek Cynic philosopher

**Di·o·ny·sus** \‚dī-ə-'nī-səs, -'nē-\ god of wine and ecstasy in Greek mythology

**Dis** \'dis\ god of the underworld in Roman mythology — compare PLUTO

**Dis·ney** \'diz-nē\ Walter Elias 1901–1966 American film producer

**Dis·rae·li** \diz-'rā-lē\ Benjamin 1804–1881 1st Earl of *Bea·cons·field* \'bē-kənz-‚fēld\ British prime minister (1868; 1874–80)

**Dix** \'diks\ Dorothea Lynde 1802–1887 American social reformer

**Dodg·son** \'däj-sən, 'däd-\ Charles Lut·widge \'lət-wij\ 1832–1898 pseudonym *Lewis Car·roll* \'kar-əl\ English mathematician and author

**Dom·i·nic** \'däm-ə-nik\ Saint *about* 1170–1221 Spanish-born founder of the Dominican order of friars

**Do·mi·tian** \də-'mish-ən\ 51–96 A.D. Roman emperor (81–96)

**Don·i·zet·ti** \‚dän-əd-'zet-ē, ‚dōn-, -ə-'zet-\ Gaetano 1797–1848 Italian composer

**Donne** \'dən\ John 1572–1631 English poet and clergyman

**Dos·to·yev·sky** \‚däs-tə-'yef-skē, -'yev-\ Fyodor Mikhaylovich 1821–1881 Russian author

**Doug·las** \'dəg-ləs\ Stephen Arnold 1813–1861 American statesman

**Doug·lass** \'dəg-ləs\ Frederick 1817–1895 American abolitionist

**Doyle** \'dȯil\ Sir Arthur Co·nan \'kō-nən, 'kȯ-\ 1859–1930 British author and physician

**Dra·co** \'drā-kō\ late 7th century B.C. Athenian lawgiver

**Drake** \'drāk\ Sir Francis 1540 (or 1543)–1596 English navigator and admiral

**Drei·ser** \'drī-sər, -zər\ Theodore 1871–1945 American author

**Drey·fus** \'drī-fəs, 'drā-\ Alfred 1859–1935 French army officer

**Dry·den** \'drīd-n\ John 1631–1700 English author

**DuBois** \dü-'bȯis, dyü-\ William Edward Burghardt 1868–1963 American educator

**Du·mas** \dü-'mä, dyü-; 'dü-‚mä, 'dyü-\ Alexandre 1802–1870 *Dumas père* \'peər\ French author

**Dumas** Alexandre 1824–1895 *Dumas fils* \'fēs\ French author

**Dun·bar** \'dən-‚bär\ Paul Laurence 1872–1906 American poet

**Dun·can** \'dəng-kən\ Isadora 1877–1927 American dancer

**Dü·rer** \'dur-ər, 'dyur-, 'duer-\ Albrecht 1471–1528 German painter and engraver

**Du·se** \'dü-zā\ Eleonora 1858–1924 Italian actress

**Dvo·řák** \də-'vȯr-‚zhäk, 'vȯr-‚zhäk\ Antonín 1841–1904 Bohemian composer

**Ea·kins** \'ā-kənz\ Thomas 1844–1916 American artist

**Ear·hart** \'eər-‚härt, 'iər-\ Amelia 1897–1937 American aviator

**Ed·dy** \'ed-ē\ Mary Baker 1821–1910 American founder of the Christian Science Church

**Ed·i·son** \'ed-ə-sən\ Thomas Alva 1847–1931 American inventor

**Ed·ward** \'ed-wərd\ name of 8 post-Norman kings of England: **I** 1239–1307 (reigned 1272–1307) *Longshanks*; **II** 1284–1327 (reigned 1307–27); **III** 1312–1377 (reigned 1327–77); **IV** 1442–1483 (reigned 1461–70; 1471–83); **V** 1470–1483 (reigned 1483); **VI** 1537–1553 (reigned 1547–53) son of Henry VIII and Jane Seymour; **VII** 1841–1910 (reigned 1901–10) *Albert Edward* son of Queen Victoria; **VIII** 1894–1972 (reigned 1936; abdicated) *Duke of Windsor* son of George V

**Edward** 1330–1376 *the Black Prince* son of Edward III; prince of Wales

**Edward** 1003?–1066 *the Confessor* king of the English (1042–66)

**Ed·wards** \'ed-wərdz\ Jonathan 1703–1758 American theologian

**Ein·stein** \'īn-‚stīn\ Albert 1879–1955 American (German-born) physicist; Nobel prize winner (1921)

**Ei·sen·how·er** \'īz-n-‚hau-ər, -‚haur\ Dwight David 1890–1969 American general; 34th president of the United States (1953–61)

**Elec·tra** \i-'lek-trə\ sister of Orestes in Greek mythology who aids him in avenging their father's murder

**El·gar** \'el-‚gär, -gər\ Sir Edward 1857–1934 English composer

**Eli** \'ē-‚lī\ early Hebrew judge and priest in the Bible

**Eli·jah** \i-'lī-jə\ or **Eli·as** \i-'lī-əs\ Hebrew prophet of the 9th century B.C.

**El·i·on** \'el-ē-ən\ Gertrude Belle 1918– American biochemist; Nobel prize winner (1988)

**El·iot** \'el-ē-ət, 'el-yət\ George 1819–1880 pseudonym of *Mary Ann Evans* English author

**Eliot** Thomas Stearns 1888–1965 British (American-born) poet and critic; Nobel prize winner (1948)

**Elis·a·beth** \i-'liz-ə-bəth\ mother of John the Baptist in the Bible

**Eli·sha** \i-'lī-shə\ Hebrew prophet in the Bible who is disciple and successor of Elijah

**Eliz·a·beth I** \i-'liz-ə-bəth\ 1533–1603 queen of England (1558–1603); daughter of Henry VIII and Anne Boleyn

**Elizabeth II** 1926– queen of Great Britain (1952– ); daughter of George VI

**El·ling·ton** \'el-ing-tən\ Edward Kennedy 1899–1974 *Duke* American bandleader and composer

**El·li·son** \'el-ə-sən\ Ralph Waldo 1914–1994 American author

**Em·er·son** \'em-ər-sən\ Ralph Waldo 1803–1882 American essayist and poet

**En·dym·i·on** \en-'dim-ē-ən\ beautiful youth loved by the moon goddess Selene in classical mythology

**Eos** \'ē-‚äs\ goddess of the dawn in Greek mythology — compare AURORA

**Ep·i·cu·rus** \‚ep-i-'kyur-əs\ 341–270 B.C. Greek philosopher

**Eras·mus** \i-'raz-məs\ Desiderius 1466?–1536 Dutch scholar

**Er·a·to** \'er-ə-,tō\ Muse of lyric and especially love poetry in Greek mythology

**Er·ik** \'er-ik\ 10th century *the Red* Norwegian navigator

**Eriksson, Leif** — see LEIF ERIKSSON

**Erin·y·es** \i-'rin-ē-,ēz\ *or* **Eu·men·i·des** \yu-'men-ə-,dēz\ the Furies in Greek mythology

**Ernst** \'eərnst, 'ərnst\ Max 1891–1976 German painter

**Eros** \'eər-,äs, 'iər-\ god of love in Greek mythology — compare CUPID

**Esau** \'ē-,sȯ\ son of Isaac and Rebekah and elder twin brother of Jacob in the Bible

**Es·ther** \'es-tər\ Hebrew woman in the Bible who as the queen of Persia delivers her people from destruction

**Eu·clid** \'yü-kləd\ *flourished about* 300 B.C. Greek geometer

**Eumenides** — see ERINYES

**Eu·rip·i·des** \yu̇-'rip-ə-,dēz\ *about* 484–406 B.C. Greek dramatist

**Eu·ro·pa** \yu̇-'rō-pə\ Phoenician princess in Greek mythology who is abducted by Zeus disguised as a white bull

**Eu·ryd·i·ce** \yu̇-'rid-ə-sē\ wife of Orpheus in Greek mythology

**Eu·ter·pe** \yu̇-'tər-pē\ Muse of music in Greek mythology

**Eve** \'ēv\ the first woman in biblical tradition; wife of Adam

**Eze·kiel** \i-'zē-kyəl, -kē-əl\ Hebrew prophet of the 6th century B.C.

**Ez·ra** \'ez-rə\ Hebrew priest, scribe, and reformer of the 5th century B.C.

**Fa·bi·us** \'fā-bē-əs\ *died* 203 B.C. *Quintus Fabius Maximus Verrucosus Cunc·ta·tor* \'kəngk-tāt-ər\ Roman general against Hannibal

**Fahd** \'fäd\ 1923– king of Saudi Arabia (1982– )

**Fahr·en·heit** \'far-ən-,hīt, 'fär-\ Daniel Gabriel 1686–1736 German physicist

**Far·a·day** \'far-ə-,dā, -əd-ē\ Michael 1791–1867 English chemist and physicist

**Far·mer** \'fär-mər\ James Leonard 1920–1999 American civil rights leader

**Far·ra·gut** \'far-ə-gət\ David Glasgow 1801–1870 American admiral

**Faulk·ner** \'fȯk-nər\ William 1897–1962 American author; Nobel prize winner (1949)

**Faust** *or* **Fau·stus** \'fau̇-stəs, 'fȯ-\ magician and astrologer in legend and literature who sells his soul to the devil for worldly experience and power

**Fawkes** \'fȯks\ Guy 1570–1606 English conspirator

**Fer·ber** \'fər-bər\ Edna 1887–1968 American writer

**Fer·di·nand I** \'fərd-n-,and\ 1016 (or 1018)–1065 *the Great* king of Castile (1035–65); of León (1037–65)

**Ferdinand V** of Castile *or* **II** of Aragon 1452–1516 *the Catholic* king of Castile (1474–1504); of Aragon (1479–1516); of Naples (1504–16); founder of the Spanish monarchy

**Fer·mi** \'feər-mē\ Enrico 1901–1954 American (Italian-born) physicist; Nobel prize winner (1938)

**Fiel·ding** \'fēl-ding\ Henry 1707–1754 English author

**Fill·more** \'fil-,mōr, -,mȯr\ Millard 1800–1874 13th president of the United States (1850–53)

**Fitz·ger·ald** \fits-'jer-əld\ Ella 1917–1996 American singer

**Fitzgerald** Francis Scott Key 1896–1940 American author

**Fitz·Ger·ald** \fits-'jer-əld\ Edward 1809–1883 English poet

**Flau·bert** \flō-'beər\ Gustave 1821–1880 French author

**Flem·ing** \'flem-ing\ Sir Alexander 1881–1955 British bacteriologist; Nobel prize winner (1945)

**Flo·ra** \'flōr-ə, 'flȯr-\ goddess of flowers in Roman mythology

**Flying Dutchman** legendary Dutch mariner condemned to sail the seas until Judgment Day

**Foch** \'fȯsh, 'fäsh\ Ferdinand 1851–1929 French general; marshal of France (1918)

**Ford** \'fōrd, 'fȯrd\ Gerald Rudolph 1913– 38th president of the United States (1974–77)

**Ford** Henry 1863–1947 American automobile manufacturer

**Fos·sey** \'fȯs-ē, 'fäs-\ Dian 1932–1985 American ethologist

**Fos·ter** \'fȯs-tər, 'fäs-\ Stephen Collins 1826–1864 American songwriter

**Fox** \'fäks\ George 1624–1691 English founder of Society of Friends

**Fran·cis I** \'fran-səs\ 1494–1547 king of France (1515–47)

**Francis II** 1768–1835 last Holy Roman emperor (1792–1806); emperor of Austria (as *Francis I*) (1804–35)

**Francis Ferdinand** 1863–1914 archduke of Austria

**Francis Joseph I** 1830–1916 emperor of Austria (1848–1916)

**Francis of As·si·si** \ə-'sē-sē, -zē, -'sis-ē\ Saint 1181 (or 1182)–1226 Italian friar; founder of Franciscan order

**Franck** \'frängk\ César Auguste 1822–1890 French (Belgian-born) organist and composer

**Fran·co** \'fräng-kō, 'frang-\ Francisco 1892–1975 Spanish general and dictator

**Frank** \'frangk\ Anne 1929–1945 Jewish (German-born) diarist during the Holocaust

**Frank·lin** \'frang-klən\ Benjamin 1706–1790 American statesman, philosopher, and inventor

**Fred·er·ick I** \'fred-rik, -ə-rik\ *about* 1123–1190 *Frederick Bar·ba·ros·sa* \,bär-bə-'räs-ə, -'rȯs-\ Holy Roman emperor (1152–90)

**Frederick II** 1194–1250 Holy Roman emperor (1215–50); king of Sicily (1198–1250)

**Frederick IX** 1899–1972 king of Denmark (1947–72)

**Frederick I** 1657–1713 king of Prussia (1701–13)

**Frederick II** 1712–1786 *the Great* king of Prussia (1740–86)

**Fré·mont** \'frē-,mänt\ John Charles 1813–1890 American general and explorer

**Freud** \'frȯid\ Sigmund 1856–1939 Austrian neurologist; founder of psychoanalysis

**Fron·te·nac et Pal·lu·au** \'fränt-n-,ak,,ä-pä-'lwȯ\ Comte de 1622–1698 French general and colonial administrator

**Frost** \'frȯst\ Robert Lee 1874–1963 American poet

**Ful·ton** \'fu̇lt-n\ Robert 1765–1815 American inventor

**Ga·bri·el** \'gā-brē-əl\ one of the four archangels named in Hebrew tradition — compare MICHAEL, RAPHAEL, URIEL

**Ga·ga·rin** \gə-'gär-ən\ Yu·ry \'yu̇r-ē\ Alekseyevich 1934–1968 Russian cosmonaut; 1st man in space (1961)

**Gage** \'gāj\ Thomas 1721–1787 British general in America

**Gains·bor·ough** \'gānz-,bər-ə, -bə-rə, -brə\ Thomas 1727–1788 English painter

**Gal·a·had** \'gal-ə-,had\ knight of the Round Table in medieval legend who finds the Holy Grail

**Gal·a·tea** \,gal-ə-'tē-ə\ a female figure carved by Pygmalion in Greek mythology and given life by Aphrodite in response to the sculptor's prayer

**Ga·len** \'gā-lən\ 129–*about* 199 A.D. Greek physician and writer

**Ga·li·lei** \,gal-ə-'lā-,ē\ Ga·li·leo \,gal-ə-'lē-ō, -'lā-\ 1564–1642 usually called *Galileo* Italian astronomer and physicist

**Gall** \'gȯl\ 1840?–1894 Sioux Indian leader

**Ga·lois** \gal-'wä\ Évariste 1811–1832 French mathematician

**Gals·wor·thy** \'gȯlz-,wər-thē\ John 1867–1933 English author; Nobel prize winner (1932)

**Ga·ma, da** \də-'gam-ə, -'gäm-\ Vasco *about* 1460–1524 Portuguese navigator and explorer

**Gan·dhi** \'gän-dē, 'gan-\ Indira Nehru 1917–1984 Indian prime minister (1966–77; 1980–84); daughter of Jawaharlal Nehru

**Gandhi** Mohandas Karamchand 1869–1948 *Ma·hat·ma* \mə-'hät-mə, -'hat-\ Indian nationalist leader

**Gan·y·mede** \'gan-i-,mēd\ cupbearer of Zeus in Greek mythology

**Gar·field** \'gär-,fēld\ James Abram 1831–1881 20th president of the United States (1881)

**Gar·i·bal·di** \,gar-ə-'bȯl-dē\ Giuseppe 1807–1882 Italian patriot

**Gar·ri·son** \'gar-ə-sən\ William Lloyd 1805–1879 American abolitionist

**Gar·vey** \'gär-vē\ Marcus Moziah 1887–1940 Jamaican black leader

**Gates** \'gāts\ Horatio *about* 1728–1806 American Revolutionary general

**Gates** William Henry III 1955– American computer software manufacturer

**Gau·guin** \gō-'gaⁿ\ (Eugène-Henri-) Paul 1848–1903 French painter

**Gauss** \'gau̇s\ Karl Friedrich 1777–1855 German mathematician and astronomer

**Gau·ta·ma Bud·dha** \,gau̇t-ə-mə-'bu̇d-ə,-'bu̇d-\ *about* 563–*about* 483 B.C. Indian founder of Buddhism

**Ga·wain** \gə-'wän, 'gä-,wän, 'gau̇-ən\ nephew of King Arthur and knight of the Round Table in medieval legend

**Gay** \'gā\ John 1685–1732 English author

**Gei·sel** \'gī-zəl\ Theodor Seuss 1904–1991 pseudonym *Dr. Seuss* \'süs\ American author and illustrator

**Gen·ghis Khan** \,jeng-gə-'skän, ,geng-\ *about* 1162–1227 Mongol conqueror

**George** \'jȯrj\ Saint *about* 3d century Christian martyr; patron saint of England

**George** name of 6 kings of Great Britain: **I** 1660–1727 (reigned 1714–27); **II** 1683–1760 (reigned 1727–60); **III** 1738–1820 (reigned 1760–1820); **IV** 1762–1830 (reigned 1820–30); **V** 1865–1936 (reigned 1910–36); **VI** 1895–1952 (reigned 1936–52)

**George I** 1845–1913 king of Greece (1863–1913)

**George II** 1890–1947 king of Greece (1922–23; 1935–47)

**George** David Lloyd — see LLOYD GEORGE

**Ge·ron·i·mo** \jə-'rän-ə-,mō\ 1829–1909 Apache Indian leader

**Gersh·win** \'gərsh-wən\ George 1898–1937 American composer

**Gib·bon** \'gib-ən\ Edward 1737–1794 English historian

**Gide** \'zhēd\ André 1869–1951 French author; Nobel prize winner (1947)

**Gid·e·on** \'gid-ē-ən\ Hebrew hero in the Bible

**Gil·bert** \'gil-bərt\ Sir William Schwenck 1836–1911 English librettist and poet; collaborated with Sir Arthur S. Sullivan

**Gil·les·pie** \gə-'les-pē\ John Birks 1917–1993 *Dizzy* American jazz musician

**Gins·burg** \'ginz-bərg\ Ruth Bader 1933– American jurist

**Giot·to** \'jȯt-tō, 'jō-tō, jē-'ät-ō\ 1266/67 (or 1276)–1337 *Giotto di Bondone* Florentine painter, architect, and sculptor

**Glad·stone** \'glad-,stōn, *chiefly British* -stən\ William Ewart 1809–1898 British prime minister (1868–74; 1880–85; 1886; 1892–94)

**Glenn** \'glen\ John Herschel 1921– American astronaut; 1st American to orbit the earth (1962)

**God·dard** \'gäd-ərd\ Robert Hutchings 1882–1945 American physicist

**Go·di·va** \gə-'dī-və\ Saxon lady noted in legend for riding naked through the streets of Coventry to relieve the town of a burdensome tax levied by her husband

**Goeb·bels** \'gərb-əlz, 'gœb-əls\ (Paul) Joseph 1897–1945 German Nazi propagandist

**Goe·thals** \'gō-thəlz\ George Washington 1858–1928 American general and engineer

**Goe·the** \'gər-tə, 'gœ̅-tə\ Johann Wolfgang von 1749–1832 German author

**Gogh, van** \van-'gō, -'gäk, -kȯk\ Vincent 1853–1890 Dutch painter

**Go·gol** \'gȯ-gəl, 'gō-,gȯl\ Nikolay Vasilyevich 1809–1852 Russian author

**Gol·ding** \'gōld-ing\ William Gerald 1911–1993 English author; Nobel prize winner (1983)

**Gold·smith** \'gōld-,smith, 'gōl-\ Oliver 1730–1774 British author

**Go·li·ath** \gə-'lī-əth\ Philistine giant in the Old Testament killed by David with a sling

**Gom·pers** \'gäm-pərz\ Samuel 1850–1924 American (British-born) labor leader

**Goo·dall** \'gu̇d-,ȯl\ Jane 1934– British ethologist

**Good·year** \'gu̇d-,yiər, 'gu̇j-,iər\ Charles 1800–1860 American inventor

**Gor·ba·chev** \,gȯr-bə-'chȯf\ Mikhail Sergeyevich 1931– Soviet politician; 1st secretary of Communist party (1985–91); president of the U.S.S.R. (1990–91)

**Gore** \'gōr, 'gȯr\ Albert, Jr. 1948– vice president of the United States (1993–2001)

---

\ə\ abut \ᵊ\ kitten \ər\ further \a\ ash \ā\ ace
\ä\ mop, mar \au̇\ out \ch\ chin \e\ bet \ē\ easy
\g\ go \i\ hit \ī\ ice \j\ job \ŋ\ sing \ō\ go
\ȯ\ law \ȯi\ boy \th\ thin \t̶h\ the \ü\ loot \u̇\ foot
\y\ yet \zh\ vision   *see also* Guide to Pronunciation

**Gor·gas** \'gór-gǝs\ William Crawford 1854–1920 American army surgeon

**Gor·ky** \'gór-kē\ Maksim 1868–1936 pseudonym of *Aleksey Maksimovich Pesh·kov* \'pesh-,kóf, -,kóv\ Russian author

**Gou·nod** \'gü-,nō\ Charles-François 1818–1893 French composer

**Go·ya y Lu·cien·tes** \'gói-ǝ-,ē-,lü-sē-,en-,täs\ Francisco José de 1746–1828 Spanish painter

**Grac·chus** \'grak-ǝs\ Gaius Sempronius 153–121 B.C. and his brother Tiberius Sempronius 163–133 B.C. *the Grac·chi* \'grak-,ī\ Roman statesmen

**Gra·ham** \'grā-ǝm, 'gra-ǝm, 'gram\ Martha 1893–1991 American dancer and choreographer

**Grant** \'grant\ Ulysses S. 1822–1885 originally *Hiram Ulysses Grant* American general; 18th president of the United States (1869–77)

**Gray** \'grā\ Thomas 1716–1771 English poet

**Gre·co, El** \el-'grek-ō, -'grāk-, -'grēk-\ 1541–1614 *Doménikos Theotokópoulos* Spanish (Cretan-born) painter

**Gree·ley** \'grē-lē\ Horace 1811–1872 American journalist and politician

**Greene** \'grēn\ Graham 1904–1991 British author

**Greene** Nathanael 1742–1786 American Revolutionary general

**Greg·o·ry** \'greg-rē, -ǝ-rē\ name of 16 popes: especially **I** Saint *about* 540–604 A.D. *the Great* (pope 590–604); **VII** Saint (*Hil·de·brand* \'hil-dǝ-,brand\) 1020–1085 (pope 1073–85); **XIII** 1502–1585 (pope 1572–85)

**Grey** \'grā\ Lady Jane 1537–1554 English noblewoman beheaded as a possible rival for the throne of Mary I

**Grey** Zane 1875–1939 originally *Pearl Zane* American author

**Grieg** \'grēg, 'grig\ Edvard Hagerup 1843–1907 Norwegian composer

**Grimm** \'grim\ Jacob 1785–1863 and his brother Wilhelm 1786–1859 German philologists and fairy tale writers

**Guin·e·vere** \'gwin-ǝ-,viǝr, 'gwen-\ wife of King Arthur and mistress of Lancelot in Arthurian legend

**Gun·ther** \'günt-ǝr\ Burgundian king and husband of Brunhild in Germanic legend

**Gu·ten·berg** \'güt-n-,bǝrg\ Johannes *between* 1390 *and* 1400–1468 German inventor of printing from movable type

**Ha·dri·an** \'hā-drē-ǝn\ 76–138 A.D. Roman emperor (117–138)

**Ha·gar** \'hā-,gär, -gǝr\ mistress of Abraham and mother of Ishmael in the Bible

**Hag·gai** \'hag-ē-,ī, 'hag-,ī\ *or* **Ag·ge·us** \a-'gē-ǝs\ Hebrew prophet of the 6th century B.C.

**Hai·le Se·las·sie** \,hī-lē-sǝ-'las-ē, -'läs-\ 1892–1975 emperor of Ethiopia (1930–36; 1941–74)

**Hale** \'hāl\ Edward Everett 1822–1909 American clergyman and author

**Hale** Nathan 1755–1776 American Revolutionary hero

**Hal·sey** \'hól-sē, -zē\ William Frederick 1882–1959 American admiral

**Ham** \'ham\ son of Noah and ancestor of the Hamitic peoples in biblical tradition

**Ha·man** \'hā-mǝn\ Old Testament enemy of the Jews hanged for plotting their destruction

**Ha·mil·car Bar·ca** \hǝ-'mil-,kär-'bär-kǝ, 'ham-ǝl-\ 270?–229 (or 228) B.C. Carthaginian general; father of Hannibal

**Ham·il·ton** \'ham-ǝl-tǝn, -ǝlt-n\ Alexander 1755–1804 American statesman

**Hamilton** Edith 1867–1963 American classicist

**Ham·mu·ra·bi** \,ham-ǝ-'räb-ē\ *died* 1750 B.C. king of Babylon (1792–50)

**Ham·sun** \'häm-sǝn\ Knut 1859–1952 pseudonym of *Knut Pedersen* Norwegian author; Nobel prize winner (1920)

**Han·cock** \'han-,käk\ John 1737–1793 American statesman

**Han·del** \'han-dl\ George Frideric 1685–1759 British (German-born) composer

**Han·dy** \'han-dē\ William Christopher 1873–1958 American blues musician

**Han·ni·bal** \'han-ǝ-bǝl\ 247–183 B.C. Carthaginian general

**Har·de·ca·nute** \,härd-i-kǝ-'nüt, -'nyüt\ *about* 1019–1042 king of the English (1040–42); king of Denmark (1028–42)

**Har·ding** \'härd-ing\ Warren Gamaliel 1865–1923 29th president of the United States (1921–23)

**Har·dy** \'härd-ē\ Thomas 1840–1928 English author

**Har·old I** \'har-ǝld\ *died* 1040 *Harold Hare·foot* \'haǝr-,fut, 'heǝr-\ king of the English (1035–40)

**Harold II** *about* 1022–1066 king of the English (1066)

**Har·ris** \'har-ǝs\ Joel Chandler 1848–1908 American author

**Har·ri·son** \'har-ǝ-sǝn\ Benjamin 1833–1901 23d president of the United States (1889–93); grandson of W. H. Harrison

**Harrison** William Henry 1773–1841 American general; 9th president of the United States (1841)

**Harte** \'härt\ Francis Brett 1836–1902 *Bret* American author

**Har·vey** \'här-vē\ William 1578–1657 English physician and anatomist

**Haw·thorne** \'hó-,thórn\ Nathaniel 1804–1864 American author

**Haydn** \'hīd-n\ (Franz) Joseph 1732–1809 Austrian composer

**Hayes** \'hāz\ Rutherford Birchard 1822–1893 19th president of the United States (1877–81)

**Haz·litt** \'haz-lǝt, 'häz-\ William 1778–1830 English essayist

**Hearst** \'hǝrst\ William Randolph 1863–1951 American newspaper publisher

**Hec·ate** \'hek-ǝt-ē\ goddess associated especially with the underworld, night, and witchcraft in Greek mythology

**Hec·tor** \'hek-tǝr\ son of Priam and Trojan hero slain by Achilles in Greek mythology

**Hec·u·ba** \'hek-yǝ-bǝ\ wife of Priam and mother of Hector and Paris in Greek mythology

**He·gel** \'hā-gǝl\ Georg Wilhelm Friedrich 1770–1831 German philosopher

**Hei·deg·ger** \'hī-,deg-ǝr, 'hīd-i-gǝr\ Martin 1889–1976 German philosopher

**Hei·ne** \'hī-nǝ *also* -nē\ Heinrich 1797–1856 German author

**Hel·en of Troy** \,hel-ǝ-nǝv-'trói\ wife of Menelaus whose abduction by Paris causes the Trojan War in Greek mythology

**He·li·os** \'hē-lē-,ōs, -ǝs\ god of the sun in Greek mythology — compare SOL

**Hell·man** \'hel-mǝn\ Lillian 1905–1984 American dramatist

**Hem·ing·way** \'hem-ing-,wā\ Ernest Miller 1899–1961 American author; Nobel prize winner (1954)

**Hen·ry** \'hen-rē\ name of 8 kings of England: **I** 1068–1135 (reigned 1100–1135); **II** 1133–1189 (reigned 1154–89); **III** 1207–1272 (reigned 1216–72); **IV** 1366–1413 (reigned 1399–1413); **V** 1387–1422 (reigned 1413–22); **VI** 1421–1471 (reigned 1422–61; 1470–71); **VII** 1457–1509 (reigned 1485–1509); **VIII** 1491–1547 (reigned 1509–47)

**Henry** name of 4 kings of France: **I** *about* 1008–1060 (reigned 1031–60); **II** 1519–1559 (reigned 1547–59); **III** 1551–1589 (reigned 1574–89); **IV** 1553–1610 *Henry of Navarre* (reigned 1589–1610)

**Henry** O. — see William Sydney PORTER

**Henry** Patrick 1736–1799 American statesman and orator

**Hen·son** \'hen-sǝn\ Matthew Alexander 1866–1955 American arctic explorer

**He·phaes·tus** \hi-'fes-tǝs, -'fēs-\ god of fire and of metalworking in Greek mythology — compare VULCAN

**He·ra** \'hir-ǝ, 'hē-rǝ\ sister and wife of Zeus and goddess of women and marriage in Greek mythology — compare JUNO

**Her·bert** \'hǝr-bǝrt\ Victor 1859–1924 American (Irish-born) composer and conductor

**Her·cu·les** \'hǝr-kyǝ-,lēz\ *or* **Her·a·cles** *also* **Her·a·kles** \'her-ǝ-,klēz\ hero in classical mythology noted for his strength and for performing 12 labors imposed on him by Hera

**Her·maph·ro·di·tus** \,hǝr-,maf-rǝ-'dīt-ǝs\ son of Hermes and Aphrodite who in Greek mythology is bodily joined with a nymph

**Her·mes** \'hǝr-,mēz, -mēz\ god of commerce, eloquence, invention, travel, and theft who serves as herald and messenger for the other gods in Greek mythology — compare MERCURY

**He·ro** \'hē-rō, 'hiǝr-ō\ priestess of Aphrodite loved by Leander

**Her·od** \'her-ǝd\ 73–4 B.C. *the Great* Roman king of Judea (37–4)

**Herod An·ti·pas** \'ant-ǝ-,pas, -pǝs\ 21 B.C.–39 A.D. Roman tetrarch of Galilee (4 B.C.–39 A.D.); son of Herod the Great

**He·rod·o·tus** \hi-'räd-ǝ-tǝs\ *about* 484–*between* 430 *and* 420 B.C. Greek historian

**Her·rick** \'her-ik\ Robert 1591–1674 English poet

**He·si·od** \'hē-sē-ǝd, 'hes-ē-\ *flourished about* 800 B.C. Greek poet

**Hes·se** \'hes-ǝ\ Hermann 1877–1962 German author

**Hes·tia** \'hes-tē-ǝ; 'hes-chǝ, 'hesh-\ goddess of the hearth and domestic activity in Greek mythology — compare VESTA

**Hey·er·dahl** \'hā-ǝr-,däl, 'hī-\ Thor 1914– Norwegian explorer and author

**Hi·a·wa·tha** \,hī-ǝ-'wó-thǝ, ,hē-ǝ-, -'wäth-ǝ\ legendary Iroquois Indian chief

**Hick·ok** \'hik-,äk\ James Butler 1837–1876 *Wild Bill* American scout and United States marshal

**Hildebrand** — see GREGORY VII

**Hil·la·ry** \'hil-ǝ-rē\ Sir Edmund Percival 1919– New Zealand mountaineer and explorer

**Hil·ton** \'hilt-n\ James 1900–1954 English novelist

**Hin·den·burg** \'hin-dǝn-,bǝrg, -,bùrg\ Paul von 1847–1934 German field marshal; president of Germany (1925–34)

**Hip·poc·ra·tes** \hip-'äk-rǝ-,tēz\ *about* 460–*about* 377 B.C. *father of medicine* Greek physician

**Hi·ro·hi·to** \,hir-ō-'hē-tō\ 1901–1989 emperor of Japan (1926–89)

**Hit·ler** \'hit-lǝr\ Adolf 1889–1945 German (Austrianborn) chancellor and führer (1933–45)

**Hobbes** \'häbz\ Thomas 1588–1679 English philosopher

**Hodg·kin** \'häj-kin\ Dorothy Mary Crowfoot 1910–1994 British physicist; Nobel prize winner (1964)

**Ho·garth** \'hō-,gärth\ William 1697–1764 English painter and engraver

**Hol·bein** \'hōl-,bīn, 'hól-\ Hans *the Elder* 1465?–1524 and *the Younger* 1497?–1543 German painters

**Hol·i·day** \'häl-ǝ-,dā\ Eleanora 1915–1959 *Billie* American jazz singer

**Holmes** \'hōmz, 'hōlmz\ Oliver Wendell 1809–1894 American physician and author

**Holmes** Oliver Wendell 1841–1935 American jurist; son of the preceding

**Ho·mer** \'hō-mǝr\ 9th–8th? century B.C. Greek epic poet

**Homer** Winslow 1836–1910 American painter

**Hook·er** \'hük-ǝr\ Thomas 1586?–1647 English Puritan clergyman and a founder of Connecticut

**Hoo·ver** \'hü-vǝr\ Herbert Clark 1874–1964 31st president of the United States (1929–33)

**Hoover** John Edgar 1895–1972 American criminologist; director of the Federal Bureau of Investigation (1924–72)

**Hop·kins** \'häp-kǝnz\ Gerard Manley 1844–1889 English poet

**Hop·per** \'häp-ǝr\ Grace 1906–1992 American admiral, mathematician, and computer scientist

**Hor·ace** \'hór-ǝs, 'här-\ 65–8 B.C. Roman poet

**Ho·ra·tius** \hǝ-'rā-shē-ǝs, -shǝs\ hero in Roman legend noted for his defense of a bridge over the Tiber against the Etruscans

**Ho·sea** \hō-'zē-ǝ, -'zā-\ *or* **Osee** \'ō-zē, ō-'zā-ǝ\ Hebrew prophet of the 8th century B.C.

**Hous·man** \'haù-smǝn\ Alfred Edward 1859–1936 English classical scholar and poet

**Hous·ton** \'hyü-stǝn, 'yü-\ Samuel 1793–1863 American general; president of the Republic of Texas (1836–38; 1841–44)

**Howe** \'haù\ Elias 1819–1867 American inventor

**Howe** Julia 1819–1910 née *Ward* American suffragist and reformer

**How·ells** \'haù-ǝlz\ William Dean 1837–1920 American author

**Hud·son** \'hǝd-sǝn\ Henry *died* 1611 English navigator

**Hudson** William Henry 1841–1922 English naturalist and author

**Hugh Ca·pet** \'kā-pǝt, 'kap-ǝt, ka-'pā\ *about* 938–996 A.D. king of France (987–996)

**Hughes** \'hyüz *also* 'yüz\ Charles Evans 1862–1948 chief justice of the United States Supreme Court (1930–41)

**Hughes** (James) Langston 1902–1967 American author

**Hu·go** \'hyü-gō, yü-\ Victor-Marie 1802–1885 French author

**Hume** \'hyüm *also* 'yüm\ David 1711–1776 Scottish philosopher and historian

**Huss** *or* **Hus** \'hǝs, 'hùs\ John *or* Jan 1372 (or 1373)–1415 Bohemian religious reformer

**Hus·sein I** \hü-'sān\ 1935–1999 king of Jordan (1952–99)

**Hussein** Saddam al-Tikriti 1937– leader of Iraq (1979– )

**Hux·ley** \'hək-slē\ Aldous Leonard 1894–1963 English author

**Hy·ge·ia** \hī-'jē-ə, -yə\ goddess of health in Greek mythology

**Hy·men** \'hī-mən\ god of marriage in Greek mythology

**Hy·pe·ri·on** \hī-'pir-ē-ən\ a Titan and the father of Eos, Selene, and Helios in Greek mythology

**Ib·sen** \'ib-sən, 'ip-\ Henrik 1828–1906 Norwegian author

**Ic·a·rus** \'ik-ə-rəs\ son of Daedalus who falls into the sea when the wax of his artificial wings melts as he flies too near the sun

**Ig·na·tius** \ig-'nā-shē-əs, -shəs\ Saint 1491–1556 *Ignatius of Loy·o·la* \'lȯi-'ō-lə\ Spanish founder of the Society of Jesus

**In·no·cent** \'in-ə-sənt\ name of 13 popes: especially **II** *died* 1143 (pope 1130–43); **III** 1160 (or 1161)–1216 (pope 1198–1216); **IV** *died* 1254 (pope 1243–54); **XI** 1611–1689 (pope 1676–89)

**Iph·i·ge·nia** \if-ə-jə-'nī-ə\ daughter of Agamemnon offered by him as a sacrifice but saved and made a priestess of Artemis

**Iris** \'ī-rəs\ goddess of the rainbow and a messenger of the gods in Greek mythology

**Ir·ving** \'ər-ving\ Washington 1783–1859 American author

**Isaac** \'ī-zik, -zək\ son of Abraham and father of Jacob in the Bible

**Is·a·bel·la I** \iz-ə-'bel-ə\ 1451–1504 queen of Castile (1474–1504) and of Aragon (1479–1504); wife of Ferdinand V of Castile

**Isa·iah** \ī-'zā-ə\ Hebrew prophet of the 8th century B.C.

**Iseult** — see ISOLDE

**Ish·ma·el** \'ish-mē-əl, -mā-\ outcast son of Abraham and Hagar in the Bible

**Isis** \'ī-səs\ ancient Egyptian nature goddess

**Isol·de** \i-'zōl-də\ *or* **Iseult** \is-'ült, iz-\ Irish princess married to King Mark of Cornwall and loved by Tristram

**Ivan III** \ē-'vän, 'ī-vən\ **Va·si·lye·vich** \və-'sil-yə-,vich\ 1440–1505 *Ivan the Great* grand duke of Russia (1462–1505)

**Ivan IV Vasilyevich** 1530–1584 *Ivan the Terrible* ruler of Russia (1533–84)

**Ives** \'īvz\ Charles Edward 1874–1954 American composer

**Jack·son** \'jak-sən\ Andrew 1767–1845 American general; 7th president of the United States (1829–37)

**Jackson** Jesse Louis 1941–     American clergyman and civil rights leader

**Jackson** Mahalia 1911–1972 American gospel singer

**Jackson** Thomas Jonathan 1824–1863 *Stonewall Jackson* American Confederate general

**Ja·cob** \'jā-kəb\ son of Isaac and Rebekah and younger twin brother of Esau in the Bible

**James** \'jāmz\ one of the 12 apostles and brother of the apostle John in the Bible

**James** *the Less* one of the 12 apostles in the Bible

**James** name of 2 kings of Great Britain: **I** 1566–1625 (reigned 1603–25); king of Scotland as *James VI* (reigned 1567–1603); **II** 1633–1701 (reigned 1685–88)

**James** Henry 1843–1916 British (American-born) author

**James** William 1842–1910 American psychologist and philosopher; brother of Henry James

**Ja·nus** \'jā-nəs\ god of gates and doors and of beginnings and endings in Roman mythology who is conventionally portrayed as having two opposite faces

**Ja·pheth** \'jā-fəth\ son of Noah and ancestor of the Medes and Greeks in biblical tradition

**Ja·son** \'jās-n\ hero in Greek mythology noted for his successful quest of the Golden Fleece

**Jay** \'jā\ John 1745–1829 American jurist and statesman; 1st chief justice of the United States Supreme Court (1789–95)

**Jef·fer·son** \'jef-ər-sən\ Thomas 1743–1826 3d president of the United States (1801–09)

**Jen·ner** \'jen-ər\ Edward 1749–1823 English physician

**Jer·e·mi·ah** \jer-ə-'mī-ə\ Hebrew prophet of the 6th and 7th centuries B.C.

**Je·rome** \jə-'rōm\ Saint *about* 347–419 (or 420) A.D. church father and biblical translator

**Je·sus** \'je-zəs, -zəz\ *about* 6 B.C.–*about* 30 A.D. *Jesus Christ* source of the Christian religion and Savior in the Christian faith

**Jez·e·bel** \'jez-ə-,bel\ queen of Israel and wife of Ahab who is notable for her wickedness in the Bible

**Joan of Arc** \jō-nə-'värk\ Saint 1412–1431 *the Maid of Orleans* French national heroine

**Job** \'jōb\ Old Testament patriarch who endures afflictions with fortitude and faith

**Jo·cas·ta** \jō-'kas-tə\ queen of Thebes in Greek mythology who unknowingly marries her son Oedipus

**Jo·el** \'jō-əl\ Hebrew prophet of the Old Testament

**John** \'jän\ *the Baptist* forerunner and baptizer of Jesus in the Bible

**John** one of the 12 apostles and the traditional author of the fourth Gospel, three Epistles, and the Book of Revelation

**John** name of 21 popes: especially **XXIII** (*Angelo Giuseppe Roncalli*) 1881–1963 (pope 1958–63)

**John** 1167–1216 *John Lack·land* \'lak-,land\ king of England (1199–1216)

**John of Gaunt** \-'gȯnt, -'gänt\ 1340–1399 Duke of Lancaster; son of Edward III of England

**John·son** \'jän-sən\ Andrew 1808–1875 17th president of the United States (1865–69)

**Johnson** John Arthur 1878–1946 *Jack* American boxer

**Johnson** Lyndon Baines 1908–1973 36th president of the United States (1963–69)

**Johnson** Philip Cortelyou 1906–     American architect

**Johnson** Samuel 1709–1784 *Dr. Johnson* English lexicographer and author

**Jol·liet** *or* **Jo·liet** \zhȯl-'yā\ Louis 1645–1700 French explorer

**Jo·nah** \'jō-nə\ Hebrew prophet who in the Bible spends three days in the belly of a great fish

**Jon·a·than** \'jän-ə-thən\ son of Saul and friend of David in the Bible

**Jones** \'jōnz\ John Paul 1747–1792 originally *John Paul* American (Scottish-born) naval officer

**Jon·son** \'jän-sən\ Benjamin 1572–1637 *Ben* English author

**Jop·lin** \'jäp-lən\ Scott 1868–1917 American pianist and composer

**Jor·dan** \'jȯrd-n\ Michael Jeffrey 1963–     American basketball player

**Jo·seph** \'jō-zəf *also* -səf\ a son of Jacob who in the Bible rises to high office in Egypt after being sold into slavery

**Joseph** *about* 1840–1904 Nez Percé Indian chief

**Joseph** Saint husband of Mary, the mother of Jesus

**Jo·se·phine** \'jō-zə-,fēn *also* -sə-\ 1763–1814 1st wife of Napoléon I; empress of France (1804–09)

**Joseph of Ar·i·ma·thea** \-,ar-ə-mə-'thē-ə\ member of the Sanhedrin who in the Gospels places the body of Jesus in his own tomb

**Jo·se·phus** \jō-'sē-fəs\ Flavius *about* 37–*about* 100 A.D. Jewish historian

**Josh·ua** \'jäsh-wə, -ə-wə\ Hebrew leader and successor of Moses during the settlement of the Israelites in Canaan

**Joyce** \'jȯis\ James Augustine 1882–1941 Irish author

**Ju·dah** \'jüd-ə\ son of Jacob and ancestor of one of the 12 tribes of Israel in the Bible

**Ju·das** \'jüd-əs\ *or* **Judas Is·car·i·ot** \-is-'kar-ē-ət\ one of the 12 apostles and betrayer of Jesus in the Bible

**Judas Mac·ca·bae·us** \'jüd-ə-,smak-ə-'bē-əs\ *died* 161 B.C. Jewish patriot

**Ju·lian** \'jül-yən\ *about* 331–363 A.D. *the Apostate* Roman emperor (361–363)

**Jung** \'yung\ Carl Gustav 1875–1961 Swiss psychologist

**Ju·no** \'jü-nō\ the queen of heaven, wife of Jupiter, and goddess of light, birth, women, and marriage in Roman mythology — compare HERA

**Ju·pi·ter** \'jü-pət-ər\ the chief god, husband of Juno, and the god of light, of the sky and weather, and of the state in Roman mythology — compare ZEUS

**Jus·tin·i·an I** \jə-'stin-ē-ən\ 483–565 A.D. *the Great* Byzantine emperor (527–565)

**Ju·ve·nal** \'jü-vən-l\ 55 to 60–*about* 127 A.D. Roman satirist

**Kaf·ka** \'käf-kə, 'kaf-\ Franz 1883–1924 Czech-born author

**Kalb** \'kälp, 'kalb\ Johann 1721–1780 Baron *de Kalb* \di-'kalb\ German general in American Revolutionary army

**Kant** \'kant, 'känt\ Immanuel 1724–1804 German philosopher

**Keats** \'kēts\ John 1795–1821 English poet

**Kel·ler** \'kel-ər\ Helen Adams 1880–1968 American deaf and blind lecturer

**Kel·vin** \'kel-vən\ 1st Baron 1824–1907 *William Thomson* British mathematician and physicist

**Kempis** Thomas a — see THOMAS A KEMPIS

**Ken·ne·dy** \'ken-əd-ē\ John Fitzgerald 1917–1963 35th president of the United States (1961–63); brother of R. F. Kennedy

**Kennedy** Robert Francis 1925–1968 American politician

**Ke·o·kuk** \'kē-ə-,kək\ 1780?–1848 American Indian chief

**Kep·ler** \'kep-lər\ Johannes 1571–1630 German astronomer

**Ke·ren·sky** \'ker-ən-skē\ Aleksandr Fyodorovich 1881–1970 Russian revolutionary

**Key** \'kē\ Francis Scott 1779–1843 American lawyer and author of "The Star-Spangled Banner"

**Keynes** \'kānz\ John Maynard 1883–1946 1st Baron *Keynes of Tilton* English economist — **Keynes·ian** \'kān-zē-ən\ *adj or n*

**Khayyám** Omar — see OMAR KHAYYÁM

**Khru·shchev** \krüsh-'chȯf, -'ȯf, -'chȯv, -'ȯv, -'chef, -'ef, 'krüsh-\ Ni·ki·ta \nə-'kēt-ə\ Sergeyevich 1894–1971 premier of U.S.S.R. (1958–64)

**Khu·fu** \'kü-,fü\ *or Greek* **Che·ops** \'kē-,äps\ 26th century B.C. king of Egypt and pyramid builder

**Kidd** \'kid\ William *about* 1645–1701 *Captain Kidd* Scottish pirate

**Kier·ke·gaard** \'kir-kə-,gärd, -,gär, -,gȯr\ Søren Aabye 1813–1855 Danish philosopher and theologian

**King** \'king\ Ernest Joseph 1878–1956 American admiral

**King** Martin Luther, Jr. 1929–1968 American clergyman and civil rights leader; Nobel prize winner (1964)

**Kip·ling** \'kip-ling\ (Joseph) Rud·yard \'rəd-yərd, 'rəj-ərd\ 1865–1936 English author

**Kis·sin·ger** \'kis-n-jər\ Henry Alfred 1923–     American (German-born) scholar and government official; United States secretary of state (1973–77); Nobel prize winner (1973)

**Klee** \'klā\ Paul 1879–1940 Swiss painter

**Knox** \'näks\ John *about* 1514–1572 Scottish religious reformer

**Koch** \'kȯk, 'kȯk, 'kōk, 'kōk, 'käk, 'käk\ Robert 1843–1910 German bacteriologist; Nobel prize winner (1905)

**Kohl** \'kōl\ Helmut 1930–     chancellor of Germany (1990–     )

**Koś·ciusz·ko** \,käs-ē-'əs-,kō, kȯsh-'chùsh-kō\ Tadeusz 1746–1817 Polish general in American Revolutionary army

**Krish·na** \'krish-nə\ deity or deified hero of later Hinduism worshiped as an incarnation of Vishnu

**Kriss Kringle** — see SANTA CLAUS

**Ku·blai Khan** \,kü-blə-'kän, -,blī-\ 1215–1294 founder of Mongol dynasty in China; grandson of Genghis Khan

**La·fa·yette** \,läf-ē-'et, ,laf-\ Marquis de 1757–1834 French general in American Revolutionary army

**La Fon·taine** \lə-,fän-'tän, -,fōⁿ¯-'ten\ Jean de 1621–1695 French writer of fables

**La·ius** \'lā-əs, 'lī-\ king of Thebes who in Greek mythology is slain by his son Oedipus

**La·marck** \lə-'märk\ Chevalier de 1744–1829 French naturalist

**Lamb** \'lam\ Charles 1775–1834 English author

**Lan·ce·lot** \'lan-sə-,lät\ knight of the Round Table and lover of Queen Guinevere in Arthurian legend

**Lange** \'lang\ Dorothea 1895–1965 American photographer

**Lang·land** \'lang-lənd\ William *about* 1330–*about* 1400 English poet

**Lang·ley** \'lang-lē\ Samuel Pierpont 1834–1906 American astronomer and airplane pioneer

**La·oc·o·ön** \lā-'äk-ə-,wän\ Trojan priest in Greek mythology killed by sea serpents after warning against the wooden horse

**Lao-tzu** \'laùd-'zə\ 6th century B.C. Chinese philosopher

**La·place** \lə-'pläs\ Pierre-Simon 1749–1827 Marquis *de Laplace* French astronomer and mathematician

---

\ə\ **abut**   \ᵊ\ **kitten**   \ər\ **further**   \a\ **ash**   \ā\ **ace**
\ä\ **mop, mar**   \aù\ **out**   \ch\ **chin**   \e\ **bet**   \ē\ **easy**
\g\ **go**   \i\ **hit**   \ī\ **ice**   \j\ **job**   \ŋ\ **sing**   \ō\ **go**
\ȯ\ **law**   \ȯi\ **boy**   \th\ **thin**   \th̲\ **the**   \ü\ **loot**   \ù\ **foot**
\y\ **yet**   \zh\ **vision**   *see also* Guide to Pronunciation

**La Roche·fou·cauld** \lä-ˌrōsh-ˌfü-ˈkō, -ˌrōsh-\ François 1613–1680 Duc *de la Rochefoucauld* French author and moralist

**La Salle** \lə-ˈsal\ Sieur de 1643–1687 *René-Robert Cavelier* French explorer in North America

**La·voi·sier** \ləv-ˈwäz-ē-ˌā\ Antoine-Laurent 1743–1794 French chemist

**Law·rence** \ˈlȯr-əns, ˈlär-\ David Herbert 1885–1930 English author

**Lawrence** Sir Thomas 1769–1830 English painter

**Lawrence** Thomas Edward 1888–1935 *Lawrence of Arabia* British archaeologist, soldier, and author

**Laz·a·rus** \ˈlaz-rəs, -ə-rəs\ brother of Mary and Martha who in the Bible is raised by Jesus from the dead

**Lazarus** beggar in the biblical parable of the rich man and the beggar

**Le·an·der** \lē-ˈan-dər\ youth in Greek mythology who swims the Hellespont nightly to visit his lover Hero

**Le·da** \ˈlēd-ə\ Spartan princess in Greek mythology who is visited by Zeus in the form of a swan

**Lee** \ˈlē\ Ann 1736–1784 English mystic and founder of Shaker society in the United States

**Lee** Henry 1756–1818 *Light-Horse Harry* American general

**Lee** Robert Edward 1807–1870 American Confederate general

**Leeu·wen·hoek** *or* **Leu·wen·hoek** \ˈlā-vən-ˌhůk\ Antonie van 1632–1723 Dutch naturalist

**Leib·niz** \ˈlīb-nəts, ˈlīp-nits\ Gottfried Wilhelm 1646–1716 German philosopher and mathematician

**Leif Er·iks·son** \ˈlā-ˈver-ik-sən, ˈlē-ˈfer-\ *flourished* 1000 Norwegian mariner; son of Erik the Red

**Le·nin** \ˈlen-ən\ 1870–1924 originally *Vladimir Ilyich Ul·ya·nov* \ül-ˈyän-əf, -ˌȯf, -ˌȯv\ Russian Communist leader

**Leo** \ˈlē-ō\ name of 13 popes: especially **I** Saint *died* 461 A.D. (pope 440–461); **III** Saint *died* 816 A.D. (pope 795–816); **XIII** 1810–1903 (pope 1878–1903)

**Le·o·nar·do da Vin·ci** \lē-ə-ˈnär-dō-də-ˈvin-chē, ˌlā-\ 1452–1519 Italian painter, sculptor, architect, and engineer

**Le·on·ca·val·lo** \ˌlā-ˌȯn-kə-ˈväl-ō\ Ruggiero 1858–1919 Italian composer and librettist

**Le·on·i·das** \lē-ˈän-əd-əs\ *died* 480 B.C. Greek hero; king of Sparta (490?–480)

**Lep·i·dus** \ˈlep-əd-əs\ Marcus Aemilius *died* 13 (or 12) B.C. Roman triumvir

**Le·vi** \ˈlē-ˌvī\ son of Jacob and ancestor of one of the 12 tribes of Israel in the Bible

**Lew·is** \ˈlü-əs\ John Llewellyn 1880–1969 American labor leader

**Lewis** Meriwether 1774–1809 American explorer (with William Clark)

**Lewis** (Harry) Sinclair 1885–1951 American author; Nobel prize winner (1930)

**Lin·coln** \ˈliŋ-kən\ Abraham 1809–1865 16th president of the United States (1861–65)

**Lind·bergh** \ˈlind-ˌbərg, ˈlin-\ Charles Augustus 1902–1974 American aviator

**Lin·nae·us** \lə-ˈnē-əs, -ˈnā-\ Carolus 1707–1778 *Carl von Lin·né* \lə-ˈnā\ Swedish botanist

**Lip·pi** \ˈlip-ē\ Fra Fi·lip·po \fə-ˈlip-ō\ *about* 1406–1469 Florentine painter

**Lis·ter** \ˈlis-tər\ Joseph 1827–1912 English surgeon

**Liszt** \ˈlist\ Franz 1811–1886 Hungarian pianist and composer

**Liv·ing·stone** \ˈliv-iŋ-stən\ David 1813–1873 Scottish explorer and missionary in Africa

**Livy** \ˈliv-ē\ 59 B.C.–17 A.D. *Titus Livius* Roman historian

**Lloyd George** \ˈlȯid-ˈjȯrj\ David 1863–1945 1st Earl of *Dwy·for* \ˈdü-ē-ˌvȯr\ British prime minister (1916–22)

**Locke** \ˈläk\ John 1632–1704 English philosopher

**Lo·hen·grin** \ˈlō-ən-ˌgrin\ son of Parsifal and knight of the Holy Grail in German legend

**Lon·don** \ˈlən-dən\ John Griffith 1876–1916 *Jack* American author

**Long·fel·low** \ˈlȯŋg-ˌfel-ō\ Henry Wads·worth \ˈwädz-wərth, -ˌwərth\ 1807–1882 American poet

**Lo·re·lei** \ˈlȯr-ə-ˌlī, ˈlȯr-\ siren in German legend whose beauty and song lures sailors to destruction on a reef in the Rhine

**Lot** \ˈlät\ nephew of Abraham in biblical tradition whose wife is turned into a pillar of salt for looking back on doomed Sodom

**Lou·is** \ˈlü-ē, ˈlü-əs\ name of 18 kings of France: especially **IX** Saint 1214–1270 (reigned 1226–70); **XI** 1423–1483 (reigned 1461–83); **XII** 1462–1515 (reigned 1498–1515); **XIII** 1601–1643 (reigned 1610–43); **XIV** 1638–1715 (reigned 1643–1715); **XV** 1710–1774 (reigned 1715–74); **XVI** 1754–1793 (reigned 1774–92); **XVII** 1785–1795 (nominally reigned 1793–95); **XVIII** 1755–1824 (reigned 1814–15; 1815–24)

**Louis** \ˈlü-əs\ Joe 1914–1981 originally *Joseph Louis Barrow* American boxer

**Louis Napoléon** — see NAPOLÉON III

**Louis Phi·lippe** \fi-ˈlēp\ 1773–1850 *the Citizen King* king of the French (1830–48)

**Low·ell** \ˈlō-əl\ Amy 1874–1925 American poet and critic

**Lowell** James Russell 1819–1891 American author

**Loyola** — see IGNATIUS

**Lu·cre·tius** \lü-ˈkrē-shē-əs, -shəs\ *about* 96–*about* 55 B.C. *Titus Lucretius Carus* Roman poet and philosopher

**Luke** \ˈlük\ physician and companion of the apostle Paul and the traditional author of the third Gospel and the Book of Acts

**Lu·ther** \ˈlü-thər\ Martin 1483–1546 German Reformation leader

**Ly·on** \ˈlī-ən\ Mary 1797–1849 American educator

**Lyt·ton** \ˈlit-n\ 1st Baron 1803–1873 *Edward George Earle Bul·wer-Lytton* \ˌbůl-wər-\ English author

**Mac·Ar·thur** \mə-ˈkär-thər\ Douglas 1880–1964 American general

**Ma·cau·lay** \mə-ˈkȯ-lē\ Thomas Babington 1800–1859 1st Baron *Macaulay* English historian, author, and statesman

**Mc·Car·thy** \mə-ˈkärth-ē\ Joseph Raymond 1908–1957 American politician

**Mc·Clel·lan** \mə-ˈklel-ən\ George Brinton 1826–1885 American general

**Mc·Clin·tock** \mə-ˈklin-tək\ Barbara 1902–1992 American botanist; Nobel prize winner (1983)

**Mc·Cor·mick** \mə-ˈkȯr-mik\ Cyrus Hall 1809–1884 American inventor of a mechanical reaper

**Mc·Cul·lers** \mə-ˈkəl-ərz\ Carson 1917–1967 née *Smith* American writer

**Ma·chi·a·vel·li** \ˌmak-ē-ə-ˈvel-ē\ Niccolò 1469–1527 Italian political philosopher

**Mc·Kin·ley** \mə-ˈkin-lē\ William 1843–1901 25th president of the United States (1897–1901)

**Mad·i·son** \ˈmad-ə-sen\ James 1751–1836 4th president of the United States (1809–17)

**Mae·ter·linck** \ˈmāt-ər-ˌliŋk *also* ˈmet-, ˈmat-\ Count Maurice 1862–1949 Belgian author; Nobel prize winner (1911)

**Ma·gel·lan** \mə-ˈjel-ən\ Ferdinand *about* 1480–1521 Portuguese navigator and explorer

**Mah·ler** \ˈmäl-ər\ Gustav 1860–1911 Austrian composer

**Ma·jor** \ˈmā-jər\ John 1943– prime minister of Great Britain (1990–97)

**Malcolm X** \ˌmal-kə-ˈmeks\ 1925–1965 American civil rights leader

**Mal·o·ry** \ˈmal-rē, -ə-rē\ Sir Thomas *flourished* 1470 English author

**Mal·thus** \ˈmal-thəs\ Thomas Robert 1766–1834 English economist

**Man·de·la** \man-ˈdel-ə\ Nelson Rolihlahla 1918– South African black political leader; president of South Africa (1994– )

**Ma·net** \ma-ˈnā\ Édouard 1832–1883 French painter

**Mann** \ˈman\ Horace 1796–1859 American educator

**Mann** \ˈmän, ˈman\ Thomas 1875–1955 American (German-born) author; Nobel prize winner (1929)

**Mao Tse-tung** \ˌmaůd-zə-ˈdůŋ, ˌmaů-zə-, ˌmaůt-sə-\ 1893–1976 Chinese Communist leader

**Ma·rat** \mə-ˈrä\ Jean-Paul 1743–1793 French (Swiss-born) revolutionary

**Mar·co·ni** \mär-ˈkō-nē\ Guglielmo 1874–1937 Italian physicist and inventor; Nobel prize winner (1909)

**Marcus Aurelius** — see ANTONINUS

**Ma·ria The·re·sa** \mə-ˌrē-ə-tə-ˈrā-sə, -ˈrā-zə\ 1717–1780 wife of Emperor Francis I; queen of Hungary and Bohemia

**Ma·rie An·toi·nette** \mə-ˌrē-ˌan-twə-ˈnet, -tə-ˈnet\ 1755–1793 daughter of Maria Theresa and wife of Louis XVI of France

**Mark** \ˈmärk\ evangelist believed to be the author of the second Gospel

**Mar·lowe** \ˈmär-ˌlō\ Christopher 1564–1593 English dramatist

**Mar·quette** \mär-ˈket\ Jacques 1637–1675 *Père* \ˌpiэr, ˌpeər\ *Marquette* Jesuit missionary and French explorer in America

**Mars** \ˈmärz\ god of war in Roman mythology — compare ARES

**Mar·shall** \ˈmär-shəl\ George Catlett 1880–1959 American general and diplomat

**Marshall** John 1755–1835 American jurist; chief justice of the United States Supreme Court (1801–35)

**Marshall** Thurgood 1908–1993 American jurist

**Martel** Charles — see CHARLES MARTEL

**Mar·tha** \ˈmär-thə\ sister of Lazarus and Mary and friend of Jesus in the Bible

**Mar·tial** \ˈmär-shəl\ *about* 40–*about* 103 A.D. Roman epigrammatist

**Mar·tin** \ˈmärt-n, mär-ˈtaⁿ\ Saint *about* 316–397 A.D. *Martin of Tours* \-ˈtůr\ a patron saint of France

**Marx** \ˈmärks\ Karl Heinrich 1818–1883 German political philosopher and socialist

**Mary** \ˈmeər-ē, ˈmaər-ē, ˈma-rē\ mother of Jesus

**Mary** sister of Lazarus and Martha in the Bible

**Mary I** 1516–1558 *Mary Tudor; Bloody Mary* queen of England (1553–58)

**Mary II** 1662–1694 joint British sovereign with William III

**Mary Mag·da·lene** \-ˈmag-də-ˌlēn, -ˌmag-də-ˈlē-nē\ woman in the Bible who is healed of evil spirits by Jesus and who later sees the risen Christ

**Mary Stuart** 1542–1587 *Mary, Queen of Scots* queen of Scotland (1542–67)

**Ma·sca·gni** \mä-ˈskän-yē, ma-\ Pietro 1863–1945 Italian composer

**Mase·field** \ˈmās-ˌfēld\ John 1878–1967 English author

**Mason** \ˈmās-n\ George 1725–1792 American statesman

**Mas·sa·soit** \ˌmas-ə-ˈsȯit\ *died* 1661 American Indian chief

**Mas·se·net** \ˌmas-n-ˈā, ma-ˈsnā\ Jules-Émile-Frédéric 1842–1912 French composer

**Math·er** \ˈmath-ər, ˈmath-\ Cotton 1663–1728 American clergyman and author

**Mather** Increase 1639–1723 American clergyman and author; father of Cotton Mather

**Ma·tisse** \ma-ˈtēs, mə-\ Henri 1869–1954 French painter

**Mat·thew** \ˈmath-yü\ one of the 12 apostles and the traditional author of the first gospel

**Maugham** \ˈmȯm\ (William) Somerset 1874–1965 English author

**Mau·pas·sant** \ˌmō-pə-ˈsäⁿ\ (Henri-René-Albert-) Guy de 1850–1893 French author

**Max·i·mil·ian** \ˌmak-sə-ˈmil-yən\ 1832–1867 emperor of Mexico (1864–67); brother of Francis Joseph I of Austria

**Maximilian I** 1459–1519 Holy Roman emperor (1493–1519)

**Maximilian II** 1527–1576 Holy Roman emperor (1564–76)

**Max·well** \ˈmak-ˌswel, -swəl\ James Clerk \ˈklärk\ 1831–1879 Scottish physicist

**Ma·za·rin** \ˌmaz-ə-ˈraⁿ\ Jules 1602–1661 French cardinal and statesman

**Maz·zi·ni** \mät-ˈsē-nē, mäd-ˈzē-\ Giuseppe 1805–1872 Italian patriot and revolutionary

**Mead** Margaret 1901–1978 American anthropologist

**Mea·ny** \ˈmē-nē\ George 1894–1980 American labor leader

**Me·dea** \mə-ˈdē-ə\ enchantress in Greek mythology who helps Jason to win the Golden Fleece and kills her children when he deserts her

**Medici** Catherine de — see CATHERINE DE MÉDICIS

**Medici** Lorenzo de' 1449–1492 *Lorenzo the Magnificent* Florentine ruler, statesman, and patron of the arts

**Me·du·sa** \mi-ˈdü-sə, -ˈdyü-, -zə\ a Gorgon in Greek mythology slain by Perseus

**Mel·pom·e·ne** \mel-ˈpäm-ə-nē\ Muse of tragedy in Greek mythology

**Mel·ville** \ˈmel-ˌvil\ Herman 1819–1891 American author

**Men·del** \ˈmen-dl\ Gregor Johann 1822–1884 Austrian botanist

**Men·de·le·yev** \ˌmen-də-ˈlā-əf\ Dmitry Ivanovich 1834–1907 Russian chemist

**Men·dels·sohn–Bar·thol·dy** \ˈmen-dl-sən-bär-ˈtȯl-dē, -ˈthȯl-\ (Jakob Ludwig) Felix 1809–1847 German composer, pianist, and conductor

**Men·e·la·us** \ˌmen-l-ˈā-əs\ king of Sparta, brother of Agamemnon, and husband of Helen of Troy in Greek mythology

**Meph·is·toph·e·les** \ˌmef-ə-ˈstäf-ə-ˌlēz\ a chief devil in the Faust legend

**Mer·ca·tor** \mər-ˈkāt-ər\ Gerhardus 1512–1594 *Gerhard Kremer* Flemish cartographer

**Mer·cu·ry** \'mər-kyə-rē, -kə-rē, -krē\ god of commerce, eloquence, travel, and theft who serves as herald and messenger of the other gods in Roman mythology

**Mer·e·dith** \'mer-əd-əth\ George 1828–1909 English author

**Mer·lin** \'mər-lən\ prophet and magician in Arthurian legend

**Me·tho·di·us** \mə-'thōd-ē-əs\ Saint *about* 825–884 A.D. Apostle to the Slavs; brother of Cyril

**Me·thu·se·lah** \mə-'thüz-lə, -'thyüz-, ə-lə\ an ancestor of Noah who lived 969 years according to biblical tradition

**Met·ter·nich** \'met-ər-nik, -nik\ Klemens Wenzel Nepomuk Lothar 1773–1859 Fürst *von Metternich* Austrian statesman

**Mey·er·beer** \'mī-ər-biər, -,beər\ Giacomo 1791–1864 German composer

**Mfume** \əm-'fü-mā\ Kweisi 1948– American civil rights leader

**Mi·cah** \'mī-kə\ Hebrew prophet of the 8th century B.C.

**Mi·chael** \'mī-kəl\ one of the four archangels named in Hebrew tradition — compare GABRIEL, RAPHAEL, URIEL

**Mi·chel·an·ge·lo** \,mī-kə-'lan-jə-,lō, ,mik-ə-'lan-, ,mē-kə-'län-\ 1475–1564 *Michelangelo di Lodovico Buonarroti Simoni* Italian sculptor, painter, architect, and poet

**Mich·e·ner** \'mich-nər, -ə-nər\ James Albert 1907–1997 American author

**Mi·das** \'mīd-əs\ legendary king of Phrygia having the power to turn everything he touched into gold

**Mil·lay** \mil-'ā\ Edna St. Vincent 1892–1950 American poet

**Mil·ler** \'mil-ər\ Arthur 1915– American author

**Mil·let** \mē-'yā, mi-'lā\ Jean-François 1814–1875 French painter

**Milne** \'miln, 'mil\ Alan Alexander 1882–1956 English author

**Mil·ti·a·des** \mil-'tī-ə-,dēz\ *about* 544–?489 B.C. Athenian general

**Mil·ton** \'milt-n\ John 1608–1674 English poet

**Mi·ner·va** \mə-'nər-və\ goddess of wisdom in Roman mythology — compare ATHENE

**Mi·nos** \'mī-nəs\ a just king of Crete in Greek mythology who upon his death is made supreme judge of the underworld

**Min·o·taur** \'min-ə-,tòr, 'mī-nə-\ monster in Greek mythology shaped half like a man and half like a bull

**Min·u·it** \'min-yə-wət\ Peter 1580–1638 Dutch colonial administrator in America

**Mi·ró** \mē-'rō\ Joan \zhü-'än\ 1893–1983 Spanish painter

**Mitch·ell** \'mich-əl\ Maria 1818–1889 American astronomer

**Mith·ras** \'mith-rəs\ Persian god of light who was the savior hero of an oriental mystery cult for men flourishing in the late Roman empire — **Mith·ra·ic** \mith-'rā-ik\ *adj* — **Mith·ra·ism** \'mith-rə-,iz-əm\ *n* — **Mith·ra·ist** \mith-'rā-əst, 'mith-rā-,ist\ *n*

**Mit·ter·rand** \,mē-ter-'ä<sup>n</sup>\ François-Maurice 1916–1996 president of France (1981–95)

**Mne·mos·y·ne** \ni-'mäs-n-ē\ goddess of memory and mother of the Muses by Zeus in Greek mythology

**Mo·dred** \'mō-drəd, 'mäd-rəd\ knight of the Round Table and rebellious nephew of King Arthur in Arthurian legend

**Mohammed** — see MUHAMMAD

**Mo·lière** \mōl-'yeər, 'mōl-,\ 1622–1673 pseudonym of *Jean-Baptiste Poque·lin* \pō-'kla<sup>n</sup>, -kə-'la<sup>n</sup>\ French actor and dramatist

**Mol·och** \'mäl-ək, 'mō-,läk\ *or* **Mol·ech** \'mäl-ək, 'mō-,lek\ a Semitic deity to whom children were sacrificed

**Mo·lo·tov** \'mäl-ə-,tof, 'mòl-, 'mōl-, -,tóv\ Vyacheslav Mikhaylovich 1890–1986 Soviet statesman

**Mo·net** \mō-'nā\ Claude 1840–1926 French painter

**Mon·roe** \mən-'rō\ James 1758–1831 5th president of the United States (1817–25)

**Mon·taigne** \män-'tān, mō<sup>n</sup>-'ten<sup>y</sup>\ Michel Eyquem de 1533–1592 French essayist

**Mont·calm de Saint-Véran** \mänt-'käm-də-,sa<sup>n</sup>-vā-'rä<sup>n</sup>, -'kälm-\ Marquis de 1712–1759 French field marshal in Canada

**Mon·tes·quieu** \,mänt-əs-'kyü, -'kyər, -'kyœ\ Baron de *La Brède et de* 1689–1755 French political philosopher

**Mon·tes·so·ri** \,mänt-ə-'sōr-ē, -'sór-\ Maria 1870–1952 Italian physician and educator

**Mon·te·ver·di** \,mänt-ə-'veərd-ē, -'vərd-\ Claudio Giovanni Antonio 1567–1643 Italian composer

**Mon·te·zu·ma II** \,mänt-ə-'zü-mə\ 1466–1520 last Aztec emperor of Mexico (1502–20)

**Moore** \'mòr, 'mor, 'mùr\ Marianne Craig 1887–1972 American poet

**Moore** Thomas 1779–1852 Irish poet

**Mor·de·cai** \'mòrd-i-,kī\ cousin of Esther who in the Bible saves the Jews from the destruction planned by Haman

**More** \'mòr, 'mor\ Sir Thomas 1478–1535 *Saint* English statesman and author

**Mor·gan** \'mòr-gən\ Sir Henry 1635–1688 English buccaneer

**Morgan** John Pierpont 1837–1913 American financier

**Mor·pheus** \'mòr-fē-əs, -,fyüs, -,füs\ god of dreams in Greek mythology

**Mor·ris** \'mòr-əs, 'mär-\ William 1834–1896 English poet, artist, and socialist

**Mor·ri·son** \'mòr-ə-sən\ Toni 1931– originally *Chloe Anthony Wofford* American author; Nobel prize winner (1993)

**Morse** \'mòrs\ Samuel Finley Breese 1791–1872 American artist and inventor of the electrical telegraph

**Mo·ses** \'mō-zəz *also* -zəs\ Hebrew prophet and lawgiver who in the Bible is the liberator of the Israelites from Egypt

**Moses** Anna Mary 1860–1961 *Grandma Moses* American painter

**Mo·zart** \'mōt-,särt\ Wolfgang Amadeus 1756–1791 Austrian composer

**Mu·bar·ak** \mù-'bär-ək\ Muhammad Hosni 1929– president of Egypt (1981– )

**Mu·ham·mad** \mō-'ham-əd, -häm- *also* mü-\ *or* **Mo·ham·med** \mō-'häm-əd\ *about* 570–632 A.D. Arab prophet and founder of Islam

**Mu·ham·mad** \mù-'häm-əd, 'ham-\ Elijah 1897–1975 originally *E. Poole* American religious leader

**Muir** \'myùr\ John 1838–1914 American (Scottish-born) naturalist

**Mul·ro·ney** \məl-'rü-nē\ (Martin) Brian 1939– prime minister of Canada (1984–93)

**Mus·so·li·ni** \,mü-sə-'lē-nē, ,mùs-ə-\ Be·ni·to \bə-'nēt-ō\ 1883–1945 *Il Du·ce* \ēl-'dü-chā\ Italian Fascist premier (1922–43)

**My·ron** \'mī-rən\ *flourished about* 480–440 B.C. Greek sculptor

**Na·bo·kov** \nə-'bò-kəf, -,kòf\ Vladimir Vladimirovich 1899–1977 American (Russian-born) author

**Na·hum** \'nā-əm, -həm\ Hebrew prophet of the 7th century B.C.

**Na·o·mi** \nā-'ō-mē\ mother-in-law of the biblical heroine Ruth

**Na·pier** \'nā-pē-ər, -,piər; nə-'piər\ John 1550–1617 Laird of *Mer·chis·ton* \'mər-kə-stən\ Scottish mathematician

**Na·po·léon I** \nə-'pōl-yən, -'pō-lē-ən\ *or* **Napo·léon Bo·na·parte** \'bō-nə-,pärt\ 1769–1821 emperor of the French (1804–15) — **Na·po·le·on·ic** \nə-,pō-lē-'än-ik\ *adj*

**Napoléon III** 1808–1873 *Louis-Napoléon* emperor of the French (1852–71); son of Louis Bonaparte and nephew of Napoléon I

**Nar·cis·sus** \när-'sis-əs\ beautiful youth in Greek mythology punished by being made to pine away for his own reflection before being transformed into the narcissus flower

**Nas·ser** \'näs-ər, 'nas-\ Ga·mal \gə-'mäl\ Ab·del \'ab-dl\ 1918–1970 Egyptian politician; president of Egypt (1956–70)

**Na·tion** \'nā-shən\ Car·ry \'kar-ē\ Amelia 1846–1911 American temperance agitator

**Neb·u·cha·drez·zar** \,neb-yə-kə-'drez-ər, ,neb-ə-kə-\ *or* **Neb·u·chad·nez·zar** \-kəd-'nez-\ *about* 630–562 B.C. king of Babylon (605–562) B.C.; conqueror of Jerusalem

**Ne·he·mi·ah** \,nē-ə-'mī-ə, ,nē-hə-\ Hebrew leader of the 5th century B.C.

**Neh·ru** \'neər-,ü, 'nā-,rü\ Ja·wa·har·lal \jə-'wä-hər-,läl\ 1889–1964 Indian nationalist; 1st prime minister (1947–64)

**Nel·son** \'nel-sən\ Horatio 1758–1805 Viscount *Nelson* British admiral

**Nem·e·sis** \'nem-ə-səs\ goddess of reward and punishment in Greek mythology

**Nep·tune** \'nep-,tün, -,tyün\ god of the sea in Roman mythology

**Ne·ro** \'nē-,rō, 'niər-,ō\ 37–68 A.D. Roman emperor (54–68)

**Nes·tor** \'nes-tər\ wise old counselor of the Greeks during the Trojan War in Greek mythology

**New·man** \'nü-mən, 'nyü-\ John Henry 1801–1890 English cardinal and author

**New·ton** \'nüt-n, 'nyüt-\ Sir Isaac 1642–1727 English mathematician and physicist

**Nich·o·las** \'nik-ləs, -ə-ləs\ Saint 4th century Christian bishop

**Nicholas I** 1796–1855 czar of Russia (1825–55)

**Nicholas II** 1868–1918 czar of Russia (1894–1917)

**Nietz·sche** \'nē-chə, -chē\ Friedrich Wilhelm 1844–1900 German philosopher

**Night·in·gale** \'nīt-n-,gāl, -ing-\ Florence 1820–1910 English nurse and philanthropist

**Ni·jin·sky** \nə-'zhin-skē, -'jin-\ Vas·lav \'vät-släf\ 1890–1950 Russian dancer

**Ni·ke** \'nī-kē\ goddess of victory in Greek mythology

**Nim·itz** \'nim-əts\ Chester William 1885–1966 American admiral

**Nim·rod** \'nim-,räd\ ruler in the Bible renowned as a mighty hunter

**Ni·o·be** \'nī-ə-bē, nī-'ō-bē\ a daughter of Tantalus in Greek mythology who while weeping for her slain children is turned into a stone from which her tears continue to flow

**Nix·on** \'nik-sən\ Richard Mil·hous \'mil-,haùs\ 1913–1994 37th president of the United States (1969–74)

**No·ah** \'nō-ə\ Old Testament patriarch and builder of the ark in which he, his family, and living creatures of every kind survive the Flood

**No·bel** \nō-'bel\ Alfred Bernhard 1833–1896 Swedish manufacturer, inventor, and philanthropist

**Nor·man** \'nòr-mən\ Jessye 1945– American soprano

**Nos·tra·da·mus** \,näs-trə-'dä-məs, ,nōs-trə-'däm-əs\ 1503–1566 French physician, astrologer, and seer

**Noyes** \'noiz\ Alfred 1880–1958 English poet

**Oba·di·ah** \,ō-bə-'dī-ə\ Hebrew prophet of Old Testament times

**Ober·on** \'ō-bə-,rän, -rən\ king of the fairies in medieval folklore and in Shakespeare's *A Midsummer Night's Dream*

**O'·Ca·sey** \ō-'kā-sē\ Sean 1880–1964 Irish dramatist

**Oce·anus** \ō-'sē-ə-nəs\ god of the great outer sea that in Greek mythology encircles the earth

**O'·Con·nor** \ō-'kän-ər\ (Mary) Flannery 1925–1964 American author

**O'Connor** \ō-'kän-ər\ Sandra Day 1930– American jurist

**Octavian** — see AUGUSTUS

**Odin** \'ōd-n\ *or* **Wo·den** \'wōd-n\ a chief god, the god of war, and the patron of heroes in Norse mythology

**Odys·seus** \ō-'dish-,üs, -'dis-,yüs, -'dis-ē-əs\ *or* **Ulys·ses** \yü-'lis-ēz\ king of Ithaca in Greek mythology who after the Greek victory in the Trojan War wanders for ten years before reaching home

**Oe·di·pus** \'ed-ə-pəs, 'ēd-\ son of the king and queen of Thebes who in Greek mythology unknowingly kills his father and marries his mother as foretold by an oracle

**Of·fen·bach** \'òf-ən-,bäk, -,bäk\ Jacques 1819–1880 French composer

**Ogle·thorpe** \'ō-gəl-,thòrp\ James Edward 1696–1785 English general, philanthropist, and founder of Georgia

**O'·Keeffe** \ō-'kēf\ Georgia 1887–1986 American painter

**Olaf I** \'ō-ləf, -ləv\ *about* 964–1000 king of Norway (995–1000)

**Olaf II** 995?–1030 *Saint Olaf* king of Norway (1 28)

**Olav V** 1903–1991 king of Norway (1957–91

**Omar Khay·yám** \,ō-,mär-,kī-'äm, -'yän -'yam\ 1048?–1122 Persian poet and astrono

**O'·Neill** \ō-'nēl\ Eugene Gladstone 1 American dramatist; Nobel prize winner (

**Ores·tes** \ə-'res-tēz, ò-\ son of Agam Clytemnestra who in Greek mythology father's murder by slaying his mother

**Or·pheus** \'òr-,fyüs, -fē-əs\ poet an Greek mythology who almost rescues ice from Hades by charming Pluto with his lyre

---

**Or·well** \'ȯr-,wel, -wəl\ George 1903–1950 pseudonym of *Eric Blair* English author — **Or·well·ian** \ȯr-'wel-ē-ən\ *adj*

**Osce·o·la** \,äs-ē-'ō-lə, ,ō-sē-\ *about* 1800–1838 Seminole Indian chief

**Osee** \'ō-zē, ō-'zā-ə\ — see HOSEA

**Osi·ris** \ō-'sī-rəs\ great god of the underworld and judge of the dead in ancient Egyptian mythology

**Otis** \'ōt-əs\ James 1725–1783 American Revolutionary statesman

**Ot·to** \'ät-ō\ 912–973 A.D. *the Great* Holy Roman emperor (936–973)

**Ov·id** \'äv-əd\ 43 B.C.–? 17 A.D. Roman poet

**Ow·en** \'ō-ən\ Robert 1771–1858 Welsh social reformer

**Paine** \'pān\ Thomas 1737–1809 American (English-born) political philosopher and author

**Pa·le·stri·na** \,pal-ə-'strē-nə\ Giovanni Pierluigi da *about* 1525–1594 Italian composer

**Pal·las** \'pal-əs\ *or* **Pallas Athene** — see ATHENE

**Pan** \'pan\ god of forests, pastures, flocks, and shepherds in Greek mythology who is represented as having the legs, ears, and horns of a goat

**Pan·da·rus** \'pan-də-rəs\ procurer of Cressida for Troilus during the Trojan War according to medieval legend

**Pan·do·ra** \pan-'dōr-ə, -'dȯr-\ curious woman in Greek mythology who opens a box and lets loose a swarm of evils upon mankind

**Pank·hurst** \'pangk-,hərst\ Emmeline 1858–1928 née *Goulden* English suffragist

**Par·a·cel·sus** \,par-ə-'sel-səs\ Philippus Aureolus 1493–1541 Swiss-born alchemist and physician

**Par·is** \'par-əs\ son of Priam whose abduction of Helen of Troy leads to the Trojan War in Greek mythology

**Park** \'pärk\ Mungo 1771–1806 Scottish explorer of the Niger

**Park·man** \'pärk-mən\ Francis 1823–1893 American historian

**Parks** \'pärks\ Rosa Lee 1913–    American civil rights activist

**Par·nell** \pär-'nel\ Charles Stewart 1846–1891 Irish nationalist

**Pas·cal** \pas-'kal, pás-kál\ Blaise 1623–1662 French mathematician and philosopher

**Pas·ter·nak** \'pas-tər-,nak\ Boris Leonidovich 1890–1960 Russian author; Nobel prize winner (1958)

**Pas·teur** \pas-'tər\ Louis 1822–1895 French chemist and microbiologist

**Pat·rick** \'pa-trik\ Saint 5th century A.D. bishop and patron saint of Ireland

**Pa·tro·clus** \pə-'trō-kləs, -'träk-ləs\ warrior in Greek mythology who is slain during the Trojan War by Hector and avenged by his friend Achilles

**Pat·ton** \'pat-n\ George Smith 1885–1945 American general

**Paul** \'pȯl\ Saint *died between* 62 *and* 68 A.D. *apostle to the Gentiles* Christian missionary and author of several New Testament epistles — **Paul·ine** \'pȯ-[?]\ *adj*

[?] name of 6 popes: especially **III** 1468–1549 [?]534–49); **V** 1552–1621 (pope 1605–21); **VI** [?] *Battista Montini*) 1897–1978 (pope 1963–

[?]n \'pȯl-'bən-yən\ giant lumberjack in [?]

[?] Linus Carl 1901–1994 American [?]nner (1954, 1962)

[?]-lóv\ Ivan Petrovich 1849– [?]; Nobel prize winner

[?]ə\ Anna 1882–1931

[?] 1920 American

[?] Greek my-

[?]ho in

[?]his

**Per·ry** \'per-ē\ Matthew Calbraith 1794–1858 American commodore

**Perry** Oliver Hazard 1785–1819 American naval officer; brother of Matthew Perry

**Per·seph·o·ne** \pər-'sef-ə-nē\ daughter of Zeus and Demeter who in Greek mythology is abducted by Pluto and made his wife and queen

**Per·seus** \'pər-,süs, -sē-əs\ a son of Zeus and Danaë and slayer of Medusa in Greek mythology

**Per·shing** \'pər-shing, -zhing\ John Joseph 1860–1948 American general

**Pé·tain** \pā-'ta^n\ Philippe 1856–1951 French general; marshal of France; premier of Vichy France (1940–44)

**Pe·ter** \'pēt-ər\ Saint *died about* 64 A.D. *Si·mon Peter* \'sī-mən-\ one of the 12 apostles in the Bible

**Peter I** 1672–1725 *the Great* czar of Russia (1682–1725)

**Peter the Hermit** *about* 1050–1115 French preacher of the 1st Crusade

**Pe·trarch** \'pē-,trärk, 'pe-\ 1304–1374 Italian *Francesco Pe·trar·ca* \pā-'trär-kə\ Italian poet — **Pe·trarch·an** \pē-'trär-kən, pe-\ *adj*

**Phae·dra** \'fē-drə\ wife of Theseus in Greek mythology who falls in love with her stepson Hippolytus

**Pha·ë·thon** \'fā-ət-n; 'fā-ə-tən, -,thän\ youth in Greek mythology who is allowed by his father Helios to drive the sun-chariot across the sky but loses control and is struck down with a thunderbolt by Zeus

**Phid·i·as** \'fid-ē-əs\ *flourished about* 490–430 B.C. Greek sculptor

**Phil·ip** \'fil-əp\ one of the 12 apostles in the Bible

**Philip** 1639?–1676 *Metacomet* American Indian chief

**Philip** name of 6 kings of France: especially **II** *or* **Philip Augustus** 1165–1223 (reigned 1179–1223); **IV** 1268–1314 (reigned 1285–1314) *the Fair*; **VI** 1293–1350 (reigned 1328–50)

**Philip** name of 5 kings of Spain: especially **II** 1527–1598 (reigned 1556–98); **V** 1683–1746 (reigned 1700–24; 1724–46)

**Philip II** 382–336 B.C. king of Macedon (359–336); father of Alexander the Great

**Philip** Prince 1921–    consort of Elizabeth II of Great Britain; 3d Duke of *Edinburgh*

**Phoebe** — see ARTEMIS

**Phoebus** — see APOLLO

**Pi·cas·so** \pi-'käs-ō, -'kas-\ Pablo 1881–1973 Spanish painter and sculptor in France

**Pick·ett** \'pik-ət\ George Edward 1825–1875 American Confederate general

**Pierce** \'piərs\ Franklin 1804–1869 14th president of the United States (1853–57)

**Pilate** — see PONTIUS PILATE

**Pin·dar** \'pin-dər, -,där\ *about* 522–438 B.C. Greek poet

**Pi·ran·del·lo** \,pir-ən-'del-ō\ Luigi 1867–1936 Italian author; Nobel prize winner (1934)

**Pi·sis·tra·tus** *or* **Pei·sis·tra·tus** \pī-'sis-trət-əs, pə-\ *died* 527 B.C. tyrant of Athens

**Pitt** \'pit\ William 1708–1778 Earl of Chatham; British statesman

**Pitt** William 1759–1806 British prime minister (1783–1801; 1804–06); son of the preceding

**Pi·us** \'pī-əs\ name of 12 popes: especially **VII** 1742–1823 (pope 1800–23); **IX** 1792–1878 (pope 1846–78); **X** 1835–1914 (pope 1903–14); **XI** 1857–1939 (pope 1922–39); **XII** 1876–1958 (pope 1939–58)

**Pi·zar·ro** \pə-'zär-ō\ Francisco *about* 1475–1541 Spanish conqueror of Peru

**Planck** \'plängk\ Max Karl Ernst Ludwig 1858–1947 German physicist; Nobel prize winner (1918)

**Pla·to** \'plāt-ō\ *about* 428–348 (or 347) B.C. Greek philosopher

**Plau·tus** \'plȯt-əs\ Titus Maccius *about* 254–184 B.C. Roman dramatist

**Pliny** \'plin-ē\ 23–79 A.D. *the Elder* Roman scholar

**Pliny** 61 (or 62)–*about* 113 A.D. *the Younger* Roman author; nephew of the preceding

**Plu·tarch** \'plü-,tärk\ *about* 46–*after* 119 A.D. Greek biographer

**Plu·to** \'plüt-ō\ god of the dead and the underworld in Greek mythology — compare DIS

**Po·ca·hon·tas** \,pō-kə-'hänt-əs\ *about* 1595–1617 American Indian friend to the colonists at Jamestown; daughter of Powhatan

**Poe** \'pō\ Edgar Allan 1809–1849 American author

**Polk** \'pōk\ James Knox 1795–1849 11th president of the United States (1845–49)

**Pol·lux** \'päl-əks\ immortal twin of Castor in classical mythology

**Po·lo** \'pō-lō\ Mar·co \'mär-kō\ 1254–1324 Venetian traveler

**Pol·y·hym·nia** \,päl-i-'him-nē-ə\ Muse of sacred song and later of learning in Greek mythology

**Poly·phe·mus** \,päl-ə-'fē-məs\ Cyclops in Greek mythology whom Odysseus blinds in order to escape from his cave

**Pom·pa·dour** \'päm-pə-,dōr, -,dȯr, -,dùr\ Madame de 1721–1764 mistress of Louis XV of France

**Pom·pey** \'päm-pē\ 106–48 B.C. *the Great* Roman general and statesman

**Ponce de Le·ón** \,päns-də-'lē-ən, ,pän-sə-,dā-lē-'ōn\ Juan 1460–1521 Spanish explorer

**Pon·ti·ac** \'pänt-ē-,ak\ *about* 1720–1769 Ottawa Indian chief

**Pon·tius Pi·late** \,pän-chəs-'pī-lət, ,pän-\ *died after* 36 A.D. Roman procurator of Judea (26–*about* 36)

**Pope** \'pōp\ Alexander 1688–1744 English poet

**Por·ter** \'pōrt-ər, 'pȯrt-\ Cole Albert 1891–1964 American composer and songwriter

**Porter** David Dixon 1813–1891 American admiral

**Porter** Katherine Anne 1890–1980 American author

**Porter** William Sydney 1862–1910 pseudonym *O. Hen·ry* \ō-'hen-rē, 'ō-\ American author

**Po·sei·don** \pə-'sīd-n\ god of the sea in Greek mythology — compare NEPTUNE

**Pot·ter** \'pät-ər\ Beatrix 1866–1943 British author and illustrator

**Pound** \'paùnd\ Ezra Loomis 1885–1972 American poet

**Pound·mak·er** \'paùnd-,mā-kər\ 1826–1886 Cree Indian chief

**Pow·ell** \'paù-əl\ Adam Clayton 1908–1972 American clergyman and politician

**Powell** Colin Luther 1937–    American general; United States secretary of state (2001–   )

**Pow·ha·tan** \,paù-ə-'tan, paùl-'hat-n\ 1550?–1618 chief of a confederacy of Algonquian-speaking Indians and father of Pocahontas

**Prax·it·e·les** \prak-'sit-l-,ēz\ *flourished* 370–330 B.C. Athenian sculptor

**Pri·am** \'prī-əm, -,am\ king of Troy during the Trojan War and father of Hector and Paris in Greek mythology

**Price** \'prīs\ (Mary) Leontyne 1927–    American soprano

**Priest·ley** \'prēst-lē\ Joseph 1733–1804 English clergyman and chemist

**Pro·crus·tes** \prə-'krəs-tēz, pə-, prō-\ robber in Greek mythology who forces travelers to fit one of two unequally long beds by stretching their bodies or cutting off their legs

**Pro·kof·iev** \prə-'kȯf-yəf, -,yef, -,yev\ Sergey Sergeyevich 1891–1953 Russian composer

**Pro·me·theus** \prə-'mē-thyüs, -thüs, -thē-əs\ Titan in Greek mythology whom Zeus tortures for giving fire to humans

**Pro·tag·o·ras** \prō-'tag-ə-rəs\ *about* 485–410 B.C. Greek philosopher and teacher

**Pro·teus** \'prō-,tyüs, -,tüs; 'prōt-ē-əs\ sea god in Greek mythology capable of assuming different forms

**Proust** \'prüst\ Marcel 1871–1922 French novelist

**Psy·che** \'sī-kē\ beautiful princess in classical mythology loved by Cupid

**Ptol·e·my** \'täl-ə-mē\ name of 15 kings of Egypt 323–30 B.C.

**Ptolemy** 2d century A.D. Alexandrian astronomer, geographer, and mathematician

**Puc·ci·ni** \pü-'chē-nē\ Giacomo 1858–1924 Italian composer

**Puck** — see ROBIN GOODFELLOW

**Pu·las·ki** \pə-'las-kē, pyü-\ Kazimierz 1747–1779 Polish soldier in American Revolution

**Pu·lit·zer** \'pùl-ət-sər, 'pyü-lət-sər\ Joseph 1847–1911 American (Hungarian-born) journalist

**Push·kin** \'push-kən\ Aleksandr Sergeyevich 1799–1837 Russian author

**Pyg·ma·lion** \pig-'māl-yən, -'mā-lē-ən\ sculptor in Greek mythology who creates Galatea

**Pyr·a·mus** \'pir-ə-məs\ legendary Babylonian youth who dies for the love of Thisbe

**Py·thag·o·ras** \pə-'thag-ə-rəs, pī-\ *about* 580–*about* 500 B.C. Greek philosopher and mathematician

**Pyth·i·as** \'pith-ē-əs\ condemned Sicilian in Greek legend whose life is spared when his devoted friend Damon offers to take his place

**Quayle** \'kwāl\ James Danforth 1947–    vice president of the United States (1989–93)

**Quin·til·ian** \kwin-'til-yən\ *about* 35–*about* 100 A.D. Roman rhetorician

[pronunciation key, partially obscured:]
\ə\ ash  \ā\ ace  \a\ ...  \e\ bet  \ē\ easy  \i\ ...  \n\ sing  \ō\ go  \ù\ foot  \ü\ loot  ...the Guide to Pronunciation

**Ra** \'rä, 'rȯ\ god of the sun and chief deity of ancient Egypt

**Ra·be·lais** \'rab-ə-ˌlā, ˌrab-ə-'lā\ François *about* 1483–1553 French author

**Ra·bin** \rä-'bēn\ Yitzhak 1922–1995 prime minister of Israel (1974–77; 92–95)

**Ra·chel** \'rā-chəl\ one of the wives of Jacob in the Bible

**Rach·ma·ni·noff** \räk-'män-ə-ˌnȯf, rak-'man-, -ˌnȯv\ Sergey Vasilyevich 1873–1943 Russian composer, pianist, and conductor

**Ra·cine** \ra-'sēn, rə-\ Jean-Baptiste 1639–1699 French dramatist

**Ra·leigh** *or* **Ra·legh** \'rȯl-ē, 'räl- *also* 'ral-\ Sir Walter 1554–1618 English navigator, courtier, and historian

**Ra·ma** \'räm-ə\ deity or deified hero of later Hinduism worshiped as an incarnation of Vishnu

**Ram·say** \'ram-zē\ Sir William 1852–1916 British chemist; Nobel prize winner (1904)

**Ram·ses** \'ram-ˌsēz\ *or* **Ram·e·ses** \'ram-ə-ˌsēz\ name of 11 kings of Egypt: especially **II** (reigned 1304–1237 B.C.); **III** (reigned 1198–1166 B.C.)

**Ran·dolph** \'ran-ˌdȯlf\ Asa Philip 1889–1979 American labor leader

**Ra·pha·el** \'raf-ē-əl, 'rā-fē-\ one of the four archangels named in Hebrew tradition — compare GABRIEL, MICHAEL, URIEL

**Ra·pha·el** \'raf-ē-əl, 'rā-fē-, 'räf-ē-\ 1483–1520 Italian painter

**Ras·pu·tin** \ra-'spyüt-n, -'spüt-, -'spu̇t-\ Grigory Yefimovich 1872–1916 Russian monk

**Ra·vel** \'ra-vel, ra-\ Mau·rice \mȯ-'rēs\ Joseph 1875–1937 French composer

**Rea·gan** \'rā-gən, 'rē-\ Ronald Wilson 1911–    40th president of the United States (1981–89)

**Re·bek·ah** *or* **Re·bec·ca** \ri-'bek-ə\ wife of Isaac in the Bible

**Red Cloud** \'red-ˌklau̇d\ 1822–1909 Sioux Indian chief

**Red Jack·et** \'red-ˌjak-ət\ 1756?–1830 *Sagoyewatha* Seneca Indian chief

**Reed** \'rēd\ Walter 1851–1902 American army surgeon

**Rehn·quist** \'ren-ˌkwist\ William Hubbs 1924–  Am. jurist; chief justice United States Supreme Court (1986–  )

**Re·marque** \rə-'märk\ Erich Maria 1898–1970 American (German-born) author

**Rem·brandt van Rijn** *or* **Ryn** \'rem-ˌbrant-vän-'rīn\ 1606–1669 Dutch painter

**Re·mus** \'rē-məs\ legendary founder of Rome slain by his twin brother Romulus

**Re·noir** \ren-'wär, 'ren-ˌwär\ Pierre-Auguste 1841–1919 French painter

**Re·vere** \ri-'viər\ Paul 1735–1818 American patriot and silversmith

**Reyn·olds** \'ren-ldz, -lz\ Sir Joshua 1723–1792 English painter

**Rhodes** \'rōdz\ Cecil John 1853–1902 British administrator and financier in South Africa

**Rich·ard** \'rich-ərd\ name of 3 kings of England: **I** 1157–1199 (reigned 1189–99) *the Lion-Hearted;* **II** 1367–1400 (reigned 1377–99); **III** 1452–1485 (reigned 1483–85)

**Rich·ard·son** \'rich-ərd-sən\ Samuel 1689–1761 English author

**Ri·che·lieu** \'rish-əl-ˌü, -ˌyü; rē-shə-'lyœ̄\ Duc de 1585–1642 French cardinal and statesman

**Ride** \'rīd\ Sally Kristen 1951–    American astronaut

**Rim·sky-Kor·sa·kov** \rim-skē-'kȯr-sə-ˌkȯf, -ˌkȯv, -ˌkȯr-sə-\ Nikolay Andreyevich 1844–1908 Russian composer

**Ri·ve·ra** \ri-'ver-ə\ Diego 1886–1957 Mexican painter

**Rob·ert I** \'räb-ərt\ 1274–1329 *the Bruce* \'brüs\ king of Scotland (1306–29)

**Robe·son** \'rōb-sən\ Paul Bustill 1898–1976 American actor and singer

**Robes·pierre** \'rōbz-ˌpiər, -ˌpyeər; ˌrō-bes-'pyeər\ Maximilien-François-Marie-Isidore de 1758–1794 French revolutionary

**Rob·in Good·fel·low** \ˌräb-ən-'gu̇d-ˌfel-ō\ *or* **Puck** \'pək\ mischievous sprite in English folklore

**Rob·in Hood** \ˌräb-ən-'hu̇d\ legendary English outlaw noted for his skill in archery and for his robbing the rich to help the poor

**Rob·in·son** \'räb-ən-sən\ Edwin Arlington 1869–1935 American poet

**Robinson** John Roosevelt 1919–1972 *Jackie* American baseball player

**Ro·cham·beau** \ˌrō-sham-'bō\ Comte de 1725–1807 French general in American Revolution

**Rocke·fel·ler** \'räk-i-ˌfel-ər, 'räk-ˌfel-\ John Davison father 1839–1937 and son 1874–1960 American oil magnates and philanthropists

**Ro·din** \rō-ˌdan, -, -ˌdaⁿn\ (François-) Auguste(-René) 1840–1917 French sculptor

**Ro·land** \'rō-lənd\ stalwart defender of the Christians against the Saracens in the Charlemagne legends

**Röl·vaag** \'rȯl-ˌväg\ Ole \'ō-la\ Ed·vart \'ed-ˌvärt\ 1876–1931 American (Norwegian-born) educator and author

**Ro·ma·nov** *or* **Ro·ma·noff** \rō-'män-əf, 'rō-mə-ˌnäf\ Michael 1596–1645 1st czar of Russia (1613–45)

**Rom·mel** \'räm-əl\ Erwin 1891–1944 German field marshal

**Rom·u·lus** \'räm-yə-ləs\ legendary founder of Rome who slew his twin brother Remus

**Rönt·gen** *or* **Roent·gen** \'rent-gən, 'rənt-, -jən\ Wilhelm Conrad 1845–1923 German physicist; Nobel prize winner (1901)

**Roo·se·velt** \'rō-zə-vəlt *(Roosevelts' usual pronunciation),* -ˌvelt *also* \'rü-\ (Anna) Eleanor 1884–1962 American humanitarian and writer; wife of Franklin Delano Roosevelt

**Roosevelt** Franklin Del·a·no \'del-ə-ˌnō\ 1882–1945 32d president of the United States (1933–45)

**Roosevelt** Theodore 1858–1919 26th president of the United States (1901–09); Nobel prize winner (1906)

**Root** \'rüt, 'ru̇t\ Elihu 1845–1937 American lawyer and statesman; Nobel prize winner (1912)

**Ross** \'rȯs\ Betsy 1752–1836 reputed maker of first American flag

**Ros·set·ti** \rō-'zet-ē, -'set-\ Christina Georgina 1830–1894 English poet; sister of Dante Gabriel Rossetti

**Rossetti** Dante Gabriel 1828–1882 English painter and poet

**Ros·si·ni** \rȯ-'sē-nē, rə-\ Gioacchino Antonio 1792–1868 Italian composer

**Ros·tand** \rȯ-'stäⁿ, 'räs-ˌtand\ Edmond 1868–1918 French author

**Roth·schild** \'rōths-ˌchīld, 'rȯth-, 'rȯs-; *German* 'rōt-ˌshilt\ Mayer Amschel 1744–1812 German financier

**Rothschild** Nathan Mayer 1777–1836 financier in London; son of the preceding

**Rous·seau** \rü-'sō, 'rü-\ Jean-Jacques 1712–1778 French (Swiss-born) philosopher and author

**Ru·bens** \'rü-bənz\ Peter Paul 1577–1640 Flemish painter

**Ru·bin·stein** \'rü-bən-ˌstīn\ An·ton \ˌän-'tȯn\ 1829–1894 Russian pianist and composer

**Ru·dolph** \'rü-ˌdȯlf\ Wilma Glodean 1940–1994 American athlete

**Rumford** Count — see THOMPSON

**Ru·pert** \'rü-pərt\ Prince 1619–1682 English (German-born) royalist general and admiral

**Rus·kin** \'rəs-kən\ John 1819–1900 English art critic

**Rus·sell** \'rəs-əl\ Bertrand Arthur William 3d Earl 1872–1970 English mathematician and philosopher; Nobel prize winner (1950)

**Ruth** \'rüth\ Moabite woman in the Bible who is an ancestor of King David

**Ruth** George Herman 1895–1948 *Babe Ruth* or *the Babe* American baseball player

**Ruth·er·ford** \'rəth-ər-fərd, 'rəth-ə-, 'rəth-\ Ernest 1871–1937 British physicist; Nobel prize winner (1908)

**Sā·dāt** \sə-'dat, -'dät\ Anwar el- 1918–1981 president of Egypt (1970–81); Nobel prize winner (1978)

**Saint–Gau·dens** \sānt-'gȯd-nz, sənt-\ Augustus 1848–1907 American (Irish-born) sculptor

**Saint–Saëns** \saⁿ-'säⁿs\ (Charles-) Camille 1835–1921 French composer

**Sal·a·din** \'sal-əd-ən, ˌsal-ə-'dēn\ 1137 (or 1138)–1193 sultan of Egypt and Syria

**Sal·in·ger** \'sal-ən-jər\ Jerome David 1919–  American author

**Salk** \'sȯk, 'sȯlk\ Jonas Edward 1914–1995 American physician

**Sa·lo·me** \sə-'lō-mē\ niece of Herod Antipas who in the Bible is given the head of John the Baptist as a reward for her dancing

**Sa·mo·set** \'sam-ə-ˌset, sə-'mäs-ət\ *died about* 1653 American Indian leader and friend of the Pilgrims

**Sam·son** \'sam-sən, 'samp-\ brawny, long-haired Hebrew hero in the Bible who wreaks havoc among the Philistines

**Sam·u·el** \'sam-yəl, -yə-wəl\ Hebrew judge in the Bible who anoints Saul and then David king

**Sand** \'sand, 'sä⁼d, 'sä⁼nd, 'sä⁼\ George 1804–1876 pseudonym of *Amandine-Aurore-Lucie Dudevant* French author

**Sand·burg** \'sand-ˌbərg, 'san-\ Carl 1878–1967 American author

**Sang·er** \'sang-ər\ Margaret 1883–1966 née *Higgins* American birth-control leader

**San·ta Claus** \'sant-ə-ˌklȯz, -ˌklȯs\ *or* **Kriss Krin·gle** \'kris-ˌkring-gəl\ a fat jolly old man of modern folklore who sports a white beard and a red suit and who delivers presents to good children at Christmastime

**Sap·pho** \'saf-ō\ *flourished about* 610–*about* 580 B.C. Greek poet

**Sa·rah** \'ser-ə, 'sar-ə, 'sä-rə\ wife of Abraham and mother of Isaac in the Bible

**Sar·gent** \'sär-jənt\ John Singer 1856–1925 American painter

**Sar·tre** \'särtr\ Jean-Paul 1905–1980 French philosopher and author

**Sat·urn** \'sat-ərn\ a god of agriculture in Roman mythology

**Saul** \'sȯl\ 1st king of Israel in the Bible

**Saul** *or* **Saul of Tarsus** the apostle Paul

**Sa·vo·na·ro·la** \ˌsav-ə-nə-'rō-lə, sə-ˌvän-ə-'rō-\ Girolamo \ji-'rȯl-ə-ˌmō\ 1452–1498 Italian friar and reformer

**Scar·lat·ti** \skär-'lät-ē\ (Pietro) Alessandro 1660–1725 and his son (Giuseppe) Domenico 1685–1757 Italian composers

**Sche·he·ra·zade** \shə-ˌher-ə-'zäd, -'zäd-ə, -'zäd-ē\ fictional wife of the sultan of India and narrator of the tales in the *Arabian Nights' Entertainments*

**Schil·ler** \'shil-ər\ (Johann Christoph) Friedrich von 1759–1805 German author

**Schin·dler** \'shind-lər\ Oskar 1908–1974 German hero of the Holocaust

**Scho·pen·hau·er** \'shō-pən-ˌhau̇-ər, -ˌhau̇r\ Arthur 1788–1860 German philosopher

**Schu·bert** \'shü-bərt, -ˌbert\ Franz Peter 1797–1828 Austrian composer

**Schu·mann** \'shü-ˌmän, -mən\ Robert 1810–1856 German composer

**Schweit·zer** \'shwīt-sər, 'swīt-, 'shvīt-\ Albert 1875–1965 French Protestant clergyman, philosopher, physician, and music scholar; Nobel prize winner (1952)

**Scip·io** \'sip-ē-ˌō, 'skip-\ **Aemilianus Af·ri·ca·nus** \ˌaf-rə-'kan-əs\ **Numantinus** Publius Cornelius 185 (or 184)–129 B.C. *Scipio the Younger* Roman general

**Scipio Africanus** Publius Cornelius 236–184 (or 183) B.C. *Scipio the Elder* Roman general

**Scott** \'skät\ Dred \'dred\ 1795?–1858 American slave

**Scott** Sir Walter 1771–1832 Scottish author

**Scott** Winfield 1786–1866 American general

**Se·at·tle** *or* **Se·atlh** \sē-'at-l\ 1786?–1866 American Indian chief

**Se·le·ne** \sə-'lē-nē, -nə\ goddess of the moon in Greek mythology

**Se·leu·cus I Ni·ca·tor** \sə-'lü-kəs-nī-'kät-ər\ 358 (to 354)–281 B.C. ruler (306–281) of a Greek dynasty in Syria

**Sen·e·ca** \'sen-i-kə\ Lucius Annaeus 4 B.C.?–65 A.D. Roman philosopher, statesman, and dramatist

**Sen·nach·er·ib** \sə-'nak-ə-rəb\ *died* 681 B.C. king of Assyria (704–681)

**Se·quoya** \si-'kwȯi-ə\ *about* 1760–1843 Cherokee Indian scholar

**Se·ton** \'sēt-n\ Saint Elizabeth Ann Bayley 1774–1821 *Mother Seton* American religious leader

**Sew·ard** \'sü-ərd, 'sü̇-ərd, 'su̇rd\ William Henry 1801–1872 American statesman; secretary of state (1861–69)

**Shake·speare** \'shāk-ˌspiər\ William 1564–1616 English dramatist and poet

**Shaw** \'shȯ\ George Bernard 1856–1950 British author

**Shaw** Robert Gould 1837–1863 American soldier

**Shel·ley** \'shel-ē\ Mary Woll·stone·craft \'wu̇l-stən-ˌkraft\ 1797–1851 English novelist; wife of Percy Bysshe Shelley

**Shelley** Percy Bysshe \\'bish\\ 1792–1822 English poet

**Shem** \\'shem\\ eldest son of Noah and ancestor of the Semitic peoples in biblical tradition

**Shep·ard** \\'shep-ərd\\ Alan Bartlett 1923–1998 American astronaut; 1st American in space (1961)

**Sher·i·dan** \\'sher-əd-n\\ Philip Henry 1831–1888 American general

**Sheridan** Richard Brins·ley \\'brinz-lē\\ 1751–1816 Irish dramatist

**Sher·man** \\'shər-mən\\ John 1823–1900 American statesman; brother of William Tecumseh Sherman

**Sherman** William Tecumseh 1820–1891 American general

**Shiva** — see SIVA

**Si·be·lius** \\sə-'bāl-yəs, -'bā-lē-əs\\ Jean 1865–1957 Finnish composer

**Sid·ney** \\'sid-nē\\ Sir Philip 1554–1586 English poet

**Sieg·fried** \\'sig-,frēd, 'sēg-\\ or **Sig·urd** \\'sig-ûrd, -ərd\\ hero in Germanic legend noted for slaying a dragon guarding a gold hoard

**Si·kor·sky** \\sə-'kȯr-skē\\ Igor Ivan 1889–1972 American (Russian-born) aeronautical engineer

**Si·mon** \\'sī-mən\\ — see PETER

**Simon** or **Simon the Zealot** one of the 12 apostles in the Bible

**Sind·bad the Sailor** \\'sin-,bad\\ citizen of Baghdad whose adventures are narrated in the *Arabian Nights' Entertainments*

**Sis·y·phus** \\'sis-i-fəs\\ king of Corinth in Greek mythology condemned to roll a heavy stone up a hill in Hades only to have it roll down again as it nears the top — **Sis·y·phe·an** \\,sis-i-'fē-ən\\ *adj*

**Sit·ting Bull** \\,sit-ing-'bûl\\ *about* 1831–1890 Sioux Indian leader

**Si·va** \\'shiv-ə, 'siv-; 'shē-və, 'sē-\\ or **Shi·va** \\'shiv-ə, 'shē-və\\ god of destruction in the Hindu sacred triad — compare BRAHMA, VISHNU — **Si·va·ism** \\-,iz-əm\\ *n*

**Smith** \\'smith\\ Adam 1723–1790 Scottish economist

**Smith** Bessie 1894 (or 1898)–1937 American blues singer

**Smith** John *about* 1580–1631 English colonist in America

**Smith** Joseph 1805–1844 American founder of the Mormon Church

**Smol·lett** \\'smäl-ət\\ Tobias George 1721–1771 British author

**Soc·ra·tes** \\'säk-rə-,tēz\\ *about* 470–399 B.C. Greek philosopher

**Sol** \\'säl\\ god of the sun in Roman mythology — compare HELIOS

**Sol·o·mon** \\'säl-ə-mən\\ son of David and 10th-century B.C. king of Israel noted for his wisdom

**Soph·o·cles** \\'säf-ə-,klēz\\ *about* 496–406 B.C. Greek dramatist

**Sou·sa** \\'sü-zə, 'sü-sə\\ John Philip 1854–1932 American bandmaster and composer

**Sou·they** \\saü-thē, 'səth-ē\\ Robert 1774–1843 English author

**Spaatz** \\'späts\\ Carl 1891–1974 American general

**Spar·ta·cus** \\'spärt-ə-kəs\\ *died* 71 B.C. Roman gladiator from Thrace and leader of a slave rebellion

**Spen·ser** \\'spen-sər\\ Edmund 1552–1599 English poet

**Spiel·berg** \\'spēl-bərg\\ Steven 1947– American filmmaker

**Spi·no·za** \\spin-'ō-zə\\ Baruch 1632–1677 Dutch philosopher of Portuguese-Jewish ancestry

**Squan·to** \\'skwän-tō, 'skwȯn-\\ *died* 1622 American Indian friend of the Pilgrims

**Sta·lin** \\'stäl-ən, 'stal-, -,ēn\\ Joseph 1879–1953 *Iosif Vissarionovich Dzhu·gash·vi·li* \\jü-gəsh-'vē-lē\\ Soviet leader

**Stan·dish** \\'stan-dish\\ Myles or Miles 1584?–1656 English colonist in America

**Stan·ley** \\'stan-lē\\ Sir Henry Morton 1841–1904 British explorer

**Stan·ton** \\'stant-n\\ Elizabeth Cady 1815–1902 American suffragist

**Steele** \\'stēl\\ Sir Richard 1672–1729 English author

**Stein** \\'stīn\\ Gertrude 1874–1946 American author

**Stein·beck** \\'stīn-,bek\\ John Ernst 1902–1968 American author; Nobel prize winner (1962)

**Stein·metz** \\'stīn-,mets, 'shtīn-\\ Charles Proteus 1865–1923 American (German-born) electrical engineer and inventor

**Sten·dhal** \\sten-'däl, stan-, *French* staⁿ-'däl\\ 1783–1842 pseudonym of *Marie-Henri Beyle* \\'bel\\ French author

**Ste·phen** \\'stē-vən\\ Saint *died about* 36 A.D. Christian martyr

**Stephen** *about* 1097–1154 *Stephen of Blois* king of England (1135–54)

**Sterne** \\'stərn\\ Laurence 1713–1768 English (Irish-born) author

**Steu·ben** \\'stü-bən, 'styü-, 'shtȯi-\\ Baron Friedrich Wilhelm von 1730–1794 Prussian-born general in American Revolutionary army

**Ste·ven·son** \\'stē-vən-sən\\ Adlai Ewing 1900–1965 American statesman

**Stevenson** Robert Louis Balfour 1850–1894 Scottish author

**Sto·ker** \\'stō-kər\\ Abraham 1847–1912 *Bram* Irish author

**Stowe** \\'stō\\ Harriet Elizabeth 1811–1896 née *Beecher* American author

**Stra·di·va·ri** \\,strad-ə-'vär-ē, -'var-, -'ver-\\ Antonio 1644–1737 *Antonius Strad·i·var·i·us* \\,strad-ə-'var-ē-əs, -'ver-\\ Italian violin maker

**Strauss** \\'straüs, 'shtraüs\\ Johann father 1804–1849 and his sons Johann 1825–1899 and Josef 1827–1870 Austrian composers

**Strauss** Ri·chard \\'rik-,ärt, 'rik-\\ 1864–1949 German composer

**Stra·vin·sky** \\strə-'vin-skē\\ Igor \\'ē-,gȯr\\ Fyodorovich 1882–1971 American (Russian-born) composer

**Stu·art** \\'stü-ərt, 'styü-, 'styü-, 'styürt\\ — see CHARLES I (Great Britain); MARY STUART

**Stuart** Charles — see CHARLES EDWARD

**Stuart** Gilbert Charles 1755–1828 American painter

**Stuart** James Ewell Brown 1833–1864 *Jeb Stuart* American Confederate general

**Stuy·ve·sant** \\'stī-və-sənt\\ Peter *about* 1610–1672 Dutch colonial administrator in America

**Sue·to·ni·us** \\swē-'tō-nē-əs, sü-ə-'tō-\\ *about* 69–*after* 122 A.D. Roman biographer and historian

**Sü·ley·man** or **Su·lei·man I** \\'sü-lā-,män, -li-\\ 1494 (or 1495)–1566 *the Magnificent* Ottoman sultan (1520–66)

**Sul·la** \\'səl-ə\\ 138–78 B.C. Roman general and statesman

**Sul·li·van** \\'səl-ə-vən\\ Sir Arthur Seymour 1842–1900 English composer and collaborator with Sir William S. Gilbert

**Sullivan** Louis Henri 1856–1924 American architect

**Sum·ner** \\'səm-nər\\ Charles 1811–1874 American statesman

**Sun Yat–sen** \\'sûn-'yät-'sen\\ 1866–1925 Chinese statesman

**Swift** \\'swift\\ Jonathan 1667–1745 English (Irish-born) author

**Swin·burne** \\'swin-,bərn, -bərn\\ Algernon Charles 1837–1909 English poet

**Tac·i·tus** \\'tas-ət-əs\\ Cornelius *about* 56–*about* 120 A.D. Roman historian

**Taft** \\'taft\\ William Howard 1857–1930 27th president of the United States (1909–13); chief justice of the United States Supreme Court (1921–30)

**Tall·chief** \\'tȯl-,chēf\\ Maria 1925– American dancer

**Tal·ley·rand–Pé·ri·gord** \\'tal-ē-,rand-,per-ə-'gȯr, -,ran-, *French* tàl-e-'räⁿ, tàl-'räⁿ\\ Charles-Maurice de 1754–1838 French statesman

**Tam·er·lane** \\'tam-ər-,lān\\ or **Tam·bur·laine** \\'tam-bər-,lān\\ 1336–1405 *Timur Lenk* Turkic conqueror

**Tan** \\'tan\\ Amy 1952– American author

**Tan·cred** \\'tan-krəd\\ 1078?–1112 Norman crusader

**Ta·ney** \\'tȯ-nē\\ Roger Brooke 1777–1864 American jurist; chief justice of the United States Supreme Court (1836–64)

**Tan·ta·lus** \\'tant-l-əs\\ king in Greek mythology condemned to stand up to his chin in a pool of water in Hades and beneath fruit-laden boughs only to have the water or fruit recede at each attempt to eat or drink

**Tay·lor** \\'tā-lər\\ Zachary 1784–1850 American general; 12th president of the United States (1849–50)

**Tchai·kov·sky** \\chī-'kȯf-skē, chə-, -'kȯv-\\ Pyotr Ilich 1840–1893 Russian composer

**Te·cum·seh** \\tə-'kəm-sə, -'kəmp-, -sē\\ or **Te·cum·tha** \\tə-'kəm-thə\\ or **Ti·kam·the** \\ti-'käm-thə\\ 1768–1813 Shawnee Indian chief

**Tek·a·kwitha** \\,tek-ə-'kwith-ə\\ or **Teg·a·kwitha** \\,teg-\\ or **Teg·a·kouita** \\,teg-ə-'kwit-ə\\ Ka·teri \\'kät-ə-rē\\ 1656–1680 *Lily of the Mohawks* beatified Mohawk Indian religious

**Te·lem·a·chus** \\tə-'lem-ə-kəs\\ son of Odysseus and Penelope who aids his father in the slaying of his mother's suitors

**Ten·ny·son** \\'ten-ə-sən\\ Alfred 1809–1892 1st Baron *Tennyson* known as *Alfred, Lord Tennyson* English poet

**Ter·ence** \\'ter-əns\\ 186 (or 185)–?159 B.C. Roman dramatist

**Te·re·sa** \\tə-'rē-sə, -'rā-\\ Mother 1910–1997 Albanian religious in India; Nobel prize winner (1979)

**Terp·sich·o·re** \\,tərp-'sik-ə-rē\\ Muse of dancing and choral song in Greek mythology

**Thack·er·ay** \\'thak-rē, -ə-rē\\ William Makepeace 1811–1863 English author

**Tha·les** \\'thā-,lēz\\ 625?–?547 B.C. Greek philosopher

**Tha·lia** \\thə-'lī-ə\\ Muse of comedy and pastoral poetry in Greek mythology

**Thatch·er** \\'thach-ər\\ Margaret Hilda 1925– née *Roberts* British prime minister (1979–90)

**The·mis·to·cles** \\thə-'mis-tə-,klēz\\ *about* 524–*about* 460 B.C. Athenian general and statesman

**The·oc·ri·tus** \\thē-'äk-rət-əs\\ *about* 310–250 B.C. Greek poet

**The·od·o·ric** \\thē-'äd-ə-rik\\ 454?–526 A.D. *the Great* king of the Ostrogoths (493–526)

**The·o·do·sius I** \\,thē-ə-'dō-shəs, -shē-əs\\ 347–395 A.D. *the Great* Roman general and emperor (379–395)

**The·re·sa** or **Te·re·sa of Avi·la** \\tə-'rē-sə, -'rā-sə, -'rä-zə . . . -'äv-ē-,lä\\ Saint 1515–1582 Spanish Carmelite nun and mystic

**The·seus** \\'thē-,süs, -sē-əs\\ hero in Greek mythology who slays Procrustes and the Minotaur and conquers the Amazons

**Thes·pis** \\'thes-pəs\\ 6th century B.C. Greek poet

**The·tis** \\'thēt-əs\\ sea goddess and mother of Achilles in Greek mythology

**This·be** \\'thiz-bē\\ legendary Babylonian maiden who dies for the love of Pyramus

**Thom·as** \\'täm-əs\\ apostle in the Bible who demands proof of Christ's resurrection

**Thomas** Clarence 1948– American jurist

**Thomas** Dyl·an \\'dil-ən\\ 1914–1953 British poet

**Thomas à Becket** — see BECKET

**Thomas a Kem·pis** \\ə-'kem-pəs, ä-'kem-\\ 1379 (or 1380)–1471 Dutch ecclesiastic and author

**Thomp·son** \\'täm-sən, 'tämp-\\ Benjamin 1753–1814 Count *Rum·ford* \\'rəm-fərd, 'rəmp-\\ British (American-born) physicist and statesman

**Thor** \\'thȯr\\ god of thunder, weather, and crops in Norse mythology

**Tho·reau** \\thə-'rō, thȯ-; 'thȯr-ō\\ Henry David 1817–1862 American author

**Thorpe** \\'thȯrp\\ James Francis 1888–1953 *Jim* American athlete

**Thu·cyd·i·des** \\thü-'sid-ə-,dēz, thyü-\\ *died about* 401 B.C. Greek historian

**Thur·ber** \\'thər-bər\\ James Grover 1894–1961 American author

**Ti·be·ri·us** \\tī-'bir-ē-əs\\ 42 B.C.–37 A.D. Roman emperor (14–37)

**Tikamthe** — see TECUMSEH

**Tim·o·thy** \\'tim-ə-thē\\ a disciple of the apostle Paul

**Tin·to·ret·to** \\,tin-tə-'ret-ō\\ *about* 1518–1594 *Jacopo Robusti* Italian painter

**Ti·ta·nia** \\tə-'tän-yə, -'tān-, ti-'tän-\\ queen of the fairies and wife of Oberon in Shakespeare's *A Midsummer Night's Dream*

**Ti·tian** \\'tish-ən\\ *about* 1488–1576 *Tiziano Vecellio* Italian painter

**Ti·to** \\'tēt-ō\\ 1892–1980 originally *Josip Broz* known as *Marshal Tito* Yugoslavian leader (1943–80)

**Ti·tus** \\'tīt-əs\\ a disciple of the apostle Paul

**Titus** 39–81 A.D. Roman emperor (79–81)

**Tocque·ville** \\'tōk-,vil, 'tȯk-, 'täk-, -,vēl, -vəl\\ Alexis-Charles-Henri Clérel de 1805–1859 French statesman and author

**Tol·kien** \\'tȯl-,kēn, 'tōl-, 'täl-\\ John Ronald Reuel 1892–1973 English author

**Tol·stoy** \\tōl-'stȯi, tōl-', täl-', 'tȯl-, 'tōl-,, 'täl-\\ Count Lev Nikolayevich 1828–1910 Russian author

**Tou·louse–Lau·trec(–Mon·fa)** \\tü-,lüz-lō-'trek (-mōⁿ-'fä)\\ Henri-Marie-Raymond de 1864–1901 French painter

**Tous·saint–Lou·ver·ture** \\tü-,seⁿ-,lü-ver-'tūēr\\ *about* 1743–1803 Haitian general and liberator

**Tra·jan** \\'trā-jən\\ 53–117 A.D. Roman emperor (98–117)

**Tris·tram** \\'tris-trəm\\ or **Tris·tan** \\'tris-tən, -,tän, -,tan\\ hero in medieval romance who drinks a love potion and falls in love with the Irish princess Isolde

**Tri·ton** \\'trīt-n\\ a sea god in Greek mythology who is half man and half fish

**Troi·lus** \\'trȯi-ləs, 'trō-ə-ləs\\ son of Priam who in medieval legend loves Cressida but loses her to Diomedes

**Trots·ky** \'trät-skē, 'tròt-\ Leon 1879–1940 originally *Lev Davidovich Bronshtein* Russian Communist leader

**Tru·deau** \'trü-dō, trü-'\ Pierre Elliott 1919–2000 prime minister of Canada (1968–79; 1980–84)

**Tru·man** \'trü-mən\ Harry S. 1884–1972 33d president of the United States (1945–53)

**Truth** \'trüth\ Sojourner *about* 1797–1883 American abolitionist

**Tub·man** \'təb-mən\ Harriet *about* 1820–1913 American abolitionist

**Tur·ner** \'tər-nər\ Joseph Mallord William 1775–1851 English painter

**Turner** Nat 1800–1831 American leader of a slave rebellion

**Tut·ankh·a·men** \,tü-,tang-'käm-ən, -,täng-\ *or* **Tut·ankh·a·ten** \-,teng-'kät-ən\ *about* 1370–1352 B.C. king of Egypt (1361–1352 B.C.)

**Tu·tu** \'tü-,tü\ Desmond Mpilo 1931– South African clergyman and political activist; Nobel prize winner (1984)

**Twain** Mark — see CLEMENS

**Tweed** \'twēd\ William Marcy 1823–1878 *Boss Tweed* American politician

**Ty·ler** \'tī-lər\ John 1790–1862 10th president of the United States (1841–45)

**Ulysses** — see ODYSSEUS

**Up·dike** \'əp-,dīk\ John Hoyer 1932– American author

**Ura·nia** \yu̇-'rā-nē-ə, -nyə\ Muse of astronomy in Greek mythology

**Ura·nus** \'yur-ə-nəs, yu̇-'rā-nəs\ the sky personified as a god and the father of the Titans in Greek mythology

**Ur·ban** \'ər-bən\ name of 8 popes: especially **II** 1035–1099 (pope 1088–99)

**Uri·el** \'yu̇r-ē-əl\ one of the four archangels named in Hebrew tradition — compare GABRIEL, MICHAEL, RAPHAEL

**Va·le·ri·an** \və-'lir-ē-ən\ *died* 260 A.D. Roman emperor (253–260)

**Van Bu·ren** \van-'byu̇r-ən, vən-\ Martin 1782–1862 8th president of the United States (1837–41)

**Van Dyck** *or* **Van·dyke** \van-'dīk, vən-\ Sir Anthony 1599–1641 Flemish-born painter in England

**Ve·ga** \'vā-gə\ Lo·pe \'lō-pā\ de 1562–1635 Spanish dramatist

**Ve·láz·quez** \və-'las-kəs\ Diego Rodríguez de Silva 1599–1660 Spanish painter

**Ve·nus** \'vē-nəs\ goddess of love and beauty in Roman mythology — compare APHRODITE

**Ver·di** \'veərd-ē\ Giuseppe 1813–1901 Italian composer

**Vergil** — see VIRGIL

**Verne** \'vərn, 'vern\ Jules \'jülz, 'zhēl\ 1828–1905 French author

**Ve·ro·ne·se** \,ver-ə-'nā-sē, -'nā-zē\ Paolo 1528–1588 Italian painter

**Ves·puc·ci** \ve-'spü-chē\ Ame·ri·go \,äm-ə-'rē-gō\ 1454–1512 *Amer·i·cus Ves·pu·cius* \ə-'mer-ə-kəs,-,ves-'pyü-shəs, -shē-əs\ Italian navigator and namesake of America

**Ves·ta** \'ves-tə\ goddess of the hearth in Roman mythology — compare HESTIA

**Vic·tor Em·man·u·el I** \'vik-tər-i-'man-yə-wəl, -'man-yəl\ 1759–1824 king of Sardinia (1802–21)

**Victor Emmanuel II** 1820–1878 king of Sardinia (1849–61); 1st king of Italy (1861–78)

**Victor Emmanuel III** 1869–1947 king of Italy (1900–46)

**Vic·to·ria** \vik-tōr-ē-ə, -'tòr-\ 1819–1901 *Alexandrina Victoria* queen of Great Britain (1837–1901)

**Vil·lon** \vē-'ōⁿ, -'yōⁿ\ François 1431–*after* 1463 French poet

**Vin·cent de Paul** \,vin-sənt-də-'pòl\ Saint 1581–1660 French priest and founder of the Vincentians

**Vinci, da** Leonardo — see LEONARDO DA VINCI

**Vir·gil** *also* **Ver·gil** \'vər-jəl\ 70–19 B.C. Roman poet — **Vir·gil·ian** *also* **Ver·gil·ian** \vər-'jil-ē-ən\ *adj*

**Vish·nu** \'vish-nü\ god of preservation in the Hindu sacred triad — compare BRAHMA, SIVA

**Vi·val·di** \vi-'väl-dē, -'vòl-\ Antonio 1678–1741 Italian composer

**Vol·taire** \vōl-'taər, vòl-, väl-, -'teər\ 1694–1778 originally *François-Marie Arouet* French author

**Vul·can** \'vəl-kən\ god of fire and metalworking in Roman mythology — compare HEPHAESTUS

**Wag·ner** \'väg-nər\ (Wilhelm) Ri·chard \'rik-,ärt, 'rik-\ 1813–1883 German composer

**Wal·cott** \'wòl-kət, -,kät\ Derek Alton 1930– West Indian author; Nobel prize winner (1992)

**Walk·er** \'wòk-ər\ Alice Malsenior 1944– American author

**Wal·len·berg** \'wäl-ən-,bərg\ Raoul 1912–1947? Swedish diplomat and hero of the Holocaust

**Wal·pole** \'wòl-,pōl, 'wäl-\ Horace 1717–1797 4th Earl of *Or·ford* \'òr-fərd\ English author

**Wal·ton** \'wòlt-n\ Izaak \'ī-zik, -zək\ 1593–1683 English author

**War·ren** \'wòr-ən, 'wär-\ Earl 1891–1974 American jurist; chief justice of the United States Supreme Court (1953–69)

**Wash·ing·ton** \'wòsh-ing-tən, 'wäsh-\ Book·er \'bu̇k-ər\ Tal·ia·ferro \'täl-ə-vər\ 1856–1915 American educator

**Washington** George 1732–1799 American general; 1st president of the United States (1789–97)

**Watt** \'wät\ James 1736–1819 Scottish inventor

**Wayne** \'wān\ Anthony 1745–1796 *Mad Anthony* American Revolutionary general

**We·ber** \'vā-bər\ Carl Maria von 1786–1826 German composer and conductor

**Web·ster** \'web-stər\ Daniel 1782–1852 American statesman

**Webster** Noah 1758–1843 American lexicographer

**Welles** \'welz\ (George) Orson 1915–1985 American film director and producer

**Wel·ling·ton** \'wel-ing-tən\ 1st Duke of 1769–1852 *Arthur Wellesley; the Iron Duke* British general and statesman

**Wel·ty** \'wel-tē\ Eudora 1909– American author

**Wells** \'welz\ Herbert George 1866–1946 English author

**Wes·ley** \'wes-lē, 'wez-\ John 1703–1791 English founder of Methodism

**West** \'west\ Benjamin 1738–1820 American painter in England

**Wes·ting·house** \'wes-ting-,hau̇s\ George 1846–1914 American inventor

**Whar·ton** \'hwòrt-n, 'wòrt-\ Edith Newbold 1862–1937 American author

**Wheat·ley** \'wēt-lē, 'hwēt-\ Phillis *about* 1753–1784 American (African-born) poet

**Whis·tler** \'hwis-lər, 'wis-\ James Abbott McNeill 1834–1903 American artist

**Whit·man** \'hwit-mən, 'wit-\ Walt 1819–1892 American poet

**Whit·ney** \'hwit-nē, 'wit-\ Eli 1765–1825 American inventor

**Whit·ti·er** \'hwit-ē-ər, 'wit-\ John Greenleaf 1807–1892 American poet

**Wie·sel** \vē-'zel, wē-\ Elie 1928– American (Romanian-born) author

**Wilde** \'wīld\ Oscar Fingal O'Flahertie Wills 1854–1900 Irish author

**Wil·der** \'wīl-dər\ Thornton Niven 1897–1975 American author

**Wil·hel·mi·na** \,wil-,hel-'mē-nə, ,wil-ə-'mē-\ 1880–1962 queen of the Netherlands (1890–1948)

**Wil·kins** \'wil-kənz\ Roy 1901–1981 American civil rights leader

**Wil·lard** \'wil-ərd\ Emma 1787–1870 née *Hart* American educator

**Wil·liam** \'wil-yəm\ name of 4 kings of England: **I** *about* 1028–1087 (reigned 1066–87) *the Conqueror;* **II** *about* 1056–1100 (reigned 1087–1100) *Ru·fus* \'rü-fəs\; **III** 1650–1702 (reigned 1689–1702); **IV** 1765–1837 (reigned 1830–37)

**William I** 1533–1584 *the Silent* prince of Orange and founder of the Dutch Republic

**William I** 1797–1888 king of Prussia (1861–88) and emperor of Germany (1871–88)

**William II** 1859–1941 emperor of Germany and king of Prussia (1888–1918; abdicated)

**Wil·liam Tell** \,wil-yəm-'tel\ legendary Swiss patriot sentenced to shoot an apple from his son's head

**Wil·liams** \'wil-yəmz\ Roger 1603?–1683 American (English-born) clergyman and founder of Rhode Island

**Williams** Tennessee 1911–1983 *Thomas Lanier Williams* American dramatist

**Williams** William Carlos 1883–1963 American author

**Wil·son** \'wil-sən\ August 1945– American dramatist

**Wilson** (Thomas) Wood·row \'wu̇d-rō\ 1856–1924 28th president of the United States (1913–21); Nobel prize winner (1919)

**Windsor** Duke of — see EDWARD VIII

**Win·throp** \'win-thrəp, 'wint-\ John 1588–1649 English colonist in America; 1st governor of Massachusetts Bay Colony

**Wo·den** \'wōd-n\ — see ODIN

**Wolfe** \'wu̇lf\ James 1727–1759 British general

**Wolfe** Thomas Clayton 1900–1938 American author

**Woll·stone·craft** \'wu̇l-stən-,kraft\ Mary 1759–1797 English feminist and author

**Wol·sey** \'wu̇l-zē\ Thomas *about* 1475–1530 English cardinal and statesman

**Woolf** \'wu̇lf\ Virginia 1882–1941 née *Stephen* English author

**Words·worth** \'wərdz- wərth, -,wərth\ William 1770–1850 English poet

**Wo·vo·ka** \wō-'vō-kə\ 1858?–1932 *Jack Wilson* Paiute Indian mystic

**Wren** \'ren\ Sir Christopher 1632–1723 English architect

**Wright** \'rīt\ Frank Lloyd 1867–1959 American architect

**Wright** Or·ville \'òr-vəl\ 1871–1948 and his brother Wilbur 1867–1912 American pioneers in aviation

**Wright** Richard 1908–1960 American author

**Wyc·liffe** \'wik-,lif, -ləf\ John *about* 1330–1384 English reformer and Bible translator

**Wy·eth** \'wī-əth\ Andrew Newell 1917– American painter

**Xa·vi·er** \'zāv-yər, 'zā-vē-ər, ig-'zā-\ Saint Francis 1506–1552 Spanish *Francisco Javier* Spanish Jesuit missionary

**Xen·o·phon** \'zen-ə-fən\ *about* 431–*about* 352 B.C. Greek historian and soldier

**Xer·xes I** \'zərk-,sēz\ *about* 519–465 B.C. *the Great* son of Darius I; king of Persia (486–465)

**Yeats** \'yāts\ William Butler 1865–1939 Irish author

**Yelt·sin** \'yelt-sən, 'yel-sin\ Boris Nikolayevich 1931– president of Russian Federation (1991–99)

**Young** \'yəng\ Brig·ham \'brig-əm\ 1801–1877 American Mormon leader

**Young** Whitney Moore 1921–1971 American civil rights leader

**Za·har·i·as** \zə-'har-ē-əs\ Mildred Ella Didrikson 1914–1956 *Babe* American athlete

**Zech·a·ri·ah** \,zek-ə-'rī-ə\ Hebrew prophet of the 6th century B.C.

**Zeng·er** \'zeng-ər, 'zeng-gər\ John Peter 1697–1746 American (German-born) journalist and printer

**Ze·no** \'zē-nō\ *about* 335–*about* 263 B.C. Greek philosopher and founder of Stoic school

**Zeph·a·ni·ah** \,zef-ə-'nī-ə\ Hebrew prophet of the 7th century B.C.

**Zeph·y·rus** \'zef-ə-rəs\ god of the west wind in Greek mythology

**Zeus** \'züs\ chief god, ruler of the elements, and husband of Hera in Greek mythology — compare JUPITER

**Zo·la** \'zō-lə, 'zō-,lä, zō-'lä\ Émile 1840–1902 French author

**Zo·ro·as·ter** \'zòr-ə-,was-tər, 'zòr-\ *or* **Zar·a·thu·shtra** \,zar-ə-'thüsh-trə, -'thəsh-\ *about* 628–*about* 551 B.C. founder of a Persian religion

**Zwing·li** \'zwing-lē, 'swing-, -glē; 'tsfing-lē\ Huldrych 1484–1531 Swiss Reformation leader

# Geographical Names

This section constitutes a pronouncing dictionary of commonly encountered current and historical place names. It complements the general vocabulary by entering many derived adjectives and nouns of geographical names, such as **Florentine** at **Florence** and **Libyan** at **Libya**.

In the entries, the letters N, S, W, and E, either singly or combined, are not part of a place name but indicate location, such as "N of Nicobar Islands" for "north of" or "SE Greece" for "southeastern". All heights and distances are given in metric units. The only abbreviations used in this section are U.S. for United States and U.S.S.R. for Union of Soviet Socialist Republics.

**Aa·chen** \'äk-ən\ *or French* **Aix–la–Cha·pelle** \,äk-,slä-shə-'pel, ,ek-\ city W Germany WSW of Cologne

**Aarhus** — see ÅRHUS

**Aba·dan** \,äb-ə-'dän, ,ab-ə-'dan\ city W Iran on Abadan Island in delta of Shatt al Arab

**Abe·o·ku·ta** \,ab-ē-'ō-kət-ə\ city SW Nigeria S of Ibadan

**Ab·er·deen** \,ab-ər-'dēn\ **1** *or* **Ab·er·deen·shire** \-,shiər, -shər\ former country NE Scotland **2** city NE Scotland — **Ab·er·do·ni·an** \-'dō-nē-ən\ *adjective or noun*

**Ab·i·djan** \,ab-i-'jän\ city, seat of government of Ivory Coast

**Abruz·zi** \ä-'brüt-sē\ region central Italy on the Adriatic E of Latium; capital, L'Aquila

**Abu Dha·bi** \,äb-ü-'däb-ē\ city, capital of United Arab Emirates

**Abu·ja** \ä-'bü-jä\ city, capital of Nigeria

**Ab·ys·sin·ia** \,ab-ə-'sin-ē-ə, -'sin-yə\ — see ETHIOPIA — **Ab·ys·sin·i·an** \-ē-ən, -yən\ *adjective or noun*

**Aca·dia** \ə-'kād-ē-ə\ *or French* **Aca·die** \ȧ-kȧ-'dē\ NOVA SCOTIA — an early name

**Acadia National Park** section of coast of Maine including areas on Mount Desert Island & Isle au Haut

**Aca·pul·co** \,äk-ə-'pül-kō, ,ak-\ city S Mexico on the Pacific

**Ac·ar·na·nia** \,ak-ər-'nā-nē-ə, -'nā-nyə\ district W Greece on Ionian Sea

**Accad** — see AKKAD

**Ac·cra** \ə-'krä\ city, capital of Ghana

**Achaea** \ə-'kē-ə\ *or* **Acha·ia** *or Greek* **Akhaïa** \ə-'kī-ə, -'kä-ə, -'kä-yə\ district S Greece in N Peloponnese

**Ach·er·on** \'ak-ə-,rän, -rən\ a river of Hades in Greek mythology

**Acon·ca·gua** \,ak-ən-'käg-wə, ,äk-, -əng-\ mountain 6960 meters W Argentina; highest in the Andes & western hemisphere

**Açores** — see AZORES

**Ac·ti·um** \'ak-shē-əm, 'ak-tē-\ promontory & ancient town W Greece in NW Acarnania

**Ada·na** \'äd-ə-nə, -,nä; ə-'dän-ə\ city S Turkey

**Ad·dis Aba·ba** \,ad-ə-'sab-ə-bə\ city, capital of Ethiopia

**Ad·e·laide** \'ad-l-,ād\ city, capital of South Australia

**Aden** \'äd-n, 'äd-, 'ad-\ **1** former British protectorate S Arabia E of Yemen **2** former British colony in SW Aden Protectorate **3** city & port S Yemen; formerly capital of People's Democratic Republic of Yemen

**Aden, Gulf of** arm of Indian Ocean between Yemen (Arabia) & Somalia (Africa)

**Adi·ge** \'äd-ə-jā\ river 410 kilometers long N Italy flowing SE into the Adriatic

**Ad·i·ron·dack** \,ad-ə-'rän-,dak\ mountains NE New York; highest Mount Marcy 1629 meters

**Ad·mi·ral·ty** \'ad-mrəl-tē, -mə-rəl-\ **1** island SE Alaska in N Alexander Archipelago **2** islands W Pacific N of New Guinea in Bismark Archipelago; belong to Papua New Guinea

**Adri·at·ic** \,ā-drē-'at-ik, ,ad-rē-\ sea arm of Mediterranean between Italy & Balkan Peninsula

**Ae·ge·an** \i-'jē-ən\ sea arm of Mediterranean between Asia Minor & Greece

**Ae·gi·na** \i-'jī-nə\ *or Greek* **Aí·yi·na** \'ā-yē-,nä\ island & ancient state SE Greece in Saronic Gulf

**Ae·o·lis** \'ē-ə-ləs\ *or* **Ae·o·lia** \ē-'ō-lē-ə, -'ōl-yə\ ancient country NW Asia Minor

**Afars and the Issas, French Territory of the** — see DJIBOUTI 1

**Af·ghan·i·stan** \af-'gan-ə-,stan\ country W Asia E of Iran; capital, Kabul

**Af·ri·ca** \'af-ri-kə\ continent of eastern hemisphere S of Mediterranean

**Aga·na** \ə-'gän-yə\ town, capital of Guam

**Agra** \'äg-rə\ city N India in W Uttar Pradesh

**Agri Dagi** *or* **Aghri Dagh** — see ARARAT

**Aguas·ca·lien·tes** \,äg-wə-,skäl-yen-,tās\ **1** state central Mexico **2** city, its capital, NE of Guadalajara

**Agul·has, Cape** \ə-'gəl-əs\ headland Republic of South Africa; most southerly point of Africa, at 34°50' S latitude

**Agulhas Current** warm current of the Indian Ocean flowing SW along SE coast of Africa

**Ahag·gar** \ə-'häg-ər, ,ä-hə-'gär\ *or* **Hog·gar** \'häg-ər, hə-'gär\ mountains S Algeria in W central Sahara; highest peak 3000 meters

**Ah·mad·abad** \'äm-əd-ə-,bäd\ city W India in Gujarat

**Ah·waz** \ä-'wäz\ city SW Iran

**Aisne** \'ān\ river 265 kilometers long N France flowing from Argonne Forest into the Oise

**Aix–la–Chapelle** — see AACHEN

**Aj·mer** \,əj-'miər, -'meər\ city NW India in central Rajasthan SW of Delhi

**Aki·ta** \ä-'kēt-ə, 'äk-i-,tä\ city Japan in N Honshu on Sea of Japan

**Ak·kad** *or* **Ac·cad** \'ak-,ad, 'äk-,äd\ **1** N division of ancient Babylonia **2** *or* **Aga·de** \ə-'gäd-ə\ ancient city, its capital

**Ak·ron** \'ak-rən\ city NE Ohio

**Al·a·bama** \,al-ə-'bam-ə\ state SE U.S.; capital, Montgomery — **Al·a·bam·i·an** \-'bam-ē-ən\ *or* **Al·a·bam·an** \-'bam-ən\ *adjective or noun*

**Åland** \'ō-,länd\ *or* **Ah·ven·an·maa** \'äk-və-,nän-,mä, 'ä-və-\ archipelago SW Finland in Baltic Sea

**Alas·ka** \ə-'las-kə\ **1** peninsula SW Alaska SW of Cook Inlet **2** state of U.S. in NW North America; capital, Juneau **3** mountain range S Alaska extending from Alaska Peninsula to Yukon boundary — **Alas·kan** \-kən\ *adjective or noun*

**Alaska, Gulf of** inlet of Pacific off S Alaska between Alaska Peninsula on W & Alexander Archipelago on E

**Al·ba Lon·ga** \,al-bə-'lóng-gə\ ancient city central Italy in Latium SE of Rome

**Al·ba·nia** \al-'bā-nē-ə, -nyə\ country S Europe in Balkan Peninsula on Adriatic; capital, Tirane

**Al·ba·ny** \'ól-bə-nē\ city, capital of New York

**Al·be·marle** \'al-bə-,märl\ sound inlet of Atlantic in NE North Carolina

**Al·bert, Lake** \'al-bərt\ lake E Africa between Uganda & Democratic Republic of the Congo in course of Nile

**Al·ber·ta** \al-'bərt-ə\ province W Canada; capital, Edmonton — **Al·ber·tan** \-bərt-n\ *adjective or noun*

**Albert Nile** — see NILE

**Al·bi·on** \'al-bē-ən\ **1** island of Great Britain **2** ENGLAND

**Al·bu·quer·que** \'al-bə-,kər-kē, -byə-\ city central New Mexico

**Al·da·bra** \'al-də-brə\ island (atoll) Seychelles, in NW Indian Ocean N of Madagascar

**Al·der·ney** \'ól-dər-nē\ island in English Channel — see CHANNEL

**Alep·po** \ə-'lep-ō\ city N Syria

**Aleu·tian** \ə-'lü-shən\ islands SW Alaska extending in an arc 2735 kilometers W from Alaska Peninsula

**Al·ex·an·der** \,al-ig-'zan-dər, ,el-\ archipelago SE Alaska

**Al·ex·an·dria** \,al-ig-'zan-drē-ə, ,el-\ **1** city N Virginia **2** city N Egypt on Mediterranean — **Al·ex·an·dri·an** \-drē-ən\ *adjective or noun*

**Al·ge·ria** \al-'jir-ē-ə\ country NW Africa on Mediterranean; capital, Algiers — **Al·ge·ri·an** \-ē-ən\ *adjective or noun*

**Al·giers** \al-'jiərz\ **1** Algeria especially as one of former Barbary States **2** city, capital of Algeria — **Al·ge·rine** \,al-jə-'rēn\ *adjective or noun*

**Al·i·garh** \,al-i-'gär\ city N India in NW Uttar Pradesh N of Agra

**Al Jīzah** — see GIZA

**Al·lah·abad** \,al-ə-hə-,bad, -,bäd\ city N India in S Uttar Pradesh W of Varanasi

**Al·le·ghe·ny** \,al-ə-'gā-nē\ mountains of Applachian system E U.S. in Pennsylvania, Maryland, Virginia, & West Virginia

**Al·len·town** \'al-ən-,taùn\ city E Pennsylvania

**Al·ma-Ata** \,al-mə-ə-'tä\ *or* **Al·ma·ty** \əl-'mä-tē\ city, capital of Kazakhstan

**Alps** \'alps\ mountain system central Europe — see MONT BLANC

**Al·sace** \al-'sas, -sȧs, 'al-,\ *or German* **El·sass** \'el-,zäs\ *or ancient* **Al·sa·tia** \al-'sā-shē-ə, -shə\ region & former province NE France between Rhine River & Vosges Mountains — **Al·sa·tian** \al-'sā-shən\ *adjective or noun*

**Al·sace–Lor·raine** \-lə-'rän, -ló-'rän\ region N France W of the Rhine including Alsace & part of Lorraine

**Al·ta·mi·ra** \,al-tə-'mir-ə\ caverns N Spain WSW of Sandander

**Al·tay** *or* **Al·tai** \al-'tī, 'al-,tī\ mountain system central Asia between Outer Mongolia & W China & between Kazakhstan & Russia in Asia; highest peak about 4570 meters

**Al·to Adi·ge** \,äl-tō-'äd-i-jä\ *or* **South Ti·rol** \-tə-'rōl, -'tī-,rōl, -,tī-'; -'tir-əl\ district N Italy in S Tirol in N Trentino-Alto Adige region

**Al·to Pa·ra·ná** \al-tō-,par-ə-'nä\ upper course of the Paraná

**Ama·ga·sa·ki** \am-ə-gə-'säk-ē\ city Japan in W central Honshu on Osaka Bay

**Am·a·ril·lo** \am-ə-'ril-ō, -'ril-ə\ city NW Texas

**Am·a·zon** \'am-ə-,zän, -zən\ *or Portuguese and Spanish* **Ama·zo·nas** \am-ə-'zō-nəs\ river about 6436 kilometers long N South America flowing from Peruvian Andes into Atlantic in N Brazil

**Am·a·zo·nia** \am-ə-'zō-nē-ə\ region N South America; basin of the Amazon

**Amer·i·ca** \ə-'mer-ə-kə\ **1** either continent (North America or South America) of western hemisphere **2** *or* **the Amer·i·cas** \-kəz\ lands of western hemisphere including North, Central & South America & West Indies **3** UNITED STATES OF AMERICA

**American Samoa** *or* **Eastern Samoa** islands SW central Pacific; capital, Pago Pago (on Tutuila Island)

**American Samoa National Park** reservation at three locations in American Samoa

**Am·man** \ä-'män, -'man\ city, capital of Jordan

**Amoy** — see XIAMEN

**Am·rit·sar** \əm-'rit-sər\ city N India in NW Punjab

**Am·ster·dam** \'am-stər-,dam, 'amp-\ city, official capital of the Netherlands

**Amu Dar'·ya** \äm-ü-'där-yə\ *or ancient* **Ox·us** \'äk-səs\ river about 2539 kilometers long in central & W Asia flowing from the Pamirs into Aral Sea

**Amur** \ä-'mu̇r\ river about 2874 kilometers long E Asia formed by junction of Shilka & Argun rivers flowing into the Pacific at N end of Tatar Strait & forming part of boundary between China & Russia in Asia

**An·a·hein** \'an-ə-,hīm\ city SW California E of Long Beach

**Aná·huac** \ə-'nä-,wäk\ the central plateau of Mexico

**An·a·to·lia** \an-ə-'tō-lē-ə, -'tōl-yə\ — see ASIA MINOR — **An·a·to·li·an** \-ən, -yən\ *adjective or noun*

**An·chor·age** \'ang-kə-rij, -krij\ city S central Alaska; largest in state

**An·co·hu·ma** \ang-kə-'hü-mə, -'hyü-\ mountain peak 6388 meters W Bolivia; highest in Illampu massif

**An·co·na** \ang-'kō-nə, an-\ city central Italy, capital of Marche

**An·da·lu·sia** \an-də-'lü-zhē-ə, -zhə\ *or Spanish* **An·da·lu·cía** \an-də-'lü-'sē-ə\ region S Spain including Sierra Nevada & valley of the Guadalquivir — **An·da·lu·sian** \an-də-'lü-zhən\ *adjective or noun*

**An·da·man** \'an-də-mən, -,man\ **1** islands India in Bay of Bengal S of Myanmar & N of Nicobar Islands; in **Andaman and Nic·o·bar** \'nik-ə-,bär\ territory **2** sea arm of Bay of Bengal S of Myanmar — **An·da·man·ese** \an-də-mə-'nēz, -'nēs\ *adjective or noun*

**An·des** \'an-dēz, -,dēz\ mountain system W South America extending from Panama to Tierra del Fuego — see ACONCAGUA — **An·de·an** \'an-dē-ən, an-\ *adjective* — **An·dine** \'an-,dēn, -,dīn\ *adjective*

**An·dhra Pra·desh** \än-drə-prə-'däsh, -'desh\ state S India N of Tamil Nadu bordering on Bay of Bengal; capital, Hyderabad

**An·dor·ra** \an-'dȯr-ə, -'där-ə\ country SW Europe in E Pyrenees between France & Spain; capital, Andorra la Vella — **An·dor·ran** \-ən\ *adjective or noun*

**An·dros** **1** \'an-drəs\ island, largest of Bahamas **2** \'an-drəs, -,dräs\ island Greece in N Cyclades SE of Euboea

**An·gel Falls** \,än-jəl\ waterfall 979 meters SE Venezuela on Auyán-tepuí Mountain

**An·gers** \äⁿ-'zhā\ city W France ENE of Nantes

**Ang·kor** \'ang-,kȯr\ ruins of ancient city NW Cambodia

**An·gle·sey** \'ang-gəl-sē\ island & former county NW Wales

**An·glo–Egyp·tian Sudan** \,ang-glō-i-,jip-shən\ former territory NE Africa under joint British & Egyptian rule; since 1956 has formed republic of Sudan

**An·go·la** \ang-'gō-lə, an-\ *or formerly* **Portuguese West Africa** country SW Africa S of mouth of Congo River; until 1975 a dependency of Portugal; capital, Luanda — **An·go·lan** \-lən\ *adjective or noun*

**An·gus** \'ang-gəs\ former county E Scotland

**An·hui** *or* **An·hwei** \'än-'hwā, -'wā\ province E China W of Jiangsu; capital, Hefei

**An·i·ak·chak Crater** \,an-ē-'ak-,chak\ volcanic crater SW Alaska on Alaska Peninsula; crater 10 kilometers in diameter

**An·jou** \'an-,jü, äⁿ-'zhü\ region & former province NW France in valley of the Loire SE of Brittany; chief city, Angers

**An·ka·ra** \'ang-kə-rə, 'äng\ *or formerly* **An·go·ra** \ang-'gȯr-ə, an-, -'gȯr-\ city, capital of Turkey in N central Anatolia

**An·na·ba** \ə-'näb-ə\ *or formerly* **Bône** \'bōn\ city NE Algeria

**An·nam** \a-'nam, ə-; 'an-,am\ region & former kingdom E Indochina in central Vietnam; capital, Hue

**An·nap·o·lis** \ə-'nap-ləs, -ə-ləs\ city, capital of Maryland

**An·shan** \'än-'shän\ city NE China in E central Liaoning

**An·ta·nan·a·ri·vo** \,an-tə-,nan-ə-'rē-vō\ *or formerly* **Ta·nan·a·rive** \tə-'nan-ə-,rēv\ city, capital of Madagascar

**Ant·arc·ti·ca** \ant-'ärk-ti-kə, 'ant-, -'ärt-i-\ body of land around the South Pole; plateau covered by great ice cap

**Antarctic Peninsula** *or formerly* **Palm·er Peninsula** \,päm-ər-, ,päl-mər-\ peninsula about 1126 kilometers long W Antarctica S of S end of South America

**An·ti·gua** \an-'tē-gə\ island British West Indies in the Leewards; with Barbuda constitutes independent country of **Antigua and Barbuda**; capital, Saint Johns

**An·ti–Leb·a·non** \'ant-i-'leb-ə-nən, -,nän\ mountains SW Asia on Lebanon-Syria border — see HERMON (Mount)

**An·til·les** \an-'til-ēz\ the West Indies excluding Bahamas — see GREATER ANTILLES, LESSER ANTILLES — **An·til·le·an** \-'til-ē-ən\ *adjective*

**An·ti·och** \'ant-ē-,äk\ city of ancient Syria on the Orontes; site at modern Antakya, Turkey

**An·trim** \'an-trəm\ traditional county E Northern Ireland; includes Belfast

**Antung** — see DANDONG

**Ant·werp** \'ant-wərp\ city N Belgium on the Scheldt

**An·yang** \'än-'yäng\ city E China in N Henan

**An·zio** \'an-zē-ō, 'än-\ *or ancient* **An·ti·um** \'an-shē-əm\ Mediterranean seaport Italy in Latium SSE of Rome

**Ao·mo·ri** \'au̇-mə-rē\ city N Japan in NE Honshu on Mutsu Bay

**Aorangi** — see COOK (Mount)

**Aos·ta** \ä-'ȯs-tə\ city NW Italy

**Ap·en·nines** \'ap-ə-,nīnz\ mountain chain Italy extending length of the peninsula; highest peak Monte Corno (NE of Rome) 2914 meters — **Ap·en·nine** \-,nīn\ *adjective*

**Apia** \ə-'pē-ə\ town, capital of Western Samoa on Upolu Island

**Apo, Mount** \'äp-ō\ volcano Philippines in SE Mindanao 2954 meters; highest peak in the Philippines

**Ap·pa·la·chia** \,ap-ə-'lā-chə, -'lach-ə, -'lā-shə\ region E U.S. including Appalachian Mountains from S central New York to central Alabama

**Ap·pa·la·chian** \,ap-ə-'lā-chən, -'lach-ən, -'lā-shən\ mountain system E North America extending from S Quebec to central Alabama — see MITCHELL (Mount)

**Apu·lia** \ə-'pyül-yə, -'pyü-lē-ə\ — see PUGLIA — **Apu·lian** \ə-'pyül-yən, -'pyü-lē-ən\ *adjective or noun*

**'Aqa·ba, Gulf of** \'äk-ə-bə, 'ak-\ arm of Red Sea E of Sinai Peninsula

**Aquid·neck Island** \ə-'kwid-,nek\ *or* **Rhode Island** \'rōd\ island SE Rhode Island in Narragansett Bay

**Aqui·taine** \'ak-wə-,tān\ old region of SW France comprising later Guienne; chief city, Toulouse

**Aqui·ta·nia** \,ak-wə-'tā-nyə, -nē-ə\ a Roman division of SW Gaul

**Ara·bia** \ə-'rā-bē-ə\ peninsula of SW Asia including Saudi Arabia, Yemen, Oman, & Persian Gulf States

**Ara·bi·an** \ə-'rā-bē-ən\ **1** desert E Egypt between Red Sea & the Nile **2** sea NW section of Indian Ocean between Arabia & India

**Ara·ca·ju** \,ar-ə-kə-'zhü\ city E Brazil NE of Salvador

**Arad** \ä-'räd\ city W Romania

**Ar·a·fu·ra** \,ar-ə-'fu̇r-ə\ sea between N Australia & W New Guinea

**Ar·a·gon** \'ar-ə-,gän, -gən\ region NE Spain bordering on France — **Ar·a·go·nese** \,ar-ə-gə-'nēz, -'nēs\ *adjective or noun*

**Arak** \är-'äk, ə-'rak\ city W Iran SW of Tehran

**Ar·al Sea** \'ar-əl\ *or Russian* **Aral·sko·ye Mo·re** \ə-,ral-skə-yə-'mȯr-ə, yə\ *or formerly* **Lake Aral** lake W Asia between Kazakhstan & Uzbekistan

**Ar·a·rat** \'ar-ə-,rat\ *or Turkish* **Ag·ri Da·gi** *or* **Agh·ri Dagh** \ä-rē-dä-'ē, äg-rē-däg-'e\ mountain 5165 meters E Turkey near border of Iran

**Ar·bil** *or* **Ir·bil** *or* **Er·bil** \är-'bēl\ city N Iraq

**Ar·ca·dia** \är-'kād-ē-ə\ mountain region S Greece in central Peloponnese

**Arch·es National Park** \'är-chəz\ reservation E Utah

**Arc·tic** \'ärk-tik, 'ärt-ik\ **1** ocean N of arctic circle **2** Arctic regions **3** archipelago N Canada in N & E Northwest Territories

**Ar·da·bil** *or* **Ar·de·bil** \,är-də-'bēl\ city NW Iran

**Ar·dennes** \är-'den\ wooded plateau NE France, W Luxemburg, & SE Belgium E of the Meuse

**Are·qui·pa** \,ar-ə-'kē-pə\ city S Peru

**Ar·gen·ti·na** \,är-jən-'tēn-ə\ country S South America between the Andes & the Atlantic S of the Pilcomayo; a republic; capital, Buenos Aires — **Argen·tine** \'är-jən-,tēn\ *adjective or noun* — **Argen·tin·ean** *or* **Ar·gen·tin·i·an** \,är-jən-'tin-ē-ən\ *adjective or noun*

**Ar·go·lis** \,är-gə-lis\ district S Greece in E Peloponnese

**Ar·gonne** \'är-,gän, 'är-,\ *or* **Argonne Forest** wooded plateau NE France S of the Ardennes between Meuse & Aisne rivers

**Ar·gos** \,är-gäs, -gəs\ ancient Greek city & state S Greece in Argolis; site at present town of Argos

**Ar·gyll** \är-'gīl, 'är-,\ *or* **Ar·gyll·shire** \-,shiər, -,shər\ former county W Scotland

**År·hus** *or* **Aar·hus** \'ȯr-,hüs\ city & port Denmark in E Jutland

**Ar·i·zo·na** \,ar-ə-'zō-nə\ state SW U.S.; capital, Phoenix — **Ar·i·zo·nan** \-nən\ *or* **Ar·i·zo·nian** \-nē-ən, -nyən\ *adjective or noun*

**Ar·kan·sas** \'är-kən-,sȯ; *1 is also* är-'kan-zəs\ **1** river 2333 kilometers long SW central U.S. flowing SE into the Mississippi **2** state S central U.S.; capital, Little Rock — **Ar·kan·san** \är-'kan-zən\ *adjective or noun*

**Ar·khan·gelsk** \är-'kan-,gelsk\ *or* **Arch·an·gel** \'är-,kān-jəl\ city N Russia in Europe, on the Northern Dvina

**Ar·ling·ton** \'är-ling-tən\ city N Texas E or Fort Worth

**Ar·magh** \är-'mä, 'är-,\ traditional county S Northern Ireland

**Ar·me·nia** \är-'mē-nē-ə, -nyə\ **1** region W Asia in mountainous area SE of Black Sea & SW of Caspian Sea divided between Iran, Turkey, Armenia (country), & Azerbaijan **2** country E Europe, capital, Yerevan; a constituent republic of U.S.S.R. 1936–91 — see LESSER ARMENIA — **Ar·me·ni·an** \-nē-ən, -nyən\ *adjective or noun*

**Arn·hem Land** \'ärn-,hem, 'är-nəm\ region N Australia on N coast of Northern Territory

**Ar·no** \'är-nō\ river 241 kilometers long central Italy flowing through Florence into Ligurian Sea

**Aru·ba** \ə-'rü-bə\ island Netherlands Antilles off coast of NW Venezuela NW of Curaçao; chief town, Oranjestad

**Arun·a·chal Pra·desh** \,är-ə-,näch-əl-prə-'däsh, -desh\ *or formerly* **North East Frontier Agency** state NE India N of Assam; capital, Itanagar

**Asa·hi·ka·wa** \,äs-ə-hē-'kä-wə\ *or* **Asa·hi·ga·wa** \-'gä-wə\ city Japan in central Hokkaido

**Ashan·ti** \ə-'shant-ē, -'shänt-\ *or* **Asan·te** \ə-'sänt-ē\ region central Ghana

**Ashkh·a·bad** \'ash-kə-,bad, -,bäd\ city, capital of Turkmenistan

**Asia** \'ā-zhə, -shə\ continent eastern hemisphere N of equator — see EURASIA

**Asia Mi·nor** \-'mī-nər\ *or* **An·a·to·lia** \,an-ə-'tō-lē-ə, -'tōl-yə\ peninsula in modern Turkey between Black Sea on N & the Mediterranean on S

**Asir** \a-'siər\ province S Saudi Arabia on Red Sea SE of Hejaz

**As·ma·ra** \az-'mär-ə, -'mar-ə\ city N Ethiopia, capital of Eritrea

**As·sam** \ə-'sam, a-; 'as-,am\ state NE India on edge of the Himalaya NW of Myanmar; capital, Dispur — **As·sam·ese** \,as-ə-'mēz, -'mēs\ adjective or noun

**As·syr·ia** \ə-'sir-ē-ə\ ancient empire W Asia extending along the middle Tigris & over foothills to the E; early capital Calah, later capital Nineveh — **As·syr·i·an** \-ən\ adjective or noun

**As·tra·khan** \'as-trə-,kan, -kən\ city Russia in Europe, on the Volga at head of its delta

**Asun·ción** \ə-,sün-sē-'ōn, ä-\ city, capital of Paraguay

**As·wân** \a-'swän, ä-\ city S Egypt on the Nile near site of **Aswân High Dam** which forms Lake Nasser

**As·yût** \,as-ē-'üt, ,äs-\ city central Egypt on the Nile

**Ata·ca·ma** \,at-ə-'käm-ə\ **1** desert N Chile between Copiapó & Peru border **2** — see PUNA DE ATACAMA

**Atchaf·a·laya** \ə-,chaf-ə-'lī-ə, ,chaf-\ river 362 kilometers long S Louisiana flowing S into Gulf of Mexico; receives waters of Red & Mississippi rivers

**Ath·a·bas·ca** \,ath-ə-'bas-kə\ river 1231 kilometers long NE Alberta flowing into Lake Athabasca

**Athabasca, Lake** lake W central Canada on Alberta-Saskatchewan border

**Ath·ens** \'ath-ənz\ city, capital of Greece — **Athe·nian** \ə-'thē-nē-ən, -nyən\ adjective or noun

**At·lan·ta** \ət-'lant-ə, at-\ city, capital of Georgia

**At·lan·tic** \ət-'lant-ik, at-\ ocean separating North America & South America from Europe & Africa

**At·lan·tis** \ət-'lant-əs, at-\ fabled island that was traditionally placed W of Strait of Gibraltar and that sank into sea

**At·las** \'at-ləs\ mountains NW Africa extending from SW Morocco to N Tunisia

**At·ti·ca** \'at-i-kə\ region E Greece; chief city, Athens

**Auck·land** \'ȯ-klənd\ city N New Zeland on NW North Island

**Augs·burg** \'ȯgz-,bərg, 'aȯgz-,bȯrg\ city S Germany in S Bavaria NW of Munich

**Au·gus·ta** \ȯ-'gəst-ə, ə-\ city, capital of Maine

**Aus·tin** \'ȯs-tən, 'äs-\ city, capital of Texas

**Austral** — see TUBUAI

**Aus·tral·asia** \,ȯs-trə-'lā-shə, ,äs-, -'lā-shə\ Australia, Tasmania, New Zealand & Melanesia — **Aus·tral·asian** \-zhən, -shən\ adjective or noun

**Aus·tra·lia** \ȯ-'strāl-yə, ä-, ə-\ **1** continent of eastern hemisphere SE of Asia **2** or in full **Commonwealth of Australia** dominion of the Commonwealth including continent of Australia & island of Tasmania; capital, Canberra — **Aus·tra·lian** \-yən\ adjective or noun

**Australian Alps** mountain range SE Australia in E Victoria & SE New South Wales; part of Great Dividing Range

**Australian Capital Territory** district SE Australia including two areas, one containing Canberra (capital of Australia) & the other on Jervis Bay; surrounded by New South Wales

**Aus·tria** \'ȯs-trē-ə, 'äs-\ country central Europe; capital, Vienna — **Aus·tri·an** \-ən\ adjective or noun

**Aus·tria–Hun·ga·ry** \-'həng-gə-rē\ dual monarchy 1867–1918 central Europe including what is now Austria, Hungary, the Czech Republic, Bukovina & Transylvania in Romania, Slovenia, Croatia, Galicia in Poland, & part of NE Italy — **Aus·tro–Hun·gar·i·an** \'ȯs-trō-,həng-'gar-ē-ən, 'äs-, -'ger-\ adjective or noun

**Aus·tro·ne·sia** \,ȯs-trə-'nē-zhə, ,äs-, -'nē-shə\ **1** islands of the S Pacific **2** area extending from Madagascar through Malay Peninsula & Archipelago to Hawaii & Easter Island — **Aus·tro·ne·sian** \-zhən, -shən\ adjective or noun

**Au·vergne** \ō-'veˑərn, -'veˑərn-yə, -'vərn\ **1** region & former province S central France; capital, Clermont (now Clermont-Ferrand) **2** mountains S central France in Massif Central; highest peak 1886 meters

**Ave·lla·ne·da** \,av-ə-zhə-'nä-də\ city E Argentina on Río de la Plata E of Buenos Aires

**Avon** \'ā-vən, 'av-ən, in the United States also 'ā-,vän\ **1** river 154 kilometers long central England rising in Northamptonshire & flowing WSW past Stratford-upon-Avon into the Severn **2** county SW England including Bristol

**Ayers Rock** \'aˑərz-, 'eˑərz-\ outcrop central Australia in SW Northern Territory SW of Alice Springs

**Ayr** \'aˑər, 'eˑər\ or **Ayr·shire** \-,shiˑər, -shər\ former county SW Scotland

**Azer·bai·jan** \,az-ər-,bī-'jän, ,äz-\ country SE Europe, capital, Baku; a constituent republic of U.S.S.R. 1936–91

**Azores** \'ā-,zȯrz, -,zȯrz, ə-\ or Portuguese **Aço·res** \ə-'sȯr-ēsh\ islands N Atlantic belonging to Portugal & lying 1290 kilometers W of Portuguese coast — **Azor·e·an** or **Azor·i·an** \ā-'zȯr-ē-ən, ə-, -'zȯr\ adjective or noun

**Az·ov, Sea of** \'az-,ȯf, 'äz-, -,äv\ gulf of Black Sea between Ukraine & Russia

**Baalbek** — see HELIOPOLIS

**Ba·bel·thu·ap** \,bäb-əl-'tü-,äp\ island W Pacific; chief island of Palau

**Bab·y·lon** \'bab-ə-lən, -,län\ ancient city, capital of Babylonia; site about 89 kilometers S of Baghdad near the Euphrates — **Bab·y·lo·nian** \,bab-ə-'lō-nyən, -nē-ən\ adjective or noun

**Bab·y·lo·nia** \,bab-ə-'lō-nyə, -nē-ə\ ancient country W Asia in valley of lower Euphrates and Tigris rivers; capital, Babylon — **Bab·y·lo·nian** \-nyən, -nē-ən\ adjective or noun

**Ba·co·lod** \bäk-'ō-,lȯd\ city Philippines on Negros

**Bac·tria** \'bak-trē-ə\ ancient country W Asia between the Hindu Kush & upper Oxus in present NE Afghanistan — **Bac·tri·an** \-ən\ adjective or noun

**Ba·den–Würt·tem·berg** \,bäd-n-'wərt-əm-,bərg, -'wȯrt-; ,vert-əm-,berk\ state SW Germany W of Bavaria; capital, Stuttgart

**Bad·lands National Park** \'bad-,landz-, -,lanz-\ reservation SW South Dakota E of Black Hills

**Baf·fin** \'baf-ən\ island NE Canada in Arctic Archipelago N of Hudson Strait

**Baffin Bay** inlet of the Atlantic between W Greenland & E Baffin Island

**Bagh·dad** or **Bag·dad** \'bag-,dad\ city, capital of Iraq on the middle Tigris

**Ba·guio** \,bäg-ē-'ō\ city, former summer capital of the Philippines in NW central Luzon

**Ba·ha·ma** \bə-'häm-ə, by outsiders also -'hä-mə\ islands in N Atlantic SE of Florida; an independent member of the Commonwealth; capital, Nassau — **Ba·ha·mi·an** \-'hä-mē-ən, -'häm-ē-ən\ or **Ba·ha·man** \-'hä-mən, -'häm-ən\ adjective or noun

**Bahia** — see SALVADOR

**Bah·rain** \bä-'rän\ islands in Persian Gulf off coast of Arabia forming an independent country; capital, Manama

**Bai·kal** or **Bay·kal** \bī-'kȯl, -'käl\ lake Russia in Asia, in mountains N of Mongolia

**Baile Atha Cliath** — see DUBLIN

**Ba·ja** \'bä-hä\ BAJA CALIFORNIA

**Ba·ja California** \,bä-hä-\ **1** peninsula NW Mexico W of Gulf of California **2** state NW Mexico in N Baja California Peninsula; capital, Mexicali

**Baja California Sur** \'sùr\ state NW Mexico in S Baja California Peninsula; capital, La Paz

**Bakh·ta·ran** \,bäk-tə-'rän\ city W Iran

**Ba·ku** \bä-'kü\ city, capital of Azerbaijan on W coast of Caspian Sea

**Bakwanga** — see MBUJI-MAYI

**Bal·a·ton** \'bal-ə-,tän, 'bȯl-ə-,tōn\ lake W Hungary

**Balboa Heights** \bal-,bō-ə-\ town Panama; former administrative center for Canal Zone

**Bâle** — see BASEL

**Bal·e·ar·ic** \,bal-ē-'ar-ik\ islands E Spain in the W Mediterranean — see MAJORCA, MINORCA, IBIZA

**Ba·li** \'bäl-ē\ island Indonesia off E end of Java — **Ba·li·nese** \,bäl-i-'nēz, ,bal-, -'nēs\ adjective or noun

**Bal·kan** \'bȯl-kən\ **1** mountains N Bulgaria extending from Yugoslavia border to Black Sea; highest 2375 meters **2** peninsula SE Europe between Adriatic & Ionian seas on the W & Aegean & Black seas on the E

**Bal·kans** or **Balkan States** \'bȯl-kənz\ countries occupying the Balkan Peninsula: Slovenia, Croatia, Bosnia and Herzegovina, Macedonia, Yugoslavia, Romania, Bulgaria, Albania, Greece, Turkey (in Europe)

**Bal·khash** or **Bal·qash** \bal-'kash, bäl-'käsh\ lake E Kazakhstan

**Bal·tic** \'bȯl-tik\ sea arm of the Atlantic N Europe E of Scandinavian Peninsula

**Bal·ti·more** \'bȯl-tə-,mōr, -,mór; 'bȯl-tə-mər, 'bȯl-mər\ city N central Maryland

**Ba·lu·chi·stan** \bə-,lü-chə-'stan\ arid region S Asia bordering on Arabian Sea in SW Pakistan & SE Iran — **Ba·lu·chi** \bə-'lü-chē\ noun

**Ba·ma·ko** \,bäm-ə-'kō\ city, capital of Mali on the Niger

**Ban·dar** — see MACHILIPATNAM

**Ban·dar Lam·pung** \,bən-dər-'läm-pùng\ city & port Indonesia in S Sumatra

**Ban·dar Se·ri Be·ga·wan** \,bən-dər-,ser-ē-bə-'gä-wən\ town, capital of Brunei

**Ban·dung** \'bän-,dùng\ city Indonesia in W Java SE of Jakarta

**Banff** \'bamf, 'bampf\ or **Banff·shire** \-,shiˑər, -shər\ former county NE Scotland

**Ban·ga·lore** \'bang-gə-,lōr, -,lòr\ city S India W of Madras, capital of Karnataka

**Bang·kok** \'bang-,käk, bang-'\ city, capital of Thailand on Chao Phraya River

**Ban·gla·desh** \,bäng-glə-'desh, ,bang-, -'däsh\ country S Asia E of India; formerly part of Pakistan; an independent republic since 1971; capital, Dhaka — see EAST PAKISTAN

**Ban·gui** \bänⁿ-'gē\ city, capital of Central African Republic

**Ban·jul** \'bän-,jül\ or formerly **Bath·urst** \'bath-,ərst, -ərst\ city, capital of Gambia

**Bao·ding** or **Pao·ting** \baù-'ding\ city NE China in Hebei SW of Beijing

**Bao·tou** or **Pao–t'ou** \baù-'tō\ city N China in SW Inner Mongolia

**Bar·ba·dos** \bär-'bäd-əs, -ōz, -äs, -ōs\ island British West Indies in Lesser Antilles E of Windward Islands; an independent dominion of the Commonwealth since 1966; capital, Bridgetown — **Bar·ba·di·an** \-'bäd-ē-ən\ adjective or noun

**Bar·ba·ry States** \'bär-bə-rē, -brē\ the states of Morocco, Algeria, Tunisia, & Tripolitania while under Turkish flag

**Bar·bu·da** \bär-'büd-ə\ island British West Indies in the Leewards — see ANTIGUA

**Bar·ce·lo·na** \,bär-sə-'lō-nə\ city NE Spain on the Mediterranean; chief city of Catalonia

**Ba·reil·ly** or **Ba·re·li** \bə-'rä-lē\ city N India in NW central Uttar Pradesh

**Ba·rents** \'bär-əns, 'bär-\ sea comprising part of Arctic Ocean between Spitsbergen & Novaya Zemlya

**Ba·ri** \'bär-ē\ city SE Italy, capital of Puglia on the Adriatic

**Bar·king** \'bär-king\ borough of E Greater London, England

**Bar·na·ul** \,bär-nə-'ül\ city S Russia in Asia, on the Ob

**Bar·net** \'bär-nət\ borough of N Greater London, England

**Ba·ro·da** \bə-'rōd-ə\ city W India in SE Gujarat

**Bar·qui·si·me·to** \,bär-kə-sə-'mät-ō\ city NW Venezuela

**Ban·ran·qui·lla** \,bar-ən-'kē-ə, -'kē-yə\ city N Colombia on the Magdalena

**Barren Grounds** treeless plains N Canada W of Hudson Bay

**Bar·row, Point** \'bar-ō\ most northerly point of Alaska & of United States at about 71°25' N latitude

**Ba·sel** \'bäz-əl\ or French **Bâle** \'bäl\ city NW Switzerland

**Ba·si·lan** \bä-'sē-,län\ **1** island S Philippines **2** city on the island

**Bas·il·don** \'baz-əl-dən\ town SE England in Essex

**Ba·si·li·ca·ta** \bə-,zil-ə-'kät-ə, -,sil-\ region S Italy on Gulf of Taranto; capital, Potenza

**Basque Provinces** \'bask\ region N Spain on Bay of Biscay including Álava, Guipúzcoa, & Vizcaya provinces

**Bas·ra** \'bäs-rə, 'bəs-, 'bas-\ city S Iraq on Shatt al Arab

**Bass** \'bas\ strait separating Tasmania & continent of Australia

**Bas·sein** \bə-'sān\ city S Myanmar

**Basse·terre** \bäs-'ter\ town, capital of Saint Kitts and Nevis

**Bas·tille** \ba-'stēl\ medieval fortress, Paris; used as prison until destroyed by mobs on July 14, 1789

**Basutoland** — see LESOTHO

**Ba·taan** \bə-'tan, -'tän\ peninsula Philippines in W Luzon on W side of Manila Bay

**Batavia** — see JAKARTA

**Bathurst** — see BANJUL

**Bat·on Rouge** \,bat-n-'rüzh\ city, capital of Louisiana

**Ba·var·ia** \bə-'ver-ē-ə, -'var-\ or German **Bay·ern** \'bī-ərn\ state SE Germany bordering on the Czech Republic & Austria; capital, Munich — **Ba·var·i·an** \bə-'ver-ē-ən, -'var-\ adjective or noun

**Ba·ya·mon** \,bī-ə-'mōn\ city NE central Puerto Rico

**Baykal** — see BAIKAL

**Beard·more** \'biərd-,mōr, -,mȯr\ glacier Antarctica, one of world's largest

**Beau·fort** \'bō-fərt\ sea comprising part of Arctic Ocean NE of Alaska & NW of Canada

**Beau·mont** \'bō-,mänt, bō-'\ city SE Texas

**Bech·u·a·na·land** \,bech-'wän-ə-,land, -ə-'wän-\ **1** region S Africa N of Orange River **2** — see BOTSWANA — **Bech·u·a·na** \,bech-'wän-ə, -ə-'wän-\ *adjective or noun*

**Bed·ford·shire** \'bed-fərd-,shiər, -shər\ *or* **Bedford** county SE England

**Bedloe's** — see LIBERTY

**Bei·jing** \'bā-'jiŋ\ *or* **Pe·king** \'pē-'kiŋ, 'pā-\ city, capital of China

**Bei·rut** \bā-'rüt\ *or ancient* **Be·ry·tus** \bə-'rīt-əs\ city, capital of Lebanon

**Be·la·rus** \,bē-lə-'rüs, 'byel-ə\ country central Europe; capital, Minsk

**Belau** — see PALAU

**Be·lém** \bə-'lem\ *or* **Pa·rá** \pə-'rä\ city N Brazil on Pará River

**Bel·fast** \'bel-,fast, bel-'\ city, capital of Northern Ireland

**Belgian Congo** — see CONGO 2

**Bel·gium** \'bel-jəm\ *or French* **Bel·gique** \bel-zhēk\ *or Flemish* **Bel·gië** \'bel-gē-ə\ country W Europe; capital, Brussels — **Bel·gian** \'bel-jən\ *adjective or noun*

**Bel·grade** \'bel-,grād, -,gräd, -,grad, bel-'\ *or* **Be·o·grad** \'beü-,gräd\ city, capital of Yugoslavia on the Danube

**Be·lize** \bə-'lēz\ *or Spanish* **Be·li·ce** \bā-'lē-sā\ **1** *or formerly* **British Hon·du·ras** \hän-'dúr-əs, -'dyúr-\ country Central America on the Caribbean; capital, Belmopan **2** city E Belize on the Caribbean

**Bel·mo·pan** \,bel-mō-'pän\ city, capital of Belize

**Be·lo Ho·ri·zon·te** \'bā-lō-,hór-ə-'zänt-ē, 'bel-ō-, -,här-\ city E Brazil N of Rio de Janeiro

**Bel·lo·rus·sian Soviet Socialist Republic** \,bel-ō-'rəsh-ən\ *or* **Bye·lo·rus·sian Soviet Socialist Republic** \bē-,el-ō-\ former constituent republic of U.S.S.R.; became independent Belarus 1991 — **Belorussian** *adjective or noun*

**Beloye More** — see WHITE SEA

**Be·ne·lux** \'ben-l-,əks\ economic union comprising Belgium, Luxembourg, & the Netherlands; formed 1947

**Ben·gal** \ben-'gól, beŋ-\ region S Asia including delta of Ganges & Brahmaputra rivers; divided between West Bengal, India, & Bangladesh — see EAST BENGAL, WEST BENGAL — **Ben·gal·ese** \,beŋ-gə-'lēz, ,ben-, -'lēs\ *adjective or noun*

**Bengal, Bay of** arm of Indian Ocean between India & Myanmar

**Ben·gha·zi** \ben-'gäz-ē, beŋ-, -'gaz-\ city NE Libya; formerly a capital of Libya

**Ben·guela Current** \ben-'gwel-ə, 'beŋ-, -'gel-\ cold current of the Atlantic Ocean flowing N along SW coast of Africa

**Be·nin** \bə-'nin, -'nēn; 'ben-ən\ **1** *or formerly* **Da·ho·mey** \də-'hō-mē\ country W Africa on Gulf of Guinea; a republic; capital, Porto-Novo **2** city SW Nigeria — **Ben·i·nese** \bə-,nin-'ēz, -,nēn-, ,ben-i-'nēz, -'nēs\ *adjective or noun*

**Benin, Bight of** the N section of Gulf of Guinea

**Ben Nev·is** \ben-'nev-əs\ mountain 1343 meters W Scotland in the Grampians; highest in Great Britain

**Be·no·ni** \bə-'nō-nē\ city NE Republic of South Africa

**Ber·ga·mo** \'beər-gə-,mō, 'bər-\ city N Italy in Lombardy NE of Milan

**Ber·gen** \'bər-gən, 'beər-\ city SW Norway

**Be·ring** \'biər-iŋ, 'beər-\ **1** sea arm of the N Pacific between Alaska & NE Siberia **2** strait 85 kilometers wide between North America (Alaska) and Asia (Russia)

**Berke·ley** \'bər-klē\ city W California on San Francisco Bay N of Oakland

**Berk·shire** \'bərk-,shiər, -shər, *for 2 British usually* 'bärk-\ **1** hills W Massachusetts; highest peak Mount Greylock 1064 meters **2** county S England W of London

**Ber·lin** \bər-'lin, ,bər-\ city, official capital of Germany; divided 1945–90 into East Berlin & West Berlin — **Ber·lin·er** \-'lin-ər\ *noun*

**Berlin, East** former city, capital of East Germany 1945–90

**Berlin, West** former city, West Germany; an enclave lying wholly within East Germany

**Ber·mu·da** \bər-'myüd-ə, ,bər-\ islands W Atlantic ESE of Cape Hatteras; a British colony; capital,

Hamilton — **Ber·mu·dan** \-'myüd-n\ *or* **Ber·mu·di·an** \-'myüd-ē-ən\ *adjective or noun*

**Bern** \'bərn, 'beərn\ city, capital of Switzerland — **Ber·nese** \bər-'nēz, ,bər-, -'nēs\ *adjective or noun*

**Ber·wick** \'ber-ik\ *or* **Ber·wick·shire** \-,shiər, -shər\ former county SE Scotland

**Berytus** — see BEIRUT

**Bes·kids** \'bes-,kidz, be-'skēdz\ mountain ranges central Europe in the W Carpathians including West Beskids (in Poland, NW Slovakia, & E Czech Republic W of Tatra Mountains) & East Beskids (in NE Slovakia)

**Bes·sa·ra·bia** \,bes-ə-'rā-bē-ə\ region SE Europe between Dniester & Prut rivers now chiefly in Moldova — **Bes·sa·ra·bi·an** \-bē-ən\ *adjective or noun*

**Beth·le·hem** \'beth-li-,hem, -lē-həm, -lē-əm\ town of ancient Palestine in Judea SW of Jerusalem in area occupied by Israel since 1967

**Bex·ley** \'bek-slē\ borough of E Greater London, England

**Bezwada** — see VIJAYAWADA

**Bhav·na·gar** \faù-'nəg-ər\ city W India in S Gujarat

**Bho·pal** \bō-'päl\ city N central India NW of Nagpur, capital of Madhya Pradesh

**Bhu·tan** \bü-'tan, -'tän\ country S Asia in the Himalaya on NE border of India; a protectorate of India; capital, Thimphu — **Bhu·ta·nese** \,büt-n-'ēz, -'ēs\ *adjective or noun*

**Bi·af·ra, Bight of** \bē-'af-rə, bī-, -'äf-\ the E section of Gulf of Guinea in W Africa

**Bia·ly·stok** \bē-,äl-i-,stók\ city NE Poland

**Bie·le·feld** \'bē-lə-,felt\ city NW central Germany E of Münster

**Big Bend National Park** reservation SW Texas on Rio Grande

**Big Thicket** wilderness area E Texas NE of Houston

**Bi·har** \bi-'här\ state E India bordering on Nepal; capital, Patna

**Bi·ki·ni** \bə-'kē-nē\ island (atoll) W Pacific in Marshall Islands

**Bil·bao** \bil-'bä-,ō, -'baù, -'bä-ō\ city N Spain

**Bil·lings** \'bil-iŋz\ city S central Montana; largest in state

**Bio·ko** \bē-'ō-(,)kō\ *or formerly* **Fer·nan·do Póo** \fər-,nan-(,)dō-'pō\ island Equatorial Guinea in Bight of Biafra

**Bir·ken·head** \'bər-kən-,hed, ,bər-kən-'\ borough NW England in Merseyside

**Bir·ming·ham** \'bər-miŋ-,ham, *British usually* -miŋ-əm\ **1** city N central Alabama **2** city W central England in Warwickshire

**Bisayas** — see VISAYAN

**Bis·cay, Bay of** \'bis-,kā, -kē\ inlet of the Atlantic between W coast of France & N coast of Spain

**Bis·cayne National Park** \bis-'kān-, 'bis-,\ reservation S Florida

**Bish·kek** \bish-'kek\ *or formerly* **Frun·ze** \'frün-zə\ city, capital of Kyrgyzstan

**Bis·marck** \'biz-,märk\ **1** city, capital of North Dakota **2** archipelago W Pacific N of E end of New Guinea

**Bis·sau** \bis-'aù\ city, capital of Guinea-Bissau

**Bi·thyn·ia** \bə-'thin-ē-ə\ ancient country NW Asia Minor bordering on Sea of Marmara and Black Sea — **Bi·thyn·i·an** \-ē-ən\ *adjective or noun*

**Black·burn** \'blak-bərn, -,bərn\ borough NW England in Lancashire

**Black Forest** *or German* **Schwarz·wald** \'shfärts-,vält, 'shwórt-,swóld\ forested mountain region SW Germany along E bank of the upper Rhine

**Black Hills** mountains W South Dakota & NE Wyoming; highest Harney Peak 2207 meters

**Black·pool** \'blak-,pül\ borough NW England in Lancashire

**Black Sea** *or ancient* **Pon·tus Eux·i·nus** \,pän-təs-yük-'sī-nəs\ *or* **Pon·tus** \'pän-təs\ sea between Europe & Asia connected with Aegean Sea through the Bosporus, Sea of Marmara, & Dardanelles

**Blan·tyre** \'blan-,tīr\ city S Malawi

**Bloem·fon·tein** \'blüm-fən-,tān, -,fän-\ city, judicial capital of the Republic of South Africa

**Blue Nile** river 1368 kilometers long Ethiopia & Sudan flowing NNW into the Nile at Khartoum

**Blue Ridge** E range of the Appalachians E U.S. extending from S Pennsylvania to N Georgia

**Bo·bo–Diou·las·so** \'bō-,bō-dyü-'las-ō\ town W Burkina Faso

**Bo·chum** \'bō-kəm\ city W Germany in valley of the Ruhr

**Boe·o·tia** \bē-'ō-shē-ə, -shə\ district E central Greece NW of Attica; chief ancient city, Thebes — **Boe·o·tian** \-shē-ən, -shən\ *adjective or noun*

**Bo·go·tá** \,bō-gə-'tó, -'tä\ city, capital of Colombia

**Bo Hai** *or* **Po Hai** \'bō-'hī\ *or* **Gulf of Chih·li** \'chē-lē, 'jiər-'lē\ arm of Yellow Sea NE China N of Shandong Peninsula

**Bo·he·mia** \bō-'hē-mē-ə\ region W Czech Republic; once a kingdom & later a province; chief city, Prague

**Boi·se** \'bói-sē, -zē\ city, capital of Idaho

**Bokhara** — see BUKHARA

**Boks·burg** \'bäks-,bərg\ city NE Republic of South Africa

**Bo·liv·ia** \bə-'liv-ē-ə\ country W central South America; administrative capital, La Paz; constitutional capital, Sucre — **Bo·liv·ian** \-ē-ən\ *adjective or noun*

**Bo·lo·gna** \bə-'lōn-yə, -'lōn-ə\ city N Italy N of Florence, capital of Emilia-Romagna

**Bol·ton** \'bōlt-n\ town NW England in Greater Manchester

**Bom·bay** \bäm-'bā\ **1** former state W India; divided 1960 into Gujarat & Maharashtra states **2** city, capital of Maharashtra

**Bône** — see ANNABA

**Bo·nin** \'bō-nən\ *or* **Oga·sa·wa·ra** \ō-,gäs-ə-'wär-ə\ islands Japan in W Pacific SE of Honshu

**Bonn** \'bän, 'bón\ city W Germany on the Rhine SSE of Cologne; formerly capital of West Germany

**Boo·thia** \'bü-thē-ə\ peninsula N Canada W of Baffin Island; its N tip is most northerly point on North American mainland

**Bor·deaux** \bór-'dō\ city SW France on the Garonne

**Bor·ders** \'bórd-ərz\ region SE Scotland; established 1975

**Bor·neo** \'bór-nē-,ō\ island Malay Archipelago SW of the Philippines

**Bos·nia** \'bäz-nē-ə\ region S Europe; with Herzegovina constitutes country of **Bosnia and Herzegovina**; capital, Sarajevo (in Bosnia) — **Bos·ni·an** \-nē-ən\ *adjective or noun*

**Bos·po·rus** \'bäs-pə-rəs, -prəs\ *or ancient* **Bosporus Thra·ci·us** \-'thrā-shē-əs, -shəs\ strait about 31 kilometers long between Turkey in Europe & Turkey in Asia connecting Sea of Marmara & Black Sea

**Bos·ton** \'bó-stən\ city, capital of Massachusetts — **Bos·to·nian** \bó-'stō-nē-ən, -nyən\ *adjective or noun*

**Bot·a·ny Bay** \'bät-n-ē, 'bät-nē\ inlet of S Pacific SE Australia in New South Wales S of Sydney

**Both·nia, Gulf of** \'bäth-nē-ə\ arm of Baltic Sea between Sweden & Finland

**Bo·tswa·na** \bät-'swän-ə\ country S Africa N of Molopo River; formerly British protectorate of Bechuanaland; now an independent republic; capital, Gaborone

**Boulder Dam** — see HOOVER DAM

**Bourgogne** — see BURGUNDY

**Bourne·mouth** \'bórn-məth, 'bórn-, 'bùrn-\ town S England in Dorset on English Channel

**Brad·ford** \'brad-fərd\ city N England in West Yorkshire

**Brah·ma·pu·tra** \,bräm-ə-'pü-trə, -'pyü-\ river 2900 kilometers long S Asia flowing from the Himalaya in Tibet to Ganges delta

**Bra·ila** \brə-'ē-lə\ city E Romania

**Bra·sí·lia** \brə-'zil-yə\ city, capital of Brazil in Federal District in E Goiás state

**Bra·sov** \bräsh-'óv\ city central Romania

**Bra·ti·sla·va** \,brat-ə-'släv-ə, ,brät-\ city, capital of Slovakia

**Bratsk** \'brätsk\ city S central Russia in Asia, NNE of Irkutsk

**Braunschweig** — see BRUNSWICK

**Bra·zil** \brə-'zil\ country E & central South America; a federal republic; capital, Brasília — **Bra·zil·ian** \brə-'zil-yən\ *adjective or noun*

**Brazil Current** warm current of the Atlantic Ocean flowing S along coast of Brazil

**Braz·za·ville** \'braz-ə-,vil, 'bräz-ə-,vēl\ city, capital of Republic of the Congo Republic on W bank of Pool Malebo in lower Congo River

**Brec·on** \'brek-ən\ or **Breck·nock** \'brek-ˌnäk, -nək\ or **Brec·on·shire** or **Breck·nock·shire** \-ˌshiər, -shər\ former county SE Wales

**Bre·men** \'brem-ən, 'brā-mən\ **1** state NW Germany **2** city, its capital

**Bren·ner** \'bren-ər\ pass 1371 meters in the Alps between Austria & Italy

**Brent** \'brent\ borough of W Greater London, England

**Bre·scia** \'bresh-ə, 'brā-shə\ city N Italy in Lombardy ENE of Milan

**Breslau** — see WROCLAW

**Brest** \'brest\ **1** city NW France in Brittany **2** city SW Belarus

**Bret·on, Cape** \kāp-'bret-n, kə-'bret-, -'brit-\ headland Canada; most easterly point of Cape Breton Island & of Nova Scotia

**Bridge·port** \'brij-ˌpōrt, -ˌpȯrt\ city SW Connecticut

**Bridge·town** \'brij-ˌtaun\ city, capital of Barbados

**Brigh·ton** \'brīt-n\ town S England in East Sussex on English Channel

**Bris·bane** \'briz-bən, -ˌbān\ city E Australia, capital of Queensland

**Bris·tol** \'bris-tl\ **1** city SW England in Avon **2** channel between S Wales & SW England

**Brit·ain** \'brit-n\ **1** the island of Great Britain **2** UNITED KINGDOM

**British Columbia** province W Canada on Pacific coast; capital, Victoria

**British Commonwealth** — see COMMONWEALTH OF NATIONS

**British Guiana** — see GUYANA

**British Honduras** — see BELIZE 1

**British India** the part of India formerly under direct British administration

**British Indian Ocean Territory** British colony in Indian Ocean comprising Chagos Archipelago & formerly Aldabra, Farquhar, & Desroches islands (returned to Seychelles 1976)

**British Isles** island group W Europe comprising Great Britain, Ireland, & adjacent islands

**British Solomon Islands** former British protectorate comprising the Solomon Islands (except Bougainville, Buka, & adjacent small islands) & Santa Cruz Islands; capital, Honiara

**British Somaliland** former British protectorate E Africa bordering on Gulf of Aden; capital, Hargeisa; since 1960 part of Somalia

**British Virgin Islands** E islands of Virgin Islands group; a British dependency; capital, Road Town (on Tortola Island)

**British West Indies** islands of the West Indies belonging to the Commonwealth & including Jamaica, Trinidad and Tobago, & the Bahama, Cayman, Windward, Leeward, & British Virgin islands

**Brit·ta·ny** \'brit-n-ē\ or French **Bre·tagne** \brə-'tán³\ region & former province NW France SW of Normandy

**Brno** \'bər-nō\ city SE Czech Republic, chief city of Moravia

**Brom·ley** \'bräm-lē\ borough of SE Greater London, England

**Bronx** \'brängs, 'brängks\ or **The Bronx** borough of New York City on mainland NE of Manhattan Island

**Brook·lyn** \'bruk-lən\ borough of New York City at SW end of Long Island

**Brooks Range** \'bruks\ mountains N Alaska

**Bruges** \'brüzh, 'brüēzh\ or Flemish **Brug·ge** \'brüēg-ə\ city NW Belgium

**Bru·nei** \brün-'ī, 'brü-ˌnī\ sultanate NE Borneo; formerly a British protectorate; capital, Bandar Seri Begawan

**Bruns·wick** \'brənz-wik\ or German **Braun·schweig** \'braun-ˌshwīg, -ˌshfīk\ city central Germany W of Berlin

**Brus·sels** \'brəs-əlz\ city, capital of Belgium

**Bryansk** \brē-'änsk\ city W Russia in Europe, SW of Moscow

**Bryce Canyon National Park** \'brīs\ reservation S Utah NE of Zion National Park

**Bu·ca·ra·man·ga** \ˌbü-kə-rə-'mäng-gə\ city N Colombia NNE of Bogotá

**Bu·cha·rest** \'bü-kə-ˌrest, 'byü-\ city, capital of Romania

**Buck·ing·ham·shire** \'bək-ing-əm-ˌshiər, -shər, in the United States also -ˌham-\ or **Buckingham** county SE central England

**Bu·da·pest** \'büd-ə-ˌpest also 'byüd-, 'bùd-, -ˌpesht\ city, capital of Hungary

**Bue·nos Ai·res** \ˌbwā-nə-'saər-ēz, ˌbō-nə-, -'seər-, -'sīr-\ city, capital of Argentina on Rio de la Plata

**Buf·fa·lo** \'bəf-ə-ˌlō\ city W New York on Lake Erie

**Bu·jum·bu·ra** \ˌbü-jəm-'bùr-ə\ or formerly **Usum·bu·ra** \ˌü-səm-'bùr-ə\ city, capital of Burundi

**Bu·ka·vu** \bü-'käv-ü\ city E Democratic Republic of the Congo

**Bu·kha·ra** \bü-'kär-ə, -'kar-, -'här-, -'har-\ or **Bo·khara** \bō-\ city Uzbekistan, E of the Amu Dar'ya

**Bu·la·wa·yo** \ˌbül-ə-'wä-ō, -'wī-\ city SW Zimbabwe

**Bul·gar·ia** \ˌbəl-'gar-ē-ə, bùl-, -'ger-\ country SE Europe on Black Sea; capital, Sofia

**Bur·gun·dy** \'bər-gən-dē\ or French **Bour·gogne** \bür-'gòn³\ region E France; a former kingdom, duchy, & province — **Bur·gun·di·an** \bər-'gən-dē-ən, ˌbər-\ adjective or noun

**Bur·ki·na Fa·so** \bùr-ˌkē-nə-'fäs-ō, bər-\ or formerly **Upper Vol·ta** \'vōl-tə, 'vȯl-, 'väl-\ country W Africa N of Ivory Coast, Ghana, & Togo; a republic; capital, Ouagadougou

**Bur·ling·ton** \'bər-ling-tən\ city NW Vermont; largest in state

**Burma** — see MYANMAR

**Bur·sa** \bùr-'sä, 'bər-sə\ city NW Turkey in Asia, near Sea of Marmara

**Bu·run·di** \bù-'rün-dē\ or formerly **Urun·di** \ù-'rün-dē\ country E central Africa; capital, Bujumbura — see RUANDA-URUNDI

**Bute** \'byüt\ **1** island SW Scotland in Firth of Clyde **2** or **Bute·shire** \-ˌshiər, -shər\ former county SW Scotland

**Byd·goszcz** \'bid-ˌgȯshch, -ˌgȯsh\ or German **Brom·berg** \'bräm-ˌberg, 'brȯm-ˌberk\ city NW central Poland

**Byelorussian Soviet Socialist Republic** — see BELORUSSIAN SOVIET SOCIALIST REPUBLIC

**Byzantium** — see ISTANBUL

**Caen** \'kä³\ city NW France

**Caer·nar·von·shire** \kär-'när-vən-ˌshiər, -shər\ or **Caernarvon** former county NW Wales

**Cae·sa·rea** \ˌsē-zə-'rē-ə, ˌses-ə-, ˌsez-ə-\ ancient city W Palestine in Samaria on the Mediterranean; Roman capital of Palestine

**Ca·glia·ri** \'käl-yə-rē\ city Italy, capital of Sardinia

**Cai·ro** \'kī-rō\ city, capital of Egypt — **Cai·rene** \kī-'rēn\ adjective or noun

**Caith·ness** \'käth-nəs\ former county N Scotland

**Ca·la·bria** \kə-'lä-brē-ə, -'läb-rē-\ **1** district of ancient Italy comprising area forming heel of peninsula of Italy; now S part of Puglia **2** or ancient **Brut·ti·um** \'brùt-ē-əm, 'brət-\ region S Italy occupying toe of peninsula of Italy; capital, Catanzaro — **Ca·la·bri·an** \kə-'lä-brē-ən, -'läb-rē-\ adjective or noun

**Cal·cut·ta** \kal-'kət-ə\ city E India on Hugli River, capital of West Bengal — **Cal·cut·tan** \-'kət-n\ adjective or noun

**Cal·e·do·nia** \ˌkal-ə-'dō-nyə, -nē-ə\ — see SCOTLAND — **Cal·e·do·nian** \-nyən, -nē-ən\ adjective or noun

**Cal·ga·ry** \'kal-gə-rē\ city SW Alberta

**Ca·li** \'käl-ē\ city W Colombia

**Cal·i·cut** \'kal-i-kət\ or **Ko·zhi·kode** \'kō-zhə-ˌkōd\ city SW India

**Cal·i·for·nia** \ˌkal-ə-'fȯr-nyə\ state SW U.S.; capital, Sacramento — **Cal·i·for·nian** \-nyən\ adjective or noun

**California, Gulf of** arm of the Pacific NW Mexico

**California Current** cold current of the Pacific Ocean flowing SE along W coast of North America

**Cal·lao** \kə-'yä-ō, kə-'yaù\ city W Peru SW of Lima

**Cal·va·ry** \'kalv-rē, -ə-rē\ or Hebrew **Gol·go·tha** \'gäl-gə-thə, gäl-'gäth-ə\ place outside ancient Jerusalem where Christ was crucified

**Ca·ma·güey** \ˌkam-ə-'gwā\ city E central Cuba

**Cam·bay, Gulf of** \kam-'bā\ inlet of Arabian Sea India N of Bombay

**Cam·ber·well** \'kam-bər-ˌwel, -wəl\ city SE Australia in S Victoria E of Melbourne

**Cam·bo·dia** \kam-'bōd-ē-ə\ or formerly **Democratic Kam·pu·chea** \-ˌkam-pù-'chē-ə\ country SE Asia bordering on Gulf of Thailand; capital, Phnom Penh — **Cam·bo·di·an** \-ē-ən\ adjective or noun

**Cam·bria** \'kam-brē-ə\ — see WALES

**Cam·bridge** \'kām-brij\ **1** city E Massachusetts W of Boston **2** city E England in Cambridgeshire

**Cam·bridge·shire** \'kām-brij-ˌshiər, -shər\ or **Cambridge** or formerly **Cambridgeshire and Isle of Ely** \'ē-lē\ county E England

**Cam·den** \'kam-dən\ **1** city SW New Jersey **2** borough of N Greater London, England

**Cam·er·oon** or French **Cam·er·oun** \ˌkam-ə-'rün\ country W equatorial Africa; capital, Yaoundé — **Cam·er·oo·nian** \-'rü-nē-ən, -'rü-nyən\ adjective or noun

**Cam·er·oons** \ˌkam-ə-'rünz\ region W Africa on NE Gulf of Guinea formerly belonging to the British and French but now divided between Nigeria & Cameroon

**Cam·pa·nia** \kam-'pā-nyə, -nē-ə\ region S Italy bordering on Tyrrhenian Sea; capital, Naples — **Cam·pa·nian** \-nyən, -nē-ən\ adjective or noun

**Cam·pe·che** \kam-'pē-chē, käm-'pä-chä\ state SE Mexico in W Yucatán Peninsula; capital, Campeche

**Cam·pi·nas** \kam-'pē-nəs\ city SE Brazil N of São Paulo

**Cam·po·bas·so** \ˌkäm-pō-'bäs-ˌō\ city central Italy

**Cam·po Gran·de** \ˌkam-pü-'gran-də, -dē\ city SW Brazil

**Cam·pos** \'kam-pəs\ city SE Brazil NE of Rio de Janeiro

**Ca·naan** \'kā-nən\ ancient region corresponding vaguely to later Palestine — **Ca·naan·ite** \'kā-nə-ˌnīt\ adjective or noun

**Can·a·da** \'kan-ə-də\ country N North America; dominion of the Commonwealth; capital, Ottawa — **Ca·na·di·an** \kə-'nād-ē-ən\ adjective or noun

**Canadian Shield** or **Lau·ren·tian Plateau** \lȯ-'ren-chən\ plateau region E Canada & NE U.S. extending from Mackenzie Basin E to Davis Strait & S to S Quebec, S central Ontario, NE Minnesota, NW Wisconsin, NW Michigan, and NE New York including the Adirondacks

**Canal Zone** or **Panama Canal Zone** strip of territory Panama; under U.S. control through 1999 for administration of the Panama Canal

**Ca·nary** \kə-'neər-ē\ islands in the Atlantic off NW coast of Africa belonging to Spain; capital, Las Palmas

**Ca·nav·er·al, Cape** \kə-'nav-rəl, -ə-rəl\ or 1963–73 officially **Cape Ken·ne·dy** \-'ken-ə-dē\ headland E Florida in the Atlantic on Canaveral Peninsula E of Indian River

**Can·ber·ra** \'kan-bə-rə, -ˌbrə, -ˌber-ə\ city, capital of Australia in Australian Capital Territory

**Can·ter·bury** \'kant-ər-ˌber-ē, 'kant-ə-, -bə-rē, -brē\ **1** city SE Australia in E New South Wales **2** city SE England in Kent

**Can·ton** \'kant-n\ city NE Ohio

**Canton** — see GUANGZHOU

**Can·yon·lands National Park** \'kan-yən-ˌlandz, -ˌlanz\ reservation SE Utah

**Cape Bret·on Island** \kāp-ˌbret-n, kə-ˌbret-, -ˌbrit-\ island SE Canada in NE Nova Scotia

**Cape of Good Hope 1** — see GOOD HOPE (Cape of) **2** or **Cape Province** or before 1910 **Cape Colony** former province S Republic of South Africa; capital, Cape Town

**Ca·per·na·um** \kə-'pər-nē-əm, -nā-\ city of ancient Palestine on NW shore of Sea of Galilee

**Cape Town** \'kā-ˌtaun\ city Republic of South Africa, its legislative capital

**Cape Verde** \'vərd\ **1** islands in the N Atlantic off W Africa; a republic; capital, Praia; until 1975 belonged to Portugal **2** — see VERT (Cape)

**Cape York Peninsula** \'yȯrk\ peninsula NE Australia in N Queensland

**Capitol Reef National Park** reservation S central Utah

**Cap·pa·do·cia** \ˌkap-ə-'dō-shə, -shē-ə\ ancient country & Roman province E Asia Minor; capital, Caesarea Mazaca

**Ca·pri** \kä-'prē, kə-; 'käp-rē, 'kap-\ island Italy S of Bay of Naples

**Ca·ra·cas** \kə-'rak-əs, -'räk-\ city, capital of Venezuela

**Car·diff** \'kärd-əf\ city, capital of Wales in South Glamorgan

**Car·di·gan·shire** \'kärd-i-gən-ˌshiər, -shər\ or **Cardigan** former county W Wales on Cardigan Bay

**Ca·rib·be·an** \ˌkar-ə-'bē-ən, kə-'rib-ē-ən\ sea arm of the Atlantic bounded on N & E by West Indies, on S by South America, & on W by Central America

**Ca·rin·thia** \kə-'rin-thē-ə, -'rint-\ **1** region central Europe in E Alps in S Austria & Slovenia **2** region S Austria; capital, Klagenfurt

**Car·low** \'kär-ˌlō\ county SE Ireland in Leinster

**Carls·bad Caverns** \'kärlz-ˌbad\ limestone caves SE New Mexico in **Carlsbad Caverns National Park**

**Car·mar·then·shire** \kär-'mär-thən-ˌshiər, kər-, kə-, -shər\ or **Carmarthen** former county S Wales

**Carmel, Mount** \'kär-məl\ mountain ridge N Israel; highest point 545 meters

**Ca·ro·li·na** \,kar-ə-'lī-nə\ English colony on E coast of North America founded 1663 & divided 1729 into North Carolina & South Carolina (the **Carolinas**) — **Car·o·lin·i·an** \-'lin-ē-ən\ adjective or noun

**Ca·ro·li·na** \,kär-ə-'lē-nə\ city NE central Puerto Rico

**Car·o·line** \'kar-ə-,līn, -lən\ islands W Pacific E of S Philippines; formerly part of Trust Territory of the Pacific Islands

**Car·pa·thi·an** \kär-'pā-thē-ən\ mountains E central Europe along boundary between Slovakia & Poland & in N & central Romania; highest Gerlachovka 2655 meters

**Carpathian Ruthenia** — see RUTHENIA

**Car·pen·tar·ia, Gulf of** \,kär-pən-'ter-ē-ə, -'tar-\ inlet of Arafura Sea N of Australia

**Car·son City** \'kärs-n\ city, capital of Nevada

**Car·ta·ge·na** \,kärt-ə-'gā-nə, -'hā-\ **1** city NW Colombia **2** city SE Spain

**Car·thage** \'kär-thij\ ancient city N Africa NE of modern Tunis; capital of an empire that included at greatest extent much of NW Africa, E Spain, & Sicily — **Car·tha·gin·ian** \,kär-thə-'jin-yən, -'jin-ē-ən\ adjective or noun

**Ca·sa·blan·ca** \,kas-ə-'blang-kə, ,käz-\ or Arabic **Dar el Bei·da** \,där-,el-bā-'dä\ city W Morocco on the Atlantic

**Cas·cade Range** \kas-'kād, 'kas-'kād\ mountains NW U.S. in Washington, Oregon, & N California — see RAINIER (Mount)

**Cas·pi·an Sea** \'kas-pē-ən\ salt lake between Europe & Asia about 28 meters below sea level

**Cas·tile** \kas-'tēl\ or Spanish **Cas·ti·lla** \kä-'stē-l'ä, -'stē-yä\ region & ancient kingdom central & N Spain

**Cas·tries** \ka-'strē, 'kas-,trēz\ city, capital of St. Lucia

**Cat·a·lo·nia** \,kat-l-'ō-nyə, -nē-ə\ or Spanish **Ca·ta·lu·ña** \,kät-l-'ü-nyə\ region NE Spain bordering on France & the Mediterranean; chief city, Barcelona — **Cat·a·lo·nian** \-'ō-nyən, -nē-ən\ adjective or noun

**Ca·ta·nia** \kə-'tān-yə, -'tän-\ city Italy in E Sicily at foot of Mount Etna

**Ca·tan·za·ro** \,kät-,än-'zär-,ō, -,änd-\ city S Italy

**Ca·thay** \kə-'thā, ka-\ CHINA — an old name

**Cats·kill** \'kat-,skil\ mountains in Appalachian system SE New York W of the Hudson

**Cau·ca·sia** \kò-'kā-zhə, -shə\ or **Caucasus** region SE Europe between Black & Caspian seas

**Cau·ca·sus** \'kò-kə-səs\ mountain system in Caucasia — see ELBRUS (Mount)

**Cav·an** \'kav-ən\ county NE Ireland (republic) in Ulster

**Cay·enne** \kī-'en, kā-\ city, capital of French Guiana

**Cay·man** \kā-'man, 'kā-, attributively 'kā-mən\ islands British West Indies NW of Jamaica; a British colony; capital, Georgetown (on Grand Cayman Island)

**Ce·bu** \sā-'bü\ **1** island E central Philippines in Visayan Islands **2** city on E coast of Cebu Island

**Ce·dar Rapids** \'sēd-ər\ city E Iowa

**Celebes** — see SULAWESI

**Celestial Empire** the former Chinese Empire

**Cel·le** \'tsel-ə, 'sel-ə\ city N central Germany NE of Hannover

**Cel·tic** \'kel-tik, 'sel-\ sea inlet of the Atlantic in British Isles SE of Ireland, SW of Wales, & W of Cornwall

**Central** region central Scotland; established 1975

**Central African Republic** country N central Africa; formerly the French territory of **Uban·gi-Sha·ri** \ü-'bang-gē-'shär-ē, yü-, -'bang-ē-\; capital, Bangui

**Central America** narrow portion of North America from S border of Mexico to South America — **Central American** adjective or noun

**Ce·ram** or **Se·ram** \'sā-,räm\ island E Indonesia in central Moluccas

**Cé·vennes** \sā-'ven\ mountain range S France W of the Rhone in SE Massif Central; highest peak Mount Mézenc 1754 meters

**Cey·lon** \si-'län, sā-\ **1** island in Indian Ocean off S India **2** — see SRI LANKA — **Cey·lon·ese** \,sā-lə-'nēz, ,sē-lə-, ,sel-ə-, -'nēs\ adjective or noun

**Chad** or French **Tchad** \'chad\ country N central Africa; a republic; capital, N'Djamana — **Chad·ian** \'chad-ē-ən\ adjective or noun

**Chad, Lake** shallow lake N central Africa at junction of boundaries of Chad, Niger, & Nigeria

**Cha·gos** \'chä-gəs\ archipelago central Indian Ocean; comprises British Indian Ocean Territory — see DIEGO GARCIA

**Chal·cid·i·ce** \kal-'sid-ə-sē\ peninsula NE Greece in E Macedonia

**Chal·dea** \kal-'dē-ə\ ancient region SW Asia on Euphrates River & Persian Gulf — **Chal·de·an** \-'dē-ən\ adjective or noun — **Chal·dee** \'kal-,dē\ noun

**Champlain, Lake** \sham-'plān\ lake between New York & Vermont extending N into Quebec

**Chan·di·garh** \'chən-dē-gər\ city N India N of Delhi, capital of Punjab & of Haryana

**Chang** \'chäng\ or **Yang·tze** \'yang-'sē; 'yangt-sē, 'yangkt-\ river 5525 kilometers long central China flowing into East China Sea

**Changan** — see XI'AN

**Ch'ang·chia·k'ou** — see ZHANGJIAKOU

**Ch'ang·chou** — see ZHANGZHOU

**Chang·chun** \'chäng-'chùn\ city NE China, capital of Jilin

**Chang·de** or **Chang·te** \'chäng-'də\ city SE central China in N Hunan

**Chang·sha** \'chäng-'shä\ city SE central China, capital of Hunan

**Channel** **1** — see SANTA BARBARA **2** islands in English Channel including Jersey, Guernsey, & Alderney & belonging to Great Britain; capital, Saint Helier

**Channel Islands National Park** reservation SW California

**Cha·pa·la** \chə-'päl-ə\ lake W central Mexico SE of Guadalajara

**Charles** \'chärlz\ river 76 kilometers long E Massachusetts flowing into Boston harbor

**Charles, Cape** cape E Virginia N of entrance to Chesapeake Bay

**Charles·ton** \'chärl-stən\ city, capital of West Virginia

**Char·lotte** \'shär-lət\ city S North Carolina

**Charlotte Ama·lie** \ə-'mäl-yə\ city, capital of Virgin Islands of the U.S.; on Saint Thomas Island

**Char·lotte·town** \'shär-lət-,taùn\ city, capital of Prince Edward Island, Canada

**Chat·ta·noo·ga** \,chat-ə-'nü-gə, ,chat-n-'ü-\ city SE Tennessee

**Che·bok·sa·ry** \,cheb-,äk-'sär-ē\ city central Russia in Europe, on the Volga W of Kazan

**Chekiang** — see ZHEJIANG

**Chelsea** — see KENSINGTON AND CHELSEA

**Che·lya·binsk** \chel-'yä-bənsk\ city W Russia in Asia, S of Sverdlovsk

**Chemnitz** \'kem-,nits, -nəts\ or 1953–90 **Karl-Marx-Stadt** \,kärl-'märk-,shtät, -,stät\ city E Germany SE of Leipzig

**Chen·chiang** — see ZHENJIANG

**Cheng·chou** — see ZHENGZHOU

**Cheng·du** or **Ch'eng·tu** \'chəng-'dü\ city SW central China, capital of Sichuan

**Cher·so·nese** \'kər-sə-,nēz, -,nēs\ any of several peninsulas (as the Gallipoli & Crimea peninsulas)

**Ches·a·peake Bay** \'ches-,pēk, -ə-,pēk\ inlet of the Atlantic in Virginia & Maryland

**Chesh·ire** \'chesh-ər, 'chesh-,iər\ or **Ches·ter** \'ches-tər\ county W England bordering on Wales

**Chev·i·ot** \'chev-ē-ət, 'chē-vē-ət\ hills along English-Scottish border

**Chey·enne** \shī-'an, -'en\ city, capital of Wyoming

**Chia·mu–ssu** — see JIAMUSI

**Chia·pas** \chē-'äp-əs\ state SE Mexico; capital, Tuxtla Gutiérrez

**Chi·ba** \'chē-bə\ city E Japan in Honshu on Tokyo Bay E of Tokyo

**Chi·ca·go** \shə-'käg-ō, -'kòg-\ city NE Illinois — **Chi·ca·go·an** \-'käg-ə-wən, -'kòg-\ noun

**Chi·chén It·zá** \chə-,chen-ət-'sä\ ruined Mayan city SE Mexico in Yucatán ESE of Mérida

**Ch'i–ch'i·ha·erh** — see QIQIHAR

**Chihli, Gulf of** — see BO HAI

**Chi·hua·hua** \chə-'wä-wä, shə-, -wə\ **1** state N Mexico bordering on U.S. **2** city, its capital

**Chile** \'chil-ē\ country SW South America; capital, Santiago — **Chil·ean** \'chil-ē-ən, chə-'lā-ən\ adjective or noun

**Chim·bo·ra·zo** \,chim-bə-'räz-ō, ,shim-\ mountain 6267 meters W central Ecuador

**Chim·kent** \chim-'kent\ city S Kazakhstan N of Tashkent

**Chi·na** \'chī-nə\ **1** country E Asia; capital, Beijing — see TAIWAN **2** sea section of the W Pacific E & SE of China; divided at Taiwan Strait into **East China** & **South China** seas

**Chinan** — see JINAN

**Chin–chou** or **Chinchow** — see JINZHOU

**Chi·os** \'kī-,äs\ island Greece in the Aegean off W coast of Turkey

**Chi·si·nau** \,kē-shē-'naù\ or 1940–91 **Ki·shi·nev** \'kish-i-,nef\ city, capital of Moldova

**Chi·ta** \chit-'ä\ city S Russia in Asia, E of Lake Baikal

**Chit·ta·gong** \'chit-ə-,gäng, -,gòng\ city SE Bangladesh on Bay of Bengal

**Chkalov** — see ORENBURG

**Chong·jin** \'chòng-jin\ city & port NE North Korea on Sea of Japan

**Chong·ju** \'chòng-jü\ city central South Korea

**Chong·qing** or **Ch'ung–ch'ing** \'chùng-'ching\ or **Chung·king** \'chùng-'king\ city SW central China in SE Sichuan

**Chon·ju** \'jən-jü\ city W South Korea

**Cho·sen** \'chō-'sen\ — see KOREA

**Christ·church** \'krīs-,chərch, 'krīst-\ city New Zealand on E coast of South Island

**Christ·mas** \'kris-məs\ **1** island E Indian Ocean SW of Java; administered by Australia **2** — see KIRITIMATI

**Ch'üan–chou** or **Chuanchow** — see QUANZHOU

**Chu–chou** or **Chuchow** — see ZHUZHOU

**Ci·li·cia** \sə-'lish-ə, -'lish-ē-ə\ ancient country SE Asia Minor on coast S of Taurus Mountains

**Cin·cin·na·ti** \,sin-sə-'nat-ē, -'nat-ə\ city SW Ohio

**Cis·al·pine Gaul** \sis-,al-,pīn\ the part of Gaul lying S & E of the Alps

**Citlaltepetl** — see ORIZABA

**Città del Vaticano** — see VATICAN CITY

**Ciu·dad Gua·ya·na** \,sē-ù-,thä-gwə-'yän-ə, -,thäth-\ city E Venezuela

**Ciu·dad Juá·rez** \,sē-ù-,thä-'hwär-əs, -ù-,dad-, -'wär-\ or **Juárez** \'hwär-əs, 'wär-\ city N Mexico in Chihuahua on Rio Grande opposite El Paso, Texas

**Ciudad Trujillo** — see SANTO DOMINGO

**Clack·man·nan** \klak-'man-ən\ or **Clack·man·nan·shire** \-,shiər, -shər\ former county central Scotland

**Clare** \'klaər, 'kleər\ county W Ireland in Munster

**Cler·mont–Fer·rand** \,kler-,mōⁿ-fə-'räⁿ\ city S central France

**Cleve·land** \'klēv-lənd\ **1** city NE Ohio **2** county N England N of North Yorkshire

**Cluj–Na·po·ca** \'klüzh-'näp-ō-kə\ city NW central Romania

**Clwyd** \'klüid\ county NE Wales; established 1974

**Clyde** \'klīd\ river 170 kilometers long SW Scotland flowing into **Firth of Clyde** (estuary)

**Clydes·dale** \'klīdz-,dāl\ valley of upper Clyde, Scotland

**Cnossus** — see KNOSSOS

**Coa·hui·la** \,kō-ə-'wē-lə, kwä-'wē-lə\ state N Mexico bordering on U.S.; capital, Saltillo

**Coast Mountains** mountain range W British Columbia; the N continuation of Cascade Range

**Coast Ranges** chain of mountain ranges W North America extending along Pacific coast W of Sierra Nevada & Cascade Range & through Vancouver Island into S Alaska to Kenai Peninsula & Kodiak Island

**Co·cha·bam·ba** \,kō-chə-'bäm-bə\ city W central Bolivia

**Co·chin China** \,kō-chən-\ region S Vietnam

**Cod, Cape** \'käd\ peninsula SE Massachusetts

**Coim·ba·tore** \,kòim-bə-'tòr, -'tór\ city S India in W Tamil Nadu

**Col·chis** \'käl-kəs\ ancient country bordering on Black Sea S of Caucasus Mountains; district now in W Republic of Georgia

**Co·li·ma** \kə-'lē-mə\ **1** state SW Mexico **2** city, its capital

**Co·logne** \kə-'lōn\ or German **Köln** \'kœln\ city W Germany on the Rhine

**Co·lom·bia** \kə-'ləm-bē-ə\ country NW South America; capital, Bogotá — **Co·lom·bi·an** \-bē-ən\ adjective or noun

**Co·lom·bo** \kə-'ləm-bō\ city, capital of Sri Lanka

**Co·lón** \kə-'lōn\ city Panama on the Caribbean

**Colón Archipelago** — see GALAPAGOS ISLANDS

**Col·o·ra·do** \ˌkäl-ə-'rad-ō, -'räd-\ **1** river about 2350 kilometers long SW U.S. & NW Mexico flowing from N Colorado into Gulf of California **2** desert SE California **3** plateau region SW U.S. W of Rocky Mountains **4** state W U.S.; capital, Denver — **Col·o·rad·an** \-'rad-n, -'räd-n\ or **Co·lo·ra·do·an** \-'rad-ə-wən, -'räd-\ adjective or noun

**Colorado Springs** city central Colorado

**Co·lum·bia** \kə-'ləm-bē-ə\ **1** river 1953 kilometers long SW Canada & NW U.S. rising in SE British Columbia & flowing S & W into the Pacific **2** plateau in Columbia River Basin in E Washington, E Oregon, & SW Idaho **3** city, capital of South Carolina

**Co·lum·bus** \kə-'ləm-bəs\ **1** city W Georgia **2** city, capital of Ohio

**Commonwealth of Independent States** association of the former constituent republics of the U.S.S.R. except for Lithuania, Latvia, & Estonia; formed 1991

**Commonwealth of Nations** or the **Commonwealth** or formerly **British Commonwealth** political organization consisting of nations loyal to the British monarch

**Co·mo, Lake** \'kō-mō\ lake N Italy in Lombardy

**Com·o·ro** \'käm-ə-ˌrō\ islands off SE Africa NW of Madagascar; formerly a French possession; a republic (except for Mayotte Island remaining French) since 1975; capital, Moroni

**Com·stock Lode** \ˌkäm-ˌstäk-\ gold & silver deposit at Virginia City, Nevada, discovered 1859

**Con·a·kry** \'kän-ə-krē\ city, capital of Guinea

**Con·cep·ción** \kən-ˌsep-sē-'ōn, -'sep-shən\ city S central Chile

**Con·cord** \'käng-kərd\ **1** city, capital of New Hampshire **2** town E Massachusetts NW of Boston

**Con·go** \'käng-gō\ **1** or **Zaire** \zä-'iər\ river more than 4344 kilometers long W equatorial Africa flowing into the Atlantic **2** or **Democratic Republic of the Congo** or 1971–97 **Zaire** or 1908–60 **Belgian Congo** country central Africa comprising most of Congo River Basin E of lower Congo River; a republic; capital, Kinshasa **3** or **Republic of the Congo** or formerly **Middle Congo** country W central Africa W of lower Congo River; capital, Brazzaville — **Con·go·lese** \ˌkäng-gə-'lēz, -'lēs\ adjective or noun

**Con·nacht** \'kän-ˌôt\ province W Ireland

**Con·nect·i·cut** \kə-'net-i-kət\ **1** river 655 kilometers long NE U.S. flowing S from N New Hampshire into Long Island Sound **2** state NE U.S.; capital, Hartford

**Con·stan·tine** \'kän-stən-ˌtēn\ city NE Algeria

**Constantinople** — see ISTANBUL

**Con·stan·tsa** \kən-'stän-sə, -'stänt-\ city SE Romania

**Cook** \'kuk\ **1** inlet of the Pacific S Alaska W of Kenai Peninsula **2** islands S Pacific SW of Society Islands belonging to New Zealand; capital, Avarua (on Rarotonga Island) **3** strait New Zealand between North Island & South Island

**Cook, Mount** or formerly **Ao·rangi** \aú-'räng-ē\ mountain 3764 meters New Zealand in W central South Island in Southern Alps; highest in New Zealand

**Co·pen·ha·gen** \ˌkō-pən-'hā-gən, -'häg-ən\ city, capital of Denmark

**Coquilhatville** — see MBANDAKA

**Cor·al** \'kór-əl, 'kär-\ sea arm of the W Pacific NE of Australia

**Cór·do·ba** \'kórd-ə-bə, -ə-və\ **1** or **Cor·do·va** \'kórd-ə-və\ or ancient **Cor·du·ba** \'kórd-yə-bə, 'kórd-ú-bə\ city S Spain on the Guadalquivir **2** city N central Argentina

**Cor·fu** \kór-'fü; 'kór-ˌfü, -ˌfyü\ island NW Greece in Ionian Islands

**Cor·inth** \'kór-ənth, 'kär-, -əntth\ **1** region of ancient Greece occupying most of Isthmus of Corinth & part of NE Peloponnese **2** ancient city, its capital; site SW of present city of Corinth — **Co·rin·thi·an** \kə-'rin-thē-ən, 'rint-\ adjective or noun

**Corinth, Gulf of** inlet of Ionian Sea central Greece N of the Peloponnese

**Corinth, Isthmus of** neck of land connecting the Peloponnese with rest of Greece

**Cork** \'kórk\ **1** county S Ireland in Munster **2** city S Ireland in County Cork

**Corn·wall** \'kórn-ˌwól, -wəl\ or since 1974 **Cornwall and Isles of Scil·ly** \'sil-ē\ county SW England

**Cor·o·man·del** \ˌkór-ə-'man-dl, ˌkär-\ coast region SE India on Bay of Bengal

**Cor·pus Chris·ti** \ˌkór-pə-'skris-tē\ city S Texas

**Cor·reg·i·dor** \kə-'reg-ə-ˌdór\ island Philippines at entrance to Manila Bay

**Cor·si·ca** \'kór-si-kə\ or French **Corse** \kórs\ island France in the Mediterranean N of Sardinia — **Cor·si·can** \'kór-si-kən\ adjective or noun

**Cos·ta Bra·va** \ˌkäs-tə-'bräv-ə, ˌkós-, ˌkōs-\ coast region NE Spain on the Mediterranean extending NE from Barcelona

**Costa del Sol** \-del-'sól, -'sōl\ coast region S Spain on the Mediterranean extending E from Gibraltar

**Cos·ta Ri·ca** \ˌkäs-tə-'rē-kə, ˌkós-, ˌkōs-\ country Central America between Nicaragua & Panama; a republic; capital, San José — **Cos·ta Ri·can** \-'rē-kən\ adjective or noun

**Côte d'A·zur** \ˌkōt-də-'zúr\ region SE France on Mediterranean coast; part of the Riviera

**Côte d'Ivoire** — see IVORY COAST

**Co·to·nou** \ˌkōt-ə-'nü\ city S Benin

**Cots·wold** \'kät-ˌswōld\ hills SW central England in Gloucestershire

**Cov·en·try** \'käv-ən-trē, 'kəv-\ city central England in West Midlands

**Co·zu·mel** \ˌkō-zə-'mel\ island SE Mexico off NE coast of Quintana Roo

**Cracow** — see KRAKOW

**Cra·io·va** \krä-'yō-və\ city S Romania

**Cra·ter** \'krāt-ər\ lake SW Oregon in Cascade Range; main feature of **Crater Lake National Park** — see MAZAMA (Mount)

**Crete** \'krēt\ island Greece in E Mediterranean; capital, Iráklion — **Cre·tan** \'krēt-n\ adjective or noun

**Cri·mea** \krī-'mē-ə, krə-\ peninsula E Europe, extending into Black Sea — **Cri·me·an** \krī-'mē-ən, krə-\ adjective

**Cro·atia** \krō-'ā-shə, -shē-ə\ country S Europe; formerly a constituent republic of Yugoslavia; capital, Zagreb

**Croy·don** \'króid-n\ borough of S Greater London, England

**Cu·ba** \'kyü-bə\ island SW in the West Indies; a republic; capital, Havana — **Cu·ban** \-bən\ adjective or noun

**Cú·cu·ta** \'kü-kət-ə\ city N Colombia

**Cu·lia·cán** \ˌkül-yə-'kän\ city NW Mexico, capital of Sinaloa

**Cu·ma·ná** \ˌkü-mə-'nä\ city NE Venezuela

**Cum·ber·land** \'kəm-bər-lənd\ former county NW England — see CUMBRIA

**Cumberland Plateau** mountain region E U.S.; part of S Appalachian Mountains W of Tennessee River extending from S West Virginia to NE Alabama

**Cum·bria** \'kəm-brē-ə\ county NW England including former counties of Cumberland & Westmorland — **Cum·bri·an** \-ən\ adjective or noun

**Cumbrian Mountains** range NW England chiefly in Cumbria

**Cu·ra·çao** \'kür-ə-ˌsō, 'kyúr-, -ˌsaú\ island Netherlands Antilles in the S Caribbean; chief town, Willemstad

**Cu·ri·ti·ba** \ˌkúr-ə-'tē-bə\ city S Brazil SW of São Paulo

**Cush** \'kəsh, 'kúsh\ ancient country NE Africa in upper Nile valley S of Egypt — **Cush·ite** \-ˌīt\ noun — **Cush·it·ic** \ˌkəsh-'it-ik, kúsh-\ adjective

**Cut·tack** \'kət-ək\ city E India in Orissa

**Cyc·la·des** \'sik-lə-ˌdēz\ islands Greece in S Aegean

**Cymru** — see WALES

**Cy·prus** \'sī-prəs\ island E Mediterranean S of Turkey; a republic of the Commonwealth; capital, Nicosia — **Cyp·ri·ot** \'sip-rē-ət, -rē-ˌät\ or **Cyp·ri·ote** \-ˌōt, -ət\ adjective or noun

**Cy·re·na·ica** \ˌsir-ə-'nā-ə-kə, ˌsī-rə-\ **1** ancient region N Africa on coast W of Egypt; capital, Cyrene **2** region E Libya; formerly a province — **Cy·re·na·i·can** \-kən\ adjective or noun

**Czecho·slo·va·kia** \ˌchek-ə-slō-'väk-ē-ə, -'vak-\ former country central Europe; capital, Prague; divided 1993 into Czech Republic & Slovakia — **Czecho·slo·vak** \-'slō-ˌväk, -ˌvak\ adjective or noun — **Czecho·slo·va·ki·an** \-slō-'väk-ē-ən, -'vak-\ adjective or noun

**Czech Republic** country central Europe; capital, Prague

**Cze·sto·cho·wa** \ˌchen-stə-'kō-və\ city S Poland

**Dacca** — see DHAKA

**Da·cia** \'dā-shə, -shē-ə\ ancient country & Roman province SE Europe roughly equivalent to Romania & Bessarabia

**Da·dra and Na·gar Ha·ve·li** \də-'drä-ən-ˌnag-ər-ə-ˌvel-ē\ territory India bordering on Gujarat & Maharashtra

**Da·ho·mey** \də-'hō-mē\ — see BENIN — **Da·ho·man** \-mən\ or **Da·ho·me·an** or **Da·ho·mey·an** \-mē-ən\ adjective or noun

**Da·kar** \'dak-ˌär, də-'kär\ city, capital of Senegal

**Da·ko·ta** \də-'kōt-ə\ or **James** \'jāmz\ river 1142 kilometers long North Dakota and South Dakota flowing S into the Missouri

**Dakota Territory** territory 1861–89 NW U.S. divided 1889 into states of North Dakota & South Dakota (the **Da·ko·tas**)

**Da·lian** or **Ta·lien** \'däl-'yen\ or **Lü·da** or **Lü·ta** \'lüe-'dä\ or **Dai·ren** \'dī-'ren\ city NE China in S Liaoning

**Dal·las** \'dal-əs, 'da-lis\ city NE Texas

**Dal·ma·tia** \dal-'mā-shə, -shē-ə\ region W Balkan Peninsula on the Adriatic — **Dal·ma·tian** \-shən\ adjective or noun

**Da·man and Diu** \də-'män-ən-'dē-ˌü, -'man-\ territory W India on Gulf of Cambay

**Da·mas·cus** \də-'mas-kəs\ city, capital of Syria

**Da·ma·vand** \'dam-ə-ˌvand\ or **Dem·a·vend** \'dem-ə-ˌvend\ mountain 5771 meters N Iran NE of Tehran

**Da Nang** \dä-'näng, 'dä-\ or formerly **Tou·rane** \tü-'rän\ city S Vietnam in Annam SE of Hue

**Dan·dong** \'dän-'dúng\ or **An·tung** \'än-'dúng\ or **Tan·tung** \'dän-'dúng\ city NE China in SE Liaoning at mouth of the Yalu

**Dan·ube** \'dan-yüb\ or German **Do·nau** \'dō-ˌnaú\ river 2850 kilometers long S Europe flowing from S Germany into Black Sea — **Da·nu·bi·an** \da-'nyü-bē-ən\ adjective

**Danzig** — see GDANSK

**Dar·da·nelles** \ˌdärd-n-'elz\ or **Hel·les·pont** \'hel-ə-ˌspänt\ strait NW Turkey connecting Sea of Marmara & the Aegean

**Dar el Beida** — see CASABLANCA

**Dar es Sa·laam** \ˌdär-ˌes-sə-'läm\ city, capital of Tanzania

**Darien, Isthmus of** — see PANAMA (Isthmus of)

**Dar·ling** \'där-ling\ river 2739 kilometers long SE Australia in Queensland & New South Wales flowing SW into the Murray

**Dar·win** \'där-wən\ city Australia, capital of Northern Territory

**Da·tong** or **Ta·tung** \'dä-'túng\ city NE China in N Shanxi

**Da·vao** \'däv-ˌaú, dä-'vaú\ city S Philippines in E Mindanao on Davao Gulf

**Da·vis** \'dā-vəs\ strait between SW Greenland & E Baffin Island connecting Baffin Bay & the Atlantic

**Day·ton** \'dāt-n\ city SW Ohio

**Dead Sea** \'ded\ salt lake between Israel & Jordan; 400 meters below the level of the Mediterranean

**Dear·born** \'diər-ˌbórn, -bərn\ city SE Michigan SW of Detroit

**Death Valley** \'deth\ arid valley E California & S Nevada containing lowest point in U.S. (86 meters below sea level); most of area included in **Death Valley National Monument**

**De·bre·cen** \'deb-rət-ˌsen\ city E Hungary

**Dec·can** \'dek-ən, -ˌan\ plateau region S India

**Del·a·ware** \'del-ə-ˌwaər, -ˌwear, -wər\ **1** river 451 kilometers long E U.S. flowing S from New York into Delaware Bay **2** state E U.S.; capital, Dover — **Del·a·war·ean** or **Del·a·war·ian** \ˌdel-ə-'waər-ē-ən, -'wer-\ adjective or noun

**Delaware Bay** inlet of the Atlantic between SW New Jersey & E Delaware

**Del·hi** \'del-ē\ **1** territory N India W of Uttar Pradesh **2** city, its capital — see NEW DELHI

**De·los** \'dē-ˌläs\ island Greece in central Cyclades — **De·lian** \'dē-lē-ən, 'dēl-yən\ adjective or noun

**Del·phi** \'del-ˌfī\ ancient town central Greece in Phocis on S slope of Mount Parnassus

**Democratic Kampuchea** — see CAMBODIA

**Democratic Republic of the Congo** — see CONGO 2

**Denali, Denali National Park** — see MCKINLEY (Mount)

**Den·bigh·shire** \'den-bē-ˌshiər, -shər\ or **Denbigh** former county N Wales

**Den·mark** \'den-ˌmärk\ country N Europe occupying most of Jutland & adjacent islands; capital, Copenhagen

**Den·ver** \'den-vər\ city, capital of Colorado

**Der·by** \'där-bē, *chiefly in the United States* 'dər-bē\ borough N central England in Derbyshire

**Der·by·shire** \'där-bē-,shiər, -shər, *United States also* 'dər-\ *or* **Derby** county N central England

**Der·ry** \'der-ē\ *or* **Lon·don·der·ry** \,lən-dən-'der-ē, 'lən-dən-,\ traditional county NW Northern Ireland

**Des Moines** \di-'mȯin\ city, capital of Iowa

**De·troit** \di-'trȯit\ **1** river 50 kilometers long between SE Michigan & Ontario connecting Lake Saint Clair & Lake Erie **2** city SE Michigan

**Dev·on** \'dev-ən\ *or* **De·von·shire** \-,shiər, -shər\ county SW England

**Dha·ka** *or* **Dac·ca** \'dak-ə, 'däk-\ city, capital of Bangladesh

**Dhau·la·gi·ri, Mount** \,daü-lə-'giər-ē\ mountain 8172 meters W central Nepal in the Himalaya

**Di·a·mond Bar** \'dī-mənd-,bär, 'dī-ə-\ city S California

**Di·e·go Gar·cia** \dē-,ā-gō-,gär'sē-ə\ island in Indian Ocean; chief island of Chagos Archipelago

**Di·jon** \dē-'zhōⁿ\ city E France N of Lyon

**Di·nar·ic Alps** \də-,nar-ik-\ range of the E Alps in W Balkan Peninsula

**Diospolis** — see THEBES 1

**District of Co·lum·bia** \kə-'ləm-bē-ə\ federal district E U.S. coextensive with city of Washington

**Djakarta** — see JAKARTA

**Dji·bou·ti** *or* **Ji·bu·ti** \jə-'büt-ē\ **1** *or formerly* **French Somaliland** *or later* **French Territory of the Afars and the Is·sas** \ä-'fär, -'färz . . . ē-'sä, -'säz\ republic E Africa on Gulf of Aden **2** city, its capital

**Dnie·per** \'nē-pər\ river 2285 kilometers long flowing from Valdai Hills, Russia through Belarus & Ukraine into Black Sea

**Dnies·ter** \'nēs-tər\ river 1411 kilometers long W Ukraine & E Moldova flowing SE from the Carpathians into Black Sea

**Dni·pro·pe·trovs'k** *or* **Dne·pro·pe·trovsk** \də-,nyep-rə-pē-'trȯfsk\ city E Ukraine

**Do·dec·a·nese** \dō-'dek-ə-,nēz, 'dō-di-kə-, -,nēs\ islands Greece in the SE Aegean — see RHODES

**Do·ha** \'dō-hä\ city & port, capital of Qatar on Persian Gulf

**Do·lo·mites** \'dō-lə-,mīts, 'däl-ə-\ *or Italian* **Do·lo·mi·ti** \,dō-lə-'mēt-ē\ range of the E Alps in NE Italy

**Dom·i·ni·ca** \,däm-ə-'nē-kə\ island British West Indies in the Leewards; capital, Roseau

**Do·min·i·can Republic** \də-,min-i-kən\ *or formerly* **San·to Do·min·go** \,sant-əd-ə-'ming-gō\ country West Indies in E Hispaniola; a republic; capital, Santo Domingo — **Do·min·i·can** \də-'min-i-kən\ *adjective or noun*

**Don** \'dän\ river 1969 kilometers long S Russia in Europe flowing into Sea of Azov

**Donau** — see DANUBE

**Don·e·gal** \,dän-i-'gȯl, ,dən-\ county NW Ireland (republic) in Ulster

**Do·nets Basin** \də-,nets-\ *or Russian* **Do·net·skiy Bas·seyn** \də-'nyet-skē-bas-'yän\ *or* **Don·bass** *or* **Don·bas** \'dän-,bas\ region E Ukraine SW of Donets River

**Do·netsk** \də-'netsk\ city E Ukraine in Donets Basin

**Dor·set** \'dȯr-sət\ *or* **Dor·set·shire** \-,shiər, -shər\ county S England on English Channel

**Dort·mund** \'dȯrt-,mùnt, -mənd\ city W Germany in the Ruhr

**Dou·a·la** \dü-'äl-ə\ city SW Cameroon

**Doug·las** \'dəg-ləs\ town Great Britain, capital of Isle of Man

**Dou·ro** \'dōr-ü, 'dȯr-\ *or Spanish* **Due·ro** \'dweər-ō\ *or ancient* **Du·ri·us** \'dùr-ē-əs, 'dyùr-\ river 895 kilometers long N Spain & N Portugal flowing into the Atlantic

**Do·ver** \'dō-vər\ **1** city, capital of Delaware **2** borough SE England in Kent on Strait of Dover

**Dover, Strait of** channel between SE England & N France; the most easterly section of English Channel

**Down** \'daún\ traditional county SE Northern Ireland

**Dra·kens·berg** \'dräk-ənz-,bərg\ mountain range N Republic of South Africa & Lesotho; highest peak Thabana Ntlenyana 3482 meters

**Dres·den** \'drez-dən\ city E Germany in Saxony

**Dry Tor·tu·gas** \-,tȯr-'tü-gəz\ island group S Florida; site of **Dry Tortugas National Park**

**Du·bayy** *or* **Du·bai** \dü-'bī\ city United Arab Emirates on Persian Gulf

**Dub·lin** \'dəb-lən\ *or Gaelic* **Bai·le Atha Cli·ath** \blä-'klē-ə\ **1** county E Ireland in Leinster **2** city, capital of Ireland (republic) in County Dublin

**Dud·ley** \'dəd-lē\ borough W central England in West Midlands

**Duis·burg** \'dü-əs-,bərg; 'düz-,bərg, 'dyüz-; *German* 'dües-,bùrk\ city W Germany at junction of Rhine & Ruhr rivers

**Du·luth** \də-'lüth\ city NE Minnesota

**Dum·fries** \,dəm-'frēs\ *or* **Dum·fries·shire** \-'frēs-,shiər, -'frēsh-, -shər\ former county S Scotland; incorporated 1975 in **Dumfries and Gallo·way** \-'gal-ə-,wā\ region

**Dun·bar·ton** \,dən-'bärt-ən\ *or* **Dun·bar·ton·shire** \-,shiər, -shər\ *or* **Dum·bar·ton** \,dəm-\ *or* **Dum·bar·ton·shire** \,dəm-\ former county W central Scotland

**Dun·dee** \,dən-'dē\ city E Scotland in Tayside

**Dun·e·din** \,də-'nēd-n\ city New Zealand in SE South Island

**Du·que de Ca·xi·as** \,dü-kə-də-kə-'shē-əs\ city SE Brazil NW of Rio de Janeiro

**Du·ran·go** \dù-'rang-gō, dyù-\ **1** state NW central Mexico **2** city, its capital

**Dur·ban** \'dər-bən\ city E Republic of South Africa

**Dur·ham** \'dər-əm, 'də-rəm, 'dùr-əm\ county N England on North Sea

**Du·shan·be** \dü-'sham-bē, dyü-, -'shäm-\ city, capital of Tajikistan

**Düs·sel·dorf** \'düs-əl-,dȯrf, 'dyüs-, 'dùs-\ city W Germany, capital of North Rhine-Westphalia

**Dutch Borneo** — see KALIMANTAN

**Dutch Guiana** — see SURINAME

**Dy·fed** \'dəv-ed, -əd\ county SW Wales; established 1974

**Dzaudzhikau** — see VLADIKAVKAZ

**Dzer·zhinsk** \dər-'zhinsk\ city central Russia in Europe, ENE of Moscow

**Ea·ling** \'ē-ling\ borough of W Greater London, England

**East An·glia** \'ang-glē-ə\ region E England including Norfolk & Suffolk

**East Bengal** the part of Bengal now in Bangladesh

**East China Sea** — see CHINA

**Eas·ter** \'ē-stər\ island SE Pacific about 3218 kilometers W of Chilean coast; belongs to Chile

**Eastern Cape** province SE Republic of South Africa

**Eastern Ghats** \'gȯts\ chain of low mountains SE India along coast

**Eastern Samoa** — see AMERICAN SAMOA

**East Germany** the German Democratic Republic — see GERMANY

**East Indies** collective name for India, Indochina, and the Malay Archipelago — **East Indian** *adjective or noun*

**East London** city S Republic of South Africa

**East Lo·thi·an** \'lō-thē-ən\ former county SE Scotland — see LOTHIAN

**East Pakistan** the former E division of Pakistan comprising E portion of Bengal; now the independent republic of Bangladesh

**East Prussia** region N Europe on the Baltic; formerly a part of Germany; divided 1945 between Poland & U.S.S.R. (Russia & Lithuania)

**East Ri·ding** \'rīd-ing\ former administrative county N England in SE Yorkshire

**East River** strait SE New York connecting upper New York Bay & Long Island Sound & separating Manhattan Island and Long Island

**East Sus·sex** \'səs-iks, *United States also* -,eks\ county SE England

**Ebro** \'ā-brō\ river 909 kilometers long NE Spain flowing into the Mediterranean

**Ec·ua·dor** \'ek-wə-,dȯr\ country W South America; a republic; capital, Quito — **Ec·ua·dor·an** \,ek-wə-'dȯr-ən, -'dȯr-\ *or* **Ec·ua·dor·ean** *or* **Ec·ua·dor·ian** \-ē-ən\ *adjective or noun*

**Ede** \'ā-,dā\ city SW Nigeria

**Ed·in·burgh** \'ed-n-,bər-ə, -,bə-rə, -,bə-rə, -brə\ city, capital of Scotland

**Ed·mon·ton** \'ed-mən-tən\ city, capital of Alberta

**Edom** \'ēd-əm\ *or* **Id·u·maea** *or* **Id·u·mea** \,ij-ə-'mē-ə\ ancient country SW Asia S of Judea & Dead Sea — **Edom·ite** \'ēd-ə-,mīt\ *noun*

**Egypt** \'ē-jəpt\ country NE Africa & Sinai Peninsula of SW Asia bordering on Mediterranean & Red seas; capital, Cairo

**Eire** — see IRELAND 2

**Elam** \'ē-ləm\ ancient country SW Asia at head of Persian Gulf E of Babylonia; capital, Susa (Shushan) — **Elam·ite** \'ē-lə-,mīt\ *noun*

**El·ba** \'el-bə\ island Italy E of N Corsica off coast of Tuscany; chief town, Portoferraio

**Elbe** \'el-bə, 'elb\ *or Czech* **La·be** \'lä-be\ *or ancient* **Al·bis** \'al-bəs\ river 1165 kilometers long N Czech Republic & N Germany flowing NW into North Sea

**El·bert, Mount** \'el-bərt\ mountain 4399 meters W central Colorado; highest in Colorado & the Rocky Mountains

**El·brus, Mount** \el-'brüz\ mountain 5642 meters S Russia in Europe, in NW Caucasus Mountains

**El·burz** \el-'bùrz\ mountains N Iran

**El Gîza** — see GIZA

**Elis** \'ē-ləs\ ancient country in NW Peloponnese, Greece

**Elisabethville** — see LUBUMBASHI

**Eliz·a·beth** \i-'liz-ə-bəth\ city NE New Jersey on Newark Bay

**Ellás** — see GREECE

**Elles·mere** \'elz-,miər\ island N Canada in N Northwest Territories

**Ellice** — see TUVALU

**El Paso** \el-'pas-ō\ city W Texas on Rio Grande

**El Sal·va·dor** \el-'sal-və-,dȯr, -,sal-və-'\ country Central America bordering on the Pacific; capital, San Salvador

**Elsass** — see ALSACE

**Ely, Isle of** \'ē-lē\ district E England in Cambridgeshire — see CAMBRIDGESHIRE

**Emi·lia–Ro·ma·gna** \ā-,mēl-yə-rō-'män-yə\ region N Italy on the Adriatic S of the Po; capital, Bologna

**En·field** \'en-,fēld\ borough of N Greater London, England

**En·gland** \'ing-glənd *also* ing-lənd\ country S Great Britain; a division of United Kingdom; capital, London

**English Channel** arm of the Atlantic between S England & N France

**En·se·na·da** \,en-sə-'näd-ə\ city NW Mexico in Baja California

**Ephra·im** \'ē-frē-əm\ **1** hilly region N Jordan E of River Jordan **2** — see ISRAEL — **Ephra·im·ite** \'ē-frē-ə-,mīt\ *noun*

**Epi·rus** \i-'pī-rəs\ region NW Greece on Ionian Sea

**Equatorial Guinea** *or formerly* **Spanish Guinea** country W Africa on Bight of Biafra including Mbini & Bioko; capital, Malabo

**Erbil** — see ARBIL

**Ere·bus, Mount** \'er-ə-bəs\ volcano 3794 meters Antarctica on Ross Island in SW Ross Sea

**Er·furt** \'eər-fərt, -,fùrt\ city central Germany WSW of Leipzig

**Erie** \'iər-ē\ **1** city NW Pennsylvania **2** canal New York between Hudson River at Albany & Lake Erie at Buffalo; built 1817–25; now superseded by New York State Barge Canal

**Erie, Lake** lake E central North America in U.S. & Canada; one of the Great Lakes

**Er·in** \'er-ən\ IRELAND

**Er·i·trea** \,er-ə-'trē-ə, -'trā-\ country NE Africa on Red Sea; capital, Asmara

**Er Rif** *or* **Er Riff** \er-'rif\ mountain region N Morocco on Mediterranean coast E of Strait of Gibraltar

**Erz·ge·bir·ge** \'erts-gə-,bir-gə\ mountains E central Germany & NW Czech Republic

**Escaut** — see SCHELDT

**Es·fa·han** \,es-fä-'hän\ *or* **Is·fa·han** \,is-\ city W central Iran

**Es·ki·se·hir** \,es-ki-shə-'hiər\ city W central Turkey

**España** — see SPAIN

**Española** — see HISPANIOLA

**Es·sen** \'es-n\ city W Germany in the Ruhr

**Es·sex** \'es-iks\ county SE England on North Sea

**Es·to·nia** \e-'stō-nē-ə, -nyə\ country E Europe on Baltic Sea; a constituent republic (**Estonian Republic**) of U.S.S.R. 1940–91; capital, Tallinn

**Ethi·o·pia** \,ē-thē-'ō-pē-ə\ **1** ancient country NE Africa S of Egypt **2** *or* **Ab·ys·sin·ia** \,ab-ə-'sin-yə, -'sin-ē-ə\ country E Africa; a republic since 1975; capital, Addis Ababa

**Et·na** \'et-nə\ volcano 3323 meters Italy in NE Sicily

**Eto·bi·coke** \et-'ō-bik-,ō\ city Canada in SE Ontario

**Etru·ria** \i-'trùr-ē-ə\ ancient country central Italy coextensive with modern Tuscany & part of Umbria

**Eu·boea** \yù-'bē-ə\ island E Greece NE of Attica & Boeotia

\ə\ abut \ᵊ\ kitten \ər\ further \a\ ash \ā\ ace
\ä\ mop, mar \aú\ out \ch\ chin \e\ bet \ē\ easy
\g\ go \i\ hit \ī\ ice \j\ job \ŋ\ sing \ō\ go
\ȯ\ law \ȯi\ boy \th\ thin \th\ the \ü\ loot \ù\ foot
\y\ yet \zh\ vision *see also* Guide to Pronunciation

**Eu·phra·tes** \yu̇-'frāt-ēz\ river 3596 kilometers long SW Asia flowing from E Turkey & uniting with the Tigris to form the Shatt al Arab

**Eur·asia** \yu̇-'rā-zhə, -shə\ landmass comprising Europe & Asia — **Eur·asian** \-zhən, -shən\ *adjective or noun*

**Eu·rope** \'yu̇r-əp\ continent of the eastern hemisphere between Asia & the Atlantic

**European Union** *or formerly* **European Communities** *or* **European Community** economic, scientific, & political organization consisting of Belgium, France, Italy, Luxembourg, Netherlands, Germany, Denmark, Greece, Ireland, United Kingdom, Spain, Portugal, Austria, Finland, & Sweden

**Ev·ans·ville** \'ev-ənz-,vil\ city SW Indiana

**Ev·er·est, Mount** \'ev-rəst, -ə-rəst\ mountain 8848 meters S Asia in the Himalaya on border between Nepal & Tibet; highest in the world

**Ev·er·glades** \'ev-ər-,glādz\ swamp region S Florida now partly drained; SW part forms **Everglades National Park**

**Eyre, Lake** \'aər, 'eər\ intermittent lake central Australia in N South Australia

**Faer·oe** *or* **Far·oe** \'faər-ō, 'fear-\ islands NE Atlantic NW of the Shetlands belonging to Denmark; capital, Tórshavn — **Faero·ese** \,far-ə-'wēz, ,fer-, -'wēs\ *adjective or noun*

**Fai·sa·la·bad** \,fī-,säl-ə-'bäd, -,sal-ə-'bad\ *or formerly* **Ly·all·pur** \lē-,äl-'pu̇r\ city NE Pakistan W of Lahore

**Falk·land Islands** \'fȯ-klənd-, 'fȯl-\ *or Spanish* **Is·las Mal·vi·nas** \,ēz-läz-mäl-'vē-näs\ islands SW Atlantic E of S end of Argentina; a British colony; capital, Stanley

**Far East** the countries of E Asia & the Malay Archipelago — usually considered as comprising the Asian countries bordering on the Pacific but sometimes as including also India, Sri Lanka, Bangladesh, Tibet, & Myanmar — **Far Eastern** *adjective*

**Far·go** \'fär-gō\ city E North Dakota; largest in state

**Fear, Cape** \'fiər\ cape SE North Carolina at mouth of Cape Fear River

**Federated Malay States** former British protectorate (1895–1945) comprising states of Negri Sembilan, Pahang, Perak, and Selangor; now part of Malaysia

**Fengtien** — see SHENYANG

**Fer·man·agh** \fər-'man-ə\ traditional county SW Northern Ireland

**Fernando Póo** — see BIOKO

**Fer·ra·ra** \fə-'rär-ə\ city N Italy NE of Bologna

**Fez** \'fez\ *or* **Fès** \'fes\ city N central Morocco

**Fife** \'fīf\ *or* **Fife·shire** \-,shiər, -shər\ region E Scotland; until 1975 a county

**Fi·ji** \'fē-jē\ islands SW Pacific; a dominion of the Commonwealth; capital, Suva — **Fi·ji·an** \-jē-ən\ *adjective or noun*

**Fin·is·terre, Cape** \,fin-ə-'steər, -'ster-ē\ cape NW Spain

**Fin·land** \'fin-lənd\ *or Finnish* **Suo·mi** \'swȯ-mē\ *or* **Suo·men Ta·sa·val·ta** \'swȯ-mən-'tas-ə-,val-tə\ country NE Europe on Gulf of Bothnia and Gulf of Finland; a republic; capital, Helsinki — **Fin·land·er** \'fin-lənd-ər\ *noun*

**Finland, Gulf of** arm of the Baltic between Finland & Estonia

**Fiume** — see RIJEKA

**Flan·ders** \'flan-dərz\ region W Belgium & N France on North Sea

**Flat·tery, Cape** \'flat-ə-rē\ cape NW Washington at entrance to Strait of Juan de Fuca

**Flint** \'flint\ city SE Michigan

**Flint·shire** \'flint-,shiər, -shər\ *or* **Flint** former county N Wales

**Flor·ence** \'flȯr-əns, 'flär-\ *or Italian* **Fi·ren·ze** \fē-'rent-sā\ *or ancient* **Flo·ren·tia** \flə-'ren-chə, -chē-ə\ city central Italy, capital of Tuscany — **Flor·en·tine** \'flȯr-ən-,tēn, 'flär-, -,tīn\ *adjective or noun*

**Flo·res** \'flȯr-əs, 'flȯr-\ island Indonesia in Lesser Sunda Islands

**Flo·ri·a·nó·po·lis** \,flȯr-ē-ə-'näp-ə-ləs, ,flȯr-\ city S Brazil on an island NE of Pôrto Alegre

**Flor·i·da** \'flȯr-əd-ə, 'flär-\ state SE U.S.; capital, Tallahassee — **Flo·rid·i·an** \flə-'rid-ē-ən\ *or* **Flor·i·dan** \'flȯr-əd-ən, 'flär-\ *adjective or noun*

**Florida, Straits of** channel between Florida Keys on NW & Cuba & Bahamas on S & E connecting Gulf of Mexico & the Atlantic

**Florida Keys** chain of islands off S tip of Florida

**Fog·gia** \'fȯ-jə, -jä\ city SE Italy in Puglia

**Foochow** — see FUZHOU

**For·a·ker, Mount** \'fȯr-i-kər, 'fär-\ mountain 5304 meters S central Alaska in Alaska Range

**For·mo·sa** \fȯr-'mō-sə, fər-, -zə\ — see TAIWAN — **For·mo·san** \-sən, -zən\ *adjective or noun*

**For·ta·le·za** \,fȯrt-l-'ā-zə\ city NE Brazil NW of Recife

**Fort–de–France** \,fȯrd-ə-'fräⁿs\ city French West Indies, capital of Martinique on W coast

**Forth** \'fȯrth, 'fȯrth\ river 187 kilometers long S central Scotland flowing E into North Sea through **Firth of Forth** (estuary)

**Fort Knox** \'näks\ military reservation N central Kentucky SSW of Louisville; location of U.S. Gold Bullion Depository

**Fort–Lamy** — see N'DJAMENA

**Fort Lau·der·dale** \'lȯd-ər-,dāl\ city SE Florida

**Fort Wayne** \'wān\ city NE Indiana

**Fort Worth** \'wərth\ city NE Texas

**Foxe Basin** \'fäks\ inlet of the Atlantic N Canada W of Baffin Island

**France** \'frans\ country W Europe between the English Channel & the Mediterranean; a republic; capital, Paris

**Frank·fort** \'frangk-fərt\ city, capital of Kentucky

**Frank·furt** \'frangk-fərt, 'frängk-,fu̇rt\ *or in full* **Frankfurt am Main** \-,äm-'mīn\ *or* **Frankfort on the Main** city SW central Germany on Main River

**Frank·lin** \'frang-klən\ former district N Canada in Northwest Territories including Arctic Islands & Boothia & Melville peninsulas

**Fra·ser** \'frā-zər, -zhər\ river 1368 kilometers long Canada in S central British Columbia flowing into the Pacific

**Fred·er·ic·ton** \'fred-rik-tən, -ə-rik-\ city, capital of New Brunswick

**Free State** *or formerly* **Or·ange Free State** \'ȯr-inj, 'är-, -ənj\ province E central Republic of South Africa

**Free·town** \'frē-,tau̇n\ city, capital of Sierra Leone

**Fre·mont** \'frē-,mänt\ city W California

**French Equatorial Africa** former country W central Africa N of Congo River comprising a federation of Chad, Gabon, Middle Congo, & Ubangi–Shari territories

**French Guiana** country N South America on the Atlantic; a dependency of France; capital, Cayenne

**French Guinea** — see GUINEA

**French Indochina** — see INDOCHINA

**French Morocco** — see MOROCCO

**French Polynesia** islands in S Pacific belonging to France & including Society, Marquesas, Tuamotu, Gambier, & Tubuai groups; capital, Papeete

**French Somaliland** — see DJIBOUTI

**French Sudan** — see MALI

**French Territory of the Afars and the Issas** — see DJIBOUTI

**French Togo** — see TOGO

**French West Indies** islands of the West Indies belonging to France & including Guadeloupe, Martinique, Désirade, Les Saintes, Marie Galante, Saint Barthélemy, & part of Saint Martin

**Fres·no** \'frez-nō\ city S central California

**Friendly Islands** — see TONGA

**Fri·sian** \'frizh-ən, 'frē-zhən\ islands N Europe in North Sea including **West Frisian** islands off N Netherlands, **East Frisian** islands off NW Germany, & **North Frisian** islands off N Germany and W Denmark

**Fri·u·li–Ve·ne·zia Giu·lia** \frē-'ü-lē-və-,net-sē-ə-'jü-yə\ region N Italy; capital, Udine

**Frunze** — see BISHKEK

**Fu·ji** \'fü-jē, 'fyü-\ *or* **Fu·ji·ya·ma** \,fü-jē-'äm-ə, ,fyü-, -'yäm-\ *or* **Fu·ji·no·ya·ma** \-jē-nō-'yäm-ə\ *or* **Fu·ji·san** \-'sän\ mountain 3776 meters Japan in S central Honshu; highest in Japan

**Fu·ji·sa·wa** \,fü-jē-'sä-wə\ city Japan in SE Honshu

**Fu·jian** \'fü-'jän, -jē-'än\ *or* **Fu·kien** \'fü-'kyen, -kē-'en\ province SE China on Formosa Strait; capital, Fuzhou

**Fu·ku·o·ka** \,fü-kə-'wō-kə\ city Japan in N Kyushu

**Fu·ku·ya·ma** \,fü-kə-'yäm-ə\ city Japan in SW Honshu

**Fulham** — see HAMMERSMITH AND FULHAM

**Fu·na·ba·shi** \,fü-nə-'bäsh-ē\ city Japan in SE Honshu on Tokyo Bay

**Fu·na·fu·ti** \,fü-nə-'füt-ē, ,fyü-, -'fyüt-\ city, capital of Tuvalu

**Fun·dy, Bay of** \'fən-dē\ inlet of the Atlantic SE Canada between New Brunswick & Nova Scotia

**Fu·shun** \'fü-'shu̇n\ city NE China in NE Liaoning

**Fu·zhou** \'fü-'jō\ *or* **Foo·chow** \'fü-'jō, -'chau̇\ *or formerly* **Min·how** \'min-'hō\ city SE China, capital of Fujian

**Ga·bon** \ga-'bōⁿ\ country W equatorial Africa; capital, Libreville — **Gab·o·nese** \,gab-ə-'nēz, -'nēs\ *adjective or noun*

**Ga·bo·rone** \,gäb-ə-'rōn\ city, capital of Botswana

**Gads·den Purchase** \'gadz-dən\ tract of land S of Gila River in present Arizona & New Mexico purchased 1853 by the U.S. from Mexico

**Ga·lá·pa·gos Islands** \gə-'läp-ə-gəs, -'lap-\ *or* **Co·lón Archipelago** \kə-'lōn\ island group Ecuador in the Pacific about 965 kilometers W of mainland

**Ga·lati** \gə-'läts, -'lät-sē\ city E Romania on the Danube

**Ga·la·tia** \gə-'lā-shə, -shē-ə\ ancient country & Roman province central Asia Minor in region centering on modern Ankara, Turkey — **Ga·la·tian** \-shən\ *adjective or noun*

**Ga·li·cia** \gə-'lish-ə, -'lish-ē-ə\ **1** region E central Europe now divided between Poland & Ukraine **2** region NW Spain on the Atlantic — **Ga·li·cian** \-shən\ *adjective or noun*

**Gal·i·lee** \'gal-ə-,lē\ hilly region N Israel — **Gal·i·le·an** \,gal-ə-'lē-ən\ *adjective or noun*

**Galilee, Sea of** *or* **Lake of Gen·nes·a·ret** \gə-'nes-ə-,ret, -rət\ *or* **Sea of Ti·be·ri·as** \tī-'bir-ē-əs\ lake N Israel on Syrian border traversed by Jordan River

**Gal·lip·o·li** \gə-'lip-ə-lē\ *or Turkish* **Ge·li·bo·lu Ya·ri·ma·da·si** \,gel-ə-bə-'lü-,yär-ə-,mäd-ə-'sē\ peninsula Turkey in Europe, between the Dardanelles & Saros Gulf

**Gal·lo·way** \'gal-ə-,wā\ district SW Scotland — see DUMFRIES

**Gal·way** \'gȯl-,wā\ county W Ireland in Connacht

**Gam·bia** \'gam-bē-ə\ country W Africa; a republic; capital, Banjul — **Gam·bi·an** \-ən\ *adjective or noun*

**Gand** — see GHENT

**Gan·ges** \'gan-jēz\ river about 2505 kilometers long N India flowing from the Himalaya SE & E to unite with the Brahmaputra & empty into Bay of Bengal through a vast delta — **Gan·get·ic** \gan-'jet-ik\ *adjective*

**Gan·su** *or* **Kan·su** \'gän-'sü\ province NW China; capital, Lanzhou

**Gar·da, Lake** \'gärd-ə\ lake N Italy NW of Verona

**Garden Grove** city SW California

**Ga·ronne** \gə-'rän, -'rȯn\ river 574 kilometers long SE France flowing into Gironde Estuary

**Gary** \'gaər-ē, 'geər-\ city NW Indiana on Lake Michigan

**Gas·co·ny** \'gas-kə-nē\ *or French* **Gas·cogne** \gá-'skōⁿʸ\ region and former province SW France

**Gas·pé** \gas-'pā, 'gas-\ peninsula SE Quebec E of mouth of the Saint Lawrence — **Gas·pe·sian** \ga-'spē-zhən\ *adjective or noun*

**Gates·head** \'gāts-,hed\ borough N England in Tyne and Wear county

**Gates of the Arctic National Park** reservation N central Alaska in Brooks Range

**Gaul** \'gȯl\ *or Latin* **Gal·lia** \'gal-ē-ə\ ancient country W Europe chiefly comprising region occupied by modern France & Belgium but at one time including also Po valley in N Italy — see CISALPINE GAUL, TRANSALPINE GAUL

**Gau·teng** \'gau̇-,teng\ province central NE Republic of South Africa

**Ga·za Strip** \'gäz-ə, 'gaz-, 'gāz-\ district S Palestine on the Mediterranean; chief town, Gaza

**Ga·zi·an·tep** \,gäz-ē-,än-'tep, -än-\ city S Turkey

**Gdansk** \gə-'dänsk, -'dansk\ *or German* **Dan·zig** \'dan-sig, 'dän-\ city N Poland on Gulf of Danzig

**Gdyn·ia** \gə-'din-ē-ə\ city N Poland

**Gebel Musa** — see MUSA (Gebel)

**Gee·long** \jə-'lȯng\ city SE Australia in S Victoria

**Gel·sen·kir·chen** \gel-zən-'kir-kən\ city W Germany in the Ruhr W of Dortmund

**Ge·ne·ral San Mar·tín** \hä-nä-,räl-,san-mär-'tēn\ city E Argentina NW of Buenos Aires

**Ge·ne·va** \jə-'nē-və\ city SW Switzerland on Lake of Geneva — **Ge·ne·van** \-vən\ *adjective or noun*

**Geneva, Lake of** *or* **Lake Le·man** \'lē-mən, 'lem-ən, lə-'man\; *ancient* **Le·man·nus** \li-'man-əs\ *or* **Le·ma·nus** \li-'män-əs\ lake on border between SW Switzerland & E France traversed by the Rhone

**Gen·oa** \'jen-ə-wə\ *or Italian* **Ge·no·va** \'je-nō-vä\ city NW Italy, capital of Liguria — **Gen·o·ese** \,jen-ə-'wēz, -'wēs\ *or* **Gen·o·vese** \-ə-'vēz, -'vēs\ *adjective or noun*

**George·town** \'jórj-,taún\ **1** a W section of Washington, District of Columbia **2** city, capital of Guyana

**George Town** *or* **Pe·nang** \pə-'nang\ city Malaysia, on an island in Peninsular Malaysia

**Geor·gia** \'jór-jə\ **1** state SE U.S.; capital, Atlanta **2** country SE Europe on Black Sea S of Caucasus Mountains; a constituent republic of U.S.S.R. 1936–91; capital, Tbilisi — **Geor·gian** \'jór-jən\ *adjective or noun*

**Georgia, Strait of** channel Canada & U.S. between Vancouver Island & mainland NW of Puget Sound

**Georgian Bay** inlet of Lake Huron in S Ontario

**Ger·man·town** \'jər-mən-,taún\ a NW section of Philadelphia, Pennsylvania

**Ger·ma·ny** \'jərm-nē, -ə-nē\ country central Europe bordering on North & Baltic seas; divided into two republics 1940–90: the Federal Republic of Germany (capital, Bonn) & the German Democratic Republic (capital, East Berlin); capital, Berlin

**Ger·mis·ton** \'jər-mə-stən\ city NE Republic of South Africa E of Johannesburg

**Gha·na** \'gän-ə, 'gan-ə\ *or formerly* **Gold Coast** country W Africa on Gulf of Guinea; a republic of the Commonwealth; capital, Accra — **Gha·na·ian** \gä-'nā-ən, ga-, -yən; 'nī-ən\ *or* **Gha·ni·an** \'gän-ē-ən, 'gän-yən, 'gan-\ *adjective or noun*

**Ghats** \'góts\ two mountain chains S India — see EASTERN GHATS, WESTERN GHATS

**Ghent** \'gent\ *or Flemish* **Gent** \'gent\ *or French* **Gand** \'gäⁿ\ city NW central Belgium

**Gi·bral·tar** \jə-'ból-tər\ British colony & fortress on S coast of Spain including Rock of Gibraltar

**Gibraltar, Rock of** headland on S coast of Spain in Gibraltar colony at E end of Strait of Gibraltar; highest point 426 meters — see PILLARS OF HERCULES

**Gibraltar, Strait of** passage between Spain & Africa connecting the Atlantic & the Mediterranean

**Gi·fu** \'gē-,fü\ city Japan in central Honshu

**Gi·jón** \hē-'hōn\ city & port NW Spain on Bay of Biscay

**Gi·la** \'hē-lə\ river 805 kilometers long SW New Mexico and S Arizona flowing W into the Colorado

**Gil·bert** \'gil-bərt\ islands Kiribati in W Pacific; until 1975 formed with Ellice Islands the British colony of **Gilbert and El·lice Islands** \'el-əs\ — see KIRIBATI

**Gil·e·ad** \'gil-ē-əd\ mountain region NE Palestine E of Jordan River; now in NW Jordan — **Gil·e·ad·ite** \-ē-ə-,dīt\ *noun*

**Gi·ronde** \jə-'ränd, zhə-; zhē-'rōⁿd\ estuary W France formed by junction of Garonne & Dordogne rivers

**Gi·za** \'gē-zə\ *or* **El Gi·za** \el-\ *or* **Al Jī·zah** \al-jē-zə\ city N Egypt on the Nile SW of Cairo

**Gla·cier Bay** \,glā-shər-\ inlet SE Alaska at S end of Saint Elias Range in **Glacier Bay National Park**

**Glacier National Park** — see WATERTON–GLACIER INTERNATIONAL PEACE PARK

**Glades** \'glādz\ EVERGLADES

**Gla·mor·gan** \glə-'mór-gən\ *or* **Gla·mor·gan·shire** \-,shiər, ər\ former county SE Wales — see MID GLAMORGAN, SOUTH GLAMORGAN, WEST GLAMORGAN

**Glas·gow** \'glas-kō, 'glas-gō, 'glaz-gō\ city S central Scotland on the Clyde — **Glas·we·gian** \glas-'wē-jən\ *adjective or noun*

**Glen·dale** \'glen-,dāl\ city S California NE of Los Angeles

**Glouces·ter·shire** \'gläs-tər-,shiər, 'glós-, -shər\ *or* **Gloucester** county SW central England

**Gnossus** — see KNOSSOS

**Goa** \'gō-ə\ state India on W coast belonging before 1962 to Portugal; capital, Panaji

**Go·bi** \'gō-bē\ desert E central Asia in Mongolia & N China

**Godthåb** — see NUUK

**Godwin Austen** — see K2

**Goi·â·nia** \gói-'an-ē-ə\ city SE central Brazil SW of Brasília

**Go·lan Heights** \,gō-,län-, -,lən-\ hilly region between NE Israel & SW Syria

**Gol·con·da** \gäl-'kän-də\ ruined city central India W of Hyderabad

**Gold Coast 1** coast region W Africa on N shore of Gulf of Guinea E of Ivory Coast **2** — see GHANA

**Golden Gate** strait W California connecting San Francisco Bay and the Pacific

**Golden Horn** inlet of the Bosporus, Turkey in Europe; harbor of Istanbul

**Golgotha** — see CALVARY

**Gomel** — see HOMYEL

**Go·mor·rah** \gə-'mär-ə, -'mór-\ city, ancient Palestine in plain of Jordan

**Good Hope, Cape of** \,gud-'hōp\ cape S Republic of South Africa

**Go·rakh·pur** \'gór-ək-,púr, 'gór-\ city NE India in E Uttar Pradesh N of Varanasi

**Gorki** *or* **Gor'kii** *or* **Gor'kiy** *or* **Gorky** — see NIZHNIY NOVGOROD

**Gor·lov·ka** \gór-'lóf-kə, -'lóv-\ city E Ukraine in Donets Basin

**Go·shen** \'gō-shən\ district of ancient Egypt E of Nile delta

**Gö·te·borg** \,yərt-ə-'bór-ē, *Swedish* ,yȫ-tə-'bóry\ *or* **Goth·en·burg** \'gäth-ən-,bərg\ city SW Sweden

**Got·land** \'gät-,land, -lənd\ island Sweden in the Baltic; capital, Visby

**Göt·ting·en** \'gót-ing-ən, 'get-, 'gœt-\ city central Germany SSW of Brunswick

**Gram·pi·an** \'gram-pē-ən\ **1** hills N central Scotland — see BEN NEVIS **2** region NE central Scotland; established 1975

**Gra·na·da** \grə-'näd-ə\ city S Spain in Andalusia

**Grand Banks** shoal area in the W Atlantic SE of Newfoundland

**Grand Canyon** gorge of Colorado River NW Arizona; area largely in **Grand Canyon National Park**

**Grand Canyon of the Snake** — see HELLS CANYON

**Grande, Rio** — see RIO GRANDE

**Grand Rapids** city SW Michigan

**Grand Te·ton National Park** \'tē-,tän\ reservation NW Wyoming S of Yellowstone National Park

**Grau·bün·den** \graú-'bin-dən, -'bún-, -'buen-\ *or French* **Gri·sons** \grē-'zōⁿ\ canton E Switzerland

**Gravenhage, 's** — see HAGUE (The)

**Graz** \'gräts\ city S Austria, capital of Styria

**Great Australian Bight** wide bay on S coast of Australia

**Great Barrier Reef** coral reef Australia off NE coast of Queensland

**Great Basin** region W U.S. between Sierra Nevada & Wasatch mountains including most of Nevada & parts of California, Idaho, Utah, Wyoming, and Oregon; has no drainage to ocean

**Great Basin National Park** reservation E Nevada

**Great Bear** lake Canada in W Northwest Territories draining through Great Bear River into Mackenzie River

**Great Brit·ain** \'brit-n\ **1** island W Europe NW of France comprising England, Scotland, & Wales **2** UNITED KINGDOM

**Great Dividing Range** mountain system E Australia & Tasmania extending S from Cape York Peninsula — see KOSCIUSKO (Mount)

**Greater An·til·les** \an-'til-ēz\ group of islands of the West Indies including Cuba, Hispaniola, Jamaica, & Puerto Rico — see LESSER ANTILLES

**Greater London** metropolitan county SE England comprising City of London & 32 surrounding boroughs

**Greater Manchester** metropolitan county NW England including city of Manchester

**Greater Sunda** — see SUNDA

**Great Lakes 1** chain of five lakes (Superior, Michigan, Huron, Erie, & Ontario) central North America in U.S. & Canada **2** group of lakes E central Africa including Rudolf, Albert, Victoria, Tanganyika, & Malawi

**Great Plains** elevated plains region W central U.S. & W Canada E of the Rockies; chiefly W of the 100th meridian extending from W Texas to NE British Columbia & NW Alberta

**Great Rift Valley** \'rift\ depression SW Asia & E Africa extending with several breaks from valley of the Jordan S to central Mozambique

**Great Salt** lake N Utah having strongly saline waters & no outlet

**Great Slave** lake NW Canada in S Northwest Territories drained by Mackenzie River

**Great Smoky** mountains between W North Carolina & E Tennessee partly in **Great Smoky Mountains National Park**; highest Clingmans Dome 2025 meters

**Greece** \'grēs\ *or ancient* **Hel·las** \'hel-əs\ *or Greek* **El·lás** \e-'läs\ country S Europe at S end of Balkan Peninsula; a republic; capital, Athens

**Green** \'grēn\ **1** mountains E North America in the Appalachians extending from S Quebec S through Vermont into W Massachusetts **2** river 1175 kilometers long W U.S. flowing from Wind River Range in W Wyoming S into the Colorado in SE Utah

**Green Bay 1** inlet of NW Lake Michigan about 195 kilometers long in NW Michigan & NE Wisconsin **2** city NE Wisconsin

**Green·land** \'grēn-lənd, -,land\ island in the N Atlantic off NE North America belonging to Denmark; capital, Nuuk

**Greens·boro** \'grēnz-,bər-ə, -,bə-rə\ city N central North Carolina

**Green·wich** \'grin-ij, 'gren-, -ich\ SE borough of Greater London, England

**Green·wich Village** \,gren-ich-, ,grin-, -ij-\ section of New York City in Manhattan on lower W side

**Gre·na·da** \grə-'näd-ə\ island British West Indies in S Windwards; an independent country since 1974; capital, Saint George's

**Gren·a·dines** \,gren-ə-'dēnz\ islands British West Indies; divided between Grenada & Saint Vincent and the Grenadines

**Gre·no·ble** \grə-'nō-bəl\ city SE France

**Grisons** — see GRAUBÜNDEN

**Gro·ning·en** \'grō-ning-ən\ city NE Netherlands

**Groz·ny** \'gróz-nē, 'gräz-\ city S Russia in Europe, N of Caucasus Mountains

**Gua·da·la·ja·ra** \,gwäd-ə-lə-'här-ə\ city W central Mexico, capital of Jalisco

**Gua·dal·ca·nal** \gwäd-l-kə-'nal, ,gwäd-ə-kə-\ island W Pacific in the SE Solomons

**Gua·dal·qui·vir** \,gwäd-l-'kwiv-ər, -,ki-'viər\ river 656 kilometers long S Spain flowing into the Atlantic

**Gua·da·lupe Mountains National Park** \'gwäd-l-,üp\ reservation W Texas

**Gua·de·loupe** \'gwäd-l-,üp\ two islands, Basseterre (or Guadeloupe proper) & Grande-Terre, separated by a narrow channel in French West Indies in central Leewards; capital, Basseterre (on Basse-terre Island)

**Gua·di·a·na** \,gwäd-ē-'än-ə, -'an-\ river 829 kilometers long S Spain & SE Portugal flowing into the Atlantic

**Guaíra** *or* **Guayra** — see SETE QUEDAS

**Guam** \'gwäm\ island W Pacific in S Marianas belonging to U.S.; capital, Agana — **Gua·ma·ni·an** \gwä-'mä-nē-ən\ *adjective or noun*

**Gua·na·ba·coa** \,gwän-ə-bə-'kō-ə\ city W Cuba

**Gua·na·ba·ra Bay** \,gwän-ə-'bar-ə, -'bär-\ inlet of the Atlantic SE Brazil on which city of Rio de Janeiro is situated

**Gua·na·jua·to** \,gwän-ə-'hwät-ō, -'wät-\ **1** state central Mexico **2** city, its capital

**Guang·xi Zhuang·zu** \'gwäng-'shē-je-'wäng-'zü\ *or* **Kwang·si–Chuang** \'gwäng-se-chə-'wäng\ region & former province S China; capital, Nanning

**Guang·zhou** *or* **Kuang–chou** \'gwäng-'jō\ *or* **Can·ton** \'kan-,tän, kan-'\ city SE China, capital of Guangdong

**Guan·ta·na·mo Bay** \gwän-'tän-ə-,mō\ inlet of the Caribbean in SE Cuba; site of U.S. naval station

**Gua·te·ma·la** \,gwät-ə-'mä-lə\ **1** country Central America; a republic **2** *or* **Guatemala City** city, its capital — **Gua·te·ma·lan** \-lən\ *adjective or noun*

**Gua·ya·quil** \,gwī-ə-'kēl, -'kil\ city W Ecuador

**Guern·sey** \'gərn-zē\ island in English Channel — see CHANNEL

**Guer·re·ro** \gə-'reər-ō\ state S Mexico on the Pacific; capital, Chilpancingo

**Gui·a·na** \gē-'an-ə, -'än-ə; gī-'an-ə\ region N South America on the Atlantic bounded on W & S by Orinoco, Negro, & Amazon rivers; includes Guyana, French Guiana, Suriname, & adjacent parts of Brazil & Venezuela — **Gui·a·nan** \-ən\ *adjective or noun*

**Gui·lin** \'gwē-'lin\ *or* **Kwei·lin** *or* **Kuei–lin** \'gwā-'lin\ city S China in NE Guangxi Zhuangzu

**Guin·ea** \'gin-ē\ **1** region W Africa on the Atlantic extending along coast from Gambia to Angola **2** *or formerly* **French Guinea** country W Africa N of Sierra Leone & Liberia; a republic; capital, Conakry — **Guin·ean** \'gin-ē-ən\ *adjective or noun*

**Guinea, Gulf of** arm of the Atlantic W central Africa

**Guin·ea–Bis·sau** \,gin-ē-bis-'aú\ *or formerly* **Portuguese Guinea** country W Africa; a republic since 1974; capital, Bissau

**Gui·yang** \'gwē-'yäng\ *or* **Kuei–yang** \'gwā-'yäng\ city S China, capital of Guizhou

**Gui·zhou** \'gwē-'jō\ *or* **Kuei–chou** \'gwā-'jō\ *or* **Kwei·chow** \'gwā-'chaú\ province S China S of Sichuan; capital, Guiyang

**Gu·ja·rat** *or* **Gu·je·rat** \,güj-ə-'rät, ,gúj-ə-\ state W India N & E of Gulf of Cambay; capital, Gandhinagar

**Guj·ran·wa·la** \,güj-rən-'wäl-ə, ,gúj-\ city NE Pakistan

**Gulf States** states of U.S. bordering on Gulf of Mexico: Florida, Alabama, Mississippi, Louisiana, and Texas

**Gulf Stream** warm current of the Atlantic Ocean flowing from Gulf of Mexico NE along coast of U.S. to Nantucket Island and thence eastward

**Gun·tur** \gún-'túr\ city E India in central Andhra Pradesh

**Gus·ta·vo A. Ma·de·ro** \gùs-'täv-,ō-,ä-mə-'der-,ō\ city central Mexico N of Mexico City

**Guy·ana** \gī-'an-ə\ *or formerly* **British Guiana** country N South America on the Atlantic; a republic in the Commonwealth since 1970; capital, Georgetown

**Gwa·li·or** \'gwäl-ē-,ór\ city N central India in NW Andhra Pradesh SSE of Agra

**Gwent** \'gwent\ county SE Wales; established 1974

**Gwyn·edd** \'gwin-eth\ county NW Wales; established 1974

**Habana, La** — see HAVANA

**Ha·chi·o·je** \,häch-ē-'ō-jē\ city Japan in SE central Honshu W of Tokyo

**Hack·ney** \'hak-nē\ borough of N Greater London, England

**Hague, The** \thə-'häg\ *or Dutch* **'s Gra·ven·ha·ge** \,skräv-ən-'häg-ə, ,skräv-\ city SW Netherlands; a capital of the Netherlands

**Haidarabad** — see HYDERABAD

**Hai·fa** \'hī-fə\ city NW Israel

**Hai·kou** \'hī-'kaú, -'kō\ city SE China, capital of Hainan

**Hai·nan** \'hī-'nän\ island SE China in South China Sea; a province; capital, Haikou

**Hai·phong** \'hī-'fóng\ city N Vietnam in Tonkin

**Hai·ti** \'hāt-ē\ **1** — see HISPANIOLA **2** country West Indies in W Hispaniola; a republic; capital, Port-au-Prince — **Hai·tian** \'hā-shən\ *adjective or noun*

**Ha·ko·da·te** \,häk-ə-'dät-ē\ city & port Japan in SW Hokkaido

**Ha·le·a·ka·la Crater** \,häl-ē-,äk-ə-'lä\ crater more than 762 meters deep Hawaii in E Maui Island in **Haleakala National Park**

**Hal·i·car·nas·sus** \,hal-ə-kär-'nas-əs\ ancient city SW Asia Minor in SW Caria on Aegean Sea

**Hal·i·fax** \'hal-ə-,faks\ **1** city, capital of Nova Scotia **2** city N England in West Yorkshire

**Hal·le** \'häl-ə\ city E central Germany NW of Leipzig

**Hal·ma·he·ra** \,häl-mə-'her-ə, ,häl-\ island E Indonesia; largest of the Moluccas

**Ha·ma** \'häm-,ä\ city W Syria

**Ha·ma·dan** \,häm-ə-'dan, -'dän\ city W Iran

**Ha·ma·ma·tsu** \,häm-ə-'mät-sü\ city Japan in S Honshu

**Ham·burg** \'ham-,bərg, 'häm-,bùrg\ city N Germany on the Elbe — **Ham·burg·er** \-,bər-gər, -,bùr-\ *noun*

**Ham·hung** \'häm-,hùng\ city E central North Korea

**Ham·il·ton** \'ham-əl-tən, -əlt-n\ **1** city S Ontario **2** town, capital of Bermuda

**Ham·mer·smith and Ful·ham** \'ham-ər-,smith-ənd-'fúl-əm\ borough of SW Greater London, England

**Ham·mond** \'ham-ənd\ city NW Indiana

**Hamp·shire** \'hamp-,shiər, 'ham-, -shər\ **1** former county S England comprising present counties of Hampshire & Isle of Wight **2** county S England on English Channel

**Hamp·ton** \'hamp-tən, 'ham-\ city SE Virginia

**Hampton Roads** channel SE Virginia through which James & Elizabeth rivers flow into Chesapeake Bay

**Hang·zhou** \'häng-'jō\ *or* **Hang–chou** \-'jō\ *or* **Hang·chow** \'häng-'chaú, 'häng-jō\ city E China, capital of Zhejiang

**Han·kow** \'häng-'kaú, -'kō; 'häng-'kō\ former city E central China — see WUHAN

**Han·o·ver** *or* **Han·o·ver** \'han-,ō-vər, 'han-ə-vər; *German* hä-'nō-vər\ city N central Germany, capital of Lower Saxony

**Ha·noi** \ha-'nói, hə-, hä-\ city, capital of Vietnam in Tonkin

**Han·yang** \'hän-'yäng\ former city E central China — see WUHAN

**Ha·ra·re** \hə-'rä-,rā\ *or formerly* **Salis·bury** \'sólz-,ber-ē, 'salz-, -bə-rē, -brē\ city, capital of Zimbabwe

**Har·bin** \'här-bən, här-'bin\ *or* **Ha–erh–pin** \'hä-'er-'bin\ *or formerly* **Pin·kiang** \'bin-jē-'äng\ city NE China, capital of Heilongjiang

**Har·in·gey** \'har-ing-gā\ borough of N Greater London, England

**Har·lem** \'här-ləm\ section of New York City in N Manhattan

**Har·ris·burg** \'har-əs-,bərg\ city, capital of Pennsylvania

**Har·row** \'har-ō\ borough of NW Greater London, England

**Hart·ford** \'härt-fərd\ city, capital of Connecticut

**Har·tle·pool** \'härt-lē-,pül\ borough N England in Cleveland

**Ha·ry·a·na** \,hə-rē-'än-ə\ state N India formed 1966 from S part of state of Punjab; capital, Chandigarh

**Harz** \'härts\ mountains central Germany between Elbe & Leine rivers

**Hat·ter·as, Cape** \'hat-ə-rəs, 'ha-trəs\ cape, North Carolina on Cape Hatteras Island

**Ha·vana** \hə-'van-ə\ *or Spanish* **La Ha·ba·na** \lä-ä-'vän-ə, lä-'vän-ə\ city, capital of Cuba

**Hav·ant** \'hav-ənt\ town S England in Hampshire

**Ha·ver·ing** \'hāv-ring, -ə-ring\ borough of NE Greater London, England

**Ha·waii** \hə-'wä-ē, -'wī-, -'wó-, -yē\ **1** *or formerly* **Sand·wich Islands** \san-,wich-, ,sand-\ group of islands central Pacific belonging to U.S. **2** island, largest of the group **3** state of U.S. comprising Hawaiian Islands except Midway; capital, Honolulu

**Hawaii Volcanoes National Park** reservation Hawaii on Hawaii Island including Mauna Loa & Kilauea

**He·bei** \'həb-'ā\ *or* **Hopeh** *or* **Hopei** \'hō-'bā\ province NE China; capital, Shijiazhuang

**Heb·ri·des** \'heb-rə-,dēz\ islands W Scotland in the Atlantic comprising **Outer Hebrides** (to W) and **Inner Hebrides** (to E) — see WESTERN ISLES — **Heb·ri·de·an** \,heb-rə-'dē-ən\ *adjective or noun*

**He·fei** *or* **Ho·fei** \'həf-'ā\ *or formerly* **Lu·chow** \'lü-jō\ city E China, capital of Anhui W of Nanjing

**Hei·long·jiang** *or* **Hei·lung·kiang** \'hā-'lùng-'jyäng\ province NE China in N Manchuria; capital, Harbin

**He·jaz** \hej-'az, hij-\ region W Saudi Arabia on Red Sea

**Hel·e·na** \'hel-ə-nə\ city, capital of Montana

**He·li·op·o·lis** \,hē-lē-'äp-ə-ləs\ **1** either of two cities of ancient Egypt near modern Cairo **2** city of ancient Syria; site at modern town of **Baal·bek** \'bä-əl-,bek, 'bäl-,bek\ in E Lebanon N of Damascus

**Hellas** — see GREECE

**Hellespont** — see DARDANELLES

**Hells Canyon** \'helz\ *or* **Grand Canyon of the Snake** canyon of Snake River on Idaho-Oregon boundary

**Hel·sin·ki** \'hel-,sing-kē, hel-'\ *or Swedish* **Hel·sing·fors** \'hel-sing-,fórz\ city, capital of Finland

**Helvetia** — see SWITZERLAND

**He·nan** \'hən-'än\ *or* **Ho·nan** \'hō-'nän\ province E central China; capital, Zhengzhou

**Heng·yang** \'həng-'yäng\ city SE central China in SE Hunan

**Henry, Cape** \'hen-rē\ headland E Virginia S of entrance to Chesapeake Bay

**Her·e·ford and Wor·ces·ter** \'her-ə-fərd-n-'wùs-tər, *in the United States also* 'hər-fərd-\ county W England bordering on Wales

**Her·e·ford·shire** \'her-ə-fərd-,shiər, -shər, *in the United States also* 'hər-fərd-\ *or* **Hereford** former county W England — see HEREFORD AND WORCESTER

**Her·mon, Mount** \'hər-mən\ mountain 2814 meters on Lebanon-Syria border; highest in Anti-Lebanon Mountains

**Her·mo·si·llo** \,er-mə-'sē-ō, -,yō\ city NW Mexico, capital of Sonora

**Hert·ford·shire** \'här-fərd-,shiər, *also* 'härt-, *in the United States also* 'hərt-\ *or* **Hertford** county SE England

**Her·ze·go·vi·na** \,hert-sə-gō-'vē-nə,,hərt-\ *or* **Her·ce·go·vi·na** \'hert-sä-,gō-vē-nä\ region S Europe S of Bosnia; now part of Bosnia and Herzegovina

**Hesse** \'hes, 'hes-ē\ *or German* **Hes·sen** \'hes-n\ state central Germany E of the Rhine & N of the Main; capital, Wiesbaden

**Hi·a·le·ah** \,hī-ə-'lē-ə\ city SE Florida

**Hi·ber·nia** \hī-'bər-nē-ə\ — see IRELAND — **Hi·ber·ni·an** \-ən\ *adjective or noun*

**Hi·dal·go** \hid-'al-gō\ state central Mexico; capital, Pachuca

**Hi·ga·shi·ōsa·ka** \hē-,gä-shē-ō-'säk-ə\ city Japan in S Honshu E of Osaka

**High·land** \'hī-lənd\ region NW Scotland; established 1975

**High·lands** \'hī-ləndz, -lənz\ the mountainous N part of Scotland lying N & W of the Lowlands

**High Plains** the Great Plains especially from Nebraska southward

**High Tatra** — see TATRA

**Hil·ling·don** \'hil-ing-dən\ borough of W Greater London, England

**Hi·ma·chal Pra·desh** \hi-,mäch-əl-prə-'desh, -'däsh\ state NW India comprising two areas NW of Uttar Pradesh; capital, Simla

**Hi·ma·la·ya, the** \him-ə-'lā-ə; hə-'mäl-yə, -'mäl-ə-yə\ *or the* **Hi·ma·la·yas** \-əz, -yəz\ mountain system S Asia on border between India & Tibet & in Kashmir, Nepal, & Bhutan — see EVEREST (Mount) — **Hi·ma·la·yan** \,him-ə-'lā-ən; hə-'mäl-yən, -'mäl-ə-yən\ *adjective*

**Hi·me·ji** \hi-'mej-ē\ city Japan in W Honshu WNW of Kobe

**Hin·du Kush** \,hin-dú-'kúsh, -'kəsh\ mountain range central Asia SW of the Pamirs on border of Kashmir & in Afghanistan

**Hin·du·stan** \,hin-dü-'stan, -də-, -'stän\ **1** region N India N of the Deccan **2** historical name for India (country)

**Hip·po** \'hip-ō\ ancient city N Africa; chief town of Numidia

**Hi·ra·ka·ta** \,hir-ə-'kät-ə\ city Japan on Honshu

**Hi·ro·shi·ma** \,hir-ə-'shē-mə, hə-'rō-shə-mə\ city Japan in SW Honshu on Inland Sea

**Hispalis** — see SEVILLE

**His·pa·nia** \his-'pän-ē-ə, -'pän-yə, -'pan-\ — see SPAIN

**His·pan·io·la** \,his-pən-'yō-lə\ *or Spanish* **Es·pa·ño·la** \,es-,pän-'yō-lə\ *or formerly* **Hai·ti** \'hāt-ē\ *or* **San·to Do·min·go** \,sant-əd-ə-'ming-gō\ island West Indies in Greater Antilles divided between Haiti on W & Dominican Republic on E

**Ho·bart** \'hō-,bärt\ city Australia, capital of Tasmania

**Ho Chi Minh City** \,hō-,chē-'min-, -,shē-\ *or formerly* **Sai·gon** \sī-'gän, 'sī-,\ city S Vietnam

**Hofei** — see HEFEI

**Hoggar** — see AHAGGAR

**Hoh·hot** \'hō-'hōt\ *or* **Hu·he·hot** \'hü-,hä-'hōt\ *or* **Hu·ho·hao·t'e** \'hü-'hō-'haú-'tə\ city N China, capital of Inner Mongolia

**Hok·kai·do** \hä-'kïd-ō\ *or formerly* **Ye·zo** \'yez-ō\ island N Japan N of Honshu

**Hol·land** \'häl-ənd\ **1** medieval county of Holy Roman Empire bordering on North Sea & comprising area now forming North & South Holland provinces of the Netherlands **2** — see NETHERLANDS — **Hol·land·er** \-ən-dər\ *noun*

**Holland, Parts of** district & former administrative county E England in SE Lincolnshire

**Hol·ly·wood** \'häl-ē-,wúd\ **1** section of Los Angeles, California, NW of downtown district **2** city SE Florida

**Hol·stein** \'hōl-,stīn, -,stēn\ region NW Germany S of Jutland Peninsula adjoining Schleswig — see SCHLESWIG-HOLSTEIN

**Holy Land** PALESTINE

**Homs** \'hōmz, 'hùms\ city W Syria

**Ho·myel'** \'hó-,myel, kó-\ *or* **Go·mel** \gó-'mel, -'myel\ *or* **Ho·mel** \hó-\ city SE Belarus

**Honan** — see HENAN

**Hon·du·ras** \hän-'dur-əs, -'dyur-\ country Central America; a republic; capital, Tegucigalpa — **Hon·du·ran** \-ən\ or **Hon·du·ra·ne·an** or **Hon·du·ra·ni·an** \,hän-dù-'rā-nē-ən, -dyù-\ adjective or noun

**Hong Kong** \'häng-,käng, -'käng; 'hóng-,kòng, -'kòng\ territory on coast of SE China including Hong Kong Island & Kowloon Peninsula; formerly a British colony; capital, Victoria

**Ho·no·lu·lu** \,hän-l-'ü-lü, ,hōn-l-\ city, capital of Hawaii on Oahu Island

**Hon·shu** \'hän-shü\ or **Hon·do** \'hän-dō\ island Japan; largest of the four chief islands

**Hood, Mount** \'hud\ mountain 3424 meters NW Oregon in Cascade Range

**Hoo·ver Dam** \,hü-vər-\ or **Boul·der Dam** \,bōl-dər-\ dam 221 meters high in Colorado River between Arizona & Nevada — see MEAD (Lake)

**Hopeh** or **Hopei** — see HEBEI

**Ho·reb** \'hōr-,eb, 'hór-\ or **Si·nai** \'sī-,nī also -nē-,ī\ mountain where according to the Bible the Law was given to Moses; generally thought to be on Sinai Peninsula

**Horn, Cape** \'hórn\ headland S Chile on Horn Island in Tierra del Fuego; the most southerly point of South America at 56° S latitude

**Hos·pi·ta·let** \,äs-,pit-l-'et, ,häs-\ city NE Spain

**Hot Springs National Park** reservation SW central Arkansas adjoining city of Hot Springs

**Houns·low** \'haunz-,lō\ borough of SW Greater London, England

**Hous·ton** \'hyü-stən, 'yü-\ city SE Texas

**How·rah** \'haù-rə\ city E India in West Bengal on Hugli River opposite Calcutta

**Hsia–men** — see XI'AMEN

**Hsiang–t'an** — see XIANGTAN

**Huai·nan** \hü-ī-'nän, 'hwī-\ city E China in N central Anhui

**Huang** or **Hwang** \'hwäng\ or **Yellow** river 4671 kilometers long N China flowing into Bo Hai

**Huas·ca·rán** \,wäs-kə-'rän\ mountain 6768 meters W Peru

**Hu·bei** \'hü-'bā\ or **Hu·peh** \'hü-'bē\ or **Hu·pei** \'hü-,bā, -'pā\ province E central China; capital, Wuhan

**Hu·bli–Dhar·war** \,hùb-lē-,där-'wär\ city SW India in W Karnataka

**Hud·ders·field** \'həd-ərz-,fēld\ town N England in West Yorkshire NE of Manchester

**Hud·son** \'həd-sən\ **1** river 492 kilometers long E New York flowing S into New York Bay **2** bay inlet of the Atlantic in N Canada **3** strait NE Canada connecting Hudson Bay & the Atlantic

**Hue** \'hwā, 'wā, hü-'ā, hyü-'ā\ city central Vietnam in Annam

**Hu·gli** or **Hoo·ghly** \'hü-glē\ river about 195 kilometers long E India flowing S into Bay of Bengal; most westerly channel of the Ganges in its delta

**Huhehot** or **Hu·ho·hao·t'e** — see HOHHOT

**Hull** \'həl\ or **Kings·ton upon Hull** \'king-stən, 'kingk-\ city N England in Humberside

**Hum·ber** \'həm-bər\ estuary E England formed by the Ouse & the Trent & flowing into North Sea

**Hum·ber·side** \'həm-bər-,sīd\ county E England; area formerly in Yorkshire

**Hum·boldt** \'həm-,bōlt\ glacier NW Greenland

**Humboldt Current** — see PERU CURRENT

**Hu·nan** \'hü-'nän\ province SE central China; capital, Changsha

**Hun·ga·ry** \'həng-grē, -gə-rē\ country central Europe; capital, Budapest

**Hun·ting·don** \'hənt-ing-dən\ or **Hun·ting·don·shire** \-,shiər, -shər\ or **Huntingdon and Pe·ter·bor·ough** \'pēt-ər-,bər-ə, -,bə-rə, -,bə-rə, -,brə\ former county E central England; since 1974 part of Cambridgeshire

**Hunt·ing·ton Beach** city SW California

**Hunts·ville** \'hənts-,vil, -vəl\ city N Alabama

**Hu·ron, Lake** \'hyùr-ən, 'yùr-, -,än\ lake E central North America in U.S. & Canada; one of the Great Lakes

**Hy·der·abad** \'hīd-rə-,bad, -ə-rə-, -,bäd\ **1** or **Hai·dar·abad** \same\ city S central India; capital of Andhra Pradesh **2** city SE Pakistan on the Indus

**Hy·met·tus** \hī-'met-əs\ mountain ridge 1026 meters central Greece E & SE of Athens

**Ia·si** \'yäsh, 'yäsh-ē\ city NE Romania

**Iba·dan** \ē-'bäd-n, -'bad-\ city SW Nigeria

**Ibe·ri·an** \ī-'bir-ē-ən\ peninsula SW Europe occupied by Spain & Portugal

**Ibi·za** \ē-'vē-thə, -'bē-\ island Spain in Balearic Islands SW of Majorca

**Ice·land** \'ī-slənd, -,sland\ island SE of Greenland between Arctic & Atlantic oceans; a republic; capital, Reykjavik — **Ice·land·er** \-slən-dər, -,slan-dər\ noun

**Ichi·ka·wa** \i-'chē-,kä-wə\ city Japan in SE Honshu E of Tokyo

**Ida** \'īd-ə\ **1** mountain 2456 meters Greece in central Crete **2** mountain 1767 meters NW Turkey in Asia SE of ancient Troy

**Ida·ho** \'īd-ə-,hō\ state NW U.S.; capital, Boise — **Ida·ho·an** \,īd-ə-'hō-ən\ adjective or noun

**Idumaea** or **Idumea** — see EDOM

**If·ni** \'if-nē\ former territory SW Morocco on the Atlantic; administered by Spain 1934–69; capital, Sidi Ifni

**Igua·zú** or **Igua·çu** \,ē-gwä-'sü\ river 1199 kilometers long S Brazil flowing W into the Alto Paraná; contains **Iguazú Falls** (waterfall about 4 kilometers wide composed of numerous cataracts averaging 61 meters in height)

**IJs·sel** or **Ijs·sel** or **Ys·sel** \'ī-səl\ river 113 kilometers long E Netherlands flowing out of Rhine N into IJsselmeer

**IJs·sel·meer** \,ī-səl-'meər\ or **Lake Ijs·sel** \'ī-səl\ freshwater lake N Netherlands separated from North Sea by a dike; part of former Zuider Zee (inlet of North Sea)

**Ika·ria** \,ē-kə-'rē-ə\ or ancient **Icar·ia** \ī-'ker-ē-ə, -'kar-; ik-'er-, -'ar-\ island Greece central Aegean W of Samos

**Ilium** or **Ilion** — see TROY

**Illam·pu** \ē-'äm-pü, -'yäm-\ or **So·ra·ta** \sə-'rät-ə\ mountain W Bolivia in the Andes E of Lake Titicaca — see ANCOHUMA

**Il·li·nois** \,il-ə-'nói also -'nóiz\ state N central U.S.; capital, Springfield — **Il·li·nois·an** \-'nói-ən, -'nóiz-\ adjective or noun

**Il·lyr·ia** \il-'ir-ē-ə\ ancient country S Europe and Balkan Peninsula on the Adriatic — **Il·lyr·i·an** \-ē-ən\ adjective or noun

**Ilo·ilo** \,ē-lə-'wē-lō\ city central Philippines on S coast of Panay Island

**In·chon** \'in-,chän\ city South Korea on Yellow Sea

**In·de·pen·dence** \,in-də-'pen-dəns\ city W Missouri E of Kansas City

**In·dia** \'in-dē-ə\ **1** or **Indian Subcontinent** peninsula region S Asia S of the Himalaya between Bay of Bengal & Arabian Sea **2** or **Bha·rat** \'bər-ət, 'bə-rət\ country comprising major portion of the peninsula; a republic of the Commonwealth; capital, New Delhi **3** or **Indian Empire** before 1947 those parts of the Indian Subcontinent under British rule or protection

**In·di·an** \'in-dē-ən\ **1** ocean E of Africa, S of Asia, W of Australia, & N of Antarctica **2** — see THAR

**In·di·ana** \,in-dē-'an-ə\ state E central U.S.; capital, Indianapolis — **In·di·an·an** \-'an-ən\ or **In·di·an·i·an** \-'an-ē-ən\ adjective or noun

**In·di·a·nap·o·lis** \,in-dē-ə-'nap-ləs, -ə-ləs\ city, capital of Indiana

**Indian River** lagoon 266 kilometers long E Florida between mainland & coastal islands

**Indian Territory** former territory S U.S. in present state of Oklahoma

**In·dies** \'in-dēz\ **1** EAST INDIES **2** WEST INDIES

**In·do·chi·na** \'in-dō-'chī-nə\ **1** peninsula SE Asia including Myanmar, Malay Peninsula, Thailand, Cambodia, Laos, & Vietnam **2** or **French Indochina** former country SE Asia comprising area now forming Cambodia, Laos, & Vietnam — **In·do·Chi·nese** \-chī-'nēz, -'nēs\ adjective or noun

**In·do·ne·sia** \,in-də-'nē-zhə, -shə\ country SE Asia in Malay Archipelago comprising Sumatra, Java, S & E Borneo, Sulawesi, W New Guinea, & many smaller islands; a republic; capital, Jakarta — see NETHERLANDS EAST INDIES — **In·do·ne·sian** \-zhən, -shən\ adjective or noun

**In·dore** \in-'dōr, -'dòr\ city W central India in W Madhya Pradesh

**In·dus** \'in-dəs\ river about 2896 kilometers long S Asia flowing from Tibet NW & SSW through Pakistan into Arabian Sea

**In·land** \'in-,land, -lənd\ sea inlet of the Pacific in SW Japan between Honshu Island on N and Shikoku Island and Kyushu Island on S

**Inner Hebrides** — see HEBRIDES

**Inner Mongolia** region N China in SE Mongolia & W Manchuria; capital, Hohhot

**Inns·bruck** \'inz-,brùk, 'ins-\ city W Austria in Tirol

**Inside Passage** protected shipping route between Puget Sound, Washington, & Skagway, Alaska

**In·ver·ness** \,in-vər-'nes\ or **In·ver·ness·shire** \-'nes-,shiər, -'nesh-, -shər\ former county NW Scotland

**Io·ni·an** \ī-'ō-nē-ən\ **1** sea arm of the Mediterranean between SE Italy & W Greece **2** islands W Greece in Ionian Sea

**Io·wa** \'ī-ə-wə\ state N central U.S.; capital, Des Moines — **Io·wan** \-wən\ adjective or noun

**I–pin** — see YIBIN

**Ipoh** \'ē-pō\ city Malaysia NNW of Kuala Lumpur

**Ips·wich** \'ip-swich\ town SE England in Suffolk

**Iran** \i-'ran, -'rän; ī-'ran\ or formerly **Per·sia** \'pər-zhə\ country SW Asia S of Caspian Sea; capital, Tehran — **Irani** \i-'ran-ē, -'rän-\ adjective or noun — **Ira·nian** \i-'ran-ē-ən, -'rän-, -'rān-\ adjective or noun

**Iraq** \i-'räk, -'rak\ country SW Asia in Mesopotamia; a republic; capital, Baghdad — **Iraqi** \-'räk-ē, -'rak-\ adjective or noun

**Irbīl** — see ARBIL

**Ire·land** \'īr-lənd\ **1** or Latin **Hi·ber·nia** \hī-'bər-nē-ə\ island W Europe in the Atlantic; one of the British Isles **2** or **Irish Republic** or **Ei·re** \'er-ə\ country occupying major portion of the island; a republic; capital, Dublin

**Irian** — see NEW GUINEA

**Iri·an Ja·ya** \,ir-ē-,än-'jä-yä\ or **West Irian** or **West New Guinea** \'gin-ē\ or formerly **Neth·er·lands New Guinea** \'neth-ər-ləndz\ territory of Indonesia comprising W half of New Guinea

**Irish** \'ī-rish\ sea arm of the Atlantic between Great Britain & Ireland

**Ir·kutsk** \iər-'kütsk, ,ər-\ city S Russia in Asia, near Lake Baikal

**Ir·ra·wad·dy** \,ir-ə-'wäd-ē\ river 2092 kilometers long Myanmar flowing S into Bay of Bengal

**Ir·tysh** \iər-'tish, ,ər-\ river about 4441 kilometers long central Asia flowing NW & N from Altay Mountains in China, through Kazakhstan, and into the Ob in Russia

**Isfahan** — see ESFAHAN

**Is·lam·abad** \is-'läm-ə-,bäd, iz-'lam-ə-,bad\ city, capital of Pakistan in NE Pakistan

**Isle of Man** — see MAN (Isle of)

**Isle Roy·ale** \'īl-'rói-əl, -'róil\ island Michigan in Lake Superior in **Isle Royale National Park**

**Is·ling·ton** \'iz-ling-tən\ borough of N Greater London, England

**Is·ma·ilia** \,iz-mä-ə-'lē-ə\ city NE Egypt on Suez Canal

**Is·ra·el** \'iz-rē-əl\ **1** ancient kingdom Palestine comprising lands occupied by the Hebrew people **2** or **Northern Kingdom** or **Ephra·im** \'ē-frē-əm\ the N part of the Hebrew kingdom after about 933 B.C. — see JUDAH **3** country SW Asia in Palestine; a republic established 1948; capital, Jerusalem — **Is·rae·li** \iz-'rā-lē\ adjective or noun

**Is·tan·bul** \,is-təm-'bül, -,täm-, -,tam-, -,tän-\ or formerly **Con·stan·ti·no·ple** \,kän-,stant-n-'ō-pəl\ or ancient **By·zan·tium** \bə-'zan-shəm, -shē-əm; -'zant-ē-əm\ city NW Turkey on Sea of Marmara & both sides of the Bosporus; former capital of Turkey

**Is·tria** \'is-trē-ə\ peninsula S central Europe extending into the N Adriatic; belongs to Croatia & Slovenia except for Trieste (to Italy) — **Is·tri·an** \-trē-ən\ adjective or noun

**Italian Somaliland** former country E Africa now part of Somalia

**It·a·ly** \'it-l-ē\ **1** peninsula about 1220 kilometers long S Europe extending into the Mediterranean between Adriatic & Tyrrhenian seas **2** country including the peninsula of Italy, Sicily, & Sardinia; a republic; capital, Rome

**Itas·ca, Lake** \ī-'tas-kə\ lake NW central Minnesota; source of the Mississippi

**Ith·a·ca** \'ith-i-kə\ island W Greece in Ionian Islands

**Iva·no·vo** \i-'vän-ə-və\ city central Russia in Europe, WNW of Nizhniy Novgorod

---

\ə\ abut \ə\ kitten \ər\ further \a\ ash \ā\ ace \ä\ mop, mar \aù\ out \ch\ chin \e\ bet \ē\ easy \g\ go \i\ hit \ī\ ice \j\ job \ŋ\ sing \ō\ go \ò\ law \òi\ boy \th\ thin \ṯh\ the \ü\ loot \ù\ foot \y\ yet \zh\ vision *see also* Guide to Pronunciation

**Ivory Coast** *or French* **Côte d'Ivoire** \,kōt-dēv-'wär\ country W Africa on Gulf of Guinea; a republic; official capital, Yamoussoukro; seat of government, Abidjan

**Iwo** \'ē-wō\ city SW Nigeria NE of Ibadan

**Iwo Ji·ma** \,ē-wō-'jē-mə\ island Japan in W Pacific in Volcano Islands about 1221 kilometers S of Tokyo

**Izhevsk** \'ē-,zhefsk\ city E central Russia in Europe NE of Kazan

**Iz·mir** \iz-'miər\ *or formerly* **Smyr·na** \'smər-nə\ city W Turkey

**Ja·bal·pur** \'jäb-əl-,pu̇r\ city central India in central Madhya Pradesh

**Jack·son** \'jak-sən\ city, capital of Mississippi

**Jack·son·ville** \'jak-sən-,vil\ city NE Florida

**Jadotville** — see LIKASI

**Jaf·fa** \'jaf-ə, 'yaf-ə\ *or ancient* **Jop·pa** \'jäp-ə\ twin city of Tel Aviv, Israel

**Jai·pur** \'jī-,pu̇r\ city NW India, capital of Rajasthan

**Ja·kar·ta** *or* **Dja·kar·ta** \jə-'kär-tə\ *or formerly* **Ba·ta·via** \bə-'tä-vē-ə, -'tä-\ city, capital of Indonesia in NW Java

**Ja·la·pa** \hə-'läp-ə\ city E Mexico, capital of Veracruz

**Ja·lis·co** \hə-'lis-kō\ state W central Mexico; capital, Guadalajara

**Ja·mai·ca** \jə-'mā-kə\ island West Indies in Greater Antilles; a dominion of the Commonwealth; capital, Kingston — **Ja·mai·can** \-kən\ *adjective or noun*

**James** \'jāmz\ **1** river in North Dakota & South Dakota — see DAKOTA **2** river 547 kilometers long Virginia flowing E into Chesapeake Bay

**James Bay** the S extension of Hudson Bay between NE Ontario & W Quebec

**James·town** \'jām-,staȯn\ ruined village E Virginia on James River; first permanent English settlement in America (1607)

**Jam·mu and Kashmir** \'jəm-,ü\ state N India; capital, Srinagar; winter capital, Jammu

**Jam·na·gar** \jäm-'nəg-ər\ *or formerly* **Na·va·na·gar** \,näv-ə-'nəg-ər\ city W India in W Gujarat

**Jam·shed·pur** \jäm-,shed-,pu̇r\ city E India in S Bihar

**Ja·pan** \jə-'pan, ji-, ja-\ *or Japanese* **Nip·pon** \nip-'än\ *or* **Ni·hon** \'nē-'hȯn\ country E Asia comprising Honshu, Hokkaido, Kyushu, Shikoku, & other islands in the W Pacific; an empire; capital, Tokyo

**Japan, Sea of** arm of the Pacific between Japan & Asian mainland

**Japan Current** *or Japanese* **Ku·ro·shio** \ku̇r-ō-'shē-,ō\ warm current of the Pacific Ocean flowing from E coast of Philippines N along E coast of Japan and thence eastward

**Jas·per National Park** \'jas-pər\ reservation W Alberta on E slope of Rocky Mountains

**Ja·va** \'jäv-ə, 'jav-ə\ island Indonesia SW of Borneo; chief city, Jakarta — **Ja·van** \-ən\ *adjective or noun*

**Jebel Musa** — see MUSA (Jebel)

**Jef·fer·son City** \'jef-ər-sən\ city, capital of Missouri

**Je·rez** \hə-'rās\ *or in full* **Je·rez de la Fron·te·ra** \hə-'rez-də-lə-,frən-'ter-ə\ city SW Spain

**Jer·i·cho** \'jer-i-,kō\ ancient city E Palestine N of Dead Sea

**Jer·sey** \'jər-zē\ **1** island in English Channel — see CHANNEL **2** NEW JERSEY — **Jer·sey·ite** \-zē-,īt\ *noun*

**Jersey City** city NE New Jersey on Hudson River

**Je·ru·sa·lem** \jə-'rü-sə-ləm, -sləm; -'rüz-ə-ləm, -'rüz-ləm\ city NW of Dead Sea divided 1948–67 between Israel & Jordan; capital of Israel since 1950 & formerly of ancient kingdoms of Israel & Judah

**Jhan·si** \'jän-sē\ city N India in SE Uttar Pradesh SW of Kanpur

**Jia·mu·si** \jē-'ä-'mü-'sē\ *or* **Chia–mu–ssu** \jē-'ä-'mü-'sü\ *or* **Kia·mu·sze** \jē-'ä-'mü-'sə\ city NE China in N Heilongjiang

**Jiang·su** *or* **Kiang·su** \jē-'äng-'sü\ province E China; capital, Nanjing

**Jiang·xi** *or* **Kiang·si** \jē-'äng-shē\ province SE China; capital, Nanchang

**Jibuti** — see DJIBOUTI

**Jid·da** *or* **Jed·da** \'jed-ə\ city W Saudi Arabia in Hejaz on Red Sea; port for Mecca

**Ji·lin** *or* **Ki·rin** \'kē-'rin\ **1** province NE China; capital, Changchun **2** city in Jilin province

**Ji·nan** *or* **Chi·nan** *or* **Tsi·nan** \jē-'nän\ city E China, capital of Shandong

**Jin·zhou** *or* **Chin–chou** *or* **Chin·chow** \'jin-'jō\ city NE China in SW Liaoning

**João Pes·soa** \,zhau̇ⁿ-pə-'sō-ə, ,zhau̇ⁿm-\ city NE Brazil N of Recife

**Jodh·pur** \'jäd-pər, -,pu̇r\ city NW India in central Rajasthan

**Jo·han·nes·burg** \jō-'han-əs-,bərg, -'hän-\ city NE Republic of South Africa

**Jo·hore Bah·ru** \jə-'hōr-'bä-rü, -'hȯr-\ city Malaysia in S Peninsular Malaysia opposite Singapore Island

**Jor·dan** \'jȯrd-n\ **1** river 320 kilometers long Israel & Jordan rising in Syria & flowing S from Anti-Lebanon Mountains into Dead Sea **2** *or formerly* **Trans·jor·dan** \trans-, tranz-, 'trans-, 'tranz-\ country SW Asia in NW Arabia; capital, Amman — **Jor·da·ni·an** \jȯr-'dā-nē-ən\ *adjective or noun*

**Juan de Fu·ca** \,hwän-də-'fyü-kə, ,wän-\ strait 161 kilometers long between Vancouver Island, British Columbia, & Olympic Peninsula, Washington

**Juan Fer·nán·dez** \,hwän-fər-'nan-dəs, ,wän-\ group of three islands SE Pacific 645 kilometers W of Chile; belongs to Chile

**Juárez** — see CIUDAD JUÁREZ

**Ju·dah** \'jüd-ə\ ancient kingdom S Palestine; capital, Jerusalem — see ISRAEL

**Ju·dea** *or* **Ju·daea** \jü-'dē-ə, -'dā-\ ancient region Palestine constituting the S division (Judah) of the country under Persian, Greek, & Roman rule — **Ju·de·an** \-ən\ *adjective or noun*

**Ju·go·sla·via** \,yü-gō-'släv-ē-ə\ — see YUGOSLAVIA — **Ju·go·slav** \,yü-gō-'släv, -'slav\ *or* **Ju·go·sla·vi·an** \-'släv-ē-ən\ *adjective or noun*

**Juiz de Fo·ra** \zhwēzh-də-'fȯr-ə, -'fȯr-\ city E Brazil N of Rio de Janeiro

**Jul·lun·dur** \'jəl-ən-dər\ city N India in Punjab SE of Amritsar

**Ju·neau** \'jü-nō, jü-'\ city, capital of Alaska

**Jung·frau** \'yu̇ng-,frau̇\ mountain 4158 meters SW central Switzerland in Bernese Alps

**Ju·ra** \'ju̇r-ə\ mountain range extending along boundary between France & Switzerland N of Lake Geneva

**Jut·land** \'jət-lənd\ **1** peninsula N Europe extending into North Sea & comprising mainland of Denmark & N portion of Schleswig-Holstein, Germany **2** the mainland of Denmark

**Ka·bul** \'käb-əl, kä-'bu̇l\ city, capital of Afghanistan

**Kadiyevka** — see STAKHANOV

**Kae·song** \'kā-,sȯng\ city North Korea SE of Pyongyang

**Ka·go·shi·ma** \,käg-ə-'shē-mə, kä-'gō-shə-mə\ city Japan in S Kyushu

**Kai·feng** \'kī-'fəng\ city E central China in NE Henan

**Ka Lae** \kä-'lä-ā\ *or* **South Cape** *or* **South Point** most southerly point of Hawaii & of U.S.

**Kal·a·ha·ri** \,kal-ə-'här-ē\ desert region S Africa N of Orange River in S Botswana & NW Republic of South Africa

**Kalgan** — see ZHANGJIAKOU

**Ka·li·man·tan** \,kä-li-'man-,tan, -tan, ,käl-ə-'män-,tän\ **1** BORNEO — its Indonesian name **2** the S & E portion of Borneo belonging to Indonesia; formerly (as **Dutch Borneo**) of Netherlands East Indies

**Ka·li·nin** \kə-'lē-nən, -'lēn-yən\ city Russia in Europe on the Volga

**Ka·li·nin·grad** \kə-'lē-nən-,grad, -,nyən-\ *or German* **Kö·nigs·berg** \'kä-nigz-,bərg, 'kȯrn-igz-, -,beȯrg, *German* 'kœ̄-niks-,berk\ city Russia in an exclave between Poland and Lithuania

**Ka·lu·ga** \kə-'lü-gə\ city Russia in Europe WNW of Oka

**Kam·chat·ka** \kam-'chat-kə\ peninsula 1207 kilometers long NE Russia in Asia between Sea of Okhotsk & Bering Sea

**Kam·pa·la** \käm-'päl-ə\ city, capital of Uganda

**Kampuchea, Democratic** — see CAMBODIA

**Ka·nan·ga** \kə-'näng-gə\ *or formerly* **Lu·lua·bourg** \lü-'lü-ə-,bu̇rg, -,bu̇r\ city S central Democratic Republic of the Congo

**Ka·na·za·wa** \kə-'näz-ə-wə, ,kan-ə-'zä-wə\ city Japan in W Honshu N of Nagoya near Sea of Japan

**Kan·chen·jun·ga** \,kan-chən-'jəng-gə, -'ju̇ng-\ mountain 8586 meters Nepal & Sikkim (India) in the Himalaya; third highest in the world

**Kan·da·har** \'kan-də-,här\ city SE Afghanistan

**Ka·no** \'kän-ō\ city N central Nigeria

**Kan·pur** \'kän-,pu̇r\ city N India in S Uttar Pradesh on the Ganges

**Kan·sas** \'kan-zəs\ state W central U.S.; capital, Topeka — **Kan·san** \-zən\ *adjective or noun*

**Kansas City** **1** city NE Kansas adjoining Kansas City, Missouri **2** city W Missouri

**Kansu** — see GANSU

**Kao·hsiung** \'kau̇-shē-'u̇ng, 'gau̇-\ city China in SW Taiwan

**Ka·ra** \'kär-ə\ sea arm of Arctic Ocean off N coast of Russia E of Novaya Zemlya

**Ka·ra·chi** \kə-'räch-ē\ city S Pakistan on Arabian Sea

**Karafuto** — see SAKHALIN

**Ka·ra·gan·da** \,kar-ə-gən-'dä\ city central Kazakhstan

**Ka·raj** \kə-'räj\ city N Iran NW of Tehran

**Kar·a·ko·ram** \,kar-ə-'kȯr-əm, -'kȯr-\ mountain system S central Asia in N Kashmir & NW Tibet connecting the Himalaya & the Pamirs

**Ka·re·lia** \kə-'rē-lē-ə, -'rēl-yə\ region NE Europe between Gulf of Finland & White Sea; now chiefly in Russia — **Ka·re·lian** \-'rē-lē-ən, -'rēl-yən\ *adjective or noun*

**Karl–Marx–Stadt** — see CHEMNITZ

**Karls·ru·he** \'kärlz-,rü-ə\ city SW Germany

**Kar·na·ta·ka** \kär-'nät-ə-kə\ *or formerly* **My·sore** \mī-'sōr, -'sȯr\ state S India; capital, Bangalore

**Kar·roo** \kə-'rü\ plateau region W Republic of South Africa W of Drakensberg Mountains; divided into **Little** (*or* **Southern**) **Karroo**, **Great** (*or* **Central**) **Karroo**, **North Karroo**

**Kashi** \'kash-ē, 'käsh-\ *or* **Kash·gar** \'kash-,gär, 'käsh-\ city W China in SW Xinjiang Uygur

**Ka·shi·wa** \kä-shē-,wä\ city Japan on Honshu

**Kash·mir** \'kash-,miər, 'kazh-, kazh-, kazh-'\ former princely state N Indian Subcontinent; now part of Jammu and Kashmir — **Kash·miri** \kash-'miər-ē, kazh-\ *adjective or noun*

**Kas·sel** \'kas-əl, 'käs-\ city central Germany WNW of Erfurt

**Ka·thi·a·war** \,kät-ē-ə-'wär\ peninsula W India in Gujarat N of Gulf of Cambay

**Kath·man·du** *or* **Kat·man·du** \,kat-,man-'dü, ,kät-,män-\ city, capital of Nepal

**Kat·mai, Mount** \'kat-,mī\ volcano 2047 meters S Alaska in **Katmai National Park and Preserve**

**Ka·to·wi·ce** \,kät-ə-'vēt-sə\ city S Poland WNW of Krakow

**Kat·te·gat** \'kat-i-,gat\ arm of North Sea between Sweden & E coast of Jutland Peninsula of Denmark

**Kau·ai** \'kau̇-,ī\ island Hawaii NW of Oahu

**Kau·nas** \'kau̇-nəs, -näs\ *or Russian* **Kov·no** \'kȯv-nō\ city central Lithuania

**Ka·wa·goe** \kə-'wäg-,ȯi\ city Japan on SE central Honshu

**Ka·wa·gu·chi** \kä-wə-'gü-chē, kä-'wäg-u̇-chē\ city Japan in E Honshu N of Tokyo

**Ka·wa·sa·ki** \,kä-wə-'säk-ē\ city Japan in E Honshu S of Tokyo

**Kay·se·ri** \,kī-zə-'rē\ city central Turkey

**Ka·zakh·stan** \kə-,zak-'stan; kə-'zäk-'stän, ,kä-\ country NW central Asia; capital, Alma-Ata; a constituent republic (**Ka·zakh Soviet Socialist Republic** \kə-'zäk, -'zak\) of U.S.S.R. 1936–91

**Ka·zan** \kə-'zan, -'zän, -'zän-yə\ city E central Russia in Europe

**Kazan Retto** — see VOLCANO ISLANDS

**Kee·lung** \'kē-'lu̇g\ city & port N Taiwan

**Kee·wa·tin** \kē-'wāt-n\ former district N Canada in E Northwest Territories NW of Hudson Bay

**Kej·im·ku·jik National Park** \,kej-mə-'kü-jik, -ə-mə-\ reservation E Canada in SW Nova Scotia

**Ke·me·ro·vo** \'kem-ə-rə-və, -,rō-və, -rə-,vō\ city S Russia in Asia in Kuznetsk Basin

**Ke·nai** \'kē-,nī\ peninsula S Alaska E of Cook Inlet; site of **Kenai Fjords National Park**

**Ke·ni·tra** \kə-'nē-trə\ *or formerly* **Port Lyau·tey** \,pȯr-lē-,ō-'tā, -'ō-\ city N Morocco

**Kennedy, Cape** — see CANAVERAL (Cape)

**Ken·sing·ton and Chel·sea** \'ken-zing-tən-ən-'chel-sē, 'ken-sing-\ royal borough of W Greater London, England

**Kent** \'kent\ county SE England — **Kent·ish** \'kent-ish\ *adjective*

**Ken·tucky** \kən-'tək-ē\ state E central U.S.; capital, Frankfort — **Ken·tuck·i·an** \-ē-ən\ *adjective or noun*

**Ken·ya** \'ken-yə, 'kēn-\ **1** mountain 5199 meters central Kenya **2** country E Africa S of Ethiopia; a republic; capital, Nairobi — **Ken·yan** \-yən\ *adjective or noun*

**Ker·a·la** \'ker-ə-lə\ state SW India bordering on Arabian Sea; capital, Trivandrum

**Ker·gue·len** \'kər-gə-lən, ,kər-gə-'len\ **1** archipelago S Indian Ocean belonging to France **2** chief island of the archipelago

**Ker·man** \kər-'män, ker-\ city SE central Iran

**Ker·ry** \'ker-ē\ county SW Ireland in Munster

**Kes·te·ven, Parts of** \ke-'stē-vən\ district & former administrative county E England in SW Lincolnshire

**Kha·ba·rovsk** \kə-'bär-əfsk\ city SE Russia in Asia on the Amur

**Khan·ka** \'kang-kə\ lake E Asia between Russia & China

**Khar·kiv** \'kär-kəf, 'kär-\ or **Khar·kov** \'kär-,kóf, -kòv, -kəf\ city NE Ukraine

**Khar·toum** \kär-'tüm\ city, capital of Sudan

**Kher·son** \keər-'sòn\ city S Ukraine

**Khy·ber** \'kī-bər\ pass 53 kilometers long on border between Afghanistan & Pakistan WNW of Peshawar

**Kiamusze** — see JIAMUSI

**Kiangsi** — see JIANGXI

**Kiangsu** — see JIANGSU

**Ki·bo** \'kē-bō\ mountain peak 5895 meters NE Tanzania; highest peak of Kilimanjaro & highest point in Africa

**Kiel** \'kēl\ city N Germany, capital of Schleswig-Holstein

**Kiel Canal** — see NORD-OSTSEE KANAL

**Kiel·ce** \kē-'elt-sä\ city S Poland S of Warsaw

**Ki·ev** or Russian **Ki·yev** \'kē-,ef, -,ev, -əf, -,yef, -,yev, -yəf\ city, capital of Ukraine

**Ki·ga·li** \ki-'gäl-ē\ city, capital of Rwanda

**Ki·lau·ea** \,kē-,laù-'ā-ə\ volcanic crater Hawaii on Hawaii Island on E slope of Mauna Loa in Hawaii Volcanoes National Park

**Kil·dare** \kil-'daər, -'deər\ county E Ireland in Leinster

**Kil·i·man·ja·ro** \,kil-ə-mən-'jär-ō, -'jar-\ mountain NE Tanzania; highest in Africa — see KIBO

**Kil·ken·ny** \kil-'ken-ē\ county SE Ireland in Leinster

**Kil·lar·ney, Lakes of** \kil-'är-nē\ three lakes SW Ireland in Kerry

**Kim·ber·ley** \'kim-bər-lē\ city Republic of South Africa

**Kin·car·dine** \kin-'kärd-n\ or **Kin·car·dine·shire** \-,shiər, -shər\ former county E Scotland

**Kings Canyon National Park** \'kingz-\ reservation SE central California in Sierra Nevada N of Sequoia National Park

**Kings·ton** \'king-stən\ city, capital of Jamaica

**Kingston upon Hull** — see HULL

**Kingston upon Thames** \'temz\ royal borough of SW Greater London, England

**Kin·ross** \kin-'ròs\ or **Kin·ross·shire** \-'ròs-,shiər, -shər, -'ròsh-\ former county E central Scotland

**Kin·sha·sa** \kin-'shäs-ə\ or formerly **Lé·o·pold·ville** \'lē-ə-,pōld-,vil, 'lā-\ city, capital of Democratic Republic of the Congo

**Kirghiz Soviet Socialist Republic** or **Kirgiz Soviet Socialist Republic** — see KYRGYZSTAN

**Kir·i·bati** \'kir-ə-,bas\ islands W Pacific including the Gilberts; an independent member of the Commonwealth; capital, Tarawa

**Kirin** — see JILIN

**Ki·riti·mati** \kə-'ris-məs\ or formerly **Christ·mas** \'kris-məs\ island in Line Islands; largest atoll in the Pacific

**Kirk·cud·bright** \kər-'kü-brē\ or **Kirk·cud·bright·shire** \-,shiər, -shər\ former county S Scotland

**Kir·kuk** \kiər-'kük\ city NE Iraq

**Ki·rov** \'kē-,ròf, -,ròv, -rəf\ city central Russia in Europe N of Kazan

**Ki·ro·vo·hrad** \,kē-rə-və-'hrät\ or **Ki·ro·vo·grad** \ki-'rō-və-,grad\ city S central Ukraine

**Ki·san·ga·ni** \,kē-sən-'gän-ē\ or formerly **Stanley·ville** \'stan-lē-,vil\ city NE Democratic Republic of the Congo

**Kishinev** — see CHISINAU

**Ki·ta·kyu·shu** \kē-,tä-kē-'ü-shü\ city Japan in N Kyushu

**Kitch·e·ner** \'kich-nər, -ə-nər\ city Canada in SE Ontario

**Klon·dike** \'klän-,dīk\ region NW Canada in central Yukon Territory in valley of Klondike River E of Dawson

**Knos·sos** or **Cnos·sus** \kə-'näs-əs, 'näs-əs\ **Gnos·sus** \gə-'näs-əs, 'näs-əs\ ruined city, capital of ancient Crete near N coast

**Knox·ville** \'näks-,vil, -vəl\ city E Tennessee

**Ko·be** \'kō-bē, -,bā\ city Japan in S Honshu

**Ko·buk Valley National Park** \kō-'bük-\ reservation NW Alaska N of arctic circle

**Ko·chi** \'kō-chē\ city Japan on S coast of Shikoku

**Ko·di·ak** \'kōd-ē-,ak\ island S Alaska E of Alaska Peninsula

**Kokand** — see QÜQON

**Ko·la** \'kō-lə\ peninsula NW Russia in Europe between Barents & White seas

**Ko·lar Gold Fields** \kō-'lär\ city S India in SE Karnataka NE of Bangalore

**Kol·ha·pur** \'kō-lə-,pùr\ city W India in SW Maharashtra SSE of Bombay

**Köln** — see COLOGNE

**Ko·mo·do** \kə-'mōd-ō\ island Indonesia in the Lesser Sundas W of Flores Island

**Königsberg** — see KALININGRAD

**Kon·ya** \kòn-'yä\ city SW central Turkey

**Koo·te·nay National Park** \'küt-n-,ā, -n-ē\ reservation SE British Columbia

**Ko·rea** \kə-'rē-ə, especially South kō-\ or Japanese **Cho·sen** \'chō-'sen\ former kingdom E Asia between Yellow Sea & Sea of Japan; capital, Seoul; divided after World War II at 38th parallel into republics of **North Korea** (capital, Pyongyang) & **South Korea** (capital, Seoul)

**Kos·ci·us·ko, Mount** \,käz-ē-'əs-kō\ mountain 2228 meters SE Australia in SE New South Wales; highest in Great Dividing Range & in Australia

**Ko·shi·ga·ya** \kō-'shē-gä-yə, ,kō-shig-'ä-yə\ city Japan on Honshu

**Kos·tro·ma** \,käs-trə-'mä\ city central Russia in Europe on the Volga

**Ko·ta Bha·ru** \kōt-ə-'bär-,ü, -ü\ city Malaysia in N Peninsular Malaysia

**Kovno** — see KAUNAS

**Kow·loon** \'kaù-'lün\ city Hong Kong on Kowloon Peninsula opposite Hong Kong Island

**Kozhikode** — see CALICUT

**Krak·a·toa** \,krak-ə-'tō-ə\ or **Krak·a·tau** \-'taù\ island & volcano Indonesia between Sumatra & Java

**Kra·kow** or **Cra·cow** \'kräk-,aù, 'krak-, 'kräk-, -ō, Polish 'kräk-,üf\ city S Poland

**Kras·no·dar** \'kras-nə-,där\ city S Russia in Europe in N Caucasus

**Kras·no·yarsk** \,kras-nə-'yärsk\ city S central Russia in Asia on the upper Yenisey

**Kre·feld** \'krā-,felt\ city W Germany on the Rhine WSW of Essen

**Kru·ger National Park** \'krü-gər\ game reserve NE Republic of South Africa on Mozambique border

**Kru·gers·dorp** \'krü-gərz-,dòrp, 'krüe-ərz-\ city NE Republic of South Africa

**Kry·vyy Rih** \kri-,vē-'rik\ or **Kri·voy Rog** \,kri-,vòi-'ròg, -'ròk\ city SE central Ukraine

**K2** \'kā-'tü\ or **God·win Aus·ten** \'gòd-wən-'òs-tən, 'gäd-, -'äs-\ mountain 8611 meters N Kashmir in Karakoram Range; second highest in the world

**Kua·la Lum·pur** \,kwäl-ə-'lùm-,pùr, -'ləm-\ city, capital of Malaysia in Peninsular Malaysia

**Kuang–chou** — see GUANGZHOU

**Kuei–chou** — see GUIZHOU

**Kuei–yang** — see GUIYANG

**Ku·ma·mo·to** \,küm-ə-'mōt-ō\ city Japan in W Kyushu

**Ku·ma·si** \kü-'mäs-ē, -'mas-\ city S central Ghana

**Kun·lun** \'kün-'lün\ mountain system W China extending E from the Pamirs to SE Qinghai; highest peak 7726 meters

**Kun·ming** \'kùn-'ming\ or formerly **Yun·nan** \yü-'nän\ or **Yun·nan·fu** \-'fü\ city S China, capital of Yunnan

**Ku·ra·shi·ki** \kü-'rä-shē-kē, ,kùr-ə-'shē-kē\ city Japan in W Honshu WSW of Okayama

**Kur·di·stan** \,kùrd-ə-'stan, ,kərd-\ region SW Asia chiefly in E Turkey, NW Iran, and N Iraq

**Ku·re** \'kùr-ē, 'kyùr-ē, 'kü-rā\ city Japan in SW Honshu on Inland Sea SE of Hiroshima

**Kur·gan** \kùr-'gan, -'gän\ city W Russia in Asia, SE of Yekaterinburg

**Ku·ril** or **Ku·rile** \'kyùr-,ēl, kyù-'rēl\ islands Russia in the Pacific between S Kamchatka Peninsula & NE Hokkaido Island

**Kur·nool** \kər-'nül\ city S India in W Andhra Pradesh SSW of Hyderabad

**Kuroshio** — see JAPAN CURRENT

**Kursk** \'kùrsk\ city SW Russia in Europe, N of Kharkiv, Ukraine

**Ku·wait** \kü-'wät\ **1** country SW Asia in Arabia at head of Persian Gulf **2** city, its capital — **Ku·waiti** \-'wät-ē\ adjective or noun

**Kuybyshev** — see SAMARA

**Kuz·netsk Basin** \kùz-'netsk\ or **Kuz·bass** or **Kuz·bas** \'kùz-,bas\ basin of Tom River S Russia in Asia, extending from Tomsk to Novokuznetsk

**Kwa·ja·lein** \'kwäj-ə-lən, -,lān\ island (atoll) W Pacific in Ralik Chain of Marshall Islands

**Kwang·ju** \'gwäng-jü, 'kwäng-\ city SW South Korea

**Kwangsi–Chuang** — see GUANGXI ZHUANGZU

**Kwang·tung** \'gwäng-'düng, 'kwäng-, -'tùng\ province SE China bordering on South China Sea & Gulf of Tonkin; capital, Canton

**Kwa·Zu·lu–Na·tal** \kwä-'zü-lü-nä-'täl\ province E Republic of South Africa between Drakensberg Mountains & Indian Ocean

**Kweichow** — see GUIZHOU

**Kweilin** or **Kuei–lin** — see GUILIN

**Kyo·to** \kē-'ōt-ō\ city Japan in W central Honshu; formerly capital of Japan

**Kyr·gyz·stan** \,kir-gi-'stan, -'stän; 'kir-gi-,\ country W central Asia; capital, Bishkek; a constituent republic (**Kir·ghiz Soviet Socialist Republic** or **Kir·giz Soviet Socialist Republic** \kiər-,gēz-\) of U.S.S.R. 1936–91

**Kyu·shu** \kē-'ü-shü\ island Japan S of W end of Honshu

**Labe** — see ELBE

**Lab·ra·dor** \'lab-rə-,dòr\ **1** peninsula E Canada between Hudson Bay & the Atlantic divided between Quebec & Newfoundland **2** the part of the peninsula belonging to Newfoundland — **Lab·ra·dor·ean** or **Lab·ra·dor·ian** \,lab-rə-'dòr-ē-ən, -'dòr-\ adjective or noun

**Labrador Current** cold current flowing S from Baffin Bay through Davis Strait to Newfoundland

**Lac·ca·dive** \'lak-ə-,dēv, -,dīv\ islands India in Arabian Sea N of Maldive Islands

**Lac·e·dae·mon** \,las-ə-'dē-mən\ — see SPARTA — **Lac·e·dae·mo·nian** \,las-əd-i-'mō-nē-ən, -nyən\ adjective or noun

**La·co·nia** \lə-'kō-nē-ə, -nyə\ ancient country S Greece in SE Peloponnese; capital, Sparta — **La·co·nian** \-nē-ən, -nyən\ adjective or noun

**Lad·o·ga** \'lad-ə-gə, 'läd-\ lake W Russia, near Finland border

**La·gos** \'lā-,gäs\ city, former capital of Nigeria

**La Habana** — see HAVANA

**La·hon·tan, Lake** \lə-'hänt-n\ prehistoric lake NW Nevada & NE California

**La·hore** \lə-'hōr, -'hòr\ city Pakistan in E Punjab province

**Lake Clark National Park** \läk-'klärk-\ reservation S central Alaska WSW of Anchorage

**Lake District** region NW England in Cumbria & NW Lancashire containing many lakes & mountains

**Lak·shad·weep** \lək-'shäd-,wēp, ,lək-shəd-'\ territory India comprising the Laccadive Islands

**Lam·beth** \'lam-bəth, -,beth\ borough of S Greater London, England

**La·nai** \lə-'nī\ island Hawaii W of Maui

**Lan·ark** \'lan-ərk\ or **Lan·ark·shire** \-,shiər, -shər\ former county S central Scotland; chief city, Glasgow

**Lan·ca·shire** \'lang-kə-,shiər, -shər\ or **Lan·cas·ter** \'lang-kə-stər\ county NW England — **Lan·cas·tri·an** \lang-'kas-trē-ən, lan-\ adjective or noun

**Land's End** \'land-'zend, 'lan-\ or ancient **Bo·le·ri·um** \bə-'lir-ē-əm\ cape SW England at SW tip of Cornwall

**Lan·gue·doc** \,lang-gə-'däk; 'län-gə-,dòk, ,läⁿg-\ region & former province S France on the Mediterranean W of Provence

**Lan·sing** \'lan-sing\ city, capital of Michigan

**La·nús** \lə-'nüs\ city E Argentina S of Buenos Aires

**Lan·zhou** or **Lan–chou** \'län-'jō\ city W central China, capital of Gansu

**Laoighis** \'lāsh, 'lēsh\ or **Leix** \'lāsh, 'lēsh\ or formerly **Queen's** \'kwēnz\ county central Ireland in Leinster

**Laos** \'laùs, 'lā-,äs, 'lā-ōs\ country SE Asia in Indochina NE of Thailand; a republic; capital, Vientiane

**La Paz** \lə-'paz, -'päz, -'päs\ city, administrative capital of Bolivia

**Lap·land** \'lap-,land, -lənd\ region N Europe above the arctic circle in N Norway, N Sweden, N Finland, & Kola Peninsula of Russia — **Lap·land·er** \-,lan-dər, -lən-\ noun

**La Pla·ta** \lə-'plät-ə\ city E Argentina SE of Buenos Aires

**L'Aqui·la** \'läk-wi-lə, 'lak-\ city central Italy NE of Rome

**Las Pal·mas** \lä-'späl-məs\ city Spain in the Canary Islands on Grand Canary Island

**La Spe·zia** \lä-'spet-sē-ə\ city NW Italy in Liguria SE of Genoa

**Las·sen Peak** \'las-n\ volcano 3187 meters N California at S end of Cascade Range in **Lassen Volcanic National Park**

**Las Ve·gas** \läs-'vā-gəs\ city SE Nevada

**Lat·a·kia** \,lat-ə-'kē-ə\ city NW Syria

**Latin America** **1** Spanish America and Brazil **2** all of the Americas S of the U.S. — **Latin-American** adjective — **Latin American** noun

**La·tium** \'lā-shē-əm, -shəm\ or Italian **La·zio** \'lät-sē-ō\ region central Italy on Tyrrhenian Sea; capital, Rome

**Lat·via** \'lat-vē-ə\ country E Europe on Baltic Sea; capital, Riga; a constituent republic (**Latvian Republic**) of U.S.S.R. 1940–91

**Lau·ren·tian Mountains** \lо̇-'ren-chən-\ range E Canada in S Quebec N of the Saint Lawrence on S edge of Canadian Shield

**Laurentian Plateau** — see CANADIAN SHIELD

**La·val** \lə-'val\ city S Quebec NW of Montreal

**Leb·a·non** \'leb-ə-nən, -,nän\ **1** or ancient **Lib·a·nus** \'lib-ə-nəs\ mountains Lebanon running parallel to coast; highest 3088 meters **2** country SW Asia on the Mediterranean; a republic; capital, Beirut — **Leb·a·nese** \,leb-ə-'nēz, -'nēs\ adjective or noun

**Leeds** \'lēdz\ city N England in West Yorkshire

**Lee·ward** \'lē-wərd\ **1** islands Hawaii extending WNW from main islands of the group **2** islands S Pacific in W Society Islands **3** islands West Indies in N Lesser Antilles

**Le Ha·vre** \lə-'hävr\ city N France on English Channel

**Leices·ter** \'les-tər\ city central England in Leicestershire ENE of Birmingham

**Leices·ter·shire** \'les-tər-,shiər, -shər\ or **Leicester** county central England

**Lein·ster** \'len-stər\ province E Ireland

**Leip·zig** \'līp-sig, -sik\ city E central Germany in Saxony

**Lei·trim** \'lē-trəm\ county NW Ireland in Connacht

**Leix** — see LAOIGHIS

**Leman, Lake** or **Lemannus** or **Lemanus** — see GENEVA (Lake of)

**Lemberg** — see L'VIV

**Lem·nos** \'lem-,näs, -nəs\ or Greek **Lím·nos** \'lēm-,nо̇s\ island Greece in the N Aegean

**Le·na** \'lē-nə, 'lā-\ river 4345 kilometers long E central Russia in Asia, flowing NE & N into Arctic Ocean

**Leningrad** — see SAINT PETERSBURG

**Le·ón** \lā-'ōn\ **1** city central Mexico in Guanajuato **2** region & ancient kingdom NW Spain

**Léopoldville** — see KINSHASA

**Le Puglie** — see PUGLIA

**Les·bos** \'lez-,bäs, -bəs\ or **Myt·i·le·ne** \,mit-l-'ē-nē\ island Greece in the Aegean off NW coast of Asia Minor

**Le·so·tho** \lə-'sō-tō, -'sü-,tü\ country S Africa surrounded by Republic of South Africa; formerly British territory of **Ba·su·to·land** \bə-'süt-ə-,land\, now an independent monarchy in the Commonwealth; capital, Maseru

**Lesser An·til·les** \an-'til-ēz\ islands in the West Indies including Virgin, Leeward, & Windward islands, Barbados, Trinidad, Tobago, & islands in the S Caribbean N of Venezuela — see GREATER ANTILLES

**Lesser Armenia** region S Turkey corresponding to ancient Cilicia

**Lesser Sunda** — see SUNDA

**Le·vant** \lə-'vant\ the countries bordering on the E Mediterranean — **Lev·an·tine** \'lev-ən-,tīn, -,tēn, lə-'van-\ adjective or noun

**Lew·i·sham** \'lü-ə-shəm\ borough of SE Greater London, England

**Lew·is with Har·ris** \,lü-ə-swoth-'har-əs, -swoth-\ island NW Scotland in Outer Hebrides

**Lex·ing·ton** \'lek-sing-tən\ city N central Kentucky

**Ley·te** \'lāt-ē\ island Philippines in Visayan Islands S of Samar

**Lha·sa** \'läs-ə, 'las-\ city SW China, capital of Tibet

**Liao·ning** \lē-'aù-'ning\ province NE China in S Manchuria; capital, Shenyang

**Liao·yang** \lē-'aù-'yäng\ city NE China in central Liaoning NE of Anshan

**Libanus** — see LEBANON

**Li·be·ria** \lī-'bir-ē-ə\ country W Africa on the Atlantic; a republic; capital, Monrovia — **Li·be·ri·an** \-ē-ən\ adjective or noun

**Lib·er·ty** \'lib-ərt-ē\ or formerly **Bed·loe's** \'bed-,lōz\ or **Bed·loe** \-lō\ island SE New York in Upper New York Bay; the Statue of Liberty is on it

**Li·bre·ville** \'lē-brə-,vil, -,vēl\ city, capital of Gabon

**Lib·ya** \'lib-ē-ə\ **1** the part of Africa N of the Sahara between Egypt & Gulf of Sidra — an ancient name **2** northern Africa W of Egypt — an ancient name **3** or **Libyan Arab Republic** country N Africa on the Mediterranean W of Egypt; a republic; capital, Tripoli — **Lib·y·an** \'lib-ē-ən\ adjective or noun

**Libyan** desert N Africa W of the Nile in Libya, Egypt, & Sudan

**Li·do** \'lēd-ō\ island Italy in Adriatic Sea

**Liech·ten·stein** \'lik-tən-,stīn, -,shtīn\ country W Europe between Austria & Switzerland; a principality; capital, Vaduz — **Liech·ten·stein·er** \-,stī-nər, -,shtī-\ noun

**Li·ège** \lē-'ezh, -'āzh\ or Flemish **Luik** \'līk\ city E Belgium

**Lif·fey** \'lif-ē\ river 81 kilometers long E Ireland flowing into Dublin Bay

**Li·gu·ria** \lə-'gyùr-ē-ə\ region NW Italy; capital, Genoa — **Li·gu·ri·an** \-ē-ən\ adjective or noun

**Ligurian** sea arm of the Mediterranean N of Corsica

**Li·ka·si** \li-'käs-ē\ or formerly **Ja·dot·ville** \zhad-ō-'vēl\ city SE Democratic Republic of the Congo

**Lille** \'lēl\ city N France

**Li·lon·gwe** \li-'lóng-wā\ city, capital of Malawi

**Li·ma** \'lē-mə\ city, capital of Peru

**Lim·burg** \'lim-,bərg\ or French **Lim·bourg** \'lim-,bərg, laⁿ-'bür\ province NE Belgium

**Lim·er·ick** \'lim-rik, -ə-rik\ county SW Ireland in Munster

**Límnos** — see LEMNOS

**Lim·po·po** \lim-'pō-pō\ river about 1770 kilometers long Africa flowing from NE Republic of South Africa into Indian Ocean in Mozambique

**Lin·coln** \'ling-kən\ city, capital of Nebraska

**Lin·coln·shire** \'ling-kən-,shiər, -shər\ or **Lincoln** county E England

**Lind·sey, Parts of** \'lin-zē\ district & former administrative county E England in N Lincolnshire

**Line** \'līn\ islands Kiribati S of Hawaii, formerly divided between U.S. & Great Britain

**Lip·a·ri** \'lip-ə-rē\ islands Italy off NE Sicily

**Li·petsk** \'lē-,petsk\ city S central Russia in Europe, N of Voronezh

**Lis·bon** \'liz-bən\ or Portuguese **Lis·boa** \lēzh-'vō-ə\ city, capital of Portugal

**Lith·u·a·nia** \,lith-ə-'wā-nē-ə, ,lith-yə-, -nyə\ country E Europe; capital, Vilnius; a constituent republic (**Lithuanian Republic**) of U.S.S.R. 1940–91

**Lit·tle Rock** \'lit-l-,räk\ city, capital of Arkansas

**Liv·er·pool** \'liv-ər-,pül\ city NW England in Merseyside

**Li·vo·nia** \lə-'vō-nē-ə, -nyə\ **1** city SE Michigan **2** region E Europe on Baltic Sea in Latvia & Estonia

**Lju·blja·na** \lē-,ü-blē-'än-ə\ city central Slovenia on Sava River

**Lla·no Es·ta·ca·do** \'lan-ō-,es-tə-'käd-ō, 'län-\ or **Staked Plain** \'stäkt-, 'stāk-\ plateau region SE New Mexico & NW Texas

**Lodz** \'lüj, 'lädz\ city central Poland WSW of Warsaw

**Lo·fo·ten** \'lō-,fōt-n\ islands NW Norway

**Lo·gan, Mount** \'lō-gən\ mountain 5951 meters NW Canada in Saint Elias Range; highest in Canada & second highest in North America

**Loire** \lə-'wär\ river 1020 kilometers long central France flowing NW & W into Bay of Biscay

**Lo·mas de Za·mo·ra** \'lō-,mäz-də-zə-'mо̇r-ə, -'mо̇r-\ city E Argentina SW of Buenos Aires

**Lom·bar·dy** \'läm-bärd-ē, -bərd-\ region N Italy of Po River; capital, Milan

**Lo·mé** \lō-'mā\ city, capital of Togo

**Lo·mond, Loch** \'lō-mənd\ lake S central Scotland

**Lon·don** \'lən-dən\ **1** city S Ontario, Canada **2** city, capital of England & of United Kingdom on the Thames; comprises **City of London** & 12 inner boroughs of Greater London — **Lon·don·er** \-də-nər\ noun

**Londonderry** — see DERRY

**Long Beach** city SW California S of Los Angeles

**Long·ford** \'lóng-fərd\ county E central Ireland in Leinster

**Long Island** island 191 kilometers long SE New York S of Connecticut

**Long Island Sound** inlet of the Atlantic between Connecticut & Long Island, New York

**Lon·gueuil** \lóng-'gäl\ city Canada in S Quebec E of Montreal

**Lor·raine** \lə-'rān, lо̇-\ region NE France around upper Moselle & Meuse rivers — see ALSACE-LORRAINE

**Los An·ge·les** \lо̇-'san-jə-ləs also -'sang-gə-ləs\ city SW California

**Lo·thi·an** \'lō-thē-ən\ region SE Scotland S of Firth of Forth; established 1975; includes Edinburgh

**Lou·ise, Lake** \lü-'ēz\ lake SW Alberta in Banff National Park

**Lou·i·si·ana** \lù-,ē-zē-'an-ə, ,lü-ə-zē-, ,lü-zē-\ state S U.S.; capital, Baton Rouge — **Lou·i·si·an·ian** \-'an-ē-ən, -'an-yən\ or **Lou·i·si·an·an** \-'an-ən\ adjective or noun

**Louisiana Purchase** area W central U.S. between Rocky Mountains & the Mississippi purchased 1803 from France

**Lou·is·ville** \'lü-i-,vil, -vəl\ city N Kentucky on the Ohio River

**Lourenço Marques** — see MAPUTO

**Louth** \'laúth\ county E Ireland in Leinster

**Low Countries** region W Europe comprising modern Belgium, Luxembourg, & the Netherlands

**Lower California** — see BAJA CALIFORNIA

**Lower Canada** former province, Canada in S & E parts of present-day Quebec

**Lower Saxony** or German **Nie·der·sach·sen** \,nēd-ər-'zäk-sən\ state NW Germany; capital, Hannover

**Low·lands** \'lō-ləndz, -lənz, -,landz, -,lanz\ the central & E part of Scotland lying between the Highlands & the Southern Uplands

**Lu·an·da** \lü-'an-də\ city, capital of Angola

**Lub·bock** \'ləb-ək\ city NW Texas

**Lü·beck** \'lü-,bek, 'lē-\ city N Germany NE of Hamburg

**Lu·blin** \'lü-blən, -,blēn\ city E Poland SE of Warsaw

**Lu·bum·ba·shi** \,lü-büm-'bäsh-ē\ or formerly **Elisabethville** \i-'liz-ə-bəth-,vil\ city SE Democratic Republic of the Congo

**Lu·cerne, Lake of** \lü-'sərn\ lake central Switzerland

**Luchow** — see HEFEI

**Luck·now** \'lək-,naú\ city N India, capital of Uttar Pradesh

**Lüda** — see DALIAN

**Lu·dhi·a·na** \,lüd-ē-'än-ə\ city NW India in Punjab SE of Amritsar

**Luik** — see LIÈGE

**Luluabourg** — see KANANGA

**Lu·sa·ka** \lü-'säk-ə\ city, capital of Zambia

**Lü·shun** \'lü-'shún\ or **Port Ar·thur** \'är-thər\ city NE China in S Liaoning

**Lusitania** — see PORTUGAL

**Lü·ta** — see DALIAN

**Lu·ton** \'lüt-n\ town SE central England in Bedfordshire

**Lux·em·bourg** or **Lux·em·burg** \'lək-səm-,bərg, 'lük-səm-,bürg\ **1** country W Europe bordered by Belgium, France, & Germany; a grand duchy **2** city, its capital — **Lux·em·bourg·er** \-,bər-gər, -,bür-\ noun — **Lux·em·bourg·ian** \,lək-səm-'bər-gē-ən, ,lük-səm-'bür-\ adjective

**Lu·zon** \lü-'zän\ island N Philippines

**L'viv** \lə-'vē-ü, -'vēf\ or **L'vov** \lə-'vо̇f, -'vо̇v\ or Polish **Lwów** \lə-'vüf, -'vüv\ or German **Lem·berg** \'lem-,bərg, -,berg\ city W Ukraine

**Lyallpur** — see FAISALABAD

**Ly·cia** \'lish-ə, 'lish-ē-ə\ ancient district & Roman province SW Asia Minor

**Lyd·ia** \'lid-ē-ə\ ancient country W Asia Minor on the Aegean; capital, Sardis — **Lyd·i·an** \-ē-ən\ adjective or noun

**Lyon** \'lyōⁿ\ or **Ly·ons** \lē-'ōⁿ, 'lī-ənz\ or ancient **Lug·du·num** \lùg-'dü-nəm, ,ləg-\ city SE central France

**Maas** — see MEUSE

**Ma·cao** or Portuguese **Ma·cau** \mə-'kaú\ **1** Portuguese territory on coast of SE China W of Hong

Kong **2** city, its capital — **Mac·a·nese** \,mak-ə-'nēz, -'nēs\ *noun*

**Macassar** — see UJUNG PANDANG

**Mac·e·do·nia** \,mas-ə-'dō-nyə, -nē-ə\ **1** region S Europe in Balkan Peninsula in NE Greece, country of Macedonia, and SW Bulgaria including territory of ancient kingdom of Macedonia (**Mac·e·don** \'mas-əd-ən, -ə,dän\) **2** country S central Balkan Peninsula; formerly a constituent republic of Yugoslavia; capital, Skopje — **Mac·e·do·nian** \,mas-ə-'dō-nyən, -nē-ən\ *adjective or noun*

**Ma·ceió** \,mas-ā-'ō\ city NE Brazil

**Mac·gil·li·cud·dy's Reeks** \mə-,gil-ə-,kəd-ēz-'rēks\ mountains SW Ireland in Kerry; highest Carrantuohill 1040 meters

**Ma·chi·da** \mə-'chē-də, 'mä-chi-,dä\ city Japan on Honshu

**Ma·chi·li·pat·nam** \,mäch-ə-lə-'pət-nəm\ *or* **Ban·dar** \'bənd-ər\ city SE India in E Andhra Pradesh

**Ma·chu Pic·chu** \,mäch-ü-'pēk-chü\ site SE Peru of ancient Inca city NW of Cuzco

**Mac·ken·zie** \mə-'ken-zē\ **1** river 1800 kilometers long NW Canada flowing from Great Slave Lake NW into Beaufort Sea **2** former district NW Canada in W Northwest Territories in basin of Mackenzie River

**Ma·khach·ka·la** \mə-,käch-kə-'lä\ city S Russia in Europe, on the Caspian

**Mack·i·nac, Straits of** \'mak-ə-,nó\ channel N Michigan connecting Lake Huron & Lake Michigan

**McKinley, Mount** \mə-'kin-lē\ *or* **De·na·li** \də-'näl-ē\ mountain 6194 meters S central Alaska in Alaska Range; highest in U.S. & North America; in **Denali National Park**

**Ma·con** \'mā-kən\ city central Georgia

**Mad·a·gas·car** \,mad-ə-'gas-kər\ *or formerly* **Mal·a·gasy Republic** \,mal-ə-,gas-ē\ island W Indian Ocean off SE Africa; a republic; capital, Antananarivo — **Mad·a·gas·can** \,mad-ə-'gas-kən\ *adjective or noun*

**Ma·dei·ra** \mə-'dir-ə, -'der-\ **1** river 3239 kilometers long W Brazil flowing NE into the Amazon **2** islands in the N Atlantic N of the Canaries belonging to Portugal; capital, Funchal **3** island; chief of the Madeira group — **Ma·dei·ran** \-ən\ *adjective or noun*

**Mad·hya Pra·desh** \,mäd-yə-prə-'desh, -'dāsh\ state central India; capital, Bhopal

**Mad·i·son** \'mad-ə-sən\ city, capital of Wisconsin

**Ma·dras** \mə-'dras, -'dräs\ **1** — see TAMIL NADU **2** city SE India, capital of Tamil Nadu

**Ma·drid** \mə-'drid\ city, capital of Spain

**Ma·du·ra** \'maj-ə-rə\ island Indonesia NE of Java

**Ma·du·rai** \,mäd-ə-'rī\ *or* **Ma·du·ra** \'maj-ə-rə\ city S India in S Tamil Nadu

**Mag·de·burg** \'mäg-də-,bùrg, 'mag-də-,bərg\ city central Germany WSW of Berlin

**Magellan, Strait of** \mə-'jel-ən\ strait at S end of South America between mainland & Tierra del Fuego Archipelago

**Mageröy** — see NORTH CAPE

**Mag·gio·re, Lake** \mə-'jór-ē, -'jór-\ lake N Italy & S Switzerland

**Mag·ni·to·gorsk** \mag-'nēt-ə-,górsk\ city SW Russia in Asia, on Ural River

**Ma·hal·la el Ku·bra** \mə-,hal-ə-el-'kü-brə\ city N Egypt in Nile Delta

**Ma·ha·rash·tra** \,mä-hə-'räsh-trə\ state W India on Arabian Sea; capital, Bombay

**Ma·hi·lyow** *or* **Mo·gi·lev** \mə-gil-'yóf\ city E Belarus

**Main** \'mīn, 'mān\ river 523 kilometers long S central Germany flowing W into the Rhine

**Maine** \'mān\ state NE U.S.; capital, Augusta

**Mainz** \'mīns\ city W Germany on the Rhine, capital of Rhineland-Palatinate

**Ma·jor·ca** \mə-'jór-kə, -'yór-\ *or Spanish* **Mal·lor·ca** \mə-'yór-kə\ island Spain; largest of the Balearic Islands — **Ma·jor·can** \-'jór-kən, -'yór-\ *adjective or noun*

**Ma·ka·lu** \'mək-ə-,lü\ mountain 8481 meters NE Nepal in the Himalaya

**Makassar** *or* **Makassar** — see UJUNG PANDANG

**Ma·ke·yev·ka** *or* **Ma·ki·yiv·ka** \mə-'kā-əf-kə, -yəf-\ city E Ukraine in Donets Basin

**Mal·a·bar Coast** \'mal-ə-,bär\ region SW India on Arabian Sea in Karnataka & Kerala states

**Ma·la·bo** \mä-'läb-ō\ *or formerly* **San·ta Isa·bel** \,san-tə-'iz-ə-bel\ city, capital of Equatorial Guinea

**Ma·lac·ca, Strait of** \mə-'lak-ə, -'läk-\ channel between S Malay Peninsula & island of Sumatra

**Má·la·ga** \'mal-ə-gə\ city S Spain in Andalusia

**Ma·lang** \mə-'läng\ city Indonesia in E Java

**Ma·la·wi** \mə-'lä-wē, -'laù-ē\ *or formerly* **Ny·asa·land** \nī-'as-ə-,land, nē-\ country SE Africa on Lake Malawi; a former British protectorate; independent republic since 1964; capital, Lilongwe

**Malawi, Lake** *or* **Lake Nya·sa** \'nyä-sä, nī-'as-ə\ lake SE Africa in Malawi, Mozambique, & Tanzania

**Ma·lay** \mə-'lā, 'mā-lā\ *or formerly* **Malaysia** **1** archipelago SE Asia including Sumatra, Java, Borneo, Sulawesi, Moluccas, & Timor; usually considered as including the Philippines & sometimes New Guinea **2** peninsula SE Asia divided between Thailand & Malaysia

**Ma·laya, Federation of** \mə-'lā-ə, mä-\ former country SE Asia on Malay Peninsula; since 1963 part of Malaysia

**Ma·lay·sia** \mə-'lā-zhə, -shə, -zhē-ə, -shē-ə\ **1** — see MALAY 1 **2** country SE Asia; a limited constitutional monarchy; capital, Kuala Lumpur — **Ma·lay·sian** \mə-'lā-zhən, -shən\ *adjective or noun*

**Mal·dive** \'mól-,dēv, -,dīv\ islands in Indian Ocean S of the Laccadives; formerly a sultanate under British protection; since 1965 **Republic of Maldives**; capital, Male — **Mal·div·i·an** \mól-'div-ē-ən\ *adjective or noun*

**Ma·li** \'mäl-ē, 'mal-ē\ *or formerly* **French Sudan** country W Africa; a republic; capital, Bamako — **Ma·li·an** \-ē-ən\ *adjective or noun*

**Malmö** \'mal-,mər, 'mal-,mœ̄\ city SW Sweden

**Mal·ta** \'mól-tə\ **1** islands in the Mediterranean S of Sicily; a former British colony; an independent republic since 1964; capital, Valletta **2** island, chief of the group

**Maluku** — see MOLUCCAS

**Malvinas, Islas** — see FALKLAND ISLANDS

**Mam·moth Cave** \,mam-əth-\ limestone caverns SW central Kentucky in **Mammoth Cave National Park**

**Man, Isle of** \'man\ island British Isles in Irish Sea; capital, Douglas; has own legislature & laws

**Ma·na·do** \mə-'näd-,ō\ city & port Indonesia on NE Sulawesi

**Ma·na·gua** \mə-'näg-wə\ city, capital of Nicaragua

**Ma·na·ma** \mə-'nam-ə\ city, capital of Bahrain

**Ma·naus** \mə-'naùs\ city W Brazil on Rio Negro 19 kilometers above its junction with the Amazon

**Man·ches·ter** \'man-,ches-tər, -chə-stər\ city NW England in Lancashire — see GREATER MANCHESTER

**Man·chu·kuo** \'man-,chü-'kwō, man-'chü-,\ former country (1931–45) E Asia in Manchuria & E Inner Mongolia; capital, Changchun

**Man·chu·ria** \man-'chúr-ē-ə\ region NE China S of the Amur — **Man·chu·ri·an** \man-'chúr-ē-ən\ *adjective or noun*

**Man·da·lay** \,man-də-'lā\ city central Myanmar

**Man·hat·tan** \man-'hat-n, mən-\ **1** island SE New York in New York City **2** borough of New York City comprising chiefly Manhattan Island

**Manihiki** — see NORTHERN COOK

**Ma·nila** \mə-'nil-ə\ city, capital of Philippines

**Ma·ni·pur** \,man-ə-'pùr, ,mən-\ state NE India between Assam & Myanmar; capital, Imphal

**Man·i·to·ba** \,man-ə-'tō-bə\ province central Canada; capital, Winnipeg — **Man·i·to·ban** \-'tō-bən\ *adjective or noun*

**Man·i·tou·lin** \,man-ə-'tü-lən\ island 129 kilometers long S Ontario in Lake Huron

**Ma·ni·za·les** \,man-ə-'zäl-əs, -'zal-\ city W central Colombia

**Man·nar, Gulf of** \mə-'när\ inlet of Indian Ocean between Sri Lanka & S tip of India

**Mann·heim** \'man-,hīm, 'män-\ city SW Germany on the Rhine NW of Stuttgart

**Man·za·nil·lo** \,man-zə-'nē-ō, -yō\ city SW Mexico in Colima on the Pacific

**Ma·pu·to** \mä-'pü-tō\ *or formerly* **Lou·ren·ço Mar·quez** \lə-,ren-sō,-mär-'kes, -'märks, -'märk\ city, capital of Mozambique

**Mar·a·cai·bo** \,mar-ə-'kī-bō\ city NW Venezuela

**Maracaibo, Lake** the S extension of Gulf of Venezuela in NW Venezuela

**Ma·ra·cay** \,mar-ə-'kī\ city N Venezuela

**Mar·a·thon** \'mar-ə-,thän, -thən\ plain E Greece in Attica NE of Athens

**Marche** \'märsh\ region central Italy on the Adriatic; capital, Ancona

**Mar del Pla·ta** \,mär-del-'plät-ə\ city & port E Argentina

**Mar·i·ana** \,mar-ē-'an-ə, ,mer-\ islands W Pacific N of Caroline Islands including the Northern Marianas and Guam

**Ma·ri·a·nao** \,mär-ē-ə-'naù\ city W Cuba W of Havana

**Mariana Trench** ocean trench W Pacific extending from SE of Guam to NW of Mariana Islands; deepest in world

**Maritime Alps** section of the W Alps SE France & NW Italy extending N from Mediterranean coast

**Maritime Provinces** the Canadian provinces of New Brunswick, Nova Scotia, & Prince Edward Island and sometimes thought to include Newfoundland

**Ma·ri·u·pol'** \,mar-ē-'ü-,pól\ *or 1949–89* **Zhda·nov** \zhe-'dä-nəf, 'shtä-\ city E Ukraine on Sea of Azov

**Mark·ham, Mount** \'mär-kəm\ mountain 4351 meters Antarctica E of Ross Ice Shelf

**Mar·ma·ra, Sea of** *or* **Sea of Mar·mo·ra** \'mär-mə-rə\ *or ancient* **Pro·pon·tis** \prə-'pänt-əs\ sea NW Turkey connected with Black Sea by the Bosporus & with Aegean Sea by the Dardanelles

**Marne** \'märn\ river 525 kilometers long NE France flowing W into the Seine

**Mar·que·sas** \mär-'kā-zəz, -zəs, -səz, -səs\ islands S Pacific N of Tuamotu Archipelago in French Polynesia — **Mar·que·san** \-zən, -sən\ *adjective or noun*

**Mar·ra·kech** \mə-'räk-ish, ,mar-ə-'kesh\ *or formerly* **Mo·roc·co** \mə-'räk-ō\ city central Morocco

**Mar·seille** \mär-'sā\ *or* **Mar·seilles** \mär-'sā, -'sälz\ *or ancient* **Mas·sil·ia** \mə-'sil-ē-ə\ city SE France

**Mar·shall** \'mär-shəl\ islands W Pacific E of the Carolines; since 1986 an independent republic in association with the U.S.; capital, Majuro

**Mar·tha's Vineyard** \,mär-thəz-\ island SE Massachusetts off SW coast of Cape Cod WNW of Nantucket

**Mar·ti·nique** \,märt-n-'ēk\ island West Indies in the Windwards; an overseas department of France; capital, Fort-de-France

**Mary·land** \'mer-ə-lənd\ state E U.S.; capital, Annapolis — **Mary·land·er** \-lən-dər, -,lan-\ *noun*

**Ma·san** \'mäs-,än\ city South Korea E of Pusan

**Mas·e·ru** \'maz-ə-,rü\ city, capital of Lesotho

**Mash·had** \mə-'shad\ city NE Iran

**Ma·son–Dix·on Line** \,mās-n-'dik-sən\ boundary between Maryland & Pennsylvania; was in part boundary between free & slave states

**Mas·qat** \'məs-,kät\ *or* **Mus·cat** \-,kät, -kət\ town E Arabia, capital of Oman

**Mas·sa·chu·setts** \,mas-ə-'chü-səts, ,mas-'chü-,zəts\ state NE U.S.; capital, Boston

**Mas·sif Cen·tral** \ma-,sēf-,sen-'träl, -,sä°-'träl\ plateau central France W of the Rhone-Saône valley — see AUVERGNE, CÉVENNES

**Mat·a·be·le·land** \,mat-ə-'bē-lē-,land\ region SW Zimbabwe; chief town, Bulawayo

**Ma·to Gros·so** \,mat-ə-'grō-sō\ plateau region SW Brazil in E central Mato Grosso state

**Mat·su·do** \mät-'sü-dō\ city Japan in SE Honshu NE of Tokyo

**Ma·tsu·shi·ma** \,mät-sü-'shē-mə, mät-'sü-shi-mə\ group of islets Japan off N Honshu NE of Sendai

**Ma·tsu·ya·ma** \,mät-sə-'yäm-ə\ city Japan in W Shikoku

**Mat·ter·horn** \'mat-ər-,hórn, 'mät-\ mountain 4478 meters in Pennine Alps on border between Switzerland & Italy

**Maui** \'maù-ē\ island Hawaii NW of Hawaii Island

**Mau·na Kea** \,maù-nə-'kā-ə\ extinct volcano 4205 meters Hawaii in N central Hawaii Island

**Mau·na Loa** \,maù-nə-'lō-ə\ volcano 4170 meters Hawaii in S central Hawaii Island in Hawaii Volcanoes National Park

**Mau·re·ta·nia** *or* **Mau·ri·ta·nia** \,mór-ə-'tā-nē-ə, ,mär-, -nyə\ ancient country NW Africa in modern Morocco & W Algeria — **Mau·re·ta·ni·an** \-nē-ən, -nyən\ *adjective or noun*

**Mauritania** country NW Africa on the Atlantic N of Senegal River; a republic; capital, Nouakchott — **Mauritanian** *adjective or noun*

**Mau·ri·tius** \mȯ-'rish-əs, -'rish-ē-əs\ island in Indian Ocean E of Madagascar; a dominion of the Commonwealth; capital, Port Louis — **Mau·ri·tian** \-'rish-ən\ *adjective or noun*

**May, Cape** \'mā\ cape S New Jersey at entrance to Delaware Bay

**Mayo** \'mā-ō\ county NW Ireland in Connacht

**Ma·yon** \mä-'yōn\ volcano 2462 meters Philippines in SE Luzon

**Ma·za·ma, Mount** \mə-'zäm-ə\ prehistoric mountain SW Oregon the collapse of whose summit formed Crater Lake in Crater Lake National Park

**Ma·za·tlán** \,mäz-ə-'tlän, ,mäs-\ city W Mexico in Sinaloa on the Pacific

**Mba·bane** \em-bə-'bän\ city, capital of Swaziland

**Mban·da·ka** \em-,bän-'däk-ə\ *or formerly* **Co·qui·lhat·ville** \,kō-kē-'at-,vil\ city W Democratic Republic of the Congo

**Mbi·ni** \em-'bē-nē\ *or formerly* **Río Mu·ni** \,rē-ō-'mü-nē\ mainland portion of Equatorial Guinea on Gulf of Guinea

**Mbuji–Mayi** \em-,bü-jē-'mī-,ē\ *or formerly* **Ba·kwan·ga** \bə-'kwäng-gə\ city S Democratic Republic of the Congo

**Mc-** — see MAC- entries

**Mead, Lake** \'mēd\ reservoir NW Arizona & SE Nevada formed by Hoover Dam in Colorado River

**Meath** \'mēth, 'mēth\ county E Ireland in Leinster

**Mec·ca** \'mek-ə\ city W Saudi Arabia, capital of Hejaz

**Me·dan** \mā-'dän\ city Indonesia in NE Sumatra

**Me·de·llín** \,med-l-'ēn, ,mā-thə-'yēn\ city NW Colombia

**Me·dia** \'mēd-ē-ə\ ancient country & province of Persian Empire

**Me·di·na** \mə-'dē-nə\ city W Saudi Arabia

**Mediolanum** — see MILAN

**Med·i·ter·ra·nean** \,med-ə-tə-'rā-nē-ən, -nyən\ sea 3700 kilometers long between Europe & Africa connecting with the Atlantic through Strait of Gibraltar

**Mee·rut** \'mā-rət, 'mir-ət\ city N India in NW Uttar Pradesh

**Me·gha·la·ya** \,mā-gə-'lā-ə\ state NE India; created 1972 out of SW part of Assam; capital, Shillong

**Méjico** — see MEXICO

**Mek·nes** \mek-'nes\ city N Morocco

**Me·kong** \'mā-'kȯng, -'käng\ river about 4200 kilometers long SE Asia flowing from E Tibet S & SE into South China Sea in S Vietnam

**Mel·a·ne·sia** \,mel-ə-'nē-zhə, -shə\ islands of the Pacific NE of Australia & S of Micronesia including Bismarck Archipelago, the Solomons, Vanuatu, New Caledonia, & the Fijis

**Mel·bourne** \'mel-bərn\ city SE Australia, capital of Victoria

**Me·los** *or Greek* **Mí·los** \'mē-,läs\ island Greece in SW Cyclades — **Me·li·an** \'mē-lē-ən\ *adjective or noun*

**Mel·ville** \'mel-,vil\ island N Canada in N Northwest Territories in Parry Islands

**Me·mel** \'mā-məl\ city W Lithuania

**Mem·phis** \'mem-fəs, 'memp-\ **1** city SW Tennessee **2** ancient city N Egypt S of modern Cairo

**Men·do·ci·no, Cape** \,men-də-'sē-nō\ headland NW California

**Menorca** — see MINORCA

**Mer·cia** \'mər-shə, -shē-ə\ ancient Anglo-Saxon kingdom central England — **Mer·cian** \'mər-shən\ *adjective or noun*

**Mé·ri·da** \'mer-əd-ə\ city SE Mexico, capital of Yucatán

**Mer·i·on·eth·shire** \,mer-ē-'än-əth-,shiər, -shər\ *or* **Merioneth** former county NW Wales

**Mer·sey** \'mər-zē\ river 113 kilometers long NW England flowing NW & W into Irish Sea through a large estuary

**Mer·sey·side** \'mər-zē-,sīd\ metropolitan county NW England; includes Liverpool

**Mer·ton** \'mərt-n\ borough of SW Greater London, England

**Me·sa** \'mā-sə\ city SW central Arizona E of Phoenix

**Me·sa·bi Range** \mə-'säb-ē\ region NE Minnesota that contains iron ore

**Me·sa Verde National Park** \,mā-sə-'vərd-ē, -'vərd\ reservation SW Colorado containing prehistoric cliff dwellings

**Mes·o·po·ta·mia** \,mes-ə-pə-'tā-mē-ə, -myə\ **1** region SW Asia between Euphrates & Tigris rivers **2** the entire Tigris-Euphrates valley — **Mes·o·po·ta·mian** \-mē-ən, -myən\ *adjective or noun*

**Mes·si·na** \mə-'sē-nə\ city Italy in NE Sicily

**Messina, Strait of** channel between NE Sicily & SW tip of peninsula of Italy

**Meuse** \'myüz, 'myərz, *French* mœz\ *or Dutch* **Maas** \'mäs\ river 933 kilometers long W Europe flowing from NE France into North Sea in the Netherlands

**Mex·i·cali** \,mek-si-'kal-ē\ city NW Mexico, capital of Baja California

**Mex·i·co** \'mek-si-,kō\ *or Spanish* **Mé·ji·co** \'me-hē-kō\ **1** country S North America; a republic **2** *or* **Mexico City** city, its capital, in Federal District **3** state S central Mexico; capital, Toluca

**Mexico, Gulf of** inlet of the Atlantic SE North America

**Mi·ami** \mī-'am-ē, -'am-ə\ city SE Florida

**Mich·i·gan** \'mish-i-gən\ state N central U.S.; capital, Lansing — **Mich·i·gan·der** \,mish-i-'gan-dər\ *noun* — **Mich·i·gan·ite** \'mish-i-gə-,nīt\ *noun*

**Michigan, Lake** lake N central U.S.; one of the Great Lakes

**Mi·cho·acán** \,mē-chə-wä-'kän\ state SW Mexico on the Pacific; capital, Morelia

**Mi·cro·ne·sia** \,mī-krə-'nē-zhə, -shə\ islands of the W Pacific E of the Philippines & N of Melanesia including Caroline, Kiribati, Mariana, & Marshall groups — **Mi·cro·ne·sian** \-zhən, -shən\ *adjective or noun*

**Middle Congo** — see CONGO 3

**Middle East** the countries of SW Asia & N Africa — usually considered as including the countries extending from Libya on the W to Afghanistan on the E — **Middle Eastern** *or* **Mid·east·ern** \'mid-'ē-stərn\ *adjective*

**Mid·dles·brough** \'mid-lz-brə\ town N England in Cleveland; formerly a county borough in North Riding, Yorkshire

**Mid·dle·sex** \'mid-l-,seks\ former county SE England including NW part of present Greater London

**Mid Gla·mor·gan** \'mid-glə-'mȯr-gən\ county SE Wales

**Mi·di** \mē-'dē\ the south of France

**Mid·i·an** \'mid-ē-ən\ ancient region NW Arabia E of Gulf of Aqaba — **Mid·i·an·ite** \-ē-ə-,nīt\ *noun*

**Mid·lands** \'mid-ləndz, -lənz\ the central counties of England — see WEST MIDLANDS

**Mid·lo·thi·an** \mid-'lō-thē-ən\ former county SE Scotland; chief city, Edinburgh

**Mid·way** \'mid-,wā\ islands (atoll) central Pacific in Hawaiian group 2098 kilometers WNW of Honolulu belonging to U.S.; not included in state of Hawaii

**Mid·west** *or* **Middle West** \'mid-'west\ region N central U.S. including area around Great Lakes & in upper Mississippi valley from Ohio on the E to North & South Dakota, Nebraska, & Kansas on the W — **Mid·west·ern** \'mid-'wes-tərn\ *or* **Middle Western** *adjective* — **Mid·west·ern·er** \'mid-'wes-tər-nər, -tə-nər\ *or* **Middle Westerner** *noun*

**Mi·lan** \mə-'lan, -'län\ *or Italian* **Mi·la·no** \mi-'län-ō\ *or ancient* **Me·di·o·la·num** \,med-ē-ō-'lä-nəm\ city NW Italy, capital of Lombardy — **Mil·a·nese** \,mil-ə-'nēz, -'nēs\ *adjective or noun*

**Mílos** — see MELOS

**Mil·wau·kee** \mil-'wȯ-kē\ city SE Wisconsin

**Mi·nas Basin** \,mī-nəs-\ landlocked bay central Nova Scotia; NE extension of Bay of Fundy

**Min·da·nao** \,min-də-'nä-ō, -'naù\ island S Philippines

**Min·do·ro** \min-'dȯr-ō, -'dȯr-\ island central Philippines

**Minhow** — see FUZHOU

**Min·ne·ap·o·lis** \,min-ē-'ap-ləs, -ə-ləs\ city SE Minnesota

**Min·ne·so·ta** \,min-ə-'sōt-ə\ state N central U.S.; capital, Saint Paul — **Min·ne·so·tan** \-'sōt-n\ *adjective or noun*

**Mi·nor·ca** \mə-'nȯr-kə\ *or Spanish* **Me·nor·ca** \mā-\ island Spain in Balearic Islands — **Mi·nor·can** \mə-'nȯr-kən\ *adjective or noun*

**Minsk** \'minsk\ city, capital of Belarus

**Mi·que·lon** \'mik-ə-,län, *French* mēk-'lōⁿ, mēk-ə-\ island off S coast of Newfoundland belonging to France — see SAINT PIERRE

**Mission Vie·jo** \-vē-'ā-hō\ city SW California

**Mis·sis·sau·ga** \,mis-ə-'sȯg-ə\ city Canada in S Ontario

**Mis·sis·sip·pi** \,mis-ə-'sip-ē, mis-'sip-ē\ **1** river 3765 kilometers long central U.S. flowing into Gulf of Mexico — see ITASCA (Lake) **2** state S U.S.; capital, Jackson

**Mis·sou·ri** \mə-'zùr-ē, -'zùr-ə\ **1** river 3968 kilometers long W U.S. flowing from SW Montana to the Mississippi in E Missouri **2** state central U.S.; capital, Jefferson City — **Mis·sou·ri·an** \-'zùr-ē-ən\ *adjective or noun*

**Mitch·ell, Mount** \'mich-əl\ mountain 2037 meters W North Carolina in Black Mountains of the Appalachians; highest in U.S. E of the Mississippi

**Mi·ya·za·ki** \,mē-,äz-'äk-ē, -,yäz-; mē-'äz-ə-kē, -'yäz-\ city Japan in SE Kyushu

**Mi·zo·ram** \mi-'zȯr-əm\ state NE India; capital, Aizawl

**Mo·ab** \'mō-,ab\ region Jordan E of Dead Sea; in biblical times a kingdom

**Mo·bile** \mō-'bēl, 'mō-,bēl\ city SW Alabama on Mobile Bay

**Moçambique** — see MOZAMBIQUE

**Mo·de·na** \'mȯd-n-ə, -n-,ä\ city N Italy SW of Venice

**Moe·sia** \'mē-shə, -shē-ə\ ancient country & Roman province S of the Danube in modern Bulgaria & Serbia

**Mog·a·di·shu** \,mäg-ə-'dish-ü, -'dēsh-\ *or* **Mog·a·di·scio** \-ō\ city, capital of Somalia

**Mogilev** — see MAHILYOW

**Mo·hen·jo–Da·ro** \mō-,hen-jō-'där-ō\ prehistoric city Pakistan in Indus valley NE of modern Karachi

**Mo·ja·ve** *or* **Mo·ha·ve** \mə-'häv-ē\ desert S California SE of S end of Sierra Nevada

**Mo·ji** \'mō-jē\ city Japan in N Kyushu

**Mol·da·via** \mäl-'dāv-ē-ə, -vyə\ **1** region E Europe in NE Romania & Moldova W of the Dniester **2** — see MOLDOVA — **Mol·da·vian** \-vē-ən, -vyən\ *adjective or noun*

**Mol·do·va** \mäl-'dō-və, mȯl-\ country E Moldavia region; capital, Chisinau; formerly a constituent republic of U.S.S.R.

**Mo·li·se** \'mȯ-li-,zā\ region central Italy on the Adriatic; capital, Campobasso

**Mol·o·kai** \,mäl-ə-'kī, ,mō-lə-\ island Hawaii ESE of Oahu

**Molotov** — see PERM

**Mo·luc·cas** \mə-'lək-əz\ *or* **Spice Islands** \'spīs\ *or Indonesian* **Ma·lu·ku** \mə-'lü-kü\ islands Indonesia E of Sulawesi — **Mo·luc·ca** \mə-'lək-ə\ *adjective* — **Mo·luc·can** \-ən\ *adjective or noun*

**Mom·ba·sa** \mäm-'bäs-ə\ city S Kenya on Mombasa Island

**Mo·na·co** \'män-ə-,kō *also* mə-'näk-ō\ country W Europe on Mediterranean coast of France; a principality; capital, Monaco — **Mo·na·can** \'mä-ə-kən, mə-'näk-ən\ *adjective or noun* — **Mon·e·gasque** \,män-i-'gask\ *noun*

**Mon·a·ghan** \'män-ə-hən, -,han\ county NE Ireland (republic) in Ulster

**Mön·chen·glad·bach** \,mœn-kən-'glät-,bäk\ city W Germany

**Mon·go·lia** \män-'gōl-yə, mäng-, -'gō-lē-ə\ **1** region E Asia E of Altay Mountains; includes Gobi Desert **2** INNER MONGOLIA **3** *or* **Outer Mongolia** country E Asia comprising major portion of Mongolia; capital, Ulaanbaatar

**Mon·mouth·shire** \'män-məth-,shiər, 'mən-, -shər\ *or* **Monmouth** former county SE Wales bordering on England

**Mon·ro·via** \mən-'rō-vē-ə, ,mən-\ city, capital of Liberia

**Mon·tana** \män-'tan-ə\ state NW U.S.; capital, Helena — **Mon·tan·an** \-ən\ *adjective or noun*

**Mont Blanc** \mōⁿ-'bläⁿ\ mountain 4807 meters SE France on Italian border; highest in the Alps

**Mon·te·ne·gro** \,mänt-ə-'nē-grō, -'nā-\ part of Yugoslavia on the Adriatic; capital, Cetinje — **Mon·te·ne·grin** \-grən\ *adjective or noun*

**Mon·ter·rey** \,mänt-ə-'rā\ city NE Mexico, capital of Nuevo León

**Mon·te·vi·deo** \,mänt-ə-və-'dā-ō, -'vid-ē-,ō\ city, capital of Uruguay

**Mont·gom·ery** \mənt-'gəm-rē, mänt-, mən-, män-, -'gäm-, -ə-rē\ city, capital of Alabama

**Mont·gom·ery·shire** \-,shiər, -shər\ *or* **Montgomery** former county E Wales

**Mont·pe·lier** \mänt-'pēl-yər, -'pil-\ city, capital of Vermont

**Mon·tre·al** \,män-trē-'ȯl, ,mən-\ city S Quebec on Montreal Island in the Saint Lawrence

**Mont–Saint–Mi·chel** \mōⁿ-saⁿ-mē-'shel\ islet NW France off coast of Brittany in Gulf of Saint-Malo

**Mont·ser·rat** \,män-sə-'rat\ island British West Indies in the Leewards; capital, Plymouth

**Mo·ra·via** \mə-'rā-vē-ə\ region E Czech Republic; chief city, Brno

**Mor·ay** \'mər-ē, 'mə-rē\ *or* **Mor·ay·shire** \-,shiər, -shər\ former county NE Scotland

**Mo·rea** \mə-'rē-ə\ PELOPONNESE — an old name — **Mo·re·an** \-'rē-ən\ *adjective or noun*

**Mo·re·los** \mə-'rā-ləs\ state S central Mexico; capital, Cuernavaca

**Mo·roc·co** \mə-'räk-ō\ **1** country NW Africa; a kingdom; capital, Rabat; formerly divided into **French Morocco** (capital, Rabat), **Spanish Morocco** (capital, Tetuán) & **International Zone** of Tangier **2** — see MARRAKECH — **Mo·roc·can** \-'räk-ən\ *adjective or noun*

**Mo·ro·ni** \mò-'rō-nē\ city, capital of Comoro

**Morris Jes·up, Cape** \-'jes-əp, ,mär-\ headland N Greenland in Arctic Ocean

**Mos·cow** \'mäs-,kaú, -,kō\ *or Russian* **Mos·kva** \mäsk-'vä\ city, capital of Russia, on Moskva River

**Mo·selle** \mō-'zel\ *or German* **Mo·sel** \'mō-zəl\ river about 545 kilometers long E France & W Germany flowing from Vosges Mountains into the Rhine at Koblenz

**Mo·sul** \mō-'sül, 'mō-səl\ city N Iraq on the Tigris

**Moul·mein** \múl-'mān, mōl-, -'mīn\ city S Myanmar at mouth of the Salween

**Mount Rainier National Park** — see RAINIER (Mount)

**Mo·zam·bique** \,mō-zəm-'bēk\ *or Portuguese* **Mo·çam·bi·que** \,mü-səm-'bē-kə\ **1** channel SE Africa between Mozambique & Madagascar **2** *or formerly* **Portuguese East Africa** country SE Africa; formerly a dependency of Portugal; capital, Maputo

**Mpu·ma·lan·ga** \əm-,pü-mä-'läng-gä\ province NE Republic of South Africa

**Mukden** — see SHENYANG

**Mul·tan** \múl-'tän\ city NE Pakistan SW of Lahore

**Mu·nich** \'myü-nik\ *or German* **Mün·chen** \'mͷn-kən\ city S Germany, capital of Bavaria

**Mun·ster** \'mən-stər\ province S Ireland

**Mün·ster** \'mən-stər, 'mün-, 'myün-, 'mͷn-\ city W Germany NNE of Dortmund

**Mur·cia** \'mər-shə, -shē-ə\ **1** region, province, & ancient kingdom SE Spain **2** city, its capital, NE of Granada — **Mur·cian** \-shən\ *adjective or noun*

**Mur·mansk** \múr-'mansk, -'mänsk\ city NW Russia in Europe, on Barents Sea

**Mur·ray** \'mər-ē, 'mə-rē\ river 2589 kilometers long SE Australia flowing W from E Victoria into Indian Ocean in South Australia — see DARLING

**Mur·rum·bidg·ee** \,mər-əm-'bij-ē, ,mə-rəm-\ river 1578 kilometers long SE Australia in New South Wales flowing W into the Murray

**Mu·sa, Ge·bel** \,jeb-əl-'mü-sə\ mountain group NE Egypt in S Sinai Peninsula; highest Gebel Katherina 2637 meters — see HOREB

**Mu·sa, Je·bel** \,jeb-əl-'mü-sə\ mountain 846 meters N Morocco opposite Rock of Gibraltar — see PILLARS OF HERCULES

**Muscat** — see MASQAT

**Muscat and Oman** — see OMAN

**Mus·co·vy** \mə-'skō-vē; 'məs-kə-vē, -,kō-\ **1** the principality of Moscow (founded 1295) which in 15th century came to dominate Russia **2** RUSSIA — an old name

**Myan·mar** \'myän-,mär\ *or formerly* **Bur·ma** \'bər-mə\ country SE Asia; capital, Yangon

**My·ce·nae** \mī-'sē-nē\ ancient city S Greece in NE Peloponnese N of Argos

**My·ko·la·yiv** \,mē-kə-'lä-yif\ *or* **Ni·ko·la·yev** \,nē-kə-'lä-yif\ city S Ukraine

**My·sia** \'mish-ə, 'mish-ē-ə\ ancient country NW Asia Minor bordering on the Propontis

**My·sore** \mī-'sòr, -'sòr\ **1** — see KARNATAKA **2** city in S Karnataka

**Myt·i·le·ne** \,mit-'l-ē-nē\ **1** ancient city Greece on E coast of Lesbos Island; site at modern town of Mytilene **2** — see LESBOS

**Nab·a·taea** *or* **Nab·a·tea** \,nab-ə-'tē-ə\ ancient Arab kingdom SE of Palestine — **Nab·a·tae·an** *or* **Nab·a·te·an** \-'tē-ən\ *adjective or noun*

**Na·be·rezh·nye Chel·ny** \näb-ə-'rezh-nə-'chel-nē, -nyə-\ city E Russia in Europe

**Na·ga·land** \'näg-ə-,land\ state E India N of Manipur in Naga hills; capital, Kohima

**Na·ga·no** \nä-'gän-ō\ city Japan in SE Honshu NW of Tokyo

**Na·ga·sa·ki** \,näg-ə-'säk-ē, ,nag-ə-'sak-ē\ city Japan in W Kyushu

**Na·goya** \nə-'gòi-ə, 'näg-ə-,yä\ city Japan in S central Honshu

**Nag·pur** \'näg-,púr\ city E central India in NE Maharashtra

**Na·ha** \'nä-hä\ city Japan in Ryukyu Islands; capital of Okinawa

**Na·huel Hua·pí** \nä-,wel-wä-'pē\ lake SW Argentina in the Andes

**Nairn** \'naərn, 'neərn\ *or* **Nairn·shire** \-,shiər, -shər\ former county NE Scotland

**Nai·ro·bi** \nī-'rō-bē\ city, capital of Kenya

**Najd** — see NEJD

**Na·mib·ia** \nə-'mib-ē-ə\ *or formerly* **South–West Africa** country SW Africa, on the Atlantic; administered by South Africa 1919–90; capital, Windhoeck

**Nan·chang** \'nän-'chäng\ city SE China, capital of Jiangxi

**Nan·cy** \'nan-sē, nän-sē\ city NE France

**Nanjing** *or* **Nan·king** \'nan-'king, 'nän-\ city E China on the Chang, capital of Jiangsu

**Nan·ning** \'nän-'ning\ city S China, capital of Guangxi Zhuangzu

**Nantes** \'nants\ city NW France

**Nan·tuck·et** \nan-'tək-ət\ island SE Massachusetts S of Cape Cod

**Na·ples** \'nā-pəlz\ *or Italian* **Na·po·li** \'näp-ə-lē\ *or ancient* **Ne·ap·o·lis** \nē-'ap-ə-ləs\ city S Italy on Bay of Naples — **Ne·a·pol·i·tan** \,nē-ə-'päl-ət-n\ *adjective or noun*

**Na·ra** \'när-ə\ city Japan in W central Honshu E of Osaka

**Nar·ra·gan·sett Bay** \,nar-ə-'gan-sət\ inlet of the Atlantic SE Rhode Island

**Nash·ville** \'nash-,vil, -vəl\ city, capital of Tennessee

**Nas·sau** \'nas-,ò\ city, capital of Bahamas on New Providence Island

**Na·tal** \nə-'tal, -'täl\ **1** city NE Brazil **2** former province E Republic of South Africa; capital, Pietermaritzburg; now part of KwaZulu-Natal

**Na·u·ru** \nä-'ü-rü\ island (atoll) W Pacific; formerly a joint British, New Zealand, & Australian trust territory; an independent republic in the Commonwealth since 1968

**Na·varre** \nə-'vär\ *or Spanish* **Na·var·ra** \nə-'vär-ə\ **1** region & former kingdom N Spain & SW France in W Pyrenees **2** province N Spain W of Aragon; capital, Pamplona

**Nax·ci·van** \,nək-ē-chi-'vän\ exclave of Azerbaijan separated from the rest of the country by Armenia

**Nax·os** \'nak-səs, -,säs\ island Greece in the Aegean; largest of the Cyclades

**Na·ya·rit** \,nī-ə-'rēt\ state W Mexico on the Pacific; capital, Tepic

**Naz·a·reth** \'naz-rəth, -ə-rəth\ town of ancient Palestine in central Galilee; now a city of N Israel

**N'Dja·me·na** \en-'jäm-ə-nə\ *or formerly* **Fort–La·my** \,fòr-lə-'mē\ city, capital of Chad

**Neagh, Lough** \'nä\ lake Northern Ireland; largest in British Isles

**Near East** the countries of NE Africa & SW Asia — **Near Eastern** *adjective*

**Ne·bras·ka** \nə-'bras-kə\ state central U.S.; capital, Lincoln — **Ne·bras·kan** \-kən\ *adjective or noun*

**Neg·ev** \'neg-,ev\ *or* **Neg·eb** \-,eb\ desert region S Israel

**Ne·gros** \'nā-grōs\ island S central Philippines in Visayan Islands

**Neis·se** \'nī-sə\ river 256 kilometers long N Europe flowing from N Czech Republic N into the Oder; forms part of boundary between Poland & Germany — see ODER

**Nejd** \'nejd, 'nezhd\ *or* **Najd** \'najd, 'nazhd\ region central & E Saudi Arabia; capital, Riyadh

**Ne·pal** \nə-'pòl, -'päl, -'pal\ country Asia on NE border of India in the Himalaya; a kingdom; capital, Kathmandu — **Nep·a·lese** \,nep-ə-'lēz, -'lēs\ *adjective or noun* — **Ne·pali** \nə-'pòl-ē, -'päl-, -'pal-\ *adjective or noun*

**Neth·er·lands** \'neth-ər-lənz, -ləndz\ **1** *or Dutch* **Ne·der·land** \'nād-ər-,länt\ *also* **Holland** country NW Europe on North Sea; a kingdom; official capital, Amsterdam, de facto capital, The Hague **2** LOW COUNTRIES — an historical usage — **Neth·er·land** \'neth-ər-lənd\ *adjective* — **Neth·er·land·er** \-,lan-dər, -lən-\ *noun* — **Neth·er·land·ish** \-dish\ *adjective*

**Netherlands An·til·les** \an-'til-ēz\ islands of the West Indies belonging to the Netherlands: Bonaire, Curaçao, and formerly Aruba, Saba, Saint Eustatius, & S part of Saint Martin; capital, Willemstad (on Curaçao)

**Netherlands East Indies** *or* **Netherlands India** *or* **Dutch East Indies** former Dutch possessions in the East Indies including Indonesia

**Netherlands New Guinea** — see IRIAN JAYA

**Ne·va** \'nē-və, 'nä-\ river 65 kilometers long W Russia in Europe, flowing from Lake Ladoga into Gulf of Finland at St. Petersburg

**Ne·vada** \nə-'vad-ə, -'väd-ə\ state W U.S.; capital, Carson City — **Ne·vad·an** \-'vad-n, -'väd-n\ *or* **Ne·vad·i·an** \-'vad-ē-ən, -'väd-\ *adjective or noun*

**Ne·vis** \'nē-vəs\ island British West Indies in the Leewards — see SAINT KITTS

**Nevis, Ben** — see BEN NEVIS

**New Am·ster·dam** \'am-stər-'dam, 'amp-\ town founded 1625 on Manhattan Island by the Dutch; renamed New York 1664 by the British

**New·ark** \'nü-ərk, 'nú-, 'nyü-, 'nyú-\ city NE New Jersey

**New Bed·ford** \'bed-fərd\ city SE Massachusetts

**New Brit·ain** \'brit-n\ island W Pacific, largest in Bismarck Archipelago

**New Bruns·wick** \'brənz-wik\ province SE Canada; capital, Fredericton

**New Cal·e·do·nia** \,kal-ə-'dō-nyə, -nē-ə\ island SW Pacific SW of Vanuatu; an overseas department of France; capital, Nouméa

**New·cas·tle** \'nü-,kas-əl, 'nyü-\ city SE Australia in E New South Wales

**New·cas·tle up·on Tyne** \nü-'kas-əl-ə-,pón-'tīn, nyü-, -,pän-, -pən-, 'nü-, 'nyü-,\ city N England in Tyne and Wear

**New Del·hi** \-'del-ē\ city, capital of India S of city of (Old) Delhi

**New England** section of U.S. comprising states of Maine, New Hampshire, Vermont, Massachusetts, Rhode Island, & Connecticut — **New En·gland·er** \-'ing-glən-dər *also* -'ing-lən-\ *noun*

**New·found·land** \'nü-fən-dlənd, 'nyü-, -lənd, -,dland, -,land; nü-fən-'dland, ,nyü-, -'land\ **1** island Canada in the Atlantic E of Gulf of Saint Lawrence **2** province E Canada comprising Newfoundland & Labrador; capital, Saint John's — **New·found·land·er** \-ər\ *noun*

**New France** the possessions of France in North America before 1763

**New Guin·ea** \-'gin-ē\ *or Indonesian* **Iri·an** \,ir-ē-'än\ **1** island W Pacific N of E Australia divided between Irian Jaya & Papua New Guinea **2** the NE portion of the island of New Guinea together with Bismarck Archipelago, Bougainville, Buka, & adjacent small islands; now part of Papua New Guinea — **New Guin·ean** \-'gin-ē-ən\ *adjective or noun*

**New·ham** \'nü-əm, 'nyü-\ borough of E Greater London, England

**New Hamp·shire** \'ham-shər, 'hamp-, -,shiər\ state NE U.S.; capital, Concord — **New Hamp·shire·man** \-mən\ *noun* — **New Hamp·shir·ite** \-,īt\ *noun*

**New Ha·ven** \'hā-vən\ city S Connecticut

**New Hebrides** — see VANUATU

**New Jer·sey** \'jər-zē\ state E U.S.; capital, Trenton — **New Jer·sey·ite** \-,īt\ *noun*

**New Mex·i·co** \'mek-si-,kō\ state SW U.S.; capital, Santa Fe — **New Mex·i·can** \-si-kən\ *adjective or noun*

**New Neth·er·land** \'neth-ər-lənd\ former Dutch colony (1613–64) North America along Hudson & lower Delaware rivers; capital, New Amsterdam

**New Or·leans** \'òr-lē-ənz; 'òrl-ənz, -yənz; òr-'lēnz\ city SE Louisiana

**New·port** \'nü-,pòrt, 'nyü-, -,pòrt\ city SE Wales

**New·port News** \,nü-,pòrt-'nüz, -,pórt-, -pərt-, ,nyü . . . 'nyüz\ city SE Virginia

**New Prov·i·dence** \-'präd-əns, -ə-,dens\ island NW central Bahamas; chief town, Nassau

**New South Wales** state SE Australia; capital, Sydney

**New Spain** former Spanish possessions in North America, Central America, West Indies, & the Philippines; capital, Mexico City

**New Sweden** former Swedish colony (1638–55) North America on W bank of Delaware River

**New York** \'yòrk\ **1** state NE U.S.; capital, Albany **2** *or* **New York City** city SE New York; includes Bronx, Brooklyn, Manhattan, Queens, & Staten Island — **New York·er** \'yòr-kər\ *noun*

---

\ə\ abut \ᵊ\ kitten \ər\ further \a\ ash \ā\ ace \ä\ mop, mar \au̇\ out \ch\ chin \e\ bet \ē\ easy \g\ go \i\ hit \ī\ ice \j\ job \ŋ\ sing \ō\ go \ò\ law \òi\ boy \th\ thin \t͟h\ the \ü\ loot \ú\ foot \y\ yet \zh\ vision *see also* Guide to Pronunciation

**New Zea·land** \'zē-lənd\ country SW Pacific ESE of Australia; a dominion of the Commonwealth; capital, Wellington — **New Zea·land·er** \-lən-dər\ *noun*

**Ni·ag·a·ra Falls** \nī-'ag-rə, -ə-rə\ falls New York & Ontario in **Niagara River** (flowing N from Lake Erie into Lake Ontario); divided by Goat Island into Horseshoe, or Canadian, Falls (48 meters high) & American Falls (51 meters high)

**Nia·mey** \nē-'äm-ā, nyä-'mā\ city, capital of Niger

**Ni·caea** \nī-'sē-ə\ *or* **Nice** \'nīs\ ancient city W Bithynia; site at modern village of Iznik in NW Turkey — **Ni·cae·an** \nī-'sē-ən\ *adjective or noun* — **Ni·cene** \'nī-,sēn, nī-'sēn\ *adjective*

**Ni·ca·ra·gua** \,nik-ə-'räg-wə\ **1** lake 164 kilometers long S Nicaragua **2** country Central America; capital, Managua — **Ni·ca·ra·guan** \-wən\ *adjective or noun*

**Nice** \'nēs\ *or ancient* **Ni·caea** \nī-'sē-ə\ city SE France

**Nic·o·bar** \'nik-ə-,bär\ islands India in Bay of Bengal S of the Andamans — see ANDAMAN

**Nic·o·sia** \,nik-ə-'sē-ə\ city, capital of Cyprus

**Niedersachsen** — see LOWER SAXONY

**Ni·ger** \'nī-jər\ **1** river 4183 kilometers long W Africa flowing into Gulf of Guinea **2** country W Africa N of Nigeria; a republic; capital, Niamey

**Ni·ge·ria** \nī-'jir-ē-ə\ country W Africa on Gulf of Guinea; a republic in the Commonwealth; capital, Abuja — **Ni·ge·ri·an** \-ē-ən\ *adjective or noun*

**Nihon** — see JAPAN

**Nii·ga·ta** \nē-'gät-ə, 'nē-gə-,tä\ city Japan in N Honshu on Sea of Japan

**Nii·hau** \'nē-,hau\ island Hawaii WSW of Kauai

**Nikolayev** — see MYKOLAYIV

**Nile** \'nīl\ river about 6693 kilometers long E Africa flowing from Lake Victoria in Uganda N into the Mediterranean in Egypt; in various sections called specifically **Vic·to·ria** \vik-'tōr-ē-ə, -'tȯr-\, *or* **Som·er·set** \'sam-ər-,set, -,set\, **Nile** between Lake Victoria & Lake Albert, **Al·bert** \'al-bərt\ **Nile** between Lake Albert & Lake No, & **White Nile** from Lake No to Khartoum — see BLUE NILE

**Nil·gi·ri** \'nil-gə-rē\ hills S India in W Tamil Nadu

**Nîmes** \'nēm\ city S France NW of Marseille

**Nin·e·veh** \'nin-ə-və\ ancient city, capital of Assyria; ruins in Iraq

**Ning·xia Hui·zu** \'ning-shē-'ä-'hwēd-'zü\ *or* **Ningsia Hui** \'ning-shē-'ä-'hwē\ region N China; before 1954 part of former province of **Ningsia**

**Nip·i·gon, Lake** \'nip-ə-,gän\ lake Canada in W Ontario N of Lake Superior

**Nip·pon** \nip-'än\ — see JAPAN — **Nip·pon·ese** \,nip-ə-'nēz, -'nēs\ *adjective or noun*

**Niš** *or* **Nish** \'nish\ city E Yugoslavia in E Serbia

**Ni·shi·no·mi·ya** \,nish-ə-'nō-mē-,ä, -, yä\ city Japan in central Honshu E of Kobe

**Ni·te·rói** \,nēt-ə-'rȯi\ city SE Brazil on Guanabara Bay opposite Rio de Janeiro

**Nizh·niy Nov·go·rad** *or* **Nizh·ni Novgorod** *or* **Nizh·ny Novgorod** \,nizh-nē-'näv-gə-,räd, -'nȯv-gə-rət\ *or* **Gor·ki** *or* **Gor·kii** *or* **Gor'kiy** *or* **Gorky** \'gȯr-kē\ city central Russia in Europe, on the Volga E of Moscow

**Nizh·ny Ta·gil** *or* **Nizh·ni Tagil** \,nizh-nē-tə-'gil\ city W Russia, in the Urals

**Nord–Ost·see Kanal** \'nȯrt-,ȯst-'zā-\ *or* **Kiel Canal** \'kēl-\ ship canal 98 kilometers long N Germany connecting Baltic & North seas

**Nor·folk** \'nȯr-fək, *in the United States also* -,fȯk\ **1** city SE Virginia **2** county E England on North Sea

**Nor·i·cum** \'nȯr-i-kəm, 'när-\ ancient country & Roman province S central Europe S of the Danube in modern Austria & Germany

**Nor·man·dy** \'nȯr-mən-dē\ *or French* **Nor·man·die** \nȯr-män̄-'dē\ region & former province NW France NE of Brittany; capital, Rouen

**North 1** river estuary of the Hudson between NE New Jersey & SE New York **2** sea arm of the Atlantic E of Great Britain **3** island N New Zealand

**North America** continent of western hemisphere NW of South America & N of the equator — **North American** *adjective or noun*

**North·amp·ton** \nȯrth-'am-tən, -'ham-, -'amp-, -'hamp-\ borough central England in Northamptonshire

**North·amp·ton·shire** \-,shiər, -shər\ *or* **North·ampton** county central England

**North Cape 1** headland New Zealand at N end of North Island **2** headland NE Norway on **Ma·ger·öy** \,mäg-ə-'rȯi\ Island

**North Car·o·li·na** \,kar-ə-'lī-nə\ state E U.S.; capital, Raleigh — **North Car·o·lin·ian** \-'lin-ē-ən, -'lin-yən\ *adjective or noun*

**North Cas·cades National Park** \kas-'kādz, 'kas-\ reservation N Washington

**North Da·ko·ta** \də-'kōt-ə\ state N U.S.; capital, Bismarck — **North Da·ko·tan** \-'kōt-n\ *adjective or noun*

**North East Frontier Agency** — see ARUNACHAL PRADESH

**North–East New Guinea** the NE section of Papua New Guinea on New Guinea mainland

**Northern** province NE Republic of South Africa

**Northern Cape** province W Republic of South Africa

**Northern Cook** \'kuk\ *or* **Ma·ni·hi·ki** \,män-ə-'hē-kē\ islands S central Pacific N of Cook Islands

**Northern Ireland** region N Ireland; a division of United Kingdom; capital, Belfast

**Northern Kingdom** — see ISRAEL

**Northern Mariana** the Mariana Islands except for Guam; a U.S. commonwealth

**Northern Rhodesia** — see ZAMBIA

**Northern Territory** territory N & central Australia; capital, Darwin

**North Korea** — see KOREA

**North Rhine–Westphalia** *or German* **Nord·rhein–West·fa·len** \'nȯrt-,rīn-,vest-'fä-lən\ state W Germany; capital, Düsseldorf

**North Ri·ding** \'rī-ding\ former administrative county N England in N Yorkshire

**North Slope** region N Alaska between Brooks Range & Arctic Ocean

**North·um·ber·land** \nȯr-'thəm-bər-lənd\ county N England — **North·um·bri·an** \-'thəm-brē-ən\ *adjective or noun*

**North·um·bria** \nȯr-'thəm-brē-ə\ ancient country Great Britain between the Humber & Firth of Forth — **North·um·bri·an** \-brē-ən\ *adjective or noun*

**North Vietnam** — see VIETNAM

**North West** province N Republic of South Africa

**Northwest Territories** territory N Canada comprising the Arctic Archipelago, the mainland N of 60° between Yukon Territory & Hudson Bay, & the islands in Hudson Bay

**North York** \'yȯrk\ city Canada in SE Ontario

**North York·shire** \'yȯrk-,shiər, -shər\ county N England

**Nor·way** \'nȯr-,wā\ country N Europe in Scandinavia; a kingdom; capital, Oslo

**Nor·we·gian** \nȯr-'wē-jən\ sea between Atlantic & Arctic oceans W of Norway

**Nor·wich** \'nȯr-wich; 'nȯr-ich, 'när-\ city E England in Norfolk

**Not·ting·ham** \'nät-ing-əm, *in the United States also* -,ham\ city N central England in Nottinghamshire

**Not·ting·ham·shire** \-,shiər, -shər\ *or* **Nottingham** county N central England

**Nouak·chott** \nü-'äk-,shät\ city, capital of Mauritania

**Nou·méa** \nü-'mā-ə\ city, capital of New Caledonia

**No·va Igua·çu** \,nō-və-,ē-gwə-'sü\ city SE Brazil NW of Rio de Janeiro

**No·va Sco·tia** \,nō-və-'skō-shə\ province SE Canada; capital, Halifax — **No·va Sco·tian** \-'skō-shən\ *adjective or noun*

**No·va·ya Zem·lya** \,nō-və-yə-,zem-lē-'ä\ two islands N of Russia in Europe, in Arctic Ocean between Barents & Kara seas

**Nov·go·rod** \'näv-gə-,räd, 'nȯv-gə-rət\ city W Russia in Europe, SSE of St. Petersburg

**No·vi Sad** \,nō-vē-'säd\ city N Yugoslavia

**No·vo·kuz·netsk** \,nō-vō-kúz-'netsk\ city S Russia in Asia at end of Kuznetsk Basin

**No·vo·si·birsk** \,nō-vō-sə-'biərsk\ city S Russia in Asia, on the Ob

**Nu·bia** \'nü-bē-ə, 'nyü-\ region NE Africa in Nile valley in S Egypt & N Sudan — **Nu·bi·an** \-bē-ən\ *adjective or noun*

**Nubian** desert NE Sudan E of the Nile

**Nue·vo Le·ón** \,nü-,ā-vō-lā-'ōn\ state N Mexico; capital, Monterrey

**Nu·ku·a·lo·fa** \,nü-kə-wə-'lō-fə\ seaport, capital of Tonga

**Nu·mid·ia** \nü-'mid-ē-ə, nyü-\ ancient country N Africa E of Mauretania in modern Algeria; chief city, Hippo — **Nu·mid·i·an** \-ē-ən\ *adjective or noun*

**Nu·rem·berg** \'nur-əm-,bərg, 'nyur-\ *or German* **Nürn·berg** \'nurn-,berk\ city S central Germany in N Bavaria

**Nuuk** \'nük\ *or* **Godt·håb** \'gȯt-,hȯp\ town, capital of Greenland on SW coast

**Nyasa, Lake** — see MALAWI (Lake)

**Nyasaland** — see MALAWI

**Oa·hu** \ə-'wä-hü\ island Hawaii; site of Honolulu

**Oak·land** \'ō-klənd\ city W California on San Francisco Bay E of San Francisco

**Oa·xa·ca** \wə-'hä-kə\ **1** state SE Mexico **2** city, its capital

**Ob** \'äb, 'ȯb\ river about 3680 kilometers long W central Russia in Asia flowing NW & N into **Gulf of Ob** (inlet of Arctic Ocean)

**Oce·a·nia** \,ō-shē-'an-ē-ə, -'än-ē-ə\ lands of the central & S Pacific: Micronesia, Melanesia, Polynesia including New Zealand, & sometimes Australia & Malay Archipelago — **Oce·a·ni·an** \-'an-ē-ən, -'än-ē-ən\ *adjective or noun*

**Oden·se** \'ōd-n-sə, 'ü-ən-zə\ city central Denmark on Fyn Island

**Oder** \'ōd-ər\ *or* **Odra** \'ō-drə\ river 912 kilometers long central Europe flowing from E Czech Republic NW into Baltic Sea; forms part of boundary between Poland & Germany — see NEISSE

**Odes·sa** \ō-'des-ə\ city S Ukraine on Black Sea

**Of·fa·ly** \'ȯf-ə-lē, 'äf-\ county central Ireland in Leinster

**Ogasawara** — see BONIN

**Og·bo·mo·sho** \,äg-bə-'mō-shō\ city W Nigeria

**Ohio** \ō-'hī-ō\ **1** river 1569 kilometers long E U.S. flowing from W Pennsylvania into the Mississippi **2** state E central U.S.; capital, Columbus — **Ohio·an** \ō-'hī-ə-wən\ *adjective or noun*

**Oi·ta** \'ȯi-,tä, ō-'ēt-ə\ city Japan in NE Kyushu

**Oka·ya·ma** \,ō-kə-'yäm-ə\ city Japan in W Honshu on Inland Sea

**Oka·za·ki** \,ō-kə-'zäk-ē\ city Japan in S central Honshu

**Okee·cho·bee, Lake** \,ō-kē-'chō-bē\ lake S central Florida

**Oke·fe·no·kee** \,ō-kē-fə-'nō-kē\ swamp SE Georgia & NE Florida

**Okhotsk, Sea of** \ō-'kätsk\ inlet of the Pacific E Russia in Asia, W of Kamchatka Peninsula & Kuril Islands

**Oki·na·wa** \,ō-kə-'nä-wə, -'naú-ə\ **1** islands Japan in central Ryukyus; capital, Naha **2** island, chief of group — **Oki·na·wan** \-'nä-wən, -'naú-ən\ *adjective or noun*

**Okla·ho·ma** \,ō-klə-'hō-mə\ state S U.S.; capital, Oklahoma City — **Okla·ho·man** \-mən\ *adjective or noun*

**Oklahoma City** city, capital of Oklahoma

**Old·ham** \'ōl-dəm\ city NW England in Greater Manchester

**Old Point Comfort** cape SE Virginia N of entrance to Hampton Roads

**Ol·du·vai Gorge** \'ȯl-də-,vī\ canyon N Tanzania SE of Serengeti Plain; site of fossil beds

**Olives, Mount of** *or* **Ol·i·vet** \'äl-ə-,vet, ,äl-ə-'\ mountain ridge W Jordan on E side of Jerusalem

**Olym·pia** \ə-'lim-pē-ə, ō-\ **1** city, capital of Washington **2** plain S Greece in NW Peloponnese

**Olym·pic** \ə-'lim-pik, ō-\ mountains NW Washington on Olympic Peninsula, partly in **Olympic National Park**; highest Mt. Olympus 2428 meters

**Olym·pus** \ə-'lim-pəs, ō-\ mountains NE Greece in Thessaly; home of the gods in Greek mythology

**Oma·ha** \'ō-mə-,hȯ, -,hä\ city E Nebraska

**Oman** \ō-'män, -'man\ *or formerly* **Mus·cat and Oman** \'məs-,kat, -kət\ country SW Asia in SE Arabia; a sultanate; capital, Masqat — see UNITED ARAB EMIRATES

**Oman, Gulf of** arm of Arabian Sea between Oman & SE Iran

**Om·dur·man** \,äm-dər-'man, -'män\ city central Sudan on left bank of the Nile opposite Khartoum

**Omi·ya** \'ō-mē-ə, ,ō-mē-ä\ city Japan in SE Honshu NW of Tokyo

**Omsk** \'ȯmsk, 'ȯmpsk, 'ämsk, 'ämpsk\ city S Russia in Asia, at confluence of Irtysh & Om rivers

**On·ta·ke** \ȯn-'täk-ā\ mountain 1118 meters Japan in central Honshu NNW of Nagoya

**On·tar·io** \än-'ter-ē-,ō\ province E Canada; capital, Toronto — **On·tar·i·an** \-ē-ən\ *adjective or noun*

**Ontario, Lake** lake E central North America in U.S. & Canada; one of the Great Lakes

**Ophir** \'ō-fər\ a biblical land rich in gold; probably in Arabia

**Opor·to** \ō-'port-ō, -'pòrt-\ *or Portuguese* **Pôr·to** \'pòr-tü\ city NW Portugal

**Ora·dea** \o-'räd-ē-ə\ city NW Romania

**Oran** \ō-'rän\ city NW Algeria

**Or·ange** \'òr-inj, 'är-, -ənj\ river 2090 kilometers long S Africa flowing W from Drakensberg Mountains into the Atlantic

**Orange Free State** — see FREE STATE

**Ordzhonikidze** — see VLADIKAVKAZ

**Or·e·gon** \'òr-i-gən, 'är-, -,gän\ state NW U.S.; capital, Salem — **Or·e·go·nian** \,òr-i-'gō-nē-ən, ,är-, -nyən\ *adjective or noun*

**Oregon Trail** pioneer route to the Pacific Northwest about 3220 kilometers long from vicinity of Independence, Missouri, to Vancouver, Washington

**Orel** \ō-'rel, òr-'yól\ city SW Russia in Europe, S of Moscow

**Oren·burg** \'òr-ən-,bərg, 'òr-, -,bùrg\ *or formerly* **Chkalov** \chə-'käl-əf\ city E Russia in Europe, on Ural River

**Ori·no·co** \,òr-ə-'nō-kō, ,òr-\ river 2061 kilometers long Venezuela flowing into the Atlantic

**Oris·sa** \ò-'ris-ə\ state E India; capital, Bhubaneswar

**Ori·za·ba** \,òr-ə-'zäb-ə, ,òr-\ **1** *or* **Ci·tlal·te·petl** \sēt-,läl-'tä-,pet-l\ inactive volcano 5700 meters SE Mexico on Puebla-Veracruz border; highest point in Mexico & third highest in North America **2** city E Mexico in Veracruz state

**Ork·ney** \'òrk-nē\ islands N Scotland; a county

**Or·lan·do** \òr-'lan-dō\ city central Florida

**Or·léans** \òr-lā-'ä"\ city N central France

**Osa·ka** \ō-'säk-ə\ city Japan in S Honshu

**Osh·a·wa** \'äsh-ə-,wä\ city Canada in SE Ontario on Lake Ontario ENE of Toronto

**Os·lo** \'äz-lō, 'äs-\ city, capital of Norway

**Os·sa, Mount** \'äs-ə\ mountain 1978 meters NE Greece in E Thessaly near Mount Pelion

**Ostra·va** \'ò-strə-və\ city E Czech Republic in Moravia

**Otran·to, Strait of** \ō-'tran-tō, 'ō-trən-,tō\ strait between SE Italy & Albania

**Ot·ta·wa** \'ät-ə-,wä, -wə, -,wò\ city, capital of Canada in SE Ontario on Ottawa River

**Oua·ga·dou·gou** \,wäg-ə-'dü-,gü\ city, capital of Burkina Faso

**Ouj·da** \uzh-'dä\ city NE Morocco near Algerian border

**Outer Hebrides** — see HEBRIDES

**Outer Mongolia** — see MONGOLIA

**Ovie·do** \,ō-vē-'ā-thō\ city NW Spain

**Ox·ford** \'äks-fərd\ city central England in Oxfordshire

**Ox·ford·shire** \'äks-fərd-,shiər, -shər\ *or* **Oxford** county central England

**Oxus** — see AMU DAR'YA

**Ozark Plateau** \'ō-,zärk\ eroded tableland N Arkansas, S Missouri, & NE Oklahoma

**Pa·cif·ic** \pə-'sif-ik\ ocean extending from arctic circle to Antarctica & from W North America & W South America to E Asia & Australia

**Pacific Islands, Trust Territory of the** islands in W Pacific in association with the U.S.: the Carolines, the Marshalls, & until 1978 the Northern Marianas

**Pa·dang** \'pä-,däng\ city & port Indonesia in W Sumatra

**Pa·dre** \'päd-rē, 'pad-\ island about 182 kilometers long S Texas in Gulf of Mexico

**Padus** — see PO

**Pa·go Pa·go** \päng-gō-'päng-gō, ,päng-ō-'päng-ō, ,päg-ō-'päg-ō\ town, capital of American Samoa on Tutuila Island

**Pa·kan·ba·ru** \,päk-ən-'bär-ü\ city Indonesia in central Sumatra

**Pak·i·stan** \'pak-i-,stan, ,päk-i-'stän\ country S Asia in Indian Subcontinent NW of India; until 1971 included also an eastern division E of India; a republic; capital, Islamabad — see EAST PAKISTAN — **Pak·i·stani** \-'stan-ē, -'stän-ē\ *adjective or noun*

**Pal·at·i·nate** \pə-'lat-n-ət\ *or German* **Pfalz** \'pfälts, 'fälts\ either of two districts SW Germany once ruled by counts palatine of the Holy Roman Empire: **Rhenish Palatinate** *or* **Rhine Palatinate** *or German* **Rhein·pfalz** \'rīn-,pfälts, -,fälts\ (on the Rhine E of Saarland) & **Upper Palatinate** (on the Danube around Regensburg) — see RHINELAND-PALATINATE

**Pa·lau** \pə-'laú\ *or* **Be·lau** \bə-\ islands W Pacific; since 1994 an independent republic in association with the U.S.; capital, Koror

**Pa·la·wan** \pə-'lä-wən, -,wän\ island W Philippines between South China & Sulu seas

**Pa·lem·bang** \,päl-əm-'bäng\ city Indonesia in SE Sumatra

**Pa·ler·mo** \pə-'lər-mō, -'leər-\ city Italy, capital of Sicily

**Pal·es·tine** \'pal-ə-,stīn, -,stēn\ region SW Asia between Syrian Desert & the Mediterranean now divided between Israel & Jordan — **Pal·es·tin·ian** \,pal-ə-'stin-ē-ən, -'stin-yən\ *adjective or noun*

**Pal·ma** \'päl-mə\ *or* **Palma de Ma·llor·ca** \-,dä-mə-'yòr-kə, -məl-\ city Spain on Majorca

**Palmer Peninsula** — see ANTARCTIC PENINSULA

**Pa·mirs** \pə-'miərz\ elevated mountainous region central Asia in E Tajikistan & on borders of Xinjiang Uygur, Kashmir, & Afghanistan; many peaks over 6100 meters

**Pam·li·co** \'pam-li-,kō\ sound inlet of the Atlantic E North Carolina between mainland & offshore islands

**Pam·plo·na** \pam-'plō-nə\ city N Spain in Navarre

**Pan·a·ma** \'pan-ə-,mä, -,mò, ,pan-ə-'\ **1** country S Central America; a republic **2** *or* **Panama City** city, its capital on the Pacific **3** canal 82 kilometers long Panama connecting Atlantic & Pacific oceans — **Pan·a·ma·ni·an** \,pan-ə-'mä-nē-ən\ *adjective or noun*

**Panama, Isthmus of** *or formerly* **Isthmus of Dar·i·en** \,dar-ē-'en\ strip of land central Panama connecting North America & South America

**Panama Canal Zone** — see CANAL ZONE

**Pa·nay** \pə-'nī\ island Philippines in Visayan Islands; chief city, Iloilo

**Pan·de·mo·ni·um** \,pan-də-'mō-nē-əm\ the capital of Hell in John Milton's Paradise Lost

**Panjab** — see PUNJAB

**Paoting** — see BAODING

**Pao·t'ou** — see BAOTOU

**Papal States** — see STATES OF THE CHURCH

**Pa·pee·te** \päp-ē-'ät-ē; pə-'pät-ē, -'pēt-\ city Society Islands on Tahiti, capital of French Polynesia

**Pap·ua, Territory of** \'pap-yə-wə, 'päp-ə-wə\ former British territory comprising SE New Guinea & offshore islands; now part of Papua New Guinea

**Papua New Guinea** country combining former territories of Papua & New Guinea; formerly a United Nations trust territory administered by Australia; independent since 1975; capital, Port Moresby

**Pará** — see BELÉM

**Par·a·guay** \'par-ə-,gwī, -,gwä\ **1** river 2549 kilometers long central South America flowing from Brazil S into the Paraná in Paraguay **2** country central South America; a republic; capital, Asunción — **Par·a·guay·an** \,par-ə-'gwī-ən, -'gwä-ən\ *adjective or noun*

**Par·a·mar·i·bo** \,par-ə-'mar-ə-,bō\ city, capital of Suriname

**Pa·ra·ná** \,par-ə-'nä\ **1** river about 4875 kilometers long central South America flowing S from Brazil into Rio de la Plata in Argentina **2** city NE Argentina

**Par·is** \'par-əs\ city, capital of France — **Pa·ri·sian** \pə-'rizh-ən, -'rēzh-\ *adjective or noun*

**Par·ma** \'pär-mə\ **1** city NE Ohio **2** city N Italy in Emilia-Romagna SE of Milan

**Par·nas·sus, Mount** \pär-'nas-əs\ massif central Greece N of Gulf of Corinth; highest point 2457 meters

**Par·os** \'par-,äs, 'per-\ island Greece in central Cyclades — **Par·i·an** \'par-ē-ən, 'per-\ *adjective*

**Par·ra·mat·ta** \,par-ə-'mat-ə\ city SE Australia in New South Wales NW of Sydney

**Par·thia** \'pär-thē-ə\ ancient country SW Asia in NE modern Iran — **Par·thi·an** \-thē-ən\ *adjective or noun*

**Pas·a·de·na** \,pas-ə-'dē-nə\ city SW California E of Glendale

**Pat·a·go·nia** \,pat-ə-'gō-nyə, -nē-ə\ barren region South America S of about 40° S latitude in S Argentina & S tip of Chile; sometimes considered to include Tierra del Fuego — **Pat·a·go·nian** \-nyən, -nē-ən\ *adjective or noun*

**Pat·er·son** \'pat-ər-sən\ city NE New Jersey

**Pat·mos** \'pat-məs\ island Greece in the Dodecanese SSW of Samos

**Pat·na** \'pət-nə\ city NE India on the Ganges, capital of Bihar

**Pat·ras** \pə-'tras, 'pa-trəs\ city W Greece in N Peloponnese on Gulf of Patras

**Pearl Harbor** inlet Hawaii on S coast of Oahu W of Honolulu

**Pee·bles** \'pē-bəlz\ *or* **Pee·bles·shire** \'pē-bəl-,shiər, -shər\ former county SE Scotland

**Peking** — see BEIJING

**Pe·li·on, Mount** \'pē-lē-ən\ mountain 1551 meters NE Greece in E Thessaly near Mount Ossa

**Pel·o·pon·nese** \'pel-ə-pə-,nēz, -,nēs\ *or* **Pel·o·pon·ne·sus** \,pel-ə-pə-'nē-səs\ *or* **Pel·o·pon·ne·sos** \-'nē-səs\ peninsula forming S part of mainland of Greece — **Pel·o·pon·ne·sian** \,pel-ə-pə-'nē-zhən, -shən\ *adjective or noun*

**Pe·lo·tas** \pə-'lòt-əs\ city S Brazil SW of Pôrto Alegre

**Pem·broke·shire** \'pem-brùk-,shiər, -shər\ *or* **Pembroke** former county SW Wales

**Penang** — see GEORGE TOWN

**Pen·de·li·kón** \,pen-,del-ə-'kòn\ *or* **Pen·te·li·kon** \,pen-,tel-ē-'kän\ mountain 1109 meters E Greece NE of Athens

**Peninsular Malaysia** territory W Malaysia comprising that part of Malaysia contained on Malay Peninsula

**Pen·nine Chain** \'pen-,īn\ mountains N England; highest Cross Fell 893 meters

**Penn·syl·va·nia** \,pen-səl-'vā-nyə, -nē-ə\ state E U.S.; capital, Harrisburg

**Pen·za** \'pen-zə\ city S central Russia in Europe

**People's Democratic Republic of Yemen** — see YEMEN

**Pe·o·ria** \pē-'òr-ē-ə, -'ōr-\ city N central Illinois

**Per·ga·mum** \'pər-gə-məm\ *or* **Per·ga·mus** \-məs\ ancient Greek kingdom including most of Asia Minor; at its height 263–133 B.C.; capital, Pergamum (in what is now W Turkey)

**Perm** \'pərm, 'peərm\ *or formerly* **Mo·lo·tov** \'mäl-ə-,tóf, 'mòl-, 'mōl-, -,tòv\ city E Russia in Europe

**Pernambuco** — see RECIFE

**Per·pi·gnan** \per-pē-'nyä"\ city S France SE of Toulouse

**Per·sep·o·lis** \pər-'sep-ə-ləs\ city of ancient Persia; site in SW Iran NE of Shiraz

**Persia** — see IRAN

**Per·sian** \'pər-zhən\ gulf arm of Arabian Sea between Iran & Arabia

**Persian Gulf States** Kuwait, Bahrain, Qatar, & United Arab Emirates

**Perth** \'pərth\ **1** city, capital of Western Australia **2** *or* **Perth·shire** \-,shiər, -shər\ former county central Scotland

**Pe·ru** \pə-'rü\ country W South America; a republic; capital, Lima — **Pe·ru·vi·an** \pə-'rü-vē-ən\ *adjective or noun*

**Peru Current** *or* **Hum·boldt Current** \'həm-,bōlt\ cold current of the S Pacific flowing N & NW along coast of N Chile, Peru, & Ecuador

**Pe·ru·gia** \pə-'rü-jə, -jē-ə\ city central Italy SE of Florence

**Pe·sha·war** \pə-'shä-wər, -'shaú-ər\ city N Pakistan ESE of Khyber Pass

**Pe·ta·re** \pet-'är-,ā\ city N Venezuela

**Pe·ter·bor·ough, Soke of** \,sō-kəv-'pēt-ər-,bər-ə, -,bə-rə, -,brə\ former administrative county E central England in Northamptonshire and later in Huntingdonshire; since 1974 part of Cambridgeshire

**Pe·tra** \'pē-trə, 'pe-trə\ ancient city NW Arabia; site in SW Jordan

**Petrified Forest National Park** reservation E Arizona

**Petrograd** — see SAINT PETERSBURG

**Pe·tro·pav·lovsk** \,pe-trə-'pav-,lòfsk\ city N Kazakhstan

**Pe·tro·za·vodsk** \,pe-trə-zə-'vätsk\ city NW Russia in Europe, on Lake Onega

**Pfalz** — see PALATINATE

**Phil·a·del·phia** \,fil-ə-'del-fyə, -fē-ə\ city SE Pennsylvania — **Phil·a·del·phian** \-fyən, -fē-ən\ *adjective or noun*

**Phi·lae** \'fī-lē\ former island S Egypt in the Nile above Aswân; now submerged in Lake Nasser

**Phil·ip·pines** \,fil-ə-'pēnz, 'fil-ə-,\ *or* **Republic of the Philippines** republic, an archipelago approximately 805 kilometers off SE coast of Asia; capital, Manila — **Phil·ip·pine** \-'pēn, -,pēn\ *adjective*

**Phi·lis·tia** \fə-'lis-tē-ə\ ancient country SW Palestine on the coast; the land of the Philistines

---

\ə\ abut \'ə\ kitten \ər\ further \a\ ash \ā\ ace \ä\ mop, mar \aú\ out \ch\ chin \e\ bet \ē\ easy \g\ go \i\ hit \ī\ ice \j\ job \ŋ\ sing \ō\ go \ò\ law \òi\ boy \th\ thin \t̶h\ the \ü\ loot \ù\ foot \y\ yet \zh\ vision *see also* Guide to Pronunciation

**Phnom Penh** \pə-'nóm-'pen, 'nóm-, pə-'näm-, 'näm-\ city, capital of Cambodia

**Phoe·ni·cia** \fi-'nish-ə, -'nēsh-, -ē-ə\ ancient country SW Asia on the Mediterranean in modern Syria & Lebanon

**Phoe·nix** \'fē-niks\ city, capital of Arizona

**Phry·gia** \'frij-ə, 'frij-ē-ə\ ancient country W central Asia Minor

**Pia·cen·za** \pyä-'chen-sə, ,pē-ə-'chen-\ city N Italy SE of Milan

**Pic·ar·dy** \'pik-ərd-ē\ *or French* **Pi·car·die** \pē-kär-dē\ region & former province N France N of Normandy; capital, Amiens

**Pied·mont** \'pēd-,mänt\ **1** plateau region E U.S. E of the Appalachians between SE New York & NE Alabama **2** *or Italian* **Pie·mon·te** \pyä-'mōn-tā\ region NW Italy W of Lombardy; capital, Turin — **Pied·mon·tese** \,pēd-mən-'tēz, -mān-, -'tēs\ *adjective or noun*

**Pierre** \'piər\ city, capital of South Dakota

**Pie·ter·mar·itz·burg** \,pēt-ər-'mar-əts-,bərg\ city E Republic of South Africa

**Pikes Peak** \'pīks\ mountain 4301 meters E central Colorado in a range of the Rockies

**Pillars of Her·cu·les** \'hər-kyə-,lēz\ two promontories at E end of Strait of Gibraltar: Rock of Gibraltar (in Europe) & Jebel Musa (in Africa)

**Pin·dus** \'pin-dəs\ mountains W Greece W of Thessaly; highest point 2480 meters

**Pinkiang** — see HARBIN

**Pi·rae·us** \pī-'rē-əs\ *or Greek* **Pi·rai·évs** \,pē-rē-'efs\ city E Greece on Saronic Gulf; port for Athens

**Pi·sa** \'pē-zə, *Italian* 'pē-sä\ city W central Italy W of Florence

**Pit·cairn** \'pit-,kaərn, -,keərn\ island S Pacific SE of Tuamotu Archipelago; a British colony

**Pitts·burgh** \'pits-,bərg\ city SW Pennsylvania

**Pla·ta, Río de la** \,rē-ō-,del-ə-'plät-ə\ estuary of Paraná & Uruguay rivers between Uruguay & Argentina

**Plov·div** \'plòv-,dif, -,div\ city S Bulgaria

**Plym·outh** \'plim-əth\ city SW England in Devonshire

**Po** \'pō\ *or ancient* **Pa·dus** \'pād-əs\ river 652 kilometers N Italy flowing into the Adriatic

**Po Hai** — see BO HAI

**Po·land** \'pō-lənd\ country central Europe on Baltic Sea; a republic; capital, Warsaw

**Pol·y·ne·sia** \,päl-ə-'nē-zhə, -shə\ islands of the central & S Pacific including Hawaii, the Line, Tuvala, Phoenix, Tonga, Cook, & Samoa Islands, French Polynesia, & often New Zealand

**Pom·er·a·nia** \,päm-ə-'rā-nē-ə, -'rā-nyə\ region N Europe on Baltic Sea; formerly in Germany, now mostly in Poland

**Pom·peii** \päm-'pā, -'pā-,ē\ ancient city S Italy SE of Naples destroyed 79 A.D. by eruption of Vesuvius — **Pom·pe·ian** \-'pā-ən\ *adjective or noun*

**Po·na·pe** \'pō-nə-,pā\ island W Pacific in the E Carolines

**Pon·ce** \'pòn-sā\ city S Puerto Rico

**Pon·di·cher·ry** \,pän-də-'cher-ē, -'sher-\ territory SE India SSW of Madras; a settlement of French India before 1954

**Pon·ta Del·ga·da** \,pänt-ə-del-'gäd-ə, -'gad-\ city Portugal in the Azores on São Miguel Island

**Pont·char·train, Lake** \,pän-chər-,trān, ,pän-chər-'\ lake SE Louisiana E of the Mississippi & N of New Orleans

**Pon·ti·a·nak** \,pän-tē-'ä-,näk\ city Indonesia on SW coast of Borneo

**Pon·tine Marshes** \,pän-,tīn, -,tēn\ district central Italy in SW Latium; marshes now reclaimed

**Pon·tus** \'pänt-əs\ **1** ancient country & Roman province NE Asia Minor **2** *or* **Pontus Euxinus** — see BLACK SEA — **Pon·tic** \'pänt-ik\ *adjective or noun*

**Poole** \'pül\ town S England in Dorset on English Channel

**Pool Ma·le·bo** \mä-'lā-bō\ expansion of Congo River between Democratic Republic of the Congo and Republic of the Congo

**Poona** — see PUNE

**Po·po·ca·te·petl** \,pō-pə-,kat-ə-'pet-l\ volcano 5450 meters SE central Mexico in Puebla

**Port Arthur** — see LÜSHUN

**Port–au–Prince** \,pōrt-ō-'prins, ,pòrt-\ -'prans, -'praⁿs\ city, capital of Haiti

**Port Eliz·a·beth** \l-'iz-ə-bəth, i-'liz-\ city S Republic of South Africa

**Port Jack·son** \'jak-sən\ inlet of S Pacific SE Australia in New South Wales; harbor of Sydney

**Port·land** \'pōrt-lənd, 'pòrt-\ city NW Oregon

**Port Lou·is** \'lü-əs, 'lü-ē, lü-'ē\ city, capital of Mauritius

**Port Lyautey** — see KENITRA

**Port Mores·by** \'mōrz-bē, 'mórz-\ city, capital of Papua New Guinea

**Pôrto** — see OPORTO

**Pôr·to Ale·gre** \,pōrt-ə-'leg-rə, ,pòrt-\ city S Brazil

**Port of Spain** city NW Trinidad, capital of Trinidad and Tobago

**Por·to–No·vo** \,pōrt-ə-'nō-vō, ,pòrt-\ city, capital of Benin

**Porto Rico** — see PUERTO RICO

**Port Phil·lip Bay** \'fil-əp\ inlet of S Pacific SE Australia in Victoria; harbor of Melbourne

**Port Said** \sä-'ēd, 'sīd\ city NE Egypt on the Mediterranean at N end of Suez Canal

**Ports·mouth** \'pōrt-sməth, 'pòrt-\ **1** city SE Virginia **2** city S England in Hampshire

**Port Su·dan** \sü-'dan, -'dän\ city NE Sudan

**Por·tu·gal** \'pōr-chi-gəl, 'pòr-\ *or ancient* **Lu·si·ta·nia** \,lü-sə-'tā-nē-ə, -nyə\ country SW Europe; a republic; capital, Lisbon

**Portuguese East Africa** — see MOZAMBIQUE

**Portuguese Guinea** — see GUINEA-BISSAU

**Portuguese India** former Portuguese possession on W coast of India including Goa, Daman, & Diu; annexed to India 1962

**Portuguese West Africa** — see ANGOLA

**Port–Vi·la** \,pór-'vē-lä, -vē-'lä\ *or* **Vi·la** \'vē-lä, vē-'lä\ seaport, capital of Vanuatu

**Po·ten·za** \pə-'tent-sə; -'ten-sə, -zə\ city S Italy

**Po·to·mac** \pə-'tō-mək, -mik\ river 462 kilometers long flowing from West Virginia into Chesapeake Bay & forming boundary between Maryland & Virginia

**Po·wys** \'pō-əs\ county E central Wales; established 1974

**Poz·nan** \'pòz-,nan-yə, 'póz-, -,nän-yə, -,nan, -,nän\ city W central Poland

**Prague** \'präg\ *or Czech* **Pra·ha** \'prä-hä\ city, capital of Czech Republic and formerly of Czechoslovakia

**Praia** \'prī-ə\ town, capital of Cape Verde

**Prairie Provinces** the Canadian provinces of Alberta, Manitoba, & Saskatchewan

**Pres·ton** \'pres-tən\ town NW England in Lancashire

**Pre·to·ria** \pri-'tōr-ē-ə, -'tòr-\ city Republic of South Africa, administrative capital of the Republic

**Prib·i·lof** \'prib-ə-,lòf\ islands Alaska in Bering Sea

**Prince Al·bert National Park** \'al-bərt\ reservation Canada in central Saskatchewan

**Prince Ed·ward Island** \-'ed-wərd\ island SE Canada in Gulf of Saint Lawrence; a province; capital, Charlottetown

**Prince Ru·pert's Land** \'rü-pərts\ historical region N & W Canada comprising drainage basin of Hudson Bay granted 1670 by King Charles II to Hudson's Bay Company

**Prín·ci·pe** \'prin-sə-pə\ island W Africa in Gulf of Guinea — see SÃO TOMÉ

**Pro·ko·pyevsk** \prə-'kóp-yəfsk\ city S Russia in Asia, NW of Novokuznetsk

**Propontis** — see MARMARA (Sea of)

**Pro·vence** \prə-'väⁿs\ region & former province SE France on the Mediterranean

**Prov·i·dence** \'präv-əd-əns, -ə-,dens\ city, capital of Rhode Island

**Prus·sia** \'prəsh-ə\ former kingdom &, later, state Germany; capital, Berlin — **Prus·sian** \-ən\ *adjective or noun*

**Pu·chon** \'pü-,chòn\ city NW South Korea

**Pu·eb·la** \pü-'eb-lə, 'pweb-, pyü-'eb-\ **1** state SE central Mexico **2** city, its capital

**Puer·to Ri·co** \,pōrt-ə-'rē-kō, ,pòrt-, ,pwert-\ *or formerly* **Por·to Ri·co** \,pōrt-, ,pòrt-\ island West Indies E of Hispaniola; a self-governing commonwealth associated with U.S.; capital, San Juan — **Puer·to Ri·can** \-'rē-kən\ *adjective or noun*

**Pu·get Sound** \,pyü-jət-\ arm of the Pacific W Washington

**Pu·glia** \'pül-yä\ *or* **Apu·lia** \ä-'pül-yä\ *or* **Le Puglie** \lə-'pül-yä\ region SE Italy bordering on the Adriatic Sea & Gulf of Taranto; capital, Bari

**Pu·na de Ata·ca·ma** \'pü-nə-,dä-,at-ə-'käm-ə, -,ät-\ plateau region NW Argentina NW of San Miguel de Tucumán

**Pu·ne** *or* **Poo·na** \'pü-nə\ city W India in Maharashtra ESE of Bombay

**Pun·jab** *or* **Pan·jab** \,pən-'jäb, -'jab, 'pən-,\ **1** region NW Indian Subcontinent in Pakistan & N India in valley of the Indus **2** *or* **Pun·jabi Su·ba** \pən-,jäb-ē-'sü-bə, -,jäb-\ state NW India in E Punjab region; capital, Chandigarh — see HARYANA **3** *or formerly* **West Punjab** province NE Pakistan

**Pu·rus** \pə-'rüs\ river about 3380 kilometers long NW central South America in SE Peru & NW Brazil flowing into the Amazon

**Pu·san** \'pü-,sän\ city South Korea on Korea Strait

**Pyong·yang** \pē-'óng-,yäng, pē-'əng-, -,yang\ city, capital of North Korea

**Pyr·e·nees** \'pir-ə-,nēz\ mountains on French-Spanish border extending from Bay of Biscay to the Mediterranean; highest Pico de Aneto (Pic de Néthou) 3404 meters

**Qa·tar** \'kät-ər, 'gät-, 'gət-\ country E Arabia on peninsula extending into Persian Gulf; an independent emirate; capital, Doha

**Qing·dao** \'ching-'daù\ *or* **Tsing·tao** \'ching-'daù, 'tsing-, 'sing-\ city E China in E Shandong

**Qing·hai** *or* **Tsing·hai** \'ching-'hī\ province W China W of Gansu; capital, Xining

**Qi·qi·har** \'chē-'chē-'här\ *or* **Ch'i–ch'i–ha–erh** \'chē-'chē-'hä-'ər\ city NE China in W Heilongjiang

**Qom** \'kùm\ city NW central Iran

**Quan·zhou** *or* **Ch'üan–chou** *or* **Chuan–chow** \chə-'wän-'jō\ city SE China in Fujian on Taiwan Strait

**Que·bec** \kwi-'bek, ki-\ *or French* **Qué·bec** \kā-bek\ **1** province E Canada **2** city, its capital, on the Saint Lawrence

**Queens** \'kwēnz\ borough of New York City on Long Island E of borough of Brooklyn

**Queen's** — see LAOIGHIS

**Queens·land** \'kwēnz-,land, -lənd\ state NE Australia; capital, Brisbane — **Queens·land·er** \-ər\ *noun*

**Que·moy** \kwi-'mói, ki-, 'kwē-,\ island E China in Taiwan Strait

**Que·ré·ta·ro** \kə-'ret-ə-,rō\ **1** state central Mexico **2** city, its capital

**Quet·ta** \'kwet-ə\ city Pakistan in N Baluchistan

**Que·zon City** \'kā-,són\ city Philippines in Luzon NE of Manila; former (1948–76) official capital of the Philippines

**Quil·mes** \'kēl-,mäs, -,mes\ city E Argentina SE of Buenos Aires

**Quin·ta·na Roo** \kēn-,tän-ə-'rō\ state SE Mexico in E Yucatán; capital, Chetumal

**Qui·to** \'kē-tō\ city, capital of Ecuador

**Qŭ·qon** \kə-'kän\ *or* **Ko·kand** \kə-'känt\ city E Uzbekistan SE of Tashkent

**Ra·bat** \rə-'bät\ city, capital of Morocco

**Rad·nor·shire** \'rad-nər-,shiər, -,nór-, -shər\ *or* **Rad·nor** former county E Wales

**Ra·dom** \'räd-,óm\ city E central Poland

**Rai·nier, Mount** \rə-'niər, rā-\ mountain 4392 meters W central Washington in **Mount Rainier National Park**; highest in Cascade Mountains

**Ra·ja·sthan** \'räj-ə-,stän\ **1** state NW India bordering on Pakistan; capital, Jaipur **2** RAJPUTANA

**Raj·kot** \'räj-,kōt\ city W India in Gujarat

**Raj·pu·ta·na** \,räj-pə-'tän-ə\ region NW India S of Punjab now largely included in Rajasthan state

**Ra·leigh** \'rò-lē, 'ral-ē\ city, capital of North Carolina

**Ran·chi** \'rän-chē\ city E India NW of Calcutta

**Rand** — see WITWATERSRAND

**Range·ley Lakes** \'rānj-lē-\ chain of lakes W Maine & N New Hampshire

**Rangoon** — see YANGON

**Rasht** \'rasht\ city NW Iran

**Rat** islands SW Alaska in W Aleutians

**Ra·wal·pin·di** \,rä-wəl-'pin-dē, ,raùl-'pin-, ,ról-'pin-\ city NE Pakistan NNW of Lahore

**Read·ing** \'red-ing\ town S England in Berkshire

**Re·ci·fe** \rə-'sē-fə\ *or formerly* **Per·nam·bu·co** \,pər-nəm-'bü-kō, -'byü-\ ,per-nəm-'bü-\ city NE Brazil

**Red** \'red\ **1** river 1638 kilometers long flowing E on Oklahoma-Texas boundary & into the Atchafalaya & the Mississippi in Louisiana **2** sea between Arabia & NE Africa

**Red·bridge** \'red-brij\ borough of NE Greater London, England

**Redwood National Park** reservation NW California

**Reg·gio** \'rej-ō, 'rej-ē-,ō\ **1** or **Reggio di Ca·la·bria** \-,dē-kə-'läb-rē-ə\ city S Italy on Strait of Messina **2** or **Reggio nel·l'Emi·lia** \-,nel-ə-'mēl-yə\ city N Italy NW of Bologna

**Re·gi·na** \ri-'jī-nə\ city, capital of Saskatchewan

**Reims** or **Rheims** \'rēmz, French 'ra\*ⁿ\*s\ city NE France

**Ren·frew** \'ren-,frü\ or **Ren·frew·shire** \-,shiər, -shər\ former county SW Scotland

**Rennes** \'ren\ city NW France

**Ré·union** \rē-'yün-yən\ island W Indian Ocean E of Madagascar; an overseas department of France; capital, Saint-Denis

**Revel** — see TALLINN

**Rey·kja·vik** \'rāk-yə-,vik, 'rāk-ə-,, -,vēk\ city, capital of Iceland

**Rey·no·sa** \rā-'nōs-ə\ city NE Mexico in Tamaulipas

**Rheinpfalz** — see PALATINATE

**Rhine** or German **Rhein** \'rīn\ or French **Rhin** \'ra\*ⁿ\* or Dutch **Rijn** \'rīn\ or ancient **Rhe·nus** \'rē-nəs\ river 1319 kilometers long W Europe flowing from SE Switzerland to North Sea in the Netherlands — **Rhen·ish** \'ren-ish, 'rē-nish\ adjective or noun

**Rhine·land** \'rīn-,land, -lənd\ or German **Rhein·land** \'rīn-,länt\ the part of Germany W of the Rhine — **Rhine·land·er** \'rīn-,lan-dər, -lən-\ noun

**Rhineland–Palatinate** or German **Rhein·land–Pfalz** \-'pfälts, -'fälts\ state W Germany chiefly W of the Rhine; capital, Mainz

**Rhode Is·land** \rō-'dī-lənd\ **1** or officially **Rhode Island and Providence Plantations** state NE U.S.; capital, Providence **2** — see AQUIDNECK ISLAND — **Rhode Is·land·er** \-lən-dər\ noun

**Rhodes** \'rōdz\ **1** island Greece in the SE Aegean; chief island of the Dodecanese **2** city, its capital

**Rhodesia** — see ZIMBABWE — **Rho·de·sian** \-zhən, -zhē-ən\ adjective or noun

**Rhon·dda** \'rän-də, 'rän-thə, 'hrän-thə\ town SE Wales

**Rhone** or French **Rhône** \'rōn\ or ancient **Rhod·a·nus** \'räd-n-əs\ river 813 kilometers long Switzerland & SE France

**Ri·bei·rão Prê·to** \,rē-və-'raüⁿ-'prā-tü\ city SE Brazil NNW of São Paulo

**Rich·mond** \'rich-mənd\ **1** — see STATEN ISLAND **2** city, capital of Virginia **3** or **Richmond upon Thames** royal borough of SW Greater London, England

**Rid·ing Mountain National Park** \,rīd-ing-\ reservation Canada in SW Manitoba

**Rift Valley** GREAT RIFT VALLEY

**Ri·ga** \'rē-gə\ city, capital of Latvia

**Ri·je·ka** or **Ri·e·ka** \rē-'ek-ə, -'yek-\ or Italian **Fiu·me** \'fyü-,mā, fē-'ü-\ city W Croatia

**Rio** \'rē-ō\ RIO DE JANEIRO

**Rio de Ja·nei·ro** \'rē-ō-,dā-zhə-'neər-ō, -,dē-, -də-, -jə-'neər-\ city SE Brazil on Guanabara Bay

**Río de Oro** \,rē-ō-dē-'ōr-ō, -'òr-\ territory NW Africa comprising S zone of Western Sahara

**Rio Grande** \,rē-ō-'grand, -'grand-ē\ or Mexican **Río Bra·vo** \-'bräv-ō\ river 3033 kilometers long SW U.S. forming part of U.S.-Mexico boundary & flowing into Gulf of Mexico

**Río Muni** — see MBINI

**Riv·er·side** \'riv-ər-,sīd\ city S California

**Riv·i·era** \,riv-ē-'er-ə\ coast region SE France & NW Italy

**Ri·yadh** \rē-'äd, -'yäd\ city, capital of Saudi Arabia

**Ro·a·noke** \'rō-ə-,nōk, 'rō-,nōk\ island North Carolina S of entrance to Albemarle Sound

**Rob·son, Mount** \'räb-sən\ mountain 3954 meters W Canada in E British Columbia; highest in the Canadian Rockies

**Roch·es·ter** \'räch-ə-stər, 'räch-,es-tər\ city W New York

**Rock·ford** \'räk-fərd\ city N Illinois

**Rocky Mountains** \,räk-ē\ mountains W North America extending SE from N Alaska to central New Mexico — see ELBERT (Mount), ROBSON (Mount)

**Rocky Mountain National Park** reservation N Colorado

**Ro·ma·nia** \rü-'mā-nē-ə, rō-\ or **Ru·ma·nia** \rü-'mā-nē-ə\ country SE Europe on Black Sea; capital, Bucharest

**Rome** \'rōm\ **1** or Italian **Ro·ma** \'rō-mä\ city, capital of Italy **2** the Roman Empire

**Ron·ces·va·lles** \,rón-səs-'vī-əs\ commune N Spain

**Roo·de·poort–Ma·rais·burg** \'rōd-ə-,pòrt-mə-'rā-,bərg, 'rō-i-,pòrt-, -,pòrt-\ city NE Republic of South Africa

**Ro·sa·rio** \rō-'zär-ē-,ō, -'sär-\ city E central Argentina

**Ros·com·mon** \rä-'skäm-ən\ county central Ireland in Connacht

**Ro·seau** \rō-'zō\ seaport, capital of Dominica

**Ross** \'ròs\ sea arm of S Pacific extending into Antarctica E of Victoria Land

**Ross and Crom·ar·ty** \'kräm-ərt-ē\ former county N Scotland

**Ros·tock** \'räs-,täk, 'rò-,stòk\ city NE Germany near Baltic coast

**Ros·tov** \rə-'stòf, -'stòv\ city S Russia in Europe, on the Don

**Rot·ter·dam** \'rät-ər-,dam\ city SW Netherlands

**Rou·baix** \rü-'bā\ city N France NE of Lille

**Rou·en** \rü-'äⁿ, rü-'äⁿn\ city N France on the Seine

**Rox·burgh** \'räks-,bər-ə, -,bə-rə, -brə\ or **Rox·burgh·shire** \-,shiər, -shər\ former county SE Scotland

**Ru·an·da–Urun·di** \rü-,än-də-ù-'rün-dē\ former trust territory E central Africa bordering on Lake Tanganyika & administered by Belgium; divided 1962 into independent nations of Burundi (formerly Urundi) & Rwanda (formerly Ruanda) — see BURUNDI, RWANDA

**Ru·dolf, Lake** \'rü-,dälf\ lake N Kenya in Great Rift Valley

**Ruhr** \'rúr\ industrial district W Germany E of the Rhine in valley of Ruhr River

**Ru·me·lia** \rü-'mēl-yə, -'mē-lē-ə\ a division of the old Ottoman Empire including Albania, Macedonia, & Thrace

**Run·ny·mede** \'rən-ē-,mēd\ meadow S England in Surrey on S bank of the Thames where Magna Charta was signed 1215

**Rupert's Land** PRINCE RUPERT'S LAND

**Ru·se** \'rü-sā\ city NE Bulgaria

**Rush·more, Mount** \'rəsh-,mōr, -,mòr\ mountain 1707 meters W South Dakota in Black Hills SW of Rapid City

**Rus·sia** \'rəsh-ə\ **1** former empire largely coextensive with later U.S.S.R.; capital, Petrograd (Saint Petersburg) **2** UNION OF SOVIET SOCIALIST REPUBLICS **3** country N Asia (**Russia in Asia**) & E Europe (**Russia in Europe**) bordering on Arctic & Pacific oceans & Baltic & Black seas; capital, Moscow; a constituent republic (**Russian Soviet Federated Socialist Republic** or **Soviet Russia**) of U.S.S.R. 1922–91

**Ru·the·nia** \rü-'thē-nyə, -nē-ə\ or **Car·pa·thi·an Ruthenia** \kär-'pā-thē-ən\ region W Ukraine W of the N Carpathians — **Ru·the·nian** \rü-'thē-nyən, -nē-ən\ adjective or noun

**Rut·land** \'rət-lənd\ or **Rut·land·shire** \-,shiər, -shər\ former county E central England

**Ru·wen·zo·ri** \,rü-ən-'zōr-ē, -'zòr-\ mountain group E central Africa between Uganda & Democratic Republic of the Congo; highest Margherita Peak (highest peak of Mount Stanley) 5109 meters

**Rwan·da** or formerly **Ru·an·da** \rü-'än-də\ country E central Africa, until 1962 part of Ruanda-Urundi trust territory; a republic; capital, Kigali — **Rwan·dan** \rü-'än-dən\ adjective or noun

**Rya·zan** \,rē-ə-'zan-yə, -'zan\ city W Russia in Europe, SE of Moscow

**Ry·binsk** \'rib-ənsk\ or formerly **Shcher·ba·kov** \,shcher-bə-'kòf, ,sher-, -'kòv\ city central Russia in Europe, NNE of Moscow

**Ryu·kyu** \rē-'ü-kyü, -'yü-, -kü\ islands W Pacific extending in an arc from Kyushu, Japan, to Taiwan, China; belong to Japan — **Ryu·kyu·an** \-kyü-ən, -kü-ən\ adjective or noun

**Saar** \'sär, 'zär\ **1** river 121 kilometers long Europe flowing from Vosges Mountains in E France into the Moselle in Germany **2** or **Saar·land** \'sär-,land, 'zär-\ district W Europe in valley of Saar River; a state of W Germany; capital, Saarbrücken

**Sa·ba** \'säb-ə\ island West Indies in Netherlands Antilles; capital, The Bottom

**Sachsen** — see SAXONY

**Sac·ra·men·to** \,sak-rə-'ment-ō\ **1** river about 515 kilometers long N California flowing S into Suisun Bay **2** city, capital of California

**Sa·ga·mi** \sə-'gäm-ē\ sea inlet of Pacific in central Honshu, Japan

**Sa·ga·mi·ha·ra** \sə-,gäm-ē-'här-ə\ city Japan on Honshu

**Sag·ue·nay** \'sag-ə-,nā, ,sag-ə-'\ river 169 kilometers long Canada in S Quebec flowing from Lake Saint John E into the Saint Lawrence

**Sa·hara** \sə-'har-ə, -'her-, -'här-\ desert region N Africa N of Sudan region extending from Atlantic coast to Red Sea, or, as sometimes considered, to the Nile — **Sa·har·an** \-ən\ adjective

**Saigon** — see HO CHI MINH CITY

**Saint Ber·nard** \,sānt-bər-'närd, -bə-\ either of two mountain passes in the Alps: the **Great Saint Bernard** (2468 meters between Italy & Switzerland E of Mont Blanc) & the **Little Saint Bernard** (2188 meters between France & Italy S of Mont Blanc)

**Saint Cath·a·rines** \'kath-rənz, -ə-rənz\ city Canada in SE Ontario

**Saint Clair, Lake** \'klaər, 'kleər\ lake SE Michigan & SE Ontario connected by **Saint Clair River** (about 65 kilometers long) with Lake Huron & draining by Detroit River into Lake Erie

**Saint Croix** \sānt-'kròi, sənt-\ **1** river 208 kilometers long Canada & U.S. on border between New Brunswick & Maine **2** island West Indies; largest of Virgin Islands of the U.S.

**Saint Eli·as, Mount** \sānt-l-'ī-əs\ mountain 5489 meters on Alaska-Canada boundary in **Saint Elias Range**

**Saint George's** \'jòr-jəz\ **1** channel British Isles between SW Wales & Ireland **2** town, capital of Grenada

**Saint Gott·hard** \sānt-'gät-ərd, -'gäth-, sənt-, ,saⁿ-gə-'tär\ **1** pass S central Switzerland in Saint Gotthard Range of the Alps **2** tunnel 15 kilometers long near the pass

**Saint He·le·na** \,sānt-l-'ē-nə, ,sānt-hə-'lē-\ island S Atlantic; a British colony; capital, Jamestown

**Saint Hel·ens** \sānt-'hel-ənz, sənt-\ town NW England in Merseyside ENE of Liverpool

**Saint Helens, Mount** volcano about 2550 meters SW Washington

**Saint John** \sānt-'jän, sənt-\ city Canada in S New Brunswick

**Saint John's** \sānt-'jänz, sənt-\ city Canada, capital of Newfoundland

**Saint Kitts** \'kits\ or **Saint Chris·to·pher** \'kris-tə-fər\ island British West Indies in the Leewards; with Nevis constitutes country of **Saint Kitts and Nevis**; capital, Basseterre (on Saint Kitts)

**Saint Law·rence** \sānt-'lòr-əns, sənt-, -'lär-\ river 1225 kilometers long E Canada in Ontario & Quebec bordering on U.S. in New York & flowing from Lake Ontario NE into the **Gulf of Saint Lawrence** (inlet of the Atlantic) **2** seaway Canada & U.S. in & along the Saint Lawrence between Lake Ontario & Montreal

**Saint Lou·is** \sānt-'lü-əs, sənt-\ city E Missouri on the Mississippi

**Saint Lu·cia** \sānt-'lü-shə, sənt-\ island British West Indies in the Windwards S of Martinique; capital, Castries

**Saint Paul** \'pòl\ city, capital of Minnesota

**Saint Pe·ters·burg** \'pēt-ərz-,bərg\ **1** city W Florida **2** or 1914–24 **Pet·ro·grad** \'pe-trə-,grad\ or 1924–91 **Le·nin·grad** \'len-ən-,grad\ city W Russia, on Gulf of Finland

**Saint Pierre** \sānt-'piər, sənt-, -pē-'eər, French saⁿ-'pyer\ **1** island in the Atlantic off S Newfoundland; with nearby island of Miquelon constitutes French territory of **Saint Pierre and Miquelon** **2** town, capital of Saint Pierre and Miquelon

**Saint Thom·as** \'täm-əs\ **1** island West Indies, one of Virgin Islands of the U.S.; chief town, Charlotte Amalie **2** — see SÃO TOMÉ

**Saint Vin·cent** \sānt-'vin-sənt, sənt-\ island British West Indies in the central Windwards; with N Grenadines constitutes independent country of **Saint Vincent and the Grenadines**; capital, Kingstown (on Saint Vincent)

**Sai·pan** \sī-'pan, -'pän, 'sī-,\ island W Pacific in S central Marianas

**Sa·kai** \sä-'kī, 'sä-\ city Japan in S Honshu on Osaka Bay

**Sa·kha·lin** \'sak-ə-ˌlēn, -lən; ˌsak-ə-'lēn\ *or formerly* **Sa·ghal·ien** \'sag-ə-ˌlēn, ˌsag-ə-'\ *or Japanese* **Ka·ra·fu·to** \kä-'räf-ə-ˌtō\ island Russia in W Pacific N of Hokkaido, Japan; until 1945 divided between Japan & U.S.S.R.

**Sal·a·man·ca** \ˌsal-ə-'mang-kə, ˌsäl-ə-'mäng-\ city W Spain

**Sal·a·mis** \'sal-ə-məs\ **1** ancient city Cyprus on E coast **2** island Greece in Saronic Gulf off Attica

**Sa·lé** \sa-'lā\ city & port NW Morocco

**Sa·lem** \'sā-ləm\ **1** city, capital of Oregon **2** city S India in N Tamil Nadu SW of Madras

**Sa·ler·no** \sə-'lər-nō, -'leər-\ city S Italy on Gulf of Salerno

**Sal·ford** \'sȯl-fərd\ city NW England in Greater Manchester

**Salisbury** — see HARARE

**Salonika** — see THESSALONÍKI

**Salop** — see SHROPSHIRE

**Sal·ta** \'säl-tə\ city NW Argentina

**Salt Lake City** city, capital of Utah

**Sal·va·dor** \'sal-və-ˌdȯr, ˌsal-və-'\ *or formerly* **São Salvador** \saü̇n-\ *or* **Ba·hia** \bä-'ē-ə\ city NE Brazil on the Atlantic — **Sal·va·dor·an** \ˌsal-və-'dȯr-ən, -'dór-\ *or* **Sal·va·do·re·an** *or* **Sal·va·do·ri·an** \-ē-ən\ *adjective or noun*

**Sal·ween** \'sal-ˌwēn\ river about 2415 kilometers long SE Asia flowing S into Gulf of Martaban in Myanmar

**Salz·burg** \'sȯlz-ˌbərg, 'sälz-, 'salz-, 'sȯlts-, -ˌbu̇rg, *German* 'zälts-ˌbu̇rk\ city W Austria

**Sa·mar** \'säm-ˌär\ island central Philippines in Visayan Islands

**Sa·ma·ra** \sə-'mär-ə\ *or 1935–91* **Kuy·by·shev** \'kwē-bə-ˌshef, 'kü-ē-, -ˌshev\ city W Russia, on the Volga

**Sa·mar·ia** \sə-'mer-ē-ə, -'mar-\ **1** district of ancient Palestine W of the Jordan between Galilee & Judea **2** ancient city, its capital & capital of the Northern Kingdom (Israel)

**Sam·a·rin·da** \ˌsam-ə-'rin-də\ city Indonesia in E Borneo

**Sam·ar·kand** \'sam-ər-ˌkand\ city E Uzbekistan

**Sam·ni·um** \'sam-nē-əm\ ancient country S central Italy SE of Latium — **Sam·nite** \'sam-ˌnīt\ *adjective or noun*

**Sa·moa** \sə-'mō-ə\ islands SW central Pacific N of Tonga Islands; divided at longitude 171° W into American, or Eastern, Samoa & Western Samoa — **Sa·mo·an** \-ən\ *adjective or noun*

**Sa·mos** \'sā-ˌmäs\ island Greece in the Aegean off coast of Turkey N of the Dodecanese — **Sa·mi·an** \-mē-ən\ *adjective or noun*

**Sam·o·thrace** \'sam-ə-ˌthrās\ island Greece in the NE Aegean

**San·aa** *or* **San·'a** \san-ˌä, sän-'ä\ city SW Arabia, capital of Yemen & formerly of Yemen Arab Republic

**San An·to·nio** \ˌsan-ən-'tō-nē-ˌō\ city S Texas

**San Ber·nar·di·no** \ˌsan-bər-nə-'dē-nō, -nər-'dē-\ city S California

**San Cris·tó·bal** \ˌsan-kris-'tō-bəl\ city W Venezuela

**Sanc·ti Spí·ri·tus** \ˌsäng-tē-'spir-ə-ˌtüs, ˌsängk-\ city W central Cuba

**San Di·ego** \ˌsan-dē-'ā-gō\ city SW California

**Sandwich Islands** — see HAWAII

**San Fran·cis·co** \ˌsan-frən-'sis-kō\ city W California

**San Isi·dro** \ˌsan-ə-'sē-drō\ city E Argentina NW of Buenos Aires

**San Joa·quin** \ˌsan-wä-'kēn, -wȯ-\ river 563 kilometers long central California flowing NW into the Sacramento

**San Jo·se** \ˌsan-ə-'zā\ city W California SE of San Francisco

**San Jo·sé** \ˌsan-ō-'zā, -ō-'zä, -hō-'zä\ city, capital of Costa Rica

**San Juan** \san-'hwän, -'wän\ city, capital of Puerto Rico

**San Lu·is Po·to·sí** \ˌsän-lü-ˌē-ˌspōt-ə-'sē\ **1** state central Mexico **2** city, its capital

**San Ma·ri·no** \ˌsan-mə-'rē-nō\ **1** country S Europe on peninsula of Italy ENE of Florence near Adriatic Sea; a republic **2** town, its capital

**San Mi·guel de Tu·cu·mán** \ˌsan-mig-ˌel-də-ˌtü-kə-'män\ *or* **Tu·cu·mán** \ˌtü-kə-'män\ city NW Argentina

**San Pe·dro Su·la** \ˌsan-ˌpā-drō-'sü-lə\ city NW Honduras

**San Sal·va·dor** \san-'sal-və-ˌdȯr\ **1** *or formerly* **Wat·lings** \'wät-lingz\ island central Bahama Islands **2** city, capital of El Salvador

**San·ta Ana** \ˌsant-ə-'an-ə\ **1** city SW California ESE of Long Beach **2** city NW El Salvador

**San·ta Bar·ba·ra** \-'bär-brə, -bə-rə\ *or* **Channel** islands California in the Pacific off SW coast

**San·ta Clara** \-'klar-ə, -'kler-ə\ city W central Cuba

**San·ta Cla·ri·ta** \ˌklə-'rēt-ə\ city S California

**San·ta Cruz** \-'krüz\ city E Bolivia

**San·ta Cruz de Te·ne·rife** \-də-ˌten-ə-'rēf-ā, -'rēf, -'rif\ city Spain in W Canary Islands on Tenerife Island

**San·ta Fe** \ˌsant-ə-'fā\ **1** city, capital of New Mexico **2** city central Argentina

**Santa Fe Trail** pioneer route to the Southwest about 1930 kilometers long used especially 1821–80 from vicinity of Kansas City, Missouri, to Santa Fe, New Mexico

**Santa Isabel** — see MALABO

**San·ta Mar·ta** \ˌsant-ə-'märt-ə\ city N Colombia

**San·tan·der** \ˌsän-ˌtän-'deər, ˌsan-ˌtan-\ city N Spain WNW of Bilbao

**San·ti·a·go** \ˌsant-ē-'äg-ō, ˌsänt-\ **1** city, capital of Chile **2** *or* **Santiago de los Ca·ba·lle·ros** \-də-ˌlōs-ˌkäb-ə-'yeər-ōs\ city N central Dominican Republic

**Santiago de Cu·ba** \-də-'kyü-bə\ city SE Cuba

**San·to Do·min·go** \ˌsant-əd-ə-'ming-gō\ **1** — see HISPANIOLA **2** — see DOMINICAN REPUBLIC **3** *or formerly* **Ciu·dad Tru·ji·llo** \sē-ü-ˌthä-trü-'hē-ō, ˌsē-ü-ˌdad-\ city, capital of Dominican Republic

**San·tos** \'sant-əs\ city SE Brazil

**São Lu·ís** \ˌsaü̇n-lü-'ēs\ city NE Brazil on Maranhão Island

**Saône** \'sōn\ river E France flowing into the Rhone

**São Pau·lo** \saü̇n-'paú-lü, saü̇nm-, -lō\ city SE Brazil

**São Salvador** — see SALVADOR

**São To·mé** *or* **São Tho·mé** \ˌsaü̇nt-ə-'mā, ˌsaü̇nt-\ *or* **Saint Thom·as** \sänt-'täm-əs\ island W Africa in Gulf of Guinea; with Príncipe Island, forms republic of **São Tomé and Príncipe** capital, São Tomé; until 1975 a Portuguese colony

**Sap·po·ro** \'säp-ə-ˌrō; sə-'pōr-ō, -'pȯr-\ city Japan on W Hokkaido

**Saragossa** — see ZARAGOZA

**Sa·ra·je·vo** \ˌsär-ə-ye-ˌvȯ\ city, capital of Bosnia and Herzegovina

**Sa·ransk** \sə-'ränsk, -'ransk\ city central Russia in Europe

**Sa·ra·tov** \sə-'rät-əf\ city S central Russia in Europe, on the Volga

**Sar·din·ia** \sär-'din-ē-ə, -'din-yə\ island Italy in the Mediterranean S of Corsica; a region; capital, Cagliari — **Sar·din·ian** \-'din-ē-ən, -'din-yən\ *adjective or noun*

**Sar·dis** \'särd-əs\ ancient city W Asia Minor, capital of Lydia

**Sar·gas·so Sea** \sär-ˌgas-ō-\ area of comparatively still water in the N Atlantic lying chiefly between 25° & 35° N latitude & 40° & 70° W longitude

**Sa·ron·ic Gulf** \sə-ˌrän-ik-\ inlet of the Aegean SE Greece between Attica & the Peloponnese

**Sas·katch·e·wan** \sə-'skach-ə-wən, sa-, -ˌwän\ province W Canada; capital, Regina

**Sas·ka·toon** \ˌsas-kə-'tün\ city Canada in central Saskatchewan

**Sas·sa·ri** \'säs-ə-rē\ city Italy in NW Sardinia

**Sau·di Arabia** \ˌsau̇d-ē-ə-'rā-bē-ə, ˌsȯd-ē-, säˌu̇d-ē-\ country SW Asia occupying largest part of Arabian Peninsula; a kingdom; capital, Riyadh — **Saudi** *adjective or noun* — **Saudi Arabian** *adjective or noun*

**Sault Sainte Ma·rie Canals** \ˌsü-ˌsänt-mə-'rē\ *or* **Soo Canals** \ˌsü-\ three ship canals, two in U.S. (Michigan) & one in Canada (Ontario), at rapids in Saint Marys River connecting Lake Superior & Lake Huron

**Sa·vaii** \sə-'vī-ˌē\ island, largest in Western Samoa

**Sa·van·nah** \sə-'van-ə\ city E Georgia

**Sa·voy** \sə-'vȯi\ *or French* **Sa·voie** \sȧ-'vwȧ\ region SE France SW of Switzerland bordering on Italy — **Sa·voy·ard** \sə-'vȯi-ˌärd, ˌsav-ˌȯi-'ärd; ˌsav-ˌwä-'yär, -'yärd\ *adjective or noun*

**Sax·o·ny** \'sak-sə-nē, 'sak-snē\ *or German* **Sach·sen** \'zäk-sən\ region & former state E Germany N of the Erzgebirge — see LOWER SAXONY

**Sca·fell Pike** \skȯ-'fel\ mountain 978 meters NW England in Cumbria; highest in Cumbrian Mountains & in England

**Scan·di·na·via** \ˌskan-də-'nā-vē-ə, -vyə\ **1** peninsula N Europe occupied by Norway & Sweden **2** Denmark, Norway, Sweden, & sometimes also Iceland & Finland

**Scar·bor·ough** \'skär-ˌbər-ə, -ˌbə-rə, -bər-ə, -brə\ city Canada in SE Ontario

**Scheldt** \'skelt\ *or* **Schel·de** \'skel-də\ *or French* **Es·caut** \es-kō\ *or ancient* **Scal·dis** \'skal-dəs\ river 434 kilometers long W Europe flowing from N France through Belgium into North Sea in Netherlands

**Schleswig–Hol·stein** \ˌshles-wig-'hōl-ˌstīn, ˌsles-, -vik-'hȯl-\ state N Germany consisting of Holstein & part of Schleswig; capital, Kiel

**Schwarzwald** — see BLACK FOREST

**Schweiz** — see SWITZERLAND

**Scil·ly** \'sil-ē\ islands SW England off Land's End in county of Cornwall and Isles of Scilly

**Sco·tia** \'skō-shə\ SCOTLAND — the Medieval Latin name

**Scot·land** \'skät-lənd\ *or Latin* **Cal·e·do·nia** \ˌkal-ə-'dō-nyə, -nē-ə\ country N Great Britain; a division of United Kingdom of Great Britain and Northern Ireland; capital, Edinburgh

**Scran·ton** \'skrant-n\ city NE Pennsylvania

**Scyth·ia** \'sith-ē-ə, 'sith-\ ancient country comprising parts of Europe & Asia in regions N & NE of Black Sea & E of Aral Sea — **Scyth·i·an** \-ē-ən\ *adjective or noun*

**Se·at·tle** \sē-'at-l\ city W Washington

**Seine** \'sān, 'sen\ river 776 kilometers long N France flowing NW into English Channel

**Sel·kirk** \'sel-ˌkərk\ **1** range of the Rocky Mountains SE British Columbia; highest peak, Mount Sir Sandford 3522 meters **2** *or* **Sel·kirk·shire** \-ˌshiər, -shər\ former county SE Scotland

**Se·ma·rang** \sə-'mär-ˌäng\ city Indonesia in central Java

**Se·mey** \'sem-ā\ *or* **Sem·i·pa·la·tinsk** \ˌsem-i-pə-'lä-ˌtinsk\ city NE Kazakhstan

**Sen·dai** \sen-'dī, 'sen-\ city Japan in NE Honshu

**Sen·e·gal** \ˌsen-i-'gȯl\ **1** river 1633 kilometers long W Africa flowing W into the Atlantic **2** country W Africa; a republic; capital, Dakar — **Sen·e·ga·lese** \ˌsen-i-gə-'lēz, -'lēs\ *adjective or noun*

**Seoul** \'sōl\ city, capital of South Korea

**Se·quoia National Park** \si-'kwȯi-ə\ reservation SE central California; includes Mount Whitney

**Seram** — see CERAM

**Ser·bia** \'sər-bē-ə\ region Balkan Peninsula; capital, Belgrade; with Montenegro constitutes Yugoslavia

**Ser·en·ge·ti Plain** \ˌser-ən-'get-ē\ area N Tanzania including **Serengeti National Park**

**Se·te Que·das** \ˌsāt-ə-'kā-thəsh\ *or formerly* **Guaí·ra** *or* **Guay·ra** \gwī-'rä\ former cataract in Alto Paraná on Brazil-Paraguay boundary; now submerged in dam-created lake

**Se·vas·to·pol** \si-'vas-tə-ˌpōl, -ˌpȯl, -pəl; ˌsev-ə-'stō-pəl, -'stȯl-\ city SW Crimea

**Sev·ern** \'sev-ərn\ river 290 kilometers long Wales & England flowing from E central Wales into Bristol Channel

**Se·ville** \sə-'vil\ *or Spanish* **Se·vi·lla** \sā-'vē-ä, -yä\ *or ancient* **His·pa·lis** \'his-pə-ləs\ city SW Spain

**Sey·chelles** \sā-'shel, -'shelz\ islands W Indian Ocean NE of Madagascar; formerly a British colony; became independent 1976; capital, Victoria (on Mahé Island)

**'s Gravenhage** — see HAGUE (The)

**Shaan·xi** \'shän-'shē\ *or* **Shen·si** \'shen-'sē, 'shən-'shē\ province N central China; capital, Xi'an

**Shan·dong** \'shän-'dȯng\ *or* **Shan·tung** \'shan-'təng\ **1** peninsula E China extending into Yellow Sea **2** province E China including Shandong Peninsula; capital, Jinan

**Shang·hai** \shang-'hī\ city E China in SE Jiangsu

**Shan·non** \'shan-ən\ river 370 kilometers long W Ireland flowing S & W into the Atlantic

**Shan·tou** \'shän-'tō\ *or* **Swa·tow** \'swä-'taü\ city SE China in E Guangdong

**Shan·xi** \'shän-'shē\ *or* **Shan·si** \'shän-'sē, -'shē\ province N China bordering on Yellow River; capital, Taiyuan

**Shas·ta, Mount** \'shas-tə\ mountain 4317 meters N California in Cascade Range

**Shatt al Ar·ab** \,shat-,al-'ar-əb\ river 193 kilometers long SE Iraq formed by confluence of Euphrates & Tigris rivers & flowing SE into Persian Gulf

**Shcherbakov** — see RYBINSK

**She·ba** \'shē-bə\ ancient country S Arabia

**She·chem** \'shē-kəm, -,kem\ ancient city central Palestine in Samaria; site at present city of Nābulus in Jordan

**Shef·field** \'shef-,ēld\ city N England in South Yorkshire

**Shen·an·do·ah National Park** \,shen-ən-'dō-ə, ,shan-ə-'dō-ə\ reservation N Virginia in Blue Ridge Mountains

**Shen·yang** \'shən-'yäng\ or **Muk·den** \'mùk-dən, 'mək-; 'mùk-'den\ or formerly **Feng·tien** \'fəng-tē-'en\ city NE China, capital of Liaoning

**Sher·wood Forest** \,shər-,wùd-\ ancient royal forest central England chiefly in Nottinghamshire

**Shet·land** \'shet-lənd\ **1** islands N Scotland NE of the Orkneys **2** or **Zet·land** \'zet-\ county comprising the Shetland Islands

**Shi·jia·zhuang** or **Shih–chia–chuang** or **Shih·kia·chwang** \'shiər-jē-'äj'wäng, 'shē-jē-\ city NE China, capital of Hebei

**Shi·ko·ku** \shi-'kō-kü\ island S Japan E of Kyushu

**Shi·raz** \shi-'räz\ city SW Iran

**Shi·zu·o·ka** \shiz-ə-'wō-kə, ,shē-zə-'ō-kə\ city Japan in central Honshu SW of Tokyo

**Sho·la·pur** \'shō-lə-,pùr\ city W India in SE Maharashtra SE of Bombay

**Shreve·port** \'shrēv-,pōrt, -,pórt\ city NW Louisiana

**Shrop·shire** \'shräp-shər, -,shir\ or officially 1974–80 **Sal·op** \'sal-əp, -,äp\ county W England bordering on Wales

**Shushan** — see SUSA

**Si·al·kot** \sē-'äl-,kōt\ city NE Pakistan NNE of Lahore

**Siam** — see THAILAND

**Siam, Gulf of** — see THAILAND (Gulf of)

**Sian** — see XI'AN

**Siangtan** — see XIANGTAN

**Si·be·ria** \sī-'bir-ē-ə\ region N Asia in Russia between the Urals & the Pacific — **Si·be·ri·an** \-ē-ən\ adjective or noun

**Si·chuan** \'sē-'chwän\ or **Sze·chwan** \'sech-'wän, 'sesh-\ province SW China; capital, Chengdu

**Sic·i·ly** \'sis-ə-lē, 'sis-lē\ or Italian **Si·ci·lia** \sē-'chēl-yä\ island S Italy SW of toe of peninsula of Italy; a region; capital, Palermo — **Si·cil·ian** \sə-'sil-yən\ adjective or noun

**Si·er·ra Le·one** \sē-,er-ə-lē-'ōn, ,sir-ə-\ country W Africa on the Atlantic; a dominion of the Commonwealth; capital, Freetown — **Si·er·ra Le·on·ean** \-'ō-nē-ən\ adjective or noun

**Si·er·ra Ma·dre** \sē-,er-ə-'mäd-rē\ mountain system Mexico including **Sierra Madre Oc·ci·den·tal** \-,äk-sə-,den-'täl\ range W of the central plateau, **Sierra Madre Ori·en·tal** \-,ōr-ē-,en-'täl, -,ór-\ range E of the plateau, & **Sierra del Sur** \sē-,er-ə-,del-'sùr\ range to the S

**Sierra Ne·vada** \-nə-'vad-ə, -'väd-\ **1** mountain range E California & W Nevada — see WHITNEY (Mount) **2** mountain range S Spain; highest peak Mulhacén 3477 meters, highest in Spain

**Sik·kim** \'sik-əm, -,im\ region SE Asia on S slope of the Himalaya between Nepal & Bhutan; a state of Republic of India since 1975; capital, Gangtok

**Si·le·sia** \sī-'lē-zhə, sə-, -zhē-ə, -shə, shē-ə\ region E central Europe in valley of the upper Oder bordering on Sudeten Mountains; formerly chiefly in Germany now chiefly in NE Czech Republic & SW Poland — **Si·le·sian** \-zhən, -shən\ adjective or noun

**Sim·birsk** \sim-'birsk\ or 1924–91 **Ul·ya·novsk** \ül-'yän-əfsk\ city central Russia in Europe

**Sim·coe, Lake** \'sim-kō\ lake Canada in SE Ontario

**Sim·fe·ro·pol** \,sim-fə-'rò-pəl, ,simp-, -'rō-\ city S central Crimea Peninsula

**Sim·la** \'sim-lə\ town N India, capital of Himachal Pradesh

**Sim·plon** \'sim-,plän\ **1** pass between Italy & Switzerland in Lepontine Alps **2** tunnel 19.8 kilometers long near the pass

**Si·nai** \'sī-,nī\ **1** — see HOREB **2** peninsula extension of continent of Asia NE Egypt between Red Sea & the Mediterranean

**Si·na·loa** \,sē-nə-'lō-ə, ,sin-ə-\ state W Mexico on Gulf of California; capital, Culiacán

**Sind** \'sind\ province S Pakistan in lower Indus River valley; chief city Karachi

**Sin·ga·pore** \'sing-ə-,pōr, -gə-, -,pór\ **1** island off S end of Malay Peninsula; a republic in the Commonwealth **2** city, its capital — **Sin·ga·por·ean** \,sing-ə-'pōr-ē-ən, -gə-, -'pór-\ adjective or noun

**Sining** — see XINING

**Sinkiang–Uighur** — see XINJIANG UYGUR

**Sion** — see ZION

**Siracusa** — see SYRACUSE

**Sjæl·land** \'shel-,än\ or **Zea·land** \'zē-lənd\ island, largest of islands of Denmark; site of Copenhagen

**Skag·ge·rak** \'skag-ə-,rak\ arm of North Sea between S Norway & N Denmark

**Skop·je** \'skóp-yā\ city N Macedonia

**Sky·ros** \'skī-rəs, -,räs\ or Greek **Skí·ros** \'skē-,rós\ island Greece in Northern Sporades E of Euboea

**Sla·vo·nia** \slə-'vō-nē-ə, -nyə\ region E Croatia between Sava, Drava, & Danube rivers — **Sla·vo·nian** \-ne-ən, -nyən\ adjective or noun

**Sli·go** \'slī-gō\ county N Ireland (republic) in Connacht

**Slo·va·kia** \slō-'väk-ē-ə, -'vak-\ country central Europe; capital, Bratislava

**Slo·ve·nia** \slō-'vē-nē-ə, -nyə\ country S Europe N & W of Croatia; formerly a constituent republic of Yugoslavia; capital, Ljubljana — **Slo·ve·nian** \-nē-ən, -nyən\ adjective or noun

**Smo·lensk** \smō-'lensk\ city W Russia in Europe, WSW of Moscow

**Smyrna** — see IZMIR

**Snow·don** \'snōd-n\ massif 1085 meters NW Wales; highest point in Wales

**Snow·do·nia** \snō-'dō-nē-ə, -nyə\ mountainous district NW Wales centering around Snowdon

**So·chi** \'sō-chē\ city S Russia in Europe, on Black Sea

**So·ci·e·ty** \sə-'sī-ət-ē\ islands S Pacific in French Polynesia; capital, Papeete (on Tahiti)

**So·co·tra** \sə-'kō-trə\ island Yemen in Indian Ocean E of Gulf of Aden; capital, Tamridah

**So·fia** \'sō-fē-ə, 'sò-, 'sō-'\ city, capital of Bulgaria

**So·ho** \'sō-,hō\ district of central London, England, in Westminster

**So·li·hull** \,sō-li-'həl\ town central England in West Midlands

**Sol·o·mon** \'säl-ə-mən\ **1** islands W Pacific E of New Guinea divided between Papua New Guinea & British Solomon Islands **2** sea arm of Coral Sea W of the Solomons

**So·ma·lia** \sō-'mäl-ē-ə, sə-, -'mäl-yə\ or **So·ma·li Republic** \-'mäl-ē\ country E Africa on Gulf of Aden & Indian Ocean; a republic; capital, Mogadishu — **So·ma·li·an** \-'mäl-ē-ən, -'mäl-yən\ adjective or noun

**So·ma·li·land** \sō-'mäl-ē-,land, sə-\ region E Africa comprising Somalia, Djibouti, & part of E Ethiopia

**Som·er·set** \'səm-ər-,set, -sət\ or **Som·er·set·shire** \-,shiər, -shər\ county SW England

**Somerset Nile** — see NILE

**Song·nam** \'sòng-'näm\ city NW South Korea

**So·no·ra** \sə-'nōr-ə, -'nór-\ state NW Mexico bordering on U.S.; capital, Hermosillo

**So·nor·an** \sə-'nōr-ən, -'nór-\ or **Sonora** desert SW U.S. & NW Mexico in S Arizona, SE California, & N Sonora

**Soo Canals** — see SAULT SAINTE MARIE CANALS

**Soochow** — see SUZHOU

**Sorata** — see ILLAMPU

**So·ro·ca·ba** \,sōr-ə-'kab-ə, ,sòr-\ city SE Brazil W of São Paulo

**Sos·no·wiec** \säs-'nō-,vyets\ city SW Poland

**South** \'saùth\ island S New Zealand

**South Africa, Republic of** country S Africa; an independent republic; until 1961 (as **Union of South Africa**) a British dominion; administrative capital, Pretoria; legislative capital, Cape Town; judicial capital, Bloemfontein

**South America** continent of western hemisphere SE of North America & chiefly S of the equator — **South American** adjective or noun

**South·amp·ton** \saùth-'am-tən, -'ham-, -'amp-, -'hamp-\ city S England in Hampshire

**South Australia** state S Australia; capital, Adelaide — **South Australian** adjective or noun

**South Bend** \'bend\ city N Indiana

**South Cape** or **South Point** — see KA LAE

**South Car·o·li·na** \,kar-ə-'lī-nə\ state SE U.S.; capital, Columbia — **South Car·o·lin·i·an** \-'lin-ē-ən, -'lin-yən\ adjective or noun

**South China Sea** — see CHINA

**South Da·ko·ta** \də-'kōt-ə\ state NW central U.S.; capital, Pierre — **South Da·ko·tan** \-'kōt-n\ adjective or noun

**South·end–on–Sea** \,saù-,thend-än-'sē, -ón-\ resort SE England in Essex E of London

**Southern Alps** mountain range New Zealand in W South Island extending almost the length of the island

**Southern Rhodesia** — see ZIMBABWE

**Southern Yemen** — see YEMEN

**South Gla·mor·gan** \glə-'mòr-gən\ county SE Wales; established 1974; includes Cardiff

**South Korea** — see KOREA

**South Seas** the areas of the Atlantic, Indian, & Pacific oceans in the southern hemisphere; especially, the S Pacific

**South Shields** \'shēldz, 'shēlz\ city N England in Tyne and Wear

**South Tirol** — see ALTO ADIGE

**South Vietnam** — see VIETNAM

**South·wark** \'səth-ərk, 'saùth-wərk\ borough of S Greater London, England

**South–West Africa** — see NAMIBIA

**South York·shire** \'yórk-,shiər, -shər\ metropolitan county N England

**Soviet Central Asia** formerly used name for the portion of central & SW Asia belonging to U.S.S.R. & comprising the Kirgiz, Tadzhik, Turkmen, & Uzbek republics and sometimes thought to include all or part of Kazakh Republic also

**Soviet Russia 1** — see RUSSIA **2** — see UNION OF SOVIET SOCIALIST REPUBLICS

**Soviet Union** — see UNION OF SOVIET SOCIALIST REPUBLICS

**Spain** \'spān\ or Spanish **Es·pa·ña** \ā-'spän-yä\ or ancient **His·pa·nia** \his-'pān-ē-ə, -'pän-yə, -'pan-\ country SW Europe in Iberian Peninsula; a kingdom; capital, Madrid

**Spanish America 1** the Spanish-speaking countries of America **2** the parts of America settled & formerly governed by the Spanish

**Spanish Guinea** — see EQUATORIAL GUINEA

**Spanish Main** \'mān\ **1** the mainland of Spanish America especially along N coast of South America **2** the Caribbean Sea & adjacent waters especially when region was infested with pirates

**Spanish Morocco** — see MOROCCO

**Spanish Sahara** former Spanish territory NW Africa SW of Morocco comprising Río de Oro & Saguia el Hamra — see WESTERN SAHARA

**Spar·ta** \'spärt-ə\ or **Lac·e·dae·mon** \,las-ə-'dē-mən\ ancient city S Greece in Peloponnese, capital of Laconia

**Spey·er** \'shpī-ər, 'spī-; 'shpīr, 'spīr\ or **Spires** \'spīrz\ city SW Germany on Rhine N of Karlsruhe

**Spice Islands** — see MOLUCCAS

**Spits·ber·gen** \'spits-,bər-gən\ islands in Arctic Ocean N of Norway; chief island, West Spitsbergen — see SVALBARD

**Split** \'split\ or **Spljet** \'spl'yet, splē-'et\ or Italian **Spa·la·to** \'späl-ə-,tō\ city S Croatia

**Spo·kane** \spō-'kan\ city E Washington

**Spor·a·des** \'spòr-ə-,dēz, 'spär-\ two island groups Greece in the Aegean: the **Northern Sporades** (chief island, Skyros, E of Euboea) & **Southern Sporades** (including Samos, Icaria, & the Dodecanese, off SW Turkey)

**Spring·field** \'spring-,fēld\ **1** city, capital of Illinois **2** city SW Massachusetts **3** city SW Missouri

**Springs** \'springz\ city NE Republic of South Africa

**Sri Lan·ka** \srē-'läng-kə, 'srē-\ or formerly **Cey·lon** \si-'län, sā-\ country coextensive with island of Ceylon; an independent republic in the Commonwealth; capital, Colombo

**Sri·na·gar** \sri-'nəg-ər\ city, summer capital of Jammu and Kashmir, in W Kashmir on Jhelum River

**Staf·ford·shire** \'staf-ərd-,shiər, -shər\ or **Stafford** county W central England

**Staked Plain** — see LLANO ESTACADO

**Sta·kha·nov** \stə-'kän-əf\ or formerly **Ka·di·yev·ka** \kə-'dē-yəf-kə\ city E Ukraine in Donets Basin

**Stalingrad** — see VOLGOGRAD

**Stam·ford** \'stam-fərd, 'stamp-\ city SW Connecticut

---

\ə\ abut \ᵊ\ kitten \ər\ further \a\ ash \ā\ ace \ä\ mop, mar \aù\ out \ch\ chin \e\ bet \ē\ easy \g\ go \i\ hit \ī\ ice \j\ job \ŋ\ sing \ō\ go \ó\ law \ói\ boy \th\ thin \th\ the \ü\ loot \ù\ foot \y\ yet \zh\ vision    *see also* Guide to Pronunciation

**Stan·ley** \'stan-lē\ town, capital of Falkland Islands
**Stanley, Mount** — see RUWENZORI
**Stanleyville** — see KISANGANI
**Stat·en Island** \'stat-n\ **1** island SE New York SW of mouth of the Hudson **2** or formerly **Rich·mond** \'rich-mənd\ borough of New York City including Staten Island
**States of the Church** or **Papal States** temporal domain of the popes in central Italy 755–1870
**Stavropol** — see TOL'YATTI
**Stir·ling** \'stər-liŋ\ or **Stir·ling·shire** \-,shiər, -shər\ former county central Scotland
**Stock·holm** \'stäk-,hōlm, -,hōm\ city, capital of Sweden
**Stock·port** \'stäk-,pōrt, -,pòrt\ town NW England in Greater Manchester
**Stock·ton** \'stäk-tən\ city central California
**Stoke on Trent** \,stō-kón-'trent, -,kän-\ city central England in Staffordshire
**Stone·henge** \'stōn-,henj, stōn-'henj\ assemblage of megaliths S England in Wiltshire on Salisbury Plain; erected by a prehistoric people
**Stone Mountain** mountain 514 meters NW Georgia E of Atlanta
**Straits Settlements** former British crown colony SE Asia on Strait of Malacca comprising Singapore Island & George Town & Malacca settlements on Malay Peninsula
**Stras·bourg** \'sträs-,bùrg, 'sträz-, -,bərg\ city NE France
**Strat·ford–upon–Avon** \'strat-fərd\ town central England in Warwickshire
**Strath·clyde** \strath-'klīd\ region SW Scotland; includes Glasgow
**Strom·bo·li** \'sträm-bə-lē\ volcano 926 meters Italy in Lipari Islands on Stromboli Island
**Stutt·gart** \'shtùt-,gärt, 'stùt-, -,stət-\ city SW Germany, capital of Baden-Württemberg
**Styr·ia** \'stir-ē-ə\ region central & SE Austria; capital, Graz
**Styx** \'stiks\ chief river of Hades in Greek mythology
**Süchow** **1** — see XUZHOU **2** — see YIBIN
**Su·cre** \'sü-krā\ city, constitutional capital of Bolivia
**Su·dan** \sü-'dan, -'dän\ **1** region N Africa S of the Sahara between the Atlantic & the upper Nile **2** country NE Africa S of Egypt; a republic; capital, Khartoum — see ANGLO-EGYPTIAN SUDAN — **Su·da·nese** \,süd-n-'ēz, -'ēs\ adjective or noun
**Su·de·ten** \sü-'dāt-n\ **1** mountains central Europe between Czech Republic & Poland **2** or **Su·de·ten·land** \sü-'dāt-n-,land\ region NE Czech Republic in Sudeten Mountains
**Su·ez** \sü-'ez, 'sü-,ez\ **1** city NE Egypt at S end of Suez Canal on **Gulf of Suez** (arm of Red Sea) **2** canal 163 kilometers long NE Egypt across Isthmus of Suez
**Suez, Isthmus of** neck of land NE Egypt between Mediterranean & Red seas connecting Africa & Asia
**Suf·folk** \'səf-ək\ county E England on North Sea
**Su·i·ta** \sü-'ēt-ə\ city Japan in S Honshu N of Osaka
**Su·la·we·si** \,sü-lə-'wä-sē\ or **Ce·le·bes** \'sel-ə-,bēz, sə-'lē-bēz\ island Indonesia E of Borneo
**Su·lu** \'sü-lü\ archipelago SW Philippines SW of Mindanao — see BASILAN
**Su·ma·tra** \sü-'mä-trə\ island W Indonesia S of Malay Peninsula — **Su·ma·tran** \-trən\ adjective or noun
**Su·mer** \'sü-mər\ the S division of ancient Babylonia — **Su·me·ri·an** \sü-'mer-ē-ən, -'mir-\ adjective or noun
**Sun·da** \'sün-də\ **1** islands Malay Archipelago comprising the **Greater Sunda Islands** (Sumatra, Borneo, Java, Sulawesi, & adjacent islands) & the **Lesser Sunda Islands** (extending from Bali to Timor); with exception of N Borneo belongs to Indonesia **2** strait between Java & Sumatra
**Sun·der·land** \'sən-dər-lənd\ seaport N England in Tyne and Wear
**Suomi** or **Suomen Tasavalta** — see FINLAND
**Su·pe·ri·or, Lake** \sù-'pir-ē-ər\ lake E central North America in U.S. & Canada; largest of the Great Lakes
**Su·ra·ba·ya** \,sùr-ə-'bī-ə\ city Indonesia in NE Java
**Su·ra·kar·ta** \,sùr-ə-'kärt-ə\ city Indonesia in central Java
**Su·rat** \'sùr-ət, sə-'rat\ city W India in SE Gujarat
**Su·ri·na·me** \,sùr-ə-'näm-ə\ or **Su·ri·nam** \'sùr-ə-,nam, ,sùr-ə-'näm\ or formerly **Dutch Guiana** country N South America between Guyana & French Guiana; capital, Paramaribo

**Sur·rey** \'sər-ē, 'sə-rē\ **1** county SE England SW of London **2** city Canada in SW British Columbia
**Su·sa** \'sü-zə\ or biblical **Shu·shan** \'shü-shən, -,shan\ ancient city, capital of Elam; ruins in SW Iran
**Sus·sex** \'səs-iks\ former county SE England on English Channel — see EAST SUSSEX, WEST SUSSEX
**Suth·er·land** \'səth-ər-lənd\ or **Suth·er·land·shire** \-,shiər, -shər\ former county N Scotland
**Sut·ton** \'sət-n\ borough of S Greater London, England
**Su·va** \'sü-və\ city, capital of Fiji on Viti Levu Island
**Su·won** \'sü-,wän\ city NW South Korea S of Seoul
**Su·zhou** \'sü-'jō\ or **Soo·chow** \'sü-jō, -'chaù\ or formerly **Wu·hsien** \'wü-shē-'en\ city E China in Jiangsu W of Shanghai
**Sval·bard** \'sfäl-,bär\ islands in Arctic Ocean including Spitsbergen & Bear Island; under Norwegian administration
**Sverdlovsk** — see YEKATERINBURG
**Swan·sea** \'swän-zē\ city SE Wales
**Swatow** — see SHANTOU
**Swa·zi·land** \'swäz-ē-,land\ country SE Africa between Republic of South Africa & Mozambique; an independent kingdom; capital, Mbabane — **Swa·zi** \'swäz-ē\ adjective or noun
**Swe·den** \'swēd-n\ country N Europe on Scandinavian Peninsula bordering on Baltic Sea; a kingdom; capital, Stockholm
**Swit·zer·land** \'swit-sər-lənd\ or Latin **Hel·ve·tia** \hel-'vē-shə, -shē-ə\ or French **Suisse** \'swēēs\ or German **Schweiz** \shfīts\ or Italian **Sviz·ze·ra** \'zvēt-sä-rä\ country W Europe in the Alps; a republic; capital, Bern
**Syd·ney** \'sid-nē\ city SE Australia, capital of New South Wales
**Syr·a·cuse** \'sir-ə-,kyüs, -,kyüz\ **1** city central New York **2** ancient city Italy in SE Sicily; site at modern city of **Si·ra·cu·sa** \,sē-rə-'kü-zə\
**Syr·ia** \'sir-ē-ə\ **1** ancient region SW Asia bordering on the Mediterranean **2** former French mandate (1920–44) including present Syria & Lebanon **3** country S of Turkey; a republic; capital, Damascus — **Syr·i·an** \'sir-ē-ən\ adjective or noun
**Syrian Desert** desert region N Saudi Arabia, SE Syria, W Iraq, & NE Jordan
**Szcze·cin** \'shchet-,sēn\ city NW Poland on the Oder
**Szechwan** — see SICHUAN
**Ta·bas·co** \tə-'bas-kō\ state SE Mexico SW of Yucatán Peninsula; capital, Villahermosa
**Ta·ble Bay** \tā-bəl-\ harbor of Cape Town, Republic of South Africa
**Ta·briz** \tə-'brēz\ city NW Iran
**Ta·co·ma** \tə-'kō-mə\ city W Washington
**Tae·gu** \ta-'gü, tī-\ city South Korea NNW of Pusan
**Tae·jon** \ta-'jòn, tī-\ city South Korea NW of Taegu
**Ta·gan·rog** \'tag-ən-,räg\ city SW Russia in Europe, W of Rostov
**Ta·gus** \'tā-gəs\ or Spanish **Ta·jo** \'tä-hō\ or Portuguese **Te·jo** \'tä-zhü\ river 1007 kilometers long Spain & Portugal flowing W into the Atlantic
**Ta·hi·ti** \tə-'hēt-ē\ island S Pacific in French Polynesia in Society Islands; chief town, Papeete — **Ta·hi·tian** \-'hē-shən\ adjective or noun
**Tai·chung** \'tī-'chùŋ\ city China in W Taiwan
**Tai·nan** \'tī-'nän\ city China in SW Taiwan
**Tai·pei** \'tī-'pā, -'bā\ or formerly **Dai·ho·ku** \'dī-'hō-,kü\ city, capital of (Nationalist) Republic of China in N Taiwan
**Tai·wan** \'tī-'wän\ or **For·mo·sa** \fòr-'mō-sə, fər-, -zə\ **1** island China off SE coast; since 1949 seat of government of (Nationalist) Republic of China; capital, Taipei **2** strait between Taiwan & China mainland connecting East China & South China seas — **Tai·wan·ese** \,tī-wə-'nēz, -'nēs\ adjective or noun
**Tai·yuan** \'tī-yü-'än\ or formerly **Yang·ku** \'yäŋ-'kü\ city N China, capital of Shanxi
**Tai·zhou** or **T'ai–chou** \'tī-'jō\ city E China in central Jiangsu NW of Shanghai
**Ta·jik·i·stan** \tä-'jik-i-,stan, -'jēk-\ country W central Asia; capital, Dushanbe; a constituent republic (**Ta·dzhik·i·stan** \same\ or **Ta·dzhik Soviet Socialist Republic** \tä-'jik, -'jēk\) of U.S.S.R. 1929–91
**Ta·ka·ma·tsu** \,täk-ə-'mät-sü, tä-'käm-ət-,sü\ city Japan in NE Shikoku
**Ta·kat·su·ki** \tə-'kät-sü-kē\ city Japan in S Honshu NNE of Osaka
**Ta·kli·ma·kan** or **Ta·kla Ma·kan** \,täk-lə-mə-'kän\ desert W China in Xinjiang Uygur

**Ta·lien** — see DALIAN
**Tal·la·has·see** \,tal-ə-'has-ē\ city, capital of Florida
**Tal·linn** \'tal-ən, 'täl-\ or formerly **Re·vel** \'rā-vəl\ city, capital of Estonia
**Ta·mau·li·pas** \,täm-,aù-'lē-pəs, təm-\ state NE Mexico; capital, Ciudad Victoria
**Tam·bov** \täm-'bòf, -'bòv\ city S central Russia in Europe, SE of Moscow
**Tam·il Na·du** \,tam-əl-'näd-ü\ or formerly **Ma·dras** \mə-'dras, -'dräs\ state S India on Bay of Bengal; capital, Madras
**Tam·pa** \'tam-pə\ city W Florida on Tampa Bay
**Tam·pe·re** \'tam-pə-,rä, 'täm-\ city SW Finland
**Tam·pi·co** \tam-'pē-kō\ city E Mexico in S Tamaulipas
**Tananarive** — see ANTANANARIVO
**Tan·gan·yi·ka** \,tan-gən-'yē-kə, ,taŋ-gən-, -gə-'nē-\ former country E Africa S of Kenya; became part of Tanzania 1964
**Tanganyika, Lake** lake E Africa between Tanzania & Democratic Republic of the Congo
**Tang·shan** \'täŋ-'shäŋ\ city NE China in E Hebei
**Tan·ta** \'tänt-ə\ city N Egypt in central Nile delta
**Tan–tung** — see DANDONG
**Tan·za·nia** \,tan-zə-'nē-ə, ,tän-\ country E Africa on Indian Ocean; a republic formed 1964 by union of Tanganyika & Zanzibar; capital, Dar es Salaam — **Tan·za·ni·an** \-'nē-ən\ adjective or noun
**Taor·mi·na** \taùr-'mē-nə\ city Italy in NE Sicily
**Ta·ran·to** \'tär-ən-,tō, tə-'rant-ō\ or ancient **Ta·ren·tum** \tə-'rent-əm\ city SE Italy on Gulf of Taranto
**Ta·ra·wa** \tə-'rä-wə\ island, capital of Kiribati
**Ta·rim** \'dä-'rēm, 'tä-\ river 2011 kilometers long W China in Xinjiang Uygur flowing into a marshy depression
**Tar·lac** \'tär-,läk\ city Philippines in central Luzon
**Tar·shish** \'tär-shish\ ancient maritime country referred to in the Bible & often identified with Tartessus
**Tar·sus** \'tär-səs\ ancient city of S Asia Minor, capital of Cilicia; now a city of S Turkey
**Tar·tes·sus** or **Tar·tes·sos** \tär-'tes-əs\ ancient kingdom on SW coast of Spain near mouth of the Guadalquivir — see TARSHISH
**Tash·kent** \tash-'kent\ city, capital of Uzbekistan
**Tas·man** \'taz-mən\ sea comprising the part of the S Pacific between SE Australia & New Zealand
**Tas·ma·nia** \taz-'mā-nē-ə, -nyə\ or earlier **Van Die·men's Land** \van-'dē-mənz\ island SE Australia S of Victoria; a state; capital, Hobart — **Tas·ma·nian** \-nē-ən, -nyən\ adjective or noun
**Ta·tra** \'tä-trə\ or **High Tatra** or Czech **Vy·so·ké Ta·try** \,vis-ə-,kä-'tä-trē\ mountains N Slovakia & S Poland in central Carpathian Mountains
**Tatung** — see DATONG
**Tau·rus** \'tòr-əs\ mountains S Turkey parallel to Mediterranean coast; highest more than 3660 meters
**Tay·side** \'tā-,sīd\ region E central Scotland
**Tbi·li·si** \tə-'bē-lə-sē, tə-bə-'lē-sē\ or **Tif·lis** \'tif-ləs, tə-'flēs\ city, capital of Republic of Georgia
**Tchad** — see CHAD
**Te·gu·ci·gal·pa** \tə-,gü-si-'gal-pə\ city, capital of Honduras
**Teh·ran** or **Te·he·ran** \,tā-ə-'ran, -'rän\ city, capital of Iran
**Tel·a·nai·pura** \,tel-ə-'nī-,pùr-ə\ city & port Indonesia in Sumatra
**Tel Aviv** \,tel-ə-'vēv\ city W Israel on the Mediterranean
**Ten·nes·see** \,ten-ə-'sē, 'ten-ə-,\ state E central U.S.; capital, Nashville — **Ten·nes·se·an** or **Ten·nes·see·an** \,ten-ə-'sē-ən\ adjective or noun
**Te·re·si·na** \,ter-ə-'zē-nə\ city NE Brazil
**Té·tou·an** \,tā-'twän\ or **Te·tuán** \te-'twän, ,tet-ə-'wän\ city N Morocco
**Tex·as** \'tek-səs, -siz\ state S U.S.; capital, Austin — **Tex·an** \-sən\ adjective or noun
**Thai·land** \'tī-,land, -lənd\ or formerly **Si·am** \sī-'am\ country SE Asia on Gulf of Thailand; capital, Bangkok — **Thai·land·er** \'tī-,lan-dər, -lən-dər\ noun
**Thailand, Gulf of** or formerly **Gulf of Siam** arm of South China Sea between Indochina & Malay Peninsula
**Thames** \'temz\ river 338 kilometers long S England flowing E from the Cotswolds in Gloucestershire into the North Sea
**Thar** \'tär\ or **Indian** desert E Pakistan & NW Republic of India E of Indus River
**Thebes** \'thēbz\ **1** or ancient **The·bae** \'thē-bē\ or later **Di·os·po·lis** \dī-'äs-pə-ləs\ ancient city S

Egypt, capital of Upper Egypt on the Nile on site including modern towns of Karnak & Luxor  **2** ancient city E Greece NNW of Athens on site of modern village of Thivai — **The·ban** \'thē-bən\ adjective or noun

**Theodore Roosevelt National Park** reservation W North Dakota

**Thes·sa·lo·ní·ki** \,thes-ä-lō-'nē-kē\ or **Sa·lon·i·ka** \sə-'län-i-kə\ or **Sal·o·ni·ki** \,sal-ə-'nē-kē\ or **Thes·sa·lo·ni·ca** \,thes-ə-lə-'nī-kə, -'län-i-kə\ city N Greece in Macedonia — **Thes·sa·lo·nian** \-'lō-nē-ən, -'lō-nyən\ adjective or noun

**Thes·sa·ly** \'thes-ə-lē\ region central Greece between Pindus Mountains & the Aegean — **Thes·sa·lian** \thə-'sā-lē-ən, -'sāl-yən\ adjective or noun

**Thim·phu** \'thim-pü\ city, capital of Bhutan

**Thousand** islands Canada & U.S. in the Saint Lawrence in Ontario & New York

**Thrace** \'thrās\ or ancient **Thra·cia** \'thrā-shə, -shē-ə\ region SE Europe in Balkan Peninsula N of the Aegean now divided between Greece & Turkey; in ancient times extended N to the Danube — **Thra·cian** \'thrā-shən\ adjective or noun

**Thunder Bay** city Canada in SW Ontario

**Thur·rock** \'thər-ək, 'thə-rək\ district SE England in Essex

**Tian·jin** \tē-'än-'jin\ or **Tien·tsin** \tē-'ent-'sin, 'tint-\ city NE China in Hebei

**Tian Shan** \tē-'än-'shän\ or **Tien Shan** \tē-'en-'shän\ mountain system central Asia extending NE from Pamirs into Xinjiang Uygur; highest Pobeda Peak (in Kyrgyzstan) 7439 meters

**Ti·ber** \'tī-bər\ or Italian **Te·ve·re** \'tā-vā-rā\ or ancient **Ti·ber·is** \'tī-bə-rəs\ river 405 kilometers long central Italy flowing through Rome into Tyrrhenian Sea

**Tiberias, Sea of** — see GALILEE

**Ti·bes·ti** \tə-'bes-tē\ mountains N central Africa in central Sahara in NW Chad; highest 3415 meters

**Ti·bet** \tə-'bet\ or **Xi·zang** \'shēd-'zäng\ autonomous region SW China on high plateau N of the Himalaya; capital, Lhasa

**Tier·ra del Fue·go** \tē-'er-ə-,del-fü-'ā-gō, -fyü-\  **1** archipelago off S South America S of Strait of Magellan  **2** chief island of the group; divided between Argentina & Chile

**Tiflis** — see TBILISI

**Ti·gris** \'tī-grəs\ river 1899 kilometers long Turkey & Iraq flowing SSE & uniting with the Euphrates to form the Shatt al Arab

**Ti·jua·na** \,tē-ə-'wän-ə, tē-'wän-ə\ city NW Mexico on U.S. border in Baja California

**Til·burg** \'til-,bərg\ city S Netherlands

**Tim·buk·tu** \,tim-,bək-'tü, tim-'bək-tü\ or **Tom·bouc·tou** \tōⁿ-bük-'tü\ town W Africa in Mali near Niger River

**Ti·mi·soa·ra** \,tē-mish-ə-'wär-ə, -mish-'wär-\ city SW Romania

**Ti·mor** \'tē-,mȯr, tē-'\ island Indonesia SE of Sulawesi; W half formerly belonged to Netherlands, E half to Portugal

**Tip·pe·rary** \,tip-ə-'rear-ē\ county S Ireland in Munster

**Ti·ra·ne** or **Ti·ra·na** \ti-'rän-ə\ city, capital of Albania

**Ti·rol** or **Ty·rol** \tə-'rōl; 'tī-,rōl, tī-'; 'tir-əl\ or Italian **Ti·ro·lo** \tē-'rō-lō\ region in E Alps in W Austria & NE Italy — **Ti·ro·le·an** \tə-'rō-lē-ən, tī-; ,tir-ə-'; ,tī-rə-\ or **Tir·o·lese** \,tir-ə-'lēz, ,tī-rə-, -'lēs\ adjective or noun

**Ti·ruch·chi·rap·pal·li** \,tir-ə-chə-'räp-ə-lē\ city S India in Tamil Nadu

**Ti·ti·ca·ca, Lake** \,tit-i-'käk-ə\ lake on Bolivia-Peru boundary at altitude of 3810 meters

**Tlax·ca·la** \tlä-'skäl-ə\ state SE central Mexico; capital, Tlaxcala

**To·ba·go** \tə-'bā-gō\ island West Indies NE of Trinidad; a territory of Trinidad and Tobago

**To·go** \'tō-gō\ or **To·go·land** \-,land\ region W Africa on Gulf of Guinea between Benin & Ghana; until 1918 a German protectorate; then divided into two trust territories: **British Togoland** (in W, since 1957 part of Ghana) & **French Togo** (in E, since 1958 the **Republic of Togo**; capital, Lomé) — **To·go·land·er** \-,lan-dər\ noun — **To·go·lese** \,tō-gō-'lēz, -'lēs\ adjective or noun

**To·ko·ro·za·wa** \,tō-kə-'rō-zə-,wä\ city Japan on Honshu

**To·ku·shi·ma** \,tō-kə-'shē-mə\ city Japan in E Shikoku

**To·kyo** \'tō-kē-,ō\ city, capital of Japan in SE Honshu on Tokyo Bay — **To·kyo·ite** \tō-kē-,ō-,īt\ noun

**To·le·do** \tə-'lēd-ō, -'lēd-ə\  **1** city NW Ohio  **2** city central Spain SW of Madrid

**To·lu·ca** \tə-'lü-kə\ city central Mexico, capital of Mexico state

**Tol'·yat·ti** or **To·gliat·ti** \tȯl-'yät-ē\ or formerly **Stav·ro·pol** \stav-'rȯ-pəl, -'rō-\ city Russia in Europe, NW of Samara

**Tombouctou** — see TIMBUKTU

**Tomsk** \'tämsk, 'tämpsk, 'tȯmsk, 'tȯmpsk\ city S central Russia in Asia

**Ton·ga** \'täng-gə, 'täng-ə\ or **Friendly Islands** islands SW Pacific E of Fiji Islands; a kingdom in the Commonwealth; capital, Nukualofa — **Ton·gan** \-gən, -ən\ adjective or noun

**Tong·hua** or **T'ung·hua** \'tȯng-'hwä, -'wä\ city NE China in SW Jilin

**To·pe·ka** \tə-'pē-kə\ city, capital of Kansas

**Tor·bay** \'tȯr-'bā, 'tȯr-\ town SW England in Devonshire

**Torino** — see TURIN

**To·ron·to** \tə-'ränt-ō, -'ränt-ə\ city, capital of Ontario

**Tor·rance** \'tȯr-əns, 'tär-\ city SW California

**Tor·re·ón** \,tȯr-ē-'ōn\ city N Mexico in SW Coahuila

**Tor·res** \'tȯr-əs\ strait between New Guinea & Cape York Peninsula, Australia

**Tor·tu·ga** \tȯr-'tü-gə\ island Haiti off N coast; a resort of pirates in 17th century

**To·run** \'tȯr-,ün-yə, -,ün\ city N Poland on the Vistula

**Toscana** — see TUSCANY

**Tou·lon** \tü-'lōⁿ\ city SE France ESE of Marseille

**Tou·louse** \tü-'lüz\ city S France on the Garonne

**Tou·raine** \tü-'rän, -'ren\ region NW central France; chief city Tours

**Tourane** — see DA NANG

**Tours** \'tùr\ city NW central France

**Tow·er Hamlets** \'taů-ər-, 'taùr-\ borough of E Greater London, England

**To·ya·ma** \tō-'yäm-ə\ city Japan in W central Honshu

**To·yo·ha·shi** \,tȯi-ə-'häsh-ē\ city Japan in S Honshu

**To·yo·na·ka** \,tȯi-ə-'nä-kə\ city Japan on Honshu

**To·yo·ta** \tȯi-'ōt-ə\ city Japan on Honshu

**Tra·fal·gar, Cape** \trə-'fal-gər, Spanish ,trä-fäl-'gär\ headland SW Spain at W end of Strait of Gibraltar

**Trans·al·pine Gaul** \trans-,al-,pīn-, tranz-\ the part of Gaul included in modern France & Belgium

**Transjordan** — see JORDAN

**Trans·vaal** \trans-'väl, tranz-\ former province NE Republic of South Africa between Vaal & Limpopo rivers; capital, Pretoria

**Tran·syl·va·nia** \,trans-əl-'vā-nyə, -nē-ə\ region W Romania — **Tran·syl·va·nian** \-nyən, -nē-ən\ adjective or noun

**Transylvanian Alps** a S extension of Carpathian Mountains in central Romania

**Treb·i·zond** \'treb-ə-,zänd\ Greek empire 1204–1461, an offshoot of Byzantine Empire; at greatest extent included Crimea, Georgia, & N coast of Black Sea E of Sakarya River; capital, Trebizond (modern Trabon, in Turkey)

**Tren·ti·no–Al·to  Adi·ge** \tren-'tē-,nō-,äl-,tō-'äd-i-jä\ region N Italy; capital, Trento

**Tren·to** \'tren-,tō\ city NE Italy

**Tren·ton** \'trent-ⁿ\ city, capital of New Jersey

**Trier** \'triər\ or **Treves** \'trēvz\ city SW Germany on the Moselle

**Tri·este** \trē-'est, trē-'es-tē\ city NE Italy on the Adriatic

**Trin·i·dad** \'trin-ə-,dad\ island West Indies off NE coast of Venezuela; with Tobago forms (since 1962) the country of **Trinidad and Tobago**; capital, Port of Spain — **Trin·i·da·di·an** \,trin-ə-'dād-ē-ən, -'dad-\ adjective or noun

**Trip·o·li** \'trip-ə-lē\  **1** city, capital of Libya  **2** city NW Lebanon  **3** Tripolitania when it was one of the Barbary States

**Tri·pol·i·ta·nia** \,trip-,äl-ə-'tān-yə, ,trip-ə-lə-\ region NW Libya; chief city, Tripoli

**Tri·pu·ra** \'trip-ə-rə\ state E India between Bangladesh & Assam; capital, Agartala

**Tris·tan da Cu·nha** \,tris-tən-də-'kü-nə\ island S Atlantic, chief of the Tristan da Cunha Islands belonging to British colony of Saint Helena

**Tri·van·drum** \triv-'an-drəm\ city S India NW of Cape Comorin, capital of Kerala

**Tro·as** \'trō-,as\ or **Tro·ad** \-,ad\ territory surrounding ancient city of Troy in NW Mysia

**Tro·bri·and** \'trō-brē-,änd\ islands SW Pacific in Solomon Sea belonging to Papua New Guinea

**Troy** \'trȯi\ or **Il·i·um** \'il-ē-əm\ or **Il·i·on** \'il-ē-,än, -ē-ən\ or ancient **Troia** \'trȯi-ə, 'trȯ-yə\ or **Tro·ja** \'trō-jə, -yə\ ancient city NW Asia Minor SW of the Dardanelles

**Trucial States** or **Trucial Oman** — see UNITED ARAB EMIRATES

**Tru·ji·llo** \trü-'hē-ō, -yō\ city NW Peru

**Truk** \'trək, 'trük\ islands W Pacific in central Carolines; chief town, Moen (on Moen Island)

**Tsaritsyn** — see VOLGOGRAD

**Tsinan** — see JINAN

**Tsinghai** — see QINGHAI

**Tsingtao** — see QINGDAO

**Tu·a·mo·tu** \,tü-ə-'mō-tü\ archipelago S Pacific in French Polynesia E of Society Islands

**Tu·bai** \tüb-'wä-ē\ or **Aus·tral** \'ȯs-trəl, 'äs-\ islands S Pacific in French Polynesia S of Tahiti

**Tuc·son** \'tü-,sän, 'tü-,\ city SE Arizona

**Tucumán** — see SAN MIGUEL DE TUCUMÁN

**Tu·la** \'tü-lə\ city W Russia in Europe, S of Moscow

**Tul·sa** \'təl-sə\ city NE Oklahoma

**T'ung·hua** — see TONGHUA

**Tu·nis** \'tü-nəs, 'tyü-\  **1** city, capital of Tunisia  **2** Tunisia especially as one of the former Barbary States — **Tu·ni·sian** \tü-'nē-zhən, tyü-, -zhē-ən\ -'nizh-ən, -ē-ən\ adjective or noun

**Tu·ni·sia** \tü-'nē-zhə, tyü-, -zhē-ə; -'nizh-ə, -ē-ə\ country N Africa on the Mediterranean E of Algeria; a republic; capital, Tunis — **Tu·ni·sian** \-zhən, -zhē-ən; -ən, -ē-ən\ adjective or noun

**Tu·rin** \'tùr-ən, 'tyùr-; tù-'rin, tyù-\ or Italian **To·ri·no** \tȯ-'rē-nō\ city NW Italy on the Po, capital of Piedmont

**Tur·key** \'tər-kē\ country W Asia (**Turkey in Asia**) & SE Europe (**Turkey in Europe**) between Mediterranean & Black seas; a republic; capital, Ankara

**Turk·men·i·stan** \,tərk-'men-ə-,stan\ country central Asia bordering on Afghanistan, Iran, & Caspian Sea; a constituent republic (**Turk·men Soviet Socialist Republic** \,tərk-mən-\) of U.S.S.R. 1925–91; capital, Ashkhabad — **Turk·me·ni·an** \,tərk-'mē-nē-ən\ adjective

**Turks and Cai·cos** \,tərk-sən-'kā-kəs\ two groups of islands (Turks Islands & Caicos Islands) British West Indies at SE end of Bahamas; a British colony

**Tur·ku** \'tùr-kü\ city SW Finland

**Tus·ca·ny** \'təs-kə-nē\ or Italian **To·sca·na** \tō-'skän-ə\ region NW central Italy; capital, Florence

**Tu·tu·ila** \,tüt-ə-'wē-lə\ island S Pacific, chief of American Samoa group

**Tu·va·lu** \tü-'väl-ü, -'vär-\ or formerly **El·lice** \'el-əs\ islands W Pacific N of Fiji; an independent member of the Commonwealth; capital, Funafuti — see GILBERT

**Tyne and Wear** \'tī-nən-'dwiər, -'wiər\ metropolitan county N England; includes Newcastle upon Tyne

**Tyre** \'tīər\ ancient city, capital of Phoenicia; now a town of S Lebanon — **Tyr·i·an** \'tir-ē-ən\ adjective or noun

**Tyrol** — see TIROL — **Tyrolean** adjective or noun — **Tyrolese** adjective or noun

**Ty·rone** \tir-'ōn\ traditional county W central Northern Ireland

**Tyr·rhe·ni·an** \tə-'rē-nē-ən\ sea, part of the Mediterranean SW of Italy, N of Sicily, & E of Sardinia & Corsica

**Tyu·men** \tyü-'men\ city W Russia in Asia, ENE of Yekaterinburg

**Tzu–kung** — see ZIGONG

**Tzu–po** — see ZIBO

**Ubangi–Shari** — see CENTRAL AFRICAN REPUBLIC

**Udi·ne** \'üd-i-,nā\ city NE Italy NE of Venice

**Ufa** \ü-'fä\ city E Russia in Europe, NE of Samara

**Ugan·da** \ü-'gan-də, -'gän-\ country E Africa N of Lake Victoria; a republic in the Commonwealth; capital, Kampala — **Ugan·dan** \-dən\ adjective or noun

**Ujung Pan·dang** \ü-,jùng-pän-'däng\ or formerly **Ma·cas·sar** or **Ma·kas·ar** or **Ma·kas·sar** \mə-'kas-ər\ city Indonesia in SW Sulawesi

**Ukraine** \yü-'krān, 'yü-\ country E Europe on N coast of Black Sea; capital, Kiev; a constituent republic of U.S.S.R. 1923–91

**Ulaan·baa·tar** or **Ulan Ba·tor** \,ü-,län-'bä-,tòr\ or formerly **Ur·ga** \'ùr-gə\ city, capital of Mongolia

**Ulan–Ude** \,ü-,län-ü-'dā\ city S Russia in Asia, E of Lake Baikal

**Ul·san** \'ùl-'sän\ city SE South Korea

**Ul·ster** \'əl-stər\ **1** region N Ireland comprising Northern Ireland & N Republic of Ireland; a province until 1921 **2** province N Republic of Ireland comprising counties Donegal, Cavan, & Monaghan **3** NORTHERN IRELAND

**Ulyanovsk** — see SIMBIRSK

**Um·bria** \'əm-brē-ə\ region central Italy in the Apennines; capital, Perugia — **Um·bri·an** \-brē-ən\ adjective or noun

**Un·ga·va** \,ən-'gav-ə\ **1** bay inlet of Hudson Strait NE Canada **2** peninsula region NE Canada in N Quebec

**Union of South Africa** — see SOUTH AFRICA (Republic of)

**Union of Soviet Socialist Republics** or **Soviet Union** or **Soviet Russia** country (1922–91) E Europe & N Asia; a union of 15 constituent republics; capital, Moscow

**United Arab Emir·ates** \i-'mir-əts, ā-, -'miər-,āts\ or formerly **Tru·cial States** \'trü-shəl-\ or **Trucial Oman** country E Arabia on Persian Gulf; a republic composed of seven emirates; capital, Abu Dhabi

**United Arab Republic** former name (1961–71) of Egypt & previously (1958–61) of union of Egypt & Syria

**United Kingdom** or in full **United Kingdom of Great Britain and Northern Ireland** country W Europe in British Isles comprising England, Scotland, Wales, Northern Ireland, Channel Islands, & Isle of Man; capital, London

**United Nations** international territory; a small area in New York City in E central Manhattan; seat of permanent headquarters of the United Nations

**United States of America** or **United States** country North America bordering on Atlantic, Pacific, & Arctic oceans & including Hawaii; a federal republic; capital, Washington

**Upper Canada** former province, Canada in S part of present-day Ontario

**Upper Volta** — see BURKINA FASO — **Upper Voltan** \'vält-n, 'vōlt-, 'vòlt-\ adjective or noun

**Ural** \'yùr-əl\ **1** mountains W central Russia extending about 2640 kilometers S from point near Kara Sea; usually considered dividing line between Europe & Asia; highest 1894 meters **2** river 2534 kilometers long Russia flowing from S end of Ural Mountains into Caspian Sea

**Uralsk** \yù-'ralsk\ city W Kazakhstan

**Ura·wa** \ù-'rä-wə\ city Japan in central Honshu N of Tokyo

**Ur·mia** \'ùr-mē-ə\ city NW Iran

**Uru·guay** \'ùr-ə-,gwī, 'yùr-; 'yùr-ə-,gwä\ **1** river 1609 kilometers long SE South America rising in Brazil & flowing into Río de la Plata **2** country SE South America; a republic; capital, Montevideo — **Uru·guay·an** \,ùr-ə-'gwī-ən, ,yùr-; ,yùr-ə-'gwä-\ adjective or noun

**Ürüm·qi** \'ue-'rüem-'chē\ or **Urum·chi** \ù-'rùm-chē, ,ùr-əm-'chē\ or **Wu·lu·mu·ch'i** \'wü-'lü-'mü-'chē\ city NW China, capital of Xinjiang Uygur

**Urundi** — see BURUNDI

**Us·pa·lla·ta** \,ü-spə-'yät-ə, -'zhät-\ mountain pass 3855 meters S South America in the Andes between Argentina & Chile

**Usumbura** — see BUJUMBURA

**Utah** \'yü-,tò, -,tä\ state W U.S.; capital, Salt Lake City — **Utah·an** \'yü-,tòn, -,tä-ən, -,tä-ən, -,tän\ adjective or noun — **Utahn** \-,tò-ən, -,tòn, -,tä-ən, -,tän\ noun

**Utrecht** \'yü-,trekt\ city central Netherlands

**Utsu·no·mi·ya** \,üt-sə-'nō-mē-,ä, -,yä\ city Japan in central Honshu N of Tokyo

**Ut·tar Pra·desh** \,üt-ər-prə-'desh, -'dāsh\ state N India bordering on Tibet & Nepal; capital, Lucknow

**Uz·bek·i·stan** \üz-,bek-i-'stan, ,əz-, -'stän\ country W central Asia between Aral Sea & Afghanistan; capital, Tashkent; a constituent republic (**Uz·bek Soviet Socialist Republic** \'üz-,bek, 'əz-, ùz-'\) of U.S.S.R. 1924–91

**Va·duz** \vä-'düts\ town, capital of Liechtenstein

**Va·len·cia** \və-'len-chə, -chē-ə, -'len-sē-ə\ **1** region & ancient kingdom E Spain between Andalusia & Catalonia **2** city, its capital, on the Mediterranean **3** city N Venezuela WSW of Caracas

**Val·la·do·lid** \,val-əd-ə-'lid, -'lē\ city NW central Spain

**Val·le d'Ao·sta** \,väl-ā-dä-'ós-tə\ region NW Italy bordering on France & Switzerland; capital, Aosta

**Val·let·ta** \və-'let-ə\ city, capital of Malta

**Val·pa·rai·so** \,val-pə-'rī-zō, -'rä-\ or Spanish **Val·pa·ra·í·so** \,väl-pä-rä-'ē-sō\ city central Chile on the Pacific WNW of Santiago

**Van·cou·ver** \van-'kü-vər\ **1** island W Canada in SW British Columbia **2** city SW British Columbia

**Van Diemen's Land** — see TASMANIA

**Va·nu·a·tu** \,vän-ü-'ä-,tü\ or formerly **New Hebrides** \-'heb-rə-,dēz\ islands SW Pacific W of Fiji; an independent member of the Commonwealth; capital, Port-Vila

**Va·ra·na·si** \və-'rän-ə-sē\ city N India in SE Uttar Pradesh

**Var·na** \'vär-nə\ city & port E Bulgaria on Black Sea

**Vat·i·can City** \,vat-i-kən-\ or Italian **Cit·tà del Va·ti·ca·no** \chēt-'tä-del-,vä-tē-'kä-nō\ independent papal state within commune of Rome, Italy; created 1929

**Ve·ne·to** \'ven-ə-,tō, 'vā-nə-\ region NE Italy; capital, Venice

**Ven·e·zu·e·la** \,ven-əz-ə-'wā-lə, -əz-'wā-, -'wē-\ country N South America; capital, Caracas — **Ven·e·zu·e·lan** \-lən\ adjective or noun

**Ven·ice** \'ven-əs\ or Italian **Ve·ne·zia** \və-'net-sē-ä\ city N Italy on islands in Lagoon of Venice — **Ve·ne·tian** \və-'nē-shən\ adjective or noun

**Ve·ra·cruz** \,ver-ə-'krüz, -'krüs\ **1** state E Mexico; capital, Jalapa **2** city E Mexico in Veracruz state on Gulf of Mexico

**Ver·ee·ni·ging** \fə-'rā-nə-ging, -nək-əng\ city NE Republic of South Africa S of Johannesburg

**Ver·mont** \vər-'mänt\ state NE U.S.; capital, Montpelier — **Ver·mont·er** \-ər\ noun

**Ve·ro·na** \və-'rō-nə\ city N Italy W of Venice

**Ver·sailles** \vər-'sī, ver-\ city N France; suburb of Paris

**Vert, Cape** \'vərt\ or **Cape Verde** \'vərd\ promontory W Africa in Senegal; most westerly point of Africa

**Ve·su·vi·us** \və-'sü-vē-əs\ volcano 1277 meters S Italy near Bay of Naples

**Vi·cen·te Ló·pez** \vi-,sent-ə-'lō-,pez\ city E Argentina N of Buenos Aires

**Vi·cen·za** \vi-'chen-sə\ city NE Italy W of Venice

**Vic·to·ria** \vik-'tōr-ē-ə, -'tòr-\ **1** city, capital of British Columbia on Vancouver Island **2** island N Canada in Arctic Archipelago S of Melville Sound **3** state SE Australia; capital, Melbourne **4** city, capital of Hong Kong — **Vic·to·ri·an** \-ē-ən\ adjective or noun

**Victoria, Lake** lake E Africa in Tanzania, Kenya, & Uganda

**Victoria Falls** waterfall 108 meters high S Africa in the Zambezi on border between Zambia & Zimbabwe

**Victoria Nile** — see NILE

**Vi·en·na** \vē-'en-ə\ or German **Wien** \vēn\ or ancient **Vin·dob·o·na** \vin-'däb-ə-nə\ or **Vin·dob·na** \-'däb-nə\ city, capital of Austria on the Danube — **Vi·en·nese** \,vē-ə-'nēz, -'nēs\ adjective or noun

**Vien·tiane** \vyen-'tyän\ city, capital of Laos

**Viet·nam** \vē-'et-'näm, -vyet-, ,vē-ət-, -'nam\ country SE Asia in Indochina; capital, Hanoi; established 1945–46 & divided 1954–75 at 17th parallel into republics of **North Vietnam** (capital, Hanoi) & **South Vietnam** (capital, Saigon)

**Vi·go** \'vē-,gō\ city & port NW Spain

**Vi·ja·ya·wa·da** \,vij-ə-yə-'wäd-ə\ or formerly **Bez·wa·da** \bez-'wäd-ə\ city SE India in E Andhra Pradesh

**Vila** — see PORT-VILA

**Vil·ni·us** \'vil-nē-əs\ or Polish **Wil·no** \'vil-nō\ or Russian **Vil·na** \'vil-nə\ or **Vil·no** \-nō\ city, capital of Lithuania

**Vin·land** \'vin-lənd\ a portion of the coast of North America visited and so called by Norse voyagers about 1000 A.D.; perhaps Newfoundland

**Vin·ni·tsa** \'vin-ət-sə\ city W central Ukraine

**Vin·son Massif** \'vin-sən\ mountain 4897 meters W Antarctica in Sentinel Range of Ellsworth Mountains; highest in Antarctica

**Vir·gin·ia** \vər-'jin-yə, -'jin-ē-ə\ state E U.S.; capital, Richmond — **Vir·gin·ian** \-yən, -ē-ən\ adjective or noun

**Virginia Beach** city SE Virginia

**Vir·gin Islands** \vər-jən-\ island group West Indies E of Puerto Rico — see BRITISH VIRGIN ISLANDS, VIRGIN ISLANDS OF THE UNITED STATES

**Virgin Islands National Park** reservation Saint John, Virgin Islands of the United States

**Virgin Islands of the United States** the W islands of the Virgin Islands group including Saint Croix, Saint John, & Saint Thomas; capital, Charlotte Amalie (on Saint Thomas)

**Vi·sa·yan** \və-'sī-ən\ or **Bi·sa·yas** \bə-'sī-əz\ islands central Philippines including Bohol, Cebu, Leyte, Masbate, Negros, Panay, & Samar

**Vish·a·kha·pat·nam** \vish-,äk-ə-'pət-nəm\ city & port E India in Andhra Pradesh

**Vis·tu·la** \'vis-chə-lə, 'vish-; 'vis-tə-lə\ or Polish **Wis·la** \'vē-slä\ river 1086 kilometers long Poland flowing N from the Carpathians into Gulf of Danzig

**Vi·ti Le·vu** \,vēt-ē-'lev-ü\ island SW Pacific; largest of the Fiji group

**Vi·to·ria** \vi-'tōr-ē-ə, -'tòr-\ city N Spain

**Vi·tó·ria** \vi-'tōr-ē-ə, -'tòr-\ city E Brazil NE of Rio de Janeiro

**Vit·syebsk** \'vēts-yipsk\ or **Vi·tebsk** \'vē-,tipsk\ city NE Belarus

**Vlad·i·kav·kaz** \,vlad-ə-,käf-'käz, -'kaz\ or 1932–43 & 1955–91 **Or·dzho·ni·kid·ze** \,òr-jän-ə-'kid-zə\ or 1944–54 **Dzau·dzhi·kau** \dzaù-'jē-,kaù, zaù-\ city S Russia, in the Caucasus

**Vlad·i·vos·tok** \,vlad-ə-və-'stäk, -'väs-,täk\ city SE Russia in Asia, on Sea of Japan

**Volcano Islands** or **Ka·zan Ret·to** \,käz-,än-'ret-ō\ island chain Japan in W Pacific S of Bonin Islands — see IWO JIMA

**Vol·ga** \'väl-gə, 'vòl-, 'vōl-\ river 3689 kilometers long W Russia flowing into Caspian Sea

**Vol·go·grad** \'väl-gə-,grad, 'vòl-, 'vōl-\ or formerly **Sta·lin·grad** \'stäl-ən-,grad, 'stal-\ or earlier **Tsa·ri·tsyn** \tsə-'rēt-sən, sə-\ city S Russia in Europe, on the Volga

**Vol·ta** \'väl-tə, 'vōl-, 'vòl-\ river about 1610 kilometers long Ghana flowing into Bight of Benin and including Lake Volta (reservoir)

**Vo·ro·nezh** \və-'rò-nish\ city SW Russia in Europe, near Don River

**Vo·ro·shi·lov·grad** \,vòr-ə-'shē-ləf-,grad, ,vär-, -ləv-\ city E Ukraine in Donets Basin

**Vosges** \'vōzh\ mountains NE France on W side of valley of the Rhine; highest 1424 meters

**Voy·a·geurs National Park** \vòi-ə-'zhərz\ reservation N Minnesota on Rainy Lake

**Vysoké Tatry** — see TATRA

**Wa·ka·ya·ma** \,wäk-ə-'yäm-ə\ city Japan in SW Honshu SW of Osaka

**Wake** \'wāk\ island N Pacific N of Marshall Islands; belongs to U.S.

**Wa·la·chia** or **Wal·la·chia** \wä-'lä-kē-ə\ region S Romania between Transylvanian Alps & the Danube

**Wales** \'wālz\ or Welsh **Cym·ru** \'kəm-rē\ or Latin **Cambria** principality SW Great Britain; a division of United Kingdom; capital, Cardiff

**Wal·la·sey** \'wäl-ə-sē\ town NW England in Merseyside

**Wal·lis** \'wäl-əs\ islands SW Pacific NE of Fiji; with Futuna Islands constitute a French overseas territory (**Wallis and Futuna Islands**)

**Wal·sall** \'wòl-,sól, -səl\ town W central England in West Midlands

**Wal·tham Forest** \,wòl-thəm-\ borough of NE Greater London, England

**Wands·worth** \'wändz-wərth, 'wänz-\ borough of SW Greater London, England

**Wan·ne–Eick·el** \,vän-ə-'ī-kəl\ city W Germany in the Ruhr

**War·ley** \'wòr-lē\ town W central England in West Midlands

**War·ren** \'wòr-ən, 'wär-\ city SE Michigan

**War·saw** \'wòr-,sò\ or Polish **War·sza·wa** \vär-'shäv-ə\ city, capital of Poland

**War·wick·shire** \'wär-ik-,shiər, -shər\ or **Warwick** county central England

**Wa·satch** \'wò-,sach\ range of the Rockies SE Idaho & N central Utah; highest Mount Timpanogos 3660 meters (in Utah)

**Wash·ing·ton** \'wòsh-ing-tən, 'wäsh-\ **1** state NW U.S.; capital, Olympia **2** city, capital of U.S.; coextensive with District of Columbia — **Wash·ing·to·nian** \,wòsh-ing-'tō-nē-ən, ,wäsh-, -nyən\ adjective or noun

**Washington, Mount** mountain 1917 meters N New Hampshire; highest in White Mountains

**Wa·ter·bury** \'wȯt-ər-ˌber-ē, 'wȯt-ə-, 'wät-\ city W central Connecticut

**Wa·ter·ford** \'wȯt-ər-fərd, 'wät-\ county S Ireland in Munster

**Wa·ter·ton–Glacier International Peace Park** \'wȯt-ər-tən-, 'wät-\ international park, comprising **Waterton Lakes National Park** in S Alberta, Canada, and **Glacier National Park** in NW Montana

**Watlings** — see SAN SALVADOR

**Wed·dell** \wə-'del, 'wed-l\ sea arm of the S Atlantic E of Antarctic Peninsula

**Wei·mar Republic** \'vī-ˌmär, 'wī-\ the German republic 1919–33

**Wel·land** \'wel-ənd\ canal 44 kilometers long SE Ontario connecting Lake Erie & Lake Ontario

**Wel·ling·ton** \'wel-ing-tən\ city, capital of New Zealand

**Wes·sex** \'wes-iks\ ancient Anglian kingdom S England; capital, Winchester

**West Australian Current** warm current flowing N off W coast of Australia

**West Bengal** state E India; capital, Calcutta

**West Brom·wich** \'brəm-ij, 'bräm-, -ich\ town W central England in West Midlands

**Western Australia** state W Australia; capital, Perth

**Western Cape** province SW Republic of South Africa

**Western Ghats** \'gȯts\ chain of low mountains SW India

**Western Isles** the Outer Hebrides constituting since 1975 a regional division of W Scotland

**Western Sahara** or formerly **Spanish Sahara** region NW Africa divided 1975 between Mauritania which gave up its claim in 1979 & Morocco which thereafter occupied the entire territory

**Western Samoa** islands Samoa W of 171° W; an independent state in the Commonwealth since 1962; capital, Apia

**West Germany** — see GERMANY

**West Gla·mor·gan** \glə-'mȯr-gən\ county S Wales

**West Indies** islands lying between SE North America & N South America & comprising the Greater Antilles, Lesser Antilles, & Bahamas — **West Indian** adjective or noun

**West Irian** — see IRIAN JAYA

**West Lo·thi·an** \'lō-thē-ən\ former county SE Scotland — see LOTHIAN

**West·meath** \west-'mēth, wes-, -'mēth\ county E central Ireland in Leinster

**West Midlands** metropolitan county W central England

**West·min·ster** \'west-ˌmin-stər, 'wes-\ or **City of Westminster** borough of W central Greater London, England

**West·mor·land** \'west-mər-lənd, 'wes-\ former county NW England

**West New Guinea** — see IRIAN JAYA

**West Pakistan** the former W division of Pakistan now coextensive with Pakistan

**West·pha·lia** \west-'fāl-yə, -'fā-lē-ə, wes-\ region NW Germany E of the Rhine; now part of North Rhine-Westphalia — **West·pha·lian** \-'fāl-yən, -'fā-lē-ən\ adjective or noun

**West Punjab** — see PUNJAB 3

**West Quod·dy Head** \'kwäd-ē\ cape; most easterly point of Maine & of U.S.

**West Ri·ding** \'rīd-ing\ former administrative county N England in W & SW Yorkshire

**West Sus·sex** \'səs-iks\ county SE England

**West Virginia** state E U.S.; capital, Charleston — **West Virginian** adjective or noun

**West York·shire** \'yȯrk-ˌshiər, -shər\ metropolitan county NW England

**Wex·ford** \'weks-fərd\ county SE Ireland in Leinster

**White** mountains N New Hampshire in the Appalachians — see WASHINGTON

**White·horse** \'hwīt-ˌhȯrs, 'wīt-\ city NW Canada, capital of Yukon Territory

**White Nile** — see NILE

**White Sea** or **Be·lo·ye Mo·re** \ˌbel-ə-yə-'mȯr-yə\ sea inlet of Barents Sea NW Russia

**Whit·ney, Mount** \'hwit-nē, 'wit-\ mountain 4418 meters SE central California in Sierra Nevada in Sequoia National Park; highest in U.S. outside of Alaska

**Wich·i·ta** \'wich-ə-ˌtȯ\ city S Kansas

**Wick·low** \'wik-lō\ county E Ireland in Leinster

**Wien** — see VIENNA

**Wies·ba·den** \'vēs-ˌbäd-n, 'vis-\ city W Germany on the Rhine W of Frankfurt, capital of Hesse

**Wight, Isle of** \'wīt\ island & county S England in English Channel

**Wig·town** \'wig-tən, -ˌtaun\ or **Wig·town·shire** \-ˌshiər, -shər\ former county SW Scotland

**Wil·helms·ha·ven** \ˌvil-helmz-'häf-ən, 'vil-əmz-ˌ\ city NW Germany NW of Bremen

**Wil·lem·stad** \'vil-əm-ˌstät\ city, capital of Netherlands Antilles on Curaçao Island

**Wil·ming·ton** \'wil-ming-tən\ city N Delaware; largest in state

**Wilno** — see VILNIUS

**Wilt·shire** \'wilt-ˌshiər, 'wil-chər, 'wilt-shər\ county S England

**Wind Cave National Park** reservation SW South Dakota in Black Hills

**Win·der·mere** \'win-dər-ˌmiər, -də-\ lake NW England in Lake District

**Wind·hoek** \'vint-ˌhuk\ city, capital of Namibia

**Wind·sor** \'win-zər\ city S Ontario on Detroit River

**Wind·ward** \'win-dwərd\ islands West Indies in the S Lesser Antilles extending S from Martinique but not including Barbados, Tobago, or Trinidad

**Win·ni·peg** \'win-ə-ˌpeg\ city, capital of Manitoba

**Winnipeg, Lake** lake S central Manitoba

**Win·ni·pe·sau·kee, Lake** \ˌwin-ə-pə-'sȯ-kē\ lake central New Hampshire

**Win·ston–Sa·lem** \ˌwin-stən-'sā-ləm\ city N central North Carolina

**Wis·con·sin** \wis-'kän-sən\ state N central U.S.; capital, Madison — **Wis·con·sin·ite** \-sə-ˌnīt\ noun

**Wisla** — see VISTULA

**Wit·wa·ters·rand** \'wit-ˌwȯt-ərz-ˌrand, -ˌwät-, -ˌränd, -ˌränt\ or **Rand** \'rand, 'ränd, 'ränt\ ridge of gold-bearing rock NE Republic of South Africa

**Wol·lon·gong** \'wul-ən-ˌgäng, -ˌgȯng\ city SE Australia in E New South Wales S of Sydney

**Wol·ver·hamp·ton** \'wul-vər-ˌham-tən, -ˌhamp-\ town W central England in West Midlands NW of Birmingham

**Won·san** \'wən-ˌsän\ city North Korea on E coast

**Worces·ter** \'wus-tər\ city E central Massachusetts

**Worces·ter·shire** \'wus-tər-ˌshiər, -tə-, -shər\ or **Worcester** former county W central England — see HEREFORD AND WORCESTER

**Wran·gell, Mount** \'rang-gəl\ volcano 4317 meters S Alaska in Wrangell Range; highest volcano in U.S.

**Wrangell–Saint Eli·as National Park** \-ˌsänt-i-'lī-əs-\ reservation S central Alaska E of Anchorage

**Wro·claw** \'vrȯt-ˌsläf, -ˌsläv\ or German **Bres·lau** \'bres-ˌlau\ city SW Poland in Silesia

**Wu·chang** \'wü-'chäng\ former city E central China — see WUHAN

**Wu·han** \'wü-'hän\ city S China, capital of Hubei; formed from former separate cities of Hankow, Hanyang, & Wuchang

**Wuhsien** — see SUZHOU

**Wu–lu–mu–ch'i** — see ÜRÜMQI

**Wup·per·tal** \'vup-ər-ˌtäl\ city W Germany in Ruhr Valley ENE of Düsseldorf

**Würt·tem·berg** \'wərt-əm-ˌbərg, 'wurt-; 'vurt-əm-ˌberk\ region SW Germany between Baden & Bavaria; chief city, Stuttgart; now part of Baden-Württemberg

**Wy·o·ming** \wī-'ō-ming\ state NW U.S.; capital, Cheyenne — **Wy·o·ming·ite** \-ming-ˌīt\ noun

**Xia·men** \'shē-'ä-mən\ or **Hsia–men** \'shē-'än\ or formerly **Amoy** \ä-'mȯi\ city SE China in S Fujian on two islands

**Xi'·an** or **Si·an** \'shē-'än\ or formerly **Chang·an** \'chäng-'än\ city E central China, capital of Shaanxi

**Xiang·tan** or **Hsiang–t'an** or **Siang·tan** \shē-'äng-'tän\ city SE China in Hunan

**Xi·ning** or **Si·ning** \shē-'ning\ city NW China, capital of Qinghai

**Xin·jiang Uy·gur** or **Sin·kiang–Ui·ghur** \'shin-jē-'äng-'wē-gər\ region & former province W China; capital, Uürümqi

**Xizang** — see TIBET

**Xu·zhou** \'shü-'jō\ or **Hsü–chou** or **Süchow** \'shü-'jō, 'sü-; 'sü-'chau\ city E China in NW Jiangsu

**Ya·kutsk** \yə-'kütsk\ city E central Russia in Asia

**Ya·lu** \'yäl-ü\ or **Am·nok** \'am-ˌnäk\ river 806 kilometers long SE Manchuria, China & North Korea flowing into Korea Bay

**Ya·mous·sou·kro** \ˌyä-mü-'sü-krō\ town central Ivory Coast, official capital of the country

**Yangku** — see TAIYUAN

**Yan·gon** \ˌyän-'gōn\ or formerly **Ran·goon** \ran-'gün, rang-\ city, capital of Myanmar

**Yangtze** — see CHANG

**Yao** \'yau\ city Japan in S Honshu E of Osaka

**Yaoun·dé** \yaun-'dā\ city, capital of Cameroon

**Yap** \'yap, 'yäp\ island W Pacific in the W Carolines

**Ya·ro·slavl** \ˌyär-ə-'släv-əl\ city central Russia in Europe, NE of Moscow

**Ye·ka·te·rin·burg** \yi-'kat-ə-rən-ˌbərg, yi-ˌkät-ə-rən-'bürk\ or 1924–91 **Sverd·lovsk** \sverd-'lȯfsk\ city W Russia, in central Ural Mountains

**Yellow** 1 — see HUANG   2 sea section of East China Sea between N China & Korea

**Yel·low·knife** \'yel-ə-ˌnīf\ town Canada, capital of Northwest Territories

**Yel·low·stone National Park** \'yel-ə-ˌstōn\ reservation NW Wyoming, E Idaho, & S Montana

**Ye·men** \'yem-ən\ country S Arabia bordering on Red Sea & Gulf of Aden; a republic formed 1990 by merger of **Yemen Arab Republic** (capital, Sanaa) with **People's Democratic Republic of Yemen** or **Southern Yemen** (capital, Aden); capital, Sanaa — **Ye·me·ni** \'yem-ə-nē\ adjective or noun — **Ye·men·ite** \-ə-ˌnīt\ noun

**Yen·i·sey** or **Yen·i·sei** \ˌyen-ə-'sā\ river 4129 kilometers long central Russia, flowing N into Arctic Ocean

**Ye·re·van** \ˌyer-ə-'vän\ city, capital of Armenia

**Yezo** — see HOKKAIDO

**Yi·bin** \'yē-'bēn\ or **I–pin** \'ē-'bēn, -'pin\ or formerly **Sü·chow** \'shü-'jō, 'sü-; 'sü-'chau\ city central China in S Sichuan

**Yog·ya·kar·ta** \ˌyȯg-yə-'kär-tə\ city Indonesia in S Java

**Yo·ho National Park** \'yō-hō\ reservation W Canada in SE British Columbia on Alberta boundary

**Yo·ko·ha·ma** \ˌyō-kə-'häm-ə\ city Japan in SE Honshu on Tokyo Bay S of Tokyo

**Yo·ko·su·ka** \yō-'kō-sə-kə, -'kō-skə\ city Japan in E Honshu W of entrance to Tokyo Bay

**Yon·kers** \'yäng-kərz\ city SE New York N of New York City

**York** \'yȯrk\ city N England in North Yorkshire

**York·shire** \'yȯrk-ˌshiər, -shər\ or **York** former county N England comprising city of York & administrative counties of East Riding, North Riding, & West Riding — see CLEVELAND, HUMBERSIDE, NORTH YORKSHIRE, SOUTH YORKSHIRE, WEST YORKSHIRE

**York, Cape** cape NE Australia in Queensland at N tip of Cape York Peninsula

**Yo·sem·i·te Falls** \yō-'sem-ət-ē\ waterfall E California in Yosemite valley in Yosemite National Park; includes two falls, the upper 436 meters & the lower 98 meters, connected by a series of cascades; total drop 739 meters

**Yosemite National Park** reservation E central California in Sierra Nevada

**Youngs·town** \'yəng-ˌstaun\ city NE Ohio

**Yssel** — see IJSSEL

**Yu·ca·tán** \ˌyü-kə-'tan, -'tän\ 1 peninsula SE Mexico & N Central America including Belize & N Guatemala   2 state SE Mexico; capital, Mérida

**Yu·go·sla·via** or **Ju·go·sla·via** \ˌyü-gō-'släv-ē-ə\ country S Europe on the Adriatic consisting of Serbia & Montenegro and formerly also of Slovenia, Croatia, Bosnia and Herzegovina, & N Macedonia; capital, Belgrade — **Yu·go·slav** \ˌyü-gō-'släv, -'slav\ or **Yu·go·sla·vi·an** \-'släv-ē-ən\ adjective or noun

**Yu·kon** \'yü-ˌkän\ 1 river 3184 kilometers long NW Canada & Alaska flowing into Bering Sea   2 or **Yukon Territory** territory NW Canada; capital, Whitehorse

**Yun·nan** \yü-'nän\ 1 province SW China bordering on Myanmar & Indochina; capital, Kunming   2 — see KUNMING

**Yunnanfu** — see KUNMING

**Zab·rze** \'zäb-zhä\ city SW Poland in Silesia

**Za·ca·te·cas** \ˌzak-ə-'tā-kəs, -'tek-əs\ 1 state N central Mexico   2 city; its capital

**Zag·a·zig** \'zag-ə-ˌzig\ city N Egypt NNE of Cairo

**Za·greb** \'zäg-ˌreb\ city, capital of Croatia

**Za·he·dan** \ˌzä-hi-'dän\ city E Iran

**Zaire** \zä-'iər\ 1 river in Africa — see CONGO 1   2 country in Africa — see CONGO 2

**Zam·be·zi** *or* **Zam·be·si** \zam-'bē-zē\ river about 2735 kilometers long SE Africa flowing from NW Zambia into Mozambique Channel

**Zam·bia** \'zam-bē-ə\ country S Africa N of the Zambezi; formerly the British protectorate of **Northern Rhodesia**; an independent republic since 1964; capital, Lusaka

**Zam·bo·an·ga** \,zam-bə-'wäng-gə\ city S Philippines in SW Mindanao

**Zan·zi·bar** \'zan-zə-,bär\ island Tanzania off NE Tanganyika coast; formerly a sultanate & British protectorate including also Pemba & other islands; became independent 1963; united 1964 with Tanganyika forming Tanzania

**Za·po·rizh·zhya** *or* **Za·po·ro·zh'ye** \,zäp-ə-'rò-zhə\ city SE Ukraine

**Za·ra·go·za** \,zar-ə-'gō-zə\ *or* **Sar·a·gos·sa** \,sar-ə-'gäs-ə\ city NE Spain in W Aragon

**Zealand** — see SJÆLLAND

**Zetland** — see SHETLAND

**Zhang·jia·kou** \'jäng-jē-'ä-'kō\ *or* **Ch'ang–chia–k'ou** \'chäng-jē-'ä-'kō\ *or* **Kal·gan** \'kal-'gan\ city NE China in NW Hebei NW of Beijing

**Zhang·zhou** *or* **Chang–chou** \'jäng-'jō\ city SE China in S Fujian

**Zhdanov** — see MARIUPOL'

**Zhe·jiang** *or* **Che–kiang** \'jəj-ē-'äng\ province E China bordering on East China Sea; capital, Hangzhou

**Zheng·zhou** *or* **Cheng–chou** \'jəng-'jō\ city NE central China, capital of Henan

**Zhen·jiang** *or* **Chen–chiang** \'jən-jē-'äng\ city E China in NW central Jiangsu

**Zhu·zhou** *or* **Chu–chou** *or* **Chu·chow** \'jü-'jō\ city SE China in E Hunan

**Zhy·to·myr** *or* **Zhi·to·mir** \zhi-'tò-,miər\ city W Ukraine

**Zi·bo** *or* **Tzu–po** \'dzə-'bō, 'zə-\ city E China in central Shandong

**Zi·gong** *or* **Tzu–kung** *or* **Tze–kung** \'dzə-'gung, 'zə-\ city S central China in S Sichuan

**Zim·ba·bwe** \zim-'bäb-wā, -wē\ *or before 1979* **Rho·de·sia** \rō-'dē-zhə, -zhē-ə\ *or* **Southern Rhodesia** country S Africa S of Zambezi River; an independent member of the Commonwealth; capital, Harare — **Zim·ba·bwe·an** \-ən\ *adjective or noun*

**Zi·on** \'zī-ən\ *or* **Si·on** \'sī-ən\ **1** the stronghold of Jerusalem conquered by David **2** a hill in Jerusalem occupied in ancient times by the Jewish Temple **3** JERUSALEM **4** ISRAEL

**Zion National Park** reservation SW Utah

**Zla·to·ust** \,zlät-ə-'üst\ city W Russia in Asia in the S Urals

**Zom·ba** \'zäm-bə\ city S Malawi

**Zui·der Zee** \,zīd-ər-'zā, -'zē\ former inlet of North Sea N Netherlands now (as IJsselmeer) partly reclaimed — see IJSSELMEER

**Zu·lu·land** \'zü-lü-,land\ territory E Republic of South Africa on Indian Ocean

**Zu·rich** \'zùr-ik\ city N Switzerland on Lake of Zurich

**Zwick·au** \'tsfik-,aù, 'zwik-\ city E Germany S of Leipzig

# A Handbook of Style

# Punctuation

The English writing system uses punctuation marks to separate groups of words for meaning and emphasis; to convey an idea of the variations of pitch, volume, pauses, and intonations of speech; and to help avoid contextual ambiguity. The use of the standard English punctuation marks is discussed in the following pages; examples are provided to illustrate the general rules.

## ' Apostrophe

1. Indicates the possessive case of nouns and indefinite pronouns. The possessive case of almost all singular nouns may be formed by adding 's. Traditionally, however, only the apostrophe is added when the s would not be pronounced in normal speech. The possessive case of plural nouns ending in s or in an \s\ or \z\ sound is generally formed by adding an apostrophe only; the possessive of irregular plurals is formed by adding 's.

> her mother-in-law's car
>
> anyone's guess
>
> the boy's mother
>
> the boys' mothers
>
> Degas's drawings
>
> Knox's products
>
> Aristophanes' play
>
> for righteousness' sake
>
> the Stephenses' house
>
> children's laughter

2. Marks omission of letters in contracted words.

> didn't
>
> o'clock
>
> hang 'em up

3. Marks omission of digits in numbers.

> class of '83

4. Is often used to form plurals of letters, figures, punctuated abbreviations, symbols, and words referred to as words.

> Dot your *i*'s and cross your *t*'s.
>
> His *1*'s and his *7*'s looked alike.
>
> Two of the junior faculty have Ph.D's.
>
> She has trouble pronouncing her *the*'s.

## [ ] Brackets

1. Set off interpolated editorial matter within quoted material.

> He wrote, "I ain't [sic] going."
>
> Vaulting ambition, which o'erleaps itself
> And falls on the other [side].
>
> > —Shakespeare

2. Function as parentheses within parentheses.

> Bowman Act (22 Stat., ch. 4, § [or sec.] 4, p. 50)

3. Set off phonetic symbols and transcriptions.

> [t] in British *duty*
>
> the word is pronounced [ˈek-sə-jənt]

## : Colon

1. Introduces a clause or phrase that explains, illustrates, amplifies, or restates what has gone before.

> The sentence was poorly constructed: it lacked
> both unity and coherence.

2. Directs attention to an appositive.

> He had only one pleasure: eating.

3. Introduces a series.

> Three abstained: England, France, and Belgium.

4. Introduces lengthy quoted material set off from the rest of a text by indentation but not by quotation marks.

> I quote from the text of Chapter One:

5. Separates elements in page references, in bibliographical and biblical citations, and in set formulas used to express ratios and time.

   *Journal of the American Medical Association* 48:356

   Stendhal, *Love* (New York: Penguin, 1975)

   John 4:10      a ratio of 3:5      8:30 a.m.

6. Separates titles and subtitles (as of books).

   *Battle Cry of Freedom: The Era of the Civil War*

7. Follows the salutation in formal correspondence.

   Dear Sir or Madam:

   Ladies and Gentlemen:

8. Punctuates headings in memorandums and formal correspondence.

   TO:      VIA:

   SUBJECT:      REFERENCE:

# Comma   ,

1. Separates main clauses joined by a coordinating conjunction (such as *and, but, or, nor,* or *for*), and sometimes short parallel clauses not joined by conjunctions.

   She knew very little about him, and he volunteered nothing.

   I came, I saw, I conquered.

2. Sets off an adverbial clause or a long adverbial phrase that precedes or interrupts the main clause.

   When she discovered the answer, she reported it to us.

   The report, after being read aloud, was put up for consideration.

3. Sets off transitional words and expressions (such as *on the contrary, on the other hand*), conjunctive adverbs (such as *consequently, furthermore, however*), and expressions that introduce an illustration or example (such as *namely, for example*).

   My partner, on the other hand, remains unconvinced.

   The regent's whim, however, threw the negotiations into chaos.

   She responded as completely as she could; that is, she answered each of the individual questions specifically.

4. Sets off contrasting and opposing expressions within sentences.

   The cost is not $65.00, but $56.65.

   He changed his style, not his ethics.

5. Separates words, phrases, or clauses in series. (Many omit the comma before the conjunction introducing the last item in a series when no ambiguity results.)

   He was young, eager, and restless.

   It requires one to travel constantly, to have no private life, and to live on almost nothing.

   Be sure to pack a flashlight, a sweater and an extra pair of socks.

6. Separates coordinate adjectives modifying a noun. However, a comma is not used between two adjectives when the first modifies the combination of the second adjective and the word or phrase it modifies.

   The harsh, damp, piercing wind cut through his jacket.

   a low common denominator

7. Sets off parenthetical elements such as nonrestrictive clauses and phrases.

   Our guide, who wore a blue beret, was an experienced traveler.

   We visited Gettysburg, site of the famous battle.

   The book's author, Marie Jones, was an accomplished athlete.

8. Introduces a direct quotation, terminates a direct quotation that is neither a question nor an exclamation, and sets off split quotations. The comma is not used with quotations that are tightly integrated into the sentences in which they appear (e.g., as subject or predicate nominatives) or those that do not represent actual dialogue.

   Mary said, "I am leaving."

   "I am leaving," Mary said.

   "I am leaving," Mary said with determination, "even if you want me to stay."

   "The computer is down" was the reply she feared.

   The fact that he said he was about to "faint from hunger" doesn't mean he actually fainted.

9. Sets off words in direct address, absolute phrases, and mild interjections.

   You may go, John, if you wish.

   I fear their encounter, his temper being what it is.

   Ah, that's my idea of an excellent dinner.

10. Separates a tag question from the rest of the sentence.

    It's a fine day, isn't it?

11. Indicates the omission of a word or words used in a parallel construction earlier in the sentence. When the meaning of the sentence is quite clear without the comma, the comma is omitted.

    Common stocks are preferred by some investors; bonds, by others.

    He was in love with her and she with him.

12. Is used to avoid ambiguity that might arise from adjacent words.

    To Mary, Jane was someone special.

13. Is used to divide digits in numbers into groups of three; however, it is generally not used in pagination, in dates, or in street numbers, and sometimes not used in numbers with four digits.

    Smithville, pop. 100,000

    4,550 cars

    *but*

    page 1411      4507 Main St.

    3600 rpm      the year 1983

14. Punctuates an inverted name.

    Morton, William A.

15. Separates a surname from a following title or degree and often from the words "Junior" and "Senior" and their abbreviations.

    Sandra H. Cobb, Vice President

    Jesse Ginsburg, D.D.M.

16. Sets off geographical names (such as state or country from city), elements of dates, and addresses. When just the month and the year are given in a date, the comma is usually omitted.

    Shreveport, Louisiana, is the site of a large air base.

    On Sunday, June 23, 1940, he was wounded.

Number 10 Downing Street, London, is a famous address.

She began her career in April 1993 at a modest salary.

17. Follows the salutation in informal correspondence, and follows the complimentary close of a letter.

Dear Mark,

Affectionately,

Very truly yours,

# — Dash

1. Usually marks an abrupt change or break in the continuity of a sentence.

When in 1960 the stockpile was sold off—indeed, dumped as surplus—natural rubber sales were hard hit.—Barry Commoner

2. Is sometimes used in place of commas or parentheses when special emphasis is required.

The presentations—and especially the one by Ms. Dow—impressed the audience.

3. Introduces a statement that explains, summarizes, or expands on what precedes it.

Oil, steel, and wheat—these are the sinews of industrialization.

The motion was then tabled—that is, removed indefinitely from consideration.

4. Often precedes the attribution of a quotation.

My foot is on my native heath. . . .—Sir Walter Scott

5. Sets off an interrupting clause or phrase. The dash takes the place of a comma that would ordinarily set off the clause, but an exclamation point or question mark is retained.

If we don't succeed—and the critics say we won't— then the whole project is in jeopardy.

They are demanding that everything—even the marsh-land!—be transferred to the new trust.

Your question—it was *your* question, wasn't it, Mr. Jones?—just can't be answered.

# . . . . . . . Ellipsis (or Suspension Points)

1. Indicates the omission of one or more words within a quoted passage. When four dots are used, the ellipsis indicates the omission of one or more sentences within the passage or the omission of words at the end of a sentence. The first or the last of the four dots is a period.

In the little world in which children have their existence, . . . there is nothing so finely perceived and so finely felt as injustice.—Charles Dickens

Security is mostly a superstition. . . . Avoiding danger is no safer in the long run than outright exposure. . . . Life is either a daring adventure or nothing.—Helen Keller

2. Usually indicates omission of one or more lines of poetry when ellipsis is extended the length of the line.

I think that I shall never see
A poem lovely as a tree
. . . . . . . . . . . . . . . .
Poems are made by fools like me,
But only God can make a tree.
—Joyce Kilmer

3. Indicates halting speech or an unfinished sentence in dialogue.

"I'd like to . . . that is . . . if you don't mind. . . ."

# ! Exclamation Point

1. Ends an emphatic phrase or sentence.

Get out of here!

Her notorious ostentation—she flew her friends to Bangkok for her birthday parties!—was feasted on by the popular press.

2. Ends an emphatic interjection.

Encore!

All of this proves—at long last!—that we were right from the start.

# - Hyphen

The hyphen is often used between parts of a compound. The styling of such words varies; when in doubt, see the entry in the dictionary at its own place or in a list of undefined words at an individual prefix. For unentered compounds, advice will be found in *Merriam-Webster's Manual for Writers and Editors* or a comparable guide.

1. Is often used between a prefix and root, especially whenever the root is capitalized, when two identical vowels come together, or when the resulting word could be confused with another identically spelled word.

pre-Renaissance

co-opted

anti-inflationary

re-cover a sofa

*but*

recover from an illness

2. Is used in some compounds, especially those containing prepositions.

president-elect            sister-in-law

good-for-nothing        over-the-counter

falling-out                   write-off

3. Is often used in compound modifiers in attributive position.

traveling in a fast-moving van

She has gray-green eyes.

a come-as-you-are party

4. Suspends the first element of a hyphenated compound or a prefix (hyphenated or not) when the second element or base word is part of a following hyphenated compound or derived form.

a six- or eight-cylinder engine

pre- and postadolescent trauma

5. Marks division of a word at the end of a line.

The ruling pas-
sion of his life

6. Is used in writing out compound numbers between 21 and 99.

 thirty-four

 one hundred thirty-eight

7. Is often used between the numerator and the denominator in writing out fractions, especially when they are used as modifiers. However, fractions used as nouns are often written as open compounds, especially when either the numerator or the denominator already contains a hyphen.

 a two-thirds majority of the vote

 three fifths of her paycheck

 one seventy-second of an inch

8. Serves as an equivalent of *through* or (*up*) *to and including* when used between indicators of range such as numbers and dates. (In typeset material the longer en dash is used.)

 pages 40–98

 the years 1980–89

9. Serves as the equivalent of *to, and,* or *versus* in indicating linkage or opposition. (In typeset material the longer en dash is used.)

 the New York–Paris flight

 the Hardy–Weinberg law

 the Lincoln–Douglas Debates

 The final score was 7–2.

# Hyphen, Double ⸗

Is used at the end-of-line division of a hyphenated compound to indicate that the compound is hyphenated and not closed.

self ⸗ [end of line] seeker

 *but*

self- [end of line] same

# Parentheses ( )

1. Enclose words, numbers, phrases, or clauses that provide examples, explanations, or supplementary material that does not essentially alter the meaning of the sentence.

 Three old destroyers (all now out of commission) will be scrapped.

 He has followed the fortunes of the modern renaissance (*al-Nahdad* ) in the Arabic-speaking world.

2. Enclose numerals that confirm a written number in a text.

 Delivery will be made in thirty (30) days.

3. Enclose numbers or letters in a series.

 We must set forth (1) our long-term goals, (2) our immediate objectives, and (3) the means at our disposal.

4. Enclose abbreviations that follow their spelled-out forms or spelled-out forms that follow their abbreviations.

 a ruling by the Federal Communications Commission (FCC)

 the manufacture and disposal of PVC (polyvinyl chloride)

5. Indicate alternative terms.

 Please indicate the lecture(s) you would like to attend.

6. Enclose publication data in footnotes and endnotes.

 Marguerite Yourcenar, *The Dark Brain of Piranesi and Other Essays* (New York: Farrar, Straus and Giroux, 1985), p. 9.

7. Are used with other punctuation marks in the following ways:

If the parenthetic expression is an independent sentence standing alone, its first word is capitalized and a period is included *inside* the last parenthesis. However, if the parenthetic expression, even if it could stand alone as a sentence, occurs within a sentence, it is uncapitalized and has no sentence period but may have an exclamation point, a question mark, a period for an abbreviation, or quotation marks within the closing parenthesis.

 The discussion was held in the boardroom. (The results are still confidential.)

 Although we liked the restaurant (their Italian food was the best), we seldom went there.

 After waiting in line for an hour (why do we do these things?), we finally left.

 Years ago, someone (I wish I could remember who!) told me about it.

 What was once informally known as A.B.D. status is now often recognized by the degree of Master of Philosophy (M. Phil.).

 He was depressed ("I must resign") and refused to do anything.

No punctuation mark should be placed directly before parenthetical material in a sentence; if a break is required, punctuation should be placed *after* the final parenthesis.

 I'll get back to you tomorrow (Friday), when I have more details.

# Period .

1. Ends sentences or sentence fragments that are neither interrogatory nor exclamatory.

 Not bad.

 Give it your best.

 I gave it my best.

 He asked if she had given it her best.

2. Follows some abbreviations and contractions.

 Dr.    A.D.    ibid.    i.e.

 Jr.    etc.    cont.

3. Is normally used with an individual's initials.

 F. Scott Fitzgerald

 T. S. Eliot

4. Is used after numerals and letters in vertical enumerations and outlines.

 Required skills are:
  1. Shorthand
  2. Typing
  3. Transcription

 I. Objectives
  A. Economy
   1. low initial cost
   2. low maintenance cost
  B. Ease of operation

# ?  Question Mark

1. Ends a direct question.

How did she do it?

"How did she do it?" he asked.

2. Ends a question that is part of a larger sentence, but not an indirect question.

How did she do it? was the question on each person's mind.

He wondered, Will it work?

He wondered whether it would work.

3. Indicates the writer's ignorance or uncertainty.

Geoffrey Chaucer, English poet (1342?–1400)

# "  "  Quotation Marks, Double

1. Enclose direct quotations but not indirect quotations.

She said, "I am leaving."

She said that she was leaving.

2. Enclose words or phrases borrowed from others, words used in a special way, and words of marked informality when introduced into formal writing.

Much of the population in the hellish future he envisions is addicted to "derms," patches that deliver potent drug doses instantaneously through the skin.

He called himself "emperor," but he was really just a dictator.

He was arrested for smuggling "smack."

3. Enclose titles of poems, short stories, articles, lectures, chapters of books, short musical compositions, and radio and TV programs.

Robert Frost's "After Apple-Picking"

Cynthia Ozick's "Rosa"

The third chapter of *Treasure Island* is entitled "The Black Spot."

"All the Things You Are"

Debussy's "Clair de lune"

NBC's "Today Show"

4. Are used with other punctuation marks in the following ways:

The period and the comma fall *within* the quotation marks.

"I am leaving," she said.

It was unclear how she maintained such an estate on "a small annuity."

The colon and semicolon fall *outside* the quotation marks.

There was only one thing to do when he said "I may not run": promise him a large campaign contribution.

He spoke of his "little cottage in the country"; he might better have called it a mansion.

The dash, the question mark, and the exclamation point fall *within* the quotation marks when they refer to the quoted matter only; they fall *outside* when they refer to the whole sentence.

"I can't see how—" he started to say.

He asked, "When did she leave?"

What is the meaning of "the open door"?

The sergeant shouted "Halt!"

Save us from his "mercy"!

5. Are not used with *yes* or *no* except in direct discourse.

She said yes to all our requests.

6. Are not used with lengthy quotations set off from the text.

He took the title for his biography of Thoreau from a passage in *Walden*:

I long ago lost a hound, a bay horse, and a turtle-dove, and am still on their trail. . . . I have met one or two who had heard the hound, and the tramp of the horse, and even seen the dove disappear behind a cloud, and they seemed as anxious to recover them as if they had lost them themselves.

However, the title *A Hound, a Bay Horse, and a Turtle-Dove* probably puzzled some readers.

# '  '  Quotation Marks, Single

1. Enclose a quotation within a quotation in American usage. When both single and double quotation marks occur at the end of a sentence, the period typically falls within *both* sets of marks.

The witness said, "I distinctly heard him say, 'Don't be late,' and then heard the door close."

The witness said, "I distinctly heard him say, 'Don't be late.' "

2. Are sometimes used in place of double quotation marks, especially in British usage. In this case a quotation within a quotation is set off by double quotation marks.

The witness said, 'I distinctly heard him say, "Don't be late," and then heard the door close.'

# ;  Semicolon

1. Links independent clauses not joined by a coordinating conjunction.

Some people have the ability to write well; others do not.

2. Links clauses joined by a conjunctive adverb (such as *consequently, furthermore, however*).

Speeding is illegal; furthermore, it is very dangerous.

3. Often occurs before expressions that introduce expansions or series (such as *for example, for instance, that is, e.g.,* or *i.e.*).

As a manager she tried to do the best job she could; that is, to keep her project on schedule and under budget.

4. Separates phrases that contain commas.

The country's resources consist of large ore deposits; lumber, waterpower, and fertile soils; and a strong, rugged people.

Send copies to our offices in Portland, Maine; Springfield, Illinois; and Savannah, Georgia.

5. Is placed outside quotation marks and parentheses.

They again demanded "complete autonomy"; the demand was again rejected.

# Virgule (or Slash)   /

1. Separates alternatives.

   high-heat and/or high-speed applications

   . . . sit hour after hour . . . and finally year after year
   in a catatonic/frenzied trance rewriting the Bible
   —William Saroyan

2. Replaces the word *to* or *and* between related terms that are compounded.

   the fiscal year 1983/1984

   in the May/June issue

3. Divides run-in lines of poetry.

   Say, sages, what's the charm on earth/Can turn death's
   dart aside?—Robert Burns

4. Divides elements in dates and divides numerators and denominators in fractions.

   offer expires 5/19/94

   Fifteen and 44/100 dollars

5. Often represents *per* or *to* when used with units of measure or to indicate the terms of a ratio.

   9 ft/sec

   29 mi/gal

   risk/reward trade-off

6. Sets off phonemes and phonemic transcription.

   /b/ as in *but*

# Capitalization

Capitals are used for two broad purposes in English: they mark a beginning (as of a sentence) and they signal a proper noun, pronoun, or adjective. The following principles, each with examples, describe the most common uses of capital letters.

## Beginnings

1. The first word of a sentence or sentence fragment is capitalized.

   The play lasted nearly three hours.

   How are you feeling?

   Bravo!

2. The first word of a sentence contained within parentheses is capitalized if it does not occur within another sentence. The first word of a parenthetical sentence within another sentence is not capitalized.

   The discussion was held in the boardroom. (The results are still confidential.)

   Although we liked the restaurant (their Italian food was the best), we seldom ate there.

   After waiting in line for an hour (why do we do these things?), we finally left.

3. The first word of a direct quotation is capitalized. However, if the quotation is interrupted in the middle of a sentence, the second part does not begin with a capital. When a quotation, whether a sentence fragment or a complete sentence, is syntactically dependent on the sentence in which it occurs, the quotation does not begin with a capital.

   The President said, "We have rejected this report entirely."

   "We have rejected this report entirely," the President said, "and we will not comment on it further."

   The President made it clear that "there is no room for compromise."

4. The first word of a sentence within a sentence is usually capitalized when it represents a direct question, a motto or aphorism, or spoken or unspoken dialogue. The first word following a colon may be either lowercased or capitalized if it introduces a complete sentence. While the former is more usual, the latter is common when the sentence is fairly lengthy and distinctly separate from the preceding clause.

   The question, as Disraeli said, is this: Is man an ape or an angel?

   My first thought was, How can I avoid this assignment?

   The advantage of this particular system is clear: it's inexpensive.

   The situation is critical: This company cannot hope to recoup the fourth-quarter losses that were sustained in five operating divisions.

5. The first word of a line of poetry is traditionally capitalized; however, in much twentieth-century poetry the line beginnings are lowercased.

   The best lack all conviction, while the worst
   Are full of passionate intensity.

   —W. B. Yeats

6. The first words of run-in enumerations that form complete sentences are capitalized, as are usually the first words of vertical lists and enumerations.

However, enumerations of words or phrases run in with the introductory text are generally lowercased.

   Do the following tasks at the end of the day:
   1. Clear your desktop of papers. 2. Cover office machines. 3. Straighten the contents of your desk drawers, cabinets, and bookcases.

   This is the agenda:
   Call to order
   Roll call
   Minutes of the previous meeting
   Treasurer's report

   On the agenda will be (1) call to order, (2) roll call, (3) minutes of the previous meeting, (4) treasurer's report. . . .

7. The first word in an outline heading is capitalized.

   I. Editorial tasks

   II. Production responsibilities
      A. Cost estimates
      B. Bids

8. The first word of the salutation of a letter and the first word of a complimentary close are capitalized.

   Dear Mary,

   Ladies and Gentlemen:

   Sincerely yours,

## Proper Nouns, Pronouns, and Adjectives

Capitals are used with almost all proper nouns—that is, nouns that name particular persons, places, or things (including abstract entities), distinguishing them from others of the same class—and proper adjectives—that is, adjectives that take their meaning from what is named by the proper noun. The essential distinction in the use of capitals and lowercase letters at the beginnings of words lies in this individualizing significance of capitals as against the generalizing significance of lowercase. The following subject headings are in alphabetical order.

### ARMED FORCES

1. Branches and units of the armed forces are capitalized, as are easily recognized short forms of full branch and unit designations. However, the words *army*, *navy*, etc., are lowercased when used in their plural forms or when they are not part of an official title.

   United States Army

   a contract with the Army

   Corps of Engineers

   a bridge built by the Engineers

   allied armies

AWARDS

2. Names of awards and prizes are capitalized.

the Nobel Prize in Chemistry

Distinguished Service Cross

Academy Award

DERIVATIVES OF PROPER NAMES

3. Derivatives of proper names are capitalized when used in their primary sense. However, if the derived term has taken on a specialized meaning, it is usually not capitalized.

Roman customs

Shakespearean comedies

Edwardian era

*but*

quixotic

herculean

bohemian tastes

GEOGRAPHICAL REFERENCES

4. Divisions of the earth's surface and names of distinct areas, regions, places, or districts are capitalized, as are most derivative adjectives and some derivative nouns and verbs.

The Eastern Hemisphere

Midwest

Tropic of Cancer

Springfield, Massachusetts

the Middle Eastern situation

an Americanism

*but*

french fries

a japan finish

manila envelope

5. Popular names of localities are capitalized.

| | |
|---|---|
| the Corn Belt | the Loop |
| The Big Apple | the Gold Coast |
| the Pacific Rim | |

6. Words designating global, national, regional, or local political divisions are capitalized when they are essential elements of specific names. However, they are usually lowercased when they precede a proper name or stand alone. (In legal documents, these words are often capitalized regardless of position.)

| | |
|---|---|
| the British Empire | Washington State |
| New York City | Ward 1 |
| *but* | |
| the fall of the empire | the state of Washington |
| the city of New York | fires in three wards |

7. Generic geographical terms (such as *lake, mountain, river, valley*) are capitalized if they are part of a specific proper name.

| | |
|---|---|
| Hudson Bay | Long Island |
| Niagara Falls | Crater Lake |
| the Shenandoah Valley | |

8. Generic terms preceding names are usually capitalized.

Lakes Michigan and Superior

Mounts Whitney and Rainier

9. Generic terms following names are usually lowercased, as are singular or plural generic terms that are used descriptively or alone.

the Himalaya and Andes mountains

the Atlantic coast of Labrador

the Hudson valley

the river valley

the valley

10. Compass points are capitalized when they refer to a geographical region or when they are part of a street name, but they are lowercased when they refer to simple direction.

up North

back East

the Northwest

West Columbus Avenue

Park Avenue South

*but*

west of the Rockies

the east coast of Florida

11. Adjectives derived from compass points and nouns designating the inhabitants of some geographical regions are capitalized. When in doubt, see the entry in the dictionary.

a Southern accent

Northerners

12. Terms designating public places are capitalized if they are part of a proper name.

Brooklyn Bridge

Lincoln Park

the St. Regis Hotel

Independence Hall

*but*

Wisconsin and Connecticut avenues

the Plaza and St. Regis hotels

GOVERNMENTAL AND JUDICIAL BODIES

13. Full names of legislative, deliberative, executive, and administrative bodies are capitalized, as are short forms of these names. However, nonspecific noun and adjective references to them are usually lowercased.

the U.S. House of Representatives

the House

the Federal Bureau of Investigation

*but*

both houses of Congress

a federal agency

14. Names of international courts, the U.S. Supreme Court, and other higher courts are capitalized. However, names of city and county courts are usually lowercased.

The International Court of Arbitration

the Supreme Court of the United States

the Supreme Court

the United States Court of Appeals for the Second Circuit

the Michigan Court of Appeals

Lawton municipal court

Newark night court

## HISTORICAL PERIODS AND EVENTS

15.  Names of congresses, councils, and expositions are capitalized.

the Yalta Conference

the Republican National Convention

16.  Names of historical events, some historical periods, and some cultural periods and movements are capitalized. When in doubt, consult the entry in the dictionary, especially for periods.

the Boston Tea Party

the Renaissance

Prohibition

the Augustan Age

the Enlightenment

*but*

the space age

neoclassicism

17.  Numerical designations of historical time periods are capitalized when they are part of a proper name; otherwise they are lowercased.

the Third Reich

the Roaring Twenties

*but*

the eighteenth century

the eighties

18.  Names of treaties, laws, and acts are capitalized.

Treaty of Versailles

The Clean Air Act of 1990

## ORGANIZATIONS

19.  Names of firms, corporations, schools, and organizations and their members are capitalized. However, common nouns occurring after the names of two or more organizations are lowercased. The word *the* at the beginning of such names is only capitalized when the full legal name is used.

Thunder's Mouth Press

University of Wisconsin

European Community

Rotary International

Kiwanians

American and United airlines

20.  Words such as *group, division, department, office,* or *agency* that designate a corporate and organizational unit are capitalized only when used with its specific name.

in the Editorial Department of Merriam-Webster

*but*

a notice to all department heads

## PEOPLE

21.  Names of persons are capitalized. However, the capitalization of particles such as *de, della, der, du, l', la, ten,* and *van* varies widely, especially in names of people in English-speaking countries.

Noah Webster

W.E.B. Du Bois

Daphne du Maurier

Wernher von Braun

Anthony Van Dyck

22.  Titles preceding the name of a person and epithets used instead of a name are capitalized. However, titles following a name or used alone are usually lowercased.

President Roosevelt

Professor Kaiser

Queen Elizabeth

Old Hickory

the Iron Chancellor

*but*

Henry VIII, king of England

23.  Corporate titles are capitalized when used with an individual's name; otherwise, they are lowercased.

Lisa Dominguez, Vice President

The sales manager called me.

24.  Words of family relationship preceding or used in place of a person's name are capitalized; however, these words are lowercased if they are part of a noun phrase used in place of a name.

Cousin Julia

I know when Mother's birthday is.

*but*

I know when my mother's birthday is.

25.  Words designating peoples, nationalities, religious groups, tribes, races, and languages are capitalized. Other terms used to refer to groups of people are often lowercased. Designations based on color are usually lowercased.

| | |
|---|---|
| Canadians | Iroquois |
| Ibo | African-American |
| Latin | Indo-European |
| highlander (an inhabitant of a highland) | |
| Highlander (an inhabitant of the Highlands of Scotland) | |
| black | white |

## PERSONIFICATIONS

26.  Personifications are capitalized.

She dwells with Beauty—Beauty that must die;
And Joy, whose hand is ever at his lips
Bidding adieu.

—John Keats

obey the commands of Nature

## PRONOUNS

27.  The pronoun I is capitalized. For pronouns referring to the Deity, see rule 29 below.

. . . no one but I myself had yet printed any of my work.—Paul Bowles

## RELIGIOUS TERMS

28.  Words designating the Deity are capitalized.

An anthropomorphic, vengeful Jehovah became a spiritual, benevolent Supreme Being.—A.R. Katz

29.  Personal pronouns referring to the Deity are usually capitalized, even when they closely follow their antecedent. However, many writers never capitalize such pronouns.

All Thy works, O Lord, shall bless Thee.

—*Oxford American Hymnal*

God's in his heaven—
All's right with the world!
—Robert Browning

30.  Traditional designations of revered persons, such as prophets, apostles, and saints, are often capitalized.

our Lady

the Prophet

the Lawgiver

31.  Names of religions, creeds and confessions, denominations, and religious orders are capitalized, as is the word *Church* when used as part of a proper name.

Judaism

Apostles' Creed

the Thirty-nine Articles of the Church of England

Society of Jesus

Hunt Memorial Church

*but*

the local Baptist church

32.  Names for the Bible or parts, versions, or editions of it and names of other sacred books are capitalized but not italicized. Adjectives derived from the names of sacred books are irregularly capitalized or lowercased; when in doubt, see the entry in the dictionary.

| | |
|---|---|
| Authorized Version | New English Bible |
| Old Testament | Pentateuch |
| Apocrypha | Gospel of Saint Mark |
| Talmud | Koran |
| biblical | Koranic |

## SCIENTIFIC TERMS

33.  Names of planets and their satellites, asteroids, stars, constellations and groups of stars, and other unique celestial objects are capitalized. However, the words *sun*, *earth*, and *moon* are usually lowercased unless they occur with other astronomical names.

| | |
|---|---|
| Venus | Ganymede |
| Sirius | the Pleiades |

the Milky Way

enjoying the beauty of the moon

probes heading for the Moon and Mars

34.  New Latin genus names in zoology and botany are capitalized; the second term in binomial scientific names, identifying the species, is not.

a cabbage butterfly (*Pieris rapae*)

a common buttercup (*Ranunculus acris*)

35.  New Latin names of all groups above genus in zoology and botany (such as class or family) are capitalized; however, their derivative adjectives and nouns are not.

| | | |
|---|---|---|
| Gastropoda | *but* | gastropod |
| Mantidae | *but* | mantid |

36.  Names of geological eras, periods, epochs, and strata and names of prehistoric divisions are capitalized.

| | |
|---|---|
| Silurian period | Pleistocene epoch |
| Age of Reptiles | Neolithic age |

## SEASONS, MONTHS, DAYS

37.  Names of months, days of the week, and holidays and holy days are capitalized.

| | |
|---|---|
| January | Ramadan |
| Tuesday | Thanksgiving |
| Yom Kippur | Easter |

38.  Names of seasons are not capitalized except when personified.

last spring

the sweet breath of Spring

## TITLES OF PRINTED MATTER AND WORKS OF ART

39.  Words in titles are capitalized, with the exception of internal conjunctions, prepositions, and articles. In some publications, prepositions of five or more letters are capitalized also.

*Of Mice and Men*

"The Man Who Would Be King"

"To His Coy Mistress"

*Slouching Towards Bethlehem*

40.  Capitalization of the titles of movies, plays, paintings, sculpture, and musical compositions follow similar conventions. For more details, see the Italicization section below.

41.  Major sections of books, long articles, or reports are capitalized when they are referred to within the same material.

See the Appendix for further information.

The Introduction explains the scope of this book.

discussed later in Chapter 4

42.  Nouns used with numbers or letters to designate major reference headings are capitalized. Nouns designating minor elements are typically lowercased.

| | |
|---|---|
| Volume V | Table 3 |
| page 101 | note 10 |

## TRADEMARKS

43.  Registered trademarks and service marks are capitalized.

| | |
|---|---|
| Express Mail | Orlon |
| Kleenex | Walkman |

## VEHICLES

44.  Names of ships, aircraft, and spacecraft are capitalized.

*Titanic*

Lindbergh's *Spirit of St. Louis*

*Apollo 13*

# Italicization

The following are usually italicized in print and underlined in manuscript and typescript.

1. Words and passages that are to be emphasized.

   This was their fatal error: there *was* no cache of supplies in the now-abandoned depot.

2. Titles of books, magazines, newspapers, plays, long poems, movies, paintings, sculpture, and long musical compositions (but not musical compositions identified by the name of their genre).

   Dickens's *Bleak House*

   *National Geographic*

   *Christian Science Monitor*

   Shakespeare's *Othello*

   Eliot's *The Waste Land*

   the movie *Back to the Future*

   Gainsborough's *Blue Boy*

   Mozart's *Don Giovanni*

       *but*

   Schubert's Sonata in B-flat Major, D. 960

   NOTE: In the plurals of such italicized titles, the *s* or *es* endings are usually in roman type.

   hidden under a stack of *New Yorker*s

3. Names of ships, aircraft, and spacecraft.

   *Titanic*

   Lindbergh's *Spirit of St. Louis*

   *Apollo 13*

4. Words, letters, and figures when referred to as such.

   The *g* in *align* is silent.

   The first *2* and the last *0* are barely legible.

5. Unfamiliar words when first introduced and defined in a text.

   Heart failure is often accompanied by *edema,* an accumulation of fluid which tends to produce swelling of the lower extremities.

6. Foreign words and phrases that have not been naturalized in English. In general, any word entered in the main A–Z vocabulary of this dictionary need not be italicized.

   *c'est la vie*

   *aere perennius*

   *che sarà, sarà*

   *sans peur et sans reproche*

       *but*

   pasta       ad hoc      ex officio

7. New Latin scientific names of genera, species, subspecies, races, and varieties (but not groups of higher rank, such as phyla, classes, or orders) in botanical or zoological names.

   a thick-shelled American clam (*Mercenaria mercenaria*)

   a mallard (*Anas platyrhynchos*)

       *but*

   the family Hominidae

8. Case titles in legal citations, both in full and shortened form; "v." for "versus" is set in either roman or italic.

   *Jones* v. *Ohio*

   *Smith et al v. Jones*

   the *Jones* case

   *Jones*

# Documentation of Sources

Writers and editors use various methods to indicate the source of a quotation or piece of information borrowed from another work. In works published for the general public and traditionally in scholarly works in the humanities, footnotes or endnotes have been preferred. In this system, sequential numbers within the text refer the reader to notes at the bottom of the page or at the end of the article, chapter, or book; these notes contain full bibliographical information on the works cited. In scholarly works in the social and natural sciences, and increasingly in the humanities as well, parenthetical references within the text refer the reader to an alphabetically arranged list of sources at the end of the work. The system of footnotes or endnotes is the more flexible, in that it allows for commentary on the work or subject and can also be used for brief peripheral discussions not tied to any specific work. However, style manuals tend to encourage the use of parenthetical references in addition to or instead of footnotes or endnotes, since for most kinds of material they are efficient and convenient for both writer and reader. In a carefully documented work, a bibliography or list of sources normally follows the entire text (including any endnotes) regardless of which system is used.

Though different publishers and journals have adopted slightly varying styles, the following examples illustrate standard styles for references, notes, and bibliographic entries. For more extensive treatment than can be provided here, *Merriam-Webster's Manual for Writers and Editors*, *The Chicago Manual of Style*, *The MLA Style Manual*, or the *Publication Manual of the American Psychological Association* may be consulted.

## Footnotes and Endnotes

Footnotes and endnotes are indicated by superscript Arabic numerals placed immediately after the material to be documented. The numbering is consecutive throughout an article or monograph; in a book, it usually starts over with each new chapter or section. Footnotes appear at the bottom of the page; endnotes, which take the same form as footnotes, are gathered at the end of the article, chapter, or book. Endnotes are generally preferred over footnotes by writers and publishers because they are easier to handle when preparing both manuscript and printed pages, though they can be less convenient for the reader. All of the examples shown reflect humanities citation style. All of the cited works appear again in the Lists of Sources section below.

## Books

| | |
|---|---|
| One author | [1]Elizabeth Bishop, *The Complete Poems: 1927–1979* (New York: Farrar, Straus & Giroux, 1983), 46. |
| Two or more authors | [2]Bert Holldobler and Edward O. Wilson, *The Ants* (Cambridge, Mass.: Belknap–Harvard Univ. Press, 1990), 119. |
| | [3]Randolph Quirk et al., *A Comprehensive Grammar of the English Language* (London: Longman, 1985), 135. |
| Edition and/or translation | [4]Arthur S. Banks, ed., *Political Handbook of the World: 1992* (Binghamton, N.Y.: CSA Publications, 1992), 293–95. |
| | [5]Simone de Beauvoir, *The Second Sex*, trans. and ed. H. M. Parshley (New York: Knopf, 1953; Random House, 1974), 446. |
| Second or later edition | [6]Albert C. Baugh and Thomas Cable, *A History of the English Language*, 3d ed. (Englewood Cliffs, N.J.: Prentice Hall, 1978), 14. |
| Article in a collection or festschrift | [7]Ernst Mayr, "Processes of Speciation in Animals," in *Mechanisms of Speciation*, ed. C. Barigozzi (New York: Alan R. Liss, 1982), 1–3. |
| Work in two or more volumes | [8]Ronald M. Nowak, *Walker's Mammals of the World*, 5th ed. (Baltimore: Johns Hopkins Univ. Press, 1991), 2:661. |
| Corporate author | [9]Commission on the Humanities, *The Humanities in American Life* (Berkeley: Univ. of California Press, 1980), 46. |
| Book lacking publication data | [10]*Photographic View Album of Cambridge* [England], n.p., n.d., n.pag. |
| Subsequent reference | [11]Baugh and Cable, 18–19. |

# Articles

[12]Stephen Jay Gould and Niles Eldredge, "Punctuated Equilibria: The Tempo and Mode of Evolution Reconsidered," *Paleobiology* 3 (1977): 121.

[13]Roseann Duenas Gonzalez, "Teaching Mexican American Students to Write: Capitalizing on the Culture," *English Journal* 71.7 (Nov. 1982): 22–24.

[14]John Lukacs, "The End of the Twentieth Century," *Harper's,* Jan. 1993: 40.

[15]Richard Preston, "A Reporter at Large: Crisis in the Hot Zone," *New Yorker,* 26 Oct. 1992: 58.

[16]William J. Broad, "Big Science Squeezes Small-Scale Researchers," *New York Times,* 29 Dec. 1992: C1.

[17]George Steiner, review of *Oeuvres en Prose Complètes, Tome 3,* by Charles Péguy, *Times Literary Supplement,* 25 Dec. 1992: 3.

Journal paginated consecutively throughout annual volume

Journal paginated consecutively only within each issue

Monthly magazine

Weekly magazine

Newspaper

Signed review

# Parenthetical References

Parenthetical references are highly abbreviated bibliographical citations that appear within the text itself, enclosed in parentheses. Such references direct the reader to a detailed bibliography or list of sources at the end of the work, often removing the need for footnotes or endnotes. The parenthetical references usually include only the author's last name and a page reference. (In the social and natural sciences, the year of publication is included after the author's name, and the page number is often omitted.) Any element of the reference that is clear from the context may be omitted. To distinguish among cited works published by the same author, the author's name may be followed by the specific work's title, which is usually shortened. (If the author-date system is being used, a lowercase letter can be added after the year—e.g., 1992a, 1992b—to distinguish between works published in the same year.) Each of the following references is keyed to an entry in the Lists of Sources section below.

Humanities style

(Quirk et al., 135)
(Baugh and Cable, *History,* 14)
(Commission on the Humanities, 46)

Sciences style

(Mayr 1982, 1–3)
(Nowak 1991, 2:661)
(Gould and Eldredge 1977)

# Lists of Sources

A bibliography or list of sources in alphabetical order usually appears at the end of the work. The following lists of cited works illustrate standard styles employed in, respectively, the humanities and the social and natural sciences. The principal differences between the two styles are these. In the sciences, (1) an initial is generally used instead of the author's first name, (2) the date is placed directly after the author's name, (3) all words in titles are lowercased except the first word and the first word of any subtitle as well as proper nouns and adjectives, and (4) article titles are not set off by quotation marks. (In some scientific publications, book and journal titles are not italicized.)

Humanities style

Baugh, Albert C., and Thomas Cable. *A History of the English Language.* 3d ed. Englewood Cliffs, N.J.: Prentice Hall, 1978.

Beauvoir, Simone de. *The Second Sex.* Trans. and ed. H. M. Parshley. New York: Alfred A. Knopf, 1953. Reprint. New York: Random House, 1974.

Bishop, Elizabeth. *The Complete Poems: 1927–1979.* New York: Farrar, Straus & Giroux, 1983.

Commission on the Humanities. *The Humanities in American Life.* Berkeley: University of California Press, 1980.

Gonzalez, Roseann Duenas. "Teaching Mexican American Students to Write: Capitalizing on the Culture." *English Journal* 71.7 (November 1982): 22–24.

Lukacs, John. "The End of the Twentieth Century." *Harper's,* January 1993: 39–58.

*Photographic View Album of Cambridge* [England]. N.d., n.p., n. pag.

Quirk, Randolph, Sidney Greenbaum, Geoffrey Leech, and Jan Svartvik. *A Comprehensive Grammar of the English Language.* London: Longman, 1985.

Steiner, George. Review of *Oeuvres en Prose Complètes, Tome 3,* by Charles Péguy. *Times Literary Supplement,* 25 December 1992: 3–4.

Sciences style

Banks, A. S., ed. 1992. *Political handbook of the world: 1992.* Binghamton, N.Y.: CSA Publications.

Broad, W. J. 1992. Big science squeezes small-scale researchers. *New York Times,* 29 Dec.: C1+.

Gould, S. J., and N. Eldredge. 1977. Punctuated equilibria: The tempo and mode of evolution reconsidered. *Paleobiology* 3: 115–151.

Holldobler, B., and E. O. Wilson. 1990. *The ants.* Cambridge, Mass.: Belknap–Harvard Univ. Press.

Mayr, E. 1982. Processes of speciation in animals. In C. Barigozzi, ed., *Mechanisms of speciation.* New York: Alan R. Liss: 1–19.

Nowak, R.M. 1991. *Walker's mammals of the world.* 5th ed. 2 vols. Baltimore: Johns Hopkins Univ. Press.

Preston, R. 1992. A reporter at large: Crisis in the hot zone. *New Yorker,* 26 Oct.: 58–81.